12.95

Chaplin and
American Culture

Don Gresswell Ltd., London, N.21 Cat. No. 1208   DG 02242 / 71

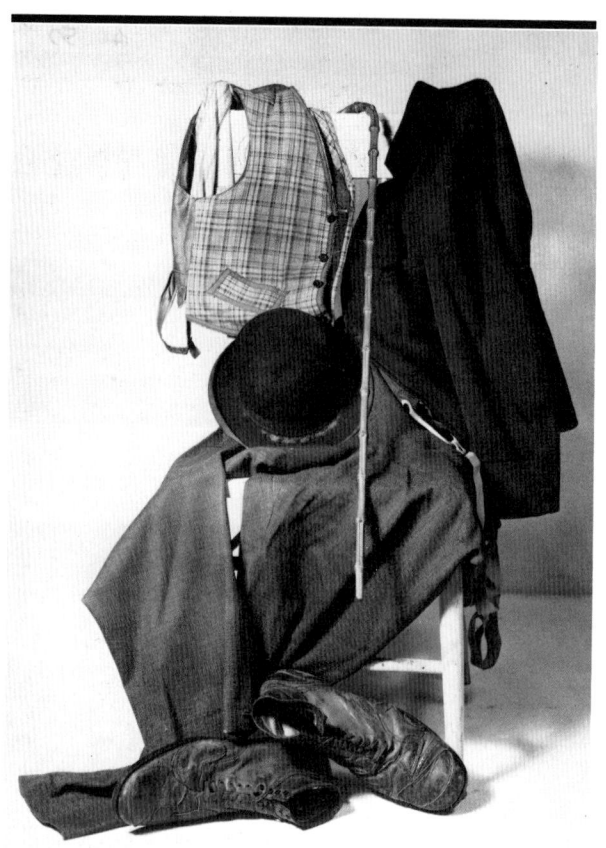

CHAPLIN
and American Culture

The Evolution of a Star Image

Charles J. Maland

PRINCETON UNIVERSITY PRESS

Princeton, New Jersey

Library of Congress Cataloging-in-Publication Data
Maland, Charles J.
Chaplin and American culture : the evolution of a
star image / Charles J. Maland.
p. cm.
Bibliography: p.
Includes index.
ISBN 0-691-09440-3 (alk. paper)
1. Chaplin, Charlie, 1889–1977. 2. Comedians—United
States—Biography. 3. Motion picture producers
and directors—United States—Biography. 4. Celebrities—
United States. 5. United States—Civilization—20th
century. 6. Fame. I. Title.
PN2287.C5M264 1989
791.43′028′0924—dc19
[B] 88-20916

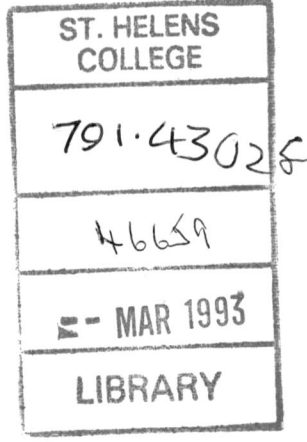

To Nancy—again
To Jonathan
and
To the memory of
Marvin Felheim

Contents

CONTENTS

CONTENTS

Illustrations

ILLUSTRATIONS AND CREDITS

CREDITS

In the following list, the numerals are the figure numbers. Any items not credited are from private collections.

Acme News pictures, 20, 21
Emporia Gazette, 11
IBM Corporation, 34, 35
Frank Interlandi, 30
Rollin Kirby, 12
Liberty, 13
London Daily Herald, 29
Motion Picture Magazine, 1, 2, 3, 4, 5, 6
New York Herald Tribune, 7
Joanna T. Steichen, 10
Tribune Media Services (*Chicago Tribune*),
    22, 28, 31
United Artists, 9, 14, 15, 16, 17, 18, 24, 25, 26, 27
Washington Evening Star, 19
Wisconsin Center for Film and Theater Research,
    frontispiece, 20
Wide World Photo (Associated Press), 23

Preface

Sometimes accidents of history divide lives into eerily symmetrical parts.

Such was surely the case with Charles Spencer Chaplin, whose place in American culture was marked by four twenty-year milestones. In 1912 the young English music-hall comedian, then unknown to most Americans, arrived in New York on the *SS Oceanic* for his second Canadian and U.S. tour.[1] Twenty years later, this same Charles Chaplin, now the world's most famous movie star, returned to the United States following a sixteen-month world trip. From the Thames to Tokyo, from Berlin to Bali, Chaplin had been celebrated by court and commoner alike. In 1952, however, two days after Chaplin and his family had set sail for Europe, the U.S. attorney general's office announced that Chaplin's reentry permit had been revoked and that if he wished to return to the United States, he would have to prove his political and moral worth. Chaplin chose exile, settling in Switzerland. Yet twenty years after he left the United States in this climate of hostility, he returned as a conquering (or at least semi-rehabilitated) hero, acclaimed by some during this 1972 visit as the greatest genius the movies had ever known. Americans apparently sought to restore Chaplin to his preeminent position of stardom in recompense for a previous generation's vilifications.

This fluctuating public reputation suggested by Chaplin's trips to and from America every twenty years is grounded in an intriguing relationship, one between Charles Chaplin—a complex, talented, and often enigmatic man—and the United States—a country that during Chaplin's residence moved fitfully and somewhat reluctantly into the world community. Although the London-born Chaplin was indelibly shaped by a Victorian world view and the performance tradition of English music halls, he also lived in the United States for nearly forty years, established himself as a star working in the American film industry, and learned that his success and failure were closely tied to his relationship with American culture.

Although many books and countless articles have been written about Chaplin, none has concentrated primarily on explaining the relationship between Chaplin and the United States.[2] This study seeks to fill that gap by tracing the dynamic interplay between Chaplin and American culture from 1913 to the 1980s and by focusing particularly on Chaplin's star image, which rose so quickly early in his career, fell so dramatically in the 1940s and 1950s, and then rose again from the 1960s on.

In carrying out this goal, the book embraces both a major and a minor theme. The major theme contends that a Chaplin *star image*, fashioned by Chaplin himself, by certain ideological and signifying practices within the film industry, by the press, and by representatives of other social institutions, was established and then evolved in American culture from World War I to the present. The star image consists of the complex and shifting set of meanings, attitudes, and mental pictures associated in the public mind with a recognized motion-picture performer—both the real person and the persona he or she plays in films. Thus Chaplin's star image consists of the changing qualities and traits associated with Charles Spencer Chaplin and the changing qualities and traits associated with the characters Chaplin played in his films, particularly his Charlie persona.[3] The book traces the complex evolution of that star image in the United States and the dynamic relationship between Chaplin and American culture. On the one hand, it focuses on how Chaplin, through his actions, words, and films, contributed to his star image. On the other, it explores how American society—through the activities of reviewers, press publicists, editorialists, moralists and censorship groups, governmental agencies, and intellectuals—helped to make Chaplin a star, to sustain that stardom, gradually to politicize it, and eventually, by the early 1950s, to nearly destroy his star image. Subsequently, the book traces how that image was reconstituted in the 1960s and especially in the 1970s, when it once again took on positive, though sometimes different, associations, allowing Chaplin and his film to experience a revival.

The minor, yet closely related, theme holds that the shifts in Chaplin's star image are intimately related to historical developments in the United States between World War I and the present. These developments include both internal advances in the film industry, like the transition to sound, and external political and social events, like the on-set of the Great Depression and the Cold War.[4] The consideration of such historical factors illuminates the study of Chaplin's star image by showing not only how these developments affected Chaplin but also how they influenced the standards and character of critical discourse

through which the reviewers, critics, and general audience responded
to him and his work.

A few words about method indicate how these themes are developed. The notion of stardom, as Richard Dyer has noted in *Stars*, his
excellent inquiry into stardom, may be examined from two different,
though related, perspectives. An ideological or sociological approach
focuses on stardom as a dominant and probably symptomatic characteristic of modern society. A textual or semiotic approach concentrates
on stardom as a part of the way films create meaning. The two approaches, Dyer argues, are interdependent. One can understand the
social significance of stars only if one understands how their meaning
or signification is realized in films (and in newspapers, magazines, advertisements, and other media texts that publicize or comment on
them). Conversely, since all texts are created in contexts, and since a
star image changes over time, the textual approach to the study of
stardom must be informed by a contextual approach sensitive to historical change.[5]

What is the apparatus by which stars are created and sustained in a
culture? Dyer observes that in the second decade of this century certain well-defined institutional practices that helped build and maintain
stars grew up within the American film industry. In particular, the star
image emerges from the interplay of four kinds of media texts already
evident in that period. First, the films themselves create a cumulative
and evolving star image: in a star's films one can discern continuities
and variations in costume, gesture, narrative concerns, and character
development. Second, studio promotional materials concerning the
stars and their films—sent to fan magazines, journalists, and movie-
theater owners—contribute to the star image. Third, publicity—"What
the press finds out" about stars—helps fashion their image. As Dyer
notes, publicity seems, but may not be, more "authentic" than promotion. Finally, criticism and commentary on the stars and their films,
from daily newspaper reviews to critical biographies, also play a part.
This book examines all four kinds of texts—films, promotion, publicity, and commentary—in exploring the growth of Chaplin's star image.[6]

As we shall see, Chaplin, functioning within this flux of surrounding
media texts, managed to obtain an unusual amount of control over the
production and distribution of his films because of the rapid and unprecedented popularity of his early work. Consequently, by the 1920s
he had managed to gain control over his star image to a degree almost
unheard of in the American film industry in the 1920s, 1930s, and
1940s. This control included the promotion of, and often even the

publicity about, his life and films. (By the mid-1920s he was so popular that he could select who would interview him and in what circumstances.) Yet in the 1930s and especially in the 1940s he began to lose control over what Dyer terms the publicity about his films. In addition, commentary about Chaplin and his films became much more divided during that same period, as the filmmaker struggled with the technological challenge of sound and with the place of political issues in his films. This inability to control the press response to him and his work eventually damaged Chaplin's star image by linking it to moral and political activities that alienated large and sometimes vocal segments of the American public.

An examination of how a star image evolves also benefits from the work of Hans Robert Jauss, probably the most historically oriented of the literary reception theorists. In his essay "Literary History as a Challenge to Literary Theory," Jauss criticizes in particular two assumptions of traditional literary history: that an objective and eternal truth can be discovered in texts and that texts rather unproblematically represent or reflect the historical reality from which they emerge. As an alternative, Jauss proposes that literary history should be "methodologically grounded and written anew," based on "an aesthetics of reception and influence." For Jauss, literary works (and for our purposes, narrative feature films) have no intrinsic history and meaning except to the extent that successive audiences respond to them.[7] Thus the history of a body of works by a writer or by a filmmaker like Chaplin must take into account the background against which the work first appeared; the "horizon of expectations" against which it was experienced by its audience; the response (critical and otherwise) that it generated; and the changes that appeared in succeeding works, due partly to responses the artist received from other artists, from reviewers, from other sectors of the intelligentsia, and from the audience at large. If we keep in mind that the "horizon of expectations" of the audience is influenced by broad social and political factors in addition to more purely aesthetic ones, this model of reception helps clarify how an artist's career unfolds temporally and how a culture's response to an artist's work is cumulative, shifting, and multifaceted.[8]

THIS BOOK is divided into five parts. Part One, "To the Top," traces the process by which Chaplin first became a star and then managed to sustain that stardom through 1919. Part Two, "At the Top: Charlie and the 1920s," concentrates on Chaplin's star image from 1920 until the release of *City Lights* (1931). Part Three, "The Challenge of Progressive Politics," treats the period between the stock market crash and

World War II, when three factors had an especially powerful impact on Chaplin's relationship with American Culture: the pressure on Chaplin to make dialogue films, the Great Depression, and the rise of fascism. If Chaplin's star image reached its height of popularity in the 1920s and 1930s, it became politicized and plummeted to its nadir in the late 1940s and early 1950s. Part Four, "Unraveling," examines the decline of Chaplin's star image in America between 1942 and 1952, and his response to that decline. Part Five, "The Exile and America," discusses the guarded restoration of Chaplin's star image from the mid-1950s to the present. An epilogue tracing the way Chaplin's Charlie persona has become "commodified" in the 1980s, particularly in the highly successful advertisement campaign for IBM microcomputers, concludes the study.

The contours of this project support the belief that the most illuminating historical criticism and analysis, exemplified by Edmund Wilson's work on Dickens, is a criticism that shows the artist as a human being grounded in a particular time and place, struggling to understand self and society and to embody that understanding in the work of art. It is a criticism rarely practiced on a filmmaker, for few who have worked in the dominant film industry have ever managed the creative control that Chaplin enjoyed for most of his career. Yet the lives and work of these few artists who, like Chaplin, have functioned successfully in the cinema can sustain such an examination. F. O. Matthiessen's suggestive comment in *American Renaissance* that the work of artists is "the most sensitive index to cultural history," since artists can articulate only what they are and what they have been made "by the society of which (they are) a willing or unwilling part," undergirds this approach to Chaplin.[9] If what follows illuminates the dynamic interplay between Chaplin and American culture, it will have achieved what it set out to do.

Knoxville, Tennessee
May 1988

Acknowledgments

The assistance, generosity, and friendship of many people and institutions have helped bring this book into being. Although it is impossible to list everyone who influenced this work, I acknowledge the following with pleasure.

Thanks first to John Mitchell and Ron Palosaari, who in the late 1960s convinced me that the movies were an art, industry, and social force worth examining.

The University of Tennessee has supported this book in a number of ways. A summer research grant from the Graduate School assisted initial research efforts. Later grants from the John C. Hodges Fund in the English Department also sustained my work, as did Joseph Trahern, department head during the time I was working on the book. I also thank the graduate and undergraduate students in my course on Chaplin and American Culture; their probing of and enthusiasm for Chaplin's work helped me think about the subject that gradually transformed itself into this book.

A number of archives, libraries, and other institutions provided me with invaluable information and generous assistance as I prepared this study. They include the University of Tennessee Libraries and especially Director Don Hunt, Judy Webster, Angie LeClercq, and the reference and interlibrary loan staffs; the British Film Institute Library, London; Barbara Humphreys and Emily Sieger of the Motion Picture Section of the Library of Congress, Washington, D.C., Charles Silver of the Museum of Modern Art Film Department, New York; three collections in the New York Public Library system—the Lincoln Center Library (Billy Rose Collection), the Main Library, and the Newspaper Library; the Wisconsin Center for Film and Theater Research, Madison; and the American Film Institute Library, Beverly Hills. The U.S. government provided me with its files on Chaplin following my Freedom of Information Act request. IBM Corporation generously provided information about its personal computer advertising campaign featuring Charlie.

ACKNOWLEDGMENTS

I benefited constantly from the work of three Chaplin scholars, in particular. David Robinson's fine biography provided information from Chaplin's papers that is available nowhere else. The bibliographies of Timothy Lyons and Wes Gehring were of great assistance, as was their encouragement through correspondence. I thank these three scholars for their painstaking work.

Various others offered important counsel at key stages of the project or read and commented on the manuscript. For their assistance, I would like to thank Neal Gabler, Michael Lofaro, John Raeburn, Robert Ray, and Janet Staiger. At Princeton University Press, Joanna Hitchcock provided generous support for the project early on, as did Marilyn Campbell. Elizabeth Gretz helped me to avoid factual errors and stylistic lapses through her careful copyediting.

Special thanks go to three people: to Nancy Klein Maland, whose support for and assistance on this project have been, as with my previous work, unfailing; to Jonathan Maland, who is three years younger than the idea for this book and thus had to live with it since infancy (thank goodness he likes Charlie!); and to the late Marvin Felheim, whose dedication to teaching and scholarship was an inspiration to generations of students, not least those of us in the American Culture Program at the University of Michigan in the early 1970s. Grateful for the vital and indispensable contributions each of these three people have made to me, I am pleased to dedicate this book to them.

Abbreviations

BRC   Billy Rose Collection, Lincoln Center Branch, New York Public Library, New York

CHC   David Bordwell, Janet Staiger, and Kristin Thompson, *The Classical Hollywood Cinema: Film Style and Mode of Production to 1960* (New York: Columbia University Press, 1985)

CHLA   David Robinson, *Chaplin: His Life and Art* (New York: McGraw-Hill, 1985)

MA   Charles Spencer Chaplin, *My Autobiography* (New York: Simon and Schuster, 1964)

NYT   *New York Times*

RLC   Robinson Locke Collection, in the Billy Rose Collection, Lincoln Center Branch, New York Public Library, New York

SAC   special agent in charge (FBI)

UAC   United Artists Collection, Wisconsin Center for Film and Theater Research, Wisconsin State Historical Library, Madison

ONE

To the Top

1

Chaplin, the Early Films, and
the Rise to Stardom

The Rough-Edged Diamond:
Charlie at Keystone

On 12 May 1913 Alf Reeves, manager of a Fred Karno music-hall company touring in America, received a telegram at the Nixon Theater in Philadelphia:

> IS THERE A MAN NAMED CHAFFIN IN YOUR COMPANY OR SOMETHING LIKE THAT STOP IF SO WILL HE COMMUNICATE WITH KESSEL AND BAUMAN 24 LONGACRE BUILDING BROADWAY NEW YORK

Reeves, suspecting that the telegram must be referring to one of his featured players, Charles Chaplin, showed it to him. When Chaplin learned that the Longacre Building primarily housed legal offices, he surmised that he had inherited some money and immediately arranged a trip to New York City. But he soon learned otherwise. Adam Kessel, Jr., and Charles O. Bauman were owners of the New York Motion Pictures Company. The telegram had been sent by Mack Sennett, head of one of their subsidiaries—a film production company in Los Angeles called Keystone. Sennett had seen Chaplin perform in 1911 at the American Music Hall and thought that Chaplin might do as a replacement for Ford Sterling, a leading Keystone comedian who was threatening to leave. Though Chaplin had no previous experience in film, he was lured to accept the offer by a princely salary: $150 weekly for three months, raised to $175 weekly for the rest of the year. Before joining Keystone, however, Chaplin had to complete his Karno tour. After his last performance, in Kansas City on November 28, an eager yet anxious Chaplin parted with his Karno associates and took a train to California. Little did he know that within three years he would be one of the most famed and highly paid men in America.[1]

Chaplin arrived in Los Angeles at a propitious time in the development of the American film industry. Though motion pictures had been projected in America since 1896, the movie industry did not experience its first significant growth until the nickelodeon boom of

1906–1907.[2] In an attempt to cash in on the enormous potential profits offered by this expansion, a group of manufacturers of motion-picture technology, headed by Thomas Edison, formed the Motion Picture Patents Company. By controlling nearly all of the key patents on motion-picture film, cameras, and projectors, the Trust—as the group was popularly known—kept tight control on the industry for several years. But a group of renegade production companies, including Keystone, emerged and by 1912 had formed a strong and organized independent movement. These Independents gradually began to weaken the hegemony of the Trust, and this in turn laid the groundwork for the ascendance of the studio system in the late 1910s and the 1920s.[3]

Chaplin's timing was fortunate because in the previous several years, the film industry, groping toward the star system that would later dominate it, had begun to market films by featuring particular actors. Thanks partly to the stability created by the Trust after its foundation in 1908, the industry was able, in the words of one scholar, "to turn investment away from patent litigation and into product development." Actors were one aspect of production that quickly received attention. (I use the term "actors" to refer to both men and women.) As early as February 1910, an author in *Nickelodeon* noted that movie audiences were demanding "a better acquaintance with those they see upon the screen," and by 1912—the year before Chaplin's arrival on the Keystone lot—a "star system" was beginning to establish itself. Although the film industry was starting to standardize its technology and method of telling stories, the star system provided a way for one company to differentiate its product from that of other companies.[4]

But Chaplin did not become a full-fledged star immediately. In fact, it would probably be more accurate to say that although he gained a considerable following among moviegoers during his year at Keystone, he did not actually become a star until after he signed with a new company, Essanay, in early 1915.

The construction of the star image did begin at Keystone, however, primarily as a result of the films themselves rather than promotion of them or publicity and commentary about them. Chaplin appeared in thirty-five films for Keystone in 1914. The first, *Making a Living*, was released on February 2; the last, *His Prehistoric Past*, on December 7. Although most of the films were one-reelers (about ten minutes long), several were only about five minutes, and one, *Tillie's Punctured Romance*, featuring Marie Dressler, took up six reels. Chaplin appeared in his "tramp" or "Charlie" costume very early—in his second film, *Kid*

Auto Races at Venice.[5] By his twelfth film, *Caught in a Cabaret*, he had finally persuaded Sennett to let him co-direct (with Mabel Normand, his costar). Chaplin then went on to direct or co-direct (with Mabel Normand, four more times) twenty of his last twenty-three films at Keystone. The year was a frenetic, educational one for Chaplin. He learned moviemaking by doing.

A look at some characteristics of the Keystone films, particularly of the persona Chaplin played, indicates the kind of star image that Chaplin began to develop during his year there. That image was shaped in part by the studio in which Chaplin worked: Sennett's studio was famous for its iconoclastic nose-thumbing at propriety and its frantic Keystone cop chases. Chaplin himself, accustomed to the more polished acting and pantomime of the English music hall, felt uneasy with the hectic, broad Keystone style (MA, pp. 147–50). Even though he began to differentiate himself through the creation of a character and to achieve some level of independence by directing his own films, Chaplin still created a persona that was tempered by the Keystone stamp.

Generalizing about Chaplin's persona at Keystone is nearly impossible, largely because he was much less conscious of the character he played (and less able to control that persona, given his position as Sennett's employee) than he became in later years. Though viewers today associate Chaplin's screen persona with a distinct outfit and props—derby and cane, tight-fitting coat and baggy pants, floppy shoes—this costume was not his trademark during the early Keystone days. In his first film Chaplin played a dandy; he wore a top hat, a double-breasted frock coat, and a monocle, and he sported a handlebar mustache. In *Mabel at the Wheel*, his tenth Keystone film, he wore a top hat, long overcoat, black gloves, spats, and a goatee. Even after he began directing himself, Chaplin's costume varied. The top hat appeared again, for example, in *Mabel's Married Life* (his nineteenth Keystone film). Sometimes his occupation in a film determined his clothing: coatless, Chaplin wore a waiter's apron over his vest in *Caught in a Cabaret*. As the Keystone year passed, however, the costume became more conventional. By his final Keystone, the Charlie persona must have been widely known to a growing audience, for in that film—*His Prehistoric Past*—Charlie wore his derby and big shoes with his caveman's skins, which suggests that the derby and shoes were already trademark enough.

Much has been written about the essential appeal of Charlie's costume and character, and these discussions often revolve around conceptions of contrast that Chaplin, in his autobiography, recalled using when trying to describe his new character to Sennett after piecing together the costume: "You know this fellow is many-sided, a tramp, a gentleman, a poet, a dreamer, a lonely fellow, always hopeful of romance and adventure. He would have you believe he is a scientist, a musician, a duke, a polo player. However, he is not above picking up cigarette butts or robbing a baby of its candy. And, of course, if the situation warrants it, he will kick a lady in the rear—but only in extreme anger" (MA, p. 144). In writing this passage Chaplin was either disingenuous or forgetful, because such a multifaceted and complex conception of Charlie's character was not apparent during the Keystone year. In fact, it would be relatively accurate to say that Chaplin's description would fit his Keystone persona well if the first half were deleted and the second half—about picking up cigarette butts, stealing candy from babies, and kicking ladies—were emphasized.

The Charlie persona that emerged from the Keystone films was often mean, crude, and brutish. Examples from the films abound. In *Between Showers*, for example, Charlie pokes Ford Sterling in the backside with an umbrella and thumbs his nose to a cop. In *A Film Johnnie*, he gets ejected from a movie theater for disruptive behavior, and in *Mabel at the Wheel*, he sticks a pin in Mabel's thigh and her boyfriend's buttocks. As a waiter in *Caught in a Cabaret*, he dusts off some food with a dirty rag, then drops the food on the floor, steps on it, puts it back on the plate, and serves it. As a dentist's odd-job man in *Laughing Gas*, he hits a man on the mouth with a brick, causing the man to spit out a mouthful of teeth. In the same film, he poses as a dentist and clambers onto a woman in the chair; when she resists, he pulls the woman's nose with a forceps and kisses her. Though the Keystone films also contain a number of the graceful and clever comic touches that would become a Chaplin trademark, the humor in these films is generally broad and sometimes bawdy slapstick. The gentle and tender character apparent in later Chaplin films—*City Lights*, for example—is at this point nowhere to be found.

Given this screen persona, what evidence exists in the press that Chaplin was becoming a name to reckon with in the film industry? One way to approach this question is to examine how representative film magazines of the day recognized Charlie (or Chaplin) in their reviews of films he appeared in. *Moving Picture World* reviewed at least seventeen of Chaplin's Keystones, and its varying levels of awareness of Chaplin suggest the degree to which he was becoming known while at Keystone. Without naming him specifically, the magazine noted his performance in its review of Chaplin's first Keystone, *Making a Living*: "The clever player who takes the role of a nervy and very shifty sharper in this picture is a comedian of the first water, who acts like one of Nature's own naturals."[6] There were no references to Chaplin in March or April. In a May issue, however, a review of *Caught in a Cabaret* stated, "Charles Chaplin was the leading funmaker" (9 May 1914: 821). This mention would suggest that Chaplin's name was becoming familiar, but that may not have been true: in a number of later reviews, Chaplin's name was misspelled. The review of *Mabel's Married Life* states, "Charles Chapman and Mabel Normand are at their best" (27 June 1914: 65). In a review of *Recreation*, the name is misspelled "Chaplain" (29 August 1914: 1242), and in the September 19 and 26 issues, the spelling reverts to "Chapman." By the time *Those Love Pangs* was reviewed in October, *Moving Picture World* had finally learned to spell Chaplin's name correctly (17 October 1914: 337). Even then, however, reviews suggest that he was not as established and settled a performer as Mabel Normand or Mack Swain. Note the review of *His Musical Career*: "Chas Chaplin and Ambrose disport themselves in this number as a pair of piano movers" (14 November 1914: 932). Ambrose was the name of the character Mack Swain played in the Keystone films at that time; reviewers and apparently audiences regularly referred to Ambrose and to Mabel, but Chaplin had not yet become known as Charlie or the tramp or the little fellow, at least not until near the end of his year at Keystone.

A similar indication that Chaplin's popularity began to grow near the end of this year comes from *Motion Picture Magazine*. The periodical featured a regular section called "Green Room Jottings," which consisted of one- or two-sentence references to people, primarily actors, in the movie business. The first reference to Chaplin appeared in the August 1914 "Jottings," in which readers learned that "Charles Chaplin (Keystone) has been an 'actor man' for sixteen years, yet he is now only twenty-four years young."[7] That same issue contained a rather bizarre caricature of Chaplin on a page with nine other figures, including Ford Sterling, John Barrymore, and—the largest in size— V. A. Potel, the "Funny Man at G. M. Anderson's Essanay Camp" (p. 131). The Chaplin sketch showed him with brawny shoulders, barrel chest, bulging biceps, and tiny waist and legs, a bulldog at his side (see Figure 1). To George Edwards, the artist, Chaplin seemed to suggest a young athlete or acrobat. Mustache, derby, and cane played no part in his star image here.

In its October 1914 issue *Motion Picture Magazine* announced the results of its "Great Player Contest," in which over eleven million ballots had ostensibly been cast by readers before the cutoff date of August 20. Earle Williams, Clara K. Young, and Mary Pickford topped the list

1. Cartoon from August 1914,
before Chaplin became
identified as Charlie.

of the one hundred leading vote getters. Mabel Normand, in fortieth place, was the highest-ranking Keystone star; the name of Charles Chaplin did not appear (p. 128). In the December issue another caricature of Chaplin appeared, this time in baggy pants, tight coat, and top hat, and carrying a cane (p. 130); in addition, there was a full-page collage containing five pictures of Chaplin's face in closeup. This was significantly more attention than he had received in the August issue.

The January issue provided a stark contrast to the "Great Player Contest" of the previous October, for in it, the results of the "Great Cast Contest" were announced (p. 126). The contest featured twelve categories, including leading man, leading woman, old man, old woman, villain, and so on. In the male comedian category, Charles Chaplin came out on top, accumulating 10,390 votes and edging out John Bunny, in second place with 9,510 votes. Even more striking, perhaps, is the fact that only Mary Maurice, who won the "old woman" category, received more votes than Chaplin. Since voting took place during the third week in November, it is apparent that by the last months of the Keystone period, Chaplin's films had become very popular. The "Great Cast Contest" was also held the following year, and by November of 1915, Chaplin had garnered 1.9 million votes, with Ford Sterling a distant second at 1.4 million votes (p. 124). Even if we are skeptical of the numbers and the voting procedures, the fact remains that by late 1914, readers of the magazine were learning about Chaplin in terms that were full of praise.

These two magazines do give us a good general picture of how Chaplin's reputation began to grow during 1914, but it is important to make a distinction here between Charlie and Chaplin. Evidence suggests that Chaplin's screen persona did become popular with viewers by the end of the Keystone period. But Chaplin himself had not yet become a star: there was little discussion in the press of the man who was responsible for the creation of the character. Recalling in 1916 his experiences near the end of his Keystone contract, Chaplin wrote: "It was odd, walking up and down the streets, eating in cafes, hearing Charlie Chaplin talked about, seeing Charlie Chaplin on every hand and never being recognized as Charlie Chaplin. I had a feeling that all the world was crosseyed, or that I was a disembodied spirit. But that did not last long."[8] Up to the end of the Keystone period, then, the star image of "Charlie Chaplin" revolved almost entirely around a character on the movie screen.

One does not really become a star until publicists and journalists focus on and the audience gets interested in the personality of the actor behind the mask, and it seems likely that Sennett and Keystone, realizing how popular Chaplin was becoming and how high his salary demands might go when it was time to renew his contract, were careful not to exploit the private life of the performer. Despite their efforts, when Chaplin's contract ran out at the end of 1914, other studios became interested in signing him up. Nineteen-fifteen was to be the year in which Chaplin would become a bona fide movie star.

"Chaplinitis": Charlie at Essanay

As Chaplin's Keystone contract neared its end, Mack Sennett had to decide what he and his associates would be willing to pay to keep Chaplin on. Sennett knew that audiences around America were lining up to see the Charlie films, but Chaplin did, too. Chaplin himself remembered asking Sennett to increase his salary to $1,000 per week, a request Sennett denied, protesting that even *he* did not make that much money (MA, p. 159). After Chaplin and Keystone failed to come to terms, Chaplin signed a one-year contract with Essanay on 2 January 1915. The terms included a $10,000 bonus for signing and $1,250 per week. The first of three large and increasingly publicized contracts for Chaplin, it ushered in a remarkable twelve months for the actor— the year of what one writer called a national case of "Chaplinitis."[9]

Chaplin's stardom grew during the Essanay period partly because the persona he had begun to create the year before became in 1915 part of a widespread craze not unlike the Davy Crockett phenomenon of the mid-1950s. Of course, Chaplin's Essanay films (thirteen released in 1915), all of which featured Charlie, contributed to the enthusiasm. (The new dimensions added to the persona during this period will be discussed in the following section.) In addition, however, the Charlie persona was proliferating throughout American culture. Manifestations of this included advertisers' use of Chaplin's character to sell toys and other paraphernalia, imitators of Chaplin, and cartoons about Chaplin.

Throughout 1915 and particularly in the last half of the year, Chaplin's name or Charlie's picture was used to sell all sorts of products. *Motion Picture Magazine* ran a picture of Charlie in its July issue to help advertise its August issue, which concluded its article on Chaplin (p. 171). The July issue also offered a free portrait of Chaplin in his Charlie costume to anyone who ordered a back issue of the magazine (p. 177). The September issue contained an advertisement by the Kirkham Company headed "Charlie Chaplin's Surprise—the Funniest Novelty Ever" (p. 159). Though it was not entirely clear exactly what the novelty was, for ten cents a Chaplin fan could find out. By the October issue, the Fisher Novelty Company was offering a "Charlie Chaplin Squirt Ring" for fifteen cents; a picture of Charlie with derby and mustache topped the ring (p. 164). By the December issue, the Nuidea Company was offering a "Charlie Chaplin Outfit," consisting of a Charlie Chaplin mustache, an imitation gold tooth, a $1,000 bankroll of stage money, and a medallion coin with a "life-like image" of Charlie on it—all for only a dime plus two cents postage (p. 158). The fact that entrepreneurs were appropriating the Charlie persona to merchandise their wares stresses how popular that persona had become.

It has been said that imitation is the sincerest form of flattery. If that is the case, Chaplin was flattered by an overwhelming number of Americans in 1915. Evidence of such imitation appeared frequently in the popular press. In June, *Motion Picture Magazine* reported that "the Chaplin mustache is spreading—not the mustache, but its popularity." The same month, the *Cleveland Plain Dealer* reported that "Cleveland has been getting so full of imitators of Charlie Chaplin that the management of Luna Park decided to offer a prize to the best imitator and out they flocked." (A young man named Leslie T. Hope, later known as Bob Hope, won one such competition in Cleveland.) Indeed, Chaplin look-alike competitions were thriving throughout the country; the

New York World reported in mid-July 1915 that over thirty theaters in the city were sponsoring Chaplin amateur nights.[10]

Chaplin imitations went well beyond amateur night at the local movie house and were found on the screen itself. In the film industry this imitation was not primarily a form of flattery. Rather, like the advertisements, it aimed at cashing in on the success of Charlie. In 1915 film actors imitating Chaplin abounded. The most prominent—and possibly the most blatantly exploitative—was Billie Ritchie, who had also worked for Karno, preceding Chaplin in a Karno sketch called "The Mumming Birds." Though Ritchie went so far as to accuse Chaplin of imitating *him*, he was really quite shameless in copying Chaplin's costume and even his plots: for example, two weeks after Chaplin's *Work* was released, Ritchie came out with *The Curse of Work*.[11] Another Chaplin imitator, Steve Duros, who was hired by theater owners in Columbus, Ohio, to dress like Charlie and walk the streets, was featured in a November issue of *Motion Picture Magazine*.[12]

Cartoons were the third manifestation of the national case of Chaplinitis. These were the first in a long line of cartoons, editorial and otherwise, that attested over the years to Chaplin's star status and reflected the press's various reactions to him. At least as early as April 1915, there appeared a regular comic strip entitled "Charlie Chaplin's Comic Capers."[13] More important for the purposes of this discussion are the single-frame cartoons alluding to Charlie. Sketches of Charlie—and also of Chaplin—began to be printed regularly in the fan magazines after the first few months of 1915. One of the most important and interesting appeared in *Motion Picture Magazine* (June 1915: 152). Headed "Charles Chaplin, Essanay Mirth Provoker," it presented a mini-biography of Chaplin himself (see Figure 2), distinguishing between the filmic persona and the man behind the mustache. It slotted Chaplin in the typical rags-to-riches category so central to the American success myth: "From a penniless immigrant stranded in New York—to a small-time comedy acrobat—to the highest paid movie actor—is the story of Chaplin's rapid rise to success." Small matter that the description bore little relation to reality; it made good copy and began to factor Chaplin the man into the calculus of the Chaplin star image.

Another cartoon, featuring a sketch of Charlie only, raised some questions about the whole Chaplin phenomenon. The August 1915 issue of *Motion Picture Magazine* commented on Chaplin's huge salary in what appeared to be negative terms. (see Figure 3). Here Charlie was sneering at someone—his competitors? Keystone? the audi-

2. Chaplin, the success story, June 1915.

ence?—while doggedly protecting his bag of money labeled "Highest Salary."

Yet another cartoon commented on Charlie's popularity without presenting the Chaplin star image. The *Cleveland Leader* of 17 May 1915 showed two boys standing outside a movie theater. One of them, alluding to the world war, asked, "Jimmie, would you rather be the President or the Kaiser?" Jimmie replied, "Aw Fudge—I'd ten thousand times rather be Charley Chaplin."

The Chaplin phenomenon, two other cartoons suggest, was also creating cultural divisions. The first, from *Motion Picture Magazine* (October 1915: 148) showed how the Chaplin star image was fostering a generation gap: a child becomes convinced of his uncle's astonishing ignorance when the uncle has to ask who Charlie Chaplin is (see Figure 4). The second, though appearing in the April 1917 issue of *Motion Picture Magazine* (p. 129), after the first tidal wave of Chaplinitis, reflected a problem that began to be much discussed in 1915 and 1916. The cartoon shows a Sunday morning Bible class, in which a young boy sits daydreaming about Charlie (see Figure 5); though it does not editorialize against the boy (in fact, the apearance of the red-nosed genteel teacher makes her seem as much the target of satire as the boy), a number of Americans would have seen the cartoon as an accurate expression of the threat to decency and morality posed by the whole Chaplin phenomenon.

If Chaplin's star image was spread by films, advertisements, imitators, and cartoons, it was also extended in 1915 by articles about the man himself, a topic not discussed during the Keystone period. As the author of "Chaplinitis" put it, after Chaplin signed the Essanay contract, "the world went mad. From New York to San Francisco, from Maine to California, came the staccato tapping of the telegraph key. 'Who is this man Chaplin? What are his ambitions? What's his theory of humor? Is he married, or single? How does he like American life? Does he eat eggs for breakfast? Is he conceited?' The newspapers wanted to know; the country demanded information."[14] The country's appetite for learning more about the funny little man in the movies was for a time insatiable.

What picture of Chaplin the man emerged from the profiles of him in 1915? Richard Dyer has suggested that the American success myth, which holds that the society is so open that anyone can rise to the top,[15] is frequently associated with stars: they become symbols of the myth. If closely examined, the 1915 articles on Chaplin together draw a portrait of the man entirely consistent with Dyer's observation.

Chaplin's humble beginnings and his personal quality of humility are stressed. "Unknown a few months ago," one article stated, Chaplin "is now said to be the highest salaried funny man in the film world." He has, continued the article, a "violet-like reluctance" to talk about himself. "There's nothing worth while talking about," it quotes Chaplin as saying. "I am no one—just a plain fellow." A second essay called him "a little Englishman, quiet, unassuming." Yet another article reinforced that view: "Personally he is said to be extremely modest, retiring, declining to assume he has accomplished much worth making a fuss about." Though Chaplin the man later would be described as being dominated by hubris, the early Chaplin was termed humble.[16]

This humility, according to one article, was "one of the best things that can be said about anybody and one of the real proofs of greatness." Greatness, or extraordinary talent or ability, was the second characteristic of Chaplin's stressed. The author of "Chaplinitis" was one of the first writers to call Chaplin a "genius" at his work, though as time passed that term came to be regularly associated with Chaplin's star image. "Once in every century," the article commented, "a man is born who is able to color and influence his world." In the twentieth

3. Controversy over Chaplin's Essanay
salary, August 1915.

century, "Charles Chaplin is doing it with pantomime and personality." The genius and greatness attributed to Chaplin were, according to one of the articles, "proof that talent will come to the top despite adverse circumstances."[17] The assumptions about humility and greatness embedded in the profiles of Chaplin enabled a generation raised on Horatio Alger novels to feel secure that its attitude toward success had again been proven in the real world.

Thanks to the national bout with "Chaplinitis," a Chaplin star image, combining the persona created in the films with the man who created it, was firmly anchored in the United States by the end of 1915 (see Figure 6). The man was portrayed as humble and unassuming, yet imbued with greatness. The persona, while immensely popular, was nevertheless in a state of flux. If the crude and mischievous persona from the Keystone era had helped to initiate Chaplin's stardom, it also met with resistance in certain sectors of American culture.

The Genteel Tradition and the "Vulgar" Charlie

Not everyone was caught up in the Chaplin craze. In fact, a significant minority found Chaplin's films a social menace. Because the individual voices raised against Chaplin represented larger social forces, it is necessary, in order to put his dilemma in context, to say a few words about the broader social canvas.

14

American historians, taking a cue from George Santayana's famous essay, "The Genteel Tradition in American Philosophy," have looked upon the first two decades of this century as a time in which the Genteel Tradition gradually lost its dominance.[18] Briefly, the Genteel Tradition was a segment of society that emerged in America in the nineteenth century after the growth of a democratic ethos and the appearance of a new business class had displaced the traditional elite from positions of wealth and power. These displaced elites—the American "gentility"—placed high value on refined manners, a polished and elegant life style, and cultivation of the high arts. They came to perceive themselves as the custodians of American culture, at least in part to compensate for their eroding economic and social status.

Leaders of the American gentility felt that because theirs was an enlightened minority which understood and appreciated culture, it must, in Charles Alexander's words, "try to elevate the national mind by promoting the creative spirit and love of beauty," even as it struggled to keep beauty from being corrupted by the uncomprehending masses and the philistine new rich.[19] One of its most cherished assumptions about art was that it had an essential moral dimension: art should teach proper moral conduct.

Proponents of the Genteel Tradition regarded the movies with mixed feelings. On the one hand, the movies seemed to belong to the "uncomprehending masses"—those who had no appreciation for "real" art or culture. On the other hand, since the movies communicated so powerfully to so many people, some saw film as a great opportunity for educating the masses, if only the proper hands could gain control of the medium. This dual view is encapsulated in a comment from an essay in *The Outlook* in early 1914, about the same time that Chaplin's first film was being released: "The very potency of the motion picture for degrading taste and morals is the measure of its powers for enlightenment." If the movies could be properly regulated, another spokesman argued, they could ideally function as "a grand social worker," enabling the genteel elite to spread its values to others lower on the social scale and hence to extend its social control.[20] As the popularity of movies with working- and middle-class Americans continued to grow, genteel custodians of culture thus began to criticize what they perceived as the danger of movies and to urge reform.

As we have noted, the character Chaplin played in his Keystone films was often abrasive and crude, however funny. Such a character was a likely target of genteel critics, particularly given Chaplin's mass popularity. A 1914 review of *The Property Man* in *Moving Picture World* indicates the dilemma some observers faced: "Some of the funniest

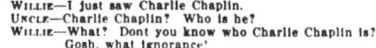

WILLIE—I just saw Charlie Chaplin.
UNCLE—Charlie Chaplin? Who is he?
WILLIE—What? Dont you know who Charlie Chaplin is?
Gosh, what ignorance!

THE SUNDAY MORNING BIBLE CLASS

4 (*left*). Chaplinitis and the generation gap, October 1915.
5 (*right*). Charlie competes with Sunday School, April 1917.

things in the picture are vulgar," wrote the critic. "They are too vulgar to describe; but are too funny to pass for vulgarity when only seen."[21]

Although this commentator was generous enough to allow that Chaplin was funny despite his vulgarity—it would be difficult for a movie reviewer to react otherwise—more genteel observers were not so tolerant. One attack on Chaplin by a custodian of culture appeared in a 1915 letter to the editor of the *New Orleans American*.[22] The purpose of the letter, in its author's words, was "to justify the stand taken by so many of the better class and better educated people in New Orleans, who find that the [Chaplin] films are not worth going to see." Why were the films unworthy? The writer pulled no punches: because of the "grotesque and vulgar antics of that product of the slums of Whitecastle." Instead of debasing public taste by presenting the low comedy of Chaplin and his ilk, the author urged, theater owners should present more inspiring programs: travel films, filmed opera, and adaptations of classic novels, poems, and plays.

Others, including religious leaders, joined in the anti-Chaplin chorus. A headline in the *Detroit News* indicates the form such criticism often took: "Low Grade Persons Only Like Charlie Chaplin and Mary Pickford, Says Pastor."[23] The article gave an account of the denunciations of these two movie stars by a prominent Detroit minister. Reactions like this one give an idea of the threat that moralists believed Chaplin's Keystone persona posed to genteel moral standards.

How did Chaplin respond to these criticisms? "The New Charlie Chaplin," a 1916 article in *Motion Picture Magazine*, suggests not only that Chaplin was aware of these challenges to his popularity but also that he was consciously beginning to shift and mold his star image in

16

response to them.[24] The article is J. B. Hirsch's account of a meeting between Chaplin and W. W. Barrett, a member of the executive staff of the National Board of Censorship. This organization, formed in 1909 to encourage "quality" movies and safeguard the public from immorality in films, arranged for a representative to meet with Chaplin and discuss with him the content and future of his movies. The article presents a dramatic account of how the Genteel Tradition put pressure on filmmakers; it also shows how Chaplin's star image was beginning to evolve.

According to Hirsch's article, Barrett visited Chaplin not only because the National Board was concerned about some questionable aspects of Chaplin's movies but also because its members believed that there were "great possibilities in the comedian's future work, both as a helpful influence in the community and as a factor in the artistic development of the Motion Picture" (p. 115). In the essay, Chaplin defended himself against charges of vulgarity: "It is because of my music-hall training and experiences that I . . . work into my acting little threads of vulgarisms." Linking his humor to a venerable tradition, Chaplin added, "This Elizabethan style of humor, this crude form of farce and slapstick comedy . . . was due entirely to my early environment, and I am now trying to steer clear from this sort of humor and adapt myself to a more subtle and finer shade of acting" (pp. 115, 117). The essay portrays Chaplin as apparently contrite, or at least as being careful not to antagonize a group that could limit his popularity.

This "new Charlie Chaplin," wrote Hirsch, has "burst the tawdry chrysalis of the . . . English music-hall manner" in favor of "a new fame, to be built on the basis of a more delicate art that will not countenance the broad sallies his old technique demanded" (p. 115). The essay recounts one of the first recorded instances of Chaplin's conflicts with pressure groups in America, conflicts that were to become more frequent as his career progressed. In this early example, Chaplin bowed to the pressure group and assured it that he would evolve as an artist in directions that would prove suitable to the National Board of Censorship and to the American public. At a time when the middle classes were beginning to attend movies in ever increasing numbers, the Chaplin described in the article was thinking about altering the character of his movies to make them more palatable to this larger audience.[25]

This essay is also interesting because it shows how Chaplin's star image was changing after he had been in the limelight for over a year. The picture of Chaplin that accompanies the article—"as he appears in real life," according to the caption—portrays a youthful-looking, handsome man wearing a dinner jacket and bow tie and gazing seriously at the viewer. The text reinforces the image. Barrett found Chaplin to be quite different from his film persona: "a neat and stylishly dressed young man; as charming and affable a boy . . . as anyone would wish to meet." In a list of features that corresponds in several ways to the list of qualities Richard Dyer associates with stardom, Hirsch describes Chaplin as a "hard worker, who writes, acts, produces and manages; an unusually intelligent man, modest, not in the least affected by his great popularity, and very keen, businesslike and thrifty—not at all like the usual actor of the 'get-rich-quick' variety." (Chaplin's thriftiness, even stinginess in certain respects, did not fit the star pattern of conspicuous consumption; it nonetheless was consistent with the Horatio Alger tradition and a quality often associated with his star image throughout his career.) Finally, Barrett saw in Chaplin an ambitious artist: "He has shaped for himself the slogan 'Art for Art's sake,' and he has dreams of unmeasured possibilities for the future of the films—all from an artistic point of view" (p. 115).

This new view of Chaplin as the unaffected yet serious artist appeared in another 1916 article, "The Real Charlie Chaplin," by Stanley W. Todd.[26] Todd claimed that those interested in knowing Chaplin rather than Charlie are "certain to encounter some surprises" (p. 41). According to Todd, Chaplin was known to his friends "as a serious-minded young fellow whose accession to affluence has not spoiled his democracy or ambitions." Chaplin also constantly sought to improve himself, telling Todd that "no man or woman should be satisfied with having won a fortune or fame in one line of work. I expect to be at it fifty years from now" (p. 44). This affirmation of hard work was a cardinal virtue of the Genteel Tradition, as was another of Chaplin's qualities reported in Todd's article: interest in high culture and the fine arts. Todd told his readers that Chaplin had read Shakespeare "from beginning to end" and was familiar with "the works of George Eliot and other noted writers" (p. 44). Chaplin, who had little formal education, was already compensating for that lack by talking with the press about his intellectual aspirations, and the press dutifully reported them.

These articles portray a star concerned about cleaning up his image and presenting a picture of his private life that would make him acceptable even to genteel Americans. The potentially damaging clash between the American gentility and the "vulgar" persona created by Chaplin was partly averted when the man behind the persona began to present himself as a hard-working, serious, aspiring artist. But there was another significant element in this new view of Chaplin: the films

6. Chaplin's star image, blending person and persona, became firmly
defined in the Essanay period. This sketch appeared
in November 1915.

19

he made during the Essanay period, from early 1915 to early 1916. How did they portray Charlie in this period when the American gentility was attacking the vulgarity of Chaplin's films?

Romance and Pathos: The "Refining" of Charlie

The Essanay films contributed to this "new" star image. Chaplin made fourteen films at Essanay: the first in the company's Chicago studios; the next five in G. M. Anderson's ill-equipped Niles studios, near San Francisco; and the remainder in Hollywood. The first seven were released within three months; thereafter, Chaplin slowed his work pace and made about one film a month. Although no neat progression from film to film is apparent, Chaplin clearly did try out new ideas, some of which broadened the appeal of his films, during this period.

At first, however, Chaplin seemed to be repeating himself. As Theodore Huff points out, a number of the Essanays resemble the Keystones. *A Night Out* treats the comic misadventures of two drunks and is in much the same vein as *The Rounders*. *In the Park* and *By the Sea* both show the flirtatious and slightly lecherous Charlie being chased by a policeman, as did a number of the Keystone films, including *Twenty Minutes of Love*. *The Champion* is a boxing story similar to that in *The Knockout*, though *The Champion* was more successful at the box office, while both *Work* and *Shanghaied* continue the slapstick comedy prominent in Keystone movies. Reaching back even earlier than the Keystone films, *A Night in the Show* draws from an old Karno sketch entitled, "A Night in an English Music Hall."

Despite these continuities, Chaplin also changed during the Essanay period. The most significant alteration was in the portrayal of Charlie's relationships with the heroines of the films. During the Keystone period, Charlie was most often at odds with women, at least in part because of the feisty screen persona of Mabel Normand, who often appeared opposite Chaplin. A fairly typical example is *Getting Acquainted*, in which Charlie, unhappily married to a demanding wife, flirts with the wife of another man until a policeman breaks up the affair.

Beginning with his second Essanay film, however, Chaplin was paired with a new actress, Edna Purviance, who was to remain his leading lady through his first United Artists film, *A Woman of Paris* (1923). For several reasons, the heroines in Chaplin's films began to change, as did Charlie's relationships with them. First, Purviance's appearance and demeanor—more youthful, passive, rounded, delicate, and innocent than Normand's—prompted a shift toward a gentler interaction between Charlie and the heroine. Second, Chaplin and Purviance themselves began to develop a relationship outside of work almost immediately after she began to act in his films. Chaplin tells us in his autobiography that after they had moved to Los Angeles (immediately after making *The Tramp*), they dined nearly every night at the Los Angeles Athletic Club, where Chaplin had rented an apartment (MA, p. 204). As would often happen during his career, Chaplin's feelings for other people worked themselves into the characterizations and narratives of his films. Third, Chaplin's awareness of criticism from genteel quarters also encouraged him to think about altering his films to broaden their appeal; one way to accomplish this was to idealize the heroine and involve Charlie in a romance with her. Fourth, the switch from one- to two-reel films gave Chaplin the opportunity to develop Charlie's relationship with another character more fully. Finally, as film historians have shown, signifying practices in the film industry were changing. In the movement from primitive to classical Hollywood in the early 1910s, the goals and desires of central characters began to structure film narratives. One of the most common of these desires was for a romantic relationship.[27]

The shift in Chaplin's portrayal of women and of Charlie during the Essanay period occurred gradually. In several of the early Essanay films, the portrayal of women is indistinguishable from that in the Keystones. Women are either objects of Charlie's lust, targets of his antics, or inconsequential to the narrative. In *A Night Out*, for example, Edna's husband discovers her in bed with a drunken, sleeping Charlie. Though Charlie does give Edna a discreet kiss at the end of *The Champion*, her role is not important in the film. Charlie's involvement with women in both *In the Park* and *By the Sea* consists almost entirely of his attempts to pursue the wives or sweethearts of other men. And Edna's part as the maid in *Work* is relatively unimportant. In these films, Charlie is often as irreverent and "vulgar" as he was at Keystone. *Variety*'s review of *Work*, Chaplin's eighth Essanay, was similar to the kind of criticism he often received in his Keystone days: "The Essanay release of the Charlie Chaplin picture for this week is *Work* in two reels. It is the usual Chaplin work of late, mussy, messy and dirty." Charging that "the Censor Board is passing matter in the Chaplin films that could not possibly get by in other pictures," the reviewer joined the genteel chorus of Chaplin critics.[28]

By the time *Work* was released, however, Chaplin had already begun displaying an emergent gentility and greater attention to characterization in his work, although sometimes these were only brief moments in otherwise knockabout films. In *A Jitney Elopement*, for example, Chaplin used an iris out (a circular lab effect that closes down to emphasize a detail) when Charlie sniffs a flower under Edna's window, just after we learn that Edna is being made to marry someone else against her wishes. The use of the flower and the attempt at pathos both foreshadowed aspects of Chaplin's work that would recur often, most notably in the final shots of *City Lights*. The moment provided one of the first examples of Charlie's stretching to do something different and more serious in his work, though it was not at all sustained in this particular film.

Chaplin's next film, *The Tramp*, concentrated more on trying to achieve pathos. It, along with *The Bank*, represented Chaplin's most careful attempts to move in directions that would make his films more acceptable to genteel audiences. The two films share several elements. First, Charlie still exhibits some of the cruelty and "vulgarity" he had become known for during the Keystone period, usually while working with other men. Second, Charlie becomes romantically attracted to the character played by Edna Purviance. Third, after Charlie's feelings become known, the audience learns that Edna already has a suitor—larger, more handsome, or of a higher social class than Charlie. Fourth, Charlie becomes caught between social groups and opts to side with Edna. Finally, Charlie's hopes are dashed when he learns that his relationship with Edna will not succeed, and he thus evokes pathos.

The sympathy both films elicit, as well as the romanticizing of women in them, gives them a more gentle quality, more breadth of feeling, than the Keystone films. Largely because of this shifting treatment of women and Charlie's relationship to them, Chaplin's films began to appeal to a broader audience.

Why was this so? The appeal stemmed in part from a portrayal of the underside of romantic relationships in a patriarchal society. If we use Janice Radway's definition of patriarchy as "a social system where women are constituted only in and by their relationships with more powerful men," Chaplin's tales of Charlie's pure and unrequited love for a woman take on added significance. Some men in his audience could identify and empathize with his *failures* in love: in a society that was becoming increasingly bureaucratized and hierarchical, losing a woman to a man of higher status or wealth was not an uncommon experience for men. Similarly, women could identify with Charlie's tenderness toward his beloved, even his renunciation. Radway has recently found through interviews with female readers of romance novels that tenderness is among the masculine qualities they prize most.[29]

22

Charlie's reticence and complete devotion once he falls in love project tenderness at the start of the relationship but prove heartrending when he realizes he must renounce his love. Although in later films Chaplin handles his romantic relationships and pathos more effectively, it is important to reiterate here that Chaplin's romances increased his appeal to men who had been rejected in love because of inadequate wealth, prestige, or power; to women who admired his tender and nurturing spirit; and to viewers with genteel sensibilities for whom the romance helped to negate the "vulgarity" that worried them.

In addition to romance and pathos, *The Tramp* and *The Bank* contain yet another similarity that reinforced a value dear to the Genteel Tradition. In both films Charlie feels deeply discouraged but shakes off that discouragement with an energetic resilience. The final shots of both show Charlie walking in long shot away from the camera, which emphasizes the depth of the frame and Charlie's isolation; he then springs forward with a sprightly step, straightening and walking off as if renewed. Though it is difficult to describe the movement adequately, its effect is clear: Charlie will not let his disappointment overwhelm him. He will move on with as much vitality and inventiveness as before, accepting a contingent universe in which suffering is a part of life. This determination to go on in spite of the odds, in spite of travail and disappointment, was a cardinal value of the Genteel Tradition. Even if Charlie did not always act with propriety, this quality endeared him to respectable audiences as much as did any other.

Thus, elements of Chaplin's films during the Essanay period made them more palatable to his genteel opposition. The films show a learning filmmaker cautiously moving in directions that deepened his work and broadened its audience appeal. Chaplin seems to have been conscious of the new directions he was taking and concerned about whether the experiment was working. When Charles McGuirk left Chaplin after a day on the set, Chaplin called after him: "Say, did you see *The Tramp*? I know I took an awful chance. But did it get across?"[30] For an increasing number of viewers, it did.

Chaplin also showed an increasing tendency to include other "serious" elements in these films, the most prominent of which was a clear depiction of class conflict and difference. In *Work* the class differences between Charlie and Edna on the one hand and the owners of the home on the other are particulary clear, just as in *The Bank*. Charlie and his janitor friend stand in contrast to the bank owners and other wealthy bank patrons. *Police*, the final Essanay film, contains an interesting satire on reformers: in it, a do-gooder tries to move Charlie toward righteousness and ends up stealing his watch. The same film interestingly shows Charlie caught between the law and the lawless, as he would be again in later films, including *The Pilgrim* and *Modern Times*. John McCabe tells us that during the final months of his Essanay contract Chaplin began working on a film called *Life* (never finished) that would draw on his own painful childhood experiences and "show the tragicomic world of flophouses, grimy alleys, and living 'on the beg.' "[31]

By the end of the Essanay period Chaplin's star image was composed of the softening, more romantic Charlie and the serious, hardworking, ambitious, and modest young filmmaker who aspired to high art. A new, more serious Chaplin was emerging, one who asked film writer Terry Ramsaye to refer to him as Charles, not Charlie.[32] The young music-hall comedian had been vaulted to fame in Hollywood. He also had faced the genteel moralists of America and had begun to make films that, in certain ways, were more palatable to them. But his Essanay days were approaching an end, and new challenges, both aesthetic and cultural, were to confront him as he moved to a new studio and America moved toward more active involvement in World War I.

2

The Perils of Popularity

Chaplin's Star Image in the
Mutual Period

On the evening of 20 February 1916 Chaplin, visiting New York for contract negotiations after fulfilling his Essanay contract, attended a benefit concert at the New York Hippodrome. Asked to appear on the stage and direct a Sousa march, he agreed. Though his performance initially received only perfunctory applause, when he briefly imitated Charlie's walk on the third curtain call, the audience erupted. This reaffirmation of his stardom could not have hurt Chaplin as he entered serious negotiations with John R. Freuler of the Mutual Film Corporation. Reaching an agreement on the 25th, the two parties signed the staggering contract on February 27. It required Chaplin to make twelve comic films. In return, Chaplin would receive $10,000 per week and a $150,000 bonus for signing.[1] Remembering the atmosphere of those days in his autobiography, Chaplin wrote: "Like an avalanche, money and success came with increasing momentum; it was all bewildering, frightening—but wonderful" (MA, p. 174).

About this same time Chaplin unknowingly became involved in the first of a series of autobiographical books that would eventually contribute to his star image. Nearly a year earlier, during the Chaplinitis craze, Rose Wilder Lane of the *San Francisco Bulletin* had interviewed him for a series of biographical articles. The pieces, padded with colorful but invented details, subsequently appeared in the *Bulletin*, and by July 1916 Bobbs-Merrill Publishers wired Chaplin for pictures to supplement a book about his life, a reprint of Lane's series, to be titled *Charlie Chaplin's Own Story*.

The book contained, among other details, highly unflattering pictures of Chaplin's father and some early Chaplin employers. Consequently, Chaplin's lawyer, Nathan Burkan, began proceedings to prevent publication. The publisher countered by offering Chaplin authorship, with "editorial assistance" by Lane, as well as 5 percent of the sales price. When Chaplin continued to refuse, Lane wrote Chaplin that the "publicity value of the book" was very high, but all efforts to persuade him were fruitless. Although a few advance copies of the book did leak out, by December 1916 Bobbs-Merrill agreed that the book would not be sold without Chaplin's approval. This never came, and therefore Chaplin's first "autobiography" never saw the light of day or significantly affected his star image.[2]

Before this controversy, however, Chaplin began at Mutual, and released his first comedy in the middle of May. By October 1917 his twelfth film, *The Adventurer*, was finished. The eighteen-month period was a remarkably prolific and creative one for Chaplin. He had both the time and the creative independence to make films as he wished, and it paid off. Some critics look back on this as Chaplin's most successful period—Theodore Huff calls 1916–1917 "Chaplin's most fertile years, his most sustained creative period"—and Chaplin himself remembered the Mutual years as "the happiest period of my career."[3]

Nevertheless, from the time he signed his huge Mutual contract, Chaplin generated some resentment, much of which revolved around questions of high salary and worth, in the popular press. Granted, the American success ethic presumes that the talented rise to the top and deserve the rewards they win, and the rise of movie stars to the top has been framed in terms of the traditional American success story from the beginning of the star system. But $670,000? Some were skeptical, much as today some question the salaries paid to top professional athletes.

This general resentment over huge salaries for movie stars was reflected in Alfred A. Cohn's article in *Photoplay*, which, though published the month after Chaplin signed his Mutual contract, seems to have been written before Chaplin signed with Mutual.[4] Titled "What They Really Get—NOW," the piece argued essentially that the star salaries were grossly inflated in an era of unemployment, concern about the instability threatened by the war in Europe, and other worrisome economic trends. Cohn mentions Chaplin specifically, and argues that the comedian's $175,000 earnings in 1916 were unreasonably high. If Cohn considered the Essanay salary exorbitant, what would he have thought about the Mutual agreement?

The attitude of another journalist (and probably of many of his readers) toward Chaplin's new salary appeared in the May 1916 issue of *Photoplay*. Titled "C. Chaplin: Millionaire-Elect," it compared statistics to inform readers about Chaplin's accumulating wealth. According to the essay, except for John Hayes Hammond, president of U.S. Steel, "Chaplin's salary is likely the biggest salary grabbed off by any public person outside of royalty."[5] Compared to the public sector, Chaplin's salary represented 17 percent of the total salaries paid to 96 senators and 435 representatives of the U.S. Congress, and 93 percent of the Senate's payroll alone. If the nine Supreme Court justices pooled their earnings, the combined total would amount to 19.5 percent of Chaplin's salary. The author's resentment is clear from the tone of the article; note the use of "grabbed off" instead of "earned" in the quotation above. But he also reflected a tension in American cultural values. If the talented rise to the top, and if, in a business like the movie industry, the star's films make a profit despite the huge salary paid out, isn't the star entitled to what he or she can earn in the marketplace? Such at least was the author's conclusion: though the size of the salary might seem "wildly extravagant," it did fall "into its proper relation in the scale of receipts and disbursements when the profits made out of Chaplin pictures [were] considered."

Chaplin seems about this time to have become more sensitive to the importance of good publicity. In July he told a reporter that "publicity is one of the most essential things in the career of a man, whatever his profession, whose popularity depends in no small way upon keeping himself before the public." It was the press, Chaplin continued, that sustained the "spark of interest" that the public has for the performer.[6] This concern about the importance of publicity helped keep Chaplin at the forefront of the public imagination after the signing of the Mutual contract, even though the faddishness, imitations, and commercialization of the Charlie persona waned compared to the heady days of mid-1915. As we shall see in subsequent chapters, Chaplin's attitude toward the press and his willingness to cultivate it varied considerably throughout his career. By 1953 he blamed much of his problematic situation on a hostile press and claimed it had always treated him badly. During the Mutual years, however, the facts suggest otherwise.

One of the most notable developments in Chaplin's star image in this period was the growing tendency in the press to treat Chaplin not just as a movie star and director but also as a serious artist, something highly unusual in the upstart, brash medium of motion pictures. The tendency, as we saw in Chapter 1, was established in the January 1916 article in *Motion Picture Magazine* by J. B. Hirsch, "The New Charlie Chaplin." But perhaps more important in helping Chaplin gain intellectual legitimacy was an article in the venerable *Harper's Weekly* by the prominent stage actress Minnie Maddern Fiske in May 1916.[7] Though Chaplin had begun to claim early on—partly to compensate for his lack of formal education—that he read the classics and was interested in the life of the mind, it was an important breakthrough for Chaplin's reputation to have an established artist praise him in a prominent national magazine, where serious critical attention was much more significant for his star image than yet another article in a movie fan magazine.

Fiske opened her brief essay by asserting that "a constantly increasing body of cultured, artistic people are beginning to regard . . . Charles Chaplin as an extraordinary artist, as well as a comic genius." The universal popularity of Chaplin's films, she said, required critics to account for the basis of his success. This could be located in "the old, familiar secret of inexhaustible imagination, governed by the unfailing precision of a perfect technique."

Significantly, Fiske challenged genteel critics (and many readers of *Harper's*, one suspects) over the issue of Chaplin's alleged "vulgarity." The point was moot, she argued. "Chaplin is vulgar," she admitted, but "there is vulgarity in the comedies of Aristophanes, and in those of Plautus and Terence and the Elizabethans, not excluding Shakespeare. Rabelais is vulgar, Fielding and Smollett and Swift are vulgar. . . . Vulgarity and distinguished art can exist together." And they did in Chaplin's work. Although Chaplin had to function within the trying context of an art still in its infancy, he had done well and would do better: "Those of us who believe that Charles Chaplin is essentially a great comic artist look forward to fine achievements. . . . [W]e are confident that he will attain the artistic stature to which it seems he is entitled." The praise was surely gratifying to Chaplin; he repaid it when, in his autobiography, he called the "ebullient, humorous and intelligent" Fiske one of the American actresses he most admired (MA, p. 261). Even more important for the growth of Chaplin's star image, the article informed the custodians of culture that Chaplin was a name worth taking into account in discussions of important American artists.

A similar defense of Chaplin appeared in another prestigious but more recently established journal of opinion, *New Republic*. When its first issue appeared in November 1914, it described itself as "A Journal of Opinion which seeks to meet the challenge of a new time." Politically liberal and culturally sympathetic to the attack on the Genteel Tradition in the arts, *New Republic* represented a younger and considerably different constituency than *Harper's*. Yet it, too, stamped its approval on Chaplin in Harvey O'Higgins's "Charlie Chaplin's Art," published in early 1917.[8] An American writing from Europe, O'Higgins noted that "Chaplin is as preeminent a favorite in Paris . . . as he is here." Chaplin's films, he argued, had "become more and more delicate and finished" than they had been in the early Keystone period. It is significant that he also defended Chaplin's art as a democratic art, much as cultural nationalists like Van Wyck Brooks, writing in the pages of the same magazine, were simultaneously calling for a revitalization of American literature and culture. To O'Higgins, Chaplin was "an example of how the best can be the most successful, of how a real talent can triumph over the most appalling limitations put upon its expression, and of how the popular eye can recognize such a talent without the aid of pundits of culture and even in spite of their anathemas" (all quotes p. 18). In writings like those of Fiske and O'Higgins, Chaplin began to establish a clientele among the American intelligentsia, a following that became more pronounced in the 1920s and that he sustained through much of his career.

The Further "Refining" of Charlie

When O'Higgins noted that Chaplin's films were becoming more "delicate and finished," he might also have added "more serious." During the Mutual period Chaplin continued to explore the more serious issues in his comedies that he had begun in such Essanay films as *The Bank* and *Police*, and in the unfinished *Life*. One Chaplin critic, Wes Gehring, has even argued that in the Mutual period one can discover "a consistent, viable political stance in Chaplin's work," which Gehring aligns with the American Progressive movement. To defend this thesis, he notes that in eleven of his twelve Mutual films Chaplin focused on five different issues important to the Progressives: "urban corruption; the plight of the urban poor; the idle rich . . . ; elitism; and alcohol." Although this argument is sometimes strained—as when a film like *One A.M.* is read as "a comic nightmare" and a "commentary on the misuse of alcohol"—it is clear that in his films Chaplin often represented class divisions or the squalid conditions of urban poverty that corresponded to the same reality in American society in his day. As Joris Ivens has observed, in some of Chaplin's films "the real feeling of human misery in filthy surroundings was completely communicated."[9]

Yet the Mutual films were by no means tracts. There is no consistent political thread weaving through their fabric, and though the Progressive issues Gehring mentions form a backdrop in the films, they are never the primary focus of narrative concern. The attempts of middle-class elites to instruct and control the behavior of the urban lower classes—efforts that are identified by American historians as a central strand of American Progressivism—are not central in the Chaplin Mutuals. Indeed, at times the middle-class reformers, like the preacher at the opening of *Easy Street*, are satirical targets rather than sympathetically treated figures.

I would argue that the Mutual films generally are unified by placing Charlie in a particular setting and creating comedy through his interactions with objects (like escalators or alarm clocks) and people (like those he waits on in *The Rink*) in the settings. Chaplin the director also continues in many of these films to develop romantic relationships between Charlie and Edna, though the endings do not always lead to Charlie's failure in love, as occurred in *The Bank*. To get a sense of Chaplin's achievements and handling of Charlie in this period, we can focus on three of the "serious" Mutual films: *The Vagabond*, *Easy Street*, and *The Immigrant*, the third, ninth, and eleventh of Chaplin's Mutuals. The three films have at least one thing in common: in each of the three Charlie and the characters played by Edna Purviance—a gypsy waif, a social worker, and a freshly arrived American immigrant—are united in the end.

In *The Vagabond*, Charlie plays an itinerant street musician who falls in love with the Edna character, who has been captured by a brutal gypsy (Eric Campbell). Though Charlie and Edna manage to escape midway through the film, the plot is complicated when a painter seeking inspiration "discovers" Edna as she walks through the woods and asks to paint her portrait. He does, and she begins to be attracted to the talented artist. Returning to the wagon, where Charlie has been fixing a meal, Edna showers all her attentions on the artist, a scene even more somber because of the elaborate and careful preparations Charlie has made as his way of showing his affection to Edna. The pangs of unrequited love are captured most effectively in a medium two-shot of Edna and Charlie that lasts about fourteen seconds—an unusually long take in the early Chaplin films. In it, as Edna on the right of the frame looks longingly after the departing artist, Charlie glances slowly back and forth between the artist and Edna's reaction. After the artist leaves to arrange for his portrait of Edna to be exhibited, Charlie pathetically and ineffectually tries to compete with his rival by sketching his own picture of her. The film moves toward its resolution by drawing on a plot device from nineteenth-century novels: Edna turns out to be the stolen child of a wealthy woman, who comes in a limousine to claim Edna after discovering her identity when the painting is displayed. Learning of the situation, Charlie politely gives a genteel handshake to Edna's mother, tenderly embraces Edna, and magnanimously shakes hands with the artist. The film appears to be heading toward an ending similar to *The Tramp* and *The Bank*: the car drives off, leaving Charlie alone. Facing the camera, he somberly leans against the wagon, then tries to move forward with his sprightly resilient walk. But he fails. Turning away, he drags himself back to the wagon and leans with his forehead on his forearm in the most moving shot of the film.

Where could Chaplin go from here? If Charlie's sheer will to overcome disappointment failed to work as it had worked in earlier films, how could the story end? Walter Kerr tells us that a sequence was originally planned in which Charlie committed suicide by jumping in a pond, but Chaplin realized that such a scene would never do.[10] Instead, Edna has a change of heart and orders the chauffeur to turn around. As Charlie sits on the wagon steps, head in hands, the car returns, Edna hustles Charlie into it, and everyone leaves together. Chaplin tempers the film's strong sense of isolation and the pain of rejection through the conventional, classical Hollywood closed ending.

The importance of the quest for romantic love in Chaplin's films from the Mutual period on cannot be minimized if we are to understand their immense and lasting popularity. Had Chaplin stayed within the framework of Keystone slapstick, he would never have survived in Hollywood as long as he did: either audiences would have tired of the persona or Chaplin would have exhausted the creative pantomimic spark he had honed in the British musical halls, or both. But by adding to comedy the element of romantic love, whether requited or not, Chaplin tapped deeply into one source of what has made narrative art popular for centuries.

Though feminist critics have persuasively argued that this myth of romantic love can be a powerful cultural tool to justify, manage, and perpetuate a patriarchal society, in Chaplin's films, romance functions somewhat differently. In general, Charlie's social class and physical strength are inferior to his male rivals. Neither a Heathcliff nor a Rhett Butler, Charlie never sweeps a woman off her feet with his appearance; he's tender and vulnerable. The relationship between Charlie and his heroine is therefore always tentative, not based on qualities traditionally associated with masculinity: strength, physical attractiveness, and wealth. If women are commonly dominated by men in the myth of romance, Charlie himself is also threatened by those same men, and moviegoers who have experienced some form of domination in their lives (this includes nearly all moviegoers), find the conflicts of romance depicted in Chaplin's films very real indeed. The question of how romance functions in the Chaplin films will recur, but suffice it to say here that by the time Chaplin made *The Vagabond*, he was already working creatively within the tradition of romance and adapting it to his own aesthetic uses.[11]

The importance of romance in Chaplin's Mutual films can also be seen by looking briefly at *Easy Street* and *The Immigrant*. These two films also demonstrate that it is nearly impossible to find a consistent political and social perspective in the Chaplin Mutual films. In *Easy Street* Charlie falls in love with a social reformer working at an urban mission; to win her approval he becomes a policeman and helps rid a decrepit neighborhood of a domineering bully. After saving the reformer from a drug fiend, Charlie ends up winning her affections and establishing himself as a respected and somewhat genteel authority figure in the community—the neighborhood cop. In contrast to the position of authority he earned in *Easy Street*, Charlie, like Edna, is a jobless newcomer arriving in America in *The Immigrant*. This film includes a scene in a restaurant that is extremely funny, partly because neither Charlie nor Edna has the money to pay for the food they have ordered. Only an artist, who admires Edna's beauty and offers her money to pose, saves them from a dire fate. At the end of this film, Charlie is pulling Edna into the office of a justice of the peace to get married, despite their tenuous financial condition. Though the couple achieved a kind of respectable gentility at the end of *Easy Street* and still remains in urban poverty at the close of *The Immigrant*, the romance between Charlie and Edna is a constant in the two films, as are a somber social background and Charlie's skill at generating humor through his interactions with objects and people. The Mutual period is clearly a maturing and creative one for Chaplin.

That maturation process reached its first flowering in *A Dog's Life*, Chaplin's first film for First National Exhibitors Circuit, the company he signed with after completing his Mutual contract. Chaplin had agreed upon terms with First National on 17 June 1917, amid another splash of publicity. Even though Mutual had offered Chaplin a million dollars to make twelve more comedies, Chaplin resisted, commissioning his brother Sydney to enter into negotiations with the newly formed First National, headed by J. D. Williams. First National was composed of a group of prominent theater owners in larger cities who wanted to combat the growing influence of producer Adolph Zukor. They planned to do so by signing up popular stars who would make films that First National could distribute. They offered Chaplin a million dollars, plus a bonus of $75,000 upon signing, to make eight comedies, with Chaplin himself bearing the production costs. First National would pay Chaplin $125,000 as he began each comedy; if the comedy ended up longer than two reels, Chaplin would receive $15,000 for each additional reel after the film was completed. Though the contract was not as lucrative as his Mutual contract, it offered

Chaplin more creative control over the films he made and more time to make them than he had experienced at Mutual.

The whole signing was pervaded by a businesslike aura. General Manager Williams of First National told reporters about his company's expectations: "The whole idea of the contract is to do away with quantity and substitute quality. Chaplin has pledged himself to establish a reputation for perfect pictures. He fully realizes that the production of unsatisfactory comedies at this time would cost him anywhere from a quarter million to a half million dollars on his next contract."[12] But, the press reported, Chaplin had no intention of making films that lost money. As he told an interviewer a few months earlier, making movies was a tremendous responsibility: "I get depressed thinking of it. You see, it's like this. I should hate to think that my pictures weren't making money for the firm releasing them. My pride couldn't stand that."[13]

Surely Chaplin held up his end of the bargain with *A Dog's Life*. Released in April 1918, it was a three-reel film, about 50 percent longer than any of his Mutuals, and though it might be fair to call it his most ambitious offering to that time, it continued developing some of the characteristics of the "serious" Mutuals discussed above. Like a number of the Mutuals, its background was one of urban poverty. It, too, presented a romance between Charlie and Edna. But it also was more self-conscious, with a more sophisticated thematic and structural unity. In his autobiography Chaplin recalled that with *A Dog's Life* he "was beginning to think of comedy in a structural sense" and that the central motif that unified his structure was "paralleling the life of a dog with that of a tramp" (MA, p. 209). Indeed, the title is perfectly appropriate, for it plays on the clichéd metaphor—"it's a dog's life"— which suggests how difficult human existence is. The film makes the metaphor concrete by showing the travails of Charlie and a dog named Scraps.[14]

From the film's opening Chaplin uses visual and narrative parallels to connect Charlie and Scraps. When we first see Charlie, he is lying asleep outdoors against a fence, his prone body near the bottom of the frame, head facing left. The first shot of Scraps is graphically almost identical: he, too, is asleep outdoors, curled in a pail at the lower part of the frame, his head also facing left. At the beginning of the film Charlie is disturbed by a policeman who chases him away; the same policeman frightens Scraps a few moments later. After Charlie awakens, he wanders into an employment agency and is taken advantage of by other job seekers; when Scraps starts his day, a pack of dogs attacks him. Following these parallels, Charlie and Scraps meet as

Charlie saves Scraps from the pack, a gesture Scraps returns later in the film by digging up a wallet filled with money for Charlie.

If Charlie and Scraps are living a dog's life, so is Edna. Consistent with the film's focus, Edna finds herself thrust into a system of exploitation—the sexual exploitation of a dance hall. Edna first appears singing a slow and melancholy song that contrasts starkly to the frenetic dances of the other performers. After the song, the hall owner orders her to flirt with the male customers and do whatever is necessary to make him some money. When she refuses, she's fired—out on the streets like Charlie. Fortunately, Charlie has been enriched by Scraps's discovery of the wallet just before Edna is let go, and he befriends her with the same tenderness and gentle affection that he had shown in some of his earlier films and that he would show again in most of the later Charlie features. And as with *The Vagabond*, *The Immigrant*, and *Easy Street*, Charlie and Edna are united at the end. The plot device of the discovered money enables Charlie, Edna, and Scraps to settle down on a little farm, their escape from the dog's life of urban poverty.

An important Chaplin film, *A Dog's Life* reiterated several tendencies evident in the Mutual films, particularly the romance between Charlie and Edna, and the "serious" theme underlying the comedy. It solidified the persona of the increasingly complex Charlie. It reinforced the tendency of the press to present Chaplin as a serious artist. And it pointed forward to later Chaplin films in two particularly significant ways. The relationship between Charlie and Scraps looks almost like a trial run of the one between Charlie and the kid in *The Kid* (1920). And the ending of the film, in which a brightly lit rural setting provides an oasis in the desert of urban difficulties, anticipates a number of films in which a pastoral setting or a "folk" world offers some characters a vision of hope and serenity in contrast to the harsh urban world. This pastoral world is especially noticeable at the ending of *A Woman of Paris*, in the Austerlich countryside in *The Great Dictator*, and in Henri Verdoux's country home in *Monsieur Verdoux*, but one can also detect it in a different form in the blind girl's apartment in *City Lights* and in the daydream shared by Charlie and the gamin in *Modern Times*. This tendency to juxtapose two sets of values in the films would by the 1940s profoundly affect Chaplin's star image, because the contrasts began to imply distinct social and political commitments. For the time being, however, the creative freedom offered by the First National contract enabled Chaplin to move toward greater flexibility and complexity in his films. With *A Dog's Life* he moved forward confidently in developing his art and created films that ensured the continuity and growth of his star image.

Chaplin the "Slacker"?

Despite these shifts in his films, however, Chaplin's reputation continued to face challenges. Though he seemed to be overcoming charges of vulgarity and greediness as he made his First National films, another began to rear its head: the question of Chaplin's military status during World War I. When the war broke out in Europe in August 1914, Chaplin was midway through his first year at Keystone, and the conflict seemed distant to him, as it did to most Americans. He was not yet particularly well known, and American neutrality was strongly established. Few Americans were concerned about the relationship between a British movie actor and his country far across the ocean.

But that situation changed as Chaplin's fame grew, as the United States moved away from neutrality, and as the movie industry's role in the war effort entered public debate. In tracing how and when the country moved from neutrality to involvement, one might note that after the war broke out in Europe, the United States imported a number of German films, like *Behind German Lines* and *The German Side of the War*, presenting the German perspective on the war; such films were shown in American theaters as late as 1916. Beginning with the sinking of the British liner *Lusitania* in May 1915, however, tolerance for such German films—indeed for Germany itself—diminished. Despite official government disapproval, films urging preparedness or even celebrating the British war effort began to appear. For example, *The Battle Cry of Peace* (1915), director J. Stuart Blackton later recalled, "was propaganda for the United States to enter the war. . . . It was against the administration because at that time Mr. Wilson was arguing for neutrality and peace." The shift from a neutralist or pacifist attitude to a pro-involvement view developed inexorably in America between 1915 and April 1917, when the United States entered the war. By that time, in the words of one film historian, the transition "to out-and-out pro-war passion was already complete."[15]

After America joined the Allies, government legislation helped suppress pacifism and encourage pro-war sentiment. The Espionage Act of 15 June 1917 set maximum fines of $10,000 and twenty years' imprisonment for anyone who interfered with the draft or encouraged disloyalty. The Espionage Act of May 1918 extended these penalties to cover a wide variety of activities, including obstructing the sale of

35

U.S. bonds or speaking critically about the government, Constitution, or flag of the United States.

Simultaneously, the government sought to build morale through the Committee on Public Information, headed by George Creel. Established by an act of Congress in May 1917, it sought through various means, including movies, to influence public opinion in favor of the American war effort, both at home and abroad.[16]

Within this context, it is not surprising that Chaplin's attitude toward the war and his military status became an issue. As a prominent movie star from 1915 on and as a young British male eligible for the draft, Chaplin inevitably drew the attention of some citizens. As early as his Keystone days, Chaplin began to be criticized in England for not being in uniform and fighting for his country. In addition to receiving threatening letters, some enclosing white feathers (a symbol of "slackers" during World War I), Chaplin was also the target of occasional public attacks. In an effort to defuse the antagonism he had aroused, Chaplin contributed money to the British cause.

When it became known that his 1916 Mutual contract contained a clause that forbade him from leaving the United States without company permission, however, Chaplin received another barrage of criticism from the British press.[17] One newspaper account reported in June 1916 that signs were beginning to appear at some British movie theaters reading, "No Chaplin Here," protesting Chaplin's lack of involvement in the British war effort.[18]

After America entered the war, publicity about and criticism of Chaplin's nonparticipation became more widespread in the United States. Theodore Huff writes that Chaplin received thousands of letters at his studio, many of them abusive, demanding that he enlist. *Variety* reported two months after the U.S. entry that not only was Chaplin being called a "slacker" by his fellow citizens but he was also being observed by U.S. government officials who had been told that Chaplin had refused a British War Office demand that he return to England. The article reported that the Secret Service was keeping Chaplin under surveillance because he had reportedly told someone about plans to move to South America, bringing along his assets in gold.[19]

Such public charges, regardless of their veracity, were clearly a threat to Chaplin's star image. Partly to stem the tide, Chaplin's studio released a press announcement saying that Chaplin had registered for the selective service draft in Los Angeles on June 5. According to stories, he actually visited the recruiting station but was rejected for being underweight.[20]

Not everyone attacked Chaplin for failing to enlist. In fact, some quoted in the press felt that Chaplin would be much more useful to the war effort making movies. In July 1917 the *New York Telegraph* reported on an article in a British magazine that demanded Chaplin join up, thus demonstrating his pride in his British origins. The reporter for the *Telegraph* objected: Wasn't Chaplin able to communicate to many more people by making movies or even by making public appearances in support of the British cause than by fighting in the trenches?[21] Many soldiers agreed with him. A wounded British officer told an American audience in 1918 that Chaplin "made us laugh when it often seemed that nothing else could. And I for one hope that the authorities will realize he is of far greater value as a gloom chaser than as a fighter." After hearing such testimony from many sources, Chaplin used the same argument when he wrote to a British correspondent early in 1918: "I only wish that I could join the English army and fight for my mother country. But I have received so many letters from soldiers at the front, as well as civilians, asking me to continue making pictures that I have come to the conclusion that my work lies here in Los Angeles. At the same time, if any country thinks it needs me in the trenches more than soldiers need my pictures, I am ready to go."[22]

Chaplin was never drafted, but his letter makes clear that he took seriously the questions about his involvement. Just as he and the press had earlier "cleaned up" his image when confronted by genteel critics, here he used the press to help manage the war controversy.

If the press helped Chaplin avoid the image of slacker, it also helped him establish the image of patriot. In early 1918 the U.S. government announced the third Liberty Loan Drive for April and May, aimed at raising $3 billion to support the war effort. Chaplin was invited to join a large group of speakers, including several movie stars, who would encourage groups gathered in large cities to purchase bonds. He agreed and made a number of appearances in the Northeast and the South in April.

As might be expected, his appearances drew huge crowds and raised large amounts of money; his participation also solidified and even enhanced his star image. He began in Washington, D.C., to help open the drive. On the first anniversary of America's entry into the war, April 6, he appeared with Douglas Fairbanks, Mary Pickford, and Marie Dressler, parading down Pennsylvania Avenue before huge crowds, after which each star was assigned to a large booth on the White House ellipse to take Liberty Loan subscriptions. The newspapers said the next day that Chaplin and Fairbanks had to run through the crowds to get to their booths after the parade. Mary Pickford was delayed 45 minutes trying to get to hers. Over $3 million in Liberty bonds were reported sold.[23]

From Washington Chaplin moved to New York, perhaps his most spectacular appearance on the tour. The New York rally took place at noon on April 8, on the steps of the U.S. Sub-Treasury Building, at the corner of Broad and Wall streets, in the center of the financial district. At least 20,000 people gathered to see Chaplin and Fairbanks. One newspaper reported Chaplin's brief speech. "Now listen, I have never made a speech before in my life," Chaplin began to a cheering and laughing crowd,

> but I believe I can make one now. You people out there—I want you to forget all about percentages in this third Liberty Loan. Human life is at stake and no one ought to worry about what rate of interest the bonds are going to bring or what he can make by purchasing them. Money is needed—money to support the great army and navy of Uncle Sam. This very minute the Germans occupy a position of advantage, and we have to get the dollars. It ought to go over so that we can drive that old devil, the Kaiser, out of France.

Fairbanks followed with a brief speech, and the celebration concluded with Fairbanks lifting Chaplin aloft, who in turn raised a derby into the air (see Figure 7). The audience loved it.[24]

After New York Chaplin took a southern swing while Fairbanks and Pickford took a northern route. On the tour Chaplin spoke to large crowds in Richmond, Virginia; Lexington, Kentucky; Macon and Atlanta, Georgia; Nashville and Memphis, Tennessee; and finally New Orleans. The pattern was nearly the same everywhere: Chaplin would be met by large crowds at the train station. He would appear at large auditoriums (Atlanta and Nashville) or even outdoors in parks (Memphis and New Orleans) to give brief impassioned speeches about buying bonds to support the war. Finally, to help entertain the audiences and hasten the pace of selling, he would perform some "Charlie antics."

According to the prominently placed newspaper accounts, Chaplin was a hit with the crowds and successful as a bond seller. An Atlanta reporter judged Chaplin's April 17 speech as "excellent and effective," then described the pandemonium that broke loose when Chaplin did his Charlie walk.[25] In Nashville Chaplin filled Ryman Auditorium on April 18; thousands had to be turned away. After appearing at Overton Park in Memphis on a cold, damp day, Chaplin was ordered to bed by a doctor.[26] He soon went on to New Orleans where, Huff records, a former government official demanded to be listed above the "vulgar" movie comedian on posters. He was, and drew an audience of 400; Chaplin drew 40,000.[27] By April 30 Chaplin was back in New York, leading a rally at City Hall Park that raised well over $100,000, and then concluded his efforts with a brief address at the Astor Hotel on May 1. By May 3 he was on his way back to California after the long and exhausting tour.[28]

Besides supporting the war effort through the Liberty Loan tour, Chaplin also bought $350,000 worth of Liberty bonds during the first three drives and made two films about the war.[29] The first, titled *The Bond* and sponsored by the Liberty Loan Committee, is a brief film encouraging people to buy bonds. It is an allegory showing how the bonds of marriage, love, and friendship are capable of creating a powerful mallet strong enough to knock out the Kaiser. The Liberty Loan Committee distributed it without charge throughout the country.

More substantial was *Shoulder Arms*, Chaplin's second film for First National and one of the most remembered American entertainment films dealing with World War I. The film opens in boot camp, where Charlie, in uniform, tries to adapt himself to military discipline and training, not always successfully. Charlie moves to the trenches, then volunteers for a special mission that enables him to meet Edna, playing a French peasant girl who embodies the fate of "poor France." Together they concoct a scheme and capture a large group of German soldiers—or so it seems. Chaplin ends the film as he ended *The Bank*: Charlie wakes from his dreams of accomplishment. All the action and comedy had taken place in his mind as he slept after an exhausting day in boot camp.

In some ways *Shoulder Arms* was a departure for Chaplin. It was the longest movie he had directed up to that time, and it contained more action, particularly in the final reel, than was common for a Chaplin film. In addition, the film is interesting for the way it places Charlie in a typical war situation. Unlike many of the Hollywood films of the day, it did not portray the Germans as "vicious Huns" or go out of its way to stir up hatred. The German soldiers are for the most part nonentities, though one leader is a comic butt because of his tiny stature and authoritarian treatment of his troops, and another lustful leader threatens Edna. Chaplin's aim was rather to use comedy and a gentle tenderness to appeal to his audience. Incidents in the boot camp, as when Charlie tries to march and handle a rifle, and in the trenches, as when he launches a Limburger cheese grenade or floats in the flooded dugout bedroom, provide good examples of Chaplin's comic imagination at work. The most poignant scene comes when Charlie, after

7. Chaplin and Fairbanks on Wall Street during
Liberty Loan Drive, April 1918.

receiving no mail during mail call, looks over the shoulder of another soldier reading his mail. Though we don't see the contents of the letter, we know what they are by watching the shifting emotions at play on Charlie's face as he reads along. This is a shot that surely touched soldiers abroad and their loved ones at home as they sought a few moments of respite from the strain of the war.

It is unlikely, however, that the film had much direct effect on soldier morale, because it was not completed until late October 1918, only a couple of weeks before the Armistice was signed. Nevertheless, Chaplin's contribution to the war effort was significant: not only did he lend his celebrity status and his energies toward raising large amounts of money (and indeed contributing sizable sums of his own), but he also through this and earlier films provided pleasure and reminders of home for soldiers abroad who saw them. Blackton, writing for *Photoplay* in June 1918, described Chaplin's effect on the soldiers.

40

"It was my impression," Blackton wrote concerning a visit to the trenches, "that the buoyancy of the American soldier even during the dark days of the war was in large part due to the diverting influence of the motion picture." The most important and popular of the diversions, he added, were the films of Charlie Chaplin.[30] Many would doubtless have agreed with critic Julian Johnson's assessment that "in a shrapnel-smashed world, Mr. Chaplin is today the greatest single lightener of the iron burden" wrought by the war.[31]

In response to the significant social challenge to his popularity posed by the issue of his war involvement, Chaplin supported the dominant attitudes in American society of his day, thus sustaining and even enhancing his star image. Though in his autobiography he remembers the war as a time of "barbarism" in which a "religion of war" brought on "an avalanche of mad destruction and brutal slaughter," his behavior in 1918 was suitable, even exemplary, to the vast majority of Americans who supported the war effort (MA, pp. 213, 218). The ultimate short-term result added the characteristic of patriotism to the Chaplin star image. In later years, when his conflicts with certain pockets of the American public and press led him to be branded as a dangerous threat to the country, few remembered these days of Chaplin's contributions to the U.S. war effort. For the time being, however, the image of Chaplin as slacker had been turned aside.

The First Marriage and Divorce

The huge crowds Chaplin drew during the Liberty Loan tour reaffirmed his status as a leading movie star. That stardom, as the fan magazines were fond of pointing out, made the young, handsome Chaplin one of the country's most eligible bachelors. Up to this point, Chaplin's relationships with women had not played a large part in the public perception of his star image. Between 1918 and 1920, however, that changed. In relatively rapid succession the twenty-nine-year-old Chaplin met a seventeen-year-old movie actress, married her after learning of her pregnancy, and divorced her. The first of Chaplin's four marriages and three divorces, this experience caused Chaplin personal pain and created another distressing public conflict for him, making 1919 and 1920 two of the most trying years—both privately and professionally—in his young life.

Because Chaplin's relationships with women increasingly came to affect his star image, it will be useful to say a few words about the basis of his attitudes toward women. Chaplin's attraction to particularly young women and his unstable relationships with the first two women he married seems rooted in his earlier personal experience. Without being unduly psychological, one might note that Chaplin's parents separated when he was very young, partly due to his father's alcoholism. Chaplin and his half brother Sydney remained with their mother for a time but were forced into the Lambeth workhouse in 1896 when their mother became unable to support them. David Auerbach has reasonably suggested that the vulnerable seven-year-old Chaplin felt betrayed by his mother, deprived of her love and support when he needed it most. At the same time he came to feel some guilt about being unable to help her then or in the subsequent decade, when she was in and out of sanitariums. Auerbach hypothesizes that this ambivalence led to Chaplin's tendency to view women in two opposite ways: as ideal, romantic young beauties or as threatening viragos.[32] In his relationships with women, he was irresistibly drawn to those who fit his conception of the former.

This attraction was solidified in his mind through his relationship with Hetty Kelly, which he dwells on at some length in his autobiography. Chaplin was nineteen and a relatively successful music-hall comedian in England when he met Kelly, a fifteen-year-old dancer in a troupe appearing on the same bill as Chaplin. Captivated by her youthful beauty, Chaplin first arranged to meet her on a Sunday afternoon. Both shy, they went for strolls several times, but when Chaplin impulsively mentioned marriage, Kelly drew back and they stopped seeing one another. Chaplin later wrote that "the episode was but a childish infatuation to her, but to me it was the beginning of a spiritual development, a reaching out for beauty." In another context, he added: "Although I had met her but five times . . . that brief encounter affected me for a long time."[33]

Chaplin seems never to have gotten over Kelly. When he was in New York for the signing of his Mutual contract, after experiencing for the first time the attentions of rabid movie fans on his train trip from California, he learned that Kelly was in New York visiting a friend (in the intervening years she had married a wealthy American). Feeling a paradoxical loneliness amid all the attention, Chaplin stole away from his hotel and walked to the building where she was staying, too shy to call but hoping he would meet her going into or coming out of the building. He didn't.

Later, on his trip to London in 1921, he hoped he would be able to see her but was shocked to learn that she had died. The one meeting he had really desired on the trip was denied him.[34] This experience of unrequited love seems to have shaped an image of the ideal woman—young, beautiful, almost ethereal—in Chaplin's mind, which drew him to women whose appearance matched it yet made it impossible for any woman to live up to his demands and expectations.

Such, at least, was the pattern played out in Chaplin's relationship with young Mildred Harris, a movie actress whom Chaplin had first met at a party given by Samuel Goldwyn in mid-1918. Harris was only seventeen at the time, already an experienced movie actress, having appeared in films since 1914. As Chaplin tells it, she pursued him, asking for a ride home as he prepared to leave the party. They began to see one another—"dinners, dances, moonlit nights and ocean drives"—and in October Harris told Chaplin she believed she was pregnant. On the 23rd of that month they were married in a quiet ceremony in Los Angeles.[35]

The marriage was probably doomed from the start. Chaplin remembers feeling ambivalent about the entire situation. On the one hand he felt that the "union had no vital basis"; on the other, "now that I was married I wanted to be and wanted the marriage to be a success." But for a number of reasons the relationship never had a chance. Chaplin became upset about a contract Harris signed with Louis B. Mayer, and the couple argued about her career. (Though Chaplin claimed that she didn't obtain favorable terms in the contract, he may also have felt threatened by a working spouse.) And Chaplin, perceiving himself as something of an intellectual, felt that she was too simple for him. Perhaps most damaging to the relationship was the death of their child in July 1919; it lived only three days. In Chaplin's words, this loss "began the withering of our marriage" (MA, pp. 237–39). By the fall of 1919 the couple had separated, Chaplin moving back into the Los Angeles Athletic Club.

Despite the separation the Chaplins—Mildred at least—tried to keep up appearances. In January 1920 she told a newspaper reporter that "I intend to have a happy home and realize that the trouble with most love affairs after marriage is that the romance dies out and is supplanted by commonplace things. I am determined that this should never be."[36] But her hopes were in vain. In April the newspapers reported a fight between Chaplin and Mayer in a Los Angeles restaurant. Apparently Chaplin had taken offense when Mayer suggested that Chaplin's settlement offer to his wife was embarrassingly small. On August 3 the *New York Times* reported that Harris's lawyers had filed divorce papers for her on the basis of cruelty. The next day they printed a clarification. Harris, who was then visiting New York, had expressed surprise when she learned the papers had been filed. She also told reporters that the charges would be "mental cruelty" and denied any reports that Chaplin had been physically violent with her.[37]

The divorce was finally granted in November 1920, with Harris winning a settlement of $100,000 and some community property.

How did the press respond? Since the marriage and divorce of one of Hollywood's biggest stars would seem to be a "perfect" story, one would expect it to be plastered on the front pages of newspapers across the country. But such was not the case. The press seemed unusually restrained and discreet in its reporting of the first Chaplin divorce. The *New York Times* carried one story in March on the Chaplins' domestic troubles (on page 10), two stories in August—the first on the filing of the divorce, the second something of a retraction (both on page 14)—and failed even to report the divorce settlement, even though Chaplin was in New York City when the divorce was granted.

The *Times* was also sympathetic to Chaplin when it editorialized on August 11 concerning the filing of the divorce. The editorial quoted Harris's allegation that Chaplin ignored her by taking long, contemplative walks, even in the rain. According to Harris, "the harder it rained, the longer he walked and harder he thought." The editorialist treated the charge as absurd and, though finding such a tendency rare in Hollywood, defended Chaplin's right to think. "If thought on the part of a movie artist has such devastating consequences," the editorial concluded rhetorically, "what would happen if movie audiences started to think?"[38]

For the most part this gentle treatment was typical of how the press handled the situation. As personally painful as the whole relationship was for Chaplin and Harris, they were not, except for the ridicule Harris suffered in the *Times* editorial, as victimized by the press as Chaplin would be in 1927 and 1928 during his second divorce and even more so during the Joan Barry affair in the 1940s.

Why was this? One important reason relates to the state of Chaplin's star image, which in 1918 and 1919 contained fewer negative connotations and contradictions than it would later. American culture associated Chaplin first with the irreverent, funny, sympathetic, and increasingly romantic Charlie. They next pictured Chaplin himself as an aspiring, talented, and still relatively humble filmmaker. A crucial third reason is that Chaplin, after the Liberty Loan tour, was associated with patriotism and with supporting dominant opinions. With such positive qualities linked to the star image, a divorce seemed like an unfortunate anomaly. Though the breakup would later be considered a more serious and negative element of Chaplin's star image, the press and the public in 1919 thought it forgivable. For the most part an aura of magic still surrounded Chaplin's star image.

Troubles at First National

But what happened to Chaplin's film career between the time he met Harris and the time he divorced her? What kind of films did he make? If the press was relatively quiet about his divorce, what did they write about him generally? The two "Harris years" were for Chaplin artistically distracted, if not arid, years. Though the press continued to portray Chaplin the man as an intriguing and serious artist, significant numbers of film reviewers and commentators were displeased with the two films he made during this period, and there was even speculation that Chaplin's greatness might be on the wane.

The two films were *Sunnyside* and *A Day's Pleasure* (released in June and November 1919), which Chaplin worked on from about the time he married Harris until the time they separated. In addition to the pressures of the relationship, several other factors made it difficult for Chaplin to concentrate on his work. First, Chaplin had to worry about expenses for his new film studio, begun in November 1917 and completed three months later. Building his own studio was one of Chaplin's shrewdest acts of foresight, enabling him to control his productions and own the rights to his films, an independence almost unheard of in Hollywood, before or after. Nonetheless, it cost him a lot of money and considerable anxiety.

Second, Chaplin was beginning to be restive, chafing at the bonds imposed by the First National contract. He had hoped to honor his eight-picture contract in no more than eighteen months, but by the time that period had elapsed, he had completed only two films. The agreement seemed even more constricting because in early 1919 Chaplin entered into negotiations with D. W. Griffith, Douglas Fairbanks, Mary Pickford, and William S. Hart (who later withdrew) to form a company, United Artists, that would distribute films they each independently produced. As will be discussed in more detail in Chapter 3, since film companies like Adolph Zukor's Paramount were beginning to integrate film production, distribution, and exhibition in single organizations, Chaplin and the other prominent film figures feared that competition for their talents, and thus the amount of money they could command for their services, could drop precipitously. In April the United Artists' contracts of incorporation were signed, an event that for Chaplin made finishing his six remaining First National films seem even more onerous. When First National executives refused to renegotiate his contract (both *A Dog's Life* and *Shoulder Arms* had done very well at the box office, and Chaplin hoped for more favorable terms), the ruthless attitude of the executives,

Chaplin wrote, "embittered me" and "impeded the progress of my work" (MA, p. 224). All these concerns made it hard for Chaplin to work fruitfully on his films.

The pressures show in the films. *Sunnyside* displeased critics when it was released and generally continued to do so long after. The film is poorly structured by the standards of the classical Hollywood cinema that were then solidifying. In the middle of a film about Charlie's difficulties as a hotel employee, for example, Charlie gets bumped on the head and has a dream about dancing through a sylvan forest with some wood nymphs. With no apparent connection to the narrative, the scene seems nothing more than an homage by Chaplin to Nijinsky, whom Chaplin had met some time earlier.

Despite this structural weakness, *Sunnyside* is at times interesting thematically.[39] A central element of the film is its criticism of small-town hypocrisy. The opening shot irises out to a long shot of the church in the village of Sunnyside early on a Sunday morning, then irises in and back out to a sign, "Love Thy Neighbor," hanging over the bed of the hotel owner, Charlie's boss. Except for time spent piously reading his Bible, this ostensibly religious man spends the entire film unceremoniously kicking Charlie in the hindside. He never exhibits the behavior urged by the sign over his bed. It is significant that Chaplin's attack came out the same year as Sherwood Anderson's *Winesburg, Ohio*, and the year before Sinclair Lewis's *Main Street*, both assaults on what the authors saw as twisted and hypocritical lives lived in small-town America. Chaplin's social criticism in this early 1919 film was at times uncharacteristically harsh, given his previous films.

Also interesting is *Sunnyside*'s half-hearted romance. Ever since Edna Purviance had joined Chaplin early in his Essanay period, some element of romance had become commonplace in his films. But the romance in *Sunnyside* is handled so cynically that a viewer is tempted to read it autobiographically.[40] Chaplin's quest for love in earlier films like *The Bank* or *The Vagabond* seems to have worn thin after his relationship with Harris had ended in marriage: when he introduces Edna as the somewhat foolish farmer's daughter in *Sunnyside*, he does so with the perfunctory title, "And Now, the Romance." Though he does attempt to achieve some pathos later in the film, when Charlie unsuccessfully tries to imitate the dress and manners of the city slicker who dominates Edna's attentions—reminiscent of the way he tried to sketch Edna after the artist painted her in *The Vagabond*—the romance is hard-edged, tinged with a bitter cynicism uncommon in Chaplin's previous films. To critics and audiences used to his earlier work, *Sunnyside* was an unwelcome departure.

A Day's Pleasure was also received harshly. Like *Sunnyside*, it has no real romance. Instead, Charlie plays a married man taking his wife and two boys—both of whom wear Chaplinesque derbies—for a day of what they hope will be pleasure. Their hopes are in vain, of course. The film consists of three sequences: starting the car, riding on a boat, and driving home. Chaplin seems to have begun by trying to create a comedy that would draw sustenance from the increasing popularity of automobile driving in America ("Everybody's doing it," one title says). But inspiration and vitality are absent. Except for a few amusing moments, as when Charlie tries to set up a deck chair or when he escapes from a puddle of tar by stepping out of his shoes and into a policeman's fallen hat, the film is flat and even, at times, mean spirited. Charlie uses a plump woman for a gangplank when he scurries on the boat, and tries to fish her out of the water with a sharply hooked pole. In one of the few instances of racial stereotyping in his films, Chaplin has the black trombonist in the boat's band roll his eyes in the worst minstrel tradition, then puts him in whiteface to suggest the musician's nausea. In a fight with another seasick man on the boat, Charlie is as cruel as he was in his Keystone era, ending his fight with several strategically aimed punches to the man's groin.

The typical critical response to these two films was summed up by one film magazine when it wrote that "*Sunnyside* was anything but sunny. *A Day's Pleasure* was certainly not a pleasure." *Variety*, long a relatively reliable litmus test for the popularity of films and filmmakers, was also hard on both the films. *Sunnyside* suggested that the Chaplin comic well "was running dry," for at no time was it "up to the Chaplin standard." Nor did *A Day's Pleasure* "measure up to the standard of his old offerings." Instead, it was "just a series of episodes, padded to the extreme."[41] In two years Chaplin, working at a much slower pace than he (and his fans) had grown used to, had completed only two short and relatively unsuccessful films while competitors like Buster Keaton and Harold Lloyd were appearing frequently in comic shorts. A star needs to stay in the public eye if he is to maintain his position of stardom, and Chaplin had not consistently done so through new films during these years.

Nevertheless, though his reviews were bad, not all of his press between 1918 and the start of 1920 was so harsh. In fact, Chaplin's star image stayed as high as it did during that time more because of promotion and publicity about Chaplin himself than because of his films. The two most important essays praising Chaplin appeared in *Ladies' Home Journal*, in August 1918, and the following month in *Photoplay*.

The first article, "Mr. Charles Spencer Chaplin: The Man You Don't

47

Know," was written by Rob Wagner, a former teacher and artist who became Chaplin's publicity man during World War I. Clearly intent on promoting Chaplin, the piece turns the comedian into something of a saint. The "real Chaplin" loves and is loved by children, according to Wagner, and is a versatile creative genius at filmmaking, the maker of "essentially one-man pictures." He is an aesthete who responds deeply to music. He is intellectual, an "omniverous reader" whose "tastes run to philosophy and the modern English realists." He works tremendously hard when engaged on a film, "yet for the fame that comes with them he cares very little." To top it all off, despite the fortune he has made, "the modesty of his material wants are strongly expressed in his personal life." The Chaplin portrayed by this article—one of the first profiles of Chaplin to appear in a large circulation, national mass magazine—shines in his devotion to art, his unparalleled creative versatility, and his limited material desires.[42]

A second, equally complimentary profile was the article in *Photoplay* by Julian Johnson, one of the best of early movie writers. The title and subtitle of the essay, based on some discussions Johnson and Chaplin had at a Los Angeles restaurant, suggest its main purpose: "Charles, Not Charlie: Concerning a serious-minded man whose screen personality is better known than any other being in the world."[43] Johnson sought to cut through all the contradictory information about Chaplin appearing in the popular press. To do so, he writes, one must begin by distinguishing clearly between Chaplin the man and Charlie the movie character.

The article paints a sympathetic and admirable portrait of the "real" Charles Spencer Chaplin. According to Johnson, Charles dislikes crowds, largely because the only emotion he sees on the faces is curiosity, nothing that can lead to serious interchange between humans. He dresses conservatively, with "the unostentatious attire of good breeding." He is a cautious businessman whose "charities are carefully chosen." Though Chaplin has little formal education, he is rapidly becoming a man of culture. He "talks with the clean, well-bred speech of an Englishman," and his studio is the "most artistic" ever built in Hollywood.

These qualities, writes Johnson, reflect "the innate taste and refinement of a man slowly rising to self-won culture after early vicissitudes and almost no schooling." This "innate taste" is moving Chaplin toward an interest in more serious, ambitious films. "The serious bits in all of his plays are the episodes he likes most," writes Johnson, Chaplin's favorite being the episode in *The Bank* in which Charlie discovers the bouquet he had given Edna tossed into a wastebasket. "In the ensuing bit of almost motionless pantomime," writes Johnson in a comment that typifies the desire of some critics to raise Chaplin's aesthetic standing, "Chaplin struck a note of tragedy which in its depth and universality was really Shakespearean."[44]

One factor contributing to this perspective of Chaplin as a serious and talented artist was the degree to which Chaplin was beginning to entertain and be entertained by famous artists and other figures from around the world, many of them more anxious to meet the famous comedian than he was to meet them. In his autobiography Chaplin describes at considerable length his meetings during this period with Pavlova, Nijinsky, Paderewski, pianist Leopold Godowsky, Jascha Heifetz, Lord and Lady Mountbatten, Constance Collier, and Sir Herbert Beerbohm Tree. Chaplin was internationally recognized and in demand. By associating with artists and other notables, he was apparently legitimizing his own status as an important artist, particularly since many of them sought out the great Chaplin rather than vice versa.

Other articles, and indeed the comedian himself, echoed this tendency to view Chaplin as a serious artist. *Moving Picture World* carried an article that stressed how much attention Chaplin was getting in a wide variety of magazines. It claimed that only the Kaiser and President Wilson had received more attention than Chaplin in the public press over the previous two years. Furthermore, a wide number of "high brow" journals like the *New Republic*, *New Statesman*, *Century*, and *Smart Set* were praising Chaplin's work.[45] Chaplin himself, during a visit to New York City on the Liberty Loan tour, told a reporter that he was a "high-lowbrow," an artist interested in both serious and popular art. While there, he added, he hoped very much to see the production of Ibsen's play *A Doll's House*.[46] Film writer Elsie Codd, after visiting Chaplin on the set of *Sunnyside*, reported that Chaplin was interested in writing a screenplay on a "deep psychological problem." She added: "I have never seen a man more intensely *alive*."[47]

Chaplin also fostered this image by writing an article that appeared in *American Magazine* in November 1918. In "What People Laugh At," Chaplin wrote as a comic theorist, seeking to explain the sources of his comedy. Though some of the essay deals with examples of how he got ideas for films by observing the world around him, in other sections Chaplin makes pithy observations about comedy and human experience, as when he writes: "Restraint is a great word, not only for actors but for everybody to remember. Restraint of tempers, appetites, desires, bad habits, and so on [is valuable to cultivate]."[48] The unschooled music-hall comedian had become a somber comic theorist in barely five years.

At the turn of the decade, however, two articles questioned whether the recent failed films or the positive profiles were more important to the star image. *Theater Magazine* published an article in late 1919 that asked, "Is the Charlie Chaplin Vogue Passing?" A genteel attack on Chaplin written in a huffy tone, the author recalled that two years earlier it "would have been deemed treasonable to cast the smallest of critical stones at Chaplin." Ascribing Chaplin's success to simple repetition, the critic charged that "the appeal of every Chaplin picture is to the lowest human instincts," a familiar charge of genteel critics since the Keystone days. To this, the essay added that the Chaplin comedies were based on "the psychological principle that pain is diverting" and that their appeal was "an extremely unintellectual one." "I strenuously object to incompetent persons styling Charles Chaplin a great artist," the essay concluded, "when he's nothing of the sort."[49]

Another piece, this one more sympathetic despite the concerns it raised, appeared in early 1920. The April issue of *Photoplay* opened with "A Letter to a Genius," addressed to Chaplin, on its title page. After registering its disappointment over Chaplin's films since *Shoulder Arms*, the letter concluded (perhaps "implored" might be a better word): "We are not commanding nor advising nor even criticizing; we speak because we need you—because you made this turbulent God's marble a better thing to live on—because since you have been out of sorts the world has gone lame and happiness has moved away. Come back, Charlie!"[50] Such a statement suggested how profoundly Chaplin's work in the 1910s had affected moviegoers. Despite the conflicts over the alleged vulgarity in Chaplin's films, despite his huge salaries, despite the war controversy, despite his divorce and the two weak films made as his marriage was dissolving, Chaplin's star image still evoked hope from his followers.

As the decade ended, then, Chaplin's star image had already begun to evolve. Initially it was based almost entirely on the character of Charlie, which first appeared in the Keystone years. There Charlie had been crude, at times cruel, and often very funny. During the Essanay contract, however, and even more during the Mutual years, Charlie tempered that cruelty and became known for both his amusing antics and, increasingly, his yearnings for romance and friendship with an idealized woman. Though he was nearly always vulnerable both physically and fiscally, he maintained his dignity and the purity of his desires.

But beginning with the Essanay years, the real person, Charles

Spencer Chaplin, began to figure into the equation of his star image. Most of the press first portrayed him as the modest and talented beneficiary of American opportunity, a kind of Horatio Alger hero with comic talents. Later, as doubts and misgivings were raised about his huge salaries or his war involvement or his divorce, the press in general came to Chaplin's defense and portrayed him not just as the modest man of success but as the serious, ambitious, and versatile artist. At the end of this period, even the term "genius" surfaced.

By 1920, contradictions and strains already characterized the star image. Charlie was often penniless; Chaplin was an enterprising man making millions. Charlie's ardor for Edna was intense and unyielding; Chaplin's marriage quickly disintegrated. Charlie often mixed with the down and out; Chaplin mixed with the rich and famous. Yet despite these conflicts and tensions, by the end of the decade, Chaplin had found many defenders in the press who hoped he would regain the artistic form he had seemed to lose in *Sunnyside* and *A Day's Pleasure*. As the 1920s were beginning and his divorce settlement was being worked out, Chaplin himself was feverishly engrossed in a new film about Charlie, an orphan, and a cold world that challenged them both. Much of his future, in the coming decade and beyond, depended on it.

TWO

**At the Top: Charlie
and the 1920s**

3

From *The Kid*
to *The Gold Rush*

Finishing Up at First National

As we have seen, Chaplin's rise in 1914 and 1915 was meteoric. But the history of stardom in America is filled with stories of stars and celebrities whose popularity lasted a few years, a few months, or even a few weeks. As Chaplin himself found during 1919, when his marriage was breaking up and his creative juices seemed to stop flowing, patience and fidelity were not virtues possessed by all of the moviegoing public. Sustaining his star image was no easy task.

Yet Chaplin managed to maintain his popularity in the first half of the 1920s, and he did so by managing his star image—both his comic persona and the way he presented himself to the press—in a much more sophisticated way than observers have sometimes granted. Through his films, his writings, his dealings with the press, and even his interactions with a branch of the young intelligentsia, Chaplin solidified his status in the 1920s as the world's premiere comic film performer and director.

One crucial way a star image is sustained is, of course, through films. For most stars the personae they play contribute centrally to their star images. In Chaplin's case, however, because he not only acted in films but also wrote and directed them, the films are important to his star image both in respect to the Charlie character and to the kind of filmmaker and artist Chaplin was perceived to be. Charlie seemed less warm and romantic in *Sunnyside* and *A Day's Pleasure*, but the artist implied by the films also seemed less skilled and ambitious. Both changes threatened his star image. Yet in Chaplin's next film, *The Kid* (1920), as well as in two of the remaining three films on his First National contract (*The Idle Class* and *The Pilgrim*), Chaplin managed to resurrect and deepen Charlie while implicitly presenting Chaplin as a renewed filmmaker.

The renewal began with *The Kid*. In his autobiography Chaplin recalled telling a friend that as *The Kid* developed, he was beginning to blend "slapstick with sentiment" (MA, p. 235). More accurately, Chap-

55

lin returned in *The Kid* to the mixture of comedy and pathos evident in films like *The Vagabond* and *The Bank* but entirely absent in *A Day's Pleasure*. Chaplin apparently realized that the sentiment was one of the sources of popularity of his films. Furthermore, he added other characteristics to the film, including some pointed social criticism and some "artistic" stylistic devices, that helped viewers and critics to see the film as a stunning artistic achievement.

The opening title emphasized what Chaplin was after: "A comedy with a smile—and perhaps a tear." The narrative structure was simple. A woman, abandoned by the artist who fathered her child, leaves the infant in a luxurious car outside a mansion, hoping he will be offered the life she cannot provide. The car is stolen and the child abandoned again, only to be discovered by Charlie, who decides to heed the note left with the child, which asks the finder to love and care for the "orphan." Five years pass. The baby is now "the kid," who breaks windows so his adoptive father can make a living by repairing them. Their scenes together display a deep bond of affection. When the central conflict arises—a threat by county officials to take the child away from Charlie because of his poverty and humble setting—the effect is striking and generates the most powerful moments of pathos in the movie. Though the officials initially fail, Charlie and the child are forced to go into hiding. The child's birth mother, who has become a wealthy and successful actress and has subsequently devoted herself to charity work in the slums, learns the boy's true identity when she is shown the note she originally pinned on his blanket. She offers a reward for his return, and an unscrupulous flophouse owner steals the child from Charlie. Falling asleep on his doorstep after an exhausting search for the boy, Charlie dreams of heaven (a much more integrated dream sequence than was found in *Sunnyside*). There an initial social harmony quickly degenerates due to jealousy and envy. Awakened by an apparently hostile policeman, Charlie is dragged to a car, then taken to the elegant home of the mother/actress. He and the kid are reunited.

The Kid is important to Chaplin's star image partly because of its vivid portrayal of cruel people and venal social institutions that make it difficult for the poor but noble Charlie to survive. The ironic opening scene shows the mother, whose "only sin is motherhood," being turned out of the charity hospital, babe in arms. The bars of the gate she passes through visually equate the hospital with a prison. Shortly thereafter, Chaplin cuts to the callous father, apparently an artist, who accidentally knocks a picture of his former lover into a fireplace, retrieves it, then matter-of-factly tosses it back to be burned.[1] Parallel to the hospital is the county orphan asylum, which on the advice of a "country doctor" who treats the child, decides that he would be better off in an orphanage than with Charlie who has nurtured him from infancy. Those living in the Victorian urban squalor of Charlie's neighborhood also exhibit cruelty. The kid gets accosted by a neighborhood bully, and when the kid seems to be getting the upper hand, the bully's monstrous brother threatens to attack Charlie. Later, it is the flophouse owner who kidnaps the boy to collect a $1000 reward.

The film portrays a bleak social background, and the method of the film is one that would increasingly characterize Chaplin's work: it juxtaposes two moral universes, a negative one associated with various ills of society and a positive one embodied in Charlie and his closest relationships. In contrast to the harsh and uncaring society in this film are the woman, the kid, and Charlie. The reference to the charity hospital in the first scene is an important one, for the film's positive moral universe is related to charity in two senses. One definition of charity, providing help or relief to the poor, is acted out by the mother. Although she achieves success as an actress quickly, she is not corrupted by wealth. In fact, as one title puts it, for her charity is not a "duty" but a "joy."

In developing her character, Chaplin at least twice used stylistic devices that helped identify him as a "serious" filmmaker. In the first scene Chaplin associates the mother with Christ through a nondiegetic insert: as she walks away from the hospital, Chaplin cuts to an image of Christ carrying the cross up Calvary.[2] Even before Eisenstein, Chaplin was experimenting with intellectual montage. Second, some prints of the film emphasize the mother's goodness with a shot of her standing with her infant outside a church as a young woman and older man come outside in their wedding procession. Though the mother is unmarried, the church window behind her creates a halolike effect around her head.[3] Such attention to style and symbol helped foster the "serious" image that Chaplin was seeking to convey.

Charlie's relationship with the child exhibits a second kind of charity: the feeling of benevolence and good will toward another. Throughout the film, in both comic and sentimental scenes, Charlie and the kid demonstrate their deep emotional bond. When Charlie cares for the infant in his comic improvised nursery, when the two perfect their window-breaking and repairing service, even when Charlie cleans his boy's face or the boy cooks for his father, we see how close they have become.

Their bond is the central human tie in the film, and the dramatic climax occurs when the asylum director, his driver, and a policeman forceably separate Charlie and the kid. This climax is heightened through the use of film style in several ways. One medium shot of the child backed into a corner makes him look almost like a trapped animal. A medium two-shot of the boy and Charlie embracing, bleary-eyed Charlie looking into the camera, captures the intensity of their bond. After the two are separated, Chaplin cross-cuts between the child in the back of the asylum truck and Charlie being restrained in his apartment: the boy imploringly reaches out his arms and mouths the words, "I want my daddy, oh please." Their deep bond is indestructible, and it is a bitter social irony that the officials believe their brand of charity, the same kind that ignominiously turned the child's mother out of the hospital at the opening of the film, will be more humane than the one already animating the relationship between the kid and Charlie.

Chaplin's dream sequence, effectively integrated in the narrative, provided another indication of Chaplin as "serious" filmmaker. The dream follows the boy's separation from Charlie; in it, Charlie imagines a limited view of heaven, set entirely in the street outside his flat but cheerfully painted and garlanded. The inhabitants are Charlie's neighbors, dressed in white and sporting wings. They fly, including even a little dog, play harps, and dance in the streets, but the utopia cannot last. Three devils slip by a sleeping guardian at the pearly gates and enter to plant seeds of discord. One devil tempts a dark-haired young beauty (played by Lita Gray, who would become the second Mrs. Chaplin in 1924) to "vamp" Charlie, entices Charlie to pursue her, then prods her "sweetheart"—who happens to be none other than the monstrous bully whose younger brother picked the fight with the kid—into jealousy. A fight ensues, a winged policeman intercedes, and when Charlie tries to fly away, the policeman shoots him down. Not only does the scene provide some comic relief, but it also closes off Charlie's escape: evil exists even in his dreams of heaven.

The ending is a tentatively happy one: although the kid and Charlie are reunited through the other charitable character, the woman, the conclusion is not as closed as film viewers in the 1920s were accustomed to. Rather, its tentativeness is similar to the close of *City Lights*. Dragged by a policeman to a luxurious car, Charlie is driven to the woman's home, which resembles the house in front of which she abandoned her infant in the opening scenes of the film. As the policeman leads Charlie to the front door, the boy accompanies his mother out to greet him. He embraces Charlie, which cements the central relationship of the film. But then, as Charlie, the kid, and the mother step into the entry and close the door, the camera remains discreetly outside and Chaplin fades to darkness. Just how the relationship among the three will work itself out remains a mystery. Charity in both senses is affirmed in the film, but the presence of evil in the world, even in the world of dreams, makes any overly optimistic inference about the conclusion uncertain at best.

Response to Chaplin's blend of slapstick, sentiment, and serious art was striking, among both the public and the critics. The film, according to one source, grossed around $2.5 million, with Chaplin's share over $1 million. Robinson, who had access to Chaplin's records, says that Chaplin convinced First National to advance him $1.5 million and to pay him 50 percent of the net after the advance was recovered. By 1924 the film had played in fifty countries around the globe. Such success enabled Chaplin to retain the financial security he had built up in his three previous contracts, despite the fact that *The Kid* cost him over $500,000 to make.[4]

Critics also responded positively to the film. The thoughtful reviewer for *Exceptional Photoplays* suggested that Chaplin "can bring tears or laughter to the largest audience in the world with less apparent effort than any other actor on the screen." During an era when the values of genteel Americans were being challenged, the reviewer defends Chaplin from the charge of being "very lowbrow, very vulgar, very unesthetic." Rather, he says, Chaplin's slapstick is rooted in a venerable tradition, of the sort that appeared in Aristophanes, Cervantes, Shakespeare, and Goethe. *The Kid* is "a criticism of life" and a celebration of the kid and his father's love: "it is the charm of their relation against egotism and unconcern of the rest of the world which makes the picture so fascinating."[5] Typical of a number of reviews, this one stresses that Chaplin the artist was doing much more than just making another comedy.

In the *New Republic* Francis Hackett called *The Kid* a "triumph," a film of "integrity." In contrast to the typically low standards of Hollywood, he added, Chaplin's "wisdom, his sincerity, his integrity ... should go some way to revolutionize motion picture production in this country. From an industry *The Kid* raises production to an art."[6] The review underlines how Chaplin's star image was beginning to be contrasted to, and placed on an aesthetic level above, regular Hollywood films. The *New York Times* and *Variety* also praised the film, and *Theatre Magazine* wrote that the film "certainly outdoes in humor and the special brand of Chaplin pathos, anything this popular film star has yet produced."[7] This blend of comedy and pathos was already becoming a firmly fixed characteristic of the Chaplin films, so much so that viewers were easily noticing and even expecting it.

Chaplin completed his First National contract by making *The Idle*

Class, Pay Day, and *The Pilgrim.* Of the three, *Pay Day* did the least to enhance his star image. A potboiling blend of *One A.M.* and *The Rounders,* focusing on Charlie's drinking and his escape from a domineering wife, the film seems done simply to help fulfill the burdensome First National obligation. The fact that it took him only thirty working days to complete the film, about the same pace he had used at Essanay, helps confirm this suspicion.[8]

Both *The Idle Class* and *The Pilgrim,* however, show Chaplin seriously engaged in defining his central persona. In *The Idle Class,* furthermore, he drew on autobiographical elements, just as he had in *The Kid,* only here the personal content referred to more recent events than the childhood memories fueling the earlier film. Chaplin worked on *The Idle Class* after returning from the premiere of *The Kid* in New York, where he was feted by the wealthy and constantly surrounded by adoring fans whenever he was out in public. In the film, Chaplin plays two roles: the familiar Charlie and an isolated wealthy drunkard, Mr. Charles.[9] The film's title refers to both characters: one's idleness contributes to his poverty, the other's idleness results from his prosperity. The wealthy man, unlike Chaplin, is an alcoholic. Yet similar to Chaplin after his divorce, he is lonely, a part of but somewhat alienated from high society, and estranged from his wife.

In contrast, Charlie, though a down-and-out underdog, is nevertheless a dreamer. This is most evident in Charlie's daydream, which hearkens back to his wish-fulfillment dreams in *The Bank* and *Shoulder Arms.* The dream comes after Charlie sees the rich man's wife gallop past on a runaway horse. In rapid succession, Charlie imagines saving the woman, falling in love with her, marrying her, and fathering her children—a respectable, middle-class dream for such a social outcast, and an obvious wish fulfillment that also points forward to *The Gold Rush.* Unsurprisingly, though, Charlie awakens quickly. Later he does for a time romance the rich man's wife at a costume party, where his regular clothing constitutes his costume. He is soon on the run again, however, when the husband escapes from his suit-of-armor costume, and Charlie's true identity is uncovered. Before he leaves, Charlie gives a parting kick to the hindside of the wife's wealthy father. If the real Charles is now wealthy, polished, and somewhat isolated, the persona Charlie can still thumb his nose at the upper classes from the underside of society.

Following *The Idle Class* Chaplin, who had worked almost constantly since arriving on the Keystone lot in 1913, took a European trip and wrote a book on his travels, *My Trip Abroad,* to be discussed later in this chapter. Back in America, he ground out the indifferent *Pay Day,* and then turned to *The Pilgrim*. In a departure from his regular practice, Chaplin worked from a written script and completed the film more quickly than was his custom: forty-five working days. Finished in September 1922 and released in January 1923, *The Pilgrim* was a four-reeler that First National accepted as the final two films of his contract.[10] Like *The Idle Class*, *The Pilgrim* shows a serious Chaplin at work exploring the contours of his comic persona.

In it, as in *The Kid*, Charlie plays a social pariah whose intuitive goodness opposes the flaws of respectable society, a contrast generating satire on genteel piety attuned to the zeitgeist of the 1920s. As the film opens, Charlie has escaped from prison (an allusion to breaking free from the First National contract?) and steals a minister's clothing: Charlie becomes a chaplain. After he takes a train to Devil's Gulch, Texas, where a new minister has been expected, the film follows Charlie's comic misadventures at the train station, a church service, a genteel home, and a saloon, where Charlie retrieves some money stolen from his host family. The story ends when the town sheriff, appreciating Charlie's honesty in returning the money, sets him free along the Texas–Mexico border.

In addition to the comedy arising from Charlie's struggles to act like a minister (you can take Charlie out of prison, but you can't take the prison out of Charlie), the narrative creates humor through its satire of the small town. In contrast to the idealized, white-picket-fence image that M-G-M would later exploit in the Andy Hardy series, Chaplin's small town is much more similar to those described by American writers who "revolted against the village" in the first decades of the twentieth century: writers like Edwin Arlington Robinson, Edgar Lee Masters, Sherwood Anderson, and Sinclair Lewis.[11] Two examples should suffice. While walking to church with the deacon, Charlie discovers that the apparently temperate deacon keeps a bottle of whiskey in his back pocket. Later, when visiting the Brown family (Edna Purviance plays their daughter in her final leading comic role for Chaplin), Charlie the minister is accosted by the small son of a couple who arrive for a brief visit. The little rogue jabs people with a knitting needle, rains a barrage of punches on Charlie and his own father, pours fishbowl water on Charlie, and plasters his father's face with a sticky sheet of flypaper. When his parents leave the room, the urchin tries to follow Charlie into the kitchen and gets a swift kick in the rear. In many of the Keystone and Essanay films, Charlie had used the kick gratuitously, which alienated some viewers, but here the kick is underplayed and justified by the narrative. We clearly side with Charlie as he tries to defend himself against the behavior of the uncontrolled child.

As in *The Kid*, Charlie's morality is clearly underlined in the film. He is attracted to Edna, but his romance is cut short when an acquaintance from prison weasels himself an invitation to spend the night at the Brown residence and steals their savings. Selflessly, Charlie recovers the money and returns it to the Browns, but his cover has been blown. The sheriff, who cannot avert his eyes, must arrest Charlie the wanted escapee, but he hasn't the heart to lock up a person who has performed such an act of kindness and virtue. He therefore takes Charlie to the Texas–Mexico border and suggests that he pick some flowers across the border (and outside the sheriff's jurisdiction). Puzzled for a time about the strange request, Charlie finally understands. Standing in Mexico, he lifts his eyes and raises his arms to the skies in a gesture of freedom. Immediately, he's caught in an outlaw gun battle. Scampering back to the American side, Charlie wavers indecisively. Where should he go? Texas, offering social order and the Brown's daughter, is impossible because he will be returned to prison. Mexico, tempting him with freedom, is lawless and anarchic. In the final shot, a fitting conclusion to Chaplin's First National years, Charlie waddles away from the camera, one foot on each side of the border. There is no easy and comfortable spot for Chaplin's Charlie to plant himself. In like manner, Chaplin himself, after an increasingly rich and self-consciously creative period at First National, was now at a crossroads, finally ready to embark on independent production. But in what direction and to what end?

Interviews and Writings in the
Early 1920s

If Chaplin's films during these final years at First National contributed to his star image, so did the interviews he granted and his own writings. One of the first interviews of Chaplin after his divorce from Mildred Harris in November 1920 was also one of the most important, for it presented an image of Chaplin the serious artist to a culturally influential audience and reinforced the serious undertones evident in films like *A Dog's Life*, *Sunnyside*, and *The Kid* (the latter released two months after the interview).

The title of the interview captured its thrust: "The Hamlet-Like Nature of Charlie Chaplin."[12] Conducted by Benjamin De Casseres, the interview has a tone and substance that would have been almost unthinkable just three years earlier, when Chaplin was still working at the frenetic pace of nearly a film a month. It is an interview given by someone who is becoming used to constant attention and adulation yet is not particularly satisfied with the situation. Similarly, it is an interview with someone impatient with the role of funny man and drawn instead to the world of ideas and a dark view of life.

Near the opening of the interview, De Casseres outlined the contours of his picture of Chaplin: "In many hours' easy conversational talk with Chaplin I discovered a spirit of a very rare vintage—a poet, an esthete; a dynamic and ultra-advanced thinker; a man with a thousand surprising facets; a man of many accomplishments; a man infinitely sad and melancholy; a man as delicate as violin strings that register the world-wail and the world-melody; a Puck, a Hamlet, an Ariel—and a Voltaire." In the interchange that follows, Chaplin's comments suggest that he was increasingly becoming interested in ideas. Though he had very little schooling and as late as age thirteen could barely read or write, Chaplin had begun to feel the need to educate himself as early as his first trip to America (MA, p. 123). This lack of formal education bothered Chaplin: he once wrote that "I wanted to know not for the love of knowledge but as a defense against the world's contempt for the ignorant." Although Raoul Sobel and David Francis are probably accurate when they argue that Chaplin's grasp of ideas was superficial, Chaplin apparently began to read more, after he slowed his working pace, and would then allude in interviews to the authors and works he was encountering, which gave an aura of high art to his image and his films.[13] At a time when the movies were struggling for respectability (and a broader audience), this was shrewd of Chaplin, as well as potentially profitable. By presenting himself as interested in ideas, he was differentiating his star image from that of competitors like Buster Keaton or Harold Lloyd (see Figure 8).

In this interview Chaplin displayed his learning several times. He talks of his dissatisfaction at being pressured into the role of Charlie: "Solitude is the only relief. The dream-world is then the great reality; the real world an illusion. I go to my library and live with the great abstract thinkers—Spinoza, Schopenhauer, Nietzsche and Walter Pater." He also indicated a desire "to retire to some Italian lake with my beloved violin, my Shelley and Keats, and live under an assumed name a life purely imaginative and intellectual."

In addition, Chaplin stresses his stardom by mentioning celebrities he has encountered, like Caruso and Heifetz. A little rankled that Caruso had called him the "Caruso of the Movies"—and more rankled at waiting in Caruso's dressing room for attention from the great tenor—Chaplin tells the interviewer that he called Caruso the "Chaplin of the

Operatic Stage." When Heifetz dined at Chaplin's house, according to the interview, Chaplin played "a bit of Bach" for him. By mentioning how he mingled and even showed up leading artists from other arts, Chaplin sought to reaffirm his status as star.

The interview also presented a relatively common notion about stardom: that it's lonely at the top. At times, Chaplin told De Casseres, "I am oppressed . . . . by what is known among the Romantics as world-weariness." Later, asked about what it felt like to rocket from poverty to wealth, Chaplin replied, "Nothing fails like success. I mean by that that money never satisfied a spiritual or intellectual need. . . . I doubt whether a rich man ever has a real friend—for how when one is fixed for life in this world's goods can one tell friend, enemy or fawner? I always understand poor artists; rich ones always seem to me a contradiction in terms." Such comments cumulatively draw the star closer to the stargazers by suggesting that despite the star's privileged status, his life is still beset with problems and difficulties.

While this *Times* interview did much to present Chaplin as a serious, popular, and at times melancholy artist, Chaplin's most detailed "advertisement for himself" was his account of his 1921 European journey, *My Trip Abroad*.[14] The trip itself lasted from September 4 to October 18, with stopovers in New York City both before and after. He traveled to London, to Paris (twice), and to Berlin. Chaplin's account was mainly dictated to a young newsman, Monta Bell, during the return by train from New York to Los Angeles. In general, the book recounts his activities while on the trip, and though at times repetitious, it provides another interesting picture of Chaplin's presentation of himself early in the 1920s. The fact that it was first published as a series of articles in *Photoplay* before being sold in book form meant both that Chaplin was paid twice for his efforts and that a wider readership was ensured.

The book reiterated some of the star characteristics evident in the 1920 *Times* interview and added others. It first gives a vivid picture of how wearing it was to be surrounded constantly by people. Early in the trip, before leaving New York City, Chaplin writes of putting on his "prop" smile for reporters and crowds as a way to survive the constant attention: this is another picture of the paradoxical loneliness of the star that he had alluded to in the *Times* interview.

Another aspect of *My Trip Abroad* is its definition of Chaplin's stardom by listing the celebrities he met while on his trip. He tells of meeting Carl Sandburg in Chicago; Max Eastman, Douglas Fairbanks, and Mary Pickford in New York; H. G. Wells, J. M. Barrie, and Nathan Burke in England; Waldo Frank, Sir Phillip Sassoon, and Dudley Field

8. Chaplin in 1920—the image of the serious
artist begins to establish itself.

Malone in Paris; and many others. In addition, Chaplin claims to have
either turned down or been afraid to go to affairs attended by George
Bernard Shaw or Lloyd George.

But more evident in this book than in any earlier work is Chaplin's
interest in politics and the direction of his political sympathies. Although Chaplin's only extensive political involvements before his 1921
trip had been the Liberty Loan tour and the making of *Shoulder Arms*,
both of which showed Chaplin reaffirming the opinions dominant in
the United States, *My Trip Abroad* shows Chaplin flirting with or at
least open to the leftist political ideas that would later become closely
associated with his star image.

One indication of this is Chaplin's reference to Soviet Russia in the
book. The first mention comes when a reporter asks him if he is a
Bolshevik. Chaplin's answer: "I am an artist. I am interested in life.
Bolshevism is a new phase of life. I must be interested in it" (p. 8).
When reporters continue to badger him about Bolshevism, Lenin, and
Russia, Chaplin backs off, telling them, "I am an artist, not a politi-
cian," almost precisely the defense he would use in 1947 when the
opening of *Monsieur Verdoux* stirred up considerable controversy (p.

45). Later in the book he wrote that if given the opportunity, he would like to meet Trotsky and Lenin. Perhaps because he had had dinner with Max Eastman and some of his other leftist friends just before leaving for his trip, Chaplin had socialism, Russia, and the Bolshevik Revolution on his mind and wasn't afraid to tell reporters or inform readers of his book about these political encounters or thoughts.

Chaplin's comments about Bolshevism and their impact on his star image in 1920 and 1921 must be understood in the context of the Red Scare of 1919 and 1920. While the October 1917 Bolshevik Revolution in Russia raised the hopes of socialists throughout Europe and America, it also raised fears and generated negative reaction among those Americans who perceived socialist ideology to be a threat to their wealth and status or a challenge to American individualism. Though public and private propaganda during World War I was aimed primarily at Germany, after the end of the war cultural hatreds and anxieties were refocused by conservative attacks against radicalism, specifically the "Red menace." Several bombings in 1919, including one in the front of Attorney General A. Mitchell Palmer's home, intensified these fears and were attributed to the "Reds." In late 1919 the United States government deported over 250 alien residents to the Soviet Union, even though most had committed no offense and were not Communists. On New Year's Day in 1920, Palmer orchestrated a nationwide raid of radicals (many of whom were American citizens and avowed non-Communists) that led to the arrest of some 6,000 people. Despite the systematic violation of the civil rights of those arrested, few spoke out against Palmer's tactics.[15] Chaplin's openness about what Bolshevism represented probably sounded dangerous to many Americans who either actively participated in or passively acquiesced to attacks on the "Red menace."

In addition to this series of references to Bolshevism, Chaplin offers a more general picture of his political sympathies in a number of places in his book. These remarks form one of the book's most interesting dimensions, showing Chaplin grappling with a central and extremely unusual life experience: his meteoric rise from relative poverty to extreme wealth, his shift from lower to upper class, and the effect of this on his view of the world. Throughout *My Trip Abroad* Chaplin consistently reveals a social consciousness and a sympathy for the lower class, particularly those who are suffering most.

For example, describing his days on the ship, Chaplin tells of attempting to play cricket with some of the ship's crew and becoming upset when the first-class passengers crowd in to gawk at the movie star. His subsequent arrival in London and particularly his visit back to his old neighborhood make Chaplin reflect on the poverty out of which he arose. At one point he indicates that he wishes he could do something to solve a social problem like unemployment (p. 49). At another he writes sympathetically about encountering a blind man he had known as a child on the streets of London. At yet another, when his cousin Aubrey points out that a passing truck driver is a fallen aristocrat, Chaplin replies that the fall is probably for the best. The truck driver, in Chaplin's view, is a "true aristocrat," part of the "real elite, not the Blue Book variety," because he now is "loving adventure, ... doing something all the time, and loving the doing" (p. 142). In these instances, as well as in his comments on the death penalty and prison reform (p. 152), Chaplin exhibits a sympathy for the outcasts of society, a populist skepticism about the wealthy, and an awareness of social problems affecting the poor.

The conclusion suggests that Chaplin wishes to leave his reader with an image of his genuine social concern. His final thoughts relate to his desire for world disarmament, and he quotes Tennyson:

> When shall all men's good
> Be each man's rule and universal peace
> Shine like a shaft of light across the land,
> And like a lane of beams athwart the sea?

Such an allusion, despite the slight misquotation, not only stresses Chaplin's social conscience; it also reiterates his desire to be considered a learned man. Both were strong characteristics of the star image he was projecting in the first half of the 1920s.

Two other documents from 1922 reiterate Chaplin's image in this era: an interview in *Literary Digest* and an article by Chaplin, "In Defense of Myself," in *Collier's*.[16] In the interview, Chaplin attacks the British class system: he knew, the interviewer tells us, "that the very people who were clamoring and beseeching him to their tables and receptions would not before have given him a considered glance. . . . They wanted to see, not him, but the symbol of success." Chaplin also talked to his interviewer of "his bitter youth and his loneliness and his struggles" and seemed to the interviewer "the loneliest, saddest man I ever knew." This invites comparison with the image of the lonely husband Chaplin played in *The Idle Class* and supports the contention that Chaplin was at this point working more often in an autobiographical vein than he had in his earlier years.

"In Defense of Myself," besides giving an interesting and perceptive discussion of his screen persona's essence and its appeal to the movie audience, stresses the seriousness of "quality comedy" (and hence the seriousness of Chaplin the artist). Genuine and lasting humor, Chaplin writes, goes beyond "broad and slapstick kind of comedy":

> The true spirit of humor does not revolve about physical mishaps or even incongruities of dress and behavior. These may be the outward paraphernalia of humor, like the motley of the fool, but humor itself is woven deeper into the fabric of life. I began to look upon humor as a kind of gentle and benevolent custodian of the mind which prevents one from being overwhelmed and driven to the point of insanity by the apparent seriousness of life.

Thus the star image of Chaplin in the early 1920s, forged by the interplay of Charlie's role in films like *The Kid* and Chaplin's writings and interviews, blended a number of themes: humor, populism, social and political awareness, serious aesthetic and intellectual aspirations, and a loneliness engendered by a popularity that made intimate human contact almost impossible. In his next two films Chaplin moved a long way toward solidifying this star image and asserting his position as the preeminent artist in the American film industry.

Branching Out: *A Woman of Paris*

After completing his First National contract, Chaplin was finally able to contemplate his first film for United Artists, the distributing company he had formed with Fairbanks, Pickford, and Griffith in 1919. And as those thoughts began to shape into firmer plans, Chaplin startled his partners: his new film would not be a comedy but rather a sophisticated romantic melodrama, and would star not Chaplin but rather Edna Purviance and Adolphe Menjou. The result, *A Woman of Paris*, was released in October 1923. Before examining this film, however, it is important to discuss Chaplin's economic situation as he moved into independent production at United Artists, for this presented him with both constraints and opportunities and had a bearing on the development of his star image.

As we have already seen, Chaplin became a wealthy and famous star in part because he had the good luck to enter the film industry just as companies were beginning to market their films by emphasizing the actors who appeared in them. From 1913 to 1919 the star system institutionalized itself, and Chaplin, like Pickford and Fairbanks, was a prime beneficiary of that shift. However, by late 1918 two companies, Adolph Zukor's Paramount Pictures and the First National Exhibitors Circuit, had gained considerable control over the distribution of movies. Paramount, a distributing company, signed contracts with a number of production companies (e.g., Famous Players–Lasky) that gave it exclusive rights to distribute their pictures and then required theater owners to rent its films in large blocks. First National, an association of theater owners, had formed partly to counter Paramount's growing power; it hoped to obtain outstanding films made by independent producers for their member theaters. In addition to signing Chaplin to his million-dollar contract for eight films, First National made a similar agreement with Mary Pickford.[17]

United Artists arose in early 1919 when, at a January convention of the First National Exhibitors Circuit in Los Angeles, rumors began flying about an impending mammoth merger in the industry. According to an account in *Moving Picture World*, one such story was that "First National is going to form a combination with Famous Players [a Paramount production branch], Artcraft, Goldwyn, Metro, Fox, and after that they'll tell the stars just where to get off in the matter of salary."[18] Any such merger of Paramount and First National was certain to constitute a threat to the salaries of Chaplin and other big stars. Significantly, Chaplin himself attended the convention to ask the First National directors for extra funds for production costs, since both *A Dog's Life* and *Shoulder Arms* were longer than the two-reel films for which he had contracted.[19] When he was turned down, even treated with indifference, he and his brother Sydney decided that something must be done. On January 14 Chaplin held a meeting at his house with Fairbanks, William S. Hart, Griffith, and a representative for Pickford, who was ill. By the next afternoon, all had become signatories to the articles of agreement that established the United Artists' Association.[20]

In essence, United Artists, by distributing collectively the films Fairbanks, Pickford, Hart, Griffith, and Chaplin would independently produce, was designed to protect the independence that they had managed to attain in the film industry. (Hart, though involved in the planning stages, withdrew and remained at Famous Players–Lasky when offered $200,000 per film.)[21] Though Fairbanks, Pickford, and Griffith had all begun releasing films through United Artists by 1920—with some other producers joining them—Chaplin was tied to his First National contract through the release of *The Pilgrim* in 1923. As film historians have shown, Chaplin's years at First National were key years in the consolidation of the American film industry, during which three important shifts were occurring: studio production began to dominate the market; producers began to wrest creative control from directors, resulting in a "central producer" mode of production; and principles of scientific management and systematic division of labor became commonplace in the production of movies.[22]

The dimensions of Chaplin's emerging star image that stressed his serious side and his concern for high art were cultivated at least in part to counter this trend of "assembly-line "movie production and to differentiate his "product" and those of others at United Artists from the films made by the major studios. Chaplin had this in mind when, in February 1923, he, along with Pickford, Fairbanks, Harold Lloyd, and Griffith, signed what they told reporters was a "declaration of independence from producers and exhibitors of 'machine-made' films." In a joint statement, the filmmakers warned that the powerful corporate combinations "will dwarf the artistic growth of the motion picture." They also claimed a desire "to protect the independent producer and the independent exhibitor against these commercial combinations."[23] In this case, as well as later in his career, Chaplin's use of the press to emphasize an aspect of his star image—his individual artistic vision—stemmed at least in part from distinct economic motivations.

Since United Artists lost money in each of its first three full years of operation (1920–1922) and since Paramount and First National had if anything increased their strength in the market, the success of this declaration of independence and the links with independent exhibitors were crucial if Chaplin and his colleagues were to survive in the competitive marketplace and still retain creative and financial control over their films. It was in this context that Chaplin contemplated his first film for United Artists.

Chaplin's writings and interviews in 1922 indicate that he was becoming restless with comedies featuring Charlie. As early as 1920 he told an interviewer that his "world-weariness" was partly "a reaction from my innate sense of humor, disgust of the character that circumstances has forced me to create."[24] He also was interested in directing a film that would star Edna Purviance, who was becoming less appropriate in appearance for the ingenue type that Chaplin liked in his comedies as a romantic companion for Charlie. Thus, when Peggy Hopkins Joyce, with whom Chaplin had a brief affair in 1922, suggested a film based on Henri Letellier, a wealthy Parisian bon vivant, Chaplin began working on a film called *Public Opinion*. It would star Purviance and, in the Letellier part, Adolphe Menjou, who reportedly resembled him.[25] From this germ grew *A Woman of Paris*, which more than any other film established Chaplin's reputation as a serious film director and artist quite apart from his performing talents.

Chaplin stresses his artistic concerns in the opening titles, which contain a statement warning viewers that he will not appear in the film and that it is the first "serious drama" he has written and produced. He also sets the tone by subtitling the film "a drama of fate." What follows is a simple narrative, focusing on Marie St. Claire (Edna Purviance), Jean Millet (Carl Miller), and Pierre Revel (Adolphe Menjou). Marie and Jean, from the same village in France, have decided to leave for Paris and marry despite the objections of their fathers. When Jean's father is suddenly stricken ill, eventually dying, Jean misses his appointment to leave with Marie on the train. Marie, however, believes he has rejected her. A year passes and we learn that Marie has become the kept woman of Pierre Revel, a wealthy and eligible Parisian bachelor. Her life with Pierre is one of pleasure and luxury, but she begins to reevaluate their relationship when Pierre announces his upcoming marriage of convenience and when she accidentally meets Jean, who has moved to Paris with his mother and is eking out a living as a painter. He proposes, though his mother disapproves, and the remainder of the film traces Marie's attempts to choose between luxury or marriage, while fate conspires to keep her from realizing happiness. Ultimately, Jean's misapprehension about Marie's feelings leads him to suicide. The stricken Marie renounces her life with Pierre and, after reconciling with Jean's mother, retires with her to the countryside, where they dedicate their lives to the care of orphans.

In many ways, the film is most un-Chaplinesque, at least as reviewers, critics, and audiences had come to define that term from his previous films. Probably the most important shifts are the film's general lack of broad comedy and its restrained acting style. Discussing the film with an interviewer, Chaplin stressed his concern for such restraint: "In real life great emotions are repressed. There are no such great emotional splurges as we often see on the stage and on the screen. . . . It is this realism that is worthwhile striving for—a realism that will portray emotions intelligently and at the same time keep the audience interested in the story."[26] Perhaps the best example of underplayed emotion in the film comes when Jean's mother learns of her son's death. Instead of broad and uncontrolled grief, Chaplin sought, and actress Lydia Knott achieved, a stunned numbness—the kind of formal feeling that, wrote Emily Dickinson, follows great pain.[27]

The restraint and subtlety of acting is combined with a more expressive use of film style. Early in the film Chaplin shows the influence of German Expressionism, as looming shadows of both fathers precede them when they first appear. He uses the interplay of light and shadow again at the train station, a device frequently noted by the reviewers. In that scene Chaplin presents Marie in a medium shot, and, as her eyes blur with grief after surmising that Jean has abandoned her, the shadows of a moving train pass by her. She walks toward the camera and passes to the right of it in closeup: Chaplin implies the existence of the fateful train to Paris without once showing it. Two other subtle uses of film style are the cutaway to a close-up of a smoking pipe lying on the carpet, indicating to viewers the incapacitation or death of Jean's father, and Jean's discovery of a man's shirt collar in Marie's dresser, a visual suggestion of Pierre's frequent presence in her apartment. Chaplin also managed to titillate audiences without unduly offending censors when he showed the feet and lower legs of a woman being "unwrapped" at a Latin Quarter party and when, by framing the masseur and keeping Marie's body just below the bottom of the frame, he presented a nearly nude Marie getting a massage. Although the narrative is linear and quite simple, Chaplin tells the story with a kind of visual sophistication that was rarely evident in his earlier films.

Despite the lack of sustained comedy in the film and the more sophisticated use of film style, *A Woman of Paris* does resemble some of Chaplin's earlier comic narratives—*The Kid*, most obviously—in the way it contrasts two distinctly different ways of life, both of which embody moral universes that generate narrative conflict. The two perspectives in *A Woman of Paris* represent the urban haves and have-nots, a contrast that Chaplin would return to in a later comedy, *City Lights*. The urban haves are represented by Pierre, Marie (after she becomes his mistress), and their acquaintances. The urban have-nots are represented by Jean and his mother after they move to Paris, where he has become a talented but struggling painter. Throughout the film Chaplin skillfully uses mise-en-scène,[28] particularly sets (Marie's apartment versus Jean's) and costumes (Pierre's versus Jean's; Marie's versus Jean's mother's) to juxtapose the two worlds.

This contrast, particularly the one between Pierre and Jean, poses the central question of the film: will Marie favor Pierre or Jean, after Jean again declares his love for Marie? As one title puts it: "In the mind of Marie St. Clair is the problem—marriage or luxury." Costume becomes important here, for the Marie whom Jean loves is the one he knew before they went to Paris. She poses for him wearing a long, white, low-cut dress and a feathery hat; Jean, however, paints her in the dark, high-necked dress and subdued hat she was wearing the night they were to have left for Paris. Significantly, when Marie agrees to reconcile with Pierre after Jean has temporarily come between them, she puts on the same costume, and she is wearing it when Jean commits suicide in despair after he believes he has been rejected by Marie.

Whereas the earlier Chaplin films that posed moral contrasts usually drew a clear melodramatic line between good (Charlie) and evil (the wealthy, the physically imposing, the snobbish, etc.), that line is fuzzier here. Jean's dedication to art and his basic decency are beyond question, but his strained relationship with his father and later, his mother, keep us from identifying him exclusively with good. And though Marie's "friends" Paulette and Fifi surely suggest that the wealthy are hypocritical, dishonest, and spiteful in their dealings with one another, Pierre's charm, love of the good life, and tolerance of Marie keep us from fully identifying him with evil. After the climactic event of the film—Jean's suicide at the base of the nude statue in the café's entrance—Marie reconciles with Jean's mother. They are bound by their mutual grief. The closing scene, which is introduced by the title, "Time heals, and experience teaches that the secret of happiness is in service to others," reminds one of the affirmation of charity in *The Kid*. Marie and Jean's mother have dedicated themselves to running a small orphanage in a bucolic rural setting, ninety kilometers from Paris.

By the end of the film, the meaning of Chaplin's subtitle, "a drama of fate," is clear. At several crucial points in the narrative pure coincidence or accident conspire to keep Jean and Marie apart. The death of Jean's father just as Jean prepares to leave with Marie to Paris constitutes the first. The second comes when Jean's mother arrives home unexpectedly, just in time to overhear Jean propose marriage to Marie. Then the tables are turned when Marie, coming to visit Jean unannounced, overhears Jean tell his mother that the proposal came at a moment of weakness and that he would never marry Marie, even though we know he really feels differently. Fate even seems to lend a hand in the final shots of the film. Pierre, riding with a friend back toward Paris and telling him he doesn't know what has happened to Marie St. Clair, drives past a horse-drawn cart traveling in the other direction. Though Pierre is unaware of it, Marie is riding in the cart with one of her orphan children. Thus she passes her former lover, though neither is aware of it. The feeling that humans are victims of fate pervades the film.

A Woman of Paris is also interesting because of the submerged autobiography in the film. Just as he had in *The Kid*, Chaplin used his personal experience in constructing the narrative. But whereas *The Kid* was informed primarily by childhood experiences and memories, *A Woman of Paris*, like *The Idle Class*, drew on dilemmas Chaplin was undergoing as a private man and public celebrity after he had become widely known and admired.[29] This tendency to express sides of his personality through the characters of his films became increasingly common in Chaplin's films from the time his United Artists period began until its culmination in *Limelight*, the most obviously autobiographical of Chaplin's films.

Although the autobiography may be more buried in *A Woman of Paris*, it is nevertheless there.[30] Chaplin claims in his autobiography that he made the film partly because he was still interested in Edna Purviance's career, even though they had become "emotionally estranged" shortly before Chaplin's first marriage (MA, p. 296). In some ways, Marie's story is Edna's. Edna came from a rural area—Lovecraft, Paradise Valley, Nevada—and agreed to come to a big city, Los Angeles, with a budding young artist, the twenty-six-year-old Chaplin, in 1915. Later, after Chaplin's fame had grown, she, like Marie, became the mistress of a wealthy man (Chaplin) whose engagement to another woman (Mildred Harris) she read about in the newspapers. The central difference between Marie and Edna is that Marie breaks free of Pierre while Edna remained on Chaplin's payroll for the rest of her life (MA, p. 496).

As these parallels suggest, Chaplin projected himself into two characters in the film: the struggling dedicated artist, Jean, and the wealthy cosmopolitan cynic, Pierre. Much of the complexity of the film, and its refusal to move into a tempting melodramatic mold, stems from the fact that Chaplin apparently felt drawn toward both of the characters, which left him unable to commit himself fully to either. One of Chaplin's dedications in the early 1920s was to movies as art—indeed, he would not have risked making a film like *A Woman of Paris* if he had not had aspirations toward serious art. That dedication drew him toward Jean, even though Jean's case was weakened when Chaplin cast a rather weak actor—at least in comparison to Adolphe Menjou—in Jean's role. On the other hand, Chaplin himself was increasingly cast in the role of celebrity and bon vivant in the early 1920s, particularly after his European tour. He no longer had to seek out other celebrities: they sought him. It is evident that Chaplin invested some of his own experience in Pierre, and the way he is presented in the film, in part due to Adolphe Menjou's engaging performance, makes it clear that Chaplin found it impossible to condemn a man that the conventions of melodrama would surely have cast in the role of villain. This autobiographical subtext of *A Woman of Paris*, though not much apparent to viewers and critics in 1923, casts important light on how Chaplin, consciously or unconsciously, was drawing on his own experience as he sought to establish himself as a serious artist in his first genuinely independent feature-length production. It is probably fair to suggest that Chaplin even projected himself into Marie's character in the scene in which Pierre tries to console the melancholy

Marie by telling her that she has everything. Marie's answer, "Not everything," underscores the hints in Chaplin's writings in the early 1920s that his life, despite his fame and fortune, was less than satisfactory.

Nevertheless, Chaplin's desire to be recognized as a serious artist and director in *A Woman of Paris* was certainly satisfied, at least as far as critics and reviewers were concerned. The *New York Times* reviewer wrote on the day after the film opened that it "fascinated an interesting and curious throng last night at the Lyric Theater." To this reviewer Chaplin proved himself to be "a bold, resourceful, imaginative, ingenious, careful, studious, and daring artist."[31] The following Sunday the *Times* again praised the production: "mostly it is the detail to which much studious thought and attention has been given, that is responsible for the great charm of this unusually fine production."[32]

Other reviewers were equally enthusiastic. In the *New York Herald Tribune*, for example, Harriette Underhill wrote, "we could say volumes and write columns, but the few words to which we are limited seem inadequate, no matter how we choose them. Charles Chaplin is a great artist!" And the film, Underhill added, was "the perfect motion picture."[33] Robert Sherwood held that Chaplin "proves to the satisfaction of everyone that he is the first genius of the silent drama."[34] One of the few hesitancies expressed, somewhat amusingly, appeared in *Photoplay*. Warning its readers that the film was "for the sophisticated rather than for a strictly family audience," *Photoplay's* reviewer suggested that "any fifteen-year-old child who appreciates it should be taken home and spanked." Though the reviewer believed that the film was not "great," it did prove that Chaplin "is one of the greatest of all directors."[35] Even the *New Republic's* demanding Stark Young, who the previous year had called on Chaplin to become more ambitious in developing his art, praised *A Woman of Paris*: "not a great drama, this Woman of Paris, but for these forward achievements of Mr. Chaplin's an exciting spot on the horizon."[36]

These reviews failed to note any autobiographical elements in the work, perhaps because *A Woman of Paris* was such a departure from Chaplin's previous films that its obvious differences drew the attention of reviewers. Viewers of Chaplin films in 1923 had been led to expect a comedy that featured Charlie and included both romance and pathos. There had also been some indication, through Chaplin's interviews in the early 1920s and *My Trip Abroad*, that Chaplin was becoming a restive funny man, concerned with issues more serious than slapstick. To the extent that audiences and reviewers were aware of this, *A Woman of Paris* helped include Chaplin the serious intellect and talented director within his star image.

Because of viewers' expectations about Chaplin as a comic film-maker, however, it was almost inevitable that the film would not become a box-office hit. Nevertheless, it seemed to fool *Variety*, the trade publication whose reviews sought in part to gauge box-office potential. The *Variety* reviewer, calling it "a serious sincere effort" and "a candidate for honors and dollars entirely independent of the drawing power Chaplin built up in other fields," raved about the film. Judging Chaplin "a new genius both as a producer and director," the reviewer thought the film "a cinch for the biggest houses."[37] This enthusiasm was not entirely realized. Domestically, the film grossed $634,000, which was surely higher than the gross for a run-of-the-mill studio picture but about the same as the *least* successful United Artists films of Griffith, Pickford, and Fairbanks up through 1923.[38]

So Chaplin made his point and firmly established himself among critics and more sophisticated viewers as a serious and ambitious artist, without suffering too much financially. Yet by the time the film opened, he was telling people that *A Woman of Paris* was an experiment, a deviation from the kind of films that had made him and would keep him an independently wealthy man. In an interview appearing the Sunday after *A Woman of Paris* opened, Chaplin stated that "unless my feelings undergo a marked change, I am going right back to comedy—back to one of the kind of films with which the public identifies me."[39] He reiterated this intention to return to comedy to a group of school children in Detroit a week later, and by the spring of 1924 he had begun production on a full-length feature comedy/romance/epic.[40]

Creating an Epic: *The Gold Rush*

"This is the picture that I want to be remembered by," Chaplin stated on one of the newspaper advertisements provided in the pressbook for *The Gold Rush*.[41] Surely Chaplin had great ambitions for the film, which he hoped would surpass even *The Kid* as a serious comedy featuring Charlie as the central character. After *A Woman of Paris* had established him as a serious director and producer, Chaplin's next step was to outdo any of his comic competitors—Harold Lloyd, Harry Langdon, and Buster Keaton, among others—in the creation of a full-length feature comedy. And he did. Starting to shoot in February 1924, Chaplin completed in fourteen months a ten-reel feature film, longer than any of his competitors' films to that time. After the August

1925 release of *The Gold Rush*, Chaplin reached the height of his reputation up to that time as a film artist and comic performer for American film viewers. Besides the film itself, Chaplin's skill as a publicist
and purveyor to the press of particular star qualities helped him to
achieve this fame.

The film, of course, accounts for some of his popularity. Chaplin
remembers telling himself that his "next film must be an epic" as he
cast about for ideas after completing *A Woman of Paris* (MA, p. 303).
He also labeled his next work a "dramatic comedy" in the film's promotional material. These comments are entirely appropriate, for the
resulting film returns to and in some ways surpasses in effectiveness
the characteristics that audiences of Chaplin's films had come to expect in his work: "serious" concerns, comedy, and pathos.

The epic elements of the film relate partly to the film's unlikely
source: the Donner party disaster, in which a group of pioneers was
snowbound while trying to cross the Sierra Nevadas in 1846 and 1847.
According to C. F. McGlashlin's *The Story of the Donner Party*, a book
that Chaplin most likely read, only forty-eight of the ninety survived,
some of them resorting to cannibalism.[42] This tenacious human struggle to overcome the threats of nature provided one epic conflict at the
foundation of *The Gold Rush*. The fact that Chaplin did considerable
location shooting in Truckee, California, near the Donner party
statue, emphasizes this source of the film's epic stature.[43]

But Chaplin did not set the film in California in the 1840s. Rather,
perhaps influenced by some stereoscopic slides he had seen at the
home of Douglas Fairbanks, he made the Klondike in 1898, during
the height of the gold mania that drew many dreamers, entrepreneurs, and get-rich-quick schemers to Alaska in search of their fortunes, the setting. Significantly Chaplin, living in the middle of the
consumption-oriented 1920s, rooted his film in a time equally known
for its materialism. The fact that *The Gold Rush* appeared in the same
year as two literary works that explored the abiding, almost pathological lure of wealth and success in America—*The Great Gatsby* and *An
American Tragedy*—and just a year after Erich von Stroheim's *Greed*,
suggests that a number of artists were perceiving and responding to
the same cultural currents. And by setting his film during a gold rush,
Chaplin enriched its epic and metaphorical possibilities.

However, after the opening shots, which show hundreds of fortune
hunters laboring slowly up the Chilkoot Pass—one of them collapsing
of exhaustion and ignored by his compatriots—the film does not really
have much of an epic scope. On the contrary: after this opening, the
cast of characters, except for a large group of extras and bit characters

at the dance hall, is really quite small. It consists principally of Charlie, Big Jim (his fellow prospector), Black Larsen (a villain who dies midway through the film), Georgia (a dance-hall girl who falls in love with Charlie), and Jack (a rival to Charlie for Georgia's affections). Through the interactions of this smaller cast of characters arise both the comedy and the dramatic pathos, both of which were familiar to Chaplin fans.

In creating the comedy, Chaplin drew once again on his pantomimic skills honed in the English music halls. Anything he ever did in film is equalled by a number of his comic routines here, particularly Charlie's attempts to escape the sights of the shotgun that Jim and Black Larsen struggle over; the boiled shoe Thanksgiving dinner, replete with spaghetti shoestrings; and the "Oceana Roll" that Charlie performs for Georgia and his other dinner guests in his dream. In a final scene, the cabin set—a raised stage that rested on a fulcrum and tipped back and forth through the use of a pulley system—generates the comic climax. The cabin is ostensibly blown to the edge of a precipice, after which it tilts back and forth depending on which side Charlie and Jim are standing.[44]

But it may be the pathos generated by the relationship between Georgia and Charlie that constituted the film's most lasting contribution to the shaping of Chaplin's comic persona and his persistent appeal to viewers. In *The Gold Rush* Charlie is not like what Joan Mellen has called the "Big Bad Wolves" of American movies: the typical masculine stereotype of a strong, attractive, self-confident, and engaging man, represented in *The Gold Rush* by Jack.[45] Rather, Charlie is physically unimposing, even somewhat ridiculous in appearance, and often bumbling. Edgar Morin perceptively notes that in contrast to the typical romantic hero in movies, the comic hero portrayed so convincingly by Chaplin relates to women in quite a different manner. Whereas the relationship between the typical hero and women is sexual, the relationship between the comic hero and women is desexualized. Yet, says Morin, the comic hero is often in love: "his love is sublime because it is not founded on sexual domination and appropriation: it is a total gift of himself, like infantile or canine love." Though the comic hero may not seem to have as much to give, he is willing to give it all.[46]

In *The Gold Rush* Chaplin's idealized love for Georgia—his yearning for human intimacy and his contrasting fear of isolation—is symbolized by an important prop, a picture of Georgia. He initially gets the torn picture from the floor of the dance hall shortly after he first sees her. Later we learn, as does Georgia, that Charlie keeps it under the pillow of his bed. Even after he has struck it rich near the end of the film, Charlie retains the picture, now framed on a side table in his sleeping quarters. The film suggests that human fulfillment comes not from riches but ultimately from close human ties.[47]

This need for close bonds with others and the difficulty of achieving them lead directly to the two scenes of most profound pathos in *The Gold Rush*. They occur close to one another, three-quarters of the way through the film. The first comes on New Year's Eve, traditionally a time when people gather with friends to reflect on the past and look toward the future. Charlie, having invited the dance-hall girls to dine with him, has worked hard to earn some money to prepare a feast for them. They're late, but Chaplin dissolves from a shot of a table empty except for Charlie to one of the table surrounded by the women. Charlie entertains his guests with the Oceana Roll, but as he finishes and is being congratulated, Chaplin again dissolves to Charlie asleep at the otherwise empty table. The warmth of the crowded frame shifts to the coldness of the nearly empty one, and elicits strong empathy from the viewer. As in *The Bank*, *Shoulder Arms*, and *The Idle Class*, Charlie's accomplishments take place only in his dreams. But here, because of the situation and the characterization, the effect is deeper and richer than in the earlier films.

Only a few moments after this scene, the second prominent situation of pathos appears. Noticing that it is nearly midnight and his party a failure, the despairing Charlie makes his way to the dance hall. Just as he reaches the building, Chaplin frames Charlie in an extremely powerful way: he stands in the frigid winter air, alone, outside a window, while inside the dance hall people embrace, celebrate, and collectively ring in the new year. Literally an outsider looking in, Charlie is both spatially and psychologically distant from the festive crowd. The effect of these two scenes must be experienced to be fully apprehended.

The final scene of *The Gold Rush*, superficially a happy ending and arguably forced, fashioned with the box office in mind, is actually much more aesthetically complex than it first appears. After Charlie and Jim find their gold, they become millionaires and are leaving the Klondike on a ship. Jim seems happy after striking it rich, but Charlie still seems empty and incomplete without Georgia. For reporters, Charlie changes back into his prospecting clothes. He tumbles down a stairway to find himself at Georgia's feet, and—when she thinks he is a stowaway—is protected by her. They whisper, apparently decide to marry, and are being photographed by a newspaperman as the film ends.

This final scene does give the audience its "happy ending," realizing the romance Charlie has desired. But it is more complicated in two ways. First, Chaplin was again working in submerged autobiography. Like Charlie, Chaplin went from rags to riches in an extremely short time, finding his gold mine in the movie industry. Just as Charlie had to get into his old clothes at the end of the film to satisfy reporters and win Georgia, so Chaplin had to get into his tramp costume to satisfy movie audiences. Also like Charlie, Chaplin often found himself a lonely, isolated man, both before he struck it rich (notably in the Hetty Kelly incident) and after. The pressbook for *The Gold Rush* shows that Chaplin was conscious of the parallels between Charlie and himself: one proposed newspaper headline reads "Chaplin Comedy an Auto-biography: The Material Success of Charlie Chaplin at Last Has Never Satisfied His Soul."[48] With one marriage failed and the second marriage already on the rocks, as will be discussed in Chapter 4, the melancholic Chaplin must have yearned for a relationship of trust and mutual affection shorn of role playing and status, though his desire for control in his dealings with others made it hard for him to achieve such a relationship.

The film's ending is also more complicated by Chaplin's self-referential look at what he was doing in his role as film director and producer. At the very end of the original version of the film, Charlie and Georgia are posing for the photographer. Just before the picture is snapped, however, Charlie turns and kisses Georgia. In a title, the photographer replies: "Oh! You've spoilt the picture." If we take the photographer to be the filmmaker's spokesman, we see Chaplin the self-conscious director telling alert viewers that he knows the happy ending, the embrace, and the kiss in one sense "spoil" the film: after all the hunger, brutality, and cruelty in the film narrative, a coincidental gold strike and even more coincidental reconcilation of lovers seems implausible if not contradictory. Yes, it is, Chaplin hints in his conclusion, and like Murnau's *The Last Laugh* a year earlier, a happy ending is subtly undercut by a self-referential gesture.[49]

The Gold Rush works as epic, as comedy, as conveyer of dramatic pathos, as submerged autobiography, and as self-referential exploration of happy endings. Charlie had surely endeared himself to a large mass audience and added to Chaplin's star status. But the promotion of the film, the most elaborate and systematic effort Chaplin had overseen to that time, also contributed to his star image and suggests how Chaplin sought to shape that image in the mid-1920s.

To place the promotion of *The Gold Rush* in context, a few words should be said about advertising in the film industry. Film historians have shown that advertising became important early. Advertising was important to the development of the film industry not simply because it directed people to individual films but also because it helped set up the ground rules for what was acceptable and even expected in film production. In the first decade of the century, film production companies like Edison advertised to distributors and exhibitors by using catalogues that listed and "pitched" their films. By the next decade, fan magazines emphasizing stars appeared on the scene. As the studio system began to establish itself, studios set up publicity departments, which in turn provided newspaper reviewers and theater owners with information like pressbooks that would help advertise locally. According to one film historian, the early catalogue advertisements "exhibit many of the exchange-values the industry has consistently promoted as the qualities in their films: novelty, specific popular genres, brand names, 'realism,' authenticity, spectacle, stars, and certain creators of the product whose skills as artists were considered acknowledged."[50] If we can add to this list a tendency to hyperbolize the qualities of a particular star or story or set design, we have a pretty good idea of the kind and degree of characteristics which were typically emphasized in advertisements for Hollywood films. With this list in mind, the promotion for *The Gold Rush* seems in many ways typical, in a few ways unusual.

Perhaps the most important piece of promotion literature for *The Gold Rush* was the program prepared for the film's opening at Grauman's Chinese Theater.[51] Besides listing the events that preceded the feature—which included an overture by Grauman's Egyptian Orchestra, with Julius K. Johnson at the "Mighty Egyptian Organ," and a "Festival of Dancing Ice Skaters"—the text of the program gives an idea of Chaplin's artistic reputation as he wished to project it. Hyperbole is used to stress Chaplin's apparently unique talent for movies: "Chaplin was the biggest man on the lot from the time he made his first comedy." A variation on that theme—and one that Chaplin and his publicists often referred to throughout the 1920s after his association with United Artists began—was the assertion that his films were more serious and of much higher quality than the typical studio-made film. As opposed to the "factory system of movies," *The Gold Rush* "was never restricted by definite schedule or time clock methods, but inspired by Chaplin with a passion for perfection as his only taskmaster." Chaplin's being is invested with a kind of transcendence: "Within a short time after his entry into pictures directors complained to the powers-to-be [*sic*] that Chaplin wanted his own way and could not 'take direction.' It was great talent trying to assert itself and climb out of the embryo into the uniform of the greatest actor in the world. He was conscious of ability in his soul, as great talent ever is." Finally, expanding some of the publicity statements that accompanied *A Woman of Paris*, the program emphasizes how painstakingly Chaplin works and how much money he has been willing to spend to make films that satisfy his artistic genius. Syd Grauman writes that on the day he visited the set, only three set-ups were completed, though each was "shot at least twenty times." A section called "What Was Used in Making" employs numbers to express the epic scope of the film: 500 workmen used 239,577 board feet of lumber, 2,000 feet of garden hose, and 7,000 feet of rope. The snow was simulated by using 285 tons of salt, 100 barrels of flour, and four carloads of confetti for blizzards. In Richard Dyer's terms, to be a star, one must be portrayed as extraordinary, and the program stresses this dimension of Chaplin through its emphasis on star, novelty, and spectacle.

The pressbook, assembled by a United Artists publicity staff under the guidance of Chaplin and his own staff to help exhibitors promote the film, reiterates many of these themes (see Figure 9). One of the proposed headlines to pass on to newspapers was "Opening Scenes Cost $50,000," which uses budget figures to sell the film, a ploy with which contemporary film viewers are familiar. Two more—"One Man Power in Chaplin Picture" and "*The Gold Rush* Is Chaplin's Greatest"— implied that Chaplin's name alone sold tickets, as indeed it did by 1925. The pressbook suggested that exhibitors encourage the sponsorship of a Chaplin walking contest for children, and it included a number of telegrams of congratulation from Hollywood luminaries like Fairbanks, Pickford, William Hart, and Norma Talmadge (all of whom had been or were associated with United Artists). Among the other telegrams was an interesting tribute from rival Buster Keaton, who called the film "the most impressive comedy ever made." The pressbook even carried reviews and articles that could be signed by the newspaper's movie reviewer. One, describing a visit to the Chaplin's set, was modestly headed, "Chaplin's Genius Supreme on Set in Famous Studio." If anything, the pressbook was even more extreme than the program in promoting the film and stressing Chaplin's genius. And though the promotion for *The Gold Rush* emphasized a number of the same qualities found in other Hollywood advertising, it was helping to shape and reinforce a distinct star image for Chaplin: the independent, even solitary creative genius, admired by the greats of the industry, who was willing to spend whatever money and effort necessary to achieve perfection in his films.

Some of the reviews of the film, one in particular, were as enthu-

9. The long-familiar Charlie helps advertise
The Gold Rush in 1925.

siastic as the promotion material. In its prerelease review of the film, *Variety* was extravagant: "*The Gold Rush* is a distinct triumph for Charlie Chaplin from both artistic and commercial standpoints, and is a picture sure to create a veritable riot at theater box offices. It is the greatest and most elaborate comedy ever filmed and will stand for years to come as the biggest hit in its field, just as *The Birth of a Nation* still withstands its many competitors in the dramatic field."[52] If such a review seemed too good to be true from the box-office weathervane of trade journals, it was. A month later, at the New York opening of the film, *Variety* reviewed the film again, this time more circumspectly. *The Gold Rush* "may have impressed Chaplin's friends on the coast to that degree," the New York reviewer wrote, "but as shown at the Strand, New York, it does not live up to the rave from the west. It's just a good Chaplin comedy." Despite these qualifications, however,

83

the reviewer adds that "in any kind of show, it will draw a heavy gross."[53]

Ivan St. Johns in *Photoplay* followed the line established by the second *Variety* review: "That it is a great development in the comedy field, or that it brings a new comedy era to the screen certainly is not true. It is simply ten reels of a very good Chaplin comedy, which ought to be enough for anybody, but it is no more."[54] In the *New York Times* Mordaunt Hall judged the film "by all means Chaplin's supreme effort, as back of the ludicrous touches there is a truth, a glimpse into the disappointments of Chaplin's early life."[55]

Two points are worth noting here. First, as Hall's comment suggests, some observers were beginning to see hints of Chaplin's autobiography woven into the fabric of his films, a blending that helped his star image in the 1920s but hindered him later on. Second, the reviews show that Chaplin was becoming so highly regarded by the reviewers that their role was not to judge whether his films were good enough to recommend but rather to decide where on the spectrum of Chaplin's greatness a particular film belonged. Like the promotion and the film itself, the reviews of *The Gold Rush* showed a star at the height of his popularity.

Cultivating the Intelligentsia

As well as making films that were consistently successful with mass audiences and daily newspaper reviewers, Chaplin also managed by the mid-1920s to do something no other Hollywood star had: win the respect of American intellectuals. This occurred during a period of literary renaissance in America, which Malcolm Cowley would later call the "second flowering" of American literature. It was stimulated in part by a lively group of literary, political, and cultural magazines—like the *Dial*, the *New Republic*, and *Vanity Fair*—the most important of which were centered in New York City. As Chaplin's fame enabled him to make contacts there, his relationships with some of these intellectuals, as well as their friendships among themselves, eventually led to frequent praise for Chaplin in their articles and books as the first and only important American screen artist. Public kudos from such circles gave Chaplin's star image a legitimacy among the intelligentsia rarely attained by an American filmmaker before the studio system broke up. A look at the activities and writings of Max Eastman, Waldo Frank, Stark Young, Gilbert Seldes, Edmund Wilson, and John Peale Bishop demonstrates the dynamics that enabled Chaplin to become a darling of the younger and generally antigenteel intellectuals in the 1920s.[56]

The best place to start is the fall of 1919, an unhappy time in Chaplin's life: his infant son had died in July after living only three days, his marriage with Mildred Harris was unraveling, and he was feeling oppressed by his First National contract (*A Day's Pleasure* would be released in December). For some reason he decided to attend a political lecture by Max Eastman in the Philharmonic Auditorium. Eastman was, in his own words, "about the only Socialist agitator who had opposed the World War and supported the Russian revolution, and yet managed to stay out of jail."[57] After the lecture, Chaplin visited Eastman backstage, praised his "restraint," contributed a modest $25 to his magazine, the *Liberator*, and invited him to dinner. Their friendship grew, and they remained good friends until Eastman's politics turned to the right in the late 1930s and the 1940s.

This friendship helped Chaplin meet other Greenwich Village intellectuals when he took a trip to New York City in November 1920 (MA, p. 247). Perhaps partly because his divorce had just become final and work on *The Kid* was nearly completed, Chaplin was ready to make new acquaintances. He visited the editorial offices of *Vanity Fair*, where he met, among others, its young managing editor, Edmund Wilson. On the same trip, he began to encounter a number of other young intellectuals and artists, including some of the Provincetown Players. In his autobiography Chaplin also recalled meeting on this visit both critic Waldo Frank (who had already written on him—not entirely positively) and poet Hart Crane (who later wrote a poem, "Chaplinesque," inspired by *The Kid*) (MA, p. 248). All in all, Chaplin's 1920 visit provided the film star with a nucleus of intellectual acquaintances who helped advance his career through their writings and their influence on others throughout the decade and after.[58]

Although Eastman later wrote a good deal about Chaplin, sometimes repeating his stories of their acquaintance from book to book, he did not write much on Chaplin in the 1920s.[59] Eastman's influence was more personal, for in addition to the interactions already noted, Chaplin also visited Eastman in New York City on his way to and from Europe in 1921, referring to him in *My Trip Abroad* as "one of my best friends."[60]

Waldo Frank wrote considerably about Chaplin both before and after he met the comedian, but more positively after he had met Chaplin personally. Frank, six years younger than Eastman and nearly the same age as Chaplin, had earned an M.A. from Yale and was the founder and editor of the *Seven Arts* in its short (1916–1917) but influential life. His first reference to Chaplin was in a *Seven Arts* article in 1917, "Valedictory to a Theatrical Season." He wrote: "Chaplin is an extremely brilliant clown but also an unhealthy one," a comment that sounds much like those the genteel critics of Chaplin's "vulgarity" were making at much the same time. Later, in *Our America* (1919) Frank made similar observations, acclaiming Chaplin as "our most significant and most authentic dramatic artist" but objecting to the "sophistications in Chaplin's work that are not healthy."[61]

Yet meeting the star seemed to make people revise their negative opinion of him. Chaplin recalls his 1920 meeting with Frank in his autobiography, calling him "the first to write seriously about me" and adding, "naturally, we became very good friends" (MA, p. 248), a comment that underlines Chaplin's tendency to surround himself with admirers. Frank also remembers the meeting and recalls that Chaplin thanked him for his positive comments in *Our America*; in Frank's view, Chaplin was grateful to have a "highbrow" take his work seriously. After they became personally acquainted, Frank's writings strongly defended Chaplin the artist. When he reprinted his 1917 essay in *Salvos* (1924), Frank appended a note: "The injustice which this essay does to Mr. Chaplin by a total disregard for the pure aesthetic virtue of his art, I have righted. . . . Mr. Chaplin's art is far from unhealthy. His art is indeed a symbol of health in a complexly morbid world."[62] Frank had begun to identify the comic world created by Chaplin as a viable alternative to the materialism of American culture.

The next year Frank published his first piece focused entirely on Chaplin, the essay that contributed most of any by Frank to Chaplin's star image. Titled "Funny-Legs," it appeared in the first volume of the *New Yorker*, a new magazine aimed at a sophisticated urban audience. The article stressed Chaplin's worldwide fame: Frank reported that when Chaplin visited a circus in Paris while on his European tour, the audience feverishly chanted, "Charlot!" In addition to remarking on "the intellectuals of New York and Paris [who turned Chaplin's] stunts into logarithmic mazes as if he were Einstein," Frank portrayed Chaplin as an enigmatic, questing genius. He recounted a long evening spent discussing Schopenhauer and Spinoza with Chaplin. Sometime during the night, according to Frank, Chaplin reflected on his dissatisfactions in spite of his fame: "I don't know . . . I may retire. I may study Sanskrit." Chaplin is a man of masks, in Frank's view, a man of many faces and possibilities, who is trying to find answers to life. His quests leave him "lost in a world of which he is the king, and which he does not love and which distrusts him, knowing him different from it."[63] The essay provides an admiring, penetrating personal view of

Chaplin and stresses, among other qualities, Chaplin's melancholia and his interest in the life of the mind.

Another intellectual to take Chaplin's work seriously in this period was Stark Young (b. 1881), a native Mississippian who earned an M.A. from Columbia University in 1902 and who taught literature at the universities of Mississippi and Texas and Amherst College from 1904 to 1921. Thereafter, he moved to New York City and served on the editorial staffs of *Theater Arts Monthly* and the *New Republic*, where he was drama critic. Young was a demanding and fastidious critic with classical tastes, yet in 1922 he published an open letter to Chaplin, "Dear Mr. Chaplin," in the *New Republic*, which praised Chaplin's achievements, particularly his comic persona ("You have created one of the great clowns of all time") and his acting style ("The greatest actor in English you are easily. You have a technique completely finished").[64]

Yet Young's letter was not simply a tribute to Chaplin's brilliance; it also urged Chaplin to become more ambitious, to "go on to a larger field." Because Chaplin was such a gifted artist, Young suggested, he should break out of the "one thing" he had so far done—silent comedies—and do *Liliom* or *He Who Gets Slapped* or *Peer Gynt*. Or even better, Young advised Chaplin, "You could do new things written by you or for you, things in which you would use your full endowment, comic and otherwise." Like Frank, Young observed an unfulfilled yearning in the mask of Charlie, "a poetry and a music and a poignancy that eats into you." Tap that in your art, Young advised, and you will satisfy that most demanding of critics: yourself. Written after profiles of Chaplin that, as we have seen, portrayed Chaplin as the lonely and "Hamlet-like" artist, this article not only helped legitimate Chaplin as an important artist to *New Republic* readers but also helped to reinforce that dimension of Chaplin's star image that portrayed him as a serious, ambitious, and versatile artist.

Young's praise apparently did not fall on deaf ears. Shortly after the open letter was published, Chaplin began *A Woman of Paris*. When visiting New York City for the opening of that film, Chaplin asked Young to dinner, in part to thank him for his praise and in part, it seems, to seek more positive publicity about his new film. Young came away from the dinner even more impressed with Chaplin than before. In a letter to Julian Huxley, he rhapsodized: "A very remarkable person, as well as an extraordinary artist. Talks amazingly. . . . I found him a very congenial mind . . . the most interesting person I have seen in a long time except Duse."[65] As we have seen, Young did subsequently praise *A Woman of Paris*. Despite their divergent political opinions—

Young later became a contributor to the famous Southern Agrarian manifesto, *I'll Take My Stand*—Chaplin always remained high in Young's esteem.

Another admirer of Chaplin, though from a perspective quite different from Young's, was Gilbert Seldes (b. 1893). A contemporary and friend of Edmund Wilson (b. 1895) and John Peale Bishop (b. 1899), Seldes was a Phi Beta Kappa graduate of Harvard University in 1914, a correspondent during World War I, and an editor for the *Dial* from 1920 to 1923. Most important for our purposes, Seldes was the author of the first sustained examination and defense of American popular culture, *The Seven Lively Arts* (1924).[66] Like Frank, Seldes was interested in what moved the "real America," and he sought to discover this in a variety of American popular entertainments: ragtime, jazz, Ziegfeld productions, the satire of Mr. Dooley and Ring Lardner, circus clowns, popular dance, and even Krazy Kat comic strips. Unlike high culture, Seldes argued, these popular amusements did not seek to uplift or express the sublime and tragic. Nevertheless, in their desire to entertain, they often were as imaginative and as stimulating as high culture. And one of the most imaginative and stimulating of popular artists in America was Chaplin.

Seldes treated Chaplin briefly in his book's first chapter, which focused on the Keystone films. But his central examination of Chaplin's art appeared in Chapter 3, " 'I Am Here Today': Charlie Chaplin." Seldes found it miraculous that "a figure wholly in the tradition of the great clowns," which required "creative energy, freshness, inventiveness, change," should arise in the 1910s and 1920s in America, "for neither the time nor the country in which Charlie works is exceptionally favorable to such a phenomenon" (p. 41). Like many young American intellectuals coming to maturity during or after World War I, Seldes, by defending Chaplin against charges of vulgarity, was challenging what he perceived as the outmoded values of his genteel elders.

Demonstrating his awareness of the French admiration for Chaplin, Seldes distinguished between the person, Charlie Chaplin, and the mask, Charlot, just as Frank did in his *New Yorker* essay the following year. (Both Seldes and Frank lived in France for periods in the early 1920s, and they probably helped transmit the French influence on the American intellectual acceptance of Chaplin.) The name Charlot, wrote Seldes, "will serve for that figure on the screen, the created image which is, and at the same time is more than Charlie Chaplin, and is less" (p. 43). Beginning as a comic persona familiar to children, then to "the people," after which he became "universally known and admired" with films like *The Bank* and *Shoulder Arms*, Chaplin finally was considered, after *The Kid*, as a "great artist," not just a comic persona. For Seldes, as for many others after him, the making of *The Kid* marked a new stage in the development of Chaplin the artist.

Yet Seldes especially admired early films like *The Pawnshop*. Unlike Young, Seldes urged Chaplin to continue in the vein of comic vitality that he established in the short films: "the surest way to be wrong about Charlie is to forget the Keystones" (p. 52). In fact, Seldes took a direct and extended swipe at Young's open letter to Chaplin in his own essay. To Young's suggestion that Chaplin appeal to "a more cultured audience," Seldes responded: "Oh Lord! these are the phrases which are offered as bribes to the one man who has destroyed the world and created it in his own image" (p. 53). Rather than having Chaplin become serious and develop his "literary" side, Seldes, referring to the French name for Charlie, urged him to remember the early Charlot, the one announced by the billboards outside the nickel movie theaters: "I am here today." To Seldes, this terse phrase constituted "the beginning before time and the end without end of his wisdom and his loveliness" (p. 54). Thus, as well as praising Chaplin's artistry in the 1920s, Seldes celebrated the comic inventiveness of the early Charlot.

One of Seldes's intellectual compatriots in the early 1920s was Edmund Wilson. Though Wilson is known to us today as the magisterial man of letters who authored monuments like *Axel's Castle* and who generally abhorred popular culture, he was also an early advocate of Chaplin. Wilson first publicly discussed Chaplin in a review of *The Seven Lively Arts*. The review may partly have been a favor to Seldes, who once got Wilson a job as press agent for the Swedish Ballet when it was visiting the United States.[67] Not long after, Seldes sent a copy of *The Seven Lively Arts* to Wilson, who—without giving up his disdain for much popular art—wrote a fairly positive review of the book, calling it "a valuable and enormously entertaining book on the vulgar arts."[68]

Shortly after reviewing Seldes's book, Wilson did meet Chaplin again, thanks to his job with the Swedish Ballet. In February 1924 Wilson, having written a comic ballet for the troupe, traveled to California to try to persuade Chaplin to appear in it. Wilson visited the set of *The Gold Rush*, and talked with Chaplin there and then again at his home. Though Chaplin seemed amused at Wilson's ballet, later published as *Cronkhite's Clocks*, he "explained that he always had to do everything himself, invent and play his own character." Wilson came away from the experience impressed: "[Chaplin] was good mannered and perfectly natural. . . . When one talked to him, one found that his instant reactions were as fresh, as authentically personal, as those of a poet like E. E. Cummings."[69] Wilson admired Chaplin for his creative independence, something Wilson himself always sought.

The following year Wilson wrote his only extended piece on Chaplin, a review of *The Gold Rush* for the *New Republic*.[70] Wilson began by noting that gags were the most important part of silent film comedy and by giving examples of gags from the films of Keaton, Lloyd, and Fairbanks. But the only comedian, he wrote, "doing anything really distinguished with this comedy of gags is, of course, Charlie Chaplin." To Wilson, Chaplin's ability to extend gags through the use of situation and pantomime—as in the tilting cabin scene of *The Gold Rush*—constituted one of his central artistic accomplishments. Wilson also praised Chaplin for his creation of "deliberately ironic or pathetic situations," but, in his characteristically probing manner, suggested that the "straight situations and the gags rather jar together." Although Wilson was accurate in noting that "Chaplin has gained in reputation with the critics and the sophisticated public," he was probably less accurate when he suggested that he was losing some of his original popular audience: *The Gold Rush* was a great popular success, grossing over $4 million in its first several years, giving Chaplin $2 million in profits, United Artists $1 million.[71]

Wilson was prescient, however, when he suggested that Chaplin's films, when compared with those of Lloyd or Keaton, *looked* old-fashioned, even more so than old-fashioned movies. To Wilson, Chaplin's gift was "primarily the actor's, not the artist's or director's." Particularly after sound was introduced in Hollywood and Chaplin continued to make nondialogue films, reviewers frequently pointed out that even given Chaplin's enormous gift with pantomime, his films were stylistically primitive. Although Wilson's charge did not become a widely shared part of Chaplin's star image for some time, it is an early expression of an idea that would later plague Chaplin as he attempted to sustain his star image in the 1940s and 1950s.

Despite his reservations, however, Wilson concluded that Chaplin's recent comedies, like *The Kid* and *The Gold Rush*, "with their gags and their overtones of tragedy, their adventures half absurd, half realistic, their mythical hero, now a figure of poetry, now a type out of the funny papers, represent the height of his achievement." Thus the man whose reputation as a discriminating reviewer and critic was growing bestowed his critical approval on Chaplin.

Chaplin's reputation among the young intellectual elite in America is also evidenced in the writings of John Peale Bishop, a classmate of Wilson's at Princeton who also knew Seldes. An editor of *Vanity Fair* for a time, Bishop was primarily known in the 1920s and 1930s as a critic of contemporary literature. He wrote two thoughtful essays on movies in the mid-1920s, however—reflecting the growing legitimacy of movies as a subject of aesthetic discourse—and Chaplin figured in both of them.

The first, "The Movies as an Art: *The Last Laugh*," appeared in *Vanity Fair* in June 1925, a few months before the opening of *The Gold Rush*.[72] The essay is structured as a dialogue between a screenwriter and a critic, and the debate suggests something about the divergent attitudes toward the movies in America at the time. Intellectuals were beginning to admit that the German Expressionists and, later, Soviets like Eisenstein were capable of making genuinely artistic films while American studio films were simply light or vulgar entertainments. In fact, it is probably fair to say that the regular reviewing of movies in the more intellectual journals—almost unheard of in the mid-1920s but commonplace by the mid-1930s—resulted in part from these kinds of foreign films, which differed in varying degrees from the standard Hollywood product. They seemed to such writers more challenging, visually "artistic," and complex than American films.[73]

In Bishop's essay, the critic defended the more elitist position—that only foreign films like *The Last Laugh* can genuinely be considered art—while the screenwriter defended American films. Notably, however, the screenwriter often used Chaplin as an example of the best in American movies, and even the critic had positive comments on Chaplin's work. When the critic praised the visual economy of *The Last Laugh*, the screenwriter replied that Chaplin's films, even his early ones, were also "virtually without titles." Even though the critic thought *The Last Laugh* superior to any Chaplin film, he admitted that the best of Chaplin's work possessed a "comic poetry" in a high vein.

Bishop's other essay, "Sex Appeal in the Movies," which appeared in the *New Republic* in 1927, countered the notion that sex appeal sells movies. He argued that, on the contrary, the actors who had managed to remain popular for a considerable time in the movies were those who projected characters that were not particularly sexual. Though Bishop mentioned Pickford, Keaton, and others, he spent more time discussing Chaplin. The crux of his remarks were that if the Chaplin persona was in love, the woman he loved remained "mysterious and remote," and if he was married, as in *Pay Day*, the persona interacted with his wife like a "capricious little boy doing his best to arrange things amicably with a severe parent." Though his analysis was convincing, more important here is the implicit status Chaplin had assumed by November 1927. At one point Bishop referred to Chaplin's "middle period," after the Mutual films but before *A Woman of Paris*,

10. Portrait of Chaplin in 1925 by photographer Edward Steichen; reprinted by permission of Joanna T. Steichen. Print courtesy International Museum of Photography, George Eastman House, Rochester.

and he also stated, almost as if it were a given that no one would argue about, that Chaplin "alone of all the actors of the screen actually arrives at creating a separate world." The assumption of the essay, one that Chaplin surely relished, was that Chaplin was the unquestioned king of comedy in Hollywood and the premiere actor in the movie industry.

If we collect these treatments of Chaplin by Frank, Young, Seldes, Wilson, and Bishop, we can see that Wilson was accurate when he observed in 1925 that Chaplin's reputation among critics and more sophisticated movie viewers had grown considerably in the first half of the decade. Out of Frank's divided view of Chaplin emerged—after Frank met and became friendly with the star—a glowing, almost reverent picture of the melancholy film artist. His meeting with Stark Young at a critical time—the New York City release of *A Woman of Paris*—earned Chaplin a well-placed friend who remained a devoted admirer for the rest of his life. Chaplin's meetings with Wilson; Seldes's defense of popular art, particularly Chaplin's; and the mutual friendship of Wilson, Seldes, and Bishop helped Chaplin get critical attention from these three intellectuals. These were by no means the only American intellectuals to write on Chaplin in the early and mid-1920s, nor did they always agree on what constituted his central artistic contributions. What is important is that they discussed his work seriously and thus gave Chaplin's star image an artistic status higher than any other American film artist of the era. Photographs of Chaplin by prominent photographers only reinforced this status (see Figure 10).

Chaplin's star image had solidifed. Though Charlie still constituted an important part of that image, he had become more than a slapstick anarchist: he was also associated with romantic, often unrequited, yearnings and the pathos engendered by loneliness, suffering, or rejection. In addition, especially after *My Trip Abroad*, *The Kid*, and *A Woman of Paris*, Chaplin the man began to figure prominently in the star image. This man had artistic and intellectual aspirations, he at times worked his own experiences into his films (especially his experiences of childhood suffering and adult loneliness), and he was willing to take risks like *A Woman of Paris* to demonstrate that his creative versatility extended beyond performance. The success of *The Gold Rush* and the positive attention of the intelligentsia (thanks in part to Chaplin's personal charm and even calculated shrewdness) underlined Chaplin's growing reputation in the mid-1920s as the foremost star and serious film artist in Hollywood.

4

Struggling through the Twenties

Chaplin and Lita Grey

In his autobiography Chaplin says that while in New York City for the premiere of *The Gold Rush*, he had an unexplained "collapse" that so frightened him he wanted to make out a will (MA, p. 305). Though he recovered quickly, the collapse was symbolically apt, for it ushered in a difficult half decade for Chaplin the star. The period, in Chaplin's own words, "was one of great professional prosperity but also of private grief."[1] Between 1925 and the release of *City Lights* (1931), Chaplin suffered through a second divorce and serious tax problems, struggled with the aesthetic challenge of sound films, and witnessed the onset of the Great Depression. All posed challenges to what seemed in 1925 to be Chaplin's unassailable public reputation.

The second divorce provided the first test for Chaplin's star image. Following his divorce from Mildred Harris, Chaplin's private life in the early 1920s generated little negative publicity. Nearly everyone who knew Chaplin in these years and wrote about him testified that he was an extremely engaging, charming, and magnetic personality. This, combined with the star status he had achieved in the film industry and the fact that he was again a bachelor, made him very attractive to women. Between 1921 and 1924 his name was linked with a number of women, among them Peggy Hopkins Joyce (the original "Gold digger"), Claire Sheridan (the sculptor and cousin of Winston Churchill), and Pola Negri (the movie star).[2] As might be expected, the fan magazines and newspaper syndicates were interested in these relationships, and some sources even alleged that Sheridan and Negri were both engaged to Chaplin at one time or another in the early 1920s.

However, Chaplin's relationship with Lillita McMurray—whose stage name was Lita Grey—was probably the most wrenching, destructive, and unfortunate relationship he had with a woman in his life. The circumstances of their marriage in November 1924 and their subsequent divorce, which became official in August 1927, not only caused both of them extreme mental grief and anguish but also posed Chaplin with the first serious threat to his star image since his rise to

preeminent stardom. Furthermore, it planted some of the seeds of acrimony among the public that would grow and later blossom when his
reputation was seriously sagging in the 1940s.

Telling the full story of the courtship, marriage, separation, and divorce of Chaplin and Grey is an impossible task. Chaplin does not
mention Grey by name in his autobiography, where he disposes of
their entire relationship tersely: "During the filming of *The Gold Rush*
I married for the second time. Because we have two grown sons of
whom I am very fond, I will not go into any details. For two years we
were married and tried to make a go of it, but it was hopeless and
ended in a great deal of bitterness" (MA, p. 305).

Lita Grey, however, discusses their relationship in great detail, using
fourteen of the twenty-two chapters of her memoirs to explain from
her point of view how their relationship developed from the time she
visited Chaplin's studio in hopes of getting the lead in *The Gold Rush*
until the divorce settlement. Any account will necessarily be tinged by
the fact that only one side of the story has been told.

Despite this, it is possible to outline what occurred and to describe
in particular the tremendous strain Chaplin experienced for a variety
of reasons in January and February of 1927. Grey first met Chaplin
through a neighbor, Chuck Riesner, who served as Chaplin's assistant
director in the early 1920s. Through Riesner, the twelve-year-old Lillita got a job as an extra in *The Kid*. Chaplin was so impressed by her
appearance that he soon cast her as the angel temptress in the heaven
sequence of the film. A short time later, Lillita and her mother played
brief roles as maids in *The Idle Class*. Early in 1924 Grey auditioned
and won the role of Georgia in *The Gold Rush*. She signed a contract
in March. Chaplin was attracted to her, a feeling that she reciprocated,
and by the fall of 1924 she was pregnant with Chaplin's child. In November they were married in Enpalme, Mexico. That same month
Chaplin announced that Georgia Hale had replaced Grey in *The Gold
Rush*, for Lita wished to devote full time to her new role as Chaplin's
wife. Charles Chaplin, Jr., was born on 5 May 1925, though Chaplin
managed to keep the birth a secret until it was announced (with an
altered birth certificate, according to Grey) on June 28.[3] Though the
marriage began intolerably, according to Grey, she and Chaplin had a
brief period of rapprochement after the birth of the baby. By the summer of 1925 she was again pregnant, and gave birth on 30 March 1926
to their second son, Sydney, named for Chaplin's half brother.

In the spring and summer of 1926 the marriage deteriorated. Grey
writes that Chaplin would take her to an occasional party or premiere
"for appearances' sake," but otherwise would have virtually nothing to

do with her or their sons: with *The Circus* well under way, he apparently was completely absorbed by it, as he tended to be in the midst of a film production. Grey, finding the situation hopeless, asked Chaplin for a divorce in the fall. Chaplin told her to take a vacation to think things over, which she did, sailing for Hawaii with her mother and oldest son in November. Upon returning, she decided to separate immediately, and on December 2 newspapers reported in front-page stories that Chaplin's wife had left him and had taken their children with her. A day later, they reported that the split had been declared permanent and that Grey asked for $1 million in alimony payments.[4]

In January 1927 the Chaplin divorce case became a national controversy. On January 10 Grey's lawyer and uncle, Edwin McMurray, filed a divorce complaint against Chaplin, Chaplin's studio, United Artists, Alf Reeves (Chaplin's business manager), and a number of banks that held Chaplin's assets. Grey's uncle wrote the complaint without letting her see it until just before it was filed. Though her most damaging complaints were included in the document, she says in her memoirs that a number of them were also "cleverly, shockingly enlarged upon or distorted." By January 12 copies of the complaint were being sold on the street corners of Los Angeles. As Grey observed, "by the liberal standards of the 1960's, phrases like these might seem comparatively tame. But in 1927 such words as 'abnormal,' 'unnatural,' 'degenerate' and 'indecent'—especially as applied to the world-beloved Charlie Chaplin—struck several million sensation seekers with bombshell force."[5] The Chaplin image was under siege.

In addition to the divorce complaint, Chaplin was also worried at the time about an unauthorized biography of him, written by a former employee, Jim Tully, who had worked for Chaplin for eighteen months during the production of *The Gold Rush*. One of the reasons Chaplin left for New York City in January was to visit the offices of *Pictorial Review*, which had announced that the four-part Chaplin profile would appear from January through April. If his pleas to halt publication fell on deaf ears, Chaplin was prepared to use his considerable legal means—once successful with *Charlie Chaplin's Own Story* in 1916— to prevent dissemination of the series. After learning of the articles and worrying about how the possibly negative publicity would affect the impending divorce, Chaplin's lawyers sued Tully on January 8, then sought an injunction against *Pictorial Review* on January 14 to prevent publication of the remaining issues. On February 3 the courts refused to issue the injunction, and the articles were published as scheduled under the title, "Charlie Chaplin: His *Real* Life Story."[6]

If the divorce complaint and unauthorized biography were not

11. "The Gold Rush": Cartoonist William Cargill
dramatizes Chaplin's plight over divorce and tax
problems, January 1927. Reprinted by
permission of *Emporia Gazette*.

enough, Chaplin learned shortly after arriving in New York City that
federal tax authorities were claiming he owed a huge sum in back
taxes. The *New York Times* reported on January 18 that government
tax officials, like Lita Grey's lawyers, were seeking a lien against Chaplin's assets, in this case to ensure payment of back taxes. On the 22nd
the government claimed that Chaplin owed $1.135 million in personal
income taxes, going back as far as 1918. Chaplin's money was placed
into receivership by January 20. Not until January 28 was he able to
free any of his New York funds, but that same day the government
filed another lien, this one against United Artists. The financial pressures on the independent filmmaker, with both his wife and the government claiming over a million dollars, must have been overwhelming. Although the tax problem dropped out of the news (Chaplin
didn't settle with the government until 10 February 1928), coming as
it did in the middle of the divorce controversy, it surely added to the
strain.[7] The cartoon that originally appeared in the *Emporia Gazette*
suggests graphically how Chaplin must have felt in this rush for his
gold (see Figure 11).

On January 16 Chaplin's doctor reported that Chaplin was "suffering from a serious nervous breakdown."[8] With his funds placed in receivership and charges of abnormality emanating from certain quarters, the Chaplin story remained hot and constant news throughout January and into February. Thereafter, occasional stories continued to appear through the summer, with Chaplin's answer to the divorce complaint and his counter-complaint reported on June 3, and Grey's answer to Chaplin's cross-complaint covered on July 2. After all the buildup by the press in January, the coverage of settlement itself was relatively quiet. On August 22, Lita Grey—who had been seeking $1.25 million—was awarded $825,000: $625,000 for herself, plus a $100,000 trust fund for each son. Chaplin was ordered to pay Grey $375,000 immediately, $100,000 a year in 1928 and 1929, and $50,000 in 1930. He was also ordered to pay $10,000 in expenses to Grey for the separation period, $22,000 receivers' costs, $2,100 court costs, and $1,000 per month for the children for five years while the trust funds were being set up. Chaplin himself was not in the courtroom when the decision was announced.[9] For the next four months, Chaplin's name was barely mentioned in the *New York Times*. It must have been a relief.

Mixed Reviews: The Press and the Second Divorce

How did the public and press handle this separation and divorce? Despite Chaplin's enormous popularity, he had often been charged with "vulgarity" earlier in his career by genteel Americans. In the 1920s, despite a relatively broad political consensus, American life was characterized by deep cultural divisions, as manifested by such controversial issues as Prohibition, immigration restriction, and the Scopes trial. Such issues all embodied splits in American culture: traditionalism versus modernism, rural versus urban values, fundamentalist religious versus secular viewpoints, and nativist versus cultural pluralist perspectives. Although Chaplin's popularity was widespread, traditionalists who supported Prohibition, favored immigration restriction, and opposed the teaching of evolution in the schools could find much to criticize about Chaplin. The "puritanism" that Van Wyck Brooks and other cultural critics denounced in the 1910s and 1920s may have been misnamed; however, there is no doubt that conservative moralists, fueled by the Fatty Arbuckle scandal in 1921 and the unsolved death of William Desmond Taylor in 1922, were as concerned about the possible harmful effects of movies in the 1920s as they had been in the preceding decade. Such individuals were not likely to forgive Chaplin his indiscretions simply because he was a famous star.

The incident that stimulated the most debate and denunciation of Chaplin was Grey's divorce complaint, filed January 10. Even as staid and conservative a newspaper as the *Chicago Tribune* reported on the spectacular details with glee. They reprinted what Grey allegedly heard Chaplin tell his entourage on his wedding night: "Well, boys, this is better than the penitentiary but it won't last long." They quoted Grey's claim that she was a "virtuous and innocent girl" when she was engaged to Chaplin. They reported that Grey accused Chaplin of "soliciting, urging, and demanding throughout their entire married life, that the defendant submit to acts which were revolting and degrading; shocking to her sensibilities and abhorrent to her conception of decency." And they wrote that, according to Grey, Chaplin had withheld support for the Chaplin babies since November 30 except for paying one milk bill of $27 and had not even visited the children at Christmas.[10]

The first wave of public response to these allegations was critical of Chaplin. His alleged failure to provide food for his children presented a concrete image that drove women's clubs around the country into action. A spokesperson for one such group told reporters: "If Chaplin thinks he can starve his child-wife into submission, he is reckoning without the women of Hollywood. Thirty women, representing twenty clubs, met Thursday, and we already have begun to raise money to properly feed and care for Mrs. Chaplin's little boys."[11] Among other reactions in the first days after the complaint was filed, the mayor of Quebec banned all posters and advertisements for Chaplin films. He stated that he would have banned the films, too, but could not because the local censorship board was responsible for that. The next day, the La Salle, Illinois, League of Women Voters called for a ban on Chaplin films; the mayor of Seattle asked his censorship board to rule on banning Chaplin's films; and the mayor of Lynn, Massachusetts, ordered that no Chaplin films were to be shown while the divorce proceedings were going on.[12] Another example of the public outcry was a letter to a film columnist a week after the story broke. Mrs. R. T. Niles wrote to protest an article defending Chaplin. She charged that Chaplin "has an unfortunate habit of getting himself mixed up with young women whom he subsequently marries—probably to keep out of prison or from being deported." She concluded, "Is this man to be permitted to run riot for the rest of his life amid the foolish little girls of this country?"[13]

But Chaplin also had his defenders, both among the public and in the press (see Figure 12). A few days after the first criticisms from women's clubs, the Miami Beach Women's Club publicly asked Miami theater owners not to ban Chaplin's films but instead to play as many of them as possible in a gesture of support for Chaplin. Their spokesperson, Mrs. Clayton Sedgwick Cooper, said her group aimed to counteract "silly agitation which women's clubs have taken in regard to Chaplin's pictures." The same day that the city of Pasadena banned Chaplin's films, the Theater Owners Chamber of Commerce praised his talents as a filmmaker. At the end of January a letter to the editor of the *New York Herald Tribune* added a defense of Chaplin. Its author, Alice Carpenter, wrote: "There is no one, man or woman, in the movie world who has done more to lift the pictures to a high plane, or who deserves to a greater extent the loyal sympathy and support of our people than Mr. Chaplin, now suffering from the unbalanced actions of a willful girl." In February, the Motion Picture Theater Owners of America, meeting in New York City, passed a resolution praising Chaplin, and the Green Room Club of New York City presented him with a gold plaque honoring his talents.[14]

The motivations for these defenses of Chaplin are not always clear, but several seem likely. On the one hand, the defense by the Miami Beach Women's Club could be seen as a liberal response to the conservative moralism of those women's clubs who urged the banning of Chaplin's films. On the other, their position could also be seen as simply a variation of conservative moralism, but one that defended Chaplin because it was his wife's fault that the marriage had foundered. For the theater owners, the motivations were clearer: Chaplin's films drew well and made them money. If Chaplin were discredited as Arbuckle had been several years earlier, one of their most dependable box-office draws would be lost.

Beginning with some early pieces on the editorial pages, the press also defended Chaplin. On January 15, the *New York Morning Telegraph* ran an editorial, "The Chaplin Films," defending Chaplin and criticizing the bans on his films. "The public must hear the full story if it is inclined to meddle in the personal marital problems of a movie star," the editor declared, adding that "the masses seem to relish scandal when it invades the movie lot or struts back stage." It backed New York City mayor Jimmy Walker's refusal to ban Chaplin films. About the same time, the editorial page of the *New York Telegraph* commented approvingly on Will Hays's refusal to step into the controversy: "What is gained," it asked, "by rushing into print with attacks on anyone before that person has had his day in court, or, at least, [been] given an opportunity to tell his story for public analysis?"[15]

A number of journalists who had earlier written positively about Chaplin's films also supported him in print. Among them was Har-

WHAT REMAINS UNTOUCHED

12. Cartoonist Rollin Kirby in *Theatre Arts* defends Chaplin the
artist during the 1927 divorce publicity.

riette Underhill, film columnist for the *New York Herald Tribune*.
Shortly after the divorce story broke, she wrote a column praising
Chaplin's filmmaking talents: "The reason everyone has loved Charlie
Chaplin's pictures is because his soul *is* photographed. Charles Chaplin is a superior soul. He is filled with ideals. . . . He is a public benefactor and he belongs to his public. Mr. Chaplin never should marry.
He probably realizes this himself." Though her column was not really
a commentary on the divorce case, it did urge readers to keep cool
heads and not to prejudge it. Underhill's piece generated considerable

reader response, including the castigation by Mrs. Niles cited above and a number of defenses of Chaplin, some of which were printed in the column the following week.[16]

The trade magazines and columnists also came to his defense. *Moving Picture World*, in "The Spotlight Turns Yellow," gave a telling subtitle to its article: "Reformers for hire are only eager to seize on Chaplin, but the world will judge him as an artist and a victim." The essay defends Chaplin as an idealist and lover of beauty, writing hopefully that Chaplin "was, and is, wistful and very human. So we think that the public will be fair simply because it likes Chaplin."[17] H. L. Mencken, that boisterous observer of the American scene, apparently enjoyed the public's display of fickleness, for he wrote in a *Baltimore Sun* column that "the very morons who worshipped Charlie Chaplin six weeks ago now prepare to dance around the stake while he is burned."[18] Mencken was no particular admirer of either Chaplin or the movies, but he found his cynical view of the American "booboisie" reinforced in its denunciations of Chaplin.

Not surprisingly, the *New Yorker* also defended Chaplin in Ralph Barton's satiric "Picking on Charlie Chaplin." In the essay Barton wrote that Chaplin

> is probably more important than anybody else on earth. . . . What other man on earth has been loved, respected and admired, at the same time, by French intellectuals, isolated Esquimaux, Iowa Babbits, jazz-maddened New Yorkers, Bulgarian peasants, Scotch Presbyterians, New Guinea cannibals, German scientists, English statesmen, real estate brokers, dentists, kindergarten teachers, and the entire race of artists? The fellow is, let us admit it with a befitting hysteria, unique in history.[19]

Much as Chaplin's comic films were used to justify his failure to serve as a soldier in World War I, Chaplin's star status here is used to excuse his marital problems. A similar defense of Chaplin appeared in a cartoon printed in *Liberty* magazine (see Figure 13). It accused Lita Grey of cultivating the women's clubs and manipulating the press to exaggerate how difficult her life had become after separating from Chaplin.

Artists and intellectuals generally rose in defense of Chaplin, which suggests something of the split then evident in American culture between conservative moralists and a more cosmopolitan, educated, and urban audience that felt the attacks simply reinforced Brooks's view of the "puritanism" endemic in American culture. One might add that French intellectuals were also vocal in expressing their opinions in fa-

IT WILL ALL COME OUT OF THE ALIMONY. Mrs. Charles Spencer Chaplin poses for a few photo-graphs in the kitchen with the baby, to show the palpitating public how she has been obliged to take up menial duties while waiting for her husband to come across.

13. *Liberty* cartoon (1927) satirizes Chaplin's wife, the women's clubs, and the press during the second divorce.

vor of Chaplin, perhaps even more actively than American intellectuals: the *Boston Evening Transcript* carried an article, "Paris Still Pays Honor to 'Charlot,'" which described organized efforts by French intellectuals to defend Chaplin.[20]

Tully's articles, which appeared during and immediately after the greatest publicity surrounding the divorce, also contributed to Chaplin's star image. Although it is difficult to say whether Chaplin's fears about the articles were justified, he did have some reason to be uneasy, for he had fired Tully when he refused to delete some passages uncomplimentary to Chaplin from a book he was about to publish. Perhaps suspecting that the articles would be a vindictive retaliation for the firing, and knowing that due to the separation and pending divorce, publicity was imminent, Chaplin felt he had no alternative but to seek to halt publication.

However, the articles themselves, which appeared between January and April 1927 in *Pictorial Review*, are neither denunciation nor hagiography; both critics and defenders of Chaplin found support for their positions in them. The first installment, while containing praise, also included more negative passages than the other three. Take, for instance, this description: "Complex and weirdly strange, a rider of stormy moods, he is a complex human riddle that even a Havelock Ellis might never solve" (Jan., p. 8). This installment also called Chaplin "notoriously close with money" and completely unwilling to acknowledge any influence of others on his acting style and comic persona (Jan., p. 29). Chaplin only visited his mother "a few times in as many years" after he brought her to California in 1921, Tully wrote, a charge disputed by Lita Grey in her book. And in one final, cutting passage, Tully, who presented himself as a man of common stock but superior aesthetic taste, wrote that Chaplin is "plentifully supplied with the littleness of big men" (Jan., p. 30).

But in the subsequent issues, and even in certain details of the January piece, Chaplin was portrayed more positively. From the first, Tully portrayed Chaplin as physically attractive and engaging, even magnetic, at social occasions. In the February article, Tully wrote that Chaplin often liked to "chatter on philosophical and sociological subjects" with him, that he could be the "most ingratiating of men," that he was capable of strong pity and kindness, and that he was a brilliant artist completely absorbed in his work (Feb., pp. 19–20). The March issue reiterated Chaplin's pity for the down and out, his artistry, and his enormous capacity for work as it recounted shooting on location in Truckee for *The Gold Rush*. And in the brief final installment, Tully called Chaplin "one of the two greatest men in motion pictures"—the other was James Cruze, director of *The Covered Wagon* (Apr., p. 104).

Compared to the nearly idolatrous picture of Chaplin that had dominated the early 1920s, Tully's was probably more balanced and reasonable. In fact, it appears that the public and press were generally split in their response to the divorce case. Even though we lack Chaplin's version of his relationship with Grey, it seems on balance that he emerged from the whole incident with much less damage to his star image than one might have expected. This may have to do at least in part with the dynamics of stardom. A man as wealthy as Chaplin was able to spend considerable money on his defense. More subtly, however, a star's fans are interested not just in his films but also in his private life: as Richard Dyer has suggested, one of the central concerns of fan magazines is "the *problems* of love."[21] Following this line of argument, the movie fan, by empathizing with the difficulties the star has in searching for personal happiness and love, adds another level to the identification with the star that began with his or her presentation in the movies. The press's treatment of Chaplin's divorce case may even, paradoxically, have enabled some of his fans to identify more strongly with Chaplin by allowing them vicariously to share the burdens of the "real" person. In any case, viewed with hindsight, Chaplin's reputation foundered surprisingly little in 1927 because of the press coverage surrounding his divorce difficulties. Although his marriage with Lita Grey was over, Chaplin's honeymoon with the American public was apparently continuing. After his struggles with taxes, Tully, and Grey, Chaplin had to return his attention to the film that was well under way when the problems began.

The Burdens of Being Funny:
The Circus

Shortly after the opening of *The Gold Rush* in August 1925, Chaplin was back at work, planning another film. His choice of subject was crucial. On the one hand, in only one of his two previous films had his Charlie persona appeared. Chaplin's Olympian status among critics, as well as his own aspirations, encouraged him to follow Stark Young's advice from 1922 and take on something new and more ambitious. On the other hand, *The Gold Rush* had done far better at the box office than had *A Woman of Paris*, and Chaplin was both jealous enough of his independence and shrewd enough to know that keeping the Charlie persona at the center of his films would be an economically sound decision.

Chaplin was thus pulled in two directions about his new project: should he stick with Charlie or abandon him? In November an article in the *New York Times* commented on Chaplin's plans. It reported that Chaplin had toyed with the idea of making a film called *The Suicide Club* but had discarded that idea in favor of another film—contents unknown—called *The Dandy*. After completing that film, Chaplin would make *The Clown*, in which Charlie would appear in the costume of a circus clown except for his shoes, cane, and bowler. "This story," continued the article, "was described as another dramatic comedy, and in its method something after the style of *The Gold Rush*, except that it was to have a tragic ending—the funmaker impersonated by Chaplin is supposed to die in the tanbark while the spectators are applauding the comic pantomime."[22] These descriptions suggest that Chaplin was compromising by planning one non-Charlie film, then a second featuring a close relative of Charlie.

As it turned out, however, Chaplin returned more quickly than the *Times* article suggested he would to the formula that succeeded in *The Gold Rush*. *The Dandy* disappeared into the rapidly filling bin of discarded Chaplin ideas and projects, and *The Clown* evolved into *The*

Circus. The tragic ending of *The Clown* was deferred (it sounds much like the conclusion of Chaplin's 1952 film, *Limelight*). And instead of being disguised as a circus clown, Charlie looks quite familiar in *The Circus*, clad in much the same way he appeared in most scenes of *The Gold Rush* and in many earlier Charlie comedies.

For some reason, reviewers suggested when the film was released that *The Circus* (1928) was somewhat archaic. In the *New York Times*, Mordaunt Hall praised it and noted that it was "more like his earlier films than either *The Kid* or *The Gold Rush*."[23] In the *New Republic* Chaplin's old friend Young used almost the same phrasing, calling *The Circus* "purer in the old-style Chaplin than *The Kid* or *The Gold Rush*."[24] It is true that some gags recall those of earlier Chaplin films, as when Charlie quickly gulps down a baby's hot dog when his father is not looking, reminiscent of the lunch wagon scene in *A Dog's Life*.

Nevertheless, in *The Circus* Chaplin also very carefully builds on the success of *The Gold Rush* by following the narrative structure and the essential blend of comedy and pathos he had established in this earlier film. One could almost say that Chaplin was self-consciously creating his own genre, one that ensured his popularity and respect among a diverse audience and sustained his star image.

Consider the similarities between *The Gold Rush* and *The Circus*. In both films the central character is Charlie, dressed the same in nearly every scene. In both works Charlie is thrust into a new social situation—the Klondike, a circus—in which he must learn to function. In both settings human beings exhibit cruelty to others. In *The Gold Rush* both Black Larsen and Jack cause problems for Charlie; in *The Circus* the circus owner is an unreasonable and often cruel character.

Both films develop a romance between Charlie and a heroine that creates joy and sorrow, and here they are especially similar. Charlie's joyous enthusiasm in Hank's cabin in *The Gold Rush*—he jumps around, swings from the rafters, and beats the feathers out of a pillow when Georgia accepts his invitation to a New Year's Eve dinner—is analogous to the scene in *The Circus* when Charlie dances gleefully after he believes that Merna loves him. Both films also create moments of pathos that stem from Charlie's unrequited love. The pathos that arises in *The Gold Rush* when Charlie wakes up from his dream of a successful party with Georgia, followed by his walk to the dance hall and his isolated look into the window at the others' celebration, functions in much the same way, albeit more powerfully, as the scene in *The Circus* in which Charlie overhears Merna tell the fortune-teller that she is in love with Rex, the tightrope walker. Chaplin shows Charlie's reaction in medium close-up, followed by a long shot of Charlie alone in the dressing room. The isolation of Charlie in the frame recalls the similar isolation when Charlie stands alone outside of the Monte Carlo dance hall in *The Gold Rush*.

Both films also frequently use animals to generate comedy. *The Gold Rush* uses bears, dogs, and a mule, and for a time Big Jim even imagines Charlie to be a chicken. In *The Circus*, Charlie often has an intransigent circus mule chasing him. He swallows a horse pill whole trying to blow it through a tube into a horse's throat. He has a comic scene when locked in with a lion, a circumstance exacerbated by a barking dog outside the cage. And in the comic climax of the film, monkeys clamber all over Charlie as he tries to walk the tightrope.

This final scene suggests yet another similarity. In both films, the final long *comic* scene places Charlie in extreme danger, either balancing tenuously in a cabin at the edge of a precipice or walking a tightrope, high above the circus crowd, when he doesn't really know how. Taken collectively, these similarities in the areas of central character, setting, handling of romance, use of animals to generate comedy, and climactic comic scenes suggest that however different the films are in other ways, they possess a very similar structure, one with which Chaplin's approving audience was becoming familiar and with which Chaplin's star image was becoming associated.

There are, of course, dissimilarities in the two films. (A central dynamic of popular cinema generally is the equipoise between similarity and differentiation from film to film.) One of the most prominent differences lies in the conclusions. Most simply, in *The Gold Rush* Charlie gets the girl and in *The Circus*, he does not. More precisely, he realizes in *The Circus* that he is not right for Merna and that Rex is, so he sacrifices his own desires for the well-being of the other two. The final shots of *The Circus* contrast significantly to the final shots of *The Gold Rush*. At the end of *The Circus*, Charlie picks up a torn paper with a star on it that had once been the center of the hoop Merna jumped through in the film's first shot. He looks at it, apparently musing on how transitory stardom is (even he himself had been a star "funny man" in the circus for a time). He then crumples it into a ball, begins walking away from the camera, tosses the ball into the air, and kicks it sideways as it falls toward the ground. After a few heavily burdened steps, he takes a sprightly bounce, much like at the end of *The Tramp*, and walks away from the camera with renewed resolve. One of Charlie's increasingly central characteristics—his ability to endure pain and grief without letting it destroy him—is revealed in this final scene. A social outsider, Charlie nevertheless does not let disappointments destroy his affirmation of life.

However different from the final scene of *The Gold Rush*, this conclusion does resemble the ending of that film in its hints of self-referentiality. Viewed from the perspective of Chaplin's unhappy second marriage, the angry divorce proceedings, and other problems that confronted Chaplin as he was working on the film (among them the pressure to follow *The Gold Rush* with another worthy of his reputation), Charlie's act of crumpling up and discarding the star suggests that Chaplin himself was at times doubtful that the pressures of stardom were healthy for him or his art. The ending of *The Circus* thus employs self-referentiality much as the ending of *The Gold Rush* does.[25]

The Circus is also self-referential in the sense of alluding to one's autobiography. Chaplin explores the contradictions of his own being in ways that recall *A Woman of Paris*. A number of people who knew Chaplin in the mid-1920s have noted how variable his moods were. Tully, in his *Pictorial Review* articles, for example, wrote that Chaplin had "moods that change like early March weather in his native England."[26] Lita Grey stressed the doubleness of the Charles Spencer Chaplin she knew: "I saw him in every conceivable mood, from the peak of elation to the nadir of prolonged depression. I was witness to his compassion and his cruelty, to his explosive rages and about-face kindness, to his wisdom and his ignorance, to his limitless ability to love and his incredible insensitivities."[27]

Doubleness in *The Circus* is expressed primarily through Charlie and the ringmaster, Chaplin's shadow self. Charlie expresses the joyous, resilient, amusing, compassionate side of Chaplin. We have already seen Chaplin's compassion for the poor and down and out expressed in *My Trip Abroad*. Tully also recalls that when he was "a hungry writer with more ambition than capacity," Chaplin gave him a hundred dollars that had helped him a great deal.[28] Though self-sacrifice was not a new trait of Charlie's in *The Circus*, his sacrifice of his own love for Merna's happiness, a decision that dooms him to a loneliness that Chaplin himself had experienced, was an act crucial to Charlie's character and crucial, too, one could argue, to Chaplin's best self-image.

If this image of a charitable, compassionate, self-sacrificing Charlie was not new, what *was* relatively new in *The Circus* was Chaplin's willingness to confront the harsher side of his being. As one critic has shrewdly noted, the ringmaster in *The Circus* is the first in a long line of shadow selves that appear in later Chaplin films. Allan Garcia played the ringmaster, who resembles a number of other Chaplin characters, including the millionaire in *City Lights* and the factory owner in *Modern Times* (the latter also played by Garcia). The ringmaster's costume in *The Circus*, which consists of a top hat, riding boots, jodhpurs, and a whip, is similar to the costumes worn by the Hynkel character in *The Great Dictator* and by Calvero when he does his "flea act" in *Limelight*. And the ringmaster's cruelty is not unlike the darker side of Monsieur Verdoux in the film of that title.[29]

The ringmaster is like Chaplin both professionally and personally. Professionally, his comic enterprise, the circus, functions as a metaphor for another comic enterprise, the movie studio concerned with making Chaplinesque comedies. Many accounts of Chaplin on the set stress his complete control and his desire for perfection; in Tully's words, "Never did a despot dominate a country as Chaplin rules his studio."[30] Like Chaplin, the ringmaster is a demanding perfectionist: in the tryout he is constantly directing his clowns. In fact, his first line in the film, spoken to Merna—"you missed the hoop again"—mirrors Chaplin's tendency to control his set completely and to make sure a shot was perfect before moving on.

But the ringmaster also resembles Chaplin's darker personal side. The character denies his daughter food because she fails to perform up to his expectations. Later in the film he physically abuses her, and he summarily fires a group of men working under him when they seek higher pay. Although we only have Lita Grey's version of their marriage and divorce, if her account is at all accurate, Chaplin was at times incredibly cruel to his second wife from the day they were married— or perhaps even from the day he learned she was pregnant. Although the ringmaster does reluctantly approve of his daughter's marriage ex post facto—perhaps an acknowledgment by Chaplin that his own darker side could be brightened—he exhibits a human cruelty that Chaplin seemed to be discovering both in himself and in others as he struggled through some of his difficulties in the mid-1920s. This would become an increasing concern as he observed the human sufferings of the Depression and World War II.

These autobiographical links were not frequently drawn by critics of *The Circus* in 1928. However, Tully's charges about Chaplin's moodiness and despotism and more generally circulating stories about Chaplin's perfectionism did have some effect on his star image. Comments like Tully's transferred a potentially noxious germ to the body of Chaplin's star image, but for the time, at least, the illness remained latent. Not until the 1940s did the germ, in combination with others, come to infect the entire star image. On the other hand, the stories of Chaplin's perfectionism could be, and in the 1920s were, read more positively, as the true indication of Chaplin's demanding genius. As long as the resulting films were satisfying to audiences, his high standards were generally considered a positive quality.

How did *The Circus* fare with the critics and the public? *The Circus* did very well with both groups. Surveying the reviews, *Literary Digest* gathered the impression that Chaplin's "critical admirers are killing the fatted calf to celebrate his return to his own field of pure clowning."[31] Critic Robert Sherwood had high praise for Chaplin: "Chaplin doesn't have to play *Hamlet*. He doesn't have to play any part created by any other genius from Shakespeare down." Countering those who thought Chaplin should abandon Charlie for more serious subjects, Sherwood, echoing comments by Seldes earlier in the decade, wrote that Charlie "is just as important, just as true, as all the melancholy princes who ever discovered that there is something rotten in Denmark."[32] To Alexander Bakshy, writing in the *Nation*, Chaplin was "again at his very best" in *The Circus*, and Young, in spite of some reservations about Chaplin's makeup and the handling of pathos in the film, also found the film a triumph.[33]

The critical reception of the film suggests that the expectations Chaplin had raised through his previous films were well satisfied by *The Circus*. More and more, it seemed that Chaplin was forming his own genre. Or, to put it another way, he was establishing an aesthetic contract with his audience, promising them a consistent central character, a romance tinged with pathos, inventive humor, and some serious themes or concerns (often, like many Hollywood films, based on moral contrasts rooted in individual characters) underlying the work. In exchange, viewers offered their dollars for tickets and their critical adulation. To them, Chaplin satisfied his end of the aesthetic contract in *The Circus*.

The film also did well at the box office, nearly as well as *The Gold Rush*. The United Artists balance sheets of domestic film rentals through the end of 1931 show that *The Gold Rush* had accumulated $2.15 million in rentals, while *The Circus* had garnered $1.82 million.[34] For some reason, Chaplin later did not remember *The Circus* as very successful, perhaps because he associated the making of it with an unpleasant period of his life. His attitude is suggested by the fact that he did not revive the film until 1969 (*The Gold Rush* was revived much earlier, in 1942) and that he mentions it only once in his autobiography, and then only in the context of his mother's final illness (MA, p. 288). It is too bad that *The Circus* has faded from public consciousness, for it is a fascinating film that shows Chaplin dealing successfully with interesting thematic material. It is also historically significant as the last film Chaplin had the luxury of making in the silent era.

Charlie and the Threat of the Talkies

Two events of almost equally cataclysmic effect took place during the time that Chaplin was at work on his next film, *City Lights*. First, the interest in talking films, generated by public enthusiasm for *Don Juan* (1926), *The Jazz Singer* (1927), and other films using Warner's Vitaphone and Fox's Movietone systems, led nearly the entire film industry to transform to sound film production and exhibition between the spring of 1928 and the end of the decade.[35] Second, in October 1929 the crash of the stock market diminished or wiped out the assets of many Americans and eventually led to an economic depression of such magnitude that by 1933 a quarter to a third of the nonfarm work force in the United States was unemployed. Both the internal factor, the technological development of sound, and the external factor, the national economic catastrophe of the depression, had far-reaching effects not only on the American film industry but also on Chaplin's evolving star image.

However, only the challenge of sound films significantly affected *City Lights*. The plot contours of *City Lights* were laid out well before the crash. Talking with *Times* reviewer Mordaunt Hall in July 1929, Chaplin said that the central characters in the film were Charlie, a blind girl, and a wealthy "Jekyll and Hyde inebriate" who when drunk, recognized Charlie, but otherwise did not—exactly the central dramatis personae and situation of the completed film.[36] Though the depression subsequently had a profound effect on Chaplin's film, life, relationship to his audience, and even to some extent on the way his films were approached by critics—as will be related in upcoming chapters—*City Lights* is not a film of the depression but rather a film of the 1920s.

Though the crash had no large effect on *City Lights*, it can be documented that the threat of sound films clearly did challenge and worry Chaplin. Less than six months after *The Jazz Singer* premiered and three months after *The Circus* opened, a nervous group at United Artists, including Chaplin, Griffith, Pickford, Fairbanks, Norma Talmadge, and Barrymore, gathered in one of the studio bungalows and waited to let their fans hear they had voices. They were all participating in a special radio broadcast called the Dodge Brothers Hour, broadcast both to fifty-five NBC radio affiliates nationwide and to a number of movie theaters in the larger cities throughout the United States. Though the program included music by the Paul Whiteman Orchestra and a pitch for the new six-cylinder Dodge by the president of Dodge Motors, most listeners had tuned in to hear the voices of their favorite silent movie stars. Talmadge gave a short discourse on fashion, Griffith spoke about love, Fairbanks gave a typically optimistic pep talk to America's youth, and Chaplin—what else?—told a couple of jokes.[37]

To the extent that the silent stars considered this a test of their abilities to survive in the increasingly popular medium of talking films, the reports of the broadcast had to be worrisome. *Variety* solicited the comments of movie-theater owners around the country about how their audiences responded to the radio hookup that had interrupted their regular programs. Their responses were almost uniformly sobering. The Boston audience started "the razz" within ten minutes and forced the owner to go back to the regularly scheduled movies. A number of theaters reported that their business was off. None felt it was up. A Baltimore theater owner probably voiced the consensus among owners and much of the audience when he told the *Variety* reporter that he felt it was a mistake to take audiences behind the scenes and let them listen to entertainers "whose talents are essentially visual."[38]

"Entertainers whose talents are essentially visual." If Chaplin read these words or heard them reported by his staff, as he most likely did, they must have unsettled him. Although the theater owners had no specific criticism of Chaplin's performance in their summaries of audience response, neither did they have any praise, while they did for John Barrymore. More significantly, a *Variety* reporter who talked with Chaplin after the broadcast wrote "that he nearly died while doing it, through mike fright, and was worried as to how he did."[39] This was not Chaplin's first encounter with radio: a few years earlier he had broadcast on New York's WOR. Afterward, he told the studio director that he was so certain he had lost "about nine pounds" that he would be willing to sign a statement to that effect.[40] If Chaplin participated in the Dodge broadcast as a way to try out his voice with a movie audience without having to risk the large investment of a film, there is little doubt that this helped discourage him from adding dialogue to his next picture.

The threat of sound was a vexing one for Chaplin, for although *The Circus* did well at the box office, he was still confronted with considerable financial pressures. Not only did his divorce settlement require him to come up with $825,000 in several payments through 1930, but his income tax dispute with the federal government was finally settled the month before the broadcast, and not in his favor. The settlement required $1,670,000 of Chaplin: $1,073,000 in personal income taxes and the rest in corporate taxes from the Charles Chaplin Film Corporation.[41] In deciding whether to accept or reject dialogue in his next film, Chaplin had economic considerations in mind.

It was not an easy decision, for Chaplin halted activity and postponed production during the spring and summer of 1928 to think about it.[42] By October, however, he had cast Virginia Cherrill in the role of the blind girl, and by the spring of 1929 he was ready to cast his lot as a partial aesthetic conservative: though he would not resist recorded sound tracks per se, he would resist pressure to have his characters, particularly Charlie, speak. The clearest evidence of Chaplin's growing resolve to resist dialogue appeared in "Charlie Chaplin Attacks the Talkies," which appeared in *Motion Picture Magazine* in May 1929. When asked about his attitude toward talkies, Chaplin replied to the interviewer, "You can tell 'em I loathe them." Chaplin's other comments elaborated on this theme:

> They are spoiling the oldest art in the world, the art of pantomime.
> They are ruining the great beauty of silence.
> They are defeating the meaning of the screen, the appeal that has created the star system, the fan system, the vast popularity of the whole—the appeal of beauty.[43]

A couple of months later, in the midst of production, Chaplin told Mordaunt Hall that he might have "an incidental song, the patter of dancing feet, now and again the tones of a trombone or a cornet and the inevitable synchronized musical score" but that he would not have sound effects or dialogue. Hall, who had talked with Chaplin about sound in 1928, found that Chaplin "was even more strongly opposed to giving shadows a voice" than he had been the year before.[44] Though Chaplin would include a musical score ("music, like pictures, is a universal language," he told the *Motion Picture* interviewer), sound effects, and especially dialogue, were out.

Chaplin decided to resist dialogue in his next film for several reasons. First, since the foreign revenues on Chaplin's films were even larger than the domestic grosses, having Charlie speak English would mean partially cutting him off from non–English speaking audiences. Second, many intellectuals, both American and European, sharply criticized talking films on aesthetic grounds and praised the artistry that arose from the limitations of silent film style. Given the primitive quality of the first silent films and the beauty of the best films made in the late silent period, their resistance was understandable. And given Chaplin's concern for support from the intelligentsia, his decision to resist dialogue made sense.[45] Third, Chaplin had already shown that he was nervous about using his voice in public and uncertain about associating his voice with the Charlie persona: since Charlie's essential appeal resulted from his pantomime, Chaplin logically surmised that making Charlie a talking as well as a miming character could undercut his appeal.

Probably the most important reason that Chaplin decided to resist spoken dialogue in *City Lights*—and also a key reason for his continuing popularity through *Modern Times* in 1936—was that he was shrewd enough to know that he had in his previous films established what we have called an "aesthetic contract" with his audience. Central to the nature of Hollywood films from the 1910s to the present is the notion of story types or genres. Though the term "genre" is a thorny one, genre critics have usefully suggested that audiences of popular films often prefer films that are a blend of convention and innovation, standardization and differentiation: the audience responds first to convention (established and familiar characters, themes, actions, and iconography) and then looks for something fresh or interesting to take place within that conventional structure.[46]

As the above comparison of *The Circus* and *The Gold Rush* demonstrated, Chaplin had by the late 1920s created a kind of personal genre (not unlike what Hitchcock did later in another vein) consisting of the central comic persona, a romance, pantomimic comedy, situations of pathos leading to empathy for that comic persona, and a contrast in value systems or moral perspectives. Although Chaplin's personal genre must be understood as fitting comfortably within the contours of 1920s "persona comedy" (Lloyd, Keaton, Langdon, etc.) and the narrative conventions of classical Hollywood cinema, it was also distinctive enough, especially because of the Charlie persona, to be perceived as identifiably different and attractive by viewers. And because Chaplin, unlike other Hollywood movie comedians, owned his studio, he had the luxury after the introduction of sound of deciding the extent to which he would continue making films within his personal genre. It became clear to him that having Charlie talk would violate a central tenet of Chaplin's aesthetic contract: Charlie the silent, pantomimic character capable of evoking both laughter and tears.

Though Chaplin had decided firmly by 1929 that *City Lights* would be a nondialogue film, production history was troubled. Sound films came more and more to dominate the industry in 1929 and 1930, and the top-grossing film of 1930 was *Animal Crackers*, a dialogue comedy starring that most un-Chaplinesque group (except perhaps Harpo), the Marx Brothers. During this time Chaplin, who had become an ever more meticulous and deliberate perfectionist on the set and was sometimes even irregular about coming to the studio at all, had an extremely difficult time working consistently. Going over the shooting schedule in some of Chaplin's papers recently made available, Kevin Brownlow noted that in the first 534 working days after shooting of

City Lights began, shooting took place on only 166 days: the others were "off" days, even though the cast and crew were on the set and being paid. Such details suggest that Chaplin's decision to stay with nondialogue films caused him considerable anxiety.[17] The technological change was posing a distinct threat to the star image.

Farewell to the Twenties:
City Lights

Once the troubled shooting schedule and the scoring of *City Lights* (1931) were completed, however, its promotion campaign, the completed film itself, and its critical reviews all suggest that Chaplin fulfilled his aesthetic contract with his audience and preserved his star image in a remarkably effective way. The pressbook prepared for *City Lights* skillfully sought to reinforce the image of Charlie and of Chaplin's films that had been built up through *The Circus*. One full-page ad was headed, "The King of Comedy in the Supreme Laugh Sensation of the Century."[48] It stressed that Chaplin would continue to offer comedy and pathos: the film, it claimed, "plays on your funny bone and the heart strings." Since part of Chaplin's star image emphasized his versatility and complete creative control, one headline showed how that control was extended in the sound era: "Chaplin Writes Songs in Film." Promotion headlines also stressed Chaplin's negative response to talkies: "Comedian Defies Movie Trend in Making *City Lights*: Thinks It His Best." Another headline made bold claims: "*City Lights* Is Expected to Change Trend of Film World. . . . Movie Prophets Predict Avalanche of Talkless Pictures as a Result" (the prophets were wrong). While these two headlines sought to present Chaplin as an aesthetic purist, they also hinted at the aesthetic conservatism that would later become an important element of his star image and that damaged it for many people.

Somewhat uncharacteristically, at least compared to the promotion campaigns for *The Gold Rush* and *The Circus*, the pressbook contained an article about Chaplin's personal life. It was headed, "Tennis and Running Keep Chaplin Healthy." Perhaps the promoters wanted the audience to know that Chaplin was still fit and robust despite his age. Pictures and sketches in the pressbook, some of which were later included in Chaplin's *My Life in Pictures* (pp. 236–37), stressed the familiar costume, mustache, and manner of the old Charlie. Time may have passed, the promotion material seemed to say, but Chaplin has stayed the same, except that he has added musical composition to his varied and considerable talents.

Though no full analysis of *City Lights* is possible in this limited space (Molyneaux's book provides a close reading), it is useful to highlight three characteristics of the film. First, the film fulfills Chaplin's aesthetic contract—that is, it continues the familiar development of Chaplin's comic/romantic/pathetic narratives that his audience had become familiar and pleased with in his previous two comic feature films. Second, Chaplin again works submerged autobiography into *City Lights*, much as he had in some previous films from *The Kid* on. And third, *City Lights* shows Chaplin as a cultural critic, casting a critical eye on urban American culture in the 1920s from the perspective of the Victorian world view that so profoundly shaped his sensibility.

We noted earlier that film genres, including Chaplin's "personal genre," consist of "regularized variety": the interplay of repetition and variation. *City Lights* exhibits many of the narrative and comic conventions of *The Gold Rush* and *The Circus* and also adds variations, thus honoring the contract Chaplin had made with his audience. Charlie again appears at the center of the film with his familiar costume and demeanor. As in the other two films, he is apparently not gainfully employed (he does work for a time, but not very successfully). He falls in love with a beautiful woman, which leads to comic and pathetic situations, both of which are related to one of the film's innovations—the woman is blind. Comedy results when she unknowingly tosses water in his face or winds the yarn of his underwear into a ball; probably the most powerful pathos comes when Charlie is released from prison: alone, haggard, and penniless. To a lesser extent than the other films, animals help create comic situations, as when the elephants pass by the street-cleaning Charlie.

There are also variations from *The Gold Rush* and *The Circus* in *City Lights*. Largely because of the film's urban setting, humor comes more than usual from Charlie's interactions with people, at times in elegant settings. Like the other two films, Chaplin sets up alternative moral universes, each representing a set of cultural values, but in *City Lights* this is handled somewhat differently. In the previous two films, Charlie represented the "good" values, Black Larsen and the ringmaster the "evil" values. In *City Lights*, however, Charlie moves back and forth between two worlds: the upper-class luxury of the millionaire and the urban, almost folk world of the flower girl and her grandmother. Charlie acts with charity in both worlds, but the film also morally affirms the flower girl's world and criticizes the millionaire's. The ending of *City Lights*, like the endings of the previous two films, concentrates on the outcome of the relationship between Charlie and the girl. However, whereas Charlie is united with Georgia in *The Gold Rush* and sacrifices his love for Merna in *The Circus*, in *City Lights* Chaplin leaves the relationship between the flower girl and Charlie (and the audience itself) poised in a delicate and sublimely indecisive manner, leading to what for several reasons is one of the most memorable endings in movie history. Using innovation within the boundaries of convention, Chaplin fulfills his audience's expectations.

A second characteristic of *City Lights* is the continuation of sub-merged autobiography that Chaplin began working into his films during the 1920s. The two worlds that Charlie moves between—the urban poor and the urban wealthy—equate with the two worlds that Chaplin experienced at different periods of his life: his poverty during his London childhood and his later wealth. The plain and simple mise-en-scène of the flower girl's apartment recalls Jean's apartment in *A Woman of Paris*, just as the luxurious mise-en-scène that surrounds the millionaire in *City Lights* resembles the life of Pierre and Marie in Paris. Chaplin was familiar with both worlds. Even more specifically autobiographical are the similarities between Chaplin the man and the millionaire in the film.[49] Both the millionaire's extremely erratic behavior, a key element of the plot and theme, and his ability to dominate a party resemble the vital yet moody and almost schizophrenic Chaplin of the mid-1920s, described by Tully and Grey in their accounts of Chaplin. Since Chaplin does not portray the millionaire as sympathetically as he did Pierre in *A Woman of Paris*, it may be that his awareness of his behavior during his second marriage made him more critical of this melancholy and occasionally cruel side of his own being. His apparent consciousness of that behavior, as well as his longing for the almost pastoral Victorian world of the flower girl and her mother, help give *City Lights* a decidedly personal resonance.

In addition to these autobiographical implications, *City Lights* contains serious criticism of American urban life. This characteristic of the film perpetuates a dimension of the Chaplin star image that began to emerge in the early 1920s: the serious artist concerned with more than just providing laughs. If *The Pilgrim* was a less systematic and developed critique of the small town, in *City Lights* Chaplin turned his attention to what he saw as the disturbing quality of life in prosperous urban America. Although it is not apparently set in the depression, *City Lights* might fruitfully be paired with F. Scott Fitzgerald's short story, "Babylon Revisited," for both of these 1931 works directly or obliquely take a searching look at the glittering way of life of wealthy Americans in the Jazz Age and find it lacking.

Although Chaplin had from early in his career shown a sympathy for the dispossessed and had even occasionally, as in *The Immigrant* or

The Pilgrim, satirically attacked society, *City Lights* begins a series of four films (through *Monsieur Verdoux*) in which sober cultural or political concerns increasingly dominate the narratives while the comedy becomes less central. As cultural criticism, *City Lights* is thematically quite direct: it presents Chaplin's response to the social world in which he had moved in the 1920s—the world of the urban upper class—and contrasts it to an idealized urban folk world, rooted in Chaplin's memory, which serves as the film's moral alternative to the superficiality, rootlessness, and moral emptiness of the urban upper classes.

It is important to note, however, that this theme is subtly developed: although Chaplin had satiric aims in the film, he took pains not to be too topical. Chaplin's images do not attack city life overtly or polemically; rather, the film presents a subtler denunciation.[50] The fact that neither the city nor the central characters are ever specifically named (the characters are simply called the girl, the millionaire, and the tramp) gives the film a broader mythic appeal, as opposed, for example, to a work like *The Grapes of Wrath*, which is securely rooted in a specific time and place.[51] Using this more general approach, *City Lights* nevertheless is Chaplin's somber commentary on the 1920s, the decade of his greatest success, his pinnacle of stardom.

The film's opening shot emphasizes its overriding concern with modern urban life: behind the words "City Lights," which are formed by bright lights, a city landscape bustles with rushing people and passing vehicles, accompanied by a jazz theme. The sound track early identifies the city as American: in the opening statue-dedication sequence, characters come to attention when the "Star-Spangled Banner" is played—even Charlie, whose pants are skewered by the sword of one of the statues. That scene also sets up a contrast between the city respectables and the disreputables like Charlie. The respectables are represented by the mayor, a woman's club spokesperson, and the sculptor responsible for the ridiculous public statuary that is being dedicated. Their voices are approximated by a kazoo; Chaplin uses the aural device to satirize them (from the start, *City Lights* is never a silent film) and to contrast them with Charlie.

After the opening two scenes set up Charlie's character and his alienation from much of urban society, Chaplin moves toward the central contrast in the film: in the third and fifth scenes he introduces the other two key figures in the movie, the flower girl and the millionaire.[52] The girl lives in a simple second-story apartment with her grandmother. Apparently lit by natural light, it has sparse furnishings, though some of them, including the canary and the potted flowers on the window sill, derive from nature. A central possession in the home is the family album, which Charlie looks at and describes to the flower girl: it associates her way of life with family unity and social tradition. Significantly, this warm and fulfilling way of life is also threatened by the city. Charlie accidentally learns midway through the film that the flower girl and her grandmother are in danger of being evicted because they do not have enough money to pay their rent.

In contrast, the millionaire moves through the glamour and glitter of the Jazz Age. If the flower is the central image associated with the girl's world, money is the millionaire's key image. His home is sumptuously decorated, and in the evenings, during parties, illuminated artificially. Its elaborate furnishings contrast to the simplicity of the girl's, both in quantity and in splendor. Structurally parallel to the girl's cherished photograph album is the millionaire's picture of his estranged wife, which he tosses to the floor after looking at it early in the film. (As we have seen, being estranged from a wife was hardly unusual for Chaplin, as well.) In contrast to the sedate yet struggling world of the flower girl, the millionaire is constantly active (giving parties or going to night clubs) frequently suicidal (particularly when drunk), and apparently made of money, for he never seems to worry about it. If the flower girl's world is one in which human relationships are important and human compassion is lasting, the millionaire's world is one of short-term and superficial human relationships: significantly, it is only when he's drunk that the millionaire knows and is generous to Charlie. His life alternates between frenetic activity and despair.

This contrast between the two worlds provides the basic rhythm of the plot, which alternates between pathos and comedy. The flower girl's world is a passive one: Charlie must visit her for that plot strand to progress. This element of the story—his kindness to her, her misapprehension that Charlie is wealthy, and the development of their romance—leads to the central moments of pathos in the film. On the other hand, the primary comic scenes arise either from Charlie's interactions with the millionaire or from his attempts to make money for the girl's operation by taking jobs: the waterfront scene, the nightclub scene, the party scene, and the boxing scene. This is the more active world and the source of most of the film's comedy.

But amid the humor, Chaplin weaves a satirical critique of the millionaire. A man alone, the millionaire flings away the picture of his estranged wife. The night club and party scenes, as well as his trip to Europe, show him as a man constantly on the move but going nowhere. His drinking is presented as a desire for escape, yet ultimately it only leads him back to suicidal thoughts. The contradiction of his generosity to Charlie when drunk and indignant rejection of him when sober is more than a narrative device to further the plot and generate comedy; the contradiction is Chaplin's comment on the superficiality of the millionaire's world and the emptiness of his values.

The flower girl's world serves as a counterpoint in Chaplin's cultural critique. We have already noted that her life is associated with simplicity, nature, and poverty. It is a world that the millionaire knows nothing about; the glare of the city lights blind him to the sufferings of the less fortunate. It is true that, as one critic suggests, *City Lights* endorses the flower girl's "more remote, gratifying and likable folk world."[53] But were it not for Charlie's good fortune and concern for the flower girl, she and her grandmother would be turned out on the streets for failing to pay their rent. The good are victimized and nearly powerless in this film; the flawed are powerful and oblivious.

After presenting the urban upper-class world as gaudy, prosperous, and superficially appealing, yet morally hollow at the core, Chaplin offers the flower girl a choice in the famous, inconclusive conclusion of *City Lights*. Charlie, just released from prison, where he had served a term for stealing the money that enabled the girl to pay her rent and to get the operation that restored her sight, is as bedraggled in costume, makeup, and manner as his audience had ever seen him. After harassment from two pea-shooting newsboys, Charlie trudges by the floral shop run by the now-prosperous flower girl and her grandmother. Looking through her store window, the girl observes him picking up a wilted flower by the curb but, never having seen him, does not know who he is. Their eyes meet, and the flower girl, taking pity on him, offers him money—the central image of the millionaire's world. Charlie refuses and, painfully aware of his appearance, tries to scurry by. The flower girl comes outside the door and offers him a flower. Their hands meet, and through her sensitive touch she realizes that Charlie is her benefactor. "You?" she says in a title. Charlie replies in anticipation, "You can see now?" Their exchange invites us to reflect on the double meaning of "see"—to visualize and to understand—for the flower girl sees through her eyes but understands through her touch. An indescribable expression of wonder, disappointment, and gratitude, complicated by tears blurring in her eyes, covers the flower girl's face, but Chaplin cuts back to a close-up of Charlie. Is his expression anticipation? Hopelessness? Bittersweet recognition of the absurdity of life? Happiness? Before it is clear, the shot fades out.

Chaplin leaves his audience suspended. He has presented the world of a millionaire who is not only unhappy but even mean-spirited. He has also shown a tramp and blind flower girl from another world who are charitable and, for most of the film at least, victimized. Then at the conclusion Chaplin twists the plot and gives the flower girl a choice. Will she opt for the appealing yet hollow world of the millionaire, the world of money, the world of the prosperous 1920s that her restored sight has made a possibility? Or will she return, like the woman of Paris, to the world from whence she came, the world of flowers, the world where charity leads to self-sacrifice and lasting human ties? We will never know, and one of the reasons this scene is so emotionally powerful is that Chaplin himself knew the attractions of both worlds and, though wanting ideally to choose the flower world, knew that he sometimes chose the other. Some of our most powerful and penetrating cultural criticism in narrative art arises when the creator confronts commonly shared dilemmas that he feels deeply in his own being. *City Lights* is just such a work, and by posing the alternatives so effectively, Chaplin was continuing to foster his image as a serious comedian.

How did the public and critics react to the film and to a filmmaker whose work had not appeared on the screen for three long years? The public evidently responded very positively. When *City Lights* opened at the Cohan Theater in New York City, it initially played continuously from 9 A.M. through a midnight show every night but Sunday. It grossed over a half-million dollars at this one theater during its twelve-week run. Another indicator of how well *City Lights* did comes from the United Artists' corporate records: by the end of 1931, the ledgers reveal, *City Lights* had already accumulated more domestic rentals than *The Circus* and over 90 percent of the domestic rentals that *The Gold Rush* had garnered since 1925.[54] These results, one might add, came during the depths of the depression.

The press was for the most part even more enthusiastic. Paul Rotha wrote in his first edition of *The Film Till Now* that *City Lights* had more advance publicity than any film in history up to that time. If the *New York Times* coverage was typical, he may be right: Mordaunt Hall was doing articles on *City Lights* as early as July and August 1929, and as the opening approached, the *Times* gave Chaplin prominent space in two Sunday issues in January. The newspaper reviews were generally raves. Typical was Hall's, titled "Chaplin Hilarious in *City Lights*," which described the audience's enthusiasm on opening night, praised the boxing scene and the ending, and summed up: "It was a joyous evening. Mr. Chaplin's shadow has grown no less."[55] The *Herald Tribune* was equally enthusiastic, calling the picture "a very brilliant film, a genuinely hilarious comedy which shows the Great Man of the Cinema

121

in his happiest and most characteristic moods." *City Lights* was, the reviewer wrote, "a magnificent comedy" that blended "hilarity with pathos" so skillfully that it deserved to be called "an historic comedy."[56] Chaplin had, for this reviewer at least, fulfilled his aesthetic contract.

Some of the reviewers in the weeklies or monthlies, including Chaplin's advocate Seldes, also thought the film superb. Writing in the *New Republic*, Seldes found it "beyond question" that Chaplin had "created one of his masterpieces." It is, he wrote, "magnificently organized, deeply thought out and felt, and communicated with an unflagging energy and a masterly technique." Accurately noting the film's alternation between comedy and romance—another staple of Chaplin's personal genre—Seldes too singled out the ending as especially effective, as "infinitely sad and altogether appropriate. For in this picture Chaplin has not for a moment suggested that our laughter hides our tears; only that at the end of our laughter, there will be nothing but tears for the gayest of us."[57]

Thus, despite all the uncertainty Chaplin had shown during the production of the film, as well as the bravado he had exhibited in defending the nondialogue, pantomimic film in the years before its release, *City Lights* joined the long line of Chaplin star vehicles. There was little indication that Chaplin's star had fallen, even though the industry had transformed itself to talking films and the nation itself was in the throes of the depression.

There were storm clouds on the horizon, however. Some respondents, although a decided minority, had reservations about *City Lights* and Chaplin's future. *Variety* issued one warning. Though acknowledging that Chaplin "is still the consummate pantomimist," *Variety* thought that Chaplin might suffer a little by sticking with nondialogue films. "There will always be room for Chaplin," they admitted, but sound films will likely "make him slightly less important in the general public eye as time goes on." As the quality of sound films improved, *Variety* suggested between the lines, Chaplin was in danger of making himself an anachronism.[58] This was a criticism that Chaplin would have to, and did, confront in his next film, *Modern Times* (1936).

But perhaps the most negative (as well as most prophetic) review of *City Lights* came from an old defender of Chaplin, Alexander Bakshy, whose review, "Charlie Chaplin Falters," appeared in the *Nation*. Resisting the "fervent acclaim" given the film, Bakshy judged it "the feeblest of his longer pictures," and for a very specific reason: Chaplin was trying too hard to be serious and evoke pity. Chaplin's comic character—"a round peg in a square hole"—could generate pity by itself, wrote Bakshy, which made a sentimental plot unnecessary and even counterproductive. "Chaplin's growing seriousness, his desire to be more than a mere comedian," Bakshy objected, has "deceived him into holding sentiment more precious than fun."[59] Thoughout the 1920s, large numbers of Americans had come to perceive Chaplin as a serious, even brilliant artist. That Chaplin aspired to fill this role is evident from his films of the period. That it had become a distinct part of his star image is evident from Bakshy's comment. As the depression deepened, however, and as Chaplin prepared to leave for a world tour following the opening of *City Lights*, his dual perception of himself as a serious cultural critic and as a comedian were about to become a central issue in his art and life. And as it did so, his star image continued its evolution.

THREE

The Challenge of Progressive Politics

5

The Depression, the World Tour,
and *Modern Times*

A Comedian Sees—and Comments
on—the World

Chaplin's film career after *City Lights*, particularly the evolution of his star image, is explicable only if one keeps in mind the historical circumstances in which Chaplin made his films and the cultural climate in which critics and audiences responded to them. Andrew Sarris spoke persuasively and well several years ago when he lamented the tendency "to look at Chaplin's entire career as a single slab of personal achievement and thus to flatten out the temporal perspective by which each of the films was viewed at the time." If we are able to flesh out rather than flatten out this temporal perspective, we should have a much firmer conception of how and why Chaplin's star image evolved, particularly after he began to face the challenge of progressive politics.[1]

If *City Lights* is best considered Chaplin's postscript on the 1920s, his world tour in 1931 and 1932 was his introduction to the depression, to the political debates it engendered, and to the challenges it posed to him as a filmmaker and world-renowned public figure. The tour reiterated both to him and to the world that his status as an artist and celebrity was undiminished, but it also vividly demonstrated to him how widespread the effects of the depression were and encouraged him to comment on political and economic affairs, something he did both on his tour and in his account of it, *A Comedian Sees the World* (1933). In the years following his return, Chaplin witnessed the depths of the American depression, the election of Franklin D. Roosevelt and the passage of his first New Deal policies, Upton Sinclair's 1934 EPIC (End Poverty in California) campaign, and the growing conflict between the producers and aspiring unionists in Hollywood. Within this national and local context, he conceived and filmed *Modern Times*, which both before and after its release generated a great deal of controversy concerning its social and political implications.

Chaplin's world tour, which began the same month that *City Lights* opened in New York City and lasted fifteen months, was an experience that modified his world view and affected his subsequent career. He wrote extensively about the trip, publishing his reflections both in a high circulation magazine and later as a book, and this too affected the American star image of Chaplin as a celebrity. The trip itself, the press's coverage of it, and Chaplin's account of it provide a basis for understanding Chaplin's next film and constitute a starting point for the politicization of Chaplin's star image.

Like his European tour in 1921, Chaplin drew huge crowds on his 1931 trip whenever his arrival in a new city was made public. Unlike the previous journey, however, Chaplin spent considerable time in various locations and saw much of the world. His itinerary included England, Germany, France (Paris, Normandy, Nice), Austria, Italy (Venice and Rome), Spain, Switzerland (St. Moritz), Ceylon, Singapore, Java, Bali, and Japan.[2]

Though short reports about his tour were carried relatively frequently in the American press, probably the most publicized incident occurred in early May, when Chaplin was charged with refusing to participate in a command performance for the King of England.[3] Chaplin quickly denied the allegations. He stated that he had only been asked by a music-hall manager to appear in a charity program and, refusing, had sent a $1,000 check for the benefit fund instead (the same amount he earned in his last two years in England before going to America). The incident clearly raised Chaplin's ire, as his comments indicate: "They say I have a duty to England. I wonder just what that duty is? No one wanted me or cared for me in England seventeen years ago. I had to go to America for my chance, and I got it there. Only then did England take the slightest interest in me." Such a comment delighted American cartoonists and editorialists, for it reaffirmed the dearly held myth of America as the land of opportunity.[4]

In the same press conference Chaplin also commented on public affairs in what was, up to this point in his career, an unusually candid and testy way: "Patriotism is the greatest insanity the world has ever suffered. I have been all over Europe in the last few months. Patriotism is rampant everywhere, and the result is going to be another war. I hope they send the old men to the front the next time, for it is the old men who are the real criminals in Europe today."[5] Although such a comment was unlikely to antagonize many in the early 1930s—in both Europe and America the memory of World War I was as strong as the isolationist desire to avoid another one—such overt political comments by a movie star could easily jeopardize his status in another context. Evidence suggests that during his trip Chaplin became increasingly willing to comment on political and economic issues.

128

This is in part because Chaplin met even more prominent political figures and commentators on this trip than in 1921. If one only goes through *A Comedian Sees the World*, the list that can be compiled of such people is impressive.[6] In England he met and talked with Ramsay MacDonald, Lloyd George, Winston Churchill (the present, past, and future prime ministers), Gandhi, George Bernard Shaw, H. G. Wells, Aldous Huxley, Sir Phillip Sassoon, and many members of Parliament. In Germany he dined with members of the Reichstag and the nephew of the Kaiser. In France he met the permanent secretary of the French Cabinet. In Belgium he was decorated by the King—and so on through the trip. It is apparent that political affairs were more on his mind in this trip than in the previous one.

In fact, a close examination of *A Comedian Sees the World* reveals the star image Chaplin sought to present in the early 1930s. One of the first themes in the memoir is Chaplin's awareness of being a celebrity and his skill at coping with that fact. At one point Chaplin warns his readers that "the tourist's opinions of countries he visits are usually in error, especially a celebrity's, who sees things through a glamour of excitement." Reading of the crowds Chaplin had to wade through at nearly every stop on the tour, one knows clearly what he means. The constant attention of the press is another indication of Chaplin's celebrity status, but Chaplin, referring to the press's behavior after he had visited MacDonald, shows how he has learned to deal with it: "I have a technique now for such interviews. I usually answer in monosyllables, and to foolish questions just smile."[7] The persona of this memoir is a celebrity who has, despite becoming weary of and exhausted from the constant adulation, become able to function within its structure.

The book's political references are perhaps its most interesting dimension. Chaplin wrote of his vague longings to help the underprivileged in *My Trip Abroad*, but specific references to political affairs were relatively rare in that book in comparison with *A Comedian Sees the World*. Here, Chaplin frequently records his political discussions with the powerful and prominent and often offers his prescriptions for the economic dislocations of the depression. Probably the most detailed is his account of a speech he gave at a dinner given by Lady Astor that included members of each political party in Parliament. Speakers were asked what they would do if given the power of a Mussolini to help England in its present situation. Chaplin spoke first and proposed, among other changes, the following:

1. Reduce the government
2. Create a government Bureau of Economics that would control prices, interests, and profits
3. Amalgamate England's colonies "into an economic unity"

4. Support "internationalism, world cooperation of trade, the abolition of the gold standard"

5. Reduce hours of labor and provide a "comfortable amount" to all men and women over twenty-one

6. "Stand for private enterprise so far as it would not deter the progress or well-being of the majority"[8]

While the list is something of a hodgepodge—the first two points, for example, seem contradictory—it gives some idea of Chaplin's thinking about the depression in the early part of his trip.

Later interchanges provide more insight into Chaplin's politics. At a "dialectic evening" with Winston Churchill and some young members of Parliament, Chaplin responded to criticism of Gandhi by saying that "Gandhis or Lenins do not start revolutions. They are forced up by the masses and usually voice the want of the people." He also added, however, "I believe we should go with evolution to avoid revolution, and there's every evidence that the world needs a drastic change." In Berlin, Chaplin's comments to Albert Einstein about the necessity for fewer working hours, more printing of money, and price controls prompted Einstein's famous statement, "You're not a comedian, you're an economist." Meeting with Gandhi in London's East End, Chaplin queried him about his opposition to machine technology and defended the machine as a way to provide modern man with more leisure.[9] Though it would be difficult to reconcile all of Chaplin's political comments in the memoir, most are consistent with the core "progressive" beliefs that, according to Richard Pells, were shared among the American Left between the Progressive Era and World War II: faith in the capacity to reform people by affecting their technological and social environment; admiration for organizational efficiency; and a yearning to harmonize liberty and art with technological progress and community participation.[10]

Two tangential political themes in the book are especially relevant here: Chaplin's attitude toward America and his comments on the relationship between his art and politics. Within the decade, people would be charging that Chaplin had only scorn for his adopted country. The memoir, however, presents a mixed picture of the United States. Some details are critical. While visiting the south of France, Chaplin encountered a number of American expatriates and recounted their inability to live in America because of its "prohibition and Blue Laws and all the don'ts of organized puritanisms." For a man who had been hounded by certain sectors of the population during his 1927 divorce, such a perspective was not surprising. Later, Chaplin commented indirectly on conditions in America when he mentioned meeting two young Americans who, to avoid living unemployed back home, had settled in Bali, where the amount of five dollars a day was perfectly adequate to live on. Describing his return to the United States, however, Chaplin is more positive. He writes at the end of his memoir that America's "youthful spirit born of prosperity and success has worn off and in its place there are a maturity and sobriety." (The first half of this comment seems quite consistent with the central concerns of *City Lights*.) In his closing paragraph Chaplin reports his feeling "that in America lies the hope of the whole world. For whatever takes place in the transition of this epoch-making time, America will be equal to it."[11]

Chaplin's attitude toward art and its relationship to politics is important because, as we shall see, artists were increasingly being pressured by critics and by some of the public to be "socially conscious" in their art during the early years of the depression. For the most part, Chaplin's comments on the subject in his memoir suggest that he was opposed to the notion of "socially conscious art." The subject comes up both directly, as in a reference to a meeting with George Bernard Shaw, and indirectly.

Recounting the meeting with Shaw, Chaplin wrote that he admired Shaw's intellect but was uncomfortable with his view "that all art should be propaganda." Chaplin's view was quite different, for he preferred "to think the object of art is to intensify feeling, color or sound." This intensification "gives a fuller range to the art in expressing life, in spite of the moral aspect of it."[12] Although the distinctions are not especially sharp in this formulation, it does seem that Chaplin did not, at this point in his career, believe that art should be aimed primarily at providing moral or political instruction to its audience.

Other comments from the memoir support this position. In discussing his unrequited love affair with Hetty Kelly, Chaplin connects art with love. For him that failed affair "was the beginning of a spiritual development, a reaching out for beauty," and the "beautiful" was consistently linked with the creation of art. If we think of the pathos that stems from unrequited or jeopardized love in his films, we get a fuller understanding of what he means by art's intensification of feeling and art's relationship to love. At another point, while visiting Italy, he was impressed by the comment of an Italian: "Art is the treatment applied to work, and has nothing to do with subject matter." Chaplin here stresses the importance of style over subject matter. Finally, as he nears the end of his book, he makes an offhand remark about the remarkably ritualized Japanese tea ceremony: "To the practical western world the tea ceremony might seem quaint and trivial. Yet if we consider the highest object of life is the pursuit of the beautiful, what is more rational than applying it to the commonplace?"[13] Life at its best, Chaplin is arguing in this passage, aspires toward art, and art itself is concerned much more with style than with content. What is so remarkable about these comments is that Chaplin was quickly confronted with other views as the 1930s wore on, and his next three films showed an increasing concern with subject matter or content, sometimes so overtly that Chaplin began to be attacked for his inadequate, primitive style and didactic messages. But at the time he wrote this memoir, Chaplin leaned toward a more aesthetic than sociological view of art.

All in all, *A Comedian Sees the World* gives us a vivid picture of Chaplin at his height as a celebrity to that point, confronted for the first time in a serious way with the strains engendered by the depression. Because the press coverage of the tour concentrated on the famous people Chaplin met and talked with, Chaplin's star image afterward was even more sterling than before. Instead of simply being known as a major figure in world cinema, he began to be rated by some as one of the most important people in the world. A feature in the *New York Times* from January 1932—even before Chaplin completed his trip—gives an idea of how important a public figure he had become in the press and, by extension, in many sectors of the public imagination.

The article, "Ten Men Who Stand as Symbols," discusses ten people whose "personalities have caught the imagination of mankind": the Prince of Wales, Mussolini, Stalin, the Pope, Henry Ford, Gandhi, Charles Lindbergh, Albert Einstein, George Bernard Shaw, and Chaplin. These "Decemviri of Individuality" were important, argued the author, because each person had enabled people to visualize something that was important to humanity. The two artists of the group, Chaplin and Shaw, were both "rebels against routine." Chaplin's particular appeal, according to the author, was the ability of his comic persona to reconcile disparities in human class, manners, and personality. He was "the highbrow who happens to be a hobo, the duke who was only born a dustman, the utterly genteel who is utterly shabby." Significantly, the author seemed to blend Chaplin and Charlie: Chaplin himself was something of a dustman turned duke in his private life, and the description also relates to oppositions in Charlie's character. Here Chaplin's star image overtly blends the man and his filmic creation, something that later—particularly in a film like *Monsieur Verdoux*—would seriously damage his reputation. Nevertheless, the article aimed not to bury Chaplin but to praise him: "as Homer was a father of poetry, so is 'Charlie' a father of laughter." Chaplin was "the standard by which others are estimated."[14]

High tributes to Chaplin were common in the early 1930s, and he was often grouped with celebrities in the press. For example, a *Vanity Fair* page from the early 1930s, featuring celebrities who played the violin, pictured Mussolini, Upton Sinclair, Einstein, and Chaplin. When a newspaper ran an article called "Distorted Faces of Celebrities," it included caricatures of the faces of Ramsay MacDonald, Lloyd George, and Chaplin.[15] In these instances Chaplin was associated with politicians but not necessarily with politics. Though he mixed with world political leaders on his world tour—the first time that Chaplin met frequently with politicians—his own political views were generally not a focus of articles in the early 1930s, even though he was beginning to make more public comments about social issues than he had previously. From the mid-1930s on, however, his political views did interest the press, and they eventually became an inextricable part of his star image.

Critics, Artists, and
Depression America

The period between Chaplin's return to the United States in 1932 and the release of *Modern Times* in 1936 was absolutely crucial to the evolution of his star image. During this period Chaplin, like many other artists, began to feel more pointedly the challenge of progressive politics.

Chaplin returned from his world tour in May 1932 to an America approaching the depths of the depression. Since President Herbert Hoover had taken office in 1929, industrial production had declined more than half. At the start of the summer of 1932, according to *Iron Age*, steel plants were running at 12 percent capacity, with no immediate improvement in sight. Industrial construction, falling from $949 million to $74 million in three years, had nearly halted. Unemployment estimates for nonfarm jobs ranged from a quarter to a third of the work force, many of whom had no source of income or relief. In parts of Los Angeles not far from Hollywood, people unable to pay their utility bills were cooking on wood fires outside their apartments. As many as two million people, whose plight was soon to be documented in Warner Brothers' *Wild Boys of the Road*, were wandering around the country in search of work or sometimes just a warm meal.[16]

The presidential primaries were already in full swing when Chaplin returned. A couple of weeks earlier, in the California Democratic primary, Speaker of the House John Nance Gardner from Texas, aided by newspaper magnate William Randolph Hearst (a Chaplin acquaintance), had run well ahead of the favorite, New York governor Franklin D. Roosevelt. However, at the June Democratic national convention in Chicago, the patrician Roosevelt marshaled enough support to win the nomination in the fourth roll call. Flying to Chicago to address the convention, Roosevelt pledged "a new deal for the American people." Roosevelt ran a relatively moderate campaign—far too moderate for many leftists—and won a landslide victory. He captured every state south and west of Pennsylvania and accumulated a 472–59 margin in the electoral college.[17]

Though Roosevelt came into office in early 1933 with no firm or ideologically based plan for pulling the country out of the depression, he did begin dramatically. Within his first two weeks he had engineered a "bank holiday" that closed and helped restore confidence in banks. He had proposed and persuaded Congress to pass strong economic measures that included budget cuts, and he had recommended that Congress end Prohibition. After his first, famed "Hundred Days," Roosevelt and a sympathetic Congress had begun to lay the groundwork for the New Deal and to reassure many Americans that the country was not in ruins. When Congress passed a second group of laws in 1935, including the Social Security Act and the Wagner Act, Roosevelt garnered even more support, and in November 1936—nine months after the opening of *Modern Times*—he easily won reelection. From a mood of despair the country had moved in four years to a mood of cautious optimism. And though the irate "economic royalists" who were Roosevelt's target in the 1936 campaign may not have admitted it at the time, his policies helped to save a tottering capitalist system.[18]

Hollywood felt the effects of the depression much as many other parts of the country did. Within the movie colony itself, the movement of political sentiment to the left was more belated and never quite as widespread as it was among artists centered in New York City and its environs. This was due in part to the fact that the depression affected the movie industry more gradually than it hit heavy industry or construction: it was easier for a person to scrape up a dime for a movie ticket during hard times than it was for an investor to finance a skyscraper. By 1932, however, the film industry too was struggling. Estimates suggest that attendance had dropped to sixty million tickets a week from eighty million in 1929. Paramount, which had made $18 million in 1930 and $6 million in 1931, had a $21 million deficit in 1932. The next year it went into backruptcy, Fox underwent reorganization, and RKO was placed in receivership. The depression had reached the movies.[19]

Political activity in Hollywood was in part stimulated by actions the movie producers took at almost precisely the time Roosevelt called the bank holiday. At a meeting of the executives of the Motion Picture Producers and Distributors Association (MPPDA), the producers agreed on March 9 to impose a blanket wage cut on employees. On March 12 one of the only strong unions in Hollywood, IATSE (International Alliance of Theatrical Stage Employees, which covered electricians, engineers, grips, and the musicians' union), refused the cut, which led to the closing of the studios on March 13. The producers hurriedly met with members of the IATSE and ironed out an agreement acceptable to both nonunion and union employees. The IATSE members emerged united and strong, providing a model for unorganized groups like the screenwriters. Union organizing thereafter became an important political activity in Hollywood.[20]

The 1934 gubernatorial campaign in California provided another political focus for Hollywood. That year, over 700,000 workers in California, half of them in Los Angeles County, were unemployed, and strife between citrus growers and migrant workers was rampant. Socialist Upton Sinclair, famed for his muckraking novel *The Jungle* (1907), decided to run for governor under the EPIC (End Poverty in California) campaign and won the Democratic party nomination in late August. Prominent businessmen, including many studio chiefs, were appalled at the prospect of trying to conduct business in a state with a socialist governor. The studio executives were particularly worried because a year earlier, in a curious book done with the cooperation of studio chief William Fox (*Upton Sinclair Presents William Fox*), Sinclair had advocated either national ownership or at least firm federal regulation of the movie industry.

The studio heads worked hard to defeat Sinclair. Besides making and distributing deceptive anti-Sinclair newsreels, they publicly threatened to move to Florida if Sinclair were elected. Sinclair in response mockingly told audiences that if the studios moved to Florida, a bite on the nose of a starlet by a vicious Florida mosquito could cost a studio $50,000 per day in lost production costs. And even if they did move, said Sinclair, he might just "put the state into making pictures . . . I'll ask Charlie Chaplin to run part of the show."[21]

The studios' anti-Sinclair tactics spawned a leftist counter-offensive in Hollywood. Dorothy Thompson and Gene Fowler, among others, combined with writers from around the state to found the California Authors' League for Sinclair. Chaplin was one of the Hollywood figures who supported Sinclair, partly because of personal acquaintance. Chaplin had known him for some time: in his autobiography, Chaplin later wrote that his interest in socialism stemmed from his acquaintance with Sinclair (MA, p. 350), and Sinclair had even submitted a script to Chaplin called *The Hypnotist* in 1918, though nothing had come of it. Recalling the EPIC campaign in his autobiography, Sinclair wrote that Chaplin agreed to speak at a Sinclair rally in Hollywood, though no firm evidence exists that the speech ever took place. Nevertheless, it does seem clear that Chaplin supported Sinclair's candidacy. Active support for Sinclair was for many Hollywood figures a first taste of political involvement, and often not the last. Even though Sinclair eventually lost by some 230,000 votes (a third-party candidate split the vote on the left), the EPIC campaign served as an early event in the politicization of Hollywood that would increase considerably in the late 1930s.[22]

The economic breakdown of the early 1930s and the ensuing political controversies had a powerful impact on many American artists and intellectuals. Perhaps the earliest and most profound effects were to weaken what Malcolm Cowley in *Exile's Return* termed the "religion of art," so widely held by expatriate artists in the 1920s, and to heighten the awareness of artists and intellectuals concerning the social and political dilemmas of the age. With the effects of the depression so vividly apparent in the cities where many of the artists and intellectuals gathered, this growth of political consciousness is no surprise.[23]

However, merely being conscious of the social and political currents of the age was not enough for many. Artists and intellectuals were pressured, particularly by the Left, to exercise their awareness by treating social realities in their work and identifying explicitly with the interests of the dispossessed. The attack on playwright/novelist Thornton Wilder by *New Masses* critic Mike Gold in 1930 provides a vivid and famous picture of such pressure. Reviewing four novels and a volume of plays by Wilder in the *New Republic*, Gold accused Wilder of creating "an historical junkshop" of a world, with characters brooding over their "little lavender tragedies" with "tender irony." Because Wilder had no guiding social philosophy, except perhaps an outdated and socially irrelevant "Anglo-Catholicism," asserted Gold, he spoke for the values of the leisure classes: "the air of good breeding, the decorum, priestliness, glossy high finish as against intrinsic qualities, conspicuous inutility, caste feeling, love of the archaic." In contrast, Gold urged authors to depict a real world where the working class struggled with real social problems, and to write from an ideological perspective

136

sympathetic to workers and attuned to a Marxist view of history and the class struggle.[24]

Gold's interest in the relationship between art and reality from a leftist perspective gradually became shared by a number of American intellectuals, including some film critics and reviewers. Myron Lounsbury, in his history of American film criticism before World War II, identified two varieties of film criticism—the "social radical" and the "modern liberal"—affected by these leftist pressures in the 1930s. Social radical criticism, which appeared in such periodicals as *Experimental Cinema*, *New Theater*, and *New Masses*, was closer to Gold's perspective, more overtly supportive of radical social change and the place of the cinema as a mass art to encourage it. The modern liberal approach, which appeared in such journals as the *Nation* and the *New Republic*, shared the social radical's assumption that cinema reflects and shapes the values of its audiences, but tended to support more gradual social reform. The modern liberal critic likewise approved of films that attempted to grapple with the realities of contemporary life in its narrative.[25] Although social radical criticism in the early 1930s was more likely to denounce American capitalism (and Hollywood as an expression of it) in the early 1930s, the two strains of American film criticism became more similar after the beginning of the Popular Front period and the achievements of the New Deal in the mid-1930s. Both groups encouraged filmmakers like Chaplin to make his films more politically relevant to the problems of the age and to show his commitment in a time of social turmoil.

Some of the most accomplished social radical film criticism in the early 1930s was written by Harry Alan Potamkin. Born in 1900, Potamkin began a career in the 1920s as a poet but became a devoted writer on film after experiencing the vitality of French film culture during a trip to Paris in 1926. Though his writings on film in the late 1920s reveal an aestheticism characteristic of that era, the stock market crash and the onset of the depression, as well as the example of Soviet films that were beginning to be shown in the West in the late 1920s as an alternative to Hollywood, shifted Potamkin's focus. In the words of Lewis Jacobs, Potamkin's criticism in the 1930s "was generated by a social consciousness that responded to the crisis of the Depression with a critical approach that was sociological, tempered by a Marxist viewpoint. The compulsion to 'change the world' linked Potamkin's aesthetic sensibility with political and economic insights into a synthesis that directed his criticism in the last years leftward, toward social reform."[26] From around 1930 until his untimely death in 1933, Potamkin wrote a vigorous and challenging social/ideological criticism whose assumptions became widespread in the leftist press in the middle and latter part of the decade.

Potamkin's assumption that movies should grapple with the realities of the depression shaped his comments on Chaplin. In a 1931 essay on the growth of film criticism in the United States, he criticized Seldes and others like him who in the 1920s created a "cult of Charlie Chaplin which has never allowed a decent study of a man of talent who has not realized the great work that might have been expected of him." A 1932 essay expressed his view of Chaplin's weakness more explicitly. There Potamkin, challenging the critical consensus of the 1920s, objected to the "overdose of maudlin pathos" in Chaplin's previous three films. For Potamkin *City Lights* peaked in the opening scenes, then abandoned its serious concerns: "Its major motif, the relation between the millionaire and 'the classic hobo,' becomes subsidiary to the minor motif of the blind girl and Chaplin. The author-director-producer-star has weakened. He has fallen very far beneath the indications of *The Kid*, its social satire, its insistence on the major relationship, as against the formula romantic relationship."[27] In this view, Chaplin had abdicated his responsibility to concentrate on serious social concerns like the extremes of wealth and poverty and had focused instead on the wish fulfillment of romance and the emotional balm of pathos.

A similar analysis of Chaplin's work was advanced in 1934 by another social radical critic, Lorenzo Turrent Rozas. His essay, "Charlie Chaplin's Decline," originally published in Spanish in a Mexican Communist literary monthly, appeared in *Living Age* in June 1934. This was during the difficult period when Chaplin was working on the screenplay for *Modern Times*, four months before shooting began. It is not unlikely that Chaplin, accustomed to lavish praise of his films, looked carefully at an article in a popular magazine that argued his reputation was sliding. In the essay Rozas criticized *The Gold Rush* in much the same terms that Potamkin had used in objecting to *City Lights*. Rozas admitted that *The Gold Rush* was "one of the harshest criticisms ever made of capitalism in its last stage," but he nevertheless charged that the romantic ending was an evasion and salve for audiences.

Although generally praising the criticism of a corrupt society implicit in *The Gold Rush* and other Chaplin films, Rozas argued that Chaplin, like Kropotkin, was an anarchist, a position that led one "inexorably to defeat" because the anarchist "finally becomes involved with the society he repudiates." Rozas, expressing the Marxist view of the stages of economic development, held that "Chaplin and his art triumphed in the boom days of Yankee capitalism," but with the onset of the depression, Chaplin became "an accomplice of capitalism." At present, he continued, Chaplin was "in his decadence—alone, seated in the limited arena of his art. He explores the horizon. There is no road for him to follow. To insist on the old one is impossible, and to go where the workers are now marching is also impossible. To do that he would have to throw away the ballast of his millions."[28] Believing it unlikely that Chaplin would choose the "road of Marx and Lenin," Rozas charged that in hard times Chaplin's films were really harmful, because they "disorientate and confuse men who are struggling for the final victory of the disinherited." Like Potamkin, Rozas thought that Chaplin's commitments to pathos and to the individuality of the Charlie character weakened his art in the changed political and economic climate. Both critics implicitly suggested that a movement in the direction of social realism and overt commitment to radical politics would be useful and enriching to Chaplin's art. Their work was part of the broader challenge of progressive politics that confronted Chaplin and many other artists in the period.

Although building an airtight case of influence is difficult, there is evidence that suggests Chaplin was influenced by social radical criticism. In his autobiography, Chaplin wrote that as he cast about for a new film idea after returning from his world tour, "I was depressed by the remark of a young critic who said that *City Lights* was very good, but that it verged on the sentimental, and that in my future films I should try to approximate realism. I found myself agreeing with him" (MA, p. 383). It is not unlikely that the "young critic" Chaplin spoke of was either Potamkin or Rozas.

Direct influence or not, it is indisputable that many artists felt widespread pressures in the early and mid-1930s to demonstrate their social and political commitments in their works. Because of the temper of the times, it is also understandable from a psychological as well as a political and social perspective why so many artists, even many in Hollywood by the mid- and late 1930s, devoted themselves to political causes. In the 1930s, identification with some social or political group helped to mitigate alienation in a period of economic distress. It also protected one from being charged with outmoded individualism, lack of sympathy for common people, or aestheticism. For an artist like Chaplin, who knew loneliness and was already sympathetic to the dispossessed, this political climate was, as we shall see, ineluctably affecting.[29]

Chaplin's Public Politics
before 1936

What political views were associated with Chaplin's star image before the depression? Looking at the period before the crash, it is fair to say that although Chaplin mixed with a number of political leftists in his travels, he really had little active political involvement, and the press did not frequently discuss that dimension of his star image.

The issue did, however, occasionally arise before 1929. Recall Chaplin's statement to the press during his 1921 European tour that as an artist interested in life, he must be interested in Bolshevism. Before leaving on that trip, he had held a press conference at the Ritz-Carlton Hotel in New York. There a surprised reporter found that Chaplin was interested in social problems like "government ownership of railroads, socialism, unemployment, and the relations of capital and labor." Doubting the "soundness" of Chaplin's opinions but not his "sincerity," the skeptical reporter quoted rather moderate comments by Chaplin. For example, Chaplin urged that management must cooperate with labor if the country was to be prosperous. The reporter's surprise indicates that he did not expect Chaplin to comment on politics, particularly from a leftist perspective: it was not a part of his star image in the early 1920s.[30]

This early indication of social awareness and the politics of what John Diggins has called the American "lyrical left" probably stems both from Chaplin's own sympathy for social outcasts and from his associations with artists he met in Los Angeles and New York. Besides meeting Upton Sinclair in the late 1910s, Chaplin also became acquainted about the same time with two men who edited leftist magazines: Max Eastman, editor of the *Liberator*, as discussed in Chapter 3, and Frank Harris, editor of *Pearson's*. He met the Englishman Harris in New York at the end of 1920. Eastman and Harris, different in many ways, were both socialists at the time, and both had publicly opposed American involvement in World War I. Chaplin made small contributions to each magazine, after a personal solicitation by Eastman and a published appeal in Harris's magazine. Although Eastman remained a friend at least until his politics moved to the right (by the 1950s he was writing for William F. Buckley's *National Review*), he felt Chaplin's political views superficial: "Charlie liked radical ideas; he liked to talk about transforming the world; but he didn't like to pay for the talk, much less the transformation." These comments were written after Eastman had become more conservative, but it is probably true that Chaplin's politics were not firmly formed in the 1910s

and 1920s: he may have been drawn, after the fact, to those who opposed World War I, but he himself had actively supported American
involvement by raising money for war bonds and by making *The Bond*
and *Shoulder Arms*, activities that both supported the system and
helped to build his public image. These actions were more firmly associated with Chaplin's star image before the crash than any fixed political positions.[31]

By the time he finished his 1931–1932 tour, however, Chaplin was
beginning to speak out more often on political affairs, and reporters
found them newsworthy. Stopping in Vancouver at the end of his
journey on 13 June 1932, Chaplin held a press conference. There,
echoing Einstein's recent comments to him, he told reporters, "I am
reputedly a comedian but after seeing the financial conditions of the
world I have decided I am as much an economist as financiers are
comedians." Chaplin was joining a growing chorus of critics who
would have agreed with his view that these financiers "would have to
take less profit" if economic conditions were to improve.[32]

Chaplin's fame made his political opinions newsworthy. As he wrote
in *A Comedian Sees the World*, he was surprised "to see how seriously my
views were taken. Popularity . . . endowed my opinions with importance." One indication of this was an article that appeared in a rather
unlikely section of the *New York Times*, the financial page, two weeks
after his Vancouver comments. This piece reported the economic
views Chaplin had expressed at another press conference. He suggested that the gold standard should be abolished as a basis of currency, that currency then be expanded, and that an international currency be established to help Germany pay off its war reparation debts.
He also boasted that "leading economists" he had met on his tour
could find "nothing wrong" with his plan. Though these prescriptions
for economic ills may seem eccentric or cranky today, it bears noting
that the United States did, at Roosevelt's urging, go off the gold standard the following April, to the chagrin of many conservatives.[33]
Chaplin's economic views thus reflected some of the current thinking
of how to get out of the economic collapse.

Chaplin did not speak out on political issues as frequently between
1933 and the release of *Modern Times* in 1936 as he had during and
immediately after his world tour, but most indications suggest that he
became a Roosevelt convert publicly sympathetic to the New Deal. Alistair Cooke, who as a young English college student in America met
Chaplin and spent considerable time with him in the summers of 1933
and 1934, notes that Chaplin was sympathetic to the Labour party in
England and that he praised Roosevelt's New Deal measures. Chap-

lin's support of the New Deal and the Democratic party is reiterated directly and indirectly in a number of sources. In October 1933, Chaplin made a speech in support of Roosevelt's National Recovery Administration (NRA) over a CBS radio affiliate. He supported Upton Sinclair's EPIC campaign as the 1934 Democratic candidate for the governor of California. And in November 1934, he made the statement to reporters that his upcoming film would *not* satirize the NRA, because he was "a great admirer of President Roosevelt and in entire sympathy with his policy,"[34] though of course given Roosevelt's growing popularity, this position was not unusual.

Although his autobiography admittedly looked back three decades to this period, Chaplin's longest and most detailed political affirmation in the book praised the United States during Roosevelt's early years. Calling it "the most inspiring era in American history," Chaplin added that opponents of the New Deal called its reforms "socialism." Whether or not the New Deal was socialist, Chaplin recalled, "it saved capitalism from complete collapse. It also inaugurated some of the finest reforms in the history of the United States. It was inspiring to see how quickly the American citizen reacted to constructive government" (MA, pp. 379–80). The fact that Chaplin gave $500 to Roosevelt's 1936 reelection campaign also indicates his mainstream sympathy for the Democratic party in the mid-1930s.[35]

However, the popular artist in a mass art form like the movies takes a chance when he or she speaks out on current issues. By identifying himself with specific political opinions or economic prescriptions, Chaplin risked alienating some of his audience. Since the star image includes both the private person and the movie persona on the screen, if Chaplin gave some of his audience reason to dislike him, Charlie (and the box-office prospects of his films) could also suffer. Although the press did not often directly attack Chaplin's politics in these years, Chaplin's image was beginning to be associated with leftist politics. One indication of this is newsman Karl Kitchen's report on an evening he spent with Chaplin in March 1935. In a casual comment, Kitchen notes that Chaplin "has long had the reputation of being a 'parlor pink,' and during one of the earlier Red Scares, he was reported to have remarked that even if the country went Bolshevist he would not care, as he would become 'the people's artist.' " Such an observation, made when leftist views were more widespread, was not too damaging. After World War II and the shift in the political climate, however, such "evidence" was used against Chaplin. In assessing his discussion with Chaplin, moreover, Kitchen observed that it was dubious "whether Chaplin is sincere when he discusses certain phases of socialism."[36] Like the New York reporter in 1921, Kitchen minimized Chaplin's seriousness about politics.

In trying to pinpoint Chaplin's political views as they appeared in the early and mid-1930s, it is most accurate to say that he became an enthusiastic New Dealer after becoming alerted to the dilemmas of the depression by his world tour. It is also accurate to say that Chaplin was beginning to think of politics in Manichaean terms—"progressives" versus "conservatives" or "the common man" versus the "financiers"— and clearly sided with the former. However, as his political interests and allegiances grew in these years, he was faced with a dilemma. Given his view of art as something separate from politics, as was indicated by his comments in *A Comedian Sees the World*, as well as his increasing interest in politics, Chaplin had to grapple with the question of how aesthetics and politics related. Such an issue may seem vague when stated in the abstract, but it became very concrete indeed to Chaplin as he thought about his new film. How would this new political awareness affect the aesthetic contract he had forged with his audience? And how would the resulting film, *Modern Times*, affect his star image?

Modern Times: Production, Publicity, and Promotion

Modern Times, in many ways one of Chaplin's most interesting and fascinating films, can be most profitably examined here as a case study of ambivalence about the relationship between aesthetics and ideology. The ambivalence is evident in the finished film itself, but it is also apparent in the film's production, the publicity surrounding it, the promotional material Chaplin's staff created to market it, and even the critical response to it. It seemed that Chaplin, his staff, his audience, and the reviewers were unsure of the place of political concerns within Chaplin's personal genre and star image, even though the times seemed to encourage them. As he contemplated *Modern Times*, we have seen that there was some pressure on (and compulsion in) Chaplin the artist, like many other artists in the depression, to make a political commitment and to express that commitment through his art. However, this conflicted with Chaplin's earlier, averred belief that art and propaganda did not mix.

The information Chaplin provided the press about his new film suggests something of his uncertainty. As early as August 1933, even before *A Comedian Sees the World* began to appear, Chaplin's business manager Alf Reeves announced that Chaplin would begin production on a new film the next month. According to Reeves, Paulette Goddard was to play "a tomboy character in the picture, which will be laid in the lower part of any big city with factories." The following month a report came from Los Angeles that Chaplin had reopened his studios and planned to begin shooting on the new film in sixty days. Yet progress was very slow. Charles Chaplin, Jr., recalls that his father had begun working on the project shortly after returning from his world tour, but that even as late as the spring of 1934, "his dark moods became more pronounced, his flashes of anger more frequent" as he worked on the script. "Fear of failure," according to his son, "was plaguing him." Not only did Chaplin have to worry whether the public would accept another nondialogue film—he had decided to keep Charlie mute yet again—but the subject matter of the film and its political thrust also presented a perplexing dilemma.[37]

After shooting began in October 1934, the kinds of issues discussed in published reports about the film showed how much the "aesthetic discourse" about Chaplin had shifted from the 1910s and 1920s. Before 1920, film reviews were rarely much more than a brief plot description or statement of the reviewer's impression of the film. In such a context, the central question was, depending on the reviewer's orientation, either "was it funny?" or "was it vulgar?" In the 1920s, Chaplin began making longer films and receiving more attention from the intelligentsia. Movie reviews in general were beginning to appear more regularly in elite, intellectual journals. In such a context, reporters and others who wrote on Chaplin's films seemed primarily interested in whether Chaplin would make a purely comic film like the early shorts (as Seldes urged) or whether he would blend comedy and pathos, as in *The Kid* or *The Gold Rush*. Already what Jauss calls the "horizon of expectations" within which Chaplin's films were received had changed.[38]

But it is evident that changes in the social and political sphere, particularly a wrenching shift like the depression, can influence changes in the critical and aesthetic sphere, and thus can affect the way aesthetic works are received and the way star images evolve. By the time *Modern Times* was in production, the "horizon of expectations" had shifted again, and the central critical question was whether Chaplin would make a "purely entertaining" film or a "socially conscious" film. Reports during the making of the film conflicted, sometimes dramatically.

For example, one early article (30 August 1934) gave a fairly accurate overall description of the film: "Its locale will be the industrial quarter of a great city and its main action will be outlined against a varying background of factories, workshops, waterfronts, and dance halls." Within this setting, the description went on, Charlie would befriend a "waif" played by Paulette Goddard. Some months later, when Chaplin denied a rumor that the film would satirize the NRA, a second article quoted Chaplin as saying that it would be "a comedy picture with no endeavor to comment or satirize on social or political affairs." The following March, further along in the shooting, another reporter who spoke with Chaplin found the same thing: "It does not, he told me, contain any political inferences." Yet the same article reported that the working title of the film was "The Masses," which surely had political implications, given the fact that *New Masses* was the name of the newspaper of the American Communist party in the 1930s. (Chaplin later denied that this ever was the working title.) Furthermore, the plot description Chaplin gave mentioned a "high-pressure factory," an employee who gets fired, an arrest at a Communist parade, and a final rally.[39] Chaplin apparently wanted it both ways: he wanted to show in his work that his political sympathies were in the right place, but for those in his audience who didn't share those sympathies, he wanted to claim that the film was pure entertainment, without political implications.

Chaplin's dilemma intensified when he received a well-publicized visit in the summer of 1935 from Boris Z. Shumiatsky, president and general manager of the Soviet motion picture industry. Shumiatsky and a small Soviet delegation had visited Hollywood and received some publicity on their tour. Shortly before he returned to the Soviet Union, Shumiatsky summed up his attitude toward the American film industry by praising a number of its artists, including Chaplin, as well as its sophisticated technology. But he also criticized Hollywood films that dealt with "subjects of an ephemeral and seasonal nature." Film was such an important art form, Shumiatsky told the press, that more American filmmakers should make films that "represent the life of America" and "the serious problems facing the people of this country."[40]

Such ideas were already familiar to Chaplin; what made the visit significant was that Chaplin showed Shumiatsky a rough cut of *Modern Times.* Though this made no news in the American press at the time of the screening, some of Shumiatsky's subsequent writings about the film in *Pravda* found their way to the *New Masses* and the *Daily Worker,* and then to the *New York Times,* which caused Chaplin a good deal of worry and consternation. In November, the *Times* reported that Chaplin's new film "has been put down as a document that takes sides in the social struggle." The *Times* quoted Shumiatsky's claim in *New*

Masses that Chaplin's film showed "honestly and truthfully how the American working class is carrying on the struggle against capitalism although he himself, to be sure, does not believe in the successful outcome of this struggle." The *Daily Worker* carried translations of several articles by Shumiatsky. One of them quoted his view that *Modern Times* was "a sharp satire on the capitalist system in which he derides capitalist rationalization, crisis, the decrepit morality of bourgeois society, prison, and war." Shumiatsky claimed that his criticisms of the film led Chaplin to say at their parting, "I am very pleased we met. But this meeting will cost me many weeks of labor on my film." According to Shumiatsky, his comments encouraged Chaplin to change the ending. In its final form, Shumiatsky predicted, the ending would indicate "a stage in the ideological growth of a remarkable artist" in which Chaplin would present "the conviction that it is necessary to fight for a better life for all humanity, with a conviction of the necessity for active struggle."[41]

It is quite possible that Shumiatsky's discussions with Chaplin about the film did contribute to production delays. The film was originally scheduled for an October 11 release date, then expected in December, then in mid-January, until it was finally released the first week in February 1936. Nevertheless, any public report that a Soviet film authority had told Chaplin how to make his film was doubly unacceptable to Chaplin and his staff. Not only did Chaplin's ego demand that he be perceived as the sole creator of his movies, but the suggestion that a Soviet official dictated the changes would have been poison to the financial success of his film in the United States, even in the depression years.

So Chaplin and his staff struck back, boosted by a defense from the prominent Hollywood columnist, Terry Ramsaye, in *Motion Picture Herald*. Ramsaye noted in the opening of a December 1935 article that *Modern Times* was "becoming a subject of international discussion, by reason of the zeal of Reds and the red and pink press which would have us believe that the picture has by Russian influence been converted into a document for their cause." Speaking through Alf Reeves, Chaplin denied the charges. "The Russian story," Reeves told reporters, "reads deep, terrible social meanings to sequences that Mr. Chaplin considers funny." In a denial repeated in similar terms throughout the production of the film, Reeves continued, "I can assure you that this picture is intended as entertainment, and perhaps it might be said, too, that Mr. Chaplin's purpose in making this picture is to make money." Although admitting that the film's ending had changed, he concluded, "it is not true that anybody can ever tell Mr. Chaplin anything about such matters—he, as you know, has very much his own way and he has his own ideas—always."[42] Like Ramsaye, Chaplin and his people sensed that the *Daily Worker* aimed to make some political hay about the upcoming film, and Chaplin clearly wanted no part of it: anything that might jeopardize the box-office reception quickly set him on edge. If one weighs all this prerelease publicity from the early plot descriptions to the Shumiatsky visit and its aftermath, it is hard to avoid the conclusion that Chaplin was ambivalent: he both wanted and did not want to make a socially relevant film.

The promotion campaign designed for *Modern Times* played down the political implications of the film and concentrated instead on its "entertainment" value and the return of the familiar Charlie after a five-year absence. The opening instructions to theater owners in the pressbook presented Charlie as a valuable commodity in the finest capitalist tradition: "Remember that the most valuable theatrical property in the world is being entrusted to your care. Ordinary advertising and publicity campaigns should be dwarfed when arranged alongside your campaign on Charlie Chaplin."[43]

The pressbook also contained a variety of suggestions about how to market the film:

1. Hire a Chaplin look-alike to wear a sandwich sign saying, "I'm back again."
2. Put a false cardboard factory front on the theater.
3. Have coloring contests or dot puzzles, available to theaters for purchase in bulk from United Artists, for children.
4. Rent from United Artists banners, puzzles, a gilded Chaplin shoe, Chaplin doorknob hangers, derby hats, *Modern Times* tire covers (for rear spare tires), or a neon marquee figure of Charlie.
5. Publish in newspaper ads an article (enclosed in pressbook) in which great people pay tribute to Chaplin's genius (many of these statements came from the 1931 world tour).
6. Publish in newspapers five caricatures of Charlie (enclosed) by famous newspaper cartoonists.

The pictures on the posters and stills did have one innovation from earlier pressbooks: Charlie was often featured in the pictures *with* the gamin (Charlie alone had dominated the photographs and posters in earlier pressbooks). This sharing of attention in the promotion may be autobiographically significant, for Paulette Goddard, who played the waif, became Chaplin's third wife and was a close and stable companion, as well as the only Chaplin wife who had successful movie roles outside of Chaplin films. It could also be read as an indication that

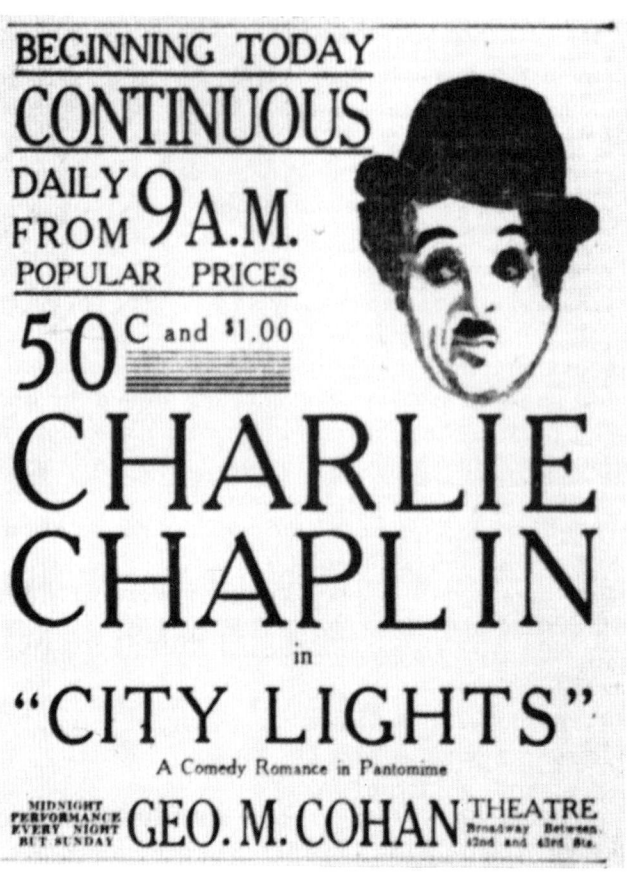

14. Advertisement for *City Lights* (1931).

Chaplin's compulsion to receive sole credit for his productions was moderating, or even as a tempering of his individualism.

Though the pressbook's pictures and posters paired Charlie and the gamin at times, newspaper advertisements often concentrated solely on the familiar image of Charlie to market the film. In fact, some ads for *Modern Times* used a sketch of Charlie's face that was nearly identical to an ad for *City Lights* (see Figures 14 and 15). On the whole, the promotion of *Modern Times* downplayed any political significance in the film and instead suggested that Chaplin would again be fulfilling the aesthetic contract he established with his audience in *The Gold Rush* and even earlier. Chaplin's growing interest in politics, as well as the intelligentsia's pressures on him to produce socially relevant art, thus

15. This advertisement for *Modern Times* (1936) presents
Charlie without the gamin, but with an expression nearly
identical to a *City Lights* ad (Fig. 14).

did battle with the promotion material on the film and his public statements about the movie as it was in production. This relatively conservative promotional campaign may have been the safest way to lure
conservative viewers into the theater, but what did they see, how did
they respond, and what effect did the film have on Chaplin's star image?

Modern Times: Political Ambiguity
and Critical Response

As already discussed, Chaplin's previous three feature films before
Modern Times had each featured Charlie and blended comedy, ro-

mance, and pathos in a relatively similar way, establishing an aesthetic contract between Chaplin and his audience. *Modern Times* also contains these three elements. The comedy of the film often hearkens back to earlier Chaplin films. For example, Charlie's skating in the department store toy department and his antics as a waiter near the end of the film both recall *The Rink* (1916). Other comic scenes—as Charlie's disruptive dance around the factory after the assembly-line work has driven him mad, or his performance during the gibberish song at the film's conclusion—rank among the finest pantomime Chaplin ever achieved. Like the other films, *Modern Times* has a romance, here between Charlie and the gamin (played by Chaplin's protégé, Paulette Goddard). The film contains some pathos, too, but unlike other Chaplin films, most of the pathos that exists here involves the plight of the gamin, not Charlie. What makes *Modern Times* decidedly different from Chaplin's previous three films are the political references and social realism that keep intruding into Charlie's world. One could argue that this constitutes a violation of Chaplin's aesthetic contract.

These topical allusions to social disorder and the problems of the depression, however, are intermittent and sometimes uneasily juxtaposed with the more conventional elements of Chaplin's personal genre. The allusions could be considered Chaplin's attempt to provide variety within the regularities of his typical structure—a common strategy of popular genre films. But the ambiguity of the film's political implications could also be seen as rooted in Chaplin's own ambivalence about how to reconcile Charlie with the new social and political dilemmas of the time.

The background to the opening credits of *Modern Times* is a clock face whose hands are approaching six o'clock, which is followed by a new work shift heading toward a factory. The political ambiguities of the film begin with a title that precedes the first shots of the film itself: "A story of industry, of individual enterprise, of humanity crusading in the pursuit of happiness." Does "industry" refer to the quality of hard work or to a sector of the economy? The next two phrases both could have quite patriotic associations to some American viewers. "Individual enterprise" could suggest the kind of ambition or active energy that has often been associated with and prized by middle-class Americans. "The pursuit of happiness" alludes to the Declaration of Independence, as patriotic a reference as one could ask for. On the other hand, to a depression viewer with leftist political sympathies, both phrases could carry more critical implications. "Individual enterprise" could be seen as a negative reference to one of the ideological tenets that drove the United States into the depression and something that needed to be replaced by social solidarity. "The pursuit of happiness" could easily be read ironically, for Charlie's pursuit seems thwarted at nearly every turn.

After the opening title, Chaplin uncharacteristically introduces viewers to the setting by using a stylistic device that calls attention to itself. In fact, as would have been clear to many leftist viewers of the intelligentsia, Chaplin used what Eisenstein called an "intellectual montage," a juxtaposition of two shots that creates a third conception that would not exist if the two shots were not joined.[44] *Modern Times* associates workers and animals in its opening. The first shot is of a herd of milling sheep, which dissolves to a mass of workers walking up subway steps on the way to work. This is followed by another dissolve to workers heading toward a factory and another shot of the workers inside the factory itself.

Unfortunately, because the viewer is given little context at the beginning of *Modern Times*, it is hard to determine the significance of the intellectual montage. Is it a criticism of workers, who behave like mindless sheep? Is it a criticism of a political and economic system that treats workers as sheep? In Eisenstein's film, the meaning of an intellectual montage is generally clear from what has preceded it in the narrative and carries virtually no ambiguity. In *Modern Times*, however, the intellectual montage promises social significance without first establishing a clear perspective: it is intriguing without being precise. And given the varied, perhaps even contradictory, view of workers and unions presented in the film, the montage never comes clearly into focus.

The film moves on to depict the owner of the Electro Steel Company and the workers who suffer under him, a portrayal consistent with popular leftist stereotypes of wealthy capitalists and oppressed workers in the 1930s. Sitting alone in his office as his workers sweat on the assembly line, the owner plays with a picture puzzle, then turns to the funny papers. Besides being lazy, frivolous, and simple-minded, the owner is insidious in his desire to squeeze as much production as he can out of his workers. Significantly, the first recorded words in any Chaplin film are the owner's, when he gives an order via loudspeaker to a lackey on the factory floor: "Section Five. Speed 'er up." Later he says over another loudspeaker: "Attention foremen. Trouble on line five. Check on the nut tightener [Charlie]. Nuts coming through loose on line five." And later still, as the working day is almost over: "Mac. Section Five, more speed."[45] The owner's willingness to try the Bellows Feeding Machine as another way to enhance productivity also defines his character. His obsession with efficient, assembly-line productivity ultimately drives Charlie mad. This part of the film supports Shumiatsky's claim that *Modern Times* is an attack on capitalist rationalization of production. In general, the portrayals of the factory owner and of the harassed workers who toil under him are ones that leftists in the audience would have relished.

As the narrative develops, however, other political dimensions emerge. One of the most prominent is the social realism that critics had urged on Chaplin, which is evident in a number of scenes. One of the first is Charlie's walk past a closed-down factory just after he gets out of prison. He picks up a red flag that has fallen from a truck bed and, waving to return it, finds himself at the head of a demonstration of workers who have just rounded the corner (see Figure 16). Though Charlie's action is innocuous, the response of the police is not: they beat back the demonstrators with their billy clubs and jail Charlie as a Communist agitator. (Ironically, Charlie seems more at home in the secure prison than the chaotic world of depression America; with his picture of Lincoln on the cell wall and his daily paper, he seems quite satisfied with his fate.)

Other instances of social realism include more violent encounters between police and workers; the suggestion in the department store burglary that hard times drive the working class to crime in order to eat; the gamin's theft of bananas to feed her siblings and unemployed father; and her father's situation itself. When introducing the father, Chaplin grants him a sympathetic close-up; it indicates the frustrating toll that unemployment had on people living in a society where not working was an indication of personal inadequacy rather than societal failure. The father's death at a demonstration of unemployed workers represents a degree of social realism rarely seen on American movie screens in the depression. This depiction was a primary reason that a social radical critic like Kyle Crichton could write in his *New Masses* review, "I came away stunned at the thought that such a film had been made and was being distributed. . . . To anyone who has studied the set-up, financial and ideological, of Hollywood, *Modern Times* is not so much a fine motion picture as an historical event."[46]

In addition to the ambiguous prologue title, the intellectual montage, the stereotypic owner and workers, and the social realism, however, *Modern Times* contains hints of Chaplin's Victorian roots. This suggestion is clearest in the gamin's situation after her father's death. In an action reminiscent of *The Kid*, the county juvenile division issues a warrant for her arrest (because she is still a minor). The authorities' persistent threat to the budding relationship between Charlie and the gamin in the last phase of the film provides a melodramatic situation,

16. Charlie the inadvertent radical in *Modern Times*, 1936.

rooted in Chaplin's apprentice years in the English theater, similar to
the one he had used well for emotional effect in *The Kid*. Here Chaplin's aesthetic view that the intensification of emotion is important to
art is evident.

The film also guardedly affirms American middle-class values, particularly its optimism. When Charlie sits reading the newspaper in
prison, with headlines like "Strikes and Riots: Breadlines Broken by
Unruly Mobs," he looks toward the camera and shakes his head disapprovingly in a way that many Americans did during the depression,

trying to shake away the negative effects of the "news." A more specific but complicated affirmation of middle-class values comes in the dream Charlie and the gamin have as they sit outside a middle-class home. Chaplin here parodies the happy American household when a husband and wife kiss outside their house as he goes off to work, with the wife skipping back inside for another apparently joyous day of housework. When Charlie asks the gamin if she could imagine them in such a house, however, the ensuing dream suggests that their aspirations are remarkably similar to that of the parodied couple. And later, after Charlie gets his job as a department store night watchman, the gamin luxuriates in an elegant white fur coat and dreams dreams like any middle-class consumer of the depression.

One could argue that the film is trying to undercut these dreams as foolish and unrealizable for the lower classes in the depression: the contrast between the dream house and the shack in which the girl and Charlie later live supports such an analysis. Less consistent with such a leftist analysis, though, is the subtle criticism of unions throughout the film, particularly evident when a strike is called immediately after a factory has reopened and Charlie has obtained a job that would enable him and the gamin to have some means of support.

Even more clearly, the conclusion of the film seems tailored to please the middle-class optimist. After having successfully eluded the juvenile authorities at the café, but losing their secure jobs in doing so, Charlie and the gamin are sitting beside a road the next morning. She, weeping, asks in a title, "What's the use of trying?" Charlie's response would have pleased Horatio Alger: "Buck up—never say die. We'll get along." The reassured girl responds, "you betcha" (if my lip reading is accurate), and the two stand, then walk down the road in the early morning light. Although little in the film gives grounds for such optimism—one leftist critic mocked Chaplin's title as a "bromidic optimistic caption"—classical Hollywood tendencies toward a closed happy ending encouraged it.[47] Furthermore, one could even argue that this simple affirmation of effort amid difficult circumstances had become not only an essential element of Charlie's character and the "personal genre" but perhaps even a central tenet for Chaplin himself, who had been forced to cope with difficulties in his personal and professional life yet managed to keep forging on. Charlie's final sprightly steps in *The Circus* and his encouraging affirmation of life to the suicidal millionaire in *City Lights* are both closely related, in substance if not exactly in tone, to Charlie's final words of encouragement in *Modern Times*. Despite the greater political awareness and references central to

Modern Times, the conclusion brings the viewer back to the familiar, the safe, and the ordinary that popular films so often embrace.

The quiet and perhaps groundless optimism of the conclusion thus was thrown into the same pot with the other ingredients of the film to make an unusual political stew. The reactions of critics to the film suggest that they perceived many elements in it. But their reviews also demonstrate that although there were enough different flavors to please everyone at least to some extent, they were not blended well enough to satisfy anyone fully.

In general, the reviews of *Modern Times* reveal how the critical discourse about movies had shifted since Chaplin's earlier films. Critics now focused on two questions, one old, one new: (1) is the film funny; and (2) is it socially significant, and if so, what is its political line? The first question had been asked by critics since Chaplin appeared on the scene; the second was more recent, in part, as we have seen, a product of the stress on socially relevant art engendered by the depression. While some reviewers affirmed the humor and denied the social significance, others—generally those critics who could be associated with Lounsbury's social radical or modern liberal critical traditions—argued that the film was both funny and socially aware. Kate Cameron's review in the *New York Daily News* typified the first group: "It had been hinted that Chaplin had gone serious on us and that he had a message of serious social import to deliver to the world in *Modern Times*. No such thing has happened, thank goodness. . . . There is nothing of real significance in Chaplin's work except his earnest desire, and his great ability, to entertain." Predictably, those critics who denied the social significance of the film seemed generally more conservative, both politically and aesthetically, than those who did not. They tended to believe that films should be "entertaining" and that "social significance" had no place in such entertainments. They saw *Modern Times* as another contribution to Chaplin's established mode of filmmaking, a fulfillment of his aesthetic contract. To these reviewers Charlie the comic persona loomed much larger than Chaplin the filmmaker in their conception of Chaplin's star image.

But to the modern liberal and social radical critics, the relevant questions and discussion focused not so much on Charlie as on Chaplin, the serious artist. What attitude toward the current social crises would he take? Richard Watts, Jr., who wrote in his first *Herald Tribune* review that the film was a social statement, responded to conservative letters opposing his opinion in a second review: "The people I disagree with most heartily are those who insist that *Modern Times* is merely rough-and-ready farce and that we who see a certain sociological interest and significance in some of it are bleak fellows who insist on seeing sermons in stones." Elaborating, Watts continued, "Its suggestion of ideas is intermittent and rather vague, but they are definitely Left Wing in their sympathy and interest."[48]

Watts's assertion that Chaplin's politics were leftist is important, for this view was shared by the leftist press in general. Three good examples are Crichton's review in *New Masses*, Charmion von Wiegand's longer treatment, "Little Man, What Now?" in *New Theater*, and Edward Newhouse's "Charlie's Critics," published in *Partisan Review* two months after the picture opened. All three can be considered social radical critics. Von Wiegand's essay noted that the posh audience at the New York City premiere was fully amused with the film but did not identify as closely with Charlie in his moments of suffering as a less wealthy morning audience some days later. The review also argued that "as a creative genius," Chaplin "is so sensitive to his environment that he has acutely felt the impact of the changes which are occurring in the body of our society." Though praising Chaplin for grappling "with the fundamental problems of our times" in the film, von Wiegand charges that he could not really do so when his central character was "still the optimistic, lovable Charlie—a clown." Like much of the leftist press, von Wiegand was thankful that Chaplin had made his art more socially oriented but also wished that he had been more explicit in his affirmations. In addition, the review implies, as did others, that Chaplin the intellectual and artist ought be the focus of Chaplin's star image, and that Charlie, however amusing, was something of a political liability in the new, trying era.

In his *Partisan Review* essay, Newhouse agreed that the film was leftist but directly responded to von Wiegand's urgings that Chaplin become a revolutionary.

> That would not only be fine but miraculous, and I don't think he will ever make it. . . . Chaplin has had his chances to learn about the revolution and there is no evidence he took much advantage of them. For all that, we must look at *Modern Times* as something that came out of Hollywood. That is what makes Chaplin great and his picture a tremendous achievement. Chaplin is an individualist, he is a romantic, but not romantic enough to have closed his eyes to the most fundamental cruelties of bourgeois society. To film these things beautifully and bitterly is a contribution as important as that of Dreiser in literature.

Although the Left could not fully agree on *Modern Times*, it did respect Chaplin the artist and intellectual for facing up to and presenting contemporary social problems like hunger, unemployment, and police brutality.[49] To these reviewers, Chaplin was beginning to break his aesthetic contract, and this was in many ways to the good.

What the reviews indicate is that with the release of *Modern Times* Chaplin's star image had become inextricably associated in the public mind with politics. Whether the reviewers decried or welcomed this, and whether they accepted or rejected the film's political implications, they agreed it was an issue worth writing about: it had become a part of the critical discourse of the 1930s. From this point until Chaplin's exile and beyond, his political and social views were never separate from his star image, and Charlie the persona became a less dominant dimension of that image. The pressures of the depression had affected both Chaplin and the critics who wrote on films, and the horizon of expectations for those watching Chaplin films entered a new phase.

Chaplin's new film did not succeed at the box office as some might have expected. Although *Variety* predicted that *Modern Times* would be "box office with a capital B," *Modern Times* grossed only $1.4 million domestically, at least a half-million dollars less than each of Chaplin's previous three films. Even *City Lights*, released during a deeper part of the depression than *Modern Times*, fared much better. In fact, *Modern Times* did not even cover its production costs until it went into foreign distribution, something highly unusual for a Chaplin feature film up to that time.

Though it would be unfair to call *Modern Times* a box-office disaster, its disappointing performance seems linked to at least two factors. Even though the film fulfilled the central concerns of the aesthetic contract, its foray into social significance probably diminished its popularity. Chaplin's ambivalence about the place of political themes in his art had led to a confusing mixture in *Modern Times*. The film criticized the domination of humans by machines. It presented social realities with sometimes uncompromising directness. And it occasionally offered rather typical American optimism to help face those problems. Though the mixture was fascinating, *Modern Times* was also apparently threatening to viewers who wanted pure Hollywood entertainment, untainted by messages and politics, in their movies.

Another explanation for the disappointing reception of *Modern Times* is suggested by Otis Ferguson's grousing remark in the *New Republic* that "*Modern Times* is about the last thing they should have called the Chaplin picture."[50] Chaplin's refusal to make a dialogue film, nearly a decade after sound films were introduced, made *Modern Times* a stylistic anachronism. Though Ferguson was one of the few critics to complain about the style—Chaplin movies were so established a genre that they received special treatment by critics—some movie viewers probably passed up *Modern Times* because it was a "silent" film. By maintaining what seemed to be an old-fashioned film style and simultaneously venturing into previously unfamiliar areas of social significance, Chaplin was risking his preeminence as a star in Hollywood and America.

6

The Popular Front,
The Great Dictator, and the
Second Front, 1936–1942

The Popular Front and American
Antifascism

Although Chaplin's uncertainty about the relationship between politics and art generated, as we have seen, a certain ambiguity in *Modern Times*, his thoughts on the subject gradually became clearer after the release of the film, which led his political commitments to become a more significant aspect of his star image. A contributing factor to this change in his image was his decision, after much resistance and brooding, to capitulate fully to sound and make a dialogue film. Equally important was the shift of the political climate in America and Hollywood in the last half of the 1930s toward a greater awareness of the international threat of fascism, which gave Chaplin a cause he felt he could and must fully embrace. Antifascism became the most passionate and public political commitment of Chaplin's life, one that would have an inestimable effect on his star image.

In the middle and later years of the 1930s, the attention of Americans gradually turned away from the domestic concerns of the depression to international concerns about fascism. The popularity of President Roosevelt had something to do with this shift: even though the depression had not "ended" by 1936, most Americans felt that conditions had improved and that the future was more hopeful than the recent past. Perhaps more important to the shift in political attention were the international events that thrust themselves on Americans with accelerating urgency. From the time of Adolf Hitler's rise to power in 1933, the rearmament of Germany in the mid-1930s, and the systematic denial of civil and human rights for German Jews during the same period, the character of fascism and the threat it posed became increasingly apparent. Similarly, the Italian invasion of Ethiopia in 1935 was an early example of fascist expansionism. When both Italy and Germany provided arms and other support for Franco's attack on the Spanish Loyalists during the Spanish Civil War (1936–

1939), the threat became more concrete and the lines of division more clearly drawn. Although the Munich Pact of 1938 temporarily averted war, it also raised questions about the futility of appeasement. After the European political situation was thrown into disarray by the Nazi–Soviet Nonaggression Pact of 24 August 1939, Hitler felt confident enough to invade Poland at the beginning of September. By September 3, England had declared war on Germany, and a riveted American population sympathetic to the Allied cause (84 percent in favor, according to a Gallup poll) both concentrated on the international situation and debated whether America should intervene or isolate itself from the tragic struggles in Europe. Richard Pells has summed up the movement in the era well: "inexorably, the crisis in Europe and the Far East supplanted the depression as the decade's major concern."[1]

Another aspect of this shift in attention was a change in the Communist party's political strategy. In 1935 the Seventh World Congress of the Communist International, concerned about the growing threat that Hitler posed to the Soviet Union, officially called for a "Popular Front" to combat the fascist threat. This call had varying effects in different countries, but it led the Communist Party of the United States (CPUSA) to tone down its rhetoric. Instead of calling themselves "revolutionaries," Party members would more likely refer to themselves as "progressives," which placed them within a much larger group of antifascists. Instead of celebrating the "proletariat," a member would celebrate "the people." Instead of dismissing the New Deal as "social fascism"—just another disguised variety of the rotten capitalist system—a member might have even praised its willingness to fight for the interests of the common people. These shifts meant that the drama of social conflict, although still apparent, was couched in new terms: instead of "revolutionary socialists" doing battle with "oppressive capitalists," American Communists in the late 1930s found themselves engulfed in a struggle between "progressives" and "reactionaries."

As it moderated its rhetoric, the CPUSA also began to identify itself with various American traditions. Instead of quoting Marx, Engels, and Lenin, the Party was much more likely to cite Paine, Jefferson, or Lincoln. Earl Browder, general secretary, indicated something of the change when he asserted that the Party was "really the only party entitled by its program and work to designate itself as 'sons and daughters of the American revolution.' " One slogan used by the Party during the Popular Front period was "Communism Is Twentieth-Century Americanism," a theme put into symbolic action when in 1937, on the anniversary of Paul Revere's ride, a Young Communist League chapter in New York hired a man in colonial garb to ride a horse down Wall Street. He also carried a sign: "The DAR [Daughters of the American Revolution] forgets but the YCL remembers." To Communists, at least in America, the Popular Front clearly meant identifying with national traditions.[2]

This shift in rhetoric and attitude toward national traditions had a political effect. Although the Party kept its distance from Roosevelt in the 1936 presidential election and continued to urge the formation of a Farmer–Labor party while acknowledging its preference for Roosevelt over Landon, by the 1938 elections it had abandoned its hopes for a third party and argued that such a strategy could only serve to fragment the Left and aid the forces of reaction. By this time, it had committed itself fully to cooperation with other antifascists. This led to widespread cooperation and increasing unity among groups on the political left and center who agreed on the seriousness of the fascist threat. Although some advocates of the Popular Front also sought to counter the efforts of conservatives who wished to stifle unionism and social reform measures, this was not a primary thrust of the Popular Front: it rather tended to downplay domestic issues that, had they been emphasized, would likely have divided those who could otherwise cooperate against fascism. In the domestic sphere at least, the Popular Front thus had conservative political implications.[3]

Perhaps the most vivid and, for understanding Chaplin's next film, the most relevant way to discuss the political atmosphere of the Popular Front period is to examine one of its most active areas: Hollywood. Except for New York City, Hollywood was the most important center of international awareness and activism in the United States during the mid- and later 1930s—and with good reason. Not only was Hollywood already an unusually cosmopolitan community thanks to the many European filmmakers and artists who came to work there during the twenties, but the Los Angeles area in general became the destination of thousands of Jewish refugees fleeing from Hitler from 1933 on. The list of artists and filmmakers who escaped Hitler and came to Hollywood is impressively long. It includes such people as actors Peter Lorre and Luise Ranier; composers Max Steiner, Erich Korngold, and Hanns Eisler; directors William Dieterle, Billy Wilder, and Fritz Lang; and writers Thomas and Heinrich Mann, Lion Feuchtwanger, Franz Werfel, and Bertolt Brecht. Because so many of the arrivals after 1935 came for political reasons, and because a number of "international salons" regularly functioned to bring together the refugees with other Hollywood residents, the political awareness of fascism became more pronounced and thus the Popular Front activity more lively in Hollywood than in most other parts of the country.[4] Chaplin came to know a number of the emigrés and exiles—Salka Viertel, Eisler, Feuchtwanger, and others—and was influenced by their politics, as will be discussed in Chapter 8 (MA, p. 434).

Probably the most prominent manifestation of Popular Front antifascism in Hollywood was the Hollywood Anti-Nazi League, which flourished between 1936 and 1939. The first important anti-Nazi gathering in Hollywood was a hundred-dollar-a-plate banquet at the Victor Hugo Restaurant in April 1936 attended by many movie luminaries. Following more organizational activity by Dorothy Parker, Donald Ogden Stewart, Fritz Lang, and Frederick March, among others, the official establishment of the Hollywood League against Nazism (shortly after renamed the Hollywood Anti-Nazi League) was held at the Wilshire Ebel Theater on 23 July 1936. By the fall the League was buying full-page ads in *Variety* and other trade magazines, using such headlines as "The Menace of Hitlerism in America," and announcing a mass meeting at the Shrine Auditorium. The meeting was attended by over 10,000 people. It has been estimated that at its peak the League had about 4,000 to 5,000 members representing a wide range of political views. In its four years of existence, the League held meetings, demonstrations, banquets, and parties; raised money for the Loyalists in Spain; published a newspaper (*Hollywood Now*) that reported on the dangers of fascism, both at home and abroad; and even sponsored two radio shows each week: "Dots and Dashes from Abroad" and "The Voice of the League." Leni Reifenstahl, the director of *Triumph of the Will*, and Vittorio Mussolini, the dictator's son and the head of the Italian film studio, Cinecitta—both of whom had been invited to Hollywood by conservative producers, were snubbed by the group. The League generally helped set up an atmosphere of vigorous antifascism in Hollywood in the three years before the war broke out in Europe.[5]

Another antifascist organization to spring up in Hollywood during these years was the Motion Picture Democratic Committee (MPDC). This group grew up partly as a reaction against the actions of studio heads and other businessmen during the 1934 EPIC campaign. It became active again in June 1938 to work for the election of the progressive Democratic candidate for governor of California, Culbert Olson. Due in part to the considerable funds that it raised, the MPDC helped to elect Olson, despite the fact that 1938 state and local elections generally turned out to be quite anti-Roosevelt. During the next year the MPDC continued its support of Olson and spent considerable time affirming such national causes as the La Follette Committee on

Labor and challenging others, like the newly established House Committee on Un-American Activities. The MPDC was more willing to question the Soviet Union than the Anti-Nazi League was (the 1939 MPDC Declaration of Policy affirmed "categorical opposition to any and all forms of minority dictatorship," right or left) and was more actively involved in electoral politics. However, like the Hollywood Anti-Nazi League, the MPDC was faced with a serious intellectual challenge when the Nazi–Soviet Nonaggression Pact was announced on 24 August 1939.[6]

The pact had a profound and shocking effect on Communist party members, liberals, and everyone in between. Its ultimate effect, particularly after the Soviet Union attacked Finland in late November 1939, was to dismantle the Popular Front and drive a wedge between radicals and liberals in Hollywood who had been cooperating for several years. Party members and their sympathizers who defended the Soviet's actions as pragmatic generally began calling for peace and attacking Roosevelt's foreign policy as war-mongering. In defending an isolationist foreign policy for the United States, they suddenly found themselves aligned with conservatives of various stripes with whom they had little else in common. On the other hand, many liberals drew themselves even closer to Roosevelt and moved toward a pro-Allies, interventionist position. This division made groups like the Anti-Nazi League and the MPDC unworkable, and within a short time both organizations, shorn of their unity and effectiveness, vanished from the scene. Not until the Wehrmacht attacked the Soviet Union on 22 June 1941 did the CPUSA shift back to an antifascist, interventionist political line. At that point an uneasy resurgence of the Popular Front took place.[7]

After the war broke out—and during the time Chaplin was shooting *The Great Dictator*—American public opinion gradually began shifting from an isolationist to an interventionist position. This was partly due to German successes on the battlefield. Two weeks after the war broke out in September 1939 (and just after Chaplin began shooting his new film), 82 percent of Americans polled expected the Allies to win. Only 7 percent expected that the Germans would win. However, in July 1940, more than a month after the fall of France (and while Chaplin was editing *The Great Dictator*), only 43 percent believed that England would win; 24 percent thought a German victory more likely. Furthermore, that same month, 69 percent said they believed that a German victory would affect them personally, whereas the previous March, before the fall of France and Belgium, only 47 percent held such a view. Despite a strong yearning, rooted in the painful memories of World War I, to keep out of another large-scale war, the American public was moving in 1940 toward a feeling that some sort of action in favor of the Allies was becoming essential despite the often vociferous opposition by midwestern isolationists and members of the CPUSA to any involvement.[8]

Within this context of antifascism, an increased participation in the political process by many Hollywood figures, and growing support for interventionism, Chaplin was contemplating and then shooting his next film. We have already seen that Chaplin was generally favorable to Roosevelt and the New Deal from the early 1930s. Furthermore, he, like many other Hollywood figures with liberal political inclinations, was influenced by the antifascist atmosphere of the 1936–1939 era. He attended Anti-Nazi League meetings and became more aware of the fascist threat. After the outbreak of the war and the early successes of the Germans, he also attended meetings of the Committee to Defend America by Aiding the Allies, a group whose name indicates its position. But unlike his politicized Hollywood colleagues, Chaplin possessed a financial independence that enabled him to make a film on a controversial political issue if he chose. And such ideas were percolating in his mind as he began to plan a film to follow *Modern Times*.[9]

The Great Dictator: Preparation, Production, and Promotion

A number of eerie similarities make one wonder if Chaplin was fated to make a film about Hitler. The two were born within four days of one another in April 1889. They were raised in similar circumstances of childhood poverty. Both at times demanded strict control over their subordinates when, as adults, they achieved positions of power. Probably the most widely discussed similarity, the physical resemblance of Hitler and Chaplin's persona Charlie, centered on their mustaches. Since Chaplin's interest in creating overtly political films coincided almost exactly with Hitler's consolidation of power in Germany and growing international notoriety, it is understandable that Chaplin gradually decided that his next film after *Modern Times* would satirize the German leader. Throughout the reverses of fortune and the shifts in political alliances in those volatile years of 1938–1940, Chaplin remained firmly committed to his conception: in October 1940, *The Great Dictator* opened in New York City.

Before he decided to make a "Hitler film," Chaplin had to consider whether he would continue to resist dialogue films. Because nearly a decade had passed since sound films had been introduced, Chaplin was seeming more than ever like an anachronism in the film industry. Two Sundays after *Modern Times* opened in 1936, the *New York Times* carried an uncharacteristically critical article on him, titled "The Curious Mr. Chaplin." In addition to charging that Chaplin was parsimonious, contradictory, egotistic, and difficult—even unreasonable—to work with, the article suggested that Chaplin "clings tenaciously to youth" because "he resents and fears growing old." That resentment and fear, according to the article, "has caused him to fortify himself in the past and to refuse to concede anything to the contemporary medium." In comments that must have been disturbing to the comedian (the *Times* generally gave him a great deal of attention, praise, and advance publicity for his features), the article called him a "lone wolf" who, to the current film industry, represented only "the Hollywood that was."[10]

For the rest of 1936 and into the following year Chaplin apparently did little work on a new film project. From shortly after the opening of *Modern Times* until early June, he and Paulette Goddard took a trip to the Far East, during which, according to Chaplin, they were married (MA, p. 385). Upon returning, Chaplin again agonized about the question of whether to make another nondialogue film. "To continue with a feeling that the art of pantomime was gradually becoming obsolete," he recalled years later, "was a discouraging thought" (MA, p. 385). The decision to abandon the pantomime so central to the comic persona that had enriched him was a difficult one. On the other hand, Chaplin's growing desire to comment on current social and political issues made dialogue films seem much more attractive.

By September 1937, Chaplin announced that his next film would be a talking one. Shortly after the announcement Frank Nugent paid tribute in the *New York Times* to the "little tramp" who was "the colossus of the cinema." He also seemed a bit relieved at Chaplin's decision. After *Modern Times*, he wrote, "it was useless to pretend that the sound revolution had passed over his head leaving him as firmly enthroned as ever." To compensate, Nugent suggested, Chaplin was to become "a producer with certain politico-sociological messages to deliver," an observation that emphasizes how Chaplin's star image was becoming linked to politics. A *Times* editorial the next day commented that "a note of sadness sighs through the announcement that Charlot is no more."[11]

Though the editorialists did not know it at the time, Chaplin shortly thereafter began to work on a film that would pit a caricature of Hitler against a close relative of Charlie. At least two people, Ivor Montagu and Alexander Korda, seem to have influenced Chaplin's decision to

make an anti-Hitler satire.[12] Before he decided to forge ahead with a
Hitler story, however, Chaplin had cast about for a film that would
star Paulette Goddard. At one point in 1937, he was enthusiastic about
having her do a film version of the novel *Regency*, by D. L. Murray,
but that idea came to nothing. When an impatient Goddard signed a
contract with David O. Selznick, Chaplin decided he needed a change
of scenery and in February 1938 left Hollywood to spend several
months in Pebble Beach, California. There he worked on another
story, this one about a young millionaire who takes a cruise to China
and falls in love with a beautiful White Russian employed at a dance
hall. It was to have starred Goddard and Gary Cooper, but it too fell
by the wayside as the Hitler idea kept crossing his mind. "How could
I throw myself into feminine whimsey or think of romance or the
problems of love," Chaplin recalled, "when madness was being stirred
up by a hideous grotesque—Adolf Hitler?"[13]

Chaplin as usual sought to keep the persistent press from learning
much about his film, but some information about it leaked out even
before shooting began. These leaks give us some indication of how the
story evolved. A report in November 1938 said that Chaplin would
play a prisoner in a concentration camp who would speak gibberish
because he didn't speak the same language as the others. (Apparently
Chaplin did for a time toy with the idea of using language in much
the same way as he had with Charlie's song in *Modern Times*.) By February 1939, articles reported that the new film would be called *The
Dictators* and that Chaplin would play a local dictator who would use
"Teutonic speech." About the same time Frank Nugent came back to
New York City from the West Coast and summed up a story Chaplin
had written called "The Dictator: The Story of a Little Fish in a Shark-
Infested World." In the story, two dictators—Hinkle and Mussemup—
tangle, and another character played by Chaplin is mistaken for Hinkle, taken to the city of Vanilla in the country of Ostrich, and gives a
speech calling for world peace. As the crowd becomes stirred by his
words, the character, much like the soldier in *Shoulder Arms*, wakes up
in a concentration camp: his actions have just been a dream.[14]

Making film satires about contemporary political subjects can be a
hazardous preoccupation: when political currents shift, the filmmaker's attitude toward his subject (and the film's appeal to its audience)
can change radically. Chaplin came to know these dilemmas. According to one newspaper account, he had completed the script by the start
of April 1939, then did shooting of miniatures and sound tests starting
in June.[15] However, the Nazi–Soviet Pact in August and the outbreak
of World War II in September delayed shooting and confronted

Chaplin with serious questions. First of all, this film would be Chaplin's most expensive to make, because of the large cast, the elaborate sets, and the recorded, synchronized dialogue. If *Modern Times* failed to earn production costs in domestic rentals, and if most European markets were closed to Chaplin and South American markets were threatened as well because of the war, would *The Great Dictator* be a poor investment? Second, if the American government remained officially neutral on the European war, would government pressure be brought to bear against the production of anti-Nazi films? Third, if American public opinion remained radically divided between isolationist and interventionist positions, would a satirical attack on Hitler and Nazism risk alienating a large potential segment of the audience? And finally, what position would Chaplin himself take vis-à-vis the Nazis: if he loathed them, did he loathe them enough to urge Americans to take up arms against them? And if so, would that notion be incorporated into the film?

These were all difficult questions, particularly since no one could foresee the scope or duration of the war. Ten days after the Germans invaded Poland, the *New York Times* reported that, despite denials by Chaplin, "there are indications that he will postpone *The Dictators* until the future can be appraised with more assuredness."[16] After a brief delay, however, Chaplin went ahead with the shooting, which was essentially finished in late March 1940. During the time Chaplin was cutting and scoring the film, Hitler launched an offensive on Belgium and France. The same day that the fall of Belgium was reported in the *Times*, in fact, another article noted that several early antifascist films, including *Mortal Storm*, *Four Sons*, and *The Great Dictator*, were pending but that their release was uncertain. According to the article, several United Artists executives predicted that releasing Chaplin's new film in the present political situation could only result in "disaster for the screen." Chaplin, however, issued a statement: "The report that I have withdrawn the film is entirely without foundation. I am cutting it now and as soon as it can be synchronized, it will be released. More than ever now the world needs to laugh. At a time like this, laughter is a safety valve for our sanity."[17] Already financially involved in the film to the tune of at least $1.5 million, Chaplin had little choice but to go ahead with his plans. A September release was announced.

That release date was pushed back to mid-October, and as the film's release drew near, articles about its topicality began to appear. One of the most detailed was an interview with and profile of Chaplin in the *New York Times Magazine* on September 8. There Chaplin, the serious political intellect, emphasized his opinion of Hitler: "Leaders with

MR. EXHIBITOR ... Here is the picture that has never before been equalled in advance interest and entertainment importance. Here is the picture that is actually a national event ...the picture with the greatest combination of star and theme in the history of the screen. Here is the picture upon which every newspaper and magazine in the country has lavished full page space, climaxing a steadily sustained publicity build-up of more than two years. Here is the picture the world is waiting for ...

CHARLIE CHAPLIN
in
"THE GREAT DICTATOR"

17. Plea to exhibitors in *The Great Dictator* pressbook: Chaplin the social critic.

tenth-rate minds have captured the new instruments of propaganda and are using these instruments to destroy good, civilized, kind, behavior," he told interviewer Robert van Gelder. "I'm the clown, and what can I do that is more effective than to laugh at these fellows who are putting humanity to the goose-step?" The article also contained a description of Chaplin's working methods and, with the accompanying pictures of Chaplin from *The Great Dictator* and other films, generally prepared readers for the monumental upcoming opening.[18]

Chaplin and United Artists were also preparing promotional material as the opening neared. The pressbook for *The Great Dictator*, more than any earlier Chaplin pressbook, announced the fact that the film had a "message." Consider the opening appeal to the exhibitor on page one: "Here is the picture that is actually a national event . . . the picture with the greatest combination of star and theme in the history of the screen." *The Great Dictator*, it added, is "a history-making comedy based on the most vital topic in the history of the world" (see Figure 17). The program that accompanied the pressbook stressed Chaplin's brilliance and his commitment. One statement, after noting that

Chaplin was born less than one hundred hours before Hitler and that Chaplin spent a childhood of "almost Dickensian destitution," asserted that Chaplin's features to 1936 "are all classics of cinematic comedy, the acknowledged masterpieces of the man whom George Bernard Shaw called 'the only genius in motion pictures.' " It added that in *The Great Dictator*, however, "Chaplin is more than genius. He is an institution, the idol of millions of all races and creeds, the champion of the pathetic and oppressed. And, at a time when the world is sore and sick at heart, the little man with the funny moustache is something of a saviour, bringing with him at a time we need it most the invaluable therapy of laughter." Note the transformations here. In the midst of hyperbole common in Hollywood publicity, both persona Charlie and Chaplin himself are portrayed as internationalist spokesmen for humanity.

Accompanying pictures and posters showed Chaplin as the Jewish barber posing with Hannah, Chaplin as the dictator playing with the balloon globe, and a somber and posed Chaplin, wearing suit and tie, shot from a low angle. This picture was accompanied by a text that gave Chaplin yet more extravagant praise and again stressed his progressive political commitment: "Admiration for the little tramp . . . . is confined to no race, class, or creed. Essentially, Charlie Chaplin belongs to the little guy—the men, the women, and the children who make up the overwhelming portion of the population of all the countries of the world." The pressbook and accompanying program emphasized not only that Chaplin would talk in the film (preparing audiences for a fundamental departure from previous Chaplin films), but also that he would have a progressive message to convey.[19]

The advance publicity evidently was successful, for massive crowds on opening night gathered at both the Capitol and the Astor theaters in New York City to get a glimpse of Chaplin and Goddard, who attended both premieres. Newspapers and trade journals reported on the extravaganza, with some using pictures of Chaplin and Goddard nearly crushed by the crowds as they made their way toward the theater entrances. Others, like *Motion Picture Daily*, printed a number of pictures of prominent figures who had attended. (These included such industry luminaries as Harry Warner, president of Warner Brothers; Adolph Zukor, board chairman of Paramount; and Spyros Skouras, head of National Theatres.)[20] Despite the risk of making such a film and the controversy it was sure to engender, the opening night, at least, was a genuine media event.

The Great Dictator and the
Aesthetic Contract

The Great Dictator is Chaplin's most overtly political and topical film. It involved itself with the times more than any other of his works, and explored a subject that was weighing heavily on the minds of most Americans when the film was released. One way to underline the film's relevance is to look at the books that were featured in the *New York Times Book Review* the Sunday before *The Great Dictator* opened in October 1940. Ernest Hemingway's antifascist novel of commitment, *For Whom the Bell Tolls*, was reviewed. So was Edmund Wilson's study of Marxism, *To the Finland Station*, which he concluded with a sense of disillusionment that contrasted with his enthusiasm for that tradition earlier in the 1930s. A contemporary report on political conditions in Europe, Claire Booth Luce's *Europe in the Spring*, was given prominent attention, as were two books that sought to define the democratic values that could be used to counter fascism: Eleanor Roosevelt's *The Moral Basis of Democracy* and the interventionist Lewis Mumford's *Faith for Living*. The same day that *The Great Dictator* opened, two headlines on page one of the *Times* indicated the state of the current crisis. "London Is Rocked by Heaviest Raid, RAF Keeps Berlin Awake Six Hours," wrote one. A second showed that the interventionist/isolationist division in America had not disappeared: "Lindbergh Assails Present Leaders—Asks Voters to Back 'Strength and Peace' Instead of 'Weakness and War.' "[21] Whereas the attention of the American people was focused primarily on domestic affairs when *Modern Times* was released, these books and headlines indicate how fully that attention had shifted toward international affairs and the fascist threat. *The Great Dictator*, with its satiric attack on fascism and its affirmation of an alternative set of values, was exploring issues of central concern to Americans at the time of its release.

The topicality of the satire in *The Great Dictator*, which would have been clearly evident to most informed viewers in 1940, manifested itself through references to people, places, and historical events. Adenoid Hynkel (Hitler), the Phooey (Der Führer), is aided by his loyal sycophants, Minister of War Herring (Goering) and Minister of the Interior Garbitsch (Goebbels). The appearance and demeanor of the actors emphasized the satirical references. Chaplin, of course, bore a close physical resemblance to Hitler. In addition, though, Billy Gilbert's bulk brought Hermann Goering to mind, while Henry Daniell's suave and sleek manner created an effective analogue for the German minister of propaganda. After Chaplin's performance, probably the

170

strongest satirical acting was by Jack Oakie as Benzino Napoloni, Chaplin's caricature of Mussolini, also referred to as "Il Digaditch" (Il Duce). His rivalry with "Hinkie" helps deflate the expanded egos of the two tyrants.

Hynkel is from Tomania, a blend of the word for food poisoning and the suffix "mania"—madness. Napoloni's country is Bacteria—another poison infecting the world's body politic. In the military review scene, Napoloni refers to the name of his capital city: "Aroma." The historical setting of the film is extremely clear—from near the end of World War I to the Nazis' invasion of Austria in 1938. To strengthen the specificity of the setting, Chaplin presents several documentary montages. They include headlines with specific historical references as well as documentary newsreel footage, some of Nazi party rallies. Early in the film, headlines move the film from the Armistice to the rise of Hitler by referring to the Dempsey–Tunney fight, Lindbergh's transatlantic flight, and the onset of the depression. Later, two headlines refer to the Nazi persecution of Jews: "Ghettoes Raided" and "Jewish Property Confiscated."

The film's topicality is also rooted in specific events. One is the Nuremberg Nazi party rallies of 1933 and 1938, which are called to mind during Hynkel's speech at the start of the film and the barber's speech at the end. Another reference is to Mussolini's visit to Germany in September 1937, when he cemented his friendship with Hitler thanks to Hitler's flattery and the impressive display of German military might at a military review. The Anschluss, Hitler's annexation of Austria (called "Osterlich" in the film) in 1938, is a final reference.

This last event is significant, for Chaplin was becoming deeply concerned about the fate of Jewish refugees while he was working on the film. In mid-1939 the *New York Times* reported that Chaplin instructed United Artists to pay his share of the European rentals earned by *The Great Dictator* to a Vienna Jewish organization aiding Jews emigrating from Central Europe. These monies never went to the organization, for by the time the film was ready, no European nation except perhaps Switzerland could have shown the film, and the Vienna organization was defunct. But Chaplin persisted. On 28 July 1940, it was reported that he was among a number of people who had collectively deposited $6 million in a Milan, Italy, bank to support Austrian Jews who were being forced from Austria by the beginning of August. When the film shows that Hannah's dream of escaping her persecutors by moving to Osterlich is delusory, Chaplin is basing the film on concrete historical circumstances.[22]

In its use of this pointedly topical satire, *The Great Dictator* was atypical for Chaplin. Many of his earlier films had, of course, scored satirical points against various targets. Except for *Shoulder Arms*, however, that satire had almost never been directed toward matters of prevailing public debate. After *The Great Dictator*, however, Chaplin was much more willing to include specific historical references in his films, as we shall see. This departure from his aesthetic contract would have distinct effects on his star image.

In what other ways did *The Great Dictator* either fulfill or depart from Chaplin's aesthetic contract? Of course, the most significant stylistic departure from previous Chaplin films was the inclusion of dialogue. For the first time, excluding the brief gibberish song in *Modern Times*, audiences heard Chaplin's voice and those of his fellow players. Although *The Great Dictator* still has its share of effective pantomime, as when Charlie's surrogate, the barber, shaves a customer or when Hynkel does his "globe ballet," dialogue is an integral part of the film. Audiences had to get used to hearing Chaplin speak, both as the blustering Hynkel and as the timid barber.

Concerning two other characteristics of Chaplin's aesthetic contract—romance and pathos—the film is equivocal. There is a romance of sorts between the Jewish barber and Hannah. Because Paulette Goddard played Hannah, many viewers would have noted the continuity between this film and *Modern Times*. Yet the romance is less central to the narrative than in the earlier Chaplin feature comedies. The same is probably true of pathos. Though some scenes are poignant—the scene of the barber and Hannah overlooking the burning ghetto is perhaps the best example—the pathos is not directed toward the Charlie persona (or his surrogate) the way it was in *The Gold Rush*, *The Circus*, and *City Lights*. The differences in the handling of both the romance and the pathos in *The Great Dictator* represent, if not a violation of the aesthetic contract, at least an attenuation of it.

On one hand, the topicality, the addition of dialogue, and the handling of romance and pathos in *The Great Dictator* all represented to audiences shifts from the Chaplin films many knew. On the other, perhaps the central similarity between *The Great Dictator* and the earlier comic features that had established the terms of the aesthetic contract was the clear contrast between a "good" moral universe and an evil one, embodied by a contrast between Charlie and another character (the county officials in *The Kid*, both Jack and Black Larsen in *The Gold Rush*, the ringmaster in *The Circus*, and the millionaire in *City Lights*).

The Great Dictator centers on such a contrast. The opening credits emphasize it, for there Chaplin groups the actors under two categories: "People of the Palace" and "People of the Ghetto." The narra-

tive structure is itself one of Chaplin's most balanced: it contains a prologue set in World War I that shows the Jewish barber fighting as a
patriotic albeit ineffective Tomanian soldier and an epilogue set after
the start of World War II that shows the barber again, but this time,
disguised as Hynkel, urging his countrymen not to fight. Within this
frame, the stories of the barber and Hynkel, of life in the ghetto and
life in the palace, are regularly intercut: Hynkel and his cohorts are
on the screen 47 minutes, the barber and the others of the ghetto 46
minutes.[23]

The settings in which the barber and Hynkel live help emphasize
the moral contrast. The barber has a shop on a modest city street. The
courtyard between his shop and the Jaeckels' home, as well as the merchants who sell their wares on the sidewalks, give the city a European
feeling, but the furnishings in the Jaeckels' home and the costumes
and manner of the people in the ghetto give it a folk flavor, similar to
the flower girl's home in *City Lights* or Jean's flat in *A Woman of Paris*.
These settings all suggest a warmth and simplicity associated with positive (and often threatened) values in Chaplin's films. In contrast, the
dictator moves in a setting of opulence. When he gives a speech to the
sons and daughters of the Double Cross, he stands on a massive platform, prominently displaying symbols of propaganda, high above the
thousands who are listening. In his palace Hynkel has a huge office
that dwarfs anyone who enters. His surroundings suggest his egotism:
he has a bust of himself on his desk, his file cabinets are false-fronted
mirrors that he preens before, and he sometimes goes briefly into a
room and poses for a sculptor and painter who work simultaneously
on tributes to the Phooey. All in all, Hynkel's settings suggest a callous
and egotistical leader who lives in splendor, far removed from his people, whom he manipulates and for whom he shows consistent disdain
(see Figure 18).

The characterizations of Hynkel and the barber (both played by
Chaplin), as well as of those who surround them—particularly Garbitsch and Napoloni in Hynkel's case, and Hannah and Schultz in the
barber's—also develop the moral contrast. A central feature of the
film is what Paul Goodman called its "invective" against Hynkel's qualities: his megalomania, narcissism, compulsion to dominate, and disregard for human life.[24] But though villains in earlier Chaplin films
exhibited similar qualities, Hynkel is different in that he is clearly associated with a historical and specific ideology: fascism. Thus the core
of Chaplin's invective against Hynkel is a historical and specific antifascism. This progressivism, grown and nourished during the Popular
Front period and extending beyond it for most non-Communist anti-

fascists even after the Nazi–Soviet Pact, envisioned a polar political spectrum that placed "fascism" at one end and "democracy" at the opposite.

The ideology of fascism is expressed most clearly in the film by Garbitsch's brief address near the end.

> Victory shall come to the worthy. Today, democracy, liberty, and equality are words to fool the people. No nation can progress with such ideas. They stand in the way of action. Therefore we frankly abolish them. In the future each man will serve the interests of the state with absolute obedience. Let him who refuses beware. The rights of citizenship will be taken away from all Jews and non-Aryans. They are inferior and therefore enemies of the state. It is the duty of all true Aryans to hate and despise them.

This speech explicitly expresses Chaplin's understanding of the fascism that his film opposed.

Typical of Chaplin's aesthetic contract, a humane code of values provides an alternative. In contrast to the power-hungry Hynkel and his henchmen, the barber, Hannah, and the other citizens of the ghetto simply want to live and let live. Hannah, a victim of modern civilization—she is an orphan whose father was killed in World War I—enunciates this philosophy to the barber: "Life could be wonderful if people could be left alone." But the physical layout of the ghetto shows that Hannah's dream cannot be realized. When on the sidewalks, the Jews are vulnerable to attacks from Hynkel's storm troopers, depending on the whims of the Phooey's policies. Early in the film, they have some protection within the courtyard between the barber's shop and Mr. Jaeckel's house; however, even this sanctuary is violated as the film progresses. Shortly after Chaplin cuts to a shot of a caged bird hanging by the Jaeckels' front door, soldiers raid the courtyard, capture the barber and the "traitor" Schultz, and send them to a concentration camp. The others have no alternative but to emigrate to Osterlich. The innocent, the kind, the tolerant, and the compassionate seem endlessly victimized.

Described in this way, the conflicts in the film seem to lead to a dark conclusion. If, as the film suggests is the case, the good are weak and the evil are powerful, is the world doomed? A central aesthetic and political question raised by *The Great Dictator* is this: how ought the good, and the advocates of democracy who empathize with them, respond to the cruelties of the fascists? This was a very real dilemma for Americans when *The Great Dictator* was being shot and released, for in

18. Chaplin as Hynkel in *The Great Dictator*, 1940.

the late 1930s, many antifascists were also pacifists or at least extremely reluctant to support any American involvement in another European war. Like the people of the ghetto, many Americans, though much less directly affected, were agonizing about how to respond to the threats of the dictators.

Several details in *The Great Dictator* suggest an answer. Early in the film Hannah uses her frying pan to smash the heads of two storm troopers who have been harassing the barber. It gives her a feeling of release and catharsis. As the scene closes, she tells the barber, "That did me a lot of good. You sure got nerve the way you fought back. That's what we should all do: fight back. We can't fight alone, but we can lick 'em together."[25] Although an American viewer in October

1940 could take this as an affirmation that the Allies supported by the United States could counter the fascist threat, active resistance by Jews to Hynkel and his supporters in the context of the film itself seems futile: those forces of darkness are too organized, too well armed, and too powerful to overcome. What perspective and tactics, then, does Chaplin defend?

The famous ending—the part of the film that elicited the most debate when the film was released and that has drawn considerable critical attention since—suggests an answer.[26] Following Garbitsch's comments, quoted above, the disguised barber, at Schultz's urging, walks up to the microphones and delivers a speech of three and a half uninterrupted minutes that counters Hynkel's speech near the opening of the film. Chaplin, who had resisted dialogue long after the rest of Hollywood had accommodated itself to the new technology, here finally affirmed the power of the word. This was a turnabout, for both *Modern Times* (in the phonograph record sales pitch) and an earlier scene in *The Great Dictator* (when the inventor demonstrates his bulletproof uniform), use the line, "actions speak louder than words," indicating Chaplin's aesthetic resistance to the dictates of dialogue in pictures. However, in this final speech, Chaplin resolved his dilemma about the relationship of politics and aesthetics, and in doing so broke the irksome bonds of silence imposed on him by Charlie's pantomime.

Although the speech contains contradictions and inconsistencies, when read closely, its essential kernel defends the democracy of progressive politics in its struggle with fascism. As he concludes, the barber appeals directly to the Tomanian soldiers and implores that they not fight for the dictator but rather take power from him and return it to "the people." The barber does not specifically beat the drums of war against the fascists—he is, after all, urging the Tomanian soldiers to abandon their dictator, in which case any war would be over. He does clearly imply, however, that if the perverted dictators can be stopped in no other way, it may be necessary to fight for the well-being of the world, so that the kindness and decency of the people of the ghetto can survive and flourish.

Ultimately, one word sums up Chaplin's strategy for concluding his most overtly political film: "hope." As Garbitsch is introducing him, the barber hears Schultz urging him to speak: "It's our only hope." Pensively, the barber repeats the word, "hope," then makes his way to the microphones. The speech is an expression of hope despite what Chaplin saw as a world gone mad. The fact that it is followed by the soldiers' cheers and the barber's comments, via radio waves, to Hannah about seeing a better world on the horizon only reinforces the point. Chaplin's political sentiments and message rang clear in the film: he had met the challenge of progressive politics.

Although the presentation of contrasting moral perspectives was integral to Chaplin's aesthetic contract, the manner in which the "good" universe was defended in the conclusion was not. The ending was a stark departure from Chaplin's general practice and from the classical Hollywood system of filmmaking in the 1930s in three ways. First, the ending explicitly defended a topical and controversial political position. It was much more explicitly ideological than any previous Chaplin ending and hastened the tendency of Americans to associate Chaplin's star image with a progressive political perspective.

Second, the ending was not "closed": it failed to resolve all the narrative conflicts. Through a steady diet of Hollywood films in the depression, audiences were taught to expect neatly presented plot conflicts that were clearly and unambiguously resolved. This Chaplin did not do. Though the convention of mistaken identity that made the ending possible was an old one, this error is never cleared up. Hynkel, dressed as a duck hunter, is arrested by storm troopers when he claims to be the dictator. The barber, with his dictator's uniform, fools the troops into believing he is Hynkel. Chaplin faced an extremely difficult task in convincing the audience in the theater that the barber's gentle speech will deceive, much less be accepted by, the assembled crowd. And by leaving the final expression of hope balancing precariously on the tightrope of unresolved mistaken identity, Chaplin violated his audience's expectations. This change in their typical experience of moviegoing made many viewers uneasy, as we shall see, though few would have been able to articulate exactly why this was so.

Third, and even more significantly, by having the barber deliver a long, uninterrupted speech with shots of unusually long duration, the film style violated stylistic conventions audiences were familiar with from many American films. Though long speeches were not unheard of in Hollywood films of the era, they were generally broken up by cutting to different camera angles and distances of the speaker or, more commonly, by using a shot/reverse shot (cutting back and forth between the speaker and the character who was listening to him). One analyst who has looked closely at the American film style in the 1930s has estimated that a typical film then averaged a cut every seven seconds.[27]

The barber's speech is shot in a way that deviates widely from these conventions. During the speech itself, which lasts three and a half minutes (followed by two and a half minutes focusing primarily on Hannah, with the barber's voice occasionally urging hope for the future), Chaplin uses only three shots:

1. Medium close-up shot of the barber: 78 seconds
2. Dissolve to full shot of Hannah: 9 seconds
3. Dissolve to medium shot of the barber, dollying after 60 seconds to medium close-up: 122 seconds

Juxtaposed with the typical 1930s cutting rhythm of one shot every 7 seconds, Chaplin's violation of convention becomes starkly evident. As a number of writers on the classical Hollywood film have noted, the aim of its style is to draw attention away from itself to the narrative, and to tell that story in as functional, efficient, and engaging a manner as possible.[28] By using such long takes, with nothing varied in the background to draw the audience's attention away from the barber's impassioned face, Chaplin interrupted the relatively smooth and rapid flow of images that characterized the classical style. Thus, not only did Chaplin deviate in a number of ways throughout the film from the aesthetic contract he had forged with his audience through his comic features, but his ending also, through a violation of the ideological, narrative, and stylistic conventions of Hollywood films, disrupted the satiric fiction he had been creating. The close of *The Great Dictator* was not simply an unsatisfactory ending for many contemporary viewers and critics. It was also, despite Chaplin's courage and conviction in presenting this conclusion, the beginning of the decline of his enormous public popularity in America.

Critical, National, and International Reaction to *The Great Dictator*

As one would expect when the world's most famous movie star made a film about the world's most infamous political figure, the reaction to *The Great Dictator* was enormous—in fact, the most widespread of any film Chaplin ever made. That is true whether one measures reaction by the film's box-office success, the number of critical reviews it generated, or the official responses to the film by governmental officials.

For all of Chaplin's worry during production concerning the box-office prospects of *The Great Dictator*, the film was an overwhelming financial success. Opening at two theaters in New York City, it enjoyed a fifteen-week run there, a good indication of its appeal to audiences. Although it was not released until after the end of World War II in many European countries, it earned over $5 million in rentals worldwide, more than any other Chaplin film, which generated its maker a profit of $1.5 million on an investment of $2 million. *The Great Dictator* was more than just a financial success in 1940: when Bosley Crowther did an article in 1942 on the top ten moneymaking films in the previous half decade, *The Great Dictator* was third on his list. When one recalls that *Gone with the Wind* was made during that period and that roughly 2,400 other American films were released during the same time span, the box-office appeal of *The Great Dictator* becomes even more impressive.[29]

The critical reviews generated by *The Great Dictator* are extremely interesting to read, and there are a lot of them: because the film was so topical, it was even reviewed in places where movies were normally not given much attention. The critic for the *New York Times* suggested how important the film was when, after the excitement of its premiere, he wrote that "for the first time within memory, the most eagerly awaited picture of the year was a comedy."[30]

Reading through the reviews, one gains two somewhat contrary impressions. The first is that Chaplin was approaching the high point of his career as a star and public figure: the young comedian who was surprised in 1915 that anyone would be interested in his opinions or take them seriously had matured into a fifty-one-year-old man who had come to see it as his responsibility to comment on the world's most pressing public issue, and he was being recognized for it. But one also senses in reading the reviews that Chaplin's star was beginning to fall. Although the critics respected and were intrigued by what he attempted in the film, many felt the film engaged too directly with politics. Because of the ideology and aura of "entertainment" deeply embedded in the classical Hollywood system of filmmaking, overt treatment of controversial political issues was taboo. When a filmmaker violated that taboo, even in order to attack an ideology like fascism that was being widely assailed in the country at the time the film was released, the filmmaker was certain to alienate a substantial number of critics and to make many viewers uneasy. The ending particularly disturbed reviewers, for there the ideological violation was accompanied, as we have seen, by a violation of narrative and stylistic conventions of the classical Hollywood system. Since in his previous features Chaplin had for the most part adhered to the conventions of the closed ending and the continuity style, his substitution of direct address for closed ending and of extremely long takes for the much more common shot/reverse shot made Chaplin even more vulnerable to attack from critics. Henceforth, no movie fan would be able to separate the dimension of politics from the star image of Charles Spencer Chaplin. Furthermore, the persona of Charlie, and all the engaging

179

qualities that made him the object of identification and comment, began to weaken as an integral part of the Chaplin star image.

If anything like a critical consensus can be gleaned from the newspaper reviews, it is that although the film was an important one that ought not be missed, the ending was unsuccessful and a mistake. Generally, the more conservative the critic or newspaper, the more negative the review. For example, Archer Winston wrote in the *New York Post* that although he enjoyed the comedy in the film, "the speech is so completely out of key with all that has preceded it that it makes you squirm. Even if you understand perfectly well the noble motives for it. . . . nevertheless, it is an artistic boner of the first water." Two days later, also in the *Post*, Sidney Skolsky recommended the film but added, Chaplin "wrote the final speech himself, and this is where the picture failed completely." The *New York Sun* observed that "Mr. Chaplin, who has been going in more and more heavily for social significance during his last two pictures, now goes completely overboard. He turns his show into drama that is closer to tragedy than comedy. . . . a great disappointment." Hearst's *Journal-American* judged that the film was "at its best when Chaplin devotes himself to comedy," and Ed Sullivan, whose political conservatism would lead him to attack Chaplin often after 1940, dismissed the film in the *Daily News* by writing that "every comic wants to play Hamlet, but no clown should play Hamlet." The *Herald Tribune*, generally sympathetic to Chaplin's work, wrote that "the pattern of [Chaplin's] new motion picture is definitely disconcerting. *The Great Dictator* is aflame with Chaplin's genius but the flame flickers badly."[31]

Other critics, generally those who were more sympathetic to Chaplin's progressive politics, were gentler with the film but still critical at times. Given the situation in Europe, a thesis proposed in William Boehnel's review in the *World Telegram* was certainly arguable: "Hitler and all he represents are beyond the kidding stage. [*The Great Dictator*] is propaganda first and entertainment afterward." Yet Boehnel still defended the film: "If it falters now and again as entertainment, the things it says and does must be honored." In the *Philadelphia Record* Elsie Finn wrote that although the final speech "is delivered in too Hitlerish a manner, it's the film's logical conclusion." And in what might have been the two most important reviews—those in *Variety* and the *New York Times*—Chaplin was luckier. "The preachment is strong, notably in the six-minute speech at the finish," wrote *Variety*, "but the comedy, which Chaplin has woven around the dictators, at whose expense he makes fun (partly with a sneer), is extremely entertaining." With prescience, the reviewer added, "The box-office potentialities are excellent." Bosley Crowther's sympathy for socially significant films led him to praise it as "a superlative accomplishment by a great and true artist . . . unquestionably the most significant—if not the most entertaining—film that Chaplin has ever made." To Chaplin's credit, wrote Crowther, "He is actually making a most profound and tragic comment upon a truly evil state of affairs."[32]

One of the most interesting reviews of *The Great Dictator* appeared in the *Daily Worker*, the CPUSA newspaper. The film was released well after the Nazi–Soviet Pact but before the Nazis attacked Russia: precisely during that period when Party members had abandoned the cooperative antifascism of the Popular Front period and were generally working against American involvement in the world war. Given his responsibility to defend that political line in his review, the *Daily Worker* reviewer, David Platt, had his work cut out for him. His review in the *Worker* was titled, "Chaplin in *The Great Dictator* Achieves a Triumph of Satire." The two subtitles reveal the tension built into the review: "Masterpiece of Comedy Lashes All Oppression" and "Picture Ends With Eloquent Plea for Peace." The astonishing element of the review is its argument that *The Great Dictator*'s conclusion is "a tremendous contribution to peace." The film has nothing for the "Roosevelts and Churchills and little Hitlers in industry" who are trying to plunge America into "the dark age of war," wrote Platt. Rather, it is "a genuine people's film against war and fascism." This is a most torturously twisting review of *The Great Dictator*. Platt had the unenviable responsibility of being antifascist (but not too much so) and antiwar at the same time. By distorting the film, he managed to accomplish this.[33]

Despite widespread attention, *The Great Dictator* was thus much less successful with reviewers than it was at the box office. This somewhat critical response by reviewers can be understood in at least two ways. First, because Chaplin's film had so much prerelease publicity, because it treated such a topical issue, and because of Chaplin's high status as a filmmaker, the expectations of reviewers were probably higher and their standards more critical. The higher the expectation, the more likely one is to be disappointed.

Reception theory provides another reason for the negative critical response to *The Great Dictator*. In Jauss's terms, the "aesthetic distance" between *The Great Dictator* and the critics was greater than for any Chaplin film at least since *A Woman of Paris*. Hence the hesitant, ambivalent, or outright negative responses: the unsettling new political dimension in the film was hard for many to bear. Whereas much of Chaplin's work could easily be considered the "entertainment art" (*Unterhaltungskunst*) that Jauss devalues, this film was in certain ways less predictable and more disturbing to viewers. The work initiated a change in the horizon of expectations through which viewers would encounter Chaplin's subsequent work, and those shifts would create difficulties for the sustenance of Chaplin's star image.[34]

In any case, the attack by reviewers on the film's ending was more than Chaplin expected or could tolerate. Just a week after the film's New York City opening, but before the film went into general release, Chaplin publicly responded to the reviews in a letter to the *New York Times*. Countering those who argued that Hitler was no longer funny, Chaplin writes that it is not only possible but necessary to laugh at Hitler during these troubled times, because laughter is "health-giving." To those who find the ending inappropriate, he adds: "To me it is a logical ending to the story. To me it is the speech the barber would have made—even had to make. . . . May I not end my comedy on a note which reflects, honestly and realistically, the world in which we live, and may I not be excused for pleading for a better world?" Such comments show how Chaplin's aesthetic views had changed during the depression decade. From a view that art and politics lie in distinctly different realms, Chaplin, like many American artists influenced by the 1930s, was arguing that it was an artist's right, if not responsibility, to "reflect" the problems of the world and to "plead" for a better one. (It is also worth mentioning that as well as defending his political views, Chaplin was trying to protect his film's economic prospects.)[35]

The reaction to the film by the weekly magazines and monthly journals, most of which came out after Chaplin's letter, reveal much the same response found in the daily newspapers. One of the only purely positive reviews appeared in *Catholic World*. Although it was quite short, it was filled with praise: in the reviewer's words, "More devastating than any bomb invented, his caricature of tyrants will long outlive their tyranny." Much more common were charges that although the film was funny, the comedy and the serious social comment did not blend successfully. In the *New Republic* Otis Ferguson gave a mixed review. On the positive side, it was "a good picture," containing not just laughter but also "warmth and grace" (the qualities Ferguson associated with previous Chaplin films and the Charlie of old). He also found, however, "the symbiosis of comedy and earnestness an unhappy state of union, detrimental to both." In his view, "for the world's first funny man to prove that he too can write a *New Republic* editorial" was not particularly impressive, since Chaplin's came "several years later": denouncing Hitler took more prescience and courage in 1937 than in 1940. And the ending? To Ferguson, the "exhortation to the downtrodden of the world . . . is not only a bad case of overwriting but dramatically and even inspirationally futile." Philip Hartung's review in *Commonweal* followed similar lines: "When the world's best comedian takes himself and the world's woes too seriously, he goes sour." Likewise, the *Nation* ("the picture leaves one . . . with a curious mixture of enthusiasm and disappointment") and *Newsweek* praised parts of the film but on the whole were, with most other reviewers, uneasy.[36]

Saturday Review, in an editorial, attacked Chaplin's topicality most vigorously of all. "The root problem in *The Great Dictator*," according to its author, "is simply that Hitler and his doings are no longer funny." By tying his film to a particular time and place, Chaplin gave up the "universality" so central to his earlier movies. The editorialist believed he saw a lesson in the Chaplin episode. Rejecting the 1930s notion of socially aware, committed art, he wrote: "Our comedians will render good service to the national morale if they can give us something to laugh at in the years ahead; but they had better pick out material that would have been just as recognizable, just as funny, before Hitler was ever born." The tone of American cultural life was beginning to shift in a direction that ultimately would challenge Chaplin's progressive politics in a fundamental way. Looking back from nearly a half century, it seems more than a little significant that even the liberal journals that would have been sympathetic to the film's politics were criticizing it in their film reviews.[37]

The film continued to generate controversy and gain publicity for a long time after its release. In March 1941, Fritz Hippler, head of the Cinema Department of the German Reich's Ministry of Propaganda, answered President Roosevelt's comment to the Motion Picture Academy a week earlier that dictators fear the propaganda effect of American movies. Scoffing at the notion, Hippler remarked that "if it is true that the American movie has carried 'the ideals of a free nation' throughout the world, then America's ideal must be light amusement, song hits and tap dancing." He added that Germany's ban on American films resulted from the recent release of a number of "provocative films" that included *The Mad Dog of Europe*, *The Mortal Storm*, and *The Great Dictator*. The controversy continued throughout 1941: in July the *Daily Mirror* reported that Paulette Goddard had become the target of a smear campaign by domestic Nazi and fascist groups. Reviewers who commented on the film in its second or third runs in 1941 and 1942—after American involvement in the war seemed likely or had even begun—were more willing than the earlier reviewers, however, to endorse the film. In May 1941 the *St. Louis Dispatch* wrote: "If the rages of Adolph Hitler at times go beyond the limits of burlesque and become genuinely frightening and insane, it is because Chaplin has that to say about Hynkel or Hitler." Early in 1942 the *Dallas Morning News*, noting that the final speech "was roundly condemned eighteen months ago," added that "now, with *The Great Dictator* assuming a new seriousness, the oration does not seem off key."[38]

The film also came to the attention of various governmental officials, in part because it was so clearly antifascist at a time when the government was still officially neutral. Isolationists did not like *The Great Dictator*. In mid-1941, Senators Burton Wheeler and Gerald Nye, both members of the isolationist America First Committee, expressed their indignation over Hollywood's antifascist films (though there were only a few) and argued that they were promoting America's involvement into the war. Wheeler accused the film industry and the Roosevelt administration of carrying on "a violent propaganda campaign intending to incite the American people to the point where they will become involved in this war." To counter the threat they perceived, Nye joined Bennett Clark in proposing a resolution approved by the Senate on 1 August 1941, which was to investigate "any propaganda disseminated by motion pictures and radio or any other activity of the motion-picture industry to influence public sentiment in the direction of participation by the United States in the present European war." This resolution established the Senate Subcommittee on War Propaganda. Its members accused a number of films of being "war mongering documents," among them *Pastor Hall*, *Foreign Correspondent*, *Blackout*, *That Hamilton Woman*, *So Ends Our Night*, and *The Great Dictator*. Chaplin himself was subpoenaed in September to testify on *The Great Dictator* in October. Senator Clark told the press that the subcommittee "wished to ascertain Chaplin's motives" in making the film. The *Washington Evening Star* published a cartoon shortly after the announcement satirizing the fears of the subcommittee and defending Chaplin (see Figure 19). Although the legal files of United Artists show that Chaplin's lawyers prepared some information about *The Great Dictator* requested by the subcommittee, Chaplin never was called to testify: after a delay, Pearl Harbor interrupted the subcommittee's activities, and soon after it disbanded.[39]

In part because its antifascism was so pronounced, *The Great Dictator* caused the Roosevelt administration considerable difficulty in its relations with Latin America, many of whose nations had sizable German immigrant populations. The issue of showing or not showing *The Great Dictator* became hotly contested in many of the countries as time went on. After Germany overran most of Europe, many believed that Latin America would be the next area of Nazi aggression. Chaplin recalled meeting with Roosevelt for forty minutes at the White House after the

19. *Washington Evening Star* cartoon (September 1941) on Chaplin the "premature antifascist": FDR cited the cartoon to help mock the Senate Subcommittee's position.

President requested a print of the film. According to Chaplin, Roosevelt's only response to him specifically about the film was: "Sit down, Charlie, your picture is giving us a lot of trouble in the Argentine" (MA, p. 405). All through 1941 and 1942 the *New York Times* carried brief articles about whether or not various Latin American countries were showing the film. To list only the *Times* references, in January 1941 a cut version of the film was shown in Chile while it was banned in Paraguay and shown in its entirety in Nicaragua. In February it was shown in Costa Rica over the protests of both Germany and Italy. In March it played in Ecuador. As late as March 1942 Paraguay lifted its ban on the film, and it finally played in May. While all this was going on in Latin America, the *Times* reported that the film was getting a very strong response in England in February 1941 and a rental was being negotiated by the Soviet Union after the Nazi invasion made the film politically acceptable.[40]

The Great Dictator remained newsworthy. Shortly after Rome was liberated in June 1944, *The Great Dictator* played there. Probably because the country's devastating experiences of war were so recent, the Italian audience had a hard time laughing during the film. After the film, according to an American observer, the audience left "the cinema subdued and, it seemed, stunned." A similar reaction greeted the first showing of the film to a selected group of Germans in 1946.[41] No previous Chaplin film had generated such controversy or elicited such a strong reaction, and the fact that even its foreign releases garnered U.S. publicity suggests that Chaplin's star image was increasingly becoming associated with a certain political stance. As America became more involved in the fight against fascism, Chaplin himself was moving toward an active involvement in politics that would make this link even stronger.

Chaplin and the Second Front

Having expressed his progressive politics on film, Chaplin also reaffirmed them in 1941 and 1942 through overt political activity. Even though he had long been uncomfortable as a public speaker and had rarely spoken to large crowds except during the Liberty Loan tour of 1918—which usually involved very short, often comic, exhortations—Chaplin's hesitance about public speaking diminished after *The Great Dictator*. This was in part because he had something he wanted to say and in part because after having said so much in *The Great Dictator*, he no longer felt compelled to protect the pantomime of Charlie. Furthermore, Chaplin was goaded by the hate mail he received from domestic fascist sympathizers while he was making and helping to promote *The Great Dictator*. After the Nazis attacked the Soviet Union in June 1941 and the United States entered the war in December, Chaplin was even more willing to contribute to the war against fascism. Though it has become customary over the years, even ritualistic, to dismiss Chaplin's politics as unformed or contradictory or superficial, Chaplin's activities in 1941 and especially 1942 suggest that he made a concerted effort to contribute to the war as a progressive antifascist. This activity, which supplemented his political affirmations in *The Great Dictator*, wedded progressive politics even more closely to his star image.[42]

One of Chaplin's first public addresses after the release of *The Great Dictator* was to read its final speech in Washington, D.C., the evening before Roosevelt's third inauguration. Scheduled as one of a number of artists to perform at Constitution Hall, Chaplin arrived at Union Station the afternoon of 19 January 1941, to perform that evening. Upon his arrival, he told reporters, "I feel everyone has given the Nazis' momentary victories too much importance. . . . We should all be made more cognizant of human decency." When asked his views on Roosevelt, Chaplin replied, "He is the hope of us all. He is the hope of the world."[43] That evening, to a packed audience, Chaplin appeared with Nelson Eddy, Mickey Rooney, Raymond Massey, Ethel Barrymore, and others.[44]

The following day Chaplin stood at the Capitol Plaza to hear Roosevelt deliver his inaugural address, in which the President promised that the torch of liberty would remain burning brightly. As Chaplin left and moved toward the entrance of the Senate Office Building, however, he heard a small portion of the large crowd shout, "Heil, Hitler." According to a report, Chaplin "obviously had a retort ready, but friends quickly took his arms and guided him—almost forcibly— through the crowd."[45]

Later that year Chaplin read the speech again, this time at the hall of the Daughters of the American Revolution in Washington for a radio hookup (MA, p. 161). The same day he met with Roosevelt and had the conversation about Argentina mentioned above. One could of course argue that reading this speech was not particularly dangerous for Chaplin's public reputation: after all, he had already firmly associated himself with the positions it articulated. Shortly after America entered the war allied with the Soviet Union, however, Chaplin began to leave his *Great Dictator* speech at home and deliver more extemporaneous public addresses, this time in favor of the opening of a second front in Europe.

Chaplin's first step in this direction was to join several groups that aimed to foster Soviet–American unity during the war or to send humanitarian aid to the Soviets after the Nazis invaded. One of the earliest pieces of evidence demonstrating such activity is a full-page advertisement paid for by Russian War Relief and appearing in the 10 October 1941 issue of the *New York Times*. The advertisement's headline was "Russia's 'Scorched Earth' Calls to America's Green Fields" (the "scorched earth" referred to the Soviet policy of burning any of their own houses and fields that had to be abandoned in the face of the oncoming Nazis). Below this was an announcement of a Russian War Relief benefit scheduled for Madison Square Garden on October 27, as well as a list of the organization's supporters, who, according to the ad, were "moved not only by their humanitarianism but actuated by their common-sense Americanism." Around three hundred names appeared on the list. In addition to Chaplin, it included many actors (among them, Dame May Whitty, Gale Sondergaard, Basil Rathbone, Nigel Bruce, Helen Hayes, Alfred Lunt), film directors (Rouben Mamoulian, John Huston, Frank Capra, Lewis Milestone), writers (Elmer Rice, Thomas Mann, Lion Feuchtwanger, Brooks Atkinson), and intellectuals (Robert Lynd).[46]

A headline in the *Times* the same day suggests how the second front policy would gradually, by the middle of 1942, gain a broad level of support among the American populace. The headline read "Nazis Claim Vast Victory." The accompanying articles discussed the furious battles as the Nazis attacked and moved even closer to Moscow. The articles reported that, according to Soviet radio, German forces had "been halted in the terrific drives on Moscow from the south and southwest." As newspapers reported daily on the carnage in Russia, the dogged resistance of the Soviet military and populace, and the ferocity of the battles with the Nazis, more and more people, including important U.S. government officials, began to believe that it would be sound military strategy to have Great Britain and the United States establish a second front in western Europe that would force the Nazis to split their forces.

On a national level, the drive to support a second front policy was strongest in the United States between May and November of 1942. In the opening months of the year, several prominent spokesmen delivered well-publicized speeches in favor of such a policy. On February 26 the popular Soviet ambassador to the United States, Maxim Litvinoff, made a plea in a speech to the Overseas Press Club for a second front to be established by the spring. On April 23 a prominent British statesman, Lord Beaverbrook, spoke to a meeting of the American Newspaper Publishers Association and also defended a second front policy. He argued that by opening the second front, the chances for a quick defeat of the Axis powers would be at hand. Among American statesmen, both Wendell Willkie, the 1940 Republican presidential candidate, and Joseph E. Davies, the former U.S. ambassador to the Soviet Union, also came out publicly for the policy in the spring.[47]

By summer, the policy seemed to be the U.S. government's as well. When the Soviet foreign minister Molotov visited Washington in June, he bluntly asked Roosevelt and his aides if the United States could undertake an offensive that would drive off forty German divisions. According to Cordell Hull, who attended the meeting, when General George C. Marshall answered that it could be done, Roosevelt "authorized Mr. Molotov to inform Mr. Stalin that we expect the formation of a second front this year." Although the Soviets were forced to wait until 1944 before the American and British forces invaded western Europe, the Allies did invade North Africa in November 1942. At this point, the American perspective changed, and headlines like the ones on the front page of the *New York Times*—"American Forces Land in French Africa; British Naval, Air Units Assisting Them; Effective Second Front, Roosevelt Says"—helped to mute calls for a second front after the end of the year.[48]

As Ralph Levering has shown, partly because of broad coverage in the media during that time, the second front policy—despite a tradition in the United States of antipathy toward the Soviet Union—was supported by a significant majority of the American public by the middle of 1942. In July a Gallup poll showed that 60 percent of the people who had opinions about the second front policy favored it. It seemed to many a pragmatic policy when the Nazis exhibited so much strength in eastern and central Europe. Support for the policy was strongest among people with leftist or middle-of-the-road political views, while few conservatives, according to Levering, "spoke out either for or against a second front in 1942." (These conservatives, though hesitant to come out publicly in favor of the Soviet Union on any issue, nevertheless did not want to seem unpatriotic by coming out against a second front.) A *Time* magazine cover of Dmitri Shostakovich on July 20, accompanied by an article supporting the policy, as well as the popularity during the summer of two books that supported the Soviet Union—Joseph Davies's *Mission to Moscow* and young James Reston's pro-interventionist *Prelude to Victory*—also helped through sales and reviews to spur pro–second front opinion in the country.[49]

Chaplin, of course, had ideological reasons for supporting the second front policy: its main aim was to help defeat the Germans, and his antifascism was well served by supporting it. But Chaplin had also over the years met and enjoyed the company of Soviet visitors to Hollywood. We have already mentioned Chaplin's friendship with Sergei Eisenstein when the Soviet director was in California in 1930 and Chaplin's acquaintance, while cutting *Modern Times*, with Boris Shumiatsky and his colleagues. It also seems that the Soviet national response to Chaplin blossomed after the visit with Shumiatsky. In April 1938 the Soviet film industry, with Shumiatsky as spokesman, sent an official letter of greeting to Chaplin on his fiftieth birthday.[50] After *Modern Times* and *The Great Dictator*, the Soviets generally became much more positive about the humanitarianism in his films, and Chaplin often became the recipient of official praise from the Soviet Union, as we shall see. Chaplin's second front activities stemmed at least in part from his fondness for some of the Soviet "celebrities" that he had met in Hollywood and from his gratitude for Soviet praise of his films.

Between May and December 1942, Chaplin was a featured or sole speaker for at least six rallies, most of which were fund-raisers for Russian War Relief. At a time when many figures in Hollywood were enlisting in the armed forces or contributing to the war effort in other ways, like visiting USOs, Chaplin made his contribution through speech making.[51]

He first became involved as a speaker in a way that was unusual for a star of his stature: as a second choice, a substitute. On 17 May 1942, he received a phone call from a Russian War Relief official in San Francisco, who asked if he could fill in for Joseph E. Davies, who was to have been the featured speaker at a rally on May 18 in San Francisco's Civic Center but had fallen ill. Chaplin agreed and took the train to San Francisco. In his autobiography, Chaplin recalled that because of his full schedule, he had little time to plan a speech. That evening, after hearing a number of short speeches that he felt were too tentative in support of the policy, he stepped up to give his allotted four-minute speech, but went on extemporaneously for forty minutes when the crowd became enthusiastic. If his memory is accurate, he urged the audience to embrace the alliance more fully as a way to overcome the fascist threat, and was greeted at the end of his speech by seven minutes of applause (MA, pp. 407–9). The leftist San Francisco newspaper, *People's World*, reported that "it was Chaplin whose warmth and sincere entreaty for military action in Europe evoked the deepfelt response of the audience." According to the article, Chaplin and the audience then drafted a mass telegram urging President Roosevelt to open a second front as soon as possible.[52]

After the meeting Chaplin remembers dining with Dudley Field Malone and John Garfield. According to Chaplin, Garfield praised him for his courage in giving the speech. This disturbed Chaplin, for as he put it later, "I did not wish to be valorous or caught up in a political cause célèbre. I had only spoken what I sincerely felt and thought was right" (MA, p. 409). Though the comment left a "depressing pall" over Chaplin for the rest of the evening, he recovered enough to give another speech at a Russian War Relief rally in the Los Angeles Shrine Auditorium on May 25.[53] Though no transcript or detailed descriptions of the speech are available, it seems reasonable to surmise that the central thrust of his comments in Los Angeles mirrored his speech in San Francisco.

Chaplin's next public address in favor of the opening of a second front was via telephone on July 22, transmitted from Los Angeles to Madison Square Park in New York City, where the CIO sponsored a "Support the President Rally for a Second Front Now," which drew 60,000 people. Since the CIO's Greater New York Industrial Union

Council later published the speech as a brochure, along with a brief description of the occasion, we have an accurate transcript, which Chaplin later reprinted in his autobiography.[54] The crowd, who gathered on a beautiful day to support Roosevelt's call for the immediate opening of a second front, heard such speakers as U.S. senators James M. Mead and Claude Pepper, New York mayor Fiorello LaGuardia, and New York CIO president Joseph Curran.

According to an eyewitness account, when Chaplin's speech began to be broadcast, "The great crowd, previously warned not to interrupt with applause, hushed and strained for every word. Thus they listened for fourteen minutes to Charles Chaplin, the great people's artist of America, as he spoke to them by telephone from Hollywood." Chaplin opened dramatically: "On the battlefields of Russia democracy will live or die. The fate of the Allied nations is in the hands of the Communists." He went on to say that the Soviet Union's back was to the wall—the wall of democracy. If the Nazis prevailed, Chaplin argued, they would turn to America and Great Britain with promises that would be attractive to appeasers, even as they tried to "take away our liberty and enslave our minds." If that were to happen, Chaplin predicted in a passage that recalled *The Great Dictator*: "Human progress will be lost. There will be no minority rights, no workers' rights, no citizen's rights." How could this dire future be prevented? By opening a second front immediately and aiming "for victory in the spring." With a stirring challenge—"Remember [that] great achievements throughout history have been the conquest of what seemed the impossible"—Chaplin ended his call for a second front that would preserve democracy in the face of Nazi tyranny. It is worth noting here that nowhere in the speech does Chaplin either endorse or criticize the Soviet system; rather, he calls for support of the Soviet Union to help defeat the Nazi aggressors.

Chaplin's next public appearance to speak in favor of a second front was at Carnegie Hall in New York City on Friday evening, 16 October 1942. Sponsored by the Artist's Front to Win the War, the dinner was attended by 3,000 people, who heard such people as Sam Jaffee, I. F. Stone, Joris Ivens, Carl Van Doren, and Lillian Hellman speak before Orson Welles introduced Chaplin as the featured speaker (see Figure 20). Chaplin opened his half-hour speech in a way that would come back to haunt him: "Dear Comrades. Yes, I mean comrades. When one sees the magnificent fight the Russian people are putting up, it is a pleasure and a privilege to use the word 'comrade.' " From there he made comments on a number of topics. He praised Roosevelt "for the wonderful job he is doing," comparing him to Washington, Jefferson,

20. Chaplin and Orson Welles meet before Chaplin's Carnegie Hall speech in favor of a second front, October 1942.

and Lincoln and saying that he had done more for the "little people" than any American president except Lincoln. Turning to the second front theme, he said that "every self-respecting citizen in the United States wants a second front now. . . . The American people want to get this bloody job done and get it done now." In another comment open to later criticism, Chaplin praised Roosevelt for releasing early from prison the former general secretary of the CPUSA, Earl Browder. Chaplin also, according to a report in the *Herald Tribune*, said that he "found it a privilege to pay Uncle Sam" his taxes and expressed a lack of concern about reports that "after the war Communism may spread over world" because "I can live on $25,000 a year." Finally, he pleased the assembly in an encore by returning to the podium, raising two fingers in a "V," and telling the cheering crowd that the gesture stood "for victory and for '2'—second front." Compared to the telephone broadcast in July, this speech, though similar in ideological thrust— support of the Soviet allies and a second front policy—also contained many more comments than the earlier talk that, when reported in newspapers, gave political conservatives a sense that Chaplin had really become a radical sympathizer of the Soviet system.[55]

A little more than a month after the Carnegie Hall speech, Chaplin traveled to Chicago to speak at Orchestra Hall for a "Salute Our Russian Ally" rally, held on the ninth anniversary of the establishment of Soviet–American relations. There an estimated 2,600 people paid from 55 cents to $1.10 to hear Chaplin speak, with funds going to Russian War Relief. The brief report on the speech by the conservative *Chicago Tribune* makes it sound similar in tone and approach to Chaplin's October message. After the "Star-Spangled Banner" and the Soviet national anthem were played, Carl Sandburg and Rear Admiral H. P. Taylor spoke. Then Chaplin opened his remarks with "Ladies, Gentlemen, Friends, and Comrades," once again stressing a word that for him indicated support of the Soviet–American alliance. According to the *Tribune*'s report, Chaplin criticized the head of the Boston American Legion for protesting labor leader Harry Bridges's speech at Harvard and also told the audience that "no longer is the world shocked at the word 'communism.' " Such a comment likely did, however, shock the *Tribune*'s editorial staff and more than a few of its readers.[56]

Chaplin's final speech in favor of the Soviet–American alliance against fascism was at a dinner in his honor on 3 December 1942, at the Pennsylvania Hotel in New York City. It was given by the "Arts to Russia Week" committee of Russian War Relief. Chaplin was lauded as an artist who was fighting "to keep culture and the arts alive in a world of free peoples." Among the greetings to Chaplin were cables from Moscow sent by Shostakovich, Eisenstein, and the writer Alexei Tolstoi. Another cable, from Soviet war correspondent Ilya Ehrenburg, read in part: "All your life on the screen you have defended the little man against the malevolent and soulless machine. We are glad to see you taking a stand against Nazism. It isn't humans who've fallen upon us but ersatz-men, brutal, repulsive automatons. We defend against them our lives, our right to smile, our right to freedom and happiness. We are glad that you, Dear Chaplin, are with us." In his own brief remarks, Chaplin asked the seven hundred listeners to abandon their prejudices against Soviet political and economic ideals, "since our Allies do not object to our own ideals and form of government." According to the report in the *New York Times*, he also said that "Communism happens to be what the Russians are fighting for and from the way they are fighting they must like it pretty well. I am not a Communist, but I feel pretty pro-Communist."[57]

This gathering made it clear that the Soviets had embraced Chaplin as a "people's artist," whether he sought the title or not, and that Chaplin himself was willing to praise publicly the Soviet effort against the Nazis. Throughout his six speeches in 1942, Chaplin gradually, perhaps imperceptibly to him, moved from a focus on the necessity to oppose the Nazi threat to a tendency to praise the Soviet allies and urge closer ties with them. In the context of the war effort in 1942, such praise was not uncommon; in fact, it was quite typical of those who held progressive political views at the time. But when the political climate changed, Chaplin would be called upon to answer for his actions.

Thus Chaplin concluded the most active political period of his life. We have seen that Chaplin's political views during this time cannot be understood without understanding the historical context in which they formed: the pressures placed on artists during the depression to commit themselves to a socially conscious art, the growth of the Popular Front, and the intricacies of political alliances during the second front period. Although Chaplin would stay interested and even sporadically active, when he was not working on a film, in American politics until he left the country in 1952, he would never again speak to the large and enthusiastic groups he spoke to in 1942, in part because of the changing climate of opinion, in part because his star image was beginning to take on political associations controversial to more conservative Americans. A foreshadowing of that change was a 21 December 1942 column by the conservative gadfly Westbrook Pegler. Responding to Chaplin's December 3 speech, Pegler, using a dichotomous logic that would become common during the Cold War, wrote that "Chaplin lately has said that he was pro-Communist which means only that he is anti-American." In Pegler's view, Chaplin, "after years of sly pretending, when an open profession of his political faith would have hurt his business, now that he has all the money he needs and has lost his way with the public, has frankly allied himself with the pro-Communist actors and writers of the theater and the movies, who call themselves artists, but who are mostly hams and hacks."[58] Pegler ignored the fact that *The Great Dictator* was Chaplin's most successful film at the box office (hardly an indication that he had "lost his way with the public"), and he practiced a kind of guilt by association that Chaplin's candid public comments about communism during the second front period encouraged. Darkly foreshadowing what was to come for Chaplin in the years ahead, Pegler remarked in his column, "in common, I am sure, with many other Americans, I would like to know why Charlie Chaplin has been allowed to stay in the United States about 40 years without becoming a citizen." As a Scripps-Howard columnist, widely syndicated in some six hundred newspapers, Pegler was writing for such a broad audience that one might fairly say this column began the assault on Chaplin's progressive politics that would within a decade result in his exile.

FOUR

Unraveling

7

Joan Barry, the Press, and
the Tarnished Image

The Affair

Because stardom depends on winning and maintaining the good
graces of an audience, and because public taste and cultural values
shift over time, nearly every star's career is a story of his or her rise
and fall. Chaplin's career is no exception. Chaplin's fall—following
what was, for the movies, an unprecedented period of popularity—
may be the most dramatic in the history of stardom in America, related as it is to the vagaries of history, the complex impulses of the
star's personality, and shifting ideological currents in the United
States. Charles Chaplin, Jr., recalling how gratified his father was with
the ovation he received after delivering *The Great Dictator* speech at
Roosevelt's preinaugural concert in 1941, has written that "my father's
appearance at the gathering, the heartfelt applause at his earnest
words, might be called the pinnacle of his public success in this country. From then on the path led downward by subtle degrees until it
ended in his self-imposed exile."[1] In a decline that was not even "subtle" at times, Chaplin's star image suffered badly in the 1940s and
early 1950s. So badly, in fact, that when he left the country for the
London premiere of *Limelight* in September 1952, the attorney general's office revoked his reentry permit and stated Chaplin would have
to prove his moral and political worthiness before returning to the
country in which he had lived for nearly forty years.

The third of June, 1943, was a turning point in the unraveling of
Chaplin's star image. That day, nearly six months after his last speech
urging the opening of a second front in Europe, a young aspiring actress named Joan Barry filed a paternity suit against him that claimed
he was the father of the baby she expected in October. The story made
front-page headlines and filled the Los Angeles papers and many
others across the country throughout most of the month. This case fell
within the jurisdiction of the California state courts, but by August the
U.S. attorney's office in California had begun an investigation of the
Barry–Chaplin relationship, assisted vigorously by the Los Angeles of-

fice of the Federal Bureau of Investigation. The subsequent trials, both federal and state, also generated widespread publicity and contributed to the tarnishing of Chaplin's star image.

In a sense, the story of Chaplin's affair with Barry begins with his separation and divorce from Paulette Goddard. The estrangement began as *The Great Dictator* was being completed, and Chaplin's son Charles remembers that although both Goddard and Chaplin attended the October 1940 premieres of the film at the Capitol and Astor theaters in New York City, they did not travel together: Goddard came from Mexico, where she had been visiting painter Diego Rivera for the second time in six months. By early December she had moved into the empty beach house of her agent, Myron Selznick, and then became extremely busy, appearing in eight films in 1941 and 1942 alone. With no fanfare and almost no press coverage (in contrast to Chaplin's second divorce), she and Chaplin mutually agreed upon a divorce, which Goddard eventually received in Mexico on 4 June 1942.[2]

In May 1941, some months after *The Great Dictator*'s success and Chaplin's performance at Roosevelt's preinaugural concert, a young woman named Joan Barry returned to Los Angeles from Mexico City, bearing a letter of introduction from A. C. Blumenthal—an associate of J. Paul Getty—to Tim Durant, a close friend of Chaplin's since the late 1930s (see Figure 21). In early June, a few days after they first met, Durant asked Barry if she would like to meet Chaplin. With another woman, Durant and Barry dined with Chaplin at Perino's Restaurant in Los Angeles. The affair began around this time.[3]

Barry had just turned twenty-two. She had been born Mary Louise Gribble on 24 May 1919 in Detroit, Michigan. Her father, Jim Gribble, whom Barry described as a veteran of World War I suffering from shell shock, committed suicide before she was born, and her mother later remarried a man named Berry. They moved to New York City, where she attended elementary and secondary school before moving to California in 1938, hoping to become a movie actress. She told the FBI that at various times she had used the names Mary Louise Berry, Joan Barratt, Mary L. Barratt, Joanne Berry, JoAnne Berry, and Joan Barry, trying out the variations at least in part to find a suitable name for the movies.[4]

Her record in Los Angeles had been a checkered one. Twice caught shoplifting dresses from department stores in 1938, she was released after the first theft but booked after the second, receiving a suspended ninety-day jail sentence and a year's probation. FBI files reveal that "a local businessman became acquainted with Berry in September, 1938,

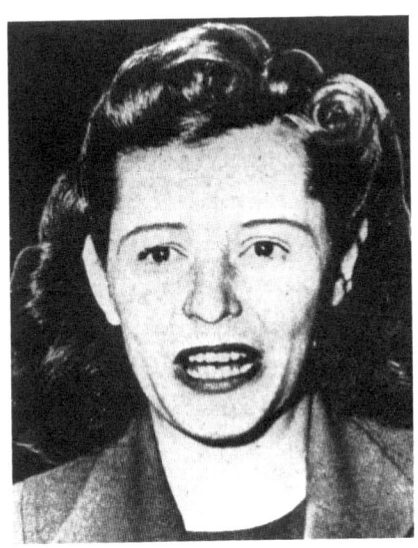

21. Joan Barry in March 1944.

and kept her in a local apartment house and hotel over a period of several years." Barry also told FBI agents that she knew J. Paul Getty before meeting Chaplin and had spent the early part of 1941 in Mexico City with Getty. According to her story, Getty persuaded A. C. Blumenthal to write letters of introduction for her to various people in Hollywood, including Chaplin's friend Tim Durant, in hopes of enabling her to break into the movies.[5]

After their first meeting at Perino's, Barry, escorted by Durant, attended one of Chaplin's tennis afternoons the following Sunday, and their relationship began to develop, though their versions of who pursued whom differ significantly. Chaplin claims that Barry called him the first two or three times after the Sunday party and made it clear that she was available to him. In his words, "Persistence is the road to accomplishment. Thus she achieved her object and I began to see her often" (MA, p. 414). In contrast, Barry later contended to FBI agents that Chaplin was the aggressor. After telling them that she and Chaplin first made love in his home, she added, "Chaplin's success in this regard was due to his verbal persuasiveness. I have been told, and from my personal experiences with him I know it to be true, that he is very proud of his success with women along these lines. This verbal persuasiveness of Chaplin's was his violent insistence that he was madly in love with me. He began calling me his favorite name for his lady loves, 'Hunchy.' "[6]

Both versions contain a degree of self-justification, and the truth probably lies somewhere in between. Barry, hoping for a movie career, did probably throw herself at Chaplin, and Chaplin, unencumbered and lonely following his separation from Goddard, likely played his part, too. In any case, Barry signed a movie contract with Chaplin on 23 June 1941 and read for the part of Bridget in a play called *Shadow and Substance*, to which Chaplin soon bought the rights. Barry's six-month contract paid her $75 a week and gave Chaplin the option to renew the contract after six months at $100 a week if he desired. He enrolled her in Max Reinhardt's acting school and began writing the script.[7]

The liaison continued intermittently through much of 1941 and into 1942, though Barry told FBI agents that she continued to see other men and even went to Tulsa in May 1942 to see Getty. That same month, Chaplin and Barry mutually agreed to cancel her contract (Barry hoped that a screen test with M-G-M would land her a job), though she continued on the payroll through September. Chaplin also made his first speech in favor of the second front that May, and much of his time over the next several months centered on his political commitments. Though the stories of what happened between Chaplin and Barry are widely contradictory, both parties agreed that Chaplin gave Barry and her mother train fare and some extra money to return to New York City. Chaplin later claimed that Barry had been negligent in her acting lessons and had decided she didn't want to be an actress, and that the money was a way of completely severing their ties. Barry said that "one day out of a clear blue sky" Chaplin told her she could go to New York. She and her mother left October 2. Toward the end of that month, a few days after Chaplin's second front speech at Carnegie Hall, Chaplin and Barry met one evening, apparently on Barry's initiative, and Barry went for a short time to Chaplin's suite at the Waldorf-Astoria, after which, she and Chaplin took a cab and he dropped her off at the Hotel Pierre, where she was staying. What exactly happened during this evening became a matter of great conjecture during the trials. It is clear that both returned separately to Los Angeles and that Barry made another trip to Tulsa to visit Getty for a week or ten days in November.[8]

The relationship had become extremely tenuous and sporadic, and by the end of December Chaplin wanted to be rid of the whole affair. At 1:00 A.M. on December 23, after her knocks and rings had gone unanswered, Barry forced herself into Chaplin's home by breaking two windows. Gun in hand, she went to Chaplin's second-floor bedroom, where she held him at gunpoint and threatened suicide. This incident—corroborated by Chaplin, Barry's courtroom testimony, and Chaplin's sons—was not settled until the morning, when Chaplin managed to get the gun from Barry and persuaded her to leave. At the end of the month, inebriated, she again tried to see Chaplin. On the morning of 1 January 1943, after having taken an overdose of barbiturates, she was arrested on the street by the Beverly Hills police department. (She was without money and had been evicted from her hotel because she could not pay her bill.) Charged with vagrancy, she was given a suspended sentence on the 2nd and placed on probation, the terms of which required that she pay some hotel bills and leave Beverly Hills. On January 5 she left for New York City by train, stopping first in Tulsa before going on.[9]

The affair seemed to be settled until Barry, pregnant, returned to Los Angeles in May. She tried to see Chaplin in order to claim that she was pregnant with his child. On 7 May 1943, following Chaplin's complaint, she was arrested by the Beverly Hills police for violating the terms of her probation and jailed. When the judge at her May 12 hearing learned that she was pregnant, he ordered her moved from the county jail to a sanitarium for health reasons. Later that month, after Barry's mother returned from New York to be with her daughter, Barry twice went uninvited to Chaplin's house—the second time around June 1—to discuss her plight. By her own admission she still hoped that she and Chaplin could be married. When Chaplin, by now deeply involved in a relationship with Oona O'Neill, refused to consider this, Barry and her mother decided to "go public." They asked two gossip columnists they had previously contacted, Hedda Hopper and Florabel Muir, to tell Barry's side of the story. When Barry filed the paternity suit naming Chaplin as the father of her child on June 3, the millstones of publicity had already begun grinding away at Chaplin's star image.[10]

Chaplin, Barry, and the Courts

Though Chaplin eventually became embroiled in federal charges, he first was faced with a civil violation that fell within the jurisdiction of the California state courts. Barry sued Chaplin on 3 June 1943. The following day Chaplin was served papers ordering him to appear in California Superior Court on June 17 to answer the charges. Chaplin denied the paternity charges and his lawyers worked out an arrangement whereby any trial would be postponed until after the birth of the child so Chaplin, Barry, and the baby (later born on October 3 and christened Carole Ann) could have blood tests. Through her lawyers,

Barry agreed to drop the paternity suit if blood tests proved that Chaplin could not have been the father of the child.[11] But in exchange Chaplin had to pay: for Barry's promise, he agreed to put up a sum of $2,500, plus $100 per week to support Barry; $500 more thirty days before the child was born; $1,000 when it was born; $500 monthly for four months after the child was born; $1,000 when the blood tests were taken; and $5,500 in attorney fees and court costs. Action on the paternity suit was then delayed until early 1944.[12]

However, in part due to the widespread publicity it was receiving, the Chaplin case soon came to the attention of federal authorities. Fred N. Howser, the U.S. district attorney of Los Angeles County, told the press that he was investigating two allegations: that Chaplin had paid for two abortions performed on Barry, and that the Beverly Hills police department was acting on Chaplin's behalf when Barry was arrested in January and May. By 24 June 1943, the FBI was also becoming involved, for that day R. B. Hood, the Special Agent in Charge of the Los Angeles office sent a memo to Hoover on "Information Concerning Charles Chaplin." This document contained information about Barry's dealing with Getty, the details of Chaplin's marriage to Oona O'Neill a week earlier, and an informant's denial that Chaplin was "Communistically inclined." The memo did not indicate, however, what charges would be investigated against Chaplin and Barry.[13]

By August, the abortion issue had been discarded, and the FBI, which often investigates cases handled by the U.S. Department of Justice, was beginning an investigation of Chaplin for possible violation of the Mann Act, which forbade paying for anyone's transportation across state lines for sexual purposes. Popularly known as the "White Slave Traffic Act," the law had been passed during the Progressive Era to stamp out organized prostitution but was sometimes used to threaten or harass wealthy or famous individuals. Trying to capitalize on the fact that Chaplin paid Barry's train fares both to and from New York City in October 1942, the FBI and the U.S. district attorney's office suspected that they might have a case. This was initiated after Special Agent Hood learned from the U.S. district attorney's office that Chaplin had paid for Barry's trip. He wrote a memo to Hoover on August 14, upon which Hoover wrote, "Shouldn't we run this down? If a White Slave violation, we ought to go after it vigorously." By August 17, FBI interoffice memos in Washington were referring to the case like this: "Charles Chaplin; Joan Barry, Victim—White Slave Traffic." And on August 20 Hoover ordered his communications section to telegram the Los Angeles office and ask them to report on developments and to "expedite investigation." The federal government was deeply involved in the case and would continue to be until the following May.[14]

Throughout the fall the U.S. district attorney's office in Los Angeles County and the FBI kept up their investigations. The FBI at first concentrated on obtaining evidence against Chaplin for violation of the Mann Act. Three reports from the Los Angeles office to Washington in October and November focused on that charge. Two were reports of the investigation by Agent H. Frank Angell (8 October 1943, 61 pages; and 9 November 1943, 45 pages); the third was a seven-page summary of Gerith von Ulm's biography of Chaplin (which contains considerable information about Chaplin's various affairs) by Special Agent Hood for the Washington office.[15] These reports, based on newspaper clippings, inquiries by FBI agents in Los Angeles and New York City, and the testimony of informants, began the attempt to provide the U.S. district attorney with evidence to use against Chaplin for Mann Act violations.

About the same time the November 9 report was filed, however, the investigation expanded. That day an interoffice memo in Washington reported on a telephone call from Special Agent Hood. He had met with the new U.S. district attorney, Charles Carr, who had taken over the Mann Act case in Los Angeles, and had learned that Carr was a little concerned about "the lack of a commercial angle" and about "Gribble's [Barry's] reputation." Both, he felt, could make it difficult to convict Chaplin for Mann Act violations. Carr was also interested, Hood continued, in Chaplin's role when Barry was arrested in early January and then ordered out of Beverly Hills, since one informant alleged that Barry's lawyer in the case was also Chaplin's. Carr thought that in this area "there may be a violation of the Civil Rights Statute."[16]

Soon thereafter, the FBI began to help Carr obtain information about the exact details of Barry's arrest on 1 January 1943, her suspended sentence the following day, and her whereabouts the next six months. The files from this part of the investigation contain some strange, almost paranoiac information. At one point, for example, the FBI speculates that Chaplin, through his lawyer, was trying to use his political influence in Washington to have the case dropped. This information was passed on directly from Hoover to Assistant Attorney General Tom Clark. Another set of memos discussed the possibility that Chaplin might flee the country, perhaps to the Soviet Union, if the investigations continued. When Hoover learned of this rumor, he wrote at the bottom of Hood's telegram: "Give immediate attention. Don't let this fellow do a run out." Hood responded by notifying FBI offices in San Diego, El Paso, Seattle, and Butte (!) to place stops at border stations in case Chaplin tried to leave the country. Looking for further negative information on Chaplin, another memo observed that Chaplin might have been buying black-market meat and having it delivered to his home.[17]

The central thread of FBI files from November through January concerns the possibility of a civil rights case to go along with the Mann Act charge. District Attorney Carr was hesitant about whether to go ahead with the civil rights charge; in fact, he slowed down the investigation of the case somewhat until Attorney General Biddle and Assistant Attorney General Clark told him to go ahead, adding that they thought chances of prosecution on this charge were pretty good.[18] By the middle of January Carr began presenting evidence to the grand jury. Among those testifying were FBI agents, gossip columnists Hopper and Muir, and Barry herself. On 10 February 1944 the federal grand jury handed down four indictments against Chaplin. The story made the front page of the next day's *New York Times*.[19]

The indictments all revolved around Mann Act charges or alleged violations of Barry's civil rights. The central indictment, and the only one to name Chaplin alone, alleged violation of Title 18, Section 398, of the U.S. Code (the Mann Act), and charged that Chaplin "did knowingly, wilfully, unlawfully, and feloniously transport and cause to be transported" Joan Barry "with the intent and purpose . . . of having [her] . . . engage in illicit sex relations with him." The indictment contained two counts: one for the train ticket to New York City and the other for the return ticket.

The remaining three indictments all named others with Chaplin and alleged that Joan Barry's right to due process, guaranteed by the Fourteenth Amendment to the Constitution, were violated in her January and May arrests. The first charged Chaplin, Beverly Hills police detective W. W. White, and municipal judge Charles Griffin of depriving Barry of her civil rights (violation of Title 18, Section 52 of the U.S. Code) when she was induced to plead guilty of vagrancy and taken to the train station in January. The second was similar: it alleged violation of Title 18, Section 51, and charged that Chaplin, his friend Robert Arden, and Detective White cooperated in denying Barry her civil rights in the same incident. Finally, in the longest and most complex indictment, alleging violation of Title 18, Section 88, seven people were accused of conspiring to deny Barry her civil rights both in the January incident and in May, when she was arrested for violating her probation and sentenced to thirty days in jail. The seven were Chaplin, Arden, Detective White, Judge Griffin, and three others: police sergeant Claude Marple, police matron Jessie Billie Reno, and

Chaplin's friend Tim Durant. If Chaplin were convicted on all four counts, he faced up to twenty-three years in prison and fines up to $26,000.[20]

After being fingerprinted (and photographed) on February 14, Chaplin was brought to trial under the Mann Act charges beginning on March 21. Both Barry and Chaplin testified. According to his lawyer, Jerry Giesler, Chaplin was excellent, "the best witness I've ever seen in a law court." Even when he was merely sitting at the counsel table, Geisler continued, "He looked helpless, friendless and wistful, as he sat there with the weight of the whole United States Government against him."[21] Apparently the jury was also impressed with Chaplin the witness and with Giesler's argument that Chaplin had no immoral intent when giving Barry train tickets. On April 4, after deliberating 6 hours and 58 minutes and going through four ballots, the jury returned a not guilty decision. Chaplin was acquitted.[22]

The three other federal indictments never came to trial. The civil rights and conspiracy charges were being prepared for trial in May, but both the Department of Justice in Washington and the U.S. district attorney's office in Los Angeles began to doubt the wisdom of bringing the case to trial because of flimsy evidence, particularly after Judge J.F.T. O'Connor, who also heard the Mann Act trial, dismissed all charges against Judge Griffin following a hearing. On May 5 Assistant Attorney General Clark directed District Attorney Carr in Los Angeles to drop all remaining charges against Chaplin and others not already cleared. Special Agent Hood, after talking with Carr, summed up Clark's justification for the decision in a May 11 memo to Hoover: "Carr said that the letter continued to the effect that he, Carr, knew the Department from the very beginning thought the cases against Subject [Chaplin] were weak, but had deferred to his judgment until the Department had a chance to go over all the evidence. Now that the evidence had been reviewed, the Department has decided that there is no case."[23] Thus Chaplin's problems with the federal court system over the Barry case were over.

Yet, the California paternity suit was not. Four months after the October 2 birth of Barry's daughter—and just after the indictments against Chaplin on federal charges had hit the newspapers—Chaplin, Barry, and Carole Ann had submitted to blood tests. Three doctors, one neutral, one hired by Barry, and one by Chaplin, analyzed the results. On 16 February 1944, the day after Chaplin's fingerprinting drew hordes of photographers, the doctors concurred that the blood tests proved Chaplin could not have been the father of the child. Chaplin, whose blood type was O (Barry's was A), could not possibly have fathered Carole Ann, whose blood type was B. Barry's lawyer, John Irwin, following the agreement he had reached with Chaplin's lawyers, was about to drop the charge. Barry, however, had other ideas. She decided to pursue the case and, after Irwin refused to continue as her lawyer, hired the rancorous seventy-seven-year-old Joseph Scott.[24]

Scott, a rangy, beetle-browed firebrand, decided that Chaplin must be brought to trial on the paternity charge and that he must be handled roughly. After Scott and Giesler took a week just to choose the jury, the case began December 19. Chaplin denied the paternity charges. Scott resorted to some name calling in the courtroom, and termed Chaplin a "pestiferous, lecherous hound," "a little runt of a Svengali" who lied "like a cheap Cockney cad," and more. The tactics, however, did not work. After deliberating four and a half hours on January 3 and nearly one more full day on January 4, the jury returned deadlocked, 7 votes to 5 in favor of Chaplin.[25]

Scott insisted on a retrial, which began 12 April 1945 and lasted through April 17. Chaplin again took the witness stand and denied the charges. In the course of the trial the prosecution called J. Paul Getty, among others, as a witness. He denied ever having sexual intercourse with Barry (he was suspected since Barry had visited Tulsa in November 1942 and in early January 1943). This jury voted 9 to 3 that Chaplin was the father and liable for child support, despite the findings of the blood tests, which at that time California did not accept as admissible evidence in paternity suit trials. Chaplin was clearly upset, but the next day Scott and Barry, who had been asking for $50,000 in fees and $1,500 per month for Carole Ann, had their turn to be disappointed. The court ordered Chaplin to pay Barry $5,000 in fees and $75 per week child support until Carole Ann reached the age of twenty-one.[26]

Chaplin and his lawyers immediately began to seek an appeal to reverse what they felt was a clear miscarriage of justice. The California state court system, however, disagreed. On June 6 Chaplin was denied a new trial on the paternity suit charges. The cases brought by Barry and by the federal government against Chaplin were finally closed. Because of the tempest of publicity Chaplin received from the time the paternity suit was filed in June 1943, however, the Joan Barry case was to lie close to the surface of the American public imagination for a long time and contributed to the decline in Chaplin's star image that would eventually separate him from the country he had called home since 1913.

Chaplin, Barry, and the
Gossip Columnists

Chaplin's legal difficulties in the Barry affair, however much they soured him on the American legal system, had little affect on his star image. However, the press coverage of those legal difficulties greatly affected his declining star image, for these reports presented Chaplin's problems in great detail to the American public. We have discussed Chaplin's first three divorces and seen that the Mildred Harris divorce received almost no press coverage; the divorce from Lita Grey, although treated prominently in the press, generated considerable sympathy for Chaplin in some quarters; and the quiet divorce from Paulette Goddard elicited no great publicity or criticism. In contrast, nearly all the press coverage of the Joan Barry affair, except for that of the small circulation left-wing press, was hostile to Chaplin. A look at coverage by the gossip columnists and the national mass press reveals how critically Chaplin was portrayed at this time.

Beginning in Hollywood as early as the 1910s, gossip columnists became particularly powerful in making and breaking movie stars. The essential function of the gossip columnist during the studio era was to chat to his or her readers about Hollywood: who would appear in a new picture, whose career was blossoming or withering, who was in love with whom, and so on. When a scandal hit, the columnist sought the "inside story" and often took sides while providing readers information about the course of events. The Barry-Chaplin situation was certain to draw the attention of the gossip columnists. Yet it also did more. To a surprising degree, not only did gossip columnists generate negative publicity against Chaplin in the Barry case, but two in particular even befriended Barry, enabling "her" story to be told, and provided the FBI with testimony that helped the federal government in its attempt to convict Chaplin on Mann Act and civil rights charges. The two primary gossip columnists to take up pens against Chaplin were Hedda Hopper (of the *Los Angeles Times*) and Florabel Muir (of the *New York Daily News*), both of whom were based in Hollywood and wrote columns widely syndicated in newspapers around the nation.[27]

Hopper, with Louella Parsons, was one of the two most prominent and powerful gossip columnists in Hollywood in the 1940s. A failed actress, she was also interested in politics and ran unsuccessfully for the Los Angeles County Central Committee in 1932 as a Republican. Her weekly column on Hollywood, which she began for the *Washington Post* in 1935, became more influential when, in 1938, the *Los An-*

geles Times picked it up in syndication. From that point on she became an important local outlet for the movie producers.[28]

Although Hopper did print friendly squibs about Chaplin as late as 1939, she came to dislike him for two reasons. First, she disagreed with his progressive politics. An avowed isolationist (even for a time after World War II broke out), she was suspicious of *The Great Dictator* and Chaplin's second front activities. As a political conservative who in her columns defended the right-wing Motion Picture Alliance for the Preservation of American Ideals, attacked the leftist Writer's Guild, and worried about the threats of domestic communism throughout the war, Hopper had little in common politically with Chaplin.[29]

Second, Hopper disliked Chaplin because he didn't truckle to gossip columnists, as so many stars and aspiring stars did. Though the fan magazines in the mid-1910s were, as we have seen, instrumental in helping to build the popularity of Chaplin's star image, by the 1920s his fame had become so widespread and his economic situation so independent that he didn't have to beat the bushes for publicity. Instead, the publicists came to him whenever he desired. For example, the *New York Times* movie columnists regularly gave Chaplin generous advance articles on all his upcoming films from *The Gold Rush* on, sometimes a year or more before the films were released. This enabled Chaplin to keep aloof in the era of gossip columnists. Since they liked power and recognition as much as many movie stars did, Chaplin's attitude easily stirred up their antagonism.

Given her distaste for Chaplin, Hopper jumped at the chance to attack him over the Barry case. She and Florabel Muir were in the thick of the case right from the beginning, not only through their columns but even through their personal interactions with Barry.

Sometime in May 1943, after Chaplin had Barry arrested for harassing him, Barry or her mother, seeking press coverage, contacted Hopper. Hopper showed great interest and won the trust of Barry and her mother so fully that by the end of the month Barry seemed to be in a three-party conversation with Chaplin and Hopper. In her long interview with FBI agents, Barry recalled that after Chaplin's attorneys put her off on Memorial Day, "I called home and they said that my mother had gone up to Hedda Hopper's, . . . and I called her there and Florabel [Muir] was there." Barry then had Chaplin's butler, Edward Chaney, drive her to Hopper's, and a few days later the paternity suit was filed. From the time of the Memorial Day visit Hopper and Muir became advocates in the press in support of Barry's case.[30]

The first key document in their case for Barry was Hopper's column of 3 June 1943: the same day Barry's lawyer filed the paternity suit.

Although the column purported to treat the "latest development on the Joan Barry–Charlie Chaplin situation," a "cozy little luncheon" at Chaplin's poolside, it also aimed to discredit Chaplin on a number of fronts. Some charges it made were entirely unrelated to the case: that Chaplin had never become a U.S. citizen; that Chaplin refused when asked to contribute to the Motion Picture Relief Fund Home; that Chaplin gave only $100 when asked to contribute to the Red Cross; that Chaplin called for a second front (presumably referring to his October 1942 appearance) when the policy "was already arranged by the American and British Governments." In a display of anti-Semitism, Hopper went on to criticize Chaplin for denying that he was Jewish. "Jews should be proud of their heritage," she wrote sanctimoniously. "Christ was a Jew." (Ironically, she was apparently unaware that Chaplin was not Jewish.) Hopper then quoted an earlier column, written when Barry's role in *Shadow and Substance* was announced, in which she congratulated Barry but warned her about Chaplin's proclivities: "There've been many Chaplin leading ladies before you. All got the same package with the same trimmings." The column concludes in a belligerent tone, asking a series of questions: "Will her child have a name? What is to become of that child and its mother, Joan Barry? Those are the questions Hollywood is asking today. Those are the questions Hollywood has a right to ask and not only hope for an answer but to demand one."[31]

Hopper struck again in her June 22 column. In it she noted that since "the Chaplin business has simmered down to a slow boil," she thought it useful to pass along the contents of a letter she received from "an important Chicago man." It read in part: "Chaplin should keep constantly in mind that he is not a citizen, merely a guest, and should conduct himself as a guest. Up to this point of exposure he had a right to become a citizen. But I doubt that he could now become one. I'm sure the laws of our country include moral turpitude as good and sufficient grounds for the deportation of an alien." The letter also criticized Chaplin's second front speeches, which involved him, according to the letter, in "matters for which he has neither been trained nor sufficiently well versed to talk intelligently." It concluded by doubting "if his native England would put up with an American guest in that country daring to be so bold." By quoting the letter at such length, Hopper was helping to establish a pattern that became more pronounced at time went by: the tendency to criticize Chaplin for both his politics and his alleged immorality, and to link the two. To increasing numbers of people after the Barry case broke, Chaplin's moral behavior was impolitic and his politics were immoral.[32]

Muir also defended Barry in her columns. Her 2 June 1944 column carried a story, like Hopper's, about Barry's luncheon with Chaplin. According to Muir, "Joan's momma is saying it would be nice—with a baby on the way—if Joan and Chaplin would wed." After the initial June publicity of the paternity suit died down, the case didn't get much coverage until Barry's baby was born in early October. Muir was at the forefront here. On October 10 she did an article called "Jane Doe Chaplin and Tests for Paternity." The article contained considerable information about the blood tests that would be done when the baby was four months old. But it also gave some prominence to the name of radio commentator Robert Arden when it outlined the Barry–Chaplin dealings the previous December and January. Muir wrote that Arden had used other names, including Rudolf Kleiger, a telling detail, for the same information later appears regularly in FBI files, which suggests that Muir was unknowingly or, more likely, knowingly providing information to the agency. Indeed, the FBI report from Los Angeles to Washington of 9 November 1943 contained in its section on Robert Arden some information from Muir given to the FBI through an unnamed "Source A."[33]

Hopper continued to criticize Chaplin in her columns in late 1943. She claimed in October, for example, that employees she visited at the Douglas Aircraft plant disliked Chaplin and, a few days later, she made veiled charges that Chaplin was guilty of casting-couch promiscuity. Just after Christmas Hopper commented that there was no truth to the rumor that Barry and Chaplin would settle the paternity suit out of court. Chaplin surely had a busy year, she added, struggling with the Barry case and "marrying a girl who just turned 18. . . . From things I learned, Charlie, who contributed $25,000 to the Communist cause and $100 to the Red Cross, soon will find himself involved with something about as serious as the Barry case." These imprecise charges about contributions would later end up in FBI files on Chaplin as a security risk, which will be discussed in Chapter 9. Hopper's final cryptic comment in this column suggests she had inside information about the Mann Act and civil rights charges that were soon to be taken before the grand jury.[34]

This was entirely likely, for both Hopper and Muir were involved in the legal proceedings against Chaplin. In early January 1944 Muir was interviewed by District Attorney Carr and FBI agents as they prepared the civil rights charges against Chaplin. When she told them that Chaplin's friends Tim Durant and Minna Wallis had secured a former lawyer of Chaplin's for Barry when she was dealing with the police in May 1943, Special Agent Hood telegrammed Hoover about the incident and said that Muir might "be used as a witness" because of that evidence. And indeed she was. On January 14 Muir, Hopper, and FBI agent Frank H. Angell, who had been writing the majority of the reports in Los Angeles for Hoover, all testified before the grand jury.[35]

Muir's support for Barry did not end here. At the end of January she was trying to help Barry control her drinking problem. Barry's lawyer, John J. Irwin, had asked Muir to talk with Barry and convince the young mother that appearing drunk in public could result in bad publicity and damage her chances in the upcoming trials. In the same meeting Muir discouraged Barry from making a trip to Mexico and then tried to get Barry's mother to take a short vacation, which Muir— aware of the tensions between Barry and her mother—thought might alleviate some of Barry's anxieties.[36]

Significantly, though Hopper criticized Chaplin once again in a January column, she did not mention him in February. On the one hand, the newspaper headlines made such references less necessary. On the other, it was also in February that the results of the blood tests, which established that Chaplin could not have been the child's father, were made public, thus perhaps quelling some of her public vitriol for Chaplin. In March, however, in a section of her column headed "Step Too Far," Hopper quoted from a "Beverly Hills scratch sheet" (Rob Wagner's *Script*, to be discussed below). "There are men and women in far corners of the world who have never heard of Jesus Christ," Wagner had written, "yet they know and love Chaplin." To which Hopper responded, "I'm wondering how the coupling of the buffoon's name with that of Diety [*sic*] will improve his standing with the public, whose good opinion he is assiduously courting for the first time." As the Mann Act trial was about to begin, Hopper sought to discredit Chaplin by suggesting that he was trying to manipulate the press to help him win his trial. In the same column she countered Wagner's assertion that "the Fascist clique is hounding" Chaplin. She asked, "Lord love us, Eddie Hoover, isn't that a new role for you and your FBI?"[37]

After the Mann Act trial began and Chaplin was eventually acquitted, Hopper wrote twice more on Chaplin. The first occasion was after a visit to the courtroom. Here she subtly attacked Chaplin's cause by stressing how slick his attorney was; the only way Chaplin could wriggle out of the charges, she implied, was to hire a famed Hollywood trial lawyer. After Chaplin's acquittal on April 4, Hopper waited nearly a week before responding. When she did, it was to charge again that the only way Chaplin could get off the hook was through deception. "Charlie Chaplin did a complete about face to members of the press during his trial," Hopper wrote. "He's always been the least cooperative star. . . . At night clubs he tells snapshot boys when to shoot and how often but at the trial he and Jerry Giesler hired a press agent. Charlie was ready, willing, and posed for everything."[38]

In one sense, of course, Hopper was right. Chaplin and Giesler had hired a press agent for the Mann Act trials, Giesler surmising accurately that Chaplin's star image was rapidly tarnishing and that it would have to be polished during the trials or Chaplin could be in for serious problems. But Hopper's treatment, coming as it did after a verdict was reached, was also an attempt to undermine the decision and persist in her attacks on Chaplin's reputation despite his acquittal.

Perhaps the most bizarre chapter in the story of Hopper's vendetta against Chaplin is contained in a four-page letter from Agent Hood to his chief, Hoover, in April. Hood takes up several topics, one particularly relevant here. Evidently a columnist for the *Hollywood Reporter* had called an FBI agent and reported the following story. Hopper had allegedly told Buddy Rogers, Mary Pickford's husband, that Chaplin's jury had been bought off, and Rogers asked for evidence. Hopper then told Rogers of a call she had received from a woman who had experienced a vision in which she had seen members of the Chaplin jury discussing a payoff from Chaplin. The woman also told Hopper that although she wasn't able to identify any of the jury members individually, she would give it more thought. On the basis of this call, Hopper was spreading the rumor. Even the zealous FBI agents in Los Angeles were skeptical: in his understated FBI prose, Hood told Hoover, "It is contemplated that no further inquiry will be made along this line unless more specific information is obtained."[39]

The same letter also provided evidence that Muir was continuing her investigation of the Barry–Chaplin case and feeding information to the FBI. Hood reminded Hoover that Muir "has followed this case from the beginning, and . . . has previously been referred to in previous communications to you." In this instance, Muir had called Agent Angell and reported to him that "rumor among the press representatives here in Los Angeles was to the effect that the government was going to dismiss the remaining charges against Chaplin, et al. because of the acquittal Chaplin received under the Mann Act charges." In this case, of course, Muir proved prophetic, for charges were dropped, but the letter also offers firm evidence that the gossip columnists were providing the FBI with information in the Barry–Chaplin investigations.[40]

Though Muir and Hopper ran out of steam concerning the Barry–

Chaplin case after Chaplin's federal charges were dropped, Hopper visited the courtroom again after the California state paternity trial began. Her resulting story, the lead in her column of December 22, typified her distaste for Chaplin. The brief reference described Chaplin as "no longer suave, simple and appealing but overacting frightfully" and contrasted him with "the center of attraction," Carole Ann: "a little innocent baby, cooing because she didn't know what it was all about."[41]

It is striking how influential Hopper and Muir were in the Barry–Chaplin situation, and not simply because of their writings. Not only did they befriend Barry, helping to put her plight before their reading public and seeking to help her control her behavior, but they also testified in her defense before the grand jury and shared information on her behalf with the FBI. Chaplin's star image, which at one time seemed unassailable, was under attack. It was also coming to be dominated much more by Chaplin the man—his views and his private activities—than by the lovable Charlie.

The Press and the Barry–Chaplin Story

The rest of the press gave the Barry–Chaplin story widespread coverage at certain crucial points. This gave it even greater prominence—often front-page headline coverage—and thus placed Chaplin's name and face before more people than the gossip columnists reached in their syndicated columns. The coverage significantly affected Chaplin's star image, for what was reported was largely negative toward Chaplin in the mass circulation press, though generally sympathetic in the small circulation leftist press. We will focus here on how a major daily newspaper, the *Chicago Tribune*, and the two most prominent U.S. mass magazines, *Time* and *Newsweek*, treated the case, in contrast to the treatment found in the leftist press.

Owned by the politically conservative McCormick family, the *Chicago Tribune* was a staid, conservative newspaper in the 1940s in both its editorial stance and its format. Of the two mass magazines, *Time*, edited by Henry Luce, had the larger circulation and was generally considered conservative in its presentation of the week's news. *Newsweek* generally tended to be more middle of the road.

It must be stressed that the *Chicago Tribune* was by no stretch of the imagination a sensationalist purveyor of yellow journalism. This being the case, one might expect that its treatment of the Barry–Chaplin story would be somewhat restrained. It is also true, however, that since Chaplin's politics contrasted sharply with the editorial line of the pa-

22. *Chicago Tribune* headline on 11 February 1944. Copyright
© 1987, Chicago Tribune Company, all rights reserved,
used with permission.

per, it had some reason to play up the story in hopes of discrediting Chaplin. Of these two contrary impulses, the latter won out.

News treatment of the Barry–Chaplin case in the *Tribune* and the two magazines peaked four times: (1) the indictment, fingerprinting, and blood-test stages in February 1944; (2) the Mann Act trials in late March and early April; (3) the first paternity suit trial in December 1944 and early January 1945; and (4) to a lesser extent, the second paternity suit trial in April 1945. Even though the coverage took place during the war years, when news from battle zones demanded press attention, the Chaplin case very often dominated the front page in the *Tribune* and figured prominently in weekly news magazine stories.

This was certainly the case when the indictment story first broke. On February 11 the lead headline in the *Tribune*, covering the entire top of page one, was "U.S. Jury Indicts Chaplin" (see Figure 22).[42] The brief story summarized the indictments, listed the penalties Chaplin might receive if convicted, and referred to Chaplin as the "white haired English alien." Four days later an equally large headline dominated page one: "Fingerprint, Book Chaplin in Barry Case." The subtitle was also conspicuous and was subtly critical: "Nervous and Testy on Appearance." For the first time, Chaplin's picture appeared in the

214

23. Chaplin fingerprinted after indictment, 1944. Wide World Photo.

photograph section, located on the back page of section one. In it, an obviously stressed Chaplin was shown being fingerprinted (see Figure 23). The photograph was the first of a number of shots used in the *Tribune*'s picture section throughout the case.

Although the weekly mass magazines, of course, wrote fewer articles than the newspapers on the Barry–Chaplin situation, *Newsweek* printed a devastating story following the indictment. The article, "Chaplin as Villain" (21 February 1944), was supplemented with five pictures: Barry on the witness stand, presumably during her grand jury testimony; an unflattering picture of Chaplin, looking inebriated while dining with Oona Chaplin; and three smaller pictures of Chaplin's previous three wives. The article called the Barry case the "biggest public relations scandal since the Fatty Arbuckle murder trial in 1921." Besides noting that Chaplin, if convicted, faced up to twenty-three years in jail, fines of $26,000, and even possible deportation, *Newsweek* revealed that Barry's situation had been publicized by Hedda Hopper and "veteran sob sister" Florabel Muir. The essay biased its audience against Chaplin when it wrote that the film industry collectively "felt no personal love for Chaplin—because of his egotism, intellectual pretensions, niggardliness, and failure to take part in Hollywood enter-

215

tainment plans for the [armed] services." Appearing less than a month before the Mann Act trials were about to begin, this article boded ill for Chaplin's star image.[43]

Almost as damaging as the coverage of the indictment was the coverage of the Mann Act trials, which seemed designed to create sympathy for Barry and antipathy for Chaplin. The *Tribune*'s first article covering the trial typified this bias. The headline covering the top of the front page on March 22 read, "Chaplin Begins Nervous Role at Bar of Law." The physical description of Chaplin in the accompanying text painted an unattractive picture. His face, according to the reporter, was "heavy jowled, lined, and dissipated." His eyes were "small" and his figure "stocky." In addition, the article stressed something that Hopper had mentioned: that Chaplin had hired a press agent to help control his client's public image. The job of Casey Shawhan, according to the article, was "to feed, wine, and placate members of the press covering the trial." By mentioning Chaplin's strategy, the *Tribune*'s reporter blunted its effectiveness.

From then to the end of the trial, the *Tribune* continued to use large headlines that spanned the top of the front page each day after testimony was given. Those headlines included "Barry–Chaplin Tryst Told" (March 24); "Judge Shields Joan's Past" (March 25); "Denies Chaplin Blackmail" (March 29); "Chaplin Takes Stand Today" (March 30); "Joan Tells Chaplin Threat" (April 1); and "U.S. Jury Acquits Chaplin!" (April 4). The only exception to this headline size came on the day after Chaplin testified. In this case, the *Tribune* printed a front-page story with a headline smaller than the rest—"Chaplin Tells His Story, Denies All." It also undercut Chaplin in the accompanying story. It mocked Chaplin's "performance" on the stand and commented ironically after describing his testimony: "Ah. The sorrow of it!" The negative bias against Chaplin in the daily accounts of the trial was accentuated by the breadth of the coverage: front-page stories, huge headlines, pictures in the photo section a number of times, and relatively long transcripts of sometimes sensationalistic testimony on the inside pages.

Though *Newsweek* ran only one article about Chaplin's testimony during the Mann Act trial, it called the testimony "the most important performance of his life," subtly suggesting that he would not be telling the truth but rather simply acting to sway the jury. *Time*'s first reference to the Barry–Chaplin affair came shortly after the Mann Act trial began, and its treatment, like *Newsweek*'s, denigrated Chaplin. According to *Time*, Barry's affair with Chaplin "fitted into a familiar pattern," which, *Time* implied, was that Chaplin pursued and later abandoned women at will. The article also described Chaplin as "a dapper grey multimillionaire of 54, widely envied in Hollywood for his unassailable arrogance and for his affairs with a succession of pretty young 'proteges.' "[44]

After Chaplin's acquittal on the Mann Act charges, the *Tribune* was relatively quiet about Chaplin until the jury was selected for Chaplin's first paternity trial in December, which, of the whole Barry affair, generated the most vituperative comments about Chaplin. The press covered it closely. During the trial, the *Tribune* gave the story front-page coverage on six of seven days, sometimes with large, full-width headlines. Again, the *Tribune* regularly reprinted testimony on inside pages during this trial, some of which was particularly juicy because of the florid, accusatory rhetoric of Barry's lawyer, Joseph Scott. One notable bias in the *Tribune*'s coverage of this case was the report on the hung jury. After consistent front-page coverage throughout the trial, the *Tribune* buried the outcome—a hung jury tipped 7–5 in Chaplin's favor—on page six.

Newsweek did not run a report on the first trial and its outcome, but *Time* carried two articles in consecutive weeks. The first, titled "Just a Peter Pan," aimed directly at Chaplin. With his "platinum hair damp against his perspiring forehead," Chaplin, it wrote, felt himself an "ill-used man." Calling the affair a "kind of profane love story the Hays Office has not allowed Hollywood to film for years," *Time*—blending the political with the sexual—reported that Chaplin had sought to inculcate in Barry proper antifascist attitudes. Then it quoted from one of Barry's letters to Chaplin: "Right you are, Charles. We should destroy soulless, unimaginative, money-mad hypocrites who boast of breeding but are more ill-mannered than the lowest serf." From the context, it is evident that *Time* believed Chaplin deserved this denunciation as much as any fascist. The next week *Time* carried a second piece, which concentrated on Scott's colorful criticisms of Chaplin. One notable quote was his assertion that Chaplin "goes around fornicating . . . with the same aplomb that the average man orders bacon and eggs for breakfast."[45] Such articles, so widely distributed, were key in helping to shape the image of Chaplin as an immoral womanizer.

The second paternity trial received less coverage in the *Tribune*. Fortunately for Chaplin—since the outcome went against him—this trial fell victim to a major story: the death of Franklin D. Roosevelt. In fact, the first two days of the retrial in April 1945 escaped notice in the *Tribune* because of Roosevelt's death. The second trial was also shorter and less flamboyant than the first. The only front-page story in the

Tribune was the April 19 report on the trial's outcome. There, a small-ish headline announced: "Rule Chaplin Must Pay $75/Week to Baby."

Much the same was true with *Newsweek* and *Time*. Just after the second trial, *Newsweek* carried just one rather straightforward report on both trials. It summarized the outcome of each, then listed the terms of the final settlement. It only strayed from this when it quoted some of Scott's denunciations of Chaplin in the first trial (repeating the "Piccadilly pimp" accusation, among others). *Time*'s final word on the matter was a short report on 30 July. The article also seemed designed to portray Chaplin in a negative light. It noted that the court had ordered Chaplin to pay his $75 per week child support payment while the case was being appealed, and also mentioned that Chaplin had estimated his net worth at $3 million but was still balking at the payments. *Time* thus reinforced the picture of Chaplin's cheapness that they had explicitly commented on in their first article.[46]

Several points can be made about the press coverage of the Barry–Chaplin story. First, its prominence in the *Chicago Tribune* was striking: the story not only received almost constant front-page coverage but even earned the day's lead headline with surprising frequency. Second, both the newspaper and especially the mass magazines tended to highlight charges and testimony and downplay the results of the trial, particularly when the outcome favored Chaplin. (Chaplin was taught a lesson learned by many public figures in America: an indictment lingers in the public mind long after an acquittal.) Third, Chaplin's star image was affected most strongly and negatively by the story of the indictments and the charges leveled against Chaplin in the trials, particularly in the first paternity suit, when Scott skewered Chaplin with his pointed language.

One can gauge how strongly the dominant press came out against Chaplin by looking briefly at the way that the leftist press understood the issues involved. Two examples will suffice: an article in *Script* and an editorial by Mike Gold in the *Daily Worker*.

Script, a small Beverly Hills publication on movies that came out twice a month, was edited by Rob Wagner, a friend and former employee of Chaplin's who held leftist political sympathies. Shortly before the Mann Act trials began, *Script* published a lead article entitled "The Press: Its Own Worst Enemy," the article Hopper responded to when she talked about the fascist charges in a "Beverly Hills scratch sheet."[47] The essay sought to demonstrate how Chaplin had become a victim of "character assassination by the press." Among other things, it pointed out how the influential *Variety* carried "a lengthy editorial in effect asking the industry to boot Chaplin out," while the same day "the newspapers carried the news that exonerated the actor of the paternity charges." The essay also inquired why federal officials would choose Chaplin as a target for civil rights charges after the paternity suit was filed, when so many paternity suits are filed with no federal involvement. The answer, it said, was that "Chaplin is a shining target for the Fascist clique in America. He is an artist, a liberal artist who also is articulate. When he apeaks, through the medium of films, his audience numbers in the hundreds of millions." In making *The Great Dictator*, Wagner argued, Chaplin made himself a threat to the fascists, even those in America "who have leanings toward Fascism, under no matter what name." And in the Barry case, these domestic fascists and fascist sympathizers found a convenient situation that enabled them to discredit Chaplin's name. The essay thus placed the federal case against Chaplin in a political perspective and suggested a link between the moral and legal attacks against Chaplin on the one hand and ulterior political yearnings to discredit him on the other. It concluded by calling on its readers to "withhold judgment of Charles Spencer Chaplin. For decency's sake."

A similar interpretation was expressed in a *Daily Worker* editorial by Mike Gold, the same critic who had excoriated Thornton Wilder and urged a politically radical art in the early 1930s. His article, "Charge It," was published after the first paternity trial had returned with a hung jury and a retrial was scheduled.[48] Gold was briefer and blunter than the *Script* essay. The Barry charge, he said, "fits into the campaign for Chaplin's destruction running for years in the Hearst, McCormick fascist press of America." Though Chaplin as the lovable tramp had alienated no one, Gold argued, as soon as he made *The Great Dictator*, he alienated the right wing in America and abroad, so that by 1945 they "hate him bitterly from Berlin to Los Angeles." The Barry trials and the press coverage of it were, for Gold, simply manifestations of this political attack on Chaplin.

This tendency to see Chaplin's problems as a result of domestic political machinations was a keynote of the leftist interpretation of the Barry case, and a view far removed from the analysis and coverage offered by the dominant press. Instead of portraying Chaplin as a moral menace, the Left was beginning to look at him as a political victim.

To say that the press coverage of the Barry case damaged Chaplin's star image is no startling news. It is significant, however, that the story's prominence in major newspapers and mass magazines, as well as the consistently negative (or at best neutral) portrayal of Chaplin in them, was very different from the press coverage of the Harris divorce, the Goddard divorce, and even the divorce from Grey, over which the press was much more split, with many columnists and reporters coming to Chaplin's defense, even though the Grey divorce, too, received widespread coverage.

One more important outcome of the trial and the press coverage of it has been for the most part overlooked. Chaplin, a proud and stubborn man, suffered great humiliation for nearly two years during the Barry charges and trials; for some of that time he was even threatened with the possibility of imprisonment. Having become an active antifascist a relatively short time before, Chaplin was prone to believe interpretations, like those in the leftist articles discussed above, that portrayed him as a victim of domestic fascist activities. In his autobiography he mentions being disappointed that his lawyer Jerry Giesler failed to follow up a letter from a Catholic priest in San Francisco who claimed to have evidence that Barry was being used by a domestic fascist group (MA, p. 426). People who see themselves as victims of political pressures often tend to become more firmly attached to their views, even to the point of martyrdom. There is considerable evidence that Chaplin's political opinions became more rigid—and perhaps more simplistically Manichaean—as a result of the Barry trials and press coverage. To understand Chaplin's political views and activities during and immediately after World War II and the effect they had both on his work and, ultimately, on his unraveling star image in America, we must examine his next film, *Monsieur Verdoux*.

8

Monsieur Verdoux and the Cold War:
Irreconcilable Differences

The Hollywood Emigrés

Though the Barry affair generated a great deal of public hostility toward Chaplin, he did get support from one group of personal friends as he battled in the courts. "During the trial," he wrote in his autobiography, "we had been surrounded by many dear friends—all of them loyal and sympathetic. Salka Viertel, the Clifford Odetses, the Hanns Eislers, the Feuchtwangers and many others" (MA, p. 434). Chaplin goes on to describe the prominent literati who often gathered at Viertel's salon in Santa Monica: Thomas Mann, Bertolt Brecht, Lion Feuchtwanger, Stephen Spender, and others. The fact that most of these people were exiles, and a number of them German refugees forced to flee by Hitler's policies, is significant: a strong case can be made that Chaplin's progressive, antifascist political and social views during the 1940s were shaped through and solidified by his interactions with this immigrant community in Hollywood and with domestic American leftists like Clifford Odets and Donald Ogden Stewart. Furthermore, though these associations may not have been widely known around the country, they certainly were in the movie community, and they gave gossip columnists like Hopper more reason to attack Chaplin's star image on political grounds. By examining Chaplin's relationships with four of this emigré group—Salka Viertel, Lion Feuchtwanger, Bertolt Brecht, and Hanns Eisler—and the general political perspective they shared during this period, we can more fully understand the shape of Chaplin's world view as he conceived, thought about, and developed the film that became *Monsieur Verdoux*.

The hegira of political refugees from Europe to America in the 1930s, and the story of the part played by these refugees in American culture since that time, has been the subject of considerable attention in the past several years.[1] One can hardly imagine the course of American intellectual life in the postwar era, for example, without the contributions of Erik Erikson, Bruno Bettelheim, Erich Fromm, Hannah Arendt, Paul Lazarsfeld, Hans Morgenthau, Erwin Panofsky, Erich

Auerbach, Roman Jakobson, and Paul Tillich. The group with which Chaplin associated in Hollywood was different from the larger refugee community in two ways: it was made up primarily of artists, and the politics of the group in general emphasized a more distinctively leftist and activist antifascism.

Of the emigrés Chaplin knew best (and mentioned in his autobiography), nearly all—understandably, given Chaplin's orientation and profession—were involved in the arts. Salka Viertel, for example, was an actress who became a screenwriter best known for a number of Greta Garbo films, including *Queen Christina* and *Anna Karenina*. She had come with her husband Berthold to California in 1927, when F. W. Murnau asked him to collaborate on a script. Before directing a number of films in Hollywood, Berthold Viertel had established himself in Germany as a poet, playwright, and novelist. Hanns Eisler, one of Chaplin's closer associates, was a composer who later wrote the national anthem of East Germany. Bertolt Brecht, the noted playwright and poet who is today the best known of this group, also collaborated with Eisler on some musical pieces. Lion Feuchtwanger, though not much remembered now, was a novelist whose work was widely read in the 1930s.

Not every German refugee in America or in the Los Angeles area was a dedicated political leftist. In fact, some Germans preferred to remain silent on political matters after arriving in the country they willingly or unwillingly had adopted. Some were even politically conservative: one right-wing group in Los Angeles, an assemblage Otto Preminger called "the FBI group," often met at the home of the wealthy Lady Elsi Mendl, for example. Nevertheless, those forced from their homelands due to the raging racial policies of Hitler were on the whole actively antifascist. And as Anthony Heilbut has observed, the artists and radicals among the refugees "saw themselves as vanguardists, anticipating a future that would transcend the cultural and political limits of the present." Heilbut called the Viertel home in Santa Monica—just up the street from the ocean—the "real salon" in Hollywood, the place peopled by "the same group of left-wing bohemian filmmakers and writers that had come together at the Romanische Café" in Berlin in the 1920s.[2] That this group of refugee artists admired the director of *Modern Times* and *The Great Dictator* was no surprise.

The leftist, antifascist political inclination of Feuchtwanger, Brecht, and the Viertels was well established. Feuchtwanger had become known in Europe and America in part for his novel *The Oppermanns* (1934), an early antifascist work that dealt with a wealthy German Jewish family forced into political awareness and opposition to Hitler. While living in France from 1933 to 1940, Feuchtwanger was, according to one scholar, "one of the chief Socialist propagandists" against the Hitler regime. Brecht and Eisler, who knew one another well, were both Marxists whose political views were established in the 1920s, with Brecht involved in trying to incorporate his political views into drama and Eisler, into music. Salka Viertel, though probably less systematically radical than the other three, was nevertheless an ardent antifascist. Not only was she active with Donald Ogden Stewart in the founding of the Hollywood Anti-Nazi League in 1936, but she also was a driving force in the establishment of the European Film Fund, a group established in 1940 that pressed studio heads to hire refugee writers on one-year contracts so they could escape Europe. In her memoir of the period, *The Kindness of Strangers*, Viertel described, somewhat tongue in cheek, the political diversity in her family: "Berthold had his own personal kind of socialism, Peter was a New Dealer, I was a 'premature anti-Fascist,' Thomas a Democrat and Hans a Trotskyite." As a whole, this group was considerably more sympathetic to the Soviet Union and more enthusiastic about the Soviet–American alliance during World War II than the group surrounding Thomas Mann, which tended to combine its antifascism with a political liberalism that was skeptical of socialist ideology.[3]

Except for the Viertels, who had lived in the Los Angeles area from the late 1920s, these Germans all arrived in Los Angeles in the early 1940s: Feuchtwanger and his wife Marta in January 1941, Brecht in July 1941, and Eisler in April 1942.[4] It was Salka Viertel who helped bring the emigrés and Chaplin together. She had first met Chaplin in the late 1930s when seated next to him at a dinner. He was then working on *The Great Dictator*, and she recalls that "he was possessed by his work, and it was captivating to watch his never-ceasing absorption, his constant improvising of situations." After Barry's paternity suit was filed, Viertel saw Chaplin "quite often," and during this period Chaplin met and also became close, in varying degrees, to Feuchtwanger, Brecht, and Eisler. Chaplin learned in this period to analyze his legal problems and his problems with the press in political terms, or even to attribute them to political causes, much as leftist journalists like Mike Gold did. As Viertel herself describes the hoopla surrounding the paternity case, "For the patriots of the Right it was the occasion to punish Chaplin for having remained a British subject, and for his flirtations with the Left."[5] (The issue of Chaplin's citizenship came up frequently in the late 1940s and 1950s; it will be treated in chapters 9 and 10.)

Feuchtwanger's biographers also stress the friendship between the Feuchtwangers and Chaplin (and Oona O'Neill Chaplin as well after she became part of Chaplin's life), which began soon after Feuchtwanger and his wife arrived in the country. A close affinity developed between the two couples and they visited one another's homes frequently. The affinity stemmed partly from Feuchtwanger's admiration for Chaplin's films (Chaplin often liked those best who liked his films most), and Chaplin's admiration for Feuchtwanger's work. (According to a *New York Times* report in 1930, Chaplin considered buying the rights to and playing the lead role in Feuchtwanger's *Jew Suss*.) But their friendship also grew, according to the biographers, because of their similar political inclinations. Feuchtwanger supported Chaplin through all his ordeals in the 1940s and 1950s and then maintained a correspondence after Chaplin exiled himself to Switzerland. Chaplin himself remembers that during a private showing of *Monsieur Verdoux*, Feuchtwanger, Thomas Mann, and several more "stood up and applauded for over a minute."[6]

Chaplin and Brecht, who had been an admirer of Chaplin's films since 1918, "saw each other frequently at Eisler's home, at Salka Viertel's salon, in Chaplin's own home, and at Hollywood gatherings." They shared an interest in politics: Brecht recalls that he and Chaplin were the only two people at a large Hollywood party in 1944 listening to a radio broadcast of the presidential election results. Nevertheless, Brecht and Chaplin never grew really close and comfortable with one another. Hanns Eisler described Brecht's manner toward Chaplin as one of "cordial, attentive respect," something like that of a devoted student toward an admired mentor. According to Eisler, Chaplin wondered at Brecht's tendency to theorize systematically but at times obtusely about art. He was also mystified when Brecht, after reading a draft of the script for *Monsieur Verdoux*, commented only that Chaplin wrote the script "Chinese fashion" (MA, p. 434). When both Chaplin and Brecht were having political problems, however, Chaplin showed his loyalty to his friend by attending the Los Angeles opening of Brecht's *Galileo* in July 1947.[7]

Brecht and Chaplin were mutual friends of composer Hanns Eisler, whom Chaplin calls a "great musician" in his autobiography (*MA*, p. 452). Eisler had admired and written about Chaplin before they met. During a tour of the United States in 1935, for example, he reported on the controversy surrounding *Modern Times* and Boris Shumiatsky's comments on the film: "The reactionary Hearst press hastened to open an attack on Chaplin, claiming he was making a Communist film." Eisler went on to say, inaccurately and somewhat illogically, that

Chaplin expressed his support of communism in an interview "because under Communism he will be recognized as the greatest actor in the world." After they met in the early 1940s, Chaplin and Eisler became close friends and often saw one another. Eisler believed that he and Brecht radicalized Chaplin. Although Chaplin tended to dominate the discussion when Eisler and Brecht saw him, Eisler told an interviewer, Chaplin soon learned that Eisler and Brecht laughed loudest and longest when his jokes had a strong social thrust. It is not unreasonable to suggest that the sharply ironic and satiric comedy that emerged in *Monsieur Verdoux* was influenced by the humor Brecht and Eisler enjoyed. This kind of humor was, according to Heilbut, one of the central and distinguishing characteristics of the German emigrés in America. "Witty, impious, quite unlike any other, Jewish or American," Heilbut writes, its tone was "sharp and biting"—an almost perfect description of some of the humor in *Monsieur Verdoux*.[8]

Thus during the difficult period in which Chaplin was struggling with the Barry case, and then with the changing and increasingly hostile political climate in the United States, he and his new wife Oona O'Neill Chaplin, who was sympathetic to his political views, found themselves isolated from most of Hollywood but gaining companionship and support from this group of leftist emigrés, outsiders in a new land. They viewed Chaplin's problems as a manifestation of fascist forces at work in America to discredit him for his political activities and views.[9]

If one sought to sum up the political views of this group, the following would be central. First, the group was avowedly and actively antifascist. Second, they were in general enthusiastic supporters of the Soviet Union (Feuchtwanger wrote a book in 1937, based on a visit there that year, in praise of the Soviet system) and thus were sympathetic to the cause of Allied unity.[10] Third, partly because they were living in an alien culture, they were ambivalent about the United States: though America had granted them asylum, it also seemed unreasonably materialistic and hypocritically intolerant. (Two German emigrés, Fritz Lang and William Dieterle, like Chaplin, ran afoul of the House Subcommittee on Un-American Activities [HUAC], headed by Martin Dies, for the "anti-American" or "prematurely anti-fascist" ideas expressed in films they directed in the late 1930s. After the war, as we shall see, a number of others had similar and more serious problems.) In an era of patriotic fervor, systematically marshaled during World War II and perpetuated after the war, this genuine ambivalence about America was out of step with dominant ideological currents. And fourth, the group tended to understand conservative opposition to their views as fascist; thus Chaplin's legal problems, particularly the federal charges brought against him, were perceived as motivated by fascist forces who hoped to punish Chaplin for his "dangerous ideas."

It is a truism of social psychology that human beings come to understand who they are and what they believe through their interactions with "significant others"—their family and closest friends. As Chaplin emerged from the Barry trials and moved toward his next film, his significant others included Salka Viertel, the Feuchtwangers, Brecht, and the Eislers. The political perspective they collectively reinforced—strong antifascism, sympathy to the Soviet allies, and skepticism about the hypocrisies of American democracy—was becoming increasingly tenuous as American views shifted in the early postwar years.

The Cooling of Progressivism in Early Postwar America

Chaplin's association with the German emigrés is significant in part because of the influence of their progressive, antifascist world view on Chaplin's first film following the Barry case, *Monsieur Verdoux* (1947). The film is for Chaplin a fascinating departure, a work of social criticism and bitter irony shaped by his experiences and associations in the first half of the 1940s. As we shall see, it elicited extreme hostility from some quarters, making it Chaplin's first real box-office failure. Many American reviewers attacked the film, although it received high critical praise when it was rereleased in 1964 and again in 1973.[11] That rejection was in part, as we shall see later in the chapter, related to the film's departure from Chaplin's aesthetic contract. But this initial critical rejection can also be explained by reference to American cultural history: *Monsieur Verdoux* is a "progressive" work (in the 1930s sense of the term) released in a different era, hostile to that political position. What had changed?

The Communist party's official policy of Popular Front cooperation with other antifascist groups ended abruptly with the Nazi–Soviet Nonaggression Pact of August 1939, and this led to a break between the CPUSA and many American liberals. However, the Nazi invasion of the Soviet Union in June 1941 and the American entry into the war the following December helped partially and temporarily to mend that rift. The Americans and Soviets became allies, and if that made many American conservatives uncomfortable, it also renewed the hopes of some American leftists. For the Left, between 1941 and 1944 there was a tempered renewal of the Popular Front spirit, and liberals and

Communists alike cooperated to support the war effort. Chaplin's speeches during 1942 promoting a second front were just one manifestation of this spirit. Besides favoring the second front policy, American liberals in this period were also generally in favor of close military cooperation among the United States, Great Britain, and the Soviet Union (the so-called Big Three); moral and material support for resistance movements in occupied countries; and the hope for "One World"—or at least the need to preserve the "grand alliance"—after the war was over.[12]

These positions all primarily related to foreign affairs: for the duration of the war, domestic reform took a back seat to the conduct of the war effort. When liberals discussed American society, they most often presented it positively as the democratic alternative to fascism. The typical liberal view was that though the Soviet Union and the United States were different, both were "good" societies fighting against an evil one. Henry Wallace, Roosevelt's Vice-President, downplayed the differences between the Soviet Union and the United States when he wrote in the pages of the *New Republic* in 1942 that Russia, an "economic democracy," and the United States, a "political democracy," were unified in their desire "for the education, the productivity and the enduring happiness of the common man."[13] Such statements exemplify how cooperation between Communists and liberals, so common in the late 1930s had revived.

The Allied victory in 1945 led to optimistic expectations not just among American liberals but among Americans generally. The United States emerged from the war confident, powerful, and vigorous. It was, after all, the major power that suffered least during the war. No battles had been fought on its soil. None of its mainland cities had been bombed. Its economy, thanks in no small part to war-time production, was booming, well recovered from the crisis of the 1930s. It even had sole possession of the devastating and terrifying atomic bomb. The United States seemed in an ideal position to reshape the postwar world according to its own purposes. To progressive liberals this meant a world in which fascism was abolished, domestic New Deal reforms were pushed forward, and cooperation between the United States and the Soviet Union would foster a cooperative and peaceful, even united, world.

Historical events often dash hopes, and so it was with this American buoyancy after 1945. By 1950 the United States had experienced a number of shocks that shifted the cultural and political climate and made it much less comfortable for progressive liberals who, like Chaplin, had publicly called during the war for cooperation between the

227

United States and the Soviet Union. For most Americans the Soviet Union, having enlarged its sphere of influence and tightened its grip on Eastern Europe, had come to be considered America's bitter adversary. As early as March 1946, in a famous speech in Fulton, Missouri, Winston Churchill warned that "an iron curtain has descended across the continent" with the Soviet side subject "to a very high and in many cases increasing measure of control from Moscow."[14] The following year President Truman, much less popular with American liberals than his charismatic predecessor had been, articulated a get-tough containment policy and vowed to go anywhere on the globe to help contain the spread of communism. The same year HUAC began its infamous investigations of Communist influence and infiltration in the United States, including Hollywood, and many Americans were asked to take loyalty oaths if they wished to retain old jobs or get new ones. In 1949 two more blows stunned those who hoped for postwar international cooperation: Mao Tse-tung's Communists took control of China and the Soviet Union successfully detonated its first atomic weapon. To cap it off, by 1950 the United States found itself engaged in yet another war after only a half decade of respite, this time in far-off Korea.

This distinct shift in the political climate led to a crisis in American liberalism. Historian Mary McAuliffe has shown that American liberals after 1946 became divided over the issue of how to respond to the Soviet Union and Stalin. To understand the change, one might draw on William O'Neill's *A Better World*, a study of the reaction of American liberal intellectuals to Stalin. O'Neill uses the term "progressives" to describe those on the left who refused to denounce Russia and the term "anti-Stalinists" to describe those who actively opposed Stalin's brand of communism, even though they considered themselves liberals (in the American sense) on other issues. O'Neill distinguishes both groups from the "anti-Communists," conservatives who made blanket denunciations of the Communist government in the Soviet Union, regardless of who was leading it.[15]

These distinctions enable one to see the crisis and direction of postwar American liberalism more clearly. The progressive attitude toward the Soviet Union dominated American liberalism in the late 1930s, but its appeal gradually lessened for a number of reasons: news of Stalin's purges in the late 1930s, the 1939 Nazi–Soviet Pact, and—after the reprieve from 1942 to the end of the war—a growing belief that Stalin's aggression in foreign policy and his ruthlessness in Soviet domestic affairs betrayed the democratic socialist ideal that many leftists had embraced during the depression. As a result, progressivism declined and anti-Stalinism grew among American liberals. Henry Wallace's Progressive party campaign in 1948 was the last hurrah of the progressive position, and that campaign steadily lost steam through 1948 as the election approached: Wallace ultimately garnered just over a million votes (less than 2 percent of the ballots cast). Truman, by defining himself as a New Deal liberal in domestic affairs and a firm anti-Stalinist in foreign affairs, managed to stage his famous narrow victory.[16]

To define this decline in progressivism another way, between 1938 and 1948 the spectrum of American political ideology shifted radically. In 1938 a dichotomy existed, weighted toward and made up of a large and ecumenical progressive Left, united by its antifascism, at one end, and a smaller political Right, often isolationist, at the other. On the left Communists, socialists, New Dealers, and other antifascists could cooperate by minimizing their ideological differences and stressing their opposition to Hitler.

By 1948, the spectrum of American political ideology began to look quite different: tripartite rather than dichotomous. To borrow from the title of Arthur Schlesinger's influential book of 1949, liberals of the Americans for Democratic Action variety began to see the United States as a "vital center," poised between the left- and right-wing totalitarianisms of communism and fascism. In essence, a Cold War ideological consensus—a paradigm of assumptions and beliefs, which Geoffrey Hodgson has usefully called "the ideology of liberal consensus"—was beginning to solidify, and its main assumptions would dominate American intellectual life until its breakdown in the early 1960s.[17]

The two cornerstone beliefs of this ideology of liberal consensus cast light on the fate of *Monsieur Verdoux* and, ultimately, of Chaplin himself. The first belief centered on domestic issues. It held, roughly, that the American economic system had evolved, softening the brutalities of late-nineteenth-century capitalism and thus becoming more democratic and offering abundance to a wider segment of the population than ever before. The growth of the economy during and after the war led many to believe that the key to democracy was productivity and technology: in this view, by enlarging the economic pie, class conflict would be defused and blue-collar workers brought into the middle class. Social problems so evident and pressing in the depression thus seemed more manageable and less threatening. In short, the ideology of liberal consensus held that the structure of American society was essentially sound, needing only minor reform to keep it fine tuned.

Concerning foreign affairs, the ideology of liberal consensus held that the only serious threat to American harmony and progress was the spectre of communism, both within American society and abroad. The United States, as leader of the "free world," must brace itself for a long struggle against communism and fight it around the world while simultaneously promoting the economic and political virtues of the American system. Truman's containment policy was a logical outgrowth—or better, a central enunciation—of this dimension of the emerging paradigm of consensus. As Hodgson sums it up: "confident to the verge of complacency about the perfectability of American society, anxious to the point of paranoia about the threat of Communism—those were the two faces of the consensus mood."[18]

Ironically, the tendency of Americans after World War II to view the Soviet Union as an unalterable enemy reflected a frame of mind rooted in the late 1930s. Progressive antifascism encouraged people to think of international politics in Manichaean terms: us (antifascists; the Allies) versus them (fascists; the Axis). After the war, particularly given Soviet conduct in Eastern Europe, it was easy for many Americans mentally to change the name of their adversary from the Nazis to the Soviets: though the villain was different, the frame of mind was almost identical.[19] Simultaneously, the economic prosperity during and after the war defused most radical criticism of capitalism, so that social criticism of American and West European societies began to seem unnecessary to some, imprudent to others, and even "un-American" to an increasingly large number. Thus many progressives followed their fellow citizens and shifted the focus of their suspicions or hatred to the Soviet Union while simultaneously embracing American society.

To some progressives, however, Chaplin included, this new Cold War mentality seemed unnecessarily belligerent in foreign affairs and too complacent in domestic affairs. Chaplin and other progressives held out an optimism about the possibilities of peace with the Soviet Union and remained doubtful that American society was achieving a harmonious utopia. Having committed himself to progressive politics in *The Great Dictator* and his second front speeches, feeling himself a victim of fascist forces in the way he was treated during the Barry trials, Chaplin set out to make a film that expressed a progressive critique of capitalist society just as the Cold War was setting in with a vengeance. The result, as one might expect, did his star image no good.

Lashing Out: *Monsieur Verdoux*

Monsieur Verdoux (1947) constituted an extreme deviation in a number of ways from the kind of feature films Chaplin had been making. As we shall see later in this chapter, both the promotion and reception of the film contributed to the unraveling of Chaplin's star image, but so, too, did the film itself. The film can best be understood in the context of Chaplin's progressive antifascism and his public humiliation during the Barry trials. These two factors led to two central themes in the film: a social critique of capitalist society and a clear (though perhaps unconscious and unintended) disparagement of women bordering on misogyny.

Briefly, *Monsieur Verdoux* is set in France during the mid-1930s, from after the onset of the depression to 1937, following the outbreak of the Spanish Civil War. The central character, Henri Verdoux (played by Chaplin), has served faithfully as a bank clerk for thirty years but has been fired from his position because of the depression. To support his crippled wife and his son, Verdoux has become a Bluebeard—using his considerable charm to marry wealthy women for their money and then killing them. In the course of the film he murders two of his wives, fails to murder a third (the lucky Annabella, played by Martha Raye) after some comic misadventures, and just misses marrying another. Ultimately, his schemes catch up with him. After he learns that the police are on his trail (he manages to poison one detective), he also loses both the fortune he has accumulated in a stock market collapse and, subsequently, his family. Turning himself in to the authorities, he is tried, found guilty of murder, and sentenced to be hanged. At the trial he argues in his own defense that "numbers sanctify": that his efforts to survive led to minimal destruction when compared to the mass wartime murders of the state, and that it is unjust for him to be tried as a criminal while a murderous soldier is honored as a hero. The final shot of the film shows Verdoux walking away from the camera as he is led by prison guards to his execution.

Even this short description suggests how far *Monsieur Verdoux* strayed from Chaplin's aesthetic contract. First, its comedy is less evident and different from Chaplin's earlier films. Except for Verdoux's ability to count bills with amazing rapidity, his backward tumble out of a window, and his escapades in the rowboat trying to murder Annabella, slapstick or visual humor is at a minimum. Instead, the humor is macabre, very often emerging from Verdoux's attempts to carry out his murderous plans.

Second, the film is essentially devoid of romance and pathos. Although Verdoux is ostensibly happily married, the two sequences in which he returns to the sunlit country cottage to visit his crippled wife and his son are lifeless and stilted. It is clear that Verdoux is much more fully alive when he is out in his business world, marrying and murdering women. Whereas the pathos in most of Chaplin's earlier comic features was evoked when Charlie was disappointed in his romantic aspirations, the viewer is given no pathetic character with whom to identify in *Monsieur Verdoux*.

Third, Chaplin departs from his practice of presenting two moral universes, one good and one evil, through the central narrative conflict, a tendency that was clear through *The Great Dictator*. Instead, he establishes two sets of disturbing moral perspectives. The first set of values is society's, which is dominated by wartime destruction, economic chaos, and the primacy of profit over human needs. Counterpoised to and emanating from this set of values are Verdoux's. A victim of the depression and a ruthlessly competitive society, he becomes ruthless and murderous himself, all the while justifying his public actions on private grounds. The audience is left with no comfortable, comforting moral perspective, unlike all previous Chaplin features starring Charlie.

Related to these deviations from Chaplin's aesthetic contract is the most significant one: a new central character. In Chaplin's own apt description, the charming, loquacious, dapper, smartly dressed Verdoux is "a paradox of virtue and vice" (MA, p. 435). He adores and provides for his invalid wife but has murdered thirteen women and plans to kill more. He will carefully avoid stepping on a caterpillar, while behind him one of his victims burns in an incinerator. He has been a gentle and law-abiding citizen for fifty years but becomes first a systematic murderer and ultimately an accusing social critic. As with the character of Alex in Stanley Kubrick's *A Clockwork Orange*, audiences simultaneously abhor Verdoux and empathize with him because his society seems even more corrupt than he is. Verdoux is a far cry from the tender, gentle, resilient Charlie that was so important in building Chaplin's star image to the heights it achieved in the 1920s. Charlie was an ideal character for the creation and sustenance of Chaplin's star image; Verdoux immediately sets up a barrier between himself and an audience expecting Charlie.

One can also go beyond the observation that Chaplin broke his aesthetic contract with his audience. As in *The Great Dictator*, he also violated conventions of the classical Hollywood cinema. In *Monsieur Verdoux* these violations related more to narrative than stylistic norms. Principally, Chaplin strayed from the Hollywood tendency to treat individual characters, not social forces, as the causal agents in a narrative.[20] Absolutely central to the narrative of *Verdoux* is the conception that larger social and economic forces, particularly economic depression and war, determine the fates of individual people. Twice in *Monsieur Verdoux* these larger social forces pressure Verdoux to alter his life significantly. First, a depression forces him out of work, which leads him to a career as a Bluebeard to support his family. Second, a stock market panic wipes out his fortune, and, also grieving over the deaths of his wife and son of unspecified causes, he loses his desire to live. He then turns himself in to the police. Viewers of Hollywood films were accustomed to see the desires of their individual heroes opposed by individual villains, with the heroes generally realizing their goals and the villains foiled. In this film, though, social forces determine the fate of the hero, who himself is both villain and hero in certain ways and who at the end of the story is led to his execution. Such a narrative method distanced much of Chaplin's potential audience from the film.

Thus Chaplin violated both his aesthetic contract and the narrative conventions of classical Hollywood cinema. Why did Chaplin discard Charlie, trading him in for the urbane, polished Verdoux? It is tempting to answer this question autobiographically: Charlie, whose essential appeal was based largely on pantomime, could not express what Chaplin felt compelled to say after committing himself to progressive politics and experiencing loneliness, acrimony, and public humiliation during the Barry affair. Chaplin's disgust with the course of civilization and his discouraging relationships with women propelled him even further away from the world of his tender resilient screen persona than he had strayed in *The Great Dictator*. He needed a Verdoux to add a more explicit dimension of social realism and criticism to his films. This new persona enabled Chaplin to express his political denunciation of contemporary Western society and to exorcise the ghosts of his failures with women. However those two aims might hurt his star image, Chaplin had deeply felt, personal reasons for the social vision he presented through *Monsieur Verdoux*.

How did the film contribute to the state of Chaplin's star image in the mid-1940s? As we have already seen, even before *Verdoux*, Chaplin's star image was becoming less associated with Charlie the persona and more linked to Chaplin the man. Chaplin the man, furthermore, was becoming endowed with different traits. In the 1920s and early 1930s he was the "genius" filmmaker of astonishing versatility or the serious intellect, sensitive to true art and sympathetic to the plight of common people. As a result of *The Great Dictator* and the publicity surrounding his second front activities and the Barry trials, however, Chaplin's star image was becoming associated with progressive politics and questionable sexual morality.

These two traits invited viewers already upset with Chaplin to make an autobiographical reading of *Monsieur Verdoux*. The film's assault on women was easily linked to Chaplin's experiences during the Barry case, and the film's political critique recalled the progressive world view that Chaplin had embraced at least since *The Great Dictator*. It is clear, however, that these lashing attacks on women and on capitalist society were not designed to soothe and satisfy a mass audience. Chaplin had been one of the most consistently popular figures in American film history up through *The Great Dictator*. But for several reasons, he did not make *Verdoux* with a careful eye on the box office. In abandoning the comic persona Charlie after being associated or even identified with him for over thirty years, Chaplin was immediately risking the greatest source of his box-office appeal. But in substituting for Charlie a Bluebeard character—and particularly in doing so not long after Chaplin himself had been portrayed by bold headlines as a despoiler of young women—the director was further risking a dangerous identification of the actor with the new character he played. Finally, in having that central character justify his murders by articulating a progressive critique of capitalism, and then releasing the film at the very time that the dominant American ideology was increasingly defending its capitalist system as the only viable alternative to communism, Chaplin was asking for trouble.

A number of analysts, including Richard Dyer, have argued that stars exist in a culture in part because they embody within their characters certain prevailing cultural values and attitudes. Stars thus may serve two ideological functions: to reinforce the dominant ideology of the culture in which the star is popular or to conceal important cultural tensions and contradictions, a process that Dyer calls displacement.[21] At least two elements of Chaplin's Charlie persona may be cited in this regard. First, Charlie's ability to maintain his human dignity and resilience in spite of his lower-class status and minimal power in society clearly touched a deep chord among the American (and world) moviegoing public. This aspect of Charlie's character functioned to displace the tension in American society between the myth that anyone working hard can make it in America and the reality that very few move from the bottom to the top of the economic pyramid.

Second, Charlie's constant yearning for romance despite the factors working against him (his size, his lack of status) also appealed to an audience conditioned to expect romance in films, even if the romances in the Chaplin films were not always worked out in the end. (A content analysis of one hundred Hollywood films made in 1941–1942 found that most leading characters—68 percent—desired romantic love over all else.)[22] This element of Charlie's character reinforced the myth of romantic love, long a staple in American and much of Western culture.

But in *Monsieur Verdoux* Chaplin's persona fulfilled neither of these star functions. Verdoux, albeit driven by circumstances, becomes a financially successful businessman/murderer, so successful that he invests in the stock market, something that could and would never have occurred to Charlie. In creating an enterprising and successful bourgeois hero, Chaplin disgarded one of the most powerful reasons for his central character's appeal in previous films. And though Verdoux, under his aliases, does engage in some manipulative "romancing," the audience knows that his ulterior motives are always murder and money, a far cry from the tender and deeply felt longing Charlie exhibited when in the presence of his beloved. Moreover, Verdoux's love for his wife shows none of the intensity or enthusiasm of feeling Charlie directed from a distance toward Georgia or Merna or the blind flower girl. Such violations of his aesthetic contract of stardom, when combined with the negative publicity he suffered during the Barry affair, made it inevitable that Chaplin would antagonize the audience that had previously worshipped him as a star.

Monsieur Verdoux: Initial Promotion and Reception

When discussing a film's production history, it is usually appropriate to consider first its promotion and then its critical and popular reception. In the case of *Monsieur Verdoux*, however, it is much more useful to consider the promotion and reception simultaneously. Not only did the promotion of the film at United Artists begin very late, largely because Chaplin refused to lift the veil of secrecy from his production, but after the bad reviews the film garnered during its New York City opening and the press-conference grilling Chaplin endured the next Monday, United Artists was forced to withdraw the film and reconceive its promotion campaign in hopes of salvaging the film. This section will discuss the checkered promotion and reception history of *Monsieur Verdoux* until the film was withdrawn after the New York City run, and the next section will consider the fate of the film after that.

Compared to the tremendous advance publicity given films like *City Lights*, *Modern Times*, and especially *The Great Dictator*, *Monsieur Verdoux* remained shrouded in mystery almost to the day of its release (11 April 1947). The other three films were all the subject of a number of articles in the *New York Times* during the production and postproduction periods, which helped to ready the audience in advance. In the case of *Monsieur Verdoux*, however, the only *Times* article of any significance preparing the way for the film was a brief report and picture spread in the March 30 magazine section. After alluding to the secrecy surrounding the project, the article quoted Chaplin's description of the film:

> I am a mass killer. I start out as a bank clerk, a respectable, dapper, middle-class Frenchman. Then the depression of 1930 costs me my job. I have a wife and child whom I love and must support. And so I turn to the business of marrying women and killing them for their money. Actually, I am a very moral man; I never let these women touch me and I hate my new job, I hate the women. I am in business and I must do my duty after the classic heroic mode.

This terse and rather misleading description is accompanied by seven production stills over a two-page spread, but the photos suggest that Chaplin did not show the film to the *Times* reporter. One caption refers to Verdoux's "periodic weddings" in the film, although in fact only one is presented—and even it isn't carried out. Another caption says that Martha Raye's character ends up dead like the rest of Verdoux's victims, which is not true.[23]

Correspondence of the United Artists publicity staff in New York City confirms that Chaplin and his studio employees failed to give the film adequate advance publicity. In an April 3 cable to United Artists executive Paul Lazarus, about a week before the film's New York opening, Tom Waller of the publicity staff in New York complained that his office was having a difficult time developing any campaign since of the entire office, only he had seen the film. Waller continued in an ominous tone: "Chaplin today requested mass meeting of press. . . . I am setting up such a mass meeting for Monday April 14. Chaplin expects this will be controversial and understands we can do nothing to protect him or picture him once he submits to mass questioning."[24] Dutifully but reluctantly, the staff announced Chaplin's first extensive press conference for publicity in his career in a press release dated April 8, followed by an April 9 release stating that the conference would be restricted to accredited members of the press.[25]

Chaplin's lack of concern about promoting his film is somewhat surprising, given how shrewdly he had handled the press at other times in his career. As we have seen, he was particularly skillful at cultivating intellectuals like Stark Young, Gilbert Seldes, Waldo Frank, and Edmund Wilson in the 1920s, relationships that bore fruit in praise-filled articles in intellectual journals and a consequent raising and broadening of his star status. Yet his inattention to promoting *Monsieur Verdoux* is explicable. In the 1920s Chaplin was still in the business of solidifying and raising his reputation; he had not yet fully shaken the image of a vulgar music-hall comedian who entertained only unsophisticated audiences. By the 1940s, he had long been a darling of both the masses and the intelligentsia, accustomed to having the press at his beck and call. His behavior before the opening of *Monsieur Verdoux* suggests two explanations. Perhaps unaware of how much the Barry affair had strained his relations with the press, Chaplin seemed to believe—at least until he arrived in New York—that when his new film was ready, the audiences and reviewers would come flocking to him as they had since the 1920s. Another, darker, explanation is that Chaplin was driven by a subconscious wish to strike back at his attackers, even if it meant that his film would fail at the box office.

Whatever Chaplin's motivations, the lack of advance publicity for *Monsieur Verdoux* and the impending press conference even merited a column in the trade publication *Motion Picture Daily* on April 11, the day the film premiered. In it columnist Red Kann reported on United Artists' "initial difficulties with Chaplin" over publicizing the film. Chaplin had apparently hoped to open the film a week earlier, on Good Friday, but United Artists officials convinced him that the film would need more buildup. Kann also reported that Chaplin had first planned to talk only with the *Times*, the *Herald Tribune*, and a representative of one wire service. When United Artists officials objected to such minimal publicity, Kann continued, "Chaplin is the one who insisted upon a general press interview. . . . UA officials did what they could to discourage the en masse cross-fire, pointing out Charlie would have to take on all comers including those who might be after answers as to why he never became an American citizen and his version of his alleged lack of cooperation in the war effort." In reply to these worries, Kann reported, Chaplin replied only, "I can handle it."[26] One wonders how much Chaplin was unconsciously assuming the role of Verdoux, whose fast-talking charm usually enables him to extricate himself from the most difficult of circumstances.

Chaplin was not as persuasive as his fictional counterpart. Had he scheduled a press conference to promote the premiere of almost any other of his feature films—except perhaps *The Circus*, which followed closely on the heels of his divorce to Lita Grey—Chaplin would likely have been warmly received. But when he stepped forward on Monday, April 14, to answer questions from the press in the packed Grand Ballroom of the Gotham Hotel, he received a frosty reception.[27] Chaplin's opening comment, tinged with apparent irony, shows that he expected trouble: "Thank you, ladies and gentlemen of the press. I am not going to waste your time. I should say—proceed with the butchery" (p. 35).

And in many ways a butchery it was. Though the press conference was purportedly designed to help promote *Monsieur Verdoux*, most of the questions concerned Chaplin's political views and activities. If one does not count restatement or elaboration of questions, about 60 percent dealt with political issues, with no reference to films at all. Of the remaining 40 percent, about half asked Chaplin specifically about *Monsieur Verdoux* and the other half asked him about films in general. The political questions were generally hostile, peppering Chaplin on a range of issues and charges. Was he a Communist? Was he a Communist sympathizer? Why hadn't he become an American citizen? Why hadn't he contributed more prominently to the recent war effort? Why wasn't he more patriotic or nationalistic? Did he know Hanns Eisler and was Eisler a Communist? Wasn't postwar Soviet expansionism comparable to prewar German expansionism? And so on.

The most insistent and vituperative reporter there was James W. Fay, who represented a publication called *Catholic War Veterans*. Fay asked Chaplin thirteen questions, none of which had anything to do with *Monsieur Verdoux* or with films in general. Fay was particularly upset that Chaplin had not become an American citizen and that he had said publicly that he was not a nationalist. In the increasingly frigid atmosphere of the Cold War, Fay represented a considerable sector of the American public when he scolded Chaplin: "I'm objecting to your particular stand that you have no patriotic feelings about this country or any other country" (p. 36).

In his responses to the political questions, Chaplin consistently defended progressive views. He stated that he was not a Communist and had never belonged to any political party but said that he did "sympathize very much with Russia" during World War II because they were "holding the front" (p. 36). He explained his second front activities in progressive terms: in the speeches he had called "for the unity of the Allied cause—which at that time was being disrupted. . . . It was very obvious to see that [the Nazis] were trying to disunite us in this country" (p. 38). When asked if Eisler was a Communist, he replied,

"I don't know whether he is a Communist or not. I know he is a fine artist and a great musician and a very sympathetic friend." To the reporter who asked him to equate German and Soviet expansionism, Chaplin declined: "Now, when you're getting my opinion on political matters and on military matters, I'm not going to be embroiled" (p. 38). To Chaplin, the times were bad ("there is a lot of hate in the world and I think these are very troublesome days," p. 41), and the only way to counter the political atmosphere was to search for the kind of world unity envisioned by the Allied cause in World War II. This progressive outlook prevented him from denouncing the Soviet Union and joining the increasingly fashionable tendency to celebrate America unconditionally.

Just as Verdoux defended actions that were sure to be denounced by audiences, Chaplin refused to cut his conscience to fit the fashion of 1947, which gave considerable material to those in the press who opposed his views. The press conference thus promoted neither *Monsieur Verdoux* nor Chaplin's public reputation; the worst fears of United Artists press representatives were realized.

One can, however, overestimate the degree to which reviewers and critics attacked *Monsieur Verdoux* on the film's initial release. At the time of the premiere, American liberals were still deeply engaged in the debate over progressive and anti-Stalinist views of foreign policy. The day *Monsieur Verdoux* opened in New York City, for example, the *Times* carried advertisements both for Henry Wallace's progressive column in the *New Republic* (he had recently become editor) and for Churchill's anti-Stalinist article in *Life* headed, "It is barely a year since I spoke in Fulton." The same issue also contained a headline: "Churchill Says Britain Saved Greece from Communism," and on the day of the press conference, a small group in the U.S. House of Representatives—angry about Wallace's public criticism of the containment policy—demanded that his passport be revoked.[28] Progressives and anti-Stalinists were still debating, and in a similar vein Chaplin and his films had both critics and defenders, with those on the left more apt to defend him.

In the press conference, for example, a number of questions implied a civil and even a sympathetic attitude toward Chaplin. Most prominent among his defenders was James Agee—author of *Let Us Now Praise Famous Men*, "Comedy's Greatest Era" (an essay that highly praised Chaplin), and *The African Queen* screenplay—who was clearly outraged by Fay and others. Sitting in the balcony, he had to be handed a microphone so Chaplin could hear his trembling voice. In his comment, Agee wondered how the questioners could "congratu-

239

late themselves upon this country as the finest on earth and as a 'free country' " while they "pry into what a man's citizenship is, try to tell him his business from hour to hour . . . and exert a public moral blackmail against him for not becoming an American citizen, for his political views, and for not entertaining troops in the . . . way they think he should." Chaplin, gratified by the support after so much antagonism, replied, "Thank you very much" (p. 41).

Just as some defended Chaplin at the press conference, so did an articulate minority defend the film, though the negative reviews dominated. One of the few laughs Chaplin got during the press conference came when he was asked for his reaction to the reviews of *Verdoux* in the New York papers. "Well, the one optimistic note," he replied, "is that they were mixed" (p. 38).

The film surely had its detractors. Reporters at the press conference and many of the reviews of the film criticized it for its "message" and for not being like Chaplin's early Charlie films. At the press conference Chaplin received comments and questions like the following:

"You have stopped being a good comedian since you've been bringing messages."

"Are you going to make any more pictures for children?"

"Are you going to make any more tramp pictures?"

"Is there any possibility that some of your old pictures like *Modern Times* will be released?"

All such questions indicated a longing for an earlier (and less threatening) Chaplin whom the questioners clearly admired, and perhaps also a sense of regret concerning the new Chaplin who was emerging in the difficult present.

The negative and mixed reviews of *Monsieur Verdoux* convey much the same attitude. Perhaps the most hostile review in the New York City daily papers was Howard Barnes's in the influential *Herald Tribune*, which opened: "In *Monsieur Verdoux* Charles Chaplin has composed what he likes to term a 'comedy of murders' with a woeful lack of humor, melodrama, or dramatic taste." In the review Barnes made a mistake common among commentators on Chaplin: he equated Chaplin with the role he was playing and assumed that Chaplin justified or even approved of Verdoux's actions. If part of a reviewer's job is to recommend or steer his or her readers away from a film, there is no mistaking Barnes's attitude toward *Monsieur Verdoux*: "It has little entertainment value, either as somber symbolism or sheer nonsense."[29]

Such unequivocal denunciation was unusual. Of the negative and mixed reviews, it was much more common for reviewers to criticize

Chaplin's message and to yearn for a return to his earlier comic style. One might say that the "aesthetic discourse" surrounding the Chaplin films was changing again. In the 1910s reviewers asked if Chaplin's films were funny and some asked if they were unacceptably vulgar. In the 1920s they tended to ask whether the blend of pathos and comedy was successful. In the 1930s they asked if Chaplin was committed to a cause, and often hoped he was. Now in the late 1940s they were asking if he had a message, and hoped he did not. The tendency of critics in the 1930s to urge artists to commit themselves politically was diminishing rapidly in the 1940s, as the shift in the political climate affected the tastes and commentary of some reviewers.

Philip Hartung's review in *Commonweal* was typical. Titled, "Unusual—To Say the Least," the review asserted that "when he goes in for pantomime . . . Chaplin is at his best" but criticized the film's "spurious social philosophy."[30] John McCarten's *New Yorker* review, "Chaplin and a Murky Message," held that when Chaplin relied on his old "antics"— presumably scenes like the one when Verdoux falls backward out of a second-floor window—"one is tempted to forgive him for having got himself involved in a film full of cloudy observations on the cosmos." The only genuine success of the film comes "along sartorial lines," wrote McCarten. "Personally I preferred him when was baggier, humbler, and funnier." McCarten wished, in Jauss's terms, for a film of much less striking "aesthetic distance," a work of "entertainment" or "culinary" art.[31]

A related criticism—that a comedian should not try to do serious roles—came from *Variety* and *Newsweek*. *Variety* wrote that "Comedians who yen to do *Hamlet* usually wind up with neo-tragic results, and *Monsieur Verdoux* runs according to form," and opened its review with this terse box-office prediction: "Chaplin will have to carry this one. And how."[32] *Newsweek*'s review, "Little Man, What Now?" was supplemented with a picture of Raye and Chaplin, captioned "Better in Pantomime." It found the funny spots "too few and much too far between," and judged firmly: "Jean Gabin, famous for his heavy roles, would never try to be a commic juggler; there is no reason why Chaplin should take it upon himself to play straight."[33] The reviewer for the *Christian Science Monitor*, in "An Assault from Mr. Chaplin," frequently used the words "sardonic" and "bitter" to describe the "keenly disappointing" film. As in many other reviews, the message came under sternest attack: "his broadsides of indictment against society (particularly the ruthlessness of business) become merely petty and meaningless, expressions of hatred, contempt, and personal bitterness."[34] This chorus of negative criticism indicates how Chaplin's star was falling, just as it indicates that most American movie reviewers were becoming much less likely to encourage or even accept social criticism in films.

Other reviews, usually from more leftist, prestigious, or elite publications, were more positive. In the *New York Times*, Bosley Crowther, usually sympathetic with realist or "message" films, gave *Monsieur Verdoux* a generally positive review. More than most reviewers, Crowther caught the paradox of the Verdoux character: "As Mr. Chaplin plays him he is both a satan and a faun—a devil in elegant clothing and a charming innocent with the manners of a dude." With this character at the center, Chaplin created a film with a message: "Mr. Chaplin . . . believes in using his talent for socking hard—socking, that is, at the evil and injustice he sees in the world and aiming directly at the midriff of general complacency." While other critics were ready to write Chaplin off as a has-been, Crowther asserted that "Mr. Chaplin is still in the game—and hitting hard."[35]

The *New Republic*, more sympathetic to progressive politics than most newspapers, also gave *Monsieur Verdoux* some positive, albeit guarded, attention. Shirley O'Hara's review of the film, while polite, was generally negative ("I am bewildered by it and disappointed"). However, in a column two weeks later, on the press conference, she defended Chaplin and criticized the behavior of her press cohorts. O'Hara wrote that Chaplin "couldn't have expected the shockingly rude, sustained impertinence of the attack" during the press conference, and that Chaplin's "patience and courtesy were astounding." She and a few others "could only be ashamed at what ugly hostile liberties can be taken in the name of freedom of the press."[36] Though panning the film, the *New Republic* defended the comedian's political liberty.

The reviews that gave Chaplin almost unqualified praise came from journals firmly associated with the Left: the *Nation*, *Partisan Review*, *PM*, and the Communist magazine *Mainstream*. The *Nation* reviewer was Chaplin's most vocal defender in the press conference, James Agee. He devoted three entire columns to his review of *Monsieur Verdoux*, and his words still convey the enthusiasm and seriousness with which he wrote them. To Agee, *Monsieur Verdoux* was Chaplin's "most ambitious film." Likewise, his theme, "the greatest and most appropriate to its time that he has yet undertaken, is the bare problem of surviving in such a world as this." Though Agee argued that Chaplin could have expressed more clearly the root causes for Verdoux's murders, he still felt that *Verdoux* was "one of the few indispensable works of our time," a work whose "grim central spirit" was conveyed with "cold nihilistic irony," a "great poem" from a "great poet."[37] To Agee,

Chaplin was neither the rakish womanizer nor the naive leftist; he was rather a major twentieth-century artist exploring issues of profound importance.

Another long and serious treatment of the film appeared in *Partisan Review* and was written by the young Robert Warshow, a perceptive analyst of popular culture who later would write influential essays on the gangster and western film genres, as well as a tribute to Chaplin's *Limelight*. Warshow's essay, which has subsequently left its mark on our contemporary understanding of Chaplin, placed *Verdoux* as the culmination of a series of films that began in the early 1930s, when the pressure of the times forced Chaplin's screen persona to "be for or against the society," a decision that would become "the determining factor in his life and the defining element of his character." Ultimately, this led Chaplin to abandon the tramp character, conclusively, in the final speech of *The Great Dictator*. The new character, Verdoux, though not as great a character as Charlie, nevertheless continued the line of development in Chaplin's art begun in the early 1930s. By 1947, "Chaplin's view of society has taken on a new savagery," which can easily be linked to Chaplin's humiliation during the Barry trials and to the increasing pressure being placed on his progressive political views. Like Agee, Warshow found the film complex and important, one that "must" be approached with a willingness to understand and enjoy it as a shifting pattern of ambiguity and irony, made up of all the complexities and contradictions not only of our society but of Chaplin's own mind and the mind of the spectator."[38]

Although Agee and Warshow were leftists, neither toed the progressive line so fully and consistently as reviewers for *PM* and *Mainstream*, which both found much to praise about *Verdoux*, especially its criticism of modern capitalist societies. *PM* twice came to Chaplin's defense after the press conference, once in an editorial by Max Lerner and once in a transcription of some of Chaplin's comments from the press conference itself.[39] In his editorial, Lerner suggests that "Chaplin has given us as elaborate and satiric 'theory of business enterprise' as Thorstein Veblen ever dared." In an attempt to deflect the growing tendency to denounce Chaplin's art because of his politics—a tendency that culminated in reactions to Chaplin's next film, *Limelight*—Lerner countered, "As for myself, I am content to take him as an artist, and to face the criticisms of our institutions that his art implies. . . . Where he makes his money and how he spends it, what he did or did not do about the war, what he thinks of Russia or Communism: these are his affairs, not ours. This hounding of him is unclean." The progressive Left in America was not yet willing to give up criticism of American

life, as Lerner's discussion showed. A few days later, *PM* defended
Chaplin again. Whereas the *Chicago Tribune* had found Chaplin stocky
and jowly in the Barry trials, *PM* found him "a short white-haired man
with small kindly wrinkles around his eyes" when he held his press
conference. Noting that only three of the New York City papers carried stories after the press conference—despite the hundreds of reporters who attended—*PM* went on to quote approvingly many of
Chaplin's press conference comments on political affairs, some of
which would seem dangerously leftist to an increasing number of
Americans as the Cold War worsened.

The longest and most thoughtful defense of *Monsieur Verdoux* was
Arnaud d'Usseau's "Chaplin's *Monsieur Verdoux*." It appeared in a new
journal called *Mainstream*, a Communist publication. The essay discussed what d'Usseau saw as the film's central achievements and analyzed why it had been so savagely attacked. In d'Usseau's view, the
film's chief accomplishment was Chaplin's social analysis, which placed
"the moral burden" of Verdoux's murders "entirely on society." Here
he quoted Shaw approvingly: "Not only does society commit more
frightful crimes than any individuals, King or commoner; it legalizes
its crimes, and forges certificates of righteousness for them, besides
torturing anyone who exposes their true character." To d'Usseau, Verdoux is the "completely integrated" bourgeois citizen, shaped by capitalist society to behave as he does. Yet in Chaplin's hands he becomes
a "tragic figure capable of evoking our profoundest sympathy." In his
analysis of the critical response to the film, d'Usseau suggests at least
three reasons why critics reacted to it with such hostility. First, Chaplin
did not honor his star persona, Charlie, hence disappointing those
seeking the familiar. Second, Chaplin parodied the success ethic by
making a mock rags-to-riches story, thus challenging cherished American beliefs. And third, some critics, in d'Usseau's view, made the valid
criticism that Chaplin's dialogue was at times weak and his film style at
times mediocre. More than anything else, however, *Monsieur Verdoux*
disturbed the critics because the central character's "behavior is a comment on those values our society celebrates." Since d'Usseau also objected to the values the film focused on—individualism, the profit motive, and the success ethic—he was sympathetic to Verdoux's analysis
and concluded: "We are grateful to be alive in Chaplin's time. He is
indeed our greatest artist."[40]

Regardless of these defenses, *Monsieur Verdoux* was a disappointment at the box office in its five-week run at the Broadway Theater in
New York City. *Variety* reported during the third week of the run that
the film was "falling back rapidly in the current frame," and the next

week it reported that the third week's receipts were $6,000 less than it had predicted, with the box office "slipping badly" in the fourth week. According to *Variety*'s figures, the film drew $27,000 in the shortened first week, $28,000 the second, then $18,000, $15,000, and $12,000 in the last three weeks of the run.[41] In contrast to the immediate and long-running success of *The Great Dictator*, the box-office response of New York City audiences to *Monsieur Verdoux* shocked Chaplin, for it was even more dismal news than the critical reviews. Part of the failure of *Verdoux* at the Broadway Theater undoubtedly had to do with in-adequate publicity buildup, but Chaplin also had to face two more un-pleasant facts: without Charlie, he had no guaranteed large audience, and if he continued to insist on inserting progressive messages into his films in the changed political atmosphere, he would have to face the financial consequences. Before doing anything else, however, he agreed with United Artists officials to withdraw the film from release and try to give it a second, and better, start.

The Campaign That Failed

It was unprecedented, indeed nearly unthinkable, that Chaplin would be forced to pull a feature film from distribution and redesign its pub-licity campaign. Given the initial response to *Verdoux*, however, he had little choice. Fortunately for those interested in the evolution of Chap-lin's star image, the United Artists Collection at the Wisconsin Center for Film and Theater Research contains considerable material on the redone publicity campaign for *Monsieur Verdoux*. Located in the files of Paul Lazarus, Jr., and Alfred Tamarin, two United Artists publicity executives, this material provides insight into Chaplin's combative mood in 1947. The reception of the film after the campaign began gives us a firm indication of the status of Chaplin's star image as the Cold War set in.[42]

As noted, Chaplin and officials at United Artists, who also had an economic stake in the film, decided to withdraw the film after its New York run ended in May 1947. They hoped to regroup and develop a new advertising campaign for a rescheduled national release in Au-gust. Even before the new campaign was prepared, however, ominous signs of pressure group resistance to the film began to appear. On May 12 *Motion Picture Daily* reported that a group in Ohio was urging theater exhibitors not to book *Monsieur Verdoux* because Chaplin had never become an American citizen. In Memphis the local censorship board decided to ban the film. Such grassroots resistance worried United Artists so much that it placed an ad disguised as an article in the July 23 issue of *Hollywood Reporter* that predicted that *Monsieur Verdoux* would do $20 million of business.[43] Soon after, however, they realized that the time was not ripe for a national release and the August date was postponed.

The new publicity campaign for *Monsieur Verdoux* began when, in late June, publicist Russell Birdwell signed a six-month contract with the Chaplin Studios to direct the publicity campaign for United Artists, in which he was assisted by Jane Turner. Birdwell wasted no time. On June 24 he wrote a letter to the editor of the *Hollywood Reporter* saying that *Monsieur Verdoux* was a controversial film that needed defending. The disputes over the film, he hoped, would "sweep *Verdoux* into a vortex of fiery condemnation and enthusiastic approval." The same day he announced the challenging, combative slogan that would provide a focus for the new campaign: "Chaplin Changes! Can You?" By June 27 Birdwell had asked Arthur Kelly to send out six thousand broadside ads using this approach to potential exhibitors.[44]

The ensuing pressbook prepared to promote the film nearly assaulted the viewer. Since Chaplin had traded his most marketable character, Charlie, for Verdoux, the publicists, in consultation with Chaplin, decided to emphasize the change and hope to sell the film at least partly on that basis. One 8½ by 11 inch advertising picture in the pressbook exemplified this approach: it showed Verdoux in medium close-up accompanied only by the campaign's theme as its caption: "Chaplin changes. Can you?" (see Figures 24 and 25). Such an overt challenge to the viewer at a time when Chaplin's public reputation had been slipping for several years seems, in retrospect, to have been a questionable approach.

Another ad in the pressbook indicated the difficulties United Artists had in selling a Chaplin film without Charlie or a close relative. It showed another medium close up of Verdoux at the center of the ad surrounded by close-up cutouts of four women who appeared in the film. The headline at the top of the page described the film as "A Strange Love Story That Hurts," and below the pictures was a more detailed description: "In *Monsieur Verdoux* there is a peculiar intensity of drama . . . an even more peculiar hysteria of laughter—and a strange love story that hurts." This appeal, like the previous one, suggested that Chaplin was doing something new but was hardly likely to generate much viewer enthusiasm.[45]

Nevertheless, this was the campaign that Birdwell, working for Chaplin, prepared for the anticipated August release. Corporate records indicate that though the film did get a few scattered August playdates in the hinterlands (in South Dakota, for example), the release was generally pushed back to September. This delay stemmed at least in part from complications arising over Chaplin's status with the House Subcommittee on Un-American Activities. Its investigators had been in Hollywood in the late spring and summer talking with a number of people, including Chaplin's friend Hanns Eisler, and it began to look as if Chaplin might be called upon to testify. Birdwell, in a decision consistent with his notion that the controversial nature of the film should be emphasized (he apparently felt that there was no such thing as bad publicity), decided to open the film in HUAC's home court—Washington, D.C. It became even easier for Birdwell to stress the controversial when Chaplin was indeed served with a subpoena to appear before HUAC—in the same group of people that included the Hollywood Ten (see Chapter 9)—and was originally scheduled to testify in late September. Birdwell responded by capitalizing on the headlines and tailoring the release around them. First, he scheduled the film to open on Thursday, September 25, the day after the HUAC probe was scheduled to open (when HUAC moved its date to October, he did not follow suit, however, but did move the opening a day to the more convenient Friday). Second, he decided to make use of the telegram Chaplin sent to all members of HUAC. It read: "I am opening my comedy, *Monsieur Verdoux*, on September 26th in five Washington, D.C. theaters and it indeed would be a pleasure to have you as my guest on opening day. Respectfully, Charlie Chaplin." United Artists sent out the telegrams September 19 and also informed the press. Finally, Birdwell decided to revise the ad campaign to portray the film as under siege by unreasonable censors.[46]

Beginning several days before *Verdoux* opened and then continuing after the premiere, Birdwell placed ads from the pressbook in the Washington papers, and added a new headline: "The Picture That Couldn't Be Stopped."[47] Instead of planning an exclusive showing of the film in one large downtown theater—as was customary with Chaplin films—he scheduled it for five theaters—the Nix, Apex, Atlas, Naylor, and Senator. Four of these were neighborhood theaters, and one a small midtown theater. By the day of the opening he exultantly cabled Chaplin that three of the four daily papers would carry rave reviews and predicted, "we will top a two and a half million gross."[48]

In Washington, at least, the strategy seemed to work. *Monsieur Verdoux* enjoyed a much better response from reviewers there than it had received in New York City. The best example was Richard Coe's *Washington Post* review, "Philosophical Clown." "*Monsieur Verdoux*," Coe wrote, "is a bold, brilliant, and bitterly amusing film"; he went on to give it one of its best newspaper reviews.[49]

24. Original ad for *Monsieur Verdoux*, 1947.

25. New, combative ad from second
Monsieur Verdoux ad campaign, 1947.

Verdoux also did much better than expected at the box office in Washington. On September 28 Birdwell telegrammed United Artists executive Paul Lazarus, Jr., that both the Pix and the Apex had broken their previous opening day and Saturday box-office records. In fact, by 3:00 P.M. the first day, the film had already garnered $12,876 in the two theaters—another record and 10 percent of what *Verdoux* had drawn in its entire five-week New York run.[50] By the end of the week, the film had earned $41,118, encouraging enough for United Artists officials to hold it over for two more weeks. What's more, Washington's interest in the film was sustained. *Variety* reported in its second week that the film was "still going strong," and in the third week that it was still holding, which was a "surprise to all."[51] It seemed that things were looking up.

Following the Washington run, however, the film slowed down. Its next play dates came around October 21 in Chicago, New Orleans, San Francisco, Seattle, Toronto, and Portland. But as the news of the first-day receipts came in, United Artists appeared to give up on the film. On October 22 Lazarus cabled Birdwell that Arthur Kelly had halted ads for the film because the grosses were so bad. By October 28, Lazarus cabled Birdwell again, this time to announce that "the picture is not going well." Birdwell fought to keep the film moving: on October 29 he cabled Kelly that he and Chaplin agreed that the film should open at all dates and not be withdrawn or it would certainly be considered a genuine flop. Kelly and Lazarus, however, had made up their minds. That the film was indeed a flop in the United States is hinted at by the fact that the next correspondence between Birdwell and Lazarus in his file is on the final day of Birdwell's contract: his December 15 cable to Lazarus thanks him for "all of your help."[52]

What happened? For several reasons—a combination of the public pressure, the difficulty of selling what was for Chaplin such an unusual film, and the growing HUAC pressure on studio executives after the Hollywood Ten trials to quell "subversive" propaganda in their pictures—*Monsieur Verdoux* received virtually no more releases in the United States in 1947 and only a modest number in 1948. At the end of 1947 United Artists tallied up the total domestic receipts for their various releases of the year: *Body and Soul* had earned $2,035,800; *Red River*, $1,584,800; Olivier's *Henry V*, $383,000; and *Monsieur Verdoux*, $162,000. The company's most profitable filmmaker in 1941 (the year of *The Great Dictator*) had created its biggest disappointment of 1947.[53] In his history of United Artists, Tino Balio notes that two years after *Monsieur Verdoux* was first released, it still had grossed only $325,000 in the United States. According to Balio, "even though the picture grossed more than $1.5 million abroad [an indication of *Verdoux*'s more positive reception outside the United States], Chaplin felt that the UA sales force was responsible for its poor domestic showing, with the result that he lost confidence in his company."[54]

It seems much more likely, however, that Chaplin was searching for a scapegoat when he castigated the United Artists sales force. He had, after all, hindered the publicity staff by withholding information before the New York release. He had insisted on a press conference. And he had approved the hiring of Birdwell to direct the second publicity campaign and had agreed to an approach whose tone was haughty, almost belligerent, nearly daring the audience to change along with the great artist Chaplin. Surely Chaplin deserves a good part of the blame for the film's publicity.

But just why did *Monsieur Verdoux* fail so badly in its domestic release? Part of the reason relates to the social structure of stardom. We have already noted the framework provided by Richard Dyer, which proposes that a star's image is created out of a variety of media documents: promotion, publicity, films, and criticism/commentary.[55]

In each of these four areas *Monsieur Verdoux* failed to sustain Chaplin's star image in positive ways. The promotion and publicity for the film were almost nonexistent until the film's New York premiere, and then the primary promotion event—the press conference—worked more against than for the film and its star. Except for the Washington promotion campaign, which stressed the controversy surrounding the film and its difference from earlier Chaplin films, the promotion and publicity of the film were almost complete failures. The film itself, by breaking Chaplin's aesthetic contract with his audience in a number of ways (especially by presenting a new central persona different in class and interests from the familiar Charlie), also undercut Chaplin's star image. And as we have seen, the reviews and commentary on the film generally rejected the film, often for that very reason: for breaking his aesthetic contract, for failing to provide what he had provided in his previous films (and what the reviewers had grown to expect). The few passionate critical defenses of *Verdoux* came from leftist critics who, in Jauss's terms, were able to bridge the "aesthetic distance" between *Verdoux* and the audience because they were much more interested in Chaplin the serious artist and progressive social commentator than in the comedy and pathos of Chaplin's pantomimic alter ego, Charlie. Chaplin dared his audience to change, and these few reviewers did. Most, however, did not.

This leads to yet another reason for the failure of *Monsieur Verdoux* in the United States. It should be noted that the London and Paris openings of the film were much more successful than the one in New York City. Upon its mid-November opening at the New Gallery and Tivoli Theatres in London, *Monsieur Verdoux* garnered very positive reviews and did quite well at the box office. The public response in Paris was even stronger: it opened there in mid-June of 1948, breaking house records that had been held by *The Best Years of Our Lives* and *For Whom the Bell Tolls*.[56]

This more positive response to *Monsieur Verdoux*, particularly in Paris, suggests how a star image is intimately related to cultural values and historical change and thus helps us to understand a broader historical reason for the failure of *Monsieur Verdoux*. American culture, which lacked any established, strong socialist tradition, embraced the assumptions of the Cold War more quickly and fully than most West European countries. Many of the Americans who saw the film (and even many who only read about it) understood Chaplin's social critique as a leftist denunciation of his host country, even though the film was set in France. This understanding emerged at a time when the tendency to celebrate American society and to disapprove of criticism of it was becoming increasingly prevalent. This tendency was demonstrated by the public efforts in various areas of the country to ban the film and by the pressures put on Hollywood studio executives to eliminate "subversive content" (too often translated as "criticism of the

United States") from their films after the HUAC investigations. Both these pressures affected United Artists officials as they decided not to give *Monsieur Verdoux* more general release after the fairly successful Washington run.

When these cultural and historical factors are combined with the negative publicity surrounding Chaplin in the American press during the Barry trials and the unsatisfactory promotion, publicity, and commentary on *Monsieur Verdoux*, it is no wonder that the rift between Chaplin and the American public was steadily widening. It was not about to close. Chaplin's progressive political activities had continued after his second front period and would continue through 1949, and both congressional denunciations and FBI investigations of his politics would continue to chip away at his declining star image. The reputation that once had seemed a pillar of marble now seemed composed of sandstone.

9

Chaplin's Politics and American
Culture, 1943–1952

Chaplin the Progressive
Activist, 1943–1949

Just as *Monsieur Verdoux* contributed to the image of Chaplin as a leftist social critic, so did his public political activities in the latter part of the decade, many of which were publicized in the press. Although Chaplin's active involvement in politics had waned after his second front speeches of 1942—largely because until the middle of 1945 the Barry trials consumed so much of his time—he did not entirely halt his political activity. In fact, contrary to those commentators who downplay or disparage his interest, Chaplin's involvements in politics between 1943 and 1949 were nearly all consistent with the position we have termed "progressive." These clustered around two sorts of activity: interactions with Soviet artists and diplomats, and involvement in domestic political issues from a progressive perspective.[1]

Chaplin's relationship with Soviet artists and diplomats from World War II on resulted in part from his second front speeches and his support for various Soviet-American friendship groups that grew up during the war. Chaplin was, for example, one of the sponsors when the founding of the National Council of American-Soviet Friendship was announced in April 1943. Similarly, when an "American–Soviet Friendship Rally" was held in Madison Square Garden on 16 November 1944, a number of Hollywood movie stars—including Chaplin, John Garfield, Rita Hayworth, Orson Welles, James Cagney, Katherine Hepburn, Gene Kelly, and Edward G. Robinson—signed a message in a gesture of support for it. The statement said that the artists added their voices in favor of the bond that existed between "our great country and our great Allies." The message added: "In this friendship lies not only the hope but the future of the world."[2] In both these cases and in other such instances, Chaplin acted consistently with his desire to encourage Soviet–American cooperation and to defeat fascism.

As a result of his public support of the Soviet–American alliance, Chaplin was invited to functions by Soviet consulate officials in Los

Angeles and honored as an artist in the Soviet Union. In May 1943, while Soviet–American relations were still in full bloom, the *New York Times* commented on Chaplin's popularity in the Soviet Union.[3] This was formally recognized in 1944 when on April 26 and 27, a Soviet cultural organization called VOKS sponsored a tribute to Chaplin in Moscow. On the first evening a large audience made up of Soviet artists, public figures, and journalists, including foreign journalists, viewed selections from Chaplin's films at the Moscow Cinema Club. On the next day film actress Vera Maretskaya opened by reading a message of greeting from Chaplin, which was followed by tributes to Chaplin's life and work by people like director Vsevolod Pudovkin, Dmitri Shostakovich, and journalist Ilya Ehrenburg. The festival closed by sending Chaplin a collective telegram, wishing him "new successes assisting in our common struggle against Hitlerism, as well as many years of work for the good of the world and also of mankind." The event was reported by the *New York Times* and *Newsweek*. Such coverage in U.S. publications of large circulation affected the evolution of Chaplin's star image, for it gave him attention that would be seen as suspicious to many Americans after the political climate changed in the late 1940s.[4]

Chaplin returned the praise in 1946 to Soviet director Sergei Eisenstein, whom Chaplin had known since Eisenstein visited Hollywood in the late 1920s. In 1946 Chaplin saw Part One of *Ivan the Terrible* and was so enthusiastic about it that he sent a telegram congratulating Eisenstein on "the greatest historic film ever made."[5] The film made such a strong impression on Chaplin that he even praised it in his autobiography as "the acme of all historical pictures," one that "dealt with history poetically" (MA, p. 323).

Of gatherings at the Soviet consulate or other events honoring Soviet artists, perhaps the most publicized and damaging to his star image was a party Chaplin attended in late May, 1946, aboard a Soviet ship in Long Beach Harbor. The evening, arranged by Soviet consul Konstantin Simonov and Soviet trade representative Alexander Graachev, included a banquet and the showing of a Soviet film called *The Bear*. Charles and Oona Chaplin attended, along with director Lewis Milestone, actor John Garfield, and their wives. The event would probably have created no stir except for an incident that took place as the Chaplins were leaving. Apparently U.S. Customs agents, checking to be sure no dutiable articles were brought ashore after the banquet, were waiting as the guests left the ship. News photographers overheard Chaplin say, in reference to the Customs officials, "Oh, I see we are under the power of the American Gestapo." Though it is quite possible the comment was made in jest, the newspapers splashed their front pages with negative Chaplin publicity. The Hearst-owned *New York Journal-American*, for example, used a headline spanning half of the front page: "Chaplin at Red Ship Revel; Slurs U.S. Customs Men." A subtitle added, "Calls Agents 'Gestapo.' " The lead sentence provides a good example of the article's anti-Chaplin slant: "Tingling with champagne, a select group of Hollywood film luminaries applauded a Russian movie about a water-drinking revolutionary at a weekend revel aboard a Soviet ship in Long Beach harbor." An accompanying photograph, which showed Chaplin greeting an unidentified man, was captioned, "And One Saw Red!"[6] This "Simonov incident," which later turned up in Chaplin's FBI internal security file, raises at least two relevant issues. First, even if he was joking, Chaplin revealed his progressive assumption that American society had its own tendencies toward fascism as he understood the term. Second, the incident reiterated how certain factions of the press could turn an innocuous event into an opportunity for negative publicity about Chaplin's politics.

Besides these interactions with Soviet officials and artists, Chaplin engaged in considerable progressive political activity after World War II. One of the first occasions was a personal act with political implications: reading Theodore Dreiser's poem, "The Road I Came," at Dreiser's funeral on 3 January 1946. The novelist, long known for his progressive political sympathies, had joined the Communist party during World War II and had become acquainted with Chaplin after meeting him at a reception held at the Soviet consulate in Los Angeles in 1943. In her memoirs, Helen Dreiser notes that she and her husband subsequently came to know the Chaplins quite well and that Dreiser "had a deep regard for Chaplin as an artist, intellectual, humanitarian, world citizen, and comedian." Chaplin apparently also spent some evenings in the last years of the war with Dreiser, Clifford Odets, and John Howard Lawson, all political progressives. Lawson, a Communist screenwriter and later one of the Hollywood Ten, eulogized Dreiser at his funeral, and Chaplin read the poem, the end of which was later inscribed on Dreiser's memorial.[7]

Participating in an acquaintance's funeral is hardly a bold political act, but Chaplin also became something of a champion of progressive causes in the late 1940s, often in defense of the civil liberties of those holding unpopular leftist views. One such act was to protest the legal proceedings against Communists Eugene Dennis, Leon Josephson, and Gerhart Eisler (brother of Hanns Eisler). The three were about to be tried in federal court on contempt of Congress charges because they had refuesed to testify before HUAC, and in June 1947, two months after the devastating opening of *Monsieur Verdoux* in New York, Chaplin joined a group of notables who urged that the trials of these three men be postponed "in order that they may have proper time to prepare their case and in order to avoid undue prejudice against them at a time when red-baiting hysteria is so violent." Ultimately, both Dennis and Josephson were given one-year prison terms after being cited for contempt of Congress, and Gerhart Eisler left the country in 1949 with deportation proceedings hanging over his head.[8] By defending these figures as the political climate was becoming increasingly uncomfortable for domestic radicals, Chaplin was sticking out his neck and endangering his already slumping star image. Although it was certainly his right to express his views about these proceedings, Chaplin was either naive about how, given the change in political climate, his actions might affect his star image, or else he was beginning to feel that his political commitments were more important to him than his stardom.

Chaplin's encounters with HUAC also showed his progressive political sympathies. In addition to being subpoenaed to testify before the committee (as will be discussed in the following section), Chaplin confronted HUAC in at least two other ways. He added his signature to an *amici curiae* brief that challenged HUAC's contempt citations against the Hollywood Ten, and he supported his friend Hanns Eisler, who testified before HUAC in May and September 1947 about his alleged Communist political leanings (at the hearings he was called, among other things, "the Karl Marx of Communism in the music field"). Eisler denied being a member of the Communist party and concluded his testimony by charging that "the Committee hopes to create a drive against every liberal, progressive, and socially conscious artist in this country."

When it began to appear in November 1947 that deportation proceedings would be instituted against Eisler and his wife, Chaplin telegrammed Pablo Picasso and asked him to organize a group of fellow artists to protest at the American Embassy in Paris against the "outrageous deportation proceedings against Hanns Eisler." Chaplin also asked Picasso to send a copy of the protest statement so he could use it for publicity in Los Angeles. In December he joined thirteen other prominent artists and scientists, including Albert Einstein and Thomas Mann, in sending a petition to Attorney General Tom Clark, that urged him to drop the deportation proceedings. When the warrant for deportation was issued in February 1948, Chaplin again interceded, promising to provide the Eislers financial support if the U.S.

government would allow them to leave the country voluntarily. They ultimately did so, leaving for Czechoslovakia on 26 March 1948.[9]

In 1948 Chaplin became enthusiastic about the presidential campaign of Henry Wallace: Wallace's call to cooperate with rather than contain the Soviet Union was as attractive to Chaplin as Wallace's desire to extend the New Deal. Although Chaplin's name is not listed in the *New York Times Index* for 1948, his first absence since the 1920s, his political involvements with the Progressive party were prominently reported in the Los Angeles press. For example, on 29 March 1948, Wallace's running mate, Senator Glen Taylor of Idaho, addressed a "Rally for Peace" in Gilmore Stadium in Los Angeles, with 12,000 attending. The *Los Angeles Times* reported that Chaplin attended and contributed $500 to the campaign. An even more enthusiastic crowd of 24,000 gathered again at the stadium in mid-May to hear Wallace himself minimize the threat posed by the Soviet Union and attack America's support of reactionary dictators. Charles and Oona Chaplin met Wallace at the home of William Wyler during this visit, and the next day the *Los Angeles Times* gave first-page coverage to the story, including a picture of the smiling Chaplin writing a $1000 check for Wallace's campaign.[10]

Wallace lost, and lost badly. Chaplin found other ways to continue his political activities, however, and in 1949 he publicly supported two peace conferences, at a time when progressivism was clearly a waning political position in the United States. From March 27 to 29, the Cultural and Scientific Conference for World Peace was held in New York City. The State Department denied visas to many West European leftists, which left primarily American progressives and Eastern bloc Communists able to attend. A number of anti-Stalinist liberals attended in order to challenge the dominant progressive viewpoint. The harsh reception given the anti-Stalinists led many Americans, even (perhaps particularly) the anti-Stalinist liberals, to perceive such peace conferences as dominated by Communists.[11] Despite the controversies swirling around the peace conferences, Chaplin made a public statement on April 5 in support of the World Congress for Peace, to be held in Paris that month, and in September the *New York Times* reported that both Chaplin and Henry Wallace had sent messages of support to the American Continental Congress on World Peace, held in Mexico City.[12]

Chaplin also lent his name to protest the Peekskill incident, which has achieved prominence in the annals of Cold War repression in the United States. The incident involved the disruption of a picnic held by leftists at Lakeland Acres picnic grounds outside Peekskill, New

York, on 27 August 1949. Prominent black athlete, actor, singer, and political activist Paul Robeson was scheduled to sing that Saturday evening, but insults by American Legionnaires and other demonstrators led to a riot that prevented him from appearing. The performance was rescheduled for Sunday, September 4, and though Robeson was able to sing that afternoon, he did so with the epithets of demonstrators ringing in his ears. Then, as the huge crowd of 25,000 was disbanding, demonstrators threw stones, broke hundreds of car windows, overturned at least eight cars, burned a cross, and threw a woman over a hedge after taking her baby from her. When Robeson sent a letter to President Truman in October demanding a federal investigation of the incident and prosecution of the guilty, Chaplin signed it and indicated his support.[13] As with so many of his activities in the 1940s, Chaplin here demonstrated both his progressive political views and his belief that domestic leftists should be allowed to hold and express their views without interference or censorship. Such a consistent and firm political position made Chaplin vulnerable to challenges and attacks by government officials and agencies, and also by conservative voluntary associations like the American Legion, as the 1940s wore on.

Chaplin and the U.S. Congress

In the later 1930s, Robert Sklar has argued, American filmmakers like Walt Disney and Frank Capra, aware of the powerful cultural mythmaking capacities of the movies, helped through their films to reaffirm traditional American cultural mythology. After America entered World War II, the film industry, with government encouragement and support, broadened this effort by going systematically into the business of affirming the American war effort and "the American way" in its pictures.[14]

In part because of the government's cooperative efforts with filmmakers, exemplified by fictional war films or such documentary films as the "Why We Fight" series, elected officials also came to believe in the power of movies. In addition to being pleased that films could affirm traditional American values, however, some officials became concerned that the opposite could also be true: that films could contain disruptive or "subversive" material that could erode dominant values. Just as the Legion of Decency placed pressure on the film industry from a religious perspective in the early 1930s, the U.S. Congress placed political pressure on the film industry to exercise care in the "content" of its films and to rid itself of anyone perceived as leftist, especially as the Cold War set in. Due to his consistently progressive stance throughout the 1940s, Chaplin became a frequent target of such congressional attacks. Since these criticisms were often publicized, they too contributed to the politicization of Chaplin's star image in the 1940s. They also indicate the pattern of hostility toward Chaplin and his star image that was developing throughout the decade.

As was noted earlier, Chaplin's politics first came under close congressional examination in the late 1930s and then again in 1941. In the late 1930s his name was mentioned, along with many others, by Martin Dies, then chairman of HUAC, as one with Communist sympathies, but nothing came of it. In 1941 the Senate's Subcommittee on War Propaganda, chaired by Senator D. W. Clark of Idaho, investigated Chaplin's *The Great Dictator* and a number of other films for their "prematurely anti-fascist" sentiments. This investigation was cut short, however, by America's entry into the war.[15]

During the war, publicity about the Barry affair certainly made Chaplin a more vulnerable and popular target for certain political factions. Two congressmen willing to make political hay by attacking Chaplin's morality were Senator William Langer of Missouri and Representative John Rankin of Mississippi. In February 1945, Langer introduced a bill on the floor of the Senate that would, if passed, have instructed the attorney general to investigate Chaplin and could have possibly led to his deportation. Although the bill was never passed, it indicated a trend. By July, Rankin joined the chorus of Chaplin denouncers. On the floor of the House that month, he criticized the Hollywood community for buying and hanging so many "loathesome" paintings and illustrations from the radical magazine *New Masses*, then added: "I am sure that some of them got into the home of Charles Chaplin, the perverted subject of Great Britain who has become famous for his forcible seduction of white girls."[16]

This was followed by more denunciation of the comedian by members of the Congress in 1947, the year of *Monsieur Verdoux*'s release and the Hollywood Ten trials. The attacks began when in a Senate hearing on 7 March 1947, Senator Langer commented that the U.S. policy of deportation was inconsistent. Why, he asked, should some people be deported when "a man like Charlie Chaplin, with his communistic leanings, with his unsavory record of lawbreaking, of rape, or the debauching of American girls 16 and 17 years of age, remains?"[17]

The hostile reaction to the release of *Monsieur Verdoux* provided some Congressmen with more ammunition for their anti-Chaplin arsenals. Rankin again attacked in June, when he announced how pleased he was that the "rotten picture by Charlie Chaplin" was being banned in Memphis. At the same time, he almost gleefully inserted into the *Congressional Record* an anti-Chaplin editorial from the *Shreveport Journal*, along with a hostile letter to the editor from a Shreveport businessman. But then his challenge to Chaplin became more concrete: "I am today demanding," announced Rankin, "that Attorney General Tom Clark institute proceedings to deport Charlie Chaplin. He has refused to become an American citizen, his very life in Hollywood is detrimental to the moral fabric of America. In that way he can be kept off the American screen, and his loathesome pictures can be kept from before the eyes of the American youth. He should be deported and got rid of at once."[18] As we shall see, Rankin's suggestion did reach Clark, who passed it on to J. Edgar Hoover, head of the FBI, who in turn incorporated the issue into the ongoing investigation of Chaplin as an internal security risk. The same call to deport Chaplin was heard again in 1949, when Senator Harry P. Cain urged that Chaplin be deported because of his Communist ties.[19] In the Cold War atmosphere, such public denunciations of the declining star's unpopular political views apparently played well to the constituents back home.

Although senators sometimes attacked Chaplin, his name was heard more often in the House of Representatives, for when HUAC was revived in 1947 under Chairman J. Parnell Thomas, Hollywood quickly became a key focus and remained one through the early 1950s.[20] Chaplin's name came up frequently, and in several contexts. He was among the initial group subpoenaed in 1947 to testify before HUAC; his name was mentioned regularly in the testimonies of witnesses who willingly or unwillingly appeared before the committee; and his name appeared in the special congressional reports written under HUAC auspices.

On 21 September 1947, five days before *Monsieur Verdoux* was released in Washington for its short but relatively successful run, HUAC subpoenaed forty-three Hollywood figures to testify as a part of its investigation of subversive content in Hollywood movies. Half of the group was made up of cooperative ("friendly") witnesses—people like Adolphe Menjou, Gary Cooper, Ronald Reagan, Walt Disney, Ayn Rand, and Sam Wood—and many of these had expected to be called. Some of the others were leftists who were at first called the Hollywood Nineteen, and ultimately the Hollywood Ten. This group of avowed progressives, some of whom were also Communists, opposed on constitutional grounds the committee's inquiries into their political opinions, were cited for contempt of Congress, and were sentenced to a year in prison on those charges. Chaplin was acquainted with or had met a number of the original Nineteen, including Bertolt Brecht, Lewis Milestone, Herbert Biberman, and John Howard Lawson. Because of his progressive political views and his association with some of the Nineteen, Chaplin, given HUAC's political aims, was in a vulnerable position.

Despite his subpoena, however, Chaplin never testified. He had most likely expected the call, for at least two reasons. First, in December 1946 the *Washington Post* reported that Chaplin would be subpoenaed to testify when HUAC reopened hearings in January. At that point the committee's chief counsel said the committee wanted to know more about "reports that motion picture money is financing a third party tentatively named the People's Front, which has an eye on running Henry Wallace for President." An article in such a prominent paper on such a subject undoubtedly came to Chaplin's attention. Second, Chaplin's friend Hanns Eisler was interrogated by FBI staff in Los Angeles in the summer of 1947 (and testified before a closed HUAC session in Los Angeles in May and then in a Washington public hearing September 24 and 26), and Chaplin probably felt that his own testimony would be inevitable, given his publicly affirmed friendship with and defenses of Eisler.[21]

After expecting to be called in the summer of 1947, Chaplin sent a telegram to committee chairman Thomas. It said, in part: "In order that you be completely up-to-date on my thinking I suggest that you view carefully my latest production *Monsieur Verdoux*. It is against war and the futile slaughter of our youth. I trust you will find its humane message distasteful. While you are preparing your engraved subpoena I will give you a hint on where I stand. I am not a Communist. I am a peace-monger." The combative tone of the telegram continued when Chaplin and United Artists decided to open *Monsieur Verdoux* the day after Hanns Eisler was scheduled to testify before HUAC in Washington. As mentioned in Chapter 8, a few days before that scheduled opening, publicist Birdwell sent a telegram in Chaplin's name to each member of HUAC that invited them to attend the premiere on September 26. None accepted Chaplin's invitation, yet for whatever reason—perhaps Chaplin's reputation, however much it was fading—HUAC decided not to call him and, according to Chaplin, sent him a courteous reply telling him that he could consider the matter closed.[22]

The reply was, however, far from the last time Chaplin's name came up in the HUAC investigations. It appeared a number of times in HUAC testimony. Several prominent anti-Communists leveled charges against him. In March 1947, at HUAC's early hearings, both Jack B.

Tenney and Walter S. Steele brought up Chaplin's name. Tenney, a California state senator, had chaired since 1941 the Joint Fact-Finding Committee on Un-American Activities, California's counterpart to HUAC, and enthusiastically shared his information.[23] When Representative Karl Mundt asked him about communism in Hollywood, Tenney answered: "We do know that many of the so-called stars in Hollywood permit their names to be used by Communist front organizations. . . . We have Garfield, John Garfield; Charlie Chaplin. Both of these gentlemen attended a party given by a Soviet writer in San Pedro harbor, and entertained him, we understand, at their homes, and in every way have given aid and comfort to Communist-front organizations."[24] Though Tenney mixed up his harbors (the ship was anchored in Long Beach Harbor), he did bring to the Committee's attention an incident that had already, as we have seen, appeared in the press and gave it a most sinister appearance.

Walter Steele was chairman of the National Security Committee of the American Coalition of Patriotic, Civic, and Fraternal Societies, a confederation of over a hundred patriotic organizations. He had first appeared before HUAC on 16 August 1938, when he branded 640 organizations, including the American Civil Liberties Union, the Boy Scouts, and the Camp Fire Girls, as "Communistic."[25] At the March hearings, Steele charged that Chaplin was a "charter member" of an organization called the People's Radio Foundation. According to Steele, the group's stated goal was to make the public aware of "worthy American civic and cultural traditions and achievements and like contributions made by nationality groups." Steele told HUAC that it was a Communist organization.[26] The story later made it into the newspapers—Ed Sullivan was one columnist who slurred Chaplin after the testimony. When Chaplin was asked about the organization in a 1948 interview with the Immigration and Naturalization Service (INS), he denied any involvement with it.[27]

A third witness to mention Chaplin in 1947 was Howard Rushmore, a former Communist who had served for a time as film critic for the *New York Daily Worker*. Converted to anticommunism after breaking with the Party, Rushmore was asked if he knew Chaplin or if Chaplin had sent articles to the *Daily Worker*. He answered no to both questions. But when asked if the *Worker* had any policy toward Chaplin, Rushmore replied, "He was what we call in the business a 'sacred cow.' . . . That is a newspaper phrase which—well, loosely, would mean that you always give favorable publicity to and a lot of it."[28] These three testimonies, given when guilt by association was a common practice, all damaged Chaplin, however false or distorted the testimony may have been and however much the testimony disregarded Chaplin's right to free association.

Chaplin's name also came up occasionally when leftists testified. For example, in 1950 Edward G. Robinson explained his contribution to the Committee for the First Amendment (a group that supported the Hollywood Ten) by saying that at one time "it was stated that Charlie Chaplin and I would be the first to receive subpoenas." Naturally, Robinson continued, he then contributed money to support others who did receive subpoenas. The following year John Garfield affirmed his presence with Chaplin at the infamous Simonov harbor party, and musician Artie Shaw explained that he signed a card allowing his name to be used as a supporter for the World Peace Congress in 1949 after he saw a number of names, including Chaplin's, on the letterhead of the request. Bishop G. Bromley Oxnam defended his involvements with the National Council of American–Soviet Friendship (he had spoken at the same "Salute to Our Russian Ally" meeting in 1942 as Chaplin had) by listing some of the sponsors, who included Chaplin, Van Wyck Brooks, Albert Einstein, Justice Learned Hand, Fiorello LaGuardia, Thomas Mann, Robert Lynd, and Ralph Barton Perry. These references reiterated Chaplin's progressive involvements during the 1940s. In addition, the testimonies by Shaw and Oxnam suggested that Chaplin, like many others during the war years, was sometimes influenced to support a cause because he saw names of other acquaintances or celebrities on the list of sponsors.[29]

Chaplin's name also came to HUAC's attention in the reports on various subjects that were prepared by aides at the behest of the committee and then made available to the public. Two in particular stand out. The first was HUAC's 1950 report on the Cultural and Scientific Conference for World Peace, held in New York City in March 1949.[30] The report opens by claiming that the conference "was actually a super-mobilization of the inveterate wheelhorses and supporters of the Communist Party and its auxiliary organizations" (p. 1). Chaplin was named twice. The first reference indicated that the French atomic scientist Frédéric Joliot-Curie had announced that Chaplin would be one of the American delegates to the World Peace Conference in Paris in April 1949 (p. 10). (Though the HUAC report was released a year after the Paris conference, it failed to note that Chaplin had not actually attended.) The second reference to Chaplin names him as one of the New York conference sponsors, a list that included an ecumenical group of leftists: Marlon Brando, Leonard Bernstein, Aaron Copland, W.E.B. DuBois, Albert Einstein, Judy Holliday, Robert and Helen Lynd, Linus Pauling, Muriel Ruykeyser, Studs Terkel, Henry Wallace, and a large number of Hollywood figures. Both Norman Mailer and F. O. Matthiessen were listed among the expected speakers (pp. 57–60). The HUAC report intimates that having one's name on such a list nearly constituted disloyalty to America.

The 1949 peace movement was a favorite target of HUAC, and in April of the next year it released its "Report on Communist 'Peace' Offensive."[31] The report's subtitle ("A Campaign to Disarm and Defeat the United States") and opening sentence ("the most dangerous hoax ever devised by the international Communist conspiracy is the current world wide 'peace' offensive") indicate its attitude. The report makes four claims about Chaplin's involvement:

1. That Chaplin was listed as a sponsor for the Cultural and Scientific Conference for World Peace, held in New York City, March 25–27, 1949 (p. 104).
2. That he was listed as one of "Americans sponsoring the World Peace Conference" in Paris in April 1949 (p. 110).
3. That he was a member of the Committee for U.S. Participation in the American Continental Congress for World Peace, held September 5–10, 1949 (p. 21).
4. That Chaplin and Henry Wallace sent greetings to that Congress, held in Mexico City (p. 23).

We have already noted Chaplin's willingness to lend his name in support of these peace conferences, in part because their general thrust coincided with his internationalist, "One World" sympathies. It is important to remember what involvement in such activities meant to most members of HUAC and to many other Americans in the Cold War era. Much like conservative critics of the nuclear freeze movement in 1984, HUAC investigators—in spite of the constitutionally guaranteed freedom of speech and assembly—tended to think of those who supported the 1949 peace conferences as dupes (at the very least), as naive instruments of Soviet foreign policy, as dangerous subversives, or worse.

Chaplin and the FBI: The Internal Security File

With all this attention paid in the U.S. Congress to Chaplin's progressive politics, it is no surprise that another organization vigilant in its attempt to ferret out what it termed Communist influence in America, the FBI, should pay some attention to Chaplin in these years.[32] Like other stars whose leftist political views have become public, including, more recently, people like Jane Fonda and John Lennon, Chaplin was closely observed by the FBI. As we have seen, the Bureau had already expended considerable time and resources in exploring Chaplin's involvement with Joan Barry. Their interest in Chaplin's politics went through two long phases, the first lasting from 1946 to 1949, the second from 1951 to Chaplin's banishment/exile in 1952. This section will trace the investigation through early 1952; the FBI's role in Chaplin's "banishment" will be discussed in Chapter 10. A summary of the Bureau's activities relating to Chaplin will highlight how this organization—one small but influential part of American culture—significantly affected Chaplin's fortunes and, more subtly, helped damage his star image.[33]

The subject of Chaplin's politics shows up very early in FBI files. The first known reference is a report from the Los Angeles field office to the Washington headquarters, dated 14 August 1922. The report indicated that Chaplin had held a reception at his home for William Z. Foster, a leader of the American Communist Party, when Foster was visiting Los Angeles. It added that the party had been attended by many of the Hollywood "parlor Bolsheviki." Copies of the report were sent by Director William J. Burns to Will Hays (the recently named head of the MPPDA), and to the Bureau's assistant director, J. Edgar Hoover. An accompanying memo to Hoover reported that "numerous movie stars are taking more than an active part in the Red movement" and evidently "endeavoring to organize a program for placing propaganda before the public via the movies."[34] One suspects that Hoover never forgot the connection between Chaplin and communism made in the letter's carelessly worded list of allegations.

During World War II, the FBI devoted little attention to investigating Chaplin's politics, except to the extent that his political views came up during the Barry investigations. Hoover did receive one report from a confidential informant in the New York office that summarized Chaplin's second front speech at the Hotel Pennsylvania on 3 December 1942, along with Russian War Relief press releases about the event. The informant's political views are clear from his comment that the speeches expressed "the usual pro-Soviet 'cultural' propaganda," a notion that was passed along in a memo summarizing the report two weeks later. It described Chaplin's speech by saying that he "defended Communism and eulogized Russia" in it.[35] This report and memo were exceptions to the rule, however; Chaplin's politics did not become the focus of FBI attention until after the war was over and the Cold War beginning.

In 1946, the Special Agent in Charge of the Los Angeles office received from Hoover a terse directive dated September 9: "It is requested that you review the references to Charles Chaplin in the films of your office and give consideration to recommending the preparations of a Security Index Card." (The security index card was filed for those who were under an active FBI investigation related to internal security matters.) This directive began a large investigation that continued off and on until 18 May 1953, some weeks after Chaplin turned in his reentry permit and decided to settle in Switzerland. At that point, Hoover directed the Los Angeles office to place Chaplin's card in the "unavailable" section.

Up through 1949 the investigation took place largely in Los Angeles, where FBI agents researched press clippings, magazine articles, and even Gerith von Ulm's biography of Chaplin; kept Chaplin periodically under observation; and interviewed a variety of informants and witnesses (whose names are most often blacked out in the released files, but who appear to include some members of the press and some of Chaplin's domestic staff) about Chaplin's political views, associations, and activities. In addition to the Los Angeles field office, others—including those in San Francisco and New York City—also played smaller parts in the investigation.

At first, however, the Los Angeles office seemed to drag its feet in responding to Hoover's September 1946 letter, for on 14 March 1947, Hoover, apparently piqued at their delay, wrote them again: "It is requested that the instructions contained in the Bureau's memorandum of September 9, 1946, be given attention at an early date."[36] Evidently the Los Angeles office knew when it had displeased its director, for the next item in the file is a fourteen-page report—the first report in the Chaplin internal security file, number 100–127090.[37]

The account contains little striking information, but it sets the tone for later reports: straightforward and factual, even when they contain unsubstantiated claims, questionable claims from informants, or downright falsehoods. One such detail that also shows up in a number of subsequent FBI reports is the claim that Chaplin was the "son of a family named THONSTEIN," which came from eastern Europe to London in 1850 (p. 1). The report implies that Chaplin is of Jewish descent, an implication later asserted as fact in a description of Chaplin at the end (p. 13). There it claims that Chaplin's "Descent" is "Jewish" and his only "Peculiarity" is that he "speaks with a Jewish accent." Despite the falsehood of these details, Chaplin is made to seem a more suspicious or secretive character in later reports because the opening page of most lists "Thonstein" as one of his aliases.

This initial piece served as the basis of a twenty-four-page, typed, single-spaced report prepared for Hoover himself by the Washington office. Completed 6 August 1947, this second report was longer in part because Chaplin had released *Monsieur Verdoux* in the intervening months and had had a number of run-ins with the press over his political sympathies. Preceding the August 6 report in the files are a number of press clippings concerning the controversy over *Monsieur Verdoux*, including positive reports from the *New York Daily Worker* and two Ed Sullivan columns that attack Chaplin's progressive politics (e.g., "During the war, instead of entertaining the troops or our wounded, Chaplin delivered nothing but political speeches for Russia, demanding a second front").[38]

The August 6 report, after a brief background introduction, was divided into eleven categories that with variations served as a basis for later reports:

1. Evidence of Membership in the Communist Party and Association with Known Communists [this section mentions that he read a poem at Dreiser's funeral]
2. Evidence of Financial Contributions to the Communist Party by Chaplin
3. Chaplin's Contacts with Russian Officials and Representatives of the Soviet Consular Service [this section mentions the Simonov incident]
4. Assistance Given by Chaplin to American–Soviet Relations
5. Additional Evidence of Pro-Soviet Activities on the Part of Chaplin [this section mentions a gossip-column squib that Chaplin was invited to a Soviet New Year's Party]
6. Affiliations with Russian War Relief
7. Affiliations with the Artists Front to Win the War
8. Activities on Behalf of a Second Front [the previous three sections detail some of Chaplin's 1942 and 1943 political activities]
9. Affiliations with the People's Radio Foundation
10. Associations with Miscellaneous Communist Front Organizations [these include a number of antifascist organizations]
11. White Slave Traffic Violation and Civil Rights and Domestic Violence Violations by Chaplin [this section includes results of FBI investigations in the Barry case on charges that Chaplin either was acquitted of or were dropped for lack of evidence]

Though it is clear that the FBI assiduously scoured press accounts and quizzed informants about Chaplin's political views in order to gather a great deal of information that establishes his progressive activity between 1942 and 1947, the report is devoid of any evidence that would suggest subversive activity.

Nevertheless, the Bureau was quite willing to share information, however inconclusive, circumstantial, or false, that could damage Chaplin's reputation. One way it affected Chaplin's public image was by providing information to gossip columnists. We have already seen in Chapter 7 how the FBI and gossip columnists Hopper and Muir worked in tandem during the Barry trials. All were investigators of sorts, and it appears that between 1943 and the early 1950s the FBI shared information with a number of gossip columnists, including Hopper, Muir, Parsons, and Sullivan.

The system seems to have worked like this. If the gossip columnists were able through their contacts to obtain information concerning Chaplin, they may have passed it along to FBI agents. It is not unlikely that some of the named and unnamed informants in the FBI reports were gossip columnists or their contacts. A 24 March 1944 FBI memo from Agent Nichols to Agent Tolson, for example, does report that columnist Florabel Muir provided a Los Angeles agent with the information that Chaplin hired a press agent during the Barry trials. (It is often difficult to determine with certainty if a columnist was an informant because informants' names are usually blacked out in the released files.)

Evidence is firmer that the FBI, in exchange, would provide information to the columnists that could be leaked through their gossip columns. For example, a memo of 14 August 1947 from Agent Nichols to Agent Rosen (both in the Washington office) shows that this practice of leaking information to gossip columnists was used. It opened: "The following might be an excellent item for Louella Parsons." "The following" turned out to be some extremely circuitous information: a report of a San Francisco FBI agent, dated 3 February 1922, that quoted a press dispatch from Berlin concerning an article in the Soviet newspaper *Pravda*, which praised Chaplin as a great comic actor and hailed him as a "Communist friend of humanity." The leak to Parsons was not an isolated case, for by August 24, another FBI memo from Assistant Director Ladd to Hoover referred to the "material prepared for Hedda Hopper" and described the same article from *Pravda*. Hoover, who often reveals hard-headed pragmatism in his memos and notations, jotted at the bottom of the memo: "Certainly a much labored effort brought forth a miserable product." Regardless of Hoover's skepticism, however, it seems apparent that the FBI was providing information to gossip columnists in 1947 that could be used to damage Chaplin's star image. And the FBI reports show conclusively that the FBI used information from gossip columns as evidence damaging to Chaplin, as when, in the August 6 report, under "Chaplin's Contacts with Russian Officials," Ed Sullivan's 6 April 1944 column was used as evidence. It claimed that the Soviet consul in Los Angeles had been authorized to turn over a Russian plane to take Chaplin to Moscow if he lost the Mann Act trial and that the Chaplins were studying Russian (p. 12).

FBI internal security files on Chaplin also show that the FBI shared its information on Chaplin with other governmental agencies. When the Immigration and Naturalization Service, responding to the calls for Chaplin's deportation by Congressman Rankin and others, wrote the FBI to ask if their investigation would conflict with the FBI's, Hoover replied that the INS inquiry "would in no way interfere with our investigation concerning him." The letter also referred to a request by John Boyd, the executive assistant to the commissioner of the INS, for information on Chaplin. In response, Hoover sent the INS a seventeen-page report that contained much of the same questionable information included in the August 6 report, and in exchange he received from Boyd the transcript of an interview Boyd conducted with Chaplin in 1947, an extremely interesting document.[39] Sharing information about Chaplin, even weak information, seems to have been a frequent practice of the FBI, and it did Chaplin's star image no good.

The Los Angeles office worked too slowly for Hoover a second time, and in February 1948 he wrote again, reminding them that he had asked nearly a year and a half earlier whether they thought it advisable that a security index card be prepared for Chaplin. In addition, he asked them to update their 13 March 1947 report. Though it is unclear what prompted Hoover's letter, it may be that a seven-page document from the Department of State, withheld in the material released to me but placed immediately before Hoover's letter in the FBI files, either requested information about Chaplin or reminded Hoover to continue the FBI's investigation of the comedian.[40]

Between February and early June 1948 the Los Angeles office responded with two letters and a short report, which primarily treated two issues: Chaplin's *Monsieur Verdoux* press conference and his November 1947 telegram to Picasso in support of Hanns Eisler. In addition to summarizing the details of the two situations, the letters and report surveyed the press response to each.[41] These three documents were followed by more activities. The Los Angeles office, after some difficulty, persuaded Hoover to ask the Treasury Department for Chaplin's income tax returns between 1941 and 1947: they hoped to find some evidence of contributions to Communist causes. They also wrote a longer report of thirty-two pages, dated 10 August 1948, and sent it to Hoover.

The August 10 report, similar in some ways to previous reports, is significant for at least two reasons.[42] First, it shows that surveillance of Chaplin's private activities was going on with some regularity and intensity. Although large portions of the released report are blackened out or withheld, usually for reasons of national security ("b1" in FOIA code), what remains does list a significant number of Chaplin's personal contacts and activities. These contacts include such minutia as dinner invitations the Chaplins exchanged with Salka Viertel and the number of telephone calls—five—Lion Feuchtwanger made to Chaplin's home in August and October 1945 (pp. 24, 26). Second, in a listing of leads to follow, the report suggests that the Washington office request a transcript of the interview Chaplin had with INS commissioner John Boyd in April 1948 (p. 31), in which Chaplin specifically defends his progressive and internationalist views.[43]

The investigation continued through 1948 and 1949. By November a security index card had been prepared for Chaplin (two years after Hoover had asked that this be considered), with the aliases of "Charlie Chaplin" and "Thonstein" included on the card. When Hoover asked Los Angeles in April 1949 to submit a report "showing the current status of this investigation," the office responded with the 5 July 1949 report, the bulk of which contains Chaplin's interview with Boyd. About a month later, Hoover responded to the report with this evaluation: "A review of this file at the Bureau reflects that no substantial information has been developed to date which would indicate that the subject has been engaged in espionage or other intelligence activities."[44] Hoover went on to ask the Los Angeles office to "submit your observations concerning further investigative steps to be taken in this case." On October 7 the office wrote Hoover to tell him that nearly all the leads had been pursued and "no new information of value has been obtained." If no significant new information were discovered after two more interviews, they recommended that the Chaplin internal security case be closed.[45]

In November 1949 pressure was placed by the U.S. attorney general's office on Hoover himself, and his Washington office, to determine whether they had a case against Chaplin. In a November 10 letter to Hoover, Assistant Attorney General Alexander M. Campbell asked to have "copies of all of the Bureau reports on Charles Chaplan [*sic*]," particularly those related to "the field of subversive activities, any Communist connections, associations or information concerning Communist Party activity, or front organization membership and/or activity."[46] The reports were sent, and on December 21, one of Hoover's assistants sent him a memo saying that the attorney general's aide asked the Bureau to "check its files to see if there is any information therein which could be used in a trial to establish that Chaplin was a member of the Communist Party or had donated funds to the Communist Party itself."[47] Hoover immediately telegrammed the Los Angeles office to see if they knew of any witnesses who could testify against Chaplin on either of those issues.[48] They replied on December 27, and on the basis of that telegram, Hoover wrote to Peyton Ford, the assistant to the attorney general: "It was determined that there are no witnesses available who could offer testimony that Chaplin has been a member of the Communist Party in the past, is now a member, or that he has contributed funds to the Communist Party."[49]

Throughout this correspondence, the national fear, bordering on hysteria, of internal Communist subversion is evident. All this attention paid to Chaplin suggests how profoundly his star image was becoming associated with progressive politics. After several years of extensive FBI investigation of Chaplin, however, it appeared that the FBI's interest in Chaplin as a security risk was waning. They simply could not find what they wanted to undermine Chaplin.

An FBI memo of 7 February 1950 supports this conclusion. It noted that Chaplin had been investigated since November 1946 and that considerable information concerning his "pro-Communist sympathies and activities" had been discovered, but that "no information . . . indicating that Chaplin has engaged in espionage activities" had been found. Accordingly, the memo recommended that the Chaplin internal security investigation be closed.[50] Thus despite the FBI's vigorous efforts during an increasing Cold War atmosphere, this investigation of Chaplin as a security risk seemed to be winding down.

The investigation was not over, however. In the middle of 1950 two reports based on information obtained from confidential FBI informants helped to keep the file active. The first was an interoffice memo from Agent Turner to Agent Hennrich summarizing a conversation about Chaplin that the informant, a double agent, reportedly had with Petr Fedotov, the Soviet acting minister of state security. Fedotov told the informant that if Chaplin would move to Moscow he would receive anything he wanted, including a villa, for life and that Stalin, an admirer of Chaplin, was "interested in the prestige and reputation of the USSR in the world and if Chaplin would move to Russia, it would be good propaganda."[51] Although no FBI action was taken other than filing the memo, it did suggest that Chaplin's name and star image was becoming a pawn in the chess game of international Cold War politics.

The second document containing information on Chaplin was more instrumental in keeping the file open. On 21 June 1950 Louis F. Budenz, former managing editor of the *Daily Worker*, told New York FBI agents who had been interviewing him that Chaplin was a "concealed Communist." Budenz, a zealous anti-Communist following his withdrawal from the Party and his 1946 HUAC testimony, later claimed to have testified more than 3,000 hours to FBI agents.[52] The comments on Chaplin were part of a much longer testimony over several months that Budenz carried out in cooperation with the New York FBI office, resulting in the naming of some four hundred "concealed Communists" in the show business community. Budenz claimed that two Party members told him in 1936 that Chaplin was "the equivalent of a member of the Party" and alleged that he had submitted *Modern Times* to the "Moscow Board of Censorship in Russia." (This fantasy likely evolved from the screening of *Modern Times* for Shumiatsky in 1935.) He also claimed that Earl Browder suggested in the early 1940s that Chaplin should not apply for citizenship because it might generate problems that could lead to his deportation. (Budenz never explains why this made Chaplin a Communist.) Finally, he alleged that Chaplin was a member of various Communist-front organizations and had contributed money to some of them, something long known to FBI agents, because progressive groups like the National Council of American–Soviet Relations and the Progressive Citizens of America were on the attorney general's list of such organizations.[53]

On the basis of this memo, Hoover instructed the Los Angeles office in January 1951 to reopen the case and bring Chaplin's activities up to date. In March he prodded the office again, giving them an April 10 deadline to submit their report because Budenz was to testify again before HUAC, possibly about Chaplin. In response the Los Angeles office sent Hoover a fourteen-page report dated 5 April 1951, certainly one of the most feeble documents in Chaplin's FBI files. It contained a report by an informant "of unknown reliability"—a catering service employee—who said that Chaplin had attended a party at the house of Clifford Odets that was also attended by Gerhart Eisler. It also claimed that Chaplin had received three books on Czechoslovakia "from Moscow, Russia, through the Progressive Book Shop" in Los Angeles. Perhaps the wildest point in the report was an allegation by an informant whom the Bureau did not consider "to be very reliable." He claimed that Chaplin and another person whose identity has been blacked out in released files were "purchasing all types of arms, including revolvers, machine guns, and rifles" and that the two had "six airplanes that they are presently utilizing to fly these arms and other war materials in and out of Mexico."[54]

Apparently Hoover agreed with what was patently obvious from the report: that the Los Angeles office had to grasp for straws in compiling the April 1951 document. Or so it seems, at any rate, for nothing of consequence appears again in the FBI files until a letter from Hoover to Los Angeles in 1952. Because it deals with events leading up to the revocation of Chaplin's reentry permit, it will be discussed in Chapter 10.

What can we conclude about the FBI's investigation of Chaplin as a security risk through mid-1952? Chaplin's political views and private activities had been subject to severe—and many would say, unconstitutional—examination for over six years without any damaging information being accumulated, even by the extreme standards of the time. In addition, the FBI and the gossip columnists were apparently sharing information that could be used to harm Chaplin's reputation. Reading these files is a sobering experience. Not only do they underline how public even the most private activities of a star can become, but they also reveal how various institutions in American culture—in this case, the press, the FBI, Congress, and other administrative agencies like the IRS and INS—can cooperate formally and informally to discredit someone like Chaplin. The FBI investigation of Chaplin's politics constitutes one more step in the decline of Chaplin's star image that had begun in a serious way during the Barry trials, even though, as we shall see, Chaplin began to downplay and moderate his political views between 1950 and 1952 as a way to seek a truce, if not a reconciliation, with American culture.

Backing Away from Politics, 1950–1952

Following the Barry trials, the box-office failure of *Monsieur Verdoux*, and the negative associations resulting from his progressive political activity, Chaplin found himself in a bind. As a popular artist whose success depended on satisfying a large audience, he seemed to have two choices: either stop making films or reconcile himself with his audience by making a film more palatable to public taste than *Monsieur Verdoux*. As he began to plan the film that became *Limelight*, he seemed to be choosing the second path, even though this meant becoming more circumspect in public about the progressive political positions that he had firmly embraced through the 1940s.

One major reason for Chaplin's turnabout was economic. United Artists, the company he had helped found and through which he had released all his films from *A Woman of Paris* on, was for several reasons on the verge of economic ruin. The foreign market, which had provided a bonanza for Hollywood studios immediately after World War II, had begun to diminish by 1948 as European countries started to set up import quotas, high taxes, and other restrictions to keep too much currency from flowing out of their countries. The domestic market was also shrinking: between 1946 and 1948, movie attendance in the United States had declined between 15 and 25 percent, and this trend continued throughout most of the 1950s. And independent production, which United Artists had been almost the only company to encourage and cultivate before World War II, was becoming increasingly commonplace after war, so that talented producers and directors who would have previously come to United Artists were making deals with other studios. All these factors meant economic difficulties for Chaplin and Mary Pickford, the major United Artists stockholders. When the company's 1948 losses totaled $517,000, the worst it had ever recorded, Chaplin had good reason to aspire to making a film more popular than *Monsieur Verdoux*.[55]

The continuing pressure of the Cold War in the United States was a broader factor that encouraged Chaplin to become more discreet about his political activities from 1950 on. In foreign affairs, after the Soviet Union successfully detonated an atomic bomb and China "fell" to the Communists in 1949, and after the Cold War became hot in Korea in May 1950, any public statements in favor of more benign relations with the Soviet Union would have alienated the speaker from large portions of the American public.

Domestically, 1949 and 1950 saw the rise of Joseph McCarthy's virulent strain of anticommunism. After redbaiting an ex-Communist journalist in November 1949, McCarthy charged Communist infiltration of the State Department in a speech to a group of Young Republicans in November and, in a more famous speech of February 1950, to an audience in Wheeling, West Virginia, at which he held up a sheet of paper that he claimed listed 205 Communists in the State Department's employ. The year 1950 also witnessed strong fears of espionage: Klaus Fuchs was sentenced to fourteen years in prison for espionage in March, the same month that Harry Gold was arrested to begin the chain of events leading to the trial and execution of Ethel and Julius Rosenberg. And after the first Alger Hiss trial ended in a hung jury in 1949, Hiss was convicted of espionage in 1950 and given a five-year jail sentence. Amid this hostile atmosphere, large numbers of formerly leftist intellectuals either revised their progressive views or decided the wiser course was to remain silent on political issues. Chaplin's political activity (or inactivity) between 1950 and 1953 must be understood in this context.[56]

Thus Chaplin had good reasons to strive for reconciliation with his American moviegoing public, not the least being that his public reputation was in a shambles. The star image that had been so widely admired up to World War II had shifted radically. If we recall the assumption that a star image is a complex of meanings and effects that changes over time, we could say that as the 1940s progressed, Chaplin the man, and an increasingly controversial Chaplin at that, came to dominate the star image to a much greater extent, with a consequent decline in the centrality of the lovable, struggling, resilient Charlie. Chaplin's gradual capitulation to sound and subsequent abandonment of Charlie undoubtedly had much to do with this shift, but so did his active engagement in progressive politics and the publicity surrounding the Barry trials. Although Chaplin didn't seem to realize before the release of *Monsieur Verdoux* how badly his stardom had slipped, he appparently did understand his miscalculation afterward. But what could he do about it? Gestures of reconciliation seem to have been his answer.

One way Chaplin tried to mend the rift with his audience was by rereleasing *City Lights* in April 1950. We might recall that one suggestion Chaplin received during his *Monsieur Verdoux* press conference was that he either make more "Charlie" films or bring back the old ones. Chaplin chose the latter when in December 1949 he allowed the private school his daughter Geraldine was attending to show *City Lights* as a fund-raiser. It was a sellout; and patrons had to be turned away. Chaplin was pleased to see both young and old in the audience loving the film. That response prompted Chaplin and United Artists to open *City Lights* in Manhattan on 8 April 1950, and as late as May 21 the *New York Times* reported that the film was still "packing in satisfied customers."[57]

Rereleasing such a quintessential "Charlie" film as *City Lights* was a good way for Chaplin to reestablish ties with his audience: the film starred Charlie, it blended comedy and pathos with extreme skill and control, and its narrative omitted the overt progressive politics found in his subsequent features. Chaplin thus not only reminded his old fans of the star image they had so fully embraced but also introduced young viewers to the image of Charlie, one they would never have expected in the era of paternity suits and political harassment.

It is not unlikely that Chaplin hoped to mend fences with the public by systematically presenting his old features, in a sense creating his stardom afresh for a new generation. This is precisely what he did with the American rerelease of his films through RBC Films in the early 1970s, when the political climate in the country had changed enough to make the culture receptive to Chaplin's stardom again. But in 1950 it wasn't that easy. First of all, not that many screens were available for revivals of classic films. Granted, the Museum of Modern Art had established a Film Department a decade earlier, and other art museums were beginning to show an interest in classic films. In addition, the number of "art houses" and college film societies was beginning to grow; however, that number was certainly not large enough to affect many viewers outside a few large cities. Even more important, the political climate was still too hostile. One indication of the resistance to the rerelease of Chaplin's films occurred in December 1950, when the *New York Times* reported that the fledgling television station WPIX canceled its scheduled showings of Chaplin shorts after a protest, on political grounds, by the Hudson County, New Jersey, branch of Catholic War Veterans, the same group that James Fay had represented at the *Monsieur Verdoux* press conference.[58]

Yet there is good evidence that by 1950 Chaplin was seeking to distance himself from domestic communism in a way he had not throughout the 1940s. In July, the *Daily People's World*, a San Francisco–based leftist newspaper, announced that Chaplin's *The Circus* would be shown two nights as a fund-raiser for the paper. Chaplin, apparently sensitive to the negative publicity that could arise if one of his films were associated with the leftist group, put his foot down. He ordered his lawyers to halt the unauthorized showing of the film, a refusal that was even noted in the *New York Times*.[59] Although such an action was not surprising from a business standpoint, given the care with which Chaplin and his associates controlled his features and especially the revenues that flowed from them, it also contained political significance, for it was one of the rare instances after Chaplin's second front days that a newspaper report about him stressed his separation from, rather than his association with, a leftist organization.

This decision to deny a leftist group permission to show *The Circus* suggests that Chaplin was trying to tone down his progressive politics. In fact, I have been unable to find any references in the American press from 1950 to 1952 in which Chaplin defends the Soviet Union, even the Soviets' conduct in fighting fascism during World War II. This must be understood at least partly as consistent with the growing disillusionment with Stalin and the Soviet Union among American liberals that began to be widespread after the beginning of the Cold War. Yet even when Chaplin *could* be coaxed into talking about his political views, his tone was not belligerent, as it had sometimes been during the 1940s. For example, the *Hollywood Reporter* of 9 March 1950 (a month after McCarthy's Wheeling speech) quoted Chaplin's position on citizenship: "As a believer in 'One World,' I wish to respectfully state that my position is unaltered and that I have not made any request, officially or unofficially, for citizenship." Though Chaplin did not compromise his progressive position in this statement, he did—with the word "respectfully"—couch it in terms more conciliatory and hence more palatable to his audience, even for some of those who would have rejected his views.

Another indication of a thaw in the freeze that had developed between Chaplin and moviegoers was the appearance of several laudatory pieces on Chaplin in American mass magazines in 1949 and 1950. These articles came after several years when almost the only items that praised Chaplin were in the leftist, relatively small circulation press. Of these new mass-magazine pieces, the two most significant were by James Agee and Al Capp. Agee's "Comedy's Greatest Era," which appeared in a September 1949 issue of *Life*, probably reached the largest audience. Agee surveyed American silent film comedy in his essay but reserved his highest praise for the character of "the tramp." In Agee's words, "the finest pantomime, the deepest emotion, the richest and most poignant poetry were in Chaplin's work. He could probably pantomime Bryce's *The American Commonwealth* and make it paralyzingly funny in the bargain." Several months later Capp, best known for his "Li'l Abner" cartoon strip, published his essay. Although Capp was known as a political satirist, he argued here that Chaplin's work transcended politics. "When the ideological passions of our time are laughable curios," he wrote, "the greatest artist that our time has produced will be recognized as Charlie Chaplin." In this *Atlantic* cover article, Capp located the roots of humor in man's inhumanity to man, which he judged one basis of Chaplin's success, but he also pinpointed the pathos that often surrounded Charlie's relationship with women. "No confused, despondent lover ever saw a Chaplin picture," Capp wrote, "who didn't come away feeling considerably cheered up."[60]

Both Agee and Capp contributed ideas that in a more receptive political climate could help salvage Chaplin's star image. Agee emphasized the Charlie persona and the brilliant pantomime in the Chaplin films, both key aspects of the aesthetic contract that had cemented Chaplin's relationship with his audience in the 1910s and 1920s. Similarly, Capp, by emphasizing the intensity of Charlie's romances and the depth of pathos evoked when the romances went unrequited, brought to the fore elements that had played important roles in popularizing Chaplin's star image. It seemed that perhaps the worst was over for him.

In addition to these articles, which reached large audiences, three books on Chaplin were published in English in 1951 and 1952: Theodore Huff's *Charlie Chaplin*, Peter Cotes and Thelma Niklaus's *The Lit-*

tle Fellow, and Robert Payne's *The Great God Pan*. Although these books were not best-sellers when released and probably had little immediate effect on Chaplin's star image, they did look forward to a time when the *auteur* approach, to be discussed in Chapter 11, would come to dominate the history and analysis of film. Huff's biography, which was reprinted in paperback in the 1960s, eventually reached a relatively wide audience and thus had some effect on Chaplin's star image.[61]

By mid-1952 Chaplin had been quiet about his progressive politics for two years, quite a contrast to the vigorous political activity he had been involved in during the 1940s. As we have seen, the Barry trials and his political involvements had generated much controversy in the press during the 1940s, which had brought Chaplin the unwanted attention of elected government officials and the FBI. Nevertheless, with positive articles and books appearing and a nonpolitical film in the works, Chaplin may have thought that his preeminent star status was reviving.

10

Limelight and Banishment: The
Futility of Reconciliation

Chaplin, the U.S. Government, and
Banishment, 1952–1953

We know that stars have often been manufactured by publicity and promotion departments with little regard for the wishes of the contract actor who embodied the role. In such cases the actor has had little control over the star image. Chaplin, however—because of his personal charm, because of his enormous early success, and because he soon owned his means of production and then wrote, directed, and produced his work—was able to shape and control his star image to a significant degree between the World Wars.

Yet even with this much creative independence and business acumen, Chaplin was unable to control his star image fully, as he would learn most graphically in 1952 and 1953. We have seen in Chapter 9 how Chaplin, aware that publicity about his politics was endangering his career, began to retreat from his progressive commitments around 1950. Around the same time he was busily at work on a film tentatively titled *Foot Lights*. As Chaplin himself recalled, "I was optimistic and still not convinced that I had completely lost the affection of the American people" (MA, p. 456). Evidence suggests that the film, which was eventually released as *Limelight* in the fall of 1952, constituted Chaplin's attempt to reconcile himself with the American moviegoing public, in part by making the film more overtly autobiographical. Yet he learned that his desires for reconciliation were not easily realized. By 1952 and 1953 his star image had become a source of controversy in Cold War debates. The situation had become so serious that by the end of 1953, Chaplin had—following the attorney general's revocation of his reentry permit—sold his studio and his Hollywood home and, severing his ties almost completely from his adopted country of nearly forty years, moved permanently into a manor in Switzerland.

Because the release and reviews of *Limelight* occurred after Chaplin's departure for Europe, we must first look at Chaplin's decision to uproot himself from the United States. I am calling what occurred a "banishment" in two senses of the word: both in the general sense of driving someone away from a country and the specific sense of a governmental action that forces one from a country or makes it extremely difficult for one to return.

Because so many misconceptions exist about the events of 1952 and 1953, and because the opening of the FBI files makes it possible to explore what kind of case the government had against Chaplin, it is important to outline what actually did transpire. In the summer of 1952, while he was finishing postproduction work on *Limelight*, Chaplin decided to travel to Europe for a family vacation and to attend the Paris and London openings of his new film. He applied to the INS for a reentry permit, which as a resident alien he would need to return to the United States following his trip. This was granted him on July 16.[1]

After setting sail from New York City aboard the *Queen Elizabeth* on September 18, however, Chaplin and his family received bad news: a spokesman for Attorney General James McGranery announced on September 19 that Chaplin's reentry permit had been revoked and that Chaplin would have to answer INS questions about his political views and moral behavior before he would be allowed to reenter the country. McGranery's spokesman told the press that his office had "a pretty good case" against Chaplin. Ten days later McGranery told the press that Chaplin "is in my judgement an unsavory character," and charged him with "making statements that would indicate a leering, sneering attitude" toward the country whose hospitality enriched him.[2] In his first public response to the situation, Chaplin told reporters that he still intended to return to America.

In contrast to the hostile treatment he had received from various government agencies and some quarters of the press in the United States, Chaplin was celebrated in England, France, and Italy in the last months of 1952. *Variety* reported that at the October 16 premiere of *Limelight* at the Odeon Theater in London, the ovation for Chaplin was "far greater than that accorded" Princess Margaret.[3] Five days later he and Oona were presented to Queen Elizabeth at a royal command performance of the film. Arriving in France in November and Italy in December, Chaplin drew equally enthusiastic crowds and, as on his world tour in 1931–1932, was celebrated by politicians and artists in both countries.

Some of the comments Chaplin made in interviews during these months also indicate that he was reformulating his political views away from his progressive tolerance of the Soviet Union to a position different and somewhat more palatable to his audience in the days of the Cold War. In his statement to the press upon his arrival in Cherbourg,

France, he said: "I am not political. . . . I am an individualist and believe in liberty. That is as far as my political convictions go." In a November interview with the Belgian newspaper *Le Peuple*, he commented, "I don't believe in any dogma. . . . It is the man, the individual who counts above all, more than anything. . . . In modern times where everything is being regimented the artist must more than ever think of the internal life of the individual, of this unique phenomenon which is a human being, the artist must create for man."[4] In both these statements Chaplin reverts to a defense of the individual against the massive institutions of modern society, a position he reasserts in his autobiography when he tries to "sum up the state of the world as I see it today": "The accumulating complexities of modern life, the kinetic invasion of the twentieth century, find the individual hemmed in by gigantic institutions that threaten from all sides, politically, scientifically, and economically. We are becoming the victims of soul-conditioning, of sanctions and permits" (MA, 470).

This defense of the individual over social institutions is similar to the anarchism that the young Marxist critic Lorenzo Rozas had perceived in Chaplin's work in his 1934 analysis and provides grounds for the assertion of some later critics that a sort of anarchism is the center of the Chaplin's sociopolitical world view.[5] The defense of the underdog against authority figures and powerful institutions had long been a trademark in his films; however, it became subordinated in his political activities during his progressive involvements from 1942 on. Only in 1952 did this resurface as a central part of Chaplin's political beliefs. Given his personal situation at the time, as he found himself caught in the cogs of bureaucratic machinery as tightly as Charlie ever was in *Modern Times*, his view was understandable.

In his autobiography Chaplin recalls having to bite his tongue when he first met the press after learning of McGranery's actions. "I would have liked to tell them that the sooner I was rid of that hate-beleaguered atmosphere the better, that I was fed up with America's insults and moral pomposity," he wrote, "but everything I possessed was in the States and I was terrified they might find a way of confiscating it." Therefore, "I came out with a pompous statement to the effect that I would return and answer their charges" (MA, p. 465). Even at this juncture Chaplin opted for reconciliation rather than denunciation: the once peerless star was hoping to halt the decline of his public reputation and protect his financial interests.

By April 1953, however, Chaplin decided that enough was enough. He had, after all, been celebrated across the European continent, feted by the wealthy, the famous, and the powerful as a (perhaps *the*) genius of the cinema. In such circumstances, the prospect of returning to America to face more interrogations about his political views and moral worth was clearly unappealing. To break ties with the United States, Chaplin had to get his assets out of the country. In January and February of 1953 Oona Chaplin accomplished this in a trip back to Los Angeles. At the same time, Chaplin acquired an estate called Manoir de Ban in Corsier-sur-Vevey, Switzerland, which would be his permanent residence until his death on Christmas morning of 1977. With these tasks completed Chaplin visited the American embassy in Switzerland on 10 April 1953 and turned in his reentry permit, thus officially giving up plans to return to the United States. The long and stormy love affair between Chaplin and America seemed to be over.

Since Chaplin did not return to the United States to answer the charges leveled against him by the attorney general's office, it has never been made clear whether he would have been refused entry had he chosen to fight the charges. However, documents from the FBI, INS, attorney general's office, and the State Department can help us answer that question, just as they provide a good picture of how actively these organizations worked on the Chaplin case in 1952 and 1953. Although, as we have seen, the FBI was the most active governmental agency investigating Chaplin through early 1952, the INS became more involved after he applied for a reentry permit. After he left the country, his case moved to the jurisdiction of the State Department, which began to provide information concerning his activities and the European response to him throughout the remainder of 1952 and 1953.

As we have seen, the April 1951 report on Chaplin as a security risk by the Los Angeles office of the FBI contained so little that Hoover apparently saw no need for further investigation. Or so it seems, at least, for nothing of consequence appears again in the FBI files until a letter from Hoover to Los Angeles in July 1952. It noted that Chaplin had recently applied for a reentry permit and had asked government officials if the permit would guarantee the right to return to the United States. With Chaplin's possible trip in mind, Hoover asked the Los Angeles office to forward any information they could accumulate "concerning the subject and his activities in relation to moving or taking a trip."[6]

On August 25 a Bureau memo notes that it had received information from the INS that Chaplin had been issued a reentry permit on July 16. It also observed that Chaplin had moved back his departure date from September 4 to "about September 10."[7] On September 9, a meeting took place between McGranery and Hoover. McGranery stated that he was thinking about how Chaplin's return to the United States could be prevented. Chaplin's planned trip abroad provided the opportunity, said McGranery, "of taking steps which would prevent his re-entry . . . because of moral turpitude." Hoover then drafted a memo dated September 11 to three of his aides instructing them to prepare immediately "a memorandum of all information in our files concerning Charlie Chaplin . . . [to] be transmitted to the Attorney General for his information."[8]

The idea of deporting Chaplin or preventing him from returning to the country was not new in September 1952. In the last chapter we noted that at least two members of Congress publicly called for Chaplin's deportation in the late 1940s. Similarly, *Variety* reported in February 1951 that Chaplin had abandoned plans to shoot some of *Limelight* in London, apparently because he could receive no firm guarantees that he would be permitted to return to the country after he left, even if he had a reentry permit.[9]

After Hoover's request, however, the preparation of material for the attorney general was given priority in the Washington office. The FBI effort was immediate and large scale. Agent Belmont's September 16 memo to Agent Ladd noted that they received Hoover's directive to write a report on Friday afternoon, September 12. Two agents immediately began to review the seven-volume Barry files and the six-volume internal security files. By Tuesday, the day of Belmont's memo, three more agents were laboring full time in the preparation of the document for McGranery. By September 18 the twenty-page summary was completed and sent out to the Attorney General. The following day Chaplin's reentry permit was revoked.[10]

But did the government have adequate grounds on which to exclude Chaplin? The evidence suggests it did not, at least as of the week following the revocation of the reentry permit. A key FBI document supports this. An FBI memo from Belmont to Ladd, dated September 30, recounts a meeting on the 29th attended by FBI Supervisor John E. Foley (the FBI's liaison representative to the INS) and three INS officials: Commissioner A. R. Mackey, Deputy Commissioner Benjamin Habberton, and Assistant Commissioner Raymond Farrell.[11] After thanking the FBI for its offer of assistance in the case, Commissioner Mackey asked Deputy Commissioner Farrell to brief Foley on the INS's progress in the case. According to Belmont's memo, "Mr. Farrell stated bluntly that at the present time INS does not have sufficient information to exclude Chaplin from the United States if he attempts to re-enter" (p. 2). Mackey broke in to say that the INS could make it difficult for Chaplin to reenter "but in the end, there is no doubt Chaplin would be admitted." Furthermore, he added, if the INS attempted to delay Chaplin's reentry, the case "might well rock INS and the Department of Justice to its foundations" (p. 2).

During the same meeting Farrell informed Foley that the INS hoped Chaplin would not attempt to return before December 24, when the recently passed Immigration and Nationality Act, which gave the State Department and its various agencies much broader powers in dealing with radicals, would go into effect.[12] "If Chaplin's lawyer was astute," Farrell told Foley, "he would have Chaplin return to the United States before the effective date of the new law." The meeting concluded with plans for the INS to press forward in trying to obtain information, perhaps via an interview with Chaplin's maid or butler, that would exclude Chaplin on a charge that he "conspired to cause one of his girl friends [Joan Barry] to abort." The INS officials feared that there could "be a great great deal of unfavorable publicity if attempts were made to exclude Chaplin on security grounds alone"—hence their interest in the abortion issue.

Thus at the end of September the INS believed they had no evidence, either on an abortion conspiracy charge or on a security charge, that could deny Chaplin reentry had he attempted to return. In a letter to Hoover on October 1 the INS officially requested the assistance of the FBI in its investigation of Chaplin, and for the next several months it tried to obtain such evidence in cooperation with the FBI. The FBI's internal security files on Chaplin between October 1952 and April 1953 contain a large number of documents, the longest of which is a 124-page report prepared by six Los Angeles FBI agents at Hoover's request for other FBI offices and for the INS.[13] The report was essentially a summary of earlier reports from Los Angeles that dealt with both the Barry case and Chaplin's political views. After a summary and some background information on Chaplin, the report's other major headings are:

A. Information Pertaining to Question of Communist Party Membership of Charles Chaplin
B. Individual Associates of Chaplin Who Are Reported to Be Communist Party Members [this section includes sections on Hanns Eisler, Lion Feuchtwanger, and Theodore Dreiser]
C. Affiliation of Charles Chaplin with Groups Declared to Be Communist Subversive Groups or Reputedly Controlled or Influenced by Communist Party

This report, and other shorter FBI reports sent by Hoover to the INS, provided the INS with allegations that could possibly have been used for the expected Chaplin hearing.

The INS needed witnesses to proceed, however. This need for reliable substantiation of the allegations in the FBI files provided the basis for a constant stream of correspondence beginning in October between the Washington and Los Angeles FBI offices, and between Hoover and various other non-FBI agencies, primarily the attorney general's office and the INS. Hoover wrote often to the Los Angeles office, instructing them to help the Los Angeles branch of the INS in seeking out FBI informants who might provide the INS with interviews for their investigation. He also told his agents to search for informants who were quoted or cited in the FBI reports that had been given to the INS.

Reading over this correspondence, one cannot help but be struck by how unsubstantiated many of the allegations were. For example, the 14 October 1952 FBI report, and others before it, claimed that Chaplin was a member of the Independent Progressive party and regularly attended its meetings. When the Los Angeles office, on Hoover's instructions, tracked down the source of that information, however, the unnamed woman informant told the FBI that she had obtained the information from another woman who had overheard it when she was a patron in a beauty salon. The FBI then contacted the second woman, who didn't have "any recollection of the information furnished regarding Chaplin's membership and attendance at IPP meetings." Another example is the charge that Chaplin received books on Czechoslovakia from the Soviet Union, in itself an improbable reason for deportation. The source for this story was a Customs agent in Los Angeles who provided the information through inspection of the mails. When contacted, he said "he had no personal recollection of the above literature being received by Chaplin."[14]

These examples, though perhaps more bizarre than others, are typical in that they turned up no witnesses for the INS. Several times in the fall and winter Hoover wrote the INS with the news that specific informants they asked about were unable to testify. One letter, of 31 October 1952, listed six specific sources requested by the INS: all were unavailable to testify. A December 9 letter bore similar news. Although it did give the INS the name of one informant, it added that he "has proven to be unreliable in the past." On 19 February 1953 Hoover again wrote the INS, telling them that the source of yet another story was from another governmental agency. When contacted, that agency could not identify specifically who originated the story. One can only conclude that the FBI had spent a tremendous number of hours and massive amounts of paper preparing long reports about

Chaplin that were based on shaky, distorted, or even downright false information.[15]

Other government agencies were brought into the Chaplin case after he left the country. On 8 October 1952, Hoover wrote to the chief of the Security Division at the State Department and sent a copy of the letter to the director of the Central Intelligence Agency (CIA). The letter informed the recipients that Chaplin had left the United States on September 17 and could "possibly be denied admittance to this country upon return." Hoover specifically stated that the FBI was not requesting any investigation of Chaplin by the State Department or the CIA, but he asked them to send "any information concerning subject's activity that may come to your attention."[16] I have found no evidence that either organization conducted a detailed investigation of Chaplin after receiving this letter; however, the U.S. Embassies in Belgium, England, France, and Switzerland all monitored Chaplin at one time or another. A letter from Belgium translated an interview Chaplin did with a leftist newspaper; the embassy in London translated several pro-Chaplin Soviet reports. The embassy in Paris provided the longest report: it photocopied several articles on Chaplin from newspapers of various political slants, translated them, and commented on how enthusiastically Chaplin was generally received in Paris.[17] For the most part, however, the FBI and the INS did the most to prepare for Chaplin's expected INS hearing, and right up until the day Chaplin turned in his reentry permit, they were unable to find solid evidence that would have excluded him from the country.

On April 15, the Department of Justice sent out a press release, a copy of which made its way into the FBI files. It stated that Chaplin had surrendered his reentry permit to State Department authorities in Geneva on April 10. The previous flood of FBI activity in the investigation of Chaplin dwindled to a trickle. On April 20 Hoover suggested to the Los Angeles office that Chaplin's security index card be removed from his file since he had given up his reentry permit. On April 30 Hoover wrote again, this time telling the Los Angeles office to complete its remaining investigation and "submit recommendations concerning subject's status on the Security Index so that this investigation can be closed." That final report, dated 10 July 1953, reiterated Chaplin's friendship with Hanns Eisler and Lion Feuchtwanger and said that John Howard Lawson was hoping to organize a campaign to have *Limelight* shown throughout the United States. Finally, on August 12 the Los Angeles office wrote Hoover that since Chaplin had turned in his reentry permit, they felt his security index card should be cancelled.[18] Although the files released by the FBI through the Freedom of Information Act contain another eighty pages of information, the last item dealing with the theft of his corpse in 1978, Chaplin's battle with the FBI was over.

Limelight: Autobiography and the Aesthetic Contract

As Chaplin had begun to contemplate and plan his next film in the late 1940s and 1950, he was confronted with a number of problems. His previous film, his first comedy since the 1910s with no persona similar to Charlie, had been a failure at the box office and with most critics. The company of which he was a major stockholder, United Artists, was experiencing serious economic difficulties, as was much of the Hollywood film industry. And his star image, which in previous decades had been dominated by Charlie (the romantic, funny, resilient representative of common people) and by Chaplin (the versatile artistic genius, masterful pantomimist, and even at times serious commentator on public affairs), had shifted in the 1940s. The Barry trials and Chaplin's involvement in progressive politics had transformed his star image so that two traits—questionable sexual conduct and progressive (in the minds of some people, even subversive) political views—came to do battle with the others.

One obvious solution would have been to make another film featuring Charlie, but two circumstances militated against that. First, Charlie was a product of nondialogue films, and Chaplin, regularly criticized by reviewers for an old-fashioned or awkward film style since *Modern Times*, would have been taking a serious risk to make a nondialogue film twenty years after the industry had shifted to talking pictures. Second, Chaplin was sixty years old in 1949: to perform the antics of the inimitable Charlie, Chaplin had to be physically capable of doing so. Despite his vigor, Chaplin would have been hard pressed to perform as Charlie for an entire grueling shooting schedule.

The issue of Chaplin's age had been raised by a critic remarkably early in Chaplin's career. In his 1922 essay, "Dear Mr. Chaplin," Stark Young had urged Chaplin to broaden and evolve as an artist because the public "uses up for its own ends what it finds and then throws it aside" and because of "the hard biological fact" of Chaplin's inevitable "physical decline from perfection."[19] Young couldn't have predicted that the introduction of sound pictures would combine with Chaplin's aging to make the antics of Charlie less possible, yet his comments were prescient: much of Chaplin's audience did abandon him, and by 1950, Chaplin knew better, given his age and appearance, than to dust off the derby, cane, baggy pants, and mustache and give Charlie a rebirth.

What, then, was the solution? Near the end of the *Monsieur Verdoux* press conference, when a questioner expressed dissatisfaction that Chaplin's recent films subordinated comedy to message, Chaplin replied: "as one gets older we are not just satisfied to go along with the same old line. We have to get excited by something before we can arouse our energy to do something. And I suppose it is one of my indulgences. I'm sorry."[20] By 1948 Chaplin's new "indulgence" was a film featuring neither Charlie nor a progressive political issue. Rather, he had become excited by a story about an aging comedian who fears he is no longer funny. He had begun working on a novel between 1948 and 1951, which eventually reached about 100,000 words,[21] and the manuscript became the source of Chaplin's next film.

The public began to learn a few details about the film quite early. In the spring of 1950 Richard Lauterbach interviewed Chaplin for an article to appear in *New York Times Magazine*. Already Chaplin had the story for his new film pretty firmly worked out. Lauterbach described it for his readers: "The script is finished. It will have music, dancing, humor, pity—everything but the tramp. Tentatively titled 'Foot Lights,' the story concerns the attempted comeback of an aging English music hall comic who falls in love with a young dancer. He has been on the top, but feels he is losing his touch and is afraid he can no longer make audiences laugh." After hearing the plot description, Lauterbach immediately asked Chaplin whether the film was autobiographical. "Everything is autobiographical," Chaplin replied, "but don't make too much of that."[22]

More than two years before the film was ready, Chaplin had let the press know its plot outline. Furthermore, it was apparent that the film would likely draw more heavily on autobiographical elements than most of Chaplin's other films, however much those earlier films may have covertly touched on autobiography. Despite the hostility that had greeted *Monsieur Verdoux*, despite the continuing investigations by various governmental bodies, and despite the unraveling of his star image, Chaplin was going ahead with his new film and would even draw on his own star image for details of character and plot. Like his other activities in 1950 and 1951, however, Chaplin's work on his new film suggested that he was seeking a reconciliation with his audience. He did so partly by returning to particular aspects of the aesthetic contract that had helped establish and sustain his stardom and partly by drawing on his own autobiography in quite explicit ways.

Though the title of the film was changed to *Limelight*, the finished

26. Chaplin as Calvero in *Limelight*, 1952.

work resembled the description Chaplin gave Lauterbach in 1950 quite closely. An aging music-hall comedian, Calvero (Chaplin), has been driven to drink as his career deteriorates (see Figure 26). At the opening of the film, he saves a young woman named Terry (Claire Bloom), after she has attempted suicide. Taking her into his apartment, Calvero nurses her back to health and encourages her to resume her ballet dancing. Her career blossoms. His declines. When he observes that she is falling in love with the young composer Neville (Sydney Chaplin), Calvero disappears for six months. At the end of

289

the film, Terry persuades Calvero to allow a benefit tribute to be held for him. Calvero agrees, performs his comic routines successfully at the benefit, and dies offstage at the end of the film after suffering a heart attack, while Terry is onstage, performing.

The film makes several gestures of reconciliation toward Chaplin's American audience. Three of these are related to the aesthetic contract that had established and sustained his star image. For the first time since *City Lights*, Chaplin made a film without an overt expression of progressive politics. Apparently he realized after the failure of *Monsieur Verdoux* that progressive messages were likely to antagonize a large number of his potential viewers, mired as they were in the atmosphere of the Cold War. Like the film industry as a whole, which had given prominence to such "social problem" films like *Gentleman's Agreement*, *Pinky*, and *Intruder in the Dust* in the half decade after World War II, Chaplin learned where it hurts producers most—the box office—that sizable portions of the audience had by 1950 become sensitive about if not hostile toward movies that criticized American society.

Omitting messages was a negative act of reconciliation: it left out something that Chaplin had begun to include from *Modern Times* on as he revised his aesthetic contract. But in *Limelight* Chaplin also made two positive gestures of reconciliation, both of which drew on key characteristics of Chaplin's original aesthetic contract. The first was to include a number of comic incidents that would remind the audience of Chaplin's gift at pantomime. In the film's first scene, the down-and-out comedian Calvero comes home drunk and creates considerable humor through pantomime as he fumbles with his key and, after getting into the hall of his boarding house, looks at the bottom of his shoes after smelling a foul odor (thus demonstrating the very "vulgarity" for which Chaplin's genteel critics had attacked him in the 1910s). Although the film also includes several of Calvero's music-hall routines, the only other genuine moments of comic pantomime come when Calvero imitates several objects (like a pansy or a Japanese tree) for Terry, and when he and Buster Keaton perform together (for the only time in their careers) as a comic violinist and comic pianist in the film's conclusion. This latter scene, played without dialogue, almost brings the audience back to the tradition of American silent comedy that flourished in the 1920s and that Chaplin and Keaton did so much to establish.

Second, in *Limelight* Chaplin returned to another convention: the focus on a romance, often unfulfilled, between the Chaplin persona and a woman. As in so many other Chaplin features, the woman in *Limelight* is flawed or vulnerable. Here Terry, the young aspiring ballerina, has a history of rheumatic fever; her temporary paralysis aligns her with the other Chaplin heroines with physical flaws, especially the blind girl in *City Lights* and Mona, Verdoux's invalid wife. As an orphan, she is similar to the gamin in *Modern Times* (and not inappropriately, given Calvero's paternal concern for her, with Jackie Coogan's character in *The Kid*). When Calvero mistakes her for a prostitute early in the film, she is even linked with the streetwalker whom Verdoux spares.

In addition to Terry's similarities to earlier women characters, the contours of the romance in *Limelight* remind one of other Chaplin films, especially *The Circus*. In both films the character played by Chaplin comes to admire the heroine and yearn for her attention. In both the heroine falls in love with someone else, after which the Chaplin persona overhears her in a discussion that leads him to believe that his love affair is doomed. And in both films the Chaplin character sacrifices his longing to love the heroine for what he believes is her well-being and happiness. Thus Chaplin provided in *Limelight* another gesture of reconciliation: a romantic dilemma that had at least the potential for that which had made Charlie so endearing in *The Kid*, *The Gold Rush*, *The Circus*, and *City Lights*.

However, both the comedy and the romantic pathos in *Limelight* were at best partial gestures for audiences who wished Charlie were back. Except for the scene with Keaton and a few of Calvero's gestures, *Limelight* is not a very funny film. In fact, Chaplin is several times faced with the problem of a story that requires performing comic scenes that the audiences in the film do not think are funny. It doubtless takes a special talent to act out an ostensibly comic scene that is not funny, but it still doesn't yield comedy.

Similarly, the handling of the romance in *Limelight* is different in one key way from that in *The Circus*. In the "overhearing" scene in *Limelight*, Neville tells Terry on her doorstep that he loves her and that her feeling for Calvero is really pity, not love. She protests, but Calvero, lying half-drunk inside the door, overhears and, having predicted earlier that she would fall in love with Neville, leaves Terry voluntarily so that the young couple's relationship can blossom. When Terry sees Calvero again six months later and tells him that she still loves him, he replies, "I know." Since Calvero controls the relationship, the pathos resulting from unrequited love is muted compared to the feelings we experience when Charlie overhears Merna declare her love for Rex in *The Circus* or when Charlie awakes from his "Oceana Roll" dream in *The Gold Rush* to find that Georgia has stood him up on New Year's Eve. The empathy Charlie almost pleads for (and very often gets) in those two films—based on our common fear of being vulnerable, lonely, and rejected—is dulled in *Limelight*, for Calvero rarely appears as vulnerable in his relationship with Terry as Charlie almost always was in the presence of a woman to whom he was attracted. Though some pathos is generated when Calvero fails in his comic routines, almost none emerges from the romance.

Clearly something new is at work in *Limelight*, something besides a return to aspects of Chaplin's old aesthetic contract. In many of his earlier comic films, particularly from *The Kid* on, Chaplin had practiced "submerged autobiography": drawing subtly and indirectly on details of his life to create his characters. In *Limelight*, the submerged becomes explicit: Chaplin makes overt autobiographical references and creates parallels to his main character that are central to the film.

This movement from submerged to explicit autobiography began with *Monsieur Verdoux*. There the central character's critique of capitalist society and his murder of women loosely paralleled Chaplin's own political views and the public's perception of his problems with women; in fact, some of the audience actually connected Verdoux's politics and attitude toward women with Chaplin's, which did his star image no good. In reflecting on the film Chaplin admitted to Lauterbach that he made a mistake by not getting audiences to feel pity and understanding for Verdoux.[23]

In *Limelight* Chaplin, aware that his private life and public activities had increasingly come to dominate his star image in the 1940s, decided to use autobiographical elements so much a part of his "biographical legend" (the term is Boris Tomashevsky's).[24] However, he would be even more explicitly autobiographical than he was in *Verdoux* and would carefully select those details so that audiences would identify both with Calvero and with Chaplin himself. He would turn autobiography to his advantage and create an aging comedian afraid of losing his audience rather than a Bluebeard with progressive politics.

Calvero and Chaplin are indeed similar in a number of ways, and these similarities constitute the most obvious and important autobiographical level of the film.[25] To list only a few, at the opening of the film Calvero has begun to fail as a comedian so much that he even dreams of performing before an empty theater. In much the same way Chaplin was coming off a film, *Monsieur Verdoux*, that many in his audience thought far from funny. Compared to Chaplin's previous box-office successes, it too played to relatively empty theaters. A second similarity between Calvero and Chaplin is the relationship each has with a young woman. Just as Calvero and Terry develop a loving bond, so did the aged Chaplin and the young Oona O'Neill marry.

Calvero even makes a joke of his relationship with Terry that acts as Chaplin's ironic reference to his own relationships with women. When Terry protests about feigning marriage, Calvero responds, "I've had five wives already. One more or less won't matter to me." Throughout the film Calvero's philosophical comments on life remind one of the intellectual Chaplin that constituted a part of his star image from the 1920s on. One could even say that Calvero's last performance at the benefit is analogous to the film; *Limelight* thus becomes Chaplin's own swan song, his own last attempt to leave his audience entertained and enlightened.[26] To underline the similarity between Calvero and Chaplin visually, a poster on Calvero's wall promotes him as the "Tramp Comedian," and over his mantel is a posed photograph of Chaplin from the 1920s, wearing a double-breasted suit, the only photograph of Chaplin to appear in one of his films.

Chaplin also encouraged an autobiographical reading of *Limelight* by his casting. Chaplin's two sons from his marriage to Lita Grey both appear in the film. Sydney has the largest role, as Neville, while Charles, Jr., appears briefly (along with Chaplin's half brother Wheeler Dryden) as the policeman in the first part of the ballet sequence. In the film's opening shots, the three oldest children of Oona O'Neill Chaplin and her husband also appear briefly. Charles, Jr., explains these appearances when he writes that Chaplin "had a very sentimental reason for making *Limelight* what he called a family affair. He said he fully expected it to be his last as well as his greatest picture."[27]

The promotion campaign for *Limelight* reinforces the view that *Limelight* was a more overtly and consciously autobiographical film than any other Chaplin had made. On the day *Limelight* opened in New York City, the large ads in both the *New York Times* and the *New York Herald Tribune* centered on something no other ad for a Chaplin film had ever done: Chaplin's own face, minus the mustache. The *Herald Tribune* ad is most direct. Four columns wide, the ad's largest letters are at the top: "Charles Chaplin." The film's title is below and to the right of center, and below that, in the center, is a large picture of Chaplin's face without makeup and without mustache. Surrounding the head are four smaller pictures and captions promising comedy, slapstick, ballet, and romance, but the looming presence of Charles Chaplin dominates. The *Times* ad also features Chaplin's face, though in a slightly more complicated fashion (see Figure 27). Below the text at the top of the ad is a picture of Chaplin looking into a mirror and putting makeup on his eyebrows. Like the *Herald Tribune* picture, Chaplin is without a mustache, but here, the artifice of the theater is suggested: Chaplin clearly is preparing himself to take on another

27. Newspaper advertisement for *Limelight* (1952), promoting Chaplin.

role.[28] For the first time since he donned Charlie's costume and began overseeing his own publicity, Chaplin himself is in the limelight—the actor, director, producer, and human being Charles Chaplin, rather than the character he plays. That this element was central to *Limelight* is reinforced by another unusual aspect of the film's promotion: for the first time ever, Chaplin allowed *Life* magazine to roam his sets while he was shooting and to come into his home and photograph him interacting with his family. The resulting eleven-page spread included both candid shots from the shooting and pictures, formal and informal, of Chaplin and his family.[29] Showing Chaplin as the happily married family man surely presented an alternative picture to the embattled man fighting a paternity suit in 1945. But it also showed that Chaplin was preparing the publicity campaign for *Limelight* very carefully after the fiasco of *Monsieur Verdoux*. *Limelight* would clearly aim at reconciliation through a return to elements of Chaplin's aesthetic contract and a conscious use of autobiography. It would remain for the reviewers and the public to judge how successful Chaplin's attempt had been.

Critical Response to *Limelight*

How did American reviewers respond to *Limelight*? The critical response reflected in part a new, emerging aesthetic discourse about movies. If the discourse of the depression decade, at least among some reviewers (those we termed "social radical" and "modern liberal"), encouraged filmmakers to make films that were realistic, dealt with socially significant subject matter, and revealed the filmmaker's devotion to progressive politics, the aesthetic discourse emerging in the 1950s was different for at least two significant reasons.

First, the expansion of the Soviet Union and the growing fears about internal subversion in the early Cold War years both helped to break down the intellectual dominance of the progressive paradigm. To critics of narrative art, this meant that judging a book or film by the degree to which it elicited a sympathy for common people or articulated a progressive "message" was a thing of the past.[30] Chaplin himself found this out, with a vengeance, in the response to *Monsieur Verdoux*. Of course, this does not mean that writers influenced by the progressive aesthetic discourse stopped writing or totally shifted their perspectives. The influential Bosley Crowther of the *New York Times*, for example, long maintained his interest in and defense of "socially significant" movies, though he was more circumspect about directly criticizing American society in his reviews of the 1950s than social radical critics like Harry Alan Potamkin had been in the 1930s. Most reviewers were less drawn to social and political analyses of movies in the 1950s than they had been in the 1930s.[31]

Second, as cultural critics in the 1940s and 1950s generally began to worry less about defending progressive art, they began to worry more about the possibly deleterious effect of "mass culture." To many important critics in this period, Richard Pells has noted, "the rise of the media was associated with the decline of a traditional elite that once dominated the arts."[32] Although television and comic books bore the largest brunt of attacks, the movies also garnered their fair share.

In this new context, characterized by a suspicion of mass culture, how were movie reviewers and critics likely to approach films, particularly one by someone as well known and as established as Chaplin? One appealing focus for reviewers and critics was the "great artist" approach, a kind of pre-auteurist auteurism that drew on the Romantic literary tradition. (The auteur approach will be discussed in Chapter 11.) It suggested that a society's greatest artists possessed heightened perceptions and a special ability to explain and comment on society through their works—and in the case of a "mass art" like film, to "rise above" the alleged limitations of the medium. The responsibility of the reviewer of a film by a great artist was to identify what insights and truths the artist was imparting and how a new work fit into the larger body of work that the artist had created throughout his or her career.

Within this context (as well as a hostile political context, discussed in the next section) emerged the reception of *Limelight*. The reviews show first that Chaplin successfully communicated to reviewers the personal dimensions of the film. Whether reviewers liked or disliked it, they noted its autobiographical elements. William Barrett wrote that Chaplin "is the real subject of the movie" (the title of his review is "Chaplin as Chaplin"). To Crowther, *Limelight* was "an extraordinarily personal film." In a fully developed exploration of this dimension, Robert Warshow's *Partisan Review* article claimed that the film was Chaplin's "apology and, so far as he is capable of such a thing, his self-examination." Philip Hartung, less enthused, suggested in *Commonweal* that "the whole picture has the effect of being a kind of Chaplin apologia." *Newsweek* asserted that the film "crackles with comments it is difficult not to regard as autobiographical." In the *New Republic* Eric Bentley observed that "the film is at best a glorious failure about a glorious failure. The name is Calvero; the portrait on his mantelpiece is that of Chaplin, young. Symbolic autobiography: an amazing conception for a movie man." Chaplin clearly succeeded in this aim.[33]

How did the reviewers judge Chaplin's new, more explicitly autobiographical, mode? Barrett's review dwelt most fully on the film as autobiography. He confessed to being perplexed about the film because Chaplin himself remained an enigma. Chaplin portrayed a character who was "almost hypnotic in its fascination," but there remained "something unexpressed and mysterious about it." Barrett was left wondering "how much of the real personality is conveyed and how much held back." Though he did not think it Chaplin's best film and certainly not his funniest, Barrett believed it Chaplin's most powerful film, evoking a feeling that was "due in good part to the fact that here, more than any of his other pictures, Charles Chaplin has come the closest to playing Charles Chaplin." Barrett reaffirmed Chaplin's status as a great, versatile artist: "not since the days when Richard Wagner flourished . . . has such a display of universal genius been attempted."[34]

In *Saturday Review* Arthur Knight was equally absorbed by the autobiographical elements and even more positive about the film. To Knight, *Limelight* was "an artistic testament" in which Chaplin summed up his "fundamental philosophies and attitudes about life, about love, about audiences, about comedy." The experience of hearing such direct expression on film of an artist's philosophy, wrote Knight, was "something unprecedented except for the movie versions of a few Shaw plays and Chaplin's own *Monsieur Verdoux*." As the film develops, it becomes "the voice of a great comedian, a great spirit, giving cinematic shape to his own ripe experience." One could hardly imagine higher praise for the film.[35]

Some of those disappointed with the film noticed that Chaplin included elements of his old aesthetic contract but wished that it had been followed more fully. The *New Yorker* was pleased with the "rewarding flashes of the sort of comedy and pathos that distinguished Mr. Chaplin's work in the past." However, the film as a whole was "furiously loquacious," so much so that "it is sometimes hard to remember he is master of pantomime, able to put more into a shrug than most actors can put into a soliloquy." Hollis Alpert's review in *Saturday Review* also endorsed the "celebrated juxtaposition of comedy and pathos" in *Limelight*, as well as the comic routine with Buster Keaton ("a pure and utter gem"). But the film had too many faults, which showed "Chaplin in his present phase, with less to say than he had before, and with less assurance in the saying of it."[36]

Bentley's somewhat negative review in the *New Republic* is a good one to conclude this discussion, because Bentley himself was writing to some extent from within the progressive paradigm, unusual in

1952. Placing the film in the historical context of a great artist, Bentley compares *Limelight* unfavorably to *Monsieur Verdoux* and *City Lights*: "If *City Lights*, for example, says all that the Chaplin of the early period had to say, *Verdoux* sums up the Chaplin of the later period, the period when he had begun to think and to lose popularity, when his love of women, laughed at in the twenties, had come to be linked, by the logic of the intellectual underworld, with his political leanings." In contrast, *Limelight* "is a return to the bosom of the bourgeoisie," expressed through the bourgeoisie's favorite form: "sentimental domestic drama." Although Bentley agreed that the film might be too talky and pretentious, his review challenged those who longed for Charlie of the good old days. "The most inept thing is to wish he would 'just stick to the Tramp' for this is to forget that an artist must develop." Bentley's review is laced with the pre-auteur auteurism noted above, and he shows how much he respected Chaplin's work by writing that despite his criticism of the film, it was still "better than 999 out of 1000 films."[37]

Overall, these mixed to good reviews—most of which were written after McGranery revoked the reentry permit but before the scheduled (January 1953) nationwide release of *Limelight*—suggest several conclusions about Chaplin's attempted reconciliation. First, a good number of the reviews clearly longed for an earlier Chaplin, for more comedy and more intense pathos, and maybe even for Charlie himself. Second, a surprising number found Chaplin's new autobiographical mode interesting and sometimes even deeply moving. Third, Chaplin the filmmaker fared well when judged by the emerging critical discourse that emphasized the "great artist" approach. Even the negative reviews expressed a strong sense that Chaplin was an important and interesting artist, one who had played a large role in the history of American movies.

Thus, by toning down his progressive politics and trying to reconcile with his audience through autobiography and a return to some of the elements of his aesthetic contract, Chaplin's star image was at least partially sustained by the reviews of *Limelight*. Their focus throughout was on several characteristics of his star image: Chaplin's versatility, his acting skill, his philosophizing mode, and the creativity of comedy and pathos that were so much a part of his films. Given the fact that most of these reviews were written a month or less after Chaplin's reentry permit had been revoked but well before he turned it in, the reaction seems quite positive. However, as we turn from the reviews of *Limelight* to the reaction in the press to Chaplin's banishment, and then to the pressure group boycotts of Chaplin and *Limelight*, another story—the politicization of Chaplin's star image—predominates.

The Press and Banishment

Despite Chaplin's gestures of reconciliation in his actions and in his new film, and despite these relatively good reviews of *Limelight*, the response of the American press to Chaplin's "banishment" was affected by (and exemplified) the popular mood in the United States in the early 1950s. Although HUAC had not directly harassed Hollywood much since the Hollywood Ten contempt citations of October 1947, several events stimulated HUAC to renew its Hollywood investigations in 1951. Between 1947 and 1951 the trial of Alger Hiss, Mao Tse-tung's victory in China, the Soviet Union's detonation of an atomic bomb, the arrest of atomic spy Klaus Fuchs in England and of Julius and Ethel Rosenberg in the United States, the passage of the McCarren Act (requiring registration of all members of the Communist party), the outbreak of the Korean War, and above all, the rise of Joseph McCarthy's vigorous brand of anticommunism (beginning with his February 1950 speech in Wheeling) all contributed to an intensified and often xenophobic anti-Communist sentiment in the United States. In the midst of this climate, HUAC, led by a new chairman, John S. Wood of Georgia, resumed its political inquisitions, sending subpoenas in March 1951 to eight film industry radicals, including Larry Parks, Howard da Silva, and Gale Sondergaard. This second wave of HUAC investigations of Hollywood ran intermittently through 1953.[38]

Furthermore, *Limelight* was released after Chaplin's reentry permit was revoked in September 1952. It premiered in New York City on 23 October 1952, then played in other cities beginning in January 1953. Given the heightened anti-Communist feeling in the United States, the renewed association of Hollywood and communism, and the revocation of Chaplin's reentry permit for unspecified reasons related to politics and morality, *Limelight* generated political controversy, despite the fact that Chaplin had not included any suggestion of progressive politics in the film. In fact, Chaplin's star image itself became highly politicized in 1952–1953, more than at any other time in his career, before or after. The reactions to Chaplin's banishment and new film became a kind of litmus test of a writer or group's own ideological leanings and identifications.

The conservative press had a field day with the news of Chaplin's woes. The *Chicago Tribune* not only gave the story front-page coverage but covered the top of the front page with a bold headline, "MOVE TO

28. *Chicago Tribune* headline on 20 September 1952. Copyright
© 1987, Chicago Tribune Company, all rights reserved,
used with permission.

BAN CHAPLIN IN U.S.," as in its handling of several stories in the Barry
case (see Figure 28). The accompanying article recounted the details
of the attorney general's actions, then slanted the story against Chaplin. It wrote that he had "scorned citizenship in this country" even
though he had "amassed millions" in it; that he had been denounced
in Congress as "left wing and radical"; that he supported "Commu-
nist-organized" peace conferences; that he had been declared father
of Joan Barry's illegitimate child (but not that blood tests had proven
he could not have been); and that he had once settled out of court
after being accused of plagiarism. The front-page story leaves the
reader no doubt about the *Tribune*'s attitude toward Chaplin: how
could one feel about a dishonest, scheming, scornful, lewd radical?[39]

Westbrook Pegler, who had targeted Chaplin as a distasteful radical
back in the second front days, went after the comedian again, even
before hearing the news of McGranery's actions, upon learning that
Chaplin was going abroad. His September 19 column was subtitled:
"He Doesn't Care If Chaplin Never Comes Back." The crux of the
column was contained in one sentence: "He has lived among us and
imposed upon us by flouting our ideals and degrading our morals and
standards in entertainment for almost half a century." To Pegler,

Chaplin was "never more than a custard-pie comedian." The following Sunday, he lauded McGranery's decision, calling it "the first honest show of initiative against the Red Front of Hollywood by the Department of Justice." Terming Chaplin a "filthy character who is a menace to young girls," Pegler helped to stir up public opinion against the departed star.[40]

Hedda Hopper, Chaplin's conservative gossip columnist nemesis, wasted no time in passing on the news. She headlined her "Looking at Hollywood" column in the same issue, "Screen Folk, Big and Little, Hail Action Against Chaplin." The opening sentence read, "There are hundreds of people in Hollywood, perhaps thousands—stars, directors, producers, and all those wonderful people we call little people, workers behind the camera, electricians, cameramen, props—who are dancing in the street for joy over Attorney General McGranery's statement that before Charlie Chaplin can return to the United States he will have to pass the board of immigration." The attack continued. Chaplin may be a good actor, "but that doesn't give him the right to go against our customs, to abhor everything we stand for, to throw our hospitality back in our faces." Forgetting Chaplin's Liberty Loan tour and discounting his second front speeches, Hopper stated: "he did nothing for either World War I or World War II." Then she closed: "I've known him for many years. I abhor what he stands for, while I admire his talents as an actor. I would like to say, 'Good riddance to bad company.' " This vituperative attack, playing on the era's anti-Communist phobias, was one of the worst press lashings Chaplin ever received. Given the fact that Hopper mentioned she'd had a "very close check" on his reentry permit situation "for months" and that the column appeared the same day as the news of the revocation, it is likely that Hopper was again being fed government information that she could use to discredit Chaplin.[41]

Hollywood's other major gossip columnist, Louella Parsons, who was less conservative politically, also publicized Chaplin's departure. Beginning on September 22, she syndicated a five-part series on the story of Chaplin's problems with the attorney general.[42] On one hand, since she had long been known as a friend of Chaplin's, having first met him when he worked briefly in Chicago at the start of his Essanay contract, one might have expected her to defend him. On the other hand, the prevailing political atmosphere (and the fact that her employer was the Hearst newspaper chain) put pressure on her to criticize Chaplin.

The articles are an important contribution to the star image of Chaplin as it solidified in 1952. They essentially paint him as a "charming, gracious" man who lost his way sometime in the 1940s. Although much of what appeared in the second, third, and fourth installments was positive regarding Chaplin, Parsons also criticized him, particularly in the fifth installment. Attacking Chaplin for his "smug statement" about being a citizen of the world, she also attributed his political views to his obstinacy and his feeling that he was a "law unto himself." She criticized him for the Simonov incident (in which he made his "American gestapo" statement), his affiliations with second front and peace organizations, and the alleged pro-Soviet inscriptions on the back of pictures he had given to the children of Maxim Litvinov, Soviet ambassador to the United States. To Parsons, Chaplin showed "nothing less than insolence" when he announced his work on *Limelight* about the time he also lent his name as a sponsor of the World Peace Congress. She also told of her final meeting with Chaplin, a cold visit to the set of *Limelight*. Of the film itself, Parsons wrote that she was "bitterly disappointed," for it had "too little comedy and I wasn't moved once." Parsons ultimately refused to defend Chaplin, saying for example that she had often urged him to become a citizen but that his "innate stubbornness" kept him from doing so.

Parsons concluded by portraying a king fallen due to his own hubris: "How very, very sad that the fantastic success story of Charles Spencer Chaplin is destined to end on such a tragic note." The series shows that Parsons was far more generous to Chaplin than Hopper. Nevertheless, it also enabled Parsons to establish a political distance from Chaplin while at the same time presenting a rise and fall morality tale, satisfying to audiences because they were not implicated in their hero's demise: he had brought his fate on himself.

If conservatives pictured Chaplin as an arrogant or stubborn comedian who showed nothing but ingratitude and scorn for the country in which he had become a wealthy and famous man, the progressive Left—what little remained of it—portrayed the banished Chaplin as a humane victim of American repression. This is best exemplified by the treatment of Chaplin's banishment in the *Daily Worker*. It first mentioned Chaplin's dilemma on September 22, and quoted from the *London Observer*'s editorial defense of Chaplin. The article's headline: "Britons Back Chaplin, Attack 'Smears' in U.S." The next day the *Worker* gave a sympathetic account of Chaplin's press conference upon arriving at Cherbourg, and on September 24 it began a three-part series on Chaplin and the reasons for his problems by David Platt. Collectively, these three articles give us a precise picture of the *Worker*'s understanding of Cold War politics, and of how its image of Chaplin could be used to further its own ideological ends, just as the conservative press had used another image of Chaplin for its purposes.[43]

The first, "Why Gov't Wants to Bar Charles Chaplin," opened by implicitly calling the U.S. position "fascist": whereas Hitler and Mussolini banned Chaplin's films, "Truman and McGranery have gone one step further. They want to ban Chaplin." The government action, wrote Platt, "climaxes a witchhunt by cultural illiterates against leading figures in the arts, sciences and professions, such as the world has not seen since the dark days of fascist dictatorships." The rest of the article recounted Chaplin's "persecution" in the United States, and was not above distortion, hyperbole, or even outright lying to make its case. It claimed that the press ganged up on him for his social satire in *The Immigrant*, though no such evidence has ever been turned up. It asserted with no specifics that "a year or two later Chaplin joined the ranks of artists and professionals who hailed the world-shaking Russian Revolution," a strained interpretation of Chaplin's 1921 comment to reporters that he had to be interested in Bolshevism, since it was a part of life and artists must be interested in life. It concluded that "the attempt to ban Chaplin is clearly a step toward depriving the American people of a vital segment of democratic culture."

The next two articles followed in the same vein. The first, "Chaplin's Films are Directed against Humbug and Injustice," accounted for Chaplin's popularity by noting his films "are on the side of the underdog and are directed against humbug, snobbery, social injustice," while also revealing "poverty and hunger in the midst of plenty." It also distorted, this time by misquoting Chaplin's 1918 comment on comedy, substituting "bloated capitalist" where Chaplin used "rich."[44] The final article, "Chaplin's *The Great Dictator* Appealed for Peace and Human Decency," argued that this film had been criticized because Chaplin was an advocate of peace in a country that wished war. To Platt, "behind the gang-up on Chaplin and *The Great Dictator* was a resentment that the film could not be used for war propaganda," which was abominable, for the film, "because of its suberb art and solid core of truth, is one of the few American films whose importance grows with the years." Grounding the Chaplin dilemma in the present, Platt concluded: "That its maker is now being barred from the U.S., which has been his home for more than 40 years, because of his antifascist convictions, shows how badly conditions have deteriorated in our country since the defeat of the fascist dictators so ably satirized in Chaplin's great film." The *Worker* thus used Chaplin's image to convey its view that Cold War America was war-mongering, undemocratic, and cruel to its greatest artists and that Chaplin was among its fore-most progressive victims.

Ultimately, except for the Communist press, Chaplin had few out-right defenders, even among liberals. Chaplin's case was the subject of a large number of newspaper articles and magazine "think pieces" in the liberal press, but nearly everyone who wrote anything sympathetic about him was very careful to criticize or at least keep a distance from his political beliefs, thus, like Parsons, protecting him or herself against the charge of being a Communist sympathizer.

The first and perhaps the least qualified defense of Chaplin ap-peared in the *New York Times*. Its editorial, "Is 'Charlot' a Menace?" appeared just two days after McGranery's action was announced.[45] After noting Chaplin's achievements and worldwide popularity, as well as the irony that he became wealthy by entertaining the common man and "puncturing the pretensions of the proud," the editorial judged that "those who have followed him through the years cannot easily regard him as a dangerous person." Although it granted that it possibly "will be shown that he has in some way been connected with or deceived by what have been described as Communist fronts," the *Times* stated that "unless there is far more evidence against him than is at the moment visible, the Department of State will not dignify itself or increase the national security if it sends him into exile."

The following Sunday Chaplin made the *Times* in three parts of the paper. The first was Crowther's defense, "Under Suspicion." Noting that Chaplin had been "perennial victim of gossip mongers and howl-ers of hate," Crowther wrote that "it is hard to imagine anybody less deserving of being an enemy of this country than this famous and ac-complished man." The second reference was an article about how the INS would proceed if Chaplin came back to face his charges. The third was a cartoon called "The Old Routine," first published in the *Omaha World-Herald*, which showed Charlie slipping on two banana peels labeled "Left-wing Activity" and "Morals Charge," landing on his backside on a sidewalk labeled "Immigration Inquiry." Although the attitude of the cartoonist toward his subject is ambiguous, the cartoon certainly perpetuated the habit of blending the creator and his crea-tion—an integral element of Chaplin's star image—and of associating left-wing politics with both.[46]

In the *New York Herald Tribune*, columnist Dorothy Thompson also came to Chaplin's defense, albeit in a somewhat strange way. She de-cided to play along with the anti-Communists and praise Chaplin for being one himself. Chaplin's central theme, Thompson argued, was "the tragic-comic fate of man, lonely against the organized mass."

Whereas communism exalted "the mass against the individual," Charlie was "the eternal nonconformist. . . . the champion not only of our rights, but of our human, individual follies." In Thompson's view, exiling Chaplin from the United States would simply aid the Communists: they would get fodder for anti-American propaganda, while the United States would lose an artist who was one of the "most effective anti-Communists alive." This conclusion may have puzzled a lot of readers, but Thompson's fear that the Chaplin affair would have international repercussions was borne out by subsequent events.[47]

Time gave the matter attention as the lead and longest story in the "People" section of its September 29 issue.[48] It reported on McGranery's action, then speculated about the grounds on which Chaplin would be charged. He had, said *Time*, "been cited as a sponsor for some Communist-front groups," and the Barry case could "leave him open to a charge of 'moral turpitude.'" Following these speculations, *Time* contrasted a defense of Chaplin from the London *Observer* to Hopper's "good riddance" attack, cited above. The brief account left one feeling that there may well have been good reasons to keep Chaplin out of the country.

Irving Kristol's "McGranery and Charlie Chaplin" was a typical anti-Stalinist liberal response to the charges against Chaplin. Appearing in *Commentary*, which Kristol edited, the essay criticized Chaplin's behavior and praised his art: "It is true that Mr. Chaplin, as an alien, is a guest in this country and that he has shown himself to be both rude and ungrateful. On the other hand, it is worth remembering that, alien though he be, Mr. Chaplin is one of the glories of *American* culture." Liberals in the early 1950s often seemed more worried about the American image abroad than almost anything else, and Kristol, writing that "according to one observer who has just returned from Europe, . . . Mr. McGranery managed with one stroke to erase a year's work by the Voice of America," was no exception. Though criticizing defenses of Chaplin in the European press as having "a sunny air about them," Kristol hoped that with a new attorney general taking office (Eisenhower had just won the presidential election, with Nixon as his running mate), the damage to the American reputation could be minimized. Instead of attacking the government's action as thought control and political repression, as a leftist in the late 1930s would likely have done, here an anti-Stalinist liberal wrung his hands about the U.S. reputation overseas and ignored the fact that Chaplin's reputation was being besmirched and his livelihood threatened for political reasons.[49]

The *Nation*, another liberal journal, also worried about the negative

AMERICAN WAY-OF-LIFE

29. Cartoon from the *Nation* (1952), which first appeared
in the *London Daily Herald*, bemoans the propaganda value
to the Soviet Union of the Chaplin banishment.

publicity the case would generate for the United States. In October it
suggested that "by threatening to bar Charlie Chaplin from coming
back to the United States the Department of Justice has gone several
leagues out of its way to invite ridicule and contempt of sensible people." The editors of the *Nation* warned that Chaplin might make
McGranery and his aides look "like a pack of fools," much as Charlie
had make the Kaiser look in *Shoulder Arms*.[50]

The negative foreign publicity that several commentators predicted
did occur: the banishment generated considerable anti-American publicity abroad. A cartoon in the *London Daily Herald*, later reprinted in
the *Nation*, suggests the international implications of Chaplin's woes
(see Figure 29).[51] By depicting a rotund, smiling Soviet cameraman in
the lower right corner, the cartoon suggests that the Soviets were happily recording the spectacle for their own purposes.

One final, rather quirky, article responding to Chaplin's banishment, William Bradford Huie's "Mr. Chaplin and the Fifth Freedom,"
appeared in the *American Mercury*.[52] Asserting that "our only real enemy is any form of tyranny over the human mind," Huie defended
Chaplin's freedom of speech and freedom of expression and criticized
the government for its action. But his defense was qualified. The article was subtitled "The Sovereign Right to Be a Fool," and a fool is
what Huie believed Chaplin to be: "a genuine twenty-four-carat, ring-
tailed stinker." The article distorts or misstates Chaplin's positions on

such subjects as citizenship, patriotism, lechery, and communism, but concludes that if all McGranery "can prove is that [Chaplin] is a stinker, they are only repeating what has been common knowledge for thirty years, and they should leave the man and his family alone." Such a "defense" was unlikely to do Chaplin's public image much good, but Chaplin could take solace in the fact that the *Mercury*'s circulation was small.

One could sum up the press's initial treatment of Chaplin's banishment by reiterating that though Chaplin's star image had become a pawn in the ideological chess game of Cold War America, it was not an even match. The Left, because the rift between liberals and progressives was widening as the Cold War intensified, was split. Liberals, unwilling to play whole-heartedly, for the most part sat out and left the game to the few remaining radicals. Those radicals, however, held far fewer pieces than the Right, and, as we shall see, the Right easily captured Chaplin's star image—at least for a time.

The *Limelight* Boycott and Chaplin's Star Image

If Chaplin's star image was somewhat harmed by the conservative press in 1952–1953, much more damaging to it and to the box-office fortunes of *Limelight* were the boycott efforts of conservative voluntary organizations that began in October 1952. Although national political figures like McCarthy and Nixon played a considerable role in generating anti-Communist feeling in America in the late 1940s and early 1950s, they were not alone. As one historian of American anticommunism in the postwar decade has argued, "Voluntary organizations played a crucial role in the development of the Red Scare. They responded to the Scare . . . by attempting to limit Communist expression in the general society."[53] Of these organizations, none was as damaging to Chaplin's public reputation as the American Legion.

The Legion, numbering 2.5 million members and another million auxiliary members, was the most influential anti-Communist pressure group to affect the movie industry in the early 1950s. Its interest in exposing Communist influence in Hollywood dated back at least to May 1949, when *American Legion Magazine* published an article, "How Communists Make Stooges out of Movie Stars," but its activity became more organized when its 1951 national convention called for the establishment of a "public information program" on the subject.[54]

Chaplin became the focus of the Legion's wrath during its next convention, held in early October 1952.⁵⁵ There a resolution was passed on October 12 urging theater owners not to show any Chaplin films (and Legion members not to attend Chaplin films if they were shown) until the matter of Chaplin's political and moral fitness to return to the country was cleared up. After the convention adjourned, it remained for local chapters to decide what actions to take if a Chaplin film were scheduled to be shown.⁵⁶

United Artists officials were worried. According to James F. O'Neil, director of publications for the Legion, two United Artists executives, Arthur Krim and Robert Benjamin, visited him in his office on October 20 concerning the Legion's anti-Chaplin resolution. They told him that they were "stuck" with *Limelight* (Chaplin being a principal stockholder in the company) and had to seek distribution for the film. O'Neil nonetheless promised to take action against *Limelight* and even threatened to take action against United Artists itself.⁵⁷

One of the first steps taken by the Legion thereafter was an article— Victor Lasky's "Whose Little Man?"—that appeared in the December issue of *American Legion Magazine*. Its vicious portrayal of Chaplin probably did much to fuel Legion zealotry in the boycott. The six pages included an opening photograph of Chaplin fingering a half-filled champagne glass. Admitting that Chaplin had become a universally popular figure, Lasky also pointed out that he had made an "inordinate" number of enemies, primarily because of Chaplin's "extreme megalomania, his total lack of interest in anything except himself—and his art." Besides displaying a "studied disinterest in personal ethics," wrote Lasky, Chaplin "added one especially unfortunate ingredient; he became a fellow-traveler of communism." He probably never became a party member, continued Lasky, for "it would be difficult even to imagine this supreme egotist submitting to the de-personalized, rigid discipline which Party members are forced to accept."⁵⁸

The essay's contents suggest that Lasky had access to FBI files. He may have obtained them from the Bureau itself or perhaps had seen reports in the hands of gossip columnists Hopper and Muir, who are both prominently mentioned in the article. The topics covered in the article also frequently appeared in Bureau files: "pro-Soviet" second front speeches; failure to entertain at USO events; the Simonov incident; friendship with and defense of Hanns Eisler; support of Wallace's presidential campaign; defense of Gerhart Eisler, Josephson, and Dennis; support of various Peace Congresses; and Rushmore's "sacred cow" allegation. The article also included a wide variety of allegations relating to the Barry trials. A strong case was created against

Chaplin by playing on the anti-Communist assumptions of the day and neglecting information (such as Chaplin's Liberty Loan tour during World War I) that would give a more complex and rounded picture of Chaplin. The article was a catalyst for and harbinger of widespread anti-Chaplin activity by individual Legion posts.

This local pressure was most pronounced in January and February 1953, and then into the spring, when *Limelight* was being scheduled for a more general nationwide release. The first bombshell came on January 15, when Fox West Coast Theaters, the largest West Coast chain of theaters, announced its cancellation of a January 21 opening of *Limelight*. President Charles Skouras made the decision after Ward Bond and Roy Brewer, two members of the Motion Picture Alliance for the Preservation of American Ideals (a Hollywood anti-Communist group that opposed the Hollywood Ten), discussed the American Legion's resolution with Skouras.[59] Two days later it was announced that Loew's, which normally distributed United Artists films, had not chosen to do so with *Limelight*, partly as a result of Legion pressure, and RKO picked it up.

Shortly thereafter, the Legion found a powerful supporter in Howard Hughes, then principal stockholder of RKO Theaters Corporation and board chairman of RKO Pictures. Hughes wrote the Hollywood Legion Post no. 43 in late January that although he had no legal control over the theater operations, he would urge the management to "take the necessary legal measures to cancel all bookings of *Limelight*."[60] This industry pressure on distributors and large theater chains set the stage for more local efforts on the part of the Legion and allied groups like the Veterans of Foreign Wars and the Catholic War Veterans.

Protests began springing up around the country and often had a significant effect on the distribution of the film. For example, in the first half of February, the Ritz Theater in Newburgh, New York, canceled a scheduled run of the film after an American Legion protest, the World Theater in Philadelphia withdrew the film four weeks before the end of its run because of Legion protests, and fifteen Legionnaires picketed two RKO theaters in the Bronx (at the Marble Hill and Fordham theaters). At the time of the Bronx picketing, *Limelight* had just begun a week-long run at sixty-seven New York City area theaters, but it was withdrawn after only three days at most of them. *Variety* reported on February 4 that Legion officials in Washington, D.C., had announced boycotts of *Limelight* when it opened at the Little and Plaza Theaters and had released a statement criticizing "Chaplin's long record of association with Communist Fronts and causes, and his openly expressed contempt for the United States." The film was also withdrawn in Columbus, Ohio, and New Orleans. One contemporary journalist writing on the boycotts contended that normally a Chaplin film would have played at about 2,500 theaters by the end of February but as of February 15 it had only played at about 150. After examining how broadly and systematically the Legion protested and picketed against *Limelight* because of questions raised about its maker, one begins to understand Chaplin's statement to the London press after he turned in his reentry permit that he had been the victim of "reactionary" forces.[61]

Given the positive and mixed national reviews of *Limelight*, there is little doubt that the boycott had a considerable effect on the box-office fortunes of *Limelight*. This is particularly evident when one looks at how the film did in its fall 1952 New York City run—before the Legion's boycott activities were organized. These initial box-office figures from *Variety* suggested that *Limelight* would make a lot of money. In their review of the film two weeks before the New York opening, *Variety* had predicted that despite the length, "It's all Chaplin and deserving of stout b.o." *Limelight* then opened at the Astor and Trans-Lux 60th theaters in Manhattan and did strong business the first week ("Sock 45½G at 2 Locations," according to the *Variety* headline). The run continued through October and November, and the film brought in around $35,000 per week for at least three more weeks. Though receipts sagged in early December, they bounced back to nearly $50,000 the week of Christmas. Ultimately, *Limelight*, perhaps buoyed by some good reviews, ran twelve weeks in its initial run and did extremely well given the political and social climate.[62]

After Legion pressure began to be applied in January and February 1953, however, the door slammed shut. Although *Limelight* did manage to get some bookings in cities like Toronto, Seattle, and Chicago, the overall performance was extremely disappointing for Chaplin and United Artists. After ranking a lowly eleventh in *Variety's* box-office receipts for January—and never higher than eighth for any individual week—the film did not even make the top twelve in February, when the nationwide release occurred and the highest grosses were expected. The disappointing February performance in the New York City neighborhood theaters, where the film was withdrawn from most after three days, led *Variety* to predict that *Limelight's* total take for distributors would be no higher than a million dollars. Considering the fact that the film made some $5 million worldwide, its U. S. box-office performance, influenced by the Legion's campaign, was very weak.

Relatively few viewers were even given the opportunity to see Chaplin's gesture of reconciliation.[63]

These pressure tactics did not go unnoticed in the press. Some liberal publications evinced a sympathy that had been evident in some of the reviews of *Limelight*. This sympathy can be best understood by placing it in a broader context of opposition to the tactics of HUAC and McCarthy. In the early 1950s a minority opposition did exist, however quiet or aberrant it might have been considered at the time. When many intellectuals were celebrating America for its democracy and freedom and tolerating or even embracing McCarthyism, some refused to go along with the tide. In the words of Richard Pells, intellectuals like Dwight Macdonald, Henry Steele Commager, Lillian Hellman, Arthur Miller, Mary McCarthy, and I. F. Stone "resisted not simply the tactics of but the rationale for McCarthyism"—sometimes by publicly denouncing the rationale in print, sometimes by refusing to name names before HUAC.[64]

Though none of these figures spoke out concerning the Legion's actions against *Limelight*, its tactics did raise the anticensorship hackles of other writers and journalists. These defenses of Chaplin reflected different degrees of dissent, but together they formed a nucleus of sympathy that later helped to regenerate Chaplin's star image in the 1960s and 1970s. For example, *Commonweal* quoted Justice Learned Hand: "I believe that that community is already in process of dissolution where each man begins to eye his neighbor as a possible enemy, where non-conformity with the accepted creed, political as well as religious, is a mark of disaffection." Even though *Commonweal* covered itself by admitting that Chaplin had "no doubt" said "some things which are, perhaps deservedly, unpopular in the country" and that his conduct "has shocked many people," it did take the Legion to task in an era when such a challenge made one vulnerable to harsh criticism. Even more unusual than these defenses was the position taken by a veteran's organization. On February 7 the *Times* published a letter from Bernard Storder, chairman of the Motion Picture Section of the American Veterans Committee. It read in part: "As citizens and as veterans we condemn this latest attempt at thought control by the Legion as a gross violation of the basic democratic principle of the freedom of the arts from interference by pressure groups." To counter the Legion pressure, his group urged *Times* readers to request that theater owners show the film. The position of the AVC, however, was the exception among veterans' groups rather than the rule; most were sympathetic to the Legion campaign.[65]

Chaplin's decision to turn in his reentry permit was the last phase of the 1952–1953 controversy and returned editors and journalists, on the right and left, to their typewriters. The *New York Times*, which had defended Chaplin since the day after the revocation of his reentry permit, was a little harder on the comedian in its editorial, "Mr. Chaplin Bows Out." Reminding its readers of its earlier support of Chaplin, the *Times* stated that "Chaplin's evident unwillingness to return deprives him of the opportunity to fight the charges against him . . . and, unfortunately, will give great encouragement to those who believe in the 'purge' technique for American artistic and cultural life." As in *Commonweal*'s attack on the Legion tactics, the *Times* editors also distanced themselves from Chaplin, writing that "we hold no brief for Mr. Chaplin's private life or public views" and coming close to implying that he might have had trouble with the immigration officials had he chosen to return.[66]

The conservatives also commented. Representative is Robert Ruark's syndicated column, entitled "Chaplin's Worst Sin," which appeared after Chaplin's decision. The "worst sin" was failing to become a citizen of the United States after residing so long in the country. Had Chaplin done so, Ruark believed, he would have been spared many of his problems, and surely the reentry issue would have disappeared or at least have been framed in different terms. Yet Ruark's distaste for Chaplin is clear; referring to the Barry case, Ruark called him "a bounder of the worst sort" and "a little blighter." Of Chaplin's refusal to face an INS hearing Ruark judged that "tacitly he must stand as convicted" of the Communist charges. The conclusion belittled the artist who had been a public figure, and often a public idol, for many of the almost forty years he had lived in the country: "I think the loss is small, any way you figure it. And that no great injustice has been done anybody."[67]

Such small-minded commentary is perhaps a fitting way to conclude this look at the state of Chaplin's star image as he decided to settle abroad. In the midst of the charges and countercharges, the attacks and the defenses, one quality came to dominate Chaplin's star image: the progressive political activism. Chaplin's alleged moral turpitude played a minor role. Except for a few reviews, Chaplin the great filmmaker and actor was neglected, and Charlie was forgotten. The star image was out of Chaplin's hands. Despite his gestures of reconciliation in the early 1950s—both his relative temperance in political matters and his appeals in *Limelight*—American culture rejected him. Although the liberal community did some ineffectual hand-wringing, organized pressure-group activity on the right, particularly by the American Legion, made it certain that Chaplin—the man whom Shaw had called the only genius the movies had produced, and the man who had created the mythic persona so profoundly central to the movies—would receive no hearing. Since the Left was declining and in disarray, radical support of Chaplin had little influence on the cultural debate—and what effect it had was negative. By the early 1950s, the Right was in the saddle in the United States, and Chaplin, both the real human being and the star image that surrounded his name, became one of its victims.

FIVE

The Exile and America

11

The Exiled Monarch and the Guarded
Restoration, 1953–1977

Running Battles: Chaplin, American Culture,
and the Later 1950s

Between 1953 and his death in 1977, Chaplin lived outside the United States, and his star image affected American culture considerably less than it had during the years he lived and worked in the country. However, during that period his star image also recovered from its nadir in the late 1940s and early 1950s until, by the early 1970s, it enjoyed a guarded restoration. Chaplin's star image evolved from one associated with the qualities of "dangerous radical" and "womanizer" to one much more positive, which emphasized Chaplin the virtuoso filmmaker and aging family patriarch, as well as, once again, the adorable Charlie. Some of the reasons for the change include an evolving political climate in the United States, shifts in the "aesthetic discourse" about movies (in particular, the dominance of auteurism), and Chaplin's careful management of both his star image and his business interests through rereleases, the publication of his autobiography, and his 1972 return visit to the United States.

This change did not, however, happen overnight. In Chaplin's first years away from the United States he did little to endear himself with the American press and public, and the press particularly played its part in perpetuating his reputation as a misguided radical. One of Chaplin's first public statements after he turned in his reentry permit set the hostile tone for relations between Chaplin and the press through much of the 1950s. In April 1953, Chaplin visited London and issued a press release. This scathing statement, quoted in *Newsweek* a week later, enabled Chaplin to vent the frustrations that he had been harboring at least since the days of *Monsieur Verdoux*:

> It is not easy to uproot myself and my family from a country where I have lived for 40 years without a feeling of sadness. But since the end of the last war, I have been the object of vicious propaganda by powerful reactionary groups who by their influence and by the aid of America's yellow press have created an

unhealthy atmosphere in which liberal-minded individuals can be singled out and persecuted. I have therefore given up my residence in the United States.[1]

As the American Legion boycott activities and the response of the conservative press to Chaplin and his exile demonstrated, Chaplin's allegations contained large doses of truth, however inflammatory his rhetoric. Yet to most Americans, increasingly self-satisfied about the essential goodness of their institutions as the 1950s wore on—and, as a legacy of the McCarthy era, becoming intolerant of views that offered criticism of those institutions—Chaplin's comments simply supported the widely shared image of Chaplin the radical.

Neither Chaplin nor the American press seemed much concerned about mending the rift in the next several years. Chaplin himself was involved in three publicized events that hurt his reputation in America. The first was the announcement in May 1954 that Chaplin and Dmitri Shostakovich were the winners of the Soviet-sponsored World Peace Council award. The other two were meetings with Communist officials: with Chinese prime minister Chou En-lai in Geneva in 1954 and with the Soviet leaders Nikita Khrushchev and Nikolai Bulganin in London in 1956.

In each of these situations, Chaplin affirmed his commitment to world peace, a position that conservatives and anti-Stalinist liberals in the United States considered naive and dangerously left-wing. When Chaplin accepted the $14,000 peace prize in June (he later donated it to several charities), for example, he told reporters, "To promulgate a demand for peace, whether from East or West, I firmly believe is a step in the right direction."[2] In his autobiography Chaplin remembers drinking "many toasts" with Chou En-lai during their 1954 dinner. In one of them, he recalled, "I toasted the future of China and said that although I was not a Communist I wholeheartedly joined in their hope and desire for a better life for the Chinese people, and for all people" (MA, pp. 485–89). The meeting with the Soviet officials came when Chaplin received an invitation to the Soviet embassy following a goodwill address Khrushchev made in London. Chaplin recalls complimenting Khrushchev on the speech: "It had come like a ray of sunshine, and I told him so, saying that it had given hope for peace to millions throughout the world" (MA, p. 482).[3]

The American press reaction to Chaplin's continued commitment to progressive causes was mostly critical. Responding to the peace prize, the *New York Times*, which had in general defended Chaplin through his career, editorialized unequivocally against him. Titled

"Little Man, Farewell," the editorial claimed that if Chaplin "knew more about Russia, or if he were perhaps less bitter, he would be well aware that the 'peace prize' is not a peace prize at all but a prize offered to those in Russia or outside of Russia who serve the purposes of a brutal and tyrannical imperialism." Chaplin should know, the *Times* wrote, that his little tramp "could not survive and prosper in today's Russia." By accepting the prize, Chaplin "has allowed himself to be used by a sinister conspiracy of which the little man he so touchingly represented is the victim. . . . He shuffles off leftward, toward Moscow, perhaps not calling himself a Communist or a fellow traveler—but there he goes and the sag of his back, the flap of his coattails, the set of his little derby over the ears and the sadly reminiscent twirling of his cane move us almost to tears."[4] The editorial's only positive comment related to Chaplin's early films. As so often happened after *The Great Dictator* and especially after *Monsieur Verdoux*, Chaplin the aspiring social commentator was negatively compared to Charlie the silent film comic. Thus a contradiction grew up in the Chaplin star image: though dominated by the present Chaplin—an arrogant radical sympathizer—the star image also included the faded image of funny little Charlie. This subordinate dimension provided a seed for Chaplin's renaissance in the 1960s and 1970s. But in the mid-1950s Chaplin the Red dominated.

In September 1954, the *Saturday Evening Post*, the conservative family-oriented magazine with a huge circulation, lambasted Chaplin in an editorial titled "Double Play: Chaplin to Robeson to Malenkov."[5] Its opening charge is a strong one, claiming that Chaplin was "doing all he can to make the world weep bitterly and worry its head off. After living in the United States forty years, Chaplin has openly joined our enemy, the Soviet slave masters." The basis for this charge was first, that he had "dined at Geneva with Chou-en-Lai, Red gauletier in China"; second, that he had accepted a prize from the World "Peace" Council [their quotation marks], the "foremost Soviet front in the world"; and third, that he had sent a telegram to a "Culture Salute to Paul Robeson" held in New York City. To cap its argument, the *Post* quoted the Kremlin's public praise for Chaplin after he received the peace prize: "He came into our camp as simply and naturally as a tributary falls into a river, as a river falls into the ocean." The editorial makes use of the guilt by association tactics that victimized Chaplin in the late 1940s: if the Soviets like something, the logic went, it must be bad. The editorial also demonstrates the degree to which Chaplin's image was still at the mercy of Cold War politics.

Partly because of this continued press hostility, Chaplin and his films continued to be the occasional targets of pressure groups. Early in 1955 Muhlenberg College scheduled four Chaplin films to play in its "Films of Yesterday" series. When the American Legion protested, however, the college quickly buckled under the pressure and the four films were canceled.[6]

The anti-Stalinist liberal intelligentsia, however, despite its disapproval of Chaplin's progressive politics, was beginning to make itself heard after McCarthy and his tactics fell from favor. The day after the ban on the Chaplin films was announced, the American Committee for Cultural Freedom, an organization of prominent American intellectuals formed in 1951, attacked the Legion's tactics and the college's action. Within a week the college had reversed its position and decided to go ahead with the films.[7] The Legion was blocked. Though it is evident that the Legion's activities against Chaplin were not nearly so prominent in the late 1950s as they had been during the *Limelight* release, it still was able to bring some influence to bear. In fact, as we shall see, Chaplin believed that the sentiment against him in America was so powerful that he did not even attempt to release any of the films he controlled (the First National and United Artists films) until 1963.

The years from 1953 to 1957 were thus generally years of tension in the relationship between Chaplin and American culture. For most of that period, Chaplin was either contemplating or actively working on a film that would allude to the treatment he received in the United States in 1952 and earlier. Although that film, *A King in New York*, did not play in the United States in its initial run, the American press coverage of the French and British openings of the film in 1957 also contributed, generally in a negative way, to Chaplin's star image.

After beginning to script the film in the middle of 1953, Chaplin shot the film in London between May and July 1956, edited and scored it in Paris, and released it in 1957.[8] The film's narrative focuses on King Igor Shahdov (Chaplin) who, after being dethroned during a revolution in his country of Estrovia, travels to New York City with his valet, Jaume, carrying blueprints for a project that could harness atomic energy for peaceful ends. After a night on the town, he learns that his untrustworthy prime minister has stolen his securities, which leaves him in a financially precarious position. This leads him to accept invitations from New York socialites and to endorse various consumer products for money. On a visit to a progressive school, King Shahdov debates, then later befriends, a prodigy, Rupert Macabee (played by Chaplin's son, Michael), whose parents are Communists in conflict with the HUAC. When the press gets wind of the association between

Rupert and Shahdov, the former king also comes under the suspicion of HUAC and is subpoenaed to testify. En route to the hearing, Shahdov's finger is caught in a water hose. Bringing it along with him to the HUAC chambers, he gets his finger out only when water pressure builds, after which the hose showers the entire committee. Though he clears himself of any Communist associations, Shahdov decides, after a final visit to Rupert—who is devastated after having "named names" to secure his parents' release from prison—to return to Europe.

As in *Limelight*, Chaplin encouraged an autobiographical reading of *A King in New York* by playing a character far different from Charlie and similar in a number of ways to Chaplin himself. Like Chaplin, King Shahdov has to flee his country of residence and become an exile. Like Chaplin during the Barry trials, the king is surrounded by the press when he is fingerprinted upon his arrival in the United States. Like Chaplin, he is an idealist interested in promoting the cause of world peace. Like Chaplin, he is subpoenaed to testify before HUAC because of his associations with alleged Communists. Like Chaplin (in the comedian's earlier years, at least), he shows considerable interest in young women. The former king of American film comedy and the exiled king had much in common.[9]

If these autobiographical associations were unlikely to endear the film to American critics, neither did its cultural critique of the United States find favor. Although detailed analysis of its social criticism is not necessary here, the film satirized at least four aspects of American society: popular culture, progressive education, advertising, and the behavior of the press. Even though much of the film's social critique is based on a rather traditional perspective—the satirical jibes at rock music, wide-screen movies, and "creativity" in progressive schools, for example—American society in the mid-1950s was not receptive to criticism from abroad.[10] Chaplin guessed as much, for he chose not to release the film widely in the United States until 1973, a year after he returned to be honored in New York City and Los Angeles.[11]

Even without showing the film in the United States, Chaplin managed to generate negative commentary. The titles of articles reporting on the British response give an indication of the American press's hostility to Chaplin. Four reports from large circulation U.S. newspapers and magazines, all of which appeared within two weeks of the film's London press screening, are representative: "Critics Are Cool to Chaplin Film," "Unfunny Charlie Chaplin," "Critics Find Chaplin's Anti-U.S. Movie a Flop," and "The Unfunny Comic."[12] A number of these early reports wrote that the foreign, particularly British, press disliked the film. For example, the *New York Times*, which subtitled its essay, "Fails to Impress London Writers," quoted three negative reviews from British newspapers and charged that Chaplin used the film "to ridicule many aspects of American life." *Time* reported that the film "impressed most critics as being less a labor of love than one of hate." The *Nation* held that "critical response has been almost unanimous in its disappointment." In the *New York Herald Tribune* Art Buchwald wrote a column from Paris on a screening he had of the film with a French journalist and a potential U.S. independent distributor. In addition to quoting a negative review from the *London Daily Express*, Buchwald reported that the French journalist laughed just three times, that the exhibitor said only, "it stinks," and that all three left the screening room "sadly deflated."[13]

This early negative response, particularly the reports that the British press panned the film, seems at least partly a case of American journalists searching for the worst response. Although disappointment was expressed in some British reviews, *A King in New York* was also highly praised in some quarters. In the influential *London Times*, for example, Dilys Powell made the extravagant claim that "the very fact that [*A King in New York*] occurs enables the cinema . . . to take its place without question among the seats reserved for the major arts." Admitting that Chaplin's satire was characterized at times by "a dash of malice," Powell pointed out with some relish the film's paradox that "a monarch is more democratic on some of his political thinking than a republic."[14] David Robinson's recent assertion that "the British press was largely favourable and at worst respectful" to *A King in New York* may be too generous, but the British response was surely more positive than the American press granted at the time.[15]

The reviews in American newspapers and periodicals reveal some interesting similarities, which suggest that the prevailing critical discourse for discussing Chaplin films had regressed. Shunning the tendency of critics in the 1930s and early 1940s to encourage "progressive" political concerns in films, the American critics of *A King in New York* reverted to critical questions that were more characteristic of the 1910s and the 1920s. Partly because the economic prosperity of the war and postwar years had muted the calls for the restructuring of the American economy that had been more prevalent in the depression years and partly because radical critics were frequently attacked or summarily dismissed during the most frigid years of the Cold War, most American audiences and reviewers were less enthusiastic about, or even openly hostile to, the "progressive" films that earlier critics like Harry Alan Potamkin or Lewis Jacobs had called for and praised during the 1930s. The 1950s were, as noted earlier, dominated by an ideological consensus that considered American society fundamentally sound and equitable. Working within this sociopolitical consensus, few U.S. critics and reviewers would respond favorably to a film overtly critical of American institutions, and fewer still would agree that a film's political position was the standard upon which one would base an evaluation of the film.[16]

This does not mean that American reviewers were hesitant about attacking the film because it criticized the United States. In fact, some were happy to do so. *Time*, for example, opened its review by telling its readers that Chaplin was a "bitter man" and a "self exile" settled in Switzerland: "Convinced that he had been persecuted by McCarthyism, Red-liner Chaplin decided to deprive the U.S. of one of the few authentic geniuses produced by the movies." *Time* then prefaced a plot summary with a sharp critique of its politics: "Intended as satire, *King's* few funny spots are outweighed by shrill invective and heavy-footed propaganda." The *Nation*, whose editors could have been sympathetic to the film's political satire, noted that the film had a "political plot" but commented that "the really good parts of the film were strung on a line that had nothing to do with" it. Similarly, the *New Republic* minimized (or side-stepped) the validity of the political critique by finding fault with the presentation of the material: "Chaplin leads us clumsily towards the point of the film—McCarthyism—by introducing a repugnant little schoolboy, played by his son." The same review also disparaged the film's political dimension by referring to the "incredible inaccuracy of the satire." And even when a reviewer accepted the validity of some of the satire—as Marvin Felheim did in his *Reporter* review—he followed the admission by writing that "most of these evils have been much more blatantly condemned in American films" like *Storm Center*.[17]

Reviewers of *A King in New York* tended to ask whether the film was funny, as had their counterparts in the 1910s, or if the film successfully blended pathos and humor, as in the 1920s. In both cases, the reviewers generally answered no.

Saturday Review: "This film is not funny enough and not often enough"
Nation: "It is not very funny" (p. 310)
New Republic: "For about 90 seconds he is very funny. But that is the beginning and the end" (p. 22)
Newsweek: "The Unfunny Comic" (title)
Time: "Unfunny Charlie Chaplin" (title)[18]

Some reviewers did find funny incidents in the film—Felheim, for example, was pleased with the satire on American movies. The point to be stressed, however, is that the reviewers seemed to be judging a film that had no intention of being a Keystone comedy by the very standards of slapstick.

Similarly, some reviewers looked for the blend of pathos and romance Chaplin perfected between *The Kid* and *City Lights*. To Robert Fulford in the *New Republic*, "*A King in New York* . . . is dismaying from any position you choose to take. If you look for comedy, it is almost entirely missing: and when it turns up it is usually inept. If you look for pathos, you look in vain: Chaplin tries for the pathetic a dozen times, but he never comes close" (p. 22). *Saturday Review* took the same position, arguing that "Chaplin attempts to use the boy for pathos as he used a little boy in *The Kid* and the blind girl in *City Lights*. But it doesn't come off, chiefly because there are not enough gags or comic sequences to carry the serious parts" (p. 27). Thus, while Chaplin was more concerned with blending political satire and a critique of American commercial culture in the 1950s, the reviewers were measuring the film by standards applied to his films of the 1920s.

The resulting mismatch was another blow to Chaplin's star image. A number of the reviewers even turned nostalgically back to the Chaplin of earlier years and lamented the decline of an artist of genius. "There are flashes of the old Charlie Chaplin," wrote Felheim, "but at the center is Mr. Chaplin. . . . Unhappily he is a sadder and an older man: the real punch is gone. His dethroned king is an ironically apt image." Similar, but perhaps harsher and thus more representative, was the *New Republic*'s analysis:

> So long as Chaplin took black-and-white subjects (like the kind tramp versus the vicious millionaire in *City Lights*), his childlike, though never childish, approach invariably worked. . . . It was only when he turned to a sort of half-baked philosophy that he began to bore his audience.
>
> Now Chaplin has put that kind of comedy behind him. He is facing . . . a world that is too big and too confusing for him. The difference now is that it is the artist, and not the character, who is lost and helpless. (p. 23)

Though one could argue that this yearning for the Charlie of earlier days contained the seeds for the eventual restoration of Chaplin's public reputation, the reviews of *A King in New York* did not indicate this. Because Chaplin's earlier feature films were not available for viewing, they remained at best vague shadows in the memories of reviewers and audiences. And although the auteur theory was flourishing as "les politique des auteurs" among the renegade French group of *Cahiers du cinema* critics by the mid-1950s, the approach had not yet taken root in the United States. Both factors would later help to restore Chaplin's public reputation, but two titles best describe the state of Chaplin's star image in the United States after the reviews of *A King in New York*. In one review, Chaplin was "a monarch in exile." In another, he was "a king in decline."

These labels continued to describe the state of Chaplin's reputation in the United States through the late 1950s, for following the European release of *A King in New York* and the generally negative reviews of it that appeared in the American press, Chaplin's name did not cease generating controversy. Probably the most prominent and widely distributed criticism of Chaplin to appear in the American press shortly after *A King in New York* was James O'Donnell's three-part essay, "Charlie Chaplin's Stormy Exile," in the widely circulated and conservative *Saturday Evening Post*.[19] Apparently in March 1958, the opening piece clearly set out to paint a negative portrait of America's fallen clown. The top left-hand corner of the article's first page, for example, contained an unflattering, jowly picture of Chaplin frowning and looking down, his double chin folded; beneath was a caption that described Chaplin as "a tragi-comedian with 'furious and hidden' grievances." The subtitle of the essay read, "Poor Charlie, once the funniest man alive, is now a stuffed shirt who has destroyed the peace of a dreamy Swiss village" (1: 19). Such details set the tone for all three articles, which complained about Chaplin's failure to pay back taxes, his parsimony, his rudeness to employees and to Vevey city officials, and his acceptance of the peace prize. Collectively, the widely read articles portrayed Chaplin as an unreasonably arrogant man, criticized his recent work (*A King* is described as "a reckless satire of not much of anything," 1: 96), and generally perpetuated the star image of the politically unwise monarch in decline.

One other incident in the late 1950s epitomizes the state of Chaplin's star image in America. Early in 1958 the Hollywood Chamber of Commerce announced a list of 1,500 celebrities whose names were to be inscribed on brass plaques and embedded in local sidewalks. Chaplin's name was absent from the list, and no official explanation was offered. After this early announcement, it took some time for the project to get under way. In 1960 it was reported again that Chaplin's name was left off the list of those who would be included in the "Walk of Fame" along about a mile of Hollywood Boulevard. This time, however, the Chamber of Commerce told reporters that some of the local property owners, who were footing the bill for the project, objected to

Chaplin's inclusion.[20] Latent hostilities against Chaplin still smoldered in the movie community, as they did in the wider culture.

Shifting Winds: The 1960s

In the 1960s, particularly between 1960 and 1964, Chaplin's star image began to take on more positive associations in the United States. At least five factors contributed to this renewal. On the broadest plane, the ideology of liberal consensus that had dominated American intellectual and political life since the late 1940s began to break down. Many came to question its basic assumptions and, increasingly, to accept those who, like Chaplin, challenged them. Second, on a more specific legal and economic level, Chaplin's representatives worked through the federal courts to clarify his ownership of his First National and United Artists films, and thus to secure his legal right to distribute them. Third, when that was completed, Chaplin arranged to show a series of his feature films in New York City. Fourth, the publication of Chaplin's autobiography in September 1964 brought the shape of his career—told from his own perspective—to the attention of readers and reviewers. Fifth, the 1967 release of Chaplin's disastrous final feature film, *A Countess from Hong Kong*, though a critical and financial failure, stressed to viewers through contrast how good his earlier films were. These factors combined to mute the negative image of Chaplin the radical and to bring Charlie—a central ingredient in the creation of Chaplin's stardom in the first place—back into the calculus of Chaplin's star image in America.

The key contextual factor to understanding the shift in Chaplin's reputation from the Eisenhower years to the election of Lyndon B. Johnson as President in 1964 was the waning intensity of anti-Communist zealotry in the United States and the growing tendency among some Americans to admit that the United States itself faced such difficult domestic problems as poverty and civil inequality. Perhaps the first important indications of the shift came in 1954, when the Supreme Court handed down its school desegregation decision, the Democrats regained control of Congress in the fall, and the Senate officially condemned the actions of Joseph McCarthy. In 1955, the Montgomery bus boycott was the first important protest of the civil rights movement.

In foreign affairs, Stalin's death in 1953 and the Soviet Union's partial condemnation of him in 1956 led many intellectuals to reassess their tendency to divide the world into simple categories of good and evil. Though the Soviet involvement in Hungary in 1956 served as a reminder that the Soviets would act decisively to protect its "sphere of influence," the Kremlin also frequently commented on the necessity for "peaceful coexistence" in a split world. Especially in the late 1950s, the Cold War seemed to experience a thaw as both Eisenhower and Khrushchev began to call for summit conferences, reciprocal visits, a curbing of the arms race, and cultural exchange programs. Although problems intensified again between 1960 and 1962, as evidenced by the Gary Powers spy plane incident, the Berlin Wall crisis, the aborted Bay of Pigs invasion, and the Cuban missile crisis, by September of 1963 (about two months before Chaplin's films began their New York rerelease run) the U.S. Senate ratified a nuclear test ban treaty that ushered in a period of relative stability in U.S.–Soviet relations.

That the monumental civil rights march on Washington, D.C., took place in August 1963 and that President Kennedy was assassinated three months later only accentuated the shifting focus of national attention from foreign to domestic affairs. As Richard Pells has described, "an increasing number of Americans were questioning, if not discarding, many of the assumptions and practices of the previous fifteen years."[21] The decline of Chaplin's public reputation and the growing tendency to regard Chaplin the star as an unwise radical had been closely related to these "assumptions and practices," now beginning to be challenged.

Chaplin also used the courts to help lay the groundwork for improvement of his star image. After settling with the IRS in late 1958 over back taxes owed for 1953,[22] thus clearing any liabilities he had in the United States, Chaplin was free to begin rereleasing his films in the United States without worrying about having the profits held up or confiscated. Rereleasing the earlier features was an attractive possibility. Doing so would present the Charlie persona to a new generation. And the number of theaters willing to present foreign films and older film "classics" was growing: according to one industry count, the number in the United States grew from 83 in 1950 to 644 in 1966.[23] This growth was creating a market for films like Chaplin's silent features.

But to tap that market, Chaplin needed to establish conclusively his sole legal ownership of the films and his right to distribute them. Since he did not own the rights to the Keystone, Essanay, and Mutual films, they had been frequently revived and even made available for sale for decades. This made it tempting for entrepreneurs, particularly after Chaplin left the country and was out of favor, to obtain and even distribute prints of other Chaplin films to which he did own the rights.

In June 1959 Chaplin, through Roy Export Company (his European-based distributing company) and Lopert Films (the company authorized by Chaplin to distribute his films in the United States), filed suit in federal district court against the International Art Production Management Company. The suit sought an injunction against International to stop its distribution of *The Gold Rush*, which they had rented to a New York City theater for the previous six weeks. The suit alleged unfair trade practices and the unlawful ownership of prints. In July the courts found in favor of Chaplin and awarded Roy Export a permanent injunction against the showing of any Chaplin First National or United Artists film in the United States with the exception of one version of *The Gold Rush*.[24] Chaplin's control of these films was thus secure.

Chaplin, sensing lingering hostility within certain segments of American culture, did not immediately schedule rerelease of the films. In the early 1960s, though, some indications of a more positive treatment of Chaplin in the American press began to appear. One of the earliest was Bosley Crowther's interview and feature in the *New York Times Magazine* in 1960, titled "The Modern—and Mellower—Times of Mr. Chaplin."[25] The article helped to revive his U.S. reputation in several ways. First, it indicated that his attitude toward the United States for the treatment he had received in the late 1940s and 1950s had softened. Crowther quoted Chaplin on his current attitude: "I cannot help but be bitter about many things that happened to me. But the country and the American people—they are great, of course." Second, Crowther outlined Chaplin's entire career, and in his summary he refused to dwell on details of Chaplin's private life that alienated him from so many Americans and focused instead on Chaplin the actor, particularly on his persona Charlie, who "represented the ever-hopeful average man in the eternal and usually hopeless struggle of the individual against the mass." A number of stills visually supported this return of Charlie. Finally, Crowther, writing that "many close investigations" failed to turn up any evidence that Chaplin was a Communist, implicitly defended Chaplin's political views (p. 59). In the article Chaplin the man thus emerges more as a victim of repressive political times than as a dangerous radical.

Chaplin's star image also benefited from Oxford University's decision in 1962 to award the aging comedian an honorary degree—a ceremony that made the front page of the *New York Times*. In an interview afterward, he told reporters that he felt no bitterness toward the United States. The *Times*'s editorial staff apparently took notice and found the changing tone significant, for a few days later they brought up the subject in an editorial titled, "Re-enter the 'Little Tramp.'"[26] In addition to noting that Chaplin had been awarded the honorary degree (along with Secretary of State Dean Rusk), it comments on the lasting image of the "little tramp": he "lives, and will live until the last of the films that show him in action have turned to dust." The editors do not fail to establish their credentials as Cold War liberals in the piece; they write that the Communists "tried to use [Chaplin] for their purposes" but that "he insisted that he never had belonged and never would belong to their humorless fraternity of the Left." However, the climax of the editorial is its conclusion, which urges the Kennedy administration to lift the ban imposed on Chaplin in 1952: "We do not believe the Republic would be in danger . . . if yesterday's unforgotten little tramp were allowed to amble down the gangplank of a steamer or plane in an American port." The imagery is significant: in defending Chaplin, the *Times* stressed Charlie, sympathetically revised Charles, and kept Chaplin the woman chaser out of the picture.

Articles like Crowther's and honors like the Oxford degree helped set the stage for the next three key events: the rerelease of Chaplin feature films in New York, which played continuously for eleven months beginning in November 1963; Chaplin's autobiography, published in 1964; and Chaplin's final film, *A Countess from Hong Kong*, released early in 1967. Although Chaplin did receive some negative response from critics and audiences concerning these events, particularly *Countess*, the tendency of each was to enhance his star image "retrospectively." That is, all three encouraged viewers and readers to look back over Chaplin's whole career and not simply to dwell on his films and activities during the years when his reputation was sliding. By looking at the entire sweep of Chaplin's work from the more favorable historical context of the mid-1960s, viewers and readers helped to revise the negative star image of Chaplin inherited from the late 1940s and 1950s. This occurred in large part by returning the factor of Charlie to the polysemy of Chaplin's star image.

Perhaps heartened by the conciliatory tone of the *Times* editorial and other positive responses from the United States, Chaplin and his business representatives arranged the first systematic rerelease of Chaplin's features, limited to one theater in New York City. From the opening of *City Lights* in the last week of November 1963 until mid-October 1964 (well past the September publication date of Chaplin's autobiography), six Chaplin programs had a successful and continuous run at the Plaza Theater. After *City Lights*, the Plaza showed the Chaplin Revue (*Shoulder Arms*, *A Dog's Life*, and *The Pilgrim*), *The Great Dictator*, *Modern Times* (double featured with *The Gold Rush* in all but the first two weeks), *Monsieur Verdoux*, and *Limelight*.[27]

Note the pattern of release: Chaplin chose to present audiences first with his Charlie persona, the trademark that did so much to establish his star image. If we accept the barber in *The Great Dictator* as a kind of surrogate Charlie, viewers were not confronted with Chaplin's later personae, Verdoux and Calvero, until the last two films of the run. If we recall the excoriation Chaplin received from nearly every quarter when *Verdoux* was released in 1947, it is remarkable to note that *Monsieur Verdoux* not only enjoyed the longest (with *City Lights*, nine weeks) and most financially successful run in the series but also received widespread critical acclaim. Something was happening to Chaplin's star image.

Opening on Friday, July 3, *Monsieur Verdoux* set a weekend box-office record for the 525-seat Plaza, garnering $13,500 in receipts for the three-day weekend. (At the ticket prices of $1.50 and $2, this indicates more than thirteen sellouts for the three days.) The film continued to do a strong business, grossing $12,500 in the seventh week, compared to $11,500 in the seventh week for *The Great Dictator*, whose gross was the second biggest of the series.[28]

The critical response, such as it was (it was not customary in 1964 for reviewers to write about revivals), was positive. In the *New York Herald Tribune* Judith Crist, praising the film's "fantastic comedy, its biting ironies . . . , and its crushing social satire," told her readers that *Verdoux* was a "classic that we are at last privileged to appreciate after its abortive debut 17 years ago." Crowther recommended the film highly and used two reviews in the *New York Times* to praise and to chide those who initially gave it a hostile reception. One of the few who had given *Verdoux* a relatively good review in 1947, Crowther was more enthusiastic in 1964, calling it "a superior sardonic comedy" and "an engrossingly wry and paradoxical film, screamingly funny in places . . . and devoted to an unusually serious and sobering argument." In a follow-up article a week later in the Sunday *Times*, Crowther told his readers that seeing *Monsieur Verdoux* was "a rare and rousing privilege that no one should miss." He also wrote about the "almost faded notoriety that was unjustly fomented against it at the time of its release" and lamented "the melancholy memories [the film] stirs of the outrage and abuse so cruelly heaped on Mr. Chaplin, who caused it to be withdrawn."[29] The article suggested that Chaplin had been a victim of the times.

In July, a *Newsweek* article seconded that view. Entitled "Charles the Great," it contained four stills of Chaplin playing Verdoux and reported on the huge gap between the film's reception in 1947 and in 1964. To *Newsweek* the enthusiastic reception of *Verdoux* was a comment on the times as much as on the film: "What has changed—at least in New York, and probably throughout the country—is the atmosphere. *Chaplin is no longer a villain*. A new generation has grown up, receptive to his artistry and eager for his gift of laughter. This very change affects the way we now view the film."[30] Chaplin's star image was evolving, distinctly taking on the image of victim instead of villain, of a man and performer unjustly attacked during the years of excessively zealous anticommunism.

This new and more positive response to *Monsieur Verdoux* provides an almost perfect case study for key assumptions of Hans Robert Jauss's aesthetic of reception. For Jauss, "a literary work [or in our case, a work of cinema] is not an object that stands by itself and that offers the same view to each reader in each period." Instead of being a kind of "monument" revealing its "timeless essence," a work is more "like an orchestration that strikes ever new resonances among its readers" as time passes.[31] The stark contrast between the reception of *Monsieur Verdoux* in 1947 and its reception in 1964 vividly illustrates Jauss's principle. In 1947 the character of Verdoux deeply offended reviewers for at least two reasons. First, Verdoux's occupation of marrying and murdering women for money almost inevitably reminded reviewers and audiences of Chaplin's own unhappy experiences with women, particularly Joan Barry. Second, Verdoux's overt social criticism of capitalist society during the depression found little sympathy in a society that had just fought a world war to defend that way of life and was swiftly moving into a Cold War climate that considered any criticism of domestic institutions misguided if not treasonous.

Jauss's concept of "aesthetic distance"—the disparity between what the initial audience of a work expects (its "horizon of expectations") and what the new work actually presents—can help us explain this vast difference in the reception of *Monsieur Verdoux*. When the aesthetic distance is large, Jauss posits, the work will disturb, puzzle, or shock the expectations of the initial audience, but it may also help change the horizon of expectations so that eventually, the aesthetic distance between the work and a later audience will diminish.[32]

Just such a process was at work during this reevaluation of *Monsieur Verdoux*. By 1964, the details of the Barry case and of Chaplin's other escapades with young women had faded from public memory and thus played no more than a minuscule role in the audience's response to the film. Chaplin had been a happily married man for twenty years. Few remembered Chaplin's political activism from the 1940s. More recalled the circumstances that drove him from the country in 1952 as a victim of the McCarthy era. Given the shifting political climate, characterized by a greater willingness to criticize American institutions, audiences in 1964 were more inclined to understand and sympathize with the social criticism in the film. The often bitterly ironic satire found in *Monsieur Verdoux* had defied audience expectations in 1947: such humor was unusual in that era not only for Chaplin but also for American film comedy in general. But sophisticated New York City audiences were more prone to accept such satire in 1964, as is evidenced both by the popularity of *Dr. Strangelove* during its New York run early in 1964 and by the attention the "black humor" novelists (Vonnegut, Southern, Friedman, Heller) were receiving at roughly the same time. The moviegoer who was interviewed by a *New York Times* reporter after having seen *Monsieur Verdoux* may have been right: he said that the film was released "seventeen years before its time."[33]

If the 1964 response to *Verdoux* indicated that American audiences were becoming more responsive to Chaplin and his films, the entire rereleased series also contributed to the shift in his star image. By running three of Chaplin's best First National films and all of the comic features through *The Great Dictator* except *The Circus*, the schedule brought to the fore the Charlie persona who originally did so much to establish Chaplin as a star in Hollywood. Then, by playing the controversial *Verdoux* and the autobiographical *Limelight*, the series enabled viewers who saw all the films to examine them as examples of how Chaplin the director and actor evolved after he felt compelled to abandon the Charlie persona. The fact that the "auteur theory," popularized by Andrew Sarris (and to be discussed below), was fast becoming an influential approach to the study of film meant that the Chaplin rereleases were well timed: they allowed *cinéastes* in New York to survey much of the director's career and identify his preoccupations and his evolution as an artist. Times had muted the political and moral objections to Chaplin the man rooted in the 1940s, and this extended series of his mature work helped to begin restoring Chaplin the serious artist and Charlie the persona to the center of Chaplin's star image.

The publication of Chaplin's autobiography in September 1964 also contributed to this shift. The publishing history of *My Autobiography* was itself news; *Time*'s review called it "one of the richest publishing coups of the century." The book was released simultaneously in eight languages and Chaplin was reportedly guaranteed a minimum royalty of $500,000 for the English-language editions alone.[34] *Publishers Weekly* announced that just in the United States, the book had accumulated advance sales of over 47,000 copies before the official publication date. Within a month it was already in its third printing, and by

Thanksgiving it was tied for first (with Douglas MacArthur's *Reminiscences*) on *Publishers Weekly*'s list of best-selling nonfiction books. By December 1964, 100,000 hardcover copies were in print, and the book remained in the top ten on the best-seller list through the middle of March 1965.[35] These figures apply only to the hardcover edition published by Simon and Schuster. The book was also a main selection of the Book-of-the-Month Club, and it remains in print even today in paperback.

That is not to say, however, that the reviews of the book were unequivocally positive. On the contrary, nearly all the reviews were mixed, with the same complaints cropping up repeatedly. One of the most common criticisms was that the last half or more of the book was a listing of famous people Chaplin had met. Aligned with that objection was the complaint that Chaplin had almost nothing of consequence to say about the films that made him famous. Reviewers also regularly attacked Chaplin's writing style, particularly his apparent tendency to leaf through a thesaurus in search of obscure vocabulary (among the most frequent targets were Chaplin's use of "esurient" and his references to the "intellectual subcutaneous texture of Greenwich Village" and to an "affluent potpourri" of celebrities). One reviewer summed up the book as "stupendously verbose"; Brendan Gill clucked at the "gross solecism" of the "my" in the title.[36]

Two reviewers for more conservative publications, *Time* and *National Review*, included political stabs at Chaplin and his book. *Time* described Chaplin as "notoriously vain, snobbish, difficult to know and to work with" and charged that he left the country "in a sneering rage." For *Time*, the book was "uneven and uncommunicative about his many loves and his vociferous left-wing politics." The reviewer for *National Review* objected to Chaplin's assertion that the New Deal years constituted "the most inspiring era in American history," and he too criticized Chaplin's brevity in discussing his leftist politics and his love life. These reviewers seemed to want Chaplin to provide evidence that would corroborate the political and moral charges against him that had flown so thick and fast in the press during the late 1940s and early 1950s.[37]

This sort of attack and innuendo was, however, the exception. One of the most striking elements about the remaining reviews is how often they chide American institutions for their mistreatment of Chaplin during the McCarthy era. To *Newsweek*, Chaplin's exile was "disgracefully, sneakily perpetrated by his adopted nation." To John Houseman, Chaplin was one of the victims of the "Red purge" that "reached a virulent and spiteful climax in Hollywood during the late forties." In

333

a second *New York Times* review, Brooks Atkinson lamented the "squalid paternity suit brought by Joan Barry and the United States Government's cowardly revocation of his re-entry permit." Perhaps no reviewer was as direct as Robert Hatch, writing in *Harper's*: "The persecution of Chaplin in the name of American patriotism and public decency is a scandal this era is saddled with forever."[38] To the extent that the reviews give an accurate indication of the state of Chaplin's star image, it is clear that Chaplin the political victim had by 1964 superseded Chaplin the dangerous Red.

As well as presenting a more generous attitude toward Chaplin's political views, the reviews, like the rereleases, brought Charlie the tramp back to the center of the Chaplin star image. *Newsweek* included a shot of Charlie from the 1910s. The titles of the reviews often mentioned the tramp:

Newsweek: "The Tramp"
Commonweal: "Real Life of the Tramp"[39]
National Review: "Only the Little Tramp Matters"
Time: "The Little Tramp: As Told to Himself"
New York Times: "Chaplin, the Biographer, Is Not So Eloquent as the Silent Little Tramp He Created"

Just as important, the reviews often centered on the significance of the Charlie persona and even quoted the passage in which Chaplin described the origin of the character. To Atkinson, "the little tramp was one of the great myths, like Pierrot or Harlequin." For Hatch, Charlie "was the most beloved folk image the world had ever known." To Gill, "Chaplin the actor and Chaplin the deviser of gags" are characterized by "genius." This theme is well summed up in Charles Poore's initial *New York Times* review. After quoting the best part of Chaplin's long description of Charlie, Poore concludes, "But why go on? The characteristics the world has seen in him cover all humanity. And that's enough to ask, this side of paradise."[40]

Paradoxically, Chaplin's final film—a critical and financial failure—also helped rebuild Chaplin's star image. Less than a year after the publication of *My Autobiography*, news began to circulate about Chaplin's preparation of another film. Gradually word came out that the movie, about a White Russian countess who falls in love with an American ambassador, would star Marlon Brando and Sophia Loren. By January 1967 *A Countess from Hong Kong* was given its world premiere in London and on 16 March 1967, its New York City benefit premiere, attended by such luminaries as Henry Fonda, Lynda Byrd Johnson, and Jacob Javits.[41]

The publicity about the film contributed to the rebuilding of Chap-

lin's star image, especially two photo essays in *Life* magazine, whose
1967 circulation was 7.4 million. "A Passionate Clown Comes Back"
appeared during the shooting schedule in 1966; "Ageless Master's
Anatomy of Comedy" came out about a week before the film's opening in New York.[42] Both articles roughly follow the format of the *Life*
spread on *Limelight* in 1952. All of them included some plot description, some comments by Chaplin about the film or about filmmaking
and comedy in general, and a good number of photographs. All three
included pictures of Chaplin with his wife and children, which stressed
his role as a happy family man. By 1966 Chaplin was more than twenty
years away from the Barry affair and more than twenty years into his
apparently happy marriage with Oona O'Neill Chaplin. The 1966–
1967 articles also emphasized Charlie, both in pictures from *City Lights*
and *The Tramp* and in Chaplin's comments about him: "I never
thought of the tramp in terms of appeal. He was myself, a comic spirit,
something within me I must express." Chaplin the proud patriarch
and "ageless master"; Charlie the tender comic spirit: these were key
dimensions in the revaluation of Chaplin's star image in the 1960s.

Nevertheless, *A Countess from Hong Kong* was an unmitigated disaster, both with the critics and at the box office, despite the fact that
Chaplin directed the picture and that two of the era's top box-office
draws, Brando and Loren, starred. The reviews were surely the most
negative Chaplin ever received. To *Time*, the film was "a substandard
shipboard farce . . . the worst ever made by Charlie Chaplin." The
Newsweek reviewer wrote that Chaplin's "old techniques are not simply
crusty and conventional but stiff and clumsy." In the *National Review*,
Hugh Kenner judged the film "one long prolix fumble, like a freshman theme," and asked, "how did Charlie get trapped inside this turkey?" "I wish I could say some nice things about the new Chaplin
movie," wrote Philip Hartung in a brief paragraph in *Commonweal*,
"but *A Countess from Hong Kong* is so old-fashioned and dull that one
can hardly believe it was made now."[43]

The box-office figures were similarly dismal. Though the Sutton
Theater tried in a *Times* advertisement to promote the film by pictur-
ing people standing in long lines by the theater marquee, *Countess*—a
new film—probably grossed less, in this much larger theater, than the
rereleased *Monsieur Verdoux* had grossed in 1964.[44] After its run was
completed around the country and *Variety* listed its 1967 box-office
grosses, *Countess* was sixty-second on its list, with just $1.1 million in
rentals. In comparison, *The Dirty Dozen* topped the list with $18.2 mil-
lion, *Georgy Girl* was seventh with $7.3 million, and *Blow-Up* fourteenth
with $5.9 million.[45]

Yet despite the negative reviews and the poor box-office showing, when one examines the reviews closely and considers the context, it seems that the reviews probably didn't much hurt Chaplin's star image, for at least two reasons. First, the film did not really get that much critical attention. The reviews of *My Autobiography* were much longer and more numerous in American mass periodicals than the reviews of *Countess*. Second, the film was a considerable departure from the kind of films that had helped to create and sustain Chaplin's star image. Except for *A Woman of Paris*, this was the only Chaplin film that did not feature Chaplin in a lead role (though he did have a Hitchcockian walk-on as a nauseated ship steward). Because Chaplin did not star in the movie, reviewers could distinguish between Chaplin the aging director and Chaplin the performer/actor/director/composer/producer—that is, Chaplin the auteur—who had made such a mark on the history of American film.

And that is to some extent what the reviewers did. Whereas hostile reviewers of Chaplin's three previous films had seemed at times to review Chaplin's political views and sexual history as much as the films themselves, the reviewers of *Countess* appeared almost anguished at having to tell readers that the film was a bomb. Hartung, for example, expressed in *Commonweal* his desire to find something good in Chaplin's new film "because I think he is one of the greatest movie makers of all times." *Newsweek* contrasted the failure of *Countess* with the previous achievement of Chaplin: "[his] vision was the poetry of an age— the age of the underdog and of poetic justice, of innocent romance and innocent beauty, of clowns and orphans and lyrical anarchy, a post-Victorian age where love conquered all." The world had changed, the reviewer went on, and Chaplin's vision stayed the same— hence the regrettable failure. In *National Review*, Hugh Kenner attributed the failure of *Countess* to the fact that Chaplin's genius was as a performer, not as a director.[46] With that perspective, one could throw out the bath water but not the baby—dismiss the film without discarding the artist. Whether the reviewers focused, like *Newsweek*, on the director Chaplin's "vision" or, like Kenner, on the performer Chaplin's artistry, they made it clear to their readers that their harsh view of *Countess* did not diminish their admiration for Chaplin's previous achievements.

Chaplin's star image in America had changed considerably from the days of *A King in New York*. The increasingly leftist political climate, characterized by a greater willingness to criticize American domestic policy, helped curb the attacks on Chaplin's politics rooted in the 1940s and 1950s and encouraged the public to think of Chaplin as a political victim instead of a political villain. Just as important, the revival of the Chaplin films in New York City, the publication of Chaplin's autobiography, and even the release of *Countess* encouraged people to think back to the beginnings of his career (instead of back only to the 1940s) and to consider again the importance of the Charlie persona in Chaplin's star image. As the 1960s drew to a close, the Chaplin cult was again growing.

A Guarded Restoration: The 1972 Return Tour

In April 1972, as the twentieth anniversary of his exile from America approached, Charles Spencer Chaplin, accompanied by Oona O'Neill Chaplin, returned to New York City and then to Los Angeles to receive accolades and an honorary Oscar. The trip elicited enormous press coverage, by far the most attention Chaplin had received in the United States for at least two decades. Coupling this visit with a widespread rerelease of his films, Chaplin and his associates helped generate a huge interest in his films and his star image. The dangerous leftist of the 1950s had become the wronged genius of the 1970s.

Interestingly, economic considerations played a large part in Chaplin's decision to break the vow he made in early 1953 never to return to the United States. The story begins in May 1971 at the Cannes film festival. There the French government awarded Chaplin with its highest public recognition, making him a Commandeur de la Légion d'Honneur. As a part of the festivities, *City Lights* was screened before an enthusiastic audience. The Charlie that the critics longed for in their reviews of *A Countess from Hong Kong* had returned—to great acclaim.

One member of the audience was a film distribution executive for Columbia Pictures, Mo Rothman, who upon leaving the theater bumped into Oliver Unger, an American independent film producer. The two agreed that distributing a package of Chaplin's films would be a wonderful and potentially profitable idea. Calling Chaplin shortly thereafter, they soon met with him and his wife in Cap d'Antibes to discuss the idea, and managed to overcome Chaplin's reluctance by pointing out that it would be a perfect way for his children to know what a great motion picture star he had been. By the fall of 1971, Chaplin and Rothman had signed an agreement. Rothman advanced Chaplin $6,000,000 against 50 percent of the income derived from the film rentals in exchange for the exclusive right to distribute nine Chaplin films. The Chaplins, along with their eight children, attended the world premiere of the rereleased films in Paris in November, and by January 1972 the series had already been scheduled to play in twenty-eight cities in the United States.[47]

Rothman, however, hoped for some special promotion. He reasoned, and Chaplin agreed, that one of the best ways for Chaplin to gain public exposure and hence to generate interest for his rereleased films was for him to visit the United States. Managing the visit, Rothman planned for Chaplin to be shielded from journalists but to be available for a series of "balcony appearances," in which still and movie photographers could capture his image and relay it to the public.[48] Given Chaplin's unfortunate experience with press conferences, particularly during the release of *Monsieur Verdoux*, the choice seemed a wise one.

The return became a major media event. On January 13 Motion Picture Academy president Daniel Taradash announced that Chaplin would attend the Oscar ceremonies in April to receive a special Oscar. Chaplin helped to defuse some possible resistance to his visit by telling an interviewer in February that the press had exaggerated his pique over the criticism he had endured in 1952 and that he was eagerly anticipating his return visit.[49] By mid-February the itinerary was planned: the Chaplins would arrive in New York City, spend several days there while attending various festivities, and then move on to Los Angeles, where the special Oscar would be awarded.

The reception in New York was all that could have been expected and more. The Chaplins arrived on April 3, where a hundred members of the press awaited them at Kennedy Airport. The next evening the Film Society of the Lincoln Center sponsored a "Salute to Charlie Chaplin." Over 2,800 people jammed Philharmonic Hall to see *The Kid* and *The Idle Class* and to catch a glimpse of Chaplin himself. Celebrities and luminaries from Paulette Goddard and Leopold Stokowski to Dick Cavett and Norman Mailer attended. When the eighty-two-year-old Chaplin first swept into the hall, Zero Mostel, high up in a tier, broke a few moments' silence by shouting, "Bravo, Charlie, bravo," and soon the entire gathering was shouting "bravo" and "*Char*lie, *Char*lie, *Char*lie!" After the screenings, Chaplin said a few words: "Thanks for the wonderful applause. . . . It's so gratifying to know that I have so many friends." Chaplin later said that the occasion made him feel like he was being "reborn."[50]

But New York was not finished with Chaplin. On April 6 Chaplin received the Handel Medallion, the city's highest cultural award, from Mayor John Lindsay. In his introduction, the mayor described Chaplin as "this compassionate man, this most decent human being, this skilled artist, this great citizen of the world"—quite a change from the terms political figures were using to describe Chaplin in 1952.[51]

The following day the Chaplins flew to Los Angeles. Arriving at 3:00 P.M., they were escorted past dozens of photographers and reporters to a waiting limousine, where two representatives of the Academy, President Taradash and Howard Koch, welcomed them. At crowded gatherings in Los Angeles, Chaplin had reunions with many friends and associates from the past, including Jackie Coogan (the kid in *The Kid*), Georgia Hale (of *The Gold Rush*), and Tim Durant.

The Oscar ceremony on April 11 was the final high point. Chaplin, reportedly afraid no one would show up for "his" night, watched the ceremonies backstage on a television monitor and showed great pleasure at recognizing old friends in the audience. Taradash presented the special award, which honored Chaplin for his "incalculable effect in making motion pictures the art form of the century." Nearly overcome by the reception, Chaplin delivered a brief speech: "I thank you so much. This is an emotional moment for me, and words are so feeble, so futile. I can only say thank you for inviting me here. You're sweet people." Thereafter Jack Lemmon, one of the emcees, handed Chaplin a hat and cane. Chaplin, giving the audience a taste of the comedy and pathos he had generated for so many millions of viewers over the years, fumbled for a moment with the familiar derby, then departed. After the ceremony Chaplin was more verbal: "It was all so *emotional* and the *audience*—I felt *their* emotion. I thought some of them might hiss, but they were so *sweet*—all those famous people, all those artists. You know, they haven't done this to me before. It surpasses everything."[52] By April 12 the Chaplins were returning to Europe.

Just how was Chaplin's public reputation in the United States affected by these ten days in 1972? One might begin answering that question by placing the visit in the context of the times. We have seen that Chaplin began in the 1960s to be looked at more as a victim of McCarthyism than as a violator of American morals and manners. The shifting political climate, which led to an increasing willingness on the part of many Americans to grant the weaknesses of their social institutions, made Charlie's nose-thumbing antics and Chaplin's progressive politics seem much more acceptable than they had been in the decade after World War II.

Even though American society in the late 1960s and early 1970s became polarized over the issues of Vietnam and urban disorder, and even though the old cold warrior Richard Nixon had been elected President in 1968 and was about to be reelected six months after

Chaplin's visit in 1972, the prevailing attitude toward communism and the Soviet Union had changed since 1952. Ironically, Nixon and his advisor Henry Kissinger would soon come to be identified with a policy advocating détente with the Soviet Union, and Nixon himself visited China and opened up a dialogue that would lead to normalized relations between the two countries. This new view of relations between the United States and leading Communist nations provides a useful framework for understanding the context of Chaplin's return in 1972 and the press's generally enthusiastic reportage of it. The culture that had sought to expunge leftist politics in the early 1950s had become more tolerant of those views by the early 1970s.[53]

Chaplin's return visit created an avalanche of publicity in the American press, the most concentrated and pervasive since the Barry case and perhaps even since his rise to stardom in 1914 and 1915. Between April 1 and May 6 alone, twelve important mass magazines and journals of opinion carried feature articles on Chaplin.[54] Unlike the coverage of the Barry trial, however, this publicity was on the whole favorable. For example, *Time*, *Newsweek*, and *Life* (in two separate articles) all carried generous stories, amply illustrated with photographs, about the New York and Los Angeles festivities.[55] The title of one of the *Life* articles, "Love Feast for Charlie," gives a good indication of how these articles presented Chaplin.

This positive treatment was typical, but Chaplin's restoration was nevertheless guarded. Another *Time* article, a two-page preview of Chaplin's visit on April 10, "Re-Enter Charlie Chaplin, Smiling and Waving," illustrates how a conservative magazine dealt with Chaplin's return. The piece was almost classic in its ambivalence, a kind of welcome mat before a closely guarded door. After describing and praising the "mute grace" of Chaplin's Tramp, the essay surveyed the "ambivalent skirmish" between Chaplin and the United States that led up to his exile and mentioned his marriage and divorce to Lita Grey, as well as the opposition of "industrialists" to *Modern Times* and of isolationists to *The Great Dictator*. Discussing Chaplin's politics, the essay called Chaplin a "fan of sentimental collectivism, of revolution seen through a scrim," but excused the views by saying they originated in the actor's childhood of poverty. Then it discounted his opinion, describing him as "a political naif who would only fellow-travel in first class." Though the government's decision to withdraw the reentry permit was "a classic in xenophobia," Chaplin's *King in New York* was a "labor of hate, a film entirely without humor" and his autobiography a work "of benign evasion" in which the "bitterness was cloaked." The article, arguing that the reconciliation between the United States and

Chaplin has been too long in coming, concluded with a kind of paean to the United States: "America of the '70s has become a better region for the artist."

Although the text of the essay refused to condone many of Chaplin's past activities, its visual imagery drew one away from Chaplin the man and toward Charlie the persona. Of the nine photographs, seven were stills from Chaplin films. The remaining two were of Chaplin as a younger man doing acrobatics and of the elderly, white-haired Chaplin smiling, thumbs in his ears and fingers waving. The pictures thus presented Chaplin as an unthreatening entertainer. This stress on Charlie was reiterated by the final sentences of the article, in which Chaplin's Oscar ceremony was called a Chaplinesque gesture, "like an entire nation shaking off its bygone disappointments and its tragic errors, kicking out its legs and setting off once more on that long and hopeful road."[56]

Newspaper editorials and editorial cartoons joined in welcoming Chaplin back to the United States. A *New York Times* editorial, "Charlie's Happy Return," appeared in February after the details of the trip were released and set the stage for Chaplin's welcome. "If a nation could collectively blush," it opened, "the United States had good reason to do so when its officialdom ruled two decades ago that Charles Chaplin could not come back to these shores until he offered proof of his 'moral worth.' " Chaplin's return, the editor concluded, signified a "welcome if long-delayed victory of art and humor over bureaucratic rigidity."[57] Consistent with shifts that began in the 1960s, the presentation of Chaplin here was as the victim of political and bureaucratic machinations.

The *Los Angeles Times*, generally much less sympathetic to Chaplin than the *New York Times* during his difficult days, nevertheless paid double editorial tribute to Chaplin on the day he was to receive his Oscar. The first was a cartoon of an Oscar statuette wearing a derby, captioned "Academy Award's Finest Hour!" (see Figure 30). The accompanying editorial, "Charlie Chaplin Returns," noted Chaplin's worldwide reputation and observed that the government's actions in 1952 were "widely and correctly interpreted as a shabby cover to bar Chaplin from the country for political reasons." Another newspaper that had often treated Chaplin harshly, the *Chicago Tribune*, featured Chaplin in an editorial cartoon on April 10. In it, Charlie wore his regular Tramp costume with the sole exception that the derby had been replaced with an Uncle Sam top hat of stars and stripes (see Figure 31). Though the lack of a caption or of any distinctive expression on the cartoon figure's face made the cartoonist's point of view un-

30. Frank Interlandi's April 1972 cartoon in the *Los Angeles Times* celebrates Chaplin's special Oscar.

clear, it seems most likely that the cartoon simultaneously observed Chaplin's new softened comments about the United States and the country's celebration of the artist.[58]

While these more conservative publications were making fresh accommodations with Chaplin, those on the left, the *Nation*, for example, saw Chaplin's return through more jaundiced eyes and used it as an opportunity to recall the unsavory McCarthy years and comment more skeptically on the present—however sympathetic they may have been to Chaplin himself. In its editorial, "Modern Times," the *Nation* commented that Chaplin's homecoming "has been a triumph—but a very melancholy one, because all the auspices were wrong. Chaplin's moral worth is not being vindicated by this visit; there is merely a conspiracy to pretend that some of that unsavory nonsense never occurred." The editorial further commented that Chaplin had returned not "because the people loved him" but because "there is a lot of money to be made out of him"—an allusion to his $5 million distribu-

31. *Chicago Tribune* editorial cartoon acknowledges
Chaplin's 1972 return trip. Copyright © 1987,
Chicago Tribune Company, all rights reserved,
used with permission.

tion contract with Rothman. All in all, "it has been a sad return—years
too late and for shabby motives. We hope it has not hurt the old man
in body or heart, and wish him a safe journey back to Switzerland."[59]

If that editorial demonstrated that the political controversies surrounding the Chaplin image were still alive—however diminished—
other evidence reinforced that suspicion. Although, the *Los Angeles
Times* published a positive editorial on April 10, the day before it chose
to print an article entitled "They Haven't Given Up—Letter Writers
Assail Chaplin." Subtitled "Bitterness Survives 20 Years," it reported
that "hundreds of letters" had "poured in" to the paper and that most
of them appeared "to have been written by elderly people and mentioned Chaplin's alleged leftist leanings."[60] Some of the letters quoted
called Chaplin a "traitor," "Comrade Charlie," and an "insane Revolutionary Zionist."

A second indication that Chaplin's name was still controversial centered on the old debate in Hollywood about whether Chaplin should

be memorialized by placing his name and a bronze star on the Hollywood Boulevard Walk of Fame, an action that, after pressure group activity, had been refused in 1959 by the Hollywood Chamber of Commerce. But about a month after Chaplin's return visit had been announced, the Chamber of Commerce reversed itself and announced that Chaplin's name would be put on "Star Boulevard." At the dedication ceremony on April 10 (the same day Chaplin received his Oscar), however, several older women passed out a sheet of paper that purported to describe "Charlie Chaplin's Red Record." Though Chaplin did not attend the dedication, it was clear that his day of triumph and celebration was not shared by all Americans. Such a conclusion was reinforced when on April 17, the former movie actor and then governor of California, Ronald Reagan, told reporters that although Chaplin may have been a "genius" filmmaker, American officials acted correctly in 1952 when they revoked his reentry permit.[61]

Despite these misgivings, however, the response of the press to Chaplin's return was, if never as consistently high as the treatment Chaplin received during the halcyon years in the 1920s, predominantly positive. Two of the longest articles from that time illustrate this well: Richard Schickel's cover essay for the April 2 *New York Times Magazine*, and Father George H. Dunne's long memoir in *Commonweal*, "I Remember Chaplin."[62] As two of the longest and most informed explorations of Chaplin and his achievements to appear in the popular press in 1972, they deserve more detailed treatment.

Schickel's article, which appeared the Sunday before Chaplin arrived in the United States, constituted a kind of prestigious prologue to his visit. Not only was it the cover article of the issue, but it also contained generous stills of Charlie from films like *One A.M.* and *A Night Out*, of Calvero from *Limelight*, and of Chaplin rubbing elbows with such notables as Winston Churchill and George Bernard Shaw.

Schickel began by observing that because Chaplin had already been so highly regarded by his peers, critics, and the literary intelligentsia, "praise, at this point, seems superfluous" (p. 12). He also pointed out how impossible it was to find an article that criticized Chaplin or even treated his work objectively without somehow apologizing for the criticism. "No entertainer in history," Schickel argued, had "so imposed himself on the consciousness of his times for so long a time" (p. 13).

Nevertheless, Schickel's essay sought to review both the strengths and the limitations of Chaplin's art. In doing so, he did much to summarize some of the most significant commentary on Chaplin by prominent American critics since the 1920s. As he examined the intelligentsia's response to Chaplin over the decades, Schickel both acknowledged the growing historical awareness of the movies in the 1970s and revealed his adherence to auteurism. From the 1920s he alluded to Gilbert Seldes's enthusiasm for *The Pawnshop* and Edmund Wilson's view that though Chaplin was a consummate actor, he was a lackluster director. From the 1930s Schickel cited Otis Ferguson's observations on the stylistic primitivism of *Modern Times*. He also referred to Robert Warshow's analysis from the 1940s concerning the inevitable destruction of the tramp after *City Lights* and James Agee's paean to Chaplin in "The Golden Age of Comedy" (1950). The general thrust of Schickel's treatment was that Chaplin's greatest years were the early ones. The later films, in his view, were seriously flawed. The ending of *The Great Dictator* was a "desperate preachment"; the ending of *Verdoux* was "bitter." *Limelight* was filled with "self-pity" and *A King of New York*, "reportedly" (Schickel apparently had not yet seen the film), with "savagery." That left only the "sheer emptiness and lack of energy" of *A Countess from Hong Kong* (p. 49).

The essay was ultimately a concise statement of an influential view of Chaplin's work that had been developing among certain segments of the public since the 1940s and among critics since the early 1960s: that Chaplin was a great comic actor whose work began to sour after *City Lights*, primarily because he wanted to deal with "big themes" in his work. Such a view was at least in part an example of how fully the progressive critical principles prevalent in the 1930s and into the 1940s had been rejected by American reviewers and critics. In Schickel's words, "One could see that [Chaplin] was increasingly bewildered by the world, increasingly unable to encompass his feelings about (and prescriptions for) it in the metaphors he employed in lieu of The Little Fellow in his films" (p. 49). Schickel did mention despising those who harassed Chaplin about his political views and his morality; he also wrote that "guilt well[ed] up" in him as he criticized Chaplin. Nonetheless, Schickel placed the zenith of Chaplin's achievement before 1935—the era of Charlie—before Chaplin's capitulation to dialogue in films and before more overt social themes entered his work.

George Dunne's "I Remember Chaplin," subtitled "a nostalgic retrospect," complemented Schickel's article. Although Dunne did not concentrate on Chaplin's films, he did briefly praise, as did Schickel, Chaplin's films before World War II. Having seen *Modern Times* again shortly before writing the article, Dunne described the experience as "a sheer delight and a moving reminder of how much the world is indebted to the unique genius of this man" (p. 303).

However, Dunne's essay is much more concerned with defending Chaplin from his political detractors by describing his meetings with

Chaplin in the late 1940s. A Catholic priest, Dunne had written what he described as an "interracial documentary play," *Trial by Fire*, which was about to open in Hollywood at a theater on Sunset Boulevard. On the evening of the dress rehearsal, Chaplin attended, probably on the recommendation of a union head who knew both Chaplin and Dunne. Chaplin gave Dunne and the rest of the group some advice about the play, and after the rehearsal, Dunne and Chaplin dined with two others at the Players Club and talked well into the evening. The following night both Charles and Oona Chaplin attended the play's opening.

The Chaplin depicted in Dunne's article was a victim of the age. Himself a liberal engaged in union and civil rights activities, Dunne recalled how he was visited by Ronald Reagan, George Murphy, and Jane Wyman during the late 1940s and warned about the Communist control of the unions he was defending. He also depicted Joseph Scott, Joan Barry's lawyer, as a "superpatriot and a militantly loyal Catholic" whose "patriotic sensibilities" were offended by Chaplin's failure to become a citizen (p. 306). These conservative Chaplin foes are the villains of Dunne's memoir.

In contrast, Chaplin, despite his fame, showed Dunne and the rest of his group an "easy, informal and friendly manner" that was "totally without affectation" (p. 307). Dunne admitted that his estimation of Chaplin might be colored by the fact that Chaplin considered *Trial by Fire* a good play. But his account of their postrehearsal discussion depicted Chaplin's politics as reasonable and humane. On the question of citizenship, Dunne recalled Chaplin's comments:

> I have been in nearly every country. . . . And I have found people everywhere, regardless of color, race or nationality, to be pretty much the same, all human beings with the same desires, the same impulses. I feel a bond with all of them. Were I to take citizenship anywhere it would be here. This is where I have made my home. This is where I have made my career and my money. I am grateful to America. . . . But the swearing of allegiance to any country seems to me a rejection of all other people in the world. And this I cannot bring myself to do. (p. 308)

Nor, in Dunne's view, should he be forced to.

Dunne concluded by trying to explain, on the basis of his evening with the comic, his understanding of Chaplin's sympathy for the Soviet Union. Noting Chaplin's "nostalgia for the pre-mechanical age," Dunne speculated that Chaplin opposed "not so much capitalism as the mechanical age." Since Chaplin lived in capitalist nations as he saw the world become more mechanized, however, he equated the two. "The flaw in his reasoning," wrote Dunne, was that the Soviet Union, however opposed to capitalism, was by no means opposed to mechanization. Chaplin, when asked why he had never visited the Soviet Union, replied, "Because . . . I am afraid I might be disillusioned" (p. 309).

This comment provided Dunne a key to understanding Chaplin:

> That said everything that needed to be said about the nature of Chaplin's interest in Communism and the Soviet Union. It grew out of an act of hope that there was an alternative to the dehumanizing kind of society organized under capitalistic auspices which threatened human values and issued in an act of faith that the Soviet experiment contained the promise of realizing such an alternative. If he lost that faith what would be left of hope? And so he refused to run the risk. (p. 309)

The evening was a memorable one for Dunne, capped only by the attendance of the Chaplins on opening night and their kind words for the author. Reflecting on the significance of his experience, Dunne can only comment on Chaplin's exile: "The loss—and the shame— were America's" (p. 309). Perhaps as well as any, this comment sums up the press's view of Chaplin's 1952 departure during his triumphant return to the United States twenty years later. Schickel and Dunne helped create the image of Chaplin as a significant and humane artist who became a victim of his age.

Rereleases and Chaplin's Star Image in the 1970s

In addition to generating monumental press coverage during his 1972 trip to the United States, Chaplin contributed to the revival of his star image in the 1970s through the rerelease of his films. Thanks to his agreement with Rothman, Chaplin's films began to show in retrospectives around America beginning late in 1971. The rereleases were extremely important in perpetuating Chaplin's star image, for Chaplin himself made no new films after 1967 and had not appeared in any significant role since 1957. The history of Hollywood films is filled with stories of faded stars, and Chaplin could have become one himself, had his films not been made available. In fact, although the return trip drew the most concentrated attention to Chaplin in the 1970s, one could easily argue that the rereleases contributed more to Chaplin's star image because they provided so much opportunity for commentary. This came from newspaper reviewers, magazine jour-nalists, and academic critics, and all of them shaped and solidified Chaplin's star image.

Until the films' systematic rerelease, few Americans outside of New York City (where the 1963–1964 Chaplin retrospective was held) had seen any of Chaplin's feature films for twenty years, except perhaps mediocre prints of *The Gold Rush*. And almost no one had been able to see the films chronologically, in the order of their creation. But begin-ning in late 1971, dozens of revival theaters and campus film societies began scheduling Chaplin film series for weekly showings or even longer runs.

This provided viewers with what was then a unique chance to see much of Chaplin's work in a relatively concentrated time. As one re-viewer noted, in these retrospectives "a lifetime of work can be seen over a period of a few months, not jammed together, as it might be at a film festival, not caught piecemeal over the years."[63] Such an oppor-tunity was relished by many *cinéastes*, because it gave them a chance to examine firsthand how Chaplin developed as an artist and to weigh the strengths and limitations of his work. Given the assumptions of the auteur theory, then a prevailing critical perspective, such showings were ideal.

But before the commentary could be generated, it was necessary to get viewers into the theaters to see the films. The enormous coverage of Chaplin's return visit helped to generate an interest in the films, as Rothman and Chaplin had surmised it would. But newspaper adver-tisements for the rereleases also helped promote the movies, in large part by featuring Charlie's image. Two examples appeared in the 5 April 1972 *New York Times* in an ad whose headline also tied in with Chaplin's return visit to the city. One half announces the showing of *City Lights*. It contains the famous closeup of Charlie holding a rose with his mixed expression of joy, fear, and expectancy. The other half announces *Modern Times*, and is dominated by a large image of the sprightly Charlie. Next to a quote from Canby's rave review, Charlie strides briskly, cane in hand, toward the viewer (see Figure 32).[64] Some versions of the ad for *Modern Times* included six identical smaller im-ages of Charlie set beside the theater names. Rothman and Chaplin knew that the persona Chaplin had created was a valuable commodity, and the promotion stressed this.

Reviewers in newspapers also helped to stir up enthusiasm for the films with their positive reviews. One of the most enthusiastic critics was Vincent Canby in the *New York Times*. *The Idle Class*, he wrote, "has

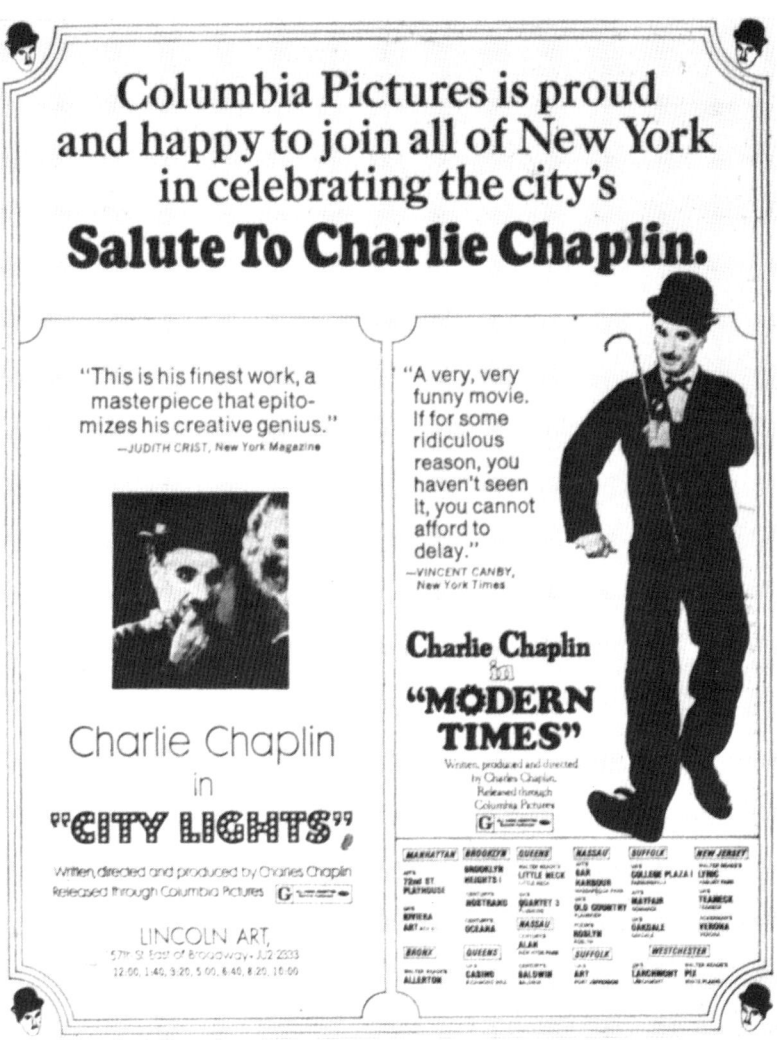

32. Newspaper ad during 1972 rerelease: the return of Charlie to center stage of the Chaplin star image.

the density of content and much of the comic resonance of the later features." *City Lights*, his favorite of the films, was "perfectly conceived as a single entity." *The Great Dictator* was, in his view, the "most passionate of low farces," a film that had taken on a "special eloquence." Although the much-criticized final speech was "still awkward," it could also "be understood as part of the development of an artist whose life

349

has always been so much a part of his work." Even *Monsieur Verdoux* was a comedy "of the highest order," both "rigorous and demanding."[65]

Gene Siskel in the *Chicago Tribune* was also enthusiastic about the rereleased films, calling *City Lights* "more elemental and elegant than today's movies." In contrast to the "ill-considered dialogue" and music that "comes across as just so much noise" in contemporary films, he found that *City Lights* used its "romantic, stirring score" as a counterpoint for its physical comedy. Siskel also appreciated *The Great Dictator*. Here, Siskel judged, Chaplin broke his silence for good reasons: "It is to his everlasting credit that he gave up his artistic principle of silence for a moral principle that compelled him to speak against Hitler and Nazism." Although the film was not, in his view, as strong as *City Lights* or *Modern Times*—largely because the slapstick was not particularly inventive—Siskel defended the often-criticized ending. He not only called it "a great humanitarian sermon" but also quoted excerpts from the final speech for nearly the last half of his review.[66]

Another representative daily reviewer to praise Chaplin was Kevin Thomas in the *Los Angeles Times*. The titles of two of his reviews indicate his perspective: "Still a Lot of Candlepower to *City Lights*" and "*Limelight* in L.A.—at Last." Although Thomas found that *Modern Times* had "the same grace and poignance" as *City Lights* but "considerably more substance," he called the ending of the latter film "one of the most affecting, justly famous conclusions in the history of the movies." He also praised *Limelight* as "an incomparable, profoundly moving portrait of the artist as an old man." Thomas marveled at Chaplin's ability "to create a world of his own on film" so successfully that in his various roles as star, director, writer, and composer, Chaplin was "sublime in his artistry." As with Canby and Siskel, Thomas filled his reviews with admiration for Chaplin.[67]

One can make several points about the image of Chaplin that emerged from the commentary of newspaper reviewers and the journalists like those who contributed to the special *Film Comment* issue on Chaplin in the fall of 1972.[68] First, they tended to look at the films as expressions of Chaplin's inner self and world view. As Canby put it, "Despite the overlay of social consciousness, all of Chaplin's movies—and not just the later ones—have been to some extent emotional autobiographies." Similarly, in the *Film Comment* issue, Emily Sieger discussed *Limelight* as Chaplin's attempt to continue developing as an artist after the aesthetic and ideological conclusions of *Monsieur Verdoux* had closed a number of options available to him. The dominance of the auteur approach in the 1960s and 1970s, the opportunity to see the rereleases systematically, and the availability of Chaplin's autobiography (Siskel and others seemed to use it for reference material in their reviews) all encouraged journalists to read the films as expressions of Chaplin's psyche and world view, as his "emotional autobiographies."

Related to this stress on an auteurist approach was the critics' tendency to discuss the development of Chaplin's "vision" by dividing that evolution into various stages. For example, in *Film Comment* William Paul, writing on *The Gold Rush*, argued that Chaplin's "vision was expanding" as he made the feature films: the "emotional expressiveness of his works" grew deeper (p. 16). The later films thus contained "a more spiritual quality," for they had progressed from the earlier stress on "the basic hungers of physical existence . . . to the expression in art of man's need to transcend these hungers" (p. 18). As one reads through the commentary, though, most of the *Film Comment* critics hold that the apogee of Chaplin's art was located sometime in the 1930s or early 1940s, after which Chaplin created complex, interesting, but less successful films. This would be consistent with Canby's view that Chaplin's greatest films began with *The Kid* and continued through *Modern Times*: these are in large part the feature-length films starring Charlie. Such attention helped create the image of Chaplin as a serious artist whose work, much as Shakespeare's or Tolstoy's, grew and evolved through time.

Perhaps most important, there was a decided tendency to stress two aspects of Chaplin's star image: the Charlie persona and Chaplin's versatility and "genius" as a filmmaker. In the *Film Comment* special issue, the most singularly positive analyses were of the films in which Charlie appeared. Films from *Monsieur Verdoux* on did not fare as well. When William Paul wrote that "the one unifying force in all Chaplin films is simply Charlie himself," he expressed a view that was explicit or implicit in nearly all the essays (p. 16). In the comments on Chaplin as filmmaker, some objections were raised. Hirsch, writing about *Monsieur Verdoux*, and David Robinson, writing from memory about *A King in New York* (it had not yet been rereleased when he wrote the piece), both criticized the stylistic primitivism or lack of attention to detail in the films. However, in general, these observers tended to reject the earlier view, expressed by people like Wilson and Ferguson, that Chaplin's style was awkward and old-fashioned. They did so not by detailed defenses of Chaplin's style but rather, as in Paul's reference to "Chaplin's unfairly criticized visual style," by briefly suggesting that Chaplin's style was suitable for his aesthetic aims. Chaplin's intuitive artistry, in their view, enabled him to present narrative concerns with appropriate stylistic means.

The stress on the Charlie persona in the *Film Comment* issue was reinforced by the illustrations. The articles were accompanied by seventeen stills, sixteen of which were of Chaplin playing his various roles. Included were one still of Chaplin as Hynkel, one as Verdoux, two as Calvero, and one as King Shahdov. The other eleven were of the Charlie persona, peering around a corner with the kid, doing a David and Goliath mime sermon in *The Pilgrim*, waving a red flag in *Modern Times*, and so on. At least as far as the *Film Comment* articles and the newspaper reviewers were concerned, the return of Chaplin to the United States in 1972 was as much a return of the symbolic power of the Charlie persona as it was of the aging, tottering comedian.

Yet another factor contributed to the evolution of Chaplin's star image: the growth of academic interest in film. Before the mid-1960s, college courses on film as an art form were nearly as rare as courses on the novel in universities before 1900. In the mid- and late 1960s a dramatic proliferation of film courses occurred. More widespread American release of European art films by directors like Bergman, Antonioni, Godard, and Fellini demonstrated that films could be as complex and ambitious as other narrative art forms. American movies (within limitations) also became more able to experiment in subject matter and film style, as television became the dominant medium of mass entertainment and film began to aim at more specialized audiences. Furthermore, college enrollments expanded dramatically as the baby boom generation came of age and as a college degree became a required credential for more and more jobs. And the social and political climate included a sense that education ought to be "relevant" to students' lives. Since moviegoing was often a regular part of those lives, film courses seemed to meet that demand for relevancy. Combined, these factors contributed to the rapid growth of film classes. Although only about 200 institutions offered film courses as late as 1969, the American Film Institute reported that by 1978, over 1,000 colleges and universities around the country were offering over 9,000 courses in film and television studies. Over 40,000 students were pursuing degrees in the field. Those figures, moreover, were probably conservative, based only on the institutions that had responded to the AFI survey.[69]

By the 1980s, a large number of people had been introduced to Chaplin's work through courses that asked them to watch his films, read about him, listen to lectures about his work and place in film history, and even write about him. In a general sense Chaplin's contemporary star image has thus been shaped in part by the academic discourse about Chaplin in the past two decades. A brief look at some of that work gives a sense of the various ways Chaplin and his films have been approached.[70]

It is most useful to begin by looking at Andrew Sarris's views on Chaplin. Sarris was in the 1960s the most influential American advocate of the auteur approach to film study. Beginning more as a journalist than as an academic, Sarris's influential "Notes on the Auteur Theory in 1962" set off a cultural debate when Pauline Kael lambasted the central conceptions of the "theory" in an article called "Circles and Squares."[71] Sarris's central notion was that film history ought to be organized by examining the films of a particular director as a coherent body of work. That group of films could then be explored to define its stylistic, narrative, and thematic patterns and preoccupations. The critic/historian could also evaluate the quality of the work and compare the director's work with that of other directors. In 1968 Sarris put this approach into practice with *The American Cinema: Directors and Directions, 1929–1968*, which became for many the reference book of auteurism in the late 1960s and early 1970s.[72]

The auteur approach was an ideal springboard for Chaplin's reputation. The auteurists tended to approve most highly of two kinds of directors: those who, during the American studio years, managed to place a "personal stamp" on their films in spite of the homogenizing pressures of the studios; and European directors who, like Renoir or Bergman or Murnau, seemed to express a distinctive style and world view through their films. The most highly valued auteurs were independent creators in the best Romantic tradition. What better candidate for laurels could there have been than Chaplin, whose stormy life personified independence, whose films featured the unique and mythic Charlie, and whose creative independence was ensured by his versatility and by his sole ownership of a movie studio?

Sarris's thumbnail sketch of Chaplin in *The American Cinema*—appearing in the "Pantheon," Sarris's section on the greatest directors—was understandably filled with praise. The reasons for this praise have helped shape the way we presently think about Chaplin. Sarris, echoing Canby, praised Chaplin first for the personal quality of his films: "Viewed as a whole, Chaplin's career is a cinematic biography on the highest level of artistic expression" (p. 41). Second, Sarris connected Chaplin's film style to the Charlie persona. Because, Sarris said, Chaplin's "other self on the screen has always been the supreme object of contemplation," he tended toward a film style that minimized heavy editing in favor of long takes that focused on Charlie and on the objects that surrounded him.

Third, Sarris minimized the significance of the ideas and social criticism in Chaplin's later features: "Chaplin dabbled in Marxian (*Modern Times*) and Brechtian (*Monsieur Verdoux*) analysis, but the solipsism of his conceptions negated the social implications of his ideas." Sarris's discounting of Chaplin's ideas was consistent with much early auteurist criticism, for at least in part, auteurism was a reaction against the kind of socially oriented film criticism rooted in the 1930s and personified in the 1940s and 1950s by the reviews of Crowther in the *New York Times*.[73] Sarris admitted as much in his introduction to *The American Cinema* by criticizing what he called the "forest critics," who wanted every movie to deal "Realistically with a Problem in Adult Terms" (p. 22).

Sarris continued to write about Chaplin and to review rereleases of his films in the years after the publication of *The American Cinema*. After his sketch there, Sarris's article on Chaplin in *Cinema: A Biographical Dictionary*, is probably his most important in developing an auteurist interpretation of Chaplin's significance.[74] In the dozen years that had elapsed since the publication of the earlier analysis, Sarris's approach to cinema had evolved. He had become less dogmatic about the auteur approach and more interested in the relationship between politics and the cinema.[75] This shift is apparent in his more recent treatment of Chaplin.

If anything, the entry views Chaplin even more favorably than the earlier piece. It opens: "Charles Chaplin is arguably the single most important artist produced by the cinema, certainly its most extraordinary performer and probably still its most universal icon" (p. 201). One reason for such high praise, especially for a dictionary of cinema, is that Sarris had come to place more value on the later, more political and autobiographical, Chaplin films. Admitting that Chaplin advocates could often be divided into those who favored the early shorts and those who favored the later, more overtly ideological, films, Sarris suggested that "it would seem that time is more on the side of his features than of his shorts." Chaplin was able, Sarris continued, to "communicate emotionally with the troubled masses through all the convulsions of War, Revolution, Inflation, Depression and Disillusion that passed blindly across his pantomimic path" (p. 202). And even though Chaplin abandoned his tramp and lost much of his audience after World War II, those who remained "gained in appreciation as they contemplated an artist who for more than half a century had used the screen as his personal diary" (p. 211). Benefiting from Chaplin's re-

releases of 1972 and thereafter, which gave Sarris and others the opportunity of seeing the Chaplin films—even *A King of New York*—as a
whole body of work, the later features began to seem more understandable. Some, especially *The Great Dictator* and *Monsieur Verdoux*,
also began to seem more important than the earlier films, even though
they are less funny. Auteurism thus combined with the rereleases and
a more liberal climate of opinion to elevate the latter part of Chaplin's
career.

In addition to the work of Sarris, the writings of Gerald Mast have
done much to shape the academic perspective on Chaplin in the past
fifteen years. On the broadest and most basic level, Mast's treatment
of Chaplin in *A Short History of the Movies* has been influential.[76] Mast
offered a more thoughtful, detailed, and probably more influential
analysis of Chaplin, however, in *The Comic Mind* (1973).[77] His treatment of Chaplin appears in chapters 6 through 8: "Chaplin: From
Keystone to Mutual," "Chaplin: First Nationals and Silent Features,"
and "Chaplin: Sound Films." Throughout, Mast devoted considerable
attention to analyses of individual films and a cross-referencing analysis of stylistic, narrative, and thematic motifs in Chaplin's films.

For our purposes, however, the center was located in an early section, "The Chaplin Career and Chaplin Clichés," of chapter 6. In it,
Mast posited a set of four clichés that he opposed about Chaplin's
work:

1. "Chaplin is a funny man without a real idea in his head."
2. The structures of Chaplin's films are flawed.
3. Chaplin's films are " 'bad' cinematically . . . Chaplin didn't
   understand composition, editing, lighting, and sound; many of his
   best bits would be as good on the stage as on a screen."
4. "Chaplin . . . reached brilliant perfection in the Mutuals and then
   got longer, duller, more banal, less unified, less funny, more
   saccharine in the later films." (64–66)

Mast countered each, and in doing so helped to shape our current
understanding of Chaplin.

Mast admitted that Chaplin often had trouble expressing ideas with
words (they "were not his medium"), but said that he did have "complex ideas about human conduct and social organizations" and "could
express them brilliantly." He generally did so not with words but with
"his face, his hands, his body" (p. 64). Examples abounded in Mast's
subsequent analysis.

Concerning structure, Mast countered that *Remembrance of Things
Past, Waiting for Godot*, and *Ulysses* could also be attacked for not telling
a neatly structured story. For Mast, such criticism was beside the point:

"Chaplin's structures are not stories but thematic investigations—putting the wandering *picaro*, the homeless tramp ... in juxtaposition with a particular social and moral environment" (p. 65). Instead of being structured primarily around the goal of telling a story—the usual "dominant" of classical Hollywood films—Chaplin's films investigated a theme implied by the film's title. The structures flowed from that aim.

Mast also defended Chaplin's film style. Giving examples of Chaplin's composition (Charlie in the house of mirrors in *The Circus*), camera movement (Charlie and the red flag in *Modern Times*), editing (the globe balloon scene in *The Great Dictator*), lighting (the audition scene in *Limelight*), and other stylistic elements, Mast argued that Chaplin's style, though not flashy or obtrusive, was functional, "exactly right for Chaplin" (p. 66).

Regarding the comparative worth of the shorts and the later features, Mast argued a position similar to Sarris's later article (in fact, he may have influenced Sarris). This view admitted that the most effective Mutual shorts were "flawless gems of comic business in a comic structure." However, though the longer features did occasionally lapse into "sentimentality, slow pacing, or overstated moralizing, they are far more impressive expressions of the human spirit" because they "work with more complex emotional and intellectual material," flawed though they may otherwise be (p. 67). To prefer the Chaplin shorts to these later films, Mast suggested, is to opt for the perfection of *The Comedy of Errors* over the complexity of *Hamlet*. Chaplin's paramount importance in film history, the centrality of the Charlie persona and his relationship to Chaplin himself, and the value and significance of Chaplin's later feature films were thus among the emphases expressed by Sarris and Mast. Because their work has been so widely read, their perspectives have shaped our current image of Chaplin.

During the 1970s, however, other approaches to the study of film challenged, proposed alternatives to, and even denounced the auteur approach to film study. One common alternative approach to film study is the formalist or neoformalist approach, which emphasizes close textual examination of the individual film. In the words of a widely used introductory film text, "form is a specific system of patterned relationships we perceive in any artwork." The task of the formalist film analyst is to examine the patterns of narrative form and cinematic style in any individual work, as well as to evaluate the film according to such criteria as originality, intensity of effect, and complexity.[78]

The neoformalist approach, and most others that propose close attention to the cinematic style of individual texts, has lowered Chaplin's reputation, particularly in relation to the films of Keaton. Formalism often prizes films in which the cinematic style calls attention to itself in interesting and original ways. Whereas Chaplin's films rarely do so (perhaps with the exception of the use of the sound track in Chaplin's three films after *The Circus*), Keaton's sometimes do, as when Keaton's title character in *Sherlock, Jr.* falls asleep in his projection booth, and his double-exposure alter ego walks through the theater and up into the screen. As the character stands immobile in the frame, the environment around him constantly changes, calling attention to the nature of cinematic form and illusion. Keaton's interest in cinematic style and his allegedly tighter narratives have led to judgments like Dwight Macdonald's: "I think he was much greater than Chaplin. He made half a dozen long films that are absolutely superb, and really work better than Chaplin's long films."[79]

A second approach that has probably dented Chaplin's reputation in the academy is, broadly speaking, one that blends an interest in semiology (the study of the way signs create meaning) with attention to ideology. Although this "approach" exists in many variations, it evolved from the work of French theorists like Christian Metz and Louis Althusser and found its strongest articulation in English on the pages of *Screen* magazine during the 1970s. Rooted in the political divisions of the late 1960s, radical dissatisfaction with capitalist society, and an awareness of the theoretical flaws of auteurism, this approach turns away from the focus on directors and the listing of film masterpieces to questions of how meaning is created in the cinema, how the industrial and economic context of commercial cinema determines its products, and the way in which ideology in films "constructs" the desires and perceptions of viewers. Some advocates of this approach denounce all commercial cinema as irrelevant and prefer to devote attention to avant-garde cinema. Others, while retaining interest in commercial films, reject the auteur approach as too Romantic, too theoretically imprecise, or too traditional to be of any assistance in answering their most pressing questions about the cinema. To the extent that these semiological and ideological approaches have found advocates in academia, Chaplin's reputation has declined not so much from attacks as from indifference.[80]

Others, however, have retained a fascination with Chaplin's life and career, and have contributed new insights or perspectives on Chaplin. Julian Smith, for example, in a critical biography of Chaplin, adopts a somewhat traditional psychoanalytical approach.[81] Though critics have long pondered the relationship between Chaplin and Charlie,

Smith proposes, rather, that Chaplin expressed various sides of his personality through different characters in the same films: in Pierre, Jean, and Marie in *A Woman of Paris*; in Charlie and the ringmaster in *The Circus*; in Charlie and the millionaire in *City Lights*, and so on. In effect, Smith examines Chaplin's films, even those that do not seem overtly autobiographical, as Chaplin's elaborate attempts to work out psychological conflicts through the various characters in his films. This approach leads one to speculate that Chaplin was much more self-conscious about and perhaps even sensitive to his own compulsions to control and dominate others. Such a view would help to alter Chaplin's star image should it become widespread.

Historical film research and scholarship, which works to uncover, study, and assess the significance of various documents in an attempt to reach a fuller understanding of a subject, has also contributed to Chaplin's public reputation in the past fifteen years. One recent area of research likely to shape the evolving view of Chaplin in the United States relates to the production histories of Chaplin's films.[82]

Two books and a documentary film series have contributed considerably to our understanding of Chaplin's production methods. Although Gerard Molyneaux did not have access to Chaplin's papers, he does a thorough production history of *City Lights* in his monograph *Charles Chaplin's "City Lights"*. Through careful research and interviews with those involved, Molyneaux reconstructs the troubled production history of the film. He clearly shows his admiration for *City Lights* in his subsequent analysis, but after examining the evidence, his conclusion about Chaplin's organizational ability is nevertheless compelling: "Chaplin's skill as a director is undistinguished and unenviable. At worst, his methods are counter-productive."[83]

One suspects that Chaplin's unplanned, intuitive method of filmmaking, rooted in his early days at Keystone, is responsible for his problems and delays in production. That suspicion is reinforced by the three-hour documentary, *The Unknown Chaplin*, compiled by Kevin Brownlow and David Gill. Consisting of outtakes and home movies from Chaplin's own archives and interviews with Chaplin associates like Lita Grey and Georgia Hale, the film gives a vivid picture of Chaplin's working methods. It contains some rich material for those interested in Chaplin, such as an entire comic scene originally meant to open *City Lights*, and also, as Anthony Slide puts it, depicts Chaplin as "overindulgent in his filmmaking," shooting scenes "with total disregard as to the amount of film he is using or even, presumably, the wear and tear on his fellow workers."[84]

A more generous interpretation of this overindulgence would posit, as Slide does at one point, that Chaplin had "a dedicated, relentless search for perfection" (p. 9). The argument would hold that because Chaplin's final results were at times so unforgettable and because he was spending his own money when shooting so much footage, criticism of Chaplin's directorial methods are beside the point. David Robinson's recent biography of Chaplin takes this more sympathetic point of view. One of the book's most valuable contributions is its production history of Chaplin's films. Blessed with Oona Chaplin's cooperation and access to Chaplin's papers, Robinson affirms Chaplin's extreme methods for many of his films (the ratio of film shot to film used for *The Great Dictator* was 41:1, for *City Lights*, 38.8:1). Yet like Slide, Robinson in the end admires Chaplin for what he terms his "indefatigable application to the quest for perfection." He also shows that Chaplin worked in a much more organized and regimented fashion in some of his later films than he had in *City Lights*.[85] If access to Chaplin's working records are extended to other scholars, it will be interesting to see what effect the resulting information will have on Chaplin's public reputation.

Thus the work of scholars and critics has continued to keep Chaplin's life and career in the public eye and has helped to shift and alter the image Americans have of Chaplin and Charlie. Several questions are raised by this recent scholarship. They lie at the center of the critical/aesthetic discourse about Chaplin in the 1970s and 1980s. Was Chaplin an inferior stylist or does his style perfectly carry out its function? Were Chaplin's features or shorts greater achievements and why? Of what quality and significance are Chaplin's later features (from *The Great Dictator* on)? To what extent are Chaplin's films indications of his psychological makeup? Were Chaplin's huge shooting ratios a manifestation of his quest for perfection or an indication that he too often had no idea of what he wanted in his films?

Though these questions are still being debated, one thing is certain: Chaplin's star image went through a drastic transformation between 1952 and the late 1970s. A complex set of factors made the shift possible. The changing political climate, which tolerated and even encouraged criticism of the United States, transformed Chaplin from a political villain to a victim of repressive times. It also encouraged critics and viewers to value more highly films like *Monsieur Verdoux* and *A King of New York*, which overtly engaged in social criticism. A shift in the prevailing critical discourse to auteurism also benefited Chaplin's star image, for his versatility, his tendency to center on a comic persona he played himself, and the increasingly autobiographical characteristics of his later features all seemed tailor-made for auteurist critics. However, Chaplin's own actions played a role. His presentation of himself as a family patriarch helped diminish the image, rooted in the 1940s and before, of Chaplin the womanizer. His business decisions, which included his rereleased films, the publication of his autobiography, and his 1972 return tour, also played a key role. Politics, economics, critical discourse, presentation of self through the filters of the media: all help to make and break stars. All helped in this case to return the exiled monarch to his throne. It remains only to examine what has happened to this star image after the death in 1977 of the person who embodied, created, and constituted it.[86]

12

Epilogue

In his elegy to the memory of William Butler Yeats, W. H. Auden wrote that when Yeats died, he "became his admirers." The line is an eloquent one, suggesting that the achievements of artists survive them when their admirers discuss and thus perpetuate the vitality of their work and the memory of their lives. In the case of stars, however, the line is incomplete. When they die, stars do in a sense become their admirers. But they also become their detractors and even, in some instances, become those who wish to "commodify" the images—that is, use the image to sell something else.

Whether through the efforts of admirers, detractors, or commodifiers, a star image very often outlives a star. We know this to be true from the stories and legends still circulating about the great nineteenth-century Shakespearean actors. In the age of mechanical and electronic reproduction, this survival is especially pronounced, for some arts can be frozen in time, the physical presence of the star preserved for future generations. It is still possible in the 1980s, for example, to observe the sprightly twenty-eight-year-old Chaplin as Charlie cleaning up Easy Street or the weathered sixty-two-year-old Chaplin as Calvero musing about the perplexities of art, aging, and declining fame. Though the person is dead, the image survives.

That the evolution of Chaplin's star image in the United States is intimately related to the shifts in American political and cultural history since World War I is as true today as it was in the 1910s and 1920s. During the 1980s, the presidential administration of Ronald Reagan has promoted an ethic that hearkens back to the 1920s. That ethic opposes increased taxation and the expansion of government in the social sphere and counters by celebrating individualism and the entrepreneurial spirit of capitalism. Most political analysts agree that the liberal coalition forged during the New Deal had fragmented by the first half of the 1980s and left the Democratic party with no unifying sense of purpose. President Reagan's polished media presence and uncanny knack of telling the public what it wanted to hear, however contradictory the stories, filled the political void left by the collapse of the New Deal coalition.

Oddly enough, when Chaplin was alive, he defended in different ways and at different times both New Deal liberalism and entrepreneurial capitalism. His progressive political positions in the 1940s were shaped by the ethos of the New Deal. On the other hand, from his early years in the movie industry and throughout his career, Chaplin, assisted by his business and legal advisors, jealously guarded the rights to his films in the best capitalist spirit.

It is not surprising, therefore, that immediately after Chaplin's death, representatives of Roy Export, owned by the Chaplin family, moved to protect the copyrights to the Charlie image and to all Chaplin movies from the First National period on. Although there was (and is) some legal disagreement concerning what happens to the rights to a character after the death of the actor who created and portrayed that character, Roy Export was upheld in its first legal test. It sued CBS News for using film clips from Chaplin features in its obituary of the comedian and was awarded $700,000 in fines by a federal district court. Despite CBS's argument that it was exercising its First Amendment right to report on a newsworthy event, the U.S. Court of Appeals allowed the decision to stand. The decision explicitly supported Roy Export's ownership of the Charlie character and implicitly endorsed the right of its Swiss-based licensing company, Bubbles, Inc., to lease that image to businesses that desired to use it for commercial or promotional purposes.[1]

It is both ironic and somehow appropriate that Chaplin's star image in the 1980s was most actively perpetuated, other than by the films themselves, by the "Big Blue"—IBM, the model of corporate America. In fact, even more than the Chaplin films, IBM's advertising campaign for its personal computers, begun in 1981 and continuing until 1987 (when the actors of the M.A.S.H. television program took over), kept the image of Charlie before the eyes of the American public. The IBM advertising campaign provides an interesting picture of one way, and for what purposes, Chaplin's star image is outliving its creator.

Before 1980, IBM was known primarily as a reliable yet staid company that provided high-quality office machines to businesses. Although it was hesitant to try the untested, mass consumer market of personal computers, in 1980 it decided to enter the fray and sent a crew of engineers to Boca Raton, Florida, to create a machine that could compete with Apple and the other computer manufacturers. By August 1981 the IBM-PC was ready to be sold to customers.[2]

But the product had to be marketed as well as engineered and manufactured. As the engineers were working in Florida, advertisers at the New York agency of Lord, Geller, Federico, Einstein (LGFE) were thinking about advertising campaigns as early as January 1981. One of LGFE's executives, Bob Tore, recalls a meeting with his colleague, Bob Mabley: "We were talking about the problems of big computers and their unfriendliness. We had the idea of showing the history of the computer shrinking—a big white box in a white, sterile room, that would get smaller and smaller. We wanted to have a person reacting to it, and with all that white background, we obviously needed a character in a black suit to stand out. That became Charlie." Mabley, who had just joined the firm in February 1981, adds his recollections:

> We wanted a figure to represent us, but with Dick Cavett doing Apple and Bill Cosby doing Texas Instruments, the field was getting a little cluttered. We knew we wanted a single, friendly person who would represent Everyman. But we didn't really see a need for on-camera dialog. That pointed to mime.
>
> We talked about Marcel Marceau for about 10 minutes and considered a few other ideas. We quickly developed criteria for who this mime should be and ended up with the conclusion that it could only be Charlie Chaplin. After that, Bob Tore and I were on a roll, and everything began to work.[3]

The idea was planted. Before it could grow to fruition, however, IBM had to secure the rights to use the Charlie image from Bubbles, Inc. Bob Mabley conceded to a reporter in 1983 that the law was inconclusive about rights to an image like Charlie's after Chaplin died. "But IBM," he added, "being who they are, wanted to be absolutely sure."[4] After negotiations, IBM signed a one-year licensing agreement with Bubbles, renewable each fall, that gave the company the exclusive right to use the Charlie image and the title "Modern Times" for advertising personal computer and office products. Bubbles retained the right to review the advertising material that used the image. IBM officials refuse to divulge how much the rights cost them, but it is known that by 1983, IBM was spending an estimated-$25 million on its PC advertising budget alone. The contract was renewed into 1987.[5]

After auditioning over thirty candidates, the agency hired an actor named Billy Scudder, born in 1940, to play the Charlie character. Scudder had been impersonating Charlie at amusement parks like Knotts Berry Farm and at parties for nearly a decade. By September 1981, the first IBM television spot using the Charlie image, "House," was aired, beginning a long and successful collaboration that soon would expand to print and radio advertisements.[6]

The campaign was by several standards remarkably successful. If success is measured by IBM-PC sales, there is no doubt: in 1983, IBM sold 850,000 units, as much as Apple had sold in four years.[7] Although subsequent sales of the PCjr were disappointing and although by 1986 IBM-compatible machines—the "clones"—were gaining a greater share of the personal computer market, there is no doubt that IBM attained a strong foothold in the market almost immediately after its PC was available and the advertising campaign had begun. Indeed the speed with which many companies began to develop and sell IBM-compatible machines indicates how fast it was becoming the industry standard.

If success is measured by what advertisers think about the campaign, the IBM–Charlie collaboration receives similarly high marks. An IBM official noted that the campaign was extremely successful at getting the public to associate a character (Charlie) with the product (personal computer): when marketing researchers asked people what character they associated with the personal computer, the answer very often was the "little tramp." This "top-of-mind awareness" or "unaided recall," the official added, was one sign of a very effective campaign.[8]

Although it is not surprising that IBM officials would praise the campaign, it has also been praised by other advertising organizations. The campaign won a number of awards in 1981, including an Andy Award, an International Broadcasting Award, and awards from the Art Directors Club and the International Film and Television Festival. "Bakery," the third of the television spots featuring Charlie, won one of *Advertising Age*'s Best Commercial Awards for 1982.[9] And by 1985 director Stuart Hagman had directed nine IBM–Charlie commercials, had been nominated five times for Directors Guild of America television commercial awards, and had won twice.[10]

Just as Charlie spawned imitators in the 1910s, IBM competitors quickly began to use the Charlie image in ads to promote their own products—perhaps the surest indication of the campaign's success. Seequa, for example, advertised its computer by showing Charlie with his pockets turned inside out: buying a Seequa, the ad promised, would cost a lot less than buying an IBM (see Figure 33). Another company, Fortune Systems, used Charlie to attack the capabilities of the IBM-PC and promote its own. The ad pictures Charlie from behind. His right hand is behind his back with fingers crossed. The accompanying caption reads, "and trust me, when your information needs grow, you can always connect all your PCs together." Here the ad alleges that Charlie is IBM's corporate liar in terms of the network-

33. One of countless computer ads making unauthorized use of Charlie's image after the IBM "Little Tramp" ad campaign.

ing capabilities of its product. Even Apple suggested Charlie's presence in a TV commercial: the ad compared the Apple IIc and the IBM-PCjr. At the end of the commercial the narrator asks viewers which machine is preferable, and a cane appears from the side of the screen and chooses the IIc. The imitation was so widespread that in one issue of *PC Magazine*, for example, twelve ads for software or peripherals directly or indirectly alluded to the IBM–Charlie campaign.[11]

As expected, however, IBM challenged the rights of other computer companies to use the image. The licensing agency that leased the image of Charlie to IBM also went into action. In mid-1984, Herbert Jacoby, a New York lawyer representing Bubbles, Inc., told a reporter,

"Almost everybody in the industry seems to want to use the tramp. . . . I must have written to 75 companies about this." Asked about what influence his letters have had, Jacoby replied, "Ninety-five percent of the companies I talk to are cooperative. . . . Only rarely does anybody tell me to go to hell."[12] For that 5 percent, Jacoby and his firm were likely to go to court. Through 1986, the relationship between IBM and Charlie remained harmonious.

Why did IBM choose Charlie? How did the ads portray his image? What qualities did the advertisements associate with Charlie, and how were they related to the selling strategy?

Those involved in creating the advertisements offer some answers to these questions. To Scudder, Charlie's essential quality is his vulnerability: "That's the key to Chaplin. He did all those tricks and mischief, but he was still vulnerable." This enables people to identify with and respond so easily and fully to Charlie, in Scudder's view. Arlene Jaffee, an LFGE writer on the campaign, stresses how the character helped to create an unthreatening mood: "I think its secret was that the whole gestalt of the campaign was so friendly, human, and communicative."[13]

It is easy to see how this quality proved attractive to IBM. One marketing analyst has observed that the Chaplin campaign "operates as a foil to the large intimidating monolith called IBM. Chaplin's antics not only allay fears about using a personal computer but about IBM itself."[14] By his very demeanor, Charlie can help reduce the computer to human scale and break down the public's fear of it. If Charlie can use one, the unarticulated logic goes, then I certainly can. In computerese, Charlie makes the computer seem "user-friendly."

A few examples of the ads themselves illustrate how Chaplin's image has been used. The first television spot, "House," emerged very much as Mabley and Tore conceived it. In the course of the ad, a gigantic box shrinks. When it becomes a manageable size, Charlie takes out an IBM-PC, scans a "how-to" book, then sits at a white table with a rose on it and begins to work on the computer. As he does so, the voice-over narrator concludes, "IBM made its personal computer to help a person be more productive, to help a person be more creative, and those are good reasons for a person to feel good." By moving from the forbiddingly large computer of the old days to the manageable PC of the present, and by associating the PC with productivity, creativity, and feeling good, IBM creates an environment in which Charlie's vulnerability and ultimate resilience can thrive. The rose, which was used frequently in later ads, is entirely consistent with the Charlie image in films like *The Bank* and *City Lights*. And by having Charlie master the

34. Charlie operates a computer: the IBM "Little Tramp" ad campaign. Note the association of Charlie and flowers, which derives from films like *City Lights*. Courtesy IBM.

PC so effortlessly, the advertisement underlines to its audience how nonthreatening and simple an IBM computer really is.

This was not the only commercial to refer to specific Chaplin films. Another put Charlie on roller skates, much as he had done in *The Rink* and later in *Modern Times*. And the term "modern times," which IBM had also leased rights to, appeared regularly. Two examples are print advertisements for the IBM-PCjr, which emphasized how a home TV can be connected to the computer, and the IBM Portable PC, which stresses its mobility. Both used the phrase in their titles: "How to Plug Your Family into Modern Times" and "How to Move with Modern Times and Take Your PC With You." Both also used the rose introduced in the first television commercial, as did ads for the IBM-PC (see Figure 34).

Though the Charlie of the IBM ad campaign resembles Chaplin's Charlie, he also differs in certain ways. As in most of Chaplin's films, Charlie wears a derby, floppy shoes, and a dark suit. For IBM, however, Charlie is cleaned up. He usually wears a pressed striped tie and pinstriped pants, and he seems to have the same tailor as the wealthy man Chaplin portrayed in *The Idle Class* (see Figure 35). Apparently the down-and-out, frazzled, threadbare Charlie of films like *A Dog's Life* was not appropriate for the corporate giant.

The commercials also very often make Charlie a small businessman (who is saved by a computer) or a hustling entrepreneur. One ad stresses how IBM computers can grow with a business by showing Charlie's success as a furniture store owner. Another print ad appropriated a phrase common about the time of the 1984 Los Angeles Olympics: "How to Go for the Gold." In it Charlie is clearing a hurdle and wears a number 6 over his suit coat; the ad goes on to plug a software game called Decathalon, which would allow an IBM-PC user to "experience the thrill of victory."[15]

Throughout the ad campaign a curious (and apparently conscious) transformation of Charlie's image took place. In 1936, Chaplin's *Modern Times* presented technology as an impersonal, harmful force. The speed of the assembly line turned Charlie into a physical wreck. A television monitor operated by the owner invaded Charlie's privacy in the rest room. The Bellows feeding machine tried to mechanize eating in the interest of factory productivity. In perhaps the most famous symbolic image, Charlie was nearly swallowed up by the cogs of a gigantic machine. One of Chaplin's themes was that technology victimized Charlie. It was an imprisoning, not liberating, force in *Modern Times*.

Though the IBM commercials have often used the title "Modern Times" to accompany Charlie's image in its advertisements, at some points their purposes obviously contradict the thrust of Chaplin's *Modern Times*. One angry computer executive for an IBM competitor, peeved when Bubbles told his company to stop using the image in its ads, charged that "Charlie would roll over in his grave if he knew they were siding with IBM." But Bob Mabley is straightforward in admitting that Charlie's frustration with technology shifts in the IBM ad campaign. "By bringing Charlie into real modern times," he commented, "we were able to show how he is finally able to conquer that frustration. It is clear that technology is now on his side." An article in *PC Magazine* states the counter-argument to Chaplin's *Modern Times* in its most blithely optimistic terms: "As many of the early PC ads and

35. To market computers, Charlie is spruced up in pinstripes
for the "Little Tramp" campaign. Courtesy IBM.

commercials implied, the Personal Computer, like a 16-bit Moses, can help to set us free."[16]

Critics could easily argue that although a personal computer enables one to store and manipulate large quantities of information, it is not necessarily a liberating force for people like data processors who "input" information eight hours a day. Critics can legitimately complain that the IBM commercials distort the image of Charlie garnered from the Chaplin films. The fact remains, however, that Roy Export has sold the image to IBM and that in doing so, the image is subject to transformation through the way it is manipulated by people other than the original creator. Chaplin, the man widely denounced as a dangerous leftist and exiled from the United States in part because of those perceived commitments in the 1940s and early 1950s, is after his death enriching his survivors through the sale of that image, in the best capitalist tradition, to one of the most massive of corporate enterprises. To compound the irony, the image is being used to sell what has become a central icon of high technology: the microcomputer.

Was IBM concerned that the allegations about Chaplin's politics might be dredged up to damage its own corporate reputation? An article in *PC Magazine* suggests that his suspect past was taken into account by IBM (the article calls *Modern Times* Chaplin's "springboard for his increasingly public socialist sentiments," which "would cause him to be hounded during the McCarthy era"). To inquiries about this issue, an IBM spokesperson replied with the official company position: IBM was confident that the public could distinguish a fictional character from the man who created that character. If that distinction were made, Chaplin's past, which IBM admitted might be suspect, should have no effect on the campaigns.[17] No available evidence suggests that details of Chaplin's past had any significant negative influence on the IBM–Charlie collaboration to sell personal computers.

As WE REACH the centenary of Chaplin's birth, what conclusions can be drawn about the evolution of Chaplin's star image in American culture? It is clear, due in part to IBM, that Chaplin's star image is still alive and evolving over a decade after his death. One direction of its evolution is also somehow characteristic of a dominant trend of the period: as the Reagan era has celebrated capitalist enterprise, so has the image of Charlie helped market the computer, a product so representative of the 1980s that *Time* named it "Man of the Year" in 1985.

Yet it would be too pessimistic—and a distortion as well—to suggest that IBM's Charlie has *become* the Chaplin star image. Those who commodify the image to sell products are joined by other admirers and detractors of the image. Other texts besides the IBM advertisements contribute to Chaplin's star image in the 1980s. Chapter 11 suggested that Chaplin and his work still draw the interest of writers and readers, as David Robinson's recent biography, *Chaplin: His Life and Art*, demonstrates. College film courses often include examinations of Chaplin's work on their syllabi. Chaplin's films are still being shown by revival houses and college film societies. And the films appear on cable channels, most prominently the Disney channel, which in the mid-1980s ran a full series of the United Artists features and some of the First National shorts. Video shops rent the films. A documentary series like *The Unknown Chaplin* even presents us with more of Chaplin's work. IBM had no monopoly on Chaplin's star image in the 1980s, however secure its license to use Charlie for selling computers.

This book has traced the evolution of Chaplin's star image in America by exploring the interactions between Chaplin and various public institutions, especially the press, the government, and pressure groups. These interactions have been placed in their historical context, which includes not only the history of the film industry and film criticism and reviewing but also the more specific history of Chaplin's relevant personal and political involvements and the broader cultural and political history of the United States. In the case of Chaplin, it seems self-evident that the evolution of his star image and the changing reception he and his films received were closely bound up with these historical currents.

After examining how Chaplin's star image has evolved in the United States since the heady days of "Chaplinitis," it is apparent that Chaplin's star image is a product of history for at least two different reasons. First, Chaplin himself lived in a historical context, both shaped by and shaping that context through his public actions and his films. His Liberty Loan and second front activities; his films and his shifting conception of character in them; his divorces and affairs; his exile and return—all took place within and were influenced by historical context. The histories of the American film industry (both its technological and its signifying practices), American society, and even international politics inform the ways in which Chaplin's star image has evolved and is evolving in the twentieth century. But Chaplin was not a passive subject fully determined by those histories, however much they constrained him or limited his choices. The evolution of Chaplin's star image also suggests that, through his actions and films, Chaplin played an important role himself in shaping that image. Whereas many stars in the studio era had minimal control over their star images, Chaplin, because he owned his means of production after 1918 and participated in so many aspects of filmmaking (including of promotion campaigns), was able to help control his star image to a degree unthinkable for most other stars. Despite the legitimate skepticism in some critical circles since the late 1960s about auteurism and romanticization of the individual artist, Chaplin clearly contributed in important ways to the shaping of his star image.

Second, the star image is a product of history because the reception of Chaplin and his films, including the prevailing critical discourse about films, is rooted in history. Those who read about Chaplin, write about Chaplin, or watch his films also function in a specific historical context. The qualities that Chaplin's admirers and detractors discover in his life and films have changed over time. The vulgarity or hilarity of Charlie, the persona, struck audiences in the 1910s. The filmmaker

Chaplin's blend of pathos and comedy seemed prominent in the 1920s and early 1930s. From the mid-1930s through the 1950s, the man's political perspectives, whether in his films or in his public activities, as well as his associations with women, seemed to dominate public attention. Thanks to Chaplin's lower, more accommodating public profile and the shrewd rerelease of his films in the past two decades, the character of Charlie began to reassume a larger role in Chaplin's star image. Simultaneously, due in part to the dominance of auteurism, Chaplin himself was again regarded as a talented artist rather than as a man with questionable political views and morality. Chaplin's star image has evolved in certain ways partly because the critical discourse about movies and their place in American culture has shifted significantly since Chaplin's career began. But to bring the argument full circle, these shifts in the critical discourse (think of the 1930s, for example) were themselves often related to the same broad social and economic forces that influenced Chaplin. Chaplin's star image can only be understood within the web of culture and history.

Further research is needed to examine how individual viewers have read and responded to Chaplin films and the ways in which groups of different social classes, genders, and ages receive him in different, patterned ways. However impossible it is to identify all the ways that Chaplin and his movies have affected Americans, people have used Chaplin's movies and his star image for a variety of purposes. To some, the movies have offered compensation: even though their lives were frustrating and bounded, Charlie offered an image of how the physically small and powerless could survive with dignity and resilience. To others, some of his movies have reinforced a sense of alienation from modern society: for them, *Monsieur Verdoux*'s sustained examination of an impersonal and ruthless society elicited a powerful response. To some, Chaplin even became a reified political position. Whether such people denounced or celebrated Chaplin depended on whether they were, in the American sense, political liberals or conservatives. Chaplin then became the victim or the villain, depending on one's views. Doubtless an exploration of individual responses to Chaplin's life and films would demonstrate that the star image has been meaningful to people in many other, and often culturally patterned, ways.[18]

Chaplin's star image thus is, as Richard Dyer suggested in his book on stars, a "structured polysemy." That is, his star image is made up of many, sometimes contradictory, qualities and meanings that evolve as the culture converses about his life, his films, and his worth. As Auden would have it, Chaplin has, since his death, become his admirers. But he has also become his detractors and his commodifiers. The future shape of his star image will depend on the quality of the cultural conversation about Chaplin, Charlie, and the films that brought both to stardom. Let the conversation continue.

Notes

1. Film historians have often cited the *Olympic* as the ship on which Chaplin arrived, but since that ship had been sent to Belfast for refurbishing on 21 September 1912, they have made a mistake. Documents from the U.S. Immigration and Naturalization Service verify that Chaplin arrived on the *Oceanic*. See Harold Manning and Timothy J. Lyons, "Charlie Chaplin's Early Life: Fact and Fiction," *Historical Journal of Film, Radio, and Television* 3, no. 1 (1983): 35–41.

2. Timothy Lyons, in his invaluable *Charles Chaplin: A Guide to References and Resources* (Boston: G. K. Hall, 1979), lists over 1,700 books and articles about Chaplin, yet concludes that "the literature has not fully explored Chaplin's life and work in the context of American culture and society" (p. 19). Although here I focus on the relationship between Chaplin and American culture, my research has led me to believe that it would be interesting and worthwhile to examine the evolution of Chaplin's star image in a number of countries, especially Great Britain, France, and the Soviet Union.

3. Throughout the book, "Charlie" will refer to Chaplin's most familiar screen persona, often called "the tramp" or "the little fellow." "Chaplin" will refer to the real person, Charles Spencer Chaplin.

4. A recent work on American film history that skillfully delineates the relationship between popular films and such internal and external historical developments is Robert Ray, *A Certain Tendency of the Hollywood Cinema, 1930–1980* (Princeton: Princeton Univ. Press, 1985). See especially the introduction and pp. 28–29. Such attention to historical factors is consistent with the neoformalist approach, to which I am indebted. As David Bordwell has observed in his brief exegesis of the neoformalist approach ("Lowering the Stakes," *Iris* 1, no. 1 [1983]: 15), "the historical emphasis of [Russian] Formalism does not exclude consideration of economics, ideology, technological change, or other historical factors."

5. Richard Dyer, *Stars* (London: British Film Institute, 1979), p. 1.

6. Dyer, *Stars*, pp. 69–72. Examining this broad variety of media texts in addition to Chaplin's films is absolutely central if one is to get a firm sense of how Chaplin's star image evolved. Tony Bennett, a scholar interested in the James Bond phenomenon, has recently drawn on Pierre Macherey's work to argue that "incrustations" which shape and do much to define the evolution of Bond, have grown up around the Bond novels and films. Bennett goes so far

as to propose that the Bond text (film or novel) "does not have any existence that is separable from such incrustations." Similarly here, Chaplin's star image evolved not simply because of his films, but also because of such "incrustations" as movie posters and press kits; feature articles about films; reviews; publicity about Chaplin's private and public activities; and the broader shifts in the social and political climate. On "incrustations," see Bennett's "Text and Social Process: The Case of James Bond," *Screen Education*, no. 41 (Winter/Spring 1982): 3–14.

7. "Literary History as a Challenge to Literary Theory," in Hans Robert Jauss, *Toward an Aesthetic of Reception*, trans. Timothy Bahti (Minneapolis: Univ. of Minnesota Press, 1982), p. 20.

8. In *Speaking of Soap Operas* (Chapel Hill: Univ. of North Carolina Press, 1985), Robert Allen observes that even though Jauss is interested in the relationship between literary history and broader historical currents, his "model of literary history is largely insular" (p. 99). He also cites (p. 182) Robert Holub's survey of German reader-response criticism, in which Iser and Jauss are strongly criticized "for their lack of sociological grounding with respect to the reader." Greater attention to the broader sociohistorical currents is necessary if we are to understand the evolution of Chaplin's star image.

9. F. O. Matthiessen, *American Renaissance* (New York: Oxford Univ. Press, 1941), p. xv.

1. CHAPLIN, THE EARLY FILMS, AND THE RISE TO STARDOM

1. The account of Chaplin's entry into the movies comes from Chaplin's *My Autobiography* (New York: Simon and Schuster, 1964), pp. 137–39; the date of his departure from the Karno company is found in Theodore Huff, *Charlie Chaplin* (1951; reprinted New York: Pyramid Books, 1964), p. 3, and corroborated by John McCabe, *Charlie Chaplin* (Garden City, New York: Doubleday, 1978), pp. 46–47. David Robinson, in *Chaplin: His Life and Art* (New York: McGraw-Hill, 1985), pp. 102–7, also treats Chaplin's introduction to the movies and reprints a part of his first contract. These three are presently the most reliable of the Chaplin biographies in English and can be supplemented by Georges Sadoul, *Vie de Charlot* (Paris: Lherminier, 1978). Hereafter, Chaplin's autobiography will be cited as MA and the Robinson biography as CHLA.

2. See Robert C. Allen, *Vaudeville and Film, 1895–1915: A Study in Media Interaction* (New York: Arno, 1980), esp. pp. 23–92.

3. On the struggles for control of the film industry from 1908 on, see Tino Balio, ed., *The American Film Industry*, 2nd ed. (Madison: Univ. of Wisconsin Press, 1985), pp. 103–251. The transformation of the film industry from the "primitive" phase to the "classical Hollywood" phase is treated most fully in David Bordwell, Janet Staiger, and Kristin Thompson, *The Classical Hollywood Cinema: Film Style and Mode of Production to 1960* (New York: Columbia Univ. Press, 1985), esp. parts. 2, 3. Hereafter, this work will be cited as CHC. Background on Keystone can be found in Mack Sennett, *King of Comedy* (New York:

Doubleday, 1954) and Kalton C. Lahue and Terry Brewer, *Kops and Custards* (Norman: Oklahoma Univ. Press, 1968).

4. Janet Staiger, "Seeing Stars," *Velvet Light Trap*, no. 20 (Summer 1983): 13; CHC, ch. 9, esp. pp. 101–2.

5. Though the persona portrayed by Chaplin in so many films has been called a number of different things—the tramp, the little tramp, the little fellow, and others—I will in this study regularly refer to the persona as "Charlie." (See the Preface, note 3.)

6. *Moving Picture World* 19 (17 February 1914): 678. The subsequent references in this paragraph come from volumes 19–22 of the same periodical. Dates and page numbers are cited parenthetically in the text.

7. *Motion Picture Magazine* 13, no. 7 (August 1914): 126. The subsequent references in the next few paragraphs come from the same volume. Issues and page numbers are cited in the text.

8. Charles Spencer Chaplin, *Charlie Chaplin's Own Story*, ed. Harry Geduld (1916; reprinted Bloomington: Indiana Univ. Press, 1985), p. 140. This book, actually written by a journalist named Rose Lee Wilder after interviews with Chaplin in 1915, was published by Bobbs-Merrill in Indianapolis but never released. See Chapter 2, below, and CHLA, pp. 180–85, for further information on the book.

9. Charles J. McGuirk, "Chaplinitis," *Motion Picture Magazine* 9, nos. 6–7 (July and August 1915): 85–89 and 121–24. The quotation is from part 1, p. 87.

10. *Motion Picture Magazine* quoted in Raoul Sobel and David Francis, *Chaplin: Genesis of a Clown* (London: Quartet Books, 1977), p. 144; *Cleveland Plain Dealer*, 9 June 1915; *New York World*, 19 June 1915 (both newspaper articles are in the Robinson Locke Collection, vol. 110, within the Billy Rose Collection, Lincoln Center Branch, New York Public Library, New York); Wes Gehring, *Charlie Chaplin: A Bio-Bibliography* (Westport, Conn.: Greenwood, 1983), p. 62. The books by Sobel and Francis and by Gehring both contain useful information about the Chaplin craze. The Robinson Locke Collection will hereafter be cited as RLC.

11. Discussions of Ritchie are found in Sobel and Francis, *Chaplin: Genesis of a Clown*, pp. 143–44, and McCabe, *Charlie Chaplin*, p. 89. McCabe also comments on another Chaplin imitator, Charles Amador, who changed his name to Charles Aplin.

12. Howard Philip Rhoades, "Who Is This?" *Motion Picture Magazine* 10, no. 10 (November 1915): 115.

13. An example of the comic strip can be found in Chaplin, *My Life in Pictures* (New York: Grosset and Dunlap, 1975), p. 16. The RLC, vol. 110, contains one such cartoon from the 5 April 1915 issue of the *Cleveland Leader*.

14. McGuirk, "Chaplinitis," part 1, p. 87.

15. Dyer, *Stars*, pp. 48–49.

16. E. V. Whitcomb, "Charlie Chaplin," *Photoplay* 7 (February 1915): 35–37; "A Real Film ABC," *Moving Picture World* (6 February 1915), both in RLC, vol.

110. The point here is not whether Chaplin actually was humble—and evidence suggests that his pride did grow as he aged—but that he was being presented as humble by the press.

17. The quotations come from the articles by Whitcomb, McGuirk, and "A Real Film ABC." See also, in RLC, vol. 110: Victor Eubank, "The Funniest Man on the Screen," *Motion Picture Magazine* (March 1915); "Charlie Chaplin, Cheerful Comedian," *Picture-Play Weekly* 1, no. 3 (24 April 1915): 1; *Chicago Tribune*, 25 April 1915.

18. Santayana's essay is included in *Winds of Doctrine* (New York: Scribner's, 1913).

19. Charles Alexander, *Here the Country Lies* (Bloomington: Indiana Univ. Press, 1980), p. 9. On the Genteel Tradition, see ibid., pp. 1–27; Henry F. May, *The End of American Innocence* (New York: Knopf, 1959); and Stow Persons, *The Decline of American Gentility* (New York: Scribner's, 1973).

20. Both quotations appear in Lary May, *Screening Out the Past* (New York: Oxford Univ. Press, 1980), pp. 59, 53.

21. Review of *The Property Man* in *Moving Picture World* 21 (15 August 1914): 961.

22. *New Orleans American*, 9 September 1915, RLC, vol. 110.

23. *Detroit News*, 13 April 1916, in RLC, vol. 110.

24. J. B. Hirsch, "The New Charlie Chaplin," *Motion Picture Magazine* 10, no. 12 (January 1916): 115–17. Page numbers for citations of this article in subquent paragraphs are given in the text.

25. Though two recent studies of movie theaters in Boston and New York dispute the traditional view that moviegoing before 1915 was almost exclusively a working-class entertainment, they do agree that by the mid-1910s, the audience was growing and much of it was middle class. See Russell Merritt, "Nickelodeon Theaters, 1905–1914," in Balio, *American Film Industry*, pp. 59–82, and Robert C. Allen, "Motion Picture Exhibition in Manhattan, 1906–1912," in *The American Movie Industry*, ed. Gorham Kindem (Carbondale: Southern Illinois Univ. Press), pp. 12–24.

26. *Motion Picture Classic* 3 (September 1916): 41–44.

27. See CHC, pp. 177–83.

28. Quoted in Gerald D. McDonald et al., *The Films of Charlie Chaplin* (New York: Bonanza Books, 1965), p. 99.

29. Janice Radway, *Reading the Romance* (Chapel Hill: Univ. of North Carolina Press, 1984), pp. 10, 147–49.

30. McGuirk, "Chaplinitis," part 1, p. 89.

31. McCabe, *Charlie Chaplin*, p. 78. Apparently, Chaplin also shot footage during the early 1920s for another film dealing with the flophouses he saw in his childhood. Kevin Brownlow's fascinating compilation film, *The Unknown Chaplin*, includes some of that footage.

32. Chaplin's request to Ramsaye is reported in the *Toledo Blade*, 10 March 1916, RLC, vol. 110.

1. Chaplin's Mutual contract negotiations and the Hippodrome evening are discussed in Robert Grau, "The More People Laughed at the Idea of Chaplin's Salary, the More They Had to Pay," *Motion Pictures Magazine* (May 1916), RLC, vol. 110; and Terry Ramsaye, *A Million and One Nights* (1926, reprinted New York: Simon and Schuster, 1964), pp. 731–36.

2. CHLA, pp. 180–85. Harry Geduld, in his introduction to the recently reprinted edition of *Charlie Chaplin's Own Story*, argues that, although there is a good deal of invented detail in the book, it does provide some useful insight into some aspects of Chaplin's life to 1916, if used judiciously. Geduld's introduction corrects some of the errors found in the book, but one wonders if he would have been more critical of the book had he had access to the information Robinson recounts in his biography.

3. Huff, *Charlie Chaplin*, p. 58; MA, p. 188.

4. *Photoplay* (March 1916), RLC, vol. 110.

5. Sobel and Francis discuss this March 1916 article in *Chaplin: Genesis of a Clown*, pp. 149–50.

6. "Newspapers Aided Chaplin to Fame," *New Orleans Daily States*, 23 July 1916, RLC, vol. 110.

7. *Harper's Weekly* 62 (6 May 1916): 494. Benjamin McArthur (p. 176) called Fiske "a leading box-office attraction from the 1890s to the 1920s."

8. *New Republic* 10 (3 February 1917): 16–18.

9. Wes Gehring, "Chaplin and the Progressive Era: The Neglected Politics of a Clown," *Indiana Social Studies Quarterly* 34 (Autumn 1981): 10–18, at 10, 11, 18. Ivens is quoted by Gehring.

10. Walter Kerr, *The Silent Clowns* (New York: Knopf, 1975), p. 88.

11. See John Cawelti's "typology of literary formulas" in *Adventure, Mystery, and Romance* (Chicago: Univ. of Chicago Press, 1976), ch. 2, and esp. pp. 41–42. Cawelti's concept of "formula" is an extremely rich one and, I would argue, useful in understanding the body of Chaplin's work: in a sense, Chaplin created, then later in his career deviated from, his own unique formula.

12. Quoted in *Moving Picture World* (21 July 1917), RLC, vol. 110.

13. Quoted in Mabel Condon, "In Chaplin's House of Glass," *Picture-Play Magazine* (December 1916), RLC, vol. 110.

14. This move to a tighter narrative structure is consistent with the general trend of Hollywood films through the 1910s. By the end of the 1910s, according to Kristin Thompson (CHC, p. 193), Hollywood narratives "came to place more emphasis upon character, and to construct tightly organized causal chains." These characteristics stemmed partly from the tendency to make longer films, which Chaplin himself began with *A Dog's Life* and continued with *The Kid* (1920).

15. Lewis Jacobs, *Rise of the American Film* (1939; reprinted New York: Teacher's College Press, 1971), pp. 251, 253. Jacobs discusses movies during World War I in considerable detail in chapter 14.

16. The fate of civil liberties during World War I is treated in Harry N.

Scheiber, *The Wilson Administration and Civil Liberties, 1917–1921* (Ithaca: Cornell Univ. Press, 1960) and William Preston, Jr., *Aliens and Dissenters: Federal Suppression of Radicals, 1903–1933* (Cambridge: Harvard University Press, 1963). The Committee on Public Information is treated in James R. Mock and Cedric Larson, *Words That Won the War* (Princeton: Princeton Univ. Press, 1939).

17. Kevin Brownlow, *The War, the West, and the Wilderness* (New York: Knopf, 1979), pp. 38–40.

18. " 'No Chaplin Here,' Say English Signs; Sore at Comedian," *New York Star*, 28 June 1916, RLC, vol. 110.

19. Huff, *Charlie Chaplin*, pp. 74–75; *Variety*, 22 June 1917, p. 20.

20. Huff, *Charlie Chaplin*, p. 75; Brownlow, *War*, p. 40; *Variety*, 22 June 1917, p. 20.

21. Burton Ormesby, "*The Weekly Dispatch* Gets Another Craving to See Chaplin in Khaki," *New York Telegraph*, 22 July 1917, RLC, vol. 110.

22. Beally quoted in *Moving Picture World* (18 May 1918, RLC, vol. 111; Chaplin letter in *Pictures and Picturegoer* (23 February 1918): p. 241.

23. *Washington Post*, 7 April 1918, p. 8.

24. "20,000 Throng Wall Street to Hear Movie Stars Tell How to Win War," *New York Herald Tribune*, 9 April 1918, p. 8; "Stirring Celebrations Help Speed Loan Drive," *NYT*, 9 April 1918, p. 4.

25. "8,000 People Buy Bonds from Charlie Chaplin," *Atlanta Constitution*, 18 April 1918, p. 1.

26. "Chaplin Sells Liberty Bonds; Meeting at Ryman Proves Grand and Glorious Success," *Nashville Banner*, 19 April 1918, p. 7; *Memphis Commercial Appeal*, 21 April 1918, pp. 1, 10.

27. Huff, *Charlie Chaplin*, p. 75.

28. *Moving Picture World* (18 May 1918), RLC, vol. 111.

29. *Memphis Commercial Appeal*, 21 April 1918, p. 10.

30. Corporal J. Stuart Blackton, "Chaplin Holds the Rhine," *Photoplay* (June 1918), RLC, vol. 111.

31. Review of *The Immigrant* in *Photoplay* 12 (September 1917): 99.

32. David Auerbach, "Charlie Chaplin: Of Crime and Genius—A Psycho-Portrait," *Encounter* 60 (May 1983): 86–92.

33. McCabe, *Charlie Chaplin*, p. 35; MA, p. 108.

34. MA, pp. 178, 267. Kelly's brother, Arthur, later became a prominent executive in the foreign offices of United Artists.

35. See Sadoul, *Vie de Charlot*, pp. 229–32 for a chronology of their relationship.

36. Marjorie Daw, "A Little Journey to the Home of Mr. and Mrs. Charles Chaplin," *Detroit Journal*, 31 January 1920, RLC, vol. 111.

37. Huff, *Charlie Chaplin*, p. 78; *NYT*, 3 August 1920, p. 14; *NYT*, 4 August 1920, p. 14.

38. *NYT*, 11 August 1920, p. 8.

39. One of the few critics who likes the film, Gerald Mast, places it in the cat-

egory of Chaplin's ironic comedies, culminating in *Monsieur Verdoux*, in which Chaplin takes "cynical, unpleasant material" and makes it funny. Mast argues that "in the course of the film, Chaplin has booted the rural idyll itself in the pants, particularly in the breach between what it supposedly believes and what it actually does." See Gerald Mast, *The Comic Mind*, 2nd ed. (Chicago: Univ. of Chicago Press, 1979), p. 92.

40. Julian Smith, in *Chaplin* (Boston: Twayne, 1984), p. 46, has perceptively suggested that Purviance's portrayal of the gullible farmer's daughter is a projection of Chaplin's recent bride: both seem to be somewhat foolish and fickle, a far cry from the characters Edna had played in the initial two First Nationals. Just as Mildred was wooed into a contract shortly after her marriage by Louis B. Mayer, Smith points out the farmer's daughter is swept off her feet by a city slicker in town for a day. Robinson (CHLA, pp. 248–50) also suggests that Chaplin's difficulties during the long production of *Sunnyside*, as well as the romantic triangle in the film, seem drawn from Chaplin's unfortunate marriage.

41. "A Letter to a Genius," *Photoplay* 17 (April 1920): 27; *Variety*, 20 June 1919, p. 53; *Variety*, 12 December 1919, p. 45.

42. *Ladies' Home Journal*, August 1918, p. 82.

43. *Photoplay* 14 (September 1918): 81.

44. Ibid., pp. 83, 117.

45. "Appeals to Brows High and Low," *Moving Picture World* (23 March 1918), RLC, vol. 111.

46. *Toledo Times*, 16 May 1918, RLC, vol. 111.

47. "Some First Impressions of Charlie Chaplin," *Pictures and Picturegoer* (11 October 1919): 444, RLC, vol. 111. Emphasis in original.

48. Charles Spencer Chaplin, "What People Laugh At," *American Magazine* 86 (November 1918): 34, 134–37.

49. *Theatre Magazine* 30 (October 1919): 249; the essay is also reprinted in *Focus on Chaplin*, ed. Donald McCaffrey (Englewood Cliffs, N.J.: Prentice-Hall, 1971), pp. 71–73.

50. *Photoplay* 17 (April 1920): 27.

3. FROM *THE KID* TO *THE GOLD RUSH*

1. Chaplin's portrayal of artists in his films is intriguingly varied. An artist saves Charlie and Edna from the waiter in *The Immigrant*, is the rival for Edna's affections in *The Vagabond*, a cad in *The Kid*, and as we shall see later in this chapter, a rather romantic but doomed character in *A Woman of Paris*.

2. A nondiegetic insert is a shot showing an object not part of the space of the narrative, which is cut into the narrative sequence.

3. Chaplin deleted this shot from the rerelease, perhaps because he felt its sentimentality too obvious and forced.

4. See Huff, *Charlie Chaplin*, p. 106; CHLA, p. 265.

5. *Exceptional Photoplays* 3 (January-February 1921): 2, 6–7; reprinted in *American Film Criticism*, ed. Stanley Kauffman (New York: Liveright, 1972), pp. 115–18.

6. *New Republic* 26 (30 March 1921): 136–37; reprinted in Kauffmann, *American Film Criticism*, pp. 118–21.

7. *Variety*, 21 January 1921, p. 40; *NYT*, 22 January 1921, p. 9; *Theatre Magazine* review quoted in *The Films of Charlie Chaplin*, ed. Gerald D. McDonald et al. (New York: Citadel, 1965), p. 167.

8. CHLA, p. 295.

9. As Julian Smith notes, Chaplin explores in *The Idle Class* "more intensely than any other the split between his person and his persona"—in other words, between Chaplin and Charlie (*Chaplin*, p. 56). From Smith's perspective in the 1980s, Chaplin increasingly began to invest his own psyche in more than one character after 1920, sometimes by playing two roles, as in *The Great Dictator*, and sometimes by expressing two sides of his complex personality through two different characters. See Chapter 11.

10. Robinson (CHLA, p. 296) notes that this is the first Chaplin film for which much written script and gag material has survived in Chaplin's records. Because the production itself was stopped for work on the story much less often than in previous films, Robinson suggests "that Chaplin was moving away from his earlier method of creating and improvising on the set and even on film, towards a greater degree of advance planning on paper." Though he would still have some huge production problems, particularly on *City Lights*, Chaplin seems somewhat belatedly to have begun moving toward the production practices that had been common in Hollywood for nearly a decade.

11. See Anthony Channell Hilfer, *The Revolt against the Village, 1915–1930* (Chapel Hill: Univ. of North Carolina Press, 1969).

12. Benjamin De Casseres, "The Hamlet-Like Nature of Charlie Chaplin," *NYT*, 12 December 1920, sec. 3, p. 5.

13. See Sobel and Francis, *Chaplin: Genesis of a Clown*, p. 79. Robinson (CHLA, pp. 131–33) transcribes a 1914 letter from Chaplin to his brother Sidney which, besides providing a fascinating picture of Chaplin's state of mind at Keystone, shows that Chaplin was not a highly educated man.

14. Charles Chaplin, *My Trip Abroad* (New York: Harper, 1922).

15. See R. K. Murray, *The Red Scare* (Minneapolis: Univ. of Minnesota Press, 1955), and Louis F. Post, *The Deportations Delirium of Nineteen-Twenty* (1923; reprinted New York: DaCapo, 1970). Post was the assistant secretary of labor who halted the wholesale deportations.

16. *Literary Digest* 72 (28 January 1922): 48; *Collier's*, 11 November 1922; reprinted in Gehring, *Charlie Chaplin*, pp. 108–14.

17. The context for the founding of United Artists is well described in Tino Balio, *United Artists* (Madison: Univ. of Wisconson Press, 1976), ch. 1. My discussion here is indebted to Balio's work.

18. A. H. Giebler, *Moving Picture World* (1 February 1919): 619. Quoted in Balio, *United Artists*, p. 3.

19. Balio, *United Artists*, p. 12; MA, pp. 221–23.

20. Balio, *United Artists*, pp. 12–13, takes this account from Giebler's article (cited in note 18).

21. Balio, *United Artists*, p. 24.

22. See CHC, esp. chs. 12–13, and George Mitchell, "The Consolidation of the American Film Industry," *Cine-Tracts*, nos. 2 (1976): 28–36, and 3/4 (1976): 63–70.

23. *NYT*, 23 February 1923, p. 16.

24. De Casseres, "The Hamlet-Like Nature of Charlie Chaplin," sec. 3, p. 5.

25. Interesting background and production information on *A Woman of Paris* can be found in Adolphe Menjou and M. M. Musselman, *It Took Nine Tailors* (New York: McGraw-Hill, 1948), ch. 14, esp. pp. 104–6.

26. "What Chaplin Thinks," *NYT*, 7 October 1923, sec. 9, p. 4.

27. Menjou and Musselman, *It Took Nine Tailors*, p. 118.

28. By mise-en-scène, I mean those elements of film style that film shares with the theater: sets and props, costumes, lighting, and acting styles. See Bordwell and Thompson, *Film Art*, 2nd ed. (New York: Random House, 1986), ch. 5.

29. There is even an oblique reference to Chaplin's childhood in *A Woman of Paris*. Marie cares for orphans at the end of the film, much as Charlie cared for the boy in *The Kid* and as Chaplin himself may have wished for when he and Sydney were in the Lambeth workhouse.

30. The following is indebted to Smith, *Chaplin*, particularly pp. 63–65.

31. *NYT*, 2 October 1923, p. 7.

32. *NYT*, 7 October 1923, sec. 9, p. 4.

33. *New York Herald Tribune*, 3 October 1923, p. 12.

34. Quoted in *Selected Film Criticism, 1921–30*, ed. Anthony Slide (Metuchen, N.J.: Scarecrow Press, 1982), p. 320.

35. *Photoplay* 25 (December 1923): 73; reprinted in Slide, *Selected Film Criticism, 1921–30*, p. 318.

36. "The Death of Zeus," *New Republic* 36 (7 November 1923): 283.

37. *Variety*, 27 September 1923, p. 25. The *Variety* reviewer's comment about the bigger houses points out that American movie audiences were not identical throughout the country. In general, the taste of viewers who attended first-run showings in the major cities was more sophisticated and less moralistic than viewers in small-town America. As we shall see in subsequent chapters, Chaplin's star image often became a subject of considerable controversy in the press, partly because of these different orientations of American viewers and writers.

38. Balio, *United Artists*, p. 45. Though this was a considerable box-office return for an average picture, one can get an idea of how disappointing it was for a Chaplin film by noting that the gross for Fairbanks's *Robin Hood* was $1.4 million the same year and for *The Gold Rush*, Chaplin's next film, $2.07 million in its first year. See United Artists Balance Sheets and Work Papers, box 1, folders 5 (1923) and 7 (1925), United Artists Collection, the Wisconsin Center for Film and Theater Research in the Wisconsin State Historical Library, Madison (hereafter cited as UAC).

39. *NYT*, 7 October 1923, sec. 9, p. 4.

40. *NYT*, 16 October 1923, p. 23.

41. Pressbooks on Chaplin's United Artists films are available in two places: the UAC, and, from *The Circus* (1928) on, the Billy Rose Collection (hereafter BRC) at the New York Public Library, Lincoln Center Branch. *The Gold Rush* pressbook is found in UAC, UA pressbook 448, reel 13.

42. C. F. McGlashlin, *History of the Donner Party* (San Francisco: A. Carlisle, 1922), p. vi. Chaplin also discussed the genesis of the film in his autobiography, pp. 304–5, though he exaggerated how many survived. See also Timothy Lyons, "The Idea in *The Gold Rush*: A Study of Chaplin's Use of the Comic Technique of Pathos-Humor," in McCaffrey, *Focus on Chaplin*, pp. 113–23.

43. Lita Grey Chaplin, with Morton Cooper, *My Life with Chaplin: An Intimate Memoir* (New York: Grove, 1966), ch. 5, discusses the shooting at Truckee, much of which was discarded after Grey was replaced as Georgia.

44. Apparently Chaplin had this scene in mind early in the conception of the film, for Lita Grey, Chaplin's second wife and the person originally cast to play Georgia, tells how proudly Chaplin showed her this particular set when he was first considering her for the role. See Grey, *My Life with Chaplin*, pp. 53–54.

45. Joan Mellen, *Big Bad Wolves: Masculinity in American Film* (New York: Pantheon, 1977).

46. See Morin, *Stars* (New York: Grove, 1960), pp. 111–12.

47. One could argue that presenting the wealthy Charlie as unhappy is another manifestation of what Robin Wood has called "the Rosebud syndrome," the ultimately conservative notion that because the rich are necessarily unhappy, we should all be satisfied being poor or of moderate means. Unlike Charles Foster Kane, though, Charlie, deprived of love for much of the film, is also unfulfilled when he is poor. Also, unlike Kane, he apparently achieves both wealth and happiness in the film's ending.

48. UA pressbook 448, reel 13, UAC.

49. Chaplin cut the ending short in his 1942 rerelease of *The Gold Rush*. In it—the version most readily available today—the final shot of the film is of Charlie and Georgia walking arm in arm up a stairway, away from the camera, a more purely "happy ending." Dennis DiNitto and William Herman have discussed the original ending in *Film and the Critical Eye* (New York: Macmillan, 1975), p. 101. One might add that this self-referentiality in Chaplin's films was more evident to reviewers in *The Circus* and *Modern Times* than in *The Gold Rush*. And it was not widely commented upon until, in our postmodern era, self-referentiality in art became widely practiced by artists and widely praised by critics. See Garret Stewart, "Modern Hard Times: Chaplin and the Cinema of Self-Reflexiveness," *Critical Inquiry* 3 (1976): 295–315.

50. A discussion of the place of advertising in the film industry is found in CHC, pp. 97–102.

51. A copy of the program is available in the RLC. This account of the promotion of *The Gold Rush* comes from this program and the pressbook of the film (UA pressbook 448, UAC).

52. *Variety*, 1 July 1925, p. 32.

53. *Variety*, 19 August 1925, p. 36.

54. *Photoplay* 28 (September 1925): 50.

55. "Here and There with Chaplin," *NYT*, 11 November 1925, sec. 7, p. 3.

56. Although this study is concentrating on Chaplin and the United States, it is worth noting that the first book-length study of Chaplin, *Charlot*, by poet, journalist, and *cinéaste* Louis Delluc, was published in France in 1921. (An English edition was published in 1922.) Delluc had been a co-founder of the world's first film society in 1920. An opening challenge in the preface of his book likely encouraged young American intellectuals who read the book to take Chaplin's work seriously: "To the creative artist of the cinema, the mask of Charlie Chaplin has just the same importance as the traditional mask of Beethoven has to the musical composer."

57. Max Eastman, *Great Companions* (New York: Farrar, Straus, and Cudahy, 1959), p. 209.

58. Edmund Wilson, *The Twenties* (New York: Farrar, Straus, and Giroux, 1975), p. 158. Chaplin posed for a photograph with the *Vanity Fair* group, sans Wilson, which is reproduced in MA, p. 247. Gorham Munson, in *The Awakening Twenties* (Baton Rouge: Louisiana State Univ. Press, 1985), ch. 13, writes that the evening Chaplin spent with Crane and Frank was in October 1923, when Chaplin was in New York to promote *A Woman of Paris*. Munson recalls missing the meeting because he was already in bed in his Greenwich Village apartment when the three came by and rang the doorbell, and he also quotes from several of Crane's letters from that period discussing the meeting. From his more detailed account, it seems clear that this is another instance of inaccuracy in Chaplin's autobiography, even though Frank and Chaplin may also have met in 1920. Munson, does, however, agree with the point being made here when he recalls "Chaplin's sympathetic interest in the intelligentsia who were speaking out against reaction in the early postwar years" and when he recounts that Chaplin contributed in 1919 to the founding of a little magazine called *The Modernist* that Munson was working on (p. 233).

59. Among others, Eastman later wrote extensively on Chaplin in *Love and Revolution* (New York: Random House, 1964), *Heroes I Have Known* (New York: Simon and Schuster, 1942), and *Great Companions*.

60. See Chaplin, *My Trip Abroad*, chs. 2, 15.

61. Both comments are taken from "Hollywood and Chaplin," in *Memoirs of Waldo Frank*, ed. Alan Trachtenberg (Amherst: Univ. of Massachusetts Press, 1973), pp. 147–54.

62. Frank, *Memoirs*, p. 154.

63. *New Yorker* 1 (23 May 1925): 9–10; the essay was reprinted in *Time Exposures* (New York: Boni and Liveright, 1926), pp. 87–92.

64. *New Republic* 31 (23 August 1922): 358–59. The ensuing quotations are from this article.

65. Letter to Julian Huxley, 2 December 1923, in *Stark Young, A Life in the Arts: Letters, 1900–1962*, ed. John Pilkington (Baton Rouge: Louisiana State

Univ. Press, 1975). Young was alluding in the letter to Eleonora Duse, the noted Italian dramatic actress who used an extremely naturalistic acting style.

66. Gilbert Seldes, *The Seven Lively Arts* (New York: Harper's, 1924).

67. Wilson, *The Twenties* p. 157.

68. Letter to Alyse Gregory, 17 April 1924, in Edmund Wilson, *Letters on Literature and Politics, 1912–1972*, ed. Elena Wilson (New York: Farrar, Straus, and Giroux, 1977), p. 114; review of *The Seven Lively Arts* (1924), collected in Edmund Wilson, *The Shores of Light* (New York: Farrar, Straus, and Young, 1952), p. 156. The review originally appeared in the *Dial*, where Seldes had served for a time as editor.

69. Wilson, *Shores of Light*, pp. 158–59.

70. The review appeared in the 2 September 1925 issue and is conveniently reprinted in Kauffmann, *American Film Criticism*, pp. 162–65.

71. Balio, *United Artists*, p. 57.

72. Both this review and the other, "Sex Appeal in the Movies," are reprinted in *The Collected Essays of John Peale Bishop*, ed. Edmund Wilson (New York: Scribner's, 1948), pp. 210–21.

73. This attitude, and the resulting desire of American studio heads to hire "artistic" directors from Europe to enhance the prestige of their films, is discussed by Allen and Gomery in *Film History: Theory and Practice* (New York: Knopf, 1985), pp. 91–105.

4. STRUGGLING THROUGH THE TWENTIES

1. Chaplin, *My Life in Pictures*, p. 228.

2. A close analysis of Chaplin's relationships with, attitudes toward, and cinematic portrayals of women would make a fascinating study. Anyone interested in his relationships with women in the early 1920s would want to look at Anita Leslie's biography, *Claire Sheridan* (New York: Doubleday, 1977); Pola Negri's autobiography, *Memoirs of a Star* (New York: Doubleday, 1970); Max Eastman's treatment of Chaplin's affair with Eastman's lover, Florence Deshon, in *Love and Revolution*, pp. 184–211 passim; and, most important, Lita Grey Chaplin's *My Life with Chaplin*.

3. Grey, *My Life with Chaplin*, p. 186. Huff, *Charlie Chaplin*, p. 166, and a number of other lesser biographers accept the altered date. Charles Chaplin, Jr.'s insightful *My Father, Charlie Chaplin* (New York: Popular Library, 1961), seems implicitly to substantiate his mother's story, for instead of writing, "I was born on June 28, 1926," he writes, "June 28, 1926, my birth certificate reads" (p. 9).

4. *NYT*, 2 December 1926, p. 1; 3 December 1926, p. 1.

5. Grey, *My Life with Chaplin*, pp. 252–55, discusses the complaint and quotes a number of the most juicy passages from it. The entire complaint and Chaplin's cross-complaint, along with a number of court orders and commentary by an old Chaplin nemesis, Ed Sullivan, were published as *Chaplin vs. Chaplin*, ed. Ed Sullivan (Los Angeles: Marvin Miller Enterprises, 1965).

6. The story of the legal tussle between Chaplin and Tully is summarized in

NYT (all 1927), 8 January, p. 19; 9 January, p. 8; 14 January, p. 15; and 3 February, p. 25. The articles themselves appeared in four installments in the January-April issues of *Pictorial Review*.

7. *NYT*, 18 January 1927, p. 1; 20 January 1927, p. 1; 23 January 1927, p. 1; 28 January 1927, p. 7; 10 February 1928, p. 26.

8. *NYT*, 16 January 1927, p. 5.

9. *NYT*, 23 August 1927, pp. 1, 8.

10. *Chicago Tribune*, 11 January 1927, pp. 1, 14.

11. Quoted in Grey, *My Life with Chaplin*, p. 260.

12. *NYT*, 12 January 1927, p. 1; *NYT*, 13 January 1927, p. 27; *Boston Advertiser*, 14 January 1927, RLC, vol. 111. The UAC contains a letter from Chaplin to the United Artists Legal Department telling them not to sue the city of Lynn in an attempt to lift the ban. He did not want more publicity at that point.

13. Grey, *My Life with Chaplin*, p. 260.

14. *NYT*, 15 January 1927, p. 1; *NYT*, 26 January 1927, p. 9; *New York Herald Tribune*, 30 January 1927; *NYT*, 11 February 1927, p. 2; *NYT*, 14 February 1927, p. 15. The Cooper quotation is taken from Sumner Smith, "The Spotlight Turns Yellow," *Moving Picture World* (22 January 1927): 252.

15. Hays was president of the Motion Pictures Producers and Distributors of America The "Hays Office" was the industry's self-censorhip body. *New York Morning Telegraph*, 15 January 1927, p. 4; "The Level Head of Will Hays," *New York Morning Telegraph*, RLC, vol. 111. The *Telegraph* seemed to be a strong defender of Chaplin; its film columnist, Herb Cruikshank, in "The Screen in Review" on January 15, offered Chaplin first-page space to give his version of the story. Cruikshank's open letter says, "The dignity of your silence has been impressive."

16. "Something More about the Much-Discussed Chaplin," *New York Herald Tribune*, 23 January 1927, sec. 6, p. 3; "A Sage Once Said, 'It Takes All Kinds to Make a World,'" *New York Herald Tribune*, 30 January 1927, sec. 6, p. 3.

17. "The Spotlight Turns Yellow," p. 252.

18. Quoted in Huff, *Charlie Chaplin*, p. 169.

19. *New Yorker* 3 (23 January 1927): 17–18.

20. *Boston Evening Transcript*, 9 April 1927, p. 3.

21. Dyer, *Stars*, pp. 52–53. Emphasis in original.

22. *NYT*, 29 November 1925, sec. 7, p. 5.

23. Quoted in *Literary Digest* 96 (24 March 1928): 41.

24. *New Republic* 38 (8 February 1928); reprinted in Kauffmann, *American Film Criticism*, pp. 201–4.

25. Kerr, *Silent Clowns*, pp. 339–43, argues in considerable detail that *The Circus* is "a comedy about the consciousness of being funny." See Smith, *Chaplin*, pp. 79–84, both on that notion and on more autobiographical issues, to which my discussion is indebted. Though both give fruitful readings of the film, I believe both undervalue it.

26. Tully, *Pictorial Review*, January 1927, p. 8.

27. Grey, *My Life with Chaplin*, p. 323.

28. Tully, *Pictorial Review*, January 1927, p. 8.

29. See Smith, *Chaplin*, pp. 82–83.

30. Tully, *Pictorial Review*, February 1928, p. 75.

31. "Bonnie Prince Charlie of the Custard Pies," *Literary Digest* 96 (24 March 1928): 36.

32. "Bonnie Prince Charlie," p. 42.

33. Bakshy's review, which appeared in the *Nation* on 29 February 1928, and Young's, which appeared in the *New Republic* on 8 February 1928, both are reprinted in Kauffmann, *American Film Criticism*, pp. 200–204.

34. O'Brien file, box 209, files 1–2, UAC. Since both films were through their initial release by this time, these figures provide a relatively accurate comparison.

35. The film industry's transformation to sound is treated in Harry Geduld, *The Birth of the Talkies* (Bloomington: Indiana Univ. Press, 1975); Douglas Gomery, "The Coming of Sound to the American Cinema: A History of the Transformation of an Industry" (Ph.D. diss. Univ. of Wisconsin, 1975); Alexander Walker, *The Shattered Silents* (New York: Morrow, 1979); and CHC, ch. 23. Balio, *United Artists*, ch. 4, treats the response of United Artists to the challenge and threat of sound films.

36. *NYT*, 14 July 1929, sec. 9, p. 4.

37. "Movie Stars Give Big Radio Program," *NYT*, 19 March 1928, p. 23.

38. *Variety*, 4 April 1928, p. 9.

39. Ibid., p. 2.

40. *NYT*, 25 November 1928, sec. 11, p. 22.

41. *NYT*, 10 February 1928, p. 26.

42. Chaplin, Jr., *My Father, Charlie Chaplin*, p. 36.

43. Gladys Hall, "Charlie Chaplin Attacks the Talkies," *Motion Picture* 37 (May 1929): 29. Three months later, the August issue of *Motion Picture* carried Al Jolson's response to Chaplin's defense of silent films. Jolson, noting that Chaplin was energetically talkative at parties they had both attended, challenged that "if Charlie wants to keep what he calls 'the great beauty of silence,' let him go lock himself in a room—become a nun's brother, or something. . . . Charlie goes on record as loathing talkies. . . . I think he'd better get to like 'em—or he'll find out the public don't like him."

44. *NYT*, 14 July 1929, sec. 9, p. 4. As *City Lights* was about to open, Chaplin again articulated his reasons for spurning dialogue in an article, "Pantomime and Comedy," *NYT*, 25 January 1931, sec. 8, p. 8.

45. A sampling of the negative response to talking pictures in 1928–1929 can be found in Geduld, *Birth of the Talkies*, app. A. See, for example, comments by George Bernard Shaw, Luigi Pirandello, Thomas Edison, and Aldous Huxley.

46. On the interplay of convention and invention in narrative formulas, see Thomas Schatz, *Hollywood Genres* (New York: Random House, 1981), esp. chs. 1–2, and Cawelti, *Adventure, Mystery, and Romance*. See also Stephen Neale,

Genre (London: British Film Institute, 1980), esp. ch. 3. His term "regularized variety" capsulizes well this dimension of genre films (p. 48).

47. This information is related in the third part of Brownlow's fascinating documentary film, *The Unknown Chaplin*. See also Gerard Molyneaux's production history of the film in *Charles Chaplin's "City Lights"* (New York: Garland, 1983), ch. 1, and CHLA, ch. 12.

48. This information on the pressbook of *City Lights* is taken from the UA pressbooks, microfilm no. 448, reel 13, UAC.

49. See Smith, *Chaplin*, pp. 93–94, on submerged autobiography in *City Lights*.

50. For a similar but more fully developed analysis on this theme, see Molyneaux, *Charles Chaplin's "City Lights,"* pp. 210 ff.

51. Looked at more pragmatically, Chaplin's decision not to root the film too securely in time and place also made the film more appealing to a wider audience, both in the United States and abroad. This lack of specificity thus served much the same purpose for Chaplin as avoiding dialogue.

52. Molyneaux provides a helpful breakdown of scenes in an appendix to *Charles Chaplin's "City Lights,"* pp. 242–48.

53. Molyneaux, *Charles Chaplin's "City Lights,"* p. 221.

54. The running times for *City Lights* are listed, among other places, in an ad in the *New York Herald Tribune*, 7 February 1931, p. 8. Balio, *United Artists*, pp. 91, lists the total grosses of the Cohan run, where he also notes that *City Lights* eventually earned Chaplin over $5 million worldwide; Balance Sheets and Associated Records, 1931 volume, UAC.

55. *NYT*, 7 February 1931, p. 11.

56. *New York Herald Tribune*, 7 February 1931, p. 8.

57. *New Republic* 66 (25 February 1931): 46–47.

58. *Variety*, 11 February 1931, p. 14.

59. *Nation* (4 March 1931): 250–51. Two other somewhat guarded reviews, one by Rob Wagner, a former Chaplin associate, the other in *Life*, are reprinted in *Selected Film Criticism, 1931–40*, ed. Anthony Slide (Metuchen, N.J.: Scarecrow, 1982), pp. 48–51. The *Life* review suggested that moralist critics of Chaplin's "vulgarity" had not disappeared: it thought "the scene in which Charley acts effeminate while a pugilist is undressing" was in "bad taste and entirely out of step with the picture" (p. 51).

5. THE DEPRESSION, THE WORLD TOUR, AND *MODERN TIMES*

1. Andrew Sarris, "Charles Spencer Chaplin," in *Cinema: A Critical Dictionary*, ed. Richard Roud (London: Secker & Warburg, 1980), 1: 208, 203.

2. A relatively detailed chronology of the trip is provided in Sadoul, *Vie de Charlot*, pp. 243–44.

3. Though first announced in the London press, the *NYT* reported it on 5 May 1931, p. 2.

4. Chaplin's quotation, the cartoon, and the comments of several American

editors, are included in "John Bull Hit by a Chaplin Pie," *Literary Digest* 109 (23 May 1931), p. 10.

5. Ibid.

6. According to Robinson (CHLA, p. 453), Chaplin wrote the memoir himself between June 1932 and February 1933. It was published in five monthly installments between September 1933 and January 1934 in *Woman's Home Companion*, vol. 61. Subsequent references to these articles will include only the month and page number of the citation.

7. January, p. 86; September, p. 87.

8. September, p. 88.

9. October, pp. 15, 17; December, p. 22. It is entirely likely that Chaplin's conversation with Gandhi had some effect on his imagination as he contemplated his next film, which is much less optimistic about machines.

10. See Richard Pells, *Radical Visions and American Dreams* (New York: Harper, 1973), p. 334.

The term "progressive" will be used regularly to describe Chaplin's political views in this and succeeding chapters. As Raymond Williams has noted in *Keywords* (London: Fontana, 1976), pp. 205–7, "progressive" emerged in the nineteenth century as a term of political position, the antonym of "conservative." Williams points out that today the term has a built-in complexity, for it is used two ways: (1) by the left to describe its position (as in "progressive-minded person") and (2) by leftists and others to distinguish advocates of moderate and orderly change from advocates of more radical and sudden change. In this second sense of the word, even a conservative could call him or herself a progressive—an advocate of gradual social evolution.

Chaplin used the term "progressive" to describe himself at times; when he did, he generally used it in two ways: to mean the opposite of conservative or to describe himself as a leftist (as we shall see, in 1947 and 1948 he also at times aligned himself with Henry Wallace's Progressive party, a more specific usage). When I use the term in this book, it will refer to a political position that is consistent with both of these implications, but it will also refer to something more specific and historically rooted. When the term became used more frequently in the United States in the second half of the 1930s, it was associated with three political issues, in descending order of importance: (1) antifascism; (2) a belief in domestic reform that benefited the "common people" or the "working class"; and (3) a sympathy for the Soviet Union. In this study, "progressive" will be used in this sense, except when it obviously refers to Wallace's party, the Progressive Citizens of America.

11. November, p. 100; January, pp. 21, 86.

12. September, p. 10. This position reiterates the one he had expressed to Flora Merrill in a February 1931 interview that appeared in the *New Work World*, which he gave the month *City Lights* opened and just before he began the world tour: "I am always suspicious of a picture with a message. Don't say that I'm a propagandist" (quoted in CHLA, p. 458).

13. September, p. 8; October, p. 104; January, p. 86.

14. P. W. Wilson, "Ten Men Who Stand as Symbols," *NYT*, 10 January 1932, sec. 5, p. 10.

15. These details, and others, come from "Sealing Wax, Cabbages, and Kings," *NYT*, 30 September 1934, sec. 9, p. 5.

16. The standard one-volume social and political history of the Roosevelt era is William E. Leuchtenburg, *Franklin D. Roosevelt and the New Deal* (New York: Harper, 1963). The economic statistics are taken from this work, pp. 1–2. Leuchtenberg's history contains a good bibliography for works published up to 1963; a more updated bibliography appears in Pells, *Radical Visions*. See also Arthur M. Schlesinger's pro–New Deal, three-volume history of the thirties, *The Age of Roosevelt* (Boston: Houghton Mifflin, 1957–60).

17. Leuchtenberg, *Franklin D. Roosevelt*, pp. 7–17 passim.

18. Ibid., chs. 3–4.

19. In *The American Film Industry* (Madison: Univ. of Wisconsin Press, 1976), editor Tino Balio briefly sketches the effects of the depression on the movie industry. See also Douglas Gomery's essay on how the NRA benefited the movie producers: "Hollywood, the National Recovery Administration, and the Question of Monopoly Power," *Journal of the University Film Association* 31, no. 2 (Spring 1979): 47–52.

20. The producers' salary reduction plan, and the political atmosphere in Hollywood generally during the classic sound era, is treated in Larry Ceplair and Steven Englund, *The Inquisition in Hollywood: Politics and the Film Community, 1930–1960* (New York: Doubleday, 1980), pp. 19–20. Nancy Lynn Schwartz, *The Hollywood Writers' Wars* (New York: Knopf, 1982), pp. 9–12, also treats the salary cuts as a crucial incident leading to a unionization move in Hollywood.

21. 23 October 1934, quoted in Leon Harris, *Upton Sinclair: American Rebel* (New York: Crowell, 1975), p. 305.

22. Harris, *Upton Sinclair*, p. 172; Upton Sinclair, *The Autobiography of Upton Sinclair* (New York: Harcourt, 1962), p. 273; Ceplair and Englund, *Inquisition Hollywood*, pp. 92–93.

23. Malcolm Cowley, *Exile's Return* (New York: Viking Press, 1951), pp. 113–31; see also Alexander, *Here the Country Lies*, p. 154.

24. *New Republic* 64 (22 October 1930): 267; for a broader treatment of the Gold-Wilder controversy and the responses it generated, see Daniel Aaron, *Writers on the Left* (New York: Harcourt, 1960), pp. 237–243.

25. Myron Lounsbury, *The Origins of American Film Criticism* (New York: Arno, 1973), chs. 4, 5, and pp. 484–86. Lounsbury ends his useful survey of American film criticism with a reading of Lewis Jacobs's *Rise of the American Film*, but it seems clear that the social film criticism of Bosley Crowther, influential *NYT* film critic from 1940 to 1967, is closely aligned with the "modern liberal" approach and more loosely related to the "social radical" position.

26. Harry Alan Potamkin, Introduction, *The Compound Cinema: The Film Writings of Harry Alan Potamkin*, ed. and intro. Lewis Jacobs (New York: Columbia Univ. Press, 1977), p. xxxi.

27. Potamkin, "Motion Picture Criticism," in *Compound Cinema*, p. 49 (originally in *The New Freeman*, 4 March 1931); "Film Cults," in *Compound Cinema*, p. 228 (originally in *Modern Thinker and Author's Review*, November 1932).

28. Lorenzo Turrent Rozas, "Charlie Chaplin's Decline," *Living Age*, no. 396 (June 1934): 319–23.

29. The importance of commitment in the 1930s has been discussed in a number of works, among them Warren Susman's "The Culture of the Thirties" (1970) and "Culture and Commitment" (1973), collected in *Culture as History* (New York: Pantheon, 1984), pp. 150–210; Pells, *Radical Visions*, ch. 4, esp. 158–69; and Charles Maland, *American Visions: The Films of Chaplin, Ford, Capra, and Welles, 1936–1941* (New York: Arno, 1977), pp. 5–9.

30. *NYT*, 30 August 1921, p. 10.

31. John Diggins, *The American Left in the Twentieth Century* (New York: Harcourt, 1973), p. 17 and passim; Eastman, *Great Companions*, p. 215; MA, pp. 242–43; Frank Harris, *Contemporary Portraits*, 4th series (New York: Brentano's, 1923), pp. 56–76.

32. *NYT*, 14 June 1932, p. 26.

33. *Women's Home Companion*, December 1933, p. 23; *NYT*, 28 June 1932, p. 26; Leuchtenberg, *Franklin D. Roosevelt*, pp. 50–51. On the international fate of the gold standard during the early years of the depression, see Gustav Cassel, *The Downfall of the Gold Standard* (New York: Oxford Univ. Press, 1936).

34. Alistair Cooke, *Six Men* (New York: Knopf, 1977), pp. 25, 27; CHLA, p. 458; *New York Herald Tribune*, 22 November 1934, p. 14.

35. *New York American*, 29 January 1937, RLC, vol. 110. Paulette Goddard, Chaplin's third wife and female lead in *Modern Times* and *The Great Dictator*, shared Chaplin's enthusiasm for the New Deal. She told a *NYT* reporter (18 October 1936) that she believed in the New Deal but that many Hollywood figures were "falling easy victims to fascism," which was "fast outdistancing communism in the film colony."

36. *NYT*, 17 March 1935, sec. 8, p. 4; the article was also discussed in the *Motion Picture Herald*, 23 March 1935, p. 49.

37. *NYT*, 29 August 1933, p. 20; *NYT*, 20 September 1933, p. 16; Chaplin, Jr., *My Father, Charlie Chaplin*, p. 81. Though Chaplin consistently told the press that Charlie would not talk in the new film, Robinson notes (CHLA, p. 466) that Chaplin and Paulette Goddard did do some sound tests in late November 1934, more than two months after shooting had begun.

38. Robert Allen and Douglas Gomery discuss the useful concept of the prevailing critical or aesthetic discourse and apply it to Murnau's *Sunrise* in *Film History: Theory and Practice*, pp. 89–108. Jauss discusses the "horizon of expectations" in "Literary History," in Jauss, *Toward an Aesthetic of Reception*, esp. pp. 25–28.

39. *NYT*, 30 August 1934, sec. 9, p. 3; *New York Herald Tribune*, 22 November 1934, p. 14; *NYT*, 17 March 1935, sec. 8, p. 4.

40. "Mr. Shumiatsky on American Films," *NYT*, 4 August 1935.

41. Boris Shumiatsky, "Charlie Chaplin's New Picture," trans. Leon Dennen,

New Masses (24 September 1935): 29–30; *NYT*, 17 November 1935; the *Daily Worker* articles are quoted in Terry Ramsaye, "Chaplin Ridicules Reds' Claim Film Aids 'Cause,' " *Motion Picture Herald*, 7 December 1935, p. 1.

42. Ramsaye, "Chaplin Ridicules," pp. 1, 2. One might augment Reeves's final comment by noting that people who worked with Chaplin often recalled that he would never immediately accept a suggestion from someone else, though he often would use such an idea later, claiming it as his own.

43. *Modern Times*, microfilm pressbooks, BRC. The New York promotion campaign, engineered by Monroe Greenthal of United Artists, followed many of the suggestions in the pressbook and was successful enough to earn praise in *Box-Office* 28 (15 February 1936): 7. According to the article, among Greenthal's other contributions were a display window in Macy's of the "original Chaplin hat, shoes, and cane" and a neon sign reading "CHARLIE CHAPLIN" on the theater marquee instead of "ROXY."

44. A good example of intellectual montage in Eisenstein's work are the cross-cuts between the massacre of the workers with the slaughter of an ox at the end of *Strike!*: the workers are being treated like animals. Chaplin undoubtedly was aware of developments in Russian cinema in the 1920s. Eisenstein frequently visited Chaplin's home in the summer and fall of 1930 when he was in Hollywood, for a time under contract with Paramount, and for a time seeking financing for a film to be made in Mexico. Eisenstein first gained entry into Chaplin's company thanks to letters that his companion, Ivor Montagu, had obtained from H. G. Wells and Shaw. In his autobiography, Eisenstein recalled Chaplin's first words of greeting when they met by Chaplin's tennis court: "Just saw *Potemkin* again. You know, in five years it hasn't aged a bit; still the same." See Sergei Eisenstein, *Immoral Memories*, trans. Herbert Marshall (Boston: Houghton-Mifflin, 1983), p. 81. Another account of the Eisenstein–Chaplin friendship, including some pictures, is provided in Montague's *With Eisenstein in Hollywood* (New York: International Publishers, 1969).

45. The facts that the owner's voice is heard only via a loudspeaker and that the sales pitch for the Bellows Feeding Machine (designed for "keeping ahead of the competition") is on a phonograph record are also significant. One important dimension of *Modern Times* not stressed here is Chaplin's implicit critique of the tyranny of sound in motion-picture art. Just as the owner's words tyrannize the workers, the technology of sound reproduction tyrannizes the makers of films. But Chaplin has the last word (no pun intended): Charlie's gibberish song and pantomime at the end of *Modern Times* communicates far more effectively and pleasingly than all the other words in the film. On Chaplin's self-reflexiveness in *Modern Times*, see Stewart's excellent essay, "Modern Hard Times."

46. *New Masses*, 18 February 1936, reprinted in Kauffmann, *American Film Criticism*, pp. 329–31. Crichton was the pen name Robert Forsythe used when writing for *New Masses*; under his own name he was an editor for *Scribner's* and *Collier's*.

47. Charmion von Wiegand, "Little Man, What Now?" *New Theater* 3 (March 1936): 36.

48. All these reviews are included in the Chaplin clippings file, BRC: *Daily News*, 6 February 1936; *Herald Tribune*, 16 February 1936; *Variety*, 12 February 1936.

49. Von Wiegand, "Little Man," pp. 6–8, 35–37; Edward Newhouse, "Charlie's Critics," *Partisan Review* 3 (April 1936): 26.

50. *New Republic* 85 (19 February 1936); reprinted in Kauffmann, *American Film Criticism*, pp. 331–34.

6. THE POPULAR FRONT, *THE GREAT DICTATOR*, AND THE SECOND FRONT

1. The Gallup Poll results were published in *Public Opinion Quarterly* 4 (1940): 102; Pells, *Radical Vision*, p. 293. American response to the international situation is treated in Leuchtenberg, *Franklin D. Roosevelt*, Chs. 9, 12, 13.

2. Daniel Bell, *Marxian Socialism in the United States*, rev. ed. (Princeton: Princeton Univ. Press, 1967), pp. 135–36; Irving Howe and Lewis Coser, *The American Communist Party* (Boston: Beacon, 1957), p. 341, and more generally, 319–55.

3. See, for example, the contrasting attitudes toward Roosevelt expressed in Joseph Freeman, "The Middle Class and the Election," *New Masses* 20 (11 August 1936): 28, and A. B. Magill, "Still Time to Unite," *New Masses* 27 (10 May 1938): 5–6. See also Pells, *Radical Vision*, ch. 7.

4. On the cosmopolitanism of Hollywood, see John Baxter, *The Hollywood Exiles* (London, 1976) and the more rigorous and specific book by John Russell Taylor, *Strangers in Paradise: The Hollywood Emigrés, 1933–50* (London: Faber & Faber, 1983). Ceplair and Englund, *Inquisition in Hollywood*, esp. pp. 94–104, also discuss Hollywood's internationalism and its effect on the politics of the Popular Front.

5. Ceplair and Englund, *Inquisition in Hollywood*, pp. 107–8.

6. Ibid., pp. 117–24.

7. See Leo Rosten, *Hollywood* (New York: Harcourt, 1941), pp. 139–44; Ceplair and Englund, *Inquisition in Hollywood*, pp. 139–99 passim; Pells, *Radical Vision*, pp. 347–51.

8. See Robert Endicott Osgood, *Ideals and Self-Interest in American Foreign Relations* (Chicago: Univ. of Chicago Press, 1963, 1953), pp. 407–10.

9. Philip Dunne, the son of the famous humorist and a screenwriter active in liberal politics from the 1930s on, recalls first meeting Chaplin at an Anti-Nazi League meeting and also later encountering him at a meeting of the Committee to Defend America by Aiding the Allies. See Philip Dunne, *Take Two* (New York: McGraw-Hill, 1980), pp. 139–40.

10. *NYT*, 16 February 1936, sec. 9, p. 1.

11. *NYT*, 15 September 1937, p. 27; 19 September 1937, sec. 11, p. 5; 20 September 1937, p. 22.

12. Montagu, who spent considerable time with Chaplin in 1930 when he was in Hollywood with Sergei Eisenstein, recalls (*With Eisenstein in Hollywood*,

p. 94) that sometime during the 1930s he sent Chaplin a Nazi propaganda book of photographs of Jews, *Juden Sehen Dich An* (Jews Are Looking at You). Though Chaplin was not Jewish, the book included a portrait of Chaplin with a caption, "Dieser ebenso langweilige wie widerwärtige kleine Zappeljude" (this little Jewish tumbler, as disgusting as he is boring). Chaplin recounts Korda's suggestion in MA, pp. 392–93.

13. Chaplin, Jr., *My Father, Charlie Chaplin*, pp. 128, 140–46; MA, p. 391.

14. Jack Oakie, who plays Napolini in the films, recalls how secret Chaplin kept the set in his memoir, *Jack Oakie's Double Takes* (San Francisco: Strawberry Hill Press, 1980), pp. 71–80; NYT, 6 November 1938, sec. 9, p. 5; 26 February 1939, sec. 9, p. 4.

15. NYT, 18 August 1940, sec. 9, p. 3.

16. NYT, 10 September 1939, sec. 9, p. 3.

17. NYT, 26 May 1940, sec. 9, p. 3.

18. NYT, 8 September 1940, sec. 7, pp. 8–11.

19. *The Great Dictator*, microfilm pressbooks and programs, BRC. On the use of the term "progressive" in this study, see Chapter 5, note 10.

20. *Motion Picture Daily*, 16 October 1940, p. 7; NYT, 16 October 1940, p. 29.

21. NYT, 13 October 1940, sec. 9, passim; NYT, 15 October 1940, p. 1.

22. On the Nuremberg Nazi party congresses, the Mussolini visit to Germany in 1937, and the details of the Austrian Anschluss, see, e.g., William Shirer, *The Rise and Fall of the Third Reich* (1959; reprinted New York: Simon and Schuster, 1980), pp. 230, 264, 382–83, and ch. 11; NYT, 15 June 1939, p. 11; NYT, 28 July 1938, p. 6.

23. Smith, *Chaplin*, p. 114.

24. Paul Goodman, "Chaplin Again, Again, and Again," *Partisan Review* 7 (November/December 1940): 58–64.

25. This speech resembles the endings of two other important American films released after the war began but before the United States entered: Steinbeck/Zanuck/Ford's *Grapes of Wrath* (1940) and Capra/Riskin's *Meet John Doe* (1941). All three express the progressive's faith that "the people" can survive adversity and even triumph in the name of democracy.

26. Among the critics who have focused on the final scene are Smith, *Chaplin*, pp. 117–89; Robert Warshow, *The Immediate Experience* (Garden City: Doubleday, 1962), p. 210; André Bazin, "Defense de *Monsieur Verdoux*," *Les Temps Modernes* (3 December 1947): 1115–22; and Maland, *American Visions*, pp. 89–94.

27. Barry Salt, "Film Style and Technology in the 1930s," *Film Quarterly* 30 (Fall 1976): 19–32.

28. See Bordwell and Thompson, *Film Art*, pp. 57–59, 163–71; CHC, chs. 1–7 passim; Noël Burch, *To the Distant Observer* (Berkeley: Univ. of California Press, 1979), pp. 61–66; Ray, *A Certain Tendency*, esp. pp. 25–65.

29. Balio, *United Artists*, p. 165; NYT, 22 March 1942, sec. 6, pp. 12–13.

30. NYT, 20 October 1940, sec. 9, p. 3.

31. *Post*, 16 October 1940; *Post*, 18 October 1940; *Journal-American*, 16 Oc-

tober 1940; *Journal-American* and *Daily News*, cited in *Daily Worker*, 19 October 1940; *Herald Tribune*, 20 October 1940; all unpaginated in Chaplin press clippings file, BRC.

32. *World Telegram*, 16 October 1940; *Philadelphia Record*, 24 October 1940; *Variety*, 16 October 1940; *NYT*, 20 October 1940, sec. 9, p. 3: all in Chaplin press clippings file, BRC.

33. *Daily Worker*, 16 October 1940. The *Worker* followed up this review with an October 19 article, "Those Peculiar Reviews," which lambasted the daily newspaper reviewers. According to the *Worker*, the critics from other newspapers attacked *The Great Dictator* "because of its peace message."

34. Jauss, "Literary History," in Jauss, *Toward an Aesthetic of Reception*, p. 25.

35. *NYT*, 27 October 1940, sec. 9, p. 5.

36. *Catholic World* 152 (December 1940): 333; *New Republic* 4 (4 November 1940), reprinted in *The Film Criticism of Otis Ferguson*, ed. Robert Wilson (Philadelphia: Temple Univ. Press, 1971), pp. 314–16; *Commonweal* 33 (November 1940): 80; *Nation* 131 (26 October 1940): 401; *Newsweek* 16 (28 October 1940): 60.

37. *Saturday Review* 23 (9 November 1940): 8.

38. *NYT*, 9 March 1941; *Daily Mirror*, 7 July 1941; *St. Louis Dispatch*, 16 March 1941; and *Dallas Morning News*, 14 February 1942: all unpaginated articles in Chaplin press clippings file, BRC.

39. The Reich protest was reported in *NYT*, 22 December 1938, p. 14. On the Senate Subcommittee on War Propaganda, see Ceplair and Englund, *Inquisition in Hollywood*, pp. 159–62, and *NYT*, 14 September 1941, p. 41. The resolution establishing the subcommittee was S.R. 152 (77th Cong., 1st sess.), introduced by Senators Clark of Missouri and Nye of North Dakota. Chaplin and United Artists' response to the subcommittee is detailed in correspondence in the O'Brien legal files, box 186, folders 6 and 7, UAC.

40. *NYT* (all 1941), 5 January, p. 34; 28 January p. 22; 30 January, p. 18; 1 February, p. 2; 16 February, p. 39; 10 March, p. 20; 24 June, p. 6; 15 March, sec. 8, p. 3; 3 May, sec. 8, p. 3.

41. *NYT*, 23 October 1944, p. 6; *NYT*, 10 August 1946, p. 16.

42. Alistair Cooke's portrait of Chaplin in *Six Men* provides a good example of how observers have minimized or downplayed the seriousness of Chaplin's political perspective.

43. *NYT*, 20 January 1941, p. 7; *Washington Post*, 20 January 1941, pp. 1, 4.

44. *NYT*, 21 January 1941, p. 1.

45. *Washington Post*, 21 January 1941, p. 1.

46. *NYT*, 10 October 1941, p. 15. On 25 September 1941, *People's World* named Chaplin as one of the original sponsors of Russian War Relief, Incorporated, though in the *Times* advertisement he is not listed as any kind of officer, honorary or otherwise.

47. Ralph Levering, *American Opinion and the Russian Alliance, 1939–1945* (Chapel Hill: Univ. of North Carolina Press, 1976), pp. 63–70.

48. *The Memoirs of Cordell Hull*, 2 vols (New York: Macmillan, 1948), 2: 1264; *NYT*, 8 November 1942, sec. 1, p. 1.

49. Levering, *American Opinion*, pp. 70–84 passim.

50. *NYT*, 23 April 1938, sec. 4, p. 2. One might note that Chaplin did not allow his United Artists films to be released in the Soviet Union until the 1930s because the Soviets were unwilling to pay the money Chaplin and United Artists thought would be fair for such a large country. Nevertheless, as early as 1930 retrospectives of Chaplin's films, using old prints, were being shown in Moscow. See *NYT*, 13 April 1930, sec. 10, p. 4.

51. One might note that both of Chaplin's sons, Sydney and Charles, Jr., enlisted in the U.S. armed forces in October 1943.

52. *People's World*, 20 May 1942, p. 1.

53. *Los Angeles Times*, 26 March 1941.

54. The Museum of Modern Art Film Department, in its "Chaplin, 1940–49" folder, has a copy of the brochure. It is reprinted in MA, pp. 410–13.

55. *New York Herald Tribune*, 17 October 1942, p. 4; *NYT*, 17 October 1942, p. 16.

56. *Chicago Tribune*, 26 November 1942, p. 23.

57. The Ehrenburg cable is included in a clipping in the "Chaplin, 1940–49" folder, Museum of Modern Art Film Department; *NYT*, 4 December 1942, p. 15.

58. Westbrook Pegler, "Fair Game," *New York World-Telegram*, 21 December 1942.

7. JOAN BARRY, THE PRESS, AND THE TARNISHED IMAGE

1. Chaplin, Jr., *My Father, Charlie Chaplin*, p. 192.

2. Ibid., pp. 187–90; Lyons, *Charles Chaplin: Guide to References and Resources*, p. 30; MA, p. 406.

3. The details of the relationship between Chaplin and Barry are impossible to recount with absolute confidence. Ironically, the files of the FBI's investigation of Chaplin surrounding the Barry case, available through the Freedom of Information Act, file no. 31–5301, probably constitute the best source. Much of the information in this section is from that file, particularly from the 11 November 1943 report of the Los Angeles office to Director J. Edgar Hoover in Washington, D.C., which runs 43 pages, and a second report from the office to Hoover, dated 25 February 1944 (66 pages). Of course, the information contained in the FBI files must be looked at critically and sifted carefully, since the aim of their investigation was to obtain information that could be used against Chaplin by the U.S. district attorney's office and since Barry's interviews with them contain inconsistencies and contradictions. But used cautiously, the files shed light on the Chaplin–Barry affair.

4. FBI report, L.A. office to Washington, 9 November 1943, p. 10.

5. FBI report, 9 November 1943, p. 11.

6. FBI report, L.A. office to Washington, 25 February 1944, p. 4.

7. FBI report, 25 February 1942, pp. 5, 9; MA, pp. 414–15. Barry and Chap-

lin differ about the timing of the *Shadow and Substance* reading. Chaplin claims the reading took place before he put her on contract; Barry remembers that Chaplin didn't even know of the play until the fall of 1942, after which he arranged the reading. Chaplin apparently exaggerated what he paid Barry, claiming that her salary was $250 a week (MA, p. 414); Barry showed FBI agents her salary check stubs to substantiate the $75 figure.

8. FBI report, 25 February 1944, pp. 13–14, 18; MA, pp. 415–18.

9. FBI report, 25 February 1944, pp. 20–21; MA, p. 419; Chaplin, Jr., *My Father, Charlie Chaplin*, pp. 204–9; Jerry Giesler, *The Jerry Giesler Story* (New York: Simon and Schuster, 1960), p. 187.

10. FBI report, 25 February 1944, pp. 23–24.

11. Although blood tests cannot prove someone *is* the father of a child, they can prove about 15 percent of the time that someone is *not* the father of a child, since parents with certain blood types cannot possibly produce a child with a third blood type. Because such a high percentage of people have one of two blood types, however, the percentage of men who can prove that they are not the father of a child is relatively low.

12. *NYT*, 11 June 1943, p. 22.

13. FBI memo, Hood to Hoover, 24 June 1943.

14. FBI memo, Hood to Hoover, 24 August 1943; FBI memo, Pennington to Rosen, 17 August 1943; FBI telegram, Hoover to SAC (special agent in charge) Los Angeles, 20 August 1943; FBI memo, SAC Los Angeles to Hoover, 25 August 1943.

15. Gerith von Ulm's biography, *Charlie Chaplin: King of Comedy* (Caldwell, Idaho: Claxton, 1940), was written partly through the cooperation of Chaplin's longtime valet and chauffeur, Kono. This cooperation makes the biography seem more like an "insider's" look at Chaplin's private life than most biographies of Chaplin.

16. FBI Memo, Pennington to Rosen, 9 November 1943.

17. FBI Memo, Davis to Rosen, 9 November 1943; memo, Hoover to Assistant Attorney General Clark, 7 December 1943; FBI memo, SAC Los Angeles Hood to Hoover, 22 December 1943; FBI teletype, SAC Los Angeles to Washington, date blacked out but apparently around 10 December 1943.

18. A telegram from Washington to SAC Los Angeles, probably about December 27 (the date is blacked out), reported on the Carr/Clark interchange on this issue and ordered that future Los Angeles investigation include the civil rights angle.

19. *NYT*, 11 February 1944, p. 1.

20. SAC Hood in Los Angeles sent copies of all four indictments to Agent Rosen in Washington on February 14; they are included in the FBI files on the case, and my quotations are taken from them.

21. Giesler, *Jerry Giesler Story*, pp. 187–88.

22. *Chicago Tribune*, 5 April 1944, p. 1.

23. FBI memo, Hood to Hoover and Rosen, 11 May 1944.

24. *NYT*, 16 February 1944, p. 19; *Chicago Tribune*, 18 February 1944, p. 1.

25. *Time* 45 (8 January 1945), p. 36; *Chicago Tribune*, 5 January 1945, p. 6.

26. *NYT*, 14 April 1945, p. 13; 18 April 1945, p. 25; 19 April 1945, p. 29.

27. An interesting biographical treatment of Hollywood's two most powerful gossip columnists, Hopper and Louella Parsons, is George Eells's *Hedda and Louella* (New York: Putnam's, 1972). Eells notes that in general, Parsons was more sympathetic to Chaplin: she repaid Chaplin for giving her the "scoop" on his marriage to Oona O'Neill by reporting in an article that the blood tests *proved* Chaplin was not the father of Barry's child. Hopper never mentioned this in her writing on Chaplin.

28. Eells, *Hedda and Louella*, pp. 130, 171.

29. Ibid., p. 173. The Motion Picture Alliance, founded in 1944, later numbered Hopper as one of its officers—see Ceplair and Englund, *Inquisition in Hollywood*, p. 211.

30. Barry's testimony is included in the FBI report, Los Angeles office to Washington, 25 February 1944; the interview took place in early January 1944.

31. *Chicago Tribune*, 3 June 1943, p. 22.

32. The FBI files include Hopper's column from the *Pittsburgh Press*, 22 June 1943. The column was apparently sent unsolicited to the FBI: an envelope addressed to Hoover and postmarked Pittsburgh, June 25, is the second photocopied page of the FBI file on Chaplin.

33. *New York Daily News*, 2 June 1943, p. 4; 10 October 1943, pp. 22–23. FBI report, Los Angeles office to Washington, 9 November 1943, pp. 36–37.

34. *Chicago Tribune*, 4 October 1943, p. 18; 6 October 1943, p. 26; 27 December 1943, p. 14.

35. FBI telegram, SAC LA Hood to Hoover, date blacked out (probably about January 5–8); FBI telegram, Hood to Hoover, 14 January 1944.

36. FBI telegram, Hood to Hoover, 31 January 1944, p. 1.

37. *Chicago Tribune*, 18 January 1944, p. 18; *Los Angeles Times*, 13 March 1944, p. 10.

38. *Chicago Tribune*, 28 March 1944, p. 15; 10 April 1944, p. 18.

39. FBI letter, Hood to Hoover, 14 April 1944.

40. In her column of April 28—two weeks after Muir's conversation with the FBI but three weeks before charges against Chaplin were dropped—Hopper wrote that the remaining federal charges against Chaplin would likely be dropped upon Attorney General Biddle's request.

41. *Chicago Tribune*, 22 December 1944, p. 15.

42. *Chicago Tribune*, 11 February 1944, p. 1. In the following paragraphs on the *Tribune*'s coverage of the Barry–Chaplin story, the dates of the articles will be cited in the text.

43. *Newsweek* 23 (21 February 1944): 46, 48.

44. *Newsweek* 23 (10 April 1944): 29; *Time* 43 (3 April 1944): 24–25.

45. *Time* 45 (1 January 1945): 15–16; 45 (8 January 1945).

46. *Newsweek* 25 (30 April 1945): 41; *Time* 45 (30 July 1944): 52.

47. *Script* 30 (4 March 1944): 1–2. Hopper's article is discussed in the previous section, above.

48. Mike Gold, "Charge It," *Daily Worker* (19 January 1945), Chaplin clippings file, BRC.

8. *MONSIEUR VERDOUX* AND THE COLD WAR

1. On the contributions of these refugees to scholarship, science, and the arts in America since their arrival, see especially Lewis A. Coser, *Refugee Scholars in America* (New Haven: Yale Univ. Press, 1984), which does not limit itself to *German* refugees, and Anthony Heilbut, *Exiled in Paradise: German Refugee Artists and Intellectuals in America, from the 1930s to the Present* (New York: Viking, 1983), which does.

2. Heilbut, *Exiled in Paradise*, pp. 108, viii.

3. Ibid., p. 35; Salka Viertel, *The Kindness of Strangers* (New York: Holt, Rinehart, 1969), p. 211; Taylor, *Strangers in Paradise*, p. 146. Another more general book on the contribution of Europeans to American cinema is Baxter, *The Hollywood Exiles*, esp. chs. 11, 12. While Brecht's political views are well known and have been much discussed, Eisler's are less so; *A Rebel in Music*, ed. Manfred Grabs (New York: International Publishers, 1978), is an interesting collection of his essays and lectures. A key theme of his writings is contained in an interview from June 1935, in which Eisler calls for "an alliance between the music intellectuals and the working class" (p. 100).

4. See Taylor, *Strangers in Paradise*, ch. 9, "The New Weimar," for a discussion of the arrival and settlement of the German refugees in Hollywood. See also James K. Lyon, *Bertolt Brecht in America* (Princeton: Princeton Univ. Press, 1980), pp. 28–31. Another treatment of Brecht's experiences in the United States is Bruce Cook, *Brecht in Exile* (New York: Holt, Rinehart, 1982).

5. Viertel, *Kindness of Strangers*, p. 290.

6. See Hilda Waldo, "Lion Feuchtwanger: A Biography," in John M. Spalek, ed., *Lion Feuchtwanger: The Man, His Ideas, His Work* (Los Angeles: Hennessey and Ingalls, 1972), p. 15; Wilhelm von Sternburg, *Lion Feuchtwanger: Ein deutsches Schriftstellerleben* (Königstein: Atheneum, 1984), pp. 300–301, 305 ff.; Volker Skierka, *Lion Feuchtwanger: Eine Biographie* (Berlin: Quadriga Verlag, 1984), pp. 242–43; *NYT*, 24 January 1930, p. 26; and Harold von Hofe, ed., *Feuchtwanger–Zweig: Briefwechsel, 1933–58* (Berlin and Weimar: Aufbau Verlag, 1984), 2: 202; MA, p. 450.

7. Lyon, *Bertolt Brecht*, pp. 84, 196; interviews with Eisler in Hans Bunge, ed., *Fragen Sie Mir über Brecht: Hanns Eisler in Gesprach* (Munich: Rogner & Bernard, 1970), pp. 58–59.

8. Eisler, *Rebel*, p. 102; Bunge, *Fragen Sie Mir ber Brecht*, pp. 58–59; Heilbut, *Exiled in Paradise*, p. ix.

9. One leftist, screenwriter Bess Taffel, remembers that when leftists in Hollywood like Eisler and Chaplin were becoming isolated after the start of the Hollywood Ten trials, the formerly large groups that gathered at the Eislers' home had dwindled to Taffel, Salka Viertel, the Feuchtwangers, the Chaplins, and their hosts. Ceplair and Englund, *Inquisition in Hollywood*, pp. 379–80. Taffel, who joined the Communist party during the height of its patriotic rhetoric

in 1943, became disillusioned when its idealism declined around 1946, and she eventually broke with the Party entirely. She saw her friends at the Eislers' as "non-Party left-wingers." Another leftist, though not a German refugee, who knew Chaplin and was sympathetic to this political perspective was screenwriter Donald Ogden Stewart, who was blacklisted in the 1950s. His memoirs, *By a Stroke of Luck* (New York: Paddington Press, 1975), particularly pp. 264 ff., provide another picture of the shape of progressive antifascism during and after World War Two.

10. Feuchtwanger's favorable book on the Soviet Union, *Moskau 37*, was published in Amsterdam in 1937.

11. Among the major reviewers who praised *Verdoux* during these rereleases were Bosley Crowther, *NYT*, 4 July 1964; Andrew Sarris, *Village Voice*, 23 July 1964; and Vincent Canby, *NYT*, 8 July 1973. In his review Canby wrote that *Playtime* (directed by Jacques Tati) and *Monsieur Verdoux* were "two of the greatest comedies of all time."

12. Ceplair and Englund, *Inquisition in Hollywood*, p. 186, call the period between 1941 and 1944 "Popular Front Redivivis." On this spirit, see also Richard Pells, *The Liberal Mind in a Conservative Age* (New York: Harper and Row, 1985), pp. 32–40.

13. "Beyond the Atlantic Charter," *New Republic* 107 (23 November 1942): 667.

14. The text of the speech is found in *Churchill: Complete Speeches*, ed. Robert Rhodes James (London: Chelsea House, 1974), 7: 7283–93.

15. Mary McAuliffe, *Crisis on the Left* (Amherst: Univ. of Massachusetts Press, 1978); William O'Neill, *A Better World* (New York: Simon and Schuster, 1982).

16. On the decline of progressive liberalism through 1948, see McAuliffe, *Crisis on the Left*, ch. 3.

17. Geoffrey Hodgson, *America in Our Time* (New York: Doubleday, 1976), esp. chs. 1–4. On the emergence of the American consensus, see also Robert Skotheim, *Totalitarianism and American Social Thought* (New York: Holt, Rinehart, 1971); Lawrence S. Wittner, *Cold War America* (New York: Praeger, 1974); and Pells, *Liberal Mind*, esp. chs. 1–3.

18. Hodgson, *America in Our Time*, pp. 75–76.

19. Pells (*Liberal Mind*, p. 97) makes almost the same point: that American intellectuals, used to "taking sides" since the Depression, found it easy to shift villains after the war. "The identity of the combatants had now changed," Pells writes, "Russia having supplanted both the 'bosses' and the Nazis as embodiments of everlasting villainy. But the intellectuals' frame of mind remained the same."

20. See CHC, esp. ch. 2.

21. See Dyer, *Stars*, pp. 28–32. See also William R. Brown, *Image Maker: Will Rogers and the American Dream* (Columbia: Univ. of Missouri Press, 1970), and Charles Eckert, "Shirley Temple and the House of Rockefeller," *Jump Cut*, no. 2 (July-August 1974): 1, 17–20. Brown argues that Rogers's image reinforced certain dominant American values at a time when they were under threat. Eck-

ert also believes that stars reaffirm dominant values, though in part through this complex process of displacement.

22. Dorothy B. Jones, "The Quantitative Analysis of Motion Picture Content," *Public Opinion Quarterly* 16 (1942): 411–28.

23. Thomas F. Brady, " 'Bluebeard' Chaplin," *NYT*, 30 March 1947, sec. 6, pp. 24–25.

24. Cable, Tom Waller to Paul Lazarus, Jr., 3 April 1947. Alfred Tamarin papers, file 6, folder 6, UAC.

25. United Artists press releases, 8 April and 9 April 1947, Alfred Tamarin papers, file 6, folder 6, UAC. The publicity staff was worried about the conference right up to the day it was held. That day Tom Waller sent a note to Paul Lazarus, Jr., which said that UA executive and old Chaplin associate Arthur Kelly had told him to downplay the press conference. To this Waller added tartly: "I reminded Mr. Kelley that twice when I saw Mr. Chaplin I advised strenuously against any mass press meeting."

26. Red Kann, "Insider's Outlook," *Motion Picture Daily* 61 (11 April 1947): 2.

27. We are fortunate that a transcript of the Chaplin press conference, with notes by George Wallach, who attended the meeting and did the taping, has been published (the article mistakenly says the press conference was held on April 12). See George Wallach, "Charlie Chaplin's *Monsieur Verdoux* Press Conference," *Film Comment* 5 (Winter 1969): 34–42. The page numbers for quotations from the press conference are cited parenthetically in the text.

28. *NYT*, 11 April 1947, pp. 1, 17, 18; 14 April 1947, p. 1.

29. *New York Herald Tribune*, 12 April 1947, p. 8.

30. *Commonweal* 47 (2 May 1947): 68.

31. *New Yorker* 23 (19 April 1947): 42; Jauss, "Literary History," in Jauss, *Toward an Aesthetic of Reception*, pp. 25–26.

32. *Variety*, 16 April 1947, p. 8.

33. *Newsweek* 29 (28 April 1947): 98.

34. John Beaufort, "An Assault from Mr. Chaplin," *Christian Science Monitor*, 19 April 1947, Chaplin clippings file, BRC.

35. *NYT*, 12 April 1947, p. 11.

36. *New Republic* 116 (21 April 1947): 38–39; 5 May 1947, p. 39; *Theater Arts* gave the film a guardedly positive review much like that of the *New Republic* in Hermane Rich Isaacs' "Expectations: Great and Small," *Theatre Arts* 31 (June 1947): 47–48.

37. James Agee, *Agee on Film* (Boston: Beacon, 1964), 1: 252–62.

38. Appearing in a journal that prized the complexity, ambiguity, and irony of writers like Kafka and Céline at the same time that it pulled away from the easy pieties of progressivism, Warshow's essay found a proper home. "*Monsieur Verdoux*" first appeared in *Partisan Review* 14 (July-August 1947): 380–89, and is collected in Warshow's *The Immediate Experience*; see pp. 208, 215, 222.

39. Max Lerner, "Chaplin—Art and Politics," *PM*, 17 April 1947, p. 2; "The Essential Quality of Civilization," *PM*, 20 April 1947, Chaplin clippings file,

BRC. The United Artists press staff even corresponded about Lerner's editorial the day before it appeared, which shows how worried they were about generating positive response to the film. See memo, Larry Beller to Tom Waller, 16 April 1947, Alfred Tamarin file, box 6, folder 6, UAC.

40. Arnaud d'Usseau, "Chaplin's *Monsieur Verdoux*," *Mainstream* 1 (Summer 1947): 308–17.

41. *Variety*, 30 April 1947, p. 13; 7 May 1947, p. 15; 14 May 1947, p. 11.

42. On the redesigned publicity campaign, see particularly the files of Paul Lazarus, Jr., box 16, folder 14, and box 17, folder 8; and of Alfred Tamarin, box 6, folder 6, all UAC.

43. *Motion Picture Daily*, 12 May 1947, p. 3; d'Usseau, "Chaplin's *Monsieur Verdoux*," p. 316; *Hollywood Reporter*, 23 July 1947, p. 5.

44. This information comes from box 16, folder 14 of the Lazarus files, UAC.

45. Chaplin clippings file, BRC.

46. United Artists publicity papers, Alfred Tamarin file, box 6, folder 6, UAC; "Moral: Chaplin Should Heckle Congress More," *Variety*, 1 October 1947, p. 4.

47. See, for example, *Washington Post*, 27 September 1947, sec. B, p. 8.

48. Cable, Birdwell to Chaplin, September 26, 1947, Paul Lazarus, Jr., file, box 16, folder 14, UAC.

49. *Washington Post*, 27 September 1947, sec. B, p. 8.

50. Telegram, Birdwell to Lazarus, 28 September 1947, Alfred Tamarin file, box 6, folder 6, UAC.

51. *Variety*, 8 October 1947, p. 4; 15 October 1947, p. 12.

52. All cables in the Paul Lazarus, Jr., files, UAC.

53. Domestic earnings, 1947, Paul Lazarus, Sr., sales correspondence, UAC.

54. Balio, *United Artists*, p. 214.

55. Dyer, *Stars*, pp. 68–72.

56. United Artists press releases, November 1947 and June 1948, Alfred Tamarin file, box 6, folder 6, UAC.

9. CHAPLIN'S POLITICS AND AMERICAN CULTURE

1. Alistair Cooke's observation, in *Six Men*, p. 27, provides a good example of this tendency: Chaplin's "much-abused 'radical philosophy'" was no more than an automatic theme song in favor of peace, humanity, 'the little man,' and other desirable abstractions—as humdrum politicians come out for mother love and lower taxes."

2. See *Daily Worker*, 6 April 1943, p. 2; 29 September 1943, pp. 2, 5; 21 November 1944, p. 11.

3. *NYT*, 9 May 1943, sec. 6, p. 10.

4. *Moscow News*, 29 April 1944, p. 4; the event was also reported in *NYT*, 28 April 1944, p. 4, and, in an insinuating tone, in *Newsweek*, 15 May 1944 (just after Chaplin's acquittal on Mann Act charges and the Justice Department's order not to continue prosecution of Chaplin on the civil rights charges). See

Grigori Alexandrov, "Chaplin's Art is Weapon in Fight against Fascism," *Moscow News*, 29 April 1944, pp. 4–5.

5. Yon Barna, *Eisenstein* (Boston: Little, Brown, 1973), p. 257.

6. *New York Journal-American*, 28 May 1946, p. 1. Garfield discussed the affair in his testimony before HUAC on 23 April 1951. According to Garfield, Simonov was a screenwriter and novelist who visited Hollywood; he gave the party on the ship as a gesture of thanks to Chaplin, Milestone, and Garfield. See Garfield testimony, HUAC hearings, Communist Infiltration of the Motion Picture Industry, vol. 2, 82nd Cong., p. 354.

7. Helen Dreiser, *My Life with Dreiser* (New York: World, 1951), pp. 281, 319–22 (the latter is an account of the funeral; it also quotes the poem). See also W. A. Swanberg, *Dreiser* (New York: Scribner's, 1965), p. 509.

8. *Daily Worker*, 4 June 1947; Gerhart Eisler, a prominent Communist before he came to the United States in the early 1940s, lived a quiet life in the United States, occasionally contributing articles to the Communist press. In 1946, however, he was charged with being a "top Communist International Agent" in the United States, and he finally left the country in April 1949, stowing away in a Polish vessel, the *Batory*. See Joseph R. Starobin, *American Communism in Crisis, 1943–1957* (Cambridge: Harvard Univ. Press, 1972), esp. pp. 304–5.

9. David Caute, *The Great Fear* (New York: Simon and Schuster, 1978), p. 503; Eisler, *Rebel in Music*, p. 152; Ceplair and Englund, *Inquisition in Hollywood*, pp. 379–80. On the Picasso telegram and the appeal to the attorney general's office, see Sadoul, *Vie de Charlot*, p. 149; Heilbut, *Exiled in Paradise*, p. 374; and *Daily Worker*, 18 January 1948, sec. 2, p. 3. In its 11 December 1947 issue, the *Hollywood Reporter* ran an article quoting the November 27 telegram. It also carried an editorial by W. R. Wilkerson that indicates how badly Chaplin's reputation was slipping. It read in part: "The wonder to us is that Washington hasn't long ago relieved Chaplin of his privilege of living in this country, working among us, banking millions of dollars while, at the same time, it becomes quite obvious that he is not satisfied with the conduct of our government and continually criticizes its actions." As we shall see, such sentiments mirrored views being expressed by members of Congress at around the same time, which fueled the FBI investigation of Chaplin's politics in the late 1940s. Indeed, Wilkerson's editorial is quoted in an 8 May 1948 letter from the FBI's Los Angeles field office to Director J. Edgar Hoover. Hanns Eisler himself eventually settled in East Germany in 1950 where he resided until his death in 1962.

10. *Los Angeles Times*, 30 March 1948, sec. 1, p. 10; 17 May 1948, sec. 1, p. 1.

11. O'Neill, *Better World*, pp. 163–69, provides an account of the Waldorf Conference sympathetic to the anti-Stalinists and critical of the progressives. More recently, anti-Stalinist Sidney Hook has described his attempts to participate in the conference in "The Communist Peace Offensive," *Partisan Review*, *50th Anniversary Edition*, ed. William Phillips (New York: Stein and Day, 1985), pp. 210–29.

12. *NYT* 5 April 1949, p. 7; 12 September 1949, p. 5.

13. On the Peekskill incident and Chaplin's involvement in it, see Philip S. Foner, *Paul Robeson Speaks* (New York: Brunner-Mazel, 1978), pp. 543–45; Dorothy Baker Gillim, *Paul Robeson: All-American* (Washington, D.C.: New Republic Books, 1976), esp. ch. 16; and Howard Fast, *Peekskill* (New York: New Century, 1950).

14. Robert Sklar, *Movie-Made America* (New York: Random House, 1975), pp. 196–97; see also Garth Jowett, *Film: The Democratic Art* (Boston: Little, Brown, 1976), ch. 12, "Hollywood Goes to War."

15. On the Dies Committee and the Clark Committee, see Ceplair and Englund, *Inquisition in Hollywood*, esp. pp. 109–11 and 155–65, passim.

16. Langer's bill, which was never passed, was reported in *Variety*, 15 February 1945; Rankin's remarks are found in *Congressional Records*, 79th Cong., 1st sess., 19 July 1945, p. 7377.

17. *Congressional Record*, 80th Cong., 1st sess., 7 March 1947, p. 1792.

18. *Congressional Record*, 80th Cong., 1st sess., 12 June 1947, p. 6895.

19. *NYT*, 14 May 1949, p. 19.

20. The literature on HUAC and the Hollywood Ten—one of HUAC's most famous cases—is enormous, but one of the best places to start is with Walter Goodman, *The Committee* (New York: Farrar, Straus, 1968). Also indispensable are the transcripts of testimonies before HUAC, some of which appear in Eric Bentley, ed., *Thirty Years of Treason* (New York: Viking, 1971), pp. 482–95. See also the *Cumulative Index to Publications of the Committee on Un-American Activities, 1938–1954* (Washington, D.C.: U.S. Government Printing Office, 1962).

21. *Washington Post*, 6 December 1946, p. 3; Ceplair and Englund, *Inquisition in Hollywood*, pp. 379–80.

22. On Chaplin's HUAC interactions, see Balio, *United Artists*, pp. 211–13; and MA, pp. 447–49. In his autobiography, Chaplin gives a shorter and less argumentative version of the telegram, but it too contains the assertion, "I am not a Communist. I am a peace-monger."

23. See Edward L. Barrett, Jr., *The Tenney Committee* (Ithaca: Cornell Univ. Press, 1951).

24. "Hearings on H.R. 1884 and H.R. 2122, Bills to Curb or Outlaw the Communist Party of the United States," HUAC 24–28 March 1947, testimony of Jack B. Tenney, p. 264.

25. Goodman, *The Committee*, pp. 29–30, 198. p. 13. Steele's testimony to the Dies Committee in 1939 and 1940 is published in "Executive Hearings Made Public," HUAC, vols. 1 and 2, pp. 278–428 and 455–706.

26. "Hearings on H.R. 1884 and H.R. 2122," pp. 107–8.

27. In his "Little Old New York" column in the *Washington Times Herald* on 16 April 1947, Sullivan accused Chaplin of "always pitching for the Kremlin": "Chaplin has been a prominent member of at least five Communist-front organizations, one of which tried desperately to get an FM broadcasting station to spread their doctrines in the New York area." Chaplin's denial of association with the group is included in the transcript of the INS interview, pp. 31–32, included in FBI report, SAC Los Angeles to Hoover, 5 July 1949.

28. "Hearings Regarding Communist Infiltration of the Motion-Picture Industry," HUAC, 20–24, 27–30 October 1947, p. 179. See Chapter 10 below for a discussion of the degree to which Chaplin was a "sacred cow" to the *Daily Worker*.

29. Robinson testimony, HUAC Hearings and Reports, 81st Cong., p. 3332; Garfield testimony, HUAC Hearings, "Communist Infiltration of Hollywood Motion-Picture Industry, Part II," 82nd Cong., p. 354; Shaw testimony, HUAC Hearings, "Investigation of Communist Activities in the New York City Area, Part I," 83rd Cong., p. 1185; Oxnam testimony, HUAC Hearings, "Testimony of Bishop G. Bromley Oxnam," 83rd Cong., p. 3599.

30. "Review of the Scientific and Cultural Conference for World Peace," 81st Cong., 26 April 1950, House Report no. 1954. Page numbers for references given in the text.

31. "Report on Communist 'Peace' Offensive," 82nd Cong., 25 April 1951, House Report no. 378. Page numbers for references given in the text.

32. The FBI was established in 1908 by Attorney General Bonaparte under the name "Bureau of Investigation." It underwent a reorganization after J. Edgar Hoover was named director in 1924 (a position he held until his death in 1972) and took its present name in 1935. Its investigative jurisdiction relates to federal cases in two areas: general investigation (as with their involvement in Chaplin's Mann Act charge) and domestic investigative intelligence (as in the present case). Thanks to the Freedom of Information Act, the FBI files on Chaplin have become available to scholars upon request. The files I have obtained concerning the investigation of Chaplin as a security risk between 1946 and 1953 contain hundreds of pages. They include such documents as letters between government agencies, interoffice memos, clippings from newspaper and magazine articles, summaries of testimony and information gathered from informants, and formal reports prepared by FBI staff for Director Hoover or for other administrative agencies. It should be stressed that the files are not complete. Many reports and letters have words or even entire sections blacked out, while at times entire pages are withheld (and a form noting this is inserted), for varying reasons, the most common of which are to protect the identity of an informant or to preserve national security.

33. For a fuller account of Chaplin's interactions with the FBI and other governmental agencies, Timothy Lyons's forthcoming *The Case against Mr. Chaplin* promises to be an important and fundamental work. Lyons has published a brief article on the subject, "The United States vs. Charlie Chaplin," *American Film* 9 (September 1984): 29–34. Robinson's recent biography also contains a brief appendix discussing the FBI investigations of Chaplin (CHLA, pp. 750–56).

34. FBI report, Los Angeles to Washington, 14 August 1922; FBI memo, "GFR" to Hoover, 28 August 1922.

35. FBI report, New York to Washington, 4 December 1942; FBI memo, Welch to Ladd, 23 December 1942.

36. FBI memo, Hoover to SAC Los Angeles, 14 March 1947.

37. FBI report, SAC Los Angeles to Hoover, dated 13 March 1947, received in April. Page references cited parenthetically in the text.

38. FBI clipping of Sullivan column in *Washington Times Herald*, 12 April 1947.

39. FBI letter, Hoover to commissioner, INS, 2 October 1947. The transcript of the INS interview is included in FBI report, SAC Los Angeles to Hoover, 5 July 1949.

40. FBI letter, Hoover to SAC Los Angeles, 21 February 1948.

41. FBI letter, SAC Los Angeles to Hoover, 25 February 1948; FBI letter, SAC Los Angeles to Hoover, 8 May 1948; FBI report, Los Angeles office to Washington office, 9 June 1948.

42. FBI report, SAC Los Angeles to Hoover, 10 August 1948. Page numbers of references cited in the text.

43. Although the interview took place in 1948, it was not made public until the late 1970s and hence had no bearing on Chaplin's star image until then. This is in contrast to some of the information accumulated by the FBI and shared with the press.

44. FBI letter, Hoover to SAC Los Angeles, 7 April 1949; FBI letter, Hoover to SAC Los Angeles, 3 August 1949.

45. FBI letter, SAC Los Angeles to Hoover, 7 October 1949.

46. Letter, Assistant Attorney General Campbell to Hoover, 10 November 1949.

47. FBI memo, Agent D. W. Ladd to Hoover, 21 December 1949.

48. FBI telegram, Hoover to SAC Los Angeles, 22 December 1949.

49. FBI telegram, SAC Los Angeles to Hoover, 27 December 1949; FBI letter, Hoover to Peyton Ford (assistant to attorney general), 29 December 1949.

50. FBI memo, Agent Turner to Agent Whitson, 7 February 1949.

51. FBI interoffice memo, Turner to Hennrich, 4 May 1950.

52. See Kenneth O'Reilly, *Hoover and the Un-Americans* (Philadelphia: Temple Univ. Press, 1983), p. 236. According to O'Reilly, Budenz, who also taught at Notre Dame and Fordam universities, earned a hefty supplementary income as a professional anti-Communist writer and lecturer: $61,000 until his retirement for health reasons in 1957.

53. FBI letter, SAC New York to Hoover, 14 July 1950, p. 4.

54. FBI report, SAC Los Angeles to Hoover, 5 April 1951, pp. 3, 5, 12.

55. On the state of United Artists and the film industry in the late 1940s, see Balio, *United Artists*, pp. 219–29. On the rise of independent production, see Janet Staiger, "Individualism versus Collectivism," *Screen* 24, nos. 4/5 (July-October 1983): 68–79, as well as her chapter on the "package unit system" of production in CHC, pp. 330–37.

56. See Caute, *Great Fear*, chs. 2, 3, and passim, and Pells, *Liberal Mind,*, esp. chs. 2, 5. In a section on three intellectuals who had been socialists in the 1930s—Dwight Macdonald, William Phillips, and Philip Rahv, Pells sums up the direction of their views: "by the end of the 1940s, their minds and their

essays were filled less with the dream of a social democracy than with the harrowing imagery of totalitarianism" (p. 83).

57. Richard Lauterbach, "The Whys of Chaplin's Appeal," *NYT Magazine*, 21 May 1950, p. 24. Lauterbach, a former editor of *Life* magazine, was preparing a biography of Chaplin but died before completing it.

58. The growth of art house screens between 1950 and 1965 is noted by Douglas Ayer et al., "Self Censorship in the Movie Industry," in *American Movie Industry*, ed. Kindem, p. 223; *NYT*, 7 December 1950, p. 52.

59. *NYT*, 31 July 1950, p. 19. The incident surrounding *The Circus* even became a focus of FBI attention: see FBI letter, SAC Los Angeles to Hoover, 2 August 1950, which reported that Chaplin "was incensed about the unauthorized use of his film" and instructed his lawyers "to take all legal steps to prevent such an exhibition and to prosecute the proposed exhibitioners to the fullest extent of the law."

60. *Life* 27 (5 September 1949): 77; "The Comedy of Charlie Chaplin," *Atlantic* 185 (February 1950): 26. Other articles during this period treating Chaplin positively include the following: *New Yorker* 26 (25 February 1950): 24; *Saturday Review* 33 (6 May 1950): 46–47; *NYT Magazine*, 21 May 1950, p. 24.

61. Huff, *Charlie Chaplin*; Peter Cotes and Thelma Niklaus, *The Little Tramp* (New York: Philosophical Library, 1951); Robert Payne, *The Great God Pan* (New York: Hermitage House, 1952). Huff's book was reprinted by Pyramid in 1964 and by 1972 had gone into its fourth printing. Arthur Knight reviewed all three of these books in two book reviews: see *Saturday Review* 34 (7 April 1951): 10–11, and 35 (26 April 1952): 13–14.

10. *LIMELIGHT* AND BANISHMENT

1. See FBI letter, Hoover to SAC Los Angeles, 16 September 1952.

2. *NYT*, 20 September 1952, pp. 1, 16; 3 October 1952, p. 1.

3. *Variety*, 22 October 1952, p. 61.

4. *NYT*, 23 September 1952, p. 21; the second passage and some other Chaplin comments are included in a letter from the American embassy in Brussels to the U.S. Department of State, 17 November 1952.

5. See Rozas, "Charlie Chaplin's Decline," and Philip G. Rosen, "The Chaplin World View," *Cinema Journal* 9 (Fall 1969): 2–12.

6. FBI letter, Hoover to SAC Los Angeles, 8 July 1952.

7. FBI memo, Foley to Keay, 25 August 1952.

8. These details are recounted in an FBI memo, Belmont to Ladd, 16 September 1952.

9. *Variety*, 14 February 1951, p. 3.

10. FBI memo, Belmont to Ladd, 16 September 1952, p. 2; FBI summary report, Washington office to McGranery, 18 September 1952.

11. FBI memo, Belmont to Ladd, 30 September 1952.

12. The act, Public Law 414, 82nd Cong., provided the INS with a powerful tool to deprive leftist citizens of their citizenship and to revoke the residence

permits of leftist aliens and deport them. In *The Great Fear*, Caute says the act "set the Congressional seal on wide-spread xenophobia" (p. 225).

13. FBI report, SAC Los Angeles to Hoover, 14 October 1952.

14. FBI letter, SAC Los Angeles to Hoover, 7 November 1952, pp. 2–3.

15. See FBI letters, all from Hoover to the commissioner and assistant commissioner, INS, 31 October and 9 December 1952 and 19 February 1953.

16. FBI letter, Hoover to chief, Division of Security, U.S. Department of State.

17. Letter, legal attaché, American embassy in London, to Hoover, 31 October 1952; letter, legal attaché, American embassy in Paris, to Hoover, 6 November 1952. (The letter from the embassy in Brussels was sent on 19 November 1952 to the Department of State and a copy was forwarded to the FBI.)

18. FBI letters, Hoover to SAC Los Angeles, 20 April 1953 and 30 April 1953; FBI report, SAC Los Angeles to Hoover, 10 July 1953; FBI letter, SAC Los Angeles to Hoover, 12 August 1953.

19. Young, *New Republic* 31 (23 August 1922): 358–59.

20. Wallach, "*Monsieur Verdoux* Press Conference," p. 39.

21. Robinson, *Chaplin: His Life and Art*, p. 550.

22. Richard Lauterbach, "The Whys of Chaplin's Appeal," *NYT Magazine*, 21 May 1950, p. 24.

23. Lauterbach, "Whys," p. 26.

24. On "biographical legend": see Boris Tomashevsky, "Literature and Biography," in *Readings in Russian Poetics*, ed. Ladislav Matejka and Krystyna Pomorska (Ann Arbor: Univ. of Michigan Press, 1978).

25. Robinson (CHLA, pp. 550–58) emphasizes how consciously autobiographical Chaplin was in preparing the film. Chaplin's unfinished novel told the story of Calvero and Terry much as it was presented in the film but supplemented it with more information about the past lives of both characters. Robinson, who calls the novel a "complex series of autobiographical reflexions," convincingly argues that Chaplin was not only reflecting on his own personal situation in the film but also on his father, his mother, and a number of other family relationships from his earlier years.

26. This analogy becomes more convincing when we learn from Charles Chaplin, Jr., that during the shooting of *Limelight*, his father told him, "I think your father is going to quit after this one. He's getting old." See Chaplin, Jr., *My Father, Charlie Chaplin*, p. 253.

27. Chaplin, Jr., *My Father, Charlie Chaplin*, p. 253.

28. *Herald Tribune*, 23 October 1952, p. 31; *NYT*, 23 October 1952, p. 39.

29. See "Chaplin at Work," *Life* 32 (17 March 1952): 117–27.

30. On the breakdown of the progressive paradigm in the postwar years, see Pells, *Liberal Mind*, esp. ch. 3, and Gene Wise, *American Historial Explanations: A Strategy for Grounded Inquiry*, 2nd ed., rev. (Minneapolis: Univ. of Minnesota Press, 1980), ch. 8.

31. See Frank Beaver, *Bosley Crowther: Social Critic of the Film* (New York: Arno, 1974). As noted in Chapter 5, note 25, Crowther is a good example of

a "modern liberal" reviewer; after 1950 the "social radical" perspective of the 1930s had almost disappeared.

32. Pells, *Liberal Mind*, p. 220. A convenient sampling of postwar writings on mass culture can be found in Bernard Rosenberg and David White, eds., *Mass Culture* (Glencoe, Ill.: The Free Press, 1957).

33. William Barrett, "Chaplin as Chaplin," *American Mercury* 75 (November 1952): 90; Crowther, *NYT*, 24 October 1952, p. 27; Warshow, in *Immediate Experience*, p. 225 (originally in *Partisan Review* [November-December 1954]); Hartung, *Commonweal* 57 (31 October 1952): 102; *Newsweek* 33 (27 October 1952): 112; Bentley, *New Republic* 127 (17 November 1952): 31. These are only a few of the many reviews that comment on *Limelight's* autobiographical elements, on which even non-American reviewers commented. See the comments by the British reviewer Gavin Lambert ("At 63 Chaplin has executed an imaginative portrait of the artist as an old man and shown his creative powers to be at their height") and André Bazin (*Limelight* is "confessional," a "portrait of the author"). See Lambert, " 'The Elegant Melancholy of Twilight': Impressions of 'Limelight,' " *Sight and Sound* 22 (January-March 1953): 123–27, and Bazin, "*Limelight*," in *What Is Cinema?* vol. 2, trans. Hugh Gray (Berkeley: Univ. of California Press, 1971), pp. 124–27.

34. Barrett, "Chaplin as Chaplin," pp. 90–95, passim. Quotes at pp. 90, 91, 95.

35. Knight, *Saturday Review* 35 (25 October 1952): 29, 30.

36. *New Yorker* 28 (25 October 1952): 141; Alpert, *Saturday Review* 35 (25 October 1952): 31–32. See also Manny Farber's review in the *Nation* 175 (25 October 1952): 393–94.

37. Bentley, *New Republic* 127 (17 November 1952): 30–31.

38. On second wave, see Ceplair and Englund, *Inquisition in Hollywood*, ch. 11.

39. *Chicago Tribune*, 20 September 1952, pp. 1, 9.

40. *New York Journal-American*, 19 September 1952, p. 3; 21 September 1952, p. 4.

41. *Chicago Tribune*, 20 September 1952, sec. 2, p. 2.

42. Though the articles appeared throughout the country, I am referring to those that appeared in the *San Francisco Examiner*, 22–26 September 1952. All the quotations in this paragraph and the next are taken from this series.

43. *Daily Worker* (all 1952), 22 September, p. 6; 23 September, p. 3; 24 September, p. 5; 25 September, p. 7; 1 October, p. 7. Quotations in the next two paragraphs are taken from the last three articles.

44. The correct statement, in Chaplin's "What People Laugh At," reads, "people as a whole get satisfaction from seeing the rich get the worst of things." Chaplin's article is excerpted in *Focus on Chaplin*, ed. McCaffrey, pp. 48–54. It originally appeared in *American Magazine* 86 (November 1918): 34, 134–37.

45. *NYT*, 21 September 1952, sec. 4, p. 10. The *Nation* editorialized almost identically in its 4 October 1952 issue (p. 287): "Whatever his political views

may be—and he says he has never been a Communist—Charlie Chaplin can hardly be regarded as an overt threat to American institutions."

46. *NYT*, 28 September 1952, sec. 2, p. 1; sec. 4, p. 10.

47. "Chaplin's Art Proclaims Him Anti-Communist," *New York Herald Tribune*, George W. Demott scrapbook, BRC.

48. *Time* 60 (29 September 1952): 34.

49. Irving Kristol, "McGranery and Charlie Chaplin," *Commentary*, 24 November 1952, p. 9. Emphasis in original. See also Pells, *Liberal Mind*, pp. 130–47, which treats the increasing celebration of American society among liberals in the early 1950s and their attendant rejection of the progressive critique of American society. Kristol's article contains seeds of both attitudes. A radical in the late 1930s and early 1940s, Kristol moved right in the 1940s and even came to defend McCarthy in a qualified way. See Alan Wald, *The New York Intellectuals* (Chapel Hill: Univ. of North Carolina Press, 1987), pp. 350–54.

50. *Nation* 175 (4 October 1952): 287.

51. Ibid., p. 288.

52. William Bradford Huie, "Mr. Chaplin and the Fifth Freedom," *American Mercury* 75 (November 1952): 123–28.

53. James Truett Selcraig, *The Red Scare in the Midwest, 1945–1955: A State and Local Study* (Ann Arbor: UMI Research Press, 1982), p. 87.

54. On the American Legion's campaign against Hollywood in the early 1950s see Selcraig, *Red Scare*, pp. 90–92, and Caute, *Great Fear*, pp. 502–4.

55. One local Legion post succeeded in getting a college showing of Chaplin shorts canceled a week *before* the convention. See *Knoxville Journal*, 6 October 1952, p. 4; 7 October 1952, pp. 1, 3; 8 October 1952, p. 10.

56. See William Murray, "*Limelight*: Chaplin and His Censors," *Nation* 176 (21 March 1952): 247. The Legion's attitude toward McGranery is indicated by its California branch, which gave him a plaque of commendation in late October for his stand against Chaplin. See *NYT*, 29 October 1952, p. 32.

57. Murray, "*Limelight*," p. 247.

58. Victor Lasky, "Whose Little Man?" *American Legion Magazine*, December 1951, pp. 28, 46–50.

59. *NYT*, 16 January 1953, p. 18. Brewer was also head of IATSE, the dominant film industry craft union. His anti-Communist strategy during the long film industry strike in 1945 is detailed in Sklar, *Movie-Made America*, pp. 256–62.

60. *NYT*, 28 January 1953, p. 23; Murray, "*Limelight*," p. 247.

61. Murray, "*Limelight*" surveys the censorship campaign of the Legion, but see also *NYT* (all 1953), 26 January, p. 15; 28 January, p. 23; 3 February, p. 21; 5 February, p. 15; and 13 February, p. 17; and *Variety* (all 1953), 21 January, p. 3; 4 February, p. 23; and 11 February, p. 5.

62. See *Variety* (all 1952), 8 October, p. 6; 29 October, p. 9; 5 November, p. 9; 12 November, p. 11; 19 November, p. 11; 26 November, p. 13; 3 December, pp. 8–9; 10 December, p. 9; 17 December, p. 9; 24 December, p. 9; 31 December, p. 9.

63. *Variety*, 4 February 1953, p. 5; 11 February 1953, p. 5; 4 March 1953, p. 4.

64. Pells, *Liberal Mind*, p. 265. In chapter 5, Pells discusses in considerable detail the varied responses of American intellectuals to the loyalty oaths, HUAC, McCarthy, and other issues that raised questions about the character of and threats to civil liberties in the United States in the late 1940s and early 1950s.

65. *Commonweal*, 6 February 1953, p. 441; *NYT*, 7 February 1953, p. 14. In the same issue (pp. 451–53), *Commonweal* also included a sympathetic and thoughtful review of *Limelight* by J. L. Tallenay, editor of a French journal, *La vie intellectuelle*, in which the review originally appeared.

66. *NYT*, 17 April 1953, p. 24.

67. Ruark's column is included in the George W. DeMott scrapbook, BRC.

11. THE EXILED MONARCH AND THE GUARDED RESTORATION

1. *Newsweek* 41 (27 April 1953): 37.

2. *Newsweek* 43 (14 June 1954): 48. A 1958 article on Chaplin in the *Saturday Evening Post* 230 (8 March 1958) reported that Chaplin refused to accept the award publicly in Berlin or London and preferred to accept it at his home, perhaps to avoid some of the negative publicity in the West that a more public ceremony could have generated.

3. See *London Times*, 25 April 1956, p. 10; and *NYT*, 25 April 1956, p. 3. In his autobiography Chaplin mistakenly reverses the visits with Chou En-lai and the Soviet leaders.

4. *NYT*, 5 June 1954, p. 16; for a similarly negative response, see also *Newsweek* 43 (14 June 1954): 48.

5. *Saturday Evening Post* 227 (4 September 1954): 10, 12. One of the few articles sympathetic to Chaplin appearing in the mid-1950s was "The Great Chaplin Chase," by Ernest Callenbach, which appeared in the *Nation* 83 (4 August 1956): 96–99. After surveying Chaplin's career, the article attributed American hostility for Chaplin to his politics, his escapades with women, and what Callenbach termed the "folk anarchism" of Chaplin's screen persona.

6. *NYT*, 7 January 1955, p. 16.

7. *NYT*, 8 January 1955, p. 9; 13 January 1955, p. 31. A similar incident occurred at the Hicksville (N.Y.) Public Library in November 1958; after letting the situation cool for a month, the library's board of trustees lifted their ban and permitted the screening of four Chaplin short films. See *NYT*, 12 November 1958, p. 39; 13 November 1958, p. 36; 19 December 1958, p. 2.

8. For brief reports on the production in the American press, see *NYT*, 20 December 1953, sec. 2, p. 5; 16 October 1954, p. 12; 26 August 1955, p. 11; 28 October 1956, sec. 2, p. 5.

9. During the time of the film's British release, Chaplin admitted to Ella Winter the parallel between himself and the deposed monarch. "There was a time," he told Winter, "when they put out the red carpet, literally, on every platform when I went from Los Angeles to New York. The crowd adored me." But both the king and Chaplin were deposed. See CHLA, pp. 592–93.

10. The roots of this conservative cultural critique appear to be autobiographical. Chaplin himself had long been accustomed to celebrity status, clearly used to the attention a king or even an ex-king would enjoy. He also increasingly came to enjoy a quiet and rather conservative home life when he was not making films. Charles Chaplin, Jr., describes this side of Chaplin in parts of *My Father, Charlie Chaplin*. After Chaplin's marriage to Oona O'Neill, this personally conservative side became even more central: his last twenty-five years were spent living in Swiss baronial splendor. In his film Chaplin gives King Shahdov both of these characteristics: enough celebrity status to warrant the attention of others and enough conservative temperament to find certain aspects of American culture amusing or even repugnant.

11. Chaplin apparently planned and budgeted the film knowing it would not be released in the United States. Robinson (CHLA, p. 590) notes that shooting took only twelve weeks, the shortest for any Chaplin feature. And given the enthusiastic welcome Chaplin received in Europe after his departure from the United States, he was probably right in assuming that he could recoup his expenditures via the European market alone.

12. *NYT*, 11 September 1957, p. 29; *New York Herald Tribune*, 11 September 1957; *Newsweek* 50 (9 September 1957): 108; *Time* 70 (23 September 1957): 48.

13. *NYT*, 11 September 1957, p. 29; *Time*, 70 (23 September 1957), p. 48; *Nation* 185 (2 November 1957), p. 310; *New York Herald Tribune*, 15 September 1957, sec. 4, p. 1.

14. "Chaplin Satirizes McCarthyism," *London Times*, 11 September 1957, p. 3.

15. CHLA p. 591; see also David Robinson, *Chaplin: The Mirror of Opinion* (Bloomington: Indiana Univ. Press, 1984), pp. 158–61.

16. Hodgson, *America in Our Time*, pp. 67, 75–76. One critic who did appreciate films with sociological or political "messages," *NYT* critic Bosley Crowther, did not attend the London premiere and consequently did not review the film. Of all the influential American critics in the mid-1950s, he was the one most likely to have responded positively to the film.

17. *Time* 70 (23 September 1947): 48; *Nation* 185 (2 November 1957): 310–11; *New Republic* 137 (7 October 1957): 22; and *Reporter* 17 (17 October 1957): 43. The commentators who criticized the film because its production values were low and its satire out of date did have a point. When the king is about to leave for his night out, for example, Chaplin cuts to some stock footage of movie marquees: one theater is playing *Three Little Words*, another is playing *Pretty Baby*, both American films released in 1950. Only the theater Shahdov walks into is playing a more recent film, *The Baby and the Battleship* (British, 1956). Though all three titles are consistent with Chaplin's satirical picture of the thinness of popular culture, the inclusion of out-of-date or foreign titles reveals a lack of concern for production values that the classical Hollywood cinema prided itself in. Similarly, since McCarthy had been censured by the Senate nearly three years earlier and HUAC was much less prone to issue con-

tempt citations than it had been between 1947 and 1953, Chaplin's satire was less topical than it was, say, in *The Great Dictator*.

18. *Saturday Review* 40 (28 September 1957): 26; *Newsweek* 50 (9 September 1957): 108. The subsequent reviews have already been cited in note 17; their page numbers are cited in the text.

19. *Saturday Evening Post* 230, part I (8 March 1958): 19–21 ff.; part II (15 March 1958): 44–45 ff.; part III (22 March 1958): 38 ff. Further references to these articles will be cited in the text with the part and page numbers in parentheses.

20. *NYT*, 21 February 1958, p. 19; *NYT*, 26 April 1960, p. 40.

21. Pells, *Liberal Mind*, p. 346. Pells treats this shifting mood of the late 1950s in chapter 6. On the circumstances leading to the downfall of Joseph McCarthy, see Eric F. Goldman, *The Crucial Decade and After, 1945–1960* (New York: Vintage, 1960), pp. 271–79.

22. *NYT*, 30 December 1958, p. 7, reported that Chaplin agreed to pay $425,000 in 1953 taxes. He claimed that since he was not in the country after September 1952, he was not liable for 1953 taxes. Though the IRS in 1956 announced that they would seek $1.1 million, the settlement was ultimately for $330,000 with interest. See CHLA, p. 593.

23. Ayer et al., "Self Censorship," in Kindem, *American Movie Industry*, p. 223.

24. *NYT*, 11 June 1959, p. 37; 24 July 1959, p. 14. *The Gold Rush* was not fully included in the decision. Chaplin had rereleased *The Gold Rush* with a recorded musical score in 1942, and his organization—perhaps partly due to the political pressures Chaplin found himself facing—failed to renew the copyright to the original film in 1952. Chaplin's organization thus still retains the copyright to the 1942 version of *The Gold Rush* but does not have rights to the 1925 version. That is one reason for the variant endings often found in that film.

25. Bosley Crowther, "The Modern—and Mellower—Times of Mr. Chaplin," *NYT Magazine*, 6 November 1960, pp. 52–60.

26. *NYT*, 28 June 1962, p. 1; 29 June 1962, p. 12; 2 July 1962, p. 28 (editorial).

27. An examination of *Variety*'s box-office grosses and the *Times* movie ads during this period establish the continuous run; generally, the Plaza ran a large ad in the *Times* at least the day before and the day of a new program's opening, then ran much smaller ads as time passed.

28. *NYT*, 7 July 1964, p. 25; *Variety*, 22 April 1964, p. 10; *Variety*, 26 August 1964, p. 13.

29. *New York Herald Tribune*, 26 July 1964, p. 26; *NYT*, 4 July 1964, p. 8; *NYT*, 12 July 1964, sec. II, p. 1.

30. *Newsweek* 64 (27 July 1964): 78. Emphasis added.

31. Jauss, "Literary History," in Jauss, *Toward an Aesthetic of Reception*, p. 21.

32. Ibid., pp. 25–26. Jauss argues that the "aesthetic distance" of a work also "provides a criterion for the determination of its aesthetic value" (p. 25): the

greater the aesthetic distance, the greater the work. Such an aesthetic seems clearly to derive from a modernist stress on originality and is problematic when applied to a commercial medium like the movies. If one accepts this tenet of Jauss's aesthetic, it is hard to avoid concluding that *Monsieur Verdoux* is Chaplin's greatest film.

33. *NYT*, 7 July 1964, p. 25. On the reception of *Strangelove*, see Charles Maland, "*Dr. Strangelove*: Nightmare Comedy and the Ideology of Liberal Consensus," in *Hollywood as Historian*, ed. Peter Rollins (Lexington: Univ. of Kentucky Press, 1983), pp. 208–10. The black humorists are treated perceptively by Morris Dickstein in *Gates of Eden* (New York: Basic, 1977), ch. 4.

34. *Time* 84 (2 October 1964): 132.

35. *Publishers Weekly* 186 (5 October 1964): 132; (26 October 1964): 74; (23 November 1964): 98; (14 December 1964): 106; 187 (15 March 1965): 98.

36. John Houseman, "Charlie's Chaplin," *Nation* 199 (12 October 1964): 223; *NYT*, 1 October 1964, p. 33; Brendan Gill, "Total Strangers," *New Yorker* 40 (12 December 1964): 237.

37. *Time* 84 (2 October 1964): 132; *National Review* 16 (December 1964): 1068.

38. *Newsweek* 64 (5 October 1964): 112; Houseman, "Charlie's Chaplin," p. 224; *NYT*, 16 October 1964, p. 36; *Harper's* 229 (October 1964): 131.

39. *Commonweal* 81 (16 October 1964): 104. Other reviews cited in notes 37 and 38.

40. Atkinson, *NYT*, 16 October 1964, p. 36; Hatch, *Harper's* 229 (October 1964): 129; Gill, *New Yorker*, 12 December 1964, p. 238; Poore, *NYT*, 1 October 1964, p. 33.

41. *NYT*, 23 July 1965, p. 19; 2 November 1965, p. 28; 17 March 1967, p. 35.

42. *Life* 60 (1 April 1966): 80–86; 62 (10 March 1967): 80–94.

43. *Time* 89 (31 March 1967): 95; *Newsweek* 69 (3 April 1967): 90; *National Review* 19 (30 May 1967): 599, 600; *Commonweal* 86 (1 April 1967): 128. It is unlikely that the negative reviews surprised Chaplin, for he had already suffered through a similar set when the film premiered in London in January. According to the *NYT*, Chaplin told reporters that the London critics who didn't like *Countess* were "bloody idiots." See *NYT*, 7 January 1967, p. 22.

44. *Monsieur Verdoux* and *Countess* both ran just over two months and grossed slightly over $20,000 in their first two weeks. At the end of two months in 1964, however, *Monsieur Verdoux* was still grossing $11,500 per week at the Plaza; *Countess* was down to about $8,500 per week at the Sutton. See *Variety*, 10 May 1967, p. 10.

45. *Variety*, 3 January 1968, p. 25.

46. Hartung, *Commonweal* 86 (1 April 1967): 90; Kenner, *National Review* 19 (30 May 1967): 600.

47. *Chicago Tribune*, 11 January 1972, sec. 2, p. 1; *NYT*, 7 April 1972, p. 24; CHLA, pp. 620–21.

48. *NYT*, 7 April 1972, p. 24.

49. *NYT*, 14 January 1972, p. 18; 9 February 1972, p. 44.

50. *NYT*, 5 April 1972, p. 38; *New Yorker*, 15 April 1972, pp. 36–37.

51. *NYT*, 7 April 1972, p. 24.

52. *NYT*, 12 April 1972, p. 9; *Los Angeles Times*, 12 April 1972, sec. 4, p. 13; *Life* 72 (21 April 1972): 90. Emphasis in original.

53. See Hodgson, *America in Our Time*, pp. 384–85, 421–28.

54. See *Reader's Guide to Periodical Literature*, vol. 32 (1972), s.v. "Chaplin, Charlie."

55. *Time* 99 (17 April 1972): 71; *Newsweek* 79 (17 April 1972): 94; Richard Meryman, "Love Feast for Charlie," and Candace Bergen, " 'I Thought They Might Hiss,' " *Life* 72 (21 April 1972): 86–90..

56. *Time* 99 (10 April 1972): 65–66.

57. *NYT*, 8 February 1972, p. 24. The *Times'* followup editorial, "Tramp's Triumph" (7 April 1972, sec. 1, p. 34), appeared after the Lincoln Center affair and was, if anything, even harder on the officials who banned Chaplin in 1952. It noted that Chaplin's admirers were on hand to greet him, but the faded officials responsible for his exile were not. "Chaplin knows the difference between the morals of a country and the moralizing of its passing politicians," wrote the editors. "We can only be grateful that he does, for otherwise we would not have had the pleasure of his return."

58. *Los Angeles Times*, 10 April 1972, sec. 2, p. 6; *Chicago Tribune*, 10 April 1972, p. 16.

59. *Nation* 214 (24 April 1972): 518–19.

60. *Los Angeles Times*, 9 April 1972, sec. 1B, p. 1.

61. *NYT*, 11 February 1972, p. 36; *Los Angeles Times*, 9 April 1972, sec. 1B, p. 1; *Los Angeles Times*, 11 April 1972, sec. 1, p. 3; *Los Angeles Times*, 18 April 1972, sec. 4, p. 18.

62. Richard Schickel, "Hail Chaplin—The Early Chaplin," *NYT Magazine*, 2 April 1972, pp. 12–13, 47–48; George H. Dunne, "I Remember Chaplin," *Commonweal* 96 (2 June 1972): 303–9. Subsequent references to these articles will be made parenthetically in the text.

63. *NYT*, 18 June 1973, p. 5.

64. *NYT*, 8 April 1972, p. 16; 7 April 1972, p. 29.

65. *NYT*, 16 April 1972, sec. 2, pp. 1, 26; 23 January 1972, sec. 2, p. 12; 18 June 1973, sec. 2, p. 5; 8 July 1973, sec. 2, p. 1.

66. *Chicago Tribune*, 25 February 1972, sec. 2, p. 13; 17 March, sec. 2, p. 1.

67. *Los Angeles Times*, 2 April 1972, Calif., p. 12; 13 December 1972, sec. 4, p. 28.

68. *Film Comment* 8 (September-October 1972): 11–26. Page numbers for quotations from this issue will be cited in the text. The *Film Comment* articles probably had a somewhat larger influence on Chaplin's image than they normally would have, because Chaplin's American distributor in the mid-1970s, RBC Films, sent out photocopies of this issue, along with a 1970 *Film Comment* article on *The Circus* by David Bordwell, to those who ordered a Chaplin series.

69. Sam L. Grogg, Jr., and Dennis R. Bohnenkamp, *AFI Guide to College Courses in Film and Television* (Washington: American Film Institute, 1978).

70. A detailed bibliographical essay on Chaplin criticism is available in Wes Gehring, *Charlie Chaplin: A Bio-Bibliography* (Westport, Conn.: Greenwood, 1983), ch. 4. See also Timothy Lyons, *Charles Chaplin: A Guide to References and Resources* (Boston: G. K. Hall, 1979).

71. The articles by Sarris and Kael are included in Gerald Mast and Marshall Cohen, *Film Theory and Criticism*, 3rd ed. (New York: Oxford Univ. Press, 1985), pp. 527–52. The articles have appeared in this widely used anthology since its first edition. See also Edward Murray, "Andrew Sarris and *Auteur* Criticism," in his *Nine American Film Critics* (New York: Ungar, 1975), pp. 38–66.

72. Andrew Sarris, *The American Cinema: Directors and Directions, 1929–1968* (New York: Dutton, 1968).

73. See Beaver, *Bosley Crowther*.

74. Richard Roud, ed., *Cinema: A Biographical Dictionary* (New York: Viking, 1980), 1: 201–12.

75. This shift is most apparent in Sarris's more recent collection of film criticism, *Politics and Cinema* (New York: Columbia Univ. Press, 1978); see esp. pp. 1–22 .

76. Gerald Mast, *A Short History of the Movies*, 2nd ed. (New York: Dutton, 1976), chs. 5, 6, and 11.

77. Mast, *Comic Mind*, pp. 61–124.

78. Bordwell and Thompson, *Film Art*, 2nd ed., pp. 34–35. In this second edition, Bordwell and Thompson have added two other possible criteria for evaluating films: coherence and intensity of effect (p. 34). It could easily be argued that some of Chaplin's films would fare considerably better if evaluated by those standards than by the standards of originality and complexity.

79. Quoted in Roud, *Cinema: A Biographical Dictionary*, p. 201.

80. For an attempt to discuss the historical context and describe the critical agenda of this semiological/ideological approach, see Sylvia Harvey, *May '68 and Film Culture* (London: British Film Institute, 1980). Some of the challenges to the auteur approach, some from semiological or ideological perspectives, are discussed or reprinted in John Caughie, ed., *Theories of Authorship* (London: Routledge and Kegan Paul, 1981), pp. 199–291.

81. Smith, *Chaplin*, passim.

82. Chaplin himself helped stimulate interest in the production history of his films when he published *My Life in Pictures*, a kind of photo album summarizing his career. The book was published in England in 1974 and in the United States in 1975.

83. Molyneaux, *Charlie Chaplin's "City Lights,"* p. 57.

84. Anthony Slide, "The American Press and Public v. Charles Spencer Chaplin," *Cineaste* 13, no. 4 (1984): 9.

85. CHLA, pp. 746, xiv.

86. Chaplin's death on Christmas Eve in 1977, and the subsequent bizarre

story of his disinterment and demands for ransom to return the body, are discussed in CHLA, pp. 627–31.

12. EPILOGUE

1. Martin Porter, "That's Why the PC Is a Tramp," *PC Magazine* 2 (July 1983): 329–34.

2. Verne Gay, "Charlie Chaplin is Alive and Well," *Marketing and Media Decisions*, 19 April 1984, p. 89; Porter, "That's Why," pp. 329–34.

3. Daniel Burstein, "Using Yesterday to Sell Tomorrow: How the Unlikely IBM–Charlie Chaplin Marriage Came to Be," *Advertising Age* 54 (11 April 1983): sec. 2, p. 4; Porter, "That's Why," p. 333.

4. Burstein, "Using Yesterday," p. 5.

5. Telephone conversation with IBM, Montvale, N.J., 11 August 1986; Gay, "Charlie," p. 94.

6. Burstein, "Using Yesterday," p. 5.

7. Gay, "Charlie," p. 88.

8. Telephone conversation with IBM, Boca Raton, Florida, 11 August 1986.

9. Burstein, "Using Yesterday," p. 5.

10. Bob Marich, "Hagman Has DGA Top Spot for His TV Work," *Advertising Age* 56 (14 March 1985): 3.

11. Paul Richter, "Estate Zealously Guards Chaplin's Little Tramp," *Los Angeles Times*, 12 June 1984, sec. 4, pp. 1, 3; Porter, "That's Why," p. 331; *PC Magazine* 1, no. 2 (1983), passim.

12. Richter, "Estate," pp. 1, 3.

13. Porter, "That's Why," p. 330; Burstein, "Using Yesterday," p. 5.

14. Gay, "Charlie," pp. 88–89.

15. The ad is reprinted in Burstein, "Using Yesterday," p. 4.

16. Porter, "That's Why," pp. 332, 334, 330.

17. Ibid., p. 330; telephone conversation with IBM, Montvale, N.J., 11 August 1986.

18. On stardom and the ideological functions of compensation, reinforcement of values, and displacement of values, see Dyer, *Stars*, pp. 22–34. An interesting collection focusing on gender and reading response is Elisabeth Flynn and Patrocinio P. Schweickart, *Gender and Reading: Essays on Readers, Texts, and Contexts* (Baltimore: Johns Hopkins Univ. Press, 1986). See particularly the essays by Crawford and Chaffin, Bleich, and Flynn. Another useful essay on reader response criticism and its application to television viewing is Robert C. Allen's in *Channels of Discourse*, ed. Robert C. Allen (Chapel Hill: Univ. of North Carolina Press, 1987), ch. 3.

Select Bibliography

This bibliography lists a selection of the works most useful in the researching of this book and is divided into four categories: newspapers and periodicals; works by or about Chaplin (including memoirs and parts of books); works on film history, film theory, and literary theory; and works on twentieth-century American cultural history. Archives consulted are listed in the Acknowledgments. My search for secondary sources dealing with Chaplin has been considerably assisted by two very useful bibliographies: Timothy Lyons, *Charles Chaplin: A Guide to References and Resources* (Boston, 1979), and Wes Gehring, *Charlie Chaplin: A Bio-Bibliography* (Westport, Conn., 1983).

NEWSPAPERS AND PERIODICALS

This listing includes only the newspapers and periodicals I consulted most systematically in my attempt to gauge the character and evolution of Chaplin's public reputation in America.

Chicago Tribune
Daily Worker
Los Angeles Times
New York Herald Tribune
New York Times
Variety
Washington Post
Commonweal
Life

Motion Picture Magazine
Moving Picture World
Nation
New Masses
New Republic
Newsweek
Photoplay
Saturday Evening Post
Time

WORKS BY OR ABOUT CHAPLIN

Auerbach, David. "Charlie Chaplin: Of Crime and Genius—A Psycho-Portrait." *Encounter* 60 (May 1983): 86–92.

Bishop, John Peale. *The Collected Essays of John Peale Bishop*. Edited by Edmund Wilson. New York, 1948.

Burke, Thomas. *City of Encounters*. Boston, 1932.

Callenbach, Ernest. "The Great Chaplin Chase." *Nation* 83 (4 August 1956): 96–99.

Chaplin, Charles. *Charlie Chaplin's Own Story.* Edited by Harry Geduld. Indianapolis, 1916. Reprinted Bloomington, 1985.

———. "In Defense of Myself." *Collier's,* 11 November 1922, reprinted in Gehring, *Charles Chaplin,* pp. 108–14.

———. "What People Laugh At." *American Magazine* 86 (November 1918): 34, 134–37.

———. *My Trip Abroad.* New York, 1922.

———. "Pantomime and Comedy." *New York Times,* 25 January 1931, sec. 8, p. 8.

———. "A Comedian Sees the World." *Woman's Home Companion* 61 (September 1933–January 1934). Five-part memoir.

———. *My Autobiography.* New York, 1964.

———. *My Life in Pictures.* New York, 1975.

Chaplin, Charles, Jr. *My Father, Charlie Chaplin.* New York, 1961.

Chaplin, Lita Grey, with Morton Cooper. *My Life with Chaplin: An Intimate Memoir.* New York, 1966.

Cooke, Alistair. *Six Men.* New York, 1977.

Dreiser, Helen. *My Life with Dreiser.* New York, 1951.

Dunne, George. "I Remember Chaplin." *Commonweal* 96 (2 June 1972): 303–309.

d'Usseau, Arnaud. "Chaplin's *Monsieur Verdoux.*" *Mainstream* 1 (Summer 1947): 308–317.

Eastman, Max. *Heroes I Have Known.* New York, 1942.

———. *Great Companions.* New York, 1959.

———. *Love and Revolution.* New York, 1964.

Eisenstein, Sergei. *Immoral Memories.* Translated by Herbert Marshall. Boston, 1983.

Film Comment 8 (September-October 1972). Special issue on Chaplin.

Frank, Waldo. *Memoirs of Waldo Frank.* Edited by Alan Trachtenberg. Amherst, 1973.

———. *Time Exposures.* New York, 1926.

Gehring, Wes. "Chaplin and the Progressive Era: The Neglected Politics of a Clown." *Indiana Social Studies Quarterly* 34 (Autumn 1981): 10–18.

———. *Charlie Chaplin: A Bio-Bibliography.* Westport, Conn., 1983.

Giesler, Jerry. *The Jerry Giesler Story.* New York, 1960.

Harris, Frank. *Contemporary Portraits.* 4th series. New York, 1923.

Huff, Theodore. *Charlie Chaplin.* 1951. Reprinted New York, 1964.

Kerr, Walter. *The Silent Clowns.* New York, 1975.

Lyons, Timothy. *Charles Chaplin: A Guide to References and Resources.* Boston, 1979.

———. "The United States vs. Charlie Chaplin." *American Film* 9 (September 1984): 29–34.

McCabe, John. *Charlie Chaplin.* Garden City, N.Y.: Doubleday, 1978.

McCaffrey, Donald, ed. *Focus on Chaplin.* Englewood Cliffs, N.J., 1971.

Macdonald, Dwight. "On Chaplin, Verdoux, and Agee." *Esquire* 63, April 1965.

MacDonald, Gerald et al., eds. *The Films of Charlie Chaplin*. New York: Citadel, 1965.

Maland, Charles J. *American Visions: The Films of Chaplin, Ford, Capra, and Welles, 1936–1941*. New York, 1977.

———. "A Documentary Note on Charlie Chaplin's Politics." *Historical Journal of Film, Radio and Television* 5, no. 2 (1985): 199–208.

———. " 'Are You Now or Have You Ever Been?': An INS Interview with Charles Chaplin." *Cineaste* 14, no. 4 (1986): 10–15.

Manning, Harold, and Timothy J. Lyons. "Charlie Chaplin's Early Life: Fact and Fiction." *Historical Journal of Film, Radio, and Television* 3, no. 1 (1983): 35–41.

Mast, Gerald. *The Comic Mind*. 2nd ed. Chicago, 1979.

Menjou, Adolphe, and M. M. Musselman. *It Took Nine Tailors*. New York, 1948.

Molyneaux, Gerard. *Charlie Chaplin's "City Lights."* New York, 1983.

Montagu, Ivor. *With Eisenstein in Hollywood*. New York, 1969.

Moss, Robert F. *Charlie Chaplin*. New York, 1975.

Munson, Gorham. *The Awakening Twenties*. Baton Rouge, 1985.

Negri, Pola. *Memoirs of a Star*. New York, 1970.

Newhouse, Edward. "Charlie's Critics." *Partisan Review* 3 (April 1936): 25–26.

Oakie, Jack. *Jack Oakie's Double Takes*. San Francisco, 1980.

Ramsaye, Terry. "Chaplin Ridicules Reds' Claim Film Aids 'Cause.' " *Motion Picture Herald* 7 December 1935, p. 1.

Robinson, David. *Chaplin: The Mirror of Opinion*. Bloomington, 1984.

———. *Chaplin*: His Life and Art. New York, 1985.

Rosen, Philip. "The Chaplin World View." *Cinema Journal* 9 (Fall 1969): 2–12.

Rozas, Lorenzo Turrent. "Charlie Chaplin's Decline." *Living Age* 396 (June 1934): 319–23.

Sadoul, Georges. *Vie de Charlot*. Paris, 1978.

Sarris, Andrew. "Charles Spencer Chaplin." *Cinema: A Critical Dictionary*. Edited by Richard Roud. Vol. 1. London, 1980.

Schickel, Richard. "Hail Chaplin—The Early Chaplin." *New York Times Magazine*, 2 April 1972, pp. 12–13, 47–48.

Seldes, Gilbert. *The Seven Lively Arts*. New York, 1924.

Sinclair, Upton. *The Autobiography of Upton Sinclair*. New York, 1962.

Shumiatsky, Boris. "Charlie Chaplin's New Picture." *New Masses*, 24 September 1935, pp. 29–30.

Slide, Anthony. "The American Press and Public versus Charles Spencer Chaplin." *Cineaste* 13, no. 4 (1984): 6–9.

Smith, Julian. *Chaplin*. Boston, 1984.

Sobel, Raoul, and David Francis. *Chaplin: Genesis of a Clown*. London, 1977.

Stewart, Donald Ogden. *By a Stroke of Luck*. New York, 1975.

Stewart, Garret. "Modern Hard Times: Chaplin and the Cinema of Self-Reflexiveness." *Critical Inquiry* 3 (1976): 295–315.

Sullivan, Ed, ed. *Chaplin vs. Chaplin*. Los Angeles, 1965.

Tyler, Parker. *Chaplin: Last of the Clowns*. New York, 1972 (reprint), 1947.

Viertel, Salka. *The Kindness of Strangers*. New York, 1969.

von Ulm, Gerith. *Charlie Chaplin: King of Comedy*. Caldwell, Idaho, 1940.

von Wiegand, Charmion. "Little Man, What Now?" *New Theater* 3 (March 1936): 6–8.

Wallach, George. "Charlie Chaplin's *Monsieur Verdoux* Press Conference." *Film Comment*, 5 (Winter 1969): 34–42.

WORKS ON FILM HISTORY, FILM THEORY, AND LITERARY THEORY

Agee, James. *Agee on Film*. Vol. 1. Boston, 1964.

Allen, Robert C. *Vaudeville and Film, 1895–1915: A Study in Media Interaction*. New York, 1980.

———. *Speaking of Soap Operas*. Chapel Hill, 1985.

———, ed. *Channels of Discourse*. Chapel Hill, 1987.

Allen, Robert C. and Douglas Gomery. *Film History: Theory and Practice*. New York, 1985.

Balio, Tino. *United Artists*. Madison, 1976.

Balio, Tino, ed. *The American Film Industry*. 2nd ed. Madison, 1985.

Baxter, John. *The Hollywood Exiles*. London, 1976.

Beaver, Frank. *Bosley Crowther: Social Critic of the Film*. New York, 1974.

Bennett, Tony. "Text and Social Process: The Case of James Bond." *Screen Education* 41 (Winter/Spring 1982): 3–14.

Bennett, Tony, and Janet Woollacott. *Bond and Beyond: The Political Career of a Popular Hero*. London, 1987.

Bordwell, David, and Kristin Thompson. *Film Art*. 2nd ed. New York, 1986.

Bordwell, David, Janet Staiger, and Kristin Thompson. *The Classical Hollywood Cinema: Film Style and Mode of Production to 1960*. New York, 1985. Abbreviated in notes as CHC.

Brownlow, Kevin. *The War, the West, and the Wilderness*. New York, 1979.

Burch, Noël. *To the Distant Observer*. Berkeley, 1979.

Caughie, John, ed. *Theories of Authorship*. London, 1981.

Cawelti, John. *Adventure, Mystery, and Romance*. Chicago, 1976.

Ceplair, Larry, and Steven Englund. *The Inquisition in Hollywood: Politics and the Film Community, 1930–1960*. New York, 1980.

DiNitto, Dennis, and William Herman. *Film and the Critical Eye*. New York, 1975.

Dunne, Philip. *Take Two*. New York, 1980.

Dyer, Richard. *Stars*. London, 1979.

Eckert, Charles. "Shirley Temple and the House of Rockefeller." *Jump Cut* no. 2 (July-August 1974): 1, 17–20.

Eells, George. *Hedda and Louella*. New York, 1972.

Eisler, Hanns. *A Rebel in Music*. Edited by Manfred Grabs. New York, 1978.

Ferguson, Otis. *The Film Criticism of Otis Ferguson*. Edited by Robert Wilson. Philadelphia, 1971.

Geduld, Harry. *The Birth of the Talkies*. Bloomington, 1975.

Gomery, Douglas. "The Coming of Sound to the American Cinema: A History of the Transformation of an Industry." Ph.D. dissertation, University of Wisconsin, 1975.

Haralovich, Mary Beth. "The Social History of Film: Heterogeneity and Mediation." *Wide Angle* 8, no. 2 (1986): 4–14.

Harvey, Sylvia. *May '68 and Film Culture*. London, 1980.

Jacobs, Lewis. *Rise of the American Film*. New York, 1939.

Jauss, Hans Robert. *Toward an Aesthetic of Reception*. Translated by Timothy Bahti. Minneapolis, 1982.

Jowett, Garth. *Film: The Democratic Art*. Boston, 1976.

Kauffmann, Stanley, ed. *American Film Criticism*. New York, 1972.

Kindem, Gorham, ed. *The American Movie Industry*. Carbondale, Ill., 1982.

Lounsbury, Myron. *The Origins of American Film Criticism*. New York, 1973.

McArthur, Benjamin. *Actors and American Culture, 1800–1920*. Philadelphia, 1984.

Mast, Gerald. *A Short History of the Movies*. 2nd ed. New York, 1976.

Mast, Gerald, and Marshall Cohen. *Film Theory and Criticism*. 3rd ed. New York, 1985.

May, Lary. *Screening Out the Past*. New York, 1980.

Mellen, Joan. *Big Bad Wolves: Masculinity in American Film*. New York, 1977.

Mitchell, George. "The Consolidation of the American Film Industry." *Cine-Tracts* nos. 2 (1976): 28–36; and 3/4 (1976): 63–70.

Morin, Edgar. *The Stars*. Translated by Richard Howard. New York, 1960.

Murray, Edward. *Nine American Film Critics*. New York, 1975.

Neale, Stephen. *Genre*. London, 1980.

Potamkin, Harry Alan. *The Compound Cinema: The Film Writings of Harry Alan Potamkin*. Edited by Lewis Jacobs. New York, 1977.

Poteet, George H. *Film Criticism in Popular American Periodicals, 1933–67*. New York, 1977.

Radway, Janice. *Reading the Romance*. Chapel Hill, 1984.

Ray, Robert. *A Certain Tendency of the Hollywood Cinema, 1930–1980*. Princeton, 1985.

Rosten, Leo. *Hollywood*. New York, 1941.

Sarris, Andrew. *The American Cinema: Directors and Directions, 1929–1968*. New York, 1968.

———. *Politics and Cinema*. New York, 1978.

Schatz, Thomas. *Hollywood Genres*. New York, 1981.

Schwartz, Nancy Lynn. *The Hollywood Writers' Wars*. New York, 1982.

Sklar, Robert. *Movie-Made America*. New York, 1976.

Slide, Anthony, ed. *Selected Film Criticism, 1921–30*. Metuchen, N.J., 1982.

———. *Selected Film Criticism, 1931–40*. Metuchen, N.J., 1982.

Staiger, Janet. "Seeing Stars." *Velvet Light Trap* no. 20 (Summer 1983): 13–17.

———. "Individualism versus Collectivism." *Screen* 24, nos. 4/5 (July-October 1983): 68–79.

Taylor, John Russell. *Strangers in Paradise: The Hollywood Emigrés, 1933–50*. London, 1983.

Tomashevsky, Boris. "Literature and Biography." In *Readings in Russian Poetics*, ed. Ladislav Matejka and Krystyna Pomorska. Ann Arbor, 1978.

Walker, Alexander. *The Shattered Silents*. New York, 1979.

Warshow, Robert. *The Immediate Experience*. New York, 1962.

Williams, Raymond. *Keywords*. London, 1976.

WORKS ON TWENTIETH-CENTURY AMERICAN CULTURAL HISTORY

Aaron, Daniel. *Writers on the Left*. New York, 1961.

Alexander, Charles. *Here the Country Lies*. Bloomington, 1980.

Barrett, Edward L., Jr. *The Tenney Committee*. Ithaca, 1951.

Belfrage, Cedric. *The American Inquisition*. New York, 1973.

Bell, Daniel. *Marxian Socialism in the United States*. Rev. ed. Princeton, 1967.

Bentley, Eric, ed. *Thirty Years of Treason*. New York, 1971.

Caute, David. *The Great Fear*. New York, 1978.

Cook, Bruce. *Brecht in Exile*. New York, 1982.

Coser, Lewis. *Refugee Scholars in America*. New Haven, 1984.

Cowley, Malcolm. *Exile's Return*. Rev. ed. New York, 1951.

Diggins, John. *The American Left in the Twentieth Century*. New York, 1973.

Foner, Philip S. *Paul Robeson Speaks*. New York, 1978.

Gillim, Dorothy Baker. *Paul Robeson: All American*. Washington, D.C., 1976.

Goldman, Eric. *The Crucial Decade and After, 1945–1960*. New York, 1960.

Goodman, Walter. *The Committee*. New York, 1968.

Harris, Leon. *Upton Sinclair: American Rebel*. New York, 1975.

Heilbut, Anthony. *Exiled in Paradise: German Refugee Artists and Intellectuals in America, from the 1930s to the Present*. New York, 1983.

Hilfer, Anthony Channell. *The Revolt against the Village, 1915–1930*. Chapel Hill, 1969.

Hodgson, Geoffrey. *America in Our Time*. New York, 1976.

Howe, Irving, and Lewis Coser. *The American Communist Party*. Boston, 1957.

Leuchtenberg, William. *Franklin D. Roosevelt and the New Deal*. New York, 1963.

Levering, Ralph. *American Opinion and the Russian Alliance, 1939–1945*. Chapel Hill, 1976.

Lyon, James K. *Bertolt Brecht in America*. Princeton, 1980.

McAuliffe, Mary. *Crisis on the Left*. Amherst, 1978.

Manchester, William. *The Glory and the Dream*. New York, 1974.

May, Henry F. *The End of American Innocence*. New York, 1959.

O'Neill, William. *A Better World*. New York, 1982.

O'Reilly, Kenneth. *Hoover and the Un-Americans*. Philadelphia, 1983.

Pells, Richard. *Radical Visions and American Dreams*. New York, 1973.

———. *The Liberal Mind in a Conservative Age*. New York, 1985.

Skotheim, Robert. *Totalitarianism and American Social Thought*. New York, 1971.

Starobin, Joseph R. *American Communism in Crisis, 1943–1957*. Cambridge, 1972.

Susman, Warren. "The Culture of the Thirties" and "Culture and Commitment." In *Culture as History*. New York, 1984. pp. 150–210.

Wald, Alan. *The New York Intellectuals*. Chapel Hill, 1987.

Wilson, Edmund. *The Shores of Light*. New York, 1952.

———. *The Twenties*. New York, 1975.

———. *Letters on Literature and Politics, 1912–1972*. New York, 1977.

Wise, Gene. *American Historical Explanations: A Strategy for Grounded Inquiry*. 2nd ed., rev. Minneapolis, 1980.

Wittner, Lawrence S. *Cold War America*. New York, 1974.

Young, Stark. *Stark Young, A Life in the Arts: Letters, 1900–1962*. Edited by John Pilkington. Baton Rouge, 1975.

Index

Webster's Contemporary
School & Office Dictionary

Webster's Contemporary School & Office Dictionary

Created in Cooperation with the Editors of
MERRIAM-WEBSTER

FEDERAL
STREET
PRESS

A Division of Merriam-Webster, Incorporated
Springfield, Massachusetts

This 2008 edition published by
Federal Street Press
A Division of Merriam-Webster, Incorporated
P.O. Box 281
Springfield, MA 01102

Federal Street Press books are available for bulk purchase for
sales promotion and premium use.
For details write the manager of special sales,
Federal Street Press, P.O. Box 281, Springfield, MA 01102

ISBN 13   978-1-59695-047-4

ISBN 10   1-59695-047-1

Printed in the United States of America

08 09 10 11 12   5 4 3 2 1

CONTENTS

PREFACE

The 70,000 plus definitions that you will find in this dictionary cover the words most frequently used in English language speech and writing. You will find a wealth of information in this volume about meaning, spelling, pronunciation, etymology, and synonyms.

A Foreign Words and Phrases section covers words and phrases from other languages that often occur in English texts but have not become part of the standard English vocabulary.

In addition, an in-depth Biographical Names section offers information about individuals from history and contemporary culture as well as biblical, legendary and mythological characters. A fully up-to-date Geographical Names section identifies places of importance in the United States and the world, as well as providing current population figures.

This dictionary was created by the editors of Merriam-Webster, a company that has been publishing dictionaries and other language reference books for more than 170 years.

The dictionary contains so much information, that it is necessary to condense much of it to accommodate the limitations of the printed page. This section provides information on the conventions used throughout the dictionary, from the styling of entries and pronunciation to how we present information on usage and meaning. An understanding of the information contained in these notes will make the dictionary both easier and more rewarding to use.

ENTRIES

A boldface letter or a combination of such letters, including punctuation marks and diacritics where needed, that is set flush with the left-hand margin of each column of type is a main entry. The main entry may consist of letters set solid, of letters joined by a hyphen or a diagonal, or of letters separated by one or more spaces:

alone . . . *adj*
avant–garde . . . *n*
and/or . . . *conj*
assembly language *n*
av·a·lanche . . . *n*

The material in lightface type that follows each main entry on the same line and on succeeding indented lines presents information about the main entry.

The main entries follow one another in alphabetical order letter by letter: *bill of attainder* follows *billion; Day of Atonement* follows *daylight saving time*. Those containing an Arabic numeral are alphabetized as if the numeral were spelled out: *4-H* comes between *fourfold* and *Four Hundred; 3-D* comes between *three* and *three-dimensional*. Those that often begin with the abbreviation *St.* in common usage have the abbreviation spelled out: *Saint Valentine's Day*. Main entries that begin with *Mc* are alphabetized just as they are spelled.

A pair of guide words is printed at the top of each page. These indicate that the entries falling alphabetically between the words at the top of the outer column of each page are found on that page.

The guide words are usually the alphabetically first and the alphabetically last entries on the page:

alpha rhythm · ambition

Occasionally the last printed entry is not the alphabetically last entry. Any boldface word—a main entry with definition, a variant, an inflected form, a defined or undefined run-on, or a run-in entry—may be used as a guide word.

On page 27, for example, *ascertain* is the last main entry, but *ascertainable*, an undefined run-on entry at *ascertain*, is the alphabetically last entry and is therefore the second guide word. The alphabetically last entry is not used, however, if it follows alphabetically the first guide word on the succeeding page. Thus on page 41 *bears* is not a guide word because it follows alphabetically the entry *bear* which is the first guide word on page 42.

When one main entry has exactly the same written form as another, the two are distinguished by superscript numerals preceding each word:

¹**melt** . . . *vb*
²**melt** *n*
¹**pine** . . . *n*
²**pine** *vb*

Full words come before parts of words made up of the same letters; solid compounds come before hyphenated compounds; hyphenated compounds come before open compounds; and lowercase entries come before those with an initial capital:

²**super** *n*
super- . . . *prefix*
run·down . . . *n*
run–down . . . *adj*
run down *vb*
dutch . . . *adv*
Dutch . . . *n*

The centered dots within entry words indicate division points at which a hyphen may be put at the end of a line of print or writing. Thus the noun *cap·puc·ci·no* may be ended on one line and continued on the next in this manner:

                           cap-
puccino
                         cappuc-
cino
                         cappucci-
no

Centered dots are not shown after a single initial letter or before a single terminal letter because typesetters seldom cut off a single letter:

abyss . . . *n*
flighty . . . *adj*
idea . . . *n*

Nor are they usually shown at the second and succeeding homographs unless they differ among themselves:

¹sig·nal . . . *n*
²signal *vb*
³signal *adj*
   but
¹min·ute . . . *n*
²mi·nute . . . *adj*

There are acceptable alternative end-of-line divisions just as there are acceptable variant spellings and pronunciations, but no more than one division is shown for any entry in this dictionary.

A double hyphen at the end of a line in this dictionary (as in the definition at ¹**pug 1**) stands for a hyphen that is retained when the word is written as a unit on one line. This kind of fixed hyphen is always represented in boldface words in this dictionary with an en dash, longer than an ordinary hyphen.

When a main entry is followed by the word *or* and another spelling, the two spellings are equal variants. Both are standard, and either one may be used according to personal inclination:

ocher *or* ochre

If two variants joined by *or* are out of alphabetical order, they remain equal variants. The one printed first is, however, slightly more common than the second:

¹plow *or* plough

When another spelling is joined to the main entry by the word *also*, the spelling after *also* is a secondary variant and occurs less frequently than the first:

absinthe *also* absinth

Secondary variants belong to standard usage and may be used according to personal inclination. Once the word *also* is used to signal a secondary variant, all following secondary variants are joined by *or*:

²wool·ly *also* wool·ie *or* wooly

Variants whose spelling puts them alphabetically more than a column away from the main entry are entered at their own alphabetical places as well as at the applicable main entry:

²gage *var of* GAUGE
¹gauge *also* gage
²gauge *also* gage

Variants having a usage label appear only at their own alphabetical places:

me·tre . . . *chiefly Brit var of* METER

To show all the stylings that are found for English compounds would require space that can be better used for other information. So this dictionary limits itself to a single styling for a compound:

peace·mak·er
pell–mell
boom box

When a compound is widely used and one styling predominates, that styling is shown. When a compound is uncommon or when the evidence indicates that two or three stylings are approximately equal in frequency, the styling shown is based on the comparison of other similar compounds.

A main entry may be followed by one or more derivatives or by a homograph with a different functional label. These are run-on entries. Each is introduced by a long dash and each has a functional label. They are not defined, however, since their meanings are readily understood from the meaning of the root word:

fear·less . . . *adj* . . . — fear·less·ly *adv* —
   fear·less·ness *n*
hic·cup . . . *n* . . . — hiccup *vb*

A main entry may be followed by one or more phrases containing the entry word or an inflected form of it. These are also run-on entries. Each is introduced by a long dash but there is no functional label. They are, however, defined since their meanings are more than the sum of the meanings of their elements:

¹set . . . *vb* . . . — set sail : . . .
¹hand . . . *n* . . . — at hand : . . .

Defined phrases of this sort are run on at the entry defining the first major word in the phrase. When there are variants, however, the run-on appears at the entry defining the first major invariable word in the phrase:

¹seed . . . *n* . . . — go to seed *or* run to seed
   1 : . . .

Boldface words that appear within parentheses (as **co·ca** at **co·caine** and **jet engine** and **jet propulsion** at **jet–propelled**) are run-in entries.

Attention is called to the definition of *vocabulary entry* on page 556. The term *dictionary entry* includes all vocabulary entries as well as all boldface entries in the back sections headed "Foreign Words & Phrases," "Biographical Names," and "Geographical Names."

PRONUNCIATION

The matter between a pair of reversed slashes \ \ following the entry word indicates the pronunciation. The symbols used are explained in the chart at the end of this section.

A hyphen is used in the pronunciation to show syllabic division. These hyphens sometimes coincide with the centered dots in the entry word that indicate end-of-line division:

ab·sen·tee \,ab-sən-'tē\

Sometimes they do not:

met·ric \'me-trik\

A high-set mark ' indicates major (primary) stress or accent; a low-set mark , indicates minor (secondary) stress or accent:

heart·beat \'härt-,bēt\

The stress mark stands at the beginning of the syllable that receives the stress.

A syllable with neither a high-set mark nor a low-set mark is unstressed:

¹**struc·ture** \'strək-chər\

The presence of variant pronunciations indicates that not all educated speakers pronounce words the same way. A second-place variant is not to be regarded as less acceptable than the pronunciation that is given first. It may, in fact, be used by as many educated speakers as the first variant, but the requirements of the printed page are such that one must precede the other:

apri·cot \'a-prə-,kät, 'ā-\
fore·head \'fȯr-əd, 'fȯr-,hed\

Symbols enclosed by parentheses represent elements that are present in the pronunciation of some speakers but are absent from the pronunciation of other speakers, or elements that are present in some but absent from other utterances of the same speaker:

¹**om·ni·bus** \'äm-ni-(,)bəs\
ad·di·tion·al \ə-'di-sh(ə-)nəl\

Thus, the above parentheses indicate that some people say \'äm-ni-,bəs\ and others say \'äm-ni-bəs\; some \ə-'di-shə-nəl\, others \ə-'di-shnəl\.

When a main entry has less than a full pronunciation, the missing part is to be supplied from a pronunciation in a preceding entry or within the same pair of reversed slashes:

cham·pi·on·ship \-,ship\
pa·la·ver \pə-'la-vər, -'lä-\

The pronunciation of the first three syllables of *championship* is found at the main entry *champion*. The hyphens before and after \'lä\ in the pronunciation of *palaver* indicate that both the first and the last parts of the pronunciation are to be taken from the immediately preceding pronunciation.

In general, no pronunciation is indicated for open compounds consisting of two or more English words that have own-place entry:

witch doctor *n*

Only the first entry in a sequence of numbered homographs is given a pronunciation if their pronunciations are the same:

¹**re·ward** \ri-'wȯrd\ *vb*
²**reward** *n*

The absent but implied pronunciation of derivatives and compounds run on after a main entry is a combination of the pronunciation at the main entry and the pronunciation of the other element as given at its alphabetical place in the vocabulary:

— **quick·ness** *n*
— **hold with**

Thus, the pronunciation of *quickness* is the sum of the pronunciations given at *quick* and *-ness;* that of *hold with*, the sum of the pronunciations of the two elements that make up the phrase.

FUNCTIONAL LABELS

An italic label indicating a part of speech or another functional classification follows the pronunciation or, if no pronunciation is given, the main entry. The eight traditional parts of speech are indicated as follows:

bold . . . *adj*
forth·with . . . *adv*
¹**but** . . . *conj*

ge·sund·heit . . . *interj*
bo·le·ro . . . *n*
²**un·der** . . . *prep*
¹**it** . . . *pron*
slap . . . *vb*

Other italicized labels used to indicate functional classifications that are not traditional parts of speech include:

AT *abbr*
self- *comb form*
un- . . . *prefix*
-ial *adj suffix*
²**-ly** *adv suffix*
²**-er** . . . *n suffix*

-ize *vb suffix*
Fe *symbol*
may . . . *verbal auxiliary*

Functional labels are sometimes combined:

afloat . . . *adj or adv*

INFLECTED FORMS

NOUNS

The plurals of nouns are shown in this dictionary when suffixation brings about a change of final *-y* to *-i-*, when the noun ends in a consonant plus *-o* or in *-ey*, when the noun ends in *-oo*, when the noun has an irregular plural or an uninflected plural or a foreign plural, when the noun is a compound that pluralizes any element but the last, when a final consonant is doubled, when the noun has variant plurals, and when it is believed that the dictionary user might have reasonable doubts about the spelling of the plural or when the plural is spelled in a way contrary to what is expected:

²**spy** *n, pl* **spies**
si·lo . . . *n, pl* **silos**
val·ley . . . *n, pl* **valleys**
²**shampoo** *n, pl* **shampoos**
mouse . . . *n, pl* **mice**
moose . . . *n, pl* **moose**
cri·te·ri·on . . . *n, pl* **-ria**
son–in–law . . . *n, pl* **sons–in–law**
¹**quiz** . . . *n, pl* **quiz·zes**
¹**fish** . . . *n, pl* **fish** *or* **fish·es**

pi . . . *n, pl* **pis**
³**dry** *n, pl* **drys**

Cutback inflected forms are used when the noun has three or more syllables:

ame·ni·ty . . . *n, pl* **-ties**

The plurals of nouns are usually not shown when the base word is unchanged by suffixation, when the noun is a compound whose second element is readily recognizable as a regular free form entered at its own place, or when the noun is unlikely to occur in the plural:

night . . . *n*
fore·foot . . . *n*
mo·nog·a·my . . . *n*

Nouns that are plural in form and that are regularly construed as plural are labeled *n pl*:

munch·ies . . . *n pl*

Nouns that are plural in form but that are not always construed as plurals are appropriately labeled:

lo·gis·tics . . . *n sing or pl*

VERBS

The principal parts of verbs are shown in this dictionary when suffixation brings about a doubling of a final consonant or an elision of a final *-e* or a change of final *-y* to *-i-*, when final *-c* changes to *-ck* in suffixation, when the verb ends in *-ey*, when the inflection is irregular, when there are variant inflected forms, and when it is believed that the dictionary user might have reasonable doubts about the spelling of an inflected form or when the inflected form is spelled in a way contrary to what is expected:

²**snag** *vb* **snagged; snag·ging**
¹**move** . . . *vb* **moved; mov·ing**
¹**cry** . . . *vb* **cried; cry·ing**
¹**frol·ic** . . . *vb* **frol·icked; frol·ick·ing**
¹**sur·vey** . . . *vb* **sur·veyed; sur·vey·ing**
¹**drive** . . . *vb* **drove** . . . **driv·en** . . . **driv·ing**
²**bus** *vb* **bused** *or* **bussed; bus·ing** *or* **bus·sing**

²**visa** *vb* **vi·saed** . . . **vi·sa·ing**
²**chagrin** *vb* **cha·grined** . . . **cha·grin·ing**

The principal parts of a regularly inflected verb are shown when it is desirable to indicate the pronunciation of one of the inflected forms:

learn . . . *vb* **learned** \'lərnd, 'lərnt\; **learn·ing**
¹**al·ter** \'ȯl-tər\ *vb* **al·tered; al·ter·ing** \-t(ə-)riŋ\

Cutback inflected forms are usually used when the verb has three or more syllables, when it is a two-syllable word that ends in *-l* and has variant spellings, and when it is a compound whose second element is readily recognized as an irregular verb:

elim·i·nate . . . *vb* **-nat·ed; -nat·ing**
²**quarrel** *vb* **-reled** *or* **-relled; -rel·ing** *or* **-rel·ling**
¹**re·take** . . . *vb* **-took** . . . **-tak·en** . . . **-tak·ing**

The principal parts of verbs are usually not shown when the base word is unchanged by suffixation or when the verb is a compound whose second element is readily recognizable as a regular free form entered at its own place:

¹jump . . . *vb*
pre·judge . . . *vb*

Another inflected form of English verbs is the third person singular of the present tense, which is regularly formed by the addition of *-s* or *-es* to the base form of the verb. This inflected form is not shown except at a handful of entries (as *have* and *do*) for which it is in some way unusual.

ADJECTIVES & ADVERBS

The comparative and superlative forms of adjectives and adverbs are shown in this dictionary when suffixation brings about a doubling of a final consonant or an elision of a final *-e* or a change of final *-y* to *-i*, when the word ends in *-ey*, when the inflection is irregular, and when there are variant inflected forms:

¹red . . . *adj* red·der; red·dest
¹tame . . . *adj* tam·er; tam·est
¹kind·ly . . . *adj* kind·li·er; -est
hors·ey *also* horsy . . . *adj* hors·i·er; -est
¹good . . . *adj* bet·ter . . . best
¹far . . . *adv* far·ther . . . *or* fur·ther . . .
far·thest *or* fur·thest . . .

The superlative forms of adjectives and adverbs of two or more syllables are usually cut back:

³fancy *adj* fan·ci·er; -est
¹ear·ly . . . *adv* ear·li·er; -est

The comparative and superlative forms of regularly inflected adjectives and adverbs are shown when it is desirable to indicate the pronunciation of the inflected forms:

¹young \'yəŋ\ *adj* youn·ger \'yəŋ-gər\; youn·gest \'yəŋ-gəst\

The inclusion of inflected forms in *-er* and *-est* at adjective and adverb entries means nothing more about the use of *more* and *most* with these adjectives and adverbs than that their comparative and superlative degrees may be expressed in either way: *lazier* or *more lazy; laziest* or *most lazy.*

At a few adjective entries only the superlative form is shown:

²mere *adj, superlative* mer·est

The absence of the comparative form indicates that there is no evidence of its use.

The comparative and superlative forms of adjectives and adverbs are usually not shown when the base word is unchanged by suffixation, when the inflected forms of the word are identical with those of a preceding homograph, or when the word is a compound whose second element is readily recognizable as a regular free form entered at its own place:

¹near . . . *adv*
³good *adv*
un·wor·thy . . . *adj*

Inflected forms are not shown at undefined run-ons.

CAPITALIZATION

Most entries in this dictionary begin with a lowercase letter. A few of these have an italicized label *often cap*, which indicates that the word is as likely to be capitalized as not and that it is as acceptable with an uppercase initial as it is with one in lowercase. Some entries begin with an uppercase letter, which indicates that the word is usually capitalized. The absence of an initial capital or of an *often cap* label indicates that the word is not ordinarily capitalized:

salm·on . . . *n*
gar·gan·tuan . . . *adj, often cap*
Mo·hawk . . . *n*

The capitalization of entries that are open or hyphenated compounds is similarly indicated

by the form of the entry or by an italicized label:

dry goods . . . *n pl*
french fry *n, often cap 1st F*
un—Amer·i·can . . . *adj*
Par·kin·son's disease . . . *n*
lazy Su·san . . . *n*
Jack Frost *n*

A word that is capitalized in some senses and lowercase in others shows variations from the form of the main entry by the use of italicized labels at the appropriate senses:

Trin·i·ty . . . *n* . . . 2 *not cap*
To·ry . . . *n* . . . 3 *often not cap*
ti·tan . . . *n* 1 *cap*
re·nais·sance . . . *n* . . . 1 *cap* . . . 2 *often cap*

ETYMOLOGY

This dictionary gives the etymologies for a number of the vocabulary entries. These etymologies are inside square brackets preceding the definition. Meanings given in roman type within these brackets are not definitions of the entry, but are meanings of the Middle English, Old English, or non-English words within the brackets.

The etymology gives the language from which words borrowed into English have come. It also gives the form of the word in that language or a representation of the word in our alphabet if the form in that language differs from that in English:

philo·den·dron . . . [NL, fr. Gk, neut. of *philodendros* loving trees . . .]

¹sav·age . . . [ME, *sauvage,* fr. AF, *salvage, savage,* LL *salvaticus,* alter. of L *silvaticus* of the woods, wild . . .]

An etymology beginning with the name of a language (including ME or OE) and not giving the foreign (or Middle English or Old English) form indicates that this form is the same as the form of the entry word:

le·gume . . . [F]

¹jour·ney . . . [ME, fr. OF . . .]

An etymology beginning with the name of a language (including ME or OE) and not giving the foreign (or Middle English or Old English) meaning indicates that this meaning is the same as the meaning expressed in the first definition in the entry:

ug·ly . . . *adj* . . . [ME, fr. ON *uggligr* . . .] **1** : FRIGHTFUL, DIRE

USAGE

Three types of status labels are used in this dictionary—temporal, regional, and stylistic—to signal that a word or a sense of a word is not part of the standard vocabulary of English.

The temporal label *obs* for "obsolete" means that there is no evidence of use since 1755:

³post *n* **1** *obs*

The label *obs* is a comment on the word being defined. When a thing, as distinguished from the word used to designate it, is obsolete, appropriate orientation is usually given in the definition:

cat·a·pult . . . *n* **1** : an ancient military machine for hurling missiles

The temporal label *archaic* means that a word or sense once in common use is found today only sporadically or in special contexts:

¹mete . . . *vb* . . . **1** *archaic*

¹thou . . . *pron, archaic*

A word or sense limited in use to a specific region of the U.S. has an appropriate label. The adverb *chiefly* precedes a label when the word has some currency outside the specified region, and a double label is used to indicate considerable currency in each of two specific regions:

²wash *n* . . . **8** *West*

do·gie . . . *n, chiefly West*

crul·ler . . . *n* . . . **2** *Northern & Midland*

Words current in all regions of the U.S. have no label.

A word or sense limited in use to one of the other countries of the English-speaking world has an appropriate regional label:

chem·ist . . . *n* . . . **2** *Brit*

loch . . . *n, Scot*

²wireless *n* . . . **1** *chiefly Brit*

The label *dial* for "dialect" indicates that the pattern of use of a word or sense is too complex for summary labeling: it usually includes several regional varieties of American English or of American and British English:

²mind *vb* **1** *chiefly dial*

The stylistic label *slang* is used with words or senses that are especially appropriate in contexts of extreme informality:

³can . . . *vb* . . . **2** *slang*

²grand *n* . . . *slang*

There is no satisfactory objective test for slang, especially with reference to a word out of context. No word, in fact, is invariably slang, and many standard words can be given slang applications.

The stylistic labels *offensive* and *disparaging* are used for those words or senses that in common use are intended to hurt or that are likely to give offense even when they are used without such an intent:

dumb . . . *adj* **1** *often offensive*

half–breed . . . *n, often disparaging*

Definitions are sometimes followed by verbal illustrations that show a typical use of the word in context. These illustrations are enclosed in angle brackets, and the word being illustrated is usually replaced by a lightface swung dash. The swung dash stands for the boldface entry word, and it may be followed by an italicized suffix:

> ¹**jump** . . . *vb* . . . **5** . . . ⟨∼ town⟩
> **all–around** . . . *adj* **1** . . . ⟨best ∼ performance⟩
> ¹**can·on** . . . *n* . . . **3** . . . ⟨the ∼*s* of good taste⟩
> **en·joy** . . . *vb* . . . **2** . . . ⟨∼*ed* the concert⟩

The swung dash is not used when the form of the boldface entry word is changed in suffixation, and it is not used for compounds:

> ²**deal** *vb* . . . **2** . . . ⟨*dealt* him a blow⟩
> **drum up** *vb* **1** . . . ⟨*drum up* business⟩

Definitions are sometimes followed by usage notes that give supplementary information about such matters as idiom, syntax, and semantic relationship. A usage note is introduced by a lightface dash:

> ²**cry** *n* . . . **5** . . . — usu. used in the phrase *a far cry*
> ²**drum** *vb* . . . **4** . . . — usu. used with *out*
> ¹**jaw** . . . *n* . . . **2** . . . — usu. used in pl.
> ¹**ada·gio** . . . *adv or adj* . . . — used as a direction in music
> **hajji** . . . *n* . . . — often used as a title

Sometimes a usage note is used in place of a definition. Some function words (as conjunctions and prepositions) have chiefly grammatical meaning and little or no lexical meaning; most interjections express feelings but are otherwise untranslatable into lexical meaning; and some other words (as honorific titles) are more amenable to comment than to definition:

> **or** . . . *conj* — used as a function word to indicate an alternative
> ¹**at** . . . *prep* **1** — used to indicate a point in time or space
> **auf Wie·der·seh·en** . . . *interj* . . . — used to express farewell
> **sir** . . . *n* . . . **2** — used as a usu. respectful form of address

SENSE DIVISION

A boldface colon is used in this dictionary to introduce a definition:

> **equine** . . . *adj* . . . : of or relating to the horse

It is also used to separate two or more definitions of a single sense:

> **no·ti·fy** . . . *vb* . . . **1** : to give notice of : report the occurrence of

Boldface Arabic numerals separate the senses of a word that has more than one sense:

> **add** . . . *vb* **1** : to join to something else so as to increase in number or amount **2** : to say further . . . **3** : to combine (numbers) into one sum

A particular semantic relationship between senses is sometimes suggested by the use of one of the two italic sense dividers *esp* or *also*.

The sense divider *esp* (for *especially*) is used to introduce the most common meaning included in the more general preceding definition:

> **crys·tal** . . . *n* . . . **2** : something resembling crystal (as in transparency); *esp* : a clear colorless glass of superior quality

The sense divider *also* is used to introduce a meaning related to the preceding sense by an easily understood extension of that sense:

> **chi·na** . . . *n* : porcelain ware; *also* : domestic pottery in general

The order of senses is historical: the sense known to have been first used in English is entered first. This is not to be taken to mean, however, that each sense of a multisense word developed from the immediately preceding sense. It is altogether possible that sense 1 of a word has given rise to sense 2 and sense 2 to sense 3, but frequently sense 2 and sense 3 may have developed independently of one another from sense 1.

When an italicized label follows a boldface numeral, the label applies only to that specific numbered sense. It does not apply to any other boldface numbered senses:

> **craft** . . . *n* . . . **3** *pl usu* **craft**
> ¹**fa·ther** . . . *n* . . . **2** *cap* . . . **5** *often cap*
> **dul·ci·mer** . . . *n* . . . **2** *or* **dul·ci·more**
> \-ˌmōr\
> ²**lift** *n* . . . **5** *chiefly Brit*

At *craft* the *pl* label applies to sense 3 but to none of the other numbered senses. At *father* the *cap* label applies only to sense 2 and the *often cap* label only to sense 5. At *dulcimer* the variant spelling and pronunciation apply only to sense 2, and the *chiefly Brit* label at *lift* applies only to sense 5.

Explanatory Notes

CROSS-REFERENCE

Four different kinds of cross-references are used in this dictionary: directional, synonymous, cognate, and inflectional. In each instance the cross-reference is readily recognized by the lightface small capitals in which it is printed.

A cross-reference following a lightface dash and beginning with *see* is a directional cross-reference. It directs the dictionary user to look elsewhere for further information:

eu·ro . . . *n* . . . —see MONEY table

A cross-reference following a boldface colon is a synonymous cross-reference. It may stand alone as the only definition for an entry or for a sense of an entry; it may follow an analytical definition; it may be one of two or more synonymous cross-references separated by commas:

pa·pa . . . *n* : FATHER
¹**par·tic·u·lar** . . . *adj* . . . 4 : attentive to details : PRECISE
²**main** *adj* 1 : CHIEF, PRINCIPAL
¹**fig·ure** . . . *n* . . . 6 : SHAPE, FORM, OUTLINE

A synonymous cross-reference indicates that an entry, a definition at the entry, or a specific sense at the entry cross-referred to can be substituted as a definition for the entry or the sense in which the cross-reference appears.

A cross-reference following an italic *var of* ("variant of") is a cognate cross-reference:

pick·a·back . . . *var of* PIGGYBACK

Occasionally a cognate cross-reference has a limiting label preceding *var of* as an indication that the variant is not standard American English:

aero·plane . . . *chiefly Brit var of* AIRPLANE

A cross-reference following an italic label that identifies an entry as an inflected form (as of a noun or verb) is an inflectional cross-reference:

calves *pl of* CALF
woven *past part of* WEAVE

Inflectional cross-references appear only when the inflected form falls at least a column away from the entry cross-referred to.

SYNONYMS

A bold italic Synonyms preceded by a small black diamond figure near the end of an entry introduces words that are synonymous with the word being defined:

alone . . . *adj* . . . ◆ *Synonyms* LONELY, LONESOME, LONE, SOLITARY

Synonyms are not definitions although they may often be substituted for each other in context.

COMBINING FORMS, PREFIXES, & SUFFIXES

An entry that begins or ends with a hyphen is a word element that forms part of an English compound:

-wise . . . *adv comb form* . . . ⟨slant*wise*⟩
ex- . . . *prefix* . . . 2 . . . ⟨*ex*-president⟩
-let *n suffix* 1 . . . ⟨book*let*⟩

Combining forms, prefixes, and suffixes are entered in this dictionary for two reasons: to make understandable the meaning of many undefined run-ons and to make recognizable the meaningful elements of words that are not entered in the dictionary.

LISTS OF UNDEFINED WORDS

Many words that begin with the prefixes or combining forms *anti-, in-, non-, over-, re-, self-, semi-, sub-, super-,* and *un-* are self-explanatory combinations of the prefix or combining form

and a word entered elsewhere in the dictionary, and they are listed undefined at the bottom of the page or spread on which they would normally appear if defined.

ABBREVIATIONS & SYMBOLS

Abbreviations and symbols for chemical elements are included as main entries in the vocabulary:

RSVP *abbr* . . . please reply
Ca *symbol* calcium

Abbreviations have been normalized to one form. In practice, however, there is considerable variation in the use of periods and in capitalization (as *vhf, v.h.f.,* and *V.H.F.* for the entry VHF), and stylings other than those given in this dictionary are often acceptable.

ABBREVIATIONS IN THIS WORK

ab	about	*G, Ger*	German	*OIt*	Old Italian
abbr	abbreviation	*Gk*	Greek	*ON*	Old Norse
abl	ablative	*Gmc*	Germanic	*OPers*	Old Persian
acc	accusative	*Heb*	Hebrew	*orig*	originally
A.D.	anno Domini	*Hung*	Hungarian	*part*	participle
adj	adjective	*Icel*	Icelandic	*Pers*	Persian
adv	adverb	*imit*	imitative	*perh*	perhaps
AF	Anglo-French	*imper*	imperative	*Pg*	Portuguese
alter	alteration	*interj*	interjection	*pl*	plural
Am, Amer	American	*Ir*	Irish	*Pol*	Polish
AmerF	American French	*irreg*	irregular	*pp*	past participle
AmerInd	American Indian	*It, Ital*	Italian	*prep*	preposition
AmerSp	American Spanish	*Jp*	Japanese	*pres*	present, president
Ar	Arabic	*K*	Kelvin	*prob*	probably
Aram	Aramaic	*km*	kilometers	*pron*	pronoun,
B.C.	before Christ	*L*	Latin		pronunciation
Brit	British	*LaF*	Louisiana French	*prp*	present participle
C	Celsius	*LG*	Low German	*pseud*	pseudonym
ca	circa	*LGk*	Late Greek	*r*	reigned
Calif	California	*LHeb*	Late Hebrew	*Russ*	Russian
Canad	Canadian	*lit*	literally	*Sc*	Scotch, Scots
CanF	Canadian French	*LL*	Late Latin	*Scand*	Scandinavian
cap	capital, capitalized	*m*	meters	*ScGael*	Scottish Gaelic
Celt	Celtic	*masc*	masculine	*Scot*	Scottish
cen	central	*MD*	Middle Dutch	*sing*	singular
cent	century	*ME*	Middle English	*Skt*	Sanskrit
Chin	Chinese	*MexSp*	Mexican Spanish	*Slav*	Slavic
comb	combining	*MF*	Middle French	*So*	South
compar	comparative	*MGk*	Middle Greek	*Sp, Span*	Spanish
conj	conjunction	*mi*	miles	*St*	Saint
D	Dutch	*ML*	Medieval Latin	*superl*	superlative
Dan	Danish	*modif*	modification	*Sw*	Swedish
dat	dative	*MS*	manuscript	*syn*	synonym, synonymy
deriv	derivative	*Mt*	Mount	*trans*	translation
dial	dialect	*n*	noun	*Turk*	Turkish
dim	diminutive	*neut*	neuter	*US*	United States
E	English	*NewEng*	New England	*USSR*	Union of Soviet
Egypt	Egyptian	*NGk*	New Greek		Socialist Republics
Eng	English	*NHeb*	New Hebrew	*usu*	usually
esp	especially	*NL*	New Latin	*var*	variant
est	estimated	*No*	North	*vb*	verb
F	Fahrenheit, French	*Norw*	Norwegian	*vi*	verb intransitive
fem	feminine	*n pl*	noun plural	*VL*	Vulgar Latin
fl	flourished	*obs*	obsolete	*vt*	verb transitive
fr	from	*OE*	Old English	*W*	Welsh
ft	feet	*OF*	Old French		

PRONUNCIATION SYMBOLS

ə	abut, collect, suppose	ȯi	toy
ˈə, ˌə	humdrum	p	pepper, lip
ᵊ	(in ᵊl, ᵊn) battle, cotton; (in lᵊ, mᵊ, rᵊ) French table, prisme, titre	r	rarity
		s	source, less
ər	operation, further	sh	shy, mission
a	map, patch	t	tie, attack
ā	day, fate	th	thin, ether
ä	bother, cot, father	th	then, either
är	car, heart	ü	boot, few \ˈfyü\
au̇	now, out	u̇	put, pure \ˈpyu̇r\
b	baby, rib	u̇r	boor, tour
ch	chin, catch	ue̶	French rue, German füllen, fühlen
d	did, adder	v	vivid, give
e	set, red	w	we, away
er	bare, fair	y	yard, cue \ˈkyü\
ē	beat, easy	ʸ	indicates that a preceding \l\, \n\, or \w\ is modified by having the tongue approximate the position for \y\, as in French digne \dēnʸ\
f	fifty, cuff		
g	go, big		
h	hat, ahead		
hw	whale	z	zone, raise
i	tip, banish	zh	vision, pleasure
ir	near, deer	\	slant line used in pairs to mark the beginning and end of a transcription: \ˈpen\
ī	site, buy		
j	job, edge		
k	kin, cook	ˈ	mark at the beginning of a syllable that has primary (strongest) stress: \ˈshə-fəl-ˌbȯrd\
ḵ	German Bach, Scots loch		
l	lily, cool		
m	murmur, dim	ˌ	mark at the beginning of a syllable that has secondary (next-strongest) stress: \ˈshə-fəl-ˌbȯrd\
n	nine, own		
ⁿ	indicates that a preceding vowel is pronounced through both nose and mouth, as in French bon \bōⁿ\	-	mark of a syllable division in pronunciations (the mark of end-of-line division in boldface entries is a centered dot ·)
ŋ	sing, singer, finger, ink	( )	indicate that what is symbolized between sometimes occurs and sometimes does not occur in the pronunciation of the word: **bakery** \ˈbā-k(ə-)rē\ = \ˈbā-kə-rē, ˈbā-krē\
ō	bone, hollow		
ȯ	saw		
ȯr	boar, port		
œ	French bœuf, feu, German Hölle, Höhle		

¹a \'ā\ *n, pl* **a's** *or* **as** \'āz\ *often cap* **1** : the 1st letter of the English alphabet **2** : a grade rating a student's work as superior
²a \ə, (')ā\ *indefinite article* : ONE, SOME — used to indicate an unspecified or unidentified individual ⟨there's ∼ man outside⟩
³a *abbr, often cap* **1** absent **2** acre **3** alto **4** answer **5** are **6** area
AA *abbr* **1** Alcoholics Anonymous **2** antiaircraft **3** associate in arts
AAA *abbr* American Automobile Association
A and M *abbr* agricultural and mechanical
A and R *abbr* artists and repertory
aard·vark \'ärd-,värk\ *n* [obs. Afrikaans, fr. Afrikaans *aard* earth + *vark* pig] : a large burrowing African mammal that feeds on ants and termites with its long sticky tongue

aardvark

¹ab \'ab\ *n* : an abdominal muscle
²ab *abbr.* about
AB *abbr* **1** able-bodied seaman **2** airman basic **3** [NL *artium baccalaureus*] bachelor of arts
ABA *abbr* American Bar Association
aback \ə-'bak\ *adv* : by surprise ⟨taken ∼⟩
aba·cus \'a-bə-kəs\ *n, pl* **aba·ci** \-,sī, -,kē\ *or* **aba·cus·es** : an instrument for making calculations by sliding counters along rods or grooves
¹abaft \ə-'baft\ *prep* : to the rear of
²abaft *adv* : toward or at the stern : AFT
ab·a·lo·ne \,a-bə-'lō-nē, 'a-bə-,\ *n* : any of a genus of large edible sea mollusks with a flattened slightly spiral shell with holes along the edge
¹aban·don \ə-'ban-dən\ *vb* [ME *abandounen*, fr. AF *abanduner*, fr. (*mettre*) *a bandun* to hand over, put in someone's control] : to give up completely : FORSAKE, DESERT — **aban·don·ment** *n*
²abandon *n* : a thorough yielding to natural impulses; *esp* : EXUBERANCE
aban·doned \ə-'ban-dənd\ *adj* : morally unrestrained
♦ *Synonyms* PROFLIGATE, DISSOLUTE, REPROBATE
abase \ə-'bās\ *vb* **abased; abas·ing** : HUMBLE, DEGRADE — **abase·ment** *n*
abash \ə-'bash\ *vb* : to destroy the composure of : EMBARRASS — **abash·ment** *n*
abate \ə-'bāt\ *vb* **abat·ed; abat·ing** **1** : to put an end to ⟨∼ a nuisance⟩ **2** : to decrease in amount, number, or degree
abate·ment \ə-'bāt-mənt\ *n* **1** : DECREASE **2** : an amount abated; *esp* : a deduction from a tax
ab·at·toir \'a-bə-,twär\ *n* [F] : SLAUGHTERHOUSE
ab·ba·cy \'a-bə-sē\ *n, pl* **-cies** : the office or term of office of an abbot or abbess
ab·bé \a-'bā, 'a-,\ *n* : a member of the French secular clergy — used as a title
ab·bess \'a-bəs\ *n* : the superior of a convent for nuns

ab·bey \'a-bē\ *n, pl* **abbeys** **1** : MONASTERY **2** : CONVENT **3** : an abbey church
ab·bot \'a-bət\ *n* [ME *abbod*, fr. OE, fr. LL *abbat-, abbas*, fr. LGk *abbas*, fr. Aramaic *abbā* father] : the superior of a monastery for men
abbr *abbr* abbreviation
ab·bre·vi·ate \ə-'brē-vē-,āt\ *vb* **-at·ed; -at·ing** : SHORTEN, CURTAIL; *esp* : to reduce to an abbreviation
ab·bre·vi·a·tion \ə-,brē-vē-'ā-shən\ *n* **1** : the act or result of abbreviating **2** : a shortened form of a word or phrase used for brevity esp. in writing
¹ABC \,ā-(,)bē-'sē\ *n, pl* **ABC's** *or* **ABCs** \-'sēz\ **1** : ALPHABET — usu. used in pl. **2** : RUDIMENTS — usu. used in pl.
²ABC *abbr* American Broadcasting Company
Ab·di·as \ab-'dī-əs\ *n* : OBADIAH
ab·di·cate \'ab-di-,kāt\ *vb* **-cat·ed; -cat·ing** : to give up (as a throne) formally — **ab·di·ca·tion** \,ab-di-'kā-shən\ *n*
ab·do·men \'ab-də-mən, ab-'dō-\ *n* **1** : the cavity in or area of the body between the chest and the pelvis **2** : the part of the body posterior to the thorax in an arthropod — **ab·dom·i·nal** \ab-'dä-mə-n³l\ *adj* — **ab·dom·i·nal·ly** *adv*
ab·duct \ab-'dəkt\ *vb* : to take away (a person) by force : KIDNAP — **ab·duc·tion** \-'dək-shən\ *n* — **ab·duc·tor** \-tər\ *n*
abeam \ə-'bēm\ *adv or adj* : on a line at right angles to a ship's keel
abed \ə-'bed\ *adv or adj* : in bed
Abe·na·ki \,a-bə-'nä-kē\ *also* **Ab·na·ki** \ab-'nä-kē\ *n, pl* **Abenaki** *or* **Abenakis** *also* **Abnaki** *or* **Abnakis** : a member of a group of American Indian peoples of northern New England and southern Quebec
ab·er·ra·tion \,a-bə-'rā-shən\ *n* **1** : deviation esp. from a moral standard or normal state **2** : failure of a mirror or lens to produce exact point-to-point correspondence between an object and its image **3** : unsoundness of mind : DERANGEMENT — **ab·er·rant** \a-'ber-ənt\ *adj*
abet \ə-'bet\ *vb* **abet·ted; abet·ting** [ME *abetten*, fr. AF *abeter*, fr. *beter* to bait] **1** : INCITE, ENCOURAGE **2** : to assist or support in the achievement of a purpose ⟨∼ a fugitive⟩ — **abet·tor** *or* **abet·ter** \-'be-tər\ *n*
abey·ance \ə-'bā-əns\ *n* : a condition of suspended activity — **abey·ant** \-ənt\ *adj*
ab·hor \ab-'hór, əb-\ *vb* **ab·horred; ab·hor·ring** [ME *abhorren*, fr. L *abhorrēre*, fr. *ab-* + *horrēre* to shudder] : LOATHE, DETEST — **ab·hor·rence** \-əns\ *n*
ab·hor·rent \-ənt\ *adj* : LOATHSOME, DETESTABLE ⟨∼ crimes⟩
abide \ə-'bīd\ *vb* **abode** \-'bōd\ *or* **abid·ed; abid·ing** **1** : BEAR, ENDURE **2** : DWELL, REMAIN, LAST — **abide by** : to conform or acquiesce to ⟨*abide by* the law⟩
abil·i·ty \ə-'bi-lə-tē\ *n, pl* **-ties** : the quality of being able : POWER, SKILL
-ability *also* **-ibility** *n suffix* : capacity, fitness, or tendency to act or be acted on in a (specified) way ⟨flamm*ability*⟩
ab·ject \'ab-,jekt, ab-'jekt\ *adj* : low in spirit, hope, or state ⟨∼ poverty⟩ — **ab·jec·tion** \ab-'jek-shən\ *n* — **ab·ject·ly** *adv* — **ab·ject·ness** *n*
ab·jure \ab-'júr\ *vb* **ab·jured; ab·jur·ing** **1** : to renounce solemnly : RECANT **2** : to abstain from — **ab·ju·ra·tion** \,ab-jə-'rā-shən\ *n*
abl *abbr* ablative
ab·late \a-'blāt\ *vb* **ab·lat·ed; ab·lat·ing** : to remove or become removed esp. by cutting, abrading, or vaporizing
ab·la·tion \a-'blā-shən\ *n* **1** : surgical cutting and removal **2** : loss of a part (as the outside of a nose cone) by melting or vaporization
ab·la·tive \'ab-lə-tiv\ *adj* : of, relating to, or constituting a grammatical case (as in Latin) expressing typically the relation of separation and source — **ablative** *n*
ablaze \ə-'blāz\ *adj or adv* : being on fire : BLAZING

able \'ā-bəl\ *adj* **abler** \-b(ə-)lər\; **ablest** \-b(ə-)ləst\ [ME, fr. AF, fr. L *habilis* apt, fr. *habēre* to hold, possess] **1** : having sufficient power, skill, or resources to accomplish an object **2** : marked by skill or efficiency — **ably** \-blē\ *adv*

-able *also* **-ible** *adj suffix* **1** : capable of, fit for, or worthy of (being so acted upon or toward) ⟨break*able*⟩ ⟨collect*ible*⟩ **2** : tending, given, or liable to ⟨knowledge*able*⟩ ⟨perish*able*⟩

able-bod·ied \,ā-bəl-'bä-dēd\ *adj* : having a sound strong body

abloom \ə-'blüm\ *adj* : BLOOMING

ab·lu·tion \ə-'blü-shən, a-\ *n* : the washing of one's body or part of it

ABM \,ā-(,)bē-'em\ *n*, *pl* **ABM's** *or* **ABMs** : ANTIBALLISTIC MISSILE

Abnaki *var of* ABENAKI

ab·ne·gate \'ab-ni-,gāt\ *vb* **-gat·ed; -gat·ing 1** : DENY, RENOUNCE **2** : SURRENDER, RELINQUISH ⟨~ her powers⟩ — **ab·ne·ga·tion** \,ab-ni-'gā-shən\ *n*

ab·nor·mal \ab-'nór-məl\ *adj* : deviating from the normal or average — **ab·nor·mal·i·ty** \,ab-nór-'ma-lə-tē\ *n* — **ab·nor·mal·ly** *adv*

¹aboard \ə-'bórd\ *adv* **1** : ALONGSIDE **2** : on, onto, or within a car, ship, or aircraft **3** : in or into a group or association ⟨welcome new workers ~⟩

²aboard *prep* : ON, ONTO, WITHIN

abode \ə-'bōd\ *n* **1** : STAY, SOJOURN **2** : HOME, RESIDENCE

abol·ish \ə-'bä-lish\ *vb* : to do away with : ANNUL ⟨~ slavery⟩ — **ab·o·li·tion** \,a-bə-'li-shən\ *n*

ab·o·li·tion·ism \,a-bə-'li-shə-,ni-zəm\ *n* : advocacy of the abolition of slavery — **ab·o·li·tion·ist** \-'li-sh(ə-)nist\ *n or adj*

A–bomb \'ā-,bäm\ *n* : ATOMIC BOMB — **A–bomb** *vb*

abom·i·na·ble \ə-'bä-mə-nə-bəl\ *adj* : ODIOUS, LOATHSOME, DETESTABLE

abominable snow·man \-'snō-mən, -,man\ *n, often cap A&S* : a mysterious creature with human or apelike characteristics reported to exist in the high Himalayas

abom·i·nate \ə-'bä-mə-,nāt\ *vb* **-nat·ed; -nat·ing** [L *abominari*, lit., to deprecate as an ill omen, fr. *ab-* away + *omen* omen] : LOATHE, DETEST

abom·i·na·tion \ə-,bä-mə-'nā-shən\ *n* **1** : something abominable **2** : DISGUST, LOATHING

ab·orig·i·nal \,a-bə-'ri-jə-nəl\ *adj* : ORIGINAL, INDIGENOUS, PRIMITIVE

ab·orig·i·ne \,a-bə-'ri-jə-nē\ *n* : a member of the original race of inhabitants of a region : NATIVE

aborn·ing \ə-'bór-niŋ\ *adv* : while being born or produced

¹abort \ə-'bórt\ *vb* **1** : to cause or undergo abortion **2** : to terminate prematurely ⟨~ a spaceflight⟩ — **abor·tive** \-'bór-tiv\ *adj*

²abort *n* : the premature termination of a mission or of a procedure relating to an aircraft or spacecraft

abor·tion \ə-'bór-shən\ *n* : the spontaneous or induced termination of a pregnancy after, accompanied by, resulting in, or closely followed by the death of the embryo or fetus

abor·tion·ist \-sh(ə-)nist\ *n* : one who induces abortions

abound \ə-'baùnd\ *vb* **1** : to be plentiful : TEEM **2** : to be fully supplied

¹about \ə-'baùt\ *adv* **1** : reasonably close to; *also* : on the verge of ⟨~ to join the army⟩ **2** : on all sides **3** : NEARBY

²about *prep* **1** : on every side of **2** : near to **3** : CONCERNING

about–face \-'fās\ *n* : a reversal of direction or attitude — **about–face** *vb*

¹above \ə-'bəv\ *adv* **1** : in the sky; *also* : in or to heaven **2** : in or to a higher place; *also* : higher on the same page or on a preceding page

²above *prep* **1** : in or to a higher place than : OVER ⟨storm clouds ~ the bay⟩ **2** : superior to ⟨he thought her far ~ him⟩ **3** : more than : EXCEEDING **4** : as distinct from ⟨~ the noise⟩

above·board \-,bórd\ *adv or adj* : without concealment or deception : OPENLY

abp *abbr* archbishop

abr *abbr* abridged; abridgment

ab·ra·ca·dab·ra \,a-brə-kə-'da-brə\ *n* **1** : a magical charm or incantation against calamity **2** : GIBBERISH

abrade \ə-'brād\ *vb* **abrad·ed; abrad·ing 1** : to wear away by friction **2** : to wear down in spirit : IRRITATE — **abra·sion** \-'brā-zhən\ *n*

¹abra·sive \ə-'brā-siv\ *n* : a substance (as pumice) for abrading, smoothing, or polishing

²abrasive *adj* : tending to abrade : causing irritation ⟨~ relationships⟩ — **abra·sive·ly** *adv* — **abra·sive·ness** *n*

abreast \ə-'brest\ *adv or adj* **1** : side by side **2** : up to a standard or level esp. of knowledge ⟨kept ~ of the news⟩

abridge \ə-'brij\ *vb* **abridged; abridg·ing** [ME *abregen*, fr. AF *abreger*, fr. LL *abbreviare*, fr. L *ad* to + *brevis* short] : to lessen in length or extent : SHORTEN — **abridg·ment** *or* **abridge·ment** *n*

abroad \ə-'bród\ *adv or adj* **1** : over a wide area **2** : away from one's home **3** : outside one's country

ab·ro·gate \'a-brə-,gāt\ *vb* **-gat·ed; -gat·ing** : ANNUL, REVOKE — **ab·ro·ga·tion** \,a-brə-'gā-shən\ *n*

abrupt \ə-'brəpt\ *adj* **1** : broken or as if broken off **2** : SUDDEN, HASTY ⟨an ~ turn⟩ **3** : so quick as to seem rude ⟨an ~ reply⟩ **4** : DISCONNECTED **5** : STEEP — **abrupt·ly** *adv*

abs *abbr* absolute

ab·scess \'ab-,ses\ *n*, *pl* **ab·scess·es** [L *abscessus*, lit., act of going away, fr. *abscedere* to go away, fr. *abs-, ab-* away + *cedere* to go] : a localized collection of pus surrounded by inflamed tissue — **ab·scessed** \-,sest\ *adj*

ab·scis·sa \ab-'si-sə\ *n*, *pl* **abscissas** *also* **ab·scis·sae** \-'si-(,)sē\ : the horizontal coordinate of a point in a plane coordinate system obtained by measuring parallel to the x-axis

ab·scis·sion \ab-'si-zhən\ *n* **1** : the act or process of cutting off **2** : the natural separation of flowers, fruits, or leaves from plants — **ab·scise** \ab-'sīz\ *vb*

ab·scond \ab-'skänd\ *vb* : to depart secretly and hide oneself

ab·sence \'ab-səns\ *n* **1** : the state or time of being absent **2** : WANT, LACK **3** : INATTENTION

¹ab·sent \'ab-sənt\ *adj* **1** : not present **2** : LACKING **3** : INATTENTIVE

²ab·sent \ab-'sent\ *vb* : to keep (oneself) away

³ab·sent \'ab-sənt\ *prep* : in the absence of : WITHOUT

ab·sen·tee \,ab-sən-'tē\ *n* : one that is absent or keeps away

absentee ballot *n* : a ballot submitted (as by mail) in advance of an election by a voter who is unable to be present at the polls

ab·sen·tee·ism \,ab-sən-'tē-,i-zəm\ *n* : chronic absence (as from work or school)

ab·sent–mind·ed \,ab-sənt-'mīn-dəd\ *adj* : unaware of one's surroundings or actions : INATTENTIVE — **ab·sent–mind·ed·ly** *adv* — **ab·sent–mind·ed·ness** *n*

ab·sinthe *also* **ab·sinth** \'ab-,sinth\ *n* [F] : a liqueur flavored esp. with wormwood and anise

ab·so·lute \'ab-sə-,lüt, ,ab-sə-'lüt\ *adj* **1** : free from imperfection or mixture **2** : free from control, restriction, or qualification ⟨~ power⟩ **3** : lacking grammatical connection with any other word in a sentence ⟨~ construction⟩ **4** : POSITIVE ⟨~ proof⟩ **5** : relating to the fundamental units of length, mass, and time **6** : FUNDAMENTAL, ULTIMATE — **ab·so·lute·ly** *adv*

absolute pitch *n* **1** : the position of a tone in a standard scale independently determined by its rate of vibration **2** : the ability to sing a note asked for or to name a note heard

absolute value *n* : a nonnegative number equal to a given real number with any negative sign removed

absolute zero *n* : a theoretical temperature marked by a complete absence of heat and motion and equivalent to exactly -273.15°C or -459.67°F

ab·so·lu·tion \,ab-sə-'lü-shən\ *n* : the act of absolving; *esp* : a remission of sins pronounced by a priest in the sacrament of reconciliation

ab·so·lut·ism \'ab-sə-,lü-,ti-zəm\ *n* **1** : the theory that a ruler or government should have unlimited power **2** : government by an absolute ruler or authority

ab·solve \ab-'zälv, -'sälv\ *vb* **ab·solved; ab·solv·ing** : to set free from an obligation or the consequences of guilt

ab·sorb \ab-'sórb, -'zórb\ *vb* **1** : to take in and make part of an existent whole **2** : to suck up or take in in the manner of a sponge **3** : to engage (one's attention) : ENGROSS **4** : to receive without recoil or echo ⟨a ceiling that $\sim$_s_ sound⟩ **5** : ASSUME, BEAR ⟨$\sim$ all costs⟩ **6** : to transform (radiant energy) into a different form esp. with a resulting rise in temperature — **ab·sorb·ing** _adj_ — **ab·sorb·ing·ly** _adv_

ab·sor·bent _also_ **ab·sor·bant** \əb-'sȯr-bənt, '-zȯr-\ _adj_ : able to absorb ⟨$\sim$ cotton⟩ — **ab·sor·ben·cy** \-bən-sē\ _n_ — **absorbent** _also_ **absorbant** _n_

ab·sorp·tion \əb-'sȯrp-shən, -'zȯrp-\ _n_ **1** : a process of absorbing or being absorbed **2** : concentration of attention — **ab·sorp·tive** \-tiv\ _adj_

ab·stain \əb-'stān\ _vb_ : to refrain from an action or practice — **ab·stain·er** _n_ — **ab·sten·tion** \-'sten-chən\ _n_

ab·ste·mi·ous \ab-'stē-mē-əs\ _adj_ : sparing in use of food or drink : TEMPERATE — **ab·ste·mi·ous·ly** _adv_ — **ab·ste·mi·ous·ness** _n_

ab·sti·nence \'ab-stə-nəns\ _n_ : voluntary refraining esp. from eating certain foods, drinking liquor, or engaging in sexual intercourse — **ab·sti·nent** \-nənt\ _adj_

abstr _abbr_ abstract

¹**ab·stract** \ab-'strakt, 'ab-ˌstrakt\ _adj_ **1** : considered apart from a particular instance **2** : expressing a quality apart from an object ⟨_whiteness_ is an $\sim$ word⟩ **3** : having only intrinsic form with little or no pictorial representation ⟨$\sim$ painting⟩ — **ab·stract·ly** _adv_ — **ab·stract·ness** _n_

²**ab·stract** \'ab-ˌstrakt; _2 also_ ab-'strakt\ _n_ **1** : SUMMARY, EPITOME **2** : an abstract thing or state

³**ab·stract** \ab-'strakt, 'ab-ˌstrakt; _2 usu_ 'ab-ˌstrakt\ _vb_ **1** : REMOVE, SEPARATE **2** : to make an abstract of : SUMMARIZE **3** : to draw away the attention of **4** : STEAL — **ab·stract·ed·ly** \ab-'strak-təd-lē, 'ab-ˌstrak-\ _adv_

abstract expressionism _n_ : art that expresses the artist's attitudes and emotions through abstract forms — **abstract expressionist** _n_

ab·strac·tion \ab-'strak-shən\ _n_ **1** : the act of abstracting : the state of being abstracted **2** : an abstract idea **3** : an abstract work of art

ab·struse \ab-'strüs\ _adj_ : hard to understand : RECONDITE — **ab·struse·ly** _adv_ — **ab·struse·ness** _n_

ab·surd \əb-'sərd, -'zərd\ _adj_ [MF _absurde_, fr. L _absurdus_, fr. _ab-_ from + _surdus_ deaf, stupid] : RIDICULOUS, UNREASONABLE — **ab·sur·di·ty** \-'sər-də-tē, -'zər-\ _n_ — **ab·surd·ly** _adv_

abun·dant \ə-'bən-dənt\ _adj_ [ME, fr. AF, fr. L _abundant-, abundans_, prp. of _abundare_ to abound, fr. _ab-_ from + _unda_ wave] : more than enough : amply sufficient ♦ **Synonyms** COPIOUS, PLENTIFUL, AMPLE, BOUNTIFUL — **abun·dance** \-dəns\ _n_ — **abun·dant·ly** _adv_

¹**abuse** \ə-'byüs\ _n_ **1** : a corrupt practice **2** : MISUSE ⟨drug $\sim$⟩ **3** : coarse and insulting speech **4** : MISTREATMENT ⟨child $\sim$⟩

²**abuse** \ə-'byüz\ _vb_ **abused; abus·ing 1** : to put to a wrong use : MISUSE **2** : to use excessively ⟨$\sim$ alcohol⟩ **3** : MISTREAT **4** : to attack in words : REVILE — **abus·er** _n_ — **abu·sive** \-'byü-siv\ _adj_ — **abu·sive·ly** _adv_ — **abu·sive·ness** _n_

abut \ə-'bət\ _vb_ **abut·ted; abut·ting** : to touch along a border : border on

abut·ment \ə-'bət-mənt\ _n_ : the part of a structure (as a bridge) that supports weight or withstands lateral pressure

abut·ter \ə-'bə-tər\ _n_ : one that abuts; _esp_ : the owner of a contiguous property

abuzz \ə-'bəz\ _adj_ : filled or resounding with activity or excitement ⟨an office $\sim$ with rumors⟩

abys·mal \ə-'biz-məl\ _adj_ **1** : immeasurably deep : BOTTOMLESS **2** : absolutely wretched ⟨$\sim$ living conditions of the poor⟩ — **abys·mal·ly** _adv_

abyss \ə-'bis\ _n_ **1** : the bottomless pit in old accounts of the universe **2** : an immeasurable depth

abys·sal \ə-'bi-səl\ _adj_ : of or relating to the bottom waters of the ocean depths

ac _abbr_ account

-ac _n suffix_ : one affected with ⟨hypochondri_ac_⟩

Ac _symbol_ actinium

AC _abbr_ **1** air-conditioning **2** alternating current **3** [L _ante Christum_] before Christ **4** [L _ante cibum_] before meals **5** area code

aca·cia \ə-'kā-shə\ _n_ : any of a genus of leguminous trees or shrubs with round white or yellow flower clusters and often feathery leaves

acad _abbr_ academic; academy

ac·a·deme \'a-kə-ˌdēm, ˌa-kə-'\ _n_ : SCHOOL; _also_ : academic environment

¹**ac·a·dem·ic** \ˌa-kə-'de-mik\ _n_ : a person who is academic in background, outlook, or methods

²**academic** _adj_ **1** : of, relating to, or associated with schools or colleges **2** : literary or general rather than technical **3** : theoretical rather than practical — **ac·a·dem·i·cal·ly** \-mi-k(ə-)lē\ _adv_

ac·a·de·mi·cian \ˌa-kə-də-'mi-shən, ə-ˌka-də-\ _n_ **1** : a member of a society of scholars or artists **2** : ACADEMIC

ac·a·dem·i·cism \ˌa-kə-'de-mə-ˌsi-zəm\ _also_ **acad·e·mism** \ə-'ka-də-ˌmi-zəm\ _n_ **1** : a formal academic quality **2** : purely speculative thinking

acad·e·my \ə-'ka-də-mē\ _n, pl_ **-mies** [Gk _Akadēmeia_, school of philosophy founded by Plato, fr. _Akadēmeia_, gymnasium where Plato taught, fr. _Akadēmos_ Greek mythological hero] **1** : a school above the elementary level; _esp_ : a private high school **2** : a society of scholars or artists

acan·thus \ə-'kan-thəs\ _n, pl_ **acanthus 1** : any of a genus of prickly herbs of the Mediterranean region **2** : an ornamentation (as on a column) representing the leaves of the acanthus

a cap·pel·la _also_ **a ca·pel·la** \ˌä-kə-'pe-lə\ _adv or adj_ [It _a cappella_ in chapel style] : without instrumental accompaniment

acc _abbr_ accusative

ac·cede \ak-'sēd\ _vb_ **ac·ced·ed; ac·ced·ing 1** : to become a party to an agreement **2** : to express approval **3** : to enter upon an office ♦ **Synonyms** AGREE, ACQUIESCE, ASSENT, CONSENT, SUBSCRIBE

ac·cel·er·ate \ik-'se-lə-ˌrāt, ak-\ _vb_ **-at·ed; -at·ing 1** : to bring about earlier **2** : to speed up : QUICKEN — **ac·cel·er·a·tion** \-ˌse-lə-'rā-shən\ _n_

ac·cel·er·a·tor \ik-'se-lə-ˌrā-tər, ak-\ _n_ **1** : one that accelerates **2** : a pedal for controlling the speed of a motor-vehicle engine **3** : an apparatus for imparting high velocities to charged particles

ac·cel·er·om·e·ter \ik-ˌse-lə-'rä-mə-tər, ak-\ _n_ : an instrument for measuring acceleration or vibrations

¹**ac·cent** \'ak-ˌsent, ak-'sent\ _vb_ : STRESS, EMPHASIZE

²**ac·cent** \'ak-ˌsent\ _n_ **1** : prominence given to one syllable of a word esp. by stress **2** : a distinctive manner of pronunciation ⟨a foreign $\sim$⟩ **3** : a mark (as ´, `, ˆ) over a vowel used usu. to indicate a difference in pronunciation from a vowel not so marked — **ac·cen·tu·al** \ak-'sen-chə-wəl\ _adj_

ac·cen·tu·ate \ak-'sen-chə-ˌwāt\ _vb_ **-at·ed; -at·ing** : STRESS, EMPHASIZE — **ac·cen·tu·a·tion** \-ˌsen-chə-'wā-shən\ _n_

ac·cept \ik-'sept, ak-\ _vb_ **1** : to receive willingly **2** : to agree to **3** : to assume an obligation to pay

ac·cept·able \ik-'sep-tə-bəl, ak-\ _adj_ : capable or worthy of being accepted — **ac·cept·abil·i·ty** \ik-ˌsep-tə-'bi-lə-tē, ak-\ _n_

ac·cep·tance \ik-'sep-təns, ak-\ _n_ **1** : the act of accepting **2** : the state of being accepted or acceptable **3** : an accepted bill of exchange

ac·cep·ta·tion \ˌak-ˌsep-'tā-shən\ _n_ : the generally understood meaning of a word

¹**ac·cess** \'ak-ˌses\ _n_ **1** : capacity to enter or approach **2** : a way of approach : ENTRANCE

²**access** _vb_ : to get at : gain access to

ac·ces·si·ble \ik-'se-sə-bəl, ak-, ek-\ _adj_ **1** : capable of being reached ⟨$\sim$ by train⟩ **2** : capable of being used or seen ⟨$\sim$ archives⟩ **3** : capable of being understood ⟨an $\sim$ film⟩ — **ac·ces·si·bil·i·ty** \-ˌse-sə-'bi-lə-tē\ _n_

ac·ces·sion \ik-'se-shən, ak-\ _n_ **1** : increase by something added **2** : something added **3** : the act of coming to a high office or position

ac·ces·so·ry _also_ **ac·ces·sa·ry** \ik-'se-sə-rē, ak-\ _n, pl_ **-ries 1** : a person who though not present abets or assists in the commission of an offense **2** : something helpful but not essential ♦ **Synonyms** APPURTENANCE, ADJUNCT, APPENDAGE, APPENDIX — **accessory** _adj_

ac·ci·dent \'ak-sə-dənt\ _n_ **1** : an event occurring by chance or unintentionally **2** : CHANCE ⟨met by $\sim$⟩ **3** : a nonessential property

¹**ac·ci·den·tal** \ˌak-sə-'den-tᵊl\ _adj_ **1** : happening unexpectedly or by chance **2** : happening without intent or through carelessness ♦ **Synonyms** CASUAL, FORTU-

ITOUS, INCIDENTAL, CHANCE — **ac·ci·den·tal·ly** \-'den-t⁹l-ē\ *also* **ac·ci·dent·ly** \-'dent-lē\ *adv*

²accidental *n* : a musical note foreign to a key indicated by a signature

ac·claim \ə-'klām\ *vb* **1** : APPLAUD, PRAISE **2** : to declare by acclamation ✦ *Synonyms* EXTOL, LAUD, COMMEND, HAIL — **acclaim** *n*

ac·cla·ma·tion \ˌa-klə-'mā-shən\ *n* **1** : loud eager applause **2** : an overwhelming affirmative vote by shouting or applause rather than by ballot

ac·cli·mate \'a-klə-ˌmāt, ə-'klī-mət\ *vb* **-mat·ed; -mat·ing** : to accustom or become accustomed to a new climate or situation — **ac·cli·ma·tion** \ˌa-klə-'mā-shən, -ˌklī-\ *n*

ac·cli·ma·tise *Brit var of* ACCLIMATIZE

ac·cli·ma·tize \ə-'klī-mə-ˌtīz\ *vb* **-tized; -tiz·ing** : ACCLIMATE — **ac·cli·ma·ti·za·tion** \-ˌklī-mə-tə-'zā-shən\ *n*

ac·cliv·i·ty \ə-'kli-və-tē\ *n, pl* **-ties** : an ascending slope

ac·co·lade \'a-kə-ˌlād\ *n* [F, fr. *accoler* to embrace, ultim. fr. L *ad-* to + *collum* neck] : an expression of praise : AWARD

ac·com·mo·date \ə-'kä-mə-ˌdāt\ *vb* **-dat·ed; -dat·ing** **1** : to make fit or suitable : ADAPT, ADJUST **2** : HARMONIZE, RECONCILE **3** : to provide with something needed **4** : to hold without crowding **5** : to undergo visual accommodation

ac·com·mo·dat·ing *adj* : OBLIGING

ac·com·mo·da·tion \ə-ˌkä-mə-'dā-shən\ *n* **1** : something supplied to satisfy a need; *esp* : LODGINGS — usu. used in pl. **2** : the act of accommodating : ADJUSTMENT **3** : the automatic adjustment of the eye for seeing at different distances

ac·com·pa·ni·ment \ə-'kəm-pə-nē-mənt, -'kəmp-nē-\ *n* : something that accompanies another; *esp* : subordinate music to support a principal voice or instrument

ac·com·pa·ny \-nē\ *vb* **-nied; -ny·ing** **1** : to go or occur with : ATTEND **2** : to play an accompaniment for — **ac·com·pa·nist** \-nist\ *n*

ac·com·plice \ə-'käm-pləs, -'kəm-\ *n* : an associate in wrongdoing

ac·com·plish \ə-'käm-plish, -'kəm-\ *vb* : to bring to completion ✦ *Synonyms* ACHIEVE, EFFECT, EXECUTE, PERFORM — **ac·com·plish·er** *n*

ac·com·plished \-plisht\ *adj* **1** : EXPERT, SKILLED ⟨an ∼ pianist⟩ **2** : established beyond doubt ⟨an ∼ fact⟩

ac·com·plish·ment \ə-'käm-plish-mənt, -'kəm-\ *n* **1** : COMPLETION **2** : something completed or effected **3** : an acquired excellence or skill

¹ac·cord \ə-'kórd\ *vb* [ME, fr. AF *acorder*, fr. VL **accordare*, fr. L *ad-* to + *cord-, cor* heart] **1** : GRANT, CONCEDE **2** : AGREE, HARMONIZE — **ac·cor·dant** \-'kór-d⁹nt\ *adj*

²accord *n* **1** : AGREEMENT, HARMONY **2** : willingness to act ⟨gave of their own ∼⟩

ac·cor·dance \ə-'kór-d⁹ns\ *n* **1** : ACCORD **2** : the act of granting

ac·cord·ing·ly \ə-'kór-diŋ-lē\ *adv* **1** : in accordance **2** : CONSEQUENTLY, SO

according to *prep* **1** : in conformity with ⟨paid *according to* ability⟩ **2** : as stated or attested by ⟨*according to* you⟩

¹ac·cor·di·on \ə-'kór-dē-ən\ *n* [G *Akkordion*, fr. *Akkord* chord] : a portable keyboard instrument with a bellows and reeds — **ac·cor·di·on·ist** \-ə-nist\ *n*

²accordion *adj* : folding like the bellows of an accordion ⟨∼ pleats⟩

ac·cost \ə-'kóst\ *vb* [MF *accoster*, ultim. fr. L *ad-* to + *costa* rib, side] : to approach and speak to esp. aggressively

¹ac·count \ə-'kaúnt\ *n* **1** : a statement of business transactions **2** : a formal business arrangement for regular dealings or services **3** : a statement of reasons, causes, or motives **4** : VALUE, IMPORTANCE **5** : a sum of money deposited in a bank and subject to withdrawal by the depositor — **on account of** : BECAUSE OF — **on no account** : under no circumstances — **on one's own account** : on one's own behalf

²account *vb* **1** : CONSIDER ⟨I ∼ him lucky⟩ **2** : to give an explanation — used with *for*

ac·count·able \ə-'kaún-tə-bəl\ *adj* **1** : ANSWERABLE, RESPONSIBLE **2** : EXPLICABLE — **ac·count·abil·i·ty** \-ˌkaún-tə-'bi-lə-tē\ *n*

ac·coun·tant \ə-'kaún-t⁹nt\ *n* : a person skilled in accounting — **ac·coun·tan·cy** \-t⁹n-sē\ *n*

account executive *n* : a business executive in charge of a client's account

ac·count·ing \ə-'kaún-tiŋ\ *n* : the art or system of keeping and analyzing financial records

ac·cou·tre *or* **ac·cou·ter** \ə-'kü-tər\ *vb* **-cou·tred** *or* **-cou·tered; -cou·tring** *or* **-cou·ter·ing** \-'kü-t(ə-)riŋ\ : EQUIP, OUTFIT

ac·cou·tre·ment *or* **ac·cou·ter·ment** \ə-'kü-trə-mənt, -'kü-tər-\ *n* [F] **1** : an accessory item — usu. used in pl. **2** : an identifying characteristic

ac·cred·it \ə-'kre-dət\ *vb* **1** : to endorse or approve officially **2** : CREDIT — **ac·cred·i·ta·tion** \-ˌkre-də-'tā-shən\ *n*

ac·cre·tion \ə-'krē-shən\ *n* **1** : growth or enlargement esp. by addition from without **2** : a product of accretion

accretion disk *n* : a disk of usu. gaseous matter surrounding and gradually accumulating onto a massive celestial object

ac·crue \ə-'krü\ *vb* **ac·crued; ac·cru·ing** **1** : to come by way of increase **2** : to be added by periodic growth — **ac·cru·al** \-əl\ *n*

acct *abbr* account; accountant

ac·cul·tur·a·tion \ə-ˌkəl-chə-'rā-shən\ *n* : cultural modification of an individual or group by borrowing and adapting traits from another culture

ac·cu·mu·late \ə-'kyü-myə-ˌlāt\ *vb* **-lat·ed; -lat·ing** [L *accumulare*, fr. *ad-* to + *cumulare* to heap up] : to heap or pile up ✦ *Synonyms* AMASS, GATHER, COLLECT, STOCKPILE — **ac·cu·mu·la·tion** \-ˌkyü-myə-'lā-shən\ *n* — **ac·cu·mu·la·tive** \-'kyü-myə-lə-tiv\ *adj* — **ac·cu·mu·la·tor** \-'kyü-myə-ˌlā-tər\ *n*

ac·cu·rate \'a-kyə-rət\ *adj* : free from error : EXACT, PRECISE — **ac·cu·ra·cy** \-rə-sē\ *n* — **ac·cu·rate·ly** *adv* — **ac·cu·rate·ness** *n*

ac·cursed \ə-'kərst, -'kər-səd\ *or* **ac·curst** \ə-'kərst\ *adj* **1** : being under a curse **2** : DAMNABLE, EXECRABLE

ac·cu·sal \ə-'kyü-zəl\ *n* : ACCUSATION

ac·cu·sa·tive \ə-'kyü-zə-tiv\ *adj* : of, relating to, or being a grammatical case marking the direct object of a verb or the object of a preposition — **accusative** *n*

ac·cu·sa·to·ry \ə-'kyü-zə-ˌtór-ē\ *adj* : expressing accusation ⟨an ∼ tone⟩

ac·cuse \ə-'kyüz\ *vb* **ac·cused; ac·cus·ing** : to charge with an offense : BLAME — **ac·cu·sa·tion** \ˌa-kyə-'zā-shən\ *n* — **ac·cus·er** *n*

ac·cused \ə-'kyüzd\ *n, pl* **accused** : the defendant in a criminal case

ac·cus·tom \ə-'kəs-təm\ *vb* : to make familiar through use or experience

ac·cus·tomed \ə-'kəs-təmd\ *adj* : USUAL, CUSTOMARY ⟨with ∼ grace⟩; *also* : being in the habit ⟨∼ed to winning⟩

¹ace \'ās\ *n* [ME *as* a die face marked with one spot, fr. AF, fr. L, unit, a copper coin] **1** : a playing card bearing a single large pip in its center **2** : a point (as in tennis) won on a serve that goes untouched **3** : a golf score of one stroke on a hole **4** : a combat pilot who has downed five or more enemy planes **5** : one that excels **6** : the best pitcher on a baseball team

²ace *vb* **aced; ac·ing** **1** : to score an ace against (an opponent) or on (a golf hole) **2** : to defeat decisively **3** : to perform extremely well in or on ⟨aced the quiz⟩

³ace *adj* : of first rank or quality

ACE in·hib·i·tor \ˌā-ˌsē-ē-in-'hi-bə-tər, 'ās-\ *n* : any of a group of drugs that lower blood pressure by relaxing the arteries

acer·bic \ə-'sər-bik, a-\ *adj* : acid in temper, mood, or tone ⟨∼ wit⟩

acer·bi·ty \ə-'sər-bə-tē\ *n, pl* **-ties** : SOURNESS, BITTERNESS

acet·amin·o·phen \ə-ˌsē-tə-'mi-nə-fən\ *n* : a crystalline compound used in chemical synthesis and in medicine to relieve pain and fever

ac·e·tate \'a-sə-ˌtāt\ *n* **1** : a salt or ester of acetic acid **2** : a textile fiber made from cellulose and acetic acid; *also* : a fabric or plastic made of this fiber

ace·tic acid \ə-ˌsē-tik-\ *n* : a colorless pungent liquid acid that is the chief acid of vinegar and is used esp. in making chemical compounds

ac·e·tone \'a-sə-ˌtōn\ *n* : a volatile flammable fragrant liquid compound used in making other chemical compounds and as a solvent

ace·tyl·cho·line \ə-ˌsē-tᵊl-ˈkō-ˌlēn\ n : a compound that is released at nerve endings of the autonomic nervous system and is active in the transmission of nerve impulses

acet·y·lene \ə-ˈse-tᵊl-ən, -tᵊl-ˌēn\ n : a colorless flammable gas used as a fuel (as in welding and soldering)

ace·tyl·sal·i·cyl·ic acid \ə-ˈsē-tᵊl-ˌsa-lə-ˌsi-lik-\ n : ASPIRIN 1

ache \ˈāk\ vb **ached; ach·ing 1** : to suffer a usu. dull persistent pain ⟨an *aching* back⟩ **2** : LONG, YEARN ⟨*aching* to go home⟩ — **ache** n — **ach·ing·ly** \ˈā-kiŋ-lē\ adv

achieve \ə-ˈchēv\ vb **achieved; achiev·ing** [ME *acheven*, fr. AF *achever* to finish, fr. *a-* to (fr. L *ad-*) + *chef* end, head, fr. L *caput*] : to gain by work or effort ♦ *Synonyms* ACCOMPLISH, ATTAIN, REALIZE — **achiev·able** \-ˈchē-və-bəl\ adj — **achieve·ment** n — **achiev·er** n

Achil·les' heel \ə-ˌki-lēz-\ n [fr. the story that the Greek warrior Achilles was vulnerable only in the heel] : a vulnerable point

Achil·les tendon \ə-ˌki-lēz-\ n : the tendon joining the muscles in the calf of the leg to the bone of the heel

ach·ro·mat·ic \ˌa-krə-ˈma-tik\ adj : giving an image almost free from extraneous colors ⟨∼ lens⟩

achy \ˈā-kē\ adj **ach·i·er; ach·i·est** : afflicted with aches — **ach·i·ness** n

¹**ac·id** \ˈa-səd\ adj **1** : sour or biting to the taste; *also* : sharp or sour in manner **2** : of or relating to an acid — **acid·i·ty** \ə-ˈsi-də-tē\ n — **acid·ly** adv

²**acid** n **1** : a sour substance **2** : a usu. water-soluble chemical compound that has a sour taste, reacts with a base to form a salt, and reddens litmus **3** : LSD — **acid·ic** \ə-ˈsi-dik\ adj

acid·i·fy \ə-ˈsi-də-ˌfī\ vb **-fied; -fy·ing 1** : to make or become acid **2** : to change into an acid — **acid·i·fi·ca·tion** \-ˌsi-də-fə-ˈkā-shən\ n

ac·i·do·sis \ˌa-sə-ˈdō-səs\ n, pl **-do·ses** \-ˌsēz\ : an abnormal state of reduced alkalinity of the blood and body tissues

acid precipitation n : precipitation with above normal acidity that is caused esp. by atmospheric pollutants

acid rain n : acid precipitation in the form of rain

acid test n : a severe or crucial test

acid·u·lous \ə-ˈsi-jə-ləs\ adj : somewhat acid or harsh in taste or manner

ack abbr acknowledge; acknowledgment

ac·knowl·edge \ik-ˈnä-lij, ak-\ vb **-edged; -edg·ing 1** : to recognize the rights or authority of **2** : to admit as true **3** : to express thanks for; *also* : to report receipt of ⟨∼ a letter⟩ **4** : to recognize as valid — **ac·knowl·edg·ment** or **ac·knowl·edge·ment** n

ACL \ˌā-ˌsē-ˈel\ n : ANTERIOR CRUCIATE LIGAMENT

ACLU abbr American Civil Liberties Union

ac·me \ˈak-mē\ n [Gk *akmē*] : the highest point

ac·ne \ˈak-nē\ n [Gk *aknē*, MS var. of *akmē*, lit., point] : a skin disorder marked by inflammation of skin glands and hair follicles and by pimple formation esp. on the face

ac·o·lyte \ˈa-kə-ˌlīt\ n **1** : one who assists a member of the clergy in a liturgical service **2** : FOLLOWER

ac·o·nite \ˈa-kə-ˌnīt\ n **1** : MONKSHOOD **2** : the dried root of a common Eurasian monkshood used formerly as a drug

acorn \ˈā-ˌkȯrn, -kərn\ n : the nut of the oak

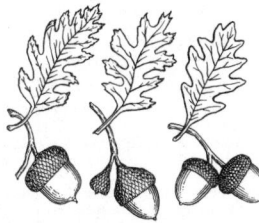

acorn: three different kinds of oak tree

acorn squash n : an acorn-shaped dark green winter squash with a ridged surface and yellow to orange flesh

acous·tic \ə-ˈkü-stik\ or **acous·ti·cal** \-sti-kəl\ adj **1** : of or relating to the sense or organs of hearing, to sound, or to the science of sounds **2** : deadening sound ⟨∼ tile⟩ **3** : operated by or utilizing sound waves **4** : having a sound that is not electronically modified ⟨∼ guitar⟩ — **acous·ti·cal·ly** \-k(ə-)lē\ adv

acous·tics \ə-ˈkü-stiks\ n sing or pl **1** : the science of sound **2** : the qualities in a room that make it easy or hard for a person in it to hear distinctly

ac·quaint \ə-ˈkwānt\ vb [ME, ultim. fr. L *ad-* + *cognoscere* to know] **1** : to cause to know personally **2** : INFORM

ac·quain·tance \ə-ˈkwān-tᵊns\ n **1** : personal knowledge **2** : a person with whom one is acquainted — **ac·quain·tance·ship** n

acquaintance rape n : rape committed by someone known to the victim

ac·qui·esce \ˌa-kwē-ˈes\ vb **-esced; -esc·ing** : to accept, comply, or submit without open opposition ♦ *Synonyms* CONSENT, AGREE, ASSENT, ACCEDE — **ac·qui·es·cence** \-ˈe-sᵊns\ n — **ac·qui·es·cent** \-sᵊnt\ adj — **ac·qui·es·cent·ly** adv

ac·quire \ə-ˈkwī(-ə)r\ vb **ac·quired; ac·quir·ing** : to gain possession of : GET — **ac·quir·able** \-ˈkwī-rə-bəl\ adj

acquired adj **1** : gained by or as a result of effort or experience **2** : caused by environmental forces and not passed from parent to offspring in the genes ⟨∼ characteristics⟩

acquired immune deficiency syndrome n : AIDS

acquired immunodeficiency syndrome n : AIDS

ac·quire·ment \ə-ˈkwī(-ə)r-mənt\ n **1** : ATTAINMENT, ACCOMPLISHMENT **2** : the act of acquiring

ac·qui·si·tion \ˌa-kwə-ˈzi-shən\ n **1** : ACQUIREMENT **2** : something acquired

ac·quis·i·tive \ə-ˈkwi-zə-tiv\ adj : eager to acquire : GREEDY — **ac·quis·i·tive·ly** adv — **ac·quis·i·tive·ness** n

ac·quit \ə-ˈkwit\ vb **ac·quit·ted; ac·quit·ting 1** : to pronounce not guilty **2** : to conduct (oneself) usu. satisfactorily — **ac·quit·tal** \ə-ˈkwi-tᵊl\ n

acre \ˈā-kər\ n **1** pl : LANDS, ESTATE **2** — see WEIGHT table

acre·age \ˈā-k(ə-)rij\ n : area in acres

ac·rid \ˈa-krəd\ adj **1** : sharp and biting in taste or odor **2** : deeply bitter : CAUSTIC — **acrid·i·ty** \a-ˈkri-də-tē\ n — **ac·rid·ly** adv — **ac·rid·ness** n

ac·ri·mo·ny \ˈa-krə-ˌmō-nē\ n, pl **-nies** : harsh or biting sharpness of language or feeling — **ac·ri·mo·ni·ous** \ˌa-krə-ˈmō-nē-əs\ adj — **ac·ri·mo·ni·ous·ly** adv — **ac·ri·mo·ni·ous·ness** n

ac·ro·bat \ˈa-krə-ˌbat\ n [F *acrobate*, fr. Gk *akrobatēs*, fr. *akros* topmost + *bainein* to go] : a performer of gymnastic feats — **ac·ro·bat·ic** \ˌa-krə-ˈba-tik\ adj — **ac·ro·bat·i·cal·ly** \-ti-k(ə-)lē\ adv

ac·ro·bat·ics \ˌa-krə-ˈba-tiks\ n sing or pl : the performance of an acrobat

ac·ro·nym \ˈa-krə-ˌnim\ n : a word (as *radar*) or abbreviation (as *FBI*) formed from the initial letter or letters of each of the successive parts or major parts of a compound term

ac·ro·pho·bia \ˌa-krə-ˈfō-bē-ə\ n : abnormal dread of being in a high place : fear of heights

acrop·o·lis \ə-ˈkrä-pə-ləs\ n [Gk *akropolis*, fr. *akros* topmost + *polis* city] : the upper fortified part of an ancient Greek city

¹**across** \ə-ˈkrȯs\ adv **1** : to or on the opposite side **2** : so as to be understandable ⟨get the point ∼⟩

²**across** prep **1** : to or on the opposite side of ⟨ran ∼ the street⟩ **2** : on so as to cross or pass at an angle ⟨a log ∼ the road⟩

across–the–board adj **1** : placed to win if a competitor wins, places, or shows ⟨an ∼ bet⟩ **2** : including all classes or categories ⟨an ∼ wage increase⟩

acros·tic \ə-ˈkrȯs-tik\ n : a composition usu. in verse in which the initial or final letters of the lines taken in order form a word or phrase — **acrostic** adj

acryl·ic \ə-ˈkri-lik\ n **1** : ACRYLIC RESIN **2** : a paint in which the vehicle is acrylic resin **3** : a quick-drying synthetic textile fiber

acrylic resin n : a glassy thermoplastic used for cast and molded parts or as coatings and adhesives

¹**act** \ˈakt\ n **1** : a thing done : DEED **2** : STATUTE, DECREE **3** : a main division of a play; *also* : an item on a va-

riety program   **4** : an instance of insincere behavior : PRETENSE

²**act** *vb* **1** : to perform by action esp. on the stage; *also* : FEIGN, SIMULATE, PRETEND   **2** : to take action   **3** : to conduct oneself : BEHAVE   **4** : to perform a specified function   **5** : to produce an effect

³**act** *abbr* **1** active **2** actual

ACT *abbr* Australian Capital Territory

actg *abbr* acting

ACTH \ₐā-(ₐ)sē-(ₐ)tē-ʹāch\ *n* : a protein hormone of the pituitary gland that stimulates the adrenal cortex

act·ing \ʹak-tiŋ\ *adj* : doing duty temporarily or for another ⟨~ president⟩

ac·tin·i·um \ak-ʹti-nē-əm\ *n* : a radioactive metallic chemical element

ac·tion \ʹak-shən\ *n* **1** : a legal proceeding   **2** : the manner or method of performing   **3** : ACTIVITY   **4** : ACT, DEED   **5** : the accomplishment of a thing usu. over a period of time, in stages, or with the possibility of repetition   **6** *pl* : CONDUCT   **7** : COMBAT, BATTLE   **8** : the events of a literary plot   **9** : an operating mechanism ⟨the ~ of a gun⟩; *also* : the way it operates ⟨stiff ~⟩

ac·tion·able \ʹak-sh(ə-)nə-bəl\ *adj* : affording ground for an action or suit at law — **ac·tion·ably** \-blē\ *adv*

ac·ti·vate \ʹak-tə-ₓvāt\ *vb* **-vat·ed; -vat·ing**   **1** : to spur into action; *also* : to make active, reactive, or radioactive   **2** : to treat (as carbon) so as to improve adsorptive properties   **3** : to set up (a military unit) formally; *also* : to call to active duty — **ac·ti·va·tion** \ₐak-tə-ʹvā-shən\ *n* — **ac·ti·va·tor** \ʹak-tə-ₓvā-tər\ *n*

ac·tive \ʹak-tiv\ *adj* **1** : causing or involving action or change   **2** : asserting that the grammatical subject performs the action represented by the verb ⟨~ voice⟩   **3** : BRISK, LIVELY   **4** : erupting or likely to erupt ⟨~ volcano⟩   **5** : presently in operation or use   **6** : tending to progress or to cause degeneration ⟨~ tuberculosis⟩ — **active** *n* — **ac·tive·ly** *adv* — **ac·tive·ness** *n*

ac·tive–ma·trix \ʹak-tiv-ₓmā-triks\ *adj* : of, relating to, or being an LCD in which each pixel is individually controlled

ac·tive·wear \ʹak-tiv-ₓwer\ *n* : clothing designed for recreation or informal wear

ac·tiv·ism \ʹak-ti-ₓvi-zəm\ *n* : a doctrine or practice that emphasizes vigorous action for political ends — **ac·tiv·ist** \-vist\ *n or adj*

ac·tiv·i·ty \ak-ʹti-və-tē\ *n, pl* **-ties**   **1** : the quality or state of being active   **2** : forceful or energetic action   **3** : an occupation in which one is engaged

ac·tor \ʹak-tər\ *n* : a person who acts in a play or motion picture

ac·tress \ʹak-trəs\ *n* : a woman who is an actor

Acts \ʹakts\ *or* **Acts of the Apostles** *n* — see BIBLE table

ac·tu·al \ʹak-chə-wəl, -shə-\ *adj* : really existing : REAL — **ac·tu·al·i·ty** \ₐak-chə-ʹwa-lə-tē, -shə-\ *n* — **ac·tu·al·i·za·tion** \ₐak-chə-wə-lə-ʹzā-shən, -shə-\ *n* — **ac·tu·al·ize** \ʹak-chə-wə-ₓlīz, -shə-\ *vb*

ac·tu·al·ly \ʹak-chə-wə-lē, -shə-\ *adv* : in fact or in truth : REALLY

ac·tu·ary \ʹak-chə-ₓwer-ē, -shə-\ *n, pl* **-ar·ies** : a person who calculates insurance risks and premiums — **ac·tu·ar·i·al** \ₐak-chə-ʹwer-ē-əl, -shə-\ *adj*

ac·tu·ate \ʹak-chə-ₓwāt\ *vb* **-at·ed; -at·ing**   **1** : to put into action   **2** : to move to action — **ac·tu·a·tion** \ₐak-chə-ʹwā-shən, -shə-\ *n* — **ac·tu·a·tor** \ʹak-chə-ₓwā-tər, -shə-\ *n*

act up *vb* **1** : MISBEHAVE   **2** : to function improperly

acu·ity \ə-ʹkyü-ə-tē\ *n, pl* **-ities** : keenness of perception

acu·men \ə-ʹkyü-mən\ *n* : mental keenness and penetration   ◆ *Synonyms* DISCERNMENT, INSIGHT, PERCIPIENCE, PERSPICACITY

acu·pres·sure \ʹa-kyu̇-ₓpre-shər\ *n* : a finger massage of those points on the body stimulated in acupuncture

acu·punc·ture \-ₓpəŋk-chər\ *n* : an orig. Chinese practice of inserting thin needles through the skin at specific points esp. to cure disease or relieve pain — **acu·punc·tur·ist** \ₐa-kyu̇-ʹpəŋk-chə-rist\ *n*

acute \ə-ʹkyüt\ *adj* **acut·er; acut·est** [ME, fr. L *acutus*, pp. of *acuere* to sharpen, fr. *acus* needle]   **1** : SHARP, POINTED   **2** : containing less than 90 degrees ⟨an ~ angle⟩   **3** : sharply perceptive; *esp* : mentally keen   **4** : SEVERE ⟨~ distress⟩; *also* : having a sudden onset, sharp rise, and short duration ⟨~ inflammation⟩   **5** : of, marked by, or

being an accent mark having the form ´ — **acute·ly** *adv* — **acute·ness** *n*

acy·clo·vir \(ₐ)ā-ʹsī-klō-ₓvir\ *n* : a drug used esp. to treat the genital form of herpes simplex

ad \ʹad\ *n* : ADVERTISEMENT

AD *abbr* **1** after date   **2** [L *anno Domini*] in the year of our Lord — often printed in small capitals and often punctuated   **3** assistant director   **4** athletic director

ad·age \ʹa-dij\ *n* : an old familiar saying : PROVERB, MAXIM

¹**ada·gio** \ə-ʹdä-j(ē-ₓ)ō, -zh(ē-ₓ)ō\ *adv or adj* [It] : at a slow tempo — used as a direction in music

²**adagio** *n, pl* **-gios**   **1** : an adagio movement   **2** : a ballet duet or trio displaying feats of lifting and balancing

¹**ad·a·mant** \ʹa-də-mənt, -ₓmant\ *n* [ME, fr. AF, fr. L *adamant-, adamas* hardest metal, diamond, fr. Gk] : a stone believed to be impenetrably hard — **ad·a·man·tine** \ₐa-də-ʹman-ₓtēn, -ₓtīn\ *adj*

²**adamant** *adj* : INFLEXIBLE, UNYIELDING — **ad·a·man·cy** \ʹa-də-mən-sē\ *n* — **ad·a·mant·ly** *adv*

Ad·am's apple \ʹa-dəmz-\ *n* : the projection in front of the neck formed by the largest cartilage of the larynx

adapt \ə-ʹdapt\ *vb* **1** : to make suitable or fit (as for a new use or for a different situation)   **2** : to adjust to environmental conditions   ◆ *Synonyms* ADJUST, ACCOMMODATE, CONFORM — **adapt·abil·i·ty** \ə-ₓdap-tə-ʹbi-lə-tē\ *n* — **adapt·able** *adj* — **ad·ap·ta·tion** \ₐa-ₓdap-ʹtā-shən\ *n* — **ad·ap·ta·tion·al** \-sh(ə-)nəl\ *adj* — **adap·tive** \ə-ʹdap-tiv\ *adj* — **ad·ap·tiv·i·ty** \ₐa-ₓdap-ʹti-və-tē\ *n*

adapt·er *also* **adap·tor** \ə-ʹdap-tər\ *n* **1** : one that adapts   **2** : a device for connecting two dissimilar parts of an apparatus   **3** : an attachment for adapting apparatus for uses not orig. intended

adaptive optics *n sing or pl* : a telescopic system that improves image resolution by compensating for distortions from atmospheric turbulence

ADC *abbr* **1** aide-de-camp   **2** Aid to Dependent Children

add \ʹad\ *vb* **1** : to join to something else so as to increase in number or amount   **2** : to say further ⟨let me ~ this⟩   **3** : to combine (numbers) into one sum

ADD *abbr* attention deficit disorder

ad·dend \ʹa-ₓdend\ *n* : a number to be added to another

ad·den·dum \ə-ʹden-dəm\ *n, pl* **-da** \-də\ [L] : something added; *esp* : a supplement to a book

¹**ad·der** \ʹa-dər\ *n* [ME, alter. (by false division of *a naddre*) of *naddre*, fr. OE *nædre*]   **1** : a poisonous European viper or a related snake   **2** : any of various harmless No. American snakes (as the hognose snake)

²**add·er** \ʹa-dər\ *n* : one that adds; *esp* : a device that performs addition

¹**ad·dict** \ə-ʹdikt\ *vb* **1** : to devote or surrender (oneself) to something habitually or excessively   **2** : to cause addiction to a substance in (as a person) — **ad·dic·tive** \-ʹdik-tiv\ *adj*

²**ad·dict** \ʹa-(ₓ)dikt\ *n* : one who is addicted esp. to a substance

ad·dic·tion \ə-ʹdik-shən\ *n* **1** : the quality or state of being addicted   **2** : compulsive need for and use of a habit-forming substance (as heroin, nicotine, or alcohol) characterized by well-defined physiological symptoms upon withdrawal; *also* : persistent compulsive use of a substance known by the user to be harmful

ad·di·tion \ə-ʹdi-shən\ *n* **1** : the act or process of adding; *also* : something added   **2** : the operation of combining numbers to obtain their sum   ◆ *Synonyms* ACCRETION, INCREMENT, ACCESSION, AUGMENTATION

ad·di·tion·al \ə-ʹdi-sh(ə-)nəl\ *adj* : coming by way of addition : ADDED, EXTRA

ad·di·tion·al·ly \ə-ʹdi-sh(ə-)nə-lē\ *adv* : in or by way of addition : FURTHERMORE

¹**ad·di·tive** \ʹa-də-tiv\ *adj* **1** : of, relating to, or characterized by addition   **2** : produced by addition — **ad·di·tiv·i·ty** \ₐa-də-ʹti-və-tē\ *n*

²**additive** *n* : a substance added to another in small quantities to effect a desired change in properties ⟨food ~s⟩

ad·dle \ʹa-dᵊl\ *vb* **ad·dled; ad·dling**   **1** : to throw into confusion : MUDDLE   **2** : to become rotten ⟨*addled* eggs⟩

addn *abbr* addition

addnl *abbr* additional

add–on \ʹad-ₓȯn, -ₓän\ *n* : something (as a feature or accessory) added esp. as an enhancement

¹ad·dress \ə-'dres\ *vb* **1** : to direct the attention of (oneself) **2** : to direct one's remarks to : deliver an address to **3** : to mark directions for delivery on **4** : to identify (as a memory location) by an address
²ad·dress \ə-'dres, 'a-ˌdres\ *n* **1** : skillful management **2** : a formal speech : LECTURE **3** : the place where a person or organization may be communicated with **4** : the directions for delivery placed on mail; *also* : the designation of a computer account from which one can send or receive e-mail **5** : a location (as in a computer's memory) where particular data is stored; *also* : URL
ad·dress·ee \ˌa-ˌdre-'sē, ə-ˌdre-'sē\ *n* : one to whom something is addressed
ad·duce \ə-'düs, -'dyüs\ *vb* **ad·duced; ad·duc·ing** : to offer as argument, reason, or proof ✦ *Synonyms* ADVANCE, ALLEGE, CITE, SUBMIT — **ad·duc·er** *n*
-ade *n suffix* **1** : act : action ⟨block*ade*⟩ **2** : product; *esp* : sweet drink ⟨lime*ade*⟩
ad·e·nine \'a-də-ˌnēn\ *n* : a purine base that codes genetic information in the molecular chain of DNA and RNA
ad·e·noid \'a-də-ˌnȯid, 'ad-ˌnȯid\ *n* : an enlarged mass of tissue near the opening of the nose into the throat — usu. used in pl. — **adenoid** *or* **ad·e·noi·dal** \ˌa-də-'nȯi-dᵊl\ *adj*
aden·o·sine tri·phos·phate \ə-'de-nə-ˌsēn-trī-'fäs-ˌfāt\ *n* : ATP
ad·e·no·vi·rus \ˌa-dᵊn-ō-'vī-rəs\ *n* : any of a family of viruses causing infections of the respiratory tract, conjunctiva, and gastrointestinal tract
¹ad·ept \'a-ˌdept\ *n* : EXPERT
²adept \ə-'dept\ *adj* : highly skilled : EXPERT — **adept·ly** *adv* — **adept·ness** *n*
ad·e·quate \'a-di-kwət\ *adj* : equal to or sufficient for a specific requirement — **ad·e·qua·cy** \-kwə-sē\ *n* — **ad·e·quate·ly** *adv* — **ad·e·quate·ness** *n*
ad·here \ad-'hir\ *vb* **ad·hered; ad·her·ing 1** : to give support : maintain loyalty **2** : to stick fast : CLING — **ad·her·ence** \-'hir-əns\ *n* — **ad·her·ent** \-ənt\ *adj or n*
ad·he·sion \ad-'hē-zhən\ *n* **1** : the act or state of adhering **2** : the union of bodily tissues abnormally grown together after inflammation; *also* : the newly formed uniting tissue **3** : the molecular attraction between the surfaces of bodies in contact
¹ad·he·sive \-'hē-siv, -ziv\ *adj* **1** : tending to adhere : STICKY **2** : prepared for adhering
²adhesive *n* : an adhesive substance
adhesive tape *n* : tape coated on one side with an adhesive mixture; *esp* : one used for covering wounds
¹ad hoc \'ad-'häk, -'hōk\ *adv* [L, for this] : for the case at hand apart from other applications
²ad hoc *adj* : concerned with or formed for a particular purpose ⟨an *ad hoc* committee⟩ ⟨*ad hoc* solutions⟩
adi·a·bat·ic \ˌa-dē-ə-'ba-tik\ *adj* : occurring without loss or gain of heat — **adi·a·bat·i·cal·ly** \-ti-k(ə-)lē\ *adv*
adieu \ə-'dü, -'dyü\ *n, pl* **adieus** *or* **adieux** \ə-'düz, -'dyüz\ : FAREWELL — often used interjectionally
ad in·fi·ni·tum \ˌad-ˌin-fə-'nī-təm\ *adv or adj* : without end or limit
ad in·ter·im \ad-'in-tə-rəm, -ˌrim\ *adv* : for the intervening time — **ad interim** *adj*
adi·os \ˌa-dē-'ōs, ˌä-\ *interj* [Sp *adiós*, lit., to God] — used to express farewell
ad·i·pose \'a-də-ˌpōs\ *adj* : of or relating to animal fat : FATTY
adj *abbr* **1** adjective **2** adjutant
ad·ja·cent \ə-'jā-sᵊnt\ *adj* : situated near or next ✦ *Synonyms* ADJOINING, CONTIGUOUS, ABUTTING, JUXTAPOSED, CONTERMINOUS — **ad·ja·cent·ly** *adv*
ad·jec·tive \'a-jik-tiv\ *n* : a word that typically serves as a modifier of a noun — **ad·jec·ti·val** \ˌa-jik-'tī-vəl\ *adj* — **ad·jec·ti·val·ly** *adv*
ad·join \ə-'jȯin\ *vb* : to be situated next to
ad·join·ing *adj* : touching or bounding at a point or line
ad·journ \ə-'jərn\ *vb* **1** : to suspend indefinitely or until a stated time **2** : to transfer to another place — **ad·journ·ment** *n*
ad·judge \ə-'jəj\ *vb* **ad·judged; ad·judg·ing 1** : JUDGE, ADJUDICATE **2** : to hold or pronounce to be : DEEM **3** : to award by judicial decision
ad·ju·di·cate \ə-'jü-di-ˌkāt\ *vb* **-cat·ed; -cat·ing** : to settle judicially — **ad·ju·di·ca·tion** \ə-ˌjü-di-'kā-shən\ *n*
ad·junct \'a-ˌjəŋkt\ *n* : something joined or added to an-

other but not essentially a part of it ✦ *Synonyms* APPENDAGE, APPURTENANCE, ACCESSORY, APPENDIX — **adjunct** *adj*
ad·jure \ə-'jur\ *vb* **ad·jured; ad·jur·ing** : to command solemnly : urge earnestly ✦ *Synonyms* BEG, BESEECH, IMPLORE — **ad·ju·ra·tion** \ˌa-jə-'rā-shən\ *n*
ad·just \ə-'jəst\ *vb* **1** : to bring to agreement : SETTLE **2** : to cause to conform : ADAPT, FIT **3** : REGULATE ⟨~ a watch⟩ — **ad·just·able** *adj* — **ad·just·er** *also* **ad·jus·tor** \ə-'jəs-tər\ *n* — **ad·just·ment** \ə-'jəst-mənt\ *n*
ad·ju·tant \'a-jə-tənt\ *n* : one who assists; *esp* : an officer who assists a commanding officer by handling correspondence and keeping records
ad·ju·vant \'a-jə-vənt\ *n* : one that helps or facilitates; *esp* : something that enhances the effectiveness of medical treatment — **adjuvant** *adj*
¹ad–lib \'ad-'lib\ *vb* **ad–libbed; ad–lib·bing** : IMPROVISE — **ad–lib** *n*
²ad–lib *adj* : spoken, composed, or performed without preparation
ad lib \'ad-'lib\ *adv* [NL *ad libitum*] **1** : at one's pleasure **2** : without limit
adm *abbr* administration; administrative
ADM *abbr* admiral
ad·man \'ad-ˌman\ *n* : one who writes, solicits, or places advertisements
admin *abbr* administration; administrative
ad·min·is·ter \əd-'mi-nə-stər\ *vb* **1** : MANAGE, SUPERINTEND **2** : to mete out : DISPENSE ⟨~ punishment⟩ **3** : to give ritually or remedially ⟨~ quinine for malaria⟩ **4** : to perform the office of administrator — **ad·min·is·tra·ble** \-strə-bəl\ *adj* — **ad·min·is·trant** \-strənt\ *n*
ad·min·is·tra·tion \əd-ˌmi-nə-'strā-shən\ *n* **1** : the act or process of administering **2** : MANAGEMENT **3** : the officials directing the government of a country **4** : the term of office of an administrative officer or body — **ad·min·is·tra·tive** \ad-'mi-nə-ˌstrā-tiv\ *adj* — **ad·min·is·tra·tive·ly** *adv*
ad·min·is·tra·tor \ad-'mi-nə-ˌstrā-tər\ *n* : one that administers; *esp* : one who settles an intestate estate
ad·mi·ra·ble \'ad-m(ə-)rə-bəl\ *adj* : worthy of admiration : EXCELLENT — **ad·mi·ra·bil·i·ty** \ˌad-m(ə-)rə-'bi-lə-tē\ *n* — **ad·mi·ra·ble·ness** *n* — **ad·mi·ra·bly** \-blē\ *adv*
ad·mi·ral \'ad-m(ə-)rəl\ *n* [ME, ultim. fr. Ar *amīr-al-* commander of the (as in *amīr-al-baḥr* commander of the sea)] : a commissioned officer in the navy ranking next below a fleet admiral
ad·mi·ral·ty \'ad-m(ə-)rəl-tē\ *n* **1** *cap* : a British government department formerly having authority over naval affairs **2** : the court having jurisdiction over questions of maritime law
ad·mire \əd-'mī(-ə)r\ *vb* **ad·mired; ad·mir·ing** [MF *admirer*, fr. L *admirari*, fr. *ad-* to + *mirari* to wonder] : to regard with high esteem — **ad·mi·ra·tion** \ˌad-mə-'rā-shən\ *n* — **ad·mir·er** *n* — **ad·mir·ing·ly** \-'mī-riŋ-lē\ *adv*
ad·mis·si·ble \ad-'mi-sə-bəl\ *adj* : that can be or is worthy to be admitted or allowed : ALLOWABLE ⟨~ evidence⟩ — **ad·mis·si·bil·i·ty** \-ˌmi-sə-'bi-lə-tē\ *n*
ad·mis·sion \əd-'mi-shən\ *n* **1** : the act of admitting **2** : the privilege of being admitted **3** : a fee paid for admission **4** : the granting of an argument **5** : the acknowledgment of a fact
ad·mit \əd-'mit\ *vb* **ad·mit·ted; ad·mit·ting 1** : PERMIT, ALLOW **2** : to recognize as genuine or valid **3** : to allow to enter ⟨*admitted* to the club⟩ **4** : to accept into a hospital as an inpatient
ad·mit·tance \əd-'mi-tᵊns\ *n* : the act or process of admitting : permission to enter
ad·mit·ted·ly \əd-'mi-təd-lē\ *adv* : as has been or must be admitted **2** : it must be admitted
ad·mix \ad-'miks\ *vb* : to mix in
ad·mix·ture \ad-'miks-chər\ *n* **1** : something added in mixing **2** : MIXTURE
ad·mon·ish \əd-'mä-nish\ *vb* : to warn gently : reprove with a warning ✦ *Synonyms* CHIDE, REPROACH, REBUKE, REPRIMAND, REPROVE — **ad·mon·ish·er** *n* — **ad·mon·ish·ing·ly** *adv* — **ad·mon·ish·ment** *n* — **ad·mo·ni·tion** \ˌad-mə-'ni-shən\ *n* — **ad·mon·i·to·ry** \ad-'mä-nə-ˌtȯr-ē\ *adj*
ad nau·se·am \ad-'nȯ-zē-əm\ *adv* [L] : to a sickening or excessive degree

ado \ə-'dü\ *n* **1** : heightened fuss or concern **2** : TROUBLE

adobe \ə-'dō-bē\ *n* **1** : sun-dried brick; *also* : clay for making such bricks **2** : a structure made of adobe bricks

ad·o·les·cence \ˌa-də-'les-ᵊns\ *n* : the process or period of growth between childhood and maturity — **ad·o·les·cent** \-ᵊnt\ *adj or n*

adopt \ə-'däpt\ *vb* **1** : to take (a child of other parents) as one's own child **2** : to take up and practice as one's own **3** : to accept formally and put into effect — **adopt·able** \-'däp-tə-bəl\ *adj* — **adopt·er** *n* — **adop·tion** \-'däp-shən\ *n*

adop·tive \ə-'däp-tiv\ *adj* : made or acquired by adoption ⟨the ~ father⟩ — **adop·tive·ly** *adv*

ador·able \ə-'dȯr-ə-bəl\ *adj* **1** : worthy of adoration **2** : extremely charming ⟨an ~ child⟩ — **ador·able·ness** *n* — **ador·ably** \-blē\ *adv*

adore \ə-'dȯr\ *vb* **adored; ador·ing** [ME *adouren*, fr. AF *aurer, adourer*, fr. L *adorare*, fr. *ad-* to + *orare* to speak, pray] **1** : WORSHIP **2** : to regard with loving admiration ⟨~s his wife⟩ **3** : to be extremely fond of ⟨~s pecan pie⟩ — **ad·o·ra·tion** \ˌa-də-'rā-shən\ *n*

adorn \ə-'dȯrn\ *vb* : to enhance the appearance of esp. with ornaments ⟨blouses ~ed with sequins⟩ — **adorn·ment** *n*

ad·re·nal \ə-'drē-nᵊl\ *adj* : of, relating to, or being a pair of endocrine organs (**adrenal glands**) that are located near the kidneys and produce several hormones and esp. epinephrine

adren·a·line \ə-'dre-nə-lən\ *n* : EPINEPHRINE

adrift \ə-'drift\ *adv or adj* **1** : afloat without motive power or moorings **2** : without guidance or purpose

adroit \ə-'drȯit\ *adj* [F, fr. OF, fr. *a-* to + *droit* right] **1** : dexterous with one's hands **2** : SHREWD, RESOURCEFUL
+ **Synonyms** CANNY, CLEVER, CUNNING, INGENIOUS — **adroit·ly** *adv* — **adroit·ness** *n*

ad·sorb \ad-'sȯrb, -'zȯrb\ *vb* : to take up (as molecules of gases) and hold on the surface of a solid or liquid — **ad·sorp·tion** \-'sȯrp-shən, -'zȯrp-\ *n*

ad·u·la·tion \ˌa-jə-'lā-shən\ *n* : excessive admiration or flattery — **ad·u·late** \'a-jə-ˌlāt\ *vb* — **ad·u·la·tor** \-ˌlā-tər\ *n* — **ad·u·la·to·ry** \-lə-ˌtȯr-ē\ *adj*

¹adult \ə-'dəlt, 'a-ˌ\ *adj* [L *adultus*, pp. of *adolescere* to grow up, fr. *ad-* to + *alescere* to grow] : fully developed and mature — **adult·hood** *n*

²adult *n* : one that is adult; *esp* : a human being after an age (as 18) specified by law

adul·ter·ant \ə-'dəl-tə-rənt\ *n* : something used to adulterate another

adul·ter·ate \ə-'dəl-tə-ˌrāt\ *vb* **-at·ed; -at·ing** [L *adulterare*, fr. *ad-* to + *alter* other] : to make impure by mixing in a foreign or inferior substance — **adul·ter·a·tion** \-ˌdəl-tə-'rā-shən\ *n*

adul·tery \ə-'dəl-t(ə-)rē\ *n, pl* **-ter·ies** : sexual unfaithfulness of a married person — **adul·ter·er** \-tər-ər\ *n* — **adul·ter·ess** \-t(ə-)rəs\ *also* **adul·tress** \-trəs\ *n* — **adul·ter·ous** \-t(ə-)rəs\ *adj*

ad·um·brate \'a-dəm-ˌbrāt\ *vb* **-brat·ed; -brat·ing** **1** : to foreshadow vaguely : INTIMATE **2** : to suggest or disclose partially **3** : SHADE, OBSCURE — **ad·um·bra·tion** \ˌa-dəm-'brā-shən\ *n*

adv *abbr* **1** adverb **2** advertisement

ad va·lor·em \ˌad-və-'lȯr-əm\ *adj* [L, according to the value] : imposed as a percentage of the value ⟨an *ad valorem* tax⟩

¹ad·vance \əd-'vans\ *vb* **ad·vanced; ad·vanc·ing** **1** : to assist the progress of ⟨~ a cause⟩ **2** : to bring or move forward ⟨~ a pawn⟩ **3** : to promote in rank **4** : to make earlier in time **5** : PROPOSE **6** : LEND **7** : to raise in rate : INCREASE — **ad·vance·ment** *n*

²advance *n* **1** : a forward movement **2** : IMPROVEMENT **3** : a rise esp. in price or value **4** : OFFER — **in advance** : BEFOREHAND

³advance *adj* : made, sent, or furnished ahead of time ⟨~ payment⟩

ad·van·tage \əd-'van-tij\ *n* **1** : superiority of position **2** : BENEFIT, GAIN **3** : the 1st point won in tennis after deuce — **ad·van·ta·geous** \ˌad-van-'tā-jəs\ *adj* — **ad·van·ta·geous·ly** *adv*

ad·vent \'ad-ˌvent\ *n* **1** *cap* : a penitential period beginning four Sundays before Christmas **2** *cap* : the coming of Christ **3** : a coming into being or use

ad·ven·ti·tious \ˌad-vən-'ti-shəs\ *adj* **1** : ACCIDENTAL, INCIDENTAL **2** : arising or occurring sporadically or in other than the usual location ⟨~ buds⟩ — **ad·ven·ti·tious·ly** *adv*

¹ad·ven·ture \əd-'ven-chər\ *n* **1** : a risky undertaking **2** : a remarkable and exciting experience — **ad·ven·tur·ous** \-ch(ə-)rəs\ *adj*

²adventure *vb* **-ven·tured; -ven·tur·ing** \-'ven-ch(ə-)riŋ\ **1** : RISK, HAZARD ⟨~ their capital in foreign trade⟩ **2** : to engage in adventure

ad·ven·tur·er \əd-'ven-ch(ə-)rər\ *n* **1** : a person who engages in new and risky undertakings **2** : a person who follows a military career for adventure or profit **3** : a person who tries to gain wealth by questionable means

ad·ven·ture·some \əd-'ven-chər-səm\ *adj* : inclined to take risks

ad·ven·tur·ess \əd-'ven-ch(ə-)rəs\ *n* : a female adventurer

ad·verb \'ad-ˌvərb\ *n* : a word that typically serves as a modifier of a verb, an adjective, or another adverb — **ad·ver·bi·al** \ad-'vər-bē-əl\ *adj* — **ad·ver·bi·al·ly** *adv*

¹ad·ver·sary \'ad-vər-ˌser-ē\ *n, pl* **-sar·ies** : FOE

²adversary *adj* : involving antagonistic parties or interests

ad·verse \ad-'vərs, 'ad-ˌvərs\ *adj* **1** : acting against or in a contrary direction ⟨~ winds⟩ **2** : UNFAVORABLE ⟨~ criticism⟩ — **ad·verse·ly** *adv*

ad·ver·si·ty \ad-'vər-sə-tē\ *n, pl* **-ties** : hard times : MISFORTUNE

ad·vert \ad-'vərt\ *vb* : REFER ⟨~ to a previous remark⟩

ad·ver·tise \'ad-vər-ˌtīz\ *vb* **-tised; -tis·ing** **1** : INFORM, NOTIFY **2** : to call public attention to esp. in order to sell — **ad·ver·tis·er** *n*

ad·ver·tise·ment \ˌad-vər-'tīz-mənt; əd-'vər-təs-mənt\ *n* **1** : the act of advertising **2** : a public notice intended to advertise something

ad·ver·tis·ing \'ad-vər-ˌtī-ziŋ\ *n* : the business of preparing advertisements

ad·vice \əd-'vīs\ *n* **1** : recommendation with regard to a course of action : COUNSEL **2** : INFORMATION, REPORT

ad·vis·able \əd-'vī-zə-bəl\ *adj* : proper to be done : EXPEDIENT ⟨~ to stay fit⟩ — **ad·vis·abil·i·ty** \-ˌvī-zə-'bi-lə-tē\ *n*

ad·vise \əd-'vīz\ *vb* **ad·vised; ad·vis·ing** **1** : to give advice to : COUNSEL **2** : INFORM, NOTIFY **3** : CONSULT, CONFER ⟨~ with your friends⟩ — **ad·vis·er** *also* **ad·vi·sor** \-'vī-zər\ *n*

ad·vised \əd-'vīzd\ *adj* : thought out : CONSIDERED ⟨well-*advised*⟩ — **ad·vis·ed·ly** \-'vī-zəd-lē\ *adv*

ad·vise·ment \əd-'vīz-mənt\ *n* **1** : careful consideration ⟨take the matter under ~⟩ **2** : the act of advising

ad·vi·so·ry \əd-'vī-zə-rē\ *adj* **1** : having or exercising power to advise **2** : containing or giving advice

¹ad·vo·cate \'ad-və-kət, -ˌkāt\ *n* [ultim. fr. L *advocare* to summon, fr. *ad-* + *vocare* to call] **1** : one who pleads another's cause **2** : one who argues or pleads for a cause or proposal — **ad·vo·ca·cy** \-və-kə-sē\ *n*

²ad·vo·cate \-ˌkāt\ *vb* **-cat·ed; -cat·ing** : to plead in favor of — **ad·vo·ca·tion** \ˌad-və-'kā-shən\ *n*

advt *abbr* advertisement

adze *also* **adz** \'adz\ *n* : a tool with a curved blade set at right angles to the handle that is used in shaping wood

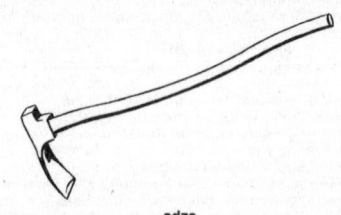

adze

AEC *abbr* Atomic Energy Commission

ae·gis \'ē-jəs\ *n* **1** : SHIELD, PROTECTION ⟨under the ~ of the constitution⟩ **2** : PATRONAGE, SPONSORSHIP ⟨under the ~ of the museum⟩

ae·o·li·an harp \ē-'ō-lē-ən-\ *n* : a box with strings that produce musical sounds when the wind blows on them

ae·on or **eon** \'ē-ən, -,än\ n : an indefinitely long time : AGE
aer·ate \'aer-,āt\ vb **aer·at·ed; aer·at·ing 1 :** to supply, impregnate, or combine with a gas and esp. air **2 :** to supply (blood) with oxygen by respiration — **aer·a·tion** \,er-'ā-shən\ n — **aer·a·tor** \'er-,ā-tər\ n
¹ae·ri·al \'er-ē-əl\ adj **1 :** inhabiting, occurring in, or done in the air **2 :** AIRY **3 :** of or relating to aircraft
²aer·i·al \'er-ē-əl\ n : ANTENNA 2
ae·ri·al·ist \'er-ē-ə-list\ n : a performer of feats above the ground esp. on a trapeze
ae·rie \'er-ē, 'ir-ē\ n : a highly placed nest (as of an eagle)
aer·o·bat·ics \,er-ə-'ba-tiks\ n sing or pl : spectacular flying feats and maneuvers
aer·o·bic \,er-'rō-bik\ adj **1 :** living or active only in the presence of oxygen ⟨∼ bacteria⟩ **2 :** involving or increasing oxygen consumption; also : of or relating to aerobics — **aer·o·bi·cal·ly** \-bi-k(ə-)lē\ adv
aer·o·bics \-biks\ n sing or pl : strenuous exercises that produce a marked temporary increase in respiration and heart rate; also : a system of physical conditioning involving these
aero·drome \'er-ə-,drōm\ n, chiefly Brit : AIRPORT
aero·dy·nam·ics \,er-ō-dī-'na-miks\ n : the science dealing with the forces acting on bodies in motion in a gas (as air) — **aero·dy·nam·ic** \-mik\ also **aero·dy·nam·i·cal** \-mi-kəl\ adj — **aero·dy·nam·i·cal·ly** \-mi-k(ə-)lē\ adv
aero·naut \'er-ə-,nȯt\ n [F aéronaute, ultim. fr. Gk aēr air + nautēs sailor] : one who operates or travels in an airship or balloon
aero·nau·tics \,er-ə-'nȯ-tiks\ n : the science of aircraft operation — **aero·nau·ti·cal** \-ti-kəl\ also **aero·nau·tic** \-tik\ adj
aero·pho·bia \,er-ō-'fō-bē-ə\ n : fear or strong dislike of flying
aero·plane \'er-ə-,plān\ chiefly Brit var of AIRPLANE
aero·sol \'er-ə-,säl, -,sȯl\ n **1 :** a suspension of fine solid or liquid particles in a gas; also, pl : the particles themselves **2 :** a substance (as an insecticide) dispensed from a pressurized container as an aerosol
aero·space \'er-ō-,spās\ n : the earth's atmosphere and the space beyond — **aerospace** adj
aery \'er-ē\ adj **aer·i·er; -est :** having an aerial quality : ETHEREAL ⟨∼ visions⟩
aes·thete also **es·thete** \'es-,thēt\ n : a person having or affecting sensitivity to beauty esp. in art
aes·thet·ic also **es·thet·ic** \es-'the-tik\ adj **1 :** of or relating to aesthetics **2 :** appreciative of the beautiful — **aes·thet·i·cal·ly** also **es·thet·i·cal·ly** \-ti-k(ə-)lē\ adv
aes·thet·ics also **es·thet·ics** \-tiks\ n : a branch of philosophy dealing with the nature, creation, and appreciation of beauty
ae·ti·ol·o·gy chiefly Brit var of ETIOLOGY
AF abbr **1** air force **2** audio frequency
¹afar \ə-'fär\ adv : from, at, or to a great distance
²afar n : a great distance
AFB abbr air force base
AFC abbr **1** American Football Conference **2** automatic frequency control
AFDC abbr Aid to Families with Dependent Children
af·fa·ble \'a-fə-bəl\ adj : courteous and agreeable in conversation — **af·fa·bil·i·ty** \,a-fə-'bi-lə-tē\ n — **af·fa·bly** \'a-fə-blē\ adv
af·fair \ə-'fer\ n [ME afere, fr. AF fr. afaire, fr. a faire to do] **1 :** something that relates to or involves one : CONCERN **2 :** a romantic or sexual attachment of limited duration
¹af·fect \ə-'fekt, a-\ vb **1 :** to be fond of using or wearing **2 :** SIMULATE, ASSUME, PRETEND
²affect vb : to produce an effect on : INFLUENCE
³af·fect \'a-,fekt\ n : EMOTION; also : an observable display of emotion ⟨an expressionless ∼⟩
af·fec·ta·tion \,a-,fek-'tā-shən\ n : an attitude or behavior that is assumed by a person but not genuinely felt
af·fect·ed \ə-'fek-təd\ adj **1 :** given to or marked by affectation **2 :** artificially assumed to impress others — **af·fect·ed·ly** adv
af·fect·ing \ə-'fek-tiŋ\ adj : arousing pity, sympathy, or sorrow ⟨an ∼ story⟩ — **af·fect·ing·ly** adv
af·fec·tion \ə-'fek-shən\ n : tender attachment — **af·fec·tion·ate** \-sh(ə-)nət\ adj — **af·fec·tion·ate·ly** adv

af·fec·tive \a-'fek-tiv\ adj : relating to, influencing, or expressing an emotion or feeling : EMOTIONAL ⟨an ∼ disorder⟩
af·fer·ent \'a-fə-rənt, -,fer-ənt\ adj : bearing or conducting inward toward a more central part and esp. a nerve center (as the central nervous system)
af·fi·ance \ə-'fī-əns\ vb **-anced; -anc·ing :** BETROTH, ENGAGE
af·fi·da·vit \,a-fə-'dā-vət\ n [ML, he has made an oath] : a sworn statement in writing
¹af·fil·i·ate \ə-'fi-lē-,āt\ vb **-at·ed; -at·ing :** to associate as a member or branch — **af·fil·i·a·tion** \-,fi-lē-'ā-shən\ n
²af·fil·i·ate \ə-'fi-lē-ət\ n : an affiliated person or organization
af·fin·i·ty \ə-'fi-nə-tē\ n, pl **-ties 1 :** KINSHIP, RELATIONSHIP **2 :** attractive force : ATTRACTION, SYMPATHY
affinity card n : a credit card issued in affiliation with an organization (such as a charity or an airline) the use of which benefits the organization or possessor of the card
af·firm \ə-'fərm\ vb **1 :** CONFIRM **2 :** to assert positively **3 :** to make a solemn and formal declaration or assertion in place of an oath ✦ **Synonyms** AVER, AVOW, AVOUCH, DECLARE, ASSERT — **af·fir·ma·tion** \,a-fər-'mā-shən\ n
¹af·fir·ma·tive \ə-'fər-mə-tiv\ adj : asserting that the fact is so : POSITIVE
²affirmative n **1 :** an expression of affirmation or assent **2 :** the side that upholds the proposition stated in a debate
affirmative action n : an active effort to improve the employment or educational opportunities of members of minority groups and women
¹af·fix \ə-'fiks\ vb : ATTACH, ADD
²af·fix \'a-,fiks\ n : one or more sounds or letters attached to the beginning or end of a word that produce a derivative word or an inflectional form
af·fla·tus \ə-'flā-təs\ n : divine inspiration
af·flict \ə-'flikt\ vb : to cause pain and distress to ✦ **Synonyms** RACK, TRY, TORMENT, TORTURE — **af·flic·tion** \-'flik-shən\ n
af·flic·tive \ə-'flik-tiv\ adj : causing affliction : DISTRESSING ⟨∼ emotions⟩ — **af·flic·tive·ly** adv
af·flu·ence \'a-,flü-ən(t)s, a-'flü-\ n : abundant supply; also : WEALTH, RICHES — **af·flu·ent** \-ənt\ adj
af·ford \ə-'fȯrd\ vb **1 :** to manage to bear or bear the cost of without serious harm or loss **2 :** PROVIDE, FURNISH ⟨the roof ∼ed a fine view⟩
af·for·es·ta·tion \ə-,fȯr-ə-'stā-shən\ n : the act or process of establishing a forest — **af·for·est** \a-'fȯr-əst, -'fär-\ vb
af·fray \ə-'frā\ n : FIGHT, FRAY
af·fright \ə-'frīt\ vb, archaic : FRIGHTEN, ALARM — **affright** n
af·front \ə-'frənt\ vb **1 :** INSULT **2 :** CONFRONT ⟨∼ death⟩ — **affront** n
af·ghan \'af-,gan\ n **1** cap : a native or inhabitant of Afghanistan **2 :** a blanket or shawl of colored wool knitted or crocheted in sections — **Afghan** or **Af·ghani** \af-'ga-nē, -'gä-\ adj
Afghan hound n : any of a breed of tall slim swift hunting dogs with a coat of silky thick hair and a long silky top-knot
afi·cio·na·do \ə-,fi-sh(ē-)ə-'nä-dō, -sē-ə-\ n, pl **-dos** [Sp, fr. pp. of aficionar to inspire affection] : DEVOTEE, FAN
afield \ə-'fēld\ adv or adj **1 :** to, in, or on the field **2 :** away from home **3 :** out of the way : ASTRAY
afire \ə-'fī(-ə)r\ adj or adv : being on fire : BURNING
AFL abbr American Football League
aflame \ə-'flām\ adj or adv : FLAMING
AFL–CIO abbr American Federation of Labor and Congress of Industrial Organizations
afloat \ə-'flōt\ adj or adv **1 :** borne on or as if on the water **2 :** CIRCULATING ⟨rumors were ∼⟩ **3 :** ADRIFT
aflut·ter \ə-'flə-tər\ adj **1 :** FLUTTERING **2 :** nervously excited ⟨∼ at the news⟩
afoot \ə-'fu̇t\ adv or adj **1 :** on foot **2 :** in action : in progress
afore·men·tioned \ə-'fȯr-'men-chənd\ adj : mentioned previously
afore·said \-,sed\ adj : said or named before
afore·thought \-,thȯt\ adj : PREMEDITATED ⟨with malice ∼⟩

a for·ti·o·ri \ˌä-ˌfòr-tē-'òr-ē\ *adv* [NL, lit., from the stronger (argument)] : with even greater reason

afoul of \ə-'faúl-əv\ *prep* **1** : in or into conflict with **2** : in or into collision or entanglement with

Afr *abbr* Africa; African

afraid \ə-'frād\ *adj* **1** : FRIGHTENED, FEARFUL **2** : filled with concern or regret ⟨∼ I won't be able to go⟩

A–frame \'ā-ˌfrām\ *n* : a building having triangular front and rear walls with the roof reaching to the ground

afresh \ə-'fresh\ *adv* : ANEW, AGAIN

Af·ri·can \'a-fri-kən\ *n* **1** : a native or inhabitant of Africa **2** : a person of African ancestry — **African** *adj*

Af·ri·can–Amer·i·can \-ə-'mer-ə-kən\ *n* : an American of African and esp. of black African descent — **African–American** *adj*

Af·ri·can·ized bee \'a-frə-kə-ˌnīzd-\ *n* : a highly aggressive hybrid honeybee accidentally produced from Brazilian and African stocks that has spread from So. America into Mexico and the southern U.S.

Africanized honeybee *n* : AFRICANIZED BEE

African violet *n* : a tropical African plant widely grown indoors for its velvety fleshy leaves and showy purple, pink, or white flowers

Af·ri·kaans \ˌa-fri-'käns\ *n* : a language developed from 17th century Dutch that is one of the official languages of the Republic of So. Africa

Afro *n, pl* **Afros** : a hairstyle of tight curls in a full evenly rounded shape

Af·ro–Amer·i·can \ˌa-frō-ə-'mer-ə-kən\ *n* : AFRICAN= AMERICAN — **Afro–American** *adj*

aft \'aft\ *adv* : near, toward, or in the stern of a ship or the tail of an aircraft

AFT *abbr* American Federation of Teachers

¹af·ter \'af-tər\ *adv* : AFTERWARD, SUBSEQUENTLY

²after *prep* **1** : behind in place **2** : later than ⟨∼ dinner⟩ **3** : in pursuit or search of ⟨he's ∼ your job⟩

³after *conj* : following the time when ⟨we will come ∼ we make plans⟩

⁴after *adj* **1** : LATER ⟨in ∼ years⟩ **2** : located toward the rear

af·ter·birth \'af-tər-ˌbərth\ *n* : the placenta and membranes of the fetus that are expelled after childbirth

af·ter·burn·er \-ˌbər-nər\ *n* : a device incorporated in the tail pipe of a turbojet engine for injecting fuel into the hot exhaust gases and burning it to provide extra thrust

af·ter·care \-ˌker\ *n* : the care, nursing, or treatment of a convalescent patient

af·ter·deck \-ˌdek\ *n* : the rear half of the deck of a ship

af·ter·ef·fect \-ə-ˌfekt\ *n* : an effect that follows its cause after an interval

af·ter·glow \-ˌglō\ *n* : a glow remaining where a light has disappeared

af·ter·im·age \-ˌim-ij\ *n* : a usu. visual sensation continuing after the stimulus causing it has ended

af·ter·life \-ˌlīf\ *n* : an existence after death

af·ter·math \-ˌmath\ *n* **1** : a second-growth crop esp. of hay **2** : CONSEQUENCES, EFFECTS ♦ *Synonyms* AFTEREFFECT, UPSHOT, RESULT, OUTCOME

af·ter·noon \ˌaf-tər-'nün\ *n* : the time between noon and evening

af·ter·shave \'af-tər-ˌshāv\ *n* : a usu. scented lotion for the face after shaving

af·ter·taste \-ˌtāst\ *n* : a sensation (as of flavor) continuing after the stimulus causing it has ended

af·ter–tax \'af-tər-'taks\ *adj* : remaining after payment of taxes and esp. of income tax ⟨an ∼ profit⟩

af·ter·thought \-ˌthót\ *n* : an idea occurring later

af·ter·ward \-wərd\ *or* **af·ter·wards** \-wərdz\ *adv* : at a later time

Ag *symbol* [L *argentum*] silver

AG *abbr* **1** adjutant general **2** attorney general

again \ə-'gen, -'gin\ *adv* **1** : once more : ANEW ⟨come see us ∼⟩ **2** : on the other hand ⟨we may, and ∼ we may not⟩ **3** : in addition : BESIDES

against \ə-'genst\ *prep* **1** : in opposition to **2** : directly opposite to : FACING **3** : as defense from **4** : so as to touch or strike ⟨threw him ∼ the wall⟩; *also* : TOUCHING

¹aga·pe \ä-'gä-pā, 'ä-gə-ˌpā\ *n* [LL, fr. Gk *agapē*, lit., love] : unselfish unconditional love for another

²agape \ə-'gāp\ *adj or adv* : having the mouth open in wonder or surprise : GAPING

agar \'ä-ˌgär\ *n* **1** : a jellylike substance extracted from a red alga and used esp. as a gelling and stabilizing agent in foods **2** : a culture medium containing agar

agar–agar \ˌä-ˌgär-'ä-ˌgär\ *n* : AGAR

ag·ate \'a-gət\ *n* **1** : a striped or clouded quartz **2** : a playing marble of agate or of glass

aga·ve \ə-'gä-vē\ *n* : any of a genus of spiny-leaved plants (as a century plant) related to the amaryllis

agcy *abbr* agency

¹age \'āj\ *n* **1** : the length of time during which a being or thing has lived or existed **2** : the time of life at which some particular qualification is achieved; *esp* : MAJORITY **3** : the latter part of life **4** : a long time **5** : a period in history

²age *vb* **aged; ag·ing** *or* **age·ing 1** : to grow old or cause to grow old **2** : to become or cause to become mature or mellow

-age *n suffix* **1** : aggregate : collection ⟨track*age*⟩ **2** : action : process ⟨haul*age*⟩ **3** : cumulative result of ⟨break*age*⟩ **4** : rate of ⟨dos*age*⟩ **5** : house or place of ⟨orphan*age*⟩ **6** : state : rank ⟨vassal*age*⟩ **7** : fee : charge ⟨post*age*⟩

aged \'ā-jəd *for 1;* 'ājd *for 2*\ *adj* **1** : of advanced age **2** : having attained a specified age ⟨a man ∼ 40 years⟩

age·ism \'ā-ˌji-zəm\ *n* : discrimination against persons of a particular age and esp. the elderly — **age·ist** \-jist\ *n*

age·less \'āj-ləs\ *adj* **1** : not growing old or showing the effects of age **2** : TIMELESS, ETERNAL ⟨∼ truths⟩

agen·cy \'ā-jən-sē\ *n, pl* **-cies 1** : one through which something is accomplished : INSTRUMENTALITY **2** : the office or function of an agent **3** : an establishment doing business for another **4** : an administrative division (as of a government) ♦ *Synonyms* MEANS, MEDIUM, VEHICLE

agen·da \ə-'jen-də\ *n* : a list of things to be done : PROGRAM

agent \'ā-jənt\ *n* **1** : one that acts **2** : MEANS, INSTRUMENT **3** : a person acting or doing business for another **4** : a computer program designed to automate certain tasks (as gathering information online) ♦ *Synonyms* ATTORNEY, DEPUTY, PROXY, DELEGATE

Agent Orange *n* : an herbicide widely used in the Vietnam War that is composed of 2,4-D and 2,4,5-T and contains a toxic contaminant

agent pro·vo·ca·teur \ˌä-ˌzhäⁿ-prō-ˌvä-kə-'tər, 'ä-jənt-\ *pl* **agents provocateurs** \'ä-ˌzhäⁿ-prō-ˌväk-ə-'tər, 'ä-jəntsprō-\ [F] : a person hired to infiltrate a group and incite its members to illegal action

age of consent : the age at which one is legally competent to give consent esp. to marriage or to sexual intercourse

age–old \'āj-'ōld\ *adj* : having existed for ages : ANCIENT

ag·er·a·tum \ˌa-jə-'rā-təm\ *n, pl* **-tum** *also* **-tums** : any of a genus of tropical American plants that are related to the daisies and have small showy heads of usu. blue or white flowers

age spots *n pl* : benign flat spots of dark pigmentation on the skin occurring esp. among older people

Ag·ge·us \a-'gē-əs\ *n* : HAGGAI

¹ag·glom·er·ate \ə-'glä-mə-ˌrāt\ *vb* **-at·ed; -at·ing** [L *agglomerare* to heap up, join, fr. *ad-* to + *glomer-, glomus* ball] : to gather into a mass : CLUSTER — **ag·glom·er·a·tion** \-ˌglä-mə-'rā-shən\ *n*

²ag·glom·er·ate \-rət\ *n* : rock composed of volcanic fragments

ag·glu·ti·nate \ə-'glü-t⁼n-ˌāt\ *vb* **-nat·ed; -nat·ing 1** : to cause to adhere : gather into a group or mass **2** : to cause (as red blood cells or bacteria) to collect into clumps — **ag·glu·ti·na·tion** \-ˌglü-t⁼n-'ā-shən\ *n*

ag·gran·dise *Brit var of* AGGRANDIZE

ag·gran·dize \ə-'gran-ˌdīz, 'a-grən-\ *vb* **-dized; -diz·ing** : to make great or greater ⟨∼ an estate⟩ — **ag·gran·dize·ment** \ə-'gran-dəz-mənt, -dīz-; ˌa-grən-'dīz-\ *n*

ag·gra·vate \'a-grə-ˌvāt\ *vb* **-vat·ed; -vat·ing 1** : to make more severe : INTENSIFY **2** : IRRITATE — **ag·gra·va·tion** \ˌa-grə-'vā-shən\ *n*

¹ag·gre·gate \'a-gri-gət\ *adj* : formed by the gathering of units into a body

²ag·gre·gate \-ˌgāt\ *vb* **-gat·ed; -gat·ing** : to collect into one mass

³ag·gre·gate \-gət\ *n* : a mass or body of units or parts somewhat loosely associated with one another; *also* : the whole amount

ag·gre·ga·tion \,a-gri-'gā-shən\ *n* **1** : a group, body, or mass composed of many distinct parts **2** : the collecting of units or parts into a mass or whole

ag·gres·sion \ə-'gre-shən\ *n* **1** : an unprovoked attack **2** : the practice of making attacks **3** : hostile, injurious, or destructive behavior or outlook esp. when caused by frustration — **ag·gres·sor** \-'gre-sər\ *n*

ag·gres·sive \ə-'gre-siv\ *adj* **1** : tending toward or exhibiting aggression; *esp* : marked by combative readiness **2** : marked by driving energy or initiative : ENTERPRISING **3** : more intensive or comprehensive esp. in dosage or extent — **ag·gres·sive·ly** *adv* — **ag·gres·sive·ness** *n*

ag·grieve \ə-'grēv\ *vb* **aggrieved; ag·griev·ing** **1** : to cause grief to **2** : to inflict injury on : WRONG

ag·gro \'a-,grō\ *adj* : aggressive or aggressively daring in style or manner ⟨∼ music⟩ ⟨∼ surfing⟩

aghast \ə-'gast\ *adj* : struck with amazement or horror

ag·ile \'a-jəl\ *adj* : able to move quickly and easily — **ag·ile·ly** *adv* — **agil·i·ty** \ə-'ji-lə-tē\ *n*

ag·i·ta \'a-jə-tə\ *n* [southern It dial. pron. of It *acido*, lit., heartburn, acid] : a feeling of agitation or anxiety

ag·i·tate \'a-jə-,tāt\ *vb* **-tat·ed; -tat·ing** **1** : to move with an irregular rapid motion **2** : to stir up : EXCITE **3** : to discuss earnestly **4** : to attempt to arouse public feeling — **ag·i·ta·tion** \,a-jə-'tā-shən\ *n* — **ag·i·ta·tor** \'a-jə-,tā-tər\ *n*

ag·it·prop \'a-jət-,präp\ *n* [Russ] : political propaganda promulgated esp. through the arts

agleam \ə-'glēm\ *adj* : GLEAMING ⟨eyes ∼ with tears⟩

aglit·ter \ə-'gli-tər\ *adj* : GLITTERING

aglow \ə-'glō\ *adj* : GLOWING

ag·nos·tic \ag-'näs-tik\ *adj* [Gk *agnōstos* unknown, unknowable, fr. *a-* un- + *gnōstos* known] : of or relating to the belief that the existence of any ultimate reality (as God) is unknown and prob. unknowable — **agnostic** *n* — **ag·nos·ti·cism** \-'näs-tə-,si-zəm\ *n*

ago \ə-'gō\ *adj or adv* : earlier than the present time ⟨10 years ∼⟩

agog \ə-'gäg\ *adj* [MF *en gogues* in mirth] : full of excitement : EAGER

a–go–go \ä-'gō-,gō\ *adj* [*Whisky à Gogo*, café and disco in Paris, France, fr. F *à gogo* galore] : GO-GO

ag·o·nise *Brit var of* AGONIZE

ag·o·nize \'a-gə-,nīz\ *vb* **-nized; -niz·ing** : to suffer or cause to suffer agony — **ag·o·niz·ing·ly** *adv*

ag·o·ny \'a-gə-nē\ *n, pl* **-nies** [ME *agonie*, fr. L *agonia*, fr. Gk *agōnia* struggle, anguish, fr. *agōn* gathering, contest for a prize] : extreme pain of mind or body ♦ **Synonyms** SUFFERING, DISTRESS, MISERY

ago·ra \,ä-gə-'rä\ *n, pl* **ago·rot** \-'rōt\ — see *shekel* at MONEY table

ag·o·ra·pho·bia \,a-gə-rə-'fō-bē-ə\ *n* : abnormal fear of being in a helpless, embarrassing, or inescapable situation characterized esp. by avoidance of open or public places — **ag·o·ra·pho·bic** \-'fō-bik, -'fä-\ *adj or n*

agr *abbr* agricultural; agriculture

agrar·i·an \ə-'grer-ē-ən\ *adj* **1** : of or relating to land or its ownership ⟨∼ reforms⟩ **2** : of or relating to farmers or farming interests — **agrarian** *n* — **agrar·i·an·ism** *n*

agree \ə-'grē\ *vb* **agreed; agree·ing** **1** : ADMIT, CONCEDE ⟨∼s that he was wrong⟩ **2** : to be similar : CORRESPOND ⟨both copies ∼⟩ **3** : to express agreement or approval **4** : to be in harmony **5** : to settle by common consent **6** : to be fitting or healthful : SUIT ⟨this climate ∼s with her⟩

agree·able \ə-'grē-ə-bəl\ *adj* **1** : PLEASING, PLEASANT ⟨an ∼ fragrance⟩ **2** : ready to consent ⟨I'm ∼ to their proposal⟩ **3** : being in harmony : CONSONANT — **agree·able·ness** *n* — **agree·ably** \-blē\ *adv*

agree·ment \ə-'grē-mənt\ *n* **1** : harmony of opinion or action **2** : mutual understanding or arrangement; *also* : a document containing such an arrangement

ag·ri·busi·ness \'a-grə-,biz-nəs, -nəz\ *n* : an industry engaged in the manufacture and sale of farm equipment and supplies and in the production, processing, storage, and sale of farm commodities

agric *abbr* agricultural; agriculture

ag·ri·cul·ture \'a-gri-,kəl-chər\ *n* : FARMING, HUSBANDRY — **ag·ri·cul·tur·al** \,a-gri-'kəl-ch(ə-)rəl\ *adj* — **ag·ri·cul·tur·ist** \-ch(ə-)rist\ *or* **ag·ri·cul·tur·al·ist** \-ch(ə-)rə-list\ *n*

agron·o·my \ə-'grä-nə-mē\ *n* : a branch of agriculture

that deals with the raising of crops and the care of the soil — **ag·ro·nom·ic** \,a-grə-'nä-mik\ *adj* — **agron·o·mist** \ə-'grä-nə-mist\ *n*

aground \ə-'graünd\ *adv or adj* : on or onto the bottom or shore ⟨ran ∼⟩

agt *abbr* agent

ague \'ā-gyü\ *n* : a fever (as malaria) with recurrent chills and sweating

ahead \ə-'hed\ *adv or adj* **1** : in or toward the front **2** : into or for the future ⟨plan ∼⟩ **3** : in or toward a more advantageous position

ahead of *prep* **1** : in front or advance of **2** : in excess of : ABOVE

ahoy \ə-'hói\ *interj* — used in hailing ⟨ship ∼⟩

AI *abbr* artificial intelligence

¹aid \'ād\ *vb* : to provide with what is useful in achieving an end : ASSIST

²aid *n* **1** : ASSISTANCE **2** : ASSISTANT

AID *abbr* Agency for International Development

aide \'ād\ *n* : a person who acts as an assistant; *esp* : a military officer assisting a superior

aide–de–camp \,ād-di-'kamp, -'kän\ *n, pl* **aides–de–camp** \,ādz-di-\ [F] : AIDE

AIDS \'ādz\ *n* [*a*cquired *i*mmuno*d*eficiency *s*yndrome] : a serious disease of the human immune system that is characterized by severe reduction in the numbers of helper T cells and increased vulnerability to life-threatening illnesses and that is caused by infection with HIV commonly transmitted in infected blood esp. during illicit intravenous drug use and in bodily secretions (as semen) during sexual intercourse

AIDS–related complex *n* : a group of symptoms (as fever, weight loss, and lymphadenopathy) that is associated with the presence of antibodies to HIV and is followed by the development of AIDS in a certain proportion of cases

AIDS virus *n* : HIV

ai·grette \ā-'gret, 'ā-,\ *n* [F, plume, egret] : a plume or decorative tuft for the head

ail \'āl\ *vb* **1** : to be the matter with : TROUBLE **2** : to be unwell

ai·lan·thus \ā-'lan-thəs\ *n* : any of a genus of Asian trees or shrubs with pinnate leaves and ill-scented greenish flowers; *esp* : TREE OF HEAVEN

ai·le·ron \'ā-lə-,rän\ *n* : a movable part of an airplane wing used in banking

ail·ment \'āl-mənt\ *n* : a bodily disorder

¹aim \'ām\ *vb* [ME, fr. AF *aesmer & esmer*; AF *aesmer*, fr. *a-* to (fr. L *ad-*) + *esmer* to estimate, fr. L *aestimare*] **1** : to point a weapon at an object **2** : to direct one's efforts : ASPIRE **3** : to direct to or toward a specified object or goal

²aim *n* **1** : the pointing of a weapon at an object **2** : the ability to hit a target **3** : OBJECT, PURPOSE ⟨my ∼ is to win⟩ — **aim·less** \-ləs\ *adj* — **aim·less·ly** *adv* — **aim·less·ness** *n*

AIM *abbr* American Indian Movement

ain't \'ānt\ **1** : are not **2** : is not **3** : am not — though disapproved by many and more common in less educated speech, used in both speech and writing to catch attention and to gain emphasis

Ai·nu \'ī-nü\ *n, pl* **Ainu** *or* **Ainus** **1** : a member of an indigenous people of northern Japan **2** : the language of the Ainu people

¹air \'er\ *n* **1** : the gaseous mixture surrounding the earth **2** : a light breeze **3** : MELODY, TUNE **4** : the outward appearance of a person or thing : MANNER **5** : an artificial manner **6** : COMPRESSED AIR ⟨∼ sprayer⟩ **7** : AIRCRAFT ⟨traveled by ∼⟩ **8** : AVIATION ⟨∼ safety⟩ **9** : the medium of transmission of radio waves; *also* : RADIO, TELEVISION

²air *vb* **1** : to expose to the air **2** : to expose to public view

air bag *n* : a bag designed to inflate automatically to protect automobile occupants in case of collision

air·boat \'er-,bōt\ *n* : a shallow-draft boat driven by an airplane propeller

air·borne \-,bórn\ *adj* : done or being in the air

air brake *n* **1** : a brake operated by a piston driven by compressed air **2** : a surface projected into the airflow to lower an airplane's speed

air·brush \'er-,brəsh\ *n* : a device for applying a fine spray (as of paint) by compressed air — **airbrush** *vb* air con·di·tion·er \ˌer-kən-'di-sh(ə-)nər\ n : an apparatus for filtering air and controlling its humidity and temperature — air–con·di·tion \-'di-shən\ vb

air·craft \'er-ˌkraft\ n, pl aircraft : a vehicle for traveling through the air

aircraft carrier n : a warship with a deck on which airplanes can be launched and landed

air·drop \'er-ˌdräp\ n : delivery of cargo or personnel by parachute from an airplane in flight — air–drop vb

Aire·dale terrier \'er-ˌdāl-\ n : any of a breed of large terriers with a hard wiry coat

air·fare \'er-ˌfer\ n : fare for travel by airplane

air·field \-ˌfēld\ n : AIRPORT

air·flow \-ˌflō\ n : the motion of air relative to a body in it

air·foil \-ˌfȯi(-ə)l\ n : an airplane surface designed to produce reaction forces from the air through which it moves

air force n : the military organization of a nation for air warfare

air·frame \'er-ˌfrām\ n : the structure of an aircraft, rocket, or missile without the power plant; also : AIRCRAFT

air·freight \-'frāt\ n : freight transport by aircraft in volume; also : the charge for this service

air gun n 1 : a gun operated by compressed air 2 : a hand tool that works by compressed air; esp : AIRBRUSH

air·head \'er-ˌhed\ n : a mindless or stupid person

air lane n : AIRWAY 1

air·lift \'er-ˌlift\ n : transportation (as of supplies or passengers) by aircraft — airlift vb

air·line \-ˌlīn\ n : a transportation system using airplanes

air·lin·er \-ˌlī-nər\ n : a large passenger airplane operated by an airline

air lock n : an airtight chamber separating areas of different pressure

air·mail \'er-ˌmāl\ n : the system of transporting mail by aircraft; also : mail so transported — airmail vb

air·man \-mən\ n 1 : AVIATOR, PILOT 2 : an enlisted man in the air force in one of the three ranks below sergeant

airman basic n : an enlisted man of the lowest rank in the air force

airman first class n : an enlisted man in the air force with a rank just below that of sergeant

air mass n : a large horizontally homogeneous body of air

air·mo·bile \'er-ˌmō-bəl, -ˌbēl\ adj : of, relating to, or being a military unit whose members are transported to combat areas usu. by helicopter

air·plane \-ˌplān\ n : a powered heavier-than-air aircraft that has fixed wings from which it derives lift

air·play \-ˌplā\ n : the playing of a musical recording on the air by a radio station

air pocket n : a condition of the atmosphere (as a local downdraft) that causes an airplane to drop suddenly

air police n : the military police of an air force

air·port \'er-ˌpȯrt\ n : a place from which aircraft operate that usu. has paved runways and a terminal

air rage n : an airline passenger's uncontrolled anger that is usu. expressed in aggressive or violent behavior

air raid n : an attack by armed airplanes on a surface target

air·ship \'er-ˌship\ n : a lighter-than-air aircraft having propulsion and steering systems

air·sick \-ˌsik\ adj : affected with motion sickness associated with flying — air·sick·ness n

air·space \-ˌspās\ n : the space above a nation and under its jurisdiction

air·speed \-ˌspēd\ n : the speed of an object (as an airplane) with relation to the surrounding air

air·strip \-ˌstrip\ n : a runway without normal airport facilities

air·tight \'er-ˌtīt\ adj 1 : so tightly sealed that no air can enter or escape 2 : leaving no opening for attack

air–to–air adj : launched from one airplane in flight at another; also : involving aircraft in flight

air·waves \'er-ˌwāvz\ n pl : AIR 9

air·way \-ˌwā\ n 1 : a regular route for airplanes 2 : AIRLINE

air·wor·thy \-ˌwər-thē\ adj : fit for operation in the air ⟨an ~ plane⟩ — air·wor·thi·ness n

airy \'er-ē\ adj air·i·er; -est 1 : LOFTY ⟨~ perches⟩ 2 : lacking in reality : EMPTY 3 : DELICATE 4 : BREEZY

aisle \'īl\ n [ME ele, fr. AF ele, lit., wing, fr. L ala] 1 : the side of a church nave separated by piers from the nave proper 2 : a passage between sections of seats

ajar \ə-'jär\ adj or adv : partly open

AK abbr Alaska

aka abbr also known as

AKC abbr American Kennel Club

akim·bo \ə-'kim-bō\ adj or adv : having the hand on the hip and the elbow turned outward

akin \ə-'kin\ adj 1 : related by blood 2 : similar in kind

Al symbol aluminum

AL abbr 1 Alabama 2 American League 3 American Legion

1-al adj suffix : of, relating to, or characterized by ⟨directional⟩

2-al n suffix : action : process ⟨rehearsal⟩

Ala abbr Alabama

al·a·bas·ter \'a-lə-ˌbas-tər\ n 1 : a compact fine-textured usu. white and translucent gypsum often carved into objects (as vases) 2 : a hard translucent calcite

à la carte \ˌa-lə-'kärt, ˌä-\ adv or adj [F] : with a separate price for each item on the menu

alac·ri·ty \ə-'la-krə-tē\ n : cheerful readiness : BRISKNESS

à la mode \ˌa-lə-'mōd, ˌä-\ adj [F, according to the fashion] 1 : FASHIONABLE, STYLISH 2 : topped with ice cream

1alarm \ə-'lärm\ also ala·rum \ə-'lär-əm, -'ler-\ n [ME alarme, fr. MF, fr. OIt all'arme, lit., to arms] 1 : a warning signal or device 2 : the terror caused by sudden danger

2alarm also alarum vb 1 : to warn of danger 2 : FRIGHTEN

alarm·ist \ə-'lär-mist\ n : a person who alarms others esp. needlessly

alas \ə-'las\ interj — used to express unhappiness, pity, or concern

al·ba·core \'al-bə-ˌkȯr\ n, pl -core or -cores : a large tuna that is a source of canned tuna

Al·ba·nian \al-'bā-nē-ən\ n : a native or inhabitant of Albania

al·ba·tross \'al-bə-ˌtrȯs, -ˌträs\ n, pl -tross or -tross·es : any of a family of large web-footed seabirds

al·be·do \al-'bē-(ˌ)dō\ n, pl -dos : the fraction of incident radiation that is reflected by a body or surface

al·be·it \ȯl-'bē-ət, al-\ conj : even though : ALTHOUGH

al·bi·no \al-'bī-nō\ n, pl -nos : a person or animal lacking coloring matter in the skin, hair, and eyes — al·bi·nism \'al-bə-ˌni-zəm\ n

al·bum \'al-bəm\ n 1 : a book with blank pages used for making a collection (as of stamps or photographs) 2 : one or more recordings (as on tape or disk) produced as a single unit

al·bu·men \al-'byü-mən\ n 1 : the white of an egg 2 : ALBUMIN

al·bu·min \al-'byü-mən\ n : any of numerous water-soluble proteins of blood, milk, egg white, and plant and animal tissues

al·bu·min·ous \al-'byü-mə-nəs\ adj : containing or resembling albumen or albumin

al·bu·ter·ol \al-'byü-tə-ˌrȯl, -ˌrōl\ n : a drug used as an aerosol or in tablet form to treat asthma

alc abbr alcohol

al·cal·de \al-'käl-dē\ n : the chief administrative and judicial officer of a Spanish or Spanish-American town

al·ca·zar \al-'kä-zər, -'ka-\ n [Sp alcázar, fr. Ar al-qaṣr castle] : a Spanish fortress or palace

al·che·my \'al-kə-mē\ n : medieval chemistry chiefly concerned with efforts to turn base metals into gold — al·che·mist \'al-kə-mist\ n

al·co·hol \'al-kə-ˌhȯl\ n [NL, fr. ML, powdered antimony, fr. Sp, fr. Ar al-kuḥul the powdered antimony] 1 : a colorless flammable liquid that is the intoxicating agent in fermented and distilled liquors 2 : any of various carbon compounds similar to alcohol 3 : beverages containing alcohol

1al·co·hol·ic \ˌal-kə-'hȯ-lik, -'hä-\ adj 1 : of, relating to, caused by, or containing alcohol 2 : affected with alcoholism — al·co·hol·i·cal·ly \-li-k(ə-)lē\ adv

2alcoholic n : a person affected with alcoholism

al·co·hol·ism \'al-kə-ˌhȯ-ˌli-zəm\ n : continued excessive and usu. uncontrollable use of alcoholic drinks; also : a complex chronic psychological and nutritional disorder associated with such use

al·cove \'al-ˌkōv\ n 1 : a nook or small recess opening off a larger room 2 : a niche or arched opening (as in a wall)

ald *abbr* alderman
al·der \'òl-dər\ *n* : any of a genus of trees or shrubs related to the birches and growing in wet areas
al·der·man \'òl-dər-mən\ *n* : a member of a city legislative body
ale \'āl\ *n* : an alcoholic beverage brewed from malt and hops that is usu. more bitter than beer
ale·a·tor·ic \ˌā-lē-ə-'tòr-ik\ *adj* : characterized by chance or random elements ⟨∼ music⟩
ale·a·to·ry \'ā-lē-ə-ˌtòr-ē\ *adj* : ALEATORIC
alee \ə-'lē\ *adv* : on or toward the lee
ale·house \'āl-ˌhaủs\ *n* : a place where ale is sold to be drunk on the premises
¹alert \ə-'lərt\ *adj* [It *all' erta*, lit., on the ascent] **1** : watchful against danger **2** : quick to perceive and act — **alert·ly** *adv* — **alert·ness** *n*
²alert *n* **1** : ALARM 1 **2** : the period during which an alert is in effect
³alert *vb* **1** : WARN **2** : to make aware of
Aleut \ˌa-lē-'üt, ə-'lüt\ *n* **1** : a member of a people of the Aleutian and Shumagin islands and the western part of Alaska Peninsula **2** : the language of the Aleuts
ale·wife \'āl-ˌwīf\ *n, pl* **ale·wives** \-ˌwīvz\ : a food fish related to the herring that is abundant esp. along the Atlantic coast

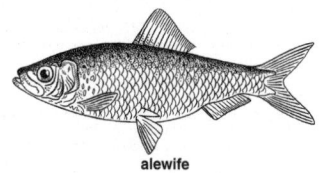

alewife

Al·ex·an·dri·an \ˌa-lig-'zan-drē-ən\ *adj* **1** : HELLENISTIC **2** : of or relating to Alexander the Great
al·ex·an·drine \-'zan-drən\ *n, often cap* : a line of six iambic feet
al·fal·fa \al-'fal-fə\ *n* : a leguminous plant widely grown for hay and forage
al·fres·co \al-'fres-kō\ *adj or adv* [It] : taking place in the open air
alg *abbr* algebra
al·ga \'al-gə\ *n, pl* **al·gae** \'al-(ˌ)jē\ : any of a group of lower plants having chlorophyll but no vascular system and including seaweeds and related freshwater plants — **al·gal** \-gəl\ *adj*
al·ge·bra \'al-jə-brə\ *n* [ML, fr. Ar *al-jabr*] : a generalization of arithmetic in which letters representing numbers are combined according to the rules of arithmetic — **al·ge·bra·ic** \ˌal-jə-'brā-ik\ *adj* — **al·ge·bra·i·cal·ly** \-'brā-ə-k(ə-)lē\ *adv*
Al·gon·qui·an \al-'gän-kwē-ən, -'gäŋ-\ *or* **Al·gon·quin** \-kwən\ *n* **1** *usu* **Algonquin** : a member of an American Indian people of the Ottawa River valley **2** *usu* **Algonquian** : a family of American Indian languages of eastern and central No. America
al·go·rithm \'al-gə-ˌri-thəm\ *n* : a procedure for solving a problem esp. in mathematics or computing — **al·go·rith·mic** \ˌal-gə-'rith-mik\ *adj* — **al·go·rith·mi·cal·ly** \-mi-k(ə-)lē\ *adv*
¹alias \'ā-lē-əs, 'āl-yəs\ *adv* [L, otherwise, fr. *alius* other] : otherwise called
²alias *n* : an assumed name
¹al·i·bi \'a-lə-ˌbī\ *n* [L, elsewhere, fr. *alius* other] **1** : a plea offered by an accused person of not having been at the scene of an offense **2** : an excuse (as for failure)
²alibi *vb* **-bied; -bi·ing 1** : to furnish an excuse for **2** : to offer an excuse
¹alien \'ā-lē-ən, 'āl-yən\ *adj* **1** : belonging to another : FOREIGN **2** : EXOTIC 1
²alien *n* **1** : a foreign-born resident who has not been naturalized **2** : EXTRATERRESTRIAL
alien·able \'āl-yə-nə-bəl, 'ā-lē-ə-nə-\ *adj* : transferable to the ownership of another ⟨∼ property⟩
alien·ate \'ā-lē-ə-ˌnāt, 'āl-yə-\ *vb* **-at·ed; -at·ing 1** : to make hostile : ESTRANGE **2** : to transfer (property) to another — **alien·ation** \ˌā-lē-ə-'nā-shən, ˌāl-yə-\ *n*

alien·ist \'ā-lē-ə-nist, 'āl-yə-\ *n* : PSYCHIATRIST
¹alight \ə-'līt\ *vb* **alight·ed** *also* **alit** \ə-'lit\; **alight·ing 1** : to get down (as from a vehicle) **2** : to come to rest from the air ♦ **Synonyms** SETTLE, LAND, PERCH
²alight *adj* : lighted up
align *also* **aline** \ə-'līn\ *vb* **1** : to bring into line **2** : to array on the side of or against a cause — **align·er** *n* — **align·ment** *also* **aline·ment** *n*
¹alike \ə-'līk\ *adv* : EQUALLY ⟨denounced by teachers and students ∼⟩
²alike *adj* : LIKE ⟨∼ in their beliefs⟩ ♦ **Synonyms** AKIN, ANALOGOUS, SIMILAR, COMPARABLE
al·i·ment \'a-lə-mənt\ *n* : NOURISHMENT 1 — **aliment** *vb*
al·i·men·ta·ry \ˌa-lə-'men-t(ə-)rē\ *adj* : of, relating to, or functioning in nourishment or nutrition
alimentary canal *n* : the tube that extends from the mouth to the anus and functions in the digestion and absorption of food and the elimination of residues
al·i·mo·ny \'a-lə-ˌmō-nē\ *n, pl* **-nies** [L *alimonia* sustenance, fr. *alere* to nourish] : an allowance made to one spouse by the other for support pending or after legal separation or divorce
A–line \'ā-ˌlīn\ *adj* : having a flared bottom and a close-fitting top ⟨an ∼ skirt⟩
alive \ə-'līv\ *adj* **1** : having life **2** : being in force or operation **3** : SENSITIVE ⟨∼ to the danger⟩ **4** : ALERT, BRISK **5** : ANIMATED ⟨streets ∼ with traffic⟩ — **alive·ness** *n*
alk *abbr* alkaline
al·ka·li \'al-kə-ˌlī\ *n, pl* **-lies** *or* **-lis 1** : a substance (as a hydroxide) that has a bitter taste and neutralizes acids **2** : a mixture of salts in the soil of some dry regions in such amount as to make ordinary farming impossible — **al·ka·line** \-kə-lən, -ˌlīn\ *adj* — **al·ka·lin·i·ty** \ˌal-kə-'li-nə-tē\ *n*
al·ka·loid \'al-kə-ˌlòid\ *n* : any of various usu. basic and bitter organic compounds found esp. in seed plants
al·kane \'al-ˌkān\ *n* : a hydrocarbon in which each carbon atom is bonded to 4 other atoms
al·kyd \'al-kəd\ *n* : any of numerous synthetic resins used esp. for protective coatings and in paint
¹all \'òl\ *adj* **1** : the whole of ⟨sat up ∼ night⟩ **2** : every member of ⟨∼ EVERY ⟨∼ manner of problems⟩ **4** : any whatever ⟨beyond ∼ doubt⟩ **5** : nothing but ⟨∼ ears⟩ **6** : being more than one person or thing ⟨who ∼ is coming⟩
²all *adv* **1** : WHOLLY ⟨sat ∼ alone⟩ **2** : selected as the best — used in combination ⟨*all*-state champs⟩ **3** : so much ⟨∼ the better for it⟩ **4** : for each side ⟨the score is two ∼⟩
³all *pron sing or pl* **1** : the whole number, quantity, or amount ⟨∼ of it is gone⟩ **2** : EVERYBODY, EVERYTHING ⟨∼ are members⟩ ⟨that is ∼⟩
⁴all *n* : the whole of one's resources ⟨gave his ∼⟩
Al·lah \'ä-lə, 'a-; 'ä-ˌlä, ä-'lä\ *n* [Ar *allāh*] : GOD 1 — used in Islam
all along *adv* : all the time ⟨knew it *all along*⟩
all–Amer·i·can \ˌòl-ə-'mer-ə-kən\ *adj* **1** : selected as the best in the U.S. **2** : composed wholly of American elements **3** : typical of the U.S. — **all–American** *n*
all–around \ˌòl-ə-'raủnd\ *adj* **1** : considered in all aspects ⟨best ∼ performance⟩ **2** : competent in many fields : VERSATILE ⟨an ∼ athlete⟩
al·lay \ə-'lā\ *vb* **1** : ALLEVIATE **2** : CALM ♦ **Synonyms** LIGHTEN, RELIEVE, EASE, ASSUAGE
all clear *n* : a signal that a danger has passed
al·lege \ə-'lej\ *vb* **al·leged; al·leg·ing 1** : to assert without proof **2** : to offer as a reason — **al·le·ga·tion** \ˌa-li-'gā-shən\ *n* — **al·leged** \ə-'lejd, -'le-jəd\ *adj* — **al·leg·ed·ly** \ə-'le-jəd-lē\ *adv*
al·le·giance \ə-'lē-jəns\ *n* **1** : loyalty owed by a citizen to a government **2** : loyalty to a person or cause
al·le·go·ry \'a-lə-ˌgòr-ē\ *n, pl* **-ries** : the expression through symbolism of truths or generalizations about human experience — **al·le·gor·i·cal** \ˌa-lə-'gòr-i-kəl\ *adj* — **al·le·gor·i·cal·ly** \-k(ə-)lē\ *adv*
¹al·le·gro \ə-'le-grō, -'lā-\ *n, pl* **-gros** : an allegro movement
²allegro *adv or adj* [It, merry] : at a brisk lively tempo — used as a direction in music
al·lele \ə-'lēl\ *n* : any of the alternative forms of a gene that may occur at a given site on a chromosome — **al·le·lic** \-'lē-lik, -'le-\ *adj*

al·le·lu·ia \ˌa-lə-ˈlü-yə\ *interj* : HALLELUJAH
Al·len wrench \ˈa-lən-\ *n* [*Allen* Manufacturing Company, Hartford, Conn.] : an L-shaped hexagonal metal bar of which either end fits the socket of a screw or bolt
al·ler·gen \ˈa-lər-jən\ *n* : something that causes allergy — al·ler·gen·ic \ˌa-lər-ˈje-nik\ *adj*
al·ler·gist \ˈa-lər-jist\ *n* : a specialist in allergies
al·ler·gy \ˈa-lər-jē\ *n, pl* -gies [G *Allergie*, fr. Gk *allos* other + *ergon* work] : exaggerated or abnormal reaction (as by sneezing) to substances or situations harmless to most people — al·ler·gic \ə-ˈlər-jik\ *adj*
al·le·vi·ate \ə-ˈlē-vē-ˌāt\ *vb* -at·ed; -at·ing : RELIEVE, LESSEN ⟨~ pain⟩ ✦ *Synonyms* LIGHTEN, MITIGATE, ALLAY — al·le·vi·a·tion \ə-ˌlē-vē-ˈā-shən\ *n*
al·ley \ˈa-lē\ *n, pl* alleys 1 : a garden or park walk 2 : a place for bowling 3 : a narrow passageway esp. between buildings
al·ley–oop \ˌa-lē-ˈyüp\ *n* : a basketball play in which a player catches a pass above the basket and immediately dunks the ball
al·ley·way \ˈa-lē-ˌwā\ *n* : ALLEY 3
all–fired \ˈȯl-ˌfī(-ə)rd\ *adv* : EXTREMELY, EXCESSIVELY ⟨~ stubborn⟩
All·hal·lows \ȯl-ˈha-lōz\ *n, pl* Allhallows : ALL SAINTS' DAY
all hours *n pl* : a very late time ⟨stayed up until *all hours*⟩
al·li·ance \ə-ˈlī-əns\ *n* : a union to promote common interests ✦ *Synonyms* LEAGUE, COALITION, CONFEDERACY, FEDERATION
al·li·ga·tor \ˈa-lə-ˌgā-tər\ *n* [Sp *el lagarto* the lizard] : either of two large short-legged reptiles resembling crocodiles but having a shorter and broader snout
alligator pear *n* : AVOCADO
al·lit·er·ate \ə-ˈli-tə-ˌrāt\ *vb* -at·ed; -at·ing 1 : to form an alliteration 2 : to arrange so as to make alliteration
al·lit·er·a·tion \ə-ˌli-tə-ˈrā-shən\ *n* : the repetition of initial sounds in adjacent words or syllables — al·lit·er·a·tive \-ˈli-tə-ˌrā-tiv\ *adj*
al·lo·cate \ˈa-lə-ˌkāt\ *vb* -cat·ed; -cat·ing : ALLOT, ASSIGN — al·lo·ca·tion \ˌa-lə-ˈkā-shən\ *n*
al·lot \ə-ˈlät\ *vb* al·lot·ted; al·lot·ting : to distribute as a share ✦ *Synonyms* ASSIGN, APPORTION, ALLOCATE — al·lot·ment *n*
all–out \ˈȯl-ˈaut\ *adj* : made with maximum effort
¹all over *adv* : EVERYWHERE
²all over *prep* 1 : in eagerly affectionate, attentive, or aggressive pursuit 2 : in or into a state marked by excessive criticism
al·low \ə-ˈlau\ *vb* 1 : to assign as a share ⟨~ time for rest⟩ 2 : to count as a deduction 3 : to make allowance ⟨~ for expansion⟩ 4 : ADMIT, CONCEDE ⟨~ed that the situation was serious⟩ 5 : PERMIT ⟨~s the dog to roam⟩ — al·low·able *adj*
al·low·ance \-əns\ *n* 1 : an allotted share 2 : money given regularly for expenses 3 : a taking into account of extenuating circumstances
al·loy \ˈa-ˌlȯi, ə-ˈlȯi\ *n* 1 : a substance composed of metals melted together 2 : an admixture that lessens value — al·loy \ə-ˈlȯi, ˈa-ˌlȯi\ *vb*
all right *adv* 1 — used interjectionally esp. to express agreement or resignation or to indicate the resumption of a discussion ⟨*all right*, let's go⟩ 2 : beyond doubt 3 : SATISFACTORILY ⟨does *all right* in school⟩ — all right *adj*
All Saints' Day *n* : a Christian feast on November 1 in honor of all saints
All Souls' Day *n* : a day of prayer observed by some Christian churches on November 2 for the souls of the faithful departed
all·spice \ˈȯl-ˌspīs\ *n* : the berry of a West Indian tree related to the European myrtle; *also* : the mildly pungent and aromatic spice made from it
all–star \ˈȯl-ˌstär\ *n* : a member of a team of star performers — all–star *adj*
all–ter·rain vehicle *n* : a small motor vehicle with three or four wheels for use on a wide range of terrain
all told *adv* : with everything or everyone counted ⟨expecting eight guests *all told*⟩
al·lude \ə-ˈlüd\ *vb* al·lud·ed; al·lud·ing [L *alludere*, lit., to play with] : to refer indirectly — al·lu·sion \-ˈlü-zhən\ *n* — al·lu·sive \-ˈlü-siv\ *adj* — al·lu·sive·ly *adv* — al·lu·sive·ness *n*

al·lure \ə-ˈlur\ *vb* al·lured; al·lur·ing : CHARM, ENTICE — allure *n* — al·lur·ing·ly *adv*
al·lu·vi·um \ə-ˈlü-vē-əm\ *n, pl* -vi·ums *or* -via \-vē-ə\ : soil material (as clay) deposited by running water — al·lu·vi·al \-vē-əl\ *adj or n*
all–wheel \ˈȯl-ˈwēl\ *adj* : acting independently on or by means of all four wheels of a vehicle
al·ly \ə-ˈlī, ˈa-ˌlī\ *vb* al·lied; al·ly·ing : to enter into an alliance — al·ly \ˈa-ˌlī, ə-ˈlī\ *n*
-ally *adv suffix* : ²-LY ⟨specifically⟩
al·ma ma·ter \ˌal-mə-ˈmä-tər\ *n* [L, fostering mother] 1 : an educational institute that one has attended 2 : the song or hymn of an alma mater
al·ma·nac \ˈȯl-mə-ˌnak, ˈal-\ *n* 1 : a publication esp. of astronomical and meteorological data 2 : a usu. annual publication of miscellaneous information
al·man·dite \ˈal-mən-ˌdīt\ *n* : a deep red garnet
al·mighty \ȯl-ˈmī-tē\ *adj* 1 *often cap* : having absolute power over all ⟨*Almighty* God⟩ 2 : relatively unlimited in power — al·might·i·ness *n*
Almighty *n* : GOD 1
al·mond \ˈä-mənd, ˈa-; ˈal-\ *n* : a small tree related to the peach; *also* : the edible nutlike kernel of its fruit
al·mo·ner \ˈal-mə-nər, ˈä-mə-\ *n* : a person who distributes alms
al·most \ˈȯl-ˌmōst, ȯl-ˈmōst\ *adv* : very nearly but not exactly
alms \ˈämz, ˈälmz\ *n, pl* alms [ME *almesse*, *almes*, fr. OE *ælmesse*, *ælmes*, fr. L *eleemosyna* alms, fr. Gk *eleēmosynē* pity, alms, fr. *eleēmōn* merciful, fr. *eleos* pity] : something given freely to relieve the poor
alms·house \-ˌhaus\ *n* : POORHOUSE
al·oe \ˈa-lō\ *n* 1 : any of a large genus of succulent chiefly southern African plants related to the lilies 2 *pl* : the dried juice of the leaves of an aloe used esp. formerly as a laxative
aloe vera \-ˈver-ə, -ˈvir-\ *n* : an aloe with leaves that yield a jellylike emollient extract used esp. in cosmetics; *also* : this extract
aloft \ə-ˈlȯft\ *adv* 1 : high in the air 2 : in flight
alo·ha \ə-ˈlō-ə, ä-ˈlō-hä\ *interj* [Hawaiian] — used to greet or bid farewell
alone \ə-ˈlōn\ *adj* 1 : separated from others 2 : not including anyone or anything else : ONLY ⟨she ~ knows why⟩ ✦ *Synonyms* LONELY, LONESOME, LONE, SOLITARY — alone *adv*
¹along \ə-ˈlȯŋ\ *prep* 1 : in a line matching the direction of ⟨sail ~ the coast⟩ 2 : at a point on or during ⟨stopped ~ the way⟩
²along *adv* 1 : FORWARD, ON ⟨move ~⟩ 2 : as a companion ⟨bring her ~⟩ 3 : at an advanced point ⟨plans are far ~⟩
along·shore \ə-ˈlȯŋ-ˈshȯr\ *adv or adj* : along the shore or coast ⟨walked ~⟩
¹along·side \-ˌsīd\ *adv* : along or by the side
²alongside *prep* 1 : along or by the side of 2 : in association with
alongside of *prep* : ALONGSIDE
aloof \ə-ˈlüf\ *adj* : removed or distant physically or emotionally — aloof·ly *adv* — aloof·ness *n*
al·o·pe·cia \ˌa-lə-ˈpē-sh(ē-)ə\ *n* : BALDNESS
aloud \ə-ˈlaud\ *adv* : with the speaking voice ⟨read ~⟩
alp \ˈalp\ *n* : a high rugged mountain
al·pac·a \al-ˈpa-kə\ *n* : a domesticated mammal esp. of Peru that is related to the llama; *also* : its woolly hair or a thin cloth made from this hair
al·pha \ˈal-fə\ *n* 1 : the 1st letter of the Greek alphabet — A or α 2 : something first : BEGINNING
al·pha·bet \ˈal-fə-ˌbet\ *n* : the set of letters or characters used in writing a language
al·pha·bet·i·cal \ˌal-fə-ˈbe-ti-kəl\ *or* al·pha·bet·ic \-ˈbe-tik\ *adj* 1 : arranged in the order of the letters of the alphabet 2 : of or employing an alphabet — al·pha·bet·i·cal·ly \-ti-k(ə-)lē\ *adv*
al·pha·bet·ize \ˈal-fə-bə-ˌtīz\ *vb* -ized; -iz·ing : to arrange in alphabetical order — al·pha·bet·iz·er *n*
al·pha·nu·mer·ic \ˌal-fə-nü-ˈmer-ik, -nyü-\ *adj* : consisting of letters and numbers and often other symbols ⟨an ~ code⟩; *also* : being a character in an alphanumeric system
alpha particle *n* : a positively charged particle identical

with the nucleus of a helium atom that is ejected at high speed in certain radioactive transformations

alpha rhythm *n* : ALPHA WAVE

alpha wave *n* : an electrical rhythm of the brain often associated with a state of wakeful relaxation

Al·pine \'al-ˌpīn\ *adj* **1** : relating to, located in, or resembling the Alps **2** *often not cap* : of, relating to, or growing on upland slopes above timberline **3** : of or relating to competitive ski events consisting of slalom and downhill racing

al·ready \ȯl-'re-dē\ *adv* : by this time : PREVIOUSLY

al·right \ȯl-'rīt\ *adv* : ALL RIGHT

al·so \'ȯl-sō\ *adv* : in addition : TOO

al·so–ran \-ˌran\ *n* **1** : a horse or dog that finishes out of the money in a race **2** : a contestant that does not win

alt *abbr* **1** alternate **2** altitude

Alta *abbr* Alberta

al·tar \'ȯl-tər\ *n* **1** : a structure on which sacrifices are offered or incense is burned **2** : a table used as a center of ritual or worship

altar server *n* : a boy or girl who assists the celebrant at a church service

¹al·ter \'ȯl-tər\ *vb* **al·tered; al·ter·ing** \-t(ə-)riŋ\ **1** : to make or become different **2** : CASTRATE, SPAY — **al·ter·able** \'ȯl-tə-rə-bəl\ *adj* — **al·ter·a·tion** \ˌȯl-tə-'rā-shən\ *n*

²alter *abbr* alteration

al·ter·ca·tion \ˌȯl-tər-'kā-shən\ *n* : a noisy or angry dispute

al·ter ego \ˌȯl-tər-'ē-gō\ *n* [L, lit., second I] : a second self; *esp* : a trusted friend

al·ter·i·ty \ȯl-'ter-ə-tē\ *n* : the quality or state of being radically alien to the conscious self or a particular cultural orientation

¹al·ter·nate \'ȯl-tər-nət, 'al-\ *adj* **1** : arranged or succeeding by turns **2** : every other **3** : being an alternative ⟨an ∼ route⟩ — **al·ter·nate·ly** *adv*

²al·ter·nate \-ˌnāt\ *vb* **-nat·ed; -nat·ing** : to occur or cause to occur by turns — **al·ter·na·tion** \ˌȯl-tər-'nā-shən, ˌal-\ *n*

³alternate *n* : SUBSTITUTE

alternating current *n* : an electric current that reverses its direction at regular intervals

al·ter·na·tive \ȯl-'tər-nə-tiv, al-\ *adj* **1** : offering a choice ⟨several ∼ plans⟩ **2** : different from the usual or conventional — **alternative** *n*

alternative medicine *n* : any of various systems of healing (as homeopathy) not typically practiced in conventional Western medicine

al·ter·na·tor \'ȯl-tər-ˌnā-tər, 'al-\ *n* : an electric generator for producing alternating current

al·though *also* **al·tho** \ȯl-'thō\ *conj* : in spite of the fact that : even though

al·tim·e·ter \al-'ti-mə-tər, 'al-tə-ˌmē-tər\ *n* : an instrument for measuring altitude

al·ti·tude \'al-tə-ˌtüd, -ˌtyüd\ *n* **1** : angular distance above the horizon **2** : vertical distance : HEIGHT **3** : the perpendicular distance in a geometric figure from the vertex to the base, from the vertex of an angle to the side opposite, or from the base to a parallel side or face

al·to \'al-tō\ *n, pl* **altos** [It, lit., high, fr. L *altus*] : the lower female voice part in a 4-part chorus; *also* : a singer having this voice or part

¹al·to·geth·er \ˌȯl-tə-'ge-thər\ *adv* **1** : WHOLLY ⟨stopped raining ∼⟩ **2** : in all ⟨spent $100 ∼⟩ **3** : on the whole ⟨∼ their efforts were successful⟩

²altogether *n* : NUDE ⟨posed in the ∼⟩

al·tru·ism \'al-trü-ˌi-zəm\ *n* [F *altruisme*, fr. *autrui* other people, fr. OF, oblique case form of *autre* other, fr. L *alter*] : unselfish interest in the welfare of others — **al·tru·ist** \-ist\ *n* — **al·tru·is·tic** \ˌal-trü-'is-tik\ *adj* — **al·tru·is·ti·cal·ly** \-ti-k(ə-)lē\ *adv*

al·um \'a-ləm\ *n* : either of two colorless crystalline aluminum-containing compounds used esp. as an emetic and as an astringent and styptic

alu·mi·na \ə-'lü-mə-nə\ *n* : the oxide of aluminum occurring in nature as corundum and in bauxite

al·u·min·i·um \ˌal-yə-'mi-nē-əm\ *n, chiefly Brit* : ALUMINUM

alu·mi·nize \ə-'lü-mə-ˌnīz\ *vb* **-nized; -niz·ing** : to treat with aluminum

alu·mi·num \ə-'lü-mə-nəm\ *n* : a silver-white malleable ductile light metallic element that is the most abundant metal in the earth's crust

aluminum oxide *n* : ALUMINA

alum·na \ə-'ləm-nə\ *n, pl* **-nae** \-(ˌ)nē\ : a woman graduate or former student of a college or school

alum·nus \ə-'ləm-nəs\ *n, pl* **-ni** \-ˌnī\ [L, foster son, pupil, fr. *alere* to nourish] : a graduate or former student of a college or school

al·ways \'ȯl-wēz, -wəz, -(ˌ)wāz\ *adv* **1** : at all times : INVARIABLY **2** : FOREVER

Alz·hei·mer's disease \'älts-ˌhī-mərz-, 'alts-\ *n* : a degenerative brain disease of unknown cause that is characterized esp. by progressive mental deterioration and memory loss

am *pres 1st sing of* BE

¹Am *abbr* America; American

²Am *symbol* americium

¹AM \'ā-ˌem\ *n* : a broadcasting system using amplitude modulation; *also* : a radio receiver for broadcasts made by such a system

²AM *abbr* **1** ante meridiem — often not cap. and often punctuated **2** [NL *artium magister*] master of arts

AMA *abbr* American Medical Association

amah \'ä-(ˌ)mä\ *n* : a female servant in eastern Asia; *esp* : a Chinese nurse

amain \ə-'mān\ *adv, archaic* : with full force or speed

amal·gam \ə-'mal-gəm\ *n* **1** : an alloy of mercury with another metal used in making dental cements **2** : a mixture of different elements

amal·gam·ate \ə-'mal-gə-ˌmāt\ *vb* **-at·ed; -at·ing** : to unite or merge into one body — **amal·ga·ma·tion** \-ˌmal-gə-'mā-shən\ *n*

aman·u·en·sis \ə-ˌman-yə-'wen-səs\ *n, pl* **-en·ses** \-ˌsēz\ : one employed to write from dictation or to copy what another has written : SECRETARY

am·a·ranth \'a-mə-ˌranth\ *n* **1** : any of a large genus of coarse herbs sometimes grown for their showy flowers **2** : a flower that never fades

am·a·ran·thine \ˌa-mə-'ran-thən, -ˌthīn\ *adj* **1** : relating to or resembling an amaranth **2** : UNDYING

am·a·ryl·lis \ˌa-mə-'ri-ləs\ *n* : any of various plants related to the lilies; *esp* : an autumn-flowering South African bulbous herb widely grown for its large showy red to whitish flowers

amass \ə-'mas\ *vb* : ACCUMULATE

am·a·teur \'a-mə-(ˌ)tər, -ˌtūr, -ˌtyūr, -ˌchūr, -chər\ *n* [F, fr. L *amator* lover, fr. *amare* to love] **1** : a person who engages in a pursuit for pleasure and not as a profession **2** : a person who is not expert — **am·a·teur·ish** \ˌa-mə-'tər-ish, -'tūr-, -'tyūr-, -'chər-\ *adj* — **am·a·teur·ism** \'a-mə-(ˌ)tər-i-zəm, -ˌtūr-, -ˌtyūr-, -ˌchūr-, -ˌchər-\ *n*

am·a·tive \'a-mə-tiv\ *adj* : indicative of love : AMOROUS — **am·a·tive·ly** *adv* — **am·a·tive·ness** *n*

am·a·to·ry \'a-mə-ˌtȯr-ē\ *adj* : of or expressing sexual love

amaze \ə-'māz\ *vb* **amazed; amaz·ing** : to fill with wonder — **ASTOUND** ◆ **Synonyms** ASTONISH, SURPRISE, DUMBFOUND — **amaze·ment** *n* — **amaz·ing·ly** *adv*

am·a·zon \'a-mə-ˌzän, -zən\ *n* **1** *cap* : a member of a race of female warriors of Greek mythology **2** : a tall strong often masculine woman — **am·a·zo·ni·an** \ˌa-mə-'zō-nē-ən\ *adj, often cap*

amb *abbr* ambassador

am·bas·sa·dor \am-'ba-sə-dər\ *n* : a representative esp. of a government — **am·bas·sa·do·ri·al** \-ˌba-sə-'dȯr-ē-əl\ *adj* — **am·bas·sa·dor·ship** *n*

am·ber \'am-bər\ *n* : a yellowish or brownish fossil resin used esp. for ornamental objects; *also* : the color of this resin

am·ber·gris \'am-bər-ˌgris, -ˌgrēs\ *n* : a waxy substance from the sperm whale used in making perfumes

am·bi·dex·trous \ˌam-bi-'dek-strəs\ *adj* : using both hands with equal ease — **am·bi·dex·trous·ly** *adv*

am·bi·ence *or* **am·bi·ance** \'am-bē-əns, äⁿ-'byäⁿs\ *n* : a pervading atmosphere

¹am·bi·ent \'am-bē-ənt\ *adj* : existing on all sides

²ambient *n* : music intended to serve as an unobtrusive accompaniment to other activities

am·big·u·ous \am-'bi-gyə-wəs\ *adj* : capable of being understood in more than one way — **am·bi·gu·i·ty** \ˌam-bə-'gyü-ə-tē\ *n* — **am·big·u·ous·ly** *adv*

am·bi·tion \am-'bi-shən\ *n* [ME, fr. MF or L; MF, fr. L *ambition-, ambitio* lit., act of soliciting for votes, fr. *ambire* to go around] : eager desire for success or power

am·bi·tious \-shəs\ *adj* : characterized by ambition — **am·bi·tious·ly** *adv* — **am·bi·tious·ness** *n*

am·biv·a·lence \am-'bi-və-ləns\ *n* : simultaneous attraction toward and repulsion from a person, object, or action — **am·biv·a·lent** \-lənt\ *adj*

¹**am·ble** \'am-bəl\ *vb* **am·bled; am·bling** \-b(ə-)liŋ\ : to go at an amble

²**amble** *n* : an easy gait esp. of a horse

am·bro·sia \am-'brō-zh(ē-)ə\ *n* : the food of the Greek and Roman gods — **am·bro·sial** \-zh(ē-)əl\ *adj*

am·bu·lance \'am-byə-ləns\ *n* : a vehicle equipped for carrying the injured or sick

am·bu·lant \'am-byə-lənt\ *adj* : AMBULATORY

¹**am·bu·la·to·ry** \'am-byə-lə-,tōr-ē\ *adj* **1** : of, relating to, or adapted to walking **2** : able to walk or move about

²**ambulatory** *n, pl* **-ries** : a sheltered place (as in a cloister) for walking

am·bus·cade \'am-bə-,skād\ *n* : AMBUSH

am·bush \'am-,büsh\ *n* : a trap in which concealed persons wait to attack by surprise — **ambush** *vb*

amdt *abbr* amendment

ameba, ameboid *var of* AMOEBA, AMOEBOID

ame·lio·rate \ə-'mēl-yə-,rāt\ *vb* **-rat·ed; -rat·ing** : to make or grow better : IMPROVE — **ame·lio·ra·tion** \-,mēl-yə-'rā-shən\ *n*

amen \(,)ā-'men, (,)ä-\ *interj* — used esp. at the end of prayers to affirm or express approval

ame·na·ble \ə-'mē-nə-bəl, -'me-\ *adj* **1** : ANSWERABLE ⟨~ to the law⟩ **2** : COMPLIANT

amend \ə-'mend\ *vb* **1** : to change for the better : IMPROVE **2** : to alter formally in phraseology — **amend·able** \-'men-də-bəl\ *adj*

amend·ment \ə-'mend-mənt\ *n* **1** : correction of faults **2** : the process of amending a parliamentary motion or a constitution; *also* : the alteration so proposed or made

amends \ə-'mendz\ *n sing or pl* : compensation for injury or loss

ame·ni·ty \ə-'me-nə-tē, -'mē-\ *n, pl* **-ties** **1** : AGREEABLE-NESS **2** : a gesture observed in social relationships **3** : something that serves as a comfort or convenience

Amer *abbr* America; American

amerce \ə-'mərs\ *vb* **amerced; amerc·ing** **1** : to penalize by a fine determined by the court **2** : PUNISH — **amerce·ment** *n*

Amer·i·ca·na \ə-,mer-ə-'ka-nə, -'kä-\ *n pl* : materials concerning or characteristic of America, its civilization, or its culture

American Indian *n* : a member of any of the aboriginal peoples of No. and So. America except the Eskimos

Amer·i·can·ism \ə-'mer-ə-kə-,ni-zəm\ *n* **1** : a characteristic feature of English as used in the U.S. **2** : attachment or loyalty to the traditions, interests, or ideals of the U.S. **3** : a custom or trait peculiar to the U.S. or to Americans

Amer·i·can·ize \ə-'mer-ə-kə-,nīz\ *vb* : to make or become American — **Amer·i·can·i·za·tion** \ə-,mer-ə-kə-nə-'zā-shən\ *n*

Amer·i·can·ness \ə-'mer-ə-kən-nəs\ *n* : the quality or state of being American

American plan *n* : a hotel plan whereby the daily rates cover the cost of room and three meals

American Sign Language *n* : a sign language for the deaf in which meaning is conveyed by a system of hand gestures and placement

am·er·i·ci·um \,am-ə-'rish-ē-əm, -'ris-\ *n* : a radioactive metallic chemical element produced artificially from plutonium

AmerInd *abbr* American Indian

Am·er·in·di·an \,a-mə-'rin-dē-ən\ *n* : AMERICAN INDIAN — **Amerindian** *adj*

am·e·thyst \'a-mə-thəst\ *n* [ME *amatiste*, fr. AF & L; AF, fr. L *amethystus*, fr. Gk *amethystos*, lit., remedy against drunkenness, fr. *a-* not + *methyein* to be drunk, fr. *methy* wine] : a gemstone consisting of clear purple or bluish-violet quartz

ami·a·ble \'ā-mē-ə-bəl\ *adj* **1** : AGREEABLE ⟨an ~ comedy⟩ **2** : having a friendly and sociable disposition — **ami·a·bil·i·ty** \,ā-mē-ə-'bi-lə-tē\ *n* — **ami·a·ble·ness** *n* — **ami·a·bly** \'ā-mē-ə-blē\ *adv*

am·i·ca·ble \'a-mi-kə-bəl\ *adj* : FRIENDLY, PEACEABLE ⟨an ~ settlement of differences⟩ — **am·i·ca·bil·i·ty** \,a-mi-kə-'bi-lə-tē\ *n* — **am·i·ca·bly** \'a-mi-kə-blē\ *adv*

amid \ə-'mid\ *or* **amidst** \-'midst\ *prep* : in or into the middle of : AMONG

amid·ships \ə-'mid-,ships\ *adv* : in or near the middle of a ship

ami·no acid \ə-'mē-nō-\ *n* : any of numerous nitrogen-containing acids that include some which are used by cells to build proteins

amir *var of* EMIR

¹**amiss** \ə-'mis\ *adv* **1** : WRONGLY **2** : ASTRAY ⟨something had gone ~⟩ **3** : IMPERFECTLY

²**amiss** *adj* **1** : WRONG **2** : out of place

am·i·ty \'a-mə-tē\ *n, pl* **-ties** : FRIENDSHIP; *esp* : friendly relations between nations

am·me·ter \'a-,mē-tər\ *n* : an instrument for measuring electric current esp. in amperes

am·mo \'a-mō\ *n* : AMMUNITION

am·mo·nia \ə-'mō-nyə\ *n* [NL, fr. L *sal ammoniacus* sal ammoniac (ammonium chloride), fr. Gk *ammōniakos* of Ammon, fr. *Ammōn* Ammon, an Egyptian god near one of whose temples it was extracted] **1** : a colorless gaseous compound of nitrogen and hydrogen used in refrigeration and in the making of fertilizers and explosives **2** : a solution (**ammonia water**) of ammonia in water

am·mo·ni·um \ə-'mō-nē-əm\ *n* : an ion or chemical group derived from ammonia by combination with hydrogen

ammonium chloride *n* : a white crystalline volatile salt used in batteries and as an expectorant

am·mu·ni·tion \,am-yə-'ni-shən\ *n* **1** : projectiles fired from guns **2** : explosive items used in war **3** : material for use in attack or defense

Amn *abbr* airman

am·ne·sia \am-'nē-zhə\ *n* **1** : abnormal loss of memory **2** : the selective overlooking of events or acts not favorable to one's purpose — **am·ne·si·ac** \-zhē-,ak, -zē-\ *or* **am·ne·sic** \-zik, -sik\ *adj or n*

am·nes·ty \'am-nə-stē\ *n, pl* **-ties** : an act granting a pardon to a group of individuals — **amnesty** *vb*

am·nio·cen·te·sis \,am-nē-ō-,sen-'tē-səs\ *n, pl* **-te·ses** \-,sēz\ : the surgical insertion of a hollow needle through the abdominal wall and uterus of a pregnant female esp. to obtain fluid used to check the fetus for chromosomal abnormality and fetal sex

am·ni·ot·ic fluid \,am-nē-'ä-tik-\ *n* : the watery fluid in which the embryo or fetus is immersed

amoe·ba *also* **ame·ba** \ə-'mē-bə\ *n, pl* **-bas** *or* **-bae** \-(,)bē\ : any of various tiny one-celled protozoans that lack permanent cell organs and occur esp. in water and soil — **amoe·bic** \-bik\ *adj*

amoe·boid *also* **ame·boid** \-,bȯid\ *adj* : resembling an amoeba esp. in moving or readily changing shape

amok \ə-'mək, -'mäk\ *or* **amuck** \-'mək\ *adv* : in a violent, frenzied, or uncontrolled manner ⟨run ~⟩

among \ə-'məŋ\ *also* **amongst** \-'məŋst\ *prep* **1** : in or through the midst of **2** : in the number, class, or company of **3** : in shares to each of **4** : by common action of

amon·til·la·do \ə-,män-tə-'lä-dō\ *n, pl* **-dos** [Sp] : a medium dry sherry

amor·al \ā-'mȯr-əl\ *adj* **1** : neither moral nor immoral; *esp* : being outside the sphere to which moral judgments apply **2** : lacking moral sensibility — **amor·al·ly** *adv*

am·o·rous \'a-mə-rəs\ *adj* **1** : inclined to love **2** : being in love **3** : of or indicative of love — **am·o·rous·ly** *adv* — **am·o·rous·ness** *n*

amor·phous \ə-'mȯr-fəs\ *adj* **1** : SHAPELESS, FORMLESS **2** : not crystallized

am·or·tize \'a-mər-,tīz, ə-'mȯr-\ *vb* **-tized; -tiz·ing** : to extinguish (as a mortgage) usu. by payment on the principal at the time of each periodic interest payment — **amor·ti·za·tion** \,a-mər-tə-'zā-shən, ə-,mȯr-\ *n*

Amos \'ā-məs\ *n* — see BIBLE table

¹**amount** \ə-'maunt\ *vb* **1** : to be equivalent **2** : to reach a total : add up

²**amount** *n* **1** : the total number or quantity **2** : a principal sum plus the interest on it

amour \ə-'mur, ä-, a-\ *n* **1** : a love affair esp. when illicit **2** : LOVER

amour pro·pre \,a-,mur-'prōpr³, ,ä-, -'prȯpr³\ *n* [F] : SELF-ESTEEM

¹**amp** \'amp\ *n* **1** : AMPERE **2** : AMPLIFIER; *also* : a unit consisting of an electronic amplifier and a loudspeaker

²amp vb : EXCITE, ENERGIZE ⟨tried to ~ up the crowd⟩
am·per·age \'am-p(ə-)rij\ n : the strength of a current of electricity expressed in amperes
am·pere \'am-,pir\ n : a unit of electric current equivalent to a steady current produced by one volt applied across a resistance of one ohm
am·per·sand \'am-pər-,sand\ n [alter. of and per se and, spoken form of the phrase & per se and, lit., (the character) & by itself (stands for the word) and] : a character & used for the word and
am·phet·amine \am-'fe-tə-,mēn, -mən\ n : a compound or one of its derivatives that stimulates the central nervous system and is used esp. to treat hyperactive children and to suppress appetite
am·phib·i·an \am-'fi-bē-ən\ n 1 : an amphibious organism; esp : any of a class of vertebrate animals (as frogs and salamanders) intermediate between fishes and reptiles 2 : an airplane that can land on and take off from either land or water
am·phib·i·ous \am-'fi-bē-əs\ adj [Gk amphibios, lit., living a double life, fr. amphi- on both sides + bios mode of life] 1 : able to live both on land and in water 2 : adapted for both land and water 3 : made by joint action of land, sea, and air forces invading from the sea; also : trained for such action
am·phi·bole \'am-fə-,bōl\ n : any of a group of rock-forming minerals of similar crystal structure
am·phi·the·ater \'am-fə-,thē-ə-tər\ n 1 : an oval or circular structure with rising tiers of seats around an arena 2 : a very large auditorium
am·pho·ra \'am-fə-rə\ n, pl -rae \-,rē\ or -ras : an ancient Greek jar or vase with two handles that rise almost to the level of the mouth
am·ple \'am-pəl\ adj **am·pler** \-plər\; **am·plest** \-pləst\ 1 : LARGE, CAPACIOUS 2 : enough to satisfy : ABUNDANT — **am·ply** \-plē\ adv
am·pli·fy \'am-plə-,fī\ vb -fied; -fy·ing 1 : to expand by extended treatment 2 : to increase in magnitude or strength; esp : to make louder — **am·pli·fi·ca·tion** \,am-plə-fə-'kā-shən\ n — **am·pli·fi·er** \'am-plə-,fī(-ə)r\ n
am·pli·tude \-,tüd, -,tyüd\ n 1 : ample extent : FULLNESS 2 : the extent of a vibratory movement (as of a pendulum) 3 : the height or depth of an oscillation (as of an alternating current or a radio wave) compared to its average value
amplitude modulation n : modulation of the amplitude of a radio carrier wave in accordance with the strength of the signal; also : a broadcasting system using such modulation
am·poule or **am·pule** also **am·pul** \'am-,pyül, -pül\ n : a small sealed bulbous glass vessel used to hold a solution for hypodermic injection
am·pu·tate \'am-pyə-,tāt\ vb -tat·ed; -tat·ing : to cut off ⟨~ a leg⟩ — **am·pu·ta·tion** \,am-pyə-'tā-shən\ n
am·pu·tee \,am-pyə-'tē\ n : one who has had a limb amputated
AMSLAN abbr American Sign Language
amt abbr amount
amuck var of AMOK
am·u·let \'am-yə-lət\ n : an ornament worn as a charm against evil
amuse \ə-'myüz\ vb amused; amus·ing : to entertain in a light or playful manner : DIVERT — **amuse·ment** n — **amusing** adj — **amus·ing·ly** adv
amusement park n : a commercially operated park having various devices (as a roller coaster) for entertainment and booths for selling refreshments
AMVETS \'am-,vets\ abbr American Veterans (of World War II)
am·y·lase \'a-mə-,lās, -,lāz\ n : any of several enzymes that accelerate the breakdown of starch and glycogen
an \ən, (')an\ indefinite article : A — used before words beginning with a vowel sound
¹-an or **-ian** also **-ean** n suffix 1 : one that belongs to ⟨American⟩ ⟨crustacean⟩ 2 : one skilled in or specializing in ⟨phonetician⟩
²-an or **-ian** also **-ean** adj suffix 1 : of or belonging to ⟨American⟩ 2 : characteristic of : resembling ⟨Mozartean⟩
AN abbr airman (Navy)
an·a·bol·ic steroid \,a-nə-'bä-lik-\ n : any of a group of

synthetic steroid hormones sometimes abused by athletes in training to increase the size and strength of their muscles
anach·ro·nism \ə-'na-krə-,ni-zəm\ n 1 : the error of placing a person or thing in the wrong period 2 : one that is chronologically out of place — **anach·ro·nis·tic** \ə-,na-krə-'nis-tik\ adj — **anach·ro·nous** \-'na-krə-nəs\ adj
an·a·con·da \,a-nə-'kän-də\ n : a large So. American snake that suffocates and kills its prey by constriction
anad·ro·mous \ə-'na-drə-məs\ adj : ascending rivers from the sea for breeding ⟨shad are ~⟩
anae·mia, anae·mic chiefly Brit var of ANEMIA, ANEMIC
an·aer·obe \'a-nə-,rōb\ n : an anaerobic organism
an·aer·o·bic \,a-nə-'rō-bik\ adj : living, active, occurring, or existing in the absence of free oxygen
an·aes·the·sia, an·aes·thet·ic chiefly Brit var of ANESTHESIA, ANESTHETIC
ana·gram \'a-nə-,gram\ n : a word or phrase made by transposing the letters of another word or phrase
¹anal \'ā-nᵊl\ adj 1 : of, relating to, situated near, or involving the anus 2 : of, relating to, or characterized by the stage of psychosexual development in psychoanalytic theory during which one is concerned esp. with feces 3 : of, relating to, or characterized by personality traits (as frugality and neatness) considered typical of fixation at the anal stage of development — **anal·ly** adv
²anal abbr 1 analogy 2 analysis; analytic
an·al·ge·sia \,a-nᵊl-'jē-zhə\ n : insensibility to pain — **anal·ge·sic** \-'jē-zik, -sik\ adj
an·al·ge·sic \-'jē-zik, -sik\ n : an agent for producing analgesia
analog computer n : a computer that operates with numbers represented by directly measurable quantities (as voltages)
anal·o·gous \ə-'na-lə-gəs\ adj : similar in one or more respects — **anal·o·gous·ly** adv
an·a·logue or **an·a·log** \'a-nə-,lòg, -,lag\ n 1 : something that is analogous to something else 2 : an organ similar in function to one of another animal or plant but different in structure or origin
anal·o·gy \ə-'na-lə-jē\ n, pl -gies 1 : inference that if two or more things agree in some respects they will probably agree in others 2 : a likeness in one or more ways between things otherwise unlike — **an·a·log·i·cal** \,a-nə-'lä-ji-kəl\ adj — **an·a·log·i·cal·ly** \-k(ə-)lē\ adv
anal—re·ten·tive \'ā-nᵊl-ri-'ten-tiv\ adj : ANAL 3
an·a·lyse chiefly Brit var of ANALYZE
anal·y·sis \ə-'na-lə-səs\ n, pl -y·ses \-,sēz\ [NL, fr. Gk. fr. analyein to break up, fr. ana- up + lyein to loosen] 1 : separation of a thing into the parts or elements of which it is composed 2 : an examination of a thing to determine its parts or elements; also : a statement showing the results of such an examination 3 : PSYCHOANALYSIS — **an·a·lyst** \'a-nə-list\ n — **an·a·lyt·ic** \,a-nə-'li-tik\ or **an·a·lyt·i·cal** \-ti-kəl\ adj — **an·a·lyt·i·cal·ly** adv
an·a·lyte \'a-nə-,līt\ n : a chemical substance that is the subject of chemical analysis
an·a·lyze \'a-nə-,līz\ vb -lyzed; -lyz·ing : to make an analysis of
an·a·pest \'a-nə-,pest\ n : a metrical foot of two unaccented syllables followed by one accented syllable — **an·a·pes·tic** \,a-nə-'pes-tik\ adj or n
an·ar·chism \'a-nər-,ki-zəm\ n : the theory that all government is undesirable — **an·ar·chist** \-kist\ n or adj — **an·ar·chis·tic** \,a-nər-'kis-tik\ adj
an·ar·chy \'a-nər-kē\ n 1 : a social structure without government or law and order 2 : utter confusion — **an·ar·chic** \a-'när-kik\ adj — **an·ar·chi·cal·ly** \-ki-k(ə-)lē\ adv
anas·to·mo·sis \ə-,nas-tə-'mō-səs\ n, pl -mo·ses \-,sēz\ 1 : the union of parts or branches (as of blood vessels) 2 : NETWORK
anat abbr anatomical; anatomy
anath·e·ma \ə-'na-thə-mə\ n 1 : a solemn curse 2 : a person or thing accursed; also : one intensely disliked
anath·e·ma·tize \-,tīz\ vb -tized; -tiz·ing : to pronounce an anathema on : CURSE
anat·o·mise Brit var of ANATOMIZE
anat·o·mize \ə-'na-tə-,mīz\ vb -mized; -miz·ing : to dissect so as to examine the structure and parts; also : ANALYZE
anat·o·my \ə-'na-tə-mē\ n, pl -mies [LL anatomia dissec-

tion, fr. Gk *anatomē*, fr. *anatemnein* to dissect, fr. *ana-* up + *temnein* to cut] **1** : a branch of science dealing with the structure of organisms **2** : structural makeup esp. of an organism or any of its parts **3** : a separating into parts for detailed study : ANALYSIS — **an·a·tom·i·cal** \,a-nə-'tä-mi-kəl\ *or* **an·a·tom·ic** \-mik\ *adj* — **an·a·tom·i·cal·ly** \-mi-k(ə-)lē\ *adv* — **anat·o·mist** \ə-'na-tə-mist\ *n*

anc *abbr* ancient

-ance *n suffix* **1** : action or process ⟨further*ance*⟩ : instance of an action or process ⟨perform*ance*⟩ **2** : quality or state : instance of a quality or state ⟨protuber*ance*⟩ **3** : amount or degree ⟨conduct*ance*⟩

an·ces·tor \'an-,ses-tər\ *n* [ME *ancestre*, fr. AF, fr. L *antecessor* predecessor, fr. *antecedere* to go before, fr. *ante-* before + *cedere* to go] : one from whom an individual is descended

an·ces·tress \'an-,ses-trəs\ *n* : a female ancestor

an·ces·try \'an-,ses-trē\ *n* **1** : line of descent : LINEAGE **2** : ANCESTORS — **an·ces·tral** \an-'ses-trəl\ *adj*

an·cho \'än-chō\ *n, pl* **anchos** : a poblano chili pepper esp. when mature and dried to a reddish black

¹**an·chor** \'aŋ-kər\ *n* **1** : a heavy metal device attached to a ship that catches hold of the bottom and holds the ship in place **2** : something that serves to hold an object firmly **3** : ANCHORPERSON **4** : a large store that attracts customers and other businesses to a shopping mall

anchor 1: different styles

²**anchor** *vb* : to hold or become held in place by or as if by an anchor

an·chor·age \'aŋ-k(ə-)rij\ *n* : a place suitable for ships to anchor

an·cho·rite \'aŋ-kə-,rīt\ *n* : HERMIT

an·chor·man \'aŋ-kər-,man\ *n* **1** : the member of a team who competes last **2** : an anchorperson who is a man

an·chor·per·son \-,pər-sən\ *n* : a broadcaster who reads the news and introduces the reports of other broadcasters

an·chor·wom·an \-,wù-mən\ *n* **1** : a woman who competes last **2** : an anchorperson who is a woman

an·cho·vy \'an-,chō-vē, an-'chō-\ *n, pl* **-vies** *or* **-vy** : any of a family of small herringlike fishes often used as food

an·cien ré·gime \äⁿs-yäⁿ-rā-'zhēm\ *n* **1** : the political and social system of France before the Revolution of 1789 **2** : a system no longer prevailing

¹**an·cient** \'ān-shənt\ *adj* **1** : having existed for many years ⟨~ customs⟩ **2** : belonging to times long past; *esp* : belonging to the period before the Middle Ages

²**ancient** *n* **1** : an aged person **2** *pl* : the peoples of ancient Greece and Rome; *esp* : the classical authors of Greece and Rome

an·cil·lary \'an-sə-,ler-ē\ *adj* **1** : SUBORDINATE, SUBSIDIARY ⟨a factory's ~ plants⟩ **2** : AUXILIARY, SUPPLEMENTARY ⟨~ evidence⟩ — **ancillary** *n*

-ancy *n suffix* : quality or state ⟨flamboy*ancy*⟩

and \'and, (')and\ *conj* **1** — used to indicate connection or addition esp. of items within the same class or type or to join words or phrases of the same grammatical rank or function **2** — used to join one finite verb to another so that together they are equivalent to an infinitive of purpose ⟨come ~ see me⟩

¹**an·dan·te** \än-'dän-,tā, -tē\ *adv or adj* [It, lit., going, prp. of *andare* to go] : moderately slow — used as a direction in music

²**andante** *n* : an andante movement

and·iron \'an-,dī(-ə)rn\ *n* : one of a pair of metal supports for firewood in a fireplace

and/or \'and-'ȯr\ *conj* — used to indicate that either *and*

or *or* may apply ⟨men ~ women means men *and* women or men *or* women⟩

an·dro·gen \'an-drə-jən\ *n* : a male sex hormone (as testosterone)

an·drog·y·nous \an-'drä-jə-nəs\ *adj* **1** : having the characteristics of both male and female **2** : suitable for either sex ⟨~ clothing⟩ — **an·drog·y·ny** \-nē\ *n*

an·droid \'an-,drȯid\ *n* : a mobile robot usu. with a human form

an·ec·dot·al \,a-nik-'dō-t^əl\ *adj* **1** : relating to or consisting of anecdotes **2** : based on reports of an unscientific nature — **an·ec·dot·al·ly** *adv*

an·ec·dote \'an-ik-,dōt\ *n, pl* **-dotes** *also* **-dota** \,a-nik-'dō-tə\ [F, fr. Gk *anekdota* unpublished items, fr. *a-* not + *ekdidonai* to publish] : a brief story of an interesting, amusing, or biographical incident

ane·mia \ə-'nē-mē-ə\ *n* **1** : a condition in which blood is deficient in quantity, in red blood cells, or in hemoglobin and which is marked by pallor, weakness, and irregular heart action **2** : lack of vitality — **ane·mic** \ə-'nē-mik\ *adj*

an·e·mom·e·ter \,a-nə-'mä-mə-tər\ *n* : an instrument for measuring the force or speed of the wind

anem·o·ne \ə-'ne-mə-nē\ *n* : any of a large genus of herbs related to the buttercups that have showy flowers without petals but with conspicuous often colored sepals

anent \ə-'nent\ *prep* : CONCERNING

an·es·the·sia \,a-nəs-'thē-zhə\ *n* : loss of bodily sensation

an·es·the·si·ol·o·gy \-,thē-zē-'ä-lə-jē\ *n* : a branch of medical science dealing with anesthesia and anesthetics — **an·es·the·si·ol·o·gist** \-jist\ *n*

¹**an·es·thet·ic** \,a-nəs-'the-tik\ *adj* : of, relating to, or capable of producing anesthesia

²**anesthetic** *n* : an agent that produces anesthesia

anes·the·tist \ə-'nes-thə-tist\ *n* : one who administers anesthetics

anes·the·tize \ə-'nes-thə-,tīz\ *vb* **-tized; -tiz·ing** : to subject to anesthesia

an·eu·rysm *also* **an·eu·rism** \'an-yə-,ri-zəm\ *n* : an abnormal blood-filled bulge of a blood vessel

anew \ə-'nü, -'nyü\ *adv* **1** : over again ⟨begin ~⟩ **2** : in a new form ⟨this film tells the story ~⟩

an·gel \'ān-jəl\ *n* [ME, fr. OE *engel* & AF *angele*, both fr. L *angelus*, fr. Gk *angelos*, lit., messenger] **1** : a spiritual being superior to man **2** : an attendant spirit **3** : a winged figure of human form in art **4** : MESSENGER, HARBINGER ⟨~ of death⟩ **5** : a person held to resemble an angel **6** : a financial backer — **an·gel·ic** \an-'je-lik\ *or* **an·gel·i·cal** \-li-kəl\ *adj* — **an·gel·i·cal·ly** \-k(ə-)lē\ *adv*

an·gel·fish \'än-jəl-,fish\ *n* : any of several brightly colored tropical fishes that are flattened from side to side

an·gel·i·ca \an-'je-li-kə\ *n* : a biennial herb related to the carrot whose roots and fruit furnish a flavoring oil

¹**an·ger** \'aŋ-gər\ *vb* : to make angry

²**anger** *n* [ME, affliction, anger, fr. ON *angr* grief] : a strong feeling of displeasure ♦ **Synonyms** WRATH, IRE, RAGE, FURY, INDIGNATION

an·gi·na \an-'jī-nə\ *n* : a disorder (as of the heart) marked by attacks of intense pain; *esp* : ANGINA PECTORIS — **an·gi·nal** \an-'jī-n^əl\ *adj*

angina pec·to·ris \-'pek-t(ə-)rəs\ *n* : a heart disease marked by brief attacks of sharp chest pain caused by deficient oxygenation of heart muscles

an·gio·gen·e·sis \,an-jē-ō-'je-nə-səs\ *n* : the formation of blood vessels — **an·gio·gen·ic** \-'je-nik\ *adj*

an·gio·gram \'an-jē-ə-,gram\ *n* : a radiograph made by angiography

an·gi·og·ra·phy \,an-jē-'ä-grə-fē\ *n* : the use of radiography to make blood vessels visible after injection of a substance opaque to radiation

an·gio·plas·ty \'an-jē-ə-,plas-tē\ *n* : surgical repair of a blood vessel esp. by using an inflatable catheter to unblock arteries clogged by atherosclerotic deposits

an·gio·sperm \-,spərm\ *n* : FLOWERING PLANT

¹**an·gle** \'aŋ-gəl\ *n* **1** : a sharp projecting corner **2** : the figure formed by the meeting of two lines in a point **3** : a point of view **4** : a special technique or plan : GIMMICK — **an·gled** *adj*

²**angle** *vb* **an·gled; an·gling** \-g(ə-)liŋ\ : to turn, move, or direct at an angle

³**angle** *vb* **an·gled; an·gling** \-g(ə-)liŋ\ : to fish with a hook and line — **an·gler** \-glər\ *n* — **an·gling** \-gliŋ\ *n*

an·gle·worm \'aŋ-gəl-ˌwərm\ *n* : EARTHWORM

An·gli·can \'aŋ-gli-kən\ *adj* 1 : of or relating to the established episcopal Church of England 2 : of or relating to England or the English nation — **Anglican** *n* — **An·gli·can·ism** \-kə-ˌni-zəm\ *n*

an·gli·cize \'aŋ-glə-ˌsīz\ *vb* **-cized; -ciz·ing** *often cap* 1 : to make English (as in habits, speech, character, or outlook) 2 : to borrow (a foreign word or phrase) into English without changing form or spelling and sometimes without changing pronunciation — **an·gli·ci·za·tion** \ˌaŋ-glə-sə-'zā-shən\ *n, often cap*

An·glo \'aŋ-glō\ *n, pl* **Anglos** : a non-Hispanic white inhabitant of the U.S.; *esp* : one of English origin and descent

An·glo-cen·tric \ˌaŋ-glō-'sen-trik\ *adj* : centered on or favoring England or things English

An·glo–French \ˌaŋ-glō-'french\ *n* : the French language used in medieval England

An·glo·phile \'aŋ-glə-ˌfī(-ə)l\ *also* **An·glo·phil** \-ˌfil\ *n* : one who greatly admires England and things English

An·glo·phobe \'aŋ-glə-ˌfōb\ *n* : one who is averse to England and things English

An·glo–Sax·on \ˌaŋ-glō-'sak-sən\ *n* 1 : a member of any of the Germanic peoples who invaded England in the 5th century A.D. 2 : a member of the English people 3 : Old English — **Anglo–Saxon** *adj*

an·go·ra \aŋ-'gór-ə, an-\ *n* 1 : yarn or cloth made from the hair of an Angora goat or rabbit 2 *cap* : any of a breed of cats, goats, or rabbits with a long silky coat

an·gry \'aŋ-grē\ *adj* **an·gri·er; -est** : feeling or showing anger ✦ **Synonyms** ENRAGED, WRATHFUL, IRATE, INDIGNANT, MAD — **an·gri·ly** \-grə-lē\ *adv*

angst \'äŋst\ *n* [G] : a feeling of anxiety

ang·strom \'aŋ-strəm\ *n* : a unit of length equal to one ten-billionth of a meter

an·guish \'aŋ-gwish\ *n* : extreme pain or distress esp. of mind — **an·guished** \-gwisht\ *adj*

an·gu·lar \'aŋ-gyə-lər\ *adj* 1 : sharp-cornered 2 : having one or more angles 3 : being thin and bony — **an·gu·lar·i·ty** \ˌaŋ-gyə-'ler-ə-tē\ *n*

An·gus \'aŋ-gəs\ *n* : any of a breed of usu. black hornless beef cattle originating in Scotland

an·hy·drous \an-'hī-drəs\ *adj* : free from water

an·i·line \'a-nᵊl-ən\ *n* : an oily poisonous liquid used in making dyes, medicines, and explosives

an·i·mad·vert \ˌa-nə-ˌmad-'vərt\ *vb* : to remark critically : express censure — **an·i·mad·ver·sion** \-'vər-zhən\ *n*

¹**an·i·mal** \'a-nə-məl\ *n* 1 : any of a kingdom of living things typically differing from plants in capacity for active movement, in rapid response to stimulation, and in lack of cellulose cell walls 2 : a lower animal as distinguished from human beings; *also* : MAMMAL

²**animal** *adj* 1 : of, relating to, or derived from animals 2 : of or relating to the physical as distinguished from the mental or spiritual ✦ **Synonyms** CARNAL, FLESHLY, SENSUAL

an·i·mal·cule \ˌa-nə-'mal-kyül\ *n* : a tiny animal usu. invisible to the naked eye

¹**an·i·mate** \'a-nə-mət\ *adj* : having life

²**an·i·mate** \-ˌmāt\ *vb* **-mat·ed; -mat·ing** 1 : to impart life to 2 : to give spirit and vigor to 3 : to make appear to move ⟨~ a cartoon for motion pictures⟩ — **an·i·mat·ed** *adj* — **an·i·mat·ed·ly** *adv*

an·i·ma·tion \ˌa-nə-'mā-shən\ *n* 1 : VIVACITY, LIVELINESS 2 : a motion picture made from a series of drawings simulating motions by means of slight progressive changes

an·i·ma·tron·ic \ˌa-nə-mə-'trä-nik\ *adj* : of, relating to, or being an electrically animated mechanical figure (as a puppet)

an·i·mism \'a-nə-ˌmi-zəm\ *n* : attribution of conscious life to objects in and phenomena of nature or to inanimate objects — **an·i·mist** \-mist\ *n* — **an·i·mis·tic** \ˌa-nə-'mis-tik\ *adj*

an·i·mos·i·ty \ˌa-nə-'mä-sə-tē\ *n, pl* **-ties** : ILL WILL, RESENTMENT

an·i·mus \'a-nə-məs\ *n* : deep-seated resentment and hostility

an·ion \'a-ˌnī-ən, -ˌnī-ˌän\ *n* : a negatively charged ion

an·ise \'a-nəs\ *n* : an herb related to the carrot with aromatic seeds (**aniseed** \-sēd\) used in flavoring

an·is·ette \ˌa-nə-'set, -'zet\ *n* [F] : a usu. colorless sweet liqueur flavored with aniseed

ankh \'äŋk\ *n* : a cross having a loop for its upper vertical arm and serving esp. in ancient Egypt as an emblem of life

an·kle \'aŋ-kəl\ *n* : the joint or region between the foot and the leg

an·kle·bone \'aŋ-kəl-ˌbōn\ *n* : the bone that in human beings bears the weight of the body and with the tibia and fibula forms the ankle joint

an·klet \'aŋ-klət\ *n* 1 : something (as an ornament) worn around the ankle 2 : a short sock reaching slightly above the ankle

ann *abbr* 1 annals 2 annual

an·nals \'a-nᵊlz\ *n pl* 1 : a record of events in chronological order 2 : historical records — **an·nal·ist** \-nᵊl-ist\ *n*

an·neal \ə-'nēl\ *vb* 1 : to make (as glass or steel) less brittle by heating and then cooling 2 : STRENGTHEN, TOUGHEN

¹**an·nex** \ə-'neks, 'a-ˌneks\ *vb* 1 : to attach as an addition 2 : to incorporate (as a territory) within a political domain — **an·nex·a·tion** \ˌa-ˌnek-'sā-shən\ *n*

²**an·nex** \'a-ˌneks, -niks\ *n* : a subsidiary or supplementary structure

an·nexe *chiefly Brit var of* ANNEX

an·ni·hi·late \ə-'nī-ə-ˌlāt\ *vb* **-lat·ed; -lat·ing** : to destroy completely — **an·ni·hi·la·tion** \-ˌnī-ə-'lā-shən\ *n*

an·ni·ver·sa·ry \ˌa-nə-'vər-sə-rē\ *n, pl* **-ries** : the annual return of the date of a notable event and esp. a wedding

an·no Do·mi·ni \ˌa-nō-'dä-mə-nē, -'dō-, -ˌnī\ *adv, often cap* *A* [ML, in the year of the Lord] — used to indicate that a time division falls within the Christian era

an·no·tate \'a-nə-ˌtāt\ *vb* **-tat·ed; -tat·ing** : to furnish with notes — **an·no·ta·tion** \ˌa-nə-'tā-shən\ *n* — **an·no·ta·tor** \'a-nə-ˌtā-tər\ *n*

an·nounce \ə-'naúns\ *vb* **an·nounced; an·nounc·ing** 1 : to make known publicly 2 : to give notice of the arrival or presence of — **an·nounce·ment** *n*

an·nounc·er \ə-'naún-sər\ *n* : a person who introduces radio or television programs, makes commercial announcements, or gives station identification

an·noy \ə-'nói\ *vb* : to disturb or irritate esp. by repeated acts : VEX ✦ **Synonyms** IRK, BOTHER, PESTER, TEASE, HARASS — **an·noy·ing·ly** *adv*

an·noy·ance \ə-'nói-əns\ *n* 1 : the act of annoying 2 : the state of being annoyed 3 : NUISANCE ⟨the delay was a minor ~⟩

¹**an·nu·al** \'an-yə-wəl\ *adj* 1 : covering the period of a year ⟨~ rainfall⟩ 2 : occurring once a year : YEARLY 3 : completing the life cycle in one growing season ⟨~ plants⟩ — **an·nu·al·ly** *adv*

²**annual** *n* 1 : a publication appearing once a year 2 : an annual plant

annual ring *n* : the layer of wood produced by a single year's growth of a woody plant

an·nu·i·tant \ə-'nü-ə-tənt, -'nyü-\ *n* : a beneficiary of an annuity

an·nu·i·ty \ə-'nü-ə-tē, -'nyü-\ *n, pl* **-i·ties** : an amount payable annually; *also* : the right to receive such a payment

an·nul \ə-'nəl\ *vb* **an·nulled; an·nul·ling** : to make legally void — **an·nul·ment** *n*

an·nu·lar \'an-yə-lər\ *adj* : ring-shaped

an·nun·ci·ate \ə-'nən-sē-ˌāt\ *vb* **-at·ed; -at·ing** : ANNOUNCE

an·nun·ci·a·tion \ə-ˌnən-sē-'ā-shən\ *n* 1 *cap* : March 25 observed as a church festival commemorating the announcement of the Incarnation 2 : ANNOUNCEMENT

an·nun·ci·a·tor \ə-'nən-sē-ˌā-tər\ *n* : one that annunciates; *specif* : a usu. electrically controlled signal board or indicator

an·ode \'a-ˌnōd\ *n* 1 : the positive electrode of an electrolytic cell 2 : the negative terminal of a battery 3 : the electron-collecting electrode of an electron tube — **an·od·ic** \a-'nä-dik\ *also* **an·od·al** \-'nō-dᵊl\ *adj*

an·od·ize \'a-nə-ˌdīz\ *vb* **-ized; -iz·ing** : to subject (a metal) to electrolytic action as the anode of a cell in order to coat with a protective or decorative film

an·o·dyne \'a-nə-ˌdīn\ *n* : something that relieves pain : a soothing agent

anoint \ə-'nȯint\ *vb* **1** : to apply oil to esp. as a sacred rite **2** : CONSECRATE — **anoint·ment** *n*
anom·a·lous \ə-'nä-mə-ləs\ *adj* : deviating from a general rule : ABNORMAL
anom·a·ly \ə-'nä-mə-lē\ *n, pl* **-lies** : something anomalous : IRREGULARITY
¹anon \ə-'nän\ *adv* : SOON
²anon *abbr* anonymous; anonymously
anon·y·mous \ə-'nä-nə-məs\ *adj* : of unknown or undeclared origin or authorship — **an·o·nym·i·ty** \ˌa-nə-'ni-mə-tē\ *n* — **anon·y·mous·ly** *adv*
anoph·e·les \ə-'nä-fə-ˌlēz\ *n* [NL, genus name, fr. Gk *anōphelēs* useless, fr. *a-* not + *ophelos* advantage, help] : any of a genus of mosquitoes that includes all mosquitoes which transmit malaria to human beings
an·o·rec·tic \ˌa-nə-'rek-tik\ *adj* : ANOREXIC — **anorectic** *n*
an·orex·ia \ˌa-nə-'rek-sē-ə\ *n* **1** : loss of appetite esp. when prolonged **2** : ANOREXIA NERVOSA
anorexia ner·vo·sa \-nər-'vō-sə\ *n* : a serious disorder in eating behavior marked esp. by a pathological fear of weight gain leading to faulty eating patterns, malnutrition, and usu. excessive weight loss
an·orex·ic \ˌa-nə-'rek-sik\ *adj* **1** : lacking or causing loss of appetite **2** : affected with or as if with anorexia nervosa — **anorexic** *n*
¹an·oth·er \ə-'nə-thər\ *adj* **1** : some other ⟨do it ∼ time⟩ **2** : being one in addition : one more ⟨∼ piece of pie⟩
²another *pron* **1** : an additional one : one more **2** : one that is different from the first or present one
ans *abbr* answer
¹an·swer \'an-sər\ *n* **1** : something spoken or written in reply to a question **2** : a solution of a problem
²answer *vb* **1** : to speak or write in reply to **2** : to be responsible **3** : to be adequate — **an·swer·er** *n*
an·swer·able \'an-sə-rə-bəl\ *adj* **1** : subject to taking blame or responsibility **2** : capable of being refuted
answering machine *n* : a machine that receives telephone calls by playing a recorded message and usu. by recording messages from callers
answering service *n* : a commercial service that answers telephone calls for its clients
¹ant \'ant\ *n* : any of a family of small social insects related to the bees and living in communities usu. in earth or wood
²ant *abbr* antonym
Ant *abbr* Antarctica
ant- — see ANTI-
¹-ant *n suffix* **1** : one that performs or promotes (a specified action) ⟨coolant⟩ **2** : thing that is acted upon (in a specified manner) ⟨inhalant⟩
²-ant *adj suffix* **1** : performing (a specified action) or being (in a specified condition) ⟨propellant⟩ **2** : promoting (a specified action or process) ⟨expectorant⟩
ant·ac·id \ant-'a-səd\ *n* : an agent that counteracts acidity — **antacid** *adj*
an·tag·o·nism \an-'ta-gə-ˌni-zəm\ *n* **1** : active opposition or hostility **2** : opposition in physiological action — **an·tag·o·nis·tic** \-ˌta-gə-'nis-tik\ *adj*
an·tag·o·nist \-nist\ *n* : ADVERSARY, OPPONENT
an·tag·o·nize \an-'ta-gə-ˌnīz\ *vb* **-nized; -niz·ing** : to provoke the hostility of
ant·arc·tic \ant-'ärk-tik, -'är-tik\ *adj, often cap* : of or relating to the south pole or the region near it
antarctic circle *n, often cap A&C* : the parallel of latitude that is approximately 66½ degrees south of the equator
¹an·te \'an-tē\ *n* : a poker stake put up before the deal to build the pot; *also* : an amount paid : PRICE
²ante *vb* **an·ted; an·te·ing** **1** : to put up (an ante) **2** : PAY
ant·eat·er \'ant-ˌē-tər\ *n* : any of several mammals (as an aardvark) that feed mostly on ants or termites
an·te·bel·lum \ˌan-ti-'be-ləm\ *adj* : existing before a war; *esp* : existing before the U.S. Civil War of 1861-65
an·te·ced·ent \ˌan-tə-'sē-dⁿnt\ *n* **1** : a noun, pronoun, phrase, or clause referred to by a personal or relative pronoun **2** : a preceding event or cause **3** *pl* : the significant conditions of one's earlier life **4** *pl* : ANCESTORS — **antecedent** *adj*
an·te·cham·ber \'an-ti-ˌchäm-bər\ *n* : ANTEROOM
an·te·date \'an-ti-ˌdāt\ *vb* **1** : to date (a paper) as of an earlier day than that on which the actual writing or signing is done **2** : to precede in time

an·te·di·lu·vi·an \ˌan-ti-də-'lü-vē-ən, -dī-\ *adj* **1** : of the period before the biblical flood **2** : ANTIQUATED
an·te·lope \'an-tə-ˌlōp\ *n, pl* **-lope** *or* **-lopes** [ME, fabulous heraldic beast, prob. fr. MF *antelop* savage animal with sawlike horns, fr. ML *anthalopus*, fr. LGk *antholops*] **1** : any of various deerlike ruminant mammals that chiefly inhabit Africa and have a slender build and horns extending upward and backward **2** : PRONGHORN
an·te me·ri·di·em \'an-ti-mə-'ri-dē-əm\ *adj* [L] : being before noon
an·ten·na \an-'te-nə\ *n, pl* **-nae** \-(ˌ)nē\ *or* **-nas** [ML, fr. L, sail yard] **1** : one of the long slender paired segmented sensory organs on the head of an arthropod (as an insect or crab) **2** *pl usu* **-nas** : a metallic device (as a rod or wire) for sending out or receiving radio waves
an·te·pe·nult \ˌan-ti-'pē-ˌnȯlt\ *also* **an·te·pen·ul·ti·ma** \-ˌpi-'nȯl-tə-mə\ *n* : the 3d syllable of a word counting from the end — **an·te·pen·ul·ti·mate** \-ˌpi-'nȯl-tə-mət\ *adj or n*
an·te·ri·or \an-'tir-ē-ər\ *adj* **1** : situated before or toward the front **2** : situated near or nearer to the head **3** : coming before in time ♦ **Synonyms** PRECEDING, PREVIOUS, PRIOR, ANTECEDENT
anterior cruciate ligament *n* : a cross-shaped ligament of the knee that connects the tibia and femur
an·te·room \'an-ti-ˌrüm, -ˌrüm\ *n* : a room forming the entrance to another and often used as a waiting room
an·them \'an-thəm\ *n* **1** : a sacred vocal composition **2** : a song or hymn of praise or gladness
an·ther \'an-thər\ *n* : the part of a stamen of a seed plant that produces and contains pollen
ant·hill \'ant-ˌhil\ *n* : a mound thrown up by ants or termites in digging their nest
an·thol·o·gy \an-'thä-lə-jē\ *n, pl* **-gies** [NL *anthologia* collection of epigrams, fr. MGk, fr. Gk, flower gathering, fr. *anthos* flower + *logia* collecting, fr. *legein* to gather] : a collection of literary selections — **an·thol·o·gist** \-jist\ *n* — **an·thol·o·gize** \-ˌjīz\ *vb*
an·thra·cite \'an-thrə-ˌsīt\ *n* : a hard glossy coal that burns without much smoke
an·thrax \'an-ˌthraks\ *n* : an infectious and usu. fatal bacterial disease of warm-blooded animals (as cattle and sheep) that is transmissible to humans; *also* : a bacterium causing anthrax
an·thro·po·cen·tric \ˌan-thrə-pə-'sen-trik\ *adj* : interpreting or regarding the world in terms of human values and experiences
an·thro·poid \'an-thrə-ˌpȯid\ *n* **1** : any of several large tailless apes (as a gorilla) **2** : a person resembling an ape — **anthropoid** *adj*
an·thro·pol·o·gy \ˌan-thrə-'pä-lə-jē\ *n* : the science of human beings and esp. of their physical characteristics, their origin and ancestry, their environment and social relations, and their culture — **an·thro·po·log·i·cal** \-pə-'lä-ji-kəl\ *adj* — **an·thro·pol·o·gist** \-'pä-lə-jist\ *n*
an·thro·po·mor·phism \ˌan-thrə-pə-'mȯr-ˌfi-zəm\ *n* : an interpretation of what is not human or personal in terms of human or personal characteristics : HUMANIZATION — **an·thro·po·mor·phic** \-fik\ *adj*
an·ti \'an-ˌtī, -tē\ *n, pl* **antis** : one who is opposed
anti- \ˌan-ti, -tē, -ˌtī\ *or* **ant-** *or* **anth-** *prefix* **1** : opposite in kind, position, or action **2** : opposing : hostile toward **3** : counteractive **4** : preventive of : curative of

antiaging	antigovernment
anti-AIDS	anti-HIV
antiaircraft	anti-imperialism
antialcohol	anti-imperialist
anti-American	antiknock
antianxiety	antilabor
antiapartheid	antimalarial
antibacterial	antimicrobial
anticapitalist	antinausea
anti-Catholic	antipoverty
anticholesterol	antislavery
anticlerical	antispasmodic
anticolonial	antistatic
anticommunism	antisubmarine
anticommunist	antitank
antidemocratic	antitumor
antidiscrimination	antiviral
antiestablishment	antiwar
antifascist	

an·ti·abor·tion \ˌan-tē-ə-'bȯr-shən, ˌan-ˌtī-\ *adj* : opposed to abortion — **an·ti·abor·tion·ist** \-shə-nist\ *n*

an·ti·bal·lis·tic missile \ˌan-ti-bə-'lis-tik-, ˌan-ˌtī-\ *n* : a missile for intercepting and destroying ballistic missiles

an·ti·bi·ot·ic \-bī-'ä-tik, -bē-\ *n* : a substance produced by or derived by chemical alteration of a substance produced by a microorganism (as a fungus or bacterium) that in dilute solution inhibits or kills another microorganism — **antibiotic** *adj*

an·ti·body \'an-ti-ˌbä-dē\ *n* : any of a large number of proteins of high molecular weight produced normally by specialized B cells after stimulation by an antigen and acting specifically against the antigen in an immune response

¹an·tic \'an-tik\ *n* [It *antico* ancient thing or person, fr. *antico* ancient, fr. L *antiquus*] : an often wildly playful or funny act or action

²antic *adj* **1** *archaic* : GROTESQUE **2** : PLAYFUL

an·ti·can·cer \ˌan-ti-'kan-sər, ˌan-ˌtī-\ *adj* : used against or tending to arrest or prevent cancer ⟨~ drugs⟩

An·ti·christ \'an-ti-ˌkrīst\ *n* **1** : one who denies or opposes Christ **2** : a false Christ

an·tic·i·pate \an-'ti-sə-ˌpāt\ *vb* **-pat·ed; -pat·ing** **1** : to foresee and provide for beforehand ⟨~s problems⟩ **2** : to look forward to — **an·tic·i·pa·tion** \-ˌti-sə-'pā-shən\ *n* — **an·tic·i·pa·to·ry** \-'ti-sə-pə-ˌtȯr-ē\ *adj*

an·ti·cli·max \ˌan-ti-'klī-ˌmaks\ *n* : something (as the ending of a story) that is strikingly less important or dramatic than expected — **an·ti·cli·mac·tic** \-klī-'mak-tik\ *adj*

an·ti·cline \'an-ti-ˌklīn\ *n* : an arch of layers of rock in the earth's crust

an·ti·co·ag·u·lant \ˌan-ti-kō-'a-gyə-lənt\ *n* : a substance that hinders the clotting of blood — **anticoagulant** *adj*

an·ti·cy·clone \ˌan-ti-'sī-ˌklōn\ *n* : a system of winds that rotates about a center of high atmospheric pressure — **an·ti·cy·clon·ic** \-sī-'klä-nik\ *adj*

an·ti·de·pres·sant \ˌan-ti-di-'pres-ᵊnt, ˌan-ˌtī-\ *n* : a drug used to relieve psychic depression — **antidepressant** *adj*

an·ti·dote \'an-ti-ˌdōt\ *n* : a remedy to counteract the effects of poison

an·ti·drug \'an-ˌtī-ˌdrəg\ *adj* : acting against or opposing illicit drugs

an·ti·fer·til·i·ty \ˌan-ti-fər-'ti-lə-tē\ *adj* : tending to reduce or destroy fertility — CONTRACEPTIVE ⟨~ agents⟩

an·ti·freeze \'an-ti-ˌfrēz\ *n* : a substance added to a liquid to lower its freezing temperature

an·ti·fun·gal \ˌan-tē-'fəŋ-gəl, ˌan-ˌtī-\ *n* : FUNGICIDE — **antifungal** *adj*

an·ti·gen \'an-ti-jən\ *n* : any substance (as a toxin) foreign to the body that induces an immune response — **an·ti·gen·ic** \ˌan-ti-'je-nik\ *adj* — **an·ti·ge·nic·i·ty** \-jə-'ni-sə-tē\ *n*

an·ti·grav·i·ty \ˌan-ti-'gra-və-tē, ˌan-ˌtī-\ *adj* : reducing or canceling the effect of gravity

an·ti·he·ro \'an-ti-ˌhē-rō, 'an-ˌtī-\ *n* : a protagonist who is notably lacking in heroic qualities (as courage)

an·ti·his·ta·mine \ˌan-ti-'his-tə-ˌmēn, ˌan-ˌtī-, -mən\ *n* : any of various drugs used in treating allergies and colds — **antihistamine** *adj*

an·ti·hy·per·ten·sive \-ˌhī-pər-'ten-siv\ *n* : a substance that is effective against high blood pressure — **antihypertensive** *adj*

an·ti·in·flam·ma·to·ry \-in-'fla-mə-ˌtȯr-ē\ *adj* : counteracting inflammation — **anti-inflammatory** *n*

an·ti·in·tel·lec·tu·al \-ˌin-tə-'lek-chə-wəl\ *adj* : opposing or hostile to intellectuals or to an intellectual view or approach

an·ti·lock \'an-ti-ˌläk, 'an-ˌtī-\ *adj* : being a braking system designed to prevent the wheels from locking

an·ti·log·a·rithm \ˌan-ti-'lȯ-gə-ˌri-thəm, ˌan-ˌtī-, -'lä-\ *n* : the number corresponding to a given logarithm ⟨if the logarithm in base *x* of *a* equals *b* then the antilogarithm in base *x* of *b* equals *a*⟩

an·ti·ma·cas·sar \ˌan-ti-mə-'ka-sər\ *n* : a cover to protect the back or arms of furniture

an·ti·mat·ter \'an-ti-ˌma-tər, 'an-ˌtī-\ *n* : matter composed of antiparticles

an·ti·mo·ny \'an-tə-ˌmō-nē\ *n* : a brittle silvery white metallic chemical element used esp. in alloys

an·ti·neu·tron \ˌan-ti-'nü-ˌträn, ˌan-ˌtī-, -'nyü-\ *n* : the antiparticle of the neutron

an·ti·no·mi·an \ˌan-ti-'nō-mē-ən\ *n* : one who denies the validity of moral laws

an·tin·o·my \an-'ti-nə-mē\ *n, pl* **-mies** : a contradiction between two seemingly true statements

an·ti·nov·el \'an-ti-ˌnä-vəl, 'an-ˌtī-\ *n* : a work of fiction that lacks all or most of the traditional features of the novel

an·ti·nu·cle·ar \ˌan-ti-'nü-klē-ər, -'nyü-\ *adj* : opposing the use or production of nuclear power

an·ti·ox·i·dant \ˌan-tē-'äk-sə-dənt, ˌan-ˌtī-\ *n* : a substance that inhibits oxidation — **antioxidant** *adj*

an·ti·par·ti·cle \'an-ti-ˌpär-ti-kəl, 'an-ˌtī-\ *n* : a subatomic particle identical to another subatomic particle in mass but opposite to it in electric and magnetic properties

an·ti·pas·to \ˌan-ti-'pas-tō, ˌän-ti-'päs-\ *n, pl* **-ti** \-(ˌ)tē\ : any of various typically Italian hors d'oeuvres

an·tip·a·thy \an-'ti-pə-thē\ *n, pl* **-thies** **1** : settled aversion or dislike **2** : an object of aversion — **an·ti·pa·thet·ic** \ˌan-ti-pə-'the-tik\ *adj*

an·ti·per·son·nel \ˌan-ti-ˌpər-sə-'nel, ˌan-ˌtī-\ *adj* : designed for use against military personnel ⟨~ mine⟩

an·ti·per·spi·rant \-'pər-spə-rənt\ *n* : a preparation used to reduce perspiration

an·tiph·o·nal \an-'ti-fə-nᵊl\ *adj* : performed by two alternating groups — **an·tiph·o·nal·ly** *adv*

an·ti·pode \'an-tə-ˌpōd\ *n, pl* **an·tip·o·des** \an-'ti-pə-ˌdēz\ [ME *antipodes*, pl., persons dwelling at opposite points on the globe, fr. L, fr. Gk, fr. pl. of *antipod-, antipous* with feet opposite, fr. *anti-* against + *pod-, pous* foot] : the parts of the earth diametrically opposite — usu. used in pl. — **an·tip·o·dal** \an-'ti-pə-dᵊl\ *adj* — **an·tip·o·de·an** \(ˌ)an-ˌti-pə-'dē-ən\ *adj*

an·ti·pol·lu·tion \ˌan-ti-pə-'lü-shən\ *adj* : designed to prevent, reduce, or eliminate pollution ⟨~ laws⟩

an·ti·pope \'an-ti-ˌpōp\ *n* : one elected or claiming to be pope in opposition to the pope canonically chosen

an·ti·pro·ton \ˌan-ti-'prō-ˌtän\ *n* : the antiparticle of the proton

an·ti·psy·chot·ic \ˌan-tē-sī-'kä-tik\ *n* : any of the powerful tranquilizers used to treat psychosis — **antipsychotic** *adj*

an·ti·quar·i·an \ˌan-tə-'kwer-ē-ən\ *adj* **1** : of or relating to antiquities **2** : dealing in old books — **antiquarian** *n* — **an·ti·quar·i·an·ism** *n*

an·ti·quary \'an-tə-ˌkwer-ē\ *n, pl* **-quar·ies** : a person who collects or studies antiquities

an·ti·quat·ed \'an-tə-ˌkwā-təd\ *adj* : OUT-OF-DATE, OLD-FASHIONED

¹an·tique \an-'tēk\ *n* : an object made in a bygone period

²antique *adj* **1** : belonging to antiquity **2** : OLD-FASHIONED **3** : of a bygone style or period

³antique *vb* **-tiqued; -tiqu·ing** **1** : to finish or refinish in antique style : give an appearance of age to **2** : to shop around for antiques — **an·tiqu·er** *n*

an·tiq·ui·ty \an-'ti-kwə-tē\ *n, pl* **-ties** **1** : ancient times **2** : great age **3** *pl* : relics of ancient times **4** *pl* : matters relating to ancient culture

an·ti·ret·ro·vi·ral \ˌan-tē-'re-trō-ˌvī-rəl, ˌan-ˌtī-\ *adj* : effective against retroviruses ⟨~ drugs⟩ — **antiretroviral** *n*

antis *pl of* ANTI

an·ti—Sem·i·tism \ˌan-ti-'se-mə-ˌti-zəm, ˌan-ˌtī-\ *n* : hostility toward Jews as a religious or social minority — **an·ti—Sem·ite** \-'se-ˌmīt\ *n* — **an·ti—Se·mit·ic** \-sə-'mi-tik\ *adj*

an·ti·sep·tic \ˌan-tə-'sep-tik\ *adj* **1** : killing or checking the growth of germs that cause decay or infection **2** : scrupulously clean : ASEPTIC **3** : coldly impersonal ⟨an ~ greeting⟩ — **antiseptic** *n* — **an·ti·sep·ti·cal·ly** *adv*

an·ti·se·rum \'an-ti-ˌsir-əm, 'an-ˌtī-\ *n* : a serum containing antibodies

an·ti·so·cial \ˌan-ti-'sō-shəl\ *adj* **1** : disliking the society of others **2** : contrary or hostile to the well-being of society ⟨crime is ~⟩; *esp* : deviating sharply from the social norm — **an·ti·so·cial·ly** *adv*

an·tith·e·sis \an-'ti-thə-səs\ *n, pl* **-e·ses** \-ˌsēz\ **1** : the opposition or contrast of ideas **2** : the direct opposite

an·ti·thet·i·cal \ˌan-tə-'the-ti-kəl\ *also* **an·ti·thet·ic** \-tik\ *adj* : constituting or marked by antithesis — **an·ti·thet·i·cal·ly** \-ti-k(ə-)lē\ *adv*

an·ti·tox·in \ˌan-ti-'täk-sən\ *n* : an antibody that is able to neutralize a particular toxin or disease-causing agent; *also* : an antiserum containing an antitoxin

an·ti·trust \ˌan-ti-ˈtrəst\ *adj* : of or relating to legislation against trusts; *also* : consisting of laws to protect trade and commerce from unlawful restraints and monopolies or unfair business practices

an·ti·ven·in \-ˈve-nən\ *n* : an antitoxin to a venom; *also* : a serum containing such antitoxin

ant·ler \ˈant-lər\ *n* [ME *aunteler,* fr. AF *antiler,* fr. VL **anteocularis* located before the eye, fr. L *ante-* before + *oculus* eye] : one of the paired deciduous solid bone processes on the head of a deer; *also* : a branch of this — **ant·lered** \-lərd\ *adj*

ant lion *n* : any of various insects having a long-jawed larva that digs a conical pit in which it lies in wait for insects (as ants) on which it feeds

an·to·nym \ˈan-tə-ˌnim\ *n* : a word of opposite meaning

ant·sy \ˈant-sē\ *adj* 1 : RESTLESS, IMPATIENT ⟨~ children⟩ 2 : APPREHENSIVE ⟨~ investors⟩

anus \ˈā-nəs\ *n* [L] : the lower or posterior opening of the alimentary canal

an·vil \ˈan-vəl\ *n* 1 : a heavy iron block on which metal is shaped 2 : INCUS

anx·i·ety \aŋ-ˈzī-ə-tē\ *n, pl* **-et·ies** 1 : painful uneasiness of mind usu. over an anticipated ill 2 : abnormal apprehension and fear often accompanied by physiological signs (as sweating and increased pulse), by doubt about the nature and reality of the threat itself, and by self-doubt

anx·ious \ˈaŋk-shəs\ *adj* 1 : uneasy in mind : WORRIED ⟨~ parents⟩ 2 : earnestly wishing : EAGER ⟨~ to leave⟩ — **anx·ious·ly** *adv*

¹any \ˈe-nē\ *adj* 1 : one chosen at random 2 : of whatever number or quantity

²any *pron* 1 : any one or ones ⟨take ~ of the books you like⟩ 2 : any amount ⟨~ of the money not used is to be returned⟩

³any *adv* : to any extent or degree : AT ALL ⟨could not walk ~ farther⟩

any·body \-ˌbä-dē, -bə-\ *pron* : ANYONE

any·how \-ˌhaù\ *adv* 1 : in any way 2 : NEVERTHELESS; *also* : in any case

any·more \ˌe-nē-ˈmór\ *adv* 1 : any longer ⟨won't bother you ~⟩ 2 : at the present time

any·one \ˈe-nē-(ˌ)wən\ *pron* : any person

any·place \-ˌplās\ *adv* : ANYWHERE 1

any·thing \-ˌthiŋ\ *pron* : any thing whatever

any·time \ˈe-nē-ˌtīm\ *adv* : at any time whatever

any·way \-ˌwā\ *adv* : ANYHOW

any·where \-ˌhwer\ *adv* 1 : in or to any place 2 : to any extent ⟨not ~ near done⟩

any·wise \-ˌwīz\ *adv* : in any way whatever

A–OK \ˌā-ō-ˈkā\ *adv or adj* : very definitely OK

A1 \ˈā-ˈwən\ *adj* : of the finest quality

aor·ta \ā-ˈór-tə\ *n, pl* **-tas** *or* **-tae** \-tē\ : the main artery that carries blood from the heart — **aor·tic** \-tik\ *adj*

ap *abbr* 1 apostle 2 apothecaries'

AP *abbr* 1 American plan 2 Associated Press

apace \ə-ˈpās\ *adv* : SWIFTLY

Apache \ə-ˈpa-chē\ *n, pl* **Apache** *or* **Apach·es** \-ˈpa-chēz, -ˈpa-shəz\ : a member of an American Indian people of the southwestern U.S.; *also* : any of the languages of the Apache people — **Apach·e·an** \ə-ˈpa-chē-ən\ *adj or n*

apanage *var of* APPANAGE

apart \ə-ˈpärt\ *adv* 1 : separately in place or time 2 : ASIDE 3 : in two or more parts : to pieces

apart·heid \ə-ˈpär-ˌtāt, -ˌtīt\ *n* [Afrikaans] : a policy of racial segregation formerly practiced in the Republic of So. Africa

apart·ment \ə-ˈpärt-mənt\ *n* : a room or set of rooms occupied as a dwelling; *also* : a building divided into individual dwelling units

ap·a·thy \ˈa-pə-thē\ *n* 1 : lack of emotion 2 : lack of interest : INDIFFERENCE — **ap·a·thet·ic** \ˌa-pə-ˈthe-tik\ *adj* — **ap·a·thet·i·cal·ly** \-ti-k(ə-)lē\ *adv*

ap·a·tite \ˈa-pə-ˌtīt\ *n* : any of a group of minerals that are phosphates of calcium and occur esp. in phosphate rock and in bones and teeth

apato·sau·rus \ə-ˌpa-tə-ˈsór-əs\ *n* : BRONTOSAURUS

APB *abbr* all points bulletin

¹ape \ˈāp\ *n* 1 : any of the larger tailless primates (as a baboon or gorilla); *also* : MONKEY 2 : MIMIC, IMITATOR; *also* : a large uncouth person

²ape *vb* **aped; ap·ing** : IMITATE, MIMIC

ape–man \ˈāp-ˌman\ *n* : a primate intermediate in character between Homo sapiens and the higher apes

aper·çu \ˌa-pər-ˈsü\ *n, pl* **aperçus** \-ˈsüz\ : an immediate impression; *esp* : INSIGHT

aper·i·tif \ˌä-ˌper-ə-ˈtēf\ *n* : an alcoholic drink taken as an appetizer

ap·er·ture \ˈa-pər-ˌchùr, -chər\ *n* : OPENING, HOLE

apex \ˈā-ˌpeks\ *n, pl* **apex·es** *or* **api·ces** \ˈā-pə-ˌsēz, ˈa-\ : the highest point : PEAK

apha·sia \ə-ˈfā-zh(ē-)ə\ *n* : loss or impairment of the power to use or comprehend words — **apha·sic** \-zik\ *adj or n*

aph·e·lion \a-ˈfēl-yən\ *n, pl* **-elia** \-yə\ [NL, fr. *apo-* away from + Gk *hēlios* sun] : the point in an object's orbit most distant from the sun

aphid \ˈā-fəd\ *n* : any of numerous small insects that suck the juices of plants

aphis \ˈā-fəs, ˈa-\ *n, pl* **aphi·des** \-fə-ˌdēz\ : APHID

aph·o·rism \ˈa-fə-ˌri-zəm\ *n* : a short saying stating a general truth : MAXIM — **aph·o·ris·tic** \ˌa-fə-ˈris-tik\ *adj*

aph·ro·di·si·ac \ˌa-frə-ˈdi-zē-ˌak, -ˈdē-zē-\ *n* : an agent that excites sexual desire — **aphrodisiac** *adj*

api·ary \ˈā-pē-ˌer-ē\ *n, pl* **-ar·ies** : a place where bees are kept — **api·a·rist** \-pē-ə-rist\ *n*

api·cal \ˈā-pi-kəl, ˈa-\ *adj* : of, relating to, or situated at an apex — **api·cal·ly** \-k(ə-)lē\ *adv*

apiece \ə-ˈpēs\ *adv* : for each one

aplen·ty \ə-ˈplen-tē\ *adj* : being in plenty or abundance

aplomb \ə-ˈpläm, -ˈpləm\ *n* [F, lit., perpendicularity, fr. MF, fr. *a plomb,* lit., according to the plummet] : complete composure or self-assurance

APO *abbr* army post office

Apoc *abbr* 1 Apocalypse 2 Apocrypha

apoc·a·lypse \ə-ˈpä-kə-ˌlips\ *n* 1 : a writing prophesying a cataclysm in which evil forces are destroyed 2 *cap* — see BIBLE table — **apoc·a·lyp·tic** \-ˌpä-kə-ˈlip-tik\ *also* **apoc·a·lyp·ti·cal** \-ti-kəl\ *adj*

Apoc·ry·pha \ə-ˈpä-krə-fə\ *n* 1 *not cap* : writings of dubious authenticity 2 : books included in the Septuagint and Vulgate but excluded from the Jewish and Protestant canons of the Old Testament — see BIBLE table 3 : early Christian writings not included in the New Testament

apoc·ry·phal \-fəl\ *adj* 1 : not canonical : SPURIOUS 2 *often cap* : of or resembling the Apocrypha — **apoc·ry·phal·ly** *adv* — **apoc·ry·phal·ness** *n*

apo·gee \ˈa-pə-(ˌ)jē\ *n* [F *apogée,* fr. NL *apogaeum,* fr. Gk *apogaion,* fr. *apo* away from + *gē, gaia* earth] : the point at which an orbiting object is farthest from the body being orbited

apo·lit·i·cal \ˌā-pə-ˈli-ti-kəl\ *adj* 1 : having an aversion for or no interest in political affairs 2 : having no political significance — **apo·lit·i·cal·ly** \-k(ə-)lē\ *adv*

apol·o·get·ic \ə-ˌpä-lə-ˈje-tik\ *adj* : expressing apology — **apol·o·get·i·cal·ly** \-ti-k(ə-)lē\ *adv*

apo·lo·gia \ˌa-pə-ˈlō-j(ē-)ə\ *n* : APOLOGY; *esp* : an argument in support or justification

apol·o·gise *Brit var of* APOLOGIZE

apol·o·gize \ə-ˈpä-lə-ˌjīz\ *vb* **-gized; -giz·ing** : to make an apology : express regret — **apol·o·gist** \-jist\ *n*

apol·o·gy \ə-ˈpä-lə-jē\ *n, pl* **-gies** 1 : a formal justification : DEFENSE 2 : an expression of regret for a wrong

ap·o·plexy \ˈa-pə-ˌplek-sē\ *n* : STROKE 3 — **ap·o·plec·tic** \ˌa-pə-ˈplek-tik\ *adj*

ap·o·pto·sis \ˌa-pəp-ˈtō-səs, -pə-ˈtō-\ *n, pl* **-pto·ses** \-ˌsēz\ : a genetically directed process of cell self-destruction

aport \ə-ˈpórt\ *adv* : on or toward the left side of a ship

apos·ta·sy \ə-ˈpäs-tə-sē\ *n, pl* **-sies** : a renunciation or abandonment of a former loyalty (as to a religion) — **apos·tate** \ə-ˈpäs-ˌtāt, -tət\ *adj or n*

a pos·te·ri·o·ri \ˌä-pō-ˌstir-ē-ˈór-ē\ *adj* [L, lit., from the latter] : relating to or derived by reasoning from observed facts — **a posteriori** *adv*

apos·tle \ə-ˈpä-səl\ *n* 1 : one of the group composed of Jesus' 12 original disciples and Paul 2 : the first prominent missionary to a region or group 3 : a person who initiates or first advocates a great reform — **apos·tle·ship** *n*

ap·os·tol·ic \ˌa-pə-ˈstä-lik\ *adj* 1 : of or relating to an apostle or to the New Testament apostles 2 : of or relating to a succession of spiritual authority from the apostles 3 : PAPAL

¹apos·tro·phe \ə-ˈpäs-trə-(ˌ)fē\ *n* : the rhetorical addressing of a usu. absent person or a usu. personified thing (as in "O grave, where is thy victory?")

²**apostrophe** *n* : a punctuation mark ' used esp. to indicate the possessive case or the omission of a letter or figure

apos·tro·phise *Brit var of* APOSTROPHIZE

apos·tro·phize \ə-'päs-trə-ˌfīz\ *vb* **-phized; -phiz·ing** : to address as if present or capable of understanding

apothecaries' weight *n* : a system of weights based on the troy pound and ounce and used chiefly by pharmacists — see WEIGHT table

apoth·e·cary \ə-'pä-thə-ˌker-ē\ *n, pl* **-car·ies** [ME *apothecarie*, fr. ML *apothecarius*, fr. LL, shopkeeper, fr. L *apotheca* storehouse, fr. Gk *apothēkē*, fr. *apotithenai* to put away] : DRUGGIST

ap·o·thegm \'a-pə-ˌthem\ *n* : APHORISM

apo·the·o·sis \ə-ˌpä-thē-'ō-səs, ˌa-pə-'thē-ə-səs\ *n, pl* **-o·ses** \-ˌsēz\ **1** : DEIFICATION **2** : the perfect example

¹**app** \'ap\ *n* : APPLICATION 6

²**app** *abbr* **1** apparatus **2** appendix

ap·pall *also* **ap·pal** \ə-'pȯl\ *vb* **ap·palled; ap·pall·ing** : to overcome with horror : DISMAY

Ap·pa·loo·sa \ˌa-pə-'lü-sə\ *n* : any of a breed of saddle horses developed in western No. America and usu. having a white or solid-colored coat with small spots

ap·pa·nage *also* **a·pa·nage** \'a-pə-nij\ *n* **1** : provision (as a grant of land) made by a sovereign or legislative body for dependent members of the royal family **2** : a rightful adjunct

ap·pa·ra·tus \ˌa-pə-'ra-təs, -'rä-\ *n, pl* **-tus·es** *or* **-tus** [L] **1** : a set of materials or equipment for a particular use **2** : a complex machine or device : MECHANISM **3** : the organization of a political party or underground movement

¹**ap·par·el** \ə-'per-əl\ *vb* **-eled** *or* **-elled; -el·ing** *or* **-el·ling** **1** : CLOTHE **2** : ADORN

²**apparel** *n* : CLOTHING, DRESS

ap·par·ent \ə-'per-ənt\ *adj* **1** : open to view : VISIBLE **2** : EVIDENT, OBVIOUS **3** : appearing as real or true : SEEMING

ap·par·ent·ly \-lē\ *adv* : it seems apparent

ap·pa·ri·tion \ˌa-pə-'ri-shən\ *n* : a supernatural appearance : GHOST

ap·peal \ə-'pēl\ *vb* **1** : to take steps to have (a case) reheard in a higher court **2** : to plead for help, corroboration, or decision **3** : to arouse a sympathetic response — **appeal** *n*

ap·pear \ə-'pir\ *vb* **1** : to become visible **2** : to come formally before an authority **3** : SEEM **4** : to become evident **5** : to come before the public

ap·pear·ance \ə-'pir-əns\ *n* **1** : outward aspect : LOOK **2** : the act of appearing **3** : PHENOMENON

ap·pease \ə-'pēz\ *vb* **ap·peased; ap·peas·ing** **1** : to cause to subside : ALLAY **2** : PACIFY, CONCILIATE; *esp* : to buy off by concessions — **ap·pease·ment** *n* — **ap·peas·able** \-'pē-zə-bəl\ *adj*

ap·pel·lant \ə-'pe-lənt\ *n* : one who appeals esp. from a judicial decision

ap·pel·late \ə-'pe-lət\ *adj* : having power to review decisions of a lower court

ap·pel·la·tion \ˌa-pə-'lā-shən\ *n* : NAME, DESIGNATION

ap·pel·lee \ˌa-pə-'lē\ *n* : one against whom an appeal is taken

ap·pend \ə-'pend\ *vb* : to attach esp. as something additional : AFFIX

ap·pend·age \ə-'pen-dij\ *n* **1** : something appended to a principal or greater thing **2** : a projecting part (as an antenna) of an animal or plant body; *esp* : an arm, leg, or similar part ✦ **Synonyms** ACCESSORY, ADJUNCT, APPENDIX, APPURTENANCE

ap·pen·dec·to·my \ˌa-pən-'dek-tə-mē\ *n, pl* **-mies** : surgical removal of the intestinal appendix

ap·pen·di·ci·tis \ə-ˌpen-də-'sī-təs\ *n* : inflammation of the intestinal appendix

ap·pen·dix \ə-'pen-diks\ *n, pl* **-dix·es** *or* **-di·ces** \-də-ˌsēz\ [L] **1** : supplementary matter added at the end of a book **2** : a narrow blind tube usu. about three or four inches long that extends from the cecum in the lower right-hand part of the abdomen

ap·per·tain \ˌa-pər-'tān\ *vb* : to belong as a rightful part or privilege

ap·pe·tis·er, ap·pe·tis·ing *Brit var of* APPETIZER, APPETIZING

ap·pe·tite \'a-pə-ˌtīt\ *n* [ME *apetit*, fr. AF, fr. L *appetitus*, fr. *appetere* to strive after, fr. *ad-* to + *petere* to go to] **1** : natural desire for satisfying some want or need esp. for food **2** : TASTE, PREFERENCE

ap·pe·tiz·er \'a-pə-ˌtī-zər\ *n* : a food or drink taken just before a meal to stimulate the appetite

ap·pe·tiz·ing \-ziŋ\ *adj* : tempting to the appetite — **ap·pe·tiz·ing·ly** *adv*

appl *abbr* applied

ap·plaud \ə-'plȯd\ *vb* : to show approval esp. by clapping

ap·plause \ə-'plȯz\ *n* : approval publicly expressed (as by clapping)

ap·ple \'a-pəl\ *n* : a rounded fruit with firm white flesh and a seedy core; *also* : a tree that bears this fruit

ap·ple·jack \-ˌjak\ *n* : a liquor distilled from fermented cider

ap·plet \'a-plət\ *n* : a short computer program esp. for performing a simple specific task

ap·pli·ance \ə-'plī-əns\ *n* **1** : INSTRUMENT, DEVICE **2** : a piece of household equipment (as a stove or toaster) operated by gas or electricity

ap·pli·ca·ble \'a-pli-kə-bəl, ə-'pli-kə-\ *adj* : capable of being applied : RELEVANT — **ap·pli·ca·bil·i·ty** \ˌa-pli-kə-'bi-lə-tē, ə-ˌpli-kə-\ *n*

ap·pli·cant \'a-pli-kənt\ *n* : one who applies ⟨a job ∼⟩

ap·pli·ca·tion \ˌa-plə-'kā-shən\ *n* **1** : the act of applying **2** : assiduous attention **3** : REQUEST; *also* : a form used in making a request **4** : something placed or spread on a surface **5** : capacity for use **6** : a program (as a word processor) that performs one of a computer's major tasks

ap·pli·ca·tor \'a-plə-ˌkā-tər\ *n* : a device for applying a substance (as medicine or polish)

ap·plied \ə-'plīd\ *adj* : put to practical use ⟨∼ art⟩

ap·pli·qué \ˌa-plə-'kā\ *n* [F] : a fabric decoration cut out and fastened to a larger piece of material — **appliqué** *vb*

ap·ply \ə-'plī\ *vb* **ap·plied; ap·ply·ing** **1** : to put to practical use **2** : to place in contact : put or spread on a surface **3** : to employ with close attention **4** : to have reference or connection **5** : to submit a request

ap·point \ə-'pȯint\ *vb* **1** : to fix or set officially ⟨∼ a day for trial⟩ **2** : to name officially **3** : to fit out : EQUIP

ap·poin·tee \ə-ˌpȯin-'tē, ˌa-\ *n* : a person appointed

ap·poin·tive \ə-'pȯin-tiv\ *adj* : subject to appointment

ap·point·ment \ə-'pȯint-mənt\ *n* **1** : the act of appointing **2** : an arrangement for a meeting **3** *pl* : FURNISHINGS, EQUIPMENT **4** : a nonelective office or position

ap·por·tion \ə-'pȯr-shən\ *vb* : to distribute proportionately : ALLOT — **ap·por·tion·ment** *n*

ap·po·site \'a-pə-zət\ *adj* : APPROPRIATE, RELEVANT — **ap·po·site·ly** *adv* — **ap·po·site·ness** *n*

ap·po·si·tion \ˌa-pə-'zi-shən\ *n* : a grammatical construction in which a noun or pronoun is followed by another that has the same referent (as *the poet* and *Burns* in "a biography of the poet Burns")

ap·pos·i·tive \ə-'pä-zə-tiv, a-\ *adj* : of, relating to, or standing in grammatical apposition — **appositive** *n*

ap·praise \ə-'prāz\ *vb* **ap·praised; ap·prais·ing** : to set a value on — **ap·prais·al** \-'prā-zəl\ *n* — **ap·prais·er** *n*

ap·pre·cia·ble \ə-'prē-shə-bəl\ *adj* : large enough to be recognized and measured — **ap·pre·cia·bly** *adv*

ap·pre·ci·ate \ə-'prē-shē-ˌāt\ *vb* **-at·ed; -at·ing** **1** : to value justly **2** : to be aware of **3** : to be grateful for **4** : to increase in value — **ap·pre·ci·a·tion** \-ˌprē-shē-'ā-shən\ *n*

ap·pre·cia·tive \ə-'prē-shə-tiv, -shē-ˌāt-\ *adj* : having or showing appreciation — **ap·pre·cia·tive·ly** *adv*

ap·pre·hend \ˌa-pri-'hend\ *vb* **1** : ARREST **2** : to become aware of **3** : to look forward to with dread **4** : UNDERSTAND — **ap·pre·hen·sion** \-'hen-chən\ *n*

ap·pre·hen·sive \-'hen-siv\ *adj* : viewing the future with anxiety — **ap·pre·hen·sive·ly** *adv* — **ap·pre·hen·sive·ness** *n*

¹**ap·pren·tice** \ə-'pren-təs\ *n* **1** : a person learning a craft under a skilled worker **2** : BEGINNER — **ap·pren·tice·ship** *n*

²**apprentice** *vb* **-ticed; -tic·ing** : to bind or set at work as an apprentice

ap·prise \ə-'prīz\ *vb* **ap·prised; ap·pris·ing** : INFORM ⟨*apprised* him of his rights⟩

ap·proach \ə-'prōch\ *vb* **1** : to move nearer to ⟨∼ the bench⟩ **2** : to be almost the same as **3** : to make ad-

vances to esp. for the purpose of creating a desired result **4** : to take preliminary steps toward ⟨∼ the subject carefully⟩ — **approach** *n* — **ap·proach·able** *adj*
ap·pro·ba·tion \ˌa-prə-'bā-shən\ *n* : APPROVAL
¹**ap·pro·pri·ate** \ə-'prō-prē-ˌāt\ *vb* **-at·ed; -at·ing 1** : to take possession of **2** : to set apart for a particular use
²**ap·pro·pri·ate** \ə-'prō-prē-ət\ *adj* : fitted to a purpose or use : SUITABLE ✦ *Synonyms* PROPER, FIT, APT, BEFITTING — **ap·pro·pri·ate·ly** *adv* — **ap·pro·pri·ate·ness** *n*
ap·pro·pri·a·tion \ə-ˌprō-prē-'ā-shən\ *n* : something (as money) set aside by formal action for a specific use
ap·prov·al \ə-'prü-vəl\ *n* : an act of approving — **on approval** : subject to a prospective buyer's acceptance or refusal
ap·prove \ə-'prüv\ *vb* **ap·proved; ap·prov·ing 1** : to have or express a favorable opinion of **2** : to accept as satisfactory : RATIFY ⟨∼ the treaty⟩
approx *abbr* approximate; approximately
¹**ap·prox·i·mate** \ə-'präk-sə-mət\ *adj* : nearly correct or exact ⟨an ∼ count⟩ — **ap·prox·i·mate·ly** *adv*
²**ap·prox·i·mate** \-ˌmāt\ *vb* **-mat·ed; -mat·ing** : to come or bring near or close — **ap·prox·i·ma·tion** \ə-ˌpräk-sə-'mā-shən\ *n*
appt *abbr* appoint; appointed; appointment
ap·pur·te·nance \ə-'pərt-nəns, -'pər-tə-nəns\ *n* : something that belongs to or goes with another thing ✦ *Synonyms* ACCESSORY, ADJUNCT, APPENDAGE, APPENDIX — **ap·pur·te·nant** \ə-'pərt-nənt, -'pər-tə-nənt\ *adj*
Apr *abbr* April
APR *abbr* annual percentage rate
apri·cot \'a-prə-ˌkät, 'ā-\ *n* [alter. of earlier *abrecock*, ultim. fr. Ar *al-birqūq*, ultim. fr. L (*persicum*) *praecox*, lit., early-ripening (peach)] : an oval orange-colored fruit resembling the related peach and plum in flavor; *also* : a tree bearing apricots
April \'ā-prəl\ *n* [ME, fr. AF & L; AF *avrill*, fr. L *Aprilis*] : the 4th month of the year
a pri·o·ri \ˌä-prē-'òr-ē\ *adj* [L, from the former] **1** : characterized by or derived by reasoning from self-evident propositions **2** : independent of experience — **a priori** *adv*
apron \'ā-prən\ *n* [ME, alter. (fr. misdivision of *a napron*) of *napron*, fr. MF *naperon*, dim. of *nape* cloth, modif. of L *mappa* napkin] **1** : a garment tied over the front of the body to protect the clothes **2** : a paved area for parking or handling airplanes — **aproned** *adj*
¹**ap·ro·pos** \ˌa-prə-'pō, 'a-prə-ˌpō\ *adv* [F *à propos*, lit., to the purpose] **1** : OPPORTUNELY **2** : in passing : INCIDENTALLY
²**apropos** *adj* : being to the point
apropos of *prep* : with regard to
apse \'aps\ *n* : a projecting usu. semicircular and vaulted part of a building (as a church)
¹**apt** \'apt\ *adj* **1** : well adapted : SUITABLE **2** : having an habitual tendency : LIKELY **3** : quick to learn — **apt·ly** *adv* — **apt·ness** \'apt-nəs\ *n*
²**apt** *abbr* **1** apartment **2** aptitude
ap·ti·tude \'ap-tə-ˌtüd, -ˌtyüd\ *n* **1** : natural ability : TALENT **2** : capacity for learning **3** : APPROPRIATENESS
aqua \'a-kwə, 'ä-\ *n* : a light greenish blue color
aqua·cul·ture \'a-kwə-ˌkəl-chər, 'ä-\ *n* : the cultivation of aquatic organisms (as fish or shellfish) for human use esp. as food — **aqua·cul·tur·ist** \-chə-rist\ *n*
aqua·ma·rine \ˌa-kwə-mə-'rēn, ˌä-\ *n* **1** : a bluish green gem **2** : a pale blue to light greenish blue
aqua·naut \'a-kwə-ˌnòt, 'ä-\ *n* : a person who lives in an underwater shelter for an extended period
aqua·plane \-ˌplān\ *n* : a board towed behind a motorboat and ridden by a person standing on it — **aquaplane** *vb*
aqua re·gia \ˌa-kwə-'rē-j(ē-)ə\ *n* [NL, lit., royal water] : a mixture of nitric and hydrochloric acids that dissolves gold or platinum
aquar·i·um \ə-'kwer-ē-əm\ *n, pl* **-i·ums** *or* **-ia** \-ē-ə\ **1** : a container (as a glass tank) in which living aquatic animals or plants are kept **2** : a place where aquatic animals and plants are kept and shown
Aquar·i·us \ə-'kwer-ē-əs\ *n* [L, lit., water carrier] **1** : a zodiacal constellation between Capricorn and Pisces usu. pictured as a man pouring water : the 11th sign of the zodiac in astrology; *also* : one born under this sign

¹**aquat·ic** \ə-'kwä-tik, -'kwa-\ *adj* **1** : growing or living in or frequenting water **2** : performed in or on water
²**aquatic** *n* : an aquatic animal or plant
aqua·vit \'ä-kwə-ˌvēt\ *n* : a clear liquor flavored with caraway seeds
aqua vi·tae \ˌa-kwə-'vī-tē, ˌä-\ *n* [ME, fr. ML, lit., water of life] : a strong alcoholic liquor (as brandy)
aq·ue·duct \'a-kwə-ˌdəkt\ *n* **1** : a conduit for carrying running water **2** : a structure carrying a canal over a river or hollow **3** : a passage in a bodily part

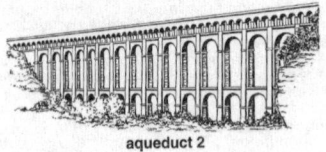

aqueduct 2

aque·ous \'ā-kwē-əs, 'a-\ *adj* **1** : WATERY **2** : made of, by, or with water
aqueous humor *n* : a clear fluid occupying the space between the lens and the cornea of the eye
aqui·fer \'a-kwə-fər, 'ä-\ *n* : a water-bearing stratum of permeable rock, sand, or gravel
aq·ui·line \'a-kwə-ˌlīn, -lən\ *adj* **1** : of or resembling an eagle **2** : hooked like an eagle's beak ⟨an ∼ nose⟩
ar *abbr* arrival; arrive
Ar *symbol* argon
AR *abbr* Arkansas
-ar *adj suffix* : of or relating to ⟨molecul*ar*⟩ : being ⟨spectacul*ar*⟩ : resembling ⟨oracul*ar*⟩
Ar·ab \'a-rəb\ *n* **1** : a member of a Semitic people of the Arabian peninsula in southwestern Asia **2** : a member of an Arabic-speaking people — **Arab** *adj* — **Ara·bi·an** \ə-'rā-bē-ən\ *adj or n*
ar·a·besque \ˌa-rə-'besk\ *n* : a design of interlacing lines forming figures of flowers, foliage, and sometimes animals — **arabesque** *adj*
¹**Ar·a·bic** \'a-rə-bik\ *n* : a Semitic language of southwestern Asia and northern Africa
²**Arabic** *adj* **1** : of or relating to the Arabs, Arabic, or the Arabian peninsula in southwestern Asia **2** : expressed in or making use of Arabic numerals
Arabic numeral *n* : any of the number symbols 0, 1, 2, 3, 4, 5, 6, 7, 8, 9
ar·a·ble \'a-rə-bəl\ *adj* : fit for or used for the growing of crops ⟨∼ land⟩
arach·nid \ə-'rak-nəd\ *n* : any of a class of usu. 8-legged arthropods comprising the spiders, scorpions, mites, and ticks — **arachnid** *adj*
Ar·a·ma·ic \ˌa-rə-'mā-ik\ *n* : an ancient Semitic language
ar·a·mid \'a-rə-məd, -ˌmid\ *n* : any of several light but very strong heat-resistant synthetic materials used esp. in textiles and plastics
Arap·a·ho *or* **Arap·a·hoe** \ə-'ra-pə-ˌhō\ *n, pl* **-ho** *or* **-hos** *or* **-hoe** *or* **-hoes** : a member of an American Indian people of the western U.S.
ar·bi·ter \'är-bə-tər\ *n* : one having power to decide : JUDGE
ar·bi·trage \'är-bə-ˌträzh\ *n* [F, fr. MF, arbitration] : the purchase and sale of the same or equivalent securities in different markets in order to profit from price discrepancies
ar·bi·tra·geur \ˌär-bə-(ˌ)trä-'zhər\ *or* **ar·bi·trag·er** \'är-bə-ˌträ-zhər\ *n* : one who practices arbitrage
ar·bit·ra·ment \är-'bi-trə-mənt\ *n* **1** : the act of deciding a dispute **2** : the judgment given by an arbitrator
ar·bi·trary \'är-bə-ˌtrer-ē\ *adj* **1** : AUTOCRATIC, DESPOTIC **2** : determined by will or caprice : selected at random — **ar·bi·trari·ly** \ˌär-bə-'trer-ə-lē\ *adv* — **ar·bi·trari·ness** \'är-bə-ˌtrer-ē-nəs\ *n*
ar·bi·trate \'är-bə-ˌträt\ *vb* **-trat·ed; -trat·ing 1** : to act as arbitrator **2** : to act on as arbitrator **3** : to submit for decision to an arbitrator — **ar·bi·tra·tion** \ˌär-bə-'trā-shən\ *n*
ar·bi·tra·tor \'är-bə-ˌträ-tər\ *n* : one chosen to settle differences between two parties in a controversy
ar·bor \'är-bər\ *n* [ME *erber, herber* garden, fr. AF, fr.

herbe herb, grass] : a shelter formed of or covered with vines or branches

ar·bo·re·al \är-'bòr-ē-əl\ *adj* **1** : of, relating to, or resembling a tree **2** : living in trees ⟨~ monkeys⟩

ar·bo·re·tum \,är-bə-'rē-təm\ *n, pl* **-retums** *or* **-re·ta** \-tə\ [L, plantation of trees, fr. *arbor* tree] : a place where trees and plants are grown for scientific and educational purposes

ar·bor·vi·tae \,är-bər-'vī-tē\ *n* : any of various evergreen trees and shrubs with scalelike leaves that are related to the cypresses

ar·bour *chiefly Brit var of* ARBOR

ar·bu·tus \är-'byü-təs\ *n* : TRAILING ARBUTUS

¹arc \'ärk\ *n* **1** : a sustained luminous discharge of electricity (as between two electrodes) **2** : a continuous portion of a curved line (as part of the circumference of a circle)

²arc *vb* **arced** \'ärkt\; **arc·ing** \'är-kiŋ\ : to form an electric arc

ARC *abbr* **1** AIDS-related complex **2** American Red Cross

ar·cade \är-'kād\ *n* **1** : an arched or covered passageway; *esp* : one lined with shops **2** : a row of arches with their supporting columns **3** : an amusement center having coin-operated games

ar·cane \är-'kān\ *adj* : SECRET, MYSTERIOUS

¹arch \'ärch\ *n* **1** : a curved structure spanning an opening (as a door) **2** : something resembling an arch **3** : ARCHWAY

²arch *vb* **1** : to cover with an arch **2** : to form or bend into an arch

³arch *adj* **1** : CHIEF, EMINENT ⟨my ~ enemy⟩ **2** : ROGUISH, MISCHIEVOUS; *also* : deliberately playful or impudent ⟨~ comments⟩ — **arch·ly** *adv* — **arch·ness** *n*

⁴arch *abbr* architect; architectural; architecture

ar·chae·ol·o·gy *or* **ar·che·ol·o·gy** \,är-kē-'ä-lə-jē\ *n* : the study of past human life as revealed by relics left by ancient peoples — **ar·chae·o·log·i·cal** \-ə-'lä-ji-kəl\ *adj* — **ar·chae·ol·o·gist** \-'ä-lə-jist\ *n*

ar·cha·ic \är-'kā-ik\ *adj* **1** : having the characteristics of the language of the past and surviving chiefly in specialized uses ⟨~ words⟩ **2** : belonging to an earlier time : ANTIQUATED — **ar·cha·i·cal·ly** \-i-k(ə-)lē\ *adv*

arch·an·gel \'är-,kān-jəl\ *n* : a chief angel

arch·bish·op \ärch-'bi-shəp\ *n* : a bishop of high rank

arch·bish·op·ric \-shə-(,)prik\ *n* : the jurisdiction or office of an archbishop

arch·con·ser·va·tive \(,)ärch-kən-'sər-və-tiv\ *n* : an extreme conservative — **archconservative** *adj*

arch·dea·con \-'dē-kən\ *n* : a church official who assists a diocesan bishop in ceremonial or administrative functions

arch·di·o·cese \-'dī-ə-səs, -,sēz\ *n* : the diocese of an archbishop

arch·duke \-'dük, -'dyük\ *n* **1** : a sovereign prince **2** : a prince of the imperial family of Austria

Ar·che·an \är-'kē-ən\ *adj* : of, relating to, or being the earliest eon of geologic history — **Archean** *n*

arch·en·e·my \,ärch-'e-nə-mē\ *n, pl* **-mies** : a principal enemy

Ar·cheo·zo·ic \,är-kē-ə-'zō-ik\ *adj* : ARCHEAN — **Archeozoic** *n*

ar·chery \'är-chə-rē\ *n* : the art or practice of shooting with bow and arrows — **ar·cher** \'är-chər\ *n*

ar·che·type \'är-ki-,tīp\ *n* : the original pattern or model of all things of the same type — **ar·che·typ·al** \,är-kə-'tī-pəl\ *adj*

arch·fiend \,ärch-'fēnd\ *n* : a chief fiend; *esp* : SATAN

ar·chi·epis·co·pal \,är-kē-ə-'pis-kə-pəl\ *adj* : of or relating to an archbishop

ar·chi·man·drite \,är-kə-'man-,drīt\ *n* : a dignitary in an Eastern church ranking below a bishop

ar·chi·pel·a·go \,är-kə-'pe-lə-,gō, ,är-chə-\ *n, pl* **-goes** *or* **-gos** : a group of islands

ar·chi·tect \'är-kə-,tekt\ *n* **1** : a person who plans buildings and oversees their construction **2** : a person who designs and guides a plan or undertaking

ar·chi·tec·ture \'är-kə-,tek-chər\ *n* **1** : the art or science of planning and building structures **2** : a method or style of building **3** : the manner in which the elements (as of a design) or components (of a computer) are arranged or

organized — **ar·chi·tec·tur·al** \,är-kə-'tek-chə-rəl, -'tek-shrəl\ *adj* — **ar·chi·tec·tur·al·ly** *adv*

ar·chi·trave \'är-kə-,träv\ *n* : the supporting horizontal member just above the columns in a building in the classical style of architecture

ar·chive \'är-,kīv\ *n* **1** : a place for keeping public records; *also* : public records — often used in pl. **2** : a repository esp. of information

ar·chi·vist \'är-kə-vist, -,kī-\ *n* : a person in charge of archives

ar·chon \'är-,kän, -kən\ *n* : a chief magistrate of ancient Athens

arch·ri·val \'ärch-'rī-vəl\ *n* : a principal rival

arch·way \'ärch-,wā\ *n* : a passageway under an arch; *also* : an arch over a passage

arc lamp *n* : a gas-filled electric lamp that produces light when a current arcs between incandescent electrodes

¹arc·tic \'ärk-tik, 'är-tik\ *adj* [ME *artik*, fr. L *arcticus*, fr. Gk *arktikos*, fr. *arktos* bear, Ursa Major, north] **1** *often cap* : of or relating to the north pole or the region near it **2** : FRIGID

²arc·tic \'är-tik, 'ärk-tik\ *n* : a rubber overshoe that reaches to the ankle or above

arctic circle *n, often cap A&C* : the parallel of latitude that is approximately 66½ degrees north of the equator

-ard *also* **-art** *n suffix* : one that is characterized by performing some action, possessing some quality, or being associated with some thing esp. conspicuously or excessively ⟨bragg*art*⟩ ⟨dull*ard*⟩

ar·dent \'är-dⁿnt\ *adj* **1** : characterized by warmth of feeling : PASSIONATE **2** : FIERY, HOT ⟨an ~ sun⟩ **3** : GLOWING ⟨~ eyes⟩ — **ar·dent·ly** *adv*

ar·dor \'är-dər\ *n* **1** : warmth of feeling : ZEAL **2** : sexual excitement

ar·dour *chiefly Brit var of* ARDOR

ar·du·ous \'är-jə-wəs, -dyü-wəs\ *adj* : DIFFICULT, LABORIOUS — **ar·du·ous·ly** *adv* — **ar·du·ous·ness** *n*

¹are *pres 2d sing or pres pl of* BE

²are \'er\ *n* — see METRIC SYSTEM table

ar·ea \'er-ē-ə\ *n* **1** : a flat surface or space **2** : the amount of surface included (as within the lines of a geometric figure) **3** : range or extent of some thing or concept : FIELD **4** : REGION

area code *n* : a usu. 3-digit number that identifies each telephone service area in a country (as the U.S. or Canada)

are·na \ə-'rē-nə\ *n* [L *harena, arena* sand, sandy place] **1** : an enclosed area used for public entertainment **2** : a sphere of activity or competition

ar·gen·tite \'är-jən-,tīt\ *n* : a dark gray or black mineral of metallic luster that is an important ore of silver

ar·gon \'är-,gän\ *n* [Gk, neut. of *argos* idle, lazy, fr. *a-* not + *ergon* work; fr. its relative inertness] : a colorless odorless gaseous chemical element found in the air and used for filling electric lamps

ar·go·sy \'är-gə-sē\ *n, pl* **-sies** **1** : a large merchant ship **2** : FLEET

ar·got \'är-gət, -,gō\ *n* : the language of a particular group or class

argu·able \'är-gyü-ə-bəl\ *adj* : open to argument, dispute, or question

ar·gu·ably \'är-gyü-(ə)blē\ *adv* : as may be argued or shown by argument

ar·gue \'är-gyü\ *vb* **ar·gued; ar·gu·ing** **1** : to give reasons for or against something **2** : to contend in words : DISPUTE **3** : DEBATE **4** : to persuade by giving reasons

ar·gu·ment \'är-gyə-mənt\ *n* **1** : a reason offered in proof **2** : discourse intended to persuade **3** : QUARREL

ar·gu·men·ta·tion \,är-gyə-mən-'tā-shən\ *n* : the art of formal discussion

ar·gu·men·ta·tive \,är-gyə-'men-tə-tiv\ *adj* : inclined to argue

ar·gyle *also* **ar·gyll** \'är-,gī(-ə)l\ *n, often cap* : a geometric knitting pattern of varicolored diamonds on a single background color; *also* : a sock knit in this pattern

aria \'är-ē-ə\ *n* : an accompanied elaborate vocal solo forming part of a larger work

ari·a·ry \,ä-rē-'ä-rē\ *n, pl* **ariary** — see MONEY table

ar·id \'a-rəd\ *adj* : very dry; *esp* : having insufficient rainfall to support agriculture — **arid·i·ty** \ə-'ri-də-tē\ *n*

Ar·i·es \'er-,ēz, -ē-,ēz\ *n* [L, lit., ram] **1** : a zodiacal constellation between Pisces and Taurus pictured as a ram **2** : the 1st sign of the zodiac in astrology; *also* : one born under this sign

aright \ə-'rīt\ *adv* : RIGHT, CORRECTLY

arise \ə-'rīz\ *vb* **arose** \-'rōz\; **aris·en** \-'ri-z°n\; **aris·ing** \-'rī-ziŋ\ **1** : to get up **2** : ORIGINATE **3** : ASCEND
✦ *Synonyms* RISE, DERIVE, SPRING, ISSUE

ar·is·toc·ra·cy \ₐa-rə-'stä-krə-sē\ *n, pl* **-cies** **1** : government by a noble or privileged class; *also* : a state so governed **2** : the governing class of an aristocracy **3** : UPPER CLASS — **aris·to·crat** \ə-'ris-tə-ₐkrat\ *n* — **aris·to·crat·ic** \ə-ₐris-tə-'kra-tik\ *adj*

arith *abbr* arithmetic; arithmetical

arith·me·tic \ə-'rith-mə-ₐtik\ *n* **1** : a branch of mathematics that deals with computations usu. with nonnegative real numbers **2** : COMPUTATION, CALCULATION — **arith·met·ic** \ₐer-ith-'me-tik\ *or* **ar·ith·met·i·cal** \-ti-kəl\ *adj* — **ar·ith·met·i·cal·ly** \-ti-k(ə-)lē\ *adv* — **arith·me·ti·cian** \ə-ₐrith-mə-'ti-shən\ *n*

arithmetic mean *n* : the sum of a set of numbers divided by the number of numbers in the set

Ariz *abbr* Arizona

ark \'ärk\ *n* **1** : a boat held to resemble that of Noah's at the time of the Flood **2** : the sacred chest in a synagogue representing to Hebrews the presence of God; *also* : the repository for the scrolls of the Torah

Ark *abbr* Arkansas

¹arm \'ärm\ *n* [ME, fr. OE *earm*] **1** : a human upper limb and esp. the part between the shoulder and wrist; *also* : a corresponding limb of a 2-footed vertebrate **2** : something resembling an arm in shape or position ⟨an ∼ of a chair⟩ ⟨the eight ∼s of an octopus⟩ **3** : POWER, MIGHT ⟨the ∼ of the law⟩ — **armed** \'ärmd\ *adj* — **arm·less** *adj*

²arm *vb* [ME, fr. AF *armer*, fr. L *armare*, fr. *arma* weapons, tools] : to furnish with weapons

³arm *n* **1** : WEAPON **2** : a branch of the military forces **3** *pl* : the hereditary heraldic devices of a family

ar·ma·da \är-'mä-də, -'mā-\ *n* : a fleet of warships

ar·ma·dil·lo \ₐär-mə-'di-lō\ *n, pl* **-los** [Sp, fr. dim. of *armado* armed one] : any of several small burrowing mammals with the head and body protected by an armor of bony plates

Ar·ma·ged·don \ₐär-mə-'ge-d°n\ *n* : a final conclusive battle between the forces of good and evil; *also* : the site or time of this

ar·ma·ment \'är-mə-mənt\ *n* **1** : military strength **2** : arms and equipment (as of a tank or combat unit) **3** : the process of preparing for war

ar·ma·ture \'är-mə-ₐchùr, -chər\ *n* **1** : a protective covering or structure (as the spines of a cactus) **2** : the rotating part of an electric generator or motor; *also* : the movable part in an electromagnetic device (as a loudspeaker)

arm·chair \'ärm-ₐcher\ *n* : a chair with armrests

armed forces *n pl* : the combined military, naval, and air forces of a nation

Ar·me·nian \är-'mē-nē-ən\ *n* **1** : a native or inhabitant of Armenia **2** : the Indo-European language of the Armenians

arm·ful \'ärm-ₐfül\ *n, pl* **armfuls** *or* **arms·ful** \'ärmz-ₐfül\ : as much as the arm or arms can hold

arm·hole \'ärm-ₐhōl\ *n* : an opening for the arm in a garment

ar·mi·stice \'är-mə-stəs\ *n* : temporary suspension of hostilities by mutual agreement : TRUCE

arm·let \'ärm-lot\ *n* : a band worn around the upper arm

ar·mor \'är-mər\ *n* **1** : protective covering **2** : armored forces and vehicles — **ar·mored** \-mərd\ *adj*

ar·mor·er \'är-mər-ər\ *n* **1** : a person who makes arms and armor **2** : a person who services firearms

ar·mo·ri·al \är-'mȯr-ē-əl\ *adj* : of or bearing heraldic arms

ar·mory \'är-mə-rē\ *n, pl* **ar·mor·ies** **1** : a place where arms are stored **2** : a factory where arms are made

ar·mour, ar·moury *chiefly Brit var of* ARMOR, ARMORY

arm·pit \'ärm-ₐpit\ *n* : the hollow under the junction of the arm and shoulder

arm·rest \-ₐrest\ *n* : a support for the arm

ar·my \'är-mē\ *n, pl* **armies** **1** : a body of men organized for war **2** *often cap* : the complete military organization of a country for land warfare **3** : a great number **4** : a body of persons organized to advance a cause

army ant *n* : any of various nomadic social ants

ar·my·worm \'är-mē-ₐwərm\ *n* : any of numerous moths whose larvae move about destroying crops

aro·ma \ə-'rō-mə\ *n* : a usu. pleasing odor : FRAGRANCE — **ar·o·mat·ic** \ₐar-ə-'ma-tik\ *adj*

aro·ma·ther·a·py \ə-ₐrō-mə-'ther-ə-pē\ *n* : massage with a preparation of fragrant oils extracted from herbs, flowers, and fruits

arose *past of* ARISE

¹around \ə-'raùnd\ *adv* **1** : in a circle or in circumference ⟨a tree five feet ∼⟩ **2** : in or along a circuit ⟨the road goes ∼ by the lake⟩ **3** : on all sides ⟨nothing for miles ∼⟩ **4** : NEARBY ⟨wait ∼ awhile⟩ **5** : from one place to another ⟨travels ∼ on business⟩ **6** : in an opposite direction ⟨turn ∼⟩ **7** — used with some verbs to indicate continued action ⟨joking ∼⟩ **8** : APPROXIMATELY ⟨cost ∼ $5⟩

²around *prep* **1** : SURROUNDING ⟨trees ∼ the house⟩ **2** : to or on another side of ⟨∼ the corner⟩ **3** : NEAR ⟨stayed right ∼ home⟩ **4** : along the circuit of ⟨go ∼ the world⟩

arouse \ə-'raùz\ *vb* **aroused; arous·ing** **1** : to awaken from sleep **2** : to stir up : EXCITE — **arous·al** \-'raù-zəl\ *n*

ar·peg·gio \är-'pe-jē-ₐō, -'pe-jō\ *n, pl* **-gios** [It fr. *arpeggiare* to play on the harp, fr. *arpa* harp] : a chord whose notes are performed in succession and not simultaneously

arr *abbr* **1** arranged **2** arrival; arrive

ar·raign \ə-'rān\ *vb* **1** : to call before a court to answer to an indictment **2** : to accuse of wrong or imperfection — **ar·raign·ment** *n*

ar·range \ə-'rānj\ *vb* **ar·ranged; ar·rang·ing** **1** : to put in order **2** : PLAN ⟨∼ an interview⟩ **3** : to adapt (a musical composition) to voices or instruments other than those for which it was orig. written **4** : to come to an agreement about : SETTLE — **ar·range·ment** *n* — **ar·rang·er** *n*

ar·rant \'a-rənt\ *adj* : being notoriously without moderation : EXTREME

ar·ras \'a-rəs\ *n, pl* **arras** **1** : TAPESTRY **2** : a wall hanging or screen of tapestry

¹ar·ray \ə-'rā\ *vb* **1** : to dress esp. splendidly **2** : to arrange in order (as in an array)

²array *n* **1** : a regular arrangement **2** : rich apparel **3** : a large or varied group

ar·rears \ə-'rirz\ *n pl* **1** : a state of being behind in the discharge of obligations ⟨in ∼ with the rent⟩ **2** : overdue debts

¹ar·rest \ə-'rest\ *vb* **1** : STOP, CHECK **2** : to take into legal custody

²arrest *n* **1** : the act of stopping; *also* : the state of being stopped **2** : the taking into custody by legal authority

ar·rhyth·mia \ā-'rith-mē-ə\ *n* : an alteration of the heartbeat's rhythm

ar·riv·al \ə-'rī-vəl\ *n* **1** : the act of arriving **2** : one that arrives

ar·rive \ə-'rīv\ *vb* **ar·rived; ar·riv·ing** **1** : to reach a destination **2** : to make an appearance ⟨the guests have *arrived*⟩ **3** : to attain success

ar·ro·gant \'er-ə-gənt\ *adj* : offensively exaggerating one's own importance — **ar·ro·gance** \-gəns\ *n* — **ar·ro·gant·ly** *adv*

ar·ro·gate \-ₐgāt\ *vb* **-gat·ed; -gat·ing** : to claim or seize without justification as one's right — **ar·ro·ga·tion** \ₐar-ə-'gā-shən\ *n*

ar·row \'er-ō\ *n* **1** : a missile shot from a bow and usu. having a slender shaft, a pointed head, and feathers at the butt **2** : a pointed mark used to indicate direction

ar·row·head \'er-ō-ₐhed\ *n* : the pointed end of an arrow

arrowhead

ar·row·root \-,rüt, -,rüt\ *n* : an edible starch from the roots of any of several tropical American plants; *also* : a plant yielding arrowroot

ar·royo \ə-'rȯi-ə, -ō\ *n, pl* **-royos** [Sp] **1** : a watercourse in a dry region **2** : a water-carved gully or channel

ar·se·nal \'ärs-nəl, 'är-sə-nəl\ *n* [ultim. fr. Ar *dār ṣinā'a* house of manufacture] **1** : a place for making and storing arms and military equipment **2** : STORE, REPERTOIRE

ar·se·nic \'ärs-nik, 'är-sə-nik\ *n* **1** : a solid brittle poisonous chemical element of grayish metallic luster **2** : a very poisonous oxygen compound of arsenic used in making insecticides

ar·son \'är-s°n\ *n* : the willful or malicious burning of property — **ar·son·ist** \-ist\ *n*

¹art \'ärt\ *n* **1** : skill acquired by experience or study **2** : a branch of learning; *esp* : one of the humanities **3** : an occupation requiring knowledge or skill **4** : the use of skill and imagination in the production of things of beauty; *also* : works so produced **5** : ARTFULNESS

²art *adj* : produced as an artistic effort ⟨an ~ film⟩

³art *abbr* **1** article **2** artificial **3** artillery

-art — see -ARD

ar·te·fact *chiefly Brit var of* ARTIFACT

ar·te·ri·al \är-'tir-ē-əl\ *adj* **1** : of or relating to an artery; *also* : relating to or being the oxygenated blood found in most arteries **2** : of, relating to, or being a route for through traffic

ar·te·ri·ole \är-'tir-ē-,ōl\ *n* : any of the small terminal branches of an artery that ends in capillaries — **ar·te·ri·o·lar** \-,tir-ē-'ō-lər\ *adj*

ar·te·rio·scle·ro·sis \är-,tir-ē-ō-sklə-'rō-səs\ *n* : a chronic disease in which arterial walls are abnormally thickened and hardened — **ar·te·rio·scle·rot·ic** \-'rä-tik\ *adj or n*

ar·tery \'är-tə-rē\ *n, pl* **-ter·ies** **1** : one of the tubular vessels that carry blood from the heart **2** : a main channel of transportation or communication

ar·te·sian well \är-'tē-zhən-\ *n* : a well from which the water flows to the surface by natural pressure; *also* : a deep well

art·ful \'ärt-fəl\ *adj* **1** : performed with, showing, or using art or skill **2** : CRAFTY — **art·ful·ly** *adv* — **art·ful·ness** *n*

ar·thri·tis \är-'thrī-təs\ *n, pl* **-thri·ti·des** \-'thri-tə-,dēz\ : inflammation of the joints — **ar·thrit·ic** \-'thri-tik\ *adj or n*

ar·thro·pod \'är-thrə-,päd\ *n* : any of a phylum of invertebrate animals comprising those (as insects, spiders, or crabs) with segmented bodies and jointed limbs — **arthropod** *adj*

ar·thros·co·py \är-'thräs-kə-pē\ *n, pl* **-pies** : visual examination of the interior of a joint (as the knee) with a special surgical instrument; *also* : surgery on a joint using arthroscopy — **ar·thro·scope** \'är-thrə-,skōp\ *n* — **ar·thro·scop·ic** \,är-thrə-'skä-pik\ *adj*

ar·ti·choke \'är-tə-,chōk\ *n* [It dial. *articiocco*, ultim. fr. Ar *al-khurshūf*] : a tall thistlelike herb related to the daisies; *also* : its edible flower head

ar·ti·cle \'är-ti-kəl\ *n* [ME, fr. AF, fr. L *articulus* joint, division, dim. of *artus* joint, limb] **1** : a distinct part of a written document **2** : a nonfictional prose composition forming an independent part of a publication **3** : a word (as *an*, *the*) used with a noun to limit or give definiteness to its application **4** : a member of a class of things; *esp* : COMMODITY

¹ar·tic·u·lar \är-'ti-kyə-lər\ *adj* : of or relating to a joint ⟨~ cartilage⟩

¹ar·tic·u·late \är-'ti-kyə-lət\ *adj* **1** : divided into meaningful parts : INTELLIGIBLE **2** : able to speak; *also* : expressing oneself readily and effectively ⟨an ~ orator⟩ **3** : JOINTED — **ar·tic·u·late·ly** *adv* — **ar·tic·u·late·ness** *n*

²ar·tic·u·late \-,lāt\ *vb* **-lat·ed; -lat·ing** **1** : to utter distinctly **2** : to unite by or as if by joints — **ar·tic·u·la·tion** \-,ti-kyə-'lā-shən\ *n*

ar·ti·fact \'är-tə-,fakt\ *n* : something made or modified by humans usu. for a purpose; *esp* : an object remaining from another time or culture ⟨prehistoric ~s⟩

ar·ti·fice \'är-tə-fəs\ *n* **1** : TRICK; *also* : TRICKERY **2** : an ingenious device; *also* : INGENUITY

ar·ti·fi·cer \är-'ti-fə-sər, 'är-tə-fə-sər\ *n* : a skilled worker

ar·ti·fi·cial \,är-tə-'fi-shəl\ *adj* **1** : produced by art rather than nature; *also* : made by humans to imitate nature **2**

: not genuine : FEIGNED — **ar·ti·fi·ci·al·i·ty** \-,fi-shē-'a-lə-tē\ *n* — **ar·ti·fi·cial·ly** *adv* — **ar·ti·fi·cial·ness** *n*

artificial insemination *n* : introduction of semen into the uterus or oviduct by other than natural means

artificial intelligence *n* : the capability of a machine and esp. a computer to imitate intelligent human behavior

artificial respiration *n* : the rhythmic forcing of air into and out of the lungs of a person whose breathing has stopped

ar·til·lery \är-'ti-lə-rē\ *n, pl* **-ler·ies** **1** : crew-served mounted firearms (as guns) **2** : a branch of the army armed with artillery — **ar·til·ler·ist** \-rist\ *n*

ar·ti·san \'är-tə-zən, -sən\ *n* : a worker who practices a trade or handicraft

art·ist \'är-tist\ *n* **1** : one who practices an art; *esp* : one who creates objects of beauty **2** : ARTISTE

ar·tiste \är-'tēst\ *n* : a skilled public performer

ar·tis·tic \är-'tis-tik\ *adj* : showing taste and skill — **ar·tis·ti·cal·ly** \-ti-k(ə-)lē\ *adv*

art·ist·ry \'är-tə-strē\ *n* : artistic quality or ability

art·less \'ärt-ləs\ *adj* **1** : lacking art or skill **2** : free from artificiality : NATURAL **3** : free from guile : SINCERE — **art·less·ly** *adv* — **art·less·ness** *n*

art nou·veau \,är-nü-'vō, ,ärt-\ *n, often cap A&N* [F, lit., new art] : a late 19th century design style characterized by sinuous lines and leaf-shaped forms

art·work \'ärt-,wərk\ *n* : an artistic production or work

arty \'är-tē\ *adj* **art·i·er; -est** : showily or pretentiously artistic — **art·i·ly** \'är-tə-lē\ *adv* — **art·i·ness** *n*

aru·gu·la \ə-'rü-gə-lə\ *n* : a yellowish-flowered herb related to the mustards with edible leaves used esp. in salads

ar·um \'a-rəm\ *n* : any of a family of plants (as the jack-in-the-pulpit or a skunk cabbage) with flowers in a fleshy enclosed spike

ARV *abbr* American Revised Version

¹-ary *n suffix* : thing or person belonging to or connected with ⟨functionary⟩

²-ary *adj suffix* : of, relating to, or connected with ⟨budgetary⟩

Ary·an \'a-rē-ən, 'er-e-; 'är-yən\ *adj* **1** : INDO-EUROPEAN **2** : NORDIC — **Aryan** *n*

¹as \əz, (,)az\ *adv* **1** : to the same degree or amount : EQUALLY ⟨~ green as grass⟩ **2** : for instance ⟨various trees, ~ oak or pine⟩ **3** : when considered in a specified relation ⟨my opinion ~ distinguished from his⟩

²as *conj* **1** : in the same amount or degree in which ⟨green ~ grass⟩ **2** : in the same way that ⟨farmed ~ his father before him had farmed⟩ **3** : WHILE, WHEN ⟨spoke to me ~ I was leaving⟩ **4** : THOUGH ⟨improbable ~ it seems⟩ **5** : SINCE, BECAUSE ⟨~ I'm not wanted, I'll go⟩ **6** : that the result is ⟨so guilty ~ to leave no doubt⟩

³as *pron* **1** : THAT — used after *same* or *such* ⟨it's the same price ~ before⟩ **2** : a fact that ⟨he's rich, ~ you know⟩

⁴as *prep* : in the capacity or character of ⟨this will serve ~ a substitute⟩

As *symbol* arsenic

AS *abbr* **1** American Samoa **2** Anglo-Saxon **3** associate in science

asa·fet·i·da *or* **asa·foe·ti·da** \,a-sə-'fe-tə-dē, -'fē-\ *n* : an ill-smelling plant gum formerly used in medicine

ASAP *abbr* as soon as possible

as·bes·tos \as-'bes-təs, az-\ *n* : a noncombustible grayish mineral that occurs in fibrous form and has been used as a fireproof material

as·cend \ə-'send\ *vb* **1** : to move upward : MOUNT, CLIMB **2** : to succeed to : OCCUPY ⟨he ~ed the throne⟩

as·cen·dan·cy *also* **as·cen·den·cy** \ə-'sen-dən-sē\ *n* : controlling influence : DOMINATION

¹as·cen·dant *also* **as·cen·dent** \ə-'sen-dənt\ *n* : a dominant position

²ascendant *also* **ascendent** *adj* **1** : moving upward **2** : DOMINANT

as·cen·sion \ə-'sen-chən\ *n* : the act or process of ascending

Ascension Day *n* : the Thursday 40 days after Easter observed in commemoration of Christ's ascension into heaven

as·cent \ə-'sent\ *n* **1** : the act of mounting upward : CLIMB **2** : degree of upward slope

as·cer·tain \,a-sər-'tān\ *vb* : to learn with certainty — **as·cer·tain·able** *adj*

as·cet·ic \ə-'se-tik\ adj : practicing self-denial esp. for spiritual reasons : AUSTERE — **ascetic** n — **as·cet·i·cism** \-'se-tə-,si-zəm\ n

ASCII \'as-kē\ n [American Standard Code for Information Interchange] : a computer code for representing alphanumeric information

ascor·bic acid \ə-'skȯr-bik-\ n : VITAMIN C

as·cot \'as-kət, -,kät\ n [Ascot Heath, racetrack near Ascot, England] : a broad neck scarf that is looped under the chin

as·cribe \ə-'skrīb\ vb **as·cribed; as·crib·ing** : to refer to a supposed cause, source, or author : ATTRIBUTE — **as·crib·able** adj — **as·crip·tion** \-'skrip-shən\ n

asep·tic \ā-'sep-tik\ adj : free or freed from disease-causing germs

asex·u·al \ā-'sek-shə-wəl\ adj **1** : lacking sex or functional sex organs **2** : occurring or formed without the production and union of two kinds of gametes ⟨∼ reproduction⟩ **3** : devoid of sexuality — **asex·u·al·ly** adv

as for prep : with regard to : CONCERNING ⟨as for the others, they were late⟩

¹**ash** \'ash\ n **1** : any of a genus of trees related to the olive and having winged seeds and bark with grooves and ridges **2** : the tough elastic wood of an ash

²**ash** n **1** : the solid matter left when material is burned **2** : fine mineral particles from a volcano **3** pl : the remains of the dead human body after cremation or disintegration

ashamed \ə-'shāmd\ adj **1** : feeling shame **2** : restrained by anticipation of shame ⟨∼ to say anything⟩ — **ashamed·ly** \-'shā-məd-lē\ adv

ash·en \'a-shən\ adj : resembling ashes (as in color); esp : deadly pale

ash·lar \'ash-lər\ n : hewn or squared stone; also : masonry of such stone

ashore \ə-'shȯr\ adv : on or to the shore

as how conj : THAT ⟨allowed as how she was glad to be here⟩

ash·ram \'äsh-rəm\ n : a religious retreat esp. of a Hindu sage

ash·tray \'ash-,trā\ n : a receptacle for tobacco ashes

Ash Wednesday n : the 1st day of Lent

ashy \'a-shē\ adj **ash·i·er; -est** : ASHEN

Asian \'ā-zhən\ adj : of, relating to, or characteristic of the continent of Asia or its people — **Asian** n

¹**aside** \ə-'sīd\ adv **1** : to or toward the side **2** : out of the way : AWAY ⟨putting ∼ savings⟩

²**aside** n : an actor's words heard by the audience but supposedly not by other characters on stage

aside from prep **1** : BESIDES ⟨aside from being pretty, she's intelligent⟩ **2** : with the exception of ⟨aside from one D his grades are excellent⟩

as if conj **1** : as it would be if ⟨it's as if nothing had changed⟩ **2** : as one would if ⟨he acts as if he'd never been away⟩ **3** : THAT ⟨it seems as if nothing ever happens around here⟩

as·i·nine \'a-sə-,nīn\ adj [L asininus, fr. asinus ass] : STUPID, FOOLISH — **as·i·nin·i·ty** \a-sə-'ni-nə-tē\ n

ask \'ask\ vb **asked** \'askt\; **ask·ing 1** : to call on for an answer ⟨she ∼ed him about his trip⟩ **2** : UTTER ⟨∼ a question⟩ **3** : to make a request of ⟨∼ him for help⟩ **4** : to make a request for ⟨∼ help of her⟩ **5** : to set as a price ⟨∼ed $800 for the car⟩ **6** : INVITE

askance \ə-'skans\ adv **1** : with a side glance **2** : with distrust

askew \ə-'skyü\ adv or adj : out of line : AWRY

ASL abbr American Sign Language

¹**aslant** \ə-'slant\ adv or adj : in a slanting direction

²**aslant** prep : over or across in a slanting direction

asleep \ə-'slēp\ adv or adj **1** : in or into a state of sleep **2** : DEAD **3** : NUMB **4** : INACTIVE

as long as conj **1** : provided that ⟨do as you like as long as you get home on time⟩ **2** : INASMUCH AS, SINCE ⟨as long as you're up, turn on the light⟩

aso·cial \(,)ā-'sō-shəl\ adj : ANTISOCIAL

as of prep : AT, DURING, FROM, ON ⟨takes effect as of July 1⟩

asp \'asp\ n : a small poisonous African snake

as·par·a·gus \ə-'sper-ə-gəs\ n : a tall branching perennial herb related to the lilies; also : its edible young stalks

as·par·tame \'as-pər-,tām, ə-'spär-\ n : a crystalline low-calorie sweetener

ASPCA abbr American Society for the Prevention of Cruelty to Animals

as·pect \'as-,pekt\ n **1** : a position facing a particular direction **2** : APPEARANCE, LOOK **3** : PHASE

as·pen \'as-pən\ n : any of several poplars with leaves that flutter in the slightest breeze

as per \'az-,pər\ prep : in accordance with ⟨as per instructions⟩

as·per·i·ty \a-'sper-ə-tē\ n, pl **-ties 1** : ROUGHNESS **2** : harshness of temper

as·per·sion \ə-'spər-zhən\ n : a slanderous or defamatory remark

as·phalt \'as-,fȯlt\ also **as·phal·tum** \as-'fȯl-təm\ n : a dark substance found in natural beds or obtained as a residue in petroleum refining and used esp. in paving streets

asphalt jungle n : a big city or a specified part of a big city

as·pho·del \'as-fə-,del\ n : any of several Old World herbs related to the lilies and bearing flowers in long erect spikes

as·phyx·ia \as-'fik-sē-ə\ n : a lack of oxygen or excess of carbon dioxide in the body that results in unconsciousness and often death and is usu. caused by interruption of breathing

as·phyx·i·ate \-sē-,āt\ vb **-at·ed; -at·ing** : SUFFOCATE — **as·phyx·i·a·tion** \-,fik-sē-'ā-shən\ n

as·pic \'as-pik\ n [F, lit., asp] : a savory meat jelly

as·pi·rant \'as-pə-rənt, ə-'spī-rənt\ n : one who aspires
♦ **Synonyms** CANDIDATE, APPLICANT, SEEKER

¹**as·pi·rate** \'as-pə-rət\ n **1** : an independent sound \h\ or a character (as the letter h) representing it **2** : a consonant having aspiration as its final component

²**as·pi·rate** \'as-pə-,rāt\ vb **-rat·ed; -rat·ing** : to draw, remove, or take up or into by suction

as·pi·ra·tion \,as-pə-'rā-shən\ n **1** : the pronunciation or addition of an aspirate; also : the aspirate or its symbol **2** : a drawing of something in, out, up, or through by or as if by suction **3** : a strong desire to achieve something noble; also : an object of this desire

as·pire \ə-'spī(-ə)r\ vb **as·pired; as·pir·ing 1** : to seek to attain or accomplish a particular goal **2** : to rise aloft

as·pi·rin \'as-pə-rən\ n, pl **aspirin** or **aspirins 1** : a white crystalline drug used to relieve pain and fever **2** : a tablet of aspirin

as regards also **as respects** prep : in regard to : with respect to

ass \'as\ n **1** : any of several long-eared mammals smaller than the related horses; esp : one of Africa ancestral to the donkey **2** : a stupid person

as·sail \ə-'sāl\ vb : to attack violently — **as·sail·able** adj — **as·sail·ant** n

as·sas·sin \ə-'sa-sᵊn\ n [ML assassinus, fr. Ar ḥashshāshīn, pl. of ḥashshāsh worthless person, lit., hashish-user, fr. ḥashīsh hashish] : a murderer esp. for hire or fanatical reasons

as·sas·si·nate \ə-'sa-sə-,nāt\ vb **-nat·ed; -nat·ing** : to murder by sudden or secret attack — **as·sas·si·na·tion** \-,sa-sə-'nā-shən\ n

as·sault \ə-'sȯlt\ n **1** : a violent attack **2** : an unlawful attempt or threat to do harm to another — **assault** vb — **as·sault·ive** \ə-'sȯl-tiv\ adj

assault rifle n : a military automatic rifle with a large-capacity magazine

¹**as·say** \'a-,sā, a-'sā\ n : analysis to determine the quantity of one or more components present in a sample (as of an ore or drug)

²**as·say** \a-'sā, 'a-,sā\ vb **1** : TRY, ATTEMPT **2** : to subject (as an ore or drug) to an assay **3** : JUDGE **3**

as·sem·blage \ə-'sem-blij, 3 & 4 also ,as-,äm-'bläzh\ n **1** : a collection of persons or things : GATHERING **2** : the act of assembling **3** : an artistic composition made from scraps, junk, and odds and ends **4** : the art of making assemblages

as·sem·ble \ə-'sem-bəl\ vb **-bled; -bling 1** : to collect into one place : CONGREGATE **2** : to fit together the parts of **3** : to meet together : CONVENE

as·sem·bly \ə-'sem-blē\ n, pl **-blies 1** : a gathering of persons : MEETING **2** cap : a legislative body; esp : the lower house of a legislature **3** : a signal for troops to assemble **4** : the fitting together of parts (as of a machine)

assembly language *n* : a computer language consisting of mnemonic codes corresponding to machine-language instructions

as·sem·bly–line \ə-'sem-blē-ˌlīn\ *adj* : made by or as if by an assembly line; *esp* : lacking originality or creativity

assembly line *n* : an arrangement of machines, equipment, and workers in which work passes from operation to operation in a direct line

as·sem·bly·man \ə-'sem-blē-mən\ *n* : a member of a legislative assembly

as·sem·bly·wom·an \-ˌwù-mən\ *n* : a woman who is a member of a legislative assembly

as·sent \ə-'sent\ *vb* : AGREE, CONCUR — **assent** *n*

as·sert \ə-'sərt\ *vb* **1** : to state positively **2** : to demonstrate the existence of ✦ **Synonyms** DECLARE, AFFIRM, PROTEST, AVOW, CLAIM — **as·ser·tive** \-'sər-tiv\ *adj* — **as·ser·tive·ly** *adv* — **as·ser·tive·ness** *n*

as·ser·tion \ə-'sər-shən\ *n* : a positive statement

as·sess \ə-'ses\ *vb* **1** : to fix the rate or amount of **2** : to impose (as a tax) at a specified rate **3** : to evaluate for taxation — **as·sess·ment** *n* — **as·ses·sor** \-'se-sər\ *n*

as·set \'a-ˌset\ *n* **1** *pl* : the entire property of a person or company that may be used to pay debts **2** : ADVANTAGE, RESOURCE ⟨my wit is my chief ∼⟩

as·sev·er·ate \ə-'se-və-ˌrāt\ *vb* **-at·ed; -at·ing** : to assert earnestly — **as·sev·er·a·tion** \-ˌse-və-'rā-shən\ *n*

as·sid·u·ous \ə-'si-jə-wəs\ *adj* : steadily attentive : DILIGENT — **as·si·du·i·ty** \ˌa-sə-'dü-ə-tē, -'dyü-\ *n* — **as·sid·u·ous·ly** *adv* — **as·sid·u·ous·ness** *n*

as·sign \ə-'sīn\ *vb* **1** : to transfer (property) to another **2** : to appoint to or as a duty ⟨∼ a lesson⟩ **3** : FIX, SPECIFY ⟨∼ a limit⟩ **4** : ASCRIBE ⟨∼ a reason⟩ — **as·sign·able** *adj*

as·sig·na·tion \ˌa-sig-'nā-shən\ *n* : an appointment for a meeting; *esp* : TRYST

assigned risk *n* : a poor risk (as an accident-prone motorist) that an insurance company is forced to insure by state law

as·sign·ment \ə-'sīn-mənt\ *n* **1** : the act of assigning **2** : something assigned

as·sim·i·late \ə-'si-mə-ˌlāt\ *vb* **-lat·ed; -lat·ing** **1** : to take up and absorb as nourishment; *also* : to absorb into a cultural tradition **2** : COMPREHEND **3** : to make or become similar — **as·sim·i·la·tion** \-ˌsi-mə-'lā-shən\ *n*

¹**as·sist** \ə-'sist\ *vb* : HELP, AID — **as·sis·tance** \-'sis-təns\ *n*

²**assist** *n* **1** : an act of assistance **2** : the action of a player who enables a teammate to make a putout (as in baseball) or score a goal (as in hockey or basketball)

as·sis·tant \ə-'sis-tənt\ *n* : a person who assists : HELPER

as·sis·ted living \ə-'sis-təd-\ *n* : a system of housing and limited care for senior citizens who need assistance with daily activities but do not require care in a nursing home

as·sis·tive \ə-'sis-tiv\ *adj* : providing aid or assistance ⟨∼ technology⟩

as·size \ə-'sīz\ *n* [ME *assise*, fr. AF, session, legal action, fr. *asseer, asseoir* to seat, fr. VL **assedēre*, fr. L *assidēre* to sit beside] : a judicial inquest **2** *pl* : the former regular sessions of superior courts in English counties

assn *abbr* association

assoc *abbr* associate; associated; association

¹**as·so·ci·ate** \ə-'sō-shē-ˌāt, -sē-\ *vb* **-at·ed; -at·ing** **1** : to join in companionship or partnership **2** : to connect in thought

²**as·so·ci·ate** \-shē-ət, -sē-; -shət\ *n* **1** : a fellow worker : PARTNER **2** : COMPANION **3** *often cap* : a degree conferred esp. by a junior college ⟨∼ in arts⟩ — **associate** *adj*

as·so·ci·a·tion \ə-ˌsō-shē-'ā-shən, -sē-\ *n* **1** : the act of associating **2** : an organization of persons : SOCIETY

as·so·cia·tive \ə-'sō-shē-ˌā-tiv, -sē-; -shə-tiv\ *adj* **1** : of, relating to, or involved in association esp. of ideas or images **2** : of, having, or being the property of producing the same mathematical value regardless of how an expression's elements are grouped as long as their order is the same

as·so·nance \'a-sə-nəns\ *n* : repetition of vowels esp. as an alternative to rhyme in verse — **as·so·nant** \-nənt\ *adj or n*

as soon as *conj* : immediately at or shortly after the time that ⟨we'll start *as soon as* they arrive⟩

as·sort \ə-'sòrt\ *vb* **1** : to distribute into like groups : CLASSIFY **2** : HARMONIZE

as·sort·ed \-'sòr-təd\ *adj* : consisting of various kinds

as·sort·ment \-'sòrt-mənt\ *n* : a collection of assorted things or persons

asst *abbr* assistant

as·suage \ə-'swāj\ *vb* **as·suaged; as·suag·ing** **1** : to make (as pain or grief) less : EASE **2** : SATISFY ✦ **Synonyms** ALLEVIATE, RELIEVE, LIGHTEN, MITIGATE

as·sume \ə-'süm\ *vb* **as·sumed; as·sum·ing** **1** : to take upon oneself **2** : to pretend to have or be **3** : to take as granted or true though not proved

as·sump·tion \ə-'səmp-shən\ *n* **1** : the taking up of a person into heaven **2** *cap* : August 15 observed in commemoration of the Assumption of the Virgin Mary **3** : a taking upon oneself **4** : PRETENSION **5** : SUPPOSITION

as·sur·ance \ə-'shùr-əns\ *n* **1** : PLEDGE **2** *chiefly Brit* : INSURANCE **3** : SECURITY **4** : SELF-CONFIDENCE; *also* : AUDACITY

as·sure \ə-'shùr\ *vb* **as·sured; as·sur·ing** **1** : INSURE **2** : to give confidence to **3** : to state confidently to **4** : to make certain the coming or attainment of

as·sured \ə-'shùrd\ *n, pl* **assured** *or* **assureds** : INSURED

as·ta·tine \'as-tə-ˌtēn\ *n* : an unstable radioactive chemical element

as·ter \'as-tər\ *n* : any of various mostly fall-blooming leafy-stemmed composite herbs with daisylike purple, white, pink, or yellow flower heads

as·ter·isk \'as-tə-ˌrisk\ *n* [L *asteriscus*, fr. Gk *asteriskos*, lit., little star, dim. of *astēr* star] : a character * used as a reference mark or as an indication of the omission of letters or words

astern \ə-'stərn\ *adv or adj* **1** : in, at, or toward the stern **2** : BACKWARD

as·ter·oid \'as-tə-ˌròid\ *n* : any of the numerous small celestial bodies found esp. between Mars and Jupiter

asth·ma \'az-mə\ *n* : a chronic lung disorder marked by recurrent episodes of labored breathing, a feeling of tightness in the chest, and coughing — **asth·mat·ic** \az-'ma-tik\ *adj or n*

as though *conj* : AS IF

astig·ma·tism \ə-'stig-mə-ˌti-zəm\ *n* : a defect in a lens or an eye causing improper focusing and blurred vision — **as·tig·mat·ic** \ˌas-tig-'ma-tik\ *adj*

astir \ə-'stər\ *adj* **1** : being in action : MOVING **2** : being out of bed

as to *prep* **1** : ABOUT, CONCERNING ⟨uncertain *as to* what went on⟩ **2** : ACCORDING TO ⟨graded *as to* size⟩

as·ton·ish \ə-'stä-nish\ *vb* : to strike with sudden and usu. great wonder : AMAZE — **as·ton·ish·ing·ly** *adv* — **as·ton·ish·ment** *n*

as·tound \ə-'staùnd\ *vb* : to fill with bewilderment or wonder — **as·tound·ing·ly** *adv*

¹**astrad·dle** \ə-'stra-dᵊl\ *adv* : on or above and extending onto both sides

²**astraddle** *prep* : ASTRIDE

as·tra·khan \'as-trə-kən, -ˌkan\ *n, often cap* **1** : karakul of Russian origin **2** : a cloth with a usu. wool, curled, and looped pile resembling karakul

as·tral \'as-trəl\ *adj* : of, relating to, or coming from the stars

astray \ə-'strā\ *adv or adj* **1** : off the right path or route **2** : into error

¹**astride** \ə-'strīd\ *adv* **1** : with one leg on each side **2** : with legs apart

²**astride** *prep* : with one leg on each side of

¹**as·trin·gent** \ə-'strin-jənt\ *adj* : able or tending to shrink body tissues — **as·trin·gen·cy** \-jən-sē\ *n*

²**astringent** *n* : an astringent agent or substance

astrol *abbr* astrologer; astrology

as·tro·labe \'as-trə-ˌlāb\ *n* : an instrument formerly used for observing the positions of celestial bodies

as·trol·o·gy \ə-'strä-lə-jē\ *n* : divination based on the supposed influence of the stars upon human events — **as·trol·o·ger** \-jər\ *n* — **as·tro·log·i·cal** \ˌas-trə-'lä-ji-kəl\ *adj* — **as·tro·log·i·cal·ly** \-kə-lē\ *adv*

astron *abbr* astronomer; astronomy

as·tro·naut \'as-trə-ˌnòt\ *n* : a traveler in a spacecraft

as·tro·nau·tics \ˌas-trə-'nò-tiks\ *n* : the science of the construction and operation of spacecraft — **as·tro·nau·tic** \-tik\ *or* **as·tro·nau·ti·cal** \-ti-kəl\ *adj*

as·tro·nom·i·cal \ˌas-trə-ˈnä-mi-kəl\ *also* **as·tro·nom·ic** \-mik\ *adj* **1** : of or relating to astronomy **2** : extremely large ⟨an ~ amount of money⟩

astronomical unit *n* : a unit of length used in astronomy equal to the mean distance of the earth from the sun or about 93 million miles (150 million kilometers)

as·tron·o·my \ə-ˈsträ-nə-mē\ *n, pl* **-mies** : the science of objects and matter beyond the earth's atmosphere — **as·tron·o·mer** \-mər\ *n*

as·tro·phys·ics \ˌas-trō-ˈfi-ziks\ *n* : astronomy dealing esp. with the physical properties and dynamic processes of celestial objects — **as·tro·phys·i·cal** \-zi-kəl\ *adj* — **as·tro·phys·i·cist** \-ˈfi-zə-sist\ *n*

as·tute \ə-ˈstüt, -ˈstyüt, a-\ *adj* [L *astutus*, fr. *astus* craft] : shrewdly discerning; *also* : WILY — **as·tute·ly** *adv* — **as·tute·ness** *n*

asun·der \ə-ˈsən-dər\ *adv or adj* **1** : into separate pieces ⟨torn ~⟩ **2** : separated in position from each other

ASV *abbr* American Standard Version

¹**as well as** *conj* : and in addition : and moreover ⟨brave *as well as* loyal⟩

²**as well as** *prep* : in addition to : BESIDES ⟨the coach, *as well as* the team, is ready⟩

asy·lum \ə-ˈsī-ləm\ *n* [ME, fr. L, fr. Gk *asylon*, neut. of *asylos* inviolable, fr. *a-* not + *sylon* right of seizure] **1** : a place of refuge **2** : protection given to esp. political fugitives **3** : an institution for the care of the needy or sick and esp. of the insane

asym·met·ri·cal \ˌā-sə-ˈme-tri-kəl\ *or* **asym·met·ric** \-trik\ *adj* : not symmetrical — **asym·met·ri·cal·ly** \-tri-kə-lē\ *adv* — **asym·me·try** \(ˌ)ā-ˈsi-mə-trē\ *n*

asymp·tom·at·ic \ˌā-ˌsimp-tə-ˈma-tik\ *adj* : presenting no symptoms of disease ⟨an ~ infection⟩

as·ymp·tote \ˈa-səmp-ˌtōt\ *n* : a straight line that is approached ever more closely by a curve that never coincides with it — **as·ymp·tot·ic** \ˌa-səmp-ˈtä-tik\ *adj* — **as·ymp·tot·i·cal·ly** \-ti-k(ə-)lē\ *adv*

¹**at** \ət, (ˈ)at\ *prep* **1** — used to indicate a point in time or space ⟨be here ~ 3 o'clock⟩ **2** — used to indicate a goal ⟨swung ~ the ball⟩ **3** — used to indicate position or condition ⟨~ rest⟩ **4** — used to indicate means, cause, or manner ⟨sold ~ auction⟩

²**at** *also* **att** \ˈät\ *n, pl at also* **att** — see *kip* at MONEY table

At *symbol* astatine

AT *abbr* automatic transmission

at all *adv* : in any way : in any circumstances ⟨not *at all* likely⟩

at·a·vism \ˈa-tə-ˌvi-zəm\ *n* : appearance in an individual of a character typical of an ancestral form; *also* : such an individual or character — **at·a·vis·tic** \ˌa-tə-ˈvis-tik\ *adj*

atax·ia \ə-ˈtak-sē-ə\ *n* : an inability to coordinate muscular movements

ate *past of* EAT

¹**-ate** *n suffix* **1** : one acted upon (in a specified way) ⟨distill*ate*⟩ **2** : chemical compound or complex derived from a (specified) compound or element ⟨acet*ate*⟩

²**-ate** *n suffix* **1** : office : function : rank : group of persons holding a (specified) office or rank ⟨episcop*ate*⟩ **2** : state : dominion : jurisdiction ⟨emir*ate*⟩

³**-ate** *adj suffix* **1** : acted on (in a specified way) : being in a (specified) state ⟨temper*ate*⟩ ⟨degener*ate*⟩ **2** : marked by having ⟨vertebr*ate*⟩

⁴**-ate** *vb suffix* : cause to be modified or affected by ⟨pollin*ate*⟩ : cause to become ⟨activ*ate*⟩ : furnish with ⟨aer*ate*⟩

ate·lier \ˌa-tᵊl-ˈyā\ *n* **1** : an artist's or designer's studio **2** : WORKSHOP

athe·ist \ˈā-thē-ist\ *n* : one who denies the existence of God — **athe·ism** \-ˌi-zəm\ *n* — **athe·is·tic** \ˌā-thē-ˈis-tik\ *adj*

ath·e·nae·um *or* **ath·e·ne·um** \ˌa-thə-ˈnē-əm\ *n* : LIBRARY 1

ath·ero·scle·ro·sis \ˌa-thə-rō-sklə-ˈrō-səs\ *n* : arteriosclerosis characterized by the deposition of fatty substances in and the hardening of the inner layer of the arteries — **ath·ero·scle·rot·ic** \-ˈrä-tik\ *adj*

athirst \ə-ˈthərst\ *adj* **1** *archaic* : THIRSTY **2** : EAGER, LONGING

ath·lete \ˈath-ˌlēt\ *n* [ME, fr. L *athleta*, fr. Gk *athlētēs*, fr. *athlein* to contend for a prize, fr. *athlon* prize, contest] : a person who is trained to compete in athletics

athlete's foot *n* : ringworm of the feet

ath·let·ic \ath-ˈle-tik\ *adj* **1** : of or relating to athletes or

athletics **2** : VIGOROUS, ACTIVE **3** : STURDY, MUSCULAR — **ath·let·i·cal·ly** \-ti-kə-lē\ *adv* — **ath·let·i·cism** \-tə-ˌsi-zəm\ *n*

ath·let·ics \ath-ˈle-tiks\ *n sing or pl* : exercises and games requiring physical skill, strength, and endurance

athletic supporter *n* : an elastic pouch used to support the male genitals and worn esp. during athletic activity

¹**athwart** \ə-ˈthwórt\ *prep* **1** : ACROSS **2** : in opposition to

²**athwart** *adv* : obliquely across

atilt \ə-ˈtilt\ *adv or adj* **1** : in a tilted position **2** : with lance in hand

-ation *n suffix* : action or process ⟨flirt*ation*⟩ : something connected with an action or process ⟨discolor*ation*⟩

Atl *abbr* Atlantic

at–large \ˈat-ˈlärj\ *adj* : of or being a political representative who is elected to serve an entire area rather than one of its subdivisions

at·las \ˈat-ləs\ *n* : a book of maps

atm *abbr* atmosphere; atmospheric

ATM *n* : a computerized electronic machine that performs basic banking functions

at·mo·sphere \ˈat-mə-ˌsfir\ *n* **1** : the gaseous envelope of a celestial body; *esp* : the mass of air surrounding the earth **2** : a surrounding influence **3** : a unit of pressure equal to the pressure of air at sea level or about 14.7 pounds per square inch (10 newtons per square centimeter) **4** : an intriguing or singular tone, effect, or appeal — **at·mo·spher·ic** \ˌat-mə-ˈsfir-ik, -ˈsfer-\ *adj* — **at·mo·spher·i·cal·ly** \-i-k(ə-)lē\ *adv*

at·mo·spher·ics \ˌat-mə-ˈsfir-iks, -ˈsfer-\ *n pl* : radio noise from atmospheric electrical phenomena

atoll \ˈa-ˌtól, -ˌtäl, ˈā-\ *n* : a coral island consisting of a reef surrounding a lagoon

at·om \ˈa-təm\ *n* [ME, fr. L *atomus*, fr. Gk *atomos*, fr. *atomos* indivisible, fr. *a-* not + *temnein* to cut] **1** : a tiny particle : BIT **2** : the smallest particle of a chemical element that can exist alone or in combination

atom·ic \ə-ˈtä-mik\ *adj* **1** : of or relating to atoms; *also* : NUCLEAR 2 ⟨~ energy⟩ **2** : extremely small

atomic bomb *n* : a very destructive bomb utilizing the energy released by splitting the atom

atomic clock *n* : a very precise clock regulated by the natural vibration of atoms or molecules (as of cesium)

atomic number *n* : the number of protons in the nucleus of an element

atomic weight *n* : the mass of one atom of an element

at·om·ise *chiefly Brit var of* ATOMIZE, ATOMIZER

at·om·ize \ˈa-tə-ˌmīz\ *vb* **-ized; -iz·ing** : to reduce to minute particles

at·om·iz·er \ˈa-tə-ˌmī-zər\ *n* : a device for dispensing a liquid (as perfume) as a mist

atom smasher *n* : ACCELERATOR 3

aton·al \ā-ˈtōn-ᵊl\ *adj* : marked by avoidance of traditional musical tonality — **ato·nal·i·ty** \ˌā-tō-ˈna-lə-tē\ *n* — **aton·al·ly** \ā-ˈtōn-ə-lē\ *adv*

atone \ə-ˈtōn\ *vb* **atoned; aton·ing** **1** : to make amends **2** : EXPIATE

atone·ment \ə-ˈtōn-mənt\ *n* **1** : the reconciliation of God and mankind through the death of Jesus Christ **2** : reparation for an offense : SATISFACTION

¹**atop** \ə-ˈtäp\ *adv or adj* : on, to, or at the top

²**atop** *prep* : on top of

ATP \ˌā-ˌtē-ˈpē\ *n* [adenosine *t*riphosphate] : a compound that occurs widely in living tissue and supplies energy for many cellular processes by undergoing enzymatic hydrolysis

atri·um \ˈā-trē-əm\ *n, pl* **atria** \-trē-ə\ *also* **atri·ums** **1** : the central room of a Roman house; *also* : an open patio or court in the center of a building (as a hotel) **2** : an anatomical cavity or passage; *esp* : one of the chambers of the heart that receives blood from the veins — **atri·al** \-əl\ *adj*

atro·cious \ə-ˈtrō-shəs\ *adj* **1** : savagely brutal, cruel, or wicked **2** : very bad : ABOMINABLE — **atro·cious·ly** *adv* — **atro·cious·ness** *n*

atroc·i·ty \ə-ˈträ-sə-tē\ *n, pl* **-ties** **1** : ATROCIOUSNESS **2** : an atrocious act or object ⟨the *atrocities* of war⟩

at·ro·phy \ˈa-trə-fē\ *n, pl* **-phies** : decrease in size or wasting away of a bodily part or tissue — **atrophy** *vb*

at·ro·pine \ˈa-trə-ˌpēn\ *n* : a drug from belladonna and related plants used esp. to relieve spasms and to dilate the pupil of the eye

¹att *var of* AT

²att *abbr* **1** attached **2** attention **3** attorney

at·tach \ə-'tach\ *vb* **1** : to seize legally in order to force payment of a debt **2** : to bind by personal ties **3** : FASTEN, CONNECT **4** : to be fastened or connected

at·ta·ché \ˌa-tə-'shā, ˌa-ˌta-, ə-ˌta-\ *n* [F] : a technical expert on the diplomatic staff of an ambassador

at·ta·ché case \ə-'ta-shā-, ˌa-tə-'shā-\ *n* : a small thin suitcase used esp. for carrying business papers; *also* : BRIEFCASE

at·tach·ment \ə-'tach-mənt\ *n* **1** : legal seizure of property **2** : connection by ties of affection and regard **3** : a device attached to a machine or implement **4** : a connection by which one thing is attached to another

¹at·tack \ə-'tak\ *vb* **1** : to set upon with force or words : ASSAIL, ASSAULT **2** : to set to work on

²attack *n* **1** : an offensive action **2** : a fit of sickness **3** : a scoring action in a game

³attack *adj* : designed, planned, or used for a military attack

at·tain \ə-'tān\ *vb* **1** : ACHIEVE, ACCOMPLISH **2** : to arrive at : REACH — **at·tain·abil·i·ty** \-'tā-nə-'bi-lə-tē\ *n* — **at·tain·able** *adj*

at·tain·der \ə-'tān-dər\ *n* : extinction of the civil rights of a person upon sentence of death or outlawry

at·tain·ment \ə-'tān-mənt\ *n* **1** : the act of attaining **2** : ACCOMPLISHMENT

at·taint \ə-'tānt\ *vb* : to condemn to loss of civil rights

at·tar \'a-tər\ *n* [Pers *'aṭir* perfumed, fr. Ar, fr. *'iṭr* perfume] : a fragrant floral oil

at·tempt \ə-'tempt\ *vb* : to make an effort toward : TRY — **attempt** *n*

at·tend \ə-'tend\ *vb* **1** : to look after : TEND **2** : to be present with **3** : to be present at **4** : to apply oneself **5** : to pay attention **6** : to direct one's attention

at·ten·dance \ə-'ten-dəns\ *n* **1** : the act or fact of attending **2** : the number of persons present; *also* : the number of times a person attends

¹at·ten·dant \ə-'ten-dənt\ *n* : one that attends another to render a service

²attendant *adj* : ACCOMPANYING ⟨~ circumstances⟩

at·ten·tion \ə-'ten-chən\ *n* **1** : the act or state of applying the mind to an object **2** : CONSIDERATION **3** : an act of courtesy **4** : a position of readiness assumed on command by a soldier — **at·ten·tive** \-'ten-tiv\ *adj* — **at·ten·tive·ly** *adv* — **at·ten·tive·ness** *n*

attention deficit disorder *n* : a behavioral syndrome esp. of children that is marked by hyperactivity, impulsive behavior, and inattention

attention–deficit/hyperactivity disorder *n* : ATTENTION DEFICIT DISORDER

attention span *n* : the length of time during which one is able to concentrate or remain interested

at·ten·u·ate \ə-'ten-yə-ˌwāt\ *vb* **-at·ed; -at·ing** **1** : to make or become thin **2** : WEAKEN ⟨sorrows ~ with time⟩ — **attenuate** \-wət\ *adj* — **at·ten·u·a·tion** \-ˌten-yə-'wā-shən\ *n*

at·test \ə-'test\ *vb* **1** : to certify as genuine by signing as a witness **2** : MANIFEST ⟨her record ~s her integrity⟩ **3** : TESTIFY ⟨~ to a belief⟩ — **at·tes·ta·tion** \ˌa-ˌtes-'tā-shən\ *n*

at·tic \'a-tik\ *n* : the space or room in a building immediately below the roof

¹at·tire \ə-'tī(-ə)r\ *vb* **at·tired; at·tir·ing** : to put garments on : DRESS, ARRAY

²attire *n* : DRESS, CLOTHES

at·ti·tude \'a-tə-ˌtüd, -ˌtyüd\ *n* **1** : POSTURE **2** : a mental position or feeling with regard to a fact or state **3** : the position of something in relation to something else **4** : a negative or hostile state of mind **5** : a cocky or arrogant manner

at·ti·tu·di·nise *Brit var of* ATTITUDINIZE

at·ti·tu·di·nize \ˌa-tə-'tü-də-ˌniz, -'tyü-\ *vb* **-nized; -niz·ing** : to assume an affected mental attitude : POSE

attn *abbr* attention

at·tor·ney \ə-'tər-nē\ *n, pl* **-neys** : a legal agent qualified to act for persons in legal proceedings

attorney general *n, pl* **attorneys general** *or* **attorney generals** : the chief legal representative and adviser of a nation or state

at·tract \ə-'trakt\ *vb* **1** : to draw to or toward oneself : cause to approach **2** : to draw by emotional or aesthetic appeal ✦ *Synonyms* CHARM, FASCINATE, ALLURE, CAPTIVATE, ENCHANT — **at·trac·tive** \-'trak-tiv\ *adj* — **at·trac·tive·ly** *adv* — **at·trac·tive·ness** *n*

at·trac·tant \ə-'trak-tənt\ *n* : a substance (as a pheromone) that attracts specific animals (as insects)

at·trac·tion \ə-'trak-shən\ *n* **1** : the act or power of attracting; *esp* : personal charm **2** : an attractive quality, object, or feature **3** : a force tending to draw particles together

attrib *abbr* attributive

¹at·tri·bute \'a-trə-ˌbyüt\ *n* **1** : an inherent characteristic **2** : a word ascribing a quality; *esp* : ADJECTIVE

²at·trib·ute \ə-'tri-ˌbyüt, -byət\ *vb* **-ut·ed; -ut·ing** **1** : to explain as to cause or origin ⟨~ the illness to fatigue⟩ **2** : to regard as a characteristic ✦ *Synonyms* ASCRIBE, CREDIT, CHARGE, IMPUTE — **at·trib·ut·able** *adj* — **at·tri·bu·tion** \ˌa-trə-'byü-shən\ *n*

at·trib·u·tive \ə-'trib-yə-tiv\ *adj* : joined directly to a modified noun without a linking verb ⟨*red* in *red hair* is an ~ adjective⟩ — **attributive** *n* — **at·trib·u·tive·ly** *adv*

at·tri·tion \ə-'tri-shən\ *n* **1** : the act of wearing away by or as if by rubbing **2** : a reduction in numbers as a result of resignation, retirement, or death

at·tune \ə-'tün, -'tyün\ *vb* : to bring into harmony : TUNE — **at·tune·ment** *n*

atty *abbr* attorney

ATV \ˌā-ˌtē-'vē\ *n* : ALL-TERRAIN VEHICLE

atyp·i·cal \ā-'ti-pi-kəl\ *adj* : not typical : IRREGULAR — **atyp·i·cal·ly** \-k(ə-)lē\ *adv*

Au *symbol* [L *aurum*] gold

au·burn \'ȯ-bərn\ *adj* : reddish brown — **auburn** *n*

au cou·rant \ˌō-kü-'räⁿ\ *adj* [F, lit., in the current] : UP-TO-DATE, STYLISH

¹auc·tion \'ȯk-shən\ *n* [L *auction-, auctio,* fr. *augēre* to increase] : public sale of property to the highest bidder

²auction *vb* **auc·tioned; auc·tion·ing** \-shə-niŋ\ : to sell at auction

auc·tion·eer \ˌȯk-shə-'nir\ *n* : an agent who conducts an auction

aud *abbr* audit; auditor

au·da·cious \ȯ-'dā-shəs\ *adj* **1** : DARING, BOLD **2** : INSOLENT — **au·da·cious·ly** *adv* — **au·da·cious·ness** *n* — **au·dac·i·ty** \-'da-sə-tē\ *n*

au·di·ble \'ȯ-də-bəl\ *adj* : capable of being heard — **au·di·bil·i·ty** \ˌȯ-də-'bi-lə-tē\ *n* — **au·di·bly** \'ȯ-də-blē\ *adv*

²audible *n* : a play called at the line of scrimmage — **audible** *vb*

au·di·ence \'ȯ-dē-əns\ *n* **1** : a formal interview **2** : an opportunity of being heard **3** : an assembly of listeners or spectators

¹au·dio \'ȯ-dē-ˌō\ *adj* **1** : of or relating to frequencies (as of radio waves) corresponding to those of audible sound waves **2** : of or relating to sound or its reproduction and esp. high-fidelity reproduction **3** : relating to or used in the transmission or reception of sound

²audio *n* **1** : the transmission, reception, or reproduction of sound **2** : the section of television or motion-picture equipment that deals with sound

au·di·ol·o·gy \ˌȯ-dē-'ä-lə-jē\ *n* : a branch of science dealing with hearing and esp. with the treatment of individuals having trouble with hearing — **au·di·o·log·i·cal** \-ə-'lä-ji-kəl\ *adj* — **au·di·ol·o·gist** \-'ä-lə-jist\ *n*

au·dio·phile \'ȯ-dē-ō-ˌfī(-ə)l\ *n* : one who is enthusiastic about high-fidelity sound reproduction

au·dio·tape \'ȯ-dē-ō-ˌtāp\ *n* : a tape recording of sound

au·dio·vi·su·al \ˌȯ-dē-ō-'vi-zhə-wəl\ *adj* : of, relating to, or making use of both hearing and sight

au·dio·vi·su·als \-wəlz\ *n pl* : audiovisual teaching materials (as videotapes)

¹au·dit \'ȯ-dət\ *n* : a formal examination and verification of financial accounts

²audit *vb* **1** : to perform an audit on or for **2** : to attend (a course) without expecting formal credit

¹au·di·tion \ȯ-'di-shən\ *n* **1** : HEARING **2** : a trial performance to appraise an entertainer's merits

²audition *vb* **-tioned; -tion·ing** \-'di-shə-niŋ\ : to give an audition to; *also* : to give a trial performance

au·di·tor \'ȯ-də-tər\ *n* **1** : LISTENER **2** : a person who audits

au·di·to·ri·um \ˌȯ-də-'tȯr-ē-əm\ *n, pl* **-ri·ums** *or* **-ria**

\-rē-ə\ **1** : the part of a public building where an audience sits **2** : a hall or building used for public gatherings
au·di·to·ry \'ȯ-də-ˌtȯr-ē\ *adj* : of or relating to hearing or to the sense or organs of hearing ⟨~ stimuli⟩
auditory tube *n* : EUSTACHIAN TUBE
auf Wie·der·seh·en \auf-'vē-dər-ˌzän\ *interj* [G] — used to express farewell
Aug *abbr* August
au·ger \'ȯ-gər\ *n* : a tool for boring

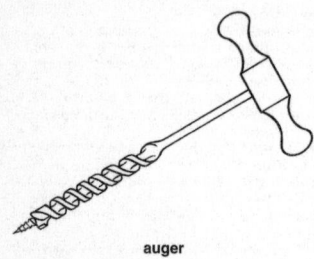

auger

aught \'ȯt, 'ät\ *n* : ZERO, CIPHER
aug·ment \ȯg-'ment\ *vb* : ENLARGE, INCREASE — **aug·men·ta·tion** \ˌȯg-mən-'tā-shən\ *n*
au gra·tin \ō-'gra-tᵊn, ȯ-, -'grä-\ *adj* [F, lit., with the burnt scrapings from the pan] : covered with bread crumbs or grated cheese and browned
¹**au·gur** \'ȯ-gər\ *n* : DIVINER, SOOTHSAYER
²**augur** *vb* **1** : to foretell esp. from omens **2** : to give promise of : PRESAGE
au·gu·ry \'ȯ-gyə-rē, -gə-\ *n, pl* **-ries** **1** : divination from omens **2** : OMEN, PORTENT
au·gust \ȯ-'gəst\ *adj* : marked by majestic dignity or grandeur — **au·gust·ly** *adv* — **au·gust·ness** *n*
August \'ȯ-gəst\ *n* [ME, fr. OE, fr. L *Augustus*, fr. *Augustus* Caesar] : the 8th month of the year
au jus \ō-'zhü, -'zhüs, -'jüs; ō-zhœ\ *adj* [F] : served in the juice obtained from roasting
auk \'ȯk\ *n* : any of several stocky black-and-white diving seabirds that breed in colder parts of the northern hemisphere
auld \'ȯl, 'ȯld, 'äl, 'äld\ *adj, chiefly Scot* : OLD
aunt \'ant, 'änt\ *n* **1** : the sister of one's father or mother **2** : the wife of one's uncle
aunt·ie \'an-tē, 'än-\ *n* : AUNT
au pair \ō-'per\ *n* [F, on even terms] : a usu. young foreign person who does domestic work for a family in return for room and board and to learn the family's language
au·ra \'ȯr-ə\ *n* **1** : a distinctive atmosphere surrounding a given source **2** : a luminous radiation
au·ral \'ȯr-əl\ *adj* : of or relating to the ear or to the sense of hearing
aurar *pl of* EYRIR
au·re·ole \'ȯr-ē-ˌōl\ *or* **au·re·o·la** \ȯ-'rē-ə-lə\ *n* : HALO, NIMBUS
au re·voir \ˌō-rə-'vwär\ *n* [F, lit., till seeing again] : GOOD= BYE
au·ri·cle \'ȯr-i-kəl\ *n* : an atrium of the heart
au·ric·u·lar \ȯ-'ri-kyə-lər\ *adj* **1** : told privately ⟨~ confession⟩ **2** : known or recognized by the sense of hearing
au·ro·ra \ə-'rȯr-ə\ *n, pl* **auroras** *or* **au·ro·rae** \-ˌē\ : a luminous phenomenon of streamers or arches of light appearing in the upper atmosphere esp. of a planet's polar regions — **au·ro·ral** \-əl\ *adj*
aurora aus·tra·lis \-ȯ-'strä-ləs\ *n* : an aurora that occurs in earth's southern hemisphere
aurora bo·re·al·is \-ˌbȯr-ē-'a-ləs\ *n* : an aurora that occurs in earth's northern hemisphere
AUS *abbr* Army of the United States
aus·pice \'ȯ-spəs\ *n, pl* **aus·pic·es** \-spə-səz, -ˌsēz\ [L *auspicium*, fr. *auspic-, auspex* diviner by birds, fr. *avis* bird + *specere* to look, look at] **1** : observation of birds by an augur **2** *pl* : kindly patronage and protection **3** : a prophetic sign or omen
aus·pi·cious \ȯ-'spi-shəs\ *adj* **1** : promising success

: PROPITIOUS **2** : FORTUNATE, PROSPEROUS ⟨an ~ year⟩ — **aus·pi·cious·ly** *adv* — **aus·pi·cious·ness** *n*
aus·tere \ȯ-'stir\ *adj* **1** : STERN, SEVERE, STRICT **2** : ABSTEMIOUS **3** : UNADORNED ⟨~ style⟩ — **aus·tere·ly** *adv* — **aus·ter·i·ty** \-'ster-ə-tē\ *n*
aus·tral \'ȯs-trəl\ *adj* : SOUTHERN
Aus·tro·ne·sian \ˌȯs-trə-'nē-zhən\ *adj* : of, relating to, or constituting a family of languages spoken in the area extending from Madagascar eastward through the Malay Peninsula to Hawaii and Easter Island
auth *abbr* **1** authentic **2** author **3** authorized
au·then·tic \ə-'then-tik, ȯ-\ *adj* : GENUINE, REAL — **au·then·ti·cal·ly** \-ti-k(ə-)lē\ *adv* — **au·then·tic·i·ty** \ˌȯ-ˌthen-'ti-sə-tē\ *n*
au·then·ti·cate \ə-'then-ti-ˌkāt, ȯ-\ *vb* **-cat·ed; -cat·ing** : to prove genuine — **au·then·ti·ca·tion** \-ˌthen-ti-'kā-shən\ *n*
au·thor \'ȯ-thər\ *n* [ME *auctour*, fr. AF *auctor, autor*, fr. L *auctor* originator, author, fr. *augēre* to increase] **1** : one that originates or creates **2** : one that writes or composes a literary work
au·thor·ess \'ȯ-thə-rəs\ *n* : a woman author
au·tho·ri·sa·tion, au·tho·rise *Brit var of* AUTHORIZATION, AUTHORIZE
au·thor·i·tar·i·an \ə-ˌthär-ə-'ter-ē-ən, ȯ-, -ˌthȯr-\ *adj* **1** : characterized by or favoring the principle of blind obedience to authority **2** : characterized by or favoring concentration of political power in an authority not responsible to the people — **authoritarian** *n*
au·thor·i·ta·tive \ə-'thär-ə-ˌtā-tiv, ȯ-, -'thȯr-\ *adj* — supported by, proceeding from, or being an authority — **au·thor·i·ta·tive·ly** *adv* — **au·thor·i·ta·tive·ness** *n*
au·thor·i·ty \ə-'thär-ə-tē, ȯ-, -'thȯr-\ *n, pl* **-ties** **1** : a citation used in support of a statement or in defense of an action; *also* : the source of such a citation **2** : one appealed to as an expert **3** : power to influence thought or behavior **4** : freedom granted : RIGHT **5** : persons in command; *esp* : GOVERNMENT **6** : convincing force
au·tho·rize \'ȯ-thə-ˌrīz\ *vb* **-rized; -riz·ing** **1** : SANCTION ⟨custom *authorized* by time⟩ **2** : to give legal power to — **au·tho·ri·za·tion** \ˌȯ-thə-rə-'zā-shən\ *n*
au·thor·ship \'ȯ-thər-ˌship\ *n* **1** : the state of being an author **2** : the source of a piece of writing, music, or art
au·tism \'ȯ-ˌti-zəm\ *n* : a disorder that appears by age three and is characterized esp. by impaired ability to communicate with others and form normal social relationships and by repetitive patterns of behavior — **au·tis·tic** \ȯ-'tis-tik\ *adj*
¹**au·to** \'ȯ-tō\ *n, pl* **autos** : AUTOMOBILE
²**auto** *abbr* automatic
au·to·bahn \'ȯ-tō-ˌbän, 'au̇-\ *n* : a German, Swiss, or Austrian expressway
au·to·bi·og·ra·phy \ˌȯ-tə-bī-'ä-grə-fē\ *n* : the biography of a person narrated by that person — **au·to·bi·og·ra·pher** \-fər\ *n* — **au·to·bi·o·graph·i·cal** \-ˌbī-ə-'gra-fi-kəl\ *adj* — **au·to·bi·o·graph·i·cal·ly** \-k(ə-)lē\ *adv*
au·toch·tho·nous \ȯ-'täk-thə-nəs\ *adj* : INDIGENOUS, NATIVE ⟨a ~ people⟩
au·to·clave \'ȯ-tō-ˌklāv\ *n* : an apparatus (as for sterilizing) using superheated high-pressure steam
au·toc·ra·cy \ȯ-'tä-krə-sē\ *n, pl* **-cies** : government by one person having unlimited power — **au·to·crat** \'ȯ-tə-ˌkrat\ *n* — **au·to·crat·ic** \ˌȯ-tə-'kra-tik\ *adj* — **au·to·crat·i·cal·ly** \-ti-k(ə-)lē\ *adv*
au·to·ex·po·sure \ˌȯ-tō-ik-'spō-zhər\ *n* : a camera system that automatically adjusts the exposure according to ambient light
¹**au·to·graph** \'ȯ-tə-ˌgraf\ *n* **1** : an original manuscript **2** : a person's signature written by hand
²**autograph** *vb* : to write one's signature on
au·to·im·mune \ˌȯ-tō-i-'myün\ *adj* : of, relating to, or caused by antibodies or lymphocytes that attack molecules, cells, or tissues of the organism producing them ⟨~ diseases⟩ — **au·to·im·mu·ni·ty** \-i-'myü-nə-tē\ *n*
au·to·mate \'ȯ-tə-ˌmāt\ *vb* **-mat·ed; -mat·ing** **1** : to operate automatically using mechanical or electronic devices **2** : to convert to automatic operation — **au·to·ma·tion** \ˌȯ-tə-'mā-shən\ *n*
automated teller machine *n* : ATM
¹**au·to·mat·ic** \ˌȯ-tə-'ma-tik\ *adj* **1** : INVOLUNTARY **2** : made so that certain parts act in a desired manner at the

proper time : SELF-ACTING — au·to·mat·i·cal·ly \-ti-k(ə-)lē\ adv
²automatic n : an automatic device; esp : an automatic firearm
automatic teller n : ATM
automatic teller machine n : ATM
au·tom·a·ton \ȯ-'tä-mə-tən, -ˌtän\ n, pl -atons or -a·ta \-ə-tə, -ə-ˌtä\ 1 : an automatic machine; esp : ROBOT 2 : an individual who acts mechanically
au·to·mo·bile \'ȯ-tə-mō-ˌbēl, ˌȯ-tə-mə-'bēl\ n : a usu. 4-wheeled automotive vehicle for passenger transportation
au·to·mo·tive \ˌȯ-tə-'mō-tiv\ adj 1 : of or relating to automobiles, trucks, or buses 2 : SELF-PROPELLED
au·to·nom·ic nervous system \ˌȯ-tə-'nä-mik-\ n : a part of the vertebrate nervous system that governs involuntary actions and that consists of the sympathetic nervous system and the parasympathetic nervous system
au·ton·o·mous \ȯ-'tä-nə-məs\ adj : having the right or power of self-government — au·ton·o·mous·ly adv — au·ton·o·my \-mē\ n
au·top·sy \'ȯ-ˌtäp-sē, 'ȯ-təp-\ n, pl -sies [Gk autopsia act of seeing with one's own eyes, fr. autos self + opsis sight] : examination of a dead body usu. with dissection sufficient to determine the cause of death or extent of change produced by disease — autopsy vb
au·tumn \'ȯ-təm\ n : the season between summer and winter — au·tum·nal \ȯ-'təm-nəl\ adj
aux abbr auxiliary
¹aux·il·ia·ry \ȯg-'zil-yə-rē, -'zi-lə-rē\ adj 1 : providing help 2 : functioning in a subsidiary capacity 3 : accompanying a verb form to express person, number, mood, or tense 〈~ verbs〉
²auxiliary n, pl -ries 1 : an auxiliary person, group, or device 2 : an auxiliary verb
aux·in \'ȯk-sən\ n : a plant hormone that stimulates growth in length
av abbr 1 avenue 2 average 3 avoirdupois
AV abbr 1 ad valorem 2 audiovisual 3 Authorized Version
¹avail \ə-'vāl\ vb : to be of use or advantage : HELP, BENEFIT
²avail n : USE 〈effort was of no ~〉
avail·able \ə-'vā-lə-bəl\ adj 1 : USABLE 〈~ resources〉 2 : ACCESSIBLE 〈~ in any drugstore〉 — avail·abil·i·ty \-ˌvā-lə-'bi-lə-tē\ n
av·a·lanche \'a-və-ˌlanch\ n : a mass of snow, ice, earth, or rock sliding down a mountainside
avant–garde \ˌä-ˌvänt-'gärd, -ˌvänt-\ n [F, vanguard] : those esp. in the arts who create or apply new or experimental ideas and techniques — avant–garde adj
av·a·rice \'a-və-rəs\ n : excessive desire for wealth : GREED — av·a·ri·cious \ˌa-və-'ri-shəs\ adj
avast \ə-'vast\ vb imper — a nautical command to stop or cease
av·a·tar \'a-və-ˌtär\ n [Skt avatāra descent] : INCARNATION
avaunt \ə-'vȯnt\ adv : AWAY, HENCE
avdp abbr avoirdupois
ave abbr avenue
Ave Ma·ria \ˌä-vā-mə-'rē-ə\ n : HAIL MARY
avenge \ə-'venj\ vb avenged; aveng·ing : to take vengeance for — aveng·er n
av·e·nue \'a-və-ˌnü, -ˌnyü\ n 1 : a way or route to a place or goal : PATH 2 : a broad street
aver \ə-'vər\ vb averred; aver·ring : ALLEGE, ASSERT; also : DECLARE
¹av·er·age \'a-və-rij, 'a-vrij\ n [earlier, proportionally distributed charge for damage at sea, modif. of MF avarie damage to ship or cargo, fr. It avaria, fr. Ar 'awārīyah damaged merchandise] 1 : ARITHMETIC MEAN 2 : a ratio of successful tries to total tries esp. in athletics 〈batting ~ of .303〉
²average adj 1 : equaling or approximating an arithmetic mean 2 : being about midway between extremes 3 : not out of the ordinary : COMMON
³average vb av·er·aged; av·er·ag·ing 1 : to be at or come to an average 2 : to be, do, or get usually 3 : to find the average of
averse \ə-'vərs\ adj : having an active feeling of dislike or reluctance 〈~ to exercise〉
aver·sion \ə-'vər-zhən\ n 1 : a feeling of repugnance for

something with a desire to avoid it 2 : something decidedly disliked
avert \ə-'vərt\ vb 1 : to turn aside or away 〈~ the eyes〉 2 : to ward off
avg abbr average
avi·an \'ā-vē-ən\ adj [L avis bird] : of, relating to, or derived from birds
avi·ary \'ā-vē-ˌer-ē\ n, pl -ar·ies : a place for keeping birds confined
avi·a·tion \ˌā-vē-'ā-shən, ˌa-\ n 1 : the operation of heavier-than-air aircraft 2 : aircraft manufacture, development, and design
avi·a·tor \'ā-vē-ˌā-tər, 'a-\ n : an airplane pilot
avi·a·trix \ˌā-vē-'ā-triks, ˌa-\ n, pl -trix·es \-trik-səz\ or -tri·ces \-trə-ˌsēz\ : a woman airplane pilot
av·id \'a-vəd\ adj 1 : craving eagerly : GREEDY 2 : enthusiastic in pursuit of an interest — avid·i·ty \ə-'vi-də-tē, a-\ n — av·id·ly adv — av·id·ness n
avi·on·ics \ˌā-vē-'ä-niks, ˌa-\ n pl : electronics designed for use in aerospace vehicles — avi·on·ic \-nik\ adj
avo \'ä-(ˌ)vü\ n, pl avos — see pataca at MONEY table
av·o·ca·do \ˌa-və-'kä-dō, ˌä-\ n, pl -dos also -does [modif. of Sp aguacate, fr. Nahuatl āhuacatl, avocado, testicle] : a pulpy green- to purple-skinned nutty-flavored fruit of a tropical American tree; also : this tree
av·o·ca·tion \ˌa-və-'kā-shən\ n : HOBBY
av·o·cet \'a-və-ˌset\ n : any of several long-legged shorebirds with webbed feet and slender upward-curving bills
avoid \ə-'vȯid\ vb 1 : to keep away from : SHUN 2 : to prevent the occurrence of 3 : to refrain from — avoidable adj — avoid·ably adv — avoid·ance \ə-'vȯi-dəns\ n
av·oir·du·pois \ˌa-vər-də-'pȯiz\ n [ME avoir de pois goods sold by weight, fr. AF, lit., goods of weight] 1 : AVOIRDUPOIS WEIGHT 2 : WEIGHT, HEAVINESS; esp : personal weight
avoirdupois weight n : a system of weights based on a pound of 16 ounces and an ounce of 16 drams (28 grams) — see WEIGHT table
avouch \ə-'vaùch\ vb 1 : to declare positively : AVER 2 : to vouch for
avow \ə-'vaù\ vb : to declare openly — avow·al \-'vaù(-ə)l\ n
avun·cu·lar \ə-'vəŋ-kyə-lər\ adj : of, relating to, or resembling an uncle
await \ə-'wāt\ vb : to wait for : EXPECT
¹awake \ə-'wāk\ vb awoke \-'wōk\ also awaked \-'wākt\; awo·ken \-'wō-kən\ or awaked also awoke; awak·ing : to bring back to consciousness : wake up
²awake adj : not asleep; also : ALERT
awak·en \ə-'wā-kən\ vb awak·ened; awak·en·ing \-'wā-kə-niŋ\ : AWAKE
¹award \ə-'wȯrd\ vb 1 : to give by judicial decision 〈~ damages〉 2 : to give in recognition of merit or achievement
²award n 1 : a final decision : JUDGMENT 2 : something awarded : PRIZE
aware \ə-'wer\ adj : having perception or knowledge : CONSCIOUS, INFORMED — aware·ness n
awash \ə-'wȯsh, -'wäsh\ adj 1 : washed by waves or tide 2 : AFLOAT 3 : FLOODED
¹away \ə-'wā\ adv 1 : from this or that place 〈go ~〉 2 : out of the way 3 : in another direction 〈turn ~〉 4 : out of existence 〈fade ~〉 5 : from one's possession 〈give ~〉 6 : without interruption 〈chatter ~〉 7 : at a distance in space or time 〈far ~〉 〈~ back in 1910〉
²away adj 1 : ABSENT 2 : distant in space or time 〈a lake 10 miles ~〉
¹awe \'ȯ\ n 1 : profound and reverent dread of the supernatural 2 : respectful fear inspired by authority
²awe vb awed; aw·ing : to inspire with awe
aweigh \ə-'wā\ adj : just clear of the bottom 〈anchors ~〉
awe·some \'ȯ-səm\ adj 1 : expressive of awe 〈~ tribute〉 2 : inspiring awe
awe·struck \-ˌstrək\ also awe·strick·en \-ˌstri-kən\ adj : filled with awe
aw·ful \'ȯ-fəl\ adj 1 : inspiring awe 2 : extremely disagreeable 3 : very great 〈an ~ lot of money〉 — aw·ful·ly adv
awhile \ə-'hwī(-ə)l\ adv : for a while
awhirl \ə-'hwərl\ adj : being in a whirl
awk·ward \'ȯ-kwərd\ adj 1 : CLUMSY 〈~ with needle and

thread⟩ **2** : UNGRACEFUL ⟨∼ writing⟩ **3** : difficult to explain : EMBARRASSING **4** : difficult to deal with — **awk·ward·ly** adv — **awk·ward·ness** n

awl \'ȯl\ n : a pointed instrument for making small holes

aw·ning \'ȯ-niŋ\ n : a rooflike cover (as of canvas) extended over or in front of a place as a shelter

AWOL \'ā-ˌwȯl, ˌā-ˌdə-bəl-yü-ˌō-'el\ n : a person who is absent without leave — **AWOL** adj or adv

awry \ə-'rī\ adv or adj **1** : ASKEW **2** : AMISS

ax or **axe** \'aks\ n : a chopping or cutting tool with an edged head fitted parallel to a handle

ax·i·al \'ak-sē-əl\ adj **1** : of, relating to, or functioning as an axis **2** : situated around, in the direction of, on, or along an axis — **ax·i·al·ly** adv

ax·i·om \'ak-sē-əm\ n [L axioma, fr. Gk axiōma, lit., something worthy, fr. axioun to think worthy, fr. axios worth, worthy] **1** : a statement generally accepted as true : MAXIM **2** : a proposition regarded as a self-evident truth — **ax·i·om·at·ic** \ˌak-sē-ə-'ma-tik\ adj — **ax·i·om·at·i·cal·ly** \-ti-k(ə-)lē\ adv

ax·is \'ak-səs\ n, pl **ax·es** \-ˌsēz\ **1** : a straight line around which a body rotates **2** : a straight line or structure with respect to which a body or figure is symmetrical **3** : one of the reference lines of a system of coordinates **4** : an alliance between major powers

ax·le \'ak-səl\ n : a shaft on which a wheel revolves

ax·on \'ak-ˌsän\ n : the long thin usu. unbranched part of a nerve cell that usu. conducts impulses away from the cell body

ayah \'ī-ə\ n [Hindi & Urdu āyā, fr. Pg aia, fr. L avia grandmother] : a nurse or maid native to India

aya·tol·lah \ˌī-ə-'tō-lə\ n [Pers āyatollāh, lit., sign of God, fr. Ar aya sign, miracle + allāh God] : an Islamic religious leader — used as a title of respect

¹aye also **ay** \'ā\ adv : ALWAYS, EVER

²aye also **ay** \'ī\ adv : YES

³aye also **ay** \'ī\ n, pl **ayes** : an affirmative vote

AZ abbr Arizona

aza·lea \ə-'zāl-yə\ n : any of numerous rhododendrons with funnel-shaped blossoms and usu. deciduous leaves

az·i·do·thy·mi·dine \ə-ˌzī-dō-'thī-mə-ˌdēn\ n : AZT

az·i·muth \'a-zə-məth\ n : horizontal direction expressed as an angular distance from a fixed point

AZT \ˌā-(ˌ)zē-'tē\ n : an antiviral drug used to treat AIDS

Az·tec \'az-ˌtek\ n : a member of a Nahuatl-speaking people that founded the Mexican empire and were conquered by Hernan Cortes in 1519 — **Az·tec·an** adj

azure \'a-zhər\ n : the blue of the clear sky — **azure** adj

¹b \'bē\ n, pl **b's** or **bs** \'bēz\ often cap **1** : the 2d letter of the English alphabet **2** : a grade rating a student's work as good

²b abbr, often cap **1** bachelor **2** bass **3** bishop **4** book **5** born

B symbol boron

Ba symbol barium

BA abbr **1** bachelor of arts **2** batting average

bab·ble \'ba-bəl\ vb **bab·bled; bab·bling 1** : to talk enthusiastically or excessively **2** : to utter meaningless sounds — **babble** n — **bab·bler** \-b(ə-)lər\ n

babe \'bāb\ n **1** : BABY **2** slang : GIRL, WOMAN

ba·bel \'bā-bəl, 'ba-\ n, often cap [fr: the Tower of Babel, Gen 11:4–9] : a place or scene of noise and confusion; also : a confused sound ✦ **Synonyms** HUBBUB, RACKET, DIN, UPROAR, CLAMOR

ba·boon \ba-'bün\ n [ME babewin, fr. MF babouin, baboue grimace] : any of several large apes of Asia and Africa with doglike muzzles

ba·bush·ka \bə-'büsh-kə, -'bùsh-\ n [Russ, grandmother, dim. of baba old woman] : a kerchief for the head

¹ba·by \'bā-bē\ n, pl **babies 1** : a very young child : INFANT **2** : the youngest or smallest of a group **3** : a childish person — **baby** adj — **ba·by·hood** n — **ba·by·ish** adj

²baby vb **ba·bied; ba·by·ing** : to tend or treat often with excessive care

baby boom n : a marked rise in birthrate — **baby boom·er** \-'bü-mər\ n

baby's breath n : any of a genus of herbs that are related to the pinks and have small delicate flowers

ba·by·sit \'bā-bē-ˌsit\ vb **-sat** \-ˌsat\; **-sit·ting** : to care for children usu. during a short absence of the parents — **ba·by·sit·ter** n

bac·ca·lau·re·ate \ˌba-kə-'lȯr-ē-ət\ n **1** : the degree of bachelor conferred by colleges and universities **2** : a sermon delivered to a graduating class

bac·ca·rat \ˌbä-kə-'rä, ˌba-\ n : a card game in which three hands are dealt and players may bet either or both hands against the dealer's

bac·cha·nal \ˌba-kə-nᵊl, ˌba-kə-'nal, ˌbä-kə-'näl\ n **1** : ORGY **2** : REVELER

bac·cha·na·lia \ˌba-kə-'nāl-yə\ n, pl **bacchanalia** : a drunken orgy — **bac·cha·na·lian** \-'nāl-yən\ adj or n

bach·e·lor \'bach-lər, 'ba-chə-lər\ n **1** : a person who has received the usu. lowest degree conferred by a 4-year college **2** : an unmarried man — **bach·e·lor·hood** n

bach·e·lor·ette \ˌbach-lə-'ret, ˌba-chə-\ n : an unmarried woman

bachelor's button n : a European plant related to the daisies and having usu. blue, pink, or white flower heads

ba·cil·lus \bə-'si-ləs\ n, pl **-li** \-ˌlī\ [NL, fr. ML, small staff, dim. of L baculus staff] : any of a genus of rod-shaped bacteria; also : a disease-producing bacterium — **bac·il·lary** \'ba-sə-ˌler-ē\ adj

¹back \'bak\ n **1** : the rear or dorsal part of the human body; also : the corresponding part of a lower animal **2** : the part or surface opposite the front **3** : a player in the backfield in football — **back·less** \-ləs\ adj

²back adv **1** : to, toward, or at the rear **2** : AGO **3** : so as to be restrained or retarded **4** : to, toward, or in a former place or state **5** : in return or reply

³back adj **1** : located at or in the back; also : REMOTE **2** : OVERDUE ⟨∼ rent⟩ **3** : moving or operating backward **4** : not current ⟨∼ issues of a magazine⟩

⁴back vb **1** : SUPPORT, UPHOLD **2** : to go or cause to go backward or in reverse **3** : to furnish with a back : form the back of — **back·er** n

back·ache \'bak-ˌāk\ n : a pain in the lower back

back·bench·er \-'ben-chər\ n : a rank-and-file member of a British legislature

back·bite \-ˌbīt\ vb **-bit** \-ˌbit\; **-bit·ten** \-ˌbi-tᵊn\; **-bit·ing** \-ˌbī-tiŋ\ : to say mean or spiteful things about someone who is absent — **back·bit·er** n

back·board \-ˌbȯrd\ n : a board placed at or serving as the back of something

back·bone \-ˌbōn\ n **1** : the bony column in the back of a vertebrate that is the chief support of the trunk and consists of a jointed series of vertebrae enclosing and protecting the spinal cord **2** : firm resolute character **3** : the primary high-speed hardware and transmission lines of a telecommunication network

back·drop \'bak-ˌdräp\ n : a painted cloth hung across the rear of a stage

back·field \-ˌfēld\ n : the football players whose positions are behind the line

¹back·fire \-ˌfī(-ə)r\ n : a loud noise caused by the improperly timed explosion of fuel in the cylinder of an internal combustion engine

²back·fire *vb* **1** : to make or undergo a backfire **2** : to have a result opposite to what was intended

back·flip \-ˌflip\ *n* : a backward somersault esp. in the air

back·gam·mon \ˈbak-ˌga-mən\ *n* : a game played with pieces on a double board in which the moves are determined by throwing dice

back·ground \ˈbak-ˌgraúnd\ *n* **1** : the scenery behind something **2** : the setting within which something takes place; *also* : the sum of a person's experience, training, and understanding

back·hand \ˈbak-ˌhand\ *n* : a stroke (as in tennis) made with the back of the hand turned in the direction of movement; *also* : the side on which such a stroke is made — **back·hand** *vb*

back·hand·ed \ˈbak-ˈhan-dəd\ *adj* **1** : INDIRECT, DEVIOUS; *esp* : SARCASTIC ⟨a ∼ compliment⟩ **2** : using or made with a backhand

back·hoe \ˈbak-ˌhō\ *n* : an excavating machine having a bucket that is drawn toward the machine

back·ing \ˈba-kiŋ\ *n* **1** : something forming a back **2** : SUPPORT, AID; *also* : a body of supporters

back·lash \ˈbak-ˌlash\ *n* **1** : a sudden violent backward movement or reaction **2** : a strong adverse reaction

¹back·log \-ˌlòg, -ˌläg\ *n* **1** : a large log at the back of a hearth fire **2** : an accumulation of tasks unperformed or materials not processed

²backlog *vb* : to accumulate in reserve

back of *prep* : BEHIND

back order *n* : a business order yet to be fulfilled because stock is unavailable — **back–order** *vb*

back out *vb* : to withdraw esp. from a commitment or contest

¹back·pack \ˈbak-ˌpak\ *n* : a camping pack supported by an aluminum frame and carried on the back

²backpack *vb* : to hike with a backpack — **back·pack·er** *n*

back·ped·al \ˈbak-ˌpe-dᵊl\ *vb* : RETREAT

back·rest \-ˌrest\ *n* : a rest for the back

back·side \-ˌsīd\ *n* : BUTTOCKS

back·slap \-ˌslap\ *vb* : to display excessive cordiality — **back·slap·per** *n*

back·slide \-ˌslīd\ *vb* **-slid** \-ˌslid\; **-slid** *or* **-slid·den** \-ˌslid⁻ᵊn\; **-slid·ing** \-ˌslī-diŋ\ : to lapse morally or in religious practice — **back·slid·er** *n*

back·space \-ˌspās\ *vb* : to move back a space in a text with the press of a key — **backspace** *n*

back·spin \-ˌspin\ *n* : a backward rotary motion of a ball

¹back·stage \ˈbak-ˌstāj\ *adj* **1** : relating to or occurring in the area behind a stage **2** : of or relating to the private lives of theater people **3** : of or relating to the inner working or operation

²back·stage \ˈbak-ˈstāj\ *adv* **1** : in or to a backstage area **2** : SECRETLY ⟨worked ∼ to gain support⟩

back·stairs \-ˌsterz\ *adj* : SECRET, FURTIVE; *also* : SORDID, SCANDALOUS

¹back·stop \-ˌstäp\ *n* : something serving as a stop behind something else; *esp* : a screen or fence to keep a ball from leaving the field of play

²backstop *vb* **1** : SUPPORT **2** : to serve as a backstop to

back·sto·ry \-ˌstór-ē\ *n* : a story that tells what led up to the main story or plot (as of a film)

back·stretch \ˈbak-ˈstrech\ *n* : the side opposite the homestretch on a racecourse

back·stroke \-ˌstrōk\ *n* : a swimming stroke executed on the back — **back·strok·er** \-ˌstrō-kər\ *n*

back talk *n* : impudent, insolent, or argumentative replies

back·track \ˈbak-ˌtrak\ *vb* **1** : to retrace one's course **2** : to reverse a position or stand

back·up \-ˌəp\ *n* **1** : one that serves as a substitute or alternative **2** : a copy of computer data — **back up** *vb*

¹back·ward \ˈbak-wərd\ *or* **back·wards** \-wərdz\ *adv* **1** : toward the back **2** : with the back foremost ⟨ride ∼⟩ **3** : in a reverse or contrary direction or way ⟨count ∼⟩ **4** : toward the past; *also* : toward a worse state

²backward *adj* **1** : directed, turned, or done backward **2** : DIFFIDENT, SHY **3** : retarded in development — **back·ward·ly** *adv* — **back·ward·ness** *n*

back·wash \ˈbak-ˌwósh, -ˌwäsh\ *n* : a backward flow or movement (as of water or air) produced by a propelling force (as the motion of oars)

back·wa·ter \-ˌwò-tər, -ˌwä-\ *n* **1** : water held or turned

back in its course **2** : an isolated or backward place or condition

back·woods \-ˈwùdz\ *n pl* **1** : wooded or partly cleared areas far from cities **2** : a remote or isolated place

ba·con \ˈbā-kən\ *n* : salted and smoked meat from the sides or back of a pig

bacteria *pl of* BACTERIUM

bac·te·ri·cid·al \bak-ˌtir-ə-ˈsī-dᵊl\ *adj* : destroying bacteria — **bac·te·ri·cide** \-ˈtir-ə-ˌsīd\ *n*

bac·te·ri·ol·o·gy \bak-ˌtir-ē-ˈä-lə-jē\ *n* **1** : a science dealing with bacteria **2** : bacterial life and phenomena — **bac·te·ri·o·log·ic** \-ə-ˈlä-jik\ *or* **bac·te·ri·o·log·i·cal** \-ə-ˈlä-ji-kəl\ *adj* — **bac·te·ri·ol·o·gist** \-ˈä-lə-jist\ *n*

bac·te·rio·phage \bak-ˈtir-ē-ə-ˌfāj\ *n* : any of various viruses that attack specific bacteria

bac·te·ri·um \bak-ˈtir-ē-əm\ *n*, *pl* **-ria** \-ē-ə\ [NL, fr. Gk *baktērion* staff] : any of a group of single-celled microorganisms including some that cause disease and others that are valued esp. for their chemical effects (as fermentation) — **bac·te·ri·al** \-ē-əl\ *adj*

bad \ˈbad\ *adj* **worse** \ˈwərs\; **worst** \ˈwərst\ **1** : below standard : POOR; *also* : UNFAVORABLE ⟨a ∼ report⟩ **2** : SPOILED, DECAYED **3** : WICKED; *also* : not well⸗ behaved : NAUGHTY **4** : DISAGREEABLE ⟨a ∼ taste⟩; *also* : HARMFUL **5** : DEFECTIVE, FAULTY ⟨∼ wiring⟩; *also* : not valid ⟨a ∼ check⟩ **6** : UNWELL, ILL **7** : SORRY, REGRETFUL ⟨feels ∼ about forgetting to call⟩ ♦ **Synonyms** EVIL, WRONG, IMMORAL, INIQUITOUS — **bad·ly** *adv* — **bad·ness** *n*

bade *past and past part of* BID

badge \ˈbaj\ *n* : a device or token usu. worn as a sign of status

¹bad·ger \ˈba-jər\ *n* : any of several sturdy burrowing mammals with long claws on their forefeet

²badger *vb* : to harass or annoy persistently

ba·di·nage \ˌba-də-ˈnäzh\ *n* [F] : playful talk back and forth : BANTER

bad·land \ˈbad-ˌland\ *n* : a region marked by intricate erosional sculpturing and scanty vegetation — usu. used in pl.

bad·min·ton \ˈbad-ˌmi-tᵊn, -ˌmin-tᵊn\ *n* : a court game played with light rackets and a shuttlecock volleyed over a net

bad–mouth \ˈbad-ˌmaùth\ *vb* : to criticize severely

Bae·de·ker \ˈbā-di-kər, ˈbe-\ *n* : GUIDEBOOK

¹baf·fle \ˈba-fəl\ *vb* **baf·fled; baf·fling** \-fə-liŋ\ : FRUSTRATE, THWART, FOIL; *also* : PERPLEX — **baf·fle·ment** *n*

²baffle *n* : a device (as a wall or screen) to deflect, check, or regulate flow (as of liquid or sound) — **baf·fled** \ˈba-fəld\ *adj*

¹bag \ˈbag\ *n* **1** : a flexible usu. closable container (as for storing or carrying) **2** : something that bulges and sags like a bag ⟨∼s under the eyes⟩

²bag *vb* **bagged; bag·ging 1** : DISTEND, BULGE **2** : to put in a bag **3** : to get possession of; *esp* : to take in hunting ♦ **Synonyms** TRAP, SNARE, CATCH, CAPTURE, COLLAR

ba·gasse \bə-ˈgas\ *n* [F] : plant residue (as of sugarcane) left after a product (as juice) has been extracted

bag·a·telle \ˌba-gə-ˈtel\ *n* [F] : TRIFLE 1

ba·gel \ˈbā-gəl\ *n* [Yiddish *beygl*] : a firm doughnut-shaped roll usu. made by boiling and then baking

bag·gage \ˈba-gij\ *n* **1** : the traveling bags and personal belongings of a traveler : LUGGAGE **2** : intangible things that get in the way ⟨emotional ∼⟩

bag·gies \ˈba-gēz\ *n pl* : baggy pants or shorts

bag·gy \ˈba-gē\ *adj* **bag·gi·er; -est** : puffed out or hanging like a bag — **bag·gi·ly** \-gə-lē\ *adv* — **bag·gi·ness** \-gē-nəs\ *n*

bag·man \ˈbag-mən\ *n* : a person who collects or distributes illicitly gained money on behalf of another

ba·gnio \ˈban-yō\ *n, pl* **bagnios** [It *bagno*, lit., public bath] : BROTHEL

bag of waters : a double-walled fluid-filled sac that encloses and protects the fetus in the womb and that breaks releasing its fluid during the process of birth

bag·pipe \ˈbag-ˌpīp\ *n* : a musical wind instrument consisting of a bag, a tube with valves, and sounding pipes — often used in pl. — **bag·pip·er** \-ˌpī-pər\ *n*

ba·guette \ba-ˈget\ *n* [F, lit., rod] **1** : a gem having the shape of a narrow rectangle; *also* : the shape itself **2** : a long thin loaf of French bread

baht \'bät\ *n, pl* baht *also* bahts — see MONEY table

¹bail \'bāl\ *n* : a container for ladling water out of a boat

²bail *vb* : to dip and throw out water from a boat — **bail·er** *n*

³bail *n* : security given to guarantee a prisoner's appearance when legally required; *also* : one giving such security or the release secured

⁴bail *vb* : to release under bail; *also* : to procure the release of by giving bail — **bail·able** \'bā-lə-bəl\ *adj*

⁵bail *n* : the arched handle (as of a pail or kettle)

bai·liff \'bā-ləf\ *n* **1** : an aide of a British sheriff who serves writs and makes arrests; *also* : a minor officer of a U.S. court **2** : an estate or farm manager esp. in Britain : STEWARD

bai·li·wick \'bā-li-ˌwik\ *n* : one's special province or domain ◆ *Synonyms* TERRITORY, FIELD, SPHERE

bail·out \'bā-ˌlaut\ *n* : a rescue from financial distress

bairn \'bern\ *n, chiefly Scot* : CHILD

¹bait \'bāt\ *vb* **1** : to persecute by continued attacks **2** : to harass with dogs usu. for sport ⟨~ a bear⟩ **3** : to furnish (as a hook) with bait **4** : ALLURE, ENTICE **5** : to give food and drink to (as an animal) ◆ *Synonyms* BADGER, HECKLE, HOUND

²bait *n* **1** : a lure for catching animals (as fish) **2** : LURE, TEMPTATION ◆ *Synonyms* SNARE, TRAP, DECOY, COME-ON, ENTICEMENT

bait·fish \'bāt-ˌfish\ *n* : a small fish that attracts and is a food source for a larger fish; *also* : a fish used for bait

bal·za \'bäl-(ˌ)zä\ *n, pl* baiza *or* baizas — see *rial* at MONEY table

baize \'bāz\ *n* : a coarse feltlike fabric

¹bake \'bāk\ *vb* baked; bak·ing **1** : to cook or become cooked in dry heat esp. in an oven **2** : to dry and harden by heat ⟨~ bricks⟩ — **bak·er** *n*

²bake *n* : a social gathering featuring baked food

baker's dozen *n* : THIRTEEN

bak·ery \'bā-k(ə-)rē\ *n, pl* -er·ies : a place for baking or selling baked goods

bake sale *n* : a fund-raising event at which usu. homemade foods are sold

bake·shop \'bāk-ˌshäp\ *n* : BAKERY

bake·ware \-ˌwer\ *n* : dishes used for baking and serving food

baking powder *n* : a powder that consists of a carbonate, an acid, and a starch and that makes the dough rise in baking cakes and biscuits

baking soda *n* : SODIUM BICARBONATE

bak·sheesh \'bak-ˌshēsh\ *n* : payment (as a tip or bribe) to expedite service

bal *abbr* balance

bal·a·lai·ka \ˌba-lə-'lī-kə\ *n* [Russ] : a triangular 3-stringed instrument of Russian origin played by plucking or strumming

¹bal·ance \'ba-ləns\ *n* [ME, fr. AF, fr. VL *bilancia*, fr. LL *bilanc-, bilanx* having two scalepans, fr. L *bi* two + *lanc-, lanx* plate] **1** : a weighing device : SCALE **2** : a weight, force, or influence counteracting the effect of another **3** : an oscillating wheel used to regulate a timepiece **4** : a state of equilibrium **5** : REMAINDER, REST; *esp* : an amount in excess esp. on the credit side of an account — **bal·anced** \-lənst\ *adj*

²balance *vb* bal·anced; bal·anc·ing **1** : to compute the balance of an account **2** : to arrange so that one set of elements equals another; *also* : to equal or equalize in weight, number, or proportions **3** : WEIGH **4** : to bring or come to a state or position of balance; *also* : to bring into harmony or proportion

bal·boa \bal-'bō-ə\ *n* — see MONEY table

bal·brig·gan \bal-'bri-gən\ *n* : a knitted cotton fabric used esp. for underwear

bal·co·ny \'bal-kə-nē\ *n, pl* -nies **1** : a platform projecting from the side of a building and enclosed by a railing **2** : a gallery inside a building

¹bald \'bold\ *adj* **1** : lacking a natural or usual covering (as of hair) **2** : UNADORNED, PLAIN ⟨the ~ truth⟩ ◆ *Synonyms* BARE, BARREN, NAKED, NUDE — **bald·ly** *adv* — **bald·ness** *n*

bal·da·chin \'bol-də-kən, 'bal-\ *or* bal·da·chi·no \ˌbal-də-'kē-nō\ *n, pl* -chins *or* -chinos : a canopylike structure over an altar

bald cypress *n* : either of two coniferous trees of southern U.S. swamps; *also* : their hard red wood

bald eagle *n* : a large brown eagle of No. America that when mature has white head and neck feathers and a white tail

bal·der·dash \'bol-dər-ˌdash\ *n* : NONSENSE

bald·ing \'bol-diŋ\ *adj* : becoming bald

bal·dric \'bol-drik\ *n* : a belt worn over the shoulder to carry a sword or bugle

¹bale \'bāl\ *n* : a large or closely packed bundle

²bale *vb* baled; bal·ing : to pack in a bale — **bal·er** *n*

ba·leen \bə-'lēn\ *n* : a horny substance attached in plates to the upper jaw of some large whales (**baleen whales**)

bale·ful \'bāl-fəl\ *adj* : DEADLY, HARMFUL; *also* : OMINOUS ◆ *Synonyms* SINISTER, MALEFIC, MALEFICENT, MALIGN

¹balk \'bok\ *n* **1** : HINDRANCE, CHECK, SETBACK **2** : an illegal motion of the pitcher in baseball while in position

²balk *vb* **1** : BLOCK, THWART **2** : to stop short and refuse to go on **3** : to commit a balk in sports ◆ *Synonyms* FRUSTRATE, BAFFLE, FOIL, THWART — **balky** \'bo-kē\ *adj*

¹ball \'bol\ *n* **1** : a rounded body or mass (as an object used in a game or as a missile); *also* : a roundish protuberant part of the body ⟨the ~ of the foot⟩ **2** : a game played with a ball **3** : a pitched baseball that misses the strike zone and is not swung at by the batter ⟨foul ~⟩ — **on the ball** : COMPETENT, KNOWLEDGEABLE, ALERT

²ball *vb* : to form into a ball

³ball *n* : a large formal dance

bal·lad \'ba-ləd\ *n* **1** : a narrative poem of strongly marked rhythm suitable for singing **2** : a simple song : AIR **3** : a slow romantic song

bal·lad·eer \ˌba-lə-'dir\ *n* : a singer of ballads

¹bal·last \'ba-ləst\ *n* **1** : heavy material used to stabilize a ship or control a balloon's ascent **2** : crushed stone laid in a railroad bed or used in making concrete

²ballast *vb* : to provide with ballast ◆ *Synonyms* BAL-ANCE, STABILIZE, STEADY

ball bearing *n* : a bearing in which the revolving part turns upon steel balls that roll easily in a groove; *also* : one of the balls in such a bearing

ball·car·ri·er \'bol-ˌker-ē-ər\ *n* : the football player carrying the ball in an offensive play

ball·er \'bo-lər\ *n* : an implement for shaping food into a ball ⟨melon ~⟩

bal·le·ri·na \ˌba-lə-'rē-nə\ *n* : a female ballet dancer

bal·let \'ba-ˌlā, ba-'lā\ *n* **1** : dancing in which fixed poses and steps are combined with light flowing movements often to convey a story; *also* : a theatrical art form using ballet dancing **2** : a company of ballet dancers

bal·let·o·mane \ba-'le-tə-ˌmān\ *n* : a devotee of ballet

bal·lis·tic missile \bə-'lis-tik-\ *n* : a missile that is guided during ascent and that falls freely during descent

bal·lis·tics \-tiks\ *n sing or pl* **1** : the science of the motion of projectiles (as bullets) in flight **2** : the flight characteristics of a projectile — **ballistic** *adj*

ball of fire : an unusually energetic person

¹bal·loon \bə-'lün\ *n* **1** : a bag filled with gas or heated air so as to rise and float in the atmosphere usu. carrying a suspended load **2** : an inflatable bag used as a toy or decoration — **bal·loon·ist** *n*

²balloon *vb* **1** : to swell or puff out **2** : to travel in a balloon **3** : to increase rapidly

balcony 1

¹bal·lot \'ba-lət\ *n* [It *ballotta* small ball used in secret voting, fr. It dial., dim. of *balla* ball] **1** : a piece of paper used to cast a vote   **2** : the action or a system of voting; *also* : the right to vote

²ballot *vb* : to decide by ballot : VOTE

¹ball·park \'bȯl-ˌpärk\ *n* : a park in which ball games are played

²ballpark *adj* : approximately correct ⟨∼ estimate⟩

ball·point \'bȯl-ˌpȯint\ *n* : a pen whose writing point is a small rotating metal ball that inks itself from an inner container

ball·room \'bȯl-ˌrüm, -ˌrum\ *n* : a large room for dances

ballroom dance *n* : any of various dances (as the tango, two-step, and waltz) in which couples perform set moves

bal·ly·hoo \'ba-lē-ˌhü\ *n, pl* **-hoos** : extravagant statements and claims made for publicity — ballyhoo *vb*

balm \'bäm, 'bälm\ *n* **1** : a fragrant healing or soothing lotion or ointment   **2** : any of several spicy fragrant herbs of the mint family   **3** : something that comforts or soothes

balmy \'bä-mē, 'bäl-\ *adj* balm·i·er; -est **1** : gently soothing : MILD   **2** : FOOLISH, ABSURD ♦ *Synonyms* SOFT, BLAND, MILD, GENTLE — balm·i·ness *n*

ba·lo·ney \bə-'lō-nē\ *n* : NONSENSE

bal·sa \'bȯl-sə\ *n* : the extremely light strong wood of a tropical American tree; *also* : the tree

bal·sam \'bȯl-səm\ *n* **1** : a fragrant aromatic and usu. resinous substance oozing from various plants; *also* : a preparation containing or smelling like balsam   **2** : a balsam-yielding tree (as balsam fir)   **3** : a common garden ornamental plant — bal·sam·ic \bȯl-'sa-mik\ *adj*

balsam fir *n* : a resinous No. American evergreen tree that is widely used for pulpwood and as a Christmas tree

balsamic vinegar *n* : an aged Italian vinegar made from white grapes

Balt \'bȯlt\ *n* : a native or inhabitant of Lithuania, Latvia, or Estonia

Bal·ti·more oriole \'bȯl-tə-ˌmȯr-\ *n* : a common American oriole in which the male is brightly colored with orange, black, and white

bal·us·ter \'ba-lə-stər\ *n* [F *balustre*, fr. It *balaustro*, fr. *balaustra* wild pomegranate flower, fr. L *balaustium*; fr. its shape] : an upright support for a rail (as of a staircase)

bal·us·trade \'ba-lə-ˌsträd\ *n* : a row of balusters topped by a rail

bam·boo \bam-'bü\ *n, pl* bamboos : any of various woody mostly tall tropical grasses including some with strong hollow stems used for building, furniture, or utensils

bamboo curtain *n, often cap B&C* : a political, military, and ideological barrier in eastern Asia

bam·boo·zle \bam-'bü-zəl\ *vb* -boo·zled; -boo·zling : TRICK, HOODWINK

¹ban \'ban\ *vb* banned; ban·ning : PROHIBIT, FORBID

²ban *n* **1** : CURSE   **2** : a legal or formal prohibition ⟨a ∼ on beef imports⟩

³ban \'bän\ *n, pl* ba·ni \'bä-nē\ — see *leu* at MONEY table

ba·nal \bə-'näl, -'nal; 'bä-nᵊl\ *adj* [F] : COMMONPLACE, TRITE — ba·nal·i·ty \bā-'na-lə-tē\ *n*

ba·nana \bə-'na-nə\ *n* : a treelike tropical plant bearing thick clusters of yellow or reddish finger-shaped fruit; *also* : this fruit

¹band \'band\ *n* **1** : something that binds, ties, or goes around   **2** : a strip or stripe that can be distinguished (as by color or texture) from nearby matter   **3** : a range of wavelengths (as in radio)

²band *vb* **1** : to tie up, finish, or enclose with a band   **2** : to gather together or unite esp. for some common end — band·er *n*

³band *n* : a group of persons, animals, or things; *esp* : a group of musicians organized for playing together

¹ban·dage \'ban-dij\ *n* : a strip of material used esp. in dressing wounds

²bandage *vb* ban·daged; ban·dag·ing : to dress or cover with a bandage

Band-Aid \'ban-ˌdād\ *adj* : offering, making use of, or serving as a temporary or expedient remedy or solution

ban·dan·na *or* ban·dana \ban-'da-nə\ *n* : a large colored figured handkerchief

B and B *abbr* bed-and-breakfast

band·box \'band-ˌbäks\ *n* : a usu. cylindrical box for carrying clothing

band·ed \'ban-dəd\ *adj* : having or marked with bands

ban·de·role *or* ban·de·rol \'ban-də-ˌrōl\ *n* : a long narrow forked flag or streamer

ban·dit \'ban-dət\ *n* [It *bandito*, fr. *bandire* to banish] **1** *pl also* ban·dit·ti \ban-'di-tē\ : an outlaw who lives by plunder; *esp* : a member of a band of marauders   **2** : ROBBER — ban·dit·ry \'ban-də-trē\ *n*

ban·do·lier *or* ban·do·leer \ˌban-də-'lir\ *n* : a belt slung over the shoulder esp. to carry ammunition

band saw *n* : a saw in the form of an endless steel belt running over pulleys

band·stand \'band-ˌstand\ *n* : a usu. roofed platform on which a band or orchestra performs outdoors

b and w *abbr* black and white

band·wag·on \'band-ˌwa-gən\ *n* **1** : a wagon carrying musicians in a parade   **2** : a movement that attracts growing support

band·width \-'width\ *n* : the capacity for data transfer of an electronic communication system

¹ban·dy \'ban-dē\ *vb* ban·died; ban·dy·ing **1** : to exchange (as blows or quips) esp. in rapid succession   **2** : to use in a glib or offhand way

²bandy *adj* : curved outward ⟨∼ legs⟩

bane \'bān\ *n* **1** : POISON   **2** : WOE, HARM; *also* : a source of this — bane·ful *adj*

¹bang \'baŋ\ *vb* **1** : BUMP ⟨fell and ∼ed his knee⟩   **2** : to strike, thrust, or move usu. with a loud noise

²bang *n* **1** : a resounding blow   **2** : a sudden loud noise

³bang *adv* **1** : DIRECTLY, RIGHT ⟨ran ∼ up against more trouble⟩

⁴bang *n* : a fringe of hair cut short (as across the forehead) — usu. used in pl.

⁵bang *vb* : to cut (as hair) to produce bangs

ban·gle \'baŋ-gəl\ *n* **1** : BRACELET   **2** : a loose-hanging ornament

bang-up \'baŋ-ˌəp\ *adj* : FIRST-RATE, EXCELLENT ⟨a ∼ job⟩

bani *pl of* ³BAN

ban·ish \'ba-nish\ *vb* **1** : to require by authority to leave a country   **2** : to drive out : EXPEL ♦ *Synonyms* EXILE, OSTRACIZE, DEPORT, RELEGATE — ban·ish·ment *n*

ban·is·ter \'ba-nə-stər\ *n* **1** : a handrail with its supporting posts   **2** : HANDRAIL   **3** : BALUSTER

ban·jo \'ban-jō\ *n, pl* banjos *also* banjoes : a musical instrument with a long neck, a drumlike body, and usu. five strings — ban·jo·ist \-ist\ *n*

¹bank \'baŋk\ *n* **1** : a piled-up mass (as of cloud or earth)   **2** : an undersea elevation   **3** : rising ground bordering a lake, river, or sea   **4** : the sideways slope of a surface along a curve or of a vehicle as it rounds a curve

²bank *vb* **1** : to form a bank about   **2** : to cover (as a fire) with fuel to keep inactive   **3** : to build (a curve) with the roadbed or track inclined laterally upward from the inside edge   **4** : to pile or heap in a bank; *also* : to arrange in a tier   **5** : to incline (an airplane) laterally

³bank *n* [ME, fr. MF *or* It; MF *banque*, fr. *banca*, lit., bench, of Gmc origin] **1** : an establishment concerned esp. with the custody, loan, exchange, or issue of money, the extension of credit, and the transmission of funds   **2** : a stock of or a place for holding something in reserve ⟨a blood ∼⟩

⁴bank *vb* **1** : to conduct the business of a bank   **2** : to deposit money or have an account in a bank — bank·er *n* — bank·ing *n*

⁵bank *n* : a group of objects arranged close together in a row or tier) ⟨a ∼ of file drawers⟩

bank·book \'baŋk-ˌbuk\ *n* : the depositor's book in which a bank records deposits and withdrawals

bank·card \-ˌkärd\ *n* : a card (as a credit card or an ATM card) issued by a bank

bank·note \-ˌnōt\ *n* : a promissory note issued by a bank and circulating as money

bank·roll \-ˌrōl\ *n* : supply of money : FUNDS

¹bank·rupt \'baŋk-(ˌ)rəpt\ *n* [modif. of MF *banquerote* bankruptcy, fr. It *bancarotta*, fr. *banca* bank + *rotta* broken] : an insolvent person; *esp* : one whose property is turned over by court action to a trustee to be handled for the benefit of his creditors — bankrupt *vb*

²bankrupt *adj* **1** : reduced to financial ruin; *esp* : legally declared a bankrupt   **2** : wholly lacking in or deprived of some essential ⟨morally ∼⟩ — bank·rupt·cy \'baŋk-(ˌ)rəpt-sē\ *n*

banner • barkeeper

¹ban·ner \'ba-nər\ *n* **1** : a piece of cloth attached to a staff and used by a leader as his standard **2** : FLAG **3** : an advertisement that runs usu. across the top of a Web page
²banner *adj* : distinguished from all others esp. in excellence ⟨a ~ year⟩
ban·nock \'ba-nək\ *n* : a flat oatmeal or barley cake usu. cooked on a griddle
banns \'banz\ *n pl* : public announcement esp. in church of a proposed marriage
ban·quet \'baŋ-kwət\ *n* [MF, fr. It *banchetto*, fr. dim. of *banca* bench] : a ceremonial dinner — **banquet** *vb*
ban·quette \baŋ-'ket\ *n* : a long upholstered bench esp. along a wall
ban·shee \'ban-shē\ *n* [Ir *bean sídhe* & ScGael *bean sìth*, lit., woman of fairyland] : a female spirit in Gaelic folklore whose wailing warns a family that one of them will soon die
ban·tam \'ban-təm\ *n* **1** : any of numerous small domestic fowls that are often miniatures of standard breeds **2** : a small but pugnacious person
¹ban·ter \'ban-tər\ *vb* : to speak to in a witty and teasing manner
²banter *n* : good-natured witty joking
Ban·tu \'ban-,tü\ *n, pl* **Bantu** *or* **Bantus** **1** : a group of languages spoken in central and southern Africa **2** : a member of a group of African peoples who speak Bantu
ban·yan \'ban-yən\ *n* : a large tropical Asian tree whose aerial roots grow downward to the ground and form new trunks
ban·zai \bän-'zī\ *n* : a Japanese cheer or cry of triumph
bao·bab \'baú-,bab, 'bä-ə-\ *n* : a tropical African tree with short swollen trunk and sour edible fruits resembling gourds
bap·tism \'bap-,ti-zəm\ *n* **1** : a Christian sacrament signifying spiritual rebirth and symbolized by the ritual use of water **2** : an act of baptizing — **bap·tis·mal** \bap-'tiz-məl\ *adj*
baptismal name *n* : GIVEN NAME
Bap·tist \'bap-tist\ *n* : a member of any of several Protestant denominations emphasizing baptism by immersion of believers only
bap·tis·tery *or* **bap·tis·try** \'bap-tə-strē\ *n, pl* **-ter·ies** *or* **-tries** : a place esp. in a church used for baptism
bap·tize \bap-'tīz, 'bap-,tīz\ *vb* **bap·tized; bap·tiz·ing** [ME, fr. AF *baptiser*, fr. L *baptizare*, fr. Gk *baptizein* to dip, baptize, fr. *baptein* to dip] **1** : to administer baptism to; *also* : CHRISTEN **2** : to purify esp. by an ordeal
¹bar \'bär\ *n* **1** : a long narrow piece of material (as wood or metal) used esp. for a lever, fastening, or support **2** : BARRIER, OBSTACLE **3** : the railing in a law court at which prisoners are stationed; *also* : the legal profession or the whole body of lawyers **4** : a stripe, band, or line much longer than wide **5** : a counter at which food or esp. drink is served; *also* : BARROOM **6** : a vertical line across the musical staff
²bar *vb* **barred; bar·ring** **1** : to fasten, confine, or obstruct with or as if with a bar or bars **2** : to mark with bars : STRIPE **3** : to shut or keep out : EXCLUDE **4** : FORBID, PREVENT
³bar *prep* : EXCEPT ⟨the most popular actor, ~ none⟩
⁴bar *abbr* barometer; barometric
Bar *abbr* Baruch
barb \'bärb\ *n* **1** : a sharp projection extending backward (as from the point of an arrow) **2** : a biting critical remark — **barbed** \'bärbd\ *adj* — **barb·less** \'bärb-ləs\ *adj*
bar·bar·ian \bär-'ber-ē-ən\ *adj* **1** : of, relating to, or being a land, culture, or people alien to and usu. believed to be inferior to another's **2** : lacking refinement, learning, or artistic or literary culture — **barbarian** *n* — **bar·bar·i·an·ism** \-ē-ə-,ni-zəm\ *n*
bar·bar·ic \bär-'ber-ik\ *adj* **1** : BARBARIAN **2** : marked by a lack of restraint : WILD **3** : PRIMITIVE, UNSOPHISTICATED
bar·ba·rism \'bär-bə-,ri-zəm\ *n* **1** : the social condition of barbarians; *also* : the use or display of barbarian or barbarous acts, attitudes, or ideas **2** : a word or expression that offends standards of correctness or purity
bar·ba·rous \'bär-bə-rəs\ *adj* **1** : lacking culture or refinement **2** : using linguistic barbarisms **3** : mercilessly harsh or cruel — **bar·bar·i·ty** \bär-'ber-ə-tē\ *n* — **bar·ba·rous·ly** *adv* — **bar·ba·rous·ness** *n*

¹bar·be·cue \'bär-bi-,kyü\ *vb* **-cued; -cu·ing** **1** : to cook on a rack or revolving spit over or before a source of heat **2** : to cook in a highly seasoned vinegar sauce
²barbecue *n* : a social gathering at which barbecued food is served
bar·bell \'bär-,bel\ *n* : a bar with adjustable weights attached to each end used for exercise and in weight-lifting competition
bar·ber \'bär-bər\ *n* [ME, fr. AF *barbour*, fr. *barbe* beard, fr. L *barba*] : one whose business is cutting and dressing hair and shaving and trimming beards
bar·ber·ry \'bär-,ber-ē\ *n* : any of a genus of spiny shrubs bearing yellow flowers and oblong red berries
bar·bi·tu·rate \bär-'bi-chə-rət\ *n* : any of various compounds (as a salt or ester) formed from an organic acid (**bar·bi·tu·ric acid** \,bär-bə-'tür-ik-, -'tyúr-\); *esp* : one used as a sedative or hypnotic
bar·ca·role *or* **bar·ca·rolle** \'bär-kə-,rōl\ *n* : a Venetian boat song characterized by a beat suggesting a rowing rhythm; *also* : a piece of music imitating this
bar chart *n* : BAR GRAPH
bar code *n* : a set of printed and variously spaced bars and sometimes numerals that is designed to be scanned to provide information about the object it labels — **bar·cod·ed** \'bär-,kō-dəd\ *adj* — **bar coding** *n*
bard \'bärd\ *n* : POET
¹bare \'ber\ *adj* **bar·er; bar·est** **1** : NAKED **2** : UNCONCEALED, EXPOSED **3** : EMPTY **4** : leaving nothing to spare : MERE **5** : PLAIN, UNADORNED ⟨the ~ facts⟩
♦ *Synonyms* NUDE, BALD — **bare·ness** *n*
²bare *vb* **bared; bar·ing** : to make or lay bare : UNCOVER
bare·back \-,bak\ *or* **bare·backed** \-'bakt\ *adv or adj* : without a saddle
bare·faced \-'fāst\ *adj* **1** : having the face uncovered; *esp* : BEARDLESS **2** : not concealed : OPEN — **bare·faced·ly** \-'fā-səd-lē, -'fāst-lē\ *adv*
bare·foot \-,fút\ *or* **bare·foot·ed** \-'fú-təd\ *adv or adj* : with bare feet
bare·hand·ed \-'han-dəd\ *adv or adj* **1** : without gloves **2** : without tools or weapons
bare·head·ed \-'he-dəd\ *adv or adj* : without a hat
bare·ly \'ber-lē\ *adv* **1** : PLAINLY, MEAGERLY ⟨a ~ furnished room⟩ **2** : by a narrow margin : only just ⟨~ enough money⟩
bar·fly \'bär-,flī\ *n* : a drinker who frequents bars
¹bar·gain \'bär-gən\ *n* **1** : AGREEMENT **2** : an advantageous purchase **3** : a transaction, situation, or event regarded in the light of its results
²bargain *vb* **1** : to negotiate over the terms of an agreement; *also* : to come to terms **2** : BARTER
bar·gain–base·ment \'bär-gən-'bās-mənt\ *adj* : markedly inexpensive
¹barge \'bärj\ *n* **1** : a broad flat-bottomed boat usu. moved by towing **2** : a motorboat supplied to a flagship (as for an admiral) **3** : a ceremonial boat elegantly furnished — **barge·man** \-mən\ *n*
²barge *vb* **barged; barg·ing** **1** : to carry by barge **2** : to move or thrust oneself clumsily or rudely
bar graph *n* : a graphic technique for comparing amounts by rectangles whose lengths are proportional to the amounts they represent
ba·ris·ta \bə-'rēs-tə\ *n* : a person who makes and serves coffee to the public
bari·tone \'ber-ə-,tōn\ *n* [F *baryton* or It *baritono*, fr. Gk *barytonos* deep sounding, fr. *barys* heavy + *tonos* tone] : a male voice between bass and tenor; *also* : a man with such a voice
bar·i·um \'ber-ē-əm\ *n* : a silver-white metallic chemical element that occurs only in combination
¹bark \'bärk\ *vb* **1** : to make the short loud cry of a dog **2** : to speak or utter in a curt loud tone : SNAP
²bark *n* : the sound made by a barking dog
³bark *n* : the tough corky outer covering of a woody stem or root
⁴bark *vb* **1** : to strip the bark from **2** : to rub the skin from : ABRADE
⁵bark *n* : a ship of three or more masts with the aft mast fore-and-aft rigged and the others square-rigged
bar·keep \'bär-,kēp\ *also* **bar·keep·er** \-,kē-pər\ *n* : BARTENDER

bark·er \'bär-kər\ *n* : a person who stands at the entrance esp. to a show and tries to attract customers to it

bar·ley \'bär-lē\ *n* : a cereal grass with seeds used as food and in making malt liquors; *also* : its seed

bar mitz·vah \bär-'mits-və\ *n, often cap B&M* [Heb *bar miṣwāh*, lit., son of the (divine) law] **1** : a Jewish boy who at about 13 years of age assumes religious responsibilities **2** : the ceremony recognizing a boy as a bar mitzvah

barn \'bärn\ *n* [ME *bern*, fr. OE *bereærn*, fr. *bere* barley + *ærn* house, store] : a building used esp. for storing hay and grain and for housing livestock or farm equipment

bar·na·cle \'bär-ni-kəl\ *n* : any of numerous small marine crustaceans free-swimming when young but permanently fixed (as to rocks, whales, or ships) when adult

barn·storm \'bärn-ˌstórm\ *vb* : to travel through the country making brief stops to entertain (as with shows or flying stunts) or to campaign for political office

barn·yard \-ˌyärd\ *n* : a usu. fenced area adjoining a barn

baro·graph \'ber-ə-ˌgraf\ *n* : a recording barometer

ba·rom·e·ter \bə-'räm-ə-tər\ *n* : an instrument for measuring atmospheric pressure — **baro·met·ric** \ˌbar-ə-'me-trik\ *adj*

bar·on \'ber-ən\ *n* : a member of the lowest grade of the British peerage — **ba·ro·ni·al** \bə-'rō-nē-əl\ *adj* — **bar·ony** \'ber-ə-nē\ *n*

bar·on·age \'ber-ə-nij\ *n* : PEERAGE

bar·on·ess \'ber-ə-nəs\ *n* **1** : the wife or widow of a baron **2** : a woman holding a baronial title in her own right

bar·on·et \'ber-ə-nət\ *n* : a man holding a rank of honor below a baron but above a knight — **bar·on·et·cy** \-sē\ *n*

ba·roque \bə-'rōk, -'räk\ *adj* : marked by the use of complex forms, bold ornamentation, and the juxtapositioning of contrasting elements

ba·rouche \bə-'rüsh\ *n* [G *Barutsche*, fr. It *biroccio*, ultim. fr. LL *birotus* two-wheeled, fr. L *bi-* two + *rota* wheel] : a 4-wheeled carriage with a high driver's seat in front and a folding top

bar·racks \'ber-əks\ *n sing or pl* : a building or group of buildings for lodging soldiers

bar·ra·cu·da \ˌber-ə-'kü-də\ *n, pl* **-da** *or* **-das** : any of several large slender predaceous sea fishes including some used for food

bar·rage \bə-'räzh, -'räj\ *n* : a heavy concentration of fire (as of artillery)

barred \'bärd\ *adj* : STRIPED

¹bar·rel \'ber-əl\ *n* **1** : a round bulging cask with flat ends of equal diameter **2** : the amount contained in a barrel **3** : a cylindrical or tubular part ⟨gun ~⟩ — **bar·reled** \-əld\ *adj*

²barrel *vb* **-reled** *or* **-relled**; **-rel·ing** *or* **-rel·ling** **1** : to pack in a barrel **2** : to travel at high speed

bar·rel·head \-ˌhed\ *n* : the flat end of a barrel — **on the barrelhead** : asking for or granting no credit ⟨paid cash *on the barrelhead*⟩

barrel roll *n* : an airplane maneuver in which a complete revolution about the longitudinal axis is made

¹bar·ren \'ber-ən\ *adj* **1** : STERILE, UNFRUITFUL **2** : unproductive of results ⟨a ~ scheme⟩ **3** : lacking interest or charm **4** : lacking inspiration or ideas — **bar·ren·ness** \-nəs\ *n*

²barren *n* : a tract of barren land

bar·rette \bä-'ret, bə-\ *n* : a clasp or bar for holding the hair in place

¹bar·ri·cade \'ber-ə-ˌkād, ˌber-ə-'kād\ *vb* **-cad·ed; -cad·ing** : to block, obstruct, or fortify with a barricade

²barricade *n* [F, fr. MF, fr. F. *barriquer* to barricade, fr. *barrique* barrel] **1** : a hastily thrown-up obstruction or fortification **2** : BARRIER, OBSTACLE

bar·ri·er \'ber-ē-ər\ *n* : something that separates, demarcates, or serves as a barricade ⟨racial ~s⟩

barrier island *n* : a long broad sandy island lying parallel to a shore

barrier reef *n* : a coral reef roughly parallel to a shore and separated from it usu. by a lagoon

bar·ring \'bär-iŋ\ *prep* : excluding by exception : EXCEPTING

bar·rio \'bär-ē-ˌō, 'ber-\ *n, pl* **-ri·os** **1** : a district of a city or town in a Spanish-speaking country **2** : a Spanish-speaking quarter in a U.S. city

bar·ris·ter \'ber-ə-stər\ *n* : a British counselor admitted to plead in the higher courts

bar·room \'bär-ˌrüm, -ˌrùm\ *n* : a room or establishment whose main feature is a bar for the sale of liquor

¹bar·row \'ber-ō\ *n* : a large burial mound of earth and stones

²barrow *n* **1** : WHEELBARROW **2** : a cart with a boxlike body and two shafts for pushing it

Bart *abbr* baronet

bar·tend·er \'bär-ˌten-dər\ *n* : a person who serves liquor at a bar

bar·ter \'bär-tər\ *vb* : to trade by exchange of goods — **barter** *n* — **bar·ter·er** *n*

Ba·ruch \'bär-ˌük, bə-'rük\ *n* — see BIBLE table

bas·al \'bā-səl\ *adj* **1** : situated at or forming the base **2** : BASIC

basal metabolism *n* : the turnover of energy in a fasting and resting organism using energy solely to maintain vital cellular activity, respiration, and circulation as measured by the rate at which heat is given off

ba·salt \bə-'sólt, 'bā-ˌsólt\ *n* : a dark fine-grained igneous rock — **ba·sal·tic** \bə-'sól-tik\ *adj*

¹base \'bās\ *n, pl* **bas·es** \'bā-səz\ **1** : BOTTOM, FOUNDATION **2** : a side or face on which a geometrical figure stands; *also* : the length of a base **3** : a main ingredient or fundamental part **4** : the point of beginning an act or operation **5** : a place on which a force depends for supplies **6** : a number (as 5 in 5⁷) that is raised to a power; *esp* : a number that when raised to a power equal to the logarithm of a number yields the number itself ⟨the logarithm of 100 to ~ 10 is 2 since $10^2 = 100$⟩ **7** : the number of units in a given digit's place of a number system that is required to give the numeral 1 in the next higher place ⟨the decimal system uses a ~ of 10⟩; *also* : such a system using an indicated base ⟨convert from ~ 10 to ~ 2⟩ **8** : any of the four stations at the corners of a baseball diamond **9** : a chemical compound (as lime or ammonia) that reacts with an acid to form a salt, has a bitter taste, and turns litmus blue ✦ *Synonyms* BASIS, GROUND, GROUNDWORK, FOOTING, FOUNDATION — **base·less** *adj*

²base *vb* **based; bas·ing** **1** : to form or serve as a base for **2** : ESTABLISH

³base *adj* **1** : of low value and inferior quality : DEBASED, ALLOYED **2** : CONTEMPTIBLE, IGNOBLE **3** : MENIAL, DEGRADING ✦ *Synonyms* LOW, VILE, DESPICABLE, WRETCHED — **base·ly** *adv* — **base·ness** *n*

base·ball \'bās-ˌból\ *n* : a game played with a bat and ball by two teams on a field with four bases arranged in a diamond; *also* : the ball used in this game

baseball cap *n* : a cap of the kind worn by baseball players that has a rounded crown and a long visor

base·board \-ˌbórd\ *n* : a line of boards or molding covering the joint of a wall and the adjoining floor

base-born \-'bórn\ *adj* **1** : MEAN, IGNOBLE **2** : of humble birth **3** : of illegitimate birth

base exchange *n* : a post exchange at a naval or air force base

base hit *n* : a hit in baseball that enables the batter to reach base safely with no error made and no base runner forced out

BASE jumping \'bās-\ *n* [building, antenna, span, earth] : the activity of parachuting from a high structure or cliff

base·line \'bās-ˌlīn\ *n* **1** : a line serving as a basis esp. to calculate or locate something **2** : the area within which a baseball player must keep when running between bases

base·ment \-mənt\ *n* **1** : the part of a building that is wholly or partly below ground level **2** : the lowest or fundamental part of something

base on balls : an advance to first base given to a baseball player who receives four balls

base runner *n* : a baseball player who is on base or is attempting to reach a base

¹bash \'bash\ *vb* **1** : to strike violently : HIT **2** : to smash by a blow **3** : to attack physically or verbally

²bash *n* **1** : a heavy blow **2** : a festive social gathering : PARTY

bash·ful \'bash-fəl\ *adj* : inclined to shrink from public attention — **bash·ful·ly** \-fə-lē\ *adv* — **bash·ful·ness** *n*

ba·sic \'bā-sik\ *adj* **1** : of, relating to, or forming the base or essence : FUNDAMENTAL **2** : concerned with fundamental scientific principles : not applied **3** : of, relating

to, or having the character of a chemical base ✦ **Syno-nyms** UNDERLYING, BASAL, PRIMARY — **ba·sic·i·ty** \bā-'si-sə-tē\ *n*
BA·SIC \'bā-sik\ *n* [Beginner's *A*ll-purpose *S*ymbolic *I*nstruction *C*ode] : a simplified language for programming a computer
ba·si·cal·ly \'bā-si-k(ə-)lē\ *adv* 1 : at a basic level 2 : for the most part 3 : in a basic manner
ba·sil \'bā-zəl, 'ba-, -səl\ *n* : any of several mints with fragrant leaves used in cooking; *also* : the leaves
ba·sil·i·ca \bə-'si-li-kə, -'zi-\ *n* [L, fr. Gk *basilikē*, fr. fem. of *basilikos* royal, fr. *basileus* king] 1 : an early Christian church building consisting of nave and aisles with clerestory and apse 2 : a Roman Catholic church given ceremonial privileges
bas·i·lisk \'ba-sə-ˌlisk, 'ba-zə-\ *n* [ME, fr. L *basiliscus*, fr. Gk *basiliskos*, fr. dim. of *basileus* king] : a legendary reptile with fatal breath and glance
ba·sin \'bā-sᵊn\ *n* 1 : an open usu. circular vessel with sloping sides for holding liquid (as water) 2 : a hollow or enclosed place containing water; *also* : the region drained by a river
ba·sis \'bā-səs\ *n, pl* **ba·ses** \-ˌsēz\ 1 : FOUNDATION, BASE 2 : a fundamental principle
bask \'bask\ *vb* 1 : to expose oneself to comfortable heat 2 : to enjoy something warmly comforting ⟨~*ing* in his friends' admiration⟩
bas·ket \'bas-kət\ *n* : a container made of woven material (as twigs or grasses); *also* : any of various lightweight usu. wood containers
bas·ket·ball \-ˌbȯl\ *n* : a game played on a court by two teams who try to throw an inflated ball through a raised goal; *also* : the ball used in this game — **bas·ket·ball·er** \-ˌbȯ-lər\ *n*
basket case *n* 1 : a person who has all four limbs amputated 2 : a person who is mentally incapacitated or worn out (as from nervous tension)
basket weave *n* : a textile weave resembling the checkered pattern of a plaited basket
bas·ma·ti rice \ˌbäz-'mä-tē-\ *n* : an aromatic long-grain rice originating in southern Asia
bas mitzvah *var of* BAT MITZVAH
Basque \'bask\ *n* 1 : a member of a people inhabiting a region bordering on the Bay of Biscay in northern Spain and southwestern France 2 : the language of the Basque people — **Basque** *adj*
bas–re·lief \ˌbä-ri-'lēf\ *n* [F] : a sculpture in relief with the design raised very slightly from the background

bas-relief

¹bass \'bas\ *n, pl* **bass** *or* **bass·es** : any of numerous sport and food bony fishes (as a striped bass)
²bass \'bās\ *adj* : of low pitch
³bass \'bās\ *n* 1 : a deep sound or tone 2 : the lower half of the musical pitch range 3 : the lowest part in a 4-part chorus; *also* : a singer having this voice or part
bas·set hound \'ba-sət-\ *n* : any of an old breed of short-legged hunting dogs of French origin having long ears and a short smooth coat
bas·si·net \ˌba-sə-'net\ *n* : a baby's bed that resembles a basket and often has a hood over one end
bas·so \'ba-sō, 'bä-\ *n, pl* **bassos** *or* **bas·si** \'bä-ˌsē\ [It] : a bass singer
bas·soon \bə-'sün\ *n* : a musical wind instrument lower in pitch than the oboe

bass·wood \'bas-ˌwud\ *n* : any of several New World lindens or their wood
bast \'bast\ *n* : BAST FIBER
¹bas·tard \'bas-tərd\ *n* 1 : an illegitimate child 2 : an offensive or disagreeable person
²bastard *adj* 1 : ILLEGITIMATE 2 : of an inferior or nontypical kind, state, or form; *also* : SPURIOUS — **bas·tardy** *n*
bas·tard·ise *Brit var of* BASTARDIZE
bas·tard·ize \'bas-tər-ˌdīz\ *vb* **-ized; -iz·ing** : to reduce from a higher to a lower state : DEBASE
¹baste \'bāst\ *vb* **bast·ed; bast·ing** : to sew with long stitches so as to keep temporarily in place
²baste *vb* **bast·ed; bast·ing** : to moisten (as meat) at intervals with liquid while cooking
bast fiber *n* : a strong woody plant fiber obtained chiefly from phloem and used esp. in making ropes
bas·ti·na·do \ˌbas-tə-'nā-dō, -'nä-\ *or* **bas·ti·nade** \ˌbas-tə-'nād, -'näd\ *n, pl* **-na·does** *or* **-nades** 1 : a blow or beating esp. with a stick 2 : a punishment consisting of beating the soles of the feet
bas·tion \'bas-chən\ *n* : a projecting part of a fortification; *also* : a fortified position
¹bat \'bat\ *n* 1 : a stout stick : CLUB 2 : a sharp blow 3 : an implement (as of wood) used to hit a ball (as in baseball) 4 : a turn at batting — usu. used in the phrase *at bat*
²bat *vb* **bat·ted; bat·ting** : to hit with or as if with a bat
³bat *n* : any of an order of night-flying mammals with forelimbs modified to form wings
⁴bat *vb* **bat·ted; bat·ting** : WINK, BLINK
batch \'bach\ *n* 1 : a quantity (as of bread) baked at one time 2 : a quantity of material for use at one time or produced at one operation
bate \'bāt\ *vb* **bat·ed; bat·ing** : MODERATE, REDUCE
bath \'bath, 'bäth\ *n, pl* **baths** \'bathz, 'baths, 'bäthz, 'bäths\ 1 : a washing of the body 2 : water for washing the body 3 : a liquid in which objects are immersed so that it can act on them 4 : BATHROOM 5 : a financial loss ⟨took a ~ in the market⟩
bathe \'bāth\ *vb* **bathed; bath·ing** 1 : to wash in liquid and esp. water; *also* : to apply water or a medicated liquid to ⟨*bathed* her eyes⟩ 2 : to take a bath; *also* : to take a swim 3 : to wash along, over, or against so as to wet 4 : to suffuse with or as if with light — **bath·er** *n*
bath·house \'bath-ˌhaus, 'bäth-\ *n* 1 : a building equipped for bathing 2 : a building containing dressing rooms for bathers
bathing suit *n* : SWIMSUIT
ba·thos \'bā-ˌthäs\ *n* [Gk, lit., depth] 1 : the sudden appearance of the commonplace in otherwise elevated matter or style 2 : insincere or overdone pathos — **ba·thet·ic** \bə-'the-tik\ *adj*
bath·robe \'bath-ˌrōb, 'bäth-\ *n* : a loose often absorbent robe worn before and after bathing or as a dressing gown
bath·room \-ˌrüm, -ˌrum\ *n* : a room containing a bathtub or shower and usu. a sink and toilet
bath·tub \-ˌtəb\ *n* : a usu. fixed tub for bathing
ba·tik \bə-'tēk, 'ba-tik\ *n* [Javanese *batik*] 1 : an Indonesian method of hand-printing textiles by coating with wax the parts not to be dyed; *also* : a design so executed 2 : a fabric printed by batik
ba·tiste \bə-'tēst\ *n* : a fine sheer fabric of plain weave
bat·man \'bat-mən\ *n* : an orderly of a British military officer
bat mitz·vah \bät-'mits-və\ *also* **bas mitzvah** \bäs-\ *n, often cap* B&M [Heb *bath miṣwāh*, lit., daughter of the (divine) law] 1 : a Jewish girl who at about 13 years of age assumes religious responsibilities 2 : the ceremony recognizing a girl as a bat mitzvah
ba·ton \bə-'tän\ *n* : STAFF, ROD; *esp* : a stick with which the leader directs an orchestra or band
bats·man \'bats-mən\ *n* : a batter esp. in cricket
bat·tal·ion \bə-'tal-yən\ *n* 1 : a large body of troops organized to act together : ARMY 2 : a military unit composed of a headquarters and two or more units (as companies)
¹bat·ten \'ba-tᵊn\ *vb* 1 : to grow or make fat 2 : THRIVE
²batten *n* : a strip of wood used esp. to seal or strengthen a joint
³batten *vb* : to fasten with battens
¹bat·ter \'ba-tər\ *vb* : to beat or damage with repeated blows

²**batter** *n* : a soft mixture (as for cake) basically of flour and liquid

³**batter** *n* : one that bats; *esp* : the player whose turn it is to bat

battering ram *n* **1** : an ancient military machine for battering down walls **2** : a heavy metal bar with handles used to batter down doors

bat·tery \'ba-tə-rē\ *n, pl* **-ter·ies** **1** : BEATING; *esp* : unlawful beating or use of force on a person **2** : a grouping of artillery pieces for tactical purposes; *also* : the guns of a warship **3** : a group of electric cells for furnishing electric current; *also* : a single electric cell ⟨a flashlight ∼⟩ **4** : a number of similar items grouped or used as a unit ⟨a ∼ of tests⟩ **5** : the pitcher and catcher of a baseball team

bat·ting \'ba-tiŋ\ *n* : layers or sheets of cotton or wool (as for lining quilts)

batting cage *n* : a screen around the back and sides of the home plate area to stop baseballs during practice

¹**bat·tle** \'ba-t³l\ *n* [ME *batel*, fr. AF *bataille* battle, battalion, fr. LL *battalia* combat, alter. of *battualia* fencing exercises, fr. L *battuere* to beat] : a general military engagement; *also* : an extended contest or controversy

²**battle** *vb* **bat·tled; bat·tling** : to engage in battle : CONTEND, FIGHT

bat·tle–ax *or* **battle–axe** \'ba-t³l-₁aks\ *n* **1** : a long-handled ax formerly used as a weapon **2** : a quarrelsome domineering woman

battle fatigue *n* : COMBAT FATIGUE

bat·tle·field \'ba-t³l-₁fēld\ *n* : a place where a battle is fought

bat·tle·ment \-mənt\ *n* : a decorative or defensive parapet on top of a wall

bat·tle·ship \-₁ship\ *n* : a warship of the most heavily armed and armored class

bat·tle·wag·on \-₁wa-gən\ *n* : BATTLESHIP

bat·ty \'ba-tē\ *adj* **bat·ti·er; -est** : CRAZY, FOOLISH

bau·ble \'bȯ-bəl\ *n* : TRINKET

baud \'bȯd, *Brit* 'bȯd\ *n, pl* **baud** *also* **bauds** : a unit of data transmission speed

baulk *chiefly Brit var of* BALK

baux·ite \'bȯk-₁sīt\ *n* : a clayey mixture that is the chief ore of aluminum

bawd \'bȯd\ *n* **1** : MADAM **2** **2** : PROSTITUTE

bawdy \'bȯ-dē\ *adj* **bawd·i·er; -est** : OBSCENE, LEWD — **bawd·i·ly** \'bȯ-də-lē\ *adv* — **bawd·i·ness** \-dē-nəs\ *n*

¹**bawl** \'bȯl\ *vb* : to cry or cry out loudly; *also* : to scold harshly

²**bawl** *n* : a long loud cry : BELLOW

¹**bay** \'bā\ *adj* : reddish brown

²**bay** *n* **1** : a bay-colored animal **2** : a reddish brown color

³**bay** *n* **1** : a section or compartment of a building or vehicle **2** : a compartment projecting outward from the wall of a building and containing a window (**bay window**)

⁴**bay** *vb* : to bark with deep long tones

⁵**bay** *n* **1** : the position of one unable to escape and forced to face danger **2** : a baying of dogs

⁶**bay** *n* : an inlet of a body of water (as the sea) usu. smaller than a gulf

⁷**bay** *n* : LAUREL; *also* : a shrub or tree resembling the laurel

bay·ber·ry \'bā-₁ber-ē\ *n* : a hardy deciduous shrub of coastal eastern No. America bearing small hard berries coated with a white wax used for candles; *also* : its fruit

bay leaf *n* : the dried leaf of the European laurel used in cooking

¹**bay·o·net** \'bā-ə-nət, ₁bā-ə-'net\ *n* : a daggerlike weapon made to fit on the muzzle end of a rifle

²**bayonet** *vb* **-net·ed** *also* **-net·ted; -net·ing** *also* **-net·ting** : to use or stab with a bayonet

bay·ou \'bī-yü, -ō\ *n* [Louisiana French, fr. Choctaw *bayuk*] : a marshy or sluggish body of water

bay rum *n* : a fragrant liquid used esp. as a cologne or after-shave lotion

ba·zaar \bə-'zär\ *n* **1** : a group of shops : MARKETPLACE **2** : a fair for the sale of articles usu. for charity

ba·zoo·ka \bə-'zü-kə\ *n* [*bazooka* (a crude musical instrument made of pipes and a funnel)] : a weapon consisting of a tube that launches an explosive rocket able to pierce armor

¹**BB** \'bē-(₁)bē\ *n* : a small round shot pellet

²**BB** *abbr* base on balls

BBB *abbr* Better Business Bureau

BBC *abbr* British Broadcasting Corporation

bbl *abbr* barrel; barrels

BC *abbr* **1** before Christ — often printed in small capitals and often punctuated **2** British Columbia

B cell *n* [bone-marrow-derived *cell*] : any of the lymphocytes that secrete antibodies when mature

B complex *n* : VITAMIN B COMPLEX

bd *abbr* **1** board **2** bound

bdl *or* **bdle** *abbr* bundle

bdrm *abbr* bedroom

be \'bē\ *vb, past 1st & 3d sing* **was** \'wəz, 'wäz\; *2d sing* **were** \'wər\; *pl* **were**; *past subjunctive* **were**; *past part* **been** \'bin\; *pres part* **be·ing** \'bē-iŋ\; *pres 1st sing* **am** \əm, 'am\; *2d sing* **are** \ər, 'är\; *3d sing* **is** \'iz, əz\; *pl* **are**; *pres subjunctive* **be** **1** : to equal in meaning or symbolically ⟨God *is* love⟩; *also* : to have a specified qualification or relationship ⟨leaves *are* green⟩ ⟨this fish *is* a trout⟩ **2** : to have objective existence ⟨I think, therefore I *am*⟩; *also* : to have or occupy a particular place ⟨here *is* your pen⟩ **3** : to take place : OCCUR ⟨the meeting *is* tonight⟩ **4** — used with the past participle of transitive verbs as a passive voice auxiliary ⟨the door *was* opened⟩ **5** — used as the auxiliary of the present participle in expressing continuous action ⟨he *is* sleeping⟩ **6** — used as an auxiliary with the past participle of some intransitive verbs to form archaic perfect tenses **7** — used as an auxiliary with *to* and the infinitive to express futurity, prearrangement, or obligation ⟨you *are* to come when called⟩

Be *symbol* beryllium

¹**beach** \'bēch\ *n* : a sandy or gravelly part of the shore of an ocean or lake

²**beach** *vb* : to run or drive ashore

beach buggy *n* : DUNE BUGGY

beach·comb·er \'bēch-₁kō-mər\ *n* : a person who searches along a shore for something of use or value

beach·head \'bēch-₁hed\ *n* : a small area on an enemy-held shore occupied in the initial stages of an invasion

bea·con \'bē-kən\ *n* **1** : a signal fire **2** : a guiding or warning signal (as a lighthouse) **3** : a radio transmitter emitting signals for guidance of aircraft

¹**bead** \'bēd\ *n* [ME *bede* prayer, prayer bead, fr. OE *bed*, *gebed* prayer] **1** *pl* : a series of prayers and meditations made with a rosary **2** : a small piece of material pierced for threading on a line (as in a rosary) **3** : a small globular body **4** : a narrow projecting rim or band — **bead·ing** *n* — **beady** *adj*

²**bead** *vb* : to form into a bead

bea·dle \'bē-d³l\ *n* : a usu. English parish officer whose duties include keeping order in church

bea·gle \'bē-gəl\ *n* : a small short-legged smooth-coated hound

beak \'bēk\ *n* : the bill of a bird and esp. of a bird of prey; *also* : a pointed projecting part — **beaked** \'bēkt\ *adj*

bea·ker \'bē-kər\ *n* **1** : a large widemouthed drinking cup **2** : a widemouthed thin-walled laboratory vessel

¹**beam** \'bēm\ *n* **1** : a large long piece of timber or metal **2** : the bar of a balance from which the scales hang **3** : the breadth of a ship at its widest part **4** : a ray or shaft of light **5** : a collection of nearly parallel rays (as X-rays) or particles (as electrons) **6** : a constant radio signal transmitted for the guidance of pilots; *also* : the course indicated by this signal

²**beam** *vb* **1** : to send out light **2** : BROADCAST **3** : to transmit (data) electronically **4** : to smile with joy

¹**bean** \'bēn\ *n* : the edible seed borne in pods by some leguminous plants; *also* : a plant or a pod bearing beans

²**bean** *vb* : to strike on the head with an object

bean·bag \'bēn-₁bag\ *n* : a cloth bag partially filled typically with dried beans and used as a toy

bean·ball \'bēn-₁bȯl\ *n* : a pitch thrown at a batter's head

bean curd *n* : TOFU

bean·ie \'bē-nē\ *n* : a small round tight-fitting skullcap

beano \'bē-nō\ *n, pl* **beanos** : BINGO

¹**bear** \'ber\ *n, pl* **bears** **1** *or pl* **bear** : any of a family of large heavy mammals with shaggy hair and small tails **2** : a gruff or sullen person **3** : one who sells (as securities) in expectation of a price decline — **bear·ish** *adj*

2**bear** *vb* **bore** \ˈbȯr\; **borne** \ˈbȯrn\ *also* **born** \ˈbȯrn\; **bear·ing** **1** : CARRY **2** : to be equipped with **3** : to give as testimony ⟨~ witness to the facts of the case⟩ **4** : to give birth to; *also* : PRODUCE, YIELD ⟨a tree that ~*s* regularly⟩ **5** : ENDURE, SUSTAIN ⟨~ pain⟩ ⟨*bore* the weight on piles⟩; *also* : to exert pressure or influence **6** : to go in an indicated direction ⟨~ to the right⟩ — **bear·able** *adj* — **bear·er** *n*

1**beard** \ˈbird\ *n* **1** : the hair that grows on the face of a man **2** : a growth of bristly hairs (as on a goat's chin) — **beard·ed** \ˈbir-dəd\ *adj* — **beard·less** *adj*

2**beard** *vb* : to confront boldly

bearing *n* **1** : manner of carrying oneself : COMPORTMENT **2** : a supporting object, purpose, or point **3** : a machine part in which another part (as an axle or pin) turns **4** : an emblem in a coat of arms **5** : the position or direction of one point with respect to another or to the compass; *also* : a determination of position **6** *pl* : comprehension of one's situation **7** : connection with or influence on something; *also* : SIGNIFICANCE

bear market *n* : a market in which securities or commodities are persistently declining in value

bear·skin \ˈber-ˌskin\ *n* : an article (as a hat) made of the skin of a bear

beast \ˈbēst\ *n* **1** : ANIMAL 1; *esp* : a 4-footed mammal **2** : a contemptible person

1**beast·ly** \ˈbēst-lē\ *adj* **beast·li·er; -est** **1** : BESTIAL **2** : ABOMINABLE, DISAGREEABLE — **beast·li·ness** \-nəs\ *n*

2**beastly** *adv* : VERY ⟨a ~ cold day⟩

1**beat** \ˈbēt\ *vb* **beat; beat·en** \ˈbē-tᵊn\ *or* **beat; beat·ing** **1** : to strike repeatedly **2** : TREAD **3** : to affect or alter by beating ⟨~ metal into sheets⟩ **4** : to sound (as an alarm) on a drum **5** : OVERCOME; *also* : SURPASS **6** : to act or arrive before ⟨~ his brother home⟩ **7** : THROB — **beat·er** *n*

2**beat** *n* **1** : a single stroke or blow esp. of a series; *also* : PULSATION **2** : a rhythmic stress in poetry or music or the rhythmic effect of these **3** : a regularly traversed course

3**beat** *adj* **1** : EXHAUSTED **2** : of or relating to beatniks

4**beat** *n* : BEATNIK

be·atif·ic \ˌbē-ə-ˈti-fik\ *adj* : giving or indicative of great joy or bliss

be·at·i·fy \bē-ˈa-tə-ˌfī\ *vb* **-fied; -fy·ing** **1** : to make supremely happy **2** : to declare to have attained the blessedness of heaven and authorize the title "Blessed" for — **be·at·i·fi·ca·tion** \-ˌa-tə-fə-ˈkā-shən\ *n*

be·at·i·tude \bē-ˈa-tə-ˌtüd, -ˌtyüd\ *n* **1** : a state of utmost bliss **2** : any of the declarations made in the Sermon on the Mount (Mt 5:3–12) beginning "Blessed are"

beat·nik \ˈbēt-nik\ *n* : a usu. young and artistic person who rejects the mores of established society

beau \ˈbō\ *n, pl* **beaux** \ˈbōz\ *or* **beaus** [F, fr. *beau* beautiful, fr. L *bellus* pretty] **1** : a man of fashion : DANDY **2** : SUITOR, LOVER

beau geste \bō-ˈzhest\ *n, pl* **beaux gestes** *or* **beau gestes** \bō-ˈzhest\ [F] : a graceful or magnanimous gesture

beau ide·al \ˌbō-ī-ˈdē(-ə)l\ *n, pl* **beau ideals** [F] : the perfect type or model

Beau·jo·lais \ˌbō-zhō-ˈlā\ *n* : a light fruity red wine

beau monde \bō-ˈmänd, -ˈmōⁿd\ *n, pl* **beau mondes** \-ˈmänz, -ˈmändz\ *or* **beaux mondes** \bō-ˈmōⁿd\ [F] : the world of high society and fashion

beau·te·ous \ˈbyü-tē-əs\ *adj* : BEAUTIFUL — **beau·te·ous·ly** *adv*

beau·ti·cian \byü-ˈti-shən\ *n* : COSMETOLOGIST

beau·ti·ful \ˈbyü-ti-fəl\ *adj* : characterized by beauty : LOVELY ◆ ***Synonyms*** PRETTY, FAIR, COMELY — **beau·ti·ful·ly** \-f(ə-)lē\ *adv*

beautiful people *n pl, often cap B&P* : wealthy or famous people whose lifestyle is usu. expensive and well-publicized

beau·ti·fy \ˈbyü-tə-ˌfī\ *vb* **-fied; -fy·ing** : to make more beautiful — **beau·ti·fi·ca·tion** \ˌbyü-tə-fə-ˈkā-shən\ *n* — **beau·ti·fi·er** *n*

beau·ty \ˈbyü-tē\ *n, pl* **beauties** : qualities that give pleasure to the senses or exalt the mind : LOVELINESS; *also* : something having such qualities

beauty shop *n* : an establishment where hairdressing, facials, and manicures are done

beaux arts \bō-ˈzär\ *n pl* [F] : FINE ARTS

bea·ver \ˈbē-vər\ *n, pl* **beavers** : a large fur-bearing herbivorous rodent that builds dams and underwater houses of mud and sticks; *also* : its fur

beaver

be·calm \bi-ˈkäm, -ˈkälm\ *vb* : to keep (as a ship) motionless by lack of wind

be·cause \bi-ˈkȯz, -ˈkəz\ *conj* : for the reason that ⟨ran away ~ they were afraid⟩

because of *prep* : by reason of

beck \ˈbek\ *n* : a beckoning gesture; *also* : SUMMONS

beck·on \ˈbe-kən\ *vb* : to summon or signal esp. by a nod or gesture; *also* : ATTRACT

be·cloud \bi-ˈklau̇d\ *vb* : OBSCURE

be·come \bi-ˈkəm\ *vb* **-came** \-ˈkām\; **-come; -com·ing** **1** : to come to be ⟨~ tired⟩ **2** : to suit or be suitable to ⟨her dress ~*s* her⟩

becoming *adj* : SUITABLE, FIT; *also* : ATTRACTIVE — **be·com·ing·ly** *adv*

1**bed** \ˈbed\ *n* **1** : an article of furniture to sleep on **2** : a plot of ground prepared for plants **3** : FOUNDATION, BOTTOM **4** : LAYER, STRATUM

2**bed** *vb* **bed·ded; bed·ding** **1** : to put or go to bed **2** : to fix in a foundation : EMBED **3** : to plant in beds **4** : to lay or lie flat or in layers

bed–and–breakfast *n* : an establishment offering lodging and breakfast

be·daub \bi-ˈdȯb\ *vb* : SMEAR

be·daz·zle \bi-ˈda-zəl\ *vb* : to confuse by or as if by a strong light; *also* : FASCINATE — **be·daz·zle·ment** *n*

bed·bug \ˈbed-ˌbəg\ *n* : a wingless bloodsucking bug infesting houses and esp. beds

bed·clothes \ˈbed-ˌklōthz\ *n pl* : materials for making up a bed

bed·ding \ˈbe-diŋ\ *n* **1** : BEDCLOTHES **2** : FOUNDATION

be·deck \bi-ˈdek\ *vb* : ADORN

be·dev·il \bi-ˈde-vəl\ *vb* **1** : HARASS, TORMENT **2** : CONFUSE, MUDDLE

be·dew \bi-ˈdü, -ˈdyü\ *vb* : to wet with or as if with dew

bed·fast \ˈbed-ˌfast\ *adj* : BEDRIDDEN

bed·fel·low \-ˌfe-lō\ *n* **1** : one sharing the bed of another **2** : a close associate : ALLY

be·di·zen \bi-ˈdī-zᵊn, -ˈdi-\ *vb* : to dress or adorn with showy or vulgar finery

bed·lam \ˈbed-ləm\ *n* [*Bedlam,* popular name for the Hospital of St. Mary of Bethlehem, London, an insane asylum, fr. ME *Bedlem* Bethlehem] **1** *often cap* : an insane asylum **2** : a scene of uproar and confusion

bed·ou·in *also* **bed·u·in** \ˈbe-də-wən\ *n, pl* **bedouin** *or* **bedouins** *also* **beduin** *or* **beduins** *often cap* [ME *Bedoyne,* fr. MF *bedoïn,* fr. Ar *badawī* desert dweller] : a nomadic Arab of the Arabian, Syrian, or No. African deserts

bed·pan \ˈbed-ˌpan\ *n* : a shallow vessel used by a bedridden person for urination or defecation

bed·post \-ˌpōst\ *n* : the post of a bed

be·drag·gled \bi-ˈdra-gəld\ *adj* : soiled and disordered as if by being drenched

bed·rid·den \ˈbed-ˌri-dᵊn\ *adj* : kept in bed by illness or weakness

1**bed·rock** \-ˈräk\ *n* : the solid rock underlying surface materials (as soil)

2**bedrock** *adj* : solidly fundamental, basic, or reliable ⟨traditional ~ values⟩

bed·roll \ˈbed-ˌrōl\ *n* : bedding rolled up for carrying

bed·room \-ˌrüm, -ˌru̇m\ *n* : a room containing a bed and used esp. for sleeping

bed·side \-ˌsīd\ *n* : the place beside a bed esp. of a sick or dying person

bed·sore \-ˌsȯr\ *n* : an ulceration of tissue deprived of adequate blood supply by prolonged pressure

bed·spread \-ˌspred\ *n* : a usu. ornamental cloth cover for a bed

bed·stead \-ˌsted\ *n* : the framework of a bed

bed·time \-ˌtīm\ *n* : time for going to bed

bed–wet·ting \-ˌwe-tiŋ\ *n* : involuntary discharge of urine esp. in bed during sleep — **bed–wet·ter** *n*

¹**bee** \'bē\ *n* : any of numerous 4-winged insects (as honeybees or bumblebees) that feed on nectar and pollen and that sometimes produce honey or have a painful sting

²**bee** *n* : a gathering of people for a specific purpose ⟨a quilting ∼⟩

beech \'bēch\ *n, pl* **beech·es** *or* **beech** : any of a genus of hardwood trees with smooth gray bark and small sweet triangular nuts; *also* : its wood — **beech·en** \'bē-chən\ *adj*

beech·nut \'bēch-ˌnət\ *n* : the nut of a beech

¹**beef** \'bēf\ *n, pl* **beefs** \'bēfs\ *or* **beeves** \'bēvz\ **1** : the flesh of a steer, cow, or bull; *also* : the dressed carcass of a beef animal **2** : a steer, cow, or bull esp. when fattened for food **3** : MUSCLE, BRAWN **4** *pl* **beefs** : COMPLAINT

²**beef** *vb* **1** : STRENGTHEN — usu. used with *up* ⟨∼*ed* up security⟩ **2** : COMPLAIN

beef·eat·er \'bē-ˌfē-tər\ *n* : a yeoman of the guard of an English monarch

beef·steak \-ˌstāk\ *n* : a slice of beef suitable for broiling or frying

beefy \'bē-fē\ *adj* **beef·i·er; -est** : THICKSET, BRAWNY

bee·hive \'bē-ˌhīv\ *n* : HIVE 1, HIVE 3

bee·keep·er \-ˌkē-pər\ *n* : a person who raises bees — **bee·keep·ing** *n*

bee·line \-ˌlīn\ *n* : a straight direct course

been *past part of* BE

beep·er \'bē-pər\ *n* : PAGER; *esp* : one that beeps

beer \'bir\ *n* : an alcoholic beverage brewed from malt and hops — **beery** *adj*

beer belly *n* : POTBELLY

bees·wax \'bēz-ˌwaks\ *n* : WAX 1

beet \'bēt\ *n* : a garden plant with edible leaves and a thick sweet root used as a vegetable, as a source of sugar, or as forage; *also* : its root

¹**bee·tle** \'bē-t²l\ *n* : any of an order of insects having four wings of which the stiff outer pair covers the membranous inner pair when not in flight

²**beetle** *vb* **bee·tled; bee·tling** : to jut out : PROJECT

be·fall \bi-'fȯl\ *vb* **-fell** \-'fel\; **-fall·en** \-'fȯ-lən\ : to happen to : OCCUR

be·fit \bi-'fit\ *vb* : to be suitable to

be·fog \bi-'fȯg, -'fäg\ *vb* : OBSCURE; *also* : CONFUSE

¹**be·fore** \bi-'fȯr\ *adv or adj* **1** : in front **2** : EARLIER

²**before** *prep* **1** : in front of ⟨stood ∼ him⟩ **2** : earlier than ⟨got there ∼ me⟩ **3** : in a more important category than ⟨put quality ∼ quantity⟩

³**before** *conj* **1** : earlier than the time that ⟨he got here ∼ I did⟩ **2** : more willingly than ⟨she'd starve ∼ she'd steal⟩

be·fore·hand \bi-'fȯr-ˌhand\ *adv or adj* : in advance

be·foul \bi-'fau̇(-ə)l\ *vb* : SOIL

be·friend \bi-'frend\ *vb* : to act as friend to

be·fud·dle \bi-'fə-d²l\ *vb* : MUDDLE, CONFUSE

beg \'beg\ *vb* **begged; beg·ging 1** : to ask as a charity; *also* : ENTREAT **2** : EVADE; *also* : assume as established, settled, or proved ⟨∼ the question⟩

be·get \bi-'get\ *vb* **-got** \-'gät\; **-got·ten** \-'gä-t²n\ *or* **-got; -get·ting** : to become the father of : SIRE

¹**beg·gar** \'be-gər\ *n* : one that begs; *esp* : a person who begs as a way of life

²**beggar** *vb* : IMPOVERISH

beg·gar·ly \'be-gər-lē\ *adj* **1** : contemptibly mean or inadequate **2** : marked by unrelieved poverty ⟨a ∼ life⟩

beg·gary \'be-gə-rē\ *n* : extreme poverty

be·gin \bi-'gin\ *vb* **be·gan** \-'gan\; **be·gun** \-'gən\; **be·gin·ning 1** : to do the first part of an action : COMMENCE **2** : to come into being : ARISE; *also* : FOUND **3** : ORIGINATE, INVENT — **be·gin·ner** *n*

beg off *vb* : to ask to be excused from something

be·gone \bi-'gȯn\ *vb* : to go away : DEPART — used esp. in the imperative

be·go·nia \bi-'gōn-yə\ *n* : any of a genus of tropical herbs widely grown for their showy leaves and waxy flowers

be·grime \bi-'grīm\ *vb* **be·grimed; be·grim·ing** : to make dirty

be·grudge \bi-'grəj\ *vb* **1** : to give or concede reluctantly **2** : to be reluctant to grant or allow — **be·grudg·ing·ly** \-'grə-jiŋ-lē\ *adv*

be·guile \-'gī(-ə)l\ *vb* **be·guiled; be·guil·ing 1** : DECEIVE **2** : to while away **3** : to engage the interest of by guile

be·guine \bi-'gēn\ *n* [AmerF *béguine,* fr. F *béguin* flirtation] : a vigorous popular dance of the islands of Saint Lucia and Martinique

be·gum \'bā-gəm, 'bē-\ *n* : a Muslim woman of high rank

be·half \bi-'haf, -'häf\ *n* : BENEFIT, SUPPORT, DEFENSE

be·have \bi-'hāv\ *vb* **be·haved; be·hav·ing 1** : to bear, comport, or conduct oneself in a particular and esp. a proper way **2** : to act, function, or react in a particular way

be·hav·ior \bi-'hā-vyər\ *n* : way of behaving; *esp* : personal conduct — **be·hav·ior·al** \-vyə-rəl\ *adj* — **be·hav·ior·al·ly** \-rə-lē\ *adv*

be·hav·ior·ism \bi-'hā-vyə-ˌri-zəm\ *n* : a school of psychology concerned with the objective evidence of behavior without reference to conscious experience

be·hav·ior·ist \-vyə-rist\ *n* **1** : a person who supports behaviorism **2** : a person who studies behavior

be·hav·iour, be·hav·iour·ism *chiefly Brit var of* BEHAVIOR, BEHAVIORISM

be·head \bi-'hed\ *vb* : to cut off the head of

be·he·moth \bi-'hē-məth, 'bē-ə-ˌmäth\ *n* : a huge powerful animal described in Job 40:15–24; *also* : something of monstrous size or power

be·hest \bi-'hest\ *n* **1** : COMMAND **2** : an urgent prompting

¹**be·hind** \bi-'hīnd\ *adv or adj* **1** : BACK, BACKWARD ⟨look ∼⟩ **2** : LATE, SLOW

²**behind** *prep* **1** : in or to a place or situation in back of or to the rear of ⟨look ∼ you⟩ ⟨the staff stayed ∼ the troops⟩ **2** : inferior to (as in rank) : BELOW ⟨three games ∼ the first-place team⟩ **3** : in support of : SUPPORTING ⟨we're ∼ you all the way⟩

be·hind·hand \bi-'hīnd-ˌhand\ *adj* : being in arrears
 ✦ *Synonyms* TARDY, LATE, OVERDUE, BELATED

be·hold \bi-'hōld\ *vb* **-held** \-'held\; **-hold·ing 1** : to have in sight : SEE **2** — used imperatively to direct the attention — ✦ *Synonyms* VIEW, OBSERVE, NOTICE, ESPY — **be·hold·er** *n*

be·hold·en \bi-'hōl-dən\ *adj* : OBLIGATED, INDEBTED

be·hoove \bi-'hüv\ *vb* **be·hooved; be·hoov·ing** : to be necessary, proper, or advantageous for

be·hove *chiefly Brit var of* BEHOOVE

beige \'bäzh\ *n* : a pale dull yellowish brown — **beige** *adj*

be·ing \'bē-iŋ\ *n* **1** : EXISTENCE; *also* : LIFE **2** : the qualities or constitution of an existent thing **3** : a living thing; *esp* : PERSON

be·la·bor \bi-'lā-bər\ *vb* : to assail (as with words) tiresomely or at length

be·la·bour *chiefly Brit var of* BELABOR

be·lat·ed \bi-'lā-təd\ *adj* : DELAYED, LATE

be·lay \bi-'lā\ *vb* **1** : to wind (a rope) around a pin or cleat in order to hold secure **2** : QUIT, STOP — used in the imperative

belch \'belch\ *vb* **1** : to expel (gas) from the stomach through the mouth **2** : to gush forth ⟨a volcano ∼*ing* lava⟩ — **belch** *n*

bel·dam *or* **bel·dame** \'bel-dəm\ *n* [ME *beldam* grandmother, fr. AF *bel* beautiful + ME *dam* lady, mother] : an old woman

be·lea·guer \bi-'lē-gər\ *vb* **1** : BESIEGE **2** : HARASS ⟨∼*ed* parents⟩

bel·fry \'bel-frē\ *n, pl* **belfries** : a tower for a bell (as on a church); *also* : the part of the tower in which the bell hangs

Belg *abbr* Belgian; Belgium

Bel·gian endive \'bel-jən\ *n* : the blanched shoot of chicory

Belgian waffle *n* : a waffle having large depressions and usu. topped with fruit and whipped cream

be·lie \bi-'lī\ *vb* **-lied; -ly·ing 1** : MISREPRESENT **2** : to show (something) to be false **3** : to run counter to

be·lief \bə-'lēf\ *n* **1** : CONFIDENCE, TRUST **2** : something (as a tenet or creed) believed ✦ *Synonyms* CONVICTION, OPINION, PERSUASION, SENTIMENT

be·lieve \bə-ˈlēv\ *vb* **be·lieved; be·liev·ing** **1** : to have religious convictions **2** : to have a firm conviction about something : accept as true **3** : to hold as an opinion : SUPPOSE — **be·liev·able** \-ˈlē-və-bəl\ *adj* — **be·liev·ably** \-blē\ *adv* — **be·liev·er** *n*
be·like \bi-ˈlīk\ *adv, archaic* : PROBABLY
be·lit·tle \bi-ˈli-tᵊl\ *vb* **-lit·tled; -lit·tling** : to make seem little or less; *also* : DISPARAGE
¹**bell** \ˈbel\ *n* **1** : a hollow metallic device that makes a ringing sound when struck **2** : the sounding or stroke of a bell (as on shipboard to tell the time); *also* : time so indicated **3** : something with the flared form of a typical bell
²**bell** *vb* : to provide with a bell
bel·la·don·na \ˌbe-lə-ˈdä-nə\ *n* [It, lit., beautiful lady] : a medicinal extract (as atropine) from a poisonous European herb related to the potato; *also* : this herb
bell–bot·toms \ˈbel-ˈbä-təmz\ *n pl* : pants with wide flaring bottoms — **bell–bottom** *adj*
bell·boy \ˈbel-ˌbȯi\ *n* : BELLHOP
belle \ˈbel\ *n* : an attractive and popular girl or woman
belles let·tres \bel-ˈletrᵊ\ *n pl* [F] : literature that is an end in itself and not practical or purely informative — **bel·le·tris·tic** \ˌbe-lə-ˈtris-tik\ *adj*
bell·hop \ˈbel-ˌhäp\ *n* : a hotel or club employee who takes guests to rooms, carries luggage, and runs errands
bel·li·cose \ˈbe-li-ˌkōs\ *adj* : WARLIKE, PUGNACIOUS ◆ ***Synonyms*** BELLIGERENT, QUARRELSOME, COMBATIVE, CONTENTIOUS — **bel·li·cos·i·ty** \ˌbe-li-ˈkä-sə-tē\ *n*
bel·lig·er·en·cy \bə-ˈli-jə-rən-sē\ *n* **1** : the status of a nation engaged in war **2** : BELLIGERENCE, TRUCULENCE
bel·lig·er·ent \-rənt\ *adj* **1** : waging war **2** : aggressively self-assertive ◆ ***Synonyms*** BELLICOSE, PUGNACIOUS, COMBATIVE, CONTENTIOUS, WARLIKE — **bel·lig·er·ence** \-rəns\ *n* — **belligerent** *n* — **bel·lig·er·ent·ly** *adv*
bel·low \ˈbe-lō\ *vb* **1** : to make the deep hollow sound characteristic of a bull **2** : to shout in a deep voice — **bellow** *n*
bel·lows \-lōz, -ləz\ *n sing or pl* : a closed device with sides that can be spread apart and then pressed together to draw in air and expel it through a tube
bell·weth·er \ˈbel-ˈwe-t͟hər, -ˌwe-\ *n* : one that takes the lead or initiative; *also* : an indicator of trends
¹**bel·ly** \ˈbe-lē\ *n, pl* **bellies** [ME *bely* bellows, belly, fr. OE *belg* bag, skin] **1** : ABDOMEN 1; *also* : POTBELLY **2** : the underpart of an animal's body
²**belly** *vb* **bel·lied; bel·ly·ing** : BULGE
¹**bel·ly·ache** \ˈbe-lē-ˌāk\ *n* : pain in the abdomen : STOMACHACHE
²**bellyache** *vb* : COMPLAIN
belly button *n* : the human navel
belly dance *n* : a usu. solo dance emphasizing movement of the belly — **belly dance** *vb* — **belly dancer** *n*
belly laugh *n* : a deep hearty laugh
be·long \bi-ˈlȯŋ\ *vb* **1** : to be suitable or appropriate; *also* : to be properly situated ⟨shoes ~ in the closet⟩ **2** : to be the property ⟨this ~*s* to me⟩; *also* : to be attached (as through birth or membership) ⟨~ to a club⟩ **3** : to form an attribute or part ⟨this wheel ~*s* to the cart⟩ **4** : to be classified ⟨whales ~ among the mammals⟩
be·long·ings \-ˈlȯŋ-iŋz\ *n pl* : GOODS, EFFECTS, POSSESSIONS
be·loved \bi-ˈləvd, -ˈlə-vəd\ *adj* : dearly loved — **beloved** *n*
¹**be·low** \bi-ˈlō\ *adv* **1** : in or to a lower place or rank **2** : on earth **3** : in hell
²**below** *prep* **1** : lower than ⟨~ sea level⟩ **2** : inferior to (as in rank)
be·low·decks \bi-ˌlō-ˈdeks, -ˈlō-ˌdeks\ *adv* : inside the superstructure of a boat or down to a lower deck
¹**belt** \ˈbelt\ *n* **1** : a strip (as of leather) worn about the waist **2** : a flexible continuous band to communicate motion or convey material **3** : a region marked by some distinctive feature; *esp* : one suited to a particular crop
²**belt** *vb* **1** : to encircle or secure with a belt **2** : to beat with or as if with a belt **3** : to mark with an encircling band **4** : to sing loudly
³**belt** *n* **1** : a jarring blow : WHACK **2** : DRINK ⟨a ~ of whiskey⟩
belt·er \ˈbel-tər\ *n* : a singer with a powerful voice
belt–tightening *n* : a reduction in spending
belt·way \ˈbelt-ˌwā\ *n* : a highway around a city
be·lu·ga \bə-ˈlü-gə\ *n* [Russ] **1** : a large white sturgeon of the Black Sea, Caspian Sea, and their tributaries that is a source of caviar; *also* : caviar from beluga roe **2** : a whale of arctic and subarctic waters that is white when mature
bel·ve·dere \ˈbel-və-ˌdir\ *n* [It, lit., beautiful view] : a structure (as a summerhouse) designed to command a view
be·mire \bi-ˈmī(-ə)r\ *vb* : to cover or soil with or sink in mire
be·moan \bi-ˈmōn\ *vb* : LAMENT, DEPLORE ◆ ***Synonyms*** BEWAIL, GRIEVE, MOAN, WEEP
be·muse \bi-ˈmyüz\ *vb* : BEWILDER, CONFUSE
¹**bench** \ˈbench\ *n* **1** : a long seat for two or more persons **2** : the seat of a judge in court; *also* : the office or dignity of a judge **3** : COURT; *also* : JUDGES **4** : a table for holding work and tools ⟨a carpenter's ~⟩
²**bench** \ˈbench\ *vb* **1** : to furnish with benches **2** : to seat on a bench **3** : to remove from or keep out of a game
¹**bench·mark** \ˈbench-ˌmärk\ *n* **1** *usu* **bench mark** : a mark on a permanent object serving as an elevation reference in topographical surveys **2** : a point of reference for measurement; *also* : STANDARD
²**benchmark** *vb* : to study (as a competitor's business practices) in order to improve one's own performance
bench press *n* : an exercise in which a weight is raised by a person lying on a bench — **bench–press** *vb*
bench warrant *n* : a warrant issued by a presiding judge or by a court against a person guilty of contempt or indicted for a crime
¹**bend** \ˈbend\ *vb* **bent** \ˈbent\; **bend·ing** **1** : to draw (as a bow) taut **2** : to curve or cause a change of shape in ⟨~ a bar⟩ **3** : to make fast : SECURE **4** : DEFLECT **5** : to turn in a certain direction ⟨*bent* his steps toward town⟩ **6** : APPLY ⟨*bent* themselves to the task⟩ **7** : SUBDUE **8** : to curve downward **9** : YIELD, SUBMIT
²**bend** *n* **1** : an act or process of bending **2** : something bent; *esp* : CURVE **3** *pl* : a painful and sometimes fatal disorder caused by release of gas bubbles in the tissues upon too rapid decrease in air pressure after a stay in a compressed atmosphere
³**bend** *n* : a knot by which a rope is fastened (as to another rope)
bend·er \ˈben-dər\ *n* : SPREE ⟨hungover after a weekend ~⟩
¹**be·neath** \bi-ˈnēth\ *adv* : BELOW ⟨the mountains and the town ~⟩ ◆ ***Synonyms*** UNDER, UNDERNEATH
²**beneath** *prep* **1** : BELOW, UNDER ⟨stood ~ a tree⟩ **2** : unworthy of ⟨considered such behavior ~ her⟩ **3** : concealed by ⟨a warm heart ~ a gruff manner⟩
bene·dic·tion \ˌbe-nə-ˈdik-shən\ *n* : the invocation of a blessing esp. at the close of a public worship service
ben·e·fac·tion \-ˈfak-shən\ *n* : a charitable donation ◆ ***Synonyms*** CONTRIBUTION, ALMS, BENEFICENCE, OFFERING
ben·e·fac·tor \ˈben-ə-ˌfak-tər\ *n* : one that confers a benefit and esp. a benefaction
ben·e·fac·tress \-ˌfak-trəs\ *n* : a woman who is a benefactor
ben·e·fice \ˈbe-nə-fəs\ *n* : an ecclesiastical office to which the revenue from an endowment is attached
be·nef·i·cence \bə-ˈne-fə-səns\ *n* **1** : beneficent quality **2** : BENEFACTION
be·nef·i·cent \-sənt\ *adj* : doing or producing good (as by acts of kindness or charity); *also* : BENEFICIAL
ben·e·fi·cial \ˌbe-nə-ˈfi-shəl\ *adj* : being of benefit or help : HELPFUL ◆ ***Synonyms*** ADVANTAGEOUS, PROFITABLE, FAVORABLE, PROPITIOUS — **ben·e·fi·cial·ly** *adv*
ben·e·fi·cia·ry \ˌbe-nə-ˈfi-shē-ˌer-ē, -ˈfi-shə-rē\ *n, pl* **-ries** : one that receives a benefit (as the income of a trust or the proceeds of an insurance)
¹**ben·e·fit** \ˈbe-nə-ˌfit\ *n* **1** : ADVANTAGE ⟨the ~*s* of exercise⟩ **2** : useful aid : HELP; *also* : material aid or service provided or due (as in sickness or unemployment) as a right in addition to regular pay **3** : a performance or event to raise funds
²**benefit** *vb* **-fit·ed** \-ˌfi-təd\ *also* **-fit·ted; -fit·ing** *also* **-fit·ting** **1** : to be useful or profitable to **2** : to receive benefit
be·nev·o·lence \bə-ˈne-və-ləns\ *n* **1** : charitable nature **2**

: an act of kindness : CHARITY — be·nev·o·lent \-lənt\ adj — be·nev·o·lent·ly adv

be·night·ed \bi-'nī-təd\ adj 1 : overtaken by darkness or night 2 : living in ignorance

be·nign \bi-'nīn\ adj [ME benigne, fr. AF, fr. L benignus] 1 : of a gentle disposition; also : showing kindness 2 : of a mild kind; esp : not malignant ⟨~ tumors⟩ ✦ Synonyms BENIGNANT, KIND, KINDLY, GOOD-HEARTED — be·nig·ni·ty \-'nig-nə-tē\ n — be·nign·ly adv

be·nig·nant \-'nig-nənt\ adj : BENIGN 1 ✦ Synonyms KIND, KINDLY, GOOD-HEARTED

ben·i·son \'be-nə-sən, -zən\ n : BLESSING, BENEDICTION

¹bent \'bent\ n 1 : strong inclination or interest; also : TALENT 2 : power of endurance ✦ Synonyms TALENT, APTITUDE, GIFT, FLAIR, KNACK, GENIUS

²bent adj 1 : changed by bending : CROOKED ⟨~ branches⟩ 2 : strongly inclined : DETERMINED ⟨~ on going⟩

bent grass n : any of a genus of stiff velvety grasses used esp. for lawns and pastures

ben·thic \'ben-thik\ adj : of, relating to, or occurring at the bottom of a body of water

ben·ton·ite \'ben-tə-ˌnīt\ n : an absorptive clay used esp. as a filler (as in paper)

bent·wood \'bent-ˌwüd\ adj : made of wood bent into shape ⟨a ~ rocker⟩

be·numb \bi-'nəm\ vb 1 : DULL, DEADEN 2 : to make numb esp. by cold

ben·zene \'ben-ˌzēn\ n : a colorless volatile flammable liquid hydrocarbon used in organic synthesis and as a solvent — ben·ze·noid \-zə-ˌnóid\ adj or n

ben·zine \'ben-ˌzēn\ n : any of various flammable petroleum distillates used as solvents or as motor fuels

ben·zo·ate \'ben-zə-ˌwāt\ n : a salt or ester of benzoic acid

ben·zo·ic acid \ben-'zō-ik-\ n : a white crystalline acid used as a preservative and antiseptic and in synthesizing chemicals

ben·zo·in \'ben-zə-wən, -ˌzóin\ n : a balsamic resin from trees of southern Asia used esp. in medicine and perfumes

be·queath \bi-'kwēth, -'kwēth\ vb [ME bequethen, fr. OE becwethan, fr. be- + cwethan to say] 1 : to leave by will 2 : to hand down

be·quest \bi-'kwest\ n 1 : the action of bequeathing 2 : something bequeathed : LEGACY

be·rate \-'rāt\ vb : to scold harshly

Ber·ber \'bər-bər\ n : a member of any of various peoples living in northern Africa west of Tripoli

ber·ceuse \ber-'sœz, -'süz\ n, pl ber·ceuses \same or -'sü-zəz\ [F, fr. bercer to rock] 1 : LULLABY 2 : a musical composition that resembles a lullaby

¹be·reaved \bi-'rēvd\ adj : suffering the death of a loved one — be·reave·ment n

²bereaved n, pl bereaved : one who is bereaved

be·reft \-'reft\ adj 1 : deprived of or lacking something — usu. used with of 2 : BEREAVED ⟨a ~ mother⟩

be·ret \bə-'rā\ n : a round soft cap with no visor

berg \'bərg\ n : ICEBERG

beri·beri \ˌber-ē-'ber-ē\ n : a deficiency disease marked by weakness, wasting, and nerve damage and caused by lack of thiamine

berke·li·um \'bər-klē-əm\ n : an artificially produced radioactive chemical element

berm \'bərm\ n : a narrow shelf or path at the top or bottom of a slope; also : a mound or bank of earth

Bermuda grass n : a creeping grass often used for lawns and pastures

Ber·mu·das \bər-'myü-dəz\ n pl : BERMUDA SHORTS

Bermuda shorts n pl : knee-length walking shorts

ber·ry \'ber-ē\ n, pl berries 1 : a small pulpy fruit (as a strawberry) 2 : a simple fruit (as a grape, tomato, or cucumber) with the wall of the ripened ovary thick and pulpy 3 : the dry seed of some plants (as coffee)

ber·serk \bər-'sərk, -'zərk\ adj [ON berserkr warrior frenzied in battle, prob. fr. ber- bear + serkr shirt] : FRENZIED, CRAZED — berserk adv

¹berth \'bərth\ n 1 : adequate distance esp. for a ship to maneuver 2 : the place where a ship is anchored or a vehicle rests 3 : ACCOMMODATIONS 4 : JOB, POSITION ✦ Synonyms POST, SITUATION, OFFICE, APPOINTMENT

²berth vb 1 : to bring or come into a berth 2 : to allot a berth to

ber·yl \'ber-əl\ n : a hard silicate mineral occurring as colorless hexagonal crystals when pure

be·ryl·li·um \bə-'ri-lē-əm\ n : a light strong metallic chemical element used as a hardener in alloys

be·seech \bi-'sēch\ vb -sought \-'sót\ or -seeched; -seech·ing : to beg urgently : ENTREAT ✦ Synonyms IMPLORE, PLEAD, SUPPLICATE, IMPORTUNE

be·seem \bi-'sēm\ vb, archaic : BEFIT

be·set \-'set\ vb -set; -set·ting 1 : TROUBLE, HARASS 2 : ASSAIL; also : SURROUND

be·set·ting adj : persistently present

¹be·side \bi-'sīd\ prep 1 : by the side of ⟨sit ~ me⟩ 2 : BESIDES 3 : not relevant to ⟨~ the point⟩

²beside adv, archaic : BESIDES

¹be·sides \bi-'sīdz\ prep 1 : other than ⟨no one ~ us⟩ 2 : together with

²besides adv 1 : as well : ALSO 2 : MOREOVER

be·siege \bi-'sēj\ vb : to lay siege to; also : to press with requests — be·sieg·er n

be·smear \-'smir\ vb : SMEAR

be·smirch \-'smərch\ vb : SMIRCH, SOIL

be·som \'bē-zəm\ n : BROOM

be·sot \bi-'sät\ vb be·sot·ted; be·sot·ting 1 : INFATUATE 2 : to make dull esp. by drinking

be·spat·ter \-'spa-tər\ vb : SPATTER

be·speak \bi-'spēk\ vb -spoke \-'spōk\; -spo·ken \-'spō-kən\; -speak·ing 1 : PREARRANGE 2 : ADDRESS 3 : REQUEST 4 : INDICATE, SIGNIFY 5 : FORETELL

be·sprin·kle \bi-'spriŋ-kəl\ vb : SPRINKLE

¹best \'best\ adj, superlative of GOOD 1 : excelling all others 2 : most productive (as of good or satisfaction) 3 : LARGEST, MOST

²best adv, superlative of WELL 1 : in the best way 2 : MOST

³best n : something that is best

⁴best vb : to get the better of : OUTDO

bes·tial \'bes-chəl\ adj 1 : of or relating to beasts 2 : resembling a beast esp. in brutality or lack of intelligence

bes·ti·al·i·ty \ˌbes-chē-'a-lə-tē, ˌbēs-\ n, pl -ties 1 : the condition or status of a lower animal 2 : display or gratification of bestial traits or impulses 3 : sexual relations between a human being and a lower animal

bes·ti·ary \'bes-chē-ˌer-ē\ n, pl -ar·ies : a medieval allegorical or moralizing work on the appearance and habits of animals

be·stir \bi-'stər\ vb : to rouse to action

best man n : the principal groomsman at a wedding

be·stow \bi-'stō\ vb 1 : PUT, PLACE, STOW 2 : to present as a gift — be·stow·al n — be·stow·er n

be·stride \bi-'strīd\ vb -strode \-'strōd\; -strid·den \-'stri-dᵊn\; -strid·ing : to ride, sit, or stand astride

¹bet \'bet\ n 1 : something that is wagered, risked, or pledged usu. between two parties on the outcome of a contest; also : the making of such a bet 2 : OPTION ⟨the back road is your best ~⟩

²bet vb bet also bet·ted; bet·ting 1 : to stake on the outcome of an issue or a contest ⟨~ $2 on the race⟩ 2 : to make a bet with 3 : to lay a bet

³bet abbr between

be·ta \'bā-tə\ n 1 : the 2d letter of the Greek alphabet — B or β 2 : a nearly complete form of a new product (as software)

beta–block·er \-ˌblä-kər\ n : any of a group of drugs that decrease the rate and force of heart contractions and lower high blood pressure

be·ta–car·o·tene \-'ker-ə-ˌtēn\ n : an isomer of carotene found in dark green and dark yellow vegetables and fruits

be·take \bi-'tāk\ vb -took \-'tük\; -tak·en \-'tā-kən\; -tak·ing : to cause (oneself) to go

beta particle n : a high-speed electron; esp : one emitted by a radioactive nucleus

beta ray n 1 : BETA PARTICLE 2 : a stream of beta particles

beta test n : a field test of the beta version of a product esp. by outside testers and prior to commercial release — beta test vb

be·tel \'bē-tᵊl\ n : a climbing pepper of southern Asia whose leaves are chewed together with lime and betel nut as a stimulant

betel nut n : the astringent seed of an Asian palm that is chewed with betel leaves

bête noire \‚bet-'nwär, ‚bāt-\ *n, pl* **bêtes noires** *same or* -'nwärz\ [F, lit., black beast] : a person or thing strongly disliked or avoided

beth·el \'be-thəl\ *n* [Heb *bēth'ēl* house of God] : a place of worship esp. for seamen

be·think \bi-'think\ *vb* -**thought** \-'thȯt\; -**think·ing** : REMEMBER; *also* : PONDER

be·tide \bi-'tīd\ *vb* : to happen to

be·times \bi-'tīmz\ *adv* : in good time : EARLY ✦ *Synonyms* SOON, SEASONABLY, TIMELY

be·to·ken \bi-'tō-kən\ *vb* 1 : PRESAGE 2 : to give evidence of ✦ *Synonyms* INDICATE, ATTEST, BESPEAK, TESTIFY

be·tray \bi-'trā\ *vb* 1 : to lead astray; *esp* : SEDUCE 2 : to deliver to an enemy 3 : ABANDON 4 : to prove unfaithful to 5 : to reveal unintentionally; *also* : SHOW, INDICATE ✦ *Synonyms* MISLEAD, DELUDE, DECEIVE, BEGUILE — **be·tray·al** *n* — **be·tray·er** *n*

be·troth \bi-'trȯth, -'trōth\ *vb* : to promise to marry — **be·troth·al** *n*

be·trothed *n* : the person to whom one is betrothed

¹**bet·ter** \'be-tər\ *adj, comparative of* GOOD 1 : greater than half 2 : improved in health 3 : more attractive, favorable, or commendable 4 : more advantageous or effective ⟨a ∼ solution⟩ 5 : improved in accuracy or performance

²**better** *vb* 1 : to make or become better 2 : SURPASS, EXCEL

³**better** *adv, comparative of* WELL 1 : in a superior manner 2 : to a higher or greater degree; *also* : MORE

⁴**better** *n* 1 : something better; *also* : a superior esp. in merit or rank 2 : ADVANTAGE

⁵**better** *verbal auxiliary* : had better ⟨you ∼ hurry⟩

better half *n* : SPOUSE

bet·ter·ment \'be-tər-mənt\ *n* : IMPROVEMENT

bet·tor *or* **bet·ter** \'be-tər\ *n* : one that bets

¹**be·tween** \bi-'twēn\ *prep* 1 : by the common action of ⟨earned $10,000 ∼ the two of them⟩ 2 : in the interval separating ⟨an alley ∼ two buildings⟩; *also* : in intermediate relation to 3 : in point of comparison of ⟨choose ∼ two cars⟩

²**between** *adv* : in an intervening space or interval

be·twixt \bi-'twikst\ *adv or prep* : BETWEEN

¹**bev·el** \'be-vəl\ *n* 1 : a device for adjusting the slant of the surfaces of a piece of work 2 : the angle or slant that one surface or line makes with another when not at right angles

²**bevel** *vb* -**eled** *or* -**elled**; -**el·ing** *or* -**el·ling** 1 : to cut or shape to a bevel 2 : INCLINE, SLANT

bev·er·age \'bev-rij\ *n* : a drinkable liquid

bevy \'be-vē\ *n, pl* **bev·ies** 1 : a large group or collection 2 : a group of animals and esp. quail

be·wail \bi-'wāl\ *vb* : LAMENT ✦ *Synonyms* DEPLORE, BEMOAN, GRIEVE, MOAN, WEEP

be·ware \-'wer\ *vb* : to be on one's guard : be wary of

be·wil·der \bi-'wil-dər\ *vb* : PERPLEX, CONFUSE ✦ *Synonyms* MYSTIFY, DISTRACT, PUZZLE — **be·wil·der·ment** *n*

be·witch \-'wich\ *vb* 1 : to affect by witchcraft 2 : CHARM, FASCINATE ✦ *Synonyms* ENCHANT, ATTRACT, CAPTIVATE — **be·witch·ment** *n*

bey \'bā\ *n* 1 : a former Turkish provincial governor 2 : the former native ruler of Tunis or Tunisia

¹**be·yond** \bē-'änd\ *adv* 1 : FARTHER ⟨extends to the river and ∼⟩ 2 : BESIDES

²**beyond** *prep* 1 : on or to the farther side of 2 : out of the reach or sphere of 3 : BESIDES

be·zel \'bē-zəl, 'be-\ *n* 1 : a rim that holds a transparent covering (as on a watch) 2 : the faceted part of a cut gem that rises above the setting

bf *abbr* boldface

BG *or* **B Gen** *abbr* brigadier general

Bh *symbol* bohrium

bhang \'baṅ\ *n* [Hindi *bhāṅg*] : HEMP; *also* : a mildly intoxicating preparation made from hemp leaves

Bi *symbol* bismuth

BIA *abbr* Bureau of Indian Affairs

bi·an·nu·al \(‚)bī-'an-yə-wəl\ *adj* : occurring twice a year — **bi·an·nu·al·ly** *adv*

¹**bi·as** \'bī-əs\ *n* 1 : a line diagonal to the grain of a fabric 2 : PREJUDICE, BENT

²**bias** *adv* : on the bias : DIAGONALLY ⟨cut cloth ∼⟩

³**bias** *vb* **bi·ased** *or* **bi·assed**; **bi·as·ing** *or* **bi·as·sing** : PREJUDICE

bi·ath·lon \bī-'ath-lən, -‚län\ *n* : a composite athletic contest consisting of cross-country skiing and target shooting with a rifle

¹**bib** \'bib\ *n* : a cloth or plastic shield tied under the chin to protect the clothes while eating

²**bib** *abbr* Bible; biblical

bi·be·lot \'bē-bə-‚lō\ *n, pl* **bibelots** *same or* -‚lōz\ : a small household ornament or decorative object

bi·ble \'bī-bəl\ *n* [ME, fr. OF, fr. ML *biblia*, fr. Gk, pl. of *biblion* book, dim. of *byblos* papyrus, book, fr. *Byblos*, ancient Phoenician city from which papyrus was exported] 1 *cap* : the sacred scriptures of Christians comprising the Old and New Testaments 2 *cap* : the sacred scriptures of Judaism; *also* : those of some other religion 3 : a publication that is considered authoritative for its subject — **bib·li·cal** \'bi-bli-kəl\ *adj*

bib·li·og·ra·phy \‚bi-blē-'ä-grə-fē\ *n, pl* -**phies** 1 : the history or description of writings or publications 2 : a list of writings (as on a subject or of an author) — **bib·li·og·ra·pher** \-fər\ *n* — **bib·li·o·graph·ic** \-ə-'gra-fik\ *also* **bib·li·o·graph·i·cal** \-fi-kəl\ *adj*

bib·lio·phile \'bi-blē-ə-‚fī(-ə)l\ *n* : a lover of books

bib·u·lous \'bi-byə-ləs\ *adj* 1 : highly absorbent 2 : fond of alcoholic beverages

bi·cam·er·al \'bī-'ka-mə-rəl\ *adj* : having or consisting of two legislative branches

bicarb \(‚)bī-'kärb, 'bī-‚\ *n* : SODIUM BICARBONATE

bi·car·bon·ate \(‚)bī-'kär-bə-‚nät, -nət\ *n* : an acid carbonate

bicarbonate of soda : SODIUM BICARBONATE

bi·cen·te·na·ry \‚bī-sen-'te-nə-rē, bī-'sen-t²n-‚er-ē\ *n* : BICENTENNIAL — **bicentenary** *adj*

bi·cen·ten·ni·al \‚bī-sen-'te-nē-əl\ *n* : a 200th anniversary or its celebration — **bicentennial** *adj*

bi·ceps \'bī-‚seps\ *n, pl* **biceps** *also* **bi·ceps·es** [NL, fr. L, two-headed, fr. *bi-* two + *caput* head] : a muscle (as in the front of the upper arm) having two points of origin

¹**bick·er** \'bi-kər\ *n* : ALTERCATION

²**bicker** *vb* : to engage in a petty quarrel

bi·coast·al \bī-'kōs-t²l\ *adj* : living or working on both the east and west coasts of the U.S.

bi·con·cave \‚bī-(‚)kän-'kāv, (‚)bī-'kän-‚kāv\ *adj* : concave on both sides

bi·con·vex \‚bī-(‚)kän-'veks, (‚)bī-'kän-‚veks\ *adj* : convex on both sides

bi·cus·pid \bī-'kəs-pəd\ *n* : PREMOLAR

¹**bi·cy·cle** \'bī-‚si-kəl\ *n* : a light 2-wheeled vehicle with a saddle, pedals, and handlebars for steering

²**bicycle** *vb* -**cy·cled**; -**cy·cling** \-‚si-k(ə-)liṅ, -‚sī-\ : to ride a bicycle — **bi·cy·cler** \-k(ə-)lər\ *n* — **bi·cy·clist** \-k(ə)list\ *n*

¹**bid** \'bid\ *vb* **bade** \'bad, 'bād\ *or* **bid**; **bid·den** \'bi-d²n\ *or* **bid** *also* **bade**; **bid·ding** 1 : COMMAND, ORDER 2 : INVITE 3 : to give expression to ⟨*bade* a tearful farewell⟩ 4 : to make a bid : OFFER — **bid·der** *n*

²**bid** *n* 1 : the act of one who bids; *also* : an offer for something 2 : INVITATION 3 : an announcement in a card game of what a player proposes to accomplish 4 : an attempt to win or gain ⟨a ∼ for mayor⟩

bid·da·ble \'bi-də-bəl\ *adj* 1 : OBEDIENT, DOCILE 2 : capable of being bid

bid·dy \'bi-dē\ *n, pl* **biddies** : HEN; *also* : a young chicken

bide \'bīd\ *vb* **bode** \'bōd\ *or* **bid·ed**; **bided**; **bid·ing** 1 : to wait for 2 : WAIT, TARRY 3 : DWELL

bi·det \bi-'dā\ *n* : a bathroom fixture used esp. for bathing the external genitals and the anal region

bi·di·rec·tion·al \‚bī-də-'rek-sh(ə-)nəl\ *adj* : involving, moving, or taking place in two usu. opposite directions — **bi·di·rec·tion·al·ly** *adv*

bi·en·ni·al \bī-'e-nē-əl\ *adj* 1 : taking place once in two years 2 : lasting two years 3 : producing leaves the first year and fruiting and dying the second year — **biennial** *n* — **bi·en·ni·al·ly** *adv*

bi·en·ni·um \bī-'e-nē-əm\ *n, pl* -**niums** *or* -**nia** \-ə\ [L, fr. *bi-* two + *annus* year] : a period of two years

bier \'bir\ *n* : a stand bearing a coffin or corpse

bi·fo·cal \'bī-‚fō-kəl\ *adj* : having two focal lengths

bifocals \-‚kəlz\ *n pl* : eyeglasses with lenses that have one

BOOKS OF THE BIBLE

HEBREW BIBLE

LAW	PROPHETS		WRITINGS
Genesis	Joshua	Obadiah	Psalms
Exodus	Judges	Jonah	Proverbs
Leviticus	1 & 2 Samuel	Micah	Job
Numbers	1 & 2 Kings	Nahum	Song of Songs
Deuteronomy	Isaiah	Habakkuk	Ruth
	Jeremiah	Zephaniah	Lamentations
	Ezekiel	Haggai	Ecclesiastes
	Hosea	Zechariah	Esther
	Joel	Malachi	Daniel
	Amos		Ezra
			Nehemiah
			1 & 2 Chronicles

CHRISTIAN CANON—OLD TESTAMENT

ROMAN CATHOLIC	PROTESTANT	ROMAN CATHOLIC	PROTESTANT
Genesis	Genesis	Wisdom	
Exodus	Exodus	Sirach	
Leviticus	Leviticus	Isaiah	Isaiah
Numbers	Numbers	Jeremiah	Jeremiah
Deuteronomy	Deuteronomy	Lamentations	Lamentations
Joshua	Joshua	Baruch	
Judges	Judges	Ezekiel	Ezekiel
Ruth	Ruth	Daniel	Daniel
1 & 2 Samuel	1 & 2 Samuel	Hosea	Hosea
1 & 2 Kings	1 & 2 Kings	Joel	Joel
1 & 2 Chronicles	1 & 2 Chronicles	Amos	Amos
Ezra	Ezra	Obadiah	Obadiah
Nehemiah	Nehemiah	Jonah	Jonah
Tobit		Micah	Micah
Judith		Nahum	Nahum
Esther	Esther	Habakkuk	Habakkuk
Job	Job	Zephaniah	Zephaniah
Psalms	Psalms	Haggai	Haggai
Proverbs	Proverbs	Zechariah	Zechariah
Ecclesiastes	Ecclesiastes	Malachi	Malachi
Song of Songs	Song of Solomon	1 & 2 Maccabees	

PROTESTANT APOCRYPHA

1 & 2 Esdras	Baruch
Tobit	Prayer of Azariah and the Song
Judith	of the Three Holy Children
Additions to Esther	Susanna
Wisdom of Solomon	Bel and the Dragon
Ecclesiasticus or the Wisdom of Jesus	The Prayer of Manasses
Son of Sirach	1 & 2 Maccabees

CHRISTIAN CANON—NEW TESTAMENT

Matthew	Ephesians	James
Mark	Philippians	1 & 2 Peter
Luke	Colossians	1, 2, 3 John
John	1 & 2 Thessalonians	Jude
Acts of the Apostles	1 & 2 Timothy	Revelation *or*
Romans	Titus	Apocalypse
1 & 2 Corinthians	Philemon	
Galatians	Hebrews	

part that corrects for near vision and one for distant vision

bi·fold \'bī-ˌfōld\ *adj* : designed to fold twice ⟨~ doors⟩

bi·fur·cate \'bī-fər-ˌkāt, bī-'fər-\ *vb* **-cat·ed; -cat·ing** : to divide into two branches or parts — **bi·fur·ca·tion** \ˌbī-fər-'kā-shən\ *n*

big \'big\ *adj* **big·ger; big·gest 1** : large in size, amount, or scope **2** : PREGNANT; *also* : SWELLING **3** : IMPORTANT, IMPOSING **4** : NOBLE, GENEROUS **5** : POPULAR — **big·ness** *n* — **big on** : strongly favoring or liking

big·a·my \'bi-gə-mē\ *n* : the act of marrying one person while still legally married to another — **big·a·mist** \-mist\ *n* — **big·a·mous** \-məs\ *adj*

big bang theory *n* : a theory in astronomy: the universe originated in an explosion (**big bang**) from a single point of nearly infinite energy density

big brother *n* **1** : an older brother **2** : a man who befriends a delinquent or friendless boy **3** *cap both Bs* : the leader of an authoritarian state or movement

big cheese *n* : ³BOSS

big crunch *n* : a hypothetical event in which all matter in the universe collapses to a single point of nearly infinite energy density

Big Dipper *n* : the seven principal stars of Ursa Major in a form resembling a dipper

big·foot \'big-ˌfút\ *n* : SASQUATCH

big·horn sheep \'big-ˌhȯrn\ *n* : a wild sheep of mountainous western No. America

bight \'bīt\ *n* **1** : a curve in a coast; *also* : the bay formed by such a curve **2** : a slack part in a rope

big–name \'big-'nām\ *adj* : widely popular ⟨a ~ performer⟩ — **big name** *n*

big·ot \'bi-gət\ *n* : one who regards or treats members of a group with hatred and intolerance ♦ **Synonyms** FANATIC, ENTHUSIAST, ZEALOT — **big·ot·ed** \-gə-təd\ *adj* — **big·ot·ry** \-trē\ *n*

big screen *n* : the motion picture medium as contrasted to television

big shot \'big-ˌshät\ *n* : an important person

big time \-ˌtīm\ *n* **1** : a high-paying vaudeville circuit requiring only two performances a day **2** : the top rank of an activity or enterprise — **big–tim·er** *n*

big top *n* **1** : the main tent of a circus **2** : CIRCUS

big·wig \'big-ˌwig\ *n* : BIG SHOT

bike \'bīk\ *n* **1** : BICYCLE **2** : MOTORCYCLE

bik·er *n* : MOTORCYCLIST; *esp* : one who is a member of an organized gang

bike·way \'bīk-ˌwā\ *n* : a thoroughfare for bicycles

bi·ki·ni \bə-'kē-nē\ *n* [F, fr. *Bikini*, atoll in the Marshall Islands] : a woman's brief 2-piece bathing suit

bi·lat·er·al \bī-'la-tə-rəl\ *adj* **1** : having or involving two sides **2** : affecting reciprocally two sides or parties — **bi·lat·er·al·ism** \-tə-rə-ˌli-zəm\ *n* — **bi·lat·er·al·ly** *adv*

bile \'bī(-ə)l\ *n* **1** : a bitter greenish fluid secreted by the liver that aids in the digestion of fats **2** : an ill-humored mood

bilge \'bilj\ *n* **1** : the part of a ship that lies between the bottom and the point where the sides go straight up **2** : stale or worthless remarks or ideas

bi·lin·gual \bī-'liŋ-gwəl\ *adj* : expressed in, knowing, or using two languages

bil·ious \'bil-yəs\ *adj* **1** : marked by or suffering from disordered liver function **2** : IRRITABLE, ILL-TEMPERED — **bil·ious·ness** *n*

bilk \'bilk\ *vb* : CHEAT, SWINDLE

¹bill \'bil\ *n* : the jaws of a bird together with their horny covering; *also* : a mouthpart (as of a turtle) resembling these — **billed** \'bild\ *adj*

²bill *vb* : to caress fondly

³bill *n* **1** : an itemized statement of particulars; *also* : INVOICE **2** : a written document or note **3** : a printed advertisement (as a poster) announcing an event **4** : a draft of a law presented to a legislature for enactment **5** : a written statement of a legal wrong suffered or of some breach of law **6** : a piece of paper money

⁴bill *vb* **1** : to enter in or prepare a bill; *also* : to submit a bill or account to **2** : to advertise by bills or posters

bill·board \-ˌbȯrd\ *n* : a flat surface on which advertising bills are posted

¹bil·let \'bi-lət\ *n* **1** : an order requiring a person to pro-

vide lodging for a soldier; *also* : quarters assigned by or as if by such an order **2** : POSITION, APPOINTMENT

²billet *vb* : to assign lodging to by billet

bil·let–doux \ˌbi-lā-'dü\ *n, pl* **billets–doux** *same or* -'düz\ [F *billet doux*, lit., sweet letter] : a love letter

bill·fold \'bil-ˌfōld\ *n* : WALLET

bil·liards \'bil-yərdz\ *n* : any of several games played on an oblong table by driving balls against each other or into pockets with a cue

bil·lings·gate \'bi-liŋz-ˌgāt, *Brit usu* -git\ *n* [*Billingsgate*, old gate and fish market, London, England] : coarsely abusive language

bil·lion \'bil-yən\ *n* **1** : a thousand millions **2** *Brit* : a million millions — **billion** *adj* — **bil·lionth** \-yənth\ *adj or n*

bill of attainder : a legislative act that imposes punishment without a trial

bill of health : a usu. favorable report following an examination

bill of sale : a legal document transferring ownership of goods

¹bil·low \'bi-lō\ *n* **1** : WAVE; *esp* : a great wave **2** : a rolling mass (as of fog or flame) like a great wave — **bil·lowy** \'bi-lə-wē\ *adj*

²billow *vb* : to rise and roll in waves; *also* : to swell out ⟨~*ing* sails⟩

bil·ly \'bi-lē\ *n, pl* **billies** : BILLY CLUB

billy club *n* : a heavy usu. wooden club; *esp* : a police officer's club

bil·ly goat \'bi-lē-\ *n* : a male goat

bi·met·al \'bī-ˌme-t²l\ *adj* : BIMETALLIC — **bimetal** *n*

bi·me·tal·lic \ˌbī-mə-'ta-lik\ *adj* : made of two different metals — often used of devices having a bonded expansive part — **bimetallic** *n*

bi·met·al·lism \bī-'me-t²l-ˌi-zəm\ *n* : the use of two metals at fixed ratios to form a standard of value for a monetary system

¹bi·month·ly \bī-'mənth-lē\ *adj* **1** : occurring every two months **2** : occurring twice a month : SEMIMONTHLY — **bimonthly** *adv*

²bimonthly *n* : a bimonthly publication

bin \'bin\ *n* : a box, crib, or enclosure used for storage

bi·na·ry \'bī-nə-rē, -ˌner-ē\ *adj* **1** : consisting of two things or parts **2** : relating to, being, or belonging to a system of numbers having 2 as its base ⟨the ~ digits 0 and 1⟩ **3** : involving a choice between or condition of two alternatives only (as on-off, yes-no) — **binary** *n*

binary star *n* : a system of two stars revolving around each other

binary system *n* : BINARY STAR

bin·au·ral \bī-'nȯr-əl\ *adj* : of or relating to sound reproduction involving the use of two separated microphones and two transmission channels to achieve a stereophonic effect

bind \'bīnd\ *vb* **bound** \'baúnd\; **bind·ing 1** : TIE; *also* : to restrain as if by tying **2** : to put under an obligation; *also* : to constrain with legal authority **3** : BANDAGE **4** : to unite into a mass **5** : to compel as if by a pledge ⟨a handshake ~*s* the deal⟩ **6** : to strengthen or decorate with a band **7** : to fasten together and enclose in a cover ⟨~ books⟩ **8** : to exert a tying, restraining, or compelling effect — **bind·er** *n*

bind·ing \'bīn-diŋ\ *n* : something (as a ski fastening, a cover, or an edging fabric) used to bind

bin·dle \'bin-d²l\ *n* : a bundle of clothes or bedding

¹binge \'binj\ *n* **1** : SPREE **2** : an act of excessive consumption (as of food)

²binge *vb* **binged; binge·ing** *or* **bing·ing** : to go on a binge — **bing·er** *n*

bin·go \'biŋ-gō\ *n, pl* **bingos** : a game of chance played with cards having numbered squares corresponding to numbered balls drawn at random and won by covering five squares in a row

bin·na·cle \'bi-ni-kəl\ *n* [alter. of ME *bitakle*, fr. Pg or Sp; Pg *bitácola* & Sp *bitácula*, fr. L *habitaculum* dwelling place, fr. *habitare* to inhabit] : a container holding a ship's compass

¹bin·oc·u·lar \bī-'nä-kyə-lər, bə-\ *adj* : of, relating to, or adapted to the use of both eyes — **bin·oc·u·lar·ly** *adv*

²bin·oc·u·lar \bə-'nä-kyə-lər, bī-\ *n* **1** : a binocular optical instrument (as a microscope) **2** : a hand-held optical instrument composed of two telescopes and a focusing device — usu. used in pl.

bi·no·mi·al \bī-'nō-mē-əl\ *n* **1** : a mathematical expression consisting of two terms connected by the sign plus (+) or minus (–) **2** : a biological species name consisting of two terms — **binomial** *adj*

bio·chem·is·try \ˌbī-ō-'ke-mə-strē\ *n* : chemistry that deals with the chemical compounds and processes occurring in living things — **bio·chem·i·cal** \-mi-kəl\ *adj or n* — **bio·chem·ic·al·ly** \-k(ə-)lē\ *adv* — **bio·chem·ist** \-mist\ *n*

bio·de·grad·able \-di-'grä-də-bəl\ *adj* : capable of being broken down esp. into innocuous products by the actions of living things (as microorganisms) ⟨a ~ detergent⟩ — **bio·de·grad·abil·i·ty** \-ˌgrä-də-'bi-lə-tē\ *n* — **bio·deg·ra·da·tion** \-ˌde-grə-'dä-shən\ *n* — **bio·de·grade** \-di-'grād\ *vb*

bio·di·ver·si·ty \-də-'vər-sə-tē, -dī-\ *n* : biological diversity in an environment as indicated by numbers of different species of plants and animals

bio·en·gi·neer·ing \-ˌen-jə-'nir-iŋ\ *n* **1** : the application of engineering principles to medicine and biology **2** : GENETIC ENGINEERING

bio·eth·ics \-'e-thiks\ *n* : the ethics of biological research and its applications esp. in medicine — **bio·eth·i·cal** \-'e-thi-kəl\ *adj* — **bio·eth·i·cist** \-'e-thə-sist\ *n*

bio·feed·back \-'fēd-ˌbak\ *n* : the technique of making unconscious or involuntary bodily processes (as heartbeats or brain waves) perceptible to the senses (as by use of an oscilloscope) in order to manipulate them by conscious mental control

biog *abbr* biographer; biographical; biography

bio·ge·og·ra·phy \ˌbī-ō-jē-'ä-grə-fē\ *n* : a science that deals with the geographical distribution of plants and animals — **bio·ge·og·ra·pher** *n*

bi·og·ra·phy \bī-'ä-grə-fē, bē-\ *n, pl* **-phies** : a written history of a person's life; *also* : such writings in general — **bi·og·ra·pher** *n* — **bio·graph·i·cal** \ˌbī-ə-'gra-fi-kəl\ *also* **bi·o·graph·ic** \-fik\ *adj*

bio·in·for·mat·ics \ˌbī-ō-in-fər-'ma-tiks\ *n* : the storage, classification, and analysis of biological information using computers

biol *abbr* biologic; biological; biologist; biology

bi·o·log·i·cal \ˌbī-ə-'lä-ji-kəl\ *also* **bi·o·log·ic** \-jik\ *adj* **1** : of, relating to, or produced by biology or life and living processes **2** : connected by direct genetic relationship rather than by adoption or marriage ⟨her ~ father⟩ — **bi·o·log·i·cal·ly** \-ji-k(ə-)lē\ *adv*

biological clock *n* : an inherent timing mechanism in a living system that is inferred to exist in order to explain the timing of various physiological and behavioral states and processes

biological warfare *n* : warfare in which harmful living organisms (**biological weapons**) are used against an enemy esp. to cause large-scale death or disease

bi·ol·o·gy \bī-'ä-lə-jē\ *n* [G *Biologie*, fr. Gk *bios* mode of life + *logos* word, discourse] **1** : a science that deals with living beings and life processes **2** : the life processes of an organism or group — **bi·ol·o·gist** \bī-'ä-lə-jist\ *n*

bio·mass \'bī-ō-ˌmas\ *n* **1** : the amount of living matter (as in a unit area) **2** : plant materials and animal waste used esp. as fuel

bio·med·i·cal \ˌbī-ō-'me-di-kəl\ *adj* : of, relating to, or involving biological, medical, and physical science

bi·on·ic \bī-'ä-nik\ *adj* : having normal biological capability or performance enhanced by or as if by electronic or mechanical devices

bio·phys·ics \ˌbī-ō-'fi-ziks\ *n* : a branch of science concerned with the application of physical principles and methods to biological problems — **bio·phys·i·cal** \-zi-kəl\ *adj* — **bio·phys·i·cist** \-'fi-zə-sist\ *n*

bio·pic \'bī-ō-ˌpik\ *n* : a biographical movie

bi·op·sy \'bī-ˌäp-sē\ *n, pl* **-sies** : the removal of tissue, cells, or fluids from the living body for examination

bio·rhythm \'bī-ō-ˌri-thəm\ *n* : an innately determined rhythmic biological process (as sleep); *also* : the internal mechanism controlling such a process

bio·sci·ence \-'sī-əns\ *n* : BIOLOGY 1; *also* : LIFE SCIENCE

bio·sphere \'bī-ə-ˌsfir\ *n* **1** : the part of the world in which life can exist **2** : living organisms together with their environment

bio·tech \'bī-ō-ˌtek\ *n* : BIOTECHNOLOGY

bio·tech·nol·ogy \ˌbī-ō-tek-'nä-lə-jē\ *n* : the manipulation (as through genetic engineering) of living organisms to produce useful products; *also* : biological science so applied

bio·ter·ror·ism \-'ter-ər-ˌi-zəm\ *n* : terrorism involving the use of biological weapons — **bio·ter·ror·ist** \-ist\ *adj or n*

bi·ot·ic \bī-'ä-tik\ *adj* : of, relating to, or caused by living organisms

bi·o·tin \'bī-ə-tən\ *n* : a vitamin of the vitamin B complex found esp. in yeast, liver, and egg yolk and active in growth promotion

bi·o·tite \'bī-ə-ˌtīt\ *n* : a dark mica containing iron, magnesium, potassium, and aluminum

bi·par·ti·san \bī-'pär-tə-zən\ *adj* : marked by or involving cooperation, agreement, and compromise between two major political parties — **bi·par·ti·san·ship** \-ˌship\

bi·par·tite \-'pär-ˌtīt\ *adj* **1** : being in two parts **2** : shared by two ⟨~ treaty⟩

bi·ped \'bī-ˌped\ *n* : a 2-footed animal — **bi·ped·al** \(ˌ)bī-'pe-dᵊl\ *adj*

bi·plane \'bī-ˌplān\ *n* : an aircraft with two wings placed one above the other

bi·po·lar \bī-'pō-lər\ *adj* : having or involving the use of two poles — **bi·po·lar·i·ty** \ˌbī-pō-'ler-ə-tē\ *n*

bipolar disorder *n* : any of several psychological disorders of mood characterized usu. by alternating episodes of depression and mania

bi·ra·cial \bī-'rā-shəl\ *adj* : of, relating to, or involving members of two races

¹birch \'bərch\ *n* **1** : any of a genus of mostly short-lived deciduous shrubs and trees with membranous outer bark and pale close-grained wood; *also* : this wood **2** : a birch rod or bundle of twigs for flogging — **birch** or **birch·en** \'bər-chən\ *adj*

²birch *vb* : WHIP, FLOG

¹bird \'bərd\ *n* : any of a class of warm-blooded egg-laying vertebrates having the body feathered and the forelimbs modified to form wings

²bird *vb* : to observe or identify wild birds in their native habitat — **bird·er** *n*

bird·bath \'bərd-ˌbath, -ˌbäth\ *n* : a usu. ornamental basin set up for birds to bathe in

bird·house \-ˌhaus\ *n* : an artificial nesting place for birds; *also* : AVIARY

bird·ie \'bər-dē\ *n* : a score of one under par on a hole in golf

bird·lime \-ˌlīm\ *n* : a sticky substance smeared on twigs to snare small birds

bird of paradise : any of numerous brilliantly colored plumed birds of the New Guinea area

bird of prey : a carnivorous bird that feeds wholly or chiefly on carrion or on meat taken by hunting

bird·seed \'bərd-ˌsēd\ *n* : a mixture of small seeds (as of hemp or millet) used for feeding birds

bird's-eye \'bərdz-ˌī\ *adj* **1** : marked with spots resembling birds' eyes ⟨~ maple⟩ **2** : seen from above as if by a flying bird ⟨~ view⟩; *also* : CURSORY

bi·ret·ta \bə-'re-tə\ *n* : a square cap with three ridges on top worn esp. by Roman Catholic clergymen

birr \'bir, 'bər\ *n, pl* **birr** — see MONEY table

¹birth \'bərth\ *n* **1** : the act or fact of being born or of bringing forth young **2** : LINEAGE, DESCENT **3** : ORIGIN, BEGINNING — **birth** *vb*

²birth *adj* : BIOLOGICAL 2 ⟨~ parents⟩

birth canal *n* : the channel formed by the cervix, vagina, and vulva through which the fetus passes during birth

birth control *n* : control of the number of children born esp. by preventing or lessening the frequency of conception

birth·day \'bərth-ˌdā\ *n* : the day or anniversary of one's birth

birth defect *n* : a physical or biochemical defect present at birth and inherited or environmentally induced

birth·mark \'bərth-ˌmärk\ *n* : an unusual mark or blemish on the skin at birth

birth·place \-ˌplās\ *n* : place of birth or origin

birth·rate \-ˌrāt\ *n* : the number of births per number of individuals in a given area or group during a given time

birth·right \-ˌrīt\ *n* : a right, privilege, or possession to which one is entitled by birth ♦ *Synonyms* LEGACY, PATRIMONY, HERITAGE, INHERITANCE

birth·stone \-ˌstōn\ *n* : a gemstone associated symbolically with the month of one's birth

bis·cuit \'bis-kət\ *n* [ME *bisquite*, fr. AF *besquit*, fr. (*pain*) *besquit* twice-cooked bread] **1** : a crisp flat cake; *esp*, *Brit* : CRACKER 2 **2** : a small quick bread made from dough that has been rolled and cut or dropped from a spoon

bi·sect \'bī-ˌsekt\ *vb* : to divide into two usu. equal parts; *also* : CROSS, INTERSECT — **bi·sec·tion** \'bī-ˌsek-shən\ *n* — **bi·sec·tor** \-tər\ *n*

bi·sex·u·al \bī-'sek-shə-wəl\ *adj* **1** : possessing characters of or having sexual desire for both sexes **2** : of, relating to, or involving both sexes — **bisexual** *n* — **bi·sex·u·al·i·ty** \ˌbī-ˌsek-shə-'wal-ə-tē\ *n*

bish·op \'bi-shəp\ *n* [ME *bisshop*, fr. OE *bisceop*, fr. LL *episcopus*, fr. Gk *episkopos*, lit., overseer, fr. *epi-* on, over + *skeptesthai* to look] **1** : a member of the clergy ranking above a priest and typically governing a diocese **2** : any of various Protestant church officials who superintend other clergy **3** : a chess piece that can move diagonally across any number of adjoining unoccupied squares

bish·op·ric \'bi-shə-prik\ *n* **1** : DIOCESE **2** : the office of bishop

bis·muth \'biz-məth\ *n* : a heavy brittle grayish white metallic chemical element used in alloys and medicine

bi·son \'bī-sᵊn, -zᵊn\ *n, pl* **bison** : BUFFALO 2

bisque \'bisk\ *n* : a thick cream soup

bis·tro \'bēs-trō, 'bis-\ *n, pl* **bistros** [F] **1** : a small or unpretentious restaurant **2** : BAR; *also* : NIGHTCLUB

¹bit \'bit\ *n* **1** : the biting or cutting edge or part of a tool **2** : the part of a bridle that is placed in a horse's mouth

²bit *n* **1** : a morsel of food; *also* : a small piece or quantity of something **2** : a small coin; *also* : a unit of value equal to 12½ cents **3** : something small or trivial **4** : an indefinite usu. small degree or extent ⟨a ~ tired⟩

³bit *n* [*binary digit*] : a unit of computer information equivalent to the result of a choice between two alternatives; *also* : its physical representation

¹bitch \'bich\ *n* **1** : a female canine; *esp* : a female dog **2** : a malicious, spiteful, or overbearing woman

²bitch *vb* : COMPLAIN

¹bite \'bīt\ *vb* **bit** \'bit\; **bit·ten** \'bi-tᵊn\ *also* **bit**; **bit·ing** \'bī-tiŋ\ **1** : to grip with teeth or jaws; *also* : to wound or sting with or as if with fangs **2** : to cut or pierce with or as if with an edged instrument **3** : to cause to smart or sting **4** : CORRODE **5** : to take bait

²bite *n* **1** : the act or manner of biting **2** : FOOD **3** : a wound made by biting; *also* : a penetrating effect

bite–size \'bīt-ˌsīz\ *adj* **1** : of a size that can be eaten in one bite **2** : being or made small or brief esp. so as to be easily manageable

biting *adj* : SHARP, CUTTING

bit·map \'bit-ˌmap\ *n* : an array of binary data representing a bitmapped image or display

bit·mapped \'bit-ˌmapt\ *adj* : of, relating to, or being a digital image or display for which an array of binary data specifies the value of each pixel

bit·ter \'bi-tər\ *adj* **1** : being or inducing the one of the basic taste sensations that is acrid, astringent, or disagreeable and is suggestive of hops **2** : marked by intensity or severity (as of distress or hatred) **3** : extremely harsh or cruel — **bit·ter·ly** *adv* — **bit·ter·ness** *n*

bit·tern \'bi-tərn\ *n* : any of various small or medium-sized herons

bit·ters \'bi-tərz\ *n sing or pl* : a usu. alcoholic solution of bitter and often aromatic plant products used in mixing drinks and as a mild tonic

¹bit·ter·sweet \'bi-tər-ˌswēt\ *n* **1** : a poisonous nightshade with purple flowers and reddish berries **2** : a woody vine with yellow capsules that open when ripe to show scarlet seed covers

²bittersweet *adj* : being at once both bitter and sweet

bi·tu·mi·nous coal \bə-'tü-mə-nəs-, bī-, -'tyü-\ *n* : a coal that when heated yields considerable volatile waste matter

bi·valve \'bī-ˌvalv\ *n* : any of a class of mollusks (as clams or scallops) of two separate parts that open and shut — **bivalve** *adj*

¹biv·ouac \'bi-və-ˌwak\ *n* [F, fr. LG *biwacht*, fr. *bi* at + *wacht* guard] : a temporary encampment or shelter

²bivouac *vb* **-ouacked; -ouack·ing** : to form a bivouac : CAMP

¹bi·week·ly \ˌbī-'wē-klē\ *adj* **1** : occurring twice a week **2** : occurring every two weeks : FORTNIGHTLY — **biweek·ly** *adv*

²biweekly *n* : a biweekly publication

bi·year·ly \-'yir-lē\ *adj* **1** : BIANNUAL **2** : BIENNIAL

bi·zarre \bə-'zär\ *adj* : ODD, ECCENTRIC, FANTASTIC ⟨~ costumes⟩ — **bi·zarre·ly** *adv*

bi·zar·ro \bə-'zär-ō\ *adj* : characterized by a bizarre, fantastic, or unconventional approach

bk *abbr* **1** bank **2** book

Bk *symbol* berkelium

bkg *abbr* banking

bkgd *abbr* background

bks *abbr* barracks

bkt *abbr* **1** basket **2** bracket

bl *abbr* **1** bale **2** barrel **3** blue

blab \'blab\ *vb* **blabbed; blab·bing** : TATTLE, GOSSIP

¹black \'blak\ *adj* **1** : of the color black; *also* : very dark **2** : SWARTHY **3** : of or relating to various groups of dark-skinned people **4** : of or relating to the African-American people or their culture **5** : SOILED, DIRTY **6** : lacking light ⟨a ~ night⟩ **7** : WICKED, EVIL ⟨~ magic⟩ **8** : DISMAL, GLOOMY ⟨a ~ outlook⟩ **9** : SULLEN ⟨a ~ mood⟩ — **black·ish** *adj* — **black·ly** *adv* — **black·ness** *n*

²black *n* **1** : a black pigment or dye; *also* : something (as clothing) that is black **2** : the characteristic color of soot or coal **3** : a person of a dark-skinned race **4** : AFRICAN=AMERICAN

³black *vb* : BLACKEN

black·a·moor \'bla-kə-ˌmùr\ *n* : a dark-skinned person

black–and–blue \ˌbla-kən-'blü\ *adj* : darkly discolored from blood effused by bruising

black–and–white \ˌbla-kən-'hwīt\ *n* : SQUAD CAR

black·ball \'blak-ˌból\ *vb* **1** : to vote against; *esp* : to exclude from membership by casting a negative vote **2** : OSTRACIZE — **black·ball** *n*

black bass *n* : any of several freshwater sunfishes native to eastern and central No. America

black bear *n* : a usu. black-furred bear of No. America forests

¹black belt \'blak-ˌbelt\ *n, often cap both Bs* : an area densely populated by blacks

²black belt \-'belt\ *n* : one who holds the rating of expert (as in judo or karate); *also* : the rating itself

black·ber·ry \-ˌber-ē\ *n* : the usu. black or purple juicy but seedy edible fruit of various brambles; *also* : a plant bearing this fruit

black·bird \-ˌbərd\ *n* : any of various birds (as the red-winged blackbird) of which the male is largely or wholly black

black·board \-ˌbórd\ *n* : a smooth usu. dark surface used for writing or drawing on with chalk

black·body \'bla-ˈbä-dē\ *n* : a body or surface that completely absorbs incident radiation with no reflection

black box *n* **1** : a usu. complicated electronic device whose components and workings are unknown or mysterious to the user **2** : a device used in aircraft to record cockpit conversations and flight data

black death *n* : an epidemic of bacterial plague and esp. bubonic plague that spread rapidly in Europe and Asia in the 14th century

black·en \'bla-kən\ *vb* **black·ened; black·en·ing 1** : to make or become black **2** : DEFAME, SULLY ⟨~ed her reputation⟩

black·ened *adj* : coated with spices and quickly seared in a very hot skillet ⟨~ swordfish⟩

black eye *n* : a discoloration of the skin around the eye from bruising

black–eyed Su·san \ˌblak-ˌīd-'sü-zᵊn\ *n* : a coarse No. American plant that is related to the daisies and has deep yellow to orange flower heads with dark conical centers

Black·foot \'blak-ˌfùt\ *n, pl* **Black·feet** *or* **Blackfoot** : a member of an American Indian people of Montana, Alberta, and Saskatchewan

black·guard \'bla-gərd, -ˌgärd\ *n* : SCOUNDREL, RASCAL

black·head \'blak-ˌhed\ *n* : a small usu. dark oily mass plugging the outlet of a skin gland

black hole *n* : a celestial object with a gravitational field so strong that light cannot escape from it

black·ing \'bla-kiŋ\ *n* : a substance applied to something to make it black

¹**black·jack** \'blak-ˌjak\ *n* **1** : a leather-covered club with a flexible handle **2** : a card game in which the object is to be dealt cards having a higher count than the dealer but not exceeding 21

²**blackjack** *vb* : to hit with or as if with a blackjack

black light *n* : invisible ultraviolet light

black·list \'blak-ˌlist\ *n* : a list of persons who are disapproved of and are to be punished or boycotted — **blacklist** *vb*

black·mail \'blak-ˌmāl\ *n* : extortion by threats esp. of public exposure; *also* : something so extorted — **blackmail** *vb* — **black·mail·er** *n*

black market *n* : illicit trade in goods; *also* : a place where such trade is carried on

Black Mass *n* : a travesty of the Christian Mass ascribed to worshipers of Satan

Black Muslim *n* : a member of a chiefly black group that professes Islamic religious belief

black nationalist *n*, *often cap B&N* : a member of a group of militant blacks who advocate separatism from whites and the formation of self-governing black communities — **black nationalism** *n*, *often cap B&N*

black–on–black *adj* : involving a black person against another black person ⟨~ crime⟩

black·out \'blak-ˌaút\ *n* **1** : a period of darkness due to electrical power failure **2** : a transitory loss or dulling of vision or consciousness **3** : the prohibition or restriction of the telecasting of a sports event — **black out** *vb*

black pepper *n* : a spice that consists of the dried berry of a pepper plant ground with the black husk still on

black power *n* : the mobilization of the political and economic power of black Americans esp. to compel respect for their rights and improve their condition

black sheep *n* : a member of a group who is disreputable or not regarded favorably

black·smith \'blak-ˌsmith\ *n* : a smith who forges iron — **black·smith·ing** *n*

black·strap molasses \'blak-ˌstrap-\ *n* : a thick dark molasses obtained from successive processing of raw sugar

black·thorn \-ˌthórn\ *n* : a European thorny plum

black–tie \'blak-'tī\ *adj* : characterized by or requiring semiformal evening clothes consisting of a usu. black tie and tuxedo for men and a formal dress for women

black·top \'blak-ˌtäp\ *n* : a dark tarry material (as asphalt) used esp. for surfacing roads — **blacktop** *vb*

black widow *n* : a venomous New World spider having the female black with an hourglass-shaped red mark on the underside of the abdomen

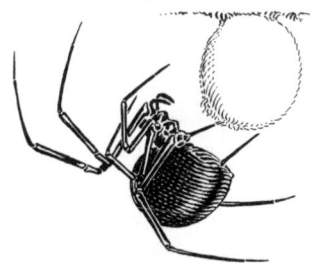

black widow

blad·der \'bla-dər\ *n* : a sac in which liquid or gas is stored; *esp* : one in a vertebrate into which urine passes from the kidneys

¹**blade** \'blād\ *n* **1** : a leaf of a plant and esp. of a grass; *also* : the flat part of a leaf as distinguished from its stalk **2** : something (as the flat part of an oar or an arm of a propeller) resembling the blade of a leaf **3** : the cutting part of an instrument or tool **4** : SWORD; *also* : SWORDSMAN **5** : a dashing fellow ⟨a gay ~⟩ **6** : the runner of an ice skate — **blad·ed** \'blā-dəd\ *adj*

²**blade** *vb* **blad·ed; blad·ing** : to skate on in-line skates — **blad·er** \'blā-dər\ *n*

blain \'blān\ *n* : an inflammatory swelling or sore

¹**blame** \'blām\ *vb* **blamed; blam·ing** [ME, fr. AF *blamer*,

blasmer, fr. L *blasphemare* to blaspheme, fr. Gk *blasphēmein*] **1** : to find fault with **2** : to hold responsible or responsible for ✦ **Synonyms** CENSURE, DENOUNCE, CONDEMN, CRITICIZE — **blam·able** *adj*

²**blame** *n* **1** : CENSURE, REPROOF **2** : responsibility for fault or error ✦ **Synonyms** GUILT, FAULT, CULPABILITY, ONUS — **blame·less** *adj* — **blame·less·ly** *adv* — **blame·less·ness** *n*

blame·wor·thy \-ˌwər-thē\ *adj* : deserving blame — **blame·wor·thi·ness** *n*

blanch \'blanch\ *vb* : to make or become white or pale : BLEACH

blanc·mange \blə-'mänj, -'mänᶻh\ *n* : a dessert made from gelatin or a starchy substance and milk usu. sweetened and flavored

bland \'bland\ *adj* **1** : smooth in manner : SUAVE ⟨a ~ smile⟩ **2** : gently soothing ⟨a ~ diet⟩; *also* : INSIPID ✦ **Synonyms** GENTLE, MILD, SOFT, BALMY — **bland·ly** *adv* — **bland·ness** *n*

blan·dish·ment \'blan-dish-mənt\ *n* : flattering or coaxing speech or action : CAJOLERY

¹**blank** \'blaŋk\ *adj* **1** : showing or causing an appearance of dazed dismay; *also* : EXPRESSIONLESS **2** : free from writing or marks; *also* : having spaces to be filled in **3** : DULL, EMPTY ⟨~ moments⟩ **4** : ABSOLUTE, DOWNRIGHT ⟨a ~ refusal⟩ **5** : not shaped in final form — **blank·ly** *adv* — **blank·ness** *n*

²**blank** *n* **1** : an empty space **2** : a form with spaces for the entry of data **3** : an unfinished form (as of a key) **4** : a cartridge with propellant and a seal but no projectile

³**blank** *vb* **1** : to cover or close up : OBSCURE **2** : to keep from scoring

blank check *n* **1** : a signed check with the amount unspecified **2** : complete freedom of action

¹**blan·ket** \'blaŋ-kət\ *n* **1** : a heavy woven often woolen covering **2** : a covering layer ⟨a ~ of snow⟩

²**blanket** *vb* : to cover with a blanket

³**blanket** *adj* : covering a group or class ⟨~ insurance⟩; *also* : applicable in all instances ⟨~ rules⟩

blank verse *n* : unrhymed iambic pentameter

blare \'bler\ *vb* **blared; blar·ing** : to sound loud and harsh; *also* : to proclaim loudly — **blare** *n*

blar·ney \'blär-nē\ *n* [*Blarney stone*, a stone in Blarney Castle, near Cork, Ireland, held to bestow skill in flattery on those who kiss it] : skillful flattery : BLANDISHMENT

bla·sé \blä-'zā\ *adj* [F] : apathetic to pleasure or excitement as a result of excessive indulgence; *also* : SOPHISTICATED

blas·pheme \blas-'fēm, 'blas-ˌ\ *vb* **blas·phemed; blas·phem·ing** **1** : to speak of or address with irreverence **2** : to utter blasphemy — **blas·phem·er** *n*

blas·phe·my \'blas-fə-mē\ *n, pl* **-mies** **1** : the act of expressing lack of reverence for God **2** : irreverence toward something considered sacred — **blas·phe·mous** \-məs\ *adj*

¹**blast** \'blast\ *n* **1** : a violent gust of wind; *also* : its effect **2** : sound made by a wind instrument **3** : a current of air forced at high pressure through a hole in a furnace (**blast furnace**) **4** : a sudden withering esp. of plants : BLIGHT **5** : EXPLOSION; *also* : the shock wave of an explosion

²**blast** *vb* : to shatter by or as if by an explosion

blast off *vb* : TAKE OFF **4** — used esp. of rocket-propelled vehicles — **blast-off** \'blast-ˌóf\ *n*

bla·tant \'blā-tᵊnt\ *adj* : offensively obtrusive : vulgarly showy ✦ **Synonyms** VOCIFEROUS, BOISTEROUS, CLAMOROUS, OBSTREPEROUS — **bla·tan·cy** \-tᵊn-sē\ *n* — **bla·tant·ly** *adv*

blath·er \'bla-thər\ *vb* : to talk foolishly at length — **blath·er** *n*

blath·er·skite \'bla-thər-ˌskīt\ *n* : a person who blathers

¹**blaze** \'blāz\ *n* **1** : FIRE **2** : intense direct light accompanied by heat **3** : something (as a dazzling display or sudden outburst) suggesting fire ⟨a ~ of autumn leaves⟩ ✦ **Synonyms** GLARE, GLOW, FLAME

²**blaze** *vb* **blazed; blaz·ing** **1** : to burn brightly; *also* : to flare up **2** : to be conspicuously bright : GLITTER

³**blaze** *vb* **blazed; blaz·ing** : to make public or conspicuous

⁴**blaze** *n* **1** : a usu. white stripe on the face of an animal **2** : a trail marker; *esp* : one made on a tree

⁵**blaze** *vb* **blazed; blaz·ing** : to mark (as a tree or trail) with blazes

blaze orange *n* : a very bright orange used in clothing for visibility

blaz·er \'blā-zər\ *n* : a sports jacket often with notched collar and pockets that are stitched on

¹**bla·zon** \'blā-z°n\ *n* **1** : COAT OF ARMS **2** : ostentatious display

²**blazon** *vb* **1** : to publish widely : PROCLAIM **2** : DECK, ADORN

bldg *abbr* building

bldr *abbr* builder

¹**bleach** \'blēch\ *vb* : WHITEN, BLANCH

²**bleach** *n* : a preparation used in bleaching

bleach·ers \'blē-chərz\ *n sing or pl* : a usu. uncovered stand of tiered seats for spectators

bleak \'blēk\ *adj* **1** : desolately barren and often windswept **2** : lacking warm or cheering qualities — **bleak·ly** *adv* — **bleak·ness** *n*

blear \'blir\ *adj* : dim with water or tears ⟨~ eyes⟩

bleary \'blir-ē\ *adj* **1** : dull or dimmed esp. from fatigue or sleep **2** : poorly outlined or defined ⟨a ~ view⟩

bleat \'blēt\ *n* : the cry of a sheep or goat or a sound like it — **bleat** *vb*

bleed \'blēd\ *vb* **bled** \'bled\; **bleed·ing** **1** : to lose or shed blood **2** : to be wounded; *also* : to feel pain or distress **3** : to flow or ooze from a wounded surface; *also* : to draw fluid from ⟨~ a tire⟩ **4** : to extort money from

bleed·er \'blē-dər\ *n* : one that bleeds; *esp* : HEMOPHILIAC

bleeding heart *n* **1** : a garden plant related to the poppies that has usu. deep pink or white drooping heart-shaped flowers **2** : a person who shows extravagant sympathy esp. for an object of alleged persecution

¹**blem·ish** \'ble-mish\ *vb* : to spoil by a flaw : MAR

²**blemish** *n* : a noticeable flaw

¹**blench** \'blench\ *vb* [ME, to deceive, blench, fr. OE *blencan* to deceive] : FLINCH, QUAIL ✦ **Synonyms** SHRINK, RECOIL, WINCE, START

²**blench** *vb* : to grow or make pale

¹**blend** \'blend\ *vb* **blend·ed; blend·ing** **1** : to mix thoroughly **2** : to prepare (as coffee) by mixing different varieties **3** : to combine into an integrated whole **4** : HARMONIZE ✦ **Synonyms** FUSE, MERGE, MINGLE, COALESCE — **blend·er** *n*

²**blend** *n* : a product of blending ✦ **Synonyms** COMPOUND, COMPOSITE, ALLOY, MIXTURE

blended family *n* : a family that includes children of a previous marriage of one spouse or both

bless \'bles\ *vb* **blessed** \'blest\ *also* **blest** \'blest\; **bless·ing** [ME, fr. OE *blētsian*, fr. *blōd* blood; fr. the use of blood in consecration] **1** : to consecrate by religious rite or word **2** : to sanctify with the sign of the cross **3** : to invoke divine care for **4** : PRAISE, GLORIFY **5** : to confer happiness upon

bless·ed \'ble-səd\ *also* **blest** \'blest\ *adj* **1** : HOLY **2** : BEATIFIED **3** : DELIGHTFUL — **bless·ed·ly** *adv* — **bless·ed·ness** *n*

bless·ing \'ble-siŋ\ *n* **1** : the act or words of one who blesses; *also* : APPROVAL **2** : a thing conducive to happiness **3** : grace said at a meal

blew *past of* BLOW

¹**blight** \'blīt\ *n* **1** : a plant disease or injury marked esp. by withering and death of parts; *also* : an organism causing blight **2** : an impairing or frustrating influence; *also* : a deteriorated condition ⟨urban ~⟩

²**blight** *vb* : to affect with or suffer from blight

blimp \'blimp\ *n* : an airship that maintains its form by pressure of contained gas

¹**blind** \'blīnd\ *adj* **1** : lacking or grossly deficient in ability to see; *also* : intended for blind persons **2** : not based on reason, evidence, or knowledge ⟨~ faith⟩ **3** : not intelligently controlled or directed ⟨~ chance⟩ **4** : performed solely by using aircraft instruments ⟨a ~ landing⟩ **5** : hard to discern or make out : HIDDEN ⟨a ~ seam⟩ **6** : lacking an opening or outlet ⟨a ~ alley⟩ — **blind·ly** *adv* — **blind·ness** \'blīnd-nəs\ *n*

²**blind** *vb* **1** : to make blind **2** : DAZZLE **3** : DARKEN; *also* : HIDE

³**blind** *n* **1** : something (as a shutter) to hinder vision or keep out light **2** : a place of concealment **3** : SUBTERFUGE

blind date *n* : a date between persons who have not previously met; *also* : either of these persons

blind·er \'blīn-dər\ *n* : either of two flaps on a horse's bridle to prevent it from seeing to the side

blind·fold \'blīnd-ˌfōld\ *vb* : to cover the eyes of with or as if with a bandage — **blindfold** *n*

¹**blink** \'bliŋk\ *vb* **1** : WINK **2** : TWINKLE **3** : EVADE, IGNORE

²**blink** *n* **1** : GLIMMER, SPARKLE **2** : a usu. involuntary shutting and opening of the eye

blink·er \'bliŋ-kər\ *n* : a blinking light used as a signal

blin·tze \'blint-sə\ *or* **blintz** \'blints\ *n* [Yiddish *blintse*] : a thin rolled pancake with a filling usu. of cream cheese

blip \'blip\ *n* **1** : a spot on a radar screen ✦ ABERRATION 1

bliss \'blis\ *n* : complete happiness : JOY ✦ **Synonyms** BEATITUDE, BLESSEDNESS — **bliss·ful** \-fəl\ *adj* — **bliss·ful·ly** *adv*

¹**blis·ter** \'blis-tər\ *n* **1** : a raised area of skin containing watery fluid; *also* : an agent that causes blisters **2** : something (as a raised spot in paint) suggesting a blister **3** : a disease of plants marked by large raised patches on the leaves

²**blister** *vb* : to develop a blister; *also* : to cause blisters

blithe \'blīth, 'blīth\ *adj* **blith·er; blith·est** : happily lighthearted ✦ **Synonyms** MERRY, JOVIAL, JOLLY, JOCUND — **blithe·ly** *adv* — **blithe·some** \-səm\ *adj*

blitz \'blits\ *n* **1** : an intensive series of air raids **2** : a fast intensive campaign **3** : a rush of the passer by the defensive linebackers in football — **blitz** *vb*

blitz·krieg \-ˌkrēg\ *n* [G, fr. *Blitz* lightning + *Krieg* war] : a sudden violent enemy attack

bliz·zard \'bli-zərd\ *n* : a long severe snowstorm

blk *abbr* **1** black **2** block

bloat \'blōt\ *vb* : to swell by or as if by filling with water or air

blob \'bläb\ *n* : a small lump or drop of a thick consistency

bloc \'bläk\ *n* [F, lit., block] : a combination of individuals or groups (as nations) working for a common purpose

¹**block** \'bläk\ *n* **1** : a solid piece of substantial material (as wood or stone) **2** : HINDRANCE, OBSTRUCTION; *also* : interruption of normal function of body or mind ⟨heart ~⟩ **3** : a frame enclosing one or more pulleys and having a hook or strap by which it may be attached **4** : a piece of material with a hand-cut design on its surface from which copies are to be made **5** : a large building divided into separate units (as apartments or offices) **6** : a row of houses or shops **7** : a city square; *also* : the distance along one of the sides of such a square **8** : a quantity of things considered as a unit ⟨a ~ of seats⟩

²**block** *vb* **1** : OBSTRUCT, CHECK **2** : to outline roughly ⟨~ out a design⟩ **3** : to provide or support with a block ✦ **Synonyms** BAR, IMPEDE, HINDER, OBSTRUCT

block·ade \blä-'kād\ *n* : the isolation of a place usu. by troops or ships — **blockade** *vb* — **block·ad·er** *n*

block·age \'blä-kij\ *n* : an act or instance of obstructing : the state of being blocked

block·bust·er \'bläk-ˌbəs-tər\ *n* : one that is very large, successful, expensive, or dramatic ⟨a ~ movie⟩

block·head \'bläk-ˌhed\ *n* : DOLT, DUNCE

block·house \-ˌhau̇s\ *n* : a small strong building used as a shelter (as from enemy fire) or observation post

¹**blond** *or* **blonde** \'bländ\ *adj* : fair in complexion; *also* : of a light or bleached color ⟨~ mahogany⟩ — **blond·ish** \'blän-dish\ *adj*

²**blond** *or* **blonde** *n* : a person having blond hair

blood \'bləd\ *n* **1** : a usu. red liquid that circulates in the heart, arteries, and veins of animals **2** : LIFEBLOOD; *also* : LIFE **3** : LINEAGE, STOCK **4** : KINSHIP; *also* : KINDRED **5** : the taking of life **6** : TEMPER, PASSION **7** : DANDY 1 — **blood·less** *adj* — **bloody** *adj*

blood·bath \'bləd-ˌbath, -ˌbäth\ *n* : MASSACRE

blood count *n* : the determination of the number of blood cells in a specific volume of blood; *also* : the number of cells so determined

blood-cur·dling \'bləd-kərd-liŋ, -ˌkər-d°l-iŋ\ *adj* : arousing fright or horror

blood·ed \'blə-dəd\ *adj* **1** : having blood of a specified kind ⟨warm-*blooded* animals⟩ **2** : entirely or largely purebred ⟨~ horses⟩

blood group *n* : one of the classes into which human beings can be separated by the presence or absence in their blood of specific antigens

53

bloodhound • blue screen

blood·hound \'blǝd-ˌhaủnd\ n : any of a breed of large powerful hounds with long drooping ears, a wrinkled face, and keen sense of smell

blood·let·ting \-ˌle-tiŋ\ n 1 : PHLEBOTOMY 2 : BLOOD-SHED

blood·line \-ˌlīn\ n : a sequence of direct ancestors esp. in a pedigree

blood·lust \-ˌlǝst\ n : desire for bloodshed

blood·mo·bile \-ˌmō-ˌbēl\ n : a motor vehicle equipped for collecting blood from donors

blood poisoning n : invasion of the bloodstream by virulent microorganisms from a focus of infection accompanied esp. by chills, fever, and prostration

blood pressure n : pressure of the blood on the walls of blood vessels and esp. arteries

blood·root \'blǝd-ˌrüt, -ˌrủt\ n : a plant related to the poppy that has a red root and sap, a solitary leaf, and a white flower in early spring

blood·shed \-ˌshed\ n : wounding or taking of life : CARNAGE, SLAUGHTER

blood·shot \-ˌshät\ adj : inflamed to redness ⟨~ eyes⟩

blood·stain \-ˌstān\ n : a discoloration caused by blood — **blood·stained** \-ˌstānd\ adj

blood·stone \-ˌstōn\ n : a green quartz sprinkled with red spots

blood·stream \-ˌstrēm\ n : the flowing blood in a circulatory system

blood·suck·er \-ˌsǝ-kǝr\ n : an animal that sucks blood; esp : LEECH — **blood·suck·ing** adj

blood test n : a test of the blood (as to detect disease-causing agents)

blood thinner n : a drug used to prevent the clotting of blood

blood·thirsty \'blǝd-ˌthǝr-stē\ adj : eager to shed blood — **blood·thirst·i·ly** \-ˌthǝr-stǝ-lē\ adv — **blood·thirst·i·ness** \-stē-nǝs\ n

blood type n : BLOOD GROUP — **blood·typ·ing** n

blood vessel n : a vessel (as a vein or artery) in which blood circulates in the body

Bloody Mary \-'mer-ē\ n, pl **Bloody Marys** : a drink made essentially of vodka and tomato juice

¹bloom \'blüm\ n 1 : FLOWER 1; also : flowers or amount of flowers (as of a plant) 2 : the period or state of flowering 3 : a state or time of beauty and vigor 4 : a powdery coating esp. on fruits and leaves 5 : rosy color; also : an appearance of freshness or health — **bloomy** adj

²bloom vb 1 : to produce or yield flowers 2 : MATURE 3 : to glow esp. with healthy color ♦ **Synonyms** FLOWER, BLOSSOM

bloo·mers \'blü-mǝrz\ n pl [Amelia Bloomer †1894 Am. reformer] : a woman's garment of short loose pants gathered at the knee

bloop·er \'blü-pǝr\ n 1 : a fly ball hit barely beyond a baseball infield 2 : an embarrassing public blunder

¹blos·som \'blä-sǝm\ n 1 : the flower of a plant 2 : the period or state of flowering

²blossom vb : FLOWER, BLOOM

¹blot \'blät\ n 1 : SPOT, STAIN ⟨ink ~s⟩ 2 : BLEMISH ♦ **Synonyms** STIGMA, BRAND, SLUR

²blot vb blot·ted; blot·ting 1 : SPOT, STAIN 2 : OBSCURE, ECLIPSE ⟨~ out the sun⟩ 3 obs : MAR; esp : DISGRACE 4 : to dry or remove with or as if with an absorbing material 5 : to make a blot

blotch \'bläch\ n : a usu. large and irregular spot or mark (as of ink or color) — **blotch** vb — **blotchy** adj

blot·ter \'blä-tǝr\ n 1 : a piece of blotting paper 2 : a book for preliminary records (as of sales or arrests)

blot·ting paper n : a spongy paper used to absorb ink

blouse \'blaủs, 'blaủz\ n 1 : a loose outer garment like a smock 2 : a usu. loose garment reaching from the neck to about the waist

¹blow \'blō\ vb blew \'blü\; blown \'blōn\; blow·ing 1 : to be in motion; esp : to move forcibly ⟨the wind blew⟩ 2 : to send forth a current of gas (as air) 3 : to act on with a current of gas or vapor; esp : to drive with such a current 4 : to clear with a current of air 5 : to sound or cause to sound ⟨~ a horn⟩ 6 : PANT, GASP; also : to expel moist air in breathing ⟨the whale blew⟩ 7 : BOAST; also : BLUSTER 8 : ERUPT, EXPLODE 9 : MELT — used of an electrical fuse 10 : to shape or form by blown or injected air ⟨~ glass⟩ 11 : to shatter or destroy by or as

if by explosion 12 : to make breathless by exertion 13 : to spend recklessly 14 : BOTCH ⟨blew her lines⟩ — **blow·er** n

²blow n 1 : a usu. strong blowing of air : GALE 2 : BOASTING, BRAG 3 : an act or instance of blowing

³blow vb blew \'blü\; blown \'blōn\; blow·ing : FLOWER, BLOOM

⁴blow n 1 : a forcible stroke ⟨a ~ to the head⟩ 2 : COMBAT ⟨come to ~s⟩ 3 : a severe and usu. unexpected calamity

blow-by-blow adj : minutely detailed ⟨~ account⟩

blow–dry \-ˌdrī\ vb : to dry and usu. style hair with a blow-dryer

blow–dryer \-ˌdrī(-ǝ)r\ n : a hand-held hair dryer

blow-fly \'blō-ˌflī\ n : any of a family of dipteran flies (as a bluebottle) that deposit their eggs or maggots on meat or in wounds

blow·gun \-ˌgǝn\ n : a tube from which an arrow or a dart may be shot by the force of the breath

blow·out \'blō-ˌaủt\ n 1 : a bursting of something (as a tire) because of pressure of the contents (as air) 2 : a depression created by the wind in sand or soil

blow·sy also **blow·zy** \'blaủ-zē\ adj : DISHEVELED, SLOVENLY

blow·torch \'blō-ˌtȯrch\ n : a small portable burner whose flame is made hotter by a blast of air or oxygen

blow-up \'blō-ˌǝp\ n 1 : EXPLOSION 2 : an outburst of temper 3 : a photographic enlargement

blowy \'blō-ē\ adj : WINDY

BLT \ˌbē-ˌel-'tē\ n : a bacon, lettuce, and tomato sandwich

¹blub·ber \'blǝ-bǝr\ vb : to cry noisily

²blubber n 1 : the fat of large sea mammals (as whales) 2 : a noisy crying

¹blud·geon \'blǝ-jǝn\ n : a short often loaded club

²bludgeon vb : to strike with or as if with a bludgeon

¹blue \'blü\ adj blu·er; blu·est [ME, fr. AF blef, blew, of Gmc origin] 1 : of the color blue; also : BLUISH 2 : MELANCHOLY; also : DEPRESSING 3 : PURITANICAL 4 : INDECENT — **blue·ness** n

²blue n 1 : a color between green and violet in the spectrum : the color of the clear daytime sky 2 : something (as clothing or the sky) that is blue

blue baby n : a baby with bluish skin due to faulty circulation caused by a heart defect

blue·bell \-ˌbel\ n : any of various plants with blue bell-shaped flowers

blue·ber·ry \'blü-ˌber-ē, -bǝ-rē\ n : the edible blue or blackish berry of various plants of the heath family; also : one of these shrubs

blue·bird \-ˌbǝrd\ n : any of three small No. American thrushes that are blue above and reddish-brown or pale blue below

blue·bon·net \'blü-ˌbä-nǝt\ n : either of two low-growing annual lupines of Texas with silky foliage and blue flowers

blue·bot·tle \'blü-ˌbä-tᵊl\ n : any of several blowflies with iridescent blue bodies or abdomens

blue cheese n : cheese having veins of greenish-blue mold

blue–col·lar \'blü-'kä-lǝr\ adj : of, relating to, or being the class of workers whose duties call for work clothes

blue·fish \-ˌfish\ n : a marine sport and food fish that is bluish above and silvery below

blue·grass \-ˌgras\ n 1 : KENTUCKY BLUEGRASS 2 : country music played on stringed instruments having free improvisation and close harmonies

blue jay \-ˌjā\ n : a crested bright blue No. American jay

blue jeans n pl : pants usu. made of blue denim

blue·nose \'blü-ˌnōz\ n : a person who advocates a rigorous moral code

blue·point \-ˌpȯint\ n : a small oyster typically from the south shore of Long Island, New York

blue·print \-ˌprint\ n 1 : a photographic print in white on a blue ground used esp. for copying mechanical drawings and architects' plans 2 : a detailed plan of action — **blueprint** vb

blues \'blüz\ n pl 1 : MELANCHOLY 2 : music in a style marked by recurrent minor intervals and melancholy lyrics

blue screen n : a technique in which a subject is filmed in front of a blue background so as to allow the creation of a composite with other footage

blue·stock·ing \'blü-ˌstä-kiŋ\ *n* : a woman having intellectual interests

blu·et \'blü-ət\ *n* : a low No. American herb with dainty bluish flowers

blue whale *n* : a very large baleen whale that may reach a weight of 150 tons (135 metric tons) and a length of 100 feet (30 meters)

¹**bluff** \'bləf\ *adj* **1** : having a broad flattened front **2** : rising steeply with a broad flat front **3** : OUTSPOKEN, FRANK ◆ *Synonyms* ABRUPT, BLUNT, BRUSQUE, CURT, GRUFF

²**bluff** *n* : a high steep bank : CLIFF

³**bluff** *vb* : to frighten or deceive by pretense or a mere show of strength

⁴**bluff** *n* : an act or instance of bluffing; *also* : one who bluffs

blu·ing *or* **blue·ing** \'blü-iŋ\ *n* : a preparation used in laundering to counteract yellowing of white fabrics

blu·ish \'blü-ish\ *adj* : somewhat blue

¹**blun·der** \'blən-dər\ *vb* **1** : to move clumsily or unsteadily **2** : to make a stupid or needless mistake

²**blunder** *n* : an avoidable and usu. serious mistake

blun·der·buss \'blən-dər-ˌbəs\ *n* [obs. D *donderbus*, fr. D *donder* thunder + obs. D *bus* gun] : an obsolete short-barreled firearm with a flaring muzzle

¹**blunt** \'blənt\ *adj* **1** : not sharp : DULL **2** : lacking in tact : BLUFF ⟨∼ criticism⟩ ◆ *Synonyms* BRUSQUE, CURT, GRUFF, ABRUPT, CRUSTY — **blunt·ly** *adv* — **blunt·ness** *n*

²**blunt** *vb* : to make or become dull

¹**blur** \'blər\ *n* **1** : a smear or stain that obscures **2** : something vaguely perceived; *esp* : something moving too quickly to be clearly perceived — **blur·ry** \-ē\ *adj*

²**blur** *vb* **blurred; blur·ring** : DIM, CLOUD, OBSCURE

blurb \'blərb\ *n* : a short publicity notice (as on a book jacket)

blurt \'blərt\ *vb* : to utter suddenly and impulsively

blush \'bləsh\ *n* **1** : a reddening of the face (as from modesty or confusion) : FLUSH **2** : a cosmetic used to tint the face pink — **blush** *vb* — **blush·ful** *adj*

blus·ter \'bləs-tər\ *vb* **1** : to blow in stormy noisy gusts **2** : to talk or act with noisy swaggering threats — **bluster** *n* — **blus·tery** \-tə-rē\ *adj*

blvd *abbr* boulevard

B lymphocyte *n* : B CELL

BM *abbr* bowel movement

B movie *n* : a cheaply produced motion picture

BO *abbr* **1** best offer **2** body odor **3** box office **4** branch office

boa \'bō-ə\ *n* **1** : a large snake (as the **boa con·stric·tor** \-kən-ˈstrik-tər\ or the related anaconda) that suffocates and kills its prey by constriction **2** : a fluffy scarf usu. of fur or feathers

boar \'bȯr\ *n* : a male swine; *also* : WILD BOAR

¹**board** \'bȯrd\ *n* **1** : the side of a ship **2** : a thin flat length of sawed lumber; *also* : material (as cardboard) or a piece of material formed as a thin flat firm sheet **3** *pl* : STAGE 1 **4** : a table spread with a meal; *also* : daily meals esp. when furnished for pay **5** : a table at which a council or magistrates sit **6** : a group or association of persons organized for a special responsibility (as the management of a business or institution); *also* : an organized commercial exchange **7** : a sheet of insulating material carrying circuit elements and inserted in an electronic device **8** : BULLETIN BOARD

²**board** *vb* **1** : to go or put aboard ⟨∼ a boat⟩ **2** : to cover with boards **3** : to provide or be provided with meals and often lodging — **board·er** *n*

board game *n* : a game of strategy (as checkers or chess) played by moving pieces on a board

board·ing·house \'bȯr-diŋ-ˌhau̇s\ *n* : a house at which persons are boarded

board·walk \'bȯrd-ˌwȯk\ *n* : a promenade (as of planking) along a beach

boast \'bōst\ *vb* **1** : to praise oneself **2** : to mention or assert with excessive pride **3** : to prize as a possession; *also* : HAVE ⟨the house ∼s a fireplace⟩ — **boast** *n* — **boast·ful** \-fəl\ *adj* — **boast·ful·ly** *adv*

boat \'bōt\ *n* : a small vessel for travel on water; *also* : SHIP — **boat** *vb*

boat·er \'bō-tər\ *n* **1** : one that travels in a boat **2** : a stiff straw hat

boat·man \'bōt-mən\ *n* : a man who operates, works on, or deals in boats

boat people *n pl* : refugees fleeing by boat

boat·swain *or* **bo·sun** \'bō-sⁿn\ *n* : a subordinate officer of a ship in charge of the hull and related equipment

¹**bob** \'bäb\ *vb* **bobbed; bob·bing** **1** : to move up and down jerkily or repeatedly **2** : to emerge, arise, or appear suddenly or unexpectedly

²**bob** *n* : a bobbing movement

³**bob** *n* **1** : a knob, knot, twist, or curl esp. of ribbons, yarn, or hair **2** : a short haircut of a woman or child **3** : FLOAT 2 **4** : a weight hanging from a line

⁴**bob** *vb* **bobbed; bob·bing** : to cut hair in a bob

⁵**bob** *n*, *pl* **bob** *slang Brit* : SHILLING

bob·bin \'bä-bən\ *n* : a cylinder or spindle for holding or dispensing thread (as in a sewing machine)

bob·ble \'bä-bəl\ *vb* **bob·bled; bob·bling** : FUMBLE — **bobble** *n*

bob·by \'bä-bē\ *n*, *pl* **bobbies** [*Bobby*, nickname for Sir *Robert* Peel, who organized the London police force] *Brit* : a police officer

bobby pin *n* : a flat wire hairpin with prongs that press close together

bob·cat \'bäb-ˌkat\ *n* : a small usu. rusty-colored No. American lynx

bob·o·link \'bä-bə-ˌliŋk\ *n* : an American migratory songbird related to the meadowlarks

bob·sled \'bäb-ˌsled\ *n* **1** : a short sled usu. used as one of a joined pair **2** : a racing sled with two pairs of runners, a steering wheel, and a hand brake — **bobsled** *vb*

bob·white \(ˌ)bäb-ˈhwīt\ *n* : any of a genus of quail; *esp* : a popular game bird of eastern and central No. America

boc·cie *or* **boc·ci** *or* **boc·ce** \'bä-chē\ *n* : Italian lawn bowling played on a long narrow court

bock \'bäk\ *n* : a strong dark beer usu. sold in early spring

bod \'bäd\ *n* : BODY

¹**bode** \'bōd\ *vb* **bod·ed; bod·ing** : to indicate by signs : PRESAGE

²**bode** *past of* BIDE

bo·de·ga \bō-ˈdä-gə\ *n* [Sp, fr. L *apotheca* storehouse] : a usu. small store specializing in Hispanic groceries

bod·ice \'bä-dəs\ *n* [alter. of *bodies*, pl. of *body*] : the usu. close-fitting part of a dress above the waist

bodi·less \'bä-di-ləs\ *adj* : lacking a body or material form

¹**bodi·ly** \'bä-dⁿl-ē\ *adj* : of or relating to the body ⟨∼ contact⟩ ⟨∼ organs⟩

²**bodily** *adv* **1** : in the flesh **2** : as a whole ⟨lifted the crate up ∼⟩

bod·kin \'bäd-kən\ *n* **1** : DAGGER **2** : a pointed implement for punching holes in cloth **3** : a blunt needle for drawing tape or ribbon through a loop or hem

body \'bä-dē\ *n*, *pl* **bod·ies** **1** : the physical whole of a living or dead organism; *also* : the trunk or main mass of an organism as distinguished from its appendages **2** : a human being : PERSON **3** : the main part of something **4** : a mass of matter distinct from other masses **5** : GROUP **6** : VISCOSITY, FIRMNESS **7** : richness of flavor — used esp. of wines — **bod·ied** \'bä-dēd\ *adj*

body·build·ing \'bä-dē-ˌbil-diŋ\ *n* : the developing of the body through exercise and diet — **body·build·er** \-dər\ *n*

body English *n* : bodily motions made in a usu. unconscious effort to influence the movement of a propelled object (as a ball)

body·guard \'bä-dē-ˌgärd\ *n* : a personal guard; *also* : RETINUE

body language *n* : movements (as with the hands) or posture used as a means of communication

body stocking *n* : a sheer close-fitting one-piece garment for the torso that often has sleeves and legs

body·work \'bä-dē-ˌwərk\ *n* : the making or repairing of vehicle bodies

Boer \'bȯr, 'bu̇r\ *n* [D, lit., farmer] : a South African of Dutch or Huguenot descent

¹**bog** \'bäg, 'bȯg\ *n* : wet, spongy, poorly drained, and usu. acid ground — **bog·gy** *adj*

²**bog** *vb* **bogged; bog·ging** : to sink into or as if into a bog

bo·gey *also* **bo·gie** *or* **bo·gy** \'bu̇-gē, 'bō- *for 1*; 'bō- *for 2*\ *n*, *pl* **bogeys** *also* **bogies** **1** : SPECTER, HOBGOBLIN; *also* : a source of fear or annoyance **2** : a score of one over par on a hole in golf

bo·gey·man \'bù-gē-ˌman, 'bō-, 'bü-\ *n* : an imaginary monster used in threatening children

bog·gle \'bä-gəl\ *vb* **bog·gled; bog·gling** : to overwhelm or be overwhelmed with fright or amazement

bo·gus \'bō-gəs\ *adj* : SPURIOUS, SHAM

Bo·he·mi·an \bō-'hē-mē-ən\ *n* **1** : a native or inhabitant of Bohemia **2** *often not cap* : VAGABOND, WANDERER **3** *often not cap* : a person (as a writer or artist) living an unconventional life — **bohemian** *adj, often cap*

bohr·i·um \'bòr-ē-əm\ *n* : an artificially produced radioactive chemical element

¹boil \'bòi(-ə)l\ *n* : an inflamed swelling on the skin containing pus

²boil *vb* **1** : to heat or become heated to a temperature (**boil·ing point**) at which vapor is formed and rises in bubbles ⟨water ~*s* and changes to steam⟩; *also* : to act on or be acted on by a boiling liquid ⟨~ eggs⟩ **2** : to be in a state of seething agitation

³boil *n* **1** : the act or state of boiling **2** : a boiled dish (as of seafood) **3** : a gathering where boiled food is served

boil·er \'bòi-lər\ *n* **1** : a container in which something is boiled **2** : a strong vessel used in making steam **3** : a tank holding hot water

boil·er·mak·er \'bòi-lər-ˌmā-kər\ *n* : whiskey with a beer chaser

bois·ter·ous \'bòi-st(ə-)rəs\ *adj* : noisily turbulent or exuberant — **bois·ter·ous·ly** *adv*

bok choy \'bäk-'chòi\ *n* : a Chinese vegetable related to the mustards that forms a loose head of green leaves with long thick white stalks

bo·la \'bō-lə\ *or* **bo·las** \-ləs\ *n, pl* **bolas** \-ləz\ *also* **bo·las·es** [AmerSp *bolas,* fr. Sp *bola* ball] : a cord with weights attached to the ends for hurling at and entangling an animal

bold \'bōld\ *adj* **1** : COURAGEOUS, INTREPID **2** : IMPUDENT **3** : STEEP **4** : ADVENTUROUS, FREE ⟨a ~ thinker⟩ ♦ **Synonyms** DAUNTLESS, BRAVE, VALIANT — **bold·ly** *adv* — **bold·ness** \'bōld-nəs\ *n*

bold·face \'bōld-ˌfās\ *n* : a heavy-faced type; *also* : printing in boldface — **bold–faced** \-'fāst\ *adj*

bole \'bōl\ *n* : the trunk of a tree

bo·le·ro \bə-'ler-ō\ *n, pl* **-ros** **1** : a Spanish dance or its music **2** : a short loose jacket open at the front

bo·li·var \bə-'lē-ˌvär, 'bä-lə-vər\ *n, pl* **-va·res** \ˌbä-lə-'vär-ˌäs, ˌbō-\ *or* **-vars** — see MONEY table

Bo·liv·i·an \bə-'li-vē-ən\ *n* : a native or inhabitant of Bolivia — **Bolivian** *adj*

bo·li·vi·a·no \bə-ˌli-vē-'ä-(ˌ)nō\ *n, pl* **-nos** — see MONEY table

boll \'bōl\ *n* : a seed pod (as of cotton)

boll weevil *n* : a small usu. grayish or brown weevil that infests the cotton plant both as a larva and as an adult

boll·worm \'bōl-ˌwɔrm\ *n* : any of several moths and esp. the corn earworm whose larvae feed on cotton bolls

bo·lo·gna \bə-'lō-nē\ *n* [short for *Bologna sausage,* fr. *Bologna,* Italy] : a large smoked sausage of beef, veal, and pork

Bol·she·vik \'bōl-shə-ˌvik\ *n, pl* **Bolsheviks** *also* **Bol·she·vi·ki** \ˌbōl-shə-'vi-kē\ [Russ *bol'shevik,* fr. *bol'shiĭ* larger] **1** : a member of the party that seized power in Russia in the revolution of November 1917 **2** : COMMUNIST — **Bolshevik** *adj*

bol·she·vism \'bōl-shə-ˌvi-zəm\ *n, often cap* : the doctrine or program of the Bolsheviks advocating violent overthrow of capitalism

¹bol·ster \'bōl-stər\ *n* : a long pillow or cushion

²bolster *vb* : to support with or as if with a bolster; *also* : REINFORCE

¹bolt \'bōlt\ *n* **1** : a missile (as an arrow) for a crossbow or catapult **2** : a flash of lightning : THUNDERBOLT **3** : a sliding bar used to fasten a door **4** : a roll of cloth or wallpaper of specified length **5** : a rod with a head at one end and a screw thread at the other used with a nut to fasten objects together **6** : a metal cylinder that drives the cartridge into the chamber of a firearm

²bolt *vb* **1** : to move suddenly (as in fright or hurry) : START, DASH **2** : to break away (as from association) ⟨~ from a political platform⟩ **3** : to produce seed prematurely **4** : to secure or fasten with a bolt **5** : to swallow hastily or without chewing

³bolt *n* : an act of bolting

bo·lus \'bō-ləs\ *n, pl* **bo·lus·es** **1** : a large pill **2** : a soft mass of chewed food

¹bomb \'bäm\ *n* **1** : a fused explosive device designed to detonate under specified conditions (as impact) **2** : an aerosol or foam dispenser (as of insecticide or hair spray) : SPRAY CAN **3** : FAILURE, FLOP **4** : a long pass, shot, or hit

²bomb *vb* **1** : to attack with bombs **2** : FAIL ⟨~ed at the audition⟩

bom·bard \bäm-'bärd\ *vb* **1** : to attack esp. with artillery or bombers **2** : to assail persistently **3** : to subject to the impact of rapidly moving particles (as electrons) — **bom·bard·ment** *n*

bom·bar·dier \ˌbäm-bər-'dir\ *n* : a bomber-crew member who releases the bombs

bom·bast \'bäm-ˌbast\ *n* [ME, cotton padding, fr. MF *bombace,* fr. ML *bombax* cotton, alter. of L *bombyx* silkworm, silk, fr. Gk] : pretentious wordy speech or writing — **bom·bas·tic** \bäm-'bas-tik\ *adj* — **bom·bas·ti·cal·ly** \-ti-k(ə-)lē\ *adv*

bom·ba·zine \ˌbäm-bə-'zēn\ *n* **1** : a twilled fabric with silk warp and worsted filling **2** : a silk fabric in twill weave dyed black

bomb·er \'bä-mər\ *n* : one that bombs; *esp* : an airplane for dropping bombs

bomb·proof \'bäm-ˌprüf\ *adj* : safe against the explosive force of bombs

bomb·shell \'bäm-ˌshel\ *n* **1** : BOMB 1 **2** : one that stuns, amazes, or completely upsets

bona fide \'bō-nə-ˌfīd, 'bä-; ˌbō-nə-'fī-dē, -də\ *adj* [L, in good faith] **1** : made in good faith ⟨a *bona fide* agreement⟩ **2** : GENUINE, REAL ⟨a *bona fide* bargain⟩

bo·nan·za \bə-'nan-zə\ *n* [Sp, lit., calm sea, fr. ML *bonacia,* alter. of L *malacia,* fr. Gk *malakia,* lit., softness, fr. *malakos* soft] **1** : something yielding a rich return **2** : EXTRAVAGANZA

bon·bon \'bän-ˌbän\ *n* : a candy with a creamy center and a soft covering (as of chocolate)

¹bond \'bänd\ *n* **1** : FETTER **2** : a binding or uniting force or tie ⟨~*s* of friendship⟩ **3** : an agreement or obligation often made binding by a pledge of money or goods **4** : a person who acts as surety for another **5** : an interest-bearing certificate of public or private indebtedness **6** : the state of goods subject to supervision pending payment of taxes or duties due

²bond *vb* **1** : to assure payment of duties or taxes on (goods) by giving a bond **2** : to insure against losses caused by the acts of ⟨~ a bank teller⟩ **3** : to make or become firmly united as if by bonds ⟨~ iron to copper⟩ **4** : to form a close relationship ⟨~*ed* with her stepmother⟩

bond·age \'bän-dij\ *n* : SLAVERY, SERVITUDE

bond·hold·er \'bänd-ˌhōl-dər\ *n* : one that owns a government or corporation bond

bond·ing \'bän-diŋ\ *n* **1** : the formation of a close personal relationship esp. through frequent or constant association **2** : the attaching of a material (as porcelain) to a tooth surface esp. for cosmetic purposes

bond·man \'bänd-mən\ *n* : SLAVE, SERF

¹bonds·man \'bändz-mən\ *n* : SURETY 3

²bondsman *var of* BONDMAN

bond·wom·an \'bänd-ˌwù-mən\ *n* : a female slave or serf

¹bone \'bōn\ *n* **1** : a hard largely calcareous tissue forming most of the skeleton of a vertebrate animal; *also* : one of the pieces of bone making up a vertebrate skeleton **2** : a hard animal substance (as ivory or baleen) similar to true bone **3** : something made of bone — **bone·less** *adj* — **bony** *also* **bon·ey** \'bō-nē\ *adj*

²bone *vb* **boned; bon·ing** : to free from bones ⟨~ a chicken⟩

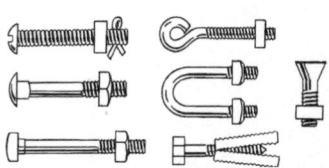

¹bolt 5: different styles

bone black *n* : the black carbon residue from calcined bones used esp. as a pigment
bone marrow *n* : MARROW
bone-meal \'bōn-ˌmēl\ *n* : crushed or ground bone used esp. as fertilizer or feed
bon-er \'bō-nər\ *n* : a stupid and ridiculous blunder
bone up *vb* 1 : CRAM 3 2 : to refresh one's memory ⟨*boned up* on the speech before giving it⟩
bon-fire \'bän-ˌfī(-ə)r\ *n* [ME *bonefire* a fire of bones, fr. *bon* bone + *fire*] : a large fire built in the open air
bon-go \'bäŋ-gō\ *n, pl* **bongos** *also* **bongoes** [AmerSp *bongó*] : one of a pair of small tuned drums played with the hands
bon-ho-mie \ˌbä-nə-'mē\ *n* [F *bonhomie*, fr. *bonhomme* good-natured man, fr. *bon* good + *homme* man] : good-natured easy friendliness
bo-ni-to \bə-'nē-tō\ *n, pl* **-tos** *or* **-to** : any of several medium-sized tunas
bon mot \bōⁿ-'mō\ *n, pl* **bons mots** *same*\ *or* **bon mots** *same*\ [F, lit., good word] : a clever remark
bon-net \'bä-nət\ *n* : a covering (as a cap) for the head; *esp* : a hat for a woman or infant tied under the chin
bon-ny \'bä-nē\ *adj* **bon-ni-er; -est** *chiefly Brit* : ATTRACTIVE, FAIR; *also* : FINE, EXCELLENT
bon-sai \bōn-'sī, 'bän-ˌ\ *n, pl* **bonsai** [Jp] : a potted plant (as a tree) dwarfed and trained to an artistic shape; *also* : the art of growing such a plant
bo-nus \'bō-nəs\ *n* : something in addition to what is expected
bon vi-vant \ˌbän-vē-'vänt, ˌbōⁿ-vē-'väⁿ\ *n, pl* **bons vivants** \ˌbän-vē-'vänts, ˌbōⁿ-vē-'väⁿ\ *or* **bon vivants** *same*\ [F, lit., good liver] : a person having cultivated, refined, and sociable tastes esp. in food and drink
bon voy-age \ˌbōⁿ-ˌvȯi-'äzh, ˌbän-; ˌbōⁿ-ˌvwä-'yäzh\ *n* : FAREWELL — often used as an interjection
bony fish *n* : any of a class of fishes (as eels or sturgeons) with a bony rather than a cartilaginous skeleton
bonze \'bänz\ *n* : a Buddhist monk
boo \'bü\ *n, pl* **boos** : a shout of disapproval or contempt — **boo** *vb*
boo-by \'bü-bē\ *n, pl* **boobies** : an awkward foolish person : DOPE
booby hatch *n* : a psychiatric hospital
booby prize *n* : an award for the poorest performance in a contest
booby trap *n* : a trap for the unwary; *esp* : a concealed explosive device set to go off when some harmless-looking object is touched — **booby–trap** *vb*
boo-dle \'bü-dᵊl\ *n* 1 : bribe money 2 : a large amount of money
¹**book** \'bùk\ *n* 1 : a set of sheets bound into a volume 2 : a long written or printed narrative or record 3 : a major division of a long literary work 4 *cap* : BIBLE — **in one's book** : in one's own opinion
²**book** *vb* 1 : to engage, reserve, or schedule by or as if by writing in a book ⟨~ seats on a plane⟩ 2 : to enter charges against in a police register
book-case \-ˌkās\ *n* : a piece of furniture consisting of shelves to hold books
book-end \-ˌend\ *n* : a support to hold up a row of books
book-ie \'bù-kē\ *n* : BOOKMAKER
book-ish \'bù-kish\ *adj* 1 : fond of books and reading 2 : inclined to rely unduly on book knowledge
book-keep-er \'bùk-ˌkē-pər\ *n* : a person who records the accounts or transactions of a business — **book-keep-ing** *n*
book-let \'bùk-lət\ *n* : PAMPHLET
book-mak-er \'bùk-ˌmā-kər\ *n* : a person who determines odds and receives and pays off bets — **book-mak-ing** *n*
book-mark \-ˌmärk\ *or* **book-mark-er** \-ˌmär-kər\ *n* 1 : a marker for finding a place in a book 2 : a shortcut to a previously viewed location (as a Web site) on a computer — **bookmark** *vb*
book-mo-bile \'bùk-mō-ˌbēl\ *n* : a truck that serves as a traveling library
book-plate \'bùk-ˌplāt\ *n* : a label pasted in a book to show who owns it
book-sell-er \'bùk-ˌse-lər\ *n* : one that sells books; *esp* : the proprietor of a bookstore
book-shelf \-ˌshelf\ *n* : a shelf for books

book-worm \'bùk-ˌwərm\ *n* : a person unusually devoted to reading and study
¹**boom** \'büm\ *vb* 1 : to make a deep hollow sound : RESOUND 2 : to grow or cause to grow rapidly esp. in number, value, esteem, or importance
²**boom** *n* 1 : a booming sound or cry 2 : a rapid expansion or increase esp. of economic activity
³**boom** *n* [D, tree, beam] 1 : a long spar used to extend the bottom of a sail 2 : a line of floating timbers used to obstruct passage or catch floating objects 3 : a beam projecting from the upright pole of a derrick to support or guide the object lifted 4 : a long usu. horizontal supporting arm (as for a microphone)
boom box *n* : a large portable radio and often tape or CD player
boo-mer-ang \'bü-mə-ˌraŋ\ *n* [Dharuk (an Australian aboriginal language) *bumarin*⁹] : a bent or angular club that can be so thrown as to return near the starting point
boom-ing \'bü-miŋ\ *adj* 1 : making a loud deep sound ⟨a ~ voice⟩ 2 : powerfully executed ⟨hit a ~ serve⟩
¹**boon** \'bün\ *n* [ME *bone* prayer, request, the favor requested, fr. ON *bōn* request] : BENEFIT, BLESSING ♦ **Synonyms** FAVOR, GIFT, LARGESS, PRESENT
²**boon** *adj* [ME *bon*, fr. AF, good] : CONVIVIAL ⟨a ~ companion⟩
boon-docks \'bün-ˌdäks\ *n pl* [Tagalog (language of the Philippines) *bundok* mountain] 1 : rough country filled with dense brush 2 : a rural area
boon-dog-gle \'bün-ˌdä-gəl, -ˌdȯ-\ *n* : a useless or wasteful project or activity
boor \'bùr\ *n* 1 : YOKEL 2 : a rude or insensitive person ♦ **Synonyms** CHURL, LOUT, CLOWN, CLODHOPPER — **boor-ish** *adj*
boost \'büst\ *vb* 1 : to push up from below 2 : INCREASE, RAISE ⟨~ prices⟩ 3 : AID, PROMOTE ⟨voted a bonus to ~ morale⟩ — **boost** *n* — **boost-er** *n*
¹**boot** \'büt\ *n, chiefly dial* : something to equalize a trade — **to boot** : BESIDES
²**boot** *vb, archaic* : AVAIL, PROFIT
³**boot** *n* 1 : a covering for the foot and leg 2 : a protective sheath (as of a flower) 3 *Brit* : an automobile trunk 4 : KICK; *also* : a discharge from employment 5 : a navy or marine corps trainee
⁴**boot** *vb* 1 : KICK 2 : to eject or discharge summarily 3 : to load or become loaded into a computer from a disk 4 : to start or become ready for use esp. by booting a program ⟨~ up the computer⟩
boot-black \'büt-ˌblak\ *n* : a person who shines shoes
boot camp *n* 1 : a navy or marine corps training camp 2 : a facility with a rigorous disciplinary program for young offenders
boo-tee *or* **boo-tie** \'bü-tē\ *n* : an infant's knitted or crocheted sock
booth \'büth\ *n, pl* **booths** \'büthz, 'büths\ 1 : a small enclosed stall (as at a fair) 2 : a small enclosure giving privacy to a person ⟨voting ~⟩ ⟨telephone ~⟩ 3 : a restaurant accommodation having a table between backed benches
boot-leg \'büt-ˌleg\ *vb* : to make, transport, or sell (as liquor) illegally — **boot-leg** *adj or n* — **boot-leg-ger** *n*
boot-less \'büt-ləs\ *adj* : USELESS ♦ **Synonyms** FUTILE, VAIN, ABORTIVE, FRUITLESS — **boot-less-ly** *adv* — **boot-less-ness** *n*
¹**boo-ty** \'bü-tē\ *n, pl* **booties** : PLUNDER, SPOIL
²**booty** *also* **boo-tie** \'bü-tē\ *n, pl* **booties** *slang* : BUTTOCKS
¹**booze** \'büz\ *vb* **boozed; booz-ing** : to drink liquor to excess — **booz-er** *n*
²**booze** *n* : intoxicating liquor — **boozy** *adj*
bop \'bäp\ *vb* **bopped; bop-ping** : HIT, SOCK — **bop** *n*
BOQ *abbr* bachelor officers' quarters
bor *abbr* borough
bo-rate \'bȯr-ˌāt\ *n* : a salt or ester of boric acid
bo-rax \'bȯr-ˌaks\ *n* : a crystalline borate of sodium that occurs as a mineral and is used as a flux and cleanser
bor-del-lo \bȯr-'de-lō\ *n, pl* **-los** [It] : BROTHEL
¹**bor-der** \'bȯr-dər\ *n* 1 : EDGE, MARGIN 2 : BOUNDARY, FRONTIER ♦ **Synonyms** RIM, BRIM, BRINK, FRINGE, PERIMETER
²**border** *vb* **bor-dered; bor-der-ing** 1 : to put a border on 2 : ADJOIN 3 : VERGE

border collie *n, often cap B* : any of a British breed of medium-sized long-haired sheepdogs

bor·der·land \'bȯr-dǝr-,land\ *n* **1** : territory at or near a border **2** : an outlying or intermediate region often not clearly defined

bor·der·line \-,līn\ *adj* : being in an intermediate position or state; *esp* : not quite up to what is standard or expected ⟨~ intelligence⟩

¹bore \'bȯr\ *vb* **bored; bor·ing** **1** : to make a hole in with or as if with a drill **2** : to make (as a well) by boring or digging away material ♦ **Synonyms** PERFORATE, DRILL, PRICK, PUNCTURE — **bor·er** *n*

²bore *n* **1** : a hole made by or as if by boring **2** : a cylindrical cavity : the diameter of a hole or tube; *esp* : the interior diameter of a gun barrel or engine cylinder

³bore *past of* BEAR

⁴bore *n* : a tidal flood with a high abrupt front

⁵bore *n* : one that causes boredom

⁶bore *vb* **bored; bor·ing** : to weary with tedious dullness

bo·re·al \'bȯr-ē-ǝl\ *adj* : of, relating to, or located in northern regions

bore·dom \'bȯr-dǝm\ *n* : the condition of being bored

bo·ric acid \'bȯr-ik-\ *n* : a white crystalline weak acid that contains boron and is used esp. as an antiseptic

born \'bȯrn\ *adj* **1** : brought into life by birth **2** : NATIVE ⟨American-*born*⟩ **3** : having special natural abilities or character from birth ⟨a ~ leader⟩

born–again *adj* : having experienced a revival of a personal faith or conviction ⟨a ~ believer⟩ ⟨a ~ liberal⟩

borne *past part of* BEAR

bo·ron \'bȯr-,än\ *n* : a chemical element that occurs in nature only in combination (as in borax)

bor·ough \'bǝr-ō\ *n* [ME *burgh*, fr. OE *burg* fortified town] **1** : a British town that sends one or more members to Parliament; *also* : an incorporated British urban area **2** : an incorporated town or village in some U.S. states; *also* : any of the five political divisions of New York City **3** : a civil division of the state of Alaska corresponding to a county in most other states

bor·row \'bär-ō\ *vb* **1** : to take or receive (something) temporarily and with intent to return ⟨~ed my car⟩ **2** : to take into possession or use from another source : DERIVE, APPROPRIATE ⟨~ a metaphor⟩

borscht \'bȯrsht\ *or* **borsch** \'bȯrsh\ *n* [Yiddish *borsht* & Ukrainian & Russ *borshch*] : a soup made mainly from beets

bosh \'bäsh\ *n* [Turk *boş* empty] : foolish talk or action : NONSENSE

bosky \'bäs-kē\ *adj* : covered with trees or shrubs

¹bos·om \'bu̇-zǝm, 'bü-\ *n* **1** : the front of the human chest; *esp* : the female breasts **2** : the seat of secret thoughts and feelings **3** : the part of a garment covering the breast — **bos·omed** \-zǝmd\ *adj*

²bosom *adj* : CLOSE, INTIMATE

¹boss \'bäs, 'bȯs\ *n* : a knoblike ornament : STUD

²boss *vb* : to ornament with bosses

³boss \'bȯs\ *n* **1** : one (as a foreman or manager) exercising control or supervision **2** : a politician who controls votes or dictates policies — **bossy** *adj*

⁴boss \'bȯs\ *vb* : to act as or in the manner of a boss

bosun *var of* BOATSWAIN

bot *abbr* botanical; botanist; botany

bot·a·ny \'bä-tǝ-nē, 'bät-nē\ *n, pl* **-nies** **1** : a branch of biology dealing with plants and plant life **2** : plant life (as of a given region); *also* : the biology of a plant or plant group — **bo·tan·i·cal** \bǝ-'ta-ni-kǝl\ *adj or n* — **bo·tan·i·cal·ly** \-kǝ-lē\ *adv* — **bot·a·nist** *n* — **bot·a·nize** \'bät-ǝ-,nīz\ *vb*

botch \'bäch\ *vb* : to foul up hopelessly : BUNGLE — **botch** *n*

¹both \'bōth\ *pron* : both ones : the one as well as the other

²both *conj* — used as a function word to indicate and stress the inclusion of each of two or more things specified by coordinated words, phrases, or clauses ⟨~ New York and London⟩

³both *adj* : being the two : affecting the one and the other

both·er \'bä-thǝr\ *vb* **1** : PESTER, TROUBLE ⟨was ~ed by bees⟩ **2** : to concern oneself : make an effort ⟨didn't ~ asking⟩ ♦ **Synonyms** VEX, ANNOY, IRK, PROVOKE — **bother** *n* — **both·er·some** \-sǝm\ *adj*

¹bot·tle \'bä-t³l\ *n* **1** : a container (as of glass) with a narrow neck and usu. no handles **2** : the quantity held by a bottle **3** : intoxicating liquor

²bottle *vb* **bot·tled; bot·tling** **1** : to confine as if in a bottle : RESTRAIN ⟨*bottled* up his anger⟩ **2** : to put into a bottle

bot·tle·neck \'bä-t³l-,nek\ *n* **1** : a narrow passage or point of congestion **2** : something that obstructs or impedes

¹bot·tom \'bä-tǝm\ *n* **1** : an under or supporting surface; *also* : BUTTOCKS **2** : the surface on which a body of water lies **3** : the lowest part or place; *also* : an inferior position ⟨start at the ~⟩ **4** : BOTTOMLAND **5** : BASIS, SOURCE ⟨get to the ~ of this mystery⟩ **6** : a quark with a charge of -⅓ and a measured energy of approximately 5 billion electron volts — **bottom** *adj* — **bot·tom·less** *adj*

²bottom *vb* **1** : to furnish with a bottom **2** : to reach the bottom **3** : to reach a point where a decline is halted or reversed — usu. used with *out*

bot·tom·land \'bä-tǝm-,land\ *n* : low land along a river

bottom line *n* **1** : the essential point : CRUX **2** : the final result : OUTCOME

bot·u·lism \'bä-chǝ-,li-zǝm\ *n* : an acute paralytic disease caused by a bacterial toxin (**bot·u·li·num toxin** \,bä-chǝ-'lī-nǝm-\) esp. in tainted food

bou·doir \'bü-,dwär, 'bu̇-, ,bü-', ,bu̇-'\ *n* [F, fr. *bouder* to pout] : a woman's dressing room or bedroom

bouf·fant \bü-'fänt, 'bü-,fänt\ *adj* [F] : puffed out ⟨~ hairdos⟩

bough \'bau̇\ *n* : a usu. large or main branch of a tree

bought *past and past part of* BUY

bouil·la·baisse \,bü-yǝ-'bäs\ *n* [F] : a highly seasoned fish stew made with at least two kinds of fish

bouil·lon \'bü-,yän; 'bu̇l-,yän, -yǝn\ *n* : a clear soup made usu. from beef

boul·der *also* **bowl·der** \'bōl-dǝr\ *n* : a large detached rounded or worn mass of rock — **boul·dered** \-dǝrd\ *adj*

bou·le·vard \'bu̇-lǝ-,värd, 'bü-\ *n* [F, modif. of MD *bolwerc* bulwark] : a broad often landscaped thoroughfare

bounce \'bau̇ns\ *vb* **bounced; bounc·ing** **1** : to cause to rebound ⟨~ a ball⟩ **2** : to rebound after striking **3** : to issue (a check) from an account with insufficient funds — **bounce** *n* — **bouncy** \'bau̇n-sē\ *adj*

bounc·er \'bau̇n-sǝr\ *n* : a person employed in a public place to remove disorderly persons

¹bound \'bau̇nd\ *adj* : intending to go

²bound *n* **1** : LIMIT, BOUNDARY — **bound·less** *adj* — **bound·less·ness** *n*

³bound *vb* **1** : to set limits to **2** : to form the boundary of **3** : to name the boundaries of

⁴bound *past and past part of* BIND

⁵bound *adj* **1** : constrained by or as if by bonds : CONFINED, OBLIGED **2** : enclosed in a binding or cover **3** : RESOLVED, DETERMINED; *also* : SURE

⁶bound *n* **1** : LEAP, JUMP **2** : REBOUND, BOUNCE

⁷bound *vb* : SPRING, BOUNCE

bound·ary \'bau̇n-drē\ *n, pl* **-aries** : something that marks or fixes a limit or extent (as of territory) ♦ **Synonyms** BORDER, FRONTIER, MARCH

bound·en \'bau̇n-dǝn\ *adj* : BINDING

boun·te·ous \'bau̇n-tē-ǝs\ *adj* **1** : GENEROUS **2** : ABUNDANT — **boun·te·ous·ly** *adv* — **boun·te·ous·ness** *n*

boun·ti·ful \'bau̇n-ti-fǝl\ *adj* **1** : giving freely **2** : PLENTIFUL — **boun·ti·ful·ly** *adv* — **boun·ti·ful·ness** *n*

boun·ty \'bau̇n-tē\ *n, pl* **bounties** [ME *bounte* goodness, fr. AF *bunté*, fr. L *bonitas*, fr. *bonus* good] **1** : GENEROSITY **2** : something given liberally **3** : a reward, premium, or subsidy given usu. for doing something

bou·quet \bō-'kā, bü-\ *n* [F, fr. MF, thicket, bunch of flowers, fr. OF (dial. of Normandy and Picardy) *bosquet* thicket, fr. *bosc* forest] **1** : flowers picked and fastened together in a bunch **2** : a distinctive aroma (as of wine) ♦ **Synonyms** SCENT, FRAGRANCE, PERFUME, REDOLENCE

bour·bon \'bǝr-bǝn\ *n* : a whiskey distilled from a corn mash

bour·geois \'bu̇rzh-,wä, bu̇rzh-'wä\ *n, pl* **bourgeois** \same or -,wäz, -'wäz\ [MF, fr. OF *burgeis* townsman, fr. *burc, borg* town, fr. L *burgus* fortified place, fr. Gmc origin] : a middle-class person — **bourgeois** *adj*

bour·geoi·sie \,bu̇rzh-,wä-'zē\ *n* : a social order dominated by bourgeois

bourne *also* **bourn** \'bȯrn, 'bu̇rn\ *n* : BOUNDARY; *also* : DESTINATION

bourse \'bu̇rs\ *n* : a European stock exchange
bout \'bau̇t\ *n* **1** : CONTEST, MATCH **2** : OUTBREAK, AT-TACK ⟨a ~ of measles⟩ **3** : SESSION
bou·tique \bü-'tēk\ *n* : a small fashionable specialty shop
bou·ton·niere \ˌbü-tᵊn-'iər\ *n* : a flower or bouquet worn in a buttonhole
¹bo·vine \'bō-ˌvīn, -ˌvēn\ *adj* **1** : of or relating to bovines **2** : having qualities (as placidity or dullness) characteristic of oxen or cows
²bovine *n* : any of a group of mammals including oxen, buffalo, and their close relatives
bovine spon·gi·form encephalopathy \-'spän-ji-ˌfȯrm-\ *n* : MAD COW DISEASE
¹bow \'bau̇\ *vb* **1** : SUBMIT, YIELD **2** : to bend the head or body (as in submission, courtesy, or assent) **3** : DEBUT ⟨the play ~s next month⟩
²bow *n* : an act or posture of bowing
³bow \'bō\ *n* **1** : BEND, ARCH; *esp* : RAINBOW **2** : a weapon for shooting arrows; *also* : ARCHER **3** : a knot formed by doubling a line into two or more loops **4** : a wooden rod strung with horsehairs for playing an instrument of the violin family
⁴bow \'bō\ *vb* **1** : BEND, CURVE **2** : to play (an instrument) with a bow
⁵bow \'bau̇\ *n* : the forward part of a ship — **bow** *adj*
bowd·ler·ise *Brit var of* BOWDLERIZE
bowd·ler·ize \'bōd-lə-ˌrīz, 'bau̇d-\ *vb* **-ized; -iz·ing** : to expurgate by omitting parts considered vulgar
bow·el \'bau̇(-ə)l\ *n* **1** : INTESTINE; *also* : one of the divisions of the intestine — usu. used in pl. **2** *pl* : the inmost parts ⟨the ~s of the earth⟩
bow·er \'bau̇(-ə)r\ *n* : a shelter of boughs or vines : ARBOR
¹bowl \'bōl\ *n* **1** : a concave vessel used to hold liquids **2** : a drinking vessel **3** : a bowl-shaped part or structure — **bowl·ful** \-ˌfu̇l\ *n*
²bowl *n* **1** : a ball for rolling on a level surface in bowling **2** : a cast of the ball in bowling
³bowl *vb* **1** : to play a game of bowling; *also* : to roll a ball in bowling **2** : to travel (as in a vehicle) rapidly and smoothly **3** : to strike or knock down with a moving object
bowlder *var of* BOULDER
bow·legged \'bō-ˌle-gəd\ *adj* : having legs that bow outward at or below the knee — **bow·leg** \'bō-ˌleg\ *n*
¹bowl·er \'bō-lər\ *n* : a person who bowls
²bowl·er \'bō-lər\ *n* : DERBY **3**
bow·line \'bō-lən, -ˌlīn\ *n* : a knot used to form a loop that neither slips nor jams
bowl·ing \'bō-liŋ\ *n* : any of various games in which balls are rolled on a green or alley at an object or a group of objects
bow·man \'bō-mən\ *n* : ARCHER
bow·sprit \'bau̇-ˌsprit\ *n* : a spar projecting forward from the prow of a ship
bow·string \'bō-ˌstriŋ\ *n* : the cord connecting the two ends of a shooting bow
¹box \'bäks\ *n, pl* **box** *or* **box·es** : an evergreen shrub or small tree used esp. for hedges
²box *n* **1** : a rigid typically rectangular receptacle often with a cover; *also* : the quantity held by a box **2** : a small compartment (as for a group of theater patrons); *also* : a boxlike receptacle or division **3** : a usu. rectangular space demarcated for a particular purpose ⟨the batter's ~⟩ **4** : PREDICAMENT — **boxy** \'bäk-sē\ *adj*
³box *vb* : to enclose in or as if in a box
⁴box *n* : a punch or slap esp. on the ear
⁵box *vb* **1** : to strike with the hand **2** : to engage in boxing with
box·car \'bäks-ˌkär\ *n* : a roofed freight car usu. with sliding doors in the sides
box cutter *n* : a small cutting tool with a retractable razor blade
¹box·er \'bäk-sər\ *n* **1** : a person who engages in boxing **2** *pl* : BOXER SHORTS
²boxer *n* : any of a German breed of compact medium-sized dogs with a short usu. fawn or brindled coat
boxer shorts *n pl* : men's loose-fitting shorts worn as underwear
box·ing \'bäk-siŋ\ *n* : the sport of fighting with the fists
box office *n* : an office (as in a theater) where admission tickets are sold

box turtle *n* : any of several No. American land turtles able to withdraw completely into their shell
box·wood \'bäks-ˌwu̇d\ *n* : the tough hard wood of the box; *also* : a box tree or shrub
boy \'bȯi\ *n* **1** : a male child : YOUTH **2** : SON — **boy·hood** \-ˌhu̇d\ *n* — **boy·ish** *adj* — **boy·ish·ly** *adv* — **boy·ish·ness** *n*
boy·cott \'bȯi-ˌkät\ *vb* [Charles C. *Boycott* †1897 Eng. land agent in Ireland who was ostracized for refusing to reduce rents] : to refrain from having any dealings with — **boycott** *n*
boy·friend \'bȯi-ˌfrend\ *n* **1** : a male friend **2** : a frequent or regular male companion in a romantic relationship
Boy Scout *n* : a member of any of various national scouting programs (as the Boy Scouts of America)
boy·sen·ber·ry \'bȯi-zᵊn-ˌber-ē, 'bȯis-\ *n* : a large reddish-black fruit with a raspberry flavor; *also* : the hybrid bramble bearing it developed by crossing blackberries and raspberries
bo·zo \'bō-ˌzō\ *n, pl* **bozos** : a foolish or incompetent person
bp *abbr* **1** bishop **2** birthplace
BP *abbr* **1** batting practice **2** blood pressure **3** boiling point
bpl *abbr* birthplace
BPOE *abbr* Benevolent and Protective Order of Elks
br *abbr* **1** branch **2** brass **3** brown
¹Br *abbr* Britain; British
²Br *symbol* bromine
BR *abbr* bedroom
bra \'brä\ *n* : BRASSIERE
¹brace \'brās\ *vb* **braced; brac·ing** **1** *archaic* : to make fast : BIND **2** : to tighten preparatory to use; *also* : to get ready for : prepare oneself **3** : INVIGORATE **4** : to furnish or support with a brace; *also* : STRENGTHEN **5** : to set firmly **6** : to gain courage or confidence
²brace *n, pl* **brac·es 1** *or pl* **brace** : two of a kind ⟨a ~ of dogs⟩ **2** : a crank-shaped device for turning a bit **3** : something (as a tie, prop, or clamp) that distributes, directs, or resists pressure or weight **4** *pl* : SUSPENDERS **5** : an appliance for supporting a body part (as the shoulders) **6** *pl* : a dental appliance used to exert pressure to straighten misaligned teeth **7** : one of two marks { } used to connect words or items to be considered together
brace·let \'brā-slət\ *n* [ME, fr. MF, dim. of *bras* arm, fr. L *bracchium*, fr. Gk *brachīōn*] : an ornamental band or chain worn around the wrist
bra·ce·ro \brä-'ser-ō\ *n, pl* **-ros** : a Mexican laborer admitted to the U.S. esp. for seasonal farm work
brack·en \'bra-kən\ *n* : a large coarse fern; *also* : a growth of such ferns
¹brack·et \'bra-kət\ *n* **1** : a projecting framework or arm designed to support weight; *also* : a shelf on such framework **2** : one of a pair of punctuation marks [ ] used esp. to enclose interpolated matter **3** : a continuous section of a series; *esp* : one of a graded series of income groups
²bracket *vb* **1** : to furnish or fasten with brackets **2** : to place within brackets; *also* : to separate or group with or as if with brackets
brack·ish \'bra-kish\ *adj* : somewhat salty — **brack·ish·ness** *n*
bract \'brakt\ *n* : an often modified leaf on or at the base of a flower stalk
brad \'brad\ *n* : a slender nail with a small head
brae \'brā\ *n, chiefly Scot* : a hillside esp. along a river
brag \'brag\ *vb* **bragged; brag·ging** : to talk or assert boastfully — **brag** *n* — **brag·ger** *n*
brag·ga·do·cio \ˌbra-gə-'dō-shē-ˌō, -sē-, -chē-\ *n, pl* **-cios 1** : BRAGGART, BOASTER **2** : empty boasting **3** : arrogant pretension : COCKINESS
brag·gart \'bra-gərt\ *n* : one who brags
Brah·man *or* **Brah·min** \'brä-mən *for 1*; 'brā-, 'brȧ-, 'brä- *for 2*\ *n* **1** : a Hindu of the highest caste traditionally assigned to the priesthood **2** : any of a breed of large vigorous humped cattle developed in the southern U.S. from Indian stock **3** *usu* **Brahmin** : a person of high social standing and cultivated intellect and taste
Brah·man·ism \'brä-mə-ˌni-zəm\ *n* : orthodox Hinduism
¹braid \'brād\ *vb* **1** : to form (strands) into a braid : PLAIT; *also* : to make from braids **2** : to ornament with braid
²braid *n* **1** : a length of braided hair **2** : a cord or ribbon

of three or more interwoven strands; *esp* : a narrow ornamental one

braille \\'brāl\ *n*, *often cap* : a system of writing for the blind that uses characters made up of raised dots

a	b	c	d	e	f	g	h	i	j
1	2	3	4	5	6	7	8	9	0

k	l	m	n	o	p	q	r	s	t

u	v	w	x	y	z	Capital Sign	Numeral Sign

braille alphabet

¹**brain** \\'brān\ *n* 1 : the part of the vertebrate central nervous system enclosed in the skull and continuous with the spinal cord that is composed of neurons and supporting structures and is the center of thought and nervous system control; *also* : a centralized mass of nerve tissue in an invertebrate 2 : INTELLECT, INTELLIGENCE — often used in pl. — **brained** \\'brānd\ *adj* — **brain·less** *adj* — **brainy** *adj*

²**brain** *vb* 1 : to kill by smashing the skull 2 : to hit on the head

brain·child \\'brān-ˌchīl(-ə)ld\ *n* : a product of one's creative imagination

brain death *n* : final cessation of activity in the central nervous system esp. as indicated by a flat electroencephalogram — **brain–dead** \-ˌded\ *adj*

brain drain *n* : the departure of educated or professional people from one country, sector, or field to another usu. for better pay or living conditions

brain·storm \-ˌstȯrm\ *n* : a sudden inspiration or idea — **brainstorm** *vb*

brain·teas·er \-ˌtē-zər\ *n* : a challenging puzzle

brain·wash·ing \\'brān-ˌwȯ-shiŋ, -ˌwä-\ *n* 1 : a forcible indoctrination to induce someone to give up basic political, social, or religious beliefs and attitudes and to accept contrasting regimented ideas 2 : persuasion by propaganda or salesmanship — **brain·wash** *vb*

brain wave *n* 1 : BRAINSTORM 2 : rhythmic fluctuations of voltage between parts of the brain; *also* : a current produced by brain waves

braise \\'brāz\ *vb* **braised; brais·ing** : to cook slowly in fat and little moisture in a closed pot

¹**brake** \\'brāk\ *n* : a common bracken fern

²**brake** *n* : rough or wet land heavily overgrown (as with thickets or reeds)

³**brake** *n* : a device for slowing or stopping motion esp. by friction — **brake·less** *adj*

⁴**brake** *vb* **braked; brak·ing** 1 : to slow or stop by or as if by a brake 2 : to apply a brake

brake·man \\'brāk-mən\ *n* : a train crew member who inspects the train and assists the conductor

bram·ble \\'bram-bəl\ *n* : any of a large genus of prickly shrubs (as a blackberry) related to the roses; *also* : any rough prickly shrub or vine — **bram·bly** \-b(ə-)lē\ *adj*

bran \\'bran\ *n* : the edible broken husks of cereal grain sifted from flour or meal

¹**branch** \\'branch\ *n* [ME, fr. AF *branche*, fr. LL *branca* paw] 1 : a natural subdivision (as a bough or twig) of a plant stem 2 : a division (as of an antler or a river) related to a whole like a plant branch to its stem 3 : a discrete element of a complex system ⟨the executive ∼⟩; *esp* : a division of a family descended from one ancestor — **branched** \\'brancht\ *adj*

²**branch** *vb* 1 : to develop branches 2 : DIVERGE 3 : to extend activities ⟨the business is ∼*ing* out⟩

¹**brand** \\'brand\ *n* 1 : a piece of charred or burning wood 2 : a mark made (as by burning) usu. to identify; *also* : a mark of disgrace : STIGMA 3 : a class of goods identified as the product of a particular firm or producer 4 : a distinctive kind ⟨my own ∼ of humor⟩

²**brand** *vb* 1 : to mark with a brand 2 : STIGMATIZE ⟨was ∼*ed* a traitor⟩

bran·dish \\'bran-dish\ *vb* : to shake or wave menacingly ⟨∼ a knife⟩ ✦ **Synonyms** FLOURISH, FLASH, FLAUNT

brand–new \\'bran-'nü, -'nyü\ *adj* : conspicuously new and unused

bran·dy \\'bran-dē\ *n*, *pl* **brandies** [short for *brandywine*, fr. D *brandewijn*, fr. MD *brantwijn*, fr. *brant* distilled + *wijn* wine] : a liquor distilled from wine or fermented fruit juice — **brandy** *vb*

brash \\'brash\ *adj* 1 : IMPETUOUS, AUDACIOUS 2 : aggressively self-assertive — **brash·ly** *adv* — **brash·ness** *n*

brass \\'bras\ *n* 1 : an alloy of copper and zinc; *also* : an object of brass 2 : brazen self-assurance 3 : persons of high rank (as in the military) — **brassy** *adj*

bras·siere \brə-'zir\ *n* : a woman's close-fitting undergarment designed to support the breasts

brat \\'brat\ *n* : an ill-behaved child — **brat·ti·ness** *n* — **brat·ty** *adj*

bra·va·do \brə-'vä-dō\ *n*, *pl* **-does** *or* **-dos** 1 : blustering swaggering conduct 2 : a show of bravery

¹**brave** \\'brāv\ *adj* **brav·er; brav·est** [MF, fr. It & Sp *bravo* courageous, wild, prob. fr. L *barbarus* barbarous] 1 : showing courage 2 : EXCELLENT, SPLENDID ✦ **Synonyms** BOLD, INTREPID, COURAGEOUS, VALIANT — **brave·ly** *adv*

²**brave** *vb* **braved; brav·ing** : to face or endure bravely

³**brave** *n* : an American Indian warrior

brav·ery \\'brā-və-rē\ *n*, *pl* **-er·ies** : COURAGE

bra·vo \\'brä-vō\ *n*, *pl* **bravos** : a shout of approval — often used as an interjection in applauding

bra·vu·ra \brə-'vyür-ə, -'vür-\ *n* 1 : a florid brilliant musical style 2 : self-assured brilliant performance — **bravura** *adj*

brawl \\'brȯl\ *n* : a noisy quarrel ✦ **Synonyms** FRACAS, ROW, RUMPUS, SCRAP, FRAY, MELEE — **brawl** *vb* — **brawl·er** *n*

brawn \\'brȯn\ *n* : strong muscles; *also* : muscular strength — **brawn·i·ness** *n* — **brawny** *adj*

bray \\'brā\ *n* : the characteristic harsh cry of a donkey — **bray** *vb*

braze \\'brāz\ *vb* **brazed; braz·ing** : to solder with an alloy (as brass) that melts at a lower temperature than the metals being joined — **braz·er** *n*

¹**bra·zen** \\'brā-zᵊn\ *adj* 1 : made of brass 2 : sounding harsh and loud 3 : of the color of brass 4 : marked by contemptuous boldness ⟨a ∼ rebuff⟩ — **bra·zen·ly** *adv* — **bra·zen·ness** *n*

²**brazen** *vb* : to face boldly or defiantly

¹**bra·zier** \\'brā-zhər\ *n* : a worker in brass

²**brazier** *n* 1 : a vessel holding burning coals (as for heating) 2 : a device on which food is grilled

Bra·zil nut \brə-'zil-\ *n* : a triangular oily edible nut borne in large capsules by a tall So. American tree; *also* : the tree

¹**breach** \\'brēch\ *n* 1 : a breaking of a law, obligation, tie (as of friendship), or standard (as of conduct) 2 : an interruption or opening made by or as if by breaking through ✦ **Synonyms** VIOLATION, TRANSGRESSION, INFRINGEMENT, TRESPASS

²**breach** *vb* 1 : to make a breach in 2 : to leap out of water ⟨whales ∼*ing*⟩

¹**bread** \\'bred\ *n* 1 : baked food made basically of flour or meal 2 : FOOD

²**bread** *vb* : to cover with bread crumbs

bread·bas·ket \\'bred-ˌbas-kət\ *n* : a major cereal-producing region

bread·fruit \-ˌfrüt\ *n* : a round usu. seedless fruit resembling bread in color and texture when baked; *also* : a tall tropical tree related to the mulberry and bearing breadfruit

bread·stuff \-ˌstəf\ *n* : GRAIN, FLOUR

breadth \\'bredth, 'bretth\ *n* 1 : WIDTH 2 : comprehensive quality : SCOPE ⟨∼ of knowledge⟩

bread·win·ner \\'bred-ˌwi-nər\ *n* : a member of a family whose wages supply its livelihood

¹**break** \\'brāk\ *vb* **broke** \\'brōk\; **bro·ken** \\'brō-kən\; **break·ing** 1 : to separate into parts usu. suddenly or violently; *also* : to render inoperable ⟨*broke* his watch⟩ 2 : TRANSGRESS ⟨∼ a law⟩ 3 : to force a way into, out of, or through 4 : to disrupt the order or unity of ⟨∼ ranks⟩ ⟨∼ up a gang⟩; *also* : to bring to submission or helplessness 5 : EXCEED, SURPASS ⟨∼ a record⟩ 6 : RUIN 7 : to make known ⟨∼ the bad news⟩ 8 : HALT, INTERRUPT; *also* : to act or change abruptly (as a course or activity) 9 : to come esp. suddenly into being or no-

tice ⟨as day ~s⟩ **10** : to fail under stress **11** : HAPPEN, DEVELOP ⟨report news as it ~s⟩ — **break·able** *adj or n* — **break into 1** : to begin with a sudden throwing off of restraint ⟨*broke into* tears⟩ **2** : to make entry or entrance into ⟨*break into* show business⟩

²**break** *n* **1** : an act of breaking **2** : a result of breaking; *esp* : an interruption of continuity ⟨coffee ~⟩ ⟨a ~ for the commercial⟩ **3** : a stroke of luck

break·age \'brā-kij\ *n* **1** : loss due to things broken **2** : the action of breaking **3** : articles or amount broken

break·down \'brāk-₁daůn\ *n* **1** : functional failure; *esp* : a physical, mental, or nervous collapse **2** : DISINTEGRA-TION **3** : DECOMPOSITION **4** : ANALYSIS, CLASSIFICA-TION — **break down** *vb*

break·er \'brā-kər\ *n* **1** : one that breaks **2** : a wave that breaks into foam (as against the shore)

break·fast \'brek-fəst\ *n* : the first meal of the day — **breakfast** *vb*

break in *vb* **1** : to enter a building by force **2** : INTER-RUPT; *also* : INTRUDE **3** : TRAIN — **break–in** \'brāk-₁in\ *n*

break·neck \'brāk-'nek\ *adj* : very fast or dangerous ⟨~ speed⟩

break out *vb* **1** : to develop or erupt suddenly or with force **2** : to develop a skin rash

break·through \'brāk-₁thrü\ *n* **1** : an act or instance of breaking through an obstruction or defensive line **2** : a sudden advance in knowledge or technique ⟨a scientific ~⟩

break·up \-₁əp\ *n* **1** : DISSOLUTION **2** : a division into smaller units — **break up** *vb*

break·wa·ter \'brāk-₁wȯ-tər, -₁wä-\ *n* : a structure protect-ing a harbor or beach from the force of waves

bream \'brim, 'brēm\ *n, pl* **bream** *or* **breams** : any of var-ious small freshwater sunfishes

breast \'brest\ *n* **1** : either of the pair of mammary glands extending from the front of the chest esp. in pubescent and adult human females **2** : the front part of the body between the neck and the abdomen **3** : the seat of emo-tion and thought

breast·bone \'brest-₁bōn\ *n* : STERNUM

breast–feed \-₁fēd\ *vb* : to feed (a baby) from a mother's breast

breast·plate \-₁plāt\ *n* : a metal plate of armor for the breast

breast·stroke \-₁strōk\ *n* : a swimming stroke executed by extending both arms forward and then sweeping them back with palms out while kicking backward and out-ward with both legs

breast·work \-₁wərk\ *n* : a temporary fortification

breath \'breth\ *n* **1** : the act or power of breathing **2** : a slight breeze **3** : air inhaled or exhaled in breathing **4** : spoken sound **5** : SPIRIT — **breath·less** *adj* — **breath·less·ly** *adv* — **breath·less·ness** *n* — **breathy** \'bre-thē\ *adj*

breathe \'brēth\ *vb* **breathed; breath·ing 1** : to inhale and exhale **2** : LIVE **3** : to halt for rest **4** : to utter soft-ly or secretly — **breath·able** *adj*

breath·er \'brē-thər\ *n* **1** : one that breathes **2** : a short rest

breath·tak·ing \'breth-₁tā-kiŋ\ *adj* **1** : making one out of breath **2** : EXCITING, THRILLING ⟨~ beauty⟩ — **breath·tak·ing·ly** *adv*

brec·cia \'bre-chē-ə, -chə\ *n* : a rock composed of sharp fragments held in fine-grained material

breech \'brēch\ *n* **1** *pl* *usu* 'bri-chəz\ : pants ending near the knee **2** : BUTTOCKS, RUMP **3** : the part of a firearm at the rear of the barrel

¹**breed** \'brēd\ *vb* **bred** \'bred\; **breed·ing 1** : BEGET; *also* : ORIGINATE **2** : to propagate sexually; *also* : MATE **3** : BRING UP, NURTURE **4** : to produce (fissionable mate-rial) from material that is not fissionable **♦ Synonyms** GENERATE, REPRODUCE, PROCREATE, PROPAGATE — **breed·er** *n*

²**breed** *n* **1** : a strain of similar and presumably related plants or animals usu. developed in domestication **2** : KIND, SORT, CLASS

breeding *n* **1** : ANCESTRY **2** : training in polite social in-teraction **3** : sexual propagation of plants or animals

¹**breeze** \'brēz\ *n* **1** : a light wind **2** : CINCH, SNAP — **breeze·less** *adj*

²**breeze** *vb* **breezed; breez·ing** : to progress quickly and easily

breeze·way \'brēz-₁wā\ *n* : a roofed open passage connect-ing two buildings (as a house and garage)

breezy \'brē-zē\ *adj* **1** : swept by breezes **2** : briskly in-formal ⟨~ prose⟩ — **breez·i·ly** \'brē-zə-lē\ *adv* — **breez-i·ness** \-zē-nəs\ *n*

breth·ren \'breth-rən, 'bre-thə-; 'bre-thərn\ *pl of* BROTH-ER — used esp. in formal or solemn address

Brethren *n pl* : members of one of several Protestant de-nominations originating chiefly in a German religious movement and stressing personal religious experience

bre·via·ry \'brē-vyə-rē, -vē-₁er-ē\ *n, pl* **-ries** *often cap* : a book of prayers, hymns, psalms, and readings used by Roman Catholic priests

brev·i·ty \'bre-və-tē\ *n, pl* **-ties 1** : shortness or concise-ness of expression **2** : shortness of duration

brew \'brü\ *vb* **1** : to prepare (as beer) by steeping, boil-ing, and fermenting **2** : to prepare (as tea) by steeping in hot water — **brew** *n* — **brew·er** *n* — **brew·ery** \'brü-ə-rē, 'brů(-ə)r-ē\ *n*

¹**bri·ar** *also* **bri·er** \'brī-ər\ *n* : a plant (as a bramble or rose) with a thorny or prickly usu. woody stem; *also* : a mass or twig of these — **bri·ary** \'brī-ər-ē\ *adj*

²**briar** *n* : a tobacco pipe made from the root or stem of a European heath

¹**bribe** \'brīb\ *n* [ME, morsel given to a beggar, bribe, fr. AF, morsel] : something (as money or a favor) given or promised to a person to influence conduct

²**bribe** *vb* **bribed; brib·ing** : to influence by offering a bribe — **brib·able** *adj* — **brib·er** *n* — **brib·ery** \'brī-bə-rē\ *n*

bric–a–brac \'brī-kə-₁brak\ *n pl* [F] : small ornamental ar-ticles

¹**brick** \'brik\ *n* : a block molded from moist clay and hard-ened by heat used esp. for building

²**brick** *vb* : to close, cover, or pave with bricks

brick·bat \'brik-₁bat\ *n* **1** : a piece of a hard material (as a brick) esp. when thrown as a missile **2** : an uncompli-mentary remark

brick·lay·er \'brik-₁lā-ər\ *n* : a person who builds or paves with bricks — **brick·lay·ing** *n*

¹**brid·al** \'brī-d²l\ *n* [ME *bridale*, fr. OE *brydealu*, fr. *bryd* bride + *ealu* ale] : MARRIAGE, WEDDING

²**bridal** *adj* : of or relating to a bride or a wedding

bride \'brīd\ *n* : a woman just married or about to be mar-ried

bride·groom \'brīd-₁grüm, -₁grům\ *n* : a man just married or about to be married

brides·maid \'brīdz-₁mād\ *n* : a woman who attends a bride at her wedding

¹**bridge** \'brij\ *n* **1** : a structure built over a depression or obstacle for use as a passageway **2** : something (as the upper part of the nose) resembling a bridge in form or function **3** : a curved piece raising the strings of a musi-cal instrument **4** : the forward part of a ship's super-structure from which it is navigated **5** : an artificial re-placement for missing teeth

²**bridge** *vb* **bridged; bridg·ing** : to build a bridge over — **bridge·able** *adj*

³**bridge** *n* : a card game for four players developed from whist

bridge·head \-₁hed\ *n* : an advanced position seized in enemy territory

bridge·work \-₁wərk\ *n* : dental bridges

¹**bri·dle** \'brī-d²l\ *n* **1** : headgear with which a horse is con-trolled **2** : CURB, RESTRAINT

²**bridle** *vb* **bri·dled; bri·dling 1** : to put a bridle on; *also* : to restrain with or as if with a bridle **2** : to show hostil-ity or scorn usu. by tossing the head

Brie \'brē\ *n* : a soft cheese with a whitish rind and a pale yellow interior

¹**brief** \'brēf\ *adj* **1** : short in duration or extent **2** : CON-CISE; *also* : CURT — **brief·ly** *adv* — **brief·ness** *n*

²**brief** *n* **1** : a concise statement or document; *esp* : one summarizing a law client's case or a legal argument **2** *pl* : short snug underpants

³**brief** *vb* : to give final instructions or essential information to

brief·case \'brēf-₁kās\ *n* : a flat flexible case for carrying papers

brier *var of* BRIAR

¹brig \'brig\ *n* : a 2-masted square-rigged sailing ship
²brig *n* : the place of confinement for offenders on a naval ship
³brig *abbr* brigade
bri·gade \bri-'gād\ *n* **1** : a military unit composed of a headquarters, one or more units of infantry or armored forces, and supporting units **2** : a group organized for a particular purpose (as fire fighting)
brig·a·dier general \'bri-gə-ˌdir-\ *n* : a commissioned officer (as in the army) ranking next below a major general
brig·and \'bri-gənd\ *n* : BANDIT — **brig·and·age** \-gən-dij\ *n*
brig·an·tine \'bri-gən-ˌtēn\ *n* : a 2-masted square-rigged ship with a fore-and-aft mainsail
Brig Gen *abbr* brigadier general
bright \'brīt\ *adj* **1** : SHINING, RADIANT **2** : ILLUSTRIOUS, GLORIOUS **3** : INTELLIGENT, CLEVER; *also* : LIVELY, CHEERFUL ♦ *Synonyms* BRILLIANT, LUSTROUS, BEAMING — **bright** *adv* — **bright·ly** *adv* — **bright·ness** *n*
bright·en \'brī-tᵊn\ *vb* : to make or become bright or brighter — **bright·en·er** *n*
¹bril·liant \'bril-yənt\ *adj* [F *brillant*, prp. of *briller* to shine, fr. It *brillare*] **1** : very bright **2** : STRIKING, DISTINCTIVE **3** : very intelligent ♦ *Synonyms* RADIANT, LUSTROUS, BEAMING, LUCID, BRIGHT, LAMBENT — **bril·liance** \-yəns\ *n* — **bril·lian·cy** \-yən-sē\ *n* — **bril·liant·ly** *adv*
²brilliant *n* : a gem cut in a particular form with many facets
¹brim \'brim\ *n* : EDGE, RIM ♦ *Synonyms* BRINK, BORDER, VERGE, FRINGE — **brim·less** *adj*
²brim *vb* **brimmed; brim·ming** : to be or become full often to overflowing
brim·ful \-'fúl\ *adj* : full to the brim
brim·stone \'brim-ˌstōn\ *n* : SULFUR
brin·dled \'brin-dᵊld\ *adj* : having dark streaks or flecks on a gray or tawny ground ⟨a ∼ Great Dane⟩
brine \'brīn\ *n* **1** : water saturated with salt **2** : OCEAN — **brin·i·ness** *n* — **briny** \'brī-nē\ *adj*
bring \'briŋ\ *vb* **brought** \'brȯt\; **bring·ing** \'briŋ-iŋ\ **1** : to cause to come with one **2** : INDUCE, PERSUADE, LEAD **3** : PRODUCE, EFFECT **4** : to sell for ⟨∼ a good price⟩ — **bring·er** *n*
bring about *vb* : to cause to take place
bring up *vb* **1** : to give a parent's fostering care to **2** : to come or bring to a sudden halt **3** : to call to notice
brink \'briŋk\ *n* **1** : an edge at the top of a steep place **2** : the point of onset
brio \'brē-ō\ *n* : VIVACITY, SPIRIT
bri·quette *or* **bri·quet** \bri-'ket\ *n* : a compacted often brick-shaped mass of fine material ⟨a charcoal ∼⟩
bris *also* **briss** \'bris\ *n* : the Jewish rite of circumcision
brisk \'brisk\ *adj* **1** : ALERT, LIVELY **2** : INVIGORATING ⟨∼ weather⟩ **3** : highly active ⟨a ∼ business⟩ ♦ *Synonyms* AGILE, SPRY, NIMBLE — **brisk·ly** *adv* — **brisk·ness** *n*
bris·ket \'bris-kət\ *n* : the breast or lower chest of a quadruped; *also* : a cut of beef from the brisket
bris·ling \'briz-liŋ, 'bris-\ *n* : SPRAT 1
¹bris·tle \'bris-əl\ *n* : a short stiff coarse hair — **bris·tle·like** \'bri-səl-ˌlīk\ *adj* — **bris·tly** *adj*
²bristle *vb* **bris·tled; bris·tling** **1** : to stand stiffly erect **2** : to show angry defiance ⟨*bristled* at the charges⟩ **3** : to appear as if covered with bristles
Brit *abbr* Britain; British
Bri·tan·nic \bri-'ta-nik\ *adj* : BRITISH
britch·es \'bri-chəz\ *n pl* : BREECHES, TROUSERS
Brit·ish \'bri-tish\ *n pl* : the people of Great Britain or the Commonwealth — **British** *adj* — **Brit·ish·ness** *n*
British thermal unit *n* : the quantity of heat needed to raise the temperature of one pound of water one degree Fahrenheit
Brit·on \'bri-tᵊn\ *n* **1** : a member of a people inhabiting Britain before the Anglo-Saxon invasion **2** : a native or inhabitant of Great Britain
brit·tle \'bri-tᵊl\ *adj* **brit·tler; brit·tlest** : easily broken : FRAGILE ♦ *Synonyms* CRISP, CRUMBLY, FRIABLE — **brit·tle·ness** *n*
bro \'brō\ *n, pl* **bros** **1** : BROTHER 1 **2** : SOUL BROTHER
¹broach \'brōch\ *n* : a pointed tool
²broach *vb* **1** : to pierce (as a cask) in order to draw the contents **2** : to open up (a subject) for discussion

broad \'brȯd\ *adj* **1** : WIDE **2** : SPACIOUS ⟨the ∼ plains⟩ **3** : CLEAR, OPEN ⟨∼ daylight⟩ **4** : OBVIOUS ⟨a ∼ hint⟩ **5** : COARSE, CRUDE ⟨∼ stories⟩ **6** : tolerant in outlook **7** : GENERAL ⟨a ∼ rule⟩ **8** : dealing with essential points — **broad·ly** *adv* — **broad·ness** *n*
broad·band \'brȯd-ˌband\ *n* : a system of high-speed telecommunication in which a frequency range is divided into multiple independent channels for simultaneous transmission of signals
¹broad·cast \'brȯd-ˌkast\ *vb* **broadcast** *also* **broad·cast·ed; broad·cast·ing** **1** : to scatter or sow broadcast **2** : to make widely known **3** : to transmit a broadcast — **broad·cast·er** *n*
²broadcast *adv* : to or over a wide area
³broadcast *n* **1** : the transmission of sound or images by radio or television **2** : a single radio or television program
broad·cloth \-ˌklȯth\ *n* **1** : a smooth dense woolen cloth **2** : a fine soft cloth of cotton, silk, or synthetic fiber
broad·en \'brȯd-ᵊn\ *vb* : WIDEN
broad·loom \-ˌlüm\ *adj* : woven on a wide loom esp. in a solid color
broad–mind·ed \-'mīn-dəd\ *adj* : tolerant of varied opinions — **broad–mind·ed·ly** *adv* — **broad–mind·ed·ness** *n*
¹broad·side \-ˌsīd\ *n* **1** : a sheet of paper printed usu. on one side (as an advertisement) **2** : all of the guns on one side of a ship; *also* : their simultaneous firing **3** : a volley of abuse or denunciation
²broadside *adv* **1** : with one side forward : SIDEWAYS **2** : from the side ⟨the car was hit ∼⟩
broad–spectrum *adj* : effective against a wide range of organisms ⟨∼ antibiotics⟩
broad·sword \'brȯd-ˌsȯrd\ *n* : a broad-bladed sword
broad·tail \-ˌtāl\ *n* : a karakul esp. with flat and wavy fur
bro·cade \brō-'kād\ *n* : a usu. silk fabric with a raised design
broc·co·li \'brä-kə-lē\ *n* [It, pl. of *broccolo* flowering top of a cabbage, dim. of *brocco* small nail, sprout, fr. L *broccus* projecting] : the stems and immature usu. green or purple flower heads of either of two garden vegetable plants closely related to the cabbage; *also* : either of the plants
bro·chette \brō-'shet\ *n* : SKEWER
bro·chure \brō-'shúr\ *n* [F, fr. *brocher* to sew, fr. MF, fr. prick, fr. OF *brochier*, fr. *broche* pointed tool] : PAMPHLET, BOOKLET
bro·gan \'brō-gən, brō-'gan\ *n* : a heavy shoe
brogue \'brōg\ *n* **1** : a dialect or regional pronunciation; *esp* : an Irish accent
broil \'brȯil\ *vb* : to cook by exposure to radiant heat : GRILL — **broil** *n*
broil·er \'brȯi-lər\ *n* **1** : a utensil for broiling **2** : a young chicken fit for broiling
broil·ing \'brȯi(-ə)-liŋ\ *adj* : extremely hot ⟨a ∼ sun⟩
¹broke \'brōk\ *past of* BREAK
²broke *adj* : PENNILESS
¹bro·ken \'brō-kən\ *past part of* BREAK
²broken *adj* **1** : SHATTERED ⟨∼ glass⟩ **2** : having gaps or breaks : INTERRUPTED, DISRUPTED **3** : SUBDUED, CRUSHED ⟨a ∼ spirit⟩ **4** : BANKRUPT **5** : imperfectly spoken ⟨∼ English⟩ — **bro·ken·ly** *adv*
bro·ken·heart·ed \ˌbrō-kən-'här-təd\ *adj* : overcome by grief or despair
bro·ker \'brō-kər\ *n* : an agent who negotiates contracts of purchase and sale — **broker** *vb*
bro·ker·age \'brō-kə-rij\ *n* **1** : the business of a broker **2** : the fee or commission charged by a broker
bro·me·li·ad \brō-'mē-lē-ˌad\ *n* : any of several tropical American ornamental plants related to the pineapple that usu. grow on trees
bro·mide \'brō-ˌmīd\ *n* : a compound of bromine and another element or chemical group including some (as potassium bromide) used as sedatives
bro·mid·ic \brō-'mi-dik\ *adj* : TRITE, UNORIGINAL
bro·mine \'brō-ˌmēn\ *n* [F *brome* bromine, fr. Gk *brōmos* stink] : a deep red liquid corrosive chemical element that gives off an irritating vapor
bronc \'bräŋk\ *n* : an unbroken or partly broken range horse of western No. America; *also* : MUSTANG
bron·chi·al \'bräŋ-kē-əl\ *adj* : of, relating to, or affecting the bronchi or their branches
bron·chi·tis \brän-'kī-təs, bräŋ-\ *n* : inflammation of the bronchi and their branches — **bron·chit·ic** \-'ki-tik\ *adj*

bron·chus \'bräŋ-kəs\ *n, pl* **bron·chi** \'bräŋ-ˌkī, -ˌkē\ : either of the main divisions of the trachea each leading to a lung

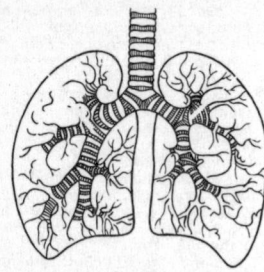

bronchi

bron·co \'bräŋ-kō\ *n, pl* **broncos** [MexSp, fr. Sp, rough, wild] : BRONC

bron·to·sau·rus \ˌbrän-tə-'sȯr-əs\ *also* **bron·to·saur** \'brän-tə-ˌsȯr\ *n* [NL, fr. Gk *brontē* thunder + *sauros* lizard] : any of a genus of large 4-footed sauropod dinosaurs of the Jurassic

Bronx cheer \'bräŋks-\ *n* : RASPBERRY 2

¹**bronze** \'bränz\ *vb* **bronzed; bronz·ing** : to give the appearance of bronze to

²**bronze** *n* **1** : an alloy of copper and tin and sometimes other elements; *also* : something made of bronze **2** : a yellowish brown color — **bronzy** \'brän-zē\ *adj*

brooch \'brōch, 'brüch\ *n* : an ornamental clasp or pin

¹**brood** \'brüd\ *n* : a family of young animals or children and esp. of birds

²**brood** *adj* : kept for breeding ⟨a ∼ mare⟩

³**brood** *vb* **1** : to sit on eggs to hatch them; *also* : to shelter (hatched young) with the wings **2** : to think anxiously or gloomily about something — **brood·ing·ly** *adv*

brood·er \'brü-dər\ *n* **1** : one that broods **2** : a heated structure for raising young birds

¹**brook** \'brük\ *n* : a small natural stream

²**brook** *vb* : TOLERATE, BEAR ⟨would ∼ no interference with his plan⟩

brook·let \'brü-klət\ *n* : a small brook

brook trout *n* : a common speckled cold-water char of No. America

broom \'brüm, 'brům\ *n* **1** : any of several shrubs of the legume family with long slender branches and usu. yellow flowers **2** : an implement with a long handle (**broomstick** \-ˌstik\) used for sweeping

broth \'brȯth\ *n, pl* **broths** \'brȯths, 'brȯthz\ **1** : liquid in which meat or sometimes vegetable food has been cooked **2** : a fluid culture medium

broth·el \'brä-thəl, 'brȯ-\ *n* : a house of prostitution

broth·er \'brə-thər\ *n, pl* **brothers** *also* **breth·ren** \'brethrən, 'bre-thə-; 'bre-thərn\ **1** : a male having one or both parents in common with another individual **2** : a man who is a religious but not a priest **3** : KINSMAN; *also* : SOUL BROTHER — **broth·er·li·ness** \-lē-nəs\ *n* — **broth·er·ly** *adj*

broth·er·hood \'brə-thər-ˌhůd\ *n* **1** : the state of being brothers or a brother **2** : ASSOCIATION, FRATERNITY **3** : the whole body of persons in a business or profession

broth·er–in–law \'brə-thə-rən-ˌlȯ, 'brə-thərn-ˌlȯ\ *n, pl* **brothers–in–law** \'brə-thər-zən-\ : the brother of one's spouse; *also* : the husband of one's sister or of one's spouse's sister

brougham \'brü-(ə)m, 'brō(-ə)m\ *n* : a light closed horse-drawn carriage with the driver outside in front

brought *past and past part of* BRING

brou·ha·ha \'brü-ˌhä-ˌhä\ *n* : HUBBUB, UPROAR

brow \'braů\ *n* **1** : the eyebrow or the ridge on which it grows; *also* : FOREHEAD **2** : the projecting upper part of a steep place

brow·beat \'braů-ˌbēt\ *vb* **-beat; -beat·en** \-ˌbē-tᵊn\ *or* **-beat; -beat·ing** : to intimidate by sternness or arrogance

¹**brown** \'braůn\ *adj* : of the color brown; *also* : of dark or tanned complexion

²**brown** *n* : a color like that of coffee or chocolate that is a blend of red and yellow darkened by black — **brown·ish** *adj*

³**brown** *vb* : to make or become brown

brown bag·ging \-'ba-giŋ\ *n* : the practice of carrying one's lunch usu. in a brown bag — **brown bag·ger** *n*

brown bear *n* : any of various large typically brown-furred bears including the grizzly bear

brown·ie \'braů-nē\ *n* **1** : a legendary cheerful elf who performs good deeds at night **2** *cap* : a member of a program of the Girl Scouts for girls in the first through third grades **3** : a small square or rectangle of chocolate cake

brown·nose \'braůn-ˌnōz\ *vb* : to ingratiate oneself with — **brownnose** *n*

brown·out \'braů-ˌnaůt\ *n* : a period of reduced voltage of electricity caused esp. by high demand and resulting in reduced illumination

brown rice *n* : hulled but unpolished rice that retains most of the bran layers

brown·stone \'braůn-ˌstōn\ *n* : a dwelling faced with reddish-brown sandstone

¹**browse** \'braůz\ *vb* **browsed; brows·ing** **1** : to feed on browse; *also* : GRAZE **2** : to read or look over something in a casual way **3** : to access (a network) with a browser

²**browse** *n* : tender shoots, twigs, and leaves fit for food for cattle

brows·er \'braů-zər\ *n* : a computer program for accessing sites or information on a network (as the World Wide Web)

bru·in \'brü-ən\ *n* : BEAR

¹**bruise** \'brüz\ *vb* **bruised; bruis·ing** **1** : to inflict a bruise on; *also* : to become bruised **2** : to break down (as leaves or berries) by pounding

²**bruise** *n* : a surface injury to flesh : CONTUSION

bruis·er \'brü-zər\ *n* : a big husky man

bruit \'brüt\ *vb* : to make widely known by common report ⟨word of his dismissal was ∼ed about⟩

brunch \'brənch\ *n* : a meal that combines a late breakfast and an early lunch

bru·net *or* **bru·nette** \brü-'net\ *adj* [F *brunet*, masc., *brunette*, fem., brownish, fr. OF, fr. *brun* brown, of Gmc origin] : having brown or black hair and usu. a relatively dark complexion — **brunet** *or* **brunette** *n*

brunt \'brənt\ *n* : the main shock, force, or stress esp. of an attack; *also* : the greater burden

bru·schet·ta \brü-'she-tə, -'ske-\ *n* : an appetizer of grilled bread with toppings

¹**brush** \'brəsh\ *n* **1** : BRUSHWOOD **2** : scrub vegetation or land covered with it

²**brush** *n* **1** : a device composed of bristles set in a handle and used esp. for cleaning or painting **2** : a bushy tail (as of a fox) **3** : an electrical conductor that makes contact between a stationary and a moving part (as of a motor) **4** : a quick light touch in passing

³**brush** *vb* **1** : to treat (as in cleaning or painting) with a brush **2** : to remove with or as if with a brush; *also* : to dismiss in an offhand manner **3** : to touch gently in passing

⁴**brush** *n* : SKIRMISH ⟨a ∼ with the law⟩ ◆ **Synonyms** ENCOUNTER, RUN-IN

brush fire *n* **1** : a fire involving low-growing plants **2** : a minor conflict or crisis

brush–off \'brəsh-ˌȯf\ *n* : a curt offhand dismissal

brush up *vb* : to renew one's skill

brush·wood \'brəsh-ˌwůd\ *n* **1** : small branches of wood esp. when cut **2** : a thicket of shrubs and small trees

brusque \'brəsk\ *adj* [F *brusque*, fr. It *brusco*, fr. ML *bruscus* a plant with stiff twigs used for brooms] : CURT, BLUNT, ABRUPT ⟨a ∼ answer⟩ ◆ **Synonyms** GRUFF, BLUFF, CRUSTY, SHORT — **brusque·ly** *adv*

brus·sels sprout \'brəs-əlz-\ *n, often cap B* : one of the edible green heads borne on the stalk of a plant closely related to the cabbage; *also, pl* : this plant

bru·tal \'brü-tᵊl\ *adj* **1** : befitting a brute : UNFEELING, CRUEL **2** : HARSH, SEVERE ⟨∼ weather⟩ **3** : unpleasantly accurate — **bru·tal·i·ty** \brü-'ta-lə-tē\ *n* — **bru·tal·ly** *adv*

bru·tal·ise *Brit var of* BRUTALIZE

bru·tal·ize \'brü-tᵊl-ˌīz\ *vb* **-ized; -iz·ing** **1** : to make brutal **2** : to treat brutally

¹**brute** \'brüt\ *adj* [ME, fr. MF *brut* rough, fr. L *brutus* brutish, lit., heavy] **1** : of or relating to beasts **2** : BRUTAL **3** : UNREASONING; *also* : purely physical ⟨∼ strength⟩

²**brute** *n* **1** : BEAST 1 **2** : a brutal person

brut·ish \'brü-tish\ *adj* **1** : BRUTE 1 **2** : strongly sensual; *also* : showing little intelligence

BS *abbr* bachelor of science

BSA *abbr* Boy Scouts of America

bskt *abbr* basket

Bt *abbr* baronet

btry *abbr* battery

Btu *abbr* British thermal unit

bu *abbr* bushel

¹**bub·ble** \'bə-bəl\ *n* **1** : a globule of gas in a liquid **2** : a thin film of liquid filled with gas **3** : something lacking firmness or solidity — **bub·bly** *adj*

²**bubble** *vb* **bub·bled; bub·bling** : to form, rise in, or give off bubbles

bub·kes \'bəp-kəs, 'büp-\ *n pl* [Yiddish] : the least amount ⟨didn't win ∼⟩

bu·bo \'bü-bō, 'byü-\ *n, pl* **buboes** : an inflammatory swelling of a lymph gland

bu·bon·ic plague \bü-'bä-nik-, byü-\ *n* : plague caused by a bacterium transmitted to human beings by flea bites and marked esp. by chills and fever and by buboes usu. in the groin

buc·ca·neer \ˌbə-kə-'nir\ *n* : PIRATE

¹**buck** \'bək\ *n, pl* **bucks** **1** *or pl* **buck** : a male animal (as a deer or antelope) **2** : DANDY **3** : DOLLAR

²**buck** *vb* **1** : to spring with an arching leap ⟨a ∼*ing* horse⟩ **2** : to charge against something; *also* : to strive for advancement sometimes without regard to ethical behavior

buck·board \-ˌbȯrd\ *n* : a 4-wheeled horse-drawn wagon with a floor of long springy boards

buck·et \'bə-kət\ *n* **1** : PAIL **2** : an object resembling a bucket in collecting, scooping, or carrying something — **buck·et·ful** *n*

bucket seat *n* : a low separate seat for one person (as in an automobile)

buck·eye \'bə-ˌkī\ *n* : any of various trees or shrubs related to the horse chestnut; *also* : the large nutlike seed of such a shrub or tree

buck fever *n* : nervous excitement of an inexperienced hunter at the sight of game

¹**buck·le** \'bə-kəl\ *n* : a clasp (as on a belt) for two loose ends

²**buckle** *vb* **buck·led; buck·ling** **1** : to fasten with a buckle **2** : to apply oneself with vigor **3** : to crumple up : BEND, COLLAPSE

³**buckle** *n* : BEND, FOLD, KINK

buck·ler \'bə-klər\ *n* : SHIELD

buck·ram \'bə-krəm\ *n* : a coarse stiff cloth used esp. for binding books

buck·saw \'bək-ˌsȯ\ *n* : a saw set in a usu. H-shaped frame for sawing wood

buck·shot \'bək-ˌshät\ *n* : lead shot that is from .24 to .33 inch (about 6.1 to 8.4 millimeters) in diameter

buck·skin \-ˌskin\ *n* **1** : the skin of a buck **2** : a soft usu. suede-finished leather — **buckskin** *adj*

buck·tooth \-'tüth\ *n* : a large protruding front tooth — **buck-toothed** \-'tütht\ *adj*

buck·wheat \-ˌhwēt\ *n* : either of two plants grown for their triangular seeds which are used as a cereal grain; *also* : these seeds

bu·col·ic \byü-'kä-lik\ *adj* [L *bucolicus*, fr. Gk *boukolikos*, fr. *boukolos* cowherd] : PASTORAL, RURAL

¹**bud** \'bəd\ *n* **1** : an undeveloped plant shoot (as of a leaf or a flower); *also* : a partly opened flower **2** : an asexual reproductive structure that detaches from the parent and forms a new individual **3** : something not yet fully developed ⟨nipped in the ∼⟩

²**bud** *vb* **bud·ded; bud·ding** **1** : to form or put forth buds; *also* : to reproduce by asexual buds **2** : to be or develop like a bud **3** : to reproduce a desired variety (as of peach) by inserting a bud in a plant of a different variety

Bud·dhism \'bü-ˌdi-zəm, 'bu-\ *n* : a religion of eastern and central Asia growing out of the teachings of Gautama Buddha — **Bud·dhist** \'bü-dist, 'bu-\ *n or adj*

bud·dy \'bə-dē\ *n, pl* **buddies** **1** : COMPANION; *also* : FRIEND **2** : FELLOW

budge \'bəj\ *vb* **budged; budg·ing** : MOVE, SHIFT; *also* : YIELD

bud·ger·i·gar \'bə-jə-rē-ˌgär\ *n* : a small brightly colored Australian parrot often kept as a pet

¹**bud·get** \'bə-jət\ *n* [ME *bowgette*, fr. MF *bougette*, dim. of *bouge* leather bag, fr. L *bulga*] **1** : STOCK, SUPPLY **2** : a financial report containing estimates of income and expenses; *also* : a plan for coordinating income and expenses **3** : the amount of money available for a particular use — **bud·get·ary** \'bə-jə-ˌter-ē\ *adj*

²**budget** *vb* **1** : to allow for in a budget **2** : to draw up a budget

³**budget** *adj* : INEXPENSIVE

bud·gie \'bə-jē\ *n* : BUDGERIGAR

¹**buff** \'bəf\ *n* **1** : a yellow to orange yellow color **2** : FAN, ENTHUSIAST

²**buff** *adj* : of the color buff

³**buff** *vb* : POLISH, SHINE

buf·fa·lo \'bə-fə-ˌlō\ *n, pl* **-lo** *or* **-loes** *also* **-los** **1** : WATER BUFFALO **2** : a large shaggy-maned No. American wild bovine mammal that has short horns and heavy forequarters with a large muscular hump

buffalo soldier *n* : an African-American soldier serving in the western U.S. after the Civil War

¹**buf·fer** \'bə-fər\ *n* : something or someone that protects or shields (as from physical damage or a financial blow)

²**buffer** *n* : one that buffs

¹**buf·fet** \'bə-fət\ *n* : BLOW, SLAP

²**buffet** *vb* **1** : to strike with the hand; *also* : to pound repeatedly **2** : to struggle against or on ♦ **Synonyms** BEAT, BATTER, DRUB, POMMEL, PUMMEL, THRASH

³**buf·fet** \(ˌ)bə-'fā, bü-\ *n* **1** : SIDEBOARD **2** : a counter for refreshments; *also* : a meal at which people serve themselves informally

buff leather *n* : a strong supple oil-tanned leather

buf·foon \(ˌ)bə-'fün\ *n* [MF *bouffon*, fr. It *buffone*] : CLOWN 2 — **buf·foon·ery** \-'fü-nə-rē\ *n* — **buf·foon·ish** \-'fü-nish\ *adj*

¹**bug** \'bəg\ *n* **1** : an insect or other creeping or crawling invertebrate animal; *esp* : an insect pest (as the cockroach or bedbug **2** : any of an order of insects with sucking mouthparts and incomplete metamorphosis that includes many plant pests **3** : an unexpected flaw or imperfection ⟨a ∼ in a computer program⟩ **4** : a disease-producing germ; *also* : a disease caused by it **5** : a concealed listening device — **bug·gy** \'bə-gəl\ *adj*

²**bug** *vb* **bugged; bug·ging** **1** : BOTHER, ANNOY **2** : to plant a concealed microphone in

³**bug** *vb* **bugged; bug·ging** *of the eyes* : PROTRUDE, BULGE

bug·a·boo \'bə-gə-ˌbü\ *n, pl* **-boos** : BOGEY 1

bug·bear \'bəg-ˌber\ *n* : BOGEY 1; *also* : a source of dread

bug·gy \'bə-gē\ *n, pl* **buggies** : a light horse-drawn carriage; *also* : a carriage for a baby

bu·gle \'byü-gəl\ *n* [ME, buffalo, instrument made of buffalo horn, bugle, fr. AF, fr. L *buculus*, dim. of *bos* head of cattle] : a valveless brass instrument resembling a trumpet and used esp. for military calls — **bu·gler** *n*

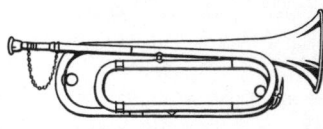

bugle

bug out *vb* **1** : to flee in panic **2** : to depart in a hurry

¹**build** \'bild\ *vb* **built** \'bilt\; **build·ing** **1** : to form or have formed by ordering and uniting materials ⟨∼ a house⟩; *also* : to bring into being or develop **2** : to produce or create gradually ⟨∼ an argument on facts⟩ **3** : INCREASE, ENLARGE; *also* : ENHANCE **4** : to engage in building — **build·er** *n*

²**build** *n* : form or mode of structure; *esp* : PHYSIQUE

build·ing \'bil-diŋ\ *n* **1** : a usu. roofed and walled structure (as a house) for permanent use **2** : the art or business of constructing buildings

build-up \'bild-ˌəp\ *n* : the act or process of building up; *also* : something produced by this

built-in \'bilt-'in\ *adj* **1** : forming an integral part of a structure **2** : INHERENT
bulb \'bəlb\ *n* **1** : an underground resting stage of a plant (as a lily or an onion) consisting of a short stem base bearing one or more buds enclosed in overlapping leaves; *also* : a fleshy plant structure (as a tuber) resembling a bulb **2** : a plant having or growing from a bulb **3** : a rounded more or less bulb-shaped object or part (as for an electric lamp) — **bul·bous** \'bəl-bəs\ *adj*
¹**bulge** \'bəlj\ *vb* **bulged; bulg·ing** : to become or cause to become protuberant
²**bulge** *n* : a swelling projecting part
bu·li·mia \bü-'lē-mē-ə, byü-, -'li-\ *n* **1** : an abnormal and constant craving for food **2** : a serious eating disorder chiefly of females that is characterized by compulsive overeating usu. followed by self-induced vomiting or laxative or diuretic abuse — **bu·lim·ic** \-'lē-mik, -'li-\ *adj or n*
¹**bulk** \'bəlk\ *n* **1** : MAGNITUDE, VOLUME **2** : material that forms a mass in the intestine; *esp* : FIBER 2 **3** : a large mass **4** : the major portion
²**bulk** *vb* **1** : to cause to swell or bulge **2** : to appear as a factor : LOOM
bulk·head \'bəlk-,hed\ *n* **1** : a partition separating compartments **2** : a structure built to cover a shaft or a cellar stairway
bulky \'bəl-kē\ *adj* **bulk·i·er; -est** : having bulk; *esp* : being large and unwieldy
¹**bull** \'bul\ *n* **1** : a male bovine animal; *also* : a usu. adult male of various large animals (as the moose, elephant, or whale) **2** : one who buys securities or commodities in expectation of a price increase — **bull·ish** *adj*
²**bull** *adj* **1** : of, relating to, or suggestive of a bull : MALE **2** : large of its kind ⟨a ~ lathe⟩
³**bull** *n* [ME *bulle*, fr. ML *bulla*, fr. L, bubble, amulet] **1** : a papal letter **2** : DECREE
⁴**bull** *n, slang* : NONSENSE
⁵**bull** *abbr* bulletin
¹**bull·dog** \'bul-,dog\ *n* : any of a breed of compact muscular short-haired dogs of English origin
²**bulldog** *vb* **1** : to throw (a steer) by seizing the horns and twisting the neck
bull·doze \-,dōz\ *vb* **1** : to move, clear, or level with a tractor-driven machine (**bull·doz·er**) having a broad blade for pushing **2** : to force as if by using a bulldozer
bul·let \'bu-lət\ *n* [MF *boulette* small ball & *boulet* missile, dims. of *boule* ball, fr. L *bulla* bubble] : a missile to be shot from a firearm
bul·le·tin \'bu-lə-t³n\ *n* **1** : a brief public report intended for immediate release on a matter of public interest **2** : a periodical publication (as of a college)
bulletin board *n* **1** : a board for posting notices **2** : a public forum on a computer network in which users write or read messages or download files
bul·let·proof \'bu-lət-,prüf\ *adj* **1** : impenetrable to bullets **2** : not subject to correction, alteration, or modification **3** : INVINCIBLE
bull·fight \'bul-,fīt\ *n* : a spectacle in which people ceremonially fight with and usu. kill bulls in an arena — **bull·fight·er** *n*
bull·frog \-,frog, -,fräg\ *n* : a large deep-voiced frog
bull·head \-,hed\ *n* : any of several common large-headed freshwater catfishes of the U.S.
bull·head·ed \-'he-dəd\ *adj* : stupidly stubborn : HEADSTRONG
bul·lion \'bul-yən\ *n* : gold or silver esp. in bars or ingots
bull market *n* : a market in which securities or commodities are persistently rising in value
bull·ock \'bu-lək\ *n* : a young bull; *also* : STEER
bull pen *n* : a place on a baseball field where pitchers warm up; *also* : the relief pitchers of a baseball team
bull session *n* : an informal discussion
bull's-eye \'bulz-,ī\ *n, pl* **bull's-eyes** : the center of a target; *also* : a shot that hits the bull's-eye
¹**bul·ly** \'bu-lē\ *n, pl* **bullies** : a person habitually cruel to others who are weaker
²**bully** *adj* : EXCELLENT, FIRST-RATE — often used interjectionally ⟨~ for you⟩
³**bully** *vb* **bul·lied; bul·ly·ing** : to behave as a bully toward : DOMINEER ✦ *Synonyms* BROWBEAT, INTIMIDATE, HECTOR

bul·rush \'bul-,rəsh\ *n* : any of several large rushes or sedges of wetlands
bul·wark \'bul-(,)wərk, -,work; 'bəl-(,)wərk\ *n* **1** : a wall-like defensive structure **2** : a strong support or protection
¹**bum** \'bəm\ *adj* **1** : of poor quality ⟨~ advice⟩ **2** : disabled by damage or injury ⟨a ~ knee⟩
²**bum** *vb* **bummed; bum·ming 1** : to spend time unemployed and wandering; *also* : LOAF **2** : to obtain by begging
³**bum** *n* **1** : LOAFER **2** : one whose time is devoted to a recreational activity ⟨a ski ~⟩ **3** : TRAMP 1
bum·ble \'bəm-bəl\ *vb* **bum·bled; bum·bling 1** : to speak in a stuttering and faltering manner **2** : to proceed unsteadily **3** : BUNGLE
bum·ble·bee \'bəm-bəl-,bē\ *n* : any of numerous large hairy social bees
bum·mer \'bə-mər\ *n* **1** : an unpleasant experience **2** : FAILURE
¹**bump** \'bəmp\ *n* **1** : a local bulge; *esp* : a swelling of tissue **2** : a sudden forceful blow or impact — **bumpy** *adj*
²**bump** *vb* **1** : to strike or knock forcibly; *also* : to move by or as if by bumping **2** : to collide with
¹**bump·er** \'bəm-pər\ *n* **1** : a cup or glass filled to the brim **2** : something unusually large — **bumper** *adj*
²**bump·er** \'bəm-pər\ *n* : a device for absorbing shock or preventing damage; *esp* : a usu. metal bar at either end of an automobile
bump·kin \'bəmp-kən\ *n* : an awkward and unsophisticated country person
bump·tious \'bəmp-shəs\ *adj* : obtusely and often noisily self-assertive
bun \'bən\ *n* : a sweet biscuit or roll
¹**bunch** \'bənch\ *n* **1** : SWELLING **2** : CLUSTER, GROUP — **bunchy** *adj*
²**bunch** *vb* : to form into a group or bunch
bun·co *or* **bun·ko** \'bəŋ-kō\ *n, pl* **buncos** *or* **bunkos** : a swindling scheme — **bunco** *vb*
¹**bun·dle** \'bən-d³l\ *n* **1** : several items bunched and fastened together; *also* : something wrapped for carrying **2** : a considerable amount : LOT **3** : a small band of mostly parallel nerve or muscle fibers **4** : a package offering related products or services at a single price
²**bundle** *vb* **bun·dled; bun·dling** : to gather or tie in a bundle
bundling *n* : a former custom of a courting couple's occupying the same bed without undressing
bung \'bəŋ\ *n* : the stopper in the bunghole of a cask
bun·ga·low \'bəŋ-gə-,lō\ *n* [Hindi & Urdu *banglā*, lit., (house) in the Bengal style] : a one-storied house with a low-pitched roof
bun·gee cord \'bən-jē-\ *n* : a long elastic cord used esp. as a fastening or shock-absorbing device
bungee jump *vb* : to jump from a height while attached to a bungee cord — **bungee jumper** *n*
bung·hole \'bəŋ-,hōl\ *n* : a hole for emptying or filling a cask
bun·gle \'bəŋ-gəl\ *vb* **bun·gled; bun·gling** : to do badly : BOTCH — **bungle** *n* — **bun·gler** *n*
bun·ion \'bən-yən\ *n* : an inflamed swelling of the first joint of the big toe
¹**bunk** \'bəŋk\ *n* : BED; *esp* : a built-in bed that is often one of a tier
²**bunk** *n* : BUNKUM, NONSENSE
bunk bed *n* : one of two single beds usu. placed one above the other
bun·ker \'bəŋ-kər\ *n* **1** : a bin or compartment for storage (as for coal on a ship) **2** : a protective embankment or dugout **3** : a sand trap or embankment constituting a hazard on a golf course
bun·kum *or* **bun·combe** \'bəŋ-kəm\ *n* [*Buncombe* County, N.C.; fr. a remark made by its congressman, who defended an irrelevant speech by claiming that he was speaking to Buncombe] : insincere or foolish talk
bun·ny \'bə-nē\ *n, pl* **-nies** : RABBIT
bunny slope *n* : a gentle incline used by novice skiers — called also *bunny hill*
Bun·sen burner \'bən-sən-\ *n* : a gas burner usu. consisting of a straight tube with air holes at the bottom
¹**bunt** \'bənt\ *vb* **1** : ¹BUTT **2** : to push or tap a baseball lightly without swinging the bat
²**bunt** *n* : an act or instance of bunting; *also* : a bunted ball

¹bun·ting \'bən-tiŋ\ *n* : any of numerous small stout-billed finches

²bunting *n* : a thin fabric used esp. for flags; *also* : FLAGS

¹buoy \'bü-ē, 'bȯi\ *n* 1 : a floating object anchored in water to mark something (as a channel) 2 : a float consisting of a ring of buoyant material to support a person who has fallen into the water

²buoy *vb* 1 : to mark by a buoy 2 : to keep afloat 3 : to raise the spirits of

buoy·an·cy \'bȯi-ən-sē, 'bü-yən-\ *n* 1 : the tendency of a body to float or rise when submerged in a fluid 2 : the power of a fluid to exert an upward force on a body placed in it 3 : resilience of spirit — buoy·ant \-ənt, -yənt\ *adj*

¹bur *var of* BURR

²bur *abbr* bureau

burbs \'bərbz\ *n pl* : SUBURBS

¹bur·den \'bər-dᵊn\ *n* 1 : LOAD; *also* : CARE, RESPONSIBILITY 2 : something oppressive : ENCUMBRANCE 3 : CARGO; *also* : capacity for cargo

²burden *vb* : LOAD, OPPRESS — bur·den·some \-səm\ *adj*

³burden *n* 1 : REFRAIN, CHORUS 2 : a main theme or idea : GIST

bur·dock \'bər-ˌdäk\ *n* : any of a genus of coarse composite herbs with globe-shaped flower heads surrounded by prickly bracts

bu·reau \'byūr-ō\ *n, pl* bureaus *also* bu·reaux \-ōz\ [F, desk, cloth covering for desks, fr. OF *burel* woolen cloth, ultim. fr. L *burra* shaggy cloth] 1 : a chest of drawers 2 : an administrative unit (as of a government department) 3 : a branch of a publication or wire service in an important news center

bu·reau·cra·cy \byū-'rä-krə-sē\ *n, pl* -cies 1 : a body of appointive government officials 2 : government marked by specialization of functions under fixed rules and a hierarchy of authority; *also* : an unwieldy administrative system burdened with excessive complexity and lack of flexibility — bu·reau·crat \'byūr-ə-ˌkrat\ *n* — bu·reau·crat·ic \ˌbyūr-ə-'kra-tik\ *adj*

bur·geon \'bər-jən\ *vb* : to put forth fresh growth (as from buds) : grow vigorously : FLOURISH

burgh \'bər-ō\ *n* : a Scottish town

bur·gher \'bər-gər\ *n* 1 : TOWNSMAN 2 : a prosperous solid citizen

bur·glary \'bər-glə-rē\ *n, pl* -glar·ies : forcible entry into a building esp. at night with the intent to commit a crime (as theft) — bur·glar \-glər\ *n* — bur·glar·ize \'bər-glə-ˌrīz\ *vb*

bur·gle \'bər-gəl\ *vb* bur·gled; bur·gling : to commit burglary on

bur·go·mas·ter \'bər-gə-ˌmas-tər\ *n* : the chief magistrate of a town in some European countries

bur·gun·dy \'bər-gən-dē\ *n, pl* -dies *often cap* 1 : a red or white table wine from the Burgundy region of France 2 : a blended red wine

buri·al \'ber-ē-əl\ *n* : the act or process of burying

bur·ka *or* bur·qa \'bür-kə\ *n* : a loose garment that covers the face and body and is worn in public by certain Muslim women

burl \'bərl\ *n* : a hard woody often flattened hemispherical outgrowth on a tree

bur·lap \'bər-ˌlap\ *n* : a coarse fabric usu. of jute or hemp used esp. for bags

¹bur·lesque \(ˌ)bər-'lesk\ *n* [*burlesque*, adj., comic, droll, fr. F, fr. It *burlesco*, fr. *burla* joke, fr. Sp] 1 : a witty or derisive literary or dramatic imitative work 2 : broadly humorous theatrical entertainment consisting of several items (as songs, skits, or dances)

²burlesque *vb* bur·lesqued; bur·lesqu·ing : to make ludicrous by burlesque ✦ *Synonyms* CARICATURE, PARODY, TRAVESTY

bur·ly \'bər-lē\ *adj* bur·li·er; -est : strongly and heavily built : HUSKY ✦ *Synonyms* MUSCULAR, BRAWNY, BEEFY, HEFTY

¹burn \'bərn\ *vb* burned \'bərnd, 'bərnt\ *or* burnt \'bərnt\; burn·ing 1 : to be on fire 2 : to feel or look as if on fire 3 : to alter or become altered by or as if by the action of fire or heat 4 : to use as fuel ⟨~ coal⟩; *also* : to destroy by fire ⟨~ trash⟩ 5 : to cause or make by fire ⟨~ a hole⟩; *also* : to affect as if by heat 6 : to record digital data or music on (an optical disk) using a laser ⟨~ a CD⟩

²burn *n* : an injury or effect produced by or as if by burning

burn·er \'bər-nər\ *n* : the part of a fuel-burning or heat=producing device where the flame or heat is produced

bur·nish \'bər-nish\ *vb* : to make shiny esp. by rubbing : POLISH — bur·nish·er *n* — bur·nish·ing *adj or n*

bur·noose *or* bur·nous \(ˌ)bər-'nüs\ *n* : a hooded cloak worn esp. by Arabs

burn·out \'bərn-ˌaùt\ *n* 1 : the cessation of operation of a jet or rocket engine 2 : exhaustion of one's physical or emotional strength; *also* : a person suffering from burnout

burp \'bərp\ *n* : an act of belching — burp *vb*

burp gun *n* : a small submachine gun

burr \'bər\ *n* 1 *usu* bur : a rough or prickly envelope of a fruit; *also* : a plant that bears burs 2 : roughness left in cutting or shaping metal 3 : a trilled \r\ as used by some speakers in northern England and Scotland 4 : WHIR — bur·ry *adj*

bur·ri·to \bə-'rē-tō\ *n* [AmerSp, fr. Sp, little donkey, dim. of *burro*] : a flour tortilla rolled around a filling and baked

bur·ro \'bər-ō, 'bùr-\ *n, pl* burros [Sp] : a usu. small donkey

¹bur·row \'bər-ō\ *n* : a hole in the ground made by an animal (as a rabbit)

²burrow *vb* 1 : to form by tunneling; *also* : to make a burrow 2 : to progress by or as if by digging — bur·row·er *n*

bur·sar \'bər-sər\ *n* : a treasurer esp. of a college

bur·si·tis \(ˌ)bər-'sī-təs\ *n* : inflammation of the serous sac (bur·sa \'bər-sə\) of a joint (as the elbow or shoulder)

¹burst \'bərst\ *vb* burst *or* burst·ed; burst·ing 1 : to fly apart or into pieces 2 : to show one's feelings suddenly; *also* : PLUNGE ⟨~ into song⟩ 3 : to enter or emerge suddenly : SPRING 4 : to be filled to the breaking point

²burst *n* 1 : a sudden outbreak : SPURT 2 : EXPLOSION 3 : result of bursting

bury \'ber-ē\ *vb* bur·ied; bury·ing 1 : to deposit in the earth; *also* : to inter with funeral ceremonies 2 : CONCEAL, HIDE 3 : SUBMERGE, ENGROSS — usu. used with *in* ⟨*buried* himself in work⟩

¹bus \'bəs\ *n, pl* bus·es *also* bus·ses [short for *omnibus*, fr. F, fr. L, for all, dat. pl. of *omnis* all] : a large motor vehicle for carrying passengers

²bus *vb* bused *or* bussed; bus·ing *or* bus·sing 1 : to travel or transport by bus 2 : to work as a busboy

³bus *abbr* business

bus·boy \'bəs-ˌbȯi\ *n* : a waiter's helper

bus·by \'bəz-bē\ *n, pl* busbies : a military full-dress fur hat

bush \'bùsh\ *n* 1 : SHRUB 2 : rough uncleared country 3 : a thick tuft ⟨a ~ of hair⟩ — bushy *adj*

bushed \'bùsht\ *adj* : TIRED, EXHAUSTED

bush·el \'bù-shəl\ *n* — see WEIGHT table

bush·ing \'bù-shiŋ\ *n* : a usu. removable cylindrical lining for an opening of a mechanical part to limit the size of the opening, resist wear, or serve as a guide

bush·mas·ter \'bùsh-ˌmas-tər\ *n* : a large venomous pit viper of Central and So. America

bush·whack \-ˌhwak\ *vb* 1 : AMBUSH 2 : to clear a path through esp. by chopping down bushes and branches — bush·whack·er *n*

busi·ness \'biz-nəs, -nəz\ *n* 1 : OCCUPATION; *also* : TASK, MISSION 2 : a commercial or industrial enterprise; *also* : TRADE ⟨~ is good⟩ 3 : AFFAIR, MATTER 4 : personal concern

busi·ness·man \-ˌman\ *n* : a man engaged in business esp. as an executive

busi·ness·per·son \-ˌpər-sᵊn\ *n* : a businessman or businesswoman

busi·ness·wom·an \-ˌwù-mən\ *n* : a woman engaged in business esp. as an executive

bus·kin \'bəs-kən\ *n* 1 : a laced boot reaching halfway to the knee 2 : tragic drama

buss \'bəs\ *n* : KISS — buss *vb*

¹bust \'bəst\ *n* [F *buste*, fr. It *busto*, fr. L *bustum* tomb] 1 : sculpture representing the upper part of the human figure 2 : the part of the human torso between the neck and the waist; *esp* : the breasts of a woman

²bust *vb* bust·ed; bust·ing 1 : BREAK, SMASH; *also* : BURST 2 : to ruin financially 3 : TAME 4 : DEMOTE 5 *slang* : ARREST; *also* : RAID

³bust *n* 1 : a drinking session 2 : a complete failure : FLOP 3 : a business depression 4 : PUNCH, SOCK 5 *slang* : a police raid; *also* : ARREST

¹bus·tle \'bə-səl\ *vb* bus·tled; bus·tling : to move or work in a brisk busy manner

²**bustle** *n* : briskly energetic activity

³**bustle** *n* : a pad or frame worn to support the fullness at the back of a woman's skirt

¹**busy** \'bi-zē\ *adj* **busi·er; -est** **1** : engaged in action : not idle **2** : being in use ⟨~ telephones⟩ **3** : full of activity ⟨~ streets⟩ **4** : MEDDLING — **busi·ly** \'bi-zə-lē\ *adv*

²**busy** *vb* **bus·ied; busy·ing** : to make or keep busy : OC-CUPY

busy·body \'bi-zē-ˌbä-dē\ *n* : MEDDLER

busy·work \-ˌwərk\ *n* : work that appears productive but only keeps one occupied

¹**but** \'bət\ *conj* **1** : except for the fact ⟨would have protested ~ that he was afraid⟩ **2** : THAT ⟨there's no doubt ~ he won⟩ **3** : without the certainty that ⟨never rains ~ it pours⟩ **4** : on the contrary ⟨not one, ~ two job offers⟩ **5** : YET ⟨poor ~ proud⟩ **6** : with the exception of ⟨none ~ the strongest attempt it⟩

²**but** *prep* : other than : EXCEPT ⟨this letter is nothing ~ an insult⟩; *also* : with the exception of ⟨no one here ~ me⟩

bu·tane \'byü-ˌtān\ *n* : either of two gaseous hydrocarbons used as a fuel

butch \'bủch\ *adj* : notably masculine in appearance or manner

¹**butch·er** \'bủ-chər\ *n* [ME *bocher*, fr. AF, fr. *buc* he-goat] **1** : one who slaughters animals or dresses their flesh; *also* : a dealer in meat **2** : one that kills brutally or needlessly **3** : one that botches — **butch·ery** \-chə-rē\ *n*

²**butcher** *vb* **1** : to slaughter and dress for meat ⟨~ hogs⟩ **2** : to kill barbarously **3** : BOTCH

but·ler \'bət-lər\ *n* [ME *buteler*, fr. AF *butiller*, † fr. OF *botele* bottle] : the chief male servant of a household

¹**butt** \'bət\ *vb* : to strike with the head or horns

²**butt** *n* : a blow or thrust with the head or horns

³**butt** *n* : a large cask

⁴**butt** *n* **1** : TARGET **2** : an object of abuse or ridicule

⁵**butt** *n* **1** : BUTTOCKS **2** : a large, thicker, or bottom end of something

⁶**butt** *vb* **1** : ABUT — used with *on* or *against* **2** : to place or join edge to edge without overlapping

butte \'byüt\ *n* : an isolated steep hill

¹**but·ter** \'bə-tər\ *n* [ME, fr. OE *butere*, fr. L *butyrum* butter, fr. Gk *boutyron*, fr. *bous* cow + *tyros* cheese] **1** : a solid edible emulsion of fat obtained from cream by churning **2** : a substance resembling butter — **but·tery** *adj*

²**butter** *vb* : to spread with or as if with butter

but·ter–and–eggs \ˌbə-tər-ᵊn-ˈnegz\ *n sing or pl* : a common perennial herb related to the snapdragon that has showy yellow and orange flowers

butter bean *n* **1** : LIMA BEAN **2** : WAX BEAN **3** : a green shell bean

but·ter·cream \'bə-tər-ˌkrēm\ *n* : a sweet butter-based mixture used esp. as a filling or frosting

but·ter·cup \'bə-tər-ˌkəp\ *n* : any of a genus of herbs having usu. yellow flowers with five petals and sepals

but·ter·fat \-ˌfat\ *n* : the natural fat of milk and chief constituent of butter

but·ter·fin·gered \-ˌfiŋ-gərd\ *adj* : likely to let things fall or slip through the fingers — **but·ter·fin·gers** \-gərz\ *n sing or pl*

but·ter·fly \-ˌflī\ *n* : any of a group of slender day-flying insects with broad often brightly-colored wings

but·ter·milk \-ˌmilk\ *n* : the liquid remaining after butter is churned

but·ter·nut \-ˌnət\ *n* : the sweet egg-shaped nut of an American tree related to the walnut; *also* : this tree

butternut squash *n* : a smooth buff-colored cylindrical winter squash

but·ter·scotch \-ˌskäch\ *n* : a candy made from brown sugar, corn syrup, and water; *also* : the flavor of such candy

but·tock \'bə-tək\ *n* **1** : the back of a hip that forms one of the fleshy parts on which a person sits **2** *pl* : the seat of the body : RUMP

¹**but·ton** \'bə-tᵊn\ *n* **1** : a small knob secured to an article (as of clothing) and used as a fastener by passing it through a buttonhole or loop **2** : something that resembles a button **3** : PUSH BUTTON **4** : a hidden sensitivity that can be manipulated to produce a desired response **5** : a usu. box-shaped computer icon that initiates a software function

²**button** *vb* : to close or fasten with or as if with buttons

¹**but·ton·hole** \'bə-tᵊn-ˌhōl\ *n* : a slit or loop for a button to pass through

²**buttonhole** *vb* : to detain in conversation by or as if by holding on to the outer garments of

¹**but·tress** \'bə-trəs\ *n* [ME *butres*, fr. AF (*arche*) *boteraz* thrusting (arch), ultim. fr. *buter* to thrust] **1** : a projecting structure to support a wall **2** : PROP, SUPPORT

²**buttress** *vb* : PROP, SUPPORT

bu·tut \bủ-ˈtüt\ *n*, *pl* **bututs** *or* **butut** — see *dalasi* at MONEY table

bux·om \'bək-səm\ *adj* : healthily plump; *esp* : full-bosomed

¹**buy** \'bī\ *vb* **bought** \'bȯt\; **buy·ing** **1** : to obtain for a price : PURCHASE; *also* : BRIBE **2** : to accept as true — **buy·er** *n*

²**buy** *n* **1** : PURCHASE 1, 2 **2** : an exceptional value : BARGAIN

¹**buzz** \'bəz\ *vb* **1** : to make a buzz **2** : to fly fast and close to

²**buzz** *n* **1** : a low humming sound **2** : RUMOR, GOSSIP

buz·zard \'bə-zərd\ *n* : any of various usu. large birds of prey and esp. the turkey vulture

buzz·er \'bə-zər\ *n* : a device that signals with a buzzing sound

buzz saw *n* : CIRCULAR SAW

buzz·word \'baz-ˌwərd\ *n* : a voguish word or phrase often from technical jargon

BVM *abbr* Blessed Virgin Mary

BWI *abbr* British West Indies

bx *abbr* box

BX *abbr* base exchange

¹**by** \'bī, bə\ *prep* **1** : NEAR ⟨stood ~ the window⟩ **2** : through or through the medium of : VIA ⟨left ~ the door⟩ **3** : PAST ⟨drove ~ the house⟩ **4** : DURING, AT ⟨studied ~ night⟩ **5** : no later than ⟨get here ~ 3 p.m.⟩ **6** : through the means or direct agency of ⟨~ force⟩ **7** : in conformity with; *also* : ACCORDING TO ⟨did it ~ the book⟩ **8** : with respect to ⟨a doctor ~ profession⟩ **9** : to the amount or extent of ⟨won ~ a nose⟩ **10** — used to express relationship in multiplication, in division, and in measurements ⟨divide *a* ~ *b*⟩ ⟨multiply ~ 6⟩ ⟨15 feet ~ 20 feet⟩

²**by** \'bī\ *adv* **1** : near at hand; *also* : IN ⟨stop ~⟩ **2** : PAST ⟨saw him go ~⟩ **3** : ASIDE, APART

bye \'bī\ *n* : a position of a participant in a tournament who advances to the next round without playing

by–elec·tion *also* **bye–election** \'bī-ə-ˌlek-shən\ *n* : a special election held between regular elections in order to fill a vacancy

by·gone \'bī-ˌgȯn\ *adj* : gone by : PAST — **bygone** *n*

by·law *also* **bye·law** \'bī-ˌlȯ\ *n* : a rule adopted by an organization for managing its internal affairs

by–line \'bī-ˌlīn\ *n* : a line at the beginning of a news story or magazine article giving the writer's name

BYO *abbr* bring your own

BYOB *abbr* bring your own beer; bring your own booze; bring your own bottle

¹**by·pass** \'bī-ˌpas\ *n* : a passage to one side or around a blocked or congested area; *also* : a surgical procedure establishing this ⟨a coronary ~⟩

²**bypass** *vb* : to avoid by means of a bypass

by·path \-ˌpath, -ˌpäth\ *n* : BYWAY

by·play \'bī-ˌplā\ *n* : action engaged in on the side (as of a stage) while the main action proceeds

by–prod·uct \-ˌprä-(ˌ)dəkt\ *n* : a sometimes unexpected product or result produced in addition to the main product or result

by·stand·er \-ˌstan-dər\ *n* : one present but not participating **♦ Synonyms** ONLOOKER, WITNESS, SPECTATOR, EYEWITNESS

byte \'bīt\ *n* : a unit of computer information consisting of a group of 8 bits

by·way \'bī-ˌwā\ *n* **1** : a little-traveled side road **2** : a secondary aspect

by·word \-ˌwərd\ *n* **1** : PROVERB **2** : one that is noteworthy or notorious

Byz·an·tine \'biz-ᵊn-ˌtēn, 'bī-, -ˌtīn; bə-ˈzan-, bī-\ *adj* **1** : of, relating to, or characteristic of the ancient city of Byzantium or the Byzantine Empire **2** *often not cap* : intricately involved and often devious

¹**c** \'sē\ *n, pl* **c's** *or* **cs** \'sēz\ *often cap* **1** : the 3d letter of the English alphabet **2** : one hundred in Roman numerals **3** *slang* : a sum of $100 **4** : a grade rating a student's work as fair

²**c** *abbr, often cap* **1** calorie **2** carat **3** Celsius **4** cent **5** centigrade **6** centimeter **7** century **8** chapter **9** circa **10** cocaine **11** copyright

C *symbol* carbon

ca *abbr* circa

Ca *symbol* calcium

CA *abbr* **1** California **2** chartered accountant **3** chief accountant **4** chronological age

cab \'kab\ *n* **1** : a light closed horse-drawn carriage **2** : TAXICAB **3** : the covered compartment for the engineer and controls of a locomotive; *also* : a similar compartment (as on a truck) — **cab** *vb*

CAB *abbr* Civil Aeronautics Board

ca·bal \kə-'bäl, -'bal\ *n* [F *cabale*, fr. ML *cabbala* cabala, fr. Heb *qabbālāh*, lit., received (lore)] **1** : a secret group of plotters or political conspirators **2** : CLUB, GROUP ⟨∼ of artists⟩

cabala *var of* KABALLAH

ca·bana \kə-'ban-yə, -'ba-nə\ *n* : a shelter at a beach or swimming pool

cab·a·ret \ˌka-bə-'rā\ *n* : NIGHTCLUB

cab·bage \'ka-bij\ *n* [ME *caboche*, fr. MF dial., lit., head, noggin] : a vegetable related to the mustard with a dense head of leaves

cab·bie *or* **cab·by** \'ka-bē\ *n, pl* **cabbies** : a driver of a cab

cab·er·net sau·vi·gnon \ˌka-bər-'nā-sō-vē-'nyōⁿ\ *n* : a dry red wine made from a single variety of black grape

cab·in \'ka-bən\ *n* **1** : a private room on a ship; *also* : a compartment below deck on a boat for passengers or crew **2** : an aircraft or spacecraft compartment for passengers, crew, or cargo **3** : a small simple one-story house

cabin boy *n* : a boy working as servant on a ship

cabin class *n* : a class of accommodations on a passenger ship superior to tourist class and inferior to first class

cabin cruiser *n* : CRUISER 3

cab·i·net \'kab-nit\ *n* **1** : a case or cupboard for holding or displaying articles **2** : the advisory council of a head of state (as a president or sovereign)

cab·i·net·mak·er \-ˌmā-kər\ *n* : a woodworker who makes fine furniture — **cab·i·net·mak·ing** *n*

cab·i·net·work \-ˌwərk\ *n* : the finished work of a cabinet-maker

¹**ca·ble** \'kā-bəl\ *n* **1** : a very strong rope, wire, or chain **2** : a bundle of insulated wires usu. twisted around a central core **3** : CABLEGRAM **4** : CABLE TELEVISION

²**cable** *vb* **ca·bled; ca·bling** : to telegraph by cable

cable car *n* : a vehicle moved by an endless cable

ca·ble·cast \'kā-bəl-ˌkast\ *n* : a cable television transmission — **cablecast** *vb*

ca·ble·gram \'kā-bəl-ˌgram\ *n* : a message sent by a submarine telegraph cable

cable modem *n* : a modem for connecting a computer to a network over a cable television line

cable television *n* : a system of television reception in which signals from distant stations are sent by cable to the receivers of paying subscribers

cab·o·chon \'ka-bə-ˌshän\ *n* : a gem or bead cut in convex form and highly polished but not given facets; *also* : this style of cutting — **cabochon** *adv*

ca·boose \kə-'büs\ *n* : a car usu. at the rear of a freight train for the use of the train crew and railroad workers

cab·ri·o·let \ˌka-brē-ə-'lā\ *n* [F] **1** : a light 2-wheeled one-horse carriage **2** : a convertible coupe

cab·stand \'kab-ˌstand\ *n* : a place where cabs wait for passengers

ca·cao \kə-'kaù, -'kā-ō\ *n, pl* **cacaos** [Sp, fr. Nahuatl *cacahuatl*] : a So. American tree whose seeds (**cacao beans**)

are the source of cocoa and chocolate; *also* : its dried fatty seeds

cac·cia·to·re \ˌkä-chə-'tōr-ē\ *adj* [It] : cooked with tomatoes and herbs ⟨chicken ∼⟩

cache \'kash\ *n* [F] : a hiding place esp. for preserving provisions; *also* : something hidden or stored in a cache — **cache** *vb*

ca·chet \ka-'shā\ *n* [F] **1** : a seal used esp. as a mark of official approval **2** : a feature or quality conferring prestige; *also* : PRESTIGE **3** : a design, inscription, or advertisement printed or stamped on mail

cack·le \'ka-kəl\ *vb* **cack·led; cack·ling 1** : to make the sharp broken cry characteristic of a hen **2** : to laugh or chatter noisily — **cackle** *n* — **cack·ler** *n*

ca·coph·o·ny \ka-'kä-fə-nē\ *n, pl* **-nies** : harsh or discordant sound — **ca·coph·o·nous** \-nəs\ *adj*

cac·tus \'kak-təs\ *n, pl* **cac·ti** \-ˌtī\ *or* **cac·tus·es** *also* **cactus** : any of a large family of drought-resistant flowering plants with succulent stems and with leaves replaced by scales or prickles

cad \'kad\ *n* : a man who deliberately disregards another's feelings — **cad·dish** \'ka-dish\ *adj* — **cad·dish·ly** *adv* — **cad·dish·ness** *n*

ca·dav·er \kə-'da-vər\ *n* : a dead body

ca·dav·er·ous \kə-'da-və-rəs\ *adj* : suggesting a corpse esp. in gauntness or pallor ✦ **Synonyms** WASTED, EMACIATED, GAUNT — **ca·dav·er·ous·ly** *adv*

cad·die *or* **cad·dy** \'ka-dē\ *n, pl* **caddies** [Sc, errand boy, modif. of F *cadet* military cadet] : a person who assists a golfer esp. by carrying the clubs — **caddie** *or* **caddy** *vb*

cad·dy \'ka-dē\ *n, pl* **caddies** [Malay *kati* a unit of weight] : a small box, can, or chest; *esp* : one to keep tea in

ca·dence \'kād-ᵊns\ *n* : the measure or beat of a rhythmical flow : RHYTHM — **ca·denced** \-ᵊnst\ *adj*

ca·den·za \kə-'den-zə\ *n* [It] : a brilliant sometimes improvised passage usu. toward the close of a musical composition

ca·det \kə-'det\ *n* [F, fr. Occitan (Gascony) *capdet* chief, fr. L *capitellum*, fr. L *caput* head] **1** : a younger son or brother **2** : a student in a service academy

Ca·dette \kə-'det\ *n* : a member of a Girl Scout program for girls in sixth through ninth grades

cadge \'kaj\ *vb* **cadged; cadg·ing** : SPONGE, BEG ⟨∼ a free meal⟩ — **cadg·er** *n*

cad·mi·um \'kad-mē-əm\ *n* : a bluish-white metallic chemical element used esp. in protective platings

cad·re \'ka-ˌdrā, 'kä-, -drē\ *n* [F] **1** : FRAMEWORK **2** : a central unit esp. of trained personnel able to assume control and train others **3** : a group of indoctrinated leaders active in promoting the interests of a revolutionary party

ca·du·ceus \kə-'dü-sē-əs, -'dyü-, -shəs\ *n, pl* **-cei** \-sē-ˌī\ [L] **1** : the staff of a herald; *esp* : a representation of a staff with two entwined snakes and two wings at the top **2** : an insignia bearing a caduceus and symbolizing a physician

cae·cum *var of* CECUM

Cae·sar \'sē-zər\ *n* **1** : any of the Roman emperors succeeding Augustus Caesar — used as a title **2** *often not cap* : a powerful ruler : AUTOCRAT, DICTATOR; *also* : the civil or temporal power

caesarean *also* **caesarian** *var of* CESAREAN

cae·si·um *chiefly Brit var of* CESIUM

cae·su·ra \si-'zhùr-ə\ *n, pl* **-suras** *or* **-su·rae** \-'zhùr-(ˌ)ē\ : a break in the flow of sound usu. in the middle of a line of verse

ca·fé \ka-'fā\ *n* [F, lit., coffee] **1** : RESTAURANT **2** : BARROOM **3** : NIGHTCLUB

ca·fé au lait \ˌka-ˌfā-ō-'lā\ *n* : coffee with hot milk in about equal parts

caf·e·te·ria \ˌka-fə-'tir-ē-ə\ *n* [AmerSp *cafetería* coffee-house] : a restaurant in which the customers serve themselves or are served at a counter

caf·feine \ka-'fēn, 'ka-ˌfēn\ *n* : a stimulating alkaloid found esp. in coffee and tea

caf·fein·at·ed \'ka-fə-ˌnā-təd\ *adj* **1** : stimulated by or as if by caffeine **2** : containing caffeine

caf·fe lat·te \'kä-fä-'lä-tä\ *n* [It] : espresso mixed with hot or steamed milk

caf·tan \kaf-'tan, 'kaf-ˌtan\ *n* [Russ *kaftan*, fr. Turk, fr. Pers *qaftān*] : an ankle-length garment with long sleeves worn in countries of the eastern Mediterranean

¹cage \'kāj\ *n* **1** : an openwork enclosure for confining an animal **2** : something resembling a cage

²cage *vb* **caged; cag·ing** : to put or keep in or as if in a cage

ca·gey *also* **ca·gy** \'kā-jē\ *adj* **ca·gi·er; -est** : wary of being trapped or deceived : SHREWD ⟨a ∼ dealer⟩ — **ca·gi·ly** \-jə-lē\ *adv* — **ca·gi·ness** \-jē-nəs\ *n*

CAGS *abbr* Certificate of Advanced Graduate Study

ca·hoot \kə-'hüt\ *n* : PARTNERSHIP, LEAGUE — usu. used in pl. ⟨officials in ∼s with the underworld⟩

cai·man *also* **cayman** \'kā-mən; kā-'man, kī-\ *n* : any of several Central and So. American reptiles closely related to alligators and crocodiles

cairn \'karn\ *n* : a heap of stones serving as a memorial or a landmark

cais·son \'kā-ˌsän, 'käs-³n\ *n* **1** : a usu. 2-wheeled vehicle for artillery ammunition **2** : a watertight chamber used in underwater construction work or as a foundation

caisson disease *n* : ²BEND 3

cai·tiff \'kā-təf\ *adj* [ME *caitif*, fr. AF *caitif, chaitif* wretched, despicable, fr. L *captivus* captive] : being base, cowardly, or despicable — **caitiff** *n*

ca·jole \kə-'jōl\ *vb* **ca·joled; ca·jol·ing** [F *cajoler*] : to persuade or coax esp. with flattery or false promises — **ca·jole·ment** *n* — **ca·jol·ery** \-'jō-lə-rē\ *n*

Ca·jun \'kā-jən\ *n* : a Louisianian descended from French-speaking immigrants from Acadia (Nova Scotia) — **Cajun** *adj*

¹cake \'kāk\ *n* **1** : a baked or fried breadlike food usu. in a small flat shape **2** : a sweet baked food made from batter or dough usu. containing flour, sugar, shortening, and a leaven (as baking powder) **3** : a hardened or compacted substance ⟨a ∼ of soap⟩ **4** : something easily done ⟨the quiz was ∼⟩

²cake *vb* **caked; cak·ing** **1** : ENCRUST **2** : to form or harden into a cake

cake·walk \'kāk-ˌwȯk\ *n* **1** : a stage dance typically involving a high prance with backward tilt **2** : a one-sided contest or an easy task

cal *abbr* **1** calendar **2** caliber

Cal *abbr* **1** California **2** calorie

cal·a·bash \'ka-lə-ˌbash\ *n* : the fruit of a gourd; *also* : a utensil made from its hard shell

cal·a·boose \'ka-lə-ˌbüs\ *n* [Sp *calabozo* dungeon] : JAIL

ca·la·di·um \kə-'lā-dē-əm\ *n* : any of a genus of tropical American ornamental plants related to the arums

cal·a·mari \ˌkä-lə-'mär-ē\ *n* [It] : squid used as food

cal·a·mine \'ka-lə-ˌmīn\ *n* : a lotion of oxides of zinc and iron

ca·lam·i·ty \kə-'la-mə-tē\ *n, pl* **-ties** **1** : great distress or misfortune **2** : an event causing great harm or loss and affliction : DISASTER ⟨an economic ∼⟩ — **ca·lam·i·tous** \-təs\ *adj* — **ca·lam·i·tous·ly** *adv* — **ca·lam·i·tous·ness** *n*

calc *abbr* calculate; calculated

cal·car·e·ous \kal-'kar-ē-əs\ *adj* : resembling calcium carbonate in hardness; *also* : containing calcium or calcium carbonate

cal·cif·er·ous \kal-'si-fə-rəs\ *adj* : producing or containing calcium carbonate

cal·ci·fy \'kal-sə-ˌfī\ *vb* **-fied; -fy·ing** : to make or become calcareous — **cal·ci·fi·ca·tion** \ˌkal-sə-fə-'kā-shən\ *n*

cal·ci·mine \'kal-sə-ˌmīn\ *n* : a thin water paint used esp. on plastered surfaces — **calcimine** *vb*

cal·cine \kal-'sīn\ *vb* **cal·cined; cal·cin·ing** : to heat to a high temperature but without fusing to drive off volatile matter and often to reduce to powder — **cal·ci·na·tion** \ˌkal-sə-'nā-shən\ *n*

cal·cite \'kal-ˌsīt\ *n* : a crystalline mineral consisting of calcium carbonate — **cal·cit·ic** \kal-'si-tik\ *adj*

cal·ci·um \'kal-sē-əm\ *n* : a silver-white soft metallic chemical element occurring only in combination

calcium carbonate *n* : a substance found in nature as limestone and marble and in plant ashes, bones, and shells

cal·cu·late \'kal-kyə-ˌlāt\ *vb* **-lat·ed; -lat·ing** [L *calculare*, fr. *calculus* pebble (used in reckoning)] **1** : to determine by mathematical processes : COMPUTE **2** : to reckon by exercise of practical judgment : ESTIMATE **3** : to design or adapt for a purpose **4** : COUNT, RELY — **cal·cu·la·ble** \-lə-bəl\ *adj* — **cal·cu·la·tor** \-ˌlā-tər\ *n*

cal·cu·lat·ed \-ˌlā-təd\ *adj* **1** : undertaken after estimating the chance of success or failure ⟨a ∼ risk⟩ **2** : planned purposefully : DELIBERATE ⟨a ∼ strategy⟩

cal·cu·lat·ing \-ˌlā-tiŋ\ *adj* : marked by shrewd consideration esp. of self-interest — **cal·cu·lat·ing·ly** *adv*

cal·cu·la·tion \ˌkal-kyə-'lā-shən\ *n* **1** : the process or an act of calculating **2** : the result of an act of calculating **3** : studied care; *also* : cold heartless planning to promote self-interest

cal·cu·lus \'kal-kyə-ləs\ *n, pl* **-li** \-ˌlī\ *also* **-lus·es** [L, pebble (used in reckoning)] **1** : a method of computation or calculation in a special notation (as of logic) **2** : a branch of mathematics concerned with the rate of change of functions and with methods of finding lengths, areas, and volumes **3** : a concretion usu. of mineral salts esp. in hollow organs or ducts

cal·de·ra \kal-'der-ə, kȯl-, -'dir-\ *n* [Sp, lit., cauldron] : a large crater usu. formed by the collapse of a volcanic cone

cal·dron *var of* CAULDRON

¹cal·en·dar \'ka-lən-dər\ *n* **1** : an arrangement of time into days, weeks, months, and years; *also* : a sheet or folder containing such an arrangement for a period **2** : an orderly list

²calendar *vb* : to enter in a calendar

¹cal·en·der \'ka-lən-dər\ *vb* : to press (as cloth or paper) between rollers or plates so as to make smooth or glossy or to thin into sheets

²calender *n* : a machine for calendering

ca·lends \'ka-ləndz, 'kā-\ *n sing or pl* : the first day of the ancient Roman month

ca·len·du·la \kə-'len-jə-lə\ *n* : any of a genus of yellow-flowered herbs related to the daisies

¹calf \'kaf, 'kȧf\ *n, pl* **calves** \'kavz, 'kȧvz\ : the young of the domestic cow; *also* : the young of various large mammals (as the elephant or whale) **2** : CALFSKIN

²calf *n, pl* **calves** \'kavz, 'kȧvz\ : the fleshy back of the leg below the knee

calf·skin \'kaf-ˌskin, 'kȧf-\ *n* : leather made of the skin of a calf

cal·i·ber *or* **cal·i·bre** \'ka-lə-bər\ *n* [MF *calibre*, fr. It *calibro*, fr. Ar *qālib* shoemaker's last] **1** : degree of mental capacity, excellence, or importance **2** : the diameter of a projectile **3** : the diameter of the bore of a gun

cal·i·brate \'ka-lə-ˌbrāt\ *vb* **-brat·ed; -brat·ing** : to adjust precisely

cal·i·bra·tion \ˌka-lə-'brā-shən\ *n* : a set of graduated marks indicating values or positions — usu. used in pl.

cal·i·co \'ka-li-ˌkō\ *n, pl* **-coes** *or* **-cos** **1** : printed cotton fabric **2** : a mottled or spotted animal — **calico** *adj*

Calif *abbr* California

Cal·i·for·nia poppy \ˌka-lə-'fȯr-nyə-\ *n* : a widely cultivated herb with usu. yellow or orange flowers that is related to the poppies

cal·i·for·ni·um \ˌka-lə-'fȯr-nē-əm\ *n* : an artificially prepared radioactive chemical element

cal·i·per \'ka-lə-pər\ *n* **1** : any of various instruments having two arms, legs, or jaws used esp. to measure diameter or thickness — usu. used in pl. **2** : a device for pressing a frictional material against the sides of a rotating wheel or disk

ca·liph \'kā-ləf, 'ka-\ *n* : a successor of Muhammad as head of Islam — used as a title — **ca·liph·ate** \-lə-ˌfāt, -fət\ *n*

cal·is·then·ics \ˌka-ləs-'the-niks\ *n sing or pl* [Gk *kalos* beautiful + *sthenos* strength] : bodily exercises usu. done without apparatus — **cal·is·then·ic** *adj*

calk \'kȯk\ *var of* CAULK

¹call \'kȯl\ *vb* **1** : SHOUT, CRY; *also* : to utter a characteristic note or cry **2** : to utter in a loud clear voice ⟨∼ed out my name⟩ **3** : to announce authoritatively **4** : SUMMON ⟨was ~*ed* to testify⟩ **5** : to make a request or demand ⟨~ for an investigation⟩ **6** : to halt (as a baseball game) because of unsuitable conditions **7** : to demand payment of (a loan); *also* : to demand surrender of (as a bond) for redemption **8** : to get or try to get in communication by telephone **9** : to make a brief visit **10** : to speak of or address by name : give a name to **11** : to estimate or consider for practical purposes ⟨~ it ten miles⟩ **12** : to temporarily transfer control of computer processing to (as a subroutine or procedure) — **call·er** *n*

²call *n* **1** : SHOUT **2** : the cry of an animal (as a bird) **3** : a request or a command to come or assemble : INVITATION, SUMMONS **4** : DEMAND, CLAIM; *also* : REQUEST **5** : a brief usu. formal visit **6** : an act of calling on the telephone **7** : DECISION ⟨a tough ~⟩ **8** : a temporary transfer of control of computer processing to a particular set of instructions

call·la lily \ˈkä-lə-\ *n* : a plant related to the arums and grown for its large white lilylike bract that surrounds a fleshy spike of small yellow flowers

call·back \ˈkȯl-ˌbak\ *n* : a calling back; *esp* : RECALL 5

call–board \-ˌbȯrd\ *n* : a board for posting notices (as of rehearsal calls)

call down *vb* : REPRIMAND

call girl *n* : a prostitute with whom appointments are made by phone

cal·lig·ra·phy \kə-ˈli-grə-fē\ *n* : artistic or elegant handwriting; *also* : the art of producing such writing — **cal·lig·ra·pher** \-fər\ *n* — **cal·li·graph·ic** \ˌka-lə-ˈgraf-ik\ *adj*

call–in \ˈkȯl-ˌin\ *adj* : allowing listeners to engage in broadcast telephone conversations ⟨a ~ show⟩

call in *vb* **1** : to order to return or be returned **2** : to summon to one's aid **3** : to report by telephone

call·ing \ˈkȯ-liŋ\ *n* **1** : a strong inner impulse toward a particular course of action **2** : the activity in which one customarily engages as an occupation

cal·li·ope \kə-ˈlī-ə-(ˌ)pē, ˈka-lē-ˌōp\ *n* [fr. *Calliope,* chief of the Muses, fr. L, fr. Gk *Kalliopē*] : a keyboard musical instrument similar to an organ and made up of a series of whistles

cal·li·per *chiefly Brit var of* CALIPER

call number *n* : a combination of characters assigned to a library book to indicate its place on a shelf

call off *vb* : CANCEL ⟨*called off* the trip⟩

cal·los·i·ty \ka-ˈlä-sə-tē\ *n, pl* **-ties** : the quality or state of being callous **2** : CALLUS 1

¹cal·lous \ˈka-ləs\ *adj* **1** : being thickened and hardened ⟨~ skin⟩ **2** : feeling no emotion or sympathy — **callous·ly** *adv* — **cal·lous·ness** *n*

²callous *vb* : to make callous

cal·low \ˈka-lō\ *adj* [ME *calu* bald, fr. OE] : lacking adult sophistication ⟨a ~ youth⟩ — **cal·low·ness** *n*

call–up \ˈkȯl-ˌəp\ *n* : an order to report for active military service

call up *vb* : to summon for active military duty

cal·lus \ˈka-ləs\ *n* **1** : a callous area on skin or bark **2** : tissue that is converted into bone in the healing of a bone fracture — **callus** *vb*

call–waiting *n* : a telephone service by which during a call in progress an incoming call is signaled (as by a click)

¹calm \ˈkäm, ˈkälm\ *n* **1** : a period or a condition free from storms, high winds, or rough water **2** : complete or almost complete absence of wind **3** : a state of tranquility

²calm *vb* : to make or become calm

³calm *adj* : marked by calm : STILL, UNRUFFLED — **calm·ly** *adv* — **calm·ness** *n*

cal·o·mel \ˈka-lə-məl, -ˌmel\ *n* : a chloride of mercury used esp. as a fungicide

ca·lor·ic \kə-ˈlȯr-ik\ *adj* **1** : of or relating to heat **2** : of, relating to, or containing calories — **ca·lo·ric·al·ly** \-i-k(ə-)lē\ *adv*

cal·o·rie *also* **cal·o·ry** \ˈka-lə-rē\ *n, pl* **-ries** : a unit for measuring heat; *esp* : one for measuring the value of foods for producing heat and energy in the human body equivalent to the amount of heat required to raise the temperature of one kilogram of water one degree Celsius

cal·o·rim·e·ter \ˌka-lə-ˈri-mə-tər\ *n* : an apparatus for measuring quantities of heat — **cal·o·rim·e·try** \-trē\ *n*

cal·u·met \ˈkal-yə-ˌmet, -mət\ *n* : an American Indian ceremonial pipe

calumet

ca·lum·ni·ate \kə-ˈləm-nē-ˌāt\ *vb* **-at·ed; -at·ing** : to make false and malicious statements about ✦ **Synonyms** DEFAME, MALIGN, LIBEL, SLANDER, TRADUCE — **ca·lum·ni·a·tion** \-ˌləm-nē-ˈā-shən\ *n* — **ca·lum·ni·a·tor** \-ˈləm-nē-ˌā-tər\ *n*

cal·um·ny \ˈka-ləm-nē\ *n, pl* **-nies** : false and malicious accusation — **ca·lum·ni·ous** \kə-ˈləm-nē-əs\ *adj*

calve \ˈkav, ˈkáv\ *vb* **calved; calv·ing** : to give birth to a calf

calves *pl of* CALF

Cal·vin·ism \ˈkal-və-ˌni-zəm\ *n* : the theological system of John Calvin and his followers — **Cal·vin·ist** \-nist\ *n or adj* — **Cal·vin·is·tic** \ˌkal-və-ˈnis-tik\ *adj*

ca·lyp·so \kə-ˈlip-sō\ *n, pl* **-sos** : a style of music originating in the British West Indies and having lyrics that usu. satirize local personalities and events

ca·lyx \ˈkā-liks, ˈka-\ *n, pl* **ca·lyx·es** *or* **ca·ly·ces** \ˈkā-lə-ˌsēz, ˈka-\ : the usu. green or leaflike outer part of a flower consisting of sepals

cal·zo·ne \kal-ˈzōn, -ˈzō-nē\ *n* : a baked or fried turnover of pizza dough stuffed with cheese and various fillings

¹cam \ˈkam\ *n* : a rotating or sliding piece in a mechanical linkage by which rotary motion is transformed into linear motion or vice versa

²cam *n* : CAMERA

ca·ma·ra·de·rie \ˌkäm-ˈrä-də-rē, ˌkam-, -ˈra-\ *n* [F] : friendly feeling and goodwill among comrades

cam·bi·um \ˈkam-bē-əm\ *n, pl* **-bi·ums** *or* **-bia** \-bē-ə\ : a thin cellular layer between xylem and phloem of most higher plants from which new tissues develop — **cam·bi·al** \-əl\ *adj*

Cam·bri·an \ˈkam-brē-ən, ˈkäm-\ *adj* : of, relating to, or being the earliest period of the Paleozoic era — **Cambrian** *n*

cam·bric \ˈkām-brik\ *n* : a fine thin white linen or cotton fabric

cam·cord·er \ˈkam-ˌkȯr-dər\ *n* : a small portable combined camera and VCR

came *past of* COME

cam·el \ˈka-məl\ *n* : either of two large hoofed cud-chewing mammals used esp. in desert regions of Asia and Africa for carrying and riding

camel hair *also* **camel's hair** *n* **1** : the hair of a camel or a substitute for it **2** : cloth made of camel hair or of camel hair and wool

ca·mel·lia \kə-ˈmēl-yə\ *n* : any of a genus of shrubs and trees related to the tea plant and grown in warm regions and greenhouses for their showy roselike flowers

Cam·em·bert \ˈka-məm-ˌber\ *n* : a soft cheese with a grayish rind and yellow interior

cam·eo \ˈka-mē-ˌō\ *n, pl* **-eos** **1** : a gem carved in relief; *also* : a small medallion with a profiled head in relief **2** : a brief appearance esp. by a well-known actor in a play or movie

cam·era \ˈkam-rə, ˈka-mər-ə\ *n* : a device with a lightproof chamber fitted with a lens through which the image of an object is projected onto a surface for recording (as on film) or for conversion into electrical signals (as for television broadcast) — **cam·era·man** \-ˌman, -mən\ *n* — **cam·era·wom·an** *n*

cam·i·sole \ˈka-mə-ˌsōl\ *n* : a short sleeveless garment for women

camomile *var of* CHAMOMILE

cam·ou·flage \ˈka-mə-ˌfläzh, -ˌfläj\ *n* [F] **1** : the disguising of military equipment with paint, nets, or foliage; *also* : the disguise itself **2** : deceptive behavior — **camouflage** *vb*

¹camp \ˈkamp\ *n* **1** : a place where tents or buildings are erected for usu. temporary shelter **2** : a collection of

tents or other shelters **3** : a program offering recreational activities (as boating and hiking) for a limited time ⟨summer ∼⟩ **4** : a body of persons encamped **5** : a training session for athletes outside of the regular season — **camp·ground** \-₁graùnd\ *n* — **camp·site** \-₁sīt\ *n*
²**camp** *vb* **1** : to make or occupy a camp **2** : to live in a camp or outdoors
³**camp** *n* **1** : exaggerated effeminate mannerisms **2** : something so outrageous, inappropriate, or theatrical as to be considered amusing — **camp** *adj* — **camp·i·ly** \'kam-pə-lē\ *adv* — **camp·i·ness** \-pē-nəs\ *n* — **campy** \-pē\ *adj*
⁴**camp** *vb* : to engage in camp : exhibit the qualities of camp
cam·paign \kam-'pān\ *n* **1** : a series of military operations forming one distinct stage in a war **2** : a series of activities designed to bring about a particular result ⟨advertising ∼⟩ — **campaign** *vb* — **cam·paign·er** *n*
cam·pa·ni·le \₁kam-pə-'nē-lē\ *n, pl* **-ni·les** *or* **-ni·li** \-'nē-lē\ : a usu. freestanding bell tower
cam·pa·nol·o·gy \₁kam-pə-'nä-lə-jē\ *n* : the art of bell ringing — **cam·pa·nol·o·gist** \-jist\ *n*
camp·er \'kam-pər\ *n* **1** : one who camps **2** : a portable dwelling (as a specially equipped vehicle) for use during casual travel and camping
Camp Fire Girl *n* : a member of a national organization of girls from ages 5 to 18
camp follower *n* **1** : a civilian (as a prostitute) who follows a military unit to attend or exploit its personnel **2** : a follower of a group who is not an adherent; *esp* : a politician who joins a movement solely for personal gain
cam·phor \'kam-fər\ *n* : a gummy volatile aromatic compound obtained from an evergreen Asian tree (**camphor tree**) and used esp. in medicine
camp meeting *n* : a series of evangelistic meetings usu. held outdoors
camp·o·ree \₁kam-pə-'rē\ *n* : a gathering of Boy Scouts or Girl Scouts from a given geographic area
cam·pus \'kam-pəs\ *n* [L, plain] : the grounds and buildings of a college or school; *also* : grounds resembling a campus ⟨hospital ∼⟩
cam·shaft \'kam-₁shaft\ *n* : a shaft to which a cam is fastened
¹**can** \kən, 'kan\ *vb, past* **could** \kəd, 'kúd\; *pres sing & pl* **can 1** : to be able to **2** : may perhaps ⟨∼ he still be alive⟩ **3** : be permitted by conscience or feeling to ⟨you ∼ hardly blame her⟩ **4** : have permission to ⟨you ∼ go now⟩
²**can** \'kan\ *n* **1** : a usu. cylindrical container or receptacle ⟨garbage ∼⟩ ⟨coffee ∼⟩ **2** : JAIL **3** : TOILET
³**can** \'kan\ *vb* **canned; can·ning 1** : to put in a can : preserve by sealing in airtight cans or jars **2** *slang* : to discharge from employment **3** *slang* : to put a stop or an end to — **can·ner** *n*
Can *or* **Canad** *abbr* Canada; Canadian
Can·a·da goose \'ka-nə-də-\ *n* : a common wild goose of No. America
ca·naille \kə-'nī, -'näl\ *n* [F, fr. It *canaglia*, fr. *cane* dog] : RABBLE, RIFFRAFF
ca·nal \kə-'nal\ *n* **1** : a tubular passage in the body : DUCT **2** : an artificial waterway (as for boats or irrigation)
can·a·lize \'kan-ᵊl-₁īz\ *vb* **-lized; -liz·ing 1** : to provide with a canal or make into or like a channel **2** : to provide with an outlet; *esp* : to direct into preferred channels — **ca·nal·i·za·tion** \₁kan-ᵊl-ə-'zā-shən\ *n*
can·a·pé \'ka-nə-pē, -₁pā\ *n* [F, lit., sofa, fr. ML *canopeum, canapeum* mosquito net] : a piece of bread or toast or a cracker topped with a savory food
ca·nard \kə-'närd\ *n* : a false or unfounded report, story or belief
ca·nary \kə-'ner-ē\ *n, pl* **ca·nar·ies** [fr. the *Canary* islands] **1** : a usu. sweet wine similar to Madeira **2** : a usu. yellow or greenish finch often kept in a cage as a pet
ca·nas·ta \kə-'nas-tə\ *n* [Sp, lit., basket] : rummy played with two full decks of cards plus four jokers
canc *abbr* canceled
can·can \'kan-₁kan\ *n* : a woman's dance of French origin characterized by high kicking
¹**can·cel** \'kan-səl\ *vb* **-celed** *or* **-celled; -cel·ing** *or* **-cel·ling** [ME *cancellen*, fr. AF *canceller, chanceller,* fr. LL *cancellare,* fr. L, to make like a lattice, fr. *cancelli* lattice] **1** : to destroy the force or validity of : ANNUL **2**

: to match in force or effect : OFFSET **3** : to cross out : DELETE **4** : to remove (a common divisor) from a numerator and denominator; *also* : to remove (equivalents) on opposite sides of an equation or account **5** : to mark (a postage stamp or check) so that it cannot be reused **6** : to neutralize each other's strength or effect — **can·cel·la·tion** \₁kan-sə-'lā-shən\ *n* — **can·cel·er** *or* **can·cel·ler** *n*
²**cancel** *n* **1** : CANCELLATION **2** : a deleted part
can·cer \'kan-sər\ *n* [L, lit., crab] **1** *cap* : a zodiacal constellation between Gemini and Leo usu. pictured as a crab **2** *cap* : the 4th sign of the zodiac in astrology; *also* : one born under this sign **3** : a malignant tumor that tends to spread in the body; *also* : an abnormal state marked by such tumors **4** : a malignant evil that spreads destructively — **can·cer·ous** \-sə-rəs\ *adj* — **can·cer·ous·ly** *adv*
can·de·la·bra \₁kan-də-'lä-brə, -'la-\ *n* : an ornamental branched candlestick or lamp with several lights
can·de·la·brum \-brəm\ *n, pl* **-bra** *also* **-brums** : CANDELABRA
can·did \'kan-dəd\ *adj* **1** : FRANK, STRAIGHTFORWARD ⟨a ∼ critique⟩ **2** : relating to photography of subjects acting naturally or spontaneously without being posed — **can·did·ly** *adv* — **can·did·ness** *n*
can·di·da·cy \'kan-də-də-sē\ *n, pl* **-cies** : the state of being a candidate
can·di·date \'kan-də-₁dāt, 'ka-nə-, -dət\ *n* [L *candidatus,* fr. *candidatus* clothed in white, fr. *candidus* white; fr. the white toga worn by office seekers in ancient Rome] : one who seeks or is proposed for an office, honor, or membership ⟨a ∼ for governor⟩
can·di·da·ture \'kan-də-də-₁chúr, 'ka-nə-\ *n, chiefly Brit* : CANDIDACY
can·died \'kan-dēd\ *adj* : preserved in or encrusted with sugar
¹**can·dle** \'kan-dᵊl\ *n* : a usu. slender mass of tallow or wax molded around a wick that is burned to give light
²**candle** *vb* **can·dled; can·dling** : to examine (as eggs) by holding between the eye and a light — **can·dler** *n*
can·dle·light \'kan-dᵊl-₁līt\ *n* **1** : the light of a candle; *also* : any soft artificial light **2** : the time when candles are lit : TWILIGHT
can·dle·lit \-₁lit\ *adj* : illuminated by candlelight ⟨a ∼ dinner⟩
Can·dle·mas \'kan-dᵊl-məs\ *n* : February 2 observed as a church festival in commemoration of the presentation of Christ in the temple
can·dle·stick \-₁stik\ *n* : a holder with a socket for a candle
can·dle·wick \-₁wik\ *n* : a soft cotton yarn; *also* : embroidery made with this yarn usu. in tufts
can·dor \'kan-dər\ *n* : FRANKNESS, OUTSPOKENNESS
can·dour *chiefly Brit var of* CANDOR
C and W *abbr* country and western
¹**can·dy** \'kan-dē\ *n, pl* **candies** [ME *sugre candy,* fr. MF *sucre candi,* fr. OF *sucre* sugar + AF *qandi* candied, fr. *qand* crystallized sugar] **1** : a confection made from sugar often with flavoring and filling **2** : something that appeals in a light or frivolous way
²**candy** *vb* **can·died; can·dy·ing** : to encrust in sugar often by cooking in a syrup
candy strip·er \-'strī-pər\ *n* : a teenage volunteer worker at a hospital
¹**cane** \'kān\ *n* **1** : a slender hollow or pithy stem (as of a reed or bramble) **2** : a tall woody grass or reed (as sugarcane or sorghum) **3** : a walking stick; *also* : a rod for flogging
²**cane** *vb* **caned; can·ing 1** : to beat with a cane **2** : to weave or make with cane — **can·er** *n*
cane·brake \'kān-₁brāk\ *n* : a thicket of cane
¹**ca·nine** \'kā-₁nīn\ *n* **1** : a pointed tooth between the outer incisor and the first premolar **2** : a canine mammal (as a domestic dog)
²**canine** *adj* [L *caninus,* fr. *canis* dog] : of or relating to dogs or to the family to which they belong
can·is·ter \'ka-nə-stər\ *n* : an often cylindrical container
can·ker \'kaŋ-kər\ *n* : a spreading sore that eats into tissue — **can·ker·ous** \-kə-rəs\ *adj*
can·ker·worm \-₁wərm\ *n* : either of two moths and esp. their larvae that are pests of fruit and shade trees
can·na \'ka-nə\ *n* : any of a genus of tropical herbs with large leaves and racemes of bright-colored flowers

can·na·bis \'ka-nə-bəs\ *n* : any of the psychoactive preparations (as marijuana) or chemicals (as THC) derived from hemp; *also* : HEMP

canned \'kand\ *adj* : prepared in standardized form for general use or wide distribution ⟨~ music⟩

can·nery \'ka-nə-rē\ *n, pl* **-ner·ies** : a factory for the canning of foods

can·ni·bal \'ka-nə-bəl\ *n* [NL *Canibalis* a member of a Caribbean Indian people, fr. Sp *Canibal*] : one that eats the flesh of its own kind — **can·ni·bal·ism** \-bə-ˌli-zəm\ *n* — **can·ni·bal·is·tic** \-bə-'lis-tik\ *adj*

can·ni·bal·ise *Brit var of* CANNIBALIZE

can·ni·bal·ize \'ka-nə-bə-ˌlīz\ *vb* **-ized; -iz·ing** **1** : to take usable parts from (as an inoperative machine) to construct or repair another machine **2** : to practice cannibalism

can·non \'ka-nən\ *n, pl* **cannons** *or* **cannon** [ME *canon*, fr. AF, fr. It *cannone*, lit., large tube, fr. *canna* reed, tube, fr. L, cane, reed] : a large heavy gun; *esp* : one mounted on a carriage

can·non·ade \ˌka-nə-'nād\ *n* : a heavy fire of artillery — **cannonade** *vb*

can·non·ball \'ka-nən-ˌból\ *n* : a usu. round solid missile for a cannon

can·non·eer \ˌka-nə-'nir\ *n* : an artillery gunner

can·not \'ka-ˌnät; kə-'nät\ : can not — **cannot but** : to be unable to do otherwise than ⟨we *cannot but* wonder why⟩

can·nu·la \'kan-yə-lə\ *n, pl* **-las** *or* **-lae** \-ˌlē\ : a small tube for insertion into a body cavity or into a duct or vessel

can·ny \'ka-nē\ *adj* **can·ni·er; -est** : PRUDENT, SHREWD — **can·ni·ly** \'kan-ᵊl-ē\ *adv* — **can·ni·ness** \'ka-nē-nəs\ *n*

ca·noe \kə-'nü\ *n* : a light narrow boat with sharp ends and curved sides that is usu. propelled by paddles — **canoe** *vb* — **ca·noe·ist** *n*

ca·no·la \kə-'nō-lə\ *n* : a rape plant producing seeds that are low in a toxic acid and yield an edible oil (**canola oil**) high in monounsaturated fatty acids; *also* : this oil

¹can·on \'ka-nən\ *n* **1** : a regulation decreed by a church council; *also* : a provision of canon law **2** : an official or authoritative list (as of works of literature) **3** : an accepted principle ⟨the ~s of good taste⟩

²canon *n* : a member of the clergy on the staff of a cathedral

ca·non·i·cal \kə-'nä-ni-kəl\ *adj* **1** : of, relating to, or forming a canon **2** : conforming to a general rule or acceptable procedure : ORTHODOX **3** : of or relating to a canon of a cathedral — **ca·non·i·cal·ly** \-k(ə-)lē\ *adv*

can·on·ize \'ka-nə-ˌnīz\ *vb* **can·on·ized** \-ˌnīzd\; **can·on·iz·ing** **1** : to declare (a deceased person) an officially recognized saint **2** : GLORIFY, EXALT — **can·on·i·za·tion** \ˌka-nə-nə-'zā-shən\ *n*

canon law *n* : the law governing a church

can·o·py \'ka-nə-pē\ *n, pl* **-pies** [ME *canope*, fr. ML *canopeum* mosquito net, fr. L *conopeum*, fr. Gk *kōnōpion*, fr. *kōnōps* mosquito] **1** : an overhanging cover, shelter, or shade **2** : the uppermost spreading layer of a forest **3** : a transparent cover for an airplane cockpit **4** : the fabric part of a parachute — **canopy** *vb*

¹cant \'kant\ *vb* : to give a slant to

²cant *n* **1** : an oblique or slanting surface **2** : TILT, SLANT

³cant *vb* **1** : to beg in a whining manner **2** : to talk hypocritically

⁴cant *n* **1** : the special idiom of a profession or trade : JARGON **2** : insincere speech; *esp* : insincerely pious words or statements

Cant *abbr* Canticle of Canticles

can·ta·bi·le \kän-'tä-bə-ˌlā\ *adv or adj* [It] : in a singing manner — used as a direction in music

can·ta·loupe *also* **can·ta·loup** \'kant-ᵊl-ˌōp\ *n* : MUSKMELON; *esp* : one with orange flesh and rough skin

can·tan·ker·ous \kan-'taŋ-kə-rəs\ *adj* : difficult to deal with : ILL-NATURED ⟨a ~ mule⟩ — **can·tan·ker·ous·ly** *adv* — **can·tan·ker·ous·ness** *n*

can·ta·ta \kən-'tä-tə\ *n* [It] : a choral composition usu. sung to instrumental accompaniment

can·teen \kan-'tēn\ *n* [F *cantine* bottle case, canteen (store), fr. It *cantina* wine cellar] **1** : a flask for carrying liquids **2** : a place of recreation and entertainment for military personnel **3** : a small cafeteria or counter at which snacks are served

can·ter \'kan-tər\ *n* : a horse's 3-beat gait resembling but smoother and slower than a gallop — **canter** *vb*

Can·ter·bury bell \'kant-ər-ˌber-ē-\ *n* : any of several plants related to the bluebell that are cultivated for their showy flowers

can·ti·cle \'kan-ti-kəl\ *n* : SONG; *esp* : any of several liturgical songs taken from the Bible

Canticle of Canticles *n* : SONG OF SONGS

¹can·ti·le·ver \'kant-ᵊl-ˌē-vər\ *n* : a projecting beam or structure supported only at one end; *also* : either of a pair of such structures projecting toward each other so that when joined they form a bridge

²cantilever *vb* **1** : to support by a cantilever ⟨a ~ed shelf⟩ **2** : to build as a cantilever **3** : to project as a cantilever

can·tle \'kant-ᵊl\ *n* : the upwardly projecting rear part of a saddle

can·to \'kan-ˌtō\ *n, pl* **cantos** [It, fr. L *cantus* song] : one of the major divisions of a long poem

can·ton \'kant-ᵊn, 'kan-ˌtän\ *n* : a small territorial division of a country; *esp* : one of the political divisions of Switzerland — **can·ton·al** \'kant-ᵊn-əl, kan-'tän-ᵊl\ *adj*

can·ton·ment \kan-'tōn-mənt, -'tän-\ *n* : usu. temporary quarters for troops

can·tor \'kan-tər\ *n* **1** : a choir leader **2** : a synagogue official who sings liturgical music and leads the congregation in prayer

can·vas *also* **can·vass** \'kan-vəs\ *n* **1** : a strong cloth formerly much used for making tents and sails **2** : a set of sails **3** : a group of tents **4** : a piece of cloth prepared as a surface for a painting; *also* : a painting on this surface **5** : the canvas-covered floor of a boxing or wrestling ring

can·vas·back \'kan-vəs-ˌbak\ *n* : a No. American wild duck with red head and gray back

¹can·vass *also* **can·vas** \'kan-vəs\ *vb* **can·vassed; can·vas·sing** : to go through (a district) or to (persons) to solicit votes or orders for goods or to determine public opinion or sentiment — **can·vass·er** *n*

²canvass *n* : an act or instance of canvassing

can·yon \'kan-yən\ *n* : a deep narrow valley with high steep sides

¹cap \'kap\ *n* **1** : a covering for the head esp. with a visor and no brim; *also* : something resembling such a covering esp. on a tip, knob or end ⟨a bottle ~⟩ **2** : a container holding an explosive charge (as for a toy gun) **3** : an upper limit (as on expenditures)

²cap *vb* **capped; cap·ping** **1** : to provide or protect with a cap **2** : to form a cap over : CROWN **3** : OUTDO, SURPASS **4** : to bring to a conclusion ⟨~ off dinner with coffee⟩

³cap *abbr* **1** capacity **2** capital **3** capitalize; capitalized

CAP *abbr* Civil Air Patrol

ca·pa·ble \'kā-pə-bəl\ *adj* : having ability, capacity, or power to do something : ABLE, COMPETENT — **ca·pa·bil·i·ty** \ˌkā-pə-'bi-lə-tē\ *n* — **ca·pa·bly** *adv*

ca·pa·cious \kə-'pā-shəs\ *adj* : able to contain much — **ca·pa·cious·ly** *adv* — **ca·pa·cious·ness** *n*

ca·pac·i·tance \kə-'pa-sə-təns\ *n* : the property of an electric nonconductor that permits the storage of energy

ca·pac·i·tor \kə-'pa-sə-tər\ *n* : an electronic circuit device for temporary storage of electrical energy

¹ca·pac·i·ty \kə-'pa-sə-tē\ *n, pl* **-ties** **1** : legal qualification or fitness ⟨~ to stand trial⟩ **2** : the ability to contain, receive, or accommodate ⟨seating ~⟩ **3** : the maximum amount or number that can be contained — see METRIC SYSTEM table, WEIGHT table **4** : ABILITY **5** : position or character assigned or assumed

²capacity *adj* : equaling maximum capacity ⟨a ~ crowd⟩

cap–a–pie *or* **cap–à–pie** \ˌka-pə-'pē\ *adv* [MF] : from head to foot : at all points

ca·par·i·son \kə-'par-ə-sən\ *n* **1** : an ornamental covering for a horse **2** : TRAPPINGS, ADORNMENT — **caparison** *vb*

¹cape \'kāp\ *n* **1** : a point of land jutting out into water **2** *often cap* : CAPE COD COTTAGE

²cape *n* : a sleeveless garment hanging from the neck over the shoulders — **caped** *adj*

Cape Cod cottage \'kāp-'käd-\ *n* : a compact rectangular dwelling of one or one-and-a-half stories usu. with a steep gable roof

¹ca·per \'kā-pər\ *n* : the greenish flower bud or young berry of a Mediterranean shrub pickled for use as a relish; *also* : this shrub

²**caper** vb **ca·pered; ca·per·ing** : to leap about in a playful manner

³**caper** n 1 : a frolicsome leap 2 : a capricious escapade 3 : an illegal or questionable act

cape·skin \'kāp-ˌskin\ n : a light flexible leather made from sheepskins

cap·ful \'kap-ˌfül\ n, pl **cap·fuls** also **caps·ful** \'kaps-\ : as much as a cap will hold

cap·il·lar·i·ty \ˌka-pə-'lar-ə-tē\ n, pl **-ties** : the action by which the surface of a liquid where it is in contact with a solid (as in a slender tube) is raised or lowered depending on the relative attraction of the molecules of the liquid for each other and for those of the solid

¹**cap·il·lary** \'ka-pə-ˌler-ē\ adj 1 : resembling a hair 2 : having a very small bore ⟨∼ tube⟩ 3 : of or relating to capillaries or to capillarity

²**capillary** n, pl **-lar·ies** : any of the tiny thin-walled blood vessels that carry blood between the smallest arteries and their corresponding veins

¹**cap·i·tal** \'ka-pət-ᵊl\ n : the top part or piece of an architectural column

¹**capital: different styles**

²**capital** adj 1 : conforming to the series A, B, C rather than a, b, c ⟨∼ letters⟩ ⟨∼ G⟩ 2 : punishable by death ⟨a ∼ crime⟩ 3 : most serious ⟨a ∼ error⟩ 4 : first in importance or position : CHIEF; also : being the seat of government ⟨the ∼ city⟩ 5 : of or relating to capital ⟨∼ expenditures⟩; esp : relating to or being assets that add to the long-term net worth of a corporation 6 : FIRST-RATE, EXCELLENT

³**capital** n 1 : accumulated wealth esp. as used to produce more wealth 2 : the total face value of shares of stock issued by a company 3 : persons holding capital 4 : ADVANTAGE, GAIN 5 : a letter larger than the ordinary small letter and often different in form 6 : the capital city of a state, province or country; also : a city preeminent in some activity ⟨the fashion ∼⟩

capital gain n : the increase in value of an asset (as stock or real estate) between the time it is bought and the time it is sold

capital goods n pl : machinery, tools, factories, and commodities used in the production of goods

cap·i·tal·ise Brit var of CAPITALIZE

cap·i·tal·ism \'ka-pət-ᵊl-ˌi-zəm\ n : an economic system characterized by private or corporate ownership of capital goods and by prices, production, and distribution of goods that are determined mainly by competition in a free market

¹**cap·i·tal·ist** \-ist\ n 1 : a person who has capital esp. invested in business 2 : a person of great wealth : PLUTOCRAT 3 : a believer in capitalism

²**capitalist** or **cap·i·tal·is·tic** \ˌka-pət-ᵊl-'is-tik\ adj 1 : owning capital 2 : practicing or advocating capitalism 3 : marked by capitalism — **cap·i·tal·is·ti·cal·ly** \-ti-k(ə-)lē\ adv

cap·i·tal·iza·tion \ˌka-pət-ᵊl-ə-'zā-shən\ n 1 : the act or process of capitalizing 2 : the total amount of money used as capital in a business

cap·i·tal·ize \'ka-pət-ᵊl-ˌīz\ vb **-ized; -iz·ing** 1 : to write or print with an initial capital or in capitals 2 : to convert into or use as capital 3 : to supply capital for 4 : to gain by turning something to advantage : PROFIT

cap·i·tal·ly \'ka-pət-ᵊl-ē\ adv : ADMIRABLY, EXCELLENTLY

cap·i·ta·tion \ˌka-pə-'tā-shən\ n : a direct uniform tax levied on each person

cap·i·tol \'ka-pət-ᵊl\ n : the building in which a legislature holds its sessions

ca·pit·u·late \kə-'pi-chə-ˌlāt\ vb **-lat·ed; -lat·ing** 1 : to surrender esp. on conditions agreed upon 2 : to cease resisting : ACQUIESCE ◆ **Synonyms** SUBMIT, YIELD, SUCCUMB, CAVE, DEFER — **ca·pit·u·la·tion** \-ˌpi-chə-'lā-shən\ n

ca·pon \'kā-ˌpän, -pən\ n : a castrated male chicken

cap·puc·ci·no \ˌka-pə-'chē-nō, ˌkä-\ n [It, lit., Capuchin; fr. the likeness of its color to that of a Capuchin's habit] : espresso mixed with foamy hot milk or cream and often flavored with cinnamon

ca·pric·cio \kə-'prē-chē-ˌō, -chō\ n, pl **-cios** [It, lit., whim, prank] : an instrumental piece in free form usu. lively in tempo and brilliant in style

ca·price \kə-'prēs\ n [F, fr. It capriccio] 1 : a sudden whim or fancy 2 : an inclination to do things impulsively 3 : CAPRICCIO — **ca·pri·cious** \-'pri-shəs\ adj — **ca·pri·cious·ly** adv — **ca·pri·cious·ness** n

Cap·ri·corn \'ka-pri-ˌkȯrn\ n 1 : a zodiacal constellation between Sagittarius and Aquarius usu. pictured as a goat 2 : the 10th sign of the zodiac in astrology; also : one born under this sign

cap·ri·ole \'ka-prē-ˌōl\ n : ³CAPER 1; also : an upward leap of a horse with a backward kick at the height of the leap — **capriole** vb

caps abbr 1 capitals 2 capsule

cap·sa·i·cin \kap-'sā-ə-sən\ n : a colorless compound found in various capsicums that gives hot peppers their hotness

cap·si·cum \'kap-si-kəm\ n : PEPPER 2

cap·size \'kap-ˌsīz, kap-'sīz\ vb **cap·sized; cap·siz·ing** : UPSET, OVERTURN

cap·stan \'kap-stən, -ˌstan\ n 1 : a machine for moving or raising heavy weights that consists of a vertical drum which can be rotated and around which cable is turned 2 : a rotating shaft that drives recorder tape

cap·su·lar \'kap-sə-lər\ adj : of, relating to, or resembling a capsule

cap·su·lat·ed \-ˌlā-təd\ adj : enclosed in a capsule

¹**cap·sule** \'kap-səl, -sül\ n 1 : a membrane or sac enclosing a body part (as of a joint) 2 : a case bearing spores or seeds 3 : a shell usu. of gelatin that is used for packaging something (as a drug); also : such a shell together with its contents 4 : a small pressurized compartment or vehicle (as for space flight)

²**capsule** adj 1 : very brief 2 : very compact

Capt abbr captain

¹**cap·tain** \'kap-tən\ n 1 : a commander of a body of troops 2 : a commissioned officer in the army, air force, or marine corps ranking next below a major 3 : an officer in charge of a ship 4 : a commissioned officer in the navy ranking next below a rear admiral or a commodore 5 : a leader of a side or team 6 : a dominant figure — **cap·tain·cy** n

²**captain** vb : to be captain of : LEAD

cap·tion \'kap-shən\ n 1 : a heading esp. of an article or document : TITLE 2 : the explanatory matter accompanying an illustration 3 : a motion-picture subtitle — **caption** vb

cap·tious \'kap-shəs\ adj : marked by an inclination to find fault — **cap·tious·ly** adv — **cap·tious·ness** n

cap·ti·vate \'kap-tə-ˌvāt\ vb **-vat·ed; -vat·ing** : to attract and hold irresistibly by some special charm or art — **cap·ti·va·tion** \ˌkap-tə-'vā-shən\ n — **cap·ti·va·tor** \'kap-tə-ˌvā-tər\ n

cap·tive \'kap-tiv\ adj 1 : made prisoner esp. in war 2 : kept within bounds : CONFINED 3 : held under control — **captive** n — **cap·tiv·i·ty** \kap-'ti-və-tē\ n

cap·tor \'kap-tər\ n : one that captures

¹**cap·ture** \'kap-chər\ n 1 : the act of capturing 2 : one that has been captured

²**capture** vb **cap·tured; cap·tur·ing** 1 : to take captive : WIN, GAIN ⟨∼ the crown⟩ 2 : to preserve in a relatively permanent form ⟨∼ the moment on film⟩

Ca·pu·chin \'ka-pyə-shən\ n : a member of an austere branch of the order of St. Francis of Assisi engaged in missionary work and preaching

car \'kär\ n 1 : a vehicle moving on wheels 2 : the compartment of an elevator 3 : the part of a balloon or airship that carries passengers or equipment

car·a·cole \'kar-ə-ˌkōl\ n : a half turn to right or left executed by a mounted horse — **caracole** vb

car·a·cul \'kar-ə-kəl\ n : the pelt of a karakul lamb after the curl begins to loosen

ca·rafe \kə-'raf, -'räf\ n 1 : a bottle with a flaring lip used esp. to hold wine 2 : a usu. glass pitcher for pouring coffee

car·am·bo·la \ˌkar-əm-ˈbō-lə\ n 1 : a 5-angled green to yellow edible tropical fruit of star-shaped cross section 2 : a tropical Asian tree widely cultivated for carambolas

car·a·mel \ˈkar-ə-məl, ˈkär-məl\ n 1 : an amorphous substance obtained by heating sugar and used for flavoring and coloring 2 : a firm chewy candy

car·a·pace \ˈkar-ə-ˌpās\ n : a protective case or shell on the back of some animals (as turtles or crabs)

¹car·at var of KARAT

²car·at \ˈkar-ət\ n : a unit of weight for precious stones equal to 200 milligrams

car·a·van \ˈkar-ə-ˌvan\ n 1 : a group of travelers journeying together through desert or hostile regions 2 : a group of vehicles traveling in a file

car·a·van·sa·ry \ˌkar-ə-ˈvan-sə-rē\ or **car·a·van·se·rai** \-sə-ˌrī\ n, pl **-ries** or **-rais** or **-rai** [Pers kārvānsarāī, fr. kārvān caravan + sarāī palace, inn] 1 : an inn in eastern countries where caravans rest at night 2 : HOTEL, INN

car·a·vel \ˈkar-ə-ˌvel\ n : a small 15th and 16th century ship with a broad bow, high narrow poop, and usu. three masts

car·a·way \ˈkar-ə-ˌwā\ n : an aromatic herb related to the carrot with fruits (**caraway seed**) used in seasoning and medicine; also : its fruit

car·bide \ˈkär-ˌbīd\ n : a compound of carbon with another element

car·bine \ˈkär-ˌbēn, -ˌbīn\ n : a short-barreled lightweight rifle

car·bo·hy·drate \ˌkär-bō-ˈhī-ˌdrāt, -drət\ n : any of various compounds composed of carbon, hydrogen, and oxygen (as sugars and starches)

car·bol·ic acid \ˌkär-ˈbä-lik-\ n : PHENOL

car·bon \ˈkär-bən\ n 1 : a nonmetallic chemical element occurring in nature esp. as diamond and graphite and as a constituent of coal, petroleum, and limestone 2 : a sheet of carbon paper; also : CARBON COPY 1 — **car·bon·less** \-ləs\ adj

car·bo·na·ceous \ˌkär-bə-ˈnā-shəs\ adj : relating to, containing, or composed of carbon

¹car·bon·ate \ˈkär-bə-ˌnāt, -nət\ n : a salt or ester of carbonic acid

²car·bon·ate \-ˌnāt\ vb **-at·ed; -at·ing** : to combine or infuse with carbon dioxide ⟨carbonated beverages⟩ — **car·bon·a·tion** \ˌkär-bə-ˈnā-shən\ n

carbon black n : any of various black substances consisting chiefly of carbon and used esp. as pigments

carbon copy n 1 : a copy made by carbon paper 2 : DUPLICATE

carbon dating n : the determination of the age of old material (as an archaeological specimen) by its content of carbon 14

carbon dioxide n : a heavy colorless gas that does not support combustion and is formed in animal respiration and in the combustion and decomposition of organic substances

carbon 14 n : a heavy radioactive form of carbon used esp. in dating old materials (as archaeological specimens)

car·bon·ic acid \ˌkär-ˈbä-nik-\ n : a weak acid that decomposes readily into water and carbon dioxide

car·bon·if·er·ous \ˌkär-bə-ˈni-fə-rəs\ adj 1 : producing or containing carbon or coal 2 cap : of, relating to, or being the period of the Paleozoic era between the Devonian and the Permian — **Carboniferous** n

carbon monoxide n : a colorless odorless very poisonous gas formed by the incomplete burning of carbon

carbon paper n : a thin paper coated with a pigment and used for making copies

carbon tet·ra·chlo·ride \-ˌte-trə-ˈklōr-ˌīd\ n : a colorless nonflammable toxic liquid used esp. as a solvent

carbon 12 n : the most abundant isotope of carbon having a nucleus of 6 protons and 6 neutrons and used as a standard for measurements of atomic weight

car·boy \ˈkär-ˌbȯi\ n [Pers qarāba, fr. Ar qarrāba demijohn] : a large container for liquids

car·bun·cle \ˈkär-ˌbəŋ-kəl\ n : a painful inflammation of the skin and underlying tissue that discharges pus from several openings

car·bu·re·tor \ˈkär-bə-ˌrā-tər, -byə-\ n : an apparatus for premixing vaporized fuel and air and supplying the mixture to an internal combustion engine

car·bu·ret·tor also **car·bu·ret·ter** \ˌkär-byə-ˈre-tər, ˈkär-byə-\ chiefly Brit var of CARBURETOR

car·case Brit var of CARCASS

car·cass \ˈkär-kəs\ n : a dead body; esp : one of an animal dressed for food

car·cin·o·gen \kär-ˈsi-nə-jən\ n : a substance or agent causing cancer — **car·ci·no·gen·ic** \ˌkärs-ᵊn-ō-ˈje-nik\ adj — **car·ci·no·ge·nic·i·ty** \-jə-ˈni-sə-tē\ n

car·ci·no·ma \ˌkärs-ᵊn-ˈō-mə\ n, pl **-mas** also **-ma·ta** \-tə\ : a malignant tumor of epithelial origin — **car·ci·no·ma·tous** \-təs\ adj

¹card \ˈkärd\ vb : to comb with a card : cleanse and untangle before spinning — **card·er** n

²card n : an instrument for combing fibers (as wool or cotton)

³card n 1 : PLAYING CARD 2 pl : a game played with playing cards; also : card playing 3 : an emotional issue used to one's advantage (as in a political campaign) 4 : a usu. clownishly amusing person : WAG 5 : a flat stiff usu. small piece of paper, cardboard, or plastic often bearing pictures or information 6 : PROGRAM; esp : a sports program — **in the cards** : INEVITABLE

⁴card vb 1 : to list or schedule on a card 2 : SCORE 3 : to ask for identification (as at a bar)

⁵card abbr cardinal

car·da·mom \ˈkär-də-məm\ n : the aromatic capsular fruit of an Indian herb related to the ginger whose seeds are used as a spice or condiment and in medicine; also : this plant

card·board \ˈkärd-ˌbȯrd\ n : a material thicker than paper and made from cellulose fiber

card–car·ry·ing \ˈkärd-ˌkar-ē-iŋ\ adj : being a regularly enrolled member of an organization (as a political party)

card catalog n : a catalog (as of books) in which the entries are arranged systematically on cards

car·di·ac \ˈkär-dē-ˌak\ adj [L cardiacus, fr. Gk kardiakos, fr. kardia heart] 1 : of, relating to, or located near the heart 2 : of, relating to, or affected with heart disease ⟨~ patients⟩

car·di·gan \ˈkär-di-gən\ n : a sweater or jacket usu. without a collar and with a full-length opening in the front

¹car·di·nal \ˈkärd-nəl, ˈkär-dᵊn-əl\ n 1 : an ecclesiastical official of the Roman Catholic Church ranking next below the pope 2 : a crested No. American finch that is nearly completely red in the male

²cardinal adj [ME, fr. LL cardinalis, fr. L serving as a hinge, fr. cardo hinge] 1 : of basic importance : CHIEF, MAIN, PRIMARY 2 : very serious ⟨a ~ sin⟩ — **car·di·nal·ly** adv

car·di·nal·ate \ˈkärd-nə-lət, -ˈkär-dᵊn-ə-lət, -ˌlāt\ n : the office, rank, or dignity of a cardinal

cardinal flower n : a No. American plant that bears a spike of brilliant red flowers

cardinal number n : a number (as 1, 5, 82, 357) that is used in simple counting and answers the question "how many?" — compare ORDINAL NUMBER

cardinal point n : one of the four principal compass points north, south, east, and west

car·dio \ˈkär-dē-ō\ adj : CARDIOVASCULAR 2

car·di·ol·o·gy \ˌkär-dē-ˈä-lə-jē\ n : the study of the heart and its action and diseases — **car·di·ol·o·gist** \-jist\ n

car·dio·pul·mo·nary resuscitation \ˌkär-dē-ō-ˈpu̇l-mə-ˌner-ē-\ n : a procedure to restore normal breathing after cardiac arrest that includes the clearance of air passages to the lungs, mouth-to-mouth method of artificial respiration, and heart massage by the exertion of pressure on the chest

car·dio·vas·cu·lar \-ˈvas-kyə-lər\ adj 1 : of or relating to the heart and blood vessels 2 : causing a temporary increase in heart rate ⟨a ~ workout⟩

card–sharp \-ˌshärp\ or **card–sharp·er** \ˈkärd-ˌshär-pər\ n : a cheater at cards

¹care \ˈker\ n 1 : a disquieted state of uncertainty and responsibility : ANXIETY 2 : watchful attention : HEED 3 : CHARGE, SUPERVISION ⟨under a doctor's ~⟩ 4 : a person or thing that is an object of anxiety or solicitude

²care vb **cared; car·ing** 1 : to feel anxiety 2 : to feel interest 3 : to give care 4 : to have a liking, fondness, taste, or inclination 5 : to be concerned about ⟨~ what happens⟩

CARE abbr Cooperative for American Relief to Everywhere

ca·reen \kə-ˈrēn\ vb 1 : to put (a ship or boat) on a beach esp. in order to clean or repair its hull   2 : to sway from side to side   3 : CAREER

¹ca·reer \kə-'rir\ *n* [MF *carrière*, fr. Old Occitan *carriera* street, fr. ML *carraria* road for vehicles, fr. L *carrus* car]   1 : COURSE, PASSAGE; *also* : speed in a course ⟨ran at full ∼⟩   2 : an occupation or profession followed as a life's work

²career *vb* : to go at top speed esp. in a headline manner

care·free \'ker-,frē\ *adj* : free from care or worry

care·ful \-fəl\ *adj* care·ful·ler; care·ful·lest   1 : using or taking care : VIGILANT   2 : marked by solicitude, caution, or prudence — care·ful·ly *adv* — care·ful·ness *n*

care·giv·er \-,gi-vər\ *n* : a person who provides direct care (as for children, elderly people, or the chronically ill)

care·less \-ləs\ *adj*   1 : free from care : UNTROUBLED   2 : UNCONCERNED, INDIFFERENT ⟨∼ of the consequences⟩   3 : not taking care   4 : not showing or receiving care — care·less·ly *adv* — care·less·ness *n*

care package *n* : a package of useful or pleasurable items given as a gift to another

¹ca·ress \kə-'res\ *vb* : to touch or stroke tenderly or lovingly — ca·ress·er *n*

²caress *n* : a tender or loving touch or embrace

car·et \'ker-ət\ *n* [L, there is lacking, fr. *carēre* to lack, be without]   : a mark ^ used to indicate the place where something is to be inserted

care·tak·er \'ker-,tā-kər\ *n*   1 : one in charge usu. as occupant in place of an absent owner   2 : one temporarily fulfilling the functions of an office

care·worn \-,wórn\ *adj* : showing the effects of grief or anxiety

car·fare \'kär-,fer\ *n* : passenger fare (as on a streetcar or bus)

car·go \'kär-gō\ *n, pl* cargoes *or* cargos : the goods carried in a ship, airplane, or vehicle : FREIGHT

Ca·rib·be·an \,ker-ə-'bē-ən, kə-'ri-bē-ən\ *adj* : of or relating to the eastern and southern West Indies or the Caribbean Sea

car·i·bou \'ker-ə-,bü\ *n, pl* caribou *or* caribous : a large circumpolar gregarious deer of northern taiga and tundra that usu. has large branched antlers usu. in both sexes — used esp. for one of the New World

car·i·ca·ture \'ker-i-kə-,chùr\ *n*   1 : distorted representation to produce a ridiculous effect   2 : a representation esp. in literature or art having the qualities of caricature — caricature *vb* — car·i·ca·tur·ist \-ist\ *n*

car·ies \'ker-ēz\ *n, pl* caries : tooth decay

car·il·lon \'ker-ə-,län\ *n* : a set of tuned bells sounded by hammers controlled from a keyboard

car·i·ous \'ker-ē-əs\ *adj* : affected with caries

car·jack·ing \'kär-ja-kiŋ\ *n* : the theft of an automobile by force or intimidation — car·jack·er *n*

car·load \'kär-,lōd\ *n* : a load that fills a car

car·mi·na·tive \kär-'mi-nə-tiv\ *adj* : expelling gas from the stomach or intestines — carminative *n*

car·mine \'kär-mən, -,mīn\ *n* : a vivid red

car·nage \'kär-nij\ *n* : great destruction of life : SLAUGHTER

car·nal \'kär-nºl\ *adj* [ME, fr. LL *carnalis*, fr. L *carn-, caro* flesh]   1 : of or relating to the body   2 : relating to or given to sensual pleasures and appetites — car·nal·i·ty \kär-'na-lə-tē\ *n* — car·nal·ly *adv*

car·na·tion \kär-'nā-shən\ *n* : a cultivated pink of any of numerous usu. double-flowered varieties derived from an Old World species

car·nau·ba wax \kär-'nó-bə-, -'naù-; ,kär-nə-'ü-bə-\ *n* : a brittle yellowish wax from a Brazilian palm that is used esp. in polishes

car·ne·lian \kär-'nēl-yən\ *n* : a hard red chalcedony used as a gem

car·ni·val \'kär-nə-vəl\ *n* [It *carnevale*, alter. of *carnelevare*, lit., removal of meat]   1 : a season of merrymaking just before Lent   2 : a boisterous merrymaking   3 : a traveling enterprise offering amusements   4 : an organized program of entertainment

car·ni·val·esque \,kär-nə-və-'lesk\ *adj* : suggestive of a carnival

car·niv·o·ra \kär-'ni-və-rə\ *n pl* : carnivorous mammals

car·ni·vore \'kär-nə-,vór\ *n* : a flesh-eating animal; *esp* : any of an order of mammals (as dogs, cats, bears, minks, and seals) feeding mostly on animal flesh

car·niv·o·rous \kär-'ni-və-rəs\ *adj*   1 : feeding on animal tissues   2 : of or relating to the carnivores — car·niv·o·rous·ly *adv* — car·niv·o·rous·ness *n*

car·ny *or* car·ney *or* car·nie \'kär-nē\ *n, pl* carnies *or* carneys   1 : CARNIVAL 3   2 : one who works with a carnival

car·ol \'ker-əl\ *n* : a song of joy or devotion — carol *vb* — car·ol·er *or* car·ol·ler *n*

car·om \'ker-əm\ *n*   1 : a shot in billiards in which the cue ball strikes two other balls   2 : a rebounding esp. at an angle — carom *vb*

car·o·tene \'ker-ə-,tēn\ *n* : any of several orange to red pigments (as beta-carotene) formed esp. in plants and used as a source of vitamin A

ca·rot·en·oid \kə-'rä-tə-,nóid\ *n* : any of various usu. yellow to red pigments (as carotenes) found widely in plants and animals

ca·rot·id \kə-'rä-təd\ *adj* : of, relating to, or being the chief artery or pair of arteries that pass up the neck and supply the head — carotid *n*

ca·rous·al \kə-'raú-zəl\ *n* : CAROUSE

ca·rouse \kə-'raùz\ *n* [MF *carrousse*, fr. *carous*, adv., all out (in *boire carous* to empty the cup), fr. G *garaus*] : a drunken revel — carouse *vb* — ca·rous·er *n*

car·ou·sel *also* car·rou·sel \,ker-ə-'sel, 'kar-ə-,sel\ *n*   1 : MERRY-GO-ROUND   2 : a circular conveyor

¹carp \'kärp\ *vb* : to find fault : CAVIL, COMPLAIN — carp *n* — carp·er *n*

²carp *n, pl* carp *or* carps : a large variable Asian freshwater fish of sluggish waters often raised for food

¹car·pal \'kär-pəl\ *adj* : of or relating to the wrist or the bones of the wrist

²carpal *n* : a carpal element or bone

carpal tunnel syndrome *n* : a condition characterized esp. by weakness, pain, and disturbances of sensation (as numbness) in the hand and fingers and caused by compression of a nerve in the wrist

car·pe di·em \'kär-pe-'dē-,em, -'dī-\ *n* [L, lit., pluck the day] : enjoyment of the present without concern for the future

car·pel \'kär-pəl\ *n* : one of the highly modified leaves that together form the ovary of a flower of a seed plant

car·pen·ter \'kär-pən-tər\ *n* : one who builds or repairs wooden structures — carpenter *vb* — car·pen·try \-trē\ *n*

car·pet \'kär-pət\ *n* : a heavy fabric used as a floor covering — carpet *vb*

car·pet·bag \-,bag\ *n* : a traveling bag common in the 19th century

car·pet·bag·ger \-,ba-gər\ *n* : a Northerner in the South after the American Civil War usu. seeking private gain under the reconstruction governments

car·pet·ing \'kär-pə-tiŋ\ *n* : material for carpets; *also* : CARPETS

car pool *n* : an arrangement in which a group of people commute together by car; *also* : a group having this arrangement — car·pool \-,pül\ *vb*

car·port \'kär-,pórt\ *n* : an open-sided automobile shelter

car·pus \'kär-pəs\ *n* : the wrist or its bones

car·ra·geen·an *or* car·ra·geen·in \,ker-ə-'gē-nən\ *n* : a colloid extracted esp. from a dark purple branching seaweed and used in foods esp. to stabilize and thicken them

car·rel \'ker-əl\ *n* : a table often partitioned or enclosed for individual study in a library

car·riage \'ker-ij\ *n*   1 : the act of carrying   2 : manner of holding the body   3 : a wheeled vehicle   4 *Brit* : a railway passenger coach   5 : a movable part of a machine for supporting some other moving part ⟨a typewriter ∼⟩

carriage trade *n* : trade from well-to-do or upper-class people

car·ri·er \'ker-ē-ər\ *n*   1 : one that carries   2 : a person or organization in the transportation business   3 : AIRCRAFT CARRIER   4 : one whose system carries the causative agents of a disease but who is immune to the disease   5 : an individual having a gene for a trait or condition that is not expressed outwardly   6 : an electromagnetic wave whose amplitude or frequency is varied in order to convey a radio or television signal

carrier pigeon *n* : a pigeon used esp. to carry messages

car·ri·on \'ker-ē-ən\ *n* : dead and decaying flesh

car·rot \'ker-ət\ *n* : the elongated usu. orange root of a common garden plant that is eaten as a vegetable; *also* : this plant

carrousel *var of* CAROUSEL

¹car·ry \ka-rē, ᵏker-ē\ *vb* **car·ried; car·ry·ing** [ME *carien*, fr. AF *carier*, fr. *carre* vehicle, fr. L *carrus*] **1** : to move while supporting : TRANSPORT, CONVEY, TAKE **2** : to influence by mental or emotional appeal **3** : to get possession or control of : CAPTURE, WIN **4** : to transfer from one place (as a column) to another ⟨∼ a number in adding⟩ **5** : to have or wear on one's person; *also* : to bear within one **6** : INVOLVE, IMPLY **7** : to hold or bear (oneself) in a specified way **8** : to keep in stock for sale **9** : to sustain the weight or burden of : SUPPORT **10** : to prolong in space, time, or degree **11** : to keep on one's books as a debtor **12** : to succeed in (an election) **13** : to win adoption (as in a legislature) **14** : PUBLISH, PRINT **15** : to reach or penetrate to a distance

²carry *n* **1** : the range of a gun or projectile or of a struck or thrown ball **2** : PORTAGE **3** : an act or method of carrying ⟨fireman's ∼⟩

car·ry·all \-ᵢȯl\ *n* : a capacious bag or case

carry away *vb* : to arouse to a high and often excessive degree of emotion

carrying charge *n* : a charge added to the price of merchandise sold on the installment plan

car·ry–on \-ᵢȯn, -ᵢän\ *n* : a piece of luggage suitable for being carried aboard an airplane by a passenger — **carry–on** *adj*

carry on *vb* **1** : CONDUCT, MANAGE **2** : to behave in a foolish, excited, or improper manner **3** : to continue in spite of hindrance or discouragement

carry out *vb* **1** : to bring to a successful conclusion **2** : to put into execution

car·sick \ᵏkär-ᵢsik\ *adj* : affected with motion sickness esp. in an automobile — **car sickness** *n*

¹cart \ᵏkärt\ *n* **1** : a heavy 2-wheeled wagon **2** : a small wheeled vehicle

²cart *vb* : to convey in or as if in a cart — **cart·er** *n*

cart·age \ᵏkär-tij\ *n* : the act of or rate charged for carting

carte blanche \ᵏkärt-ᵏblä\"sh\ *n, pl* **cartes blanches** *same or* -ᵏblä\"sh\ [F, lit., blank document] : full discretionary power

car·tel \kär-ᵏtel\ *n* : a combination of independent business enterprises designed to limit competition ◆ **Synonyms** POOL, SYNDICATE, MONOPOLY, TRUST

car·ti·lage \ᵏkär-tə-lij\ *n* : a usu. translucent somewhat elastic tissue that composes most of the skeleton of young vertebrate embryos and later is mostly converted to bone in higher vertebrates — **car·ti·lag·i·nous** \ᵢkär-tə-ᵏla-jə-nəs\ *adj*

cartilaginous fish *n* : any of a class of fishes (as a shark or ray) having the skeleton wholly or largely composed of cartilage

car·tog·ra·phy \kär-ᵏtä-grə-fē\ *n* : the making of maps — **car·tog·ra·pher** *n* — **car·to·graph·ic** \ᵢkär-tə-ᵏgra-fik\ *adj*

car·ton \ᵏkär-tᵊn\ *n* : a cardboard box or container

car·toon \kär-ᵏtün\ *n* **1** : a preparatory sketch (as for a painting) **2** : a drawing intended as humor, caricature, or satire **3** : COMIC STRIP — **cartoon** *vb* — **car·toon·ist** *n*

car·tridge \ᵏkär-trij\ *n* **1** : a tube containing a complete charge for a firearm **2** : a container of material for insertion into an apparatus **3** : a small case containing a phonograph needle and transducer that is attached to a tonearm **4** : a case containing a magnetic tape or disk **5** : a case for holding integrated circuits containing a computer program

cart·wheel \ᵏkärt-ᵢhwēl\ *n* **1** : a large coin (as a silver dollar) **2** : a lateral handspring with arms and legs extended

carve \ᵏkärv\ *vb* **carved; carv·ing 1** : to cut with care or precision ; shape by cutting **2** : to cut into pieces or slices **3** : to slice and serve meat at table — **carv·er** *n*

cary·at·id \ᵢker-ē-ᵏa-təd\ *n, pl* **-ids** *or* **-i·des** \-ᵃta-tə-ᵢdēz\ : a sculptured draped female figure used as an architectural column

CAS *abbr* certificate of advanced study

ca·sa·ba \kə-ᵏsä-bə\ *n* : any of several muskmelons with a yellow rind and sweet flesh

¹cas·cade \ᵢkas-ᵏkād\ *n* **1** : a steep usu. small waterfall **2** : something arranged in a series or succession of stages so that each stage derives from or acts upon the product of the preceding

²cas·cade *vb* **cas·cad·ed; cas·cad·ing 1** : to fall, pass, or connect in or as if in a cascade

cas·cara \ka-ᵏska-rə\ *n* : the dried bark of a small Pacific coastal tree of the U.S. and southern Canada used as a laxative; *also* : this tree

¹case \ᵏkās\ *n* [ME *cas*, fr. AF, fr. L *casus* fall, chance, fr. *cadere* to fall] **1** : a particular instance or situation **2** : an inflectional form of a noun, pronoun, or adjective indicating its grammatical relation to other words; *also* : such a relation whether indicated by inflection or not **3** : what actually exists or happens : FACT **4** : a suit or action in law : CAUSE **5** : a convincing argument **6** : an instance of disease or injury; *also* : PATIENT **7** : INSTANCE, EXAMPLE — **in case** : as a precaution — **in case of** : in the event of

²case *n* [ME *cas*, fr. AF *case*, *chase*, fr. L *capsa*] **1** : a box or container for holding something; *also* : a box with its contents **2** : an outer covering **3** : a divided tray for holding printing type **4** : CASING 2

³case *vb* **cased; cas·ing 1** : to enclose in or cover with a case **2** : to inspect esp. with intent to rob

ca·sein \ᵏkā-ᵢsēn, kā-ᵏ\ *n* : any of several phosphorus-containing proteins occurring in or produced from milk

case·ment \ᵏkās-mənt\ *n* : a window that opens like a door

case·work \-ᵢwərk\ *n* : social work that involves the individual person or family — **case·work·er** *n*

¹cash \ᵏkash\ *n* [MF or It; MF *casse* money box, fr. It *cassa*, fr. L *capsa* chest, case] **1** : ready money **2** : money or its equivalent paid at the time of purchase or delivery

²cash *vb* : to pay or obtain cash for

ca·shew \ᵏka-shü, kə-ᵏshü\ *n* : an edible kidney-shaped nut of a tropical American tree related to the sumacs; *also* : the tree

¹ca·shier \ka-ᵏshir\ *vb* : to dismiss from service; *esp* : to dismiss in disgrace

²cash·ier \ka-ᵏshir\ *n* **1** : a bank official responsible for moneys received and paid out **2** : a person who receives and records payments

cashier's check *n* : a check drawn by a bank upon its own funds and signed by its cashier

cash in *vb* **1** : to convert into cash ⟨*cash in* bonds⟩ **2** : to settle accounts and withdraw from a gambling game or business deal **3** : to obtain financial profit or advantage

cash·less \ᵏkash-ləs\ *adj* : relying on monetary transactions that use electronic means rather than cash

cash·mere \ᵏkazh-ᵢmir, ᵏkash-\ *n* : fine wool from the undercoat of an Indian goat (**cashmere goat**) or a yarn spun of this; *also* : a soft twilled fabric orig. woven from this yarn

cash out *vb* : to convert noncash assets into cash

cash register *n* : a business machine that usu. has a money drawer, indicates each sale, and records the money received

cash–strapped \ᵏkash-ᵢstrapt\ *adj* : lacking sufficient money

cas·ing \ᵏkā-siŋ\ *n* **1** : something that encases **2** : the frame of a door or window

ca·si·no \kə-ᵏsē-nō\ *n, pl* **-nos** [It, fr. *casa* house] **1** : a building or room for social amusements; *esp* : one used for gambling **2** *also* **cas·si·no** : a card game in which players win cards by matching those on the table

cask \ᵏkask\ *n* : a barrel-shaped container usu. for liquids; *also* : the quantity held by such a container

cas·ket \ᵏkas-kət\ *n* **1** : a small box (as for jewels) **2** : COFFIN

casque \ᵏkask\ *n* : HELMET

cas·sa·va \kə-ᵏsä-və\ *n* : any of several tropical spurges with rootstocks yielding a nutritious starch from which tapioca is prepared; *also* : the rootstock or its starch

cas·se·role \ᵏka-sə-ᵢrōl\ *n* **1** : a dish in which food may be baked and served **2** : food cooked and served in a casserole

cas·sette *also* **ca·sette** \kə-ᵏset\ *n* **1** : a lightproof container for photographic plates or film **2** : a plastic case containing magnetic tape

cas·sia \ᵏka-shə\ *n* **1** : a dried coarse cinnamon bark **2** : any of a genus of leguminous herbs, shrubs, and trees of warm regions including several which yield senna

cas·sit·er·ite \kə-ᵏsi-tə-ᵢrīt\ *n* : a dark mineral that is the chief tin ore

cas·sock \ᵏka-sək\ *n* : an ankle-length garment worn esp. by Roman Catholic and Anglican clergy

cas·so·wary \'ka-sə-,wer-ē\ *n, pl* **-war·ies** : any of a genus of large flightless birds closely related to the emu

¹cast \'kast\ *vb* **cast; cast·ing** **1** : THROW, FLING **2** : DIRECT ⟨~ a glance⟩ **3** : to deposit (a ballot) formally **4** : to throw off, out, or away : DISCARD, SHED **5** : COMPUTE; *esp* : to add up **6** : to assign the parts of (a play) to actors; *also* : to assign to a role or part **7** : to shape (a substance) by pouring in liquid or plastic form into a mold and letting harden without pressure **8** : to make (as a knot or stitch) by looping or catching up

²cast *n* **1** : THROW, FLING **2** : a throw of dice **3** : the set of actors in a dramatic production **4** : something formed in or as if in a mold; *also* : a rigid surgical casing (as for protecting and supporting a fractured bone) **5** : TINGE, HUE **6** : APPEARANCE, LOOK ⟨features of delicate ~⟩ **7** : something thrown out or off, shed, or expelled ⟨worm ~s⟩

cas·ta·net \,kas-tə-'net\ *n* [Sp *castañeta*, fr. *castaña* chestnut, fr. L *castanea*] : a rhythm instrument consisting of two small wooden, ivory, or plastic shells held in the hand and clicked together

cast-away \'kas-tə-,wā\ *adj* **1** : thrown away : REJECTED **2** : cast adrift or ashore as a survivor of a shipwreck — **castaway** *n*

caste \'kast\ *n* [Pg *casta*, lit., race, lineage, fr. fem. of *casto* pure, chaste, fr. L *castus*] **1** : one of the hereditary social classes in Hinduism **2** : a division of a society based on wealth, inherited rank, or occupation **3** : social position : PRESTIGE **4** : a system of rigid social stratification

cas·tel·lat·ed \'kas-tə-,lā-təd\ *adj* : having battlements like a castle

cast·er \'kas-tər\ *n* **1** *or* **cas·tor** : a small container to hold salt or pepper at the table **2** : a small wheel that turns freely and is used to support and move furniture, trucks, and equipment

cas·ti·gate \'kas-tə-,gāt\ *vb* **-gat·ed; -gat·ing** : to punish or criticize severely — **cas·ti·ga·tion** \,kas-tə-'gā-shən\ *n* — **cas·ti·ga·tor** \'kas-tə-,gā-tər\ *n*

cast·ing \'kas-tiŋ\ *n* **1** : CAST 7 **2** : something cast in a mold

casting vote *n* : a deciding vote cast by a presiding officer to break a tie

cast iron *n* : a hard brittle alloy of iron, carbon, and silicon cast in a mold

cas·tle \'ka-səl\ *n* **1** : a large fortified building or set of buildings **2** : a large or imposing house **3** : ³ROOK

castle in the air : an impracticable project

cast-off \'kast-,óf\ *adj* : thrown away or aside — **cast-off** *n*

cas·tor oil \'kas-tər-\ *n* : a thick yellowish oil extracted from the poisonous seeds of an herb (**castor–oil plant**) and used as a lubricant and purgative

cas·trate \'kas-,trāt\ *vb* **cas·trat·ed; cas·trat·ing** : to deprive of sex glands and esp. testes — **cas·tra·tion** \kas-'trā-shən\ *n* — **cas·tra·tor** \-ər\ *n*

ca·su·al \'ka-zhə-wəl\ *adj* **1** : resulting from or occurring by chance **2** : OCCASIONAL, INCIDENTAL ⟨~ employment⟩ **3** : OFFHAND, NONCHALANT ⟨a ~ approach to cooking⟩ **4** : designed for informal use ⟨~ clothing⟩ — **ca·su·al·ly** *adv* — **ca·su·al·ness** *n*

ca·su·al·ty \'ka-zhəl-tē, 'ka-zhə-wəl-\ *n, pl* **-ties** **1** : serious or fatal accident **2** : a military person lost through death, injury, sickness, or capture or through being missing in action **3** : a person or thing injured, lost, or destroyed

ca·su·ist·ry \'ka-zhə-wə-strē\ *n, pl* **-ries** : specious argument : RATIONALIZATION — **ca·su·ist** \-wist\ *n* — **ca·su·is·tic** \,ka-zhə-'wis-tik\ *or* **ca·su·is·ti·cal** \-ti-kəl\ *adj*

ca·sus bel·li \,kä-səs-'be-,lē, ,kä-səs-'be-,lī\ *n, pl* **ca·sus belli** \,kä-,süs-, ,kä-\ [NL, occasion of war] : a cause or pretext for a declaration of war

¹cat \'kat\ *n* **1** : a carnivorous mammal long domesticated as a pet and for catching rats and mice **2** : any of a family of animals (as the lion, lynx, or leopard) including the domestic cat **3** : a malicious woman **4** : GUY

²cat *abbr* catalog

ca·tab·o·lism \kə-'ta-bə-,li-zəm\ *n* : destructive metabolism involving the release of energy and resulting in the breakdown of complex materials — **cat·a·bol·ic** \,ka-tə-'bä-lik\ *adj*

cat·a·clysm \'ka-tə-,kli-zəm\ *n* : a violent change or up-

heaval — **cat·a·clys·mal** \,ka-tə-'kliz-məl\ *or* **cat·a·clys·mic** \-'kliz-mik\ *adj*

cat·a·comb \'ka-tə-,kōm\ *n* : an underground burial place with galleries and recesses for tombs

cat·a·falque \'ka-tə-,falk, -,fólk, -,fók\ *n* : an ornamental structure sometimes used in solemn funerals to hold the body

cat·a·lep·sy \'ka-tə-,lep-sē\ *n, pl* **-sies** : a trancelike state characterized esp. by loss of voluntary motion — **cat·a·lep·tic** \,ka-tə-'lep-tik\ *adj or n*

¹cat·a·log *or* **cat·a·logue** \'ka-tə-,lóg\ *n* **1** : LIST, REGISTER **2** : a systematic list of items with descriptive details; *also* : a book containing such a list

²catalog *or* **catalogue** *vb* **-loged** *or* **-logued; -log·ing** *or* **-logu·ing** **1** : to make a catalog of **2** : to enter in a catalog — **cat·a·log·er** *or* **cat·a·logu·er** *n*

ca·tal·pa \kə-'tal-pə\ *n* : any of a genus of broad-leaved trees with showy flowers and long slim pods

ca·tal·y·sis \kə-'ta-lə-səs\ *n, pl* **-y·ses** \-,sēz\ : a change and esp. increase in the rate of a chemical reaction brought about by a substance (**cat·a·lyst** \'ka-tə-list\) that is itself unchanged at the end of the reaction — **cat·a·lyt·ic** \,ka-tə-'li-tik\ *adj* — **cat·a·lyt·i·cal·ly** \-ti-k-(ə-)lē\ *adv*

catalytic converter *n* : an automobile exhaust-system component in which a catalyst changes harmful gases into mostly harmless products

cat·a·lyze \'ka-tə-,līz\ *vb* **-lyzed; -lyz·ing** : to bring about the catalysis of (a chemical reaction)

cat·a·ma·ran \,ka-tə-mə-'ran\ *n* [Tamil (a language of southern India) *kaṭṭumaram*, fr. *kaṭṭu* to tie + *maram* tree] : a boat with twin hulls

cat·a·mount \'ka-tə-,maúnt\ *n* : COUGAR; *also* : LYNX

cat·a·pult \'ka-tə-,pəlt, -,púlt\ *n* **1** : an ancient military machine for hurling missiles **2** : a device for launching an airplane (as from an aircraft carrier) — **catapult** *vb*

cat·a·ract \'ka-tə-,rakt\ *n* **1** : a cloudiness of the lens of the eye obstructing vision **2** : a large waterfall; *also* : steep rapids in a river

ca·tarrh \kə-'tär\ *n* : inflammation of a mucous membrane esp. of the nose and throat — **ca·tarrh·al** \-əl\ *adj*

ca·tas·tro·phe \kə-'tas-trə-(,)fē\ *n* [Gk *katastrophē*, fr. *katastrephein* to overturn, fr. *kata-* down + *strephein* to turn] **1** : a great disaster or misfortune **2** : utter failure — **cat·a·stroph·ic** \,ka-tə-'strä-fik\ *adj* — **cat·a·stroph·i·cal·ly** \-fi-k(ə-)lē\ *adv*

cat·a·ton·ic \,ka-tə-'tä-nik\ *adj* : of, relating to, or marked by schizophrenia characterized esp. by stupor, negativism, rigidity, purposeless excitement, and bizarre posturing — **catatonic** *n*

cat·bird \'kat-,bərd\ *n* : an American songbird with a catlike mewing call

cat·boat \'kat-,bōt\ *n* : a single-masted sailboat with a single large sail extended by a long boom

cat·call \-,kól\ *n* : a loud cry made esp. to express disapproval — **catcall** *vb*

¹catch \'kach, 'kech\ *vb* **caught** \'kót\; **catch·ing** [ME *cacchen*, fr. AF *cacher, chacher, chacer* to hunt, ultim. fr. L *captare* to chase] **1** : to capture esp. after pursuit **2** : TRAP **3** : to discover unexpectedly ⟨*caught* in the act⟩ **4** : to become suddenly aware of **5** : to take hold of : SNATCH ⟨~ at a straw⟩ **6** : INTERCEPT **7** : to get entangled **8** : to become affected with or by ⟨~ fire⟩ ⟨~ cold⟩ **9** : to seize and hold firmly; *also* : FASTEN **10** : OVERTAKE **11** : to be in time for ⟨~ a train⟩ **12** : to take in and retain **13** : to look at or listen to

²catch *n* **1** : something caught **2** : the act of catching; *also* : a game consisting of throwing and catching a ball **3** : something that catches or checks or holds immovable ⟨a door ~⟩ **4** : one worth catching esp. as a mate **5** : FRAGMENT, SNATCH **6** : a concealed difficulty or complication

catch·all \'kach-,ól, 'kech-\ *n* : something to hold a variety of odds and ends

catch–as–catch–can *adj* : using any means available

catch·er \'ka-chər, 'ke-\ *n* : one that catches; *esp* : a player positioned behind home plate in baseball

catch·ing *adj* **1** : INFECTIOUS, CONTAGIOUS **2** : ALLURING, CATCHY

catch·ment \'kach-mənt, 'kech-\ *n* **1** : something that catches water **2** : the action of catching water

catch on *vb* **1** : UNDERSTAND **2** : to become popular

catch·pen·ny \'kach-ˌpe-nē, 'kech-\ *adj* : using sensationalism or cheapness for appeal ⟨a ~ newspaper⟩

catch·phrase \-ˌfrāz\ *n* : a word or expression frequently used to represent or characterize a person, group, idea, or point of view

catch-22 \-ˌtwen-tē-'tü\ *n, pl* **catch-22's** *or* **catch-22s** *often cap* C [fr. *Catch-22*, a paradoxical rule found in the novel *Catch-22* (1961) by Joseph Heller] : a problematic situation for which the only solution is denied by a circumstance inherent in the problem or by a rule; *also* : the circumstance or rule that denies a solution

catchup *var of* KETCHUP

catch up *vb* : to travel or work fast enough to overtake or complete

catch·word \'kach-ˌwərd, 'kech-\ *n* 1 : GUIDE WORD 2 : CATCHPHRASE

catchy \'ka-chē, 'ke-\ *adj* **catch·i·er; -est** 1 : likely to catch the interest or attention 2 : TRICKY ⟨a ~ question⟩

cat·e·chism \'ka-tə-ˌki-zəm\ *n* : a summary or test (as of religious doctrine) usu. in the form of questions and answers — **cat·e·chist** \-ˌkist\ *n* — **cat·e·chize** \-ˌkīz\ *vb*

cat·e·chu·men \ˌka-tə-'kyü-mən\ *n* : a religious convert receiving training before baptism

cat·e·gor·i·cal \ˌka-tə-'gȯr-i-kəl\ *adj* 1 : ABSOLUTE, UNQUALIFIED ⟨a ~ denial⟩ 2 : of, relating to, or constituting a category — **cat·e·gor·i·cal·ly** \-i-k(ə-)lē\ *adv*

cat·e·go·rise *Brit var of* CATEGORIZE

cat·e·go·rize \'ka-ti-gə-ˌrīz\ *vb* **-rized; -riz·ing** : to put into a category : CLASSIFY — **cat·e·go·ri·za·tion** \ˌka-ti-gə-rə-'zā-shən\ *n*

cat·e·go·ry \'ka-tə-ˌgȯr-ē\ *n, pl* **-ries** : a division used in classification; *also* : CLASS, GROUP, KIND

ca·ter \'kā-tər\ *vb* [obs. *cater* buyer of provisions, fr. ME *catour*, short for *acatour*, fr. AF, fr. *acater*, *achater* to buy] 1 : to provide a supply of food 2 : to supply what is wanted — **ca·ter·er** *n*

catercorner *or* **cater–cornered** *var of* KITTY-CORNER

cat·er·pil·lar \'ka-tər-ˌpi-lər\ *n* [ME *catyrpel*, fr. OF *catepelose*, lit., hairy cat] : a wormlike often hairy insect larva esp. of a butterfly or moth

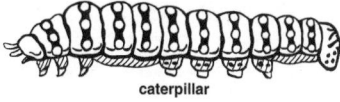

caterpillar

cat·er·waul \'ka-tər-ˌwȯl\ *vb* : to make a harsh cry — **caterwaul** *n*

cat·fish \'kat-ˌfish\ *n* : any of an order of chiefly freshwater stout-bodied fishes with slender tactile processes around the mouth

cat·gut \-ˌgət\ *n* : a tough cord made usu. from sheep intestines

ca·thar·sis \kə-'thär-səs\ *n, pl* **ca·thar·ses** \-ˌsēz\ 1 : an act of purging or purification 2 : elimination of a complex by bringing it to consciousness and affording it expression

¹**ca·thar·tic** \kə-'thär-tik\ *adj* : of, relating to, or producing catharsis

²**cathartic** *n* : PURGATIVE

ca·the·dral \kə-'thē-drəl\ *n* : the principal church of a diocese

cath·e·ter \'ka-thə-tər\ *n* : a tube for insertion into a bodily passage or cavity usu. for injecting or drawing off material or for keeping a passage open

cath·e·ter·i·za·tion \ˌka-thə-tə-rə-'zā-shən\ *n* : the use of or introduction of a catheter — **cath·e·ter·ize** \'ka-thə-tə-ˌrīz\ *vb*

cath·ode \'ka-ˌthōd\ *n* 1 : the negative electrode of an electrolytic cell 2 : the positive terminal of a battery 3 : the electron-emitting electrode of an electron tube — **cath·od·al** \'ka-ˌthō-dᵊl\ *adj* — **ca·thod·ic** \ka-'thä-dik\ *adj*

cathode–ray tube *n* : a vacuum tube in which a beam of electrons is projected on a phosphor-coated screen to produce a luminous spot

cath·o·lic \'kath-lik, 'ka-thə-\ *adj* [ME *catholik* relating to the church universal, ultim. fr. Gk *katholikos* universal,

general, fr. *katholou* in general] 1 *cap* : of or relating to Catholics and esp. Roman Catholics 2 : GENERAL, UNIVERSAL

Cath·o·lic \'kath-lik, 'ka-thə-\ *n* : a member of a church claiming historical continuity from the ancient undivided Christian church; *esp* : a member of the Roman Catholic Church — **Ca·thol·i·cism** \kə-'thä-lə-ˌsi-zəm\ *n*

cath·o·lic·i·ty \ˌka-thə-'li-sə-tē\ *n, pl* **-ties** 1 *cap* : the character of being in conformity with a Catholic church 2 : liberality of sentiments or views 3 : comprehensive range

cat·ion \'kat-ˌī-ən\ *n* : the ion in an electrolyte that migrates to the cathode; *also* : a positively charged ion

cat·kin \'kat-kən\ *n* : a long flower cluster (as of a willow) bearing crowded flowers and prominent bracts

cat·like \-ˌlīk\ *adj* : resembling a cat or its behavior; *esp* : STEALTHY

cat·nap \-ˌnap\ *n* : a very short light nap — **catnap** *vb*

cat·nip \-ˌnip\ *n* : an aromatic mint that is esp. attractive to cats

cat–o'–nine–tails \ˌka-tə-'nīn-ˌtālz\ *n, pl* **cat–o'–nine–tails** : a whip made of usu. nine knotted cords fastened to a handle

CAT scan \'kat-\ *n* [computerized *axial tomography*] : an image made by computed tomography

CAT scanner *n* : a medical instrument consisting of integrated X-ray and computing equipment that is used to make CAT scans

cat's cradle *n* : a game played with a string looped on the fingers in such a way as to resemble a small cradle

cat's–eye \'kats-ˌī\ *n, pl* **cat's–eyes** : any of various iridescent gems

cat's–paw \-ˌpȯ\ *n, pl* **cat's–paws** : a person used by another as a tool

cat·suit \'kat-ˌsüt\ *n* : a close-fitting one-piece garment that covers the torso and the legs

catsup *var of* KETCHUP

cat·tail \'kat-ˌtāl\ *n* : any of a genus of tall reedlike marsh plants with furry brown spikes of tiny flowers

cat·tle \'ka-tᵊl\ *n pl* : LIVESTOCK; *esp* : domestic bovines (as cows, bulls, or calves) — **cat·tle·man** \-mən, -ˌman\ *n*

cat·ty \'ka-tē\ *adj* **cat·ti·er, -est** : slyly spiteful — **cat·ti·ly** \'ka-tə-lē\ *adv* — **cat·ti·ness** *n*

catty–corner *or* **catty–cornered** *var of* KITTY-CORNER

CATV *abbr* community antenna television

cat·walk \'kat-ˌwȯk\ *n* : a narrow walk (as along a bridge)

Cau·ca·sian \kȯ-'kā-zhən\ *adj* : of or relating to the white race of humankind — **Caucasian** *n* — **Cau·ca·soid** \'kȯ-kə-ˌsȯid\ *adj or n*

cau·cus \'kȯ-kəs\ *n* : a meeting of a group of persons belonging to the same political party or faction usu. to decide upon policies and candidates — **caucus** *vb*

cau·dal \'kȯ-dᵊl\ *adj* : of, relating to, or located near the tail or the hind end of the body — **cau·dal·ly** *adv*

cau·dil·lo \kaù-'thē-(ˌ)yō, -'thēl-\ *n, pl* **-llos** : a Spanish or Latin-American military dictator

caught \'kȯt\ *past and past part of* CATCH

caul \'kȯl\ *n* : the inner fetal membrane of higher vertebrates esp. when covering the head at birth

caul·dron \'kȯl-drən\ *n* : a large kettle

cau·li·flow·er \'kȯ-li-ˌflaü(-ə)r\ *n* [It *cavolfiore*, fr. *cavolo* cabbage + *fiore* flower] : a garden plant closely related to cabbage and grown for its compact edible head of undeveloped flowers; *also* : this head used as a vegetable

cauliflower ear *n* : an ear deformed from injury and excessive growth of scar tissue

¹**caulk** *or* **calk** \'kȯk\ *vb* [ME, fr. AF *cauker, calcher* to trample, fr. L *calcare*, fr. *calx* heel] : to stop up and make tight against leakage (as a boat or its seams) — **caulk·er** *n*

²**caulk** *or* **calk** *also* **caulk·ing** *or* **calk·ing** *n* : material used to caulk

caus·al \'kȯ-zəl\ *adj* 1 : expressing or indicating cause 2 : relating to or acting as a cause — **cau·sal·i·ty** \kȯ-'za-lə-tē\ *n* — **caus·al·ly** *adv*

cau·sa·tion \kȯ-'zā-shən\ *n* 1 : the act or process of causing 2 : the means by which an effect is produced

¹**cause** \'kȯz\ *n* 1 : REASON, MOTIVE 2 : something that brings about a result; *esp* : a person or thing that is the agent of bringing something about 3 : a suit or action in court : CASE 4 : a question or matter to be decided 5 : a

principle or movement earnestly supported — **cause-less** *adj*

²**cause** *vb* **caused; caus·ing :** to be the cause or occasion of — **caus·a·tive** \'kȯ-zə-tiv\ *adj* — **caus·er** *n*

cause cé·lè·bre \kōz-sā-'lebrᵊ, ˌkȯz-\ *n, pl* **causes célèbres** *same*\ [F, lit., celebrated case] **1 :** a legal case that excites widespread interest **2 :** a notorious person, thing, incident, or episode

cau·se·rie \ˌkōz-'rē, ˌkō-zə-\ *n* [F] **1 :** an informal conversation **:** CHAT **2 :** a short informal essay

cause·way \'kȯz-ˌwā\ *n* : a raised way or road across wet ground or water

¹**caus·tic** \'kȯ-stik\ *adj* **1 :** CORROSIVE **2 :** SHARP, INCISIVE ⟨∼ wit⟩

²**caustic** *n* **1 :** a substance that burns or destroys organic tissue by chemical action **2 :** SODIUM HYDROXIDE

cau·ter·ize \'kȯ-tə-ˌrīz\ *vb* **-ized; -iz·ing :** to burn or sear usu. to prevent infection or bleeding — **cau·ter·i·za·tion** \ˌkȯ-tə-rə-'zā-shən\ *n*

¹**cau·tion** \'kȯ-shən\ *n* **1 :** ADMONITION, WARNING **2 :** prudent forethought to minimize risk **3 :** one that astonishes — **cau·tion·ary** \-shə-ˌner-ē\ *adj*

²**caution** *vb* **:** to advise caution to

cau·tious \'kȯ-shəs\ *adj* **:** marked by or given to caution **:** CAREFUL — **cau·tious·ly** *adv* — **cau·tious·ness** *n*

cav *abbr* **1** cavalry **2** cavity

cav·al·cade \ˌka-vəl-'kād\ *n* **1 :** a procession of riders or carriages; *also* **:** a procession of vehicles **2 :** a dramatic sequence or procession

¹**cav·a·lier** \ˌka-və-'lir\ *n* [MF, fr. It *cavaliere*, fr. Old Occitan *cavalier*, fr. LL *caballarius* horseman, fr. L *caballus* horse] **1 :** a mounted soldier **:** KNIGHT **2** *cap* **:** an adherent of Charles I of England **3 :** GALLANT

²**cavalier** *adj* **1 :** DEBONAIR **2 :** DISDAINFUL, HAUGHTY ⟨a ∼ attitude toward money⟩ — **cav·a·lier·ly** *adv*

cav·al·ry \'ka-vəl-rē\ *n, pl* **-ries :** troops mounted on horseback or moving in motor vehicles — **cav·al·ry·man** \-mən, -ˌman\ *n*

¹**cave** \'kāv\ *n* **:** a natural underground chamber open to the surface

²**cave** *vb* **caved; cav·ing 1 :** to collapse or cause to collapse **2 :** to cease to resist **:** SUBMIT — usu. used with *in*

ca·ve·at \'ka-vē-ˌät, -ˌat; 'kä-vē-ˌät\ *n* [L, let him beware] **:** WARNING

caveat emp·tor \-'emp-tər, -ˌtȯr\ *n* [NL, let the buyer beware] **:** a principle in commerce: without a warranty the buyer takes a risk

cave–in \'kā-ˌvin\ *n* **1 :** the action of caving in **2 :** a place where earth has caved in

cave·man \'kāv-ˌman\ *n* **1 :** a cave dweller esp. of the Stone Age **2 :** a man who acts in a rough or crude manner

cav·ern \'ka-vərn\ *n* **:** CAVE; *esp* **:** one of large or unknown size — **cav·ern·ous** *adj* — **cav·ern·ous·ly** *adv*

cav·i·ar *also* **cav·i·are** \'ka-vē-ˌär, 'kä-\ *n* **:** the salted roe of a large fish (as sturgeon) used as an appetizer

cav·il \'ka-vəl\ *vb* **-iled** *or* **-illed; -il·ing** *or* **-il·ling :** to make frivolous objections or raise trivial objections to — **cavil** *n* — **cav·il·er** *or* **cav·il·ler** *n*

cav·ing \'kā-viŋ\ *n* **:** the sport of exploring caves **:** SPELUNKING

cav·i·ta·tion \ˌka-və-'tā-shən\ *n* **:** the formation of partial vacuums in a liquid by a swiftly moving solid body (as a propeller) or by high-intensity sound waves

cav·i·ty \'ka-və-tē\ *n, pl* **-ties 1 :** an unfilled space within a mass **:** a hollow place **2 :** an area of decay in a tooth

ca·vort \kə-'vȯrt\ *vb* **:** PRANCE, CAPER

ca·vy \'kā-vē\ *n, pl* **cavies :** GUINEA PIG 1

caw \'kȯ\ *vb* **:** to utter the harsh call of the crow or a similar cry — **caw** *n*

cay \'kē, 'kā\ *n* **:** ⁴KEY

cay·enne pepper \ˌkī-'en-, ˌkā-\ *n* **:** a condiment consisting of ground dried fruits or seeds of a hot pepper

cayman *var of* CAIMAN

Ca·yu·ga \kā-'ü-gə, kī-\ *n, pl* **Cayuga** *or* **Cayugas :** a member of an American Indian people of New York

Cay·use \'kī-ˌyüs, kī-'\ *n* **1** *pl* **Cayuse** *or* **Cayuses :** a member of an American Indian people of Oregon and Washington **2** *pl* **cayuses***, not cap West* **:** a native range horse

Cb *symbol* columbium

CB \'sē-'bē\ *n* **:** CITIZENS BAND; *also* **:** the radio set used for citizens-band communications

CBC *abbr* Canadian Broadcasting Corporation

CBD *abbr* cash before delivery

CBS *abbr* Columbia Broadcasting System

CBW *abbr* chemical and biological warfare

cc *abbr* cubic centimeter

CC *abbr* **1** carbon copy **2** community college **3** country club

CCD \ˌsē-ˌsē-'dē\ *n* **:** CHARGE-COUPLED DEVICE

CCTV *abbr* closed-circuit television

CCU *abbr* **1** cardiac care unit **2** coronary care unit **3** critical care unit

ccw *abbr* counterclockwise

cd *abbr* cord

Cd *symbol* cadmium

¹**CD** \ˌsē-'dē\ *n* **:** CERTIFICATE OF DEPOSIT

²**CD** *n* **:** a small optical disk usu. containing recorded music or computer data; *also* **:** the content of a CD

³**CD** *abbr* Civil Defense

CDR *abbr* commander

CD–ROM \ˌsē-ˌdē-'räm\ *n* **:** a CD containing computer data that cannot be altered

CDT *abbr* central daylight (saving) time

Ce *symbol* cerium

CE *abbr* **1** chemical engineer **2** civil engineer **3** Corps of Engineers

cease \'sēs\ *vb* **ceased; ceas·ing :** to come or bring to an end **:** STOP

cease–fire \'sēs-'fī(-ə) r\ *n* **:** a suspension of active hostilities

cease·less \'sēs-ləs\ *adj* **:** being without pause or stop **:** CONTINUOUS — **cease·less·ly** *adv* — **cease·less·ness** *n*

ce·cum *also* **cae·cum** \'sē-kəm\ *n, pl* **ce·ca** \-kə\ **:** the blind pouch at the beginning of the large intestine into which the small intestine opens — **ce·cal** *also* **cae·cal** \-kəl\ *adj*

ce·dar \'sē-dər\ *n* **:** any of numerous coniferous trees (as a juniper) noted for their fragrant durable wood; *also* **:** this wood

cede \'sēd\ *vb* **ced·ed; ced·ing 1 :** to yield or give up esp. by treaty **2 :** ASSIGN, TRANSFER — **ced·er** *n*

ce·di \'sā-dē\ *n* — see MONEY table

ce·dil·la \si-'di-lə\ *n* **:** a mark placed under the letter *c* (as *ç*) to show that the *c* is to be pronounced like *s*

ceil·ing \'sē-liŋ\ *n* **1 :** the overhead inside lining of a room **2 :** the height above the ground of the base of the lowest layer of clouds when over half of the sky is obscured **3 :** the greatest height at which an airplane can operate efficiently **4 :** a prescribed upper limit ⟨price ∼⟩

cel·an·dine \'se-lən-ˌdīn, -ˌdēn\ *n* **:** a yellow-flowered herb related to the poppies

cel·e·brant \'se-lə-brənt\ *n* **:** one who celebrates; *esp* **:** a priest officiating at the Eucharist

cel·e·brate \'se-lə-ˌbrāt\ *vb* **-brat·ed; -brat·ing 1 :** to perform (as a sacrament) with appropriate rites **2 :** to honor (as a holiday) by solemn ceremonies or by refraining from ordinary business **3 :** to observe a notable occasion with festivities — **cel·e·bra·tion** \ˌse-lə-'brā-shən\ *n* — **cel·e·bra·tor** \'se-lə-ˌbrā-tər\ *n* — **cel·e·bra·to·ry** \-brə-ˌtȯr-ē, ˌse-lə-'brā-tə-rē\ *adj*

celebrated *adj* **:** widely known and often referred to ⟨a ∼ author⟩ ◆ **Synonyms** DISTINGUISHED, RENOWNED, NOTED, FAMOUS, ILLUSTRIOUS, NOTORIOUS

ce·leb·ri·ty \sə-'le-brə-tē\ *n, pl* **-ties 1 :** the state of being celebrated **:** RENOWN **2 :** a celebrated person

ce·ler·i·ty \sə-'ler-ə-tē\ *n* **:** SPEED, RAPIDITY

cel·ery \'se-lə-rē\ *n, pl* **-er·ies :** a European herb related to the carrot and widely grown for the crisp edible stems of its leaves

celery cabbage *n* **:** CHINESE CABBAGE 2

ce·les·ta \sə-'les-tə\ *or* **ce·leste** \sə-'lest\ *n* **:** a keyboard instrument with hammers that strike steel plates

ce·les·tial \sə-'les-chəl\ *adj* **1 :** HEAVENLY, DIVINE **2 :** of or relating to the sky — **ce·les·tial·ly** *adv*

celestial navigation *n* **:** navigation by observation of the positions of stars

celestial sphere *n* **:** an imaginary sphere of infinite radius against which the celestial bodies appear to be projected

cel·i·ba·cy \'se-lə-bə-sē\ n **1** : the state of being unmarried; *esp* : abstention by vow from marriage **2** : abstention from sexual intercourse

cel·i·bate \'se-lə-bət\ n : one who lives in celibacy — **celibate** *adj*

cell \'sel\ n **1** : a small room (as in a convent or prison) usu. for one person; *also* : a small compartment, cavity, or bounded space **2** : a tiny mass of protoplasm that usu. contains a nucleus, is enclosed by a membrane, and forms the smallest structural unit of living matter capable of functioning independently **3** : a container holding an electrolyte either for generating electricity or for use in electrolysis **4** : a single unit in a device for converting radiant energy into electrical energy — **celled** \'seld\ *adj*

cel·lar \'se-lər\ n **1** : BASEMENT 1 **2** : the lowest place in the standings (as in an athletic league) **3** : a stock of wines

cel·lar·ette *or* **cel·lar·et** \ˌse-lə-'ret\ n : a case or cabinet for a few bottles of wine or liquor

cell body n : the nucleus-containing central part of a neuron exclusive of its processes

cel·lo \'che-lō\ n, pl **cellos** : a bass member of the violin family tuned an octave below the viola — **cel·list** \-list\ n

cel·lo·phane \'se-lə-ˌfān\ n : a thin transparent material made from cellulose and used as a wrapping

cell phone n : a portable cordless telephone for use in a cellular system

cel·lu·lar \'sel-yə-lər\ *adj* **1** : of, relating to, or consisting of cells ⟨∼ proteins⟩ **2** : of, relating to, or being a radiotelephone system in which a geographical area is divided into small sections each served by a transmitter of limited range

cel·lu·lite \'sel-yə-ˌlīt\ n : deposits of lumpy fat within connective tissue (as in the thighs, hips, and buttocks)

cel·lu·lose \'sel-yə-ˌlōs\ n : a complex carbohydrate of the cell walls of plants used esp. in making paper or rayon — **cel·lu·los·ic** \ˌsel-yə-'lō-sik\ *adj or n*

Cel·si·us \'sel-sē-əs\ *adj* : relating to or having a scale for measuring temperature on which the interval between the triple point and the boiling point of water is divided into 99.99 degrees with 0.01° being the triple point and 100.00° the boiling point; *also* : CENTIGRADE

Celt \'kelt, 'selt\ n : a member of any of a group of peoples (as the Irish or Welsh) of western Europe — **Celt·ic** *adj*

cem·ba·lo \'chem-bə-ˌlō\ n, pl **-ba·li** \-ˌlē\ *or* **-balos** [It] : HARPSICHORD

¹ce·ment \si-'ment\ n **1** : CONCRETE; *also* : a powder that is produced from a burned mixture chiefly of clay and limestone and that is used in mortar and concrete **2** : a binding element or agency **3** : CEMENTUM; *also* : a substance for filling cavities in teeth

²cement vb **1** : to unite by or as if by cement **2** : to cover with concrete — **ce·ment·er** n

ce·men·tum \si-'men-təm\ n : a specialized external bony layer covering the dentin of the part of a tooth normally within the gum

cem·e·tery \'se-mə-ˌter-ē\ n, pl **-ter·ies** [ME *cimitery*, fr. AF *cimiterie*, fr. LL *coemeterium*, fr. Gk *koimētērion* sleeping chamber, burial place, fr. *koiman* to put to sleep] : a burial ground : GRAVEYARD

cen·o·bite \'se-nə-ˌbīt\ n : a member of a religious group living together in a monastic community — **cen·o·bit·ic** \ˌse-nə-'bi-tik\ *adj*

ceno·taph \'se-nə-ˌtaf\ n [F *cénotaphe*, fr. L *cenotaphium*, fr. Gk *kenotaphion*, fr. *kenos* empty + *taphos* tomb] : a tomb or a monument erected in honor of a person whose body is elsewhere

Ce·no·zo·ic \ˌsē-nə-'zō-ik, ˌse-\ *adj* : of, relating to, or being the era of geologic history that extends from about 65 million years ago to the present — **Cenozoic** n

cen·ser \'sen-sər\ n : a vessel for burning incense (as in a religious ritual)

¹cen·sor \'sen-sər\ n **1** : a person who inspects printed matter or motion pictures with power to suppress anything objectionable **2** : one of two early Roman magistrates whose duties included taking the census — **cen·so·ri·al** \sen-'sòr-ē-əl\ *adj*

²censor vb : to subject to censorship

cen·so·ri·ous \sen-'sōr-ē-əs\ *adj* : marked by or given to censure : CRITICAL — **cen·so·ri·ous·ly** *adv* — **cen·so·ri·ous·ness** n

cen·sor·ship \'sen-sər-ˌship\ n **1** : the action of a censor esp. in stopping the transmission or publication of matter considered objectionable **2** : the office of a Roman censor

¹cen·sure \'sen-chər\ n **1** : the act of blaming or condemning sternly **2** : an official reprimand

²censure vb **cen·sured; cen·sur·ing** : to find fault with and criticize as blameworthy — **cen·sur·able** *adj* — **cen·sur·er** n

cen·sus \'sen-səs\ n **1** : a periodic governmental count of population **2** : COUNT, TALLY — **cen·sus** vb

¹cent \'sent\ n [F, hundred, fr. L *centum*] **1** : a monetary unit equal to ¹⁄₁₀₀ of a basic unit of value — see *birr, dollar, euro, gulden, leone, lilangeni, lira, nakfa, pound, rand, rupee, shilling* at MONEY table **2** : a coin, token, or note representing one cent **3** : a former monetary unit equal to ¹⁄₁₀₀ Dutch gulden

²cent *abbr* **1** centigrade **2** central **3** century

cen·tas \'sen-ˌtäs\ n, pl **cen·tai** \-ˌtī\ *or* **cen·tu** \-ˌtü\ — see *litas* at MONEY table

cen·taur \'sen-ˌtòr\ n : any of a race of creatures in Greek mythology half man and half horse

¹cen·ta·vo \sen-'tä-(ˌ)vō\ n, pl **-vos** — see *boliviano, colón, cordoba, lempira, peso, quetzal, sucre* at MONEY table

²cen·ta·vo \-'tä-(ˌ)vü, -(ˌ)vō\ n, pl **-vos** **1** — see *escudo, metical, real* at MONEY table **2** : a former monetary unit equal to ¹⁄₁₀₀ Portuguese escudo

cen·te·nar·i·an \ˌsen-tə-'ner-ē-ən\ n : a person who is 100 or more years old

cen·te·na·ry \sen-'te-nə-rē, 'sen-tə-ˌner-ē\ n, pl **-ries** : CENTENNIAL — **centenary** *adj*

cen·ten·ni·al \sen-'te-nē-əl\ n : a 100th anniversary or its celebration — **centennial** *adj*

¹cen·ter \'sen-tər\ n **1** : the point that is equally distant from all points on the circumference of a circle or surface of a sphere; *also* : MIDDLE 1 **2** : the point about which an activity concentrates or from which something originates **3** : a region of concentrated population **4** : a middle part **5** *often cap* : political figures holding moderate views esp. between those of conservatives and liberals **6** : a player occupying a middle position (as in football or basketball)

²center vb **1** : to place or fix at or around a center or central area **2** : to give a central focus or basis : CONCENTRATE **3** : to have a center : FOCUS

cen·ter·board \'sen-tər-ˌbórd\ n : a retractable keel used esp. in sailboats

cen·ter·piece \-ˌpēs\ n **1** : an object in a central position; *esp* : an adornment in the center of a table **2** : one that is of central importance or interest in a larger whole

cen·tes·i·mal \sen-'te-sə-məl\ *adj* : marked by or relating to division into hundredths

¹cen·tes·i·mo \chen-'te-zə-ˌmō\ n, pl **-mi** \-(ˌ)mē\ : a former monetary unit equal to ¹⁄₁₀₀ Italian lira

²cen·tes·i·mo \sen-'te-sə-ˌmō\ n, pl **-mos** — see *balboa, peso* at MONEY table

cen·ti·grade \'sen-tə-ˌgrād, 'sän-\ *adj* : relating to, conforming to, or having a thermometer scale on which the interval between the freezing and boiling points of water is divided into 100 degrees with 0° representing the freezing point and 100° the boiling point ⟨10° ∼⟩ — compare CELSIUS

cen·ti·gram \-ˌgram\ n — see METRIC SYSTEM table

cen·ti·li·ter \'sen-ti-ˌlē-tər\ n — see METRIC SYSTEM table

cen·time \'sän-ˌtēm\ n **1** : a former monetary unit of any of several countries (as Belgium, France, and Luxembourg) equal to ¹⁄₁₀₀ franc **2** — see *dinar, dirham, franc, gourde* at MONEY table

cen·ti·me·ter \'sen-tə-ˌmē-tər, 'sän-\ n — see METRIC SYSTEM table

centimeter–gram–second *adj* : of, relating to, or being a system of units based on the centimeter as the unit of length, the gram as the unit of mass, and the second as the unit of time

cen·ti·mo \'sen-tə-ˌmō\ n, pl **-mos** **1** — see *bolivar, colón, dobra, guarani, sol* at MONEY table **2** : a former monetary unit equal to ¹⁄₁₀₀ peseta

cen·ti·pede \'sen-tə-ˌpēd\ n [L *centipeda*, fr. *centum* hundred + *pes* foot] : any of a class of long flattened segmented arthropods with one pair of legs on each segment except the first which has a pair of poison fangs

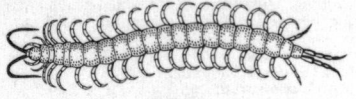

centipede

¹cen·tral \'sen-trəl\ adj 1 : constituting a center 2 : ES-SENTIAL, PRINCIPAL ⟨the novel's ~ character⟩ 3 : situated at, in, or near the center 4 : centrally placed and superseding separate units ⟨~ heating⟩ — cen·tral·ly adv

²central n : a central controlling office

cen·tral·ise Brit var of CENTRALIZE

cen·tral·ize \'sen-trə-,līz\ vb -ized; -iz·ing : to bring to a central point or under central control — cen·tral·i·za·tion \,sen-trə-lə-'zā-shən\ n — cen·tral·iz·er \'sen-trə-,līzər\ n

central nervous system n : the part of the nervous system which integrates nervous function and activity and which in vertebrates consists of the brain and spinal cord

cen·tre chiefly Brit var of CENTER

cen·trif·u·gal \sen-'tri-fyə-gəl, -fi-\ adj [NL centrifugus, fr. centr- center + L fugere to flee] 1 : proceeding or acting in a direction away from a center or axis 2 : using or acting by centrifugal force

centrifugal force n : the apparent force felt by an object moving in a curved path and acting outward from a center of rotation

cen·tri·fuge \'sen-trə-,fyüj\ n : a machine using centrifugal force (as for separating substances of different densities or for removing moisture)

cen·trip·e·tal \sen-'tri-pə-t°l\ adj [NL centripetus, fr. centr- center + L petere seek] : proceeding or acting in a direction toward a center or axis

centripetal force n : the force needed to keep an object revolving about a point moving in a circular path

cen·trist \'sen-trist\ n 1 often cap : a member of a center party 2 : one who holds moderate views

cen·tu·ri·on \sen-'tùr-ē-ən, -'tyùr-\ n : an officer commanding a Roman century

cen·tu·ry \'sen-chə-rē\ n, pl -ries 1 : a subdivision of a Roman legion 2 : a group or sequence of 100 like things 3 : a period of 100 years

century plant n : a Mexican agave maturing and flowering only once in many years and then dying

CEO \,sē-(,)ē-'ō\ n : the executive with the chief decision-making authority in an organization or business

ce·phal·ic \sə-'fa-lik\ adj 1 : of or relating to the head 2 : directed toward or situated on or in or near the head

ce·ram·ic \sə-'ra-mik\ n 1 pl : the art or process of making articles from a nonmetallic mineral (as clay) by firing 2 : a product produced by ceramics — ceramic adj

ce·ram·ist \sə-'ra-mist\ or ce·ram·i·cist \sə-'ra-mə-sist\ n : one who engages in ceramics

¹ce·re·al \'sir-ē-əl\ adj [L cerealis, fr. Ceres, the Roman goddess of agriculture] : relating to grain or to the plants that produce it; also : made of grain

²cereal n 1 : a grass (as wheat) yielding grain suitable for food; also : its grain 2 : a food and esp. a breakfast food prepared from the grain of a cereal

cer·e·bel·lum \,ser-ə-'be-ləm\ n, pl -bellums or -bel·la \-lə\ [ML, fr. L, dim. of cerebrum brain] : a part of the brain that projects over the medulla and is concerned esp. with coordination of muscular action and with bodily balance — cer·e·bel·lar \-lər\ adj

ce·re·bral \sə-'rē-brəl, 'ser-ə-\ adj 1 : of or relating to the brain, intellect, or cerebrum 2 : appealing to or involving the intellect — ce·re·bral·ly adv

cerebral cortex n : the surface layer of gray matter of the cerebrum that functions chiefly in coordination of sensory and motor information

cerebral palsy n : a disorder caused by brain damage usu. before, during, or shortly after birth and marked esp. by defective muscle control

cer·e·brate \'ser-ə-,brāt\ vb -brat·ed; -brat·ing : THINK — cer·e·bra·tion \,ser-ə-'brā-shən\ n

ce·re·brum \sə-'rē-brəm, 'ser-ə-\ n, pl -brums or -bra

\-brə\ [L, brain] : the enlarged front and upper part of the brain that contains the higher nervous centers

cere·ment \'ser-ə-mənt, 'sir-mənt\ n : a shroud for the dead

¹cer·e·mo·ni·al \,ser-ə-'mō-nē-əl\ adj : of, relating to, or forming a ceremony; also : stressing careful attention to detail — cer·e·mo·ni·al·ly adv

²ceremonial n : a ceremonial act or system : RITUAL, FORM

cer·e·mo·ni·ous \,ser-ə-'mō-nē-əs\ adj 1 : devoted to forms and ceremony 2 : CEREMONIAL 3 : according to formal usage or procedure 4 : marked by ceremony — cer·e·mo·ni·ous·ly adv — cer·e·mo·ni·ous·ness n

cer·e·mo·ny \'ser-ə-,mō-nē\ n, pl -nies 1 : a formal act or series of acts prescribed by law, ritual, or convention 2 : a conventional act of politeness 3 : a mere outward form with no deeper significance 4 : FORMALITY

ce·re·us \'sir-ē-əs\ n : any of various cacti of the western U.S. and tropical America

ce·rise \sə-'rēs\ n [F, lit., cherry] : a moderate red color

ce·ri·um \'sir-ē-əm\ n : a malleable metallic chemical element used esp. in alloys

cer·met \'sər-,met\ n : a strong alloy of a heat-resistant compound and a metal used esp. for turbine blades

cert abbr certificate; certification; certified; certify

¹cer·tain \'sər-t°n\ adj 1 : FIXED, SETTLED 2 : of a specific but unspecified character ⟨~ people in authority⟩ 3 : DEPENDABLE, RELIABLE 4 : INDISPUTABLE, UNDENIABLE 5 : assured in mind or action — cer·tain·ly adv

²certain pron : certain ones

cer·tain·ty \-tē\ n, pl -ties 1 : something that is certain 2 : the quality or state of being certain

cer·tif·i·cate \sər-'ti-fi-kət\ n 1 : a document testifying to the truth of a fact 2 : a document testifying that one has fulfilled certain requirements (as of a course) 3 : a document giving evidence of ownership or debt ⟨a stock ~⟩

certificate of deposit : a money-market bond redeemable without penalty only on maturity

cer·ti·fi·ca·tion \,sər-tə-fə-'kā-shən\ n 1 : the act of certifying : the state of being certified 2 : a certified statement

certified mail n : first class mail for which proof of delivery may be secured but no indemnity value is claimed

certified public accountant n : an accountant who has met the requirements of a state law and has been granted a certificate

cer·ti·fy \'sər-tə-,fī\ vb -fied; -fy·ing 1 : VERIFY, CONFIRM 2 : to endorse officially 3 : to guarantee (a bank check) as good by a statement to that effect stamped on its face 4 : to recognize as having met specific qualifications within a field ⟨certified teachers⟩ ♦ Synonyms AC-CREDIT, APPROVE, SANCTION, ENDORSE — cer·ti·fi·able \-ə-bəl\ adj — cer·ti·fi·ably \-blē\ adv — cer·ti·fi·er n

cer·ti·tude \'sər-tə-,tüd, -,tyüd\ n : the state of being or feeling certain

ce·ru·le·an \sə-'rü-lē-ən\ adj : AZURE

ce·ru·men \sə-'rü-mən\ n : EARWAX

cer·vi·cal \'sər-vi-kəl\ adj : of or relating to a neck or cervix

cervical cap n : a contraceptive device in the form of a thimble-shaped molded cap that fits snugly over the uterine cervix and blocks sperm from entering the uterus

cer·vix \'sər-viks\ n, pl cer·vi·ces \-və-,sēz\ or cer·vix·es 1 : NECK; esp : the back part of the neck 2 : a constricted portion of an organ or part; esp : the narrow outer end of the uterus

ce·sar·e·an or cae·sar·e·an also ce·sar·i·an or cae·sar·i·an \si-'zer-ē-ən\ n, often cap : CESAREAN SECTION — ce-sarean or caesarean also cesarian or caesarian adj

cesarean section also caesarean section n, often cap C [fr. the legendary association of such a delivery with the Roman cognomen Caesar] : surgical incision of the walls of the abdomen and uterus for delivery of offspring

ce·si·um \'sē-zē-əm\ n : a silver-white soft ductile chemical element

ces·sa·tion \se-'sā-shən\ n : a temporary or final ceasing (as of action)

ces·sion \'se-shən\ n : a yielding (as of rights) to another

cess·pool \'ses-,pül\ n 1 : an underground pit or tank for receiving household sewage 2 : a filthy or corrupt situation

ce·ta·cean \si-'tā-shən\ n : any of an order of aquatic

mostly marine mammals that includes whales, porpoises, dolphins, and related forms — **cetacean** *adj*

cf *abbr* [L *confer*] compare

Cf *symbol* californium

CF *abbr* cystic fibrosis

CFC *abbr* chlorofluorocarbon

cg *abbr* centigram

CG *abbr* **1** coast guard **2** commanding general

cgs *abbr* centimeter-gram-second

ch *abbr* **1** chain **2** champion **3** chapter **4** church

CH *abbr* **1** clearinghouse **2** courthouse **3** customhouse

Cha·blis \sha-ˈblē, shə-, shä-; ˈsha-ˌblē\ *n, pl* **Cha·blis** \-ˈblēz, -(ˌ)blēz\ **1** : a dry sharp white Burgundy wine **2** : a white California wine

cha–cha \ˈchä-ˌchä\ *n* : a fast rhythmic ballroom dance of Latin American origin

chafe \ˈchāf\ *vb* **chafed; chaf·ing 1** : IRRITATE, VEX **2** : FRET **3** : to warm by rubbing **4** : to rub so as to wear away; *also* : to make sore by rubbing

cha·fer \ˈchā-fər\ *n* : any of various scarab beetles

1chaff \ˈchaf\ *n* **1** : debris (as husks) separated from grain in threshing **2** : something comparatively worthless — **chaffy** *adj*

2chaff *n* : light jesting talk : BANTER

3chaff *vb* : to tease good-naturedly

chaf·fer \ˈcha-fər\ *vb* : BARGAIN, HAGGLE — **chaf·fer·er** *n*

chaf·finch \ˈcha-ˌfinch\ *n* : a common European finch with a cheerful song

chaf·ing dish \ˈchā-fiŋ-\ *n* : a utensil for cooking food at the table

1cha·grin \shə-ˈgrin\ *n* : mental uneasiness or annoyance caused by failure, disappointment, or humiliation

2chagrin *vb* **cha·grined** \-ˈgrind\; **cha·grin·ing** : to cause to feel chagrin

1chain \ˈchān\ *n* [ME *cheyne*, fr. AF *chaene*, fr. L *catena*] **1** : a flexible series of connected links **2** : a chainlike surveying instrument; *also* : a unit of length equal to 66 feet (about 20 meters) **3** *pl* : BONDS, FETTERS **4** : a series of things linked together ⟨mountain ∼*s*⟩; *also* : a group of usu. identical enterprises with a single owner ⟨fast-food ∼*s*⟩ ✦ **Synonyms** TRAIN, STRING, SEQUENCE, SUCCESSION, SERIES

2chain *vb* : to fasten, bind, or connect with a chain; *also* : FETTER

chain gang *n* : a gang of convicts chained together

chain letter *n* : a letter sent to several persons with a request that each send copies to an equal number of persons

chain mail *n* : flexible armor of interlocking metal rings

chain reaction *n* **1** : a series of events in which each event initiates the succeeding one **2** : a chemical or nuclear reaction yielding products that cause further reactions of the same kind

chain saw *n* : a portable power saw that has teeth linked together to form an endless chain — **chain·saw** \ˈchān-ˌsó\ *vb*

chain–smoke \ˈchān-ˈsmōk\ *vb* : to smoke esp. cigarettes continuously

1chair \ˈcher\ *n* [ME *chaiere*, fr. AF, fr. L *cathedra*, fr. Gk *kathedra*, fr. *kata-* down + *hedra* seat] **1** : a seat with a back for one person **2** : ELECTRIC CHAIR **3** : an official seat; *also* : an office or position of authority or dignity **4** : CHAIRMAN

2chair *vb* : to act as chairman of

chair·lift \ˈcher-ˌlift\ *n* : a motor-driven conveyor for skiers consisting of seats hung from a moving cable

chair·man \-mən\ *n* : the presiding officer of a meeting, committee, or event — **chair·man·ship** *n*

chair·per·son \-ˌpər-sən\ *n* : CHAIRMAN

chair·wom·an \-ˌwù-mən\ *n* : a woman who serves as chairman

chaise \ˈshāz\ *n* : a 2-wheeled horse-drawn carriage with a folding top

chaise longue \ˈshāz-ˈlòŋ\ *n, pl* **chaise longues** *same or* -ˈlòŋz\ [F, lit., long chair] : a long reclining chair

chaise lounge \-ˈlaúnj\ *n* : CHAISE LONGUE

chal·ced·o·ny \kal-ˈse-dᵊn-ē\ *n, pl* **-nies** : a translucent quartz of various colors

chal·co·py·rite \ˌkal-kə-ˈpī-ˌrīt\ *n* : a yellow mineral constituting an important copper ore

cha·let \sha-ˈlā\ *n* **1** : a herdsman's cabin in the Swiss mountains **2** : a building in the style of a Swiss cottage with a wide roof overhang

chal·ice \ˈcha-ləs\ *n* : a drinking cup; *esp* : the eucharistic cup

1chalk \ˈchók\ *n* **1** : a soft limestone **2** : chalk or chalky material esp. when used as a crayon — **chalky** *adj*

2chalk *vb* **1** : to rub or mark with chalk **2** : to record with or as if with chalk — usu. used with *up*

chalk·board \ˈchók-ˌbórd\ *n* : BLACKBOARD

chalk up *vb* **1** : ASCRIBE, CREDIT **2** : ATTAIN, ACHIEVE ⟨*chalk up* a victory⟩

1chal·lenge \ˈcha-lənj\ *vb* **chal·lenged; chal·leng·ing** [ME *chalengen* to accuse, fr. AF *chalenger*, fr. L *calumniari* to accuse falsely, fr. *calumnia* calumny] **1** : to order to halt and prove identity **2** : to take exception to : DISPUTE ⟨∼ a ruling⟩ **3** : to issue an invitation to compete ⟨*challenged* me to another game⟩ **4** : to stimulate by presenting difficulties ⟨a job that ∼*s* her⟩ — **chal·leng·er** *n*

2challenge *n* **1** : a summons to a duel **2** : an invitation to compete in a sport **3** : a calling into question **4** : an exception taken to a juror **5** : a sentry's command to halt and prove identity **6** : a stimulating or interesting task or problem

challenged *adj* : presented with difficulties (as by a disability)

chal·lis \ˈsha-lē\ *n, pl* **chal·lises** \-lēz\ : a lightweight clothing fabric of wool, cotton, or synthetic yarns

cham·ber \ˈchām-bər\ *n* **1** : ROOM; *esp* : BEDROOM **2** : an enclosed space or cavity **3** : a hall for meetings of a legislative body **4** : a judge's consultation room — usu. used in pl. **5** : a legislative or judicial body; *also* : a council for a business purpose **6** : the part of a firearm that holds the cartridge or powder charge during firing — **cham·bered** \-bərd\ *adj*

cham·ber·lain \ˈchām-bər-lən\ *n* **1** : a chief officer in the household of a king or nobleman **2** : TREASURER

cham·ber·maid \-ˌmād\ *n* : a maid who takes care of bedrooms

chamber music *n* : music intended for performance by a few musicians before a small audience

chamber of commerce : an association of businesspeople for promoting commercial and industrial interests in the community

cham·bray \ˈsham-ˌbrā\ *n* : a lightweight clothing fabric of white and colored threads

cha·me·leon \kə-ˈmēl-yən\ *n* [ME *camelion*, fr. MF, fr. L *chamaeleon*, fr. Gk *chamaileōn*, fr. *chamai* on the ground + *leōn* lion] : a small lizard whose skin changes color esp. according to its surroundings

chameleon

1cham·fer \ˈcham-fər\ *vb* **1** : to cut a furrow in (as a column) : GROOVE **2** : to make a chamfer on : BEVEL

2chamfer *n* : a beveled edge

cham·ois \ˈsha-mē\ *n, pl* **cham·ois** *same or* -mēz\ **1** : a small goatlike ruminant mammal of Europe and the Caucasus region of Russia **2** *also* **cham·my** \ˈsha-mē\ : a soft leather made esp. from the skin of the sheep or goat **3** : a cotton fabric made in imitation of chamois leather

cham·o·mile *or* **cam·o·mile** \ˈka-mə-ˌmī(-ə)l, -ˌmēl\ *n* : any of a genus of strong-scented herbs related to the daisies and having flower heads that yield a bitter substance used esp. in tonics and teas

1champ \ˈchamp, ˈchämp\ *vb* **1** : to chew noisily **2** : to show impatience of delay or restraint

2champ \ˈchamp\ *n* : CHAMPION

cham·pagne \sham-ˈpān\ *n* : a white effervescent wine

¹**cham·pi·on** \'cham-pē-ən\ n 1 : a militant advocate or defender 2 : one that wins first prize or place in a contest 3 : one that is acknowledged to be better than all others

²**champion** vb : to protect or fight for as a champion
♦ *Synonyms* BACK, ADVOCATE, UPHOLD, SUPPORT

cham·pi·on·ship \-,ship\ n 1 : the position or title of a champion 2 : the act of championing : DEFENSE 3 : a contest held to determine a champion

¹**chance** \'chans\ n 1 : something that happens without apparent cause 2 : the unpredictable element in existence : LUCK, FORTUNE 3 : OPPORTUNITY 4 : the likelihood of a particular outcome in an uncertain situation : PROBABILITY 5 : RISK 6 : a raffle ticket — **chance** adj — **by chance** : in the haphazard course of events

²**chance** vb **chanced; chanc·ing** 1 : to take place by chance : HAPPEN 2 : to come casually and unexpectedly — used with upon 3 : to leave to chance 4 : to accept the risk of

chan·cel \'chan-səl\ n : the part of a church including the altar and choir

chan·cel·lery or **chan·cel·lory** \'chan-sə-lə-rē\ n, pl **-ler·ies** or **-lor·ies** 1 : the position or office of a chancellor 2 : the building or room where a chancellor works 3 : the office or staff of an embassy or consulate

chan·cel·lor \'chan-sə-lər\ n 1 : a high state official in various countries 2 : the head of a university 3 : a judge in the equity court in various states of the U.S. 4 : the chief minister of state in some European countries — **chan·cel·lor·ship** n

chan·cery \'chan-sə-rē\ n, pl **-cer·ies** 1 : a record office for public or diplomatic archives 2 : any of various courts of equity in the U.S. and Britain 3 : a chancellor's court or office 4 : the office of an embassy 5 : the business office of a diocese

chan·cre \'shaŋ-kər\ n [F, fr. OF, fr. L *cancer*] : a primary sore or ulcer at the site of entry of an infective agent (as of syphilis)

chan·croid \'shaŋ-,krȯid\ n : a sexually transmitted disease caused by a bacterium and characterized by chancres that differ from those of syphilis in lacking hardened margins

chancy \'chan-sē\ adj **chanc·i·er; -est** 1 Scot : AUSPICIOUS 2 : RISKY

chan·de·lier \,shan-də-'lir\ n : a branched lighting fixture suspended from a ceiling

chan·dler \'chand-lər\ n [ME *chandeler* a maker or seller of candles, fr. AF, fr. *chandele* candle, fr. L *candela*] : a dealer in provisions and supplies of a specified kind ⟨ship's ∼⟩ — **chan·dlery** n

¹**change** \'chānj\ vb **changed; chang·ing** 1 : to make or become different : ALTER 2 : to replace with another 3 : to give or receive an equivalent sum in notes or coins of usu. smaller denominations or of another currency 4 : to put fresh clothes or covering on ⟨∼ a bed⟩ 5 : to put on different clothes 6 : EXCHANGE — **change·able** adj — **chang·er** n

²**change** n 1 : the act, process, or result of changing 2 : a fresh set of clothes 3 : money given in exchange for other money of higher denomination 4 : money returned when a payment exceeds the sum due 5 : coins esp. of small denominations — **change·ful** adj

change·ling \'chānj-liŋ\ n : a child secretly exchanged for another in infancy

change of life : MENOPAUSE

change·over \'chānj-,ō-vər\ n : CONVERSION, TRANSITION

change ringing n : the art or practice of ringing a set of tuned bells in continually varying order

¹**chan·nel** \'cha-nᵊl\ n 1 : the bed of a stream 2 : the deeper part of a waterway 3 : STRAIT 4 : a means of passage or transmission 5 : a range of frequencies of sufficient width for a single radio or television transmission 6 : a usu. tubular enclosed passage : CONDUIT 7 : a long gutter, groove, or furrow

²**channel** vb **-neled** or **-nelled; -nel·ing** or **-nel·ling** 1 : to make a channel in 2 : to direct into or through a channel

chan·nel·ize \'cha-nə-,līz\ vb **-ized; -iz·ing** : CHANNEL — **chan·nel·i·za·tion** \,cha-nə-lə-'zā-shən\ n

chan·son \shäⁿ-'sōⁿ\ n, pl **chan·sons** \same or -'sōⁿz\ : SONG; esp : a cabaret song

¹**chant** \'chant\ vb 1 : SING; esp : to sing a chant 2 : to utter or recite in the manner of a chant 3 : to celebrate or praise in song — **chant·er** n

²**chant** n 1 : a repetitive melody in which several words are sung to one tone : SONG; esp : a liturgical melody 2 : a manner of singing or speaking in musical monotones

chan·te·relle \,shan-tə-'rel\ n : a fragrant edible mushroom

chan·teuse \shäⁿ-'tərz, shan-'tüz\ n, pl **chan·teuses** \same or -'tər-zəz, -'tü-zəz\ [F] : a woman who is a concert or nightclub singer

chan·tey or **chan·ty** \'shan-tē, 'chan-\ n, pl **chanteys** or **chanties** : a song sung by sailors in rhythm with their work

chan·ti·cleer \,chan-tə-'klir, ,shan-\ n : ROOSTER

Chanukah var of HANUKKAH

cha·os \'kā-,äs\ n 1 often cap : the confused unorganized state existing before the creation of distinct forms 2 : the inherent unpredictability in the behavior of a complex natural system (as the atmosphere or the beating heart) 3 : complete disorder ♦ *Synonyms* CONFUSION, JUMBLE, SNARL, MUDDLE, DISARRAY — **cha·ot·ic** \kā-'ä-tik\ adj — **cha·ot·i·cal·ly** \-ti-k(ə-)lē\ adv

chaos theory n : a branch of mathematical and physical theory concerned with chaotic systems

¹**chap** \'chap\ vb **chapped; chap·ping** : to dry and crack open usu. from wind and cold ⟨chapped lips⟩

²**chap** n : a jaw with its fleshy covering — usu. used in pl.

³**chap** n, chiefly Brit : FELLOW

⁴**chap** abbr chapter

chap·ar·ral \,sha-pə-'ral\ n 1 : a dense impenetrable thicket of shrubs or dwarf trees 2 : an ecological community esp. of southern California composed of shrubby plants

chap·book \'chap-,bȯk\ n : a small book of ballads, tales, or tracts

cha·peau \sha-'pō\ n, pl **cha·peaus** \-'pōz\ or **cha·peaux** \-'pō, -'pōz\ [MF] : HAT

cha·pel \'cha-pəl\ n [ME, fr. AF *chapele*, fr. ML *cappella*, fr. LL *cappa* cloak; fr. the cloak of St. Martin of Tours preserved as a sacred relic in a chapel built for that purpose] 1 : a private or subordinate place of worship 2 : an assembly at an educational institution usu. including devotional exercises 3 : a place of worship used by a Christian group other than an established church

¹**chap·er·one** or **chap·er·on** \'sha-pə-,rōn\ n [F *chaperon*, lit., hood, fr. MF, head covering, fr. *chape* cape, fr. LL *cappa*] 1 : a person (as a matron) who accompanies young unmarried women in public for propriety 2 : an older person who accompanies young people at a social gathering to ensure proper behavior

²**chaperone** or **chaperon** vb **-oned; -on·ing** 1 : ESCORT, GUIDE 2 : to act as a chaperone to or for ⟨∼ a dance⟩ ⟨∼ teenagers⟩ — **chap·er·on·age** \-,rō-nij\ n

chap·fall·en \'chap-,fȯ-lən, 'chäp-\ adj 1 : having the lower jaw hanging loosely 2 : DEJECTED, DEPRESSED

chap·lain \'cha-plən\ n 1 : a member of the clergy officially attached to a special group (as the army) 2 : a person chosen to conduct religious exercises (as for a club) — **chap·lain·cy** \-sē\ n

chap·let \'cha-plət\ n 1 : a wreath for the head 2 : a string of beads : NECKLACE

chap·man \'chap-mən\ n, Brit : an itinerant dealer : PEDDLER

chaps \'shaps, 'chaps\ n pl [MexSp *chaparreras*] : leather leggings resembling pants without a seat that are worn esp. by western ranch hands

chap·ter \'chap-tər\ n 1 : a main division of a book 2 : a body of canons (as of a cathedral) 3 : a local branch of a society or fraternity

¹**char** \'chär\ n, pl **char** or **chars** : any of a genus of trouts (as the common brook trout) with small scales

²**char** vb **charred; char·ring** 1 : to burn or become burned to charcoal 2 : SCORCH

³**char** vb **charred; char·ring** : to work as a cleaning woman

char·ac·ter \'ker-ik-tər\ n [ME *caracter*, fr. L *character*, fr. Gk *charaktēr*, fr. *charassein* to scratch, engrave] 1 : a graphic symbol (as a letter) used in writing or printing 2 : a symbol that represents information; also : a representation of such a character that may be accepted by a computer **3** : a distinguishing feature : ATTRIBUTE **4** : the complex of mental and ethical traits marking a person or a group **5** : a person marked by conspicuous often peculiar traits **6** : one of the persons in a novel or play **7** : REPUTATION **8** : moral excellence

¹char·ac·ter·is·tic \ˌker-ik-tə-'ris-tik\ n : a distinguishing trait, quality, or property

²characteristic adj : serving to mark individual character ✦ Synonyms INDIVIDUAL, PECULIAR, DISTINCTIVE — char·ac·ter·is·ti·cal·ly \-ti-k(ə-)lē\ adv

char·ac·ter·ize \'ker-ik-tə-ˌrīz\ vb -ized; -iz·ing **1** : to describe the character of **2** : to be characteristic of — char·ac·ter·i·za·tion \ˌker-ik-tə-rə-'zā-shən\ n

cha·rades \shə-'rādz\ n sing or pl : a game in which some of the players try to guess a word or phrase from the actions of another player who may not speak

char·coal \'chär-ˌkōl\ n **1** : a porous carbon prepared from vegetable or animal substances **2** : a piece of fine charcoal used in drawing; also : a drawing made with charcoal

chard \'chärd\ n : SWISS CHARD

char·don·nay \ˌshar-dᵊn-'ā\ n, often cap [F] : a dry white wine made from a single variety of white grape

¹charge \'chärj\ n **1** : a quantity (as of fuel or ammunition) required to fill something to capacity **2** : a store or accumulation of force **3** : an excess or deficiency of electrons in a body **4** : THRILL, KICK **5** : a task or duty imposed **6** : CARE, RESPONSIBILITY **7** : one given into another's care **8** : instructions from a judge to a jury **9** : COST, EXPENSE, PRICE; also : a debit to an account **10** : ACCUSATION, INDICTMENT **11** : ATTACK, ASSAULT

²charge vb charged; charg·ing **1** : to load or fill to capacity **2** : to give an electric charge to; also : to restore the activity of (a storage battery) by means of an electric current **3** : to impose a task or responsibility on **4** : COMMAND, ORDER **5** : ACCUSE **6** : to rush against : rush forward in assault **7** : to make liable for payment; also : to record a debt or liability against **8** : to fix as a price — charge·able adj

charge–coupled device n : a semiconductor device used esp. as an optical sensor

char·gé d'af·faires \shär-ˌzhä-də-'fer\ n, pl chargés d'affaires \-ˌzhä-, -ˌzhäz-\ [F] : a diplomat who substitutes for an ambassador or minister

¹char·ger \'chär-jər\ n : a large platter

²charg·er n **1** : a device or a worker that charges something **2** : WARHORSE 1

char·i·ot \'cher-ē-ət\ n : a 2-wheeled horse-drawn vehicle of ancient times used esp. in war and in races — char·i·o·teer \ˌcher-ē-ə-'tir\ n

cha·ris·ma \kə-'riz-mə\ n : a personal quality of leadership arousing popular loyalty or enthusiasm — char·is·mat·ic \ˌkar-əz-'ma-tik\ adj

char·i·ta·ble \'cher-ə-tə-bəl\ adj **1** : liberal in giving to needy people **2** : merciful or lenient in judging others ✦ Synonyms BENEVOLENT, PHILANTHROPIC, ALTRUISTIC, HUMANITARIAN — char·i·ta·ble·ness n — char·i·ta·bly \-blē\ adv

char·i·ty \'cher-ə-tē\ n, pl -ties **1** : goodwill toward or love of humanity **2** : an act or feeling of generosity **3** : the giving of aid to the poor; also : ALMS **4** : an institution engaged in relief of the poor **5** : leniency in judging others ✦ Synonyms MERCY, CLEMENCY, LENITY

char·la·tan \'shär-lə-tən\ n : a person making usu. showy pretenses to knowledge or ability : FRAUD, FAKER

Charles·ton \'chärl-stən\ n : a lively dance in which the knees are swung in and out and the heels are turned sharply outward on each step

char·ley horse \'chär-lē-ˌhòrs\ n : a muscular pain, cramping, or stiffness from a strain or bruise

¹charm \'chärm\ n [ME charme, fr. AF, fr. L carmen song, fr. canere to sing] **1** : a practice or expression believed to have magic power **2** : something worn about the person to ward off evil or bring good fortune : AMULET **3** : a trait that fascinates or allures **4** : physical grace or attraction **5** : a small ornament worn on a bracelet or chain **6** : a quark with a charge of +⅔ and a measured energy of approximately 1.5 billion electron volts

²charm vb **1** : to affect by or as if by a magic spell **2** : to protect by or as if by charms **3** : FASCINATE, ENCHANT

✦ Synonyms ALLURE, CAPTIVATE, BEWITCH, ATTRACT — charm·er n

charmed \'chärmd\ adj : extremely lucky or prosperous ⟨a ~ life⟩

charm·ing \'chär-miŋ\ adj : PLEASING, DELIGHTFUL — charm·ing·ly adv

char·nel house \'chär-nᵊl-\ n : a building or chamber in which bodies or bones are deposited

¹chart \'chärt\ n **1** : MAP **2** : a sheet giving information in the form of a table, list, or diagram; also : GRAPH

²chart vb **1** : PLAN ⟨~ a course⟩ **2** : to make a chart of **3** : CHRONICLE ⟨~ed his adventures⟩

¹char·ter \'chär-tər\ n **1** : an official document granting rights or privileges (as to a colony, town, or college) from a sovereign or a governing body **2** : CONSTITUTION **3** : a written instrument from a society creating a branch **4** : a mercantile lease of a ship

²charter vb **1** : to grant a charter to **2** Brit : CERTIFY ⟨~ed engineer⟩ **3** : to hire, rent, or lease for temporary use ⟨~ a bus⟩ — char·ter·er n

charter member n : an original member of an organization

char·treuse \shär-'trüz, -'trüs\ n : a brilliant yellow green

char·wom·an \'chär-ˌwù-mən\ n : a cleaning woman esp. in large buildings

chary \'cher-ē\ adj chari·er; -est [ME, sorrowful, dear, fr. OE cearig sorrowful, fr. caru sorrow] **1** : CAUTIOUS, CIRCUMSPECT **2** : SPARING — char·i·ly \-ə-lē\ adv

¹chase \'chās\ n **1** : PURSUIT; also : HUNTING **2** : QUARRY **3** : a tract of unenclosed land used as a game preserve

²chase vb chased; chas·ing **1** : to follow rapidly : PURSUE **2** : HUNT **3** : to seek out ⟨chasing down clues⟩ **4** : to cause to depart or flee : drive away **5** : RUSH, HASTEN

³chase vb chased; chas·ing **1** : to decorate (a metal surface) by embossing or engraving

⁴chase n : FURROW, GROOVE

chas·er n **1** : one that chases **2** : a mild drink (as beer) taken after hard liquor

chasm \'ka-zəm\ n : GORGE 2

chas·sis \'cha-sē, 'sha-sē\ n, pl chas·sis \-sēz\ : the supporting frame of a structure (as an automobile or television set)

chaste \'chāst\ adj chast·er; chast·est **1** : innocent of unlawful sexual intercourse : VIRTUOUS, PURE **2** : CELIBATE **3** : pure in thought : MODEST **4** : severe or simple in design — chaste·ly adv — chaste·ness n

chas·ten \'chā-sᵊn\ vb : to correct through punishment or suffering : DISCIPLINE; also : PURIFY — chas·ten·er n

chas·tise \chas-'tīz\ vb chas·tised; chas·tis·ing [ME chastisen, alter. of chasten] **1** : to punish esp. bodily **2** : to censure severely : CASTIGATE — chas·tise·ment \-mənt, 'chas-təz-\ n

chas·ti·ty \'chas-tə-tē\ n : the quality or state of being chaste; esp : sexual purity

cha·su·ble \'cha-zə-bəl, -sə-\ n : the outer vestment of the priest at mass

chat \'chat\ n **1** : light familiar informal talk **2** : online discussion in a chat room — chat vb

châ·teau \sha-'tō\ n, pl châ·teaus \-'tōz\ or châ·teaux \-'tō, -'tōz\ [F, fr. OF chastel, fr. L castellum castle, dim. of castra camp] **1** : a feudal castle in France **2** : a large country house **3** : a French vineyard estate

chat·e·laine \'shat-tə-ˌlān\ n **1** : the mistress of a chateau **2** : a clasp or hook for a watch, purse, or keys

chat room n : a real-time online interactive discussion group

chat·tel \'cha-tᵊl\ n **1** : an item of tangible property other than real estate **2** : SLAVE, BONDMAN

chat·ter \'cha-tər\ vb **1** : to utter speechlike but meaningless sounds **2** : to talk idly, incessantly, or fast **3** : to click repeatedly or uncontrollably — chatter n — chat·ter·er n

chat·ter·box \'cha-tər-ˌbäks\ n : one who talks incessantly

chat·ty \'cha-tē\ adj chat·ti·er; -est : TALKATIVE — chat·ti·ly \-tə-lē\ adv — chat·ti·ness \-tē-nəs\ n

¹chauf·feur \'shō-fər, shō-'fər\ n [F, lit., stoker, fr. chauffer to heat] : a person employed to drive an automobile

²chauffeur vb **1** : to do the work of a chauffeur **2** : to transport in the manner of a chauffeur ⟨~ed the kids to school⟩

chaunt *var of* CHANT

chau·vin·ism \'shō-və-ˌni-zəm\ *n* [F *chauvinisme*, fr. Nicolas *Chauvin*, fictional soldier of excessive patriotism and devotion to Napoleon] **1** : excessive or blind patriotism **2** : an attitude of superiority toward members of the opposite sex — **chau·vin·ist** \-nist\ *n or adj* — **chau·vin·is·tic** \ˌshō-və-'nis-tik\ *adj* — **chau·vin·is·ti·cal·ly** \-ti-k(ə-)lē\ *adv*

cheap \'chēp\ *adj* **1** : INEXPENSIVE **2** : costing little effort to obtain ⟨∼ tickets⟩ **3** : worth little : SHODDY, TAWDRY ⟨∼ workmanship⟩ **4** : worthy of scorn **5** : STINGY — **cheap** *adv* — **cheap·ly** *adv* — **cheap·ness** *n*

cheap·en \'chē-pən\ *vb* **1** : to make or become cheap or cheaper in price or value **2** : to make tawdry

cheap·skate \'chēp-ˌskāt\ *n* : a miserly or stingy person; *esp* : one who tries to avoid paying a fair share of costs

¹cheat \'chēt\ *vb* **1** : to deprive of something through fraud or deceit ⟨∼ed workers of their pay⟩ **2** : to practice fraud or trickery **3** : to violate rules dishonestly ⟨∼ at cards⟩ **4** : to be sexually unfaithful — **cheat·er** *n*

²cheat *n* **1** : the act of deceiving : FRAUD, DECEPTION **2** : one that cheats : a dishonest person

¹check \'chek\ *n* **1** : exposure of a chess king to an attack **2** : a sudden stoppage of progress **3** : a sudden pause or break **4** : something that stops or restrains **5** : a standard for testing or evaluation **6** : EXAMINATION, INVESTIGATION **7** : the act of testing or verifying **8** : a written order to a bank to pay money **9** : a ticket or token showing ownership or identity **10** : a slip indicating an amount due **11** : a pattern in squares; *also* : a fabric in such a pattern **12** : a mark typically ✓ placed beside an item to show that it has been noted **13** : CRACK, SPLIT

²check *vb* **1** : to put (a chess king) in check **2** : to slow down or stop : BRAKE **3** : to restrain the action or force of : CURB **4** : to compare with a source, original, or authority : VERIFY **5** : to inspect or test for satisfactory condition **6** : to mark with a check as examined **7** : to consign for shipment for one holding a passenger ticket **8** : to mark into squares **9** : to leave or accept for safekeeping in a checkroom **10** : to prove to be consistent or truthful **11** : CRACK, SPLIT

check·book \'chek-ˌbu̇k\ *n* : a book containing blank checks

¹check·er \'che-kər\ *n* : a piece in the game of checkers

²checker *vb* **1** : to variegate with different colors or shades **2** : to vary with contrasting elements ⟨a ∼ed career⟩ **3** : to mark into squares

³checker *n* : one that checks; *esp* : an employee who checks out purchases in a store

check·er·ber·ry \'che-kər-ˌber-ē\ *n* : WINTERGREEN 1; *also* : the spicy red fruit of this plant

check·er·board \-ˌbȯrd\ *n* : a board of 64 squares of alternate colors used in various games

check·ered \'che-kərd\ *adj* : marked by inconsistent fortune or recurring problems ⟨his ∼ past⟩

check·ers \'che-kərz\ *n* : a checkerboard game for 2 players each with 12 pieces

check in *vb* : to report one's presence or arrival (as at a hotel)

check·list \'chek-ˌlist\ *n* : a list of things to be checked or done; *also* : a comprehensive list

check·mate \'chek-ˌmāt\ *vb* [ME *chekmaten*, fr. *chekmate*, interj. used to announce checkmate, fr. AF *eschec mat*, fr. Ar *shāh māt*, fr. Pers, lit., the king is left unable to escape] **1** : to thwart completely : DEFEAT, FRUSTRATE **2** : to attack (an opponent's king) in chess so that escape is impossible — **checkmate** *n*

check·off \'chek-ˌȯf\ *n* : the deduction of union dues from a worker's paycheck by the employer

check·out \'chek-ˌau̇t\ *n* **1** : the action or an instance of checking out **2** : a counter at which checking out is done **3** : the process of examining and testing something as to readiness for intended use

check out *vb* **1** : to settle one's account (as at a hotel) and leave **2** : to total or have totaled the cost of purchases in a store and to make or receive payment for them

check·point \'chek-ˌpȯint\ *n* : a point at which a check is performed

check·room \-ˌrüm, -ˌru̇m\ *n* : a room at which baggage, parcels, or clothing is left for safekeeping

checks and balances *n pl* : a system allowing each branch of a government to restrict the actions of another branch (as by a veto)

check·up \'chek-ˌəp\ *n* : EXAMINATION; *esp* : a general physical examination

ched·dar \'che-dər\ *n, often cap* : a hard mild to sharp white or yellow cheese of smooth texture

cheek \'chēk\ *n* **1** : the fleshy side part of the face **2** : IMPUDENCE, BOLDNESS, AUDACITY **3** : BUTTOCK 1 — **cheeked** \'chēkt\ *adj*

cheek·bone \'chēk-ˌbōn\ *n* : the bone or bony ridge below the eye

cheeky \'chē-kē\ *adj* **cheek·i·er; -est** : IMPUDENT, SAUCY — **cheek·i·ly** \-kə-lē\ *adv* — **cheek·i·ness** \-kē-nəs\ *n*

cheep \'chēp\ *vb* : to utter faint shrill sounds : PEEP — **cheep** *n*

¹cheer \'chir\ *n* [ME *chere* face, cheer, fr. AF, face, fr. ML *cara*, prob. fr. Gk *kara* head, face] **1** : state of mind or heart : SPIRIT **2** : ANIMATION, GAIETY **3** : hospitable entertainment : WELCOME **4** : food and drink for a feast **5** : something that gladdens **6** : a shout of applause or encouragement

²cheer *vb* **1** : to give hope or courage to : COMFORT **2** : to make glad **3** : to urge on esp. by shouts **4** : to applaud with shouts **5** : to grow or be cheerful — usu. used with *up* — **cheer·er** *n*

cheer·ful \'chir-fəl\ *adj* **1** : having or showing good spirits **2** : conducive to good spirits : pleasant and bright — **cheer·ful·ly** *adv* — **cheer·ful·ness** *n*

cheer·lead·er \'chir-ˌlē-dər\ *n* : a person who directs organized cheering esp. at a sports event — **cheer·lead·ing** *n*

cheer·less \'chir-ləs\ *adj* : BLEAK, DISPIRITING ⟨a ∼ office⟩ — **cheer·less·ly** *adv* — **cheer·less·ness** *n*

cheery \'chir-ē\ *adj* **cheer·i·er; -est** : CHEERFUL ⟨∼ music⟩ — **cheer·i·ly** \-ə-lē\ *adv* — **cheer·i·ness** \-ē-nəs\ *n*

cheese \'chēz\ *n* : the curd of milk usu. pressed into cakes and cured for use as food

cheese·burg·er \-ˌbər-gər\ *n* : a hamburger topped with cheese

cheese·cake \-ˌkāk\ *n* **1** : a dessert consisting of a creamy filling usu. containing cheese baked in a shell **2** : photographs of shapely scantily clad women

cheese·cloth \-ˌklȯth\ *n* : a lightweight coarse cotton gauze

cheese·par·ing \-ˌper-iŋ\ *n* : miserly economizing — **cheeseparing** *adj*

cheese·steak \-ˌstāk\ *n* : a sandwich of thinly sliced beef topped with melted cheese

cheesy \'chē-zē\ *adj* **chees·i·er; -est** **1** : resembling, suggesting, or containing cheese **2** : CHEAP 3 ⟨∼ motels⟩

chee·tah \'chē-tə\ *n* [Hindi *cītā* leopard, fr. Skt *citraka*, fr. *citra* bright, variegated] : a large long-legged swift-moving spotted cat of Africa and southwestern Asia

chef \'shef\ *n* : COOK; *esp* : one who manages a kitchen (as of a restaurant)

chef d'oeu·vre \shā-'dœvrᵊ\ *n, pl* **chefs d'oeuvre** *same*\ : MASTERPIECE

chem *abbr* chemical; chemist; chemistry

¹chem·i·cal \'ke-mi-kəl\ *adj* **1** : of, relating to, used in, or produced by chemistry ⟨∼ reactions⟩ **2** : acting or operated or produced by chemicals — **chem·i·cal·ly** \-k(ə-)lē\ *adv*

²chemical *n* **1** : a substance obtained by a chemical process or producing a chemical effect **2** : DRUG

chemical engineering *n* : engineering dealing with the industrial application of chemistry — **chemical engineer** *n*

chemical warfare *n* : warfare using incendiary mixtures, smokes, or irritant, burning, or asphyxiating gases

chemical weapon *n* : a weapon used in chemical warfare

che·mise \shə-'mēz\ *n* **1** : a woman's one-piece undergarment **2** : a loose straight-hanging dress

chem·ist \'ke-mist\ *n* **1** : one trained in chemistry **2** *Brit* : PHARMACIST

chem·is·try \'ke-mə-strē\ *n, pl* **-tries** **1** : the science that deals with the composition, structure, and properties of substances and of the changes they undergo **2** : chemical composition or properties ⟨the ∼ of gasoline⟩ **3** : a strong mutual attraction; *also* : harmonious interaction among people (as on a team)

che·mo \'kē-mō\ *n* : CHEMOTHERAPY
che·mo·ther·a·py \ˌkē-mō-'ther-ə-pē\ *n* : the use of chemicals in the treatment or control of disease — **che·mo·ther·a·peu·tic** \-ˌther-ə-'pyü-tik\ *adj*
che·nille \shə-'nēl\ *n* [F, lit., caterpillar, fr. OF, fr. L *canicula*, dim. of *canis* dog] : a fabric with a deep fuzzy pile often used for bedspreads and rugs
cheque *chiefly Brit var of* ¹CHECK 7
che·quer *chiefly Brit var of* CHECKER
cher·ish \'cher-ish\ *vb* 1 : to hold dear : treat with care and affection 2 : to keep deeply in mind ⟨∼ a memory⟩ — **cher·ish·able** *adj* — **cher·ish·er** *n*
Cher·o·kee \'cher-ə-ˌkē\ *n, pl* **Cherokee** *or* **Cherokees** : a member of an American Indian people orig. of Tennessee and No. Carolina; *also* : their language
che·root \shə-'rüt\ *n* : a cigar cut square at both ends
cher·ry \'cher-ē\ *n, pl* **cherries** [ME *chery*, fr. AF *cherise, cirice* (taken as a plural), fr. LL *ceresia*, fr. L *cerasus* cherry tree, fr. Gk *kerasos*] 1 : the small fleshy pale yellow to deep blackish red fruit of a tree related to the roses; *also* : the tree or its wood 2 : a moderate red
chert \'chərt, 'chat\ *n* : a rock resembling flint and consisting essentially of fine crystalline quartz and fibrous chalcedony — **cherty** *adj*
cher·ub \'cher-əb\ *n* 1 *pl* **cher·u·bim** \'cher-ə-ˌbim\ : an angel of the 2d highest rank 2 *pl* **cherubs** : a chubby rosy person — **che·ru·bic** \chə-'rü-bik\ *adj*
chess \'ches\ *n* : a game for 2 played on a chessboard with each player having 16 pieces — **chess·man** \-ˌman, -mən\ *n*
chess·board \'ches-ˌbórd\ *n* : a checkerboard used in the game of chess
chest \'chest\ *n* 1 : a box, case, or boxlike receptacle for storage or shipping 2 : the part of the body enclosed by the ribs and sternum — **chest·ed** \'ches-təd\ *adj* — **chest·ful** \'chest-ˌfúl\ *n*
ches·ter·field \'ches-tər-ˌfēld\ *n* : an overcoat with a velvet collar
chest·nut \'ches-(ˌ)nət\ *n* 1 : the edible nut of any of a genus of trees related to the beeches and oaks; *also* : this tree or its wood 2 : a grayish to reddish brown 3 : an old joke or story
chet·rum \'che-trəm\ *n, pl* **chetrums** *or* **chetrum** — see *ngultrum* at MONEY table
che·val glass \shə-'val-\ *n* : a full-length mirror that may be tilted in a frame
che·va·lier \ˌshe-və-'lir, shə-'val-ˌyā\ *n* : a member of one of various orders of knighthood or of merit
chev·i·ot \'she-vē-ət\ *n, often cap* 1 : a twilled fabric with a rough nap 2 : a sturdy soft-finished cotton fabric
chev·ron \'she-vrən\ *n* : a sleeve badge of one or more V-shaped or inverted V-shaped stripes worn to indicate rank or service (as in the armed forces)
¹**chew** \'chü\ *vb* : to crush or grind with the teeth — **chewable** *adj* — **chew·er** *n* — **chewy** \'chü-ē\ *adj* — **chew on** : to think about : PONDER ⟨*chew* on the proposals⟩ — **chew the fat** : to make conversation : CHAT
²**chew** *n* 1 : an act of chewing 2 : something for chewing
Chey·enne \shī-'an, -'en\ *n, pl* **Cheyenne** *or* **Cheyennes** [AmerF, fr. Dakota *šahíyena*] : a member of an American Indian people of the western plains of the U.S.; *also* : their language
chg *abbr* 1 change 2 charge
chi \'kī\ *n* : the 22d letter of the Greek alphabet — X or χ
Chi·an·ti \kē-'än-tē, -'an-\ *n* : a dry usu. red wine
chiar·oscu·ro \kē-ˌär-ə-'skür-ō, -'skyùr-\ *n, pl* **-ros** [It, fr. *chiaro* clear, light + *oscuro* obscure, dark] 1 : pictorial representation in terms of light and shade without regard to color 2 : the arrangement or treatment of light and dark parts in a pictorial work of art
¹**chic** \'shēk\ *n* : STYLISHNESS
²**chic** *adj* : cleverly stylish : SMART; *also* : currently fashionable
Chi·ca·na \chi-'kä-nə *also* shi-\ *n* : an American woman or girl of Mexican descent — **Chicana** *adj*
chi·cane \shi-'kān\ *n* : CHICANERY
chi·ca·nery \-'kā-nə-rē\ *n, pl* **-ner·ies** : TRICKERY, DECEPTION
Chi·ca·no \chi-'kä-nō\ *n, pl* **-nos** : a usu. male American of Mexican descent — **Chicano** *adj*

chi·chi \'shē-(ˌ)shē, 'chē-(ˌ)chē\ *adj* [F] 1 : SHOWY, FRILLY 2 : ARTY, PRECIOUS 3 : CHIC — **chichi** *n*
chick \'chik\ *n* 1 : a young chicken; *also* : a young bird 2 *slang* : GIRL, WOMAN
chick·a·dee \'chi-kə-(ˌ)dē\ *n* : any of several small grayish American birds with black or brown caps
Chick·a·saw \'chi-kə-ˌsó\ *n, pl* **Chickasaw** *or* **Chickasaws** : a member of an American Indian people of Mississippi and Alabama
¹**chick·en** \'chi-kən\ *n* 1 : a common domestic fowl esp. when young; *also* : its flesh used as food 2 : COWARD
²**chicken** *adj* 1 : COWARDLY 2 *slang* : insistent on petty esp. military discipline
chicken feed *n, slang* : an insignificant sum of money
chick·en·heart·ed \ˌchi-kən-'här-təd\ *adj* : TIMID, COWARDLY
chicken out *vb* : to lose one's courage
chicken pox *n* : an acute contagious viral disease esp. of children characterized by a low fever and blisters
chicken wire *n* : a light wire netting of hexagonal mesh
chick·pea \'chik-ˌpē\ *n* : an Asian herb of the legume family cultivated for its short pods with one or two edible seeds; *also* : its seed
chick·weed \'chik-ˌwēd\ *n* : any of several low-growing small-leaved weeds related to the pinks
chi·cle \'chi-kəl\ *n* : a gum from the latex of a tropical tree used as the chief ingredient of chewing gum
chic·o·ry \'chi-kə-rē\ *n, pl* **-ries** : a usu. blue-flowered herb related to the daisies and grown for its root and for use in salads; *also* : its dried ground root used to flavor or adulterate coffee
chide \'chīd\ *vb* **chid** \'chid\ *or* **chid·ed** \'chī-dəd\; **chid** *or* **chid·den** \'chid-ᵊn\ *or* **chided**; **chid·ing** : to speak disapprovingly to ♦ *Synonyms* REPROACH, REPROVE, REPRIMAND, ADMONISH, SCOLD, REBUKE
¹**chief** \'chēf\ *adj* 1 : highest in rank 2 : most important ♦ *Synonyms* PRINCIPAL, MAIN, LEADING, MAJOR — **chief·ly** *adv*
²**chief** *n* 1 : the leader of a body or organization : HEAD 2 : the principal or most valuable part — **chief·dom** *n*
chief master sergeant *n* : a noncommissioned officer of the highest rank in the air force
chief of staff 1 : the ranking officer of a staff in the armed forces 2 : the ranking office of the army or air force
chief of state : the formal head of a national state as distinguished from the head of the government
chief petty officer *n* : an enlisted man in the navy ranking next below a senior chief petty officer
chief·tain \'chēf-tən\ *n* : a chief esp. of a band, tribe, or clan — **chief·tain·cy** \-sē\ *n* — **chief·tain·ship** *n*
chief warrant officer *n* : a warrant officer of senior rank
chif·fon \shi-'fän, 'shi-,\ *n* [F, lit., rag, fr. *chiffe* old rag] : a sheer fabric esp. of silk
chif·fo·nier \ˌshi-fə-'nir\ *n* : a high narrow chest of drawers
chig·ger \'chi-gər\ *n* : a bloodsucking larval mite that causes intense itching
chi·gnon \'shēn-ˌyän\ *n* [F, fr. MF *chaignon* chain, collar, nape] : a knot of hair worn at the back of the head
Chi·hua·hua \chə-'wä-ˌwä\ *n* : any of a breed of very small large-eared dogs that originated in Mexico

Chihuahua

chil·blain \'chil-,blān\ *n* : a sore or inflamed swelling (as on the feet or hands) caused by exposure to cold

child \'chī(-ə)ld\ *n, pl* **chil·dren** \'chil-drən\ **1** : an unborn or recently born person **2** : a young child between the periods of infancy and youth **3** : a male or female offspring : SON, DAUGHTER **4** : one strongly influenced by another or by a place or state of affairs — **child·ish** *adj* — **child·ish·ly** *adv* — **child·ish·ness** *n* — **child·less** *adj* — **child·less·ness** *n* — **child·like** *adj*

child·bear·ing \'chīld-,ber-iŋ\ *n* : CHILDBIRTH — **childbearing** *adj*

child·birth \-,bərth\ *n* : the act or process of giving birth to offspring

child·hood \-,hüd\ *n* : the state or time of being a child

¹**child·proof** \-,prüf\ *adj* **1** : made to prevent opening or use by children ⟨~ lighters⟩ **2** : made safe for children

²**childproof** *vb* : to make childproof ⟨~ a house⟩

child's play *n* : a simple task or act

chili *also* **chile** *or* **chil·li** \'chi-lē\ *n, pl* **chil·ies** *also* **chil·es** *or* **chilis** *or* **chil·lies** **1** : any of various pungent peppers related to the tomato **2** : a thick sauce of meat and chilies **3** : CHILI CON CARNE

chili con car·ne \,chi-lē-kän-'kär-nē\ *n* [AmerSp *chile con carne* chili with meat] : a spiced stew of ground beef and chilies or chili powder usu. with beans

chili powder *n* : a seasoning made of ground chilies and other spices

chili sauce *n* : a spiced tomato sauce usu. made with red and green peppers

¹**chill** \'chil\ *n* **1** : a feeling of coldness accompanied by shivering **2** : moderate coldness **3** : a check to enthusiasm or warmth of feeling

²**chill** *adj* **1** : moderately cold **2** : COLD, RAW **3** : DISTANT, FORMAL ⟨a ~ reception⟩ **4** : DEPRESSING, DISPIRITING

³**chill** *vb* **1** : to make or become cold or chilly **2** : to make cool esp. without freezing **3** : RELAX — **chill·er** *n*

chill·ing \'chi-liŋ\ *adj* : gravely disturbing or frightening ⟨a ~ scene⟩

chilly \'chi-lē\ *adj* **chill·i·er; -est** **1** : noticeably cold **2** : unpleasantly affected by cold **3** : lacking warmth of feeling ⟨a ~ reception⟩ — **chill·i·ness** *n*

chimaera *chiefly Brit var of* CHIMERA

¹**chime** \'chīm\ *n* **1** : a set of bells musically tuned **2** : the sound of a set of bells — usu. used in pl. **3** : a musical sound suggesting bells

²**chime** *vb* **chimed; chim·ing** **1** : to make bell-like sounds **2** : to indicate (as the time of day) by chiming **3** : to be or act in accord : be in harmony

chime in *vb* : to break into or join in a conversation

chi·me·ra \kī-'mir-ə, kə-\ *n* [L *chimaera*, fr. Gk *chimaira* she-goat, chimera] **1** : an imaginary monster made up of incongruous parts **2** : an illusion or fabrication of the mind; *esp* : an impossible dream

chi·me·ri·cal \kī-'mer-i-kəl\ *also* **chi·me·ric** \-ik\ *adj* **1** : FANTASTIC, IMAGINARY **2** : inclined to fantastic schemes

chim·ney \'chim-nē\ *n, pl* **chimneys** **1** : a vertical structure extending above the roof of a building for carrying off smoke **2** : a glass tube around a lamp flame

chimp \'chimp\ *n* : CHIMPANZEE

chim·pan·zee \,chim-,pan-'zē, chim-'pan-zē\ *n* : an African ape related to the much larger gorilla

¹**chin** \'chin\ *n* : the part of the face below the lower lip including the prominence of the lower jaw — **chin·less** *adj*

²**chin** *vb* **chinned; chin·ning** : to raise (oneself) while hanging by the hands until the chin is level with the support

chi·na \'chī-nə\ *n* : porcelain ware; *also* : domestic pottery in general

Chi·na·town \-,taùn\ *n* : the Chinese quarter of a city

chinch bug \'chinch-\ *n* : a small black and white bug destructive to cereal grasses

chin·chil·la \chin-'chi-lə\ *n* **1** : either of two small So. American rodents with soft pearl-gray fur; *also* : this fur **2** : a heavy long-napped woolen cloth

chine \'chīn\ *n* : BACKBONE, SPINE; *also* : a cut of meat including all or part of the backbone

Chi·nese \chī-'nēz, -'nēs\ *n, pl* **Chinese** **1** : a native or inhabitant of China **2** : any of a group of related languages of China — **Chinese** *adj*

Chinese cabbage *n* **1** : BOK CHOY **2** : an Asian garden plant related to the cabbage and widely grown in the U.S. for its tight elongate cylindrical heads of pale green to cream-colored leaves

Chinese checkers *n* : a game in which each player in turn transfers a set of marbles from a home point to the opposite point of a pitted 6-pointed star

Chinese gooseberry *n* : a subtropical vine that bears kiwifruit; *also* : KIWIFRUIT

Chinese lantern *n* : a collapsible translucent cover for a light

¹**chink** \'chiŋk\ *n* : a small crack or fissure

²**chink** *vb* : to fill the chinks of : stop up

³**chink** *n* : a slight sharp metallic sound

⁴**chink** *vb* : to make a slight sharp metallic sound

chi·no \'chē-nō\ *n, pl* **chinos** **1** : a usu. khaki cotton twill **2** *pl* : an article of clothing made of chino

Chi·nook \shə-'nùk, chə-, -'nük\ *n, pl* **Chinook** *or* **Chinooks** : a member of an American Indian people of Oregon

chintz \'chints\ *n* : a usu. glazed printed cotton cloth

chintzy \'chint-sē\ *adj* **chintz·i·er; -est** **1** : decorated with or as if with chintz **2** : GAUDY, CHEAP **3** : STINGY — **chintz·i·ness** *n*

chin–up \'chin-,əp\ *n* : the act of chinning oneself

¹**chip** \'chip\ *n* **1** : a small usu. thin and flat piece (as of wood) cut or broken off **2** : a thin crisp morsel of food **3** : a counter used in games (as poker) **4** *pl, slang* : MONEY **5** : a flaw left after a chip is broken off **6** : INTEGRATED CIRCUIT **7** : a very small slice of silicon containing electronic circuits — **chip off the old block** : a child that resembles his or her parent

²**chip** *vb* **chipped; chip·ping** **1** : to cut or break chips from **2** : to break off in small pieces at the edges **3** : to play a chip shot

chip in *vb* : CONTRIBUTE

chip·munk \'chip-,məŋk\ *n* [earlier *chitmunk*, prob. fr. Ojibwa *ačitamo·n?* red squirrel] : any of a genus of small striped No. American and Asian rodents closely related to the squirrels and marmots

chi·pot·le \chə-'pōt-lā\ *n* : a smoked and usu. dried jalapeño pepper

chipped beef \'chipt-\ *n* : smoked dried beef sliced thin

¹**chip·per** \'chi-pər\ *n* : one that chips

²**chipper** *adj* : LIVELY, CHEERFUL

Chip·pe·wa \'chi-pə-,wò, -,wä, -,wä, -wə\ *n, pl* **Chippewa** *or* **Chippewas** : OJIBWA

chip shot *n* : a short usu. low shot to the green in golf

chi·rog·ra·phy \kī-'rä-grə-fē\ *n* : HANDWRITING, PENMANSHIP — **chi·ro·graph·ic** \,kī-rə-'gra-fik\ *adj*

chi·rop·o·dy \kə-'rä-pə-dē, shə-\ *n* : PODIATRY — **chi·rop·o·dist** \-dist\ *n*

chi·ro·prac·tic \'kī-rə-,prak-tik\ *n* : a system of therapy based esp. on manipulation of body structures — **chi·ro·prac·tor** \-tər\ *n*

chirp \'chərp\ *n* : a short sharp sound characteristic of a small bird or cricket — **chirp** *vb* — **chirpy** \'chər-pē\ *adj*

¹**chis·el** \'chi-zəl\ *n* : a metal tool with a sharpened edge at one end used to chip, carve, or cut into a solid material (as wood or stone)

²**chisel** *vb* **-eled** *or* **-elled; -el·ing** *or* **-el·ling** **1** : to work with or as if with a chisel **2** : to obtain by shrewd often unfair methods; *also* : CHEAT — **chis·el·er** *n*

¹**chit** \'chit\ *n* [ME *chitte* kitten, cub] **1** : CHILD **2** : a pert young woman

²**chit** *n* [Hindi *ciṭṭhī* letter, note] : a signed voucher for a small debt

chit-chat \'chit-,chat\ *n* : casual or trifling conversation — **chitchat** *vb*

chi·tin \'kī-tᵊn\ *n* : a sugar polymer that forms part of the hard outer integument esp. of insects — **chi·tin·ous** *adj*

chit·ter·lings *or* **chit·lins** \'chit-lənz\ *n pl* : the intestines of hogs esp. when prepared as food

chi·val·ric \shə-'val-rik\ *adj* : relating to chivalry : CHIVALROUS

chiv·al·rous \'shi-vəl-rəs\ *adj* **1** : of or relating to chivalry **2** : marked by honor, courtesy, and generosity **3** : marked by especial courtesy to women — **chiv·al·rous·ly** *adv* — **chiv·al·rous·ness** *n*

chiv·al·ry \'shi-vəl-rē\ *n, pl* **-ries** **1** : mounted men-at-arms **2** : the system or practices of knighthood **3** : the spirit or character of the ideal knight

chive \'chīv\ *n* : an herb related to the onion that has slender leaves used for flavoring; *also* : its leaves

chla·myd·ia \klə-'mi-dē-ə\ *n, pl* **-i·ae** \-dē-,ē\ **1** : any of a genus of bacteria that cause various diseases of the eye and urogenital tract **2** : a disease or infection caused by chlamydiae

chlo·ral hydrate \'klȯr-əl-\ *n* : a white crystalline compound used as a hypnotic and sedative

chlor·dane \'klȯr-,dān\ *n* : a highly chlorinated persistent insecticide

chlo·ride \'klȯr-,īd\ *n* : a compound of chlorine with another element or group

chlo·ri·nate \'klȯr-ə-,nāt\ *vb* **-nat·ed; -nat·ing** : to treat or combine with chlorine or a chlorine compound — **chlo·ri·na·tion** \,klȯr-ə-'nā-shən\ *n* — **chlo·ri·na·tor** \'klȯr-ə-,nā-tər\ *n*

chlo·rine \'klȯr-,ēn\ *n* : a nonmetallic chemical element that is found alone as a strong-smelling greenish-yellow irritating gas and is used as a bleach, oxidizing agent, and disinfectant

chlorine monoxide *n* : a reactive radical that plays a major role in stratospheric ozone depletion

chlo·rite \'klȯr-,īt\ *n* : a usu. green mineral found with and resembling mica

chlo·ro·flu·o·ro·car·bon \,klȯr-ə-'flȯr-ə-,kär-bən, -'flu̇r-\ *n* : any of several gaseous compounds that contain carbon, chlorine, fluorine, and sometimes hydrogen and are used esp. as solvents, refrigerants, and aerosol propellants

¹chlo·ro·form \'klȯr-ə-,fȯrm\ *n* : a colorless heavy fluid with etherlike odor used as a solvent

²chloroform *vb* : to treat with chloroform to produce anesthesia or death

chlo·ro·phyll \-,fil\ *n* : the green coloring matter of plants that functions in photosynthesis

chlo·ro·plast \'klȯr-ə-,plast\ *n* : a cytoplasmic organelle that contains chlorophyll and is the site of photosynthesis

chm *abbr* chairman

chock \'chäk\ *n* : a wedge for steadying something or for blocking the movement of a wheel — **chock** *vb*

chock·a·block \'chä-kə-,bläk\ *adj* : very full : CROWDED

chock–full \'chək-'fu̇l, 'chäk-\ *adj* : full to the limit : CRAMMED

choc·o·late \'chä-k(ə-)lət, 'chȯ-\ *n* [Sp, fr. Nahuatl *chocolātl*] **1** : a food prepared from ground roasted cacao beans; *also* : a drink prepared from this **2** : a candy made of or with a coating of chocolate **3** : a dark brown color — **choc·o·laty** *or* **choc·o·lat·ey** \-k(ə-)lə-tē\ *adj*

Choc·taw \'chäk-,tȯ\ *n, pl* **Choctaw** *or* **Choctaws** : a member of an American Indian people of Mississippi, Alabama, and Louisiana; *also* : their language

¹choice \'chȯis\ *n* **1** : the act of choosing : SELECTION **2** : the power or opportunity of choosing : OPTION **3** : the best part **4** : a person or thing selected **5** : a variety offered for selection

²choice *adj* **choic·er; choic·est** **1** : worthy of being chosen **2** : selected with care **3** : of high quality

choir \'kwī(-ə)r\ *n* **1** : an organized company of singers (as in a church service) **2** : the part of a church occupied by the singers or by the clergy

choir·boy \'kwī(-ə)r-,bȯi\ *n* : a boy member of a choir

choir·mas·ter \-,mas-tər\ *n* : the director of a choir (as in a church)

¹choke \'chōk\ *vb* **choked; chok·ing** **1** : to hinder breathing (as by obstructing the trachea) : STRANGLE **2** : to check the growth or action of **3** : CLOG, OBSTRUCT **4** : to enrich the fuel mixture of (a motor) by restricting the carburetor air intake **5** : to perform badly in a critical situation

²choke *n* **1** : the act of choking **2** : a narrowing in size toward the muzzle in the bore of a gun **3** : a valve for choking a gasoline engine

choke hold *n* **1** : a hold that involves strong choking pressure **2** : absolute control

chok·er \'chō-kər\ *n* : something (as a necklace) worn tightly around the neck

cho·ler \'kä-lər, 'kō-\ *n* : a tendency toward anger : IRASCIBILITY

chol·era \'kä-lə-rə\ *n* : any of several bacterial diseases usu. marked by severe vomiting and dysentery

cho·ler·ic \'kä-lə-rik, kə-'ler-ik\ *adj* **1** : IRASCIBLE **2** : ANGRY, IRATE

cho·les·ter·ol \kə-'les-tə-,rȯl\ *n* : a physiologically important waxy steroid alcohol found in animal tissues and in high concentrations implicated as a cause of arteriosclerosis

chomp \'chämp, 'chȯmp\ *vb* : to chew or bite on something heavily

chon \'chän\ *n, pl* **chon** — see *won* at MONEY table

choose \'chüz\ *vb* **chose** \chōz\; **cho·sen** \'chō-z³n\; **choos·ing** \'chü-ziŋ\ **1** : to select esp. after consideration **2** : DECIDE **3** : to have a preference for — **choos·er** *n*

choosy *or* **choos·ey** \'chü-zē\ *adj* **choos·i·er; -est** : very particular in making choices

¹chop \'chäp\ *vb* **chopped; chop·ping** **1** : to cut by repeated blows **2** : to cut into small pieces : MINCE **3** : to strike (a ball) with a short quick downward stroke

²chop *n* **1** : a sharp downward blow or stroke **2** : a small cut of meat often including part of a rib **3** : a short abrupt motion (as of a wave)

³chop *n* **1** : an official seal or stamp **2** : a mark on goods to indicate quality or kind; *also* : QUALITY, GRADE

chop·house \'chäp-,hau̇s\ *n* : RESTAURANT

chop·per \'chä-pər\ *n* **1** : one that chops **2** *pl, slang* : TEETH **3** : HELICOPTER

chop·pi·ness \'chä-pē-nəs\ *n* : the quality or state of being choppy

¹chop·py \'chä-pē\ *adj* **chop·pi·er; -est** **1** : rough with small waves **2** : JERKY, DISCONNECTED — **chop·pi·ly** \-pə-lē\ *adv*

²choppy *adj* **chop·pi·er; -est** : CHANGEABLE, VARIABLE ⟨a ∼ wind⟩

chops \'chäps\ *n pl* **1** : the fleshy covering of the jaws **2** : expertise in a particular field or activity ⟨acting ∼⟩

chop·stick \'chäp-,stik\ *n* : one of a pair of sticks used chiefly in Asian countries for lifting food to the mouth

chop su·ey \chäp-'sü-ē\ *n, pl* **chop sueys** : a dish made of vegetables (as bean sprouts, bamboo shoots, water chestnuts, onions, mushrooms) and meat or fish and served with rice

cho·ral \'kȯr-əl\ *adj* : of, relating to, or sung by a choir or chorus or in chorus — **cho·ral·ly** *adv*

cho·rale \kə-'ral, -'räl\ *n* **1** : a hymn or psalm sung in church; *also* : a harmonization of a traditional melody **2** : CHORUS, CHOIR

¹chord \'kȯrd\ *n* [alter. of ME *cord*, short for *accord*] : three or more musical tones sounded simultaneously

²chord *n* **1** : CORD 2 **2** : a straight line joining two points on a curve

chore \'chȯr\ *n* [ME *char* turn, piece of work, fr. OE *chierr*] **1** *pl* : the daily light work of a household or farm **2** : a routine task or job **3** : a difficult or disagreeable task

cho·rea \kə-'rē-ə\ *n* : any of various nervous disorders marked by spasmodic uncontrolled movements

cho·re·og·ra·phy \,kȯr-ē-'ä-grə-fē\ *n, pl* **-phies** : the art of composing and arranging dances and esp. ballets — **cho·reo·graph** \'kȯr-ē-ə-,graf\ *vb* — **cho·re·og·ra·pher** \,kȯr-ē-'ä-grə-fər\ *n* — **cho·reo·graph·ic** \,kȯr-ē-ə-'gra-fik\ *adj* — **cho·reo·graph·i·cal·ly** \-fi-k(ə-)lē\ *adv*

cho·ris·ter \'kȯr-ə-stər\ *n* : a singer in a choir

chor·tle \'chȯr-t³l\ *vb* **chor·tled; chor·tling** : to laugh or chuckle esp. in satisfaction or exultation — **chortle** *n*

¹cho·rus \'kȯr-əs\ *n* **1** : an organized company of singers : CHOIR **2** : a group of dancers and singers (as in a musical comedy) **3** : a part of a song repeated at intervals **4** : a composition to be sung by a chorus; *also* : group singing **5** : sounds uttered by a number of persons or animals together ⟨a ∼ of boos⟩

²chorus *vb* : to sing or utter in chorus

chose *past of* CHOOSE

cho·sen \'chō-z³n\ *adj* : selected or marked for special favor or privilege

chou·croute \shü-'krüt\ *n* **1** : SAUERKRAUT **2** *or* **choucroute gar·nie** \-gär-'nē\ : sauerkraut cooked and served with meat

¹chow \'chau̇\ *n* : FOOD

²chow *vb* : EAT — often used with *down*

³chow *n* : CHOW CHOW

chow–chow \'chau̇-,chau̇\ *n* : chopped mixed pickles in mustard sauce

chow chow \'chaủ-ˌchaủ\ *n* : any of a breed of thick-coated muscular dogs of Chinese origin with a blue-black tongue and a short tail curled close to the back

chow·der \'chaủ-dər\ *n* : a soup or stew made from seafood or vegetables and containing milk or tomatoes

chow mein \'chaủ-'mān\ *n* : a seasoned stew of shredded or diced meat, mushrooms, and vegetables that is usu. served with fried noodles

chrism \'kri-zəm\ *n* : consecrated oil used esp. in baptism, confirmation, and ordination

Christ \'krīst\ *n* [ME *Crist*, fr. OE, fr. L *Christus*, fr. Gk *Christos*, lit., anointed] : Jesus esp. as the Messiah — Christ·like *adj* — Christ·ly *adj*

chris·ten \'kri-sᵃn\ *vb* 1 : BAPTIZE 2 : to name at baptism 3 : to name or dedicate (as a ship) by a ceremony suggestive of baptism — chris·ten·ing *n*

Chris·ten·dom \'kri-sᵃn-dəm\ *n* 1 : CHRISTIANITY 2 : the part of the world in which Christianity prevails

¹Chris·tian \'kris-chən\ *n* : an adherent of Christianity

²Christian *adj* 1 : of or relating to Christianity 2 : based on or conforming with Christianity 3 : of or relating to a Christian 4 : professing Christianity

Chris·ti·an·i·ty \ˌkris-chē-'a-nə-tē\ *n* : the religion derived from Jesus Christ, based on the Bible as sacred scripture, and professed by Christians

Chris·tian·ize \'kris-chə-ˌnīz\ *vb* -ized; -iz·ing : to make Christian

Christian name *n* : GIVEN NAME

Christian Science *n* : a religion and system of healing founded by Mary Baker Eddy and taught by the Church of Christ, Scientist — Christian Scientist *n*

chris·tie or chris·ty \'kris-tē\ *n, pl* christies : a skiing turn made by shifting body weight forward and skidding into a turn with parallel skis

Christ·mas \'kris-məs\ *n* : December 25 celebrated as a church festival in commemoration of the birth of Christ and observed as a legal holiday

Christmas club *n* : a savings account in which regular deposits are made to provide money for Christmas shopping

Christ·mas·tide \'kris-məs-ˌtīd\ *n* : the season of Christmas

chro·mat·ic \krō-'ma-tik\ *adj* 1 : of or relating to color 2 : proceeding by half steps of the musical scale — chro·mat·i·cism \-tə-ˌsi-zəm\ *n*

chro·mato·graph \krō-'ma-tə-ˌgraf\ *n* : an instrument used in chromatography

chro·ma·tog·ra·phy \ˌkrō-mə-'tä-grə-fē\ *n* : the separation of a complex mixture into its component compounds as a result of the different rates at which the compounds travel through or over a stationary substance due to differing affinities for the substance — chro·mato·graph·ic \krō-ˌma-tə-'gra-fik\ *adj* — chro·mato·graph·i·cal·ly \-fi-k(ə-)lē\ *adv*

chrome \'krōm\ *n* 1 : CHROMIUM 2 : a chromium pigment 3 : something plated with an alloy of chromium

chro·mi·um \'krō-mē-əm\ *n* : a bluish white metallic element used esp. in alloys and chrome plating

chro·mo·some \'krō-mə-ˌsōm, -ˌzōm\ *n* [G *Chromosom*, fr. Gk *chrōma* color, pigment + *sōma* body] : any of the rod-shaped or threadlike DNA-containing structures of cellular organisms that contain most or all of the genes of the organism — chro·mo·som·al \ˌkrō-mə-'sō-məl, -'zō-\ *adj*

chro·mo·sphere \'krō-mə-ˌsfir\ *n* : the lower part of a star's atmosphere

chron *abbr* 1 chronicle 2 chronological; chronology

Chron *abbr* Chronicles

chron·ic \'krä-nik\ *adj* : marked by long duration or frequent recurrence ⟨a ~ disease⟩; *also* : HABITUAL ⟨a ~ grumbler⟩ — chron·i·cal·ly \-ni-k(ə-)lē\ *adv*

chronic fatigue syndrome *n* : a disorder of unknown cause that is characterized by persistent profound fatigue

¹chron·i·cle \'krä-ni-kəl\ *n* : HISTORY, NARRATIVE

²chronicle *vb* -cled; -cling : to record in or as if in a chronicle — chron·i·cler *n*

Chronicles *n* — see BIBLE table

chro·no·graph \'krä-nə-ˌgraf\ *n* : an instrument for measuring and recording time intervals with accuracy — chro·no·graph·ic \ˌkrä-nə-'gra-fik\ *adj* — chro·nog·ra·phy \krə-'nä-grə-fē\ *n*

chro·nol·o·gy \krə-'nä-lə-jē\ *n, pl* -gies 1 : the science that deals with measuring time and dating events 2 : a chronological list or table 3 : arrangement of events in the order of their occurrence — chron·o·log·i·cal \ˌkrän-ᵊl-'ä-ji-kəl\ *adj* — chron·o·log·i·cal·ly \-k(ə-)lē\ *adv* — chro·nol·o·gist \krə-'nä-lə-jist\ *n*

chro·nom·e·ter \krə-'nä-mə-tər\ *n* : a very accurate timepiece

chrys·a·lid \'kri-sə-ləd\ *n* : CHRYSALIS

chrys·a·lis \'kri-sə-ləs\ *n, pl* chry·sal·i·des \kri-'sa-lə-ˌdēz\ *or* chrys·a·lis·es : an insect pupa in a firm case without a cocoon

chry·san·the·mum \kri-'san-thə-məm\ *n* [L, fr. Gk *chrysanthemon*, fr. *chrysos* gold + *anthemon* flower] : any of various plants related to the daisies including some grown for their showy brightly colored flowers or for medicinal products or insecticides; *also* : a flower of a chrysanthemum

chub \'chəb\ *n, pl* chub *or* chubs : any of various small freshwater fishes related to the carp

chub·by \'chə-bē\ *adj* chub·bi·er; -est : PLUMP ⟨a ~ child⟩ — chub·bi·ness *n*

¹chuck \'chək\ *vb* 1 : to give a pat or tap 2 : TOSS 3 : DISCARD; *also* : EJECT 4 : to have done with ⟨~ed his job⟩

²chuck *n* 1 : a light pat under the chin 2 : TOSS

³chuck *n* 1 : a cut of beef including most of the neck and the parts around the shoulder blade and the first three ribs 2 : a device for holding work or a tool in a machine (as a lathe)

chuck·hole \'chək-ˌhōl\ *n* : POTHOLE

chuck·le \'chə-kəl\ *vb* chuck·led; chuck·ling : to laugh in a quiet hardly audible manner — chuckle *n*

chuck wagon *n* : a wagon equipped with a stove and food supplies

¹chug \'chəg\ *n* : a dull explosive sound made by or as if by a laboring engine

²chug *vb* chugged; chug·ging : to move or go with chugs

chuk·ka \'chə-kə\ *n* : a usu. ankle-length leather boot

chuk·ker \'chə-kər\ *also* chuk·ka \'chə-kə\ *n* : a playing period of a polo game

¹chum \'chəm\ *n* : a close friend

²chum *vb* chummed; chum·ming 1 : to room together 2 : to be a close friend

chum·my \'chə-mē\ *adj* chum·mi·er; -est : quite friendly — chum·mi·ly \-mə-lē\ *adv* — chum·mi·ness \-mē-nəs\ *n*

chump \'chəmp\ *n* : FOOL, BLOCKHEAD

chunk \'chəŋk\ *n* 1 : a short thick piece 2 : a sizable amount

chunky \'chəŋ-kē\ *adj* chunk·i·er; -est 1 : STOCKY 2 : containing chunks

church \'chərch\ *n* [ME *chirche*, fr. OE *cirice*, ultim. fr. LGk *kyriakon*, fr. Gk, neut. of *kyriakos* of the lord, fr. *kyrios* lord, master] 1 : a building esp. for Christian public worship 2 *often cap* : the whole body of Christians 3 : DENOMINATION 4 : CONGREGATION 5 : public divine worship

church·go·er \'chərch-ˌgō-ər\ *n* : one who habitually attends church — church·go·ing *adj or n*

church·less \'chərch-ləs\ *adj* : not affiliated with a church

church·man \'chərch-mən\ *n* 1 : CLERGYMAN 2 : a member of a church

church·war·den \'chərch-ˌwòr-dᵊn\ *n* : WARDEN 5

church·yard \-ˌyärd\ *n* : a yard that belongs to a church and is often used as a burial ground

churl \'chərl\ *n* 1 : a medieval peasant 2 : RUSTIC 3 : a rude ill-bred person — churl·ish *adj* — churl·ish·ly *adv* — churl·ish·ness *n*

¹churn \'chərn\ *n* : a container in which milk or cream is agitated in making butter

²churn *vb* 1 : to stir in a churn; *also* : to make (butter) by such stirring 2 : to shake around violently

churn out *vb* : to produce mechanically or in large quantity

chute \'shüt\ *n* 1 : an inclined surface, trough, or passage down or through which something may pass ⟨a coal ~⟩ ⟨a mail ~⟩ 2 : PARACHUTE

chut·ney \'chət-nē\ *n, pl* chutneys : a thick sauce containing fruits, vinegar, sugar, and spices

chutz·pah \'hut-spə, 'kut-, -(ˌ)spä\ *n* : supreme self-confidence

CIA *abbr* Central Intelligence Agency

cía *abbr* [Sp *compañía*] company

ciao \'chaù\ *interj* — used to express greeting or farewell

ci·ca·da \sə-'kā-də\ *n* : any of a family of stout-bodied insects related to the aphids and having wide blunt heads and large transparent wings

ci·ca·trix \'si-kə-ˌtriks\ *n, pl* **ci·ca·tri·ces** \ˌsi-kə-'trī-ˌsēz\ [L] : a scar resulting from formation and contraction of fibrous tissue in a wound

ci·ce·ro·ne \ˌsi-sə-'rō-nē, ˌchē-chə-\ *n, pl* **-ni** \-(ˌ)nē\ : a guide who conducts sightseers

CID *abbr* Criminal Investigation Department

ci·der \'sī-dər\ *n* : juice pressed from fruit (as apples) and used as a beverage, vinegar, or flavoring

cie *abbr* [F *compagnie*] company

ci·gar \si-'gär\ *n* [Sp *cigarro*] : a roll of tobacco for smoking

cig·a·rette \ˌsi-gə-'ret, 'si-gə-ˌret\ *n* [F, dim. of *cigare* cigar] : a slender roll of cut tobacco enclosed in paper for smoking

cig·a·ril·lo \ˌsi-gə-'ri-lō, -'rē-ō\ *n, pl* **-los** [Sp] 1 : a very small cigar 2 : a cigarette wrapped in tobacco rather than paper

ci·lan·tro \si-'län-trō, -'lan-\ *n* : leaves of coriander used as a flavoring or garnish; *also* : the coriander plant

cil·i·ate \'si-lē-ˌāt\ *n* : any of a group of protozoans characterized by cilia

cil·i·um \'si-lē-əm\ *n, pl* **cil·ia** \-lē-ə\ 1 : a minute short hairlike process; *esp* : one of a cell 2 : EYELASH

C in C *abbr* commander in chief

cinch \'sinch\ *n* 1 : a girth for a pack or saddle 2 : a sure or an easy thing — **cinch** *vb*

cin·cho·na \siŋ-'kō-nə\ *n* : any of a genus of So. American trees related to the madder; *also* : the bitter quinine-containing bark of a cinchona

cinc·ture \'siŋk-chər\ *n* : BELT, SASH

cin·der \'sin-dər\ *n* 1 : SLAG 2 *pl* : ASHES 3 : a hot piece of partly burned wood or coal 4 : a fragment of lava from an erupting volcano — **cin·dery** *adj*

cinder block *n* : a building block made of cement and coal cinders

cin·e·ma \'si-nə-mə\ *n* 1 : a motion-picture theater 2 : MOVIES — **cin·e·mat·ic** \ˌsi-nə-'ma-tik\ *adj*

cin·e·ma·theque \ˌsi-nə-mə-'tek\ *n* : a small movie house specializing in avant-garde films

cin·e·ma·tog·ra·phy \ˌsi-nə-mə-'tä-grə-fē\ *n* : motion-picture photography — **cin·e·ma·tog·ra·pher** *n* — **cin·e·mat·o·graph·ic** \-ˌma-tə-'gra-fik\ *adj*

cine·phile \'si-nə-ˌfī(-ə)l\ *n* : a lover of motion pictures

cin·e·plex \'si-nə-ˌpleks\ *n* : a complex that houses several movie theaters

cin·er·ar·i·um \ˌsi-nə-'rer-ē-əm\ *n, pl* **-ia** \-ē-ə\ : a place to receive the ashes of the cremated dead — **cin·er·ary** \'si-nə-ˌrer-ē\ *adj*

cin·na·bar \'si-nə-ˌbär\ *n* 1 : a red mineral that is the only important ore of mercury 2 : a deep vivid red

cin·na·mon \'si-nə-mən\ *n* : a spice prepared from the highly aromatic bark of any of several Asian trees related to the true laurel; *also* : a tree that yields cinnamon

cinque·foil \'siŋk-ˌfòi(-ə)l, 'saŋk-\ *n* : any of a genus of plants related to the roses with leaves having five lobes

¹ci·pher \'sī-fər\ *n* [ME, fr. ML *cifra*, fr. Ar *ṣifr* empty, zero] 1 : ZERO, NAUGHT 2 : a method of secret writing

²cipher *vb* : to compute arithmetically

cir *or* **circ** *abbr* circular

cir·ca \'sər-kə\ *prep* : ABOUT ⟨~ 1600⟩

cir·ca·di·an \sər-'kā-dē-ən\ *adj* : being, having, characterized by, or occurring in approximately 24-hour intervals (as of biological activity)

¹cir·cle \'sər-kəl\ *n* 1 : a closed curve every point of which is equally distant from a fixed point within it 2 : something circular 3 : an area of action or influence 4 : CYCLE 5 : a group bound by a common tie ⟨sewing ~⟩

²circle *vb* **cir·cled; cir·cling** 1 : to enclose in a circle 2 : to move or revolve around; *also* : to move in a circle

cir·clet \'sər-klət\ *n* : a small circle; *esp* : a circular ornament

cir·cuit \'sər-kət\ *n* 1 : a boundary around an enclosed space 2 : a course around a periphery 3 : a regular tour (as by a judge) around an assigned territory 4 : the complete path of an electric current; *also* : an assemblage of electronic components 5 : LEAGUE; *also* : a chain of theaters

circuit board *n* : BOARD 7

circuit breaker *n* : a switch that automatically interrupts the current of an overloaded circuit

circuit court *n* : a court that sits at two or more places within one judicial district

cir·cu·i·tous \ˌsər-'kyü-ə-təs\ *adj* 1 : having a circular or winding course 2 : not being forthright or direct in language or action

cir·cuit·ry \'sər-kə-trē\ *n, pl* **-ries** : the plan or the components of an electric circuit

cir·cu·ity \ˌsər-'kyü-ə-tē\ *n, pl* **-ities** : INDIRECTION

¹cir·cu·lar \'sər-kyə-lər\ *adj* 1 : having the form of a circle : ROUND 2 : moving in or around a circle 3 : CIRCUITOUS 4 : intended for circulation ⟨a ~ letter⟩ — **cir·cu·lar·i·ty** \ˌsər-kyə-'ler-ə-tē\ *n*

²circular *n* : a paper (as a leaflet) intended for wide distribution

cir·cu·lar·ise *Brit var of* CIRCULARIZE

cir·cu·lar·ize \'sər-kyə-lə-ˌrīz\ *vb* **-ized; -iz·ing** 1 : to send circulars to 2 : to poll by questionnaire 3 : to make circular

circular saw *n* : a power saw with a round cutting blade

cir·cu·late \'sər-kyə-ˌlāt\ *vb* **-lat·ed; -lat·ing** 1 : to move or cause to move in a circle, circuit, or orbit 2 : to pass from place to place or from person to person — **cir·cu·la·tion** \ˌsər-kyə-'lā-shən\ *n*

cir·cu·la·to·ry \'sər-kyə-lə-ˌtòr-ē\ *adj* : of or relating to circulation or the circulatory system

circulatory system *n* : the system of blood, blood vessels, lymphatic vessels, and heart concerned with the circulation of the blood and lymph

cir·cum·am·bu·late \ˌsər-kəm-'am-byə-ˌlāt\ *vb* **-lat·ed; -lat·ing** : to circle on foot esp. as part of a ritual

cir·cum·cise \'sər-kəm-ˌsīz\ *vb* **-cised; -cis·ing** [ME, fr. L *circumcisus*, pp. of *circumcidere*, lit., to cut around, fr. *circum* around + *caedere* to cut] : to cut off the foreskin of — **cir·cum·ci·sion** \ˌsər-kəm-'si-zhən\ *n*

cir·cum·fer·ence \sər-'kəm-f(ə-)rəns\ *n* 1 : the perimeter of a circle 2 : the external boundary or surface of a figure or object

cir·cum·flex \'sər-kəm-ˌfleks\ *n* : the mark ˆ over a vowel

cir·cum·lo·cu·tion \ˌsər-kəm-lō-'kyü-shən\ *n* : the use of unnecessary words in expressing an idea

cir·cum·lu·nar \-'lü-nər\ *adj* : revolving about or surrounding the moon

cir·cum·nav·i·gate \-'na-və-ˌgāt\ *vb* : to go completely around (as the earth) esp. by water — **cir·cum·nav·i·ga·tion** \-ˌna-və-'gā-shən\ *n*

cir·cum·po·lar \-'pō-lər\ *adj* 1 : continually visible above the horizon ⟨a ~ star⟩ 2 : surrounding or found near a pole of the earth ⟨a ~ current⟩

cir·cum·scribe \'sər-kəm-ˌskrīb\ *vb* 1 : to constrict the range or activity of 2 : to draw a line around — **cir·cum·scrip·tion** \ˌsər-kəm-'skrip-shən\ *n*

cir·cum·spect \'sər-kəm-ˌspekt\ *adj* : careful to consider all circumstances and consequences : PRUDENT — **cir·cum·spec·tion** \ˌsər-kəm-'spek-shən\ *n*

cir·cum·stance \'sər-kəm-ˌstans\ *n* 1 : a fact or event that must be considered along with another fact or event 2 : surrounding conditions 3 : CHANCE, FATE 4 *pl* : situation with regard to wealth 5 : CEREMONY

cir·cum·stan·tial \ˌsər-kəm-'stan-chəl\ *adj* 1 : consisting of or depending on circumstances 2 : INCIDENTAL 3 : containing full details — **cir·cum·stan·tial·ly** *adv*

cir·cum·vent \ˌsər-kəm-'vent\ *vb* : to check or defeat esp. by stratagem — **cir·cum·ven·tion** \-'vent-shən\ *n*

cir·cus \'sər-kəs\ *n* 1 : a usu. traveling show that features feats of physical skill, wild animal acts, and performances by clowns 2 : a circus performance; *also* : the equipment, livestock, and personnel of a circus

cirque \'sərk\ *n* : a deep steep-walled mountain basin usu. forming the blunt end of a valley

cir·rho·sis \sə-'rō-səs\ *n, pl* **-rho·ses** \-ˌsēz\ [NL, fr. Gk *kirrhos* orange-colored] : fibrosis of the liver — **cir·rhot·ic** \-'rä-tik\ *adj or n*

cir·rus \'sir-əs\ *n, pl* **cir·ri** \'sir-ˌī\ : a wispy white cloud usu. of minute ice crystals at high altitudes

cis·lu·nar \(ˌ)sis-'lü-nər\ *adj* : lying between the earth and the moon or the moon's orbit

cis·sy *Brit var of* SISSY

cis·tern \'sis-tərn\ *n* : an often underground tank for storing water

cit *abbr* **1** citation; cited **2** citizen

cit·a·del \'si-tə-dəl, -ˌdel\ *n* **1** : a fortress commanding a city **2** : STRONGHOLD

ci·ta·tion \sī-'tā-shən\ *n* **1** : an official summons to appear (as before a court) **2** : QUOTATION **3** : a formal statement of the achievements of a person; *also* : a specific reference in a military dispatch to meritorious performance of duty

cite \'sīt\ *vb* **cit·ed; cit·ing** **1** : to summon to appear before a court **2** : QUOTE **3** : to refer to esp. in commendation or praise

cit·i·fied \'si-ti-ˌfīd\ *adj* : of, relating to, or characterized by an urban style of living

cit·i·zen \'si-tə-zən\ *n* **1** : an inhabitant of a city or town **2** : a person who owes allegiance to a government and is entitled to its protection — **cit·i·zen·ship** *n*

cit·i·zen·ry \-rē\ *n, pl* **-ries** : a whole body of citizens

citizens band *n* : a range of radio frequencies set aside for private radio communications

cit·ric acid \'si-trik-\ *n* : a sour organic acid obtained from lemon and lime juices or by fermentation of sugars and used chiefly as a flavoring

cit·ron \'si-trən\ *n* **1** : the oval lemonlike fruit of a citrus tree; *also* : the tree **2** : a small hard-fleshed watermelon used esp. in pickles and preserves

cit·ro·nel·la \ˌsi-trə-'ne-lə\ *n* : a lemon-scented oil obtained from a fragrant grass of southern Asia and used in perfumes and as an insect repellent

cit·rus \'si-trəs\ *n, pl* **citrus** *or* **cit·rus·es** : any of a genus of often thorny evergreen trees or shrubs grown in warm regions for their fruits (as the orange, lemon, lime, and grapefruit); *also* : the fruit

city \'si-tē\ *n, pl* **cit·ies** [ME *citie* large or small town, fr. AF *cité*, fr. ML *civitas*, fr. L, citizenship, state, city of Rome, fr. *civis* citizen] **1** : an inhabited place larger or more important than a town **2** : a municipality in the U.S. governed under a charter granted by the state; *also* : an incorporated municipal unit of the highest class in Canada

city manager *n* : an official employed by an elected council to direct the administration of a city government

city–state \'si-tē-ˌstāt\ *n* : an autonomous state consisting of a city and surrounding territory

civ *abbr* **1** civil; civilian **2** civilization

civ·et \'si-vət\ *n* : a yellowish strong-smelling substance obtained from a catlike Old World mammal (**civet cat**) and used in making perfumes

civ·ic \'si-vik\ *adj* : of or relating to a city, citizenship, or civil affairs

civ·ics \-viks\ *n* : a social science dealing with the rights and duties of citizens

civ·il \'si-vəl\ *adj* **1** : of or relating to citizens or to the state as a political body **2** : COURTEOUS, POLITE **3** : of or relating to legal proceedings in connection with private rights and obligations ⟨the ~ code⟩ **4** : of or relating to the general population : not military or ecclesiastical

civil defense *n* : protective measures and emergency relief activities conducted by civilians in case of enemy attack or natural disaster

civil disobedience *n* : refusal to obey governmental commands esp. as a nonviolent means of protest

civil engineer *n* : an engineer whose training or occupation is in the design and construction esp. of public works (as roads or harbors) — **civil engineering** *n*

ci·vil·ian \sə-'vil-yən\ *n* : a person not on active duty in a military, police, or fire-fighting force

civ·i·li·sa·tion, civ·i·lise *chiefly Brit var of* CIVILIZATION, CIVILIZE

ci·vil·i·ty \sə-'vi-lə-tē\ *n, pl* **-ties** **1** : POLITENESS, COURTESY **2** : a polite act or expression

civ·i·li·za·tion \ˌsi-və-lə-'zā-shən\ *n* **1** : a relatively high level of cultural and technological development **2** : the culture characteristic of a time or place — **civ·i·li·za·tion·al** \-shə-n³l\ *adj*

civ·i·lize \'si-və-ˌlīz\ *vb* **-lized; -liz·ing** **1** : to raise from a primitive state to an advanced and ordered stage of cultural development **2** : REFINE — **civ·i·lized** *adj*

civil liberty *n* : freedom from arbitrary governmental interference specifically by denial of governmental power — usu. used in pl.

civ·il·ly \'si-vəl-lē\ *adv* **1** : in terms of civil rights, matters, or law ⟨~ dead⟩ **2** : in a civil manner : POLITELY

civil rights *n pl* : the nonpolitical rights of a citizen; *esp* : those guaranteed by the 13th and 14th amendments to the Constitution and by acts of Congress

civil servant *n* : a member of a civil service

civil service *n* : the administrative service of a government

civil war *n* : a war between opposing groups of citizens of the same country

civ·vies \'si-vēz\ *n pl* : civilian clothes as distinguished from a military uniform

CJ *abbr* chief justice

ck *abbr* **1** cask **2** check

cl *abbr* **1** centiliter **2** class

Cl *symbol* chlorine

¹clack \'klak\ *vb* **1** : CHATTER, PRATTLE **2** : to make or cause to make a clatter

²clack *n* **1** : rapid continuous talk : CHATTER **2** : a sound of clacking ⟨the ~ of a typewriter⟩

clad \'klad\ *adj* **1** : CLOTHED, COVERED **2** : being or consisting of coins made of outer layers of one metal bonded to a core of a different metal

¹claim \'klām\ *vb* [ME, fr. AF *claimer, clamer,* fr. L *clamare* to cry out, shout] **1** : to ask for as one's own; *also* : to take as the rightful owner **2** : to call for : REQUIRE **3** : to state as a fact : MAINTAIN

²claim *n* **1** : a demand for something due ⟨an insurance ~⟩ **2** : a right to something usu. in another's possession **3** : an assertion open to challenge **4** : something claimed (as a tract of land)

claim·ant \'klā-mənt\ *n* : a person making a claim

clair·voy·ant \klar-'vȯi-ənt\ *adj* [F, fr. *clair* clear + *voyant* seeing] **1** : able to see beyond the range of ordinary perception **2** : having the power of discerning objects not present to the senses — **clair·voy·ance** \-əns\ *n* — **clairvoyant** *n*

clam \'klam\ *n* **1** : any of numerous bivalve mollusks including many that are edible **2** : DOLLAR

clam 1

clam·bake \-ˌbāk\ *n* : a party or gathering (as at the seashore) at which food is cooked usu. on heated rocks covered by seaweed

clam·ber \'klam-bər\ *vb* : to climb awkwardly — **clamber·er** *n*

clam·my \'kla-mē\ *adj* **clam·mi·er; -est** : being damp, soft, sticky, and usu. cool — **clam·mi·ness** *n*

clam·or \'kla-mər\ *n* **1** : a noisy shouting **2** : a loud continuous noise **3** : insistent public expression (as of support or protest) — **clamor** *vb* — **clam·or·ous** *adj*

clam·our *chiefly Brit var of* CLAMOR

¹clamp \'klamp\ *n* : a device that holds or presses parts together firmly

²clamp *vb* : to fasten with or as if with a clamp

clamp down *vb* : to impose restrictions : become repressive — **clamp·down** \'klamp-ˌdaȯn\ *n*

clam·shell \'klam-ˌshel\ *n* **1** : the shell of a clam **2** : a bucket or grapnel (as on a dredge) having two hinged jaws

clam up *vb* : to become silent

clan \'klan\ *n* [ME, fr. ScGael *clann* offspring, clan, fr. Old Irish *cland* plant, offspring, fr. L *planta* plant] : a group (as in the Scottish Highlands) made up of households whose heads claim descent from a common ancestor — **clan·nish** *adj* — **clan·nish·ness** *n* clan·des·tine \klan-'des-tən\ *adj* : held in or conducted with secrecy

clang \'klaŋ\ *n* : a loud metallic ringing sound — clang *vb*

clan·gor \'klaŋ-ər, -gər\ *n* : a resounding clang or medley of clangs

clan·gour *chiefly Brit var of* CLANGOR

clank \'klaŋk\ *n* : a sharp brief metallic ringing sound — clank *vb*

¹clap \'klap\ *vb* clapped; clap·ping 1 : to strike noisily 2 : APPLAUD

²clap *n* 1 : a loud noisy crash 2 : the noise made by clapping the hands

³clap *n* : GONORRHEA

clap·board \'kla-bərd, -ˌbórd; 'klap-ˌbórd\ *n* : a narrow board thicker at one edge than the other used for siding — clap·board *vb*

clap·per \'kla-pər\ *n* : one that claps; *esp* : the tongue of a bell

clap·trap \'klap-ˌtrap\ *n* : pretentious nonsense

claque \'klak\ *n* [F, fr. *claquer* to clap] 1 : a group hired to applaud at a performance 2 : a group of sycophants

clar·et \'kler-ət\ *n* [ME, fr. AF (*vin*) *claret* clear wine] : a dry red wine

clar·i·fy \'kler-ə-ˌfī\ *vb* -fied; -fy·ing : to make or become clear — clar·i·fi·ca·tion \ˌkler-ə-fə-'kā-shən\ *n*

clar·i·net \ˌkler-ə-'net\ *n* : a single-reed woodwind instrument in the form of a cylindrical tube with a moderately flaring end — clar·i·net·ist *or* clar·i·net·tist \-'ne-tist\ *n*

clar·i·on \'kler-ē-ən\ *adj* : brilliantly clear ⟨a ~ call⟩

clar·i·ty \'kler-ə-tē\ *n* : CLEARNESS

¹clash \'klash\ *vb* 1 : to make or cause to make a clash 2 : CONFLICT, COLLIDE

²clash *n* 1 : a noisy usu. metallic sound of collision 2 : a hostile encounter 3 : a sharp conflict ⟨a ~ of opinions⟩

clasp \'klasp\ *n* 1 : a device (as a hook) for holding objects or parts together 2 : EMBRACE, GRASP — clasp *vb*

¹class \'klas\ *n* [F *classe*, fr. L *classis* group called to military service, fleet, class] 1 : a group of students meeting regularly in a course; *also* : a group graduating together 2 : a course of instruction; *also* : the period when such a course is taught 3 : social rank; *also* : high quality 4 : a group of the same general status or nature; *esp* : a major category in biological classification that is above the order and below the phylum 5 : a division or rating based on grade or quality — class·less *adj*

²class *vb* : CLASSIFY

class action *n* : a legal action undertaken in behalf of the plaintiffs and all others having an identical interest in the alleged wrong

¹clas·sic \'kla-sik\ *adj* 1 : serving as a standard of excellence; *also* : TRADITIONAL 2 : CLASSICAL 2 3 : notable esp. as the best example 4 : AUTHENTIC ⟨a ~ folk dance⟩

²classic *n* 1 : a work of enduring excellence and esp. of ancient Greece or Rome; *also* : its author 2 : a traditional event ⟨a football ~⟩

clas·si·cal \'kla-si-kəl\ *adj* 1 : CLASSIC 2 : of or relating to the ancient Greek and Roman classics 3 : of or relating to a form or system of primary significance before modern times ⟨~ economics⟩ 4 : concerned with a general study of the arts and sciences — clas·si·cal·ly \-k(ə-)lē\ *adv*

clas·si·cism \'kla-sə-ˌsi-zəm\ *n* 1 : the principles or style of the literature or art of ancient Greece and Rome 2 : adherence to traditional standards believed to be universally valid — clas·si·cist \-sist\ *n*

clas·si·fied \'kla-sə-ˌfīd\ *adj* : withheld from general circulation for reasons of national security

clas·si·fieds \-ˌfīdz\ *n pl* : advertisements grouped by subject

clas·si·fy \'kla-sə-ˌfī\ *vb* -fied; -fy·ing : to arrange in or assign to classes — clas·si·fi·able *adj* — clas·si·fi·ca·tion \ˌkla-sə-fə-'kā-shən\ *n* — clas·si·fi·er *n*

class·mate \'klas-ˌmāt\ *n* : a member of the same class (as in a college)

class·room \-ˌrüm-, -ˌrüm\ *n* : a place where classes meet

classy \'kla-sē\ *adj* class·i·er; -est : ELEGANT, STYLISH ⟨a ~ clientele⟩ — class·i·ness *n*

clat·ter \'kla-tər\ *n* : a rattling sound ⟨the ~ of dishes⟩ — clatter *vb*

clause \'klóz\ *n* 1 : a group of words having its own subject and predicate but forming only part of a compound or complex sentence 2 : a separate part of an article or document

claus·tro·pho·bia \ˌklò-strə-'fō-bē-ə\ *n* : abnormal dread of being in closed or narrow spaces — claus·tro·pho·bic \-bik\ *adj*

clav·i·chord \'kla-və-ˌkòrd\ *n* : an early keyboard instrument in use before the piano

clav·i·cle \'kla-vi-kəl\ *n* [F *clavicule*, fr. NL *clavicula*, fr. L, dim. of L *clavis* key] : COLLARBONE

cla·vier \klə-'vir; 'klä-vē-ər\ *n* 1 : the keyboard of a musical instrument 2 : an early keyboard instrument

¹claw \'klò\ *n* 1 : a sharp usu. curved nail on the toe of an animal 2 : a sharp curved process (as on the foot of an insect); *also* : a pincerlike organ at the end of a limb of some arthropods (as a lobster) — clawed \'klòd\ *adj*

²claw *vb* : to rake, seize, or dig with or as if with claws

clay \'klā\ *n* 1 : an earthy material that is plastic when moist but hard when fired and is used in making pottery; *also* : finely divided soil consisting largely of such clay 2 : EARTH, MUD 3 : a plastic substance used for modeling 4 : the mortal human body — clay·ey \'klā-ē\ *adj*

clay·more \'klā-ˌmòr\ *n* : a large 2-edged sword formerly used by Scottish Highlanders

clay pigeon *n* : a saucer-shaped target thrown from a trap in trapshooting

¹clean \'klēn\ *adj* 1 : free from dirt, disease, or pollution ⟨~ air⟩ 2 : PURE ⟨the ~ thrill of one's first flight⟩; *also* : HONORABLE 3 : THOROUGH ⟨made a ~ sweep⟩ 4 : TRIM ⟨a ~ edge⟩ ⟨a ship with ~ lines⟩; *also* : EVEN 5 : habitually neat — clean *adv* — clean·ly \'klēn-lē\ *adv* — clean·ness \'klēn-nəs\ *n*

²clean *vb* : to make or become clean — clean·able \'klē-nə-bəl\ *adj* — clean·er *n*

clean–cut \'klēn-'kət\ *adj* 1 : cut so that the surface or edge is smooth and even 2 : sharply defined or outlined 3 : giving an effect of wholesomeness

clean·ly \'klen-lē\ *adj* clean·li·er; -est 1 : careful to keep clean 2 : habitually kept clean — clean·li·ness *n*

clean room \'klēn-ˌrüm, -ˌrùm\ *n* : an uncontaminated room maintained for the manufacture or assembly of objects (as precision parts)

cleanse \'klenz\ *vb* cleansed; cleans·ing : to make clean — cleans·er *n*

¹clean·up \'klēn-ˌəp\ *n* 1 : an act or instance of cleaning 2 : a very large profit

²cleanup *adj* : being 4th in the batting order of a baseball team — cleanup *adv*

clean up *vb* : to make or score a large business profit

¹clear \'klir\ *adj* [ME *clere*, fr. AF *cler*, fr. L *clarus*] 1 : BRIGHT, LUMINOUS; *also* : UNTROUBLED, SERENE 2 : CLOUDLESS 3 : CLEAN, PURE; *also* : TRANSPARENT 4 : easily heard, seen, or understood 5 : capable of sharp discernment; *also* : free from doubt 6 : INNOCENT ⟨a ~ conscience⟩ 7 : free from restriction, obstruction, or entanglement — clear *adv* — clear·ness *n*

²clear *vb* 1 : to make or become clear 2 : to go away : DISPERSE 3 : to free from accusation or blame; *also* : to certify as trustworthy 4 : EXPLAIN 5 : to get free from obstruction 6 : SETTLE 7 : NET ⟨~ed a profit⟩ 8 : to get rid of : REMOVE 9 : to jump or go by without touching; *also* : PASS ⟨the bill ~ed the legislature⟩

³clear *n* : a clear space or part

clear·ance \'klir-əns\ *n* 1 : an act or process of clearing 2 : the distance by which one object clears another 3 : AUTHORIZATION

clear–cut \'klir-'kət\ *adj* 1 : sharply outlined 2 : DEFINITE, UNEQUIVOCAL ⟨a ~ victory⟩

clear–cut·ting \-ˌkə-tiŋ\ *n* : removal of all the trees in a stand of timber — clear–cut \-ˌkət\ *vb*

clear·head·ed \-'he-dəd\ *adj* : having a clear understanding : PERCEPTIVE

clear·ing \'klir-iŋ\ *n* 1 : a tract of land cleared of wood and brush 2 : the passage of checks and claims through a clearinghouse

clear·ing·house \-ˌhaús\ *n* : an institution maintained by banks for making an exchange of checks and claims held by each bank against other banks; *also* : an informal channel for information or assistance

clear·ly \'klir-lē\ *adv* 1 : in a clear manner 2 : it is clear

cleat \'klēt\ *n* : a piece of wood or metal fastened on or projecting from something to give strength, provide a grip, or prevent slipping

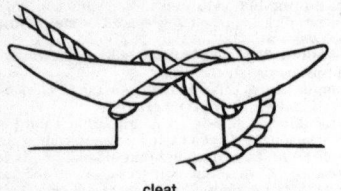

cleat

cleav·age \'klē-vij\ *n* 1 : a splitting apart : SPLIT 2 : the depression between a woman's breasts esp. when exposed by a low-cut dress

¹**cleave** \'klēv\ *vb* **cleaved** \'klēvd\ *or* **clove** \'klōv\; **cleaved; cleav·ing** : ADHERE, CLING

²**cleave** *vb* **cleaved** \'klēvd\ *also* **cleft** \'kleft\ *or* **clove** \'klōv\; **cleaved** *also* **cleft** *or* **clo·ven** \'klō-vən\; **cleav·ing** 1 : to divide by force : split asunder 2 : DIVIDE

cleav·er \'klē-vər\ *n* : a heavy chopping knife for cutting meat

clef \'klef\ *n* : a sign placed on the staff in music to show what pitch is represented by each line and space

cleft \'kleft\ *n* : FISSURE, CRACK

cleft lip *n* : a birth defect in which the upper lip is vertically split

cleft palate *n* : a split in the roof of the mouth that appears as a birth defect

clem·a·tis \'kle-mə-təs; kli-'ma-təs\ *n* : any of a genus of vines or herbs related to the buttercups that have showy usu. white or purple flowers

clem·en·cy \'kle-mən-sē\ *n, pl* **-cies** 1 : disposition to be merciful 2 : mildness of weather

clem·ent \'kle-mənt\ *adj* 1 : MERCIFUL, LENIENT ⟨a ∼ judge⟩ 2 : TEMPERATE, MILD ⟨∼ weather for this time of year⟩

clem·en·tine \'kle-mən-ˌtēn\ *n* : a small citrus fruit that is probably a hybrid between a tangerine and an orange

clench \'klench\ *vb* 1 : CLINCH 1 2 : to hold fast 3 : to set or close tightly

clere·sto·ry \'klir-ˌstȯr-ē\ *n* : an outside wall of a room or building that rises above an adjoining roof and contains windows

cler·gy \'klər-jē\ *n* : a body of religious officials authorized to conduct services

cler·gy·man \-mən\ *n* : a member of the clergy

cler·gy·per·son \-ˌpər-sᵊn\ *n* : a member of the clergy

cler·ic \'kler-ik\ *n* : a member of the clergy

cler·i·cal \'kler-i-kəl\ *adj* 1 : of or relating to the clergy 2 : of or relating to a clerk

cler·i·cal·ism \'kler-i-kə-ˌli-zəm\ *n* : a policy of maintaining or increasing the power of a religious hierarchy

clerk \'klərk, *Brit* 'klärk\ *n* 1 : CLERIC 2 : an official responsible for correspondence, records, and accounts; *also* : a person employed to perform general office work 3 : a store salesperson — **clerk** *vb* — **clerk·ship** *n*

clev·er \'kle-vər\ *adj* 1 : showing skill or resourcefulness 2 : marked by wit or ingenuity — **clev·er·ly** *adv* — **clev·er·ness** *n*

clev·is \'kle-vəs\ *n* : a U-shaped shackle used for fastening

¹**clew** \'klü\ *n* 1 : CLUE 2 : a metal loop on a lower corner of a sail

²**clew** *vb* : to haul (a sail) up or down by ropes through the clews

cli·ché \klē-'shā\ *n* [F] : a trite phrase or expression — **cli·chéd** \-'shād\ *adj*

¹**click** \'klik\ *vb* 1 : to make or cause to make a click 2 : to fit or work together smoothly 3 : to select or make a selection on a computer by pressing a button on a control device (as a mouse) — **click·able** \'kli-kə-bəl\ *adj*

²**click** *n* 1 : a slight sharp noise 2 : an instance of clicking ⟨a mouse ∼⟩

click·er \'kli-kər\ *n* : REMOTE CONTROL 2

cli·ent \'klī-ənt\ *n* 1 : DEPENDENT 2 : a person who engages the professional services of another; *also* : PATRON,

CUSTOMER 3 : a computer in a network that uses the services (as access to files) provided by a server

cli·en·tele \ˌklī-ən-'tel, ˌklē-\ *n* : a body of clients and esp. customers

cliff \'klif\ *n* : a high steep face of rock, earth, or ice

cliff–hang·er \-ˌhaŋ-ər\ *n* 1 : an adventure serial or melodrama usu. presented in installments each of which ends in suspense 2 : a contest whose outcome is in doubt up to the very end

cli·mac·ter·ic \klī-'mak-tə-rik\ *n* 1 : a major turning point or critical stage 2 : MENOPAUSE; *also* : a corresponding period in the male

cli·mate \'klī-mət\ *n* [ME *climat*, fr. MF, fr. LL *clima*, fr. Gk *klima* inclination, latitude, climate, fr. *klinein* to lean] 1 : a region having specific climatic conditions 2 : the average weather conditions at a place over a period of years 3 : the prevailing set of conditions (as temperature and humidity) indoors 4 : a prevailing atmosphere or environment ⟨the ∼ of opinion⟩ — **cli·mat·ic** \klī-'ma-tik\ *adj* — **cli·mat·i·cal·ly** \-ti-k(ə-)lē\ *adv*

cli·ma·tol·o·gy \ˌklī-mə-'tä-lə-jē\ *n* : the science that deals with climates — **cli·ma·to·log·i·cal** \-mə-tə-'lä-ji-kəl\ *adj* — **cli·ma·to·log·i·cal·ly** \-k(ə-)lē\ *adv* — **cli·ma·tol·o·gist** \-mə-'tä-lə-jist\ *n*

¹**cli·max** \'klī-ˌmaks\ *n* [L, fr. Gk *klimax*, lit., ladder, fr. *klinein* to lean] 1 : a series of ideas or statements so arranged that they increase in force and power from the first to the last; *also* : the last member of such a series 2 : the highest point 3 : ORGASM — **cli·mac·tic** \klī-'mak-tik\ *adj*

²**climax** *vb* : to come or bring to a climax

¹**climb** \'klīm\ *vb* 1 : to rise to a higher point 2 : to go up or down esp. by use of hands and feet; *also* : to ascend in growing — **climb·er** *n*

²**climb** *n* 1 : a place where climbing is necessary 2 : the act of climbing ; ascent by climbing

clime \'klīm\ *n* : CLIMATE

¹**clinch** \'klinch\ *vb* 1 : to turn over or flatten the end of something sticking out ⟨∼ a nail⟩; *also* : to fasten by clinching 2 : to make final : SETTLE 3 : to hold a boxing opponent 4 : to hold fast or firmly

²**clinch** *n* 1 : a fastening by means of a clinched nail, rivet, or bolt 2 : an act or instance of clinching in boxing

clinch·er \'klin-chər\ *n* : one that clinches; *esp* : a decisive fact, argument, act, or remark

cling \'kliŋ\ *vb* **clung** \'kləŋ\; **cling·ing** 1 : to adhere as if glued; *also* : to hold or hold on tightly 2 : to have a strong emotional attachment — **clingy** \'kliŋ-ē\ *adj*

cling·stone \'kliŋ-ˌstōn\ *n* : any of various fruits (as some peaches) whose flesh adheres strongly to the pit

clin·ic \'kli-nik\ *n* 1 : a medical class in which patients are examined and discussed 2 : a group meeting for teaching a certain skill and working on individual problems ⟨a reading ∼⟩ 3 : a facility (as of a hospital) for diagnosis and treatment of outpatients

clin·i·cal \'kli-ni-kəl\ *adj* 1 : of, relating to, or typical of a clinic; *esp* : involving direct observation of the patient ⟨∼ studies⟩ 2 : scientifically dispassionate — **clin·i·cal·ly** \-k(ə-)lē\ *adv*

cli·ni·cian \kli-'ni-shən\ *n* : a person qualified in the clinical practice of medicine, psychiatry, or psychology as distinguished from one specializing in laboratory or research techniques or in theory

¹**clink** \'kliŋk\ *vb* : to make or cause to make a sharp short metallic sound

²**clink** *n* : a clinking sound

clin·ker \'kliŋ-kər\ *n* : stony matter fused together : SLAG

¹**clip** \'klip\ *vb* **clipped; clip·ping** : to fasten with a clip

²**clip** *n* 1 : a device that grips, clasps, or hooks 2 : a cartridge holder for a rifle

³**clip** *vb* **clipped; clip·ping** 1 : to cut or cut off with shears 2 : CURTAIL, DIMINISH 3 : HIT, PUNCH 4 : to illegally block (an opponent) in football

⁴**clip** *n* 1 : a 2-bladed instrument for cutting esp. the nails 2 : a sharp blow 3 : a rapid pace

clip art *n* : ready-made usu. copyright-free illustrations

clip·board \'klip-ˌbȯrd\ *n* 1 : a small writing board with a spring clip at the top for holding papers 2 : a section of computer memory that temporarily stores data esp. to facilitate its movement or duplication

clip joint *n, slang* : an establishment (as a nightclub) that makes a practice of defrauding its customers

clip·per \'kli-pər\ *n* **1** : an implement for clipping esp. the hair or nails — usu. used in pl. **2** : a fast sailing ship

clip·ping \'kli-piŋ\ *n* : a piece clipped from something (as a newspaper)

clique \'klēk, 'klik\ *n* [F] : a small exclusive group of people : COTERIE — **cliqu·ey** \'klē-kē, 'kli-\ *adj* — **cliqu·ish** \-kish\ *adj*

cli·to·ris \'kli-tə-rəs\ *n, pl* **cli·to·ris·es** : a small erectile organ at the anterior or ventral part of the vulva homologous to the penis — **cli·to·ral** \-rəl\ *adj*

clk *abbr* clerk

clo *abbr* clothing

¹cloak \'klōk\ *n* **1** : a loose outer garment **2** : something that conceals

²cloak *vb* : to cover or hide with a cloak

cloak–and–dagger *adj* : involving or suggestive of espionage

clob·ber \'klä-bər\ *vb* **1** : to pound mercilessly; *also* : to hit with force : SMASH **2** : to defeat overwhelmingly

cloche \'klōsh\ *n* [F, lit., bell] : a woman's small close-fitting hat

¹clock \'kläk\ *n* : a timepiece not intended to be carried on the person

²clock *vb* **1** : to time (a person or a performance) by a timing device **2** : to register (as speed) on a mechanical recording device — **clock·er** *n*

³clock *n* : an ornamental figure on a stocking or sock

clock·wise \'kläk-ˌwīz\ *adv* : in the direction in which the hands of a clock move — **clockwise** *adj*

clock·work \-ˌwərk\ *n* **1** : the machinery that runs a mechanical device (as a clock or toy) **2** : the precision or regularity associated with a clock

clod \'kläd\ *n* **1** : a lump esp. of earth or clay **2** : a dull or insensitive person

clod·hop·per \-ˌhä-pər\ *n* **1** : an uncouth rustic **2** : a large heavy shoe

¹clog \'kläg\ *n* **1** : a weight attached esp. to an animal to impede motion **2** : a thick-soled shoe

²clog *vb* **clogged; clog·ging 1** : to impede with a clog : HINDER **2** : to obstruct passage through **3** : to become filled with extraneous matter

cloi·son·né \ˌklói-zə-'nā\ *adj* : a colored decoration made of enamels poured into the divided areas in a design outlined with wire or metal strips

¹clois·ter \'klói-stər\ *n* [ME *cloistre*, fr. AF, fr. ML *claustrum*, fr. L, bar, bolt, fr. *claudere* to close] **1** : a monastic establishment **2** : a covered usu. colonnaded passage on the side of a court — **clois·tral** \-strəl\ *adj*

²cloister *vb* : to shut away from the world

clone \'klōn\ *n* [Gk *klōn* twig, slip] **1** : the collection of genetically identical cells or organisms produced asexually from a single ancestral cell or organism; *also* : an individual grown from a single cell and genetically identical to it ⟨a sheep ∼⟩ **2** : a group of replicas of a biological molecule (as DNA) **3** : one that appears to be a copy of an original form — **clon·al** \'klō-nᵊl\ *adj* — **clone** *vb*

clop \'kläp\ *n* : a sound made by or as if by a hoof or wooden shoe against pavement — **clop** *vb*

¹close \'klōz\ *vb* **closed; clos·ing 1** : to bar passage through : SHUT **2** : to suspend the operations (as of a school) **3** : END, TERMINATE **4** : to bring together the parts or edges of; *also* : to fill up **5** : GRAPPLE ⟨∼ with the enemy⟩ **6** : to enter into an agreement — **clos·able** *or* **close·able** *adj*

²close \'klōz\ *n* : CONCLUSION, END

³close \'klōs\ *adj* **clos·er; clos·est 1** : having no openings **2** : narrowly restricting or restricted **3** : limited to a privileged class **4** : SECLUDED; *also* : SECRETIVE **5** : RIGOROUS ⟨keep ∼ watch⟩ **6** : SULTRY, STUFFY **7** : STINGY **8** : having little space between items or units **9** : fitting tightly; *also* : SHORT ⟨∼ haircut⟩ **10** : NEAR ⟨at ∼ range⟩ **11** : INTIMATE ⟨∼ friends⟩ **12** : ACCURATE **13** : decided by a narrow margin ⟨a ∼ game⟩ — **close** *adv* — **close·ly** *adv* — **close·ness** *n*

closed–circuit \'klōzd-'sər-kət\ *adj* : used in, shown on, or being a television installation in which the signal is transmitted by wire to a limited number of receivers

closed shop *n* : an establishment having only members of a labor union on the payroll

close·fist·ed \'klōz-'fis-təd, 'klōs-\ *adj* : STINGY

close–knit \'klōs-'nit\ *adj* : closely bound together by social, cultural, economic, or political ties

close·mouthed \'klōz-'maủthd, 'klōs-'maủtht\ *adj* : cautious or reticent in speaking

close·out \'klōz-ˌaủt\ *n* : a sale of a business's entire stock at low prices

close out *vb* **1** : to dispose of by a closeout **2** : to dispose of a business : SELL OUT

clos·er \'klō-zər\ *n* : one that closes; *esp* : a relief pitcher who specializes in finishing games

¹clos·et \'klä-zət, 'klȯ-\ *n* **1** : a small room for privacy **2** : a small compartment for household utensils or clothing **3** : a state or condition of secrecy ⟨came out of the ∼⟩

²closet *vb* : to take into a private room for an interview

close–up \'klōs-ˌəp\ *n* **1** : a photograph or movie shot taken at close range **2** : an intimate view or examination

clo·sure \'klō-zhər\ *n* **1** : an act of closing : the condition of being closed **2** : something that closes **3** : CLOTURE

clot \'klät\ *n* : a mass formed by a portion of liquid (as blood) thickening and sticking together — **clot** *vb*

cloth \'klȯth\ *n, pl* **cloths** \'klȯthz, 'klȯths\ **1** : a pliable fabric made usu. by weaving or knitting natural or synthetic fibers and filaments **2** : TABLECLOTH **3** : distinctive dress of the clergy; *also* : CLERGY

clothe \'klōth\ *vb* **clothed** *or* **clad** \'klad\; **cloth·ing 1** : DRESS; *also* : to provide with clothes **2** : to express by suitably significant language ⟨policies *clothed* in rhetoric⟩

clothes \'klōthz, 'klȯz\ *n pl* **1** : CLOTHING **2** : BED-CLOTHES

clothes·horse \-ˌhȯrs\ *n* **1** : a frame on which to hang clothes **2** : a conspicuously dressy person

¹clothes·line \-ˌlīn\ *n* : a rope or cord on which clothes are hung to dry

²clothesline *vb* : to knock down by catching by the neck with one's outstretched arm

clothes moth *n* : any of several small pale moths whose larvae eat wool, fur, and feathers

clothes·pin \'klōthz-ˌpin, 'klȯz-\ *n* : a device for fastening clothes on a line

clothes·press \-ˌpres\ *n* : a receptacle for clothes

cloth·ier \'klōth-yər, 'klō-thē-ər\ *n* : a maker or seller of clothing

cloth·ing \'klō-thiŋ\ *n* : garments in general

clo·ture \'klō-chər\ *n* : the closing or limitation (as by calling for a vote) of debate in a legislative body

¹cloud \'klaủd\ *n* [ME, rock, cloud, fr. OE *clūd*] **1** : a visible mass of particles of condensed vapor (as water or ice) suspended in the atmosphere **2** : a usu. visible mass of minute airborne particles; *also* : a mass of obscuring matter in interstellar space **3** : CROWD, SWARM ⟨a ∼ of mosquitoes⟩ **4** : something having a dark or threatening aspect ⟨a ∼ of suspicion⟩ **5** : something that obscures or blemishes ⟨a ∼ of ambiguity⟩ — **cloud·i·ness** \'klaủ-dē-nəs\ *n* — **cloud·less** *adj* — **cloudy** *adj*

²cloud *vb* **1** : to darken or hide with or as if with a cloud **2** : OBSCURE ⟨∼ed in mystery⟩ **3** : TAINT, SULLY ⟨a ∼ed reputation⟩

cloud·burst \-ˌbərst\ *n* : a sudden heavy rainfall

cloud·let \-lət\ *n* : a small cloud

cloud nine *n* : a feeling of extreme well-being or elation — usu. used with *on*

¹clout \'klaủt\ *n* **1** : a blow esp. with the hand **2** : PULL, INFLUENCE

²clout *vb* : to hit forcefully

¹clove \'klōv\ *n* : one of the small bulbs that grows at the base of the scales of a large bulb ⟨a ∼ of garlic⟩

²clove *past of* CLEAVE

³clove *n* [ME *clowe*, fr. AF *clou (de girofle)*, lit., nail of clove, fr. L *clavus* nail] : the dried flower bud of a tropical tree used esp. as a spice

clo·ven \'klō-vən\ *past part of* CLEAVE

cloven foot *n* : CLOVEN HOOF — **cloven–foot·ed** \-'fủ-təd\ *adj*

cloven hoof *n* : a foot (as of a sheep) with the front part divided into two parts — **cloven–hoofed** \-'hủft, -'hủvd\ *adj*

clo·ver \'klō-vər\ *n* : any of a genus of leguminous herbs with usu. 3-parted leaves and dense flower heads

clo·ver·leaf \-ˌlēf\ *n, pl* **cloverleafs** \-ˌlēfs\ *or* **clo·ver-**

leaves \-ˌlēvz\ : an interchange between two major highways that from above resembles a 4-leaf clover

¹**clown** \'klaůn\ n   1 : BOOR   2 : a fool or comedian in an entertainment (as a circus)   3 : a person given to joking and buffoonery — **clown·ish** adj — **clown·ish·ly** adv — **clown·ish·ness** n

²**clown** vb : to act like a clown

cloy \'klȯi\ vb : to disgust or nauseate with excess of something orig. pleasing — **cloy·ing·ly** adv

clr abbr clear

¹**club** \'kləb\ n   1 : a heavy wooden stick or staff used as a weapon; also : BAT   2 : any of a suit of playing cards marked with a black figure resembling a clover leaf   3 : a group of persons associated for a common purpose; also : the meeting place of such a group   4 : CLUB SANDWICH

²**club** vb **clubbed; club·bing**   1 : to strike with a club   2 : to unite or combine for a common cause   3 : to patronize nightclubs

club·foot \'kləb-ˈfůt\ n : a misshapen foot twisted out of position from birth; also : this deformed condition — **club·foot·ed** \-ˈfů-təd\ adj

club·house \'kləb-ˌhaůs\ n   1 : a house occupied by a club   2 : locker rooms used by an athletic team   3 : a building at a golf course with locker rooms and usu. a pro shop and a restaurant

club sandwich n : a sandwich of three slices of bread with two layers of meat (as turkey) and lettuce, tomato, and mayonnaise

club soda n : SODA WATER

cluck \'klək\ n : the call of a hen esp. to her chicks — **cluck** vb

¹**clue** \'klü\ n   1 : something that guides through an intricate procedure or maze; esp : a piece of evidence leading to the solution of a problem   2 : IDEA, NOTION ⟨has no ~ what he's doing⟩

²**clue** vb **clued; clue·ing** or **clu·ing** : to provide with a clue; also : to give information to ⟨~ me in⟩

¹**clump** \'kləmp\ n   1 : a group of things clustered together   2 : a heavy tramping sound

²**clump** vb : to tread clumsily and noisily

clum·sy \'kləm-zē\ adj **clum·si·er; -est**   1 : lacking dexterity, nimbleness, or grace   2 : not tactful or subtle — **clum·si·ly** \-zə-lē\ adv — **clum·si·ness** \-zē-nəs\ n

clung past and past part of CLING

clunk·er \'kləŋ-kər\ n   1 : a dilapidated automobile   2 : a notable failure

¹**clus·ter** \'kləs-tər\ n : GROUP, BUNCH

²**cluster** vb : to grow or gather in a cluster

¹**clutch** \'kləch\ vb : to grasp with or as if with the hand

²**clutch** n   1 : the claws or a hand in the act of grasping; also : CONTROL, POWER   2 : a device for gripping an object   3 : a coupling used to connect and disconnect a driving and a driven part of a mechanism; also : a lever or pedal operating such a coupling   4 : a crucial situation

³**clutch** adj : made, done, or successful in a crucial situation

⁴**clutch** n   1 : a nest or batch of eggs; also : a brood of chicks   2 : GROUP, BUNCH

¹**clut·ter** \'klə-tər\ vb : to fill or cover with a disorderly scattering of things

²**clutter** n : a crowded mass

cm abbr centimeter

Cm symbol curium

CM abbr [Commonwealth of the Northern Mariana Islands] Northern Mariana Islands

cmdr abbr commander

cml abbr commercial

CMSgt abbr chief master sergeant

CNO abbr chief of naval operations

CNS abbr central nervous system

co abbr   1 company   2 county

Co symbol cobalt

CO abbr   1 Colorado   2 commanding officer   3 conscientious objector

c/o abbr care of

¹**coach** \'kōch\ n [MF coche, ultim. fr. Hung kocsi (szekér), lit., (wagon) of Kocs (town in Hungary)]   1 : a large closed 4-wheeled carriage with an elevated outside front seat for the driver   2 : a railroad passenger car esp. for day travel   3 : BUS   4 : a private tutor; also : one who instructs or trains ⟨an acting ~⟩ ⟨a soccer ~⟩

²**coach** vb : to instruct, direct, or prompt as a coach

coach·man \-mən\ n : a man who drives a coach or carriage

co·ad·ju·tor \ˌkō-ə-'jü-tər, kō-'a-jə-tər\ n : ASSISTANT; esp : an assistant bishop having the right of succession

co·ag·u·lant \kō-'a-gyə-lənt\ n : something that produces coagulation

co·ag·u·late \-ˌlāt\ vb **-lat·ed; -lat·ing** : CLOT — **co·ag·u·la·tion** \kō-ˌa-gyə-'lā-shən\ n

¹**coal** \'kōl\ n   1 : EMBER   2 : a black solid combustible mineral used as fuel

²**coal** vb   1 : to supply with coal   2 : to take in coal

co·a·lesce \ˌkō-ə-'les\ vb **co·a·lesced; co·a·lesc·ing** : to grow together; also : FUSE ✦ **Synonyms** MERGE, BLEND, MINGLE, MIX — **co·a·les·cence** \-ᵊns\ n

coal·field \'kōl-ˌfēld\ n : a region rich in coal deposits

coal gas n : gas from coal; esp : gas distilled from bituminous coal and used for heating

co·a·li·tion \ˌkō-ə-'li-shən\ n : UNION; esp : a temporary union for a common purpose — **co·a·li·tion·ist** n

coal oil n : KEROSENE

coal tar n : tar distilled from bituminous coal and used in dyes and drugs

co–an·chor \'kō-'aŋ-kər\ n : a newscaster who shares the duties of head broadcaster

coarse \'kȯrs\ adj **coars·er; coars·est**   1 : of ordinary or inferior quality   2 : composed of large parts or particles ⟨~ sand⟩   3 : CRUDE ⟨~ manners⟩   4 : ROUGH, HARSH — **coarse·ly** adv — **coarse·ness** n

coars·en \'kȯr-sᵊn\ vb : to make or become coarse

¹**coast** \'kōst\ n [ME cost, fr. AF coste, fr. L costa rib, side]   1 : SEASHORE   2 : a slide down a slope   3 : the immediate area of view — used in the phrase the coast is clear — **coast·al** adj

²**coast** vb   1 : to sail along the shore   2 : to move (as downhill on a sled) without effort

coast·er n   1 : one that coasts   2 : a shallow container or a plate or mat to protect a surface

coaster brake n : a brake in the hub of the rear wheel of a bicycle

coast guard n : a military force employed in guarding or patrolling a coast — **coast·guards·man** \'kōst-ˌgärdz-mən\ n

coast·line \'kōst-ˌlīn\ n : the outline or shape of a coast

¹**coat** \'kōt\ n   1 : an outer garment for the upper part of the body   2 : an external growth (as of fur or feathers) on an animal   3 : a covering layer ⟨a ~ of paint⟩ — **coat·ed** \'kō-təd\ adj

²**coat** vb : to cover usu. with a finishing or protective coat

coat·ing \'kō-tiŋ\ n : COAT, COVERING

coat of arms : the heraldic bearings (as of a person) usu. depicted on an escutcheon

coat of mail : a garment of metal scales or rings worn as armor

co·au·thor \'kō-'ȯ-thər\ n : a joint or associate author — **coauthor** vb

coax \'kōks\ vb : WHEEDLE; also : to gain by gentle urging or flattery

co·ax·i·al \'kō-'ak-sē-əl\ adj : having coincident axes — **co·ax·i·al·ly** adv

coaxial cable n : a cable that consists of a tube of electrically conducting material surrounding a central conductor

cob \'käb\ n   1 : a male swan   2 : CORN-COB   3 : a short-legged stocky horse

co·balt \'kō-ˌbȯlt\ n [G Kobalt, alter. of Kobold, lit., goblin; fr. its occurrence in silver ore, believed to be due to goblins] : a tough shiny silver-white magnetic metallic chemical element found with iron and nickel

cob·ble \'kä-bəl\ vb **cob·bled; cob·bling** : to make or put together roughly or hastily ⟨~ together a solution⟩

cob·bler \'kä-blər\ n   1 : a mender or maker of shoes   2 : a deep-dish fruit pie with a thick crust

cob·ble·stone \'kä-bəl-ˌstōn\ n : a naturally rounded stone larger than a pebble and smaller than a boulder

co·bra \'kō-brə\ n [Pg cobra (de capello), lit., hooded snake] : any of several venomous snakes of Asia and Africa that when excited expand the skin of the neck into a broad hood

cob·web \'käb-ˌweb\ n [ME coppeweb, fr. coppe spider, fr. OE ātorcoppe]   1 : SPIDERWEB; also : a thread spun by a spider or insect larva **2** : something flimsy or entangling — **cob·web·by** \-ˌwe-bē\ *adj*

co·caine \kō-'kān, 'kō-ˌkān\ *n* : a drug obtained from the leaves of a So. American shrub (**co·ca** \'kō-kə\) that can result in severe psychological dependence and is sometimes used in medicine as a local anesthetic and illegally as a stimulant of the central nervous system

coc·cus \'kä-kəs\ *n, pl* **coc·ci** \'käk-ˌsī\ : a spherical bacterium

coc·cyx \'käk-siks\ *n, pl* **coc·cy·ges** \'käk-sə-ˌjēz\ *also* **coc·cyx·es** \'käk-sik-səz\ : the end of the spinal column beyond the sacrum esp. in humans

co·chi·neal \'kä-chə-ˌnēl\ *n* : a red dye made from the dried bodies of females of a tropical American insect (**cochineal insect**)

co·chlea \'kō-klē-ə, 'kä-\ *n, pl* **co·chle·as** *or* **co·chle·ae** \-klē-ˌē, -ˌī\ : the usu. spiral part of the inner ear containing nerve endings which carry information about sound to the brain — **co·chle·ar** \-klē-ər\ *adj*

¹cock \'käk\ *n* **1** : the adult male of a bird and esp. of the common domestic chicken **2** : VALVE, FAUCET **3** : LEADER **4** : the hammer of a firearm; *also* : the position of the hammer when ready for firing

²cock *vb* **1** : to draw back the hammer of a firearm **2** : to set or draw back in readiness for some action ⟨∼ your arm to throw⟩ **3** : to turn or tilt usu. to one side ⟨∼ one's head⟩

³cock *n* : a small pile (as of hay)

cock·ade \kä-'käd\ *n* : an ornament worn on the hat as a badge

cock·a·tiel \ˌkä-kə-'tēl\ *n* : a small crested gray parrot often kept as a cage bird

cock·a·too \'kä-kə-ˌtü\ *n, pl* **-toos** [D *kaketoe*, fr. Malay *kakatua*] : any of various large noisy crested parrots chiefly of Australia

cock·a·trice \'kä-kə-trəs, -ˌtrīs\ *n* : a legendary serpent with a deadly glance

cock·crow \'käk-ˌkrō\ *n* : DAWN

cocked hat \'käkt-\ *n* : a hat with the brim turned up on two or three sides

cock·er·el \'kä-kə-rəl\ *n* : a young male domestic chicken

cock·er spaniel \'kä-kər-\ *n* [*cocking* woodcock hunting] : any of a breed of small spaniels with long ears, square muzzle, and silky coat

cock·eyed \'kä-'kīd\ *adj* **1** : turned or tilted to one side **2** : slightly crazy : FOOLISH

cock·fight \'käk-ˌfīt\ *n* : a contest of gamecocks usu. fitted with metal spurs

¹cock·le \'kä-kəl\ *n* : any of several weedy plants related to the pinks

²cockle *n* : a bivalve mollusk with a heart-shaped shell

cock·le·shell \-ˌshel\ *n* **1** : the shell of a cockle **2** : a light flimsy boat

cock·ney \'käk-nē\ *n, pl* **cockneys** : a native of London and esp. of the East End of London; *also* : the dialect of a cockney

cock·pit \'käk-ˌpit\ *n* **1** : a pit for cockfights **2** : a space or compartment in a vehicle from which it is steered, piloted, or driven

cock·roach \'käk-ˌrōch\ *n* [Sp *cucaracha*] : any of an order or suborder of active nocturnal insects including some which infest houses and ships

cock·sure \'käk-'shùr\ *adj* **1** : perfectly sure : CERTAIN **2** : COCKY

cock·tail \'käk-ˌtāl\ *n* **1** : an iced drink made of liquor and flavoring ingredients **2** : an appetizer (as tomato juice) served as a first course of a meal

cocky \'kä-kē\ *adj* **cock·i·er; -est** : marked by overconfidence : PERT, CONCEITED — **cock·i·ly** \-kə-lē\ *adv* — **cock·i·ness** \-kē-nəs\ *n*

co·coa \'kō-kō\ *n* **1** : CACAO **2** : chocolate deprived of some of its fat and powdered; *also* : a drink made of this heated with water or milk

cocoa butter *n* : a pale vegetable fat obtained from cacao beans

co·co·nut \'kō-kə-(ˌ)nət\ *n* : a large edible hard-shelled fruit produced by a tall tropical palm (**coconut palm**)

co·coon \kə-'kün\ *n* **1** : a case usu. of silk formed by some insect larvae for protection during the pupal stage **2** : something that offers protection or isolation

cod \'käd\ *n, pl* **cod** *also* **cods** : a bottom-dwelling bony

fish of the North Atlantic that is an important food fish; *also* : a related fish of the Pacific Ocean

COD *abbr* **1** cash on delivery **2** collect on delivery

co·da \'kō-də\ *n* : a closing section in a musical composition that is formally distinct from the main structure

cod·dle \'kä-dᵊl\ *vb* **cod·dled; cod·dling** **1** : to cook slowly in water below the boiling point **2** : PAMPER

¹code \'kōd\ *n* [ME, fr. MF, fr. L *caudex, codex* trunk of a tree, document formed orig. from wooden tablets] **1** : a systematic statement of a body of law **2** : a system of principles or rules ⟨moral ∼⟩ **3** : a system of signals **4** : a system of symbols (as in secret communication) with special meanings **5** : GENETIC CODE

²code *vb* **cod·ed; cod·ing** : to put into the form or symbols of a code

co·deine \'kō-ˌdēn\ *n* : a narcotic drug made from opium and used esp. as an analgesic and cough suppressant

co·dex \'kō-ˌdeks\ *n, pl* **co·di·ces** \'kō-də-ˌsēz, 'kä-\ : a manuscript book (as of the Scriptures or classics)

cod·fish \'käd-ˌfish\ *n* : COD

cod·ger \'kä-jər\ *n* : an odd or cranky and usu. elderly fellow

cod·i·cil \'kä-də-səl, -ˌsil\ *n* : a legal instrument modifying an earlier will

cod·i·fy \'kä-də-ˌfī, 'kō-\ *vb* **-fied; -fy·ing** : to arrange in a systematic form — **cod·i·fi·ca·tion** \ˌkä-də-fə-'kä-shən, ˌkō-\ *n*

co·ed \'kō-ˌed\ *n* : a female student in a coeducational institution — **coed** *adj*

co·ed·u·ca·tion \ˌkō-ˌe-jə-'kä-shən\ *n* : the education of male and female students at the same institution — **co·ed·u·ca·tion·al** \-shə-nəl\ *adj* — **co·ed·u·ca·tion·al·ly** *adv*

co·ef·fi·cient \ˌkō-ə-'fi-shənt\ *n* **1** : a constant factor as distinguished from a variable in a mathematical term **2** : a number that serves as a measure of some property (as of a substance, device, or process)

coe·len·ter·ate \si-'len-tə-ˌrāt, -rət\ *n* : any of a phylum of radially symmetrical invertebrate animals including the corals, sea anemones, and jellyfishes

co·equal \kō-'ē-kwəl\ *adj* : equal with another — **coequal** *n* — **co·equal·i·ty** \ˌkō-ē-'kwä-lə-tē\ *n* — **co·equal·ly** *adv*

co·erce \kō-'ərs\ *vb* **co·erced; co·erc·ing** **1** : RESTRAIN, REPRESS **2** : COMPEL **3** : ENFORCE — **co·er·cion** \-'ər-zhən, -shən\ *n* — **co·er·cive** \-'ər-siv\ *adj*

co·eval \kō-'ē-vəl\ *adj* : of the same age — **coeval** *n*

co·ex·ist \ˌkō-ig-'zist\ *vb* **1** : to exist together or at the same time **2** : to live in peace with each other — **co·ex·is·tence** \-'zis-təns\ *n*

co·ex·ten·sive \ˌkō-ik-'sten-siv\ *adj* : having the same scope or extent in space or time

C of C *abbr* Chamber of Commerce

cof·fee \'kò-fē\ *n* [It & Turk; It *caffè*, fr. Turk *kahve*, fr. Ar *qahwa*] : a drink made from the roasted and ground seeds of a fruit of a tropical shrub or tree; *also* : these seeds (**coffee beans**) or a plant producing them

cof·fee·house \-ˌhaùs\ *n* : a place where refreshments (as coffee) are sold

coffee klatch \-ˌklach\ *n* : KAFFEE-KLATSCH

cof·fee·pot \-ˌpät\ *n* : a pot for brewing or serving coffee

coffee shop *n* : a small restaurant

coffee table *n* : a low table customarily placed in front of a sofa

cof·fer \'kò-fər\ *n* : a chest or box used esp. for valuables

cof·fer·dam \-ˌdam\ *n* : a watertight enclosure from which water is pumped to expose the bottom of a body of water and permit construction

cof·fin \'kò-fən\ *n* : a box or chest for burying a corpse

C of S *abbr* chief of staff

¹cog \'käg\ *n* : a tooth on the rim of a wheel or gear — **cogged** \'kägd\ *adj*

²cog *abbr* cognate

co·gen·e·ra·tion \ˌkō-ˌje-nə-'rä-shən\ *n* : the simultaneous generation of electricity and heat from the same fuel

co·gent \'kō-jənt\ *adj* : having power to compel or constrain : CONVINCING ⟨a ∼ argument⟩ — **co·gen·cy** \-jən-sē\ *n*

cog·i·tate \'kä-jə-ˌtāt\ *vb* **-tat·ed; -tat·ing** : THINK, PONDER — **cog·i·ta·tion** \ˌkä-jə-'tä-shən\ *n* — **cog·i·ta·tive** \'kä-jə-ˌtä-tiv\ *adj*

cog·nac \'kōn-ˌyak\ *n* : a French brandy
cog·nate \'käg-ˌnāt\ *adj* 1 : of the same or similar nature 2 : RELATED; *esp* : related by descent from the same ancestral language — **cognate** *n*
cog·ni·tive \'käg-nə-tiv\ *adj* : of, relating to, or being conscious intellectual activity (as thinking, remembering, reasoning, or using language) — **cog·ni·tion** \käg-'nishən\ *n* — **cog·ni·tive·ly** *adv*
cog·ni·zance \'käg-nə-zəns\ *n* 1 : apprehension by the mind : AWARENESS 2 : NOTICE, HEED — **cog·ni·zant** \'käg-nə-zənt\ *adj*
cog·no·men \käg-'nō-mən, 'käg-nə-\ *n, pl* **cognomens** *or* **cog·no·mi·na** \käg-'nä-mə-nə, -'nō-\ : NAME; *esp* : NICKNAME
co·gno·scen·te \ˌkän-yə-'shen-tē\ *n, pl* **-scen·ti** \-tē\ [obs. It] : CONNOISSEUR
cog·wheel \'käg-ˌhwēl\ *n* : a wheel with cogs or teeth
co·hab·it \kō-'ha-bət\ *vb* : to live together as a couple — **co·hab·i·ta·tion** \-ˌha-bə-'tā-shən\ *n*
co·here \kō-'hir\ *vb* **co·hered; co·her·ing** : to stick together
co·her·ent \kō-'hir-ənt\ *adj* 1 : having the quality of cohering 2 : logically consistent ⟨a ∼ explanation⟩ — **co·her·ence** \-əns\ *n* — **co·her·ent·ly** *adv*
co·he·sion \kō-'hē-zhən\ *n* 1 : a sticking together 2 : molecular attraction by which the particles of a body are united — **co·he·sive** \-siv\ *adj* — **co·he·sive·ly** *adv* — **co·he·sive·ness** *n*
co·ho \'kō-ˌhō\ *n, pl* **cohos** *or* **coho** : a rather small Pacific salmon with light-colored flesh
co·hort \'kō-ˌhȯrt\ *n* 1 : a group of warriors or followers 2 : COMPANION, ACCOMPLICE
coif \'kȯif; 2 *usu* 'kwäf\ *n* 1 : a close-fitting hat 2 : COIFFURE
coif·feur \kwä-'fər\ *n* [F] : HAIRDRESSER
coif·feuse \kwä-'fərz, -'fəz, -'füz, -'fyüz\ *n* : a female hairdresser
coif·fure \kwä-'fyùr\ *n* : a manner of arranging the hair
¹**coil** \'kȯi(-ə)l\ *vb* : to wind in a spiral shape
²**coil** *n* : a series of rings or loops (as of coiled rope, wire, or pipe) : RING, LOOP
¹**coin** \'kȯin\ *n* [ME, wedge, corner, image on a coin, fr. AF *coing*, fr. L *cuneus* wedge] 1 : a piece of metal issued by government authority as money 2 : metal money
²**coin** *vb* 1 : to make (a coin) esp. by stamping : MINT 2 : CREATE, INVENT ⟨∼ a phrase⟩ — **coin·er** *n*
coin·age \'kȯi-nij\ *n* 1 : the act or process of coining 2 : COINS
co·in·cide \ˌkō-ən-'sīd, 'kō-ən-ˌsīd\ *vb* **-cid·ed; -cid·ing** 1 : to occupy the same place in space or time 2 : to correspond or agree exactly
co·in·ci·dence \kō-'in-sə-dəns\ *n* 1 : exact agreement 2 : occurrence together apparently without reason; *also* : an event that so occurs
co·in·ci·dent \-sə-dənt\ *adj* 1 : of similar nature 2 : occupying the same space or time — **co·in·ci·den·tal** \kō-ˌin-sə-'den-tᵊl\ *adj*
co·i·tus \'kō-ə-təs\ *n* [L, fr. *coire* to come together] : SEXUAL INTERCOURSE 1 — **co·i·tal** \-tᵊl\ *adj*
¹**coke** \'kōk\ *n* : a hard gray porous fuel made by heating soft coal to drive off most of its volatile material
²**coke** *n* : COCAINE
²**col** *abbr* 1 colonial; colony 2 column
²**col** *or* **coll** *abbr* 1 collect, collected, collection 2 college, collegiate
Col *abbr* 1 Colonel 2 Colorado 3 Colossians
COL *abbr* 1 colonel 2 cost of living
co·la \'kō-lə\ *n* : a carbonated soft drink usu. containing sugar, caffeine, caramel, and special flavoring
col·an·der \'kə-lən-dər, 'kä-\ *n* : a perforated utensil for draining food
¹**cold** \'kōld\ *adj* 1 : having a low or decidedly subnormal temperature 2 : lacking warmth of feeling 3 : suffering or uncomfortable from lack of warmth — **cold·ly** *adv* — **cold·ness** *n* — **in cold blood** : with premeditation : DELIBERATELY
²**cold** *n* 1 : a condition marked by low temperature; *also* : cold weather 2 : a chilly feeling 3 : a bodily disorder popularly associated with chilling; *esp* : COMMON COLD
³**cold** *adv* 1 : TOTALLY, FINALLY ⟨stopped them ∼⟩ 2 : without notice or preparation

cold–blood·ed \'kōld-'blə-dəd\ *adj* 1 : lacking normal human feelings 2 : having a body temperature not internally regulated but close to that of the environment 3 : sensitive to cold
cold cuts *n pl* : sliced assorted cold cooked meats
cold feet *n pl* : doubt or fear that prevents action
cold front *n* : an advancing edge of a cold air mass
cold shoulder *n* : cold or unsympathetic behavior — **cold–shoul·der** *vb*
cold sore *n* : a group of fluid-filled blisters appearing in or about the mouth in the oral form of herpes simplex
cold sweat *n* : concurrent perspiration and chill usu. associated with fear, pain, or shock
¹**cold turkey** *n* : abrupt complete cessation of the use of an addictive drug
²**cold turkey** *adv* 1 : without a period of adjustment 2 : without preparation
cold war *n* : a conflict characterized by the use of means short of sustained overt military action
cole·slaw \'kōl-ˌslȯ\ *n* [D *koolsla*, fr. *kool* cabbage + *sla* salad] : a salad made of raw cabbage
col·ic \'kä-lik\ *n* 1 : sharp sudden abdominal pain 2 : a condition marked by recurrent episodes of crying and irritability in an otherwise healthy infant — **col·icky** \'kä-li-kē\ *adj*
col·i·se·um \ˌkä-lə-'sē-əm\ *n* : a large structure esp. for athletic contests
co·li·tis \kō-'lī-təs\ *n* : inflammation of the colon
col·lab·o·rate \kə-'la-bə-ˌrāt\ *vb* **-rat·ed; -rat·ing** 1 : to work jointly with others (as in writing a book) 2 : to cooperate with an enemy force occupying one's country — **col·lab·o·ra·tion** \-ˌla-bə-'rā-shən\ *n* — **col·lab·o·ra·tive** \-'la-bə-ˌrā-tiv, -b(ə-)rə-\ *adj* — **col·lab·o·ra·tor** \-'la-bə-ˌrā-tər\ *n*
col·lage \kə-'läzh\ *n* [F, lit., gluing] : an artistic composition of fragments (as of printed matter) pasted on a surface; *also* : a work that combines various elements into a cohesive whole
col·la·gen \'kä-lə-jən\ *n* : any of a group of fibrous proteins widely found in vertebrate connective tissue
¹**col·lapse** \kə-'laps\ *vb* **col·lapsed; col·laps·ing** 1 : to shrink together abruptly 2 : DISINTEGRATE; *also* : to fall in : give way 3 : to break down physically or mentally; *esp* : to fall helpless or unconscious 4 : to fold down compactly — **col·laps·ible** *adj*
²**collapse** *n* : BREAKDOWN
¹**col·lar** \'kä-lər\ *n* 1 : a band, strip, or chain worn around the neck or the neckline of a garment 2 : something resembling a collar — **col·lar·less** *adj*
²**collar** *vb* : to seize by the collar; *also* : ARREST, GRAB ⟨∼ a fugitive⟩
col·lar·bone \-ˌbōn\ *n* : the bone of the shoulder that joins the breastbone and the shoulder blade
col·lard \'kä-lərd\ *n* : a stalked smooth-leaved kale — usu. used in pl.
col·late \kə-'lāt; 'kä-ˌlāt, 'kō-\ *vb* **col·lat·ed; col·lat·ing** 1 : to compare (as two texts) carefully and critically 2 : to assemble in proper order
¹**col·lat·er·al** \kə-'la-tə-rəl\ *adj* 1 : associated but of secondary importance 2 : descended from the same ancestors but not in the same line 3 : PARALLEL 4 : of, relating to, or being collateral used as security; *also* : secured by collateral
²**collateral** *n* : property (as stocks) used as security for the repayment of a loan
col·la·tion \kä-'lā-shən, kō-\ *n* 1 : a light meal 2 : the act, process, or result of collating
col·league \'kä-ˌlēg\ *n* : an associate esp. in a profession
¹**col·lect** \'kä-likt, -ˌlekt\ *n* : a short prayer comprising an invocation, petition, and conclusion
²**col·lect** \kə-'lekt\ *vb* 1 : to bring or come together into one body or place : GATHER 2 : to accumulate (as coins) as a hobby 3 : to gain control of ⟨∼ his thoughts⟩ 4 : to receive payment of — **col·lect·ible** *or* **col·lect·able** *adj or n* — **col·lec·tor** \-'lek-tər\ *n*
³**col·lect** \kə-'lekt\ *adv or adj* : to be paid for by the receiver
col·lect·ed \kə-'lek-təd\ *adj* 1 : gathered together ⟨his ∼ poems⟩ 2 : SELF-POSSESSED, CALM
col·lec·tion \kə-'lek-shən\ *n* 1 : the act or process of col-

lecting ⟨garbage ∼⟩ **2** : something collected ⟨a stamp ∼⟩ **3** : GROUP, AGGREGATE

¹**col·lec·tive** \kə-'lek-tiv\ *adj* **1** : of, relating to, or denoting a group of individuals considered as a whole **2** : involving all members of a group as distinct from its individuals ⟨∼ action⟩ **3** : shared or assumed by all members of the group ⟨a ∼ groan⟩ — **col·lec·tive·ly** *adv*

²**collective** *n* **1** : GROUP **2** : a cooperative unit or organization

collective bargaining *n* : negotiation between an employer and a labor union

col·lec·tiv·ise *chiefly Brit var of* COLLECTIVIZE

col·lec·tiv·ism \kə-'lek-ti-ˌvi-zəm\ *n* : a political or economic theory advocating collective control esp. over production and distribution

col·lec·tiv·ize \-ˌvīz\ *vb* **-ized; -iz·ing** : to organize under collective control — **col·lec·tiv·i·za·tion** \-ˌlek-ti-və-'zā-shən\ *n*

col·leen \kä-'lēn, 'kä-ˌlēn\ *n* : an Irish girl

col·lege \'kä-lij\ *n* [ME, endowed body of clergy or scholars, fr. AF, fr. L *collegium* society, fr. *collega* colleague, fr. *com-* with + *legare* to depute] **1** : a building used for an educational or religious purpose **2** : an institution of higher learning or division of a university granting a bachelor's degree; *also* : an institution offering instruction esp. in a vocational or technical field ⟨barber ∼⟩ **3** : an organized body of persons having common interests or duties ⟨∼ of cardinals⟩ — **col·le·giate** \kə-'lē-jət\ *adj*

col·le·gi·al·i·ty \kə-ˌlē-jē-'a-lə-tē\ *n* : the relationship of colleagues

col·le·gian \kə-'lē-jən\ *n* : a college student or recent college graduate

col·le·gi·um \kə-'le-gē-əm, -'lā-\ *n, pl* **-gia** \-gē-ə\ *or* **-giums** : a group in which each member has approximately equal power

col·lide \kə-'līd\ *vb* **col·lid·ed; col·lid·ing** **1** : to come together with solid impact **2** : to come into conflict : CLASH

col·lid·er \kə-'lī-dər\ *n* : a particle accelerator in which two beams of particles are made to collide

col·lie \'kä-lē\ *n* : any of a breed of large dogs developed in Scotland for herding sheep that occur in rough-coated and smooth-coated varieties

col·lier \'käl-yər\ *n* **1** : a coal miner **2** : a ship for carrying coal

col·liery \'käl-yə-rē\ *n, pl* **-lier·ies** : a coal mine and its associated buildings

col·li·mate \'kä-lə-ˌmāt\ *vb* **-mat·ed; -mat·ing** : to make (as light rays) parallel

col·li·sion \kə-'li-zhən\ *n* : an act or instance of colliding

col·lo·ca·tion \ˌkä-lə-'kä-shən\ *n* : the act or result of placing or arranging together; *esp* : a noticeable arrangement or conjoining of linguistic elements (as words)

col·loid \'kä-ˌlöid\ *n* : a substance in the form of submicroscopic particles that when in solution or suspension do not settle out; *also* : such a substance together with the medium in which it is dispersed — **col·loi·dal** \kə-'löi-d³l\ *adj*

colloq *abbr* colloquial

col·lo·qui·al \kə-'lō-kwē-əl\ *adj* : of, relating to, or characteristic of conversation and esp. of familiar and informal conversation

col·lo·qui·al·ism \-'lō-kwē-ə-ˌli-zəm\ *n* : a colloquial expression

col·lo·qui·um \kə-'lō-kwē-əm\ *n, pl* **-quiums** *or* **-quia** \-ə\ : CONFERENCE, SEMINAR

col·lo·quy \'kä-lə-kwē\ *n, pl* **-quies** : a usu. formal conversation or conference

col·lu·sion \kə-'lü-zhən\ *n* : secret agreement or cooperation for an illegal or deceitful purpose — **col·lu·sive** \-siv\ *adj*

Colo *abbr* Colorado

co·logne \kə-'lōn\ *n* [*Cologne*, Germany] : a perfumed liquid — **co·logned** \-'lōnd\ *adj*

Co·lom·bi·an \kə-'ləm-bē-ən\ *n* : a native or inhabitant of Colombia — **Colombian** *adj*

¹**co·lon** \'kō-lən\ *n, pl* **colons** *or* **co·la** \-lə\ : the part of the large intestine extending from the cecum to the rectum — **co·lon·ic** \kō-'lä-nik\ *adj*

²**colon** *n, pl* **colons** : a punctuation mark : used esp. to direct attention to following matter (as a list)

co·lón *also* **co·lone** \kə-'lōn\ *n, pl* **co·lo·nes** \-'lō-ˌnäs\ — see MONEY table

col·o·nel \'kər-n³l\ *n* [alter. of *coronel*, fr. MF, fr. It *colonnello* column of soldiers, colonel, ultim. fr. L *columna* column] : a commissioned officer (as in the army) ranking next below a brigadier general

¹**co·lo·nial** \kə-'lō-nē-əl\ *adj* **1** : of, relating to, or characteristic of a colony; *also* : possessing or composed of colonies **2** *often cap* : of or relating to the original 13 colonies forming the U.S.

²**colonial** *n* **1** : a member or inhabitant of a colony **2** : a house built in the style of the American colonial period

co·lo·nial·ism \-ə-ˌli-zəm\ *n* : control by one power over a dependent area or people; *also* : a policy advocating or based on such control — **co·lo·nial·ist** \-list\ *n or adj*

col·o·nise *Brit var of* COLONIZE

col·o·nist \'kä-lə-nist\ *n* **1** : COLONIAL **2** : one that colonizes or settles in a new country

col·o·nize \'kä-lə-ˌnīz\ *vb* **-nized; -niz·ing** **1** : to establish a colony in or on **2** : SETTLE — **col·o·ni·za·tion** \ˌkä-lə-nə-'zā-shən\ *n* — **col·o·niz·er** *n*

col·on·nade \ˌkä-lə-'näd\ *n* : an evenly spaced row of columns usu. supporting the base of a roof structure

colonnade

co·lo·nos·co·py \ˌkō-lə-'näs-kə-pē\ *n, pl* **-pies** : endoscopic examination of the colon — **co·lon·o·scope** \kō-'lä-nə-ˌskōp\ *n*

col·o·ny \'kä-lə-nē\ *n, pl* **-nies** **1** : a body of people living in a new territory; *also* : the territory inhabited by these people **2** : a localized population of organisms ⟨a ∼ of bees⟩ **3** : a group with common interests situated in close association ⟨a writers' ∼⟩; *also* : the area occupied by such a group

col·o·phon \'kä-lə-fən, -ˌfän\ *n* **1** : an inscription placed at the end of a book with facts relative to its production **2** : a distinctive symbol used by a printer or publisher

¹**col·or** \'kä-lər\ *n* **1** : a phenomenon of light (as red or blue) or visual perception that enables one to differentiate otherwise identical objects; *also* : a hue as contrasted with black, white, or gray **2** : APPEARANCE **3** : complexion tint **4** *pl* : FLAG; *also* : military service ⟨a call to the ∼*s*⟩ **5** : VIVIDNESS, INTEREST — **col·or·ful** *adj* — **col·or·less** *adj*

²**color** *vb* **1** : to give color to; *also* : to change the color of **2** : BLUSH

Col·o·ra·do potato beetle \ˌkä-lə-'ra-dō-, -'rä-\ *n* : a black-and-yellow striped beetle that feeds on the leaves of the potato

col·or·ation \ˌkä-lə-'rä-shən\ *n* : use or arrangement of colors

col·or·a·tu·ra \ˌkä-lə-rə-'tùr-ə, -'tyùr-\ *n* **1** : elaborate ornamentation in vocal music **2** : a soprano specializing in coloratura

col·or–blind \'kä-lər-ˌblīnd\ *adj* **1** : partially or totally unable to distinguish one or more chromatic colors **2** : not influenced by differences of race — **color blindness** *n*

co·lo·rec·tal \ˌkō-lō-'rek-t³l\ *adj* : relating to or affecting the colon and rectum ⟨∼ cancer⟩

col·ored \'kä-lərd\ *adj* **1** : having color **2** : SLANTED, BIASED

col·or·fast \'kə-lər-ˌfast\ *adj* : having color that does not fade or run — **col·or·fast·ness** *n*

col·or·ize \'kä-lə-ˌrīz\ *vb* **-ized; -iz·ing** : to add color to by means of a computer — **col·or·i·za·tion** \ˌkə-lə-rə-'zā-shən\ *n*

co·los·sal \kə-'lä-səl\ *adj* : of very great size or degree ⟨a ∼ feat⟩

Co·los·sians \kə-'lä-shənz\ *n* — see BIBLE table

co·los·sus \kə-'lä-səs\ n, pl co·los·si \-ˌsī\ [L] : a gigantic statue; also : something of immense size or power

col·our chiefly Brit var of COLOR

col·por·teur \'käl-ˌpȯr-tər\ n [F] : a peddler of religious books

colt \'kōlt\ n : FOAL; also : a young male horse, ass, or zebra — colt·ish adj

col·um·bine \'kä-ləm-ˌbīn\ n [ME, fr. AF, fr. ML columbina, fr. L, fem. of columbinus dovelike, fr. columba dove] : any of a genus of plants with showy spurred flowers that are related to the buttercups

co·lum·bi·um \kə-'ləm-bē-əm\ n : NIOBIUM

Columbus Day \kə-'ləm-bəs-\ n : the 2d Monday in October or formerly October 12 observed as a legal holiday in many states in commemoration of the landing of Columbus

col·umn \'kä-ləm\ n 1 : one of two or more vertical sections of a printed page; also : one in a usu. regular series of articles (as in a newspaper) 2 : a supporting pillar; esp : one consisting of a usu. round shaft, a capital, and a base 3 : something resembling a column ⟨a ∼ of water⟩ 4 : a long row (as of soldiers) 5 : a statistical category tracked vertically (as on a spreadsheet) — col·um·nar \kə-'ləm-nər\ adj

col·um·nist \'kä-ləm-nist\ n : a person who writes a newspaper or magazine column

com abbr 1 comedy; comic 2 comma 3 commercial organization

co·ma \'kō-mə\ n : a state of deep unconsciousness caused by disease, injury, or poison — co·ma·tose \'kō-mə-ˌtōs, 'kä-\ adj

Co·man·che \kə-'man-chē\ n, pl Comanche or Comanches : a member of an American Indian people ranging from Wyoming and Nebraska south into New Mexico and Texas

¹comb \'kōm\ n 1 : a toothed instrument for arranging the hair or for separating and cleaning textile fibers 2 : a fleshy crest on the head of a fowl 3 : HONEYCOMB

²comb vb 1 : to pass a comb through 2 : to search through systematically

³comb abbr combination; combining

com·bat \kəm-'bat, 'käm-ˌbat\ vb -bat·ed or -bat·ted; -bat·ing or -bat·ting 1 : FIGHT, CONTEND 2 : to struggle against : OPPOSE — com·bat \'käm-ˌbat\ n — com·bat·ant \kəm-'ba-tᵊnt, 'käm-bə-tənt\ n — com·bat·ive \kəm-'ba-tiv\ adj

combat fatigue n : a traumatic psychological reaction occurring under wartime conditions (as combat) that cause intense stress

comb·er \'kō-mər\ n 1 : one that combs 2 : a long curling wave of the sea

com·bi·na·tion \ˌkäm-bə-'nā-shən\ n 1 : a result or product of combining 2 : a sequence of letters or numbers chosen in setting a lock 3 : the act or process of combining; also : the quality or state of being combined

¹com·bine \kəm-'bīn\ vb com·bined; com·bin·ing : to become one : UNITE

²com·bine \'käm-ˌbīn\ n 1 : a combination esp. of business or political interests 2 : a machine that harvests and threshes grain while moving over a field

comb·ings \'kō-miŋz\ n pl : loose hairs or fibers removed by a comb

combining form n : a linguistic form that occurs only in compounds or derivatives

com·bo \'käm-bō\ n, pl combos : a small jazz or dance band

comb–over \'kōm-ˌō-vər\ n : a hairstyle in which hair from the side of the head is combed over a bald spot

com·bus·ti·ble \kəm-'bəs-tə-bəl\ adj 1 : capable of being burned 2 : easily excited — com·bus·ti·bil·i·ty \-ˌbəs-tə-'bi-lə-tē\ n — combustible n

com·bus·tion \kəm-'bəs-chən\ n 1 : an act or instance of burning 2 : slow oxidation (as in the animal body)

comdg abbr commanding

comdr abbr commander

comdt abbr commandant

come \'kəm\ vb came \'käm\; come; com·ing \'kə-miŋ\ 1 : APPROACH 2 : ARRIVE 3 : to reach the point of being or becoming ⟨∼ to a boil⟩ 4 : AMOUNT ⟨the bill came to $10⟩ 5 : to take place 6 : ORIGINATE, ARISE ⟨wine ∼s from grapes⟩ 7 : to be available ⟨∼s in three sizes⟩ 8 : REACH, EXTEND ⟨grass that ∼s to our knees⟩ — come across 1 : to make a specified impression ⟨came across as rude⟩ 2 : to find esp. by chance ⟨came across an intriguing story⟩ — come clean : CONFESS — come into : ACQUIRE, ACHIEVE — come of age : MATURE — come to grips with : to meet or deal with frankly — come to pass : HAPPEN — come to terms : to reach an agreement

come·back \'kəm-ˌbak\ n 1 : RETORT 2 : a return to a former position or condition — come back vb

co·me·di·an \kə-'mē-dē-ən\ n 1 : an actor in comedy 2 : a comic person; esp : an entertainer specializing in comedy

co·me·di·enne \-ˌmē-dē-'en\ n : a woman who is a comedian

come·down \'kəm-ˌdaun\ n : a descent in rank or dignity

com·e·dy \'kä-mə-dē\ n, pl -dies [ME, narrative that ends happily, fr. ML comoedia, fr. L, play with a happy ending, fr. Gk kōmōidia, fr. kōmos revel + aeidein to sing] 1 : a light amusing play with a happy ending 2 : a literary work treating a comic theme or written in a comic style 3 : humorous entertainment — co·me·dic \kə-'mē-dik\ adj

come·ly \'kəm-lē\ adj come·li·er; -est : ATTRACTIVE, HANDSOME — come·li·ness n

come off vb 1 : APPEAR, SEEM ⟨comes off as crass⟩ 2 : SUCCEED 3 : to have recently ended ⟨is coming off surgery⟩

come–on \'kə-ˌmȯn, -ˌmän\ n : INDUCEMENT, LURE

come out vb 1 : to come into public view 2 : to declare oneself 3 : TURN OUT 6 ⟨everything came out all right⟩ — come out with : SAY 1

com·er \'kə-mər\ n 1 : one that comes ⟨all ∼s⟩ 2 : a promising beginner

¹co·mes·ti·ble \kə-'mes-tə-bəl\ adj : EDIBLE

²comestible n : FOOD — usu. used in pl.

com·et \'kä-mət\ n [ME comete, fr. OE cometa, fr. L, fr. Gk komētēs, lit., long-haired, fr. komē hair] : a small bright celestial body that develops a long tail when near the sun

come to vb : to regain consciousness

come·up·pance \kə-'mə-pəns\ n : a deserved rebuke or penalty

com·fit \'kəm-fət\ n : a candied fruit or nut

¹com·fort \'kəm-fərt\ vb 1 : to give strength and hope to 2 : CONSOLE

²comfort n 1 : CONSOLATION 2 : freedom from pain, trouble, or anxiety; also : something that gives such freedom

com·fort·able \'kəm-fər-tə-bəl, 'kəmf-tər-\ adj 1 : providing comfort or security 2 : feeling at ease — com·fort·ably \-blē\ adv

com·fort·er \'kəm-fər-tər\ n 1 : one that comforts 2 : QUILT

com·frey \'kəm-frē\ n, pl comfreys : any of a genus of perennial herbs that have coarse hairy leaves and are often used in herbal remedies

com·fy \'kəm-fē\ adj : COMFORTABLE

¹com·ic \'kä-mik\ adj 1 : relating to comedy or comic strips 2 : provoking laughter or amusement ♦ Synonyms LAUGHABLE, FUNNY, FARCICAL — com·i·cal adj

²comic n 1 : COMEDIAN 2 pl : the part of a newspaper devoted to comic strips

comic book n : a magazine containing sequences of comic strips

comic strip n : a group of cartoons in narrative sequence

com·ing adj 1 : APPROACHING, NEXT 2 : gaining importance ⟨the ∼ trend⟩

co·mi·ty \'kä-mə-tē, 'kō-\ n, pl -ties : friendly civility : COURTESY

coml abbr commercial

comm abbr 1 command; commander 2 commerce; commercial 3 commission; commissioner 4 committee 5 common 6 commonwealth

com·ma \'kä-mə\ n : a punctuation mark, used esp. as a mark of separation within the sentence

¹com·mand \kə-'mand\ vb 1 : to direct authoritatively : ORDER 2 : DOMINATE, CONTROL, GOVERN 3 : to overlook from a strategic position

²command n 1 : an order given 2 : ability to control : MASTERY 3 : the act of commanding 4 : a signal that

actuates a device (as a computer); *also* : the activation of a device by means of a signal **5** : a body of troops under a commander; *also* : an area or position that one commands **6** : a position of highest authority

com·man·dant \'kä-mən-ˌdant, -ˌdänt\ *n* : an officer in command

com·man·deer \ˌkä-mən-'dir\ *vb* : to take possession of by force

com·mand·er \kə-'man-dər\ *n* **1** : LEADER, CHIEF; *esp* : an officer commanding an army or subdivision of an army **2** : a commissioned officer in the navy ranking next below a captain

commander in chief : the supreme commander of the armed forces

com·mand·ment \kə-'mand-mənt\ *n* : COMMAND, ORDER; *esp* : any of the Ten Commandments

command module *n* : a space vehicle module designed to carry the crew and reentry equipment

com·man·do \kə-'man-dō\ *n, pl* **-dos** *or* **-does** : a member of a military unit trained for surprise raids

command sergeant major *n* : a noncommissioned officer in the army ranking above a sergeant major

com·mem·o·rate \kə-'me-mə-ˌrāt\ *vb* **-rat·ed; -rat·ing** **1** : to call or recall to mind **2** : to serve as a memorial of — **com·mem·o·ra·tion** \-ˌme-mə-'rā-shən\ *n*

com·mem·o·ra·tive \kə-'mem-rə-tiv, -'me-mə-ˌrā-tiv\ *adj* : intended to commemorate an event ⟨a ∼ stamp⟩

com·mence \kə-'mens\ *vb* **com·menced; com·menc·ing** : BEGIN, START

com·mence·ment \-mənt\ *n* **1** : the act or time of a beginning **2** : the graduation exercises of a school or college

com·mend \kə-'mend\ *vb* **1** : to commit to one's care **2** : RECOMMEND **3** : PRAISE — **com·mend·able** \-'men-də-bəl\ *adj* — **com·mend·ably** \-blē\ *adv* — **com·men·da·tion** \ˌkä-mən-'dā-shən, -ˌmen-\ *n* — **com·mend·er** *n*

com·men·su·ra·ble \kə-'men-sə-rə-bəl\ *adj* : having a common measure or a common divisor

com·men·su·rate \kə-'men-sə-rət, -'men-chə-\ *adj* : equal in measure or extent; *also* : PROPORTIONAL, CORRESPONDING ⟨a job ∼ with her abilities⟩

com·ment \'kä-ˌment\ *n* **1** : an expression of opinion **2** : an explanatory, illustrative, or critical note or observation : REMARK — **comment** *vb*

com·men·tary \'kä-mən-ˌter-ē\ *n, pl* **-tar·ies** : a systematic series of comments

com·men·ta·tor \-ˌtā-tər\ *n* : one who comments; *esp* : a person who discusses news events on radio or television

com·merce \'kä-(ˌ)mərs\ *n* : the buying and selling of commodities : TRADE

¹**com·mer·cial** \kə-'mər-shəl\ *adj* : having to do with commerce; *also* : designed for profit or for mass appeal — **com·mer·cial·ly** *adv*

²**commercial** *n* : an advertisement broadcast on radio or television

com·mer·cial·ise *Brit var of* COMMERCIALIZE

com·mer·cial·ism \kə-'mər-shə-ˌli-zəm\ *n* **1** : a spirit, method, or practice characteristic of business **2** : excessive emphasis on profit

com·mer·cial·ize \-ˌlīz\ *vb* **-ized; -iz·ing** **1** : to manage on a business basis for profit **2** : to exploit for profit

com·mi·na·tion \ˌkä-mə-'nā-shən\ *n* : DENUNCIATION — **com·mi·na·to·ry** \'kä-mə-nə-ˌtör-ē\ *adj*

com·min·gle \kə-'miŋ-gəl\ *vb* : MINGLE, BLEND

com·mis·er·ate \kə-'mi-zə-ˌrāt\ *vb* **-at·ed; -at·ing** : to feel or express pity : SYMPATHIZE — **com·mis·er·a·tion** \-ˌmi-zə-'rā-shən\ *n*

com·mis·sar \'kä-mə-ˌsär\ *n* [Russ *komissar*] : a Communist party official

com·mis·sar·i·at \ˌkä-mə-'ser-ē-ət\ *n* **1** : a system for supplying troops with food **2** : a department headed by a commissar

com·mis·sary \'kä-mə-ˌser-ē\ *n, pl* **-sar·ies** : a store for equipment and provisions esp. for military personnel

¹**com·mis·sion** \kə-'mi-shən\ *n* **1** : a warrant granting certain powers and imposing certain duties **2** : a certificate conferring military rank and authority **3** : authority to act as agent for another; *also* : something to be done by an agent **4** : a body of persons charged with performing a duty **5** : the doing of some act ⟨∼ of a crime⟩; *also* : the thing done **6** : the allowance made to an agent for transacting business for another

²**commission** *vb* **1** : to give a commission to **2** : to order to be made ⟨∼ a portrait⟩ **3** : to put (a ship) into a state of readiness for service

commissioned officer *n* : an officer of the armed forces holding rank by a commission from the president

com·mis·sion·er \kə-'mi-shə-nər\ *n* **1** : a member of a commission **2** : an official in charge of a department of public service ⟨a police ∼⟩ **3** : the administrative head of a professional sport — **com·mis·sion·er·ship** *n*

com·mit \kə-'mit\ *vb* **com·mit·ted; com·mit·ting** **1** : to put into charge or trust : ENTRUST **2** : to put in a prison or mental institution **3** : TRANSFER, CONSIGN **4** : to carry into action : PERPETRATE ⟨∼ a crime⟩ **5** : to pledge or assign to some particular course or use — **com·mit·ment** *n* — **com·mit·tal** *n*

com·mit·tee \kə-'mi-tē\ *n* : a body of persons selected to consider and act or report on some matter — **com·mit·tee·man** \-mən\ *n* — **com·mit·tee·wom·an** \-ˌwu̇-mən\ *n*

commo *abbr* commodore

com·mode \kə-'mōd\ *n* [F, fr. *commode*, adj., suitable, convenient, fr. L *commodus*, fr. *com-* with + *modus* measure] **1** : a movable washstand with cupboard below **2** : TOILET **3**

com·mo·di·ous \kə-'mō-dē-əs\ *adj* : comfortably spacious : ROOMY

com·mod·i·ty \kə-'mä-də-tē\ *n, pl* **-ties** **1** : a product of agriculture or mining **2** : an article of commerce **3** : something useful or valued ⟨that valuable ∼ patience⟩

com·mo·dore \'kä-mə-ˌdȯr\ *n* **1** : a commissioned officer in the navy ranking next below a rear admiral **2** : an officer commanding a group of merchant ships **3** : the chief officer of a yacht club

¹**com·mon** \'kä-mən\ *adj* **1** : belonging to or serving the community : PUBLIC **2** : shared by a number in a group **3** : widely or generally known, found, or observed : FAMILIAR ⟨∼ knowledge⟩ **4** : VERNACULAR **3** ⟨∼ names of plants⟩ **5** : not above the average esp. in social status ✦ **Synonyms** UNIVERSAL, GENERAL, GENERIC — **com·mon·ly** *adv*

²**common** *n* **1** *pl* : the common people **2** *pl* : a dining hall **3** *pl, cap* : the lower house of the British and Canadian parliaments **4** : a piece of land subject to common use — **in common** : shared together

com·mon·al·ty \'kä-mə-nºl-tē\ *n, pl* **-ties** : the common people

common cold *n* : a contagious respiratory disease caused by a virus and characterized by a sore, swollen, and inflamed nose and throat, usu. by much mucus, and by coughing and sneezing

common denominator *n* **1** : a common multiple of the denominators of a group of fractions **2** : a common trait or theme

common divisor *n* : a number or expression that divides two or more numbers or expressions without remainder

com·mon·er \'kä-mə-nər\ *n* : one of the common people : a person having no rank of nobility

common fraction *n* : a fraction (as ½ or ¾) in which the numerator and denominator are both integers and are separated by a horizontal or slanted line

common law *n* : a group of legal practices and traditions based on judges' decisions and social customs and usu. having the same force as laws passed by legislative bodies

common logarithm *n* : a logarithm whose base is 10

common market *n* : an economic association formed to remove trade barriers among members

common multiple *n* : a multiple of each of two or more numbers or expressions

¹**com·mon·place** \'kä-mən-ˌplās\ *n* : something that is ordinary or trite

²**commonplace** *adj* : ORDINARY

common sense *n* : ordinary good sense and judgment — **com·mon·sen·si·cal** \ˌkä-mən-'sen-si-kəl\ *adj*

com·mon·weal \'kä-mən-ˌwēl\ *n* **1** *archaic* : COMMONWEALTH **2** : the general welfare

com·mon·wealth \-ˌwelth\ *n* **1** : the body of people politically organized into a state **2** : STATE; *also* : an association or federation of autonomous states

com·mo·tion \kə-'mō-shən\ *n* **1** : DISTURBANCE, UPRISING **2** : AGITATION

com·mu·nal \kə-'myü-nºl, 'käm-yə-nºl\ *adj* **1** : of or relating to a commune or community **2** : marked by collective ownership and use of property **3** : shared or used in common

¹com·mune \kə-'myün\ *vb* com·muned; com·mun·ing : to communicate intimately ⟨∼ with nature⟩

²com·mune \'käm-ˌyün; kə-'myün\ *n* **1** : the smallest administrative district in some European countries **2** : a community organized on a communal basis

com·mu·ni·ca·ble \kə-'myü-ni-kə-bəl\ *adj* : capable of being communicated ⟨∼ diseases⟩ — com·mu·ni·ca·bil·i·ty \-ˌmyü-ni-kə-'bi-lə-tē\ *n*

com·mu·ni·cant \kə-'myü-ni-kənt\ *n* **1** : a church member entitled to receive Communion **2** : one that communicates; *esp* : INFORMANT

com·mu·ni·cate \kə-'myü-nə-ˌkāt\ *vb* -cat·ed; -cat·ing **1** : to make known **2** : to pass from one to another : TRANSMIT **3** : to receive Communion **4** : to be in communication **5** : JOIN, CONNECT — com·mu·ni·ca·tor \-ˌkā-tər\ *n*

com·mu·ni·ca·tion \kə-ˌmyü-nə-'kā-shən\ *n* **1** : an act of transmitting **2** : MESSAGE **3** : exchange of information or opinions **4** : a means of communicating — com·mu·ni·ca·tive \-'myü-nə-ˌkā-tiv, -ni-kə-tiv\ *adj*

com·mu·nion \kə-'myü-nyən\ *n* **1** : a sharing of something with others **2** *cap* : a Christian sacrament in which bread and wine are consumed as the substance or symbols of Christ's body and blood in commemoration of the death of Christ **3** : intimate fellowship or rapport **4** : a body of Christians having a common faith and discipline

com·mu·ni·qué \kə-'myü-nə-ˌkā, -ˌmyü-nə-'kā\ *n* : BULLETIN 1

com·mu·nism \'käm-yə-ˌni-zəm\ *n* **1** : social organization in which goods are held in common **2** : a theory of social organization advocating common ownership of means of production and a distribution of products of industry based on need **3** *cap* : a political doctrine based on revolutionary Marxist socialism that was the official ideology of the U.S.S.R. and some other countries; *also* : a system of government in which one party controls state-owned means of production — com·mu·nist \-nist\ *n or adj, often cap* — com·mu·nis·tic \ˌkäm-yə-'nis-tik\ *adj, often cap*

com·mu·ni·ty \kə-'myü-nə-tē\ *n, pl* -ties **1** : a body of people living in the same place under the same laws; *also* : a natural population of plants and animals that interact ecologically and live in one place (as a pond) **2** : society at large **3** : joint ownership ⟨∼ of goods⟩ **4** : SIMILARITY, LIKENESS ⟨∼ of interests⟩

community college *n* : a 2-year government-supported college that offers an associate degree

community property *n* : property held jointly by husband and wife

com·mu·ta·tion \ˌkäm-yə-'tā-shən\ *n* : substitution of one form of payment or penalty for another

com·mu·ta·tive \'käm-yə-ˌtā-tiv, kə-'myü-tə-\ *adj* : of, having, or being the property that the result obtained using a mathematical operation on any two elements of a set does not differ with the order in which the elements are used ⟨*a* x *b* = *b* x *a* because multiplication is ∼⟩ — com·mu·ta·tiv·i·ty \ˌkäm-yü-tə-'ti-və-tē, kə-ˌmyü-tə-\ *n*

com·mu·ta·tor \'käm-yə-ˌtā-tər\ *n* : a device (as on a generator or motor) for changing the direction of electric current

¹com·mute \kə-'myüt\ *vb* com·mut·ed; com·mut·ing **1** : EXCHANGE **2** : to revoke (a sentence) and impose a milder penalty **3** : to travel back and forth regularly — com·mut·er *n*

²commute *n* : a trip made in commuting

comp *abbr* **1** comparative; compare **2** compensation **3** compiled; compiler **4** composition; compositor **5** compound **6** comprehensive **7** comptroller

¹com·pact \kəm-'pakt, 'käm-ˌpakt\ *adj* **1** : SOLID, DENSE **2** : BRIEF, SUCCINCT **3** : occupying a small volume by efficient use of space ⟨∼ camera⟩ — com·pact·ly *adv* — com·pact·ness *n*

²compact *vb* : to pack together : COMPRESS — com·pac·tor \'käm-ˌpak-tər, 'käm-ˌpak-\ *n*

³com·pact \'käm-ˌpakt\ *n* **1** : a small case for cosmetics **2** : a small automobile

⁴com·pact \'käm-ˌpakt\ *n* : AGREEMENT, COVENANT

com·pact disc \'käm-ˌpakt-\ *n* : CD

com·pa·dre \kəm-'pä-drā\ *n* : a close friend : BUDDY

¹com·pan·ion \kəm-'pan-yən\ *n* [ME *compainoun*, fr. AF *cumpaing, cumpaignun*, fr. LL *companion-, companio*, fr. L *com-* together + *panis* bread] **1** : an intimate friend or associate : COMRADE **2** : one that is closely connected with something similar **3** : a celestial body that appears close to another but that may not be associated with it in space — com·pan·ion·able *adj* — com·pan·ion·ship *n*

²companion *n* : COMPANIONWAY

com·pan·ion·way \-ˌwā\ *n* : a ship's stairway from one deck to another

com·pa·ny \'kəm-pə-nē\ *n, pl* -nies **1** : association with others : FELLOWSHIP; *also* : COMPANIONS **2** : GUESTS **3** : a group of persons or things **4** : an infantry unit consisting of two or more platoons and normally commanded by a captain **5** : a group of musical or dramatic performers **6** : the officers and crew of a ship **7** : an association of persons for carrying on a business ♦ *Synonyms* PARTY, BAND, TROOP, TROUPE, CORPS, OUTFIT

com·pa·ra·ble \'käm-pə-rə-bəl, *often* kəm-'par-ə-\ *adj* : capable of being compared ⟨singers of ∼ talent⟩ ♦ *Synonyms* PARALLEL, SIMILAR, LIKE, ALIKE, CORRESPONDING — com·pa·ra·bil·i·ty \ˌkäm-pə-rə-'bi-lə-tē\ *n*

¹com·par·a·tive \kəm-'per-ə-tiv\ *adj* **1** : of, relating to, or constituting the degree of grammatical comparison that denotes increase in quality, quantity, or relation **2** : RELATIVE ⟨a ∼ stranger⟩ — com·par·a·tive·ly *adv*

²comparative *n* : the comparative degree or form in a language

¹com·pare \kəm-'per\ *vb* com·pared; com·par·ing **1** : to represent as similar : LIKEN **2** : to examine for likenesses and differences **3** : to inflect or modify (an adjective or adverb) according to the degrees of comparison

²compare *n* : the possibility of comparing ⟨beauty beyond ∼⟩

com·par·i·son \kəm-'per-ə-sən\ *n* **1** : the act of comparing **2** : change in the form of an adjective or adverb to show different levels of quality, quantity, or relation

com·part·ment \kəm-'pärt-mənt\ *n* **1** : a separate division **2** : a section of an enclosed space : ROOM

com·part·men·tal·ise *Brit var of* COMPARTMENTALIZE

com·part·men·tal·ize \kəm-ˌpärt-'men-t³l-ˌīz\ *vb* -ized; -iz·ing : to separate into compartments

¹com·pass \'kəm-pəs, 'käm-\ *vb* [ME, fr. AF *cumpasser* to measure, fr. VL **compassare* to pace off, fr. L *com-* + *passus* pace] **1** : CONTRIVE, PLOT **2** : ENCIRCLE, ENCOMPASS **3** : BRING ABOUT, ACHIEVE

²compass *n* **1** : BOUNDARY, CIRCUMFERENCE **2** : an enclosed space **3** : RANGE, SCOPE **4** : a device for determining direction by means of a magnetic needle swinging freely and pointing to the magnetic north; *also* : a nonmagnetic device that indicates direction **5** : an instrument for drawing circles or transferring measurements consisting of two legs joined by a pivot

com·pas·sion \kəm-'pa-shən\ *n* : sympathetic feeling : PITY, MERCY — com·pas·sion·ate \-shə-nət\ *adj* — com·pas·sion·ate·ly *adv*

com·pat·i·ble \kəm-'pa-tə-bəl\ *adj* : able to exist or act together harmoniously ⟨∼ colors⟩ ⟨∼ drugs⟩ ♦ *Synonyms* CONSONANT, CONGENIAL, SYMPATHETIC — com·pat·i·bil·i·ty \-ˌpa-tə-'bi-lə-tē\ *n*

com·pa·tri·ot \kəm-'pā-trē-ət, -ˌät\ *n* : a fellow countryman

com·peer \'käm-ˌpir\ *n* : EQUAL, PEER

com·pel \kəm-'pel\ *vb* com·pelled; com·pel·ling : to drive or urge with force

com·pen·di·ous \kəm-'pen-dē-əs\ *adj* : concise and comprehensive; *also* : COMPREHENSIVE ⟨a ∼ almanac⟩

com·pen·di·um \kəm-'pen-dē-əm\ *n, pl* -di·ums *or* -dia \-ə\ **1** : a brief summary of a larger work or of a field of knowledge **2** : COLLECTION

com·pen·sate \'käm-pən-ˌsāt\ *vb* -sat·ed; -sat·ing **1** : to be equivalent to : make up for **2** : PAY, REMUNERATE ♦ *Synonyms* BALANCE, OFFSET, COUNTERBALANCE, COUNTERPOISE — com·pen·sa·tion \ˌkäm-pən-'sā-shən\ *n* — com·pen·sa·to·ry \kəm-'pen-sə-ˌtȯr-ē\ *adj*

com·pete \kəm-'pēt\ *vb* com·pet·ed; com·pet·ing : CONTEND, VIE ⟨∼ for the title⟩ ⟨∼ for customers⟩

com·pe·tence \'käm-pə-təns\ *n* **1** : adequate means for subsistence **2** : FITNESS, ABILITY

com·pe·ten·cy \-tən-sē\ *n, pl* -cies : COMPETENCE

com·pe·tent \-tənt\ *adj* : CAPABLE, FIT, QUALIFIED ⟨a ∼ mechanic⟩ ⟨a ∼ juror⟩

com·pe·ti·tion \ˌkäm-pə-'ti-shən\ n 1 : the act of competing : RIVALRY 2 : CONTEST, MATCH; also : one's competitors — com·pet·i·tive \kəm-'pe-tə-tiv\ adj — com·pet·i·tive·ly adv — com·pet·i·tive·ness n

com·pet·i·tor \kəm-'pe-tə-tər\ n : one that competes : RIVAL

com·pile \kəm-'pī(-ə)l\ vb com·piled; com·pil·ing [ME, fr. AF compiler, fr. L compilare to plunder] 1 : to compose out of materials from other documents 2 : to collect and edit into a volume 3 : to translate (a computer program) with a compiler 4 : to build up gradually ⟨~ a record of four wins and two losses⟩ — com·pi·la·tion \ˌkäm-pə-'lā-shən\ n

com·pil·er \kəm-'pī-lər\ n 1 : one that compiles 2 : a computer program that translates any program correctly written in a specific programming language into machine language

com·pla·cence \kəm-'plā-ᵊns\ n : COMPLACENCY — com·pla·cent \-sᵊnt\ adj — com·pla·cent·ly adv

com·pla·cen·cy \-sᵊn-sē\ n, pl -cies : SATISFACTION; esp : SELF-SATISFACTION

com·plain \kəm-'plān\ vb 1 : to express grief, pain, or discontent 2 : to make a formal accusation — com·plain·ant n — com·plain·er n

com·plaint \kəm-'plānt\ n 1 : expression of grief, pain, or dissatisfaction 2 : a bodily ailment or disease 3 : a formal accusation against a person

com·plai·sance \kəm-'plā-sᵊns, ˌkäm-plā-'zans\ n [F] : disposition to please — com·plai·sant \-sᵊnt, -'zant\ adj — com·plai·sant·ly adv

com·pleat \kəm-'plēt\ adj : PROFICIENT

com·plect·ed \kəm-'plek-təd\ adj : having a specified facial complexion ⟨dark-complected⟩

¹com·ple·ment \'käm-plə-mənt\ n 1 : something that fills up or completes; also : the full quantity, number, or amount that makes a thing complete 2 : an added word by which a predicate is made complete 3 : a group of proteins in blood that combines with antibodies to destroy antigens — com·ple·men·ta·ry \ˌkäm-plə-'men-t(ə-)rē\ adj

²com·ple·ment \-ˌment\ vb : to be complementary to : fill out

complementary medicine n : ALTERNATIVE MEDICINE

¹com·plete \kəm-'plēt\ adj com·plet·er; -est 1 : having all parts or elements 2 : brought to an end 3 : fully carried out; also : ABSOLUTE 2 ⟨~ silence⟩ — com·plete·ly adv — com·plete·ness n — com·ple·tion \-'plē-shən\ n

²complete vb com·plet·ed; com·plet·ing 1 : FINISH, CONCLUDE 2 : to make whole or perfect ⟨the hat ~s the outfit⟩

com·plet·ist \kəm-'plē-tist\ n : one who wants to make something (as a collection) complete

¹com·plex \'käm-ˌpleks\ n 1 : a whole made up of or involving intricately interrelated elements 2 : a group of repressed desires and memories that exert a dominating influence on one's personality and behavior ⟨a guilt ~⟩

²com·plex \käm-'pleks, 'käm-ˌpleks\ adj 1 : composed of two or more parts 2 : consisting of a main clause and one or more subordinate clauses ⟨~ sentence⟩ 3 : hard to separate, analyze, or solve — com·plex·i·ty \käm-'plek-sə-tē\ n — com·plex·ly adv

complex fraction n : a fraction with a fraction or mixed number in the numerator or denominator or both

com·plex·ion \kəm-'plek-shən\ n 1 : the hue or appearance of the skin esp. of the face 2 : overall appearance — com·plex·ioned \-shənd\ adj

complex number n : a number of the form a + b √-1 where a and b are real numbers

com·pli·ance \kəm-'plī-əns\ n 1 : the act of complying to a demand or proposal 2 : a disposition to yield — com·pli·ant \-ənt\ adj

com·pli·cate \'käm-plə-ˌkāt\ vb -cat·ed; -cat·ing : to make or become complex or intricate

com·pli·cat·ed \'käm-plə-ˌkā-təd\ adj 1 : consisting of parts intricately combined 2 : difficult to analyze, understand, or explain — com·pli·cat·ed·ly adv

com·pli·ca·tion \ˌkäm-plə-'kā-shən\ n 1 : the quality or state of being complicated; also : a complex feature 2 : a disease or condition that develops during and affects the course of a primary disease or condition

com·plic·i·ty \kəm-'pli-sə-tē\ n, pl -ties : the state of being an accomplice

¹com·pli·ment \'käm-plə-mənt\ n 1 : an expression of approval or admiration; esp : a flattering remark 2 pl : best wishes : REGARDS

²com·pli·ment \-ˌment\ vb : to pay a compliment to

com·pli·men·ta·ry \ˌkäm-plə-'men-t(ə-)rē\ adj 1 : containing or expressing a compliment 2 : given free as a courtesy ⟨~ ticket⟩

com·ply \kəm-'plī\ vb com·plied; com·ply·ing : CONFORM, YIELD

¹com·po·nent \kəm-'pō-nənt, 'käm-ˌpō-\ n : a component part ◆ Synonyms INGREDIENT, ELEMENT, FACTOR, CONSTITUENT

²component adj : serving to form a part of : CONSTITUENT

com·port \kəm-'pȯrt\ vb 1 : AGREE, ACCORD ⟨actions that ~ with policy⟩ 2 : CONDUCT ⟨~ oneself with dignity⟩ ◆ Synonyms BEHAVE, ACQUIT, DEPORT — com·port·ment n

com·pose \kəm-'pōz\ vb com·posed; com·pos·ing 1 : to form by putting together : FASHION 2 : to produce (as pages of type) by composition 3 : ADJUST, ARRANGE 4 : CALM, QUIET 5 : to practice composition ⟨~ music⟩ — com·pos·er n

¹com·pos·ite \käm-'pä-zət\ adj 1 : made up of distinct parts or elements 2 : of, relating to, or being a large family of flowering plants (as a daisy or aster) that bear many small flowers united into compact heads resembling single flowers

²composite n 1 : something composite 2 : a plant of the composite family ◆ Synonyms BLEND, COMPOUND, MIXTURE, AMALGAMATION

com·po·si·tion \ˌkäm-pə-'zi-shən\ n 1 : the act or process of composing; esp : arrangement esp. in artistic form 2 : the arrangement or production of type for printing 3 : general makeup 4 : a product of mixing various elements or ingredients 5 : a literary, musical, or artistic product; esp : ESSAY

com·po·si·tion·ist \-'zi-shə-nist\ n : a teacher of writing

com·pos·i·tor \kəm-'pä-zə-tər\ n : one who sets type

com·post \'käm-ˌpōst\ n : a fertilizing material consisting largely of decayed organic matter — compost vb

com·po·sure \kəm-'pō-zhər\ n : CALMNESS, SELF-POSSESSION

com·pote \'käm-ˌpōt\ n 1 : fruits cooked in syrup 2 : a bowl (as of glass) usu. with a base and stem for serving esp. fruit or compote

¹com·pound \käm-'paund, 'käm-ˌ\ vb [ME compounen, fr. AF *cumpundre, fr. L componere, fr. com- together + ponere to put] 1 : COMBINE 2 : to form by combining parts ⟨~ a medicine⟩ 3 : SETTLE ⟨~ a dispute⟩; also : to refrain from prosecuting (an offense) in return for a consideration 4 : to increase (as interest) by an amount that can itself vary; also : to add to

²com·pound \'käm-ˌpaund\ adj 1 : made up of individual parts 2 : composed of united similar parts esp. of a kind usu. independent ⟨a ~ plant ovary⟩ 3 : formed by the combination of two or more otherwise independent elements ⟨~ sentence⟩

³com·pound \'käm-ˌpaund\ n 1 : a word consisting of parts that are words 2 : something formed from a union of elements or parts; esp : a distinct substance formed by the union of two or more chemical elements ◆ Synonyms MIXTURE, COMPOSITE, BLEND, ADMIXTURE, ALLOY

⁴com·pound \'käm-ˌpaund\ n [by folk etymology fr. Malay kampung group of buildings, village] : an enclosure containing buildings

compound interest n : interest computed on the sum of an original principal and accrued interest

com·pre·hend \ˌkäm-pri-'hend\ vb 1 : UNDERSTAND 2 : INCLUDE — com·pre·hen·si·ble \-'hen-sə-bəl\ adj — com·pre·hen·sion \-'hen-chən\ n

com·pre·hen·sive \ˌkäm-pri-'hen-siv\ adj : covering completely or broadly ⟨~ insurance⟩ — com·pre·hen·sive·ly adv — com·pre·hen·sive·ness n

¹com·press \kəm-'pres\ vb 1 : to squeeze together 2 : to reduce in size as if by squeezing ◆ Synonyms CONSTRICT, CONTRACT, SHRINK — com·pres·sor \-'pre-sər\ n

²com·press \'käm-ˌpres\ n : a folded pad or cloth used to press upon a body part

compressed air n : air under pressure greater than that of the atmosphere

com·pres·sion \kəm-'pre-shən\ *n* **1** : the act or process of compressing **2** : the process of compressing the fuel mixture in an internal combustion engine **3** : conversion (as of data) in order to reduce the space occupied or the bandwidth required

com·prise \kəm-'prīz\ *vb* **com·prised; com·pris·ing** **1** : INCLUDE, CONTAIN **2** : to be made up of **3** : COMPOSE, CONSTITUTE

¹com·pro·mise \'käm-prə-ˌmīz\ *n* : a settlement of differences reached by mutual concessions

²compromise *vb* **-mised; -mis·ing** **1** : to settle by compromise **2** : to expose to suspicion or loss of reputation

comp·trol·ler \kən-'trō-lər, 'kämp-ˌtrō-\ *n* : an official who audits and supervises expenditures and accounts

com·pul·sion \kəm-'pəl-shən\ *n* **1** : an act of compelling **2** : a force that compels **3** : an irresistible persistent impulse to perform an act ✦ *Synonyms* CONSTRAINT, FORCE, VIOLENCE, DURESS — **com·pul·sive** \-siv\ *adj* — **com·pul·sive·ly** *adv* — **com·pul·so·ry** \-sə-rē\ *adj*

com·punc·tion \kəm-'pəŋk-shən\ *n* : anxiety arising from guilt : REMORSE

com·pute \kəm-'pyüt\ *vb* **com·put·ed; com·put·ing** : CALCULATE, RECKON — **com·pu·ta·tion** \ˌkäm-pyü-'tā-shən\ *n* — **com·pu·ta·tion·al** *adj*

computed tomography *n* : radiography in which a three-dimensional image of a body structure is constructed by computer from a series of plane cross-sectional images made along an axis

com·put·er \kəm-'pyü-tər\ *n* : a programmable electronic device that can store, retrieve, and process data

com·put·er·ise *chiefly Brit var of* COMPUTERIZE

com·put·er·ize \kəm-'pyü-tə-ˌrīz\ *vb* **-ized; -iz·ing** **1** : to carry out, control, or produce by means of a computer **2** : to provide with computers **3** : to store in a computer; *also* : put into a form that a computer can use — **com·put·er·i·za·tion** \-ˌpyü-tə-rə-'zā-shən\ *n*

computerized axial tomography *n* : COMPUTED TOMOGRAPHY

com·rade \'käm-ˌrad\ *n* [MF *camarade* group sleeping in one room, roommate, companion, fr. Sp *camarada*, fr. *cámara* room, fr. LL *camera*] : COMPANION, ASSOCIATE — **com·rade·ly** *adj* — **com·rade·ship** *n*

¹con \'kän\ *vb* **conned; con·ning** **1** : MEMORIZE **2** : STUDY

²con *adv* : in opposition : AGAINST

³con *n* : an opposing argument, person, or position ⟨pros and ~s⟩

⁴con *vb* **conned; con·ning** **1** : SWINDLE **2** : PERSUADE, CAJOLE

⁵con *n* : CONVICT

conc *abbr* concentrated

con·cat·e·nate \kän-'ka-tə-ˌnāt\ *vb* **-nat·ed; -nat·ing** : to link together in a series or chain — **con·cat·e·na·tion** \(ˌ)kän-ˌka-tə-'nā-shən\ *n*

con·cave \kän-'kāv, 'kän-ˌ\ *adj* : curved or rounded inward like the inside of a bowl — **con·cav·i·ty** \kän-'ka-və-tē\ *n*

con·ceal \kən-'sēl\ *vb* : to place out of sight : HIDE — **con·ceal·er** *n* — **con·ceal·ment** *n*

con·cede \kən-'sēd\ *vb* **con·ced·ed; con·ced·ing** **1** : to admit to be true **2** : GRANT, YIELD ✦ *Synonyms* ALLOW, ACKNOWLEDGE, AVOW, CONFESS

con·ceit \kən-'sēt\ *n* **1** : excessively high opinion of one's self or ability : VANITY **2** : an elaborate or strained metaphor — **con·ceit·ed** *adj* — **con·ceit·ed·ly** *adv* — **con·ceit·ed·ness** *n*

con·ceive \kən-'sēv\ *vb* **con·ceived; con·ceiv·ing** **1** : to become pregnant or pregnant with ⟨~ a child⟩ **2** : to form an idea of : THINK, IMAGINE — **con·ceiv·able** \-'sē-və-bəl\ *adj* — **con·ceiv·ably** \-blē\ *adv*

con·cel·e·brant \kän-'se-lə-brənt\ *n* : one that jointly participates in celebrating the Eucharist

¹con·cen·trate \'kän-sən-ˌtrāt\ *vb* **-trat·ed; -trat·ing** **1** : to gather into one body, mass, or force **2** : to make less dilute **3** : to fix one's powers, efforts, or attentions

²concentrate *n* : something concentrated

con·cen·tra·tion \ˌkän-sən-'trā-shən\ *n* **1** : the act or process of concentrating : the state of being concentrated; *esp* : direction of attention on a single object **2** : the amount of a component in a given area or volume

concentration camp *n* : a camp where persons (as prisoners of war or political prisoners) are confined

con·cen·tric \kən-'sen-trik\ *adj* **1** : having a common center ⟨~ circles⟩ **2** : COAXIAL

¹con·cept \'kän-ˌsept\ *n* : THOUGHT, NOTION, IDEA — **con·cep·tu·al** \kən-'sep-chə-wəl\ *adj* — **con·cep·tu·al·ly** *adv*

²concept *adj* **1** : organized around a main idea or theme ⟨a ~ album⟩ **2** : created to illustrate a concept ⟨a ~ car⟩

con·cep·tion \kən-'sep-shən\ *n* **1** : the process of conceiving or being conceived **2** : the power to form or understand ideas or concepts **3** : IDEA, CONCEPT **4** : the originating of something

con·cep·tu·al·ise *Brit var of* CONCEPTUALIZE

con·cep·tu·al·ize \-'sep-chə-wə-ˌlīz\ *vb* **-ized; -iz·ing** : to form a conception of

¹con·cern \kən-'sərn\ *vb* **1** : to relate to **2** : to be the business of **3** : INVOLVE **3** : ENGAGE, OCCUPY

²concern *n* **1** : INTEREST, ANXIETY **2** : AFFAIR, MATTER **3** : a business organization ✦ *Synonyms* CARE, WORRY, DISQUIET, UNEASE

con·cerned \-'sərnd\ *adj* **1** : ANXIOUS, UNEASY ⟨~ for their safety⟩ **2** : INVOLVED

con·cern·ing \-'sər-niŋ\ *prep* : relating to : REGARDING

con·cern·ment \kən-'sərn-mənt\ *n* **1** : something in which one is concerned **2** : IMPORTANCE, CONSEQUENCE

¹con·cert \'kän-(ˌ)sərt\ *n* **1** : agreement in a plan or design **2** : a public performance (as of music)

²con·cert \kən-'sərt\ *vb* : to plan together

con·cert·ed \kən-'sər-təd\ *adj* : mutually agreed on; *also* : performed in unison

con·cer·ti·na \ˌkän-sər-'tē-nə\ *n* : an instrument of the accordion family

concertina wire *n* : a coiled wire with sharp points for use as an obstacle

con·cert·mas·ter \'kän-sərt-ˌmas-tər\ *or* **con·cert·meis·ter** \-ˌmī-stər\ *n* : the leader of the first violins of an orchestra and assistant to the conductor

con·cer·to \kən-'cher-tō\ *n, pl* **-ti** \-(ˌ)tē\ *or* **-tos** [It] : a piece for one or more solo instruments and orchestra in three movements

con·ces·sion \kən-'se-shən\ *n* **1** : an act of conceding or yielding **2** : something yielded **3** : a grant by a government of land or of a right to use it **4** : a grant of a portion of premises for some specific purpose; *also* : the activities or enterprise carried on — **con·ces·sion·ary** \-'se-shə-ˌner-ē\ *adj*

con·ces·sion·aire \kən-ˌse-shə-'ner\ *n* : one that owns or operates a concession

conch \'käŋk, 'känch\ *n, pl* **conchs** \'käŋks\ *or* **conch·es** \'kän-chəz\ : a large spiral-shelled marine gastropod mollusk; *also* : its shell

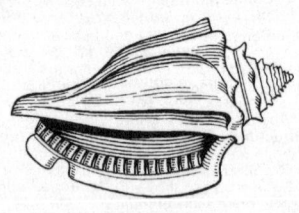

conch

con·cierge \kō^n-'syerzh\ *n, pl* **con·cierges** *same or* -'syer-zhəz\ [F] **1** : a resident in an apartment building who performs services for the tenants **2** : a usu. multilingual hotel staff member who usu. handles mail and reservations

con·cil·i·ate \kən-'si-lē-ˌāt\ *vb* **-at·ed; -at·ing** **1** : to bring into agreement : RECONCILE **2** : to gain the goodwill of — **con·cil·i·a·tion** \-ˌsi-lē-'ā-shən\ *n* — **con·cil·i·a·tor** \-'si-lē-ˌā-tər\ *n* — **con·cil·i·a·to·ry** \-'si-lē-ə-ˌtȯr-ē\ *adj*

con·cise \kən-'sīs\ *adj* : expressing much in few words : BRIEF — **con·cise·ly** *adv* — **con·cise·ness** *n*

con·clave \'kän-ˌklāv\ *n* [ME, fr. ML, fr. L, room that can be locked, fr. *com-* together + *clavis* key] : a private gathering; *also* : CONVENTION con·clude \kən-'klüd\ vb con·clud·ed; con·clud·ing 1 : to bring to a close : END 2 : DECIDE, JUDGE 3 : to bring about as a result ✦ *Synonyms* CLOSE, FINISH, TERMINATE, COMPLETE, HALT

con·clu·sion \kən-'klü-zhən\ n 1 : the logical consequence of a reasoning process 2 : TERMINATION, END 3 : OUTCOME, RESULT — con·clu·sive \-siv\ adj — con·clu·sive·ly adv — con·clu·sive·ness n

con·coct \kən-'käkt, kän-\ vb 1 : to prepare by combining raw materials 2 : DEVISE — con·coc·tion \-'käk-shən\ n

con·com·i·tant \-'kä-mə-tənt\ adj : ACCOMPANYING, ATTENDING — concomitant n

con·cord \'kän-ˌkȯrd, 'käŋ-\ n : AGREEMENT, HARMONY

con·cor·dance \kən-'kȯr-dᵊns\ n 1 : an alphabetical index of words in a book or in an author's works with the passages in which they occur 2 : AGREEMENT, COVENANT

con·cor·dant \-dᵊnt\ adj : HARMONIOUS, AGREEING

con·cor·dat \kən-'kȯr-ˌdat\ n : CONCORDANCE 2

con·course \'kän-ˌkȯrs\ n 1 : a spontaneous coming together : GATHERING 2 : an open space or hall (as in a bus terminal) where crowds gather

¹con·crete \'kän-ˌkrēt, 'kän-ˌkrēt\ adj 1 : naming a real thing or class of things : not abstract 2 : not theoretical : ACTUAL 3 : made of or relating to concrete

²con·crete \'kän-ˌkrēt, kän-'krēt\ vb con·cret·ed; con·cret·ing 1 : SOLIDIFY 2 : to cover with concrete

³con·crete \'kän-ˌkrēt, kän-'krēt\ n : a hard building material made by mixing cement, sand, and gravel with water

con·cre·tion \kän-'krē-shən\ n : a hard mass esp. when formed abnormally in the body

con·cu·bine \'käg-kyu̇-ˌbīn\ n [ME, fr. AF, fr. L concubina, fr. com- with + cubare to lie] : a woman who is not legally a wife but lives with a man and sometimes has a recognized position in his household; also : MISTRESS — con·cu·bi·nage \kän-'kyü-bə-nij\ n

con·cu·pis·cence \kän-'kyü-pə-səns\ n : ardent sexual desire : LUST

con·cur \kən-'kər\ vb con·curred; con·cur·ring 1 : to act together 2 : AGREE 3 : COINCIDE ✦ *Synonyms* UNITE, COMBINE, COOPERATE, BAND, JOIN

con·cur·rence \-'kər-əns\ n 1 : agreement in action or opinion 2 : occurrence together : CONJUNCTION

con·cur·rent \-'kər-ənt\ adj 1 : happening or operating at the same time 2 : joint and equal in authority

con·cus·sion \kən-'kə-shən\ n 1 : a hard blow or collision; also : bodily injury (as to the brain) resulting from a sudden jar 2 : AGITATION, SHAKING

con·demn \kən-'dem\ vb 1 : to declare to be wrong 2 : to convict of guilt 3 : to sentence judicially 4 : to pronounce unfit for use ⟨~ a building⟩ 5 : to declare forfeited or taken for public use ✦ *Synonyms* DENOUNCE, CENSURE, BLAME, CRITICIZE, REPREHEND — con·dem·na·tion \ˌkän-ˌdem-'nā-shən\ n — con·dem·na·to·ry \kən-'dem-nə-ˌtȯr-ē\ adj

con·den·sate \'kän-dən-ˌsāt, kən-'den-\ n : a product of condensation

con·dense \kən-'dens\ vb con·densed; con·dens·ing 1 : to make or become more compact or dense : CONCENTRATE 2 : to change from vapor to liquid ✦ *Synonyms* CONTRACT, SHRINK, COMPRESS, CONSTRICT — con·den·sa·tion \ˌkän-den-'sā-shən\ n

con·dens·er \kən-'den-sər\ n 1 : one that condenses 2 : CAPACITOR

con·de·scend \ˌkän-di-'send\ vb : to assume an air of superiority — con·de·scend·ing·ly \-'sen-diŋ-lē\ adv — con·de·scen·sion \-'sen-chən\ n

con·dign \kən-'dīn, 'kän-ˌdīn\ adj : DESERVED, APPROPRIATE ⟨~ punishment⟩

con·di·ment \'kän-də-mənt\ n : something used to make food savory; esp : a pungent seasoning (as pepper)

¹con·di·tion \kən-'di-shən\ n 1 : something essential to the occurrence of some other thing 2 : state of being 3 : social status 4 pl : state of affairs : CIRCUMSTANCES 5 : a bodily state in which something is wrong ⟨a heart ~⟩ 6 : a state of health, fitness, or working order ⟨in good ~⟩

²condition vb 1 : to put into proper condition for action or use 2 : to adapt, modify, or mold to respond in a particular way 3 : to modify so that an act or response previously associated with one stimulus becomes associated with another

con·di·tion·al \kən-'di-shə-nəl\ adj : containing, implying, or depending on a condition — con·di·tion·al·ly adv

con·di·tioned \-'di-shənd\ adj : determined or established by conditioning

con·di·tion·er \-'di-shə-nər\ n : a preparation used to improve the condition of hair

con·do \'kän-ˌdō\ n : CONDOMINIUM 3

con·dole \kən-'dōl\ vb con·doled; con·dol·ing : to express sympathetic sorrow — con·do·lence \kən-'dō-ləns\ n

con·dom \'kän-dəm, 'kən-\ n : a usu. rubber sheath worn over the penis (as to prevent pregnancy or venereal infection during sexual intercourse)

con·do·min·i·um \ˌkän-də-'mi-nē-əm\ n, pl -ums 1 : joint sovereignty (as by two or more nations) 2 : a politically dependent territory under condominium 3 : individual ownership of a unit (as an apartment) in a multiunit structure; also : a unit so owned

con·done \kən-'dōn\ vb con·doned; con·don·ing : to overlook or forgive esp. by treating (an offense) as harmless or trivial ✦ *Synonyms* EXCUSE, PARDON, FORGIVE, REMIT — con·do·na·tion \ˌkän-də-'nā-shən\ n

con·dor \'kän-dər, -ˌdȯr\ n [Sp cóndor, fr. Quechua kuntur] : a very large American vulture of the high Andes; also : a related nearly extinct vulture of southern California now resident only in captivity

con·duce \kən-'düs, -'dyüs\ vb con·duced; con·duc·ing : to lead or contribute to a particular result — con·du·cive adj

¹con·duct \'kän-(ˌ)dəkt\ n 1 : MANAGEMENT, DIRECTION 2 : BEHAVIOR

²con·duct \kən-'dəkt\ vb 1 : GUIDE, ESCORT 2 : MANAGE, DIRECT 3 : to act as a medium for conveying or transmitting 4 : BEHAVE — con·duc·tion \-'dək-shən\ n

con·duc·tance \kən-'dək-təns\ n : the readiness with which a conductor transmits an electric current

con·duc·tive \kən-'dək-tiv\ adj : having the power to conduct (as heat or electricity) — con·duc·tiv·i·ty \ˌkän-ˌdək-'ti-və-tē\ n

con·duc·tor \kən-'dək-tər\ n 1 : one that conducts; esp : a material that permits an electric current to flow easily 2 : a collector of fares in a public conveyance 3 : the leader of a musical ensemble

con·duit \'kän-ˌdü-ət, -ˌdyü-, -dȯr\ n 1 : a channel for conveying fluid 2 : a tube or trough for protecting electric wires or cables 3 : a means of transmitting or distributing

con·dyle \'kän-ˌdī(-ə)l, -dᵊl\ n : an articular prominence of a bone — con·dy·lar \-də-lər\ adj

cone \'kōn\ n 1 : the scaly usu. ovate fruit of trees of most conifers 2 : a solid figure formed by rotating a right triangle about one of its legs 3 : a solid figure that slopes evenly to a point from a usu. circular base 4 : any of the conical light-sensitive receptor cells of the retina that function in color vision 5 : something shaped like a cone

cone·flow·er \'kōn-ˌflau̇(-ə)r\ n : any of several composite plants having cone-shaped flower disks

Con·es·to·ga wagon \ˌkä-nə-'stō-gə-\ n : a broad-wheeled covered wagon used esp. for transporting freight across the prairies

Conestoga wagon

co·ney or co·ny \'kō-nē\ n, pl coneys or conies 1 : RABBIT; also : its fur 2 : PIKA

conf abbr 1 conference 2 confidential

con·fab \'kän-ˌfab, kən-'fab\ n : CONFABULATION 1

con·fab·u·la·tion \kən-ˌfab-yə-ˈlā-shən\ n 1 : CHAT; also : CONFERENCE 2 : a filling in of gaps in memory by fabrication — **con·fab·u·late** \-ˈfa-byə-ˌlāt\ vb

con·fec·tion \kən-ˈfek-shən\ n 1 : something put together from varied material 2 : a fancy dish or sweet; also : CANDY — **con·fect** \kən-ˈfekt\ vb

con·fec·tion·er \-sh(ə-)nər\ n : a maker of or dealer in confections

con·fec·tion·ery \-shə-ˌner-ē\ n, pl **-er·ies** 1 : sweet foods 2 : a confectioner's place of business

Confed abbr Confederate

con·fed·er·a·cy \kən-ˈfe-də-rə-sē\ n, pl **-cies** 1 : LEAGUE, ALLIANCE 2 cap : the 11 southern states that seceded from the U.S. in 1860 and 1861

¹con·fed·er·ate \kən-ˈfe-də-rət\ adj 1 : united in a league : ALLIED 2 cap : of or relating to the Confederacy

²confederate n 1 : ALLY, ACCOMPLICE 2 cap : an adherent of the Confederacy

³con·fed·er·ate \-ˈfe-də-ˌrāt\ vb **-at·ed; -at·ing** : to unite in a confederacy

con·fed·er·a·tion \kən-ˌfe-də-ˈrā-shən\ n 1 : an act of confederating : ALLIANCE 2 : LEAGUE

con·fer \kən-ˈfər\ vb **con·ferred; con·fer·ring** 1 : GRANT, BESTOW 2 : to exchange views : CONSULT — **con·fer·ee** \ˌkän-fə-ˈrē\ n

con·fer·ence \ˈkän-f(ə-)rəns\ n 1 : an interchange of views; esp : a meeting for this purpose 2 : an association of athletic teams

con·fer·enc·ing \ˈkän-f(ə-)rən-siŋ\ n : the holding of conferences esp. by means of electronic devices

con·fess \kən-ˈfes\ vb 1 : to acknowledge or disclose one's misdeed, fault, or sin 2 : to acknowledge one's sins to God or to a priest 3 : to receive the confession of (a penitent) ✦ **Synonyms** ADMIT, OWN, AVOW, CONCEDE, GRANT

con·fessed·ly \-ˈfe-səd-lē\ adv : by confession : ADMITTEDLY

con·fes·sion \-ˈfe-shən\ n 1 : an act of confessing (as in the sacrament of penance) 2 : an acknowledgment of guilt 3 : a formal statement of religious beliefs 4 : a religious body having a common creed — **con·fes·sion·al** adj

con·fes·sion·al \-ˈfe-shə-nəl\ n : a place where a priest hears confessions

con·fes·sor \kən-ˈfe-sər\ n 1 : one that confesses 2 : a priest who hears confessions

con·fet·ti \kən-ˈfe-tē\ n [It, pl. of confetto sweetmeat, fr. ML confectum, fr. L, neut. of confectus, pp. of conficere to prepare] : bits of colored paper or ribbon for throwing (as at weddings)

con·fi·dant \ˈkän-fə-ˌdänt, -ˌdant\ n : one to whom secrets are confided

con·fi·dante \-ˌdänt, -ˌdant\ n : CONFIDANT; esp : one who is a woman

con·fide \kən-ˈfīd\ vb **con·fid·ed; con·fid·ing** 1 : to have or show faith : TRUST ⟨~ in a friend⟩ 2 : to tell confidentially ⟨~ a secret⟩ 3 : ENTRUST

¹con·fi·dence \ˈkän-fə-dəns\ n 1 : TRUST, RELIANCE 2 : SELF-ASSURANCE, BOLDNESS 3 : a state of trust or intimacy 4 : SECRET 2 — **con·fi·dent** \-dənt\ adj — **con·fi·dent·ly** adv

²confidence adj : of or relating to swindling by false promises ⟨a ~ game⟩

con·fi·den·tial \ˌkän-fə-ˈden-shəl\ adj 1 : SECRET, PRIVATE ⟨~ information⟩ 2 : entrusted with confidences ⟨~ clerk⟩ — **con·fi·den·ti·al·i·ty** \-ˌden-shē-ˈa-lə-tē\ n — **con·fi·den·tial·ly** \-ˈden-shə-lē\ adv

con·fig·u·ra·tion \kən-ˌfig-yə-ˈrā-shən\ n : structural arrangement of parts : SHAPE

con·fig·ure \kən-ˈfi-gyər\ vb **-ured; -ur·ing** : to set up for operation esp. in a particular way

con·fine \kən-ˈfīn\ vb **con·fined; con·fin·ing** 1 : to hold within a location; also : IMPRISON 2 : to keep within limits ⟨will ~ my remarks to one subject⟩ — **con·fine·ment** n — **con·fin·er** n

con·fines \ˈkän-ˌfīnz\ n pl : BOUNDS, BORDERS

con·firm \kən-ˈfərm\ vb 1 : to give approval to : RATIFY 2 : to make firm or firmer 3 : to administer the rite of confirmation to 4 : VERIFY, CORROBORATE — **con·fir·ma·to·ry** \-ˈfər-mə-ˌtȯr-ē\ adj

con·fir·ma·tion \ˌkän-fər-ˈmā-shən\ n 1 : a religious ceremony admitting a person to full membership in a church or synagogue 2 : an act of ratifying or corroborating; also : PROOF

con·fis·cate \ˈkän-fə-ˌskāt\ vb **-cat·ed; -cat·ing** [L confiscare, fr. com- with + fiscus treasury] : to take possession of by or as if by public authority — **con·fis·ca·tion** \ˌkän-fə-ˈskā-shən\ n — **con·fis·ca·to·ry** \kən-ˈfis-kə-ˌtȯr-ē\ adj

con·fit \kōn-ˈfē\ n : a garnish of fruit or vegetables cooked in a seasoned liquid

con·fla·gra·tion \ˌkän-flə-ˈgrā-shən\ n : FIRE; esp : a large disastrous fire

¹con·flict \ˈkän-ˌflikt\ n 1 : WAR 2 : a clash between hostile or opposing elements, ideas, or forces

²con·flict \kən-ˈflikt\ vb : to show opposition or irreconcilability : CLASH

con·flu·ence \ˈkän-ˌflü-əns, kən-ˈflü-\ n 1 : a coming together at one point 2 : the meeting or place of meeting of two or more streams — **con·flu·ent** \-ənt\ adj

con·flux \ˈkän-ˌfləks\ n : CONFLUENCE

con·form \kən-ˈfȯrm\ vb 1 : to be similar or identical; also : AGREE 2 : to obey customs or standards; also : COMPLY — **con·form·able** adj — **con·form·ist** \-ˈfȯr-mist\ adj

con·for·mance \kən-ˈfȯr-məns\ n : CONFORMITY

con·for·ma·tion \ˌkän-fȯr-ˈmā-shən\ n : a forming into a whole by arranging parts

con·for·mi·ty \kən-ˈfȯr-mə-tē\ n, pl **-ties** 1 : HARMONY, AGREEMENT 2 : COMPLIANCE, OBEDIENCE

con·found \kən-ˈfau̇nd, kän-\ vb 1 : to throw into disorder or confusion 2 : CONFUSE 2 ✦ **Synonyms** BEWILDER, PUZZLE, PERPLEX, BEFOG

con·fra·ter·ni·ty \ˌkän-frə-ˈtər-nə-tē\ n : a society devoted esp. to a religious or charitable cause

con·frere \ˈkän-ˌfrer, ˈkōⁿ-\ n : COLLEAGUE, COMRADE

con·front \kən-ˈfrənt\ vb 1 : to face esp. in challenge : OPPOSE; also : to deal unflinchingly with ⟨~ed the issue⟩ 2 : to cause to face or meet — **con·fron·ta·tion** \ˌkän-frən-ˈtā-shən\ n — **con·fron·ta·tion·al** \-shə-nᵊl\ adj

Con·fu·cian \kən-ˈfyü-shən\ adj : of or relating to the Chinese philosopher Confucius or his teachings — **Con·fu·cian·ism** \-shə-ˌni-zəm\ n

con·fuse \kən-ˈfyüz\ vb **con·fused; con·fus·ing** 1 : to make mentally unclear or uncertain; also : to disturb the composure of 2 : to mix up : JUMBLE ✦ **Synonyms** MUDDLE, BEFUDDLE, ADDLE, FLUSTER — **con·fus·ed·ly** \-ˈfyü-zəd-lē\ adv — **con·fus·ing·ly** \-ˈfyü-ziŋ-lē\ adv

con·fu·sion \-ˈfyü-zhən\ n 1 : an act or instance of confusing 2 : the quality or state of being confused

con·fute \kən-ˈfyüt\ vb **con·fut·ed; con·fut·ing** : to overwhelm by argument : REFUTE — **con·fu·ta·tion** \ˌkän-fyü-ˈtā-shən\ n

cong abbr congress; congressional

con·ga \ˈkäŋ-gə\ n : a Cuban dance of African origin performed by a group usu. in single file

con·geal \kən-ˈjēl\ vb 1 : FREEZE 2 : to make or become hard or thick

con·gee \ˈkän-jē\ n : porridge made from rice

con·ge·ner \ˈkän-jə-nər\ n : one related to another; esp : a plant or animal of the same taxonomic genus as another — **con·ge·ner·ic** \ˌkän-jə-ˈner-ik\ adj

con·ge·nial \kən-ˈjē-nyəl\ adj 1 : KINDRED, SYMPATHETIC ⟨~ companions⟩ 2 : suited to one's taste or nature : AGREEABLE — **con·ge·ni·al·i·ty** \-ˌjē-nē-ˈa-lə-tē\ n — **con·ge·nial·ly** adv

con·gen·i·tal \kən-ˈje-nə-tᵊl\ adj : existing at or dating from birth ⟨~ deafness⟩ ✦ **Synonyms** INBORN, INNATE, NATURAL

con·ger eel \ˈkän-gər-\ n : a large edible marine eel of the Atlantic

con·ge·ries \ˈkän-jə-(ˌ)rēz\ n, pl **congeries** : AGGREGATION, COLLECTION

con·gest \kən-ˈjest\ vb 1 : to cause excessive fullness of the blood vessels of (as a lung) 2 : to obstruct by overcrowding — **con·ges·tion** \-ˈjes-chən\ n — **con·ges·tive** \-ˈjes-tiv\ adj

congestive heart failure n : heart failure in which the heart is unable to keep enough blood circulating in the tissues or is unable to pump out the blood returned to it by the veins

¹con·glom·er·ate \kən-ˈglä-mə-rət\ adj [L conglomerare to roll together, fr. *com-* together + *glomerare* to wind into a ball, fr. *glomer-, glomus* ball] : made up of parts from various sources

²con·glom·er·ate \-ˌrāt\ *vb* -at·ed; -at·ing : to form into a mass — con·glom·er·a·tion \-ˌglä-mə-ˈrā-shən\ *n*

³con·glom·er·ate \-rət\ *n* **1** : a mass formed of fragments from various sources; *esp* : a rock composed of fragments varying from pebbles to boulders held together by a cementing material **2** : a widely diversified corporation

con·grat·u·late \kən-ˈgra-chə-ˌlāt\ *vb* -lat·ed; -lat·ing : to express sympathetic pleasure to on account of success or good fortune : FELICITATE — con·grat·u·la·tion \-ˌgra-chə-ˈlā-shən\ *n* — con·grat·u·la·to·ry \-ˈgra-chə-lə-ˌtōr-ē\ *adj*

con·gre·gate \ˈkäŋ-gri-ˌgāt\ *vb* -gat·ed; -gat·ing [ME, fr. L *congregatus,* pp. of *congregare,* fr. *com-* together + *greg-, grex* flock] : ASSEMBLE

con·gre·ga·tion \ˌkäŋ-gri-ˈgā-shən\ *n* **1** : an assembly of persons met esp. for worship; *also* : a group that habitually so meets **2** : a religious community or order **3** : the act or an instance of congregating

con·gre·ga·tion·al \-shə-nəl\ *adj* **1** : of or relating to a congregation **2** *cap* : observing the faith and practice of certain Protestant churches which recognize the independence of each congregation in church matters — con·gre·ga·tion·al·ism \-nə-ˌli-zəm\ *n, often cap* — con·gre·ga·tion·al·ist \-list\ *n, often cap*

con·gress \ˈkäŋ-grəs\ *n* **1** : an assembly esp. of delegates for discussion and usu. action on some question **2** : the body of senators and representatives constituting a nation's legislature — con·gres·sio·nal \kən-ˈgre-shə-nəl\ *adj*

con·gress·man \ˈkäŋ-grəs-mən\ *n* : a member of a congress

con·gress·wom·an \-ˌwu̇-mən\ *n* : a woman who is a member of a congress

con·gru·ence \kən-ˈgrü-əns, ˈkäŋ-grü-\ *n* : the quality of agreeing or coinciding : CONGRUITY — con·gru·ent \kən-ˈgrü-ənt, ˈkäŋ-grü-\ *adj*

con·gru·en·cy \-sē\ *n, pl* -cies : CONGRUENCE

con·gru·ity \kän-ˈgrü-ə-tē\ *n, pl* -ities : correspondence between things — con·gru·ous \ˈkäŋ-grü-əs\ *adj*

con·ic \ˈkä-nik\ *adj* **1** : of or relating to a cone **2** : CONICAL

con·i·cal \ˈkä-ni-kəl\ *adj* : resembling a cone esp. in shape

co·ni·fer \ˈkä-nə-fər, ˈkō-\ *n* : any of an order of shrubs or trees (as the pines) that usu. are evergreen and bear cones — co·nif·er·ous \kō-ˈni-fə-rəs\ *adj*

conj *abbr* conjunction

con·jec·ture \kən-ˈjek-chər\ *n* : GUESS, SURMISE — con·jec·tur·al \-chə-rəl\ *adj* — conjecture *vb*

con·join \kən-ˈjȯin\ *vb* : to join together — con·joint \-ˈjȯint\ *adj*

con·ju·gal \ˈkän-ji-gəl\ *adj* : of or relating to marriage : MATRIMONIAL

¹con·ju·gate \ˈkän-ji-gət, -jə-ˌgāt\ *adj* **1** : united esp. in pairs : COUPLED **2** : of kindred origin and meaning ⟨*sing* and *song* are ∼⟩ — con·ju·gate·ly *adv*

²con·ju·gate \-jə-ˌgāt\ *vb* -gat·ed; -gat·ing **1** : INFLECT ⟨∼ a verb⟩ **2** : to join together : COUPLE

con·ju·ga·tion \ˌkän-jə-ˈgā-shən\ *n* **1** : an arrangement of the inflectional forms of a verb **2** : the act of conjugating : the state of being conjugated

con·junct \kän-ˈjəŋkt\ *adj* : JOINED, UNITED

con·junc·tion \kən-ˈjəŋk-shən\ *n* **1** : COMBINATION **2** : occurrence at the same time **3** : a word that joins together sentences, clauses, phrases, or words

con·junc·ti·va \ˌkän-jəŋk-ˈtī-və\ *n, pl* -vas *or* -vae \-(ˌ)vē\ : the mucous membrane lining the inner surface of the eyelids and continuing over the forepart of the eyeball

con·junc·tive \kən-ˈjəŋk-tiv\ *adj* **1** : CONNECTIVE **2** : CONJUNCT ⟨the ∼ operation of different factors⟩ **3** : being or functioning like a conjunction

³con·junc·ti·vi·tis \kən-ˌjəŋk-ti-ˈvī-təs\ *n* : inflammation of the conjunctiva

con·junc·ture \kən-ˈjəŋk-chər\ *n* **1** : CONJUNCTION, UNION **2** : JUNCTURE **3**

con·jun·to \kōn-ˈhün-tō\ *n* : Mexican-American music influenced by the music of German immigrants to Texas

con·jure \ˈkän-jər, ˈkən- *for 1, 2;* kən-ˈju̇r *for 3*\ *vb* conjured; con·jur·ing **1** : to implore earnestly or solemnly

2 : to practice magic; *esp* : to summon (as a devil) by sorcery **3** : to practice sleight of hand — con·ju·ra·tion \ˌkän-jü-ˈrā-shən, ˌkən-\ *n* — con·jur·er *or* con·ju·ror \ˈkän-jər-ər, ˈkən-\ *n*

conk \ˈkäŋk\ *vb* : BREAK DOWN; *esp* : STALL ⟨the motor ∼ed out⟩

Conn *abbr* Connecticut

con·nect \kə-ˈnekt\ *vb* **1** : JOIN, LINK **2** : to associate in one's mind **3** : to establish a communications connection ⟨∼ to the Internet⟩ — con·nect·able *adj* — con·nec·tor *n*

con·nec·tion \kə-ˈnek-shən\ *n* **1** : JUNCTION, UNION **2** : logical relationship : COHERENCE; *esp* : relation of a word to other words in a sentence **3** : family relationship **4** : BOND, LINK **5** : a person related by blood or marriage **6** : relationship in social affairs or in business **7** : an association of persons; *esp* : a religious denomination **8** : a means of communication or transport ⟨a telephone ∼⟩

¹con·nec·tive \kə-ˈnek-tiv\ *adj* : serving to connect — con·nec·tiv·i·ty \ˌkä-ˌnek-ˈti-və-tē\ *n*

²connective *n* : a word (as a conjunction) that connects words or word groups

connective tissue *n* : a tissue (as bone or cartilage) that forms a supporting framework for the body or its parts

con·nex·ion *chiefly Brit var of* CONNECTION

con·ning tower \ˈkä-niŋ-\ *n* : a raised structure on the deck of a submarine

con·nip·tion \kə-ˈnip-shən\ *n* : a fit of rage, hysteria, or alarm

con·nive \kə-ˈnīv\ *vb* con·nived; con·niv·ing [F or L; F *conniver,* fr. L *conivēre* to close the eyes, connive] **1** : to pretend ignorance of something one ought to oppose as wrong **2** : to cooperate secretly : give secret aid — con·niv·ance *n* — con·niv·er *n*

con·nois·seur \ˌkä-nə-ˈsər\ *n* : a critical judge in matters of art or taste

con·no·ta·tion \ˌkä-nə-ˈtā-shən\ *n* : a meaning in addition to or apart from the thing explicitly named or described by a word

con·no·ta·tive \ˈkä-nə-ˌtā-tiv, kə-ˈnō-tə-\ *adj* **1** : connoting or tending to connote **2** : relating to connotation

con·note \kə-ˈnōt\ *vb* con·not·ed; con·not·ing : to suggest or mean as a connotation

con·nu·bi·al \kə-ˈnü-bē-əl, -ˈnyü-\ *adj* : of or relating to marriage : CONJUGAL

con·quer \ˈkäŋ-kər\ *vb* **1** : to gain by force of arms : WIN **2** : to get the better of : OVERCOME ✦ *Synonyms* DEFEAT, SUBJUGATE, SUBDUE, OVERTHROW, VANQUISH — con·quer·or \-ər\ *n*

con·quest \ˈkän-ˌkwest, ˈkäŋ-\ *n* **1** : an act of conquering : VICTORY **2** : something conquered

con·quis·ta·dor \kȯŋ-ˈkēs-tə-ˌdȯr, kän-ˈkwis-\ *n, pl* -do·res \-ˌkēs-tə-ˈdȯr-ēz, -ˌkwis-\ *or* -dors : CONQUEROR; *esp* : a leader in the Spanish conquest of the Americas in the 16th century

cons *abbr* consonant

con·san·guin·i·ty \ˌkän-ˌsan-ˈgwi-nə-tē, -saŋ-\ *n, pl* -ties : blood relationship — con·san·guin·e·ous \-nē-əs\ *adj*

con·science \ˈkän-chəns\ *n* : consciousness of the moral right and wrong of one's own acts or motives — con·science·less *adj*

con·sci·en·tious \ˌkän-chē-ˈen-chəs\ *adj* : guided by one's own sense of right and wrong ✦ *Synonyms* SCRUPULOUS, HONORABLE, HONEST, UPRIGHT, JUST — con·sci·en·tious·ly *adv*

conscientious objector *n* : a person who refuses to serve in the armed forces or to bear arms on moral or religious grounds

¹con·scious \ˈkän-chəs\ *adj* **1** : AWARE **2** : known or felt by one's inner self **3** : mentally awake or alert : not asleep or unconscious **4** : done with awareness or purpose ⟨a ∼ decision⟩ — con·scious·ly *adv* — con·scious·ness *n*

²conscious *n* : the upper level of mental life of which a person is aware : CONSCIOUSNESS

con·script \kən-ˈskript\ *vb* : to enroll by compulsion for military or naval service — conscript \ˈkän-ˌskript\ *n* — con·scrip·tion \kən-ˈskrip-shən\ *n*

con·se·crate \ˈkän-sə-ˌkrāt\ *vb* -crat·ed; -crat·ing [ME, fr. L *consecratus,* pp. of *consecrare,* fr. *com-* together +

sacrare to set aside as sacred, fr. *sacer* sacred] **1** : to induct (as a bishop) into an office with a religious rite **2** : to make or declare sacred ⟨∼ a church⟩ **3** : to devote solemnly to a purpose — **con·se·cra·tion** \ˌkän-sə-ˈkrā-shən\ *n*
con·sec·u·tive \kən-ˈse-kyə-tiv\ *adj* : following in regular order : SUCCESSIVE — **con·sec·u·tive·ly** *adv*
con·sen·su·al \kən-ˈsen-chə-wəl\ *adj* : involving or based on mutual consent
con·sen·sus \kən-ˈsen-səs\ *n* **1** : agreement in opinion, testimony, or belief **2** : collective opinion
¹**con·sent** \kən-ˈsent\ *vb* : to give assent or approval
²**consent** *n* : approval or acceptance of something done or proposed by another
con·se·quence \ˈkän-sə-ˌkwens\ *n* **1** : RESULT **2** : IMPORTANCE ✦ *Synonyms* EFFECT, OUTCOME, AFTERMATH, UPSHOT
con·se·quent \-kwənt, -ˌkwent\ *adj* : following as a result or effect
con·se·quen·tial \ˌkän-sə-ˈkwen-chəl\ *adj* **1** : having significant consequences **2** : showing self-importance
con·se·quent·ly \ˈkän-sə-ˌkwent-lē, -kwənt-\ *adv* : as a result : ACCORDINGLY
con·ser·van·cy \kən-ˈsər-vən-sē\ *n, pl* **-cies** : an organization or area designated to conserve natural resources
con·ser·va·tion \ˌkän-sər-ˈvā-shən\ *n* : PRESERVATION; *esp* : planned management of natural resources
con·ser·va·tion·ist \-shə-nist\ *n* : a person who advocates conservation esp. of natural resources
con·ser·va·tism \kən-ˈsər-və-ˌti-zəm\ *n* : disposition to keep to established ways : opposition to change
¹**con·ser·va·tive** \kən-ˈsər-və-tiv\ *adj* **1** : PRESERVATIVE **2** : disposed to maintain existing views, conditions, or institutions **3** : MODERATE, CAUTIOUS ⟨a ∼ investment⟩ — **con·ser·va·tive·ly** *adv*
²**conservative** *n* : a person who is conservative esp. in politics
con·ser·va·tor \kən-ˈsər-və-tər, ˈkän-sər-ˌvā-\ *n* **1** : PROTECTOR, GUARDIAN **2** : one named by a court to protect the interests of an incompetent (as a child)
con·ser·va·to·ry \kən-ˈsər-və-ˌtȯr-ē\ *n, pl* **-ries** **1** : GREENHOUSE **2** : a place of instruction in one of the fine arts (as music)
¹**con·serve** \kən-ˈsərv\ *vb* **con·served; con·serv·ing** : to keep from losing or wasting : PRESERVE
²**con·serve** \ˈkän-ˌsərv\ *n* **1** : CONFECTION **2**; *esp* : a candied fruit **2** : PRESERVE; *esp* : one prepared from a mixture of fruits
con·sid·er \kən-ˈsi-dər\ *vb* [ME, fr. AF *considerer*, fr. L *considerare* to observe, think about, fr. *com-* together + *sider-, sidus* heavenly body] **1** : THINK, PONDER **2** : HEED, REGARD **3** : JUDGE, BELIEVE — **con·sid·ered** *adj*
con·sid·er·able \-ˈsi-dər-ə-bəl, -ˈsi-drə-bəl\ *adj* **1** : IMPORTANT **2** : large in extent, amount, or degree — **con·sid·er·ably** \-blē\ *adv*
con·sid·er·ate \kən-ˈsi-də-rət\ *adj* : observant of the rights and feelings of others ✦ *Synonyms* THOUGHTFUL, ATTENTIVE
con·sid·er·ation \kən-ˌsi-də-ˈrā-shən\ *n* **1** : careful thought : DELIBERATION **2** : a matter taken into account **3** : thoughtful attention **4** : JUDGMENT, OPINION **5** : RECOMPENSE
con·sid·er·ing \-ˈsi-d(ə-)riŋ\ *prep* : in view of : taking into account ⟨did well ∼ his limitations⟩
con·sign \kən-ˈsīn\ *vb* **1** : ENTRUST, COMMIT **2** : to deliver formally **3** : to send (goods) to an agent for sale — **con·sign·ee** \ˌkän-sə-ˈnē, -ˌsī-; kən-ˌsī-\ *n* — **con·sign·or** \ˌkän-sə-ˈnȯr, -ˌsī-; kən-ˌsī-\ *n*
con·sign·ment \kən-ˈsīn-mənt\ *n* : something consigned esp. in a single shipment
con·sil·ience \kən-ˈsil-yəns\ *n* : the linking together of principles from different disciplines when forming a comprehensive theory
con·sist \kən-ˈsist\ *vb* **1** : to be inherent : LIE — usu. used with *in* **2** : to be composed or made up — usu. used with *of*
con·sis·tence \kən-ˈsis-təns\ *n* : CONSISTENCY
con·sis·ten·cy \-tən-sē\ *n, pl* **-cies** **1** : COHESIVENESS, FIRMNESS **2** : agreement or harmony in parts or of different things **3** : UNIFORMITY ⟨∼ of behavior⟩ — **con·sis·tent** \-tənt\ *adj* — **con·sis·tent·ly** *adv*
con·sis·to·ry \kən-ˈsis-tə-rē\ *n, pl* **-ries** : a solemn assembly (as of Roman Catholic cardinals)
consol *abbr* consolidated
¹**con·sole** \ˈkän-ˌsōl\ *n* [F] **1** : the desklike part of an organ at which the organist sits **2** : the combination of displays and controls of a device or system **3** : a cabinet for a radio or television set resting directly on the floor **4** : a small storage cabinet between bucket seats in an automobile
²**con·sole** \kən-ˈsōl\ *vb* **con·soled; con·sol·ing** : to soothe the grief of : COMFORT, SOLACE — **con·so·la·tion** \ˌkän-sə-ˈlā-shən\ *n* — **con·so·la·to·ry** \kən-ˈsō-lə-ˌtȯr-ē, -ˈsä-\ *adj*
con·sol·i·date \kən-ˈsä-lə-ˌdāt\ *vb* **-dat·ed; -dat·ing** **1** : to unite or become united into one whole : COMBINE **2** : to make firm or secure **3** : to form into a compact mass — **con·sol·i·da·tion** \-ˌsä-lə-ˈdā-shən\ *n* — **con·sol·i·da·tor** \-ˈsä-lə-ˌdā-tər\ *n*
con·som·mé \ˌkän-sə-ˈmā\ *n* [F] : a clear soup made from well-seasoned stock
con·so·nance \ˈkän-sə-nəns\ *n* **1** : AGREEMENT, HARMONY **2** : repetition of consonants esp. as an alternative to rhyme in verse
¹**con·so·nant** \-nənt\ *adj* : having consonance, harmony, or agreement ✦ *Synonyms* CONSISTENT, COMPATIBLE, CONGRUOUS, CONGENIAL, SYMPATHETIC — **con·so·nant·ly** *adv*
²**consonant** *n* **1** : a speech sound (as \p\, \g\, \n\, \l\, \s\, \r\) characterized by constriction or closure at one or more points in the breath channel **2** : a letter other than *a, e, i, o,* and *u* — **con·so·nan·tal** \ˌkän-sə-ˈnan-tᵊl\ *adj*
¹**con·sort** \ˈkän-ˌsȯrt\ *n* **1** : a ship accompanying another **2** : SPOUSE, MATE
²**con·sort** \kən-ˈsȯrt\ *vb* **1** : to keep company **2** : ACCORD, HARMONIZE
con·sor·tium \kən-ˈsȯr-shəm, -shē-əm, -tē-\ *n, pl* **-sor·tia** \-shə-; -shē-ə, -tē-\ [L, fellowship] : an agreement or combination (as of companies) formed to undertake a large enterprise
con·spec·tus \kən-ˈspek-təs\ *n* **1** : a brief survey or summary **2** : SUMMARY
con·spic·u·ous \kən-ˈspi-kyə-wəs\ *adj* : attracting attention : PROMINENT, STRIKING ✦ *Synonyms* NOTICEABLE, REMARKABLE, OUTSTANDING — **con·spic·u·ous·ly** *adv*
con·spir·a·cy \kən-ˈspir-ə-sē\ *n, pl* **-cies** : an agreement among conspirators : PLOT
con·spir·a·tor \kən-ˈspir-ə-tər\ *n* : one who conspires — **con·spir·a·to·ri·al** \-ˌspir-ə-ˈtȯr-ē-əl\ *adj*
con·spire \kən-ˈspī(-ə)r\ *vb* **conspired; con·spir·ing** [ME, fr. AF *conspirer*, fr. L *conspirare* to be in harmony, conspire, fr. *com-* together + *spirare* to breathe] : to plan secretly an unlawful act : PLOT
const *abbr* **1** constant **2** constitution; constitutional
con·sta·ble \ˈkän-stə-bəl, ˈkən-\ *n* [ME *conestable*, fr. AF, fr. LL *comes stabuli*, lit., officer of the stable] : a public officer responsible for keeping the peace
con·stab·u·lary \kən-ˈsta-byə-ˌler-ē\ *n, pl* **-lar·ies** **1** : the police of a particular district or country **2** : a police force organized like the military
con·stan·cy \ˈkän-stən-sē\ *n, pl* **-cies** **1** : firmness of mind **2** : STABILITY
¹**con·stant** \-stənt\ *adj* **1** : STEADFAST, FAITHFUL **2** : FIXED, UNCHANGING ⟨a ∼ flow⟩ **3** : continually recurring : REGULAR ⟨a ∼ annoyance⟩ — **con·stant·ly** *adv*
²**constant** *n* : something unchanging
con·stel·la·tion \ˌkän-stə-ˈlā-shən\ *n* **1** : any of 88 groups of stars forming patterns **2** : a group of usu. related persons, qualities, or things
con·ster·na·tion \ˌkän-stər-ˈnā-shən\ *n* : amazed dismay and confusion
con·sti·pa·tion \ˌkän-stə-ˈpā-shən\ *n* : abnormally difficult or infrequent bowel movements — **con·sti·pate** \ˈkän-stə-ˌpāt\ *vb*
con·stit·u·en·cy \kən-ˈsti-chə-wən-sē\ *n, pl* **-cies** : a body of constituents; *also* : an electoral district
¹**con·stit·u·ent** \-wənt\ *n* **1** : a person entitled to vote for a representative for a district **2** : a component part
²**constituent** *adj* **1** : COMPONENT ⟨∼ parts⟩ **2** : having

power to create a government or frame or amend a constitution

con·sti·tute \'kän-stə-ˌtüt, -ˌtyüt\ *vb* **-tut·ed; -tut·ing** **1** : to appoint to an office or duty **2** : SET UP, ESTABLISH ⟨∼ a law⟩ **3** : MAKE UP, COMPOSE

con·sti·tu·tion \ˌkän-stə-'tü-shən, -'tyü-\ *n* **1** : an established law or custom **2** : the physical makeup of the individual **3** : the structure, composition, or makeup of something ⟨∼ of the sun⟩ **4** : the basic law in a politically organized body; *also* : a document containing such law

¹**con·sti·tu·tion·al** \-shə-nəl\ *adj* **1** : of or relating to the constitution of body or mind **2** : being in accord with the constitution of a state or society; *also* : of or relating to such a constitution — **con·sti·tu·tion·al·ly** *adv*

²**constitutional** *n* : an exercise (as a walk) taken for one's health

con·sti·tu·tion·al·i·ty \-ˌtü-shə-'na-lə-tē, -ˌtyü-\ *n* : the quality or state of being constitutional

con·sti·tu·tive \'kän-stə-ˌtü-tiv, -ˌtyü-, kən-'sti-chə-tiv\ *adj* **1** : CONSTRUCTIVE **2** : CONSTITUENT, ESSENTIAL

constr *abbr* construction

con·strain \kən-'strān\ *vb* **1** : COMPEL, FORCE **2** : CONFINE **3** : RESTRAIN

con·straint \-'strānt\ *n* **1** : COMPULSION; *also* : RESTRAINT **2** : repression of one's natural feelings

con·strict \-'strikt\ *vb* : to draw together : SQUEEZE — **con·stric·tion** \-'strik-shən\ *n* — **con·stric·tive** \-'strik-tiv\ *adj*

con·stric·tor \kən-'strik-tər\ *n* : a snake that coils around and compresses its prey

con·struct \kən-'strəkt\ *vb* : BUILD, MAKE — **con·struc·tor** \-'strək-tər\ *n*

con·struc·tion \kən-'strək-shən\ *n* **1** : INTERPRETATION **2** : the art, process, or manner of building; *also* : something built, created, or established : STRUCTURE **3** : syntactical arrangement of words in a sentence — **con·struc·tive** \-tiv\ *adj*

con·struc·tion·ist \-shə-nist\ *n* : a person who construes a legal document (as the U.S. Constitution) in a specific way ⟨a strict ∼⟩

con·strue \kən-'strü\ *vb* **con·strued; con·stru·ing 1** : to analyze the mutual relations of words in a sentence; *also* : TRANSLATE **2** : EXPLAIN, INTERPRET — **con·stru·able** *adj* — **con·stru·al** \-'strü-əl\ *n*

con·sub·stan·ti·a·tion \ˌkän-səb-ˌstan-chē-'ā-shən\ *n* : the actual substantial presence and combination of the body and blood of Christ with the eucharistic bread and wine

con·sul \'kän-səl\ *n* **1** : a chief magistrate of the Roman republic **2** : an official appointed by a government to reside in a foreign country to care for the commercial interests of the appointing government's citizens — **con·sul·ar** \-s-lər\ *adj* — **con·sul·ate** \-lət\ *n* — **con·sul·ship** *n*

con·sult \kən-'səlt\ *vb* **1** : to ask the advice or opinion of **2** : CONFER — **con·sul·tant** \-'səl-t³nt\ *n* — **con·sul·ta·tion** \ˌkän-səl-'tä-shən\ *n*

con·sume \kən-'süm\ *vb* **con·sumed; con·sum·ing 1** : DESTROY ⟨*consumed* by fire⟩ **2** : to spend wastefully **3** : to eat up : DEVOUR **4** : to absorb the attention of : ENGROSS — **con·sum·able** *adj* — **con·sum·er** *n*

con·sum·er·ism \kən-'sü-mə-ˌri-zəm\ *n* : the promotion of consumers' interests (as against false advertising)

consumer price index *n* : an index measuring the change in the cost of widely purchased goods and services from the cost in some base period

¹**con·sum·mate** \'kän-sə-mət, kən-'sə\ *adj* : PERFECT ⟨a ∼ team player⟩ ♦ **Synonyms** FINISHED, ACCOMPLISHED

²**con·sum·mate** \'kän-sə-ˌmāt\ *vb* **-mat·ed; -mat·ing** : to make complete : FINISH, ACHIEVE — **con·sum·ma·tion** \ˌkän-sə-'mā-shən\ *n*

con·sump·tion \kən-'səmp-shən\ *n* **1** : progressive bodily wasting away; *also* : TUBERCULOSIS **2** : the act of consuming or using up **3** : the use of economic goods

¹**con·sump·tive** \-'səmp-tiv\ *adj* **1** : tending to consume **2** : relating to or affected with consumption

²**consumptive** *n* : a person who has consumption

cont *abbr* **1** containing **2** contents **3** continent; continental **4** continued **5** control

¹**con·tact** \'kän-ˌtakt\ *n* **1** : a touching or meeting of bodies **2** : ASSOCIATION, RELATIONSHIP; *also* : CONNECTION,

COMMUNICATION **3** : a person serving as a go-between or source of information **4** : CONTACT LENS

²**contact** *vb* **1** : to come or bring into contact : TOUCH **2** : to get in communication with

contact lens *n* : a thin lens fitting over the cornea usu. to correct vision

con·ta·gion \kən-'tā-jən\ *n* [ME, fr. L *contagio*, fr. *contingere* to have contact with, pollute, fr. *com-* together + *tangere* to touch] **1** : a contagious disease; *also* : the transmission of such a disease **2** : a disease-producing agent (as a virus) **3** : transmission of an influence on the mind or emotions

con·ta·gious \-jəs\ *adj* **1** : able to be passed by contact between individuals ⟨colds are ∼⟩ ⟨∼ disease⟩; *also* : capable of passing on a contagious disease **2** : communicated or transmitted like a contagious disease; *esp* : exciting similar emotion or conduct in others

con·tain \kən-'tān\ *vb* **1** : RESTRAIN **2** : to have within : HOLD **3** : COMPRISE, INCLUDE — **con·tain·able** \-'tā-nə-bəl\ *adj* — **con·tain·ment** \-'tān-mənt\ *n*

con·tain·er \kən-'tā-nər\ *n* : RECEPTACLE

con·tam·i·nant \kən-'ta-mə-nənt\ *n* : something that contaminates

con·tam·i·nate \kən-'ta-mə-ˌnāt\ *vb* **-nat·ed; -nat·ing** : to soil, stain, or infect by contact or association — **con·tam·i·na·tion** \-ˌta-mə-'nā-shən\ *n*

contd *abbr* continued

con·temn \kən-'tem\ *vb* : to view or treat with contempt : DESPISE

con·tem·plate \'kän-təm-ˌplāt\ *vb* **-plat·ed; -plat·ing** [L *contemplari*, fr. *com-* with + *templum* space marked out for observation of auguries] **1** : to view or consider with continued attention **2** : INTEND — **con·tem·pla·tion** \ˌkän-təm-'plā-shən\ *n* — **con·tem·pla·tive** \kən-'tem-plə-tiv, 'kän-təm-ˌplā-\ *adj*

con·tem·po·ra·ne·ous \kən-ˌtem-pə-'rā-nē-əs\ *adj* : CONTEMPORARY 1

con·tem·po·rary \kən-'tem-pə-ˌrer-ē\ *adj* **1** : occurring or existing at the same time **2** : marked by characteristics of the present period — **contemporary** *n*

con·tempt \kən-'tempt\ *n* **1** : the act of despising : the state of mind of one who despises **2** : the state of being despised **3** : disobedience to or open disrespect of a court or legislature

con·tempt·ible \kən-'temp-tə-bəl\ *adj* : deserving contempt : DESPICABLE — **con·tempt·ibly** \-blē\ *adv*

con·temp·tu·ous \-'temp-chə-wəs\ *adj* : feeling or expressing contempt — **con·temp·tu·ous·ly** *adv*

con·tend \kən-'tend\ *vb* **1** : to strive against rivals or difficulties **2** : ARGUE **3** : MAINTAIN, ASSERT — **con·tend·er** *n*

¹**con·tent** \kən-'tent\ *adj* : SATISFIED

²**content** *vb* : SATISFY; *esp* : to limit (oneself) in requirements or actions

³**content** *n* : CONTENTMENT ⟨ate to his heart's ∼⟩

⁴**con·tent** \'kän-ˌtent\ *n* **1** : something contained ⟨∼s of a room⟩ **2** : subject matter or topics treated (as in a book) **3** : material (as text or music) offered by a Web site **4** : MEANING, SIGNIFICANCE **5** : the amount of material contained

con·tent·ed \kən-'ten-təd\ *adj* : SATISFIED — **con·tent·ed·ly** *adv* — **con·tent·ed·ness** *n*

con·ten·tion \kən-'ten-chən\ *n* **1** : CONTEST, STRIFE **2** : an idea or point for which a person argues — **con·ten·tious** \-chəs\ *adj* — **con·ten·tious·ly** *adv*

con·tent·ment \kən-'tent-mənt\ *n* : ease of mind : SATISFACTION

con·ter·mi·nous \kän-'tər-mə-nəs\ *adj* : having the same or a common boundary — **con·ter·mi·nous·ly** *adv*

¹**con·test** \kən-'test\ *vb* **1** : to engage in a struggle or competition : COMPETE, VIE **2** : CHALLENGE, DISPUTE ⟨∼ the accusations⟩ — **con·tes·tant** \-'tes-tənt\ *n*

²**con·test** \'kän-ˌtest\ *n* : STRUGGLE, COMPETITION

con·text \'kän-ˌtekst\ *n* [ME, fr. L *contextus* connection of words, coherence, fr. *contexere* to weave together] : the parts of a discourse that surround a word or passage and help to explain its meaning; *also* : the circumstances surrounding an act or event ⟨the ∼ of the war⟩ — **con·tex·tu·al·ly** *adv*

con·tig·u·ous \kən-'ti-gyə-wəs\ *adj* : being in contact

: TOUCHING; *also* : NEXT, ADJOINING — **con·ti·gu·i·ty** \ˌkän-tə-ˈgyü-ə-tē\ *n*

con·ti·nence \ˈkän-tə-nəns\ *n* 1 : SELF-RESTRAINT; *esp* : a refraining from sexual intercourse 2 : the ability to retain urine or feces voluntarily

¹**con·ti·nent** \ˈkän-tə-nənt\ *adj* : exercising continence

²**continent** *n* 1 : any of the great divisions of land on the globe 2 *cap* : the continent of Europe

¹**con·ti·nen·tal** \ˌkän-tə-ˈnen-tᵊl\ *adj* 1 : of or relating to a continent; *esp, often cap* : of or relating to the continent of Europe 2 *often cap* : of or relating to the colonies later forming the U.S. 3 : of or relating to cuisine based on classical European cooking

²**continental** *n* 1 *often cap* : a soldier in the Continental army 2 : EUROPEAN

continental drift *n* : a slow movement of the continents over a fluid layer deep within the earth

continental shelf *n* : a shallow submarine plain forming a border to a continent

continental slope *n* : a comparatively steep slope from a continental shelf to the ocean floor

con·tin·gen·cy \kən-ˈtin-jən-sē\ *n, pl* **-cies** : a chance or possible event

¹**con·tin·gent** \-jənt\ *adj* 1 : liable but not certain to happen : POSSIBLE 2 : happening by chance : not planned 3 : dependent on something that may or may not occur 4 : CONDITIONAL ♦ **Synonyms** ACCIDENTAL, CASUAL, INCIDENTAL, ODD

²**contingent** *n* : a quota (as of troops) supplied from an area or group

con·tin·u·al \kən-ˈtin-yə-wəl\ *adj* 1 : CONTINUOUS, UNBROKEN 2 : steadily recurring — **con·tin·u·al·ly** *adv*

con·tin·u·ance \-yə-wəns\ *n* 1 : unbroken succession 2 : the extent of continuing : DURATION 3 : adjournment of legal proceedings

con·tin·u·a·tion \kən-ˌtin-yə-ˈwā-shən\ *n* 1 : extension or prolongation of a state or activity 2 : resumption after an interruption; *also* : something that carries on after a pause or break

con·tin·ue \kən-ˈtin-yü\ *vb* **-tin·ued; -tinu·ing** 1 : to maintain without interruption 2 : ENDURE, LAST ⟨the tradition ~s⟩ 3 : to remain in a place or condition ⟨~ at this job⟩ 4 : to resume (as a story) after an intermission 5 : EXTEND ⟨~ a subscription⟩; *also* : to persist in ⟨will ~ to remind you⟩ 6 : to allow to remain 7 : to keep (a legal case) on the calendar or undecided

con·ti·nu·i·ty \ˌkän-tə-ˈnü-ə-tē, -ˈnyü-\ *n, pl* **-ties** 1 : the state of being continuous 2 : something (as a film script) that has or provides continuity

con·tin·u·ous \kən-ˈtin-yə-wəs\ *adj* : continuing without interruption — **con·tin·u·ous·ly** *adv*

con·tin·u·um \-yə-wəm\ *n, pl* **-ua** \-yə-wə\ *also* **-uums** : something that is the same throughout or consists of a series of variations or of a sequence of things in regular order

con·tort \kən-ˈtȯrt\ *vb* : to twist out of shape ⟨a ~ed face⟩ ⟨~ the truth⟩ — **con·tor·tion** \-ˈtȯr-shən\ *n*

con·tor·tion·ist \-ˈtȯr-shə-nist\ *n* : an acrobat able to twist the body into unusual postures

con·tour \ˈkän-ˌtu̇r\ *n* [F, fr. It *contorno* fr. *contornare* to round off, fr. ML, to turn around, fr. L *com-* together + *tornare* to turn on a lathe, fr. *tornus* lathe] 1 : OUTLINE 2 : SHAPE, FORM — often used in pl. ⟨the ~s of a statue⟩

contr *abbr* contract; contraction

con·tra·band \ˈkän-trə-ˌband\ *n* : goods legally prohibited in trade; *also* : smuggled goods

con·tra·cep·tion \ˌkän-trə-ˈsep-shən\ *n* : intentional prevention of conception and pregnancy — **con·tra·cep·tive** \-ˈsep-tiv\ *adj or n*

¹**con·tract** \ˈkän-ˌtrakt\ *n* 1 : a binding agreement; *also* : a document stating its terms 2 : an undertaking to win a specified number of tricks in bridge — **contract** *adj* — **con·trac·tu·al** \kən-ˈtrak-chə-wəl\ *adj* — **con·trac·tu·al·ly** *adv*

²**con·tract** \kən-ˈtrakt, 2 *usu* ˈkän-ˌtrakt\ *vb* 1 : to become affected with ⟨~ a disease⟩ 2 : to establish or undertake by contract 3 : SHRINK, LESSEN; *esp* : to draw together esp. so as to shorten ⟨~ a muscle⟩ 4 : to shorten (a word) by omitting letters or sounds in the middle — **con·tract·ible** \kən-ˈtrak-tə-bəl, ˈkän-ˌ\ *adj* — **con·trac·tion** \kən-ˈtrak-shən\ *n* — **con·trac·tor** \ˈkän-ˌtrak-tər, kən-ˈtrak-\ *n*

con·trac·tile \kən-ˈtrak-tᵊl\ *adj* : able to contract — **con·trac·til·i·ty** \ˌkän-ˌtrak-ˈti-lə-tē\ *n*

con·tra·dict \ˌkän-trə-ˈdikt\ *vb* : to assert the contrary of : deny the truth of ⟨~ a rumor⟩ — **con·tra·dic·tion** \-ˈdik-shən\ *n* — **con·tra·dic·to·ry** \-ˈdik-tə-rē\ *adj*

con·tra·dis·tinc·tion \ˌkän-trə-dis-ˈtiŋk-shən\ *n* : distinction by contrast

con·trail \ˈkän-ˌtrāl\ *n* : a streak of condensed water vapor created by an airplane or rocket at high altitudes

con·tra·in·di·cate \ˌkän-trə-ˈin-də-ˌkāt\ *vb* : to make (a treatment or procedure) inadvisable — **con·tra·in·di·ca·tion** \-ˌin-də-ˈkā-shən\ *n*

con·tral·to \kən-ˈtral-tō\ *n, pl* **-tos** : the lowest female voice; *also* : a singer having such a voice

con·trap·tion \kən-ˈtrap-shən\ *n* : CONTRIVANCE, DEVICE

con·tra·pun·tal \ˌkän-trə-ˈpən-tᵊl\ *adj* : of or relating to counterpoint

con·tra·ri·ety \ˌkän-trə-ˈrī-ə-tē\ *n, pl* **-eties** : the state of being contrary : DISAGREEMENT, INCONSISTENCY

con·trari·wise \ˈkän-ˌtrer-ē-ˌwīz, kən-ˈtrer-\ *adv* 1 : on the contrary 2 : VICE VERSA

con·trary \ˈkän-ˌtrer-ē; 4 *often* kən-ˈtrer-ē\ *adj* 1 : opposite in nature or position 2 : COUNTER, OPPOSED 3 : UNFAVORABLE — used of wind or weather 4 : unwilling to accept control or advice — **con·trar·i·an** \kən-ˈtrer-ē-ən, kän-\ *n or adj* — **con·trari·ly** \ˈkän-ˌtrer-ə-lē, kən-ˈtrer-\ *adv* — **con·trary** \in *n is* ˈkän-ˌtrer-ē, *adv is like adj*\ *n or adv*

¹**con·trast** \kən-ˈtrast\ *vb* [F *contraster*, fr. MF, to oppose, resist, fr. VL **contrastare*, fr. L *contra-* against + *stare* to stand] 1 : to show differences when compared 2 : to compare in such a way as to show differences

²**con·trast** \ˈkän-ˌtrast\ *n* 1 : diversity of adjacent parts in color, emotion, tone, or brightness ⟨the ~ of a photograph⟩ 2 : unlikeness as shown when things are compared : DIFFERENCE

con·tra·vene \ˌkän-trə-ˈvēn\ *vb* **-vened; -ven·ing** 1 : to go or act contrary to ⟨~ a law⟩ 2 : CONTRADICT ⟨~ a claim⟩

con·tre·temps \ˈkän-trə-ˌtäⁿ, kōⁿ-trə-ˈtäⁿ\ *n, pl* **con·tre·temps** \-ˌtäⁿ, -ˌtäⁿz\ [F] : an inopportune or embarrassing occurrence

contrib *abbr* contribution; contributor

con·trib·ute \kən-ˈtri-byət\ *vb* **-ut·ed; -ut·ing** : to give along with others (as to a fund); *also* : HELP, ASSIST — **con·tri·bu·tion** \ˌkän-trə-ˈbyü-shən\ *n* — **con·trib·u·tor** \kən-ˈtri-byə-tər\ *n* — **con·trib·u·to·ry** \-byə-ˌtȯr-ē\ *adj*

con·trite \ˈkän-ˌtrīt, kən-ˈtrīt\ *adj* : PENITENT, REPENTANT — **con·trite·ly** *adv* — **con·tri·tion** \kən-ˈtri-shən\ *n*

con·triv·ance \kən-ˈtrī-vəns\ *n* 1 : a mechanical device 2 : SCHEME, PLAN

con·trive \kən-ˈtrīv\ *vb* **con·trived; con·triv·ing** 1 : PLAN, DEVISE 2 : FRAME, MAKE 3 : to bring about with difficulty — **con·triv·er** *n*

con·trived \-ˈtrīvd\ *adj* : lacking in natural quality ⟨a ~ plot⟩

¹**con·trol** \kən-ˈtrōl\ *vb* **con·trolled; con·trol·ling** [ME *controllen* to verify, fr. AF *countrerouler*, fr. *countreroule* copy of an account, audit, fr. ML *contrarotulus*, fr. L *contra* against + ML *rotulus* roll] 1 : to exercise restraining or directing influence over : REGULATE 2 : DOMINATE, RULE — **con·trol·la·ble** \-ˈtrō-lə-bəl\ *adj*

²**control** *n* 1 : power to direct or regulate 2 : RESERVE, RESTRAINT 3 : a device for regulating a mechanism

con·trol·ler \kən-ˈtrō-lər, ˈkän-ˌtrō-lər\ *n* 1 : COMPTROLLER 2 : a person or thing that controls ⟨an air traffic ~⟩ ⟨a game ~⟩

con·tro·ver·sy \ˈkän-trə-ˌvər-sē\ *n, pl* **-sies** : a clash of opposing views : DISPUTE — **con·tro·ver·sial** \ˌkän-trə-ˌvər-shəl, -sē-əl\ *adj*

con·tro·vert \ˈkän-trə-ˌvərt, ˌkän-trə-ˈvərt\ *vb* : DENY, CONTRADICT — **con·tro·vert·ible** *adj*

con·tu·ma·cious \ˌkän-tü-ˈmā-shəs, -tyü-\ *adj* : stubbornly disobedient ♦ **Synonyms** REBELLIOUS, INSUBORDINATE, SEDITIOUS — **con·tu·ma·cy** \kən-ˈtü-mə-sē, -ˈtyü-; ˈkän-tyə-\ *n* — **con·tu·ma·cious·ly** *adv*

con·tu·me·ly \kän-ˈtü-mə-lē, -ˈtyü-; ˈkän-tu̇-mē-lē, -tyə-\ *n, pl* **-lies** : contemptuous treatment : INSULT

con·tu·sion \kən-ˈtü-zhən, -ˈtyü-\ *n* : BRUISE — **con·tuse** \-ˈtüz, -ˈtyüz\ *vb*

co·nun·drum \kə-ˈnən-drəm\ *n* : RIDDLE

conv *abbr* **1** convention **2** convertible

con·va·lesce \ˌkän-və-ˈles\ *vb* **-lesced; -lesc·ing :** to recover health gradually — **con·va·les·cence** \-ˈle-sᵊns\ *n* — **con·va·les·cent** \-sᵊnt\ *adj or n*

con·vec·tion \kən-ˈvek-shən\ *n* **:** circulatory motion in a fluid due to warmer portions rising and cooler denser portions sinking; *also* **:** the transfer of heat by such motion — **con·vec·tion·al** \-shə-nəl\ *adj* — **con·vec·tive** \-ˈvek-tiv\ *adj*

convection oven *n* **:** an oven with a fan that circulates hot air uniformly and continuously around the food

con·vene \kən-ˈvēn\ *vb* **con·vened; con·ven·ing :** ASSEMBLE, MEET

con·ve·nience \kən-ˈvē-nyəns\ *n* **1 :** SUITABLENESS **2 :** a laborsaving device **3 :** a suitable time ⟨at your ∼⟩ **4 :** personal comfort **:** EASE

convenience store *n* **:** a small market that is open long hours

con·ve·nient \-nyənt\ *adj* **1 :** suited to personal comfort or ease **2 :** placed near at hand — **con·ve·nient·ly** *adv*

con·vent \ˈkän-vənt, -ˌvent\ *n* [ME *covent*, fr. AF, fr. ML *conventus*, fr. L, assembly, fr. *convenire* to come together] **:** a local community or house of a religious order esp. of nuns — **con·ven·tu·al** \kän-ˈven-chə-wəl\ *adj*

con·ven·ti·cle \kən-ˈven-ti-kəl\ *n* **:** MEETING; *esp* **:** a secret meeting for worship

con·ven·tion \kən-ˈven-chən\ *n* **1 :** an agreement esp. between states on a matter of common concern **2 :** MEETING, ASSEMBLY **3 :** an assembly of persons convened for some purpose **4 :** generally accepted custom, practice, or belief

con·ven·tion·al \-chə-nəl\ *adj* **1 :** sanctioned by general custom **2 :** COMMONPLACE, ORDINARY — **con·ven·tion·al·i·ty** \-ˌven-chə-ˈna-lə-tē\ *n* — **con·ven·tion·al·ize** \-ˈven-chə-nə-ˌlīz\ *vb* — **con·ven·tion·al·ly** *adv*

con·verge \kən-ˈvərj\ *vb* **con·verged; con·verg·ing :** to approach one common center or single point ⟨*converging* paths⟩ — **con·ver·gence** \kən-ˈvər-jəns\ *n* — **con·ver·gent** \-jənt\ *adj*

con·ver·sant \kən-ˈvər-sᵊnt\ *adj* **:** having knowledge and experience — used with *with*

con·ver·sa·tion \ˌkän-vər-ˈsā-shən\ *n* **:** an informal talking together — **con·ver·sa·tion·al** \-shə-nᵊl\ *adj* — **con·ver·sa·tion·al·ly** *adv*

con·ver·sa·tion·al·ist \-shə-nᵊl-ist\ *n* **:** a person who converses a great deal or who excels in conversation

¹con·verse \ˈkän-ˌvərs\ *n* **:** CONVERSATION

²con·verse \kən-ˈvərs\ *vb* **con·versed; con·vers·ing :** to engage in conversation

³con·verse \ˈkän-ˌvərs\ *n* **:** a statement related to another statement by having its hypothesis and conclusion or its subject and predicate reversed or interchanged

⁴con·verse \kən-ˈvərs, ˈkän-ˌvers\ *adj* **:** reversed in order or relation — **con·verse·ly** *adv*

con·ver·sion \kən-ˈvər-zhən\ *n* **1 :** a change in nature or form **2 :** an experience associated with a decisive adoption of religion

¹con·vert \kən-ˈvərt\ *vb* **1 :** to turn from one belief or party to another **2 :** TRANSFORM, CHANGE **3 :** MISAPPROPRIATE **4 :** EXCHANGE — **con·vert·er** *or* **con·ver·tor** \-ˈvər-tər\ *n*

²con·vert \ˈkän-ˌvərt\ *n* **:** a person who has undergone religious conversion

¹con·vert·ible \kən-ˈvər-tə-bəl\ *adj* **:** capable of being converted

²convertible *n* **:** an automobile with a top that may be lowered or removed

con·vex \kän-ˈveks, ˈkän-ˌveks\ *adj* **:** curved or rounded outward like the exterior of a sphere or circle — **con·vex·i·ty** \kän-ˈvek-sə-tē\ *n*

con·vey \kən-ˈvā\ *vb* **1 :** CARRY, TRANSPORT ⟨a river ∼*ing* logs⟩ **2 :** TRANSFER, COMMUNICATE ⟨∼ a message⟩ — **con·vey·or** *also* **con·vey·er** \-ər\ *n*

con·vey·ance \-ˈvā-əns\ *n* **1 :** the act of conveying **2 :** a legal paper transferring ownership of property **3 :** VEHICLE

¹con·vict \kən-ˈvikt\ *vb* **:** to prove or find guilty

²con·vict \ˈkän-ˌvikt\ *n* **:** a person serving a prison sentence

con·vic·tion \kən-ˈvik-shən\ *n* **1 :** the act of convicting esp. in a court **2 :** the state of being convinced **:** BELIEF

con·vince \kən-ˈvins\ *vb* **con·vinced; con·vinc·ing :** to

bring (as by argument) to belief or action — **con·vinc·ing** *adj* — **con·vinc·ing·ly** *adv*

con·viv·ial \kən-ˈvi-vē-əl\ *adj* [LL *convivialis*, fr. L *convivium* banquet, fr. *com-* together + *vivere* to live] **:** enjoying companionship and the pleasures of feasting and drinking **:** JOVIAL, FESTIVE — **con·viv·i·al·i·ty** \-ˌvi-vē-ˈa-lə-tē\ *n* — **con·viv·ial·ly** *adv*

con·vo·ca·tion \ˌkän-və-ˈkā-shən\ *n* **1 :** a ceremonial assembly (as of the clergy) **2 :** the act of convoking

con·voke \kən-ˈvōk\ *vb* **con·voked; con·vok·ing :** to call together to a meeting

con·vo·lut·ed \ˈkän-və-ˌlü-təd\ *adj* **1 :** folded in curved or tortuous windings **2 :** INVOLVED, INTRICATE

con·vo·lu·tion \ˌkän-və-ˈlü-shən\ *n* **:** a tortuous or winding structure; *esp* **:** one of the ridges of the brain

¹con·voy \ˈkän-ˌvȯi, kən-ˈvȯi\ *vb* **:** to accompany for protection

²con·voy \ˈkän-ˌvȯi\ *n* **1 :** one that convoys; *esp* **:** a protective escort (as for ships) **2 :** the act of convoying **3 :** a group of moving vehicles

con·vulse \kən-ˈvəls\ *vb* **con·vulsed; con·vuls·ing :** to agitate violently

con·vul·sion \kən-ˈvəl-shən\ *n* **1 :** an abnormal and violent involuntary contraction or series of contractions of muscle **2 :** a violent disturbance — **con·vul·sive** \-siv\ *adj* — **con·vul·sive·ly** *adv*

cony *var of* CONEY

coo \ˈkü\ *n* **:** a soft low sound made by doves or pigeons; *also* **:** a sound like this — **coo** *vb*

COO *abbr* chief operating officer

¹cook \ˈkůk\ *n* **:** a person who prepares food for eating

²cook *vb* **1 :** to prepare food for eating **2 :** to subject to heat or fire **3 :** CONCOCT, FABRICATE — usu. used with *up* ⟨∼ up a scheme⟩ — **cook·er** *n* — **cook·ware** \-ˌwer\ *n*

cook·book \-ˌbůk\ *n* **:** a book of cooking directions and recipes

cook·ery \ˈků-kə-rē\ *n, pl* **-er·ies :** the art or practice of cooking

cook·ie *or* **cooky** \ˈků-kē\ *n, pl* **cook·ies** [D *koekje*, dim. of *koek* cake] **1 :** a small sweet flat cake **2** *cookie* **:** a file containing information about a Web site user created and read by a Web site server and stored on the user's computer

cookie–cutter *adj* **:** marked by a lack of originality or distinction ⟨∼ malls⟩

cook·out \ˈkůk-ˌaůt\ *n* **:** an outing at which a meal is cooked and served in the open

¹cool \ˈkül\ *adj* **1 :** moderately cold **2 :** not excited **:** CALM **3 :** not friendly **4 :** IMPUDENT **5 :** protecting from heat **6** *slang* **:** very good **7** *slang* **:** FASHIONABLE **✦ Synonyms** UNFLAPPABLE, COMPOSED, COLLECTED, UNRUFFLED, NONCHALANT — **cool·ly** *adv* — **cool·ness** *n*

²cool *vb* **:** to make or become cool

³cool *n* **1 :** a cool time or place **2 :** INDIFFERENCE; *also* **:** SELF-ASSURANCE, COMPOSURE ⟨kept his ∼⟩

cool·ant \ˈkü-lənt\ *n* **:** a usu. fluid cooling agent

cool·er \ˈkü-lər\ *n* **1 :** a container for keeping food or drink cool **2 :** JAIL, PRISON **3 :** a tall iced drink

coo·lie \ˈkü-lē\ *n* [Hindi & Urdu *qulī*] **:** an unskilled laborer usu. in or from the Far East

coon \ˈkün\ *n* **:** RACCOON

coon·hound \-ˌhaůnd\ *n* **:** a sporting dog trained to hunt raccoons

coon·skin \-ˌskin\ *n* **:** the pelt of a raccoon; *also* **:** something (as a cap) made of this

¹coop \ˈküp, ˈkůp\ *n* **:** a small enclosure or building usu. for poultry

²coop *vb* **:** to confine in or as if in a coop — usu. used with *up*

co–op \ˈkō-ˌäp\ *n* **:** COOPERATIVE

coo·per \ˈkü-pər, ˈků-\ *n* **:** one who makes or repairs barrels or casks — **cooper** *vb* — **coo·per·age** \-pə-rij\ *n*

co·op·er·ate \kō-ˈä-pə-ˌrāt\ *vb* **:** to act jointly or in compliance with others — **co·op·er·a·tion** \-ˌä-pə-ˈrā-shən\ *n* — **co·op·er·a·tor** \-ˈä-pə-ˌrā-tər\ *n*

¹co·op·er·a·tive \kō-ˈä-prə-tiv, -ˈä-pə-ˌrā-\ *adj* **1 :** willing to work with others **2 :** of or relating to an association formed to enable its members to buy or sell to better advantage by eliminating middlemen's profits

²**cooperative** *n* : a cooperative association

co–opt \kō-'äpt\ *vb* **1** : to choose or elect as a colleague **2** : ABSORB, ASSIMILATE; *also* : TAKE OVER ⟨a style ∼*ed* by advertisers⟩

¹**co·or·di·nate** \kō-'ȯr-də-nət\ *adj* **1** : equal in rank or order **2** : of equal rank in a compound sentence ⟨∼ clause⟩ **3** : joining words or word groups of the same rank — **co·or·di·nate·ly** *adv*

²**co·or·di·nate** \-'ȯr-də-ˌnāt\ *vb* **-nat·ed; -nat·ing 1** : to make or become coordinate ⟨∼ our schedules⟩ **2** : to work or act together harmoniously ⟨a *coordinated* wardrobe⟩ — **co·or·di·na·tion** \-ˌȯr-də-'nā-shən\ *n* — **co·or·di·na·tor** \-'ȯr-də-ˌnā-tər\ *n*

³**co·or·di·nate** \-'ȯr-də-nət\ *n* **1** : one of a set of numbers used in specifying the location of a point on a surface or in space **2** *pl* : articles (as of clothing) designed to be used together and to attain their effect through pleasing contrast

coot \'küt\ *n* **1** : a dark-colored ducklike bird related to the rails **2** : any of several No. American sea ducks **3** : a harmless simple person

coo·tie \'kü-tē\ *n* : a body louse

¹**cop** \'käp\ *n* : POLICE OFFICER

²**cop** *vb* **1** *slang* : STEAL ⟨∼ a glance⟩ **2** *slang* : ADMIT — used with *to* ⟨∼ to the charges⟩ **3** : ADOPT ⟨∼ an attitude⟩

co–pay \'kō-'pā\ *n* : CO-PAYMENT

co–pay·ment \'kō-ˌpā-mənt, ˌkō-'\ *n* : a fixed fee required of a patient by a health insurer (as an HMO) at the time of each outpatient service or filling of a prescription

¹**cope** \'kōp\ *n* : a long cloaklike ecclesiastical vestment

²**cope** *vb* **coped; cop·ing** : to struggle to overcome problems or difficulties ⟨∼ with tragedy⟩

copi·er \'kä-pē-ər\ *n* : one that copies; *esp* : a machine for making copies

co·pi·lot \'kō-ˌpī-lət\ *n* : an assistant pilot of an aircraft or spacecraft

cop·ing \'kō-piŋ\ *n* : the top layer of a wall

co·pi·ous \'kō-pē-əs\ *adj* : LAVISH, ABUNDANT ⟨a ∼ harvest⟩ — **co·pi·ous·ly** *adv* — **co·pi·ous·ness** *n*

cop–out \'käp-ˌaút\ *n* : an excuse for copping out; *also* : an act of copping out

cop out *vb* : to back out (as of an unwanted responsibility)

cop·per \'kä-pər\ *n* **1** : a malleable reddish metallic chemical element that is one of the best conductors of heat and electricity **2** : a coin or token made of copper — **cop·pery** *adj*

cop·per·head \'kä-pər-ˌhed\ *n* : a largely coppery brown pit viper esp. of the eastern and central U.S.

cop·pice \'kä-pəs\ *n* : THICKET

co·pra \'kō-prə\ *n* : dried coconut meat yielding coconut oil

copse \'käps\ *n* : THICKET

cop·ter \'käp-tər\ *n* : HELICOPTER

cop·u·la \'kä-pyə-lə\ *n* : LINKING VERB — **cop·u·la·tive** \-lə-tiv, -ˌlā-\ *adj*

cop·u·late \'kä-pyə-ˌlāt\ *vb* **-lat·ed; -lat·ing** : to engage in sexual intercourse — **cop·u·la·tion** \ˌkä-pyə-'lā-shən\ *n* — **cop·u·la·to·ry** \'kä-pyə-lə-ˌtȯr-ē\ *adj*

¹**copy** \'kä-pē\ *n, pl* **cop·ies 1** : an imitation or reproduction of an original work **2** : material to be set in type **3** : DUPLICATE ♦ *Synonyms* DUPLICATE, REPRODUCTION, FACSIMILE, REPLICA

²**copy** *vb* **cop·ied; copy·ing 1** : to make a copy of **2** : IMITATE — **copy·ist** *n*

copy·book \'kä-pē-ˌbúk\ *n* : a book formerly used to teach handwriting containing examples to be copied

copy·boy \-ˌbȯi\ *n* : a person who carries copy and runs errands (as in a newspaper office)

copy·cat \-ˌkat\ *n* : a slavish imitator

copy·desk \-ˌdesk\ *n* : the desk at which newspaper copy is edited

copy editor *n* : one who edits or prepares copy (as headlines) esp. for a newspaper

copy·read·er \-ˌrē-dər\ *n* : COPY EDITOR

¹**copy·right** \'kä-pē-ˌrīt\ *n* : the sole right to reproduce, publish, sell, or distribute a literary or artistic work

²**copyright** *vb* : to secure a copyright on

copy·writ·er \'kä-pē-ˌrī-tər\ *n* : a writer of advertising copy

co·quet *or* **co·quette** \kō-'ket\ *vb* **co·quet·ted; co·quet·ting** : FLIRT — **co·quet·ry** \'kō-kə-trē, kō-'ke-trē\ *n*

co·quette \kō-'ket\ *n* [F, fem. of *coquet*, flirtatious man, dim. of *coq* cock] : FLIRT — **co·quett·ish** *adj*

cor *abbr* corner

Cor *abbr* Corinthians

cor·a·cle \'kȯr-ə-kəl\ *n* [W *corwgl*] : a boat made of a frame covered usu. with hide or tarpaulin

cor·al \'kȯr-əl\ *n* **1** : a stony or horny material that forms the skeleton of colonies of tiny sea polyps and includes a red form used in jewelry; *also* : a coral-forming polyp or polyp colony **2** : a deep pink color — **coral** *adj*

coral snake *n* : any of several venomous chiefly tropical New World snakes brilliantly banded in red, black, and yellow or white

cor·bel \'kȯr-bəl\ *n* : a bracket-shaped architectural member that projects from a wall and supports a weight

¹**cord** \'kȯrd\ *n* **1** : a usu. heavy string consisting of several strands woven or twisted together **2** : a long slender anatomical structure (as a tendon or nerve) **3** : a small flexible insulated electrical cable used to connect an appliance with a receptacle **4** : a cubic measure used esp. for firewood and equal to a stack 4×4×8 feet **5** : a rib or ridge on cloth

²**cord** *vb* **1** : to tie or furnish with a cord **2** : to pile (wood) in cords

cord·age \'kȯr-dij\ *n* : ROPES, CORDS; *esp* : ropes in the rigging of a ship

¹**cor·dial** \'kȯr-jəl\ *adj* [ME, fr. ML *cordialis*, fr. L *cord-*, *cor* heart] : warmly receptive or welcoming : HEARTFELT, HEARTY — **cor·di·al·i·ty** \ˌkȯr-jē-'a-lə-tē, kȯr-'ja-\ *n* — **cor·dial·ly** *adv*

²**cordial** *n* **1** : a stimulating medicine or drink **2** : LIQUEUR

cor·dil·le·ra \ˌkȯr-dəl-'yer-ə, -də-'ler-\ *n* [Sp] : a series of parallel mountain ranges

cord·less \'kȯrd-ləs\ *adj* : having no cord; *esp* : powered by a battery ⟨a ∼ phone⟩ — **cord·less** *n*

cor·do·ba \'kȯr-də-bə, -və\ *n* — see MONEY table

cor·don \'kȯr-d³n\ *n* **1** : an ornamental cord or ribbon **2** : an encircling line (as of troops or police) — **cordon** *vb*

cor·do·van \'kȯr-də-vən\ *n* : a soft fine-grained leather

cor·du·roy \'kȯr-də-ˌrȯi\ *n, pl* **-roys** : a heavy ribbed fabric; *also, pl* : pants of this material

cord·wain·er \'kȯrd-ˌwā-nər\ *n* : SHOEMAKER

¹**core** \'kȯr\ *n* **1** : the central usu. inedible part of some fruits (as the apple); *also* : an inmost part of something **2** : GIST, ESSENCE

²**core** *vb* **cored; cor·ing** : to take out the core of — **cor·er** *n*

CORE \'kȯr\ *abbr* Congress of Racial Equality

co·re·op·sis \ˌkȯr-ē-'äp-səs\ *n, pl* **coreopsis** : any of a genus of widely cultivated composite herbs with showy often yellow flower heads

co·re·spon·dent \ˌkō-ri-'spän-dənt\ *n* : a person named as guilty of adultery with the defendant in a divorce suit

co·ri·an·der \'kȯr-ē-ˌan-dər\ *n* : an herb related to the carrot; *also* : its aromatic dried fruit used as a flavoring

Cor·in·thi·ans \kə-'rin-thē-ənz\ *n* — see BIBLE table

¹**cork** \'kȯrk\ *n* **1** : the tough elastic bark of a European oak (**cork oak**) used esp. for stoppers and insulation; *also* : a stopper of this **2** : a tissue of a woody plant making up most of the bark — **corky** *adj*

²**cork** *vb* : to furnish with or stop up with cork or a cork ⟨∼ a bottle⟩

cork·screw \'kȯrk-ˌskrü\ *n* : a device for drawing corks from bottles

corm \'kȯrm\ *n* : a solid bulblike underground part of a stem (as of the crocus or gladiolus)

cor·mo·rant \'kȯr-mə-rənt, -ˌrant\ *n* [ME *cormeraunt*, MF *cormorant*, fr. OF *cormareng*, fr. *corp* raven + *marenc* of the sea, fr. L *marinus*] : any of various dark-colored water birds with a long neck, hooked bill, and distensible throat pouch

¹**corn** \'kȯrn\ *n* **1** : the seeds of a cereal grass and esp. the chief cereal crop of a region (as wheat in Britain and Indian corn in the U.S.); *also* : a cereal grass **2** : sweet corn served as a vegetable

²**corn** *vb* : to salt (as beef) in brine and preservatives

³**corn** *n* : a local hardening and thickening of skin (as on a toe)

¹**corn·ball** \'korn-,bol\ *n* : an unsophisticated person; *also* : something corny

²**cornball** *adj* : CORNY ⟨~ humor⟩

corn bread *n* : bread made with cornmeal

corn·cob \-,käb\ *n* : the woody core on which the kernels of Indian corn are arranged

corn·crib \-,krib\ *n* : a crib for storing ears of Indian corn

cor·nea \'kor-nē-ə\ *n* : the transparent part of the coat of the eyeball covering the iris and the pupil — **cor·ne·al** *adj*

corn ear·worm \-'ir-,wərm\ *n* : a moth whose larva is destructive esp. to Indian corn

¹**cor·ner** \'kor-nər\ *n* [ME, fr. AF *cornere*, fr. *corne* horn, corner, fr. L *cornu* horn, point] **1** : the point or angle formed by the meeting of lines, edges, or sides **2** : the place where two streets come together **3** : a quiet secluded place **4** : a position from which retreat or escape is impossible **5** : control of enough of the available supply (as of a commodity) to permit manipulation of the price — **cor·nered** *adj* — **around the corner** : IMMINENT ⟨has a birthday just *around the corner*⟩

²**cor·ner** *vb* **1** : to drive into a corner **2** : to get a corner on ⟨~ the wheat market⟩ **3** : to turn a corner

cor·ner·stone \'kor-nər-,stōn\ *n* **1** : a stone forming part of a corner in a wall; *esp* : such a stone laid at a formal ceremony **2** : something of basic importance

cor·net \kor-'net\ *n* : a brass band instrument resembling the trumpet

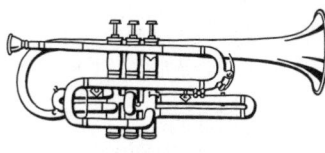

cornet

corn flour *n, Brit* : CORNSTARCH

corn·flow·er \'korn-,flaù(-ə)r\ *n* : BACHELOR'S BUTTON

cor·nice \'kor-nəs\ *n* : the horizontal projecting part crowning the wall of a building

corn·meal \'korn-,mēl\ *n* : meal ground from corn

corn·row \-,rō\ *n* : a section of hair braided flat to the scalp in rows — **cornrow** *vb*

corn·stalk \-,stök\ *n* : a stalk of Indian corn

corn·starch \-,stärch\ *n* : a starch made from corn and used in cookery as a thickening agent

corn syrup *n* : a sweet syrup obtained from cornstarch

cor·nu·co·pia \,kor-nə-'kō-pē-ə, -nyə-\ *n* [LL, fr. L *cornu copiae* horn of plenty] **1** : a horn-shaped container filled with fruits and grain emblematic of abundance **2** : ABUNDANCE

corny \'kor-nē\ *adj* **corn·i·er; -est** : tiresomely simple or sentimental

co·rol·la \kə-'rä-lə, -'rō-\ *n* : the petals of a flower

cor·ol·lary \'kor-ə-,ler-ē\ *n, pl* **-lar·ies 1** : a deduction from a proposition already proved true **2** : CONSEQUENCE, RESULT

co·ro·na \kə-'rō-nə\ *n* **1** : a colored circle often seen around and close to a luminous body (as the sun or moon) **2** : the outermost part of the atmosphere of a star (as the sun) — **co·ro·nal** \'kor-ə-n°l, kə-'rō-\ *adj*

cor·o·nal \'kor-ə-n°l\ *n* : a circlet for the head

¹**cor·o·nary** \'kor-ə-,ner-ē\ *adj* : of or relating to the heart or its blood vessels

²**coronary** *n, pl* **-nar·ies 1** : a coronary blood vessel **2** : CORONARY THROMBOSIS; *also* : HEART ATTACK

coronary thrombosis *n* : the blocking by a thrombus of one of the arteries supplying the heart tissues

cor·o·na·tion \,kor-ə-'nā-shən\ *n* : the act or ceremony of crowning a monarch

cor·o·ner \'kor-ə-nər\ *n* [ME, an officer of the crown, fr. AF, fr. *corone* crown, fr. L *corona*] : a public official who investigates causes of deaths possibly not due to natural causes

cor·o·net \,kor-ə-'net\ *n* **1** : a small crown **2** : an ornamental band worn around the temples

corp *abbr* **1** corporal **2** corporation

¹**cor·po·ral** \'kor-p(ə-)rəl\ *adj* : of or relating to the body ⟨~ punishment⟩

²**corporal** *n* : a noncommissioned officer (as in the army) ranking next below a sergeant

cor·po·rate \'kor-p(ə-)rət\ *adj* **1** : INCORPORATED; *also* : belonging to an incorporated body **2** : of or relating to large-scale business ⟨~ mergers⟩ **3** : combined into one body

cor·po·ra·tion \,kor-pə-'rā-shən\ *n* **1** : the municipal authorities of a town or city **2** : a legal creation authorized to act with the rights and liabilities of a person; *also* : COMPANY

cor·po·rat·ize \'kor-pə-rə-,tīz\ *vb* **ized; -iz·ing** : to subject to corporate control ⟨~ education⟩

cor·po·re·al \kor-'por-ē-əl\ *adj* **1** : PHYSICAL, MATERIAL **2** *archaic* : BODILY — **cor·po·re·al·i·ty** \kor-,por-ē-'a-lə-tē\ *n* — **cor·po·re·al·ly** *adv*

corps \'kor\ *n, pl* **corps** \'korz\ [F, fr. OF *cors*, fr. L *corpus* body] **1** : an organized subdivision of a country's military forces **2** : a group acting under common direction

corpse \'korps\ *n* : a dead body

corps·man \'kor-mən, 'korz-\ *n* : an enlisted man trained to give first aid

cor·pu·lence \'kor-pyə-ləns\ *n* : excessive fatness : OBESITY

cor·pu·lent \-lənt\ *adj* : OBESE

cor·pus \'kor-pəs\ *n, pl* **cor·po·ra** \-pə-rə\ [ME, fr. L] **1** : BODY; *esp* : CORPSE **2** : a body of writings or works

cor·pus·cle \'kor-pə-səl, -,pə-\ *n* **1** : a minute particle **2** : a living cell (as in blood or cartilage) not aggregated into continuous tissues — **cor·pus·cu·lar** \kor-'pəs-kyə-lər\ *adj*

cor·pus de·lic·ti \,kor-pəs-di-'lik-,tī, -tē\ *n, pl* **corpora delicti** [NL, lit., body of the crime] **1** : the substantial fact proving that a crime has been committed **2** : the body of a victim of murder

corr *abbr* **1** correct; corrected; correction **2** correspondence; correspondent; corresponding

cor·ral \kə-'ral\ *n* [Sp] : an enclosure for confining or capturing animals; *also* : an enclosure of wagons for defending a camp — **corral** *vb*

¹**cor·rect** \kə-'rekt\ *vb* **1** : to make right ⟨~ an error⟩ **2** : REPROVE, CHASTISE ⟨~ed the child⟩ — **cor·rect·able** \-'rek-tə-bəl\ *adj* — **cor·rec·tion** \-'rek-shən\ *n* — **cor·rec·tion·al** \-'rek-sh(ə-)nəl\ *adj* — **cor·rec·tive** \-'rek-tiv\ *adj*

²**correct** *adj* **1** : conforming to a conventional standard ⟨~ behavior⟩ **2** : agreeing with fact or truth ⟨a ~ answer⟩ **3** : conforming to the standards of a specific ideology ⟨environmentally ~⟩ — **cor·rect·ly** *adv* — **cor·rect·ness** *n*

cor·re·late \'kor-ə-,lāt\ *vb* **-lat·ed; -lat·ing** : to connect in a systematic way : establish the mutual relations of — **cor·re·late** \-lət, -,lāt\ *n* — **cor·re·la·tion** \,kor-ə-'lā-shən\ *n*

cor·rel·a·tive \kə-'re-lə-tiv\ *adj* **1** : reciprocally related **2** : regularly used together (as *either* and *or*) — **correlative** *n* — **cor·rel·a·tive·ly** *adv*

cor·re·spond \,kor-ə-'spänd\ *vb* **1** : to be in agreement : SUIT, MATCH **2** : to communicate by letter — **cor·re·spond·ing·ly** *adv*

cor·re·spon·dence \-'spän-dəns\ *n* **1** : agreement between particular things **2** : communication by letters; *also* : the letters exchanged

¹**cor·re·spon·dent** \-dənt\ *adj* **1** : SIMILAR **2** : FITTING, CONFORMING

²**correspondent** *n* **1** : something that corresponds **2** : a person with whom one communicates by letter **3** : a person employed to contribute news regularly from a place ⟨a war ~⟩

cor·ri·dor \'kor-ə-dər, -,dor\ *n* **1** : a passageway into which compartments or rooms open (as in a hotel or school) **2** : a narrow strip of land esp. through foreign-held territory **3** : a densely populated strip of land including two or more major cities **4** : an area identified by a common characteristic or purpose ⟨a ~ of liberalism⟩

cor·ri·gen·dum \,kor-ə-'jen-dəm\ *n, pl* **-da** \-də\ [L] : an error in a printed work discovered after printing and shown with its correction on a separate sheet

cor·ri·gi·ble \'kor-ə-jə-bəl\ *adj* : CORRECTABLE

cor·rob·o·rate \kə-'rä-bə-,rāt\ *vb* **-rat·ed; -rat·ing** [L *corroborare*, fr. *robur* strength] : to support with evidence

: CONFIRM — cor·rob·o·ra·tion \-ˌrä-bə-ˈrä-shən\ n — cor·rob·o·ra·tive \-ˈrä-bə-ˌrä-tiv, -ˈrä-brə-\ adj — cor·rob·o·ra·to·ry \-ˈrä-bə-rə-ˌtȯr-ē\ adj

cor·rode \kə-ˈrōd\ vb cor·rod·ed; cor·rod·ing : to wear or be worn away gradually (as by chemical action) — cor·ro·sion \-ˈrō-zhən\ n — cor·ro·sive \-ˈrō-siv\ adj or n

cor·ru·gate \ˈkȯr-ə-ˌgāt\ vb -gat·ed; -gat·ing : to form into wrinkles or ridges and grooves — cor·ru·gat·ed adj — cor·ru·ga·tion \ˌkȯr-ə-ˈgā-shən\ n

¹cor·rupt \kə-ˈrəpt\ vb 1 : to make evil : DEPRAVE; esp : BRIBE 2 : ROT, SPOIL — cor·rupt·ible adj — cor·rup·tion \-ˈrəp-shən\ n

²corrupt adj : morally degenerate; also : characterized by improper conduct ⟨∼ officials⟩

cor·sage \kȯr-ˈsäzh, -ˈsäj\ n [F, bust, bodice, fr. OF, bust, fr. cors body, fr. L corpus] 1 : the waist or bodice of a dress 2 : a bouquet to be worn or carried

cor·sair \ˈkȯr-ˌser\ n : PIRATE

cor·set \ˈkȯr-sət\ n : a stiffened undergarment worn for support or to give shape to the waist and hips

cor·tege also cor·tège \kȯr-ˈtezh, ˈkȯr-ˌtezh\ n [F] : PROCESSION; esp : a funeral procession

cor·tex \ˈkȯr-ˌteks\ n, pl cor·ti·ces \ˈkȯr-tə-ˌsēz\ or cor·tex·es : an outer or covering layer of an organism or one of its parts ⟨the adrenal ∼⟩ ⟨∼ of a plant stem⟩; esp : CEREBRAL CORTEX — cor·ti·cal \ˈkȯr-ti-kəl\ adj

cor·ti·co·ste·roid \ˌkȯr-ti-kō-ˈstir-ˌȯid, -ˈster-\ n : any of various steroids made in the adrenal cortex and used medically as anti-inflammatory agents

cor·ti·sone \ˈkȯr-tə-ˌsōn, -ˌzōn\ n : a corticosteroid used esp. in treating rheumatoid arthritis

co·run·dum \kə-ˈrən-dəm\ n : a very hard aluminum-containing mineral used as an abrasive or as a gem

cor·us·cate \ˈkȯr-ə-ˌskāt\ vb -cat·ed; -cat·ing : FLASH, SPARKLE — cor·us·ca·tion \ˌkȯr-ə-ˈskä-shən\ n

cor·vette \kȯr-ˈvet\ n 1 : a naval sailing ship smaller than a frigate 2 : an armed escort ship smaller than a destroyer

co·ry·za \kə-ˈrī-zə\ n : an inflammatory disorder of the upper respiratory tract; esp : COMMON COLD

cos abbr cosine

COS abbr 1 cash on shipment 2 chief of staff

co·sig·na·to·ry \kō-ˈsig-nə-ˌtȯr-ē\ n : a joint signer

co·sign·er \ˈkō-ˌsī-nər\ n : COSIGNATORY; esp : a joint signer of a promissory note

co·sine \ˈkō-ˌsīn\ n : the trigonometric function that is the ratio between the side next to an acute angle in a right triangle and the hypotenuse

¹cos·met·ic \käz-ˈme-tik\ adj [Gk kosmētikos skilled in adornment, fr. kosmein to arrange, adorn, fr. kosmos order, ornament, universe] 1 : intended to beautify the hair or complexion 2 : correcting physical defects esp. to improve appearance ⟨∼ dentistry⟩ 3 : SUPERFICIAL — cos·met·i·cal·ly \-ti-k(ə-)lē\ adv

²cosmetic n : a cosmetic preparation

cos·me·tol·o·gist \ˌkäz-mə-ˈtä-lə-jist\ n : one who gives beauty treatments — cos·me·tol·o·gy \-jē\ n

cos·mic \ˈkäz-mik\ also cos·mi·cal \-mi-kəl\ adj 1 : of or relating to the cosmos 2 : VAST, GRAND 3 : of or relating to spiritual or metaphysical ideas ⟨a ∼ thinker⟩ — cos·mi·cal·ly adv

cosmic ray n : a stream of very penetrating atomic nuclei that enter the earth's atmosphere from outer space

cos·mog·o·ny \käz-ˈmä-gə-nē\ n, pl -nies : the origin or creation of the world or universe

cos·mol·o·gy \-ˈmä-lə-jē\ n, pl -gies : a branch of astronomy dealing with the origin and structure of the universe — cos·mo·log·i·cal \ˌkäz-mə-ˈlä-ji-kəl\ adj — cos·mol·o·gist \käz-ˈmä-lə-jist\ n

cos·mo·naut \ˈkäz-mə-ˌnȯt\ n : a Soviet or Russian astronaut

cos·mo·pol·i·tan \ˌkäz-mə-ˈpä-lə-tən\ adj : belonging to all the world : not local ✦ Synonyms UNIVERSAL, GLOBAL, CATHOLIC — cosmopolitan n

cos·mos \ˈkäz-məs, 1 also -ˌmōs, -ˌmäs\ n 1 : UNIVERSE 2 : a tall garden herb related to the daisies

co·spon·sor \ˈkō-ˌspän-sər, -ˈspän-\ n : a joint sponsor — cosponsor vb

Cos·sack \ˈkä-ˌsak, -sək\ n [Pol & Ukrainian kozak, of Turkic origin] : a member of one of several autonomous communities drawn from various ethnic groups in southern Russia; also : a mounted soldier from one of these communities

¹cost \ˈkȯst\ n 1 : the amount paid or charged for something : PRICE 2 : the loss or penalty incurred in gaining something 3 pl : expenses incurred in a law suit — at all costs : regardless of consequences ⟨win at all costs⟩

²cost vb cost; cost·ing 1 : to require a specified amount in payment 2 : to cause to pay, suffer, or lose

co—star \ˈkō-ˌstär\ n : one of two leading players in a motion picture or play — co–star vb

cos·tive \ˈkäs-tiv\ adj : affected with or causing constipation

cost·ly \ˈkȯst-lē\ adj cost·li·er; -est : of great cost or value ⟨∼ gems⟩ 2 : done at great expense or sacrifice ⟨a ∼ error⟩ ✦ Synonyms DEAR, VALUABLE, EXPENSIVE — cost·li·ness n

cos·tume \ˈkäs-ˌtüm, -ˌtyüm\ n [F, fr. It, custom, dress, fr. L consuetudo custom] 1 : the style of attire characteristic of a period or country 2 : a special or fancy dress ⟨Halloween ∼s⟩ — cos·tum·er \ˈkäs-ˌtü-mər, -ˌtyü-\ n

costume jewelry n : inexpensive jewelry

cosy chiefly Brit var of COZY

¹cot \ˈkät\ n : a small house : COTTAGE

²cot n : a small often collapsible bed

cote \ˈkōt, ˈkät\ n : a small shed or coop (as for sheep or doves)

co·te·rie \ˈkō-tə-ˌrē, ˌkō-tə-ˈrē\ n [F] : an intimate often exclusive group of persons with a common interest

co·ter·mi·nous \ˌkō-ˈtər-mə-nəs\ adj : having the same scope or duration

co·til·lion \kō-ˈtil-yən, kə-\ n : a formal ball

cot·tage \ˈkä-tij\ n : a small house — cot·tag·er n

cottage cheese n : a soft uncured cheese made from soured skim milk

cot·tar or cot·ter \ˈkä-tər\ n : a peasant or farm laborer occupying a cottage and often a small holding

cotter pin n : a metal strip bent into a pin whose ends can be spread apart after insertion through a hole or slot

cot·ton \ˈkä-tᵊn\ n [ME coton, fr. AF cotun, fr. Ar quṭun] 1 : a soft fibrous usu. white substance composed of hairs attached to the seeds of various tropical plants related to the mallow; also : this plant 2 : thread or cloth made of cotton — cot·tony adj

cotton candy n : a candy made of spun sugar

cot·ton·mouth \ˈkä-tᵊn-ˌmau̇th\ n : WATER MOCCASIN

cot·ton·seed \-ˌsēd\ n : the seed of the cotton plant yielding a protein-rich meal and a fatty oil (cottonseed oil) used esp. in cooking

cot·ton·tail \-ˌtāl\ n : a No. American rabbit with a white-tufted tail

cot·ton·wood \-ˌwu̇d\ n : a poplar having seeds with cottony hairs

cot·y·le·don \ˌkä-tə-ˈlē-dᵊn\ n : the first leaf or one of the first pair or whorl of leaves developed by a seed plant

¹couch \ˈkau̇ch\ vb 1 : to lie or place on a couch 2 : to phrase in a specified manner ⟨proposals ∼ed in jargon⟩

²couch n : a piece of furniture (as a bed or sofa) that one can sit or lie on

couch·ant \ˈkau̇-chənt\ adj : lying down with the head raised ⟨coat of arms with lion ∼⟩

couch potato n : one who spends a great deal of time watching television

cou·gar \ˈkü-gər\ n, pl cougars also cougar [F couguar, fr. NL cuguacuarana, modif. of Tupi (a Brazilian Indian language) siwasuarána, fr. stwásu deer + -ran resembling] : a large powerful tawny brown wild American cat

cougar

cough \'kȯf\ *vb* : to force air from the lungs with short sharp noises; *also* : to expel by coughing — **cough** *n*
could \kəd, 'kůd\ *past of* CAN — used as an auxiliary in the past or as a polite or less forceful alternative to *can* in the present
cou·lee \'kü-lē\ *n* 1 : a small stream 2 : a dry streambed 3 : GULLY
cou·lomb \'kü-,läm, -,lōm\ *n* : a unit of electric charge equal to the electricity transferred by a current of one ampere in one second
coun·cil \'kaůn-səl\ *n* 1 : ASSEMBLY, MEETING 2 : an official body of lawmakers ⟨city ~⟩ — **coun·cil·lor** *or* **coun·cil·or** \-sə-lər\ *n* — **coun·cil·man** \-səl-mən\ *n* — **coun·cil·wom·an** \-,wů-mən\ *n*
¹**coun·sel** \'kaůn-səl\ *n* 1 : ADVICE 2 : a plan of action 3 : deliberation together 4 *pl* counsel : LAWYER
²**counsel** *vb* **-seled** *or* **-selled; -sel·ing** *or* **-sel·ling** 1 : ADVISE 2 : CONSULT
coun·sel·or *or* **coun·sel·lor** \'kaůn-sə-lər\ *n* 1 : ADVISER 2 : LAWYER 3 : one who has supervisory duties at a summer camp
¹**count** \'kaůnt\ *vb* [ME, fr. AF *cunter, counter*, fr. L *computare*, fr. *com-* with + *putare* to consider] 1 : to name or indicate one by one in order to find the total number 2 : to recite numbers in order 3 : CONSIDER, ACCOUNT 4 : RELY ⟨you can ~ on me⟩ 5 : to be of value or account ⟨~s toward your grade⟩ — **count·able** *adj*
²**count** *n* 1 : the act of counting; *also* : the total obtained by counting 2 : a particular charge in an indictment or legal declaration ⟨two ~s of murder⟩
³**count** *n* [ME, fr. AF *cunte*, fr. LL *comes*, fr. L, companion, one of the imperial court, fr. *com-* with + *ire* to go] : a European nobleman whose rank corresponds to that of a British earl
count·down \'kaůnt-,daůn\ *n* : a backward counting in fixed units (as seconds) to indicate the time remaining before an event (as the launching of a rocket) — **count down** *vb*
¹**coun·te·nance** \'kaůn-tⁿ-əns\ *n* 1 : the human face 2 : FAVOR, APPROVAL
²**countenance** *vb* **-nanced; -nanc·ing** : SANCTION, TOLERATE
¹**count·er** \'kaůn-tər\ *n* 1 : a piece (as of metal or plastic) used in reckoning or in games 2 : a level surface over which business is transacted, food is served, or work is conducted
²**count·er** *n* : a device for recording a number or amount
³**coun·ter** *vb* : to act in opposition to
⁴**coun·ter** *adv* : in an opposite direction : CONTRARY
⁵**coun·ter** *n* 1 : OPPOSITE, CONTRARY 2 : an answering or offsetting force or blow
⁶**coun·ter** *adj* : CONTRARY, OPPOSITE
coun·ter·act \,kaůn-tər-'akt\ *vb* : to lessen the force of : OFFSET — **coun·ter·ac·tive** \-'ak-tiv\ *adj*
coun·ter·at·tack \'kaůn-tər-ə-,tak\ *n* : an attack made to oppose an enemy's attack — **counterattack** *vb*
¹**coun·ter·bal·ance** \'kaůn-tər-,ba-ləns\ *n* : a weight or influence that balances another
²**counterbalance** \,kaůn-tər-'ba-ləns\ *vb* : to oppose with equal weight or influence
coun·ter·claim \'kaůn-tər-,klām\ *n* : an opposing claim esp. in law
coun·ter·clock·wise \,kaůn-tər-'kläk-,wīz\ *adv* : in a direction opposite to that in which the hands of a clock rotate — **counterclockwise** *adj*
coun·ter·cul·ture \'kaůn-tər-,kəl-chər\ *n* : a culture with values and mores that run counter to those of established society
coun·ter·es·pi·o·nage \,kaůn-tər-'es-pē-ə-,näzh, -nij\ *n* : activities intended to discover and defeat enemy espionage
¹**coun·ter·feit** \'kaůn-tər-,fit\ *adj* : SHAM, SPURIOUS; *also* : FORGED ⟨~ money⟩
²**counterfeit** *vb* 1 : to copy or imitate in order to deceive 2 : PRETEND, FEIGN — **coun·ter·feit·er** *n*
³**counterfeit** *n* : something counterfeit : FORGERY ♦ **Synonyms** FRAUD, SHAM, FAKE, IMPOSTURE, DECEIT, DECEPTION
coun·ter·in·sur·gen·cy \,kaůn-tər-in-'sər-jən-sē\ *n* : military activity designed to deal with insurgents
coun·ter·in·tel·li·gence \-in-'te-lə-jəns\ *n* : organized activities of an intelligence service designed to counter the activities of an enemy's intelligence service
coun·ter·in·tu·i·tive \-in-'tü-ə-tiv, -'tyü-\ *adj* : contrary to what would intuitively be expected
count·er·man \'kaůn-tər-,man, -mən\ *n* : one who tends a counter
coun·ter·mand \'kaůnt-ər-,mand\ *vb* : to withdraw (an order already given) by a contrary order
coun·ter·mea·sure \-,me-zhər\ *n* : an action or device designed to counter another
coun·ter·of·fen·sive \-ə-,fen-siv\ *n* : a large-scale counterattack
coun·ter·pane \-,pān\ *n* : BEDSPREAD
coun·ter·part \-,pärt\ *n* : a person or thing very closely like or corresponding to another person or thing
coun·ter·point \-,pȯint\ *n* : music in which one melody is accompanied by one or more other melodies all woven into a harmonious whole
coun·ter·poise \-,pȯiz\ *n* : COUNTERBALANCE
coun·ter·rev·o·lu·tion \,kaůn-tər-,re-və-'lü-shən\ *n* : a revolution opposed to a current or earlier one — **coun·ter·rev·o·lu·tion·ary** \-sha-,ner-ē\ *adj or n*
coun·ter·sign \'kaůn-tər-,sīn\ *n* 1 : a confirmatory signature added to a writing already signed by another person 2 : a military secret signal that must be given by a person who wishes to pass a guard — **countersign** *vb*
coun·ter·sink \-,siŋk\ *vb* **-sunk** \-,səŋk\; **-sink·ing** 1 : to form a funnel-shaped enlargement at the outer end of a drilled hole 2 : to set the head of (as a screw) at or below the surface — **countersink** *n*
coun·ter·spy \-,spī\ *n* : a spy engaged in counterespionage
coun·ter·ten·or \-,te-nər\ *n* : a tenor with an unusually high range
coun·ter·vail \,kaůn-tər-'vāl\ *vb* : COUNTERACT
coun·ter·weight \'kaůn-tər-,wāt\ *n* : COUNTERBALANCE
count·ess \'kaůn-təs\ *n* 1 : the wife or widow of a count or an earl 2 : a woman holding the rank of a count or an earl in her own right
count·ing·house \'kaůn-tiŋ-,haůs\ *n* : a building or office for keeping books and conducting business
count·less \'kaůnt-ləs\ *adj* : INNUMERABLE
coun·tri·fied *also* **coun·try·fied** \'kən-tri-,fīd\ *adj* 1 : RURAL, RUSTIC 2 : UNSOPHISTICATED 3 : played or sung in the manner of country music
¹**coun·try** \'kən-trē\ *n, pl* **countries** [ME *contree*, fr. AF *cuntree, contré*, fr. ML *contrata*, fr. L *contra* against, on the opposite side] 1 : REGION, DISTRICT 2 : FATHERLAND 3 : a nation or its territory 4 : rural regions as opposed to towns and cities 5 : COUNTRY MUSIC
²**country** *adj* 1 : RURAL 2 : of or relating to country music ⟨a ~ singer⟩
country and western *n* : COUNTRY MUSIC
country club *n* : a suburban club for social life and recreation; *esp* : one having a golf course — **country–club** *adj*
coun·try–dance \'kən-trē-,dans\ *n* : an English dance in which partners face each other esp. in rows
coun·try·man \'kən-trē-mən, 2 *often* -,man\ *n* 1 : an inhabitant of a specified country 2 : COMPATRIOT 3 : one raised or living in the country : RUSTIC
country music *n* : music derived from or imitating the folk style of the southern U.S. or of the Western cowboy
coun·try·side \'kən-trē-,sīd\ *n* : a rural area or its people
coun·ty \'kaůn-tē\ *n, pl* **counties** 1 : the domain of a count 2 : a territorial division of a country or state for purposes of local government
coup \'kü\ *n, pl* **coups** \'küz\ [F, blow, stroke] 1 : a brilliant sudden stroke or stratagem 2 : COUP D'ÉTAT
coup de grace \,kü-də-'gräs\ *n, pl* **coups de grace** \same\ [F *coup de grâce*, lit., stroke of mercy] : DEATHBLOW; *also* : a final decisive stroke or event
coup d'état \,kü-dā-'tä\ *n, pl* **coups d'état** \same or -'täz\ [F, lit., stroke of state] : a sudden violent overthrow of a government by a small group
cou·pé *or* **coupe** \kü-'pā, 2 *often* 'küp\ *n* [F *coupé*, fr. *couper* to cut] 1 : a closed horse-drawn carriage for two persons inside with an outside seat for the driver 2 *usu* **coupe** : a 2-door automobile with an enclosed body
¹**cou·ple** \'kə-pəl\ *n* 1 : two persons married, engaged, or otherwise romantically paired 2 : PAIR 3 : BOND, TIE 4 : an indefinite small number : FEW ⟨a ~ of days ago⟩
²**couple** *vb* **cou·pled; cou·pling** : to link together

cou·plet \'kə-plət\ *n* : two successive rhyming lines of verse

cou·pling \'kə-pliŋ\ (*usual for 2*), -pə-liŋ\ *n* 1 : CONNECTION 2 : a device for connecting two parts or things

cou·pon \'kü-,pän, 'kyü-\ *n* 1 : a statement attached to a bond showing interest due and designed to be cut off and presented for payment 2 : a form surrendered in order to obtain an article, service, or accommodation 3 : a printed document or slip used to submit orders or inquiries or to obtain a discount on merchandise or services

cour·age \'kər-ij\ *n* : ability to conquer fear or despair : BRAVERY, VALOR — **cou·ra·geous** \kə-'rā-jəs\ *adj* — **cou·ra·geous·ly** *adv*

cou·ri·er \'kur-ē-ər, 'kər-ē-\ *n* : one who bears messages or information esp. for the diplomatic or military services

¹**course** \'kōrs\ *n* 1 : PROGRESS, PASSAGE; *also* : direction of progress 2 : the ground or path over which something moves 3 : method of procedure : CONDUCT, BEHAVIOR 4 : an ordered series of acts or proceedings : sequence of events 5 : a series of instruction periods dealing with a subject 6 : the series of studies leading to graduation from a school or college 7 : the part of a meal served at one time — **of course** : as might be expected

²**course** *vb* **coursed; cours·ing** 1 : to hunt with dogs 2 : to run or go speedily

cours·er \'kōr-sər\ *n* : a swift or spirited horse

¹**court** \'kōrt\ *n* [ME, fr. AF, fr. L *cohort-, cohors* enclosure, group, retinue, cohort] 1 : the residence of a sovereign or similar dignitary 2 : a sovereign's formal assembly of officials and advisers as a governing power 3 : an assembly of the retinue of a sovereign 4 : an open space enclosed by a building or buildings 5 : a space walled or marked off for playing a game (as tennis or basketball) 6 : the place where justice is administered; *also* : a judicial body or a meeting of a judicial body 7 : attention intended to win favor

²**court** *vb* 1 : to try to gain the favor of 2 : WOO 3 : ATTRACT, TEMPT

cour·te·ous \'kər-tē-əs\ *adj* : marked by respect for others : CIVIL, POLITE — **cour·te·ous·ly** *adv*

cour·te·san \'kōr-tə-zən, -,zan\ *n* : PROSTITUTE

cour·te·sy \'kər-tə-sē\ *n, pl* **-sies** 1 : courteous behavior : POLITENESS 2 : a favor courteously performed

court·house \'kōrt-,haus\ *n* : a building in which courts of law are held or county offices are located

court·ier \'kōr-tē-ər\ *n* : a person in attendance at a royal court

court·ly \'kōrt-lē\ *adj* **court·li·er; -est** : REFINED, ELEGANT, POLITE ♦ *Synonyms* GALLANT, GRACIOUS — **court·li·ness** *n*

court–mar·tial \'kōrt-,mär-shəl\ *n, pl* **courts–martial** : a military or naval court for trial of offenses against military or naval law; *also* : a trial by this court — **court–martial** *vb*

court·room \-,rüm, -,rum\ *n* : a room in which a court of law is held

court·ship \-,ship\ *n* : the act of courting : WOOING

court·yard \-,yärd\ *n* : an enclosure next to a building

cous·cous \'küs-,küs\ *n* : a No. African dish of steamed semolina usu. served with meat or vegetables; *also* : the semolina itself

cous·in \'kə-zən\ *n* [ME *cosin*, fr. AF, fr. L *consobrinus*, fr. *com-* with + *sobrinus* second cousin, fr. *soror* sister] : a child of one's uncle or aunt

cou·ture \kü-'tur, -'tuer\ *n* [F] : the business of designing fashionable custom-made women's clothing; *also* : the designers and establishments engaged in this business

cou·tu·ri·er \kü-'tur-ē-ər, -ē-,ā\ *n* [F, dressmaker] : the owner of an establishment engaged in couture

cove \'kōv\ *n* : a small sheltered inlet or bay

co·ven \'kə-vən\ *n* : an assembly or band of witches

cov·e·nant \'kə-və-nənt\ *n* : a formal binding agreement : COMPACT — **cov·e·nant** \-nənt, -,nant\ *vb*

¹**cov·er** \'kə-vər\ *vb* 1 : to bring or hold within range of a firearm 2 : PROTECT, GUARD ⟨∼ed by insurance⟩ ⟨∼ third base⟩ 3 : HIDE, CONCEAL ⟨∼ up a crime⟩ 4 : to place something over or upon 5 : INCLUDE, COMPRISE 6 : to have as one's field of activity ⟨one salesman ∼s the state⟩ 7 : to buy (stocks) in order to have them for delivery on a previous short sale

²**cover** *n* 1 : something that protects or shelters 2 : LID, TOP 3 : CASE, BINDING 4 : TABLECLOTH 5 : a cloth used on a bed 6 : SCREEN, DISGUISE 7 : an envelope or wrapper for mail

cov·er·age \'kə-və-rij\ *n* 1 : the act or fact of covering 2 : the total group covered : SCOPE

cov·er·all \'kə-vər-,ol\ *n* : a one-piece outer garment worn to protect one's clothes — usu. used in pl.

cover charge *n* : a charge made by a restaurant or nightclub in addition to the charge for food and drink

cover crop *n* : a crop planted to prevent soil erosion and to provide humus

cov·er·let \'kə-vər-lət\ *n* : BEDSPREAD

¹**co·vert** \'kō-,vərt, 'kə-vərt\ *adj* 1 : HIDDEN, SECRET ⟨a ∼ operation⟩ 2 : SHELTERED — **co·vert·ly** *adv*

²**co·vert** \'kə-vərt, 'kō-\ *n* 1 : a secret or sheltered place; *esp* : a thicket sheltering game 2 : a feather covering the bases of the quills of the wings and tail of a bird

cov·er–up \'kə-vər-,əp\ *n* 1 : a device for masking or concealing 2 : a usu. concerted effort to keep an illegal or unethical act or situation from being made public

cov·et \'kə-vət\ *vb* : to desire enviously (what belongs to another) — **cov·et·ous** *adj* — **cov·et·ous·ness** *n*

cov·ey \'kə-vē\ *n, pl* **coveys** [ME, fr. AF *covee* sitting (of a hen), fr. *cover* to sit on, brood over, fr. L *cubare* to lie] 1 : a bird with her brood of young 2 : a small flock (as of quail) 3 : GROUP 1

¹**cow** \'kau\ *n* 1 : the mature female of cattle or of an animal (as the moose, elephant, or whale) of which the male is called *bull* 2 : any domestic bovine animal irrespective of sex or age

²**cow** *vb* : INTIMIDATE, DAUNT, OVERAWE

cow·ard \'kau-(ə)rd\ *n* [ME, fr. AF *cuard*, fr. *cue, coe* tail, fr. L *cauda*] : one who lacks courage or shows shameful fear or timidity — **coward** *adj* — **cow·ard·ice** \'kau-ər-dəs\ *n* — **cow·ard·ly** *adv or adj*

cow·bird \'kau-,bərd\ *n* : a small No. American blackbird that lays its eggs in the nests of other birds

cow·boy \-,boi\ *n* : one (as a mounted ranch hand) who tends cattle or horses

cow·er \'kau-(ə)r\ *vb* : to shrink or crouch down from fear or cold : QUAIL

cow·girl \'kau-,gərl\ *n* : a girl or woman who tends cattle or horses

cow·hand \'kau-,hand\ *n* : COWBOY

cow·herd \-,hərd\ *n* : one who tends cows

cow·hide \-,hid\ *n* 1 : the hide of a cow; *also* : leather made from it 2 : a coarse whip of braided rawhide

cowl \'kau(-ə)l\ *n* : a monk's hood

cow·lick \'kau-,lik\ *n* : a turned-up tuft of hair that resists control

cowl·ing \'kau-liŋ\ *n* : a usu. metal covering for the engine or another part of an airplane

cow·man \'kau-mən, -,man\ *n* : COWBOY; *also* : a cattle owner or rancher

co·work·er \'kō-,wər-kər\ *n* : a fellow worker

cow·poke \'kau-,pōk\ *n* : COWBOY

cow pony *n* : a strong and agile horse trained for herding cattle

cow·pox \'kau-,päks\ *n* : a mild disease of the cow that when communicated to humans protects against smallpox

cow·punch·er \-,pən-chər\ *n* : COWBOY

cow·slip \'kau-,slip\ *n* 1 : a yellow-flowered European primrose 2 : MARSH MARIGOLD

cox·comb \'käks-,kōm\ *n* : a conceited foolish person : FOP

cox·swain \'käk-sən, -,swän\ *n* : the steersman of a ship's boat or a racing shell

coy \'koi\ *adj* [ME, quiet, shy, fr. AF *quei, quoi, koi* quiet, fr. L *quietus*] 1 : BASHFUL, SHY 2 : marked by artful playfulness : COQUETTISH — **coy·ly** *adv* — **coy·ness** *n*

coy·ote \'ki-,ōt, ki-'ō-tē\ *n, pl* **coyotes** *or* **coyote** : a mammal of No. America smaller than the related wolves

coy·pu \'koi-pü\ *n* : NUTRIA 2

coz·en \'kə-z²n\ *vb* : CHEAT, DEFRAUD — **coz·en·age** \-ij\ *n* — **coz·en·er** *n*

¹**co·zy** \'kō-zē\ *adj* **co·zi·er; -est** : SNUG, COMFORTABLE ⟨a ∼ cabin⟩ — **co·zi·ly** \-zə-lē\ *adv* — **co·zi·ness** \-zē-nəs\ *n*

²**cozy** *n, pl* **co·zies** : a padded covering for a vessel (as a teapot) to keep the contents hot

cp *abbr* 1 compare 2 coupon

CP *abbr* **1** cerebral palsy **2** chemically pure **3** command post **4** communist party

CPA *abbr* certified public accountant

CPB *abbr* Corporation for Public Broadcasting

cpd *abbr* compound

CPI *abbr* consumer price index

Cpl *abbr* corporal

CPO *abbr* chief petty officer

CPOM *abbr* master chief petty officer

CPOS *abbr* senior chief petty officer

CPR *abbr* cardiopulmonary resuscitation

CPT *abbr* captain

CPU \ˌsē-ˌpē-ˈyü\ *n* [*central processing unit*] : the part of a computer that performs its basic operations, manages its components, and exchanges data with memory or peripherals

CQ *abbr* charge of quarters

cr *abbr* credit; creditor

Cr *symbol* chromium

¹**crab** \ˈkrab\ *n, pl* **crabs** *also* **crab** : any of various crustaceans with a short broad shell and small abdomen

²**crab** *n* : an ill-natured person

³**crab** *vb* **crabbed; crab·bing** : COMPLAIN, GROUSE

crab apple *n* : a small often highly colored sour apple; *also* : a tree that produces crab apples

crab·bed \ˈkra-bəd\ *adj* **1** : MOROSE, PEEVISH ⟨a ~ view of human nature⟩ **2** : CRAMPED, IRREGULAR ⟨~ handwriting⟩

crab·by \ˈkra-bē\ *adj* **crab·bi·er; -est** : CROSS, ILL-NATURED

crab·grass \ˈkrab-ˌgras\ *n* : a weedy grass with creeping or sprawling stems that root freely at the nodes

crab louse *n* : a louse infesting the pubic region in humans

¹**crack** \ˈkrak\ *vb* **1** : to break with a sharp sudden sound **2** : to break with or without completely separating into parts **3** : to fail in tone or become harsh ⟨her voice ~ed⟩ **4** : to subject (as a petroleum oil) to heat for breaking down into lighter products (as gasoline)

²**crack** *n* **1** : a sudden sharp noise **2** : a witty or sharp remark **3** : a narrow break or opening : FISSURE **4** : a sharp blow **5** : ATTEMPT, TRY **6** : a potent form of cocaine in small chips used illicitly for smoking

³**crack** *adj* : extremely proficient

crack·down \ˈkrak-ˌdau̇n\ *n* : an act or instance of taking positive disciplinary action ⟨a ~ on gambling⟩ — **crack down** *vb*

crack·er \ˈkra-kər\ *n* **1** : FIRECRACKER **2** : a dry thin crispy baked bread product made of flour and water

crack·er·jack \-ˌjak\ *n* : something excellent — **crackerjack** *adj*

crack·le \ˈkra-kəl\ *vb* **crack·led; crack·ling 1** : to make small sharp snapping noises **2** : to develop fine cracks in a surface — **crackle** *n* — **crack·ly** \-k(ə-)lē\ *adj*

crack·pot \ˈkrak-ˌpät\ *n* : an eccentric person

crack–up \ˈkrak-ˌəp\ *n* **1** : CRASH, WRECK; *also* : BREAKDOWN

crack up *vb* **1** : PRAISE ⟨isn't all it's *cracked up* to be⟩ **2** : to laugh or cause to laugh out loud **3** : to crash a vehicle

¹**cra·dle** \ˈkrā-dᵊl\ *n* **1** : a baby's bed or cot **2** : a framework or support (as for a telephone receiver) **3** : INFANCY ⟨from ~ to the grave⟩ **4** : a place of origin

²**cradle** *vb* **cra·dled; cra·dling 1** : to place in or as if in a cradle **2** : SHELTER, REAR

craft \ˈkraft\ *n* **1** : ART, SKILL; *also* : an occupation requiring special skill **2** : CUNNING, GUILE **3** *pl usu* **craft** : a boat esp. of small size; *also* : AIRCRAFT, SPACECRAFT

crafts·man \ˈkrafts-mən\ *n* : a skilled artisan — **crafts·man·ship** *n*

crafty \ˈkraf-tē\ *adj* **craft·i·er; -est** : CUNNING, DECEITFUL, SUBTLE — **craft·i·ly** \-tə-lē\ *adv* — **craft·i·ness** \-tē-nəs\ *n*

crag \ˈkrag\ *n* : a steep rugged cliff or rock — **crag·gy** *adj*

cram \ˈkram\ *vb* **crammed; cram·ming 1** : to pack in tight : JAM **2** : to eat greedily **3** : to study rapidly under pressure for an examination

¹**cramp** \ˈkramp\ *n* **1** : a sudden painful contraction of muscle **2** : sharp abdominal pain — usu. used in pl.

²**cramp** *vb* **1** : to affect with a cramp or cramps **2** : to restrain from free action : HAMPER

cran·ber·ry \ˈkran-ˌber-ē, -bə-rē\ *n* : the red acid berry of

any of several trailing plants related to the heaths; *also* : one of these plants

¹**crane** \ˈkrān\ *n* **1** : any of a family of tall wading birds related to the rails; *also* : any of several herons **2** : a machine for lifting and carrying heavy objects

²**crane** *vb* **craned; cran·ing** : to stretch one's neck to see better

crane fly *n* : any of a family of long-legged slender dipteran flies that resemble large mosquitoes but do not bite

cranial nerve *n* : any of the nerves that arise in pairs from the lower surface of the brain and pass through openings in the skull to the periphery of the body

cra·ni·um \ˈkrā-nē-əm\ *n, pl* **-ni·ums** *or* **-nia** \-ə-\ : SKULL; *esp* : the part enclosing the brain — **cra·ni·al** \-əl\ *adj*

¹**crank** \ˈkraŋk\ *n* **1** : a bent part of an axle or shaft or an arm at right angles to the end of a shaft by which circular motion is imparted to or received from it **2** : an eccentric person **3** : a bad-tempered person : GROUCH

²**crank** *vb* : to start or operate by or as if by turning a crank

crank·case \ˈkraŋk-ˌkās\ *n* : the housing of a crankshaft

crank out *vb* : to produce in a mechanical manner

crank·shaft \ˈkraŋk-ˌshaft\ *n* : a shaft turning or driven by a crank

cranky \ˈkraŋ-kē\ *adj* **crank·i·er; -est 1** : IRRITABLE **2** : operating uncertainly or imperfectly ⟨a ~ old tractor⟩

cran·ny \ˈkra-nē\ *n, pl* **crannies** : CREVICE, CHINK

craps \ˈkraps\ *n* : a gambling game played with two dice

crap·shoot·er \ˈkrap-ˌshü-tər\ *n* : a person who plays craps

¹**crash** \ˈkrash\ *vb* **1** : to break noisily : SMASH **2** : to damage an airplane in landing **3** : to enter or attend without invitation or without paying ⟨~ a party⟩ **4** : to suffer a sudden major failure usu. with loss of data ⟨my computer ~ed⟩

²**crash** *n* **1** : a loud sound (as of things smashing) **2** : an instance of crashing ⟨a plane ~⟩; *also* : COLLISION **3** : a sudden failure (as of a business)

³**crash** *adj* : marked by concentrated effort over the shortest possible time ⟨a ~ diet⟩

⁴**crash** *n* : coarse linen fabric used for towels and draperies

crash–land \ˈkrash-ˈland\ *vb* : to land an aircraft or spacecraft under emergency conditions usu. with damage to the craft — **crash landing** *n*

crass \ˈkras\ *adj* : GROSS, INSENSITIVE ⟨~ ignorance⟩ — **crass·ly** *adv* — **crass·ness** *n*

crate \ˈkrāt\ *n* : a container often of wooden slats — **crate** *vb*

cra·ter \ˈkrā-tər\ *n* [L, mixing bowl, crater, fr. Gk *kratēr*, fr. *kerannynai* to mix] **1** : the depression around the opening of a volcano **2** : a depression formed by the impact of a meteorite or by the explosion of a bomb or shell

cra·vat \krə-ˈvat\ *n* : NECKTIE

crave \ˈkrāv\ *vb* **craved; crav·ing 1** : to ask for earnestly : BEG **2** : to long for : DESIRE

cra·ven \ˈkrā-vən\ *adj* : COWARDLY — **craven** *n* — **cra·ven·ly** *adv*

crav·ing \ˈkrā-viŋ\ *n* : an urgent or abnormal desire

craw·fish \ˈkrȯ-ˌfish\ *n* **1** : CRAYFISH 1 **2** : SPINY LOBSTER

¹**crawl** \ˈkrȯl\ *vb* **1** : to move slowly by drawing the body along the ground **2** : to advance feebly, cautiously, or slowly **3** : to be swarming with or feel as if swarming with creeping things ⟨a place ~*ing* with ants⟩ ⟨her flesh ~ed⟩

²**crawl** *n* **1** : a very slow pace **2** : a prone speed swimming stroke

cray·fish \ˈkrā-ˌfish\ *n* **1** : any of numerous freshwater crustaceans usu. much smaller than the related lobsters **2** : SPINY LOBSTER

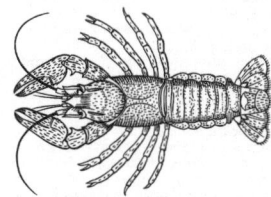

crayfish 1

cray·on \'krā-ˌän, -ən\ n : a stick of chalk or wax used for writing, drawing, or coloring; *also* : a drawing made with such material — **crayon** *vb*

¹**craze** \'krāz\ *vb* **crazed; craz·ing** [ME *crasen* to crush, craze, of Scand origin] : to make or become insane

²**craze** n : FAD, MANIA

cra·zy \'krā-zē\ *adj* **cra·zi·er; -est** 1 : mentally disordered : INSANE 2 : wildly impractical ⟨a ~ plan⟩; *also* : ERRATIC ⟨~ drivers⟩ — **cra·zi·ly** \-zə-lē\ *adv* — **cra·zi·ness** \-zē-nəs\ n

CRC *abbr* Civil Rights Commission

creak \'krēk\ *vb* : to make a prolonged squeaking or grating sound — **creak** n — **creaky** *adj*

¹**cream** \'krēm\ n 1 : the yellowish fat-rich part of milk 2 : a thick smooth sauce, confection, or cosmetic 3 : the choicest part 4 : a pale yellow color — **creamy** *adj*

²**cream** *vb* 1 : to prepare with a cream sauce 2 : to beat or blend into creamy consistency 3 : to defeat decisively

cream cheese n : a cheese made from whole milk enriched with cream

cream·ery \'krē-mə-rē\ n, *pl* **-er·ies** : an establishment where butter and cheese are made or milk and cream are prepared for sale

crease \'krēs\ n : a mark or line made by or as if by folding — **crease** *vb*

cre·ate \krē-'āt\ *vb* **cre·at·ed; cre·at·ing** : to bring into being : cause to exist : MAKE, PRODUCE — **cre·a·tive** \-'ā-tiv\ *adj* — **cre·a·tive·ness** n — **cre·a·tiv·i·ty** \ˌkrē-(ˌ)ā-'ti-və-tē\ n

cre·a·tion \krē-'ā-shən\ n 1 : the act of creating or producing ⟨~ of the world⟩ 2 : something that is created 3 : all created things : WORLD

cre·a·tion·ism \krē-'ā-shə-ˌni-zəm\ n : a doctrine or theory holding that matter, the various forms of life, and the world were created by God out of nothing — **cre·a·tion·ist** \-nist\ n *or adj*

cre·a·tor \krē-'ā-tər\ n 1 : one that creates : MAKER, AUTHOR 2 *cap* : GOD 1

crea·ture \'krē-chər\ n : a lower animal; *also* : a human being

crèche \'kresh\ n [F, manger, crib, fr. OF *creche*, of Gmc origin] : a representation of the Nativity scene

cre·dence \'krē-dᵊns\ n : mental acceptance as true or real

cre·den·tial \kri-'den-chəl\ n : something that gives a basis for credit or confidence

cre·den·za \kri-'den-zə\ n [It, lit., belief, confidence] : a sideboard, buffet, or bookcase usu. without legs

cred·i·ble \'kre-də-bəl\ *adj* : TRUSTWORTHY, BELIEVABLE — **cred·i·bil·i·ty** \ˌkre-də-'bi-lə-tē\ n — **cred·i·bly** \'kre-də-blē\ *adv*

¹**cred·it** \'kre-dət\ n [MF, fr. It *credito*, fr. L *creditum* something entrusted to another, loan, fr. *credere* to believe, entrust] 1 : the balance (as in a bank) in a person's favor 2 : time given for payment for goods sold on trust 3 : an accounting entry of payment received 4 : BELIEF, FAITH 5 : financial trustworthiness 6 : ESTEEM 7 : a source of honor or distinction 8 : a unit of academic work

²**credit** *vb* 1 : BELIEVE 2 : to give credit to

cred·it·able \'kre-də-tə-bəl\ *adj* : worthy of esteem or praise — **cred·it·ably** \-blē\ *adv*

credit card n : a card authorizing purchases on credit

cred·i·tor \'kre-də-tər\ n : a person to whom money is owed

cre·do \'krē-dō, 'krā-\ n, *pl* **credos** [ME, fr. L, I believe] : CREED

cred·u·lous \'kre-jə-ləs\ *adj* : inclined to believe esp. on slight evidence — **cred·u·lous·ly** *adv* — **cre·du·li·ty** \kri-'dü-lə-tē, -'dyü-\ n

Cree \'krē\ n, *pl* **Cree** *or* **Crees** : a member of an American Indian people of Canada

creed \'krēd\ n [ME *crede*, fr. OE *crēda*, fr. L *credo* I believe, first word of the Apostles' and Nicene Creeds] : a statement of the essential beliefs of a religious faith

creek \'krēk, 'krik\ n 1 *chiefly Brit* : a small inlet 2 : a stream smaller than a river and larger than a brook

Creek \'krēk\ n : a member of an American Indian people of Alabama, Georgia, and Florida

creel \'krēl\ n : a wicker basket esp. for carrying fish

creep \'krēp\ *vb* **crept** \'krept\; **creep·ing** 1 : CRAWL 2 : to feel as though insects were crawling on the skin 3 : to spread or grow over a surface like ivy — **creep** n — **creep·er** n

creep·ing \'krē-piŋ\ *adj* : developing or advancing by imperceptible degrees

creepy \'krē-pē\ *adj* **creep·i·er; -est** : having or producing a nervous shivery fear

cre·mate \'krē-ˌmāt\ *vb* **cre·mat·ed; cre·mat·ing** : to reduce (a dead body) to ashes with fire — **cre·ma·tion** \kri-'mā-shən\ n

cre·ma·to·ry \'krē-mə-ˌtȯr-ē, 'kre-\ n, *pl* **-ries** : a furnace for cremating; *also* : a structure containing such a furnace

crème *or* **creme** \'krem, 'krēm\ n, *pl* **crèmes** *or* **cremes** *same or* \'kremz, 'krēmz\ [F, lit., cream] : a sweet liqueur

cren·el·lat·ed *or* **cren·el·at·ed** \'kre-nə-ˌlā-təd\ *adj* : having battlements — **cren·el·la·tion** \ˌkre-nə-'lā-shən\ n

Cre·ole \'krē-ˌōl\ n 1 : a descendant of early French or Spanish settlers of the U.S. Gulf states preserving their speech and culture; *also* : a person of mixed French and Spanish and black descent speaking a dialect of French or Spanish 2 *not cap* : a language that has evolved from a pidgin but serves as the native language of a speech community

cre·o·sote \'krē-ə-ˌsōt\ n : an oily liquid obtained by distillation of coal tar and used in preserving wood

crepe *or* **crêpe** \'krāp\ n : a light crinkled fabric of any of various fibers

crêpe su·zette \ˌkrāp-sü-'zet\ n, *pl* **crêpes suzette** *same or* \ˌkrāps-\ *or* **crêpe suzettes** \-sü-'zets\ *often cap S* : a thin folded or rolled pancake in a hot orange-butter sauce that is sprinkled with a liqueur and set ablaze for serving

cre·pus·cu·lar \kri-'pəs-kyə-lər\ *adj* 1 : of, relating to, or resembling twilight 2 : occurring or active during twilight ⟨~ insects⟩

cre·scen·do \krə-'shen-dō\ *adv or adj* [It] : increasing in loudness — used as a direction in music — **crescendo** n

cres·cent \'kre-sᵊnt\ n [ME *cressant*, fr. AF fr. prp. of *crestre* to grow, increase, fr. L *crescere*] : the moon at any stage between new moon and first quarter and between last quarter and new moon; *also* : something shaped like the figure of the crescent moon with a convex and a concave edge — **cres·cen·tic** \kre-'sen-tik\ *adj*

cress \'kres\ n : any of several salad plants related to the mustards

¹**crest** \'krest\ n 1 : a tuft or process on the head of an animal (as a bird) 2 : a heraldic device 3 : an upper part, edge, or limit ⟨the ~ of a hill⟩ — **crest·ed** \'kres-təd\ *adj* — **crest·less** *adj*

²**crest** *vb* 1 : CROWN 2 : to reach the crest of 3 : to rise to a crest

crest·fall·en \'krest-ˌfȯ-lən\ *adj* : DISPIRITED, DEJECTED

Cre·ta·ceous \kri-'tā-shəs\ *adj* : of, relating to, or being the latest period of the Mesozoic era marked by great increase in flowering plants, diversification of mammals, and extinction of the dinosaurs — **Cretaceous** n

cre·tin \'krē-tᵊn\ n [F *crétin*, fr. F dial. *cretin*, lit., wretch, innocent victim, fr. L *christianus* Christian] 1 : one affected with cretinism 2 : a stupid person

cre·tin·ism \-ˌi-zəm\ n : a usu. congenital abnormal condition characterized by physical stunting and mental retardation

cre·tonne \'krē-ˌtän\ n : a strong unglazed cotton cloth for curtains and upholstery

cre·vasse \kri-'vas\ n : a deep fissure esp. in a glacier

crev·ice \'kre-vəs\ n : a narrow fissure

¹**crew** \'krü\ *chiefly Brit past of* CROW

²**crew** n [ME *crue*, fr. MF, a reinforcement, lit., increase, fr. *croistre* to grow, fr. L *crescere*] 1 : a body of people trained to work together for certain purposes 2 : a group of people who operate a ship, train, aircraft, or spacecraft 3 : the rowers and coxswain of a racing shell; *also* : the sport of rowing engaged in by a crew — **crew·man** \-mən\ n

crew cut n : a very short bristly haircut

crew·el \'krü-əl\ n : slackly twisted worsted yarn used for embroidery — **crew·el·work** \-ˌwərk\ n

¹**crib** \'krib\ n 1 : a manger for feeding animals 2 : a child's bedstead with high sides 3 : a building or bin for storage (as of grain) 4 : something used for cheating in an exam

²**crib** *vb* **cribbed; crib·bing** 1 : to put in a crib 2 : STEAL, PLAGIARIZE — **crib·ber** n

crib·bage \\'kri-bij\ *n* : a card game usu. played by two players and scored on a board (**cribbage board**)

crib death *n* : SUDDEN INFANT DEATH SYNDROME

crick \\'krik\ *n* : a painful spasm of muscles (as of the neck)

¹**crick·et** \\'kri-kət\ *n* [ME *criket*, fr. AF, of imit. origin] : any of a family of leaping insects related to the grasshoppers and noted for the chirping noises of the male

²**cricket** *n* [MF *criquet* goal stake in a bowling game] : a game played with a bat and ball by two teams on a field centering upon two wickets each defended by a batsman

cri·er \\'krī(-ə)r\ *n* : one who calls out proclamations and announcements

crime \\'krīm\ *n* : a serious offense against the public law

¹**crim·i·nal** \\'kri-mə-n³l\ *adj* **1** : involving or being a crime   **2** : relating to crime or its punishment — **crim·i·nal·i·ty** \\,kri-mə-'na-lə-tē\ *n* — **crim·i·nal·ly** *adv*

²**criminal** *n* : one who has committed a crime

crim·i·nol·o·gy \\,kri-mə-'nä-lə-jē\ *n* : the scientific study of crime and criminals — **crim·i·no·log·i·cal** \\-mə-nə-'lä-ji-kəl\ *adj* — **crim·i·nol·o·gist** \\,kri-mə-'nä-lə-jist\ *n*

¹**crimp** \\'krimp\ *vb* : to cause to become crinkled, wavy, or bent

²**crimp** *n* : something (as a curl in hair) produced by or as if by crimping

crim·son \\'krim-zən\ *n* : a deep purplish red color — **crimson** *adj*

cringe \\'krinj\ *vb* **cringed; cring·ing** : to shrink in fear : WINCE, COWER

crin·kle \\'krin-kəl\ *vb* **crin·kled; crin·kling** : to form many short bends or curves; *also* : WRINKLE — **crinkle** *n* — **crin·kly** \\-kə-lē\ *adj*

crin·o·line \\'kri-nə-lən\ *n* **1** : an open-weave cloth used for stiffening and lining   **2** : a full stiff skirt or underskirt made of crinoline

¹**crip·ple** \\'kri-pəl\ *n* : one that is disabled or deficient in a specified manner ⟨a social ∼⟩

²**cripple** *vb* **crip·pled; crip·pling** **1** : to make lame   **2** : to make useless or imperfect — **crip·pler** \\'kri-p(ə-)lər\ *n*

cri·sis \\'krī-səs\ *n, pl* **cri·ses** \\-,sēz\ [ME, fr. L, fr. Gk *krisis*, lit., decision, fr. *krinein* to decide] **1** : the turning point for better or worse in an acute disease or fever   **2** : a decisive or critical moment

crisp \\'krisp\ *adj* **1** : CURLY, WAVY   **2** : BRITTLE ⟨a ∼ potato chip⟩   **3** : FIRM, FRESH ⟨∼ lettuce⟩   **4** : being sharp and clear ⟨a ∼ photo⟩   **5** : LIVELY, SPARKLING   **6** : FROSTY, SNAPPY; *also* : INVIGORATING — **crisp** *vb* — **crisp·ly** *adv* — **crisp·ness** *n* — **crispy** *adj*

¹**criss·cross** \\'kris-,krós\ *vb* **1** : to mark with crossed lines   **2** : to go or pass back and forth

²**crisscross** *adj* : marked or characterized by crisscrossing — **crisscross** *adv*

³**crisscross** *n* : a pattern formed by crossed lines

crit *abbr* critical; criticism

cri·te·ri·on \\krī-'tir-ē-ən\ *n, pl* **-ria** \\-ē-ə\ : a standard on which a judgment may be based

crit·ic \\'kri-tik\ *n* **1** : a person who judges literary or artistic works   **2** : one inclined to find fault

crit·i·cal \\'kri-ti-kəl\ *adj* **1** : being or relating to a condition or disease involving danger of death ⟨∼ care⟩   **2** : being a crisis   **3** : inclined to criticize   **4** : relating to criticism or critics   **5** : requiring careful judgment ⟨∼ thinking⟩ — **crit·i·cal·ly** \\-k(ə-)lē\ *adv*

crit·i·cise *Brit var of* CRITICIZE

crit·i·cism \\'kri-tə-,si-zəm\ *n* **1** : the act of criticizing; *esp* : CENSURE   **2** : a judgment or review   **3** : the art of judging works of literature or art

crit·i·cize \\'kri-tə-,sīz\ *vb* **-cized; -ciz·ing** **1** : to judge as a critic : EVALUATE   **2** : to find fault : express criticism

♦ **Synonyms** BLAME, CENSURE, CONDEMN

cri·tique \\krə-'tēk\ *n* : a critical estimate or discussion

crit·ter \\'kri-tər\ *n* : CREATURE

croak \\'krōk\ *n* : a hoarse harsh cry (as of a frog) — **croak** *vb*

croak·er \\'krō-kər\ *n* **1** : an animal that croaks   **2** : a fish that produces croaking or grunting noises

Croat \\'krō-,at\ *n* : CROATIAN

Cro·atian \\krō-'ā-shən\ *n* **1** : a native or inhabitant of Croatia   **2** : a Slavic language spoken by Croatians — **Croatian** *adj*

cro·chet \\krō-'shā\ *n* : needlework done with a single thread and hooked needle — **crochet** *vb*

crock \\'kräk\ *n* : a thick earthenware pot or jar

crock·ery \\'krä-kə-rē\ *n* : EARTHENWARE

croc·o·dile \\'krä-kə-,dī(-ə)l\ *n* [ME &, L; ME *cocodrille*, AF, fr. ML *cocodrillus*, alter. of L *crocodilus*, fr. Gk *krokodilos* lizard, crocodile, fr. *krokē* shingle, pebble + *drillos* worm] : any of several thick-skinned long-bodied carnivorous reptiles of tropical and subtropical waters

cro·cus \\'krō-kəs\ *n, pl* **cro·cus·es** *also* **crocus** *or* **cro·ci** \\-,kī\ : any of a large genus of low herbs related to the irises and having brightly colored flowers borne singly in early spring

Crohn's disease \\'krōnz\ *n* : a chronic inflammatory disease of the gastrointestinal tract and esp. the ileum

crois·sant \\krò-'sänt, krwä-'säⁿ\ *n, pl* **croissants** *same or* -'sänts, -'säⁿz\ : a rich crescent-shaped roll

Cro–Ma·gnon \\krō-'mag-nən, -'man-yən\ *n* : a hominid of a tall erect race known from skeletal remains found in southern France and usu. classified as the same species as present-day humans — **Cro–Magnon** *adj*

crone \\'krōn\ *n* : HAG

cro·ny \\'krō-nē\ *n, pl* **cronies** : a close friend esp. of long standing

¹**crook** \\'krúk\ *vb* : to curve or bend sharply

²**crook** *n* **1** : a bent or curved implement   **2** : a bent or curved part; *also* : BEND, CURVE   **3** : SWINDLER, THIEF

crook·ed \\'krú-kəd\ *adj* **1** : having a crook : BENT, CURVED   **2** : DISHONEST — **crook·ed·ly** *adv* — **crook·ed·ness** *n*

croon \\'krün\ *vb* : to sing or hum in a gentle murmuring voice — **croon·er** *n*

¹**crop** \\'kräp\ *n* **1** : the handle of a whip; *also* : a short riding whip   **2** : a pouch in the throat of many birds and insects where food is received   **3** : something (as a plant product) that can be harvested; *also* : the yield at harvest

²**crop** *vb* **cropped; crop·ping** **1** : to remove the tips of : cut off short; *also* : TRIM   **2** : to feed on by cropping   **3** : to devote (land) to crops   **4** : to appear unexpectedly

crop duster *n* : a person who uses an airplane to spray crops with insecticidal dusts; *also* : an airplane so used

crop·land \\-,land\ *n* : land devoted to the production of plant crops

crop·per \\'krä-pər\ *n* : a raiser of crops; *esp* : SHARECROPPER

cro·quet \\krō-'kā\ *n* : a game in which mallets are used to drive wooden balls through a series of wickets set out on a lawn

cro·quette \\krō-'ket\ *n* [F] : a small often rounded mass of minced meat, fish, or vegetables fried in deep fat

cro·sier *or* **cro·zier** \\'krō-zhər\ *n* : a staff carried by bishops and abbots

¹**cross** \\'krós\ *n* **1** : a structure consisting of an upright beam and a crossbar used esp. by the ancient Romans for execution   **2** : a figure of the cross on which Christ was crucified used as a Christian symbol   **3** : a hybridizing of unlike individuals or strains; *also* : a product of this   **4** : a punch delivered with a circular motion over an opponent's lead

²**cross** *vb* **1** : to lie or place across; *also* : INTERSECT   **2** : to cancel by marking a cross on or by lining through   **3** : THWART, OBSTRUCT   **4** : to go or extend across : TRAVERSE   **5** : HYBRIDIZE   **6** : to meet and pass on the way

³**cross** *adj* **1** : lying across   **2** : CONTRARY, OPPOSED   **3** : marked by bad temper   **4** : HYBRID — **cross·ly** *adv*

cross·bar \\'krós-,bär\ *n* : a transverse bar or piece

cross·bow \\-,bō\ *n* : a short bow mounted crosswise at the end of a wooden stock that shoots short arrows

cross·breed \\'krós-,brēd, -'brēd\ *vb* **-bred** \\-'bred\; **-breed·ing** : HYBRIDIZE

cross–coun·try \\-'kən-trē\ *adj* **1** : extending or moving across a country   **2** : proceeding over the countryside (as fields and woods) and not by roads   **3** : of or relating to racing or skiing over the countryside instead of over a track or run — **cross–country** *adv*

cross-cur·rent \\-'kər-ənt\ *n* **1** : a current running counter to another   **2** : a conflicting tendency — usu. used in pl.

¹**cross·cut** \\-,kət\ *vb* : to cut or saw crosswise esp. of the grain of wood

²**crosscut** *adj* **1** : made or used for crosscutting ⟨a ∼ saw⟩   **2** : cut across the grain

³**crosscut** *n* : something that cuts through transversely

cross–ex·am·ine \‚krŏ-sig-'za-mən\ *vb* : to examine with questions to check the answers to previous questions — **cross–ex·am·i·na·tion** \-‚za-mə-'nā- shən\ *n* — **cross–ex·am·in·er** *n*

cross–eyed \'krŏ-‚sīd\ *adj* : having one or both eyes turned inward toward the nose

cross–fer·til·i·za·tion \-‚fər-tə-lə-'zā-shən\ *n* **1** : fertilization between sex cells produced by separate individuals or sometimes by individuals of different kinds; *also* : CROSS-POLLINATION **2** : a broadening or productive interchange (as between cultures) — **cross–fer·til·ize** \-'fərt-tə-‚līz\ *vb*

cross fire *n* **1** : crossing lines of fire in combat **2** : rapid or angry interchange

cross·hair \'krŏs-‚her\ *n* : a fine wire or thread in the eyepiece of an optical instrument used as a reference line

cross·hatch \'krŏs-‚hach\ *vb* : to mark with two series of parallel lines that intersect — **cross–hatch·ing** *n*

cross·ing \'krŏ-siŋ\ *n* **1** : a place or structure for crossing something (as a river) **2** : a point of intersection (as of a street and a railroad track)

cross·over \'krŏs-‚ō-vər\ *n* **1** : CROSSING **2** : a member of a political party who votes in the primary of the other party **3** : a broadening of the popular appeal of an artist (as a musician) by a change in the artist's style, genre, or medium **4** : an instance of breaking into another category

cross over *vb* : to achieve broader popularity by a change of medium or style

cross·piece \'krŏs-‚pēs\ *n* : a horizontal member

cross–pol·li·na·tion \‚krŏs-‚pä-lə-'nā-shən\ *n* : transfer of pollen from one flower to the stigma of another — **cross–pol·li·nate** \'krŏs-'pä-lə-‚nāt\ *vb*

cross–pur·pose \'krŏs-'pər-pəs\ *n* : a purpose contrary to another purpose ⟨working at ∼*s*⟩

cross–ques·tion \-'kwes-chən\ *vb* : CROSS-EXAMINE — **cross–question** *n*

cross–re·fer \‚krŏs-ri-'fər\ *vb* : to refer by a notation or direction from one place to another (as in a book or list) — **cross–ref·er·ence** \'krŏs-'re-frəns\ *n*

cross·road \'krŏs-‚rōd\ *n* **1** : a road that crosses a main road or runs between main roads **2** : a place where roads meet — usu. used in pl. **3** : a crucial point where a decision must be made — usu. used in pl.

cross section *n* **1** : a section cut across something; *also* : a representation made by or as if by such cutting **2** : a number of persons or things selected from a group that show the general nature of the whole group — **cross–sec·tion·al** *adj*

cross·walk \'krŏs-‚wŏk\ *n* : a marked path for pedestrians crossing a street

cross·ways \-‚wāz\ *adv* : CROSSWISE

cross·wind \-‚wind\ *n* : a wind not parallel to a course (as of an airplane)

cross·wise \-‚wīz\ *adv* : so as to cross something : ACROSS — **crosswise** *adj*

cross·word \'krŏs-‚wərd\ *n* : a puzzle in which words are put into a pattern of numbered squares in answer to clues

cros·ti·ni \krŏ-'stē-nē\ *n pl* : small slices of toasted bread served with a topping

crotch \'kräch\ *n* : an angle or area formed by the parting of two legs, branches, or members

crotch·et \'krä-chət\ *n* : an odd notion : WHIM — **crotch·ety** *adj*

crouch \'krauch\ *vb* **1** : to stoop or bend low **2** : CRINGE, COWER — **crouch** *n*

croup \'krüp\ *n* : laryngitis esp. of infants marked by a hoarse ringing cough and difficult breathing — **croupy** *adj*

crou·pi·er \'krü-pē-ər, -pē-‚ā\ *n* [F, lit., rider on the rump of a horse, fr. *croupe* rump] : an employee of a gambling casino who collects and pays bets at a gaming table

crou·ton \'krü-‚tän\ *n* [F *croûton*, dim. of *croûte* crust] : a small cube of bread toasted or fried crisp

¹**crow** \'krō\ *n* **1** : any of various large glossy black birds related to the jays **2** *cap* : a member of an American Indian people of a region in Montana and Wyoming; *also* : the language of the Crow people

²**crow** *vb* **1** : to make the loud shrill sound characteristic of the cock **2** : to utter a sound expressive of pleasure **3** : EXULT, GLOAT; *also* : BRAG, BOAST

³**crow** *n* : the cry of the cock

crow·bar \'krō-‚bär\ *n* : a metal bar usu. wedge-shaped at the end for use as a pry or lever

¹**crowd** \'kraud\ *vb* **1** : to press close **2** : to collect in numbers : THRONG **3** : CRAM, STUFF

²**crowd** *n* : a large number of people gathered together at random : THRONG

¹**crown** \'kraun\ *n* **1** : a mark of victory or honor; *esp* : the title of a champion in a sport **2** : a royal headdress **3** : the top of the head; *also* : the part of a hat that covers the top of the head **4** : the highest part (as of a tree or tooth) **5** *often cap* : sovereign power; *also* : MONARCH **6** : a formerly used British silver coin — **crowned** \'kraund\ *adj*

²**crown** *vb* **1** : to place a crown on **2** : HONOR **3** : TOP, SURMOUNT **4** : to fit (a tooth) with an artificial crown

crown vetch *n* : a Eurasian leguminous herb with umbels of pink-and-white flowers and sharp-angled pods

crow's-foot \'krōz-‚fút\ *n, pl* **crow's-feet** \-‚fēt\ : any of the wrinkles around the outer corners of the eyes — usu. used in pl.

crow's nest *n* : a partly enclosed platform high on a ship's mast for use as a lookout

crozier *var of* CROSIER

¹**CRT** \‚sē-(‚)är-'tē\ *n, pl* **CRTs** *or* **CRT's** : CATHODE-RAY TUBE; *also* : a display device incorporating a cathode-ray tube

²**CRT** *abbr* carrier route

cru·cial \'krü-shəl\ *adj* : DECISIVE ⟨a ∼ step⟩; *also* : IMPORTANT, PORTANT ⟨a ∼ question⟩

cru·ci·ate \'krü-shē-‚āt\ *adj* : CRUCIFORM

cru·ci·ble \'krü-sə-bəl\ *n* : a heat-resistant container in which material can be subjected to great heat

cru·ci·fix \'krü-sə-‚fiks\ *n* : a representation of Christ on the cross

cru·ci·fix·ion \‚krü-sə-'fik-shən\ *n* **1** *cap* : the crucifying of Christ **2** : the act of crucifying

cru·ci·form \'krü-sə-‚fȯrm\ *adj* : shaped like a cross

cru·ci·fy \'krü-sə-‚fī\ *vb* **-fied; -fy·ing** **1** : to put to death by nailing or binding the hands and feet to a cross **2** : MORTIFY **3** : TORTURE, PERSECUTE

¹**crude** \'krüd\ *adj* **crud·er; crud·est** **1** : not refined : RAW ⟨∼ oil⟩ ⟨∼ statistics⟩ **2** : lacking grace, taste, tact, or polish : RUDE — **crude·ly** *adv* — **crude·ness** *n* — **cru·di·ty** \'krü-də-tē\ *n*

²**crude** *n* : unrefined petroleum

cru·el \'krü-əl\ *adj* **cru·el·er** *or* **cru·el·ler; cru·el·est** *or* **cru·el·lest** [ME, fr. AF, fr. L *crudelis*, fr. *crudus* crude] : causing pain and suffering to others : MERCILESS — **cru·el·ly** *adv* — **cru·el·ty** \-tē\ *n*

cru·et \'krü-ət\ *n* : a small usu. glass bottle for vinegar, oil, or sauce

cruise \'krüz\ *vb* **cruised; cruis·ing** [D *kruisen* to make a cross, cruise] **1** : to sail about touching at a series of ports **2** : to travel for enjoyment **3** : to travel about the streets at random **4** : to travel at the most efficient operating speed ⟨the *cruising* speed of an airplane⟩ **5** : SURF **2** — **cruise** *n*

cruis·er \'krü-zər\ *n* **1** : SQUAD CAR **2** : a large fast moderately armored and gunned warship **3** : a motorboat equipped for living aboard

cruis·er·weight \-‚wāt\ *n* : a boxer weighing no more than 190 pounds

crul·ler \'krə-lər\ *n* **1** : a small sweet cake in the form of a twisted strip fried in deep fat **2** *Northern & Midland* : an unraised doughnut

¹**crumb** \'krəm\ *n* : a small fragment

²**crumb** *vb* **1** : to break into crumbs **2** : to cover with crumbs

crum·ble \'krəm-bəl\ *vb* **crum·bled; crum·bling** : to break into small pieces : DISINTEGRATE — **crum·bly** *adj*

crum·my *also* **crumby** \'krə-mē\ *adj* **crum·mi·er** *also* **crumb·i·er, -est** : very poor or inferior : LOUSY

crum·pet \'krəm-pət\ *n* : a small round unsweetened bread cooked on a griddle

crum·ple \'krəm-pəl\ *vb* **crum·pled; crum·pling** **1** : to crush together : RUMPLE **2** : COLLAPSE

¹**crunch** \'krənch\ *vb* : to chew with a grinding noise; *also* : to grind or press with a crushing noise

²**crunch** *n* **1** : an act of or a sound made by crunching **2** : a tight or critical situation — **crunchy** *adj*

cru·sade \krü-'sād\ *n* **1** *cap* : any of the expeditions in the 11th, 12th, and 13th centuries undertaken by Christian countries to take the Holy Land from the Muslims **2** : a reforming enterprise undertaken with zeal — **crusade** *vb* — **cru·sad·er** *n*

cruse \'krüz, 'krüs\ *n* : a jar for water or oil

¹crush \'krəsh\ *vb* **1** : to squeeze out of shape **2** : HUG, EMBRACE **3** : to grind or pound to small bits **4** : OVERWHELM, SUPPRESS

²crush *n* **1** : an act of crushing **2** : a violent crowding **3** : INFATUATION

crust \'krəst\ *n* **1** : the outside part of bread; *also* : a piece of old dry bread **2** : the cover of a pie **3** : a hard or brittle surface layer — **crust·al** *adj*

crus·ta·cean \krəs-'tā-shən\ *n* : any of a large class of mostly aquatic arthropods (as lobsters or crabs) having a firm crustlike shell — **crustacean** *adj*

crusty \'krəs-tē\ *adj* **crust·i·er; -est 1** : having or being a crust **2** : CROSS, GRUMPY

crutch \'krəch\ *n* : a supporting device; *esp* : a support fitting under the armpit for use by the disabled in walking

crux \'krəks, 'krüks\ *n, pl* **crux·es** [L, cross, torture] **1** : a puzzling or difficult problem **2** : a crucial point

¹cry \'krī\ *vb* **cried; cry·ing 1** : to call out : SHOUT **2** : to proclaim publicly : ADVERTISE **3** : WEEP

²cry *n, pl* **cries 1** : a loud outcry **2** : APPEAL, ENTREATY **3** : a fit of weeping **4** : the characteristic sound uttered by an animal **5** : DISTANCE — usu. used in the phrase *a far cry*

cry·ba·by \'krī-,bā-bē\ *n* : one who cries easily or often

cryo·gen·ic \,krī-ə-'je-nik\ *adj* : of or relating to the production of very low temperatures; *also* : involving the use of a very low temperature — **cryo·gen·i·cal·ly** \-ni-k(ə-)lē\ *adv*

cryo·gen·ics \-niks\ *n* : a branch of physics that relates to the production and effects of very low temperatures

cryo·lite \'krī-ə-,līt\ *n* : a usu. white mineral formerly used in making aluminum

crypt \'kript\ *n* : a chamber wholly or partly underground

cryp·tic \'krip-tik\ *adj* : meant to be puzzling or mysterious ⟨~ messages⟩

cryp·to·gram \'krip-tə-,gram\ *n* : a communication in cipher or code

cryp·tog·ra·phy \krip-'tä-grə-fē\ *n* : the coding and decoding of secret messages — **cryp·tog·ra·pher** \-fər\ *n*

cryp·to·sys·tem \,krip-tō-'sis-təm\ *n* : a method for coding and decoding messages

crys·tal \'kris-t°l\ *n* [ME *cristal,* fr. AF, fr. L *crystallum,* fr. Gk *krystallos* ice, crystal] **1** : transparent quartz **2** : something resembling crystal (as in transparency); *esp* : a clear colorless glass of superior quality **3** : a body that is formed by solidification of a substance and has a regular repeating arrangement of atoms and often of external plane faces ⟨a salt ~⟩ **4** : the transparent cover of a watch dial

crystal 3: snowflake crystals

crystal clear *adj* : perfectly or transparently clear

crys·tal·line \'kris-tə-lən\ *adj* **1** : made of or resembling crystal **2** : very clear or sparkling

crys·tal·lise *Brit var of* CRYSTALLIZE

crys·tal·lize \'kris-tə-,līz\ *vb* **-lized; -liz·ing 1** : to assume or cause to assume a crystalline form **2** : to take or cause to take a definite form — **crys·tal·li·za·tion** \,kris-tə-lə-'zā-shən\ *n*

crys·tal·log·ra·phy \,kris-tə-'lä-grə-fē\ *n* : the science dealing with the forms and structures of crystals — **crys·tal·log·ra·pher** *n*

cs *abbr* case; cases

Cs *symbol* cesium

CS *abbr* **1** civil service **2** county seat

CSA *abbr* Confederate States of America

C–section \'sē-,sek-shən\ *n* : CESAREAN SECTION

CSM *abbr* command sergeant major

CST *abbr* central standard time

ct *abbr* **1** carat **2** cent **3** count **4** county **5** court

CT *abbr* **1** central time **2** Connecticut

ctn *abbr* carton

ctr *abbr* **1** center **2** counter

CT scan \,sē-'tē-\ *n* : CAT SCAN

cu *abbr* cubic

Cu *symbol* [L *cuprum*] copper

cub \'kəb\ *n* : a young individual of some animals (as a fox, bear, or lion)

cub·by·hole \'kə-bē-,hōl\ *n* : a snug place (as for storing things)

Cu·ban sandwich \'kyü-bən-\ *n* : a usu. grilled and pressed sandwich served on a long split roll

¹cube \'kyüb\ *n* **1** : a solid having 6 equal square sides **2** : the result of raising a number to the third power ⟨the ~ of 3 is 27⟩

²cube *vb* **cubed; cub·ing 1** : to raise to the third power **2** : to form into a cube **3** : to cut into cubes

cube root *n* : a number whose cube is a given number

cu·bic \'kyü-bik\ *also* **cu·bi·cal** *adj* **1** : having the form of a cube **2** : being the volume of a cube whose edge is a specified unit **3** : having length, width, and height

cu·bi·cle \'kyü-bi-kəl\ *n* : a small separate space (as for sleeping, studying, or working)

cubic measure *n* : a unit (as cubic inch) for measuring volume — see METRIC SYSTEM table, WEIGHT table

cubic zir·co·nia \-,zər-'kō-nē-ə\ *also* **cubic zirconium** *n* : a synthetic gemstone resembling a diamond made from an oxide of zirconium

cub·ism \'kyü-,bi-zəm\ *n* : a style of art characterized by the abstraction of natural forms into fragmented geometric shapes — **cub·ist** \-bist\ *n or adj*

cu·bit \'kyü-bət\ *n* : an ancient unit of length equal to about 18 inches (46 centimeters)

Cub Scout *n* : a member of the program of the Boy Scouts for boys in the first through fifth grades in school

cuck·old \'kə-kəld, 'kü-\ *n* : a man whose wife is unfaithful — **cuckold** *vb*

¹cuck·oo \'kü-kü, 'ku-\ *n, pl* **cuckoos** : a largely grayish brown European bird that lays its eggs in the nests of other birds for them to hatch

²cuckoo *adj* : SILLY, FOOLISH

cu·cum·ber \'kyü-(,)kəm-bər\ *n* : the long fleshy manyseeded fruit of a vine of the gourd family that is grown as a garden vegetable; *also* : this vine

cud \'kəd\ *n* : food brought up into the mouth by some animals (as cows) from the rumen to be chewed again

cud·dle \'kə-d°l\ *vb* **cud·dled; cud·dling** : to lie close : SNUGGLE

cud·gel \'kə-jəl\ *n* : a short heavy club — **cudgel** *vb*

¹cue \'kyü\ *n* **1** : a word, phrase, or action in a play serving as a signal for the next actor to speak or act **2** : HINT — **cue** *vb*

²cue *n* : a tapered rod for striking the balls in billiards or pool

cue ball *n* : the ball a player strikes with a cue in billiards or pool

¹cuff \'kəf\ *n* **1** : a part (as of a sleeve or glove) encircling the wrist **2** : the folded hem of a trouser leg

²cuff *vb* : to strike esp. with the open hand : SLAP

³cuff *n* : a blow with the hand esp. when open

cui·sine \kwi-'zēn\ *n* : style of cooking; *also* : the food prepared

cuke \'kyük\ *n* : CUCUMBER

cul–de–sac \,kəl-di-'sak, ,kul-\ *n, pl* **culs–de–sac** *same or* ,kəlz-, ,kulz-\ *also* **cul–de–sacs** \,kəl-də-'saks, ,kul-\ [F, lit., bottom of the bag] : a street or passage closed at one end

cu·li·nary \'kə-lə-,ner-ē, 'kyü-\ *adj* : of or relating to the kitchen or cookery

¹cull \'kəl\ *vb* : to pick out from a group

²cull *n* : something rejected from a group or lot as worthless or inferior

cul·mi·nate \'kəl-mə-,nāt\ *vb* **-nat·ed; -nat·ing** : to reach the highest point — **cul·mi·na·tion** \,kəl-mə-'nā-shən\ *n*

cu·lotte \'kü-,lät, ,kyü-, kù-,lät, kyü-\ *n* [F, breeches, fr. dim. of *cul* backside] : a divided skirt; *also* : a garment having a divided skirt — often used in pl.

cul·pa·ble \'kəl-pə-bəl\ *adj* : deserving blame — **cul·pa·bil·i·ty** \,kəl-pə-'bi-lə-tē\ *n*

cul·prit \'kəl-prət\ n [AF cul. (abbr. of culpable guilty) + prest, prit ready (i.e., to prove it), fr. L praestus] : one accused or guilty of a crime

cult \'kəlt\ n 1 : formal religious veneration 2 : a religious system; also : its adherents 3 : faddish devotion; also : a group of persons showing such devotion — **cult·ish** \'kəl-tish\ adj — **cult·ist** \-tist\ n

cul·ti·va·ble \'kəl-tə-və-bəl\ adj : capable of being cultivated

cul·ti·var \'kəl-tə-ˌvär, -ˌver\ n : a plant variety originating and persisting under cultivation

cul·ti·vate \'kəl-tə-ˌvāt\ vb -vat·ed; -vat·ing 1 : to prepare for the raising of crops 2 : to foster the growth of by tilling or by labor and care ⟨∼ vegetables⟩ 3 : REFINE, IMPROVE 4 : ENCOURAGE, FURTHER — **cul·ti·va·tion** \ˌkəl-tə-'vā-shən\ n — **cul·ti·va·tor** \'kəl-tə-ˌvā-tər\ n

cul·ture \'kəl-chər\ n 1 : TILLAGE, CULTIVATION 2 : the act of developing by education and training 3 : refinement of intellectual and artistic taste 4 : the customary beliefs, social forms, and material traits of a racial, religious, or social group — **cul·tur·al** \'kəl-chə-rəl\ adj — **cul·tur·al·ly** adv — **cul·tured** \-chərd\ adj

cul·vert \'kəl-vərt\ n : a drain crossing under a road or railroad

cum abbr cumulative

cum·ber \'kəm-bər\ vb : to weigh down : BURDEN, HINDER

cum·ber·some \'kəm-bər-səm\ adj : hard to handle or manage because of size or weight — **cum·ber·some·ly** adv

cum·brous \'kəm-brəs\ adj : CUMBERSOME — **cum·brous·ly** adv — **cum·brous·ness** n

cum·in \'kə-mən, 'kyü-\ n : the seedlike fruit of a small annual herb related to the carrot that is used as a spice; also : this herb

cum·mer·bund \'kə-mər-ˌbənd, 'kəm-bər-\ n [Hindi & Urdu kamarband, fr. Pers, fr. kamar waist + band band] : a broad sash worn as a waistband

cu·mu·la·tive \'kyü-myə-lə-tiv, -ˌlā-\ adj : increasing in force or value by successive additions

cu·mu·lo·nim·bus \ˌkyü-myə-lō-'nim-bəs\ n : an anvil-shaped cumulus cloud extending to great heights

cu·mu·lus \'kyü-myə-ləs\ n, pl -**li** \-ˌlī, -ˌlē\ : a dense puffy cloud having a flat base and rounded outlines

cu·ne·i·form \kyü-'nē-ə-ˌform\ adj 1 : wedge-shaped 2 : composed of wedge-shaped characters

cun·ni·lin·gus \ˌkə-ni-'liŋ-gəs\ also **cun·ni·linc·tus** \-'liŋk-təs\ n : oral stimulation of the vulva or clitoris

¹cun·ning \'kə-niŋ\ adj 1 : SKILLFUL, DEXTEROUS 2 : marked by wiliness and trickery ⟨∼ schemes⟩ 3 : CUTE ⟨a ∼ kitten⟩ — **cun·ning·ly** adv

²cunning n 1 : SKILL 2 : SLYNESS

¹cup \'kəp\ n 1 : a small bowl-shaped drinking vessel 2 : the contents of a cup 3 : the consecrated wine of the Communion 4 : something resembling a cup : a small bowl or hollow 5 : a half pint — **cup·ful** n — **cup·like** \-ˌlīk\ adj

²cup vb cupped; cup·ping : to curve into the shape of a cup

cup·board \'kə-bərd\ n : a small closet with shelves for food or dishes

cup·cake \'kəp-ˌkāk\ n : a small cake baked in a cuplike mold

cu·pid \'kyü-pəd\ n : a winged naked figure of an infant often with a bow and arrow that represents the god Cupid

cu·pid·i·ty \kyü-'pi-də-tē\ n, pl -ties : excessive desire for money

cu·po·la \'kyü-pə-lə, -ˌlō\ n : a small structure on top of a roof or building

¹cur \'kər\ n : a mongrel dog

²cur abbr 1 currency 2 current

cu·rate \'kyür-ət\ n 1 : a member of the clergy who is in charge of a parish 2 : a member of the clergy who assists a rector or vicar — **cu·ra·cy** \-ə-sē\ n

cu·ra·tive \-ə-tiv\ adj : relating to or used in the cure of diseases ⟨∼ therapy⟩ ⟨∼ powers⟩ — **curative** n

cu·ra·tor \'kyür-ˌā-tər, kyü-'rā-\ n : CUSTODIAN; esp : one in charge of a place of exhibit (as a museum or zoo)

¹curb \'kərb\ n 1 : a bit that exerts pressure on a horse's jaws 2 : CHECK, RESTRAINT 3 : a raised edging (as of stone or concrete) along a paved street

²curb vb : to hold in or back : RESTRAIN

curb·ing \'kər-biŋ\ n 1 : the material for a curb 2 : CURB

curd \'kərd\ n : the thick protein-rich part of coagulated milk

cur·dle \'kər-dᵊl\ vb cur·dled; cur·dling : to form curds; also : SPOIL, SOUR

¹cure \'kyür\ n 1 : spiritual care 2 : recovery or relief from disease 3 : a curative agent : REMEDY 4 : a course or period of treatment

²cure vb cured; cur·ing 1 : to restore to health : HEAL, REMEDY; also : to become cured 2 : to process for storage or use ⟨∼ bacon⟩ — **cur·able** adj

cu·ré \kyü-'rā\ n [F] : a parish priest

cure–all \'kyür-ˌȯl\ n : a remedy for all ills : PANACEA

cu·ret·tage \ˌkyür-ə-'täzh\ n : a surgical scraping or cleaning of a body part (as the uterus)

cur·few \'kər-ˌfyü\ n [ME, fr. AF covrefeu, signal given to bank the hearth fire, curfew, fr. coverir to cover + fu, feu fire, fr. L focus hearth] : a regulation that specified persons (as children) be off the streets at a set hour of the evening; also : the sounding of a signal (as a bell) at this hour

cu·ria \'kyür-ē-ə, 'kur-\ n, pl **cu·ri·ae** \'kyür-ē-ˌē, 'kur-ē-ˌī\ often cap : the body of congregations, tribunals, and offices through which the pope governs the Roman Catholic Church

cu·rie \'kyür-ē\ n : a unit of radioactivity equal to 37 billion disintegrations per second

cu·rio \'kyür-ē-ˌō\ n, pl **cu·ri·os** : an object or article valued because it is strange or rare

cu·ri·ous \'kyür-ē-əs\ adj 1 : having a desire to investigate and learn 2 : STRANGE, UNUSUAL, ODD ⟨a ∼ coincidence⟩ — **cu·ri·os·i·ty** \ˌkyür-ē-'ä-sə-tē\ n — **cu·ri·ous·ness** n

cu·ri·ous·ly adv 1 : in a curious manner 2 : as is curious

cu·ri·um \'kyür-ē-əm\ n : a metallic radioactive element produced artificially

¹curl \'kərl\ vb 1 : to form into ringlets 2 : CURVE, COIL — **curl·er** n

²curl n 1 : a lock of hair that coils : RINGLET 2 : something having a spiral or twisted form — **curly** adj

cur·lew \'kər-lü, 'kərl-yü\ n, pl **curlews** or **curlew** : any of various long-legged brownish birds that have a downcurved bill and are related to the sandpipers and snipes

curli·cue \'kər-li-ˌkyü\ n : a fancifully curved or spiral figure

cur·rant \'kər-ənt\ n 1 : a small seedless raisin 2 : the acid berry of various shrubs related to the gooseberry; also : this plant

cur·ren·cy \'kər-ən-sē\ n, pl **-cies** 1 : general use or acceptance 2 : something that is in circulation as a medium of exchange : MONEY

¹cur·rent \'kər-ənt\ adj 1 : occurring in or belonging to the present ⟨the ∼ crisis⟩ 2 : used as a medium of exchange 3 : generally accepted or practiced

²current n 1 : the part of a body of fluid moving continuously in a certain direction; also : the swiftest part of a stream 2 : a flow of electric charge; also : the rate of such flow

cur·ric·u·lum \kə-'ri-kyə-ləm\ n, pl **-la** \-lə\ also **-lums** [L, running, course, fr. currere to run] : the courses offered by an educational institution

¹cur·ry \'kər-ē\ vb cur·ried; cur·ry·ing 1 : to clean the coat of (a horse) with a currycomb 2 : to treat (tanned leather) esp. by incorporating oil or grease — **curry favor** : to seek to gain favor by flattery or attention

²cur·ry n, pl **cur·ries** : a powder of pungent spices used in cooking; also : a food seasoned with curry

cur·ry·comb \-ˌkōm\ n : a comb used esp. to curry horses — **currycomb** vb

¹curse \'kərs\ n 1 : a prayer for harm to come upon one 2 : something that is cursed 3 : evil or misfortune coming as if in response to a curse

²curse vb cursed; curs·ing 1 : to call on divine power to send injury upon 2 : BLASPHEME 3 : AFFLICT ♦ Synonyms EXECRATE, DAMN, ANATHEMATIZE, OBJURGATE

cur·sive \'kər-siv\ adj : written with the strokes of the letters joined together and the angles rounded

cur·sor \'kər-sər\ n : a visual cue (as a pointer) on a computer screen that indicates position (as for data entry)

cur·so·ry \'kər-sə-rē\ adj : rapidly and often superficially done : HASTY ⟨a ∼ reading of the report⟩ — **cur·so·ri·ly** \-rə-lē\ adj

curt \\'kərt\ *adj* : rudely short or abrupt — **curt·ly** *adv* — **curt·ness** *n*

cur·tail \(ˌ)kər-'tāl\ *vb* : to cut off the end of : SHORTEN — **cur·tail·ment** *n*

cur·tain \\'kər-tᵊn\ *n* **1** : a hanging screen that can be drawn back esp. at a window **2** : the screen between the stage and auditorium of a theater — **curtain** *vb*

curt·sy *also* **curt·sey** \\'kərt-sē\ *n, pl* **curtsies** *or* **curtseys** : a courteous bow made by women chiefly by bending the knees — **curtsy** *also* **curtsey** *vb*

cur·va·ceous *also* **cur·va·cious** \ˌkər-'vā-shəs\ *adj* : having curves suggestive of a well-proportioned feminine figure

cur·va·ture \\'kər-və-ˌchùr\ *n* : a measure or amount of curving : BEND

¹**curve** \\'kərv\ *vb* **curved; curv·ing** : to bend from a straight line or course

²**curve** *n* **1** : a line esp. when curved **2** : something that bends or curves without angles ⟨a ∼ in the road⟩ **3** : a baseball pitch thrown so that it swerves esp. downward and to one side

cur·vet \(ˌ)kər-'vet\ *n* : a prancing leap of a horse — **curvet** *vb*

¹**cush·ion** \\'kù-shən\ *n* [ME cusshin, fr. AF cussin, quissin, fr. VL *coxinus*, fr. L coxa hip] **1** : a soft pillow or pad to rest on or against **2** : the springy pad inside the rim of a billiard table **3** : something soft that prevents discomfort or protects against injury

²**cushion** *vb* **1** : to provide (as a seat) with a cushion **2** : to soften or lessen the force or shock of

cusp \\'kəsp\ *n* : a pointed end or part (as of a tooth)

cus·pid \\'kəs-pəd\ *n* : a canine tooth

cus·pi·dor \\'kəs-pə-ˌdór\ *n* : SPITTOON

cus·tard \\'kəs-tərd\ *n* : a sweetened cooked mixture of milk and eggs

cus·to·di·al \ˌkəs-'tō-dē-əl\ *adj* : marked by watching and protecting rather than seeking to cure ⟨∼ care⟩

cus·to·di·an \ˌkəs-'tō-dē-ən\ *n* : one who has custody (as of a building)

cus·to·dy \\'kəs-tə-dē\ *n, pl* **-dies** : immediate charge and control

¹**cus·tom** \\'kəs-təm\ *n* **1** : habitual course of action : recognized usage **2** *pl* : taxes levied on imports **3** : business patronage

²**custom** *adj* **1** : made to personal order **2** : doing work only on order

cus·tom·ary \\'kəs-tə-ˌmer-ē\ *adj* **1** : based on or established by custom **2** : commonly practiced or observed : HABITUAL — **cus·tom·ar·i·ly** *adv*

cus·tom-built \ˌkəs-təm-'bilt\ *adj* : built to individual order

cus·tom·er \\'kəs-tə-mər\ *n* : BUYER, PURCHASER; *esp* : a regular or frequent buyer

cus·tom·house \\'kəs-təm-ˌhaùs\ *n* : the building where customs are paid

cus·tom·ise *Brit var of* CUSTOMIZE

cus·tom·ize \\'kəs-tə-ˌmīz\ *vb* **-ized; -iz·ing** : to build, fit, or alter according to individual specifications

cus·tom-made \ˌkəs-təm-'mād\ *adj* : made to individual order

¹**cut** \\'kət\ *vb* **cut; cut·ting** **1** : to penetrate or divide with a sharp edge : CLEAVE, GASH; *also* : to experience the growth of (a tooth) through the gum **2** : to hurt the feelings of **3** : to strike sharply **4** : SHORTEN, REDUCE **5** : to remove by severing or paring **6** : INTERSECT, CROSS **7** : to divide into parts **8** : to go quickly or change direction abruptly **9** : to cause to stop

²**cut** *n* **1** : something made by cutting : GASH, CLEFT **2** : SHARE **3** : a segment or section of a meat carcass **4** : an excavated channel or roadway **5** : BAND **4** **6** : a sharp stroke or blow **7** : REDUCTION ⟨a ∼ in wages⟩ **8** : the shape or manner in which a thing is cut

cut-and-dried \ˌkət-ᵊn-'drīd\ *also* **cut-and-dry** \-'drī\ *adj* : according to a plan, set procedure, or formula

cu·ta·ne·ous \kyü-'tā-nē-əs\ *adj* : of, relating to, or affecting the skin

cut·back \\'kət-ˌbak\ *n* **1** : something cut back **2** : REDUCTION

cute \\'kyüt\ *adj* **cut·er; cut·est** [short for *acute*] **1** : CLEVER, SHREWD **2** : daintily attractive : PRETTY

cu·ti·cle \\'kyü-ti-kəl\ *n* **1** : an outer layer (as of skin or a

leaf) **2** : dead or horny epidermis esp. around a fingernail — **cu·tic·u·lar** \kyü-'ti-kyə-lər\ *adj*

cut in *vb* **1** : to thrust oneself between others **2** : to interrupt a dancing couple and take one as one's partner

cut·lass \\'kət-ləs\ *n* : a short heavy curved sword

cut·ler \\'kət-lər\ *n* [ME, fr. AF *cuteler*, fr. LL *cultellarius*, fr. L *cultellus* knife] : one who makes, deals in, or repairs cutlery

cut·lery \\'kət-lə-rē\ *n* : edged or cutting tools; *esp* : implements for cutting and eating food

cut·let \\'kət-lət\ *n* : a slice of meat (as veal) for broiling or frying

cut·off \\'kət-ˌóf\ *n* **1** : the channel formed when a stream cuts through the neck of an oxbow; *also* : SHORTCUT **2** : a device for cutting off **3** *pl* : shorts orig. made from jeans with the legs cut off at the knees or higher

cut·out \\'kət-ˌaùt\ *n* : something cut out or prepared for cutting out from something else

cut out *vb* **1** : to determine or assign through necessity ⟨had her work *cut out* for her⟩ **2** : DISCONNECT **3** : to cease operating ⟨the engine *cut out*⟩ **4** : ELIMINATE ⟨*cut out* unnecessary expense⟩

cut-rate \\'kət-'rāt\ *adj* : relating to or dealing in goods sold at reduced rates

cut·ter \\'kə-tər\ *n* **1** : a tool or a machine for cutting **2** : a ship's boat for carrying stores and passengers **3** : a small armed vessel in government service **4** : a light sleigh

¹**cut·throat** \\'kət-ˌthrōt\ *n* : MURDERER

²**cutthroat** *adj* **1** : MURDEROUS, CRUEL **2** : RUTHLESS ⟨∼ competition⟩

cutthroat trout *n* : a large American trout with a red mark under the jaw

¹**cut·ting** \\'kə-tiŋ\ *n* : a piece of a plant able to grow into a new plant

²**cutting** *adj* **1** : SHARP, EDGED **2** : marked by piercing cold **3** : likely to hurt the feelings : SARCASTIC ⟨a ∼ remark⟩

cut·tle·fish \\'kə-tᵊl-ˌfish\ *n* : any of various marine mollusks having eight arms and two usu. longer tentacles and an internal shell (**cut·tle·bone** \-ˌbōn\) composed of calcium compounds

cut·up \\'kət-ˌəp\ *n* : a person who clowns or acts boisterously — **cut up** *vb*

cut·worm \-ˌwərm\ *n* : any of various smooth-bodied moth larvae that feed on plants at night

cw *abbr* clockwise

CWO *abbr* **1** cash with order **2** chief warrant officer

cwt *abbr* hundredweight

-cy \sē\ *n suffix* **1** : action : practice ⟨mendican*cy*⟩ **2** : rank : office ⟨chaplain*cy*⟩ **3** : body : class ⟨constituen*cy*⟩ **4** : state : quality ⟨accura*cy*⟩

cy·an \\'sī-ˌan, -ən\ *n* : a greenish blue color

cy·a·nide \\'sī-ə-ˌnīd, -nəd\ *n* : a poisonous compound of carbon and nitrogen with another element (as potassium)

cy·ber \\'sī-bər\ *adj* : of, relating to, or involving computers or computer networks

cyber- *comb form* : computer : computer network

cy·ber·ca·fe \\'sī-bər-ka-ˌfā\ *n* : a small restaurant offering use of computers with Internet access

cy·ber·net·ics \ˌsī-bər-'ne-tiks\ *n* : the science of communication and control theory that is concerned esp. with the comparative study of automatic control systems — **cy·ber·net·ic** *adj*

cy·ber·punk \\'sī-bər-ˌpəŋk\ *n* **1** : science fiction dealing with computer-dominated future societies **2** : HACKER **3**

cy·ber·sex \\'sī-bər-ˌseks\ *n* **1** : online sex-oriented conversations **2** : sex-oriented material available on a computer

cy·ber·space \\'sī-bər-ˌspās\ *n* : the online world of the Internet

cy·cla·men \\'sī-klə-mən\ *n* : any of a genus of plants related to the primroses and having showy nodding flowers

¹**cy·cle** \\'sī-kəl\ *n* **1** : a period of time occupied by a series of events that repeat themselves regularly and in the same order **2** : a recurring round of operations or events **3** : one complete occurrence of a periodic process (as a vibration or current alternation) **4** : a circular or spiral arrangement **5** : a long period of time : AGE **6** : BICYCLE **7** : MOTORCYCLE — **cy·clic** \\'sī-klik, 'si-\ *or* **cy·cli·cal** \kli-kəl\ — **cy·cli·cal·ly** \-k(ə-)lē\ *also* **cy·clic·ly** *adv*

²**cy·cle** \'sī-kəl\ *vb* **cy·cled; cy·cling** : to ride a cycle — **cy·clist** \'sī-klist, -kə-list\ *n*
cy·clone \'sī-ˌklōn\ *n* **1** : a storm or system of winds that rotates about a center of low atmospheric pressure and advances at 20 to 30 miles (about 30 to 50 kilometers) an hour **2** : TORNADO — **cy·clon·ic** \sī-'klä-nik\ *adj*
cy·clo·pe·dia *also* **cy·clo·pae·dia** \ˌsī-klə-'pē-dē-ə\ *n* : ENCYCLOPEDIA
cy·clo·tron \'sī-klə-ˌträn\ *n* : a device for giving high speed to charged particles by magnetic and electric fields
cy·der *Brit var of* CIDER
cyg·net \'sig-nət\ *n* : a young swan
cyl *abbr* cylinder
cyl·in·der \'si-lən-dər\ *n* : the solid figure formed by turning a rectangle about one side as an axis; *also* : a body or space of this form ⟨an engine ∼⟩ ⟨a bullet in the ∼ of a revolver⟩ — **cy·lin·dri·cal** \sə-'lin-dri-kəl\ *adj*
cym·bal \'sim-bəl\ *n* : a concave brass plate that produces a brilliant clashing sound
cyn·ic \'si-nik\ *n* : one who attributes all actions to selfish motives — **cyn·i·cal** \-ni-kəl\ *adj* — **cyn·i·cal·ly** \-k(ə-)lē\ *adv* — **cyn·i·cism** \si-nə-ˌsi-zəm\ *n*
cy·no·sure \'sī-nə-ˌshúr, 'si-\ *n* [MF & L; MF, Ursa Minor, guide, fr. L *cynosura* Ursa Minor, fr. Gk *kynosoura*, fr. *kynos oura*, lit., dog's tail] : a center of attraction
CYO *abbr* Catholic Youth Organization

cy·pher *chiefly Brit var of* CIPHER
cy·press \'sī-prəs\ *n* **1** : any of a genus of scaly-leaved evergreen trees and shrubs **2** : BALD CYPRESS **3** : the wood of a cypress
cyst \'sist\ *n* : an abnormal closed bodily sac usu. containing liquid — **cys·tic** \'sis-tik\ *adj*
cystic fibrosis *n* : a common hereditary disease marked esp. by deficiency of pancreatic enzymes, by respiratory symptoms, and by excessive loss of salt in the sweat
cy·tol·o·gy \sī-'tä-lə-jē\ *n* : a branch of biology dealing with cells — **cy·to·log·i·cal** \ˌsī-tə-'lä-ji-kəl\ *or* **cy·to·log·ic** \-jik\ *adj* — **cy·tol·o·gist** \sī-'tä-lə-jist\ *n*
cy·to·plasm \'sī-tə-ˌpla-zəm\ *n* : the protoplasm of a cell that lies external to the nucleus — **cy·to·plas·mic** \ˌsī-tə-'plaz-mik\ *adj*
cy·to·sine \'sī-tə-ˌsēn\ *n* : a chemical base that is a pyrimidine coding genetic information in DNA and RNA
CZ *abbr* Canal Zone
czar *also* **tsar** \'zär, 'tsär\ *n* [NL, fr. Russ *tsar'*, ultim. fr. L *Caesar* Caesar] : the ruler of Russia until 1917; *also* : one having great authority — **czar·ist** *also* **tsar·ist** \-ist\ *n or adj*
cza·ri·na \zä-'rē-nə\ *n* : the wife of a czar
Czech \'chek\ *n* **1** : a native or inhabitant of Czechoslovakia or the Czech Republic **2** : the language of the Czechs — **Czech** *adj*

¹**d** \'dē\ *n, pl* **d's** *or* **ds** \'dēz\ *often cap* **1** : the 4th letter of the English alphabet **2** : five hundred in Roman numerals **3** : a grade rating a student's work as poor **4** : DEFENSE
²**d** *abbr, often cap* **1** date **2** daughter **3** day **4** dead **5** deceased **6** degree **7** Democrat **8** [L *denarius, denarii*] penny; pence **9** depart; departure **10** diameter
D *symbol* deuterium
d *symbol* — used after the figure 2 or 3 to indicate the ordinal number second or third
DA *abbr* **1** deposit account **2** district attorney **3** don't answer
¹**dab** \'dab\ *n* **1** : a sudden blow or thrust : POKE; *also* : PECK **2** : a gentle touch or stroke : PAT
²**dab** *vb* **dabbed; dab·bing** **1** : to strike or touch gently : PAT **2** : to apply lightly or irregularly : DAUB — **dab·ber** *n*
³**dab** *n* **1** : DAUB **2** : a small amount
dab·ble \'da-bəl\ *vb* **dab·bled; dab·bling** **1** : to wet by splashing : SPATTER **2** : to paddle or play in or as if in water **3** : to work or involve oneself without serious effort — **dab·bler** *n*
da ca·po \dä-'kä-(ˌ)pō\ *adv or adj* [It] : from the beginning — used as a direction in music to repeat
dace \'dās\ *n, pl* **dace** : any of various small No. American freshwater fishes related to the carp
da·cha \'dä-chə\ *n* [Russ] : a Russian country house
dachs·hund \'däks-ˌhúnt\ *n* [G, fr. *Dachs* badger + *Hund* dog] : any of a breed of long-bodied short-legged dogs of German origin

dachshund

dac·tyl \'dak-t³l\ *n* [ME *dactile*, fr. L *dactylus*, fr. Gk *daktylos*, lit., finger; fr. the fact that the three syllables have the first one longest like the joints of the finger] : a metrical foot of one accented syllable followed by two unaccented syllables — **dac·tyl·ic** \dak-'ti-lik\ *adj or n*
dad \'dad\ *n* : FATHER 1
Da·da \'dä-(ˌ)dä\ *n* : a movement in art and literature based on deliberate irrationality and negation of traditional artistic values — **da·da·ism** \-ˌi-zəm\ *n, often cap* — **da·da·ist** \-ˌist\ *n or adj, often cap*
dad·dy \'da-dē\ *n, pl* **daddies** : FATHER 1
dad·dy long·legs \ˌda-dē-'lóŋ-ˌlegz\ *n, pl* **daddy longlegs** : any of an order of arachnids resembling the true spiders but having small rounded bodies and long slender legs
daemon *var of* DEMON
daf·fo·dil \'da-fə-ˌdil\ *n* : any of various bulbous herbs with usu. large flowers having a trumpetlike center
daf·fy \'da-fē\ *adj* **daf·fi·er; -est** : DAFT
daft \'daft\ *adj* : FOOLISH; *also* : INSANE — **daft·ness** *n*
dag *abbr* dekagram
dag·ger \'da-gər\ *n* **1** : a sharp pointed knife for stabbing **2** : a character † used as a reference mark or to indicate a death date
da·guerre·o·type \də-'ger-(ē-)ə-ˌtīp\ *n* : an early photograph produced on a silver or a silver-covered copper plate
dahl·ia \'dal-yə, 'däl-\ *n* : any of a genus of tuberous herbs related to the daisies and having showy flowers
¹**dai·ly** \'dā-lē\ *adj* **1** : occurring, done, or used every day or every weekday **2** : of or relating to every day ⟨∼ visitors⟩ **3** : computed in terms of one day ⟨∼ wages⟩
♦ *Synonyms* DIURNAL, QUOTIDIAN — **dai·li·ness** \-lē-nəs\ *n* — **daily** *adv*
²**daily** *n, pl* **dailies** : a newspaper published every weekday
daily double *n* : a system of betting on races in which the bettor must pick the winners of two stipulated races in one day
¹**dain·ty** \'dān-tē\ *n, pl* **dainties** [ME *deinte* high esteem, delight, fr. AF *deinté*, fr. L *dignitas* dignity, worth] : something delicious or pleasing to the taste : DELICACY
²**dainty** *adj* **dain·ti·er; -est** **1** : pleasing to the taste **2** : delicately pretty **3** : having or showing delicate taste;

also : FASTIDIOUS ✦ *Synonyms* CHOICE, DELICATE, EXQUISITE, RARE, RECHERCHÉ — **dain·ti·ly** \-ti-lē\ *adv* — **dain·ti·ness** \-tē-nəs\ *n*

dai·qui·ri \'da-kə-rē, 'dī-\ *n* [*Daiquirí,* Cuba] : a cocktail made usu. of rum, lime juice, and sugar

dairy \'der-ē\ *n, pl* **dair·ies** [ME *deyerie,* fr. *deye* dairymaid, fr. OE *dǣge* kneader of bread] **1** : CREAMERY **2** : a farm specializing in milk production

dairy·ing \'der-ē-iŋ\ *n* : the business of operating a dairy

dairy·maid \-ˌmād\ *n* : a woman employed in a dairy

dairy·man \-mən, -ˌman\ *n* : a person who operates a dairy farm or works in a dairy

da·is \'dā-əs\ *n* : a raised platform usu. above the floor of a hall or large room

dai·sy \'dā-zē\ *n, pl* **daisies** [ME *dayeseye,* fr. OE *dægesēage,* fr. *dæg* day + *ēage* eye] : any of numerous composite plants having flower heads in which the marginal flowers resemble petals

dai·sy–chain \-ˌchān\ *vb* : to link (as computer components) together in series — **daisy chain** *n*

daisy wheel *n* : a disk with spokes bearing type that serves as the printing element of an electric typewriter or printer; *also* : a printer that uses such a disk

Da·ko·ta \də-'kō-tə\ *n, pl* **Dakotas** *also* **Dakota** : a member of an American Indian people of the northern Mississippi valley; *also* : their language

dal *abbr* dekaliter

da·la·si \dä-'lä-sē\ *n, pl* **dalasi** *or* **dalasis** — see MONEY table

dale \'dāl\ *n* : VALLEY

dal·ly \'da-lē\ *vb* **dal·lied; dal·ly·ing** **1** : to act playfully; *esp* : to play amorously **2** : to waste time **3** : LINGER, DAWDLE ✦ *Synonyms* FLIRT, COQUET, TOY, TRIFLE — **dal·li·ance** \-lē-əns\ *n*

dal·ma·tian \dal-'mā-shən\ *n, often cap* : any of a breed of medium-sized dogs having a white short-haired coat with many black or brown spots

¹dam \'dam\ *n* : the female parent of an animal and esp. of a domestic animal

²dam *n* : a barrier (as across a stream) to stop the flow of water — **dam** *vb*

³dam *abbr* dekameter

¹dam·age \'da-mij\ *n* **1** : loss or harm due to injury to persons, property, or reputation **2** *pl* : compensation in money imposed by law for loss or injury ⟨bring a suit for ~*s*⟩

²damage *vb* **dam·aged; dam·ag·ing** : to cause damage to ⟨~ the furniture⟩

dam·a·scene \'da-mə-ˌsēn\ *vb* **-scened; -scen·ing** : to ornament (as iron or steel) with wavy patterns or with inlaid work of precious metals

dam·ask \'da-məsk\ *n* **1** : a firm lustrous reversible figured fabric used for household linen **2** : a tough steel having decorative wavy lines

dame \'dām\ *n* **1** : a woman of rank, station, or authority **2** : an elderly woman **3** : WOMAN

damn \'dam\ *vb* [ME *dampnen,* fr. AF *dampner,* fr. L *damnare,* fr. *damnum* damage, loss, fine] **1** : to condemn esp. to hell **2** : CURSE — **damned** *adj*

dam·na·ble \'dam-nə-bəl\ *adj* **1** : liable to or deserving punishment **2** : DETESTABLE ⟨~ weather⟩ — **dam·na·bly** \-blē\ *adv*

dam·na·tion \dam-'nā-shən\ *n* **1** : the act of damning **2** : the state of being damned

¹damp \'damp\ *n* **1** : a noxious gas **2** : MOISTURE

²damp *vb* : DAMPEN

³damp *adj* : MOIST — **damp·ness** *n*

damp·en \'dam-pən\ *vb* **1** : to check or diminish in activity or vigor ⟨~ enthusiasm⟩ **2** : to make or become damp ⟨~ a sponge⟩

damp·er \'dam-pər\ *n* **1** : a dulling or deadening influence ⟨put a ~ on the party⟩ **2** : one that damps; *esp* : a valve or movable plate (as in the flue of a stove, furnace, or fireplace) to regulate the draft

dam·sel \'dam-zəl\ *n* : MAIDEN, GIRL

dam·sel·fly \-ˌflī\ *n* : any of a group of insects that are closely related to the dragonflies but fold their wings above the body when at rest

dam·son \'dam-zən\ *n* : a plum with acid purple fruit; *also* : its fruit

Dan *abbr* Daniel

¹dance \'dans\ *vb* **danced; danc·ing** **1** : to glide, step, or move through a set series of movements usu. to music **2** : to move quickly and up and down or about **3** : to perform or take part in as a dancer — **danc·er** *n*

²dance *n* **1** : an act or instance of dancing **2** : a social gathering for dancing **3** : a piece of music (as a waltz) by which dancing may be guided **4** : the art of dancing

D & C *n* [*d*ilation *and* *c*urettage] : a surgical procedure that involves stretching the cervix and scraping the inside walls of the uterus (as to test for cancer or to perform an abortion)

dan·de·li·on \'dan-də-ˌlī-ən, -dē-\ *n* [ME *dendelyoun,* fr. AF *dent de lion,* lit., lion's tooth] : any of a genus of common yellow-flowered composite herbs

dan·der \'dan-dər\ *n* : ANGER, TEMPER

dan·di·fy \'dan-di-ˌfī\ *vb* **-fied; -fy·ing** : to cause to resemble a dandy

dan·dle \'dan-dᵊl\ *vb* **dan·dled; dan·dling** : to move up and down in one's arms or on one's knee in affectionate play ✦ *Synonyms* CARESS, FONDLE, LOVE, PET

dan·druff \'dan-drəf\ *n* : scaly white or grayish flakes of dead skin cells that come off the scalp — **dan·druffy** \-drə-fē\ *adj*

¹dan·dy \'dan-dē\ *n, pl* **dandies** **1** : a man unduly attentive to personal appearance **2** : something excellent in its class ✦ *Synonyms* FOP, COXCOMB, POPINJAY

²dandy *adj* **dan·di·er; -est** : very good : FIRST-RATE

Dane \'dān\ *n* **1** : a native or inhabitant of Denmark **2** : GREAT DANE

dan·ger \'dān-jər\ *n* [ME *daunger* control, resistance, peril, fr. AF *dangier,* fr. VL *dominiarium,* fr. L *dominium* ownership] **1** : exposure or liability to injury, harm, or evil **2** : something that may cause injury or harm ✦ *Synonyms* PERIL, HAZARD, RISK, JEOPARDY

dan·ger·ous \'dān-jə-rəs\ *adj* **1** : HAZARDOUS, PERILOUS ⟨a ~ slope⟩ **2** : able or likely to inflict injury ⟨a ~ man⟩ — **dan·ger·ous·ly** *adv*

dan·gle \'daŋ-gəl\ *vb* **dan·gled; dan·gling** **1** : to hang loosely esp. with a swinging motion : SWING **2** : to be a hanger-on or dependent **3** : to be left without proper grammatical connection in a sentence ⟨a *dangling* participle⟩ **4** : to keep hanging uncertainly **5** : to offer as an inducement

Dan·iel \'dan-yəl\ *n* — see BIBLE table

Dan·ish \'dā-nish\ *n* : the language of the Danes — **Danish** *adj*

Danish pastry *n* : a pastry made of a rich yeast-raised dough

dank \'daŋk\ *adj* : disagreeably wet or moist : DAMP — **dank·ness** *n*

dan·seuse \dänⁿ-'sərz, -'səz; dän-'süz\ *n* [F] : a female ballet dancer

dap·per \'da-pər\ *adj* **1** : SPRUCE, TRIM **2** : being alert and lively in movement and manners : JAUNTY

dap·ple \'da-pəl\ *vb* **dap·pled; dap·pling** : to mark with different-colored spots

DAR *abbr* Daughters of the American Revolution

¹dare \'der\ *vb* **dared; dar·ing** **1** : to have sufficient courage : be bold enough to **2** : CHALLENGE ⟨*dared* him to jump⟩ **3** : to confront boldly

²dare *n* : an act or instance of daring : CHALLENGE

dare·dev·il \-ˌde-vəl\ *n* : a recklessly bold person — **daredevil** *adj*

dar·ing \'der-iŋ\ *n* : venturesome boldness — **daring** *adj* — **dar·ing·ly** *adv*

¹dark \'därk\ *adj* **1** : being without light or without much light **2** : not light in color ⟨a ~ suit⟩ **3** : GLOOMY ⟨a ~ outlook⟩ **4** *often cap* : being a period of stagnation or decline ⟨the *Dark* Ages⟩ **5** : SECRETIVE ⟨~ dealings⟩ ✦ *Synonyms* DIM, DUSKY, MURKY, TENEBROUS — **dark·ly** *adv* — **dark·ness** *n*

²dark *n* **1** : absence of light : DARKNESS; *esp* : NIGHT **2** : a dark or deep color — **in the dark** **1** : in secrecy **2** : in ignorance ⟨kept *in the dark* about the plans⟩

dark·en \'där-kən\ *vb* **1** : to make or grow dark or darker **2** : DIM **3** : BESMIRCH, TARNISH **4** : to make or become gloomy or forbidding

dark horse *n* : a contestant or a political figure whose abilities and chances as a contender are not known

dark·ling \'där-kliŋ\ *adj* **1** : DARK ⟨a ~ plain⟩ **2** : MYSTERIOUS

dark·room \'därk-ˌrüm, -ˌrum\ *n* : a lightproof room in which photographic materials are processed

¹**dar·ling** \'där-liŋ\ *n* **1** : a dearly loved person **2** : FAVORITE

²**darling** *adj* **1** : dearly loved : FAVORITE **2** : very pleasing : CHARMING

darm·stadt·i·um \ˌdärm-'sta-tē-əm\ *n* : a short-lived radioactive chemical element produced artificially

¹**darn** \'därn\ *vb* : to mend with interlacing stitches — **darn·er** *n*

²**darn** *or* **darned** \'därnd\ *adv* : VERY, EXTREMELY ⟨a ∼ good job⟩

darning needle *n* **1** : a needle for darning **2** : DRAGONFLY

¹**dart** \'därt\ *n* **1** : a small missile with a point on one end and feathers on the other; *also, pl* : a game in which darts are thrown at a target **2** : something causing a sudden pain **3** : a stitched tapering fold in a garment **4** : a quick movement

²**dart** *vb* **1** : to throw with a sudden movement **2** : to thrust or move suddenly or rapidly ⟨∼ed across the street⟩ **3** : to shoot with a dart containing a usu. tranquilizing drug

dart·er \'där-tər\ *n* : any of numerous small No. American freshwater fishes related to the perches

Dar·win·ism \'där-wə-ˌni-zəm\ *n* : a theory explaining the origin and continued existence of new species of plants and animals by means of natural selection acting on chance variations — **Dar·win·ist** \-nist\ *n or adj*

¹**dash** \'dash\ *vb* **1** : SMASH **2** : to knock, hurl, or thrust violently **3** : SPLASH, SPATTER **4** : RUIN **5** : DEPRESS, SADDEN **6** : to perform or finish hastily ⟨∼ off a letter⟩ **7** : to move with sudden speed ⟨∼ed down the hall⟩

²**dash** *n* **1** : a sudden burst or splash **2** : a stroke of a pen **3** : a punctuation mark — that is used esp. to indicate a break in the thought or structure of a sentence **4** : a small addition ⟨a ∼ of salt⟩ **5** : flashy showiness **6** : animation in style and action **7** : a sudden rush or attempt ⟨made a ∼ for the door⟩ **8** : a short foot race **9** : DASHBOARD

dash·board \-ˌbord\ *n* : a panel in an automobile or aircraft below the windshield usu. containing dials and controls

dash·er \'da-shər\ *n* : a device (as in a churn) for agitating something

da·shi·ki \də-'shē-kē\ *also* **dai·shi·ki** \dī-\ *n* [modif. of Yoruba (an African language) *dàńṣíkí*] : a usu. brightly colored loose-fitting pullover garment

dash·ing \'da-shiŋ\ *adj* **1** : marked by vigorous action **2** : marked by smartness esp. in dress and manners ♦ **Synonyms** STYLISH, CHIC, FASHIONABLE, MODISH, SMART, SWANK

das·tard \'das-tərd\ *n* **1** : COWARD **2** : a person who acts treacherously — **das·tard·ly** *adj*

dat *abbr* dative

da·ta \'dā-tə, 'da-, 'dä-\ *n sing or pl* [L, pl. of *datum*] : factual information (as measurements or statistics) used as a basis for reasoning, discussion, or calculation

da·ta·base \-ˌbās\ *n* : a usu. large collection of data organized esp. for rapid search and retrieval (as by a computer) — **database** *vb*

data processing *n* : the action or process of supplying a computer with information and having the computer use it to produce a desired result

¹**date** \'dāt\ *n* [ME, fr. AF, ultim. fr. L *dactylus*, fr. Gk *daktylos*, lit., finger] : the oblong edible fruit of a tall palm; *also* : this palm

²**date** *n* [ME, fr. AF, fr. LL *data*, fr. *data* (as in *data Romae* given at Rome), fem. of L *datus*, pp. of *dare* to give] **1** : the day, month, or year of an event **2** : a statement giving the time of execution or making (as of a coin or check) **3** : the period to which something belongs **4** : APPOINTMENT; *esp* : a social engagement between two persons that often has a romantic character **5** : a person with whom one has a usu. romantic date — **to date** : up to the present moment

³**date** *vb* **dat·ed; dat·ing** **1** : to record the date of or on **2** : to determine, mark, or reveal the date, age, or period of **3** : to go on a date or dates with ⟨∼ed her for a year⟩ **4** : ORIGINATE ⟨∼s from ancient times⟩ **5** : EXTEND ⟨*dating* back to childhood⟩ **6** : to show qualities typical of a past period

dat·ed \'dā-təd\ *adj* **1** : provided with a date **2** : OLD-FASHIONED ⟨a ∼ custom⟩ ♦ **Synonyms** ANTIQUATED, ARCHAIC, OLD HAT, OUTDATED, OUTMODED, PASSÉ

date·less \'dāt-ləs\ *adj* **1** : ENDLESS **2** : having no date **3** : too ancient to be dated **4** : TIMELESS

date·line \'dāt-ˌlīn\ *n* : a line in a publication giving the date and place of composition or issue — **dateline** *vb*

date rape *n* : rape committed by the victim's date

da·tive \'dā-tiv\ *adj* : of, relating to, or constituting a grammatical case marking typically the indirect object of a verb — **dative** *n*

da·tum \'dā-təm, 'da-, 'dä-\ *n, pl* **da·ta** \-tə\ *or* **datums** : a single piece of data : FACT

dau *abbr* daughter

¹**daub** \'dȯb\ *vb* **1** : to cover with soft adhesive matter **2** : SMEAR, SMUDGE **3** : to paint crudely — **daub·er** *n*

²**daub** *n* : something daubed on : SMEAR : a crude picture

daugh·ter \'dȯ-tər\ *n* **1** : a female offspring esp. of human beings **2** : a female adopted child **3** : a human female descendant — **daughter** *adj* — **daugh·ter·less** \-ləs\ *adj*

daugh·ter–in–law \'dȯ-tə-rən-ˌlȯ\ *n, pl* **daugh·ters–in–law** \-tər-zən-\ : the wife of one's son

daunt \'dȯnt\ *vb* [ME, fr. AF *danter, daunter*, fr. L *domitare* to tame] : to lessen the courage of : INTIMIDATE, OVERWHELM

daunt·ing \'dȯn-tiŋ\ *adj* : tending to overwhelm or intimidate ⟨a ∼ task⟩

daunt·less \-ləs\ *adj* : FEARLESS, UNDAUNTED ♦ **Synonyms** BRAVE, BOLD, COURAGEOUS, LIONHEARTED — **daunt·less·ly** *adv*

dau·phin \'dȯ-fən\ *n, often cap* : the eldest son of a king of France

DAV *abbr* Disabled American Veterans

dav·en·port \'da-vən-ˌpȯrt\ *n* : a large upholstered sofa

da·vit \'dā-vət, 'da-\ *n* : a small crane on a ship used in pairs esp. to raise or lower boats

daw·dle \'dȯ-dᵊl\ *vb* **daw·dled; daw·dling** **1** : to spend time wastefully or idly **2** : LOITER — **daw·dler** *n*

¹**dawn** \'dȯn\ *vb* **1** : to begin to grow light as the sun rises **2** : to begin to appear or develop **3** : to begin to be understood ⟨the solution ∼ed on him⟩

²**dawn** *n* **1** : the first appearance of light in the morning **2** : a first appearance : BEGINNING ⟨the ∼ of a new era⟩

day \'dā\ *n* **1** : the period of light between one night and the next; *also* : DAYLIGHT, DAYTIME **2** : the period of rotation of a planet (as earth) or a moon on its axis **3** : a period of 24 hours beginning at midnight **4** : a specified day or date ⟨wedding ∼⟩ **5** : a specified time or period : AGE ⟨in olden ∼s⟩ **6** : the conflict or contention of the day **7** : the time set apart by usage or law for work ⟨the 8-hour ∼⟩

day·bed \'dā-ˌbed\ *n* : a couch that can be converted into a bed

day·book \-ˌbuk\ *n* : DIARY, JOURNAL

day·break \-ˌbrāk\ *n* : DAWN

day care *n* : supervision of and care for children or disabled adults provided during the day; *also* : a program offering day care

day·dream \'dā-ˌdrēm\ *n* : a pleasant reverie — **daydream** *vb*

day·light \'dā-ˌlīt\ *n* **1** : the light of day **2** : DAYTIME **3** : DAWN **4** : understanding of something that has been obscure **5** *pl* : CONSCIOUSNESS; *also* : WITS **6** : a perceptible space, gap, or difference

daylight saving time *n* : time usu. one hour ahead of standard time

Day of Atonement : YOM KIPPUR

day school *n* : a private school without boarding facilities

day student *n* : a student who attends regular classes at a college or preparatory school but does not live there

day·time \'dā-ˌtīm\ *n* : the period of daylight

daze \'dāz\ *vb* **dazed; daz·ing** **1** : to stupefy esp. by a blow **2** : DAZZLE — **daze** *n* — **da·zed·ly** \'dā-zəd-lē\ *adv*

daz·zle \'da-zəl\ *vb* **daz·zled; daz·zling** **1** : to overpower with light **2** : to impress greatly or confound with brilliance ⟨*dazzled* by her wit⟩ — **dazzle** *n*

dB *abbr* decibel

Db *symbol* dubnium

d/b/a *abbr* doing business as

dbl *or* **dble** *abbr* double

DC *abbr* **1** [It *da capo*] from the beginning **2** direct current **3** District of Columbia **4** doctor of chiropractic
DD *abbr* **1** days after date **2** demand draft **3** dishonorable discharge **4** doctor of divinity
D–day *n* [*D*, abbr. for *day*] : a day set for launching an operation (as an invasion)
DDS *abbr* doctor of dental surgery
DDT \,dē-(,)dē-'tē\ *n* : a persistent insecticide poisonous to many higher animals
DE *abbr* Delaware
dea·con \'dē-kən\ *n* [ME *dekene*, fr. OE *dēacon*, fr. LL *diaconus*, fr. Gk *diakonos*, lit., servant] : a subordinate officer in a Christian church
dea·con·ess \'dē-kə-nəs\ *n* : a woman chosen to assist in the church ministry
de·ac·ti·vate \dē-'ak-tə-,vāt\ *vb* : to make inactive or ineffective
¹dead \'ded\ *adj* **1** : LIFELESS **2** : DEATHLIKE, DEADLY 〈in a ~ faint〉 **3** : NUMB **4** : very tired **5** : UNRESPONSIVE **6** : EXTINGUISHED 〈~ coals〉 **7** : INANIMATE, INERT **8** : no longer active or functioning 〈a ~ battery〉 **9** : lacking power, significance, or effect 〈a ~ custom〉 **10** : OBSOLETE 〈a ~ language〉 **11** : lacking in gaiety or animation 〈a ~ party〉 **12** : QUIET, IDLE, UNPRODUCTIVE 〈~ capital〉 **13** : lacking elasticity 〈a ~ tennis ball〉 **14** : not circulating : STAGNANT 〈~ air〉 **15** : lacking warmth, vigor, or taste 〈~ wine〉 **16** : absolutely uniform 〈~ level〉 **17** : UNERRING, EXACT 〈a ~ shot〉 **18** : ABRUPT 〈a ~ stop〉 **19** : COMPLETE 〈a ~ loss〉
²dead *n*, *pl* **dead** **1** : one that is dead — usu. used collectively 〈the living and the ~〉 **2** : the time of greatest quiet 〈the ~ of the night〉
³dead *adv* **1** : UTTERLY 〈~ right〉 **2** : in a sudden and complete manner 〈stopped ~〉 **3** : DIRECTLY 〈~ ahead〉
dead·beat \-,bēt\ *n* : a person who persistently fails to pay personal debts or expenses
dead duck *n* : GONER
dead·en \'de-dᵊn\ *vb* **1** : to impair in vigor or sensation : BLUNT 〈~ pain〉 **2** : to lessen the luster or spirit of **3** : to make (as a wall) soundproof
dead end *n* **1** : an end (as of a street) without an exit **2** : a position, situation, or course of action that leads to nothing further — **dead–end** \,ded-,end\ *adj*
dead heat *n* : a contest in which two or more contestants tie (as by crossing the finish line simultaneously)
dead horse *n* : an exhausted topic or issue
dead letter *n* **1** : something that has lost its force or authority without being formally abolished **2** : a letter that cannot be delivered or returned
dead·line \'ded-,līn\ *n* : a date or time before which something must be done
dead·lock \'ded-,läk\ *n* **1** : a stoppage of action because neither faction in a struggle will give in **2** : a tie score — **deadlock** *vb*
¹dead·ly \'ded-lē\ *adj* **dead·li·er; -est** **1** : likely to cause or capable of causing death **2** : HOSTILE, IMPLACABLE **3** : very accurate : UNERRING **4** : tending to deprive of force or vitality 〈a ~ habit〉 **5** : suggestive of death **6** : very great : EXTREME — **dead·li·ness** *n*
²deadly *adv* **1** : suggesting death 〈~ pale〉 **2** : EXTREMELY 〈~ dull〉
deadly sin *n* : one of seven sins of pride, covetousness, lust, anger, gluttony, envy, and sloth held to be fatal to spiritual progress
dead meat *n* : one that is doomed
¹dead·pan \'ded-,pan\ *adj* : marked by an impassive manner or expression 〈~ humor〉 — **deadpan** *vb* — **deadpan** *adv*
²deadpan *n* : a completely expressionless face
dead reckoning *n* : the determination of the position of a ship or aircraft solely from the record of the direction and distance of its course
dead·weight \'ded-'wāt\ *n* **1** : the unrelieved weight of an inert mass **2** : a ship's load including the weight of cargo, fuel, crew, and passengers
dead·wood \-,wùd\ *n* **1** : wood dead on the tree **2** : useless personnel or material
deaf \'def\ *adj* **1** : unable to hear **2** : unwilling to hear or listen 〈~ to all suggestions〉 — **deaf·ness** *n*
deaf·en \'de-fən\ *vb* : to make deaf

¹deal \'dēl\ *n* **1** : a usu. large or indefinite quantity or degree 〈a great ~ of support〉 **2** : the act or right of distributing cards to players in a card game; *also* : HAND
²deal *vb* **dealt** \'delt\; **deal·ing** **1** : DISTRIBUTE; *esp* : to distribute playing cards to players in a game **2** : ADMINISTER, DELIVER 〈*dealt* him a blow〉 **3** : to concern itself : TREAT 〈the book ~*s* with crime〉 **4** : to take action in regard to something 〈~ with offenders〉 **5** : TRADE; *also* : to sell or distribute something as a business 〈~ in used cars〉 **6** : to reach a state of acceptance 〈~ with her child's death〉 — **deal·er** *n*
³deal *n* **1** : BARGAINING, NEGOTIATION **2** : TRANSACTION; *esp* : an agreement by contract **3** : treatment received 〈a raw ~〉 **4** : an often secret agreement or arrangement for mutual advantage **5** : BARGAIN
⁴deal *n* : wood or a board of fir or pine
deal·er·ship \'dē-lər-,ship\ *n* : an authorized sales agency 〈an auto ~〉
deal·ing \'dē-liŋ\ *n* **1** : a way of acting or of doing business **2** *pl* : friendly or business transactions
dean \'dēn\ *n* [ME *deen*, fr. AF *deien*, fr. LL *decanus*, lit., chief of ten, fr. Gk *deka* ten] **1** : a clergyman who is head of a group of canons or of joint pastors of a church **2** : the head of a division, faculty, college, or school of a university **3** : a college or secondary school administrator in charge of counseling and disciplining students **4** : DOYEN 〈the ~ of a diplomatic corps〉 — **dean·ship** *n*
dean·ery \'dē-nə-rē\ *n*, *pl* **-er·ies** : the office, jurisdiction, or official residence of a clerical dean
¹dear \'dir\ *adj* **1** : highly valued : PRECIOUS **2** : AFFECTIONATE, FOND **3** : EXPENSIVE **4** : HEARTFELT — **dear·ly** *adv* — **dear·ness** *n*
²dear *n* : a loved one : DARLING
Dear John \-'jän\ *n* : a letter (as to a soldier) in which a woman breaks off a marital or romantic relationship
dearth \'dərth\ *n* **1** : SCARCITY, FAMINE **2** : an inadequate supply : LACK 〈a ~ of jobs〉
death \'deth\ *n* **1** : the end of life **2** : the cause of loss of life **3** : a cause of ruin **4** : the state of being dead **5** : DESTRUCTION, EXTINCTION **6** : SLAUGHTER — **death·like** *adj*
death·bed \-,bed\ *n* **1** : the bed in which a person dies **2** : the last hours of life
death·blow \-,blō\ *n* : a destructive or killing stroke or event
death grip *n* : an extremely tight grip or hold
death·less \-ləs\ *adj* : IMMORTAL, IMPERISHABLE 〈~ fame〉
death·ly \-lē\ *adj* **1** : FATAL **2** : of, relating to, or suggestive of death 〈a ~ pallor〉 — **deathly** *adv*
death rattle *n* : a sound produced by air passing through mucus in the lungs and air passages of a dying person
death's–head \'deths-,hed\ *n* : a human skull emblematic of death
death·watch \'deth-,wäch\ *n* : a vigil kept over the dead or dying
deb \'deb\ *n* : DEBUTANTE
de·ba·cle \di-'bä-kəl, -'ba-\ *also* **dé·bâ·cle** *same or* dä-'bäk\ *n* [F *débâcle*] : DISASTER, FAILURE, ROUT 〈stock market ~〉
de·bar \di-'bär\ *vb* : to bar from having or doing something : PRECLUDE
de·bark \di-'bärk\ *vb* : DISEMBARK — **de·bar·ka·tion** \,dē-,bär-'kā-shən\ *n*
de·base \di-'bās\ *vb* : to lower in character, quality, or value **♦ Synonyms** DEGRADE, CORRUPT, DEPRAVE — **de·base·ment** *n*
de·bate \di-'bāt\ *vb* **de·bat·ed; de·bat·ing** **1** : to discuss a question by considering opposed arguments **2** : to take part in a debate — **de·bat·able** *adj* — **debate** *n* — **de·bat·er** *n*
de·bauch \di-'bȯch\ *vb* : SEDUCE, CORRUPT **♦ Synonyms** DEBASE, DEMORALIZE, DEPRAVE, PERVERT — **de·bauch·ery** \-'bȯ-chə-rē\ *n*
de·ben·ture \di-'ben-chər\ *n* : BOND; *esp* : one secured by the general credit of the issuer rather than a lien on particular assets
de·bil·i·tate \di-'bi-lə-,tāt\ *vb* **-tat·ed; -tat·ing** : to impair the health or strength of **♦ Synonyms** WEAKEN, DISABLE, ENFEEBLE, UNDERMINE

de·bil·i·ty \di-'bi-lə-tē\ *n, pl* **-ties** : an infirm or weakened state

¹**deb·it** \'de-bət\ *vb* : to enter as a debit : charge with or as a debit

²**debit** *n* **1** : an entry in an account showing money paid out or owed **2** : DISADVANTAGE, SHORTCOMING

debit card *n* : a card by which money may be withdrawn or the cost of purchases paid directly from the holder's bank account

deb·o·nair \,de-bə-'ner\ *adj* [ME *debonere,* fr. AF *deboneire,* fr. *de bon aire* of good family or nature] : SUAVE, URBANE; *also* : LIGHTHEARTED

de·bouch \di-'bau̇ch, -'büsh\ *vb* [F *déboucher,* fr. *dé-* out of + *bouche* mouth] : to come out into an open area : EMERGE

de·brief \di-'brēf\ *vb* **1** : to question (as a pilot back from a mission) in order to obtain useful information **2** : to review carefully upon completion

de·bris \də-'brē, dā-; 'dā-,brē\ *n, pl* **debris** \-'brēz, -,brēz\ **1** : the remains of something broken down or destroyed **2** : an accumulation of rock fragments **3** : RUBBISH

debt \'det\ *n* **1** : SIN, TRESPASS **2** : something owed : OBLIGATION **3** : a condition of owing

debt·or \'de-tər\ *n* **1** : one guilty of neglect or violation of duty **2** : one that owes a debt

de·bug \(,)dē-'bəg\ *vb* : to eliminate errors in ⟨∼ a computer program⟩

de·bunk \dē-'bəŋk\ *vb* : to expose the sham or falseness of ⟨∼ a legend⟩

¹**de·but** \'dā-,byü, dā-'byü\ *n* **1** : a first appearance **2** : a formal entrance into society

²**debut** *vb* : to make a debut; *also* : INTRODUCE

deb·u·tante \'de-byu̇-,tänt\ *n* : a young woman making her formal entrance into society

dec *abbr* **1** deceased **2** decrease

Dec *abbr* December

de·cade \'de-,kād, de-'kād\ *n* : a period of 10 years

dec·a·dence \'de-kə-dəns, di-'kā-d°ns\ *n* : DETERIORATION, DECLINE — **dec·a·dent** \'de-kə-dənt, di-'kā-d°nt\ *adj or n*

de·caf \'dē-,kaf\ *n* : decaffeinated coffee

de·caf·fein·at·ed \(,)dē-'ka-fə-nā-təd\ *adj* : having the caffeine removed ⟨∼ coffee⟩

deca·gon \'de-kə-,gän\ *n* : a plane polygon of 10 angles and 10 sides

de·cal \'dē-,kal\ *n* : a picture, design, or label made to be transferred (as to glass) from specially prepared paper

de·cal·co·ma·nia \di-,kal-kə-'mā-nē-ə\ *n* [F *décalcomanie,* fr. *décalquer* to copy by tracing (fr. *calquer* to trace, fr. It *calcare,* lit., to tread, fr. L) + *manie* mania, fr. LL *mania*] : DECAL

Deca·logue \'de-kə-,lȯg\ *n* : TEN COMMANDMENTS

de·camp \di-'kamp\ *vb* **1** : to break up a camp **2** : to depart suddenly ♦ **Synonyms** ESCAPE, ABSCOND, FLEE

de·cant \di-'kant\ *vb* : to pour (as wine) from one vessel into another

de·cant·er \di-'kan-tər\ *n* : an ornamental glass bottle for serving wine

de·cap·i·tate \di-'ka-pə-,tāt\ *vb* **-tat·ed; -tat·ing** : BEHEAD — **de·cap·i·ta·tion** \-,ka-pə-'tā-shən\ *n* — **de·cap·i·ta·tor** \-'ka-pə-,tā-tər\ *n*

deca·syl·lab·ic \,de-kə-sə-'la-bik\ *adj* : having or composed of verses having 10 syllables — **decasyllabic** *n*

de·cath·lon \di-'kath-lən, -,län\ *n* : a 10-event athletic contest

de·cay \di-'kā\ *vb* **1** : to decline from a sound or prosperous condition ⟨a ∼*ing* town⟩ **2** : to cause or undergo decomposition ⟨radium ∼*s* slowly⟩; *esp* : to break down while spoiling : ROT ⟨∼*ing* teeth⟩ — **decay** *n*

decd *abbr* deceased

¹**de·cease** \di-'sēs\ *n* : DEATH

¹**de·ceased** \-'sēst\ *adj* : no longer living; *esp* : recently dead

²**deceased** *n, pl* **deceased** : a dead person

de·ce·dent \di-'sē-d°nt\ *n* : a deceased person

de·ceit \di-'sēt\ *n* **1** : DECEPTION **2** : TRICK **3** : DECEITFULNESS ♦ **Synonyms** DISSIMULATION, DUPLICITY, GUILE

de·ceit·ful \-fəl\ *adj* : practicing or tending to practice deceit **2** : MISLEADING, DECEPTIVE ⟨a ∼ answer⟩ — **de·ceit·ful·ly** *adv* — **de·ceit·ful·ness** *n*

de·ceive \di-'sēv\ *vb* **de·ceived; de·ceiv·ing 1** : to cause to believe an untruth **2** : to use or practice deceit ♦ **Synonyms** BEGUILE, BETRAY, DELUDE, MISLEAD — **de·ceiv·er** *n*

de·cel·er·ate \dē-'se-lə-,rāt\ *vb* **-at·ed; -at·ing** : to slow down

De·cem·ber \di-'sem-bər\ *n* [ME *Decembre,* fr. OE or AF, both fr. L *December* (tenth month), fr. *decem* ten] : the 12th month of the year

de·cen·cy \'dē-s°n-sē\ *n, pl* **-cies 1** : PROPRIETY **2** : conformity to standards of taste, propriety, or quality **3** : standard of propriety — usu. used in pl.

de·cen·ni·al \di-'se-nē-əl\ *adj* **1** : consisting of 10 years **2** : happening every 10 years ⟨∼ census⟩

de·cent \'dē-s°nt\ *adj* **1** : conforming to standards of propriety, good taste, or morality **2** : modestly clothed **3** : free from immodesty or obscenity **4** : ADEQUATE ⟨∼ housing⟩ — **de·cent·ly** *adv*

de·cen·tral·i·za·tion \dē-,sen-trə-lə-'zā-shən\ *n* **1** : the distribution of powers from a central authority to regional and local authorities **2** : the redistribution of population and industry from urban centers to outlying areas — **de·cen·tral·ize** \-'sen-trə-,līz\ *vb*

de·cep·tion \di-'sep-shən\ *n* **1** : the act of deceiving **2** : the fact or condition of being deceived **3** : FRAUD, TRICK — **de·cep·tive** \-'sep-tiv\ *adj* — **de·cep·tive·ly** *adv* — **de·cep·tive·ness** *n*

deci·bel \'de-sə-,bel, -bəl\ *n* : a unit for measuring the relative loudness of sounds

de·cide \di-'sīd\ *vb* **de·cid·ed; de·cid·ing** [ME, fr. L *decidere,* lit., to cut off, fr. *de-* off + *caedere* to cut] **1** : make a final choice or judgment **2** : to bring to a definitive end ⟨one blow *decided* the fight⟩ **3** : to induce to come to a choice

de·cid·ed \di-'sī-dəd\ *adj* **1** : UNQUESTIONABLE **2** : FIRM, DETERMINED — **de·cid·ed·ly** *adv*

de·cid·u·ous \di-'si-jə-wəs\ *adj* **1** : falling off or out usu. at the end of a period of growth or function ⟨∼ leaves⟩ ⟨a ∼ tooth⟩ **2** : having deciduous parts ⟨∼ trees⟩

deci·gram \'de-sə-,gram\ *n* — see METRIC SYSTEM table

deci·li·ter \-,lē-tər\ *n* — see METRIC SYSTEM table

¹**dec·i·mal** \'de-sə-məl\ *adj* : based on the number 10 : reckoning by tens

²**decimal** *n* : any number expressed in base 10; *esp* : DECIMAL FRACTION

decimal fraction *n* : a fraction or mixed number in which the denominator is a power of 10 and that is usu. expressed with a decimal point ⟨the *decimal fraction* .25 is equivalent to the common fraction $^{25}/_{100}$⟩

decimal place *n* : the position of a digit as counted to the right of the decimal point in a decimal fraction

decimal point *n* : a period, centered dot, or in some countries a comma at the left of a decimal fraction (as .678) less than one or between a whole number and a decimal fraction in a mixed number (as 3.678)

dec·i·mate \'de-sə-,māt\ *vb* **-mat·ed; -mat·ing 1** : to take or destroy the 10th part of **2** : to cause great destruction or harm to ⟨factories *decimated* by fire⟩

dec·i·me·ter \'de-sə-,mē-tər\ *n* — see METRIC SYSTEM table

de·ci·pher \di-'sī-fər\ *vb* **1** : DECODE **2** : to make out the meaning of despite indistinctness — **de·ci·pher·able** *adj*

de·ci·sion \di-'si-zhən\ *n* **1** : the act or result of deciding **2** : promptness and firmness in deciding : DETERMINATION

de·ci·sive \-'sī-siv\ *adj* **1** : having the power to decide ⟨the ∼ vote⟩ **2** : RESOLUTE, DETERMINED **3** : CONCLUSIVE ⟨a ∼ victory⟩ — **de·ci·sive·ly** *adv* — **de·ci·sive·ness** *n*

¹**deck** \'dek\ *n* **1** : a floorlike platform of a ship; *also* : something resembling the deck of a ship **2** : a pack of playing cards

²**deck** *vb* **1** : ARRAY ⟨men ∼*ed* out in suits⟩ **2** : DECORATE **3** : to furnish with a deck **4** : KNOCK DOWN, FLOOR

deck·hand \'dek-,hand\ *n* : a sailor who performs manual duties

deck·le edge \'dek-əl-\ *n* : the rough untrimmed edge of paper — **deck·le-edged** \-'ejd\ *adj*

de·claim \di-'klām\ *vb* : to speak or deliver in the manner of a formal speech ⟨an actor ∼*ing* his lines⟩ — **dec·la-**

ma·tion \ˌde-klə-'mā-shən\ *n* — **de·clam·a·to·ry** \di-'klam-ə-ˌtȯr-ē\ *adj*

de·clar·a·tive \di-'kler-ə-tiv\ *adj* : making a declaration ⟨~ sentence⟩

de·clare \di-'kler\ *vb* **de·clared; de·clar·ing** **1** : to make known formally, officially, or explicitly : ANNOUNCE ⟨~ war⟩ **2** : to state emphatically : AFFIRM **3** : to make a full statement of ♦ **Synonyms** BLAZON, BROADCAST, PROCLAIM, PUBLISH — **dec·la·ra·tion** \ˌde-klə-'rā-shən\ *n* — **de·clar·a·to·ry** \di-'kler-ə-ˌtȯr-ē\ *adj* — **de·clar·er** *n*

de·clas·si·fy \dē-'kla-sə-ˌfī\ *vb* : to remove the security classification of ⟨~ documents⟩ — **de·clas·si·fi·ca·tion** \-ˌkla-sə-fə-'kā-shən\ *n*

de·clen·sion \di-'klen-chən\ *n* **1** : the inflectional forms of a noun, pronoun, or adjective **2** : DECLINE, DETERIORATION **3** : DESCENT, SLOPE

¹de·cline \di-'klīn\ *vb* **de·clined; de·clin·ing** **1** : to slope downward : DESCEND **2** : DROOP **3** : RECEDE ⟨morale declined⟩ **4** : WANE **5** : to withhold consent; *also* : REFUSE, REJECT ⟨~ an invitation⟩ ⟨~ to answer⟩ **6** : INFLECT **2** ⟨~ a noun⟩ — **de·clin·able** *adj* — **dec·li·na·tion** \ˌde-klə-'nā-shən\ *n*

²decline *n* **1** : a gradual sinking and wasting away **2** : a change to a lower state or level **3** : the time when something is approaching its end ⟨an empire in ~⟩ **4** : a descending slope

de·cliv·i·ty \di-'kli-və-tē\ *n, pl* **-ties** : a steep downward slope

de·code \dē-'kōd\ *vb* : to convert (a coded message) into ordinary language — **de·cod·er** *n*

dé·col·le·tage \dā-ˌkä-lə-'täzh\ *n* : the low-cut neckline of a dress

dé·col·le·té \dā-ˌkäl-'tā\ *adj* [F] **1** : wearing a strapless or low-necked gown **2** : having a low-cut neckline

de·com·mis·sion \ˌdē-kə-'mi-shən\ *vb* : to remove from service

de·com·pose \ˌdē-kəm-'pōz\ *vb* **1** : to separate into constituent parts **2** : to break down in decay : ROT — **de·com·po·si·tion** \dē-ˌkäm-pə-'zi-shən\ *n*

de·com·press \ˌdē-kəm-'pres\ *vb* : to release from pressure or compression — **de·com·pres·sion** \-'pre-shən\ *n*

decompression sickness *n* : ²BEND 3

de·con·ges·tant \ˌdē-kən-'jes-tənt\ *n* : an agent that relieves congestion (as of mucous membranes)

de·con·struc·tion \ˌdē-kən-'strak-shən\ *n* : the analysis of something (as language or literature) by the separation and individual examination of its basic elements — **de·con·struct** \-'strəkt\ *vb*

de·con·tam·i·nate \ˌdē-kən-'ta-mə-ˌnāt\ *vb* : to rid of contamination (as radioactive material) — **de·con·tam·i·na·tion** \-ˌta-mə-'nā-shən\ *n*

de·con·trol \ˌdē-kən-'trōl\ *vb* : to end control of ⟨~ prices⟩ — **decontrol** *n*

de·cor *or* **dé·cor** \dā-'kȯr, 'dā-ˌkȯr\ *n* : DECORATION; *esp* : the style and layout of interior furnishings

dec·o·rate \'de-kə-ˌrāt\ *vb* **-rat·ed; -rat·ing** **1** : to furnish with something ornamental ⟨~ a room⟩ **2** : to award a mark of honor (as a medal) to ⟨*decorated* soldiers⟩ ♦ **Synonyms** ADORN, BEAUTIFY, BEDECK, GARNISH, ORNAMENT

dec·o·ra·tion \ˌde-kə-'rā-shən\ *n* **1** : the act or process of decorating **2** : ORNAMENT **3** : a badge of honor

dec·o·ra·tive \'de-kə-rə-tiv\ *adj* : ORNAMENTAL

dec·o·ra·tor \'de-kə-ˌrā-tər\ *n* : one that decorates; *esp* : a person who designs or executes interiors and their furnishings

dec·o·rous \'de-kə-rəs, di-'kȯr-əs\ *adj* : PROPER, SEEMLY, CORRECT

de·co·rum \di-'kȯr-əm\ *n* [L] **1** : conformity to accepted standards of conduct **2** : ORDERLINESS, PROPRIETY

¹de·coy \'dē-ˌkȯi, di-'kȯi\ *n* [prob. fr. D *de kooi*, lit., the cage] **1** : something that lures or entices; *esp* : an artificial bird used to attract live birds within shot **2** : something used to draw attention away from another

²de·coy \di-'kȯi, 'dē-ˌkȯi\ *vb* : to lure by or as if by a decoy : ENTICE

¹de·crease \di-'krēs\ *vb* **de·creased; de·creas·ing** : to grow or cause to grow less : DIMINISH

²de·crease \'dē-ˌkrēs\ *n* **1** : the process of decreasing **2** : REDUCTION

¹de·cree \di-'krē\ *n* **1** : ORDER, EDICT **2** : a judicial decision

²decree *vb* **de·creed; de·cree·ing** **1** : COMMAND **2** : to determine or order judicially ♦ **Synonyms** DICTATE, ORDAIN, PRESCRIBE

dec·re·ment \'de-krə-mənt\ *n* **1** : gradual decrease **2** : the quantity lost by diminution or waste

de·crep·it \di-'kre-pət\ *adj* : broken down with age : WORN-OUT — **de·crep·i·tude** \-pə-ˌtüd, -ˌtyüd\ *n*

de·cre·scen·do \ˌdā-krə-'shen-dō\ *adv or adj* : with a decrease in volume — used as a direction in music

de·crim·i·nal·ize \dē-'kri-mə-nə-ˌlīz\ *vb* : to remove or reduce the criminal status of

de·cry \di-'krī\ *vb* : to express strong disapproval of ⟨~ welfare policies⟩

ded·i·cate \'de-di-ˌkāt\ *vb* **-cat·ed; -cat·ing** **1** : to devote to the worship of a divine being esp. with sacred rites **2** : to set apart for a definite purpose **3** : to inscribe or address as a compliment ⟨~ a novel⟩ — **ded·i·ca·tion** \ˌde-di-'kā-shən\ *n* — **ded·i·ca·tor** \'de-di-ˌkā-tər\ *n* — **ded·i·ca·to·ry** \-kə-ˌtȯr-ē\ *adj*

de·duce \di-'düs, -'dyüs\ *vb* **de·duced; de·duc·ing** **1** : to derive by reasoning : INFER **2** : to trace the course of — **de·duc·ible** *adj*

de·duct \di-'dəkt\ *vb* : SUBTRACT — **de·duct·ible** *adj*

de·duc·tion \di-'dək-shən\ *n* **1** : SUBTRACTION **2** : something that is or may be subtracted **3** : the deriving of a conclusion by reasoning : the conclusion so reached — **de·duc·tive** \-'dək-tiv\ *adj* — **de·duc·tive·ly** *adv*

¹deed \'dēd\ *n* **1** : something done **2** : FEAT, EXPLOIT **3** : a document containing some legal transfer, bargain, or contract

²deed *vb* : to convey or transfer by deed

dee·jay \'dē-ˌjā\ *n* : DISC JOCKEY

deem \'dēm\ *vb* : THINK, JUDGE ♦ **Synonyms** CONSIDER, ACCOUNT, RECKON, REGARD, VIEW

de–em·pha·size \dē-'em-fə-ˌsīz\ *vb* : to reduce in relative importance; *also* : to attach little importance to — **de–em·pha·sis** \-səs\ *n*

¹deep \'dēp\ *adj* **1** : extending far down, back, within, or outward ⟨a ~ well⟩ **2** : having a specified extension downward or backward ⟨3 feet ~⟩ **3** : difficult to understand; *also* : MYSTERIOUS, OBSCURE ⟨a ~ dark secret⟩ **4** : WISE **5** : ENGROSSED, INVOLVED ⟨~ in thought⟩ **6** : INTENSE, PROFOUND ⟨~ sleep⟩ **7** : dark and rich in color ⟨a ~ red⟩ **8** : having a low musical pitch or range ⟨a ~ voice⟩ **9** : situated well within **10** : covered, enclosed, or filled often to a specified degree — **deep·ly** *adv*

²deep *adv* **1** : DEEPLY **2** : far on : LATE ⟨~ in the night⟩

³deep *n* **1** : an extremely deep place or part; *esp* : OCEAN **2** : the middle or most intense part ⟨the ~ of winter⟩

deep·en \'dē-pən\ *vb* : to make or become deep or deeper

deep–freeze \'dēp-'frēz\ *vb* **-froze** \-'frōz\; **-fro·zen** \-'frō-z²n\ : QUICK-FREEZE

deep–fry *vb* : to cook in enough oil to cover the food being fried

deep pocket *n* **1** : one having substantial financial resources **2** *pl* : substantial financial resources

deep–root·ed \'dēp-'rü-təd, -'rü-\ *adj* : deeply implanted or established

deep–sea \'dēp-'sē\ *adj* : of, relating to, or occurring in the deeper parts of the sea ⟨~ fishing⟩

deep–seat·ed \'dēp-'sē-təd\ *adj* **1** : situated far below the surface **2** : firmly established ⟨~ convictions⟩

deer \'dir\ *n, pl* **deer** [ME, deer, animal, fr. OE *dēor* beast] : any of numerous ruminant mammals with cloven hoofs and usu. antlers esp. in the males

deer·fly \-ˌflī\ *n* : any of numerous small horseflies

deer·skin \-ˌskin\ *n* : leather made from the skin of a deer; *also* : a garment of such leather

deer tick *n* : a tick that transmits the bacterium causing Lyme disease

de–es·ca·late \dē-'es-kə-ˌlāt\ *vb* : to decrease in extent, volume, or scope : LIMIT — **de–es·ca·la·tion** \-ˌes-kə-'lā-shən\ *n*

deet \'dēt\ *n, often all cap* : a colorless oily liquid insect and tick repellent

¹def \'def\ *adj* **def·fer; def·fest** *slang* : very good : COOL

²def *abbr* **1** defendant **2** definite **3** definition

de·face \di-'fās\ *vb* : to destroy or mar the face or surface of ⟨~ a desk⟩ — **de·face·ment** *n* — **de·fac·er** *n*

de fac·to \di-'fak-tō, dā-\ *adj or adv* **1** : existing though not formally recognized ⟨a *de facto* recession⟩ **2** : actually exercising power ⟨*de facto* government⟩

de·fal·ca·tion \,dē-,fal-'kā-shən, -,fȯl-; ,dē-fəl-\ *n* : EMBEZZLEMENT

de·fame \di-'fām\ *vb* **de·famed; de·fam·ing** : to injure or destroy the reputation of by libel or slander ♦ **Synonyms** CALUMNIATE, DENIGRATE, LIBEL, MALIGN, SLANDER, VILIFY — **def·a·ma·tion** \,de-fə-'mā-shən\ *n* — **de·fam·a·to·ry** \di-'fa-mə-,tȯr-ē\ *adj*

de·fault \di-'fȯlt\ *n* **1** : failure to do something required by duty or law; *also* : failure to appear for a legal proceeding **2** : failure to compete in or to finish an appointed contest ⟨lose a race by ~⟩ **3** : a choice made without active consideration due to lack of viable alternatives **4** : a selection made automatically by a computer in the absence of a choice by the user — **default** *vb* — **de·fault·er** *n*

¹de·feat \di-'fēt\ *vb* **1** : FRUSTRATE, NULLIFY **2** : to win victory over : BEAT — **de·feat·able** \-'fē-tə-bəl\ *adj*

²defeat *n* **1** : FRUSTRATION **2** : an overthrow of an army in battle **3** : loss of a contest

de·feat·ism \-'fē-,ti-zəm\ *n* : acceptance of or resignation to defeat — **de·feat·ist** \-tist\ *n or adj*

def·e·cate \'de-fi-,kāt\ *vb* **-cat·ed; -cat·ing** **1** : to free from impurity or corruption **2** : to discharge feces from the bowels — **def·e·ca·tion** \,de-fi-'kā-shən\ *n*

¹de·fect \'dē-,fekt, di-'fekt\ *n* : BLEMISH, FAULT, IMPERFECTION

²de·fect \di-'fekt\ *vb* : to desert a cause, party, or nation esp. in order to espouse another — **de·fec·tion** \-'fek-shən\ *n* — **de·fec·tor** \-'fek-tər\ *n*

de·fec·tive \di-'fek-tiv\ *adj* : FAULTY, DEFICIENT — **defective** *n*

de·fence *chiefly Brit var of* DEFENSE

de·fend \di-'fend\ *vb* [ME, fr. AF *defendre*, fr. L *defendere*, fr. *de-* from + *-fendere* to strike] **1** : to repel danger or attack from ⟨~ the fort⟩ **2** : to act as attorney for **3** : to oppose the claim of another in a lawsuit : CONTEST **4** : to maintain against opposition ⟨~ an idea⟩ **5** : to try to retain against a challenge ⟨~ed his title⟩ — **de·fend·er** *n*

de·fen·dant \di-'fen-dənt\ *n* : a person required to make answer in a legal action or suit

de·fense \di-'fens\ *n* **1** : the act of defending : resistance against attack **2** : means, method, or capability of defending **3** : an argument in support **4** : the answer made by the defendant in a legal action **5** : a defending party, group, or team — **de·fense·less** *adj* — **de·fen·si·ble** *adj*

defense mechanism *n* : an often unconscious mental process (as repression) that assists in reaching compromise solutions to personal problems

¹de·fen·sive \di-'fen-siv\ *adj* **1** : serving or intended to defend or protect **2** : of or relating to the attempt to keep an opponent from scoring (as in a game) — **de·fen·sive·ly** *adv* — **de·fen·sive·ness** *n*

²defensive *n* : a defensive position

¹de·fer \di-'fər\ *vb* **de·ferred; de·fer·ring** [ME *deferren, differren*, fr. MF *differer*, fr. L *differre* to postpone, be different] : POSTPONE, PUT OFF

²defer *vb* **deferred; deferring** [ME *deferren, differren*, fr. MF *deferer, defferer*, fr. LL *deferre*, fr. L, to bring down, bring, fr. *de-* down + *ferre* to carry] : to submit or yield to the opinion or wishes of another — **de·fer·ral** \-əl\ *n*

def·er·ence \'de-fər-əns\ *n* : courteous, respectful, or ingratiating regard for another's wishes ♦ **Synonyms** HONOR, HOMAGE, OBEISANCE, REVERENCE — **def·er·en·tial** \,de-fə-'ren-chəl\ *adj*

de·fer·ment \di-'fər-mənt\ *n* : the act of delaying; *esp* : official postponement of military service

de·fi·ance \di-'fī-əns\ *n* **1** : CHALLENGE **2** : disposition to resist or contend

de·fi·ant \-ənt\ *adj* : full of defiance : BOLD, IMPUDENT — **de·fi·ant·ly** *adv*

de·fi·bril·la·tor \dē-'fī-brə-,lā-tər\ *n* : an electronic device that applies an electric shock to restore the rhythm of a fibrillating heart — **de·fi·bril·late** \-,lāt\ *vb* — **de·fi·bril·la·tion** \-,fī-brə-'lā-shən\ *n*

deficiency disease *n* : a disease (as scurvy or beriberi) caused by a lack of essential dietary elements and esp. a vitamin or mineral

de·fi·cient \di-'fi-shənt\ *adj* : lacking in something necessary; *also* : not up to a normal standard — **de·fi·cien·cy** \-shən-sē\ *n*

def·i·cit \'de-fə-sət\ *n* : a deficiency in amount; *esp* : an excess of expenditures over revenue

¹de·file \di-'fī(-ə)l\ *vb* **de·filed; de·fil·ing** **1** : to make filthy **2** : CORRUPT **3** : to violate the chastity of **4** : to violate the sanctity of : DESECRATE **5** : DISHONOR ♦ **Synonyms** CONTAMINATE, POLLUTE, SOIL, TAINT — **de·file·ment** *n*

²de·file \di-'fī(-ə)l, 'dē-,fī(-ə)l\ *n* : a narrow passage or gorge

de·fine \di-'fīn\ *vb* **de·fined; de·fin·ing** **1** : to set forth the meaning of ⟨~ a word⟩ **2** : to fix or mark the limits of **3** : to clarify in outline or character — **de·fin·able** *adj* — **de·fin·er** *n*

def·i·nite \'de-fə-nət\ *adj* **1** : having distinct limits : FIXED **2** : clear in meaning **3** : typically designating an identified or immediately identifiable person or thing ⟨a ~ article⟩ — **def·i·nite·ly** *adv* — **def·i·nite·ness** *n*

def·i·ni·tion \,de-fə-'ni-shən\ *n* **1** : an act of determining or settling **2** : a statement of the meaning of a word or word group; *also* : the action or process of defining **3** : the action or the power of making definite and clear : CLARITY, DISTINCTNESS

de·fin·i·tive \di-'fi-nə-tiv\ *adj* **1** : DECISIVE, CONCLUSIVE **2** : authoritative and apparently exhaustive ⟨a ~ edition⟩ **3** : serving to define or specify precisely ⟨~ laws⟩

de·flate \di-'flāt\ *vb* **de·flat·ed; de·flat·ing** **1** : to release air or gas from **2** : to reduce in size, importance, or effectiveness; *also* : to reduce from a state of inflation **3** : to become deflated

de·fla·tion \-'flā-shən\ *n* **1** : an act or instance of deflating : the state of being deflated **2** : reduction in the volume of available money or credit resulting in a decline of the general price level

de·flect \di-'flekt\ *vb* : to turn aside — **de·flec·tion** \-'flek-shən\ *n*

de·flo·ra·tion \,de-flə-'rā-shən\ *n* : rupture of the hymen

de·flow·er \dē-'flau̇(-ə)r\ *vb* : to deprive of virginity

de·fog \dē-'fȯg, -'fäg\ *vb* : to remove fog or condensed moisture from ⟨~ a windshield⟩ — **de·fog·ger** *n*

de·fo·li·ant \dē-'fō-lē-ənt\ *n* : a chemical spray or dust used to defoliate plants

de·fo·li·ate \-āt\ *vb* : to deprive of leaves esp. prematurely — **de·fo·li·a·tion** \dē-,fō-lē-'ā-shən\ *n* — **de·fo·li·a·tor** \dē-'fō-lē-,ā-tər\ *n*

de·for·es·ta·tion \dē-,fȯr-ə-'stā-shən\ *n* : the action or process of clearing an area of forests; *also* : the state of having been cleared of forests — **de·for·est** \(,)dē-'fȯr-əst, -'fär-\ *vb*

de·form \di-'fȯrm\ *vb* **1** : DISFIGURE, DEFACE **2** : to make or become misshapen or changed in shape — **de·for·ma·tion** \,dē-,fȯr-'mā-shən, ,de-fər-\ *n*

de·for·mi·ty \di-'fȯr-mə-tē\ *n, pl* **-ties** **1** : the state of being deformed **2** : a physical blemish or distortion

de·fraud \di-'frȯd\ *vb* : CHEAT

de·fray \di-'frā\ *vb* : to provide for the payment of : PAY — **de·fray·al** *n*

de·frock \(,)dē-'fräk\ *vb* : to deprive (as a priest) of the right to exercise the functions of office

de·frost \di-'frȯst\ *vb* **1** : to thaw out **2** : to free from ice — **de·frost·er** *n*

deft \'deft\ *adj* : quick and neat in action — **deft·ly** *adv* — **deft·ness** *n*

de·funct \di-'fəŋkt\ *adj* : DEAD, EXTINCT ⟨a ~ language⟩

de·fuse \dē-'fyüz\ *vb* **1** : to remove the fuse from (as a bomb) **2** : to make less harmful, potent, or tense

de·fy \di-'fī\ *vb* **de·fied; de·fy·ing** [ME, to renounce faith in, challenge, fr. AF *desfier, defier*, fr. *de-* from + *fier* to entrust, ultim. fr. L *fidere* to trust] **1** : CHALLENGE, DARE **2** : to refuse boldly to obey or to yield to : DISREGARD ⟨~ the law⟩ **3** : WITHSTAND, BAFFLE ⟨a scene that *defies* description⟩

deg *abbr* degree

de·gas \dē-'gas\ *vb* : to remove gas from

de·gen·er·a·cy \di-'je-nə-rə-sē\ *n, pl* **-cies** **1** : the state of being degenerate **2** : the process of becoming degenerate **3** : PERVERSION

¹de·gen·er·ate \di-'je-nə-rət\ *adj* : fallen or deteriorated from a former, higher, or normal condition — **de·gen·er-**

a·tion \-,je-nə-'rā-shən\ n — de·gen·er·a·tive \-'je-nə-,rā-tiv\ adj

²de·gen·er·ate \di-'je-nə-,rāt\ vb : to undergo deterioration (as in morality, intelligence, structure, or function)

³de·gen·er·ate \-rət\ n : a degenerate person; esp : a sexual pervert

de·grad·able \di-'grā-də-bəl\ adj : capable of being chemically degraded

de·grade \di-'grād\ vb 1 : to reduce from a higher to a lower rank or degree 2 : DEBASE, CORRUPT 3 : DECOMPOSE — deg·ra·da·tion \,de-grə-'dā-shən\ n

de·gree \di-'grē\ n [ME, fr. AF degré, fr. VL *degradus, fr. L de- down + gradus step, grade] 1 : a step in a series 2 : a rank or grade of official, ecclesiastical, or social position; also : the civil condition of a person 3 : the extent, intensity, or scope of something esp. as measured by a graded series 4 : one of the forms or sets of forms used in the comparison of an adjective or adverb 5 : a title conferred upon students by a college, university, or professional school on completion of a program of study 6 : a line or space of the musical staff; also : a note or tone of a musical scale 7 : a unit of measure for angles that is equal to an angle with its vertex at the center of a circle and its sides cutting off ¹⁄₃₆₀ of the circumference; also : a unit of measure for arcs of a circle that is equal to the amount of arc extending ¹⁄₃₆₀ of the circumference 8 : any of various units for measuring temperature

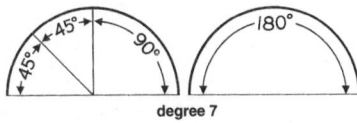

degree 7

de·horn \dē-'hȯrn\ vb : to deprive of horns

de·hu·man·ize \dē-'hyü-mə-,nīz\ vb : to deprive of human qualities, personality, or spirit — de·hu·man·i·za·tion \,dē-,hyü-mə-nə-'zā-shən\ n

de·hu·mid·i·fy \,dē-hyü-'mi-də-,fī\ vb : to remove moisture from (as the air) — de·hu·mid·i·fi·er n

de·hy·drate \dē-'hī-,drāt\ vb : to remove water from; also : to lose liquid — de·hy·dra·tion \,dē-hī-'drā-shən\ n

de·hy·dro·ge·na·tion \,dē-(,)hī-,drä-jə-'nā-shən, -drə-\ n : the removal of hydrogen from a chemical compound — de·hy·dro·ge·nate \dē-(,)hī-'drä-jə-,nāt, dē-'hī-drə-jə-\ vb

de·ice \dē-'īs\ vb : to keep free or rid of ice ⟨~ a lock⟩ — de·ic·er n

de·i·fy \'dē-ə-,fī, 'dā-\ vb -fied; -fy·ing 1 : to make a god of 2 : WORSHIP, GLORIFY — de·i·fi·ca·tion \,dē-ə-fə-'kā-shən, ,dā-\ n

deign \'dān\ vb [ME, fr. AF deigner, fr. L dignare, dignari, fr. dignus worthy] : CONDESCEND

de·ion·ize \dē-'ī-ə-,nīz\ vb : to remove ions from

de·ism \'dē-,i-zəm, 'dā-\ n, often cap : a system of thought advocating natural religion based on human morality and reason rather than divine revelation — de·ist \-ist\ n, often cap — de·is·tic \dē-'is-tik, dā-\ adj

de·i·ty \'dē-ə-tē, 'dā-\ n, pl -ties 1 : DIVINITY 2 2 cap : GOD 1 3 : a god or goddess

dé·jà vu \,dā-,zhä-'vü\ n [F, adj., already seen] : the feeling that one has seen or heard something before

de·ject·ed \di-'jek-təd\ adj : low in spirits : SAD — de·ject·ed·ly adv

de·jec·tion \di-'jek-shən\ n : lowness of spirits

de ju·re \dē-'jur-ē\ adv or adj [ML] : by legal right

deka·gram \'de-kə-,gram\ n — see METRIC SYSTEM table

deka·li·ter \-,lē-tər\ n — see METRIC SYSTEM table

deka·me·ter \-,mē-tər\ n — see METRIC SYSTEM table

del abbr delegate; delegation

Del abbr Delaware

Del·a·ware \'de-lə-,wer\ n, pl Delaware or Delawares : a member of an American Indian people orig. of the Delaware valley; also : their language

¹de·lay \di-'lā\ n 1 : the act of delaying : the state of being delayed 2 : the time for which something is delayed

²delay vb 1 : POSTPONE, PUT OFF 2 : to stop, detain, or hinder for a time 3 : to move or act slowly

de·lec·ta·ble \di-'lek-tə-bəl\ adj 1 : highly pleasing : DELIGHTFUL 2 : DELICIOUS

de·lec·ta·tion \,dē-,lek-'tā-shən\ n : DELIGHT, PLEASURE, DIVERSION

¹del·e·gate \'de-li-gət, -,gāt\ n 1 : DEPUTY, REPRESENTATIVE 2 : a member of the lower house of the legislature of Maryland, Virginia, or West Virginia

²del·e·gate \-,gāt\ vb -gat·ed; -gat·ing 1 : to entrust to another ⟨~ authority⟩ 2 : to appoint as one's delegate

del·e·ga·tion \,de-li-'gā-shən\ n 1 : the act of delegating 2 : one or more persons chosen to represent others

de·le·git·i·mize \,dē-lə-'ji-tə-,mīz\ vb : to diminish or destroy the legitimacy, prestige, or authority of

de·lete \di-'lēt\ vb de·let·ed; de·let·ing [L deletus, pp. of delēre to wipe out, destroy] : to eliminate esp. by blotting out, cutting out, or erasing ⟨~ a computer file⟩ — de·le·tion \-'lē-shən\ n

del·e·te·ri·ous \,de-lə-'tir-ē-əs\ adj : HARMFUL, NOXIOUS

delft \'delft\ n 1 : a Dutch pottery with an opaque white glaze and predominantly blue decoration 2 : glazed pottery esp. when blue and white

delft·ware \-,wer\ n : DELFT

deli \'de-lē\ n, pl del·is : DELICATESSEN

¹de·lib·er·ate \di-'li-bə-,rāt\ vb -at·ed; -at·ing : to consider carefully — de·lib·er·a·tion \-,li-bə-'rā-shən\ n — de·lib·er·a·tive \-'li-bə-,rā-tiv, -brə-tiv\ adj — de·lib·er·a·tive·ly adv

²de·lib·er·ate \di-'li-bə-rət, -'li-brət\ adj 1 : determined after careful thought 2 : done or said intentionally 3 : UNHURRIED, SLOW — de·lib·er·ate·ly adv — de·lib·er·ate·ness n

del·i·ca·cy \'de-li-kə-sē\ n, pl -cies 1 : something pleasing to eat and considered rare or luxurious 2 : FINENESS, DAINTINESS; also : FRAILTY 3 : nicety or expressiveness of touch 4 : precise perception and discrimination : SENSITIVITY 5 : sensibility in feeling or conduct; also : SQUEAMISHNESS 6 : the quality or state of requiring delicate handling

del·i·cate \'de-li-kət\ adj 1 : pleasing to the senses of taste or smell esp. in a mild or subtle way 2 : marked by daintiness or charm : EXQUISITE 3 : FASTIDIOUS, SQUEAMISH ⟨a person of ~ tastes⟩ 4 : easily damaged : FRAGILE; also : SICKLY 5 : requiring skill or tact 6 : marked by care, skill, or tact 7 : marked by minute precision : very sensitive ⟨a ~ instrument⟩ — del·i·cate·ly adv

del·i·ca·tes·sen \,de-li-kə-'te-sᵊn\ n pl [G, pl. of Delicatesse delicacy, fr. F délicatesse] 1 : ready-to-eat food products (as cooked meats and prepared salads) 2 sing, pl delicatessens : a store where delicatessen are sold

de·li·cious \di-'li-shəs\ adj : affording great pleasure : DELIGHTFUL; esp : very pleasing to the taste or smell — de·li·cious·ly adv — de·li·cious·ness n

¹de·light \di-'līt\ n 1 : great pleasure or satisfaction : JOY 2 : something that gives great pleasure — de·light·ful \-fəl\ adj — de·light·ful·ly adv

²delight vb 1 : to take great pleasure 2 : to satisfy greatly : PLEASE

de·light·ed adj : highly pleased : GRATIFIED — de·light·ed·ly adv

de·lim·it \di-'li-mət\ vb : to fix the limits of

de·lin·eate \di-'li-nē-,āt\ vb -eat·ed; -eat·ing 1 : SKETCH, PORTRAY 2 : to picture in words : DESCRIBE — de·lin·ea·tion \-,li-nē-'ā-shən\ n

de·lin·quen·cy \di-'liŋ-kwən-sē\ n, pl -cies : the quality or state of being delinquent

¹de·lin·quent \-kwənt\ n : a delinquent person

²delinquent adj 1 : offending by neglect or violation of duty or law 2 : being overdue in payment

del·i·quesce \,de-li-'kwes\ vb -quesced; -quesc·ing : MELT, DISSOLVE — del·i·ques·cent \-'kwe-sᵊnt\ adj

de·lir·i·um \di-'lir-ē-əm\ n [L, fr. delirare to be crazy, lit., to leave the furrow (in plowing), fr. de- from + lira furrow] : mental disturbance marked by confusion, disordered speech, and hallucinations; also : frenzied excitement — de·lir·i·ous \-ē-əs\ adj — de·lir·i·ous·ly adv

delirium tre·mens \-'trē-mənz, -'tre-\ n : a violent delirium with tremors that is induced by excessive and prolonged use of alcoholic liquors

de·liv·er \di-'li-vər\ vb -ered; -er·ing 1 : to set free : SAVE 2 : CONVEY, TRANSFER ⟨~ a letter⟩ 3 : to assist in giving birth or at the birth of; also : to give birth to 4 : UTTER, COMMUNICATE 5 : to send to an intended target or destination — **de·liv·er·able** \-'li-v(ə-)rə-bəl\ *adj* — **de·liv·er·ance** \-v(ə-)rəns\ *n* — **de·liv·er·er** *n*

de·liv·ery \di-'li-və-rē\ *n, pl* **-er·ies** : the act of delivering something; *also* : something delivered — **de·liv·ery·man** \-ˌman\ *n*

dell \'del\ *n* : a small secluded valley

de·louse \dē-'laús\ *vb* : to remove lice from

del·phin·i·um \del-'fi·nē-əm\ *n* : any of a genus of mostly perennial herbs related to the buttercups with tall branching spikes of irregular flowers

del·ta \'del-tə\ *n* 1 : the 4th letter of the Greek alphabet — Δ or δ 2 : something shaped like a capital Δ; *esp* : the triangular silt-formed land at the mouth of a river — **del·ta·ic** \del-'tā-ik\ *adj*

del·toid \'del-ˌtóid\ *n* : a large triangular muscle that covers the shoulder joint and raises the arm laterally

de·lude \di-'lüd\ *vb* **de·lud·ed; de·lud·ing** : MISLEAD, DECEIVE, TRICK

¹**del·uge** \'del-yüj\ *n* 1 : a flooding of land by water 2 : a drenching rain 3 : a great amount or number ⟨a ∼ of mail⟩

²**deluge** *vb* **del·uged; del·ug·ing** 1 : INUNDATE, FLOOD 2 : to overwhelm as if with a deluge

de·lu·sion \di-'lü-zhən\ *n* : a deluding or being deluded; *esp* : a persistent false psychotic belief — **de·lu·sion·al** \-'lü-zhə-nəl\ *adj* — **de·lu·sive** \-'lü-siv\ *adj*

de·luxe \di-'lúks, -'ləks, -'lüks\ *adj* : notably luxurious or elegant

delve \'delv\ *vb* **delved; delv·ing** 1 : DIG 2 : to seek laboriously for information

dely *abbr* delivery

Dem *abbr* Democrat; Democratic

de·mag·ne·tize \dē-'mag-nə-ˌtīz\ *vb* : to cause to lose magnetic properties — **de·mag·ne·ti·za·tion** \dē-ˌmag-nə-tə-'zā-shən\ *n*

dem·a·gogue *also* **dem·a·gog** \'de-mə-ˌgäg\ *n* [Gk *dēmagōgos*, fr. *dēmos* people + *agōgos* leading, fr. *agein* to lead] : a person who appeals to the emotions and prejudices of people esp. in order to gain political power — **dem·a·gogu·ery** \-ˌgä-gə-rē\ *n* — **dem·a·gogy** \-ˌgä-gē, -ˌgä-jē\ *n*

¹**de·mand** \di-'mand\ *n* 1 : an act of demanding; *also* : something claimed as due or just 2 : the ability and desire to buy goods or services; *also* : the quantity of goods wanted at a stated price 3 : a seeking or being sought after : urgent need 4 : a pressing need or requirement

²**demand** *vb* 1 : to ask for with authority : claim as due or just 2 : to ask earnestly or in the manner of a command 3 : REQUIRE, NEED ⟨a patient who ∼s constant care⟩

de·mar·cate \di-'mär-ˌkāt, 'dē-ˌmär-\ *vb* **-cat·ed; -cat·ing** 1 : DELIMIT 2 : to set apart : DISTINGUISH — **de·mar·ca·tion** \ˌdē-ˌmär-'kā-shən\ *n*

dé·marche *or* **de·marche** \dā-'märsh\ *n* : a course of action : MANEUVER

¹**de·mean** \di-'mēn\ *vb* **de·meaned; de·mean·ing** : to behave or conduct (oneself) usu. in a proper manner

²**demean** *vb* **de·meaned; de·mean·ing** : DEGRADE, DEBASE

de·mean·or \di-'mē-nər\ *n* : CONDUCT, BEARING

de·mean·our *Brit var of* DEMEANOR

de·ment·ed \di-'men-təd\ *adj* : MAD, INSANE — **de·ment·ed·ly** *adv*

de·men·tia \di-'men-chə\ *n* 1 : deterioration of cognitive functioning (as in Alzheimer's disease) 2 : INSANITY

de·mer·it \di-'mer-ət\ *n* 1 : FAULT 2 : a mark placed against a person's record for some fault or offense

de·mesne \di-'mān, -'mēn\ *n* 1 : REALM 2 : manorial land actually possessed by the lord and not held by free tenants 3 : ESTATE 4 : REGION

demi·god \'de-mi-ˌgäd\ *n* : a mythological being with more power than a mortal but less than a god

demi·john \'de-mi-ˌjän\ *n* [F *dame-jeanne*, lit., Lady Jane] : a large narrow-necked bottle usu. enclosed in wickerwork

de·mil·i·ta·rize \dē-'mi-lə-tə-ˌrīz\ *vb* : to strip of military forces, weapons, or fortifications — **de·mil·i·tar·i·za·tion** \dē-ˌmi-lə-tə-rə-'zā-shən\ *n*

demi·mon·daine \ˌde-mi-ˌmän-'dān\ *n* : a woman of the demimonde

demi·monde \'de-mi-ˌmänd\ *n* [F *demi-monde*, fr. *demi-* half + *monde* world] 1 : a class of women on the fringes

of respectable society supported by wealthy lovers 2 : a distinct isolated group having low reputation or prestige

de·min·er·al·ize \dē-'mi-nə-rə-ˌlīz\ *vb* : to remove the mineral matter from — **de·min·er·al·i·za·tion** \-ˌmi-nə-rə-lə-'zā-shən\ *n*

de·mise \di-'mīz\ *n* 1 : LEASE 2 : transfer of sovereignty to a successor ⟨∼ of the crown⟩ 3 : DEATH 4 : loss of status

demi·tasse \'de-mi-ˌtas\ *n* : a small cup of black coffee; *also* : the cup used to serve it

demo \'de-mō\ *n, pl* **demos** 1 : DEMONSTRATION 2 : a product used to show performance or merits to prospective buyers 3 : a recording used to show off a song or performer

de·mo·bi·lize \di-'mō-bə-ˌlīz, dē-\ *vb* 1 : DISBAND 2 : to discharge from military service — **de·mo·bi·li·za·tion** \di-ˌmō-bə-lə-'zā-shən, dē-\ *n*

de·moc·ra·cy \di-'mä-krə-sē\ *n, pl* **-cies** [MF *democratie*, fr. LL *democratia*, fr. Gk *dēmokratia*, fr. *dēmos* people + *kratos* strength, power] 1 : government by the people; *esp* : rule of the majority 2 : a government in which the supreme power is held by the people 3 : a political unit that has a democratic government 4 *cap* : the principles and policies of the Democratic party in the U.S. 5 : the common people esp. when constituting the source of political authority 6 : the absence of hereditary or arbitrary class distinctions or privileges

dem·o·crat \'de-mə-ˌkrat\ *n* 1 : one who believes in or practices democracy 2 *cap* : a member of the Democratic party of the U.S.

dem·o·crat·ic \ˌde-mə-'kra-tik\ *adj* 1 : of, relating to, or favoring democracy 2 *often cap* : of or relating to one of the two major political parties in the U.S. associated in modern times with policies of broad social reform and internationalism 3 : relating to or appealing to the common people ⟨∼ art⟩ 4 : not snobbish — **dem·o·crat·i·cal·ly** \-ti-k(ə-)lē\ *adv*

de·moc·ra·tize \di-'mä-krə-ˌtīz\ *vb* **-tized; -tiz·ing** : to make democratic

dé·mo·dé \ˌdā-mō-'dā\ *adj* [F] : no longer fashionable : OUT-OF-DATE

de·mo·graph·ics \ˌde-mə-'gra-fiks, ˌdē-\ *n pl* : the statistical characteristics of human populations

de·mog·ra·phy \di-'mä-grə-fē\ *n* : the statistical study of human populations and esp. their size and distribution and the number of births and deaths — **de·mog·ra·pher** \-fər\ *n* — **de·mo·graph·ic** \ˌde-mə-'gra-fik, ˌdē-\ *adj* — **de·mo·graph·i·cal·ly** \-fi-k(ə-)lē\ *adv*

dem·oi·selle \ˌdem-wə-'zel\ *n* [F] : a young woman

de·mol·ish \di-'mä-lish\ *vb* 1 : to destroy by breaking apart : RAZE 2 : SMASH 3 : to put an end to

de·mo·li·tion \ˌde-mə-'li-shən, ˌdē-\ *n* : the act of demolishing; *esp* : destruction by means of explosives

de·mon *or* **dae·mon** \'dē-mən\ *n* 1 : an evil spirit : DEVIL 2 *usu daemon* : an attendant power or spirit 3 : one that has unusual drive or effectiveness ⟨a ∼ for work⟩

de·mon·e·tize \dē-'mä-nə-ˌtīz, -'mə-\ *vb* : to stop using as money or as a monetary standard ⟨∼ silver⟩ — **de·mon·e·ti·za·tion** \dē-ˌmä-nə-tə-'zā-shən, -ˌmə-\ *n*

de·mo·ni·ac \di-'mō-nē-ˌak\ *also* **de·mo·ni·a·cal** \ˌdē-mə-'nī-ə-kəl\ *adj* 1 : possessed or influenced by a demon 2 : DEMONIC

de·mon·ic \di-'mä-nik\ *also* **de·mon·i·cal** \-ni-kəl\ *adj* : DEVILISH, FIENDISH ⟨∼ cruelty⟩

de·mon·ize \'dē-mə-ˌnīz\ *vb* **-ized; iz·ing** 1 : to convert into a demon 2 : to characterize or treat as evil or harmful

de·mon·ol·o·gy \ˌdē-mə-'nä-lə-jē\ *n* 1 : the study of demons 2 : belief in demons

de·mon·stra·ble \di-'män-strə-bəl\ *adj* 1 : capable of being demonstrated 2 : APPARENT, EVIDENT — **de·mon·stra·bly** \-blē\ *adv*

dem·on·strate \'de-mən-ˌstrāt\ *vb* **-strat·ed; -strat·ing** 1 : to show clearly 2 : to prove or make clear by reasoning or evidence 3 : to explain esp. with many examples 4 : to show publicly ⟨∼ a new car⟩ 5 : to make a public display ⟨∼ in protest⟩ — **dem·on·stra·tion** \ˌde-mən-'strā-shən\ *n* — **dem·on·stra·tor** \'de-mən-ˌstrā-tər\ *n*

¹**de·mon·stra·tive** \di-'män-strə-tiv\ *adj* 1 : demonstrating as real or true 2 : characterized by demonstration 3

: pointing out the one referred to and distinguishing it from others of the same class ⟨~ pronoun⟩ **4** : marked by display of feeling : EFFUSIVE — de·mon·stra·tive·ly *adv* — de·mon·stra·tive·ness *n*

²demonstrative *n* : a demonstrative word and esp. a pronoun

de·mor·al·ize \di-'mȯr-ə-ˌlīz\ *vb* **1** : to corrupt in morals **2** : to weaken in discipline or spirit : DISORGANIZE — de·mor·al·i·za·tion \di-ˌmȯr-ə-lə-'zā-shən\ *n*

de·mote \di-'mōt\ *vb* **de·mot·ed; de·mot·ing** : to reduce to a lower grade or rank — de·mo·tion \-'mō-shən\ *n*

de·mot·ic \di-'mä-tik\ *adj* : COMMON, POPULAR ⟨~ idiom⟩

de·mur \di-'mər\ *vb* **de·murred; de·mur·ring** [ME *demuren, demeren* to linger, fr. AF *demurer, demoerer,* fr. L *demorari,* fr. *morari* to linger, fr. *mora* delay] : to take exception : OBJECT — de·mur *n*

de·mure \di-'myu̇r\ *adj* **1** : quietly modest : DECOROUS **2** : affectedly modest, reserved, or serious : PRIM ♦ Syn·onyms SHY, BASHFUL, COY, DIFFICULT, RETIRING, UNASSERTIVE — de·mure·ly *adv*

de·mur·rer \di-'mər-ər\ *n* : a claim by the defendant in a legal action that the plaintiff does not have sufficient grounds to proceed

den \'den\ *n* **1** : LAIR 1 **2** : HIDEOUT ⟨a robber's ~⟩; *also* : a place like a hideout or a center of secret activity ⟨opium ~⟩ ⟨a ~ of iniquity⟩ **3** : a cozy private little room

Den *abbr* Denmark

de·nar \'de-ˌnär, 'dä-\ — see MONEY table

de·na·ture \dē-'nā-chər\ *vb* **de·na·tured; de·na·tur·ing** : to remove or change the natural qualities of; *esp* : to make (alcohol) unfit for drinking

den·drol·o·gy \den-'drä-lə-jē\ *n* : the study of trees — **den·drol·o·gist** \-jist\ *n*

den·gue \'deŋ-gē, -ˌgä\ *n* [Sp] : an acute infectious disease characterized by headache, severe joint pain, and rash

de·ni \'de-ˌnē, 'dä-\ *n pl* — see *denar* at MONEY table

de·ni·al \di-'nī(-ə)l\ *n* **1** : rejection of a request **2** : refusal to admit the truth of a statement or charge; *also* : assertion that something alleged is false **3** : DISAVOWAL **4** : restriction on one's own activity or desires

de·nier \'den-yər\ *n* : a unit of fineness for yarn

den·i·grate \'de-ni-ˌgrāt\ *vb* **-grat·ed; -grat·ing** [L *denigrare,* fr. *nigrare* to blacken, fr. *niger* black] : to cast aspersions on : DEFAME — den·i·gra·tion \ˌde-ni-'grā-shən\ *n*

den·im \'de-nəm\ *n* [F (*serge*) *de Nîmes* serge of Nîmes, France] **1** : a firm durable twilled usu. cotton fabric woven with colored warp and white filling threads **2** *pl* : overalls or pants of usu. blue denim

den·i·zen \'de-nə-zən\ *n* : INHABITANT

de·nom·i·nate \di-'nä-mə-ˌnāt\ *vb* : to give a name to : DESIGNATE

de·nom·i·na·tion \di-ˌnä-mə-'nā-shən\ *n* **1** : an act of denominating **2** : a value or size of a series of related values (as of money) **3** : NAME, DESIGNATION; *esp* : a general name for a category **4** : a religious organization uniting local congregations in a single body — de·nom·i·na·tion·al \-shə-nəl\ *adj*

de·nom·i·na·tor \di-'nä-mə-ˌnā-tər\ *n* : the part of a fraction that is below the line indicating division

de·no·ta·tive \'dē-nō-ˌtā-tiv, di-'nō-tə-tiv\ *adj* **1** : denoting or tending to denote **2** : relating to denotation

de·note \di-'nōt\ *vb* **1** : to mark out plainly : INDICATE **2** : to make known **3** : MEAN, NAME — de·no·ta·tion \ˌdē-nō-'tā-shən\ *n*

de·noue·ment \ˌdā-ˌnü-'mäⁿ\ *n* [F *dénouement,* lit., untying] : the final outcome of the dramatic complications in a literary work

de·nounce \di-'nau̇ns\ *vb* **de·nounced; de·nounc·ing** **1** : to pronounce esp. publicly to be blameworthy or evil **2** : to inform against : ACCUSE **3** : to announce formally the termination of (as a treaty) — de·nounce·ment *n*

de no·vo \di-'nō-vō\ *adv or adj* [L] : over again : ANEW ⟨a case tried ~⟩

dense \'dens\ *adj* **dens·er; dens·est** **1** : marked by compactness or crowding together of parts : THICK ⟨~ forest⟩ ⟨a ~ fog⟩ **2** : DULL, STUPID — dense·ly *adv* — dense·ness *n*

den·si·ty \'den-sə-tē\ *n, pl* **-ties** **1** : the quality or state of

being dense **2** : the quantity of something per unit volume, unit area, or unit length

dent \'dent\ *n* **1** : a small depressed place made by a blow or by pressure **2** : an impression or weakening effect made usu. against resistance **3** : initial progress — dent *vb*

den·tal \'den-t⁹l\ *adj* : of or relating to teeth or dentistry — den·tal·ly *adv*

dental floss *n* : a thread used to clean between the teeth

dental hygienist *n* : a person licensed to clean and examine teeth

den·tate \'den-ˌtāt\ *adj* : having pointed projections : NOTCHED

den·ti·frice \'den-tə-frəs\ *n* [ME *dentifricie,* fr. L *dentifricium,* fr. *dent-, dens* tooth + *fricare* to rub] : a powder, paste, or liquid for cleaning the teeth

den·tin \'den-t⁹n\ *or* **den·tine** \'den-ˌtēn, den-'tēn\ *n* : a calcareous material like bone but harder and denser that composes the principal mass of a tooth

den·tist \'den-tist\ *n* : a person licensed in the care, treatment, and replacement of teeth — den·tist·ry *n*

den·ti·tion \den-'ti-shən\ *n* : the number, kind, and arrangement of teeth (as of a person or animal); *also* : TEETH

den·ture \'den-chər\ *n* : a set of teeth; *esp* : a partial or complete set of false teeth

de·nude \di-'nüd, -'nyüd\ *vb* **de·nud·ed; de·nud·ing** : to strip the covering from — de·nu·da·tion \ˌdē-nü-'dā-shən, -nyü-\ *n*

de·nun·ci·a·tion \di-ˌnən-sē-'ā-shən\ *n* : the act of denouncing; *esp* : a public condemnation — de·nun·ci·a·to·ry \-'nən-sē-ə-ˌtȯr-ē\ *adj*

de·ny \di-'nī\ *vb* **de·nied; de·ny·ing** **1** : to declare untrue **2** : to refuse to recognize or acknowledge : DISAVOW **3** : to refuse to grant ⟨~ a request⟩ **4** : to reject as false ⟨~ a theory⟩

de·o·dar \'dē-ə-ˌdär\ *n* [Hindi & Urdu *devadār, deodār,* fr. Skt *devadāru,* fr. *deva* god + *dāru* wood] : a Himalayan cedar

de·odor·ant \dē-'ō-də-rənt\ *n* : a preparation that destroys or masks unpleasant odors

de·odor·ize \dē-'ō-də-ˌrīz\ *vb* : to eliminate the offensive odor of

de·ox·i·dize \dē-'äk-sə-ˌdīz\ *vb* : to remove esp. elemental oxygen from

de·oxy·ri·bo·nu·cle·ic acid \dē-ˌäk-si-ˌrī-bō-nü-ˌklē-ik-, -nyü-\ *n* : DNA

de·oxy·ri·bose \dē-ˌäk-si-'rī-ˌbōs\ *n* : a sugar with five carbon and four oxygen atoms in each molecule that is part of DNA

dep *abbr* **1** depart; departure **2** deposit **3** deputy

de·part \di-'pärt\ *vb* **1** : to go away : go away from : LEAVE **2** : DIE **3** : to turn aside : DEVIATE

de·part·ee \di-ˌpär-'tē\ *n* : a person who is departing or who has departed

de·part·ment \di-'pärt-mənt\ *n* **1** : a distinct sphere or category esp. of an activity or attribute **2** : a functional or territorial division (as of a government, business, or college) — de·part·men·tal \di-ˌpärt-'men-t⁹l, ˌdē-\ *adj* — de·part·men·tal·ly *adv*

department store *n* : a store having separate sections for a wide variety of goods

de·par·ture \di-'pär-chər\ *n* **1** : the act of going away **2** : a starting out (as on a journey) **3** : DIVERGENCE ⟨a ~ from tradition⟩

de·pend \di-'pend\ *vb* **1** : to be determined, based, or contingent ⟨life ~s on food⟩ **2** : TRUST, RELY ⟨you can ~ on me⟩ **3** : to be dependent esp. for financial support **4** : to hang down ⟨a vine ~ing from a tree⟩

de·pend·able \di-'pen-də-bəl\ *adj* : TRUSTWORTHY, RELIABLE — de·pend·abil·i·ty \-ˌpen-də-'bi-lə-tē\ *n*

de·pen·dence *also* **de·pen·dance** \di-'pen-dəns\ *n* **1** : the quality or state of being dependent; *esp* : the quality or state of being influenced by or subject to another **2** : RELIANCE, TRUST **3** : something on which one relies **4** : drug addiction; *also* : HABITUATION 2

de·pen·den·cy \-dən-sē\ *n, pl* **-cies** **1** : DEPENDENCE **2** : a territory under the jurisdiction of a nation but not formally annexed by it

¹de·pen·dent \-dənt\ *adj* **1** : hanging down **2** : determined or conditioned by another; *also* : affected with

drug dependence **3** : relying on another for support **4** : subject to another's jurisdiction **5** : SUBORDINATE 4 ⟨~ clauses⟩
²**dependent** *also* **de·pen·dant** \-dənt\ *n* : one that is dependent; *esp* : a person who relies on another for support
dependent variable *n* : a variable whose value is determined by that of one or more other variables in a function
de·pict \di-'pikt\ *vb* **1** : to represent by a picture **2** : to describe in words — **de·pic·tion** \-'pik-shən\ *n*
de·pil·a·to·ry \di-'pi-lə-ˌtōr-ē\ *n, pl* **-ries** : a preparation for removing hair, wool, or bristles
de·plane \dē-'plān\ *vb* : to get out of an airplane
de·plete \di-'plēt\ *vb* **de·plet·ed; de·plet·ing** : to exhaust esp. of strength or resources — **de·ple·tion** \-'plē-shən\ *n*
de·plor·able \di-'plȯr-ə-bəl\ *adj* **1** : LAMENTABLE ⟨a ~ death⟩ **2** : WRETCHED — **de·plor·ably** *adv*
de·plore \-'plȯr\ *vb* **de·plored; de·plor·ing** **1** : to feel or express grief for **2** : to regret strongly **3** : to consider unfortunate or deserving of disapproval
de·ploy \di-'plȯi\ *vb* : to spread out (as troops or ships) in order for battle — **de·ploy·ment** \-mənt\ *n*
de·po·nent \di-'pō-nənt\ *n* : one who gives evidence
de·pop·u·late \dē-'päp-yə-ˌlāt\ *vb* : to reduce greatly the population of — **de·pop·u·la·tion** \-ˌpä-pyə-'lā-shən\ *n*
de·port \di-'pȯrt\ *vb* **1** : CONDUCT, BEHAVE **2** : BANISH, EXILE — **de·por·ta·tion** \ˌdē-ˌpȯr-'tā-shən\ *n*
de·port·ment \di-'pȯrt-mənt\ *n* : BEHAVIOR, BEARING
de·pose \di-'pōz\ *vb* **de·posed; de·pos·ing** **1** : to remove from high office (as of king) **2** : to testify under oath or by affidavit
¹**de·pos·it** \di-'pä-zət\ *vb* **de·pos·it·ed** \-zə-təd\; **de·pos·it·ing** **1** : to place for safekeeping or as a pledge; *esp* : to put money in a bank **2** : to lay down : PLACE **3** : to let fall or sink ⟨silt ~ed by a flood⟩ — **de·pos·i·tor** \-zə-tər\ *n*
²**deposit** *n* **1** : the state of being deposited ⟨money on ~⟩ **2** : something placed for safekeeping; *esp* : money deposited in a bank **3** : money given as a pledge **4** : an act of depositing **5** : something laid down ⟨a ~ of silt⟩ **6** : a natural accumulation (as of a mineral)
de·po·si·tion \ˌde-pə-'zi-shən, ˌdē-\ *n* **1** : an act of removing from a position of authority **2** : TESTIMONY **3** : the process of depositing **4** : DEPOSIT
de·pos·i·to·ry \di-'pä-zə-ˌtōr-ē\ *n, pl* **-ries** : a place where something is deposited esp. for safekeeping
de·pot \1, *2 usu* 'dē-pō, *3 usu* 'de-pō\ *n* **1** : a place for storing goods or vehicles **2** : a place where military supplies or replacements are kept or assembled **3** : a building for railroad or bus passengers
depr *abbr* depreciation
de·prave \di-'prāv\ *vb* **de·praved; de·prav·ing** [ME, fr. AF *depraver,* fr. L *depravare* to pervert, fr. *pravus* crooked, bad] : CORRUPT, PERVERT — **de·praved** *adj* — **de·prav·i·ty** \-'pra-və-tē\ *n*
dep·re·cate \'de-pri-ˌkāt\ *vb* **-cat·ed; -cat·ing** [L *deprecari* to avert by prayer, fr. *precari* to pray] **1** : to express disapproval of **2** : BELITTLE — **dep·re·ca·tion** \ˌde-pri-'kā-shən\ *n*
dep·re·ca·to·ry \'de-pri-kə-ˌtōr-ē\ *adj* **1** : APOLOGETIC **2** : serving to deprecate : DISAPPROVING
de·pre·ci·ate \di-'prē-shē-ˌāt\ *vb* **-at·ed; -at·ing** [ME, fr. LL *depreciatus,* pp. of *depretiare,* fr. L *pretium* price] **1** : BELITTLE, DISPARAGE **2** : to lessen in price or value — **de·pre·cia·ble** \-shə-bəl\ *adj* — **de·pre·ci·a·tion** \-ˌprē-shē-'ā-shən\ *n*
dep·re·da·tion \ˌde-prə-'dā-shən\ *n* : a laying waste or plundering — **dep·re·date** \'de-prə-ˌdāt\ *vb*
de·press \di-'pres\ *vb* **1** : to press down : cause to sink to a lower position **2** : to lessen the activity or force of **3** : SADDEN, DISCOURAGE **4** : to lessen in price or value — **de·pres·sor** \-'pre-sər\ *n*
de·pres·sant \di-'pre-s°nt\ *n* : one that depresses; *esp* : a chemical substance (as a drug) that reduces bodily functional activity — **depressant** *adj*
de·pressed \-'prest\ *adj* **1** : low in spirits; *also* : affected with psychological depression **2** : suffering from economic depression
de·pres·sion \di-'pre-shən\ *n* **1** : an act of depressing : a state of being depressed **2** : a pressing down : LOWERING **3** : a state of feeling sad **4** : a psychological disorder marked esp. by sadness, inactivity, difficulty in think-

ing and concentration, and feelings of dejection **5** : a depressed area or part **6** : a period of low general economic activity with widespread unemployment
¹**de·pres·sive** \di-'pre-siv\ *adj* **1** : tending to depress **2** : characterized or affected by psychological depression
²**depressive** *n* : a person affected with or prone to psychological depression
de·pres·sur·ize \(ˌ)dē-'pre-shə-ˌrīz\ *vb* : to release pressure from
dep·ri·va·tion \ˌde-prə-'vā-shən\ *n* **1** : an act or instance of depriving : LOSS **2** : PRIVATION 2
de·prive \di-'prīv\ *vb* **de·prived; de·priv·ing** **1** : to take something away from **2** : to stop from having something
deprived *adj* : marked by deprivation esp. of the necessities of life
de·pro·gram \(ˌ)dē-'prō-ˌgram, -grəm\ *vb* : to dissuade from convictions usu. of a religious nature often by coercive means
dept *abbr* department
depth \'depth\ *n, pl* **depths** \'depths\ **1** : something that is deep; *esp* : the deep part of a body of water **2** : a part that is far from the outside or surface; *also* : the middle or innermost part **3** : ABYSS **4** : a profound or intense state ⟨the ~s of reflection⟩; *also* : the worst part ⟨during the ~s of the depression⟩ **5** : a reprehensibly low condition **6** : the distance from top to bottom or from front to back **7** : the quality of being deep **8** : the degree of intensity
depth charge *n* : an explosive device for use underwater esp. against submarines
dep·u·ta·tion \ˌde-pyə-'tā-shən\ *n* **1** : the act of appointing a deputy **2** : DELEGATION
de·pute \di-'pyüt\ *vb* **de·put·ed; de·put·ing** : DELEGATE
dep·u·tize \'de-pyə-ˌtīz\ *vb* **-tized; -tiz·ing** : to appoint or act as deputy
dep·u·ty \'de-pyə-tē\ *n, pl* **-ties** **1** : a person appointed to act for or in place of another **2** : an assistant empowered to act as a substitute in the absence of a superior **3** : a member of a lower house of a legislative assembly
der *or* **deriv** *abbr* derivation; derivative
de·rail \di-'rāl\ *vb* : to leave or cause to leave the rails — **de·rail·ment** *n*
de·rail·leur \di-'rā-lər\ *n* [F *dérailleur*] : a device for shifting gears on a bicycle by moving the chain from one set of exposed gears to another
de·range \di-'rānj\ *vb* **de·ranged; de·rang·ing** **1** : DISARRANGE, UPSET **2** : to make insane — **de·range·ment** *n*
der·by \'dər-bē, *Brit* 'där-\ *n, pl* **derbies** **1** : a horse race usu. for three-year-olds held annually **2** : a race or contest open to all **3** : a stiff felt hat with dome-shaped crown and narrow brim

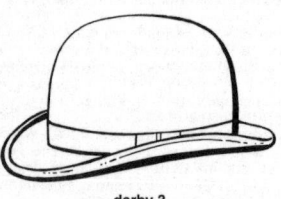

derby 3

de·reg·u·la·tion \(ˌ)dē-ˌre-gyü-'lā-shən\ *n* : the act of removing restrictions or regulations — **de·reg·u·late** \-'re-gyù-ˌlāt\ *vb*
¹**der·e·lict** \'der-ə-ˌlikt\ *adj* **1** : abandoned by the owner or occupant **2** : NEGLIGENT ⟨~ in his duty⟩
²**derelict** *n* **1** : something voluntarily abandoned; *esp* : a ship abandoned on the high seas **2** : a destitute homeless social misfit : VAGRANT, BUM
der·e·lic·tion \ˌder-ə-'lik-shən\ *n* **1** : the act of abandoning : the state of being abandoned **2** : intentional neglect ⟨~ of duty⟩
de·ride \di-'rīd\ *vb* **de·rid·ed; de·rid·ing** [L *deridēre,* fr. *ridēre* to laugh at scornfully] : RIDICULE
de ri·gueur \də-rē-'gər\ *adj* [F] : prescribed or required by fashion, etiquette, or custom : PROPER

de·ri·sion \də-'ri-zhən\ *n* : RIDICULE — **de·ri·sive** \-'rī-siv\ *adj* — **de·ri·sive·ly** *adv* — **de·ri·sive·ness** *n* — **de·ri·so·ry** \-'rī-sə-rē\ *adj*

der·i·va·tion \der-ə-'vā-shən\ *n* 1 : the formation of a word from an earlier word or root; *also* : an act of ascertaining or stating the derivation of a word 2 : ETYMOLOGY 3 : SOURCE, ORIGIN; *also* : DESCENT 4 : an act or process of deriving

de·riv·a·tive \di-'ri-və-tiv\ *n* 1 : a word formed by derivation 2 : something derived 3 : the limit of the ratio of the change of a function's value to the change in its independent variable as the latter change approaches zero — **derivative** *adj*

de·rive \di-'rīv\ *vb* **de·rived; de·riv·ing** [ME, fr. AF *deriver*, fr. L *derivare*, lit., to draw off (water), fr. *de-* from + *rivus* stream] 1 : to receive or obtain from a source 2 : to obtain from a parent substance 3 : INFER, DEDUCE 4 : to trace the derivation of 5 : to come from a certain source

der·mal \'dər-məl\ *adj* : of or relating to the skin : CUTANEOUS

der·ma·ti·tis \dər-mə-'tī-təs\ *n, pl* **-tit·i·des** \-'ti-tə-dēz\ *or* **-ti·tis·es** : inflammation of the skin

der·ma·tol·o·gy \-'tä-lə-jē\ *n* : a branch of medical science dealing with the structure, functions, and diseases of the skin — **der·ma·tol·o·gist** \-jist\ *n*

der·mis \'dər-məs\ *n* : the sensitive vascular inner layer of the skin

der·o·gate \'der-ə-gāt\ *vb* **-gat·ed; -gat·ing** 1 : to cause to seem inferior : DISPARAGE 2 : DETRACT — **der·o·ga·tion** \der-ə-'gā-shən\ *n* — **de·rog·a·tive** \di-'rä-gə-tiv\ *adj*

de·rog·a·to·ry \di-'rä-gə-tòr-ē\ *adj* : intended to lower the reputation of a person or thing : DISPARAGING — **de·rog·a·to·ri·ly** \-rä-gə-'tòr-ə-lē\ *adv*

der·rick \'der-ik\ *n* [obs. *derrick* hangman, gallows, fr. *Derick*, name of 17th cent. Eng. hangman] 1 : a hoisting apparatus : CRANE 2 : a framework over a drill hole (as for oil) for supporting machinery

der·ri·ere *or* **der·ri·ère** \der-ē-'er\ *n* : BUTTOCKS

der·ring·er \'der-ən-jər\ *n* : a short-barreled pocket pistol

der·vish \'dər-vish\ *n* [Turk *derviş*, lit., beggar, fr. Pers *darvīsh*] : a member of a Muslim religious order noted for devotional exercises (as bodily movements leading to a trance)

de·sal·i·nate \dē-'sa-lə-nāt\ *vb* **-nat·ed; -nat·ing** : DESALT — **de·sal·i·na·tion** \-sa-lə-'nā-shən\ *n*

de·sal·i·nize \dē-'sa-lə-nīz\ *vb* **-nized; -niz·ing** : DESALT — **de·sal·i·ni·za·tion** \-sa-lə-nə-'zā-shən\ *n*

de·salt \dē-'sòlt\ *vb* : to remove salt from ⟨~ seawater⟩ — **de·salt·er** *n*

des·cant \'des-kant\ *vb* 1 : to sing or play part music : SING 2 : to discourse or write at length

de·scend \di-'send\ *vb* 1 : to pass from a higher to a lower place or level : pass, move, or climb down or down along 2 : DERIVE ⟨~ed from royalty⟩ 3 : to pass by inheritance or transmission 4 : to incline, lead, or extend downward 5 : to swoop down or appear suddenly (as in an attack)

¹de·scen·dant *also* **de·scen·dent** \di-'sen-dənt\ *adj* 1 : DESCENDING 2 : proceeding from an ancestor or source

²descendant *also* **descendent** *n* 1 : one descended from another or from a common stock 2 : one deriving directly from a precursor or prototype

de·scent \di-'sent\ *n* 1 : ANCESTRY, BIRTH, LINEAGE 2 : the act or process of descending 3 : SLOPE 4 : a descending way (as a downgrade) 5 : a sudden hostile raid or assault 6 : a downward step (as in station or value) : DECLINE

de·scram·ble \dē-'skram-bəl\ *vb* : UNSCRAMBLE 2 — **de·scram·bler** \-b(ə-)lər\ *n*

de·scribe \di-'skrīb\ *vb* **de·scribed; de·scrib·ing** 1 : to represent or give an account of in words 2 : to trace the outline of — **de·scrib·able** *adj*

de·scrip·tion \di-'skrip-shən\ *n* 1 : an account of something; *esp* : an account that presents a picture to a person who reads or hears it 2 : KIND, SORT — **de·scrip·tive** \-'skrip-tiv\ *adj*

de·scry \di-'skrī\ *vb* **de·scried; de·scry·ing** 1 : to catch sight of 2 : to discover by observation or investigation

des·e·crate \'de-si-krāt\ *vb* **-crat·ed; -crat·ing** : PROFANE — **des·e·cra·tion** \de-si-'krā-shən\ *n*

de·seg·re·gate \dē-'se-gri-gāt\ *vb* : to eliminate segregation in; *esp* : to free of any law or practice requiring isolation on the basis of race — **de·seg·re·ga·tion** \-se-gri-'gā-shən\ *n*

de·sen·si·tize \dē-'sen-sə-tīz\ *vb* : to make (a sensitized or hypersensitive individual) insensitive or nonreactive to a sensitizing agent — **de·sen·si·ti·za·tion** \-sen-sə-tə-'zā-shən\ *n*

¹des·ert \'de-zərt\ *n* : dry land with few plants and little rainfall

²des·ert \'de-zərt\ *adj* : of, relating to, or resembling a desert; *esp* : being barren and without life ⟨a ~ island⟩

³de·sert \di-'zərt\ *n* 1 : the quality or fact of deserving reward or punishment 2 : a just reward or punishment

⁴de·sert \di-'zərt\ *vb* 1 : to withdraw from : ABANDON, FORSAKE — **de·sert·er** *n* — **de·ser·tion** \-'zər-shən\ *n*

de·serve \di-'zərv\ *vb* **de·served; de·serv·ing** : to be worthy of : MERIT — **de·serv·ing** *adj*

de·serv·ed·ly \-'zər-vəd-lē\ *adv* : according to merit : JUSTLY

deshabille *var of* DISHABILLE

des·ic·cate \'de-si-kāt\ *vb* **-cat·ed; -cat·ing** : DRY, DEHYDRATE — **des·ic·ca·tion** \de-si-'kā-shən\ *n* — **des·ic·ca·tor** \'de-si-kā-tər\ *n*

de·sid·er·a·tum \di-si-də-'rä-təm, -zi-, -'rā-\ *n, pl* **-ta** \-tə\ [L] : something desired as essential

¹de·sign \di-'zīn\ *vb* 1 : to conceive and plan out in the mind 2 : INTEND 3 : to devise for a specific function or end 4 : to make a pattern or sketch of 5 : to conceive and draw the plans for

²design *n* 1 : a particular purpose : deliberate planning 2 : a mental project or scheme : PLAN 3 : a secret project or scheme : PLOT 4 *pl* : aggressive or evil intent — used with *on* or *against* 5 : a preliminary sketch or plan 6 : an underlying scheme that governs functioning, developing, or unfolding : MOTIF ⟨the general ~ of the epic⟩ 7 : the arrangement of elements or details in a product or a work of art 8 : a decorative pattern ⟨a floral ~⟩ 9 : the art of executing designs

¹des·ig·nate \'de-zig-nāt, -nət\ *adj* : chosen but not yet installed ⟨ambassador ~⟩

²des·ig·nate \-nāt\ *vb* **-nat·ed; -nat·ing** 1 : to appoint and set apart for a special purpose 2 : to mark or point out : INDICATE; *also* : SPECIFY, STIPULATE 3 : to call by a name or title — **des·ig·na·tion** \de-zig-'nā-shən\ *n*

designated driver *n* : a person chosen to abstain from alcohol so as to transport others safely

designated hitter *n* : a baseball player designated at the start of the game to bat in place of the pitcher without causing the pitcher to be removed from the game

de·sign·er \di-'zī-nər\ *n* 1 : one who creates plans for a project or structure 2 : one who designs and manufactures high-fashion clothing — **designer** *adj*

designer drug *n* : a synthetic version of an illicit drug that has been chemically altered to avoid its prohibition

de·sign·ing \di-'zī-niŋ\ *adj* : CRAFTY, SCHEMING

de·sir·able \di-'zī-rə-bəl\ *adj* 1 : PLEASING, ATTRACTIVE 2 : ADVISABLE ⟨~ legislation⟩ — **de·sir·abil·i·ty** \-zī-rə-bi-lə-tē\ *n* — **de·sir·able·ness** *n* — **de·sir·ably** \-'zī-rə-blē\ *adv*

¹de·sire \di-'zī-(ə)r\ *vb* **de·sired; de·sir·ing** [ME, fr. AF *desirer*, fr. L *desiderare*, fr. *sider-, sidus* heavenly body] 1 : to long or hope for : exhibit or feel desire for 2 : REQUEST

²desire *n* 1 : a strong wish : LONGING, CRAVING 2 : sexual urge or appetite 3 : a usu. formal request for action 4 : something desired

de·sir·ous \di-'zī(-ə)r-əs\ *adj* : eagerly wishing : DESIRING ⟨~ of fame⟩

de·sist \di-'zist, -'sist\ *vb* : to cease to proceed or act

desk \'desk\ *n* [ME *deske*, fr. ML *desca*, fr. It *desco* table, fr. L *discus* dish, disc] 1 : a table, frame, or case esp. for writing and reading 2 : a counter, stand, or booth at which a person performs duties 3 : a specialized division of an organization (as a newspaper) ⟨city ~⟩

desk·top publishing \'desk-täp-\ *n* : the production of printed matter by means of a microcomputer

¹des·o·late \'de-sə-lət, -zə-\ *adj* 1 : DESERTED, ABANDONED 2 : FORSAKEN, LONELY 3 : DILAPIDATED 4

: BARREN, LIFELESS ⟨a ~ landscape⟩ **5** : CHEERLESS, GLOOMY ⟨~ memories⟩ — **des·o·late·ly** adv — **des·o·late·ness** n

²des·o·late \-ˌlāt\ vb **-lat·ed; -lat·ing** : to make desolate : lay waste : make wretched

des·o·la·tion \ˌdes-ə-ˈlā-shən, -zə-\ n **1** : the action of desolating **2** : GRIEF, SADNESS **3** : LONELINESS **4** : DEVASTATION, RUIN **5** : barren wasteland

des·oxy·ri·bo·nu·cle·ic acid \de-ˌzäk-sē-ˈrī-bō-nü-ˌklē-ik-, -nyü-\ n : DNA

¹de·spair \di-ˈsper\ vb : to lose all hope or confidence — **de·spair·ing** \-iŋ\ adj — **de·spair·ing·ly** adv

²despair n **1** : utter loss of hope **2** : a cause of hopelessness

des·patch chiefly Brit var of DISPATCH

des·per·a·do \ˌdes-pə-ˈrä-dō, -ˈrä-\ n, pl **-does** or **-dos** : a bold or reckless criminal

des·per·ate \ˈdes-pə-rət, -prət\ adj **1** : being beyond or almost beyond hope : causing despair **2** : RASH ⟨a ~ attempt⟩ **3** : extremely intense — **des·per·ate·ly** adv — **des·per·ate·ness** n

des·per·a·tion \ˌdes-pə-ˈrā-shən\ n **1** : a loss of hope and surrender to despair **2** : a state of hopelessness leading to rashness

de·spi·ca·ble \di-ˈspi-kə-bəl, ˈdes-pi-\ adj : deserving to be despised — **de·spi·ca·bly** \-blē\ adv

de·spise \di-ˈspīz\ vb **de·spised; de·spis·ing** **1** : to look down on with contempt or aversion : DISDAIN, DETEST **2** : to regard as negligible, worthless, or distasteful

de·spite \di-ˈspīt\ prep : in spite of

de·spoil \di-ˈspȯi(-ə)l\ vb : to strip of belongings, possessions, or value — **de·spoil·er** n — **de·spoil·ment** n

de·spo·li·a·tion \di-ˌspō-lē-ˈā-shən\ n : the act of plundering : the state of being despoiled

¹de·spond \di-ˈspänd\ vb : to become discouraged or disheartened

²despond n : DESPONDENCY

de·spon·den·cy \-ˈspän-dən-sē\ n : DEJECTION, HOPELESSNESS — **de·spon·dent** \-dənt\ adj — **de·spon·dent·ly** adv

des·pot \ˈdes-pət, -ˌpät\ n [MF despote, fr. Gk despotēs master, lord, autocrat] **1** : a ruler with absolute power and authority **2** : a person exercising power tyrannically — **des·pot·ic** \des-ˈpä-tik\ adj — **des·po·tism** \ˈdes-pə-ˌti-zəm\ n

des·sert \di-ˈzərt\ n : a course of sweet food, fruit, or cheese served at the close of a meal

de·stig·ma·tize \dē-ˈstig-mə-ˌtīz\ vb : to remove associations of shame or disgrace from

des·ti·na·tion \ˌdes-tə-ˈnā-shən\ n **1** : a purpose for which something is destined **2** : an act of appointing, setting aside for a purpose, or predetermining **3** : a place to which one is journeying or to which something is sent

des·tine \ˈdes-tən\ vb **des·tined; des·tin·ing** **1** : to settle in advance **2** : to designate, assign, or dedicate in advance **3** : to direct or set apart for a specific purpose or place

des·ti·ny \ˈdes-tə-nē\ n, pl **-nies** **1** : something to which a person or thing is destined : FATE, FORTUNE **2** : a predetermined course of events

des·ti·tute \ˈdes-tə-ˌtüt, -ˌtyüt\ adj **1** : lacking something needed or desirable **2** : suffering extreme poverty — **des·ti·tu·tion** \ˌdes-tə-ˈtü-shən, -ˈtyü-\ n

de·stroy \di-ˈstrȯi\ vb **1** : to put an end to : RUIN **2** : KILL

de·stroy·er \di-ˈstrȯi-ər\ n **1** : one that destroys **2** : a small speedy warship

de·struc·ti·ble \di-ˈstrək-tə-bəl\ adj : capable of being destroyed — **de·struc·ti·bil·i·ty** \-ˌstrək-tə-ˈbi-lə-tē\ n

de·struc·tion \di-ˈstrək-shən\ n **1** : RUIN **2** : the action or process of destroying something **3** : a destroying agency

de·struc·tive \di-ˈstrək-tiv\ adj **1** : causing destruction : RUINOUS **2** : designed or tending to hurt or destroy — **de·struc·tive·ly** adv — **de·struc·tive·ness** n

de·sue·tude \ˈde-swi-ˌtüd, -ˌtyüd\ n : DISUSE

des·ul·to·ry \ˈde-səl-ˌtȯr-ē\ adj : passing aimlessly from one thing or subject to another : DISCONNECTED

det abbr **1** detached; detachment **2** detail

de·tach \di-ˈtach\ vb **1** : to separate esp. from a larger mass **2** : DISENGAGE, WITHDRAW — **de·tach·able** adj

de·tached \di-ˈtacht\ adj **1** : not joined or connected : SEPARATE **2** : ALOOF, IMPARTIAL ⟨a ~ attitude⟩

de·tach·ment \di-ˈtach-mənt\ n **1** : SEPARATION **2** : the dispatching of a body of troops or part of a fleet from the main body for special service; also : the portion so dispatched **3** : a small permanent military unit of special composition **4** : indifference to worldly concerns : ALOOFNESS **5** : IMPARTIALITY

¹de·tail \di-ˈtāl, ˈdē-ˌtāl\ n [F détail, fr. OF detail slice, piece, fr. detaillier to cut in pieces, fr. taillier to cut] **1** : a dealing with something item by item ⟨go into ~⟩; also : ITEM, PARTICULAR ⟨the ~s of a story⟩ **2** : selection (as of soldiers) for special duty; also : the persons thus selected

²detail vb **1** : to report in particulars : SPECIFY **2** : to assign to a special duty

de·tailed \di-ˈtāld, ˈdē-ˌtāld\ adj : marked by abundant detail

de·tail·ing \ˈdē-ˌtāl-iŋ\ n : the meticulous cleaning and refurbishing of an automobile

de·tain \di-ˈtān\ vb **1** : to hold in or as if in custody **2** : STOP, DELAY

de·tect \di-ˈtekt\ vb : to discover the nature, existence, presence, or fact of — **de·tect·able** adj — **de·tec·tion** \-ˈtek-shən\ n — **de·tec·tor** \-ˈtek-tər\ n

¹de·tec·tive \di-ˈtek-tiv\ adj **1** : fitted or used for detection **2** : of or relating to detectives

²detective n : a person employed or engaged in detecting lawbreakers or getting information that is not readily accessible

dé·tente or **de·tente** \dā-ˈtänt\ n [F] : a relaxation of strained relations or tensions (as between nations)

de·ten·tion \di-ˈten-chən\ n **1** : the act or fact of detaining : CONFINEMENT; esp : a period of temporary custody prior to disposition by a court **2** : a forced delay

de·ter \di-ˈtər\ vb **de·terred; de·ter·ring** [L deterrēre, fr. terrēre to frighten] **1** : to turn aside, discourage, or prevent from acting (as by fear) **2** : INHIBIT

de·ter·gent \di-ˈtər-jənt\ n : a cleansing agent; esp : a chemical product similar to soap in its cleaning ability

de·te·ri·o·rate \di-ˈtir-ē-ə-ˌrāt\ vb **-rat·ed; -rat·ing** : to make or become worse in quality or condition — **de·te·ri·o·ra·tion** \-ˌtir-ē-ə-ˈrā-shən\ n

de·ter·min·able \-ˈtər-mə-nə-bəl\ adj : capable of being determined; esp : ASCERTAINABLE

de·ter·mi·nant \-mə-nənt\ n **1** : something that determines or conditions **2** : GENE

de·ter·mi·nate \di-ˈtər-mə-nət\ adj **1** : having fixed limits : DEFINITE ⟨a ~ period of time⟩ **2** : definitely settled ⟨in ~ order⟩ — **de·ter·mi·nate·ness** n

de·ter·mi·na·tion \di-ˌtər-mə-ˈnā-shən\ n **1** : the act of coming to a decision; also : the decision or conclusion reached **2** : a fixing of the extent, position, or character of something **3** : accurate measurement (as of length or volume) **4** : firm or fixed purpose — **de·ter·mi·na·tive** \-ˈtər-mə-ˌnā-tiv, -tər-mə-nə-\ adj

de·ter·mine \di-ˈtər-mən\ vb **-mined; -min·ing** **1** : to fix conclusively or authoritatively **2** : to come to a decision : SETTLE, RESOLVE **3** : to fix the form or character of beforehand : ORDAIN; also : REGULATE **4** : to find out the limits, nature, dimensions, or scope of ⟨~ a position at sea⟩ **5** : to bring about as a result

de·ter·mined \-ˈtər-mənd\ adj **1** : firmly resolved **2** : characterized by or showing determination — **de·ter·mined·ly** \-mənd-lē, -mə-nəd-lē\ adv — **de·ter·mined·ness** n

de·ter·min·ism \di-ˈtər-mə-ˌni-zəm\ n : a doctrine that acts of the will, natural events, or social changes are determined by preceding events or natural causes — **de·ter·min·ist** \-nist\ n or adj

de·ter·rence \di-ˈtər-əns\ n : the inhibition of criminal behavior by fear esp. of punishment

de·ter·rent \-ənt\ adj **1** : serving to deter **2** : relating to deterrence — **deterrent** n

de·test \di-ˈtest\ vb [L detestari, lit., to curse while calling a deity to witness, fr. de- from + testari to call to witness, fr. testis witness] : LOATHE, HATE — **de·test·able** adj — **de·tes·ta·tion** \ˌdē-ˌtes-ˈtā-shən\ n

de·throne \di-ˈthrōn\ vb : to remove from a throne : DEPOSE — **de·throne·ment** n

det·o·nate \ˈde-tᵊn-ˌāt\ vb **-nat·ed; -nat·ing** : to explode or cause to explode with violence — **det·o·na·tion** \ˌde-tᵊn-ˈā-shən\ n

det·o·na·tor \'de-t⁹n-₁ā-tər\ *n* : a device for detonating an explosive

¹de·tour \'dē-₁túr\ *n* : an indirect way replacing part of a route

²detour *vb* : to go by detour

de·tox \'dē-₁täks, di-'täks\ *n* : detoxification from an intoxicating or addictive substance — **detox** *vb*

de·tox·i·fy \dē-'täk-sə-₁fī\ *vb* **-fied; -fy·ing** **1** : to remove a poison or toxin or the effect of such from **2** : to free (as a drug user) from an intoxicating or addictive substance or from dependence on it — **de·tox·i·fi·ca·tion** \dē-₁täk-sə-fə-'kā-shən\ *n*

de·tract \di-'trakt\ *vb* **1** : to take away or diminish the value or effect of something **2** : DIVERT — **de·trac·tion** \-'trak-shən\ *n* — **de·trac·tor** \-'trak-tər\ *n*

de·train \dē-'trān\ *vb* : to leave or cause to leave a railroad train

det·ri·ment \'de-trə-mənt\ *n* : INJURY, DAMAGE; *also* : a cause of injury or damage — **det·ri·men·tal** \₁de-trə-'ment-⁹l\ *adj* — **det·ri·men·tal·ly** *adv*

de·tri·tus \di-'trī-təs\ *n, pl* **de·tri·tus** : fragments resulting from disintegration (as of rocks) : DEBRIS

deuce \'düs, 'dyüs\ *n* **1** : a two in cards or dice **2** : a tie in a tennis game with both sides at 40 **3** : DEVIL — used chiefly as a mild oath

Deut *abbr* Deuteronomy

deu·te·ri·um \dü-'tir-ē-əm, dyü-\ *n* : an isotope of hydrogen that has twice the mass of ordinary hydrogen

Deu·ter·on·o·my \₁dü-tə-'rä-nə-mē, ₁dyü-\ *n* — see BIBLE table

deut·sche mark \'dói-chə-₁märk\ *n* : a former basic monetary unit of Germany

dev *abbr* deviation

de·val·ue \dē-'val-yü\ *vb* : to reduce the international exchange value of ⟨∼ a currency⟩ — **de·val·u·a·tion** \-₁val-yə-'wā-shən\ *n*

dev·as·tate \'de-və-₁stāt\ *vb* **-tat·ed; -tat·ing** **1** : to bring to ruin **2** : to reduce to chaos or helplessness — **dev·as·tat·ing·ly** *adv* — **dev·as·ta·tion** \₁de-və-'stā-shən\ *n*

de·vel·op \di-'ve-ləp\ *vb* **1** : to unfold gradually or in detail **2** : to place (exposed photographic material) in chemicals to produce a visible image **3** : to bring out the possibilities of **4** : to make more available or usable ⟨∼ land⟩ **5** : to acquire gradually ⟨∼ a taste for olives⟩ **6** : to go through a natural process of growth, differentiation, or evolution **7** : to come into being gradually — **de·vel·op·er** *n* — **de·vel·op·ment** *n* — **de·vel·op·men·tal** \-₁ve-ləp-'men-t⁹l\ *adj* — **de·vel·op·men·tal·ly** \-'t⁹l-ē\ *adv*

de·vi·ant \'dē-vē-ənt\ *adj* : deviating esp. from some accepted norm ⟨∼ behavior⟩ — **de·vi·ance** \-əns\ *n* — **de·vi·an·cy** \-ən-sē\ *n* — **deviant** *n*

de·vi·ate \'dē-vē-₁āt\ *vb* **-at·ed; -at·ing** [LL *deviare,* fr. L *de-* from + *via* way] : to turn aside from a course, standard, principle, or topic — **de·vi·ate** \-vē-ət, -vē-₁āt\ *n* — **de·vi·a·tion** \₁dē-vē-'ā-shən\ *n*

de·vice \di-'vīs\ *n* **1** : SCHEME, STRATAGEM **2** : a piece of equipment or a mechanism for a special purpose **3** : DESIRE, INCLINATION ⟨left to my own ∼*s*⟩ **4** : an emblematic design

¹dev·il \'de-vəl\ *n* [ME *devel,* fr. OE *dēofol,* fr. LL *diabolus,* fr. Gk *diabolos,* lit., slanderer, fr. *diaballein* to throw across, slander, fr. *dia-* across + *ballein* to throw] **1** *often cap* : the personal supreme spirit of evil **2** : DEMON **3** : a wicked person **4** : an energetic, reckless, or dashing person **5** : FELLOW ⟨poor ∼⟩ ⟨lucky ∼⟩

²devil *vb* **-iled** *or* **-illed; -il·ing** *or* **-il·ling** **1** : to season highly ⟨∼*ed* eggs⟩ **2** : TEASE, ANNOY

dev·il·ish \'de-və-lish\ *adj* **1** : befitting a devil : EVIL; *also* : MISCHIEVOUS **2** : EXTREME ⟨in a ∼ hurry⟩ — **dev·il·ish·ly** *adv* — **dev·il·ish·ness** *n*

dev·il·ment \'de-vəl-mənt, -₁ment\ *n* : MISCHIEF

dev·il·ry \-rē\ *or* **dev·il·try** \-trē\ *n, pl* **-il·ries** *or* **-il·tries** **1** : action performed with the help of the devil **2** : MISCHIEF

de·vi·ous \'dē-vē-əs\ *adj* **1** : deviating from a straight line : ROUNDABOUT **2** : ERRANT **3** : TRICKY, CUNNING

¹de·vise \di-'vīz\ *vb* **de·vised; de·vis·ing** [ME, fr. AF *deviser* to divide, distinguish, invent, fr. VL *divisare,* fr. L *dividere* to divide] **1** : INVENT **2** : PLOT **3** : to give (real estate) by will

²devise *n* **1** : a disposing of real property by will **2** : a will

or clause of a will disposing of real property **3** : property given by will

de·vi·tal·ize \dē-'vī-tə-₁līz\ *vb* : to deprive of life or vitality

de·void \di-'vóid\ *adj* : being without : VOID ⟨a book ∼ of interest⟩

de·voir \də-'vwär\ *n* **1** : DUTY **2** : a formal act of civility or respect

de·volve \di-'välv\ *vb* **de·volved; de·volv·ing** : to pass (as rights or responsibility) from one to another usu. by succession or transmission — **dev·o·lu·tion** \₁de-və-'lü-shən, ₁dē-\ *n*

De·vo·ni·an \di-'vō-nē-ən\ *adj* : of, relating to, or being the period of the Paleozoic era between the Silurian and the Mississippian — **Devonian** *n*

de·vote \di-'vōt\ *vb* **de·vot·ed; de·vot·ing** **1** : to commit to wholly or chiefly **2** : to set apart for a special purpose : DEDICATE

de·vot·ed \-'vō-təd\ *adj* : characterized by loyalty and devotion : FAITHFUL

dev·o·tee \₁de-və-'tē, -'tā\ *n* : an ardent follower, supporter, or enthusiast

de·vo·tion \di-'vō-shən\ *n* **1** : religious fervor **2** : an act of prayer or private worship — usu. used in pl. **3** : a religious exercise for private use **4** : the fact or state of being dedicated and loyal ⟨∼ to music⟩; *also* : the act of devoting — **de·vo·tion·al** \-shə-nəl\ *adj*

de·vour \di-'vaú(-ə)r\ *vb* **1** : to eat up greedily or ravenously **2** : WASTE, ANNIHILATE **3** : to enjoy avidly ⟨∼ a book⟩ — **de·vour·er** *n*

de·vout \di-'vaút\ *adj* **1** : devoted to religion : PIOUS **2** : expressing devotion or piety **3** : EARNEST, SERIOUS ⟨a ∼ baseball fan⟩ — **de·vout·ly** *adv* — **de·vout·ness** *n*

dew \'dü, 'dyü\ *n* : moisture that condenses on the surfaces of cool bodies at night — **dewy** *adj*

dew·ber·ry \'dü-₁ber-ē, 'dyü-\ *n* : any of several sweet edible berries related to and resembling blackberries; *also* : a trailing bramble bearing these

dew·claw \-₁kló\ *n* : a digit on the foot of a mammal that does not reach the ground; *also* : its claw or hoof

dew·lap \-₁lap\ *n* : loose skin hanging under the neck of an animal

dew point *n* : the temperature at which the moisture in the air begins to condense

dex·ter·i·ty \dek-'ster-ə-tē\ *n, pl* **-ties** **1** : mental skill or quickness **2** : readiness and grace in physical activity; *esp* : skill and ease in using the hands

dex·ter·ous \'dek-strəs\ *adj* **1** : CLEVER **2** : done with skillfulness **3** : skillful and competent with the hands — **dex·ter·ous·ly** *adv*

dex·trose \'dek-₁strōs\ *n* : the naturally occurring form of glucose found in plants and blood

DFC *abbr* Distinguished Flying Cross

dg *abbr* decigram

DG *abbr* **1** [LL *Dei gratia*] by the grace of God **2** director general

DH \₁dē-'āch\ *n* : DESIGNATED HITTER

dhow \'daú\ *n* : an Arab sailing ship usu. having a long overhang forward and a high poop

DI *abbr* drill instructor

dia *abbr* diameter

di·a·be·tes \₁dī-ə-'bē-tēz, -təs\ *n* : an abnormal state marked by passage of excessive amounts of urine; *esp* : one (**diabetes mel·li·tus** \-'me-lə-təs\) characterized by deficient insulin, by excess sugar in the blood and urine, and by thirst, hunger, and loss of weight — **di·a·bet·ic** \-'be-tik\ *adj or n*

di·a·bol·i·cal \₁dī-ə-'bä-li-kəl\ *or* **di·a·bol·ic** \-lik\ *adj* : DEVILISH ⟨a ∼ plot⟩ — **di·a·bol·i·cal·ly** \-k(ə-)lē\ *adv*

di·a·crit·ic \₁dī-ə-'kri-tik\ *n* : a mark accompanying a letter and indicating a sound value different from that of the same letter when unmarked — **di·a·crit·i·cal** \-ti-kəl\ *adj*

di·a·dem \'dī-ə-₁dem\ *n* : CROWN; *esp* : a royal headband

di·aer·e·sis *or* **di·er·e·sis** \dī-'er-ə-səs\ *n, pl* **-eses** \-₁sēz\ : a mark ¨ placed over a vowel to show that it is to be pronounced in a separate syllable (as in *naïve*)

diag *abbr* **1** diagonal **2** diagram

di·ag·no·sis \₁dī-ig-'nō-səs\ *n, pl* **-no·ses** \-₁sēz\ : the art or act of identifying a disease from its signs and symptoms; *also* : the decision reached by diagnosis — **di·ag·nose** \'dī-ig-₁nōs\ *vb* — **di·ag·nos·tic** \₁dī-ig-'näs-tik\ *adj* — **di·ag·nos·ti·cian** \-₁näs-'ti-shən\ *n*

¹di·ag·o·nal \dī-'a-gə-nəl\ adj 1 : extending from one corner to the opposite corner in a 4-sided figure 2 : running in a slanting direction ⟨~ stripes⟩ 3 : having slanting markings or parts ⟨a ~ weave⟩ — di·ag·o·nal·ly adv

²diagonal n 1 : a diagonal line 2 : a diagonal row, pattern, or direction 3 : SLASH 3

¹di·a·gram \'dī-ə-,gram\ n : a design and esp. a drawing that makes something easier to understand — di·a·gram·ma·ble \-,gra-mə-bəl\ adj — di·a·gram·mat·ic \,dī-ə-grə-'ma-tik\ adj — di·a·gram·mat·i·cal·ly \-ti-k(ə-)lē\ adv

²diagram vb -grammed or -gramed \-,gramd\; -gram·ming or -gram·ing : to represent by a diagram

¹di·al \'dī(-ə)l\ n [ME dyal, fr. ML dialis clock wheel revolving daily, fr. L dies day] 1 : the face of a sundial 2 : the face of a timepiece 3 : a face with a pointer and numbers that indicate something ⟨the ~ of a gauge⟩ 4 : a device used for making electrical connections or for regulating operation (as of a radio)

²dial vb -aled or -alled; di·al·ing or di·al·ling 1 : to manipulate a dial so as to operate or select 2 : to make a telephone call or connection

³dial abbr dialect

di·a·lect \'dī-ə-,lekt\ n : a regional variety of a language

di·a·lec·tic \,dī-ə-'lek-tik\ n : the process or art of reasoning by discussion of conflicting ideas; also : the tension between opposing elements — di·a·lec·ti·cal \-ti-kəl\ adj

dialog box n : a window on a computer screen for choosing options or inputting information

di·a·logue \'dī-ə-,lóg\ n 1 : a conversation between two or more parties 2 : the parts of a literary or dramatic work that represent conversation

di·al·y·sis \dī-'a-lə-səs\ n, pl -y·ses \-,sēz\ 1 : the separation of substances from solution by means of their unequal diffusion through semipermeable membranes 2 : the medical procedure of removing blood from an artery, purifying it by dialysis, and returning it to a vein

diam abbr diameter

di·am·e·ter \dī-'a-mə-tər\ n [ME diametre, fr. MF, fr. L diametros, fr. Gk, fr. dia- through + metron measure] 1 : a straight line passing through the center of a figure or body; esp : one that divides a circle in half 2 : the length of a diameter

di·a·met·ric \,dī-ə-'me-trik\ or di·a·met·ri·cal \-tri-kəl\ adj 1 : of, relating to, or constituting a diameter 2 : completely opposed or opposite — di·a·met·ri·cal·ly \-k(ə-)lē\ adv

di·a·mond \'dī-mənd, 'dī-ə-\ n 1 : a hard brilliant mineral that consists of crystalline carbon and is used as a gem 2 : a flat figure having four equal sides, two acute angles, and two obtuse angles 3 : any of a suit of playing cards marked with a red diamond 4 : INFIELD; also : the entire playing field in baseball

di·a·mond·back rattlesnake \-,bak-\ n : either of two large and deadly rattlesnakes of the southern U.S.

di·an·thus \dī-'an-thəs\ n : ¹PINK 1

di·a·pa·son \,dī-ə-'pā-zᵊn, -sᵊn\ n 1 : the organ stop governing the flue pipes that form the primary basis of organ tone 2 : the entire range of musical tones

¹di·a·per \'dī-pər, 'dī-ə-\ n 1 : a cotton or linen fabric woven in a simple geometric pattern 2 : a garment for a baby drawn up between the legs and fastened about the waist

²diaper vb 1 : to ornament with diaper designs 2 : to put a diaper on

di·aph·a·nous \dī-'a-fə-nəs\ adj : of so fine a texture as to be transparent

di·a·pho·ret·ic \,dī-ə-fə-'re-tik\ adj : having the power to increase perspiration — diaphoretic n

di·a·phragm \'dī-ə-,fram\ n 1 : a sheet of muscle between the chest and abdominal cavities of a mammal 2 : a vibrating disk (as in a microphone) 3 : a cup-shaped device usu. of thin rubber fitted over the uterine cervix to act as a mechanical contraceptive barrier — di·a·phrag·mat·ic \,dī-ə-frag-'ma-tik, ,dī-,frag-\ adj

di·a·rist \'dī-ə-rist\ n : one who keeps a diary

di·a·ris·tic \,dī-ə-'ris-tik\ adj : of, relating to, or characteristic of a diary

di·ar·rhea \,dī-ə-'rē-ə\ n [ME diaria, fr. LL diarrhoea, fr. Gk diarrhoia, fr. diarrhein to flow through, fr. dia- through + rhein to flow] : abnormally frequent and watery bowel movements — di·ar·rhe·al \-'rē-əl\ adj

di·ar·rhoea chiefly Brit var of DIARRHEA

di·a·ry \'dī-ə-rē\ n, pl -ries : a daily record esp. of personal experiences; also : a book used as a diary

di·as·po·ra \dī-'as-pə-rə\ n 1 cap : the settling of scattered colonies of Jews outside Palestine after the Babylonian exile 2 cap : the Jews living outside Palestine or modern Israel 3 : the migration or scattering of a people away from an ancestral homeland

di·as·to·le \dī-'as-tə-(,)lē\ n : the stretching of the chambers of the heart during which they fill with blood — di·a·stol·ic \,dī-ə-'stä-lik\ adj

dia·ther·my \'dī-ə-,thər-mē\ n : the generation of heat in tissue by electric currents for medical purposes

di·a·tom \'dī-ə-,täm\ n : any of a class of planktonic one-celled or colonial algae with skeletons of silica

di·atom·ic \,dī-ə-'tä-mik\ adj : having two atoms in the molecule

di·a·tribe \'dī-ə-,trīb\ n : biting or abusive speech or writing

di·az·e·pam \dī-'a-zə-,pam\ n : a tranquilizer used esp. to relieve anxiety, tension, and muscle spasms

dib·ble \'di-bəl\ n : a pointed hand tool for making holes (as for planting bulbs) in the ground — dibble vb

¹dice \'dīs\ n, pl dice : DIE 1

²dice vb diced; dic·ing 1 : to cut into small cubes ⟨~ carrots⟩ 2 : to play games with dice

di·chot·o·my \dī-'kä-tə-mē\ n, pl -mies : a division or the process of dividing into two esp. mutually exclusive or contradictory groups — di·chot·o·mous \-məs\ adj

dick·er \'di-kər\ vb : BARGAIN, HAGGLE

dick·ey or dicky \'di-kē\ n, pl dickeys or dick·ies : a small fabric insert worn to fill in the neckline

di·cot·y·le·don \,dī-,kä-tə-'lēd-ᵊn\ n : any of a group of seed plants having an embryo with two cotyledons — di·cot·y·le·don·ous adj

dict abbr dictionary

¹dic·tate \'dik-,tāt\ vb dic·tat·ed; dic·tat·ing 1 : to speak or read for a person to transcribe or for a machine to record 2 : COMMAND, ORDER — dic·ta·tion \dik-'tā-shən\ n

²dic·tate \'dik-,tāt\ n : an authoritative rule, prescription, or injunction : COMMAND ⟨the ~s of conscience⟩

dic·ta·tor \'dik-,tā-tər\ n 1 : a person ruling absolutely and often brutally and oppressively 2 : one that dictates

dic·ta·to·ri·al \,dik-tə-'tór-ē-əl\ adj : of, relating to, or characteristic of a dictator or a dictatorship

dic·ta·tor·ship \dik-'tā-tər-,ship, 'dik-,tā-\ n 1 : the office of a dictator 2 : autocratic rule, control, or leadership 3 : a government or country in which absolute power is held by a dictator or a small clique

dic·tion \'dik-shən\ n 1 : choice of words esp. with regard to correctness, clearness, or effectiveness : WORDING 2 : ENUNCIATION

dic·tio·nary \'dik-shə-,ner-ē\ n, pl -nar·ies : a reference book containing words usu. alphabetically arranged along with information about their forms, pronunciations, functions, etymologies, meanings, and syntactical and idiomatic uses

dic·tum \'dik-təm\ n, pl dic·ta \-tə\ also dictums : a noteworthy, formal, or authoritative statement or observation

did past of DO

di·dac·tic \dī-'dak-tik\ adj 1 : intended to instruct, inform, or teach a moral lesson 2 : making moral observations

di·do \'dī-dō\ n, pl didoes or didos : a mischievous act : PRANK

¹die \'dī\ vb died; dy·ing \'dī-iŋ\ [ME dien, fr. or akin to ON deyja to die] 1 : to stop living : EXPIRE 2 : to pass out of existence ⟨a dying race⟩ 3 : SUBSIDE 4 ⟨the wind died down⟩ 4 : to long keenly ⟨dying to go⟩ 5 : STOP ⟨the motor died⟩

²die \'dī\ n [ME dee, fr. AF dé] 1 pl dice \'dīs\ : a small cube marked on each face with one to six spots and used usu. in pairs in games and gambling 2 pl dies \'dīz\ : a device used to shape, finish, or impress an object

die·hard \'dī-,härd\ n : one who is strongly devoted to or determined — die·hard adj

dieresis var of DIAERESIS

die·sel \'dē-zəl, -səl\ n 1 : DIESEL ENGINE 2 : a vehicle driven by a diesel engine 3 : DIESEL FUEL

diesel engine n : an internal combustion engine in whose

cylinders air is compressed to a temperature sufficiently high to ignite the fuel

diesel fuel *n* : a heavy mineral oil used as fuel in diesel engines

die·sel·ing \'dē-zə-liŋ\ *n* : the continued operation of an internal combustion engine after the ignition has been turned off

¹di·et \'dī-ət\ *n* [ME *diete*, fr. AF, fr. L *diaeta*, fr. Gk *diaita*, lit., manner of living, fr. *diaitasthai* to lead one's life] **1** : food and drink regularly consumed : FARE **2** : an allowance of food prescribed for a special reason (as to lose weight) — **di·e·tary** \-ə-,ter-ē\ *adj or n*

²diet *vb* : to eat or cause to eat or drink less or according to a prescribed rule — **di·et·er** *n*

dietary supplement *n* : a product taken orally that contains ingredients (as vitamins or amino acids) intended to supplement one's diet

di·e·tet·ics \,dī-ə-'te-tiks\ *n sing or pl* : the science or art of applying the principles of nutrition to diet — **di·e·tet·ic** *adj*

di·e·ti·tian *or* **di·e·ti·cian** \,dī-ə-'ti-shən\ *n* : a specialist in dietetics

dif *or* **diff** *abbr* difference

dif·fer \'di-fər\ *vb* **dif·fered; dif·fer·ing 1** : to be unlike **2** : VARY **3** : DISAGREE

dif·fer·ence \'di-frəns, 'di-fə-rəns\ *n* **1** : UNLIKENESS ⟨∼ in their looks⟩ **2** : distinction or discrimination in preference **3** : DISAGREEMENT; *also* : an instance or cause of disagreement ⟨unable to settle their ∼s⟩ **4** : the amount by which one number or quantity differs from another

dif·fer·ent \'di-frənt, 'di-fə-rənt\ *adj* **1** : unlike in nature or quality **2** : DISTINCT ⟨∼ age groups⟩; *also* : VARIOUS ⟨∼ members of the club⟩ **3** : ANOTHER ⟨try a ∼ channel⟩ **4** : UNUSUAL, SPECIAL — **dif·fer·ent·ly** *adv*

¹dif·fer·en·tial \,di-fə-'ren-chəl\ *adj* : showing, creating, or relating to a difference

²differential *n* **1** : the amount or degree by which things differ **2** : an arrangement of gears in an automobile that allows one wheel to turn faster than another (as in rounding curves)

differential gear *n* : DIFFERENTIAL 2

dif·fer·en·ti·ate \,di-fə-'ren-chē-,āt\ *vb* **-at·ed; -at·ing 1** : to make or become different **2** : to attain a specialized adult form and function during development **3** : to recognize or state the difference ⟨∼ between them⟩ — **dif·fer·en·ti·a·tion** \-,ren-chē-'ā-shən\ *n*

dif·fi·cult \'di-fi-(,)kəlt\ *adj* **1** : hard to do or make ⟨a ∼ climb⟩ **2** : hard to understand or deal with ⟨∼ reading⟩ ⟨a ∼ child⟩

dif·fi·cul·ty \-(,)kəl-tē\ *n*, *pl* **-ties** [ME *difficulte*, fr. AF *difficulté*, fr. L *difficilis* not easy, fr. *dis-* not + *facilis* easy] **1** : difficult nature ⟨the ∼ of a task⟩ **2** : DISAGREEMENT ⟨settled their *difficulties*⟩ **3** : OBSTACLE ⟨overcome *difficulties*⟩ **4** : TROUBLE ⟨in financial *difficulties*⟩ ✦ **Synonyms** HARDSHIP, RIGOR, VICISSITUDE

dif·fi·dent \'di-fə-dənt\ *adj* **1** : lacking confidence **2** : RESERVED **1** — **dif·fi·dence** \-dəns\ *n* — **dif·fi·dent·ly** *adv*

dif·frac·tion \di-'frak-shən\ *n* : the bending or spreading of waves (as of light) esp. when passing through narrow slits

¹dif·fuse \di-'fyüs\ *adj* **1** : VERBOSE, WORDY ⟨∼ writing⟩ **2** : not concentrated or localized ⟨∼ light⟩

²dif·fuse \di-'fyüz\ *vb* **dif·fused; dif·fus·ing 1** : to pour out or spread widely **2** : to undergo or cause to undergo diffusion **3** : to break up light by diffusion

dif·fu·sion \di-'fyü-zhən\ *n* **1** : a diffusing or a being diffused **2** : movement of particles (as of a gas) from a region of high to one of lower concentration **3** : the reflection of light from a rough surface or the passage of light through a translucent material

¹dig \'dig\ *vb* **dug** \'dəg\; **dig·ging 1** : to turn up the soil (as with a spade) **2** : to hollow out or form by removing earth ⟨∼ a hole⟩ **3** : to uncover or seek by turning up earth ⟨∼ potatoes⟩ **4** : DISCOVER ⟨∼ up information⟩ **5** : POKE, THRUST ⟨∼ a person in the ribs⟩ **6** : to work hard **7** : UNDERSTAND, APPRECIATE; *also* : LIKE, ADMIRE

²dig *n* **1** : THRUST, POKE; *also* : a cutting remark : GIBE **2** *pl* : living or working accommodations

³dig *abbr* digest

¹di·gest \'dī-,jest\ *n* : a summarized or shortened version esp. of a literary work

²di·gest \dī-'jest, də-\ *vb* **1** : to think over and arrange in

the mind **2** : to convert (food) into simpler forms that can be absorbed by the body **3** : to compress into a short summary — **di·gest·ibil·i·ty** \-,jes-tə-'bi-lə-tē\ *n* — **di·gest·ible** *adj* — **di·ges·tion** \-'jes-chən\ *n* — **di·ges·tive** \-'jes-tiv\ *adj*

di·ges·tif \,dē-zhes-'tēf\ *n* : an alcoholic drink taken after a meal

dig in *vb* **1** : to take a defensive stand esp. by digging trenches **2** : to firmly set to work **3** : to begin eating

dig·it \'di-jət\ *n* [ME, fr. L *digitus* finger, toe] **1** : any of the Arabic numerals 1 to 9 and usu. the symbol 0 **2** : FINGER, TOE

dig·i·tal \'di-jə-t²l\ *adj* **1** : of, relating to, or done with a finger or toe **2** : of, relating to, or using calculation by numerical methods or by discrete units **3** : relating to or employing communications signals in the form of binary digits ⟨a ∼ broadcast⟩ **4** : providing a readout in numerical digits ⟨a ∼ watch⟩ **5** : ELECTRONIC; *also* : characterized by computerized technology ⟨the ∼ age⟩ — **dig·i·tal·ly** *adv*

digital camera *n* : a camera that records images as digital data instead of on film

dig·i·tal·is \,di-jə-'ta-ləs\ *n* : a drug from the common foxglove that is a powerful heart stimulant; *also* : FOXGLOVE

digital versatile disc *n* : DVD

digital video disc *n* : DVD

dig·ni·fied \'dig-nə-,fīd\ *adj* : showing or expressing dignity

dig·ni·fy \-,fī\ *vb* **-fied; -fy·ing** : to give dignity, distinction, or attention to

dig·ni·tary \'dig-nə-,ter-ē\ *n*, *pl* **-tar·ies** : a person of high position or honor

dig·ni·ty \'dig-nə-tē\ *n*, *pl* **-ties 1** : the quality or state of being worthy, honored, or esteemed **2** : high rank, office, or position **3** : formal reserve of manner, language, or appearance

di·graph \'dī-,graf\ *n* : a group of two successive letters whose phonetic value is a single sound (as *ea* in *bread*)

di·gress \dī-'gres, də-\ *vb* : to turn aside esp. from the main subject or argument — **di·gres·sion** \-'gre-shən\ *n* — **di·gres·sive** \-'gre-siv\ *adj*

Di·jon mustard \'dē-,zhän-, di-'zhän-\ *n* : a mustard made from dark mustard seeds, white wine, and spices

dike \'dīk\ *n* : a bank of earth constructed to control water : LEVEE

dil *abbr* dilute

di·lap·i·dat·ed \də-'la-pə-,dā-təd\ *adj* : fallen into partial ruin or decay — **di·lap·i·da·tion** \-,la-pə-'dā-shən\ *n*

di·late \dī-'lāt, 'dī-,lāt\ *vb* **di·lat·ed; di·lat·ing** : SWELL, DISTEND, EXPAND — **dil·a·ta·tion** \,di-lə-'tā-shən\ *n* — **di·la·tion** \dī-'lā-shən\ *n*

dil·a·to·ry \'di-lə-,tȯr-ē\ *adj* **1** : DELAYING **2** : TARDY, SLOW

di·lem·ma \də-'le-mə\ *n* **1** : a usu. undesirable or unpleasant choice; *also* : a situation involving such a choice **2** : PREDICAMENT

dil·et·tante \'di-lə-,tänt, -'tant\ *n*, *pl* **-tantes** *or* **-tan·ti** \-'tän-tē, -'tan-\ [It, fr. prp. of *dilettare* to delight, fr. L *dilectare*] : a person having a superficial interest in an art or a branch of knowledge

dil·i·gent \'di-lə-jənt\ *adj* : characterized by steady, earnest, and energetic effort : PAINSTAKING — **dil·i·gence** \-jəns\ *n* — **dil·i·gent·ly** *adv*

dill \'dil\ *n* : an herb related to the carrot with aromatic leaves and seeds used as a seasoning and in pickles

dil·ly \'di-lē\ *n*, *pl* **dil·lies** : one that is remarkable or outstanding

dil·ly·dal·ly \'di-lē-,da-lē\ *vb* : to waste time by loitering or delaying

¹di·lute \dī-'lüt, də-\ *vb* **di·lut·ed; di·lut·ing** : to lessen the consistency or strength of by mixing with something else — **di·lu·tion** \-'lü-shən\ *n*

²dilute *adj* : DILUTED, WEAK

¹dim \'dim\ *adj* **dim·mer; dim·mest 1** : LUSTERLESS, DULL ⟨∼ colors⟩ **2** : not bright or distinct : OBSCURE, FAINT **3** : not seeing or understanding clearly — **dim·ly** *adv* — **dim·ness** *n*

²dim *vb* **dimmed; dim·ming 1** : to make or become dim or lusterless **2** : to reduce the light from

³dim *abbr* **1** dimension **2** diminished **3** diminutive

dime \'dīm\ *n* [ME, tenth part, tithe, fr. AF *disme, dime*, fr.

L *decima,* fr. fem. of *decimus* tenth, fr. *decem* ten] : a U.S. coin worth ¹⁄₁₀ dollar

di·men·sion \də-'men-chən, dī-\ *n* **1** : the physical property of length, breadth, or thickness; *also* : a measure of this **2** : EXTENT, SCOPE, PROPORTIONS — usu. used in pl. — **di·men·sion·al** \-'men-chə-nəl\ *adj* — **di·men·sion·al·i·ty** \-ˌmen-chə-'na-lə-tē\ *n*

di·min·ish \də-'mi-nish\ *vb* **1** : to make less or cause to appear less **2** : BELITTLE **3** : DWINDLE **4** : TAPER — **dim·i·nu·tion** \ˌdi-mə-'nü-shən, -'nyü-\ *n*

di·min·u·en·do \də-ˌmin-yə-'wen-dō\ *adv or adj* : DECRESCENDO

¹di·min·u·tive \də-'min-yə-tiv\ *n* **1** : a diminutive word or affix **2** : a diminutive individual

²diminutive *adj* **1** : indicating small size and sometimes the state or quality of being lovable, pitiable, or contemptible ⟨the ~ suffixes *-ette* and *-ling*⟩ **2** : extremely small : TINY

dim·i·ty \'di-mə-tē\ *n, pl* **-ties** : a thin usu. corded cotton fabric

dim·mer \'di-mər\ *n* : a device for controlling the amount of light from an electric lighting unit

di·mor·phic \(ˌ)dī-'mȯr-fik\ *adj* : occurring in two distinct forms — **di·mor·phism** \-ˌfi-zəm\ *n*

¹dim·ple \'dim-pəl\ *n* : a small depression esp. in the cheek or chin

²dimple *vb* **dim·pled; dim·pling** : to form dimples (as in smiling)

din \'din\ *n* : a loud confused mixture of noises

di·nar \di-'när\ *n* **1** — see MONEY table **2** — see *rial* at MONEY table

dine \'dīn\ *vb* **dined; din·ing** [ME, fr. AF *disner, diner* to eat, have a meal, fr. VL **disjejunare* to break one's fast, ultim. fr. L *jejunus* fasting] **1** : to eat dinner **2** : to give a dinner to

din·er \'dī-nər\ *n* **1** : one that dines **2** : a railroad dining car **3** : a restaurant usu. resembling a dining car

di·nette \dī-'net\ *n* : an alcove or small room used for dining

ding \'diŋ\ *vb* : to cause minor damage to a surface — **ding** *n*

din·ghy \'diŋ-ē\ *n, pl* **dinghies** **1** : a small boat **2** : LIFE RAFT

din·gle \'diŋ-gəl\ *n* : a small wooded valley

din·go \'diŋ-gō\ *n, pl* **dingoes** : a reddish brown wild dog of Australia

din·gus \'diŋ-gəs, -əs\ *n* : DOODAD

din·gy \'din-jē\ *adj* **din·gi·er; -est** : DIRTY, UNCLEAN; *also* : SHABBY — **din·gi·ness** *n*

dink \'diŋk\ *n, often all cap* [*double income, no kids*] : a couple with two incomes and no children; *also* : a member of such a couple

din·ky \'diŋ-kē\ *adj* **din·ki·er; -est** : overly small ⟨a ~ apartment⟩

din·ner \'di-nər\ *n* : the main meal of the day; *also* : a formal banquet

din·ner·ware \'di-nər-ˌwer\ *n* : tableware other than flatware

di·no \'dī-nō\ *n, pl* **dinos** : DINOSAUR

di·no·fla·gel·late \ˌdī-nō-'fla-jə-lət, -ˌlāt\ *n* : any of an order of planktonic plantlike unicellular flagellates of which some cause red tide

di·no·saur \'dī-nə-ˌsȯr\ *n* [ultim. fr. Gk *deinos* terrifying + *sauros* lizard] : any of a group of extinct long-tailed Mesozoic reptiles often of huge size

dint \'dint\ *n* **1** : FORCE ⟨by ~ of sheer grit⟩ **2** : DENT

di·o·cese \'dī-ə-səs, -ˌsēz, -ˌsēs\ *n, pl* **-ces·es** \-sə-səz, -ˌsē-zəz, -ˌsē-səz\ : the territorial jurisdiction of a bishop — **di·oc·e·san** \dī-'ä-sə-sən, ˌdī-ə-'sē-z²n\ *adj or n*

di·ode \'dī-ˌōd\ *n* : an electronic device with two electrodes or terminals used esp. as a rectifier

di·ox·in \dī-'äk-sən\ *n* : a persistent toxic hydrocarbon that occurs esp. as a by-product of industrial processes and waste incineration

¹dip \'dip\ *vb* **dipped; dip·ping** **1** : to plunge temporarily or partially under the surface (as of a liquid) **2** : to thrust in a way to suggest immersion **3** : to scoop up or out : LADLE **4** : to lower and then raise quickly ⟨~ a flag in salute⟩ **5** : to drop or slope down esp. suddenly ⟨the moon *dipped* below the crest⟩ **6** : to decrease moderately and usu. temporarily ⟨prices *dipped*⟩ **7** : to reach inside

or as if inside or below a surface ⟨*dipped* into their savings⟩ **8** : to delve casually into something; *esp* : to read superficially ⟨~ into a book⟩

²dip *n* **1** : an act of dipping; *esp* : a short swim **2** : inclination downward : DROP **3** : something obtained by or used in dipping **4** : a sauce or soft mixture into which food may be dipped **5** : a liquid into which something may be dipped (as for cleansing or coloring)

diph·the·ria \dif-'thir-ē-ə\ *n* : an acute contagious bacterial disease marked by fever and by coating of the air passages with a membrane that interferes with breathing

diph·thong \'dif-ˌthȯŋ, 'dip-\ *n* : two vowel sounds joined in one syllable to form one speech sound (as *ou* in *out*)

dip·loid \'di-ˌplȯid\ *adj* : having two haploid sets of chromosomes ⟨~ somatic cells⟩ — **diploid** *n*

di·plo·ma \də-'plō-mə\ *n* : an official record of graduation from or of a degree conferred by a school

di·plo·ma·cy \də-'plō-mə-sē\ *n* **1** : the art and practice of conducting negotiations between nations **2** : TACT

dip·lo·mat \'di-plə-ˌmat\ *n* : one employed or skilled in diplomacy — **dip·lo·mat·ic** \ˌdi-plə-'ma-tik\ *adj*

di·plo·ma·tist \də-'plō-mə-tist\ *n* : DIPLOMAT

dip·per \'di-pər\ *n* **1** : any of a genus of birds that are related to the thrushes and are skilled in diving **2** : something (as a ladle or scoop) that dips or is used for dipping **3** *cap* : BIG DIPPER **4** *cap* : LITTLE DIPPER

dipper 2

dip·so·ma·nia \ˌdip-sə-'mā-nē-ə\ *n* : an uncontrollable craving for alcoholic liquors — **dip·so·ma·ni·ac** \-nē-ˌak\ *n*

dip·stick \'dip-ˌstik\ *n* : a graduated rod for indicating depth

dip·ter·an \'dip-tə-rən\ *adj* : of, relating to, or being a fly (sense 2) — **dipteran** *n* — **dip·ter·ous** \-rəs\ *adj*

dir *abbr* **1** direction **2** director

di·ram \dē-'ram\ *n* — see *somoni* at MONEY table

dire \'dī(-ə)r\ *adj* **dir·er; dir·est** **1** : very horrible : DREADFUL ⟨~ suffering⟩ **2** : warning of disaster **3** : EXTREME ⟨~ poverty⟩

¹di·rect \də-'rekt, dī-\ *vb* **1** : ADDRESS ⟨~ a letter⟩; *also* : to impart orally : AIM ⟨~ a remark to the gallery⟩ **2** : to regulate the activities or course of : guide the supervision, organizing, or performance of **3** : to cause to turn, move, or point or to follow a certain course **4** : to point, extend, or project in a specified line or course **5** : to request or instruct with authority **6** : to show or point out the way

²direct *adj* **1** : stemming immediately from a source ⟨~ result⟩ **2** : being or passing in a straight line of descent : LINEAL ⟨~ ancestor⟩ **3** : leading from one point to another in time or space without turn or stop : STRAIGHT **4** : NATURAL, STRAIGHTFORWARD ⟨a ~ manner⟩ **5** : operating without an intervening agency or step ⟨~ action⟩ **6** : effected by the action of the people or the electorate and not by representatives ⟨~ democracy⟩ **7** : consisting of or reproducing the exact words of a speaker or writer — **direct** *adv* — **di·rect·ly** *adv* — **di·rect·ness** *n*

direct broadcast satellite *n* : a television broadcasting system in which satellite transmissions are received at the viewing location

direct current *n* : an electric current flowing in one direction only

direct deposit *n* : a method of payment in which money is transferred to the payee's account without the use of checks or cash

di·rec·tion \də-'rek-shən, dī-\ *n* **1** : MANAGEMENT, GUIDANCE **2** : COMMAND, ORDER, INSTRUCTION **3** : the course or line along which something moves, lies, or points **4** : TENDENCY, TREND — **di·rec·tion·al** \-shə-nəl\ *adj*

di·rec·tive \də-'rek-tiv, dī-\ *n* : something that directs and usu. impels toward an action or goal; *esp* : an order issued by a high-level body or official

direct mail *n* : printed matter used for soliciting business or contributions and mailed direct to individuals

di·rec·tor \də-'rek-tər, dī-\ *n* **1** : one that directs : MANAGER, SUPERVISOR, CONDUCTOR **2** : one of a group of persons who direct the affairs of an organized body — **di·rec·to·ri·al** \-,rek-'tōr-ē-əl\ *adj* — **di·rec·tor·ship** *n*

di·rec·tor·ate \-tə-rət\ *n* **1** : the office or position of director **2** : a board of directors; *also* : membership on such a board **3** : an executive staff

director's cut *n* : a version of a motion picture that is edited according to the director's wishes

di·rec·to·ry \-tə-rē\ *n, pl* **-ries** **1** : an alphabetical or classified list esp. of names and addresses **2** : FOLDER 4

dire·ful \'dī(-ə)r-fəl\ *adj* : DREADFUL; *also* : OMINOUS

dirge \'dərj\ *n* [ME *dirige* church service for the dead, fr. the first word of a LL anthem, fr. L, imper. of *dirigere* to direct] : a song of lamentation; *also* : a slow mournful piece of music

dir·ham \'dir-həm\ *n* **1** — see MONEY table **2** — see *dinar, riyal* at MONEY table

di·ri·gi·ble \'dir-ə-jə-bəl, də-'ri-jə-\ *n* : AIRSHIP

dirk \'dərk\ *n* : DAGGER 1

dirndl \'dərn-d²l\ *n* [short for G *Dirndlkleid*, fr. G dial. *Dirndl* girl + G *Kleid* dress] : a full skirt with a tight waistband

dirt \'dərt\ *n* **1** : a filthy or soiling substance (as mud, dust, or grime) **2** : loose or packed earth : SOIL **3** : moral uncleanness **4** : scandalous gossip **5** : embarrassing or incriminating information

¹**dirty** \'dər-tē\ *adj* **dirt·i·er; -est** **1** : SOILED, FILTHY **2** : INDECENT, SMUTTY ⟨∼ jokes⟩ **3** : BASE, UNFAIR ⟨a ∼ trick⟩ **4** : STORMY, FOGGY ⟨∼ weather⟩ **5** : not clear in color : DULL ⟨a ∼ red⟩ — **dirt·i·ness** *n* — **dirty** *adv*

²**dirty** *vb* **dirt·ied; dirty·ing** : to make or become dirty

dis·able \dis-'ā-bəl\ *vb* **dis·abled; dis·abling** **1** : to disqualify legally **2** : to make unable to perform by or as if by illness, injury, or malfunction — **dis·abil·i·ty** \,di-sə-'bi-lə-tē\ *n*

dis·abled *adj* : incapacitated by illness or injury; *also* : physically or mentally impaired

dis·abuse \,di-sə-'byüz\ *vb* : to free from error, fallacy, or misconception

dis·ad·van·tage \,di-səd-'van-tij\ *n* **1** : loss or damage esp. to reputation or finances **2** : an unfavorable, inferior, or prejudicial condition, quality, or circumstance — **dis·ad·van·ta·geous** \di-,sad-,van-'tā-jəs, -vən-\ *adj*

dis·ad·van·taged \-tijd\ *adj* : lacking in basic resources or conditions believed necessary for an equal position in society

dis·af·fect \,di-sə-'fekt\ *vb* : to alienate the affection or loyalty of — **dis·af·fec·tion** \-'fek-shən\ *n*

dis·agree \,di-sə-'grē\ *vb* **1** : to fail to agree **2** : to differ in opinion **3** : to cause discomfort or distress ⟨fried foods ∼ with her⟩ — **dis·agree·ment** *n*

dis·agree·able \-ə-bəl\ *adj* **1** : causing discomfort : UNPLEASANT, OFFENSIVE ⟨a ∼ odor⟩ **2** : ILL-TEMPERED, PEEVISH — **dis·agree·able·ness** *n* — **dis·agree·ably** \-blē\ *adv*

dis·al·low \,dis-ə-'laü\ *vb* : to refuse to admit or recognize : REJECT ⟨∼ a claim⟩ — **dis·al·low·ance** *n*

dis·ap·pear \,dis-ə-'pir\ *vb* **1** : to pass out of sight **2** : to cease to be : become lost — **dis·ap·pear·ance** *n*

dis·ap·point \,dis-ə-'pȯint\ *vb* : to fail to fulfill the expectation or hope of — **dis·ap·point·ment** *n*

dis·ap·pro·ba·tion \,dis-,a-prə-'bā-shən\ *n* : DISAPPROVAL

dis·ap·prov·al \,dis-ə-'prü-vəl\ *n* : adverse judgment : CENSURE

dis·ap·prove \-'prüv\ *vb* **1** : CONDEMN **2** : to feel or express disapproval ⟨∼s of smoking⟩ **3** : REJECT — **dis·ap·prov·ing·ly** \-'prü-viŋ-lē\ *adv*

dis·arm \dis-'ärm\ *vb* **1** : to take arms or weapons from **2** : to reduce the size and strength of the armed forces of a country **3** : to make harmless, peaceable, or friendly : win over ⟨a ∼*ing* smile⟩ — **dis·ar·ma·ment** \-'är-mə-mənt\ *n*

dis·ar·range \,dis-ə-'rānj\ *vb* : to disturb the arrangement or order of — **dis·ar·range·ment** *n*

dis·ar·ray \-'rā\ *n* **1** : DISORDER, CONFUSION **2** : disorderly or careless dress

dis·as·sem·ble \,dis-ə-'sem-bəl\ *vb* : to take apart

dis·as·so·ci·ate \-'sō-shē-,āt, -sē-\ *vb* : to detach from association

di·sas·ter \di-'zas-tər, -'sas-\ *n* [MF *desastre*, fr. It *disastro*, fr. *astro* star, fr. L *astrum*] : a sudden or great misfortune — **di·sas·trous** \-'zas-trəs\ *adj* — **di·sas·trous·ly** *adv*

dis·avow \,dis-ə-'vaü\ *vb* : to deny responsibility for : REPUDIATE — **dis·avow·al** \-'vaü(-ə)l\ *n*

dis·band \dis-'band\ *vb* : to break up the organization of : DISPERSE

dis·bar \dis-'bär\ *vb* : to expel from the legal profession — **dis·bar·ment** *n*

dis·be·lieve \,dis-bə-'lēv\ *vb* **1** : to hold not worthy of belief : not believe **2** : to withhold or reject belief — **dis·be·lief** \-'lēf\ *n* — **dis·be·liev·er** *n*

dis·bur·den \dis-'bər-d²n\ *vb* : to rid of a burden

dis·burse \dis-'bərs\ *vb* **dis·bursed; dis·burs·ing** **1** : to pay out : EXPEND **2** : DISTRIBUTE — **dis·burse·ment** *n*

¹**disc** *var of* DISK

²**disc** *abbr* discount

dis·card \dis-'kärd, 'dis-,kärd\ *vb* **1** : to let go a playing card from one's hand; *also* : to play (a card) from a suit other than a trump but different from the one led **2** : to get rid of as unwanted — **dis·card** \'dis-,kärd\ *n*

disc brake *n* : a brake that operates by the friction of a pair of plates pressing against the sides of a rotating disc

dis·cern \di-'sərn, -'zərn\ *vb* **1** : to detect with the eyes : DISTINGUISH **2** : DISCRIMINATE **3** : to come to know or recognize mentally — **dis·cern·ible** *adj* — **dis·cern·ment** *n*

dis·cern·ing *adj* : revealing insight and understanding

¹**dis·charge** \dis-'chärj, 'dis-,chärj\ *vb* **1** : to relieve of a charge, load, or burden : UNLOAD; *esp* : to remove the electrical energy from ⟨∼ a storage battery⟩ **2** : to let or put off ⟨∼ passengers⟩ **3** : SHOOT ⟨∼ an arrow⟩ **4** : to set free ⟨∼ a prisoner⟩ **5** : to dismiss from service or employment ⟨∼ a soldier⟩ **6** : to get rid of by paying or doing ⟨∼ a debt⟩ **7** : to give forth fluid ⟨the river ∼s into the ocean⟩

²**dis·charge** \'dis-,chärj, dis-'chärj\ *n* **1** : the act of discharging, unloading, or releasing **2** : something that discharges; *esp* : a certification of release or payment **3** : a firing off (as of a gun) **4** : a flowing out (as of blood from a wound); *also* : something that is emitted ⟨a purulent ∼⟩ **5** : release or dismissal esp. from an office or employment; *also* : complete separation from military service **6** : a flow of electricity (as through a gas)

dis·ci·ple \di-'sī-pəl\ *n* [ultim. fr. LL *discipulus* follower of Jesus in his lifetime, fr. L, pupil] **1** : one who accepts and helps to spread the teachings of another; *also* : a convinced adherent **2** *cap* : a member of the Disciples of Christ

dis·ci·pli·nar·i·an \,di-sə-plə-'ner-ē-ən\ *n* : one who enforces order

dis·ci·plin·ary \'di-sə-plə-,ner-ē\ *adj* : of or relating to discipline; *also* : CORRECTIVE ⟨take ∼ action⟩

¹**dis·ci·pline** \'di-sə-plən\ *n* **1** : PUNISHMENT **2** : a field of study : SUBJECT **3** : training that corrects, molds, or perfects **4** : control gained by obedience or training : orderly conduct **5** : a system of rules governing conduct

²**discipline** *vb* **-plined; -plin·ing** **1** : PUNISH **2** : to train or develop by instruction and exercise esp. in self-control **3** : to bring under control ⟨∼ troops⟩; *also* : to impose order upon

disc jockey or disk jockey *n* : an announcer of a radio show of popular recorded music

dis·claim \dis-'klām\ *vb* : DENY, DISAVOW — **dis·claim·er** *n*

dis·close \dis-'klōz\ *vb* : to expose to view — **dis·clo·sure** \-'klō-zhər\ *n*

dis·co \'dis-kō\ *n, pl* **discos** **1** : a nightclub for dancing to live or recorded music **2** : popular dance music characterized by hypnotic rhythm, repetitive lyrics, and electronically produced sounds

dis·col·or \dis-'kə-lər\ *vb* : to alter or change in hue or color esp. for the worse — **dis·col·or·ation** \-,kə-lə-'rā-shən\ *n*

dis·com·bob·u·late \ˌdis-kəm-ˈbä-byü-ˌlāt\ *vb* -lat·ed; -lat·ing : UPSET, CONFUSE

dis·com·fit \dis-ˈkəm-fət, *esp Southern* ˌdis-kəm-ˈfit\ *vb* : UPSET, FRUSTRATE — dis·com·fi·ture \dis-ˈkəm-fə-ˌchu̇r\ *n*

¹dis·com·fort \dis-ˈkəm-fərt\ *vb* : to make uncomfortable or uneasy

²discomfort *n* : mental or physical uneasiness

dis·com·mode \ˌdis-kə-ˈmōd\ *vb* -mod·ed; -mod·ing : INCONVENIENCE, TROUBLE

dis·com·pose \-kəm-ˈpōz\ *vb* 1 : to destroy the calmness or peace of 2 : DISARRANGE — dis·com·po·sure \-ˈpō-zhər\ *n*

dis·con·cert \ˌdis-kən-ˈsərt\ *vb* : CONFUSE, UPSET

dis·con·nect \ˌdis-kə-ˈnekt\ *vb* : to undo the connection of — dis·con·nec·tion \-ˈnek-shən\ *n*

dis·con·nect·ed *adj* : not connected; *also* : INCOHERENT — dis·con·nect·ed·ly *adv* — dis·con·nect·ed·ness *n*

dis·con·so·late \dis-ˈkän-sə-lət\ *adj* 1 : CHEERLESS 2 : hopelessly sad — dis·con·so·late·ly *adv*

dis·con·tent \ˌdis-kən-ˈtent\ *n* : uneasiness of mind : DISSATISFACTION — dis·con·tent·ed *adj*

dis·con·tin·ue \ˌdis-kən-ˈtin-yü\ *vb* 1 : to break the continuity of : cease to operate, use, or take 2 : END — dis·con·tin·u·ance \-yə-wəns\ *n* — dis·con·ti·nu·i·ty \dis-ˌkän-tə-ˈnü-ə-tē, -ˈnyü-\ *n* — dis·con·tin·u·ous \ˌdis-kən-ˈtin-yə-wəs\ *adj*

dis·cord \ˈdis-ˌkȯrd\ *n* 1 : lack of agreement or harmony : DISSENSION, CONFLICT 2 : a harsh combination of musical sounds 3 : a harsh or unpleasant sound — dis·cor·dant \dis-ˈkȯr-dᵊnt\ *adj* — dis·cor·dant·ly *adv*

dis·co·theque *or* discothèque \ˈdis-kə-ˌtek\ *n* : DISCO 1

¹dis·count \ˈdis-ˌkau̇nt\ *n* 1 : a reduction made from a regular or list price 2 : a deduction of interest in advance when lending money

²dis·count \ˈdis-ˌkau̇nt, dis-ˈkau̇nt\ *vb* 1 : to deduct from the amount of a bill, debt, or charge usu. for cash or prompt payment; *also* : to sell or offer for sale at a discount 2 : to lend money after deducting the discount ⟨~ a note⟩ 3 : DISREGARD; *also* : MINIMIZE 4 : to make allowance for bias or exaggeration 5 : to take into account (as a future event) in present calculations — dis·count·able *adj* — dis·count·er *n*

³dis·count \ˈdis-ˌkau̇nt\ *adj* : selling goods or services at a discount; *also* : sold at or reflecting a discount

dis·coun·te·nance \dis-ˈkau̇n-tə-nənts\ *vb* 1 : EMBARRASS, DISCONCERT 2 : to look with disfavor on

dis·cour·age \dis-ˈkər-ij\ *vb* -aged; -ag·ing 1 : to deprive of courage or confidence : DISHEARTEN 2 : to hinder by disfavoring 3 : to attempt to dissuade — dis·cour·age·ment *n* — dis·cour·ag·ing·ly *adv*

¹dis·course \ˈdis-ˌkȯrs\ *n* [ME *discours*, fr. ML & LL *discursus*; ML, argument, fr. LL, conversation, fr. L, act of running about, fr. *discurrere* to run about, fr. *currere* to run] 1 : CONVERSATION 2 : formal and usu. extended expression of thought on a subject

²dis·course \dis-ˈkȯrs\ *vb* dis·coursed; dis·cours·ing 1 : to express oneself in esp. oral discourse 2 : TALK, CONVERSE

dis·cour·te·ous \(ˌ)dis-ˈkər-tē-əs\ *adj* : lacking courtesy : UNCIVIL, RUDE — dis·cour·te·ous·ly *adv*

dis·cour·te·sy \-ˈkər-tə-sē\ *n* : RUDENESS; *also* : a rude act

dis·cov·er \dis-ˈkə-vər\ *vb* 1 : to make known or visible 2 : to obtain sight or knowledge of for the first time; *also* : FIND OUT — dis·cov·er·er *n*

dis·cov·ery \dis-ˈkə-və-rē\ *n, pl* -er·ies 1 : the act or process of discovering 2 : something discovered 3 : the disclosure usu. before a civil trial of pertinent facts or documents

¹dis·cred·it \(ˌ)dis-ˈkre-dət\ *vb* 1 : DISBELIEVE 2 : to cause disbelief in the accuracy or authority of 3 : DISGRACE — dis·cred·it·able *adj*

²discredit *n* 1 : loss of reputation 2 : lack or loss of belief or confidence

dis·creet \dis-ˈkrēt\ *adj* : showing good judgment; *esp* : capable of observing prudent silence — dis·creet·ly *adv*

dis·crep·an·cy \dis-ˈkre-pən-sē\ *n, pl* -cies 1 : DIFFERENCE, DISAGREEMENT 2 : an instance of being discrepant

dis·crep·ant \-pənt\ *adj* [ME *discrepaunt*, fr. L *discrepans*, prp. of *discrepare* to sound discordantly, fr. *crepare* to rat-

tle, creak] : being at variance : DISAGREEING ⟨~ conclusions⟩

dis·crete \dis-ˈkrēt, ˈdis-ˌkrēt\ *adj* 1 : individually distinct ⟨several ~ sections⟩ 2 : NONCONTINUOUS

dis·cre·tion \dis-ˈkre-shən\ *n* 1 : the quality of being discreet : PRUDENCE 2 : individual choice or judgment ⟨left the decision to his ~⟩ 3 : power of free decision or latitude of choice — dis·cre·tion·ary *adj*

dis·crim·i·nate \dis-ˈkri-mə-ˌnāt\ *vb* -nat·ed; -nat·ing 1 : DISTINGUISH, DIFFERENTIATE 2 : to make a difference in treatment on a basis other than individual merit — dis·crim·i·na·tion \-ˌkri-mə-ˈnā-shən\ *n*

dis·crim·i·nat·ing *adj* : marked by discrimination; *esp* : DISCERNING, JUDICIOUS — dis·crim·i·nat·ing·ly *adv*

dis·crim·i·na·to·ry \dis-ˈkri-mə-nə-ˌtȯr-ē\ *adj* : marked by esp. unjust discrimination ⟨~ treatment⟩

dis·cur·sive \dis-ˈkər-siv\ *adj* : passing from one topic to another : RAMBLING — dis·cur·sive·ly *adv* — dis·cur·sive·ness *n*

dis·cus \ˈdis-kəs\ *n, pl* dis·cus·es : a heavy disk that is hurled for distance in a track-and-field contest

dis·cuss \dis-ˈkəs\ *vb* [ME, fr. AF *discusser*, fr. L *discussus*, pp. of *discutere* to disperse, fr. *dis-* apart + *quatere* to shake] 1 : to argue or consider carefully by presenting the various sides 2 : to talk about — dis·cus·sion \-ˈskə-shən\ *n*

dis·cus·sant \di-ˈskə-sᵊnt\ *n* : one who takes part in a formal discussion

¹dis·dain \dis-ˈdān\ *n* : CONTEMPT, SCORN — dis·dain·ful \-fəl\ *adj* — dis·dain·ful·ly *adv*

²disdain *vb* 1 : to look on with scorn 2 : to reject or refrain from because of disdain

dis·ease \di-ˈzēz\ *n* : an abnormal bodily condition that impairs normal functioning and can usu. be recognized by signs and symptoms : SICKNESS — dis·eased \-ˈzēzd\ *adj*

dis·em·bark \ˌdi-səm-ˈbärk\ *vb* : to go or put ashore from a ship — dis·em·bar·ka·tion \di-ˌsem-ˌbär-ˈkā-shən\ *n*

dis·em·body \ˌdi-səm-ˈbä-dē\ *vb* : to deprive of bodily existence

dis·em·bow·el \-ˈbau̇-(ə)l\ *vb* : EVISCERATE 1 — dis·em·bow·el·ment *n*

dis·em·power \ˌdi-səm-ˈpau̇-(ə)r\ *vb* : to deprive of power, authority, or influence

dis·en·chant \ˌdi-sin-ˈchant\ *vb* : DISILLUSION — dis·en·chant·ment \-mənt\ *n*

dis·en·chant·ed \-ˈchan-təd\ *adj* : DISAPPOINTED, DISSATISFIED

dis·en·cum·ber \ˌdi-sᵊn-ˈkəm-bər\ *vb* : to free from something that burdens

dis·en·fran·chise \ˌdi-sin-ˈfran-ˌchīz\ *vb* : to deprive of a franchise, a legal right, or a privilege; *esp* : to deprive of the right to vote — dis·en·fran·chise·ment *n*

dis·en·gage \ˌdi-sᵊn-ˈgāj\ *vb* : RELEASE, EXTRICATE, DISENTANGLE — dis·en·gage·ment *n*

dis·en·gaged \-ˈgājd\ *adj* : IMPARTIAL, DETACHED ⟨a ~ observer⟩

dis·en·tan·gle \ˌdi-sin-ˈtaŋ-gəl\ *vb* : to free from entanglement : UNRAVEL

dis·equi·lib·ri·um \dis-ˌē-kwə-ˈli-brē-əm\ *n* : loss or lack of equilibrium

dis·es·tab·lish \ˌdis-ə-ˈsta-blish\ *vb* : to end the establishment of; *esp* : to deprive of the status of an established church — dis·es·tab·lish·ment *n*

dis·es·teem \ˌdis-ə-ˈstēm\ *n* : lack of esteem : DISFAVOR, DISREPUTE

dis·fa·vor \(ˌ)dis-ˈfā-vər\ *n* 1 : DISAPPROVAL, DISLIKE 2 : the state or fact of being no longer favored

dis·fig·ure \dis-ˈfi-gyər\ *vb* : to spoil the appearance of ⟨*disfigured* by a scar⟩ — dis·fig·ure·ment *n*

dis·fran·chise \dis-ˈfran-ˌchīz\ *vb* : DISENFRANCHISE — dis·fran·chise·ment *n*

disfunction *var of* DYSFUNCTION

dis·gorge \-ˈgȯrj\ *vb* : VOMIT; *also* : to discharge forcefully or confusedly

¹dis·grace \di-ˈskrās, dis-ˈgrās\ *vb* : to bring reproach or shame to

²disgrace *n* 1 : SHAME, DISHONOR; *also* : a cause of shame 2 : the condition of being out of favor : loss of respect — dis·grace·ful \-fəl\ *adj* — dis·grace·ful·ly *adv*

dis·grun·tle \dis-ˈgrən-tᵊl\ *vb* dis·grun·tled; dis·grun·tling : to put in bad humor

¹dis·guise \dis-'gīz\ vb dis·guised; dis·guis·ing 1 : to change the appearance of so as to conceal the identity or to resemble another 2 : HIDE, CONCEAL

²disguise n 1 : clothing put on to conceal one's identity or counterfeit another's 2 : an outward appearance that hides what something really is

¹dis·gust \dis-'gəst\ n : AVERSION, REPUGNANCE — dis·gust·ful \-fəl\ adj

²disgust vb 1 : to provoke to loathing, repugnance, or aversion : be offensive to — dis·gust·ed·ly adv — dis·gust·ing \-'gəs-tin\ adj — dis·gust·ing·ly adv

¹dish \'dish\ n [ME, fr. OE disc plate, fr. L discus quoit, disk, dish, fr. Gk diskos, fr. dikein to throw] 1 : a vessel used for serving food 2 : the food served in a dish ⟨a ∼ of berries⟩ 3 : food prepared in a particular way 4 : something resembling a dish esp. in being shallow and concave 5 : SATELLITE DISH 6 : GOSSIP 2

²dish vb 1 : to put into a dish 2 : to make concave like a dish 3 : GOSSIP

dis·ha·bille \,di-sə-'bēl\ or des·ha·bille \,de-\ n [F déshabillé] : the state of being dressed in a casual or careless manner

dis·har·mo·ny \(,)dis-'här-mə-nē\ n : lack of harmony — dis·har·mo·ni·ous \,dis-(,)här-'mō-nē-əs\ adj

dish·cloth \'dish-,klóth\ n : a cloth for washing dishes

dis·heart·en \dis-'härt-t²n\ vb : DISCOURAGE, DEJECT

dished \'disht\ adj : CONCAVE

di·shev·el \di-'she-vəl\ vb -shev·eled or -shev·elled; -shev·el·ing or -shev·el·ling [ME discheveled barehead-ed, with disordered hair, fr. AF deschevelé, fr. des- apart + chevoil hair, fr. L capillus] : to throw into disorder or disarray — di·shev·eled or di·shev·elled adj — di·shev·el·ment \-mənt\ n

dis·hon·est \dis-'sä-nəst\ adj : not honest : UNTRUSTWOR-THY, DECEITFUL — dis·hon·est·ly adv — dis·hon·es·ty \-nə-stē\ n

¹dis·hon·or \dis-'ä-nər\ n 1 : lack or loss of honor 2 : SHAME, DISGRACE 3 : a cause of disgrace 4 : the act of dishonoring a negotiable instrument when presented for payment — dis·hon·or·able \dis-'ä-nə-rə-bəl\ adj — dis·hon·or·ably \-blē\ adv

²dishonor vb 1 : DISGRACE 2 : to refuse to accept or pay ⟨∼ a check⟩

dish out vb : to give freely

dish·rag \'dish-,rag\ n : DISHCLOTH

dish·wash·er \-,wó-shər, -,wä-\ n : a person or machine that washes dishes

dish·wa·ter \-,wó-tər, -,wä-\ n : water used for washing dishes

dis·il·lu·sion \,dis-ə-'lü-zhən\ vb : to free from illusion — dis·il·lu·sion·ment n

dis·il·lu·sioned adj : DISAPPOINTED, DISSATISFIED

dis·in·cli·na·tion \dis-,in-klə-'nā-shən\ n : a preference for avoiding something : slight aversion

dis·in·cline \,dis-in-'klīn\ vb : to make unwilling

dis·in·clined adj : unwilling because of dislike or disapproval

dis·in·fect \,dis-in-'fekt\ vb : to cleanse of infection-caus-ing germs — dis·in·fec·tant \-'fek-tənt\ n — dis·in·fec·tion \-'fek-shən\ n

dis·in·for·ma·tion \,dis-in-fər-'mā-shən\ n : false information deliberately and often covertly spread

dis·in·gen·u·ous \,dis-in-'jen-yə-wəs\ adj : lacking in candor; also : giving a false appearance of simple frankness

dis·in·her·it \,dis-in-'her-ət\ vb : to deprive of the right to inherit

dis·in·te·grate \dis-'in-tə-,grāt\ vb 1 : to break or decompose into constituent parts or small particles 2 : to destroy the unity or integrity of — dis·in·te·gra·tion \-,in-tə-'grā-shən\ n

dis·in·ter \,dis-in-'tər\ vb 1 : to take from the grave or tomb 2 : UNEARTH

dis·in·ter·est·ed \(,)dis-'in-tə-rəs-təd, -,res-\ adj 1 : not interested 2 : free from selfish motive or interest : UNBI-ASED — dis·in·ter·est·ed·ness n

dis·join \(,)dis-'jóin\ vb : SEPARATE

dis·joint \(,)dis-'jóint\ vb : to disturb the orderly arrangement of; also : to separate at the joints

dis·joint·ed adj 1 : INCOHERENT ⟨∼ conversation⟩ 2 : separated at or as if at the joint

disk or disc \'disk\ n 1 : something round and flat; esp : a flat rounded anatomical structure (as the central part of the flower head of a composite plant or a pad of cartilage between vertebrae) 2 usu disc : a phonograph record 3 : a round flat plate coated with a magnetic substance on which data for a computer is stored 4 usu disc : OPTICAL DISK

disk drive n : a device for accessing or storing data on a magnetic disk

dis·kette \,dis-'ket\ n : FLOPPY DISK

disk jockey var of DISC JOCKEY

¹dis·like \(,)dis-'līk\ n : a feeling of aversion or disapproval

²dislike vb : to regard with dislike : DISAPPROVE

dis·lo·cate \'dis-lō-,kāt, dis-'lō-\ vb 1 : to put out of place; esp : to displace (a bone or joint) from normal connections ⟨∼ a shoulder⟩ 2 : DISRUPT — dis·lo·ca·tion \,dis-(,)lō-'kā-shən\ n

dis·lodge \(,)dis-'läj\ vb : to force out of a place esp. of rest, hiding, or defense

dis·loy·al \(,)dis-'lói(-ə)l\ adj : lacking in loyalty — dis·loy·al·ty n

dis·mal \'diz-məl\ adj [ME, fr. dismal, n., days marked as unlucky in medieval calendars, fr. AF, fr. ML dies mali, lit., evil days] 1 : showing or causing gloom or depression 2 : lacking merit — dis·mal·ly adv

dis·man·tle \(,)dis-'man-t²l\ vb -tled; -tling 1 : to take apart 2 : to strip of furniture and equipment — dis·man·tle·ment n

dis·may \dis-'mā\ vb : to cause to lose courage or resolution from alarm or fear : DAUNT — dismay n — dis·may·ing·ly adv

dis·mem·ber \dis-'mem-bər\ vb 1 : to cut off or separate the limbs or parts of 2 : to break up or tear into pieces — dis·mem·ber·ment n

dis·miss \dis-'mis\ vb 1 : to send away 2 : DISCHARGE 5 3 : to put aside or out of mind 4 : to put out of judicial consideration ⟨∼ed all charges⟩ — dis·miss·al n — dis·mis·sive \-'mi-siv\ adj — dis·mis·sive·ly adv

dis·mount \dis-'maùnt\ vb 1 : to get down from something (as a horse or bicycle) 2 : UNHORSE 3 : DISAS-SEMBLE

dis·obe·di·ence \,dis-ə-'bē-dē-əns\ n : neglect or refusal to obey — dis·obe·di·ent \-ənt\ adj

dis·obey \,dis-ə-'bā\ vb : to fail to obey : be disobedient

dis·oblige \,dis-ə-'blīj\ vb 1 : to go counter to the wishes of 2 : INCONVENIENCE

¹dis·or·der \dis-'ór-dər\ vb 1 : to disturb the order of 2 : to disturb the regular or normal functions of

²disorder n 1 : lack of order : CONFUSION 2 : breach of the peace or public order : TUMULT 3 : an abnormal physical or mental condition : AILMENT

dis·or·der·ly \-lē\ adj 1 : offensive to public order 2 : marked by disorder ⟨a ∼ desk⟩ — dis·or·der·li·ness n

dis·or·ga·nize \dis-'ór-gə-,nīz\ vb : to break up the regular system of : throw into disorder — dis·or·ga·ni·za·tion \dis-,ór-gə-nə-'zā-shən\ n

dis·ori·ent \(,)dis-'ór-ē-,ent\ vb : to cause to be confused or lost — dis·ori·en·ta·tion \dis-,ór-ē-ən-'tā-shən\ n

dis·own \dis-'ōn\ vb : REPUDIATE, RENOUNCE, DISCLAIM

dis·par·age \di-'sper-ij\ vb -aged; -ag·ing [ME to degrade by marriage below one's class, disparage, fr. AF despar-ager to marry below one's class, fr. parage equality, lineage, fr. per peer] 1 : to lower in rank or reputation : DEGRADE 2 : BELITTLE — dis·par·age·ment n — dis·par·ag·ing·ly adv

dis·pa·rate \'dis-pə-rət, di-'sper-ət\ adj : distinct in quality or character — dis·par·i·ty \di-'sper-ə-tē\ n

dis·pas·sion·ate \(,)dis-'pa-shə-nət\ adj : not influenced by strong feeling : CALM, IMPARTIAL — dis·pas·sion \-'pa-shən\ n — dis·pas·sion·ate·ly adv

¹dis·patch \di-'spach\ vb 1 : to send off or away with promptness or speed esp. on official business 2 : to put to death 3 : to attend to rapidly or efficiently 4 : DE-FEAT — dis·patch·er n

²dis·patch \di-'spach, 'dis-,pach\ n 1 : MESSAGE 2 : a news item sent in by a correspondent to a newspaper 3 : the act of dispatching; esp : SHIPMENT 4 : the act of putting to death 5 : promptness and efficiency in performing a task

dis·pel \di-'spel\ vb dis·pelled; dis·pel·ling 1 : to drive away by scattering : DISSIPATE

dis·pens·able \di-'spen-sə-bəl\ adj : capable of being dispensed with

dis·pen·sa·ry \di-'spen-sə-rē\ n, pl **-ries** : a place where medicine or medical or dental aid is dispensed

dis·pen·sa·tion \ˌdis-pən-'sā-shən\ n 1 : a system of rules for ordering affairs 2 : a particular arrangement or provision esp. of nature 3 : an exemption from a rule or from a vow or oath 4 : the act of dispensing 5 : something dispensed or distributed

dis·pense \di-'spens\ vb **dis·pensed; dis·pens·ing** 1 : to portion out 2 : ADMINISTER ⟨~ justice⟩ 3 : EXEMPT 4 : to make up and give out (remedies) — **dis·pens·er** n — **dispense with** 1 : SUSPEND 2 : to do without

dis·perse \di-'spərs\ vb **dis·persed; dis·pers·ing** : to break up and scatter about : SPREAD — **dis·per·sal** \-'spər-səl\ n — **dis·per·sion** \-'spər-zhən\ n

dis·pir·it \dis-'pir-ət\ vb : DEPRESS, DISCOURAGE, DISHEARTEN

dis·place \dis-'plās\ vb 1 : to remove from the usual or proper place; esp : to expel or force to flee from home or native land ⟨displaced persons⟩ 2 : to move out of position ⟨water displaced by a floating object⟩ 3 : to take the place of : REPLACE

dis·place·ment \-mənt\ n 1 : the act of displacing : the state of being displaced 2 : the volume or weight of a fluid (as water) displaced by a floating body (as a ship) 3 : the difference between the initial position of an object and a later position

¹dis·play \di-'splā\ vb [ME, fr. AF desplaier, desploier, lit., to unfold, fr. des- un- + ploier, plier to fold, fr. L plicare] : to present to view : make evident

²display n 1 : a displaying of something 2 : an electronic device (as a cathode-ray tube) that gives information in visual form; also : the visual information

dis·please \(ˌ)dis-'plēz\ vb 1 : to arouse the disapproval and dislike of 2 : to be offensive to : give displeasure

dis·plea·sure \-'ple-zhər\ n : a feeling of dislike and irritation

dis·port \di-'spórt\ vb 1 : DIVERT, AMUSE 2 : FROLIC 3 : DISPLAY

dis·pos·able \di-'spō-zə-bəl\ adj 1 : remaining after deduction of taxes ⟨~ income⟩ 2 : designed to be used once and then thrown away ⟨~ diapers⟩ — **disposable** n

dis·pos·al \di-'spō-zəl\ n 1 : CONTROL, COMMAND 2 : an orderly arrangement 3 : a getting rid of 4 : MANAGEMENT, ADMINISTRATION 5 : presenting or bestowing something ⟨~ of favors⟩ 6 : a device used to reduce waste matter (as by grinding)

dis·pose \di-'spōz\ vb **dis·posed; dis·pos·ing** 1 : to give a tendency to : INCLINE ⟨disposed to accept⟩ 2 : to put in place : ARRANGE ⟨troops disposed for withdrawal⟩ 3 : SETTLE — **dis·pos·er** n — **dispose of** 1 : to transfer to the control of another 2 : to get rid of 3 : to deal with conclusively

dis·po·si·tion \ˌdis-pə-'zi-shən\ n 1 : the act or power of disposing : DISPOSAL 2 : RELINQUISHMENT 3 : ARRANGEMENT 4 : TENDENCY, INCLINATION 5 : natural attitude toward things ⟨a cheerful ~⟩

dis·pos·sess \ˌdis-pə-'zes\ vb : to put out of possession or occupancy — **dis·pos·ses·sion** \-'ze-shən\ n

dis·praise \dis-'prāz\ vb : DISPARAGE — **dispraise** n — **dis·prais·er** n

dis·pro·por·tion \ˌdis-prə-'pór-shən\ n : lack of proportion, symmetry, or proper relation — **dis·pro·por·tion·ate** \-shə-nət\ adj

dis·prove \(ˌ)dis-'prüv\ vb : to prove to be false — **dis·proof** \-'prüf\ n

dis·pu·tant \di-'spyü-t°nt, 'dis-pyə-tənt\ n : one that is engaged in a dispute

dis·pu·ta·tion \ˌdis-pyü-'tā-shən\ n 1 : DEBATE 2 : an oral defense of an academic thesis

dis·pu·ta·tious \-shəs\ adj : inclined to dispute : ARGUMENTATIVE

¹dis·pute \di-'spyüt\ vb **dis·put·ed; dis·put·ing** 1 : ARGUE, DEBATE 2 : WRANGLE 3 : to deny the truth or rightness of 4 : to struggle against or over : OPPOSE — **dis·put·able** \di-'spyü-tə-bəl, 'dis-pyə-tə-bəl\ adj — **dis·put·er** n

²dis·pute n 1 : DEBATE 2 : QUARREL

dis·qual·i·fy \(ˌ)dis-'kwä-lə-ˌfī\ vb : to make or declare unfit or not qualified — **dis·qual·i·fi·ca·tion** \-ˌkwä-lə-fə-'kā-shən\ n

¹dis·qui·et \(ˌ)dis-'kwī-ət\ vb : to make uneasy or restless : DISTURB — **dis·qui·et·ing** adj

²disquiet n : lack of peace or tranquillity : ANXIETY

dis·qui·etude \(ˌ)dis-'kwī-ə-ˌtüd, -ˌtyüd\ n : AGITATION, ANXIETY

dis·qui·si·tion \ˌdis-kwə-'zi-shən\ n : a formal inquiry or discussion

¹dis·re·gard \ˌdis-ri-'gärd\ vb : to pay no attention to : treat as unworthy of notice or regard

²disregard n : the act of disregarding : the state of being disregarded : NEGLECT — **dis·re·gard·ful** adj

dis·re·pair \ˌdis-ri-'per\ n : the state of being in need of repair

dis·rep·u·ta·ble \dis-'re-pyü-tə-bəl\ adj : having a bad reputation

dis·re·pute \ˌdis-ri-'pyüt\ n : lack or decline of reputation : low esteem

dis·re·spect \ˌdis-ri-'spekt\ n : DISCOURTESY — **dis·re·spect·ful** adj

dis·robe \dis-'rōb\ vb : UNDRESS

dis·rupt \dis-'rəpt\ vb 1 : to break apart 2 : to throw into disorder 3 : INTERRUPT — **dis·rup·tion** \-'rəp-shən\ n — **dis·rup·tive** \-'rəp-tiv\ adj

dis·sat·is·fac·tion \di-ˌsa-təs-'fak-shən\ n : DISCONTENT

dis·sat·is·fy \di-'sa-təs-ˌfī\ vb : to fail to satisfy : DISPLEASE

dis·sect \dī-'sekt, di-\ vb 1 : to divide into parts esp. for examination and study 2 : ANALYZE — **dis·sec·tion** \-'sek-shən\ n — **dis·sec·tor** \-'sek-tər\ n

dis·sect·ed adj : cut deeply into narrow lobes ⟨a ~ leaf⟩

dis·sem·ble \di-'sem-bəl\ vb **-bled; -bling** 1 : to hide under or put on a false appearance : conceal facts, intentions, or feelings under some pretense 2 : SIMULATE — **dis·sem·bler** n

dis·sem·i·nate \di-'se-mə-ˌnāt\ vb **-nat·ed; -nat·ing** : to spread abroad as if sowing seed ⟨~ ideas⟩ — **dis·sem·i·na·tion** \-ˌse-mə-'nā-shən\ n

dis·sen·sion \di-'sen-chən\ n : disagreement in opinion : DISCORD

¹dis·sent \di-'sent\ vb 1 : to withhold assent 2 : to differ in opinion

²dissent n 1 : difference of opinion; esp : religious nonconformity 2 : a written statement in which a justice disagrees with the opinion of the majority

dis·sent·er \di-'sen-tər\ n 1 : one that dissents 2 cap : an English Nonconformist

dis·ser·ta·tion \ˌdi-sər-'tā-shən\ n : an extended usu. written treatment of a subject; esp : one submitted for a doctorate

dis·ser·vice \di-'sər-vəs\ n : INJURY, HARM, MISCHIEF

dis·sev·er \di-'se-vər\ vb : SEPARATE, DISUNITE

dis·si·dent \'di-sə-dənt\ adj [L dissidens, prp. of dissidēre to sit apart, disagree, fr. dis- apart + sedēre to sit] : disagreeing esp. with an established religious or political system, organization, or belief — **dis·si·dence** \-dəns\ n — **dissident** n

dis·sim·i·lar \di-'si-mə-lər\ adj : UNLIKE — **dis·sim·i·lar·i·ty** \di-ˌsi-mə-'ler-ə-tē\ n

dis·sim·u·late \di-'si-myə-ˌlāt\ vb : to hide under a false appearance : DISSEMBLE — **dis·sim·u·la·tion** \di-ˌsi-myə-'lā-shən\ n

dis·si·pate \'di-sə-ˌpāt\ vb **-pat·ed; -pat·ing** 1 : to break up and drive off : DISPERSE, SCATTER ⟨the breeze dissipated the fog⟩ 2 : SQUANDER 3 : to break up and vanish 4 : to be dissolute; esp : to drink alcoholic beverages to excess — **dis·si·pat·ed** adj — **dis·si·pa·tion** \ˌdi-sə-'pā-shən\ n

dis·so·ci·ate \di-'sō-shē-ˌāt\ vb **-at·ed; -at·ing** : DISCONNECT, DISUNITE — **dis·so·ci·a·tion** \di-ˌsō-shē-'ā-shən\ n — **dis·so·cia·tive** \di-'sō-shē-ˌā-tiv\ adj

dis·so·lute \'di-sə-ˌlüt\ adj : loose in morals or conduct — **dis·so·lute·ly** adv — **dis·so·lute·ness** n

dis·so·lu·tion \ˌdi-sə-'lü-shən\ n 1 : the action or process of dissolving 2 : separation of a thing into its parts 3 : DECAY; also : DEATH 4 : the termination or breaking up of (as an assembly)

dis·solve \di-'zälv\ vb 1 : to separate into component parts 2 : to pass or cause to pass into solution ⟨sugar ~s in water⟩ 3 : TERMINATE, DISPERSE ⟨~ parliament⟩ 4

: to waste or fade away ⟨his courage *dissolved*⟩ **5** : to be overcome emotionally ⟨~ in tears⟩ **6** : to resolve itself as if by dissolution
dis·so·nance \'di-sə-nəns\ *n* : DISCORD — **dis·so·nant** \-nənt\ *adj*
dis·suade \di-'swād\ *vb* **dis·suad·ed; dis·suad·ing** : to advise against a course of action : persuade or try to persuade not to do something — **dis·sua·sion** \-'swā-zhən\ *n* — **dis·sua·sive** \-'swā-siv\ *adj*
dist *abbr* **1** distance **2** district
¹**dis·taff** \'dis-,taf\ *n, pl* **distaffs** \-,tafs, -,tavz\ [ME *distaf*, fr. OE *distæf*, fr. *dis-* bunch of flax + *stæf* stick, staff] **1** : a staff for holding the flax, tow, or wool in spinning **2** : a woman's work or domain **3** : the female branch or side of a family
²**distaff** *adj* **1** : MATERNAL **2** ⟨the ~ side of the family⟩ **2** : FEMALE **1** ⟨~ executives⟩
dis·tal \'dis-t²l\ *adj* **1** : situated away from the point of attachment or origin esp. on the body **2** : of, relating to, or being the surface of a tooth that is farthest from the middle of the front of the jaw — **dis·tal·ly** *adv*
¹**dis·tance** \'dis-təns\ *n* **1** : measure of separation in space or time **2** : EXPANSE **3** : the full length ⟨go the ~⟩ **4** : spatial remoteness **5** : COLDNESS, RESERVE **6** : DIFFERENCE, DISPARITY **7** : a distant point
²**distance** *vb* **dis·tanced; dis·tanc·ing** : to leave far behind : OUTSTRIP
³**distance** *adj* : taking place via electronic media linking instructors and students ⟨~ learning⟩
dis·tant \'dis-tənt\ *adj* **1** : separate in space : AWAY **2** : FAR-OFF ⟨a ~ galaxy⟩ **3** : far apart or behind **4** : not close in relationship ⟨a ~ cousin⟩ **5** : different in kind **6** : RESERVED, ALOOF, COLD ⟨~ politeness⟩ **7** : going a long distance ⟨~ voyages⟩ — **dis·tant·ly** *adv* — **dis·tant·ness** *n*
dis·taste \(,)dis-'tāst\ *n* : DISINCLINATION, DISLIKE — **dis·taste·ful** *adj*
dis·tem·per \(,)dis-'tem-pər\ *n* : a bodily disorder usu. of a domestic animal; *esp* : a contagious often fatal virus disease of dogs
dis·tend \di-'stend\ *vb* : EXPAND, SWELL — **dis·ten·si·ble** \-'sten-sə-bəl\ *adj* — **dis·ten·sion** *or* **dis·ten·tion** \-chən\ *n*
dis·tich \'dis-(,)tik\ *n* : a unit of two lines of poetry
dis·till *also* **dis·til** \di-'stil\ *vb* **dis·tilled; dis·till·ing** **1** : to fall or let fall in drops **2** : to obtain or purify by distillation — **dis·till·er** *n* — **dis·till·ery** \-'sti-lə-rē\ *n*
dis·til·late \'dis-tə-,lāt, -lət\ *n* : a liquid product condensed from vapor during distillation
dis·til·la·tion \,dis-tə-'lā-shən\ *n* : the process of purifying a liquid by successive evaporation and condensation
dis·tinct \di-'stiŋkt\ *adj* **1** : SEPARATE, INDIVIDUAL ⟨a ~ cultural group⟩ **2** : presenting a clear unmistakable impression — **dis·tinct·ly** *adv* — **dis·tinct·ness** *n*
dis·tinc·tion \di-'stiŋk-shən\ *n* **1** : the distinguishing of a difference; *also* : the difference distinguished **2** : something that distinguishes **3** : special honor or recognition
dis·tinc·tive \di-'stiŋk-tiv\ *adj* **1** : serving to distinguish ⟨the ~ flight of the crane⟩ **2** : having or giving style or distinction — **dis·tinc·tive·ly** *adv* — **dis·tinc·tive·ness** *n*
dis·tin·guish \di-'stiŋ-gwish\ *vb* [alter. of ME *distinguen*, fr. AF *distinguer*, fr. L *distinguere*, lit., to separate by pricking] **1** : to recognize by some mark or characteristic **2** : to hear or see clearly : DISCERN **3** : to make distinctions ⟨~ between right and wrong⟩ **4** : to give prominence or distinction to; *also* : to take special notice of — **dis·tin·guish·able** *adj*
dis·tin·guished \-gwisht\ *adj* **1** : marked by eminence or excellence **2** : befitting an eminent person
dis·tort \di-'stȯrt\ *vb* **1** : to twist out of the true meaning **2** : to twist out of a natural, normal, or original shape or condition **3** : to cause to be perceived unnaturally — **dis·tor·tion** \-'stȯr-shən\ *n*
distr *abbr* distribute; distribution
dis·tract \di-'strakt\ *vb* **1** : to draw (the attention or mind) to a different object : DIVERT **2** : to stir up or confuse with conflicting emotions or motives — **dis·trac·tion** \-'strak-shən\ *n*
dis·trait \di-'strā\ *adj* : DISTRAUGHT **1**
dis·traught \di-'strȯt\ *adj* **1** : agitated with doubt or mental conflict or pain **2** : INSANE

¹**dis·tress** \di-'stres\ *n* **1** : suffering of body or mind : PAIN, ANGUISH **2** : TROUBLE, MISFORTUNE **3** : a condition of danger or desperate need — **dis·tress·ful** *adj*
²**distress** *vb* **1** : to subject to great strain or difficulties **2** : UPSET
dis·tress·ed \-'strest\ *adj* : experiencing economic decline or difficulty
dis·trib·ute \di-'stri-byüt\ *vb* **-ut·ed; -ut·ing** **1** : to divide among several or many **2** : to spread out : SCATTER; *also* : DELIVER **3** : CLASSIFY — **dis·tri·bu·tion** \,dis-trə-'byü-shən\ *n*
dis·trib·u·tive \di-'stri-byù-tiv\ *adj* **1** : of or relating to distribution **2** : of, having, or being the property of producing the same value when an operation is carried out on a whole expression and when it is carried out on each part of an expression with the results then collected together ⟨*a*(*b* + *c*) = *ab* + *ac* because multiplication is ~⟩ — **dis·trib·u·tive·ly** *adv*
dis·trib·u·tor \di-'stri-byù-tər\ *n* **1** : one that distributes **2** : one that markets goods **3** : a device for directing current to the spark plugs of an engine
dis·trict \'dis-(,)trikt\ *n* **1** : a fixed territorial division (as for administrative or electoral purposes) **2** : an area, region, or section with a distinguishing character
district attorney *n* : the prosecuting attorney of a judicial district
¹**dis·trust** \dis-'trəst\ *n* : a lack or absence of trust — **dis·trust·ful** \-fəl\ *adj* — **dis·trust·ful·ly** *adv*
²**distrust** *vb* : to have no trust or confidence in
dis·turb \di-'stərb\ *vb* **1** : to interfere with : INTERRUPT **2** : to alter the position or arrangement of; *also* : to upset the natural and esp. the ecological balance of **3** : to destroy the tranquillity or composure of : make uneasy **4** : to throw into disorder **5** : INCONVENIENCE — **dis·tur·bance** \-'stər-bəns\ *n* — **dis·turb·er** *n* — **dis·turb·ing·ly** \-'stər-biŋ-lē\ *adv*
dis·turbed \-'stərbd\ *adj* : showing symptoms of emotional illness
dis·unite \,dis-yü-'nīt\ *vb* : DIVIDE, SEPARATE
dis·uni·ty \dis-'yü-nə-tē\ *n* : lack of unity; *esp* : DISSENSION
dis·use \-'yüs\ *n* : a cessation of use or practice
dis·used \-'yüzd\ *adj* : no longer used or occupied
¹**ditch** \'dich\ *n* : a long narrow channel or trench dug in the earth
²**ditch** *vb* **1** : to enclose with a ditch; *also* : to dig a ditch in **2** : to get rid of : DISCARD **3** : to make a forced landing of an airplane on water
dith·er \'di-thər\ *n* : a highly nervous, excited, or agitated state
dit·to \'di-tō\ *n, pl* **dittos** [It *ditto, detto*, pp. of *dire* to say, fr. L *dicere*] **1** : a thing mentioned previously or above — used to avoid repeating a word **2** : a mark " or " used as a symbol for the word *ditto*
dit·ty \'di-tē\ *n, pl* **ditties** : a short simple song
dit·zy *or* **dit·sy** \'dit-sē\ *adj* **ditz·i·er** *or* **dits·i·er; -est** : eccentrically silly, giddy, or inane
di·uret·ic \,dī-yə-'re-tik\ *adj* : tending to increase urine flow — **diuretic** *n*
di·ur·nal \dī-'ər-n²l\ *adj* **1** : DAILY ⟨a ~ chore⟩ **2** : of, relating to, occurring, or active in the daytime ⟨~ animals⟩
div *abbr* **1** divided **2** dividend **3** division **4** divorced
di·va \'dē-və\ *n, pl* **divas** *or* **di·ve** \-,vä\ [It, lit., goddess, fr. L, fem. of *divus* divine, god] **1** : PRIMA DONNA **2** : a usu. glamorous and successful female performer or personality
di·va·gate \'dī-və-,gāt\ *vb* **-gat·ed; -gat·ing** : to wander or stray from a course or subject : DIVERGE — **di·va·ga·tion** \,dī-və-'gā-shən\ *n*
di·van \'dī-,van, di-'van\ *n* : COUCH, SOFA
¹**dive** \'dīv\ *vb* **dived** \'dīvd\ *or* **dove** \'dōv\; **dived; div·ing** **1** : to plunge into water headfirst **2** : SUBMERGE **3** : to come or drop down precipitously **4** : to descend in an airplane at a steep angle **5** : to plunge into some matter or activity **6** : DART, LUNGE — **div·er** *n*
²**dive** *n* **1** : the act or an instance of diving **2** : a sharp decline **3** : a disreputable bar or place of amusement
di·verge \də-'vərj, dī-\ *vb* **di·verged; di·verg·ing** **1** : to move or extend in different directions from a common point : draw apart **2** : to differ in character, form, or

opinion **3** : DEVIATE **4** : DEFLECT — **di·ver·gence** \-'vər-jəns\ *n* — **di·ver·gent** \-jənt\ *adj*
di·vers \'dī-vərz\ *adj* : VARIOUS
di·verse \dī-'vərs, də-, 'dī-,vərs\ *adj* **1** : UNLIKE **2** : composed of distinct forms or qualities — **di·verse·ly** *adv*
di·ver·si·fy \də-'vər-sə-,fī, dī-\ *vb* **-fied; -fy·ing** : to make different or various in form or quality — **di·ver·si·fi·ca·tion** \-,vər-sə-fə-'kā-shən\ *n*
di·ver·sion \də-'vər-zhən, dī-\ *n* **1** : a turning aside from a course, activity, or use : DEVIATION **2** : something that diverts or amuses : PASTIME
di·ver·si·ty \də-'vər-sə-tē, dī-\ *n, pl* **-ties** **1** : the condition of being diverse : VARIETY **2** : an instance of being diverse
di·vert \də-'vərt, dī-\ *vb* **1** : to turn from a course or purpose : DEFLECT **2** : DISTRACT **3** : ENTERTAIN, AMUSE
di·vert·ing \-'vər-tiŋ\ *adj* : providing amusement or entertainment
di·vest \dī-'vest, də-\ *vb* **1** : to deprive or dispossess esp. of property, authority, or rights **2** : to strip esp. of clothing, ornament, or equipment
¹di·vide \də-'vīd\ *vb* **di·vid·ed; di·vid·ing** **1** : SEPARATE; *also* : CLASSIFY **2** : CLEAVE, PART ⟨a ship *dividing* the waves⟩ **3** : DISTRIBUTE, APPORTION **4** : to possess or make use of in common : share in **5** : to cause to be separate, distinct, or apart from one another **6** : to separate into opposing sides or parties **7** : to mark divisions on **8** : to subject to or use in mathematical division; *also* : to be used as a divisor with respect to **9** : to branch out
²divide *n* : WATERSHED
div·i·dend \'di-və-,dend\ *n* **1** : an individual share of something distributed **2** : BONUS **3** : a number to be divided **4** : a sum or fund to be divided or distributed
di·vid·er \də-'vī-dər\ *n* **1** : one that divides (as a partition) ⟨room ~⟩ **2** *pl* : COMPASS 1
div·i·na·tion \,di-və-'nā-shən\ *n* **1** : the art or practice of using omens or magic powers to foretell the future **2** : unusual insight or intuitive perception
¹di·vine \də-'vīn\ *adj* **di·vin·er; -est** **1** : of, relating to, or being God or a god **2** : supremely good : SUPERB; *also* : HEAVENLY — **di·vine·ly** *adv*
²divine *n* **1** : CLERGYMAN **2** : THEOLOGIAN
³divine *vb* **di·vined; di·vin·ing** **1** : INFER, CONJECTURE **2** : PROPHESY **3** : DOWSE — **di·vin·er** *n*
divining rod *n* : a forked rod believed to reveal the presence of water or minerals by dipping downward when held over a vein
di·vin·i·ty \də-'vi-nə-tē\ *n, pl* **-ties** **1** : THEOLOGY **2** : the quality or state of being divine **3** : a divine being; *esp* : GOD 1
di·vis·i·ble \də-'vi-zə-bəl\ *adj* : capable of being divided — **di·vis·i·bil·i·ty** \-,vi-zə-'bi-lə-tē\ *n*
di·vi·sion \də-'vi-zhən\ *n* **1** : DISTRIBUTION, SEPARATION **2** : one of the parts or groupings into which a whole is divided **3** : DISAGREEMENT, DISUNITY **4** : something that divides or separates **5** : the mathematical operation of finding how many times one number is contained in another **6** : a large self-contained military unit **7** : an administrative or operating unit of a governmental, business, or educational organization — **di·vi·sion·al** \-'vi-zhə-nəl\ *adj*
di·vi·sive \də-'vī-siv, -'vi-siv, -'vi-ziv\ *adj* : creating disunity or dissension — **di·vi·sive·ly** *adv* — **di·vi·sive·ness** *n*
di·vi·sor \də-'vī-zər\ *n* : the number by which a dividend is divided
di·vorce \də-'vórs\ *n* **1** : an act or instance of legally dissolving a marriage **2** : SEPARATION, SEVERANCE — **divorce** *vb* — **di·vorce·ment** *n*
di·vor·cé \də-,vór-'sā\ *n* [F] : a divorced man
di·vor·cée \də-,vór-'sā, -'sē\ *n* : a divorced woman
div·ot \'di-vət\ *n* : a piece of turf dug from a golf fairway in making a stroke
di·vulge \də-'vəlj, dī-\ *vb* **di·vulged; di·vulg·ing** : REVEAL, DISCLOSE
Dix·ie·land \'dik-sē-,land\ *n* : jazz music in duple time played in a style developed in New Orleans
diz·zy \'di-zē\ *adj* **diz·zi·er; -est** [ME *disy*, fr. OE *dysig* stupid] **1** : FOOLISH, SILLY **2** : having a sensation of whirling : GIDDY **3** : causing or caused by giddiness — **diz·zi·ly** \-zə-lē\ *adv* — **diz·zi·ness** \-zē-nəs\ *n*
DJ *n, often not cap* : DISC JOCKEY

dk *abbr* **1** dark **2** deck **3** dock
dl *abbr* deciliter
DLitt *or* **DLit** *abbr* [NL *doctor litterarum*] doctor of letters; doctor of literature
DLO *abbr* dead letter office
dm *abbr* decimeter
DMD *abbr* [NL *dentariae medicinae doctor*] doctor of dental medicine
DMZ *abbr* demilitarized zone
dn *abbr* down
DNA \,dē-(,)en-'ā\ *n* : any of various nucleic acids that are usu. the molecular basis of heredity and are localized esp. in cell nuclei
DNR *abbr* do not resuscitate
¹do \'dü\ *vb* **did** \'did\; **done** \'dən\; **do·ing; does** \'dəz\ **1** : to bring to pass : ACCOMPLISH **2** : ACT, BEHAVE ⟨~ as I say⟩ **3** : to be active or busy ⟨up and ~*ing*⟩ **4** : HAPPEN ⟨what's ~*ing*?⟩ **5** : to be engaged in the study or practice of : work at ⟨he *does* tailoring⟩ **6** : COOK ⟨steak *done* rare⟩ **7** : to put in order (as by cleaning or arranging) ⟨~ the dishes⟩ **8** : DECORATE ⟨*did* the hall in blue⟩ **9** : GET ALONG ⟨~ well in school⟩ **10** : CARRY ON, MANAGE **11** : RENDER ⟨sleep will ~ you good⟩ **12** : FINISH ⟨when he had *done*⟩ **13** : EXERT ⟨*did* my best⟩ **14** : PRODUCE ⟨*did* a poem⟩ **15** : to play the part of **16** : CHEAT ⟨*did* him out of his share⟩ **17** : TRAVERSE, TOUR **18** : TRAVEL **19** : to spend or serve out a period of time ⟨*did* ten years in prison⟩ **20** : SUFFICE, SUIT **21** : to be fitting or proper **22** : USE ⟨doesn't ~ drugs⟩ **23** — used as an auxiliary verb (1) before the subject in an interrogative sentence ⟨*does* he work?⟩ and after some adverbs ⟨never *did* she say so⟩, (2) in a negative statement ⟨I *don't* know⟩, (3) for emphasis ⟨you ~ know⟩, and (4) as a substitute for a preceding predicate ⟨he works harder than I ~⟩ — **do·able** \'dü-ə-bəl\ *adj* — **do away with** **1** : to put an end to **2** : DESTROY, KILL — **do by** : to deal with : TREAT ⟨*did* right *by* her⟩ — **do for** *chiefly Brit* : to bring about the death or ruin of — **do the trick** : to produce a desired result
²do *n* **1** : AFFAIR, PARTY **2** : a command or entreaty to do something ⟨list of ~*s* and don'ts⟩ **3** : HAIRSTYLE
³do *abbr* ditto
DOA *abbr* dead on arrival
DOB *abbr* date of birth
dob·bin \'dä-bən\ *n* [Dobbin, nickname for *Robert*] **1** : a farm horse **2** : a quiet plodding horse
Do·ber·man pin·scher \'dō-bər-mən-'pin-chər\ *n* : any of a German breed of short-haired medium-sized dogs
do·bra \'dō-brə\ *n* — see MONEY table
¹doc \'däk\ *n* : DOCTOR
²doc *abbr* document
do·cent \'dō-sᵊnt, dōt-'sent\ *n* [obs. G (now *Dozent*), fr. L *docens*, prp. of *docēre* to teach] : TEACHER, LECTURER; *also* : a person who leads a guided tour
doc·ile \'dä-səl\ *adj* [L *docilis*, fr. *docēre* to teach] : easily taught, led, or managed : TRACTABLE — **do·cil·i·ty** \dä-'si-lə-tē\ *n*
¹dock \'däk\ *n* : any of a genus of coarse weedy herbs related to buckwheat
²dock *vb* **1** : to cut off the end of : cut short **2** : to take away a part of : deduct from ⟨~ a worker's wages⟩
³dock *n* **1** : an artificial basin to receive ships **2** : ²SLIP 2 **3** : a wharf or platform for loading or unloading materials or for mooring a boat
⁴dock *vb* **1** : to bring or come into dock **2** : to join (as two spacecraft) mechanically in space
⁵dock *n* : the place in a court where a prisoner stands or sits during trial
dock·age \'dä-kij\ *n* : docking facilities
dock·et \'dä-kət\ *n* **1** : a formal abridged record of the proceedings in a legal action; *also* : a register of such records **2** : a list of legal causes to be tried **3** : a calendar of matters to be acted on : AGENDA **4** : a label attached to a document containing identification or directions — **docket** *vb*
dock·hand \'däk-,hand\ *n* : LONGSHOREMAN
dock·work·er \-,wər-kər\ *n* : LONGSHOREMAN
dock·yard \-,yärd\ *n* : SHIPYARD
¹doc·tor \'däk-tər\ *n* [ME *doctour* teacher, doctor, fr. AF & ML; AF, fr. ML *doctor*, fr. L, teacher, fr. *docēre* to teach] **1** : a person holding one of the highest academic degrees

(as a PhD) conferred by a university **2** : a person skilled in healing arts; *esp* : one (as a physician, dentist, or veterinarian) academically and legally qualified to practice **3** : a person who restores or repairs things — **doc·tor·al** \'-tə-rəl\ *adj*

²**doctor** *vb* **1** : to give medical treatment to **2** : to practice medicine **3** : REPAIR **4** : to adapt or modify for a desired end **5** : to alter deceptively

doc·tor·ate \'däk-tə-rət\ *n* : the degree, title, or rank of a doctor

doc·tri·naire \ˌdäk-trə-'ner\ *n* [F] : one who attempts to put an abstract theory into effect without regard to practical difficulties — **doctrinaire** *adj*

doc·trine \'däk-trən\ *n* **1** : something that is taught **2** : DOGMA, TENET — **doc·tri·nal** \-trə-n²l\ *adj*

docu·dra·ma \'dä-kyə-ˌdrä-mə, -ˌdra-\ *n* : a drama made for television, motion pictures, or theater that deals freely with historical events

doc·u·ment \'dä-kyə-mənt\ *n* **1** : a paper that furnishes information, proof, or support of something else **2** : a computer file containing information input by a computer user usu. via a word processor — **doc·u·ment** \-ˌment\ *vb* — **doc·u·men·ta·tion** \ˌdä-kyə-mən-'tā-shən\ *n* — **doc·u·ment·er** *n*

doc·u·men·ta·ry \ˌdä-kyə-'men-tə-rē\ *adj* **1** : consisting of documents; *also* : being in writing ⟨~ proof⟩ **2** : giving a factual presentation in artistic form ⟨a ~ movie⟩ — **documentary** *n*

DOD *abbr* Department of Defense

¹**dod·der** \'dä-dər\ *n* : any of a genus of leafless parasitic twining vines that are deeply deficient in chlorophyll

²**dodder** *vb* **dod·dered; dod·der·ing** **1** : to tremble or shake usu. from age **2** : to progress feebly and unsteadily

¹**dodge** \'däj\ *n* **1** : an act of evading by sudden bodily movement **2** : an artful device to evade, deceive, or trick **3** : EXPEDIENT

²**dodge** *vb* **dodged; dodg·ing** **1** : to evade usu. by trickery **2** : to move suddenly aside; *also* : to avoid or evade by so doing — **dodg·er** *n*

do·do \'dō-dō\ *n, pl* **dodoes** *or* **dodos** [Pg *doudo,* fr. *doudo* silly, stupid] **1** : an extinct heavy flightless bird of the island of Mauritius related to the pigeons and larger than a turkey **2** : one hopelessly behind the times; *also* : a stupid person

doe \'dō\ *n, pl* **does** *or* **doe** : an adult female of various mammals (as a deer, rabbit, or kangaroo) of which the male is called **buck**

DOE *abbr* Department of Energy

do·er \'dü-ər\ *n* : one that does

does *pres 3d sing of* DO, *pl of* DOE

doff \'däf\ *vb* [ME, fr. *don* to do + *of* off] **1** : to take off (the hat) in greeting or as a sign of respect **2** : to rid oneself of

¹**dog** \'dȯg\ *n* **1** : a flesh-eating domestic mammal related to the wolves; *esp* : a male of this animal **2** : a worthless or contemptible person **3** : FELLOW, CHAP ⟨you lucky ~⟩ **4** : a mechanical device for holding something **5** : uncharacteristic or affected stylishness or dignity ⟨put on the ~⟩ **6** *pl* : RUIN ⟨gone to the ~s⟩

²**dog** *vb* **dogged; dog·ging** **1** : to hunt or track like a hound **2** : to worry as if by pursuit with dogs : PLAGUE

dog·bane \'dȯg-ˌbān\ *n* : any of a genus of mostly poisonous herbs with milky juice and often showy flowers

dog·cart \-ˌkärt\ *n* : a light one-horse carriage with two seats back to back

dog·catch·er \-ˌka-chər, -ˌke-\ *n* : a community official assigned to catch and dispose of stray dogs

dog–ear \'dȯg-ˌir\ *n* : the turned-down corner of a leaf of a book — **dog–ear** *vb* — **dog–eared** \-ˌird\ *adj*

dog·fight \'dȯg-ˌfīt\ *n* : a fight between fighter planes at close range

dog·fish \-ˌfish\ *n* : any of various small usu. bottom-dwelling sharks

dog·ged \'dȯ-gəd\ *adj* : stubbornly determined : TENACIOUS — **dog·ged·ly** *adv* — **dog·ged·ness** *n*

dog·ger·el \'dȯ-gə-rəl\ *n* : verse that is loosely styled and irregular in measure esp. for comic effect

dog·gie bag *or* **doggy bag** \'dȯ-gē-\ *n* : a container for carrying home leftover food from a restaurant meal

¹**dog·gy** *or* **dog·gie** \'dȯ-gē\ *n, pl* **doggies** : a small dog

²**dog·gy** *adj* **dog·gi·er; -est** : of or resembling a dog ⟨a ~ odor⟩

dog·house \'dȯg-ˌhau̇s\ *n* : a shelter for a dog — **in the doghouse** : in a state of disfavor

do·gie \'dō-gē\ *n, chiefly West* : a motherless calf in a range herd

dog·leg \'dȯg-ˌleg\ *n* : a sharp bend or angle (as in a road or golf fairway) — **dogleg** *vb*

dog·ma \'dȯg-mə\ *n, pl* **dogmas** *also* **dog·ma·ta** \-mə-tə\ [L, fr. Gk, fr. *dokein* to think, have an opinion] **1** : a tenet or code of tenets **2** : a doctrine or body of doctrines formally proclaimed by a church

dog·ma·tism \'dȯg-mə-ˌti-zəm\ *n* : positiveness in stating matters of opinion esp. when unwarranted or arrogant — **dog·mat·ic** \dȯg-'ma-tik\ *adj* — **dog·mat·i·cal·ly** \-ti-k(ə-)lē\ *adv*

do–good·er \'dü-ˌgu̇-dər\ *n* : an earnest often naive humanitarian or reformer

dog·tooth violet \'dȯg-ˌtüth-\ *n* : any of a genus of small spring-flowering bulbous herbs related to the lilies

dog·trot \'dȯg-ˌträt\ *n* : a gentle trot — **dogtrot** *vb*

dog·wood \'dȯg-ˌwu̇d\ *n* : any of a genus of trees and shrubs having heads of small flowers often with showy white, pink, or red bracts

doi·ly \'dȯi-lē\ *n, pl* **doilies** : a small often decorative mat

do in *vb* **1** : RUIN **2** : KILL **3** : TIRE, EXHAUST ⟨the climb *did* him *in*⟩ **4** : CHEAT

do·ings \'dü-iŋz\ *n pl* : GOINGS-ON

do–it–yourself *n* : the activity of doing or making something without professional training or help — **do–it–your·self·er** *n*

dol *abbr* dollar

dol·drums \'dōl-drəmz, 'däl-\ *n pl* **1** : a spell of listlessness or despondency **2** *often cap* : a part of the ocean near the equator known for calms **3** : a state or period of inactivity, stagnation, or slump

¹**dole** \'dōl\ *n* **1** : a distribution esp. of food, money, or clothing to the needy; *also* : something so distributed **2** : a grant of government funds to the unemployed

²**dole** *vb* **doled; dol·ing** : to give or distribute as a charity — usu. used with *out*

dole·ful \'dōl-fəl\ *adj* : full of grief : SAD — **dole·ful·ly** *adv*

dole out *vb* **1** : to give or deliver in small portions **2** : DISH OUT

doll \'däl, 'dȯl\ *n* **1** : a small figure of a human being used esp. as a child's plaything **2** : a pretty woman **3** : an attractive person — **doll·ish** \'dä-lish, 'dȯ-\ *adj*

dol·lar \'dä-lər\ *n* [Dutch or LG *daler,* fr. G *Taler,* short for *Joachimstaler,* fr. Sankt *Joachimsthal,* Bohemia, where talers were first made] **1** : any of various basic monetary units (as in the U.S. and Canada) — see MONEY table **2** : a coin, note, or token representing one dollar **3** : RINGGIT

dol·lop \'dä-ləp\ *n* **1** : LUMP, GLOB **2** : PORTION 1 — **dol·lop** *vb*

doll up *vb* **1** : to dress elegantly or extravagantly **2** : to make more attractive **3** : to get dolled up

dol·ly \'dä-lē\ *n, pl* **dollies** : a small cart or wheeled platform (as for a television or movie camera)

dol·men \'dōl-mən, 'däl-\ *n* : a prehistoric monument consisting of two or more upright stones supporting a horizontal stone slab

dolmen

do·lo·mite \'dō-lə-ˌmīt, 'dä-\ *n* : a mineral found in broad layers as a compact limestone

do·lor \'dō-lər, 'dä-\ *n* : mental suffering or anguish : SORROW — **do·lor·ous** *adj* — **do·lor·ous·ly** *adv*

do·lour *chiefly Brit var of* DOLOR

dol·phin \'däl-fən\ *n* **1** : any of various small whales with conical teeth and an elongated beaklike snout **2** : either of two active food fishes of tropical and temperate seas

dolt \'dōlt\ *n* : a stupid person — **dolt·ish** \'dōl-tish\ *adj* — **dolt·ish·ness** *n*

dom *abbr* **1** domestic **2** dominant **3** dominion

-dom *n suffix* **1** : dignity : office ⟨duke*dom*⟩ **2** : realm : jurisdiction ⟨king*dom*⟩ **3** : state or fact of being ⟨free-*dom*⟩ **4** : those having a (specified) office, occupation, interest, or character ⟨official*dom*⟩

do·main \dō-'mān\ *n* **1** : complete and absolute owner-ship of land **2** : land completely owned **3** : a territory over which dominion is exercised **4** : a sphere of knowl-edge, influence, or activity ⟨the ~ of science⟩ **5** : a sub-division of the Internet made up of computers whose URLs share a characteristic abbreviation (as *com* or *gov*)

domain name *n* : a sequence of characters (as Merriam-Webster.com) that specifies a group of online resources and forms part of its URL

dome \'dōm\ *n* **1** : a large hemispherical roof or ceiling **2** : a structure or natural formation that resembles the dome of a building **3** : a roofed sports stadium — **dome** *vb*

¹do·mes·tic \də-'mes-tik\ *adj* **1** : living near or about human habitations **2** : TAME, DOMESTICATED **3** : relat-ing and limited to one's own country or the country under consideration **4** : of or relating to the household or the family **5** : devoted to home duties and pleasures **6** : INDIGENOUS — **do·mes·ti·cal·ly** \-ti-k(ə-)lē\ *adv*

²domestic *n* : a household servant

do·mes·ti·cate \də-'mes-ti-ˌkāt\ *vb* **-cat·ed; -cat·ing** : to adapt to life in association with and to the use of humans — **do·mes·ti·ca·tion** \-ˌmes-ti-'kā-shən\ *n*

do·mes·tic·i·ty \ˌdō-ˌmes-'ti-sə-tē, də-\ *n, pl* **-ties 1** : the quality or state of being domestic or domesticated **2** : domestic activities or life

domestic violence *n* : the inflicting of injury by one fam-ily or household member on another

do·mi·cile \'dä-mə-ˌsī(-ə)l, 'dō-; 'dä-mə-səl\ *n* : a dwelling place : HOME — **domicile** *vb* — **dom·i·cil·i·ary** \ˌdä-mə-'si-lē-ˌer-ē, -ˌdō-\ *adj*

dom·i·nance \'dä-mə-nəns\ *n* **1** : AUTHORITY, CONTROL **2** : the property of one of a pair of alleles or traits that suppresses expression of the other when both are present

¹dom·i·nant \-nənt\ *adj* **1** : controlling or prevailing over all others **2** : overlooking from a high position **3** : ex-hibiting genetic dominance

²dominant *n* : a dominant gene or trait

dom·i·nate \'dä-mə-ˌnāt\ *vb* **-nat·ed; -nat·ing 1** : RULE, CONTROL **2** : to have a commanding position or control-ling power over **3** : to rise high above in a position sug-gesting power to dominate — **dom·i·na·tor** \-ˌnā-tər\ *n*

dom·i·na·tion \ˌdä-mə-'nā-shən\ *n* **1** : supremacy or pre-eminence over another **2** : exercise of mastery, ruling power, or preponderant influence

do·mi·na·trix \ˌdä-mə-'nā-triks\ *n, pl* **-trices** \-'nā-trə-ˌsēz, -nə-'trī-sēz\ : a woman who dominates her sexual partner; *also* : a dominating woman

dom·i·neer \ˌdä-mə-'nir\ *vb* **1** : to rule in an arrogant manner **2** : to be overbearing

do·mi·nie *1 usu* 'dä-mə-nē, *2 usu* 'dō-\ *n* **1** *chiefly Scot* : SCHOOLMASTER **2** : CLERGYMAN

do·min·ion \də-'min-yən\ *n* **1** : DOMAIN **2** : supreme au-thority : SOVEREIGNTY **3** *often cap* : a self-governing na-tion of the Commonwealth

dom·i·no \'dä-mə-ˌnō\ *n, pl* **-noes** *or* **-nos 1** : a long loose hooded cloak usu. worn with a half mask as a masquer-ade costume **2** : a flat rectangular block used as a piece in a game (**dominoes**)

¹don \'dän\ *vb* **donned; don·ning** [ME, fr. *don* to do + *on*] : to put on (as clothes)

²don *n* [Sp, fr. L *dominus* lord, master] **1** : a Spanish no-bleman or gentleman — used as a title prefixed to the Christian name **2** : a head, tutor, or fellow in an English university

do·ña \'dō-nyə\ *n* : a Spanish woman of rank — used as a title prefixed to the Christian name

do·nate \'dō-ˌnāt\ *vb* **do·nat·ed; do·nat·ing 1** : to make a gift of : CONTRIBUTE **2** : to make a donation

do·na·tion \dō-'nā-shən\ *n* **1** : the making of a gift esp. to a charity **2** : a free contribution : GIFT

¹done \'dən\ *past part of* DO

²done *adj* **1** : doomed to failure, defeat, or death **2** : gone by : OVER ⟨when day is ~⟩ **3** : cooked sufficiently **4** : conformable to social convention

done deal *n* : FAIT ACCOMPLI

dong \'dȯŋ, 'däŋ\ *n* — see MONEY table

don·key \'däŋ-kē, 'dəŋ-\ *n, pl* **donkeys 1** : a sturdy and patient domestic mammal classified with the asses **2** : a stupid or obstinate person

don·ny·brook \'dä-nē-ˌbru̇k\ *n, often cap* [*Donnybrook* Fair, annual Irish event known for its brawls] : an up-roarious brawl

do·nor \'dō-nər\ *n* : one that gives, donates, or presents

donut *var of* DOUGHNUT

doo·dad \'dü-ˌdad\ *n* : an often small article whose com-mon name is unknown or forgotten

doo·dle \'dü-d³l\ *vb* **doo·dled; doo·dling** : to draw or scribble aimlessly while occupied with something else — **doodle** *n* — **doo·dler** *n*

doom \'düm\ *n* **1** : JUDGMENT; *esp* : a judicial condem-nation or sentence **2** : DESTINY **3** : RUIN, DEATH — **doom** *vb*

dooms·day \'dümz-ˌdā\ *n* : JUDGMENT DAY

door \'dȯr\ *n* **1** : a barrier by which an entry is closed and opened; *also* : a similar part of a piece of furniture **2** : DOORWAY **3** : a means of access or participation : OP-PORTUNITY

door·keep·er \-ˌkē-pər\ *n* : a person who tends a door

door·knob \-ˌnäb\ *n* : a knob that when turned releases a door latch

door·man \-ˌman, -mən\ *n* : a usu. uniformed attendant at the door of a building (as a hotel)

door·mat \-ˌmat\ *n* : a mat placed before or inside a door for wiping dirt from the shoes

door·plate \-ˌplāt\ *n* : a nameplate on a door

door·step \-ˌstep\ *n* : a step or series of steps before an outer door

door·way \-ˌwā\ *n* **1** : the opening that a door closes **2** : DOOR 3

do·pa \'dō-pə\ *n* : a form of an amino acid that used esp. in the treatment of Parkinson's disease

do·pa·mine \'dō-pə-ˌmēn\ *n* : an organic compound that occurs esp. as a neurotransmitter in the brain

¹dope \'dōp\ *n* **1** : a preparation for giving a desired qual-ity **2** : an illicit, habit-forming, or narcotic drug; *esp* : MARIJUANA **3** : a stupid person **4** : INFORMATION

²dope *vb* **doped; dop·ing 1** : to treat with dope; *esp* : to give a narcotic to **2** : FIGURE OUT — usu. used with *out* **3** : to take dope — **dop·er** *n*

dop·ey *also* **dopy** \'dō-pē\ *adj* **dop·i·er; -est 1** : dulled by alcohol or a narcotic **2** : SLUGGISH **3** : STUPID — **dop·i·ness** *n*

doping *n* : the use of a substance or technique to illegally improve athletic performance

Dopp·ler effect \'dä-plər-\ *n* : a change in the frequency at which waves (as of sound) reach an observer from a source in motion with respect to the observer

do–rag \'dü-ˌrag\ *n* : a kerchief worn esp. to cover the hair

dork \'dȯrk\ *n, slang* : NERD; *also* : JERK 2

dorm \'dȯrm\ *n* : DORMITORY

dor·mant \'dȯr-mənt\ *adj* : INACTIVE; *esp* : not actively growing or functioning ⟨~ buds⟩ — **dor·man·cy** \-mən-sē\ *n*

dor·mer \'dȯr-mər\ *n* [MF *dormeor* dormitory, fr. L *dor-mitorium*, fr. *dormire* to sleep] : a window built upright in a sloping roof; *also* : the roofed structure containing such a window

dor·mi·to·ry \'dȯr-mə-ˌtȯr-ē\ *n, pl* **-ries 1** : a room for sleeping; *esp* : a large room containing a number of beds **2** : a residence hall providing sleeping rooms

dor·mouse \'dȯr-ˌmau̇s\ *n* : any of numerous Old World rodents that resemble small squirrels

dor·sal \'dȯr-səl\ *adj* : of, relating to, or located near or on the surface of the body that in humans is the back but in most other animals is the upper surface — **dor·sal·ly** *adv*

do·ry \'dȯr-ē\ *n, pl* **dories** : a flat-bottomed boat with high flaring sides and a sharp bow

DOS *abbr* disk operating system

¹dose \'dōs\ *n* [ME, fr. MF, fr. LL *dosis*, fr. Gk, lit., act of giving, fr. *didonai* to give] **1** : a measured quantity (as of medicine) to be taken or administered at one time **2** : the quantity of radiation administered or absorbed — **dos·age** \'dō-sij\ *n*

²dose *vb* **dosed; dos·ing 1** : to give in doses **2** : to give medicine to

do·sim·e·ter \dō-'si-mə-tər\ *n* : a device for measuring doses of radiations (as X-rays) — **do·sim·e·try** \-mə-trē\ *n*

dos·sier \'dós-ˌyā, ¹dó-sē-ˌā\ *n* [F, bundle of documents labeled on the back, dossier, fr. *dos* back, fr. OF, fr. L *dorsum*] : a file containing detailed records on a particular person or subject

¹**dot** \'dät\ *n* **1** : a small spot : SPECK **2** : a small round mark **3** : a precise point esp. in time ⟨be here on the ∼⟩

²**dot** *vb* **dot·ted; dot·ting 1** : to mark with a dot ⟨∼ an *i*⟩ **2** : to cover with or as if with dots — **dot·ter** *n*

DOT *abbr* Department of Transportation

dot·age \'dō-tij\ *n* : feebleness of mind esp. in old age : SENILITY

dot·ard \-tərd\ *n* : a person in dotage

dot–com \'dät-ˌkäm\ *n* : a company that markets its products or services usu. exclusively via a Web site

dote \'dōt\ *vb* **dot·ed; dot·ing 1** : to be feebleminded esp. from old age **2** : to be lavish or excessive in one's attention, affection, or fondness ⟨*doted* on her niece⟩

dot matrix *n* : a rectangular arrangement of dots from which alphanumeric characters can be formed (as by a computer printer)

Dou·ay Version \dü-¹ā-\ *n* : an English translation of the Vulgate used by Roman Catholics

¹**dou·ble** \'də-bəl\ *adj* [ME, fr. AF, fr. L *duplus*, fr. *duo* two + -*plus* multiplied by] **1** : TWOFOLD, DUAL ⟨serving a ∼ function⟩ **2** : consisting of two members or parts **3** : being twice as great or as many **4** : folded in two **5** : having more than one whorl of petals ⟨∼ roses⟩

²**double** *vb* **dou·bled; dou·bling 1** : to make, be, or become twice as great or as many **2** : to make a call in bridge that increases the trick values and penalties of (an opponent's bid) **3** : FOLD **4** : CLENCH **5** : to be or cause to be bent over **6** : to take the place of another **7** : to hit a double **8** : to turn sharply and suddenly; *esp* : to turn back on one's course

³**double** *adv* **1** : DOUBLY **2** : two together ⟨sleep ∼⟩

⁴**double** *n* **1** : something twice another in size, strength, speed, quantity, or value **2** : a base hit that enables the batter to reach second base **3** : COUNTERPART, DUPLICATE; *esp* : a person who closely resembles another **4** : UNDERSTUDY, SUBSTITUTE **5** : a sharp turn : REVERSAL **6** : FOLD **7** : a combined bet placed on two different contests **8** *pl* : a game between two pairs of players **9** : an act of doubling in a card game

double bond *n* : a chemical bond in which two atoms in a molecule share two pairs of electrons

double cross *n* : an act of betraying or cheating esp. an associate — **dou·ble–cross** \ˌdə-bəl-¹krós\ *vb* — **dou·ble–cross·er** *n*

dou·ble–deal·ing \ˌdə-bəl-¹dē-liŋ\ *n* : DUPLICITY — **dou·ble–deal·er** \-¹dē-lər\ *n* — **double–dealing** *adj*

dou·ble–deck·er \-¹de-kər\ *n* : something having two decks, levels, or layers — **dou·ble–deck** \-ˌdek\ *or* **dou·ble–decked** \-ˌdekt\ *adj*

dou·ble–dig·it \ˌdə-bəl-¹di-jət\ *adj* : amounting to 10 percent or more

dou·ble en·ten·dre \ˌdüb-ᵒl-äⁿ-¹täⁿd, ˌdə-bəl-, -¹tänd-rᵒ\ *n, pl* **double entendres** *same or* -¹tän-drəz\ [obs. F, lit., double meaning] : a word or expression capable of two interpretations with one usu. risqué

dou·ble–head·er \ˌdə-bəl-¹he-dər\ *n* : two games played consecutively on the same day

double helix *n* : a helix or spiral consisting of two strands (as of DNA) in the surface of a cylinder which coil around its axis

dou·ble–hung \ˌdə-bəl-¹həŋ\ *adj, of a window* : having an upper and a lower sash that can slide past each other

dou·ble–joint·ed \-¹jóin-təd\ *adj* : having a joint that permits an exceptional degree of freedom of motion of the parts joined ⟨a ∼ finger⟩

dou·ble–park \ˌdə-bəl-¹pärk\ *vb* : to park a vehicle beside a row of vehicles already parked parallel to the curb

double play *n* : a play in baseball by which two players are put out

double pneumonia *n* : pneumonia affecting both lungs

double standard *n* : a set of principles that applies differently and usu. more rigorously to one group of people or circumstances than to another

dou·blet \'də-blət\ *n* **1** : a man's close-fitting jacket worn in Europe esp. in the 16th century **2** : one of two similar or identical things

dou·ble take \'də-bəl-ˌtāk\ *n* : a delayed reaction to a surprising or significant situation after an initial failure to notice anything unusual

dou·ble–talk \-ˌtók\ *n* : language that appears to be meaningful but in fact is a mixture of sense and nonsense

double up *vb* : to share accommodations designed for one

double whammy *n* : a combination of two usu. adverse forces, circumstances, or effects

dou·bloon \ˌdə-¹blün\ *n* : a former gold coin of Spain and Spanish America

dou·bly \'də-blē\ *adv* **1** : in a twofold manner **2** : to twice the degree ⟨∼ glad⟩

¹**doubt** \'daút\ *vb* **1** : to be uncertain about **2** : to lack confidence in : DISTRUST **3** : to consider unlikely — **doubt·able** *adj* — **doubt·er** *n*

²**doubt** *n* **1** : uncertainty of belief or opinion **2** : a condition causing uncertainty, hesitation, or suspense ⟨the outcome was in ∼⟩ **3** : DISTRUST **4** : an inclination not to believe or accept

doubt·ful \'daút-fəl\ *adj* **1** : QUESTIONABLE ⟨∼ they knew what happened⟩ **2** : UNDECIDED ⟨the outcome of the election is ∼⟩ — **doubt·ful·ly** *adv* — **doubt·ful·ness** *n*

¹**doubt·less** \'daút-ləs\ *adv* **1** : without doubt **2** : PROBABLY

²**doubtless** *adj* : free from doubt : CERTAIN — **doubt·less·ly** *adv*

douche \'düsh\ *n* [F] **1** : a jet of fluid (as water) directed against a part or into a cavity of the body; *also* : a cleansing with a douche **2** : a device for giving douches — **douche** *vb*

dough \'dō\ *n* **1** : a mixture that consists of flour or meal and a liquid (as milk or water) and is stiff enough to knead or roll **2** : something resembling dough esp. in consistency **3** : MONEY — **doughy** \'dō-ē\ *adj*

dough·boy \-ˌbói\ *n* : an American infantryman esp. in World War I

dough·nut *also* **do·nut** \-(ˌ)nət\ *n* : a small usu. ring-shaped cake fried in fat

dough·ty \'daú-tē\ *adj* **dough·ti·er; -est** : ABLE, VALIANT ⟨a ∼ warrior⟩

Doug·las fir \'də-gləs-\ *n* : a tall evergreen timber tree of the western U.S.

dou·la \'dü-lə\ *n* : a woman who provides assistance to a mother before, during, and just after childbirth

do up *vb* **1** : to prepare (as by cleaning) for use **2** : to wrap up **3** : CLOTHE, DECORATE **4** : FASTEN

dour \'daù(-ə)r, 'dúr\ *adj* [ME, fr. L *durus* hard] **1** : STERN, HARSH **2** : OBSTINATE **3** : SULLEN — **dour·ly** *adv*

douse \'daús, ¹daúz\ *vb* **doused; dous·ing 1** : to plunge into water **2** : DRENCH **3** : EXTINGUISH ⟨∼ a match⟩

¹**dove** \'dəv\ *n* **1** : any of numerous pigeons; *esp* : a small wild pigeon **2** : an advocate of peace or of a peaceful policy — **dov·ish** \'də-vish\ *adj*

²**dove** \'dōv\ *past of* DIVE

¹**dove·tail** \'dəv-ˌtāl\ *n* : something that resembles a dove's tail; *esp* : a flaring tenon and a mortise into which it fits tightly

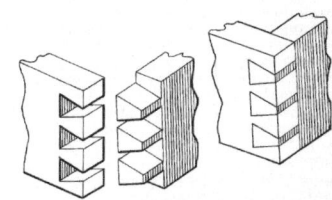

dovetail: with mortises and tenons

²**dovetail** *vb* **1** : to join by means of dovetails **2** : to fit skillfully together to form a whole ⟨our plans ∼ nicely⟩

dow·a·ger \'daú-i-jər\ *n* **1** : a widow owning property or a title from her deceased husband **2** : a dignified elderly woman

dowdy \'daú-dē\ *adj* **dowd·i·er; -est** : lacking neatness and charm : SHABBY, UNTIDY; *also* : lacking smartness

dow·el \'daú(-ə)l\ *n* **1** : a pin used for fastening together

two pieces of wood **2** : a round rod (as of wood) —
dowel *vb*

¹**dow·er** \'dau̇(-ə)r\ *n* [ME *dowere*, fr. AF *dower, douaire*, fr.
ML *dotarium*, fr. L *dot-, dos* gift, marriage portion] **1**
: the part of a deceased husband's real estate which the
law gives for life to his widow **2** : DOWRY

²**dower** *vb* : to supply with a dower or dowry : ENDOW

dow·itch·er \'dau̇-i-chər\ *n* : any of several long-billed
wading birds related to the sandpipers

¹**down** \'dau̇n\ *adv* [ME *doun*, fr. OE *dūne*, short for *adūne*,
of *dūne*, lit., from (the) hill] **1** : toward or in a lower
physical position **2** : to a lying or sitting position **3** : toward or to the ground, floor, or bottom **4** : as a down
payment ⟨paid $5 ∼⟩ **5** : on paper ⟨put ∼ what he
says⟩ **6** : in a direction that is the opposite of up **7**
: SOUTH **8** : to or in a lower or worse condition or status
9 : from a past time **10** : to or in a state of less activity
11 : into defeat ⟨voted the motion ∼⟩

²**down** *prep* : down in, on, along, or through : toward the
bottom of ⟨fell ∼ a hole⟩ ⟨lives ∼ the road⟩

³**down** *vb* **1** : to go or cause to go or come down ⟨∼ed a
warplane⟩ **2** : DEFEAT **3** : to cause (a football) to be out
of play **4** : CONSUME **3** ⟨∼ed two beers⟩

⁴**down** *adj* **1** : occupying a low position; *esp* : lying on the
ground **2** : directed or going downward **3** : being in a
state of reduced or low activity **4** : DEPRESSED, DEJECT-
ED **5** : SICK ⟨∼ with a cold⟩ **6** : FINISHED, DONE **7**
: completely mastered ⟨got her lines ∼⟩ **8** : being on
record ⟨you're ∼ for two tickets⟩

⁵**down** *n* **.1** : a low or falling period (as in activity, emotional life, or fortunes) **2** : one of a series of attempts to
advance a football **3** : a quark with a charge of -⅓ that is
one of the constituents of the proton and neutron

⁶**down** *n* : a rolling usu. treeless upland with sparse soil —
usu. used in pl.

⁷**down** *n* **1** : a covering of soft fluffy feathers; *also* : such
feathers **2** : a downlike covering or material

down·beat \'dau̇n-ˌbēt\ *n* : the downward stroke of a conductor indicating the principally accented note of a measure of music

down·burst \-ˌbərst\ *n* : a powerful downdraft usu. associated with a thunderstorm that is a hazard for low-flying
aircraft; *also* : MICROBURST

down·cast \-ˌkast\ *adj* **1** : DEJECTED **2** : directed down
⟨a ∼ glance⟩

down·draft \-ˌdraft\ *n* : a downward current of gas (as air)

down·er \'dau̇-nər\ *n* **1** : a depressant drug; *esp* : BARBI-
TURATE **2** : someone or something depressing

down·fall \'dau̇n-ˌfȯl\ *n* **1** : a sudden fall (as from high
rank) **2** : something that causes a downfall — **down·fall-
en** \-ˌfȯ-lən\ *adj*

¹**down·grade** \'dau̇n-ˌgrād\ *n* **1** : a downward slope (as of
a road) **2** : a decline toward a worse condition

²**downgrade** *vb* : to lower in quality, value, extent, or status

down·heart·ed \-'härt-əd\ *adj* : DEJECTED

¹**down·hill** \'dau̇n-'hil\ *adv* : toward the bottom of a hill —
downhill \-ˌhil\ *adj*

²**down·hill** \-ˌhil\ *n* : the sport of skiing downhill usu. in a
race against time

¹**down·load** \'dau̇n-ˌlōd\ *n* : an act or instance of down-
loading something; *also* : the item downloaded

²**download** *vb* : to transfer (data) from a computer to another device — **down·load·able** \-ˌlō-də-bəl\ *adj*

down payment *n* : a part of the full price paid at the time
of purchase or delivery with the balance to be paid later

down·play \'dau̇n-ˌplā\ *vb* : DE-EMPHASIZE ⟨∼ed the alle-
gations⟩

down·pour \'dau̇n-ˌpȯr\ *n* : a heavy rain

down·range \-'rānj\ *adv* : away from a launching site

¹**down·right** \-ˌrīt\ *adv* : THOROUGHLY

²**downright** *adj* **1** : ABSOLUTE, UTTER ⟨a ∼ lie⟩ **2**
: PLAIN, BLUNT ⟨a ∼ man⟩

down·shift \-ˌshift\ *vb* : to shift an automotive vehicle into
a lower gear

down·size \-ˌsīz\ *vb* : to reduce or undergo reduction in
size or numbers

down·spout \-ˌspau̇t\ *n* : a vertical pipe used to drain rainwater from a roof

Down syndrome \'dau̇n-\ *or* **Down's syndrome** \'dau̇nz-\
n : a birth defect characterized by mental retardation,

slanting eyes, a broad short skull, broad hands with short
fingers, and the presence of an extra chromosome

down·stage \'dau̇n-'stāj\ *adv or adj* : toward or at the
front of a theatrical stage — **down·stage** \-ˌstāj\ *n*

down·stairs \-'sterz\ *adv* : on or to a lower floor and esp.
the main or ground floor — **down·stairs** \-ˌsterz\ *adj or n*

down·stream \-'strēm\ *adv or adj* : in the direction of flow
of a stream

down·stroke \-ˌstrōk\ *n* : a downward stroke

down·swing \-ˌswin\ *n* **1** : a swing downward **2** : DOWN-
TURN

down–to–earth *adj* : PRACTICAL, REALISTIC

down·town \'dau̇n-ˌtau̇n\ *n* : the main business district of
a town or city — **downtown** \'dau̇n-'tau̇n\ *adj or adv*

down·trod·den \'dau̇n-'träd-ᵈn\ *adj* : suffering oppression

down·turn \-ˌtərn\ *n* : a downward turn esp. in economic
activity

¹**down·ward** \'dau̇n-wərd\ *or* **down·wards** \-wərdz\ *adv* **1**
: from a higher to a lower place or condition **2** : from an
earlier time **3** : from an ancestor or predecessor

²**downward** *adj* : directed toward or situated in a lower
place or condition

down·wind \'dau̇n-'wind\ *adv or adj* : in the direction that
the wind is blowing

downy \'dau̇-nē\ *adj* **down·i·er; -est** : resembling or covered with down

downy mildew *n* : any of various parasitic fungi producing whitish masses esp. on the underside of plant leaves;
also : a plant disease caused by downy mildew

downy woodpecker *n* : a small black-and-white woodpecker of No. America

dow·ry \'dau̇(-ə)r-ē\ *n, pl* **dowries** [ME *dowarie*, fr. AF,
alter. of *dower, douaire* dower] : the property that a
woman brings to her husband in marriage

dowse \'dau̇z\ *vb* **dowsed; dows·ing** : to use a divining
rod esp. to find water — **dows·er** *n*

dox·ol·o·gy \däk-'sä-lə-jē\ *n, pl* **-gies** : a usu. short hymn
of praise to God

doy·en \'dȯi-ən, 'dwä-ˌyaⁿ\ *n* : the senior or most experienced person in a group

doy·enne \dȯi-'yen, dwä-'yen\ *n* : a woman who is a doyen

doy·ley *chiefly Brit var of* DOILY

doz *abbr* dozen

doze \'dōz\ *vb* **dozed; doz·ing** : to sleep lightly — **doze** *n*

doz·en \'də-zᵊn\ *n, pl* **dozens** *or* **dozen** [ME *dozeine*, fr.
AF *duzeine*, fr. *duze* twelve, fr. L *duodecim*, fr. *duo* two +
decem ten] : a group of twelve — **doz·enth** \-zᵊnth\ *adj*

¹**DP** \ˌdē-'pē\ *n, pl* **DP's** *or* **DPs** **1** : a displaced person **2**
: DOUBLE PLAY

²**DP** *abbr* data processing

dpt *abbr* department

DPT *abbr* diphtheria-pertussis-tetanus (vaccines)

dr *abbr* **1** debtor **2** dram **3** drive **4** drum

Dr *abbr* doctor

DR *abbr* **1** dead reckoning **2** dining room

drab \'drab\ *adj* **drab·ber; drab·best** **1** : being of a light
olive-brown color **2** : DULL, MONOTONOUS, CHEERLESS
— **drab·ly** *adv* — **drab·ness** *n*

drach·ma \'drak-mə\ *n, pl* **drach·mas** *or* **drach·mai** \-ˌmī\
or **drach·mae** \-ˌ(ˌ)mē\ : the former basic monetary unit
of Greece

dra·co·ni·an \drā-'kō-nē-ən, drə-\ *adj, often cap* : CRUEL;
also : SEVERE

¹**draft** \'draft, 'dräft\ *n* **1** : the act of drawing or hauling
2 : the act or an instance of drinking or inhaling; *also*
: the portion drunk or inhaled in one such act **3** : DOSE,
POTION **4** : DELINEATION, PLAN, DESIGN; *also* : a preliminary sketch, outline, or version ⟨a rough ∼ of a
speech⟩ **5** : the act of drawing (as from a cask); *also* : a
portion of liquid so drawn **6** : the depth of water a ship
draws esp. when loaded **7** : a system for or act of selecting persons (as for sports teams or compulsory military
service); *also* : the persons so selected **8** : an order for
the payment of money drawn by one person or bank on
another **9** : a heavy demand : STRAIN **10** : a current of
air; *also* : a device to regulate air supply (as in a stove) —
on draft : ready to be drawn from a receptacle ⟨beer on
draft⟩

²**draft** *adj* **1** : used or adapted for drawing loads ⟨∼ hors-
es⟩ **2** : being or having been on draft ⟨∼ beer⟩

³**draft** *vb* **1** : to select usu. on a compulsory basis; *esp* : to

conscript for military service **2** : to draw the preliminary sketch, version, or plan of **3** : COMPOSE, PREPARE **4** : to draw off or away

draft·ee \draf-ˈtē, ˈdraf-\ *n* : a person who is drafted

drafts·man \ˈdraft-smən, ˈdräft-\ *n* : a person who draws plans (as for buildings or machinery) — **drafts·man·ly** \-lē\ *adj*

drafty \ˈdraf-tē, ˈdräf-\ *adj* **draft·i·er; -est** : exposed to or abounding in drafts of air ⟨a ∼ room⟩

¹drag \ˈdrag\ *n* **1** : a device pulled along under water for detecting or gathering **2** : something (as a harrow or sledge) that is dragged along over a surface **3** : the act or an instance of dragging **4** : something that hinders progress; *also* : something boring ⟨thinks school is a ∼⟩ **5** : STREET ⟨the main ∼⟩ **6** : clothing typical of one sex worn by a member of the opposite sex

²drag *vb* **dragged; drag·ging 1** : HAUL **2** : to move or proceed with slowness or difficulty ⟨*dragged* himself out of bed⟩ ⟨the lecture *dragged* on⟩ **3** : to force into or out of some situation, condition, or course of action **4** : PROTRACT ⟨∼ a story out⟩ **5** : to hang or lag behind **6** : to explore, search, or fish with a drag **7** : to trail along on the ground **8** : DRAW, PUFF ⟨∼ on a cigarette⟩ **9** : to move (items on a computer screen) esp. by using a mouse — **drag·ger** *n* — **drag one's feet** *also* **drag one's heels** : to act slowly or with hesitation

drag·net \-ˌnet\ *n* **1** : NET, TRAWL **2** : a network of planned actions for pursuing and catching ⟨a police ∼⟩

drag·o·man \ˈdra-gə-mən\ *n, pl* **-mans** *or* **-men** \-mən\ : an interpreter employed esp. in the Near East

drag·on \ˈdra-gən\ *n* [ME, fr. AF *dragun*, fr. L *dracon-, draco* serpent, dragon, fr. Gk *drakōn* serpent] : a fabulous animal usu. represented as a huge winged scaly serpent with a crested head and large claws

drag·on·fly \-ˌflī\ *n* : any of a group of large harmless 4-winged insects that hold the wings horizontal and unfolded in repose

¹dra·goon \drə-ˈgün, dra-\ *n* [F *dragon* dragon, dragoon, fr. MF] **1** : a heavily armed mounted soldier **2** : CAVALRYMAN

²dragoon *vb* : to force or attempt to force into submission : COERCE

drag race *n* : an acceleration contest between vehicles — **drag racer** *n*

drag·ster \ˈdrag-stər\ *n* : a usu. high-powered vehicle used in a drag race

drag strip *n* : a site for drag races

¹drain \ˈdrān\ *vb* **1** : to draw off or flow off gradually or completely **2** : to exhaust physically or emotionally ⟨∼ed by the work⟩ **3** : to make or become gradually dry or empty ⟨∼ a swamp⟩ **4** : to carry away the surface water of : discharge surface or surplus water **5** : EMPTY, EXHAUST ⟨∼ed our savings⟩ — **drain·er** *n*

²drain *n* **1** : a means (as a channel or sewer) of draining **2** : the act of draining **3** : a gradual outflow; *also* : something causing an outflow ⟨a ∼ on our savings⟩

drain·age \ˈdrā-nij\ *n* **1** : the act or process of draining; *also* : something that is drained off **2** : a means for draining : DRAIN, SEWER **3** : an area drained

drain·pipe \ˈdrān-ˌpīp\ *n* : a pipe for drainage

drake \ˈdrāk\ *n* : a male duck

¹dram \ˈdram\ *n* **1** — see WEIGHT table **2** : FLUID DRAM **3** : a small drink

²dram \ˈdräm\ *n* — see MONEY table

dra·ma \ˈdrä-mə, ˈdra-\ *n* [LL, fr. Gk, deed, drama, fr. *dran* to do, act] **1** : a literary composition designed for theatrical presentation; *also* : a production (as a film) with a serious tone or subject **2** : dramatic art, literature, or affairs **3** : a series of events involving conflicting forces — **dra·mat·ic** \drə-ˈma-tik\ *adj* — **dra·mat·i·cal·ly** \-ti-k(ə-)lē\ *adv* — **dra·ma·tist** \ˈdra-mə-tist, ˈdrä-\ *n*

dram·a·ti·sa·tion, dra·ma·tise *Brit var of* DRAMATIZATION, DRAMATIZE

dra·ma·tize \ˈdra-mə-ˌtīz, ˈdrä-\ *vb* **-tized; -tiz·ing 1** : to adapt for or be suitable for theatrical presentation **2** : to present or represent in a dramatic manner — **dram·a·ti·za·tion** \ˌdra-mə-tə-ˈzā-shən, ˌdrä-\ *n*

dra·me·dy \ˈdrä-mə-ˌdē, ˈdra-\ *n* : a comedy having dramatic moments

drank *past and past part of* DRINK

¹drape \ˈdrāp\ *vb* **draped; drap·ing 1** : to cover or adorn with or as if with folds of cloth ⟨kings *draped* in robes⟩ **2** : to cause to hang or stretch out loosely or carelessly **3** : to arrange or become arranged in flowing lines or folds

²drape *n* **1** : CURTAIN **2** : arrangement in or of folds **3** : the cut or hang of clothing

drap·er \ˈdrā-pər\ *n, chiefly Brit* : a dealer in cloth and sometimes in clothing and dry goods

drap·ery \ˈdrā-pə-rē\ *n, pl* **-er·ies 1** *Brit* : DRY GOODS **2** : a decorative fabric esp. when hung loosely and in folds; *also* : hangings of heavy fabric used as a curtain

dras·tic \ˈdras-tik\ *adj* : HARSH, RIGOROUS, SEVERE ⟨∼ punishment⟩ — **dras·ti·cal·ly** \-ti-k(ə-)lē\ *adv*

draught \ˈdräft\, **draughty** \ˈdräf-tē\ *chiefly Brit var of* DRAFT, DRAFTY

draughts \ˈdräfts\ *n, Brit* : CHECKERS

draughts·man *chiefly Brit var of* DRAFTSMAN

Dra·vid·i·an \drə-ˈvi-dē-ən\ *n* : a language family of south Asia that includes the major literary languages of southern India

¹draw \ˈdrȯ\ *vb* **drew** \ˈdrü\; **drawn** \ˈdrȯn\; **draw·ing 1** : to cause to move toward a force exerted **2** : to cause to go in a certain direction ⟨*drew* him aside⟩ **3** : to move or go steadily or gradually ⟨night ∼s near⟩ **4** : ATTRACT, ENTICE **5** : PROVOKE, ROUSE ⟨*drew* enemy fire⟩ **6** : INHALE ⟨∼ a deep breath⟩ **7** : to bring or pull out ⟨*drew* a gun⟩ **8** : to cause to come out of a container or source ⟨∼ blood⟩ ⟨∼ water for a bath⟩ **9** : EVISCERATE **10** : to require (a specified depth) to float in **11** : ACCUMULATE, GAIN ⟨∼*ing* interest⟩ **12** : to take money from a place of deposit : WITHDRAW **13** : to receive regularly ⟨∼ a salary⟩ **14** : to take (cards) from a stack or the dealer **15** : to receive or take at random ⟨∼ a winning number⟩ **16** : to bend (a bow) by pulling back the string **17** : WRINKLE, SHRINK **18** : to change shape by or as if by pulling or stretching ⟨a face *drawn* with sorrow⟩ **19** : to leave (a contest) undecided : TIE **20** : DELINEATE, SKETCH **21** : to write out in due form : DRAFT ⟨∼ up a will⟩ **22** : FORMULATE ⟨∼ comparisons⟩ **23** : INFER ⟨∼ a conclusion⟩ **24** : to spread or elongate (metal) by hammering or by pulling through dies **25** : to produce or allow a draft or current of air ⟨the chimney ∼s well⟩ **26** : to swell out in a wind ⟨all sails ∼*ing*⟩ — **draw a blank** : to be unable to think of something — **draw the line** *or* **draw a line** : to fix an arbitrary boundary between two things

²draw *n* **1** : the act, process, or result of drawing **2** : a lot or chance drawn at random **3** : a contest left undecided or deadlocked : TIE **4** : one that draws attention or patronage : ATTRACTION

draw·back \ˈdrȯ-ˌbak\ *n* : DISADVANTAGE 2

draw·bridge \-ˌbrij\ *n* : a bridge made to be raised, lowered, or turned to permit or deny passage

draw·er \ˈdrȯr, ˈdrȯ-ər\ *n* **1** : one that draws **2** *pl* : an undergarment for the lower part of the body **3** : a sliding boxlike compartment (as in a table or desk)

draw·ing \ˈdrȯ-iŋ\ *n* **1** : an act or instance of drawing; *esp* : an occasion when something is decided by drawing lots ⟨tonight's lottery ∼⟩ **2** : the act or art of making a figure, plan, or sketch by means of lines **3** : a representation made by drawing : SKETCH

drawing card *n* : DRAW 4

drawing room *n* : a formal reception room

drawl \ˈdrȯl\ *vb* : to speak or utter slowly with vowels greatly prolonged — **drawl** *n*

draw on *vb* : APPROACH ⟨night *draws* on⟩

draw out *vb* **1** : PROLONG **2** : to cause to speak freely

draw·string \ˈdrȯ-ˌstriŋ\ *n* : a string, cord, or tape for use in closing a bag or controlling fullness in garments or curtains

draw up *vb* **1** : to prepare a draft or version of **2** : to pull oneself erect **3** : to bring or come to a stop

dray \ˈdrā\ *n* : a strong low cart for carrying heavy loads

¹dread \ˈdred\ *vb* **1** : to fear greatly **2** : to feel extreme reluctance to meet or face

²dread *n* : great fear esp. of some harm to come

³dread *adj* **1** : causing great fear or anxiety **2** : inspiring awe

dread·ful \ˈdred-fəl\ *adj* **1** : inspiring dread or awe : FRIGHTENING **2** : extremely distasteful, unpleasant, or shocking — **dread·ful·ly** *adv*

dread·locks \'dred-ˌläks\ *n pl* : long braids of hair over the entire head

dread·nought \'dred-ˌnȯt\ *n* : BATTLESHIP

¹**dream** \'drēm\ *n* [ME *dreem*, fr. OE *drēam* noise, joy, and ON *draumr* dream] **1** : a series of thoughts, images, or emotions occurring during sleep **2** : a dreamlike vision : DAYDREAM, REVERIE **3** : something notable for its beauty, excellence, or enjoyable quality **4** : IDEAL — **dream·like** \-ˌlīk\ *adj* — **dreamy** *adj*

²**dream** \'drēm\ *vb* **dreamed** \'dremt, 'drēmd\ *or* **dreamt** \'dremt\; **dream·ing** **1** : to have a dream of **2** : to indulge in daydreams or fantasies : pass (time) in reverie or inaction **3** : IMAGINE — **dream·er** *n*

dream·boat \'drēm-ˌbōt\ *n, slang* : something highly desirable; *esp* : a very attractive person

dream·land \'drēm-ˌland\ *n* : an unreal delightful country that exists in imagination or in dreams

dream up *vb* : INVENT, CONCOCT

dream·world \-ˌwərld\ *n* : a world of illusion or fantasy

drear \'drir\ *adj* : DREARY

drea·ry \'drir-ē\ *adj* **drea·ri·er; -est** [ME *drery*, fr. OE *drēorig* sad, bloody, fr. *drēor* gore] **1** : DOLEFUL, SAD **2** : DISMAL, GLOOMY — **drea·ri·ly** \-ə-lē\ *adv*

¹**dredge** \'drej\ *vb* **dredged; dredg·ing** : to gather or search with or as if with a dredge — **dredg·er** *n*

²**dredge** *n* : a machine or barge for removing earth or silt

³**dredge** *vb* **dredged; dredg·ing** : to coat (food) by sprinkling (as with flour)

dregs \'dregz\ *n pl* **1** : SEDIMENT **1** **2** : the most undesirable part ⟨the ~ of humanity⟩

drench \'drench\ *vb* : to wet thoroughly

¹**dress** \'dres\ *vb* [ME, fr. AF *drescer* to direct, put right, fr. VL **directiare*, fr. L *directus* direct] **1** : to make or set straight : ALIGN **2** : to prepare for use; *esp* : BUTCHER **3** : TRIM, EMBELLISH ⟨~ a store window⟩ **4** : to put clothes on : CLOTHE; *also* : to put on or wear formal or fancy clothes **5** : to apply dressings or medicine to ⟨~ a wound⟩ **6** : to arrange (the hair) by combing, brushing, or curling **7** : to apply fertilizer to ⟨~ a field⟩ **8** : SMOOTH, FINISH ⟨~ leather⟩

²**dress** *n* **1** : APPAREL, CLOTHING ⟨casual ~⟩ **2** : a garment usu. consisting of a one-piece bodice and skirt — **dress·mak·er** \-ˌmā-kər\ *n* — **dress·mak·ing** \-ˌmā-kiŋ\ *n*

³**dress** *adj* : suitable for a formal occasion; *also* : requiring formal dress

dres·sage \drə-'säzh\ *n* [F] : the execution by a trained horse of complex movements in response to barely perceptible signals from its rider

dress down *vb* : to scold severely

¹**dress·er** \'dre-sər\ *n* : a chest of drawers or bureau with a mirror

²**dresser** *n* : one that dresses

dress·ing \'dre-siŋ\ *n* **1** : the act or process of one who dresses **2** : a sauce for adding to a dish (as a salad) **3** : a seasoned mixture usu. used as stuffing **4** : material used to cover an injury (as a wound)

dressing gown *n* : a loose robe worn esp. while dressing or resting

dressy \'dre-sē\ *adj* **dress·i·er; -est** **1** : showy in dress **2** : STYLISH, SMART

drew *past of* DRAW

¹**drib·ble** \'dri-bəl\ *vb* **drib·bled; drib·bling** **1** : to fall or flow in drops : TRICKLE **2** : DROOL **3** : to propel by successive slight taps or bounces

²**dribble** *n* **1** : a small trickling stream or flow **2** : a drizzling shower **3** : the dribbling of a ball or puck

drib·let \'dri-blət\ *n* **1** : a trifling amount **2** : a drop of liquid

dri·er *or* **dry·er** \'drī-ər\ *n* **1** : a substance that speeds drying (as of paint or ink) **2** *usu dryer* : a device for drying

¹**drift** \'drift\ *n* **1** : the motion or course of something drifting; *also* : a gradual shift of position **2** : a mass of matter (as snow or sand) piled up esp. by wind **3** : earth, gravel, and rock deposited by a glacier **4** : a general underlying design or tendency : MEANING ⟨catch my ~⟩

²**drift** *vb* **1** : to float or be driven along by or as if by a current of water or air ⟨~*ing* logs⟩ **2** : to become piled up by wind or water ⟨~*ing* snow⟩

drift·er \'drif-tər\ *n* : a person who moves about aimlessly

drift net *n* : a fishing net often miles in extent arranged to drift with the tide or current

drift·wood \'drift-ˌwu̇d\ *n* : wood drifted or floated by water

¹**drill** \'dril\ *n* **1** : a tool for boring holes **2** : the training of soldiers in marching and the handling of arms **3** : a regularly practiced exercise ⟨a shooting ~⟩

²**drill** *vb* **1** : to instruct and exercise by repetition **2** : to train in or practice military drill **3** : to bore with a drill ⟨~ a hole⟩ — **drill·er** *n*

³**drill** *n* **1** : a shallow furrow or trench in which seed is sown **2** : an agricultural implement for making furrows and dropping seed into them

⁴**drill** *n* : a firm cotton twilled fabric

drill·mas·ter \'dril-ˌmas-tər\ *n* : an instructor in military drill

drill press *n* : an upright drilling machine in which the drill is pressed to the work usu. by a hand lever

dri·ly *var of* DRYLY

¹**drink** \'driŋk\ *vb* **drank** \'draŋk\; **drunk** \'drəŋk\ *or* **drank; drink·ing** **1** : to swallow liquid : IMBIBE **2** : ABSORB **3** : to take in through the senses ⟨~ in the beautiful scenery⟩ **4** : to give or join in a toast **5** : to drink alcoholic beverages esp. to excess — **drink·able** *adj* — **drink·er** *n*

²**drink** *n* **1** : BEVERAGE; *also* : an alcoholic beverage **2** : a draft or portion of liquid **3** : excessive consumption of alcoholic beverages

¹**drip** \'drip\ *vb* **dripped; drip·ping** **1** : to fall or let fall in drops **2** : to let fall drops of moisture or liquid ⟨a *dripping* faucet⟩ **3** : to overflow with or as if with moisture ⟨clothes *dripping* with sweat⟩ ⟨stories *dripping* with irony⟩

²**drip** *n* **1** : a falling in drops **2** : liquid that falls, overflows, or is extruded in drops **3** : the sound made by or as if by falling drops

¹**drive** \'drīv\ *vb* **drove** \'drōv\; **driv·en** \'dri-vən\; **driv·ing** **1** : to urge, push, or force onward **2** : to carry through strongly ⟨~ a bargain⟩ **3** : to set or keep in motion or operation **4** : to direct the movement or course of **5** : to convey in a vehicle ⟨*drove* her to school⟩ **6** : to bring into a specified condition ⟨the noise ~*s* me crazy⟩ **7** : FORCE, COMPEL ⟨*driven* by hunger to steal⟩ **8** : to project, inject, or impress forcefully ⟨*drove* the lesson home⟩ **9** : to produce by opening a way ⟨~ a well⟩ **10** : to progress with strong momentum ⟨a *driving* rain⟩ **11** : to propel an object of play (as a golf ball) by a hard blow — **driv·er** *n*

²**drive** *n* **1** : a trip in a carriage or automobile **2** : a driving or collecting of animals ⟨a cattle ~⟩ **3** : the guiding of logs downstream to a mill **4** : the act of driving a ball; *also* : the flight of a ball **5** : DRIVEWAY **6** : a public road for driving (as in a park) **7** : the state of being hurried and under pressure **8** : an intensive campaign ⟨membership ~⟩ **9** : the apparatus by which motion is imparted to a machine **10** : an offensive or aggressive move : a military attack **11** : NEED, LONGING ⟨the ~ to succeed⟩ **12** : dynamic quality **13** : a device for reading and writing on magnetic media (as magnetic tape or disks)

drive–in \'drī-ˌvin\ *adj* : accommodating patrons while they remain in their automobiles — **drive–in** *n*

¹**driv·el** \'dri-vəl\ *vb* **-eled** *or* **-elled; -el·ing** *or* **-el·ling** **1** : DROOL, SLAVER **2** : to talk or utter stupidly, carelessly, or in an infantile way — **driv·el·er** *n*

²**drivel** *n* : NONSENSE

drive·shaft \'drīv-ˌshaft\ *n* : a shaft that transmits mechanical power

drive–through *also* **drive–thru** \'drīv-ˌthrü\ *adj* : designed for the service of patrons remaining in their automobiles — **drive–through** *also* **drive–thru** *n*

drive·way \-ˌwā\ *n* : a short private road leading from the street to a house, garage, or parking lot

¹**driz·zle** \'dri-zəl\ *n* : a fine misty rain

²**drizzle** *vb* **driz·zled; driz·zling** : to rain in very small drops

drogue \'drōg\ *n* : a small parachute for slowing down or stabilizing something (as a space capsule)

droll \'drōl\ *adj* [F *drôle*, fr. *drôle* scamp, fr. MF *drolle*, fr. MD, imp] : having a humorous, whimsical, or odd quality ⟨a ~ expression⟩ — **droll·ery** \'drō-lə-rē\ *n* — **drol·ly** *adv*

drom·e·dary \'drä-mə-ˌder-ē\ *n, pl* **-dar·ies** [ME *drome-*

darie, fr. MF *dromedaire*, fr. LL *dromedarius*, fr. L *dromad-*, *dromas*, fr. Gk, running] : CAMEL; *esp* : a domesticated one-humped camel of western Asia and northern Africa

¹**drone** \'drōn\ *n* 1 : a male honeybee 2 : one that lives on the labors of others : PARASITE 3 : an unmanned aircraft or ship guided by remote control 4 : DRUDGE

²**drone** *vb* **droned; dron·ing** : to sound with a low dull monotonous murmuring sound : speak monotonously

³**drone** *n* : a deep monotonous sound ⟨the ∼ of engines⟩

drool \'drül\ *vb* 1 : to let liquid flow from the mouth 2 : to talk foolishly — **drool** *n*

droop \'drüp\ *vb* 1 : to hang or incline downward 2 : to sink gradually 3 : LANGUISH — **droop** *n* — **droopy** *adj*

¹**drop** \'dräp\ *n* 1 : the quantity of fluid that falls in one spherical mass 2 *pl* : a dose of medicine measured by drops 3 : a small quantity of drink 4 : the smallest practical unit of liquid measure 5 : something (as a pendant or a small round candy) that resembles a liquid drop 6 : FALL 7 : a decline in quantity or quality 8 : a descent by parachute 9 : the distance through which something drops 10 : a slot into which something is to be dropped 11 : something that drops or has dropped

²**drop** *vb* **dropped; drop·ping** 1 : to fall or let fall in drops 2 : to let fall : LOWER ⟨∼ a glove⟩ ⟨*dropped* his voice⟩ 3 : SEND ⟨∼ me a note⟩ 4 : to let go : DISMISS ⟨∼ the subject⟩ 5 : MENTION ⟨∼ a suggestion⟩ 6 : to knock down : cause to fall 7 : to go lower : become less ⟨prices *dropped*⟩ 8 : SPEND, LOSE ⟨∼ $20⟩ ⟨*dropped* ten pounds⟩ 9 : to come or go unexpectedly or informally ⟨a friend *dropped* in⟩ 10 : to pass from one state into a less active one ⟨∼ off to sleep⟩ 11 : to move downward or with a current 12 : QUIT ⟨*dropped* out of the race⟩ — **drop back** : to move toward the rear — **drop behind** : to fail to keep up

drop–down \'dräp-ˌdaùn\ *adj* : PULL-DOWN

drop·kick \-'kik\ *n* : a kick made by dropping a ball to the ground and kicking it at the moment it starts to rebound — **drop–kick** *vb*

drop·let \'drä-plət\ *n* : a tiny drop

drop–off \'dräp-ˌòf\ *n* 1 : a steep or perpendicular descent 2 : a marked decline ⟨a ∼ in attendance⟩ 3 : an act or instance of delivering or depositing something ⟨∼ points along the route⟩

drop off *vb* : to fall asleep

drop out *vb* : to withdraw from participation or membership; *esp* : to leave school before graduation — **drop–out** \'dräp-ˌaút\ *n*

drop·per \'drä-pər\ *n* 1 : one that drops 2 : a short glass tube with a rubber bulb used to measure out liquids by drops

drop·pings *n pl* : MANURE, DUNG

drop·sy \'dräp-sē\ *n* [ME *dropesie*, short for *ydropesie*, fr. AF, fr. L *hydropisis*, fr. Gk *hydrōps*, fr. *hydōr* water] : EDEMA — **drop·si·cal** \-si-kəl\ *adj*

drop–top \'dräp-ˌtäp\ *n* : CONVERTIBLE

dross \'dräs\ *n* 1 : the scum that forms on the surface of a molten metal 2 : waste matter : REFUSE

drought \'draùt\ *also* **drouth** \'draùth\ *n* : a long spell of dry weather

¹**drove** \'drōv\ *n* 1 : a group of animals driven or moving in a body 2 : a large number : CROWD — usu. used in pl. ⟨tourists arriving in ∼s⟩

²**drove** *past of* DRIVE

drov·er \'drō-vər\ *n* : one who drives domestic animals usu. to market

drown \'draùn\ *vb* **drowned** \'draùnd\; **drown·ing** 1 : to suffocate by submersion esp. in water 2 : to become drowned 3 : to cover with water 4 : to cause to be muted (as a sound) by a loud noise 5 : OVERPOWER, OVERWHELM

drowse \'draùz\ *vb* **drowsed; drows·ing** : DOZE — **drowse** *n*

drowsy \'draù-zē\ *adj* **drows·i·er; -est** 1 : ready to fall asleep 2 : making one sleepy ⟨∼ music⟩ — **drows·i·ly** \-zə-lē\ *adv* — **drows·i·ness** \-zē-nəs\ *n*

drub \'drəb\ *vb* **drubbed; drub·bing** 1 : to beat severely 2 : to berate critically 3 : to defeat decisively

drudge \'drəj\ *vb* **drudged; drudg·ing** : to do hard, menial, or monotonous work — **drudge** *n* — **drudg·ery** \'drə-jə-rē\ *n*

¹**drug** \'drəg\ *n* 1 : a substance used as a medicine or in making medicine 2 : a substance (as heroin or marijuana) that can cause addiction, habituation, or a marked change in mental status

²**drug** *vb* **drugged; drug·ging** : to affect with or as if with drugs; *esp* : to stupefy with a narcotic

drug·gist \'drə-gist\ *n* : a dealer in drugs and medicines; *also* : PHARMACIST

drug·store \'drəg-ˌstòr\ *n* : a retail shop where medicines and miscellaneous articles are sold

dru·id \'drü-əd\ *n, often cap* : one of an ancient Celtic priesthood appearing in Irish, Welsh, and Christian legends as magicians and wizards

¹**drum** \'drəm\ *n* 1 : a percussion instrument usu. consisting of a hollow cylinder with a skin or plastic head stretched over one or both ends that is beaten with the hands or with a stick 2 : the sound of a drum; *also* : a similar sound 3 : a drum-shaped object (as a structure or container)

²**drum** *vb* **drummed; drum·ming** 1 : to beat a drum 2 : to sound rhythmically : THROB, BEAT 3 : to summon or enlist by or as if by beating a drum ⟨*drummed* into service⟩ 4 : EXPEL — usu. used with *out* 5 : to drive or force by steady effort ⟨∼ the facts into memory⟩ 6 : to strike or tap repeatedly so as to produce rhythmic sounds

drum·beat \'drəm-ˌbēt\ *n* : a stroke on a drum or its sound

drum major *n* : the leader of a marching band

drum ma·jor·ette \-ˌmā-jə-'rət\ *n* : a girl or woman who leads a marching band; *also* : a baton twirler who accompanies a marching band

drum·mer \'drə-mər\ *n* 1 : one that plays a drum 2 : a traveling salesman

drum·stick \'drəm-ˌstik\ *n* 1 : a stick for beating a drum 2 : the lower segment of a fowl's leg

drum up *vb* 1 : to bring about by persistent effort ⟨*drum up* business⟩ 2 : INVENT, ORIGINATE

¹**drunk** *past part of* DRINK

²**drunk** \'drəŋk\ *adj* 1 : having the faculties impaired by alcohol ⟨∼ drivers⟩ 2 : dominated by an intense feeling ⟨∼ with power⟩ 3 : of, relating to, caused by, or characterized by intoxication

³**drunk** *n* 1 : a period of excessive drinking 2 : a drunken person

drunk·ard \'drəŋ-kərd\ *n* : one who is habitually drunk

drunk·en \'drəŋ-kən\ *adj* 1 : DRUNK 2 : given to habitual excessive use of alcohol 3 : of, relating to, or resulting from intoxication ⟨a ∼ brawl⟩ 4 : unsteady or lurching as if from intoxication ⟨walked with a ∼ shuffle⟩ — **drunk·en·ly** *adv* — **drunk·en·ness** *n*

drupe \'drüp\ *n* : a partly fleshy fruit (as a plum or cherry) having one seed enclosed in a hard inner shell

¹**dry** \'drī\ *adj* **dri·er** \'drī-ər\; **dri·est** \-əst\ 1 : free or freed from water or liquid ⟨∼ fruits⟩; *also* : not being in or under water 2 : characterized by lack of water or moisture ⟨∼ climate⟩ 3 : lacking freshness : STALE 4 : devoid of natural moisture; *also* : THIRSTY 5 : no longer liquid or sticky ⟨the ink is ∼⟩ 6 : not giving milk ⟨a ∼ cow⟩ 7 : marked by the absence of alcoholic beverages ⟨a ∼ dormitory⟩ 8 : prohibiting the making or distributing of alcoholic beverages 9 : not sweet ⟨∼ wine⟩ 10 : solid as opposed to liquid ⟨∼ groceries⟩ 11 : containing or employing no liquid 12 : SEVERE; *also* : UNINTERESTING, WEARISOME 13 : not productive ⟨a writer's ∼ spell⟩ 14 : marked by a matter-of-fact, ironic, or terse manner of expression ⟨∼ humor⟩ — **dri·ly** *or* **dry·ly** *adv* — **dry·ness** *n*

²**dry** *vb* **dried; dry·ing** : to make or become dry

³**dry** *n, pl* **drys** : PROHIBITIONIST

dry·ad \'drī-əd, -ˌad\ *n* : WOOD NYMPH

dry cell *n* : a battery whose contents are not spillable

dry–clean \'drī-ˌklēn\ *vb* : to clean (fabrics) chiefly with solvents other than water — **dry cleaning** *n*

dry dock \'drī-ˌdäk\ *n* : a dock that can be kept dry during ship construction or repair

dryer *var of* DRIER

dry farm·ing *n* : farming without irrigation in areas of limited rainfall — **dry–farm** *vb* — **dry farm·er** *n*

dry goods \'drī-ˌgúdz\ *n pl* : cloth goods (as fabrics, ribbon, and ready-to-wear clothing)

dry ice *n* : solid carbon dioxide

dry measure *n* : a series of units of capacity for dry commodities — see METRIC SYSTEM table, WEIGHT table
dry rot *n* : decay of timber in which fungi consume the wood's cellulose
dry run *n* : REHEARSAL, TRIAL
dry-wall \'drī-,wól\ *n* : a wallboard consisting of fiberboard, paper, or felt over a plaster core
Ds *symbol* darmstadtium
DSC *abbr* **1** Distinguished Service Cross **2** doctor of surgical chiropody
DSM *abbr* Distinguished Service Medal
DST *abbr* daylight saving time
DTP *abbr* diphtheria, tetanus, pertussis (vaccines)
d.t.'s \dē-'tēz\ *n pl, often cap D&T* : DELIRIUM TREMENS
du-al \'dü-əl, 'dyü-\ *adj* **1** : TWOFOLD, DOUBLE **2** : having a double character or nature — **du-al-ism** \-ə-,li-zəm\ *n* — **du-al-i-ty** \dü-'a-lə-tē, dyü-\ *n*
¹dub \'dəb\ *vb* **dubbed; dub-bing 1** : to confer knighthood upon **2** : NAME, NICKNAME
²dub *n* : a clumsy person : DUFFER
³dub *vb* **dubbed; dub-bing** : to add (sound effects) to a motion picture or to a radio or television production
du-bi-ety \dü-'bī-ə-tē, dyü-\ *n, pl* **-eties 1** : UNCERTAINTY **2** : a matter of doubt
du-bi-ous \'dü-bē-əs, 'dyü-\ *adj* **1** : UNCERTAIN **2** : QUESTIONABLE **3** : feeling doubt : UNDECIDED — **du-bi-ous-ly** *adv* — **du-bi-ous-ness** *n*
dub-ni-um \'düb-nē-əm, 'dəb-\ *n* : a short-lived radioactive chemical element produced artificially
du-cal \'dü-kəl, 'dyü-\ *adj* : of or relating to a duke or dukedom
duc-at \'də-kət\ *n* : a gold coin formerly used in various European countries
duch-ess \'də-chəs\ *n* **1** : the wife or widow of a duke **2** : a woman holding the rank of duke in her own right
duchy \'də-chē\ *n, pl* **duch-ies** : the territory of a duke or duchess : DUKEDOM
¹duck \'dək\ *n, pl* **ducks** : any of various swimming birds related to but smaller than geese and swans

¹duck

²duck *vb* **1** : to thrust or plunge under water **2** : to lower the head or body suddenly : BOW; *also* : DODGE **3** : to evade a duty, question, or responsibility ⟨~ the issue⟩
³duck *n* **1** : a durable closely woven usu. cotton fabric **2** *pl* : light clothes made of duck
duck-bill \'dək-,bil\ *n* : PLATYPUS
duck-ling \-liŋ\ *n* : a young duck
duck-pin \-,pin\ *n* **1** : a small bowling pin shorter and wider in the middle than a tenpin **2** *pl but sing in constr* : a bowling game using duckpins
duck sauce *n* : a thick sweet sauce made with fruits and seasonings and used in Chinese cuisine
duct \'dəkt\ *n* **1** : a tube or canal for conveying a bodily fluid **2** : a pipe or tube through which a fluid (as air) flows — **duct-less** *adj*
duc-tile \'dək-t⁰l\ *adj* **1** : capable of being drawn out into wire or thread **2** : easily led : DOCILE — **duc-til-i-ty** \,dək-'ti-lə-tē\ *n*
ductless gland *n* : an endocrine gland
duct tape *n* : a cloth adhesive tape orig. designed for sealing certain ducts and joints — **duct tape** *vb*
dud \'dəd\ *n* **1** *pl* : CLOTHING **2** : one that fails completely; *also* : a bomb or missile that fails to explode
dude \'düd, 'dyüd\ *n* **1** : DANDY 1 **2** : a city dweller; *esp* : an Easterner in the West **3** : FELLOW, GUY — sometimes used as an informal form of address
dude ranch *n* : a vacation resort offering activities (as horseback riding) typical of western ranches

dud-geon \'də-jən\ *n* : a fit or state of indignation ⟨in high ~⟩
¹due \'dü, 'dyü\ *adj* [ME, fr. AF *deu*, pp. of *dever* to owe, fr. L *debēre*] **1** : owed or owing as a debt **2** : owed or owing as a right ⟨is ~ a fair trial⟩ **3** : APPROPRIATE, FITTING ⟨with all ~ respect⟩ **4** : SUFFICIENT, ADEQUATE **5** : REGULAR, LAWFUL ⟨~ process of law⟩ **6** : ATTRIBUTABLE, ASCRIBABLE ⟨~ to negligence⟩ **7** : PAYABLE ⟨a bill ~ today⟩ **8** : SCHEDULED ⟨~ to arrive soon⟩
²due *n* **1** : something that rightfully belongs to one ⟨give everyone their ~⟩ **2** : DEBT **3** *pl* : FEES, CHARGES
³due *adv* : DIRECTLY, EXACTLY ⟨~ north⟩
du-el \'dü-əl, 'dyü-\ *n* : a combat between two persons; *esp* : one fought with weapons in front of witnesses — **duel** *vb* — **du-el-ist** \-ə-list\ *n*
du-en-de \dü-'en-dā\ *n* [Sp dial., charm, fr. Sp, ghost, goblin, fr. *duen de casa*, prob. fr. *dueño de casa* owner of a house] : the power to attract through personal magnetism and charm
du-en-na \dü-'e-nə, dyü-\ *n* **1** : an elderly woman in charge of the younger ladies in a Spanish or Portuguese family **2** : CHAPERONE
du-et \dü-'et, dyü-\ *n* : a musical composition for two performers
due to *prep* : BECAUSE OF
duf-fel bag \'də-fəl-\ *n* : a soft oblong bag for personal belongings
duf-fer \'də-fər\ *n* : an incompetent or clumsy person
dug *past and past part of* DIG
dug-out \'dəg-,aút\ *n* **1** : a boat made by hollowing out a log **2** : a shelter dug in the ground **3** : a low shelter facing a baseball diamond that contains the players' bench
DUI *n* : the act or crime of driving while under the influence of alcohol
duke \'dük, 'dyük\ *n* **1** : a sovereign ruler of a continental European duchy **2** : a nobleman of the highest rank; *esp* : a member of the highest grade of the British peerage **3** *slang* : FIST ⟨put up your ~s⟩ — **duke-dom** *n*
dul-cet \'dəl-sət\ *adj* **1** : pleasing to the ear **2** : AGREEABLE, SOOTHING
dul-ci-mer \'dəl-sə-mər\ *n* **1** : a stringed instrument of trapezoidal shape played with light hammers held in the hands **2** *or* **dul-ci-more** \-,mór\ : an American folk instrument with three or four strings that is held on the lap and played by plucking or strumming
¹dull \'dəl\ *adj* **1** : mentally slow : STUPID **2** : slow in perception or sensibility **3** : LISTLESS **4** : slow in action : SLUGGISH ⟨a ~ market⟩ **5** : lacking intensity ⟨a ~ pain⟩; *also* : not resonant or ringing **6** : BLUNT **7** : lacking brilliance or luster ⟨a ~ finish⟩ **8** : low in saturation and lightness ⟨~ color⟩ **9** : CLOUDY, OVERCAST ⟨~ weather⟩ **10** : TEDIOUS, UNINTERESTING ⟨a ~ lecture⟩ — **dull-ness** *also* **dul-ness** *n* — **dul-ly** *adv*
²dull *vb* : to make or become dull
dull-ard \'də-lərd\ *n* : a stupid person
du-ly \'dü-lē, 'dyü-\ *adv* : in a due manner or time
dumb \'dəm\ *adj* **1** *often offensive* : lacking the power of speech **2** : SILENT **3** : STUPID — **dumb-ly** *adv*
dumb-bell \'dəm-,bel\ *n* **1** : a bar with weights at the end used for exercise **2** : one who is stupid
dumb down *vb* : to lower the level of intelligence or intellectual content of
dumb-found *also* **dum-found** \,dəm-'faúnd\ *vb* : ASTONISH, AMAZE — **dumb-found-ing-ly** \-'faún-diŋ-lē\ *adv*
dumb-wait-er \'dəm-,wā-tər\ *n* : a small elevator for conveying food and dishes from one floor to another
dum-my \'də-mē\ *n, pl* **dummies 1** : a person who cannot speak; *also* : a stupid person **2** : the exposed hand in bridge played by the declarer in addition to that player's own hand; *also* : a bridge player whose hand is a dummy **3** : an imitative substitute for something; *also* : MANNEQUIN **4** : one seeming to act alone but really acting for another **5** : a mock-up of matter to be reproduced esp. by printing
¹dump \'dəmp\ *vb* : to let fall in a pile ⟨~ laundry on the floor⟩; *also* : to get rid of carelessly ⟨~ed her boyfriend⟩
²dump *n* **1** : a place for dumping something (as refuse) **2** : a reserve supply; *also* : a place where such supplies are kept ⟨an ammunition ~⟩ **3** : a messy or objectionable place

dump·ing \'dəm-piŋ\ *n* : the selling of goods in quantity at below market price

dump·ling \'dəm-pliŋ\ *n* **1** : a small mass of boiled or steamed dough **2** : a dessert of fruit baked in biscuit dough

dumps \'dəmps\ *n pl* : a gloomy state of mind : low spirits ⟨in the ∼⟩

dump truck *n* : a truck for transporting and dumping bulk material

dumpy \'dəm-pē\ *adj* **dump·i·er; -est 1** : short and thick in build **2** : SHABBY

¹**dun** \'dən\ *n* : a brownish dark gray

²**dun** *vb* **dunned; dun·ning 1** : to make persistent demands for payment **2** : PLAGUE, PESTER — **dun** *n*

dunce \'dəns\ *n* [John *Duns* Scotus, whose once accepted writings were ridiculed in the 16th cent.] : a slow stupid person

dun·der·head \'dən-dər-ˌhed\ *n* : DUNCE, BLOCKHEAD

dune \'dün, 'dyün\ *n* : a hill or ridge of sand piled up by the wind

dune buggy *n* : a motor vehicle with oversize tires for use on sand

¹**dung** \'dəŋ\ *n* : MANURE

²**dung** *vb* : to dress (land) with dung

dun·ga·ree \ˌdəŋ-gə-'rē\ *n* **1** : a heavy coarse cotton twill; *esp* : blue denim **2** *pl* : clothes made of blue denim

dun·geon \'dən-jən\ *n* [ME *dongeon* fortress, prison, fr. AF *donjun*, fr. VL **domnion-, *domnio* keep, mastery, fr. L *dominus* lord] : a dark prison commonly underground

dung·hill \'dəŋ-ˌhil\ *n* : a manure pile

dunk \'dəŋk\ *vb* **1** : to dip or submerge temporarily in liquid **2** : to submerge oneself in water **3** : to shoot a basketball into the basket from above the rim

duo \'dü-(ˌ)ō, 'dyü-\ *n, pl* **du·os 1** : DUET **2** : PAIR 3

duo·dec·i·mal \ˌdü-ə-'de-sə-məl, ˌdyü-\ *adj* : of, relating to, or being a system of numbers with a base of 12

du·o·de·num \ˌdü-ə-'dē-nəm, ˌdyü-, dü-'ä-də-nəm, dyü-\ *n, pl* **-de·na** \-'dē-nə, -də-nə\ *or* **-denums** : the first part of the small intestine extending from the stomach to the jejunum — **du·o·de·nal** \-'dē-nᵊl, -də-nəl\ *adj*

dup *abbr* **1** duplex **2** duplicate

¹**dupe** \'düp, 'dyüp\ *n* : one who is easily deceived or cheated : FOOL

²**dupe** *vb* **duped; dup·ing** : to make a dupe of : DECEIVE, FOOL

du·ple \'dü-pəl, 'dyü-\ *adj* : having two beats or a multiple of two beats to the measure ⟨∼ time⟩

¹**du·plex** \'dü-ˌpleks, 'dyü-\ *adj* : DOUBLE

²**duplex** *n* : something duplex; *esp* : a 2-family house

¹**du·pli·cate** \'dü-pli-kət, 'dyü-\ *adj* **1** : consisting of or existing in two corresponding or identical parts or examples **2** : being the same as another

²**du·pli·cate** \'dü-pli-ˌkāt, 'dyü-\ *vb* **-cat·ed; -cat·ing 1** : to make double or twofold **2** : to make a copy of — **du·pli·ca·tion** \ˌdü-pli-'kā-shən, ˌdyü-\ *n*

³**du·pli·cate** \-kət\ *n* : a thing that exactly resembles another in appearance, pattern, or content : COPY

du·pli·ca·tor \'dü-pli-ˌkā-tər, 'dyü-\ *n* : COPIER

du·plic·i·ty \du-'pli-sə-tē, dyü-\ *n, pl* **-ties** : the disguising of true intentions by deceptive words or action — **du·plic·i·tous** \-təs\ *adj* — **du·plic·i·tous·ly** *adv*

du·ra·ble \'dür-ə-bəl, 'dyür-\ *adj* : able to exist for a long time without significant deterioration ⟨∼ goods⟩ — **du·ra·bil·i·ty** \ˌdür-ə-'bi-lə-tē, ˌdyür-\ *n*

du·rance \'dür-əns, 'dyür-\ *n* : restraint by or as if by physical force ⟨held in ∼ vile⟩

du·ra·tion \du-'rā-shən, dyü-\ *n* : the time during which something exists or lasts

du·ress \du-'res, dyü-\ *n* : compulsion by threat ⟨confession made under ∼⟩

dur·ing \'dür-iŋ, 'dyür-\ *prep* **1** : THROUGHOUT ⟨swims every day ∼ the summer⟩ **2** : at some point in ⟨broke in ∼ the night⟩

dusk \'dəsk\ *n* **1** : the darker part of twilight esp. at night **2** : partial darkness

dusky \'dəs-kē\ *adj* **dusk·i·er; -est 1** : somewhat dark in color **2** : SHADOWY — **dusk·i·ly** \-kə-lē\ *adv* — **dusk·i·ness** *n*

¹**dust** \'dəst\ *n* **1** : fine particles of matter **2** : the particles into which something disintegrates **3** : something worth-

less **4** : the surface of the ground — **dust·less** *adj* — **dusty** *adj*

²**dust** *vb* **1** : to make free of or remove dust ⟨∼ the furniture⟩ **2** : to sprinkle with fine particles ⟨popcorn ∼ed with salt⟩ **3** : to sprinkle in the form of dust **4** : to defeat badly

dust bowl *n* : a region suffering from long droughts and dust storms

dust devil *n* : a small whirlwind containing sand or dust

dust·er \'dəs-tər\ *n* **1** : one that removes dust **2** : a dress-length housecoat **3** : one that scatters fine particles; *esp* : a device for applying insecticides to crops

dust·pan \'dəst-ˌpan\ *n* : a flat-ended pan for sweepings

dust storm *n* : a violent wind carrying dust across a dry region

dutch \'dəch\ *adv, often cap* : with each person paying his or her own way ⟨go ∼⟩

Dutch \'dəch\ *n* **1 Dutch** *pl* : the people of the Netherlands **2** : the language of the Netherlands — **Dutch** *adj* — **Dutch·man** \-mən\ *n*

Dutch elm disease *n* : a fungus disease of elms characterized by yellowing of the foliage, defoliation, and death

dutch treat *n, often cap D* : an entertainment (as a meal) for which each person pays his or her own way — **dutch treat** *adv, often cap D*

du·te·ous \'dü-tē-əs, 'dyü-\ *adj* : DUTIFUL, OBEDIENT

du·ti·able \'dü-tē-ə-bəl, 'dyü-\ *adj* : subject to a duty ⟨∼ imports⟩

du·ti·ful \'dü-ti-fəl, 'dyü-\ *adj* **1** : motivated by a sense of duty ⟨a ∼ son⟩ **2** : coming from or showing a sense of duty ⟨∼ affection⟩ — **du·ti·ful·ly** *adv* — **du·ti·ful·ness** *n*

du·ty \'dü-tē, 'dyü-\ *n, pl* **duties 1** : conduct or action required by one's occupation or position **2** : assigned service or business; *esp* : active military service **3** : a moral or legal obligation **4** : TAX **5** : the service required (as of a machine) : USE ⟨a heavy-*duty* tire⟩

DV *abbr* **1** [L *Deo volente*] God willing **2** Douay Version

DVD \ˌdē-ˌvē-'dē\ *n* [*digital video disk*] : a high-capacity optical disk format; *also* : an optical disk using such a format

DVM *abbr* doctor of veterinary medicine

¹**dwarf** \'dwȯrf\ *n, pl* **dwarfs** \'dwȯrfs\ *also* **dwarves** \'dwȯrvz\ : one that is much below normal size — **dwarf·ish** *adj* — **dwarf·ism** \'dwȯr-ˌfi-zəm\ *n*

²**dwarf** *vb* **1** : to restrict the growth or development of : STUNT **2** : to cause to appear smaller ⟨*dwarfed* by comparison⟩

dwell \'dwel\ *vb* **dwelt** \'dwelt\ *or* **dwelled** \'dweld, 'dwelt\; **dwell·ing** [ME, fr. OE *dwellan* to go astray, hinder] **1** : ABIDE, REMAIN **2** : RESIDE, EXIST **3** : to keep the attention directed **4** : to write or speak insistently — used with *on* or *upon* — **dwell·er** *n*

dwell·ing \'dwe-liŋ\ *n* : RESIDENCE

DWI \ˌdē-ˌdəb-əl-(ˌ)yü-'ī\ *n* [*driving while intoxicated*] : DUI

dwin·dle \'dwin-dᵊl\ *vb* **dwin·dled; dwin·dling** : to make or become steadily less : DIMINISH

dwt *abbr* pennyweight

Dy *symbol* dysprosium

dyb·buk \'di-bək\ *n, pl* **dyb·bu·kim** \ˌdi-bù-'kēm\ *also* **dybbuks** : a wandering soul believed in Jewish folklore to enter and possess a person

¹**dye** \'dī\ *n* **1** : color produced by dyeing **2** : material used for coloring or staining

²**dye** *vb* **dyed; dye·ing 1** : to impart a new color to esp. by impregnating with a dye **2** : to take up or impart color in dyeing — **dy·er** \'dī(-ə)r\ *n*

dye·stuff \'dī-ˌstəf\ *n* : DYE 2

dying *pres part of* DIE

dyke *chiefly Brit var of* DIKE

dy·nam·ic \dī-'na-mik\ *also* **dy·nam·i·cal** \-mi-kəl\ *adj* : of or relating to physical force producing motion : ENERGETIC, FORCEFUL

¹**dy·na·mite** \'dī-nə-ˌmīt\ *n* : an explosive made of nitroglycerin absorbed in a porous material; *also* : an explosive made without nitroglycerin

²**dynamite** *vb* **-mit·ed; -mit·ing** : to blow up with dynamite

³**dynamite** *adj* : TERRIFIC, WONDERFUL

dy·na·mo \'dī-nə-ˌmō\ *n, pl* **-mos 1** : an electrical generator **2** : a forceful energetic individual

dy·na·mom·e·ter \ˌdī-nə-'mä-mə-tər\ *n* : an instrument for measuring mechanical power (as of an engine)

dy·nas·ty \'dī-nəs-tē, -ˌnas-\ *n, pl* **-ties 1** : a succession of rulers of the same family **2** : a powerful group or family that maintains its position for a long time — **dy·nas·tic** \dī-'nas-tik\ *adj*

dys·en·tery \'dis-ᵊn-ˌter-ē\ *n, pl* **-ter·ies** : a disease marked by diarrhea with blood and mucus in the feces; *also* : DIARRHEA

dys·func·tion *also* **dis·func·tion** \dis-'fəŋk-shən\ *n* **1** : impaired or abnormal functioning ⟨liver ∼⟩ **2** : abnormal or unhealthy behavior within a group ⟨family ∼⟩ — **dys·func·tion·al** \-shə-nəl\ *adj*

dys·lex·ia \dis-'lek-sē-ə\ *n* : a learning disability marked by difficulty in reading, writing, and spelling — **dys·lex·ic** \-sik\ *adj or n*

dys·pep·sia \dis-'pep-shə, -sē-ə\ *n* : INDIGESTION — **dys·pep·tic** \-'pep-tik\ *adj or n*

dys·pla·sia \dis-'plā-zh(ē-)ə\ *n* : abnormal growth or development

dys·pro·si·um \dis-'prō-zē-əm\ *n* : a metallic chemical element that forms highly magnetic compounds

dys·tro·phy \'dis-trə-fē\ *n, pl* **-phies** : a disorder involving atrophy of muscular tissue; *esp* : MUSCULAR DYSTROPHY

dz *abbr* dozen

¹**e** \'ē\ *n, pl* **e's** *or* **es** \'ēz\ *often cap* **1** : the 5th letter of the English alphabet **2** : the base of the system of natural logarithms having the approximate value 2.71828 **3** : a grade rating a student's work as poor or failing

²**e** *abbr, often cap* **1** east; eastern **2** error **3** excellent

e- *comb form* : electronic ⟨e-commerce⟩

ea *abbr* each

¹**each** \'ēch\ *adj* : being one of the class named ⟨∼ player⟩

²**each** *pron* : every individual one

³**each** *adv* : APIECE ⟨cost five cents ∼⟩

each other *pron* : each of two or more in reciprocal action or relation ⟨looked at *each other*⟩

ea·ger \'ē-gər\ *adj* : marked by urgent or enthusiastic desire or interest ⟨∼ to learn⟩ **✦ Synonyms** AVID, ANXIOUS, ARDENT, KEEN — **ea·ger·ly** *adv* — **ea·ger·ness** *n*

¹**ea·gle** \'ē-gəl\ *n* **1** : a large bird of prey related to the hawks **2** : a score of two under par on a hole in golf

²**eagle** *vb* **ea·gled; ea·gling** : to score an eagle on a golf hole

ea·glet \'ē-glət\ *n* : a young eagle

-ean — see -AN

E and OE *abbr* errors and omissions excepted

¹**ear** \'ir\ *n* **1** : the organ of hearing; *also* : the outer part of this in a vertebrate **2** : something resembling a mammal's ear in shape, position, or function **3** : an ability to understand and appreciate something heard ⟨a good ∼ for music⟩ **4** : sympathetic attention

²**ear** *n* : the fruiting spike of a cereal (as wheat or Indian corn)

ear·ache \-ˌāk\ *n* : an ache or pain in the ear

ear·drum \-ˌdrəm\ *n* : a thin membrane that receives and transmits sound waves in the ear

eared \'ird\ *adj* : having ears esp. of a specified kind or number ⟨a long-*eared* dog⟩

ear·ful \'ir-ˌfúl\ *n* : a verbal outpouring (as of news, gossip, or complaint)

earl \'ərl\ *n* [ME *erl*, fr. OE *eorl* warrior, nobleman] : a member of the British peerage ranking below a marquess and above a viscount — **earl·dom** \-dəm\ *n*

ear·lobe \'ir-ˌlōb\ *n* : the pendent part of the ear

¹**ear·ly** \'ər-lē\ *adv* **ear·li·er; -est** : at an early time (as in a period or series)

²**early** *adj* **ear·li·er; -est** **1** : of, relating to, or occurring near the beginning **2** : ANCIENT, PRIMITIVE ⟨∼ tools⟩ **3** : occurring before the usual time ⟨an ∼ breakfast⟩; *also* : occurring in the near future

¹**ear·mark** \'ir-ˌmärk\ *n* : an identification mark (as on the ear of an animal); *also* : a distinguishing mark ⟨∼s of poverty⟩

²**earmark** *vb* **1** : to mark with an earmark **2** : to designate for a specific purpose ⟨money ∼ed for education⟩

ear·muff \-ˌməf\ *n* : one of a pair of ear coverings worn to protect against cold

earn \'ərn\ *vb* **1** : to receive as a return for service **2** : DESERVE, MERIT **✦ Synonyms** GAIN, SECURE, GET, OBTAIN, ACQUIRE, WIN — **earn·er** *n*

earned run *n* : a run in baseball that scores without benefit of an error before the fielding team has had a chance to make the third putout of the inning

earned run average *n* : the average number of earned runs per game scored against a pitcher in baseball

¹**ear·nest** \'ər-nəst\ *n* : an intensely serious state of mind ⟨spoke in ∼⟩

²**earnest** *adj* **1** : seriously intent and sober ⟨an ∼ face⟩ ⟨an ∼ attempt⟩ **2** : GRAVE, IMPORTANT **✦ Synonyms** SOLEMN, SEDATE, STAID — **ear·nest·ly** *adv* — **ear·nest·ness** *n*

³**earnest** *n* **1** : something of value given by a buyer to a seller to bind a bargain **2** : PLEDGE

earn·ings \'ər-niŋz\ *n pl* **1** : something (as wages) earned **2** : the balance of revenue after deduction of costs and expenses

ear·phone \'ir-ˌfōn\ *n* : a device that reproduces sound and is worn over or in the ear

ear·piece \-ˌpēs\ *n* : a part of an instrument which is placed against or in the ear; *esp* : EARPHONE

ear·plug \-ˌpləg\ *n* : a protective device for insertion into the opening of the ear

ear·ring \-ˌriŋ\ *n* : an ornament for the earlobe

ear·shot \-ˌshät\ *n* : range of hearing

ear·split·ting \-ˌspli-tiŋ\ *adj* : intolerably loud or shrill

earth \'ərth\ *n* **1** : SOIL, DIRT **2** : LAND, GROUND **3** *often cap* : the planet on which we live that is 3d in order from the sun — see PLANET table

earth·en \'ər-thən\ *adj* : made of earth or baked clay

earth·en·ware \-ˌwer\ *n* : slightly porous opaque pottery fired at low heat

earth·ling \'ərth-liŋ\ *n* : an inhabitant of the earth

earth·ly \'ərth-lē\ *adj* : having to do with the earth esp. as distinguished from heaven — **earth·li·ness** *n*

earth·quake \-ˌkwāk\ *n* : a shaking or trembling of a portion of the earth

earth science *n* : any of the sciences (as geology or meteorology) that deal with the earth or one of its parts

earth·shak·ing \'ərth-ˌshā-kiŋ\ *adj* : of great importance : MOMENTOUS

earth·ward \-wərd\ *also* **earth·wards** \-wərdz\ *adv* : toward the earth

earth·work \'ərth-ˌwərk\ *n* : an embankment or fortification of earth

earth·worm \-ˌwərm\ *n* : a long segmented worm found in damp soil

earthy \'ər-thē\ *adj* **earth·i·er; -est** **1** : of, relating to, or consisting of earth; *also* : suggesting earth ⟨∼ flavors⟩ **2** : PRACTICAL **4** **3** : COARSE, GROSS ⟨∼ humor⟩ — **earth·i·ness** *n*

ear·wax \'ir-ˌwaks\ *n* : the yellow waxy secretion from the ear

ear·wig \-ˌwig\ *n* : any of numerous insects with slender antennae and a pair of appendages resembling forceps at the end of the body

¹**ease** \'ēz\ *n* **1** : comfort of body or mind **2** : naturalness of manner **3** : freedom from difficulty or effort **✦ Synonyms** RELAXATION, REST, REPOSE, LEISURE

²**ease** *vb* **eased; eas·ing** **1** : to relieve from distress **2** : to lessen the pressure or tension of **3** : to make or become less difficult ⟨∼ credit⟩

ea·sel \'ē-zəl\ *n* [Dutch *ezel*, lit., ass] : a frame for supporting something (as an artist's canvas)

¹east \'ēst\ *adv* : to or toward the east

²east *adj* **1** : situated toward or at the east ⟨an ∼ window⟩ **2** : coming from the east ⟨an ∼ wind⟩

³east *n* **1** : the general direction of sunrise **2** : the compass point directly opposite to west **3** *cap* : regions or countries east of a specified or implied point — **east·er·ly** \'ē-stər-lē\ *adv or adj* — **east·ward** *adv or adj* — **eastwards** *adv*

Eas·ter \'ē-stər\ *n* : a church feast observed on a Sunday in March or April in commemoration of Christ's resurrection

east·ern \'ē-stərn\ *adj* **1** *often cap* : of, relating to, or characteristic of a region designated East **2** *cap* : of, relating to, or being the Christian churches originating in the Church of the Eastern Roman Empire **3** : lying toward or coming from the east — **East·ern·er** *n*

easy \'ē-zē\ *adj* **eas·i·er; -est** **1** : marked by ease ⟨an ∼ life⟩; *esp* : not causing distress or difficulty ⟨∼ tasks⟩ **2** : MILD, LENIENT ⟨be ∼ on him⟩ **3** : GRADUAL ⟨an ∼ slope⟩ **4** : LEISURELY ⟨an ∼ pace⟩ **5** : free from pain, trouble, or worry **6** : COMFORTABLE ⟨an ∼ chair⟩ **7** : showing ease : NATURAL ⟨an ∼ manner⟩ — **eas·i·ly** \'ē-zə-lē\ *adv* — **eas·i·ness** \-zē-nəs\ *n*

easy·go·ing \ē-zē-'gō-iŋ\ *adj* : relaxed and casual in style or manner

eat \'ēt\ *vb* **ate** \'āt\; **eat·en** \'ēt-ᵊn\; **eat·ing** **1** : to take in as food : take food **2** : to use up : DEVOUR **3** : CORRODE — **eat·able** *adj or n* — **eat·er** *n*

eat·ery \'ē-tə-rē\ *n, pl* **-er·ies** : LUNCHEONETTE, RESTAURANT

eaves \'ēvz\ *n pl* : the overhanging lower edge of a roof

eaves·drop \'ēvz-ˌdräp\ *vb* : to listen secretly — **eaves·drop·per** *n*

¹ebb \'eb\ *n* **1** : the flowing back from shore of water brought in by the tide **2** : a point or state of decline

²ebb *vb* **1** : to recede from the flood **2** : DECLINE ⟨his fortunes ∼ed⟩

EBCDIC \'eb-sə-ˌdik\ *n* [extended *b*inary *c*oded *d*ecimal *in*terchange *c*ode] : a computer code for representing alphanumeric information

Ebo·la \ē-bō-lə\ *n* : an often fatal hemorrhagic fever caused by a virus (**Ebola virus**) of African origin

¹eb·o·ny \'e-bə-nē\ *n, pl* **-nies** : a hard heavy blackish wood of various tropical trees related to the persimmon

²ebony *adj* **1** : made of or resembling ebony **2** : BLACK, DARK

ebul·lient \i-'bùl-yənt, -'bəl-\ *adj* **1** : BOILING, AGITATED **2** : EXUBERANT — **ebul·lience** \-yəns\ *n*

EC *abbr* European Community

ec·cen·tric \ik-'sen-trik\ *adj* **1** : deviating from a usual or accepted pattern **2** : deviating from a circular path ⟨∼ orbits⟩ **3** : set with axis or support off center ⟨an ∼ cam⟩; *also* : being off center ✦ *Synonyms* ERRATIC, QUEER, SINGULAR, CURIOUS, ODD — **eccentric** *n* — **ec·cen·tri·cal·ly** \-tri-k(ə-)lē\ *adv* — **ec·cen·tric·i·ty** \ˌek-ˌsen-'tri-sə-tē\ *n*

Eccles *abbr* Ecclesiastes

Ec·cle·si·as·tes \i-ˌklē-zē-'as-tēz\ *n* — see BIBLE table

ec·cle·si·as·tic \i-ˌklē-zē-'as-tik\ *n* : CLERGYMAN

ec·cle·si·as·ti·cal \-ti-kəl\ *or* **ec·cle·si·as·tic** \-tik\ *adj* : of or relating to a church esp. as an institution ⟨∼ art⟩ — **ec·cle·si·as·ti·cal·ly** \-ti-k(ə-)lē\ *adv*

Ec·cle·si·as·ti·cus \i-ˌklē-zē-'as-ti-kəs\ *n* — see BIBLE table

Ecclus *abbr* Ecclesiasticus

ECG *abbr* electrocardiogram

ech·e·lon \'e-shə-ˌlän\ *n* [F *échelon*, lit., rung of a ladder] **1** : a steplike arrangement (as of troops or airplanes) **2** : a level (as of authority or responsibility) within an organization

echi·i·na·cea \ˌe-ki-'nā-sē-ə, -shə\ *n* : the dried root of three composite herbs that is used primarily in herbal remedies to boost the immune system; *also* : any of these herbs

echi·no·derm \i-'kī-nə-ˌdərm\ *n* : any of a phylum of marine animals (as starfishes and sea urchins) having similar body parts (as the arms of a starfish) arranged around a central axis and often having a calcium-containing outer skeleton

echo \'e-kō\ *n, pl* **ech·oes** *also* **ech·os** : repetition of a sound caused by a reflection of the sound waves; *also* : the reflection of a radar signal by an object — **echo** *vb* — **echo·ic** \e-'kō-ik\ *adj*

echo·lo·ca·tion \ˌe-kō-lō-'kā-shən\ *n* : a process for locating distant or invisible objects by sound reflected back to the sender (as by a bat) from the objects

echt \'ekt\ *adj* [G] : TRUE, GENUINE ⟨an ∼ New Yorker⟩

éclair \ā-'kler\ *n* [F, lit., lightning] : an oblong shell of light pastry with whipped cream or custard filling

éclat \ā-'klä\ *n* [F] **1** : a dazzling effect or success **2** : ACCLAIM

eclec·tic \e-'klek-tik\ *adj* : selecting or made up of what seems best of varied sources — **eclectic** *n* — **eclec·ti·cism** \-'klek-tə-ˌsi-zəm\ *n*

¹eclipse \i-'klips\ *n* **1** : the total or partial obscuring of one heavenly body by another; *also* : a passing into the shadow of a heavenly body **2** : a falling into obscurity or decline

²eclipse *vb* **eclipsed; eclips·ing** : to cause an eclipse of; *also* : SURPASS

eclip·tic \i-'klip-tik\ *n* : the great circle of the celestial sphere that is the apparent path of the sun

ec·logue \'ek-ˌlòg, -ˌläg\ *n* : a pastoral poem

ECM *abbr* European Common Market

ecol *abbr* ecological; ecology

E. coli \ˌē-'kō-ˌlī\ *n, pl* **E. coli** : a rod-shaped bacterium that sometimes causes intestinal illness

ecol·o·gy \i-'kä-lə-jē, e-\ *n, pl* **-gies** [G *Ökologie*, fr. Gk *oikos* house + *logos* word] **1** : a branch of science concerned with the relationships between organisms and their environment **2** : the pattern of relations between one or more organisms and the environment — **eco·log·i·cal** \ˌē-kə-'lä-ji-kəl, ˌe-\ *also* **eco·log·ic** \-jik\ *adj* — **eco·log·i·cal·ly** \-ji-k(ə-)lē\ *adv* — **ecol·o·gist** \i-'kä-lə-jist, e-\ *n*

e–com·merce \'ē-ˌkä-(ˌ)mərs\ *n* : commerce conducted via the Internet

econ *abbr* economics; economist; economy

eco·nom·ic \ˌe-kə-'nä-mik, ˌē-\ *adj* : of or relating to the production, distribution, and consumption of goods and services

eco·nom·i·cal \-'nä-mi-kəl\ *adj* **1** : THRIFTY **2** : operating with little waste or at a saving ✦ *Synonyms* FRUGAL, SPARING, PROVIDENT — **eco·nom·i·cal·ly** \-k(ə-)lē\ *adv*

eco·nom·ics \ˌe-kə-'nä-miks, ˌē-\ *n sing or pl* : a social science dealing with the production, distribution, and consumption of goods and services — **econ·o·mist** \i-'kä-nə-mist\ *n*

econ·o·mise *Brit var of* ECONOMIZE

econ·o·mize \i-'kä-nə-ˌmīz\ *vb* **-mized; -miz·ing** : to practice economy : be frugal — **econ·o·miz·er** *n*

¹econ·o·my \i-'kä-nə-mē\ *n, pl* **-mies** [MF *yconomie*, fr. ML *oeconomia*, fr. Gk *oikonomia*, fr. *oikonomos* household manager, fr. *oikos* house + *nemein* to manage] **1** : thrifty and efficient use of resources; *also* : an instance of this **2** : manner of arrangement or functioning : ORGANIZATION **3** : an economic system ⟨a money ∼⟩

²economy *adj* : ECONOMICAL ⟨∼ cars⟩

eco·sys·tem \'ē-kō-ˌsis-təm, 'e-\ *n* : the complex of an ecological community and its environment functioning as a unit in nature

eco·tour·ism \ˌe-kō-'tùr-ˌi-zəm, ˌe-\ *n* : the touring of natural habitats in a manner meant to minimize ecological impact — **eco·tour·ist** \-'tùr-ist\ *n*

ecru \'e-krü, 'ā-\ *n* [F *écru*, lit., unbleached] : BEIGE — **ecru** *adj*

ec·sta·sy \'ek-stə-sē\ *n, pl* **-sies** **1** : extreme and usu. rapturous emotional excitement **2** *often cap* : an illicit drug with hallucinogenic properties that is chemically related to amphetamine — **ec·stat·ic** \ek-'sta-tik, ik-\ *adj* — **ec·stat·i·cal·ly** \-ti-k(ə-)lē\ *adv*

Ecua *abbr* Ecuador

ec·u·men·i·cal \ˌe-kyù-'me-ni-kəl\ *adj* **1** : general in extent or influence **2** : promoting or tending toward worldwide Christian unity — **ec·u·men·i·cal·ly** \-k(ə-)lē\ *adv*

ec·ze·ma \ig-'zē-mə, 'eg-zə-mə, 'ek-sə-\ *n* : an itching skin inflammation with oozing and then crusted lesions — **ec·zem·a·tous** \ig-'ze-mə-təs\ *adj*

ed *abbr* **1** edited; edition; editor **2** education

¹-ed \d *after a vowel or* b, g, j, l, m, n, ŋ, r, t͟h, v, z, zh; əd, id *after* d, t; t *after other sounds*\ *vb suffix or adj suffix* **1** —

used to form the past participle of regular weak verbs ⟨ended⟩ ⟨faded⟩ ⟨tried⟩ ⟨patted⟩ 2 : having : characterized by ⟨cultured⟩ ⟨2-legged⟩; also : having the characteristics of ⟨bigoted⟩

²-ed vb suffix — used to form the past tense of regular weak verbs ⟨judged⟩ ⟨denied⟩ ⟨dropped⟩

Edam \'ē-dəm, -₁dam\ n : a yellow Dutch pressed cheese made in balls

ed·dy \'e-dē\ n, pl **eddies** : WHIRLPOOL — **eddy** vb

edel·weiss \'ā-d³l-₁wīs, -₁vīs\ n [G, fr. edel noble + weiss white] : a small perennial woolly composite herb that grows high in the Alps

ede·ma \i-'dē-mə\ n : abnormal accumulation of watery fluid in connective tissue or in a serous cavity — **edem·a·tous** \-'de-mə-təs\ adj

Eden \'ē-d³n\ n : PARADISE 2

¹edge \'ej\ n 1 : the cutting side of a blade 2 : SHARPNESS; also : FORCE, EFFECTIVENESS 3 : the line where something begins or ends; also : the area adjoining such an edge 4 : ADVANTAGE ⟨has an ∼ on the competition⟩ — **edged** \'ejd\ adj

²edge vb **edged; edg·ing** 1 : to give or form an edge 2 : to move or force gradually ⟨∼ into a crowd⟩ 3 : to defeat by a small margin ⟨edged out her opponent⟩ — **edg·er** n

edge·wise \'ej-₁wīz\ adv : SIDEWAYS

edg·ing \'e-jiŋ\ n : something that forms an edge or border ⟨a lace ∼⟩

edgy \'e-jē\ adj **edg·i·er; -est** 1 : SHARP ⟨an ∼ tone⟩ 2 : TENSE, NERVOUS 3 : having a bold, provocative, or unconventional quality — **edg·i·ness** n

ed·i·ble \'e-də-bəl\ adj : fit or safe to be eaten — **ed·i·bil·i·ty** \₁e-də-'bi-lə-tē\ n — **edible** n

edict \'ē-₁dikt\ n : ORDER, DECREE

ed·i·fi·ca·tion \₁e-də-fə-'kā-shən\ n : instruction and improvement esp. in morality — **ed·i·fy** \'e-də-₁fī\ vb

ed·i·fice \'e-də-fəs\ n : a usu. large building

ed·it \'e-dət\ vb 1 : to revise, assemble, or prepare for publication or release (as a motion picture) 2 : to direct the publication and policies of (as a newspaper) 3 : DELETE — **ed·i·tor** \'e-də-tər\ n — **ed·i·tor·ship** n — **ed·i·tress** \-trəs\ n

edi·tion \i-'di-shən\ n 1 : the form in which a text is published 2 : the total number of copies (as of a book) published at one time 3 : VERSION

¹ed·i·to·ri·al \₁e-də-'tȯr-ē-əl\ adj 1 : of or relating to an editor or editing 2 : being or resembling an editorial — **ed·i·to·ri·al·ly** adv

²editorial n : an article (as in a newspaper) giving the views of the editors or publishers; also : an expression of opinion resembling an editorial ⟨a television ∼⟩

ed·i·to·ri·al·ize \₁e-də-'tȯr-ē-ə-₁līz\ vb **-ized; -iz·ing** 1 : to express an opinion in an editorial 2 : to introduce opinions into factual reporting 3 : to express an opinion — **ed·i·to·ri·al·i·za·tion** \-₁tȯr-ē-ə-lə-'zā-shən\ n — **ed·i·to·ri·al·iz·er** n

EDP abbr electronic data processing

EDT abbr Eastern daylight (saving) time

educ abbr education; educational

ed·u·ca·ble \'e-jə-kə-bəl\ adj : capable of being educated

ed·u·cate \'e-jə-₁kāt\ vb **-cat·ed; -cat·ing** [ME, to rear, fr. L educatus, pp. of educare, fr. educere to lead forth, draw out] 1 : to provide with schooling 2 : to develop mentally and morally; also : to provide with information ◆ Synonyms TRAIN, DISCIPLINE, SCHOOL, INSTRUCT, TEACH — **ed·u·ca·tor** \-₁kā-tər\ n

ed·u·ca·tion \₁e-jə-'kā-shən\ n 1 : the action or process of educating or being educated 2 : a field of study dealing with methods of teaching and learning — **ed·u·ca·tion·al** \-shə-nəl\ adj — **ed·u·ca·tion·al·ly** adv

educational television n 1 : television that provides educational programming (as for students) 2 : television (as public television) that receives support from contributors

educe \i-'düs, -'dyüs\ vb **educed; educ·ing** 1 : ELICIT, EVOKE 2 : DEDUCE ◆ Synonyms EXTRACT, EVINCE, EXTORT

ed·u·tain·ment \₁e-jə-'tān-mənt\ n : entertainment that is designed to be educational

¹-ee \'ē, (₁)ē\ n suffix 1 : one that receives or benefits from (a specified action or thing) ⟨grantee⟩ ⟨patentee⟩ 2 : a person who does (a specified action) ⟨escapee⟩

²-ee n suffix 1 : a particular esp. small kind of ⟨bootee⟩ 2 : one resembling or suggestive of ⟨goatee⟩

EE abbr electrical engineer

EEC abbr European Economic Community

EEG abbr 1 electroencephalogram 2 electroencephalograph

eel \'ēl\ n : any of numerous snakelike bony fishes with a smooth slimy skin

EEO abbr equal employment opportunity

ee·rie also **ee·ry** \'ir-ē\ adj **ee·ri·er; -est** : WEIRD, UNCANNY — **ee·ri·ly** \'ir-ə-lē\ adv

eff abbr efficiency

ef·face \i-'fās, e-\ vb **ef·faced; ef·fac·ing** : to obliterate or obscure by or as if by rubbing out ◆ Synonyms ERASE, DELETE, ANNUL, CANCEL, EXPUNGE — **ef·face·able** adj — **ef·face·ment** n

¹ef·fect \i-'fekt\ n 1 : MEANING, INTENT 2 : RESULT 3 : APPEARANCE 4 : INFLUENCE 5 pl : GOODS, POSSESSIONS 6 : the quality or state of being operative : OPERATION ◆ Synonyms CONSEQUENCE, OUTCOME, UPSHOT, AFTERMATH, ISSUE

²effect vb : to cause to happen ⟨∼ repairs⟩ ⟨∼ changes⟩

ef·fec·tive \i-'fek-tiv\ adj 1 : producing a decisive or desired effect 2 : IMPRESSIVE, STRIKING 3 : ready for service or action ⟨∼ manpower⟩ 4 : being in effect — **ef·fec·tive·ly** adv — **ef·fec·tive·ness** n

ef·fec·tu·al \i-'fek-chə-wəl\ adj : producing an intended effect : ADEQUATE — **ef·fec·tu·al·ly** adv

ef·fec·tu·ate \i-'fek-chə-₁wāt\ vb **-at·ed; -at·ing** : BRING ABOUT, EFFECT

ef·fem·i·nate \ə-'fe-mə-nət\ adj : marked by qualities more typical of women than men — **ef·fem·i·na·cy** \-nə-sē\ n

ef·fen·di \e-'fen-dē\ n [Turk efendi master, fr. ModGk aphentēs, alter. of Gk authentēs] : a man of property, authority, or education in an eastern Mediterranean country

ef·fer·ent \'e-fə-rənt\ adj : bearing or conducting outward from a more central part ⟨∼ nerves⟩

ef·fer·vesce \₁e-fər-'ves\ vb **-vesced; -vesc·ing** 1 : to bubble and hiss as gas escapes 2 : to show liveliness or exhilaration — **ef·fer·ves·cence** \-'ve-s³ns\ n — **ef·fer·ves·cent** \-s³nt\ adj — **ef·fer·ves·cent·ly** adv

ef·fete \e-'fēt\ adj 1 : having lost character, vitality, or strength; also : DECADENT 2 : EFFEMINATE

ef·fi·ca·cious \₁e-fə-'kā-shəs\ adj : producing an intended effect ⟨∼ remedies⟩ ◆ Synonyms EFFECTUAL, EFFECTIVE, EFFICIENT — **ef·fi·ca·cy** \'e-fi-kə-sē\ n

ef·fi·cient \i-'fi-shənt\ adj : productive of desired effects esp. without waste — **ef·fi·cien·cy** \-shən-sē\ n — **ef·fi·cient·ly** adv

ef·fi·gy \'e-fə-jē\ n, pl **-gies** : IMAGE; esp : a crude figure of a hated person

ef·flo·res·cence \₁e-flə-'re-s³ns\ n 1 : the period or state of flowering 2 : the action or process of developing 3 : fullness of development : FLOWERING

ef·flu·ence \'e-₁flü-əns\ n : something that flows out

ef·flu·ent \'e-₁flü-ənt\ n : something that flows out; esp : a fluid (as sewage) discharged as waste — **effluent** adj

ef·flu·vi·um \e-'flü-vē-əm\ n, pl **-via** \-vē-ə\ also **-vi·ums** [L, outflow] 1 : a usu. unpleasant emanation 2 : a by-product usu. in the form of waste

ef·fort \'e-fərt\ n 1 : EXERTION, ENDEAVOR; also : a product of effort 2 : active or applied force — **ef·fort·less** adj — **ef·fort·less·ly** adv

ef·fron·tery \i-'frən-tə-rē\ n, pl **-ter·ies** : shameless boldness : IMPUDENCE ◆ Synonyms TEMERITY, AUDACITY, BRASS, GALL, NERVE, CHUTZPAH

ef·ful·gence \i-'fúl-jəns, -'fəl-\ n : radiant splendor : BRILLIANCE — **ef·ful·gent** \-jənt\ adj

ef·fu·sion \i-'fyü-zhən, e-\ n : a gushing forth; also : unrestrained utterance — **ef·fuse** \-'fyüz, e-\ vb — **ef·fu·sive** \i-'fyü-siv, e-\ adj — **ef·fu·sive·ly** adv

eft \'eft\ n : NEWT

EFT or **EFTS** abbr electronic funds transfer (system)

e.g. abbr [L exempli gratia] for example

Eg abbr Egypt; Egyptian

egal·i·tar·i·an·ism \i-₁ga-lə-'ter-ē-ə-₁ni-zəm\ n : a belief in human equality esp. in social, political, and economic affairs — **egal·i·tar·i·an** adj or n

¹egg \'eg\ vb [ME, fr. ON eggja; akin to OE ecg edge] : to urge to action — usu. used with on

²egg n [ME egge, fr. ON egg; akin to OE ǣg egg, L ovum] 1

: a rounded usu. hard-shelled reproductive body esp. of birds and reptiles from which the young hatches; *also* : the egg of the common domestic chicken as an article of food   **2** : a germ cell produced by a female

egg·beat·er \'eg-,bē-tər\ *n* : a hand-operated kitchen utensil for beating, stirring, or whipping

egg cell *n* : EGG 2

egg foo yong *or* **egg foo young** *or* **egg foo yung** \-'fü-'yəŋ\ : a fried egg patty

egg·head \-,hed\ *n* : INTELLECTUAL, HIGHBROW

egg·nog \-,näg\ *n* : a drink consisting of eggs beaten with sugar, milk or cream, and often alcoholic liquor

egg·plant \-,plant\ *n* : the edible usu. large and dark purplish fruit of a plant related to the potato; *also* : the plant

egg roll *n* : a thin egg-dough casing filled with minced vegetables and often bits of meat and usu. deep-fried

egg·shell \'eg-,shel\ *n* : the hard exterior covering of an egg

egis *var of* AEGIS

eg·lan·tine \'e-glən-,tīn, -,tēn\ *n* : SWEETBRIAR

ego \'ē-gō\ *n, pl* **egos** [L, I]   **1** : the self as distinguished from others   **2** : the one of the three divisions of the psyche in psychoanalytic theory that is the organized conscious mediator between the person and reality

ego·cen·tric \,ē-gō-'sen-trik\ *adj* : concerned or overly concerned with the self; *esp* : SELF-CENTERED

ego·ism \'ē-gō-,i-zəm\ *n*   **1** : a doctrine holding self-interest to be the motive or the valid end of action   **2** : excessive concern for oneself with or without exaggerated feelings of self-importance — **ego·ist** \-ist\ *n* — **ego·is·tic** \,ē-gō-'is-tik\ *adj* — **ego·is·ti·cal·ly** *adv*

ego·tism \'ē-gə-,ti-zəm\ *n*   **1** : the practice of talking about oneself too much   **2** : an exaggerated sense of self-importance : CONCEIT — **ego·tist** \-tist\ *n* — **ego·tis·tic** \,ē-gə-'tis-tik\ *or* **ego·tis·ti·cal** \-ti-kəl\ *adj* — **ego·tis·ti·cal·ly** *adv*

ego trip *n* : an act that enhances and satisfies one's ego

egre·gious \i-'grē-jəs\ *adj* [L *egregius* outstanding, fr. *ex, e* out of + *greg-, grex* flock, herd] : notably bad : FLAGRANT — **egre·gious·ly** *adv* — **egre·gious·ness** *n*

egress \'ē-,gres\ *n* : a way out : EXIT

egret \'ē-grət, i-'gret\ *n* : any of various herons that bear long plumes during the breeding season

egret

Egyp·tian \i-'jip-shən\ *n*   **1** : a native or inhabitant of Egypt   **2** : the language of the ancient Egyptians from earliest times to about the 3d century A.D. — **Egyptian** *adj*

ei·der \'ī-dər\ *n* : any of several northern sea ducks that yield a soft down

ei·der·down \-,daůn\ *n*   **1** : the down of the eider   **2** : a comforter filled with eiderdown

ei·do·lon \ī-'dō-lən\ *n, pl* **-lons** *or* **-la** \-lə\   **1** : PHANTOM   **2** : IDEAL

eight \'āt\ *n*   **1** : one more than seven   **2** : the 8th in a set or series   **3** : something having eight units — **eight** *adj or pron* — **eighth** \'ātth\ *adj or adv or n*

eight ball *n* : a black pool ball numbered 8 — **behind the eight ball** : in a highly disadvantageous position

eigh·teen \'āt-'tēn\ *n* : one more than 17 — **eighteen** *adj or pron* — **eigh·teenth** \-'tēnth\ *adj or n*

eighty \'ā-tē\ *n, pl* **eight·ies** : eight times 10 — **eight·i·eth** \'ā-tē-əth\ *adj or n* — **eighty** *adj or pron*

ein·stei·ni·um \īn-'stī-nē-əm\ *n* : an artificially produced radioactive element

ei·re·nic *chiefly Brit var of* IRENIC

¹ei·ther \'ē-thər, 'ī-\ *adj*   **1** : being the one and the other of two : EACH ⟨trees on ~ side⟩   **2** : being the one or the other of two ⟨take ~ road⟩

²either *pron* : the one or the other

³either *conj* — used as a function word before the first of two or more words or word groups of which the last is preceded by *or* to indicate that they represent alternatives ⟨a statement is ~ true or false⟩

ejac·u·late \i-'ja-kyə-,lāt\ *vb* **-lat·ed; -lat·ing**   **1** : to eject a fluid (as semen)   **2** : to utter suddenly : EXCLAIM — **ejac·u·la·tion** \-,ja-kyə-'lā-shən\ *n* — **ejac·u·la·to·ry** \'ja-kyə-lə-,tór-ē\ *adj*

eject \i-'jekt\ *vb* : to drive or throw out or off ♦ **Synonyms** EXPEL, OUST, EVICT, DISMISS — **ejec·tion** \-'jek-shən\ *n*

eke \'ēk\ *vb* **eked; ek·ing** : to gain, supplement, or extend usu. with effort — usu. used with *out* ⟨~ out a living⟩

EKG *abbr* [G *Elektrokardiogramm*] electrocardiogram; electrocardiograph

el *abbr* elevation

¹elab·o·rate \i-'la-bə-rət, -'la-brət\ *adj*   **1** : planned or carried out with great care   **2** : being complex and usu. ornate — **elab·o·rate·ly** *adv* — **elab·o·rate·ness** *n*

²elab·o·rate \i-'la-bə-,rāt\ *vb* **-rat·ed; -rat·ing**   **1** : to build up from simpler ingredients   **2** : to work out in detail : develop fully — **elab·o·ra·tion** \-,la-bə-'rā-shən\ *n*

élan \ā-'lä[n]\ *n* [F] : ARDOR, SPIRIT

eland \'ē-lənd, -,land\ *n, pl* **eland** *also* **elands** [Afrikaans] : either of two large African antelopes with spirally twisted horns in both sexes

elapse \i-'laps\ *vb* **elapsed; elaps·ing** : to slip by : PASS

elas·tic \i-'las-tik\ *adj*   **1** : SPRINGY   **2** : FLEXIBLE, PLIABLE ⟨an ~ bandage⟩   **3** : ADAPTABLE ⟨an ~ plan⟩ ♦ **Synonyms** RESILIENT, SUPPLE, STRETCH — **elas·tic·i·ty** \-,las-'ti-sə-tē, ,ē-,las-\ *n*

²elastic *n*   **1** : elastic material   **2** : a rubber band

elate \i-'lāt\ *vb* **elat·ed; elat·ing** : to fill with joy — **ela·tion** \-'lā-shən\ *n*

¹el·bow \'el-,bō\ *n* [ME *elbowe*, fr. OE *elboga*, fr. *el-* (akin to *eln* ell) + *boga* bow]   **1** : the joint of the arm; *also* : the outer curve of the bent arm   **2** : a bend or joint resembling an elbow in shape

²elbow *vb* : to push aside with the elbow; *also* : to make one's way by elbowing

el·bow room \'el-,bō-,rüm, -,rům\ *n* : enough space for work or operation

¹el·der \'el-dər\ *n* : ELDERBERRY 2

²elder *adj*   **1** : OLDER   **2** : EARLIER, FORMER   **3** : of higher rank : SENIOR

³elder *n*   **1** : an older individual : SENIOR   **2** : one having authority by reason of age and experience   **3** : a church officer

el·der·ber·ry \'el-dər-,ber-ē\ *n*   **1** : the edible black or red fruit of a shrub or tree related to the honeysuckle and bearing flat clusters of small white or pink flowers   **2** : a tree or shrub bearing elderberries

el·der·ly \'el-dər-lē\ *adj*   **1** : rather old; *esp* : past middle age   **2** : of, relating to, or characteristic of later life

el·dest \'el-dəst\ *adj* : of the greatest age

El Do·ra·do \,el-də-'rä-dō, -'rä-\ *n* [Sp, lit., the gilded one] : a place of vast riches, abundance, or opportunity

elec *abbr* electric; electrical; electricity

¹elect \i-'lekt\ *adj*   **1** : CHOSEN, SELECT   **2** : elected but not yet installed in office ⟨the president-*elect*⟩

²elect *n, pl* **elect**   **1** : a selected person   **2** *pl* : a select or exclusive group

³elect *vb*   **1** : to select by vote (as for office or membership)   **2** : CHOOSE, PICK

elec·tion \i-'lek-shən\ *n*   **1** : an act or process of electing   **2** : the fact of being elected

elec·tion·eer \i-,lek-shə-'nir\ *vb* : to work for the election of a candidate or party

¹elec·tive \i-'lek-tiv\ *adj*   **1** : chosen or filled by election   **2** : permitting a choice : OPTIONAL

²elective *n* : an elective course or subject of study

elec·tor \i-'lek-tər\ *n*   **1** : one qualified to vote in an election   **2** : one elected to an electoral college — **elec·tor·al** \i-'lek-tə-rəl\ *adj*

electoral college n : a body of electors who elect the president and vice president of the U.S.

elec·tor·ate \i-'lek-tə-rət\ n : a body of persons entitled to vote

elec·tric \i-'lek-trik\ adj [NL electricus produced from amber by friction, electric, fr. ML, of amber, fr. L electrum amber, fr. Gk ēlektron] **1** or **elec·tri·cal** \-tri-kəl\ : of, relating to, operated by, or produced by electricity **2** : ELECTRIFYING, THRILLING ⟨an ∼ performance⟩ — **elec·tri·cal·ly** adv

electrical storm n : THUNDERSTORM

electric chair n : a chair used to carry out the death penalty by electrocution

electric eye n : PHOTOELECTRIC CELL

elec·tri·cian \i-,lek-'tri-shən\ n : a person who installs, operates, or repairs electrical equipment

elec·tric·i·ty \i-,lek-'tri-sə-tē\ n, pl **-ties** **1** : a form of energy that occurs naturally (as in lightning) or is produced (as in a generator) and that is expressed in terms of the movement and interaction of electrons **2** : electric current

elec·tri·fy \i-'lek-trə-,fī\ vb **-fied; -fy·ing** **1** : to charge with electricity **2** : to equip for use of electric power **3** : THRILL — **elec·tri·fi·ca·tion** \i-,lek-trə-fə-'kā-shən\ n

elec·tro·car·dio·gram \i-,lek-trō-'kär-dē-ə-,gram\ n : the tracing made by an electrocardiograph

elec·tro·car·dio·graph \-,graf\ n : a device for recording the changes of electrical potential occurring during the heartbeat — **elec·tro·car·dio·graph·ic** \-,kär-dē-ə-'gra-fik\ adj — **elec·tro·car·di·og·ra·phy** \-dē-'ä-grə-fē\ n

elec·tro·chem·is·try \-'ke-mə-strē\ n : a branch of chemistry that deals with the relation of electricity to chemical changes — **elec·tro·chem·i·cal** \-'ke-mi-kəl\ adj

elec·tro·cute \i-'lek-trə-,kyüt\ vb **-cut·ed; -cut·ing** **1** : to kill (a criminal) by electricity **2** : to kill by electric shock — **elec·tro·cu·tion** \-,lek-trə-'kyü-shən\ n

elec·trode \i-'lek-,trōd\ n : a conductor used to establish electrical contact with a nonmetallic part of a circuit

elec·tro·en·ceph·a·lo·gram \i-,lek-trō-in-'se-fə-lə-,gram\ n : the tracing made by an electroencephalograph

elec·tro·en·ceph·a·lo·graph \-,graf\ n : an apparatus for detecting and recording brain waves — **elec·tro·en·ceph·a·lo·graph·ic** \-,se-fə-lə-'gra-fik\ adj — **elec·tro·en·ceph·a·log·ra·phy** \-'lä-grə-fē\ n

elec·trol·o·gist \i-,lek-'trä-lə-jist\ n : one that uses electrical means to remove hair, warts, moles, and birthmarks from the body

elec·trol·y·sis \i-,lek-'trä-lə-səs\ n **1** : the production of chemical changes by passage of an electric current through an electrolyte **2** : the destruction of hair roots with an electric current — **elec·tro·lyt·ic** \-trə-'li-tik\ adj

elec·tro·lyte \i-'lek-trə-,līt\ n : a nonmetallic electric conductor in which current is carried by the movement of ions; also : a substance whose solution or molten form is such a conductor

elec·tro·mag·net \i-,lek-trō-'mag-nət\ n : a core of magnetic material (as iron) surrounded by a coil of wire through which an electric current is passed to magnetize the core

elec·tro·mag·net·ic \-mag-'ne-tik\ adj : of, relating to, or produced by electromagnetism — **elec·tro·mag·net·i·cal·ly** adv

electromagnetic radiation n : energy in the form of electromagnetic waves; also : a series of electromagnetic waves

electromagnetic wave n : a wave (as a radio wave, an X-ray, or a wave of visible light) that consists of associated electric and magnetic effects and that travels at the speed of light

elec·tro·mag·ne·tism \i-,lek-trō-'mag-nə-,ti-zəm\ n **1** : magnetism developed by a current of electricity **2** : a natural force responsible for interactions between charged particles which result from their charge

elec·tro·mo·tive force \i-,lek-trə-'mō-tiv-\ n : the potential difference derived from an electrical source per unit quantity of electricity passing through the source

elec·tron \i-'lek-,trän\ n : a negatively charged elementary particle

elec·tron·ic \i-,lek-'trä-nik\ adj **1** : of or relating to electrons or electronics **2** : involving a computer — **elec·tron·i·cal·ly** \-ni-k(ə-)lē\ adv

electronic mail n : E-MAIL

elec·tron·ics \i-,lek-'trä-niks\ n **1** : the physics of electrons and electronic devices **2** : electronic components, devices, or equipment

electron microscope n : an instrument in which a beam of electrons is used to produce an enlarged image of a minute object

electron tube n : a device in which electrical conduction by electrons takes place within a sealed container and which is used for the controlled flow of electrons

electron volt n : a unit of energy equal to 1.60×10^{-19} joule

elec·tro·pho·re·sis \i-,lek-trə-fə-'rē-səs\ n : the movement of suspended particles through a medium (as paper or gel) by an electromotive force — **elec·tro·pho·ret·ic** \-'re-tik\ adj

elec·tro·plate \i-'lek-trə-,plāt\ vb : to coat (as with metal) by electrolysis

elec·tro·shock therapy \i-'lek-trō-,shäk-\ n : the treatment of mental disorder by applying electric current to the head and inducing convulsions

elec·tro·stat·ics \i-,lek-trə-'sta-tiks\ n : physics dealing with the interactions of stationary electric charges

el·ee·mos·y·nary \,e-li-'mäs-sə-,ner-ē\ adj : CHARITABLE

el·e·gance \'e-li-gəns\ n **1** : refined gracefulness; also : tasteful richness (as of design) **2** : something marked by elegance — **el·e·gant** \-gənt\ adj — **el·e·gant·ly** adv

ele·giac \,e-lə-'jī-ək, -,ak\ adj : of or relating to an elegy

el·e·gy \'e-lə-jē\ n, pl **-gies** : a song, poem, or speech expressing grief for one who is dead; also : a reflective poem usu. melancholy in tone

elem abbr elementary

el·e·ment \'e-lə-mənt\ n **1** pl : weather conditions; esp : severe weather ⟨boards exposed to the ∼s⟩ **2** : natural environment ⟨in her ∼⟩ **3** : a constituent part **4** pl : the simplest principles (as of an art or science) : RUDIMENTS **5** : a member of a mathematical set **6** : any of the fundamental substances that consist of atoms of only one kind ♦ **Synonyms** COMPONENT, INGREDIENT, CONSTITUENT — **el·e·men·tal** \,e-lə-'ment-ᵊl\ adj

el·e·men·ta·ry \,e-lə-'men-trē, -tə-rē\ adj **1** : SIMPLE, RUDIMENTARY; also : of, relating to, or teaching the basic subjects of education

elementary particle n : a subatomic particle of matter and energy that does not appear to be made up of other smaller particles

elementary school n : a school usu. including the first six or the first eight grades

el·e·phant \'e-lə-fənt\ n, pl **elephants** also **elephant** : any of a family of huge thickset nearly hairless mammals that have the snout lengthened into a trunk and two long curving pointed ivory tusks

el·e·phan·ti·a·sis \,e-lə-fən-'tī-ə-səs\ n, pl **-a·ses** \-,sēz\ : enlargement and thickening of tissues in response esp. to infection by minute parasitic worms

el·e·phan·tine \,e-lə-'fan-,tēn, -,tīn, 'e-lə-fən-\ adj **1** : of great size or strength **2** : CLUMSY, PONDEROUS ⟨∼ verse⟩

elev abbr elevation

el·e·vate \'e-lə-,vāt\ vb **-vat·ed; -vat·ing** **1** : to lift up : RAISE **2** : EXALT, ENNOBLE **3** : ELATE

el·e·va·tion \,e-lə-'vā-shən\ n **1** : the height to which something is raised (as above sea level) **2** : a lifting up **3** : something (as a hill or swelling) that is elevated

el·e·va·tor \'e-lə-,vā-tər\ n **1** : a cage or platform for conveying people or things from one level to another **2** : a building for storing and discharging grain **3** : a movable surface on an airplane to produce motion up or down

elev·en \i-'le-vən\ n **1** : one more than 10 **2** : the 11th in a set or series **3** : something having 11 units; esp : a football team — **eleven** adj or pron — **elev·enth** \-vənth\ adj or n

elf \'elf\ n, pl **elves** \'elvz\ : a mischievous fairy — **elf·ish** \'el-fish\ adj

ELF abbr extremely low frequency

elf·in \'el-fən\ adj : of, relating to, or resembling an elf

elic·it \i-'li-sət\ vb : to draw out or forth ♦ **Synonyms** EVOKE, EDUCE, EXTRACT, EXTORT

elide \i-'līd\ vb **elid·ed; elid·ing** : to suppress or alter by elision

el·i·gi·ble \'e-lə-jə-bəl\ adj : qualified to participate or to be chosen — **el·i·gi·bil·i·ty** \,e-lə-jə-'bi-lə-tē\ n — **eligible** n

CHEMICAL ELEMENTS

ELEMENT NAME	SYMBOL & ATOMIC NUMBER	ATOMIC WEIGHT[1]	ELEMENT NAME	SYMBOL & ATOMIC NUMBER	ATOMIC WEIGHT[1]
actinium	(Ac = 89)	227.0277	meitnerium	(Mt = 109)	(268)
aluminum	(Al = 13)	26.98154	mendelevium	(Md = 101)	(258)
americium	(Am = 95)	(243)	mercury	(Hg = 80)	200.59
antimony	(Sb = 51)	121.760	molybdenum	(Mo = 42)	95.94
argon	(Ar = 18)	39.948	neodymium	(Nd = 60)	144.24
arsenic	(As = 33)	74.92160	neon	(Ne = 10)	20.180
astatine	(At = 85)	(210)	neptunium	(Np = 93)	(237)
barium	(Ba = 56)	137.33	nickel	(Ni = 28)	58.6934
berkelium	(Bk = 97)	(247)	niobium	(Nb = 41)	92.90638
beryllium	(Be = 4)	9.012182	nitrogen	(N = 7)	14.0067
bismuth	(Bi = 83)	208.98038	nobelium	(No = 102)	(259)
bohrium	(Bh = 107)	(264)	osmium	(Os = 76)	190.23
boron	(B = 5)	10.81	oxygen	(O = 8)	15.9994
bromine	(Br = 35)	79.904	palladium	(Pd = 46)	106.42
cadmium	(Cd = 48)	112.41	phosphorus	(P = 15)	30.973761
calcium	(Ca = 20)	40.078	platinum	(Pt = 78)	195.078
californium	(Cf = 98)	(251)	plutonium	(Pu = 94)	(244)
carbon	(C = 6)	12.011	polonium	(Po = 84)	(209)
cerium	(Ce = 58)	140.116	potassium	(K = 19)	39.0983
cesium	(Cs = 55)	132.90545	praseodymium	(Pr = 59)	140.90765
chlorine	(Cl = 17)	35.453	promethium	(Pm = 61)	(145)
chromium	(Cr = 24)	51.996	protactinium	(Pa = 91)	(231)
cobalt	(Co = 27)	58.93320	radium	(Ra = 88)	(226)
copper	(Cu = 29)	63.546	radon	(Rn = 86)	(222)
curium	(Cm = 96)	(247)	rhenium	(Re = 75)	186.207
darmstadtium	(Ds = 110)	(269)	rhodium	(Rh = 45)	102.90550
dubnium	(Db = 105)	(262)	rubidium	(Rb = 37)	85.4678
dysprosium	(Dy = 66)	162.50	ruthenium	(Ru = 44)	101.07
einsteinium	(Es = 99)	(252)	rutherfordium	(Rf = 104)	(261)
erbium	(Er = 68)	167.259	samarium	(Sm = 62)	150.36
europium	(Eu = 63)	151.964	scandium	(Sc = 21)	44.95591
fermium	(Fm = 100)	(257)	seaborgium	(Sg = 106)	(266)
fluorine	(F = 9)	18.998403	selenium	(Se = 34)	78.96
francium	(Fr = 87)	(223)	silicon	(Si = 14)	28.0855
gadolinium	(Gd = 64)	157.25	silver	(Ag = 47)	107.8682
gallium	(Ga = 31)	69.723	sodium	(Na = 11)	22.989770
germanium	(Ge = 32)	72.64	strontium	(Sr = 38)	87.62
gold	(Au = 79)	196.96655	sulfur	(S = 16)	32.07
hafnium	(Hf = 72)	178.49	tantalum	(Ta = 73)	180.9479
hassium	(Hs = 108)	(277)	technetium	(Tc = 43)	(98)
helium	(He = 2)	4.002602	tellurium	(Te = 52)	127.60
holmium	(Ho = 67)	164.93032	terbium	(Tb = 65)	158.92534
hydrogen	(H = 1)	1.0079	thallium	(Tl = 81)	204.3833
indium	(In = 49)	114.818	thorium	(Th = 90)	232.0381
iodine	(I = 53)	126.90447	thulium	(Tm = 69)	168.93421
iridium	(Ir = 77)	192.217	tin	(Sn = 50)	118.71
iron	(Fe = 26)	55.845	titanium	(Ti = 22)	47.867
krypton	(Kr = 36)	83.80	tungsten	(W = 74)	183.84
lanthanum	(La = 57)	138.9055	uranium	(U = 92)	(238)
lawrencium	(Lr = 103)	(262)	vanadium	(V = 23)	50.9415
lead	(Pb = 82)	207.2	xenon	(Xe = 54)	131.29
lithium	(Li = 3)	6.941	ytterbium	(Yb = 70)	173.04
lutetium	(Lu = 71)	174.967	yttrium	(Y = 39)	88.90585
magnesium	(Mg = 12)	24.305	zinc	(Zn = 30)	65.39
manganese	(Mn = 25)	54.93805	zirconium	(Zr = 40)	91.224

[1]Weights are based on the naturally occurring isotope compositions and scaled to $^{12}C = 12$. For elements lacking stable isotopes, the mass number of the most stable nuclide is shown in parentheses.

elim·i·nate \i-'li-mə-ˌnāt\ vb -nat·ed; -nat·ing [L elimina-tus, pp. of eliminare, fr. limen threshold] **1** : REMOVE, ERADICATE **2** : to pass (wastes) from the body **3** : to leave out : IGNORE — **elim·i·na·tion** \-ˌli-mə-'nā-shən\ n

eli·sion \i-'li-zhən\ n : the omission of a final or initial sound or a word; esp : the omission of an unstressed vowel or syllable in a verse to achieve a uniform rhythm

elite \ā-'lēt, ē-\ n [F élite] **1** : the choice part; also : a superior group **2** : a typewriter type providing 12 characters to the inch — **elite** adj

elit·ism \-'lē-ˌti-zəm\ n : leadership or rule by an elite; also : advocacy of such elitism — **elit·ist** \-tist\ n or adj

elix·ir \i-'lik-sər\ n [ME, fr. ML, fr. Ar al-iksīr the elixir, fr. al the + iksīr elixir] **1** : a substance held capable of prolonging life indefinitely; also : PANACEA **2** : a sweetened alcoholic medicinal solution

Eliz·a·be·than \i-ˌli-zə-'bē-thən\ adj : of, relating to, or characteristic of Elizabeth I of England or her times

elk \'elk\ n, pl **elk** or **elks** **1** : MOOSE — used for one of the Old World **2** : a large gregarious deer of No. America, Europe, Asia, and northwestern Africa with curved antlers having many branches

elk 2

¹ell \'el\ n [ME eln, fr. OE; akin to L ulna forearm, Gk ōlenē elbow] : a former English cloth measure of 45 inches

²ell n : an extension at right angles to a building

el·lipse \i-'lips, e-\ n : a closed curve of oval shape

el·lip·sis \i-'lip-səs, e-\ n, pl **el·lip·ses** \-ˌsēz\ **1** : omission from an expression of a word clearly implied **2** : marks (as . . .) to show omission

el·lip·soid \i-'lip-ˌsȯid, e-\ n : a surface all plane sections of which are circles or ellipses — **el·lip·soi·dal** \-ˌlip-'sȯi-dᵊl\ also **ellipsoid** adj

el·lip·ti·cal \i-'lip-ti-kəl, e-\ or **el·lip·tic** \-tik\ adj **1** : of, relating to, or shaped like an ellipse **2** : of, relating to, or marked by ellipsis — **el·lip·ti·cal·ly** \-ti-k(ə-)lē\ adv

elm \'elm\ n : any of a genus of large trees that have toothed leaves and nearly circular one-seeded winged fruits and are often grown as shade trees; also : the wood of an elm

El Ni·ño \el-'nē-nyō\ n : a flow of unusually warm Pacific Ocean water moving toward and along the west coast of So. America

el·o·cu·tion \ˌe-lə-'kyü-shən\ n : the art of effective public speaking — **el·o·cu·tion·ist** \-shə-nist\ n

elon·gate \i-'lȯn-ˌgāt\ vb -gat·ed; -gat·ing : to make or grow longer ♦ **Synonyms** EXTEND, LENGTHEN, PROLONG, PROTRACT — **elon·ga·tion** \(ˌ)ē-ˌlȯn-'gā-shən\ n

elope \i-'lōp\ vb **eloped; elop·ing** : to run away esp. to be married — **elope·ment** n — **elop·er** n

el·o·quent \'e-lə-kwənt\ adj **1** : having or showing clear and forceful expression **2** : clearly showing some feeling or meaning — **el·o·quence** \-kwəns\ n — **el·o·quent·ly** adv

¹else \'els\ adv **1** : in a different or additional manner or place or at a different or additional time ⟨where ∼ can we meet⟩ **2** : OTHERWISE ⟨obey or ∼ you'll be sorry⟩

²else adj : OTHER; esp : being in addition ⟨what ∼ do you want⟩

else·where \-ˌhwer\ adv : in or to another place ⟨took my business ∼⟩

elu·ci·date \i-'lü-sə-ˌdāt\ vb -dat·ed; -dat·ing : to make clear usu. by explanation ♦ **Synonyms** CLARIFY, EXPLAIN, ILLUMINATE — **elu·ci·da·tion** \-ˌlü-sə-'dā-shən\ n

elude \ē-'lüd\ vb **elud·ed; elud·ing** **1** : EVADE **2** : to escape the notice of

elu·sive \ē-'lü-siv\ adj : tending to elude : EVASIVE — **elu·sive·ly** adv — **elu·sive·ness** n

el·ver \'el-vər\ n [alter. of eelfare migration of eels] : a young eel

elves pl of ELF

Ely·si·um \i-'li-zhē-əm, -zē-\ n, pl **-si·ums** or **-sia** \-zhē-ə, -zē-\ : PARADISE 2 — **Ely·sian** \-'li-zhən\ adj

em \'em\ n : a length approximately the width of the letter M

EM abbr **1** electromagnetic **2** electron microscope **3** enlisted man

ema·ci·ate \i-'mā-shē-ˌāt\ vb -at·ed; -at·ing : to become or cause to become very thin — **ema·ci·a·tion** \-ˌmā-shē-'ā-shən, -sē-\ n

e–mail \'ē-ˌmāl\ n **1** : a system for transmitting messages between computers on a network **2** : a message or messages sent and received through an e-mail system

emalangeni pl of LILANGENI

em·a·nate \'e-mə-ˌnāt\ vb -nat·ed; -nat·ing : to come out from a source ♦ **Synonyms** PROCEED, SPRING, RISE, ARISE, ORIGINATE — **em·a·na·tion** \ˌe-mə-'nā-shən\ n

eman·ci·pate \i-'man-sə-ˌpāt\ vb -pat·ed; -pat·ing : to set free ♦ **Synonyms** LIBERATE, RELEASE, DELIVER, DISCHARGE — **eman·ci·pa·tion** \-ˌman-sə-'pā-shən\ n — **eman·ci·pa·tor** \-'man-sə-ˌpā-tər\ n

emas·cu·late \i-'mas-kyù-ˌlāt\ vb -lat·ed; -lat·ing : to deprive of virility : CASTRATE; also : WEAKEN — **emas·cu·la·tion** \-ˌmas-kyù-'lā-shən\ n

em·balm \im-'bäm, -'bälm\ vb : to treat (a corpse) so as to protect from decay — **em·balm·er** n

em·bank·ment \im-'baŋk-mənt\ n : a raised structure (as of earth) to hold back water or carry a roadway

em·bar·go \im-'bär-gō\ n, pl **-goes** [Sp, fr. embargar to bar] : a prohibition on commerce — **embargo** vb

em·bark \im-'bärk\ vb **1** : to put or go on board a ship or airplane **2** : to make a start — **em·bar·ka·tion** \ˌem-ˌbär-'kä-shən\ n

em·bar·rass \im-'ber-əs\ vb **1** : CONFUSE, DISCONCERT **2** : to involve in financial difficulties **3** : to cause to experience self-conscious distress **4** : HINDER, IMPEDE — **em·bar·rass·ing·ly** adv — **em·bar·rass·ment** n

em·bas·sy \'em-bə-sē\ n, pl **-sies** **1** : a group of representatives headed by an ambassador **2** : the function, position, or mission of an ambassador **3** : the official residence and offices of an ambassador

em·bat·tle \im-'ba-tᵊl\ vb **1** : to arrange in order for battle; also : FORTIFY

em·bat·tled adj **1** : engaged in battle, conflict, or controversy **2** : being a site of battle, conflict, or controversy **3** : characterized by conflict or controversy ⟨an ∼ presidency⟩

em·bed \im-'bed\ vb **em·bed·ded; em·bed·ding** **1** : to enclose closely in a surrounding mass **2** : to make something an integral part of

em·bel·lish \im-'be-lish\ vb **1** : ADORN, DECORATE **2** : to add ornamental details to ♦ **Synonyms** BEAUTIFY, DECK, BEDECK, GARNISH, ORNAMENT, DRESS — **em·bel·lish·er** n — **em·bel·lish·ment** n

em·ber \'em-bər\ n **1** : a glowing or smoldering fragment from a fire **2** pl : the smoldering remains of a fire

em·bez·zle \im-'be-zəl\ vb -zled; -zling : to steal (as money) by falsifying records — **em·bez·zle·ment** n — **em·bez·zler** n

em·bit·ter \im-'bi-tər\ vb **1** : to arouse bitter feelings in **2** : to make bitter

em·bla·zon \-'blā-zᵊn\ vb **1** : to adorn with heraldic devices **2** : to display conspicuously

em·blem \'em-bləm\ n : something (as an object or picture) suggesting another object or an idea : SYMBOL — **em·blem·at·ic** \ˌem-blə-'ma-tik\ also **em·blem·at·i·cal** \-ti-kəl\ adj

em·body \im-'bä-dē\ vb **em·bod·ied; em·body·ing** **1** : INCARNATE **2** : to express in definite form **3** : to incorporate into a system or body **4** : PERSONIFY ♦ **Syno-**

nyms COMBINE, INTEGRATE — **em·bodi·ment** \-di-mənt\ *n*

em·bold·en \im-ˈbōl-dən\ *vb* : to inspire with courage

em·bo·lism \ˈem-bə-ˌli-zəm\ *n* : the obstruction of a blood vessel by a foreign or abnormal particle

em·bon·point \äⁿ-bōⁿ-ˈpwaⁿ\ *n* [F] : plumpness of person : STOUTNESS

em·boss \im-ˈbäs, -ˈbȯs\ *vb* : to ornament with raised work

em·bou·chure \ˈäm-bu̇-ˌshu̇r, ˌäm-bu̇-ˈshu̇r\ *n* [F, ultim. fr. *bouche* mouth] : the position and use of the lips, tongue, and teeth in playing a wind instrument

em·bow·er \im-ˈbau̇(-ə)r\ *vb* : to shelter or enclose in a bower

¹**em·brace** \im-ˈbrās\ *vb* **em·braced; em·brac·ing 1** : to clasp in the arms; *also* : CHERISH, LOVE **2** : ENCIRCLE **3** : TAKE UP, ADOPT ⟨*embraced* the cause⟩; *also* : WELCOME ⟨*embraced* the opportunity⟩ **4** : INCLUDE **5** : to participate in an embrace ✦ **Synonyms** COMPREHEND, INVOLVE, ENCOMPASS, EMBODY

²**embrace** *n* : an encircling with the arms

em·bra·sure \im-ˈbrā-zhər\ *n* **1** : an opening in a wall through which a cannon is fired **2** : a recess of a door or window

em·bro·ca·tion \ˌem-brə-ˈkā-shən\ *n* : LINIMENT

em·broi·der \im-ˈbrȯi-dər\ *vb* **1** : to ornament with or do needlework **2** : to elaborate with exaggerated detail

em·broi·dery \im-ˈbrȯi-də-rē\ *n, pl* **-der·ies 1** : the forming of decorative designs with needlework **2** : something embroidered

em·broil \im-ˈbrȯi(-ə)l\ *vb* **1** : to throw into confusion or disorder **2** : to involve in conflict or difficulties — **em·broil·ment** *n*

em·bryo \ˈem-brē-ˌō\ *n, pl* **embryos** : a living thing in its earliest stages of development — **em·bry·on·ic** \ˌem-brē-ˈä-nik\ *adj*

em·bry·ol·o·gy \ˌem-brē-ˈä-lə-jē\ *n* : a branch of biology dealing with embryos and their development — **em·bry·o·log·i·cal** \-brē-ə-ˈlä-ji-kəl\ *adj* — **em·bry·ol·o·gist** \-brē-ˈä-lə-jist\ *n*

em·cee \ˌem-ˈsē\ *n* : MASTER OF CEREMONIES — **emcee** *vb*

emend \ē-ˈmend\ *vb* : to correct usu. by altering the text of ✦ **Synonyms** RECTIFY, REVISE, AMEND — **emen·da·tion** \ˌē-ˌmen-ˈdā-shən\ *n*

emer *abbr* emeritus

¹**em·er·ald** \ˈem-rəld, ˈe-mə-\ *n* : a green beryl prized as a gem

²**emerald** *adj* : brightly or richly green

emerge \i-ˈmərj\ *vb* **emerged; emerg·ing** : to rise, come forth, or come out into view — **emer·gence** \-ˈmər-jəns\ *n* — **emer·gent** \-jənt\ *adj*

emer·gen·cy \i-ˈmər-jən-sē\ *n, pl* **-cies** : an unforeseen event or condition requiring prompt action ✦ **Synonyms** EXIGENCY, CONTINGENCY, CRISIS, JUNCTURE

emergency room : a hospital room for receiving and treating persons needing immediate medical care

emer·i·ta \i-ˈmer-ə-tə\ *adj* : EMERITUS — used of a woman

emer·i·tus \i-ˈmer-ə-təs\ *adj* [L] : retired from active duty ⟨professor ~⟩

em·ery \ˈe-mə-rē\ *n, pl* **em·er·ies** : a dark granular mineral consisting primarily of corundum and used as an abrasive

emet·ic \i-ˈme-tik\ *n* : an agent that induces vomiting — **emetic** *adj*

emf *n* [*electromotive force*] : POTENTIAL DIFFERENCE

em·i·grate \ˈe-mə-ˌgrāt\ *vb* **-grat·ed; -grat·ing** : to leave a place (as a country) to settle elsewhere — **em·i·grant** \-mi-grənt\ *n* — **em·i·gra·tion** \ˌe-mə-ˈgrā-shən\ *n*

émi·gré *also* **emi·gré** \ˈe-mi-ˌgrā, ˌe-mi-ˈgrā\ *n* [F] : a person who emigrates esp. because of political conditions

em·i·nence \ˈe-mə-nəns\ *n* **1** : high rank or position; *also* : a person of high rank or attainments **2** : a lofty place

em·i·nent \ˈe-mə-nənt\ *adj* **1** : CONSPICUOUS, EVIDENT **2** : DISTINGUISHED, PROMINENT ⟨an ~ physician⟩ — **em·i·nent·ly** *adv*

eminent domain *n* : a right of a government to take private property for public use

emir *or* **amir** \ə-ˈmir, ā-\ *n* [Ar *amīr* commander] : a ruler, chief, or commander in Islamic countries — **emir·ate** \ˈe-mər-ət\ *n*

em·is·sary \ˈe-mə-ˌser-ē\ *n, pl* **-sar·ies** : AGENT; *esp* : a secret agent

emis·sion \ē-ˈmi-shən\ *n* : something emitted; *esp* : substances discharged into the air

emit \ē-ˈmit\ *vb* **emit·ted; emit·ting 1** : to give off or out ⟨~ light⟩; *also* : EJECT **2** : EXPRESS, UTTER — **emit·ter** *n*

emol·lient \i-ˈmäl-yənt\ *adj* : making soft or supple; *also* : soothing esp. to the skin or mucous membrane ⟨an ~ hand lotion⟩ — **emol·lient** *n*

emol·u·ment \i-ˈmäl-yə-mənt\ *n* [ME, fr. L *emolumentum* advantage, fr. *emolere* to produce by grinding] : the product (as salary or fees) of an employment

emote \i-ˈmōt\ *vb* **emot·ed; emot·ing** : to give expression to emotion in or as if in a play

emo·ti·con \i-ˈmō-ti-ˌkän\ *n* : a group of keyboard characters (as :)) that represents a facial expression esp. in online communications

emo·tion \i-ˈmō-shən\ *n* : a usu. intense feeling (as of love, hate, or despair) — **emo·tion·al** \-shə-nəl\ *adj* — **emo·tion·al·ly** *adv*

emot·ive \i-ˈmō-tiv\ *adj* **1** : of or relating to the emotions **2** : appealing to or expressing emotion

emp *abbr* emperor; empress

empanel *var of* IMPANEL

em·pa·thy \ˈem-pə-thē\ *n* : the experiencing as one's own of the feelings of another; *also* : the capacity for this — **em·path·ic** \em-ˈpa-thik\ *adj*

em·pen·nage \ˌäm-pə-ˈnäzh, ˌem-\ *n* [F] : the tail assembly of an airplane

em·per·or \ˈem-pər-ər\ *n* : the sovereign male ruler of an empire

em·pha·sis \ˈem-fə-səs\ *n, pl* **-pha·ses** \-ˌsēz\ : particular prominence given (as to a syllable in speaking or to a phase of action)

em·pha·sise *Brit var of* EMPHASIZE

em·pha·size \-ˌsīz\ *vb* **-sized; -siz·ing** : to place emphasis on : STRESS

em·phat·ic \im-ˈfa-tik, em-\ *adj* : uttered with emphasis : STRESSED — **em·phat·i·cal·ly** \-ˈti-k(ə-)lē\ *adv*

em·phy·se·ma \ˌem-fə-ˈzē-mə, -ˈsē-\ *n* : a condition marked by abnormal expansion of the air spaces of the lungs resulting in severe breathlessness

em·pire \ˈem-ˌpī(-ə)r\ *n* **1** : a large state or a group of states under a single sovereign who is usu. an emperor; *also* : something resembling a political empire **2** : imperial sovereignty or dominion

em·pir·i·cal \im-ˈpir-i-kəl\ *also* **em·pir·ic** \-ik\ *adj* : based on observation; *also* : subject to verification by observation or experiment ⟨~ laws⟩ — **em·pir·i·cal·ly** \-i-k(ə-)lē\ *adv*

em·pir·i·cism \im-ˈpir-ə-ˌsi-zəm, em-\ *n* : the practice of relying on observation and experiment esp. in the natural sciences — **em·pir·i·cist** \-sist\ *n*

em·place·ment \im-ˈplās-mənt\ *n* **1** : a prepared position for weapons or military equipment **2** : PLACEMENT

¹**em·ploy** \im-ˈplȯi\ *vb* **1** : to make use of **2** : to use the services of **3** : OCCUPY, DEVOTE — **em·ploy·er** *n*

²**em·ploy** \im-ˈplȯi; ˈim-ˌplȯi, ˈem-\ *n* : EMPLOYMENT

em·ploy·ee *also* **em·ploye** \im-ˌplȯi-ˈē, ˌem-; im-ˈplȯi-ˌē, em-\ *n* : a person who works for another

em·ploy·ment \im-ˈplȯi-mənt\ *n* **1** : OCCUPATION, ACTIVITY **2** : the act of employing : the condition of being employed

em·po·ri·um \im-ˈpȯr-ē-əm, em-\ *n, pl* **-ri·ums** *also* **-ria** \-ē-ə\ [L, fr. Gk *emporion*, fr. *emporos* traveler, trader] : a commercial center; *esp* : a store carrying varied articles

em·pow·er \im-ˈpau̇(-ə)r\ *vb* : to give authority or power to; *also* : ENABLE — **em·pow·er·ment** \-mənt\ *n*

em·press \ˈem-prəs\ *n* **1** : the wife or widow of an emperor **2** : a sovereign female ruler of an empire

¹**emp·ty** \ˈemp-tē\ *adj* **emp·ti·er; -est** [ME, fr. OE *ǣmettig* unoccupied, fr. *ǣmetta* leisure] **1** : containing nothing ⟨~ shelves⟩ **2** : UNOCCUPIED, UNINHABITED ⟨an ~ building⟩ **3** : lacking value, force, sense, or purpose ✦ **Synonyms** VACANT, BLANK, VOID, STARK, VACUOUS — **emp·ti·ness** *n*

²**empty** *vb* **emp·tied; emp·ty·ing 1** : to make or become empty **2** : to discharge contents; *also* : to remove from what holds or encloses

³**empty** *n, pl* **empties** : an empty bottle or can

emp·ty–hand·ed \ˌemp-tē-'han-dəd\ *adj* **1** : having or bringing nothing **2** : having acquired or gained nothing

em·py·re·an \ˌem-ˌpī-'rē-ən, -pə-\ *n* **1** : the highest heaven; *also* : FIRMAMENT **2** : an ideal place or state

EMT \ˌē-(ˌ)em-'tē\ *n* [*emergency medical technician*] : a specially trained medical technician certified to provide basic medical services before and during transport to a hospital

¹emu \'ē-myü, -mü\ *n* : a swift-running flightless Australian bird smaller than the related ostrich

²emu *abbr* electromagnetic unit

em·u·late \'em-yu̇-ˌlāt\ *vb* **-lat·ed; -lat·ing** : to strive to equal or excel : IMITATE — **em·u·la·tion** \ˌem-yü-'lā-shən\ *n* — **em·u·lous** \'em-yü-ləs\ *adj*

emul·si·fi·er \i-'məl-sə-ˌfī(-ə)r\ *n* : a substance (as a soap) that helps to form and stabilize an emulsion

emul·si·fy \-ˌfī\ *vb* **-fied; -fy·ing** : to disperse (as an oil) in an emulsion — **emul·si·fi·ca·tion** \i-ˌməl-sə-fə-'kā-shən\ *n*

emul·sion \i-'məl-shən\ *n* **1** : a mixture of mutually insoluble liquids in which one is dispersed in droplets throughout the other ⟨an ~ of oil in water⟩ **2** : a light-sensitive coating on photographic film or paper

en \'en\ *n* : a length approximately half the width of the letter *M*

¹-en *also* **-n** *adj suffix* : made of : consisting of ⟨earth*en*⟩

²-en *vb suffix* **1** : become or cause to be ⟨sharp*en*⟩ **2** : cause or come to have ⟨length*en*⟩

en·able \i-'nā-bəl\ *vb* **en·abled; en·abling 1** : to make able or feasible ⟨wings that ~ one to fly⟩ **2** : to give legal power, capacity, or sanction to

en·act \i-'nakt\ *vb* **1** : to make into law **2** : to act out — **en·act·ment** *n*

enam·el \i-'na-məl\ *n* **1** : a glasslike substance used to coat the surface of metal or pottery **2** : the hard outer layer of a tooth **3** : a usu. glossy paint that forms a hard coat — **enamel** *vb*

enam·el·ware \-ˌwer\ *n* : metal utensils coated with enamel

en·am·or \i-'na-mər\ *vb* : to inflame with love

en·am·our *chiefly Brit var of* ENAMOR

en bloc \äⁿ-'bläk\ *adv or adj* : as a whole : in a mass

enc *or* **encl** *abbr* enclosure

en·camp \in-'kamp\ *vb* : to make camp — **en·camp·ment** *n*

en·cap·su·late \in-'kap-sə-ˌlāt\ *vb* **-lat·ed; -lat·ing 1** : to encase or become encased in a capsule **2** : SUMMARIZE — **en·cap·su·la·tion** \-ˌkap-sə-'lā-shən\ *n*

en·case \in-'kās\ *vb* : to enclose in or as if in a case — **en·case·ment** \-'kā-smənt\ *n*

-ence *n suffix* **1** : action or process ⟨emerg*ence*⟩ : instance of an action or process ⟨refer*ence*⟩ **2** : quality or state ⟨depend*ence*⟩

en·ceinte \äⁿ-'sant\ *adj* : PREGNANT 1

en·ceph·a·li·tis \in-ˌse-fə-'lī-təs\ *n, pl* **-lit·i·des** \-'li-tə-ˌdēz\ : inflammation of the brain — **en·ceph·a·lit·ic** \-'li-tik\ *adj*

en·ceph·a·lop·a·thy \in-ˌse-fə-'lä-pə-thē\ *n, pl* **-thies** : a disease of the brain

en·chain \in-'chān\ *vb* : FETTER, CHAIN

en·chant \in-'chant\ *vb* **1** : BEWITCH **2** : ENRAPTURE, FASCINATE ⟨was ~*ed* by his poetry⟩ — **en·chant·er** *n* — **en·chant·ing·ly** *adv* — **en·chant·ment** *n* — **en·chant·ress** \-'chan-trəs\ *n*

en·chi·la·da \ˌen-chə-'lä-də\ *n* : a tortilla rolled around a filling, covered with chili sauce, and usu. baked

en·ci·pher \in-'sī-fər, en-\ *vb* : ENCODE

en·cir·cle \in-'sər-kəl\ *vb* : to pass completely around : SURROUND — **en·cir·cle·ment** *n*

en·clave \'en-ˌklāv; 'äⁿ-ˌklāv\ *n* : a distinct territorial, cultural, or social unit enclosed within or as if within foreign territory

en·close \in-'klōz\ *vb* **1** : to shut up or in; *esp* : to surround with a fence **2** : to include along with something else in a parcel or envelope ⟨~ a check⟩ — **en·clo·sure** \-'klō-zhər\ *n*

en·code \in-'kōd, en-\ *vb* : to convert (a message) into code

en·co·mi·um \en-'kō-mē-əm\ *n, pl* **-mi·ums** *also* **-mia** \-mē-ə\ : high or glowing praise

en·com·pass \in-'kəm-pəs\ *vb* **1** : ENCIRCLE **2** : ENVELOP, INCLUDE

en·core \'än-ˌkȯr\ *n* **1** : a demand for repetition or reappearance **2** : a further performance or appearance demanded by an audience **3** : a second achievement that usu. surpasses the first — **encore** *vb*

¹en·coun·ter \in-'kau̇n-tər\ *vb* **1** : to meet as an enemy : FIGHT **2** : to meet usu. unexpectedly ⟨~ problems⟩

²encounter *n* **1** : a hostile usu. violent meeting **2** : a chance meeting **3** : an experience shared with another ⟨a romantic ~⟩

en·cour·age \in-'kər-ij\ *vb* **-aged; -ag·ing 1** : to inspire with courage and hope **2** : STIMULATE, INCITE ⟨tax cuts to ~ spending⟩ **3** : FOSTER — **en·cour·age·ment** *n* — **en·cour·ag·ing·ly** *adv*

en·croach \in-'krōch\ *vb* [ME *encrochen* to seize, fr. AF *encrocher*, fr. *croche* hook] : to enter gradually or stealthily upon another's property or rights — **en·croach·er** *n* — **en·croach·ment** *n*

en·crust *also* **in·crust** \in-'krəst\ *vb* : to provide with or form a crust

en·crus·ta·tion \(ˌ)in-ˌkrəs-'tā-shən, ˌen-\ *var of* INCRUSTATION

en·cum·ber \in-'kəm-bər\ *vb* **1** : to weigh down : BURDEN **2** : to hinder the function or activity of ⟨relations ~*ed* by mistrust⟩ — **en·cum·brance** \-brəns\ *n*

ency *or* **encyc** *abbr* encyclopedia

-en·cy *n suffix* : quality or state ⟨despond*ency*⟩

¹en·cyc·li·cal \in-'si-kli-kəl, en-\ *adj* : addressed to all the individuals of a group

²encyclical *n* : an encyclical letter; *esp* : a papal letter to the bishops of the church

en·cy·clo·pae·dia, en·cy·clo·pae·dic *chiefly Brit var of* ENCYCLOPEDIA, ENCYCLOPEDIC

en·cy·clo·pe·dia *n* [ML *encyclopaedia* course of general education, fr. Gk *enkyklios paideia* general education] : a work treating the various branches of learning — **en·cy·clo·pe·dic** \-'pē-dik\ *adj*

en·cyst \in-'sist, en-\ *vb* : to form or become enclosed in a cyst — **en·cyst·ment** *n*

¹end \'end\ *n* **1** : the part of an area that lies at the boundary; *also* : a point which marks the extent or limit of something or at which something ceases to exist **2** : a ceasing of a course (as of action or activity); *also* : DEATH **3** : the ultimate state; *also* : RESULT, ISSUE **4** : REMNANT **5** : PURPOSE, OBJECTIVE **6** : a player stationed at the extremity of a line (as in football) **7** : a share, operation, or aspect of an undertaking

²end *vb* **1** : to bring or come to an end **2** : DESTROY; *also* : DIE **3** : to form or be at the end of ♦ **Synonyms** CLOSE, CONCLUDE, TERMINATE, FINISH, COMPLETE

en·dan·ger \in-'dān-jər\ *vb* : to bring into danger; *also* : to create danger

en·dan·gered *adj* : being or relating to an endangered species

endangered species *n* : a species threatened with extinction

en·dear \in-'dir\ *vb* : to cause to become beloved or admired

en·dear·ment \-mənt\ *n* : a sign of affection : CARESS

en·deav·or \in-'de-vər\ *vb* : TRY, ATTEMPT — **endeavor** *n*

en·deav·our *chiefly Brit var of* ENDEAVOR

en·dem·ic \en-'de-mik, in-\ *adj* : restricted to a particular place ⟨~ plants⟩ ⟨an ~ disease⟩ — **endemic** *nm*

end·ing \'en-diŋ\ *n* : something that forms an end; *esp* : SUFFIX

en·dive \'en-ˌdīv\ *n* **1** : an herb related to chicory and grown as a salad plant **2** : the blanched shoot of chicory

end·less \'end-ləs\ *adj* **1** : having or seeming to have no end : ETERNAL ⟨~ debates⟩ **2** : united at the ends : CONTINUOUS ⟨an ~ belt⟩ ♦ **Synonyms** INTERMINABLE, EVERLASTING, UNCEASING, CEASELESS, UNENDING — **end·less·ly** *adv*

end·most \-ˌmōst\ *adj* : situated at the very end

end·note \-ˌnōt\ *n* : a note placed at the end of a text

en·do·crine \'en-də-krən, -ˌkrīn, -ˌkrēn\ *adj* : producing secretions that are distributed by way of the bloodstream ⟨~ glands⟩ — **endocrine** *n* — **en·do·cri·nol·o·gist** \-kri-'nä-lə-jist\ *n* — **en·do·cri·nol·o·gy** \-jē\ *n*

en·dog·e·nous \en-'dä-jə-nəs\ *adj* : caused or produced by factors inside the organism or system ⟨~ depression⟩ — **en·dog·e·nous·ly** *adv*

en·do·me·tri·um \ˌen-dō-'mē-trē-əm\ *n, pl* **-tria** \-trē-ə\

: the mucous membrane lining the uterus — **en·do·me·tri·al** \-trē-əl\ *adj*

en·dor·phin \en-'dȯr-fən\ *n* : any of a group of endogenous morphinelike proteins found esp. in the brain

en·dorse *also* **in·dorse** \in-'dȯrs\ *vb* **en·dorsed; en·dors·ing** [ME *endosen*, fr. AF *endosser* to put on, don, write on the back of, fr. *dos* back, fr. L *dorsum*] **1** : to sign one's name on the back of (as a check) **2** : APPROVE, SANCTION **3** : to recommend (as a product) usu. for financial compensation — **en·dorse·ment** *also* **in·dorse·ment** *n*

en·do·scope \'en-də-ˌskōp\ *n* : an illuminated usu. fiberoptic instrument for visualizing the interior of a hollow organ or part (as the colon or esophagus) — **en·do·scop·ic** \ˌen-də-'skä-pik\ *adj* — **en·dos·co·py** \en-'däs-kə-pē\ *n*

en·do·ther·mic \ˌen-də-'thər-mik\ *adj* : characterized by or formed with absorption of heat

en·dow \in-'daú\ *vb* **1** : to furnish with funds for support ⟨~ a school⟩ **2** : to furnish with something freely or naturally — **en·dow·ment** *n*

en·due \in-'dü, -'dyü\ *vb* **en·dued; en·du·ing** : PROVIDE, ENDOW

en·dur·ance \in-'dúr-əns, -'dyúr-\ *n* **1** : DURATION **2** : the ability to withstand hardship or stress : FORTITUDE

en·dure \in-'dúr, -'dyúr\ *vb* **en·dured; en·dur·ing 1** : LAST, PERSIST **2** : to suffer firmly or patiently : BEAR **3** : TOLERATE — **en·dur·able** *adj*

end·ways \'end-ˌwāz\ *adv or adj* **1** : LENGTHWISE **2** : with the end forward **3** : on end

end·wise \-ˌwīz\ *adv or adj* : ENDWAYS

ENE *abbr* east-northeast

en·e·ma \'e-nə-mə\ *n, pl* **enemas** *also* **ene·ma·ta** \ˌe-nə-'mä-tə, 'e-nə-mə-tə\ : injection of liquid into the rectum; *also* : material so injected

en·e·my \'e-nə-mē\ *n, pl* **-mies** [ME *enemi*, fr. AF, fr. L *inimicus*, fr. *in-* not + *amicus* friend] : one that attacks or tries to harm another : FOE; *esp* : a military opponent

en·er·get·ic \ˌe-nər-'je-tik\ *adj* : marked by energy : ACTIVE, VIGOROUS ✦ *Synonyms* STRENUOUS, LUSTY, DYNAMIC, VITAL — **en·er·get·i·cal·ly** \-ti-k(ə-)lē\ *adv*

en·er·gise *Brit var of* ENERGIZE

en·er·gize \'e-nər-ˌjīz\ *vb* **-gized; -giz·ing** : to give energy to

en·er·gy \'e-nər-jē\ *n, pl* **-gies 1** : vigorous action : EFFORT **2** : capacity for action **3** : a fundamental entity of nature usu. regarded as the capacity for performing work **4** : usable power (as heat or electricity); *also* : the resources for producing such power

energy level *n* : one of the stable states of constant energy that may be assumed by a physical system (as the electrons in an atom)

en·er·vate \'e-nər-ˌvāt\ *vb* **-vat·ed; -vat·ing** : to lessen the strength or vigor of : weaken in mind or body — **en·er·vat·ing·ly** \-ˌvā-tiŋ-lē\ *adv* — **en·er·va·tion** \ˌe-nər-'vā-shən\ *n*

en·fee·ble \in-'fē-bəl\ *vb* **-bled; -bling** : to make feeble ✦ *Synonyms* WEAKEN, DEBILITATE, SAP, UNDERMINE, CRIPPLE — **en·fee·ble·ment** *n*

en·fi·lade \'en-fə-ˌlād, -ˌläd\ *n* : gunfire directed along the length of an enemy battle line — **enfilade** *vb*

en·fold \in-'fōld\ *vb* **1** : ENVELOP **2** : EMBRACE

en·force \in-'fȯrs\ *vb* **1** : COMPEL ⟨~ obedience by threats⟩ **2** : to execute effectively ⟨~ the law⟩ — **en·force·able** *adj* — **en·force·ment** *n*

en·forc·er \in-'fȯr-sər\ *n* : one that enforces; *esp* : a player (as in ice hockey) known for rough play

en·fran·chise \in-'fran-ˌchīz\ *vb* **-chised; -chis·ing 1** : to set free (as from slavery) **2** : to admit to citizenship; *also* : to grant the vote to — **en·fran·chise·ment** \-ˌchīz-mənt, -chəz-\ *n*

eng *abbr* engine; engineer; engineering

Eng *abbr* England; English

en·gage \in-'gāj\ *vb* **en·gaged; en·gag·ing 1** : PLEDGE; *esp* : to bind by a pledge to marry **2** : EMPLOY, HIRE **3** : to attract and hold esp. by interesting; *also* : to cause to participate **4** : to commence or take part in a venture ⟨*engaged* in shady deals⟩ **5** : to bring or enter into conflict ⟨~ the enemy⟩ **6** : to connect or interlock with : MESH; *also* : to cause to mesh

en·gage·ment \in-'gāj-mənt\ *n* **1** : APPOINTMENT **2** : EMPLOYMENT **3** : a mutual promise to marry : BETROTHAL **4** : a hostile encounter

en·gag·ing *adj* : ATTRACTIVE ⟨an ~ smile⟩ — **en·gag·ing·ly** *adv*

en·gen·der \in-'jen-dər\ *vb* **1** : BEGET **2** : BRING ABOUT, CREATE ⟨~ controversy⟩ ✦ *Synonyms* GENERATE, BREED, OCCASION, PRODUCE

en·gine \'en-jən\ *n* [ME *engin*, fr. AF, fr. L *ingenium* natural disposition, talent] **1** : a mechanical device **2** : a machine for converting energy into mechanical motion **3** : LOCOMOTIVE **4** : software that performs a fundamental function esp. of a larger program — **en·gine·less** *adj*

¹en·gi·neer \ˌen-jə-'nir\ *n* **1** : a member of a military unit specializing in engineering work **2** : a designer or builder of engines **3** : one trained in engineering **4** : one that operates an engine

²engineer *vb* **1** : to lay out or manage as an engineer **2** : to guide the course of ⟨~ a rally⟩ ✦ *Synonyms* PILOT, LEAD, STEER

en·gi·neer·ing *n* : the practical applications of scientific and mathematical principles

En·glish \'iŋ-glish\ *n* **1** : the language of England, the U.S., and many areas now or formerly under British rule **2** **English** *pl* : the people of England **3** : spin imparted to a ball that is driven or rolled — **English** *adj* — **En·glish·man** \-mən\ *n* — **En·glish·wom·an** \-ˌwú-mən\ *n*

English horn *n* : a woodwind instrument longer than and having a range lower than the oboe

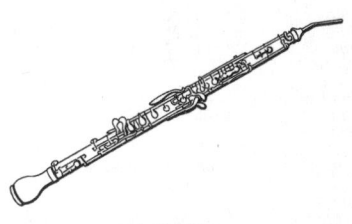

English horn

English setter *n* : any of a breed of hunting dogs with a flat silky coat of white or white with color

English sparrow *n* : HOUSE SPARROW

English system *n* : a system of weights and measures in which the foot is the principal unit of length and the pound is the principal unit of weight

engr *abbr* **1** engineer **2** engraved

en·gram \'en-ˌgram\ *n* : a hypothetical change in neural tissue postulated in order to account for persistence of memory

en·grave \in-'grāv\ *vb* **en·graved; en·grav·ing 1** : to produce (as letters or lines) by incising a surface **2** : to cut figures, letters, or designs on for printing; *also* : to print from an engraved plate ⟨~ an invitation⟩ **3** : PHOTOENGRAVE — **en·grav·er** *n*

en·grav·ing \in-'grā-viŋ\ *n* **1** : the art of one who engraves **2** : an engraved plate; *also* : a print made from it

en·gross \in-'grōs\ *vb* : to take up the whole interest or attention of ✦ *Synonyms* MONOPOLIZE, ABSORB, CONSUME

en·gulf \in-'gəlf\ *vb* : to flow over and enclose : OVERWHELM ⟨~ed in flames⟩

en·hance \in-'hans\ *vb* **en·hanced; en·hanc·ing** : to increase or improve (as in value or desirability) ✦ *Synonyms* HEIGHTEN, INTENSIFY, MAGNIFY — **en·hance·ment** *n*

enig·ma \i-'nig-mə\ *n* [L *aenigma*, fr. Gk *ainigma*, fr. *ainissesthai* to speak in riddles, fr. *ainos* fable] : something obscure or hard to understand

enig·mat·ic \ˌen-ig-'ma-tik\ *adj* : resembling an enigma ✦ *Synonyms* OBSCURE, CRYPTIC, MYSTIFYING — **en·ig·mat·i·cal·ly** \-ti-k(ə-)lē\ *adv*

en·join \in-'jȯin\ *vb* **1** : COMMAND, ORDER ⟨~ed us to desist⟩ **2** : FORBID ✦ *Synonyms* DIRECT, BID, CHARGE, COMMAND, INSTRUCT

en·joy \in-'jȯi\ *vb* **1** : to have for one's benefit or use ⟨~ good health⟩ **2** : to take pleasure or satisfaction in ⟨~ed the concert⟩ — **en·joy·able** *adj* — **en·joy·ment** *n*

enl *abbr* **1** enlarged **2** enlisted

en·large \in-ˈlärj\ *vb* **en·larged; en·larg·ing** **1** : to make or grow larger **2** : ELABORATE ✦ *Synonyms* INCREASE, AUGMENT, MULTIPLY, EXPAND — **en·large·ment** *n*

en·light·en \in-ˈlī-tᵊn\ *vb* **1** : INSTRUCT, INFORM **2** : to give spiritual insight to — **en·light·en·ment** *n*

en·list \in-ˈlist\ *vb* **1** : to secure the aid or support of **2** : to engage for service in the armed forces — **en·list·ee** \-ˌlis-ˈtē\ *n* — **en·list·ment** \-ˈlist-mənt\ *n*

en·list·ed \in-ˈlis-təd\ *adj* : of, relating to, or forming the part of a military force below commissioned or warrant officers

enlisted man *n* : a man or woman in the armed forces ranking below a commissioned or warrant officer

en·liv·en \in-ˈlī-vən\ *vb* : to give life, action, or spirit to : ANIMATE

en masse \ä⁽ⁿ⁾-ˈmas\ *adv* [F] : in a body : as a whole

en·mesh \in-ˈmesh\ *vb* : to catch or entangle in or as if in meshes

en·mi·ty \ˈen-mə-tē\ *n, pl* **-ties** : ILL WILL; *esp* : mutual hatred ✦ *Synonyms* HOSTILITY, ANTIPATHY, ANIMOSITY, RANCOR, ANTAGONISM

en·no·ble \i-ˈnō-bəl\ *vb* **-bled; -bling** : EXALT, ELEVATE; *esp* : to raise to noble rank — **en·no·ble·ment** *n*

en·nui \ˌän-ˈwē\ *n* [F] : BOREDOM

enor·mi·ty \i-ˈnór-mə-tē\ *n, pl* **-ties** **1** : an outrageous, vicious, or immoral act **2** : great wickedness **3** : IMMENSITY

enor·mous \i-ˈnór-məs\ *adj* [L *enormis*, fr. *e, ex* out of + *norma* rule] **1** : exceedingly wicked **2** : great in size, number, or degree : HUGE ✦ *Synonyms* IMMENSE, VAST, GIGANTIC, COLOSSAL, MAMMOTH, ELEPHANTINE — **enor·mous·ly** *adv*

¹**enough** \i-ˈnəf\ *adj* : SUFFICIENT

²**enough** *adv* **1** : SUFFICIENTLY **2** : FULLY, QUITE **3** : TOLERABLY

³**enough** *pron* : a sufficient number, quantity, or amount

en·quire \in-ˈkwī(-ə)r\, **en·qui·ry** \ˈin-ˌkwī(-ə)r-ē, in-ˈ; ˈinkwə-rē, ˈiŋ-\ *chiefly Brit var of* INQUIRE, INQUIRY

en·rage \in-ˈrāj\ *vb* : to fill with rage

en·rap·ture \in-ˈrap-chər\ *vb* **en·rap·tured; en·rap·tur·ing** : DELIGHT

en·rich \in-ˈrich\ *vb* **1** : to make rich or richer **2** : ORNAMENT, ADORN — **en·rich·ment** *n*

en·roll *also* **en·rol** \in-ˈrōl\ *vb* **en·rolled; en·roll·ing 1** : to enter or register on a roll or list **2** : to offer (oneself) for enrolling — **en·roll·ment** *n*

en route \än-ˈrüt, en-\ *adv or adj* : on or along the way ⟨stalled while *en route* to work⟩

ENS *abbr* ensign

en·sconce \in-ˈskäns\ *vb* **en·sconced; en·sconc·ing 1** : SHELTER, CONCEAL **2** : to settle snugly or securely ✦ *Synonyms* SECRETE, HIDE, CACHE, STASH

en·sem·ble \än-ˈsäm-bəl\ *n* [F, fr. *ensemble* together, fr. L *insimul* at the same time] : a group (as of singers, dancers, or players) or a set (as of clothes) producing a single effect

en·sheathe \in-ˈshēth\ *vb* : to cover with or as if with a sheath

en·shrine \in-ˈshrīn\ *vb* **1** : to enclose in or as if in a shrine **2** : to cherish as sacred — **en·shrine·ment** \-mənt\ *n*

en·shroud \in-ˈshraùd\ *vb* : SHROUD, OBSCURE

en·sign \ˈen-sən, *1 also* ˈen-ˌsīn\ *n* **1** : FLAG; *also* : BADGE, EMBLEM **2** : a commissioned officer in the navy ranking next below a lieutenant junior grade

en·slave \in-ˈslāv\ *vb* : to make a slave of — **en·slave·ment** *n*

en·snare \in-ˈsner\ *vb* : SNARE, TRAP ✦ *Synonyms* ENTRAP, BAG, CATCH, CAPTURE

en·sue \in-ˈsü\ *vb* **en·sued; en·su·ing** : to follow in time or as a result ⟨the birds escaped and chaos *ensued*⟩

en·sure \in-ˈshùr\ *vb* **en·sured; en·sur·ing** : INSURE, GUARANTEE

en·tail \in-ˈtāl\ *vb* **1** : to limit the inheritance of (property) to the owner's lineal descendants or to a class thereof **2** : to include or involve as a necessary step or result ⟨the sacrifices that parenting ~s⟩ — **en·tail·ment** *n*

en·tan·gle \in-ˈtaŋ-gəl\ *vb* : TANGLE, CONFUSE — **en·tan·gle·ment** *n*

en·tente \än-ˈtänt\ *n* [F] : an understanding providing for joint action; *also* : parties linked by such an entente

en·ter \ˈen-tər\ *vb* **1** : to go or come in or into **2** : to become a member of : JOIN ⟨~ the ministry⟩ **3** : BEGIN **4** : to take part in : CONTRIBUTE **5** : to go into or upon and take possession **6** : to set down (as in a list) : REGISTER ⟨~ the data⟩ **7** : to place (a complaint) before a court; *also* : to put on record ⟨~ a complaint⟩

en·ter·i·tis \ˌen-tə-ˈrī-təs\ *n* : intestinal inflammation; *also* : a disease marked by this

en·ter·prise \ˈen-tər-ˌprīz\ *n* **1** : UNDERTAKING, PROJECT **2** : readiness for daring action : INITIATIVE **3** : a business organization

en·ter·pris·ing \-ˌprī-ziŋ\ *adj* : bold and vigorous in action : ENERGETIC

en·ter·tain \ˌen-tər-ˈtān\ *vb* **1** : to treat or receive as a guest **2** : AMUSE, DIVERT ⟨~ed us with jokes⟩ **3** : to hold in mind ⟨~ed thoughts of retirement⟩ ✦ *Synonyms* HARBOR, SHELTER, LODGE, HOUSE, BILLET — **en·ter·tain·er** *n* — **en·ter·tain·ment** *n*

en·thrall *or* **en·thral** \in-ˈthról\ *vb* **en·thralled; en·thrall·ing 1** : ENSLAVE **2** : to hold spellbound

en·throne \in-ˈthrōn\ *vb* **1** : to seat on or as if on a throne **2** : EXALT

en·thuse \in-ˈthüz, -ˈthyüz\ *vb* **en·thused; en·thus·ing 1** : to make enthusiastic **2** : to show enthusiasm

en·thu·si·asm \in-ˈthü-zē-ˌa-zəm, -ˈthyü-\ *n* [Gk *enthousiasmos*, fr. *enthousiazein* to be inspired, irreg. fr. *entheos* inspired, fr. *theos* god] **1** : strong warmth of feeling : keen interest : FERVOR **2** : a cause of fervor — **en·thu·si·ast** \-ˌast, -əst\ *n* — **en·thu·si·as·tic** \in-ˌthü-zē-ˈas-tik, -ˌthyü-\ *adj* — **en·thu·si·as·ti·cal·ly** \-ti-k(ə-)lē\ *adv*

en·tice \in-ˈtīs\ *vb* **en·ticed; en·tic·ing** : ALLURE, TEMPT — **en·tice·ment** *n*

en·tire \in-ˈtī(-ə)r\ *adj* : COMPLETE, WHOLE ✦ *Synonyms* SOUND, PERFECT, INTACT, UNDAMAGED — **en·tire·ly** *adv*

en·tire·ty \in-ˈtī-rə-tē, -ˈtī(-ə)r-tē\ *n, pl* **-ties** **1** : COMPLETENESS **2** : WHOLE, TOTALITY

en·ti·tle \in-ˈtī-tᵊl\ *vb* **en·ti·tled; en·ti·tling 1** : NAME, DESIGNATE **2** : to give a right or claim to ⟨*entitled* to a fair trial⟩

en·ti·tle·ment \in-ˈtī-tᵊl-mənt\ *n* : a government program providing benefits to members of a specified group

en·ti·ty \ˈen-tə-tē\ *n, pl* **-ties** **1** : EXISTENCE, BEING **2** : something with separate and real existence

en·tomb \in-ˈtüm\ *vb* : to place in a tomb : BURY — **en·tomb·ment** *n*

en·to·mol·o·gy \ˌen-tə-ˈmä-lə-jē\ *n* : a branch of zoology that deals with insects — **en·to·mo·log·i·cal** \-mə-ˈlä-ji-kəl\ *adj* — **en·to·mol·o·gist** \-jist\ *n*

en·tou·rage \ˌän-tù-ˈräzh\ *n* [F] : RETINUE

en·tr'acte \ˈä⁽ⁿ⁾-ˌtrakt\ *n* [F] **1** : something (as a dance) performed between two acts of a play **2** : the interval between two acts of a play

en·trails \ˈen-ˌtrālz\ *n pl* : VISCERA; *esp* : INTESTINES

¹**en·trance** \ˈen-trəns\ *n* **1** : permission or right to enter **2** : the act of entering **3** : a means or place of entry

²**en·trance** \in-ˈtrans\ *vb* **en·tranced; en·tranc·ing** : CHARM, DELIGHT

en·trant \ˈen-trənt\ *n* : one that enters esp. as a competitor

en·trap \in-ˈtrap\ *vb* : ENSNARE, TRAP — **en·trap·ment** *n*

en·treat \in-ˈtrēt\ *vb* : to ask urgently : BESEECH ✦ *Synonyms* BEG, IMPLORE, PLEAD, SUPPLICATE — **en·treaty** \-ˈtrē-tē\ *n*

en·trée *or* **en·tree** \ˈän-ˌtrā\ *n* [F *entrée*] **1** : freedom of entry or access **2** : the main course of a meal in the U.S. ✦ *Synonyms* ADMISSION, ADMITTANCE, ENTRANCE

en·trench \in-ˈtrench\ *vb* **1** : to place within or surround with a trench esp. for defense; *also* : to establish solidly ⟨~ed customs⟩ **2** : ENCROACH, TRESPASS — **en·trench·ment** *n*

en·tre·pre·neur \ˌän-trə-prə-ˈnər, -ˈnùr, -ˈnyùr\ *n* [F, fr. OF, fr. *entreprendre* to undertake] : one who organizes and assumes the risk of a business or enterprise — **en·tre·pre·neur·ial** \-ˈnùr-ē-əl, -ˈnyùr-, -ˈnər-\ *adj* — **en·tre·pre·neur·ship** \-ˌship\ *n*

en·tro·py \ˈen-trə-pē\ *n, pl* **-pies** **1** : the degree of disorder in a system **2** : an ultimate state of inert uniformity

en·trust \in-ˈtrəst\ *vb* **1** : to commit something to as a trust **2** : to commit to another with confidence ✦ *Synonyms* CONFIDE, CONSIGN, RELEGATE, COMMEND

en·try \ˈen-trē\ *n, pl* **entries 1** : ENTRANCE 2 **2** : ENTRANCE 3; *also* : VESTIBULE 1 **3** : an entering in a record;

also : an item so entered **4** : a headword with its definition or identification; *also* : VOCABULARY ENTRY **5** : one entered in something (as a contest or market)

en·twine \in-'twīn\ *vb* : to twine together or around

enu·mer·ate \i-'nü-mə-ˌrāt, -'nyü-\ *vb* **-at·ed; -at·ing 1** : to determine the number of : COUNT **2** : LIST — **enu·mer·a·tion** \-ˌnü-mə-'rā-shən, -ˌnyü-\ *n*

enun·ci·ate \ē-'nən-sē-ˌāt\ *vb* **-at·ed; -at·ing 1** : to state definitely; *also* : ANNOUNCE, PROCLAIM **2** : PRONOUNCE, ARTICULATE — **enun·ci·a·tion** \-ˌnən-sē-'ā-shən\ *n*

en·ure·sis \ˌen-yù-'rē-səs\ *n* : involuntary discharge of urine : BED-WETTING

env *abbr* envelope

en·vel·op \in-'ve-ləp\ *vb* : to enclose completely with or as if with a covering — **en·vel·op·ment** *n*

en·ve·lope \'en-və-ˌlōp, 'än-\ *n* **1** : a usu. paper container for a letter **2** : WRAPPER, COVERING **3** : a conventionally accepted limit ⟨fashions that push the ∼⟩

en·ven·om \in-'ve-nəm\ *vb* **1** : to make poisonous **2** : EMBITTER

en·vi·able \'en-vē-ə-bəl\ *adj* : highly desirable — **en·vi·ably** \-blē\ *adv*

en·vi·ous \'en-vē-əs\ *adj* : feeling or showing envy — **en·vi·ous·ly** *adv* — **en·vi·ous·ness** *n*

en·vi·ron·ment \in-'vī-rən-mənt, -'vī(-ə)rn-\ *n* **1** : SURROUNDINGS **2** : the whole complex of factors (as soil, climate, and living things) that influence the form and the ability to survive of a plant or animal or ecological community — **en·vi·ron·men·tal** \-ˌvī-rən-'men-t⁹l, -ˌvīrn-\ *adj* — **en·vi·ron·men·tal·ly** \-t⁹l-ē\ *adv*

en·vi·ron·men·tal·ist \-ˌvī-rən-'men-təl-ist, -ˌvīr(-ə)n-\ *n* : a person concerned about environmental quality esp. with respect to control of pollution — **en·vi·ron·men·tal·ism** \-ˌvī-rən-'men-tə-ˌli-zəm, -ˌvī(-ə)rn-\ *n*

en·vi·rons \in-'vī-rənz\ *n pl* **1** : SUBURBS **2** : SURROUNDINGS; *also* : VICINITY

en·vis·age \in-'vi-zij\ *vb* **-aged; -ag·ing** : to have a mental picture of

en·vi·sion \in-'vi-zhən, en-\ *vb* : to picture to oneself ⟨∼s world peace⟩

en·voy \'en-ˌvói, 'än-\ *n* **1** : a diplomatic agent **2** : REPRESENTATIVE, MESSENGER

¹en·vy \'en-vē\ *n, pl* **envies** [ME *envie*, fr. AF, fr. L *invidia*, fr. *invidus* envious, fr. *invidēre* to look askance at, envy, fr. *vidēre* to see] : painful or resentful awareness of another's advantages; *also* : an object of envy

²envy *vb* **en·vied; en·vy·ing** : to feel envy toward or on account of

en·zyme \'en-ˌzīm\ *n* : any of various complex proteins produced by living cells that catalyze specific biochemical reactions at body temperatures — **en·zy·mat·ic** \ˌen-zə-'ma-tik\ *adj*

Eo·cene \'ē-ə-ˌsēn\ *adj* : of, relating to, or being the epoch of the Tertiary between the Paleocene and the Oligocene — **Eocene** *n*

EOE *abbr* equal opportunity employer

eo·lian \ē-'ō-lē-ən\ *adj* : borne, deposited, or produced by the wind

EOM *abbr* end of month

eon *var of* AEON

EP *abbr* European plan

EPA *abbr* Environmental Protection Agency

ep·au·let *also* **ep·au·lette** \ˌe-pə-'let\ *n* [F *épaulette,* dim. of *épaule* shoulder] : a shoulder ornament esp. on a coat or military uniform

épée \'e-ˌpā, ā-'pā\ *n* [F] : a fencing or dueling sword

Eph *or* **Ephes** *abbr* Ephesians

ephed·rine \i-'fe-drən\ *n* : a stimulant drug used to treat asthma and nasal congestion

ephem·era \i-'fe-mər-ə\ *n pl* : paper items (as posters or tickets) of little original value collected usu. as a hobby

ephem·er·al \i-'fe-mə-rəl\ *adj* [Gk *ephēmeros* lasting a day, daily, fr. *epi-* on +*hēmera* day] : SHORT-LIVED, TRANSITORY ✦ **Synonyms** PASSING, FLEETING, TRANSIENT, EVANESCENT — **ephem·er·al·i·ty** \i-ˌfe-mə-'ra-lə-tē\ *n*

Ephe·sians \i-'fē-zhənz\ *n* — see BIBLE table

ep·ic \'e-pik\ *n* : a long poem in elevated style narrating the deeds of a hero — **epic** *adj*

epi·cen·ter \'e-pi-ˌsen-tər\ *n* : the point on the earth's surface directly above the point of origin of an earthquake

ep·i·cure \'e-pi-ˌkyùr\ *n* : a person with sensitive and discriminating tastes esp. in food and wine

ep·i·cu·re·an \ˌe-pi-kyù-'rē-ən, -'kyùr-ē-\ *n* : EPICURE — **epicurean** *adj*

¹ep·i·dem·ic \ˌe-pə-'de-mik\ *adj* : affecting many persons at one time ⟨∼ disease⟩; *also* : excessively prevalent

²epidemic *n* : an epidemic outbreak esp. of disease

ep·i·de·mi·ol·o·gy \ˌep-ə-ˌdē-mē-'ä-lə-jē\ *n* : the study of the incidence, distribution, and control of disease in a population — **ep·i·de·mi·o·log·i·cal** \-ˌdē-mē-ə-'lä-ji-kəl\ *also* **ep·i·de·mi·o·log·ic** \-jik\ *adj* — **ep·i·de·mi·ol·o·gist** \-'ä-lə-jist\ *n*

epi·der·mis \ˌe-pə-'dər-məs\ *n* : an outer layer esp. of skin — **epi·der·mal** \-məl\ *adj*

epi·du·ral \ˌe-pi-'d(y)ùr-əl\ *adj* : administered into the space outside the membrane that envelops the spinal cord ⟨∼ anesthesia⟩ — **epidural** *n*

epi·glot·tis \ˌe-pə-'glä-təs\ *n* : a thin plate of flexible tissue protecting the tracheal opening during swallowing

ep·i·gram \'e-pə-ˌgram\ *n* : a short witty poem or saying — **ep·i·gram·mat·ic** \ˌe-pə-grə-'ma-tik\ *adj*

ep·i·lep·sy \'e-pə-ˌlep-sē\ *n, pl* **-sies** [ultim. fr. Gk *epilēpsia,* fr. *epilambanein* to seize] : a disorder marked by abnormal electrical discharges in the brain and typically manifested by sudden periods of diminished consciousness or by convulsions — **ep·i·lep·tic** \ˌe-pə-'lep-tik\ *adj or n*

ep·i·logue *also* **ep·i·log** \'e-pə-ˌlòg, -ˌläg\ *n* **1** : a concluding section of a literary work **2** : a speech addressed to the spectators by an actor at the end of a play

epi·neph·rine \ˌe-pə-'ne-frən\ *n* : an adrenal hormone used medicinally esp. as a heart stimulant, a muscle relaxant, and a vasoconstrictor

epiph·a·ny \i-'pi-fə-nē\ *n, pl* **-nies 1** *cap* : January 6 observed as a church festival in commemoration of the coming of the Magi to Jesus at Bethlehem **2** : a sudden striking understanding of something

epis·co·pa·cy \i-'pis-kə-pə-sē\ *n, pl* **-cies 1** : government of a church by bishops **2** : EPISCOPATE

epis·co·pal \i-'pis-kə-pəl\ *adj* **1** : of or relating to a bishop or episcopacy **2** *cap* : of or relating to the Protestant Episcopal Church

Epis·co·pa·lian \i-ˌpis-kə-'pāl-yən\ *n* : a member of the Protestant Episcopal Church

epis·co·pate \i-'pis-kə-pət, -ˌpāt\ *n* **1** : the rank, office, or term of a bishop **2** : a body of bishops

ep·i·sode \'e-pə-ˌsōd\ *n* [Gk *epeisodion,* fr. *epeisodios* coming in besides, fr. *eisodios* coming in, fr. *eis* into + *hodos* road, journey] **1** : a unit of action in a dramatic or literary work **2** : an incident in a course of events : OCCURRENCE ⟨a feverish ∼⟩ — **ep·i·sod·ic** \ˌe-pə-'sä-dik\ *adj*

epis·tle \i-'pi-səl\ *n* **1** *cap* : one of the letters of the New Testament **2** : LETTER — **epis·to·lary** \i-'pis-tə-ˌler-ē\ *adj*

ep·i·taph \'e-pə-ˌtaf\ *n* : an inscription in memory of a dead person

ep·i·tha·la·mi·um \ˌe-pə-thə-'lā-mē-əm\ *or* **ep·i·tha·la·mi·on** \-mē-ən\ *n, pl* **-mi·ums** *or* **-mia** \-mē-ə\ : a song or poem in honor of a bride and bridegroom

ep·i·the·li·um \ˌe-pə-'thē-lē-əm\ *n, pl* **-lia** \-lē-ə\ : a cellular membrane covering a bodily surface or lining a cavity — **ep·i·the·li·al** \-lē-əl\ *adj*

ep·i·thet \'e-pə-ˌthet, -thət\ *n* : a characterizing and often abusive word or phrase ⟨a racial ∼⟩

epit·o·me \i-'pi-tə-mē\ *n* **1** : ABSTRACT, SUMMARY **2** : EMBODIMENT — **epit·o·mize** \-ˌmīz\ *vb*

ep·och \'e-pək, -ˌpäk\ *n* : a usu. extended period : ERA, AGE — **ep·och·al** \-pə-kəl, -ˌpä-\ *adj*

ep·onym \'e-pə-ˌnim\ *n* **1** : one for whom something is or is believed to be named **2** : a name (as of a disease) based on or derived from an eponym — **epon·y·mous** \i-'pä-nə-məs\ *adj*

ep·oxy \i-'päk-sē\ *vb* **ep·ox·ied** *or* **ep·oxyed; ep·oxy·ing** : to glue, fill, or coat with epoxy resin

epoxy resin *n* : a synthetic resin used in coatings and adhesives

ep·si·lon \'ep-sə-län, -lən\ *n* : the 5th letter of the Greek alphabet — E or ε

Ep·som salts \'ep-səm-\ *n* : a bitter colorless or white magnesium salt with cathartic properties

eq *abbr* **1** equal **2** equation

equa·ble \'e-kwə-bəl, 'ē-\ *adj* : UNIFORM, EVEN; *esp* : free from unpleasant extremes — **equa·bil·i·ty** \ₑe-kwə-'bi-lə-tē, ₑē-\ *n* — **eq·ua·bly** \'e-kwə-blē, 'ē-\ *adv*

¹**equal** \'ē-kwəl\ *adj* **1** : of the same measure, quantity, value, quality, number, degree, or status as another ⟨∼ opportunity⟩ **2** : IMPARTIAL **3** : free from extremes **4** : able to cope with a situation or task — **equal·i·ty** \i-'kwä-lə-tē\ *n* — **equal·ly** *adv*

²**equal** *vb* equaled *or* equalled; equal·ing *or* equal·ling : to be or become equal to; *also* : to be identical in value to

³**equal** *n* : one that is equal

equal·ise, equal·is·er *Brit var of* EQUALIZE, EQUALIZER

equal·ize \'ē-kwə-ₗlīz\ *vb* -ized; -iz·ing : to make equal, uniform, or constant — **equal·i·za·tion** \ₑē-kwə-lə-'zā-shən\ *n* — **equal·iz·er** *n*

equals sign *or* **equal sign** *n* : a sign = indicating equivalence

equa·nim·i·ty \ₑē-kwə-'ni-mə-tē, ₑe-\ *n, pl* -ties : COMPOSURE

equate \i-'kwāt\ *vb* equat·ed; equat·ing : to make, treat, or regard as equal or comparable ⟨∼s liars with thieves⟩

equa·tion \i-'kwā-zhən\ *n* **1** : an act of equating : the state of being equated **2** : a usu. formal statement of equivalence esp. of mathematical expressions

equa·tor \i-'kwā-tər, 'ē-ₗ\ *n* : an imaginary circle around the earth that is everywhere equally distant from the two poles — **equa·to·ri·al** \ₑē-kwə-'tòr-ē-əl, ₑe-\ *adj*

equer·ry \'e-kwə-rē, i-'kwer-ē\ *n, pl* -ries **1** : an officer in charge of the horses of a prince or noble **2** : a personal attendant of a member of the British royal family

¹**eques·tri·an** \i-'kwes-trē-ən\ *adj* : of or relating to horse-back riding ⟨∼ competition⟩; *also* : representing a person on horseback ⟨an ∼ statue⟩

²**equestrian** *n* : one who rides a horse

eques·tri·enne \i-ₗkwes-trē-'en\ *n* : a female rider on horseback

equi·dis·tant \ₑē-kwə-'dis-tənt\ *adj* : equally distant

equi·lat·er·al \ₑē-kwə-'la-tə-rəl\ *adj* : having all sides or faces equal ⟨∼ triangles⟩

equi·lib·ri·um \ₑē-kwə-'li-brē-əm, ₑe-\ *n, pl* -ri·ums *or* -ria \-brē-ə\ : a state of intellectual or emotional balance; *also* : a state of balance between opposing forces or actions ✦ *Synonyms* POISE, BALANCE, EQUIPOISE

equine \'ē-ₗkwīn, 'e-\ *adj* [L *equinus*, fr. *equus* horse] : of or relating to the horse — **equine** *n*

equi·noc·tial \ₑē-kwə-'näk-shəl, ₑe-\ *adj* : relating to an equinox

equi·nox \'ē-kwə-ₗnäks, 'e-\ *n* : either of the two times each year when the sun appears directly overhead at the equator and day and night are everywhere on earth of equal length

equip \i-'kwip\ *vb* equipped; equip·ping [AF *eskiper* to load on board a ship, outfit, man, of Gmc origin] **1** : to supply with needed resources **2** : to make ready : PREPARE

equi·page \'e-kwə-pij\ *n* : a horse-drawn carriage usu. with its servants

equip·ment \i-'kwip-mənt\ *n* **1** : things used in equipping : SUPPLIES, OUTFIT **2** : the equipping of a person or thing : the state of being equipped

equi·poise \'e-kwə-ₗpòiz, 'ē-\ *n* **1** : BALANCE, EQUILIBRIUM **2** : COUNTERBALANCE

eq·ui·ta·ble \'e-kwə-tə-bəl\ *adj* : JUST, FAIR — **eq·ui·ta·bly** \-blē\ *adv*

eq·ui·ta·tion \ₑe-kwə-'tā-shən\ *n* : the act or art of riding on horseback

eq·ui·ty \'e-kwə-tē\ *n, pl* -ties **1** : JUSTNESS, IMPARTIALITY **2** : value of a property or of an interest in it in excess of claims against it

equiv *abbr* equivalent

equiv·a·lent \i-'kwi-və-lənt\ *adj* : EQUAL; *also* : virtually identical — **equiv·a·lence** \-ləns\ *n* — **equivalent** *n*

equiv·o·cal \i-'kwi-və-kəl\ *adj* **1** : AMBIGUOUS **2** : UNCERTAIN, UNDECIDED **3** : SUSPICIOUS, DUBIOUS ⟨∼ behavior⟩ ✦ *Synonyms* OBSCURE, DARK, VAGUE, ENIGMATIC — **equiv·o·cal·ly** *adv*

equiv·o·cate \i-'kwi-və-ₗkāt\ *vb* -cat·ed; -cat·ing **1** : to use misleading language **2** : to avoid giving a definite answer — **equiv·o·ca·tion** \-ₗkwi-və-'kā-shən\ *n*

¹**-er** \ər\ *adj suffix or adv suffix* — used to form the comparative degree of adjectives and adverbs of one or two

syllables ⟨hotter⟩ ⟨drier⟩ ⟨sillier⟩ and sometimes of longer ones

²**-er** \ər\ *also* -ier \ē-ər, yər\ *or* -yer \yər\ *n suffix* **1** : a person occupationally connected with ⟨furrier⟩ ⟨lawyer⟩ **2** : a person or thing belonging to or associated with ⟨old-timer⟩ **3** : a native of : resident of ⟨New Zealander⟩ **4** : one that has ⟨double-decker⟩ **5** : one that produces or yields ⟨porker⟩ **6** : one that does or performs (a specified action) ⟨batter⟩ **7** : one that is a suitable object of (a specified action) ⟨broiler⟩ **8** : one that is ⟨foreigner⟩

Er *symbol* erbium

ER *abbr* emergency room

era \'er-ə, 'e-rə, 'ir-ə\ *n* [LL *aera*, fr. L, counters, pl. of *aes* copper, money] **1** : a chronological order or system of notation reckoned from a given date as basis **2** : a period identified by some special feature ⟨the ∼ of industrialization⟩ **3** : any of the four major divisions of geologic time ✦ *Synonyms* AGE, EPOCH, PERIOD, TIME

ERA *abbr* **1** earned run average **2** Equal Rights Amendment

erad·i·cate \i-'ra-də-ₗkāt\ *vb* -cat·ed; -cat·ing [L *eradicatus*, pp. of *eradicare*, fr. *e-* out + *radix* root] : UPROOT, ELIMINATE ✦ *Synonyms* EXTERMINATE, ANNIHILATE, ABOLISH, EXTINGUISH — **erad·i·ca·ble** \-di-kə-bəl\ *adj* — **erad·i·ca·tion** \-ₗra-də-'kā-shən\ *n*

erase \i-'rās\ *vb* erased; eras·ing : to rub or scratch out (as written words); *also* : OBLITERATE ✦ *Synonyms* CANCEL, EFFACE, DELETE, EXPUNGE — **eras·er** *n* — **era·sure** \i-'rā-shər\ *n*

er·bi·um \'ər-bē-əm\ *n* : a rare metallic element found with yttrium

¹**ere** \'er\ *prep* : BEFORE

²**ere** *conj* : BEFORE

¹**erect** \i-'rekt\ *adj* **1** : not leaning or lying down : UPRIGHT **2** : being in a state of physiological erection

²**erect** *vb* **1** : BUILD **2** : to fix or set in an upright position ⟨∼ an antenna⟩ **3** : SET UP; *also* : ESTABLISH, DEVELOP

erec·tile \i-'rek-tᵊl, -'rek-ₗtī(-ə)l\ *adj* : capable of becoming erect ⟨∼ tissue⟩ ⟨∼ feathers of a bird⟩

erec·tion \i-'rek-shən\ *n* **1** : the turgid state of a previously flaccid bodily part when it becomes dilated with blood **2** : CONSTRUCTION

ere·long \er-'lòŋ\ *adv* : before long

er·e·mite \'er-ə-ₗmīt\ *n* : HERMIT

er·go \'er-gō, 'ər-\ *adv* [L] : THEREFORE

er·go·nom·ics \ₗər-gə-'nä-miks\ *n sing or pl* : an applied science concerned with designing and arranging things people use in order to improve efficiency and safety — **er·go·nom·ic** \-mik\ *adj*

er·got \'ər-gət, -ₗgät\ *n* **1** : a disease of rye and other cereals caused by a fungus; *also* : this fungus **2** : a medicinal compound or preparation derived from an ergot fungus

er·mine \'ər-mən\ *n, pl* ermines **1** : any of several weasels with winter fur mostly white; *also* : this white fur **2** : a rank or office whose official robe is ornamented with ermine

ermine 1

erode \i-'rōd\ *vb* erod·ed; erod·ing : to diminish or destroy by degrees; *esp* : to gradually eat into or wear away ⟨soil *eroded* by wind and water⟩ — **erod·ible** *also* **erod·able** \-'rō-də-bəl\ *adj*

erog·e·nous \i-'rä-jə-nəs\ *adj* **1** : sexually sensitive ⟨∼ zones⟩ **2** : of, relating to, or arousing sexual feelings

ero·sion \i-'rō-zhən\ *n* : the process or state of being eroded — **ero·sion·al** \-'rō-zhə-nəl\ *adj* — **ero·sion·al·ly** *adv*

ero·sive \i-'rō-siv\ *adj* : tending to erode — **ero·sive·ness** *n*

erot·ic \i-'rä-tik\ *adj* : relating to or dealing with sexual love : AMATORY ⟨∼ art⟩ — **erot·i·cal·ly** \-ti-k(ə-)lē\ *adv* — **erot·i·cism** \-tə-ˌsi-zəm\ *n*

err \ˈer, ˈər\ *vb* : to be or do wrong

er·rand \ˈer-ənd\ *n* : a short trip taken to do something; *also* : the object or purpose of such a trip

er·rant \ˈer-ənt\ *adj* **1** : WANDERING ⟨an ∼ knight⟩ **2** : straying outside proper bounds ⟨an ∼ throw⟩ **3** : behaving wrongly ⟨an ∼ child⟩

er·ra·ta \e-ˈrä-tə\ *n* : a list of corrigenda

er·rat·ic \i-ˈra-tik\ *adj* **1** : having no fixed course **2** : INCONSISTENT ⟨∼ dieting⟩; *also* : ECCENTRIC — **er·rat·i·cal·ly** \-ti-k(ə-)lē\ *adv*

er·ra·tum \e-ˈrä-təm\ *n, pl* **-ta** \-tə\ : CORRIGENDUM

er·ro·ne·ous \i-ˈrō-nē-əs, e-ˈrō-\ *adj* : INCORRECT — **er·ro·ne·ous·ly** *adv*

er·ror \ˈer-ər\ *n* **1** : a usu. ignorant or unintentional deviating from accuracy or truth ⟨made an ∼ in adding⟩ **2** : a defensive misplay in baseball **3** : the state of one that errs ⟨to be in ∼⟩ **4** : a product of mistake ⟨a typographical ∼⟩ — **er·ror·less** *adj*

er·satz \ˈer-ˌzäts\ *adj* [G *ersatz-*, fr. *Ersatz*, n., substitute] : being usu. an artificial and inferior substitute

erst \ˈərst\ *adv, archaic* : ERSTWHILE

¹erst·while \-ˌhwī(-ə)l\ *adv* : in the past : FORMERLY

²erstwhile *adj* : FORMER, PREVIOUS

er·u·di·tion \ˌer-ə-ˈdi-shən, ˌer-yə-\ *n* : SCHOLARSHIP, LEARNING — **er·u·dite** \ˈer-ə-ˌdīt, ˈer-yə-\ *adj*

erupt \i-ˈrəpt\ *vb* **1** : to burst forth or cause to burst forth : EXPLODE **2** : to break through a surface ⟨teeth ∼*ing* through the gum⟩ **3** : to break out with or as if with a skin rash — **erup·tion** \-ˈrəp-shən\ *n* — **erup·tive** \-tiv\ *adj*

-ery *n suffix* **1** : qualities collectively : character : -NESS ⟨snobb*ery*⟩ **2** : art : practice ⟨cook*ery*⟩ **3** : place of doing, keeping, producing, or selling (the thing specified) ⟨fish*ery*⟩ ⟨bak*ery*⟩ **4** : collection : aggregate ⟨fin*ery*⟩ **5** : state or condition ⟨slav*ery*⟩

ery·sip·e·las \ˌer-ə-ˈsi-pə-ləs, ˌir-\ *n* : an acute bacterial disease marked by fever and severe skin inflammation

er·y·the·ma \ˌer-ə-ˈthē-mə\ *n* : abnormal redness of the skin due to capillary congestion (as in inflammation)

eryth·ro·cyte \i-ˈri-thrə-ˌsīt\ *n* : RED BLOOD CELL

Es *symbol* einsteinium

¹-es \əz, iz *after* s, z, sh, ch; z *after* v *or a vowel*\ *n pl suffix* — used to form the plural of most nouns that end in *s* ⟨glass*es*⟩, *z* ⟨fuzz*es*⟩, *sh* ⟨bush*es*⟩, *ch* ⟨peach*es*⟩, or a final *y* that changes to *i* ⟨lad*ies*⟩ and of some nouns ending in *f* that changes to *v* ⟨loav*es*⟩

²-es *vb suffix* — used to form the third person singular present of most verbs that end in *s* ⟨bless*es*⟩, *z* ⟨fizz*es*⟩, *sh* ⟨hush*es*⟩, *ch* ⟨catch*es*⟩, or a final *y* that changes to *i* ⟨defies⟩

es·ca·late \ˈes-kə-ˌlāt\ *vb* **-lat·ed; -lat·ing** : to increase in extent, volume, number, intensity, or scope — **es·ca·la·tion** \ˌes-kə-ˈlā-shən\ *n*

es·ca·la·tor \ˈes-kə-ˌlā-tər\ *n* : a moving set of stairs

escallop *var of* SCALLOP

es·ca·pade \ˈes-kə-ˌpād\ *n* [F, action of escaping] : a mischievous adventure

¹es·cape \is-ˈkāp\ *vb* **es·caped; es·cap·ing** [ME, fr. AF *escaper, eschaper*, fr. VL **excappare*, fr. L *ex-* out + LL *cappa* head covering, cloak] **1** : to get free or away **2** : to avoid a threatening evil **3** : AVOID **2** ⟨∼ injury⟩ **4** : ELUDE ⟨his name ∼*s* me⟩ **5** : to be produced or uttered involuntarily by ⟨let a sob ∼ him⟩

²escape *n* **1** : flight from or avoidance of something unpleasant **2** : LEAKAGE **3** : a means of escape

³escape *adj* : providing a means or way of escape

es·cap·ee \is-ˌkā-ˈpē, ˌes-(ˌ)kā-\ *n* : one that has escaped esp. from prison

escape velocity *n* : the minimum velocity needed by a body (as a rocket) to escape from the gravitational field of a celestial body (as the earth)

es·cap·ism \is-ˈkā-ˌpi-zəm\ *n* : diversion of the mind to imaginative activity as an escape from routine — **es·cap·ist** \-pist\ *adj or n*

es·car·got \is-ˌkär-ˈgō\ *n, pl* **-gots** \-ˈgō(z)\ : a snail prepared for use as food

es·ca·role \ˈes-kə-ˌrōl\ *n* : ENDIVE 1

es·carp·ment \es-ˈkärp-mənt\ *n* **1** : a steep slope in front of a fortification **2** : a long cliff

es·chew \is-ˈchü\ *vb* : SHUN, AVOID

¹es·cort \ˈes-ˌkȯrt\ *n* : one (as a person or warship) accompanying another esp. as a protection or courtesy

²es·cort \is-ˈkȯrt, es-\ *vb* : to accompany as an escort

es·crow \ˈes-ˌkrō\ *n* [AF *escrowe* scroll, strip of parchment] : something (as a deed or a sum of money) delivered by one person to another to be delivered to a third party only upon the fulfillment of a condition; *also* : a fund or deposit serving as an escrow

es·cu·do \is-ˈkü-dō\ *n, pl* **-dos** **1** : the former basic monetary unit of Portugal **2** — see MONEY table

es·cutch·eon \is-ˈkə-chən\ *n* : the usu. shield-shaped surface on which a coat of arms is shown

Esd *abbr* Esdras

Es·dras \ˈez-drəs\ *n* — see BIBLE table

ESE *abbr* east-southeast

Es·ki·mo \ˈes-kə-ˌmō\ *n* **1** : a member of a group of peoples of northern Canada, Greenland, Alaska, and eastern Siberia **2** : any of the languages of the Eskimo peoples

Eskimo dog *n* : a sled dog of American origin

ESL *abbr* English as a second language

esoph·a·gus \i-ˈsä-fə-gəs\ *n, pl* **-gi** \-ˌgī, -ˌjī\ : a muscular tube that leads from the cavity behind the mouth to the stomach — **esoph·a·geal** \-ˌsä-fə-ˈjē-əl\ *adj*

es·o·ter·ic \ˌe-sə-ˈter-ik\ *adj* **1** : designed for or understood only by the specially initiated **2** : PRIVATE, SECRET

esp *abbr* especially

ESP \ˌē-(ˌ)es-ˈpē\ *n* : EXTRASENSORY PERCEPTION

es·pa·drille \ˈes-pə-ˌdril\ *n* [F] : a flat sandal usu. having a fabric upper and a flexible sole

es·pal·ier \is-ˈpal-yər, -ˌyā\ *n* : a plant (as a fruit tree) trained to grow flat against a support — **espalier** *vb*

es·pe·cial \is-ˈpe-shəl\ *adj* : SPECIAL, PARTICULAR — **es·pe·cial·ly** *adv*

Es·pe·ran·to \ˌes-pə-ˈrän-tō, -ˈran-\ *n* : an artificial international language based esp. on words common to the chief European languages

es·pi·o·nage \ˈes-pē-ə-ˌnäzh, -nij\ *n* [F *espionnage*] : the practice of spying

es·pla·nade \ˈes-plə-ˌnäd\ *n* : a level open stretch or area; *esp* : one for walking or driving along a shore

es·pous·al \is-ˈpau̇-zəl\ *n* **1** : BETROTHAL; *also* : WEDDING **2** : a taking up (as of a cause) as a supporter ⟨∼ of human rights⟩ — **es·pouse** \-ˈpau̇z\ *vb*

espres·so \e-ˈspre-sō\ *n, pl* **-sos** : coffee brewed by forcing steam or hot water through finely ground darkly roasted coffee beans

es·prit \i-ˈsprē\ *n* : sprightly wit

es·prit de corps \i-ˌsprē-də-ˈkȯr\ *n* [F] : the common spirit existing in the members of a group

es·py \i-ˈspī\ *vb* **es·pied; es·py·ing** : to catch sight of ◆ *Synonyms* BEHOLD, SEE, VIEW, DESCRY

Esq *or* **Esqr** *abbr* esquire

es·quire \ˈes-ˌkwī(-ə)r\ *n* [ME, fr. AF *esquier* squire, fr. LL *scutarius*, fr. L *scutum* shield] **1** : a man of the English gentry ranking next below a knight **2** : a candidate for knighthood serving as attendant to a knight **3** — used as a title of courtesy

-ess \əs, ˌes\ *n suffix* : female ⟨author*ess*⟩

¹es·say \e-ˈsā, ˈe-ˌsā\ *vb* : ATTEMPT, TRY

²es·say *n* **1** \e-ˈsā, e-ˈsā\ : ATTEMPT **2** \ˈe-ˌsā\ : a literary composition usu. dealing with a subject from a limited or personal point of view — **es·say·ist** \ˈe-ˌsā-ist\ *n*

es·sence \ˈe-sᵊns\ *n* **1** : fundamental nature or quality **2** : a substance distilled or extracted from another substance (as a plant or drug) and having the special qualities of the original substance **3** : PERFUME **4** : the most significant element or aspect of something ⟨the ∼ of the issue⟩

¹es·sen·tial \i-ˈsen-chəl\ *adj* **1** : of, relating to, or constituting an essence ⟨voting is an ∼ right of citizenship⟩ ⟨∼ oils⟩ **2** : of the utmost importance : INDISPENSABLE **3** : being a substance that must be obtained from the diet because it is not synthetically produced by the body ⟨∼ amino acids⟩ ◆ *Synonyms* IMPERATIVE, NECESSARY, NECESSITOUS — **es·sen·tial·ly** *adv*

²essential *n* : something essential

est *abbr* **1** established **2** estimate; estimated

EST *abbr* eastern standard time

¹-est \əst, ist\ *adj suffix or adv suffix* — used to form the superlative degree of adjectives and adverbs of one or two syllables ⟨fatt*est*⟩ ⟨lat*est*⟩ ⟨lucki*est*⟩ ⟨often*est*⟩ and less often of longer ones

²-est \əst, ist\ *or* **-st** \st\ *vb suffix* — used to form the archaic second person singular of English verbs (with *thou*) ⟨did*st*⟩

es·tab·lish \i-'sta-blish\ *vb* **1** : to institute permanently ⟨~ a law⟩ **2** : FOUND ⟨~ a settlement⟩; *also* : EFFECT **3** : to make firm or stable **4** : to put on a firm basis : SET UP ⟨~ a son in business⟩ **5** : to gain acceptance or recognition of ⟨the movie ~*ed* her as a star⟩; *also* : PROVE

es·tab·lish·ment \-mənt\ *n* **1** : something established **2** : a place of residence or business with its furnishings and staff **3** : an established ruling or controlling group ⟨the literary ~⟩ **4** : the act or state of establishing or being established

es·tate \i-'stāt\ *n* **1** : STATE, CONDITION; *also* : social standing : STATUS **2** : a social or political class ⟨the three ~*s* of nobility, clergy, and commons⟩ **3** : a person's possessions : FORTUNE **4** : a landed property

¹es·teem \i-'stēm\ *n* : high regard

²esteem *vb* **1** : REGARD **2** : to set a high value on ✦ *Synonyms* RESPECT, ADMIRE, REVERE

es·ter \'es-tər\ *n* : an often fragrant organic compound formed by the reaction of an acid and an alcohol

Esth *abbr* Esther

Es·ther \'es-tər\ *n* — see BIBLE table

esthete, esthetic, esthetically, esthetics *var of* AESTHETE, AESTHETIC, AESTHETICALLY, AESTHETICS

es·ti·ma·ble \'es-tə-mə-bəl\ *adj* : worthy of esteem ⟨an ~ adversary⟩

¹es·ti·mate \'es-tə-,māt\ *vb* **-mat·ed; -mat·ing 1** : to give or form an approximation (as of value, size, or cost) **2** : JUDGE, CONCLUDE ✦ *Synonyms* EVALUATE, VALUE, RATE, APPRAISE, ASSAY, ASSESS — **es·ti·ma·tor** \-,mā-tər\ *n*

²es·ti·mate \'es-tə-mət\ *n* **1** : OPINION, JUDGMENT **2** : a rough or approximate calculation **3** : a statement of the cost of work to be done

es·ti·ma·tion \,es-tə-'mā-shən\ *n* **1** : JUDGMENT, OPINION **2** : ESTIMATE **3** : ESTEEM, HONOR

es·ti·vate \'es-tə-,vāt\ *vb* **-vat·ed; -vat·ing** : to pass the summer in an inactive or resting state — **es·ti·va·tion** \,es-tə-'vā-shən\ *n*

es·trange \i-'strānj\ *vb* **es·tranged; es·trang·ing** : to alienate the affections or confidence of — **es·trange·ment** *n*

es·tro·gen \'es-trə-jən\ *n* : a steroid (as a sex hormone) that tends to cause estrus and the development of female secondary sex characteristics — **es·tro·gen·ic** \,es-trə-'je-nik\ *adj*

estrous cycle *n* : the cycle of changes in the endocrine and reproductive systems of a female mammal from the beginning of one period of estrus to the beginning of the next

es·trus \'es-trəs\ *n* : a periodic state of sexual excitability during which the female of most mammals is willing to mate with the male and is capable of becoming pregnant : HEAT — **es·trous** \-trəs\ *adj*

es·tu·ary \'es-chə-,wer-ē\ *n, pl* **-ar·ies** : an arm of the sea at the mouth of a river — **es·tu·a·rine** \-wə-,rīn, -,rēn, -rin\ *adj*

ET *abbr* eastern time

eta \'ā-tə\ *n* : the 7th letter of the Greek alphabet — H or η

ETA *abbr* estimated time of arrival

et al \et-'al\ *abbr* [L *et alii* (masc.), *et aliae* (fem.), or *et alia* (neut.)] and others

etc *abbr* et cetera

et cet·era \et-'se-tə-rə, -'se-trə\ [L] and others esp. of the same kind

etch \'ech\ *vb* [D *etsen*, fr. G *ätzen* to etch, corrode, fr. OHG *azzen* to feed] **1** : to produce (as a design) on a hard material by corroding its surface (as by acid) **2** : to delineate clearly — **etch·er** *n*

etch·ing *n* **1** : the action, process, or art of etching **2** : a design produced on or print made from an etched plate

ETD *abbr* estimated time of departure

eter·nal \i-'tər-nᵊl\ *adj* : EVERLASTING, PERPETUAL — **eter·nal·ly** *adv*

eter·ni·ty \i-'tər-nə-tē\ *n, pl* **-ties 1** : infinite duration **2** : IMMORTALITY

¹-eth \əth, ith\ *or* **-th** \th\ *vb suffix* — used to form the archaic third person singular present of verbs ⟨do*th*⟩

²-eth — see **²-TH**

eth·ane \'e-,thān\ *n* : a colorless odorless gaseous hydrocarbon found in natural gas and used esp. as a fuel

eth·a·nol \'e-thə-,nȯl\ *n* : ALCOHOL 1

ether \'ē-thər\ *n* **1** : the upper regions of space; *also* : the gaseous element formerly held to fill these regions **2** : a light flammable liquid used as an anesthetic and solvent

ethe·re·al \i-'thir-ē-əl\ *adj* **1** : CELESTIAL, HEAVENLY **2** : exceptionally delicate : AIRY, DAINTY — **ethe·re·al·ly** *adv* — **ethe·re·al·ness** *n*

Ether·net \'ē-thər-,net\ *n* : a computer network architecture for local area networks

eth·i·cal \'e-thi-kəl\ *adj* **1** : of or relating to ethics **2** : conforming to accepted and esp. professional standards of conduct ✦ *Synonyms* VIRTUOUS, MORAL, PRINCIPLED — **eth·i·cal·ly** *adv*

eth·ics \'e-thiks\ *n sing or pl* **1** : a discipline dealing with good and evil and with moral duty **2** : moral principles or practice

¹eth·nic \'eth-nik\ *adj* [ME, heathen, fr. LL *ethnicus*, fr. Gk *ethnikos* national, gentile, fr. *ethnos* nation, people] : of or relating to races or large groups of people classed according to common traits and customs — **eth·ni·cal·ly** *adv*

²ethnic *n* : a member of a minority ethnic group who retains its customs, language, or social views

eth·nol·o·gy \eth-'nä-lə-jē\ *n* : a science dealing with the races of human beings, their origin, distribution, characteristics, and relations — **eth·no·log·i·cal** \,eth-nə-'lä-ji-kəl\ *adj* — **eth·nol·o·gist** \eth-'nä-lə-jist\ *n*

ethol·o·gy \ē-'thä-lə-jē\ *n* : the scientific and objective study of animal behavior — **etho·log·i·cal** \,ē-thə-'lä-ji-kəl, ,e-\ *adj* — **ethol·o·gist** \ē-'thä-lə-jist\ *n*

ethos \'ē-,thäs\ *n* : the distinguishing character, sentiment, moral nature, or guiding beliefs of a person, group, or institution

ethyl alcohol *n* : ALCOHOL 1

eth·yl·ene \'e-thə-,lēn\ *n* : a colorless flammable gas found in coal gas or obtained from petroleum

eti·ol·o·gy \,ē-tē-'ä-lə-jē\ *n* : the causes of a disease or abnormal condition; *also* : a branch of medicine concerned with the causes and origins of diseases — **eti·o·log·ic** \,ē-tē-ə-'lä-jik\ *or* **eti·o·log·i·cal** \-ji-kəl\ *adj*

et·i·quette \'e-ti-kət, -,ket\ *n* [F *étiquette*, lit., label, list] : the forms prescribed by custom or authority to be observed in social, official, or professional life ✦ *Synonyms* PROPRIETY, DECORUM, DECENCY, DIGNITY

Etrus·can \i-'trəs-kən\ *n* **1** : the language of the Etruscans **2** : an inhabitant of ancient Etruria — **Etruscan** *adj*

et seq *abbr* [L *et sequens*] and the following one; [L *et sequentes* (masc. & fem. pl.) or *et sequentia* (neut. pl.)] and the following ones

-ette \'et, ,et, ət, it\ *n suffix* **1** : little one ⟨din*ette*⟩ **2** : female ⟨usher*ette*⟩

étude \'ā-,tüd, -,tyüd\ *n* [F, lit., study] : a musical composition for practice to develop technical skill

et·y·mol·o·gy \,e-tə-'mä-lə-jē\ *n, pl* **-gies 1** : the history of a linguistic form (as a word) shown by tracing its development and relationships **2** : a branch of linguistics dealing with etymologies — **et·y·mo·log·i·cal** \-mə-'lä-ji-kəl\ *adj* — **et·y·mol·o·gist** \-'mä-lə-jist\ *n*

Eu *symbol* europium

eu·ca·lyp·tus \,yü-kə-'lip-təs\ *n, pl* **-ti** \-,tī\ *or* **-tus·es** : any of a genus of mostly Australian evergreen trees widely grown for shade or their wood, oils, resins, and gums

Eu·cha·rist \'yü-kə-rəst\ *n* : COMMUNION 2 — **eu·cha·ris·tic** \,yü-kə-'ris-tik\ *adj, often cap*

¹eu·chre \'yü-kər\ *n* : a card game in which the side naming the trump must take three of five tricks to win

²euchre *vb* **eu·chred; eu·chring** : CHEAT, TRICK

eu·clid·e·an *also* **eu·clid·i·an** \yü-'kli-dē-ən\ *adj, often cap* : of or relating to the geometry of Euclid or a geometry based on similar axioms

eu·gen·ics \yü-'je-niks\ *n* : a science dealing with the improvement (as by selective breeding) of hereditary qualities esp. of human beings — **eu·gen·ic** \-nik\ *adj*

eu·lo·gy \'yü-lə-jē\ *n, pl* **-gies 1** : a speech in praise of some person or thing esp. in honor of a deceased person **2** : high praise — **eu·lo·gis·tic** \,yü-lə-'jis-tik\ *adj* — **eu·lo·gize** \'yü-lə-,jīz\ *vb*

eu·nuch \'yü-nək\ *n* : a castrated man

eu·phe·mism \'yü-fə-ˌmi-zəm\ *n* [Gk *euphēmismos*, fr. *euphēmos* auspicious, sounding good, fr. *eu-* good + *phēmē* speech] : the substitution of a mild or pleasant expression for one offensive or unpleasant; *also* : the expression substituted — **eu·phe·mis·tic** \ˌyü-fə-'mis-tik\ *adj* — **eu·phe·mis·ti·cal·ly** \-ti-k(ə-)lē\ *adv*

eu·pho·ni·ous \yü-'fō-nē-əs\ *adj* : pleasing to the ear — **eu·pho·ni·ous·ly** *adv*

eu·pho·ny \'yü-fə-nē\ *n, pl* **-nies** : the effect produced by words so combined as to please the ear

eu·pho·ria \yü-'fôr-ē-ə\ *n* : a marked feeling of well-being or elation — **eu·phor·ic** \-'fôr-ik\ *adj*

Eur *abbr* Europe; European

Eur·asian \yü-'rā-zhən, -shən\ *adj* **1** : of mixed European and Asian origin **2** : of or relating to Europe and Asia — **Eurasian** *n*

eu·re·ka \yü-'rē-kə\ *interj* [Gk *heurēka* I have found, fr. *heuriskein* to find; fr. the exclamation attributed to Archimedes on discovering a method for determining the purity of gold] — used to express triumph on a discovery

eu·ro \'yùr-ō\ *n, pl* **euros** : the common basic monetary unit of most countries of the European Union — see MONEY table

Eu·ro–Amer·i·can \ˌyùr-ō-ə-'mer-ə-kən\ *n* **1** : a person of mixed European and American ancestry **2** : CAUCASIAN

Eu·ro·bond \'yùr-ō-ˌbänd\ *n* : a bond of a U.S. corporation that is sold outside the U.S. but that is valued and paid for in dollars and yields interest in dollars

Eu·ro·cur·ren·cy \ˌyùr-ō-'kər-ən-sē\ *n* : moneys (as of the U.S. and Japan) held outside their countries of origin and used in the money markets of Europe

Eu·ro·dol·lar \'yùr-ō-ˌdä-lər\ *n* : a U.S. dollar held as Eurocurrency

Eu·ro·pe·an \ˌyùr-ə-'pē-ən\ *n* **1** : a native or inhabitant of Europe **2** : a person of European descent — **European** *adj* — **Eu·ro·pe·an·ize** \-ə-ˌnīz\ *vb*

European–American *n* : EURO-AMERICAN

Eu·ro·pe·an·ism \ˌyùr-ō-'pē-ə-ni-zəm\ *n* **1** : allegiance to the traditions, interests, or ideals of Europeans **2** : advocacy of political and economic integration of Europe — **eu·ro·pe·an·ist** \-nist\ *n*

European plan *n* : a hotel plan whereby the daily rates cover only the cost of the room

eu·ro·pi·um \yù-'rō-pē-əm\ *n* : a rare metallic chemical element

eu·sta·chian tube \yù-'stā-shən-\ *n, often cap E* : a tube connecting the inner cavity of the ear with the throat and equalizing air pressure on both sides of the eardrum

eu·tha·na·sia \ˌyü-thə-'nā-zhə\ *n* [Gk, easy death, fr. *eu-* good + *thanatos* death] : the act or practice of killing or permitting the death of hopelessly sick or injured persons or animals with as little pain as possible for reasons of mercy

EVA *abbr* extravehicular activity

evac·u·ate \i-'va-kyə-ˌwāt\ *vb* **-at·ed; -at·ing 1** : EMPTY **2** : to discharge wastes from the body **3** : to remove or withdraw from : VACATE — **evac·u·a·tion** \-ˌva-kyə-'wā-shən\ *n*

evac·u·ee \i-ˌva-kyə-'wē\ *n* : a person removed from a dangerous place

evade \i-'vād\ *vb* **evad·ed; evad·ing** : to manage to avoid esp. by dexterity or slyness : ELUDE, ESCAPE

eval·u·ate \i-'val-yù-ˌwāt\ *vb* **-at·ed; -at·ing** : APPRAISE, VALUE — **eval·u·a·tion** \-ˌval-yù-'wā-shən\ *n*

ev·a·nes·cent \ˌe-və-'ne-s°nt\ *adj* : tending to vanish like vapor ⟨~ pleasures⟩ ✦ **Synonyms** PASSING, TRANSIENT, TRANSITORY, MOMENTARY — **ev·a·nes·cence** \-s°ns\ *n*

evan·gel·i·cal \ˌē-ˌvan-'je-li-kəl, ˌe-vən-\ *adj* [LL *evangelium* gospel, fr. Gk *evangelion*, fr. *euangelos* bringing good news, fr. *eu-* good + *angelos* messenger] **1** : of or relating to the Christian gospel esp. as presented in the four Gospels **2** : of or relating to certain Protestant churches emphasizing the authority of Scripture and the importance of preaching as contrasted with ritual **3** : ZEALOUS ⟨~ fervor⟩ — **Evangelical** *n* — **Evan·gel·i·cal·ism** \-kə-ˌli-zəm\ *n* — **evan·gel·i·cal·ly** *adv*

evan·ge·lism \i-'van-jə-ˌli-zəm\ *n* **1** : the winning or revival of personal commitments to Christ **2** : militant or crusading zeal — **evan·ge·lis·tic** \-ˌvan-jə-'lis-tik\ *adj* — **evan·ge·lis·ti·cal·ly** *adv*

evan·ge·list \i-'van-jə-list\ *n* **1** *often cap* : the writer of any of the four Gospels **2** : a person who evangelizes; *esp* : a Protestant minister or layman who preaches at special services

evan·ge·lize \i-'van-jə-ˌlīz\ *vb* **-lized; -liz·ing 1** : to preach the gospel **2** : to convert to Christianity

evap *abbr* evaporate

evap·o·rate \i-'va-pə-ˌrāt\ *vb* **-rat·ed; -rat·ing 1** : to pass off or cause to pass off in vapor **2** : to disappear quickly **3** : to drive out the moisture from (as by heat) — **evap·o·ra·tion** \-ˌva-pə-'rā-shən\ *n* — **evap·o·ra·tor** \-ˌrā-tər\ *n*

evap·o·rite \i-'va-pə-ˌrīt\ *n* : a sedimentary rock that originates by the evaporation of seawater in an enclosed basin

eva·sion \i-'vā-zhən\ *n* **1** : a means of evading **2** : an act or instance of evading — **eva·sive** \i-'vā-siv\ *adj* — **eva·sive·ness** *n*

eve \'ēv\ *n* **1** : EVENING **2** : the period just before some important event

¹even \'ē-vən\ *adj* **1** : LEVEL, FLAT **2** : REGULAR, SMOOTH **3** : EQUAL, FAIR ⟨an ~ exchange⟩ **4** : BALANCED; *also* : fully revenged **5** : divisible by two **6** : EXACT ⟨an ~ dollar⟩ — **even·ly** *adv* — **even·ness** *n*

²even *adv* **1** : EXACTLY, PRECISELY **2** : FULLY, QUITE **3** : at the very time **4** — used as an intensive to stress identity ⟨~ I know that⟩ **5** — used as an intensive to emphasize something extreme or highly unlikely ⟨so simple ~ a child can do it⟩ **6** — used as an intensive to stress the comparative degree ⟨did ~ better⟩ **7** — used as an intensive to indicate a small or minimum degree ⟨didn't ~ try⟩

³even *vb* : to make or become even

even·hand·ed \ˌē-vən-'han-dəd\ *adj* : FAIR, IMPARTIAL — **even·hand·ed·ly** *adv*

eve·ning \'ēv-niŋ\ *n* **1** : the end of the day and early part of the night **2** *chiefly Southern & Midland* : AFTERNOON

evening primrose *n* : a coarse biennial herb with yellow flowers that open in the evening

evening star *n* : a bright planet (as Venus) seen esp. in the western sky at or after sunset

even·song \'ē-vən-ˌsóŋ\ *n, often cap* **1** : VESPERS **2** : evening prayer esp. when sung

event \i-'vent\ *n* [MF or L; MF, fr. L *eventus*, fr. *evenire* to happen, fr. *venire* to come] **1** : OCCURRENCE **2** : a noteworthy happening **3** : CONTINGENCY ⟨in the ~ of rain⟩ **4** : a contest in a program of sports — **event·ful** *adj*

even·tide \'ē-vən-ˌtīd\ *n* : EVENING

even·tu·al \i-'ven-chù-wəl\ *adj* : coming at some later time : ULTIMATE — **even·tu·al·ly** *adv*

even·tu·al·i·ty \i-ˌven-chù-'wa-lə-tē\ *n, pl* **-ties** : a possible event or outcome

even·tu·ate \i-'ven-chù-ˌwāt\ *vb* **-at·ed; -at·ing** : to result finally

ev·er \'e-vər\ *adv* **1** : ALWAYS ⟨~ faithful⟩ **2** : at any time **3** : in any way : AT ALL

ev·er·glade \'e-vər-ˌglād\ *n* : a low-lying tract of swampy or marshy land

ev·er·green \-ˌgrēn\ *adj* : having foliage that remains green ⟨most coniferous trees are ~⟩ — **evergreen** *n*

¹ev·er·last·ing \ˌe-vər-'las-tiŋ\ *adj* **1** : enduring forever : ETERNAL **2** : having or being flowers or foliage that retain form or color for a long time when dried — **ev·er·last·ing·ly** *adv*

²everlasting *n* **1** : ETERNITY ⟨from ~⟩ **2** : a plant with everlasting flowers; *also* : its flower

ev·er·more \ˌe-vər-'mór\ *adv* : FOREVER

ev·ery \'ev-rē\ *adj* [ME *everich, every*, fr. OE *ǣfre ǣlc*, fr. *ǣfre* ever + *ǣlc* each] **1** : being each one of a group **2** : all possible ⟨given ~ chance⟩; *also* : COMPLETE ⟨have ~ confidence⟩

ev·ery·body \'ev-ri-ˌbä-dē, -bə-\ *pron* : every person

ev·ery·day \'ev-rē-ˌdā\ *adj* : encountered or used routinely : ORDINARY

ev·ery·one \-(ˌ)wən\ *pron* : EVERYBODY

ev·ery·thing \'ev-rē-ˌthiŋ\ *pron* **1** : all that exists **2** : all that is relevant

ev·ery·where \'ev-rē-ˌhwer\ *adv* : in every place or part

evg *abbr* evening

evict \i-'vikt\ *vb* **1** : to put (a person) out from a property by legal process **2** : EXPEL ✦ **Synonyms** EJECT, OUST, DISMISS — **evic·tion** \-'vik-shən\ *n*

¹ev·i·dence \'e-və-dəns\ *n* 1 : an outward sign 2 : PROOF, TESTIMONY; *esp* : matter submitted in court to determine the truth of alleged facts
²evidence *vb* : PROVE, EVINCE
ev·i·dent \-dənt\ *adj* : clear to the vision and understanding ✦ Synonyms MANIFEST, DISTINCT, OBVIOUS, APPARENT, PLAIN
ev·i·dent·ly \'e-və-dənt-lē, ˌe-və-'dent-\ *adv* 1 : in an evident manner 2 : on the basis of available evidence
¹evil \'ē-vəl\ *adj* evil·er *or* evil·ler; evil·est *or* evil·lest 1 : WICKED 2 : causing or threatening distress or harm : PERNICIOUS — evil·ly *adv*
²evil *n* 1 : the fact of suffering, misfortune, and wrongdoing 2 : a source of sorrow, distress, or calamity
evil·do·er \ˌē-vəl-'dü-ər\ *n* : one who does evil
evil–mind·ed \-'mīn-dəd\ *adj* : having an evil disposition or evil thoughts — evil–mind·ed·ly *adv*
evince \i-'vins\ *vb* evinced; evinc·ing : SHOW, REVEAL
evis·cer·ate \i-'vi-sə-ˌrāt\ *vb* -at·ed; -at·ing 1 : to remove the entrails of 2 : to deprive of vital content or force — evis·cer·a·tion \-ˌvi-sə-'rā-shən\ *n*
evoke \i-'vōk\ *vb* evoked; evok·ing : to call forth or up — evo·ca·tion \ˌē-vō-'kā-shən, ˌe-və-\ *n* — evoc·a·tive \i-'vä-kə-tiv\ *adj*
evo·lu·tion \ˌe-və-'lü-shən\ *n* 1 : one of a set of prescribed movements (as in a dance) 2 : a process of change in a particular direction 3 : a theory that the various kinds of plants and animals are descended from other kinds that lived in earlier times and that the differences are due to inherited changes that occurred over many generations — evo·lu·tion·ary \-shə-ˌner-ē\ *adj* — evo·lu·tion·ist \-shə-nist\ *n*
evolve \i-'välv\ *vb* evolved; evolv·ing [L *evolvere* to unroll] : to develop or change by or as if by evolution
EW *abbr* enlisted woman
ewe \'yü\ *n* : a female sheep
ew·er \'yü-ər\ *n* : a water pitcher
¹ex \'eks\ *prep* [L] : out of : FROM
²ex *n* : a former spouse
³ex *abbr* 1 example 2 express 3 extra
Ex *abbr* Exodus
ex- \e *also occurs in this prefix where only* i *is shown below (as in "express") and* ks *sometimes occurs where only* gz *is shown (as in "exact")*\ *prefix* 1 : out of : outside 2 : former ⟨*ex-*president⟩
ex·ac·er·bate \ig-'za-sər-ˌbāt\ *vb* -bat·ed; -bat·ing : to make more violent, bitter, or severe — ex·ac·er·ba·tion \-ˌza-sər-'bā-shən\ *n*
¹ex·act \ig-'zakt\ *vb* 1 : to compel to furnish 2 : to call for as suitable or necessary — ex·ac·tion \-'zak-shən\ *n*
²exact *adj* : precisely accurate or correct — ex·act·ly *adv* — ex·act·ness *n*
ex·act·ing \ig-'zak-tiŋ\ *adj* 1 : greatly demanding ⟨an ~ taskmaster⟩ 2 : requiring close attention and precision
ex·ac·ti·tude \ig-'zak-tə-ˌtüd, -ˌtyüd\ *n* : the quality or state of being exact
ex·ag·ger·ate \ig-'za-jə-ˌrāt\ *vb* -at·ed; -at·ing [L *exaggeratus*, pp. of *exaggerare*, lit., to heap up, fr. *agger* heap] : to enlarge (as a statement) beyond normal : OVERSTATE — ex·ag·ger·at·ed·ly *adv* — ex·ag·ger·a·tion \-ˌza-jə-'rā-shən\ *n* — ex·ag·ger·a·tor \-'za-jə-ˌrā-tər\ *n*
ex·alt \ig-'zȯlt\ *vb* 1 : to raise up esp. in rank, power, or dignity 2 : GLORIFY — ex·al·ta·tion \ˌeg-ˌzȯl-'tā-shən, ˌek-ˌsȯl-\ *n*
ex·am \ig-'zam\ *n* : EXAMINATION
ex·am·ine \ig-'za-mən\ *vb* ex·am·ined; ex·am·in·ing 1 : to inspect closely 2 : QUESTION; *esp* : to test by questioning ✦ Synonyms INTERROGATE, QUERY, QUIZ, CATECHIZE — ex·am·i·na·tion \ig-ˌza-mə-'nā-shən\ *n*
ex·am·ple \ig-'zam-pəl\ *n* 1 : something forming a model to be followed or avoided 2 : a representative sample 3 : a problem to be solved in order to show the application of some rule
ex·as·per·ate \ig-'zas-pə-ˌrāt\ *vb* -at·ed; -at·ing : VEX, IRRITATE — ex·as·per·a·tion \ig-ˌzas-pə-'rā-shən\ *n*
exc *abbr* 1 excellent 2 except
ex·ca·vate \'ek-skə-ˌvāt\ *vb* -vat·ed; -vat·ing 1 : to hollow out; *also* : to form by hollowing out 2 : to dig out and remove (as earth) 3 : to reveal to view by digging away a covering — ex·ca·va·tion \ˌek-skə-'vā-shən\ *n* — ex·ca·va·tor \'ek-skə-ˌvā-tər\ *n*

ex·ceed \ik-'sēd\ *vb* 1 : to go or be beyond the limit of 2 : SURPASS — ex·ceed·ance \-'sē-d°ns\ *n*
ex·ceed·ing·ly \-'sē-diŋ-lē\ *also* ex·ceed·ing *adv* : EXTREMELY, VERY
ex·cel \ik-'sel\ *vb* ex·celled; ex·cel·ling : SURPASS, OUTDO
ex·cel·lence \'ek-sə-ləns\ *n* 1 : the quality of being excellent 2 : an excellent or valuable quality : VIRTUE 3 : EXCELLENCY 2
ex·cel·len·cy \-lən-sē\ *n, pl* -cies 1 : EXCELLENCE 2 — used as a title of honor
ex·cel·lent \-lənt\ *adj* : very good of its kind : FIRST-CLASS — ex·cel·lent·ly *adv*
ex·cel·si·or \ik-'sel-sē-ər\ *n* : fine curled wood shavings used esp. for packing fragile items
¹ex·cept \ik-'sept\ *also* ex·cept·ing *prep* : with the exclusion or exception of ⟨daily ~ Sundays⟩
²except *vb* 1 : to take or leave out 2 : OBJECT
³except *also* excepting *conj* 1 : UNLESS ⟨~ you repent⟩ 2 : ONLY ⟨I'd go, ~ it's too far⟩
ex·cep·tion \ik-'sep-shən\ *n* 1 : the act of excepting 2 : something excepted 3 : OBJECTION
ex·cep·tion·able \ik-'sep-shə-nə-bəl\ *adj* : OBJECTIONABLE
ex·cep·tion·al \ik-'sep-shə-nəl\ *adj* 1 : UNUSUAL ⟨an ~ number of rainy days⟩ 2 : SUPERIOR ⟨~ skill⟩ — ex·cep·tion·al·ly *adv*
ex·cerpt \'ek-ˌsərpt, 'eg-ˌzərpt\ *n* : a passage selected or copied : EXTRACT — excerpt \ek-'sərpt, eg-'zərpt; 'ek-ˌsərpt, 'eg-ˌzərpt\ *vb*
ex·cess \ik-'ses, 'ek-ˌses\ *n* 1 : SUPERFLUITY, SURPLUS 2 : the amount by which one quantity exceeds another 3 : INTEMPERANCE; *also* : an instance of intemperance — excess *adj* — ex·ces·sive \ik-'se-siv\ *adj* — ex·ces·sive·ly *adv*
exch *abbr* exchange; exchanged
¹ex·change \iks-'chānj\ *n* 1 : the giving or taking of one thing in return for another : TRADE 2 : a substituting of one thing for another 3 : interchange of valuables and esp. of bills of exchange or money of different countries 4 : a place where things and services are exchanged; *esp* : a marketplace for securities 5 : a central office in which telephone lines are connected for communication
²exchange *vb* ex·changed; ex·chang·ing : to transfer in return for some equivalent : BARTER, SWAP — ex·change·able \iks-'chān-jə-bəl\ *adj*
ex·che·quer \'eks-ˌche-kər\ *n* [ME *escheker*, fr. AF, chessboard, counting table, office charged with revenue collection, fr. *eschec* check (in chess), chess] : TREASURY; *esp* : a national treasury
ex·cise \'ek-ˌsīz\ *n* : a tax on the manufacture, sale, or consumption of a commodity
ex·ci·sion \ik-'si-zhən\ *n* : removal by or as if by cutting out esp. by surgical means — ex·cise \ik-'sīz\ *vb*
ex·cit·able \ik-'sī-tə-bəl\ *adj* : easily excited — ex·cit·abil·i·ty \-ˌsī-tə-'bi-lə-tē\ *n*
ex·cite \ik-'sīt\ *vb* ex·cit·ed; ex·cit·ing 1 : to stir up the emotions of : ROUSE 2 : to increase the activity of : STIMULATE ✦ Synonyms PROVOKE, PIQUE, QUICKEN — ex·ci·ta·tion \ˌek-ˌsī-'tā-shən, ˌek-sə-\ *n* — ex·cit·ed·ly *adv* — ex·cit·ing·ly *adv*
ex·cite·ment \ik-'sīt-mənt\ *n* : AGITATION, STIR
ex·claim \iks-'klām\ *vb* : to cry out, speak, or utter sharply or vehemently — ex·cla·ma·tion \ˌeks-klə-'mā-shən\ *n* — ex·clam·a·to·ry \iks-'kla-mə-ˌtȯr-ē\ *adj*
exclamation point *n* : a punctuation mark ! used esp. after an interjection or exclamation
ex·clude \iks-'klüd\ *vb* ex·clud·ed; ex·clud·ing 1 : to prevent from using or participating : BAR 2 : to put out : EXPEL — ex·clu·sion \-'klü-zhən\ *n* — ex·clu·sion·ary \-zhə-ˌner-ē\ *adj*
ex·clu·sive \iks-'klü-siv\ *adj* 1 : reserved for particular persons 2 : snobbishly aloof; *also* : STYLISH 3 : SOLE ⟨~ rights⟩; *also* : UNDIVIDED ⟨my ~ attention⟩ ✦ Synonyms CHIC, MODISH, SMART, SWANK, FASHIONABLE — exclusive *n* — ex·clu·sive·ly *adv* — ex·clu·sive·ness *n* — ex·clu·siv·i·ty \ˌeks-ˌklü-si-və-tē, iks-, -zi-\ *n*
exclusive of *prep* : not taking into account
ex·cog·i·tate \ek-'skä-jə-ˌtāt\ *vb* : to think out : DEVISE
ex·com·mu·ni·cate \ˌeks-kə-'myü-nə-ˌkāt\ *vb* : to cut off officially from the rites of the church — ex·com·mu·ni·ca·tion \-ˌmyü-nə-'kā-shən\ *n*

171   excoriate • exonerate

ex·co·ri·ate \ek-'skŏr-ē-,āt\ vb -at·ed; -at·ing : to criticize severely — ex·co·ri·a·tion \(,)ek-,skŏr-ē-'ā-shən\ n

ex·cre·ment \'ek-skrə-mənt\ n : waste discharged from the body; esp : FECES — ex·cre·men·tal \,ek-skrə-'men-t°l\ adj

ex·cres·cence \ik-'skre-s°ns\ n : OUTGROWTH; esp : an abnormal outgrowth (as a wart)

ex·cre·ta \ik-'skrē-tə\ n pl : waste matter (as feces) separated or eliminated from the body

ex·crete \ik-'skrēt\ vb ex·cret·ed; ex·cret·ing : to separate and eliminate wastes from the body esp. in urine or sweat — ex·cre·tion \-'skrē-shən\ n — ex·cre·to·ry \'ek-skrə-,tŏr-ē\ adj

ex·cru·ci·at·ing \ik-'skrü-shē-,ā-tiŋ\ adj [L excruciare to torture, fr. cruciare to crucify, fr. crux cross] : intensely painful or distressing ♦ Synonyms AGONIZING, HARROWING, TORTUROUS — ex·cru·ci·at·ing·ly adv

ex·cul·pate \'ek-(,)skəl-,pāt\ vb -pat·ed; -pat·ing : to clear from alleged fault or guilt ♦ Synonyms ABSOLVE, EXONERATE, ACQUIT, VINDICATE, CLEAR

ex·cur·sion \ik-'skər-zhən\ n 1 : EXPEDITION; esp : a pleasure trip 2 : DIGRESSION — ex·cur·sion·ist \-zhə-nist\ n

ex·cur·sive \-'skər-siv\ adj : constituting or characterized by digression

¹ex·cuse \ik-'skyüz\ vb ex·cused; ex·cus·ing [ME, fr. AF excuser, fr. L excusare, fr. causa cause, explanation] 1 : to make apology for 2 : PARDON 3 : to release from an obligation 4 : JUSTIFY — ex·cus·able adj

²excuse \ik-'skyüs\ n 1 : an act of excusing 2 : something that excuses or is a reason for excusing : JUSTIFICATION

exec n : EXECUTIVE

ex·e·cra·ble \'ek-si-krə-bəl\ adj 1 : DETESTABLE 〈~ crimes〉 2 : very bad 〈~ spelling〉

ex·e·crate \'ek-sə-,krāt\ vb -crat·ed; -crat·ing [L exsecratus, pp. of exsecrari to put under a curse, fr. ex- out of + sacer sacred] : to denounce as evil or detestable; also : DETEST — ex·e·cra·tion \,ek-sə-'krā-shən\ n

ex·e·cute \'ek-si-,kyüt\ vb -cut·ed; -cut·ing 1 : to carry out fully : put completely into effect 2 : to do what is called for by (as a law) 3 : to put to death in accordance with a legal sentence 4 : to produce by carrying out a design 5 : to do what is needed to give validity to 〈~ a deed〉 — ex·e·cu·tion \,ek-sə-'kyü-shən\ n — ex·e·cu·tion·er n

¹ex·ec·u·tive \ig-'ze-kyə-tiv\ adj 1 : of or relating to the enforcement of laws and the conduct of affairs 2 : designed for or related to carrying out plans or purposes

²executive n 1 : the branch of government with executive duties 2 : one having administrative or managerial responsibility

ex·ec·u·tor \ig-'ze-kyə-tər\ n : the person named in a will to execute it

ex·ec·u·trix \ig-'ze-kyə-,triks\ n, pl ex·ec·u·tri·ces \-,ze-kyə-'trī-,sēz\ or ex·ec·u·trix·es \-'ze-kyə-,trik-səz\ : a woman who is an executor

ex·e·ge·sis \,ek-sə-'jē-səs\ n, pl -ge·ses \-'jē-,sēz\ : explanation or critical interpretation of a text

ex·e·gete \'ek-sə-,jēt\ n : one who practices exegesis — ex·e·get·i·cal \,ek-sə-'je-ti-kəl\ adj

ex·em·plar \ig-'zem-,plär, -plər\ n 1 : one that serves as a model or example; esp : an ideal model 2 : a typical instance or example

ex·em·pla·ry \ig-'zem-plə-rē\ adj : serving as a pattern; also : COMMENDABLE 〈~ courage〉

ex·em·pli·fy \ig-'zem-plə-,fī\ vb -fied; -fy·ing : to illustrate by example : serve as an example of — ex·em·pli·fi·ca·tion \-,zem-plə-fə-'kā-shən\ n

¹ex·empt \ig-'zempt\ adj : free from some liability to which others are subject 〈~ from taxation〉

²exempt vb : to make exempt : EXCUSE — ex·emp·tion \ig-'zemp-shən\ n

¹ex·er·cise \'ek-sər-,sīz\ n 1 : EMPLOYMENT, USE 〈~ of authority〉 2 : exertion made for the sake of training or physical fitness 3 : a task or problem done to develop skill 4 pl : a public exhibition or ceremony

²exercise vb -cised; -cis·ing 1 : EXERT 〈~ control〉 2 : to train by or engage in exercise 3 : WORRY, DISTRESS — ex·er·cis·er n

ex·ert \ig-'zərt\ vb : to bring or put into action 〈~ influence〉 〈~ed himself〉 — ex·er·tion \-'zər-shən\ n

ex·fo·li·ate \eks-'fō-lē-,āt\ vb -at·ed; -at·ing : to cast off in scales, layers, or splinters — ex·fo·lia·tion \-,fō-lē-'ā-shən\ n

ex·hale \eks-'hāl\ vb ex·haled; ex·hal·ing 1 : to breathe out 2 : to give or pass off in the form of vapor — ex·ha·la·tion \,eks-hə-'lā-shən\ n

¹ex·haust \ig-'zŏst\ vb 1 : to use up wholly 2 : to tire or wear out 3 : to draw off or let out completely; also : EMPTY 4 : to develop (a subject) completely

²exhaust n 1 : the escape of used vapor or gas from an engine; also : the gas that escapes 2 : a system of pipes through which exhaust escapes

ex·haus·tion \ig-'zŏs-chən\ n : extreme weariness : FATIGUE

ex·haus·tive \ig-'zŏ-stiv\ adj : covering all possibilities : THOROUGH 〈an ~ investigation〉 — ex·haus·tive·ly adv

¹ex·hib·it \ig-'zi-bət\ vb 1 : to display esp. publicly 2 : to present to a court in legal form ♦ Synonyms DISPLAY, SHOW, PARADE, FLAUNT — ex·hi·bi·tion \,ek-sə-'bi-shən\ n — ex·hib·i·tor \ig-'zi-bə-tər\ n

²exhibit n 1 : an act or instance of exhibiting; also : something exhibited 2 : something produced and identified in court for use as evidence

ex·hi·bi·tion·ism \,ek-sə-'bi-shə-,ni-zəm\ n 1 : a perversion marked by a tendency to indecently expose one's genitals 2 : the act or practice of behaving so as to attract attention to oneself — ex·hi·bi·tion·ist \-nist\ n or adj

ex·hil·a·rate \ig-'zi-lə-,rāt\ vb -rat·ed; -rat·ing : ENLIVEN, STIMULATE — ex·hil·a·ra·tion \-,zi-lə-'rā-shən\ n

ex·hort \ig-'zŏrt\ vb : to urge, advise, or warn earnestly — ex·hor·ta·tion \,ek-,sŏr-tā-shən, ,eg-,zŏr-, -zər-\ n

ex·hume \ig-'züm, iks-'hyüm\ vb ex·humed; ex·hum·ing [ME fr. ML exhumare, fr. L ex out of + humus earth] : DISINTER — ex·hu·ma·tion \,eks-hyü-'mā-shən, ,eg-zü-\ n

ex·i·gen·cy \'ek-sə-jən-sē, ig-'zi-jən-\ n, pl -cies 1 pl : REQUIREMENTS 2 : urgent need — ex·i·gent \'ek-sə-jənt\ adj

ex·ig·u·ous \ig-'zi-gyə-wəs\ adj : scanty in amount — ex·i·gu·i·ty \,eg-zi-'gyü-ə-tē\ n

¹ex·ile \'eg-,zī(-ə)l, 'ek-,sī(-ə)l\ n 1 : BANISHMENT; also : voluntary absence from one's country or home 2 : a person driven from his or her native place

²exile vb ex·iled; ex·il·ing : BANISH, EXPEL ♦ Synonyms EXPATRIATE, DEPORT, OSTRACIZE

ex·ist \ig-'zist\ vb 1 : to have being 2 : to continue to be : LIVE

ex·is·tence \ig-'zis-təns\ n 1 : continuance in living 2 : actual or present occurrence 〈~ of a state of war〉 — ex·is·tent \-tənt\ adj

ex·is·ten·tial \,eg-zis-'ten-chəl, ,ek-sis-\ adj 1 : of or relating to existence 2 : EMPIRICAL 3 : having being in time and space 4 : of or relating to existentialism or existentialists

ex·is·ten·tial·ism \,eg-zis-'ten-chə-,li-zəm\ n : a philosophy centered on individual existence and personal responsibility for acts of free will in the absence of certain knowledge of what is right or wrong — ex·is·ten·tial·ist \-list\ adj or n

ex·it \'eg-zət, 'ek-sət\ n 1 : a departure from a stage 2 : a going out or away; also : DEATH 3 : a way out of an enclosed space 2 : a point of departure from an expressway — exit vb

exo·bi·ol·o·gy \,ek-sō-bī-'ä-lə-jē\ n : biology concerned with life originating or existing outside the earth or its atmosphere — exo·bi·ol·o·gist \-jist\ n

exo·crine gland \'ek-sə-krən-, -,krīn-, -,krēn-\ n : a gland (as a salivary gland) that releases a secretion externally by means of a canal or duct

Exod abbr Exodus

ex·o·dus \'ek-sə-dəs\ n 1 cap — see BIBLE table 2 : a mass departure : EMIGRATION

ex of·fi·cio \,ek-sə-'fi-shē-,ō\ adv or adj : by virtue of or because of an office 〈ex officio chairman〉

ex·og·e·nous \ek-'sä-jə-nəs\ adj : caused or produced by factors outside the organism or system — ex·og·e·nous·ly adv

ex·on·er·ate \ig-'zä-nə-,rāt\ vb -at·ed; -at·ing [ME, fr. L exoneratus, pp. of exonerare to unburden, fr. ex- out + onus load] : to free from blame ♦ Synonyms ACQUIT,

ABSOLVE, EXCULPATE, VINDICATE — **ex·on·er·a·tion** \-ˌzä-nə-ˈrä-shən\ *n*

ex·or·bi·tant \ig-ˈzȯr-bə-tənt\ *adj* : exceeding what is usual or proper

ex·or·cise \ˈek-ˌsȯr-ˌsīz, -sər-\ *vb* **-cised; -cis·ing** **1** : to get rid of by or as if by solemn command **2** : to free of an evil spirit — **ex·or·cism** \-ˌsi-zəm\ *n* — **ex·or·cist** \-ˌsist\ *n*

exo·sphere \ˈek-sō-ˌsfir\ *n* : the outermost region of the atmosphere

exo·ther·mic \ˌek-sō-ˈthər-mik\ *adj* : characterized by or formed with evolution of heat

ex·ot·ic \ig-ˈzä-tik\ *adj* **1** : introduced from another country ⟨~ plants⟩ **2** : strikingly, excitingly, or mysteriously different or unusual ⟨~ flavors⟩ — **exotic** *n* — **ex·ot·i·cal·ly** \-ti-k(ə-)lē\ *adv* — **ex·ot·i·cism** \-tə-ˌsi-zəm\ *n*

exp *abbr* **1** expense **2** experiment **3** export **4** express

ex·pand \ik-ˈspand\ *vb* **1** : to open up : UNFOLD **2** : EN-LARGE **3** : to develop in detail ♦ **Synonyms** AMPLIFY, SWELL, DISTEND, INFLATE, DILATE — **ex·pand·able** \-ˈspan-də-bəl\ *adj* — **ex·pand·er** *n*

ex·panse \ik-ˈspans\ *n* : a broad extent (as of land or sea)

ex·pan·sion \ik-ˈspan-chən\ *n* **1** : the act or process of expanding **2** : the quality or state of being expanded **3** : an expanded part or thing

expansion slot *n* : a socket on a motherboard for a circuit board (**expansion card**) offering additional capabilities

ex·pan·sive \ik-ˈspan-siv\ *adj* **1** : tending to expand or to cause expansion **2** : warmly benevolent, generous, or ready to talk **3** : of large extent or scope — **ex·pan·sive·ly** *adv* — **ex·pan·sive·ness** *n*

ex par·te \eks-ˈpär-tē\ *adv or adj* [ML] : from a one-sided point of view

ex·pa·ti·ate \ek-ˈspā-shē-ˌāt\ *vb* **-at·ed; -at·ing** : to talk or write at length — **ex·pa·ti·a·tion** \ek-ˌspā-shē-ˈā-shən\ *n*

¹ex·pa·tri·ate \ek-ˈspā-trē-ˌāt\ *vb* **-at·ed; -at·ing** : EXILE — **ex·pa·tri·a·tion** \ek-ˌspā-trē-ˈā-shən\ *n*

²ex·pa·tri·ate \ek-ˈspā-trē-ˌāt, -trē-ət\ *adj* : living in a foreign country — **expatriate** *n*

ex·pect \ik-ˈspekt\ *vb* **1** : SUPPOSE, THINK **2** : to look forward to : ANTICIPATE **3** : to consider reasonable, due, or necessary **4** : to consider to be obliged

ex·pec·tan·cy \-ˈspek-tən-sē\ *n, pl* **-cies** **1** : EXPECTA-TION **2** : the expected amount (as of years of life)

ex·pec·tant \-tənt\ *adj* : marked by expectation; *esp* : expecting the birth of a child — **ex·pec·tant·ly** *adv*

ex·pec·ta·tion \ˌek-ˌspek-ˈtā-shən\ *n* **1** : the act or state of expecting **2** : prospect of inheritance — usu. used in pl. **3** : something expected

ex·pec·to·rant \ik-ˈspek-tə-rənt\ *n* : an agent that promotes the discharge or expulsion of mucus from the respiratory tract — **expectorant** *adj*

ex·pec·to·rate \-ˌrāt\ *vb* **-rat·ed; -rat·ing** : SPIT — **ex·pec·to·ra·tion** \-ˌspek-tə-ˈrä-shən\ *n*

ex·pe·di·ence \ik-ˈspē-dē-əns\ *n* : EXPEDIENCY

ex·pe·di·en·cy \-ən-sē\ *n, pl* **-cies** **1** : fitness to some end **2** : use of expedient means and methods; *also* : something expedient

¹ex·pe·di·ent \-ənt\ *adj* [ME, fr. AF or L; AF, fr. L *expediens*, prp. of *expedire* to extricate, prepare, be useful, fr. *ex-* out + *ped-, pes* foot] **1** : adapted for achieving a particular end **2** : marked by concern with what is advantageous; *esp* : governed by self-interest

²expedient *n* : something expedient; *esp* : a temporary means to an end

ex·pe·dite \ˈek-spə-ˌdīt\ *vb* **-dit·ed; -dit·ing** : to carry out promptly; *also* : to speed up

ex·pe·dit·er \-ˌdī-tər\ *n* : one that expedites; *esp* : one employed to ensure efficient movement of goods or supplies in a business

ex·pe·di·tion \ˌek-spə-ˈdi-shən\ *n* **1** : a journey for a particular purpose; *also* : the persons making it **2** : efficient promptness

ex·pe·di·tion·ary \-ˈdi-shə-ˌner-ē\ *adj* : of, relating to, or constituting an expedition; *also* : sent on military service abroad

ex·pe·di·tious \-ˈdi-shəs\ *adj* : marked by or acting with prompt efficiency ♦ **Synonyms** SWIFT, FAST, RAPID, SPEEDY

ex·pel \ik-ˈspel\ *vb* **ex·pelled; ex·pel·ling** : to drive or force out : EJECT

ex·pend \ik-ˈspend\ *vb* **1** : to pay out : SPEND **2** : UTI-LIZE; *also* : USE UP — **ex·pend·able** *adj*

ex·pen·di·ture \ik-ˈspen-di-chər, -ˌchůr\ *n* **1** : the act or process of expending **2** : something expended

ex·pense \ik-ˈspens\ *n* **1** : EXPENDITURE **2** : COST **3** : a cause of expenditure **4** : SACRIFICE ⟨had a laugh at my ~⟩

ex·pen·sive \ik-ˈspen-siv\ *adj* : COSTLY, DEAR — **ex·pen·sive·ly** *adv*

¹ex·pe·ri·ence \ik-ˈspir-ē-əns\ *n* **1** : observation of or participation in events resulting in or tending toward knowledge **2** : knowledge, practice, or skill derived from observation or participation in events; *also* : the length of such participation **3** : something encountered, undergone, or lived through (as by a person or community)

²experience *vb* **-enced; -enc·ing** **1** : FIND OUT, DISCOVER **2** : to have experience of : UNDERGO

ex·pe·ri·enced *adj* : made capable through experience ⟨an ~ pilot⟩

¹ex·per·i·ment \ik-ˈsper-ə-mənt\ *n* : a controlled procedure carried out to discover, test, or demonstrate something; *also* : the process of testing — **ex·per·i·men·tal** \-ˌsper-ə-ˈmen-tᵊl\ *adj* — **ex·per·i·men·tal·ly** \-ˈmen-tᵊl-ē\ *adv*

²ex·per·i·ment \-ˌment\ *vb* : to make experiments — **ex·per·i·men·ta·tion** \ik-ˌsper-ə-mən-ˈtā-shən\ *n* — **ex·per·i·men·ter** *n*

¹ex·pert \ˈek-ˌspərt\ *adj* : showing special skill or knowledge — **ex·pert·ly** *adv* — **ex·pert·ness** *n*

²ex·pert \ˈek-ˌspərt\ *n* : an expert person : SPECIALIST

ex·per·tise \ˌek-(ˌ)spər-ˈtēz\ *n* : the skill of an expert

expert system *n* : computer software that attempts to mimic the reasoning of a human specialist

ex·pi·ate \ˈek-spē-ˌāt\ *vb* **-at·ed; -at·ing** : to give satisfaction for : ATONE — **ex·pi·a·tion** \ˌek-spē-ˈā-shən\ *n*

ex·pi·a·to·ry \ˈek-spē-ə-ˌtȯr-ē\ *adj* : serving to expiate

expiration date *n* **1** : the date after which something is no longer in effect **2** : the date after which a product is expected to decline in quality or effectiveness

ex·pire \ik-ˈspī(-ə)r, ek-\ *vb* **ex·pired; ex·pir·ing** **1** : to breathe one's last breath : DIE **2** : to come to an end **3** : to breathe out from or as if from the lungs — **ex·pi·ra·tion** \ˌek-spə-ˈrā-shən\ *n*

ex·plain \ik-ˈsplān\ *vb* [ME *explanen*, fr. L *explanare*, lit., to make level, fr. *planus* level, flat] **1** : to make clear **2** : to give the reason for — **ex·pla·na·tion** \ˌek-splə-ˈnā-shən\ *n* — **ex·plan·a·to·ry** \ik-ˈspla-nə-ˌtȯr-ē\ *adj*

ex·ple·tive \ˈek-splə-tiv\ *n* : a usu. profane exclamation

ex·pli·ca·ble \ek-ˈspli-kə-bəl, ˈek-(ˌ)spli-\ *adj* : capable of being explained

ex·pli·cate \ˈek-splə-ˌkāt\ *vb* **-cat·ed; -cat·ing** : to give a detailed explanation of — **ex·pli·ca·tion** \ˌek-spli-ˈkā-shən\ *n*

ex·plic·it \ik-ˈspli-sət\ *adj* : clearly and precisely expressed — **ex·plic·it·ly** *adv* — **ex·plic·it·ness** *n*

ex·plode \ik-ˈsplōd\ *vb* **ex·plod·ed; ex·plod·ing** [L *explodere* to drive off the stage by clapping, fr. *ex-* out + *plaudere* to clap] **1** : DISCREDIT ⟨~ a belief⟩ **2** : to burst or cause to burst violently and noisily ⟨~ a bomb⟩ ⟨the boiler *exploded*⟩ **3** : to undergo a rapid chemical or nuclear reaction with production of heat and violent expansion of gas ⟨dynamite ~s⟩ **4** : to give forth a sudden strong and noisy outburst of emotion **5** : to increase rapidly ⟨the city's population *exploded*⟩

exploded *adj* : showing the parts separated but in correct relationship to each other ⟨an ~ view of a carburetor⟩

¹ex·ploit \ˈek-ˌsplȯit\ *n* : DEED; *esp* : a notable or heroic act

²ex·ploit \ik-ˈsplȯit\ *vb* **1** : to make productive use of : UTI-LIZE **2** : to use unfairly for one's own advantage — **ex·ploi·ta·tion** \ˌek-ˌsplȯi-ˈtā-shən\ *n*

ex·plore \ik-ˈsplȯr\ *vb* **ex·plored; ex·plor·ing** **1** : to look into or travel over thoroughly **2** : to examine carefully ⟨~ a wound⟩ — **ex·plo·ra·tion** \ˌek-splə-ˈrā-shən\ *n* — **ex·plor·ato·ry** \ik-ˈsplȯr-ə-ˌtȯr-ē\ *adj* — **ex·plor·er** *n*

ex·plo·sion \ik-ˈsplō-zhən\ *n* : the act or an instance of exploding

ex·plo·sive \ik-ˈsplō-siv\ *adj* **1** : relating to or able to cause explosion **2** : tending to explode — **explosive** *n* — **ex·plo·sive·ly** *adv*

ex·po \ˈek-ˌspō\ *n, pl* **expos** : EXPOSITION 2

ex·po·nent \ik-ˈspō-nənt, ˈek-ˌspō-\ *n* **1** : a symbol written above and to the right of a mathematical expression (as 3 in a^3) to signify how many times it is to be used as a factor   **2** : INTERPRETER, EXPOUNDER   **3** : ADVOCATE, CHAMPION — **ex·po·nen·tial** \ˌek-spə-'nen-chəl\ *adj* — **ex·po·nen·tial·ly** *adv*

ex·po·nen·ti·a·tion \ˌek-spə-ˌnen-chē-'ā-shen\ *n* : the mathematical operation of raising a quantity to a power

¹**ex·port** \ek-'spórt, 'ek-ˌspórt\ *vb* : to send (as merchandise) to foreign countries — **ex·por·ta·tion** \ˌek-ˌspór-'tā-shən, -spər-\ *n* — **ex·port·er** *n*

²**ex·port** \'ek-ˌspórt\ *n*   **1** : something exported esp. for trade   **2** : the act of exporting

ex·pose \ik-'spōz\ *vb* **ex·posed; ex·pos·ing**   **1** : to deprive of shelter or protection   **2** : to submit or subject to an action or influence; *esp* : to subject (as photographic film) to radiant energy (as light)   **3** : to bring to light : DISCLOSE   **4** : to cause to be open to view

ex·po·sé \ˌek-spō-'zā\ *n* : an exposure of something discreditable

ex·po·si·tion \ˌek-spə-'zi-shən\ *n*   **1** : a setting forth of the meaning or purpose (as of a writing); *also* : discourse designed to convey information   **2** : a public exhibition

ex·pos·i·tor \ik-'spä-zə-tər\ *n* : one who explains : COMMENTATOR

ex post fac·to \ˌeks-'pōst-ˌfak-tō\ *adv or adj* : after the fact

ex·pos·tu·late \ik-'späs-chə-ˌlāt\ *vb* : to reason earnestly with a person esp. in dissuading : REMONSTRATE — **ex·pos·tu·la·tion** \-ˌspäs-chə-'lā-shən\ *n*

ex·po·sure \ik-'spō-zhər\ *n*   **1** : the fact or condition of being exposed   **2** : the act or an instance of exposing   **3** : the length of time for which a film is exposed   **4** : a section of a photographic film for one picture

ex·pound \ik-'spaúnd\ *vb*   **1** : STATE   **2** : INTERPRET, EXPLAIN — **ex·pound·er** *n*

¹**ex·press** \ik-'spres\ *adj*   **1** : EXPLICIT; *also* : EXACT, PRECISE   **2** : SPECIFIC ⟨this ∼ purpose⟩   **3** : traveling at high speed and esp. with few stops ⟨an ∼ train⟩; *also* : adapted to high speed use ⟨∼ roads⟩ — **ex·press·ly** *adv*

²**express** *adv* : by express ⟨ship it ∼⟩

³**express** *n*   **1** : a system for the prompt transportation of goods; *also* : a company operating such a service or the shipments so transported   **2** : an express vehicle

⁴**express** *vb*   **1** : to make known : SHOW, STATE ⟨∼ regret⟩; *also* : SYMBOLIZE   **2** : to squeeze out : extract by pressing   **3** : to send by express   **4** : to manifest or produce by a genetic process

ex·pres·sion \ik-'spre-shən\ *n*   **1** : UTTERANCE   **2** : something that represents or symbolizes : SIGN; *esp* : a mathematical symbol or combination of signs and symbols representing a quantity or operation   **3** : the detectable effect of a gene   **4** : a significant word or phrase; *also* : manner of expressing (as in writing or music)   **5** : facial aspect or vocal intonation indicative of feeling — **ex·pres·sion·less** *adj*

ex·pres·sion·ism \ik-'spre-shə-ˌni-zəm\ *n* : a theory or practice in art of seeking to depict the artist's subjective responses to objects and events — **ex·pres·sion·ist** \-nist\ *n or adj* — **ex·pres·sion·is·tic** \-ˌspre-shə-'nis-tik\ *adj*

ex·pres·sive \ik-'spre-siv\ *adj*   **1** : of or relating to expression   **2** : serving to express — **ex·pres·sive·ly** *adv* — **ex·pres·sive·ness** *n*

ex·press·way \ik-'spres-ˌwā\ *n* : a divided superhighway with limited access

ex·pro·pri·ate \ek-'sprō-prē-ˌāt\ *vb* **-at·ed; -at·ing** : to deprive of possession or the right to own — **ex·pro·pri·a·tion** \(ˌ)ek-ˌsprō-prē-'ā-shən\ *n*

expt *abbr* experiment

ex·pul·sion \ik-'spəl-shən\ *n* : an expelling or being expelled : EJECTION

ex·punge \ik-'spənj\ *vb* **ex·punged; ex·pung·ing** [L *expungere* to mark for deletion by dots, fr. *ex-* out + *pungere* to prick] : OBLITERATE, ERASE

ex·pur·gate \'ek-spər-ˌgāt\ *vb* **-gat·ed; -gat·ing** : to clear (as a book) of objectionable passages — **ex·pur·ga·tion** \ˌek-spər-'gā-shən\ *n*

ex·qui·site \ek-'skwi-zət, 'ek-(ˌ)skwi-\ *adj* [ME *exquisit*, fr. L *exquisitus*, pp. of *exquirere* to search out, fr. *ex* out + *quaerere* to seek]   **1** : marked by flawless form or workmanship   **2** : keenly appreciative or sensitive   **3** : pleasingly beautiful or delicate   **4** : INTENSE ⟨∼ pain⟩

ext *abbr*   **1** extension   **2** exterior   **3** external   **4** extra   **5** extract

ex·tant \'ek-stənt; ek-'stant\ *adj* : EXISTENT; *esp* : not lost or destroyed

ex·tem·po·ra·ne·ous \ek-ˌstem-pə-'rā-nē-əs\ *adj* : not planned beforehand : IMPROMPTU — **ex·tem·po·ra·ne·ous·ly** *adv*

ex·tem·po·rary \ik-'stem-pə-ˌrer-ē\ *adj* : EXTEMPORANEOUS

ex·tem·po·re \ik-'stem-pə-(ˌ)rē\ *adv* : EXTEMPORANEOUSLY

ex·tem·po·rise *Brit var of* EXTEMPORIZE

ex·tem·po·rize \ik-'stem-pə-ˌrīz\ *vb* **-rized; -riz·ing** : to do something extemporaneously

ex·tend \ik-'stend\ *vb*   **1** : to spread or stretch forth or out (as in reaching)   **2** : to exert or cause to exert to full capacity   **3** : PROFFER ⟨∼ credit⟩   **4** : PROLONG ⟨∼ a note⟩   **5** : to make greater or broader ⟨∼ knowledge⟩ ⟨∼ a business⟩   **6** : to stretch out or reach across a distance, space, or time ✦ **Synonyms** LENGTHEN, ELONGATE, PROTRACT — **ex·tend·able** *also* **ex·tend·ible** \-'sten-də-bəl\ *adj*

ex·ten·sion \ik-'sten-chən\ *n*   **1** : an extending or being extended   **2** : a program that geographically extends the educational resources of an institution   **3** : an additional part; *also* : an extra telephone connected to a line

ex·ten·sive \ik-'sten-siv\ *adj* : of considerable extent : FAR-REACHING, BROAD — **ex·ten·sive·ly** *adv*

ex·tent \ik-'stent\ *n*   **1** : the range or space over which something extends ⟨a property of large ∼⟩   **2** : the point or degree to which something extends ⟨to the fullest ∼ of the law⟩

ex·ten·u·ate \ik-'sten-yù-ˌwāt\ *vb* **-at·ed; -at·ing** : to lessen the seriousness of — **ex·ten·u·a·tion** \-ˌsten-yù-'wā-shən\ *n*

¹**ex·te·ri·or** \ek-'stir-ē-ər\ *adj*   **1** : EXTERNAL   **2** : suitable for use on an outside surface ⟨∼ paint⟩

²**exterior** *n* : an exterior part or surface

ex·ter·mi·nate \ik-'stər-mə-ˌnāt\ *vb* **-nat·ed; -nat·ing** : to get rid of completely usu. by killing off ✦ **Synonyms** EXTIRPATE, ERADICATE, ABOLISH, ANNIHILATE — **ex·ter·mi·na·tion** \-ˌstər-mə-'nā-shən\ *n* — **ex·ter·mi·na·tor** \-'stər-mə-ˌnā-tər\ *n*

¹**ex·ter·nal** \ek-'stər-n²l\ *adj*   **1** : outwardly perceivable; *also* : SUPERFICIAL   **2** : of, relating to, or located on the outside or an outer part   **3** : arising or acting from without; *also* : FOREIGN ⟨∼ affairs⟩ — **ex·ter·nal·ly** *adv*

²**external** *n* : an external feature

ex·tinct \ik-'stiŋkt\ *adj*   **1** : EXTINGUISHED; *also* : no longer active ⟨an ∼ volcano⟩   **2** : no longer existing or in use ⟨dinosaurs are ∼⟩ ⟨∼ languages⟩ — **ex·tinc·tion** \ik-'stiŋk-shən\ *n*

ex·tin·guish \ik-'stiŋ-gwish\ *vb* : to cause to stop burning; *also* : to bring to an end (as by destroying) — **ex·tin·guish·able** *adj* — **ex·tin·guish·er** *n*

ex·tir·pate \'ek-stər-ˌpāt\ *vb* **-pat·ed; -pat·ing** [L *exstirpatus*, pp. of *exstirpare*, fr. *ex-* out + *stirps* trunk, root]   **1** : to destroy completely : UPROOT ✦ **Synonyms** EXTERMINATE, ERADICATE, ABOLISH, ANNIHILATE — **ex·tir·pa·tion** \ˌek-stər-'pā-shən\ *n*

ex·tol *also* **ex·toll** \ik-'stōl\ *vb* **ex·tolled; ex·tol·ling** : to praise highly : GLORIFY

ex·tort \ik-'stórt\ *vb* [L *extortus*, pp. of *extorquēre* to wrench out, extort, fr. *ex-* out + *torquēre* to twist] : to obtain by force or improper pressure ⟨∼ a bribe⟩ — **ex·tor·tion** \-'stór-shən\ *n* — **ex·tor·tion·er** *n* — **ex·tor·tion·ist** *n*

ex·tor·tion·ate \ik-'stór-shə-nət\ *adj* : EXCESSIVE, EXORBITANT ⟨∼ prices⟩ — **ex·tor·tion·ate·ly** *adv*

¹**ex·tra** \'ek-strə\ *adj*   **1** : ADDITIONAL ⟨∼ work⟩   **2** : SUPERIOR ⟨∼ quality⟩

²**extra** *n*   **1** : a special edition of a newspaper   **2** : an added charge   **3** : an additional worker or performer (as in a motion picture)

³**extra** *adv* : beyond what is usual ⟨∼ large⟩

¹**ex·tract** \ik-'strakt, *esp for 3* 'ek-ˌstrakt\ *vb*   **1** : to draw out; *esp* : to pull out forcibly ⟨∼ a tooth⟩   **2** : to withdraw (as a juice or a constituent) by a physical or chemical process   **3** : to select for citation : QUOTE — **ex·tract·able** *adj* — **ex·trac·tion** \ik-'strak-shən\ *n* — **ex·trac·tor** \-tər\ *n*

²**ex·tract** \'ek-ˌstrakt\ *n* 1 : EXCERPT, CITATION 2 : a product (as a juice or concentrate) obtained by extracting

ex·tra·cur·ric·u·lar \ˌek-strə-kə-'ri-kyə-lər\ *adj* : lying outside the regular curriculum; *esp* : of or relating to school-connected activities (as sports) usu. carrying no academic credit

ex·tra·dite \'ek-strə-ˌdīt\ *vb* -**dit·ed; -dit·ing** : to obtain by or deliver up to extradition

ex·tra·di·tion \ˌek-strə-'di-shən\ *n* : the surrender of an alleged criminal to a different jurisdiction for trial

ex·tra·mar·i·tal \ˌek-strə-'ma-rə-tᵊl\ *adj* : of or relating to sexual intercourse by a married person with someone other than his or her spouse

ex·tra·mu·ral \-'myùr-əl\ *adj* : existing or functioning beyond the bounds of an organized unit

ex·tra·ne·ous \ek-'strā-nē-əs\ *adj* 1 : coming from without ⟨~ light⟩ 2 : not forming a vital part; *also* : IRRELEVANT — **ex·tra·ne·ous·ly** *adv*

ex·tra·net \'ek-strə-ˌnet\ *n* : a network like an intranet but also allowing access by certain outside parties

ex·traor·di·nary \ik-'strôr-də-ˌner-ē, ˌek-strə-'ôr-\ *adj* 1 : notably unusual or exceptional 2 : employed on special service ⟨an ambassador ~⟩ — **ex·traor·di·nari·ly** \-ˌstrôr-də-'ner-ə-lē, ˌek-strə-ˌôr-\ *adv*

ex·trap·o·late \ik-'stra-pə-ˌlāt\ *vb* -**lat·ed; -lat·ing** : to infer (unknown) data from known data — **ex·trap·o·la·tion** \-ˌstra-pə-'lā-shən\ *n*

ex·tra·sen·so·ry \ˌek-strə-'sen-sə-rē\ *adj* : not acting or occurring through the known senses

extrasensory perception *n* : perception (as in telepathy) of events external to the self not gained through the senses and not deducible from previous experience

ex·tra·solar \-'sō-lər\ *adj* : originating or existing outside the solar system

ex·tra·ter·res·tri·al \-tə-'res-trē-əl\ *adj* : originating or existing outside the earth or its atmosphere ⟨~ life⟩ — **extraterrestrial** *n*

ex·tra·ter·ri·to·ri·al \-ˌter-ə-'tôr-ē-əl\ *adj* : existing or taking place outside the territorial limits of a jurisdiction

ex·tra·ter·ri·to·ri·al·i·ty \-ˌtôr-ē-ˌa-lə-tē\ *n* : exemption from the application or jurisdiction of local law or tribunals ⟨diplomats enjoy ~⟩

ex·trav·a·gant \ik-'stra-vi-gənt\ *adj* 1 : EXCESSIVE ⟨~ claims⟩ 2 : unduly lavish : WASTEFUL 3 : too costly ♦ **Synonyms** IMMODERATE, EXORBITANT, EXTREME, INORDINATE, UNDUE — **ex·trav·a·gance** \-gəns\ *n* — **ex·trav·a·gant·ly** *adv*

ex·trav·a·gan·za \ik-ˌstra-və-'gan-zə\ *n* 1 : a literary or musical work marked by extreme freedom of style and structure 2 : a spectacular show

ex·tra·ve·hic·u·lar \ˌek-strə-vē-'hi-kyə-lər\ *adj* : taking place outside a vehicle (as a spacecraft) ⟨~ activity⟩

¹**ex·treme** \ik-'strēm\ *adj* 1 : very great or intense ⟨~ cold⟩ 2 : very severe or radical ⟨~ measures⟩ 3 : going to great lengths or beyond normal limits ⟨politically ~⟩ 4 : most remote ⟨the ~ end⟩ 5 : UTMOST; *also* : MAXIMUM — **ex·treme·ly** *adv*

²**extreme** *n* 1 : something located at one end or the other of a range or series 2 : EXTREMITY 4

extremely low frequency *n* : a radio frequency in the lowest range of the radio spectrum

ex·trem·ism \ik-'strē-ˌmi-zəm\ *n* : the quality or state of being extreme; *esp* : advocacy of extreme political measures — **ex·trem·ist** \-mist\ *n or adj*

ex·trem·i·ty \ik-'stre-mə-tē\ *n, pl* -**ties** 1 : the most remote part or point 2 : a limb of the body; *esp* : a human hand or foot 3 : the greatest need or danger 4 : the utmost degree 5 : a drastic or desperate measure

ex·tri·cate \'ek-strə-ˌkāt\ *vb* -**cat·ed; -cat·ing** [L *extricatus*, pp. of *extricare*, fr. *ex-* out + *tricae* trifles, perplexities] : to free from an entanglement or difficulty ♦ **Synonyms** DISENTANGLE, UNTANGLE, DISENCUMBER — **ex·tri·ca·ble** \ik-'stri-kə-bəl, ek-; 'ek-(ˌ)stri-\ *adj* — **ex·tri·ca·tion** \ˌek-strə-'kā-shən\ *n*

ex·trin·sic \ek-'strin-zik, -sik\ *adj* 1 : not forming part of or belonging to a thing 2 : EXTERNAL — **ex·trin·si·cal·ly** \-zi-k(ə-)lē, -si-\ *adv*

ex·tro·vert *also* **ex·tra·vert** \'ek-strə-ˌvərt\ *n* : a gregarious

and unreserved person — **ex·tro·ver·sion** *or* **ex·tra·ver·sion** \ˌek-strə-'vər-zhən\ *n* — **ex·tro·vert·ed** *also* **ex·tra·vert·ed** *adj*

ex·trude \ik-'strüd\ *vb* **ex·trud·ed; ex·trud·ing** 1 : to force, press, or push out 2 : to shape (as plastic) by forcing through a die — **ex·tru·sion** \-'strü-zhən\ *n* — **ex·trud·er** *n*

ex·u·ber·ant \ig-'zü-bə-rənt\ *adj* 1 : unrestrained in enthusiasm or style 2 : PROFUSE ⟨~ vegetation⟩ — **ex·u·ber·ance** \-rəns\ *n* — **ex·u·ber·ant·ly** *adv*

ex·ude \ig-'züd\ *vb* **ex·ud·ed; ex·ud·ing** [L *exsudare*, fr. *ex-* out + *sudare* to sweat] 1 : to discharge slowly through pores or cuts : OOZE 2 : to display conspicuously or abundantly ⟨~s charm⟩ — **ex·u·date** \'ek-sù-ˌdāt, -syü-\ *n* — **ex·u·da·tion** \ˌek-sù-'dā-shən, -syü-\ *n*

ex·ult \ig-'zəlt\ *vb* : REJOICE, GLORY — **ex·ul·tant** \-'zəl-tᵊnt\ *adj* — **ex·ul·tant·ly** *adv* — **ex·ul·ta·tion** \ˌek-(ˌ)səl-'tā-shən, ˌeg-(ˌ)zəl-\ *n*

ex·urb \'ek-ˌsərb, 'eg-ˌzərb\ *n* : a region outside a city and its suburbs inhabited chiefly by well-to-do families — **ex·ur·ban** \ek-'sər-bən, eg-'zər-\ *adj*

ex·ur·ban·ite \ek-'sər-bə-ˌnīt; eg-'zər-\ *n* : one who lives in an exurb

ex·ur·bia \ek-'sər-bē-ə, eg-'zər-\ *n* : the generalized region of exurbs

-ey — see -Y

¹**eye** \'ī\ *n* 1 : an organ of sight typically consisting in vertebrates of a globular structure that is located in a socket of the skull, is lined with a sensitive retina, and is normally paired 2 : VISION, PERCEPTION; *also* : faculty of discrimination ⟨an ~ for bargains⟩ 3 : POINT OF VIEW, JUDGMENT — often used in pl. ⟨in the ~s of the law⟩ 4 : something suggesting an eye (as the hole of a needle or the bud of a potato) 5 : the calm center of a cyclone — **eyed** \'īd\ *adj*

²**eye** *vb* **eyed; eye·ing** *or* **ey·ing** : to look at : WATCH

¹**eye·ball** \'ī-ˌbȯl\ *n* : the globular capsule of the vertebrate eye

²**eyeball** *vb* : to look at intently

eye·brow \-ˌbraù\ *n* : the ridge over the eye or the hair growing on it

eye·drop·per \-ˌdrä-pər\ *n* : DROPPER 2

eye·glass \-ˌglas\ *n* : a lens worn to aid vision; *also, pl* : GLASSES

eye·lash \-ˌlash\ *n* 1 : the fringe of hair edging the eyelid — usu. used in pl. 2 : a single hair of the eyelashes

eye·let \-lət\ *n* 1 : a small hole intended for ornament or for passage of a cord or lace 2 : a typically metal ring for reinforcing an eyelet : GROMMET

eye·lid \-ˌlid\ *n* : either of the movable folds of skin and muscle that can be closed over the eyeball

eye·lin·er \-ˌlī-nər\ *n* : makeup used to emphasize the contour of the eyes

eye–open·er \-ˌō-pə-nər\ *n* : something startling or surprising — **eye–open·ing** *adj*

eye·piece \-ˌpēs\ *n* : the lens or combination of lenses at the eye end of an optical instrument

eye shadow *n* : a colored cosmetic applied to the eyelids to accent the eyes

eye·sight \-ˌsīt\ *n* : SIGHT, VISION

eye·sore \-ˌsȯr\ *n* : something offensive to view

eye·strain \-ˌstrān\ *n* : weariness or a strained state of the eye

eye·tooth \-'tüth\ *n* : a canine tooth of the upper jaw

eye·wash \-ˌwȯsh, -ˌwäsh\ *n* 1 : an eye lotion 2 : misleading or deceptive statements, actions, or procedures

eye·wit·ness \-'wit-nəs\ *n* : a person who actually sees something happen

ey·rie *chiefly Brit var of* AERIE

ey·rir \'ā-ˌrir\ *n, pl* **au·rar** \'aù-ˌrär\ — see *krona* at MONEY table

Ez *or* **Ezr** *abbr* Ezra

Ezech *abbr* Ezechiel

Eze·chiel \i-'zē-kyəl\ *n* — see BIBLE table

Ezek *abbr* Ezekiel

Eze·kiel \i-'zē-kyəl\ *n* — see BIBLE table

e–zine \'ē-ˌzēn\ *n* : an online magazine

Ez·ra \'ez-rə\ *n* — see BIBLE table

¹f \'ef\ *n, pl* **f's** *or* **fs** \'efs\ *often cap* **1** : the 6th letter of the English alphabet **2** : a grade rating a student's work as failing
²f *abbr, often cap* **1** Fahrenheit **2** false **3** family **4** farad **5** female **6** feminine **7** forte **8** French **9** frequency **10** Friday
³f *symbol* focal length
F *symbol* fluorine
FAA *abbr* Federal Aviation Administration
fab \'fab\ *adj* : FABULOUS
Fa·bi·an \'fā-bē-ən\ *adj* : of, relating to, or being a society of socialists organized in England in 1884 to spread socialist principles gradually — **Fabian** *n* — **Fa·bi·an·ism** *n*
fa·ble \'fā-bəl\ *n* **1** : a legendary story of supernatural happenings **2** : a narration intended to teach a lesson; *esp* : one in which animals speak and act like people **3** : FALSEHOOD
fa·bled \'fā-bəld\ *adj* **1** : FICTITIOUS **2** : told or celebrated in fable
fab·ric \'fa-brik\ *n* [MF *fabrique,* fr. L *fabrica* workshop, structure] **1** : STRUCTURE, FRAMEWORK ⟨the ~ of society⟩ **2** : CLOTH; *also* : a material that resembles cloth
fab·ri·cate \'fa-bri-ˌkāt\ *vb* **-cat·ed; -cat·ing** **1** : INVENT, CREATE **2** : to make up for the sake of deception ⟨reporters *fabricating* news stories⟩ **3** : CONSTRUCT, MANUFACTURE — **fab·ri·ca·tion** \ˌfa-bri-'kā-shən\ *n*
fab·u·lous \'fa-byə-ləs\ *adj* **1** : resembling a fable; *also* : INCREDIBLE, MARVELOUS ⟨had a ~ time⟩ **2** : told in or based on fable — **fab·u·lous·ly** *adv*
fac *abbr* **1** facsimile **2** faculty
fa·cade *also* **fa·çade** \fə-'säd\ *n* [F *façade,* fr. It *facciata,* fr. *faccia* face] **1** : the principal face or front of a building **2** : a false, superficial, or artificial appearance ♦ ***Synonyms*** MASK, DISGUISE, FRONT, GUISE, PRETENSE, VENEER
¹face \'fās\ *n* **1** : the front part of the head **2** : PRESENCE ⟨in the ~ of danger⟩ **3** : facial expression : LOOK ⟨put a sad ~ on⟩ **4** : GRIMACE ⟨made a ~⟩ **5** : outward appearance ⟨looks easy on the ~ of it⟩ **6** : CONFIDENCE; *also* : BOLDNESS **7** : DIGNITY, PRESTIGE ⟨afraid to lose ~⟩ **8** : SURFACE; *esp* : a front, principal, bounding, or contacting surface ⟨~ of a cliff⟩ ⟨the ~*s* of a cube⟩ ⟨the ~ of a golf club⟩ — **faced** \'fāst, 'fā-səd\ *adj*
²face *vb* **faced; fac·ing** **1** : to confront brazenly **2** : to line near the edge esp. with a different material; *also* : to cover the front or surface of ⟨~ a building with marble⟩ **3** : to meet or bring in direct contact or confrontation ⟨*faced* the problem⟩ **4** : to stand or sit with the face toward ⟨~ the sun⟩ **5** : to have the front oriented toward ⟨a house *facing* the park⟩ **6** : to have as or be a prospect ⟨~ a grim future⟩ **7** : to turn the face or body in a specified direction — **face the music** : to meet the unpleasant consequences of one's actions
face·down \ˌfās-'daün\ *adv* : with the face downward ⟨cards turned ~⟩
face·less \-ləs\ *n* **1** : lacking character or individuality **2** : lacking a face
face·lift \'fās-ˌlift\ *n* **1** : plastic surgery on the face and neck to remove defects (as wrinkles) typical of aging **2** : MODERNIZATION — **face-lift** *vb*
face-off \'fās-ˌȯf\ *n* **1** : a method of beginning play by dropping a puck or ball in (as in hockey) between two opposing players each of whom attempts to control it **2** : CONFRONTATION — **face off** *vb*
fac·et \'fa-sət\ *n* [F *facette,* dim. of *face*] **1** : a small plane surface of a cut gem **2** : ASPECT, PHASE
fa·ce·tious \fə-'sē-shəs\ *adj* **1** : joking often inappropriately **2** : JOCULAR, JOCOSE ♦ ***Synonyms*** WITTY, HUMOROUS — **fa·ce·tious·ly** *adv* — **fa·ce·tious·ness** *n*
¹fa·cial \'fā-shəl\ *adj* **1** : of or relating to the face **2** : used to improve the appearance of the face
²facial *n* : a facial treatment

fac·ile \'fa-səl\ *adj* **1** : easily accomplished, handled, or attained **2** : SIMPLISTIC **3** : readily manifested and often insincere ⟨~ prose⟩ **4** : READY, FLUENT ⟨a ~ writer⟩
fa·cil·i·tate \fə-'si-lə-ˌtāt\ *vb* **-tat·ed; -tat·ing** : to make easier — **fa·cil·i·ta·tion** \-ˌsi-lə-'tā-shən\ *n* — **fa·cil·i·ta·tor** \-'si-lə-ˌtā-tər\ *n*
fa·cil·i·ty \fə-'si-lə-tē\ *n, pl* **-ties** **1** : the quality of being easily performed **2** : ease in performance : APTITUDE **3** : PLIANCY **4** : something that makes easier an action, operation, or course of conduct; *also* : REST ROOM — often used in pl. **5** : something (as a hospital) built or installed for a particular purpose
fac·ing \'fā-siŋ\ *n* **1** : a lining at the edge esp. of a garment **2** *pl* : the collar, cuffs, and trimmings of a uniform coat **3** : an ornamental or protective layer **4** : material for facing
fac·sim·i·le \fak-'si-mə-lē\ *n* [L *fac simile* make similar] **1** : an exact copy **2** : a system of transmitting and reproducing printed matter or pictures by means of signals sent over telephone lines
fact \'fakt\ *n* **1** : DEED; *esp* : CRIME ⟨accessory after the ~⟩ **2** : the quality of being actual **3** : something that exists or occurs **4** : a piece of information — **in fact** : in truth
fac·tion \'fak-shən\ *n* : a group or combination (as in a government) acting together in and usu. against a larger body : CLIQUE — **fac·tion·al·ism** \-shə-nə-ˌli-zəm\ *n*
fac·tious \'fak-shəs\ *adj* **1** : of, relating to, or caused by faction **2** : inclined to faction or the formation of factions : causing dissension ♦ ***Synonyms*** INSUBORDINATE, CONTUMACIOUS, INSURGENT, SEDITIOUS, REBELLIOUS
fac·ti·tious \fak-'ti-shəs\ *adj* : ARTIFICIAL, SHAM ⟨a ~ display of grief⟩
fac·toid \'fak-ˌtȯid\ *n* **1** : an invented fact believed to be true because of its appearance in print **2** : a brief usu. trivial fact
¹fac·tor \'fak-tər\ *n* **1** : AGENT **2** : something that actively contributes to a result ⟨a ~ in her decision⟩ **3** : GENE **4** : any of the numbers or symbols in mathematics that when multiplied together form a product; *esp* : any of the integers that divide a given integer without a remainder
²factor *vb* **1** : to work as a factor **2** : to find the mathematical factors of and esp. the prime mathematical factors of
¹fac·to·ri·al \fak-'tȯr-ē-əl\ *adj* : of, relating to, or being a factor
²factorial *n* : the product of all the positive integers from 1 to a given integer *n*
fac·to·ry \'fak-trē, -tə-rē\ *n, pl* **-ries** **1** : a trading post where resident brokers trade **2** : a building or group of buildings used for manufacturing
fac·to·tum \fak-'tō-təm\ *n* [NL, lit., do everything, fr. L *fac* do + *totum* everything] : a person (as a servant) having numerous or varied duties

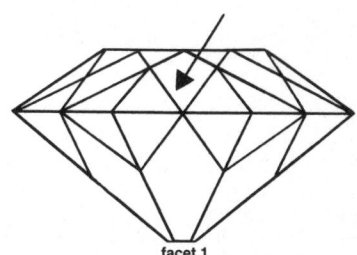

facet 1

facts of life : the physiological processes and behavior involved in sex and reproduction

fac·tu·al \'fak-chə-wəl\ *adj* : of or relating to facts; *also* : based on fact — **fac·tu·al·ly** *adv*

fac·ul·ty \'fa-kəl-tē\ *n, pl* **-ties** **1** : ability to act or do : POWER; *also* : natural aptitude **2** : one of the powers of the mind or body ⟨the ~ of hearing⟩ **3** : the teachers in a school or college or one of its divisions

fad \'fad\ *n* : a practice or interest followed for a time with exaggerated zeal : CRAZE — **fad·dish** *adj* — **fad·dish·ly** *adv* — **fad·dist** *n*

¹fade \'fād\ *vb* **fad·ed; fad·ing** **1** : WITHER **2** : to lose or cause to lose freshness or brilliance of color **3** : VANISH ⟨a *fading* memory⟩ **4** : to grow dim or faint

²fade *n* : a short haircut in which hair on top of the head stands high

FADM *abbr* fleet admiral

fae·cal, fae·ces *chiefly Brit var of* FECAL, FECES

fa·er·ie *also* **fa·ery** \'fā-rē, 'fer-ē\ *n, pl* **fa·er·ies** **1** : FAIRYLAND **2** : FAIRY

¹fag \'fag\ *vb* **fagged; fag·ging** **1** : DRUDGE **2** : TIRE, EXHAUST ⟨*fagged* by the work⟩

²fag *n* : MENIAL, DRUDGE

³fag *n* : an English public-school boy who acts as servant to another

⁴fag *vb* : to act as a fag

⁵fag *n* : CIGARETTE

fag end *n* **1** : REMNANT **2** : the extreme end **3** : the last part or coarser end of a web of cloth **4** : the untwisted end of a rope

fag·ot *or* **fag·got** \'fa-gət\ *n* : a bundle of sticks or twigs

fag·ot·ing *or* **fag·got·ing** *n* : an embroidery produced by tying threads in hourglass-shaped clusters

Fah *or* **Fahr** *abbr* Fahrenheit

Fahr·en·heit \'fer-ən-ˌhīt\ *adj* : relating to, conforming to, or having a thermometer scale with the boiling point of water at 212 degrees and the freezing point at 32 degrees above zero

fa·ience *or* **fa·ïence** \fā-'äns\ *n* [F] : earthenware decorated with opaque colored glazes

¹fail \'fāl\ *vb* **1** : to become feeble; *esp* : to decline in health **2** : to die away **3** : to stop functioning **4** : to fall short ⟨*~ed* in his duty⟩ **5** : to be or become absent or inadequate **6** : to be unsuccessful esp. in achieving a passing grade **7** : to become bankrupt **8** : DISAPPOINT **9** : NEGLECT ⟨*~ed* to lock the door⟩

²fail *n* : FAILURE ⟨without ~⟩

¹fail·ing \'fā-liŋ\ *n* : WEAKNESS, SHORTCOMING

²failing *prep* : in the absence or lack of

faille \'fī(-ə)l\ *n* : a somewhat shiny closely woven ribbed fabric (as silk)

fail-safe \'fāl-ˌsāf\ *adj* **1** : incorporating a counteractive feature for a possible source of failure **2** : having no chance of failure — **fail-safe** *n*

fail·ure \'fāl-yər\ *n* **1** : a failing to do or perform **2** : a state of inability to perform a normal function adequately ⟨heart ~⟩; *also* : an abrupt cessation of functioning ⟨a power ~⟩ **3** : a fracturing or giving way under stress **4** : a lack of success **5** : BANKRUPTCY **6** : DEFICIENCY **7** : DETERIORATION, DECAY **8** : one that has failed

¹fain \'fān\ *adj* **1** *archaic* : GLAD; *also* : INCLINED **2** : being obliged or compelled

²fain *adv* **1** : with pleasure **2** : by preference

¹faint \'fānt\ *adj* [ME *faint, feint*, fr. AF, fr. *faindre, feindre* to feign, lose heart] **1** : COWARDLY, SPIRITLESS **2** : weak, dizzy, and likely to faint **3** : lacking vigor or strength : FEEBLE ⟨~ praise⟩ **4** : hardly perceptible ⟨~ handwriting⟩ — **faint·ly** *adv* — **faint·ness** *n*

²faint *vb* : to lose consciousness

³faint *n* : the action of fainting; *also* : the resulting condition

faint·heart·ed \ˌfānt-'här-təd\ *adj* : lacking courage : TIMID

¹fair \'fer\ *adj* **1** : pleasing in appearance : BEAUTIFUL **2** : superficially pleasing : SPECIOUS **3** : CLEAN, PURE **4** : CLEAR, LEGIBLE **5** : not stormy or cloudy **6** : JUST **7** : conforming with the rules : ALLOWED; *also* : being within the foul lines ⟨~ ball⟩ **8** : open to legitimate pursuit or attack ⟨~ game⟩ **9** : PROMISING, LIKELY ⟨a ~ chance of winning⟩ **10** : favorable to a ship's course ⟨a ~ wind⟩ **11** : light in complexion : BLOND **12** : ADE-

QUATE **13** : significant in size ⟨a ~ amount of traffic⟩ — **fair·ness** *n*

²fair *adv* **1** : in a fair manner ⟨play ~⟩ **2** *chiefly Brit* : FAIRLY 4

³fair *n* **1** : a gathering of buyers and sellers at a stated time and place for trade **2** : a competitive exhibition (as of farm products) **3** : a sale of assorted articles usu. for a charitable purpose ⟨a book ~⟩ **4** : an exhibition that promotes available services ⟨a job ~⟩

fair·ground \-ˌgraund\ *n* : an area where outdoor fairs, circuses, or exhibitions are held

fair·ing \'fer-iŋ\ *n* : a structure for producing a smooth outline and reducing drag (as on an airplane)

fair·ly \'fer-lē\ *adv* **1** : HANDSOMELY **2** : in a manner of speaking ⟨~ bursting with pride⟩ **3** : without bias **4** : to a full degree or extent : PLAINLY, DISTINCTLY **5** : SOMEWHAT, RATHER ⟨a ~ easy job⟩

fair-spo·ken \'fer-'spō-kən\ *adj* : pleasant and courteous in speech

fair-trade \-'trād\ *adj* : of, relating to, or being an agreement between a producer and a seller that branded merchandise will be sold at or above a specified price — **fair-trade** *vb*

fair·way \-ˌwā\ *n* : the mowed part of a golf course between tee and green

fairy \'fer-ē\ *n, pl* **fair·ies** [ME *fairie* fairyland, enchantment, fr. AF *faerie*, fr. *fee* fairy, fr. L *Fata*, goddess of fate, fr. *fatum* fate] : an imaginary being of folklore and romance usu. having diminutive human form and magic powers — **fairy** *adj*

fairy·land \-ˌland\ *n* **1** : the land of fairies **2** : a beautiful or charming place

fairy tale *n* **1** : a children's story usu. about mythical beings (as fairies) **2** : FIB

fait ac·com·pli \ˌfāt-ˌa-ˌkōⁿ-'plē\ *n, pl* **faits accomplis** *same or* -'plēz\ [F, accomplished fact] : a thing accomplished and presumably irreversible

faith \'fāth\ *n, pl* **faiths** \'fāths, 'fāthz\ [ME *feith*, fr. AF *feid, fei*, fr. L *fides*] **1** : allegiance to duty or a person : LOYALTY **2** : belief and trust in God **3** : complete trust **4** : a system of religious beliefs — **faith·ful** \-fəl\ *adj* — **faith·ful·ly** *adv* — **faith·ful·ness** *n*

faith·less \'fāth-ləs\ *adj* **1** : DISLOYAL **2** : not to be relied on ✦ **Synonyms** FALSE, TRAITOROUS, TREACHEROUS, UNFAITHFUL — **faith·less·ly** *adv* — **faith·less·ness** *n*

fa·ji·ta \fə-'hē-tə\ *n* : a marinated strip usu. of beef or chicken grilled or broiled and served usu. with a flour tortilla and savory fillings

¹fake \'fāk\ *adj* : COUNTERFEIT, SHAM

²fake *n* **1** : IMITATION, FRAUD; *also* : IMPOSTOR **2** : a simulated move in sports (as a pretended pass)

³fake *vb* **faked; fak·ing** **1** : to treat so as to falsify **2** : COUNTERFEIT **3** : to deceive (an opponent) in a sports contest by making a fake — **fak·er** *n*

fa·kir \fə-'kir\ *n* [Ar *faqīr*, lit., poor man] **1** : a Muslim mendicant : DERVISH **2** : a wandering Hindu ascetic

fal·con \'fal-kən, 'fȯl-\ *n* **1** : a hawk trained for use in falconry **2** : any of various swift long-winged long-tailed hawks having a notched beak and usu. inhabiting open areas

fal·con·ry \'fal-kən-rē, 'fȯl-\ *n* **1** : the art of training hawks to hunt in cooperation with a person **2** : the sport of hunting with hawks — **fal·con·er** *n*

¹fall \'fȯl\ *vb* **fell** \'fel\; **fall·en** \'fȯ-lən\; **fall·ing** **1** : to descend freely by the force of gravity **2** : to hang freely **3** : to come or go as if by falling ⟨darkness *fell*⟩ **4** : to become uttered **5** : to lower or become lowered : DROP ⟨her eyes *fell*⟩ **6** : to leave an erect position suddenly and involuntarily **7** : STUMBLE, STRAY **8** : to drop down wounded or dead esp. in battle **9** : to become captured ⟨the city *fell* to the enemy⟩ **10** : to suffer ruin, defeat, or failure **11** : to commit an immoral act **12** : to move or extend in a downward direction **13** : SUBSIDE, ABATE **14** : to decline in quality, activity, quantity, or value **15** : to assume a look of shame or dejection ⟨her face *fell*⟩ **16** : to occur at a certain time **17** : to come by chance **18** : DEVOLVE ⟨the duties *fell* to him⟩ **19** : to have the proper place or station ⟨the accent ~s on the first syllable⟩ **20** : to come within the scope of something **21** : to pass from one condition to another ⟨*fell* ill⟩ **22** : to set about heartily or actively ⟨~ to work⟩ — **fall all over**

oneself *or* **fall over backward** : to display excessive eagerness — **fall flat** : to produce no response or result — **fall for** **1** : to fall in love with **2** : to become a victim of — **fall from grace** : BACKSLIDE — **fall into line** : to comply with a certain course of action — **fall short** **1** : to be deficient **2** : to fail to attain

²fall *n* **1** : the act of falling **2** : a falling out, off, or away : DROPPING **3** : AUTUMN **4** : a thing or quantity that falls ⟨a light ∼ of snow⟩ **5** : COLLAPSE, DOWNFALL **6** : the surrender or capture of a besieged place **7** : departure from virtue or goodness **8** : SLOPE **9** : WATERFALL — usu. used in pl. **10** : a decrease in size, quantity, degree, or value ⟨a ∼ in price⟩ **11** : the distance which something falls **12** : an act of forcing a wrestler's shoulders to the mat; *also* : a bout of wrestling

fal·la·cious \fə-ʹlā-shəs\ *adj* **1** : embodying a fallacy ⟨a ∼ argument⟩ **2** : MISLEADING, DECEPTIVE

fal·la·cy \ʹfa-lə-sē\ *n, pl* **-cies** **1** : a false or mistaken idea **2** : an often plausible argument using false or illogical reasoning

fall back *vb* : RETREAT, RECEDE

fall guy *n* : SCAPEGOAT

fal·li·ble \ʹfa-lə-bəl\ *adj* **1** : liable to be erroneous **2** : capable of making a mistake — **fal·li·bly** \-blē\ *adv*

fall·ing–out \ˌfó-liŋ-ʹaút\ *n, pl* **fallings–out** *or* **falling–outs** : QUARREL

falling star *n* : METEOR

fal·lo·pi·an tube \fə-ʹlō-pē-ən-\ *n, often cap F* : either of the pair of anatomical tubes that carry the eggs from the ovary to the uterus

fall·out \ʹfól-ˌaút\ *n* **1** : the often radioactive particles that result from a nuclear explosion and descend through the air **2** : a secondary and often lingering effect or result

fall out *vb* : QUARREL

¹fal·low \ʹfa-(ˌ)lō\ *n* : fallow land; *also* : the state or period of being fallow — **fallow** *vb*

²fallow *adj* **1** : left without tilling or sowing after plowing **2** : DORMANT, INACTIVE ⟨a writer's ∼ period⟩

false \ʹfóls\ *adj* **fals·er; fals·est** **1** : not genuine : ARTIFICIAL ⟨∼ teeth⟩ **2** : intentionally untrue **3** : adjusted or made so as to deceive ⟨∼ scales⟩ **4** : tending to mislead : DECEPTIVE ⟨∼ promises⟩ **5** : not true ⟨∼ concepts⟩ **6** : not faithful or loyal : TREACHEROUS **7** : not essential or permanent ⟨∼ front⟩ **8** : inaccurate in pitch **9** : based on mistaken ideas — **false·ly** *adv* — **false·ness** *n* — **fal·si·ty** \ʹfól-sə-tē\ *n*

false·hood \ʹfóls-ˌhùd\ *n* **1** : LIE **2** : absence of truth or accuracy **3** : the practice of lying

fal·set·to \fól-ʹse-tō\ *n, pl* **-tos** [It, fr. dim. of *falso* false] : an artificially high voice; *esp* : an artificial singing voice that overlaps and extends above the range of the full voice esp. of a tenor

fal·si·fy \ʹfól-sə-ˌfī\ *vb* **-fied; -fy·ing** **1** : to prove to be false **2** : to alter so as to deceive **3** : LIE; *also* : MISREPRESENT — **fal·si·fi·able** \ˌfól-sə-ʹfī-ə-bəl\ *adj* — **fal·si·fi·ca·tion** \ˌfól-sə-fə-ʹkā-shən\ *n*

fal·ter \ʹfól-tər\ *vb* **1** : to move unsteadily : STUMBLE, TOTTER **2** : to hesitate in speech : STAMMER **3** : to hesitate in purpose or action : WAVER, FLINCH **4** : to lose effectiveness ⟨a ∼*ing* business⟩ — **fal·ter·ing·ly** *adv*

fam *abbr* **1** familiar **2** family

fame \ʹfām\ *n* : public reputation : RENOWN — **famed** \ʹfāmd\ *adj*

fa·mil·ial \fə-ʹmil-yəl\ *adj* **1** : of, relating to, or suggestive of a family **2** : tending to occur in more members of a family than expected by chance alone ⟨a ∼ disorder⟩

¹fa·mil·iar \fə-ʹmil-yər\ *n* **1** : COMPANION **2** : a spirit held to attend and serve or guard a person **3** : one who frequents a place

²familiar *adj* **1** : closely acquainted : INTIMATE **2** : of or relating to a family **3** : INFORMAL **4** : FORWARD, PRESUMPTUOUS **5** : frequently seen or experienced **6** : of everyday occurrence — **fa·mil·iar·ly** *adv*

fa·mil·iar·ise *Brit var of* FAMILIARIZE

fa·mil·iar·i·ty \fə-ˌmil-ʹyer-ə-tē, -ˌmi-lē-ʹer-\ *n, pl* **-ties** **1** : close friendship : INTIMACY **2** : INFORMALITY **3** : an unduly bold or forward act or expression : IMPROPRIETY **4** : close acquaintance with something

fa·mil·iar·ize \fə-ʹmil-yə-ˌrīz\ *vb* **-ized; -iz·ing** **1** : to make known or familiar **2** : to make thoroughly acquainted

fam·i·ly \ʹfam-lē, ʹfa-mə-\ *n, pl* **-lies** [ME *familie*, fr. L *fa-*

milia household, fr. *famulus* servant] **1** : a group of individuals living under one roof and under one head : HOUSEHOLD **2** : a group of persons of common ancestry : CLAN **3** : a group of things having common characteristics; *esp* : a group of related plants or animals ranking in biological classification above a genus and below an order **4** : a social unit usu. consisting of one or two parents and their children

family planning *n* : planning intended to determine the number and spacing of one's children by using birth control

family tree *n* : GENEALOGY; *also* : a genealogical diagram

fam·ine \ʹfa-mən\ *n* **1** : an extreme scarcity of food **2** : a great shortage

fam·ish \ʹfa-mish\ *vb* **1** : STARVE **2** : to suffer for lack of something necessary

fa·mous \ʹfā-məs\ *adj* **1** : widely known **2** : honored for achievement **3** : EXCELLENT, FIRST-RATE **♦ Synonyms** RENOWNED, CELEBRATED, NOTED, NOTORIOUS, DISTINGUISHED, EMINENT, ILLUSTRIOUS

fa·mous·ly *adv* : SPLENDIDLY, EXCELLENTLY

¹fan \ʹfan\ *n* **1** : a device (as a hand-waved triangular piece or a mechanism with blades) for producing a current of air

²fan *vb* **fanned; fan·ning** **1** : to drive away the chaff from grain by winnowing **2** : to move (air) with or as if with a fan **3** : to direct a current of air upon ⟨∼ a fire⟩ **4** : to stir up to activity : STIMULATE **5** : to spread like a fan **6** : to strike out in baseball

³fan *n* : an enthusiastic follower or admirer

fa·nat·ic \fə-ʹna-tik\ *or* **fa·nat·i·cal** \-ti-kəl\ *adj* [L *fanaticus* inspired by a deity, frenzied, fr. *fanum* temple] : marked by excessive enthusiasm and often intense uncritical devotion — **fanatic** *n* — **fa·nat·i·cism** \-tə-ˌsi-zəm\ *n*

fan·ci·er \ʹfan-sē-ər\ *n* **1** : one that has a special liking or interest **2** : a person who breeds or grows some kind of animal or plant for points of excellence

fan·ci·ful \ʹfan-si-fəl\ *adj* **1** : marked by, existing in, or given to unrestrained imagination or whim rather than reason **2** : curiously made or shaped ⟨a ∼ design⟩ — **fan·ci·ful·ly** *adv*

¹fan·cy \ʹfan-sē\ *vb* **fan·cied; fan·cy·ing** **1** : LIKE **2** : IMAGINE **3** : to believe without evidence or certainty **4** : to visualize or interpret as

²fancy *n, pl* **fancies** [ME *fantasie, fantsy* imagination, image, preference, fr. AF *fantasie* illusion, fr. L *phantasia*, fr. Gk, appearance, imagination] **1** : LIKING, INCLINATION; *also* : LOVE **2** : WHIM, NOTION, IDEA ⟨a passing ∼⟩ **3** : IMAGINATION **4** : TASTE, JUDGMENT **♦ Synonyms** CAPRICE, CROTCHET, VAGARY

³fancy *adj* **fan·ci·er; -est** **1** : WHIMSICAL **2** : not plain : ORNAMENTAL, POSH **3** : of particular excellence **4** : bred esp. for a showy appearance **5** : EXCESSIVE **6** : executed with technical skill and style — **fan·ci·ly** \ʹfan-sə-lē\ *adv*

fancy dress *n* : a costume (as for a masquerade) chosen to suit a fancy

fan·cy–free \ˌfan-sē-ʹfrē\ *adj* : free from amorous attachment; *also* : free to imagine

fan·cy·work \ʹfan-sē-ˌwərk\ *n* : ornamental needlework (as embroidery)

fan·dan·go \fan-ʹdaŋ-gō\ *n, pl* **-gos** **1** : a lively Spanish or Spanish-American dance **2** : TOMFOOLERY

fane \ʹfān\ *n* **1** : TEMPLE **2** : CHURCH

fan·fare \ʹfan-ˌfer\ *n* **1** : a flourish of trumpets **2** : a showy display

fang \ʹfaŋ\ *n* : a long sharp tooth; *esp* : a grooved or hollow tooth of a venomous snake — **fanged** \ʹfaŋd\ *adj*

fan·light \ʹfan-ˌlīt\ *n* : a semicircular window with radiating bars like a fan that is set over a door or window

fan·ny \ʹfa-nē\ *n, pl* **fannies** : BUTTOCKS

fan·tail \ʹfan-ˌtāl\ *n* **1** : a fan-shaped tail or end **2** : an overhang at the stern of a ship

fan·ta·sia \fan-ʹtä-zhə, -zhē-ə, -zē-ə; ˌfan-tə-ʹzē-ə\ *n* : a musical composition free and fanciful in form

fan·ta·sise *Brit var of* FANTASIZE

fan·ta·size \ʹfan-tə-ˌsīz\ *vb* **-sized; -siz·ing** : IMAGINE, DAYDREAM

fan·tas·tic \fan-ʹtas-tik\ *also* **fan·tas·ti·cal** \-ti-kəl\ *adj* **1** : IMAGINARY, UNREAL **2** : conceived by unrestrained fancy **3** : exceedingly or unbelievably great **4** : ECCEN-

TRIC ✦ *Synonyms* CHIMERICAL, FANCIFUL, IMAGINARY — fan·tas·ti·cal·ly \-ti-k(ə-)lē\ *adv*

fan·ta·sy *also* **phan·ta·sy** \'fan-tə-sē\ *n, pl* **-sies** 1 : IMAGINATION, FANCY 2 : a product of the imagination : ILLUSION 3 : FANTASIA — **fantasy** *vb*

FAQ *abbr* frequently asked question

¹**far** \'fär\ *adv* **far·ther** \-thər\ *or* **fur·ther** \'fər-\; **far·thest** *or* **fur·thest** \-thəst\ 1 : at or to a considerable distance in space or time ⟨∼ from home⟩ 2 : by a broad interval : WIDELY, MUCH ⟨∼ better⟩ 3 : to or at a definite distance, point, or degree ⟨as ∼ as I know⟩ 4 : to an advanced point or extent ⟨go ∼ in his field⟩ — **by far** : by a considerable margin — **far and away** : DECIDEDLY — **so far** : until now

²**far** *adj* **farther** *or* **further**; **farthest** *or* **furthest** 1 : remote in space or time 2 : DIFFERENT 3 : LONG ⟨a ∼ journey⟩ 4 : being the more distant of two ⟨on the ∼ side of the lake⟩

far·ad \'fer-ˌad, -əd\ *n* : a unit of capacitance equal to the capacitance of a capacitor having a potential difference of one volt between its plates when it is charged with one coulomb of electricity

far·away \'fär-ə-ˌwä\ *adj* 1 : DISTANT, REMOTE ⟨∼ lands⟩ 2 : DREAMY

farce \'färs\ *n* 1 : a broadly satirical comedy with an improbable plot 2 : the humor characteristic of farce or pretense 3 : a ridiculous or empty display — **far·ci·cal** \'fär-si-kəl\ *adj*

far cry *n* 1 : a long distance 2 : something notably different ⟨a *far cry* from what we expected⟩

¹**fare** \'fer\ *vb* **fared**; **far·ing** 1 : GO, TRAVEL 2 : GET ALONG, SUCCEED ⟨fared well in math⟩ 3 : EAT, DINE

²**fare** *n* 1 : range of food : DIET; *also* : material provided for use, consumption, or enjoyment 2 : the price charged to transport a person 3 : a person paying a fare : PASSENGER

¹**fare·well** \fer-'wel\ *vb imper* : get along well — used interjectionally to or by one departing

²**farewell** *n* 1 : a wish of well-being at parting : GOOD-BYE 2 : LEAVE-TAKING

³**fare·well** \'fer-ˌwel\ *adj* : PARTING, FINAL ⟨a ∼ concert⟩

far–fetched \'fär-'fecht\ *adj* : not easily or naturally deduced or introduced : IMPROBABLE ⟨a ∼ story⟩

far–flung \-'fləŋ\ *adj* : widely spread or distributed ⟨a ∼ empire⟩

fa·ri·na \fə-'rē-nə\ *n* [L, meal, flour] : a fine meal (as of wheat) used in puddings or as a breakfast cereal

far·i·na·ceous \ˌfer-ə-'nä-shəs\ *adj* 1 : having a mealy texture or surface 2 : containing or rich in starch

¹**farm** \'färm\ *n* [ME *ferme* rent, lease, fr. AF, fr. *fermer* to fix, rent, fr. L *firmare* to make firm, fr. *firmus* firm] 1 : a tract of land used for raising crops or livestock 2 : a minor-league subsidiary of a major-league team

²**farm** *vb* : to use (land) as a farm ⟨∼ed 200 acres⟩; *also* : to raise crops or livestock — **farm·er** *n*

farm·hand \'färm-ˌhand\ *n* : a farm laborer

farm·house \-ˌhaùs\ *n* : a dwelling on a farm

farm·ing \'fär-miŋ\ *n* : the occupation or business of a person who farms

farm·land \'färm-ˌland\ *n* : land used or suitable for farming

farm out *vb* : to turn over (as a task) to another

farm·stead \'färm-ˌsted\ *n* : a farm with its buildings

farm·yard \-ˌyärd\ *n* : land around or enclosed by farm buildings

far–off \'fär-'òf\ *adj* : remote in time or space : DISTANT

fa·rouche \fə-'rüsh\ *adj* [F] 1 : WILD 2 : marked by shyness and lack of polish

far–out \'fär-'aùt\ *adj* : very unconventional ⟨∼ clothes⟩

far·ra·go \fə-'rä-gō, -'rä-\ *n, pl* **-goes** [L, mixed fodder, mixture] : a confused collection : MIXTURE

far–reach·ing \'fär-'rē-chiŋ\ *adj* : having a wide range or effect

far·ri·er \'fer-ē-ər\ *n* [alter. of ME *ferrour*, fr. AF, blacksmith, fr. *ferrer* to shoe (horses)] : a person who shoes horses

¹**far·row** \'fer-ō\ *vb* : to give birth to a litter of pigs

²**farrow** *n* : a litter of pigs

far–see·ing \'fär-ˌsē-iŋ\ *adj* 1 : FARSIGHTED 1 2 : FARSIGHTED 2

far·sight·ed \'fär-ˌsī-təd\ *adj* 1 : seeing or able to see to a

great distance 2 : JUDICIOUS, WISE, SHREWD 3 : affected with an eye condition in which vision is better for distant than near objects — **far·sight·ed·ness** *n*

¹**far·ther** \'fär-thər\ *adv* 1 : at or to a greater distance or more advanced point 2 : to a greater degree or extent

²**farther** *adj* 1 : more distant 2 : ADDITIONAL

far·ther·most \-ˌmōst\ *adj* : FARTHEST

¹**far·thest** \'fär-thəst\ *adj* : most distant

²**farthest** *adv* 1 : to or at the greatest distance : REMOTEST 2 : to the most advanced point 3 : by the greatest degree or extent : MOST

far·thing \'fär-thiŋ\ *n* 1 : a former British monetary unit equal to $1/4$ of a penny; *also* : a coin representing this unit 2 : something of small value

fas·cia \/ *is usu* 'fā-sh(ē-)ə, *2 is usu* 'fa-\ *n, pl* **-ci·ae** \-shē-ˌē\ *or* **-cias** 1 : a flat usu. horizontal part (as a band or board) of or on a building 2 : a sheet of connective tissue covering body structures (as muscles)

fas·ci·cle \'fa-si-kəl\ *n* 1 : a small or slender bundle (as of pine needles or nerve fibers) 2 : one of the divisions of a book published in parts — **fas·ci·cled** \-kəld\ *adj*

fas·ci·nate \'fa-sə-ˌnāt\ *vb* **-nat·ed**; **-nat·ing** [L *fascinare*, fr. *fascinum* evil spell] 1 : to transfix and hold spellbound by an irresistible power 2 : ALLURE 3 : to be irresistibly attractive — **fas·ci·na·tion** \ˌfa-sə-'nä-shən\ *n*

fas·cism \'fa-ˌshi-zəm\ *n, often cap* : a political philosophy, movement, or regime that exalts nation and often race and stands for a centralized autocratic often militaristic government — **fas·cist** \-shist\ *n or adj, often cap* — **fas·cis·tic** \fa-'shis-tik\ *adj, often cap*

¹**fash·ion** \'fa-shən\ *n* 1 : the make or form of something 2 : MANNER, WAY 3 : a prevailing custom, usage, or style 4 : the prevailing style (as in dress) ✦ *Synonyms* MODE, VOGUE, RAGE, TREND

²**fashion** *vb* 1 : MOLD, CONSTRUCT 2 : FIT, ADAPT

fash·ion·able \'fa-shə-nə-bəl\ *adj* 1 : dressing or behaving according to fashion : STYLISH 2 : of or relating to the world of fashion ⟨∼ resorts⟩ ✦ *Synonyms* CHIC, MODISH, SMART, SWANK — **fash·ion·ably** \-blē\ *adv*

¹**fast** \'fast\ *adj* 1 : firmly fixed 2 : tightly shut 3 : adhering firmly 4 : STUCK 5 : STAUNCH ⟨∼ friends⟩ 6 : characterized by quick motion, operation, or effect ⟨a ∼ trip⟩ ⟨a ∼ track⟩ 7 : indicating ahead of the correct time ⟨the clock is ∼⟩ 8 : not easily disturbed : SOUND ⟨a ∼ sleep⟩ 9 : permanently dyed; *also* : being proof against fading ⟨colors ∼ to sunlight⟩ 10 : DISSIPATED, WILD 11 : sexually promiscuous ✦ *Synonyms* RAPID, SWIFT, FLEET, QUICK, SPEEDY, HASTY

²**fast** *adv* 1 : in a firm or fixed manner ⟨stuck ∼ in the mud⟩ 2 : SOUNDLY, DEEPLY ⟨∼ asleep⟩ 3 : SWIFTLY 4 : RECKLESSLY

³**fast** *vb* 1 : to abstain from food 2 : to eat sparingly or abstain from some foods

⁴**fast** *n* 1 : the act or practice of fasting 2 : a time of fasting

fast·back \'fast-ˌbak\ *n* : an automobile having a roof with a long slope to the rear

fast·ball \-ˌbòl\ *n* : a baseball pitch thrown at full speed

fas·ten \'fa-sᵊn\ *vb* 1 : to attach or join by or as if by pinning, tying, or nailing 2 : to make fast : fix securely 3 : to become fixed or joined 4 : to focus attention ⟨∼ed onto the newest trends⟩ — **fas·ten·er** *n*

fas·ten·ing *n* : something that fastens : FASTENER

fast–food \ˌfast-'füd\ *adj* : specializing in food that is prepared and served quickly ⟨a ∼ restaurant⟩

fast–for·ward \-'fòr-ward\ *n* 1 : a function of an electronic device that advances a recording rapidly 2 : a state of rapid advancement — **fast–forward** *vb*

fas·tid·i·ous \fa-'sti-dē-əs\ *adj* 1 : overly difficult to please 2 : showing a meticulous or demanding attitude ⟨∼ workmanship⟩ ✦ *Synonyms* NICE, FINICKY, FUSSY, PARTICULAR, PERSNICKETY, SQUEAMISH — **fas·tid·i·ous·ly** *adv* — **fas·tid·i·ous·ness** *n*

fast·ness \'fast-nəs\ *n* 1 : the quality or state of being fast 2 : a fortified or secure place : STRONGHOLD

fast–talk \'fast-ˌtòk\ *vb* : to influence by persuasive and usu. deceptive talk

fast–track \'fast-ˌtrak\ *vb* : to speed up the processing or production of

fast track *n* : a course leading to rapid advancement or success

¹**fat** \'fat\ *adj* **fat·ter; fat·test** **1** : PLUMP, OBESE **2** : OILY, GREASY **3** : well filled out : BIG **4** : well stocked : ABUNDANT **5** : richly rewarding — **fat·ness** *n*

²**fat** *n* **1** : animal tissue rich in greasy or oily matter **2** : any of various energy-rich esters that occur naturally in animal fats and in plants and are soluble in organic solvents (as ether) but not in water **3** : the best or richest portion ⟨lived on the ~ of the land⟩ **4** : OBESITY **5** : excess matter

fa·tal \'fāt-ᵊl\ *adj* **1** : FATEFUL ⟨that ~ day⟩ **2** : causing death or ruin ⟨a ~ mistake⟩ — **fa·tal·ly** *adv*

fa·tal·ism \-ᵢi-zəm\ *n* : the belief that events are determined by fate — **fa·tal·ist** \-ist\ *n* — **fa·tal·is·tic** \ᵢfāt-ᵊl-'is-tik\ *adj* — **fa·tal·is·ti·cal·ly** \-ti-k(ə-)lē\ *adv*

fa·tal·i·ty \fā-'ta-lə-tē, fə-\ *n, pl* **-ties** **1** : DEADLINESS **2** : FATE **3** : death resulting from a disaster or accident; *also* : one who suffers such a death

fat·back \'fat-ᵢbak\ *n* : a fatty strip from the back of the hog usu. cured by salting and drying

fat cat *n* **1** : a wealthy contributor to a political campaign **2** : a wealthy privileged person

fate \'fāt\ *n* [ME, fr. MF or L; MF, fr. L *fatum*, lit., what has been spoken, fr. *fari* to speak] **1** : the cause or will that is held to determine events : DESTINY **2** : LOT, FORTUNE **3** : DISASTER; *esp* : DEATH **4** : END, OUTCOME **5** *pl, cap* : the three goddesses of classical mythology who determine the course of human life

fat·ed \'fā-təd\ *adj* : decreed, controlled, or marked by fate

fate·ful \'fāt-fəl\ *adj* **1** : OMINOUS, PROPHETIC **2** : IMPORTANT, DECISIVE **3** : DEADLY, DESTRUCTIVE **4** : determined by fate — **fate·ful·ly** *adv*

fath *abbr* fathom

fat·head \'fat-ᵢhed\ *n* : a stupid person — **fat·head·ed** \-'he-dəd\ *adj*

¹**fa·ther** \'fä-thər\ *n* **1** : a male parent **2** *cap* : God esp. as the first person of the Trinity **3** : FOREFATHER **4** : one deserving the respect and love given to a father **5** *often cap* : an early Christian writer accepted by the church as an authoritative witness to its teaching and practice **6** : ORIGINATOR ⟨the ~ of modern radio⟩; *also* : SOURCE **7** : PRIEST — used esp. as a title **8** : one of the leading men ⟨city ~s⟩ — **fa·ther·hood** \-ᵢhùd\ *n* — **fa·ther·less** *adj* — **fa·ther·ly** *adj*

²**father** *vb* **1** : BEGET **2** : to be the founder, producer, or author of **3** : to treat or care for as a father

father–in–law \'fä-thə-rən-ᵢlȯ\ *n, pl* **fa·thers–in–law** \-thər-zən-\ : the father of one's husband or wife

fa·ther·land \'fä-thər-ᵢland\ *n* **1** : the native land of one's ancestors **2** : one's native land

¹**fath·om** \'fa-thəm\ *n* [ME *fadme*, fr. OE *fæthm* length of the outstretched arms] : a unit of length equal to 6 feet (about 1.8 meters) used esp. for measuring the depth of water

²**fathom** *vb* **1** : to measure by a sounding line : PROBE **3** : to penetrate and come to understand — **fath·om·able** \'fa-thə-mə-bəl\ *adj*

fath·om·less \'fa-thəm-ləs\ *adj* : incapable of being fathomed

¹**fa·tigue** \fə-'tēg\ *n* [F] **1** : manual or menial work performed by military personnel **2** *pl* : the uniform or work clothing worn on fatigue and in the field **3** : weariness from labor or stress **4** : the tendency of a material to break under repeated stress

²**fatigue** *vb* **fa·tigued; fa·tigu·ing** : WEARY, TIRE

fat·ten \'fa-tᵊn\ *vb* : to make or grow fat

Fat Tuesday *n* : MARDI GRAS

¹**fat·ty** \'fa-tē\ *adj* **fat·ti·er; -est** **1** : containing fat esp. in unusual amounts **2** : GREASY

²**fatty** *n, pl* **fat·ties** : a fat person

fatty acid *n* : any of numerous acids that contain only carbon, hydrogen, and oxygen and that occur naturally in fats and various oils

fa·tu·i·ty \fə-'tü-ə-tē, -'tyü-\ *n, pl* **-ities** : FOOLISHNESS, STUPIDITY

fat·u·ous \'fa-chù-wəs\ *adj* : FOOLISH, INANE, SILLY — **fat·u·ous·ly** *adv*

fau·bourg \fō-'bùr\ *n* **1** : a suburb esp. of a French city **2** : a city quarter

fau·ces \'fȯ-ᵢsēz\ *n pl* [L, throat] : the narrow passage located between the soft palate and the base of the tongue that joins the mouth to the pharynx

fau·cet \'fȯ-sət, 'fä-\ *n* : a fixture for drawing off a liquid (as from a pipe)

¹**fault** \'fȯlt\ *n* **1** : a weakness in character : FAILING **2** : IMPERFECTION, IMPAIRMENT, DEFECT **3** : an error esp. in service in a net or racket game **4** : MISDEMEANOR; *also* : MISTAKE **5** : responsibility for something wrong **6** : a fracture in the earth's crust accompanied by a displacement of one side relative to the other — **fault·i·ly** \'fȯl-tə-lē\ *adv* — **fault·less** *adj* — **fault·less·ly** *adv* — **faulty** *adj*

²**fault** *vb* **1** : to commit a fault : ERR **2** : to fracture so as to produce a geologic fault **3** : to find a fault in

fault·find·er \'fȯlt-ᵢfīn-dər\ *n* : a person who tends to find fault or complain ♦ *Synonyms* CRITIC, CARPER, CAVILER, COMPLAINER — **fault·find·ing** *n or adj*

faun \'fȯn\ *n* : a Roman god similar to but gentler than a satyr

fau·na \'fȯ-nə\ *n, pl* **faunas** *also* **fau·nae** \-ᵢnē, -ᵢnī\ [NL, fr. L *Fauna*, sister of Faunus (the Roman god of animals)] : animals or animal life esp. of a region, period, or environment — **fau·nal** \-nəl\ *adj*

fau·vism \'fō-ᵢvi-zəm\ *n, often cap* : a movement in painting characterized by vivid colors, free treatment of form, and a vibrant and decorative effect — **fau·vist** \-vist\ *n, often cap*

faux pas \'fō-ᵢpä, fō-'\ *n, pl* **faux pas** *same or* -ᵢpäz, -'päz\ [F, lit., false step] : BLUNDER; *esp* : a social blunder

fa·va bean \'fä-və-\ *n* : the large flat edible seed of an Old World vetch; *also* : this plant

¹**fa·vor** \'fā-vər\ *n* **1** : friendly regard shown toward another esp. by a superior **2** : APPROVAL **3** : PARTIALITY **4** : POPULARITY **5** : gracious kindness; *also* : an act of such kindness **6** *pl* : effort in one's behalf : ATTENTION **7** : a token of love (as a ribbon) usu. worn conspicuously **8** : a small gift or decorative item given out at a party **9** : a special privilege **10** : sexual privileges — usu. used in pl. **11** *archaic* : LETTER **12** : BEHALF, INTEREST

²**favor** *vb* **1** : to regard or treat with favor **2** : OBLIGE **3** : ENDOW ⟨~ed by nature⟩ **4** : to treat gently or carefully : SPARE ⟨~ a lame leg⟩ **5** : PREFER **6** : SUPPORT, SUSTAIN **7** : FACILITATE ⟨darkness ~s attack⟩ **8** : RESEMBLE ⟨he ~s his father⟩

fa·vor·able \'fā-və-rə-bəl\ *adj* **1** : APPROVING **2** : HELPFUL, PROMISING, ADVANTAGEOUS ⟨~ weather⟩ — **fa·vor·ably** \-blē\ *adv*

fa·vor·ite \'fā-və-rət, -vrət\ *n* **1** : a person or a thing that is favored above others **2** : a competitor regarded as most likely to win — **favorite** *adj*

favorite son *n* : a candidate supported by the delegates of his state at a presidential nominating convention

fa·vor·it·ism \'fā-və-rə-ᵢti-zəm\ *n* : PARTIALITY, BIAS

fa·vour *chiefly Brit var of* FAVOR

¹**fawn** \'fȯn, 'fän\ *vb* **1** : to show affection ⟨a dog ~ing on its master⟩ **2** : to court favor by a cringing or flattering manner ♦ *Synonyms* GROVEL, KOWTOW, TOADY, TRUCKLE

²**fawn** *n* **1** : a young deer **2** : a light grayish brown — **fawny** \'fȯ-nē, 'fä-\ *adj*

fax \'faks\ *n* **1** : FACSIMILE 2 **2** : a device used to send or receive facsimile communications; *also* : such a communication — **fax** *vb*

fay \'fā\ *n* : FAIRY, ELF — **fay** *adj*

faze \'fāz\ *vb* **fazed; faz·ing** : to disturb the composure or courage of : DAUNT

FBI *abbr* Federal Bureau of Investigation

FCC *abbr* Federal Communications Commission

FD *abbr* fire department

FDA *abbr* Food and Drug Administration

FDIC *abbr* Federal Deposit Insurance Corporation

Fe *symbol* [L *ferrum*] iron

fe·al·ty \'fē(-ə)l-tē\ *n, pl* **-ties** : LOYALTY, ALLEGIANCE ♦ *Synonyms* FIDELITY, DEVOTION, FAITHFULNESS, PIETY

¹**fear** \'fir\ *vb* **1** : to have a reverent awe of ⟨~ God⟩ **2** : to be afraid of ⟨~s spiders⟩ **3** : to be apprehensive

²**fear** *n* **1** : an unpleasant often strong emotion caused by expectation or awareness of danger; *also* : an instance of or a state marked by this emotion **2** : anxious concern : SOLICITUDE **3** : profound reverence esp. toward God ♦ *Synonyms* DREAD, FRIGHT, ALARM, PANIC, TERROR, TREPIDATION

fear·ful \-fəl\ *adj* **1** : causing fear **2** : filled with fear **3** : showing or caused by fear **4** : extremely bad, intense, or large — **fear·ful·ly** *adv*

fear·less \-ləs\ *adj* : free from fear : BRAVE — **fear·less·ly** *adv* — **fear·less·ness** *n*

fear·some \-səm\ *adj* **1** : causing fear **2** : TIMID **3** : INTENSE 〈~ determination〉

fea·si·ble \'fē-zə-bəl\ *adj* [ME *faisible*, fr. AF *faisable*, fr. *fais-*, stem of *faire* to make, do] **1** : capable of being done or carried out 〈a ~ plan〉 **2** : SUITABLE **3** : REASONABLE, LIKELY ◆ **Synonyms** POSSIBLE, PRACTICABLE, VIABLE, WORKABLE — **fea·si·bil·i·ty** \,fē-zə-'bi-lə-tē\ *n* — **fea·si·bly** \'fē-zə-blē\ *adv*

¹feast \'fēst\ *n* **1** : an elaborate meal : BANQUET **2** : ABUNDANCE 〈a ~ of good books〉 **3** : FESTIVAL 1

²feast *vb* **1** : to take part in a feast; *also* : to give a feast for **2** : to enjoy some unusual pleasure or delight **3** : DELIGHT, GRATIFY

feat \'fēt\ *n* : DEED, EXPLOIT, ACHIEVEMENT; *esp* : an act notable for courage, skill, endurance, or ingenuity

¹feath·er \'fe-thər\ *n* **1** : any of the light horny outgrowths that form the external covering of the body of a bird **2** : the vane of an arrow **3** : PLUMAGE **4** : KIND, NATURE 〈birds of a ~〉 **5** : ATTIRE, DRESS 〈in full ~〉 **6** : CONDITION, MOOD 〈in fine ~〉 — **feath·ered** \-thərd\ *adj* — **feath·er·less** *adj* — **feath·ery** *adj* — **a feather in one's cap** : a mark of distinction : HONOR

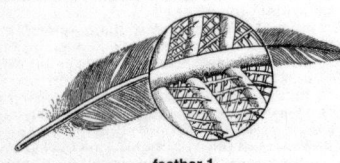

feather 1

²feather *vb* **1** : to furnish with a feather 〈~ an arrow〉 **2** : to cover, clothe, line, or adorn with or as if with feathers — **feather one's nest** : to provide for oneself financially esp. while exploiting a position of trust

feath·er·bed·ding \'fe-thər-,be-diŋ\ *n* : the requiring of an employer usu. under a union rule or safety statute to employ more workers than are needed

feath·er·edge \-,ej\ *n* : a very thin sharp edge

feath·er·weight \-,wāt\ *n* : one that is very light in weight; *esp* : a boxer weighing more than 118 but not over 126 pounds

¹fea·ture \'fē-chər\ *n* [ME *feture*, fr. AF, fr. L *factura* act of making, fr. *facere* to make] **1** : the shape or appearance of the face or its parts **2** : a part of the face : LINEAMENT **3** : a prominent part or characteristic **4** : a special attraction (as in a newspaper) **5** : something offered to the public or advertised as particularly attractive 〈a new car's ~s〉 — **fea·ture·less** *adj*

²feature *vb* **1** : to picture in the mind : IMAGINE **2** : to give special prominence to 〈the show ~s new artists〉 **3** : to play an important part

Feb *abbr* February

fe·brile \'fe-,brī(-ə)l\ *adj* : FEVERISH

Feb·ru·ary \'fe-b(y)ə-,wer-ē, 'fe-brə-\ *n* [ME *Februarie*, fr. L *Februarius*, fr. *Februa*, pl., feast of purification] : the 2d month of the year

fe·ces \'fē-,sēz\ *n pl* : bodily waste discharged from the intestine : EXCREMENT — **fe·cal** \-kəl\ *adj*

feck·less \'fek-ləs\ *adj* **1** : WEAK, INEFFECTIVE **2** : WORTHLESS, IRRESPONSIBLE

fe·cund \'fe-kənd, 'fē-\ *adj* : FRUITFUL, PROLIFIC — **fe·cun·di·ty** \fi-'kən-də-tē, fe-\ *n*

fe·cun·date \'fe-kən-,dāt, 'fē-\ *vb* **-dat·ed; -dat·ing 1** : to make fecund **2** : IMPREGNATE — **fe·cun·da·tion** \,fe-kən-'dā-shən, ,fē-\ *n*

fed *abbr* federal; federation

fed·er·al \'fe-də-rəl, -drəl\ *adj* **1** : formed by a compact between political units that surrender individual sovereignty to a central authority but retain certain limited powers **2** : of or constituting a form of government in which power is distributed between a central authority and constituent territorial units **3** : of or relating to the central govern-

ment of a federation **4** *cap* : FEDERALIST **5** *often cap* : of, relating to, or loyal to the federal government or the Union armies of the U.S. in the American Civil War — **fed·er·al·ly** *adv*

Federal *n* : a supporter of the U.S. government in the Civil War; *esp* : a soldier in the federal armies

federal district *n* : a district (as the District of Columbia) set apart as the seat of the central government of a federation

fed·er·al·ism \'fe-də-rə-li-zəm, -drə-\ *n* **1** *often cap* : the distribution of power in an organization (as a government) between a central authority and the constituent units **2** : support or advocacy of federalism **3** *cap* : the principles of the Federalists

fed·er·al·ist \-list\ *n* **1** : an advocate of federalism **2** *often cap* : an advocate of federal union between the American colonies after the Revolution and of adoption of the U.S. Constitution **3** *cap* : a member of a major political party in the early years of the U.S. favoring a strong centralized national government — **federalist** *adj, often cap*

fed·er·al·ize \'fe-də-rə-,līz, -drə-\ *vb* **-ized; -iz·ing 1** : to unite in or under a federal system **2** : to bring under the jurisdiction of a federal government

fed·er·ate \'fe-də-,rāt\ *vb* **-at·ed; -at·ing** : to join in a federation

fed·er·a·tion \,fe-də-'rā-shən\ *n* **1** : a political or societal entity formed by uniting smaller entities **2** : a federal government **3** : a union of organizations **4** : the forming of a federal union

fedn *abbr* federation

fe·do·ra \fi-'dȯr-ə\ *n* : a low soft felt hat with the crown creased lengthwise

fed up *adj* : utterly sated, tired, or disgusted

¹fee \'fē\ *n* [ME, fr. AF *fé, fief*, of Gmc origin; akin to OE *feoh* cattle, property] **1** : an estate in land held from a feudal lord **2** : an inherited or heritable estate in land **3** : a fixed charge; *also* : a charge for a service

fee·ble \'fē-bəl\ *adj* **fee·bler** \-bə-lər\; **fee·blest** \-bə-ləst\ [ME *feble*, fr. AF, fr. L *flebilis* lamentable, wretched, fr. *flēre* to weep] **1** : DECREPIT, FRAIL **2** : INEFFECTIVE, INADEQUATE 〈a ~ protest〉 — **fee·ble·ness** *n* — **fee·bly** \-blē\ *adv*

fee·ble·mind·ed \,fē-bəl-'mīn-dəd\ *adj* : lacking normal intelligence — **fee·ble·mind·ed·ness** *n*

¹feed \'fēd\ *vb* **fed** \'fed\; **feed·ing 1** : to give food to; *also* : to give as food **2** : EAT 1; *also* : PREY **3** : to furnish what is necessary to the development or function of **4** : to supply for another to use 〈~ a pass〉 〈fed the actor his lines〉 — **feed·er** *n*

²feed *n* **1** : a usu. large meal **2** : food for livestock **3** : a mechanism for feeding material to a machine

feed·back \'fēd-,bak\ *n* **1** : the return to the input of a part of the output of a machine, system, or process **2** : response esp. to one in authority about an activity or policy **3** : sound (as whistling) resulting from the retransmission of an amplified or broadcast signal

feed·lot \'fēd-,lät\ *n* : land on which cattle are fattened for market

feed·stuff \-,stəf\ *n* : FEED 2

¹feel \'fēl\ *vb* **felt** \'felt\; **feel·ing 1** : to perceive or examine through physical contact : TOUCH, HANDLE **2** : EXPERIENCE; *also* : to suffer from **3** : to ascertain by cautious trial 〈~ out public sentiment〉 **4** : to be aware of **5** : to be conscious of an inward impression, state of mind, or physical condition **6** : BELIEVE, THINK 〈say what you ~〉 **7** : to search for something with the fingers : GROPE **8** : SEEM 〈it ~s like spring〉 **9** : to have sympathy or pity

²feel *n* **1** : the sense of touch **2** : SENSATION, FEELING **3** : the quality of a thing as imparted through touch

feel·er \'fē-lər\ *n* **1** : one that feels; *esp* : a tactile organ (as on the head of an insect) **2** : a proposal or remark made to find out the views of other people

¹feel·ing \'fē-liŋ\ *n* **1** : the sense of touch; *also* : a sensation perceived by this **2** : a state of mind 〈a ~ of loneliness〉 **3** *pl* : general emotional condition : SENSIBILITIES 〈hurt their ~s〉 **4** : OPINION, BELIEF **5** : capacity to respond emotionally

²feeling *adj* **1** : SENSITIVE; *esp* : easily moved emotionally **2** : expressing emotion or sensitivity — **feel·ing·ly** *adv*

feet *pl of* FOOT

feign \'fān\ *vb* **1** : to give a false appearance of : SHAM ⟨~ illness⟩ **2** : to assert as if true : PRETEND

feint \'fānt\ *n* : something feigned; *esp* : a mock blow or attack intended to distract attention from the real point of attack — **feint** *vb*

feisty \'fī-stē\ *adj* **feist·i·er; -est** : having or showing a lively aggressiveness ⟨a ~ heroine⟩

feld·spar \'feld-,spär\ *n* : any of a group of crystalline minerals consisting of silicates of aluminum with another element (as potassium or sodium)

fe·lic·i·tate \fi-'li-sə-,tāt\ *vb* **-tat·ed; -tat·ing** : CONGRATU-LATE — **fe·lic·i·ta·tion** \-,li-sə-'tā-shən\ *n*

fe·lic·i·tous \fi-'li-sə-təs\ *adj* **1** : well chosen : APT **2** : PLEASANT, DELIGHTFUL — **fe·lic·i·tous·ly** *adv*

fe·lic·i·ty \fi-'li-sə-tē\ *n, pl* **-ties** **1** : the quality or state of being happy; *esp* : great happiness **2** : something that causes happiness **3** : a pleasing manner or quality esp. in art or language **4** : an apt expression

fe·line \'fē-,līn\ *adj* [L *felinus*, fr. *felis* cat] **1** : of or relating to cats or their kin **2** : SLY, TREACHEROUS **3** : STEALTHY — **feline** *n*

¹fell \'fel\ *n* : SKIN, HIDE, PELT

²fell *vb* **1** : to cut, beat, or knock down; *also* : KILL **2** : to sew (a seam) by folding one raw edge under the other

³fell *past of* FALL

⁴fell *adj* **1** : CRUEL, FIERCE; *also* : DEADLY — **in one fell swoop** *also* **at one fell swoop** : all at once : with a single effort

fel·lah \'fe-lə, fə-'lä\ *n, pl* **fel·la·hin** *or* **fel·la·heen** \,fe-lə-'hēn\ : a peasant or agricultural laborer in Arab countries (as Egypt or Syria)

fel·la·tio \fə-'lä-shē-,ō\ *also* **fel·la·tion** \-shən\ *n* : oral stimulation of the penis

fel·low \'fe-lō\ *n* [ME *felawe*, fr. OE *fēolaga*, fr. ON *fēlagi*, fr. *fēlag* partnership (fr. *fē* cattle, money) + *lag* act of laying] **1** : COMRADE, ASSOCIATE **2** : EQUAL, PEER **3** : one of a pair : MATE **4** : a member of an incorporated literary or scientific society **5** : MAN, BOY **6** : BOYFRIEND **7** : a person granted a stipend for advanced study

fellow man *n* : a kindred human being

fel·low·ship \'fe-lō-,ship\ *n* **1** : the condition of friendly relationship existing among persons : COMRADESHIP **2** : a community of interest or feeling **3** : a group with similar interests **4** : the position of a fellow (as of a university) **5** : the stipend granted a fellow

fellow traveler *n* : a sympathetic supporter of another's cause; *esp* : a person who sympathizes with and often furthers the ideals and program of an organized group (as the Communist party) without joining it

fel·on \'fe-lən\ *n* **1** : one who has committed a felony **2** : WHITLOW

fel·o·ny \'fe-lə-nē\ *n, pl* **-nies** : a serious crime punishable by a heavy sentence — **fe·lo·ni·ous** \fə-'lō-nē-əs\ *adj*

fel·spar *chiefly Brit var of* FELDSPAR

¹felt \'felt\ *n* **1** : a cloth made of wool and fur often mixed with natural or synthetic fibers **2** : a material resembling felt

²felt *past and past part of* FEEL

fem *abbr* **1** female **2** feminine

fe·male \'fē-,māl\ *adj* [ME, alter. of *femel*, fr. AF *femele*, fr. ML *femella*, fr. L, girl, dim. of *femina* woman] **1** : of, relating to, or being the sex that bears young; *also* : PISTILLATE **2** : characteristic of girls or women ⟨~ voices⟩

♦ Synonyms FEMININE, WOMANLY, WOMANLIKE, WOMANISH, EFFEMINATE — **female** *n*

¹fem·i·nine \'fe-mə-nən\ *adj* **1** : of the female sex; *also* : characteristic of or appropriate or peculiar to women **2** : of, relating to, or constituting the gender that includes most words or grammatical forms referring to females — **fem·i·nin·i·ty** \,fe-mə-'ni-nə-tē\ *n*

²feminine *n* : a noun, pronoun, adjective, or inflectional form or class of the feminine gender; *also* : the feminine gender

fem·i·nism \'fe-mə-,ni-zəm\ *n* **1** : the theory of the political, economic, and social equality of the sexes **2** : organized activity on behalf of women's rights and interests — **fem·i·nist** \-nist\ *n or adj*

femme fa·tale \,fem-fə-'tal\ *n, pl* **femmes fa·tales** *same or* -'talz\ [F, lit., disastrous woman] : a seductive woman

fe·mur \'fē-mər\ *n, pl* **fe·murs** *or* **fem·o·ra** \'fe-mə-rə\ : the

long leg bone extending from the hip to the knee — **fem·o·ral** \'fe-mə-rəl\ *adj*

¹fen \'fen\ *n* : low swampy land

²fen \'fən\ *n, pl* **fen** — see *yuan* at MONEY table

¹fence \'fens\ *n* [ME *fens*, short for *defens* defense] **1** : a barrier (as of wood or wire) to prevent escape or entry or to mark a boundary **2** : a person who receives stolen goods; *also* : a place where stolen goods are disposed of — **on the fence** : in a position of neutrality or indecision

²fence *vb* **fenced; fenc·ing** **1** : to enclose with a fence **2** : to keep in or out with a fence **3** : to practice fencing **4** : to use tactics of attack and defense esp. in debate — **fenc·er** *n*

fenc·ing *n* **1** : the art or practice of attack and defense with the foil, épée, or saber **2** : the fences of a property or region **3** : material used for building fences

fend \'fend\ *vb* **1** : to keep or ward off : REPEL **2** : SHIFT ⟨~ for yourself⟩

fend·er \'fen-dər\ *n* : a protective device (as a guard over the wheel of an automobile)

fen·es·tra·tion \,fe-nə-'strā-shən\ *n* : the arrangement and design of windows and doors in a building

Fe·ni·an \'fē-nē-ən\ *n* : a member of a secret 19th century Irish and Irish-American organization dedicated to overthrowing British rule in Ireland

fen·nel \'fe-nᵊl\ *n* : a garden plant related to the carrot and grown for its aromatic foliage and seeds

FEPC *abbr* Fair Employment Practices Commission

fe·ral \'fir-əl, 'fer-\ *adj* **1** : SAVAGE **2** : WILD **3** : having escaped from domestication and become wild

fer–de–lance \'fer-də-'lans\ *n, pl* **fer–de–lance** [F, lit., lance iron, spearhead] : a large venomous pit viper of Central and So. America

¹fer·ment \fər-'ment\ *vb* **1** : to cause or undergo fermentation **2** : to be or cause to be in a state of agitation or intense activity

²fer·ment \'fər-,ment\ *n* **1** : a living organism (as a yeast) causing fermentation by its enzymes; *also* : ENZYME **2** : AGITATION, TUMULT

fer·men·ta·tion \,fər-mən-'tā-shən, -,men-\ *n* **1** : chemical decomposition of an organic substance (as in the souring of milk or the formation of alcohol from sugar) by enzymatic action in the absence of oxygen often with formation of gas **2** : FERMENT 2

fer·mi·um \'fer-mē-əm, 'fər-\ *n* : an artificially produced radioactive metallic chemical element

fern \'fərn\ *n* : any of an order of vascular plants resembling seed plants in having roots, stems, and leaflike fronds but reproducing by spores instead of by flowers and seeds

fern·ery \'fər-nə-rē\ *n, pl* **-er·ies** **1** : a place for growing ferns **2** : a collection of growing ferns

fe·ro·cious \fə-'rō-shəs\ *adj* **1** : FIERCE, SAVAGE **2** : extremely intense — **fe·ro·cious·ly** *adv* — **fe·ro·cious·ness** *n*

fe·roc·i·ty \fə-'rä-sə-tē\ *n* : the quality or state of being ferocious

¹fer·ret \'fer-ət\ *n* : a partially domesticated usu. white European mammal related to the weasels

²ferret *vb* **1** : to hunt game with ferrets **2** : to drive out of a hiding place **3** : to find and bring to light by searching ⟨~ out the truth⟩

fer·ric \'fer-ik\ *adj* : of, relating to, or containing iron

ferric oxide *n* : an oxide of iron found in nature as hematite and as rust and used esp. as a pigment, for polishing, and in magnetic materials

Fer·ris wheel \'fer-əs-\ *n* : an amusement device consisting of a large upright power-driven wheel with seats that remain horizontal around its rim

fer·ro·mag·net·ic \,fer-ō-mag-'ne-tik\ *adj* : of or relating to substances that are easily magnetized

fer·rous \'fer-əs\ *adj* : of, relating to, or containing iron

fer·rule \'fer-əl\ *n* : a metal ring or cap around a slender wooden shaft to prevent splitting

¹fer·ry \'fer-ē\ *vb* **fer·ried; fer·ry·ing** [ME *ferien*, fr. OE *ferian* to carry, convey] **1** : to carry by boat across a body of water **2** : to cross by a ferry **3** : to convey from one place to another

²ferry *n, pl* **ferries** **1** : a place where persons or things are ferried **2** : FERRYBOAT

fer·ry·boat \'fer-ē-,bōt\ *n* : a boat used in ferrying

fer·tile \\'fər-t*l\\ *adj* **1** : producing plentifully : PRODUCTIVE ⟨~ soils⟩ ⟨a ~ mind⟩ **2** : capable of developing or reproducing ⟨~ seed⟩ ⟨a ~ bull⟩ ◆ *Synonyms* FRUITFUL, PROLIFIC, FECUND, PRODUCTIVE — **fer·til·i·ty** \\(,)fər-'ti-lə-tē\\ *n*

fer·til·ize \\'fər-tə-,līz\\ *vb* **-ized; -iz·ing 1** : to unite with in the process of fertilization ⟨a sperm ~s an egg⟩ **2** : to apply fertilizer to — **fer·til·i·za·tion** \\,fər-tə-lə-'zā-shən\\ *n*

fer·til·iz·er \\'fər-tə-,lī-zər\\ *n* : material (as manure or a chemical mixture) for enriching land

fer·ule \\'fer-əl\\ *n* : a rod or ruler used to punish children

fer·ven·cy \\'fər-vən-sē\\ *n, pl* **-cies** : FERVOR

fer·vent \\'fər-vənt\\ *adj* **1** : very hot : GLOWING **2** : marked by great intensity of feeling ◆ *Synonyms* IMPASSIONED, ARDENT, FERVID, FIERY, PASSIONATE — **fer·vent·ly** *adv*

fer·vid \\-vəd\\ *adj* **1** : very hot **2** : ARDENT, ZEALOUS — **fer·vid·ly** *adv*

fer·vor \\'fər-vər\\ *n* **1** : intense heat **2** : intensity of feeling or expression

fer·vour *chiefly Brit var of* FERVOR

fes·cue \\'fes-kyü\\ *n* : any of a genus of tufted perennial grasses

fes·tal \\'fes-t*l\\ *adj* : FESTIVE

fes·ter \\'fes-tər\\ *vb* **1** : to form pus **2** : PUTREFY, ROT **3** : RANKLE

fes·ti·val \\'fes-tə-vəl\\ *n* **1** : a time of celebration marked by special observances; *esp* : an occasion marked with religious ceremonies **2** : a periodic season or program of cultural events or entertainment ⟨a dance ~⟩

fes·tive \\'fes-tiv\\ *adj* **1** : of, relating to, or suitable for a feast or festival **2** : JOYFUL, GAY — **fes·tive·ly** *adv*

fes·tiv·i·ty \\fes-'ti-və-tē\\ *n, pl* **-ties 1** : FESTIVAL 1 **2** : the quality or state of being festive **3** : festive activity

¹fes·toon \\fes-'tün\\ *n* [F *feston*, fr. It *festone*, fr. *festa* festival] **1** : a decorative chain or strip hanging between two points **2** : a carved, molded, or painted ornament representing a decorative chain

²festoon *vb* **1** : to hang or form festoons on **2** : to shape into festoons

fe·ta \\'fe-tə\\ *n* : a white crumbly Greek cheese made from sheep's or goat's milk

fe·tal \\'fē-t*l\\ *adj* : of, relating to, or being a fetus

fetch \\'fech\\ *vb* **1** : to go or come after and bring or take back ⟨teach a dog to ~ a stick⟩ **2** : to bring in (as a price) **3** : to cause to come : bring out ⟨~ed tears from the eyes⟩ **4** : to give by striking ⟨~ him a blow⟩

fetch·ing *adj* : ATTRACTIVE, PLEASING ⟨a ~ smile⟩ — **fetch·ing·ly** *adv*

¹fete *or* **fête** \\'fāt, 'fet\\ *n* [F *fête*, fr. OF *feste*] **1** : FESTIVAL **2** : a large elaborate entertainment or party

²fete *or* **fête** *vb* **fet·ed** *or* **fêt·ed; fet·ing** *or* **fêt·ing 1** : to honor or commemorate with a fete **2** : to pay high honor to

fet·id \\'fe-təd\\ *adj* : having an offensive smell : STINKING

fe·tish *also* **fe·tich** \\'fe-tish\\ *n* [F & Pg; F *fétiche*, fr. Pg *feitiço*, fr. *feitiço* artificial, false, fr. L *facticius* factitious] **1** : an object (as an idol or image) believed to have magical powers (as in curing disease) **2** : an object of unreasoning devotion or concern **3** : an object whose real or fantasied presence is psychologically necessary for sexual gratification

fe·tish·ism \\-ti-,shi-zəm\\ *n* **1** : belief in or devotion to fetishes **2** : the pathological transfer of sexual interest and gratification to a fetish — **fe·tish·ist** \\-shist\\ *n* — **fe·tish·is·tic** \\,fe-ti-'shis-tik\\ *adj*

fe·tish·ize \\-ti-,shīz\\ *vb* **-ized -iz·ing** : to make a fetish of

fet·lock \\'fet-,läk\\ *n* : a projection on the back of a horse's leg above the hoof; *also* : a tuft of hair on this

fet·ter \\'fe-tər\\ *n* **1** : a chain or shackle for the feet **2** : something that confines : RESTRAINT — **fetter** *vb*

fet·tle \\'fe-t*l\\ *n* : a state of fitness or order : CONDITION ⟨in fine ~⟩

fe·tus \\'fē-təs\\ *n* : an unborn or unhatched vertebrate esp. after its basic structure is laid down; *esp* : a developing human in the uterus from usu. three months after conception to birth

feud \\'fyüd\\ *n* : a prolonged quarrel; *esp* : a lasting conflict between families or clans marked by violent attacks made for revenge — **feud** *vb*

feu·dal \\'fyü-d*l\\ *adj* **1** : of, relating to, or having the characteristics of a medieval fee **2** : of, relating to, or characteristic of feudalism

feu·dal·ism \\'fyü-də-,li-zəm\\ *n* : a system of political organization prevailing in medieval Europe in which a vassal renders service to a lord and receives protection and land in return; *also* : a similar political or social system — **feu·dal·is·tic** \\,fyü-d*l-'is-tik\\ *adj*

¹feu·da·to·ry \\'fyü-də-,tōr-ē\\ *adj* : owing feudal allegiance

²feudatory *n, pl* **-ries 1** : FIEF **2** : a person who holds lands by feudal law or usage

fe·ver \\'fē-vər\\ *n* **1** : a rise in body temperature above the normal; *also* : a disease of which this is a chief symptom **2** : a state of heightened emotion or activity **3** : CRAZE — **fe·ver·ish** *adj* — **fe·ver·ish·ly** *adv*

¹few \\'fyü\\ *pron* : not many : a small number

²few *adj* **1** : consisting of or amounting to a small number **2** : not many but some ⟨caught a ~ fish⟩ — **few·ness** *n* — **few and far between** : RARE **3**

³few *n* **1** : a small number of units or individuals ⟨a ~ of them⟩ **2** : a special limited number ⟨among the ~⟩

few·er \\'fyü-ər\\ *pron* : a smaller number of persons or things

fey \\'fā\\ *adj* **1** *chiefly Scot* : fated to die; *also* : marked by a foreboding of death or calamity **2** : able to see into the future : VISIONARY **3** : marked by an otherworldly air or attitude **4** : CRAZY, TOUCHED

fez \\'fez\\ *n, pl* **fez·zes** *also* **fez·es** : a round red felt hat that has a flat top and a tassel but no brim

ff *abbr* **1** folios **2** [*following*] and the following ones **3** fortissimo

FHA *abbr* Federal Housing Administration

fi·an·cé \\,fē-,än-'sā\\ *n* [F, fr. MF, fr. pp. of *fiancer* to promise, betroth, fr. OF *fiancier*, fr. *fiance* promise, trust, fr. *fier* to trust, ultim. fr. L *fidere*] : a man engaged to be married

fi·an·cée \\,fē-,än-'sā\\ *n* : a woman engaged to be married

fi·as·co \\fē-'as-kō\\ *n, pl* **-coes** [F] : a complete failure

fi·at \\'fē-ət, -,at, -,ät; 'fī-ət, -,at\\ *n* [L, let it be done] : an authoritative and often arbitrary order or decree

¹fib \\'fib\\ *n* : a trivial or childish lie

²fib *vb* **fibbed; fib·bing** : to tell a fib — **fib·ber** *n*

fi·ber \\'fī-bər\\ *n* **1** : a threadlike substance or structure (as a muscle cell or fine root); *esp* : a natural (as wool or flax) or artificial (as rayon) filament capable of being spun or woven **2** : indigestible material in food that stimulates the intestine to move its contents along **3** : an element that gives texture or substance **4** : basic toughness : STRENGTH — **fi·brous** \\-brəs\\ *adj*

fi·ber·board \\'fī-bər-,bōrd\\ *n* : a material made by compressing fibers (as of wood) into stiff sheets

fi·ber·fill \\-,fil\\ *n* : synthetic fibers used as a filling material (as for cushions)

fi·ber·glass \\-,glas\\ *n* : glass in fibrous form used in making various products (as insulation)

fiber optics *n* **1** *pl* : thin transparent fibers of glass or plastic that are enclosed by a less refractive material and that transmit light by internal reflection; *also* : a bundle of such fibers used in an instrument **2** : the technique of the use of fiber optics — **fiber-optic** *adj*

fibre *chiefly Brit var of* FIBER

fi·bril \\'fī-brəl, 'fi-\\ *n* : a small fiber

fi·bril·la·tion \\,fi-brə-'lā-shən, ,fī-\\ *n* : rapid irregular contractions of the heart muscle fibers resulting in a lack of synchronism between heartbeat and pulse — **fib·ril·late** \\'fi-brə-,lāt, 'fī-\\ *vb*

fi·brin \\'fī-brən\\ *n* : a white insoluble fibrous protein formed in the clotting of blood

¹fi·broid \\'fī-,broid, 'fi-\\ *adj* : resembling, forming, or consisting of fibrous tissue ⟨~ tumors⟩

²fibroid *n* : a benign tumor of the uterus

fi·bro·my·al·gia \\,fī-,brō-,mī-'al-jə\\ *n* : any of a group of rheumatic disorders affecting soft tissues (as muscles or tendons)

fi·bro·sis \\fī-'brō-səs\\ *n* : a condition marked by abnormal increase of fiber-containing tissue

fib·u·la \\'fi-byə-lə\\ *n, pl* **-lae** \\-,lē, -,lī\\ *or* **-las** : the outer and usu. the smaller of the two bones between the knee and ankle — **fib·u·lar** \\-lər\\ *adj*

FICA *abbr* Federal Insurance Contributions Act

-fication *n comb form* : making : production ⟨simpli*fication*⟩

fiche \\'fēsh\\ *n, pl* **fiche** : MICROFICHE
fi·chu \\'fi-shü\\ *n* [F] : a woman's light triangular scarf draped over the shoulders and fastened in front
fick·le \\'fi-kəl\\ *adj* : not firm or steadfast in disposition or character : INCONSTANT — **fick·le·ness** *n*
fic·tion \\'fik-shən\\ *n* **1** : something (as a story) invented by the imagination **2** : fictitious literature (as novels) — **fic·tion·al** \\-shə-nəl\\ *adj* — **fic·tion·al·ly** *adv*
fic·ti·tious \\fik-'ti-shəs\\ *adj* **1** : of, relating to, or characteristic of fiction : IMAGINARY **2** : FALSE, ASSUMED ⟨a ∼ name⟩ **3** : FEIGNED ✦ *Synonyms* CHIMERICAL, FANCIFUL, FANTASTIC, UNREAL
¹fid·dle \\'fi-dᵊl\\ *n* : VIOLIN
²fiddle *vb* **fid·dled; fid·dling 1** : to play on a fiddle **2** : to move the hands or fingers restlessly **3** : PUTTER **4** : MEDDLE, TAMPER — **fid·dler** *n*
fid·dle·head \\'fi-dᵊl-,hed\\ *n* : one of the young unfurling fronds of some ferns that are often eaten as greens
fiddler crab *n* : any of a genus of burrowing crabs with one claw much enlarged in the male

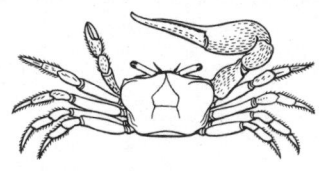

fiddler crab

fid·dle·stick \\'fi-dᵊl-,stik\\ *n* **1** : a violin bow **2** *pl* : NONSENSE — used as an interjection
fi·del·i·ty \\fə-'de-lə-tē, fī-\\ *n, pl* **-ties 1** : the quality or state of being faithful **2** : ACCURACY ⟨∼ in sound reproduction⟩ ✦ *Synonyms* ALLEGIANCE, LOYALTY, DEVOTION, FEALTY
¹fidg·et \\'fi-jət\\ *n* **1** : uneasiness or restlessness as shown by nervous movements — usu. used in pl. **2** : one that fidgets — **fidg·ety** *adj*
²fidget *vb* : to move or cause to move or act restlessly or nervously
fi·du·cia·ry \\fə-'dü-shē-,er-ē, -'dyü-, -shə-rē\\ *adj* **1** : involving a confidence or trust **2** : held or holding in trust for another ⟨∼ accounts⟩ — **fiduciary** *n*
fie \\'fī\\ *interj* — used to express disgust or disapproval
fief \\'fēf\\ *n* [F, fr. OF] : a feudal estate : FEE
¹field \\'fēld\\ *n* **1** : open country **2** : a piece of cleared land for cultivation or pasture **3** : a piece of land yielding some special product **4** : the place where a battle is fought; *also* : BATTLE **5** : an area, division, or sphere of activity ⟨the ∼ of science⟩ ⟨salesmen in the ∼⟩ **6** : an area for military exercises **7** : an area for sports **8** : a background on which something is drawn or projected ⟨a flag with white stars on a ∼ of blue⟩ **9** : a region or space in which a given effect (as magnetism) exists — **field** *adj*
²field *vb* **1** : to handle a batted or thrown baseball while on defense **2** : to put into the field **3** : to answer satisfactorily ⟨∼ a tough question⟩ — **field·er** *n*
field day *n* **1** : a day devoted to outdoor sports and athletic competition **2** : a time of extraordinary pleasure or opportunity
field event *n* : a track-and-field event (as weight-throwing) other than a race
field glass *n* : a hand-held binocular telescope — usu. used in pl.
field guide *n* : a manual for identifying natural objects, plants, or animals
field hockey *n* : a field game played between two teams of 11 players each whose object is to knock a ball into the opponent's goal with a curved stick
field marshal *n* : an officer (as in the British army) of the highest rank
field–test \\-,test\\ *vb* : to test (as a new product) in actual situations reflecting intended use — **field test** *n*
fiend \\'fēnd\\ *n* **1** : DEVIL 1 **2** : DEMON **3** : an extremely wicked or cruel person **4** : a person excessively devoted to a pursuit ⟨a golf ∼⟩ **5** : ADDICT ⟨a dope ∼⟩ — **fiend·ish** *adj* — **fiend·ish·ly** *adv*

fierce \\'firs\\ *adj* **fierc·er; fierc·est 1** : violently hostile or aggressive in temperament **2** : PUGNACIOUS **3** : INTENSE ⟨∼ pain⟩ **4** : furiously active or determined **5** : wild or menacing in appearance ✦ *Synonyms* FEROCIOUS, BARBAROUS, SAVAGE, CRUEL — **fierce·ly** *adv* — **fierce·ness** *n*
fi·ery \\'fī-ə-rē\\ *adj* **fi·er·i·er; -est 1** : consisting of fire **2** : BURNING, BLAZING **3** : FLAMMABLE **4** : hot like a fire : INFLAMED, FEVERISH **5** : RED ⟨a ∼ sunset⟩ **6** : full of emotion or spirit **7** : IRRITABLE — **fi·eri·ness** \\-rē-nəs\\ *n*
fi·es·ta \\fē-'es-tə\\ *n* [Sp] : FESTIVAL
fife \\'fīf\\ *n* [G *Pfeife* pipe, fife] : a small flute
FIFO *abbr* first in, first out
fif·teen \\fif-'tēn\\ *n* : one more than 14 — **fifteen** *adj or pron* — **fif·teenth** \\-'tēnth\\ *adj or n*
fifth \\'fifth\\ *n* **1** : one that is number five in a countable series **2** : one of five equal parts of something **3** : a unit of measure for liquor equal to ⅕ U.S. gallon (0.757 liter) — **fifth** *adj or adv*
fifth column *n* : a group of secret supporters of a nation's enemy that engage in espionage or sabotage within the country — **fifth columnist** *n*
fifth wheel *n* : one that is unnecessary and often burdensome
fif·ty \\'fif-tē\\ *n, pl* **fifties** : five times 10 — **fif·ti·eth** \\-tē-əth\\ *adj or n* — **fifty** *adj or pron*
fif·ty–fif·ty \\,fif-tē-'fif-tē\\ *adj* **1** : shared equally ⟨a ∼ proposition⟩ **2** : half favorable and half unfavorable
¹fig \\'fig\\ *n* : a soft usu. pear-shaped edible fruit of a tree related to the mulberry; *also* : a tree bearing figs
²fig *abbr* **1** figurative; figuratively **2** figure
¹fight \\'fīt\\ *vb* **fought** \\'fȯt\\; **fight·ing 1** : to contend against another in battle or physical combat **2** : BOX **3** : to put forth a determined effort **4** : STRUGGLE, CONTEND **5** : to attempt to prevent the success or effectiveness of **6** : WAGE **7** : to gain by struggle
²fight *n* **1** : a hostile encounter : BATTLE **2** : a boxing match **3** : a verbal disagreement **4** : a struggle for a goal or an objective **5** : strength or disposition for fighting ⟨full of ∼⟩
fight·er \\'fī-tər\\ *n* **1** : one that fights; *esp* : WARRIOR **2** : BOXER **3** : a fast maneuverable warplane for destroying enemy aircraft
fig·ment \\'fig-mənt\\ *n* : something imagined or made up
fig·u·ra·tion \\,fi-gyə-'rā-shən, -gə-\\ *n* **1** : FORM, OUTLINE **2** : an act or instance of representation in figures and shapes
fig·u·ra·tive \\'fi-gyə-rə-tiv, -gə-\\ *adj* **1** : EMBLEMATIC **2** : SYMBOLIC, METAPHORICAL ⟨∼ language⟩ — **fig·u·ra·tive·ly** *adv*
¹fig·ure \\'fi-gyər, -gər-\\ *n* [ME, fr. AF, fr. L *figura*, fr. *fingere* to shape] **1** : NUMERAL **2** *pl* : arithmetical calculations **3** : a written or printed character **4** : PRICE, SUM ⟨sold at a low ∼⟩ **5** : a combination of points, lines, or surfaces in geometry ⟨a circle is a closed plane ∼⟩ **6** : SHAPE, FORM, OUTLINE **7** : the graphic representation of a form esp. of a person **8** : a diagram or pictorial illustration of textual matter **9** : PATTERN, DESIGN **10** : appearance made or impression produced ⟨they cut quite a ∼⟩ **11** : a series of movements (as in a dance) **12** : PERSONAGE
²figure *vb* **fig·ured; fig·ur·ing 1** : to represent by or as if by a figure or outline **2** : to decorate with a pattern **3** : to indicate or represent by numerals **4** : REGARD, CONSIDER **5** : to be or appear important or conspicuous **6** : COMPUTE, CALCULATE
fig·ure·head \\'fi-gyər-,hed, -gər-\\ *n* **1** : a figure on the bow of a ship **2** : a head or chief in name only
figure of speech : a form of expression (as a simile or metaphor) that often compares or identifies one thing with another to convey meaning or heighten effect
figure out *vb* **1** : FIND OUT, DISCOVER **2** : SOLVE
figure skating *n* : skating that includes various jumps, spins, and dance movements
fig·u·rine \\,fi-gyə-'rēn, -gə-\\ *n* : a small carved or molded figure
fil·a·ment \\'fi-lə-mənt\\ *n* : a fine thread or threadlike object, part, or process — **fil·a·men·tous** \\,fi-lə-'men-təs\\ *adj*
fil·bert \\'fil-bərt\\ *n* : the sweet thick-shelled nut of either of two European hazels; *also* : a shrub or small tree bearing filberts

filch \'filch\ *vb* : to steal furtively

¹**file** \'fī(-ə)l\ *n* : a usu. steel tool with a ridged or toothed surface used esp. for smoothing a hard substance

²**file** *vb* **filed; fil·ing** : to rub, smooth, or cut away with a file

³**file** *vb* **filed; fil·ing** [ME, fr. ML *filare* to string documents on a string or wire, fr. *filum* file of documents, lit., thread, fr. L] 1 : to arrange in order 2 : to enter or record officially or as prescribed by law ⟨~ a lawsuit⟩ 3 : to send (copy) to a newspaper

⁴**file** *n* 1 : a device (as a folder or cabinet) by means of which papers may be kept in order 2 : a collection of papers or publications usu. arranged or classified 3 : a collection of data (as text) treated by a computer as a unit

⁵**file** *n* : a row of persons, animals, or things arranged one behind the other

⁶**file** *vb* **filed; fil·ing** : to march or proceed in file

fi·let mi·gnon \,fi-(,)lā-mēn-'yōⁿ, fi-,lā-\ *n, pl* **filets mi·gnons** \-(,)lā-mēn-'yōⁿz, -,lā-\ [F, lit., dainty fillet] : a thick slice of beef cut from the narrow end of a beef tenderloin

fil·ial \'fi-lē-əl, 'fil-yəl\ *adj* : of, relating to, or befitting a son or daughter

fil·i·bus·ter \'fi-lə-,bəs-tər\ *n* [Sp *filibustero*, lit., freebooter] 1 : a military adventurer; *esp* : an American engaged in fomenting 19th century Latin American uprisings 2 : the use of delaying tactics (as extremely long speeches) esp. in a legislative assembly; *also* : an instance of this practice — **filibuster** *vb* — **fil·i·bus·ter·er** *n*

fil·i·cide \'fi-lə-,sīd\ *n* : the murder of one's own daughter or son

fil·i·gree \'fi-lə-,grē\ *n* [F *filigrane*] : ornamental openwork (as of fine wire) — **fil·i·greed** \-,grēd\ *adj*

fil·ing \'fī-liŋ\ *n* 1 : the act or instance of using a file 2 : a small piece scraped off by a file ⟨iron ~s⟩

Fil·i·pi·no \,fi-lə-'pē-nō\ *n, pl* **Filipinos** : a native or inhabitant of the Philippines — **Filipino** *adj*

¹**fill** \'fil\ *vb* 1 : to make or become full 2 : to stop up : PLUG ⟨~ a cavity⟩ 3 : FEED, SATIATE 4 : SATISFY, FULFILL ⟨~ all requirements⟩ 5 : to occupy fully 6 : to spread through ⟨laughter ~ed the room⟩ 7 : OCCUPY ⟨~ the office of president⟩ 8 : to put a person in ⟨~ a vacancy⟩ 9 : to supply as directed ⟨~ a prescription⟩

²**fill** *n* 1 : a full supply; *esp* : a quantity that satisfies or satiates 2 : material used esp. for filling a low place

¹**fill·er** \'fi-lər\ *n* 1 : one that fills 2 : a substance added to another substance (as to increase bulk or weight) 3 : a material used for filling cracks and pores in wood before painting

²**fil·ler** \'fi-,ler\ *n, pl* **fillers** *or* **filler** — see *forint* at MONEY table

¹**fil·let** \'fi-lət, *in sense 2* fi-'lā, 'fi-(,)lā\ *also* **fi·let** \fi-'lā, 'fi-(,)lā\ *n* [ME *filet*, fr. AF, dim. of *fil* thread] 1 : a narrow band, strip, or ribbon 2 : a piece or slice of boneless meat or fish; *esp* : the tenderloin of beef

²**fil·let** \'fi-lət, *in sense 2 also* fi-'lā, 'fi-(,)lā\ *vb* 1 : to bind or adorn with or as if with a fillet 2 : to cut into fillets

fill in *vb* 1 : to provide necessary or recent information 2 : to serve as a temporary substitute

fill·ing \'fi-liŋ\ *n* 1 : material used to fill something ⟨a ~ for a tooth⟩ 2 : the yarn interlacing the warp in a fabric 3 : a food mixture used to fill pastry or sandwiches

filling station *n* : GAS STATION

fil·lip \'fi-ləp\ *n* 1 : a blow or gesture made by a flick or snap of the finger across the thumb 2 : something that serves to arouse or excite — **fillip** *vb*

fill-up \'fil-,əp\ *n* : an act or instance of filling something

fil·ly \'fi-lē\ *n, pl* **fillies** : a young female horse usu. less than four years old

¹**film** \'film\ *n* 1 : a thin skin or membrane 2 : a thin coating or layer 3 : a flexible strip of chemically treated material used in taking pictures 4 : MOTION PICTURE — **filmy** *adj*

²**film** *vb* 1 : to cover with a film 2 : to make a motion picture of

film·dom \'film-dəm\ *n* : the motion-picture industry

film·og·ra·phy \fil-'mä-grə-fē\ *n, pl* **-phies** : a list of motion pictures featuring the work of a film figure or a particular topic

film·strip \'film-,strip\ *n* : a strip of film bearing a sequence of images for projection as still pictures

¹**fils** \'fēs\ *n* [F] : SON — used after a family name to distinguish a son from his father

²**fils** \'fils\ *n, pl* **fils** — see *dinar, dirham, rial* at MONEY table

¹**fil·ter** \'fil-tər\ *n* 1 : a porous material through which a fluid is passed to separate out matter in suspension; *also* : a device containing such material 2 : a device for suppressing waves of certain frequencies; *esp* : one (as for a camera) that absorbs light of certain colors 3 : software for sorting or blocking certain online material

²**filter** *vb* 1 : to remove by means of a filter 2 : to pass through a filter — **fil·ter·able** *also* **fil·tra·ble** \-tə-rə-bəl, -trə-\ *adj* — **fil·tra·tion** \fil-'trā-shən\ *n*

filth \'filth\ *n* [ME, fr. OE *fylth*, fr. *fūl* foul] 1 : foul matter; *esp* : loathsome dirt or refuse 2 : moral corruption 3 : OBSCENITY — **filth·i·ness** *n* — **filthy** \'fil-thē\ *adj*

filthy \'fil-thē\ *adj* **filth·i·er; -est** 1 : extremely or objectionably dirty 2 ⟨~ dirty⟩ ⟨~ rich⟩

fil·trate \'fil-,trāt\ *n* : fluid that has passed through a filter

¹**fin** \'fin\ *n* 1 : a thin external process by which an aquatic animal (as a fish) moves through water 2 : a fin-shaped part (as on an airplane) 3 : FLIPPER 2 — **finned** \'find\ *adj*

²**fin** *abbr* 1 finance; financial 2 finish

fi·na·gle \fə-'nā-gəl\ *vb* **-gled; -gling** 1 : to obtain by indirect or dishonest means : WANGLE 2 : to use devious dishonest methods to achieve one's ends — **fi·na·gler** *n*

¹**fi·nal** \'fī-nᵊl\ *adj* 1 : not to be altered or undone ⟨all sales are ~⟩ 2 : ULTIMATE 3 : relating to or occurring at the end or conclusion — **fi·nal·i·ty** \fī-'na-lə-tē, fə-\ *n* — **fi·nal·ly** *adv*

²**final** *n* 1 : a deciding match or game — usu. used in pl. 2 : the last examination in a course — often used in pl.

fi·na·le \fə-'na-lē, fi-'nä-\ *n* : the close or end of something; *esp* : the last section of a musical composition

fi·nal·ise *Brit var of* FINALIZE

fi·nal·ist \'fī-nə-list\ *n* : a contestant in the finals of a competition

fi·nal·ize \'fī-nə-,līz\ *vb* **-ized; -iz·ing** : to put in final or finished form

¹**fi·nance** \fə-'nans, 'fī-,nans\ *n* [ME, ending, payment, fr. AF, fr. *finer* to end, pay, fr. *fin* end, fr. L *finis* boundary, end] 1 *pl* : money resources available esp. to a government or business 2 : management of money affairs

²**finance** *vb* **fi·nanced; fi·nanc·ing** 1 : to raise or provide funds for 2 : to furnish with necessary funds 3 : to sell or supply on credit

finance company *n* : a company that makes usu. small short-term loans usu. to individuals

fi·nan·cial \fə-'nan-chəl, fī-\ *adj* : relating to finance or financiers — **fi·nan·cial·ly** *adv*

fi·nan·cials \-shəlz\ *n pl* : financial statistics

fi·nan·cier \,fi-nən-'sir, ,fī-,nan-\ *n* 1 : a person skilled in managing public moneys 2 : a person who deals with large-scale finance and investment

finch \'finch\ *n* : any of numerous songbirds with strong conical bills

¹**find** \'fīnd\ *vb* **found** \'faůnd\; **find·ing** 1 : to meet with either by chance or by searching or study : ENCOUNTER, DISCOVER 2 : to obtain by effort or management ⟨~ time to read⟩ 3 : to arrive at : REACH ⟨the bullet *found* its mark⟩ 4 : EXPERIENCE, FEEL ⟨*found* happiness⟩ 5 : to gain or regain the use of ⟨*found* his voice again⟩ 6 : to determine and make a statement about ⟨~ a verdict⟩

²**find** *n* 1 : an act or instance of finding 2 : something found; *esp* : a valuable item of discovery

find·er \'fīn-dər\ *n* : one that finds; *esp* : VIEWFINDER

fin de siè·cle \,faⁿ-də-sē-'eklᵊ\ *adj* [F, end of century] 1 : of, relating to, or characteristic of the close of the 19th century 2 : of or relating to the end of a century

find·ing \'fīn-diŋ\ *n* 1 : the act of finding 2 : FIND 2 3 : the result of a judicial proceeding or inquiry

find out *vb* : to learn by study, observation, or search : DISCOVER

¹**fine** \'fīn\ *n* : money exacted as a penalty for an offense

²**fine** *vb* **fined; fin·ing** : to impose a fine on : punish by a fine

³**fine** *adj* **fin·er; fin·est** 1 : free from impurity 2 : very thin in gauge or texture 3 : not coarse ⟨~ sand⟩ 4 : SUBTLE, SENSITIVE ⟨a ~ distinction⟩ 5 : superior in quality or appearance 6 : ELEGANT, REFINED ⟨~ manners⟩ — **fine·ly** *adv* — **fine·ness** *n*

⁴fine *adv* **1** : very well **2** — used to express agreement

fine art *n* : art (as painting, sculpture, or music) concerned primarily with the creation of beautiful objects — usu. used in pl.

fin·ery \'fī-nə-rē\ *n, pl* **-er·ies** : ORNAMENT, DECORATION; *esp* : showy clothing and jewels

fine-spun \'fīn-'spən\ *adj* : developed with extremely or excessively fine delicacy or detail

fi·nesse \fə-'nes\ *n* **1** : refinement or delicacy of workmanship, structure, or texture **2** : CUNNING, SUBTLETY — **finesse** *vb*

fine–tune \-'tün\ *vb* : to adjust so as to bring to the highest level of performance or effectiveness

fin·fish \'fin-,fish\ *n* : FISH 2

¹fin·ger \'fiŋ-gər\ *n* **1** : any of the five divisions at the end of the hand; *esp* : one other than the thumb **2** : something that resembles or does the work of a finger **3** : a part of a glove into which a finger is inserted

²finger *vb* **fin·gered; fin·ger·ing 1** : to touch or feel with the fingers : HANDLE **2** : to perform with the fingers or with a certain fingering **3** : to mark the notes of a piece of music as a guide in playing **4** : to point out

fin·ger·board \'fiŋ-gər-,bórd\ *n* : the part of a stringed instrument against which the fingers press the strings to vary the pitch

finger bowl *n* : a small water bowl for rinsing the fingers at the table

fin·ger·ing \'fiŋ-gə-riŋ\ *n* **1** : handling or touching with the fingers **2** : the act or method of using the fingers in playing an instrument **3** : the marking of the method of fingering

fin·ger·ling \'fiŋ-gər-liŋ\ *n* : a small fish

fin·ger·nail \'fiŋ-gər-,nāl\ *n* : the nail of a finger

fin·ger·print \-,print\ *n* : the pattern of marks made by pressing the tip of a finger or thumb on a surface; *esp* : an ink impression of such a pattern taken for the purpose of identification — **fingerprint** *vb*

fin·ger·tip \-,tip\ *n* : the tip of a finger

fin·i·al \'fi-nē-əl\ *n* : an ornamental projection or end (as on a spire)

fin·ick·ing \'fi-ni-kiŋ\ *adj* : FINICKY

fin·icky \'fi-ni-kē\ *adj* : excessively particular in taste or standards

fi·nis \'fi-nəs\ *n* : END, CONCLUSION

¹fin·ish \'fi-nish\ *vb* **1** : TERMINATE **2** : to use or dispose of entirely **3** : to bring to completion : ACCOMPLISH **4** : to put a final coat or surface on **5** : to come to the end of a course or undertaking — **fin·ish·er** *n*

²finish *n* **1** : END, CONCLUSION **2** : something that completes or perfects **3** : the final treatment or coating of a surface

fi·nite \'fī-,nīt\ *adj* **1** : having definite or definable limits; *also* : having a limited nature or existence **2** : being less than some positive integer in number or measure and greater than its negative **3** : showing distinction of grammatical person and number ⟨a ∼ verb⟩

fink \'fiŋk\ *n* **1** : a contemptible person **2** : STRIKEBREAKER **3** : INFORMER

Finn \'fin\ *n* : a native or inhabitant of Finland

fin·nan had·die \,fi-nən-'ha-dē\ *n* : smoked haddock

¹Finn·ish \'fi-nish\ *adj* : of or relating to Finland, the Finns, or Finnish

²Finnish *n* : the language of the Finns

fin·ny \'fi-nē\ *adj* **1** : having or characterized by fins **2** : relating to or being fish

fiord *var of* FJORD

fir \'fər\ *n* : any of a genus of usu. large evergreen trees related to the pines; *also* : the light soft wood of a fir

¹fire \'fī(-ə)r\ *n* **1** : the light or heat and esp. the flame of something burning **2** : ENTHUSIASM, ZEAL **3** : fuel that is burning (as in a stove or fireplace) **4** : destructive burning (as of a house) **5** : the firing of weapons — **fire·less** *adj*

²fire *vb* **fired; fir·ing 1** : KINDLE, IGNITE ⟨∼ a house⟩ **2** : STIR, ENLIVEN ⟨∼ the imagination⟩ **3** : to dismiss from employment **4** : SHOOT ⟨∼ a gun⟩ ⟨∼ an arrow⟩ **5** : BAKE ⟨*firing* pottery in a kiln⟩ **6** : to apply fire or fuel to something ⟨∼ a furnace⟩

fire ant *n* : either of two small fiercely stinging So. American ants introduced into the southeastern U.S. where they are agricultural pests

fire·arm \'fī(-ə)r-,ärm\ *n* : a weapon (as a pistol) from which a shot is discharged by gunpowder

fire·ball \-,ból\ *n* **1** : a ball of fire **2** : a very bright meteor **3** : the highly luminous cloud of vapor and dust created by a nuclear explosion **4** : a highly energetic person

fire·boat \-,bōt\ *n* : a boat equipped for fighting fires

fire·bomb \-,bäm\ *n* : an incendiary bomb — **firebomb** *vb*

fire·box \-,bäks\ *n* **1** : a chamber (as of a furnace) that contains a fire **2** : a box containing a fire alarm

fire·brand \-,brand\ *n* **1** : a piece of burning wood **2** : a person who creates unrest or strife : AGITATOR

fire·break \-,brāk\ *n* : a barrier of cleared or plowed land intended to check a forest or grass fire

fire·bug \-,bəg\ *n* : a person who deliberately sets destructive fires

fire·crack·er \-,kra-kər\ *n* : a usu. paper tube containing an explosive and a fuse and set off to make a noise

fire department *n* : an organization for preventing or extinguishing fires; *also* : its members

fire engine *n* : a motor vehicle with equipment for extinguishing fires

fire escape *n* : a stairway or ladder for escape from a burning building

fire·fight·er \'fī(-ə)r-,fī-tər\ *n* : a person who fights fires; *esp* : a member of a fire department

fire·fly \-,flī\ *n* : any of various small night-flying beetles that produce flashes of light for courtship purposes

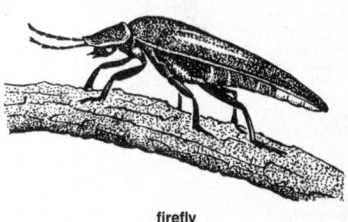

firefly

fire·house \-,haús\ *n* : FIRE STATION

fire irons *n pl* : tools for tending a fire esp. in a fireplace

fire·man \'fī(-ə)r-mən\ *n* **1** : STOKER **2** : FIREFIGHTER

fire off *vb* : to write and send

fire·place \-,plās\ *n* **1** : a framed opening made in a chimney to hold an open fire **2** : an outdoor structure of brick or stone for an open fire

fire·plug \-,pləg\ *n* : HYDRANT

fire·pow·er \-,paú(-ə)r\ *n* : the ability to deliver gunfire or warheads on a target

¹fire·proof \-'prüf\ *adj* : resistant to fire

²fireproof *vb* : to make fireproof

fire–sale \-,sāl\ *adj* : heavily discounted ⟨∼ prices⟩

fire screen *n* : a protective screen before a fireplace

¹fire·side \'fī(-ə)r-,sīd\ *n* **1** : a place near the fire or hearth **2** : HOME

²fireside *adj* : having an informal or intimate quality

fire station *n* : a building housing fire engines and usu. firefighters

fire·storm \'fī(-ə)r-,stórm\ *n* **1** : a large destructive very hot fire **2** : a sudden or violent outburst ⟨∼ of criticism⟩

fire tower *n* : a tower (as in a forest) from which a watch for fires is kept

fire·trap \'fī(-ə)r-,trap\ *n* : a building or place apt to catch on fire or difficult to escape from in case of fire

fire truck *n* : FIRE ENGINE

fire·wall \-,wól\ *n* : computer hardware or software for preventing unauthorized access to data

fire·wa·ter \'fī(-ə)r-,wó-tər, -,wä-\ *n* : intoxicating liquor

fire·wood \-,wúd\ *n* : wood used for fuel

fire·work \-,wərk\ *n* : a device designed to produce a striking display by the burning of explosive or flammable materials

firing line *n* **1** : a line from which fire is delivered against a target **2** : the forefront of an activity

¹firm \'fərm\ *adj* **1** : securely fixed in place **2** : SOLID, VIGOROUS ⟨a ∼ handshake⟩ **3** : having a solid or compact texture **4** : not subject to change or fluctuation

: STEADY 〈∼ prices〉 **5** : STEADFAST **6** : indicating firmness or resolution — **firm·ly** *adv* — **firm·ness** *n*

³**firm** *vb* : to make or become firm

³**firm** *n* [G *Firma*, fr. It, signature, ultim. fr. L *firmare* to make firm, confirm] **1** : the name under which a company transacts business **2** : a business partnership of two or more persons **3** : a business enterprise

fir·ma·ment \ˈfər-mə-mənt\ *n* : the arch of the sky : HEAVENS

firm·ware \ˈfirm-ˌwer\ *n* : computer programs contained permanently in a hardware device

¹**first** \ˈfərst\ *adj* : preceding all others as in time, order, or importance

²**first** *adv* **1** : before any other **2** : for the first time **3** : in preference to something else

³**first** *n* **1** : number one in a countable series **2** : something that is first **3** : the lowest forward gear in an automotive vehicle **4** : the winning or highest place in a competition or examination

first aid *n* : emergency care or treatment given an injured or ill person

first-born \ˈfərst-ˈbórn\ *adj* : ELDEST — **firstborn** *n*

first class *n* : the best or highest group in a classification — **first–class** *adj or adv*

first-hand \ˈfərst-ˈhand\ *adj* : coming from direct personal observation or experience — **firsthand** *adv*

first lady *n, often cap F&L* : the wife or hostess of the chief executive of a political unit (as a country)

first lieutenant *n* : a commissioned officer (as in the army) ranking next below a captain

first·ling \ˈfərst-liŋ\ *n* : one that comes or is produced first

first·ly \-lē\ *adv* : in the first place : FIRST

¹**first–rate** \-ˈrāt\ *adj* : of the first order of size, importance, or quality

²**first–rate** *adv* : very well

first sergeant *n* **1** : a noncommissioned officer serving as the chief assistant to the commander of a military unit **2** : a rank in the army below a sergeant major and in the marine corps below a master gunnery sergeant

first strike *n* : a preemptive nuclear attack

first–string \ˈfərst-ˈstriŋ\ *adj* : being a regular as distinguished from a substitute — **first–string·er** \-ˌstriŋ-ər\ *n*

firth \ˈfərth\ *n* [ME, fr. ON *fjorthr*] : ESTUARY

fis·cal \ˈfis-kəl\ *adj* [L *fiscalis*, fr. *fiscus* basket, treasury] **1** : of or relating to taxation, public revenues, or public debt **2** : of or relating to financial matters — **fis·cal·ly** *adv*

¹**fish** \ˈfish\ *n, pl* **fish** *or* **fish·es** **1** : a water-dwelling animal — usu. used in combination 〈star*fish*〉 〈shell*fish*〉 **2** : any of numerous cold-blooded water-breathing vertebrates with fins, gills, and usu. scales that include the bony fishes and usu. the cartilaginous and jawless fishes **3** : the flesh of fish used as food

²**fish** *vb* **1** : to attempt to catch fish **2** : to seek something by roundabout means 〈∼ for praise〉 **3** : to search for something underwater **4** : to engage in a search by groping **5** : to draw forth

fish–and–chips *n pl* : fried fish and french fried potatoes

fish·bowl \ˈfish-ˌbōl\ *n* **1** : a bowl for the keeping of live fish **2** : a place or condition that affords no privacy

fish·er \ˈfi-shər\ *n* **1** : one that fishes **2** : a dark brown No. American carnivorous mammal related to the weasels

fish·er·man \-mən\ *n* **1** : a person engaged in fishing **2** : a fishing boat

fish·ery \ˈfi-shə-rē\ *n, pl* **-er·ies** **1** : the business of catching fish **2** : a place for catching fish

fish·hook \ˈfish-ˌhùk\ *n* : a usu. barbed hook for catching fish

fish ladder *n* : an arrangement of pools in steps by which fish can pass over a dam in going upstream

fish·net \ˈfish-ˌnet\ *n* **1** : netting for catching fish **2** : a coarse open-mesh fabric

fish·tail \-ˌtāl\ *vb* : to have the rear end slide from side to side out of control while moving forward

fish·wife \-ˌwif\ *n* **1** : a woman who sells fish **2** : a vulgar abusive woman

fishy \ˈfi-shē\ *adj* **fish·i·er; -est** **1** : of or resembling fish **2** : QUESTIONABLE 〈the story sounds ∼ to me〉

fis·sion \ˈfi-shən, -zhən\ *n* [L *fissio*, fr. *findere* to split] **1** : a cleaving into parts **2** : a method of reproduction in which a living cell or body divides into two or more parts each of which grows into a whole new individual **3** : the splitting of an atomic nucleus resulting in the release of large amounts of energy — **fis·sion·able** \ˈfi-shə-nə-bəl, -zhə-\ *adj*

fis·sure \ˈfi-shər\ *n* : a narrow opening or crack

fist \ˈfist\ *n* **1** : the hand with fingers folded into the palm **2** : INDEX 6

fist·ful \ˈfist-ˌfùl\ *n* : HANDFUL

fist·i·cuffs \ˈfis-ti-ˌkəfs\ *n pl* : a fight with the fists

fis·tu·la \ˈfis-chə-lə\ *n, pl* **-las** *or* **-lae** : an abnormal passage leading from an abscess or hollow organ — **fis·tu·lous** \-ləs\ *adj*

¹**fit** \ˈfit\ *adj* **fit·ter; fit·test** **1** : adapted to a purpose : APPROPRIATE **2** : PROPER, RIGHT 〈a movie ∼ for children〉 **3** : PREPARED, READY **4** : physically and mentally sound — **fit·ly** *adv* — **fit·ness** *n*

²**fit** *n* **1** : a sudden violent attack (as in epilepsy) **2** : a sudden outburst

³**fit** *vb* **fit·ted** *also* **fit; fit·ting** **1** : to be suitable for or to **2** : to be correctly adjusted to or shaped for **3** : to insert or adjust until correctly in place **4** : to make a place or room for **5** : to be in agreement or accord with **6** : PREPARE **7** : ADJUST **8** : SUPPLY, EQUIP 〈*fitted* out with gear〉 **9** : BELONG — **fit·ter** *n*

⁴**fit** *n* : the fact, condition, or manner of fitting or being fitted

fit·ful \ˈfit-fəl\ *adj* : not regular : INTERMITTENT 〈∼ sleep〉 — **fit·ful·ly** *adv*

fit·ting \ˈfi-tiŋ\ *adj* : APPROPRIATE, SUITABLE — **fit·ting·ly** *adv*

²**fitting** *n* **1** : the action or act of one that fits; *esp* : a trying on of clothes being made or altered **2** : a small often standardized part 〈a plumbing ∼〉

five \ˈfīv\ *n* **1** : one more than four **2** : the 5th in a set or series **3** : something having five units; *esp* : a basketball team **4** : a 5-dollar bill — **five** *adj or pron*

¹**fix** \ˈfiks\ *vb* **1** : to make firm, stable, or fast **2** : to give a permanent or final form to **3** : AFFIX, ATTACH **4** : to hold or direct steadily 〈∼es his eyes on the horizon〉 **5** : ESTABLISH, SET **6** : ASSIGN 〈∼ the blame〉 **7** : to set in order : ADJUST **8** : PREPARE **9** : to make whole or sound again **10** : to get even with **11** : to influence by improper or illegal methods 〈∼ a race〉 — **fix·er** *n*

²**fix** *n* **1** : PREDICAMENT **2** : a determination of position (as of a ship) **3** : an accurate determination or understanding **4** : an act of improper influence **5** : a supply or dose of something (as an addictive drug) strongly desired or craved **6** : something that fixes or restores

fix·a·tion \fik-ˈsā-shən\ *n* : an obsessive or unhealthy preoccupation or attachment — **fix·ate** \ˈfik-ˌsāt\ *vb*

fix·a·tive \ˈfik-sə-tiv\ *n* : something that stabilizes or sets

fixed \ˈfikst\ *adj* **1** : securely placed or fastened : STATIONARY **2** : not volatile **3** : SETTLED, FINAL **4** : INTENT, CONCENTRATED 〈a ∼ stare〉 **5** : supplied with a definite amount of something needed (as money) — **fixed·ly** \ˈfik-səd-lē\ *adv* — **fixed·ness** \ˈfik-səd-nəs\ *n*

fix·i·ty \ˈfik-sə-tē\ *n, pl* **-ties** : the quality or state of being fixed or stable

fix·ture \ˈfiks-chər\ *n* **1** : something firmly attached as a permanent part of some other thing **2** : a familiar feature in a particular setting; *esp* : a person associated with a place or activity

¹**fizz** \ˈfiz\ *vb* : to make a hissing or sputtering sound

²**fizz** *n* : an effervescent beverage

¹**fiz·zle** \ˈfi-zəl\ *vb* **fiz·zled; fiz·zling** **1** : FIZZ **2** : to fail after a good start — often used with *out*

²**fizzle** *n* : FAILURE

fjord \fē-ˈórd\ *n* [Norw] : a narrow inlet of the sea between cliffs or steep slopes

fl *abbr* **1** [L *floruit*] flourished **2** fluid

FL *or* **Fla** *abbr* Florida

flab \ˈflab\ *n* : soft flabby body tissue

flab·ber·gast \ˈfla-bər-ˌgast\ *vb* : ASTOUND

flab·by \ˈfla-bē\ *adj* **flab·bi·er; -est** : lacking firmness : FLACCID 〈∼ muscles〉 — **flab·bi·ness** \-bē-nəs\ *n*

flac·cid \ˈflak-səd\ *adj* : lacking firmness 〈∼ muscles〉

¹**flag** \ˈflag\ *n* : any of various irises; *esp* : a wild iris

²**flag** *n* **1** : a usu. rectangular piece of fabric of distinctive design that is used as a symbol (as of a nation) or as a signaling device **2** : something used like a flag to signal or

attract attention   **3** : one of the cross strokes of a musical note less than a quarter note in value

³flag *vb* **flagged; flag·ging**   **1** : to signal with or as if with a flag; *esp* : to signal to stop ⟨~ a taxi⟩   **2** : to mark or identify with or as if with a flag   **3** : to call a penalty on

⁴flag *vb* **flagged; flag·ging**   **1** : to hang loose or limp   **2** : to become unsteady, feeble, or spiritless   **3** : to decline in interest or attraction ⟨the topic *flagged*⟩

⁵flag *n* : a hard flat stone suitable for paving

flag·el·late \'fla-jə-ˌlāt\ *vb* **-lat·ed; -lat·ing** : to punish by whipping — **flag·el·la·tion** \ˌfla-jə-'lā-shən\ *n*

fla·gel·lum \flə-'je-ləm\ *n, pl* **-la** \-lə\ *also* **-lums** : a long whiplike process that is the primary organ of motion of many microorganisms — **fla·gel·lar** \-lər\ *adj*

fla·geo·let \ˌfla-jə-'let, -'lā\ *n* [F] : a small woodwind instrument belonging to the flute class

fla·gi·tious \flə-'ji-shəs\ *adj* : grossly wicked : VILLAINOUS

flag·on \'fla-gən\ *n* : a container for liquids usu. with a handle, spout, and lid

flag·pole \'flag-ˌpōl\ *n* : a pole on which to raise a flag

fla·grant \'flā-grənt\ *adj* [L *flagrans*, prp. of *flagrare* to burn] : conspicuously bad ⟨~ abuse of power⟩ — **fla·grant·ly** *adv*

fla·gran·te de·lic·to \flə-ˌgran-tē-di-'lik-tō\ *adv* : IN FLAGRANTE DELICTO

flag·ship \'flag-ˌship\ *n*   **1** : the ship that carries the commander of a fleet or subdivision thereof and flies his flag   **2** : the most important one of a group

flag·staff \-ˌstaf\ *n* : FLAGPOLE

flag·stone \-ˌstōn\ *n* : ⁵FLAG

¹flail \'flāl\ *n* : a tool for threshing grain by hand

²flail *vb* : to strike or swing with or as if with a flail

flair \'fler\ *n* [F, lit., sense of smell, fr. OF, odor, fr. *flairier* to give off an odor, fr. VL *flagrare*, alter. of L *fragrare*]   **1** : ability to appreciate or make good use of something : BENT, TALENT   **2** : a unique style

flak \'flak\ *n, pl* **flak** [G, fr. *Fliegerabwehrkanonen*, fr. *Flieger* flyer + *Abwehr* defense + *Kanonen* cannons]   **1** : antiaircraft guns or bursting shells fired from them   **2** : CRITICISM, OPPOSITION

¹flake \'flāk\ *n*   **1** : a small loose mass or bit   **2** : a thin flattened piece or layer : CHIP — **flaky** *adj*

²flake *vb* **flaked; flak·ing** : to form or separate into flakes

³flake *n* : a markedly eccentric person : ODDBALL — **flak·i·ness** \'flā-kē-nəs\ *n* — **flaky** *adj*

flam·beau \'flam-ˌbō\ *n, pl* **flambeaux** \-ˌbōz\ *or* **flambeaus** [F, fr. MF, fr. *flambe* flame] : a flaming torch

flam·boy·ant \flam-'bȯi-ənt\ *adj* : marked by or given to strikingly elaborate or colorful display or behavior — **flam·boy·ance** \-əns\ *n* — **flam·boy·an·cy** \-ən-sē\ *n* — **flam·boy·ant·ly** *adv*

flame \'flām\ *n*   **1** : the glowing gaseous part of a fire   **2** : a state of blazing combustion   **3** : a flamelike condition   **4** : burning zeal or passion   **5** : BRILLIANCE   **6** : SWEETHEART   **7** : an angry, hostile, or abusive electronic message — **flame** *vb*

fla·men·co \flə-'meŋ-kō\ *n, pl* **-cos** [Sp, fr. *flamenco* of the Gypsies, lit., Flemish, fr. MD *Vlaminc* Fleming] : a vigorous rhythmic dance style of the Spanish Gypsies

flame·throw·er \'flām-ˌthrō-ər\ *n* : a device that expels from a nozzle a burning stream of liquid or semiliquid fuel under pressure

fla·min·go \flə-'miŋ-gō\ *n, pl* **-gos** *also* **-goes** : any of several long-legged long-necked tropical water birds with scarlet wings and a broad bill bent downward

flam·ma·ble \'fla-mə-bəl\ *adj* : easily ignited and quick=burning — **flam·ma·bil·i·ty** \ˌfla-mə-'bi-lə-tē\ *n* — **flammable** *n*

flan \'flan, 'flän\ *n* **1** : an open pie with a sweet or savory filling   **2** : custard baked with a caramel glaze

flange \'flanj\ *n* : a rim used for strengthening or guiding something or for attachment to another object

¹flank \'flaŋk\ *n*   **1** : the fleshy part of the side between the ribs and the hip; *also* : the side of a quadruped   **2** : SIDE   **3** : the right or left of a formation

²flank *vb*   **1** : to be situated on the side of : BORDER   **2** : to attack or threaten the flank of

flank·er \'flaŋ-kər\ *n* : a football player stationed wide of the formation slightly behind the line of scrimmage as a pass receiver

flan·nel \'fla-n³l\ *n*   **1** : a soft twilled wool or worsted fabric with a napped surface   **2** : a stout cotton fabric napped on one side   **3** *pl* : flannel underwear or pants

¹flap \'flap\ *n*   **1** : a stroke with something broad : SLAP   **2** : something broad, limber, or flat and usu. thin that hangs loose   **3** : the motion or sound of something broad and limber as it swings to and fro   **4** : a state of excitement or confusion

²flap *vb* **flapped; flap·ping**   **1** : to beat with something broad and flat   **2** : FLING   **3** : to move (as wings) with a beating motion   **4** : to sway loosely usu. with a noise of striking

flap·jack \'flap-ˌjak\ *n* : PANCAKE

flap·per \'fla-pər\ *n*   **1** : one that flaps   **2** : a young woman of the 1920s who showed freedom from conventions (as in conduct)

¹flare \'fler\ *n*   **1** : a blaze of light used esp. to signal or illuminate; *also* : a device for producing such a blaze   **2** : an unsteady glaring light

²flare *vb* **flared; flar·ing**   **1** : to flame with a sudden unsteady light   **2** : to become suddenly excited or angry ⟨after his harangue, I *flared* up⟩   **3** : to spread outward

flare–up \-ˌəp\ *n* : a sudden outburst or intensification

¹flash \'flash\ *vb*   **1** : to break forth in or like a sudden flame   **2** : to appear or pass suddenly or with great speed   **3** : to send out in or as if in flashes ⟨~ a message⟩   **4** : to make a sudden display (as of brilliance or feeling)   **5** : to gleam or glow intermittently   **6** : to fill by a sudden rush of water   **7** : to expose to view very briefly ⟨~ a badge⟩

✦ Synonyms GLANCE, GLINT, SPARKLE, TWINKLE — **flash·er** *n*

²flash *n*   **1** : a sudden burst of light   **2** : a movement of a flag or light in signaling   **3** : a sudden and brilliant burst (as of wit)   **4** : a brief time   **5** : SHOW, DISPLAY; *esp* : ostentatious display   **6** : one that attracts notice; *esp* : an outstanding athlete   **7** : GLIMPSE, LOOK   **8** : a first brief news report   **9** : FLASHLIGHT   **10** : a device for producing a brief and very bright flash of light for taking photographs   **11** : a quick-spreading flame or momentary intense outburst of radiant heat

³flash *adj* : of sudden origin and short duration ⟨a ~ fire⟩ ⟨a ~ flood⟩

⁴flash *adv* : by very brief exposure to an intense agent (as heat or cold) ⟨~ fry⟩ ⟨~ freeze⟩

flash·back \'flash-ˌbak\ *n*   **1** : interruption of the chronological sequence (as of a film or literary work) by an event of earlier occurrence   **2** : a past event remembered vividly

flash back *vb*   **1** : to vividly remember a past incident   **2** : to employ a flashback

flash·bulb \-ˌbəlb\ *n* : an electric bulb that can be used only once to produce a brief and very bright flash of light for taking photographs

flash card *n* : a card bearing words, numbers, or pictures briefly displayed usu. as a learning aid

flash·cube \'flash-ˌkyüb\ *n* : a cubical device incorporating four flashbulbs

flash·gun \-ˌgən\ *n* : a device for producing a bright flash of light for photography

flash·ing \'fla-shiŋ\ *n* : sheet metal used in waterproofing (as at the angle between a chimney and a roof)

flash·light \'flash-ˌlīt\ *n* : a battery-operated portable electric light

flash memory *n* : a computer memory chip not requiring connection to a power source to retain its data

flashy \'fla-shē\ *adj* **flash·i·er; -est**   **1** : momentarily dazzling   **2** : superficially attractive or impressive : SHOWY — **flash·i·ly** \-shə-lē\ *adv* — **flash·i·ness** \-shē-nəs\ *n*

flask \'flask\ *n* : a flattened bottle-shaped container ⟨a whiskey ~⟩

¹flat \'flat\ *adj* **flat·ter; flat·test**   **1** : spread out along a surface; *also* : being or characterized by a horizontal line   **2** : having a smooth, level, or even surface   **3** : having a broad smooth surface and little thickness   **4** : DOWNRIGHT, POSITIVE ⟨a ~ refusal⟩   **5** : FIXED, UNCHANGING ⟨charge a ~ rate⟩   **6** : EXACT, PRECISE ⟨in four minutes ~⟩   **7** : DULL, UNINTERESTING; *also* : INSIPID   **8** : DEFLATED ⟨a ~ tire⟩   **9** : lower than the true pitch; *also* : lower by a half step   **10** : free from gloss ⟨a ~ paint⟩   **11** : lacking depth of characterization — **flat·ly** *adv* — **flat·ness** *n*

²flat *n*   **1** : a level surface of land : PLAIN   **2** : a flat part or surface **3** : a character ♭ that indicates that a specified note is to be lowered by a half step; *also* : the resulting note **4** : something flat **5** : an apartment on one floor **6** : a deflated tire

³flat *adv* **1** : FLATLY **2** : COMPLETELY ⟨~ broke⟩ **3** : below the true musical pitch

⁴flat *vb* **flat·ted; flat·ting 1** : FLATTEN **2** : to lower in pitch esp. by a half step

flat·bed \'flat-ˌbed\ *n* : a truck or trailer with a body in the form of a platform or shallow box

flat·boat \-ˌbōt\ *n* : a flat-bottomed boat used esp. for carrying bulky freight

flat·car \-ˌkär\ *n* : a railroad freight car without sides or roof

flat·fish \-ˌfish\ *n* : any of an order of flattened marine bony fishes with both eyes on the upper side

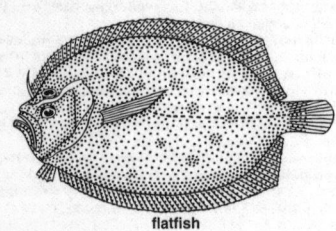

flatfish

flat·foot \-ˌfut, -ˈfut\ *n, pl* **flat·feet** \-ˌfēt, -ˈfēt\ : a condition in which the arch of the foot is flattened so that the entire sole rests upon the ground — **flat–foot·ed** \-ˈfu̇-təd\ *adj*

Flat·head \-ˌhed\ *n, pl* **Flatheads** *or* **Flathead** : a member of an American Indian people of Montana

flat·iron \-ˌī(-ə)rn\ *n* : IRON 3

flat·land \-ˌland\ *n* : land lacking significant variation in elevation

flat–out \'flat-ˌau̇t\ *adj* **1** : being or going at maximum effort or speed **2** : OUT-AND-OUT, DOWNRIGHT ⟨it was a ~ lie⟩

flat out *adv* **1** : BLUNTLY, DIRECTLY **2** : at top speed **3** *usu* **flat–out** : to the greatest degree : COMPLETELY ⟨is just *flat-out* confusing⟩

flat–panel \-ˈpa-nᵊl\ *adj* : relating to or being a thin flat video display

flat·ten \'fla-tᵊn\ *vb* : to make or become flat

flat·ter \'fla-tər\ *vb* [ME *flateren*, fr. AF *flater* to lap, flatter] **1** : to praise too much or without sincerity **2** : to represent too favorably ⟨the portrait ~s him⟩ **3** : to display to advantage **4** : to judge (oneself) favorably or too favorably — **flat·ter·er** *n*

flat·tery \'fla-tə-rē\ *n, pl* **-ter·ies** : flattering speech or attentions : insincere or excessive praise

flat·top \'flat-ˌtäp\ *n* **1** : AIRCRAFT CARRIER **2** : CREW CUT

flat·u·lent \'fla-chə-lənt\ *adj* **1** : full of gas ⟨a ~ stomach⟩ **2** : INFLATED, POMPOUS — **flat·u·lence** \-ləns\ *n*

fla·tus \'flā-təs\ *n* : gas formed in the intestine or stomach

flat·ware \'flat-ˌwer\ *n* : eating and serving utensils

flat·worm \-ˌwu̇rm\ *n* : any of a phylum of flattened mostly parasitic segmented worms (as trematodes and tapeworms)

flaunt \'flȯnt\ *vb* **1** : to display oneself to public notice **2** : to wave or flutter showily **3** : to display ostentatiously or impudently : PARADE — **flaunt** *n*

flau·ta \'flau̇-tə\ *n* : a tortilla rolled around a filling and deep-fried

flau·tist \'flȯ-tist, 'flau̇-\ *n* [It *flautista*] : FLUTIST

¹fla·vor \'flā-vər\ *n* **1** : the quality of something that affects the sense of taste or of taste and smell **2** : a substance that adds flavor **3** : characteristic or predominant quality — **fla·vored** \-vərd\ *adj* — **fla·vor·ful** *adj* — **fla·vor·less** *adj* — **fla·vor·some** *adj*

²flavor *vb* : to give or add flavor to

fla·vor·ing *n* : FLAVOR 2

fla·vour *chiefly Brit var of* FLAVOR

flaw \'flȯ\ *n* : a small often hidden defect — **flaw·less** *adj* — **flaw·less·ly** *adv* — **flaw·less·ness** *n*

flax \'flaks\ *n* : a fiber that is the source of linen; *also* : a blue-flowered plant grown for this fiber and its oily seeds

flax·en \'flak-sən\ *adj* **1** : made of flax **2** : resembling flax esp. in pale soft straw color

flay \'flā\ *vb* **1** : to strip off the skin or surface of **2** : to criticize harshly

fl dr *abbr* fluid dram

flea \'flē\ *n* : any of an order of small wingless leaping bloodsucking insects

flea·bane \-ˌbān\ *n* : any of various plants of the daisy family once believed to drive away fleas

flea–bit·ten \-ˌbi-tᵊn\ *adj* : bitten by or infested with fleas

flea market *n* : a usu. open-air market for secondhand articles and antiques

¹fleck \'flek\ *vb* : STREAK, SPOT

²fleck *n* **1** : SPOT, MARK **2** : FLAKE, PARTICLE

fledge \'flej\ *vb* **fledged; fledg·ing** : to develop the feathers necessary for flying or independent activity

fledg·ling \'flej-liŋ\ *n* **1** : a young bird just fledged **2** : an immature or inexperienced person

flee \'flē\ *vb* **fled** \'fled\; **flee·ing 1** : to run away often from danger or evil **2** : VANISH **3** : to run away from : SHUN

¹fleece \'flēs\ *n* **1** : the woolly coat of an animal and esp. a sheep **2** : a soft or woolly covering — **fleecy** *adj*

²fleece *vb* **fleeced; fleec·ing 1** : to strip of money or property by fraud or extortion **2** : SHEAR

¹fleet \'flēt\ *vb* : to pass rapidly

²fleet *n* [ME *flete*, fr. OE *flēot* ship, fr. *flēotan* to float] **1** : a group of warships under one command **2** : a group (as of ships, planes, or trucks) under one management

³fleet *adj* **1** : SWIFT, NIMBLE **2** : not enduring : FLEETING — **fleet·ness** *n*

fleet admiral *n* : an admiral of the highest rank in the navy

fleet·ing \'flē-tiŋ\ *adj* : passing swiftly

Flem·ing \'fle-miŋ\ *n* : a member of a Germanic people inhabiting chiefly northern Belgium

Flem·ish \'fle-mish\ *n* **1** : the Dutch language as spoken by the Flemings **2 Flemish** *pl* : FLEMINGS — **Flemish** *adj*

¹flesh \'flesh\ *n* **1** : the soft parts of an animal's body; *esp* : muscular tissue **2** : MEAT **3** : the physical nature of humans as distinguished from the soul **4** : human beings; *also* : living beings **5** : STOCK, KINDRED **6** : fleshy plant tissue (as fruit pulp) — **fleshed** \'flesht\ *adj*

²flesh *vb* : to make fuller or more nearly complete — usu. used with *out* ⟨*flesh out* a schedule⟩

flesh fly *n* : a dipteran fly whose maggots feed on flesh

flesh·ly \'flesh-lē\ *adj* **1** : CORPOREAL, BODILY **2** : not spiritual : WORLDLY **3** : CARNAL, SENSUAL

flesh·pot \'flesh-ˌpät\ *n* **1** *pl* : bodily comfort : LUXURY **2** : a place of lascivious entertainment — usu. used in pl.

fleshy \'fle-shē\ *adj* **flesh·i·er; -est 1** : consisting of or resembling animal flesh **2** : PLUMP, FAT

flew *past of* ¹FLY

flex \'fleks\ *vb* : to bend esp. repeatedly — **flex** *n*

flex·i·ble \'flek-sə-bəl\ *adj* **1** : capable of being flexed : PLIANT **2** : yielding to influence : TRACTABLE **3** : readily changed or changing : ADAPTABLE ♦ *Synonyms* ELASTIC, SUPPLE, RESILIENT, SPRINGY — **flex·i·bil·i·ty** \ˌflek-sə-ˈbi-lə-tē\ *n*

flex·or \'flek-sər, -ˌsȯr\ *n* : a muscle serving to bend a body part

flex·ure \'flek-shər\ *n* : TURN, FOLD

flib·ber·ti·gib·bet \ˌfli-bər-tē-ˈji-bət\ *n* : a silly flighty person

¹flick \'flik\ *n* **1** : a light sharp jerky stroke or movement **2** : a sound produced by a flick **3** : ²FLICKER

²flick *vb* **1** : to strike lightly with a quick sharp motion **2** : FLUTTER, FLIT

³flick *n* : MOVIE

¹flick·er \'fli-kər\ *vb* **1** : to move irregularly or unsteadily : FLUTTER **2** : to burn fitfully or with a fluctuating light — **flick·er·ing·ly** *adv*

²flicker *n* **1** : an act of flickering **2** : a sudden brief movement ⟨a ~ of an eyelid⟩ **3** : a momentary stirring ⟨a ~ of interest⟩ **4** : a slight indication : HINT **5** : a wavering light

³flicker *n* : a large barred and spotted No. American woodpecker with a brown back that occurs as an eastern form with yellow on the underside of the wings and tail and a western form with red in these areas

flied *past and past part of* ³FLY

fli·er \'flī(-ə)r\ *n* **1** : one that flies; *esp* : PILOT **2** : a reckless or speculative undertaking **3** *usu* **fly·er** : an advertising circular

¹**flight** \'flīt\ *n* **1** : an act or instance of flying **2** : the ability to fly **3** : a passing through air or space **4** : the distance covered in a flight **5** : swift movement **6** : a trip made by or in an airplane or spacecraft **7** : a group of similar individuals (as birds or airplanes) flying as a unit **8** : a passing (as of the imagination) beyond ordinary limits **9** : a series of stairs from one landing to another — **flight·less** *adj*

²**flight** *n* : an act or instance of running away

flight bag *n* **1** : a lightweight traveling bag with zippered outside pockets **2** : a small canvas satchel

flight line *n* : a parking and servicing area for airplanes

flighty \'flī-tē\ *adj* **flight·i·er; -est** **1** : easily upset : VOLATILE **2** : easily excited : SKITTISH **3** : CAPRICIOUS, SILLY — **flight·i·ness** \-tē-nəs\ *n*

flim-flam \'flim-,flam\ *n* : DECEPTION, FRAUD — **flim-flam·mery** \-,fla-mə-re\ *n*

flim·sy \'flim-zē\ *adj* **flim·si·er; -est** **1** : lacking strength or substance **2** : of inferior materials and workmanship **3** : having little worth or plausibility ⟨a ∼ excuse⟩ — **flim·si·ly** \-zə-lē\ *adv* — **flim·si·ness** \-zē-nəs\ *n*

flinch \'flinch\ *vb* [MF *flenchir* to bend] : to shrink from or as if from pain : WINCE — **flinch** *n*

¹**fling** \'fliŋ\ *vb* **flung** \'fləŋ\; **fling·ing** **1** : to move hastily, brusquely, or violently ⟨*flung* out of the room⟩ **2** : to kick or plunge vigorously **3** : to throw with force or recklessness; *also* : to cast as if by throwing **4** : to put suddenly into a state or condition

²**fling** *n* **1** : an act or instance of flinging **2** : a casual try : ATTEMPT **3** : a period of self-indulgence

flint \'flint\ *n* **1** : a hard dark quartz that produces a spark when struck by steel **2** : an alloy used for producing a spark in lighters — **flinty** *adj*

flint glass *n* : heavy glass containing an oxide of lead and used in lenses and prisms

flint-lock \'flint-,läk\ *n* **1** : a lock for a gun using a flint to ignite the charge **2** : a firearm fitted with a flintlock

flintlock pistol

¹**flip** \'flip\ *vb* **flipped; flip·ping** **1** : to turn by tossing ⟨∼ a coin⟩ **2** : to turn over; *also* : to leaf through **3** : FLICK, JERK ⟨∼ a light switch⟩ **4** : to lose self-control — **flip** *n*

²**flip** *adj* : FLIPPANT, IMPERTINENT

flip·pant \'fli-pənt\ *adj* : lacking proper respect or seriousness — **flip·pan·cy** \'fli-pən-sē\ *n*

flip·per \'fli-pər\ *n* **1** : a broad flat limb (as of a seal) adapted for swimming **2** : a paddlelike shoe used in skin diving

flip side *n* : the reverse and usu. less popular side of a phonograph record

¹**flirt** \'flərt\ *vb* **1** : to move erratically : FLIT **2** : to behave amorously without serious intent **3** : to show casual interest ⟨∼ed with the idea⟩; *also* : to come close to ⟨∼ with danger⟩ — **flir·ta·tion** \,flər-'tā-shən\ *n* — **flir·ta·tious** \-shəs\ *adj*

²**flirt** *n* **1** : an act or instance of flirting **2** : a person who flirts

flit \'flit\ *vb* **flit·ted; flit·ting** : to pass or move quickly or abruptly from place to place : DART — **flit** *n*

flitch \'flich\ *n* : a side of cured meat; *esp* : a side of bacon

fliv·ver \'fli-vər\ *n* : a small cheap usu. old automobile

¹**float** \'flōt\ *n* **1** : something (as a raft) that floats **2** : a cork buoying up the baited end of a fishing line **3** : a hollow ball that floats at the end of a lever in a cistern or tank and regulates the liquid level **4** : a vehicle with a platform to carry an exhibit **5** : a soft drink with ice cream floating in it

²**float** *vb* **1** : to rest on the surface of or be suspended in a fluid **2** : to move gently on or through a fluid **3** : to cause to float **4** : WANDER **5** : to offer (securities) in order to finance an enterprise **6** : to finance by floating an issue of stocks or bonds **7** : to arrange for ⟨∼ a loan⟩ — **float·er** *n*

floaty \'flō-tē\ *adj* **float·i·er –est** **1** : tending to float : BUOYANT **2** : light and billowy

¹**flock** \'fläk\ *n* **1** : a group of animals (as birds or sheep) assembled or herded together **2** : a group of people under the guidance of a leader; *esp* : CONGREGATION **3** : a large number ⟨a ∼ of tourists⟩

²**flock** *vb* : to gather or move in a flock ⟨people ∼ed to the beach⟩

floe \'flō\ *n* : a flat mass of floating ice

flog \'fläg\ *vb* **flogged; flog·ging** **1** : to beat with or as if with a rod or whip **2** : SELL ⟨∼ encyclopedias⟩ — **flog·ger** *n*

¹**flood** \'fləd\ *n* **1** : a great flow of water over the land **2** : the flowing in of the tide **3** : an overwhelming volume

²**flood** *vb* **1** : to cover or become filled with a flood **2** : to fill abundantly or excessively; *esp* : to supply an excess of fuel to **3** : to pour forth in a flood — **flood·er** *n*

flood·gate \'fləd-,gāt\ *n* : a gate for controlling a body of water : SLUICE

flood·light \-,līt\ *n* : a lamp that throws a broad beam of light; *also* : the beam itself — **floodlight** *vb*

flood·plain \-,plān\ *n* : a plain along a river or stream subject to periodic flooding

flood tide *n* **1** : a rising tide **2** : an overwhelming quantity **3** : a high point

flood·wa·ter \'fləd-,wȯ-tər, -,wä-\ *n* : the water of a flood

¹**floor** \'flȯr\ *n* **1** : the bottom of a room on which one stands **2** : a ground surface **3** : a story of a building **4** : a main level space (as in a legislative chamber) distinguished from a platform or gallery **5** : AUDIENCE **6** : the right to address an assembly **7** : a lower limit ⟨put a ∼ under wheat prices⟩ — **floor·ing** *n*

²**floor** *vb* **1** : to furnish with a floor **2** : to knock down **3** : AMAZE, DUMBFOUND **4** : to press (a vehicle's accelerator) to the floorboard esp. rapidly

floor·board \-,bȯrd\ *n* **1** : a board in a floor **2** : the floor of an automobile

floor leader *n* : a member of a legislative body who has charge of a party's organization and strategy on the floor

floor show *n* : a series of acts presented in a nightclub

floor·walk·er \'flȯr-,wȯ-kər\ *n* : a person employed in a retail store to oversee the sales force and aid customers

floo·zy *or* **floo·zie** \'flü-zē\ *n, pl* **floozies** : a usu. young woman of loose morals

flop \'fläp\ *vb* **flopped; flop·ping** **1** : FLAP **2** : to throw oneself down heavily, clumsily, or in a relaxed manner ⟨*flopped* into a chair⟩ **3** : FAIL ⟨the show *flopped*⟩ — **flop** *n* — **flop** *adv* — **flop·per** *n*

flop·house \'fläp-,haủs\ *n* : a cheap hotel

¹**flop·py** \'flä-pē\ *adj* **flop·pi·er; -est** : tending to flop; *esp* : soft and flexible — **flop·pi·ly** \-pə-lē\ *adv*

²**floppy** *n, pl* **flop·pies** : FLOPPY DISK

floppy disk *n* : a thin plastic disk with a magnetic coating on which computer data can be stored

flop sweat *n* : sweat caused by the fear of failing

flo·ra \'flȯr-ə\ *n, pl* **floras** *also* **flo·rae** \-,ē, -,ī\ [L *Flora*, Roman goddess of flowers] : plants or plant life esp. of a region or period

flo·ral \'flȯr-əl\ *adj* : of, relating to, or depicting flowers ⟨a ∼ design⟩

flo·res·cence \flȯ-'re-sᵊns, flə-\ *n* : a state or period of being in bloom or flourishing — **flo·res·cent** \-ᵊnt\ *adj*

flor·id \'flȯr-əd\ *adj* **1** : very flowery in style : ORNATE ⟨∼ prose⟩ **2** : tinged with red : RUDDY **3** : marked by emotional or sexual fervor

flo·rin \'flȯr-ən\ *n* **1** : an old gold coin first struck at Florence, Italy, in 1252 **2** : a gold coin of a European country patterned after the florin of Florence **3** : any of several modern silver coins issued in Commonwealth countries **4** : GULDEN

flo·rist \'flȯr-ist\ *n* : a person who sells flowers or ornamental plants

¹**floss** \'fläs\ *n* **1** : soft thread of silk or mercerized cotton for embroidery **2** : DENTAL FLOSS **3** : fluffy fibrous material

²**floss** *vb* : to use dental floss on (one's teeth)

flossy \ˈflä-sē\ *adj* **floss·i·er; -est 1** : of, relating to, or having the characteristics of floss **2** : STYLISH, GLAMOROUS ⟨~ hotels⟩ — **floss·i·ly** \-sə-lē\ *adv*

flo·ta·tion \flō-ˈtā-shən\ *n* : the process or an instance of floating

flo·til·la \flō-ˈti-lə\ *n* [Sp, dim. of *flota* fleet] : a fleet esp. of small ships

flot·sam \ˈflät-səm\ *n* : floating wreckage of a ship or its cargo

¹**flounce** \ˈflauns\ *vb* **flounced; flounc·ing 1** : to move with exaggerated jerky or bouncy motions **2** : to go with sudden determination

²**flounce** *n* : an act or instance of flouncing — **flouncy** \ˈflaun-sē\ *adj*

³**flounce** *n* : a strip of fabric attached by one edge; *also* : a wide ruffle

¹**floun·der** \ˈflaun-dər\ *n, pl* **flounder** *or* **flounders** : FLATFISH; *esp* : any of various important marine food fishes

²**flounder** *vb* **1** : to struggle to move or obtain footing **2** : to proceed clumsily ⟨~*ed* through the speech⟩

¹**flour** \ˈflaú(-ə)r\ *n* [ME, flower, best of anything, flour, fr. AF *flur* flower] : finely ground and sifted meal of a grain (as wheat); *also* : a fine soft powder — **floury** *adj*

²**flour** *vb* : to coat with or as if with flour

¹**flour·ish** \ˈflər-ish\ *vb* **1** : THRIVE, PROSPER **2** : to be in a state of activity or production ⟨~*ed* about 1850⟩ **3** : to reach a height of development or influence **4** : to make bold and sweeping gestures **5** : BRANDISH

²**flourish** *n* **1** : a florid bit of speech or writing; *also* : an ornamental touch or decorative detail **2** : FANFARE **3** : WAVE ⟨with a ~ of his cane⟩ **4** : showiness in doing something

¹**flout** \ˈflaút\ *vb* : to treat with contemptuous disregard ⟨~ the law⟩ — **flout·er** *n*

²**flout** *n* : TAUNT

¹**flow** \ˈflō\ *vb* **1** : to issue or move in a stream **2** : RISE ⟨the tide ebbs and ~*s*⟩ **3** : ABOUND **4** : to proceed smoothly and readily **5** : to have a smooth continuity **6** : to hang loose and billowing **7** : COME, ARISE **8** : MENSTRUATE

²**flow** *n* **1** : an act of flowing **2** : FLOOD 1, 2 **3** : a smooth uninterrupted movement **4** : STREAM; *also* : a mass of material that has flowed when molten **5** : the quantity that flows in a certain time **6** : MENSTRUATION **7** : a continuous transfer of energy — **flow·age** \ˈflō-ij\ *n*

flow·chart \ˈflō-ˌchärt\ *n* : a symbolic diagram showing step-by-step progression through a procedure

flow diagram *n* : FLOWCHART

¹**flow·er** \ˈflaú(-ə)r\ *n* [ME *flour*, fr. AF *flur, flour*, fr. L *flor-, flos*] **1** : a plant shoot modified for reproduction and bearing leaves specialized into floral organs; *esp* : one of a seed plant consisting of a calyx, corolla, stamens, and carpels **2** : a plant cultivated for its blossoms **3** : the best part or example **4** : the finest most vigorous period **5** : a state of blooming or flourishing — **flow·ered** \ˈflaú(-ə)rd\ *adj* — **flow·er·less** *adj* — **flow·er·like** \-ˌlīk\ *adj*

²**flower** *vb* **1** : DEVELOP; *also* : FLOURISH **2** : to produce flowers : BLOOM

flower girl *n* : a little girl who carries flowers at a wedding

flower head *n* : a compact cluster of small flowers without stems suggesting a single flower

flowering plant *n* : any of a major group of vascular plants (as magnolias, grasses, or roses) that produce flowers and fruit and have the seeds enclosed in an ovary

flow·er·pot \ˈflaú(-ə)r-ˌpät\ *n* : a pot in which to grow plants

flow·ery \ˈflaú(-ə)r-ē\ *adj* **1** : of, relating to, or resembling flowers **2** : full of fine words or phrases — **flow·er·i·ness** \-ē-nəs\ *n*

flown \ˈflōn\ *past and past part of* ¹FLY

fl oz *abbr* fluid ounce

flu \ˈflü\ *n* **1** : INFLUENZA **2** : any of several virus diseases marked esp. by respiratory or intestinal symptoms — **flu-like** \-ˌlīk\ *adj*

flub \ˈfləb\ *vb* **flubbed; flub·bing** : BOTCH, BLUNDER — **flub** *n*

fluc·tu·ate \ˈflək-chə-ˌwāt\ *vb* **-at·ed; -at·ing 1** : WAVER **2** : to move up and down or back and forth — **fluc·tu·a·tion** \ˌflək-chə-ˈwā-shən\ *n*

flue \ˈflü\ *n* : a passage (as in a chimney) for directing a current (as of smoke or gases)

flu·ent \ˈflü-ənt\ *adj* **1** : capable of flowing : FLUID **2** : ready or facile in speech ⟨~ in French⟩; *also* : having or showing mastery in a subject or skill **3** : effortlessly smooth and rapid ⟨~ speech⟩ — **flu·en·cy** \-ən-sē\ *n* — **flu·ent·ly** *adv*

flue pipe *n* : an organ pipe whose tone is produced by an air current striking the beveled opening of the pipe

¹**fluff** \ˈfləf\ *n* **1** : ?DOWN 1 ⟨~ from a pillow⟩ **2** : something fluffy **3** : something inconsequential **4** : BLUNDER; *esp* : actor's lapse of memory

²**fluff** *vb* **1** : to make or become fluffy ⟨~ up a pillow⟩ **2** : to make a mistake

fluffy \ˈflə-fē\ *adj* **fluff·i·er; -est 1** : covered with or resembling fluff **2** : being light and soft or airy ⟨a ~ omelet⟩ **3** : lacking in meaning or substance — **fluff·i·ly** \-fə-lē\ *adv*

¹**flu·id** \ˈflü-əd\ *adj* **1** : capable of flowing **2** : subject to change or movement **3** : showing a smooth easy style ⟨~ movements⟩ **4** : available for a different use; *esp* : LIQUID **5** ⟨~ assets⟩ — **flu·id·i·ty** \flü-ˈi-də-tē\ *n* — **flu·id·ly** *adv*

²**fluid** *n* : a substance (as a liquid or gas) tending to flow or take the shape of its container

fluid dram *or* **flu·i·dram** \ˌflü-ə-ˈdram\ *n* — see WEIGHT table

fluid ounce *n* — see WEIGHT table

¹**fluke** \ˈflük\ *n* : any of various trematode flatworms

²**fluke** *n* **1** : the part of an anchor that fastens in the ground **2** : a lobe of a whale's tail

³**fluke** *n* : a stroke of luck — **fluky** *also* **fluk·ey** \ˈflü-kē\ *adj*

flume \ˈflüm\ *n* **1** : an inclined channel for carrying water **2** : a ravine or gorge with a stream running through it

flung *past and past part of* FLING

flunk \ˈfləŋk\ *vb* : to fail esp. in an examination or course — **flunk** *n*

flun·ky *also* **flun·key** *or* **flun·kie** \ˈfləŋ-kē\ *n, pl* **flunkies** *also* **flunkeys 1** : a liveried servant; *also* : one performing menial or miscellaneous duties **2** : YES-MAN

fluo·res·cence \flò-ˈre-sᵊns\ *n* : luminescence caused by radiation absorption that ceases almost immediately after the incident radiation has stopped; *also* : the emitted radiation — **fluo·resce** \-ˈres\ *vb* — **fluo·res·cent** \-ˈresᵊnt\ *adj*

fluorescent lamp *n* : a tubular electric lamp in which light is produced by the action of ultraviolet light on a fluorescent material that coats the inner surface of the lamp

fluo·ri·date \ˈflòr-ə-ˌdāt\ *vb* **-dat·ed; -dat·ing** : to add a fluoride to (as drinking water) to reduce tooth decay — **fluo·ri·da·tion** \ˌflòr-ə-ˈdā-shən\ *n*

fluo·ride \ˈflòr-ˌīd\ *n* : a compound of fluorine

fluo·ri·nate \ˈflòr-ə-ˌnāt\ *vb* **-nat·ed; -nat·ing** : to treat or cause to combine with fluorine or a compound of fluorine — **fluo·ri·na·tion** \ˌflòr-ə-ˈnā-shən\ *n*

fluo·rine \ˈflòr-ˌēn, -ən\ *n* : a pale yellowish flammable irritating toxic gaseous chemical element

fluo·rite \ˈflòr-ˌīt\ *n* : a mineral that consists of the fluoride of calcium used as a flux and in making glass

fluo·ro·car·bon \ˌflòr-ō-ˈkär-bən\ *n* : a compound containing fluorine and carbon used chiefly as a lubricant, refrigerant, or nonstick coating; *also* : CHLOROFLUOROCARBON

fluo·ro·scope \ˈflòr-ə-ˌskōp\ *n* : an instrument for observing the internal structure of an opaque object (as the living body) by means of X-rays — **fluo·ro·scop·ic** \ˌflòr-ə-ˈskä-pik\ *adj* — **fluo·ros·co·py** \-ˈä-skə-pē\ *n*

fluo·ro·sis \ˌflù-ˈrō-səs, ˌflò-\ *n* : an abnormal condition (as spotting of the teeth) caused by fluorine or its compounds

flu·ox·e·tine \flü-ˈäk-sə-ˌtēn\ *n* : an antidepressant drug that enhances serotonin activity

flur·ry \ˈflər-ē\ *n, pl* **flurries 1** : a gust of wind **2** : a brief light snowfall **3** : COMMOTION, BUSTLE **4** : a brief outburst of activity ⟨a ~ of trading⟩ — **flurry** *vb*

¹**flush** \ˈfləsh\ *vb* : to cause (a bird) to fly away suddenly

²**flush** *n* : a hand of cards all of the same suit

³**flush** *n* **1** : a sudden flow (as of water) **2** : a surge esp. of emotion ⟨a ~ of triumph⟩ **3** : a tinge of red : BLUSH **4** : a fresh and vigorous state ⟨in the ~ of youth⟩ **5** : a passing sensation of extreme heat

⁴**flush** *vb* **1** : to flow and spread suddenly and freely **2** : to glow brightly **3** : BLUSH **4** : to wash out with a rush of fluid **5** : INFLAME, EXCITE **6** : to cause to blush

⁵**flush** *adj* **1** : of a ruddy healthy color **2** : full of life and vigor **3** : filled to overflowing : AFFLUENT **5** : readily available : ABUNDANT **6** : having an unbroken or even surface **7** : directly abutting : immediately adjacent **8** : set even with an edge of a type page or column — **flushness** *n*

⁶**flush** *adv* **1** : in a flush manner **2** : SQUARELY ⟨a blow ∼ on the chin⟩

⁷**flush** *vb* : to make flush

flus·ter \'fləs-tər\ *vb* : to put into a state of agitated confusion — **fluster** *n*

flute \'flüt\ *n* **1** : a hollow pipelike musical instrument **2** : a grooved pleat **3** : GROOVE — **flute** *vb* — **flut·ed** *adj*

flut·ing *n* : fluted decoration

flut·ist \'flü-tist\ *n* : a flute player

¹**flut·ter** \'flə-tər\ *vb* [ME *floteren* to float, flutter, fr. OE *floterian*, fr. *flotian* to float] **1** : to flap the wings rapidly **2** : to move with quick wavering or flapping motions **3** : to vibrate in irregular spasms **4** : to move about or behave in an agitated aimless manner — **flut·tery** \-tə-rē\ *adj*

²**flutter** *n* **1** : an act of fluttering **2** : a state of nervous confusion **3** : FLURRY

¹**flux** \'fləks\ *n* **1** : an act of flowing **2** : a state of continuous change **3** : a substance used to aid in fusing metals

²**flux** *vb* : ¹FUSE

¹**fly** \'flī\ *vb* **flew** \'flü\; **flown** \'flōn\; **fly·ing** **1** : to move in or pass through the air with wings **2** : to move through the air or before the wind **3** : to float or cause to float, wave, or soar in the air **4** : FLEE **5** : to fade and disappear : VANISH **6** : to move or pass swiftly ⟨time *flies*⟩ **7** : to become expended or dissipated rapidly **8** : to operate or travel in an aircraft or spacecraft **9** : to journey over by flying **10** : AVOID, SHUN **11** : to transport by flying

²**fly** *n, pl* **flies** **1** : the action or process of flying : FLIGHT **2** *pl* : the space over a theater stage **3** : a garment closing concealed by a fold of cloth **4** : the length of an extended flag from its staff or support **5** : a baseball hit high into the air **6** : the outer canvas of a tent with a double top — **on the fly** : while still in the air

³**fly** *vb* **flied**; **fly·ing** : to hit a fly in baseball

⁴**fly** *n, pl* **flies** **1** : a winged insect — usu. used in combination ⟨butter*fly*⟩ **2** : any of a large order of insects mostly with one pair of functional wings and another pair that if present are reduced to balancing organs and often with larvae without a head, eyes, or legs; *esp* : one (as a housefly) that is large and stout-bodied **3** : a fishhook dressed to suggest an insect

fly·able \'flī-ə-bəl\ *adj* : suitable for flying or being flown

fly ball *n* : ²FLY 5

fly·blown \'flī-ˌblōn\ *adj* : not pure : TAINTED, CORRUPT

fly·by \-ˌbī\ *n, pl* **flybys** **1** : a usu. low-altitude flight by an aircraft over a public gathering **2** : a flight of a spacecraft past a heavenly body (as Jupiter) close enough to obtain scientific data

fly-by-night \-ˌbī-ˌnīt\ *adj* **1** : seeking a quick profit usu. by shady acts **2** : TRANSITORY, PASSING ⟨∼ fashions⟩

fly casting *n* : the casting of artificial flies in fly-fishing or as a competitive sport

fly·catch·er \-ˌka-chər, -ˌke-\ *n* : any of various passerine birds that feed on insects caught in flight

flyer *var of* FLIER

fly–fish·ing \'flī-ˌfi-shiŋ\ *n* : a method of fishing in which an artificial fly is used for bait

flying boat *n* : a seaplane with a hull designed for floating

flying buttress *n* : a projecting arched structure to support a wall or building

flying fish *n* : any of numerous marine bony fishes capable of long gliding flights out of water by spreading their large fins like wings

flying saucer *n* : an unidentified flying object reported to be saucer-shaped or disk-shaped

flying squirrel *n* : either of two small nocturnal No. American squirrels with folds of skin connecting the forelegs and hind legs that enable them to make long gliding leaps

fly·leaf \'flī-ˌlēf\ *n, pl* **fly·leaves** \-ˌlēvz\ : a blank leaf at the beginning or end of a book

fly·pa·per \-ˌpā-pər\ *n* : paper poisoned or coated with a sticky substance for killing or catching flies

fly·speck \-ˌspek\ *n* **1** : a speck of fly dung **2** : something small and insignificant

fly·way \-ˌwā\ *n* : an established air route of migratory birds

fly·wheel \-ˌhwēl\ *n* : a heavy wheel for regulating the speed of machinery

fm *abbr* fathom

Fm *symbol* fermium

FM \'ef-ˌem\ *n* : a broadcasting system using frequency modulation; *also* : a radio receiver of such a system

fn *abbr* footnote

fo *or* **fol** *abbr* folio

FO *abbr* foreign office

¹**foal** \'fōl\ *n* : a young horse or related animal; *esp* : one under one year

²**foal** *vb* : to give birth to a foal

¹**foam** \'fōm\ *n* **1** : a mass of bubbles formed on the surface of a liquid : FROTH, SPUME **2** : material (as rubber) in a lightweight cellular form — **foamy** *adj*

²**foam** *vb* : to form foam : FROTH

fob \'fäb\ *n* **1** : a short strap, ribbon, or chain attached esp. to a pocket watch **2** : a small ornament worn on a fob

FOB *abbr* free on board

fob off *vb* **1** : to put off with a trick, excuse, or inferior substitute **2** : to pass or offer as genuine **3** : to put aside

FOC *abbr* free of charge

focal length *n* : the distance of a focus from a lens or curved mirror

fo'c'sle *var of* FORECASTLE

¹**fo·cus** \'fō-kəs\ *n, pl* **fo·ci** \-ˌsī\ *also* **fo·cus·es** [NL, fr. L, hearth] **1** : a point at which rays (as of light, heat, or sound) meet or diverge or appear to diverge; *esp* : the point at which an image is formed by a mirror, lens, or optical system **2** : FOCAL LENGTH **3** : adjustment (as of eyes or eyeglasses) that gives clear vision **4** : central point : CENTER — **fo·cal** \'fō-kəl\ *adj* — **fo·cal·ly** *adv*

²**focus** *vb* **-cused** *also* **-cussed**; **-cus·ing** *also* **-cus·sing** **1** : to bring or come to a focus ⟨∼ rays of light⟩ **2** : CENTER ⟨∼ attention on a problem⟩ **3** : to adjust the focus of

fod·der \'fä-dər\ *n* **1** : coarse dry food (as cornstalks) for livestock **2** : available material used to supply a heavy demand

foe \'fō\ *n* [ME *fo*, fr. OE *fāh*, fr. *fāh* hostile] : ENEMY

FOE *abbr* Fraternal Order of Eagles

foehn *or* **föhn** \'fərn, 'fœn, 'fän\ *n* [G *Föhn*] : a warm dry wind blowing down a mountainside

foe·man \'fō-mən\ *n* : FOE

foe·tal, foe·tus *chiefly Brit var of* FETAL, FETUS

¹**fog** \'fȯg, 'fäg\ *n* **1** : fine particles of water suspended in the lower atmosphere **2** : mental confusion — **fog·gy** *adj*

²**fog** *vb* **fogged**; **fog·ging** : to obscure or be obscured with or as if with fog

fog·horn \'fȯg-ˌhȯrn, 'fäg-\ *n* : a horn sounded in a fog to give warning

fo·gy *also* **fo·gey** \'fō-gē\ *n, pl* **fogies** *also* **fogeys** : a person with old-fashioned ideas ⟨an old ∼⟩

foi·ble \'fȯi-bəl\ *n* : a minor failing or weakness in character or behavior

foie gras \'fwä-ˌgrä\ *n* [F, lit., fat liver] : the fattened liver of an animal and esp. of a goose usu. served as a pâté

¹**foil** \'fȯi(-ə)l\ *vb* [ME, alter. of *fullen* to full cloth, fr. AF *foller*] **1** : to prevent from attaining an end : DEFEAT **2** : to bring to naught : THWART

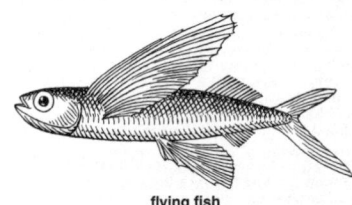

flying fish

²foil n [ME, leaf, fr. AF *fuille, foille*, fr. L *folia*, pl. of *folium* leaf] **1** : a very thin sheet of metal ⟨aluminum ~⟩ **2** : one that serves as a contrast to another ⟨acted as a ~ for a comedian⟩

³foil n : a light fencing sword with a flexible blade tapering to a blunt point

foist \'fȯist\ vb : to pass off (something false or worthless) as genuine

¹fold \'fōld\ n **1** : an enclosure for sheep **2** : a group of people with a common faith, belief, or interest

²fold vb : to house (sheep) in a fold

³fold vb **1** : to lay one part over or against another part **2** : to clasp together **3** : EMBRACE **4** : to bend (as a layer of rock) into folds **5** : to incorporate into a mixture by overturning repeatedly without stirring or beating **6** : to become doubled or pleated **7** : FAIL, COLLAPSE ⟨the business ~ed⟩

⁴fold n **1** : a doubling or folding over **2** : a part doubled or laid over another part

fold-away \'fōld-ə-ˌwā\ adj : designed to fold out of the way or out of sight

fold-er \'fōl-dər\ n **1** : one that folds **2** : a folded printed circular **3** : a folded cover or large envelope for loose papers **4** : an object in a computer operating system used to organize files or other folders

fol-de-rol \'fäl-də-ˌräl\ n **1** : a useless trifle **2** : NONSENSE

fold-out \'fōld-ˌaȯt\ n : a folded leaf (as in a magazine) larger in some dimension than the page

fo-liage \'fō-lē-ij\ n : a mass of leaves (as of a plant or forest)

fo-li-at-ed \'fō-lē-ˌā-təd\ adj : composed of or separable into layers

fo-lic acid \ˌfō-lik-\ n : a vitamin of the vitamin B complex used esp. to treat nutritional anemias

fo-lio \'fō-lē-ˌō\ n, pl **fo-li-os 1** : a leaf of a book; also : a page number **2** : the size of a piece of paper cut two from a sheet **3** : a book printed on folio pages

¹folk \'fōk\ n, pl **folk** or **folks 1** : the largest number or most characteristic part of a group of people forming a tribe or nation **2** pl : PEOPLE, PERSONS ⟨country ~⟩ ⟨old ~s⟩ **3** folks pl : the persons of one's own family

²folk adj : of, relating to, or originating among the common people ⟨~ music⟩

folk art n : the traditional anonymous art of usu. untrained people

folk-lore \'fōk-ˌlȯr\ n : customs, beliefs, stories, and sayings of a people handed down from generation to generation — **folk-lor-ic** \-ˌlȯr-ik\ adj — **folk-lor-ist** \-ist\ n

folk mass n : a mass in which traditional liturgical music is replaced by folk music

folk-sing-er \'fōk-ˌsiŋ-ər\ n : a singer of folk songs — **folk-sing-ing** n

folksy \'fōk-sē\ adj **folks-i-er; -est 1** : SOCIABLE, FRIENDLY **2** : informal, casual, or familiar in manner or style ⟨~ humor⟩

folk-way \'fōk-ˌwā\ n : a way of thinking, feeling, or acting common to a given group of people; esp : a traditional social custom

fol-li-cle \'fä-li-kəl\ n **1** : a small anatomical cavity or gland ⟨a hair ~⟩ **2** : a small fluid-filled cavity in the ovary of a mammal enclosing a developing egg — **fol-lic-u-lar** \fə-'li-kyə-lər\ adj

fol-low \'fä-lō\ vb **1** : to come or go after **2** : to proceed along ⟨~ the path⟩ **3** : to engage in as a way of life ⟨~ the sea⟩ ⟨~ a profession⟩ **4** : OBEY ⟨~ instructions⟩ **5** : PURSUE **6** : to come after in order or rank or natural sequence **7** : to keep one's attention fixed on **8** : to result from ♦ **Synonyms** SUCCEED, ENSUE, SUPERVENE — **fol-low-er** n — **follow suit 1** : to play a card of the same suit as the card led **2** : to follow an example set

¹fol-low-ing \'fä-lə-wiŋ\ adj **1** : next after : SUCCEEDING ⟨the ~ day⟩ **2** : that immediately follows ⟨trains will leave at the ~ times⟩

²following n : a group of followers, adherents, or partisans

³following prep : subsequent to : AFTER ⟨~ the lecture tea was served⟩

follow–up \'fä-lō-ˌəp\ n : a system or instance of pursuing an initial effort by supplementary action

fol-ly \'fä-lē\ n, pl **follies** [ME folie, fr. AF, fr. fol fool] **1** : lack of good sense **2** : a foolish act or idea : FOOLISH-

NESS 3 : an excessively costly or unprofitable undertaking

fo-ment \fō-'ment\ vb : INCITE

fo-men-ta-tion \ˌfō-mən-'tā-shən, -ˌmen-\ n **1** : a hot moist material (as a damp cloth) applied to the body to ease pain **2** : the act of fomenting : INSTIGATION

fond \'fänd\ adj [ME, fr. fonne fool] **1** : FOOLISH, SILLY ⟨~ pride⟩ **2** : prizing highly : DESIROUS ⟨~ of praise⟩ **3** : strongly attracted or predisposed ⟨~ of music⟩ **4** : foolishly tender : INDULGENT; also : LOVING, AFFECTIONATE **5** : CHERISHED, DEAR ⟨his ~est hopes⟩ — **fond-ly** adv — **fond-ness** n

fon-dant \'fän-dənt\ n **1** : a creamy preparation of sugar used as a basis for candies or icings

fon-dle \'fän-dᵊl\ vb **fon-dled; fon-dling** : to touch or handle lovingly : CARESS

fon-due also **fon-du** \fän-'dü, -'dyü\ n [F] : a preparation of melted cheese often flavored with white wine

¹font \'fänt\ n **1** : a receptacle for baptismal or holy water **2** : FOUNTAIN, SOURCE ⟨a ~ of information⟩

²font n : an assortment of printing type of one style and sometimes one size

food \'füd\ n **1** : material taken into an organism and used for growth, repair, and vital processes and as a source of energy; also : organic material produced by green plants and used by them as food **2** : nourishment in solid form **3** : something that nourishes, sustains, or supplies ⟨~ for thought⟩

food chain n **1** : a hierarchical arrangement of organisms in an ecological community such that each uses the next usu. lower member as a food source **2** : a hierarchy based on power or importance

food court n : an area (as within a shopping mall) set apart for food concessions

food poisoning n : a digestive illness caused by bacteria or by chemicals in food

food-stuff \'füd-ˌstəf\ n : a substance with food value; esp : a specific nutrient (as fat or protein)

¹fool \'fül\ n [ME, fr. AF fol, fr. LL follis, fr. L, bellows, bag] **1** : a person who lacks sense or judgment **2** : JESTER **3** : DUPE **4** : IDIOT

²fool vb **1** : to spend time idly or aimlessly **2** : to meddle or tamper thoughtlessly or ignorantly **3** : JOKE **4** : DECEIVE **5** : FRITTER ⟨~ed away his time⟩

fool-ery \'fü-lə-rē\ n, pl **-er-ies 1** : a foolish act, utterance, or belief **2** : foolish behavior

fool-har-dy \'fül-ˌhär-dē\ adj : foolishly daring : RASH — **fool-har-di-ness** \-dē-nəs\ n

fool-ish \'fü-lish\ adj **1** : showing or arising from folly or lack of judgment **2** : ABSURD, RIDICULOUS **3** : ABASHED — **fool-ish-ly** adv — **fool-ish-ness** n

fool-proof \'fül-ˌprüf\ adj : so simple or reliable as to leave no opportunity for error, misuse, or failure ⟨a ~ plan⟩

fools-cap \'fül-ˌskap\ n [fr. the watermark of a fool's cap formerly applied to such paper] : a size of paper typically 16×13 inches

fool's gold n : PYRITE

¹foot \'fu̇t\ n, pl **feet** \'fēt\ also **foot 1** : the end part of a leg below the ankle of a vertebrate animal **2** — see WEIGHT table **3** : a group of syllables forming the basic unit of verse meter **4** : something resembling an animal's foot in position or use **5** : the lowest part : BOTTOM **6** : the part at the opposite end from the head **7** : the part (as of a stocking) that covers the foot

²foot vb **1** : DANCE **2** : to go on foot **3** : to add up **4** : to pay or provide for paying

foot-age \'fu̇-tij\ n **1** : length expressed in feet **2** : the length of film used for a scene; also : the material contained on such footage

foot–and–mouth disease n : an acute contagious viral disease esp. of cattle

foot-ball \'fu̇t-ˌbȯl\ n **1** : any of several games played by two teams on a rectangular field with goalposts at each end in which the object is to get the ball over the goal line or between goalposts by running, passing, or kicking **2** : the ball used in football

foot-board \-ˌbȯrd\ n **1** : a narrow platform on which to stand or brace the feet **2** : a board forming the foot of a bed

foot-bridge \-ˌbrij\ n : a bridge for pedestrians

foot·ed \'fu̇-təd\ *adj* : having a foot or feet of a specified kind or number ⟨flat-*footed*⟩ ⟨four-*footed*⟩

-foot·er \'fu̇-tər\ *comb form* : one that is a specified number of feet in height, length, or breadth ⟨a six-*footer*⟩

foot·fall \'fu̇t-ˌfȯl\ *n* : the sound of a footstep

foot·hill \-ˌhil\ *n* : a hill at the foot of higher hills or mountains

foot·hold \-ˌhōld\ *n* **1** : a hold for the feet : FOOTING **2** : a position usable as a base for further advance

foot·ing *n* **1** : the placing of one's feet in a stable position **2** : the act of moving on foot **3** : a place or space for standing : FOOTHOLD **4** : position with respect to one another : STATUS **5** : BASIS

foot·less \'fu̇t-ləs\ *adj* **1** : having no feet ⟨∼ tights⟩ **2** : INEPT, INEFFECTUAL

foot·lights \-ˌlīts\ *n pl* **1** : a row of lights along the front of a stage floor **2** : the stage as a profession

foo·tling \'fu̇t-liŋ\ *adj* **1** : INEPT ⟨∼ amateurs⟩ **2** : TRIVIAL

foot·lock·er \'fu̇t-ˌlä-kər\ *n* : a small trunk designed to be placed at the foot of a bed (as in a barracks)

foot·loose \-ˌlüs\ *adj* : having no ties : FREE, UNTRAMMELED

foot·man \-mən\ *n* : a male servant who attends a carriage or waits on table, admits visitors, and runs errands

foot·note \-ˌnōt\ *n* **1** : a note of reference, explanation, or comment placed usu. at the bottom of a page **2** : COMMENTARY

foot·pad \-ˌpad\ *n* : a round somewhat flat foot on the leg of a spacecraft for distributing weight to minimize sinking into a surface

foot·path \-ˌpath, -ˌpäth\ *n* : a narrow path for pedestrians

foot·print \-ˌprint\ *n* **1** : an impression of the foot **2** : the area on a surface covered by something ⟨a tire with a wide ∼⟩

foot·race \-ˌrās\ *n* : a race run on foot

foot·rest \-ˌrest\ *n* : a support for the feet

foot·sore \-ˌsȯr\ *adj* : having sore or tender feet (as from much walking)

foot·step \-ˌstep\ *n* **1** : the mark of the foot : TRACK **2** : TREAD **3** : distance covered by a step : PACE **4** : a step on which to ascend or descend **5** : a way of life, conduct, or action

foot·stool \-ˌstül\ *n* : a low stool to support the feet

foot·wear \-ˌwer\ *n* : apparel (as shoes or boots) for the feet

foot·work \-ˌwərk\ *n* : the management of the feet (as in boxing)

fop \'fäp\ *n* : DANDY 1 — **fop·pery** \'fä-pə-rē\ *n* — **fop·pish** *adj*

¹for \fər, 'fȯr\ *prep* **1** : as a preparation toward ⟨dress ∼ dinner⟩ **2** : toward the purpose or goal of ⟨need time ∼ study⟩ ⟨money ∼ a trip⟩ **3** : so as to reach or attain ⟨run ∼ cover⟩ **4** : as being ⟨took him ∼ a fool⟩ **5** : because of ⟨cry ∼ joy⟩ **6** — used to indicate a recipient ⟨a letter ∼ you⟩ **7** : in support of ⟨fought ∼ his country⟩ **8** : directed at : AFFECTING ⟨a cure ∼ what ails you⟩ **9** — used with a noun or pronoun followed by an infinitive to form the equivalent of a noun clause ⟨∼ you to go would be silly⟩ **10** : in exchange as equal to : so as to return the value of ⟨a lot of trouble ∼ nothing⟩ ⟨pay $10 ∼ a hat⟩ **11** : CONCERNING ⟨a stickler ∼ detail⟩ **12** : CONSIDERING ⟨tall ∼ her age⟩ **13** : through the period of ⟨served ∼ three years⟩ **14** : in honor of ⟨named ∼ her grandmother⟩

²for *conj* : BECAUSE

³for *abbr* **1** foreign **2** forestry

fora *pl of* FORUM

¹for·age \'fȯr-ij\ *n* [ME, fr. AF, fr. *fuerre, foer* fodder, straw, of Gmc origin] **1** : food for animals esp. when taken by browsing or grazing **2** : a search for food or supplies

²forage *vb* **for·aged; for·ag·ing 1** : to collect forage from **2** : to search for food or supplies **3** : to get by foraging **4** : to make a search : RUMMAGE

for·ay \'fȯr-ˌā, fȯ-'rā\ *vb* : to raid esp. in search of plunder : PILLAGE — **foray** *n*

¹for·bear \fȯr-'ber\ *vb* **-bore** \-'bȯr\; **-borne** \-'bȯrn\; **-bear·ing 1** : to refrain from : ABSTAIN **2** : to be patient — **for·bear·ance** \-'ber-əns\ *n*

²forbear *var of* FOREBEAR

for·bid \fər-'bid\ *vb* **-bade** \-'bad, -'bād\ *also* **-bad** \-'bad\;

-bid·den \-'bi-dᵊn\; **-bid·ding 1** : to command against : PROHIBIT **2** : HINDER, PREVENT ♦ *Synonyms* ENJOIN, INTERDICT, INHIBIT, BAN

forbidding *adj* : DISAGREEABLE, REPELLENT ⟨a ∼ task⟩

¹force \'fȯrs\ *n* **1** : strength or energy esp. of an exceptional degree : active power **2** : capacity to persuade or convince **3** : military strength; *also, pl* : the whole military strength (as of a nation) **4** : a body (as of persons or ships) available for a particular purpose **5** : VIOLENCE, COMPULSION **6** : an influence (as a push or pull) that causes motion or a change of motion — **force·ful** \-fəl\ *adj* — **force·ful·ly** *adv* — **in force 1** : in great numbers **2** : VALID, OPERATIVE ⟨the ban remains *in force*⟩

²force *vb* **forced; forc·ing 1** : COMPEL, COERCE **2** : to cause through necessity ⟨*forced* to admit defeat⟩ **3** : to press, attain to, or effect against resistance or inertia ⟨∼ your way through⟩ **4** : to raise or accelerate to the utmost ⟨∼ the pace⟩ **5** : to produce with unnatural or unwilling effort ⟨*forced* a smile⟩ **6** : to hasten (as in growth) by artificial means

for·ceps \'fȯr-səps\ *n, pl* **forceps** [L] : a hand-held instrument for grasping, holding, or pulling objects esp. for delicate operations (as by a surgeon)

forc·ible \'fȯr-sə-bəl\ *adj* **1** : obtained or done by force **2** : showing force or energy : POWERFUL — **forc·i·bly** \-blē\ *adv*

¹ford \'fȯrd\ *n* : a place where a stream may be crossed by wading

²ford *vb* : to cross (a body of water) by wading

¹fore \'fȯr\ *adv* : in, toward, or adjacent to the front : FORWARD

²fore *adj* : being or coming before in time, order, or space

³fore *n* : something that occupies a front position

⁴fore *interj* — used by a golfer to warn anyone within range of the probable line of flight of the ball

fore–and–aft \ˌfȯr-ə-'naft\ *adj* : lying, running, or acting along the length of a structure (as a ship)

¹fore·arm \(ˌ)fȯr-'ärm\ *vb* : to arm in advance : PREPARE

²fore·arm \'fȯr-ˌärm\ *n* : the part of the arm between the elbow and the wrist

fore·bear \-ˌber\ *n* : ANCESTOR, FOREFATHER

fore·bode *also* **for·bode** \fȯr-'bōd\ *vb* **1** : to have a premonition esp. of misfortune **2** : FORETELL, PREDICT ♦ *Synonyms* AUGUR, BODE, FORESHADOW, PORTEND, PROMISE — **fore·bod·ing** *n or adj* — **fore·bod·ing·ly** *adv*

fore·cast \'fȯr-ˌkast\ *vb* **-cast** *also* **-cast·ed; -cast·ing 1** : PREDICT, CALCULATE ⟨∼ weather conditions⟩ **2** : to indicate as likely to occur — **forecast** *n* — **fore·cast·er** *n*

fore·cas·tle *or* **fo'c'sle** \'fōk-səl\ *n* **1** : the forward part of the upper deck of a ship **2** : the crew's quarters usu. in a ship's bow

fore·close \fȯr-'klōz\ *vb* **1** : to shut out : PRECLUDE **2** : to take legal measures to terminate a mortgage and take possession of the mortgaged property

fore·clo·sure \-'klō-zhər\ *n* : the act of foreclosing; *esp* : the legal procedure of foreclosing a mortgage

fore·doom \fȯr-'düm\ *vb* : to doom beforehand

fore·fa·ther \'fȯr-ˌfä-thər\ *n* **1** : ANCESTOR **2** : a person of an earlier period and common heritage

forefend *var of* FORFEND

fore·fin·ger \-ˌfiŋ-gər\ *n* : INDEX FINGER

fore·foot \-ˌfu̇t\ *n* : either of the front feet of a quadruped; *also* : the front part of the human foot

fore·front \-ˌfrənt\ *n* : the foremost part or place

foregather *var of* FORGATHER

¹fore·go \fȯr-'gō\ *vb* **-went** \-'went\; **-gone** \-'gȯn\; **-go·ing** : PRECEDE

²forego *var of* FORGO

foregoing *adj* : PRECEDING ⟨the ∼ statement can be proven⟩

fore·gone \'fȯr-ˌgȯn\ *adj* : determined in advance ⟨a ∼ conclusion⟩

fore·ground \-ˌgrau̇nd\ *n* **1** : the part of a scene or representation that appears nearest to and in front of the spectator **2** : a position of prominence

fore·hand \-ˌhand\ *n* : a stroke (as in tennis) made with the palm of the hand turned in the direction in which the hand is moving; *also* : the side on which such a stroke is made — **forehand** *adj*

fore·hand·ed \(ˌ)fȯr-'han-dəd\ *adj* : mindful of the future : PRUDENT

fore·head \'fȯr-əd, 'fȯr-ˌhed\ *n* : the part of the face above the eyes

for·eign \'fȯr-ən\ *adj* [ME *forein*, fr. AF, fr. LL *foranus* on the outside, fr. L *foris* outside] **1** : situated outside a place or country and away from one's own country **2** : born in, belonging to, or characteristic of some place or country other than the one under consideration ⟨∼ language⟩ **3** : not connected, pertinent, or characteristically present **4** : related to or dealing with other nations ⟨∼ affairs⟩ **5** : occurring in an abnormal situation in the living body ⟨a ∼ body in the eye⟩

for·eign·er \'fȯr-ə-nər\ *n* : a person belonging to or owing allegiance to a foreign country

foreign minister *n* : a governmental minister for foreign affairs

fore·know \fȯr-'nō\ *vb* **-knew** \-'nü, -'nyü\; **-known** \-'nōn\; **-know·ing** : to have previous knowledge of — **fore·knowl·edge** \'fȯr-ˌnä-lij, fȯr-'nä-\ *n*

fore·la·dy \'fȯr-ˌlā-dē\ *n* : FOREWOMAN

fore·leg \-ˌleg\ *n* : a front leg

fore·limb \-ˌlim\ *n* : a front or upper limb (as a wing, arm, fin, or leg)

fore·lock \-ˌläk\ *n* : a lock of hair growing from the front part of the head

fore·man \-mən\ *n* **1** : a spokesperson of a jury **2** : a person in charge of a group of workers

fore·mast \-ˌmast\ *n* : the mast nearest the bow of a ship

fore·most \-ˌmōst\ *adj* : first in time, place, or order : most important : PREEMINENT — **foremost** *adv*

fore·name \-ˌnām\ *n* : a first name

fore·named \-ˌnāmd\ *adj* : previously named : AFORESAID

fore·noon \-ˌnün\ *n* : MORNING

¹fo·ren·sic \fə-'ren-sik\ *adj* [L *forensis* public, forensic, fr. *forum* forum] **1** : belonging to, used in, or suitable to courts of law or to public speaking or debate **2** : relating to the application of scientific knowledge to legal problems ⟨∼ medicine⟩

²forensic *n* **1** : an argumentative exercise **2** *pl* : the art or study of argumentative discourse **3** *pl* : scientific analysis of physical evidence (as from a crime scene)

fore·or·dain \ˌfȯr-ȯr-'dān\ *vb* : to ordain or decree beforehand : PREDESTINE

fore·part \'fȯ)r-ˌpärt\ *n* **1** : the anterior part of something **2** : the earlier part of a period of time

fore·quar·ter \-ˌkwȯr-tər\ *n* : the front half of a lateral half of the body or carcass of a quadruped ⟨a ∼ of beef⟩

fore·run·ner \-ˌrə-nər\ *n* **1** : one that goes before to give notice of the approach of others : HARBINGER **2** : PREDECESSOR, ANCESTOR ♦ ***Synonyms*** PRECURSOR, HERALD

fore·sail \-ˌsāl, -səl\ *n* **1** : the lowest sail on the foremast of a square-rigged ship or schooner **2** : the principal sail forward of the foremast (as of a sloop)

foresail 1

fore·see \fȯr-'sē\ *vb* **-saw** \-'sȯ\; **-seen** \-'sēn\; **-see·ing** : to see or realize beforehand : EXPECT ♦ ***Synonyms*** FOREKNOW, DIVINE, APPREHEND, ANTICIPATE — **fore·see·able** *adj*

fore·shad·ow \-'sha-dō\ *vb* : to give a hint or suggestion of beforehand

fore·short·en \fȯr-'shȯr-t³n\ *vb* : to shorten (a detail) in a drawing or painting so that it appears to have depth

fore·sight \'fȯr-ˌsīt\ *n* **1** : the act or power of foreseeing **2** : care or provision for the future : PRUDENCE **3** : an act of looking forward; *also* : a view forward — **fore·sight·ed** \-ˌsī-təd\ *adj* — **fore·sight·ed·ly** *adv* — **fore·sight·ed·ness** *n*

fore·skin \-ˌskin\ *n* : a fold of skin enclosing the end of the penis

for·est \'fȯr-əst\ *n* [ME, fr. AF, fr. LL *forestis* (*silva*) unenclosed (woodland), fr. L *foris* outside] : a large thick growth of trees and underbrush — **for·est·ed** \'fȯr-ə-stəd\ *adj* — **for·est·land** \'fȯr-əst-ˌland\ *n*

fore·stall \fȯr-'stȯl, fȯr-\ *vb* **1** : to keep out, hinder, or prevent by measures taken in advance **2** : ANTICIPATE

forest ranger *n* : a person in charge of the management and protection of a portion of a forest

for·est·ry \'fȯr-ə-strē\ *n* : the science of growing and caring for forests — **for·est·er** \'fȯr-ə-stər\ *n*

foreswear *var of* FORSWEAR

¹fore·taste \'fȯr-ˌtāst\ *n* : an advance indication, warning, or notion

²fore·taste \fȯr-'tāst\ *vb* : to taste beforehand : ANTICIPATE

fore·tell \fȯr-'tel\ *vb* **-told** \-'tōld\; **-tell·ing** : to tell of beforehand : PREDICT ♦ ***Synonyms*** FORECAST, PROPHESY, PROGNOSTICATE

fore·thought \'fȯr-ˌthȯt\ *n* **1** : PREMEDITATION **2** : consideration for the future

fore·to·ken \fȯr-'tō-kən\ *vb* : to indicate in advance

fore·top \'fȯr-ˌtäp\ *n* : a platform near the top of a ship's foremast

for·ev·er \fȯr-'e-vər\ *adv* **1** : for a limitless time **2** : at all times : ALWAYS

for·ev·er·more \-ˌe-vər-'mȯr\ *adv* : FOREVER

fore·warn \fȯr-'wȯrn\ *vb* : to warn beforehand — **fore·warn·ing** \'wȯr-niŋ\ *n*

forewent *past of* FOREGO

fore·wing \'fȯr-ˌwiŋ\ *n* : either of the anterior wings of a 4-winged insect

fore·wom·an \'fȯr-ˌwu̇-mən\ *n* : a woman having the responsibilities of a foreman

fore·word \-ˌwərd\ *n* : PREFACE

¹for·feit \'fȯr-fət\ *n* [ME *forfait*, fr. AF, fr. pp. of *forfaire*, *forsfaire* to commit a crime, forfeit, fr. *fors* outside + *faire* to do] **1** : something forfeited : PENALTY, FINE **2** : FORFEITURE **3** : something deposited and then redeemed on payment of a fine **4** *pl* : a game in which forfeits are exacted

²forfeit *vb* : to lose or lose the right to esp. by some error, offense, or crime

for·fei·ture \'fȯr-fə-ˌchùr\ *n* **1** : the act of forfeiting **2** : something forfeited : PENALTY

for·fend \fȯr-'fend\ *vb* **1** : PREVENT **2** : PROTECT, PRESERVE

for·gath·er *or* **fore·gath·er** \fȯr-'ga-thər\ *vb* **1** : to come together : ASSEMBLE **2** : to meet someone usu. by chance

¹forge \'fȯrj\ *n* [ME, fr. AF, fr. L *fabrica*, fr. *faber* smith] : a furnace or shop with its furnace where metal is heated and worked

²forge *vb* **forged**; **forg·ing** **1** : to form (metal) by heating and hammering **2** : FASHION, SHAPE ⟨∼ an agreement⟩ **3** : to make or imitate falsely esp. with intent to defraud ⟨∼ a signature⟩ — **forg·er** *n* — **forg·ery** \'fȯr-jə-rē\ *n*

³forge *vb* **forged**; **forg·ing** : to move ahead steadily but gradually

for·get \fər-'get\ *vb* **-got** \-'gät\; **-got·ten** \-'gät-³n\ *or* **-got**; **-get·ting** **1** : to be unable to think of or recall **2** : to fail to become mindful of at the proper time **3** : NEGLECT, DISREGARD **4** : to give up hope for or expectation of — **for·get·ful** \-'get-fəl\ *adj* — **for·get·ful·ly** *adv* — **for·get·ful·ness** *n*

for·get—me—not \fər-'get-mē-ˌnät\ *n* : any of a genus of small herbs with bright blue or white flowers

forg·ing *n* : a piece of forged work

for·give \fər-'giv\ *vb* **-gave** \-'gāv\; **-giv·en** \-'gi-vən\; **-giv·ing** **1** : to give up resentment of **2** : PARDON, ABSOLVE **3** : to grant relief from payment of — **for·giv·able** *adj* — **for·give·ness** *n* — **for·giv·er** *n*

forgiving *adj* **1** : willing or able to forgive **2** : allowing room for error or weakness

for·go \fȯr-'gō\ *vb* **-went** \-'went\; **-gone** \-'gȯn\; **-go·ing** : to give up the enjoyment or advantage of : do without

fo·rint \'fȯr-int\ *n, pl* **forints** *also* **forint** — see MONEY table

¹fork \'fȯrk\ *n* **1** : an implement with two or more prongs for taking up (as in eating), pitching, or digging **2** : a forked part, tool, or piece of equipment **3** : a dividing into branches or a place where something branches; *also* : a branch of such a fork

²**fork** *vb* **1** : to divide into two or more branches **2** : to give the form of a fork to ⟨~*ing* her fingers⟩ **3** : to raise or pitch with a fork ⟨~ hay⟩ **4** : PAY, CONTRIBUTE — used with *over, out,* or *up*

forked \'fȯrkt, 'fȯr-kəd\ *adj* : having a fork : shaped like a fork ⟨~ lightning⟩

fork·lift \'fȯrk-ˌlift\ *n* : a machine for lifting heavy objects by means of steel fingers inserted under the load

for·lorn \fər-'lȯrn, fȯr-\ *adj* **1** : sad and lonely because of isolation or desertion **2** : WRETCHED **3** : nearly hopeless — **for·lorn·ly** *adv* — **for·lorn·ness** *n*

¹**form** \'fȯrm\ *n* **1** : SHAPE, STRUCTURE **2** : a body esp. of a person : FIGURE **3** : the essential nature of a thing **4** : established manner of doing or saying something **5** : FORMULA **6** : a document with blank spaces for insertion of information ⟨tax ~⟩ **7** : CEREMONY **8** : manner of performing according to recognized standards **9** : a long seat : BENCH **10** : a model of the human figure used for displaying clothes **11** : MOLD ⟨a ~ for concrete⟩ **12** : type or plates in a frame ready for printing **13** : MODE, KIND, VARIETY ⟨coal is a ~ of carbon⟩ **14** : orderly method of arrangement; *also* : a particular kind or instance of such arrangement ⟨the sonnet ~ in poetry⟩ **15** : the structural element, plan, or design of a work of art **16** : a bounded surface or volume **17** : a grade in a British school or in some American private schools **18** : RACING FORM **19** : known ability to perform; *also* : condition (as of an athlete) suitable for performing **20** : one of the ways in which a word is changed to show difference in use ⟨the plural ~ of a noun⟩ — **form·less** *adj*

²**form** *vb* **1** : to give form or shape to : FASHION, MAKE **2** : TRAIN, INSTRUCT **3** : CONSTITUTE, COMPOSE **4** : DEVELOP, ACQUIRE ⟨~ a habit⟩ **5** : to arrange in order ⟨~ a battle line⟩ **6** : to take form : ARISE ⟨clouds are ~*ing*⟩ **7** : to take a definite form, shape, or arrangement

¹**for·mal** \'fȯr-məl\ *adj* **1** : according with conventional forms and rules ⟨a ~ dinner party⟩ **2** : done in due or lawful form ⟨a ~ contract⟩ **3** : CEREMONIOUS, PRIM ⟨a ~ manner⟩ **4** : NOMINAL — **for·mal·ly** *adv*

²**formal** *n* : something (as a social event) formal in character

form·al·de·hyde \fȯr-'mal-də-ˌhīd\ *n* : a colorless pungent gas used in water solution as a preservative and disinfectant

for·mal·ise *Brit var of* FORMALIZE

for·mal·ism \'fȯr-mə-ˌli-zəm\ *n* : strict adherence to set forms

for·mal·i·ty \fȯr-'ma-lə-tē\ *n, pl* **-ties** **1** : compliance with formal or conventional rules **2** : the quality or state of being formal **3** : an established form that is required or conventional

for·mal·ize \'fȯr-mə-ˌlīz\ *vb* **-ized; -iz·ing** **1** : to give a certain or definite form to **2** : to make formal; *also* : to give formal status or approval to

¹**for·mat** \'fȯr-ˌmat\ *n* **1** : the general composition or style of a publication **2** : the general plan or arrangement of something **3** : a method of organizing data ⟨various file ~s⟩

²**format** *vb* **for·mat·ted; for·mat·ting** : to arrange (as material to be printed) in a particular format — **for·mat·ter** *n*

for·ma·tion \fȯr-'mā-shən\ *n* **1** : an act of giving form to something : DEVELOPMENT **2** : something that is formed **3** : STRUCTURE, SHAPE **4** : an arrangement of persons or things in a prescribed manner or for a certain purpose

for·ma·tive \'fȯr-mə-tiv\ *adj* **1** : giving or capable of giving form : CONSTRUCTIVE **2** : of, relating to, or characterized by important growth or formation ⟨a child's ~ years⟩

for·mer \'fȯr-mər\ *adj* **1** : PREVIOUS, EARLIER **2** : FOREGOING ⟨the ~ part of the chapter⟩ **3** : being first mentioned or in order of two or more things

for·mer·ly \-lē\ *adv* : in time past : PREVIOUSLY

form·fit·ting \'fȯrm-ˌfi-tiŋ\ *adj* : conforming to the outline of the body ⟨a ~ sweater⟩

for·mi·da·ble \'fȯr-mə-də-bəl, fȯr-'mi-\ *adj* **1** : exciting fear, dread, or awe ⟨a ~ foe⟩ **2** : imposing serious difficulties ⟨a ~ barrier⟩ — **for·mi·da·bly** \-blē\ *adv*

form letter *n* **1** : a letter on a frequently recurring topic

that can be sent to different people at different times **2** : a letter for mass circulation sent out in many printed copies

for·mu·la \'fȯr-myə-lə\ *n, pl* **-las** *or* **-lae** \-ˌlē, -ˌlī\ **1** : a set form of words for ceremonial use **2** : RECIPE, PRESCRIPTION **3** : a milk mixture or substitute for a baby **4** : a group of symbols or figures joined to express information concisely **5** : a customary or set form or method

for·mu·late \-ˌlāt\ *vb* **-lat·ed; -lat·ing** **1** : to express in a formula **2** : DESIGN, DEVISE ⟨~ a policy⟩ **3** : to prepare according to a formula — **for·mu·la·tion** \ˌfȯr-myə-'lā-shən\ *n*

for·ni·ca·tion \ˌfȯr-nə-'kā-shən\ *n* : consensual sexual intercourse between two persons not married to each other — **for·ni·cate** \'fȯr-nə-ˌkāt\ *vb* — **for·ni·ca·tor** \-ˌkā-tər\ *n*

for·sake \fər-'sāk, fȯr-\ *vb* **for·sook** \-'suk\; **for·sak·en** \-'sā-kən\; **for·sak·ing** [ME, fr. OE *forsacan*, fr. *sacan* to dispute] : to renounce or turn away from entirely

for·sooth \fər-'süth\ *adv* : in truth : INDEED

for·swear \fȯr-'swer\ *vb* **-swore** \-'swȯr\; **-sworn** \-'swȯrn\; **-swear·ing** **1** : to swear falsely : commit perjury **2** : to renounce earnestly or under oath **3** : to deny under oath

for·syth·ia \fər-'si-thē-ə\ *n, pl* **-ias** *also* **-ia** : any of a genus of shrubs related to the olive and having yellow bell-shaped flowers appearing before the leaves in early spring

¹**fort** \'fȯrt\ *n* [ME *forte*, fr. AF *fort*, fr. *fort* strong, fr. L *fortis*] **1** : a fortified place **2** : a permanent army post

¹**forte** \'fȯrt, 'fȯr-ˌtā\ *n* [F *fort*, fr. *fort,* adj., strong] : one's strong point

²**for·te** \'fȯr-ˌtā\ *adv or adj* [It, fr. *forte* strong] : LOUD — used as a direction in music

forth \'fȯrth\ *adv* **1** : FORWARD, ONWARD ⟨from that day ~⟩ **2** : out into view ⟨plants putting ~ leaves⟩

forth·com·ing \ˌfȯrth-'kə-miŋ\ *adj* **1** : coming or available soon ⟨the ~ holidays⟩ **2** : marked by openness and candor : OUTGOING

forth·right \'fȯrth-ˌrīt\ *adj* : free from ambiguity or evasiveness : going straight to the point ⟨a ~ answer⟩ — **forth·right·ly** *adv* — **forth·right·ness** *n*

forth·with \ˌfȯrth-'with\ *adv* : IMMEDIATELY

for·ti·fy \'fȯr-tə-ˌfī\ *vb* **-fied; -fy·ing** **1** : to strengthen by military defenses **2** : to give physical strength or endurance to **3** : ENCOURAGE **4** : to strengthen or enrich with a material ⟨~ bread with vitamins⟩ — **for·ti·fi·ca·tion** \ˌfȯr-tə-fə-'kā-shən\ *n*

for·tis·si·mo \fȯr-'ti-sə-ˌmō\ *adv or adj* : very loud — used as a direction in music

for·ti·tude \'fȯr-tə-ˌtüd, -ˌtyüd\ *n* : strength of mind that enables one to meet danger or bear pain or adversity with courage ♦ *Synonyms* GRIT, BACKBONE, PLUCK, GUTS

fort·night \'fȯrt-ˌnīt\ *n* [ME *fourtenight,* alter. of *fourtene night* fourteen nights] : two weeks — **fort·night·ly** \-lē\ *adj or adv*

for·tress \'fȯr-trəs\ *n* : FORT 1

for·tu·itous \fȯr-'tü-ə-təs, -'tyü-\ *adj* **1** : happening by chance **2** : FORTUNATE — **for·tu·itous·ly** *adv*

for·tu·ity \-ə-tē\ *n, pl* **-ities** : the quality or state of being fortuitous **2** : a chance event or occurrence

for·tu·nate \'fȯr-chə-nət\ *adj* **1** : bringing some good thing not foreseen **2** : LUCKY

for·tu·nate·ly \-lē\ *adv* **1** : in a fortunate manner **2** : it is fortunate that

for·tune \'fȯr-chən\ *n* **1** : prosperity attained partly through luck; *also* : CHANCE, LUCK **2** : what happens to a person : good or bad luck **3** : FATE, DESTINY **4** : RICHES, WEALTH

fortune hunter *n* : a person who seeks wealth esp. by marriage

for·tune–tell·er \-ˌte-lər\ *n* : a person who professes to foretell future events — **for·tune–tell·ing** *n or adj*

for·ty \'fȯr-tē\ *n, pl* **forties** : four times 10 — **for·ti·eth** \'fȯr-tē-əth\ *adj or n* — **forty** *adj or pron*

for·ty–five \ˌfȯr-tē-'fīv\ *n* **1** : a .45 caliber handgun — usu. written .45 **2** : a phonograph record designed to be played at 45 revolutions per minute — usu. written 45

for·ty–nin·er \-'nī-nər\ *n* : a person in the rush to California for gold in 1849

forty winks *n sing or pl* : a short sleep

fo·rum \'fȯr-əm\ *n, pl* **forums** *also* **fo·ra** \-ə\ [L] **1** : the marketplace or central meeting place of an ancient

Roman city **2** : a medium (as a publication or online service) of open discussion **3** : COURT **4** : a public assembly, lecture, or program involving audience or panel discussion

¹for·ward \'fȯr-wərd\ *adj* **1** : being near or at or belonging to the front **2** : EAGER, READY **3** : BRASH, BOLD **4** : notably advanced or developed : PRECOCIOUS **5** : moving, tending, or leading toward a position in front **6** : EXTREME, RADICAL **7** : of, relating to, or getting ready for the future — **for·ward·ness** *n*

²forward *adv* : to or toward what is ahead or in front

³forward *vb* **1** : to help onward : ADVANCE **2** : to send forward : TRANSMIT **3** : to send or ship onward

⁴forward *n* : a player who plays at the front of a team's offensive formation near the opponent's goal

for·ward·er \-wər-dər\ *n* : one that forwards; *esp* : an agent who forwards goods

for·wards \'fȯr-wərdz\ *adv* : FORWARD

forwent *past of* FORGO

¹fos·sil \'fä-səl\ *adj* [L *fossilis* obtained by digging, fr. *fodere* to dig] **1** : preserved from a past geologic age ⟨~ plants⟩ **2** : of or relating to fossil fuels

²fossil *n* **1** : a trace or impression or the remains of a plant or animal of a past geologic age preserved in the earth's crust **2** : a person whose ideas are out-of-date — **fos·sil·ize** \'fä-sə-ˌlīz\ *vb*

fossil fuel *n* : a fuel (as coal or oil) that is formed in the earth from plant or animal remains

¹fos·ter \'fȯs-tər\ *adj* [ME, fr. OE *fōstor*, fr. *fōstor* food, feeding] : affording, receiving, or sharing nourishment or parental care though not related by blood or legal ties ⟨~ parent⟩ ⟨~ child⟩

²foster *vb* **1** : to give parental care to : NURTURE **2** : to promote the growth or development of : ENCOURAGE

foster home *n* : a household in which an orphaned, neglected, or delinquent child is placed for care

fos·ter·ling \-tər-liŋ\ *n* : a foster child

Fou·cault pendulum \ˌfü-'kō-\ *n* : a device that consists of a heavy weight hung by a long wire and that swings in a constant direction which appears to change showing that the earth rotates

fought *past and past part of* FIGHT

¹foul \'faü(-ə)l\ *adj* **1** : offensive to the senses : LOATHSOME; *also* : clogged with dirt **2** : ODIOUS, DETESTABLE ⟨a ~ crime⟩ **3** : OBSCENE, ABUSIVE ⟨~ language⟩ **4** : DISAGREEABLE, STORMY ⟨~ weather⟩ **5** : TREACHEROUS, DISHONORABLE, UNFAIR **6** : marking the bounds of a playing field ⟨~ lines⟩; *also* : being outside the foul line ⟨~ ball⟩ ⟨~ territory⟩ **7** : containing marked-up corrections **8** : ENTANGLED — **foul·ly** *adv* — **foul·ness** *n*

²foul *n* **1** : an entanglement or collision in fishing or sailing **2** : an infraction of the rules in a game or sport; *also* : a baseball hit outside the foul line

³foul *vb* **1** : to make or become foul or filthy **2** : to entangle or become entangled **3** : OBSTRUCT, BLOCK **4** : to collide with **5** : to make or hit a foul

⁴foul *adv* : in a foul manner

fou·lard \fu-'lärd\ *n* : a lightweight silk of plain or twill weave usu. decorated with a printed pattern

foul-mouthed \'faü(-ə)l-'maüthd, -'maütht\ *adj* : given to the use of obscene, profane, or abusive language

foul of *prep* : AFOUL OF

foul play *n* : VIOLENCE; *esp* : MURDER

foul-up \'faü(-ə)l-ˌəp\ *n* **1** : a state of being fouled up **2** : a mechanical difficulty

foul up *vb* **1** : to spoil by mistakes or poor judgment **2** : to cause a foul-up : BUNGLE

¹found \'faünd\ *past and past part of* FIND

²found *vb* [ME, fr. AF *funder, fonder*, fr. L *fundare*, fr. *fundus* bottom] **1** : to take the first steps in building **2** : to set or ground on something solid : BASE **3** : to establish (as an institution) often with provision for future maintenance — **found·er** *n*

foun·da·tion \faün-'dā-shən\ *n* **1** : the act of founding **2** : a basis upon which something stands or is supported ⟨suspicions without ~⟩ **3** : funds given for the permanent support of an institution : ENDOWMENT; *also* : an institution so endowed **4** : supporting structure : BASE **5** : CORSET — **foun·da·tion·al** \-shə-nəl\ *adj*

foun·der \'faün-dər\ *vb* **1** : to make or become lame ⟨the

horse ~ed⟩ **2** : COLLAPSE **3** : SINK ⟨a ~ing ship⟩ **4** : FAIL

found·ling \'faünd-liŋ\ *n* : an infant found after its unknown parents have abandoned it

found·ry \'faün-drē\ *n, pl* **foundries** : a building or works where metal is cast

fount \'faünt\ *n* : SOURCE, FOUNTAIN

foun·tain \'faün-tⁿn\ *n* **1** : a spring of water **2** : SOURCE **3** : an artificial jet of water **4** : a container for liquid that can be drawn off as needed

foun·tain·head \-ˌhed\ *n* : SOURCE

fountain pen *n* : a pen with a reservoir that feeds the writing point with ink

four \'fȯr\ *n* **1** : one more than three **2** : the 4th in a set or series **3** : something having four units — **four** *adj or pron*

4x4 *also* **four–by–four** \'fȯr-bī-ˌfȯr\ *n* : a four-wheel automobile with four-wheel drive

four–flush \-ˌfləsh\ *vb* : to make a false claim : BLUFF — **four–flush·er** *n*

four·fold \-ˌfōld, -'fōld\ *adj* **1** : being four times as great or as many **2** : having four units or members — **fourfold** \-'fōld\ *adv*

4–H \'fȯr-'āch\ *adj* [fr. the fourfold aim of improving the head, heart, hands, and health] : of or relating to a program set up by the U.S. Department of Agriculture to help young people become productive citizens — **4–H'er** *n*

Four Hundred *or* **400** *n* : the exclusive social set of a community — used with *the*

four–in–hand \'fȯr-ən-ˌhand\ *n* **1** : a team of four horses driven by one person; *also* : a vehicle drawn by such a team **2** : a necktie tied in a slipknot with long ends overlapping vertically in front

four–o'clock \'fȯr-ə-ˌkläk\ *n* : a garden plant with fragrant yellow, red, or white flowers without petals that open late in the afternoon

four–post·er \ˌfȯr-'pō-stər\ *n* : a bed with tall corner posts orig. designed to support curtains or a canopy

four·score \'fȯr-'skȯr\ *adj* : being four times twenty : EIGHTY

four·some \'fȯr-səm\ *n* **1** : a group of four persons or things **2** : a golf match between two pairs of partners

four·square \-'skwer\ *adj* **1** : SQUARE **2** : marked by boldness and conviction : FORTHRIGHT — **foursquare** *adv*

four·teen \fȯr-'tēn\ *n* : one more than 13 — **fourteen** *adj or pron* — **four·teenth** \-'tēnth\ *adj or n*

fourth \'fȯrth\ *n* **1** : one that is number four in a countable series **2** : one of four equal parts of something — **fourth** *adj or adv*

fourth estate *n, often cap F&E* : the public press

fourth wall *n* : an imaginary wall that keeps performers from recognizing or directly addressing their audience

4WD *abbr* four-wheel drive

four–wheel \'fȯr-ˌhwēl\ *or* **four·wheeled** \-ˌhwēld\ *adj* : acting on or by means of four wheels of a motor vehicle ⟨~ disc brakes⟩

four–wheel drive *n* : an automotive drive mechanism that acts on all four wheels of the vehicle; *also* : a vehicle with such a drive

¹fowl \'faü(-ə)l\ *n, pl* **fowl** *or* **fowls** **1** : BIRD **2** : a cock or hen of the domestic chicken; *also* : the flesh of these used as food

²fowl *vb* : to hunt wildfowl

¹fox \'fäks\ *n, pl* **fox·es** *also* **fox** **1** : any of various flesh= eating mammals related to the wolves but smaller and with shorter legs and a more pointed muzzle; *also* : the fur of a fox **2** : a clever crafty person **3** *cap* : a member of an American Indian people formerly living in what is now Wisconsin

²fox *vb* : TRICK, OUTWIT

fox·glove \'fäks-ˌgləv\ *n* : a common plant related to the snapdragons that is grown for its showy spikes of dotted white or purple tubular flowers and as a source of digitalis

fox·hole \-ˌhōl\ *n* : a pit dug for protection against enemy fire

fox·hound \-ˌhaünd\ *n* : any of various large swift powerful hounds used in hunting foxes

fox·ing \'fäk-siŋ\ *n* : brownish spots on old paper

fox terrier *n* : a small lively terrier that occurs in varieties with smooth dense coats or with harsh wiry coats

fox terrier

fox–trot \'fäks-,trät\ *n*   **1** : a short broken slow trotting gait   **2** : a ballroom dance in duple time

foxy \'fäk-sē\ *adj* **fox·i·er; -est**   **1** : resembling or suggestive of a fox   **2** : WILY   **3** : physically attractive

foy·er \'fói(-ə)r, 'fói-,yā\ *n* [F, lit., fireplace, fr. OF *foier*, fr. VL **focarium*, fr. L *focus* hearth] : LOBBY; *also* : an entrance hallway

fpm *abbr* feet per minute

FPO *abbr* fleet post office

fps *abbr* feet per second

fr *abbr*   **1** father   **2** franc   **3** friar   **4** from

¹Fr *abbr*   **1** France; French   **2** Friday

²Fr *symbol* francium

fra·cas \'frā-kəs, 'fra-\ *n, pl* **fra·cas·es** \-kə-səz\ [F, din, row, fr. It *fracasso*, fr. *fracassare* to shatter] : BRAWL

frac·tal \'frak-t³l\ *n* : an irregular curve or shape that repeats itself at any scale on which it is examined — **fractal** *adj*

frac·tion \'frak-shən\ *n*   **1** : a numerical representation (as $\frac{1}{2}$, $\frac{3}{4}$, or 3.323) indicating the quotient of two numbers   **2** : FRAGMENT   **3** : PORTION ⟨a small ∼ of voters⟩ — **frac·tion·al** \-shə-nəl\ *adj* — **frac·tion·al·ly** *adv*

frac·tious \'frak-shəs\ *adj*   **1** : tending to be troublesome : hard to handle or control   **2** : QUARRELSOME, IRRITABLE

frac·ture \'frak-chər\ *n*   **1** : a breaking of something and esp. a bone   **2** : CRACK, CLEFT — **fracture** *vb*

frag·ile \'fra-jəl, -,jī(-ə)l\ *adj* : easily broken : DELICATE — **fra·gil·i·ty** \fra-'ji-lə-tē\ *n*

¹frag·ment \'frag-mənt\ *n* : a part broken off, detached, or incomplete

²frag·ment \-,ment\ *vb* : to break into fragments — **frag·men·ta·tion** \,frag-mən-'tā-shən, -,men-\ *n*

frag·men·tary \'frag-mən-,ter-ē\ *adj* : made up of fragments : INCOMPLETE ⟨a ∼ account⟩

fra·grant \'frā-grənt\ *adj* : having or agreeable in smell — **fra·grance** \-grəns\ *n* — **fra·grant·ly** *adv*

frail \'frāl\ *adj* [ME, fr. AF *fraile*, fr. L *fragilis* fragile, fr. *frangere* to break]   **1** : morally or physically weak   **2** : FRAGILE, DELICATE

frail·ty \'frāl-tē\ *n, pl* **frailties**   **1** : the quality or state of being frail   **2** : a fault due to weakness

¹frame \'frām\ *vb* **framed; fram·ing**   **1** : PLAN, CONTRIVE   **2** : SHAPE, CONSTRUCT   **3** : FORMULATE   **4** : DRAW UP ⟨∼ a constitution⟩   **5** : to make appear guilty   **6** : to fit or adjust for a purpose : ARRANGE   **7** : to provide with or enclose in a frame — **fram·er** *n*

²frame *n*   **1** : something made of parts fitted and joined together   **2** : the physical makeup of the body   **3** : an arrangement of structural parts that gives form or support   **4** : a supporting or enclosing border or open case (as for a window or picture)   **5** : one picture of a series (as on a length of film)   **6** : FRAME-UP

³frame *adj* : having a wood frame ⟨∼ houses⟩

frame of mind *n* : mental attitude or outlook : MOOD

frame–up \'frā-,məp\ *n*   **1** : an act or series of actions in which someone is framed   **2** : an action that is planned, contrived, or formulated

frame·work \'frām-,wərk\ *n* : a basic supporting part or structure

franc \'fraŋk\ *n*   **1** : any of various former basic monetary units (as of Belgium, France, and Luxembourg)   **2** — see MONEY table

fran·chise \'fran-,chīz\ *n* [ME, fr. AF, fr. *franchir* to free, fr. *franc* free]   **1** : a right or license granted to an individual or group ⟨a ∼ to operate a ferry⟩   **2** : a constitutional or statutory right or privilege; *esp* : the right to vote   **3** : the right of membership in a professional sports league; *also* : a team having such membership

fran·chi·see \,fran-,chī-'zē, -chə-\ *n* : one granted a franchise

fran·chis·er \'fran-,chī-zər\ *n*   **1** : FRANCHISEE   **2** : FRANCHISOR

fran·chi·sor \,fran-,chī-'zòr, -chə-\ *n* : one that grants a franchise

fran·ci·um \'fran-sē-əm\ *n* : a radioactive metallic chemical element

Fran·co–Amer·i·can \,fraŋ-kō-ə-'mer-ə-kən\ *n* : an American of French or esp. French-Canadian descent — **Franco–American** *adj*

fran·gi·ble \'fran-jə-bəl\ *adj* : BREAKABLE — **fran·gi·bil·i·ty** \,fran-jə-'bi-lə-tē\ *n*

¹frank \'fraŋk\ *adj* : marked by free, forthright, and sincere expression — **frank·ness** *n*

²frank *vb* : to mark (a piece of mail) with an official sign so that it can be mailed free; *also* : to mail free

³frank *n*   **1** : the signature or mark on a piece of mail indicating free or paid postage   **2** : the privilege of sending mail free

⁴frank *n* : FRANKFURTER

Fran·ken·stein \'fraŋ-kən-,stīn\ *n*   **1** : a monstrous creation that usu. ruins its originator   **2** : a monster in the shape of a man

frank·furt·er \'fraŋk-fər-tər, -,fər-\ *or* **frank·furt** \-fərt\ *n* : a seasoned sausage (as of beef or beef and pork)

frank·in·cense \'fraŋ-kən-,sens\ *n* : a fragrant resin burned as incense

frank·ly \'fraŋ-klē\ *adv*   **1** : in a frank manner   **2** : in truth : INDEED ⟨∼, I don't know⟩

fran·tic \'fran-tik\ *adj* : marked by uncontrolled emotion or disordered anxious activity — **fran·ti·cal·ly** \-ti-k(ə-)lē\ *adv*

frap·pé \fra-'pā\ *or* **frappe** *same or* 'frap\ *n* [F *frappé*, fr. pp. of *frapper* to strike, chill]   **1** : an iced or frozen drink   **2** : a thick milk shake — **frap·pé** \fra-'pā\ *adj*

fra·ter·nal \frə-'tər-n³l\ *adj*   **1** : of, relating to, or involving brothers   **2** : of, relating to, or being a fraternity or society   **3** : derived from two ova ⟨∼ twins⟩   **4** : FRIENDLY, BROTHERLY — **fra·ter·nal·ly** *adv*

fra·ter·ni·ty \frə-'tər-nə-tē\ *n, pl* **-ties**   **1** : a social, honorary, or professional group; *esp* : a men's student organization   **2** : BROTHERLINESS, BROTHERHOOD   **3** : persons of the same class, profession, or tastes

frat·er·nize \'fra-tər-,nīz\ *vb* **-nized; -niz·ing**   **1** : to mingle as friends   **2** : to associate on close terms with members of a hostile group — **frat·er·ni·za·tion** \,fra-tər-nə-'zā-shən\ *n*

frat·ri·cide \'fra-trə-,sīd\ *n*   **1** : one that kills a sibling or countryman   **2** : the act of a fratricide — **frat·ri·cid·al** \,fra-trə-'sī-d³l\ *adj*

fraud \'fród\ *n*   **1** : DECEIT, TRICKERY   **2** : TRICK   **3** : IMPOSTOR, CHEAT

fraud·ster \'fród-stər\ *n, chiefly Brit* : a person who engages in fraud

fraud·u·lent \'fró-jə-lənt\ *adj* : characterized by, based on, or done by fraud : DECEITFUL — **fraud·u·lence** \-ləns\ *n* — **fraud·u·lent·ly** *adv*

fraught \'fród\ *adj* : full of or accompanied by something specified ⟨∼ with danger⟩

¹fray \'frā\ *n* : FIGHT, STRUGGLE; *also* : QUARREL, DISPUTE

²fray *vb*   **1** : to wear (as an edge of cloth) by rubbing   **2** : to separate the threads at the edge of   **3** : STRAIN, IRRITATE ⟨∼ed nerves⟩

fraz·zle \'fra-zəl\ *vb* **fraz·zled; fraz·zling**   **1** : FRAY   **2** : to put in a state of extreme physical or nervous fatigue — **frazzle** *n*

¹freak \'frēk\ *n*   **1** : WHIM, CAPRICE   **2** : a strange, abnormal, or unusual person or thing   **3** *slang* : a person who uses an illicit drug **4** : an ardent enthusiast — **freak·ish** *adj* — **freaky** \'frē-kē\ *adj*

²**freak** *vb* **1** : to experience the effects (as hallucinations) of taking illicit drugs — often used with *out* **2** : to distress or become distressed — often used with *out* — **freak–out** \'frē-ˌkau̇t\ *n*

freck·le \'fre-kəl\ *n* : a small brownish spot on the skin — **freckle** *vb*

¹**free** \'frē\ *adj* **fre·er; fre·est** **1** : having liberty **2** : enjoying political or personal independence; *also* : not subject to or allowing slavery **3** : made or done voluntarily : SPONTANEOUS **4** : relieved from or lacking something unpleasant **5** : not subject to a duty, tax, or charge **6** : not obstructed : CLEAR **7** : not being used or occupied ⟨waved with my ∼ hand⟩ **8** : not fastened ⟨the ∼ end of the rope⟩ **9** : LAVISH **10** : OPEN, FRANK **11** : given without charge **12** : not literal or exact ⟨∼ translation⟩ **13** : not restricted by conventional forms ⟨∼ skating⟩ — **free·ly** *adv*

²**free** *vb* **freed; free·ing** **1** : to set free **2** : RELIEVE, RID **3** : DISENTANGLE, CLEAR ♦ **Synonyms** RELEASE, LIBERATE, DISCHARGE, EMANCIPATE, LOOSE

³**free** *adv* **1** : FREELY **2** : without charge

free·base \'frē-ˌbās\ *n* : purified cocaine smoked as crack or heated to produce vapors for inhalation — **freebase** *vb*

free·bie *or* **free·bee** \'frē-bē\ *n* : something given without charge

free·board \'frē-ˌbȯrd\ *n* : the vertical distance between the waterline and the upper edge of the side of a boat

free·boo·ter \-ˌbü-tər\ *n* [D *vrijbuiter*, fr. *vrijbuit* plunder, fr. *vrij* free + *buit* booty] : PLUNDERER, PIRATE

free-born \-'bȯrn\ *adj* **1** : not born in vassalage or slavery **2** : of, relating to, or befitting one that is freeborn

freed·man \'frēd-mən, -ˌman\ *n* : a person freed from slavery

free·dom \'frē-dəm\ *n* **1** : the quality or state of being free **2** : INDEPENDENCE **2** : EXEMPTION, RELEASE **3** : EASE, FACILITY ⟨spoke the language with ∼⟩ **4** : FRANKNESS **5** : unrestricted use **6** : a political right; *also* : FRANCHISE, PRIVILEGE

freedom fighter *n* : a person who takes part in a resistance movement against an oppressive political or social establishment

free enterprise *n* : freedom of private business to operate with little regulation by the government

free–for–all \'frē-fə-ˌrȯl\ *n* : a competition or fight open to all comers and usu. with no rules : BRAWL — **free–for–all** *adj*

free·hand \-ˌhand\ *adj* : done without mechanical aids or devices

free·hold \'frē-ˌhōld\ *n* : ownership of an estate for life usu. with the right to bequeath it to one's heirs; *also* : an estate thus owned — **free·hold·er** *n*

free·lance \-ˌlans\ *n* : one who pursues a profession (as writing) without a long-term commitment to any one employer — **free·lance** *adj or vb*

free–living \'frē-'li-viŋ\ *adj* **1** : unrestricted in pursuing personal pleasures **2** : being neither parasitic nor symbiotic ⟨∼ organisms⟩

free·load \'frē-ˌlōd\ *vb* : to impose upon another's hospitality — **free·load·er** *n*

free love *n* **1** : the practice of living openly with one of the opposite sex without marriage **2** : sexual relations without any commitments by either partner

free·man \'frē-mən, -ˌman\ *n* **1** : one who has civil or political liberty **2** : one having the full rights of a citizen

Free·ma·son \-ˌmā-sᵊn\ *n* : a member of a secret fraternal society called Free and Accepted Masons — **Free·ma·son·ry** \-rē\ *n*

free radical *n* : an esp. reactive atom or group of atoms with one or more unpaired electrons; *esp* : one that can cause bodily damage (as by altering the chemical structure of cells)

free–range \'frē-ˌrānj\ *adj* : allowed to range and forage with relative freedom ⟨∼ chickens⟩; *also* : produced by free-range animals ⟨∼ eggs⟩

free speech *n* : speech that is protected by the First Amendment to the U.S. Constitution

free spirit *n* : NONCONFORMIST

free·stand·ing \'frē-'stan-diŋ\ *adj* : standing alone or on its own foundation free of support

free·stone \'frē-ˌstōn\ *n* **1** : a stone that may be cut freely without splitting **2** : a fruit stone to which the flesh does not cling; *also* : a fruit (as a peach or cherry) having such a stone

free·think·er \-'thiŋ-kər\ *n* : one who forms opinions on the basis of reason independently of authority; *esp* : one who doubts or denies religious dogma — **free·think·ing** *n or adj*

free trade *n* : trade between nations without restrictions (as high taxes on imports)

free verse *n* : verse whose meter is irregular or whose rhythm is not metrical

free·ware \'frē-ˌwer\ *n* : software that is free or that has a small usu. optional cost

free·way \'frē-ˌwā\ *n* : an expressway without tolls

free·wheel \-'hwēl\ *vb* : to move, live, or play freely or irresponsibly

free·will \'frē-ˌwil\ *adj* : VOLUNTARY

free will *n* : voluntary choice or decision

¹**freeze** \'frēz\ *vb* **froze** \'frōz\; **fro·zen** \'frō-zᵊn\; **freez·ing** **1** : to harden or cause to harden into a solid (as ice) by loss of heat **2** : to withstand freezing **3** : to chill or become chilled with cold **4** : to damage by frost **5** : to adhere solidly by or as if by freezing **6** : to become fixed, motionless, or incapable of speech **7** : to cause to grip tightly **8** : to become clogged with ice **9** : to fix at a certain stage or level ⟨∼ wages⟩

²**freeze** *n* **1** : an act or instance of freezing **2** : the state of being frozen **3** : a state of weather marked by low temperature

freeze–dry \'frēz-ˌdrī\ *vb* : to dry in a frozen state under vacuum esp. for preservation — **freeze–dried** *adj*

freez·er \'frē-zər\ *n* : a compartment, device, or room for freezing food or keeping it frozen

¹**freight** \'frāt\ *n* **1** : payment for carrying goods **2** : CARGO **3** : BURDEN **4** : the carrying of goods by a common carrier **5** : a train that carries freight

²**freight** *vb* **1** : to load with goods for transportation **2** : BURDEN, CHARGE **3** : to ship or transport by freight

freight·er \'frā-tər\ *n* : a ship or airplane used chiefly to carry freight

French \'french\ *n* **1** : the language of France **2** : the people of France **3** : strong language — **French** *adj* — **French·man** \-mən\ *n* — **French·wom·an** \-ˌwu̇-mən\ *n*

French door *n* : a door with small panes of glass extending the full length

French dressing *n* **1** : a thin salad dressing usu. made of vinegar and oil with spices **2** : a creamy salad dressing flavored with tomatoes

french fry *n, often cap 1st F* : a strip of potato fried in deep fat until brown — **french fry** *vb, often cap 1st F*

French horn *n* : a curved brass instrument with a funnel-shaped mouthpiece and a flaring bell

French press *n* : a coffeepot in which ground beans are infused and then pressed by a plunger

French toast *n* : bread dipped in a mixture of eggs and milk and fried at a low heat

French twist *n* : a woman's hairstyle in which the hair is coiled at the rear and secured in place

fre·net·ic \fri-'ne-tik\ *adj* : FRANTIC — **fre·net·i·cal·ly** \-ti-k(ə-)lē\ *adv*

fren·zy \'fren-zē\ *n, pl* **frenzies** **1** : temporary madness or a violently agitated state **2** : intense often disordered activity — **fren·zied** \-zēd\ *adj*

freq *abbr* frequency; frequent; frequently

fre·quen·cy \'frē-kwən-sē\ *n, pl* **-cies** **1** : the fact or condition of occurring frequently **2** : rate of occurrence **3** : the number of cycles per second of an alternating current **4** : the number of waves (as of sound or electromagnetic energy) that pass a fixed point each second

frequency modulation *n* : variation of the frequency of a carrier wave according to another signal; *also* : FM

¹**fre·quent** \frē-'kwent, 'frē-kwənt\ *vb* : to associate with, be in, or resort to habitually — **fre·quent·er** *n*

²**fre·quent** \'frē-kwənt\ *adj* **1** : happening often or at short intervals ⟨making ∼ stops⟩ **2** : HABITUAL ⟨a ∼ visitor⟩ — **fre·quent·ly** *adv*

fre·quent–fli·er \'frē-kwənt-'flī-ər\ *adj* : of, relating to, or being an airline program offering awards for specified numbers of air miles traveled

fres·co \'fres-kō\ *n, pl* **frescoes** [It, fr. *fresco* fresh] : the art of painting on fresh plaster; *also* : a painting done by this method

fresh \'fresh\ *adj* **1** : VIGOROUS, REFRESHED **2** : not stale, sour, or decayed ⟨~ bread⟩ **3** : not faded **4** : not worn or rumpled **5** : not altered by processing (as freezing or canning) **6** : not containing salt **7** : free from taint : PURE **8** : fairly strong : BRISK ⟨~ breeze⟩ **9** : experienced, made, or received newly or anew **10** : ADDITIONAL, ANOTHER ⟨made a ~ start⟩ **11** : ORIGINAL, VIVID ⟨a ~ portrayal⟩ **12** : INEXPERIENCED **13** : newly come or arrived ⟨~ from school⟩ **14** : IMPUDENT — **fresh·ly** *adv* — **fresh·ness** *n*

fresh·en \'fre-shən\ *vb* : to make, grow, or become fresh

fresh·et \'fre-shət\ *n* : an overflowing of a stream (as by heavy rains)

fresh·man \'fresh-mən\ *n* **1** : a 1st-year student **2** : BEGINNER, NEWCOMER

fresh·wa·ter \-ˌwȯ-tər, -ˌwä-\ *n* : water that is not salty — **freshwater** *adj*

¹fret \'fret\ *vb* **fret·ted; fret·ting** [ME, to devour, fret, fr. OE *fretan* to devour] **1** : WEAR, CORRODE; *also* : FRAY **2** : RUB, CHAFE **3** : to make by wearing away **4** : to become irritated : WORRY, VEX **5** : GRATE; *also* : AGITATE

²fret *n* : an irritated or worried state ⟨in a ~ about the interview⟩

³fret *n* : ornamental work esp. of straight lines in symmetrical patterns

⁴fret *n* : one of a series of ridges across the fingerboard of a stringed musical instrument — **fret·ted** *adj*

fret·ful \'fret-fəl\ *adj* : IRRITABLE — **fret·ful·ly** *adv* — **fret·ful·ness** *n*

fret·saw \-ˌsȯ\ *n* : a narrow-bladed handsaw used for cutting curved outlines

fret·work \-ˌwərk\ *n* **1** : decoration consisting of frets **2** : ornamental openwork or work in relief

Fri *abbr* Friday

fri·a·ble \'frī-ə-bəl\ *adj* : easily crumbled or pulverized ⟨~ soil⟩

fri·ar \'frī(-ə)r\ *n* [ME *frere, fryer*, fr. AF *frere, friere*, lit., brother, fr. L *frater*] : a member of a religious order that orig. lived by alms

fri·ary \'frī(-ə)r-ē\ *n, pl* **-ar·ies** : a monastery of friars

¹fric·as·see \'fri-kə-ˌsē, ˌfri-kə-'sē\ *n* : a dish made of meat (as chicken) cut into pieces, stewed in stock, and served in sauce

²fricassee *vb* **-seed; -see·ing** : to cook as a fricassee

fric·tion \'frik-shən\ *n* **1** : the rubbing of one body against another **2** : the force that resists motion between bodies in contact **3** : clash in opinions between persons or groups : DISAGREEMENT — **fric·tion·al** *adj*

friction tape *n* : a usu. cloth adhesive tape impregnated with insulating material and used esp. to protect and insulate electrical conductors

Fri·day \'frī-dē, -(ˌ)dā\ *n* : the sixth day of the week

fridge \'frij\ *n* : REFRIGERATOR

fried·cake \'frīd-ˌkāk\ *n* : DOUGHNUT, CRULLER

fried rice *n* : a dish of boiled or steamed rice that is stir-fried with soy sauce and typically includes egg, meat, and vegetables

friend \'frend\ *n* **1** : one attached to another by respect or affection **2** : ACQUAINTANCE **3** : one who is not hostile **4** : one who supports or favors something ⟨a ~ of art⟩ **5** *cap* : a member of the Society of Friends : QUAKER — **friend·less** *adj* — **friend·li·ness** \-lē-nəs\ *n* — **friend·ly** *adj* — **friend·ship** \-ˌship\ *n*

frieze \'frēz\ *n* : an ornamental often sculptured band extending around something (as a building or room)

frig·ate \'fri-gət\ *n* **1** : a square-rigged warship **2** : a warship smaller than a destroyer

fright \'frīt\ *n* **1** : sudden terror : ALARM **2** : something that is ugly or shocking

fright·en \'frī-t²n\ *vb* **1** : to make afraid **2** : to drive away or out by frightening **3** : to become frightened — **fright·en·ing·ly** *adv*

fright·ful \'frīt-fəl\ *adj* **1** : TERRIFYING **2** : STARTLING **3** : EXTREME ⟨~ thirst⟩ — **fright·ful·ly** *adv* — **fright·ful·ness** *n*

frig·id \'fri-jəd\ *adj* **1** : intensely cold **2** : lacking warmth or ardor : INDIFFERENT **3** : abnormally averse to or un-

able to achieve orgasm during sexual intercourse — used esp. of women — **fri·gid·i·ty** \fri-'ji-də-tē\ *n*

frigid zone *n* : the area or region between the arctic circle and the north pole or between the antarctic circle and the south pole

frill \'fril\ *n* **1** : a gathered, pleated, or ruffled edging **2** : something unessential — **frilly** *adj*

fringe \'frinj\ *n* [ME *frenge*, fr. AF, fr. VL *frimbia, alter. of L *fimbriae* (pl.)] **1** : an ornamental border consisting of short threads or strips hanging from an edge or band **2** : something that resembles a fringe : EDGE ⟨operated on the ~s of the law⟩ **3** : something that is additional or secondary to an activity, process, or subject — **fringe** *vb*

fringe benefit *n* **1** : an employment benefit paid for by an employer without affecting basic wage rates **2** : any additional benefit

frip·pery \'fri-pə-rē\ *n, pl* **-per·ies** [MF *friperie*] **1** : FINERY **2** : pretentious display

frisk \'frisk\ *vb* **1** : to leap, skip, or dance in a lively or playful way : GAMBOL **2** : to search (a person) esp. for concealed weapons by running the hand rapidly over the clothing

frisky \'fris-kē\ *adj* **frisk·i·er; -est** : PLAYFUL — **frisk·i·ly** \-kə-lē\ *adv* — **frisk·i·ness** \-kē-nəs\ *n*

¹frit·ter \'fri-tər\ *n* : a small lump of fried batter often containing fruit or meat

²fritter *vb* **1** : to reduce or waste piecemeal **2** : to break into small fragments

fritz \'frits\ *n* : a state of disorder or disrepair — used in the phrase *on the fritz*

friv·o·lous \'fri-və-ləs\ *adj* **1** : of little importance : TRIVIAL **2** : lacking in seriousness — **fri·vol·i·ty** \fri-'vä-lə-tē\ *n* — **friv·o·lous·ly** *adv*

frizz \'friz\ *vb* : to form into small tight curls — **frizz** *n* — **frizzy** *adj*

friz·zies \'fri-zēz\ *n pl* : hair which has become difficult to manage (as due to humidity)

¹friz·zle \'fri-zəl\ *vb* **friz·zled; friz·zling** : FRIZZ, CURL — **frizzle** *n*

²frizzle *vb* **friz·zled; friz·zling** **1** : to fry until crisp and curled **2** : to cook with a sizzling noise

fro \'frō\ *adv* : BACK, AWAY — used in the phrase *to and fro*

frock \'fräk\ *n* **1** : an outer garment worn by monks and friars **2** : an outer garment worn esp. by men **3** : a woman's or girl's dress

frock coat *n* : a man's knee-length usu. double-breasted coat

frog \'frȯg, 'fräg\ *n* **1** : any of various largely aquatic smooth-skinned tailless leaping amphibians **2** : an ornamental braiding for fastening the front of a garment by a loop through which a button passes **3** : a condition in the throat causing hoarseness **4** : a small holder (as of metal, glass, or plastic) with perforations or spikes that is placed in a bowl or vase to keep cut flowers in position

frog 2

frog·man \'frȯg-ˌman, 'fräg-, -mən\ *n* : a swimmer equipped to work underwater for long periods of time

¹frol·ic \'frä-lik\ *vb* **frol·icked; frol·ick·ing** **1** : to make merry **2** : to play about happily : ROMP

²frolic *n* **1** : a playful or mischievous action **2** : FUN, MERRIMENT — **frol·ic·some** \-səm\ *adj*

from \'frəm, 'främ\ *prep* **1** — used to show a starting point ⟨a letter ~ home⟩ **2** — used to show removal or separation ⟨subtract 3 ~ 9⟩ **3** — used to show a material, source, or cause ⟨suffering ~ a cold⟩

frond \'fränd\ *n* : a usu. large divided leaf esp. of a fern or palm tree

¹front \'frənt\ *n* **1** : FOREHEAD; *also* : the whole face **2** : external and often feigned appearance **3** : a region of active fighting; *also* : a sphere of activity **4** : a political coalition **5** : the side of a building containing the main entrance **6** : the forward part or surface **7** : FRONTAGE **8** : a boundary between two dissimilar air masses **9** : a position directly before or ahead of something else **10** : a person, group, or thing used to mask the identity of the actual controlling agent

²**front** *vb* **1** : to have the principal side adjacent to something **2** : to serve as a front **3** : CONFRONT

front-age \'frən-tij\ *n* **1** : a piece of land lying adjacent (as to a street or the ocean) **2** : the length of a frontage **3** : the front side of a building

front-al \'frən-t°l\ *adj* **1** : of, relating to, or next to the forehead **2** : of, relating to, or directed at the front ⟨a ~ attack⟩ — **fron-tal-ly** *adv*

fron-tier \‚frən-'tir\ *n* **1** : a border between two countries **2** : a region that forms the margin of settled territory **3** : the outer limits of knowledge or achievement ⟨the ~s of science⟩ — **fron-tiers-man** \-'tirz-mən\ *n*

fron-tis-piece \'frən-tə‚spēs\ *n* : an illustration preceding and usu. facing the title page of a book

front man *n* : a person serving as a front or figurehead

front-ward \'frənt-wərd\ *or* **front-wards** \-wərdz\ *adv or adj* : toward the front

¹**frost** \'frȯst\ *n* **1** : freezing temperature **2** : a covering of tiny ice crystals on a cold surface — **frosty** *adj*

²**frost** *vb* **1** : to cover with frost **2** : to put icing on (as a cake) **3** : to produce a slightly roughened surface on (as glass) **4** : to injure or kill by frost

¹**frost-bite** \'frȯst-‚bīt\ *vb* **-bit** \-‚bit\; **-bit-ten** \-‚bi-t°n\; **-bit-ing** : to injure by frost or frostbite

²**frostbite** *n* : the freezing or the local effect of a partial freezing of some part of the body

frost heave *n* : an upthrust of pavement caused by freezing of moist soil

frost-ing \'frȯs-tiŋ\ *n* **1** : ICING **2** : dull finish on metal or glass

froth \'frȯth\ *n, pl* **froths** \'frȯths, 'frȯthz\ [ME, fr. ON *frotha*] **1** : bubbles formed in or on a liquid **2** : something light or worthless — **frothy** *adj*

frou-frou \'frü-‚frü\ *n* [F] **1** : a rustling esp. of a woman's skirts **2** : showy or frilly ornamentation

fro-ward \'frō-wərd\ *adj* : DISOBEDIENT, WILLFUL

frown \'fraún\ *vb* **1** : to wrinkle the forehead (as in displeasure or thought) **2** : to look with disapproval **3** : to express with a frown — **frown** *n*

frow-sy *or* **frow-zy** \'fraú-zē\ *adj* **frow-si-er** *or* **frow-zi-er**; **-est** : having a slovenly or uncared-for appearance

froze *past of* FREEZE

fro-zen \'frō-z°n\ *adj* **1** : treated, affected, or crusted over by freezing **2** : subject to long and severe cold **3** : incapable of being changed, moved, or undone : FIXED ⟨~ wages⟩ **4** : not available for present use ⟨~ capital⟩ **5** : expressing or characterized by cold unfriendliness

FRS *abbr* Federal Reserve System

frt *abbr* freight

fruc-ti-fy \'frək-tə-‚fī, 'frúk-\ *vb* **-fied; -fy-ing** **1** : to bear fruit **2** : to make fruitful or productive

fruc-tose \'frək-‚tōs, 'frúk-\ *n* : a very sweet soluble sugar that occurs esp. in fruit juices and honey

fru-gal \'frü-gəl\ *adj* : ECONOMICAL, THRIFTY — **fru-gal-i-ty** \frü-'ga-lə-tē\ *n* — **fru-gal-ly** *adv*

¹**fruit** \'früt\ *n* [ME, fr. AF *fruit, fruit,* fr. L *fructus* fruit, use, fr. *frui* to enjoy, have the use of] **1** : a product of plant growth; *esp* : a usu. edible and sweet reproductive body (as a strawberry or apple) of a seed plant **2** : a product of fertilization in a plant; *esp* : the ripe ovary of a seed plant with its contents and appendages **3** : CONSEQUENCE, RESULT — **fruit-ed** \'frü-təd\ *adj*

²**fruit** *vb* : to bear or cause to bear fruit

fruit-cake \'früt-‚kāk\ *n* : a rich cake containing nuts, dried or candied fruits, and spices

fruit fly *n* : any of various small dipteran flies whose larvae feed on fruit or decaying vegetable matter

fruit-ful \'früt-fəl\ *adj* **1** : yielding or producing fruit **2** : very productive; *also* : bringing results ⟨a ~ idea⟩ — **fruit-ful-ly** *adv* — **fruit-ful-ness** *n*

fru-ition \frü-'i-shən\ *n* **1** : ENJOYMENT **2** : the state of bearing fruit **3** : REALIZATION, ACCOMPLISHMENT ⟨guided the project to ~⟩

fruit-less \'früt-ləs\ *adj* **1** : not bearing fruit **2** : UNSUCCESSFUL ⟨a ~ attempt⟩ — **fruit-less-ly** *adv*

fruity \'frü-tē\ *adj* **fruit-i-er; -est** : resembling a fruit esp. in flavor

frumpy \'frəm-pē\ *adj* **frump-i-er; -est** : DOWDY, DRAB

frus-trate \'frəs-‚trāt\ *vb* **frus-trat-ed; frus-trat-ing** **1** : to balk or defeat in an endeavor **2** : to induce feelings of insecurity, discouragement, or dissatisfaction in **3** : to bring to nothing — **frus-trat-ing-ly** *adv* — **frus-tra-tion** \‚frəs-'trā-shən\ *n*

frus-tum \'frəs-təm\ *n, pl* **frustums** *or* **frus-ta** \-tə\ : the part of a cone or pyramid formed by cutting off the top by a plane parallel to the base

¹**fry** \'frī\ *vb* **fried; fry-ing** [ME *frien,* fr. AF *frire,* fr. L *frigere* to roast] **1** : to cook in a pan or on a griddle over heat esp. with the use of fat **2** : to undergo frying **3** : to damage or destroy by overheating esp. by high voltage

²**fry** *n, pl* **fries** **1** : a social gathering where fried food is eaten **2** : a dish of something fried; *esp, pl* : FRENCH FRIES

³**fry** *n, pl* **fry** [ME, fr. AF *frie,* fr. *freier, frier* to rub, spawn, fr. L *fricare* to rub] **1** : recently hatched fishes; *also* : very small adult fishes **2** : members of a group or class ⟨small ~⟩

fry-er \'frī-(ə)r\ *n* **1** : something (as a young chicken) suitable for frying **2** : a deep utensil for frying foods

FSLIC *abbr* Federal Savings and Loan Insurance Corporation

ft *abbr* **1** feet; foot **2** fort

FTC *abbr* Federal Trade Commission

FTP \‚ef-‚tē-'pē\ *n* [*file transfer protocol*] : a system for transferring computer files esp. via the Internet — **FTP** *vb*

fuch-sia \'fyü-shə\ *n* **1** : any of a genus of shrubs related to the evening primrose and grown for their showy nodding often red or purple flowers **2** : a vivid reddish purple color

fud-dle \'fə-d°l\ *vb* **fud-dled; fud-dling** : MUDDLE, CONFUSE

fud-dy–dud-dy \'fə-dē-‚də-dē\ *n, pl* **-dies** : one that is old-fashioned, unimaginative, or conservative

¹**fudge** \'fəj\ *vb* **fudged; fudg-ing** **1** : to exceed the proper bounds of something **2** : CHEAT; *also* : FALSIFY **3** : to fail to come to grips with

²**fudge** *n* **1** : NONSENSE **2** : a soft candy of milk, sugar, butter, and flavoring

¹**fu-el** \'fyü-əl, 'fyül\ *n* : a material used to produce heat or power by burning; *also* : a material from which nuclear energy can be liberated

²**fuel** *vb* **-eled** *or* **-elled; -el-ing** *or* **-el-ling** : to provide with or take in fuel

fuel cell *n* : a device that continuously changes the chemical energy of a fuel directly into electrical energy

fuel injection *n* : a system for injecting a precise amount of atomized fuel into an internal combustion engine — **fuel–in-ject-ed** \'fyül-in-'jek-təd\ *adj*

¹**fu-gi-tive** \'fyü-jə-tiv\ *adj* **1** : running away or trying to escape **2** : likely to vanish suddenly : not fixed or lasting

²**fugitive** *n* **1** : one who flees or tries to escape **2** : something elusive or hard to find

fugue \'fyüg\ *n* **1** : a musical composition in which different parts successively repeat the theme **2** : a disturbed state of consciousness characterized by acts that are not recalled upon recovery

füh-rer *or* **fueh-rer** \'fyúr-ər, 'fir-\ *n* [G] : LEADER; *esp* : TYRANT

¹**-ful** \fəl\ *adj suffix, sometimes* **-ful-er**; *sometimes* **-ful-lest** **1** : full of ⟨pride*ful*⟩ **2** : characterized by ⟨peace*ful*⟩ **3** : having the qualities of ⟨master*ful*⟩ **4** : tending, given, or liable to ⟨help*ful*⟩

²**-ful** \‚fúl\ *n suffix* : number or quantity that fills or would fill ⟨room*ful*⟩

ful-crum \'fúl-krəm, 'fəl-\ *n, pl* **ful-crums** *or* **ful-cra** \-krə\ [LL, fr. L *fulcire,* L bedpost] : the support on which a lever turns

ful-fill *or* **ful-fil** \fúl-'fil\ *vb* **ful-filled; ful-fill-ing** **1** : to put into effect **2** : to bring to an end **3** : SATISFY — **ful-fill-ment** *or* **ful-fil-ment** *n*

¹**full** \'fúl\ *adj* **1** : FILLED **2** : complete esp. in detail, number, or duration **3** : having all the distinguishing characteristics ⟨a ~ member⟩ **4** : MAXIMUM ⟨~ strength⟩ **5** : rounded in outline ⟨a ~ figure⟩ **6** : possessing or containing an abundance ⟨~ of wrinkles⟩ **7** : having an abundance of material ⟨~ skirt⟩ **8** : satisfied esp. with

food or drink **9** : having volume or depth of sound **10** : completely occupied with a thought or plan — **full·ness** *also* **ful·ness** *n*

²**full** *adv* **1** : VERY, EXTREMELY **2** : ENTIRELY ⟨fill a glass ∼⟩ **3** : STRAIGHT, SQUARELY ⟨hit him ∼ in the face⟩

³**full** *n* **1** : the highest or fullest state or degree **2** : the utmost extent — **in full** : to the requisite or complete amount

⁴**full** *vb* : to shrink and thicken (woolen cloth) by moistening, heating, and pressing — **full·er** *n*

full·back \'ful-ˌbak\ *n* : a football back stationed between the halfbacks

full–blood·ed \'ful-'blə-dəd\ *adj* : of unmixed ancestry : PUREBRED

full–blown \-'blōn\ *adj* **1** : being at the height of bloom **2** : fully mature or developed

full–bod·ied \-'bä-dēd\ *adj* : marked by richness and fullness

full dress *n* : the style of dress worn for ceremonial or formal occasions

full–fledged \'ful-'flejd\ *adj* **1** : fully developed **2** : having attained complete status ⟨a ∼ lawyer⟩

full house *n* : a poker hand containing three of a kind and a pair

full moon *n* : the moon with its whole disk illuminated

full–on \-,ón, -,än\ *adj* : COMPLETE, FULL-FLEDGED

full–scale \'ful-'skäl\ *adj* **1** : identical to an original in proportion and size ⟨∼ drawing⟩ **2** : involving full use of available resources ⟨a ∼ revolt⟩

full–term \-,tərm\ *adj* : retained in the uterus for the normal period of gestation before birth ⟨a ∼ baby⟩

full tilt *adv* : at high speed

full–time \'ful-'tīm\ *adj or adv* : involving or working a normal or standard schedule

ful·ly \'fú-lē\ *adv* **1** : in a full manner or degree : COMPLETELY **2** : at least ⟨∼ nine tenths of us⟩

ful·mi·nate \'fúl-mə-ˌnāt, 'fəl-\ *vb* **-nat·ed; -nat·ing** [ME, fr. ML *fulminatus*, pp. of *fulminare*, fr. L, to strike (of lightning), fr. *fulmen* lightning] : to utter or send out censure or invective : condemn severely — **ful·mi·na·tion** \ˌfúl-mə-'nā-shən, ˌfəl-\ *n*

ful·some \'fúl-səm\ *adj* **1** : COPIOUS, ABUNDANT ⟨∼ detail⟩ **2** : generous in amount or extent ⟨a ∼ victory⟩ **3** : excessively flattering ⟨∼ praise⟩

fu·ma·role \'fyü-mə-ˌrōl\ *n* : a hole in a volcanic region from which hot gases issue

fum·ble \'fəm-bəl\ *vb* **fum·bled; fum·bling 1** : to grope about clumsily **2** : to fail to hold, catch, or handle properly — **fumble** *n*

¹**fume** \'fyüm\ *n* : a usu. irritating smoke, vapor, or gas

²**fume** *vb* **fumed; fum·ing 1** : to treat with fumes **2** : to give off fumes **3** : to express anger or annoyance

fu·mi·gant \'fyü-mi-gənt\ *n* : a substance used for fumigation

fu·mi·gate \'fyü-mə-ˌgāt\ *vb* **-gat·ed; -gat·ing** : to treat with fumes to disinfect or destroy pests — **fu·mi·ga·tion** \ˌfyü-mə-'gā-shən\ *n* — **fu·mi·ga·tor** \'fyü-mə-ˌgā-tər\ *n*

¹**fun** \'fən\ *n* [E dial. *fun* to hoax] **1** : something that provides amusement or enjoyment **2** : ENJOYMENT

²**fun** *adj* : full of fun ⟨a ∼ person⟩ ⟨had a ∼ time⟩

¹**func·tion** \'fəŋk-shən\ *n* **1** : OCCUPATION **2** : special purpose **3** : the particular purpose for which a person or thing is specially fitted or used or for which a thing exists ⟨the ∼ of a hammer⟩; *also* : the natural or proper action of a bodily part in a living thing ⟨the ∼ of the heart⟩ **4** : a formal ceremony or social affair **5** : a mathematical relationship that assigns to each element of a set one and only one element of the same or another set **6** : a variable (as a quality, trait, or measurement) that depends on and varies with another ⟨height is a ∼ of age in children⟩ **7** : a computer subroutine that performs a calculation with variables provided by a program — **func·tion·al** \-shə-nəl\ *adj* — **func·tion·al·ly** *adv*

²**function** *vb* : to have or carry on a function

func·tion·ary \'fəŋk-shə-ˌner-ē\ *n, pl* **-ar·ies** : one who performs a certain function; *esp* : OFFICIAL

function word *n* : a word (as a preposition, auxiliary verb, or conjunction) expressing the grammatical relationship between other words

¹**fund** \'fənd\ *n* [L *fundus* bottom, country estate] **1** : a sum of money or resources intended for a special purpose **2** : STORE, SUPPLY **3** *pl* : available money **4** : an organization administering a special fund

²**fund** *vb* **1** : to provide funds for **2** : to convert (a short= term obligation) into a long-term interest-bearing debt — **fund·er** *n*

fun·da·men·tal \ˌfən-də-'men-t⁰l\ *adj* **1** : serving as an origin : PRIMARY **2** : BASIC, ESSENTIAL **3** : RADICAL ⟨∼ change⟩ **4** : of central importance : PRINCIPAL ⟨∼ purpose⟩ — **fundamental** *n* — **fun·da·men·tal·ly** *adv*

fun·da·men·tal·ism \-tə-ˌli-zəm\ *n* **1** *often cap* : a Protestant religious movement emphasizing the literal infallibility of the Bible **2** : a movement or attitude stressing strict adherence to a set of basic principles — **fun·da·men·tal·ist** \-list\ *adj or n*

¹**fu·ner·al** \'fyü-nə-rəl\ *adj* **1** : of, relating to, or constituting a funeral **2** : FUNEREAL 2

²**funeral** *n* : the ceremonies held for a dead person usu. before burial

fu·ner·ary \'fyü-nə-ˌrer-ē\ *adj* : of, used for, or associated with burial

fu·ne·re·al \fyú-'nir-ē-əl\ *adj* **1** : of or relating to a funeral **2** : suggesting a funeral

fun·gi·cide \'fən-jə-ˌsīd, 'fəŋ-gə-\ *n* : an agent that kills or checks the growth of fungi — **fun·gi·cid·al** \ˌfən-jə-'sī-d⁰l, ˌfəŋ-gə-\ *adj*

fun·gus \'fəŋ-gəs\ *n, pl* **fun·gi** \'fən-ˌjī, 'fəŋ-ˌgī\ *also* **fun·gus·es** \'fəŋ-gə-səz\ : any of a kingdom of parasitic spore-producing organisms (as molds, mildews, and mushrooms) formerly classified as plants — **fun·gal** \-gəl\ *adj* — **fun·gous** \-gəs\ *adj*

fu·nic·u·lar \fyú-'ni-kyə-lər, fə-\ *n* : a cable railway ascending a mountain

¹**funk** \'fəŋk\ *n* : a strong offensive smell

²**funk** *n* : a depressed state of mind

funky \'fəŋ-kē\ *adj* **funk·i·er; -est 1** : having an earthy unsophisticated style and feeling; *esp* : having the style and feeling of older black American music **2** : odd or quaint in appearance or style — **funk·i·ness** *n*

¹**fun·nel** \'fə-n⁰l\ *n* **1** : a cone-shaped utensil with a tube used for catching and directing a downward flow (as of liquid) **2** : FLUE, SMOKESTACK

²**funnel** *vb* **-neled** *also* **-nelled; -nel·ing** *also* **-nel·ling 1** : to pass through or as if through a funnel **2** : to move to a central point or into a central channel

fun·nies \'fə-nēz\ *n pl* : a comic strip or a comic section (as of a newspaper) — used with *the*

fun·ny \'fə-nē\ *adj* **fun·ni·er; -est 1** : AMUSING **2** : FACETIOUS **3** : PECULIAR **3 4** : UNDERHANDED — **funny** *adv*

funny bone *n* : a place at the back of the elbow where a blow easily compresses a nerve and causes a painful tingling sensation

fun·plex \'fən-ˌpleks\ *n* : a center containing various entertainment facilities

¹**fur** \'fər\ *n* **1** : an article of clothing made of or with fur **2** : the hairy coat of a mammal esp. when fine, soft, and thick; *also* : this coat dressed for use — **fur** *adj* — **furred** \'fərd\ *adj*

²**fur** *abbr* furlong

fur·be·low \'fər-bə-ˌlō\ *n* **1** : FLOUNCE, RUFFLE **2** : showy trimming

fur·bish \'fər-bish\ *vb* **1** : to make lustrous : POLISH **2** : to give a new look to : RENOVATE

fu·ri·ous \'fyúr-ē-əs\ *adj* **1** : FIERCE, ANGRY, VIOLENT **2** : BOISTEROUS **3** : INTENSE ⟨∼ growth⟩ — **fu·ri·ous·ly** *adv*

furl \'fərl\ *vb* **1** : to wrap or roll (as a sail or a flag) close to or around something **2** : to curl in furls — **furl** *n*

fur·long \'fər-ˌlón\ *n* [ME, fr. OE *furlang*, fr. *furh* furrow + *lang* long] : a unit of distance equal to 220 yards (about 201 meters)

fur·lough \'fər-lō\ *n* [D *verlof*, lit., permission] : a leave of absence from duty granted esp. to a soldier — **furlough** *vb*

fur·nace \'fər-nəs\ *n* : an enclosed structure in which heat is produced

fur·nish \'fər-nish\ *vb* **1** : to provide with what is needed : EQUIP **2** : SUPPLY, GIVE ⟨∼ed them with food⟩

fur·nish·ings \-ni-shiŋz\ *n pl* **1** : articles or accessories of dress **2** : FURNITURE

fur·ni·ture \'fər-ni-chər\ *n* : equipment that is necessary or desirable; *esp* : movable articles (as chairs or beds) for a room

fu·ror \\'fyur-ˌȯr\ *n* **1** : ANGER, RAGE **2** : a contagious excitement; *esp* : a fashionable craze **3** : UPROAR

fu·rore \\-ˌȯr\ *n* [It] : FUROR 2, 3

fur·ri·er \\'fǝr-ē-ǝr\ *n* : one who prepares or deals in fur

fur·ring \\'fǝr-iŋ\ *n* : wood or metal strips applied to a wall or ceiling to form a level surface or an air space

fur·row \\'fǝr-ō\ *n* **1** : a trench in the earth made by a plow **2** : a narrow groove or wrinkle — **furrow** *vb*

fur·ry \\'fǝr-ē\ *adj* **fur·ri·er; -est** **1** : resembling or consisting of fur **2** : covered with fur

¹fur·ther \\'fǝr-thǝr\ *adv* **1** : FARTHER 1 **2** : in addition : MOREOVER **3** : to a greater extent or degree

²further *vb* : to help forward — **fur·ther·ance** \\'fǝr-thǝ-rǝns\ *n*

³further *adj* **1** : FARTHER 1 **2** : ADDITIONAL ⟨~ education⟩

fur·ther·more \\'fǝr-thǝr-ˌmȯr\ *adv* : in addition to what precedes : BESIDES

fur·ther·most \\-ˌmōst\ *adj* : most distant : FARTHEST

fur·thest \\'fǝr-thǝst\ *adv or adj* : FARTHEST

fur·tive \\'fǝr-tiv\ *adj* [F or L; F *furtif*, fr. L *furtivus*, fr. *furtum* theft, fr. *fur* thief] : done by stealth : SLY — **fur·tive·ly** *adv* — **fur·tive·ness** *n*

fu·ry \\'fyur-ē\ *n, pl* **furies** **1** : intense and often destructive rage **2** : extreme fierceness or violence **3** : FRENZY

furze \\'fǝrz\ *n* : GORSE

¹fuse \\'fyüz\ *vb* **fused; fus·ing** **1** : MELT **2** : to unite by or as if by melting together — **fus·ible** *adj*

²fuse *n* : an electrical safety device having a metal wire or strip that melts and interrupts the circuit when the current becomes too strong

³fuse *n* **1** : a cord or cable that is set afire to ignite an explosive charge **2** *usu* **fuze** : a mechanical or electrical device for setting off the explosive charge of a projectile, bomb, or torpedo

⁴fuse *also* **fuze** \\'fyüz\ *vb* **fused** *also* **fuzed; fus·ing** *also* **fuz·ing** : to equip with a fuse

fu·se·lage \\'fyü-sǝ-ˌläzh, -zǝ-\ *n* : the central body portion of an aircraft

fu·sil·lade \\'fyü-sǝ-ˌläd, -ˌlād\ *n* : a number of shots fired simultaneously or in rapid succession

fu·sion \\'fyü-zhǝn\ *n* **1** : the act or process of melting or making plastic by heat **2** : union by or as if by melting **3** : the union of light atomic nuclei to form heavier nuclei with the release of huge quantities of energy

¹fuss \\'fǝs\ *n* **1** : needless bustle or excitement : COMMOTION **2** : effusive praise **3** : a state of agitation **4** : OBJECTION, PROTEST **5** : DISPUTE

²fuss *vb* : to make a fuss

fuss·bud·get \\'fǝs-ˌbǝ-jǝt\ *n* : one who fusses or is fussy about trifles

fussy \\'fǝ-sē\ *adj* **fuss·i·er; -est** **1** : IRRITABLE **2** : overly decorative ⟨a ~ wallpaper pattern⟩ **3** : requiring or giving close attention or concern to details or niceties — **fuss·i·ly** \\-sǝ-lē\ *adv* — **fuss·i·ness** \\-sē-nǝs\ *n*

fus·tian \\'fǝs-chǝn\ *n* **1** : a strong usu. cotton fabric **2** : pretentious writing or speech — **fustian** *adj*

fus·ty \\'fǝs-tē\ *adj* **fus·ti·er; -est** [prob. alter. of ME *foisted, foist* musty, fr. *foist* wine cask, fr. AF *fust, fuist* wood, tree trunk, cask] **1** : MUSTY **2** : OLD-FASHIONED

fut *abbr* future

fu·tile \\'fyü-tᵊl, 'fyü-ˌtī(-ǝ)l\ *adj* **1** : USELESS, VAIN **2** : FRIVOLOUS, TRIVIAL — **fu·tile·ly** *adv* — **fu·til·i·ty** \\fyü-'ti-lǝ-tē\ *n*

fu·ton \\'fü-ˌtän\ *n* [Jp] : a usu. cotton-filled mattress used on the floor or in a frame as a bed, couch, or chair

¹fu·ture \\'fyü-chǝr\ *adj* **1** : of, relating to, or constituting a verb tense that expresses time yet to come **2** : coming after the present

²future *n* **1** : time that is to come **2** : what is going to happen **3** : an expectation of advancement or progressive development **4** : the future tense; *also* : a verb form in it

fu·tur·ism \\'fyü-chǝ-ˌri-zǝm\ *n* : a modern movement in art, music, and literature that tries esp. to express the energy and activity of mechanical processes — **fu·tur·ist** \\'fyü-chǝ-rist\ *n*

fu·tur·is·tic \\ˌfyü-chǝ-'ris-tik\ *adj* : of or relating to the future or to futurism; *also* : very modern

fu·tu·ri·ty \\fyü-'tùr-ǝ-tē, -'tyùr-\ *n, pl* **-ties** **1** : FUTURE **2** : the quality or state of being future **3** *pl* : future events or prospects

fuze *var of* FUSE

fuzz \\'fǝz\ *n* : fine light particles or fibers (as of down or fluff)

fuzzy \\'fǝ-zē\ *adj* **fuzz·i·er; -est** **1** : having or resembling fuzz **2** : INDISTINCT ⟨~ photos⟩ **3** : being or relating to pleasant usu. sentimental emotions ⟨~ feelings⟩ — **fuzz·i·ness** \\-zē-nǝs\ *n*

fuzzy logic *n* : a system of logic in which a statement can be true, false, or any of a continuum of values in between

fwd *abbr* forward

FWD *abbr* front-wheel drive

FY *abbr* fiscal year

-fy *vb suffix* : make : form into ⟨dandi*fy*⟩

FYI *abbr* for your information

¹g \\'jē\ *n, pl* **g's** *or* **gs** \\'jēz\ *often cap* **1** : the 7th letter of the English alphabet **2** : a unit of force equal to the force exerted by gravity on a body at rest and used to indicate the force to which a body is subjected when accelerated **3** *slang* : a sum of $1000

²g *abbr, often cap* **1** game **2** gauge **3** good **4** gram **5** gravity

ga *abbr* gauge

¹Ga *abbr* Georgia

²Ga *symbol* gallium

GA *abbr* **1** general assembly **2** general average **3** general of the army **4** Georgia

gab \\'gab\ *vb* **gabbed; gab·bing** : to talk in a rapid or thoughtless manner : CHATTER — **gab** *n*

gab·ar·dine \\'ga-bǝr-ˌdēn\ *n* **1** : GABERDINE 1 **2** : a firm durable twilled fabric having diagonal ribs and made of various fibers; *also* : a garment of gabardine

gab·ble \\'ga-bǝl\ *vb* **gab·bled; gab·bling** : JABBER, BABBLE

gab·by \\'ga-bē\ *adj* **gab·bi·er; -est** : TALKATIVE, GARRULOUS

gab·er·dine \\'ga-bǝr-ˌdēn\ *n* **1** : a long loose outer garment worn in medieval times and associated esp. with Jews **2** : GABARDINE 2

gab·fest \\'gab-ˌfest\ *n* **1** : an informal gathering for general talk **2** : an extended conversation

ga·ble \\'gā-bǝl\ *n* : the vertical triangular end of a building formed by the sides of the roof sloping from the ridge down to the eaves — **ga·bled** \\-bǝld\ *adj*

gad \\'gad\ *vb* **gad·ded; gad·ding** : to be constantly active without specific purpose — usu. used with *about* — **gad·der** *n*

gad·about \\'ga-dǝ-ˌbaùt\ *n* : a person who flits about in social activity

gad·fly \\'gad-ˌflī\ *n* **1** : a fly that bites or harasses livestock **2** : a person who annoys esp. by persistent criticism

gad·get \\'ga-jǝt\ *n* : DEVICE, CONTRIVANCE — **gad·get·ry** \\'ga-jǝ-trē\ *n*

gad·o·lin·i·um \\ˌga-dǝ-'li-nē-ǝm\ *n* : a magnetic metallic chemical element

¹Gael \\'gāl\ *n* : a Celtic inhabitant of Ireland or Scotland

²Gael *abbr* Gaelic

Gael·ic \\'gā-lik\ *adj* : of or relating to the Gaels or their languages — **Gaelic** *n*

gaff \'gaf\ *n* **1** : a spear used in taking fish or turtles; *also* : a metal hook for holding or lifting heavy fish **2** : the spar supporting the top of a fore-and-aft sail **3** : rough treatment : ABUSE — **gaff** *vb*

gaffe \'gaf\ *n* : a usu. social blunder

gaf·fer \'ga-fər\ *n* **1** : an old man **2** : a lighting electrician on a motion-picture or television set

¹gag \'gag\ *vb* **gagged; gag·ging 1** : to restrict use of the mouth of with a gag **2** : to prevent from speaking freely **3** : to retch or cause to retch **4** : OBSTRUCT, CHOKE **5** : BALK **6** : to make quips — **gag·ger** *n*

²gag *n* **1** : something thrust into the mouth esp. to prevent speech or outcry **2** : an official check or restraint on free speech **3** : a laugh-provoking remark or act **4** : PRANK, TRICK

¹gage \'gāj\ *n* **1** : a token of defiance; *esp* : a glove or cap cast on the ground as a pledge of combat **2** : SECURITY

²gage *var of* GAUGE

gag·gle \'ga-gəl\ *n* [ME *gagyll*, fr. *gagelen* to cackle] **1** : a flock of geese **2** : an unorganized group

gai·ety *also* **gay·ety** \'gā-ə-tē\ *n, pl* **-eties 1** : festive activity : MERRYMAKING **2** : MERRIMENT **3** : FINERY ✦ *Synonyms* MIRTH, FESTIVITY, GLEE, HILARITY, JOLLITY

gai·ly *also* **gay·ly** \'gā-lē\ *adv* : in a gay manner

¹gain \'gān\ *n* **1** : PROFIT **2** : ACQUISITION, ACCUMULATION **3** : INCREASE

²gain *vb* **1** : to get possession of : EARN **2** : WIN ⟨~ a victory⟩ **3** : to increase in ⟨~ momentum⟩ **4** : PERSUADE **5** : to arrive at **6** : ACHIEVE ⟨~ strength⟩ **7** : to run fast ⟨the watch ~s a minute a day⟩ **8** : PROFIT **9** : INCREASE **10** : to improve in health ✦ *Synonyms* ACCOMPLISH, ATTAIN, REALIZE — **gain·er** *n*

gain·ful \'gān-fəl\ *adj* : PROFITABLE ⟨~ employment⟩ — **gain·ful·ly** *adv*

gain·say \ˌgān-'sā\ *vb* **-said** \-'sād, -'sed\; **-say·ing; -says** \-'sāz, -'sez\ [ME *gainsayen*, fr. *gain-* against + *sayen* to say] **1** : DENY, DISPUTE **2** : to speak against ✦ *Synonyms* CONTRADICT, CONTRAVENE, IMPUGN, NEGATE — **gain·say·er** *n*

gait \'gāt\ *n* : manner of moving on foot; *also* : a particular pattern or style of such moving — **gait·ed** *adj*

gai·ter \'gā-tər\ *n* **1** : a leg covering reaching from the instep to ankle, mid-calf, or knee **2** : an overshoe with a fabric upper **3** : an ankle-high shoe with elastic gores in the sides

¹gal \'gal\ *n* : GIRL

²gal *abbr* gallon

Gal *abbr* Galatians

ga·la \'gā-lə, 'ga-, 'gä-\ *n* : a festive celebration : FESTIVITY — **gala** *adj*

ga·lac·tic \gə-'lak-tik\ *adj* : of or relating to a galaxy

Ga·la·tians \gə-'lā-shənz\ *n* — see BIBLE table

gal·axy \'ga-lək-sē\ *n, pl* **-ax·ies** [ME *galaxie, galaxias*, fr. LL *galaxias*, fr. Gk, fr. *galakt-, gala* milk] **1** *often cap* : MILKY WAY GALAXY — used with *the* **2** : a very large group of stars **3** : an assemblage of brilliant or famous persons or things

gale \'gāl\ *n* **1** : a strong wind **2** : an emotional outburst ⟨~s of laughter⟩

ga·le·na \gə-'lē-nə\ *n* : a lustrous bluish gray mineral that consists of the sulfide of lead and is the chief ore of lead

¹gall \'gȯl\ *n* **1** : BILE **2** : something bitter to endure **3** : RANCOR **4** : IMPUDENCE ✦ *Synonyms* EFFRONTERY, BRASS, CHEEK, CHUTZPAH, AUDACITY, PRESUMPTION

²gall *n* : a skin sore caused by chafing

³gall *vb* **1** : CHAFE; *esp* : to become sore or worn by rubbing **2** : VEX, HARASS

⁴gall *n* : an abnormal outgrowth of plant tissue usu. due to parasites

¹gal·lant \gə-'lant, -'länt; 'ga-lənt\ *n* **1** : a young man of fashion **2** : a man who shows a marked fondness for the company of women and who is esp. attentive to them **3** : SUITOR

²gal·lant \'ga-lənt (*usual for 2, 3, 4*); gə-'lant, -'länt (*usual for 5*)\ *adj* **1** : showy in dress or bearing : SMART **2** : SPLENDID, STATELY **3** : SPIRITED, BRAVE **4** : CHIVALROUS, NOBLE **5** : polite and attentive to women — **gallant·ly** *adv*

gal·lant·ry \'ga-lən-trē\ *n, pl* **-ries 1** *archaic* : gallant appearance **2** : an act of marked courtesy **3** : courteous

attention to a woman **4** : conspicuous bravery ✦ *Synonyms* HEROISM, VALOR, PROWESS

gall·blad·der \'gȯl-ˌbla-dər\ *n* : a membranous muscular sac attached to the liver and serving to store bile

gal·le·on \'ga-lē-ən\ *n* : a large square-rigged sailing ship formerly used esp. by the Spanish

gal·le·ria \ˌga-lə-'rē-ə\ *n* [It] : a roofed and usu. glass-enclosed promenade or court

gal·lery \'ga-lə-rē\ *n, pl* **-ler·ies 1** : an outdoor balcony; *also* : PORCH, VERANDA **2** : a long narrow passage, apartment, or hall **3** : a narrow passage (as one made underground by a miner or through wood by an insect) **4** : a room where works of art are exhibited; *also* : an organization dealing in works of art **5** : a balcony in a theater, auditorium, or church; *esp* : the highest one in a theater **6** : the spectators at a sporting event (as a tennis or golf match) **7** : a photographer's studio — **gal·ler·ied** \-rēd\ *adj*

gal·ley \'ga-lē\ *n, pl* **galleys 1** : a long low ship propelled esp. by oars and formerly used esp. in the Mediterranean Sea **2** : the kitchen esp. of a ship or airplane **3** : a proof of typeset matter esp. in a single column

galley 1

Gal·lic \'ga-lik\ *adj* : of or relating to Gaul or France

gal·li·mau·fry \ˌga-lə-'mȯ-frē\ *n, pl* **-fries** [MF *galimafree* stew] : HODGEPODGE

gal·li·nule \'ga-lə-ˌnül, -ˌnyül\ *n* : any of several aquatic birds related to the rails

gal·li·um \'ga-lē-əm\ *n* : a bluish-white metallic chemical element used esp. in semiconductors

gal·li·vant \'ga-lə-ˌvant\ *vb* : to travel, roam, or move about for pleasure

gal·lon \'ga-lən\ *n* — see WEIGHT table

¹gal·lop \'ga-ləp\ *vb* **1** : to go or cause to go at a gallop **2** : to run fast — **gal·lop·er** *n*

²gallop *n* **1** : a bounding gait of a quadruped; *esp* : a fast 3-beat gait of a horse **2** : a ride or run at a gallop

gal·lows \'ga-lōz\ *n, pl* **gallows** *or* **gal·lows·es** : a frame usu. of two upright posts and a crosspiece from which criminals are hanged; *also* : the punishment of hanging

gall·stone \'gȯl-ˌstōn\ *n* : an abnormal concretion occurring in the gallbladder or bile passages

gal·lus·es \'ga-lə-səz\ *n pl* : SUSPENDERS

ga·lore \gə-'lȯr\ *adj* [Ir *go leor* enough] : ABUNDANT, PLENTIFUL

ga·losh \gə-'läsh\ *n* : a high overshoe

galv *abbr* galvanized

gal·va·nise *Brit var of* GALVANIZE

gal·va·nize \'gal-və-ˌnīz\ *vb* **-nized; -niz·ing 1** : to stimulate as if by an electric shock ⟨~ public opinion⟩ **2** : to coat (iron or steel) with zinc — **gal·va·ni·za·tion** \ˌgal-və-nə-'zā-shən\ *n* — **gal·va·niz·er** *n*

gal·va·nom·e·ter \ˌgal-və-'nä-mə-tər\ *n* : an instrument for detecting or measuring a small electric current

gam·bit \'gam-bət\ *n* [It *gambetto*, lit., act of tripping someone, fr. *gamba* leg] **1** : a chess opening in which a player risks one or more minor pieces to gain an advantage in position **2** : a calculated move : STRATAGEM ✦ *Synonyms* TRICK, ARTIFICE, GIMMICK, MANEUVER, PLAY, RUSE

¹gam·ble \'gam-bəl\ *vb* **-bled; -bling 1** : to play a game for money or property **2** : BET, WAGER **3** : VENTURE, HAZARD — **gam·bler** *n*

²gamble *n* : a risky undertaking

gam·bol \'gam-bəl\ *vb* **-boled** *or* **-bolled; -bol·ing** *or* **-bolling** : to skip about in play : FRISK — **gambol** *n*

gam·brel roof \\'gam-brəl-\ *n* : a roof with a lower steeper slope and an upper flatter one on each side

¹**game** \\'gām\ *n* 1 : AMUSEMENT, DIVERSION 2 : SPORT, FUN ⟨made ~ of the strange boy⟩ 3 : SCHEME, PROJECT 4 : a line of work : PROFESSION 5 : CONTEST 6 : animals hunted for sport or food; *also* : the flesh of a game animal

²**game** *vb* **gamed; gam·ing** 1 : to play for a stake 2 : to take dishonest advantage of

³**game** *adj* : PLUCKY, RESOLUTE — **game·ly** *adv* — **game·ness** *n*

⁴**game** *adj* : LAME ⟨a ~ leg⟩

game·cock \\'gām-ˌkäk\ *n* : a rooster trained for fighting

game fish *n* : SPORT FISH

game·keep·er \\'gām-ˌkē-pər\ *n* : a person in charge of the breeding and protection of game animals or birds on a private preserve

game show *n* : a television program on which contestants compete usu. for prizes in a game

game·some \\'gām-səm\ *adj* : MERRY ✦ **Synonyms** PLAYFUL, FROLICSOME, SPORTIVE, ANTIC

game·ster \\'gām-stər\ *n* : GAMBLER

gam·ete \\'ga-ˌmēt\ *n* : a mature germ cell — **ga·met·ic** \gə-'me-tik\ *adj*

game theory *n* : the analysis of a situation involving conflicting interests (as in business) in terms of gains and losses among opposing players

gam·in \\'ga-mən\ *n* [F] 1 : a boy who hangs around on the streets 2 : GAMINE 2

ga·mine \ga-'mēn\ *n* 1 : a girl who hangs around on the streets 2 : a small playfully mischievous girl

gam·ma \\'ga-mə\ *n* : the 3d letter of the Greek alphabet — Γ or γ

gamma globulin *n* : a blood protein fraction rich in antibodies; *also* : a solution of this from human blood donors that is given to provide immunity against some infectious diseases (as measles)

gamma ray *n* : a photon emitted by a radioactive substance; *also* : a photon of higher energy than that of an X-ray — usu. used in pl.

gam·mon \\'ga-mən\ *n, chiefly Brit* : a cured ham or side of bacon

gam·ut \\'ga-mət\ *n* : an entire range or series ✦ **Synonyms** SCALE, SPECTRUM

gamy *or* **gam·ey** \\'gā-mē\ *adj* **gam·i·er; -est** 1 : GAME, PLUCKY 2 : having the flavor of game esp. when near tainting 3 : SCANDALOUS; *also* : DISREPUTABLE — **gam·i·ness** \-mē-nəs\ *n*

¹**gan·der** \\'gan-dər\ *n* : a male goose

²**gander** *n* : LOOK, GLANCE

¹**gang** \\'gaŋ\ *n* 1 : a set of implements or devices arranged to operate together 2 : a group of persons working or associated together; *esp* : a group of criminals or young delinquents

²**gang** *vb* 1 : to attack in a gang — usu. used with *up* 2 : to form into or move or act as a gang

gang·land \\'gaŋ-ˌland\ *n* : the world of organized crime

gan·gling \\'gaŋ-gliŋ\ *adj* : loosely and awkwardly built : LANKY

gan·gli·on \\'gaŋ-glē-ən\ *n, pl* **-glia** \-ə\ *also* **-gli·ons** : a mass of nerve tissue containing cell bodies of neurons outside the central nervous system; *also* : NUCLEUS 3 — **gan·gli·on·ic** \ˌgaŋ-glē-'ä-nik\ *adj*

gan·gly \\'gaŋ-glē\ *adj* : GANGLING

gang·plank \\'gaŋ-ˌplaŋk\ *n* : a movable bridge from a ship to the shore

gang·plow \-ˌplau̇\ *n* : a plow that turns two or more furrows at one time

gan·grene \\'gaŋ-ˌgrēn, gaŋ-'grēn\ *n* : the death of soft tissues in a local area of the body due to loss of the blood supply — **gangrene** *vb* — **gan·gre·nous** \\'gaŋ-grə-nəs\ *adj*

gang·sta \\'gaŋ-stə\ *n* : a member of an urban street gang

gangsta rap *n* : rap music with usu. hostile lyrics portraying urban gang life

gang·ster \\'gaŋ-stər\ *n* : a member of a gang of criminals : RACKETEER

gang·way \\'gaŋ-ˌwā\ *n* 1 : PASSAGEWAY; *also* : GANGPLANK 2 : clear passage through a crowd

gan·net \\'ga-nət\ *n, pl* **gannets** *also* **gannet** : any of several large fish-eating usu. white and black seabirds that breed chiefly on offshore islands

gantlet *var of* GAUNTLET

gan·try \\'gan-trē\ *n, pl* **gantries** : a frame structure on side supports over or around something

GAO *abbr* General Accounting Office

gaol \\'jāl\, **gaol·er** \\'jā-lər\ *chiefly Brit var of* JAIL, JAILER

gap \\'gap\ *n* 1 : BREACH, CLEFT 2 : a mountain pass 3 : a blank space; *also* : an incomplete or deficient area 4 : a wide difference in character or attitude 5 : a problem caused by a disparity ⟨credibility ~⟩

gape \\'gāp\ *vb* **gaped; gap·ing** 1 : to open the mouth wide 2 : to open or part widely 3 : to stare with mouth open 4 : YAWN — **gape** *n*

¹**gar** \\'gär\ *n* : any of several fishes that have a long body resembling that of a pike and long narrow jaws

²**gar** *abbr* garage

GAR *abbr* Grand Army of the Republic

¹**ga·rage** \gə-'räzh, -'räj\ *n* [F, act of docking, garage, fr. *garer* to dock, fr. MF *garrer*, prob. ultim. fr. ON *vara* to beware, take care] : a shelter or repair shop for automobiles

²**garage** *vb* **ga·raged; ga·rag·ing** : to keep or put in a garage

garage sale *n* : a sale of used household or personal articles held on the seller's own premises

garb \\'gärb\ *n* 1 : style of dress 2 : outward form : APPEARANCE — **garb** *vb*

gar·bage \\'gär-bij\ *n* 1 : food waste 2 : unwanted or useless material — **gar·bage·man** \-ˌman\ *n*

gar·ble \\'gär-bəl\ *vb* **gar·bled; gar·bling** : to distort the meaning of ⟨~ a story⟩

gar·çon \gär-'sōⁿ\ *n, pl* **garçons** *same or* -'sōⁿz\ [F, boy, servant] : WAITER

¹**gar·den** \\'gär-dᵊn\ *n* 1 : a plot for growing fruits, flowers, or vegetables 2 : a public recreation area; *esp* : one for displaying plants or animals

²**garden** *vb* : to lay out or work in a garden — **gar·den·er** *n*

gar·de·nia \gär-'dē-nyə\ *n* [NL, genus name, fr. Alexander *Garden* †1791 Scot. naturalist] : any of a genus of tropical trees or shrubs that are related to the madder and have fragrant white or yellow flowers

garden–variety *adj* : COMMONPLACE, ORDINARY

gar·fish \\'gär-ˌfish\ *n* : GAR

gar·gan·tuan \gär-'gan-chə-wən\ *adj, often cap* : tremendous in size, volume, or degree ⟨~ waterfalls⟩ ✦ **Synonyms** HUGE, COLOSSAL, GIGANTIC, MAMMOTH, MONSTROUS, TITANIC

gar·gle \\'gär-gəl\ *vb* **gar·gled; gar·gling** : to rinse the throat with liquid agitated by air forced through it from the lungs — **gargle** *n*

gar·goyle \\'gär-ˌgȯi(-ə)l\ *n* 1 : a waterspout in the form of a grotesque human or animal figure projecting from the roof or eaves of a building 2 : a grotesquely carved figure

gar·ish \\'ger-ish\ *adj* : FLASHY, GLARING, SHOWY, GAUDY ⟨a ~ wardrobe⟩

¹**gar·land** \\'gär-lənd\ *n* : WREATH, CHAPLET

²**garland** *vb* : to form into or deck with a garland

gar·lic \\'gär-lik\ *n* [ME *garlek*, fr. OE *gärlēac*, fr. *gär* spear + *lēac* leek] : an herb related to the lilies and grown for its pungent bulbs used in cooking; *also* : its bulb — **gar·licky** \-li-kē\ *adj*

gar·ment \\'gär-mənt\ *n* : an article of clothing

gar·ner \\'gär-nər\ *vb* 1 : to gather into storage 2 : to acquire by effort 3 : ACCUMULATE, COLLECT

gar·net \\'gär-nət\ *n* [ME *gernet*, fr. AF *gernete*, fr. *gernet* dark red, fr. *pume gernete* pomegranate] : a transparent deep red mineral sometimes used as a gem

gar·nish \\'gär-nish\ *vb* 1 : DECORATE, EMBELLISH 2 : to add decorative or savory touches to (food) 3 : GARNISHEE — **garnish** *n*

gar·nish·ee \ˌgär-nə-'shē\ *vb* **-eed; -ee·ing** 1 : to serve with a garnishment 2 : to take (as a debtor's wages) by legal authority

gar·nish·ment \\'gär-nish-mənt\ *n* 1 : GARNISH 2 : a legal warning concerning the attachment of property to satisfy a debt; *also* : the attachment of such property

gar·ni·ture \-ni-chər, -ˌchu̇r\ *n* : EMBELLISHMENT, TRIMMING

gar·ret \\'ger-ət\ *n* : the part of a house just under the roof : ATTIC

gar·ri·son \'ger-ə-sən\ n [ME garisoun protection, fr. AF garisun healing, protection, fr. garir to heal, protect, of Gmc origin] **1** : a military post; esp : a permanent military installation **2** : the troops stationed at a garrison — **garrison** vb

garrison state n : a state organized on a primarily military basis

gar·rote or **ga·rotte** \gə-'rät, -'rōt\ n [Sp garrote] **1** : a method of execution by strangulation; also : the apparatus used **2** : an implement (as a wire with handles) for strangulation — **garrote** or **garotte** vb

gar·ru·lous \'ger-ə-ləs\ adj : TALKATIVE, WORDY — **gar·ru·li·ty** \gə-'rü-lə-tē\ n — **gar·ru·lous·ly** adv — **gar·ru·lous·ness** n

gar·ter \'gär-tər\ n : a band or strap worn to hold up a stocking or sock

garter snake n : any of a genus of harmless American snakes with longitudinal stripes on the back

1gas \'gas\ n, pl **gas·es** also **gas·ses** [NL, alter. of L chaos space, chaos] **1** : a fluid (as hydrogen or air) that tends to expand indefinitely **2** : a gas or mixture of gases used as a fuel or anesthetic **3** : a substance that can be used to produce a poisonous, asphyxiating, or irritant atmosphere **4** : GASOLINE — **gas·eous** \'ga-sē-əs, -shəs\ adj

2gas vb **gassed; gas·sing 1** : to treat with gas; also : to poison with gas **2** : to fill with gasoline ⟨~ up the car⟩

gash \'gash\ n : a deep long cut — **gash** vb

gas·ket \'gas-kət\ n : material (as rubber) or a part used to seal a joint

gas·light \'gas-,līt\ n **1** : light made by burning illuminating gas **2** : a gas flame; also : a gas lighting fixture

gas mask n : a mask with a chemical air filter used to protect the face and lungs against poison gas

gas·o·line \'ga-sə-,lēn, ,ga-sə-'lēn\ n : a flammable liquid mixture made from petroleum and used esp. as a motor fuel

gasp \'gasp\ vb **1** : to catch the breath audibly (as with shock) **2** : to breathe laboriously : PANT **3** : to utter in a gasping manner — **gasp** n

gas station n : a retail station for servicing and fueling motor vehicles

gas·tric \'gas-trik\ adj : of or relating to the stomach

gastric juice n : the acid digestive secretion of the stomach

gas·tri·tis \gas-'trī-təs\ n : inflammation of the lining of the stomach

gas·tro·en·ter·i·tis \,gas-trō-,en-tə-'rī-təs\ n : inflammation of the lining membrane of the stomach and intestines

gas·tro·en·ter·ol·o·gy \,gas-trō-,en-tə-'rä-lə-jē\ n : a branch of medicine concerned with the structure, functions, and diseases of the stomach and intestines — **gas·tro·en·ter·ol·o·gist** \-jist\ n

gas·tro·in·tes·ti·nal \,gas-trō-in-'tes-tən-ᵊl\ adj : of, relating to, affecting, or including both the stomach and intestine ⟨~ tract⟩ ⟨~ distress⟩

gas·tron·o·my \gas-'trä-nə-mē\ n [F gastronomie, fr. Gk Gastronomia, title of a 4th cent. B.C. poem, fr. gastēr belly + -nomia system of laws] : the art of good eating — **gas·tro·nom·ic** \,gas-trə-'nä-mik\ also **gas·tro·nom·i·cal** \-mi-kəl\ adj — **gas·tro·nom·i·cal·ly** \-k(ə-)lē\ adv

gas·tro·pod \'gas-trə-,päd\ n : any of a large class of mollusks (as snails and slugs) with a muscular foot and a spiral shell or none — **gastropod** adj

gas·works \'gas-,wərks\ n sing or pl : a plant for manufacturing gas

gate \'gāt\ n **1** : an opening for passage in a wall or fence **2** : a city or castle entrance often with defensive structures **3** : the frame or door that closes a gate **4** : a device (as a valve) for controlling the passage of a fluid or signal **5** : the total admission receipts or the number of people at an event

-gate \,gāt\ n comb form [Watergate, scandal that resulted in the resignation of President Richard Nixon in 1974] : usu. political scandal often involving the concealment of wrongdoing

gate–crash·er \'gāt-,kra-shər\ n : a person who enters without paying admission or attends without invitation

gate·keep·er \-,kē-pər\ n : a person who tends or guards a gate

gate·post \-,pōst\ n : the post to which a gate is hung or the one against which it closes

gate·way \-,wā\ n **1** : an opening for a gate **2** : a means of entrance or exit

1gath·er \'ga-thər\ vb **1** : to bring together : COLLECT **2** : PICK, HARVEST **3** : to pick up little by little **4** : to scoop up from a resting place ⟨~ed up the child⟩ **5** : to gain or win by gradual increase **6** : ATTRACT, ACCUMULATE ⟨~ dust⟩ **7** : to summon up ⟨~ courage to dive⟩ **8** : to gain control of ⟨~ed his wits⟩ **9** : to draw about or close to something **10** : to pull (fabric) along a line of stitching into puckers **11** : GUESS, DEDUCE, INFER **12** : ASSEMBLE **13** : to swell out and fill with pus **14** : GROW, INCREASE ✦ **Synonyms** CONGREGATE, FORGATHER — **gath·er·er** n

2gather n : a puckering in cloth made by gathering

GATT \'gat\ abbr General Agreement on Tariffs and Trade

gauche \'gōsh\ adj [F, lit., left] **1** : lacking social experience or grace; also : not tactful **2** : crudely made or done ✦ **Synonyms** CLUMSY, HEAVY-HANDED, INEPT, MALADROIT

gau·che·rie \,gō-shə-'rē\ n : a tactless or awkward action

gau·cho \'gaü-chō\ n, pl **gauchos** : a cowboy of the So. American pampas

gaud \'gód\ n : ORNAMENT, TRINKET

gaudy \'gó-dē\ adj **gaud·i·er; -est 1** : ostentatiously or tastelessly ornamented **2** : marked by showiness or extravagance : OUTLANDISH **3** : EXCEPTIONAL ⟨a ~ batting average⟩ ✦ **Synonyms** GARISH, FLASHY, GLARING, TAWDRY — **gaud·i·ly** \-də-lē\ adv — **gaud·i·ness** \-dē-nəs\ n

1gauge also **gage** \'gāj\ n **1** : measurement according to some standard or system **2** : DIMENSIONS, SIZE **3** usu **gage** : an instrument for measuring, testing, or registering

2gauge also **gage** vb **gauged** also **gaged; gaug·ing** also **gag·ing 1** : MEASURE **2** : to determine the capacity or contents of **3** : ESTIMATE, JUDGE

gaunt \'gónt\ adj **1** : excessively thin and angular ⟨a ~ face⟩ **2** : BARREN, DESOLATE ✦ **Synonyms** BONY, LANK, LANKY, LEAN, RAWBONED, SKINNY — **gaunt·ness** n

1gaunt·let also **gant·let** \'gónt-lət\ n **1** : a protective glove **2** : an open challenge (as to combat) **3** : a dress glove extending above the wrist

2gauntlet also **gantlet** n **1** : a double file of men armed with weapons (as clubs) with which to strike at an individual who is made to run between them **2** : ORDEAL **3** : a line or series of something to be greeted or managed

gauss \'gaús\ n : the centimeter-gram-second unit of magnetic flux density that is equal to 1×10^{-4} tesla

gauze \'góz\ n : a very thin often transparent fabric used esp. for draperies and surgical dressings

gauzy \'gó-zē\ adj **gauz·i·er; -est 1** : made of or resembling gauze **2** : marked by vagueness or fuzziness ⟨a ~ memory⟩

gave past of GIVE

gav·el \'ga-vəl\ n : a mallet used by a presiding officer or auctioneer

ga·votte \gə-'vät\ n : a dance of French peasant origin marked by the raising rather than sliding of the feet

gawk \'gók\ vb : to gape or stare stupidly — **gawk·er** n

gawky \'gó-kē\ adj **gawk·i·er; -est** : AWKWARD, CLUMSY — **gawk·i·ly** \-kə-lē\ adv — **gawk·i·ness** n

gay \'gā\ adj **1** : MERRY **2** : BRIGHT, LIVELY **3** : brilliant in color **4** : given to social pleasures; also : LICENTIOUS **5** : HOMOSEXUAL; also : of, relating to, or used by homosexuals ⟨a ~ bar⟩

gayety, gayly var of GAIETY, GAILY

gaz abbr gazette

gaze \'gāz\ vb **gazed; gaz·ing** : to fix the eyes in a steady intent look ✦ **Synonyms** GAPE, GAWK, GLARE, GOGGLE, PEER, STARE — **gaze** n — **gaz·er** n

ga·ze·bo \gə-'zē-bō\ n, pl **-bos 1** : BELVEDERE **2** : a free-standing roofed structure usu. open on the sides

ga·zelle \gə-'zel\ n, pl **gazelles** also **gazelle** : any of numerous small swift graceful antelopes

ga·zette \gə-'zet\ n **1** : NEWSPAPER **2** : an official journal

gaz·et·teer \,ga-zə-'tir\ n : a geographical dictionary

ga·zil·lion \gə-'zil-yən\ n : ZILLION — **gazillion** adj — **ga·zil·lionth** \-yənth\ adj

gaz·pa·cho \gəz-'pä-(,)chō, gə-'spä-\ n, pl **-chos** [Sp] : a spicy soup usu. made from raw vegetables and served cold

GB *abbr* Great Britain

GCA *abbr* ground-controlled approach

gd *abbr* good

Gd *symbol* gadolinium

GDR *abbr* German Democratic Republic

Ge *symbol* germanium

gear \'gir\ *n* **1** : CLOTHING **2** : movable property : GOODS **3** : EQUIPMENT ⟨fishing ∼⟩ **4** : a mechanism that performs a specific function ⟨steering ∼⟩ **5** : a toothed wheel **6** : working order or adjustment ⟨got her career in ∼⟩ **7** : an adjustment of transmission gears (as of an automobile or bicycle) that determines speed and direction of travel — **gear** *vb*

gear·box \'gir-,bäks\ *n* : TRANSMISSION 3

gear·shift \-,shift\ *n* : a mechanism by which transmission gears are shifted

gear·wheel \-,hwēl\ *n* : GEAR 5

gecko \'ge-kō\ *n, pl* **geck·os** *also* **geck·oes** : any of numerous small chiefly tropical insect-eating lizards

GED *abbr* **1** General Educational Development (tests) **2** general equivalency diploma

geek \'gēk\ *n* : a person of an intellectual bent who is often disliked — **geek·i·ness** *n* — **geeky** *adj*

geese *pl of* GOOSE

gee·zer \'gē-zər\ *n* : an odd or eccentric person usu. of old age

Gei·ger counter \'gī-gər-\ *n* : an electronic instrument for detecting the presence of cosmic rays or radioactive substances

gei·sha \'gā-shə, 'gē-\ *n, pl* **geisha** *or* **geishas** [Jp, fr. *gei* art + *-sha* person] : a Japanese girl or woman who is trained to provide entertaining company for men

gel \'jel\ *n* : a solid jellylike colloid (as gelatin dessert) — **gel** *vb*

gel·a·tin *also* **gel·a·tine** \'je-lə-tən\ *n* : glutinous material and esp. protein obtained from animal tissues by boiling and used as a food, in dyeing, and in photography; *also* : an edible jelly formed with gelatin — **ge·lat·i·nous** \jə-'la-tə-nəs\ *adj*

geld \'geld\ *vb* : CASTRATE

geld·ing *n* : a castrated male horse

gel·id \'je-ləd\ *adj* : extremely cold

gem \'jem\ *n* **1** : JEWEL **2** : a usu. valuable stone cut and polished for ornament **3** : something valued for beauty or perfection

Gem·i·ni \'je-mə-(,)nē, -,nī; 'ge-mə-,nē\ *n* **1** : a zodiacal constellation between Taurus and Cancer usu. pictured as twins sitting together ⟨: the 3d sign of the zodiac in astrology; *also* : one born under this sign

gem·ol·o·gy *or* **gem·mol·o·gy** \je-'mä-lə-jē, jə-\ *n* : the science of gems — **gem·olog·i·cal** \,je-mə-'lä-ji-kəl\ *adj* — **gem·ol·o·gist** *also* **gem·mol·o·gist** \-jist\ *n*

gem·stone \'jem-,stōn\ *n* : a mineral or petrified material that when cut and polished can be used in jewelry

gen *abbr* **1** general **2** genitive

Gen *abbr* Genesis

Gen AF *abbr* general of the air force

gen·darme \'zhän-,därm, 'jän-\ *n* [F, intended as sing. of *gensdarmes*, pl. of *gent d'armes*, lit., armed people] : a member of a body of soldiers esp. in France serving as an armed police force

gen·der \'jen-dər\ *n* [ME *gendre*, fr. AF *genre, gendre*, fr. L *gener-, genus* birth, race, kind, gender] **1** : any of two or more divisions within a grammatical class that determine agreement with and selection of other words or grammatical forms **2** : SEX 1

gene \'jēn\ *n* : a part of DNA or RNA that contains chemical information needed to make a particular protein (as an enzyme) controlling or influencing an inherited bodily trait (as eye color) or activity (as metabolism) or that influences or controls the activity of another gene or genes — **gen·ic** \'jē-nik, 'je-\ *adj*

ge·ne·al·o·gy \,jē-nē-'ä-lə-jē, je-, -'a-\ *n, pl* **-gies** : PEDIGREE, LINEAGE; *also* : the study of family pedigrees — **ge·ne·a·log·i·cal** \,jē-nē-ə-'lä-ji-kəl, je-\ *adj* — **ge·ne·a·log·i·cal·ly** \-k(ə-)lē\ *adv* — **ge·ne·al·o·gist** \,jē-nē-'ä-lə-jist, je-, -'a-\ *n*

gene pool *n* : the total genetic information contained in a population of interbreeding organisms

genera *pl of* GENUS

¹gen·er·al \'je-nə-rəl, 'jen-rəl\ *adj* **1** : of or relating to the whole **2** : taken as a whole **3** : relating to or covering all instances **4** : not special or specialized **5** : common to many ⟨a ∼ custom⟩ **6** : not limited in meaning : not specific **7** : holding superior rank ⟨inspector ∼⟩ **♦ Synonyms** GENERIC, UNIVERSAL

²general *n* **1** : something that involves or is applicable to the whole **2** : a commissioned officer ranking next below a general of the army or a general of the air force **3** : a commissioned officer of the highest rank in the marine corps — **in general** : for the most part

general assembly *n* **1** : a legislative assembly; *esp* : a U.S. state legislature **2** *cap G&A* : the supreme deliberative body of the United Nations

gen·er·al·i·sa·tion, gen·er·al·ise, gen·er·al·ised *Brit var of* GENERALIZATION, GENERALIZE, GENERALIZED

gen·er·al·is·si·mo \,je-nə-rə-'li-sə-,mō\ *n, pl* **-mos** [It, fr. *generale* general] : the chief commander of an army

gen·er·al·i·ty \,je-nə-'ra-lə-tē\ *n, pl* **-ties** **1** : the quality or state of being general **2** : GENERALIZATION 2 **3** : a vague or inadequate statement **4** : the greatest part : BULK

gen·er·al·i·za·tion \,je-nə-rə-lə-'zā-shən, ,jen-rə-\ *n* **1** : the act or process of generalizing **2** : a general statement, law, principle, or proposition

gen·er·al·ize \'je-nə-rə-,līz, 'jen-rə-\ *vb* **-ized; -iz·ing** **1** : to make general **2** : to draw general conclusions from **3** : to reach a general conclusion esp. on the basis of particular instances **4** : to extend throughout the body

gen·er·al·ly \'jen-rə-lē, 'jē-nə-\ *adv* **1** : in a general manner **2** : as a rule

general of the air force : a commissioned officer of the highest rank in the air force

general of the army : a commissioned officer of the highest rank in the army

general practitioner *n* : a physician or veterinarian whose practice is not limited to a specialty

gen·er·al·ship \'je-nə-rəl-,ship, 'jen-rəl-\ *n* **1** : office or tenure of office of a general **2** : LEADERSHIP **3** : military skill as a high commander

general store *n* : a retail store that carries a wide variety of goods but is not divided into departments

gen·er·ate \'je-nə-,rāt\ *vb* **-at·ed; -at·ing** : to bring into existence : PRODUCE ⟨∼ electricity⟩ **♦ Synonyms** CREATE, ORIGINATE, PROCREATE, SPAWN

gen·er·a·tion \,je-nə-'rā-shən\ *n* **1** : a body of living beings constituting a single step in the line of descent from an ancestor; *also* : the average period between generations **2** : PRODUCTION

Generation X *n* : the generation of Americans born in the 1960s and 1970s

gen·er·a·tive \'je-nə-rə-tiv, -,rā-tiv\ *adj* : having the power or function of generating, originating, producing, or reproducing ⟨∼ organs⟩

gen·er·a·tor \'je-nə-,rā-tər\ *n* : one that generates; *esp* : a machine by which mechanical energy is changed into electrical energy

ge·ner·ic \jə-'ner-ik\ *adj* **1** : not specific : GENERAL **2** : not protected by a trademark ⟨a ∼ drug⟩ **3** : of or relating to a biological genus **4** : having no particularly distinctive quality ⟨∼ towns⟩ — **generic** *n* — **ge·ner·i·cal·ly** \-i-k(ə-)lē\ *adv*

gen·er·ous \'je-nə-rəs\ *adj* **1** : free in giving or sharing ⟨∼ donors⟩ **2** : HIGH-MINDED, NOBLE **3** : ABUNDANT, AMPLE, COPIOUS ⟨a ∼ salary⟩ **♦ Synonyms** LIBERAL, BOUNTIFUL, MUNIFICENT, OPENHANDED — **gen·er·os·i·ty** \,je-nə-'rä-sə-tē\ *n* — **gen·er·ous·ly** \'je-nə-rəs-lē\ *adv* — **gen·er·ous·ness** *n*

gen·e·sis \'je-nə-səs\ *n, pl* **-e·ses** \-,sēz\ : the origin or coming into existence of something

Genesis *n* — see BIBLE table

gene-splic·ing \-,splī-siŋ\ *n* : the process of preparing recombinant DNA

gene therapy *n* : the insertion of normal or altered genes into cells esp. to replace defective genes in the treatment of genetic disorders or to provide a specialized disease-fighting function

ge·net·ic \jə-'ne-tik\ *adj* : of or relating to the origin, development, or causes of something; *also* : of, relating to, or caused by genes or genetics ⟨∼ research⟩ — **ge·net·i·cal·ly** \-ti-k(ə-)lē\ *adv*

genetic code *n* : the chemical code that is the basis of genetic inheritance and consists of units of three linked chemical groups in DNA and RNA which specify particular amino acids used to make proteins or which start or stop the process of making proteins

genetic engineering *n* : the alteration of genetic material esp. by cutting up and joining together DNA from one or more species of organism and inserting the result into an organism — **genetically engineered** *adj*

ge·net·ics \jə-'ne-tiks\ *n* : a branch of biology dealing with heredity and variation — **ge·net·i·cist** \-tə-sist\ *n*

ge·nial \'jē-nyəl, 'jē-nē-əl\ *adj* **1** : favorable to growth or comfort ⟨∼ sunshine⟩ **2** : CHEERFUL, KINDLY ⟨a ∼ host⟩ ♦ **Synonyms** AFFABLE, CONGENIAL, CORDIAL, GRACIOUS, SOCIABLE — **ge·ni·al·i·ty** \jē-nē-'a-lə-tē, jēn-'ya-\ *n* — **ge·nial·ly** *adv*

-gen·ic \'je-nik\ *adj comb form* **1** : producing : forming **2** : produced by : formed from **3** : suitable for production or reproduction by (such) a medium

ge·nie \'jē-nē\ *n, pl* **ge·nies** *also* **ge·nii** \-nē-ˌī\ [F *génie*, fr. Ar *jinnī*] : a supernatural spirit that often takes human form usu. serving the person who calls on it

gen·i·tal \'je-nə-t^əl\ *adj* **1** : concerned with reproduction ⟨∼ organs⟩ **2** : of, relating to, or characterized by the stage of psychosexual development in psychoanalytic theory in which oral and anal impulses are subordinated to adaptive interpersonal mechanisms — **gen·i·tal·ly** *adv*

gen·i·ta·lia \ˌje-nə-'tāl-yə\ *n pl* : reproductive organs; *esp* : the external genital organs — **gen·i·ta·lic** \-'ta-lik, -'tā-\ *adj*

gen·i·tals \'je-nə-t^əlz\ *n pl* : GENITALIA

gen·i·tive \'je-nə-tiv\ *adj* : of, relating to, or constituting a grammatical case marking typically a relationship of possessor or source — **genitive** *n*

gen·i·to·uri·nary \ˌje-nə-tō-'yu̇r-ə-ˌner-ē\ *adj* : of or relating to the genital and urinary organs or functions

ge·nius \'jē-nyəs\ *n, pl* **ge·nius·es** *or* **ge·nii** \-nē-ˌī\ [L, tutelary spirit, natural inclinations, fr. *gignere* to beget] **1** *pl genii* : an attendant spirit of a person or place; *also* : a person who influences another for good or evil **2** : a strong leaning or inclination **3** : a peculiar or distinctive character or spirit (as of a nation or a language) **4** *pl usu genii* : SPIRIT, GENIE **5** *pl usu geniuses* : a single strongly marked capacity or aptitude **6** : extraordinary intellectual power; *also* : a person having such power ♦ **Synonyms** GIFT, FACULTY, FLAIR, KNACK, TALENT

genl *abbr* general

geno·cide \'je-nə-ˌsīd\ *n* : the deliberate and systematic destruction of a racial, political, or cultural group

ge·nome \'jē-ˌnōm\ *n* **1** : one haploid set of chromosomes **2** : the genetic material of an organism

ge·no·mics \jē-'nō-miks\ *n* : a branch of biotechnology concerned esp. with investigating and collecting data about the structure and function of all or part of an organism's genome

-genous \jə-nəs\ *adj comb form* **1** : producing : yielding ⟨eroge*nous*⟩ **2** : having (such) an origin ⟨endoge*nous*⟩

genre \'zhän-rə, 'zhäⁿ-; 'zhäⁿr; 'jän-rə\ *n* **1** : a distinctive type or category esp. of literary composition **2** : a style of painting in which everyday subjects are treated realistically

gens \'jenz, 'gens\ *n, pl* **gen·tes** \'jen-ˌtēz, 'gen-ˌtās\ [L] : a Roman clan embracing the families of the same stock in the male line

gent *n* : GENTLEMAN

gen·teel \jen-'tēl\ *adj* **1** : ARISTOCRATIC **2** : ELEGANT, STYLISH **3** : POLITE, REFINED **4** : maintaining the appearance of superior social status **5** : marked by false delicacy, prudery, or affectation — **gen·teel·ly** *adv* — **gen·teel·ness** *n*

gen·tian \'jen-chən\ *n* : any of numerous herbs with opposite leaves and showy usu. blue flowers in the fall

gen·tile \'jen-ˌtī(-ə)l\ *n* [ME, fr. LL *gentilis* heathen, pagan, fr. L *gens*- *gens* clan, nation] **1** *often cap* : a person who is not Jewish; *esp* : a Christian as distinguished from a Jew **2** : HEATHEN, PAGAN — **gentile** *adj, often cap*

gen·til·i·ty \jen-'ti-lə-tē\ *n, pl* **-ties** **1** : good birth and family **2** : the qualities characteristic of a well-bred person **3** : good manners **4** : superior social status shown in manners or mode of life

¹gen·tle \'jen-t^əl\ *adj* **gen·tler** \'jent-lər, -t^əl-ər\; **gen·tlest** \'jent-ləst, -t^əl-əst\ **1** : belonging to a family of high social station **2** : of, relating to, or characteristic of a gentleman **3** : KIND, AMIABLE ⟨a ∼ pastor⟩ **4** : TRACTABLE, DOCILE ⟨a ∼ dog⟩ **5** : not harsh, stern, or violent **6** : SOFT, DELICATE **7** : MODERATE — **gen·tle·ness** *n* — **gen·tly** *adv*

²gentle *vb* **gen·tled; gen·tling** **1** : to make or become mild, docile, soft, or moderate **2** : MOLLIFY, PLACATE

gen·tle·folk \'jen-t^əl-ˌfōk\ *also* **gen·tle·folks** \-ˌfōks\ *n* : persons of good family and breeding

gen·tle·man \-mən\ *n* **1** : a man of good family **2** : a well-bred man **3** : MAN — used in pl. as a form of address — **gen·tle·man·ly** *adj*

gen·tle·wom·an \-ˌwu̇-mən\ *n* **1** : a woman of good family **2** : a woman attending a lady of rank **3** : a woman with very good manners : LADY

gen·tri·fi·ca·tion \ˌjen-trə-fə-'kā-shən\ *n* : the process of renewal accompanying the influx of middle-class people into deteriorating areas that often displaces earlier usu. poorer residents — **gen·tri·fy** \'jen-trə-fī\ *vb*

gen·try \'jen-trē\ *n, pl* **gentries** **1** : people of good birth, breeding, and education : ARISTOCRACY **2** : the class of English people between the nobility and the yeomanry **3** : persons of a designated class

gen·u·flect \'jen-yu̇-ˌflekt\ *vb* : to bend the knee esp. in worship — **gen·u·flec·tion** \ˌjen-yu̇-'flek-shən\ *n*

gen·u·ine \'jen-yə-wən\ *adj* **1** : AUTHENTIC, REAL ⟨a ∼ signature⟩ **2** : SINCERE, HONEST ⟨their love is ∼⟩ ♦ **Synonyms** BONA FIDE, TRUE, VERITABLE — **gen·u·ine·ly** *adv* — **gen·u·ine·ness** *n*

ge·nus \'jē-nəs\ *n, pl* **gen·era** \'je-nə-rə\ [L, birth, race, kind] : a category of biological classification that ranks between the family and the species and contains related species

geo·cen·tric \ˌjē-ō-'sen-trik\ *adj* **1** : relating to or measured from the earth's center **2** : having or relating to the earth as a center

geo·chem·is·try \-'ke-mə-strē\ *n* : a branch of geology that deals with the chemical composition of and chemical changes in the earth — **geo·chem·i·cal** \-mi-kəl\ *adj* — **geo·chem·ist** \-mist\ *n*

ge·ode \'jē-ˌōd\ *n* : a nodule of stone having a cavity lined with mineral matter

¹geo·de·sic \ˌjē-ə-'de-sik\ *adj* : made of light straight structural elements ⟨a ∼ dome⟩

²geodesic *n* : the shortest line between two points on a surface

geo·det·ic \ˌjē-ə-'de-tik\ *adj* : of, relating to, or being precise measurement of the earth and its features ⟨a ∼ survey⟩

geog *abbr* geographic; geographical; geography

ge·og·ra·phy \jē-'ä-grə-fē\ *n, pl* **-phies** **1** : a science that deals with the natural features of the earth and the climate, products, and inhabitants **2** : the natural features of a region — **ge·og·ra·pher** \-fər\ *n* — **geo·graph·ic** \ˌjē-ə-'gra-fik\ *or* **geo·graph·i·cal** \-fi-kəl\ *adj* — **geo·graph·i·cal·ly** \-fi-k(ə-)lē\ *adv*

geol *abbr* geologic; geological; geology

ge·ol·o·gy \jē-'ä-lə-jē\ *n, pl* **-gies** **1** : a science that deals with the history of the earth and its life esp. as recorded in rocks; *also* : a study of the features of a celestial body (as the moon) **2** : the geologic features of an area — **ge·o·log·ic** \ˌjē-ə-'lä-jik\ *or* **ge·o·log·i·cal** \-ji-kəl\ *adj* — **geo·log·i·cal·ly** \-ji-k(ə-)lē\ *adv* — **ge·ol·o·gist** \jē-'ä-lə-jist\ *n*

geom *abbr* geometric; geometrical; geometry

geo·mag·net·ic \ˌjē-ō-mag-'ne-tik\ *adj* : of or relating to the magnetism of the earth — **geo·mag·ne·tism** \-'mag-nə-ˌti-zəm\ *n*

geometric mean *n* : the *n*th root of the product of *n* numbers; *esp* : a number that is the second term of three consecutive terms of a geometric progression ⟨the *geometric mean* of 9 and 4 is 6⟩

geometric progression *n* : a progression (as 1, ¹/₂, ¹/₄) in which the ratio of a term to its predecessor is always the same

ge·om·e·try \jē-'ä-mə-trē\ *n, pl* **-tries** [ultim. fr. Gk *geōmetria*, fr. *geōmetrein* to measure the earth, fr. *gē* earth + *metron* measure] : a branch of mathematics dealing with the relations, properties, and measurements of solids, surfaces, lines, points, and angles — **ge·om·e·ter** \-tər\ *n* —

ge·o·met·ric \‚jē-ə-'me-trik\ or ge·o·met·ri·cal \-tri-kəl\ adj

geo·phys·ics \‚jē-ō-'fi-ziks\ n : the physics of the earth — geo·phys·i·cal \-zi-kəl\ adj — geo·phys·i·cist \-zə-sist\ n

geo·pol·i·tics \-'pä-lə-‚tiks\ n : a combination of political and geographic factors relating to a state — geo·po·lit·i·cal \-pə-'li-ti-kəl\ adj

geo·ther·mal \‚jē-ō-'thər-məl\ adj : of, relating to, or using the heat of the earth's interior

ger abbr gerund

Ger abbr German; Germany

ge·ra·ni·um \jə-'rā-nē-əm\ n [L, fr. Gk geranion, fr. geranos crane] : any of a genus of herbs with usu. deeply cut leaves and typically pink, purple, or white flowers; also : any of a related genus of herbs that are native to southern Africa and are widely grown for their clusters of showy usu. red, pink, or white flowers

ger·bil also ger·bile \'jər-bəl\ n : any of numerous Old World burrowing desert rodents with long hind legs

ge·ri·at·ric \‚jer-ē-'a-trik\ adj 1 : of or relating to geriatrics or the process of aging 2 : of, relating to, or appropriate for elderly people 3 : OLD

ge·ri·at·rics \-triks\ n : a branch of medicine dealing with the problems and diseases of old age and aging

germ \'jərm\ n 1 : a bit of living matter capable of growth and development (as into an organism) 2 : SOURCE, RUDIMENTS 3 : MICROORGANISM; esp : one causing disease

German \'jər-mən\ n 1 : a native or inhabitant of Germany 2 : the language of Germany, Austria, and parts of Switzerland — German adj — Ger·man·ic \jər-'ma-nik\ adj

ger·mane \jər-'mān\ adj [ME germain, lit., having the same parents, fr. AF, fr. L germanus, fr. germen sprout, bud] : RELEVANT, APPROPRIATE ♦ Synonyms APPLICABLE, MATERIAL, PERTINENT

ger·ma·ni·um \jər-'mā-nē-əm\ n : a grayish white hard chemical element used esp. in semiconductor and optical materials and as a catalyst

German measles n sing or pl : an acute contagious virus disease milder than typical measles but damaging to the fetus when occurring early in pregnancy

German shepherd n : any of a breed of intelligent responsive working dogs of German origin often used in police work and as guide dogs for the blind

germ cell n : an egg or sperm or one of their antecedent cells

ger·mi·cide \'jər-mə-‚sīd\ n : an agent that destroys germs — ger·mi·cid·al \‚jər-mə-'sī-dᵊl\ adj

ger·mi·nal \'jər-mə-nəl\ adj : of or relating to a germ or germ cell; also : EMBRYONIC

ger·mi·nate \'jər-mə-‚nāt\ vb -nat·ed; -nat·ing 1 : to cause to develop; begin to develop : SPROUT 2 : to come into being : EVOLVE — ger·mi·na·tion \‚jər-mə-'nā-shən\ n

ger·on·tol·o·gy \‚jer-ən-'tä-lə-jē\ n : a scientific study of aging and the problems of the aged — ge·ron·to·log·i·cal \jə-‚rän-tə-'lä-ji-kəl\ adj — ger·on·tol·o·gist \‚jer-ən-'tä-lə-jist\ n

ger·ry·man·der \'jer-ē-‚man-dər\ vb : to divide into election districts so as to give one political party an advantage — gerrymander n

ger·und \'jer-ənd\ n : a word having the characteristics of both verb and noun

ge·sta·po \gə-'stä-pō\ n, pl -pos [G, fr. Geheime Staatspolizei, lit., secret state police] : a usu. terrorist secret police organization operating against persons suspected of disloyalty

ges·ta·tion \je-'stä-shən\ n : PREGNANCY, INCUBATION — ges·tate \'jes-‚tāt\ vb

ges·tic·u·late \je-'sti-kyə-‚lāt\ vb -lat·ed; -lat·ing : to make gestures esp. when speaking — ges·tic·u·la·tion \-‚sti-kyə-'lä-shən\ n

ges·ture \'jes-chər\ n 1 : a movement usu. of the body or limbs that expresses or emphasizes an idea, sentiment, or attitude 2 : something said or done by way of formality or courtesy, as a symbol or token, or for its effect on the attitudes of others — ges·tur·al \-chə-rəl\ adj — gesture vb

ge·sund·heit \gə-'zùnt-‚hīt\ interj [G, lit., health] — used to wish good health esp. to one who has just sneezed

¹get \'get\ vb got \'gät\; got or got·ten \'gä-tᵊn\; get·ting 1 : to gain possession of (as by receiving, acquiring, earning, buying, or winning) : PROCURE, OBTAIN, FETCH 2 : to succeed in coming or going ⟨got away to the lake⟩ 3 : to cause to come or go ⟨got the car to the station⟩ 4 : BEGET 5 : to cause to be in a certain condition or position ⟨don't ~ wet⟩ 6 : BECOME ⟨~ sick⟩ 7 : PREPARE 8 : SEIZE 9 : to move emotionally; also : IRRITATE 10 : BAFFLE, PUZZLE 11 : KILL 12 : HIT 13 : to be subjected to ⟨~ the measles⟩ 14 : to receive as punishment 15 : to find out by calculation 16 : HEAR; also : UNDERSTAND ⟨got the joke⟩ 17 : PERSUADE, INDUCE 18 : HAVE ⟨he's got no money⟩ 19 : to have as an obligation or necessity ⟨you have got to come⟩ 20 : to establish communication with 21 : to be able ⟨finally got to go to med school⟩ 22 : to come to be ⟨got talking about old times⟩ 23 : to leave at once — get ahead : to achieve success — get a move on : HURRY — get away with : to avoid punishment for (as a crime) — get into : to become strongly involved or interested in ⟨got into music⟩ — get over : to reconcile oneself to ⟨get over the breakup⟩

²get \'get\ n : OFFSPRING, PROGENY

get along vb 1 : GET BY 2 : to be on friendly terms

get-away \'ge-tə-‚wā\ n 1 : ESCAPE 2 : START 3 : a usu. brief vacation

get by vb : to meet one's needs

get–to·geth·er \'get-tə-‚ge-thər\ n : an informal social gathering

get-up \'get-‚əp\ n 1 : OUTFIT, COSTUME 2 : general composition or structure

gew·gaw \'gü-‚gó, 'gyü-\ n : a showy trifle : BAUBLE, TRINKET

gey·ser \'gī-zər\ n [Icelandic Geysir, hot spring in Iceland] : a spring that intermittently shoots up hot water and steam

g–force \'jē-‚fórs\ n : the force of gravity or acceleration on a body

ghast·ly \'gast-lē\ adj ghast·li·er; -est 1 : HORRIBLE, SHOCKING 2 : resembling a ghost : DEATHLIKE, PALE ♦ Synonyms GRUESOME, GRIM, LURID, GRISLY, MACABRE

ghat \'gót\ n [Hindi & Urdu ghāṭ] : a broad flight of steps on an Indian riverbank that provides access to the water

gher·kin \'gər-kən\ n 1 : a small prickly fruit of a vine related to the cucumber used to make pickles 2 : an immature cucumber

ghet·to \'ge-tō\ n, pl ghettos or ghettoes : a quarter of a city in which members of a minority group live because of social, legal, or economic pressure

¹ghost \'gōst\ n 1 : the seat of life : SOUL 2 : a disembodied soul; esp : the soul of a dead person believed to be an inhabitant of the unseen world or to appear in bodily form to living people 3 : SPIRIT, DEMON 4 : a faint trace ⟨a ~ of a smile⟩ 5 : a false image in a photographic negative or on a television screen — ghost·ly adv

²ghost vb : GHOSTWRITE

ghost·write \-‚rīt\ vb -wrote \-‚rōt\; -writ·ten \-‚ri-tᵊn\ : to write for and in the name of another — ghost·writ·er n

ghoul \'gül\ n [Ar ghūl] : a legendary evil being that robs graves and feeds on corpses — ghoul·ish adj

GHQ abbr general headquarters

gi abbr gill

¹GI \‚jē-'ī\ adj [galvanized iron; fr. abbr. used in listing such articles as garbage cans, but taken as abbr. for government issue] 1 : provided by an official U.S. military supply department ⟨~ shoes⟩ 2 : of, relating to, or characteristic of U.S. military personnel 3 : conforming to military regulations or customs ⟨a ~ haircut⟩

²GI n, pl GIs or GI's \-'īz\ : a member or former member of the U.S. armed forces; esp : an enlisted man

³GI abbr 1 galvanized iron 2 gastrointestinal 3 general issue 4 government issue

gi·ant \'jī-ənt\ n 1 : a legendary humanlike being of great size and strength 2 : a living being or thing of extraordinary size or powers — giant adj

gi·ant·ess \'jī-ən-təs\ n : a female giant

giant panda n : PANDA 2

gib·ber \'ji-bər\ vb : to speak rapidly, inarticulately, and often foolishly

gib·ber·ish \'ji-bə-rish\ n : unintelligible or confused speech or language

¹gib·bet \'ji-bət\ n : GALLOWS

²gibbet vb 1 : to hang on a gibbet 2 : to expose to public scorn 3 : to execute by hanging

gib·bon \'gi-bən\ n : any of several tailless apes of southeastern Asia

gib·bous \'ji-bəs, 'gi-\ adj 1 : rounded like the exterior of a sphere or circle 2 : seen with more than half but not all of the apparent disk illuminated ⟨~ moon⟩ 3 : having a hump : HUMPBACKED

gibe or jibe \'jīb\ vb gibed or jibed; gib·ing or jib·ing : to utter taunting words : SNEER — gibe or jibe n

gib·lets \'jib-ləts\ n pl : the edible viscera of a fowl

Gib·son girl \'gib-sən-\ adj : of or relating to a style in women's clothing characterized by high necks, full sleeves, and slender waistlines

gid·dy \'gi-dē\ adj gid·di·er; -est 1 : DIZZY 2 : causing dizziness ⟨a ~ height⟩ 3 : not serious : FRIVOLOUS, SILLY — gid·di·ness \-dē-nəs\ n

gid·dy·ap \ˌgi-dē-'ap, -'əp\ or gid·dy·up \-'əp\ vb imper — a command (as to a horse) to go ahead or go faster

GIF \'gif, 'jif\ n [graphic interchange format] : a computer file format for digital images; also : the image itself

gift \'gift\ n 1 : a special ability : TALENT 2 : something given : PRESENT 3 : the act or power of giving

gift·ed \'gif-təd\ adj : TALENTED

¹gig \'gig\ n 1 : a long light ship's boat 2 : a light 2-wheeled one-horse carriage

¹gig 2

²gig n : a pronged spear for catching fish — gig vb

³gig n : a job for a specified time; esp : an entertainer's engagement

⁴gig n : a military demerit — gig vb

giga·byte \'ji-gə-ˌbīt, 'gi-\ n : 1024 megabytes or 1,073,741,824 bytes; also : one billion bytes

gi·gan·tic \jī-'gan-tik\ adj : exceeding the usual (as in size or force)

gig·gle \'gi-gəl\ vb gig·gled; gig·gling : to laugh with repeated short catches of the breath — giggle n — gig·gly \-gə-lē\ adj

GIGO abbr garbage in, garbage out

gig·o·lo \'ji-gə-ˌlō\ n, pl -los 1 : a man supported by a woman usu. in return for his attentions 2 : a professional dancing partner or male escort

Gi·la monster \'hē-lə-\ n : a large orange and black venomous lizard of the southwestern U.S.

¹gild \'gild\ vb gild·ed or gilt \'gilt\; gild·ing 1 : to overlay with or as if with a thin covering of gold 2 : to give an attractive but often deceptive appearance to

²gild var of GUILD

¹gill \'jil\ n — see WEIGHT table

²gill \'gil\ n : an organ (as of a fish) for obtaining oxygen from water

¹gilt \'gilt\ adj : of the color of gold

²gilt n : gold or a substance resembling gold laid on the surface of an object

³gilt n : a young female swine

¹gim·crack \'jim-ˌkrak\ n : a showy object of little use or value

²gimcrack adj : CHEAP, SHODDY

gim·let \'gim-lət\ n : a small tool with screw point and cross handle for boring holes

gim·me cap \'gi-mē-\ n : an adjustable visored cap featuring a corporate logo or slogan

gim·mick \'gi-mik\ n 1 : CONTRIVANCE, GADGET 2 : an important feature that is not immediately apparent : CATCH 3 : a new and ingenious scheme 4 : a device used to attract business or attention — gim·micky \-mi-kē\ adj

gim·mick·ry \'gi-mi-krē\ n, pl -ries : an array of or the use of gimmicks

gimpy \'gim-pē\ adj : LAME 1

¹gin \'jin\ n [ME gin, fr. AF, short for engin engine] 1 : TRAP, SNARE 2 : a machine to separate seeds from cotton — gin vb

²gin n [by shortening & alter. fr. geneva, kind of gin] : a liquor distilled from a grain mash and flavored with juniper berries

gin·ger \'jin-jər\ n : the pungent aromatic rootstock of a tropical plant used esp. as a spice and in medicine; also : the spice or the plant

ginger ale n : a carbonated soft drink flavored with ginger

gin·ger·bread \'jin-jər-ˌbred\ n 1 : a cake made with molasses and flavored with ginger 2 : lavish or superfluous ornament esp. in architecture

gin·ger·ly \'jin-jər-lē\ adj : very cautious or careful — gingerly adv

gin·ger·snap \-ˌsnap\ n : a thin brittle molasses cookie flavored with ginger

ging·ham \'giŋ-əm\ n : a clothing fabric usu. of yarn-dyed cotton in plain weave

gin·gi·vi·tis \ˌjin-jə-'vī-təs\ n : inflammation of the gums

gink·go also ging·ko \'giŋ-(ˌ)kō\ n, pl ginkgoes or ginkgos also ginkos or gingkoes 1 : a tree of eastern China with fan-shaped leaves often grown as a shade tree 2 : GINKGO BILOBA

ginkgo bi·lo·ba \-ˌbī-'lō-bə\ n : an extract of the leaves of ginkgo that is held to enhance mental functioning

gin·seng \'jin-ˌseŋ\ n : an aromatic root of a Chinese or No. American herb used esp. in Chinese medicine; also : one of these herbs

Gip·sy chiefly Brit var of GYPSY

gi·raffe \jə-'raf\ n, pl giraffes [It giraffa, fr. Ar zirāfa] : an African ruminant mammal with a very long neck and a short coat with dark blotches

gird \'gərd\ vb gird·ed or girt \'gərt\; gird·ing 1 : to encircle or fasten (as a sword) with or as if with a belt 2 : to invest esp. with power or authority 3 : PREPARE, BRACE

gird·er \'gər-dər\ n : a horizontal main supporting beam

gir·dle \'gər-dᵊl\ n 1 : something (as a belt or sash) that encircles or confines 2 : a woman's supporting undergarment that extends from the waist to below the hips — girdle vb

girl \'gərl\ n 1 : a female child 2 : a young woman 3 : SWEETHEART — girl·hood \-ˌhu̇d\ n — girl·ish adj

girl Friday n : a female assistant (as in an office) entrusted with a wide variety of tasks

girl·friend \'gərl-ˌfrend\ n 1 : a female friend 2 : a regular female companion in a romantic or sexual relationship

Girl Scout n : a member of any of the scouting programs of the Girl Scouts of the United States of America

girth \'gərth\ n 1 : a band around an animal by which something (as a saddle) may be fastened on its back 2 : a measure around something

gist \'jist\ n [AF, it lies, fr. gesir to lie, ultim. fr. L jacēre] : the main point or part

git dial var of GET

¹give \'giv\ vb gave \'gāv\; giv·en \'gi-vən\; giv·ing 1 : to make a present of 2 : to bestow by formal action 3 : to accord or yield to another 4 : to yield to force, strain, or pressure 5 : to put into the possession or keeping of another 6 : PROFFER ⟨gave her his hand⟩ 7 : DELIVER ⟨gave the bride away⟩ 8 : to present in public performance or to view 9 : PROVIDE ⟨~ a party⟩ 10 : ATTRIBUTE 11 : to make, form, or yield as a product or result ⟨cows ~ milk⟩ 12 : PAY 13 : to deliver by some bodily action ⟨gave me a push⟩ 14 : to offer as a pledge ⟨I ~ you my word⟩ 15 : DEVOTE 16 : to cause to have or receive

²give n 1 : capacity or tendency to yield to force or strain 2 : the quality or state of being springy

give–and–take \ˌgiv-ən-'tāk\ n 1 : COMPROMISE 2 : a usu. good-natured exchange (as of remarks or ideas)

give·away \'gi-və-ˌwā\ n 1 : an unintentional revelation or betrayal 2 : something given away free; esp : PREMIUM

give in vb : SUBMIT, SURRENDER

¹giv·en \'gi-vən\ adj 1 : DISPOSED, INCLINED ⟨∼ to swearing⟩ 2 : SPECIFIED, PARTICULAR ⟨at a ∼ time⟩

²given n : something taken for granted : a basic condition or assumption

³given prep : CONSIDERING

given name n : a name that precedes one's surname

give out vb 1 : EMIT 2 : BREAK DOWN 3 : to become exhausted : COLLAPSE

give up vb 1 : SURRENDER 2 : to abandon (oneself) to a feeling, influence, or activity 3 : QUIT

giz·mo also gis·mo \'giz-mō\ n, pl gizmos also gismos : GADGET

giz·zard \'gi-zərd\ n : the muscular usu. horny-lined enlargement of the alimentary canal of a bird used for churning and grinding up food

gla·cial \'glā-shəl\ adj 1 : extremely cold 2 : of or relating to glaciers 3 : being or relating to a past period of time when a large part of the earth was covered by glaciers 4 cap : PLEISTOCENE 5 : very slow ⟨a ∼ pace⟩ — gla·cial·ly adv

gla·ci·ate \'glā-shē-ˌāt\ vb -at·ed; -at·ing 1 : to subject to glacial action 2 : to produce glacial effects in or on — gla·ci·a·tion \ˌglā-shē-ˈā-shən, -sē-\ n

gla·cier \'glā-shər\ n [F, fr. MF dial. (Savoy), fr. glace ice, fr. L glacies] : a large body of ice moving slowly down a slope or spreading outward on a land surface

¹glad \'glad\ adj glad·der; glad·dest 1 : experiencing pleasure, joy, or delight 2 : PLEASED 3 : very willing ⟨was ∼ to help⟩ 4 : PLEASANT, JOYFUL 5 : CHEERFUL ⟨a ∼ morning⟩ — glad·ly adv — glad·ness n

²glad n : GLADIOLUS

glad·den \'gla-dᵊn\ vb : to make glad

glade \'glād\ n : a grassy open space surrounded by woods

glad·i·a·tor \'gla-dē-ˌā-tər\ n 1 : a person engaged in a fight to the death for public entertainment in ancient Rome 2 : a person engaging in a public fight or controversy; also : PRIZEFIGHTER — glad·i·a·to·ri·al \ˌgla-dē-ə-ˈtȯr-ē-əl\ adj

glad·i·o·lus \ˌgla-dē-ˈō-ləs\ n, pl -oli \-ˈō-(ˌ)lē, -ˌlī\ or -olus also -o·lus·es [L, fr. dim. of gladius sword] : any of a genus of chiefly African plants related to the irises and having erect sword-shaped leaves and stalks of bright colored flowers

glad·some \'glad-səm\ adj : giving or showing joy : CHEERFUL

glad·stone \'glad-ˌstōn\ n, often cap : a suitcase with flexible sides on a rigid frame that opens flat into two compartments

glam \'glam\ n : extravagantly showy glamour — glam adj

glam·or·ise Brit var of GLAMORIZE

glam·or·ize also glam·our·ize \'gla-mə-ˌrīz\ vb -ized; -iz·ing : to make or look upon as glamorous

glam·our also glam·or \'gla-mər\ n [Sc glamour magic spell, alter. of E grammar; fr. the popular association of erudition with occult practices] : an exciting and often illusory and romantic attractiveness; esp : alluring personal attraction — glam·or·ous also glam·our·ous \-mə-rəs\ adj

¹glance \'glans\ vb glanced; glanc·ing 1 : to strike and fly off to one side 2 : GLEAM 3 : to give a quick look

²glance n 1 : a quick intermittent flash or gleam 2 : a deflected impact or blow 3 : a quick look

gland \'gland\ n : a cell or group of cells that prepares and secretes a substance (as saliva or sweat) for further use in or discharge from the body

glan·du·lar \'glan-jə-lər\ adj : of, relating to, or involving glands

glans \'glanz\ n, pl glan·des \'glan-ˌdēz\ [L, lit., acorn] : a conical vascular body forming the extremity of the penis or clitoris

¹glare \'gler\ vb glared; glar·ing 1 : to shine with a harsh dazzling light 2 : to stare fiercely or angrily

²glare n 1 : a harsh dazzling light 2 : an angry or fierce stare

glaring adj : very conspicuous ⟨a ∼ error⟩ — glar·ing·ly adv

glass \'glas\ n 1 : a hard brittle amorphous usu. transparent or translucent material consisting typically of silica 2 : something made of glass; esp : TUMBLER 2 3 pl : a pair of lenses used to correct defects of vision : SPEC-

TACLES 4 : the quantity held by a glass container — glass adj — glass·ful \-ˌfu̇l\ n — glassy adj

glass-blow·ing \-ˌblō-iŋ\ n : the art of shaping a mass of glass that has been softened by heat by blowing air into it through a tube — glass-blow·er n

glass·ware \-ˌwer\ n : articles made of glass

glau·co·ma \glau̇-ˈkō-mə, glȯ-\ n : a disease of the eye marked by increased pressure within the eyeball resulting in damage to the retina and gradual loss of vision

¹glaze \'glāz\ vb glazed; glaz·ing 1 : to furnish (as a window frame) with glass 2 : to apply glaze to

²glaze n : a glassy coating or surface

gla·zier \'glā-zhər\ n : a person who sets glass in window frames

¹gleam \'glēm\ n 1 : a transient subdued or partly obscured light 2 : GLINT 3 : a faint trace ⟨a ∼ of hope⟩

²gleam vb 1 : to shine with subdued light or moderate brightness 2 : to appear briefly or faintly ♦ Synonyms FLASH, GLIMMER, GLISTEN, GLITTER, SHIMMER, SPARKLE

glean \'glēn\ vb 1 : to gather grain left by reapers 2 : to collect little by little or with patient effort — glean·able adj — glean·er n

glean·ings \'glē-niŋz\ n pl : things acquired by gleaning

glee \'glē\ n [ME, fr. OE glēo entertainment, music] 1 : JOY, HILARITY 2 : a part-song for three usu. male voices — glee·ful adj — glee·ful·ly adv

glee club n : a chorus organized for singing usu. short choral pieces

glen \'glen\ n : a narrow hidden valley

glen·gar·ry \glen-ˈga-rē\ n, pl -ries often cap : a woolen cap of Scottish origin

glib \'glib\ adj glib·ber; glib·best : speaking or spoken with careless ease — glib·ly adv

glide \'glīd\ vb glid·ed; glid·ing 1 : to move smoothly and effortlessly 2 : to descend gradually without engine power ⟨∼ in an airplane⟩ — glide n

glid·er \'glī-dər\ n 1 : one that glides 2 : an aircraft resembling an airplane but having no engine 3 : a porch seat suspended from an upright frame

¹glim·mer \'gli-mər\ vb : to shine faintly or unsteadily

²glimmer n 1 : a faint unsteady light 2 : INKLING 3 : a small amount : HINT

¹glimpse \'glimps\ vb glimpsed; glimps·ing : to take a brief look : see momentarily or incompletely

²glimpse n 1 : a faint idea : GLIMMER 2 : a short hurried look

glint \'glint\ vb 1 : to shine by reflection : SPARKLE, GLITTER, GLEAM 2 : to appear briefly or faintly — glint n

glis·san·do \gli-ˈsän-(ˌ)dō\ n, pl -di \-(ˌ)dē\ or -dos : a rapid sliding up or down the musical scale

¹glis·ten \'gli-sᵊn\ vb : to shine by reflection with a soft luster or sparkle

²glisten n : GLITTER, SPARKLE

glis·ter \'gli-stər\ vb : GLITTER

glitch \'glich\ n : MALFUNCTION; also : SNAG 2

¹glit·ter \'gli-tər\ vb 1 : to shine with brilliant or metallic luster : SPARKLE 2 : to shine with strong emotion : FLASH ⟨eyes ∼ing in anger⟩ 3 : to be brilliantly attractive esp. in a superficial way

²glitter n 1 : sparkling brilliancy, showiness, or attractiveness 2 : small glittering objects used for ornamentation — glit·tery \'gli-tə-rē\ adj

¹glitz \'glits\ n : extravagant showiness — glitzy \'glit-sē\ adj

²glitz vb : to make flashy or extravagant in appearance — often used with up

gloam·ing \'glō-miŋ\ n : TWILIGHT, DUSK

gloat \'glōt\ vb : to think about something with triumphant and often malicious delight

glob \'gläb\ n 1 : a small drop 2 : a large rounded mass

glob·al \'glō-bəl\ adj 1 : WORLDWIDE 2 : COMPREHENSIVE, GENERAL — glob·al·ly adv

glob·al·i·za·tion \ˌglō-bə-lə-ˈzā-shən\ n : the development of an increasingly integrated global economy

Global Positioning System n : GPS

global warming n : an increase in the earth's atmospheric and oceanic temperatures due to an increase in the greenhouse effect

globe \'glōb\ n 1 : BALL, SPHERE 2 : EARTH; also : a spherical representation of the earth

globe–trot·ter \'glōb-ˌträ-tər\ *n* : a person who travels widely — **globe–trot·ting** *n or adj*

glob·u·lar \'glä-byə-lər\ *adj* : having the shape of a globe or globule

glob·ule \'glä-(ˌ)byül\ *n* : a tiny globe or ball esp. of a liquid

glob·u·lin \'glä-byə-lən\ *n* : any of a class of simple proteins insoluble in pure water but soluble in dilute salt solutions that occur widely in plant and animal tissues

glock·en·spiel \'glä-kən-ˌshpēl, -ˌspēl\ *n* [G, fr. *Glocke* bell + *Spiel* play] : a percussion musical instrument consisting of a series of metal bars played with two hammers

gloom \'glüm\ *n* 1 : partial or total darkness 2 : lowness of spirits : DEJECTION 3 : an atmosphere of despondency — **gloom·i·ly** \'glü-mə-lē\ *adv* — **gloom·i·ness** \-mē-nəs\ *n* — **gloomy** \'glü-mē\ *adj*

Gloomy Gus \-'gəs\ *n, pl* **Gloomy Gus·es** : a person who is habitually gloomy

glop \'gläp\ *n* : a messy mass or mixture

glo·ri·fy \'glȯr-ə-ˌfī\ *vb* **-fied; -fy·ing** 1 : to raise to heavenly glory 2 : to light up brilliantly 3 : EXTOL 4 : to give glory to (as in worship) — **glo·ri·fi·ca·tion** \ˌglȯr-ə-fə-'kā-shən\ *n*

glo·ri·ous \'glȯr-ē-əs\ *adj* 1 : possessing or deserving glory : PRAISEWORTHY 2 : conferring glory 3 : RESPLENDENT, MAGNIFICENT ⟨a ∼ sunset⟩ 4 : DELIGHTFUL, WONDERFUL ⟨had a ∼ weekend⟩ — **glo·ri·ous·ly** *adv*

¹glo·ry \'glȯr-ē\ *n, pl* **glories** 1 : RENOWN 2 : honor and praise rendered in worship 3 : something that secures praise or renown 4 : a distinguishing quality or asset 5 : RESPLENDENCE, MAGNIFICENCE 6 : heavenly bliss 7 : a height of prosperity or achievement

²glory *vb* **glo·ried; glo·ry·ing** : to rejoice proudly : EXULT

¹gloss \'gläs, 'glȯs\ *n* 1 : LUSTER, SHEEN, BRIGHTNESS 2 : outward show

²gloss *vb* 1 : to give a false appearance of acceptableness to ⟨∼ over inadequacies⟩ 2 : to deal with too lightly or not at all

³gloss *n* [alter. of *gloze*, fr. ME *glose*, fr. AF, fr. ML *glosa, glossa*, fr. Gk *glōssa, glōtta* tongue, language, unusual word] 1 : an explanatory note (as in the margin of a text) 2 : GLOSSARY 3 : an interlinear translation 4 : a continuous commentary accompanying a text

⁴gloss *vb* : to furnish glosses for

glos·sa·ry \'glä-sə-rē, 'glȯ-\ *n, pl* **-ries** : a collection of difficult or specialized terms with their meanings — **glos·sar·i·al** \glä-'ser-ē-əl, glȯ-\ *adj*

glos·so·la·lia \ˌglä-sə-'lā-lē-ə, ˌglȯ-\ *n* [ultim. fr. Gk *glōssa* tongue, language + *lalia* chatter] : TONGUE 6

¹glossy \'glä-sē, 'glȯ-\ *adj* **gloss·i·er; -est** : having a surface luster or brightness — **gloss·i·ly** \-sə-lē\ *adv* — **gloss·i·ness** \-sē-nəs\ *n*

²glossy *n, pl* **gloss·ies** : a photograph printed on smooth shiny paper

glot·tis \'glä-təs\ *n, pl* **glot·tis·es** *or* **glot·ti·des** \-tə-ˌdēz\ : the slitlike opening between the vocal cords in the larynx — **glot·tal** \'glä-t³l\ *adj*

glove \'gləv\ *n* 1 : a covering for the hand having separate sections for each finger 2 : a padded leather covering for the hand for use in a sport

¹glow \'glō\ *vb* 1 : to shine with or as if with intense heat 2 : to have a rich warm usu. ruddy color : FLUSH, BLUSH 3 : to feel hot 4 : to show exuberance or elation ⟨∼ with pride⟩

²glow *n* 1 : brightness or warmth of color; *esp* : REDNESS 2 : warmth of feeling or emotion 3 : a sensation of warmth 4 : light such as is emitted from a heated substance

glow·er \'glaù-(ə)r\ *vb* : to stare angrily : SCOWL — **glow·er** *n*

glow·worm \'glō-ˌwərm\ *n* : any of various insect larvae or adults that give off light

glox·in·ia \gläk-'si-nē-ə\ *n* : any of a genus of tropical herbs related to the African violets; *esp* : one with showy bell-shaped or slipper-shaped flowers

gloze \'glōz\ *vb* **glozed; gloz·ing** : to make appear right or acceptable : GLOSS

glu·cose \'glü-ˌkōs\ *n* 1 : a form of crystalline sugar; *esp* : DEXTROSE 2 : a sweet light-colored syrup made from cornstarch

glue \'glü\ *n* : a jellylike protein substance made from animal materials and used for sticking things together; *also* : any of various other strong adhesives — **glue** *vb* — **gluey** \'glü-ē\ *adj*

glum \'gləm\ *adj* **glum·mer; glum·mest** 1 : broodingly morose : SULLEN 2 : DREARY, GLOOMY ⟨a ∼ countenance⟩ ✦ **Synonyms** CRABBED, DOUR, SATURNINE, SULKY

¹glut \'glət\ *vb* **glut·ted; glut·ting** 1 : OVERSUPPLY 2 : to fill esp. with food to satiety : SATIATE

²glut *n* : an excessive supply

glu·ten \'glü-t³n\ *n* : a gluey protein substance that causes dough to be sticky

glu·ti·nous \'glü-tə-nəs\ *adj* : STICKY

glut·ton \'glə-t³n\ *n* : one that eats to excess — **glut·ton·ous** \'glə-tə-nəs\ *adj* — **glut·tony** \'glə-tə-nē\ *n*

glyc·er·in *or* **glyc·er·ine** \'gli-sə-rən\ *n* : GLYCEROL

glyc·er·ol \'gli-sə-ˌrȯl, -ˌrōl\ *n* : a sweet syrupy alcohol usu. obtained from fats and used esp. as a solvent

gly·co·gen \'glī-kə-jən\ *n* : a white tasteless substance that is the chief storage carbohydrate of animals

gm *abbr* gram

GM *abbr* 1 general manager 2 guided missile

G–man \'jē-ˌman\ *n* : a special agent of the Federal Bureau of Investigation

GMT *abbr* Greenwich mean time

gnarled \'närld\ *adj* 1 : KNOTTY ⟨∼ hands⟩ 2 : GLOOMY, SULLEN

gnash \'nash\ *vb* : to grind (as teeth) together

gnat \'nat\ *n* : any of various small usu. biting dipteran flies

gnaw \'nȯ\ *vb* 1 : to consume, wear away, or make by persistent biting or nibbling 2 : to affect as if by gnawing — **gnaw·er** *n*

gneiss \'nīs\ *n* : a layered rock similar in composition to granite

gnome \'nōm\ *n* : a dwarf of folklore who lives inside the earth and guards precious ore or treasure — **gnome·like** \-ˌlīk\ *adj* — **gnom·ish** *adj*

GNP *abbr* gross national product

gnu \'nü\ *n, pl* **gnu** *or* **gnus** : WILDEBEEST

¹go \'gō\ *vb* **went** \'went\; **gone** \'gȯn, 'gän\; **go·ing; goes** \'gōz\ 1 : to move on a course : PROCEED ⟨∼ slow⟩ 2 : LEAVE, DEPART 3 : to take a certain course or follow a certain procedure ⟨reports ∼ through department channels⟩ 4 : EXTEND, RUN ⟨his land ∼es to the river⟩; *also* : LEAD ⟨that door ∼es to the cellar⟩ 5 : to be habitually in a certain state ⟨∼es barefoot⟩ 6 : to become lost, consumed, or spent; *also* : DIE 7 : ELAPSE, PASS 8 : to pass by sale ⟨*went* for a good price⟩ 9 : to become impaired or weakened ⟨his hearing started to ∼⟩ 10 : to give way under force or pressure : BREAK 11 : to move along in a specified manner ⟨it *went* well⟩ 12 : to be in general or on an average ⟨cheap, as yachts ∼⟩ 13 : to become esp. as the result of a contest ⟨the decision *went* against him⟩ 14 : to put or subject oneself ⟨∼ to great expense⟩ 15 : RESORT ⟨*went* to court to recover damages⟩ 16 : to begin or maintain an action or motion 17 : to function properly ⟨the clock doesn't ∼⟩ 18 : to be known ⟨∼es by an alias⟩ 19 : to be or act in accordance ⟨a good rule to ∼ by⟩ 20 : to come to be applied 21 : to pass by award, assignment, or lot 22 : to contribute to a result ⟨qualities that ∼ to make a hero⟩ 23 : to be about, intending, or expecting something ⟨is ∼*ing* to leave town⟩ 24 : to arrive at a certain state or condition ⟨∼ to sleep⟩ 25 : to come to be ⟨the tire *went* flat⟩ 26 : to be capable of being sung or played ⟨the tune ∼*es* like this⟩ 27 : to be suitable or becoming : HARMONIZE 28 : to be capable of passing, extending, or being contained or inserted ⟨this coat will ∼ in the trunk⟩ 29 : to have a usual or proper place or position : BELONG ⟨these books ∼ on the top shelf⟩ 30 : to be capable of being divided ⟨3 ∼*es* into 6 twice⟩ 31 : to have a tendency ⟨that ∼*es* to show that he is honest⟩ 32 : to be acceptable, satisfactory, or adequate ⟨any color will ∼ with black⟩ 33 : to empty the bladder or bowels 34 : to proceed along or according to : FOLLOW 35 : TRAVERSE 36 : BET, BID ⟨willing to ∼ $50⟩ 37 : to assume the function or obligation of ⟨∼ bail for a friend⟩ 38 : to participate to the extent of ⟨∼ halves⟩ 39 : WEIGH 40 : ENDURE, TOLERATE 41 : AFFORD ⟨can't ∼ the price⟩ 42 : SAY — used chiefly in oral narration of speech 43

go • gondola

: to engage in ⟨don't ~ telling everyone⟩ — **go at** 1 : AT-
TACK, ATTEMPT 2 : UNDERTAKE — **go back on** 1
: ABANDON 2 : BETRAY 3 : FAIL — **go by the board** : to
be discarded — **go for** 1 : to pass for or serve as 2 : to
try to secure 3 : FAVOR — **go one better** : OUTDO, SUR-
PASS — **go over** 1 : EXAMINE 2 : REPEAT 3 : STUDY,
REVIEW — **go places** : to be on the way to success — **go
steady** : to date one person exclusively — **go to bat for**
: DEFEND, CHAMPION — **go to town** 1 : to work or act
efficiently 2 : to be very successful
²**go** n, pl **goes** 1 : the act or manner of going 2 : the height
of fashion ⟨boots are all the ~⟩ 3 : a turn of affairs : OC-
CURRENCE 4 : ENERGY, VIGOR 5 : ATTEMPT, TRY ⟨give
it a ~⟩ 6 : a spell of activity ⟨finished the job at one ~⟩
— **no go** : USELESS, HOPELESS — **on the go** : constantly
active
³**go** adj : functioning properly ⟨declared all systems ~⟩
goad \'gōd\ n [ME gode, fr. OE gād spear, goad] 1 : a
pointed rod used to urge on an animal 2 : something that
urges ✦ **Synonyms** STIMULUS, IMPETUS, INCENTIVE,
SPUR, STIMULANT — **goad** vb
go–ahead \'gō-ə-ˌhed\ n : authority to proceed
goal \'gōl\ n 1 : the mark set as limit to a race; also : an
area to be reached safely in children's games 2 : AIM,
PURPOSE 3 : an area or object toward which play is directed to score; also : a successful attempt to score
goal·ie \'gō-lē\ n : GOALKEEPER
goal·keep·er \'gōl-ˌkē-pər\ n : a player who defends the
goal in various games
goal·post \-ˌpōst\ n : one of the two vertical posts with a
crossbar that constitute the goal in various games
goat \'gōt\ n, pl **goats** or **goat** : any of various hollow-
horned ruminant mammals related to the sheep that have
backward-curving horns, a short tail, and usu. straight
hair
goa·tee \gō-'tē\ n : a small trim pointed or tufted beard on
a man's chin
goat·herd \'gōt-ˌhərd\ n : a person who tends goats
goat·skin \-ˌskin\ n : the skin of a goat or a leather made
from it
¹**gob** \'gäb\ n : LUMP, MASS
²**gob** n : SAILOR
²**gob·bet** \'gä-bət\ n : LUMP, MASS
¹**gob·ble** \'gä-bəl\ vb **gob·bled; gob·bling** 1 : to swallow
or eat greedily 2 : to take eagerly : GRAB
²**gobble** vb **gob·bled; gob·bling** : to make the natural guttural noise of a male turkey
gob·ble·dy·gook also **gob·ble·de·gook** \'gä-bəl-dē-ˌgúk,
-ˌgük\ n : generally unintelligible jargon
gob·bler \'gä-blər\ n : a male turkey
go–be·tween \'gō-bə-ˌtwēn\ n : an intermediate agent
: BROKER
gob·let \'gä-blət\ n : a drinking glass with a foot and stem
gob·lin \'gä-blən\ n : an ugly or grotesque sprite that is
mischievous and sometimes evil and malicious
go·by \'gō-bē\ n, pl **gobies** also **goby** : any of numerous
spiny-finned fishes usu. having the pelvic fins united to
form a ventral sucking disk
god \'gäd, 'gód\ n 1 cap : the supreme reality; esp : the
Being worshiped as the creator and ruler of the universe
2 : a being or object believed to have supernatural attributes and powers and to require worship 3 : a thing of
supreme value 4 : an extraordinarily attractive person
god·child \'gäd-ˌchī(-ə)ld, 'gód-\ n : a person for whom another person stands as sponsor at baptism
god·daugh·ter \-ˌdó-tər\ n : a female godchild
god·dess \'gä-dəs, 'gó-\ n 1 : a female god 2 : a woman
whose charm or beauty arouses adoration
god·fa·ther \'gäd-ˌfä-thər, 'gód-\ n 1 : a man who sponsors a person at baptism 2 : the leader of an organized
crime syndicate
god·head \-ˌhed\ n 1 : divine nature or essence 2 cap
: GOD 1; also : the nature of God esp. as existing in three
persons
god·hood \-ˌhúd\ n : DIVINITY
god·less \-ləs\ adj : not acknowledging a deity or divine
law — **god·less·ness** n
god·like \-ˌlīk\ adj : resembling or having the qualities of
God or a god
god·ly \-lē\ adj **god·li·er; -est** 1 : DIVINE 2 : PIOUS, DE-
VOUT — **god·li·ness** n

god·moth·er \-ˌmə-thər\ n : a woman who sponsors a person at baptism
god·par·ent \-ˌper-ənt\ n : a sponsor at baptism
god·send \-ˌsend\ n : a desirable or needed thing or event
that comes unexpectedly
god·son \-ˌsən\ n : a male godchild
God·speed \-'spēd\ n : a prosperous journey : SUCCESS
⟨bade him ~⟩
go·fer or **go·pher** \'gō-fər\ n [alter. of go for] : an employee whose duties include running errands
go–get·ter \'gō-ˌge-tər\ n : an aggressively enterprising
person — **go–get·ting** adj or n
gog·gle \'gä-gəl\ vb **gog·gled; gog·gling** : to stare with
wide or protuberant eyes
gog·gles \'gä-gəlz\ n pl : protective glasses set in a flexible
frame that fits snugly against the face
go–go \'gō-ˌgō\ adj 1 : related to, being, or employed to
entertain in a disco ⟨~ dancers⟩ 2 : aggressively enterprising and energetic
go·ings–on \ˌgō-iŋz-'ón, -'än\ n pl : ACTIONS, EVENTS
goi·ter \'gói-tər\ n : an abnormally enlarged thyroid gland
visible as a swelling at the base of the neck — **goi·trous**
\-trəs, -tə-rəs\ adj
goi·tre chiefly Brit var of GOITER
go–kart \'gō-ˌkärt\ n : a small motorized vehicle used esp.
for racing
gold \'gōld\ n 1 : a malleable yellow metallic chemical element used esp. for coins and jewelry 2 : gold coins; also
: MONEY 3 : a yellow color
gold–brick \'gōld-ˌbrik\ n : a person who shirks assigned
work — **goldbrick** vb
gold coast n, often cap G&C : an exclusive residential district
gold digger n : a person who uses charm to extract money
or gifts from others
gold·en \'gōl-dən\ adj 1 : made of or relating to gold 2
: having the color of gold; also : BLOND 3 : SHINING,
LUSTROUS 4 : SUPERB 5 : FLOURISHING, PROSPEROUS
6 : radiantly youthful and vigorous 7 : FAVORABLE, AD-
VANTAGEOUS ⟨a ~ opportunity⟩ 8 : MELLOW, RESO-
NANT ⟨a ~ tenor⟩
gold·en–ag·er \'gōl-dən-'ā-jər\ n : an elderly and often retired person usu. engaging in club activities
golden eagle n : a large dark brown eagle with gold-col-
ored feathers on the back of the head and neck
golden hamster n : a small tawny hamster often kept as a
pet
golden handcuffs n pl : special benefits offered to an employee as an inducement to continue service
golden handshake n : a generous severance agreement
given esp. as an inducement to early retirement
golden retriever n : any of a breed of retrievers with a flat
golden coat
gold·en·rod \'gōl-dən-ˌräd\ n : any of numerous herbs related to the daisies that have tall slender stalks with many
tiny usu. yellow flower heads
golden years n pl : the advanced years in a lifetime
gold·finch \-ˌfinch\ n 1 : a small largely red, black, and
yellow Old World finch often kept in a cage 2 : any of
three small related American finches of which the males
usu. become bright yellow and black in summer
gold·fish \-ˌfish\ n : a small usu. golden-orange carp often
kept as an aquarium or pond fish
gold·smith \-ˌsmith\ n : a person who makes or deals in
articles of gold
golf \'gälf, 'gólf\ n : a game played with a small ball and
various clubs on a course having 9 or 18 holes — **golf** vb
— **golf·er** n
-gon \ˌgän\ n comb form : figure having (so many) angles
⟨hexagon⟩
go·nad \'gō-ˌnad\ n : a sperm- or egg-producing gland
: OVARY, TESTIS — **go·nad·al** \gō-'na-d°l\ adj
go·nad·o·trop·ic \gō-ˌna-də-'trä-pik\ also **go·nad·o·tro-
phic** \-'trō-fik,-'trä-\ adj : acting on or stimulating the gonads
go·nad·o·tro·pin \-'trō-pən\ also **go·nad·o·tro·phin** \-fən\
n : a gonadotropic hormone
gon·do·la \'gän-də-lə (usual for 1), gän-'dō-\ n [It. dial.
(Venice), prob. fr. MGk kontoura small vessel] 1 : a long
narrow boat used on the canals of Venice 2 : a railroad
car used for hauling loose freight (as coal) 3 : an enclo-

sure beneath an airship or balloon 4 : an enclosed car suspended from a cable and used esp. for transporting skiers

gon·do·lier \ˌgän-də-ˈlir\ *n* : a person who propels a gondola

¹gone \ˈgȯn\ *past part of* GO

²gone *adj* 1 : LOST, RUINED 2 : DEAD 3 : SINKING, WEAK 4 : INVOLVED, ABSORBED 5 : INFATUATED 6 : PREGNANT 7 : PAST

gon·er \ˈgȯ-nər\ *n* : one whose case is hopeless

gong \ˈgäŋ, ˈgȯŋ\ *n* : a metallic disk that produces a resounding tone when struck

gono·coc·cus \ˌgä-nə-ˈkä-kəs\ *n, pl* **-coc·ci** \-ˈkäk-ˌsī, -(ˌ)sē, -ˈkä-ˌkī, -(ˌ)kē\ : a pus-producing bacterium causing gonorrhea — **gono·coc·cal** \-ˈkä-kəl\ *adj*

gon·or·rhea \ˌgä-nə-ˈrē-ə\ *n* : a contagious sexually transmitted inflammation of the genital tract caused by the gonococcus — **gon·or·rhe·al** \-ˈrē-əl\ *adj*

goo \ˈgü\ *n* 1 : a viscid or sticky substance 2 : sentimental tripe — **goo·ey** \-ē\ *adj*

goo·ber \ˈgü-bər, ˈgü-\ *n, Southern & Midland* : PEANUT

¹good \ˈgud\ *adj* **bet·ter** \ˈbe-tər\; **best** \ˈbest\ 1 : of a favorable character or tendency 2 : BOUNTIFUL, FERTILE ⟨∼ land⟩ 3 : COMELY, ATTRACTIVE 4 : SUITABLE, FIT 5 : SOUND, WHOLE ⟨only one ∼ arm⟩ 6 : AGREEABLE, PLEASANT ⟨had a ∼ time⟩ 7 : SALUTARY, WHOLESOME 8 : CONSIDERABLE, AMPLE ⟨a ∼ bit of time⟩ 9 : FULL ⟨waited a ∼ hour⟩ 10 : WELL-FOUNDED 11 : TRUE ⟨holds ∼ for everybody⟩ 12 : legally valid or effectual 13 : ADEQUATE, SATISFACTORY 14 : conforming to a standard ⟨∼ English⟩ 15 : DISCRIMINATING 16 : COMMENDABLE, VIRTUOUS 17 : KIND 18 : UPPER-CLASS 19 : COMPETENT 20 : LOYAL, CLOSE — **good·ish** *adj*

²good *n* 1 : something good 2 : GOODNESS 3 : BENEFIT, WELFARE ⟨for the ∼ of mankind⟩ 4 : something that has economic utility 5 *pl* : personal property 6 *pl* : CLOTH 7 *pl* : WARES, MERCHANDISE ⟨canned ∼s⟩ 8 : good persons ⟨the ∼ die young⟩ 9 *pl* : proof of wrongdoing — **for good** : FOREVER, PERMANENTLY — **to the good** : in a position of net gain or profit ⟨$10 *to the good*⟩

³good *adv* : WELL

good–bye or **good–by** \gud-ˈbī, gə-\ *n* : a concluding remark at parting

good cholesterol *n* : HDL

good–for–noth·ing \ˈgud-fər-ˌnə-thiŋ\ *adj* : of no use or value — **good–for–nothing** *n*

Good Friday *n* : the Friday before Easter observed as the anniversary of the crucifixion of Christ

good–heart·ed \ˈgud-ˈhär-təd\ *adj* : having a kindly generous disposition — **good–heart·ed·ly** *adv* — **good–heart·ed·ness** *n*

good–look·ing \ˈgud-ˈlu̇-kiŋ\ *adj* : having an attractive appearance

good·ly \ˈgud-lē\ *adj* **good·li·er; -est** 1 : of pleasing appearance 2 : LARGE, CONSIDERABLE

good·man \ˈgud-mən\ *n, archaic* : MR.

good–na·tured \ˈgud-ˈnā-chərd\ *adj* : of a cheerful disposition — **good–na·tured·ly** \-chərd-lē\ *adv*

good·ness \-nəs\ *n* : EXCELLENCE, VIRTUE

good·wife \-ˌwīf\ *n, archaic* : MRS.

good·will \-ˈwil\ *n* 1 : BENEVOLENCE 2 : the value of the trade a business has built up over time 3 : cheerful consent 4 : willing effort

goody or **good·ie** \ˈgu̇-dē\ *n, pl* **good·ies** : something that is good esp. to eat

goody–goody \ˌgu̇-dē-ˈgu̇-dē\ *adj* : affectedly good — **goody–goody** *n*

goof \ˈgüf\ *vb* 1 : to spend time idly or foolishly 2 : BLUNDER — often used with *off* — **goof** *n*

goof·ball \ˈgüf-ˌbȯl\ *n* 1 *slang* : a barbiturate sleeping pill 2 : a goofy person

go off *vb* 1 : EXPLODE 2 : to follow a course ⟨the party *went off* well⟩

goof–off \ˈgüf-ˌȯf\ *n* : one who evades work or responsibility

goofy \ˈgü-fē\ *adj* **goof·i·er; -est** : CRAZY, SILLY — **goof·i·ness** \-fē-nəs\ *n*

goon \ˈgün\ *n* : a man hired to terrorize or kill opponents

go on *vb* 1 : to continue in a course of action 2 : to take place : HAPPEN

goose \ˈgüs\ *n, pl* **geese** \ˈgēs\ 1 : any of numerous long-

necked web-footed birds related to the swans and ducks; *also* : a female goose as distinguished from a gander 2 : a foolish person 3 *pl* **goos·es** : a tailor's smoothing iron

goose·ber·ry \ˈgüs-ˌber-ē, ˈgüz-, -bə-rē\ *n* : the acid berry of any of several shrubs related to the currant and used esp. in jams and pies

goose bumps *n pl* : roughening of the skin caused usu. by cold, fear, or a sudden feeling of excitement

goose·flesh \-ˌflesh\ *n* : GOOSE BUMPS

goose pimples *n pl* : GOOSE BUMPS

go out *vb* 1 : to become extinguished 2 : to become a candidate ⟨*went out* for the football team⟩

go over *vb* : SUCCEED

GOP *abbr* Grand Old Party (Republican)

¹go·pher \ˈgō-fər\ *n* 1 : a burrowing American land tortoise 2 : any of a family of No. American burrowing rodents with large cheek pouches opening beside the mouth 3 : any of several small ground squirrels of the prairie region of No. America

gopher 2

²gopher *var of* GOFER

go·pik \gō-ˈpēk, -ˈpik\ *n, pl* **gopik** — see *manat* at MONEY table

¹gore \ˈgȯr\ *n* : a tapering or triangular piece (as of cloth in a skirt)

²gore *vb* **gored; gor·ing** : to pierce or wound with something pointed

³gore *n* 1 : BLOOD 2 : gruesomeness depicted in vivid detail

¹gorge \ˈgȯrj\ *n* 1 : THROAT 2 : a narrow ravine 3 : a mass of matter that chokes up a passage

²gorge *vb* **gorged; gorg·ing** : to eat greedily : stuff to capacity : GLUT

gor·geous \ˈgȯr-jəs\ *adj* : resplendently beautiful

Gor·gon·zo·la \ˌgȯr-gən-ˈzō-lə\ *n* : a pungent blue cheese of Italian origin

go·ril·la \gə-ˈri-lə\ *n* [NL, fr. Gk *Gorillai*, a tribe of hairy women in an account of a voyage around Africa] : an African anthropoid ape related to but much larger than the chimpanzee

gor·man·dise *chiefly Brit var of* GORMANDIZE

gor·man·dize \ˈgȯr-mən-ˌdīz\ *vb* **-dized; -diz·ing** : to eat ravenously — **gor·man·diz·er** *n*

gorp \ˈgȯrp\ *n* : a snack consisting of high-calorie food (as raisins and nuts)

gorse \ˈgȯrs\ *n* : a spiny yellow-flowered European evergreen shrub of the legume family

gory \ˈgȯr-ē\ *adj* **gor·i·er; -est** 1 : BLOODSTAINED 2 : HORRIBLE, SENSATIONAL

gos·hawk \ˈgäs-ˌhȯk\ *n* : any of several long-tailed hawks with short rounded wings

gos·ling \ˈgäz-liŋ, ˈgȯz-\ *n* : a young goose

¹gos·pel \ˈgäs-pəl\ *n* [ME, fr. OE *gōdspel*, fr. *gōd* good + *spell* message, news] 1 : the teachings of Christ and the apostles 2 *cap* : any of the first four books of the New Testament 3 : something accepted or promoted as infallible truth

²gospel *adj* 1 : of, relating to, or emphasizing the gospel 2 : relating to or being American religious songs associated with evangelism

gos·sa·mer \ˈgä-sə-mər\ *n* [ME *gossomer*, fr. *gos* goose + *somer* summer] 1 : a film of cobwebs floating in the air 2 : something light, delicate, or tenuous

¹gos·sip \ˈgä-səp\ *n* 1 : a person who habitually reveals personal or sensational facts 2 : rumor or report of an intimate nature 3 : an informal conversation — **gos·sipy** *adj*

²gossip *vb* : to spread gossip

got *past and past part of* GET

Goth \'gäth\ *n* : a member of a Germanic people that early in the Christian era overran the Roman Empire

¹Goth·ic \'gä-thik\ *adj* **1** : of or relating to the Goths **2** : of or relating to a style of architecture prevalent in western Europe from the middle 12th to the early 16th century

²Gothic *n* **1** : the Germanic language of the Goths **2** : the Gothic architectural style or decoration

gotten *past part of* GET

Gou·da \'gü-də\ *n* : a mild Dutch milk cheese shaped in balls

¹gouge \'gaùj\ *n* **1** : a rounded troughlike chisel **2** : a hole or groove made with or as if with a gouge

²gouge *vb* **gouged; goug·ing** **1** : to cut holes or grooves in with or as if with a gouge **2** : DEFRAUD, CHEAT

gou·lash \'gü-ˌläsh, -ˌlash\ *n* [Hungarian *gulyás*] : a stew made with meat, assorted vegetables, and paprika

go under *vb* : to be overwhelmed, defeated, or destroyed : FAIL

gourd \'gòrd, 'gùrd\ *n* **1** : any of a family of tendril-bearing vines including the cucumber, squash, and melon **2** : the fruit of a gourd; *esp* : any of various inedible hard-shelled fruits used esp. for ornament or implements

gourde \'gùrd\ *n* — see MONEY table

gour·mand \'gùr-ˌmänd\ *n* **1** : one who is excessively fond of eating and drinking **2** : GOURMET

gour·met \'gùr-ˌmā, gùr-¹mā\ *n* [F, fr. MF, alter. of *gromet* boy servant, vintner's assistant] : a connoisseur of food and drink

gout \'gaùt\ *n* : a metabolic disease marked by painful inflammation and swelling of the joints — **gouty** *adj*

gov *abbr* **1** government **2** governor **3** governmental institution — used in World Wide Web addresses

gov·ern \'gə-vərn\ *vb* [ME, fr. AF *governer*, fr. L *gubernare* to steer, govern, fr. Gk *kybernan*] **1** : to control and direct the making and administration of policy in : RULE **2** : CONTROL, DIRECT, INFLUENCE **3** : DETERMINE, REGULATE **4** : RESTRAIN — **gov·ern·able** \-vər-nə-bəl\ *adj* — **gov·er·nance** \-vər-nəns\ *n*

gov·ern·ess \'gə-vər-nəs\ *n* : a woman who teaches and trains a child esp. in a private home

gov·ern·ment \'gə-vərn-mənt\ *n* **1** : authoritative direction or control : RULE **2** : the making of policy **3** : the organization or agency through which a political unit exercises authority **4** : the complex of institutions, laws, and customs through which a political unit is governed **5** : the governing body — **gov·ern·men·tal** \ˌgə-vərn-¹men-t³l\ *adj* — **gov·ern·men·tal·ly** \-t³l-ē\ *adv*

gov·er·nor \'gə-vər-nər\ *n* **1** : one that governs; *esp* : a ruler, chief executive, or head of a political unit (as a state) **2** : an attachment to a machine for automatic control of speed — **gov·er·nor·ship** *n*

govt *abbr* government

gown \'gaùn\ *n* **1** : a loose flowing outer garment **2** : an official robe worn esp. by a judge, clergyman, or teacher **3** : a woman's dress (evening ∼s) **4** : a loose robe — **gown** *vb*

gp *abbr* group

GP *abbr* general practitioner

GPO *abbr* **1** general post office **2** Government Printing Office

GPS \ˌjē-ˌpē-¹es\ *n* [Global Positioning System] : a navigation system that uses satellite signals to fix location; *also* : the signal receiver itself

GQ *abbr* general quarters

gr *abbr* **1** grade **2** grain **3** gram **4** gravity **5** gross

grab \'grab\ *vb* **grabbed; grab·bing** : to take hastily : SNATCH — **grab** *n*

¹grace \'grās\ *n* **1** : unmerited help given to people by God (as in overcoming temptation) **2** : freedom from sin through divine grace **3** : a virtue coming from God **4** — used as a title for a duke, a duchess, or an archbishop **5** : a short prayer at a meal **6** : a temporary respite (as from the payment of a debt) **7** : APPROVAL, ACCEPTANCE (in his good ∼s) **8** : CHARM **9** : ATTRACTIVENESS, BEAUTY **10** : fitness or proportion of line or expression **11** : ease of movement **12** : a musical trill or ornament — **grace·ful** \-fəl\ *adj* — **grace·ful·ly** *adv* — **grace·ful·ness** *n* — **grace·less** *adj*

²grace *vb* **graced; grac·ing** **1** : HONOR **2** : ADORN, EMBELLISH

gra·cious \'grā-shəs\ *adj* **1** : marked by kindness and courtesy (a ∼ host) **2** : GRACEFUL **3** : characterized by charm and good taste **4** : MERCIFUL — **gra·cious·ly** *adv* — **gra·cious·ness** *n*

grack·le \'gra-kəl\ *n* : any of several large American blackbirds with glossy iridescent plumage

grad *abbr* graduate; graduated

gra·da·tion \grā-¹dā-shən, grə-\ *n* **1** : a series forming successive stages **2** : a step, degree, or stage in a series **3** : an advance by regular degrees **4** : the act or process of grading

¹grade \'grād\ *n* [L *gradus* step, degree, fr. *gradi* to step, go] **1** : a position in a scale of rank, quality, or order **2** : a stage in a process or ranking **3** : a division of the school course representing one year's work; *also* : the pupils in such a division **4** : a class of persons or things of the same rank or quality **5** : a mark or rating esp. of accomplishment in school **6** : the degree of slope (as of a road); *also* : SLOPE **7** *pl* : the elementary school system

²grade *vb* **grad·ed; grad·ing** **1** : to arrange in grades : SORT **2** : to make level or evenly sloping (∼ a highway) **3** : to give a grade to (∼ a pupil in history) **4** : to assign to a grade

grade inflation *n* : the assigning of grades higher than previously assigned for given levels of achievement

grad·er \'grā-dər\ *n* **1** : a machine for leveling earth **2** : a pupil in a school grade

grade school *n* : ELEMENTARY SCHOOL

gra·di·ent \'grā-dē-ənt\ *n* : SLOPE, GRADE

grad·u·al \'gra-jə-wəl\ *adj* : proceeding or changing by steps or degrees — **grad·u·al·ly** *adv*

grad·u·al·ism \-wə-ˌli-zəm\ *n* : the policy of approaching a desired end gradually

¹grad·u·ate \'gra-jə-wət\ *n* **1** : a holder of an academic degree or diploma **2** : a graduated container for measuring contents

²graduate *adj* **1** : holding an academic degree or diploma **2** : of or relating to studies beyond the first or bachelor's degree (∼ school)

³grad·u·ate \'gra-jə-ˌwāt\ *vb* **-at·ed; -at·ing** **1** : to grant or receive an academic degree or diploma **2** : to divide into grades, classes, or intervals **3** : to admit to a particular standing or grade

grad·u·a·tion \ˌgra-jə-¹wā-shən\ *n* **1** : a mark that graduates something **2** : an act or process of graduating **3** : COMMENCEMENT 2

graf·fi·ti \grə-¹fē-(ˌ)tē\ *n* : unauthorized writing or drawing on a public surface

graf·fi·to \grə-¹fē-tō, grə-\ *n, pl* **-ti** \-(ˌ)tē\ : an inscription or drawing made on a public surface (as a wall)

¹graft \'graft\ *n* **1** : a grafted plant; *also* : the point of union in this **2** : material (as skin) used in grafting **3** : the getting of money or advantage dishonestly; *also* : the money or advantage so gained

²graft *vb* **1** : to insert a shoot from one plant into another so that they join and grow; *also* : to join one thing to another as in plant grafting (∼ skin over a burn) **2** : to get (as money) dishonestly — **graft·er** *n*

gra·ham cracker \'grā-əm-, 'gram-\ *n* : a slightly sweet cracker made chiefly of whole wheat flour

Grail \'grāl\ *n* **1** : the cup or platter used according to medieval legend by Christ at the Last Supper and thereafter the object of knightly quests **2** *not cap* : the object of an extended or difficult quest

grain \'grān\ *n* **1** : a seed or fruit of a cereal grass **2** : seeds or fruits of various food plants and esp. cereal grasses; *also* : a plant (as wheat) producing grain **3** : a small hard particle **4** : a unit of weight based on the weight of a grain of wheat — see WEIGHT table **5** : TEXTURE; *also* : the arrangement of fibers in wood **6** : natural disposition (lying goes against my ∼) — **grained** \'grānd\ *adj*

grain alcohol *n* : ALCOHOL 1

grainy \'grā-nē\ *adj* **grain·i·er; -est** **1** : resembling or having some characteristic of grain : not smooth or fine **2** *of a photograph* : appearing to be composed of grain-like particles

¹gram \'gram\ *n* [F *gramme*, fr. LL *gramma*, a small weight, fr. Gk *gramma* letter, writing, a small weight, fr. *graphein* to write] : a metric unit of mass and weight equal to ¹/₁₀₀₀ kilogram — see METRIC SYSTEM table

²gram *abbr* grammar; grammatical
-gram \ˌgram\ *n comb form* : drawing : writing : record ⟨tele*gram*⟩
gram·mar \ˈgra-mər\ *n* **1** : the study of the classes of words, their inflections, and their functions and relations in the sentence **2** : a study of what is to be preferred and what avoided in inflection and syntax **3** : speech or writing evaluated according to its conformity to grammatical rules — **gram·mar·i·an** \grə-ˈmer-ē-ən, -ˈmar-\ *n* — **gram·mat·i·cal** \-ˈma-ti-kəl\ *adj* — **gram·mat·i·cal·ly** \-k(ə-)lē\ *adv*
grammar school *n* **1** : a secondary school emphasizing Latin and Greek in preparation for college; *also* : a British college preparatory school **2** : a school intermediate between the primary grades and high school **3** : ELEMENTARY SCHOOL
gramme \ˈgram\ *chiefly Brit var of* GRAM
gram·o·phone \ˈgra-mə-ˌfōn\ *n* : PHONOGRAPH
gra·na·ry \ˈgrā-nə-rē, ˈgra-\ *n, pl* **-ries** **1** : a storehouse for grain **2** : a region producing grain in abundance
¹grand \ˈgrand\ *adj* **1** : higher in rank or importance : FOREMOST, CHIEF **2** : great in size **3** : INCLUSIVE, COMPLETE ⟨a ~ total⟩ **4** : MAGNIFICENT, SPLENDID **5** : showing wealth or high social standing **6** : IMPRESSIVE, STATELY **7** : very good : FINE ⟨had a ~ time⟩ — **grand·ly** *adv* — **grand·ness** *n*
²grand *n pl* **grand** *slang* : a thousand dollars
gran·dam \ˈgran-ˌdam, -dəm\ *or* **gran·dame** \-ˌdām, -dəm\ *n* : an old woman
grand·child \ˈgrand-ˌchī(-ə)ld\ *n* : a child of one's son or daughter
grand·daugh·ter \ˈgran-ˌdȯ-tər\ *n* : a daughter of one's son or daughter
grande dame \ˈgrän-ˈdäm\ *n, pl* **grandes dames** : a usu. elderly woman of great prestige or ability
gran·dee \gran-ˈdē\ *n* : a high-ranking Spanish or Portuguese nobleman
gran·deur \ˈgran-jər\ *n* **1** : the quality or state of being grand : MAGNIFICENCE **2** : something that is grand
grand·fa·ther \ˈgrand-ˌfä- thər\ *n* : the father of one's father or mother; *also* : ANCESTOR
grandfather clock *n* : a tall clock that stands on the floor
gran·dil·o·quence \gran-ˈdi-lə-kwəns\ *n* : pompous eloquence — **gran·dil·o·quent** \-kwənt\ *adj*
gran·di·ose \ˈgran-dē-ˌōs, ˌgran-dē-ˈōs\ *adj* : IMPRESSIVE, IMPOSING; *also* : affectedly splendid — **gran·di·ose·ly** *adv* — **gran·di·os·i·ty** \ˌgran-dē-ˈä-sə-tē\ *n*
grand jury *n* : a jury that examines accusations of crime against persons and makes formal charges on which the persons are later tried
grand mal \ˈgrän-ˌmäl; ˈgrand-ˌmal\ *n* [F, lit., great illness] : severe epilepsy
grand·moth·er \ˈgrand-ˌmə-thər\ *n* : the mother of one's father or mother; *also* : a female ancestor
grand·par·ent \-ˌper-ənt\ *n* : a parent of one's father or mother
grand piano *n* : a piano with horizontal frame and strings
grand prix \ˈgränˈ-ˈprē\ *n, pl* **grand prix** *same or* -ˈprēz\ *often cap G&P* : a long-distance auto race over a road course; *also* : a high-level competition in another sport (as sailing)
grand slam *n* **1** : a total victory or success **2** : a home run hit with three runners on base
grand·son \ˈgrand-ˌsən\ *n* : a son of one's son or daughter
grand·stand \-ˌstand\ *n* : a usu. roofed stand for spectators at a racecourse or stadium
grange \ˈgrānj\ *n* **1** : a farm or farmhouse with its various buildings **2** *cap* : one of the lodges of a national association originally made up of farmers; *also* : the association itself — **Grang·er** \ˈgrān-jər\ *n*
gran·ite \ˈgra-nət\ *n* : a hard granular igneous rock used esp. for building — **gra·nit·ic** \gra-ˈni-tik\ *adj*
gran·ite·ware \ˈgra-nət-ˌwer\ *n* : ironware with mottled enamel
gra·no·la \grə-ˈnō-lə\ *n* : a cereal made of rolled oats and usu. raisins and nuts
¹grant \ˈgrant\ *vb* **1** : to consent to : ALLOW, PERMIT **2** : GIVE, BESTOW ⟨~ed land to settlers⟩ **3** : to admit as true — **grant·er** *n* — **grant·or** \ˈgran-tər, -ˌtȯr\ *n*
²grant *n* **1** : the act of granting **2** : something granted; *esp* : a gift for a particular purpose ⟨a ~ for study abroad⟩

3 : a transfer of property by deed or writing; *also* : the instrument by which such a transfer is made **4** : the property transferred by grant — **grant·ee** \gran-ˈtē\ *n*
gran·u·lar \ˈgra-nyə-lər\ *adj* : consisting of or appearing to consist of granules — **gran·u·lar·i·ty** \ˌgra-nyə-ˈlar-ə-tē\ *n*
gran·u·late \ˈgra-nyə-ˌlāt\ *vb* **-lat·ed; -lat·ing** : to form into grains or crystals — **gran·u·la·tion** \ˌgra-nyə-ˈlā-shən\ *n*
gran·ule \ˈgra-nyül\ *n* : a small grain or particle
grape \ˈgrāp\ *n* [ME, fr. AF, grape stalk, bunch of grapes, grape, of Gmc origin] **1** : a smooth-skinned juicy edible greenish white, deep red, or purple berry that is the chief source of wine **2** : any of numerous woody vines widely grown for their bunches of grapes
grape·fruit \ˈgrāp-ˌfrüt\ *n* **1** *pl* **grapefruit** *or* **grapefruits** : a large edible yellow-skinned citrus fruit **2** : a tree bearing grapefruit
grape hyacinth *n* : any of several small bulbous herbs related to the lilies that produce clusters of usu. blue flowers in the spring
grape·shot \ˈgrāp-ˌshät\ *n* : a cluster of small iron balls formerly fired at people from short range by a cannon
grape·vine \-ˌvīn\ *n* **1** : GRAPE 2 **2** : RUMOR; *also* : an informal means of circulating information or gossip
graph \ˈgraf\ *n* : a diagram that usu. by means of dots and lines shows change in one variable factor in comparison with one or more other factors — **graph** *vb*
-graph \ˌgraf\ *n comb form* **1** : something written ⟨auto*graph*⟩ **2** : instrument for making or transmitting records ⟨seismo*graph*⟩
¹graph·ic \ˈgra-fik\ *also* **graph·i·cal** \-fi-kəl\ *adj* **1** : of or relating to the arts **(graphic arts)** of representation, decoration, and printing on flat surfaces **2** : being written, drawn, or engraved **3** : vividly described — **graph·i·cal·ly** \-fi-k(ə-)lē\ *adv*
²graphic *n* **1** : a picture, map, or graph used for illustration **2** : a pictorial image displayed on a computer screen
graphical user interface *n* : a computer program designed to allow easy user interaction esp. by having graphic menus or icons
graph·ics tablet \-fiks-\ *n* : a computer input device for entering pictorial information by drawing or tracing
graph·ite \ˈgra-ˌfīt\ *n* [G Graphit, fr. Gk graphein to write] : a soft black form of carbon used esp. for lead pencils and lubricants
grap·nel \ˈgrap-nəl\ *n* : a small anchor used esp. to recover a sunken object or to anchor a small boat
¹grap·ple \ˈgra-pəl\ *n* : the act of grappling
²grapple *vb* **grap·pled; grap·pling** **1** : to seize or hold with or as if with a hooked implement **2** : to come to grips with : WRESTLE
¹grasp \ˈgrasp\ *vb* **1** : to make the motion of seizing **2** : to take or seize firmly **3** : to enclose and hold with the fingers or arms **4** : COMPREHEND
²grasp *n* **1** : HANDLE **2** : EMBRACE **3** : HOLD, CONTROL **4** : the reach of the arms **5** : the power of seizing and holding or attaining **6** : COMPREHENSION
grasp·ing *adj* : GREEDY, AVARICIOUS
grass \ˈgras\ *n* **1** : herbage for grazing animals **2** : any of a large family of plants (as wheat, bamboo, or sugarcane) with jointed stems and narrow leaves **3** : grass-covered land **4** : MARIJUANA — **grass·like** \-ˌlīk\ *adj* — **grassy** *adj*
grass·hop·per \-ˌhä-pər\ *n* : any of numerous leaping plant-eating insects
grass·land \-ˌland\ *n* : land covered naturally or under cultivation with grasses and low-growing herbs
grass roots *n pl* : society at the local level as distinguished from the centers of political leadership
¹grate \ˈgrāt\ *vb* **grat·ed; grat·ing** **1** : to pulverize by rubbing against something rough **2** : to grind or rub against with a rasping noise **3** : IRRITATE — **grat·er** *n* — **grat·ing·ly** *adv*
²grate *n* **1** : GRATING **2** : a frame of iron bars for holding fuel while it burns
grate·ful \ˈgrāt-fəl\ *adj* **1** : THANKFUL, APPRECIATIVE; *also* : expressing gratitude **2** : PLEASING — **grate·ful·ly** *adv* — **grate·ful·ness** *n*
grat·i·fy \ˈgra-tə-ˌfī\ *vb* **-fied; -fy·ing** : to afford pleasure to — **grat·i·fi·ca·tion** \ˌgra-tə-fə-ˈkā-shən\ *n*
grat·ing \ˈgrā-tiŋ\ *n* : a framework with parallel bars or crossbars

gra·tis \'gra-təs, 'grā-\ *adv or adj* : without charge or recompense : FREE

grat·i·tude \'gra-tə-ˌtüd, -ˌtyüd\ *n* : THANKFULNESS

gra·tu·itous \grə-'tü-ə-təs, -'tyü-\ *adj* **1** : done or provided without recompense : FREE **2** : UNWARRANTED ⟨a ~ assumption⟩

gra·tu·ity \-ə-tē\ *n, pl* **-ities** : ¹⁰TIP

gra·va·men \grə-'vä-mən\ *n, pl* **-va·mens** *or* **-vam·i·na** \-'va-mə-nə\ [LL, burden] : the basic or significant part of a grievance or complaint

¹**grave** \'grāv\ *vb* **graved; grav·en** \'grā-vən\ *or* **graved; grav·ing** : SCULPTURE, ENGRAVE

²**grave** *n* : an excavation in the earth as a place of burial; *also* : TOMB

³**grave** \'grāv; *5 also* 'gräv\ *adj* **1** : IMPORTANT **2** : threatening great harm or danger **3** : DIGNIFIED, SOLEMN **4** : drab in color : SOMBER **5** : of, marked by, or being an accent mark having the form ` — **grave·ly** *adv* — **grave·ness** *n*

grav·el \'gra-vəl\ *n* : pebbles and small pieces of rock larger than grains of sand — **grav·el·ly** *adj*

Graves' disease \'grāvz-\ *n* : hyperthyroidism characterized by goiter and often protrusion of the eyeballs

grave·stone \'grāv-ˌstōn\ *n* : a burial monument

grave·yard \-ˌyärd\ *n* : CEMETERY

grav·id \'gra-vəd\ *adj* [L *gravidus*, fr. *gravis* heavy] : PREGNANT

gra·vi·me·ter \grə-'vi-mə-tər, 'gra-və-ˌmē-\ *n* : a device for measuring variations in a gravitational field

grav·i·tate \'gra-və-ˌtāt\ *vb* **-tat·ed; -tat·ing** : to move or tend to move toward something

grav·i·ta·tion \ˌgra-və-'tā-shən\ *n* **1** : a natural force of attraction that tends to draw bodies together and that occurs because of the mass of the bodies **2** : the action or process of gravitating — **grav·i·ta·tion·al** \-shə-nəl\ *adj* — **grav·i·ta·tion·al·ly** *adv*

grav·i·ty \'gra-və-tē\ *n, pl* **-ties** **1** : IMPORTANCE; *esp* : SERIOUSNESS **2** : ²MASS 5 **3** : the gravitational attraction of the mass of a celestial object (as earth) for bodies close to it; *also* : GRAVITATION 1

gra·vure \grə-'vyůr\ *n* [F] : PHOTOGRAVURE

gra·vy \'grā-vē\ *n, pl* **gravies** **1** : a sauce made from the thickened and seasoned juices of cooked meat **2** : unearned or illicit gain : GRAFT

¹**gray** *also* **grey** \'grā\ *adj* **1** : of the color gray; *also* : dull in color **2** : having gray hair **3** : CHEERLESS, DISMAL **4** : intermediate in position or character ⟨ethically ~ area⟩ — **gray·ish** *adj* — **gray·ness** *n*

²**gray** *also* **grey** *n* **1** : something of a gray color **2** : a neutral color ranging between black and white

³**gray** *also* **grey** *vb* : to make or become gray

gray·beard \'grā-ˌbird\ *n* : an old man

gray·ling \'grā-liŋ\ *n, pl* **grayling** *also* **graylings** : any of several slender freshwater food and sport fishes related to the trouts

gray matter *n* **1** : the grayish part of nervous tissue consisting mostly of the cell bodies of neurons **2** : INTELLIGENCE

gray wolf *n* : a large wolf of northern No. America and Asia that is usu. gray

gray wolf

¹**graze** \'grāz\ *vb* **grazed; graz·ing** [ME *grasen*, fr. OE *grasian*, fr. *græs* grass] **1** : to feed on herbage or pasture **2** : to feed (livestock) on grass or pasture — **graz·er** *n*

²**graze** *vb* **grazed; graz·ing** **1** : to touch lightly in passing **2** : SCRATCH, ABRADE

¹**grease** \'grēs\ *n* **1** : rendered animal fat **2** : oily material **3** : a thick lubricant — **greasy** \'grē-sē, -zē\ *adj*

²**grease** \'grēs, 'grēz\ *vb* **greased; greas·ing** : to smear or lubricate with grease

grease·paint \'grēs-ˌpānt\ *n* : theater makeup

great \'grāt\ *adj* **1** : large in size : BIG **2** : ELABORATE, AMPLE ⟨in ~ detail⟩ **3** : large in number : NUMEROUS **4** : being beyond the average : MIGHTY, INTENSE ⟨a ~ weight⟩ ⟨in ~ pain⟩ **5** : EMINENT, GRAND **6** : long continued ⟨a ~ while⟩ **7** : MAIN, PRINCIPAL ⟨a reception in the ~ hall⟩ **8** : more distant in a family relationship by one generation ⟨a *great*-grandfather⟩ **9** : markedly superior in character, quality, or skill ⟨~ at bridge⟩ **10** : EXCELLENT, FINE ⟨had a ~ time⟩ — **great·ly** *adv* — **great·ness** *n*

great ape *n* : any of a family of primates including the gorilla, orangutan, and chimpanzees

great blue heron *n* : a large crested grayish blue American heron

great circle *n* : a circle on the surface of a sphere that has the same center as the sphere; *esp* : one on the surface of the earth an arc of which is the shortest travel distance between two points

great·coat \'grāt-ˌkōt\ *n* : a heavy overcoat

Great Dane *n* : any of a breed of very tall powerful smooth-coated dogs

great·heart·ed \'grāt-'här-təd\ *adj* **1** : COURAGEOUS **2** : MAGNANIMOUS

great power *n, often cap G&P* : one of the nations that figure most decisively in international affairs

great white shark *n* : a large and dangerous shark of warm seas that has large saw-edged teeth and is whitish below and bluish or brownish above

grebe \'grēb\ *n* : any of a family of lobe-toed diving birds related to the loons

Gre·cian \'grē-shən\ *adj* : GREEK

greed \'grēd\ *n* : acquisitive or selfish desire beyond reason — **greed·i·ly** \'grē-də-lē\ *adv* — **greed·i·ness** \-dē-nəs\ *n* — **greedy** \'grē-dē\ *adj*

¹**Greek** \'grēk\ *n* **1** : a native or inhabitant of Greece **2** : the ancient or modern language of Greece

²**Greek** *adj* **1** : of, relating to, or characteristic of Greece, the Greeks, or Greek **2** : ORTHODOX 3

¹**green** \'grēn\ *adj* **1** : of the color green **2** : covered with verdure; *also* : consisting of green plants or of the leafy parts of plants ⟨a ~ salad⟩ **3** : UNRIPE; *also* : IMMATURE **4** : having a sickly appearance **5** : not fully processed or treated ⟨~ liquor⟩ ⟨~ hides⟩ **6** : INEXPERIENCED; *also* : NAIVE **7** : concerned with or supporting environmentalism — **green·ish** *adj* — **green·ness** *n*

²**green** *vb* : to make or become green

³**green** *n* **1** : a color between blue and yellow in the spectrum : the color of growing fresh grass or of the emerald **2** : something of a green color **3** : green vegetation; *esp, pl* : leafy herbs or leafy parts of a vegetable ⟨collard ~s⟩ ⟨beet ~s⟩ **4** : a grassy plot; *esp* : a smooth grassy area around the hole into which the ball must be played in golf

green·back \'grēn-ˌbak\ *n* : a U.S. legal-tender note

green bean *n* : a kidney bean that is used as a snap bean when the pods are colored green

green·belt \'grēn-ˌbelt\ *n* : a belt of parks or farmlands around a community

green card *n* : an identity card attesting the permanent resident status of an alien in the U.S.

green·ery \'grē-nə-rē\ *n, pl* **-er·ies** : green foliage or plants

green–eyed \'grē-ˌnīd\ *adj* : JEALOUS

green·gro·cer \'grēn-ˌgrō-sər\ *n, chiefly Brit* : a retailer of fresh vegetables and fruit

green·horn \-ˌhòrn\ *n* : an inexperienced person; *also* : NEWCOMER

green·house \-ˌhaús\ *n* : a glass structure for the growing of tender plants

greenhouse effect *n* : warming of a planet's atmosphere that occurs when the sun's radiation passes through the atmosphere, is absorbed by the planet, and is reradiated as radiation of longer wavelength that can be absorbed by atmospheric gases

green manure *n* : an herbaceous crop (as clover) plowed under when green to enrich the soil

green onion *n* : a young onion pulled before the bulb has enlarged and used esp. in salads; *also* : SCALLION

green pepper *n* : a sweet pepper before it turns red at maturity
green·room \'grēn-,rüm, -,rùm\ *n* : a room (as in a theater or studio) where performers can relax before, between, or after appearances
green·sward \-,swórd\ *n* : turf that is green with growing grass
green thumb *n* : an unusual ability to make plants grow
green·wash·ing \'grēn-,wò-shiŋ, -,wä-\ *n* : expressions of environmentalist concerns as a cover for products, policies, or activities deleterious to the environment
Green·wich mean time \'gri-nij-, 'gre-, -nich-\ *n* [*Greenwich*, England] : the time of the meridian of Greenwich used historically as the basis of worldwide standard time
Greenwich time *n* : GREENWICH MEAN TIME
green·wood \'grēn-,wùd\ *n* : a forest that is green with foliage
greet \'grēt\ *vb* **1** : to address with expressions of kind wishes **2** : to meet or react to in a specified manner **3** : to be perceived by — **greet·er** *n*
greet·ing *n* **1** : a salutation on meeting **2** *pl* : best wishes : REGARDS
greeting card *n* : a card that bears a message usu. sent on a special occasion
gre·gar·i·ous \gri-'ger-ē-əs\ *adj* [L *gregarius* of a flock or herd, fr. *greg-, grex* flock, herd] **1** : SOCIAL, COMPANIONABLE **2** : tending to flock together — **gre·gar·i·ous·ly** *adv* — **gre·gar·i·ous·ness** *n*
grem·lin \'grem-lən\ *n* : a cause of error or equipment malfunction conceived of as a small gnome
gre·nade \grə-'nād\ *n* [MF, lit., pomegranate, fr. LL *granata*, fr. L, fem. of *granatus* seedy, fr. *granum* grain] : a small bomb that is thrown by hand or launched (as by a rifle)
gren·a·dier \,gre-nə-'dir\ *n* : a member of a European regiment formerly armed with grenades
gren·a·dine \,gre-nə-'dēn, 'gre-nə-,dēn\ *n* : a syrup flavored with pomegranates and used in mixed drinks
grew *past of* GROW
grey *var of* GRAY
grey·hound \'grā-,haùnd\ *n* : any of a breed of tall slender dogs noted for speed and keen sight
grid \'grid\ *n* **1** : GRATING **2** : a network of conductors for distributing electric power **3** : a network of horizontal and perpendicular lines (as for locating points on a map) **4** : GRIDIRON 2; *also* : FOOTBALL
grid·dle \'gri-d°l\ *n* : a flat usu. metal surface for cooking food
griddle cake *n* : PANCAKE
grid·iron \'grid-,ī(-ə)rn\ *n* **1** : a grate for broiling food **2** : a football field
grid·lock \-,läk\ *n* : a traffic jam in which an intersection is so blocked that vehicles cannot move
grief \'grēf\ *n* **1** : emotional distress caused by or as if by bereavement; *also* : a cause of such distress **2** : DISASTER; *also* : MISHAP
griev·ance \'grē-vəns\ *n* **1** : a cause of distress affording reason for complaint or resistance **2** : COMPLAINT
grieve \'grēv\ *vb* **grieved; griev·ing** [ME *greven*, fr. AF *grever*, fr. L *gravare* to burden, fr. *gravis* heavy, grave] **1** : to cause grief or sorrow to : DISTRESS **2** : to feel grief : SORROW
griev·ous \'grē-vəs\ *adj* **1** : causing suffering, grief, or sorrow : SEVERE ⟨a ～ wound⟩ **2** : OPPRESSIVE, ONEROUS ⟨～ costs of war⟩ **3** : SERIOUS, GRAVE — **griev·ous·ly** *adv*
¹**grill** \'gril\ *vb* **1** : to broil on a grill; *also* : to fry or toast on a griddle **2** : to question intensely
²**grill** *n* **1** : a cooking utensil of parallel bars on which food is grilled **2** : a usu. informal restaurant
grille *or* **grill** \'gril\ *n* : a grating that forms a barrier or screen
grill·work \'gril-,wərk\ *n* : work constituting or resembling a grille
grim \'grim\ *adj* **grim·mer; grim·mest** **1** : CRUEL, FIERCE **2** : harsh and forbidding in appearance **3** : ghastly or repellent in character **4** : RELENTLESS — **grim·ly** *adv* — **grim·ness** *n*
gri·mace \'gri-məs, gri-'mās\ *n* : a facial expression usu. of disgust or disapproval — **grimace** *vb*
grime \'grīm\ *n* : soot, smut, or dirt adhering to or embedded in a surface; *also* : accumulated dirtiness and disorder — **grimy** *adj*
grin \'grin\ *vb* **grinned; grin·ning** : to draw back the lips so as to show the teeth esp. in amusement — **grin** *n*
¹**grind** \'grīnd\ *vb* **ground** \'graùnd\; **grind·ing** **1** : to reduce to small particles **2** : to wear down, polish, or sharpen by friction **3** : OPPRESS **4** : to press with a grating noise : GRIT ⟨～ the teeth⟩ **5** : to operate or produce by turning a crank **6** : DRUDGE; *esp* : to study hard **7** : to move with difficulty or friction ⟨gears ～*ing*⟩
²**grind** *n* **1** : dreary monotonous labor, routine, or study **2** : one who works or studies excessively
grind·er \'grīn-dər\ *n* **1** : MOLAR **2** *pl* : TEETH **3** : one that grinds **4** : SUBMARINE 2 **5** : an athlete who succeeds through hard work and determination
grind·stone \'grīnd-,stōn\ *n* : a flat circular stone of natural sandstone that revolves on an axle and is used for grinding, shaping, or smoothing
¹**grip** \'grip\ *vb* **gripped; grip·ping** **1** : to seize or hold firmly **2** : to hold the interest of strongly
²**grip** *n* **1** : GRASP; *also* : strength in gripping **2** : a firm tenacious hold **3** : UNDERSTANDING **4** : a device for gripping **5** : TRAVELING BAG
gripe \'grīp\ *vb* **griped; grip·ing** **1** : IRRITATE, VEX **2** : to cause or experience spasmodic pains in the bowels **3** : COMPLAIN — **gripe** *n*
grippe \'grip\ *n* : INFLUENZA
gris–gris \'grē-,grē\ *n, pl* **gris–gris** \-,grēz\ [F] : an amulet or incantation used chiefly by people of black African ancestry
gris·ly \'griz-lē\ *adj* **gris·li·er; -est** : HORRIBLE, GRUESOME
grist \'grist\ *n* : grain to be ground or already ground
gris·tle \'gri-səl\ *n* : CARTILAGE — **gris·tly** \'gris-lē\ *adj*
grist·mill \'grist-,mil\ *n* : a mill for grinding grain
¹**grit** \'grit\ *n* **1** : a hard sharp granule (as of sand); *also* : material composed of such granules **2** : unyielding courage — **grit·ty** *adj*
²**grit** *vb* **grit·ted; grit·ting** : GRIND, GRATE
grits \'grits\ *n pl* : coarsely ground hulled grain ⟨hominy ～⟩
griz·zled \'griz-zəld\ *adj* : streaked or mixed with gray; *also* : having gray hair
griz·zly \'griz-lē\ *adj* **griz·zli·er; -est** : GRIZZLED
grizzly bear *n* : a large powerful brownish bear of western No. America
gro *abbr* gross
groan \'grōn\ *vb* **1** : MOAN **2** : to make a harsh sound under sudden or prolonged strain ⟨the chair ～*ed* under his weight⟩ — **groan** *n*
groat \'grōt\ *n* : an old British coin worth four pennies
gro·cer \'grō-sər\ *n* [ME, fr. AF *groser* wholesaler, fr. *gros* coarse, wholesale, fr. L *grossus* coarse] : a dealer esp. in staple foodstuffs — **gro·cery** \'grōs-rē, 'grōsh-, 'grō-sə-\ *n*
grog \'gräg\ *n* [*Old Grog*, nickname of Edward Vernon †1757 Eng. admiral responsible for diluting the sailors' rum] : alcoholic liquor; *esp* : liquor (as rum) mixed with water
grog·gy \'grä-gē\ *adj* **grog·gi·er; -est** : weak and unsteady on the feet or in action — **grog·gi·ly** \-gə-lē\ *adv* — **grog·gi·ness** \-gē-nəs\ *n*
groin \'gróin\ *n* **1** : the juncture of the lower abdomen and inner part of the thigh; *also* : the region of this juncture **2** : the curved line or rib on a ceiling along which two vaults meet
grok \'gräk\ *vb* **grokked; grok·king** : to understand profoundly and intuitively
grom·met \'grä-mət, 'grə-\ *n* **1** : a ring of rope **2** : an eyelet of firm material to strengthen or protect an opening
¹**groom** \'grüm, 'grùm\ *n* **1** : a person responsible for the care of horses **2** : BRIDEGROOM
²**groom** *vb* **1** : to clean and care for (an animal) **2** : to make neat or attractive **3** : PREPARE
grooms·man \'grümz-mən, 'grùmz-\ *n* : a male friend who attends a bridegroom at his wedding
groove \'grüv\ *n* **1** : a long narrow channel **2** : a fixed routine — **groove** *vb*
groovy \'grü-vē\ *adj* **groov·i·er; -est** **1** : EXCELLENT **2** : HIP
grope \'grōp\ *vb* **groped; grop·ing** **1** : to feel about or search for blindly or uncertainly ⟨～ for the right word⟩ **2** : to feel one's way by groping

gros·beak \'grōs-ˌbēk\ *n* : any of several finches of Europe or America with large stout conical bills

gro·schen \'grō-shən\ *n, pl* **groschen** : a former Austrian monetary unit equal to ¹/₁₀₀ schilling

gros·grain \'grō-ˌgrān\ *n* [F *gros grain* coarse texture] : a silk or rayon fabric with crosswise cotton ribs

¹**gross** \'grōs\ *adj* **1** : glaringly noticeable **2** : OUT-AND-OUT, UTTER **3** : BIG, BULKY; *esp* : excessively fat **4** : GENERAL, BROAD **5** : consisting of an overall total exclusive of deductions ⟨~ earnings⟩ **6** : CARNAL, EARTHY ⟨~ pleasures⟩ **7** : UNREFINED; *also* : crudely vulgar **8** : lacking knowledge — **gross·ly** *adv* — **gross·ness** *n*

²**gross** *n* : an overall total exclusive of deductions — **gross** *vb*

³**gross** *n, pl* **gross** : a total of 12 dozen things ⟨a ~ of pencils⟩

gross domestic product *n* : the gross national product excluding the value of net income earned abroad

gross national product *n* : the total value of the goods and services produced in a nation during a year

gro·szy \'grō-shē\ *n, pl* **groszy** — see *zloty* at MONEY table

grot \'grät\ *n* : GROTTO

gro·tesque \grō-'tesk\ *adj* **1** : FANCIFUL, BIZARRE **2** : absurdly incongruous **3** : ECCENTRIC — **gro·tesque·ly** *adv*

grot·to \'grä-tō\ *n, pl* **grottoes** *also* **grottos** **1** : CAVE **2** : an artificial cavelike structure

grouch \'graüch\ *n* **1** : a fit of bad temper **2** : a habitually irritable or complaining person — **grouch** *vb* — **grouchy** *adj*

¹**ground** \'graünd\ *n* **1** : the bottom of a body of water **2** *pl* : sediment at the bottom of a liquid **3** : a basis for belief, action, or argument **4** : BACKGROUND **5** : the surface of the earth; *also* : SOIL **6** : an area with a particular use ⟨fishing ~s⟩ **7** *pl* : the area about and belonging to a building **8** : a conductor that makes electrical connection with the earth — **ground·less** *adj*

²**ground** *vb* **1** : to bring to or place on the ground **2** : to run or cause to run aground **3** : to provide a reason or justification for **4** : to furnish with a foundation of knowledge **5** : to connect electrically with a ground **6** : to restrict to the ground; *also* : prohibit from some activity

³**ground** *past and past part of* GRIND

ground ball *n* : a batted baseball that rolls or bounces along the ground

ground cover *n* : low plants that grow over and cover the soil; *also* : a plant suitable for use as ground cover

ground·ed \'graün-dəd\ *adj* : mentally and emotionally stable

ground·er \'graün-dər\ *n* : GROUND BALL

ground·hog \'graünd-ˌhȯg, -ˌhäg\ *n* : WOODCHUCK

ground·ling \'graünd-liŋ\ *n* : a spectator in the pit of an Elizabethan theater

ground rule *n* **1** : a sports rule adopted to modify play on a particular field, court, or course **2** : a rule of procedure

ground squirrel *n* : any of various burrowing squirrels of No. America and Eurasia that often live in colonies in open areas

ground swell *n* **1** : a broad deep ocean swell caused by an often distant gale or earthquake **2** *usu* **ground·swell** : a rapid spontaneous growth (as of political opinion)

ground·wa·ter \'graünd-ˌwȯ-tər, -ˌwä-\ *n* : water within the earth that supplies wells and springs

ground·work \-ˌwərk\ *n* : FOUNDATION, BASIS

ground zero *n* **1** : the point above, below, or at which a nuclear explosion occurs **2** : the center or origin of rapid, intense, or violent activity

¹**group** \'grüp\ *n* **1** : a number of individuals related by a common factor (as physical association, community of interests, or blood) **2** : a combination of atoms commonly found together in a molecule ⟨a methyl ~⟩

²**group** *vb* : to associate in groups : CLUSTER, AGGREGATE

grou·per \'grü-pər\ *n, pl* **groupers** *also* **grouper** : any of numerous large solitary bottom fishes of warm seas

group home *n* : a residence for persons requiring care or supervision

group·ie \'grü-pē\ *n* : a fan of a rock group who usu. follows the group around on concert tours; *also* : ENTHUSIAST, FAN

group therapy *n* : therapy in the presence of a therapist in which several patients discuss their personal problems

groupware \'grüp-ˌwer\ *n* : software that enables users to work jointly via a network on projects or files

¹**grouse** \'graüs\ *n, pl* **grouse** *or* **grouses** : any of various chiefly ground-dwelling game birds that have feathered legs and are usu. of reddish brown or other protective color

grouse

²**grouse** *vb* **groused; grous·ing** : COMPLAIN, GRUMBLE

grout \'graüt\ *n* : material (as mortar) used for filling spaces — **grout** *vb*

grove \'grōv\ *n* : a small wood usu. without underbrush

grov·el \'grä-vəl, 'grɔ-\ *vb* **-eled** *or* **-elled; -el·ing** *or* **-el·ling** **1** : to creep or lie with the body prostrate in fear or humility **2** : to abase oneself

grow \'grō\ *vb* **grew** \'grü\; **grown** \'grōn\; **grow·ing** **1** : to spring up and develop to maturity **2** : to be able to grow : THRIVE **3** : to take on some relation through or as if through growth ⟨tree limbs *grown* together⟩ **4** : INCREASE, EXPAND **5** : to develop from a parent source **6** : BECOME **7** : to have an increasing influence **8** : to cause to grow — **grow·er** *n*

growing pains *n pl* **1** : pains in the legs of growing children having no known relation to growth **2** : the stresses and strains attending a new project or development

growl \'graü(-ə)l\ *vb* **1** : RUMBLE **2** : to utter a deep throaty sound **3** : GRUMBLE — **growl** *n*

grown–up \'grō-ˌnəp\ *adj* : not childish : ADULT — **grown–up** *n*

growth \'grōth\ *n* **1** : stage or condition attained in growing **2** : a process of growing esp. through progressive development or increase **3** : a result or product of growing ⟨a fine ~ of hair⟩; *also* : an abnormal mass of tissue (as a tumor)

growth hormone *n* : a vertebrate hormone that is secreted by the pituitary gland and regulates growth

growth industry *n* : a business, interest, or activity that is increasingly popular, profitable, or trendy

¹**grub** \'grəb\ *vb* **grubbed; grub·bing** **1** : to clear or root out by digging **2** : to dig in the ground usu. for a hidden object **3** : to search about

²**grub** *n* **1** : a soft thick wormlike insect larva ⟨beetle ~s⟩ **2** : DRUDGE; *also* : a slovenly person **3** : FOOD

grub·by \'grə-bē\ *adj* **grub·bi·er; -est** : DIRTY, SLOVENLY — **grub·bi·ness** \-bē-nəs\ *n*

grub·stake \'grəb-ˌstāk\ *n* : supplies or funds furnished a mining prospector in return for a share in his finds

¹**grudge** \'grəj\ *vb* **grudged; grudg·ing** : to be reluctant to give : BEGRUDGE

²**grudge** *n* : a feeling of deep-seated resentment or ill will

gru·el \'grü-əl\ *n* : a thin porridge

gru·el·ing *or* **gru·el·ling** \'grü-liŋ, 'grü-ə-\ *adj* : requiring extreme effort : EXHAUSTING

grue·some \'grü-səm\ *adj* [fr. earlier *growsome*, fr. E dial. *grow, grue* to shiver] : inspiring horror or repulsion — **grue·some·ly** *adv* — **grue·some·ness** *n*

gruff \'grəf\ *adj* **1** : rough in speech or manner **2** : being deep and harsh : HOARSE — **gruff·ly** *adv*

grum·ble \'grəm-bəl\ *vb* **grum·bled; grum·bling** **1** : to mutter in discontent **2** : GROWL, RUMBLE — **grum·bler** *n*

grumpy \'grəm-pē\ *adj* **grump·i·er; -est** : moodily cross

: SURLY — **grump·i·ly** \-pə-lē\ *adv* — **grump·i·ness** \-pē-nəs\ *n*
grunge \'grənj\ *n* 1 : one that is grungy 2 : heavy metal rock music expressing alienation and discontent 3 : untidy or tattered clothing typically worn by grunge fans
grun·gy \'grən-jē\ *adj* **grun·gi·er; -est** : shabby or dirty in character or condition
grun·ion \'grən-yən\ *n* : a fish of the California coast which comes inshore to spawn at nearly full moon
grunt \'grənt\ *n* : a deep throaty sound (as that of a hog) — **grunt** *vb*
GSA *abbr* 1 General Services Administration 2 Girl Scouts of America
G suit *n* [gravity] : a suit for a pilot or astronaut designed to counteract the physiological effects of acceleration
GSUSA *abbr* Girl Scouts of the United States of America
gt *abbr* great
Gt Brit *abbr* Great Britain
gtd *abbr* guaranteed
GU *abbr* Guam
gua·ca·mo·le \ˌgwä-kə-'mō-lē\ *n* [MexSp, fr. Nahuatl *āhuacamōlli*, fr. *āhuacatl* avocado + *mōlli* sauce] : mashed and seasoned avocado
gua·nine \'gwä-ˌnēn\ *n* : a purine base that codes genetic information in the molecular chain of DNA and RNA
gua·no \'gwä-nō\ *n* [Sp, fr. Quechua *wanu* fertilizer, dung] : excrement esp. of seabirds or bats; *also* : a fertilizer composed chiefly of this excrement
gua·ra·ni \ˌgwär-ə-'nē\ *n, pl* **guaranies** *also* **guaranis** — see MONEY table
¹**guar·an·tee** \ˌger-ən-'tē\ *n* 1 : GUARANTOR 2 : GUARANTY 3 : an agreement by which one person undertakes to secure another in the possession or enjoyment of something 4 : an assurance of the quality of or of the length of use to be expected from a product offered for sale 5 : GUARANTY 4
²**guarantee** *vb* **-teed; -tee·ing** 1 : to undertake to answer for the debt, failure to perform, or faulty performance of (another) 2 : to undertake an obligation to establish, perform, or continue 3 : to give security to
guar·an·tor \ˌger-ən-'tòr\ *n* : one who gives a guarantee
¹**guar·an·ty** \'ger-ən-tē\ *n, pl* **-ties** 1 : an undertaking to answer for another's failure to pay a debt or perform a duty 2 : GUARANTEE 3 3 : GUARANTOR 4 : PLEDGE, SECURITY
²**guaranty** *vb* **-tied; -ty·ing** : GUARANTEE
¹**guard** \'gärd\ *n* 1 : a person or a body of persons on sentinel duty 2 *pl* : troops assigned to protect a sovereign 3 : a defensive position (as in boxing) 4 : the act or duty of protecting or defending 5 : PROTECTION 6 : a protective or safety device 7 : a football lineman playing between center and tackle; *also* : a basketball player stationed toward the rear — **on guard** : WATCHFUL, ALERT
²**guard** *vb* 1 : PROTECT, DEFEND 2 : to watch over 3 : to be on guard
guard·house \'gärd-ˌhaùs\ *n* 1 : a building occupied by a guard or used as a headquarters by soldiers on guard duty 2 : a military jail
guard·ian \'gär-dē-ən\ *n* 1 : CUSTODIAN 2 : one who has the care of the person or property of another — **guard·ian·ship** *n*
guard·room \'gärd-ˌrüm\ *n* 1 : a room used by a military guard while on duty 2 : a room where military prisoners are confined
guards·man \'gärdz-mən\ *n* : a member of a military body called *guard* or *guards*
gua·va \'gwä-və\ *n* : the sweet yellow or pink acid fruit of a shrubby tropical American tree used esp. for making jam and jelly; *also* : the tree
gu·ber·na·to·ri·al \ˌgü-bər-nə-'tòr-ē-əl\ *adj* : of or relating to a governor
guer·don \'gər-dᵊn\ *n* : REWARD, RECOMPENSE
Guern·sey \'gərn-zē\ *n, pl* **Guernseys** : any of a breed of usu. reddish brown dairy cattle that produce rich yellowish milk
guer·ril·la *or* **gue·ril·la** \gə-'ri-lə\ *n* [Sp *guerrilla*, fr. dim. of *guerra* war, of Gmc origin] : one who engages in irregular warfare esp. as a member of an independent unit
¹**guess** \'ges\ *vb* 1 : to form an opinion from little or no evidence 2 : BELIEVE, SUPPOSE 3 : to conjecture correctly about : DISCOVER — **guess** *n*

guest \'gest\ *n* 1 : a person to whom hospitality (as of a house or a club) is extended 2 : a patron of a commercial establishment (as a hotel) 3 : a person not a regular member of a cast who appears on a program
guest·house \'gest-ˌhaùs\ *n* : a house run as a boarding house or bed-and-breakfast
guf·faw \(ˌ)gə-'fò\ *n* : a loud burst of laughter — **guf·faw** *vb*
guid·ance \'gī-dᵊns\ *n* 1 : the act or process of guiding 2 : ADVICE, DIRECTION
¹**guide** \'gīd\ *n* 1 : one who leads or directs another's course 2 : one who shows and explains points of interest 3 : something that provides guiding information; *also* : SIGNPOST 4 : a device to direct the motion of something
²**guide** *vb* **guid·ed; guid·ing** 1 : to act as a guide to 2 : MANAGE, DIRECT 3 : to superintend the training of — **guid·able** \'gī-də-bəl\ *adj*
guide·book \'gīd-ˌbùk\ *n* : a book of information for travelers
guided missile *n* : a missile whose course may be altered during flight
guide dog *n* : a dog trained to lead the blind
guide·line \'gīd-ˌlīn\ *n* : an indication or outline of policy or conduct
guide word *n* : a term at the head of a page of an alphabetical reference work that indicates the alphabetically first or last word on that page
gui·don \'gī-ˌdän, 'gī-dᵊn\ *n* : a small flag (as of a military unit)
guild \'gild\ *n* : an association of people with common aims and interests; *esp* : a medieval association of merchants or craftsmen — **guild·hall** \-ˌhòl\ *n*
guile \'gī(-ə)l\ *n* : deceitful cunning : DUPLICITY — **guile·ful** *adj* — **guile·less** *adj* — **guile·less·ness** *n*
guil·lo·tine \'gi-lə-ˌtēn, ˌgē-ə-'tēn\ *n* [F, fr. Joseph *Guillotin* †1814 Fr. physician] : a machine for beheading persons — **guillotine** *vb*
guilt \'gilt\ *n* 1 : the fact of having committed an offense esp. against the law 2 : BLAMEWORTHINESS 3 : a feeling of responsibility for wrongdoing — **guilt·less** *adj*
guilt-trip \'gilt-ˌtrip\ *vb* : to cause feelings of guilt in
guilty \'gil-tē\ *adj* **guilt·i·er; -est** 1 : having committed a breach of conduct or a crime 2 : suggesting or involving guilt 3 : aware of or suffering from guilt — **guilt·i·ly** \-tə-lē\ *adv* — **guilt·i·ness** \-tē-nəs\ *n*
guin·ea \'gi-nē\ *n* 1 : a British gold coin no longer issued worth 21 shillings 2 : a unit of value equal to 21 shillings
guinea fowl *n* : a gray and white spotted West African bird related to the pheasants and widely raised for food; *also* : any of several related birds
guinea hen *n* : a female guinea fowl; *also* : GUINEA FOWL
guinea pig *n* 1 : a small stocky short-eared and nearly tailless So. American rodent often kept as a pet or used in lab research 2 : a subject of research or testing
guise \'gīz\ *n* 1 : a form or style of dress : COSTUME 2 : external appearance : SEMBLANCE
gui·tar \gi-'tär\ *n* : a musical instrument with usu. six strings plucked with a pick or with the fingers
gulch \'gəlch\ *n* : RAVINE
gul·den \'gül-dən, 'gùl-\ *n, pl* **guldens** *or* **gulden** 1 : the basic monetary unit of the Netherlands until 2002 2 — see MONEY table
gulf \'gəlf\ *n* [ME *goulf*, fr. MF *golfe*, fr. It *golfo*, fr. LL *colpus*, fr. Gk *kolpos* bosom, gulf] 1 : a part of an ocean or sea partly or mostly surrounded by land 2 : ABYSS, CHASM 3 : a wide separation ⟨the ∼ between generations⟩
¹**gull** \'gəl\ *n* : any of numerous mostly white or gray long-winged web-footed seabirds
²**gull** *vb* : to make a dupe of : DECEIVE
³**gull** *n* : DUPE
gul·let \'gə-lət\ *n* : ESOPHAGUS; *also* : THROAT
gull·ible \'gə-lə-bəl\ *adj* : easily duped or cheated
gul·ly \'gə-lē\ *n, pl* **gullies** : a trench worn in the earth by and often filled with running water after rains
gulp \'gəlp\ *vb* 1 : to swallow hurriedly or greedily 2 : SUPPRESS ⟨∼ down a sob⟩ 3 : to catch the breath as if in taking a long drink — **gulp** *n*
¹**gum** \'gəm\ *n* : the oral tissue that surrounds the necks of the teeth

²**gum** *n* [ME *gomme*, fr. MF, fr. L *cummi, gummi*, fr. Gk *kommi*, fr. Egyptian *qmy.t*] **1** : a sticky plant exudate; *esp* : one that hardens on drying **2** : a sticky substance **3** : a preparation usu. of a plant gum sweetened and flavored and used for chewing — **gum·my** *adj*

gum arabic *n* : a water-soluble gum obtained from several acacias and used esp. in making inks, adhesives, confections, and pharmaceuticals

gum·bo \'gəm-bō\ *n* [AmerF *gombo*, of Bantu origin] : a rich thick soup usu. thickened with okra

gum·drop \'gəm-ˌdräp\ *n* : a candy made usu. from corn syrup with gelatin and coated with sugar crystals

gump·tion \'gəmp-shən\ *n* **1** *chiefly dial* : shrewd common sense **2** : ENTERPRISE, INITIATIVE ⟨lacked the ~ to try⟩

gum·shoe \'gəm-ˌshü\ *n* : DETECTIVE — **gumshoe** *vb*

¹**gun** \'gən\ *n* **1** : CANNON **2** : a portable firearm **3** : a discharge of a gun **4** : something suggesting a gun in shape or function **5** : THROTTLE — **gunned** \'gənd\ *adj*

²**gun** *vb* **gunned; gun·ning 1** : to hunt with a gun **2** : SHOOT **3** : to open up the throttle of so as to increase speed

gun·boat \'gən-ˌbōt\ *n* : a small lightly armed ship for use in shallow waters

gun·fight \-ˌfīt\ *n* : a duel with guns — **gun·fight·er** *n*

gun·fire \-ˌfī(-ə)r\ *n* : the firing of guns

gung ho \'gəŋ-'hō\ *adj* : extremely zealous or enthusiastic

gun·man \-mən\ *n* : a man armed with a gun; *esp* : a professional killer

gun·ner \'gə-nər\ *n* **1** : a soldier or airman who operates or aims a gun **2** : one who hunts with a gun

gun·nery \'gə-nə-rē\ *n* : the use of guns; *esp* : the science of the flight of projectiles and effective use of guns

gunnery sergeant *n* : a noncommissioned officer in the marine corps ranking next below a master sergeant

gun·ny·sack \'gə-nē-ˌsak\ *n* : a sack made of a coarse heavy fabric (as burlap)

gun·point \'gən-ˌpòint\ *n* : the muzzle of a gun — **at gunpoint** : under a threat of death by being shot

gun·pow·der \-ˌpaù-dər\ *n* : an explosive powder used in guns and blasting

gun·shot \-ˌshät\ *n* **1** : shot fired from a gun **2** : the range of a gun ⟨within ~⟩

gun–shy \-ˌshī\ *adj* **1** : afraid of a loud noise **2** : markedly distrustful

gun·sling·er \-ˌsliŋ-ər\ *n* : a skilled gunman esp. in the American West

gun·smith \-ˌsmith\ *n* : one who designs, makes, or repairs firearms

gun·wale *also* **gun·nel** \'gə-n°l\ *n* : the upper edge of a ship's or boat's side

gup·py \'gə-pē\ *n*, *pl* **guppies** [R.J.L. *Guppy* †1916 Trinidadian naturalist] : a small brightly colored tropical fish

gur·gle \'gər-gəl\ *vb* **gur·gled; gur·gling** : to make a sound like that of an irregularly flowing or gently splashing liquid — **gurgle** *n*

Gur·kha \'gùr-kə, 'gər-\ *n* : a soldier from Nepal in the British or Indian army

gur·ney \'gər-nē\ *n*, *pl* **gurneys** : a wheeled cot or stretcher

gu·ru \'gùr-ü\ *n*, *pl* **gurus** [ultim. Sanskrit *guru*, fr. *guru*, adj., heavy, venerable] **1** : a personal religious and spiritual teacher in Hinduism **2** : a teacher in matters of fundamental concern **3** : EXPERT ⟨a fitness ~⟩

gush \'gəsh\ *vb* **1** : to issue or pour forth copiously or violently : SPOUT **2** : to make an effusive display of affection or enthusiasm

gush·er \'gə-shər\ *n* : one that gushes; *esp* : an oil well with a large natural flow

gushy \'gə-shē\ *adj* **gush·i·er; -est** : marked by effusive sentimentality

gus·set \'gə-sət\ *n* : a triangular insert (as in a seam of a sleeve) to give width or strength — **gusset** *vb*

gus·sy up \'gə-sē-\ *vb* **gus·sied up gus·sy·ing up 1** : in best or formal clothes **2** : to make more attractive, glamorous or fancy

¹**gust** \'gəst\ *n* **1** : a sudden brief rush of wind **2** : a sudden outburst : SURGE — **gusty** *adj*

²**gust** *vb* : to blow in gusts

gus·ta·to·ry \'gəs-tə-ˌtòr-ē\ *adj* : relating to or associated with the sense of taste

gus·to \'gəs-tō\ *n*, *pl* **gustoes** : enthusiastic enjoyment; *also* : VITALITY **4**

¹**gut** \'gət\ *n* **1** *pl* : BOWELS, ENTRAILS **2** : the alimentary canal or a part of it (as the intestine); *also* : BELLY, ABDOMEN **3** *pl* : the inner essential parts ⟨a car's ~s⟩ **4** *pl* : COURAGE, PLUCK

²**gut** *vb* **gut·ted; gut·ting 1** : EVISCERATE **2** : to destroy the inside of ⟨fire *gutted* the building⟩

gut check *n* : a test of courage, character, or determination

gutsy \'gət-sē\ *adj* **guts·i·er; -est** : marked by courage and determination

gut·ter \'gə-tər\ *n* : a groove or channel for carrying off esp. rainwater

gut·ter·snipe \-ˌsnīp\ *n* : a street urchin

gut·tur·al \'gə-tə-rəl\ *adj* **1** : sounded in the throat **2** : being or marked by an utterance that is strange, unpleasant, or disagreeable — **guttural** *n*

gut·ty \'gə-tē\ *adj* **gut·ti·er; -est 1** : GUTSY **2** : having a vigorous challenging quality

gut–wrench·ing \'gət-ˌren-chiŋ\ *adj* : causing emotional anguish

¹**guy** \'gī\ *n* : a rope, chain, or rod attached to something as a brace or guide

²**guy** *vb* : to steady or reinforce with a guy

³**guy** *n* : MAN, FELLOW; *also*, *pl* : PERSONS ⟨all the ~s came⟩

⁴**guy** *vb* : to make fun of : RIDICULE

guz·zle \'gə-zəl\ *vb* **guz·zled; guz·zling** : to drink greedily

gym \'jim\ *n* : GYMNASIUM

gym·kha·na \jim-'kä-nə\ *n* : a meet featuring sports contests; *esp* : a contest of automobile-driving skill

gym·na·si·um *for 1* jim-'nä-zē-əm, -zhəm, *for 2* gim-'nä-zē-əm\ *n*, *pl* **-na·si·ums** *or* **-na·sia** \-'nä-zē-ə, -'nä-zhə; -'nä-zē-ə\ [L, exercise ground, school, fr. Gk *gymnasion*, fr. *gymnazein* to exercise naked, fr. *gymnos* naked] **1** : a room or building for indoor sports **2** : a European secondary school that prepares students for the university

gym·nas·tics \jim-'nas-tiks\ *n* : a competitive sport developed from physical exercises designed to demonstrate strength, balance, and body control — **gym·nast** \'jim-ˌnast\ *n* — **gym·nas·tic** *adj*

gym·no·sperm \'jim-nə-ˌspərm\ *n* : any of a group of woody vascular seed plants (as conifers) that produce naked seeds not enclosed in an ovary

gyn *or* **gynecol** *abbr* gynecology

gy·nae·col·o·gy *chiefly Brit var of* GYNECOLOGY

gy·ne·col·o·gy \ˌgī-nə-'kä-lə-jē\ *n* : a branch of medicine dealing with the diseases and hygiene of women — **gy·ne·co·log·ic** \-ni-kə-'lä-jik\ *or* **gy·ne·co·log·i·cal** \-ji-kəl\ *adj* — **gy·ne·col·o·gist** \-nə-'kä-lə-jist\ *n*

gy·no·cen·tric \ˌgī-nə-'sen-trik\ *adj* : emphasizing feminine interests or a feminine point of view

gyp \'jip\ *n* **1** : CHEAT, SWINDLER **2** : FRAUD, SWINDLE — **gyp** *vb*

gyp·sum \'jip-səm\ *n* : a calcium-containing mineral used in making plaster of paris

Gyp·sy \'jip-sē\ *n*, *pl* **Gypsies** [by shortening & alter. fr. *Egyptian*] : a member of a traditionally traveling people coming orig. from India and living chiefly in Europe, Asia, and No. America; *also* : the language of the Gypsies

gypsy moth *n* : an Old World moth that was introduced into the U.S. where its caterpillar is a destructive defoliator of many trees

gy·rate \'jī-ˌrāt\ *vb* **gy·rat·ed; gy·rat·ing 1** : to revolve around a point or axis **2** : to oscillate with or as if with a circular or spiral motion — **gy·ra·tion** \jī-'rā-shən\ *n*

gyr·fal·con \'jər-ˌfal-kən, -ˌfòl-\ *n* : an arctic falcon with several color forms that is the largest of all falcons

¹**gy·ro** \'jī-rō\ *n*, *pl* **gyros** : GYROSCOPE

²**gy·ro** \'yē-ˌrō, 'zhir-ō\ *n*, *pl* **gyros** : a sandwich esp. of lamb and beef, tomato, onion, and yogurt sauce on pita bread

gy·ro·scope \'jī-rō-ˌskōp\ *n* : a wheel or disk mounted to spin rapidly about an axis that is free to turn in various directions

Gy Sgt *abbr* gunnery sergeant

gyve \'jīv, 'gīv\ *n* : FETTER — **gyve** *vb*

H

¹**h** \\'āch\\ *n, pl* **h's** *or* **hs** \\'ā-chəz\\ *often cap* : the 8th letter of the English alphabet

²**h** *abbr, often cap* **1** hard; hardness **2** heroin **3** hit **4** husband

H *symbol* hydrogen

¹**ha** \\'hä\\ *interj* — used esp. to express surprise or joy

²**ha** *abbr* hectare

Hab *abbr* Habacuc; Habakkuk

Ha·ba·cuc \\'ha-bə-ˌkək, hə-'ba-kək\\ *n* : HABAKKUK

Ha·bak·kuk \\'ha-bə-ˌkək, hə-'ba-kək\\ *n* — see BIBLE table

ha·ba·ne·ra \\ˌhä-bə-'ner-ə\\ *n* [Sp (*danza*) *habanera*, lit., dance of Havana] : a Cuban dance in slow time; *also* : the music for this dance

ha·ba·ne·ro *also* **ha·ba·ñe·ro** \\ˌ(h)ä-bə-'n(y)er-ō\\ *n* : a very hot chili pepper that is usu. orange when mature

ha·be·as cor·pus \\'hā-bē-əs-'kȯr-pəs\\ *n* [ME, fr. ML, lit., you should have the body (the opening words of the writ)] : a writ issued to bring a party before a court

hab·er·dash·er \\'ha-bər-ˌda-shər\\ *n* : a dealer in men's clothing and accessories

hab·er·dash·ery \\-ˌda-shə-rē\\ *n, pl* **-er·ies** **1** : goods sold by a haberdasher **2** : a haberdasher's shop

ha·bil·i·ment \\hə-'bi-lə-mənt\\ *n* **1** *pl* : TRAPPINGS, EQUIPMENT **2** : DRESS; *esp* : the dress characteristic of an occupation or occasion — usu. used in pl.

hab·it \\'ha-bət\\ *n* **1** : DRESS, GARB **2** : BEARING, CONDUCT **3** : PHYSIQUE **4** : mental makeup **5** : a usual manner of behavior : CUSTOM **6** : a behavior pattern acquired by frequent repetition ⟨has a ∼ of swearing⟩ **7** : ADDICTION ⟨a drug ∼⟩ **8** : mode of growth or occurrence ⟨trees with a spreading ∼⟩

hab·it·able \\'ha-bə-tə-bəl\\ *adj* : capable of being lived in — **hab·it·abil·i·ty** \\ˌha-bə-tə-'bi-lə-tē\\ *n*

hab·i·tat \\'ha-bə-ˌtat\\ *n* [L, it inhabits] : the place or environment where a plant or animal naturally occurs

hab·i·ta·tion \\ˌha-bə-'tā-shən\\ *n* **1** : OCCUPANCY **2** : a dwelling place : RESIDENCE **3** : SETTLEMENT

hab·it-form·ing \\'ha-bət-ˌfȯr-miŋ\\ *adj* : causing addiction : ADDICTIVE

ha·bit·u·al \\hə-'bi-chə-wəl\\ *adj* **1** : CUSTOMARY **2** : doing, practicing, or acting by force of habit **3** : inherent in an individual ⟨∼ grace⟩ — **ha·bit·u·al·ly** *adv* — **ha·bit·u·al·ness** *n*

ha·bit·u·ate \\hə-'bi-chə-ˌwāt\\ *vb* **-at·ed; -at·ing** **1** : ACCUSTOM **2** : to cause or undergo habituation

ha·bit·u·a·tion \\hə-ˌbi-chə-'wā-shən\\ *n* **1** : the process of making habitual **2** : psychological dependence on a drug after a period of use

ha·bi·tué *also* **ha·bi·tue** \\hə-'bi-chə-ˌwā\\ *n* [F] **1** : one who may be regularly found in or at (as a place of entertainment) **2** : DEVOTEE

ha·ci·en·da \\ˌhä-sē-'en-də\\ *n* **1** : a large estate in a Spanish-speaking country **2** : the main building of a farm or ranch

¹**hack** \\'hak\\ *vb* **1** : to cut or sever with repeated irregular blows **2** : to cough in a short dry manner **3** : to manage successfully; *also* : TOLERATE ⟨can't ∼ the pressure⟩ **4** : to gain access to a computer illegally

²**hack** *n* **1** : an implement for hacking **2** : a short dry cough **3** : a hacking blow

³**hack** *n* **1** : a horse hired or used for varied work **2** : a horse worn out in service **3** : a light easy often 3-gaited saddle horse **4** : HACKNEY, TAXICAB **5** : a person who works solely for mercenary reasons; *esp* : a writer working solely for commercial success — **hack** *adj*

⁴**hack** *vb* : to operate a taxicab

hack·er \\'ha-kər\\ *n* **1** : one that hacks; *also* : a person unskilled at something **2** : an expert at using a computer **3** : a person who illegally gains access to and sometimes tampers with information in a computer system

hack·ie \\'ha-kē\\ *n* : a taxicab driver

hack·le \\'ha-kəl\\ *n* **1** : one of the long feathers on the neck or back of a bird **2** *pl* : hairs (as on a dog's neck)

that can be erected **3** *pl* : TEMPER, DANDER

hack·man \\'hak-mən\\ *n* : HACKIE

¹**hack·ney** \\'hak-nē\\ *n, pl* **hackneys** **1** : a horse for riding or driving **2** : a carriage or automobile kept for hire

²**hackney** *vb* : to make trite

hack·neyed \\'hak-nēd\\ *adj* : lacking in freshness or originality ⟨∼ slogans⟩

hack·saw \\'hak-ˌsȯ\\ *n* : a fine-tooth saw in a frame for cutting metal

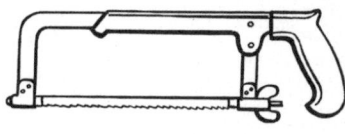

hacksaw

hack·work \\-ˌwərk\\ *n* : work done on order usu. according to a formula

had *past and past part of* HAVE

had·dock \\'ha-dək\\ *n, pl* **haddock** *also* **haddocks** : an Atlantic food fish usu. smaller than the related cod

Ha·des \\'hā-(ˌ)dēz\\ *n* **1** : the abode of the dead in Greek mythology **2** *often not cap* : HELL

haem *chiefly Brit var of* HEME

hae·ma·tite *Brit var of* HEMATITE

haf·ni·um \\'haf-nē-əm\\ *n* : a gray metallic chemical element

haft \\'haft\\ *n* : the handle of a weapon or tool

hag \\'hag\\ *n* **1** : an ugly or evil-looking old woman **2** : WITCH 1

Hag *abbr* Haggai

Hag·gai \\'ha-gē-ˌī, 'ha-ˌgī\\ *n* — see BIBLE table

hag·gard \\'ha-gərd\\ *adj* : having a worn or emaciated appearance ⟨∼ faces⟩ ♦ **Synonyms** CAREWORN, WASTED, DRAWN — **hag·gard·ly** *adv* — **hag·gard·ness** *n*

hag·gis \\'ha-gəs\\ *n* : a traditionally Scottish dish made of the heart, liver, and lungs of a sheep or a calf minced with suet, onions, oatmeal, and seasonings

hag·gle \\'ha-gəl\\ *vb* **hag·gled; hag·gling** : to argue in bargaining — **hag·gler** *n*

Ha·gi·og·ra·pha \\ˌha-gē-'ä-grə-fə, ˌhä-jē-\\ *n pl* — see WRITINGS

ha·gio·graph·ic \\ˌha-gē-ə-'gra-fik, ˌhä-, -jē-\\ *adj* : of or relating to hagiography; *esp* : excessively flattering

ha·gi·og·ra·phy \\ˌha-gē-'ä-grə-fē, ˌhä-jē-\\ *n* **1** : biography of saints or venerated persons **2** : idealizing or idolizing biography — **ha·gi·og·ra·pher** \\-fər\\ *n*

hai·ku \\'hī-(ˌ)kü\\ *n, pl* **haiku** [Jp] : an unrhymed Japanese verse form of three lines containing usu. five, seven, and five syllables respectively; *also* : a poem in this form

¹**hail** \\'hāl\\ *n* **1** : precipitation in the form of small lumps of ice **2** : something that gives the effect of falling hail

²**hail** *vb* **1** : to precipitate hail **2** : to pour down and strike like hail

³**hail** *interj* [ME, fr. ON *heill*, fr. *heill* healthy] — used to express acclamation

⁴**hail** *vb* **1** : SALUTE, GREET **2** : SUMMON

⁵**hail** *n* **1** : an expression of greeting, approval, or praise **2** : hearing distance

Hail Mary *n* : a salutation and prayer to the Virgin Mary

hail·stone \\'hāl-ˌstōn\\ *n* : a pellet of hail

hail·storm \\-ˌstȯrm\\ *n* : a storm accompanied by hail

hair \\'her\\ *n* : a threadlike outgrowth esp. from the skin of a mammal; *also* : a covering or growth of hairs of an animal or a body part — **haired** \\'herd\\ *adj* — **hair·less** *adj*

hair·breadth \\'her-ˌbredth\\ *or* **hairs·breadth** \\'herz-\\ *n* : a very small distance or margin

hair·brush \\-ˌbrəsh\\ *n* : a brush for the hair

hair·cloth \\-ˌklȯth\\ *n* : a stiff wiry fabric used esp. for upholstery

hair·cut \-ˌkət\ *n* : the act, process, or style of cutting and shaping the hair

hair·do \-ˌdü\ *n*, *pl* **hairdos** : HAIRSTYLE

hair·dress·er \-ˌdre-sər\ *n* : a person who dresses or cuts hair — **hair·dress·ing** *n*

hair·line \-ˌlīn\ *n* **1** : a very thin line **2** : the outline of the hair on the head

hair·piece \-ˌpēs\ *n* **1** : supplementary hair (as a switch) used in some women's hairdos **2** : TOUPEE

hair·pin \-ˌpin\ *n* **1** : a U-shaped pin to hold the hair in place **2** : a sharp U-shaped turn in a road — **hairpin** *adj*

hair·rais·ing \'her-ˌrā-ziŋ\ *adj* : causing terror or astonishment

hair·split·ter \-ˌspli-tər\ *n* : a person who makes excessively fine distinctions in reasoning — **hair·split·ting** \-ˌspli-tiŋ\ *adj or n*

hair·spray \'her-ˌsprā\ *n* : a liquid sprayed onto the hair to hold it in place

hair·style \-ˌstī(-ə)l\ *n* : a way of wearing the hair — **hair·styl·ing** *n*

hair·styl·ist \-ˌstī-list\ *n* : HAIRDRESSER

hair–trigger *adj* : immediately responsive to the slightest stimulus

hairy \'her-ē\ *adj* **hair·i·er; -est 1** : covered with or as if with hair **2** : tending to cause nervous tension ⟨a few ~ moments⟩ **3** : difficult to deal with — **hair·i·ness** \-ē-nəs\ *n*

hairy woodpecker *n* : a common No. American woodpecker with a white back that is larger than the similarly marked downy woodpecker

hajj \'haj\ *n* : the Islamic religious pilgrimage to Mecca

hajji \'ha-jē\ *n* : one who has made a pilgrimage to Mecca — often used as a title

hake \'hāk\ *n* : any of several marine food fishes related to the cod

ha·la·la *or* **ha·la·lah** \hə-ˈlä-lə\ *n*, *pl* **halala** *or* **halalas** *or* **halalah** *or* **halalahs** — see *riyal* at MONEY table

hal·berd \'hal-bərd, 'hȯl-\ *also* **hal·bert** \-bərt\ *n* : a weapon esp. of the 15th and 16th centuries consisting of a battle-ax and pike on a long handle

hal·cy·on \'hal-sē-ən\ *adj* [Gk *halkyōn, alkyōn* a mythical bird believed to nest at sea and to calm the waves] **1** : CALM, PEACEFUL ⟨a ~ lake⟩ **2** : being a time of happiness, success, or prosperity

¹**hale** \'hāl\ *adj* : free from defect, disease, or infirmity ✦ **Synonyms** HEALTHY, SOUND, ROBUST, WELL

²**hale** *vb* **haled; hal·ing 1** : HAUL, PULL **2** : to compel to go

ha·ler \'hä-lər\ *n*, *pl* **ha·le·ru** \'hä-lə-ˌrü\ — see *koruna* at MONEY table

¹**half** \'haf, 'häf\ *n*, *pl* **halves** \'havz, 'håvz\ **1** : either of two equal parts that compose something **2** : one of a pair

²**half** *adj* **1** : being one of two equal parts **2** : amounting to nearly half **3** : PARTIAL, INCOMPLETE — **half** *adv*

half–and–half \ˌhaf-ᵊn-'haf, ˌhäf-ᵊn-'häf\ *n* : something that is half one thing and half another

half·back \'haf-ˌbak, 'häf-\ *n* **1** : a football back stationed on or near the flank **2** : a player stationed immediately behind the forward line

half–baked \-'bākt\ *adj* **1** : poorly planned or developed; *also* : lacking common sense **2** : not thoroughly baked

half–breed \-ˌbrēd\ *n*, *often disparaging* : one of mixed racial descent — **half–breed** *adj, often disparaging*

half brother *n* : a brother related through one parent only

half–caste \'haf-ˌkast, 'häf-\ *n* : HALF-BREED — **half–caste** *adj*

half–cocked \'haf-'käkt, 'häf-\ *adj* : lacking adequate preparation

half–dol·lar \-'dä-lər\ *n* **1** : a coin representing one half of a dollar **2** : the sum of fifty cents

half·heart·ed \-'här-təd\ *adj* : lacking spirit or interest — **half·heart·ed·ly** *adv* — **half·heart·ed·ness** *n*

half–life \-ˌlīf\ *n* : the time required for half of something (as atoms or a drug) to undergo a process

half–mast \-'mast\ *n* : a point about halfway down from the top of a mast or staff

half note *n* : a musical note equal in time to one half of a whole note

half–pen·ny \'hāp-nē\ *n*, *pl* **half–pence** \'hā-pəns\ *or* **half–pennies** : a former British coin representing one half of a penny

half–pint \'haf-ˌpīnt, 'häf-\ *adj* : of less than average size — **half–pint** *n*

half sister *n* : a sister related through one parent only

half sole *n* : a shoe sole extending from the shank forward — **half–sole** *vb*

half–staff \'haf-'staf, 'häf-\ *n* : HALF-MAST

half step *n* : a musical interval equivalent to one twelfth of an octave

half–time \'haf-ˌtīm, 'häf-\ *n* : an intermission between halves of a game

half–track \-ˌtrak\ *n* : a motor vehicle propelled by an endless chain-track drive system; *esp* : such a vehicle lightly armored for military use

half–truth \-ˌtrüth\ *n* : a statement that is only partially true; *esp* : one that deliberately mixes truth and falsehood

half·way \-'wā\ *adj* **1** : midway between two points **2** : PARTIAL **1** — **halfway** *adv*

half–wit \-ˌwit\ *n* : a foolish or imbecilic person — **half–wit·ted** \-'wi-təd\ *adj* — **half–wit·ted·ness** *n*

hal·i·but \'ha-lə-bət\ *n, pl* **halibut** *also* **halibuts** [ME *halybutte*, fr. *haly, holy* holy + *butte* flatfish; fr. its being eaten on holy days] : any of several large edible marine flatfishes

ha·lite \'ha-ˌlīt, 'hā-\ *n* : ROCK SALT

hal·i·to·sis \ˌha-lə-'tō-səs\ *n* : the condition of having fetid breath

hall \'hȯl\ *n* **1** : the residence of a medieval king or noble; *also* : the house of a landed proprietor **2** : a large public building **3** : a college or university building; *also* : DORMITORY **4** : LOBBY; *also* : CORRIDOR **5** : AUDITORIUM

hal·le·lu·jah \ˌha-lə-'lü-yə\ *interj* [Heb *hallēlūyāh* praise (ye) the Lord] — used to express praise, joy, or thanks

hall·mark \'hȯl-ˌmärk\ *n* **1** : a mark put on an article to indicate origin, purity, or genuineness **2** : a distinguishing characteristic

hal·low \'ha-lō\ *vb* **1** : CONSECRATE **2** : REVERE, VENERATE ⟨our ~ed leader⟩ — **hal·lowed** \-lōd, -lə-wəd\ *adj*

Hal·low·een *also* **Hal·low·e'en** \ˌha-lə-'wēn, ˌhä-\ *n* : the evening of October 31 observed esp. by children in merrymaking and masquerading

hal·lu·ci·nate \hə-'lü-sə-ˌnāt\ *vb* **-nat·ed; -nat·ing** : to have hallucinations or experience as a hallucination

hal·lu·ci·na·tion \hə-ˌlü-sə-'nā-shən\ *n* : perception of objects with no reality due usu. to use of drugs (as LSD) or to disorder of the nervous system; *also* : something so perceived ✦ **Synonyms** DELUSION, ILLUSION, MIRAGE — **hal·lu·ci·na·to·ry** \-'lü-sə-nə-ˌtȯr-ē\ *adj*

hal·lu·ci·no·gen \hə-'lü-sə-nə-jən\ *n* : a substance that induces hallucinations — **hal·lu·ci·no·gen·ic** \-ˌlü-sə-nə-'je-nik\ *adj or n*

hall·way \'hȯl-ˌwā\ *n* **1** : an entrance hall **2** : CORRIDOR

ha·lo \'hā-lo\ *n, pl* **halos** *or* **haloes** [L *halos*, fr. Gk *halōs* threshing floor, disk, halo] **1** : a circle of light appearing to surround a shining body (as the sun) **2** : the aura of glory surrounding an idealized person or thing

¹**hal·o·gen** \'ha-lə-jən\ *n* : any of the five elements fluorine, chlorine, bromine, iodine, and astatine

²**hal·o·gen** *adj* : containing, using, or being a halogen ⟨a ~ lamp⟩

¹**halt** \'hȯlt\ *adj* : LAME 1

²**halt** *n* : STOP

³**halt** *vb* **1** : to stop marching or traveling **2** : DISCONTINUE, END ⟨~ protests⟩

¹**hal·ter** \'hȯl-tər\ *n* **1** : a rope or strap for leading or tying an animal; *also* : HEADSTALL **2** : NOOSE **3** : a brief blouse held in place by straps around the neck and across the back

²**halter** *vb* **hal·tered; hal·ter·ing 1** : to catch with or as if with a halter; *also* : to put a halter on (as a horse) **2** : HANG **3** : IMPEDE, RESTRAIN

halt·ing \'hȯl-tiŋ\ *adj* : UNCERTAIN, FALTERING — **halt·ing·ly** *adv*

halve \'hav, 'häv\ *vb* **halved; halv·ing 1** : to divide into two equal parts **2** : to reduce to one half

halv·ers \'ha-vərz, 'hä-\ *n pl* : half shares : HALVES

halves *pl of* HALF

hal·yard \'hal-yərd\ *n* : a rope or tackle for hoisting and lowering (as sails)

¹**ham** \'ham\ *n* **1** : a buttock with its associated thigh — usu. used in pl. **2** : a cut of meat and esp. pork from the thigh **3** : a showy performer **4** : an operator of an amateur radio station — **ham** *adj*

²**ham** *vb* **hammed; ham·ming** : to overplay a part : OVER-ACT

ham·burg·er \'ham-₁bər-gər\ *or* **ham·burg** \-₁bərg\ *n* [G *Hamburger* of Hamburg, Germany] **1** : ground beef **2** : a sandwich consisting of a ground-beef patty in a round roll

ham·let \'ham-lət\ *n* : a small village

¹**ham·mer** \'ha-mər\ *n* **1** : a hand tool used for pounding; *also* : something resembling a hammer in form or function **2** : the part of a gun whose striking action causes explosion of the charge **3** : a metal sphere hurled by a flexible handle for distance in a track-and-field event (**hammer throw**) **4** : ACCELERATOR 2

²**hammer** *vb* **1** : to beat, drive, or shape with repeated blows of a hammer : POUND **2** : to produce or bring about as if by repeated blows — usu. used with *out* **3** : to criticize severely

ham·mer·head \'ha-mər-₁hed\ *n* **1** : the striking part of a hammer **2** : any of a family of medium-sized sharks with eyes at the ends of lateral extensions of the flattened head

ham·mer·lock \-₁läk\ *n* : a wrestling hold in which an opponent's arm is held bent behind the back

ham·mer·toe \-₁tō\ *n* : a toe deformed by having one or more joints permanently flexed

¹**ham·mock** \'ha-mək\ *n* [Sp *hamaca*, of AmerInd origin] : a swinging couch hung by cords at each end

²**hammock** *n* : a fertile elevated area of the southern U.S. and esp. Florida with hardwood vegetation and soil rich in humus

¹**ham·per** \'ham-pər\ *vb* : IMPEDE; *also* : RESTRAIN ✦ **Synonyms** TRAMMEL, CLOG, FETTER, SHACKLE

²**hamper** *n* : a large usu. lidded basket

ham·ster \'ham-stər\ *n* [G, fr. OHG *hamustro*, of Slavic origin] : any of a subfamily of small Old World rodents with large cheek pouches

¹**ham·string** \'ham-₁striŋ\ *n* : any of several muscles at the back of the thigh or tendons at the back of the knee

²**hamstring** *vb* **-strung** \-₁strəŋ\; **-string·ing** **1** : to make ineffective or powerless ⟨*hamstrung* by guilt⟩ **2** : to cripple by cutting the leg tendons

¹**hand** \'hand\ *n* **1** : the end of a front limb when modified (as in humans) for grasping **2** : an indicator or pointer on a dial **3** : personal possession — usu. used in pl.; *also* : CONTROL **4** : SIDE 5 **5** : a pledge esp. of betrothal **6** : HANDWRITING **7** : SKILL, ABILITY; *also* : a significant part ⟨had a ~ in the victory⟩ **8** : ASSISTANCE; *also* : PARTICIPATION ⟨had no ~ in the affair⟩ **9** : an outburst of applause **10** : a single round in a card game; *also* : the cards held by a player after a deal **11** : WORKER, EMPLOYEE; *also* : a member of a ship's crew — **hand·less** *adj* — **at hand** : near in time or place — **on hand** : in present possession or readily available — **out of hand** : out of control

²**hand** *vb* **1** : to lead, guide, or assist with the hand **2** : to give, pass, or transmit with the hand

hand·bag \'hand-₁bag\ *n* : a bag for carrying small personal articles and money

hand·ball \-₁bȯl\ *n* : a game played by striking a small rubber ball against a wall with the hand

hand·bill \-₁bil\ *n* : a small printed sheet for distribution by hand

hand·book \-₁bůk\ *n* : a concise reference book : MANUAL

hand·car \-₁kär\ *n* : a small 4-wheeled railroad car propelled by hand or by a small motor

hand·clasp \-₁klasp\ *n* : HANDSHAKE

hand·craft \-₁kraft\ *vb* : to fashion by manual skill

¹**hand·cuff** \-₁kəf\ *n* : a metal fastening that can be locked around a wrist and is usu. connected with another such fastening — usu. used in pl.

²**handcuff** *vb* : MANACLE

hand·ed \'han-dəd\ *adj* : having or using such or so many hands ⟨a left-*handed* person⟩ — **hand·ed·ness** *n*

hand·ful \₁hand-₁fůl\ *n, pl* **hand·fuls** \-₁fůlz\ *also* **hands·ful** \'handz-₁fůl\ **1** : as much or as many as the hand will grasp **2** : a small number **3** : as much as one can manage

hand·gun \-₁gən\ *n* : a firearm held and fired with one hand

hand·held \-₁held\ *adj* : designed for use while being held in the hand — **handheld** *n*

¹**hand·i·cap** \'han-di-₁kap\ *n* [obs. E *handicap*, a game in

which forfeit money was held in a cap, fr. *hand in cap*] **1** : a contest in which an artificial advantage is given or disadvantage imposed on a contestant to equalize chances of winning; *also* : the advantage given or disadvantage imposed **2** : a disadvantage that makes achievement difficult

²**handicap** *vb* **-capped; -cap·ping** **1** : to give a handicap to **2** : to put at a disadvantage

hand·i·capped *adj, sometimes offensive* : having a physical or mental disability

hand·i·cap·per \-₁ka-pər\ *n* : a person who predicts the winners in a contest

hand·i·craft \'han-di-₁kraft\ *n* **1** : manual skill **2** : an occupation requiring manual skill **3** : the articles fashioned by those engaged in handicraft — **hand·i·craft·er** \-₁kraf-tər\ *n* — **hand·i·crafts·man** \-₁krafts-mən\ *n*

hand in glove *or* **hand and glove** *adv* : in an extremely close relationship

hand·i·work \'han-di-₁wərk\ *n* : work done personally or by the hands

hand·ker·chief \'haŋ-kər-chəf, -₁chēf\ *n, pl* **-chiefs** \-chəfs, -₁chēfs\ *also* **-chieves** \-₁chēvz\ : a small piece of cloth used for various personal purposes (as the wiping of the face)

¹**han·dle** \'han-dᵊl\ *n* **1** : a part (as of a tool) designed to be grasped by the hand **2** : NAME; *also* : NICKNAME — **handled** \-dᵊld\ *adj* — **off the handle** : into a state of sudden and violent anger — usu. used with *fly*

²**handle** *vb* **han·dled; han·dling** **1** : to touch, hold, or manage with the hands **2** : to have responsibility for **3** : to deal or trade in **4** : to behave in a certain way when managed or directed ⟨a car that ~s well⟩ — **han·dler** *n*

han·dle·bar \'han-dᵊl-₁bär\ *n* : a usu. bent bar with a grip at each end (as for steering a bicycle) — usu. used in pl.

hand·made \'hand-₁mād\ *adj* : made by hand or by a hand process

hand·maid·en \-₁mā-dᵊn\ *also* **hand·maid** \-₁mād\ *n* : a female attendant

hand–me–down \-me-₁daůn\ *adj* : used by one person after having been used by another — **hand–me–down** *n*

hand·out \'hand-₁aůt\ *n* **1** : a portion (as of food) given to a beggar **2** : a piece of printed information for free distribution; *also* : a prepared statement released to the press

hand over *vb* : to yield control of

hand·pick \'hand-'pik\ *vb* : to select personally ⟨a ~ed candidate⟩

hand·rail \-₁rāl\ *n* : a narrow rail for grasping as a support

hand·saw \-₁sȯ\ *n* : a saw designed to be used with one hand

hands down *adv* **1** : with little effort **2** : without question

hand·sel \'han-səl\ *n* **1** : a gift made as a token of good luck **2** : a first installment : earnest money

hand·set \'hand-₁set\ *n* : a combined telephone transmitter and receiver mounted on a handheld device

hand·shake \-₁shāk\ *n* : a clasping usu. of right hands by two people

hands–off \'handz-'ȯf\ *adj* : characterized by noninterference

hand·some \'han-səm\ *adj* **hand·som·er; -est** [ME *handsom* easy to manipulate] **1** : SIZABLE, AMPLE **2** : GENEROUS, LIBERAL **3** : pleasing and usu. impressive in appearance ✦ **Synonyms** BEAUTIFUL, LOVELY, PRETTY, COMELY, FAIR — **hand·some·ly** *adv* — **hand·some·ness** *n*

hands–on \'handz-'ȯn, -'än\ *adj* **1** : being or providing direct practical experience in the operation of something **2** : characterized by active personal involvement ⟨~ management⟩

hand·spring \'hand-₁spriŋ\ *n* : an acrobatic feat in which the body turns in a full circle from a standing position and lands first on the hands and then on the feet

hand·stand \-₁stand\ *n* : an act of supporting the body on the hands with the trunk and legs balanced in the air

hand–to–hand *adj* : involving physical contact or very close range ⟨~ fighting⟩ — **hand to hand** *adv*

hand–to–mouth *adj* : having or providing nothing to spare — **hand to mouth** *adv*

hand·wo·ven \'hand-₁wō-vən\ *adj* : produced on a hand-operated loom

hand·writ·ing \-₁rī-tiŋ\ *n* : writing done by hand; *also* : the form of writing peculiar to a person — **hand·writ·ten** \-ˌri-t³n\ *adj*

handy \'han-dē\ *adj* **hand·i·er; -est** 1 : conveniently near 2 : easily used 3 : DEXTEROUS — **hand·i·ly** \-də-lē\ *adv* — **hand·i·ness** \-dē-nəs\ *n*

handy·man \-ˌman\ *n* 1 : one who does odd jobs 2 : one competent in a variety of small skills or repair work

¹**hang** \'haŋ\ *vb* **hung** \'həŋ\ *also* **hanged; hang·ing** 1 : to fasten or remain fastened to an elevated point without support from below; *also* : to fasten or be fastened so as to allow free motion on the point of suspension 〈~ a door〉 2 : to suspend by the neck until dead; *also* : to die by hanging 3 : DROOP 〈*hung* his head in shame〉 4 : to fasten to a wall 〈~ wallpaper〉 5 : to prevent (a jury) from coming to a decision 6 : to display (pictures) in a gallery 7 : to remain stationary in the air 8 : to be imminent 9 : DEPEND 10 : to take hold for support 11 : to be burdensome 12 : to undergo delay 13 : to incline downward; *also* : to fit or fall from the figure in easy lines 14 : to be raptly attentive 15 : to pass time idly by relaxing or socializing 〈~*ing* at the mall〉 — often used with *around* or *out* — **hang out to dry** : to subject to ruin by abandonment

²**hang** *n* 1 : the manner in which a thing hangs 2 : an understanding of something 〈got the ~ of skiing〉

han·gar \'haŋ-ər\ *n* [F] : a covered and usu. enclosed area for housing and repairing aircraft

hang·dog \'haŋ-ˌdȯg\ *adj* 1 : SAD, DEJECTED 2 : SHEEPISH

hang·er \'haŋ-ər\ *n* 1 : one that hangs 2 : a device that fits inside or around a garment for hanging from a hook or rod

hang·er-on \'haŋ-ər-'ȯn, -'än\ *n, pl* **hangers-on** : one who hangs around a person or place esp. for personal gain

hang in *vb* : to persist tenaciously

hang·ing *n* 1 : an execution by strangling or snapping the neck by a suspended noose 2 : something hung

hang·man \'haŋ-mən\ *n* 1 : a public executioner 2 : a game in which players must identify an unknown word by guessing the letters that comprise it within a designated number of chances

hang·nail \-ˌnāl\ *n* : a bit of skin hanging loose at the edge of a fingernail

hang on *vb* 1 : to keep hold onto something 2 : HANG IN 3 : to await something desired

hang·out \'haŋ-ˌaȯt\ *n* : a favorite place for spending time

hang·over \-ˌō-vər\ *n* 1 : something that remains from what is past 2 : disagreeable physical effects following heavy drinking or the use of drugs

hang–up \'haŋ-ˌəp\ *n* : a source of mental or emotional difficulty

hang up *vb* 1 : to place on a hook or hanger 2 : to end a telephone conversation by breaking the connection 3 : to keep delayed or suspended

hank \'haŋk\ *n* : COIL, LOOP

han·ker \'haŋ-kər\ *vb* : to desire strongly or persistently — **han·ker·ing** *n*

han·kie *or* **han·ky** \'haŋ-kē\ *n, pl* **hankies** : HANDKERCHIEF

han·ky–pan·ky \ˌhaŋ-kē-'paŋ-kē\ *n* 1 : questionable or underhanded activity 2 : sexual dalliance

hansel *var of* HANDSEL

han·som \'han-səm\ *n* : a 2-wheeled covered carriage with the driver's seat elevated at the rear

han·ta·virus \'hän-tə-ˌvī-rəs, 'hən-, 'han-\ *n* : any of a genus of viruses including some transmitted by rodents that cause pneumonia or hemorrhagic fevers

Ha·nuk·kah *also* **Cha·nu·kah** \'kä-nə-kə, 'hä-\ *n* [Heb *ḥănukkāh* dedication] : an 8-day Jewish holiday commemorating the rededication of the Temple of Jerusalem after its defilement by Antiochus of Syria

hap \'hap\ *n* 1 : HAPPENING 2 : CHANCE, FORTUNE

¹**hap·haz·ard** \hap-'ha-zərd\ *n* : CHANCE

²**haphazard** *adj* : marked by lack of plan or order — **hap·haz·ard·ly** *adv* — **hap·haz·ard·ness** *n*

hap·less \'hap-ləs\ *adj* : UNFORTUNATE — **hap·less·ly** *adv* — **hap·less·ness** *n*

hap·loid \'hap-ˌlȯid\ *adj* : having the number of chromosomes characteristic of gametic cells — **haploid** *n*

hap·ly \'hap-lē\ *adv* : by chance

hap·pen \'ha-pən\ *vb* 1 : to occur by chance 2 : to take place 3 : CHANCE 2

¹**hap·pen·ing** *n* 1 : OCCURRENCE 2 : an event that is especially interesting, entertaining, or important

²**happening** *adj* 1 : very fashionable 2 : offering much stimulating activity 〈a ~ nightclub〉

hap·pi·ly \'ha-pə-lē\ *adv* 1 : LUCKILY 2 : in a happy manner or state 〈lived ~ ever after〉 3 : APTLY, SUCCESSFULLY

hap·pi·ness \'ha-pē-nəs\ *n* 1 : a state of well-being and contentment; *also* : a pleasurable satisfaction 2 : APTNESS

hap·py \'ha-pē\ *adj* **hap·pi·er; -est** 1 : FORTUNATE 2 : APT, FELICITOUS 3 : enjoying well-being and contentment 〈a ~ childhood〉 4 : PLEASANT 〈a ~ ending〉; *also* : PLEASED, GRATIFIED 〈~ to meet you〉 5 : quick or enthusiastic to use or do something 〈trigger-*happy*〉 〈a cliché-*happy* writer〉 ✦ **Synonyms** GLAD, CHEERFUL, LIGHTHEARTED, JOYFUL, JOYOUS

hap·py–go–lucky \ˌha-pē-gō-'lə-kē\ *adj* : CAREFREE

happy hour *n* : a period of time when the price of drinks at a bar is reduced

hara–kiri \ˌha-ri-'kir-ē, -'ka-rē\ *n* [Jp *harakiri*, fr. *hara* belly + *kiri* cutting] : ritual suicide by disembowelment

ha·rangue \hə-'raŋ\ *n* 1 : a ranting speech or writing 2 : LECTURE — **harangue** *vb* — **ha·rangu·er** *n*

ha·rass \hə-'ras, 'ha-rəs\ *vb* [F *harasser*, fr. MF, fr. *harer* to set a dog on, fr. OF *hare*, interj. used to incite dogs, of Gmc origin] 1 : EXHAUST, FATIGUE 2 : to worry and impede by repeated raids 3 : to annoy continually 4 : to create an unpleasant or hostile situation for esp. by one's verbal or physical conduct ✦ **Synonyms** HARRY, PLAGUE, PESTER, TEASE, BEDEVIL — **ha·rass·ment** *n*

har·bin·ger \'här-bən-jər\ *n* : one that announces or foreshadows what is coming : PRECURSOR; *also* : PORTENT

¹**har·bor** \'här-bər\ *n* 1 : a place of security and comfort 2 : a part of a body of water protected and deep enough to furnish anchorage : PORT

²**harbor** *vb* 1 : to give or take refuge : SHELTER 〈~ a fugitive〉 〈~*ed* in the barn〉 2 : to be the home or habitat of; *also* : LIVE 3 : to hold a thought or feeling 〈~ a grudge〉

har·bor·age \'här-bə-rij\ *n* : HARBOR

har·bour *chiefly Brit var of* HARBOR

hard \'härd\ *adj* 1 : not easily penetrated : not easily yielding to pressure 2 : high in alcoholic content 3 : containing salts that prevent lathering with soap 〈~ water〉 4 : stable in value 〈~ currency〉 5 : physically fit 6 : FIRM, DEFINITE 〈~ agreement〉; *also* : based on clear fact 〈~ evidence〉 7 : CLOSE, SEARCHING 〈a ~ look〉 8 : REALISTIC 〈good ~ sense〉 9 : OBDURATE, UNFEELING 〈a ~ heart〉 10 : difficult to bear 〈~ times〉; *also* : HARSH, SEVERE 11 : RESENTFUL 〈~ feelings〉 12 : STRICT, UNRELENTING 〈a ~ bargain〉 13 : INCLEMENT 〈a ~ winter〉 14 : intense in force or manner 〈a ~ gust of wind〉 15 : ARDUOUS, STRENUOUS 〈~ work〉 16 : sounding as in *arcing* and *geese* respectively — used of *c* and *g* 17 : TROUBLESOME 〈a ~ problem〉 18 : having difficulty in doing something 〈~ of hearing〉 19 : addictive and gravely detrimental to health 〈~ drugs〉 20 : of or relating to the natural sciences and esp. the physical sciences — **hard** *adv* — **hard·ness** *n*

hard–and–fast *adj* : rigidly binding : STRICT 〈a ~ rule〉

hard·back \'härd-ˌbak\ *n* : a hardcover book

hard·ball \-ˌbȯl\ *n* 1 : BASEBALL 2 : forceful uncompromising methods

hard–bit·ten \-'bi-t³n\ *adj* : SEASONED, TOUGH 〈~ campaigners〉

hard·board \-ˌbȯrd\ *n* : a very dense fiberboard

hard–boiled \-'bȯi(-ə)ld\ *adj* 1 *of an egg* : boiled until both white and yolk have solidified 2 : lacking sentiment : TOUGH; *also* : HARDHEADED 2

hard·bound \-ˌbaȯnd\ *adj* : HARDCOVER

hard copy *n* : copy of textual or graphic information (as from computer storage) produced on paper

hard–core \'härd-'kȯr\ *adj* 1 : extremely resistant to solution or improvement 2 : being the most determined or dedicated members of a specified group 3 : containing explicit depictions of sex acts — **hard core** *n*

hard·cov·er \-'kə-vər\ *adj* : having rigid boards on the sides covered in cloth or paper 〈~ books〉

hard disk *n* : a sealed rigid metal disk used as a computer storage device; *also* : HARD DRIVE

hard drive *n* : a data-storage device consisting of a drive and one or more hard disks

hard·en \'här-dᵊn\ *vb* **1** : to make or become hard or harder **2** : to confirm or become confirmed in disposition or action — **hard·en·er** *n*

hard·hack \'härd-ˌhak\ *n* : an American spirea with dense clusters of pink or white flowers and leaves having a hairy rusty yellow underside

hard hat *n* **1** : a protective hat worn esp. by construction workers **2** : a construction worker

hard·head·ed \'härd-'he-dəd\ *adj* **1** : STUBBORN, WILLFUL **2** : SOBER, REALISTIC ⟨some ∼ advice⟩ — **hard·head·ed·ly** *adv* — **hard·head·ed·ness** *n*

hard–heart·ed \-'här-təd\ *adj* : PITILESS, CRUEL — **hard–heart·ed·ly** *adv* — **hard–heart·ed·ness** *n*

har·di·hood \'här-dē-ˌhüd\ *n* **1** : resolute courage and fortitude **2** : VIGOR, ROBUSTNESS

hard–line \'härd-'līn\ *adj* : advocating or involving a rigidly uncompromising course of action — **hard–lin·er** \-'lī-nər\ *n*

hard–luck \-ˌlək\ *adj* : marked by or relating to bad luck ⟨∼ losing teams⟩

hard·ly \'härd-lē\ *adv* **1** : with force **2** : SEVERELY **3** : with difficulty **4** : only just : BARELY ⟨can ∼ tell the difference⟩ **5** : certainly not ⟨is ∼ a friend of mine⟩

hard–nosed \-ˌnōzd\ *adj* : TOUGH, UNCOMPROMISING; *also* : HARDHEADED 2

hard palate *n* : the bony anterior part of the palate forming the roof of the mouth

hard·pan \'härd-ˌpan\ *n* : a compact layer in soil that is impenetrable by roots

hard–pressed \-'prest\ *adj* : HARD PUT; *esp* : being under financial strain

hard put *adj* **1** : barely able **2** : faced with difficulty or perplexity

hard rock *n* : rock music marked by a heavy beat, high amplification, and usu. frenzied performances

hard–shell \'härd-ˌshel\ *or* **hard–shelled** \-ˌsheld\ *adj* **1** : having a hard shell **2** : HIDEBOUND, UNCOMPROMISING ⟨a ∼ conservative⟩

hard·ship \-ˌship\ *n* **1** : SUFFERING, PRIVATION **2** : something that causes suffering or privation

hard·tack \-ˌtak\ *n* : a saltless hard biscuit, bread, or cracker

hard·top \-ˌtäp\ *n* : an automobile having a permanent rigid top

hard·ware \-ˌwer\ *n* **1** : ware (as cutlery or tools) made of metal **2** : the physical components (as electronic devices) of a vehicle (as a spacecraft) or an apparatus (as a computer)

hard–wired \-ˌwī(-ə)rd\ *adj* **1** : connected or incorporated by or as if by permanent electrical connections **2** : genetically or innately determined or predisposed ⟨∼ reactions⟩ ⟨is ∼ to avoid change⟩

hard·wood \-ˌwu̇d\ *n* : the wood of a broad-leaved usu. deciduous tree as distinguished from that of a conifer; *also* : such a tree — **hardwood** *adj*

hard·work·ing \-'wər-kiŋ\ *adj* : INDUSTRIOUS, DILIGENT

har·dy \'här-dē\ *adj* **har·di·er; -est 1** : BOLD, BRAVE **2** : AUDACIOUS, BRAZEN **3** : ROBUST; *also* : able to withstand adverse conditions (as of weather) ⟨∼ shrubs⟩ — **har·di·ly** \-də-lē\ *adv* — **har·di·ness** \-dē-nəs\ *n*

hare \'her\ *n, pl* **hare** *or* **hares** : any of various swift timid long-eared mammals like the related rabbits but born with open eyes and fur

hare·bell \'her-ˌbel\ *n* : a slender herb with bright blue bell-shaped flowers

hare·brained \-'brānd\ *adj* : FOOLISH, ABSURD

hare·lip \-'lip\ *n, sometimes offensive* : cleft lip

ha·rem \'her-əm\ *n* [Ar *ḥarīm*, lit., something forbidden & *ḥaram*, lit., sanctuary] **1** : a house or part of a house allotted to women in a Muslim household **2** : the women and servants occupying a harem **3** : a group of females associated with one male

hark \'härk\ *vb* : LISTEN

harken *var of* HEARKEN

har·le·quin \'här-li-kən, -kwən\ *n* **1** *cap* : a character (as in comedy) with a shaved head, masked face, variegated tights, and wooden sword **2** : CLOWN 2

har·lot \'här-lət\ *n* : PROSTITUTE

¹harm \'härm\ *n* **1** : physical or mental damage : INJURY **2** : MISCHIEF, HURT — **harm·ful** \-fəl\ *adj* — **harm·ful·ly** *adv* — **harm·ful·ness** *n* — **harm·less** *adj* — **harm·less·ly** *adv* — **harm·less·ness** *n*

²harm *vb* : to cause harm to : INJURE

¹har·mon·ic \här-'mä-nik\ *adj* **1** : of or relating to musical harmony or harmonics **2** : pleasing to the ear — **har·mon·i·cal·ly** \-ni-k(ə-)lē\ *adv*

²harmonic *n* : a musical overtone

har·mon·i·ca \här-'mä-ni-kə\ *n* : a small wind instrument in which the sound is produced by metal reeds

har·mo·ni·ous \här-'mō-nē-əs\ *adj* **1** : musically concordant **2** : CONGRUOUS **3** : marked by accord in sentiment or action — **har·mo·ni·ous·ly** *adv* — **har·mo·ni·ous·ness** *n*

har·mo·nise *Brit var of* HARMONIZE

har·mo·ni·um \här-'mō-nē-əm\ *n* : a keyboard wind instrument in which the wind acts on a set of metal reeds

har·mo·nize \'här-mə-ˌnīz\ *vb* **-nized; -niz·ing 1** : to play or sing in harmony **2** : to be in harmony **3** : to bring into consonance or accord — **har·mo·ni·za·tion** \ˌhär-mə-nə-'zā-shən\ *n*

har·mo·ny \'här-mə-nē\ *n, pl* **-nies** [ME *armony*, fr. AF *armonie*, fr. L *harmonia*, fr. Gk, joint, harmony, fr. *harmos* joint] **1** : musical agreement of sounds; *esp* : the combination of tones into chords and progressions of chords **2** : a pleasing arrangement of parts; *also* : ACCORD **3** : internal calm

¹har·ness \'här-nəs\ *n* **1** : the gear other than a yoke of a draft animal **2** : something that resembles a harness

²harness *vb* **1** : to put a harness on; *also* : YOKE **2** : UTILIZE ⟨∼ one's potential⟩

¹harp \'härp\ *n* : a musical instrument consisting of a triangular frame set with strings plucked by the fingers — **harp·ist** \'här-pist\ *n*

²harp *vb* **1** : to play on a harp **2** : to dwell on a subject tiresomely — **harp·er** *n*

har·poon \här-'pün\ *n* : a barbed spear used esp. in hunting whales — **harpoon** *vb* — **har·poon·er** *n*

harp·si·chord \'härp-si-ˌkȯrd\ *n* : a keyboard instrument producing tones by the plucking of its strings with quills or with leather or plastic points

har·py \'här-pē\ *n, pl* **harpies** [L *Harpyia*, a malign creature of myth having a woman's head and a bird's body, fr. Gk] **1** : a predatory person : LEECH **2** : a shrewish woman

har·ri·dan \'her-ə-dən\ *n* : SHREW 2

¹har·ri·er \'her-ē-ər\ *n* **1** : any of a breed of medium-sized foxhounds **2** : a runner on a cross-country team

²harrier *n* : a slender long-legged hawk

¹har·row \'her-ō\ *n* : a cultivating tool that has spikes, spring teeth, or disks and is used esp. to pulverize and smooth the soil

²harrow *vb* **1** : to cultivate with a harrow **2** : TORMENT, VEX

har·rumph \hə-'rəmf\ *vb* : to comment disapprovingly as though clearing the throat

har·ry \'her-ē\ *vb* **har·ried; har·ry·ing 1** : RAID, PILLAGE **2** : to torment by or as if by constant attack ✦ **Synonyms** WORRY, ANNOY, PLAGUE, PESTER

harsh \'härsh\ *adj* **1** : disagreeably rough **2** : causing discomfort or pain **3** : unduly exacting : SEVERE — **harsh·ly** *adv* — **harsh·ness** *n*

harsh·en \'här-shən\ *vb* : to make or become harsh ⟨∼ed his voice⟩

hart \'härt\ *n, chiefly Brit* : STAG

har·um–scar·um \ˌhar-əm-'skar-əm\ *adj* : RECKLESS, IRRESPONSIBLE

¹har·vest \'här-vəst\ *n* **1** : the season for gathering in crops; *also* : the act of gathering in a crop **2** : a mature crop **3** : the product or reward of effort

²harvest *vb* **1** : to gather in a crop : REAP **2** : to gather, hunt, or kill (as deer) for human use or population control **3** : to remove cells, tissues, or organs from a living or recently deceased body esp. for transplanting — **har·vest·er** *n*

has *pres 3d sing of* HAVE

has–been \'haz-ˌbin\ *n* : one that has passed the peak of ability, power, effectiveness, or popularity

¹hash \'hash\ *vb* [F *hacher*, fr. OF *hachier*, fr. *hache* battle-ax, of Gmc origin] **1** : to chop into small pieces **2** : to talk about — often used with *over* or *out*

²hash *n* **1** : chopped meat mixed with potatoes and browned **2** : HODGEPODGE, JUMBLE

³hash *n* : HASHISH

hash browns *n pl* : boiled potatoes that have been diced, mixed with chopped onions and shortening, and fried

hash·ish \'ha-ˌshēsh, ha-'shēsh\ *n* [Ar *hashīsh*] : the intoxicating concentrated resin from the flowering tops of the female hemp plant

hasp \'hasp\ *n* : a fastener (as for a door) consisting of a hinged metal strap that fits over a staple and is secured by a pin or padlock

has·si·um \'ha-sē-əm\ *n* : an artificially produced radioactive metallic chemical element

has·sle \'ha-səl\ *n* **1** : WRANGLE; *also* : FIGHT **2** : an annoying or troublesome concern — **hassle** *vb*

has·sock \'ha-sək\ *n* : a cushion that serves as a seat or leg rest; *also* : a cushion to kneel on in prayer

haste \'hāst\ *n* **1** : rapidity of motion or action : SPEED **2** : rash or headlong action **3** : excessive eagerness — **hast·i·ly** \'hā-stə-lē\ *adv* — **hast·i·ness** \-stē-nəs\ *n* — **hasty** \'hā-stē\ *adj*

has·ten \'hā-sᵊn\ *vb* **1** : to urge on **2** : to move or act quickly : HURRY ✦ *Synonyms* SPEED, ACCELERATE, QUICKEN

hat \'hat\ *n* : a covering for the head usu. having a shaped crown and brim — **under one's hat** : SECRET ⟨kept the plans *under his hat*⟩

hat·box \'hat-ˌbäks\ *n* : a round piece of luggage esp. for carrying hats

¹hatch \'hach\ *n* **1** : a small door or opening **2** : a door or cover for access down into a compartment of a ship

²hatch *vb* **1** : to produce by incubation; *also* : INCUBATE **2** : to emerge from an egg or pupa; *also* : to give forth young **3** : ORIGINATE ⟨~ a scheme⟩ — **hatch·ery** \'ha-chə-rē\ *n*

hatch·back \'hach-ˌbak\ *n* : an automobile with a rear hatch that opens upward

hatch·et \'ha-chət\ *n* **1** : a short-handled ax with a hammerlike part opposite the blade **2** : TOMAHAWK

hatchet man *n* : a person hired for murder, coercion, or unscrupulous attack

hatch·ing \'ha-chiŋ\ *n* : the engraving or drawing of closely spaced fine lines chiefly to give an effect of shading; *also* : the pattern so created

hatch·way \'hach-ˌwā\ *n* : a hatch giving access usu. by a ladder or stairs

¹hate \'hāt\ *n* **1** : intense hostility and aversion **2** : an object of hatred — **hate·ful** \-fəl\ *adj* — **hate·ful·ly** *adv* — **hate·ful·ness** *n*

²hate *vb* **hat·ed; hat·ing** **1** : to express or feel extreme enmity **2** : to find distasteful ✦ *Synonyms* DETEST, ABHOR, ABOMINATE, LOATHE — **hat·er** *n*

ha·tred \'hā-trəd\ *n* : HATE; *also* : prejudiced hostility or animosity

hat·ter \'ha-tər\ *n* : one that makes, sells, or cleans and repairs hats

hau·berk \'hȯ-bərk\ *n* : a coat of mail

haugh·ty \'hȯ-tē\ *adj* **haugh·ti·er; -est** [obs. *haught*, fr. ME *haute*, fr. AF *halt, haut*, lit., high, fr. L *altus*] : disdainfully proud ✦ *Synonyms* INSOLENT, LORDLY, OVERBEARING, ARROGANT — **haugh·ti·ly** \-tə-lē\ *adv* — **haugh·ti·ness** \-tē-nəs\ *n*

¹haul \'hȯl\ *vb* **1** : to exert traction on : DRAW, PULL **2** : to furnish transportation : CART — **haul·er** *n*

²haul *n* **1** : PULL, TUG **2** : the result of an effort to obtain, collect, or win **3** : the length or course of a transportation route; *also* : LOAD

haul·age \'hȯ-lij\ *n* **1** : the act or process of hauling **2** : a charge for hauling

haunch \'hȯnch\ *n* **1** : ²HIP 1 **2** : HINDQUARTER 2 — usu. used in pl. **3** : HINDQUARTER 1

¹haunt \'hȯnt\ *vb* **1** : to visit often : FREQUENT **2** : to have a disquieting effect on ⟨was ~*ed* by his past⟩; *also* : to reappear continually in **3** : to visit or inhabit as a ghost — **haunt·er** *n* — **haunt·ing·ly** *adv*

²haunt \'hȯnt, *2 is usu* 'hant\ *n* **1** : a place habitually frequented **2** *chiefly dial* : GHOST

haute cou·ture \ˌōt-kü-'tùr\ *n* [F] : the establishments or designers that create exclusive and often trend-setting fashions for women; *also* : the fashions created

haute cui·sine \-kwi-'zēn\ *n* : artful or elaborate cuisine

hau·teur \hȯ-'tər, ō-, hō-\ *n* : ARROGANCE, HAUGHTINESS

¹have \'hav, həv, v; *in sense 2 before "to" usu* 'haf\ *vb* **had** \'had, həd\; **hav·ing; has** \'haz, həz, *in sense 2 before "to" usu* 'has\ **1** : to hold in possession; *also* : to hold in one's use, service, or regard ⟨*has* a good job⟩ **2** : to be compelled or forced ⟨~ to go now⟩ **3** : to stand in relationship to ⟨*has* many enemies⟩ **4** : OBTAIN; *also* : RECEIVE, ACCEPT **5** : to be marked by ⟨*has* red hair⟩ **6** : SHOW; *also* : USE, EXERCISE ⟨~ mercy⟩ **7** : EXPERIENCE; *also* : TAKE ⟨~ a look⟩ **8** : to entertain in the mind ⟨~ an idea⟩ **9** : to cause to **10** : ALLOW **11** : to be competent in **12** : to hold in a disadvantageous position; *also* : TRICK **13** : BEGET **14** : to partake of **15** — used as an auxiliary with the past participle to form the present perfect, past perfect, or future perfect — **have at** : ATTACK — **have coming** : DESERVE — **have done with** : to be finished with — **have had it** : to have endured all one will permit or can stand — **have to do with** : to have in the way of relation with or effect on

²have \'hav\ *n* : one that has material wealth

ha·ven \'hā-vən\ *n* **1** : HARBOR, PORT **2** : a place of safety **3** : a place offering favorable conditions ⟨an artist's ~⟩

have–not \'hav-ˌnät, -'nät\ *n* : one that is poor in material wealth

hav·er·sack \'ha-vər-ˌsak\ *n* [F *havresac*, fr. G *Habersack* bag for oats] : a bag similar to a knapsack but worn over one shoulder

hav·oc \'ha-vək\ *n* **1** : wide and general destruction **2** : great confusion and disorder

haw \'hȯ\ *n* : a hawthorn berry; *also* : HAWTHORN

Ha·wai·ian \hə-'wä-yən\ *n* **1** : a native or resident of Hawaii; *esp* : one of Polynesian ancestry **2** : the Polynesian language of Hawaii

¹hawk \'hȯk\ *n* **1** : any of numerous mostly small or medium-sized day-flying birds of prey (as a falcon or kite) **2** : a supporter of a war or a warlike policy — **hawk·ish** *adj*

hawk 1

²hawk *vb* : to make a harsh coughing sound in or as if in clearing the throat; *also* : to raise by hawking

³hawk *vb* : to offer goods for sale by calling out in the street — **hawk·er** *n*

hawk·weed \'hȯk-ˌwēd\ *n* : any of several plants related to the daisies usu. having yellow flowers

haw·ser \'hȯ-zər\ *n* : a large rope for towing, mooring, or securing a ship

haw·thorn \'hȯ-ˌthȯrn\ *n* : any of a genus of spiny spring-flowering shrubs or small trees related to the apple

¹hay \'hā\ *n* **1** : herbage (as grass) mowed and cured for fodder **2** : REWARD **3** *slang* : BED ⟨hit the ~⟩ **4** : a small amount of money

²hay *vb* : to cut, cure, and store for hay

hay·cock \'hā-ˌkäk\ *n* : a small conical pile of hay

hay fever *n* : an acute allergic reaction esp. to plant pollen that resembles a cold

hay·loft \'hā-ˌlȯft\ *n* : a loft for hay

hay·mow \-ˌmaù\ *n* : a mow of or for hay

hay·rick \-ˌrik\ *n* : a large sometimes thatched outdoor stack of hay

hay·seed \-ˌsēd\ *n, pl* **hayseed** *or* **hayseeds** **1** : clinging bits of straw or chaff from hay **2** : BUMPKIN, YOKEL

hay·stack \-ˌstak\ *n* : a stack of hay

hay·wire \-ˌwī(-ə)r\ *adj* : being out of order or control : CRAZY ⟨things went ~⟩

¹**haz·ard** \'ha-zərd\ *n* [ME, a dice game, fr. AF *hasard*, fr. Sp *azar*, Ar *al-zahr* the die] **1** : a source of danger **2** : CHANCE; *also* : ACCIDENT **3** : an obstacle on a golf course — **haz·ard·ous** *adj*
²**hazard** *vb* : VENTURE, RISK ⟨∼ a guess⟩
¹**haze** \'hāz\ *n* **1** : fine dust, smoke, or light vapor causing lack of transparency in the air **2** : vagueness of mind or perception
²**haze** *vb* **hazed; haz·ing** : to harass by abusive and humiliating tricks usu. by way of initiation
ha·zel \'hā-zəl\ *n* **1** : any of a genus of shrubs or small trees related to the birches and bearing edible brown nuts **(ha·zel·nuts** \-ˌnəts\) **2** : a light brown color
hazy \'hā-zē\ *adj* **haz·i·er; -est 1** : obscured or darkened by haze **2** : VAGUE, INDEFINITE ⟨a ∼ memory⟩; *also* : UNCERTAIN — **haz·i·ly** \-zə-lē\ *adv* — **haz·i·ness** \-zē-nəs\
Hb *abbr* hemoglobin
HBM *abbr* Her Britannic Majesty; His Britannic Majesty
H–bomb \'āch-ˌbäm\ *n* : HYDROGEN BOMB
HC *abbr* **1** Holy Communion **2** House of Commons
hd *abbr* head
HD *abbr* heavy-duty
hdbk *abbr* handbook
hdkf *abbr* handkerchief
HDL \ˌāch-(ˌ)dē-'el\ *n* [*h*igh-*d*ensity *l*ipoprotein] : a cholesterol-poor protein-rich lipoprotein of blood plasma correlated with reduced risk of atherosclerosis
hdwe *abbr* hardware
he \'hē\ *pron* **1** : that male one **2** : a person : the person ⟨∼ who hesitates is lost⟩
He *symbol* helium
HE *abbr* **1** Her Excellency **2** His Eminence **3** His Excellency
¹**head** \'hed\ *n* **1** : the front or upper part of the body containing the brain, the chief sense organs, and the mouth **2** : MIND; *also* : natural aptitude ⟨has a ∼ for math⟩ **3** : POISE ⟨a level ∼⟩ **4** : the obverse of a coin **5** : INDIVIDUAL; *also pl* **head** : one of a number (as of cattle) **6** : the end that is upper or higher or opposite the foot; *also* : either end of something (as a drum) whose two ends need not be distinguished **7** : a compact mass of plant parts (as leaves or flowers) **8** : the source of a stream **9** : DIRECTOR, LEADER; *also* : a leading element (as of a procession) **10** : a projecting part; *also* : the striking part of a weapon **11** : the place of leadership or honor **12** : a separate part or topic **13** : the foam on a fermenting or effervescing liquid **14** : a critical point ⟨events came to a ∼⟩ — **head·ed** \'he-dəd\ *adj* — **head·less** *adj* — **over one's head** : beyond one's comprehension or competence
²**head** *adj* : PRINCIPAL, CHIEF ⟨∼ chef⟩
³**head** *vb* **1** : to provide with or form a head; *also* : to form the head of **2** : LEAD, CONDUCT ⟨∼ed the search⟩ **3** : to get in front of esp. so as to stop; *also* : SURPASS **4** : to put or stand at the head **5** : to point or proceed in a certain direction ⟨∼ed west⟩
head·ache \'he-ˌdāk\ *n* **1** : pain in the head **2** : a baffling situation or problem — **head·achy** *also* **headachey** \-ˌā-kē\ *adj*
head·band \'hed-ˌband\ *n* : a band worn on or around the head
head·bang·er \-ˌban-ər\ *n* : one who performs or enjoys hard rock
head·board \-ˌbȯrd\ *n* : a board forming the head (as of a bed)
head cold *n* : a common cold centered in the nasal passages and adjacent mucous tissues
head·dress \'hed-ˌdres\ *n* : an often elaborate covering for the head
head·first \-'fərst\ *adv* : HEADLONG 1 ⟨dove ∼ into the water⟩ — **headfirst** *adj*
head·gear \-ˌgir\ *n* : a covering or protective device for the head
head·hunt·er \-ˌhən-tər\ *n* **1** : one that engages in headhunting **2** : a recruiter of esp. executive personnel
head–hunt·ing \-ˌhən-tiŋ\ *n* : the practice of seeking out and decapitating enemies and preserving their heads as trophies
head·ing \'he-diŋ\ *n* **1** : the compass direction in which the longitudinal axis of a ship or airplane points **2**

: something that appears at the top or beginning of something else (as a document)
head·land \'hed-lənd, -ˌland\ *n* : PROMONTORY
head·light \-ˌlīt\ *n* : a light mounted on the front of a vehicle to illuminate the road ahead
¹**head·line** \-ˌlīn\ *n* : a head of a newspaper story or article usu. printed in large type
²**headline** *vb* **1** : to provide with a headline **2** : to publicize highly **3** : to be a leading performer in
head·lock \-ˌläk\ *n* : a wrestling hold in which one encircles the opponent's head with one arm
¹**head·long** \-'lȯŋ\ *adv* **1** : with the head foremost **2** : RECKLESSLY **3** : without delay
²**head·long** \-ˌlȯŋ\ *adj* **1** : PRECIPITATE, RASH ⟨∼ flight⟩ **2** : plunging with the head foremost
head·man \'hed-'man, -ˌman\ *n* : one who is a leader : CHIEF
head·mas·ter \-ˌmas-tər\ *n* : a man who is head of a private school
head·mis·tress \-ˌmis-trəs\ *n* : a woman who is head of a private school
head of stream : strong driving force : MOMENTUM
head–on \'hed-'ȯn, -'än\ *adj* : having the front facing in the direction of initial contact or line of sight ⟨∼ collision⟩ — **head–on** *adv*
head·phone \-ˌfōn\ *n* : an earphone held on by a band over the head
head·piece \-ˌpēs\ *n* : a covering for the head
head·pin \-ˌpin\ *n* : a bowling pin that stands foremost in the arrangement of pins
head·quar·ters \-ˌkwȯr-tərz\ *n sing or pl* **1** : a place from which a commander exercises command **2** : the administrative center of an enterprise
head·rest \-ˌrest\ *n* **1** : a support for the head **2** : a pad at the top of the back of an automobile seat
head·room \-ˌrüm, -ˌrum\ *n* : vertical space in which to stand, sit, or move
head·scratcher \-ˌskra-chər\ *n* : PUZZLE, MYSTERY
head·set \-ˌset\ *n* : a pair of headphones
head·ship \-ˌship\ *n* : the position, office, or dignity of a head
heads·man \'hedz-mən\ *n* : EXECUTIONER
head·stall \'hed-ˌstȯl\ *n* : a part of a bridle or halter that encircles the head
head·stone \-ˌstōn\ *n* : a memorial stone at the head of a grave
head·strong \'hed-ˌstrȯŋ\ *adj* **1** : not easily restrained **2** : directed by ungovernable will ♦ **Synonyms** UNRULY, INTRACTABLE, WILLFUL, PERTINACIOUS, REFRACTORY, STUBBORN
heads–up \'hedz-'əp\ *n* : WARNING
head·wait·er \-'wā-tər\ *n* : the head of the dining-room staff of a restaurant or hotel
head·wa·ter \-ˌwȯ-tər, -ˌwä-\ *n* : the source of a stream — usu. used in pl.
head·way \-ˌwā\ *n* : forward motion; *also* : PROGRESS
head·wind \-ˌwind\ *n* : a wind blowing in a direction opposite to a course esp. of a ship or aircraft
head·word \'hed-ˌwərd\ *n* **1** : a word or term placed at the beginning **2** : a word qualified by a modifier
head·work \-ˌwərk\ *n* : mental work or effort : THINKING
heady \'he-dē\ *adj* **head·i·er; -est 1** : WILLFUL, RASH; *also* : IMPETUOUS **2** : INTOXICATING **3** : SHREWD
heal \'hēl\ *vb* **1** : to make or become healthy, sound, or whole **2** : CURE, REMEDY — **heal·er** *n*
health \'helth\ *n* **1** : sound physical or mental condition; *also* : overall condition of the body ⟨in poor ∼⟩ **2** : WELL-BEING **3** : a toast to someone's health or prosperity
health care *n* : efforts made to maintain or restore health — usu. hyphenated when used attributively
health club *n* : a commercial establishment providing health and fitness facilities and equipment for members
health·ful \'helth-fəl\ *adj* **1** : beneficial to health **2** : HEALTHY — **health·ful·ly** *adv* — **health·ful·ness** *n*
health maintenance organization *n* : HMO
healthy \'hel-thē\ *adj* **health·i·er; -est 1** : enjoying or typical of good health : WELL **2** : evincing or conducive to health **3** : PROSPEROUS ⟨a ∼ economy⟩; *also* : CONSIDERABLE 2 ⟨a ∼ savings⟩ — **health·i·ly** \-thə-lē\ *adv* — **health·i·ness** \-thē-nəs\ *n*

¹**heap** \'hēp\ *n* : PILE ⟨rubbish ~⟩; *also* : LOT 5 ⟨a ~ of fun⟩

²**heap** *vb* **1** : to throw or lay in a heap **2** : to give in large quantities; *also* : to load heavily

hear \'hir\ *vb* **heard** \'hərd\; **hear·ing 1** : to perceive by the ear **2** : to gain knowledge of by hearing : LEARN **3** : HEED; *also* : ATTEND **4** : to give a legal hearing to or take testimony from — **hear·er** *n*

hear·ing *n* **1** : the process, function, or power of perceiving sound; *esp* : the special sense by which noises and tones are received as stimuli **2** : EARSHOT **3** : opportunity to be heard **4** : a listening to arguments (as in a court); *also* : a session of (as of a legislative committee) in which testimony is taken from witnesses

hear·ken \'här-kən\ *vb* : to give attention : LISTEN ✦ **Synonyms** HEAR, HARK, HEED

hear·say \'hir-ˌsā\ *n* : RUMOR

hearse \'hərs\ *n* : a vehicle for carrying the dead to the grave

heart \'härt\ *n* **1** : a hollow muscular organ that by rhythmic contraction keeps up the circulation of the blood in the body; *also* : something resembling a heart in shape **2** : any of a suit of playing cards marked with a red figure of a heart; *also, pl* : a card game in which the object is to avoid taking tricks containing hearts **3** : the whole personality; *also* : the emotional or moral as distinguished from the intellectual nature **4** : COURAGE **5** : one's innermost being ⟨knew it in his ~⟩ **6** : CENTER; *also* : the essential part **7** : the younger central part of a compact leafy cluster (as of lettuce) — **heart·ed** \'här-təd\ *adj* — **by heart** : by rote or from memory

heart·ache \-ˌāk\ *n* : anguish of mind

heart attack *n* : an acute episode of heart disease due to insufficient blood supply to the heart muscle

heart·beat \'härt-ˌbēt\ *n* : one complete pulsation of the heart

heart·break \-ˌbrāk\ *n* : crushing grief

heart·break·ing \-ˌbrā-kiŋ\ *adj* : causing extreme sorrow or distress — **heart·break·er** \-ˌbrā-kər\ *n* — **heart·break·ing·ly** *adv*

heart·bro·ken \-ˌbrō-kən\ *adj* : overcome by sorrow

heart·burn \-ˌbərn\ *n* : a burning distress behind the sternum due esp. to the backward flow of acid from the stomach to the esophagus

heart disease *n* : an abnormal organic condition of the heart or of the heart and circulation

heart·en \'här-t³n\ *vb* : ENCOURAGE, CHEER

heart·felt \'härt-ˌfelt\ *adj* : deeply felt : SINCERE

hearth \'härth\ *n* **1** : an area (as of brick) in front of a fireplace; *also* : the floor of a fireplace **2** : HOME

hearth·stone \'härth-ˌstōn\ *n* **1** : stone forming a hearth **2** : HOME

heart·less \'härt-ləs\ *adj* : CRUEL

heart·rend·ing \-ˌren-diŋ\ *adj* : HEARTBREAKING

heart·sick \-ˌsik\ *adj* : very despondent — **heart·sick·ness** *n*

heart–stop·ping \-ˌstä-piŋ\ *adj* : extremely shocking or exciting

heart·strings \-ˌstriŋz\ *n pl* : the deepest emotions or affections

heart·throb \-ˌthräb\ *n* **1** : the throb of a heart **2** : sentimental emotion **3** : SWEETHEART **4** : an entertainer noted for his sex appeal

heart–to–heart *adj* : SINCERE, FRANK

heart·warm·ing \'härt-ˌwȯr-miŋ\ *adj* : inspiring sympathetic feeling

heart·wood \-ˌwu̇d\ *n* : the older harder nonliving and usu. darker wood of the central part of a tree trunk

¹**hearty** \'här-tē\ *adj* **heart·i·er; -est 1** : giving full support; *also* : JOVIAL **2** : vigorously healthy **3** : ABUNDANT; *also* : NOURISHING ✦ **Synonyms** SINCERE, WHOLEHEARTED, UNFEIGNED, HEARTFELT — **heart·i·ly** \-tə-lē\ *adv* — **heart·i·ness** \-tē-nəs\ *n*

²**hearty** *n, pl* **heart·ies** : an enthusiastic jovial fellow; *also* : SAILOR

¹**heat** \'hēt\ *vb* **1** : to make or become warm or hot **2** : EXCITE — **heat·ed·ly** *adv* — **heat·er** *n*

²**heat** *n* **1** : a condition of being hot : WARMTH **2** : a form of energy that when added to a body causes the body to rise in temperature, to fuse, to evaporate, or to expand **3** : high temperature **4** : intensity of feeling; *also* : sexual

excitement esp. in a female mammal **5** : a preliminary race for narrowing the competition **6** : pungency of flavor **7** *slang* : POLICE **8** : PRESSURE, COERCION; *also* : ABUSE, CRITICISM ⟨took ~ for my mistakes⟩

heat exchanger *n* : a device (as an automobile radiator) for transferring heat from one fluid to another without allowing them to mix

heat exhaustion *n* : a condition marked by weakness, nausea, dizziness, and profuse sweating resulting from physical exertion in a hot environment

heath \'hēth\ *n* **1** : a tract of wasteland **2** : any of a family of often evergreen shrubby plants (as a blueberry or heather) of wet acid soils — **heathy** *adj*

hea·then \'hē-thən\ *n, pl* **heathens** *or* **heathen 1** : an unconverted member of a people or nation that does not acknowledge the God of the Bible **2** : an uncivilized or irreligious person — **heathen** *adj* — **hea·then·dom** *n* — **hea·then·ish** *adj* — **hea·then·ism** *n*

heath·er \'he-thər\ *n* : a northern and alpine evergreen heath with usu. lavender flowers — **heath·ery** *adj*

heat lightning *n* : flashes of light without thunder ascribed to distant lightning reflected by high clouds

heat·stroke \'hēt-ˌstrōk\ *n* : a disorder marked esp. by high body temperature without sweating and by collapse that follows prolonged exposure to excessive heat

¹**heave** \'hēv\ *vb* **heaved** *or* **hove** \'hōv\; **heav·ing 1** : to rise or lift upward **2** : THROW **3** : to rise and fall rhythmically; *also* : PANT **4** : RETCH **5** : PULL, PUSH — **heaver** *n*

²**heave** *n* **1** : an effort to lift or raise **2** : THROW, CAST **3** : an upward motion **4** *pl* : a chronic lung disease of horses marked by difficult breathing and persistent cough

heav·en \'he-vən\ *n* **1** : FIRMAMENT — usu. used in pl. **2** *often cap* : the abode of the Deity and of the blessed dead; *also* : a spiritual state of everlasting communion with God **3** *cap* : GOD 1 **4** : a place of supreme happiness — **heav·en·ly** *adj* — **heav·en·ward** *adv or adj*

¹**heavy** \'he-vē\ *adj* **heavi·er; -est 1** : having great weight **2** : hard to bear **3** : SERIOUS **4** : DEEP, PROFOUND ⟨a ~ silence⟩ **5** : burdened with something oppressive; *also* : PREGNANT **6** : SLUGGISH **7** : DRAB; *also* : DOLEFUL **8** : DROWSY **9** : greater than the average of its kind or class **10** : very rich and hard to digest; *also* : not properly raised or leavened **11** : producing goods (as steel) used in the production of other goods — **heavi·ly** \-və-lē\ *adv* — **heavi·ness** \-vē-nəs\ *n*

²**heavy** *n, pl* **heav·ies** : a theatrical role representing a dignified or imposing person; *also* : a villain esp. in a story

heavy–du·ty \ˌhe-vē-'dü-tē, -'dyü-\ *adj* : able to withstand unusual strain

heavy–hand·ed \-'han-dəd\ *adj* **1** : CLUMSY **2** : OPPRESSIVE, HARSH

heavy–heart·ed \-'här-təd\ *adj* : SADDENED, DESPONDENT

heavy lifting *n* : a burdensome or laborious duty

heavy metal *n* : energetic and highly amplified electronic rock music

heavy·set \ˌhe-vē-'set\ *adj* : stocky and compact in build

heavy water *n* : water enriched in deuterium

heavy·weight \'he-vē-ˌwāt\ *n* : one above average in weight; *esp* : a boxer in an unlimited weight division

Heb *abbr* Hebrews

He·bra·ism \'hē-brā-ˌi-zəm\ *n* : the thought, spirit, or practice characteristic of the Hebrews — **He·bra·ic** \hi-'brā-ik\ *adj*

He·bra·ist \'hē-ˌbrā-ist\ *n* : a specialist in Hebrew and Hebraic studies

He·brew \'hē-brü\ *n* **1** : the language of the Hebrews **2** : a member of or descendant from a group of Semitic peoples; *esp* : ISRAELITE — **Hebrew** *adj*

He·brews \'hē-(ˌ)brüz\ *n* — see BIBLE table

hec·a·tomb \'he-kə-ˌtōm\ *n* : an ancient Greek and Roman sacrifice of 100 oxen or cattle

heck·le \'he-kəl\ *vb* **heck·led; heck·ling** : to harass with questions or gibes : BADGER — **heck·ler** *n*

hect·are \'hek-ˌter\ *n* — see METRIC SYSTEM table

hec·tic \'hek-tik\ *adj* **1** : being hot and flushed **2** : filled with excitement, activity, or confusion — **hec·ti·cal·ly** \-ti-k(ə-)lē\ *adv*

hec·to·gram \'hek-tə-ˌgram\ *n* — see METRIC SYSTEM table

hec·to·li·ter \'hek-tə-ˌlē-tər\ *n* — see METRIC SYSTEM table

hec·to·me·ter \'hek-tə-ˌmē-tər, hek-'tä-mə-tər\ *n* — see METRIC SYSTEM table

hec·tor \'hek-tər\ *vb* [*hector* bully, fr. *Hector,* champion of Troy in Greek legend] **1** : SWAGGER **2** : to intimidate by bluster or personal pressure

¹hedge \'hej\ *n* **1** : a fence or boundary formed of shrubs or small trees **2** : BARRIER **3** : a means of protection (as against financial loss)

²hedge *vb* **hedged; hedg·ing 1** : ENCIRCLE **2** : HINDER **3** : to protect oneself financially by a counterbalancing action **4** : to evade the risk of commitment — **hedg·er** *n*

hedge·hog \'hej-ˌhog, -ˌhäg\ *n* : a small Old World insect-eating mammal covered with spines; *also* : PORCUPINE

hedge·hop \-ˌhäp\ *vb* : to fly an airplane very close to the ground

hedge·row \-ˌrō\ *n* : a row of shrubs or trees bounding or separating fields

he·do·nism \'hē-də-ˌni-zəm\ *n* [Gk *hēdonē* pleasure] : the doctrine that pleasure is the chief good in life; *also* : a way of life based on this — **he·do·nist** \-nist\ *n* — **he·do·nis·tic** \ˌhēdə-'ni-stik\ *adj*

¹heed \'hēd\ *vb* : to pay attention

²heed *n* : ATTENTION, NOTICE — **heed·ful** \-fəl\ *adj* — **heed·ful·ly** *adv* — **heed·ful·ness** *n* — **heed·less** *adj* — **heed·less·ly** *adv* — **heed·less·ness** *n*

¹heel \'hēl\ *n* **1** : the hind part of the foot **2** : one of the crusty ends of a loaf of bread **3** : a solid attachment forming the back of the sole of a shoe **4** : a rear, low, or bottom part **5** : a contemptible person

²heel *vb* : to tilt to one side : LIST

¹heft \'heft\ *n* : WEIGHT, HEAVINESS

²heft *vb* : to test the weight of by lifting

hefty \'hef-tē\ *adj* **heft·i·er; -est 1** : marked by bigness, bulk, and usu. strength **2** : impressively large ⟨got a ∼ raise⟩

he·ge·mo·ny \hi-'je-mə-nē\ *n* : preponderant influence or authority over others : DOMINATION

he·gi·ra \hi-'jī-rə\ *n* [the *Hegira,* flight of Muhammad from Mecca in A.D. 622, fr. ML, fr. Ar *hijra,* lit., departure] : a journey esp. when undertaken to escape a dangerous or undesirable environment

heif·er \'he-fər\ *n* : a young cow; *esp* : one that has not had a calf

height \'hīt\ *n* **1** : the highest part or point **2** : the distance from the bottom to the top of something standing upright **3** : ALTITUDE

height·en \'hī-tⁿn\ *vb* **1** : to increase in amount or degree **2** : to make or become high or higher ♦ **Synonyms** ENHANCE, INTENSIFY, AGGRAVATE, MAGNIFY

Heim·lich maneuver \'hīm-lik-\ *n* [Henry J. *Heimlich* b1920 Am. surgeon] : the manual application of sudden upward pressure on the upper abdomen of a choking victim to force a foreign object from the trachea

hei·nous \'hā-nəs\ *adj* [ME, fr. AF *hainus, heinous,* fr. *haine* hate, fr. *hair* to hate] : hatefully or shockingly evil — **hei·nous·ly** *adv* — **hei·nous·ness** *n*

heir \'er\ *n* : one who inherits or is entitled to inherit property, rank, title, or office — **heir·ship** *n*

heir apparent *n, pl* **heirs apparent** : an heir whose right to succeed (as to a title) cannot be taken away if he or she survives the present holder

heir·ess \'er-əs\ *n* : a female heir esp. to great wealth

heir·loom \'er-ˌlüm\ *n* **1** : a piece of personal property that descends by inheritance **2** : something handed on from one generation to another

heir presumptive *n, pl* **heirs presumptive** : an heir whose present right to inherit could be lost through the birth of a nearer relative

heist \'hīst\ *vb* : to commit armed robbery on; *also* : STEAL — **heist** *n*

held *past and past part of* HOLD

he·li·cal \'he-li-kəl, 'hē-\ *adj* : SPIRAL

he·li·cop·ter \'he-lə-ˌkäp-tər, 'hē-\ *n* [F *hélicoptère,* fr. Gk *helik-, helix* spiral + *pteron* wing] : an aircraft that is supported in the air by one or more rotors on substantially vertical axes

he·lio·cen·tric \ˌhē-lē-ō-'sen-trik\ *adj* : having or relating to the sun as center

he·li·o·sphere \'hē-lē-ə-ˌsfir, -ō-\ *n* : the region in space influenced by the sun or solar wind

he·lio·trope \'hē-lē-ə-ˌtrōp\ *n* [L *heliotropium,* fr. Gk *hēli-otropion,* fr. *hēlios* sun + *tropos* turn; fr. its flowers' turning toward the sun] : any of a genus of herbs or shrubs related to the forget-me-nots that have small white or purple flowers

he·li·port \'he-lə-ˌpȯrt\ *n* : a landing and takeoff place for a helicopter

he·li·um \'hē-lē-əm\ *n* [NL, fr. Gk *hēlios* sun] : a very light inert gaseous chemical element occurring in various natural gases

he·lix \'hē-liks\ *n, pl* **he·li·ces** \'he-lə-ˌsēz, 'hē-\ *also* **he·lix·es** \'hē-lik-səz\ : something spiral in form

hell \'hel\ *n* **1** : a nether world in which the dead continue to exist **2** : the realm of the devil in which the damned suffer everlasting punishment **3** : a place or state of torment or destruction — **hell·ish** *adj*

hel·la·cious \he-'lā-shəs\ *adj* **1** : exceptionally powerful or violent **2** : remarkably good **3** : extremely difficult **4** : extraordinarily large

hell-bent \'hel-ˌbent\ *adj* : stubbornly determined

hell·cat \-ˌkat\ *n* **1** : WITCH 2 **2** : a violently temperamental person; *esp* : an ill-tempered woman

hel·le·bore \'he-lə-ˌbȯr\ *n* **1** : any of a genus of poisonous herbs related to the buttercups; *also* : the dried root of a hellebore **2** : a poisonous plant related to the lilies; *also* : its dried roots used in medicine and insecticides

Hel·lene \'he-ˌlēn\ *n* : GREEK

Hel·le·nism \'he-lə-ˌni-zəm\ *n* : a body of humanistic and classical ideals associated with ancient Greece — **Hel·len·ic** \he-'le-nik\ *adj* — **Hel·le·nist** \'he-lə-nist\ *n*

Hel·le·nis·tic \ˌhe-lə-'nis-tik\ *adj* : of or relating to Greek history, culture, or art after Alexander the Great

hell-for-leather *adv* : at full speed

hell·gram·mite \'hel-grə-ˌmīt\ *n* : an aquatic insect larva that is used as bait in fishing

hell·hole \'hel-ˌhōl\ *n* : a place of extreme misery or squalor

hel·lion \'hel-yən\ *n* : a troublesome or mischievous person

hel·lo \hə-'lō, he-\ *n, pl* **hellos** : an expression of greeting — used interjectionally

helm \'helm\ *n* **1** : a lever or wheel for steering a ship **2** : a position of control

hel·met \'hel-mət\ *n* : a protective covering for the head

helmet: ancient battle helmets and modern football helmet

helms·man \'helmz-mən\ *n* : the person at the helm : STEERSMAN

helms·per·son \-ˌpər-sⁿn\ *n* : HELMSMAN

hel·ot \'he-lət\ *n* **1** : SLAVE, SERF

¹help \'help\ *vb* **1** : AID, ASSIST **2** : IMPROVE, RELIEVE **3** : to be of use; *also* : PROMOTE **4** : to change for the better **5** : to refrain from; *also* : PREVENT **6** : to serve with food or drink ⟨∼ yourself⟩ — **help·er** *n*

²help *n* **1** : AID, ASSISTANCE; *also* : a source of aid **2** : REMEDY, RELIEF **3** : one who assists another **4** : EMPLOYEE — **help·ful** \-fəl\ *adj* — **help·ful·ly** *adv* — **help·ful·ness** *n* — **help·less** *adj* — **help·less·ly** *adv* — **help·less·ness** *n*

helper T cell *n* : a T cell that participates in the immune response by recognizing foreign antigens and has a protein on its surface to which HIV attaches

help·ing *n* : a portion of food

help·mate \'help-ˌmāt\ *n* **1** : HELPER **2** : WIFE

help·meet \-ˌmēt\ *n* : HELPMATE

hel·ter-skel·ter \ˌhel-tər-'skel-tər\ *adv* **1** : in undue haste or disorder **2** : HAPHAZARDLY

helve \'helv\ *n* : a handle of a tool or weapon

Hel·ve·tian \hel-'vē-shən\ *adj* : SWISS — **Helvetian** *n*

¹hem \'hem\ *n* **1** : a border of an article (as of cloth) doubled back and stitched down **2** : RIM, MARGIN

²hem *vb* **hemmed; hem·ming 1** : to make a hem in sewing; *also* : BORDER, EDGE **2** : to surround restrictively

he-man \'hē-ˌman\ *n* : a strong virile man

he-ma-tite \'hē-mə-ˌtīt\ *n* : a mineral that consists of an oxide of iron and that constitutes an important iron ore

he-ma-tol-o-gy \ˌhē-mə-'tä-lə-jē\ *n* : a branch of biology that deals with the blood and blood-forming organs — **he-ma-to-log-ic** \-tə-'lä-jik\ *also* **he-ma-to-log-i-cal** \-ji-kəl\ *adj* — **he-ma-tol-o-gist** \-'tä-lə-jist\ *n*

he-ma-to-ma \-'tō-mə\ *n, pl* **-mas** *also* **-ma-ta** \-mə-tə\ : a usu. clotted mass of blood forming as a result of a broken blood vessel

heme \'hēm\ *n* : the deep red iron-containing part of hemoglobin

hemi-sphere \'he-mə-ˌsfir\ *n* 1 : one of the halves of the earth as divided by the equator into northern and southern parts or by a meridian into eastern and western parts 2 : either of two half spheres formed by a plane through the sphere's center — **hemi-spher-ic** \ˌhe-mə-'sfir-ik, -'sfer-\ *or* **hemi-spher-i-cal** \-'sfir-i-kəl, -'sfer-\ *adj*

hem-line \'hem-ˌlīn\ *n* : the line formed by the lower edge of a garment

hem-lock \'hem-ˌläk\ *n* 1 : any of several poisonous herbs related to the carrot 2 : an evergreen tree related to the pines; *also* : its soft light wood

he-mo-glo-bin \'hē-mə-ˌglō-bən\ *n* : an iron-containing compound found in red blood cells that carries oxygen from the lungs to the body tissues

he-mo-phil-ia \ˌhē-mə-'fi-lē-ə\ *n* : a hereditary blood defect usu. of males that slows blood clotting with resulting difficulty in stopping bleeding — **he-mo-phil-i-ac** \-lē-ˌak\ *adj or n*

hem-or-rhage \'hem-rij, 'he-mə-\ *n* : a large discharge of blood from the blood vessels — **hemorrhage** *vb* — **hem-or-rhag-ic** \ˌhe-mə-'ra-jik\ *adj*

hemorrhagic fever *n* : any of a group of virus diseases characterized chiefly by sudden onset, fever, aching, and bleeding in the internal organs

hem-or-rhoid \'hem-ˌròid, 'he-mə-\ *n* : a swollen mass of dilated veins at or just within the anus — usu. used in pl.

hemp \'hemp\ *n* : a tall widely grown Asian herb that is the source of a tough fiber used in rope and of marijuana and hashish from its flowers and leaves; *also* : the fiber — **hemp-en** \'hem-pən\ *adj*

hem-stitch \'hem-ˌstich\ *vb* : to embroider (fabric) by drawing out parallel threads and stitching the exposed threads in groups to form designs

hen \'hen\ *n* : a female chicken esp. over a year old; *also* : a female bird

hence \'hens\ *adv* 1 : AWAY 2 : from this time ⟨four years ∼⟩ 3 : CONSEQUENTLY 4 : from this source or origin

hence-forth \hens-ˌfórth\ *adv* : from this point on

hence-for-ward \-'fór-wərd\ *adv* : HENCEFORTH

hench-man \'hench-mən\ *n* [ME *hengestman* groom, fr. *hengest* stallion] : a trusted follower or supporter

hen-na \'he-nə\ *n* 1 : an Old World tropical shrub with fragrant white flowers; *also* : a reddish brown dye obtained from its leaves and used esp. on hair 2 : the color of henna dye

hen-peck \'hen-ˌpek\ *vb* : to nag and boss one's husband

hep \'hep\ *adj* : HIP

hep-a-rin \'he-pə-rən\ *n* : a compound found esp. in liver that slows the clotting of blood and is used medically

he-pat-ic \hi-'pa-tik\ *adj* : of, relating to, or associated with the liver

he-pat-i-ca \hi-'pa-ti-kə\ *n* : any of a genus of herbs related to the buttercups that have lobed leaves and delicate white, pink, or bluish flowers

hep-a-ti-tis \ˌhe-pə-'tī-təs\ *n, pl* **-tit-i-des** \-'ti-tə-ˌdēz\ : inflammation of the liver; *also* : a virus disease of which this is a feature

hep-tam-e-ter \hep-'ta-mə-tər\ *n* : a line of verse containing seven metrical feet

hep-tath-lon \hep-'tath-lən, -ˌlän\ *n* : a 7-event athletic contest for women

¹**her** \'hər\ *adj* : of or relating to her or herself

²**her** *pron, objective case of* SHE

¹**her-ald** \'her-əld\ *n* 1 : an official crier or messenger 2 : HARBINGER 3 : ANNOUNCER 4 : ADVOCATE

²**herald** *vb* 1 : to give notice of 2 : HAIL, GREET; *also* : PUBLICIZE

he-ral-dic \he-'ral-dik, hə-\ *adj* : of or relating to heralds or heraldry

her-ald-ry \'her-əl-drē\ *n, pl* **-ries** 1 : the practice of devising and granting armorial insignia and of tracing genealogies 2 : INSIGNIA 3 : PAGEANTRY

herb \'ərb, 'hərb\ *n* 1 : a seed plant that lacks woody tissue and dies to the ground at the end of a growing season 2 : a plant or plant part valued for medicinal or savory qualities — **herb-a-ceous** \ˌər-'bā-shəs, ˌhər-\ *adj*

herb-age \'ər-bij, 'hər-\ *n* : green plants esp. when used or fit for grazing

her-bal \'ər-bəl, 'hər-\ *adj* : of, relating to, utilizing, or made of herbs

herb-al-ist \'ər-bə-list, 'hər-\ *n* 1 : a person who practices healing by the use of herbs 2 : a person who collects or grows herbs

her-bar-i-um \ˌər-'ber-ē-əm, ˌhər-\ *n, pl* **-ia** \-ē-ə\ 1 : a collection of dried plant specimens 2 : a place that houses an herbarium

her-bi-cide \'ər-bə-ˌsīd, 'hər-\ *n* : an agent used to destroy or inhibit plant growth — **her-bi-cid-al** \ˌər-bə-'sī-d⁺l, ˌhər-\ *adj*

her-biv-o-rous \ˌər-'bi-və-rəs, ˌhər-\ *adj* : feeding on plants — **her-bi-vore** \'ər-bə-ˌvór, 'hər-\ *n*

her-cu-le-an \ˌhər-kyə-'lē-ən, ˌhər-'kyü-lē-\ *adj, often cap* [*Hercules*, hero of Greek myth renowned for his strength] : of extraordinary power, size, or difficulty

¹**herd** \'hərd\ *n* 1 : a group of animals of one kind kept or living together 2 : a group of people with a common bond ⟨a ∼ of tourists⟩ 3 : MOB

²**herd** *vb* 1 : to assemble or move in a herd — **herd-er** *n*

herds-man \'hərdz-mən\ *n* : one who manages, breeds, or tends livestock

¹**here** \'hir\ *adv* 1 : in or at this place; *also* : NOW 2 : at or in this point, particular, or case 3 : in the present life or state 4 : to this place ⟨come ∼⟩

²**here** *n* : this place ⟨get away from ∼⟩

here-abouts \'hir-ə-ˌbaùts\ *or* **here-about** \-ˌbaút\ *adv* : in this vicinity

¹**here-af-ter** \hir-'af-tər\ *adv* 1 : after this in sequence or in time 2 : in some future time or state

²**hereafter** *n, often cap* 1 : FUTURE 2 : an existence beyond earthly life

here-by \hir-'bī\ *adv* : by means of this

he-red-i-tary \hə-'re-də-ˌter-ē\ *adj* 1 : genetically passed or passable from parent to offspring 2 : passing by inheritance; *also* : having title or possession through inheritance 3 : of a kind established by tradition

he-red-i-ty \-'re-də-tē\ *n* : the characteristics and potentialities genetically derived from one's ancestors; *also* : the passing of these from ancestor to descendant

Her-e-ford \'hər-fərd\ *n* : any of a breed of red-coated beef cattle with white faces and markings

here-in \hir-'in\ *adv* : in this

here-of \-'əv, -'äv\ *adv* : of this

here-on \-'ón, -'än\ *adv* : on this

her-e-sy \'her-ə-sē\ *n, pl* **-sies** [ME *heresie*, fr. AF, fr. LL *haeresis*, fr. LGk *hairesis*, fr. Gk, action of taking, choice, sect, fr. *hairein* to take] 1 : adherence to a religious opinion contrary to church dogma 2 : an opinion or doctrine contrary to church dogma 3 : dissent from a dominant theory, opinion, or practice — **her-e-tic** \-ˌtik\ *n* — **he-ret-i-cal** \hə-'re-ti-kəl\ *adj*

here-to \hir-'tü\ *adv* : to this document

here-to-fore \'hir-tə-ˌfór\ *adv* : up to this time

here-un-der \hir-'ən-dər\ *adv* : under this or according to this writing

here-un-to \hir-'ən-tü\ *adv* : to this

here-upon \'hir-ə-ˌpón, -ˌpän\ *adv* : on this or immediately after this

here-with \'hir-ˌwith, -'with\ *adv* 1 : with this 2 : HEREBY

her-i-ta-ble \'her-ə-tə-bəl\ *adj* : capable of being inherited

her-i-tage \'her-ə-tij\ *n* 1 : property that descends to an heir 2 : LEGACY 3 : BIRTHRIGHT

her-maph-ro-dite \(ˌ)hər-'ma-frə-ˌdīt\ *n* : an animal or plant having both male and female reproductive organs — **hermaphrodite** *adj* — **her-maph-ro-dit-ic** \(ˌ)hər-ˌma-frə-'di-tik\ *adj*

her-met-ic \hər-'me-tik\ *also* **her-met-i-cal** \-ti-kəl\ *adj* : AIRTIGHT — **her-met-i-cal-ly** \-ti-k(ə-)lē\ *adv*

her-mit \'hər-mət\ *n* [ME *heremite, eremite*, fr. AF, fr. LL *eremita*, fr. LGk *erēmitēs*, fr. Gk, adj., living in the desert, fr. erēmia desert, fr. erēmos desolate] : one who lives in solitude esp. for religious reasons

her·mit·age \-mə-tij\ *n* **1** : the dwelling of a hermit **2** : a secluded dwelling

hermit crab *n* : any of numerous crabs that occupy empty mollusk shells

her·nia \'hər-nē-ə\ *n, pl* **-ni·as** *or* **-ni·ae** \-nē-ˌē, -nē-ˌī\ : a protrusion of a bodily part (as a loop of intestine) into a pouch of the weakened wall of a cavity in which it is normally enclosed — **her·ni·ate** \-nē-ˌāt\ *vb* — **her·ni·a·tion** \ˌhər-nē-'ā-shən\ *n*

he·ro \'hē-rō\ *n, pl* **heroes** **1** : a mythological or legendary figure of great strength or ability **2** : a man admired for his achievements and qualities **3** : the chief male character in a literary or dramatic work **4** *pl usu* **heros** : SUBMARINE **2** — **he·ro·ic** \hi-'rō-ik\ *adj* — **he·ro·i·cal·ly** \-i-k(ə-)lē\ *adv*

heroic couplet *n* : a rhyming couplet in iambic pentameter

he·ro·ics \hi-'rō-iks\ *n pl* : heroic or showy behavior

her·o·in \'her-ə-wən\ *n* : an illicit addictive narcotic drug made from morphine

her·o·ine \'her-ə-wən\ *n* **1** : a woman admired for her achievements and qualities **2** : the chief female character in a literary or dramatic work

her·o·ism \'her-ə-ˌwi-zəm\ *n* **1** : heroic conduct **2** : the qualities of a hero ✦ **Synonyms** VALOR, PROWESS, GALLANTRY

her·on \'her-ən\ *n, pl* **herons** *also* **heron** : any of various long-legged long-billed wading birds with soft plumage

her·pes \'hər-pēz\ *n* : any of several virus diseases characterized by the formation of blisters on the skin or mucous membranes

herpes sim·plex \-'sim-ˌpleks\ *n* : either of two virus diseases marked in one by watery blisters above the waist (as on the mouth and lips) and in the other on the sex organs

herpes zos·ter \-'zäs-tər\ *n* : SHINGLES

her·pe·tol·o·gy \ˌhər-pə-'tä-lə-jē\ *n* : a branch of zoology dealing with reptiles and amphibians — **her·pe·tol·o·gist** \ˌhər-pə-'tä-lə-jist\ *n*

her·ring \'her-iŋ\ *n, pl* **herring** *or* **herrings** : a valuable narrow-bodied food fish of the No. Atlantic; *also* : a related fish of the No. Pacific harvested esp. for its roe

her·ring·bone \'her-iŋ-ˌbōn\ *n* : a pattern made up of rows of parallel lines with adjacent rows slanting in reverse directions; *also* : a twilled fabric with this pattern

hers \'hərz\ *pron* : one or the ones belonging to her

her·self \hər-'self\ *pron* : SHE, HER — used reflexively, for emphasis, or in absolute constructions

hertz \'hərts, 'herts\ *n, pl* **hertz** : a unit of frequency equal to one cycle per second

hes·i·tant \'he-zə-tənt\ *adj* : tending to hesitate — **hes·i·tance** \-təns\ *n* — **hes·i·tan·cy** \-tən-sē\ *n* — **hes·i·tant·ly** *adv*

hes·i·tate \'he-zə-ˌtāt\ *vb* **-tat·ed; -tat·ing** **1** : to hold back (as in doubt) **2** : PAUSE ✦ **Synonyms** WAVER, VACILLATE, FALTER, SHILLY-SHALLY — **hes·i·ta·tion** \ˌhe-zə-'tā-shən\ *n*

het·ero·dox \'he-tə-rə-ˌdäks\ *adj* **1** : differing from an acknowledged standard **2** : holding unorthodox opinions — **het·er·o·doxy** \-ˌdäk-sē\ *n*

het·er·o·ge·neous \ˌhe-tə-rə-'jē-nē-əs, -nyəs\ *adj* : consisting of dissimilar ingredients or constituents : MIXED — **het·er·o·ge·ne·ity** \-jə-'nē-ə-tē\ *n* — **het·er·o·ge·neous·ly** *adv*

het·ero·glos·sia \ˌhe-tə-rō-'glä-sē-ə, -'glō-\ *n* : a diversity of voices, styles of discourse, or points of view in a literary work

het·ero·sex·ism \ˌhe-tə-rō-'sek-si-zəm\ *n* : discrimination or prejudice by heterosexuals against homosexuals

het·ero·sex·u·al \ˌhe-tə-rō-'sek-shə-wəl\ *adj* **1** : of, relating to, or marked by sexual interest in the opposite sex; *also* : of, relating to, or involving sexual intercourse between members of opposite sex **2** : of or relating to different sexes — **heterosexual** *n* — **het·ero·sex·u·al·i·ty** \-ˌsek-shə-'wa-lə-tē\ *n*

hew \'hyü\ *vb* **hewed; hewed** *or* **hewn** \'hyün\; **hew·ing** **1** : to cut or fell with blows (as of an ax) **2** : to give shape to with or as if with an ax **3** : to conform strictly — **hew·er** *n*

HEW *abbr* Department of Health, Education, and Welfare

¹hex \'heks\ *vb* **1** : to practice witchcraft **2** : JINX

²hex *n* : SPELL, JINX

³hex *adj* : HEXAGONAL

⁴hex *abbr* hexagon

hexa·gon \'hek-sə-ˌgän\ *n* [ultim. fr. Gk *hex* six + *gōnia* angle] : a polygon having six angles and six sides — **hexag·o·nal** \hek-'sa-gən-°l\ *adj*

hex·am·e·ter \hek-'sa-mə-tər\ *n* : a line of verse containing six metrical feet

hey \'hā\ *interj* — used esp. to call attention to or express doubt, surprise, or joy

hey·day \'hā-ˌdā\ *n* : a period of greatest strength, vigor, or prosperity

hf *abbr* half

Hf *symbol* hafnium

HF *abbr* high frequency

hg *abbr* hectogram

Hg *symbol* [NL *hydrargyrum*, lit., water silver] mercury

hgt *abbr* height

hgwy *abbr* highway

HH *abbr* **1** Her Highness **2** His Highness **3** His Holiness

HHS *abbr* Department of Health and Human Services

HI *abbr* **1** Hawaii **2** humidity index

hi·a·tus \hī-'ā-təs\ *n* [L, fr. *hiare* to yawn] **1** : a break in an object : GAP **2** : a period when something is suspended or interrupted

hi·ba·chi \hi-'bä-chē\ *n* [Jp] : a charcoal brazier

hi·ber·nate \'hī-bər-ˌnāt\ *vb* **-nat·ed; -nat·ing** : to pass the winter in a torpid or resting state — **hi·ber·na·tion** \ˌhī-bər-'nā-shən\ *n* — **hi·ber·na·tor** \'hī-bər-ˌnā-tər\ *n*

hi·bis·cus \hī-'bis-kəs, hə-\ *n* : any of a genus of herbs, shrubs, and trees related to the mallows and noted for large showy flowers

hic·cup *also* **hic·cough** \'hi-(ˌ)kəp\ *n* **1** : a spasmodic breathing movement checked by sudden closing of the glottis accompanied by a peculiar sound; *also, pl* : an attack of hiccuping **2** : a slight irregularity, error, or malfunction **3** : a brief minor interruption or change — **hiccup** *vb*

hick \'hik\ *n* [*Hick*, nickname for *Richard*] : an unsophisticated provincial person — **hick** *adj*

hick·o·ry \'hi-kə-rē\ *n, pl* **-ries** : any of a genus of No. American hardwood trees related to the walnuts; *also* : the wood of a hickory — **hickory** *adj*

hi·dal·go \hi-'dal-gō\ *n, pl* **-gos** *often cap* [Sp, fr. earlier *fijo dalgo*, lit., son of something] : a member of the lower nobility of Spain

hidden tax *n* : a tax ultimately paid by someone other than the person on whom it is formally levied **2** : an economic injustice that reduces one's income or buying power

¹hide \'hīd\ *vb* **hid** \'hid\; **hid·den** \'hid-°n\ *or* **hid; hid·ing** **1** : to put or remain out of sight **2** : to conceal for shelter or protection; *also* : to seek protection **3** : to keep secret **4** : to turn away in shame or anger — **hid·er** *n*

²hide *n* : the skin of an animal

hide–and–seek \ˌhīd-°n-'sēk\ *n* : a children's game in which everyone hides from one player who tries to find them

hide·away \'hī-də-ˌwā\ *n* : HIDEOUT

hide·bound \'hīd-ˌbaùnd\ *adj* : being inflexible or conservative

hid·eous \'hi-dē-əs\ *adj* [ME *hidous*, fr. AF *hidus, hisdos*, fr. *hisde, hide* terror] **1** : offensive to one of the senses : UGLY **2** : morally offensive to : SHOCKING ✦ **Synonyms** GHASTLY, GRISLY, GRUESOME, HORRIBLE, LURID, MACABRE — **hid·eous·ly** *adv* — **hid·eous·ness** *n*

hide·out \'hīd-ˌaùt\ *n* : a place of refuge or concealment

hie \'hī\ *vb* **hied; hy·ing** *or* **hie·ing** : HASTEN

hi·er·ar·chy \'hī-ə-ˌrär-kē\ *n, pl* **-chies** : a ruling body of clergy organized into ranks **2** : persons or things arranged in a graded series — **hi·er·ar·chi·cal** \ˌhī-ə-'rär-ki-kəl\ *adj* — **hi·er·ar·chi·cal·ly** \-k(ə-)lē\ *adv*

hi·er·o·glyph·ic \ˌhī-ə-rə-'gli-fik\ *n* [MF *hiéroglyphique*, adj., ultim. fr. Gk *hieroglyphikos*, fr. *hieros* sacred + *glyphein* to carve] **1** : a character in a system of picture writing (as of the ancient Egyptians) **2** : a symbol or sign difficult to decipher

hieroglyphic 1

hi-fi \'hī-'fī\ *n* **1** : HIGH FIDELITY **2** : equipment for reproduction of sound with high fidelity
hig-gle-dy-pig-gle-dy \ˌhi-gəl-dē-'pi-gəl-dē\ *adv* : in confusion
¹**high** \'hī\ *adj* **1** : ELEVATED; *also* : TALL **2** : advanced toward fullness or culmination; *also* : slightly tainted **3** : advanced esp. in complexity ⟨*~er* mathematics⟩ **4** : long past **5** : SHRILL, SHARP **6** : far from the equator ⟨*~* latitudes⟩ **7** : exalted in character **8** : of greater degree, size, or amount than average ⟨*~* in cholesterol⟩ **9** : of relatively great importance **10** : FORCIBLE, STRONG ⟨*~* winds⟩ **11** : showing elation or excitement **12** : INTOXICATED; *also* : excited or stupefied by or as if by a drug — **high-ly** *adv*
²**high** *adv* **1** : at or to a high place or degree **2** : LUXURIOUSLY ⟨living *~*⟩
³**high** *n* **1** : an elevated place **2** : a region of high barometric pressure **3** : a high point or level **4** : the gear of a vehicle giving the highest speed **5** : an excited or stupefied state produced by or as if by a drug
high-ball \'hī-ˌbȯl\ *n* : a usu. tall drink of liquor mixed with water or a carbonated beverage
high beam *n* : a vehicle headlight with a long-range focus
high-born \'hī-'bȯrn\ *adj* : of noble birth
high-boy \-ˌbȯi\ *n* : a high chest of drawers mounted on a base with legs
high-bred \-'bred\ *adj* : coming from superior stock
high-brow \-ˌbraú\ *n* : a person of superior learning or culture — **highbrow** *adj* — **high-brow-ism** \-ˌbraú-ˌi-zəm\ *n*
high–definition *adj* : being or relating to a television system with twice as many scan lines per frame as a conventional system
high–density li-po-pro-tein \-ˌlī-pō-'prō-tēn, -ˌli-\ *n* : HDL
high-er-up \ˌhī-ər-'əp\ *n* : a superior officer or official
high-fa-lu-tin \ˌhī-fə-'lü-tᵊn\ *adj* : PRETENTIOUS, POMPOUS
high fashion *n* **1** : HIGH STYLE **2** : HAUTE COUTURE
high fidelity *n* : the reproduction of sound or image with a high degree of faithfulness to the original
high five *n* **1** : a slapping of upraised right hands by two people (as in celebration) — **high–five** *vb*
high–flown \'hī-'flōn\ *adj* **1** : EXALTED **2** : BOMBASTIC
high frequency *n* : a radio frequency between 3 and 30 megahertz
high gear *n* **1** : HIGH 4 **2** : a state of intense or maximum activity
high-hand-ed \'hī-'han-dəd\ *adj* : OVERBEARING — **high–hand-ed-ly** *adv* — **high–hand-ed-ness** *n*
high–hat \-'hat\ *adj* : SUPERCILIOUS, SNOBBISH — **high–hat** *vb*
high-land \'hī-lənd\ *n* : elevated or mountainous land
high-land-er \-lən-dər\ *n* **1** : an inhabitant of a highland **2** *cap* : an inhabitant of the Scottish Highlands
high–lev-el \'hī-'le-vəl\ *adj* **1** : being of high importance or rank **2** : being or relating to highly concentrated and environmentally hazardous nuclear waste
¹**high-light** \-ˌlīt\ *n* : an event or detail of major importance
²**highlight** *vb* **1** : EMPHASIZE **2** : to constitute a highlight of **3** : to mark (text) with a highlighter **4** : to cause to be displayed in a way that stands out on a computer screen
high-light-er \-ˌlī-tər\ *n* : a pen with transparent ink used for marking text passages
high-mind-ed \-'mīn-dəd\ *adj* : marked by elevated principles and feelings — **high-mind-ed-ness** *n*
high-ness \'hī-nəs\ *n* **1** : the quality or state of being high **2** — used as a title (as for kings)
high–pres-sure \-'pre-shər\ *adj* : using or involving aggressive and insistent sales techniques
high–rise \-'rīz\ *adj* **1** : having several stories and being equipped with elevators ⟨*~* apartments⟩ **2** : of or relating to high-rise buildings

high road *n* : HIGHWAY
high school *n* : a school usu. including grades 9 to 12 or 10 to 12
high sea *n* : the open sea outside territorial waters — usu. used in pl.
high–sound-ing \'hī-'saún-diŋ\ *adj* : POMPOUS, IMPOSING
high–spir-it-ed \-'spir-ə-təd\ *adj* : characterized by a bold or energetic spirit
high–strung \-'strəŋ\ *adj* : having an extremely nervous or sensitive temperament
high style *n* : the newest in fashion or design
high-tail \'hī-ˌtāl\ *vb* : to retreat at full speed
high tech \-'tek\ *n* : HIGH TECHNOLOGY
high technology *n* : technology involving the use of advanced devices
high–ten-sion \'hī-'ten-chən\ *adj* : having or using a high voltage
high–test \-'test\ *adj* : having a high octane number
high–tick-et \-'ti-kət\ *adj* : EXPENSIVE
high–toned \-'tōnd\ *adj* **1** : high in social, moral, or intellectual quality **2** : PRETENTIOUS, POMPOUS
high-way \'hī-ˌwā\ *n* : a main direct road
high-way-man \'hī-ˌwā-mən\ *n* : a thief who robs travelers on a road
hi-jack *also* **high-jack** \'hī-ˌjak\ *vb* : to steal esp. by stopping a vehicle on the highway; *also* : to commandeer a flying airplane — **hijack** *n* — **hi-jack-er** *n*
¹**hike** \'hīk\ *vb* **hiked; hik-ing** **1** : to move or raise with a sudden motion **2** : to take a long walk — **hik-er** *n*
²**hike** *n* **1** : a long walk **2** : RISE, INCREASE ⟨price *~*⟩
hi-lar-i-ous \hi-'ler-ē-əs, hī-\ *adj* : marked by or providing boisterous merriment — **hi-lar-i-ous-ly** *adv* — **hi-lar-i-ty** \-ə-tē\ *n*
hill \'hil\ *n* **1** : a usu. rounded elevation of land **2** : a little heap or mound (as of earth) — **hilly** *adj*
hill-bil-ly \'hil-ˌbi-lē\ *n, pl* **-lies** : a person from a backwoods area
hill-ock \'hi-lək\ *n* : a small hill
hill-side \'hil-ˌsīd\ *n* : the part of a hill between the summit and the foot
hill-top \-ˌtäp\ *n* : the top of a hill
hilt \'hilt\ *n* : a handle esp. of a sword or dagger
him \'him\ *pron, objective case of* HE
him-self \him-'self\ *pron* : HE, HIM — used reflexively, for emphasis, or in absolute constructions
¹**hind** \'hīnd\ *n, pl* **hinds** *also* **hind** : a female of a common Eurasian deer
²**hind** *adj* : REAR ⟨the dog's *~* legs⟩
¹**hin-der** \'hin-dər\ *vb* **1** : to impede the progress of **2** : to hold back ✦ **Synonyms** OBSTRUCT, BLOCK, BAR, IMPEDE
²**hind-er** \'hīn-dər\ *adj* : HIND
Hin-di \'hin-dē\ *n* : a literary and official language of northern India
hind-most \'hīnd-ˌmōst\ *adj* : farthest to the rear
hind-quar-ter \-ˌkwȯr-tər\ *n* **1** : one side of the back half of the carcass of a quadruped **2** *pl* : the part of the body of a quadruped behind the junction of hind limbs and trunk
hin-drance \'hin-drəns\ *n* **1** : the state of being hindered **2** : IMPEDIMENT 1 **3** : the action of hindering
hind-sight \'hīnd-ˌsīt\ *n* : understanding of an event after it has happened
Hindu–Arabic *adj* : relating to, being, or composed of Arabic numerals
Hin-du-ism \'hin-dü-ˌi-zəm\ *n* : a body of religious beliefs and practices native to India — **Hin-du** *n or adj*
hind wing *n* : either of the posterior wings of a 4-winged insect
¹**hinge** \'hinj\ *n* : a jointed device on which a swinging part (as a door, gate, or lid) turns
²**hinge** *vb* **hinged; hing-ing** **1** : to attach by or furnish with hinges **2** : to be contingent on a single consideration
hint \'hint\ *n* **1** : an indirect or summary suggestion **2** : CLUE **3** : a very small amount ✦ **Synonyms** DASH, SOUPÇON, SUSPICION, TINCTURE, TOUCH — **hint** *vb*
hin-ter-land \'hin-tər-ˌland\ *n* **1** : a region behind a coast **2** : a region remote from cities
¹**hip** \'hip\ *n* : the fruit of a rose
²**hip** *n* **1** : the part of the body on either side below the waist consisting of the side of the pelvis and the upper thigh **2** : HIP JOINT

³hip *adj* hip·per; hip·pest : keenly aware of or interested in the newest developments or styles — hip·ness *n*
⁴hip *vb* hipped; hip·ping : TELL, INFORM
hip·bone \'hip-'bōn, -,bōn\ *n* : the large flaring bone that makes a lateral half of the pelvis in mammals
hip–hop \'hip-,häp\ *n* 1 : a subculture esp. of inner-city youths who are devotees of rap music 2 : the stylized rhythmic music that accompanies rap — hip–hop *adj*
hip–hug·gers \'hip-,hə-gərz\ *n pl* : low-slung close-fitting pants that rest on the hips
hip joint *n* : the articulation between the femur and the hipbone
hipped \'hipt\ *adj* : having hips esp. of a specified kind ⟨broad-*hipped*⟩
hip·pie *or* hip·py \'hi-pē\ *n, pl* hippies : a usu. young person who rejects established mores and advocates nonviolence; *also* : a long-haired unconventionally dressed young person
hip·po \'hi-pō\ *n, pl* hippos : HIPPOPOTAMUS
hip·po·drome \'hi-pə-,drōm\ *n* : an arena for equestrian performances
hip·po·pot·a·mus \,hi-pə-'pä-tə-məs\ *n, pl* -mus·es *or* -mi \-,mī\ [L, fr. Gk *hippopotamos*, alter. of *hippos potamios*, lit., river horse] : a large thick-skinned aquatic mammal of sub-Saharan Africa that is related to the swine
¹hire \'hī(-ə)r\ *n* 1 : payment for labor or personal services : WAGES 2 : EMPLOYMENT 3 : one who is hired
²hire *vb* hired; hir·ing 1 : to employ for pay 2 : to engage the temporary use of for pay 3 : to take employment
hire·ling \'hī(-ə)r-liŋ\ *n* : a hired person; *esp* : one with mercenary motives
hir·sute \'hər-,süt, 'hir-\ *adj* : HAIRY
¹his \'hiz\ *adj* : of or relating to him or himself
²his *pron* : one or the ones belonging to him
His·pan·ic \hi-'spa-nik\ *adj* : of, relating to, or being a person of Latin-American descent living in the U.S. — Hispanic *n*
hiss \'his\ *vb* : to make a sharp sibilant sound; *also* : to express disapproval of by hissing — hiss *n*
hissy fit \'hi-sē-\ *n* : TANTRUM
hist *abbr* historian; historical; history
his·ta·mine \'his-tə-,mēn, -mən\ *n* : a compound widespread in animal tissues that plays a major role in allergic reactions (as hay fever)
his·to·gram \'his-tə-,gram\ *n* : a representation of statistical data by rectangles whose widths represent class intervals and whose heights usu. represent corresponding frequencies
his·tol·o·gy \his-'tä-lə-jē\ *n, pl* -gies 1 : a branch of anatomy dealing with tissue structure 2 : tissue structure or organization — his·to·log·i·cal \,his-tə-'lä-ji-kəl\ *or* his·to·log·ic \-'lä-jik\ *adj* — his·tol·o·gist \-'tä-lə-jist\ *n*
his·to·ri·an \hi-'stòr-ē-ən\ *n* : a student or writer of history
his·to·ric·i·ty \,his-tə-'ri-sə-tē\ *n* : historical actuality
his·tor·i·cal \hi-'stòr-i-kəl\ *adj* *also* his·tor·ic \-'stòr-ik\ 1 : of, relating to, or having the character of history 2 : HISTORIAN
his·to·ry \'his-tə-rē\ *n, pl* -ries [ultim. fr. L *historia*, fr. Gk, inquiry, history, fr. *histōr, istōr* knowing, learned] 1 : a chronological record of significant events often with an explanation of their causes 2 : a branch of knowledge that records and explains past events 3 : events that form the subject matter of history 4 : an established record ⟨a convict's ~ of violence⟩ — his·tor·ic \hi-'stòr-ik\ *adj* — his·tor·i·cal \-i-kəl\ *adj* — his·tor·i·cal·ly \-k(ə-)lē\ *adv*
his·tri·on·ic \,his-trē-'ä-nik\ *adj* [LL *histrionicus*, fr. L *histrio* actor] 1 : deliberately affected 2 : of or relating to actors, acting, or the theater — his·tri·on·i·cal·ly \-ni-k(ə-)lē\ *adv*
his·tri·on·ics \-niks\ *n pl* 1 : theatrical performances 2 : deliberate display of emotion for effect
¹hit \'hit\ *vb* hit; hit·ting 1 : to reach with a blow : STRIKE; *also* : to arrive with a force like a blow ⟨the storm ~⟩ 2 : to make or bring into contact : COLLIDE 3 : to affect detrimentally ⟨was ~ by the flu⟩ 4 : to make a request of 5 : to come upon 6 : to accord with : SUIT 7 : REACH, ATTAIN 8 : to indulge in often to excess — hit·ter *n*
²hit *n* 1 : an act or instance of hitting or being hit 2 : a great success 3 : BASE HIT 4 : a dose of a drug 5 : a murder committed by a gangster 6 : an instance of connecting to a particular Web site 7 : a successful match in a search (as of the Internet)

¹hitch \'hich\ *vb* 1 : to move by jerks 2 : to catch or fasten esp. by a hook or knot 3 : HITCHHIKE
²hitch *n* 1 : JERK, PULL 2 : a sudden halt 3 : a connection between something towed and its mover 4 : KNOT
hitch·hike \'hich-,hīk\ *vb* : to travel by securing free rides from passing vehicles — hitch·hik·er *n*
¹hith·er \'hi-thər\ *adv* : to this place
²hither *adj* : being on the near or adjacent side
hith·er·to \-,tü\ *adv* : up to this time
HIV \,āch-(,)ī-'vē\ *n* [*human immunodeficiency virus*] : any of several retroviruses that infect and destroy helper T cells causing the great reduction in their numbers that is diagnostic of AIDS
hive \'hīv\ *n* 1 : a container for housing honeybees 2 : a colony of bees 3 : a place swarming with busy occupants — hive *vb*
hives \'hīvz\ *n sing or pl* : an allergic disorder marked by raised itching patches on the skin or mucous membranes
hl *abbr* hectoliter
HL *abbr* House of Lords
hm *abbr* hectometer
HM *abbr* 1 Her Majesty; Her Majesty's 2 His Majesty; His Majesty's
HMO \,āch-(,)em-'ō\ *n* [*health maintenance organization*] : a comprehensive health-care organization financed by periodic fixed payments by voluntarily enrolled individuals and families
HMS *abbr* 1 Her Majesty's ship 2 His Majesty's ship
Ho *symbol* holmium
hoa·gie *also* hoa·gy \'hō-gē\ *n, pl* hoagies : SUBMARINE 2
hoard \'hòrd\ *n* : a hidden accumulation — hoard *vb* — hoard·er *n*
hoar·frost \'hòr-,fròst\ *n* : FROST 2
hoarse \'hòrs\ *adj* hoars·er; hoars·est 1 : rough and harsh in sound 2 : having a grating voice — hoarse·ly *adv* — hoarse·ness *n*
hoary \'hòr-ē\ *adj* hoar·i·er; -est 1 : gray or white with or as if with age 2 : ANCIENT — hoar·i·ness \'hòr-ē-nəs\ *n*
hoax \'hōks\ *n* : an act intended to trick or dupe; *also* : something accepted or established by fraud — hoax *vb* — hoax·er *n*
hob \'häb\ *n* : MISCHIEF, TROUBLE ⟨raising ~⟩
¹hob·ble \'hä-bəl\ *vb* hob·bled, hob·bling 1 : to limp along; *also* : to make lame 2 : FETTER
²hobble *n* 1 : a hobbling movement 2 : something used to hobble an animal
hob·by \'hä-bē\ *n, pl* hobbies : a pursuit or interest engaged in for relaxation — hob·by·ist \-ist\ *n*
hob·by·horse \'hä-bē-,hòrs\ *n* 1 : a stick with a horse's head on which children pretend to ride 2 : a toy horse mounted on rockers 3 : a topic to which one constantly reverts
hob·gob·lin \'häb-,gäb-lən\ *n* 1 : a mischievous goblin 2 : BOGEY 1
hob·nail \-,nāl\ *n* : a short large-headed nail for studding shoe soles — hob·nailed \-,nāld\ *adj*
hob·nob \-,näb\ *vb* hob·nobbed; hob·nob·bing 1 : to associate familiarly
ho·bo \'hō-bō\ *n, pl* hoboes *also* hobos : TRAMP 2
¹hock \'häk\ *n* : a joint or region in the hind limb of a quadruped just above the foot and corresponding to the human ankle
²hock *n* [D *hok* pen, prison] : ²PAWN 3 ⟨got his watch out of ~⟩; *also* : DEBT 3 — hock *vb*
hock·ey \'hä-kē\ *n* 1 : FIELD HOCKEY 2 : ICE HOCKEY
ho·cus-po·cus \,hō-kəs-'pō-kəs\ *n* 1 : SLEIGHT OF HAND 2 : nonsense or sham used to conceal deception
hod \'häd\ *n* : a long-handled carrier for mortar or bricks
hodge·podge \'häj-,päj\ *n* : a heterogeneous mixture : JUMBLE
Hodgkin's disease \'häj-kinz-\ *n* : a neoplastic disease of lymphoid tissue characterized esp. by enlargement of lymph nodes, spleen, and liver
hoe \'hō\ *n* : a long-handled implement with a thin flat blade used esp. for cultivating, weeding, or loosening the earth around plants — hoe *vb*
hoe·cake \'hō-,kāk\ *n* : a small cornmeal cake
hoe·down \-,daùn\ *n* 1 : SQUARE DANCE 2 : a gathering featuring hoedowns
¹hog \'hòg, 'häg\ *n, pl* hogs *also* hog 1 : a domestic swine

esp. when grown **2** : a selfish, gluttonous, or filthy person — **hog·gish** *adj*

²**hog** *vb* **hogged; hog·ging** : to take or hold selfishly

ho·gan \'hō-ˌgän\ *n* : a Navajo Indian dwelling usu. made of logs and mud

hog·back \'hóg-ˌbak, 'häg-\ *n* : a ridge with a sharp summit and steep sides

hog·nose snake \'hóg-ˌnōz-, 'häg-\ *or* **hog·nosed snake** \-ˌnōzd-\ *n* : any of a genus of rather small harmless stout² bodied No. American snakes that seldom bite but hiss wildly and often play dead when disturbed

hogs·head \'hógz-ˌhed, 'hägz-\ *n* **1** : a large cask or barrel **2** : a liquid measure equal to 63 U.S. gallons

hog–tie \'hóg-ˌtī, 'häg-\ *vb* **1** : to tie together the feet of ⟨∼ a calf⟩ **2** : to make helpless

hog·wash \-ˌwòsh, -ˌwäsh\ *n* **1** : SWILL, SLOP **2** : NONSENSE, BALONEY

hog wild *adj* : lacking in restraint

hoi pol·loi \ˌhòi-pə-'lòi\ *n pl* [Gk, the many] : the general populace

hoi·sin sauce \'hòi-ˌsin-\ *n* : a thick reddish sauce of soybeans, spices, and garlic used in Asian cookery

¹**hoist** \'hòist\ *vb* : RAISE, LIFT

²**hoist** *n* **1** : LIFT **2** : an apparatus for hoisting

hoke \'hōk\ *vb* **hoked; hok·ing** : FAKE — usu. used with *up*

hok·ey \'hō-kē\ *adj* **hok·i·er; -est 1** : CORNY **2** : PHONY

ho·kum \'hō-kəm\ *n* : NONSENSE

¹**hold** \'hōld\ *vb* **held** \'held\; **hold·ing 1** : POSSESS; *also* : KEEP **2** : RESTRAIN **3** : to have a grasp on **4** : to support, remain, or keep in a particular situation or position **5** : SUSTAIN; *also* : RESERVE **6** : BEAR, COMPORT **7** : to maintain in being or action : PERSIST **8** : CONTAIN, ACCOMMODATE **9** : HARBOR, ENTERTAIN; *also* : CONSIDER, REGARD **10** : to carry on by connected action; *also* : CONVOKE **11** : to occupy esp. by appointment or election **12** : to be valid **13** : HALT, PAUSE — **hold·er** *n* — **hold forth** : to speak at length — **hold to** : to adhere to : MAINTAIN — **hold with** : to agree with or approve of

²**hold** *n* **1** : STRONGHOLD **2** : CONFINEMENT; *also* : PRISON **3** : the act or manner of holding : GRIP **4** : a restraining, dominating, or controlling influence **5** : something that may be grasped as a support **6** : an order or indication that something is to be reserved or delayed — **on hold** : in a temporary state of waiting (as during a phone call); *also* : in a state of postponement ⟨plans *on hold*⟩

³**hold** *n* **1** : the interior of a ship below decks; *esp* : a ship's cargo deck **2** : an airplane's cargo compartment

hold·ing *n* **1** : land or other property owned **2** : a ruling of a court esp. on an issue of law

holding pattern *n* : a course flown by an aircraft waiting to land

hold out *vb* **1** : to continue to fight or work **2** : to refuse to come to an agreement — **hold·out** \'hōl-ˌdaút\ *n*

hold·over \'hōl-ˌdō-vər\ *n* : one that is held over

hold·up \'hōl-ˌdəp\ *n* **1** : DELAY **2** : robbery at the point of a gun

hole \'hōl\ *n* **1** : an opening into or through something **2** : a hollow place (as a pit or cave) **3** : DEN, BURROW **4** : a wretched or dingy place **5** : a unit of play from tee to cup in golf **6** : an awkward position — **hole** *vb*

hol·i·day \'hä-lə-ˌdā\ *n* [ME, fr. OE *hāligdæg*, fr. *hālig* holy + *dæg* day] **1** : a day set aside for special religious observance **2** : a day of freedom from work; *esp* : one in commemoration of an event **3** : VACATION — **holiday** *vb*

ho·li·ness \'hō-lē-nəs\ *n* : the quality or state of being holy — used as a title for various high religious officials

ho·lis·tic \hō-'lis-tik\ *adj* : relating to or concerned with integrated wholes or complete systems rather than with the analysis or treatment of separate parts ⟨∼ medicine⟩ ⟨∼ ecology⟩

hol·lan·daise \ˌhä-lən-'dāz\ *n* : a rich sauce made basically of butter, egg yolks, and lemon juice or vinegar

hol·ler \'hä-lər\ *vb* : to cry out : SHOUT — **holler** *n*

¹**hol·low** \'hä-lō\ *n* **1** : CAVITY, HOLE **2** : a surface depression

²**hollow** *adj* **hol·low·er** \'hä-lə-wər\; **hol·low·est** \-lə-wəst\ **1** : CONCAVE, SUNKEN **2** : having a cavity within **3** : lacking in real value, sincerity, or substance; *also* : FALSE **4** : MUFFLED ⟨a ∼ sound⟩ — **hol·low·ness** *n*

³**hollow** *vb* : to make or become hollow

hol·low·ware *or* **hol·o·ware** \'hä-lə-ˌwar\ *n* : vessels (as bowls or cups) with a significant depth and volume

hol·ly \'hä-lē\ *n, pl* **hollies** : either of two trees or shrubs with branches of usu. evergreen glossy spiny-margined leaves and red berries

hol·ly·hock \'hä-lē-ˌhäk, -ˌhòk\ *n* [ME *holihoc*, fr. *holi* holy + *hoc* mallow] : a biennial or perennial herb related to the mallows that is widely grown for its tall stalks of showy flowers

hol·mi·um \'hōl-mē-əm\ *n* : a metallic chemical element

ho·lo·caust \'hä-lə-ˌkóst, 'hō-\ *n* **1** : a thorough destruction esp. by fire **2** *often cap* : the killing of European Jews by the Nazis during World War II; *also* : GENOCIDE

Ho·lo·cene \'hō-lə-ˌsēn\ *adj* : of, relating to, or being the present geologic epoch — **Holocene** *n*

ho·lo·gram \'hō-lə-ˌgram, 'hä-\ *n* : a three-dimensional image produced by an interference pattern of light (as laser light)

ho·lo·graph \'hō-lə-ˌgraf, 'hä-\ *n* : a document wholly in the handwriting of its author

ho·log·ra·phy \hō-'lä-grə-fē\ *n* : the process of making a hologram — **ho·lo·graph·ic** \ˌhō-lə-'gra-fik, ˌhä-\ *adj*

Hol·stein \'hōl-ˌstēn, -ˌstīn\ *n* : any of a breed of large black-and-white dairy cattle that produce large quantities of comparatively low-fat milk

Hol·stein–Frie·sian \-'frē-zhən\ *n* : HOLSTEIN

hol·ster \'hōl-stər\ *n* [D] : a usu. leather case for a firearm

ho·ly \'hō-lē\ *adj* **ho·li·er; -est 1** : worthy of absolute devotion **2** : SACRED **3** : having a divine quality ♦ **Synonyms** HALLOWED, BLESSED, SANCTIFIED, CONSECRATED — **ho·li·ly** \-lə-lē\ *adv*

Holy Spirit *n* : the third person of the Christian Trinity

ho·ly·stone \'hō-lē-ˌstōn\ *n* : a soft sandstone used to scrub a ship's wooden decks — **holystone** *vb*

hom·age \'ä-mij, 'hä-\ *n* [ME, fr. AF *homage, omage, home*, fr. L *homo* human being] : expression of high regard; *also* : TRIBUTE 3

hom·bre \'äm-ˌbrā, 'əm-, -bre\ *n* : GUY, FELLOW

hom·burg \'häm-ˌbərg\ *n* [*Homburg*, Germany] : a man's felt hat with a stiff curled brim and a high crown creased lengthwise

homburg

¹**home** \'hōm\ *n* **1** : one's residence; *also* : HOUSE **2** : the social unit formed by a family living together **3** : a congenial environment; *also* : HABITAT **4** : a place of origin **5** : the objective in various games

²**home** *vb* **homed; hom·ing 1** : to go or return home **2** : to proceed to or toward a source of radiated energy used as a guide

home·body \'hōm-ˌbä-dē\ *n* : one whose life centers on home

home·boy \-ˌbói\ *n* **1** : a boy or man from one's neighborhood, hometown, or region **2** : a fellow member of a youth gang **3** : an inner-city youth

home·bred \-'bred\ *adj* : produced at home : INDIGENOUS

home·com·ing \-ˌkə-miŋ\ *n* **1** : a return home **2** : an annual celebration for alumni at a college or university

home computer *n* : a small inexpensive microcomputer

home economics *n* : the theory and practice of homemaking

home·girl \'hōm-ˌgərl\ *n* **1** : a girl or woman from one's neighborhood, hometown, or region **2** : a girl or woman who is a member of one's peer group **3** : an inner-city girl or woman

home·grown \'hōm-'grōn\ *adj* **1** : grown domestically ⟨∼ peaches⟩ **2** : LOCAL, INDIGENOUS ⟨a ∼ artist⟩

home·land \-ˌland\ *n* **1** : native land **2** : an area set aside to be a state for a people of a particular national, cultural, or racial origin

home·less \-ləs\ *adj* : having no home or permanent residence — **home·less·ness** *n*

home·ly \'hōm-lē\ *adj* **home·li·er; -est 1** : FAMILIAR **2** : unaffectedly natural **3** : lacking beauty or proportion — **home·li·ness** \-lē-nəs\ *n*

home·made \'hōm-ˌmād\ *adj* : made in the home, on the premises, or by one's own efforts

home·mak·er \-ˌmā-kər\ *n* : one who manages a household esp. as a wife and mother — **home·mak·ing** \-kiŋ\ *n*

ho·me·op·a·thy \ˌhō-mē-'ä-pə-thē\ *n* : a system of medical practice that treats disease esp. with minute doses of a remedy that would in healthy persons produce symptoms similar to those of the disease treated — **ho·meo·path** \'hō-mē-ə-ˌpath\ *n* — **ho·meo·path·ic** \ˌhō-mē-ə-'pa-thik\ *adj*

ho·meo·sta·sis \ˌhō-mē-ō-'stā-səs\ *n* : the maintenance of a relatively stable state of equilibrium between interrelated physiological, psychological, or social factors characteristic of an individual or group — **ho·meo·stat·ic** \-'sta-tik\ *adj*

home page *n* : the page usu. encountered first at a Web site that usu. contains hyperlinks to the other pages of the site

home plate *n* : a slab at the apex of a baseball diamond that a base runner must touch in order to score

hom·er \'hō-mər\ *n* : HOME RUN — **homer** *vb*

home·room \'hōm-ˌrüm, -ˌrüm\ *n* : a classroom where pupils report at the beginning of each school day

home run *n* : a hit in baseball that enables the batter to go around all the bases and score a run

home·school \'hōm-ˌskül\ *vb* : to teach school subjects to one's children at home — **home·school·er** \-ˌskü-lər\ *n*

home·sick \'hōm-ˌsik\ *adj* : longing for home and family while absent from them — **home·sick·ness** *n*

home·spun \-ˌspən\ *adj* **1** : spun or made at home; *also* : made of a loosely woven usu. woolen or linen fabric **2** : SIMPLE, HOMELY

¹home·stead \-ˌsted\ *n* : the home and land occupied by a family

²homestead *vb* : to acquire or settle on public land — **home·stead·er** *n*

home·stretch \-'strech\ *n* **1** : the part of a racecourse between the last curve and the winning post **2** : a final stage (as of a project)

home theater *n* : an entertainment system (as a television with surround sound and a DVD player) for the home

home video *n* : prerecorded videocassettes or videodiscs for home viewing

¹home·ward \-wərd\ *or* **home·wards** \-wərdz\ *adv* : toward home

²homeward *adj* : being or going toward home

home·work \-ˌwərk\ *n* **1** : an assignment given a student to be completed outside the classroom **2** : preparatory reading or research

¹hom·ey \'hō-mē\ *adj* **hom·i·er; -est** : characteristic of home

²homey *or* **hom·ie** \'hō-mē\ *n, pl* **homeys** *or* **homies** : HOMEBOY

ho·mi·cide \'hä-mə-ˌsīd, 'hō-\ *n* [L *homicida* murderer & *homicidium* manslaughter; both fr. *homo* human being + *caedere* to cut, kill] **1** : a person who kills another **2** : a killing of one human being by another — **hom·i·cid·al** \ˌhä-mə-'sī-dᵊl\ *adj*

hom·i·ly \'hä-mə-lē\ *n, pl* **-lies** : SERMON — **hom·i·let·ic** \ˌhä-mə-'le-tik\ *adj*

homing pigeon *n* : a racing pigeon trained to return home

hom·i·nid \'hä-mə-nəd, -ˌnid\ *n* : any of a family of primate mammals that comprise all living humans and extinct ancestral and related forms — **hominid** *adj*

hom·i·ny \'hä-mə-nē\ *n* : hulled corn with the germ removed

ho·mo·cys·te·ine \ˌhō-mō-'sis-tə-ˌēn\ *n* : an amino acid associated with an increased risk of heart disease when occurring at high levels in the blood

ho·mo·erot·ic \ˌhō-mō-i-'rä-tik\ *adj* : marked by or portraying homosexual desire — **ho·mo·erot·i·cism** \-'rä-tə-ˌsi-zəm\ *n*

ho·mo·ge·neous \ˌhō-mə-'jē-nē-əs, -nyəs\ *adj* : of the same or a similar kind; *also* : of uniform structure — **ho·mo·ge·ne·i·ty** \-jə-'nē-ə-tē\ *n* — **ho·mo·ge·neous·ly** *adv*

ho·mog·e·ni·sa·tion, ho·mog·e·nise *Brit var of* HOMOGENIZATION, HOMOGENIZE

ho·mog·e·nize \hō-'mä-jə-ˌnīz, hə-\ *vb* **-nized; -niz·ing 1** : to make homogeneous **2** : to reduce the particles in (as milk) to uniform size and distribute them evenly throughout the liquid — **ho·mog·e·ni·za·tion** \-ˌmä-jə-nə-'zā-shən\ *n* — **ho·mog·e·niz·er** *n*

ho·mo·graph \'hä-mə-ˌgraf, 'hō-\ *n* : one of two or more words spelled alike but different in origin, meaning, or pronunciation (as the *bow* of a ship, a *bow* and arrow)

ho·mol·o·gy \hō-'mä-lə-jē, hə-\ *n, pl* **-gies 1** : structural likeness between corresponding parts of different plants or animals due to evolution from a common ancestor **2** : structural likeness between different parts of the same individual — **ho·mol·o·gous** \-'mä-lə-gəs\ *adj*

hom·onym \'hä-mə-ˌnim, 'hō-\ *n* **1** : HOMOPHONE, HOMOGRAPH **2** : one of two or more words spelled and pronounced alike but different in meaning (as *pool* of water and *pool* the game)

ho·mo·pho·bia \'hō-mə-'fō-bē-ə\ *n* : irrational fear of, aversion to, or discrimination against homosexuality or homosexuals — **ho·mo·phobe** \'hō-mə-ˌfōb\ *n* — **ho·mo·pho·bic** \-'fō-bik\ *adj*

ho·mo·phone \'hä-mə-ˌfōn, 'hō-\ *n* : one of two or more words (as *to, too, two*) pronounced alike but different in meaning or derivation or spelling

Ho·mo sa·pi·ens \ˌhō-mō-'sā-pē-ənz, -'sa-\ *n* : HUMANKIND

ho·mo·sex·u·al \ˌhō-mō-'sek-shə-wəl\ *adj* : of, relating to, or marked by sexual interest in the same sex as oneself; *also* : of, relating to, or involving sexual intercourse between members of the same sex — **homosexual** *n* — **ho·mo·sex·u·al·i·ty** \-ˌsek-shə-'wa-lə-tē\ *n*

hon *abbr* honor; honorable; honorary

hone \'hōn\ *n* : WHETSTONE — **hone** *vb* — **hon·er** *n*

hone in *vb* : to move toward or direct attention to an objective

¹hon·est \'ä-nəst\ *adj* [ME, fr. AF, fr. L *honestus* honorable, fr. *honos, honor* honor] **1** : free from deception : TRUTHFUL; *also* : GENUINE, REAL **2** : REPUTABLE **3** : CREDITABLE ⟨an ~ day's work⟩ **4** : marked by integrity **5** : FRANK ♦ **Synonyms** UPRIGHT, JUST, CONSCIENTIOUS, HONORABLE, — **hon·est·ly** *adv* — **hon·es·ty** \-nə-stē\ *n*

²honest *adv* : HONESTLY; *also* : with all sincerity ⟨I didn't do it, ~⟩

hon·ey \'hə-nē\ *n, pl* **honeys** : a sweet sticky substance made by honeybees from the nectar of flowers — **hon·eyed** \-nēd\ *adj*

hon·ey·bee \'hə-nē-ˌbē\ *n* : a honey-producing bee often kept in hives

¹hon·ey·comb \-ˌkōm\ *n* : a mass of 6-sided wax cells built by honeybees; *also* : something of similar structure or appearance

²honeycomb *vb* : to make or become full of cavities like a honeycomb

hon·ey·dew \-ˌdü, -ˌdyü\ *n* : a sweetish deposit secreted on plants by aphids, scale insects, or fungi

honeydew melon *n* : a smooth-skinned muskmelon with sweet green flesh

honey locust *n* : a tall usu. spiny No. American leguminous tree with hard durable wood and long twisted pods

hon·ey·moon \'hə-nē-ˌmün\ *n* **1** : a period of harmony esp. just after marriage **2** : a holiday taken by a newly married couple — **honeymoon** *vb* — **hon·ey·moon·er** *n*

hon·ey·suck·le \'hə-nē-ˌsə-kəl\ *n* : any of a genus of shrubs with fragrant tube-shaped flowers rich in nectar

honk \'häŋk, 'hóŋk\ *n* : the cry of a goose; *also* : a similar sound (as of a horn) — **honk** *vb* — **honk·er** *n*

hon·ky–tonk \'häŋ-kē-ˌtäŋk, 'hóŋ-kē-ˌtòŋk\ *n* : a tawdry nightclub or dance hall — **honky–tonk** *adj*

¹hon·or \'ä-nər\ *n* **1** : good name : REPUTATION; *also* : outward respect **2** : PRIVILEGE **3** : a person of superior standing — used esp. as a title **4** : one who brings respect or fame ⟨an ~ to the class⟩ **5** : an evidence or symbol of distinction **6** : CHASTITY, PURITY **7** : INTEGRITY ♦ **Synonyms** HOMAGE, REVERENCE, DEFERENCE, OBEISANCE

²honor *vb* **1** : to regard or treat with honor **2** : to confer honor on **3** : to fulfill the terms of; *also* : to accept as payment — **hon·or·ee** \ˌä-nə-'rē\ *n* — **hon·or·er** *n*

hon·or·able \'ä-nə-rə-bəl\ *adj* **1** : deserving of honor **2** : of great renown **3** : accompanied with marks of honor **4** : doing credit to the possessor **5** : characterized by integrity — **hon·or·able·ness** *n* — **hon·or·ably** \-blē\ *adv*

hon·o·rar·i·um \ä-nə-'rer-ē-əm\ *n, pl* **-ia** \-ē-ə\ *also* **-i·ums** : a reward usu. for services on which custom or propriety forbids a price to be set

hon·or·ary \'ä-nə-,rer-ē\ *adj* **1** : having or conferring distinction **2** : conferred in recognition of achievement without the usual prerequisites ⟨~ degree⟩ **3** : UNPAID, VOLUNTARY ⟨an ~ chairman⟩ — **hon·or·ari·ly** \,ä-nə-'rer-ə-lē\ *adv*

hon·or·if·ic \,ä-nə-'ri-fik\ *adj* : conferring or conveying honor ⟨~ titles⟩

hon·our, hon·our·able *chiefly Brit var of* HONOR, HONORABLE

¹hood \'hůd\ *n* **1** : a covering for the head and neck and sometimes the face **2** : an ornamental fold (as at the back of an ecclesiastical vestment) **3** : a cover for parts of mechanisms; *esp* : the covering over an automobile engine — **hood·ed** \'hů-dəd\ *adj*

²hood \'hůd, 'hüd\ *n* : HOODLUM

³hood \'hůd\ *n* : an inner-city neighborhood; *also* : INNER CITY

-hood \,hůd\ *n suffix* **1** : state : condition : quality : character ⟨boy*hood*⟩ ⟨hardi*hood*⟩ **2** : instance of a (specified) state or quality ⟨false*hood*⟩ **3** : individuals sharing a (specified) state or character ⟨brother*hood*⟩

hood·ie \'hů-dē\ *n* : a hooded sweatshirt

hood·lum \'hůd-ləm, 'hůd-\ *n* **1** : THUG **2** : a young ruffian

hoo·doo \'hü-dü\ *n, pl* **hoodoos** **1** : a body of magical practices traditional esp. among blacks in the southern U.S. **2** : something that brings bad luck — **hoodoo** *vb*

hood·wink \'hůd-,wiŋk\ *vb* : to deceive by false appearance

hoo·ey \'hü-ē\ *n* : NONSENSE

hoof \'hůf, 'hüf\ *n, pl* **hooves** \'hůvz, 'hüvz\ *also* **hoofs** : a horny covering that protects the ends of the toes of ungulate mammals (as horses or cattle); *also* : a hoofed foot — **hoofed** \'hůft, 'hüft\ *adj*

¹hook \'hůk\ *n* **1** : a curved or bent device for catching, holding, or pulling **2** : something curved or bent like a hook **3** : a flight of a ball (as in golf) that curves in a direction opposite to the dominant hand of the player propelling it **4** : a short punch delivered with a circular motion and with the elbow bent and rigid

²hook *vb* **1** : CURVE, CROOK **2** : to seize or make fast with a hook **3** : STEAL **4** : to work as a prostitute

hoo·kah \'hů-kə, 'hü-\ *n* [Ar *ḥuqqa* bottle of a water pipe] : WATER PIPE

hook·er \'hů-kər\ *n* **1** : one that hooks **2** : PROSTITUTE

hook·up \'hů-,kəp\ *n* : an assemblage (as of apparatus or circuits) used for a specific purpose (as in radio)

hook·worm \'hůk-,wərm\ *n* : any of several parasitic intestinal nematode worms having hooks or plates around the mouth; *also* : infestation with or disease caused by hookworms

hoo·li·gan \'hü-li-gən\ *n* : RUFFIAN, HOODLUM — **hoo·li·gan·ism** \-gə-,ni-zəm\ *n*

hoop \'hůp, 'hüp\ *n* **1** : a circular strip used esp. for holding together the staves of a barrel **2** : a circular figure or object : RING **3** : a circle of flexible material for expanding a woman's skirt **4** : BASKETBALL — usu. used in pl.

hoop·la \'hůp-,lä, 'hůp-\ *n* [F *houp-là*, interj.] : TO-DO; *also* : BALLYHOO

hoop·ster \'hüp-stər\ *n* : a basketball player

hoo·ray \hů-'rā\ *interj* — used to express joy, approval, or encouragement

hoose·gow \'hüs-,gaú\ *n* [Sp *juzgado* panel of judges, courtroom] : JAIL

¹hoot \'hüt\ *vb* **1** : to shout or laugh usu. in contempt **2** : to make the natural throat noise of an owl — **hoot·er** *n*

²hoot *n* **1** : a sound of hooting **2** : the least bit ⟨don't give a ~⟩ **3** : something or someone amusing ⟨the play is a real ~⟩

hoot·e·nan·ny \'hü-tə-,na-nē\ *n, pl* **-nies** : a gathering at which folksingers entertain often with the audience joining in

¹hop \'häp\ *vb* **hopped; hop·ping** **1** : to move by quick springy leaps **2** : to make a quick trip **3** : to ride on esp. surreptitiously and without authorization

²hop *n* **1** : a short brisk leap esp. on one leg **2** : DANCE **3** : a short trip by air

³hop *n* : a vine related to the hemp plant whose ripe dried pistillate catkins are used esp. in flavoring malt liquors; *also, pl* : its pistillate catkins

¹hope \'hōp\ *vb* **hoped; hop·ing** : to desire with expectation of fulfillment

²hope *n* **1** : TRUST, RELIANCE **2** : desire accompanied by expectation of fulfillment; *also* : something hoped for **3** : one that gives promise for the future — **hope·ful** \-fəl\ *adj* — **hope·ful·ness** *n* — **hope·less** *adj* — **hope·less·ly** *adv* — **hope·less·ness** *n*

HOPE *abbr* Health Opportunity for People Everywhere

hope·ful·ly \'hōp-fə-lē\ *adv* **1** : in a hopeful manner **2** : it is hoped

Ho·pi \'hō-pē\ *n, pl* **Hopi** *or* **Hopis** : a member of an American Indian people of Arizona; *also* : the language of the Hopi people

hopped–up \'häpt-'əp\ *adj* **1** : being under the influence of a narcotic; *also* : full of enthusiasm or excitement **2** : having more than usual power ⟨a ~ engine⟩

hop·per \'hä-pər\ *n* **1** : a usu. immature hopping insect (as a grasshopper) **2** : a usu. funnel-shaped container for delivering material (as grain) **3** : a freight car with hinged doors in a sloping bottom **4** : a box into which a bill to be considered by a legislative body is dropped **5** : a tank holding a liquid and having a device for releasing its contents through a pipe

hop·scotch \'häp-,skäch\ *n* : a child's game in which a player tosses an object (as a stone) into areas of a figure drawn on the ground and hops through the figure to pick up the object

hor *abbr* horizontal

horde \'hórd\ *n* : THRONG, SWARM

ho·ri·zon \hə-'rī-z⁰n\ *n* [ME, fr. LL, fr. Gk *horizont-, horizōn*, fr. prp. of *horizein* to bound, fr. *horos* limit, boundary] **1** : the apparent junction of earth and sky **2** : range of outlook or experience

hor·i·zon·tal \,hór-ə-'zän-t⁰l\ *adj* : parallel to the horizon : LEVEL — **horizontal** *n* — **hor·i·zon·tal·ly** *adv*

hor·mon·al \hór-'mō-n⁰l\ *adj* : of, relating to, or effected by hormones — **hor·mon·al·ly** \-n⁰l-ē\ *adv*

hor·mone \'hór-,mōn\ *n* [Gk *hormōn*, prp. of *horman* to stir up, fr. *hormē* impulse, assault] : a product of living cells that circulates in body fluids and has a specific effect on the activity of cells remote from its point of origin

horn \'hórn\ *n* **1** : one of the hard projections of bone or keratin on the head of many hoofed mammals **2** : something resembling or suggesting a horn **3** : a brass wind instrument **4** : a usu. electrical device that makes a noise ⟨an automobile ~⟩ — **horned** \'hórnd\ *adj* — **horn·less** *adj*

horn·book \'hórn-,bůk\ *n* **1** : a child's primer consisting of a sheet of parchment or paper protected by a sheet of transparent horn **2** : a rudimentary treatise

horned toad *n* : any of several small harmless insect-eating lizards with spines on the head resembling horns and spiny scales on the body

hor·net \'hór-nət\ *n* : any of the larger social wasps

horn in *vb* : to participate without invitation : INTRUDE

horn·pipe \'hórn-,pīp\ *n* : a lively folk dance of the British Isles

horny \'hór-nē\ *adj* **horn·i·er; -est** **1** : of or made of horn; *also* : HARD, CALLOUS **2** : having horns **3** : desiring sexual gratification; *also* : excited sexually

ho·rol·o·gy \hə-'rä-lə-jē\ *n* : the science of measuring time or constructing time-indicating instruments — **ho·ro·log·i·cal** \,hór-ə-'lä-ji-kəl\ *adj* — **ho·rol·o·gist** \hə-'rä-lə-jist\ *n*

horo·scope \'hór-ə-,skōp\ *n* [ME *horoscopum*, fr. L *horoscopus*, fr. Gk *hōroskopos*, fr. *hōra* hour + *skopos* watcher] **1** : a diagram of the relative positions of planets and signs of the zodiac at a particular time for use by astrologers to foretell events of a person's life **2** : an astrological forecast

hor·ren·dous \hó-'ren-dəs\ *adj* : DREADFUL, HORRIBLE

hor·ri·ble \'hór-ə-bəl\ *adj* **1** : marked by or conducive to horror **2** : highly disagreeable — **hor·ri·ble·ness** *n* — **hor·ri·bly** \-blē\ *adv*

hor·rid \'hór-əd\ *adj* **1** : HIDEOUS **2** : REPULSIVE — **hor·rid·ly** *adv*

hor·rif·ic \hȯ-'ri-fik\ adj : having the power to horrify —
hor·rif·i·cal·ly \-fi-k(ə-)lē\ adv
hor·ri·fy \'hȯr-ə-ˌfī\ vb -fied; -fy·ing : to cause to feel horror ♦ **Synonyms** APPALL, DAUNT, DISMAY
hor·ror \'hȯr-ər\ n 1 : painful and intense fear, dread, or
dismay 2 : intense repugnance 3 : something that hor-
rifies
horror story n : an account of an unsettling or unfortunate occurrence
hors de com·bat \ˌȯr-də-kōⁿ-'bä\ adv or adj : in a disabled
condition
hors d'oeuvre \ȯr-'dərv\ n, pl **hors d'oeuvres** \same or
-'dərvz\ also **hors d'oeuvre** [F hors-d'oeuvre, lit., outside
of the work] : any of various savory foods usu. served as
appetizers
horse \'hȯrs\ n, pl **hors·es** also **horse** 1 : a large solid-
hoofed herbivorous mammal domesticated as a draft and
saddle animal 2 : a supporting framework usu. with legs
— **horse·less** adj
¹horse·back \'hȯrs-ˌbak\ n : the back of a horse
²horseback adv : on horseback
horse chestnut n : a large tree with palmate leaves, erect
conical clusters of showy flowers, and large glossy brown
seeds enclosed in a prickly bur; also : its seed
horse·flesh \'hȯrs-ˌflesh\ n : horses for riding, driving, or
racing
horse·fly \-ˌflī\ n : any of a family of large dipteran flies
with bloodsucking females
horse·hair \-ˌher\ n 1 : the hair of a horse esp. from the
mane or tail 2 : cloth made from horsehair
horse·hide \-ˌhīd\ n 1 : the dressed or raw hide of a
horse 2 : the ball used in baseball
horse latitudes n pl : either of two calm regions near 30°N
and 30°S latitude
horse·laugh \'hȯrs-ˌlaf, -ˌläf\ n : a loud boisterous laugh
horse·man \-mən\ n 1 : one who rides horseback; also
: one skilled in managing horses 2 : a breeder or raiser of
horses — **horse·man·ship** n
horse·play \-ˌplā\ n : rough boisterous play
horse·play·er \-ˌplā-ər\ n : a bettor on horse races
horse·pow·er \'hȯrs-ˌpau̇(-ə)r\ n : a unit of power equal in
the U.S. to 746 watts
horse·rad·ish \-ˌra-dish\ n : a tall white-flowered herb related to the mustards whose pungent root is used as a
condiment; also : the pungent condiment
horse·shoe \'hȯrs-ˌshü\ n 1 : a usu. U-shaped protective
metal plate fitted to the rim of a horse's hoof 2 pl : a
game in which horseshoes are pitched at a fixed object —
horse·shoe vb — **horse·sho·er** n
horseshoe crab n : any of several marine arthropods with
a broad crescent-shaped combined head and thorax
horse·tail \'hȯrs-ˌtāl\ n : any of a genus of primitive spore-
producing plants with hollow jointed stems and leaves reduced to sheaths about the joints
horse·whip \-ˌhwip\ vb : to flog with a whip made to be
used on a horse
horse·wom·an \-ˌwu̇-mən\ n 1 : a woman skilled in riding horseback or in caring for or managing horses 2 : a
woman who breeds or raises horses
hors·ey also **horsy** \'hȯr-sē\ adj **hors·i·er; -est** 1 : of, relating to, or suggesting a horse 2 : having to do with
horses or horse racing
hort abbr horticultural; horticulture
hor·ta·tive \'hȯr-tə-tiv\ adj : giving exhortation
hor·ta·to·ry \'hȯr-tə-ˌtȯr-ē\ adj : HORTATIVE
hor·ti·cul·ture \'hȯr-tə-ˌkəl-chər\ n : the science and art
of growing fruits, vegetables, flowers, and ornamental
plants — **hor·ti·cul·tur·al** \ˌhȯr-tə-'kəl-chə-rəl\ adj —
hor·ti·cul·tur·ist \-rist\ n
Hos abbr Hosea
ho·san·na \hō-'za-nə, -'zä-\ interj [Gk hōsanna, fr. Heb
hōshī'āh-nnā pray, save (us)!] — used as a cry of acclamation and adoration — **hosanna** n
¹hose \'hōz\ n, pl **hose** or **hos·es** 1 pl **hose** : STOCKING,
SOCK; also : a close-fitting garment covering the legs and
waist 2 : a flexible tube for conveying fluids (as from a
faucet)
²hose vb **hosed; hos·ing** : to spray, water, or wash with a
hose
Ho·sea \hō-'zā-ə, -'zē-\ n — see BIBLE table
ho·siery \'hō-zhə-rē, -zə-\ n : STOCKINGS, SOCKS

hosp abbr hospital
hos·pice \'häs-pəs\ n 1 : a lodging for travelers or for
young persons or the underprivileged 2 : a facility or
program for caring for dying persons
hos·pi·ta·ble \hä-'spi-tə-bəl, 'häs-(ˌ)pi-\ adj 1 : given to
generous and cordial reception of guests 2 : readily receptive — **hos·pi·ta·bly** \-blē\ adv
hos·pi·tal \'häs-ˌpi-t²l\ n [ME, fr. AF, fr. ML hospitale hos-
pice, guest house, fr. neut. of L hospitalis of a guest, fr.
hospit-, hospes guest, host] : an institution where the sick
or injured receive medical or surgical care
hos·pi·tal·ise Brit var of HOSPITALIZE
hos·pi·tal·i·ty \ˌhäs-pə-'ta-lə-tē\ n, pl **-ties** : hospitable
treatment, reception, or disposition
hos·pi·tal·ize \'häs-ˌpi-tə-ˌlīz\ vb **-ized; -iz·ing** : to place in
a hospital as a patient — **hos·pi·tal·i·za·tion** \ˌhäs-ˌpi-t²l-
ə-'zā-shən\ n
¹host \'hōst\ n [ME, fr. AF ost, fr. LL hostis, fr. L, stranger,
enemy] 1 : ARMY 2 : MULTITUDE
²host n [ME hoste host, guest, fr. AF, fr. L hospit-, hospes]
1 : one who receives or entertains guests 2 : an animal or
plant on or in which a parasite lives 3 : one into which
something (as an organ) is transplanted 4 : SERVER 2 —
host vb
³host n, often cap [ultim. fr. L hostia sacrifice] : the eucharistic bread
hos·tage \'häs-tij\ n 1 : a person kept as a pledge pending
the fulfillment of an agreement 2 : a person taken by
force to secure the taker's demands
hos·tel \'häs-t²l\ n [ME, fr. AF, fr. ML hospitale hospice]
1 : INN 2 : a supervised lodging for youth — **hos·tel·er**
or **hos·tel·ler** n
hos·tel·ry \-rē\ n, pl **-ries** : INN, HOTEL
host·ess \'hō-stəs\ n : a woman who acts as host
hos·tile \'häs-t²l, -ˌtī(-ə)l\ adj : marked by usu. overt antagonism : UNFRIENDLY — **hostile** n — **hos·tile·ly** adv
hos·til·i·ty \hä-'sti-lə-tē\ n, pl **-ties** 1 : an unfriendly state
or action 2 pl : overt acts of war
hos·tler \'häs-lər, 'äs-\ n : one who takes care of horses or
mules
hot \'hät\ adj **hot·ter; hot·test** 1 : marked by a high temperature or an uncomfortable degree of body heat 2
: giving a sensation of heat or of burning 3 : ARDENT,
FIERY 4 : sexually excited 5 : EAGER 6 : newly made
or received 7 : PUNGENT 8 : unusually lucky or favorable (〈~ dice〉 9 : recently and illegally obtained 〈~
jewels〉 — **hot** adv — **hot·ly** adv — **hot·ness** n
hot·bed \-ˌbed\ n 1 : a glass-covered bed of soil heated (as
by fermenting manure) and used esp. for raising seed-
lings 2 : an environment that favors rapid growth or development
hot–blood·ed \-'blə-dəd\ adj : easily roused or excited
hot–box \-ˌbäks\ n : a bearing (as of a railroad car) over-
heated by friction
hot button n : an emotional issue or concern that triggers
immediate intense reaction
hot·cake \-ˌkāk\ n : PANCAKE
hot dog n : a cooked frankfurter usu. served in a long split
roll
ho·tel \hō-'tel\ n [F hôtel, fr. OF hostel, fr. ML hospitale
hospice] : a building where lodging and usu. meals, entertainment, and various personal services are provided for
the public
hot flash n : a sudden brief flushing and sensation of heat
usu. associated with menopausal endocrine imbalance
hot·head·ed \'hät-'he-dəd\ adj : FIERY, IMPETUOUS —
hot·head \-ˌhed\ n — **hot·head·ed·ly** adv — **hot·head-
ed·ness** n
hot·house \-ˌhau̇s\ n : a heated greenhouse esp. for raising
tropical plants
hotline n : a telephone line for emergency use (as between
governments or to a counseling service)
hot pants n pl : very short shorts
hot pepper n : a small usu. thin-walled pepper with a pungent taste; also : a plant bearing hot peppers
hot plate n : a simple portable appliance for heating or for
cooking
hot potato n : an embarrassing or controversial issue
hot rod n : an automobile modified for high speed and fast
acceleration — **hot–rod·der** \-'rä-dər\ n
hots \'häts\ n pl : strong sexual desire — usu. used with the

hot seat *n* : a position of anxiety or embarrassment
hot-shot \'hät-ˌshät\ *n* : a showily skillful person
hot tub *n* : a large tub of hot water for one or more bathers
hot water *n* : TROUBLE, DIFFICULTY
hot-wire \'hät-ˌwī(-ə)r\ *vb* : to start (an automobile) by short-circuiting the ignition system
¹**hound** \'haùnd\ *n* 1 : : any of various hunting dogs that track prey by scent or sight 2 : FAN, ADDICT
²**hound** *vb* : to pursue relentlessly
hour \'aù(-ə)r\ *n* 1 : the 24th part of a day : 60 minutes 2 : the time of day 3 : a particular or customary time 4 : a class session — **hour-ly** *adv or adj*
hour-glass \'aù(-ə)r-ˌglas\ *n* : a glass vessel for measuring time in which sand runs from an upper compartment to a lower compartment in an hour
hou-ri \'hùr-ē\ *n* [F, fr. Pers hūrī, fr. Ar ḥūrīya] : one of the beautiful maidens of the Muslim paradise
¹**house** \'haùs\ *n, pl* **hous-es** \'haù-zəz\ 1 : a building for human habitation 2 : an animal shelter (as a den or nest) 3 : a building in which something is stored 4 : HOUSEHOLD; *also* : FAMILY 5 : a residence for a religious community or for students; *also* : those in residence 6 : a legislative body 7 : a place of business or entertainment 8 : a business organization 9 : the audience in a theater or concert hall — **house-ful** *n*
²**house** \'haùz\ *vb* **housed; hous-ing** 1 : to provide with or take shelter : LODGE 2 : STORE
house-boat \'haùs-ˌbōt\ *n* : a pleasure boat fitted for use as a dwelling or for leisurely cruising
house-boy \-ˌbòi\ *n* : a boy or man hired to act as a household servant
house-break \-ˌbrāk\ *vb* **-broke; -brok-en; -break-ing** : to train (a pet) in excretory habits acceptable in indoor living
house-break-ing \-ˌbrā-kiŋ\ *n* : the act of breaking into a dwelling with the intent of committing a felony
house-clean \-ˌklēn\ *vb* : to clean a house and its furniture — **house-clean-ing** *n*
house-coat \-ˌkōt\ *n* : a woman's often long-skirted informal garment for wear around the house
house-fly \-ˌflī\ *n* : a dipteran fly that is common about human habitations
¹**house-hold** \-ˌhōld\ *n* : those who dwell as a family under the same roof — **house-hold-er** *n*
²**household** *adj* 1 : DOMESTIC 2 : FAMILIAR, COMMON ⟨a ~ name⟩
house-keep-er \-ˌkē-pər\ *n* : a woman employed to take care of a house
house-keep-ing \-ˌkē-piŋ\ *n* : the care and management of a house or institutional property
house-lights \-ˌlīts\ *n pl* : the lights that illuminate the auditorium of a theater
house-maid \-ˌmād\ *n* : a girl or woman who is a servant employed to do housework
house-moth-er \-ˌmə-thər\ *n* : a woman acting as hostess, chaperone, and often housekeeper in a group residence
house-plant \-ˌplant\ *n* : a plant grown or kept indoors
house sparrow *n* : a Eurasian sparrow widely introduced in urban and agricultural areas
house-top \'haùs-ˌtäp\ *n* : ROOF
house-wares \-ˌwerz\ *n pl* : small articles of household equipment
house-warm-ing \-ˌwòr-miŋ\ *n* : a party to celebrate the taking possession of a house or premises
house-wife \-ˌwīf\ *n* : a married woman in charge of a household — **house-wife-ly** *adj* — **house-wif-ery** \-ˌwī-fə-rē\ *n*
house-work \-ˌwərk\ *n* : the work of housekeeping
¹**hous-ing** \'haù-ziŋ\ *n* 1 : SHELTER; *also* : dwellings provided for people 2 : something that covers or protects
²**housing** *n* : CAPARISON 1
HOV *abbr* high-occupancy vehicle
hove *past and past part of* HEAVE
hov-el \'hə-vəl, 'hä-\ *n* : a small, wretched, and often dirty house : HUT
hov-er \'hə-vər, 'hä-\ *vb* **hov-ered; hov-er-ing** 1 : FLUTTER; *also* : to move to and fro 2 : to be in an uncertain state
hov-er-craft \-ˌkraft\ *n* : a vehicle that rides on a cushion of air over a surface
¹**how** \'haù\ *adv* 1 : in what way or manner ⟨~ was it

done⟩ 2 : with what meaning ⟨~ do we interpret such behavior⟩ 3 : for what reason ⟨~ could you have done such a thing⟩ 4 : to what extent or degree ⟨~ deep is it⟩ 5 : in what state or condition ⟨~ are you⟩ — **how about** : what do you say to or think of ⟨how about coming with me⟩ — **how come** : why is it that
²**how** *conj* 1 : the way or manner in which ⟨remember ~ they fought⟩ 2 : HOWEVER ⟨do it ~ you like⟩
¹**how-be-it** \haù-'bē-ət\ *conj* : ALTHOUGH
²**howbeit** *adv* : NEVERTHELESS
how-dah \'haù-də\ *n* [Hindi &Urdu hauda, fr. Ar haudaj] : a seat or covered pavilion on the back of an elephant or camel
¹**how-ev-er** \haù-'e-vər\ *conj* : in whatever manner that
²**however** *adv* 1 : in whatever manner; *also* : to whatever degree 2 : in spite of that
how-it-zer \'haù-ət-sər\ *n* : a short cannon that shoots shells at a high angle
howl \'haù(-ə)l\ *vb* 1 : to emit a loud long doleful sound characteristic of dogs 2 : to cry loudly — **howl** *n*
howl-er \'haù-lər\ *n* 1 : one that howls 2 : a humorous and ridiculous blunder
howl-ing *adj* 1 : DESOLATE, WILD 2 : very great ⟨a ~ success⟩
how-so-ev-er \ˌhaù-sə-'we-vər\ *adv* : HOWEVER 1
hoy-den \'hòi-dᵊn\ *n* : a girl or woman of saucy, boisterous, or carefree behavior — **hoy-den-ish** *adj*
hp *abbr* horsepower
HP *abbr* high pressure
HPF *abbr* highest possible frequency
HQ *abbr* headquarters
hr *abbr* 1 here 2 hour
HR *abbr* House of Representatives
HRH *abbr* 1 Her Royal Highness 2 His Royal Highness
hryv-nia \'(h)riv-nē-ə\ *n, pl* **hryvnia** *or* **hryvnias** — see MONEY table
hrzn *abbr* horizon
Hs *symbol* hassium
HS *abbr* high school
HST *abbr* Hawaiian standard time
ht *abbr* height
HT *abbr* 1 Hawaii time 2 high-tension
HTML \ˌāch-ˌtē-ˌem-'el\ *n* [*hypertext markup language*] : a computer language used to create World Wide Web documents
http *abbr* hypertext transfer protocol
hua-ra-che \wə-'rä-chē\ *n* [MexSp] : a sandal with an upper made of interwoven leather strips
hub \'həb\ *n* 1 : the central part of a circular object (as a wheel) 2 : a center of activity; *esp* : an airport or city through which an airline routes most of its traffic
hub-bub \'hə-bəb\ *n* : UPROAR; *also* : TURMOIL
hub-cap \'həb-ˌkap\ *n* : a removable metal cap over the end of an axle
hu-bris \'hyü-brəs\ *n* : exaggerated pride or self-confidence
huck-le-ber-ry \'hə-kəl-ˌber-ē\ *n* 1 : any of a genus of American shrubs of the heath family; *also* : its edible dark blue berry 2 : BLUEBERRY
huck-ster \'hək-stər\ *n* : PEDDLER, HAWKER — **huck-ster-ism** \-stə-ˌri-zəm\ *n*
HUD *abbr* Department of Housing and Urban Development
¹**hud-dle** \'hə-dᵊl\ *vb* **hud-dled; hud-dling** 1 : to crowd together 2 : CONFER
²**huddle** *n* 1 : a closely packed group 2 : MEETING, CONFERENCE
hue \'hyü\ *n* 1 : COLOR; *also* : gradation of color 2 : the attribute of colors that permits them to be classed as red, yellow, green, blue, or an intermediate color — **hued** \'hyüd\ *adj*
hue and cry *n* : a clamor of pursuit or protest
huff \'həf\ *n* : a fit of anger or pique — **huff** *vb* — **huff-i-ly** \'hə-fə-lē\ *adv* — **huffy** \'hə-fē\ *adj*
hug \'həg\ *vb* **hugged; hug-ging** 1 : EMBRACE 2 : to stay close to — **hug** *n*
huge \'hyüj\ *adj* **hug-er; hug-est** : very large or extensive — **huge-ly** *adv* — **huge-ness** *n*
hug-ger–mug-ger \'hə-gər-ˌmə-gər\ *n* 1 : SECRECY 2 : CONFUSION, MUDDLE

Hu·gue·not \'hyü-gə-ˌnät\ *n* : a French Protestant of the 16th and 17th centuries

hu·la \'hü-lə\ *n* : a sinuous Polynesian dance usu. accompanied by chants

hulk \'həlk\ *n* **1** : a heavy clumsy ship **2** : an old ship unfit for service **3** : a bulky or unwieldy person or thing

hulk·ing \'həl-kiŋ\ *adj* : BURLY, MASSIVE

¹**hull** \'həl\ *n* **1** : the outer covering of a fruit or seed **2** : the frame or body esp. of a ship or boat

²**hull** *vb* : to remove the hulls of — **hull·er** *n*

hul·la·ba·loo \'hə-lə-bə-ˌlü\ *n, pl* **-loos** : a confused noise : UPROAR

hul·lo \ˌhə-'lō\ *chiefly Brit var of* HELLO

hum \'həm\ *vb* **hummed; hum·ming 1** : to utter a sound like that of the speech sound \m\ prolonged **2** : DRONE **3** : to be busily active **4** : to run smoothly **5** : to sing with closed lips — **hum** *n* — **hum·mer** *n*

¹**hu·man** \'hyü-mən, 'yü-\ *adj* **1** : of, relating to, being, or characteristic of humans **2** : having human form or attributes — **hu·man·ly** *adv* — **hu·man·ness** *n*

²**human** *n* : any of a species of bipedal primate mammals comprising all living persons and their recent ancestors; *also* : HOMINID — **hu·man·like** \-ˌlīk\ *n*

hu·mane \hyü-'mān, yü-\ *adj* **1** : marked by compassion, sympathy, or consideration for others **2** : HUMANISTIC — **hu·mane·ly** *adv* — **hu·mane·ness** *n*

human immunodeficiency virus *n* : HIV

hu·man·ism \'hyü-mə-ˌni-zəm, 'yü-\ *n* **1** : devotion to the humanities; *also* : the revival of classical letters characteristic of the Renaissance **2** : a doctrine or way of life centered on human interests or values — **hu·man·ist** \-nist\ *n or adj* — **hu·man·is·tic** \ˌhyü-mə-'nis-tik, ˌyü-\ *adj*

hu·man·i·tar·i·an \hyü-ˌma-nə-'ter-ē-ən, yü-\ *n* : one who practices philanthropy — **humanitarian** *adj* — **hu·man·i·tar·i·an·ism** *n*

hu·man·i·ty \hyü-'ma-nə-tē, yü-\ *n, pl* **-ties 1** : the quality or state of being human or humane **2** *pl* : the branches of learning dealing with human concerns (as philosophy) as opposed to natural processes (as physics) **3** : the human race

hu·man·ize \'hyü-mə-ˌnīz, 'yü-\ *vb* **-ized; -iz·ing** : to make human or humane — **hu·man·i·za·tion** \ˌhyü-mə-nə-'zā-shən, ˌyü-\ *n* — **hu·man·iz·er** *n*

hu·man·kind \'hyü-mən-ˌkīnd, 'yü-\ *n* : the human race

hu·man·oid \'hyü-mə-ˌnòid, 'yü-\ *adj* : having human form or characteristics — **humanoid** *n*

human pap·il·lo·ma·virus \-ˌpa-pə-'lō-mə-ˌvī-rəs\ *n* : any of numerous DNA-containing viruses that cause various human warts

¹**hum·ble** \'həm-bəl\ *adj* **hum·bler** \-bə-lər\; **hum·blest** \-bə-ləst\ [ME, fr. AF, fr. L *humilis* low, humble, fr. *humus* earth] **1** : not proud or haughty **2** : not pretentious : UNASSUMING **3** : INSIGNIFICANT ✦ *Synonyms* MEEK, MODEST, LOWLY — **hum·ble·ness** *n* — **hum·bly** *adv*

²**humble** *vb* **hum·bled; hum·bling 1** : to make humble **2** : to destroy the power or prestige of — **hum·bler** *n*

¹**hum·bug** \'həm-ˌbəg\ *n* **1** : HOAX, FRAUD **2** : NONSENSE

²**humbug** *vb* **hum·bugged; hum·bug·ging** : DECEIVE

hum·ding·er \'həm-'diŋ-ər\ *n* : a person or thing of striking excellence

hum·drum \'həm-ˌdrəm\ *adj* : MONOTONOUS, DULL — **humdrum** *n*

hu·mer·us \'hyü-mə-rəs\ *n, pl* **hu·meri** \'hyü-mə-ˌrī, -ˌrē\ : the long bone extending from shoulder to elbow

hu·mid \'hyü-məd, 'yü-\ *adj* : containing or characterized by perceptible moisture : DAMP — **hu·mid·ly** *adv*

hu·mid·i·fy \hyü-'mi-də-ˌfī\ *vb* **-fied; -fy·ing** : to make humid — **hu·mid·i·fi·ca·tion** \-ˌmi-də-fə-'kā-shən\ *n* — **hu·mid·i·fi·er** \-'mi-də-ˌfī-ər\ *n*

hu·mid·i·ty \hyü-'mi-də-tē, yü-\ *n, pl* **-ties** : the amount of atmospheric moisture

hu·mi·dor \'hyü-mə-ˌdòr, 'yü-\ *n* : a case (as for storing cigars) in which the air is kept properly humidified

hu·mil·i·ate \hyü-'mi-lē-ˌāt, yü-\ *vb* **-at·ed; -at·ing** : to injure the self-respect of : MORTIFY — **hu·mil·i·at·ing·ly** *adv* — **hu·mil·i·a·tion** \-ˌmi-lē-'ā-shən\ *n*

hu·mil·i·ty \hyü-'mi-lə-tē, yü-\ *n* : the quality or state of being humble

hum·ming·bird \'hə-miŋ-ˌbərd\ *n* : any of a family of tiny brightly colored American birds related to the swifts

hum·mock \'hə-mək\ *n* : a rounded mound : KNOLL — **hum·mocky** \-mə-kē\ *adj*

hum·mus \'hə-məs, 'hù-\ *n* [Ar *ḥummuṣ* chickpeas] : a paste of pureed chickpeas usu. mixed with sesame oil or paste

hu·mon·gous \hyü-'məŋ-gəs, -'män-\ *adj* [perh. alter. of *huge* + *monstrous*] : extremely large

¹**hu·mor** \'hyü-mər, 'yü-\ *n* **1** : TEMPERAMENT **2** : MOOD **3** : WHIM **4** : a quality that appeals to a sense of the ludicrous or incongruous; *also* : a keen perception of the ludicrous or incongruous **5** : comical or amusing entertainment — **hu·mor·ist** \'hyü-mə-rist, 'yü-\ *n* — **hu·mor·less** \'hyü-mər-ləs, 'yü-\ *adj* — **hu·mor·less·ly** *adv* — **hu·mor·less·ness** *n* — **hu·mor·ous** \'hyü-mə-rəs, 'yü-\ *adj* — **hu·mor·ous·ly** *adv* — **hu·mor·ous·ness** *n*

²**humor** *vb* : to comply with the wishes or mood of

hu·mour *chiefly Brit var of* HUMOR

hump \'həmp\ *n* **1** : a rounded protuberance (as on the back of a camel) **2** : a difficult phase or obstacle ⟨over the ~⟩ — **humped** *adj*

hump·back \'həmp-ˌbak; *1 also* -'bak\ *n* **1** : HUNCHBACK **2** : HUMPBACK WHALE — **hump·backed** *adj*

humpback whale *n* : a large baleen whale having very long flippers

hu·mus \'hyü-məs, 'yü-\ *n* : the dark organic part of soil formed from decaying matter

Hun \'hən\ *n* : a member of an Asian people that invaded Europe about A.D. 450

¹**hunch** \'hənch\ *vb* **1** : to thrust oneself forward **2** : to assume or cause to assume a bent or crooked posture

²**hunch** *n* **1** : PUSH **2** : a strong intuitive feeling about what will happen

hunch·back \'hənch-ˌbak\ *n* : a person with a crooked back; *also* : a back with a hump — **hunch·backed** *adj*

hun·dred \'hən-drəd\ *n, pl* **hundreds** *or* **hundred** : 10 times 10 — **hundred** *adj* — **hun·dredth** \-drədth\ *adj or n*

hun·dred·weight \-ˌwāt\ *n, pl* **hundredweight** *or* **hundredweights** — see WEIGHT table

¹**hung** *past and past part of* HANG

²**hung** *adj* : unable to reach a decision or verdict ⟨a ~ jury⟩

Hung *abbr* Hungarian; Hungary

Hun·gar·i·an \ˌhəŋ-'ger-ē-ən\ *n* **1** : a native or inhabitant of Hungary **2** : the language of the Hungarians — **Hungarian** *adj*

hun·ger \'həŋ-gər\ *n* **1** : a craving or urgent need for food **2** : a strong desire — **hunger** *vb* — **hun·gri·ly** *adv* — **hun·gry** *adj*

hung·over \'həŋ-'ō-vər\ *adj* : having a hangover

hung up *adj* **1** : DELAYED **2** : ENTHUSIASTIC; *also* : PREOCCUPIED — usu. used with *on* ⟨*hung up* on winning⟩

hunk \'həŋk\ *n* **1** : a large piece **2** : an attractive well-built man — **hunky** *adj*

hun·ker \'həŋ-kər\ *vb* **1** : CROUCH, SQUAT — usu. used with *down* **2** : to settle in for a sustained period — used with *down*

hun·ky-do·ry \ˌhəŋ-kē-'dòr-ē\ *adj* : quite satisfactory : FINE

¹**hunt** \'hənt\ *vb* **1** : to pursue for food or in sport; *also* : to take part in a hunt **2** : to try to find : SEEK **3** : to drive or chase esp. by harrying **4** : to traverse in search of prey — **hunt·er** *n*

²**hunt** *n* : an act, practice, or instance of hunting

Hun·ting·ton's disease \'hən-tiŋ-tənz-\ *n* : a chorea that usu. begins in middle age and leads to dementia

hunt·ress \'hən-trəs\ *n* : a woman who hunts game

hunts·man \'hənts-mən\ *n* **1** : HUNTER **2** : a person who manages a hunt and looks after the hounds

hur·dle \'hər-dᵊl\ *n* **1** : a barrier to leap over in a race **2** : OBSTACLE — **hurdle** *vb* — **hur·dler** *n*

hur·dy-gur·dy \ˌhər-dē-'gər-dē, 'hər-dē-ˌgər-dē\ *n, pl* **-gur·dies** : a musical instrument in which the sound is produced by turning a crank

hurl \'hərl\ *vb* **1** : to move or cause to move vigorously **2** : to throw down with violence **3** : FLING; *also* : PITCH — **hurl** *n* — **hurl·er** *n*

hur·ly-bur·ly \ˌhər-lē-'bər-lē\ *n* : UPROAR, TUMULT

Hu·ron \'hyür-ən, 'hyùr-ˌän\ *n, pl* **Hurons** *or* **Huron** : a member of a confederacy of American Indian peoples formerly living between Georgian Bay and Lake Ontario

hur·rah \hù-'rȯ, -'rä\ *also* **hur·ray** \hù-'rä\ *interj* — used to express joy, approval, or encouragement

hur·ri·cane \'hər-ə-ˌkān\ *n* [Sp *huracán*, of AmerInd origin] : a tropical cyclone with winds of 74 miles (118 kilometers) per hour or greater that is usu. accompanied by rain, thunder, and lightning

¹**hur·ry** \'hər-ē\ *vb* **hur·ried; hur·ry·ing** **1** : to carry or cause to go with haste **2** : to impel to a greater speed **3** : to move or act with haste — **hurried** *adj* — **hur·ried·ly** *adv*

²**hurry** *n* : extreme haste or eagerness

¹**hurt** \'hərt\ *vb* **hurt; hurt·ing** **1** : to feel or cause to feel physical or emotional pain **2** : to do harm to : DAMAGE **3** : OFFEND **4** : HAMPER **5** : to be in need — usu. used with *for* — **hurt** *adj*

²**hurt** *n* **1** : a bodily injury or wound **2** : SUFFERING **3** : HARM, WRONG — **hurt·ful** *adj* — **hurt·ful·ness** *n*

hur·tle \'hər-t⁹l\ *vb* **hur·tled; hur·tling** **1** : to move rapidly or forcefully **2** : HURL, FLING

¹**hus·band** \'həz-bənd\ *n* [ME *husbonde*, fr. OE *hūsbonda* master of a house, fr. ON *hūsbōndi*, fr. *hūs* house + *bōndi* householder] : a male partner in a marriage

²**husband** *vb* : to manage prudently

hus·band·man \'həz-bənd-mən\ *n* : FARMER

hus·band·ry \'həz-bən-drē\ *n* **1** : the control or judicious use of resources **2** : AGRICULTURE **3** : the production and care of domestic animals

¹**hush** \'həsh\ *vb* **1** : to make or become quiet or calm **2** : SUPPRESS

²**hush** *n* : SILENCE, QUIET

hush–hush \'həsh-ˌhəsh\ *adj* : SECRET, CONFIDENTIAL

¹**husk** \'həsk\ *n* **1** : a usu. thin dry outer covering of a seed or fruit **2** : an outer layer : SHELL

²**husk** *vb* : to strip the husk from — **husk·er** *n*

¹**hus·ky** \'həs-kē\ *adj* **hus·ki·er; -est** : HOARSE — **hus·ki·ly** \-kə-lē\ *adv* — **hus·ki·ness** \-kē-nəs\ *n*

²**husky** *n, pl* **huskies** **1** : a heavy-coated working dog of the New World Arctic **2** : SIBERIAN HUSKY

³**husky** *adj* **1** : BURLY, ROBUST **2** : LARGE

hus·sar \(ˌ)hə-'zär\ *n* [Hung *huszár*] : a member of any of various European cavalry units

hus·sy \'hə-zē, -sē\ *n, pl* **hussies** [alter. of *housewife*] **1** : a lewd or brazen woman **2** : a pert or mischievous girl

hus·tings \'həs-tiŋz\ *n pl* : a place where political campaign speeches are made; *also* : the proceedings in an election campaign

hus·tle \'hə-səl\ *vb* **hus·tled; hus·tling** **1** : JOSTLE, SHOVE **2** : HASTEN, HURRY **3** : to work energetically — **hustle** *n* — **hus·tler** \'həs-lər\ *n*

hut \'hət\ *n* : a small and often temporary dwelling : SHACK

hutch \'həch\ *n* **1** : a chest or compartment for storage **2** : a cupboard usu. surmounted with open shelves **3** : a pen or coop for an animal **4** : HUT

huz·zah *or* **huz·za** \(ˌ)hə-'zä\ *n* : a shout of acclaim — often used interjectionally to express joy or approbation

HV *abbr* **1** high velocity **2** high voltage

HVAC *abbr* heating, ventilating and air-conditioning

hvy *abbr* heavy

HW *abbr* hot water

hwy *abbr* highway

hy·a·cinth \'hī-ə-(ˌ)sinth\ *n* : a bulbous Mediterranean herb related to the lilies that is widely grown for its spikes of fragrant bell-shaped flowers

hy·brid \'hī-brəd\ *n* **1** : an offspring of genetically differing parents (as members of different breeds or species) **2** : one of mixed origin or composition — **hybrid** *adj* — **hy·brid·i·za·tion** \ˌhī-brə-də-'zā-shən\ *n* — **hy·brid·ize** \'hī-brə-ˌdīz\ *vb* — **hy·brid·iz·er** *n*

hy·dra \'hī-drə\ *n* : any of numerous small tubular freshwater coelenterates that are polyps having at one end a mouth surrounded by tentacles

hy·dran·gea \hī-'drān-jə\ *n* : any of a genus of shrubs related to the currants and grown for their showy clusters of white, pink, or bluish flowers

hy·drant \'hī-drənt\ *n* : a pipe with a valve and spout at which water may be drawn from a main pipe

hy·drate \'hī-ˌdrāt\ *n* : a compound formed by union of water with some other substance — **hydrate** *vb*

hy·drau·lic \hī-'drȯ-lik\ *adj* [ultim. fr. Gk *hydraulis* pipe organ using water pressure, fr. *hydōr* water + *aulos* reed instrument] **1** : operated, moved, or effected by means of water **2** : of or relating to hydraulics **3** : operated by the resistance offered or the pressure transmitted when a quantity of liquid is forced through a small orifice or through a tube **4** : hardening or setting under water

hy·drau·lics \-liks\ *n* : a science that deals with practical applications of liquid (as water) in motion

hydro \'hī-drō\ *n* : HYDROPOWER

hy·dro·car·bon \'hī-drō-ˌkär-bən\ *n* : an organic compound containing only carbon and hydrogen

hy·dro·ceph·a·lus \ˌhī-drō-'se-fə-ləs\ *n* : abnormal increase in the amount of fluid in the cranial cavity accompanied by enlargement of the skull and atrophy of the brain

hy·dro·chlo·ric acid \ˌhī-drə-ˌklȯr-ik-\ *n* : a sharp-smelling corrosive acid used in the laboratory and in industry and present in dilute form in gastric juice

hy·dro·dy·nam·ics \ˌhī-drō-dī-'na-miks\ *n* : a science that deals with the motion of fluids and the forces acting on moving bodies immersed in fluids — **hy·dro·dy·nam·ic** *adj*

hy·dro·elec·tric \ˌhī-drō-i-'lek-trik\ *adj* : of or relating to production of electricity by waterpower — **hy·dro·elec·tric·i·ty** \-ˌlek-'tri-sə-tē\ *n*

hy·dro·foil \'hī-drə-ˌfȯi(-ə)l\ *n* : a boat that has fins attached to the bottom by struts for lifting the hull clear of the water to allow faster speeds

hy·dro·gen \'hī-drə-jən\ *n* [F *hydrogène*, fr. Gk *hydōr* water + *-genēs* born; fr. the fact that water is generated by its combustion] : a gaseous colorless odorless highly flammable chemical element that is the lightest of the elements — **hy·drog·e·nous** \hī-'drä-jə-nəs\ *adj*

hy·dro·ge·nate \hī-'drä-jə-ˌnāt, 'hī-drə-\ *vb* **-nat·ed; -nat·ing** : to combine or treat with hydrogen; *esp* : to add hydrogen to the molecule of — **hy·dro·ge·na·tion** \hī-ˌdrä-jə-'nā-shən, ˌhī-drə-\ *n*

hydrogen bomb *n* : a bomb whose violent explosive power is due to the sudden release of atomic energy resulting from the fusion of light nuclei (as of hydrogen atoms)

hydrogen peroxide *n* : an unstable compound of hydrogen and oxygen used esp. as an oxidizing and bleaching agent, an antiseptic, and a propellant

hy·dro·graph·ic \ˌhī-drə-'gra-fik\ *adj* : of or relating to the description and study of bodies of water — **hy·drog·ra·pher** *n* — **hy·drog·ra·phy** \hī-'drä-grə-fē\ *n*

hy·drol·o·gy \hī-'drä-lə-jē\ *n* : a science dealing with the properties, distribution, and circulation of water — **hy·dro·log·ic** \ˌhī-drə-'lä-jik\ *or* **hy·dro·log·i·cal** \-ji-kəl\ *adj* — **hy·drol·o·gist** \hī-'drä-lə-jist\ *n*

hy·dro·ly·sis \hī-'drä-lə-səs\ *n* : a chemical decomposition involving the addition of the elements of water

hy·drom·e·ter \hī-'drä-mə-tər\ *n* : a floating instrument for determining specific gravities of liquids and hence the strength (as of alcoholic liquors)

hy·dro·pho·bia \ˌhī-drə-'fō-bē-ə\ *n* [LL, fr. Gk, fr. *hydōr* water + *phobos* fear] : RABIES

hy·dro·phone \'hī-drə-ˌfōn\ *n* : an underwater listening device

¹**hy·dro·plane** \'hī-drə-ˌplān\ *n* **1** : a powerboat designed for racing that skims the surface of the water **2** : SEAPLANE

²**hydroplane** *vb* : to skid on a wet road due to loss of contact between the tires and road

hy·dro·pon·ics \ˌhī-drə-'pä-niks\ *n* : the growing of plants in nutrient solutions — **hy·dro·pon·ic** *adj*

hy·dro·pow·er \'hī-drə-ˌpaù(-ə)r\ *n* : hydroelectric power

hy·dro·sphere \'hī-drə-ˌsfir\ *n* : the water (as vapor or lakes) of the earth

hy·dro·stat·ic \ˌhī-drə-'sta-tik\ *adj* : of or relating to fluids at rest or to the pressures they exert or transmit

hy·dro·ther·a·py \ˌhī-drə-'ther-ə-pē\ *n* : the use of water esp. externally in the treatment of disease or disability

hy·dro·ther·mal \ˌhī-drə-'thər-məl\ *adj* : of or relating to hot water

hy·drous \'hī-drəs\ *adj* : containing water

hy·drox·ide \hī-'dräk-ˌsīd\ *n* **1** : a negatively charged ion consisting of one atom of oxygen and one atom of hydrogen **2** : a compound of hydroxide with an element or group

hy·e·na \hī-'ē-nə\ *n* [ME *hyene*, fr. L *hyaena*, fr. Gk *hyaina, fr. hys* hog] : any of several large doglike carnivorous mammals of Asia and Africa

hy·giene \'hī-jēn\ *n* **1** : a science concerned with establishing and maintaining good health **2** : conditions or practices conducive to health — **hy·gien·ic** \hī-'je-nik, -jē-\ *adj* — **hy·gien·i·cal·ly** \-ni-k(ə-)lē\ *adv* — **hy·gien·ist** \hī-'jē-nist, 'hī-,jē-, hī-'je-\ *n*

hy·grom·e·ter \hī-'grä-mə-tər\ *n* : any of several instruments for measuring the humidity of the atmosphere

hy·gro·scop·ic \,hī-grə-'skä-pik\ *adj* : readily taking up and retaining moisture

hying *pres part of* HIE

hy·men \'hī-mən\ *n* : a fold of mucous membrane partly closing the opening of the vagina

hy·me·ne·al \,hī-mə-'nē-əl\ *adj* : NUPTIAL

hymn \'him\ *n* : a song of praise esp. to God — **hymn** *vb*

hym·nal \'him-nəl\ *n* : a book of hymns

hyp *abbr* hypothesis; hypothetical

¹**hype** \'hīp\ *vb* **hyped; hyp·ing 1** : STIMULATE — usu. used with *up* **2** : INCREASE — **hyped-up** *adj*

²**hype** *vb* **hyped; hyping 1** : DECEIVE **2** : PUBLICIZE

³**hype** *n* **1** : DECEPTION, PUT-ON **2** : PUBLICITY

hy·per \'hī-pər\ *adj* **1** : HIGH-STRUNG, EXCITABLE **2** : extremely active

hy·per·acid·i·ty \,hī-pər-ə-'si-də-tē\ *n* : the condition of containing excessive acid esp. in the stomach — **hy·per·ac·id** \-'a-səd\ *adj*

hy·per·ac·tive \-'ak-tiv\ *adj* : excessively or pathologically active — **hy·per·ac·tiv·i·ty** \-,ak-'ti-və-tē\ *n*

hy·per·bar·ic \,hī-pər-'ber-ik\ *adj* : of, relating to, or utilizing greater than normal pressure (as of oxygen)

hy·per·bo·la \hī-'pər-bə-lə\ *n, pl* **-las** *or* **-lae** \-(,)lē\ : a curve formed by the intersection of a double right circular cone with a plane that cuts both halves of the cone — **hy·per·bol·ic** \,hī-pər-'bä-lik\ *adj*

hy·per·bo·le \hī-'pər-bə-(,)lē\ *n* : extravagant exaggeration used as a figure of speech

hy·per·crit·i·cal \,hī-pər-'kri-ti-kəl\ *adj* : excessively critical — **hy·per·crit·i·cal·ly** \-k(ə-)lē\ *adv*

hy·per·drive \'hī-pər-,drīv\ *n* : a state of extremely heightened activity

hy·per·ex·tend \,hī-pər-ik-'stend\ *vb* : to extend beyond the normal range of motion — **hy·per·ex·ten·sion** \-'sten-shən\ *n*

hy·per·gly·ce·mia \,hī-pər-glī-'sē-mē-ə\ *n* : excess of sugar in the blood — **hy·per·gly·ce·mic** \-mik\ *adj*

hy·per·ki·net·ic \-kə-'ne-tik\ *adj* : characterized by fast-paced or frenetic activity

hy·per·link \'hī-pər-,liŋk\ *n* : a connecting element (as highlighted text) between one place in a hypertext or hypermedia document and another

hy·per·me·dia \'hī-pər-,mē-dē-ə\ *n* : a database format offering direct access to text, sound, or images related to that on display

hy·per·opia \,hī-pə-'rō-pē-ə\ *n* : a condition in which visual images come to focus behind the retina resulting esp. in defective vision for near objects — **hy·per·opic** \-'rō-pik, -'rä-\ *adj*

hy·per·sen·si·tive \-'sen-sə-tiv\ *adj* **1** : excessively or abnormally sensitive **2** : abnormally susceptible physiologically to a specific agent (as a drug) — **hy·per·sen·si·tive·ness** *n* — **hy·per·sen·si·tiv·i·ty** \-,sen-sə-'ti-və-tē\ *n*

hy·per·ten·sion \'hī-pər-,ten-chən\ *n* : high blood pressure — **hy·per·ten·sive** \,hī-pər-'ten-siv\ *adj or n*

hy·per·text \'hī-pər-,tekst\ *n* : a database format in which information related to that on display can be accessed directly from the display

hy·per·thy·roid·ism \,hī-pər-'thī-,rȯi-,di-zəm\ *n* : excessive activity of the thyroid gland; *also* : the resulting bodily condition — **hy·per·thy·roid** \-'thī-,rȯid\ *adj*

hy·per·tro·phy \hī-'pər-trə-fē\ *n, pl* **-phies** : excessive development of a body part — **hy·per·tro·phic** \,hī-pər-'trō-fik\ *adj* — **hypertrophy** *vb*

hy·per·ven·ti·late \,hī-pər-'ven-tə-,lāt\ *vb* : to breathe rapidly and deeply esp. to the point of losing an abnormal amount of carbon dioxide from the blood — **hy·per·ven·ti·la·tion** \-,ven-tə-'lā-shən\ *n*

hy·phen \'hī-fən\ *n* : a punctuation mark - used esp. to divide or to compound words or word parts — **hyphen** *vb*

hy·phen·ate \'hī-fə-,nāt\ *vb* **-at·ed; -at·ing** : to connect or divide with a hyphen — **hy·phen·ation** \,hī-fə-'nā-shən\ *n*

hyp·no·sis \hip-'nō-səs\ *n, pl* **-no·ses** \-,sēz\ : an induced state that resembles sleep and in which the subject is responsive to suggestions of the inducer (**hyp·no·tist** \'hip-nə-tist\) — **hyp·no·tism** \'hip-nə-,ti-zəm\ *n* — **hyp·no·tiz·able** \'hip-nə-,tī-zə-bəl\ *adj* — **hyp·no·tize** \-,tīz\ *vb*

¹**hyp·not·ic** \hip-'nä-tik\ *adj* **1** : inducing sleep : SOPORIFIC **2** : of or relating to hypnosis or hypnotism **3** : readily holding the attention — **hyp·not·i·cal·ly** \-ti-k(ə-)lē\ *adv*

²**hypnotic** *n* : a sleep-inducing drug

hy·po \'hī-pō\ *n, pl* **hypos** : SODIUM THIOSULFATE; *also* : a solution of sodium thiosulfate

hy·po·al·ler·gen·ic \,hī-pō-,a-lər-'je-nik\ *adj* : having little likelihood of causing an allergic response

hy·po·cen·ter \'hī-pō-,sen-tər\ *n* : the point of origin of an earthquake

hy·po·chon·dria \,hī-pə-'kän-drē-ə\ *n* [NL, fr. LL, pl., upper abdomen (formerly regarded as the seat of hypochondria), fr. Gk, lit., the parts under the cartilage (of the breastbone), fr. *hypo-* under + *chondros* cartilage] : depression of mind often centered on imaginary physical ailments — **hy·po·chon·dri·ac** \-drē-,ak\ *adj or n*

hy·poc·ri·sy \hi-'pä-krə-sē\ *n, pl* **-sies** : a feigning to be what one is not or to believe what one does not; *esp* : the false assumption of an appearance of virtue or religion — **hyp·o·crite** \'hi-pə-,krit\ *n* — **hyp·o·crit·i·cal** \,hi-pə-'kri-ti-kəl\ *adj* — **hyp·o·crit·i·cal·ly** \-k(ə-)lē\ *adv*

¹**hy·po·der·mic** \,hī-pə-'dər-mik\ *adj* : administered by or used in making an injection beneath the skin

²**hypodermic** *n* : HYPODERMIC SYRINGE; *also* : an injection made with this

hypodermic needle *n* : NEEDLE 3; *also* : HYPODERMIC SYRINGE

hypodermic syringe *n* : a small syringe with a hollow needle for injecting material into or through the skin

hypodermic syringe

hy·po·gly·ce·mia \,hī-pō-glī-'sē-mē-ə\ *n* : abnormal decrease of sugar in the blood — **hy·po·gly·ce·mic** \-mik\ *adj*

hy·pot·e·nuse \hī-'pä-tə-,nüs, -,nyüs, -,nüz, -,nyüz\ *n* : the side of a right triangle that is opposite the right angle; *also* : its length

hy·po·thal·a·mus \,hī-pō-'tha-lə-məs\ *n* : a part of the brain that lies beneath the thalamus and is a control center for the autonomic nervous system

hy·poth·e·sis \hī-'pä-thə-səs\ *n, pl* **-e·ses** \-,sēz\ : an assumption made esp. in order to test its logical or empirical consequences — **hy·po·thet·i·cal** \,hī-pə-'the-ti-kəl\ *adj* — **hy·po·thet·i·cal·ly** \-k(ə-)lē\ *adv*

hy·poth·e·size \-,sīz\ *vb* **-sized; -siz·ing** : to adopt as a hypothesis

hy·po·thy·roid·ism \,hī-pō-'thī-,rȯi-,di-zəm\ *n* : deficient activity of the thyroid gland; *also* : a resultant lowered metabolic rate and general loss of vigor — **hy·po·thy·roid** *adj*

hys·sop \'hi-səp\ *n* : a European mint sometimes used as a potherb

hys·ter·ec·to·my \,his-tə-'rek-tə-mē\ *n, pl* **-mies** : surgical removal of the uterus

hys·te·ria \hi-'ster-ē-ə, -'stir-\ *n* [NL, fr. E *hysteric*, adj., fr. L *hystericus*, fr. Gk *hysterikos*, fr. *hystera* womb; fr. the Greek notion that hysteria was peculiar to women and caused by disturbances in the uterus] **1** : a nervous disorder marked esp. by defective emotional control **2** : unmanageable fear or outburst of emotion — **hys·ter·ic** \-'ster-ik\ *n* — **hys·ter·i·cal** \-'ster-i-kəl\ *also* **hysteric** *adj* — **hys·ter·i·cal·ly** \-k(ə-)lē\ *adv*

hys·ter·ics \-'ster-iks\ *n pl* : a fit of uncontrollable laughter or crying

Hz *abbr* hertz

¹i \'ī\ *n, pl* i's *or* is \'īz\ *often cap* 1 : the 9th letter of the English alphabet 2 : one in Roman numerals
²i *abbr, often cap* island; isle
³i *symbol* imaginary unit
¹I \'ī, ə\ *pron* : the one speaking or writing
²I *abbr* interstate
³I *symbol* iodine
Ia *or* IA *abbr* Iowa
-ial *adj suffix* : ¹-AL ⟨manori*al*⟩
iamb \'ī-,am\ *or* iam·bus \ī-'am-bəs\ *n, pl* iambs \'ī-,amz\ *or* iam·bus·es : a metrical foot of one unaccented syllable followed by one accented syllable — iam·bic \ī-'am-bik\ *adj or n*
-ian — *see* -AN
-iatric *also* -iatrical *adj comb form* : of or relating to (such) medical treatment or healing ⟨pedi*atric*⟩
-iatrics *n pl comb form* : medical treatment ⟨pedi*atrics*⟩
ib *or* ibid *abbr* ibidem
ibex \'ī-,beks\ *n, pl* ibex *or* ibex·es [L] : any of several Old World wild goats with large curved horns
ibi·dem \'i-bə-,dem, i-'bī-dəm\ *adv* [L] : in the same place
-ibility — *see* -ABILITY
ibis \'ī-bəs\ *n, pl* ibis *or* ibis·es [L, fr. Gk, fr. Egypt *hbw*] : any of various wading birds related to the herons but having a downwardly curved bill
-ible — *see* -ABLE
ibu·pro·fen \ī-byü-'prō-fən\ *n* : a nonsteroidal anti-inflammatory drug used to relieve pain and fever
IC \ī-'sē\ *n* : INTEGRATED CIRCUIT
¹-ic *adj suffix* 1 : of, relating to, or having the form of : being ⟨panoram*ic*⟩ 2 : related to, derived from, or containing ⟨alcohol*ic*⟩ 3 : in the manner of : like that of : characteristic of 4 : associated or dealing with : utilizing ⟨electron*ic*⟩ 5 : characterized by : exhibiting ⟨nostalg*ic*⟩ : affected with ⟨allerg*ic*⟩ 6 : caused by 7 : tending to produce ⟨analges*ic*⟩
²-ic *n suffix* : one having the character or nature of : one belonging to or associated with : one exhibiting or affected by : one that produces
-ical *adj suffix* : -IC ⟨symmetri*cal*⟩ ⟨geologi*cal*⟩ — -ically *adv suffix*
ICBM \ī-,sē-(,)bē-'em\ *n, pl* ICBM's *or* ICBMs \-'emz\ : an intercontinental ballistic missile
ICC *abbr* Interstate Commerce Commission
¹ice \'īs\ *n* 1 : frozen water 2 : a substance resembling ice 3 : a state of coldness (as from formality or reserve) 4 : a flavored frozen dessert; *esp* : one containing no milk or cream
²ice *vb* iced; ic·ing 1 : FREEZE 2 : CHILL 3 : to cover with or as if with icing
ice age *n* : a time of widespread glaciation
ice bag *n* : a waterproof bag to hold ice for local application of cold to the body
ice·berg \'īs-,bərg\ *n* : a large floating mass of ice broken off from a glacier
iceberg lettuce *n* : any of various crisp light green lettuces that form a compact head like a cabbage
ice·boat \'īs-,bōt\ *n* : a boatlike frame on runners propelled on ice by sails
ice·bound \-,baùnd\ *adj* : surrounded, obstructed, or covered by ice
ice·box \-,bäks\ *n* : REFRIGERATOR
ice·break·er \-,brā-kər\ *n* : a ship equipped (as with a reinforced bow) to make a channel through ice
ice cap *n* : a glacier forming on relatively level land and flowing outward from its center
ice cream *n* : a frozen food containing sweetened or flavored cream or butterfat
ice hockey *n* : a game in which two teams of ice-skating players try to shoot a puck into the opponent's goal
ice·house \'īs-,haùs\ *n* : a building in which ice is made or stored

¹Ice·lan·dic \īs-'lan-dik\ *adj* : of, relating to, or characteristic of Iceland, the Icelanders, or their language
²Icelandic *n* : the language of Iceland
ice·man \'īs-,man\ *n* : one who sells or delivers ice
ice milk *n* : a sweetened frozen food made of skim milk
ice pick *n* : a hand tool ending in a spike for chipping ice
ice–skate \'īs-,skāt\ *vb* : to skate on ice — ice–skater *n*
ice storm *n* : a storm in which falling rain freezes on contact
ice water *n* : chilled or iced water esp. for drinking
ich·thy·ol·o·gy \,ik-thē-'ä-lə-jē\ *n* : a branch of zoology dealing with fishes — ich·thy·ol·o·gist \-jist\ *n*
ici·cle \'ī,si-kəl\ *n* [ME *isikel*, fr. *is* ice + *ikel* icicle, fr. OE *gicel*] : a hanging mass of ice formed by the freezing of dripping water
ic·ing \'ī-siŋ\ *n* : a sweet usu. creamy mixture used to coat baked goods
ICJ *abbr* International Court of Justice
icky \'i-kē\ *adj* ick·i·er; -est : OFFENSIVE, DISTASTEFUL — ick·i·ness *n*
icon *also* ikon \'ī-,kän\ *n* 1 : IMAGE; *esp* : a religious image painted on a wood panel 2 : a small picture on a computer display that suggests the purpose of an available function — icon·ic \ī-'kä-nik\ *adj*
icon·o·clasm \ī-'kä-nə-,kla-zəm\ *n* : the doctrine, practice, or attitude of an iconoclast
icon·o·clast \-,klast\ *n* [ML *iconoclastes*, fr. MGk *eikonoklastēs*, lit., image destroyer, fr. Gk *eikōn* image + *klan* to break] 1 : one who destroys religious images or opposes their veneration 2 : one who attacks cherished beliefs or institutions
-ics \iks\ *n sing or pl suffix* 1 : study : knowledge : skill : practice ⟨linguist*ics*⟩ ⟨electron*ics*⟩ 2 : characteristic actions or activities ⟨acrobat*ics*⟩ 3 : characteristic qualities, operations, or phenomena ⟨mechan*ics*⟩
ic·tus \'ik-təs\ *n* : the recurring stress or beat in a rhythmic or metrical series of sounds
ICU *abbr* intensive care unit
icy \'ī-sē\ *adj* ic·i·er; -est 1 : covered with, abounding in, or consisting of ice 2 : intensely cold 3 : being cold and unfriendly — ic·i·ly \'ī-sə-lē\ *adv* — ic·i·ness \-sē-nəs\ *n*
¹id \'id\ *n* [L, it] : the part of the psyche in psychoanalytic theory that is completely unconscious and concerned with instinctual needs and drives
²id *abbr* idem
¹ID \'ī-'dē\ *vb* ID'd *or* IDed; ID'ing *or* IDing : IDENTIFY
²ID *abbr* 1 Idaho 2 identification
idea \ī-'dē-ə\ *n* 1 : a plan for action : DESIGN 2 : something imagined or pictured in the mind 3 : a central meaning or purpose ♦ *Synonyms* CONCEPT, CONCEPTION, NOTION, IMPRESSION
¹ide·al \ī-'dēl\ *adj* 1 : existing only in the mind : IMAGINARY; *also* : lacking practicality 2 : of or relating to an ideal or to perfection : PERFECT
²ideal *n* 1 : a standard of excellence 2 : one regarded as a model worthy of imitation 3 : GOAL ♦ *Synonyms* ARCHETYPE, EXAMPLE, EXEMPLAR, PARADIGM, PATTERN
ide·al·ise *Brit var of* IDEALIZE
ide·al·ism \ī-'dē-ə-,li-zəm\ *n* : the practice of forming ideals or living under their influence; *also* : an idealized representation — ide·al·ist \-list\ *n* — ide·al·is·tic \ī-,dē-ə-'lis-tik\ *adj* — ide·al·is·ti·cal·ly \-ti-k(ə-)lē\ *adv*
ide·al·ize \ī-'dē-ə-,līz\ *vb* -ized; -iz·ing : to think of or represent as ideal — ide·al·i·za·tion \-,dē-ə-lə-'zā-shən\ *n*
ide·al·ly \ī-'dē-ə-lē, -'dē-ə-lē\ *adv* 1 : in idea or imagination : MENTALLY 2 : in agreement with an ideal : PERFECTLY
ide·a·tion \,ī-dē-'ā-shən\ *n* : the forming or entertaining of ideas — ide·ate \'ī-dē-,āt\ *vb* — ide·a·tion·al \,ī-dē-'ā-shə-nəl\ *adj*
idem \'ī-,dem, 'ē-, -\ *pron* [L, same] : the same as something previously mentioned
iden·ti·cal \ī-'den-ti-kəl\ *adj* 1 : being the same : essen-

tially alike ♦ **Synonyms** EQUIVALENT, EQUAL, TANTA-
MOUNT
iden·ti·fi·ca·tion \ī-ˌden-tə-fə-ˈkā-shən\ *n* **1** : an act of
identifying : the state of being identified **2** : evidence of
identity **3** : an unconscious psychological process by
which an individual models thoughts, feelings, and actions after another person or an object
iden·ti·fy \ī-ˈden-tə-ˌfī\ *vb* **-fied; -fy·ing 1** : to regard as
identical **2** : ASSOCIATE **3** : to establish the identity of
4 : to practice psychological identification — **iden·ti·fi-
able** \-ˌden-tə-ˈfī-ə-bəl\ *adj* — **iden·ti·fi·ably** \-blē\ *adv* —
iden·ti·fi·er \-ˌfī(-ə)r\ *n*
iden·ti·ty \ī-ˈden-tə-tē\ *n, pl* **-ties 1** : sameness of essential
character **2** : INDIVIDUALITY **3** : the fact of being the
same person or thing as claimed
identity crisis *n* : psychological conflict esp. in adolescence involving confusion about one's social role and
one's personality
identity theft *n* : the illegal use of someone else's personal
information to obtain money or credit
ideo·gram \ˈī-dē-ə-ˌgram, ˈi-\ *n* **1** : a picture or symbol
used in a system of writing to represent a thing or an
idea **2** : a character or symbol used in a system of writing to represent an entire word
ideo·logue *also* **idea·logue** \ˈī-dē-ə-ˌlóg\ *n* : a partisan advocate or adherent of a particular ideology
ide·ol·o·gy \ˌī-dē-ˈä-lə-jē, ˌi-\ *also* **ide·al·o·gy** \-ˈä-lə-jē,
-ˈa-\ *n, pl* **-gies 1** : the body of ideas characteristic of a
particular individual, group, or culture **2** : the asser-
tions, theories, and aims that constitute a political, social,
and economic program — **ide·o·log·i·cal** \ˌī-dē-ə-ˈlä-ji-
kəl, ˌi-\ *adj* — **ide·o·log·i·cal·ly** \-ˈlä-ji-k(ə-)lē\ *adv* — **ide-
ol·o·gist** \-dē-ˈä-lə-jist\ *n*
ides \ˈīdz\ *n sing or pl* : the 15th day of March, May, July,
or October or the 13th day of any other month in the ancient Roman calendar
id·i·o·cy \ˈi-dē-ə-sē\ *n, pl* **-cies 1** *usu offensive* : extreme
mental retardation **2** : something notably stupid or foolish
id·i·om \ˈi-dē-əm\ *n* **1** : the language peculiar to a person
or group **2** : the characteristic form or structure of a language **3** : an expression that cannot be understood from
the meanings of its separate words (as *give way*) — **id·i·o-
mat·ic** \ˌi-dē-ə-ˈma-tik\ *adj* — **id·i·o·mat·i·cal·ly** \-ti-
k(ə-)lē\ *adv*
id·i·o·path·ic \ˌi-dē-ə-ˈpa-thik\ *adj* : arising spontaneously
or from an obscure or unknown cause ⟨an ~ disease⟩
id·i·o·syn·cra·sy \ˌi-dē-ə-ˈsin-krə-sē\ *n, pl* **-sies** : personal
peculiarity — **id·i·o·syn·crat·ic** \ˌi-dē-ō-sin-ˈkra-tik\ *adj*
— **id·i·o·syn·crat·i·cal·ly** \-ˈkra-ti-k(ə-)lē\ *adv*
id·i·ot \ˈi-dē-ət\ *n* [ME, fr. AF *ydiote*, fr. L *idiota* ignorant
person, fr. Gk *idiōtēs* one in a private station, layman, ignorant person, fr. *idios* one's own, private] **1** *usu offensive* : a person affected with idiocy **2** : a foolish or stupid
person — **id·i·ot·ic** \ˌi-dē-ˈä-tik\ *adj* — **id·i·ot·i·cal·ly** \-ti-
k(ə-)lē\ *adv*
id·i·ot-proof \ˈi-dē-ət-ˌprüf\ *adj* : extremely easy to operate
or maintain
¹idle \ˈī-d³l\ *adj* **idler** \ˈī-də-lər\; **idlest** \ˈī-də-ləst\ **1**
: GROUNDLESS, WORTHLESS, USELESS ⟨~ talk⟩ **2** : not
occupied or employed : INACTIVE **3** : LAZY — **idle·ness**
n — **idly** \ˈīd-lē\ *adv*
²idle *vb* **idled; idling 1** : to spend time doing nothing **2**
: to make idle **3** : to run without being connected so that
power is not used for useful work — **idler** *n*
idol \ˈī-d³l\ *n* **1** : an image worshipped as a god; *also* : a
false god **2** : an object of passionate devotion
idol·a·ter *or* **idol·a·tor** \ī-ˈdä-lə-tər\ *n* : a worshiper of idols
idol·a·try \-trē\ *n, pl* **-tries 1** : the worship of a physical
object as a god **2** : excessive devotion — **idol·a·trous**
\-trəs\ *adj*
idol·ize \ˈī-də-ˌlīz\ *vb* **-ized; -iz·ing** : to make an idol of —
idol·i·za·tion \ˌī-də-lə-ˈzā-shən\ *n*
idyll \ˈī-d³l\ *n* **1** : a simple work of writing or poetry that
describes country life or suggests a peaceful setting **2** : a
fit subject for an idyll — **idyl·lic** \ī-ˈdi-lik\ *adj*
i.e. \ˈī-ˈē\ *abbr* [L *id est*] that is
IE *abbr* industrial engineer
-ier — see -ER
if \ˈif\ *conj* **1** : in the event that ⟨~ he stays, I leave⟩ **2**
: WHETHER ⟨ask ~ he left⟩ **3** — used as a function

word to introduce an exclamation expressing a wish ⟨~
it would only rain⟩ **4** : even though ⟨an interesting ~
untenable argument⟩ **5** : and perhaps not even ⟨few ~
any changes are expected⟩
IF *abbr* intermediate frequency
if·fy \ˈi-fē\ *adj* : full of contingencies or unknown conditions
-i·fy \ə-ˌfī\ *vb suffix* : -FY
ig·loo \ˈi-glü\ *n, pl* **igloos** [Inuit (an Eskimo language) *iglu*
house] : an Eskimo house or hut often made of snow
blocks and in the shape of a dome
ig·ne·ous \ˈig-nē-əs\ *adj* **1** : FIERY **2** : formed by solidification of molten rock
ig·nite \ig-ˈnīt\ *vb* **ig·nit·ed; ig·nit·ing** : to set afire or
catch fire — **ig·nit·able** \-ˈnī-tə-bəl\ *adj*
ig·ni·tion \ig-ˈni-shən\ *n* **1** : a setting on fire **2** : the
process or means (as an electric spark) of igniting the fuel
mixture in an engine **3** : a device that activates an ignition system
ig·no·ble \ig-ˈnō-bəl\ *adj* **1** : of common birth **2** : not
honorable : BASE, MEAN ♦ **Synonyms** DESPICABLE,
SCURVY, SORDID, VILE, WRETCHED — **ig·no·bly** *adv*
ig·no·min·i·ous \ˌig-nə-ˈmi-nē-əs\ *adj* **1** : DISHONOR-
ABLE **2** : DESPICABLE **3** : HUMILIATING, DEGRADING
♦ **Synonyms** DISREPUTABLE, DISCREDITABLE, DIS-
GRACEFUL, INGLORIOUS — **ig·no·min·i·ous·ly** *adv* — **ig-
no·mi·ny** \ˈig-nə-ˌmi-nē, ig-ˈnä-mə-nē\ *n*
ig·no·ra·mus \ˌig-nə-ˈrä-məs\ *n, pl* **-mus·es** *also* **-mi** \-mē\
[*Ignoramus*, ignorant lawyer in *Ignoramus* (1615), play by
George Ruggle] : an utterly ignorant person
ig·no·rance \ˈig-nə-rəns\ *n* : the state of being ignorant
ig·no·rant \ˈig-nə-rənt\ *adj* **1** : lacking knowledge **2** : resulting from or showing lack of knowledge or intelli-
gence **3** : UNAWARE, UNINFORMED ♦ **Synonyms** BE-
NIGHTED, ILLITERATE, UNEDUCATED, UNLETTERED,
UNTUTORED — **ig·no·rant·ly** *adv*
ig·nore \ig-ˈnór\ *vb* **ig·nored; ig·nor·ing** : to refuse to
take notice of ♦ **Synonyms** OVERLOOK, SLIGHT, NE-
GLECT
igua·na \i-ˈgwä-nə\ *n* : any of various large tropical American lizards

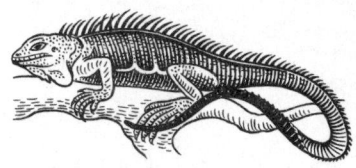

iguana

ihp *abbr* indicated horsepower
IHS \ˌī-ˌäch-ˈes\ [LL, part transliteration of Gk ΙΗΣ, abbr.
for ΙΗΣΟΥΣ *Iēsous* Jesus] — used as a Christian symbol
and monogram for *Jesus*
ikon *var of* ICON
IL *abbr* Illinois
il·e·itis \ˌi-lē-ˈī-təs\ *n* : inflammation of the ileum
il·e·um \ˈi-lē-əm\ *n, pl* **il·ea** \-lē-ə\ : the part of the small intestine between the jejunum and the large intestine
il·i·ac \ˈi-lē-ˌak\ *adj* : of, relating to, or located near the
ilium
il·i·um \ˈi-lē-əm\ *n, pl* **il·ia** \-lē-ə\ : the uppermost and largest of the three bones making up either side of the pelvis
ilk \ˈilk\ *n* : SORT, KIND
¹ill \ˈil\ *adj* **worse** \ˈwərs\; **worst** \ˈwərst\ **1** : attended or
caused by an evil intent ⟨~ deeds⟩ **2** : not normal or
sound ⟨~ health⟩; *also* : not in good health : SICK **3**
: BAD, UNLUCKY ⟨an ~ omen⟩ **4** : not right or proper
⟨~ manners⟩ **5** : UNFRIENDLY, HOSTILE ⟨~ feeling⟩
²ill *adv* **worse; worst 1** : with displeasure **2** : in a harsh
manner **3** : HARDLY, SCARCELY ⟨can ~ afford it⟩ **4**
: BADLY, UNLUCKILY **5** : in a faulty way
³ill *n* **1** : EVIL **2** : MISFORTUNE, DISTRESS **3** : AILMENT,
SICKNESS; *also* : TROUBLE
⁴ill *abbr* illustrated; illustration; illustrator
Ill *abbr* Illinois

ill·ad·vised \ˌil-əd-ˈvīzd\ *adj* : not well counseled ⟨∼ efforts⟩ — **ill·ad·vis·ed·ly** \-ˈvī-zəd-lē\ *adv*

ill·bred \-ˈbred\ *adj* : badly brought up : IMPOLITE

il·le·gal \il-ˈlē-gəl\ *adj* : not lawful; *also* : not sanctioned by official rules ✦ *Synonyms* UNLAWFUL, CRIMINAL, ILLEGITIMATE, ILLICIT, WRONGFUL — **il·le·gal·i·ty** \ˌi-li-ˈga-lə-tē\ *n* — **il·le·gal·ly** *adv*

il·leg·i·ble \il-ˈle-jə-bəl\ *adj* : not legible — **il·leg·i·bil·i·ty** \il-ˌle-jə-ˈbi-lə-tē\ *n* — **il·leg·i·bly** \il-ˈle-jə-blē\ *adv*

il·le·git·i·mate \ˌi-li-ˈji-tə-mət\ *adj* 1 : born of unmarried parents 2 : ILLOGICAL 3 : ILLEGAL — **il·le·git·i·ma·cy** \-ˈji-tə-mə-sē\ *n* — **il·le·git·i·mate·ly** *adv*

ill·fat·ed \ˈil-ˈfā-təd\ *adj* : UNFORTUNATE ⟨an ∼ expedition⟩

ill·fa·vored \-ˈfā-vərd\ *adj* : UGLY, UNATTRACTIVE

ill·got·ten \-ˈgä-tᵊn\ *adj* : acquired by improper means ⟨∼ gains⟩

ill·hu·mored \-ˈhyü-mərd, -ˈyü-\ *adj* : SURLY, IRRITABLE

il·lib·er·al \il-ˈli-bə-rəl\ *adj* : not liberal : NARROW, BIGOTED

il·lic·it \il-ˈli-sət\ *adj* : not permitted : UNLAWFUL — **il·lic·it·ly** *adv*

il·lim·it·able \il-ˈli-mə-tə-bəl\ *adj* : BOUNDLESS, MEASURELESS — **il·lim·it·ably** \-blē\ *adv*

Il·li·nois \ˌi-lə-ˈnȯi *also* -ˈnȯiz\ *n, pl* **Illinois** : a member of an American Indian people of Illinois, Iowa, and Wisconsin

il·lit·er·ate \il-ˈli-tə-rət\ *adj* 1 : having little or no education; *esp* : unable to read or write 2 : showing a lack of familiarity with the fundamentals of a particular field of knowledge — **il·lit·er·a·cy** \-ˈli-tə-rə-sē\ *n* — **illiterate** *n*

ill·man·nered \ˈil-ˈma-nərd\ *adj* : marked by bad manners : RUDE

ill·na·tured \-ˈnā-chərd\ *adj* : CROSS, SURLY — **ill·na·tured·ly** *adv*

ill·ness \ˈil-nəs\ *n* : SICKNESS

il·log·i·cal \il-ˈlä-ji-kəl\ *adj* : lacking sound reasoning; *also* : SENSELESS — **il·log·i·cal·ly** \-ji-k(ə-)lē\ *adv*

ill·starred \ˈil-ˈstärd\ *adj* : UNLUCKY 1 ⟨an ∼ venture⟩

ill·tem·pered \-ˈtem-pərd\ *adj* : CROSS

ill·treat \-ˈtrēt\ *vb* : to treat cruelly or improperly : MALTREAT — **ill·treat·ment** *n*

il·lu·mi·nate \i-ˈlü-mə-ˌnāt\ *vb* **-nat·ed; -nat·ing** 1 : to supply or brighten with light : light up 2 : to make clear : ELUCIDATE; *also* : to bring to the fore 3 : to decorate (as a manuscript) with designs or pictures in gold or colors — **il·lu·mi·nat·ing·ly** *adv* — **il·lu·mi·na·tion** \-ˌlü-mə-ˈnā-shən\ *n* — **il·lu·mi·na·tor** \-ˈlü-mə-ˌnā-tər\ *n*

il·lu·mine \i-ˈlü-mən\ *vb* **-mined; -min·ing** : ILLUMINATE

ill·us·age \ˈil-ˈyü-sij\ *n* : harsh, unkind, or abusive treatment

ill·use \-ˈyüz\ *vb* : MALTREAT, ABUSE

il·lu·sion \i-ˈlü-zhən\ *n* [ME, fr. AF, fr. LL *illusio*, fr. L, action of mocking, fr. *illudere* to mock at, fr. *ludere* to play, mock] 1 : a mistaken idea : MISCONCEPTION 2 : a misleading visual image; *also* : HALLUCINATION

il·lu·sion·ist \i-ˈlü-zhə-nist\ *n* : one that produces illusions; *esp* : a sleight-of-hand performer

il·lu·sive \i-ˈlü-siv\ *adj* : DECEPTIVE

il·lu·so·ry \i-ˈlü-sə-rē, -zə-\ *adj* : DECEPTIVE ⟨∼ hopes⟩

illust *or* **illus** *abbr* illustrated; illustration

il·lus·trate \ˈi-ləs-ˌtrāt\ *vb* **-trat·ed; -trat·ing** [L *illustrare*, fr. *lustrare* to purify, make bright] 1 : to explain by use of examples : CLARIFY; *also* : DEMONSTRATE 2 : to provide with pictures or figures that explain or decorate 3 : to serve to explain or decorate — **il·lus·tra·tor** \ˈi-lə-ˌstrā-tər\ *n*

il·lus·tra·tion \ˌi-lə-ˈstrā-shən\ *n* 1 : the act of illustrating : the condition of being illustrated 2 : an example or instance that helps make something clear 3 : a picture or diagram that explains or decorates

il·lus·tra·tive \i-ˈləs-trə-tiv, ˈi-lə-ˌstrā-\ *adj* : serving, tending, or designed to illustrate — **il·lus·tra·tive·ly** *adv*

il·lus·tri·ous \i-ˈləs-trē-əs\ *adj* : notably outstanding because of rank or achievement ✦ *Synonyms* DISTINGUISHED, EMINENT, FAMOUS, GREAT, NOTABLE, PROMINENT — **il·lus·tri·ous·ness** *n*

ill will *n* : unfriendly feeling

ILS *abbr* instrument landing system

¹im·age \ˈi-mij\ *n* 1 : a likeness or imitation of a person or thing; *esp* : STATUE 2 : a picture of an object formed by a device (as a mirror or lens) 3 : a visual representation of something ⟨a computer ∼⟩ 4 a person strikingly like another person ⟨he is the ∼ of his father⟩ 5 : a mental picture or conception : IMPRESSION, IDEA, CONCEPT 6 : a vivid representation or description

²image *vb* **im·aged; im·ag·ing** 1 : to call up a mental picture of 2 : to describe or portray in words 3 : to create a representation of 4 : REFLECT, MIRROR 5 : to make appear : PROJECT

im·ag·ery \ˈi-mij-rē\ *n, pl* **-er·ies** 1 : IMAGES; *also* : the art of making images 2 : figurative language 3 : mental images; *esp* : the products of imagination

imag·in·able \i-ˈma-jə-nə-bəl\ *adj* : capable of being imagined : CONCEIVABLE — **imag·in·ably** *adv*

imag·i·nary \i-ˈma-jə-ˌner-ē\ *adj* 1 : existing only in the imagination 2 : containing or relating to a quantity (**imaginary unit**) that is the positive square root of minus 1 ($\sqrt{-1}$)

imaginary number *n* : a complex number (as $2 + 3i$) with a nonzero term (**imaginary part**) containing the imaginary unit as a factor

imag·i·na·tion \i-ˌma-jə-ˈnā-shən\ *n* 1 : the act or power of forming a mental image of something not present to the senses or not previously known or experienced 2 : creative ability 3 : RESOURCEFULNESS 4 : a mental image : a creation of the mind — **imag·i·na·tive** \i-ˈma-jə-nə-tiv, -ˌnā-\ *adj* — **imag·i·na·tive·ly** *adv*

imag·ine \i-ˈma-jən\ *vb* **imag·ined; imag·in·ing** 1 : to form a mental picture of something not present 2 : THINK, GUESS ⟨I ∼ it will rain⟩

imag·in·ings \-ˈmaj-niŋz, -ˈma-jə-\ *n pl* : products of the imagination

im·ag·ism \ˈi-mi-ˌji-zəm\ *n, often cap* : a movement in poetry advocating free verse and the expression of ideas and emotions through clear precise images — **im·ag·ist** \-jist\ *n*

ima·go \i-ˈmā-gō, -ˈmä-\ *n, pl* **imagoes** *or* **ima·gi·nes** \-ˈmä-gə-ˌnēz, -ˈmä-\ [NL, fr. L, image] : an insect in its final adult stage — **ima·gi·nal** \i-ˈmä-gə-nᵊl, -ˈmä-\ *adj*

im·bal·ance \ˈim-ˈba-ləns\ *n* : lack of balance : the state of being out of equilibrium or out of proportion

im·be·cile \ˈim-bə-səl, -ˌsil\ *n* 1 *usu offensive* : a person affected with moderate mental retardation 2 : FOOL, IDIOT — **imbecile** *or* **im·be·cil·ic** \ˌim-bə-ˈsi-lik\ *adj* — **im·be·cil·i·ty** \ˌim-bə-ˈsi-lə-tē\ *n*

imbed *var of* EMBED

im·bibe \im-ˈbīb\ *vb* **im·bibed; im·bib·ing** 1 : to receive and retain in the mind 2 : to drink alcoholic beverages 3 : to take in or up : ABSORB — **im·bib·er** *n*

im·bri·ca·tion \ˌim-brə-ˈkā-shən\ *n* 1 : an overlapping of edges (as of tiles) 2 : a pattern showing imbrication — **im·bri·cate** \ˈim-bri-kət\ *adj*

im·bro·glio \im-ˈbrōl-yō\ *n, pl* **-glios** [It, fr. *imbrogliare* to entangle] 1 : a confused mass 2 : a complicated situation; *also* : a serious or embarrassing misunderstanding

im·brue \im-ˈbrü\ *vb* **im·brued; im·bru·ing** : STAIN ⟨*imbrued* with blood⟩

im·bue \-ˈbyü\ *vb* **im·bued; im·bu·ing** 1 : to permeate or influence as if by dyeing 2 : to tinge or dye deeply

IMF *abbr* International Monetary Fund

imit *abbr* imitative

im·i·ta·ble \ˈi-mə-tə-bəl\ *adj* : capable or worthy of being imitated or copied

im·i·tate \ˈi-mə-ˌtāt\ *vb* **-tat·ed; -tat·ing** 1 : to follow as a model : COPY 2 : RESEMBLE 3 : REPRODUCE 4 : MIMIC, COUNTERFEIT — **im·i·ta·tor** \-ˌtā-tər\ *n*

im·i·ta·tion \ˌi-mə-ˈtā-shən\ *n* 1 : an act of imitating 2 : COPY, COUNTERFEIT 3 : a literary work that reproduces the style of another author — **imitation** *adj*

im·i·ta·tive \ˈi-mə-ˌtā-tiv\ *adj* 1 : marked by imitation 2 : inclined to imitate 3 : COUNTERFEIT

im·mac·u·late \i-ˈma-kyə-lət\ *adj* 1 : being without stain or blemish : PURE 2 : spotlessly clean ⟨∼ linen⟩ — **im·mac·u·late·ly** *adv*

im·ma·nent \ˈi-mə-nənt\ *adj* 1 : INHERENT 2 : being within the limits of experience or knowledge — **im·ma·nence** \-nəns\ *n* — **im·ma·nen·cy** \-nən-sē\ *n*

im·ma·te·ri·al \ˌi-mə-ˈtir-ē-əl\ *adj* 1 : not consisting of matter : SPIRITUAL 2 : UNIMPORTANT, TRIFLING ✦ *Synonyms* BODILESS, DISEMBODIED, INCORPOREAL, INSUB-

STANTIAL, NONPHYSICAL — **im·ma·te·ri·al·i·ty** \-ˌtir-ē-'a-lə-tē\ *n*

im·ma·ture \ˌi-mə-'tür, -'tyür\ *adj* : lacking complete development : not yet mature — **im·ma·tu·ri·ty** \-'tür-ə-tē, -'tyür-\ *n*

im·mea·sur·able \(ˌ)i-'me-zhə-rə-bəl\ *adj* : not capable of being measured : indefinitely extensive : ILLIMITABLE — **im·mea·sur·ably** \-blē\ *adv*

im·me·di·a·cy \i-'mē-dē-ə-sē\ *n, pl* **-cies** 1 : the quality or state of being immediate 2 : something that is of immediate importance

im·me·di·ate \i-'mē-dē-ət\ *adj* 1 : acting directly and alone : DIRECT ⟨the ∼ cause of death⟩ 2 : being next in line or relation ⟨members of the ∼ family⟩ 3 : not distant : CLOSE 4 : made or done at once ⟨an ∼ response⟩ 5 : near to or related to the present time ⟨the ∼ future⟩ — **im·me·di·ate·ly** *adv*

im·me·mo·ri·al \ˌi-mə-'mòr-ē-əl\ *adj* : extending beyond the reach of memory, record, or tradition

im·mense \i-'mens\ *adj* [ME, fr. MF, fr. L *immensus* immeasurable, fr. *mensus,* pp. of *metiri* to measure] 1 : very great in size or degree : VAST, HUGE 2 : EXCELLENT — **im·mense·ly** *adv* — **im·men·si·ty** \-'men-sə-tē\ *n*

im·merse \i-'mərs\ *vb* **im·mersed; im·mers·ing** 1 : to plunge or dip esp. into a fluid 2 : ENGROSS, ABSORB 3 : to baptize by immersing — **im·mer·sion** \-'mər-zhən\ *n*

im·mi·grant \'i-mi-grənt\ *n* 1 : a person who immigrates 2 : a plant or animal that becomes established where it did not previously occur

im·mi·grate \'i-mə-ˌgrāt\ *vb* **-grat·ed; -grat·ing** : to come into a foreign country and take up residence — **im·mi·gra·tion** \ˌi-mə-'grā-shən\ *n*

im·mi·nent \'i-mə-nənt\ *adj* : ready to take place; *esp* : hanging threateningly over one's head — **im·mi·nence** \-nəns\ *n* — **im·mi·nent·ly** *adv*

im·mis·ci·ble \(ˌ)i-'mi-sə-bəl\ *adj* : incapable of mixing — **im·mis·ci·bil·i·ty** \-ˌmi-sə-'bi-lə-tē\ *n*

im·mis·er·a·tion \(ˌ)i-ˌmi-zə-'rā-shən\ *n* : IMPOVERISHMENT

im·mo·bile \(ˌ)i-'mō-bəl\ *adj* : incapable of being moved : FIXED — **im·mo·bil·i·ty** \ˌi-mō-'bi-lə-tē\ *n*

im·mo·bi·lize \i-'mō-bə-ˌlīz\ *vb* : to make immobile — **im·mo·bi·li·za·tion** \i-ˌmō-bə-lə-'zā-shən\ *n*

im·mod·er·ate \(ˌ)i-'mä-də-rət\ *adj* : lacking in moderation : EXCESSIVE — **im·mod·er·a·cy** \-rə-sē\ *n* — **im·mod·er·ate·ly** *adv*

im·mod·est \(ˌ)i-'mä-dəst\ *adj* : not modest : BRAZEN, INDECENT ⟨an ∼ dress⟩ ⟨∼ conduct⟩ — **im·mod·est·ly** *adv* — **im·mod·es·ty** \-də-stē\ *n*

im·mo·late \'i-mə-ˌlāt\ *vb* **-lat·ed; -lat·ing** [L *immolare,* to sprinkle with meal before sacrificing, sacrifice, fr. *mola* sacrificial barley cake, lit., millstone] : to offer in sacrifice; *esp* : to kill as a sacrificial victim — **im·mo·la·tion** \ˌi-mə-'lā-shən\ *n*

im·mor·al \(ˌ)i-'mòr-əl\ *adj* : not moral — **im·mor·al·ly** *adv*

im·mo·ral·i·ty \ˌi-mò-'ra-lə-tē, ˌi-mə-\ *n* 1 : WICKEDNESS; *esp* : UNCHASTITY 2 : an immoral act or practice

¹im·mor·tal \(ˌ)i-'mòr-tᵊl\ *adj* 1 : not mortal : exempt from death ⟨∼ gods⟩ 2 : destined to be remembered forever ⟨those ∼ words⟩ — **im·mor·tal·ly** *adv*

²immortal *n* 1 : one exempt from death 2 *pl, often cap* : the gods in Greek and Roman mythology 3 : a person whose fame is lasting ⟨an ∼ of baseball⟩

im·mor·tal·ise *Brit var of* IMMORTALIZE

im·mor·tal·i·ty \ˌi-ˌmòr-'ta-lə-tē\ *n* : the quality or state of being immortal; *esp* : unending existence

im·mor·tal·ize \i-'mòr-tᵊ-ˌlīz\ *vb* **-ized; -iz·ing** : to make immortal

im·mov·able \(ˌ)i-'mü-və-bəl\ *adj* 1 : firmly fixed, settled, or fastened : FAST, STATIONARY ⟨∼ mountains⟩ 2 : STEADFAST, UNYIELDING 3 : IMPASSIVE — **im·mov·abil·i·ty** \-ˌmü-və-'bi-lə-tē\ *n* — **im·mov·ably** \-blē\ *adv*

im·mune \i-'myün\ *adj* : EXEMPT 2 : having a special capacity for resistance (as to a disease) 3 : containing or producing antibodies — **im·mu·ni·ty** \-'myü-nə-tē\ *n*

immune response *n* : a response of the body to an antigen resulting in the formation of antibodies and cells designed to react with the antigen and render it harmless

immune system *n* : the bodily system that protects the body from foreign substances, cells, and tissues by pro-ducing the immune response and that includes esp. the thymus, spleen, lymph nodes, and lymphocytes

im·mu·nize \'i-myə-ˌnīz\ *vb* **-nized; -niz·ing** : to make immune — **im·mu·ni·za·tion** \ˌi-myə-nə-'zā-shən\ *n*

im·mu·no·de·fi·cien·cy \ˌi-myə-nō-di-'fi-shən-sē\ *n* : inability to produce the normal number of antibodies or immunologically sensitized cells esp. in response to specific antigens — **im·mu·no·de·fi·cient** \-'fi-shənt\ *adj*

im·mu·no·glob·u·lin \ˌi-myə-nō-'glä-byə-lən\ *n* : ANTIBODY

im·mu·nol·o·gy \ˌi-myə-'nä-lə-jē\ *n* : a science that deals with the immune system, immunity, and the immune response — **im·mu·no·log·ic** \-nə-'lä-jik\ *or* **im·mu·no·log·i·cal** \-ji-kəl\ *adj* — **im·mu·no·log·i·cal·ly** \-ji-k(ə-)lē\ *adv* — **im·mu·nol·o·gist** \-'nä-lə-jist\ *n*

im·mu·no·sup·pres·sion \ˌi-myə-nō-sə-'pre-shən\ *n* : suppression (as by drugs) of natural immune responses — **im·mu·no·sup·press** \-'pres\ *vb* — **im·mu·no·sup·pres·sant** \-'pre-sᵊnt\ *n or adj* — **im·mu·no·sup·pres·sive** \-'pre-siv\ *adj*

im·mu·no·ther·a·py \-'ther-ə-pē\ *n* : the treatment or prevention of disease by attempting to induce immunity

im·mure \i-'myür\ *vb* **im·mured; im·mur·ing** 1 : to enclose within or as if within walls 2 : to build into a wall; *esp* : to entomb in a wall

im·mu·ta·ble \(ˌ)i-'myü-tə-bəl\ *adj* : UNCHANGEABLE, UNCHANGING — **im·mu·ta·bil·i·ty** \-ˌmyü-tə-'bi-lə-tē\ *n* — **im·mu·ta·bly** \-'myü-tə-blē\ *adv*

¹imp \'imp\ *n* 1 : a small demon : FIEND 2 : a mischievous child

²imp *abbr* 1 imperative 2 imperfect 3 imperial 4 import; imported

¹im·pact \im-'pakt\ *vb* 1 : to press together 2 : to have an impact on

²im·pact \'im-ˌpakt\ *n* 1 : a forceful contact, collision, or onset; *also* : the impetus communicated in or as if in a collision 2 : EFFECT

im·pact·ed \im-'pak-təd\ *adj* 1 : packed or wedged in 2 : wedged between the jawbone and another tooth

im·pair \im-'per\ *vb* : to diminish in quantity, value, excellence, or strength : DAMAGE, LESSEN — **im·pair·ment** *n*

im·paired \-'pard\ *adj* : being in a less than perfect or whole condition; *esp* : disabled or functionally defective — often used in combination ⟨hearing-*impaired*⟩

im·pa·la \im-'pa-lə\ *n, pl* **impalas** *or* **impala** : a large brownish African antelope that in the male has slender curved horns with ridges

im·pale \im-'pāl\ *vb* **im·paled; im·pal·ing** : to pierce with or as if with something pointed — **im·pale·ment** *n*

im·pal·pa·ble \(ˌ)im-'pal-pə-bəl\ *adj* 1 : unable to be felt by touch : INTANGIBLE 2 : not easily seen or understood — **im·pal·pa·bly** \-blē\ *adv*

im·pan·el *or* **em·pan·el** *vb* : to enter in or on a panel : ENROLL ⟨∼ a jury⟩

im·part \im-'pärt\ *vb* 1 : to give from one's store or abundance ⟨the sun ∼s warmth⟩ 2 : to make known

im·par·tial \(ˌ)im-'pär-shəl\ *adj* : not partial : UNBIASED, JUST — **im·par·tial·i·ty** \-ˌpär-shē-'a-lə-tē\ *n* — **im·par·tial·ly** *adv*

im·pass·able \(ˌ)im-'pa-sə-bəl\ *adj* : incapable of being passed, traversed, or crossed ⟨∼ roads⟩ — **im·pass·ably** \-blē\ *adv*

im·passe \'im-ˌpas\ *n* 1 : a predicament from which there is no obvious escape 2 : an impassable road or way

im·pas·si·ble \(ˌ)im-'pa-sə-bəl\ *adj* : incapable of feeling : IMPASSIVE

im·pas·sioned \im-'pa-shənd\ *adj* : filled with passion or zeal : showing great warmth or intensity of feeling ✦ **Synonyms** PASSIONATE, ARDENT, FERVENT, FERVID

im·pas·sive \(ˌ)im-'pa-siv\ *adj* : showing no signs of feeling, emotion, or interest : EXPRESSIONLESS, INDIFFERENT ✦ **Synonyms** STOIC, PHLEGMATIC, APATHETIC, STOLID — **im·pas·sive·ly** *adv* — **im·pas·siv·i·ty** \ˌim-ˌpa-'si-və-tē\ *n*

im·pas·to \im-'pas-tō, -'päs-\ *n* : the thick application of a pigment to a canvas or panel in painting; *also* : the body of pigment so applied

im·pa·tiens \im-'pā-shənz, -shəns\ *n* : any of a genus of herbs with usu. spurred flowers and seed capsules that readily split open

im·pa·tient \(ˌ)im-'pā-shənt\ *adj* 1 : not patient : restless or short of temper esp. under irritation, delay, or opposition **2** : INTOLERANT ⟨∼ of poverty⟩ **3** : prompted or marked by impatience ⟨an ∼ reply⟩ **4** : ANXIOUS — **im·pa·tience** \-shəns\ n — **im·pa·tient·ly** adv

im·peach \im-'pēch\ vb [ME empechen to accuse, fr. AF empecher, enpechier to ensnare, impede, prosecute, fr. LL impedicare to fetter, fr. L pedica fetter, fr. ped-, pes foot] **1** : to charge (a public official) before an authorized tribunal with misconduct in office **2** : to challenge the credibility or validity of **3** : to remove from public office for misconduct — **im·peach·ment** n

im·pec·ca·ble \(,)im-'pe-kə-bəl\ adj **1** : not capable of sinning or wrongdoing **2** : FAULTLESS, IRREPROACHABLE ⟨a man of ∼ character⟩ — **im·pec·ca·bil·i·ty** \-,pe-kə-'bi-lə-tē\ n — **im·pec·ca·bly** \-'pe-kə-blē\ adv

im·pe·cu·nious \,im-pi-'kyü-nyəs, -nē-əs\ adj : having little or no money — **im·pe·cu·nious·ness** n

im·ped·ance \im-'pē-dⁿns\ n : the opposition in an electrical circuit to the flow of an alternating current

im·pede \im-'pēd\ vb **im·ped·ed; im·ped·ing** [L impedire, fr. ped-, pes foot] : to interfere with the progress of

im·ped·i·ment \im-'pe-də-mənt\ n **1** : something that impedes, hinders, or obstructs **2** : a speech defect

im·ped·i·men·ta \im-,pe-də-'men-tə\ n pl : things that impede

im·pel \im-'pel\ vb **im·pelled; im·pel·ling** : to urge or drive forward or on : FORCE; also : PROPEL

im·pel·ler also **im·pel·lor** \im-'pe-lər\ n : a rotor esp. in a pump

im·pend \im-'pend\ vb **1** : to hover or hang over threateningly : MENACE **2** : to be about to occur

im·pen·e·tra·ble \(,)im-'pe-nə-trə-bəl\ adj **1** : incapable of being penetrated or pierced ⟨an ∼ jungle⟩ **2** : incapable of being comprehended : INSCRUTABLE ⟨an ∼ mystery⟩ — **im·pen·e·tra·bil·i·ty** \-,pe-nə-trə-'bi-lə-tē\ n — **im·pen·e·tra·bly** \-'pe-nə-trə-blē\ adv

im·pen·i·tent \(,)im-'pe-nə-tənt\ adj : not penitent : not repenting of sin — **im·pen·i·tence** \-təns\ n

im·per·a·tive \im-'per-ə-tiv\ adj **1** : expressing a command, request, or encouragement ⟨∼ sentence⟩ **2** : having power to restrain, control, or direct **3** : NECESSARY ⟨an ∼ duty⟩ — **imperative** n — **im·per·a·tive·ly** adv

im·per·cep·ti·ble \,im-pər-'sep-tə-bəl\ adj : not perceptible; esp : too slight to be perceived ⟨∼ changes⟩ — **im·per·cep·ti·bly** \-blē\ adv

im·per·cep·tive \,im-pər-'sep-tiv\ adj : not perceptive ⟨an ∼ reader⟩

imperf abbr imperfect

¹im·per·fect \(,)im-'pər-fikt\ adj **1** : not perfect : DEFECTIVE, INCOMPLETE **2** : of, relating to, or being a verb tense used to designate a continuing state or an incomplete action esp. in the past — **im·per·fect·ly** adv

²imperfect n : the imperfect tense; also : a verb form in it

im·per·fec·tion \,im-pər-'fek-shən\ n : the quality or state of being imperfect; also : FAULT, BLEMISH

im·pe·ri·al \im-'pir-ē-əl\ adj **1** : of, relating to, or befitting an empire or an emperor; also : of or relating to the United Kingdom or to the Commonwealth or British Empire **2** : ROYAL, SOVEREIGN; also : REGAL, IMPERIOUS **3** : of unusual size or excellence

im·pe·ri·al·ism \im-'pir-ē-ə-,li-zəm\ n : the policy of seeking to extend the power, dominion, or territories of a nation — **im·pe·ri·al·ist** \-list\ n or adj — **im·pe·ri·al·is·tic** \-,pir-ē-ə-'lis-tik\ adj — **im·pe·ri·al·is·ti·cal·ly** \-ti-k(ə-)lē\ adv

im·per·il \im-'per-əl\ vb **-iled** or **-illed; -il·ing** or **-il·ling** : ENDANGER

im·pe·ri·ous \im-'pir-ē-əs\ adj **1** : COMMANDING, LORDLY **2** : ARROGANT, DOMINEERING **3** : IMPERATIVE, URGENT ⟨∼ problems⟩ — **im·pe·ri·ous·ly** adv

im·per·ish·able \(,)im-'per-i-shə-bəl\ adj : not perishable or subject to decay

im·per·ma·nent \(,)im-'pər-mə-nənt\ adj : not permanent : TRANSIENT — **im·per·ma·nent·ly** adv

im·per·me·able \(,)im-'pər-mē-ə-bəl\ adj : not permitting passage (as of a fluid) through its substance

im·per·mis·si·ble \,im-pər-'mi-sə-bəl\ adj : not permissible

im·per·son·al \(,)im-'pər-sə-nəl\ adj **1** : not referring to any particular person or thing **2** : not involving human emotions — **im·per·son·al·i·ty** \-,pər-sə-'na-lə-tē\ n — **im·per·son·al·ly** adv

im·per·son·ate \im-'pər-sə-,nāt\ vb **-at·ed; -at·ing** : to assume or act the character of — **im·per·son·a·tion** \-,pər-sə-'nā-shən\ n — **im·per·son·a·tor** \-'pər-sə-,nā-tər\ n

im·per·ti·nent \(,)im-'pər-tə-nənt\ adj **1** : IRRELEVANT **2** : not restrained within due or proper bounds : RUDE, INSOLENT, SAUCY — **im·per·ti·nence** \-nəns\ n — **im·per·ti·nent·ly** adv

im·per·turb·able \,im-pər-'tər-bə-bəl\ adj : marked by extreme calm, impassivity, and steadiness : SERENE

im·per·vi·ous \(,)im-'pər-vē-əs\ adj **1** : incapable of being penetrated (as by moisture) **2** : not capable of being affected or disturbed ⟨∼ to criticism⟩

im·pe·ti·go \,im-pə-'tē-gō, -'tī-\ n : a contagious skin disease characterized by vesicles, pustules, and yellowish crusts

im·pet·u·ous \im-'pe-chə-wəs\ adj **1** : marked by impulsive vehemence ⟨∼ temper⟩ **2** : marked by force and violence ⟨with ∼ speed⟩ — **im·pet·u·os·i·ty** \(,)im-,pe-chə-'wä-sə-tē\ n — **im·pet·u·ous·ly** adv

im·pe·tus \'im-pə-təs\ n [L, assault, impetus, fr. impetere to attack, fr. petere to go to, seek] **1** : a driving force : IMPULSE; also : INCENTIVE **2** : MOMENTUM

im·pi·e·ty \(,)im-'pī-ə-tē\ n, pl **-ties 1** : the quality or state of being impious **2** : an impious act

im·pinge \im-'pinj\ vb **im·pinged; im·ping·ing 1** : to strike or dash esp. with a sharp collision **2** : ENCROACH, INFRINGE — **im·pinge·ment** n

im·pi·ous \'im-pē-əs, (,)im-'pī-\ adj : not pious : IRREVERENT, PROFANE

imp·ish \'im-pish\ adj : of, relating to, or befitting an imp; esp : MISCHIEVOUS — **imp·ish·ly** adv — **imp·ish·ness** n

im·pla·ca·ble \(,)im-'pla-kə-bəl, -'plā-\ adj : not capable of being appeased, pacified, mitigated, or changed ⟨an ∼ enemy⟩ — **im·pla·ca·bil·i·ty** \-,pla-kə-'bi-lə-tē, -,plā-\ n — **im·pla·ca·bly** \-'pla-kə-blē\ adv

im·plant \im-'plant\ vb **1** : to set firmly and deeply **2** : to fix in the mind or spirit **3** : to insert in living tissue (as for growth or absorption) — **im·plant** \'im-,plant\ n — **im·plan·ta·tion** \,im-,plan-'tā-shən\ n

im·plau·si·ble \(,)im-'plô-zə-bəl\ adj : not plausible — **im·plau·si·bil·i·ty** \-,plô-zə-'bi-lə-tē\ n — **im·plau·si·bly** \-'plô-zə-blē\ adv

¹im·ple·ment \'im-plə-mənt\ n [ME, fr. AF, fr. ML implementum item making a full complement, appurtenance, tool, fr. LL, act of filling up, fr. L implēre to fill up] : TOOL, UTENSIL, INSTRUMENT

²im·ple·ment \-,ment\ vb **1** : CARRY OUT; esp : to put into practice **2** : to provide implements for — **im·ple·men·ta·tion** \,im-plə-mən-'tā-shən\ n

im·pli·cate \'im-plə-,kāt\ vb **-cat·ed; -cat·ing 1** : IMPLY **2** : INVOLVE — **im·pli·ca·tion** \,im-plə-'kā-shən\ n

im·plic·it \im-'pli-sət\ adj **1** : understood though not directly stated or expressed : IMPLIED; also : POTENTIAL **2** : COMPLETE, UNQUESTIONING, ABSOLUTE ⟨∼ faith⟩ — **im·plic·it·ly** adv

im·plode \im-'plōd\ vb **im·plod·ed; im·plod·ing 1** : to burst or collapse inward **2** : SELF-DESTRUCT — **im·plo·sion** \-'plō-zhən\ n — **im·plo·sive** \-siv\ adj

im·plore \im-'plôr\ vb **im·plored; im·plor·ing** : BESEECH, ENTREAT ♦ **Synonyms** SUPPLICATE, BEG, IMPORTUNE, PLEAD

im·ply \im-'plī\ vb **im·plied; im·ply·ing 1** : to involve or indicate by inference, association, or necessary consequence rather than by direct statement ⟨war implies fighting⟩ **2** : to express indirectly : hint at : SUGGEST

im·po·lite \,im-pə-'līt\ adj : not polite : RUDE, DISCOURTEOUS

im·pol·i·tic \(,)im-'pä-lə-,tik\ adj : not politic : UNWISE

im·pon·der·a·ble \(,)im-'pän-də-rə-bəl\ adj : incapable of being weighed or evaluated with exactness — **imponderable** n

¹im·port \im-'pôrt\ vb **1** : MEAN, SIGNIFY **2** : to bring (as merchandise) into a place or country from a foreign or external source — **im·port·er** n

²im·port \'im-,pôrt\ n **1** : IMPORTANCE, SIGNIFICANCE **2** : MEANING, SIGNIFICATION **3** : something (as merchandise) brought in from another country

im·por·tance \im-'pôr-tⁿns\ n : the quality or state of being important : MOMENT, SIGNIFICANCE ♦ **Synonyms** CONSEQUENCE, IMPORT, WEIGHT

im·por·tant \im-'pȯr-t⁰nt\ *adj* **1** : marked by importance : SIGNIFICANT **2** : giving an impression of importance — **im·por·tant·ly** *adv*

im·por·ta·tion \ˌim-ˌpȯr-'tā-shən, -pər-\ *n* **1** : the act or practice of importing **2** : something imported

im·por·tu·nate \im-'pȯr-chə-nət\ *adj* **1** : troublesomely urgent or persistent **2** : BURDENSOME, TROUBLESOME

im·por·tune \ˌim-pər-'tün, -'tyün; im-'pȯr-chən\ *vb* **-tuned; -tun·ing** : to urge or beg with troublesome persistence — **im·por·tu·ni·ty** \-pər-'tü-nə-tē, -'tyü-\ *n*

im·pose \im-'pōz\ *vb* **im·posed; im·pos·ing 1** : to establish or apply by authority ⟨∼ a tax⟩; *also* : to establish by force ⟨*imposed* a government⟩ **2** : OBTRUDE ⟨*imposed* herself on others⟩ **3** : to take unwarranted advantage of something ⟨∼ on her good nature⟩ — **im·po·si·tion** \ˌimpə-'zi-shən\ *n*

im·pos·ing *adj* : impressive because of size, bearing, dignity, or grandeur — **im·pos·ing·ly** *adv*

im·pos·si·ble \(ˌ)im-'pä-sə-bəl\ *adj* **1** : incapable of being or of occurring **2** : enormously difficult **3** : extremely undesirable : UNACCEPTABLE — **im·pos·si·bil·i·ty** \-ˌpä-sə-'bi-lə-tē\ *n* — **im·pos·si·bly** \-'pä-sə-blē\ *adv*

¹im·post \'im-ˌpōst\ *n* : TAX, DUTY

²impost *n* : a block, capital, or molding from which an arch springs

im·pos·tor *or* **im·pos·ter** \im-'päs-tər\ *n* : one that assumes an identity or title not one's own in order to deceive

im·pos·ture \im-'päs-chər\ *n* : DECEPTION; *esp* : fraudulent impersonation

im·po·tent \'im-pə-tənt\ *adj* **1** : lacking in power or strength : HELPLESS **2** : unable to copulate; *also* : STERILE — **im·po·tence** \-təns\ *n* — **im·po·ten·cy** \-tən-sē\ *n* — **im·po·tent·ly** *adv*

im·pound \im-'pau̇nd\ *vb* **1** : CONFINE, ENCLOSE ⟨∼ stray dogs⟩ **2** : to seize and hold in legal custody **3** : to collect in a reservoir ⟨∼ water⟩ — **im·pound·ment** *n*

im·pov·er·ish \im-'pä-və-rish\ *vb* : to make poor; *also* : to deprive of strength, richness, or fertility — **im·pov·er·ish·ment** *n*

im·prac·ti·ca·ble \(ˌ)im-'prak-ti-kə-bəl\ *adj* : not practicable : incapable of being put into practice or use

im·prac·ti·cal \(ˌ)im-'prak-ti-kəl\ *adj* **1** : not practical **2** : IMPRACTICABLE

im·pre·cate \'im-pri-ˌkāt\ *vb* **-cat·ed; -cat·ing** : CURSE — **im·pre·ca·tion** \ˌim-pri-'kā-shən\ *n*

im·pre·cise \ˌim-pri-'sīs\ *adj* : not precise — **im·pre·cise·ly** *adv* — **im·pre·cise·ness** *n* — **im·pre·ci·sion** \-'si-zhən\ *n*

im·preg·na·ble \im-'preg-nə-bəl\ *adj* : incapable of being taken by assault : UNCONQUERABLE, UNASSAILABLE — **im·preg·na·bil·i·ty** \(ˌ)im-ˌpreg-nə-'bi-lə-tē\ *n*

im·preg·nate \im-'preg-ˌnāt\ *vb* **-nat·ed; -nat·ing 1** : to fertilize or make pregnant **2** : to cause to be filled, permeated, or saturated — **im·preg·na·tion** \ˌim-ˌpreg-'nā-shən\ *n*

im·pre·sa·rio \ˌim-prə-'sär-ē-ˌō\ *n, pl* **-ri·os** [It, fr. *impresa* undertaking, fr. *imprendere* to undertake] **1** : the manager or conductor of an opera or concert company **2** : one who puts on an entertainment **3** : MANAGER, PRODUCER

¹im·press \im-'pres\ *vb* **1** : to apply with or produce (as a mark) by pressure : IMPRINT **2** : to press, stamp, or print in or upon **3** : to produce a vivid impression of **4** : to affect esp. forcibly or deeply — **im·press·ible** *adj*

²im·press \'im-ˌpres\ *n* **1** : a characteristic or distinctive mark **2** : IMPRESSION, EFFECT **3** : an impression or image of something formed by or as if by pressure; *also* : a product of pressure or influence

³im·press \im-'pres\ *vb* **1** : to force into naval service **2** : to get the aid or services of by forcible argument or persuasion — **im·press·ment** *n*

im·pres·sion \im-'pre-shən\ *n* **1** : a characteristic trait or feature resulting from influence : IMPRESS **2** : IMPRINT **3** : an esp. marked influence or effect on feeling, sense, or mind **4** : a single print or copy (as from type or from an engraved plate or book) **5** : all the copies of a publication (as a book) printed for one issue : PRINTING **6** : a usu. vague notion or remembrance **7** : an imitation in caricature of a noted personality as a form of entertainment

im·pres·sion·able \im-'pre-shə-nə-bəl\ *adj* : capable of being easily impressed : easily molded or influenced

im·pres·sion·ism \im-'pre-shə-ˌni-zəm\ *n, often cap* : a theory or practice in modern art of depicting the natural appearances of objects by dabs or strokes of primary unmixed colors in order to simulate actual reflected light — **im·pres·sion·is·tic** \-ˌpre-shə-'nis-tik\ *adj*

im·pres·sion·ist \im-'pre-shə-nist\ *n* **1** *often cap* : a painter who practices impressionism **2** : an entertainer who does impressions

im·pres·sive \im-'pre-siv\ *adj* : making or tending to make a marked impression ⟨an ∼ speech⟩ — **im·pres·sive·ly** *adv* — **im·pres·sive·ness** *n*

im·pri·ma·tur \ˌim-prə-'mä-ˌtu̇r\ *n* [NL, let it be printed] **1** : a license to print or publish; *also* : official approval of a publication by a censor **2** : SANCTION, APPROVAL

¹im·print \im-'print, 'im-ˌprint\ *vb* **1** : to stamp or mark by or as if by pressure : IMPRESS **2** : to fix firmly (as on the memory)

²im·print \'im-ˌprint\ *n* **1** : something imprinted or printed **2** : a publisher's name printed at the foot of a title page **3** : an indelible distinguishing effect or influence

im·pris·on \im-'pri-z⁰n\ *vb* : to put in or as if in prison : CONFINE — **im·pris·on·ment** *n*

im·prob·a·ble \(ˌ)im-'prä-bə-bəl\ *adj* : unlikely to be true or to occur — **im·prob·a·bil·i·ty** \ˌprä-bə-'bi-lə-tē\ *n* — **im·prob·a·bly** \-'prä-bə-blē\ *adv*

im·promp·tu \im-'prämp-tü, -tyü\ *adj* [F, fr. *impromptu* extemporaneously, fr. L *in promptu* in readiness] **1** : made or done on or as if on the spur of the moment **2** : EXTEMPORANEOUS, UNREHEARSED ⟨an ∼ speech⟩ — **impromptu** *adv or n*

im·prop·er \(ˌ)im-'prä-pər\ *adj* **1** : not proper, fit, or suitable **2** : INCORRECT, INACCURATE **3** : not in accord with propriety, modesty, or good manners — **im·prop·er·ly** *adv*

improper fraction *n* : a fraction whose numerator is equal to or larger than the denominator

im·pro·pri·e·ty \ˌim-prə-'prī-ə-tē\ *n, pl* **-ties 1** : an improper act or remark; *esp* : an unacceptable use of a word or of language **2** : the quality or state of being improper

im·prove \im-'prüv\ *vb* **im·proved; im·prov·ing 1** : to enhance or increase in value or quality **2** : to grow or become better ⟨your work is *improving*⟩ **3** : to make good use of ⟨∼ the time by reading⟩ — **im·prov·able** \-'prü-və-bəl\ *adj*

im·prove·ment \im-'prüv-mənt\ *n* **1** : the act or process of improving **2** : increased value or excellence of something **3** : something that adds to the value or appearance of a thing

im·prov·i·dent \(ˌ)im-'prä-və-dənt\ *adj* : not providing for the future — **im·prov·i·dence** \-dəns\ *n*

im·pro·vise \'im-prə-ˌvīz\ *vb* **-vised; -vis·ing** [F *improviser*, fr. It *improvvisare*, fr. *improvviso* sudden, fr. L *improvisus*, lit., unforeseen] **1** : to compose, recite, play, or sing on the spur of the moment : EXTEMPORIZE ⟨∼ on the piano⟩ **2** : to make, invent, or arrange offhand ⟨∼ a sail out of shirts⟩ — **im·pro·vi·sa·tion** \im-ˌprä-və-'zā-shən, ˌim-prə-və-\ *n* — **im·pro·vis·er** *or* **im·pro·vi·sor** \ˌim-prə-'vī-zər, 'im-prə-ˌvī-\ *n*

im·pru·dent \(ˌ)im-'prü-d⁰nt\ *adj* : not prudent : lacking discretion, wisdom, or good judgement — **im·pru·dence** \-d⁰ns\ *n* — **im·pru·dent·ly** *adv*

im·pu·dent \'im-pyü-dənt\ *adj* : marked by contemptuous boldness or disregard of others — **im·pu·dence** \-dəns\ *n* — **im·pu·dent·ly** *adv*

im·pugn \im-'pyün\ *vb* [ME, to assail, fr. AF *empugner*, fr. L *inpugnare*, fr. *pugnare* to fight] : to attack by words or arguments : oppose or attack as false or as lacking integrity

im·pu·is·sance \im-'pwi-s⁰ns, -'pyü-ə-səns\ *n* [ME, fr. MF] : the quality or state of being powerless : WEAKNESS

im·pulse \'im-ˌpəls\ *n* **1** : a force that starts a body into motion; *also* : the motion produced by such a force **2** : an arousing of the mind and spirit to some usu. unpremeditated action **3** : NERVE IMPULSE

im·pul·sion \im-'pəl-shən\ *n* **1** : the act of impelling : the state of being impelled **2** : a force that impels **3** : IMPULSE 2; *also* : COMPULSION 3

im·pul·sive \im-'pəl-siv\ *adj* **1** : having the power of or actually driving or impelling **2** : arising from or prone to act on impulse — **im·pul·sive·ly** *adv* — **im·pul·sive·ness** *n*

im·pu·ni·ty \im-'pyü-nə-tē\ *n* [MF or L; MF *impunité*, fr. L *impunitas*, fr. *impune* without punishment, fr. *poena* penalty, punishment] : exemption from punishment, harm, or loss

im·pure \(,)im-'pyür\ *adj* **1** : not pure : UNCHASTE, OBSCENE **2** : DIRTY, FOUL ⟨~ water⟩ **3** : ADULTERATED, MIXED — **im·pu·ri·ty** \-'pyür-ə-tē\ *n*

im·pute \im-'pyüt\ *vb* **im·put·ed; im·put·ing 1** : to lay the responsibility or blame for often falsely or unjustly **2** : to credit to a person or a cause : ATTRIBUTE — **im·put·able** \-'pyü-tə-bəl\ *adj* — **im·pu·ta·tion** \,im-pyü-'tā-shən\ *n*

¹in \'in\ *prep* **1** — used to indicate physical surroundings ⟨swim ~ the lake⟩ **2** : INTO 1 ⟨ran ~ the house⟩ **3** : DURING ⟨~ the summer⟩ **4** : WITH ⟨written ~ pencil⟩ **5** — used to indicate one's situation or state of being ⟨~ luck⟩ ⟨~ love⟩ **6** — used to indicate manner or purpose ⟨~ a hurry⟩ ⟨said ~ reply⟩ **7** : INTO 2 ⟨broke ~ pieces⟩

²in *adv* **1** : to or toward the inside ⟨come ~⟩; *also* : to or toward some destination or place ⟨flew ~ from the South⟩ **2** : at close quarters : NEAR ⟨the enemy closed ~⟩ **3** : into the midst of something ⟨mix ~ the flour⟩ **4** : to or at its proper place ⟨fit a piece ~⟩ **5** : WITHIN ⟨locked ~⟩ **6** : in vogue or season **7** : in one's presence, possession, or control ⟨the results are ~⟩

³in *adj* **1** : located inside or within **2** : that is in position, operation, or power ⟨the ~ party⟩ **3** : directed inward : INCOMING ⟨the ~ train⟩ **4** : keenly aware of and responsive to what is new and fashionable ⟨the ~ crowd⟩; *also* : extremely fashionable ⟨the ~ thing to do⟩

⁴in *n* **1** : one who is in office or power or on the inside **2** : INFLUENCE, PULL ⟨he has an ~ with the owner⟩

⁵in *abbr* **1** inch **2** inlet

In *symbol* indium

IN *abbr* Indiana

in- \(,)in\ *prefix* : not : absence of : NON-, UN-

inaccessibility	indecipherable
inaccessible	indemonstrable
inaccuracy	indestructible
inaccurate	indeterminable
inaction	indiscernible
inactive	indistinguishable
inactivity	inedible
inadmissibility	ineducable
inadmissible	ineffaceable
inadvisability	inefficacious
inadvisable	inefficacy
inapparent	inelastic
inapplicable	inelasticity
inapposite	inequitable
inapproachable	inequity
inappropriate	ineradicable
inaptitude	inerrant
inarguable	inexpedient
inartistic	inexpensive
inattentive	inexpressive
inaudible	inextinguishable
inaudibly	infeasible
inauspicious	inharmonious
inauthentic	inhospitable
incautious	injudicious
incombustible	inoffensive
incomprehension	insanitary
inconclusive	insensitive
incongruent	insensitivity
inconsistency	insignificance
inconsistent	insignificant
incoordination	insolvable
incurious	insusceptible

in·abil·i·ty \,i-nə-'bi-lə-tē\ *n* : the quality or state of being unable

in ab·sen·tia \in-ab-'sen-chə, -chē-ə\ *adv* : in one's absence

in·ac·ti·vate \(,)i-'nak-tə-,vāt\ *vb* : to make inactive — **in·ac·ti·va·tion** \(,)i-,nak-tə-'vā-shən\ *n*

in·ad·e·quate \(,)i-'na-di-kwət\ *adj* : not adequate : INSUFFICIENT — **in·ad·e·qua·cy** \-kwə-sē\ *n* — **in·ad·e·quate·ly** *adv* — **in·ad·e·quate·ness** *n*

in·ad·ver·tent \,i-nəd-'vər-t²nt\ *adj* **1** : HEEDLESS, INATTENTIVE **2** : UNINTENTIONAL ⟨an ~ omission⟩ — **in·ad·ver·tence** \-t²ns\ *n* — **in·ad·ver·ten·cy** \-t²n-sē\ *n* — **in·ad·ver·tent·ly** *adv*

in·alien·able \(,)i-'nāl-yə-nə-bəl, -'nā-lē-ə-\ *adj* : incapable of being alienated, surrendered, or transferred ⟨~ rights⟩ — **in·alien·abil·i·ty** \(,)i-,nāl-yə-nə-'bi-lə-tē, -,nā-lē-ə-\ *n* — **in·alien·ably** *adv*

in·amo·ra·ta \i-,nä-mə-'rä-tə\ *n* : a woman with whom one is in love

inane \i-'nān\ *adj* **inan·er; -est** : EMPTY, INSUBSTANTIAL; *also* : SHALLOW, SILLY ⟨~ comments⟩ — **inane·ly** *adv* — **inan·i·ty** \i-'na-nə-tē\ *n*

in·an·i·mate \(,)i-'na-nə-mət\ *adj* : not animate or animated : lacking the qualities of living things — **in·an·i·mate·ly** *adv* — **in·an·i·mate·ness** *n*

in·ap·pre·cia·ble \,i-nə-'prē-shə-bəl\ *adj* : too small to be perceived — **in·ap·pre·cia·bly** \-blē\ *adv*

in·apt \i-'napt\ *adj* **1** : not suitable **2** : INEPT — **in·apt·ly** *adv* — **in·apt·ness** *n*

in·ar·tic·u·late \,i-när-'ti-kyə-lət\ *adj* **1** : not understandable as spoken words **2** : MUTE **3** : incapable of being expressed by speech ⟨~ fear⟩; *also* : UNSPOKEN **4** : not having the power of distinct utterance or effective expression — **in·ar·tic·u·late·ly** *adv*

in·as·much as \,i-nəz-'məch-\ *conj* : seeing that : SINCE

in·at·ten·tion \,i-nə-'ten-chən\ *n* : failure to pay attention : DISREGARD — **in·at·ten·tive** \-'ten-tiv\ *adj*

¹in·au·gu·ral \i-'nȯ-gyə-rəl, -gə-\ *adj* **1** : of or relating to an inauguration **2** : marking a beginning

²inaugural *n* **1** : an inaugural address **2** : INAUGURATION

in·au·gu·rate \i-'nȯ-gyə-,rāt, -gə-\ *vb* **-rat·ed; -rat·ing 1** : to introduce into an office with suitable ceremonies : INSTALL **2** : to dedicate ceremoniously **3** : BEGIN, INITIATE — **in·au·gu·ra·tion** \-,nȯ-gyə-'rā-shən, -gə-\ *n*

in·board \'in-,bȯrd\ *adv* **1** : inside the hull of a ship **2** : close or closest to the center line of a vehicle or craft — **inboard** *adj*

in·born \'in-'bȯrn\ *adj* **1** : present from or as if from birth **2** : HEREDITARY, INHERITED ♦ *Synonyms* INNATE, CONGENITAL, NATIVE

in·bound \'in-,baůnd\ *adj* : inward bound ⟨~ traffic⟩

in·box \'in-,bäks\ *n* : a receptacle for incoming interoffice letters; *also* : a computer folder for incoming e-mail

in·bred \'in-'bred\ *adj* **1** : ingrained in one's nature as deeply as if by heredity **2** : subjected to or produced by inbreeding

in·breed·ing \'in-,brē-diŋ\ *n* **1** : the interbreeding of closely related individuals esp. to preserve and fix desirable characters of and to eliminate unfavorable characters from a stock **2** : confinement to a narrow range or a local or limited field of choice — **in·breed** \-'brēd\ *vb*

inc *abbr* **1** incomplete **2** incorporated **3** increase

In·ca \'iŋ-kə\ *n* [Sp, fr. Quechua *inka* ruler of the Inca empire] **1** : a noble or a member of the ruling family of an Indian empire of Peru, Bolivia, and Ecuador until the Spanish conquest **2** : a member of any people under Inca influence

in·cal·cu·la·ble \(,)in-'kal-kyə-lə-bəl\ *adj* **1** : not capable of being calculated; *esp* : very great **2** : not predictable — **in·cal·cu·la·bly** \-blē\ *adv*

in·can·des·cent \,in-kən-'de-s²nt\ *adj* **1** : glowing with heat **2** : SHINING, BRILLIANT — **in·can·des·cence** \-s²ns\ *n*

incandescent lamp *n* : LIGHT BULB 1

in·can·ta·tion \,in-,kan-'tā-shən\ *n* : a use of spells or verbal charms spoken or sung as a part of a ritual of magic; *also* : a formula of words used in or as if in such a ritual

in·ca·pa·ble \(,)in-'kā-pə-bəl\ *adj* : lacking ability or qualification for a particular purpose; *also* : UNQUALIFIED — **in·ca·pa·bil·i·ty** \-,kā-pə-'bi-lə-tē\ *n*

in·ca·pac·i·tate \,in-kə-'pa-sə-,tāt\ *vb* **-tat·ed; -tat·ing** : to make incapable or unfit

in·ca·pac·i·ty \,in-kə-'pa-sə-tē\ *n, pl* **-ties** : the quality or state of being incapable

in·car·cer·ate \in-'kär-sə-,rāt\ *vb* **-at·ed; -at·ing** : IMPRISON, CONFINE — **in·car·cer·a·tion** \(,)in-,kär-sə-'rā-shən\ *n*

in·car·na·dine \in-'kär-nə-,dīn, -,dēn\ *vb* **-dined; -din·ing** : REDDEN

in·car·nate \in-'kär-nət, -,nāt\ *adj* **1** : having bodily and esp. human form and substance **2** : PERSONIFIED — **in·car·nate** \-,nāt\ *vb*

in·car·na·tion \,in-,kär-'nā-shən\ *n* **1** : the embodiment of a deity or spirit in an earthly form **2** *cap* : the union of divine and human natures in Jesus Christ **3** : a person showing a trait or typical character to a marked degree **4** : the act of incarnating : the state of being incarnate

in·cen·di·ary \in-'sen-dē-ˌer-ē\ *adj* **1** : of or relating to a deliberate burning of property **2** : tending to excite or inflame **3** : designed to start fires ⟨an ~ bomb⟩ — **incendiary** *n*

1in·cense \'in-ˌsens\ *n* **1** : material used to produce a fragrant odor when burned **2** : the perfume or smoke from some spices and gums when burned

2in·cense \in-'sens\ *vb* **in·censed; in·cens·ing** : to make extremely angry

in·cen·tive \in-'sen-tiv\ *n* [ME, fr. LL *incentivum,* fr. *incentivus* stimulating, fr. L, setting the tune, fr. *incinere* to play (a tune), fr. *canere* to sing] : something that incites or is likely to incite to determination or action

in·cep·tion \in-'sep-shən\ *n* : BEGINNING, COMMENCEMENT

in·cer·ti·tude \(ˌ)in-'sər-tə-ˌtüd, -ˌtyüd\ *n* **1** : UNCERTAINTY, DOUBT, INDECISION **2** : INSECURITY, INSTABILITY

in·ces·sant \(ˌ)in-'se-sᵊnt\ *adj* : continuing or flowing without interruption ⟨~ rains⟩ — **in·ces·sant·ly** *adv*

in·cest \'in-ˌsest\ *n* [ME, fr. L *incestus* sexual impurity, fr. *incestus* impure, fr. *castus* pure] : sexual intercourse between persons so closely related that marriage is illegal — **in·ces·tu·ous** \in-'ses-chü-wəs\ *adj*

1inch \'inch\ *n* [ME, fr. OE *ynce,* fr. L *uncia* twelfth part, inch, ounce] — see WEIGHT table

2inch *vb* : to move by small degrees

in·cho·ate \in-'kō-ət, 'in-kə-ˌwāt\ *adj* : being only partly in existence or operation : INCOMPLETE, INCIPIENT

inch·worm \'inch-ˌwərm\ *n* : LOOPER

1in·ci·dence \'in-sə-dəns\ *n* : rate of occurrence or effect

1in·ci·dent \-dənt\ *n* **1** : OCCURRENCE, HAPPENING **2** : an action likely to lead to grave consequences esp. in diplomatic matters

2incident *adj* **1** : occurring or likely to occur esp. in connection with some other happening **2** : falling or striking on something ⟨~ light rays⟩

1in·ci·den·tal \ˌin-sə-'den-tᵊl\ *adj* **1** : subordinate, nonessential, or attendant in position or significance ⟨~ expenses⟩ **2** : CASUAL, CHANCE

2incidental *n* **1** *pl* : minor items (as of expense) that are not individually accounted for **2** : something incidental

in·ci·den·tal·ly \ˌin-sə-'den-tə-lē, -'dent-lē\ *adv* **1** : in an incidental manner **2** : by the way

in·cin·er·ate \in-'si-nə-ˌrāt\ *vb* **-at·ed; -at·ing** : to burn to ashes — **in·cin·er·a·tion** \-ˌsi-nə-'rā-shən\ *n*

in·cin·er·a·tor \in-'si-nə-ˌrā-tər\ *n* : a furnace for burning waste

in·cip·i·ent \in-'si-pē-ənt\ *adj* : beginning to be or become apparent

in·cise \in-'sīz\ *vb* **in·cised; in·cis·ing** **1** : to cut into **2** : CARVE, ENGRAVE

in·ci·sion \in-'si-zhən\ *n* : CUT, GASH; *esp* : a surgical cut

in·ci·sive \in-'sī-siv\ *adj* : impressively direct and decisive — **in·ci·sive·ly** *adv*

in·ci·sor \in-'sī-zər\ *n* : a front tooth typically adapted for cutting

in·cite \in-'sīt\ *vb* **in·cit·ed; in·cit·ing** **1** : to arouse to action : stir up — **in·cite·ment** *n* — **in·cit·er** *n*

in·ci·vil·i·ty \ˌin-sə-'vi-lə-tē\ *n* **1** : RUDENESS, DISCOURTESY **2** : a rude or discourteous act

incl *abbr* include; included; including; inclusive

in·clem·ent \(ˌ)in-'kle-mənt\ *adj* : SEVERE, STORMY ⟨~ weather⟩ — **in·clem·en·cy** \-mən-sē\ *n*

in·cli·na·tion \ˌin-klə-'nā-shən\ *n* **1** : PROPENSITY, BENT; *esp* : LIKING **2** : BOW, NOD ⟨an ~ of the head⟩ **3** : a tilting of something **4** : SLANT, SLOPE

1in·cline \in-'klīn\ *vb* **in·clined; in·clin·ing** **1** : BOW, BEND **2** : to be drawn toward an opinion or course of action **3** : to deviate from the vertical or horizontal : SLOPE **4** : INFLUENCE, PERSUADE — **in·clin·er** *n*

2in·cline \'in-ˌklīn\ *n* : SLOPE

inclose, inclosure *var of* ENCLOSE, ENCLOSURE

in·clude \in-'klüd\ *vb* **in·clud·ed; in·clud·ing** : to take in or comprise as a part of a whole ⟨the price ~s tax⟩ — **in·clu·sion** \in-'klü-zhən\ *n*

in·clu·sive \in-'klü-siv\ *adj* **1** : including stated limits or extremes ⟨from Monday to Friday ~⟩ **2** : broad in

scope; *esp* : covering all items, costs, or services — **in·clu·sive·ly** *adv* — **in·clu·sive·ness** *n*

incog *abbr* incognito

1in·cog·ni·to \ˌin-ˌkäg-'nē-to, in-'käg-nə-ˌtō\ *adv or adj* [It, fr. L *incognitus* unknown, fr. *cognoscere* to know] : with one's identity concealed

2incognito *n, pl* **-tos** **1** : one appearing or living incognito **2** : the state or disguise of an incognito

in·co·her·ent \ˌin-kō-'hir-ənt, -'her-\ *adj* **1** : not sticking closely or compactly together : LOOSE **2** : lacking normal clarity or intelligibility in speech or thought — **in·co·her·ence** \-əns\ *n* — **in·co·her·ent·ly** *adv*

in·come \'in-ˌkəm\ *n* : a gain usu. measured in money that derives from labor, business, or property

income tax *n* : a tax on the net income of an individual or business concern

in·com·ing \'in-ˌkə-miŋ\ *adj* : coming in ⟨the ~ tide⟩ ⟨~ freshmen⟩

in·com·men·su·rate \ˌin-kə-'men-sə-rət, -'men-chə-\ *adj* : not commensurate; *esp* : INADEQUATE

in·com·mode \ˌin-kə-'mōd\ *vb* **-mod·ed; -mod·ing** : INCONVENIENCE, DISTURB

in·com·mu·ni·ca·ble \ˌin-kə-'myü-ni-kə-bəl\ *adj* : not communicable : not capable of being communicated or imparted; *also* : UNCOMMUNICATIVE

in·com·mu·ni·ca·do \ˌin-kə-ˌmyü-nə-'kä-dō\ *adv or adj* : without means of communication; *also* : in solitary confinement ⟨a prisoner held ~⟩

in·com·pa·ra·ble \(ˌ)in-'käm-pə-rə-bəl, -prə-\ *adj* **1** : eminent beyond comparison : MATCHLESS **2** : not suitable for comparison — **in·com·pa·ra·bly** \-blē\ *adv*

in·com·pat·i·ble \ˌin-kəm-'pa-tə-bəl\ *adj* : incapable of or unsuitable for association or use together ⟨~ colors⟩ ⟨temperamentally ~⟩ — **in·com·pat·i·bil·i·ty** \ˌin-kəm-ˌpa-tə-'bi-lə-tē\ *n*

in·com·pe·tent \(ˌ)in-'käm-pə-tənt\ *adj* **1** : not legally qualified **2** : not competent : lacking sufficient knowledge, skill, or ability — **in·com·pe·tence** \-təns\ *n* — **in·com·pe·ten·cy** \-tən-sē\ *n* — **incompetent** *n*

in·com·plete \ˌin-kəm-'plēt\ *adj* : lacking a part or parts : UNFINISHED, IMPERFECT — **in·com·plete·ly** *adv* — **in·com·plete·ness** *n*

in·com·pre·hen·si·ble \ˌin-ˌkäm-prē-'hen-sə-bəl\ *adj* : impossible to comprehend : UNINTELLIGIBLE

in·con·ceiv·able \ˌin-kən-'sē-və-bəl\ *adj* **1** : impossible to comprehend **2** : UNBELIEVABLE

in·con·gru·ous \(ˌ)in-'käŋ-grü-wəs\ *adj* : not consistent with or suitable to the surroundings or associations — **in·con·gru·i·ty** \ˌin-kən-'grü-ə-tē, -ˌkän-\ *n* — **in·con·gru·ous·ly** *adv*

in·con·se·quen·tial \ˌin-ˌkän-sə-'kwen-chəl\ *adj* **1** : ILLOGICAL; *also* : IRRELEVANT **2** : of no significance : UNIMPORTANT — **in·con·se·quen·tial·ly** *adv*

in·con·se·quence \(ˌ)in-'kän-sə-ˌkwens\ *n*

in·con·sid·er·able \ˌin-kən-'si-də-rə-bəl\ *adj* : SLIGHT, TRIVIAL ⟨the cost was not ~⟩

in·con·sid·er·ate \ˌin-kən-'si-də-rət\ *adj* : HEEDLESS, THOUGHTLESS; *esp* : not respecting the rights or feelings of others — **in·con·sid·er·ate·ly** *adv* — **in·con·sid·er·ate·ness** *n*

in·con·sol·able \ˌin-kən-'sō-lə-bəl\ *adj* : incapable of being consoled — **in·con·sol·ably** \-blē\ *adv*

in·con·spic·u·ous \ˌin-kən-'spi-kyə-wəs\ *adj* : not readily noticeable — **in·con·spic·u·ous·ly** *adv*

in·con·stant \(ˌ)in-'kän-stənt\ *adj* : not constant : CHANGEABLE ♦ **Synonyms** FICKLE, CAPRICIOUS, MERCURIAL, UNSTABLE, VOLATILE — **in·con·stan·cy** \-stən-sē\ *n* — **in·con·stant·ly** *adv*

in·con·test·able \ˌin-kən-'tes-tə-bəl\ *adj* : not contestable : INDISPUTABLE — **in·con·test·ably** \-'tes-tə-blē\ *adv*

in·con·ti·nent \(ˌ)in-'känt-ᵊn-ənt\ *adj* **1** : lacking self-restraint **2** : unable to retain urine or feces voluntarily — **in·con·ti·nence** \-əns\ *n*

in·con·tro·vert·ible \ˌin-ˌkän-trə-'vər-tə-bəl\ *adj* : not open to question : INDISPUTABLE ⟨~ evidence⟩ — **in·con·tro·vert·ibly** \-blē\ *adv*

1in·con·ve·nience \ˌin-kən-'vē-nyəns\ *n* **1** : something that is inconvenient **2** : the quality or state of being inconvenient

2inconvenience *vb* **-nienced; -nienc·ing** : to subject to inconvenience

in·con·ve·nient \ˌin-kən-ˈvē-nyənt\ *adj* : not convenient : causing trouble or annoyance : INOPPORTUNE — **in·con·ve·nient·ly** *adv*

in·cor·po·rate \in-ˈkȯr-pə-ˌrāt\ *vb* **-rat·ed; -rat·ing 1** : to unite closely or so as to form one body : BLEND **2** : to form, form into, or become a corporation **3** : to give material form to : EMBODY — **in·cor·po·ra·tion** \-ˌkȯr-pə-ˈrā-shən\ *n*

in·cor·po·re·al \ˌin-kȯr-ˈpȯr-ē-əl\ *adj* : having no material body or form

in·cor·rect \ˌin-kə-ˈrekt\ *adj* **1** : INACCURATE, FAULTY ⟨an ~ transcription⟩ **2** : not true : WRONG **3** : UNBECOMING, IMPROPER — **in·cor·rect·ly** *adv* — **in·cor·rect·ness** *n*

in·cor·ri·gi·ble \(ˌ)in-ˈkȯr-ə-jə-bəl\ *adj* : incapable of being corrected, amended, or reformed — **in·cor·ri·gi·bil·i·ty** \(ˌ)in-ˌkȯr-ə-jə-ˈbi-lə-tē\ *n* — **in·cor·ri·gi·bly** \-ˈkȯr-ə-jə-blē\ *adv*

in·cor·rupt·ible \ˌin-kə-ˈrəp-tə-bəl\ *adj* **1** : not subject to decay or dissolution **2** : incapable of being bribed or morally corrupted — **in·cor·rupt·ibil·i·ty** \-ˌrəp-tə-ˈbi-lə-tē\ *n* — **in·cor·rupt·ibly** \-ˈrəp-tə-blē\ *adv*

incr *abbr* increase; increased

¹in·crease \in-ˈkrēs, ˈin-ˌkrēs\ *vb* **in·creased; in·creas·ing** [ME *encresen*, fr. AF *encreistre*, fr. L *increscere*, fr. *crescere* to grow] **1** : to become greater : GROW **2** : to multiply by the production of young ⟨rabbits ~ rapidly⟩ **3** : to make greater — **increased** *adj* — **in·creas·ing·ly** \-ˈkrē-siŋ-lē\ *adv*

²in·crease \ˈin-ˌkrēs, in-ˈkrēs\ *n* **1** : addition or enlargement in size, extent, or quantity : GROWTH **2** : something that is added to an original stock or amount (as by growth)

in·cred·i·ble \(ˌ)in-ˈkre-də-bəl\ *adj* : too extraordinary and improbable to be believed; *also* : hard to believe — **in·cred·i·bil·i·ty** \(ˌ)in-ˌkre-də-ˈbi-lə-tē\ *n* — **in·cred·i·bly** \-ˈkre-də-blē\ *adv*

in·cred·u·lous \-ˈkre-jə-ləs\ *adj* **1** : SKEPTICAL **2** : expressing disbelief — **in·cre·du·li·ty** \ˌin-kri-ˈdü-lə-tē, -ˈdyü-\ *n* — **in·cred·u·lous·ly** *adv*

in·cre·ment \ˈiŋ-krə-mənt, ˈin-\ *n* **1** : the action or process of increasing esp. in quantity or value : ENLARGEMENT **2** : something gained or added; *esp* : one of a series of regular consecutive additions — **in·cre·men·tal** \ˌiŋ-krə-ˈmen-tᵊl, ˌin-\ *adj* — **in·cre·men·tal·ly** *adv*

in·crim·i·nate \in-ˈkri-mə-ˌnāt\ *vb* **-nat·ed; -nat·ing** : to charge with or prove involvement in a crime or fault : ACCUSE — **in·crim·i·na·tion** \-ˌkri-mə-ˈnā-shən\ *n* — **in·crim·i·na·to·ry** \-ˈkri-mə-nə-ˌtȯr-ē\ *adj*

incrust *var of* ENCRUST

in·crus·ta·tion \ˌin-ˌkrəs-ˈtā-shən\ *n* **1** : CRUST; *also* : an accumulation (as of habits, opinions, or customs) resembling a crust **2** : the act of encrusting : the state of being encrusted

in·cu·bate \ˈiŋ-kyù-ˌbāt, ˈin-\ *vb* **-bat·ed; -bat·ing** : to sit on (eggs) to hatch by the warmth of the body; *also* : to keep (as an embryo) under conditions favorable for development — **in·cu·ba·tion** \ˌiŋ-kyù-ˈbā-shən, ˌin-\ *n*

in·cu·ba·tor \ˈiŋ-kyù-ˌbāt-ər, ˈin-\ *n* : one that incubates; *esp* : an apparatus providing suitable conditions (as of warmth and moisture) for incubating something (as a premature baby)

in·cu·bus \ˈiŋ-kyə-bəs, ˈin-\ *n, pl* **-bi** \-ˌbī, -ˌbē\ *also* **-bus·es** [ME, fr. LL, fr. L *incubare* to lie on] **1** : a spirit supposed to work evil on persons in their sleep **2** : NIGHTMARE **1 3** : one that oppresses like a nightmare

in·cul·cate \in-ˈkəl-ˌkāt, ˈin-(ˌ)kəl-\ *vb* **-cat·ed; -cat·ing** [L *inculcare*, lit., to tread on, fr. *calcare* to trample, fr. *calx* heel] : to teach and impress by frequent repetitions or admonitions — **in·cul·ca·tion** \ˌin-(ˌ)kəl-ˈkā-shən\ *n*

in·cul·pa·ble \(ˌ)in-ˈkəl-pə-bəl\ *adj* : free from guilt : INNOCENT

in·cul·pate \in-ˈkəl-ˌpāt, ˈin-(ˌ)kəl-\ *vb* **-pat·ed; -pat·ing** : INCRIMINATE

in·cum·ben·cy \in-ˈkəm-bən-sē\ *n, pl* **-cies 1** : something that is incumbent **2** : the quality or state of being incumbent **3** : the office or period of office of an incumbent

¹in·cum·bent \in-ˈkəm-bənt\ *n* : the holder of an office or position

²incumbent *adj* **1** : imposed as a duty **2** : occupying a specified office **3** : lying or resting on something else

in·cu·nab·u·lum \ˌin-kyə-ˈna-byə-ləm, iŋ-\ *n, pl* **-la** \-lə\ [NL, fr. L *incunabula*, pl., bands holding the baby in a cradle, fr. *cunae* cradle] : a book printed before 1501

in·cur \in-ˈkər\ *vb* **in·curred; in·cur·ring** : to become liable or subject to : bring down upon oneself

in·cur·able \(ˌ)in-ˈkyùr-ə-bəl\ *adj* **1** : not curable **2** : not likely to be changed — **incurable** *n* — **in·cur·ably** \(ˌ)in-ˈkyùr-ə-blē\ *adv*

in·cur·sion \in-ˈkər-zhən\ *n* **1** : a sudden hostile invasion : RAID **2** : an entering in or into (as an activity)

in·cus \ˈiŋ-kəs\ *n, pl* **in·cu·des** \iŋ-ˈkyü-(ˌ)dēz\ [NL, fr. L, anvil] : the middle bone of a chain of three small bones in the middle ear of a mammal

ind *abbr* **1** independent **2** index **3** industrial; industry

Ind *abbr* **1** Indian **2** Indiana

in·debt·ed \in-ˈde-təd\ *adj* **1** : owing gratitude or recognition to another **2** : owing money — **in·debt·ed·ness** *n*

in·de·cent \(ˌ)in-ˈdē-sᵊnt\ *adj* : not decent; *esp* : grossly improper or offensive — **in·de·cen·cy** \-sᵊn-sē\ *n* — **in·de·cent·ly** *adv*

in·de·ci·sion \ˌin-di-ˈsi-zhən\ *n* : a wavering between two or more possible courses of action : IRRESOLUTION

in·de·ci·sive \ˌin-di-ˈsī-siv\ *adj* **1** : INCONCLUSIVE ⟨an ~ battle⟩ **2** : marked by or prone to indecision **3** : INDEFINITE — **in·de·ci·sive·ly** *adv* — **in·de·ci·sive·ness** *n*

in·de·co·rous \(ˌ)in-ˈde-kə-rəs; ˌin-di-ˈkȯr-əs\ *adj* : conflicting with accepted standards of good conduct or good taste ✦ *Synonyms* IMPROPER, UNSEEMLY, INDECENT, UNBECOMING, INDELICATE — **in·de·co·rous·ly** *adv* — **in·de·co·rous·ness** *n*

in·deed \in-ˈdēd\ *adv* **1** : without any question : TRULY — often used interjectionally to express irony, disbelief, or surprise **2** : in reality **3** : all things considered

in·de·fat·i·ga·ble \ˌin-di-ˈfa-ti-gə-bəl\ *adj* : UNTIRING ⟨an ~ worker⟩ — **in·de·fat·i·ga·bly** \-blē\ *adv*

in·de·fea·si·ble \-ˈfē-zə-bəl\ *adj* : not capable of being annulled or voided — **in·de·fea·si·bly** \-blē\ *adv*

in·de·fen·si·ble \-ˈfen-sə-bəl\ *adj* **1** : incapable of being maintained as right or valid **2** : INEXCUSABLE ⟨~ comments⟩ **3** : incapable of being protected against physical attack

in·de·fin·able \-ˈfī-nə-bəl\ *adj* : incapable of being precisely described or analyzed — **in·de·fin·ably** \-blē\ *adv*

in·def·i·nite \(ˌ)in-ˈde-fə-nət\ *adj* **1** : not defining or identifying ⟨*an* is an ~ article⟩ **2** : not precise : VAGUE **3** : having no fixed limits — **in·def·i·nite·ly** *adv* — **in·def·i·nite·ness** *n*

in·del·i·ble \in-ˈde-lə-bəl\ *adj* [ME, fr. ML *indelibilis*, alter. of L *indelebilis*, fr. *delēre* to delete, destroy] **1** : not capable of being removed or erased **2** : making marks that cannot be erased **3** : LASTING, UNFORGETTABLE — **in·del·i·bly** \in-ˈde-lə-blē\ *adv*

in·del·i·cate \(ˌ)in-ˈde-li-kət\ *adj* : not delicate; *esp* : IMPROPER, COARSE, TACTLESS ✦ *Synonyms* INDECENT, UNSEEMLY, INDECOROUS, UNBECOMING — **in·del·i·ca·cy** \in-ˈde-lə-kə-sē\ *n*

in·dem·ni·fy \in-ˈdem-nə-ˌfī\ *vb* **-fied; -fy·ing** [L *indemnis* unharmed, fr. *in-* not + *damnum* damage] **1** : to secure against hurt, loss, or damage **2** : to make compensation to for hurt, loss, or damage — **in·dem·ni·fi·ca·tion** \-ˌdem-nə-fə-ˈkā-shən\ *n*

in·dem·ni·ty \in-ˈdem-nə-tē\ *n, pl* **-ties 1** : security against hurt, loss, or damage; *also* : exemption from incurred penalties or liabilities **2** : something that indemnifies

¹in·dent \in-ˈdent\ *vb* [ME, fr. AF *endenter*, fr. *dent* tooth, fr. L *dent-, dens*] **1** : to notch the edge of **2** : INDENTURE **3** : to set (as a line of a paragraph) in from the margin

²indent *vb* **1** : to force inward so as to form a depression **2** : to form a dent in

in·den·ta·tion \ˌin-ˌden-ˈtā-shən\ *n* **1** : NOTCH; *also* : a recess in a surface **2** : the action of indenting : the condition of being indented **3** : DENT **4** : INDENTION 2

in·den·tion \in-ˈden-chən\ *n* **1** : INDENTATION 2 **2** : the blank space produced by indenting

¹in·den·ture \in-ˈden-chər\ *n* **1** : a written certificate or agreement; *esp* : a contract binding one person (as an apprentice) to work for another for a given period of time — often used in pl. **2** : INDENTATION 1 **3** : DENT

²indenture *vb* **in·den·tured; in·den·tur·ing** : to bind (as an apprentice) by indentures in·de·pen·dence \ˌin-də-ˈpen-dəns\ n : the quality or state of being independent : FREEDOM

Independence Day n : July 4 observed as a legal holiday in the U.S. in commemoration of the adoption of the Declaration of Independence in 1776

in·de·pen·dent \ˌin-də-ˈpen-dənt\ adj 1 : SELF-GOVERNING; also : not affiliated with a larger controlling unit 2 : not requiring or relying on something else or somebody else ⟨an ∼ conclusion⟩ ⟨∼ of her parents⟩ 3 : not easily influenced : showing self-reliance and personal freedom ⟨an ∼ mind⟩ 4 : not committed to a political party ⟨an ∼ voter⟩ 5 : MAIN ⟨an ∼ clause⟩ — independent n — in·de·pen·dent·ly adv

independent variable n : a variable whose value is not determined by that of any other variable in a function

in·de·scrib·able \ˌin-di-ˈskrī-bə-bəl\ adj 1 : that cannot be described 2 : being too intense or great for description — in·de·scrib·ably \-blē\ adv

in·de·ter·mi·nate \ˌin-di-ˈtər-mə-nət\ adj 1 : VAGUE; also : not known in advance 2 : not limited in advance; also : not leading to a definite end or result — in·de·ter·mi·na·cy \-nə-sē\ n — in·de·ter·mi·nate·ly adv

¹in·dex \ˈin-ˌdeks\ n, pl in·dex·es or in·di·ces \-də-ˌsēz\ 1 : POINTER 2 : SIGN, INDICATION ⟨an ∼ of character⟩ 3 : a guide for facilitating references; esp : an alphabetical list of items treated in a printed work with the page number where each item may be found 4 : a list of restricted or prohibited material 5 pl usu indices : a number or symbol or expression (as an exponent) associated with another to indicate a mathematical operation or use or position in an arrangement or expansion 6 : a character ☞ used to direct attention (as to a note) 7 : INDEX NUMBER

²index vb 1 : to provide with or put into an index 2 : to serve as an index 3 : to regulate by indexation

in·dex·ation \ˌin-ˌdek-ˈsā-shən\ n : a system of economic control in which a body of variables (as wages and interest) rise or fall at the same rate as an index of the cost of living

index finger n : the finger next to the thumb

in·dex·ing n : INDEXATION

index number n : a number used to indicate change in magnitude (as of cost) as compared with the magnitude at some specified time

index of refraction : REFRACTIVE INDEX

in·dia ink \ˈin-dē-ə-\ n, often cap 1st I 1 : a solid black pigment used in drawing 2 : a fluid made from india ink

In·di·an \ˈin-dē-ən\ n 1 : a native or inhabitant of India or of the East Indies; also : a person of Indian descent 2 : AMERICAN INDIAN — Indian adj

Indian corn n : a tall widely grown American cereal grass bearing seeds on long ears; also : its ears or seeds

Indian meal n : CORNMEAL

Indian paintbrush n : any of a genus of herbaceous plants related to the snapdragons that have brightly colored bracts

Indian pipe n : a waxy white leafless saprophytic herb of Asia and the U.S.

Indian summer n : a period of mild weather in late autumn or early winter

In·dia paper \ˈin-dē-ə-\ n 1 : a thin absorbent paper used esp. for taking impressions (as of steel engravings) 2 : a thin tough opaque printing paper

in·di·cate \ˈin-də-ˌkāt\ vb -cat·ed; -cat·ing 1 : to point out or to 2 : to show indirectly 3 : to state briefly — in·di·ca·tion \ˌin-də-ˈkā-shən\ n — in·di·ca·tor \ˈin-də-ˌkā-tər\ n

¹in·dic·a·tive \in-ˈdi-kə-tiv\ adj 1 : of, relating to, or being a verb form that represents an act or state as a fact ⟨∼ mood⟩ 2 : serving to indicate ⟨actions ∼ of fear⟩

²indicative n 1 : the indicative mood of a language 2 : a form in the indicative mood

in·di·cia \in-ˈdi-shə, -shē-ə\ n pl 1 : distinctive marks 2 : postal markings then imprinted on mail or mailing labels

in·dict \in-ˈdīt\ vb [alter. of earlier indite, fr. ME, fr. AF to write, point out, indict, ultim. fr. L indicere to make known formally, fr. dicere to say] 1 : to charge with a fault or offense 2 : to charge with a crime by the finding of a jury — in·dict·able adj — in·dict·ment n

in·die \ˈin-dē\ n 1 : one that is independent; esp : an unaffiliated record or motion-picture production company 2 something produced by an indie — indie adj

in·dif·fer·ent \in-ˈdi-frənt, -fə-rənt\ adj 1 : UNBIASED, UNPREJUDICED 2 : of no importance one way or the other 3 : marked by no special liking for or dislike of something 4 : being neither excessive nor inadequate 5 : PASSABLE, MEDIOCRE 6 : being neither right nor wrong — in·dif·fer·ence \-frəns, -fə-rəns\ n — in·dif·fer·ent·ly adv

in·dig·e·nous \in-ˈdi-jə-nəs\ adj : produced, growing, or living naturally in a particular region

in·di·gent \ˈin-di-jənt\ adj : IMPOVERISHED, NEEDY — in·di·gence \-jəns\ n

in·di·gest·ible \ˌin-dī-ˈjes-tə-bəl, -də-\ adj : not readily digested

in·di·ges·tion \-ˈjes-chən\ n : inadequate or difficult digestion : DYSPEPSIA

in·dig·nant \in-ˈdig-nənt\ adj : filled with or marked by indignation — in·dig·nant·ly adv

in·dig·na·tion \ˌin-dig-ˈnā-shən\ n : anger aroused by something unjust, unworthy, or mean

in·dig·ni·ty \in-ˈdig-nə-tē\ n, pl -ties : an offense against personal dignity or self-respect; also : humiliating treatment

in·di·go \ˈin-di-ˌgō\ n, pl -gos or -goes [It dial., fr. L indicum, fr. Gk indikon, fr. indikos Indic, fr. Indos India] 1 : a blue dye obtained from plants or synthesized 2 : a deep reddish blue color

in·di·rect \ˌin-də-ˈrekt, -dī-\ adj 1 : not straight ⟨an ∼ route⟩ 2 : not straightforward and open ⟨∼ methods⟩ 3 : not having a plainly seen connection ⟨an ∼ cause⟩ 4 : not directly to the point ⟨an ∼ answer⟩ — in·di·rec·tion \-ˈrek-shən\ n — in·di·rect·ly adv — in·di·rect·ness n

in·dis·creet \ˌin-di-ˈskrēt\ adj : not discreet : IMPRUDENT — in·dis·creet·ly adv

in·dis·cre·tion \ˌin-di-ˈskre-shən\ n 1 : IMPRUDENCE ⟨dietary ∼⟩ 2 : something marked by lack of discretion; esp : an act deviating from accepted morality

in·dis·crim·i·nate \ˌin-di-ˈskri-mə-nət\ adj 1 : not marked by discrimination or careful distinction 2 : HAPHAZARD, RANDOM ⟨an ∼ application of a law⟩ 3 : UNRESTRAINED 4 : MOTLEY — in·dis·crim·i·nate·ly adv

in·dis·pens·able \ˌin-di-ˈspen-sə-bəl\ adj : absolutely essential : REQUISITE — indispensable n — in·dis·pens·abil·i·ty \-ˌspen-sə-ˈbi-lə-tē\ n — in·dis·pens·ably \-ˈspen-sə-blē\ adv

in·dis·posed \ˌin-di-ˈspōzd\ adj 1 : slightly ill 2 : AVERSE — in·dis·po·si·tion \(ˌ)in-ˌdis-pə-ˈzi-shən\ n

in·dis·put·able \ˌin-di-ˈspyü-tə-bəl, (ˌ)in-ˈdis-pyə-\ adj : not disputable : UNQUESTIONABLE ⟨∼ proof⟩ — in·dis·put·ably \-blē\ adv

in·dis·sol·u·ble \ˌin-di-ˈsäl-yə-bəl\ adj : not capable of being dissolved, undone, or broken : PERMANENT ⟨an ∼ contract⟩

in·dis·tinct \ˌin-di-ˈstiŋkt\ adj 1 : not sharply outlined or separable : BLURRED, FAINT, DIM 2 : not readily distinguishable : UNCERTAIN — in·dis·tinct·ly adv — in·dis·tinct·ness n

in·dite \in-ˈdīt\ vb in·dit·ed; in·dit·ing : COMPOSE ⟨∼ a poem⟩; also : to put in writing ⟨∼ a letter⟩

in·di·um \ˈin-dē-əm\ n : a malleable silvery metallic chemical element

indiv abbr individual

¹in·di·vid·u·al \ˌin-də-ˈvi-jə-wəl\ adj 1 : of, relating to, or associated with an individual ⟨∼ traits⟩ 2 : being an individual : existing as an indivisible whole : intended for one person 4 : SEPARATE ⟨∼ copies⟩ 5 : having marked individuality ⟨an ∼ style⟩ — in·di·vid·u·al·ly adv

²individual n 1 : a single member of a category : a particular person, animal, or thing 2 : PERSON ⟨a disagreeable ∼⟩

in·di·vid·u·al·ise Brit var of INDIVIDUALIZE

in·di·vid·u·al·ism \ˌin-də-ˈvi-jə-wə-ˌli-zəm\ n 1 : a doctrine that the interests of the individual are primary 2 : a doctrine holding that the individual has political or economic rights with which the state must not interfere 3 : INDIVIDUALITY

in·di·vid·u·al·ist \-list\ n 1 : one that pursues a markedly independent course in thought or action 2 : one that advocates or practices individualism — individualist or in·di·vid·u·al·is·tic \-ˌvi-jə-wə-ˈlis-tik\ adj

in·di·vid·u·al·i·ty \-ˌvi-jə-'wa-lə-tē\ *n, pl* **-ties** **1** : the sum of qualities that characterize and distinguish an individual from all others; *also* : PERSONALITY **2** : separate or distinct existence **3** : INDIVIDUAL, PERSON

in·di·vid·u·al·ize \-'vi-jə-wə-ˌlīz\ *vb* **-ized; -iz·ing** **1** : to make individual in character **2** : to treat or notice individually : PARTICULARIZE **3** : to adapt to the needs of an individual

individual retirement account *n* : IRA

in·di·vid·u·ate \ˌin-də-'vi-jə-ˌwāt\ *vb* **-at·ed; -at·ing** : to give individuality to : form into an individual — **in·di·vid·u·a·tion** \-ˌvi-jə-'wā-shən\ *n*

in·di·vis·i·ble \ˌin-də-'vi-zə-bəl\ *adj* : impossible to divide or separate — **in·di·vis·i·bil·i·ty** \-ˌvi-zə-'bi-lə-tē\ *n* — **in·di·vis·i·bly** *adv*

In·do–Ar·y·an \ˌin-dō-'er-ē-ən\ *n* : a branch of the Indo-European language family that includes Hindi and other languages of south Asia

in·doc·tri·nate \in-'däk-trə-ˌnāt\ *vb* **-nat·ed; -nat·ing** **1** : to instruct esp. in fundamentals or rudiments : TEACH **2** : to teach the beliefs and doctrines of a particular group — **in·doc·tri·na·tion** \(ˌ)in-ˌdäk-trə-'nā-shən\ *n* — **in·doc·tri·na·tor** *n*

In·do–Eu·ro·pe·an \ˌin-dō-ˌyur-ə-'pē-ən\ *adj* : of, relating to, or constituting a family of languages comprising those spoken in most of Europe and in the parts of the world colonized by Europeans since 1500 and also in Persia, the subcontinent of India, and some other parts of Asia

in·do·lent \'in-də-lənt\ *adj* [LL *indolens* insensitive to pain, fr. L *dolēre* to feel pain] **1** : slow to develop or heal ⟨∼ ulcers⟩ **2** : LAZY — **in·do·lence** \-ləns\ *n* — **in·do·lent·ly** *adv*

in·dom·i·ta·ble \in-'dä-mə-tə-bəl\ *adj* : UNCONQUERABLE ⟨∼ courage⟩ — **in·dom·i·ta·bly** \-blē\ *adv*

in·door \'in-ˌdȯr\ *adj* **1** : of or relating to the inside of a building **2** : living, located, or carried on within a building

in·doors \in-'dȯrz\ *adv* : in or into a building

indorse, indorsement *var of* ENDORSE, ENDORSEMENT

in·du·bi·ta·ble \(ˌ)in-'dü-bə-tə-bəl, -'dyü-\ *adj* : UNQUESTIONABLE — **in·du·bi·ta·bly** \-blē\ *adv*

in·duce \in-'düs, -'dyüs\ *vb* **in·duced; in·duc·ing** **1** : PERSUADE, INFLUENCE **2** : BRING ABOUT **3** : to produce (as an electric current) by induction **4** : to determine by induction; *esp* : to infer from particulars — **in·duc·er** *n*

in·duce·ment \-mənt\ *n* **1** : something that induces : MOTIVE **2** : the act or process of inducing

in·duct \in-'dəkt\ *vb* **1** : to place in office **2** : to admit as a member **3** : to enroll for military training or service — **in·duct·ee** \-ˌdək-'tē\ *n*

in·duc·tance \in-'dək-təns\ *n* : a property of an electric circuit by which a varying current produces an electromotive force in that circuit or in a nearby circuit; *also* : the measure of this property

in·duc·tion \in-'dək-shən\ *n* **1** : the act or process of inducting; *also* : INITIATION **2** : the formality by which a civilian is inducted into military service **3** : inference of a generalized conclusion from particular instances; *also* : a conclusion so reached **4** : the act of causing or bringing on or about **5** : the process by which an electric current, an electric charge, or magnetism is produced in a body by the proximity of an electric or magnetic field

in·duc·tive \in-'dək-tiv\ *adj* : of, relating to, or employing induction

in·duc·tor \in-'dək-tər\ *n* : an electrical component that acts upon another or is itself acted upon by induction

in·dulge \in-'dəlj\ *vb* **in·dulged; in·dulg·ing** **1** : to give free rein to : GRATIFY **2** : HUMOR **3** : to gratify one's taste or desire for ⟨∼ in alcohol⟩

in·dul·gence \in-'dəl-jəns\ *n* **1** : remission of temporal punishment due in Roman Catholic doctrine for sins whose eternal punishment has been remitted by reception of the sacrifice of penance **2** : the act of indulging : the state of being indulgent **3** : an indulgent act **4** : the thing indulged in **5** : SELF-INDULGENCE — **in·dul·gent** \-jənt\ *adj* — **in·dul·gent·ly** *adv*

in·du·rat·ed \'in-dyu̇-ˌrā-təd, -du̇-\ *adj* : physically or emotionally hardened — **in·du·ra·tion** \ˌin-dyu̇-'rā-shən, -du̇-\ *n*

in·dus·tri·al \in-'dəs-trē-əl\ *adj* **1** : of or relating to indus-

try **2** : HEAVY-DUTY ⟨an ∼ zipper⟩ **3** : characterized by highly developed industries — **in·dus·tri·al·ly** *adv*

in·dus·tri·al·ise *Brit var of* INDUSTRIALIZE

in·dus·tri·al·ist \-ə-list\ *n* : a person owning or engaged in the management of an industry

in·dus·tri·al·ize \in-'dəs-trē-ə-ˌlīz\ *vb* **-ized; -iz·ing** : to make or become industrial — **in·dus·tri·al·i·za·tion** \-ˌdəs-trē-ə-lə-'zā-shən\ *n*

in·dus·tri·ous \in-'dəs-trē-əs\ *adj* : DILIGENT, BUSY — **in·dus·tri·ous·ly** *adv* — **in·dus·tri·ous·ness** *n*

in·dus·try \'in-(ˌ)dəs-trē\ *n, pl* **-tries** **1** : DILIGENCE **2** : a department or branch of a craft, art, business, or manufacture; *esp* : one that employs a large personnel and capital **3** : a distinct group of productive enterprises **4** : manufacturing activity as a whole

in·dwell \(ˌ)in-'dwel\ *vb* : to exist within as an activating spirit or force

In·dy car \'in-dē-\ *n* : a single-seat, open-cockpit racing car with the engine in the rear

¹in·e·bri·ate \i-'nē-brē-ˌāt\ *vb* **-at·ed; -at·ing** : to make drunk : INTOXICATE — **in·e·bri·a·tion** \-ˌnē-brē-'ā-shən\ *n*

²in·e·bri·ate \-ət\ *n* : one that is drunk; *esp* : DRUNKARD

in·ef·fa·ble \(ˌ)in-'e-fə-bəl\ *adj* **1** : incapable of being expressed in words : INDESCRIBABLE ⟨∼ joy⟩ **2** : UNSPEAKABLE ⟨∼ disgust⟩ **3** : not to be uttered : TABOO — **in·ef·fa·bly** \-blē\ *adv*

in·ef·fec·tive \ˌi-nə-'fek-tiv\ *adj* **1** : INEFFECTUAL **2** : not able to perform efficiently or as expected : INCAPABLE — **in·ef·fec·tive·ly** *adv* — **in·ef·fec·tive·ness** *n*

in·ef·fec·tu·al \-'fek-chə-wəl\ *adj* **1** : not producing the proper or usual effect **2** : INEFFECTIVE 2 — **in·ef·fec·tu·al·ly** *adv*

in·ef·fi·cient \ˌi-nə-'fi-shənt\ *adj* **1** : not producing the desired effect **2** : wasteful of time or energy **3** : INCAPABLE, INCOMPETENT — **in·ef·fi·cien·cy** \-'fi-shən-sē\ *n* — **in·ef·fi·cient·ly** *adv*

in·el·e·gant \(ˌ)in-'e-li-gənt\ *adj* : lacking in refinement, grace, or good taste — **in·el·e·gance** \-gəns\ *n* — **in·el·e·gant·ly** *adv*

in·el·i·gi·ble \(ˌ)i-'ne-lə-jə-bəl\ *adj* : not qualified for an office or position — **in·el·i·gi·bil·i·ty** \(ˌ)i-ˌne-lə-jə-'bi-lə-tē\ *n*

in·eluc·ta·ble \ˌi-ni-'lək-tə-bəl\ *adj* : not to be avoided, changed, or resisted — **in·eluc·ta·bly** \-blē\ *adv*

in·ept \i-'nept\ *adj* **1** : lacking in fitness or aptitude : UNFIT **2** : FOOLISH **3** : being out of place : INAPPROPRIATE **4** : generally incompetent : BUNGLING — **in·ept·ly** *adv* — **in·ept·ness** *n*

in·ep·ti·tude \(ˌ)i-'nep-ti-ˌtüd, -ˌtyüd\ *n* : the quality or state of being inept; *esp* : INCOMPETENCE

in·equal·i·ty \ˌi-ni-'kwä-lə-tē\ *n* **1** : the quality of being unequal or uneven; *esp* : UNEVENNESS, DISPARITY **2** : an instance of being unequal

in·ert \i-'nərt\ *adj* [L *inert-, iners* unskilled, idle, fr. *art-, ars* skill] **1** : powerless to move **2** : SLUGGISH **3** : lacking in active properties ⟨chemically ∼⟩ — **in·ert·ly** *adv* — **in·ert·ness** *n*

in·er·tia \i-'nər-shə, -shē-ə\ *n* **1** : a property of matter whereby it remains at rest or continues in uniform motion unless acted upon by some outside force **2** : INERTNESS, SLUGGISHNESS — **in·er·tial** \-shəl\ *adj*

in·es·cap·able \ˌi-nə-'skā-pə-bəl\ *adj* : incapable of being escaped : INEVITABLE — **in·es·cap·ably** \-blē\ *adv*

in·es·ti·ma·ble \(ˌ)i-'nes-tə-mə-bəl\ *adj* **1** : incapable of being estimated or computed ⟨∼ errors⟩ **2** : too valuable or excellent to be fully appreciated — **in·es·ti·ma·bly** \-blē\ *adv*

in·ev·i·ta·ble \i-'ne-və-tə-bəl\ *adj* : incapable of being avoided or evaded : bound to happen — **in·ev·i·ta·bil·i·ty** \(ˌ)i-ˌne-və-tə-'bi-lə-tē\ *n*

in·ev·i·ta·bly \-blē\ *adv* **1** : in an inevitable way **2** : as is to be expected

in·ex·act \ˌi-nig-'zakt\ *adj* **1** : not precisely correct or true : INACCURATE **2** : not rigorous and careful — **in·ex·act·ly** *adv* — **in·ex·act·ness** *n*

in·ex·cus·able \ˌi-nik-'skyü-zə-bəl\ *adj* : impossible to excuse or justify — **in·ex·cus·ably** \-blē\ *adv*

in·ex·haust·ible \ˌi-nig-'zȯ-stə-bəl\ *adj* **1** : incapable of being used up ⟨an ∼ supply⟩ **2** : UNTIRING ⟨an ∼ hiker⟩ — **in·ex·haust·ibly** \-blē\ *adv* in·ex·o·ra·ble \(ˌ)i-'nek-sə-rə-bəl\ adj : not to be persuaded, moved, or stopped : RELENTLESS — in·ex·o·ra·bly adv

in·ex·pe·ri·ence \ˌi-nik-'spir-ē-əns\ n : lack of experience or of knowledge gained by experience — in·ex·pe·ri·enced \-ənst\ adj

in·ex·pert \(ˌ)i-'nek-ˌspərt\ adj : not expert : UNSKILLED — in·ex·pert·ly adv

in·ex·pi·a·ble \(ˌ)i-'nek-spē-ə-bəl\ adj : not capable of being atoned for

in·ex·pli·ca·ble \ˌi-nik-'spli-kə-bəl, (ˌ)i-'nek-(ˌ)spli-\ adj : incapable of being explained or accounted for — in·ex·pli·ca·bly \-blē\ adv

in·ex·press·ible \-'spre-sə-bəl\ adj : not capable of being expressed — in·ex·press·ibly \-blē\ adv

in ex·tre·mis \ˌin-ik-'strā-məs, -'strē-\ adv : in extreme circumstances; esp : at the point of death

in·ex·tri·ca·ble \ˌi-nik-'stri-kə-bəl, (ˌ)i-'nek-(ˌ)stri-\ adj 1 : forming a maze or tangle from which it is impossible to get free   2 : incapable of being disentangled or untied — in·ex·tri·ca·bly \-blē\ adv

inf abbr 1 infantry   2 infinitive

in·fal·li·ble \(ˌ)in-'fa-lə-bəl\ adj 1 : incapable of error : UNERRING   2 : SURE, CERTAIN ⟨an ∼ remedy⟩ — in·fal·li·bil·i·ty \ˌin-ˌfa-lə-'bi-lə-tē\ n — in·fal·li·bly \(ˌ)in-'fa-lə-blē\ adv

in·fa·mous \'in-fə-məs\ adj 1 : having a reputation of the worst kind   2 : DISGRACEFUL — in·fa·mous·ly adv

in·fa·my \-mē\ n, pl -mies 1 : evil reputation brought about by something grossly criminal, shocking, or brutal   2 : an extreme and publicly known criminal or evil act   3 : the state of being infamous

in·fan·cy \'in-fən-sē\ n, pl -cies 1 : early childhood   2 : a beginning or early period of existence

in·fant \'in-fənt\ n [ME enfaunt, fr. AF enfant, fr. L infant-, infans, adj., incapable of speech, young, fr. fant-, fans, prp. of fari to speak] : BABY; also : a person who is a legal minor

in·fan·ti·cide \in-'fan-tə-ˌsīd\ n : the killing of an infant

in·fan·tile \'in-fən-ˌtī(-ə)l, -tᵊl, -ˌtēl\ adj : of or relating to infants; also : CHILDISH

infantile paralysis n : POLIOMYELITIS

in·fan·try \'in-fən-trē\ n, pl -tries [MF & It; MF infanterie, fr. It infanteria, fr. infante boy, foot soldier] : soldiers trained, armed, and equipped to fight on foot — in·fan·try·man \-mən\ n

in·farct \'in-ˌfärkt\ n [L infarctus, pp. of infarcire to stuff] : an area of dead tissue (as of the heart wall) caused by blocking of local blood circulation — in·farc·tion \in-'färk-shən\ n

in·fat·u·ate \in-'fa-chə-ˌwāt\ vb -at·ed; -at·ing : to inspire with a foolish or extravagant love or admiration — in·fat·u·a·tion \-ˌfa-chə-'wā-shən\ n

in·fect \in-'fekt\ vb 1 : to contaminate with disease-producing matter   2 : to communicate a pathogen or disease to   3 : to cause to share one's feelings ⟨∼ed us with his enthusiasm⟩

in·fec·tion \in-'fek-shən\ n 1 : a disease or condition caused by a germ or parasite; also : such a germ or parasite   2 : an act or process of infecting — in·fec·tious \-shəs\ adj — in·fec·tive \-'fek-tiv\ adj

infectious mononucleosis n : an acute infectious disease characterized by fever, swelling of lymph glands, and increased numbers of lymph cells in the blood

in·fe·lic·i·tous \ˌin-fi-'li-sə-təs\ adj : not appropriate in application or expression — in·fe·lic·i·ty \-sə-tē\ n

in·fer \in-'fər\ vb in·ferred; in·fer·ring 1 : to derive as a conclusion from facts or premises   2 : GUESS, SURMISE   3 : to lead to as a conclusion or consequence   4 : HINT, SUGGEST ✦ Synonyms DEDUCE, CONCLUDE, JUDGE, GATHER — in·fer·ence \'in-frəns, -fə-rəns\ n — in·fer·en·tial \ˌin-fə-'ren-chəl\ adj

in·fe·ri·or \in-'fir-ē-ər\ adj 1 : situated lower down   2 : of low or lower degree or rank   3 : of lesser quality   4 : of little or less importance, value, or merit — inferior n — in·fe·ri·or·i·ty \(ˌ)in-ˌfir-ē-'ȯr-ə-tē\ n

in·fer·nal \in-'fər-nᵊl\ adj 1 : of or relating to hell   2 : HELLISH, FIENDISH ⟨∼ schemes⟩   3 : DAMNABLE ⟨an ∼ pest⟩ — in·fer·nal·ly adv

in·fer·no \in-'fər-nō\ n, pl -nos [It, hell, fr. LL infernus, fr.

L, lower] : a place or a state that resembles or suggests hell; also : intense heat

in·fer·tile \(ˌ)in-'fər-tᵊl\ adj : not fertile or productive : BARREN — in·fer·til·i·ty \ˌin-fər-'ti-lə-tē\ n

in·fest \in-'fest\ vb : to trouble by spreading or swarming in or over; also : to live in or on as a parasite — in·fes·ta·tion \ˌin-ˌfes-'tā-shən\ n

in·fi·del \'in-fə-dᵊl, -fə-ˌdel\ n 1 : one who is not a Christian or opposes Christianity   2 : an unbeliever esp. with respect to a particular religion

in·fi·del·i·ty \ˌin-fə-'de-lə-tē, -fī-\ n, pl -ties 1 : lack of belief in a religion   2 : unfaithfulness or an instance of it esp. in marriage

in·field \'in-ˌfēld\ n : the part of a baseball field inside the baselines — in·field·er n

in·fight·ing \'in-ˌfī-tiŋ\ n 1 : fighting at close quarters   2 : dissension or rivalry among members of a group

in·fil·trate \in-'fil-ˌtrāt, 'in-(ˌ)fil-\ vb -trat·ed; -trat·ing 1 : to enter or filter into or through something   2 : to pass into or through by or as if by filtering or permeating — in·fil·tra·tion \ˌin-(ˌ)fil-'trā-shən\ n — in·fil·tra·tor n

in·fi·nite \'in-fə-nət\ adj 1 : LIMITLESS, BOUNDLESS, ENDLESS ⟨∼ space⟩ ⟨∼ patience⟩   2 : VAST, IMMENSE; also : INEXHAUSTIBLE ⟨∼ wealth⟩   3 : greater than any preassigned finite value however large ⟨∼ number of positive integers⟩; also : extending to infinity ⟨∼ plane surface⟩ — infinite n — in·fi·nite·ly adv

in·fin·i·tes·i·mal \(ˌ)in-ˌfi-nə-'te-sə-məl\ adj : immeasurably or incalculably small — in·fin·i·tes·i·mal·ly adv

in·fin·i·tive \in-'fi-nə-tiv\ n : a verb form having the characteristics of both verb and noun and in English usu. being used with to

in·fin·i·tude \in-'fi-nə-ˌtüd, -ˌtyüd\ n 1 : the quality or state of being infinite   2 : something that is infinite esp. in extent

in·fin·i·ty \in-'fi-nə-tē\ n, pl -ties 1 : the quality of being infinite   2 : unlimited extent of time, space, or quantity : BOUNDLESSNESS   3 : an indefinitely great number or amount

in·firm \in-'fərm\ adj 1 : deficient in vitality; esp : feeble from age   2 : weak of mind, will, or character : IRRESOLUTE   3 : not solid or stable : INSECURE

in·fir·ma·ry \in-'fər-mə-rē\ n, pl -ries : a place for the care of the infirm or sick

in·fir·mi·ty \in-'fər-mə-tē\ n, pl -ties 1 : FEEBLENESS   2 : DISEASE, AILMENT   3 : a personal failing : FOIBLE

infl abbr influenced

in fla·gran·te de·lic·to \ˌin-flə-'grän-tē-di-'lik-tō, -'gran-\ adv 1 : in the very act of committing a misdeed   2 : in the midst of sexual activity

in·flame \in-'flām\ vb in·flamed; in·flam·ing 1 : KINDLE   2 : to excite to excessive or uncontrollable action or feeling; also : INTENSIFY   3 : to affect or become affected with inflammation

in·flam·ma·ble \in-'fla-mə-bəl\ adj 1 : FLAMMABLE   2 : easily inflamed, excited, or angered : IRASCIBLE

in·flam·ma·tion \ˌin-flə-'mā-shən\ n : a bodily response to injury in which an affected area becomes red, hot, and painful and congested with blood

in·flam·ma·to·ry \in-'fla-mə-ˌtȯr-ē\ adj 1 : tending to excite the senses or to arouse anger, disorder, or tumult : SEDITIOUS   2 : causing or accompanied by inflammation ⟨an ∼ disease⟩

in·flate \in-'flāt\ vb in·flat·ed; in·flat·ing 1 : to swell with air or gas ⟨∼ a balloon⟩   2 : to puff up : ELATE ⟨∼ one's ego⟩   3 : to expand or increase abnormally ⟨∼ prices⟩ — in·flat·able adj

in·fla·tion \in-'flā-shən\ n 1 : an act of inflating : the state of being inflated   2 : empty pretentiousness : POMPOSITY   3 : a continuing rise in the general price level usu. attributed to an increase in the volume of money and credit

in·fla·tion·ary \-shə-ˌner-ē\ adj : of, characterized by, or productive of inflation

in·flect \in-'flekt\ vb 1 : to turn from a direct line or course : CURVE   2 : to vary a word by inflection   3 : to change or vary the pitch of the voice

in·flec·tion \in-'flek-shən\ n 1 : the act or result of curving or bending   2 : a change in pitch or loudness of the voice   3 : the change of form that words undergo to mark

inflectional • inhaling

254

case, gender, number, tense, person, mood, or voice — **in·flec·tion·al** \-shə-nəl\ adj

in·flex·i·ble \(ˌ)in-ˈflek-sə-bəl\ adj 1 : UNYIELDING 2 : RIGID 3 : incapable of change — **in·flex·i·bil·i·ty** \-ˌflek-sə-ˈbi-lə-tē\ n — **in·flex·i·bly** \-ˈflek-sə-blē\ adv

in·flex·ion \in-ˈflek-shən\ chiefly Brit var of INFLECTION

in·flict \in-ˈflikt\ vb : AFFLICT; also : to give by or as if by striking — **in·flic·tion** \-ˈflik-shən\ n

in·flo·res·cence \ˌin-flə-ˈres-ᵊns\ n : the manner of development and arrangement of flowers on a stem; also : a flowering stem with its appendages : a flower cluster

in·flow \ˈin-ˌflō\ n : a flowing in

¹in·flu·ence \ˈin-ˌflü-əns\ n 1 : the act or power of producing an effect without apparent force or direct authority 2 : the power or capacity of causing an effect in indirect or intangible ways 3 : one that exerts influence — **in·flu·en·tial** \ˌin-flü-ˈen-chəl\ adj — **under the influence** : affected by alcohol

²influence vb -enced; -enc·ing 1 : to affect or alter by influence : SWAY 2 : to have an effect on the condition or development of : MODIFY

in·flu·en·za \ˌin-flü-ˈen-zə\ n [It, lit., influence, fr. ML influentia; fr. the belief that epidemics were due to the influence of the stars] : an acute and highly contagious virus disease marked by fever, prostration, aches and pains, and respiratory inflammation; also : any of various feverish usu. virus diseases typically with respiratory symptoms

in·flux \ˈin-ˌfləks\ n : a coming in

in·fo \ˈin-(ˌ)fō\ n : INFORMATION

in·fold \in-ˈfōld\ vb 1 : ENFOLD 2 : to fold inward or toward one another

in·fo·mer·cial \ˈin-fō-ˌmər-shəl\ n : a television program that is an extended advertisement often including a discussion or demonstration

in·form \in-ˈfȯrm\ vb 1 : to communicate knowledge to : TELL 2 : to give information or knowledge 3 : to act as an informer ✦ **Synonyms** ACQUAINT, APPRISE, ADVISE, NOTIFY

in·for·mal \(ˌ)in-ˈfȯr-məl\ adj 1 : conducted or carried out without formality or ceremony ⟨an ~ party⟩ 2 : characteristic of or appropriate to ordinary, casual, or familiar use ⟨~ clothes⟩ — **in·for·mal·i·ty** \ˌin-fȯr-ˈma-lə-tē, -fər-\ n — **in·for·mal·ly** \(ˌ)in-ˈfȯr-mə-lē\ adv

in·for·mant \in-ˈfȯr-mənt\ n : a person who gives information : INFORMER

in·for·ma·tion \ˌin-fər-ˈmā-shən\ n 1 : the communication or reception of knowledge or intelligence 2 : knowledge obtained from investigation, study, or instruction : FACTS, DATA 3 : the attribute communicated by one of two or more alternative sequences of something (as nucleotides in DNA or binary digits in a computer program) — **in·for·ma·tion·al** \-shə-nəl\ adj

information superhighway n : INTERNET

in·for·ma·tive \in-ˈfȯr-mə-tiv\ adj : imparting knowledge : INSTRUCTIVE

in·formed \in-ˈfȯrmd\ adj 1 : having or based on information ⟨an ~ decision⟩ 2 : EDUCATED, KNOWLEDGEABLE

informed consent n : consent to a medical procedure by someone who understands what is involved

in·form·er \-ˈfȯr-mər\ n : one that informs; esp : a person who informs against others for illegalities esp. for financial gain

in·fo·tain·ment \ˌin-fō-ˈtān-mənt\ n : a television program that presents information (as news) in a manner intended to be entertaining

in·frac·tion \in-ˈfrak-shən\ n [ME, fr. ML infractio, fr. L, subduing, fr. infringere to break, crush] : the act of infringing : VIOLATION

in·fra dig \ˌin-frə-ˈdig\ adj [short for L infra dignitatem] : being beneath one's dignity

in·fra·red \ˌin-frə-ˈred\ adj : being, relating to, or using radiation having wavelengths longer than those of red light — **infrared** n

in·fra·struc·ture \ˈin-frə-ˌstrək-chər\ n 1 : the underlying foundation or basic framework (as of a system or organization) 2 : the system of public works of a country, state, or region; also : the resources (as buildings or equipment) required for an activity

in·fre·quent \(ˌ)in-ˈfrē-kwənt\ adj 1 : seldom happening : RARE 2 : placed or occurring at wide intervals in space

or time ✦ **Synonyms** UNCOMMON, SCARCE, SPORADIC — **in·fre·quent·ly** adv

in·fringe \in-ˈfrinj\ vb **in·fringed; in·fring·ing** 1 : VIOLATE, TRANSGRESS ⟨~ a patent⟩ 2 : ENCROACH, TRESPASS ⟨~ on our rights⟩ — **in·fringe·ment** n

in·fu·ri·ate \in-ˈfyu̇r-ē-ˌāt\ vb -at·ed; -at·ing : to make furious : ENRAGE — **in·fu·ri·at·ing·ly** adv

in·fuse \in-ˈfyüz\ vb **in·fused; in·fus·ing** 1 : to instill a principle or quality in ⟨infused the team with confidence⟩ 2 : INSPIRE, ANIMATE 3 : to steep (as tea) without boiling — **in·fu·sion** \-ˈfyü-zhən\ n

¹-ing \iŋ\ n suffix 1 : action or process ⟨sleeping⟩ : instance of an action or process ⟨a meeting⟩ 2 : product or result of an action or process ⟨an engraving⟩ ⟨earnings⟩ 3 : something used in an action or process ⟨a bed covering⟩ 4 : something connected with, consisting of, or used in making (a specified thing) ⟨scaffolding⟩ 5 : something related to (a specified concept) ⟨offing⟩

²-ing n suffix : one of a (specified) kind

³-ing vb suffix or adj suffix — used to form the present participle ⟨sailing⟩ and sometimes to form an adjective resembling a present participle but not derived from a verb ⟨swashbuckling⟩

in·ga·ther \ˈin-ˌga-thər\ vb : to gather in : ASSEMBLE

in·ge·nious \in-ˈjēn-yəs\ adj 1 : marked by special aptitude at discovering, inventing, or contriving 2 : marked by originality, resourcefulness, and cleverness in conception or execution — **in·ge·nious·ly** adv — **in·ge·nious·ness** n

in·ge·nue or **in·gé·nue** \ˈan-jə-ˌnü, ˈän-; ˈaⁿ-zhə-, ˈäⁿ-\ n : a naive girl or young woman; esp : an actress portraying such a person

in·ge·nu·i·ty \ˌin-jə-ˈnü-ə-tē, -ˈnyü-\ n, pl -ties : skill or cleverness in planning or inventing : INVENTIVENESS

in·gen·u·ous \in-ˈjen-yə-wəs\ adj [L ingenuus native, freeborn, fr. gignere to beget] 1 : innocently straightforward ⟨her ~ curiosity⟩ 2 : lacking craft or subtlety ⟨~ comments⟩ — **in·gen·u·ous·ly** adv — **in·gen·u·ous·ness** n

in·gest \in-ˈjest\ vb : to take in for or as if for digestion — **in·ges·tion** \-ˈjes-chən\ n

in·gle·nook \ˈiŋ-gəl-ˌnu̇k\ n : a nook by a large open fireplace; also : a bench occupying this nook

in·glo·ri·ous \(ˌ)in-ˈglȯr-ē-əs\ adj 1 : SHAMEFUL 2 : not glorious : lacking fame or honor — **in·glo·ri·ous·ly** adv

in·got \ˈiŋ-gət\ n : a mass of metal cast in a form convenient for storage or transportation

¹in·grain \(ˌ)in-ˈgrān\ vb : to work indelibly into the natural texture or mental or moral constitution — **in·grained** adj

²in·grain \ˈin-ˌgrān\ adj 1 : made of fiber that is dyed before being spun into yarn 2 : made of yarn that is dyed before being woven or knitted 3 : INNATE — **ingrain** n

in·grate \ˈin-ˌgrāt\ n : an ungrateful person

in·gra·ti·ate \in-ˈgrā-shē-ˌāt\ vb -at·ed; -at·ing : to gain favor by deliberate effort

in·gra·ti·at·ing adj 1 : capable of winning favor : PLEASING ⟨an ~ smile⟩ 2 : FLATTERING ⟨an ~ manner⟩

in·grat·i·tude \(ˌ)in-ˈgra-tə-ˌtüd, -ˌtyüd\ n : lack of gratitude : UNGRATEFULNESS

in·gre·di·ent \in-ˈgrē-dē-ənt\ n : one of the substances that make up a mixture or compound : CONSTITUENT

in·gress \ˈin-ˌgres\ n : ENTRANCE, ACCESS — **in·gres·sion** \in-ˈgre-shən\ n

in·grow·ing \ˈin-ˌgrō-iŋ\ adj : growing or tending inward

in·grown \ˈin-ˌgrōn\ adj : grown in; esp : having the free tip or edge embedded in the flesh ⟨an ~ toenail⟩

in·gui·nal \ˈiŋ-gwə-nᵊl\ adj : of, relating to, or situated in or near the region of the groin ⟨an ~ hernia⟩

in·hab·it \in-ˈha-bət\ vb : to live or dwell in ⟨spiders that ~ caves⟩ — **in·hab·it·able** adj — **in·hab·i·ta·tion** \in-ˌha-bə-ˈtā-shən\ n

in·hab·i·tant \in-ˈha-bə-tənt\ n : a permanent resident in a place

in·hal·ant \in-ˈhā-lənt\ n : something (as a medicine) that is inhaled

in·ha·la·tor \ˈin-hə-ˌlā-tər\ n : a device that provides a mixture of carbon dioxide and oxygen for breathing

in·hale \in-ˈhāl\ vb **in·haled; in·hal·ing** : to breathe in — **in·ha·la·tion** \ˌin-hə-ˈlā-shən\ n

in·hal·er \in-ˈhā-lər\ n : a device by means of which medicinal material is inhaled

in·here \in-'hir\ vb in·hered; in·her·ing : to be inherent
in·her·ent \in-'hir-ənt, -'her-\ adj : established as an essential part of something : INTRINSIC ⟨risks ~ in the venture⟩ — in·her·ent·ly adv
in·her·it \in-'her-ət\ vb 1 : to receive esp. from one's ancestors 2 : to receive by genetic transmission — in·her·it·able \-ə-tə-bəl\ adj — in·her·i·tance \-ə-təns\ n — in·her·i·tor \-ə-tər\ n
in·hib·it \in-'hi-bət\ vb 1 : PROHIBIT, FORBID 2 : to hold in check : RESTRAIN — in·hib·i·tor \-bə-tər\ n — in·hib·i·to·ry \-bə-,tór-ē\ adj
in·hi·bi·tion \,in-hə-'bi-shən\ n 1 : PROHIBITION, RESTRAINT 2 : a usu. inner check on free activity, expression, or functioning
in–house \'in-,haùs, -'haùs\ adj : existing, originating, or carried on within a group or organization
in·hu·man \(,)in-'hyü-mən, -'yü-\ adj 1 : lacking pity, kindness, or mercy : SAVAGE ⟨an ~ tyrant⟩ 2 : COLD, IMPERSONAL 3 : not worthy of or conforming to the needs of human beings ⟨~ living conditions⟩ 4 : of or suggesting a nonhuman class of beings — in·hu·man·ly adv — in·hu·man·ness n
in·hu·mane \,in-hyü-'mān, -yü-\ adj : not humane : INHUMAN 1
in·hu·man·i·ty \-'ma-nə-tē\ n, pl -ties 1 : the quality or state of being cruel or barbarous 2 : a cruel or barbarous act
in·im·i·cal \i-'ni-mi-kəl\ adj 1 : being adverse often by reason of hostility ⟨forces ~ to change⟩ 2 : HOSTILE, UNFRIENDLY ⟨~ factions⟩ — in·im·i·cal·ly adv
in·im·i·ta·ble \(,)i-'ni-mə-tə-bəl\ adj : not capable of being imitated
in·iq·ui·ty \i-'ni-kwə-tē\ n, pl -ties [ME iniquite, fr. AF iniquité, fr. L iniquitas, fr. iniquus uneven, fr. aequus equal] 1 : WICKEDNESS 2 : a wicked act — in·iq·ui·tous \-təs\ adj
¹ini·tial \i-'ni-shəl\ adj 1 : of or relating to the beginning : INCIPIENT ⟨my ~ reaction⟩ 2 : being at the beginning — ini·tial·ly adv
²initial n : the first letter of a word or name
³initial vb -tialed or -tialled; -tial·ing or -tial·ling : to affix an initial to
¹ini·ti·ate \i-'ni-shē-,āt\ vb -at·ed; -at·ing 1 : START, BEGIN 2 : to induct into membership by or as if by special ceremonies 3 : to instruct in the rudiments or principles of something — ini·ti·a·tion \-,ni-shē-'ā-shən\ n
²ini·tiate \i-'ni-shē-ət\ n 1 : a person who is undergoing or has passed an initiation 2 : a person who is instructed or adept in some special field
ini·tia·tive \i-'ni-shə-tiv\ n 1 : an introductory step 2 : self-reliant enterprise ⟨showed great ~⟩ 3 : a process by which laws may be introduced or enacted directly by vote of the people
ini·tia·to·ry \i-'ni-shē-ə-,tór-ē\ adj 1 : INTRODUCTORY 2 : tending or serving to initiate ⟨~ rites⟩
in·ject \in-'jekt\ vb 1 : to force into something ⟨~ serum with a needle⟩ 2 : to introduce as an element into some situation or subject ⟨~ a note of suspicion⟩ — in·jec·tion \-'jek-shən\ n
in·junc·tion \in-'jəŋk-shən\ n 1 : ORDER, ADMONITION 2 : a court writ whereby one is required to do or to refrain from doing a specified act
in·jure \'in-jər\ vb in·jured; in·jur·ing 1 : WRONG 2 : to damage or hurt esp. physically ♦ Synonyms HARM, IMPAIR, MAR, SPOIL
in·ju·ry \'in-jə-rē\ n, pl -ries 1 : an act that damages or hurts : WRONG 2 : hurt, damage, or loss sustained — in·ju·ri·ous \in-'jùr-ē-əs\ adj
in·jus·tice \(,)in-'jəs-təs\ n 1 : violation of a person's rights : UNFAIRNESS 2 : an unjust act or deed : WRONG
¹ink \'iŋk\ n [ME enke, fr. AF encre, enke, fr. LL encaustum, fr. L encaustus burned in, fr. Gk enkaustos, fr. enkaiein to burn in] : a usu. liquid and colored material for writing and printing — inky adj
²ink vb : to put ink on; esp : SIGN
ink·blot test \'iŋk-,blät-\ n : any of several psychological tests based on the interpretation of irregular figures
ink·horn \-,hórn\ n : a small bottle (as of horn) for holding ink
in–kind \'in-'kīnd\ adj : consisting of something (as goods) other than money

ink–jet n : a computer printer that sprays electrically charged droplets of ink onto paper — ink–jet adj
in·kling \'iŋ-kliŋ\ n 1 : HINT, INTIMATION 2 : a vague idea
ink·stand \'iŋk-,stand\ n : INKWELL; also : a pen and ink stand
ink·well \-,wel\ n : a container for ink
in·laid \'in-'lād\ adj : decorated with material set into a surface
¹in·land \'in-,land, -lənd\ adj 1 chiefly Brit : not foreign : DOMESTIC ⟨~ revenue⟩ 2 : of or relating to the interior of a country ⟨the ~ states⟩
²inland n : the interior of a country
³inland adv : into or toward the interior
in–law \'in-,ló\ n : a relative by marriage
¹in·lay \(,)in-'lā, 'in-,lā\ vb in·laid \-'lād\; in·lay·ing : to set (a material) into a surface or ground material esp. for decoration
²in·lay \'in-,lā\ n 1 : inlaid work 2 : a shaped filling cemented into a tooth
in·let \'in-,let, -lət\ n 1 : a small or narrow bay 2 : an opening for intake esp. of a fluid
in–line skate n : a roller skate whose four wheels are set in a straight line — in–line skater n — in–line skating n
in·mate \'in-,māt\ n : any of a group occupying a single place of residence; esp : a person confined (as in a hospital or prison)
in me·di·as res \in-,mā-dē-əs-'rās\ adv [L, lit., into the midst of things] : in or into the middle of a narrative or plot
in·most \'in-,mōst\ adj : deepest within : INNERMOST
inn \'in\ n : HOTEL, TAVERN
in·nards \'i-nərdz\ n pl [alter. of inwards] 1 : the internal organs of a human being or animal; esp : VISCERA 2 : the internal parts of a structure or mechanism
in·nate \i-'nāt\ adj 1 : existing in, belonging to, or determined by factors present in an individual from birth : NATIVE 2 : INHERENT, INTRINSIC — in·nate·ly adv
in·ner \'i-nər\ adj 1 : situated farther in ⟨the ~ bark⟩ 2 : near a center esp. of influence ⟨the ~ circle⟩ 3 : of or relating to the mind or spirit ⟨an ~ voice⟩ 4 : being a usu. repressed part of one's psychological makeup ⟨the ~ child⟩
inner city n : the usu. older, poorer, and more densely populated section of a city — inner–city adj
in·ner–di·rect·ed \,i-nər-də-'rek-təd, -(,)dī-\ adj : directed in thought and action by one's own scale of values as opposed to external norms
inner ear n : the part of the ear that is most important for hearing, is located in a cavity in the temporal bone, and contains sense organs of hearing and of awareness of position in space
in·ner·most \'i-nər-,mōst\ adj : farthest inward : INMOST
in·ner·sole \'i-nər-'sōl\ n : INSOLE
in·ner·spring \'i-nər-'spriŋ\ adj : having coil springs inside a padded casing ⟨an ~ mattress⟩
inner tube n : an airtight rubber tube inside a tire to hold air under pressure
in·ning \'i-niŋ\ n 1 sing or pl : a division of a cricket match 2 : a baseball team's turn at bat; also : a division of a baseball game consisting of a turn at bat for each team
inn·keep·er \'in-'kē-pər\ n 1 : a proprietor of an inn 2 : a hotel manager
in·no·cence \'i-nə-səns\ n 1 : BLAMELESSNESS; also : freedom from legal guilt 2 : GUILELESSNESS, SIMPLICITY; also : IGNORANCE
in·no·cent \-sənt\ adj [ME, fr. AF, fr. L innocens, fr. nocens wicked, fr. nocēre to harm] 1 : free from guilt or sin : BLAMELESS 2 : harmless in effect or intention; also : CANDID ⟨an ~ remark⟩ 3 : free from legal guilt or fault : LAWFUL 4 : INGENUOUS 5 : UNAWARE — innocent n — in·no·cent·ly adv
in·noc·u·ous \i-'nä-kyə-wəs\ adj 1 : HARMLESS 2 : not offensive; also : INSIPID ⟨~ jokes⟩
in·nom·i·nate \i-'nä-mə-nət\ adj : having no name; also : ANONYMOUS
in·no·vate \'i-nə-,vāt\ vb -vat·ed; -vat·ing : to introduce as

or as if new : make changes — **in·no·va·tive** \-ˌvā-tiv\ *adj* — **in·no·va·tor** \-ˌvā-tər\ *n*

in·no·va·tion \ˌi-nə-'vā-shən\ *n* **1** : the introduction of something new **2** : a new idea, method, or device

in·nu·en·do \ˌin-yə-'wen-dō\ *n, pl* **-dos** *or* **-does** [L, by nodding, fr. *innuere* to nod to, make a sign to, fr. *nuere* to nod] : HINT, INSINUATION; *esp* : a veiled reflection on character or reputation

in·nu·mer·a·ble \i-'nü-mə-rə-bəl, -'nyü-\ *adj* : too many to be numbered

in·oc·u·late \i-'nä-kyə-ˌlāt\ *vb* **-lat·ed; -lat·ing** [ME, to insert a bud in a plant, fr. L *inoculare*, fr. *oculus* eye, bud] : to introduce something into; *esp* : to introduce a serum or antibody into (an organism) to treat or prevent a disease — **in·oc·u·la·tion** \-ˌnä-kyə-'lä-shən\ *n*

in·op·er·a·ble \(ˌ)in-'ä-pə-rə-bəl\ *adj* **1** : not suitable for surgery ⟨an ∼ tumor⟩ **2** : not operable ⟨∼ vehicles⟩

in·op·er·a·tive \-'ä-pə-rə-tiv, -'ä-pə-ˌrā-\ *adj* : not functioning

in·op·por·tune \(ˌ)in-ˌä-pər-'tün, -'tyün\ *adj* : INCONVENIENT, INAPPROPRIATE — **in·op·por·tune·ly** *adv*

in·or·di·nate \in-'ór-dⁿn-ət\ *adj* : exceeding reasonable limits : IMMODERATE ⟨drank an ∼ amount of water⟩ — **in·or·di·nate·ly** *adv*

in·or·gan·ic \ˌin-ˌór-'ga-nik\ *adj* : being or composed of matter of other than plant or animal origin : MINERAL

in·pa·tient \'in-ˌpā-shənt\ *n* : a hospital patient who receives lodging and food as well as treatment

in·put \'in-ˌpút\ *n* **1** : something put in **2** : power or energy put into a machine or system **3** : information fed into a computer or data processing system **4** : ADVICE, OPINION — **input** *vb*

in·quest \'in-ˌkwest\ *n* **1** : an official inquiry or examination esp. before a jury **2** : INQUIRY, INVESTIGATION

in·qui·etude \(ˌ)in-'kwī-ə-ˌtüd, -ˌtyüd\ *n* : UNEASINESS, RESTLESSNESS

in·quire \in-'kwī(-ə)r\ *vb* **in·quired; in·quir·ing 1** : to ask about : ASK **2** : INVESTIGATE, EXAMINE — **in·quir·er** *n* — **in·quir·ing·ly** *adv*

in·qui·ry \'in-ˌkwī(-ə)r-ē, in-'kwī(-ə)r-ē; 'in-kwə-rē, 'iŋ-\ *n, pl* **-ries 1** : a request for information; *also* : RESEARCH **2** : a systematic investigation of a matter of public interest

in·qui·si·tion \ˌin-kwə-'zi-shən, ˌiŋ-\ *n* **1** : a judicial or official inquiry usu. before a jury **2** *cap* : a former Roman Catholic tribunal for the discovery and punishment of heresy **3** : a severe questioning — **in·quis·i·tor** \in-'kwi-zə-tər\ *n* — **in·quis·i·to·ri·al** \-ˌkwi-zə-'tór-ē-əl\ *adj*

in·quis·i·tive \in-'kwi-zə-tiv\ *adj* **1** : given to examination or investigation **2** : unduly curious — **in·quis·i·tive·ly** *adv* — **in·quis·i·tive·ness** *n*

in re \in-'rā, -'rē\ *prep* : in the matter of

INRI *abbr* [L *Iesus Nazarenus Rex Iudaeorum*] Jesus of Nazareth, King of the Jews

in·road \'in-ˌród\ *n* **1** : INVASION, RAID **2** : an advance made usu. at the expense of another ⟨made ∼s toward getting the job⟩

in·rush \'in-ˌrəsh\ *n* : a crowding or flooding in

ins *abbr* **1** inches **2** insurance

INS *abbr* Immigration and Naturalization Service

in·sa·lu·bri·ous \ˌin-sə-'lü-brē-əs\ *adj* : UNWHOLESOME, NOXIOUS

ins and outs *n pl* **1** : characteristic peculiarities **2** : RAMIFICATIONS

in·sane \(ˌ)in-'sān\ *adj* **1** : exhibiting serious and debilitating mental disorder; *also* : used by or for the insane **2** : ABSURD **3** : greatly exceeding the ordinary, usual, or expected — **in·sane·ly** *adv* — **in·san·i·ty** \in-'sa-nə-tē\ *n*

in·sa·tia·ble \(ˌ)in-'sā-shə-bəl\ *adj* : incapable of being satisfied ⟨an ∼ thirst⟩ — **in·sa·tia·bil·i·ty** \(ˌ)in-ˌsā-shə-'bi-lə-tē\ *n* — **in·sa·tia·bly** *adv*

in·sa·tiate \(ˌ)in-'sā-shē-ət, -shət\ *adj* : INSATIABLE — **in·sa·tiate·ly** *adv*

in·scribe \in-'skrīb\ *vb* **1** : to write, engrave, or print as a lasting record **2** : ENROLL **3** : to write, engrave, or print characters upon **4** : to dedicate to someone **5** : to draw within a figure so as to touch in as many places as possible — **in·scrip·tion** \-'skrip-shən\ *n*

in·scru·ta·ble \in-'skrü-tə-bəl\ *adj* : not readily comprehensible : MYSTERIOUS — **in·scru·ta·bly** \-blē\ *adv*

in·seam \'in-ˌsēm\ *n* : the seam on the inside of the leg of a pair of pants; *also* : the length of this seam

in·sect \'in-ˌsekt\ *n* [L *insectum*, fr. *insectus*, pp. of *insecare* to cut into, fr. *secare* to cut] : any of a class of small usu. winged arthropod animals (as flies, bees, beetles, and moths) with usu. three pairs of legs as adults

in·sec·ti·cide \in-'sek-tə-ˌsīd\ *n* : an agent for destroying insects — **in·sec·ti·cid·al** \(ˌ)in-ˌsek-tə-'sīd-ᵊl\ *adj*

in·sec·tiv·o·rous \ˌin-ˌsek-'ti-və-rəs\ *adj* : feeding on insects

in·se·cure \ˌin-si-'kyúr\ *adj* **1** : UNCERTAIN **2** : not protected : UNSAFE ⟨an ∼ investment⟩ **3** : LOOSE, SHAKY ⟨an ∼ hinge⟩ **4** : not highly stable ⟨an ∼ marriage⟩; *also* : lacking assurance : ANXIOUS, FEARFUL — **in·se·cure·ly** *adv* — **in·se·cu·ri·ty** \-'kyúr-ə-tē\ *n*

in·sem·i·nate \in-'se-mə-ˌnāt\ *vb* **-nat·ed; -nat·ing** : to introduce semen into the genital tract of (a female) — **in·sem·i·na·tion** \-ˌse-mə-'nā-shən\ *n*

in·sen·sate \(ˌ)in-'sen-ˌsāt, -sət\ *adj* **1** : lacking sense or understanding; *also* : FOOLISH **2** : INANIMATE **3** : BRUTAL, INHUMAN ⟨∼ rage⟩

in·sen·si·ble \(ˌ)in-'sen-sə-bəl\ *adj* **1** : IMPERCEPTIBLE; *also* : SLIGHT, GRADUAL **2** : INANIMATE **3** : UNCONSCIOUS **4** : lacking sensory perception or ability to react ⟨∼ to pain⟩ **5** : APATHETIC, INDIFFERENT; *also* : UNAWARE ⟨∼ of their danger⟩ **6** : MEANINGLESS **7** : lacking delicacy or refinement — **in·sen·si·bil·i·ty** \-ˌsen-sə-'bi-lə-tē\ *n* — **in·sen·si·bly** \-'sen-sə-blē\ *adv*

in·sen·tient \(ˌ)in-'sen-chē-ənt\ *adj* : lacking perception, consciousness, or animation — **in·sen·tience** \-chē-əns\ *n*

in·sep·a·ra·ble \(ˌ)in-'se-prə-bəl, -pə-rə-\ *adj* **1** : incapable of being separated or disjoined **2** : very close or intimate ⟨∼ friends⟩ — **in·sep·a·ra·bil·i·ty** \-ˌse-prə-'bi-lə-tē, -pə-rə-\ *n* — **inseparable** *n* — **in·sep·a·ra·bly** \-'se-prə-blē, -pə-rə-\ *adv*

¹in·sert \in-'sərt\ *vb* **1** : to put or thrust in ⟨∼ a key in a lock⟩ ⟨∼ a comma⟩ **2** : INTERPOLATE **3** : to set in (as a piece of fabric) and make fast

²in·sert \'in-ˌsərt\ *n* : something that is inserted or is for insertion; *esp* : written or printed material inserted (as between the leaves of a book)

in·ser·tion \in-'sər-shən\ *n* **1** : something that is inserted **2** : the act or process of inserting

in·set \'in-ˌset\ *vb* **inset** *or* **in·set·ted; in·set·ting** : to set in : INSERT — **inset** *n*

¹in·shore \'in-'shór\ *adj* **1** : situated, living, or carried on near shore **2** : moving toward shore ⟨an ∼ current⟩

²inshore *adv* : to or toward shore

¹in·side \in-'sīd, 'in-ˌsīd\ *n* **1** : an inner side or surface : INTERIOR **2** : inward nature, thoughts, or feeling **3** *pl* : VISCERA, ENTRAILS **4** : a position of power, trust, or familiarity — **inside** *adj*

²inside *adv* **1** : on the inner side **2** : in or into the interior

³inside *prep* **1** : in or into the inside of ⟨∼ the house⟩ **2** : WITHIN ⟨∼ an hour⟩

inside of *prep* : INSIDE

inside out *adv* **1** : in such a manner that the inner surface becomes the outer ⟨turned the shirt *inside out*⟩ **2** : in a state of disarray or reorganization ⟨turned her life *inside out*⟩

in·sid·er \in-'sī-dər\ *n* : a person who is in a position of power or has access to confidential information

in·sid·i·ous \in-'si-dē-əs\ *adj* [L *insidiosus*, fr. *insidiae* ambush, fr. *insidēre* to sit in, sit on, fr. *sedēre* to sit] **1** : SLY, TREACHEROUS **2** : SEDUCTIVE **3** : having a gradual and cumulative effect : SUBTLE — **in·sid·i·ous·ly** *adv* — **in·sid·i·ous·ness** *n*

in·sight \'in-ˌsīt\ *n* : the power, act, or result of seeing into a situation : UNDERSTANDING, PENETRATION — **in·sight·ful** \'in-ˌsīt-fəl, in-'sīt-\ *adj*

in·sig·nia \in-'sig-nē-ə\ *also* **in·sig·ne** \-(ˌ)nē\ *n, pl* **-nia** *or* **-ni·as** : a distinguishing mark esp. of authority or honor : BADGE

in·sin·cere \ˌin-sin-'sir\ *adj* : not sincere : HYPOCRITICAL — **in·sin·cere·ly** *adv* — **in·sin·cer·i·ty** \-'ser-ə-tē\ *n*

in·sin·u·ate \in-'sin-yə-ˌwāt\ *vb* **-at·ed; -at·ing** [L *insinuare*, fr. *sinuare* to bend, curve, fr. *sinus* curve] **1** : to introduce gradually or in a subtle, indirect, or artful way **2** : to imply in a subtle or devious way — **in·sin·u·a·tion** \(ˌ)in-ˌsin-yə-'wā-shən\ *n*

in·sin·u·at·ing *adj* **1** : winning favor and confidence by imperceptible degrees **2** : tending gradually to cause doubt, distrust, or change of outlook

in·sip·id \in-'si-pəd\ *adj* **1** : lacking taste or savor **2** : DULL, FLAT — **in·si·pid·i·ty** \ˌin-sə-'pi-də-tē\ *n*

in·sist \in-'sist\ *vb* [MF or L; MF *insister*, fr. L *insistere* to stand upon, persist, fr. *sistere* to take a stand] : to take a resolute stand ⟨∼ed on paying⟩

in·sis·tence \in-'sis-təns\ *n* : the act of insisting; *also* : an insistent attitude or quality : URGENCY

in·sis·tent \in-'sis-tənt\ *adj* : disposed to insist — **in·sis·tent·ly** *adv*

in si·tu \in-'sī-tü, -'sē-\ *adv or adj* [L, in position] : in the natural or original position ⟨an *in situ* cancer⟩

in·so·far as \ˌin-sə-'fär-\ *conj* : to the extent or degree that

insol *abbr* insoluble

in·so·la·tion \ˌin-(ˌ)sō-'lā-shən\ *n* : solar radiation that has been received

in·sole \'in-ˌsōl\ *n* **1** : an inside sole of a shoe **2** : a loose thin strip placed inside a shoe for warmth or comfort

in·so·lent \'in-sə-lənt\ *adj* : contemptuous, rude, disrespectful, or bold in behavior or language — **in·so·lence** \-ləns\ *n*

in·sol·u·ble \(ˌ)in-'säl-yə-bəl\ *adj* **1** : having or admitting of no solution or explanation **2** : difficult or impossible to dissolve — **in·sol·u·bil·i·ty** \-ˌsäl-yə-'bi-lə-tē\ *n*

in·sol·vent \(ˌ)in-'säl-vənt\ *adj* **1** : unable or insufficient to pay all debts ⟨an ∼ estate⟩ **2** : IMPOVERISHED, DEFICIENT — **in·sol·ven·cy** \-vən-sē\ *n*

in·som·nia \in-'säm-nē-ə\ *n* : prolonged and usu. abnormal sleeplessness — **in·som·ni·ac** \-nē-ˌak\ *n*

in·so·much as \ˌin-sə-'məch\ *conj* : INASMUCH AS

insomuch that *conj* : to such a degree that : SO

in·sou·ci·ance \in-'sü-sē-əns, aⁿ-süs-'yäⁿs\ *n* [F] : lighthearted unconcern — **in·sou·ci·ant** \in-'sü-sē-ənt, aⁿ-süs-'yäⁿ\ *adj*

insp *abbr* inspector

in·spect \in-'spekt\ *vb* : to view closely and critically : EXAMINE ⟨∼ the gem for flaws⟩ — **in·spec·tion** \-'spek-shən\ *n* — **in·spec·tor** \-tər\ *n*

inspector general *n* : the head of a system of inspection (as of an army)

in·spi·ra·tion \ˌin-spə-'rā-shən\ *n* **1** : the act or power of moving the intellect or emotions **2** : INHALATION **3** : the quality or state of being inspired; *also* : something that is inspired **4** : an inspiring agent or influence — **in·spi·ra·tion·al** \-shə-nəl\ *adj*

in·spire \in-'spīr\ *vb* **in·spired; in·spir·ing** **1** : to influence, move, or guide by divine or supernatural inspiration **2** : to exert an animating, enlivening, or exalting influence upon ⟨a painter *inspired* by cubism⟩; *also* : AFFECT **3** : to communicate to an agent supernaturally; *also* : bring out or about **4** : INHALE **5** : INCITE **6** : to spread by indirect means — **in·spir·er** *n*

in·spir·it \in-'spir-ət\ *vb* : ENCOURAGE, HEARTEN

inst *abbr* **1** instant **2** institute; institution; institutional

in·sta·bil·i·ty \ˌin-stə-'bi-lə-tē\ *n* : lack of steadiness; *esp* : lack of emotional or mental stability

in·stal *chiefly Brit var of* INSTALL

in·stall \in-'stȯl\ *vb* **1** : to place formally in office : induct into an office, rank, or order **2** : to establish in an indicated place, condition, or status **3** : to set up for use or service — **in·stal·la·tion** \ˌin-stə-'lā-shən\ *n*

¹in·stall·ment *also* **in·stal·ment** \in-'stȯl-mənt\ *n* : INSTALLATION

²installment *also* **instalment** *n* **1** : one of the parts into which a debt or sum is divided for payment **2** : one of several parts presented at intervals

¹in·stance \'in-stəns\ *n* **1** : INSTIGATION, REQUEST **2** : EXAMPLE ⟨for ∼⟩ **3** : an event or step that is part of a process or series ♦ **Synonyms** CASE, ILLUSTRATION, SAMPLE, SPECIMEN

²instance *vb* **in·stanced; in·stanc·ing** : to mention as a case or example

¹in·stant \'in-stənt\ *n* **1** : MOMENT ⟨the ∼ we met⟩ **2** : the present or current month

²instant *adj* **1** : URGENT **2** : PRESENT, CURRENT **3** : IMMEDIATE ⟨∼ relief⟩ **4** : premixed or precooked for easy final preparation ⟨∼ cake mix⟩; *also* : immediately soluble in water ⟨∼ coffee⟩

in·stan·ta·neous \ˌin-stən-'tā-nē-əs\ *adj* : done or occurring in an instant or without delay ⟨an ∼ chemical reaction⟩ — **in·stan·ta·neous·ly** *adv*

in·stan·ter \in-'stan-tər\ *adv* : at once

in·stan·ti·ate \in-'stan-chē-ˌāt\ *vb* **-at·ed; -at·ing** : to represent (an abstraction) by a concrete example — **in·stan·ti·a·tion** \-ˌstan-chē-'ā-shən\ *n*

in·stant·ly \'in-stənt-lē\ *adv* : at once : IMMEDIATELY

in·state \in-'stāt\ *vb* : to establish in a rank or office : INSTALL

in·stead \in-'sted\ *adv* **1** : as a substitute or equivalent **2** : as an alternative : RATHER

instead of *prep* : as a substitute for or alternative to ⟨use glue *instead of* paste⟩

in·step \'in-ˌstep\ *n* : the arched part of the human foot in front of the ankle joint; *esp* : its upper surface

in·sti·gate \'in-stə-ˌgāt\ *vb* **-gat·ed; -gat·ing** : to goad or urge forward : PROVOKE, INCITE ⟨∼ a revolt⟩ — **in·sti·ga·tion** \ˌin-stə-'gā-shən\ *n* — **in·sti·ga·tor** \'in-stə-ˌgā-tər\ *n*

in·stil *chiefly Brit var of* INSTILL

in·still \in-'stil\ *vb* **1** : to cause to enter drop by drop **2** : to impart gradually

¹in·stinct \'in-ˌstiŋkt\ *n* **1** : a natural aptitude **2** : a largely inheritable and unalterable tendency of an organism to make a complex and specific response to environmental stimuli without involving reason; *also* : behavior originating below the conscious level — **in·stinc·tive** \in-'stiŋk-tiv\ *adj* — **in·stinc·tive·ly** *adv*

²instinct \in-'stiŋkt, 'in-ˌstiŋkt\ *adj* : IMBUED, INFUSED

in·stinc·tu·al \in-'stiŋk-chə-wəl\ *adj* : of, relating to, or based on instinct

¹in·sti·tute \'in-stə-ˌtüt, -ˌtyüt\ *vb* **-tut·ed; -tut·ing** **1** : to establish in a position or office **2** : ORGANIZE **3** : INAUGURATE, INITIATE

²institute *n* **1** : an elementary principle recognized as authoritative; *also, pl* : a collection of such principles and precepts **2** : an organization for the promotion of a cause : ASSOCIATION **3** : an educational institution **4** : a brief course of instruction on a particular field

in·sti·tu·tion \ˌin-stə-'tü-shən, -'tyü-\ *n* **1** : an act of originating, setting up, or founding **2** : an established practice, law, or custom **3** : a society or corporation esp. of a public character ⟨a charitable ∼⟩; *also* : ASYLUM **3** — **in·sti·tu·tion·al** \-'tü-shə-nəl, -'tyü-\ *adj* — **in·sti·tu·tion·al·ize** \-nə-ˌlīz\ *vb* — **in·sti·tu·tion·al·ly** *adv*

instr *abbr* **1** instructor **2** instrument

in·struct \in-'strəkt\ *vb* [ME, fr. L *instructus*, pp. of *instruere*, fr. *struere* to build] **1** : TEACH **2** : INFORM **3** : to give an order or a command to

in·struc·tion \in-'strək-shən\ *n* **1** : LESSON, PRECEPT **2** : COMMAND, ORDER **3** *pl* : DIRECTIONS **4** : the action, practice, or profession of a teacher — **in·struc·tion·al** \-shə-nəl\ *adj*

in·struc·tive \in-'strək-tiv\ *adj* : carrying a lesson : ENLIGHTENING

in·struc·tor \in-'strək-tər\ *n* : one that instructs; *esp* : a college teacher below professorial rank — **in·struc·tor·ship** *n*

in·stru·ment \'in-strə-mənt\ *n* **1** : a device used to produce music **2** : a means by which something is done **3** : a device for doing work and esp. precision work ⟨a drafting ∼⟩ **4** : a legal document (as a deed) **5** : a device used in navigating an airplane — **in·stru·ment** \-ˌment\ *vb*

in·stru·men·tal \ˌin-strə-'men-t³l\ *adj* **1** : acting as a crucial agent or means ⟨was ∼ in arranging the deal⟩ **2** : of, relating to, or done with an instrument **3** : relating to, composed for, or performed on a musical instrument

in·stru·men·tal·ist \-'men-tə-list\ *n* : a player on a musical instrument

in·stru·men·tal·i·ty \ˌin-strə-mən-'ta-lə-tē, -ˌmen-\ *n, pl* **-ties** **1** : the quality or state of being instrumental **2** : MEANS, AGENCY

in·stru·men·ta·tion \ˌin-strə-mən-'tā-shən, -ˌmen-\ *n* **1** : ORCHESTRATION **2** : instruments for a particular purpose

instrument panel *n* : DASHBOARD

in·sub·or·di·nate \ˌin-sə-'bȯr-də-nət\ *adj* : disobedient to authority — **in·sub·or·di·na·tion** \-ˌbȯr-də-'nā-shən\ *n*

in·sub·stan·tial \ˌin-səb-'stan-chəl\ *adj* **1** : lacking substance or reality **2** : lacking firmness or solidity

in·suf·fer·able \(ˌ)in-ˈsə-fə-rə-bəl\ *adj* : not to be endured : INTOLERABLE ⟨an ∼ bore⟩ — **in·suf·fer·ably** \-blē\ *adv*

in·suf·fi·cient \ˌin-sə-ˈfi-shənt\ *adj* : not sufficient ⟨∼ funds⟩; *also* : lacking capacity — **in·suf·fi·cien·cy** \-shən-sē\ *n* — **in·suf·fi·cient·ly** *adv*

in·su·lar \ˈin-sə-lər, -syə-\ *adj* **1** : of, relating to, or forming an island **2** : dwelling or situated on an island **3** : NARROW-MINDED — **in·su·lar·i·ty** \ˌin-sə-ˈlar-ə-tē, -syə-\ *n*

in·su·late \ˈin-sə-ˌlāt\ *vb* **-lat·ed; -lat·ing** [L *insula* island] : ISOLATE; *esp* : to separate a conductor of electricity, heat, or sound from other conducting bodies by means of a nonconductor — **in·su·la·tion** \ˌin-sə-ˈlā-shən\ *n* — **in·su·la·tor** \ˈin-sə-ˌlā-tər\ *n*

in·su·lin \ˈin-sə-lən\ *n* : a pancreatic hormone essential esp. for the metabolism of carbohydrates and the regulation of glucose levels in the blood

¹in·sult \in-ˈsəlt\ *vb* [MF or L; MF *insulter,* fr. L *insultare,* lit., to spring upon, fr. *saltare* to leap] : to treat with insolence or contempt : AFFRONT — **in·sult·ing·ly** *adv*

²in·sult \ˈin-ˌsəlt\ *n* : a gross indignity

in·su·per·a·ble \(ˌ)in-ˈsü-pə-rə-bəl\ *adj* : incapable of being surmounted, overcome, passed over, or solved — **in·su·per·a·bly** \-blē\ *adv*

in·sup·port·able \ˌin-sə-ˈpȯr-tə-bəl\ *adj* **1** : UNENDUR-ABLE **2** : UNJUSTIFIABLE

in·sur·able \in-ˈshu̇r-ə-bəl\ *adj* : capable of being or proper to be insured

in·sur·ance \in-ˈshu̇r-əns\ *n* **1** : the business of insuring persons or property **2** : coverage by contract whereby one party agrees to guarantee another against a specified loss **3** : the sum for which something is insured **4** : a means of guaranteeing protection or safety

in·sure \in-ˈshu̇r\ *vb* **in·sured; in·sur·ing 1** : to provide or obtain insurance on or for : UNDERWRITE **2** : to make certain : ENSURE

in·sured \in-ˈshu̇rd\ *n* : a person whose life or property is insured

in·sur·er \in-ˈshu̇r-ər\ *n* : one that insures; *esp* : an insurance company

in·sur·gent \in-ˈsər-jənt\ *n* **1** : a person who revolts against civil authority or an established government : REBEL **2** : a member of a political party who rebels against it — **in·sur·gence** \-jəns\ *n* — **in·sur·gen·cy** \-jən-sē\ *n* — **in·sur·gent** *adj*

in·sur·mount·able \ˌin-sər-ˈmau̇n-tə-bəl\ *adj* : INSUPERA-BLE ⟨∼ problems⟩ — **in·sur·mount·ably** \-blē\ *adv*

in·sur·rec·tion \ˌin-sə-ˈrek-shən\ *n* : an act or instance of revolting against civil authority or an established government — **in·sur·rec·tion·ist** \-shə-nist\ *n*

int *abbr* **1** interest **2** interior **3** intermediate **4** internal **5** international **6** intransitive

in·tact \in-ˈtakt\ *adj* : untouched esp. by anything that harms or diminishes

in·ta·glio \in-ˈtal-yō\ *n, pl* **-glios** [It] : an engraving cut deeply into the surface of a hard material (as stone)

in·take \ˈin-ˌtāk\ *n* **1** : an opening through which fluid enters **2** : the act of taking in **3** : something taken in

¹in·tan·gi·ble \(ˌ)in-ˈtan-jə-bəl\ *adj* : incapable of being touched : IMPALPABLE — **in·tan·gi·bly** \-blē\ *adv*

²intangible *n* **1** : an incorporeal asset **2** : an abstract quality or attribute

in·te·ger \ˈin-ti-jər\ *n* [L, adj., whole, entire] : a number (as 1, 2, 3, 12, 432) that is not a fraction and does not include a fraction, is the negative of such a number, or is 0

in·te·gral \ˈin-ti-grəl\ *adj* **1** : essential to completeness ⟨∼ to the company⟩ **2** : formed as a unit with another part **3** : composed of parts that make up a whole **4** : ENTIRE

²integral *n* : the result of a mathematical integration

in·te·grate \ˈin-tə-ˌgrāt\ *vb* **-grat·ed; -grat·ing 1** : to find a function that has a given derivative **2** : to form, coordinate, or blend into a functioning whole : UNITE **3** : to incorporate into a larger unit **4** : to end the segregation of and bring into equal membership in society or an organization; *also* : DESEGREGATE — **in·te·gra·tion** \ˌin-tə-ˈgrā-shən\ *n*

integrated circuit *n* : a group of tiny electronic components and their connections that is produced in or on a small slice of material (as silicon)

in·teg·ri·ty \in-ˈte-grə-tē\ *n* **1** : adherence to a code of val-

ues : INCORRUPTIBILITY **2** : SOUNDNESS **3** : COMPLETE-NESS

in·teg·u·ment \in-ˈte-gyə-mənt\ *n* : a covering layer (as a skin or cuticle) of an organism or one of its parts

in·tel·lect \ˈin-tə-ˌlekt\ *n* **1** : the power of knowing : the capacity for knowledge **2** : the capacity for rational or intelligent thought esp. when highly developed **3** : a person with great intellectual powers

in·tel·lec·tu·al \ˌin-tə-ˈlek-chə-wəl\ *adj* **1** : of, relating to, or performed by the intellect : RATIONAL **2** : given to study, reflection, and speculation ⟨∼ games⟩ **3** : engaged in activity requiring the creative use of the intellect — **intellectual** *n* — **in·tel·lec·tu·al·ly** *adv*

in·tel·lec·tu·al·ism \-chə-wə-ˌli-zəm\ *n* : devotion to the exercise of intellect or to intellectual pursuits

in·tel·li·gence \in-ˈte-lə-jəns\ *n* **1** : ability to learn and understand or to deal with new or trying situations **2** : mental acuteness **3** : INFORMATION, NEWS **4** : an agency engaged in obtaining information esp. concerning an enemy or possible enemy; *also* : the information so gained

intelligence quotient *n* : IQ

in·tel·li·gent \in-ˈte-lə-jənt\ *adj* [L *intelligens,* fr. *intelligere* to understand, fr. *inter* between + *legere* to select] : having or showing intelligence or intellect — **in·tel·li·gent·ly** *adv*

in·tel·li·gen·tsia \in-ˌte-lə-ˈjent-sē-ə, -ˈgent-\ *n* [Russ *intelligentsiya,* fr. L *intelligentia* intelligence] : intellectuals forming a vanguard or elite

in·tel·li·gi·ble \in-ˈte-lə-jə-bəl\ *adj* : capable of being understood or comprehended — **in·tel·li·gi·bil·i·ty** \-ˌte-lə-jə-ˈbi-lə-tē\ *n* — **in·tel·li·gi·bly** \-ˈte-lə-jə-blē\ *adv*

in·tem·per·ance \(ˌ)in-ˈtem-pə-rəns\ *n* : lack of moderation; *esp* : habitual or excessive drinking of intoxicants — **in·tem·per·ate** \-pə-rət\ *adj* — **in·tem·per·ate·ness** *n*

in·tend \in-ˈtend\ *vb* [ME *entenden, intenden,* fr. AF *entendre,* fr. L *intendere* to stretch out, direct, aim at, fr. *tendere* to stretch] **1** : to have in mind as a purpose or aim ⟨∼s to retire⟩ **2** : to design for a specified use or future ⟨programs ∼ed to help students⟩

in·ten·dant \in-ˈten-dənt\ *n* : an official (as a governor) esp. under the French, Spanish, or Portuguese monarchies

¹in·tend·ed *adj* **1** : expected to be such in the future; *esp* : BETROTHED **2** : INTENTIONAL ⟨an ∼ pun⟩

²intended *n* : an engaged person

in·tense \in-ˈtens\ *adj* **1** : existing in an extreme degree ⟨∼ pain⟩ **2** : marked by great zeal, energy, or eagerness ⟨∼ effort⟩ **3** : showing strong feeling; *also* : deeply felt — **in·tense·ly** *adv*

in·ten·si·fy \in-ˈten-sə-ˌfī\ *vb* **-fied; -fy·ing 1** : to make or become intense or more intensive **2** : to make more acute : SHARPEN ♦ **Synonyms** AGGRAVATE, HEIGHTEN, ENHANCE, MAGNIFY — **in·ten·si·fi·ca·tion** \-ˌten-sə-fə-ˈkā-shən\ *n*

in·ten·si·ty \in-ˈten-sə-tē\ *n, pl* **-ties 1** : the quality or state of being intense; *esp* : degree of strength, energy, or force

¹in·ten·sive \in-ˈten-siv\ *adj* **1** : highly concentrated **2** : serving to give emphasis — **in·ten·sive·ly** *adv*

²intensive *n* : an intensive word, particle, or prefix

intensive care *n* : continuous monitoring and treatment of seriously ill patients; *also* : an area of a hospital providing this treatment

¹in·tent \in-ˈtent\ *n* **1** : the state of mind with which an act is done : VOLITION **2** : PURPOSE, AIM ⟨the artist's ∼⟩ **3** : MEANING, SIGNIFICANCE

²intent *adj* **1** : directed with keen attention ⟨an ∼ gaze⟩ **2** : ENGROSSED; *also* : DETERMINED ⟨∼ on winning⟩ — **in·tent·ly** *adv* — **in·tent·ness** *n*

in·ten·tion \in-ˈten-chən\ *n* **1** : a determination to act in a certain way **2** : PURPOSE, AIM, END ♦ **Synonyms** INTENT, DESIGN, OBJECT, OBJECTIVE, GOAL

in·ten·tion·al \in-ˈten-chə-nəl\ *adj* : done by intention or design : INTENDED — **in·ten·tion·al·ly** *adv*

in·ter \in-ˈtər\ *vb* **in·terred; in·ter·ring** : BURY

in·ter·ac·tion \ˌin-tər-ˈak-shən\ *n* : mutual or reciprocal action or influence — **in·ter·act** \-ˈakt\ *vb*

in·ter·ac·tive \-ˈak-tiv\ *adj* **1** : mutually or reciprocally active **2** : involving the actions or input of a user ⟨∼ exhibits⟩ **3** : allowing two-way electronic communications (as between a person and a computer) — **in·ter·ac·tive·ly** *adv* — **in·ter·ac·tiv·i·ty** \-ak-ˈti-və-tē\ *n*

in·ter alia \ˌin-tər-ˈā-lē-ə, -ˈä-\ *adv* : among other things

in·ter·atom·ic \ˌin-tər-ə-'tä-mik\ *adj* : existing or acting between atoms

in·ter·breed \-'brēd\ *vb* **-bred** \-'bred\; **-breed·ing** : to breed together

in·ter·ca·la·ry \in-'tər-kə-ˌler-ē\ *adj* **1** : INTERCALATED ⟨February 29 is an ~ day⟩ **2** : INTERPOLATED

in·ter·ca·late \-ˌlāt\ *vb* **-lat·ed; -lat·ing** **1** : to insert (as a day) in a calendar **2** : to insert between or among existing elements or layers — **in·ter·ca·la·tion** \-ˌtər-kə-'lā-shən\ *n*

in·ter·cede \ˌin-tər-'sēd\ *vb* **-ced·ed; -ced·ing** : to act between parties with a view to reconciling differences

¹**in·ter·cept** \ˌin-tər-'sept\ *vb* **1** : to stop or interrupt the progress or course of **2** : to include (as part of a curve or solid) between two points, curves, or surfaces **3** : to gain possession of (an opponent's pass) — **in·ter·cep·tion** \-'sep-shən\ *n*

²**in·ter·cept** \'in-tər-ˌsept\ *n* : INTERCEPTION; *esp* : the interception of a target by an interceptor or missile

in·ter·cep·tor \in-tər-'sep-tər\ *n* : a fighter plane designed for defense against attacking bombers

in·ter·ces·sion \ˌin-tər-'se-shən\ *n* **1** : MEDIATION **2** : prayer or petition in favor of another — **in·ter·ces·sor** \-'se-sər\ *n* — **in·ter·ces·so·ry** \-'se-sə-rē\ *adj*

¹**in·ter·change** \ˌin-tər-'chānj\ *vb* **1** : to put each in the place of the other **2** : EXCHANGE **3** : to change places mutually — **in·ter·change·able** \-'chān-jə-bəl\ *adj* — **in·ter·change·ably** \-blē\ *adv*

²**in·ter·change** \'in-tər-ˌchānj\ *n* **1** : EXCHANGE **2** : a highway junction that by separated levels permits passage between highways without crossing traffic streams

in·ter·col·le·giate \ˌin-tər-kə-'lē-jət\ *adj* : existing or carried on between colleges ⟨~ sports⟩

in·ter·com \'in-tər-ˌkäm\ *n* : a two-way system for localized communication

in·ter·con·nect \ˌin-tər-kə-'nekt\ *vb* : to connect with one another — **in·ter·con·nec·tion** \-'nek-shən\ *n*

in·ter·con·ti·nen·tal \-ˌkän-tə-'nent-ᵊl\ *adj* **1** : extending among or carried on between continents ⟨~ trade⟩ **2** : capable of traveling between continents ⟨~ ballistic missiles⟩

in·ter·course \'in-tər-ˌkòrs\ *n* **1** : connection or dealings between persons or nations **2** : physical sexual contact between individuals that involves the genitalia of at least one person ⟨anal ~⟩; *esp* : SEXUAL INTERCOURSE

in·ter·de·nom·i·na·tion·al \ˌin-tər-di-ˌnä-mə-'nä-shə-nəl\ *adj* : involving different denominations

in·ter·de·part·men·tal \ˌin-tər-di-ˌpärt-'men-tᵊl, -ˌdē-\ *adj* : carried on between or involving different departments (as of a college)

in·ter·de·pen·dent \ˌin-tər-di-'pen-dənt\ *adj* : dependent upon one another — **in·ter·de·pen·dence** \-dəns\ *n*

in·ter·dict \ˌin-tər-'dikt\ *vb* **1** : to prohibit by decree **2** : to destroy, cut off, or damage (as an enemy line of supply) **3** : INTERCEPT ⟨~ed drug shipments⟩ — **in·ter·dic·tion** \-'dik-shən\ *n*

in·ter·dis·ci·plin·ary \-'di-sə-plə-ˌner-ē\ *adj* : involving two or more academic, scientific, or artistic disciplines

¹**in·ter·est** \'in-trəst; 'in-tə-rəst, -ˌrest\ *n* **1** : right, title, or legal share in something **2** : a charge for borrowed money that is generally a percentage of the amount borrowed; *also* : the return received by capital on its investment **3** : WELFARE, BENEFIT; *also* : SELF-INTEREST **4** : CURIOSITY, CONCERN **5** : readiness to be concerned with or moved by an object or class of objects **6** : a quality in a thing that arouses interest

²**interest** *vb* **1** : to persuade to participate or engage **2** : to engage the attention of

in·ter·est·ing *adj* : holding the attention — **in·ter·est·ing·ly** *adv*

¹**in·ter·face** \'in-tər-ˌfās\ *n* **1** : a surface forming a common boundary of two bodies, spaces, or phases ⟨an oil-water ~⟩ **2** : the place at which two independent systems meet and act on or communicate with each other ⟨the man-machine ~⟩ **3** : the means by which interaction or communication is achieved at an interface — **in·ter·fa·cial** \ˌin-tər-'fā-shəl\ *adj*

²**interface** *vb* **-faced; -fac·ing** **1** : to connect by means of an interface **2** : to serve as an interface

in·ter·faith \ˌin-tər-'fāth\ *adj* : involving persons of different religious faiths

in·ter·fere \ˌin-tər-'fir\ *vb* **-fered; -fer·ing** [ME *enterferen*, fr. AF (*s'*)*entreferir* to strike one another, fr. *entre* between, among + *ferir* to strike, fr. L *ferire*] **1** : to come in collision or be in opposition : CLASH **2** : to enter into the affairs of others **3** : to affect one another

in·ter·fer·ence \-'fir-əns\ *n* **1** : the act or process of interfering **2** : something that interferes : OBSTRUCTION **3** : the mutual effect on meeting of two waves resulting in areas of increased and decreased amplitude **4** : the blocking of an opponent in football to make way for the ball-carrier **5** : the illegal hindering of an opponent in sports

in·ter·om·e·ter \ˌin-tər-'rä-mə-tər\ *n* : an apparatus that uses the interference of waves (as of light) for making precise measurements — **in·ter·fer·om·e·try** \-fə-'rä-mə-trē\ *n*

in·ter·fer·on \ˌin-tər-'fir-ˌän\ *n* : any of a group of antiviral proteins of low molecular weight produced usu. by animal cells in response to a virus, a parasite in the cell, or a chemical

in·ter·ga·lac·tic \ˌin-tər-gə-'lak-tik\ *adj* : relating to or situated in the spaces between galaxies

in·ter·gen·er·a·tion·al \-ˌje-nə-'rā-shə-nəl\ *adj* : existing or occurring between generations

in·ter·gla·cial \-'glā-shəl\ *n* : a warm period between successive glaciations

in·ter·gov·ern·men·tal \-ˌgə-vərn-'men-tᵊl\ *adj* : existing or occurring between two governments or levels of government

in·ter·im \'in-tə-rəm\ *n* [L, adv., meanwhile, fr. *inter* between] : a time intervening : INTERVAL — **interim** *adj*

¹**in·te·ri·or** \in-'tir-ē-ər\ *adj* **1** : lying, occurring, or functioning within the limiting boundaries : INSIDE, INNER **2** : remote from the surface, border, or shore : INLAND

²**interior** *n* **1** : the inland part (as of a country) **2** : INSIDE **3** : the internal affairs of a state or nation **4** : a scene or view of the interior of a building

interior decoration *n* : INTERIOR DESIGN — **interior decorator** *n*

interior design *n* : the art or practice of planning and supervising the design and execution of architectural interiors and their furnishings — **interior designer** *n*

interj *abbr* interjection

in·ter·ject \in-tər-'jekt\ *vb* : to throw in between or among other things

in·ter·jec·tion \ˌin-tər-'jek-shən\ *n* : an exclamatory word (as *ouch*) — **in·ter·jec·tion·al·ly** \-shə-nə-lē\ *adv*

in·ter·lace \ˌin-tər-'lās\ *vb* **1** : to unite by or as if by lacing together : INTERWEAVE **2** : INTERSPERSE

in·ter·lard \ˌin-tər-'lärd\ *vb* : to vary by inserting or interjecting something

in·ter·leave \ˌin-tər-'lēv\ *vb* **-leaved; -leav·ing** : to arrange in alternate layers

in·ter·leu·kin \ˌin-tər-'lü-kən\ *n* : any of several proteins of low molecular weight that are produced by cells of the body and regulate the immune system and immune responses

¹**in·ter·line** \ˌin-tər-'līn\ *vb* : to insert between lines already written or printed

²**interline** *vb* : to provide (as a coat) with an interlining

in·ter·lin·ear \ˌin-tər-'li-nē-ər\ *adj* : inserted between lines already written or printed ⟨an ~ translation of a text⟩

in·ter·lin·gual \ˌin-tər-'liŋ-gwəl\ *adj* : of, relating to, or existing between two or more languages

in·ter·lin·ing \'in-tər-ˌlī-niŋ\ *n* : a lining (as of a coat) between the ordinary lining and the outside fabric

in·ter·link \ˌin-tər-'liŋk\ *vb* : to link together

in·ter·lock \ˌin-tər-'läk\ *vb* **1** : to engage or interlace together : lock together : UNITE **2** : to connect so that action of one part affects action of another part — **in·ter·lock** \'in-tər-ˌläk\ *n*

in·ter·loc·u·tor \ˌin-tər-'lä-kyə-tər\ *n* : one who takes part in dialogue or conversation

in·ter·loc·u·to·ry \-ˌtòr-ē\ *adj* : made during the progress of a legal action and not final or definite ⟨an ~ decree⟩

in·ter·lope \ˌin-tər-'lōp\ *vb* **-loped; -lop·ing** **1** : to encroach on the rights (as in trade) of others **2** : INTRUDE, INTERFERE — **in·ter·lop·er** *n*

in·ter·lude \'in-tər-ˌlüd\ *n* **1** : a usu. short simple play or

dramatic entertainment **2** : an intervening period, space, or event **3** : a piece of music inserted between the parts of a longer composition or a religious service
in·ter·mar·riage \ˌin-tər-ˈmer-ij\ *n* **1** : marriage within one's own group as required by custom **2** : marriage between members of different groups
in·ter·mar·ry \-ˈmer-ē\ *vb* **1** : to marry each other **2** : to marry within a group **3** : to become connected by intermarriage
¹**in·ter·me·di·ary** \ˌin-tər-ˈmē-dē-ˌer-ē\ *adj* **1** : INTERMEDIATE **2** : acting as a mediator
²**intermediary** *n, pl* **-ar·ies** : MEDIATOR, GO-BETWEEN
¹**in·ter·me·di·ate** \ˌin-tər-ˈmē-dē-ət\ *adj* : being or occurring at the middle place or degree or between extremes
²**intermediate** *n* **1** : one that is intermediate **2** : INTERMEDIARY
intermediate school *n* **1** : JUNIOR HIGH SCHOOL **2** : a school usu. comprising grades 4–6
in·ter·ment \in-ˈtər-mənt\ *n* : BURIAL
in·ter·mez·zo \ˌin-tər-ˈmet-sō, -ˈmed-zō\ *n, pl* **-zi** \-sē, -zē\ *or* **-zos** [It, ultim. fr. L *intermedius* intermediate] : a short movement connecting major sections of an extended musical work (as a symphony); *also* : a short independent instrumental composition
in·ter·mi·na·ble \(ˌ)in-ˈtər-mə-nə-bəl\ *adj* : ENDLESS; *esp* : wearisomely protracted — **in·ter·mi·na·bly** \-blē\ *adv*
in·ter·min·gle \ˌin-tər-ˈmiŋ-gəl\ *vb* : to mingle or mix together
in·ter·mis·sion \ˌin-tər-ˈmi-shən\ *n* **1** : INTERRUPTION, BREAK **2** : a temporary halt esp. in a public performance
in·ter·mit \-ˈmit\ *vb* **-mit·ted; -mit·ting** : DISCONTINUE; *also* : to be intermittent
in·ter·mit·tent \-ˈmi-tᵊnt\ *adj* : coming and going at intervals ✦ *Synonyms* RECURRENT, PERIODIC, ALTERNATE — **in·ter·mit·tent·ly** *adv*
in·ter·mix \ˌin-tər-ˈmiks\ *vb* : to mix together : INTERMINGLE — **in·ter·mix·ture** \-ˈmiks-chər\ *n*
in·ter·mo·lec·u·lar \-mə-ˈle-kyə-lər\ *adj* : existing or acting between molecules
in·ter·mon·tane \ˌin-tər-ˈmän-ˌtān\ *adj* : situated between mountains
¹**in·tern** \ˈin-ˌtərn, in-ˈtərn\ *vb* : to confine or impound esp. during a war — **in·tern·ee** \(ˌ)in-ˌtər-ˈnē\ *n* — **in·tern·ment** \in-ˈtərn-mənt\ *n*
²**in·tern** *also* **in·terne** \ˈin-ˌtərn\ *n* : an advanced student or recent graduate (as in medicine) gaining supervised practical experience — **in·tern·ship** *n*
³**in·tern** \ˈin-ˌtərn\ *vb* : to work as an intern
in·ter·nal \in-ˈtər-nᵊl\ *adj* **1** : INWARD, INTERIOR **2** : relating to or located in the inside of the body ⟨~ pain⟩ **3** : of, relating to, or occurring within the confines of an organized structure ⟨~ affairs⟩ **4** : of, relating to, or existing within the mind **5** : INTRINSIC, INHERENT ⟨~ evidence⟩ — **in·ter·nal·ly** *adv*
internal combustion engine *n* : an engine in which the fuel is ignited within the engine cylinder
in·ter·nal·ise *Brit var of* INTERNALIZE
in·ter·nal·ize \in-ˈtər-nə-ˌlīz\ *vb* **-ized; -iz·ing** : to incorporate (as values) within the self through learning or socialization — **in·ter·nal·i·za·tion** \-ˌtər-nə-lə-ˈzā-shən\ *n*
internal medicine *n* : a branch of medicine that deals with the diagnosis and treatment of diseases not requiring surgery
¹**in·ter·na·tion·al** \ˌin-tər-ˈna-shə-nəl\ *adj* **1** : common to or affecting two or more nations ⟨~ trade⟩ **2** : of, relating to, or constituting a group having members in two or more nations — **in·ter·na·tion·al·ly** *adv*
²**international** *n* : one that is international; *esp* : an organization of international scope
in·ter·na·tion·al·ise *Brit var of* INTERNATIONALIZE
in·ter·na·tion·al·ism \-ˈna-shə-nə-ˌli-zəm\ *n* : a policy of cooperation among nations; *also* : an attitude favoring such a policy — **in·ter·na·tion·al·ist** \-ˌlist\ *n or adj*
in·ter·na·tion·al·ize \-ˈna-shə-nə-ˌlīz\ *vb* : to make international; *esp* : to place under international control
International System of Units *n* : a system of units based on the metric system and used by international convention esp. for scientific work
in·ter·ne·cine \ˌin-tər-ˈne-ˌsēn, -ˈnē-ˌsīn\ *adj* [L *internecinus*, fr. *internecare* to destroy, kill, fr. *necare* to kill, fr.

nec-, nex violent death] **1** : DEADLY; *esp* : mutually destructive **2** : of, relating to, or involving conflict within a group ⟨~ feuds⟩
In·ter·net \ˈin-tər-ˌnet\ *n* : an electronic communications network that connects computer networks worldwide
in·ter·nist \ˈin-ˌtər-nist\ *n* : a physician who specializes in internal medicine
in·ter·nun·cio \ˌin-tər-ˈnən-sē-ˌō, -ˈnún-\ *n* [It *internunzio*] : a papal legate of lower rank than a nuncio
in·ter·of·fice \-ˈȯ-fəs\ *adj* : functioning or communicating between the offices of an organization
in·ter·per·son·al \-ˈpər-sə-nəl\ *adj* : being, relating to, or involving relations between persons — **in·ter·per·son·al·ly** *adv*
in·ter·plan·e·tary \ˌin-tər-ˈpla-nə-ˌter-ē\ *adj* : existing, carried on, or operating between planets ⟨~ space⟩
in·ter·play \ˈin-tər-ˌplā\ *n* : INTERACTION
in·ter·po·late \in-ˈtər-pə-ˌlāt\ *vb* **-lat·ed; -lat·ing** **1** : to change (as a text) by inserting new or foreign matter **2** : to insert (as words) into a text or into a conversation **3** : to estimate values of (data or a function) between two known values — **in·ter·po·la·tion** \-ˌtər-pə-ˈlā-shən\ *n*
in·ter·pose \ˌin-tər-ˈpōz\ *vb* **-posed; -pos·ing** **1** : to place between **2** : to thrust in : INTRUDE, INTERRUPT **3** : to inject between parts of a conversation or argument **4** : to come or be between ✦ *Synonyms* INTERFERE, INTERCEDE, INTERMEDIATE, INTERVENE — **in·ter·po·si·tion** \-pə-ˈzi-shən\ *n*
in·ter·pret \in-ˈtər-prət\ *vb* **1** : to explain the meaning of; *also* : to act as an interpreter : TRANSLATE **2** : to understand according to individual belief, judgment, or interest **3** : to represent artistically — **in·ter·pret·er** *n* — **in·ter·pre·tive** \-ˈtər-prə-tiv\ *adj*
in·ter·pre·ta·tion \in-ˌtər-prə-ˈtā-shən\ *n* **1** : EXPLANATION **2** : an instance of artistic interpretation in performance or adaptation — **in·ter·pre·ta·tive** \-ˈtər-prə-ˌtā-tiv\ *adj*
in·ter·ra·cial \-ˈrā-shəl\ *adj* : of, involving, or designed for members of different races
in·ter·reg·num \ˌin-tə-ˈreg-nəm\ *n, pl* **-nums** *or* **-na** \-nə\ **1** : the time during which a throne is vacant between two successive reigns or regimes **2** : a pause in a continuous series
in·ter·re·late \ˌin-tər-ri-ˈlāt\ *vb* : to bring into or have a mutual relationship — **in·ter·re·lat·ed·ness** \-ˈlā-təd-nəs\ *n* — **in·ter·re·la·tion** \-ˈlā-shən\ *n* — **in·ter·re·la·tion·ship** *n*
interrog *abbr* interrogative
in·ter·ro·gate \in-ˈter-ə-ˌgāt\ *vb* **-gat·ed; -gat·ing** : to question esp. formally and systematically — **in·ter·ro·ga·tion** \-ˌter-ə-ˈgā-shən\ *n* — **in·ter·ro·ga·tor** \-ˈter-ə-ˌgā-tər\ *n*
in·ter·rog·a·tive \ˌin-tə-ˈrä-gə-tiv\ *adj* : asking a question ⟨~ sentence⟩ — **interrogative** *n* — **in·ter·rog·a·tive·ly** *adv*
in·ter·rog·a·to·ry \ˌin-tə-ˈrä-gə-ˌtȯr-ē\ *adj* : INTERROGATIVE
in·ter·rupt \ˌin-tə-ˈrəpt\ *vb* **1** : to stop or hinder by breaking in **2** : to break the uniformity or continuity of **3** : to break in by speaking while another is speaking — **in·ter·rupt·er** *n* — **in·ter·rup·tion** \-ˈrəp-shən\ *n* — **in·ter·rup·tive** \-ˈrəp-tiv\ *adv*
in·ter·scho·las·tic \ˌin-tər-skə-ˈlas-tik\ *adj* : existing or carried on between schools
in·ter·sect \ˌin-tər-ˈsekt\ *vb* **1** : to divide by passing through or across **2** : to meet and cross (as at a point); *also* : OVERLAP — **in·ter·sec·tion** \-ˈsek-shən\ *n*
in·ter·sperse \ˌin-tər-ˈspərs\ *vb* **-spersed; -spers·ing** **1** : to place something at intervals in or among **2** : to insert at intervals among other things — **in·ter·sper·sion** \-ˈspər-zhən\ *n*
¹**in·ter·state** \ˌin-tər-ˈstāt\ *adj* : relating to, including, or connecting two or more states esp. of the U.S.
²**in·ter·state** \ˈin-tər-ˌstāt\ *n* : an interstate highway
in·ter·stel·lar \ˌin-tər-ˈste-lər\ *adj* : located or taking place among the stars
in·ter·stice \in-ˈtər-stəs\ *n, pl* **-stic·es** \-stə-ˌsēz, -stə-səz\ : a space that intervenes between things : CHINK — **in·ter·sti·tial** \ˌin-tər-ˈsti-shəl\ *adj*
in·ter·tid·al \ˌin-tər-ˈtī-dᵊl\ *adj* : of, relating to, or being the

area that is above low-tide mark but exposed to tidal flooding ⟨life in the ∼ mud⟩

in·ter·twine \-'twīn\ *vb* : to twine or cause to twine about one another : INTERLACE — **in·ter·twine·ment** *n*

in·ter·twist \-'twist\ *vb* : INTERTWINE

in·ter·ur·ban \-'ər-bən\ *adj* : connecting cities or towns

in·ter·val \'in-tər-vəl\ *n* [ME *intervalle*, fr. AF & L; AF *entreval*, fr. L *intervallum* space between ramparts, interval, fr. *inter-* between + *vallum* rampart] **1** : a space of time between events or states : PAUSE **2** : a space between objects, units, or states **3** : the difference in pitch between two tones

in·ter·vene \,in-tər-'vēn\ *vb* **-vened; -ven·ing 1** : to occur, fall, or come between points of time or between events **2** : to enter or appear as an unrelated feature or circumstance ⟨rain *intervened* and we postponed the trip⟩ **3** : to come in or between in order to stop, settle, or modify ⟨∼ in a quarrel⟩ **4** : to occur or lie between two things — **in·ter·ven·tion** \-'ven-chən\ *n*

in·ter·ven·tion·ism \-'ven-chə,ni-zəm\ *n* : interference by one country in the political affairs of another — **in·ter·ven·tion·ist** \-'ven-chə-nist\ *n or adj*

in·ter·view \'in-tər-,vyü\ *n* **1** : a formal consultation usu. to evaluate qualifications **2** : a meeting at which a writer or reporter obtains information from a person; *also* : the recorded or written account of such a meeting — **interview** *vb* — **in·ter·view·ee** \,in-tər-(,)vyü-'ē\ *n* — **in·ter·view·er** *n*

in·ter·vo·cal·ic \,in-tər-vō-'ka-lik\ *adj* : immediately preceded and immediately followed by a vowel

in·ter·weave \,in-tər-'wēv\ *vb* **-wove** \-'wōv\ *also* **-weaved; -wo·ven** \-'wō-vən\ *also* **-weaved; -weav·ing** : to weave or blend together : INTERTWINE, INTERMINGLE — **interwoven** *adj*

in·tes·tate \in-'tes-,tāt, -tət\ *adj* **1** : having made no valid will ⟨died ∼⟩ **2** : not disposed of by will ⟨∼ estate⟩

in·tes·tine \in-'tes-tən\ *n* : the tubular part of the alimentary canal that extends from stomach to anus and consists of a long narrow upper part (**small intestine**) followed by a broader shorter lower part (**large intestine**) — **in·tes·ti·nal** \-tə-nᵊl\ *adj*

in·ti·fa·da \,in-tə-'fä-də\ *n* : an armed uprising of Palestinians against Israeli occupation of the West Bank and Gaza Strip

¹in·ti·mate \'in-tə-,māt\ *vb* **-mat·ed; -mat·ing** [LL *intimare* to put in, announce, fr. L *intimus* innermost] **1** : ANNOUNCE, NOTIFY **2** : to communicate indirectly : HINT — **in·ti·ma·tion** \,in-tə-mā-shən\ *n*

²in·ti·mate \'in-tə-mət\ *adj* **1** : INTRINSIC; *also* : INNERMOST **2** : marked by very close association, contact, or familiarity **3** : marked by a warm friendship **4** : suggesting informal warmth or privacy **5** : of a very personal or private nature — **in·ti·ma·cy** \'in-tə-mə-sē\ *n* — **in·ti·mate·ly** *adv*

³in·ti·mate \'in-tə-mət\ *n* : an intimate friend, associate, or confidant

in·tim·i·date \in-'ti-mə-,dāt\ *vb* **-dat·ed; -dat·ing** : to make timid or fearful : FRIGHTEN; *esp* : to compel or deter by or as if by threats ♦ *Synonyms* COW, BULLDOZE, BULLY, BROWBEAT — **in·tim·i·dat·ing·ly** *adv* — **in·tim·i·da·tion** \-,ti-mə-'dā-shən\ *n*

intl *or* **intnl** *abbr* international

in·to \'in-tü\ *prep* **1** : to the inside of ⟨ran ∼ the house⟩ **2** : to the state, condition, or form of ⟨got ∼ trouble⟩ **3** : AGAINST ⟨ran ∼ a wall⟩

in·tol·er·a·ble \(,)in-'tä-lə-rə-bəl\ *adj* **1** : UNBEARABLE ⟨∼ pain⟩ **2** : EXCESSIVE — **in·tol·er·a·bly** \-blē\ *adv*

in·tol·er·ant \(,)in-'tä-lə-rənt\ *adj* **1** : unable or unwilling to endure **2** : unwilling to grant equality, freedom, or other social rights : BIGOTED — **in·tol·er·ance** \-rəns\ *n*

in·to·na·tion \,in-tō-'nā-shən\ *n* **1** : something that is intoned **2** : the act of intoning and esp. of chanting **3** : the manner of singing, playing, or uttering tones; *esp* : the rise and fall in pitch of the voice in speech

in·tone \in-'tōn\ *vb* **in·toned; in·ton·ing** : to utter in musical or prolonged tones : CHANT

in to·to \in-'tō-tō\ *adv* [L, on the whole] : TOTALLY, ENTIRELY

in·tox·i·cant \in-'täk-si-kənt\ *n* : something that intoxicates; *esp* : an alcoholic drink — **intoxicant** *adj*

in·tox·i·cate \-sə-,kāt\ *vb* **-cat·ed; -cat·ing 1** : to affect by a drug (as alcohol or cocaine) esp. to the point of physical or mental impairment **2** : to excite to enthusiasm or frenzy — **in·tox·i·ca·tion** \-,täk-sə-'kā-shən\ *n*

in·trac·ta·ble \(,)in-'trak-tə-bəl\ *adj* : not easily controlled

in·tra·mu·ral \-'myür-əl\ *adj* : being or occurring within the walls or limits (as of a city or college) ⟨∼ sports⟩

in·tra·mus·cu·lar \-'məs-kyə-lər\ *adj* : situated within, occurring in, or administered by entering a muscle — **in·tra·mus·cu·lar·ly** *adv*

in·tra·net \'in-trə-,net\ *n* : a network similar to the World Wide Web but having access limited to certain authorized users

intrans *abbr* intransitive

in·tran·si·gent \-jənt\ *adj* : UNCOMPROMISING ⟨an ∼ attitude⟩ — **in·tran·si·gence** \-jəns\ *n* — **intransigent** *n*

in·tran·si·tive \(,)in-'tran-sə-tiv, -zə-\ *adj* : not transitive; *esp* : not having or containing an object ⟨an ∼ verb⟩ — **in·tran·si·tive·ly** *adv* — **in·tran·si·tive·ness** *n*

in·tra·state \,in-trə-'stāt\ *adj* : existing or occurring within a state

in·tra·uter·ine device \-'yü-tə-rən-, -,rīn-\ *n* : a device inserted into and left in the uterus to prevent pregnancy

in·tra·ve·nous \,in-trə-'vē-nəs\ *adj* : being within or entering by way of the veins ⟨∼ feeding⟩; *also* : used in or using intravenous procedures ⟨∼ needles⟩ — **in·tra·ve·nous·ly** *adv*

intrench *var of* ENTRENCH

in·trep·id \in-'tre-pəd\ *adj* : characterized by resolute fearlessness, fortitude, and endurance — **in·tre·pid·i·ty** \,in-trə-'pi-də-tē\ *n*

in·tri·cate \'in-tri-kət\ *adj* [ME, fr. L *intricatus*, pp. of *intricare* to entangle, fr. *tricae* trifles, complications] **1** : having many complexly interrelated parts : COMPLICATED **2** : difficult to follow, understand, or solve — **in·tri·ca·cy** \-tri-kə-sē\ *n* — **in·tri·cate·ly** *adv*

¹in·trigue \'in-,trēg, in-'trēg\ *n* **1** : a secret scheme : MACHINATION **2** : a clandestine love affair

²in·trigue \in-'trēg\ *vb* **in·trigued; in·trigu·ing 1** : to accomplish by intrigue **2** : to carry on an intrigue; *esp* : PLOT, SCHEME **3** : to arouse the interest, desire, or curiosity of — **in·trigu·ing·ly** *adv*

in·trin·sic \in-'trin-zik, -sik\ *adj* : belonging to the essential nature or constitution of a thing — **in·trin·si·cal·ly** \-zi-k(ə-)lē, -si-\ *adv*

introd *abbr* introduction

in·tro·duce \,in-trə-'düs, -'dyüs\ *vb* **-duced; -duc·ing 1** : to lead or bring in esp. for the first time **2** : to bring into practice or use **3** : to cause to be acquainted **4** : to present for discussion **5** : PLACE, INSERT ♦ *Synonyms* INSINUATE, INTERPOLATE, INTERPOSE, INTERJECT — **in·tro·duc·tion** \-'dək-shən\ *n* — **in·tro·duc·to·ry** \-'dək-tə-rē\ *adj*

in·troit \'in-,tróit, -,trō-ət\ *n* **1** *often cap* : the first part of the traditional proper of the Mass **2** : a piece of music sung or played at the beginning of a worship service

in·tro·spec·tion \-'spek-shən\ *n* : a reflective looking inward : an examination of one's own thoughts or feelings — **in·tro·spect** \,in-trə-'spekt\ *vb* — **in·tro·spec·tive** \-'spek-tiv\ *adj* — **in·tro·spec·tive·ly** *adv*

in·tro·vert \'in-trə-,vərt\ *n* : a reserved or shy person — **in·tro·ver·sion** \,in-trə-'vər-zhən\ *n* — **introvert** *adj* — **in·tro·vert·ed** \'in-trə-,vər-təd\ *adj*

in·trude \in-'trüd\ *vb* **in·trud·ed; in·trud·ing 1** : to thrust, enter, or force in or upon **2** : ENCROACH, TRESPASS — **in·trud·er** *n* — **in·tru·sion** \-'trü-zhən\ *n* — **in·tru·sive** \-'trü-siv\ *adj* — **in·tru·sive·ness** *n*

intrust *var of* ENTRUST

in·tu·it \in-'tü-ət, -'tyü-\ *vb* : to know, sense, or understand by intuition

in·tu·ition \,in-tü-'wi-shən, -tyü-\ *n* **1** : quick and ready insight **2** : the power or faculty of knowing things without conscious reasoning — **in·tu·i·tive** \in-'tü-ə-tiv, -'tyü-\ *adj* — **in·tu·i·tive·ly** *adv*

In·u·it \'i-nü-wət, 'in-yü-\ *n* [Inuit *inuit*, pl. of *inuk* person] **1** *pl* **Inuit** *or* **Inuits** : a member of the Eskimo people of No. America and Greenland **2** : the language of the Inuit people

in·un·date \'i-nən-,dāt\ *vb* **-dat·ed; -dat·ing** : to cover with or as if with a flood : OVERFLOW — **in·un·da·tion** \ˌi-nən-'dā-shən\ n

in·ure \i-'nŭr, -'nyŭr\ vb **in·ured; in·ur·ing** [ME enuren, fr. in ure customary, fr. putten in ure to use, put into practice, part trans. of AF mettre en ovre, en uevre] 1 : to accustom to accept something undesirable 2 : to become of advantage

in utero \in-'yū-tə-ˌrō\ adv or adj [L] : in the uterus : before birth

inv abbr 1 inventor 2 invoice

in vac·uo \in-'va-kyŭ-ˌwō\ adv [L] : in a vacuum

in·vade \in-'vād\ vb **in·vad·ed; in·vad·ing** 1 : to enter for conquest or plunder 2 : to encroach upon 3 : to spread through and usu. harm ⟨germs ~ the tissues⟩ — **in·vad·er** n

¹**in·val·id** \(ˌ)in-'va-ləd\ adj : being without foundation or force in fact, reason, or law — **in·va·lid·i·ty** \ˌin-və-'li-də-tē\ n — **in·val·id·ly** adv

²**in·va·lid** \'in-və-ləd\ adj : being in ill health : SICKLY

³**invalid** \'in-və-ləd\ n : a person in usu. chronic ill health — **in·va·lid·ism** \-lə-ˌdi-zəm\ n

⁴**in·va·lid** \'in-və-ləd, -ˌlid\ vb 1 : to remove from active duty by reason of sickness or disability 2 : to make sickly or disabled

in·val·i·date \(ˌ)in-'va-lə-ˌdāt\ vb : to make invalid; esp : to weaken or make valueless — **in·val·i·da·tion** \in-ˌva-lə-'dā-shən\ n

in·valu·able \-'val-yə-bəl, -yə-wə-bəl\ adj : valuable beyond estimation

in·vari·able \-'ver-ē-ə-bəl\ adj : not changing or capable of change : CONSTANT — **in·vari·ably** \-blē\ adv

in·va·sion \in-'vā-zhən\ n : an act or instance of invading; esp : entry of an army into a country for conquest

in·va·sive \in-'vā-siv, -ziv\ adj 1 : tending to spread ⟨~ cancer cells⟩ 2 : involving entry into the living body (as by surgery) ⟨~ therapy⟩

in·vec·tive \in-'vek-tiv\ n 1 : an abusive expression or speech 2 : abusive language — **invective** adj

in·veigh \in-'vā\ vb : to protest or complain bitterly or vehemently : RAIL

in·vei·gle \in-'vā-gəl, -'vē-\ vb **in·vei·gled; in·vei·gling** [AF enveegler, aveogler to blind, hoodwink, fr. avogle, enveugle blind, fr. ML ab oculis, lit., lacking eyes] 1 : to win over by flattery : ENTICE 2 : to acquire by ingenuity or flattery

in·vent \in-'vent\ vb 1 : to think up 2 : to create or produce for the first time — **in·ven·tor** \-'ven-tər\ n

in·ven·tion \in-'ven-chən\ n 1 : INVENTIVENESS 2 : a creation of the imagination; esp : a false conception 3 : a device, contrivance, or process originated after study and experiment 4 : the act or process of inventing

in·ven·tive \in-'ven-tiv\ adj 1 : CREATIVE, INGENIOUS ⟨an ~ composer⟩ 2 : characterized by invention ⟨an ~ turn of mind⟩ — **in·ven·tive·ness** n

in·ven·to·ry \'in-vən-ˌtór-ē\ n, pl **-ries** 1 : an itemized list of current goods or assets 2 : SURVEY, SUMMARY 3 : STOCK, SUPPLY 4 : the act or process of taking an inventory — **inventory** vb

¹**in·verse** \(ˌ)in-'vərs, 'in-ˌvərs\ adj : opposite in order, nature, or effect : REVERSED — **in·verse·ly** adv

²**inverse** n : something inverse or resulting in or from inversion : OPPOSITE

in·ver·sion \in-'vər-zhən\ n 1 : a reversal of position, order, or relationship; esp : an increase of temperature with altitude through a layer of air 2 : the act or process of inverting

in·vert \in-'vərt\ vb 1 : to reverse in position, order, or relationship 2 : to turn upside down or inside out 3 : to turn inward

in·ver·te·brate \(ˌ)in-'vər-tə-brət, -ˌbrāt\ adj : lacking a backbone; also : of or relating to invertebrate animals — **invertebrate** n

¹**in·vest** \in-'vest\ vb 1 : to install formally in an office or honor 2 : to furnish with power or authority : VEST 3 : to cover completely : ENVELOP 4 : CLOTHE, ADORN 5 : BESIEGE 6 : to endow with a quality or characteristic

²**invest** vb 1 : to commit (money) in order to earn a financial return 2 : to expend for future benefits or advantages 3 : to make an investment — **in·ves·tor** \-'ves-tər\ n

in·ves·ti·gate \in-'ves-tə-ˌgāt\ vb **-gat·ed; -gat·ing** [L investigare to track, investigate, fr. vestigium footprint, track]

: to study by close examination and systematic inquiry — **in·ves·ti·ga·tion** \-ˌves-tə-'gā-shən\ n — **in·ves·ti·ga·tive** \-'ves-tə-ˌgā-tiv\ adj — **in·ves·ti·ga·tor** \-ˌgā-tər\ n

in·ves·ti·ture \in-'ves-tə-ˌchŭr, -chər\ n 1 : the act of ratifying or establishing in office 2 : something that covers or adorns

¹**in·vest·ment** \in-'vest-mənt\ n 1 : an outer layer : ENVELOPE 2 : INVESTITURE l 3 : BLOCKADE, SIEGE

²**investment** n : the outlay of money for income or profit; also : the sum invested or the property purchased

in·vet·er·ate \in-'ve-tə-rət\ adj 1 : firmly established by age or long persistence 2 : confirmed in a habit

in·vi·a·ble \(ˌ)in-'vī-ə-bəl\ adj : incapable of surviving

in·vid·i·ous \in-'vi-dē-əs\ adj 1 : tending to cause discontent, animosity, or envy 2 : ENVIOUS 3 : OBNOXIOUS ⟨~ remarks⟩ — **in·vid·i·ous·ly** adv

in·vig·o·rate \in-'vi-gə-ˌrāt\ vb **-rat·ed; -rat·ing** : to give life and energy to : ANIMATE — **in·vig·o·ra·tion** \-ˌvi-gə-'rā-shən\ n

in·vin·ci·ble \(ˌ)in-'vin-sə-bəl\ adj : incapable of being conquered, overcome, or subdued — **in·vin·ci·bil·i·ty** \-ˌvin-sə-'bi-lə-tē\ n — **in·vin·ci·bly** \-'vin-sə-blē\ adv

in·vi·o·la·ble \-'vī-ə-lə-bəl\ adj 1 : safe from violation or profanation 2 : UNASSAILABLE ⟨~ borders⟩ — **in·vi·o·la·bil·i·ty** \-ˌvī-ə-lə-'bi-lə-tē\ n

in·vi·o·late \-'vī-ə-lət\ adj : not violated or profaned : PURE

in·vis·i·ble \-'vi-zə-bəl\ adj 1 : incapable of being seen ⟨~ to the naked eye⟩ 2 : HIDDEN 3 : IMPERCEPTIBLE, INCONSPICUOUS — **in·vis·i·bil·i·ty** \-ˌvi-zə-'bi-lə-tē\ n — **in·vis·i·bly** \-'vi-zə-blē\ adv

invisible hand n : a hypothetical economic force that works for the benefit of all

in·vi·ta·tion·al \ˌin-və-'tā-shə-nəl\ adj : limited to invited participants ⟨an ~ tournament⟩ — **invitational** n

in·vite \in-'vīt\ vb **in·vit·ed; in·vit·ing** 1 : ENTICE, TEMPT 2 : to increase the likelihood of ⟨~ trouble⟩ 3 : to request the presence or participation of : ASK 4 : to request formally 5 : ENCOURAGE ⟨~ suggestions⟩ — **in·vi·ta·tion** \ˌin-və-'tā-shən\ n

in·vit·ing adj : ATTRACTIVE, TEMPTING

in vi·tro \in-'vē-trō, -'vī-, -'vi-\ adv or adj [NL, lit., in glass] : outside the living body and in an artificial environment ⟨in vitro fertilization⟩

in·vo·ca·tion \ˌin-və-'kā-shən\ n 1 : SUPPLICATION; esp : a prayer at the beginning of a service 2 : a formula for conjuring : INCANTATION

¹**in·voice** \'in-ˌvóis\ n [modif. of MF envois, pl. of envoi message] : an itemized list of goods shipped usu. specifying the price and the terms of sale : BILL

²**invoice** vb **in·voiced; in·voic·ing** : to send an invoice to or for : BILL

in·voke \in-'vōk\ vb **in·voked; in·vok·ing** 1 : to petition for help or support 2 : to appeal to or cite as authority ⟨~ a law⟩ 3 : to call forth by incantation : CONJURE ⟨~ spirits⟩ 4 : to make an earnest request for : SOLICIT 5 : to put into effect or operation 6 : to bring about : CAUSE

in·vol·un·tary \(ˌ)in-'vä-lən-ˌter-ē\ adj 1 : done contrary to or without choice 2 : COMPULSORY ⟨~ servitude⟩ 3 : not controlled by the will : REFLEX ⟨~ contractions⟩ — **in·vol·un·tari·ly** \-ˌvä-lən-'ter-ə-lē\ adv

in·vo·lute \'in-və-ˌlüt\ adj : INVOLVED, INTRICATE

in·vo·lu·tion \ˌin-və-'lü-shən\ n 1 : the act or an instance of enfolding or entangling 2 : COMPLEXITY, INTRICACY

in·volve \in-'välv\ vb **in·volved; in·volv·ing** 1 : to draw in as a participant 2 : ENVELOP 3 : to occupy (as oneself) absorbingly; esp : to commit oneself emotionally 4 : to relate closely : CONNECT 5 : to have as part of itself : INCLUDE 6 : ENTAIL, IMPLY 7 : ²AFFECT — **in·volve·ment** n

in·volved \-'välvd\ adj : INTRICATE, COMPLEX ⟨an ~ plot⟩

in·vul·ner·a·ble \(ˌ)in-'vəl-nə-rə-bəl\ adj 1 : incapable of being wounded, injured, or damaged 2 : immune to or proof against attack — **in·vul·ner·a·bil·i·ty** \-ˌvəl-nə-rə-'bi-lə-tē\ n — **in·vul·ner·a·bly** \-'vəl-nə-rə-blē\ adv

¹**in·ward** \'in-wərd\ adj 1 : situated on the inside 2 : MENTAL; also : SPIRITUAL 3 : directed toward the interior

²**inward** or **in·wards** \-wərdz\ adv 1 : toward the inside, center, or interior 2 : toward the inner being ⟨turned his thoughts ~⟩

in·ward·ly \'in-wərd-lē\ adv 1 : MENTALLY, SPIRITUALLY 2 : INTERNALLY ⟨bled ~⟩ 3 : to oneself ⟨cursed ~⟩

IOC *abbr* International Olympic Committee

io·dide \'ī-ə-ˌdīd\ *n* : a compound of iodine with another element or group

io·dine \'ī-ə-ˌdīn, -dᵊn\ *n* **1** : a nonmetallic chemical element used esp. in medicine and photography **2** : a solution of iodine used as a local antiseptic

io·dise *Brit var of* IODIZE

io·dize \'ī-ə-ˌdīz\ *vb* **io·dized; io·diz·ing** : to treat with iodine or an iodide

ion \'ī-ən, 'ī-ˌän\ *n* [Gk, neut. of *iōn*, prp. of *ienai* to go; so called because in electrolysis it goes to one of the two poles] : an electrically charged particle, atom, or group of atoms — **ion·ic** \ī-'ä-nik\ *adj*

-ion *n suffix* : act, process, state, or condition ⟨valida*tion*⟩

ion·ise *Brit var of* IONIZE

ion·ize \'ī-ə-ˌnīz\ *vb* **ion·ized; ion·iz·ing** **1** : to convert wholly or partly into ions **2** : to become ionized — **ion·iz·able** \ˌī-ə-'nī-zə-bəl\ *adj* — **ion·i·za·tion** \ˌī-ə-nə-'zā-shən\ *n* — **ion·iz·er** \'ī-ə-ˌnī-zər\ *n*

ion·o·sphere \ī-'ä-nə-ˌsfir\ *n* : the part of the earth's atmosphere extending from about 30 miles (50 kilometers) to the exosphere that contains ionized atmospheric gases — **ion·o·spher·ic** \ī-ˌä-nə-'sfir-ik, -'sfer-\ *adj*

IOOF *abbr* Independent Order of Odd Fellows

io·ta \ī-'ō-tə\ *n* [L, fr. Gk *iōta*] **1** : the 9th letter of the Greek alphabet — I or ι **2** : a very small quantity : JOT

IOU \ˌī-(ˌ)ō-'yü\ *n* : an acknowledgement of a debt

IP *abbr* innings pitched

IP address \'ī-'pē-\ *n* [*Internet p*rotocol] : the numeric address of a computer on the Internet

ip·e·cac \'i-pi-ˌkak\ *n* [Pg *ipecacuanha*] : an emetic and expectorant drug used esp. as a syrup in treating accidental poisoning; *also* : either of two tropical American plants or their rhizomes and roots used to make ipecac

IPO \ˌī-ˌpē-'ō\ *n, pl* **IPOs** : an initial public offering of a company's stock

ip·so fac·to \ˌip-sō-'fak-tō\ *adv* [NL, lit., by the fact itself] : by the very nature of the case

iq *abbr* [L *idem quod*] the same as

IQ \'ī-'kyü\ *n* : a number used to express a person's relative intelligence as determined by a standardized test

¹Ir *abbr* Irish

²Ir *symbol* iridium

IR *abbr* infrared

¹IRA \ˌī-(ˌ)är-'ā; 'ī-rə\ *n* [*i*ndividual *r*etirement *a*ccount] : a retirement savings account in which income taxes are deferred until withdrawals are made

²IRA *abbr* Irish Republican Army

irai·mbi·la·nja \ē-ˌrīm-bē-'län(d)-zə\ *n, pl* **iraimbilanja** — see *ariary* at MONEY table

iras·ci·ble \i-'ra-sə-bəl\ *adj* : marked by hot temper and easily provoked anger ♦ *Synonyms* CHOLERIC, TESTY, TOUCHY, CRANKY, CROSS — **iras·ci·bil·i·ty** \-ˌra-sə-'bi-lə-tē\ *n*

irate \ī-'rāt\ *adj* **1** : roused to ire **2** : arising from anger — **irate·ly** *adv*

ire \'ī(-ə)r\ *n* : ANGER, WRATH — **ire·ful** *adj*

Ire *abbr* Ireland

ire·nic \ī-'re-nik\ *adj* : favoring, conducive to, or operating toward peace or conciliation

ir·i·des·cence \ˌir-ə-'de-sᵊns\ *n* : a rainbowlike play of colors — **ir·i·des·cent** \-sᵊnt\ *adj*

irid·i·um \ir-'i-dē-əm\ *n* : a hard brittle heavy metallic chemical element

iris \'ī-rəs\ *n, pl* **iris·es** *also* **iri·des** \'ī-rə-ˌdēz, 'ir-ə-\ [ME, fr. L *iris* rainbow, iris plant, fr. Gk, rainbow, iris plant, iris of the eye] **1** : the colored part around the pupil of the eye **2** : any of a large genus of plants with linear basal leaves and large showy flowers

Irish \'ī-rish\ *n* **1 Irish** *pl* : the people of Ireland **2** : the Celtic language of Ireland — **Irish** *adj* — **Irish·man** \-mən\ *n* — **Irish·wom·an** \-ˌwu̇-mən\ *n*

Irish bull *n* : an incongruous statement (as "it was hereditary in his family to have no children")

Irish coffee *n* : hot sugared coffee with Irish whiskey and whipped cream

Irish moss *n* : the dried and bleached plants of a red alga that is a source of carrageenan; *also* : this red alga

Irish setter *n* : any of a breed of hunting dogs with a mahogany-red coat

irk \'ərk\ *vb* : to make weary, irritated, or bored : ANNOY

irk·some \'ərk-səm\ *adj* : tending to irk : ANNOYING — **irk·some·ly** *adv*

¹iron \'ī(-ə)rn\ *n* [ME, fr. OE *īsern, īren*] **1** : a heavy malleable magnetic metallic chemical element that rusts easily and is vital to biological processes **2** : something made of metal and esp. iron ⟨branding ~⟩; *also* (as handcuffs) used to bind or restrain ⟨put them in ~s⟩ **3** : a household device with a flat base that is heated and used for pressing cloth **4** : STRENGTH, HARDNESS

²iron *vb* **1** : to press or smooth with or as if with a heated iron **2** : to remove (as wrinkles) by ironing — **iron·er** *n*

¹iron·clad \-'klad\ *adj* **1** : sheathed in iron armor **2** : so firm or secure as to be unbreakable

²iron·clad \-ˌklad\ *n* : an armored naval vessel esp. of the 19th century

iron curtain *n* : a political, military, and ideological barrier that isolates an area; *esp, often cap* : one formerly isolating an area under Soviet control

iron·ic \ī-'rä-nik\ *also* **iron·i·cal** \-ni-kəl\ *adj* **1** : of, relating to, or marked by irony **2** : given to irony

iron·i·cal·ly \-ni-k(ə-)lē\ *adv* **1** : in an ironic manner **2** : it is ironic

iron·ing *n* : clothes ironed or to be ironed

iron lung *n* : a device for artificial respiration that encloses the chest in a chamber in which changes of pressure force air into and out of the lungs

iron out *vb* : to remove or lessen difficulties in or extremes of

iron oxide *n* : FERRIC OXIDE

iron·stone \'ī(ə)rn-ˌstōn\ *n* **1** : a hard iron-rich sedimentary rock **2** : a hard heavy durable pottery developed in England in the 19th century

iron·ware \-ˌwer\ *n* : articles made of iron

iron·weed \-ˌwēd\ *n* : any of a genus of mostly weedy plants related to the asters that have terminal heads of red, purple, or white flowers

iron·wood \-ˌwu̇d\ *n* : any of numerous trees or shrubs with exceptionally hard wood; *also* : the wood

iron·work \-ˌwərk\ *n* **1** : work in iron **2** *pl* : a mill or building where iron or steel is smelted or heavy iron or steel products are made — **iron·work·er** *n*

iro·ny \'ī-rə-nē\ *n, pl* **-nies** [L *ironia*, fr. Gk *eirōnia*, fr. *eirōn* dissembler] **1** : the use of words to express the opposite of what one really means **2** : incongruity between the actual result of a sequence of events and the expected result

Ir·o·quois \'ir-ə-ˌkwȯi\ *n, pl* **Iroquois** *same or* -ˌkwȯiz\ **1** *pl* : an American Indian confederacy orig. of New York that consisted of the Cayuga, Mohawk, Oneida, Onondaga, and Seneca and later included the Tuscarora **2** : a member of any of the Iroquois peoples

ir·ra·di·ate \i-'rā-dē-ˌāt\ *vb* **-at·ed; -at·ing** **1** : ILLUMINATE **2** : ENLIGHTEN **3** : to treat by exposure to radiation **4** : RADIATE — **ir·ra·di·a·tion** \-ˌrā-dē-'ā-shən\ *n*

¹ir·ra·tio·nal \(ˌ)i-'ra-shə-nəl\ *adj* **1** : incapable of reasoning ⟨~ beasts⟩; *also* : defective in mental power ⟨~ with fever⟩ **2** : not based on reason ⟨~ fears⟩ **3** : being or numerically equal to an irrational number — **ir·ra·tio·nal·i·ty** \(ˌ)i-ˌra-shə-'na-lə-tē\ *n* — **ir·ra·tio·nal·ly** \(ˌ)i-'ra-shə-nᵊl-ē\ *adv*

²irrational *n* : IRRATIONAL NUMBER

irrational number *n* : a real number that cannot be expressed as the quotient of two integers

ir·rec·on·cil·able \(ˌ)i-ˌre-kən-'sī-lə-bəl, -'re-kən-ˌsī-\ *adj* : impossible to reconcile, adjust, or harmonize — **ir·rec·on·cil·abil·i·ty** \(ˌ)i-ˌre-kən-ˌsī-lə-'bi-lə-tē\ *n*

ir·re·cov·er·able \ˌir-i-'kə-və-rə-bəl\ *adj* : not capable of being recovered or rectified : IRREPARABLE ⟨an ~ loss⟩ — **ir·re·cov·er·ably** \-blē\ *adv*

ir·re·deem·able \ˌir-i-'dē-mə-bəl\ *adj* **1** : not redeemable; *esp* : not terminable by payment of the principal ⟨an ~ bond⟩ **2** : not convertible into gold or silver at the will of the holder **3** : being beyond remedy : HOPELESS

ir·re·den·tism \-'den-ˌti-zəm\ *n* : a principle or policy directed toward the incorporation of a territory historically or ethnically part of another into that other — **ir·re·den·tist** \-tist\ *n or adj*

ir·re·duc·ible \ˌir-i-'dü-sə-bəl, -'dyü-\ *adj* : not reducible — **ir·re·duc·ibly** \-blē\ *adv*

ir·re·fut·able \ˌir-i-'fyü-tə-bəl, (ˌ)i-'re-fyət-\ *adj* : impossible to refute

irreg *abbr* irregular

ir·reg·u·lar \(ₐ)i-'re-gyə-lər\ *adj* **1** : not regular : not natural or uniform **2** : not conforming to the normal or usual manner of inflection ⟨~ verbs⟩ **3** : not belonging to a regular or organized army ⟨~ troops⟩ — **irregular** *n* — **ir·reg·u·lar·ly** *adv*

ir·reg·u·lar·i·ty \i-ₐre-gyə-'la-rə-tē\ *n, pl* **-ties** **1** : something that is irregular **2** : the quality or state of being irregular **3** : occasional constipation

ir·rel·e·vant \(ₐ)i-'re-lə-vənt\ *adj* : not relevant — **ir·rel·e·vance** \-vəns\ *n*

ir·re·li·gious \ir-i-'li-jəs\ *adj* : lacking religious emotions, doctrines, or practices

ir·re·me·di·a·ble \ir-i-'mē-dē-ə-bəl\ *adj* : impossible to remedy or correct

ir·re·mov·able \-'mü-və-bəl\ *adj* : not removable

ir·rep·a·ra·ble \(ₐ)i-'re-pə-rə-bəl\ *adj* : impossible to make good, undo, repair, or remedy ⟨~ damage⟩

ir·re·place·able \ir-i-'plā-sə-bəl\ *adj* : not replaceable ⟨~ antiques⟩

ir·re·press·ible \-'pre-sə-bəl\ *adj* : impossible to repress or control

ir·re·proach·able \-'prō-chə-bəl\ *adj* : not reproachable : BLAMELESS

ir·re·sist·ible \ir-i-'zis-tə-bəl\ *adj* : impossible to successfully resist — **ir·re·sist·ibly** \-blē\ *adv*

ir·res·o·lute \(ₐ)i-'re-zə-ˌlüt\ *adj* : uncertain how to act or proceed : VACILLATING — **ir·res·o·lute·ly** \-ˌlüt-lē; (ₐ)i-ˌre-zə-'lüt-\ *adv* — **ir·res·o·lu·tion** \(ₐ)i-ˌre-zə-'lü-shən\ *n*

ir·re·spec·tive of \ir-i-'spek-tiv-\ *prep* : without regard to

ir·re·spon·si·ble \-'spän-sə-bəl\ *adj* : not responsible — **ir·re·spon·si·bil·i·ty** \-ˌspän-sə-'bi-lə-tē\ *n* — **ir·re·spon·si·bly** \-'spän-sə-blē\ *adv*

ir·re·triev·able \ir-i-'trē-və-bəl\ *adj* : not retrievable : IRRECOVERABLE

ir·rev·er·ence \(ₐ)i-'re-və-rəns\ *n* **1** : lack of reverence **2** : an irreverent act or utterance — **ir·rev·er·ent** \-rənt\ *adj* — **ir·rev·er·ent·ly** *adv*

ir·re·vers·ible \ir-i-'vər-sə-bəl\ *adj* : incapable of being reversed

ir·rev·o·ca·ble \(ₐ)i-'re-və-kə-bəl\ *adj* : incapable of being revoked or recalled — **ir·rev·o·ca·bly** \-blē\ *adv*

ir·ri·gate \'ir-ə-ˌgāt\ *vb* **-gat·ed; -gat·ing** **1** : to supply (as land) with water by artificial means; *also* : to flush with liquid — **ir·ri·ga·tion** \ir-ə-'gā-shən\ *n*

ir·ri·ta·bil·i·ty \ir-ə-tə-'bi-lə-tē\ *n* **1** : the property of living things and of protoplasm that enables reaction to stimuli **2** : the quality or state of being irritable; *esp* : readiness to become annoyed or angry

ir·ri·ta·ble \'ir-ə-tə-bəl\ *adj* : capable of being irritated; *esp* : readily or easily irritated — **ir·ri·ta·bly** \-blē\ *adv*

ir·ri·tate \'ir-ə-ˌtāt\ *vb* **-tat·ed; -tat·ing** **1** : to excite to anger : EXASPERATE **2** : to make sore or inflamed — **ir·ri·tant** \'ir-ə-tənt\ *adj or n* — **ir·ri·tat·ing·ly** *adv* — **ir·ri·ta·tion** \ir-ə-'tā-shən\ *n*

ir·rupt \(ₐ)i-'rəpt\ *vb* **1** : to rush in forcibly or violently **2** : to increase suddenly in numbers ⟨rabbits ~ in cycles⟩ — **ir·rup·tion** \-'rəp-shən\ *n*

IRS *abbr* Internal Revenue Service

is *pres 3d sing of* BE

Isa *or* **Is** *abbr* Isaiah

Isa·iah \ī-'zā-ə\ *n* — see BIBLE table

Isa·ias \ī-'zā-əs\ *n* : ISAIAH

ISBN *abbr* International Standard Book Number

is·che·mia \is-'kē-mē-ə\ *n* : deficient supply of blood to a body part (as the brain) — **is·che·mic** \-mik\ *adj*

-ish *adj suffix* **1** : of, relating to, or being ⟨Finn*ish*⟩ **2** : characteristic of ⟨boy*ish*⟩ ⟨mul*ish*⟩ **3** : inclined or liable to ⟨book*ish*⟩ **4** : having a touch or trace of : somewhat ⟨purpl*ish*⟩ **5** : having the approximate age of ⟨forty*ish*⟩ **6** : somewhat near ⟨four*ish*⟩

isin·glass \'ī-zᵊn-ˌglas, 'ī-ziŋ-\ *n* **1** : a gelatin obtained from various fish **2** : mica esp. in thin sheets

isl *abbr* island

Is·lam \is-'läm, iz-, -'lam, 'is-ˌ, 'iz-ˌ\ *n* [Ar *islām* submission (to the will of God)] : the religious faith of Muslims including belief in Allah as the sole deity and in Muhammad as his prophet; *also* : the civilization built on this faith — **Is·lam·ic** \is-'lä-mik, iz-, -'la-\ *adj*

is·land \'ī-lənd\ *n* [ME *iland*, fr. OE *īgland*, fr. *īg* island + *land* land] **1** : a body of land smaller than a continent surrounded by water **2** : something resembling an island in its isolation

is·land·er \'ī-lən-dər\ *n* : a native or inhabitant of an island

isle \'ī(-ə)l\ *n* : ISLAND; *esp* : a small island

is·let \'ī-lət\ *n* : a small island

ism *n* : a distinctive doctrine, cause, or theory

-ism \ˌi-zəm\ *n suffix* **1** : act : practice : process ⟨criti*cism*⟩ **2** : manner of action or behavior characteristic of a (specified) person or thing ⟨fanatic*ism*⟩ **3** : state : condition : property ⟨dual*ism*⟩ **4** : abnormal state or condition ⟨alcohol*ism*⟩ **5** : doctrine : theory : cult ⟨Buddh*ism*⟩ **6** : adherence to a set of principles ⟨stoic*ism*⟩ **7** : prejudice or discrimination on the basis of a (specified) attribute ⟨racism⟩ ⟨sex*ism*⟩ **8** : characteristic or peculiar feature or trait ⟨colloquial*ism*⟩

iso·bar \'ī-sə-ˌbär\ *n* : a line on a map connecting places of equal barometric pressure — **iso·bar·ic** \ˌī-sə-'bär-ik, -'ber-\ *adj*

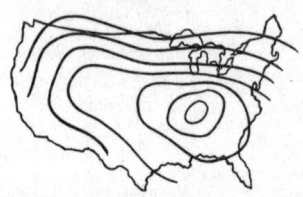

isobars

iso·late \'ī-sə-ˌlāt\ *vb* **-lat·ed; -lat·ing** [fr. *isolated* set apart, fr. F *isolé*, fr. It *isolato*, fr. *isola* island, fr. L *insula*] : to place or keep by itself : separate from others — **iso·la·tion** \ˌī-sə-'lā-shən\ *n*

isolated *adj* **1** : occurring alone or once : UNIQUE **2** : SPORADIC

iso·la·tion·ism \ˌī-sə-'lā-shə-ˌni-zəm\ *n* : a policy of national isolation by abstention from international political and economic relations — **iso·la·tion·ist** \-shə-nist\ *n or adj*

iso·mer \'ī-sə-mər\ *n* : any of two or more chemical compounds that contain the same numbers of atoms of the same elements but differ in structural arrangement and properties — **iso·mer·ic** \ˌī-sə-'mer-ik\ *adj* — **isom·er·ism** \ī-'sä-mə-ˌri-zəm\ *n*

iso·met·rics \ˌī-sə-'me-triks\ *n sing or pl* : exercise involving a series of brief and intense contractions of muscles against each other or against an immovable resistance — **iso·met·ric** *adj*

iso·prene \'ī-sə-ˌprēn\ *n* : a hydrocarbon used esp. in making synthetic rubber

isos·ce·les \ī-'sä-sə-ˌlēz\ *adj* : having two equal sides ⟨an ~ triangle⟩

iso·therm \'ī-sə-ˌthərm\ *n* : a line on a map connecting points having the same temperature

iso·ther·mal \ˌī-sə-'thər-məl\ *adj* : of, relating to, or marked by equality of temperature

iso·tope \'ī-sə-ˌtōp\ *n* [Gk *isos* equal + *topos* place] : any of the forms of a chemical element that differ chiefly in the number of neutrons in an atom — **iso·to·pic** \ˌī-sə-'tä-pik, -'tō-\ *adj* — **iso·to·pi·cal·ly** \-'tä-pi-k(ə-)lē, -'tō-\ *adv*

Isr *abbr* Israel; Israeli

Is·ra·el·ite \'iz-rē-ə-ˌlīt\ *n* : a member of the Hebrew people descended from Jacob

is·su·ance \'i-shü-wəns\ *n* : the act of issuing or giving out esp. officially

¹is·sue \'i-shü\ *n* [ME, exit, proceeds, fr. AF, fr. *issir* to come out, go out, fr. L *exire*, fr. *ire* to go] **1** : the action of going, coming, or flowing out : EGRESS, EMERGENCE **2** : EXIT, OUTLET, VENT **3** : OFFSPRING, PROGENY **4** : OUTCOME, RESULT **5** : a point of debate or controversy; *also* : the point at which an unsettled matter is ready for a decision **6** : a discharge (as of blood) from the body **7** : something coming forth from a specified source **8** : the act of officially giving out or printing : PUBLICATION; *also* : the quantity of things given out at one time

²issue *vb* **is·sued; is·su·ing** **1** : to go, come, or flow out **2** : to come forth or cause to come forth : EMERGE, DISCHARGE, EMIT **3** : ACCRUE **4** : to descend from a specified parent or ancestor **5** : to result in **6** : to put forth or distribute officially **7** : PUBLISH **8** : EMANATE, RESULT — **is·su·er** *n*

¹-ist *n suffix* **1** : one that performs a (specified) action ⟨cyc(*list*) : one that makes or produces (novel*ist*) **2** : one that plays a (specified) musical instrument (harp*ist*) **3** : one that operates a (specified) mechanical instrument or contrivance (machin*ist*) **4** : one that specializes in a (specified) art or science or skill (geolog*ist*) **5** : one that adheres to or advocates a (specified) doctrine or system or code of behavior (social*ist*) or that of a (specified) individual (Darwin*ist*)

²**-ist** *adj suffix* : -ISTIC

isth·mi·an \'is-mē-ən\ *adj* : of, relating to, or situated in or near an isthmus

isth·mus \'is-məs\ *n* : a narrow strip of land connecting two larger portions of land

¹**it** \'it, ət\ *pron* **1** : that one — used of a lifeless thing, a plant, a person or animal, or an abstract entity (~'s a big building) (~'s a shade tree) (who is ~) (beauty is everywhere and ~ is a source of joy) **2** — used as a subject of an impersonal verb that expresses a condition or action without reference to an agent (~ is raining) **3** — used as an anticipatory subject or object (~'s good to see you)

²**it** \'it\ *n* : the player in a game who performs the principal action of the game (as trying to find others in hide-and-seek)

It *abbr* Italian; Italy

ital *abbr* italic; italicized

Ital *abbr* Italian

Ital·ian \i-'tal-yən\ *n* **1** : a native or inhabitant of Italy **2** : the language of Italy — **Italian** *adj*

ital·ic \i-'ta-lik, ī-\ *adj* : relating to type in which the letters slope up toward the right (as in *"italic"*) — **italic** *n*

ital·i·cize \i-'ta-lə-ˌsīz, ī-\ *vb* **-cized; -ciz·ing** : to print in italics — **ital·i·ci·za·tion** \-ˌta-lə-sə-'zā-shən\ *n*

itch \'ich\ *n* **1** : an uneasy irritating skin sensation that evokes a desire to scratch the affected area **2** : a skin disorder accompanied by an itch **3** : a persistent desire — **itch** *vb* — **itchy** *adj*

-ite *n suffix* **1** : native : resident (suburban*ite*) **2** : adherent : follower (Le35in*ite*) **3** : product (metabo*lite*) **4** : mineral : rock (quartz*ite*)

item \'ī-təm\ *n* [L, likewise, also] **1** : a separate particular in a list, account, or series : ARTICLE **2** : a separate piece of news (as in a newspaper)

item·ise *Brit var of* ITEMIZE

item·ize \'ī-tə-ˌmīz\ *vb* **-ized; -iz·ing** : to set down in detail : LIST — **item·i·za·tion** \ˌī-tə-mə-'zā-shən\ *n*

it·er·ate \'i-tə-ˌrāt\ *vb* **-at·ed; -at·ing** : REITERATE, REPEAT

it·er·a·tion \ˌi-tə-'rā-shən\ *n* **1** : REPETITION; *esp* : a computational process in which a series of operations is repeated until a condition is met **2** : one repetition of the series of operations in iteration **3** : VERSION

itin·er·ant \ī-'ti-nə-rənt, ə-\ *adj* : traveling from place to place; *esp* : covering a circuit (an ~ preacher)

itin·er·ary \ī-'ti-nə-ˌrer-ē, ə-\ *n, pl* **-ar·ies** **1** : the route of a journey or the proposed outline of one **2** : a travel diary **3** : GUIDEBOOK

its \'its\ *adj* : of or relating to it or itself

it·self \it-'self\ *pron* : that identical one — used reflexively, for emphasis, or in absolute constructions

-ity *n suffix* : quality : state : degree (alkalin*ity*)

IUD \ˌī-(ˌ)yü-'dē\ *n* : INTRAUTERINE DEVICE

IV \ˌī-'vē\ *n, pl* **IVs** [*intravenous*] : an apparatus used to administer a fluid (as of nutrients) intravenously; *also* : a fluid administered by IV

-ive *adj suffix* : that performs or tends toward an (indicated) action (correct*ive*)

ivo·ry \'ī-vrē, -və-rē\ *n, pl* **-ries** [ME *ivorie*, fr. AF *ivoire*, *ivurie*, fr. L *eboreus* of ivory, fr. *ebur* ivory] **1** : the hard creamy-white material composing the tusks of an elephant or walrus **2** : a pale yellow color **3** : something made of ivory or of a similar substance

ivory tower *n* **1** : an impractical lack of concern with urgent problems **2** : a place of learning

ivy \'ī-vē\ *n, pl* **ivies** : a trailing woody evergreen vine with small black berries that is related to ginseng

IWW *abbr* Industrial Workers of the World

-ize *vb suffix* **1** : cause to be or conform to or resemble (American*ize*) : cause to be formed into (union*ize*) **2** : subject to a (specified) action (satir*ize*) **3** : saturate, treat, or combine with (macadam*ize*) **4** : treat like (idol*ize*) **5** : become : become like (crystall*ize*) **6** : be productive in or of : engage in a (specified) activity (philosoph*ize*) **7** : adopt or spread the manner of activity or the teaching of (Christian*ize*)

¹**j** \'jā\ *n, pl* **j's** *or* **js** \'jāz\ *often cap* : the 10th letter of the English alphabet

²**j** *abbr, often cap* **1** jack **2** journal **3** judge **4** justice

¹**jab** \'jab\ *vb* **jabbed; jab·bing** : to thrust quickly or abruptly : POKE

²**jab** *n* : a usu. short straight punch

jab·ber \'ja-bər\ *vb* : to talk rapidly, indistinctly, or unintelligibly : CHATTER — **jabber** *n* — **jab·ber·er** *n*

jab·ber·wocky \'ja-bər-ˌwä-kē\ *n* : meaningless speech or writing

ja·bot \zha-'bō, 'ja-ˌbō\ *n* : a ruffle worn down the front of a dress or shirt

jac·a·ran·da \ˌja-kə-'ran-də\ *n* : any of a genus of pinnate-leaved tropical American trees with clusters of showy blue flowers

¹**jack** \'jak\ *n* **1** : a mechanical device; *esp* : one used to raise a heavy body a short distance **2** : a male donkey **3** : a small target ball in lawn bowling **4** : a small national flag flown by a ship **5** : a small 6-pointed metal object used in a game (**jacks**) **6** : a playing card bearing the figure of a soldier or servant **7** : a socket into which a plug is inserted for connecting electric circuits

²**jack** *vb* **1** : to raise by means of a jack **2** : INCREASE (~ up prices)

jack·al \'ja-kəl\ *n* [Turk *çakal*, fr. Pers *shaqāl*] : any of several mammals of Asia and Africa related to the wolves

jack·a·napes \'ja-kə-ˌnāps\ *n* **1** : MONKEY, APE **2** : an impudent or conceited person

jack·ass \'jak-ˌas\ *n* **1** : DONKEY; *esp* : a male donkey **2** : a stupid person : FOOL

jack·boot \-ˌbüt\ *n* **1** : a heavy military boot of glossy black leather extending above the knee **2** : a laceless military boot reaching to the calf

jack·daw \'jak-ˌdȯ\ *n* : a black and gray Old World crow-like bird

jack·et \'ja-kət\ *n* [ME *jaket*, fr. AF *jackés*, pl., dim. of MF *jaque* short jacket, fr. *jacques* peasant, fr. the name *Jacques* James] **1** : a garment for the upper body usu. having a front opening, collar, and sleeves **2** : an outer covering or casing (a book ~)

Jack Frost *n* : frost or frosty weather personified

jack·ham·mer \'jak-ˌha-mər\ *n* : a pneumatic percussion tool for drilling rock or breaking pavement

jack-in-the-box *n, pl* **jack-in-the-boxes** *or* **jacks-in-the-box** : a toy consisting of a small box out of which a figure springs when the lid is raised

jack-in-the-pulpit *n, pl* **jack-in-the-pulpits** *also* **jacks-in-the-pulpit** : a No. American spring-flowering woodland herb having an upright club-shaped spadix arched over by a green and purple spathe

¹**jack·knife** \'jak-ˌnīf\ *n* **1** : a large pocketknife **2** : a dive in which the diver bends from the waist and touches the ankles before straightening out

²**jackknife** *vb* : to fold like a jackknife ⟨the trailer truck *jackknifed*⟩

jack·leg \\ˈjak-ˌleg\\ *adj* **1** : lacking skill or training **2** : MAKESHIFT

jack–of–all–trades *n, pl* **jacks–of–all–trades** : one who is able to do passable work at various tasks

jack·o'·lan·tern \\ˈja-kə-ˌlan-tərn\\ *n* : a lantern made of a pumpkin cut to look like a human face

jack·pot \\ˈjak-ˌpät\\ *n* **1** : a large sum of money formed by the accumulation of stakes from previous play (as in poker) **2** : an impressive and often unexpected success or reward

jack·rab·bit \\-ˌra-bət\\ *n* : any of several large hares of western No. America with very long ears and hind legs

Jack Russell terrier \\ˈjak-ˈrə-səl-\\ *n* : any of a breed of small terriers having a white coat with dark markings

jack·straw \\-ˌströ\\ *n* **1** *pl* : a game in which straws or thin sticks are let fall in a heap and each player in turn tries to remove them one at a time without disturbing the rest **2** : one of the pieces used in jackstraws

jack–tar \\-ˈtär\\ *n, often cap* : SAILOR

Ja·cob's ladder \\ˈjā-kəbz-\\ *n* : any of several perennial herbs related to phlox that have pinnate leaves and blue or white bell-shaped flowers

jac·quard \\ˈja-ˌkärd\\ *n, often cap* : a fabric of intricate variegated weave or pattern

¹**jade** \\ˈjād\\ *n* **1** : a broken-down, vicious, or worthless horse **2** : a disreputable woman

²**jade** *vb* **jad·ed; jad·ing** **1** : to wear out by overwork or abuse **2** : to become weary ✦ *Synonyms* EXHAUST, FATIGUE, TIRE

³**jade** *n* [F, fr. obs. Sp (*piedra de la*) *ijada*, lit., loin stone; fr. the belief that jade cures renal colic] : a usu. green gemstone that takes a high polish

jad·ed *adj* : made dull, apathetic, or cynical by experience or by surfeit

¹**jag** \\ˈjag\\ *n* : a sharp projecting part

²**jag** *n* : SPREE ⟨a crying ∼⟩

jag·ged \\ˈja-gəd\\ *adj* : sharply notched

jag·uar \\ˈja-ˌgwär\\ *n* : a black-spotted tropical American cat that is larger and stockier than the Old World leopard

jaguar

jai alai \\ˈhī-ˌlī\\ *n* [Sp, fr. Basque, fr. *jai* festival + *alai* merry] : a court game played by usu. two or four players with a ball and a curved wicker basket strapped to the wrist

jail \\ˈjāl\\ *n* [ME *jaiole*, fr. AF *gaiole, jaiole*, fr. LL *caveola*, dim. of L *cavea* cage] : PRISON; *esp* : one for persons held in lawful custody — **jail** *vb*

jail·bird \\-ˌbərd\\ *n* : a habitual criminal

jail·break \\-ˌbrāk\\ *n* : a forcible escape from jail

jail·er *also* **jail·or** \\ˈjā-lər\\ *n* : a keeper of a jail

jal·ap \\ˈja-ləp, ˈjä-\\ *n* : a powdered purgative drug from the root of a Mexican plant related to the morning glory; *also* : this root or plant

ja·la·pe·ño \\ˌhä-lə-ˈpān-(ˌ)yō\\ *n* : a small plump dark green chili pepper

ja·lopy \\jə-ˈlä-pē\\ *n, pl* **ja·lop·ies** : a dilapidated vehicle (as an automobile)

jal·ou·sie \\ˈja-lə-sē\\ *n* [F, lit., jealousy] : a blind, window, or door with adjustable horizontal slats or louvers

¹**jam** \\ˈjam\\ *vb* **jammed; jam·ming** **1** : to press into a close or tight position **2** : to cause to become wedged so as to be unworkable; *also* : to make or become unworkable through the jamming of a movable part **3** : to push forc-

ibly ⟨∼ on the brakes⟩ **4** : CRUSH, BRUISE ⟨*jammed* a finger in the door⟩ **5** : to make unintelligible by sending out interfering signals or messages **6** : to take part in a jam session — **jam·mer** *n*

²**jam** *n* **1** : a crowded mass that impedes or blocks ⟨traffic ∼⟩ **2** : a difficult state of affairs

³**jam** *n* : a food made by boiling fruit and sugar to a thick consistency

Jam *abbr* Jamaica

jamb \\ˈjam\\ *n* [ME *jambe*, fr. AF *jambe, gambe*, lit., leg] : an upright piece forming the side of an opening (as of a door)

jam·ba·laya \\ˌjəm-bə-ˈlī-ə\\ *n* [LaF] : rice cooked with ham, sausage, chicken, shrimp, or oysters and seasoned with herbs

jam·bo·ree \\ˌjam-bə-ˈrē\\ *n* : a large festive gathering

James \\ˈjāmz\\ *n* — see BIBLE table

jam–pack \\ˈjam-ˈpak\\ *vb* : to pack tightly or to excess

jam session *n* : an impromptu performance esp. by jazz musicians

Jan *abbr* January

jan·gle \\ˈjaŋ-gəl\\ *vb* **jan·gled; jan·gling** : to make a harsh or discordant sound — **jangle** *n*

jan·i·tor \\ˈja-nə-tər\\ *n* [L, doorkeeper, fr. *janus* arch, gate] : a person who has the care of a building — **jan·i·to·ri·al** \\ˌja-nə-ˈtòr-ē-əl\\ *adj*

Jan·u·ary \\ˈja-nyə-ˌwer-ē\\ *n* [ME *Januarie*, fr. L *Januarius*, first month of the ancient Roman year, fr. *Janus*, two-faced god of gates and beginnings] : the 1st month of the year

¹**ja·pan** \\jə-ˈpan\\ *n* : a varnish giving a hard brilliant finish

²**japan** *vb* **ja·panned; ja·pan·ning** : to cover with a coat of japan

Jap·a·nese \\ˌja-pə-ˈnēz, -ˈnēs\\ *n, pl* **Japanese** **1** : a native or inhabitant of Japan **2** : the language of Japan — **Japanese** *adj*

Japanese beetle *n* : a small metallic green and brown scarab beetle introduced from Japan that is a pest on the roots of grasses as a grub and on foliage and fruits as an adult

¹**jape** \\ˈjāp\\ *vb* **japed; jap·ing** **1** : JOKE **2** : MOCK

²**jape** *n* : JEST, GIBE

¹**jar** \\ˈjär\\ *vb* **jarred; jar·ring** **1** : to make a harsh or discordant sound **2** : to have a harsh or disagreeable effect **3** : VIBRATE, SHAKE

²**jar** *n* **1** : a state of conflict **2** : a harsh discordant sound **3** : JOLT **4** : a painful effect : SHOCK

³**jar** *n* : a widemouthed container usu. of glass or earthenware

jar·di·niere \\ˌjär-də-ˈnir\\ *n* : an ornamental stand for plants or flowers

jar·gon \\ˈjär-gən\\ *n* **1** : confused unintelligible language **2** : the special vocabulary of a particular group or activity **3** : obscure and often pretentious language

Jas *abbr* James

jas·mine \\ˈjaz-mən\\ *also* **jes·sa·mine** \\ˈjes-mən, ˈje-sə-\\ *n* [MF *jasmin*, fr. Ar *yāsamīn*, fr. Pers] : any of various climbing shrubs with fragrant flowers

jas·per \\ˈjas-pər\\ *n* : a usu. red, yellow, or brown opaque quartz

jaun·dice \\ˈjòn-dəs\\ *n* : yellowish discoloration of skin, tissues, and body fluids by bile pigments; *also* : an abnormal condition marked by jaundice

jaun·diced \\-dəst\\ *adj* **1** : affected with or as if with jaundice **2** : exhibiting envy, distaste, or hostility

jaunt \\ˈjònt\\ *n* : a short trip usu. for pleasure

jaun·ty \\ˈjòn-tē\\ *adj* **jaun·ti·er; -est** : sprightly in manner or appearance : LIVELY — **jaun·ti·ly** \\-tə-lē\\ *adv* — **jaun·ti·ness** \\-tē-nəs\\ *n*

jave·lin \\ˈja-və-lən\\ *n* **1** : a light spear **2** : a slender shaft thrown for distance in a track-and-field contest

¹**jaw** \\ˈjò\\ *n* **1** : either of the bony or cartilaginous structures that support the soft tissues enclosing the mouth and that usu. bear teeth **2** : the parts forming the walls of the mouth and serving to open and close it — usu. used in pl. **3** : one of a pair of movable parts for holding or crushing something — **jawed** \\ˈjòd\\ *adj*

²**jaw** *vb* : to talk abusively, indignantly, or at length

¹**jaw·bone** \\-ˌbōn\\ *n* : JAW 1

²**jawbone** *vb* : to talk forcefully and persuasively

jaw·break·er \-ˌbrā-kər\ n 1 : a word difficult to pronounce 2 : a round hard candy

jaw–drop·ping \ˈjȯ-ˌdra-piŋ\ adj : causing great surprise or astonishment

jaw·less fish \ˈjȯ-ləs-\ n : any of a group of primitive vertebrates (as lampreys) without jaws

jay \ˈjā\ n : any of various noisy brightly colored often largely blue birds smaller than the related crows

jay·bird \ˈjā-ˌbərd\ n : JAY

jay·vee \ˌjā-ˈvē\ n 1 : JUNIOR VARSITY 2 : a member of a junior varsity team

jay·walk \ˈjā-ˌwȯk\ vb : to cross a street carelessly without regard for traffic regulations — **jay·walk·er** n

¹**jazz** \ˈjaz\ n 1 : American music characterized by improvisation, syncopated rhythms, and contrapuntal ensemble playing 2 : empty talk 3 : similar but unspecified things : STUFF

²**jazz** vb : ENLIVEN ⟨∼ things up⟩

jazzy \ˈja-zē\ adj **jazz·i·er; -est** 1 : having the characteristics of jazz 2 : marked by unrestraint, animation, or flashiness

JCS abbr joint chiefs of staff

jct abbr junction

JD abbr 1 [L juris doctor] doctor of jurisprudence; doctor of law 2 [L jurum doctor] doctor of laws 3 justice department 4 juvenile delinquent

jeal·ous \ˈje-ləs\ adj 1 : demanding complete devotion 2 : suspicious of a rival or of one believed to enjoy an advantage 3 : VIGILANT — **jeal·ous·ly** adv — **jeal·ou·sy** \-lə-sē\ n

jeans \ˈjēnz\ n pl [pl. of jean twilled cloth, short for jean fustian, fr. ME Gene Genoa, Italy] : pants made of durable twilled cotton cloth

jeep \ˈjēp\ n : a small four-wheel drive general-purpose motor vehicle used in World War II

¹**jeer** \ˈjir\ vb : to speak or cry out in derision : MOCK

²**jeer** n : TAUNT

Je·ho·vah \ji-ˈhō-və\ n : GOD 1

je·hu \ˈjē-hü, -hyü\ n : a driver of a coach or cab

je·june \ji-ˈjün\ adj [L jejunus empty of food, hungry, meager] : lacking interest or significance : DULL

je·ju·num \ji-ˈjü-nəm\ n [L] : the section of the small intestine between the duodenum and the ileum — **je·ju·nal** \-ˈjü-nᵊl\ adj

jell \ˈjel\ vb 1 : to come to the consistency of jelly 2 : to take shape ⟨my idea began to ∼⟩

jel·ly \ˈje-lē\ n, pl **jellies** 1 : a food with a soft elastic consistency due usu. to the presence of gelatin or pectin; esp : a fruit product made by boiling sugar and the juice of a fruit 2 : a substance resembling jelly — **jelly** vb — **jel·ly·like** adj

jelly bean n : a bean-shaped candy

jel·ly·fish \ˈje-lē-ˌfish\ n : a marine coelenterate with a nearly transparent jellylike body and stinging tentacles

jen·net \ˈje-nət\ n 1 : a small Spanish horse 2 : a female donkey

jen·ny \ˈje-nē\ n, pl **jennies** : a female bird or donkey

jeop·ar·dy \ˈje-pər-dē\ n [ME jeopardie, fr. AF juparti, jeuparti alternative, lit., divided game] : exposure to death, loss, or injury ♦ **Synonyms** PERIL, HAZARD, RISK, DANGER — **jeop·ar·dize** \-ˌdīz\ vb

Jer abbr Jeremiah; Jeremias

jer·e·mi·ad \ˌjer-ə-ˈmī-əd, -ˌad\ n : a prolonged lamentation or complaint; also : a cautionary or angry harangue

Jer·e·mi·ah \ˌjer-ə-ˈmī-ə\ n — see BIBLE table

Jer·e·mi·as \ˌjer-ə-ˈmī-əs\ n : JEREMIAH

¹**jerk** \ˈjərk\ n 1 : a short quick pull or twist : TWITCH 2 : an annoyingly stupid or foolish person — **jerk·i·ly** \ˈjər-kə-lē\ adv — **jerky** \ˈjər-kē\ adj

²**jerk** vb 1 : to give a sharp quick push, pull, or twist 2 : to move in short abrupt motions

jer·kin \ˈjər-kən\ n : a close-fitting usu. sleeveless jacket

jerk·wa·ter \ˈjərk-ˌwȯ-tər, -ˌwä-\ adj [fr. jerkwater rural train] : of minor importance : INSIGNIFICANT ⟨∼ towns⟩

jer·ry–built \ˈjer-ē-ˌbilt\ adj : built cheaply and flimsily

jer·ry–rigged \-ˌrigd\ adj : organized or constructed in a crude or improvised manner

jer·sey \ˈjər-zē\ n, pl **jerseys** [Jersey, one of the Channel islands] 1 : a plain weft-knitted fabric 2 : a close-fitting knitted shirt 3 often cap : any of a breed of small usu. fawn-colored dairy cattle

Jersey barrier n : a concrete slab that is used with others to block or reroute traffic or to divide a highway

Je·ru·sa·lem artichoke \jə-ˈrü-sə-ləm-\ n : a No. American sunflower widely grown for its edible tubers that are used as a vegetable; also : its tubers

jess \ˈjes\ n : a leg strap by which a captive bird of prey may be controlled

jessamine var of JASMINE

jest \ˈjest\ n 1 : an act intended to provoke laughter 2 : a witty remark 3 : a frivolous mood ⟨said in ∼⟩ — **jest** vb

jest·er \ˈjes-tər\ n : a retainer formerly kept to provide casual entertainment

¹**jet** \ˈjet\ n : a velvet-black coal that takes a good polish and is often used for jewelry

²**jet** vb **jet·ted; jet·ting** : to spout or emit in a stream

³**jet** n 1 : a forceful rush (as of liquid or gas) through a narrow opening; also : a nozzle for a jet of fluid 2 : a jet-propelled airplane

⁴**jet** vb **jet·ted; jet·ting** : to travel by jet

jet lag n : a condition that is marked esp. by fatigue and irritability and occurs following a long flight through several time zones — **jet–lagged** adj

jet·lin·er \ˈjet-ˌlī-nər\ n : a jet-propelled airliner

jet·port \-ˌpȯrt\ n : an airport designed to handle jets

jet–pro·pelled \ˌjet-prə-ˈpeld\ adj : driven by an engine (**jet engine**) that produces propulsion (**jet propulsion**) by the rearward discharge of a jet of fluid (as heated air and exhaust gases)

jet·sam \ˈjet-səm\ n : jettisoned goods; esp : such goods washed ashore

jet set n : an international group of wealthy people who frequent fashionable resorts

jet stream n : a long narrow high-altitude current of high-speed winds blowing generally from the west

jet·ti·son \ˈje-tə-sən\ vb 1 : to throw (goods) overboard to lighten a ship or aircraft in distress 2 : DISCARD — **jetti·son** n

jet·ty \ˈje-tē\ n, pl **jetties** 1 : a pier built to influence the current or to protect a harbor 2 : a landing wharf

jeu d'es·prit \zhœ-des-ˈprē\ n, pl **jeux d'esprit** \same\ [F, lit., play of the mind] : a witty comment or composition

Jew \ˈjü\ n 1 : ISRAELITE 2 : one whose religion is Judaism — **Jew·ish** adj

¹**jew·el** \ˈjü-əl\ n [ME juel, fr. AF, dim. of ju, jeu game, play, fr. L jocus game, joke] 1 : an ornament of precious metal 2 : GEMSTONE, GEM

²**jewel** vb **-eled** or **-elled; -el·ing** or **-el·ling** : to adorn or equip with jewels

jewel box n : a thin plastic case for a CD or DVD

jew·el·er or **jew·el·ler** \ˈjü-ə-lər\ n : a person who makes or deals in jewelry and related articles

jew·el·ery chiefly Brit var of JEWELRY

jew·el·ry \ˈjü-əl-rē\ n : JEWELS; esp : objects of precious metal set with gems and worn for personal adornment

Jew·ry \ˈju̇r-ē, ˈju̇-ər-ē, ˈjü-rē\ n : the Jewish people

jg abbr junior grade

jib \ˈjib\ n : a triangular sail set on a line running from the bow to the mast

²**jib** vb **jibbed; jib·bing** : to refuse to proceed further

¹**jibe** var of GIBE

²**jibe** \ˈjīb\ vb **jibed; jib·ing** : to be in accord : AGREE

ji·ca·ma \ˈhē-kə-mə\ n : an edible starchy tuber of a tropical American vine of the legume family

jif·fy \ˈji-fē\ n, pl **jiffies** : MOMENT, INSTANT ⟨I'll be ready in a ∼⟩

¹**jig** \ˈjig\ n 1 : a lively dance in triple rhythm 2 : TRICK, GAME ⟨the ∼ is up⟩ 3 : a device used to hold work during manufacture or assembly

²**jig** vb **jigged; jig·ging** : to dance a jig

jig·ger \ˈji-gər\ n : a measure usu. holding 1 to 2 ounces (30 to 60 milliliters) used in mixing drinks

jig·gle \ˈji-gəl\ vb **jig·gled; jig·gling** : to move with quick little jerks — **jiggle** n

jig·saw \ˈjig-ˌsȯ\ n : SCROLL SAW 2

jigsaw puzzle n : a puzzle consisting of small irregularly cut pieces to be fitted together to form a picture

ji·had \ji-ˈhäd, -ˈhad\ n 1 : a Muslim holy war 2 : CRUSADE 2

¹**jilt** \ˈjilt\ vb : to drop (as a lover) capriciously or unfeelingly

²jilt *n* : one who jilts a lover
jim crow \'jim-'krō\ *n, often cap J&C* : discrimination against blacks esp. by legal enforcement or traditional sanctions — jim crow *adj, often cap J&C* — jim crow·ism \-'krō-ı̇-zəm\ *n, often cap J&C*
jim–dan·dy \'jim-'dan-dē\ *n* : something excellent of its kind — jim–dandy *adj*
jim·mies \'ji-mēz\ *n pl* : tiny rod-shaped bits of usu. chocolate-flavored candy often sprinkled on ice cream
¹jim·my \'ji-mē\ *n, pl* jimmies : a small crowbar
²jimmy *vb* jim·mied; jim·my·ing : to force open with a jimmy
jim·son·weed \'jim-sən-ˌwēd\ *n, often cap* : a coarse poisonous weed related to the tomato that has large trumpet-shaped white or violet flowers
¹jin·gle \'jiŋ-gəl\ *vb* jin·gled; jin·gling : to make a light clinking or tinkling sound
²jingle *n* 1 : a light clinking or tinkling sound 2 : a short verse or song with catchy repetition
jin·go·ism \'jiŋ-gō-ˌi-zəm\ *n* : extreme chauvinism or nationalism marked esp. by a belligerent foreign policy — jin·go·ist \-ist\ *n* — jin·go·is·tic \ˌjiŋ-gō-'is-tik\ *adj*
jin·rik·sha \jin-'rik-ˌshȯ\ *n* : RICKSHA
¹jinx \'jiŋks\ *n* : one that brings bad luck
²jinx *vb* : to foredoom to failure or misfortune
jit·ney \'jit-nē\ *n, pl* jitneys : a small bus that serves a regular route on a flexible schedule
jit·ter·bug \'ji-tər-ˌbəg\ *n* : a dance in which couples two-step, balance, and twirl vigorously in standardized patterns — jitterbug *vb*
jit·ters \'ji-tərz\ *n pl* : extreme nervousness — jit·tery \-tə-rē\ *adj*
¹jive \'jīv\ *n* 1 : swing music or dancing performed to it 2 : glib, deceptive, or foolish talk 3 : the jargon of jazz enthusiasts
²jive *vb* jived; jiv·ing 1 : KID, TEASE 2 : to dance to or play jive
Jn *or* Jno *abbr* John
Jo *abbr* Joel
¹job \'jäb\ *n* 1 : a piece of work 2 : something that has to be done : TASK 3 : a regular remunerative position — job·less *adj*
²job *vb* jobbed; job·bing 1 : to do occasional pieces of work for hire 2 : to hire or let by the job
Job \'jōb\ *n* — see BIBLE table
job action *n* : a protest action by workers to force compliance with demands
job·ber \'jä-bər\ *n* 1 : a person who buys goods and then sells them to other dealers : MIDDLEMAN 2 : a person who does work by the job
job·hold·er \'jäb-ˌhōl-dər\ *n* : one having a regular job
jock \'jäk\ *n* [*jockstrap*] : ATHLETE; *esp* : a school or college athlete
¹jock·ey \'jä-kē\ *n, pl* jockeys : one who rides a horse esp. as a professional in a race
²jockey *vb* jock·eyed; jock·ey·ing : to maneuver or manipulate by adroit or devious means
jock·strap \'jäk-ˌstrap\ *n* [E slang *jock* penis] : ATHLETIC SUPPORTER
jo·cose \jō-'kōs\ *adj* 1 : MERRY 2 : HUMOROUS ♦ Synonyms JOCULAR, FACETIOUS, WITTY
joc·u·lar \'jä-kyə-lər\ *adj* : marked by jesting : PLAYFUL — joc·u·lar·i·ty \ˌjäk-yə-'lar-ə-tē\ *n* — joc·u·lar·ly *adv*
jo·cund \'jä-kənd\ *adj* : marked by mirth or cheerfulness
jodh·pur \'jäd-pər\ *n* 1 *pl* : riding breeches loose above the knee and tight-fitting below 2 : an ankle-high boot fastened with a strap
Joe Blow \'jō-\ *n* : an average or ordinary man
Jo·el \'jō-əl\ *n* — see BIBLE table
Joe Six–Pack \'jō-\ *n* : a blue-collar worker
¹jog \'jäg\ *vb* jogged; jog·ging 1 : to give a slight shake or push to 2 : to go at a slow monotonous pace 3 : to run or ride at a slow trot — jog·ger *n*
²jog *n* 1 : a slight shake 2 : a jogging movement or pace
³jog *n* 1 : a projecting or retreating part of a line or surface 2 : a sharp abrupt change in direction
jog·gle \'jä-gəl\ *vb* jog·gled; jog·gling : to shake slightly — joggle *n*
john \'jän\ *n* 1 : TOILET 2 : a prostitute's client
John \'jän\ *n* — see BIBLE table

john·ny \'jä-nē\ *n, pl* johnnies : a short-sleeved gown opening in the back that is worn by hospital patients
John·ny–jump–up \ˌjä-nē-'jəmp-ˌəp\ *n* : any of various small-flowered cultivated pansies
joie de vi·vre \ˌzhwä-də-'vēvrᵊ\ *n* [F] : keen enjoyment of life
join \'jȯin\ *vb* 1 : to come or bring together so as to form a unit 2 : to come or bring into close association 3 : to become a member of 4 : ADJOIN 5 : to take part in a collective activity
join·er \'jȯi-nər\ *n* 1 : a worker who constructs articles by joining pieces of wood 2 : a gregarious person who joins many organizations
¹joint \'jȯint\ *n* 1 : the point of contact between bones of an animal skeleton with the parts that surround and support it 2 : a cut of meat suitable for roasting 3 : a place where two things or parts are connected 4 : ESTABLISHMENT; *esp* : a shabby or disreputable establishment 5 : a marijuana cigarette — joint·ed *adj*
²joint *adj* 1 : UNITED 2 : common to two or more — joint·ly *adv*
³joint *vb* 1 : to unite by or provide with a joint 2 : to separate the joints of
joist \'jȯist\ *n* : any of the small beams ranged parallel from wall to wall in a building to support a floor or ceiling

floor joists

¹joke \'jōk\ *n* : something said or done to provoke laughter; *esp* : a brief narrative with a humorous climax
²joke *vb* joked; jok·ing : to make jokes — jok·ing·ly *adv*
jok·er \'jō-kər\ *n* 1 : a person who jokes 2 : an extra card used in some card games 3 : a misleading part of an agreement that works to one party's disadvantage
jol·li·fi·ca·tion \ˌjä-li-fə-'kā-shən\ *n* : a festive celebration
jol·li·ty \'jä-lə-tē\ *n, pl* -ties : GAIETY, MERRIMENT
jol·ly \'jä-lē\ *adj* jol·li·er; -est : full of high spirits : MERRY
¹jolt \'jōlt\ *vb* 1 : to give a quick hard knock or blow to 2 : to move with a sudden jerky motion — jolt·er *n*
²jolt *n* 1 : an abrupt jerky blow or movement 2 : a sudden shock
Jon *abbr* Jonah; Jonas
Jo·nah \'jō-nə\ *n* — see BIBLE table
Jo·nas \'jō-nəs\ *n* : JONAH
¹jones \'jōnz\ *n* 1 *slang* : addiction to heroin 2 *slang* : HEROIN 3 *slang* : a craving for something
²jones *vb, slang* : to have a craving for something
jon·gleur \zhōⁿ-'glər\ *n* : an itinerant medieval minstrel
jon·quil \'jän-kwəl\ *n* [F *jonquille*, fr. Sp *junquillo*, dim. of *junco* reed, fr. L *juncus*] : a narcissus with fragrant clustered white or yellow flowers
josh \'jäsh\ *vb* : TEASE, JOKE
Josh *abbr* Joshua
Josh·ua \'jä-shə-wə\ *n* — see BIBLE table
Joshua tree *n* : a tall branched yucca of the southwestern U.S.
jos·tle \'jä-səl\ *vb* jos·tled; jos·tling 1 : to come in contact or into collision 2 : to make one's way by pushing and shoving
Jos·ue \'jä-shü-ē\ *n* : JOSHUA
¹jot \'jät\ *n* : the least bit : IOTA
²jot *vb* jot·ted; jot·ting : to write briefly and hurriedly
jot·ting \'jä-tiŋ\ *n* : a brief note
joule \'jül\ *n* : a unit of work or energy equal to the work done by a force of one newton acting through a distance of one meter
jounce \'jaůns\ *vb* jounced; jounc·ing : JOLT — jounce *n*
jour *abbr* 1 journal 2 journeyman
jour·nal \'jər-nᵊl\ *n* [ME, service book containing the day

hours, fr. AF *jurnal*, fr. *jurnal* daily, fr. L *diurnalis*, fr. *dies* day] **1** : a brief account of daily events **2** : a record of proceedings (as of a legislative body) **3** : a periodical (as a newspaper) dealing with current events **4** : the part of a rotating axle or spindle that turns in a bearing

jour·nal·ese \ˌjər-nə-ˈlēz, -ˈlēs\ *n* : a style of writing held to be characteristic of newspapers

jour·nal·ism \ˈjər-nə-ˌli-zəm\ *n* **1** : the business of writing for, editing, or publishing periodicals (as newspapers) **2** : writing designed for or characteristic of newspapers — **jour·nal·ist** \-list\ *n* — **jour·nal·is·tic** \ˌjər-nə-ˈlis-tik\ *adj*

¹jour·ney \ˈjər-nē\ *n, pl* **journeys** [ME, fr. OF *journee* day's journey, fr. *jour* day] : a traveling from one place to another

²journey *vb* **jour·neyed; jour·ney·ing** : to go on a journey : TRAVEL

jour·ney·man \-mən\ *n* **1** : a worker who has learned a trade and works for another person **2** : an experienced reliable worker

¹joust \ˈjaust\ *vb* : to engage in a joust

²joust *n* : a combat on horseback between two knights with lances esp. as part of a tournament

jo·vial \ˈjō-vē-əl\ *adj* : marked by good humor — **jo·vi·al·i·ty** \ˌjō-vē-ˈa-lə-tē\ *n* — **jo·vi·al·ly** *adv*

¹jowl \ˈjau̇(-ə)l\ *n* : loose flesh about the lower jaw or throat

²jowl *n* **1** : the lower jaw **2** : CHEEK

¹joy \ˈjȯi\ *n* [ME, fr. AF *joie*, fr. L *gaudia*] **1** : a feeling of happiness that comes from success, good fortune, or a sense of well-being **2** : a source of happiness ✦ *Synonyms* BLISS, DELIGHT, ENJOYMENT, PLEASURE — **joyless** *adj*

²joy *vb* : REJOICE

joy·ful \-fəl\ *adj* : experiencing, causing, or showing joy — **joy·ful·ly** *adv*

joy·ous \ˈjȯi-əs\ *adj* : JOYFUL — **joy·ous·ly** *adv* — **joy·ous·ness** *n*

joy·ride \ˈjȯi-ˌrīd\ *n* : a ride for pleasure often marked by reckless driving — **joyride** *vb* — **joy·rid·er** *n* — **joy·rid·ing** *n*

joy·stick \-ˌstik\ *n* : a control device (as for a computer) consisting of a lever capable of motion in two or more directions

JP *abbr* **1** jet propulsion **2** justice of the peace

JPEG \ˈjā-ˌpeg\ *n* [*J*oint *P*hotographic *E*xperts *G*roup] : a computer file format for usu. high-quality digital images

Jr *abbr* junior

jt *or* **jnt** *abbr* joint

ju·bi·lant \ˈjü-bə-lənt\ *adj* [L *jubilans*, prp. of *jubilare* to rejoice] : EXULTANT — **ju·bi·lant·ly** *adv*

ju·bi·la·tion \ˌjü-bə-ˈlā-shən\ *n* : EXULTATION

ju·bi·lee \ˈjü-bə-ˌlē, ˌjü-bə-ˈlē\ *n* [ME, fr. AF & LL; AF *jubilé*, fr. LL *jubilaeus*, fr. LGk *iōbēlaios*, fr. Heb *yōbhēl* ram's horn, trumpet, jubilee] **1** : a 50th anniversary **2** : a season or occasion of celebration

ju·co \ˈjü-ˌkō\ *n, pl* **jucos** : JUNIOR COLLEGE; *also* : an athlete at a junior college

Jud *abbr* Judith

Ju·da·ic \ju̇-ˈdā-ik\ *also* **Ju·da·ical** \-ˈdā-ə-kəl\ *adj* : of, relating to, or characteristic of Jews or Judaism

Ju·da·ism \ˈjü-də-ˌi-zəm, -dā-, -dē-\ *n* : a religion developed among the ancient Hebrews and marked by belief in one God and by the moral and ceremonial laws of the Old Testament and the rabbinic tradition

Jude \ˈjüd\ *n* — see BIBLE table

Judg *abbr* Judges

¹judge \ˈjəj\ *vb* **judged; judg·ing** **1** : to form an authoritative opinion **2** : to decide as a judge : TRY **3** : to form an estimate or evaluation about something : THINK ✦ *Synonyms* CONCLUDE, DEDUCE, GATHER, INFER

²judge *n* **1** : a public official authorized to decide questions brought before a court **2** : UMPIRE **3** : one who gives an authoritative opinion : CRITIC — **judge·ship** *n*

Judges *n* — see BIBLE table

judg·ment *or* **judge·ment** \ˈjəj-mənt\ *n* **1** : a decision or opinion given after judging; *esp* : a formal decision given by a court **2** *cap* : the final judging of mankind by God **3** : the process of forming an opinion by discerning and comparing **4** : the capacity for judging : DISCERNMENT

judg·men·tal \ˌjəj-ˈmen-təl\ *adj* **1** : of, relating to, or involving judgment **2** : characterized by a tendency to judge harshly — **judg·men·tal·ly** *adv*

judgment call *n* : a subjective decision, ruling, or opinion

Judgment Day *n* : the day of the final judging of all human beings by God

ju·di·ca·ture \ˈjü-di-kə-ˌchu̇r\ *n* **1** : the administration of justice **2** : JUDICIARY 1

ju·di·cial \ju̇-ˈdi-shəl\ *adj* **1** : of or relating to the administration of justice or the judiciary **2** : ordered or enforced by a court **3** : CRITICAL — **ju·di·cial·ly** *adv*

ju·di·cia·ry \ju̇-ˈdi-shē-ˌer-ē, -shə-rē\ *n* **1** : a system of courts of law; *also* : the judges of these courts **2** : a branch of government in which judicial power is vested — **judiciary** *adj*

ju·di·cious \ju̇-ˈdi-shəs\ *adj* : having, exercising, or characterized by sound judgment ✦ *Synonyms* PRUDENT, SAGE, SANE, SENSIBLE, WISE — **ju·di·cious·ly** *adv*

Ju·dith \ˈjü-dəth\ *n* — see BIBLE table

ju·do \ˈjü-dō\ *n* [Jp, fr. *jū* weakness, gentleness + *dō* art] : a sport derived from jujitsu that emphasizes the use of quick movement and leverage to throw an opponent — **ju·do·ist** \-ist\ *n*

ju·do·ka \ˈjü-dō-ˌkä\ *n, pl* **judoka** *or* **judokas** : one who participates in judo

¹jug \ˈjəg\ *n* **1** : a large deep container with a narrow mouth and a handle **2** : JAIL, PRISON

²jug *vb* **jugged; jug·ging** : JAIL, IMPRISON

jug-eared \ˈjəg-ˌird\ *adj* : having protuberant ears

jug·ger·naut \ˈjə-gər-ˌnȯt\ *n* [Hindi *Jagannāth*, title of Vishnu (a Hindu god), lit., lord of the world] : a massive inexorable force or object that crushes everything in its path

jug·gle \ˈjə-gəl\ *vb* **jug·gled; jug·gling** **1** : to keep several objects in motion in the air at the same time **2** : to manipulate esp. in order to achieve a desired and often fraudulent end — **jug·gler** \ˈjə-glər\ *n*

jug·u·lar \ˈjə-gyə-lər\ *adj* : of, relating to, or situated in or on the throat or neck ⟨the ∼ veins⟩

juice \ˈjüs\ *n* **1** : the extractable fluid contents of cells or tissues **2** *pl* : the natural fluids of an animal body **3** : something that supplies power; *esp* : ELECTRICITY **2**

juic·er \ˈjü-sər\ *n* : an appliance for extracting juice (as from fruit)

juice up *vb* : to give life, energy, or spirit to

juicy \ˈjü-sē\ *adj* **juic·i·er; -est** **1** : SUCCULENT **2** : rich in interest; *also* : RACY — **juic·i·ly** \-sə-lē\ *adv* — **juic·i·ness** \-sē-nəs\ *n*

ju·jit·su *also* **ju·jut·su** *or* **jiu·jit·su** \jü-ˈjit-sü\ *n* : an art of fighting employing holds, throws, and paralyzing blows

ju·ju \ˈjü-jü\ *n* : a style of African music characterized by a rapid beat, use of percussion instruments, and vocal harmonies

ju·jube \ˈjü-ˌjüb, ˈjü-jü-ˌbē\ *n* : a fruit-flavored gumdrop or lozenge

juke·box \ˈjük-ˌbäks\ *n* : a coin-operated machine that automatically plays selected recordings

Jul *abbr* July

ju·lep \ˈjü-ləp\ *n* [ME, sweetened water, fr. MF, fr. Ar *julāb*, fr. Pers *gulāb*, fr. *gul* rose + *āb* water] : a drink made of bourbon, sugar, and mint served over crushed ice

Ju·ly \ju̇-ˈlī\ *n* [ME *Julie*, fr. OE *Julius*, fr. L, fr. Gaius *Julius* Caesar] : the 7th month of the year

¹jum·ble \ˈjəm-bəl\ *vb* **jum·bled; jum·bling** : to mix in a confused mass

²jumble *n* : a disorderly mass or pile

jum·bo \ˈjəm-bō\ *n, pl* **jumbos** [*Jumbo*, a huge elephant exhibited by P.T. Barnum] : a very large specimen of its kind — **jumbo** *adj*

¹jump \ˈjəmp\ *vb* **1** : to spring into the air : leap over **2** : to give a start **3** : to rise or increase suddenly or sharply **4** : to make a sudden attack **5** : to leave hurriedly and often furtively ⟨∼ town⟩ **6** : to act or move before (as a signal) — **jump bail** : to abscond after being released from custody on bail — **jump ship 1** : to leave the company of a ship without authority **2** : to desert a cause — **jump the gun** : to begin something before the proper time

²jump *n* **1** : a spring into the air; *esp* : one made for height or distance in a track meet **2** : a sharp sudden increase **3** : an initial advantage

¹jump·er \ˈjəm-pər\ *n* : one that jumps

²jumper *n* **1** : a loose blouse **2** : a sleeveless one-piece dress worn usu. with a blouse **3** *pl* : a child's sleeveless coverall

jumping bean *n* : a seed of any of several Mexican shrubs that tumbles about because of the movements of a small moth larva inside it

jumping–off place *n*   **1** : a remote or isolated place   **2** : a place from which an enterprise is launched

jump·mas·ter \\'jəmp-ˌmas-tər\ *n* : a person who supervises parachutists

jump–start \\'jəmp-ˌstärt\ *vb* : to start (an engine or vehicle) by connection to an external power source

jump·suit \\'jəmp-ˌsüt\ *n*   **1** : a coverall worn by parachutists in jumping   **2** : a one-piece garment consisting of a blouse or shirt with attached pants or shorts

jumpy \\'jəm-pē\ *adj* **jump·i·er; -est** : NERVOUS, JITTERY

jun *abbr* junior

Jun *abbr* June

junc *abbr* junction

jun·co \\'jəŋ-kō\ *n, pl* **juncos** *or* **juncoes** : any of a genus of small common pink-billed No. American finches that are largely gray with conspicuous white tail feathers

junc·tion \\'jəŋk-shən\ *n*   **1** : an act of joining   **2** : a place or point of meeting

junc·ture \\'jəŋk-chər\ *n*   **1** : JOINT, CONNECTION   **2** : UNION   **3** : a critical time or state of affairs

June \\'jün\ *n* [ME, fr. L *Junius*] : the 6th month of the year

jun·gle \\'jəŋ-gəl\ *n* [Hindi & Urdu *jangal* forest]   **1** : a thick tangled mass of tropical vegetation; *also* : a tract overgrown with vegetation   **2** : a place of ruthless struggle for survival

¹ju·nior \\'jü-nyər\ *adj*   **1** : YOUNGER   **2** : lower in rank ⟨a ∼ partner⟩   **3** : of or relating to juniors

²junior *n*   **1** : a person who is younger or of lower rank than another   **2** : a student in the next-to-last year before graduating

junior college *n* : a school that offers studies corresponding to those of the 1st two years of college

junior high school *n* : a school usu. including grades 7–9

junior varsity *n* : a team whose members lack the experience or qualifications required for the varsity

ju·ni·per \\'jü-nə-pər\ *n* : any of numerous coniferous shrubs or trees with leaves like needles or scales and female cones like berries

¹junk \\'jəŋk\ *n*   **1** : old iron, glass, paper, or waste; *also* : discarded articles   **2** : a shoddy product   **3** : something of little meaning, worth, or significance   **4** *slang* : NARCOTICS; *esp* : HEROIN — **junky** *adj*

²junk *vb* : DISCARD, SCRAP

³junk *n* : a ship of eastern Asia with a high stern and 4-cornered sails

junk·er \\'jəŋ-kər\ *n* : something (as an old automobile) ready for scrapping

Jun·ker \\'yu̇ŋ-kər\ *n* [G] : a member of the Prussian landed aristocracy

jun·ket \\'jəŋ-kət\ *n*   **1** : a pudding of sweetened flavored milk set by rennet   **2** : a trip made by an official at public expense

junk food *n* : food that is high in calories but low in nutritional content

junk·ie *also* **junky** \\'jəŋ-kē\ *n, pl* **junkies**   **1** : a narcotics peddler or addict   **2** : one that derives inordinate pleasure from or is dependent on something ⟨a sugar ∼⟩

jun·ta \\'hu̇n-tə, 'jən-, 'hən-\ *n* [Sp, fr. *junto* joined, fr. L *junctus*, pp. of *jungere* to join] : a group of persons controlling a government esp. after a revolutionary seizure of power

Ju·pi·ter \\'jü-pə-tər\ *n* : the largest of the planets and the one 5th in order of distance from the sun — see PLANET table

Ju·ras·sic \ju̇-'ra-sik\ *adj* : of, relating to, or being the period of the Mesozoic era between the Triassic and the Cretaceous that is marked esp. by the presence of dinosaurs — **Jurassic** *n*

ju·rid·i·cal \ju̇-'ri-di-kəl\ *also* **ju·rid·ic** \-dik\ *adj*   **1** : of or relating to the administration of justice   **2** : LEGAL — **ju·rid·i·cal·ly** \-di-k(ə-)lē\ *adv*

ju·ris·dic·tion \ˌju̇r-əs-'dik-shən\ *n*   **1** : the power, right, or authority to interpret and apply the law   **2** : the authority of a sovereign power   **3** : the limits or territory within which authority may be exercised — **ju·ris·dic·tion·al** \-shə-nəl\ *adj*

ju·ris·pru·dence \-'prü-dᵊns\ *n*   **1** : the science or philosophy of law   **2** : a system of laws

ju·rist \\'ju̇r-ist\ *n* : one having a thorough knowledge of law; *esp* : JUDGE

ju·ris·tic \ju̇-'ris-tik\ *adj*   **1** : of or relating to a jurist or jurisprudence   **2** : of, relating to, or recognized in law

ju·ror \\'ju̇r-ər, -ˌȯr\ *n* : a member of a jury

¹ju·ry \\'ju̇r-ē\ *n, pl* **juries**   **1** : a body of persons sworn to inquire into a matter submitted to them and to give their verdict   **2** : a committee for judging and awarding prizes

²jury *adj* : improvised for temporary use esp. in an emergency ⟨a ∼ mast⟩

jury nullification *n* : the acquitting of a defendant by a jury in disregard of the judge's instructions and contrary to the jury's findings of fact

jury–rig \\'ju̇r-ē-ˌrig\ *vb* : to construct or arrange in a makeshift fashion

¹just \\'jəst\ *adj*   **1** : having a basis in or conforming to fact or reason : REASONABLE ⟨∼ comment⟩   **2** : CORRECT, PROPER ⟨∼ proportions⟩   **3** : morally or legally right ⟨a ∼ title⟩   **4** : DESERVED, MERITED ⟨∼ punishment⟩

♦ **Synonyms** UPRIGHT, HONORABLE, CONSCIENTIOUS, HONEST — **just·ly** *adv* — **just·ness** *n*

²just \\'jəst, 'jist\ *adv*   **1** : EXACTLY ⟨∼ right⟩   **2** : very recently ⟨has ∼ left⟩   **3** : BARELY ⟨∼ too late⟩   **4** : DIRECTLY ⟨∼ west of here⟩   **5** : ONLY ⟨∼ last year⟩   **6** : QUITE ⟨∼ wonderful⟩   **7** : POSSIBLY ⟨it ∼ might work⟩

jus·tice \\'jəs-təs\ *n*   **1** : the administration of what is just (as by assigning merited rewards or punishments)   **2** : JUDGE   **3** : the administration of law   **4** : FAIRNESS; *also* : RIGHTEOUSNESS

justice of the peace : a local magistrate empowered chiefly to try minor cases, to administer oaths, and to perform marriages

jus·ti·fy \\'jəs-tə-ˌfī\ *vb* **-fied; -fy·ing**   **1** : to prove to be just, right, or reasonable   **2** : to pronounce free from guilt or blame   **3** : to adjust spaces in a line of printed text so the margins are even — **jus·ti·fi·able** *adj* — **jus·ti·fi·ca·tion** \ˌjəs-tə-fə-'kā-shən\ *n*

jut \\'jət\ *vb* **jut·ted; jut·ting** : PROJECT, PROTRUDE

jute \\'jüt\ *n* : a strong glossy fiber from either of two tropical plants used esp. for making sacks and twine

juv *abbr* juvenile

¹ju·ve·nile \\'jü-və-ˌnī(-ə)l, -nəl\ *adj*   **1** : showing incomplete development   **2** : of, relating to, or characteristic of children or young people

²juvenile *n*   **1** : a young person; *esp* : one below the legally established age of adulthood   **2** : a young animal (as a fish or a bird) or plant   **3** : an actor or actress who plays youthful parts

juvenile delinquency *n* : violation of the law or antisocial behavior by a juvenile — **juvenile delinquent** *n*

jux·ta·pose \\'jək-stə-ˌpōz\ *vb* **-posed; -pos·ing** : to place side by side — **jux·ta·po·si·tion** \ˌjək-stə-pə-'zi-shən\ *n*

JV *abbr* junior varsity

¹k \'kā\ *n, pl* **k's** *or* **ks** \'kāz\ **1** *often cap* : the 11th letter of the English alphabet **2** *cap* : STRIKEOUT
²k *abbr* **1** karat **2** kitchen **3** knit **4** kosher — often enclosed in a circle
¹K *abbr* **1** Kelvin **2** kindergarten
²K *symbol* [NL *kalium*] potassium
kab·ba·lah *also* **kab·ba·la** *or* **ka·ba·la** *or* **ca·ba·la** \kə-'bä-lə, 'ka-bə-lə\ *n, often cap* **1** : a medieval Jewish mysticism marked by belief in creation through emanation and a cipher method of interpreting Scripture **2** : esoteric or mysterious doctrine
kabob *var of* KEBAB
Ka·bu·ki \kə-'bü-kē\ *n* : traditional Japanese popular drama with highly stylized singing and dancing
kad·dish \'kä-dish\ *n, often cap* : a Jewish prayer recited in the daily synagogue ritual and by mourners at public services after the death of a close relative
kaf·fee·klatsch \'kȯ-fē-,klach, 'kä-\ *n, often cap* [G] : an informal social gathering for coffee and conversation
kai·ser \'kī-zər\ *n* : EMPEROR; *esp* : the ruler of Germany from 1871 to 1918
Ka·lash·ni·kov \kə-'lash-nə-,kȯf\ *n* [M. T. *Kalashnikov* b1919 Soviet weapons designer] : a Soviet-designed assault rifle
kale \'kāl\ *n* : a hardy cabbage with curled leaves that do not form a head
ka·lei·do·scope \kə-'lī-də-,skōp\ *n* : a tube containing loose bits of colored material (as glass) and two mirrors at one end that shows many different patterns as it is turned — **ka·lei·do·scop·ic** \-,lī-də-'skä-pik\ *adj* — **ka·lei·do·scop·i·cal·ly** \-pi-k(ə-)lē\ *adv*
ka·ma·ai·na \,kä-mə-'ī-nə\ *n* [Hawaiian *kama'āina*, fr. *kama* child + *'āina* land] : one who has lived in Hawaii for a long time
kame \'kām\ *n* [Sc, lit., comb] : a short ridge or mound of material deposited by water from a melting glacier
ka·mi·ka·ze \,kä-mi-'kä-zē\ *n* [Jp, lit., divine wind] : a member of a corps of Japanese pilots assigned to make a suicidal crash on a target; *also* : an airplane flown in such an attack
Kan *or* **Kans** *abbr* Kansas
kan·ga·roo \,kaŋ-gə-'rü\ *n, pl* **-roos** : any of various large leaping marsupial mammals of Australia and adjacent islands with powerful hind legs and a long thick tail used as a support
kangaroo court *n* : a court or an illegal self-appointed tribunal characterized by irresponsible, perverted, or irregular procedures
ka·o·lin \'kā-ə-lən\ *n* : a fine usu. white clay used in ceramics and refractories and for the treatment of diarrhea
ka·pey·ka \kä-'pā-kä\ *n, pl* **ka·pe·ek** \kä-'pā-ək\ — see *rubel* at MONEY table
ka·pok \'kä-,päk\ *n* : silky fiber from the seeds of a tropical tree used esp. as a filling (as for life preservers)
Kap·o·si's sar·co·ma \'ka-pə-sēz-sär-'kō-mə\ *n* : a neoplastic disease associated esp. with AIDS that affects esp. the skin and mucous membranes and is characterized usu. by the formation of pink to reddish-brown or bluish plaques
kap·pa \'ka-pə\ *n* : the 10th letter of the Greek alphabet — K or κ
ka·put *also* **ka·putt** \kä-'pu̇t, kə-, -'pu̇t\ *adj* [G, fr. F *capot* not having made a trick at piquet] **1** : utterly defeated or destroyed **2** : unable to function : USELESS
kar·a·kul \'ker-ə-kəl\ *n* : the usu. curly glossy black coat of a very young lamb of a hardy Asian breed of sheep
kar·a·o·ke \,ker-ē-'ō-kē\ *n* [Jp] : a device that plays instrumental accompaniments for songs to which the user sings along
kar·at \'ker-ət\ *n* : a unit for expressing proportion of gold in an alloy equal to ¹/₂₄ part of pure gold
ka·ra·te \kə-'rä-tē\ *n* [Jp, lit., empty hand] : an art of self=

defense in which an attacker is disabled by crippling kicks and punches
kar·ma \'kär-mə\ *n, often cap* [Skt] : the force generated by a person's actions held in Hinduism and Buddhism to perpetuate reincarnation and to determine the nature of the person's next existence — **kar·mic** \-mik\ *adj*
karst \'kärst\ *n* [G] : an irregular limestone region with sinks, underground streams, and caverns
ka·ty·did \'kä-tē-,did\ *n* : any of several large green tree=dwelling American grasshoppers with long antennae

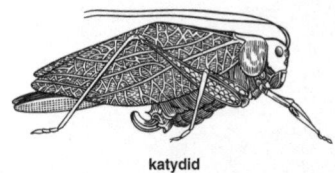

katydid

kay·ak \'kī-,ak\ *n* : an Eskimo canoe made of a skin-covered frame with a small opening and propelled by a double-bladed paddle; *also* : a similar portable boat — **kay·ak·er** *n*
kayo \(,)kā-'ō, 'kā-ō\ *n* : KNOCKOUT — **kayo** *vb*
ka·zoo \kə-'zü\ *n, pl* **kazoos** : a toy musical instrument consisting of a tube with a membrane sealing one end and a side hole to sing or hum into
KB *abbr* kilobyte
kc *abbr* kilocycle
KC *abbr* **1** Kansas City **2** King's Counsel **3** Knights of Columbus
kc/s *abbr* kilocycles per second
KD *abbr* knocked down
ke·bab *or* **ke·bob** *also* **ka·bob** \kə-'bäb\ *n* : cubes of meat cooked with vegetables usu. on a skewer
kedge \'kej\ *n* : a small anchor
¹keel \'kēl\ *n* **1** : the chief structural member of a ship running lengthwise along the center of its bottom **2** : something (as a bird's breastbone) like a ship's keel in form or use — **keeled** \'kēld\ *adj*
²keel *vb* : FAINT, SWOON — usu. used with *over*
keel·boat \'kēl-,bōt\ *n* : a shallow covered keeled riverboat for freight that is usu. rowed, poled, or towed
keel·haul \-,hȯl\ *vb* : to haul under the keel of a ship as punishment
¹keen \'kēn\ *adj* **1** : SHARP ⟨a ∼ knife⟩ **2** : SEVERE ⟨a ∼ wind⟩ **3** : ENTHUSIASTIC ⟨∼ about swimming⟩ **4** : mentally alert ⟨a ∼ mind⟩ **5** : STRONG, ACUTE ⟨∼ eyesight⟩ **6** : WONDERFUL, EXCELLENT — **keen·ly** *adv* — **keen·ness** *n*
²keen *n* : a lamentation for the dead uttered in a loud wailing voice or in a wordless cry — **keen** *vb*
¹keep \'kēp\ *vb* **kept** \'kept\; **keep·ing 1** : FULFILL, OBSERVE ⟨∼ a promise⟩ ⟨∼ a holiday⟩ **2** : GUARD ⟨∼ us from harm⟩; *also* : to take care of ⟨∼ a neighbor's children⟩ **3** : MAINTAIN ⟨∼ silence⟩ **4** : to have in one's service or at one's disposal ⟨∼ a horse⟩ **5** : to preserve a record in ⟨∼ a diary⟩ **6** : to have in stock for sale **7** : to retain in one's possession ⟨∼ what you find⟩ **8** : to carry on (as a business) : CONDUCT **9** : HOLD, DETAIN ⟨∼ him in jail⟩ **10** : to refrain from revealing ⟨∼ a secret⟩ **11** : to continue in good condition ⟨meat will ∼ in a freezer⟩ **12** : ABSTAIN, REFRAIN — **keep·er** *n*
²keep *n* **1** : FORTRESS **2** : the means or provisions by which one is kept — **for keeps 1** : with the provision that one keep what one has won ⟨play marbles *for keeps*⟩ **2** : PERMANENTLY ⟨came home *for keeps*⟩
keep–away \'kēp-ə-,wā\ *n* : a game in which players try to keep an object from one or more other players

keeping *n* : CONFORMITY ⟨in ∼ with good taste⟩
keeping room *n* : a common room used for multiple purposes
keep·sake \'kēp-ˌsāk\ *n* : MEMENTO
keep up *vb* 1 : to persevere in 2 : MAINTAIN, SUSTAIN 3 : to keep informed 4 : to continue without interruption
keg \'keg\ *n* : a small cask or barrel
keg·ger \'ke-gər\ *n* : a party featuring one or more kegs of beer
keg·ler \'keg-lər\ *n* : ¹BOWLER
kelp \'kelp\ *n* : any of various coarse brown seaweeds; *also* : a mass of these or their ashes often used as fertilizer
kel·vin \'kel-vən\ *n* : a unit of temperature equal to ¹/₂₇₃.₁₆ of the Kelvin scale temperature of the triple point of water and equal to the Celsius degree
Kelvin *adj* : relating to, conforming to, or being a temperature scale according to which absolute zero is 0 K, the equivalent of −273.15°C
ken \'ken\ *n* 1 : range of vision : SIGHT 2 : range of understanding
ken·nel \'ke-nᵊl\ *n* : a shelter for a dog or cat; *also* : an establishment for the breeding or boarding of dogs or cats — **kennel** *vb*
ke·no \'kē-nō\ *n* : a game resembling bingo
ke·no·sis \kə-'nō-səs\ *n* : the relinquishment of divine attributes by Jesus Christ in becoming human — **ke·not·ic** \-'nä-tik\ *adj*
ken·te cloth \'ken-ˌtā-\ *n* : colorfully patterned cloth traditionally woven by hand in Ghana
Ken·tucky bluegrass \kən-ˌtə-kē-\ *n* : a valuable pasture and meadow grass of both Europe and America
Ke·ogh plan \'kē-(ˌ)ō-\ *n* [Eugene James *Keogh* †1989 Am. politician] : an individual retirement account for the self-employed
ke·pi \'kā-pē, 'ke-\ *n* [F] : a military cap with a round flat top and a visor
ker·a·tin \'ker-ə-tən\ *n* : any of various sulfur-containing proteins that make up hair and horny tissues
kerb \'kərb\ *n*, *Brit* : CURB 3
ker·chief \'kər-chəf, -ˌchēf\ *n*, *pl* **kerchiefs** \-chəfs, -ˌchēfs\ *also* **kerchieves** \-ˌchēvz\ [ME *courchef*, fr. AF *coverchef, cuerchief*, fr. *coverir* to cover + *chef* head] 1 : a square of cloth worn esp. as a head covering 2 : HANDKERCHIEF
kerf \'kərf\ *n* : a slit or notch made by a saw or cutting torch
ker·nel \'kər-nᵊl\ *n* 1 : the inner softer part of a seed, fruit stone, or nut 2 : a whole seed of a cereal ⟨a ∼ of corn⟩ 3 : a central or essential part : CORE
ker·o·sene *also* **ker·o·sine** \'ker-ə-ˌsēn, ˌker-ə-'sēn\ *n* : a flammable oil produced from petroleum and used for a fuel and as a solvent
kes·trel \'kes-trəl\ *n* : any of various small falcons that usu. hover in the air while searching for prey
ketch \'kech\ *n* : a large fore-and-aft rigged boat with two masts
ketch·up *also* **catch·up** \'ke-chəp, 'ka-\ *or* **cat·sup** \'ke-chəp, 'ka-; 'kat-səp\ *n* : a seasoned tomato puree
ket·tle \'ke-tᵊl\ *n* : a metallic vessel for boiling liquids
ket·tle·drum \-ˌdrəm\ *n* : a brass, copper, or fiberglass drum with calfskin or plastic stretched across the top
¹**key** \'kē\ *n* 1 : a usu. metal instrument by which the bolt of a lock is turned; *also* : a device having the form or function of a key 2 : a means of gaining or preventing entrance, possession, or control 3 : EXPLANATION, SOLUTION 4 : one of the levers pressed by a finger in operating or playing an instrument 5 : a leading individual or principle 6 : a system of seven tones based on their relationship to a tonic; *also* : the tone or pitch of a voice 7 : a small switch for opening or closing an electric circuit ⟨a telegraph ∼⟩
²**key** *vb* 1 : SECURE, FASTEN 2 : to regulate the musical pitch of 3 : to bring into harmony or conformity 4 : to make nervous — usu. used with *up*
³**key** *adj* : BASIC, CENTRAL ⟨∼ issues⟩
⁴**key** *n* : a low island or reef (as off the southern coast of Florida)
⁵**key** *n, slang* : a kilogram esp. of marijuana or heroin
key·board \-ˌbȯrd\ *n* 1 : a row of keys (as on a piano) 2 : an assemblage of keys for operating a machine
key club *n* : a private club serving liquor and providing entertainment

key·hole \'kē-ˌhōl\ *n* : a hole for receiving a key
¹**key·note** \-ˌnōt\ *n* 1 : the first and harmonically fundamental tone of a scale 2 : the central fact, idea, or mood
²**keynote** *vb* 1 : to set the keynote of 2 : to deliver the major address (as at a convention) — **key·not·er** *n*
key·punch \'kē-ˌpənch\ *n* : a machine with a keyboard used to cut holes or notches in punch cards — **keypunch** *vb* — **key·punch·er** *n*
key·stone \-ˌstōn\ *n* : the wedge-shaped piece at the crown of an arch that locks the other pieces in place
key·stroke \-ˌstrōk\ *n* : an act or instance of depressing a key on a keyboard
key word *n* : a word that is a key; *esp usu* **key·word** : a significant word from a title or document used esp. as an indication of the content
kg *abbr* kilogram
KGB *abbr* [Russ *Komitet gosudarstvennoĭ bezopasnosti*] (Soviet) State Security Committee
kha·ki \'ka-kē, 'kä-\ *n* [Hindi & Urdu *khākī* dust-colored, fr. *khāk* dust, fr. Pers] 1 : a light yellowish brown color 2 : a khaki-colored cloth; *also* : a military uniform of this cloth
khan \'kän, 'kan\ *n* : a Mongol leader; *esp* : a successor of Genghis Khan
khe·dive \kə-'dēv\ *n* : a ruler of Egypt from 1867 to 1914 governing as a viceroy of the sultan of Turkey
khoum \'küm\ *n* — see *ouguiya* at MONEY table
kHz *abbr* kilohertz
KIA *abbr* killed in action
kib·ble \'ki-bəl\ *vb* **kib·bled; kib·bling** : to grind coarsely — **kibble** *n*
kib·butz \ki-'bu̇ts, -'büts\ *n, pl* **kib·but·zim** \-ˌbu̇t-'sēm, -ˌbüt-\ [ModHeb *qibbūṣ*] : a communal farm or settlement in Israel
ki·bitz·er \'ki-bət-sər, kə-'bit-\ *n* : one who looks on and usu. offers unwanted advice — **kib·itz** \'ki-bəts\ *vb*
ki·bosh \'kī-ˌbäsh\ *n* : something that serves as a check or stop ⟨put the ∼ on his plan⟩
¹**kick** \'kik\ *vb* 1 : to strike out or hit with the foot; *also* : to score by kicking a ball 2 : to object strongly 3 : to recoil when fired — **kick·er** *n*
²**kick** *n* 1 : a blow or thrust with the foot; *esp* : a propelling of a ball with the foot 2 : the recoil of a gun 3 : a feeling or expression of objection 4 : stimulating effect esp. of pleasure
kick·back \'kik-ˌbak\ *n* 1 : a sharp violent reaction 2 : a secret return of a part of a sum received
kick back *vb* : to assume a relaxed position or attitude
kick·box·ing \'kik-ˌbäk-siŋ\ *n* : boxing in which boxers are permitted to kick with bare feet — **kick·box·er** \-sər\ *n*
kick in *vb* 1 : CONTRIBUTE 2 *slang* : DIE 3 : to begin operating or having an effect
kick·off \'kik-ˌȯf\ *n* 1 : a kick that puts the ball in play (as in football) 2 : COMMENCEMENT ⟨campaign ∼⟩
kick off *vb* 1 : to start or resume play with a placekick 2 : to begin proceedings 3 *slang* : DIE
kick over *vb* : to begin or cause to begin to fire — used of an internal combustion engine
kick·shaw \'kik-ˌshȯ\ *n* [modif. of F *quelque chose* something] 1 : DELICACY 2 : TRINKET
kick·stand \'kik-ˌstand\ *n* : a swiveling metal bar attached to a 2-wheeled vehicle for holding it up when not in use
kick-start \'kik-ˌstärt\ *vb* : JUMP-START
kicky \'ki-kē\ *adj* : providing a kick or thrill : EXCITING
¹**kid** \'kid\ *n* 1 : a young goat 2 : the flesh, fur, or skin of a young goat; *also* : something made of kid 3 : CHILD, YOUNGSTER — **kid·dish** *adj*
²**kid** *vb* **kid·ded; kid·ding** 1 : FOOL 2 : TEASE — **kid·der** *n* — **kid·ding·ly** *adv*
kid·do \'ki-dō\ *n, pl* **kiddos** — used as a familiar form of address ⟨you're okay, ∼⟩ 2 : CHILD, KID
kid·nap \'kid-ˌnap\ *vb* **kid·napped** *also* **kid·naped** \-ˌnapt\; **kid·nap·ping** *also* **kid·nap·ing** \-ˌna-piŋ\ : to hold or carry a person away by unlawful force or by fraud and against one's will — **kid·nap·per** *also* **kid·nap·er** \-ˌna-pər\ *n*
kid·ney \'kid-nē\ *n, pl* **kidneys** : either of a pair of organs lying near the backbone that excrete waste products of the body in the form of urine
kidney bean *n* 1 : an edible seed of the common cultivated bean; *esp* : one that is large and dark red 2 : a plant bearing kidney beans

kid·skin \'kid-ˌskin\ *n* : the skin of a young goat used for leather

kiel·ba·sa \kēl-'bä-sə, kil-\ *n, pl* **-basas** *also* **-ba·sy** \-'bä-sē\ [Pol *kiełbasa*] : a smoked sausage of Polish origin

¹kill \'kil\ *vb* **1** : to deprive of life **2** : to put an end to ⟨~ competition⟩; *also* : DEFEAT ⟨~ a proposed amendment⟩ **3** : USE UP ⟨~ time⟩ **4** : to mark for omission ✦ *Synonyms* SLAY, MURDER, ASSASSINATE, EXECUTE — **kill·er** *n*

²kill *n* **1** : an act of killing **2** : an animal or animals killed (as in a hunt); *also* : an aircraft, ship, or vehicle destroyed by military action

kill·deer \'kil-ˌdir\ *n, pl* **killdeers** *or* **killdeer** [imit.] : an American plover with a plaintive penetrating cry

killer app \-'ap\ *n* : a component (as a computer application) that in itself makes something worth having or using

killer bee *n* : AFRICANIZED BEE

killer whale *n* : a small gregarious black and white flesh-eating whale with a white oval patch behind each eye

kill·ing *n* : a sudden notable gain or profit

killing field *n* : a scene of mass killing

kill·joy \'kil-ˌjȯi\ *n* : one who spoils the pleasures of others

kiln \'kil, 'kiln\ *n* [ME *kilne*, fr. OE *cyln*, fr. L *culina* kitchen] : a heated enclosure (as an oven) for processing a substance by burning, firing, or drying — **kiln** *vb*

ki·lo \'kē-lō\ *n, pl* **kilos** : KILOGRAM

ki·lo·byte \'ki-lə-ˌbīt, 'kē-\ *n* : 1024 bytes

kilo·cy·cle \'ki-lə-ˌsī-kəl\ *n* : KILOHERTZ

ki·lo·gram \'kē-lə-ˌgram, 'ki-\ *n* **1** : the basic metric unit of mass that is nearly equal to the mass of 1000 cubic centimeters of water at its maximum density — see METRIC SYSTEM table **2** : the weight of a kilogram mass under earth's gravity

ki·lo·hertz \'ki-lə-ˌhərts, 'kē-, -ˌherts\ *n* : 1000 hertz

kilo·li·ter \'ki-lə-ˌlē-tər\ *n* — see METRIC SYSTEM table

ki·lo·me·ter \ki-'lä-mə-tər, 'ki-lə-ˌmē-\ *n* : a metric unit of length equal to 1000 meters — see METRIC SYSTEM table

ki·lo·ton \'ki-lə-ˌtən, 'kē-lō-\ *n* **1** : 1000 tons **2** : an explosive force equivalent to that of 1000 tons of TNT

ki·lo·volt \-ˌvōlt\ *n* : 1000 volts

kilo·watt \'ki-lə-ˌwät\ *n* : 1000 watts

kilowatt–hour *n* : a unit of energy equal to that expended by one kilowatt in one hour

kilt \'kilt\ *n* : a knee-length pleated skirt usu. of tartan worn by men in Scotland

kil·ter \'kil-tər\ *n* : proper condition ⟨out of ~⟩

ki·mo·no \kə-'mō-nə\ *n, pl* **-nos** **1** : a loose robe with wide sleeves traditionally worn with a wide sash as an outer garment by the Japanese **2** : a loose dressing gown or jacket

kin \'kin\ *n* **1** : an individual's relatives **2** : KINSMAN

ki·na \'kē-nə\ *n, pl* **kina** — see MONEY table

ki·na·ra \kē-'nä-rə\ *n* : a candelabra with seven candlesticks used during Kwanzaa

¹kind \'kīnd\ *n* **1** : essential quality or character **2** : a group united by common traits or interests : CATEGORY; *also* : VARIETY **3** : goods or commodities as distinguished from money

²kind *adj* **1** : of a sympathetic, forbearing, or pleasant nature **2** : arising from sympathy or forbearance ⟨~ deeds⟩ ✦ *Synonyms* BENEVOLENT, BENIGN, BENIGNANT, KINDLY — **kind·ness** *n*

kin·der·gar·ten \'kin-dər-ˌgär-t⁰n\ *n* [G, lit., children's garden] : a school or class for children usu. from four to six years old

kin·der·gart·ner \-ˌgärt-nər\ *n* **1** : a kindergarten teacher **2** : a kindergarten pupil

kind·heart·ed \ˌkīnd-'här-təd\ *adj* : marked by a sympathetic nature

kin·dle \'kin-d⁰l\ *vb* **kin·dled; kin·dling** **1** : to set on fire : start burning **2** : to stir up : AROUSE **3** : ILLUMINATE, GLOW

kin·dling \'kind-liŋ, 'kin-lən\ *n* : easily combustible material for starting a fire

¹kind·ly \'kīnd-lē\ *adj* **kind·li·er; -est** **1** : of an agreeable or beneficial nature **2** : of a sympathetic or generous nature — **kind·li·ness** *n*

²kindly *adv* **1** : READILY ⟨does not take ~ to criticism⟩ **2** : SYMPATHETICALLY **3** : COURTEOUSLY, OBLIGINGLY

kind of *adv* : to a moderate degree ⟨it's *kind of* late to begin⟩

¹kin·dred \'kin-drəd\ *n* **1** : a group of related individuals **2** : one's relatives

²kindred *adj* : of a like nature or character

kine \'kīn\ *archaic pl of* COW

kin·e·ma \'ki-nə-mə\ *Brit var of* CINEMA

ki·ne·mat·ics \ˌki-nə-'ma-tiks\ *n* : a science that deals with motion apart from considerations of mass and force — **ki·ne·mat·ic** -tik\ *or* **ki·ne·mat·i·cal** \-ti-kəl\ *adj*

kin·es·the·sia \ˌki-nəs-'thē-zhə, -zhē-ə\ *or* **kin·es·the·sis** \-'thē-səs\ *n, pl* **-the·sias** *or* **-the·ses** \-ˌsēz\ : a sense that perceives bodily movement, position, and weight and is mediated by nervous receptors in tendons, muscles, and joints; *also* : sensory experience derived from this sense — **kin·es·thet·ic** \-'the-tik\ *adj*

ki·net·ic \kə-'ne-tik\ *adj* : of or relating to the motion of material bodies and the forces and energy (**kinetic energy**) associated with them

ki·net·ics \-tiks\ *n sing or pl* : a science that deals with the effects of forces upon the motions of material bodies or with changes in a physical or chemical system

kin·folk \'kin-ˌfōk\ *or* **kinfolks** *n pl* : RELATIVES

king \'kiŋ\ *n* **1** : a male sovereign **2** : a chief among competitors ⟨home-run ~⟩ **3** : the principal piece in the game of chess **4** : a playing card bearing the figure of a king **5** : a checker that has been crowned — **king·less** *adj* — **king·ly** *adj or adv* — **king·ship** *n*

king crab *n* **1** : HORSESHOE CRAB **2** : a large crab of the No. Pacific caught commercially for food

king·dom \'kiŋ-dəm\ *n* **1** : a country whose head is a king or queen **2** : a realm or region in which something or someone is dominant ⟨a cattle ~⟩ **3** : one of the three primary divisions of lifeless material, plants, and animals into which natural objects are grouped; *also* : a biological category that ranks above the phylum

king·fish·er \-ˌfi-shər\ *n* : any of numerous usu. bright-colored crested birds that feed chiefly on fish

king·pin \'kiŋ-ˌpin\ *n* **1** : HEADPIN **2** : the leader in a group or undertaking

Kings *n* — see BIBLE table

king–size \'kiŋ-ˌsīz\ *or* **king–sized** \-ˌsīzd\ *adj* **1** : longer than the regular or standard size **2** : unusually large **3** : having dimensions of about 76 by 80 inches (1.9 by 2.0 meters) ⟨a ~ bed⟩; *also* : of a size that fits a king-size bed

kink \'kiŋk\ *n* **1** : a short tight twist or curl **2** : a mental peculiarity : QUIRK **3** : CRAMP ⟨a ~ in the back⟩ **4** : an imperfection likely to cause difficulties in operation — **kinky** *adj*

kin·ship \'kin-ˌship\ *n* : RELATIONSHIP

kins·man \'kinz-mən\ *n* : RELATIVE; *esp* : a male relative

kins·wom·an \-ˌwu̇-mən\ *n* : a female relative

ki·osk \'kē-ˌäsk\ *n* **1** : a small structure with one or more open sides **2** : a stand-alone device providing information and services on a computer screen ⟨interactive ~s at the museum⟩

Ki·o·wa \'kī-ə-ˌwȯ, -ˌwä, -ˌwā\ *n, pl* **Kiowa** *or* **Kiowas** : a member of an American Indian people of Colorado, Kansas, New Mexico, Oklahoma, and Texas

kip \'kip, 'gip\ *n, pl* **kip** *or* **kips** — see MONEY table

kip·per \'ki-pər\ *n* : a fish (as a herring) preserved by salting and drying or smoking — **kipper** *vb*

kirk \'kərk, 'kirk\ *n, chiefly Scot* : CHURCH

kir·tle \'kər-t⁰l\ *n* : a long gown or dress worn by women

kis·met \'kiz-ˌmet, -mət\ *n, often cap* [Turk, fr. Ar *qisma* portion, lot] : FATE

¹kiss \'kis\ *vb* **1** : to touch or caress with the lips as a mark of affection or greeting **2** : to touch gently or lightly

²kiss *n* **1** : a caress with the lips **2** : a gentle touch or contact **3** : a bite-size candy

kiss·er \'ki-sər\ *n* **1** : one that kisses **2** *slang* : MOUTH **3** *slang* : FACE

kit \'kit\ *n* **1** : a set of articles for personal use; *also* : a set of tools or implements or of parts to be assembled **2** : a container (as a case) for a kit

kitch·en \'ki-chən\ *n* **1** : a room with cooking facilities **2** : the personnel that prepares, cooks, and serves food

kitch·en·ette \ˌki-chə-'net\ *n* : a small kitchen or an alcove containing cooking facilities

kitchen police *n* **1** : KP **2** : the work of KPs

kitch·en·ware \'ki-chən-ˌwer\ *n* : utensils and appliances for kitchen use

kite \'kīt\ *n* **1** : any of various long-winged hawks often with deeply forked tails **2** : a light frame covered with paper or cloth and designed to be flown in the air at the end of a long string

kith \'kith\ *n* [ME, fr. OE *cȳthth*, fr. *cūth* known] : familiar friends, neighbors, or relatives ⟨~ and kin⟩

kitsch \'kich\ *n* [G] : something often of poor quality that appeals to popular or lowbrow taste — **kitschy** \'ki-chē\ *adj*

kit·ten \'ki-t³n\ *n* : a young cat — **kit·ten·ish** *adj*

¹**kit·ty** \'ki-tē\ *n, pl* **kitties** : CAT; *esp* : KITTEN

²**kitty** *n, pl* **kitties** : a fund in a poker game made up of contributions from each pot; *also* : POOL

kit·ty-cor·ner *also* **cat·ty-cor·ner** *or* **cat·er·cor·ner** \'ki-tē-,kȯr-nər, 'ka-; 'ka-tə-\ *or* **kit·ty-cor·nered** *or* **cat·ty-cor·nered** *or* **cat·er·cornered** \-nərd\ *adv or adj* : in a diagonal or oblique position

ki·wi \'kē-(,)wē\ *n* **1** : any of a small genus of flightless New Zealand birds **2** : KIWIFRUIT

ki·wi·fruit \-,früt\ *n* : a brownish hairy egg-shaped fruit of a subtropical vine that has sweet bright green flesh and small edible black seeds

KJV *abbr* King James Version

KKK *abbr* Ku Klux Klan

kl *abbr* kiloliter

klatch *also* **klatsch** \'klach\ *n* [G *Klatsch* gossip] : a gathering marked by informal conversation

klep·toc·ra·cy \klep-'tä-krə-sē\ *n, pl* **-cies** : government by those who seek chiefly status and personal gain at the expense of the governed

klep·to·ma·nia \,klep-tə-'mā-nē-ə\ *n* : a persistent neurotic impulse to steal esp. without economic motive — **klep·to·ma·ni·ac** \-nē-,ak\ *n*

klieg light *or* **kleig light** \'klēg-\ *n* : a very bright lamp used in making motion pictures

klutz \'kləts\ *n* [Yiddish *klots*, lit., wooden beam] : a clumsy person — **klutzy** *adj*

km *abbr* kilometer

kn *abbr* knot

knack \'nak\ *n* **1** : a clever way of doing something **2** : natural aptitude

knap·sack \'nap-,sak\ *n* : a bag (as of canvas) strapped on the back and used esp. for carrying supplies

knave \'nāv\ *n* **1** : ROGUE **2** : JACK **6** — **knav·ery** \'nā-və-rē\ *n* — **knav·ish** \'nā-vish\ *adj*

knead \'nēd\ *vb* : to work and press into a mass with the hands; *also* : MASSAGE — **knead·er** *n*

knee \'nē\ *n* : the joint in the middle part of the leg — **kneed** \'nēd\ *adj*

knee·cap \'nē-,kap\ *n* : a thick flat triangular movable bone forming the front of the knee

knee·hole \-,hōl\ *n* : a space (as under a desk) for the knees

knee–jerk \'nē-,jərk\ *adj* : readily predictable ⟨a ~ reaction⟩

kneel \'nēl\ *vb* **knelt** \'nelt\ *or* **kneeled; kneel·ing** : to bend the knee : fall or rest on the knees

¹**knell** \'nel\ *vb* **1** : to ring esp. for a death or disaster **2** : to summon, announce, or proclaim by a knell

²**knell** *n* **1** : a stroke of a bell esp. when tolled (as for a funeral) **2** : an indication of the end or failure of something

knew *past of* KNOW

knick·ers \'ni-kərz\ *n pl* : loose-fitting short pants gathered at the knee

knick·knack \'nik-,nak\ *n* : a small trivial article intended for ornament

¹**knife** \'nīf\ *n, pl* **knives** \'nīvz\ **1** : a cutting instrument consisting of a sharp blade fastened to a handle **2** : a sharp cutting tool in a machine

²**knife** *vb* **knifed; knif·ing** : to stab, slash, or wound with a knife

¹**knight** \'nīt\ *n* **1** : a mounted warrior of feudal times serving a king **2** : a man honored by a sovereign for merit and in Great Britain ranking below a baronet **3** : a man devoted to the service of a lady **4** : a member of an order or society **5** : a chess piece having an L-shaped move — **knight·ly** *adj*

²**knight** *vb* : to make a knight of

knight·hood \'nīt-,hud\ *n* **1** : the rank, dignity, or profession of a knight **2** : CHIVALRY **3** : knights as a class or body

knish \kə-'nish\ *n* [Yiddish] : a small round or square of dough stuffed with a filling (as of meat or fruit) and baked or fried

¹**knit** \'nit\ *vb* **knit** *or* **knit·ted; knit·ting 1** : to link firmly or closely **2** : WRINKLE ⟨~ her brows⟩ **3** : to form a fabric by interlacing yarn or thread in connected loops with needles **4** : to grow together — **knit·ter** *n*

²**knit** *n* **1** : a basic knitting stitch **2** : a knitted garment or fabric

knit·wear \-,wer\ *n* : knitted clothing

knob \'näb\ *n* **1** : a rounded protuberance; *also* : a small rounded ornament or handle **2** : a rounded usu. isolated hill — **knobbed** \'näbd\ *adj* — **knob·by** \'nä-bē\ *adj*

¹**knock** \'näk\ *vb* **1** : to strike with a sharp blow **2** : BUMP, COLLIDE **3** : to make a pounding noise; *esp* : to have engine knock **4** : to find fault with

²**knock** *n* **1** : a sharp blow **2** : a pounding noise; *esp* : one caused by abnormal ignition in an automobile engine

knock·down \'näk-,daun\ *n* **1** : the action of knocking down **2** : something (as a blow) that knocks down **3** : something that can be easily assembled or disassembled

knock down *vb* **1** : to strike to the ground with or as if with a sharp blow **2** : to take apart : DISASSEMBLE **3** : to receive as income or salary : EARN **4** : to make a reduction in

knock·er \'nä-kər\ *n* : one that knocks; *esp* : a device hinged to a door for use in knocking

knock–knee \'näk-,nē\ *n* : a condition in which the legs curve inward at the knees — **knock–kneed** \-,nēd\ *adj*

knock·off \'näk-,of\ *n* : a copy or imitation of someone or something popular

knock off *vb* **1** : to stop doing something **2** : to do quickly, carelessly, or routinely **3** : to deduct from a price **4** : KILL **5** : ROB **6** : COPY, IMITATE

knock·out \'näk-,aut\ *n* **1** : a blow that fells and immobilizes an opponent (as in boxing) **2** : something sensationally striking or attractive

knock out *vb* **1** : to defeat by a knockout **2** : to make unconscious or inoperative **3** : to tire out : EXHAUST

knock·wurst *also* **knack·wurst** \'näk-,wərst, -,vurst\ *n* : a short thick heavily seasoned sausage

knoll \'nōl\ *n* : a small round hill

¹**knot** \'nät\ *n* **1** : an interlacing (as of string) forming a lump or knob and often used for fastening or tying together **2** : PROBLEM **3** : a bond of union; *esp* : the marriage bond **4** : a protuberant lump or swelling in tissue **5** : a rounded cross-grained area in lumber that is a section through the junction of a tree branch with the trunk; *also* : the woody tissue forming this junction in a tree **6** : GROUP, CLUSTER **7** : an ornamental bow of ribbon **8** : one nautical mile per hour; *also* : one nautical mile — **knot·ty** *adj*

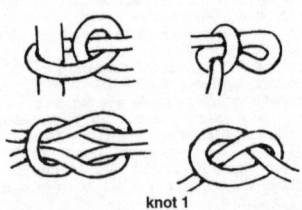

knot 1

²**knot** *vb* **knot·ted; knot·ting 1** : to tie in or with a knot **2** : ENTANGLE

knot·hole \-,hōl\ *n* : a hole in a board or tree trunk where a knot has come out

knout \'naut, 'nüt\ *n* : a whip used for flogging

know \'nō\ *vb* **knew** \'nü, 'nyü\; **known** \'nōn\; **know·ing 1** : to perceive directly : have understanding or direct cognition of; *also* : to recognize the nature of **2** : to be acquainted or familiar with **3** : to be aware of the truth of **4** : to have a practical understanding of — **know·able** *adj* — **know·er** *n* — **in the know** : possessing confidential information

know–how \'nō-,hau\ *n* : knowledge of how to do something smoothly and efficiently

knowing *adj* **1** : having or reflecting knowledge, intelligence, or information **2** : shrewdly and keenly alert **3** : DELIBERATE ⟨∼ interference⟩ ✦ *Synonyms* CLEVER, BRIGHT, SMART — **know·ing·ly** *adv*

knowl·edge \'nä-lij\ *n* **1** : understanding gained by actual experience ⟨a ∼ of carpentry⟩ **2** : range of information ⟨to the best of my ∼⟩ **3** : clear perception of truth **4** : something learned and kept in the mind

knowl·edge·able \'nä-li-jə-bəl\ *adj* : having or showing knowledge or intelligence

knuck·le \'nə-kəl\ *n* : the rounded knob at a joint and esp. at a finger joint

knuckle down *vb* : to apply oneself earnestly

knuckle under *vb* : SUBMIT, SURRENDER

knurl \'nərl\ *n* **1** : KNOB **2** : one of a series of small ridges on a metal surface to aid in gripping — **knurled** \'nərld\ *adj* — **knurly** *adj*

¹**KO** \(,)kā-'ō, 'kā-ō\ *n* : KNOCKOUT

²**KO** *vb* **KO'd; KO'·ing** : to knock out in boxing

ko·ala \kō-'ä-lə\ *n* : a gray furry Australian marsupial that has large hairy ears and feeds on eucalyptus leaves

ko·bo \'kō-(,)bō\ *n, pl* **kobo** — see *naira* at MONEY table

K of C *abbr* Knights of Columbus

kohl·ra·bi \kōl-'rä-bē\ *n, pl* **-bies** [G, fr. It *cavolo rapa*, lit., cabbage turnip] : a cabbage that forms no head but has a swollen fleshy edible stem

koi \'kói\ *n, pl* **koi** [Jp] : a carp bred for large size and a variety of colors and often stocked in ornamental ponds

ko·lin·sky \kə-'lin-skē\ *n, pl* **-skies** : the fur of various Asian minks

Ko·mo·do dragon \kə-'mō-dō-\ *n* [*Komodo* Island, Indonesia] : a carnivorous lizard of Indonesia that is the largest of all known lizards

kook \'kük\ *n* : SCREWBALL 2

kooky *also* **kook·ie** \'kü-kē\ *adj* **kook·i·er; -est** : having the characteristics of a kook : CRAZY, ECCENTRIC — **kook·i·ness** *n*

Koo·te·nai *or* **Ku·te·nai** \'kü-tə-,nä\ *n, pl* **-nai** *or* **-nais** : a member of an American Indian people of the Rocky Mountains in both the U.S. and Canada; *also* : their language

ko·peck *or* **ko·pek** \'kō-,pek\ *n* [Russ *kopeĭka*] — see *ruble* at MONEY table

ko·piy·ka \,kō-'pē-kə\ *n* — see *hryvnia* at MONEY table

ko·ra \'kór-ə\ *n* : a 21-stringed African musical instrument

Ko·ran \kə-'ran, -'rän\ *n* [Ar *qur'ān*] : a sacred book of Islam that contains revelations made to Muhammad by Allah

ko·ru·na \'kór-ə-,nä\ *n, pl* **ko·ru·ny** \-ə-nē\ *or* **korunas** *or* **ko·run** \-ən\ — see MONEY table

ko·sher \'kō-shər\ *adj* [Yiddish, fr. Heb *kāshēr* fit, proper] **1** : ritually fit for use according to Jewish law **2** : selling or serving kosher food

kow·tow \kaù-'taù, 'kaù-,taù\ *vb* [Chin *kòutóu*, fr. *kòu* to knock + *tóu* head] **1** : to show obsequious deference **2** : to kneel and touch the forehead to the ground as a sign of homage or deep respect

KP \,kā-'pē\ *n* **1** : an enlisted man detailed to help the cooks in a military mess **2** : the work of KPs

kph *abbr* kilometers per hour

Kr *symbol* krypton

kraal \'kräl, 'król\ *n* **1** : a native village in southern Africa **2** : an enclosure for domestic animals in southern Africa

kraut \'kraùt\ *n* : SAUERKRAUT

Krem·lin \'krem-lən\ *n* : the Russian government

Krem·lin·ol·o·gist \,krem-lə-'nä-lə-jist\ *n* : a specialist in the policies and practices of the government of the Soviet Union

¹**kro·na** \'krō-nə\ *n, pl* **kro·nor** \-,nór\ [Sw] — see MONEY table

²**kro·na** \'krō-nə\ *n, pl* **kro·nur** \-nər\ [Icel] — see MONEY table

kro·ne \'krō-nə\ *n, pl* **kro·ner** \-nər\ — see MONEY table

kroon \'krōn\ *n, pl* **kroo·ni** \'krō-nē\ *or* **kroons** — see MONEY table

Kru·ger·rand \'krü-gər-,rand, -,ränd\ *n* : a 1-ounce gold coin of the Republic of South Africa

kryp·ton \'krip-,tän\ *n* : a gaseous chemical element used esp. in electric lamps

KS *abbr* Kansas

kt *abbr* **1** karat **2** knight

ku·do \'kü-dō, 'kyü-\ *n, pl* **kudos** [fr. *kudos* (taken as pl.)] **1** : AWARD, HONOR **2** : COMPLIMENT, PRAISE

ku·dos \'kü-,däs, 'kyü-\ *n* : fame and renown resulting from achievement

kud·zu \'kúd-zü, 'kəd-\ *n* [Jp *kuzu*] : a fast-growing weedy leguminous vine used for forage and erosion control

ku·lak \kü-'lak, kyü-, -'läk\ *n* [Russ, lit., fist] **1** : a wealthy peasant farmer in 19th century Russia **2** : a farmer characterized by Communists as too wealthy

kum·quat \'kəm-,kwät\ *n* : any of several small citrus fruits with sweet spongy rind and acid pulp

ku·na \'kü-,nä\ *n, pl* **kuna** *or* **ku·ne** \-nä\ — see MONEY table

kung fu \,kəŋ-'fü, ,kùŋ-\ *n* : a Chinese art of self-defense resembling karate

kung pao \'kəŋ-'paú, 'kùŋ-, 'kùŋ-\ *adj* : being stir-fried or deep-fried and served in a spicy hot sauce usu. with peanuts

kur·ta \'kər-tə\ *n* : a long loose-fitting collarless shirt

ku·rus \kə-'rüsh\ *n, pl* **kurus** — see *lira* at MONEY table

kV *abbr* kilovolt

kvell \'kvel\ *vb* : to be extraordinarily proud

kvetch \'kvech, 'kfech\ *vb* : to complain habitually — **kvetch** *n*

kW *abbr* kilowatt

kwa·cha \'kwä-chə\ *n, pl* **kwacha** — see MONEY table

kwan·za \'kwän-zə\ *n, pl* **kwanzas** *or* **kwanza** — see MONEY table

Kwan·zaa *also* **Kwan·za** \'kwän-zə\ *n* [Swahili *kwanza* first] : an African-American cultural festival held from December 26 to January 1

kwash·i·or·kor \,kwä-shē-'ór-kòr, -ór-'kór\ *n* : a disease of young children caused by deficient intake of protein

kWh *abbr* kilowatt-hour

Ky *or* **KY** *abbr* Kentucky

kyat \'chät\ *n, pl* **kyats** *or* **kyat** — see MONEY table

ky·bosh *chiefly Brit var of* KIBOSH

¹**l** \'el\ *n, pl* **l's** *or* **ls** \'elz\ *often cap* **1** : the 12th letter of the English alphabet **2** : fifty in Roman numerals

²**l** *abbr, often cap* **1** lake **2** large **3** left **4** [L *libra*] pound **5** line **6** liter

¹**La** *abbr* Louisiana

²**La** *symbol* lanthanum

LA *abbr* **1** law agent **2** Los Angeles **3** Louisiana

laa·ri \'lä-rē\ *n, pl* **laari** — see *rufiyaa* at MONEY table

lab \'lab\ *n* : LABORATORY

Lab *n* : LABRADOR RETRIEVER

¹**la·bel** \'lā-bəl\ *n* **1** : a slip attached to something for identification or description **2** : a descriptive or identifying word or phrase **3** : BRAND 3

²**label** *vb* **-beled** *or* **-belled; -bel·ing** *or* **-bel·ling** **1** : to affix a label to **2** : to describe or name with a label

la·bi·al \'lā-bē-əl\ *adj* : of, relating to, or situated near the lips or labia

la·bia ma·jo·ra \'lā-bē-ə-mə-'jòr-ə\ *n pl* : the outer fatty folds of the vulva

labia mi·no·ra \-mə-'nòr-ə\ *n pl* : the inner highly vascular folds of the vulva

la·bile \'lā-,bī(-ə)l, -bəl\ *adj* **1** : UNSTABLE **2** : ADAPTABLE

la·bi·um \'lā-bē-əm\ *n, pl* **la·bia** \-ə\ [NL, fr. L, lip] : any of the folds at the margin of the vulva

¹la·bor \'lā-bər\ *n* **1** : physical or mental effort; *also* : human activity that provides the goods or services in an economy **2** : the physical efforts of giving birth; *also* : the period of such labor **3** : TASK **4** : those who do manual labor or work for wages; *also* : labor unions or their officials

²labor *vb* **1** : WORK **2** : to move with great effort **3** : to be in the labor of giving birth **4** : to suffer from some disadvantage or distress ⟨~ under a delusion⟩ **5** : to treat or work out laboriously — **la·bor·er** *n*

lab·o·ra·to·ry \'la-brə-ˌtȯr-ē, -bə-rə-\ *n, pl* **-ries** : a place equipped for making scientific experiments or tests

Labor Day *n* : the 1st Monday in September observed as a legal holiday in recognition of the working people

la·bored \'lā-bərd\ *adj* : not freely or easily done ⟨~ breathing⟩

la·bo·ri·ous \lə-'bȯr-ē-əs\ *adj* **1** : INDUSTRIOUS **2** : requiring great effort — **la·bo·ri·ous·ly** *adv*

la·bor·sav·ing \'lā-bər-ˌsā-viŋ\ *adj* : designed to replace or decrease labor

labor union *n* : an organization of workers formed to advance its members' interest in respect to wages and working conditions

la·bour *chiefly Brit var of* LABOR

lab·ra·dor·ite \'la-brə-ˌdȯr-ˌīt\ *n* : an iridescent feldspar used in jewelry

Lab·ra·dor retriever \'la-brə-ˌdȯr-\ *n* : any of a breed of strongly built retrievers having a short dense black, yellow, or chocolate coat

la·bur·num \lə-'bər-nəm\ *n* : any of a genus of leguminous shrubs or trees with hanging clusters of yellow flowers

lab·y·rinth \'la-bə-ˌrinth\ *n* : a place constructed of or filled with confusing intricate passageways : MAZE

lab·y·rin·thine \ˌla-bə-'rin-thən, -ˌthīn, -ˌthēn\ *adj* : INTRICATE, INVOLVED

lac \'lak\ *n* : a resinous substance secreted by a scale insect and used chiefly in the form of shellac

¹lace \'lās\ *vb* **laced; lac·ing 1** : TIE **2** : to adorn with lace **3** : INTERTWINE **4** : BEAT, LASH **5** : to add something that taints (as a drug) or enhances flavor (as a spice) **6** : to criticize sharply — used with *into*

²lace *n* [ME, fr. AF *lace, laz*, fr. L *laqueus* snare] **1** : a cord or string used for drawing together two edges **2** : an ornamental braid **3** : a fine openwork usu. figured fabric made of thread — **lacy** \'lā-sē\ *adj*

lac·er·ate \'la-sə-ˌrāt\ *vb* **-at·ed; -at·ing** : to tear roughly — **lac·er·a·tion** \ˌla-sə-'rā-shən\ *n*

lace·wing \'lās-ˌwiŋ\ *n* : any of various insects with delicate wing veins, long antennae, and often brilliant eyes

lacewing

lach·ry·mal *or* **lac·ri·mal** \'la-krə-məl\ *adj* **1** *usu* lacrimal : of, relating to, or being glands that produce tears **2** : of, relating to, or marked by tears

lach·ry·mose \'la-krə-ˌmōs\ *adj* **1** : TEARFUL **2** : MOURNFUL

¹lack \'lak\ *vb* **1** : to be wanting or missing **2** : to be deficient in

²lack *n* : the fact or state of being wanting or deficient : NEED

lack·a·dai·si·cal \ˌla-kə-'dā-zi-kəl\ *adj* : lacking life, spirit, or zest — **lack·a·dai·si·cal·ly** \-k(ə-)lē\ *adv*

lack·ey \'la-kē\ *n, pl* **lackeys 1** : FOOTMAN, SERVANT **2** : TOADY

lack·lus·ter \'lak-ˌləs-tər\ *adj* : DULL

la·con·ic \lə-'kä-nik\ *adj* [L *laconicus* Spartan, fr. Gk

lakōnikos; fr. the Spartan reputation for terseness of speech] : sparing of words : TERSE **♦ Synonyms** CONCISE, CURT, SHORT, SUCCINCT, BRUSQUE — **la·con·i·cal·ly** \-ni-k(ə-)lē\ *adv*

lac·quer \'la-kər\ *n* : a clear or colored usu. glossy and quick-drying surface coating — **lacquer** *vb*

lac·ri·ma·tion \ˌla-krə-'mā-shən\ *n* : secretion of tears

la·crosse \lə-'krȯs\ *n* [CanF *la crosse*, lit., the crooked stick] : a goal game in which players use a long-handled triangular-headed stick having a mesh pouch for catching, carrying, and throwing the ball

lac·tate \'lak-ˌtāt\ *vb* **lac·tat·ed; lac·tat·ing** : to secrete milk — **lac·ta·tion** \lak-'tā-shən\ *n*

lac·tic \'lak-tik\ *adj* **1** : of or relating to milk **2** : obtained from sour milk or whey

lactic acid *n* : a syrupy acid present in blood and muscle tissue and used esp. in food and medicine

lac·tose \'lak-ˌtōs\ *n* : a sugar present in milk

la·cu·na \lə-'kü-nə, -'kyü-\ *n, pl* **la·cu·nae** \-nē\ *also* **la·cunas** [L, pool, pit, gap, fr. *lacus* lake] : a blank space or missing part : GAP, DEFICIENCY

lad \'lad\ *n* **1** : YOUTH; *also* : FELLOW

lad·der \'la-dər\ *n* **1** : a structure for climbing that consists of two parallel sidepieces joined at intervals by crosspieces **2** : something resembling a ladder in having ascending steps or stages ⟨a tournament ~⟩

lad·die \'la-dē\ *n* : a young lad

lad·en \'lā-dᵊn\ *adj* : LOADED, BURDENED

lad·ing \'lā-diŋ\ *n* : CARGO, FREIGHT

la·dle \'lā-dᵊl\ *n* : a deep-bowled long-handled spoon used in taking up and conveying liquids — **ladle** *vb*

la·dy \'lā-dē\ *n, pl* **ladies** [ME, fr. OE *hlǣfdige*, fr. *hlāf* bread + *-dige* (akin to *dǣge* kneader of bread)] **1** : a woman of property, rank, or authority; *also* : a woman of superior social position or of refinement **2** : WOMAN **3** : WIFE

lady beetle *n* : LADYBUG

la·dy·bird \'lā-dē-ˌbərd\ *n* : LADYBUG

la·dy·bug \-ˌbəg\ *n* : any of various small nearly hemispherical and usu. brightly colored beetles that feed mostly on other insects

la·dy·fin·ger \-ˌfiŋ-gər\ *n* : a small finger-shaped sponge cake

lady–in–waiting *n, pl* **ladies–in–waiting** : a lady appointed to attend or wait on a queen or princess

la·dy·like \'lā-dē-ˌlīk\ *adj* : WELL-BRED

la·dy·ship \-ˌship\ *n* : the condition of being a lady : rank of lady

lady's slipper *also* **lady slipper** *n* : any of several No. American orchids with slipper-shaped flowers

¹lag \'lag\ *n* **1** : a slowing up or falling behind; *also* : the amount by which one lags **2** : INTERVAL

²lag *vb* **lagged; lag·ging 1** : to fail to keep up : stay behind **2** : to slacken gradually **♦ Synonyms** DAWDLE, DALLY, TARRY, LOITER

la·ger \'lä-gər\ *n* : a usu. dry beer slowly brewed and matured under refrigeration

lag·gard \'la-gərd\ *adj* : tending to lag ⟨~ workers⟩ — **laggard** *n* — **lag·gard·ly** *adv or adj* — **lag·gard·ness** *n*

la·gniappe \'lan-ˌyap\ *n* : something given free esp. with a purchase

la·goon \lə-'gün\ *n* : a shallow sound, channel, or pond near or connected to a larger body of water

laid *past and past part of* LAY

laid–back \'lād-'bak\ *adj* : having a relaxed style or character ⟨~ music⟩

lain *past part of* ¹LIE

lair \'ler\ *n* **1** : the resting or living place of a wild animal : DEN **2** : a usu. hidden refuge

laird \'lerd\ *n, chiefly Scot* : a landed proprietor

lais·ser–faire *chiefly Brit var of* LAISSEZ-FAIRE

lais·sez–faire \ˌle-ˌsā-'fer, ˌlā-, -ˌzā-\ *n* [F *laissez faire* let do] : a doctrine opposing governmental control of economic affairs beyond that necessary to maintain peace and property rights

la·ity \'lā-ə-tē\ *n* **1** : the people of a religious faith as distinct from its clergy **2** : the mass of people as distinct from those of a particular field

lake \'lāk\ *n* : an inland body of standing water of considerable size; *also* : a pool of liquid (as lava or pitch)

La·ko·ta \lə-'kō-tə\ *n, pl* **Lakota** *also* **Lakotas** : a member of a western division of the Dakota peoples; *also* : their language

¹**lam** \\'lam\ *vb* **lammed; lam·ming** : to flee hastily — **lam** *n*

²**lam** *abbr* laminated

Lam *abbr* Lamentations

la·ma \\'lä-mə\ *n* : a Buddhist monk of Tibet or Mongolia

la·ma·sery \\'lä-mə-ˌser-ē\ *n, pl* **-ser·ies** : a monastery for lamas

¹**lamb** \\'lam\ *n* **1** : a young sheep; *also* : its flesh used as food   **2** : an innocent or gentle person

²**lamb** *vb* : to bring forth a lamb

lam·baste *or* **lam·bast** \lam-'bāst, -'bast\ *vb* **1** : BEAT   **2** : EXCORIATE ✦ *Synonyms* CASTIGATE, FLAY, LASH

lamb·da \\'lam-də\ *n* : the 11th letter of the Greek alphabet — Λ or λ

lam·bent \\'lam-bənt\ *adj* [L *lambens*, prp. of *lambere* to lick]   **1** : FLICKERING ⟨a ~ flame⟩   **2** : softly radiant ⟨~ eyes⟩   **3** : marked by lightness or brilliance ⟨~ humor⟩ ✦ *Synonyms* EFFULGENT, INCANDESCENT, LUCENT, LUMINOUS — **lam·ben·cy** \-bən-sē\ *n* — **lam·bent·ly** *adv*

lamb·skin \\'lam-ˌskin\ *n* : a lamb's skin or a small fine-grade sheepskin or the leather made from either

¹**lame** \\'lām\ *adj* **lam·er; lam·est**   **1** : having a body part and esp. a limb so disabled as to impair freedom of movement; *also* : marked by stiffness and soreness   **2** : lacking substance : WEAK ⟨~ excuses⟩   **3** : INFERIOR, PITIFUL — **lame·ly** *adv* — **lame·ness** *n*

²**lame** *vb* **lamed; lam·ing** : to make lame : DISABLE

la·mé \lä-'mā, la-\ *n* [F] : a brocaded clothing fabric with tinsel filling threads (as of gold or silver)

lame-brain \\'lām-ˌbrān\ *n* : DOLT

lame duck *n* : an elected official continuing to hold office between an election and the inauguration of a successor — **lame–duck** *adj*

¹**la·ment** \lə-'ment\ *vb* **1** : to mourn aloud : WAIL   **2** : to express sorrow or regret for : BEWAIL — **lam·en·ta·ble** \\'la-mən-tə-bəl, lə-'men-tə-\ *adj* — **lam·en·ta·bly** \-blē\ *adv* — **lam·en·ta·tion** \ˌla-mən-'tā-shən\ *n*

²**lament** *n* **1** : a crying out in grief : WAIL   **2** : DIRGE, ELEGY   **3** : COMPLAINT

Lamentations *n* — see BIBLE table

la·mia \\'lā-mē-ə\ *n* : a female demon

lam·i·na \\'la-mə-nə\ *n, pl* **-nae** \-ˌnē\ *or* **-nas** : a thin plate or scale

¹**lam·i·nate** \\'la-mə-ˌnāt\ *vb* **-nat·ed; -nat·ing** : to make by uniting layers of one or more materials — **lam·i·na·tion** \ˌla-mə-'nā-shən\ *n*

²**lam·i·nate** \-nət\ *n* : a product manufactured by laminating

lamp \\'lamp\ *n* **1** : a vessel with a wick for burning a flammable liquid (as oil) to produce light   **2** : a device for producing light or heat

lamp·black \-ˌblak\ *n* : black soot used esp. as a pigment

lamp·light·er \-ˌlī-tər\ *n* : one that lights a lamp

lam·poon \lam-'pün\ *n* : SATIRE; *esp* : a harsh satire directed against an individual — **lampoon** *vb*

lam·prey \\'lam-prē\ *n, pl* **lampreys** : any of a family of eel-shaped jawless fishes that have well-developed eyes and a large disk-shaped sucking mouth armed with horny teeth

LAN \\'lan, ˌel-ˌa-'en\ *n* : LOCAL AREA NETWORK

la·nai \lə-'nī\ *n* [Hawaiian *lānai*] : PORCH, VERANDA

¹**lance** \\'lans\ *n* **1** : a spear carried by mounted soldiers   **2** : any of various sharp-pointed implements; *esp* : LANCET

²**lance** *vb* **lanced; lanc·ing** : to pierce or open with a lance ⟨~ a boil⟩

lance corporal *n* : an enlisted man in the marine corps ranking above a private first class and below a corporal

lanc·er \\'lan-sər\ *n* : a cavalryman of a unit formerly armed with lances

lan·cet \\'lan-sət\ *n* : a sharp-pointed and usu. 2-edged surgical instrument

¹**land** \\'land\ *n* **1** : the solid part of the surface of the earth; *also* : a part of the earth's surface ⟨fenced ~⟩ ⟨marshy ~⟩   **2** : NATION   **3** : REALM, DOMAIN — **land·less** *adj*

²**land** *vb* **1** : DISEMBARK; *also* : to touch at a place on shore   **2** : to alight or cause to alight on a surface ⟨~ a punch⟩   **3** : to bring to or arrive at a destination   **4** : to catch and bring in ⟨~ a fish⟩; *also* : GAIN, SECURE ⟨~ a job⟩

lan·dau \\'lan-ˌdaȯ\ *n* : a 4-wheeled carriage with a top divided into two sections that can be lowered, thrown back, or removed

land·ed *adj* : having an estate in land ⟨~ gentry⟩

land·er \\'lan-dər\ *n* : a space vehicle designed to land on a celestial body

land·fall \\'land-ˌfȯl\ *n* : a sighting or making of land (as after a voyage); *also* : the land first sighted

land·fill \-ˌfil\ *n* : a low-lying area on which refuse is buried between layers of earth — **landfill** *vb*

land·form \-ˌfȯrm\ *n* : a natural feature of a land surface

land·hold·er \-ˌhōl-dər\ *n* : a holder or owner of land — **land·hold·ing** \-diŋ\ *adj or n*

land·ing \\'lan-diŋ\ *n* **1** : the action of one that lands   **2** : a place for discharging or taking on passengers and cargo   **3** : a level part of a staircase

landing gear *n* : the part that supports the weight of an aircraft when it is on the ground

land·la·dy \\'land-ˌlā-dē\ *n* : a woman who is a landlord

land·locked \-ˌläkt\ *adj* **1** : enclosed or nearly enclosed by land ⟨a ~ country⟩   **2** : confined to fresh water by some barrier ⟨~ salmon⟩

land·lord \-ˌlȯrd\ *n* **1** : the owner of property leased or rented to another   **2** : a person who rents lodgings : INNKEEPER

land·lub·ber \-ˌlə-bər\ *n* : one who knows little of the sea or seamanship

land·mark \-ˌmärk\ *n* **1** : an object that marks a course or boundary or serves as a guide   **2** : an event that marks a turning point   **3** : a structure of unusual historical and usu. aesthetic interest

land·mass \-ˌmas\ *n* : a large area of land

land mine *n* **1** : a mine placed on or just below the surface of the ground and designed to be exploded by the weight of someone or something passing over it   **2** : a trap for the unwary

land·own·er \-ˌō-nər\ *n* : an owner of land

¹**land·scape** \-ˌskāp\ *n* **1** : a picture of natural inland scenery   **2** : a portion of land that can be seen in one glance

²**landscape** *vb* **land·scaped; land·scap·ing** : to modify a natural landscape) by grading, clearing, or decorative planting

land·slide \-ˌslīd\ *n* **1** : the slipping down of a mass of rocks or earth on a steep slope; *also* : the mass of material that slides   **2** : an overwhelming victory esp. in a political contest

lands·man \\'landz-mən\ *n* : a person who lives on land; *esp* : LANDLUBBER

land·ward \\'land-wərd\ *adv or adj* : to or toward the land

lane \\'lān\ *n* **1** : a narrow passageway (as between fences)   **2** : a relatively narrow way or track ⟨traffic ~⟩

lang *abbr* language

lan·guage \\'laŋ-gwij\ *n* [ME, fr. AF *langage*, fr. *langue* tongue, language, fr. L *lingua*]   **1** : the words, their pronunciation, and the methods of combining them used and understood by a community   **2** : form or style of verbal expression ⟨legal ~⟩   **3** : a system of signs and symbols and rules for using them that is used to carry information

lan·guid \\'laŋ-gwəd\ *adj* **1** : WEAK   **2** : sluggish in character or disposition : LISTLESS   **3** : SLOW — **lan·guid·ly** *adv* — **lan·guid·ness** *n*

lan·guish \\'laŋ-gwish\ *vb* **1** : to become languid   **2** : to become dispirited : PINE   **3** : to appeal for sympathy by assuming an expression of grief

lan·guor \\'laŋ-gər\ *n* **1** : a languid feeling   **2** : listless indolence or inertia ✦ *Synonyms* LETHARGY, LASSITUDE, TORPIDITY, TORPOR — **lan·guor·ous** *adj* — **lan·guor·ous·ly** *adv*

La Ni·ña \lä-'nē-nyə\ *n* : an upwelling of unusually cold ocean water along the west coast of So. America that often follows an El Niño

lank \\'laŋk\ *adj* **1** : not well filled out   **2** : hanging straight and limp

lanky \\'laŋ-kē\ *adj* **lank·i·er; -est** : ungracefully tall and thin

lan·o·lin \\'lan-ᵊl-ən\ *n* : the fatty coating of sheep's wool esp. when refined for use in ointments and cosmetics

lan·ta·na \lan-'tä-nə\ *n* : any of a genus of tropical shrubs related to the vervains with showy heads of small bright flowers

lan·tern \\'lan-tərn\ *n* [ME *lanterne*, fr. AF, fr. L *lanterna*, fr. Gk *lamptēr*, fr. *lampein* to shine]   **1** : a usu. portable

light with a protective covering **2** : the chamber in a lighthouse containing the light **3** : a projector for slides
lan·tha·num \'lan-thə-nəm\ *n* : a soft malleable metallic chemical element
lan·yard \'lan-yərd\ *n* : a piece of rope for fastening something in ships; *also* : any of various cords
¹**lap** \'lap\ *n* **1** : a loose panel of a garment **2** : the clothing that lies on the knees, thighs, and lower part of the trunk when one sits; *also* : the front part of the lower trunk and thighs of a seated person **3** : an environment of nurture ⟨the ~ of luxury⟩ **4** : CHARGE, CONTROL ⟨in the ~ of the gods⟩
²**lap** *vb* **lapped; lap·ping 1** : FOLD **2** : WRAP **3** : to lay over or near so as to partly cover
³**lap** *n* **1** : the amount by which an object overlaps another; *also* : the part of an object that overlaps another **2** : an act or instance of going over a course (as a track or swimming pool)
⁴**lap** *vb* **lapped; lap·ping 1** : to scoop up food or drink with the tip of the tongue; *also* : DEVOUR — usu. used with *up* **2** : to splash gently ⟨*lapping* waves⟩
⁵**lap** *n* **1** : an act or instance of lapping **2** : a gentle splashing sound
lap·a·ros·co·py \ˌla-pə-'räs-kə-pē\ *n, pl* **-pies 1** : visual examination of the abdomen by means of an endoscope; *also* : surgery using laparoscopy — **lap·a·ro·scope** \'la-pə-rə-ˌskōp\ *n* — **lap·a·ro·scop·ic** \ˌla-pə-rə-'skä-pik\ *adj*
lap·dog \'lap-ˌdȯg\ *n* : a small dog that may be held in the lap
la·pel \lə-'pel\ *n* : the fold of the front of a coat that is usu. a continuation of the collar
¹**lap·i·dary** \'la-pə-ˌder-ē\ *n, pl* **-dar·ies** : a person who cuts, polishes, or engraves precious stones
²**lapidary** *adj* **1** : of, relating to, or suitable for engraved inscriptions **2** : of, relating to, or suggestive of precious stones or the art of cutting them
lap·in \'la-pən\ *n* : rabbit fur usu. sheared and dyed
la·pis la·zu·li \ˌla-pəs-'la-zə-lē, -zhə-\ *n* : a usu. blue semi-precious stone often having sparkling bits of pyrite
lap·pet \'la-pət\ *n* : a fold or flap on a garment
¹**lapse** \'laps\ *n* [L *lapsus,* fr. *labi* to slip] **1** : a slight error ⟨a mental ~⟩ **2** : a fall from a higher to a lower state **3** : the termination of a right or privilege through failure to meet requirements **4** : INTERRUPTION **5** : APOSTASY **6** : a passage of time; *also* : INTERVAL ♦ **Synonyms** BLOOPER, BLUNDER, BONER, GOOF, MISTAKE, SLIP
²**lapse** *vb* **lapsed; laps·ing 1** : to commit apostasy **2** : SINK, SLIP **3** : CEASE
lap·top \'lap-ˌtäp\ *adj* : of a size that can be used conveniently on one's lap ⟨a ~ computer⟩ — **laptop** *n*
lap·wing \'lap-ˌwiŋ\ *n* : an Old World crested plover
lar·board \'lär-bərd\ *n* : ⁵PORT
lar·ce·ny \'lär-sə-nē\ *n, pl* **-nies** [ME, fr. AF *larcenie* theft, fr. L *latrocinium* robbery, fr. *latro* mercenary soldier] : THEFT — **lar·ce·nous** \-nəs\ *adj*
larch \'lärch\ *n* : any of a genus of trees related to the pines that shed their needles in the fall
¹**lard** \'lärd\ *vb* **1** : to insert strips of usu. pork fat into (meat) before cooking; *also* : GREASE **2** *obs* : ENRICH
²**lard** *n* : a soft white fat obtained by rendering fatty tissue of the hog
lar·der \'lär-dər\ *n* : a place where foods (as meat) are kept
large \'lärj\ *adj* **larg·er; larg·est 1** : having more than usual power, capacity, or scope **2** : exceeding most other things of like kind in quantity or size ⟨a ~ ♦ **Synonyms** BIG, GREAT, OVERSIZE — **large** *adv* — **large·ness** *n* — **at large 1** : UNCONFINED **2** : as a whole
large·ly \'lärj-lē\ *adv* : to a large extent
lar·gesse *or* **lar·gess** \lär-'zhes, -'jes\ *n* **1** : liberal giving **2** : a generous gift
¹**lar·go** \'lär-gō\ *adv or adj* [It, slow, broad, fr. L *largus* abundant] : at a very slow tempo — used as a direction in music
²**largo** *n, pl* **largos** : a largo movement
lari \'lä-rē\ *n, pl* **lari** — see MONEY table
lar·i·at \'lar-ē-ət\ *n* [AmerSp *la reata* the lasso, fr. Sp *la* the + AmerSp *reata* lasso, fr. Sp *reatar* to tie again] : a long rope used to catch or tether livestock : LASSO
¹**lark** \'lärk\ *n* : any of a family of small songbirds; *esp* : SKYLARK
²**lark** *n* : a source of or quest for fun or adventure

³**lark** *vb* : to engage in harmless fun or mischief — often used with *about*
lark·spur \'lärk-ˌspər\ *n* : DELPHINIUM; *esp* : any of the widely cultivated annual delphiniums
lar·va \'lär-və\ *n, pl* **lar·vae** \-(ˌ)vē\ *also* **larvas** [NL, fr. L, specter, mask] : the wingless often wormlike form in which insects hatch from the egg; *also* : any young animal (as a tadpole) that is fundamentally unlike its parent — **lar·val** \-vəl\ *adj*
lar·yn·gi·tis \ˌlar-ən-'jī-təs\ *n* : inflammation of the larynx
lar·ynx \'lar-iŋks\ *n, pl* **la·ryn·ges** \lə-'rin-ˌjēz\ *or* **lar·ynx·es** : the upper part of the trachea containing the vocal cords — **la·ryn·ge·al** \lə-'rin-jəl\ *adj*
la·sa·gna \lə-'zän-yə\ *n* [It] : boiled broad flat noodles baked with a sauce usu. of tomatoes, cheese, and meat
las·car \'las-kər\ *n* : an Indian sailor
las·civ·i·ous \lə-'si-vē-əs\ *adj* : LUSTFUL, LEWD ♦ **Synonyms** LICENTIOUS, LECHEROUS, LIBIDINOUS, SALACIOUS — **las·civ·i·ous·ness** *n*
la·ser \'lā-zər\ *n* [*light amplification by stimulated emission of radiation*] **1** : a device that produces an intense monochromatic beam of light **2** : something thrown or directed straight with high speed or intensity
laser disc *n* : OPTICAL DISK; *esp* : one containing a video recording
¹**lash** \'lash\ *vb* **1** : to move violently or suddenly **2** : WHIP **3** : to attack verbally
²**lash** *n* **1** : a stroke esp. with a whip; *also* : WHIP **2** : a stinging rebuke **3** : EYELASH
³**lash** *vb* : to bind with or as if with a line
lass \'las\ *n* : GIRL
lass·ie \'la-sē\ *n* : LASS
las·si·tude \'la-sə-ˌtüd, -ˌtyüd\ *n* **1** : WEARINESS, FATIGUE **2** : LANGUOR
las·so \'la-sō, la-'sü\ *n, pl* **lassos** *or* **lassoes** [Sp *lazo*] : a rope or long leather thong with a noose used for catching livestock — **lasso** *vb*
¹**last** \'last\ *vb* **1** : to continue in existence or operation **2** : to remain fresh or unimpaired : ENDURE **3** : to manage to continue **4** : to be enough for the needs of
²**last** *n* : a foot-shaped form on which a shoe is shaped or repaired
³**last** *vb* : to shape with a last
⁴**last** *adv* **1** : at the end **2** : most recently **3** : in conclusion
⁵**last** *adj* **1** : following all the rest : FINAL **2** : next before the present ⟨~ week⟩ **3** : most up-to-date **4** : farthest from a specified quality, attitude, or likelihood ⟨the ~ thing we want⟩ **5** : CONCLUSIVE; *also* : SUPREME — **last·ly** *adv*
⁶**last** *n* : something that is last — **at last** : FINALLY
last-ditch \'last-ˌdich\ *adj* : made as a final effort esp. to avert disaster
last laugh *n* : an ultimate satisfaction or triumph despite previous doubt or criticism
Last Supper *n* : the supper eaten by Jesus and his disciples on the night of his betrayal
lat *abbr* latitude
Lat *abbr* Latin
¹**latch** \'lach\ *vb* : to catch or get hold
²**latch** *n* : a catch that holds a door or gate closed
³**latch** *vb* : to make fast with a latch
latch·et \'la-chət\ *n* : a strap, thong, or lace for fastening a shoe or sandal
latch·key \'lach-ˌkē\ *n* : a key for opening a door latch esp. from the outside
latch·string \-ˌstriŋ\ *n* : a string on a latch that may be left hanging outside the door for raising the latch
¹**late** \'lāt\ *adj* **lat·er; lat·est 1** : coming or remaining after the due, usual, or proper time **2** : far advanced toward the close or end **3** : recently deceased **4** : made, appearing, or happening just previous to the present : RECENT — **late·ly** *adv* — **late·ness** *n*
²**late** *adv* **lat·er; lat·est 1** : after the usual or proper time; *also* : at or to an advanced point in time **2** : RECENTLY
late·com·er \'lāt-ˌkə-mər\ *n* : one who arrives late
la·teen \lə-'tēn\ *adj* : relating to or being a triangular sail extended by a long spar slung to a low mast
la·tent \'lāt-ᵊnt\ *adj* : present but not visible or active ♦ **Synonyms** DORMANT, QUIESCENT, POTENTIAL — **la·ten·cy** \-ᵊn-sē\ *n*

¹lat·er·al \'la-tə-rəl\ *adj* : situated on, directed toward, or coming from the side — **lat·er·al·ly** *adv*

²lateral *n* 1 : a branch from the main part 2 : a football pass thrown parallel to the line of scrimmage or away from the opponent's goal

la·tex \'lā-ˌteks\ *n, pl* la·ti·ces \'lā-tə-ˌsēz, 'la-\ *or* la·tex·es 1 : a milky juice produced by various plant cells (as of milkweeds, poppies, and the rubber tree) 2 : a water emulsion of a synthetic rubber or plastic used esp. in paint

lath \'lath, 'lȧth\ *n, pl* laths *or* lath : a thin narrow strip of wood used esp. as a base for plaster; *also* : a building material in sheets used for the same purpose — **lath** *vb*

lathe \'lāth\ *n* : a machine in which a piece of material is held and turned while being shaped by a tool

¹lath·er \'la-thər\ *n* 1 : a foam or froth formed when a detergent is agitated in water; *also* : foam from profuse sweating (as by a horse) 2 : DITHER

²lather *vb* : to spread lather over; *also* : to form a lather

Lat·in \'lat-ᵊn\ *n* 1 : the language of ancient Rome 2 : a member of any of the peoples whose languages derive from Latin — **Latin** *adj*

La·ti·na \lə-'tē-nə\ *n* : a woman or girl who is a native or inhabitant of Latin America; *also* : a woman or girl of Latin-American origin living in the U.S.

Latin American *n* : a native or inhabitant of any of the countries of No., Central, or So. America whose official language is Spanish or Portuguese — **Latin–American** *adj*

La·ti·no \lə-'tē-nō\ *n, pl* -nos : a native or inhabitant of Latin America; *also* : a person of Latin-American origin living in the U.S. — **Latino** *adj*

lat·i·tude \'la-tə-ˌtüd, -ˌtyüd\ *n* 1 : angular distance north or south from the earth's equator measured in degrees 2 : a region marked by its latitude 3 : freedom of action or choice

lat·i·tu·di·nar·i·an \ˌla-tə-ˌtü-də-'ner-ē-ən, -ˌtyü-\ *n* : a person who is liberal in religious belief and conduct

la·trine \lə-'trēn\ *n* : TOILET

lats \'lȧts\ *n, pl* la·ti \'lä-tē\ *or* la·tu \'lä-tü\ — see MONEY table

lat·ter \'la-tər\ *adj* 1 : more recent; *also* : FINAL 2 : of, relating to, or being the second of two things referred to

lat·ter–day *adj* 1 : of present or recent times 2 : of a later or subsequent time

Latter–day Saint *n* : a member of a religious body founded by Joseph Smith in 1830 and accepting the Book of Mormon as divine revelation : MORMON

lat·ter·ly \'la-tər-lē\ *adv* 1 : LATER 2 : of late : RECENTLY

lat·tice \'la-təs\ *n* 1 : a framework of crossed wood or metal strips; *also* : a window, door, or gate having a lattice 2 : a regular geometrical arrangement

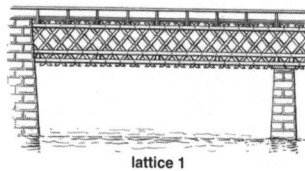

lattice 1

lat·tice·work \-ˌwərk\ *n* : LATTICE; *also* : work made of lattices

Lat·vi·an \'lat-vē-ən\ *n* 1 : a native or inhabitant of Latvia 2 : the language of the Latvians — **Latvian** *adj*

¹laud \'lȯd\ *n* : PRAISE, ACCLAIM

²laud *vb* : PRAISE, EXTOL ✦ *Synonyms* CELEBRATE, EULOGIZE, GLORIFY, MAGNIFY — **laud·able** *adj* — **laud·ably** *adv*

lau·da·num \'lȯd-ᵊn-əm\ *n* : a tincture of opium

lau·da·to·ry \'lȯ-də-ˌtōr-ē\ *adj* : of, relating to, or expressive of praise

¹laugh \'laf, 'lȧf\ *vb* [ME, fr. OE *hliehhan*] : to show mirth, joy, or scorn with a chuckle or explosive vocal sound; *also* : to become amused or derisive — **laugh·able** *adj* — **laugh·ing·ly** *adv*

²laugh *n* 1 : the act of laughing 2 : JOKE; *also* : JEER 3 *pl* : SPORT 1

laughing gas *n* : NITROUS OXIDE

laugh·ing·stock \'la-fiŋ-ˌstäk, 'lȧ-\ *n* : an object of ridicule

laugh·ter \'laf-tər, 'lȧf-\ *n* : the action or sound of laughing

¹launch \'lȯnch\ *vb* 1 : THROW, HURL; *also* : to send off ⟨~ a rocket⟩ 2 : to set afloat 3 : to set in operation : START — **launch·er** *n*

²launch *n* : an act or instance of launching

³launch *n* : a small open or half-decked motorboat

launch·pad \'lȯnch-ˌpad\ *n* : a platform from which a rocket is launched

laun·der \'lȯn-dər\ *vb* 1 : to wash or wash and iron clothing and household linens 2 : to transfer (as money of an illegal origin) through an outside party to conceal the true source — **laun·der·er** *n*

laun·dress \'lȯn-drəs\ *n* : a woman who is a laundry worker

laun·dry \'lȯn-drē\ *n, pl* laundries [fr. obs. *launder* launderer, fr. AF *lavandere*, fr. ML *lavandarius*, fr. L *lavandus* needing to be washed, fr. *lavare* to wash] 1 : a place where laundering is done 2 : clothes or linens that have been or are to be laundered — **laun·dry·man** \-mən\ *n*

lau·re·ate \'lȯr-ē-ət\ *n* : the recipient of honor for achievement in an art or science — **lau·re·ate·ship** *n*

lau·rel \'lȯ-rəl\ *n* 1 : an evergreen tree or shrub of southern Europe that is related to the sassafras and cinnamon and has glossy aromatic leaves : MOUNTAIN LAUREL 2 : a crown of laurel awarded as an honor — usu. used in pl.

lav *abbr* lavatory

la·va \'lä-və, 'la-\ *n* [It] : melted rock coming from a volcano; *also* : such rock that has cooled and hardened

la·vage \lə-'väzh\ *n* [F] : WASHING; *esp* : the washing out (as of an organ) esp. for medicinal reasons

lav·a·to·ry \'la-və-ˌtōr-ē\ *n, pl* -ries 1 : a fixed washbowl with running water and drainpipe 2 : BATHROOM

lave \'lāv\ *vb* laved; lav·ing : WASH

lav·en·der \'la-vən-dər\ *n* 1 : a Mediterranean mint or its dried leaves and flowers used to perfume clothing and bed linen 2 : a pale purple color

¹lav·ish \'la-vish\ *adj* [ME *laves, lavage*, prob. fr. MF *lavasse, lavache* downpour, fr. *laver* to wash] 1 : expending or bestowing profusely 2 : expended or produced in abundance ⟨~ gifts⟩ 3 : marked by excess ⟨~ decor⟩ — **lav·ish·ly** *adv* — **lav·ish·ness** *n*

²lavish *vb* : to expend or give freely

law \'lȯ\ *n* 1 : a rule of conduct or action established by custom or laid down and enforced by a governing authority; *also* : the whole body of such rules 2 : the control brought about by enforcing rules 3 *cap* : the revelation of the divine will set forth in the Old Testament; *also* : the first part of the Jewish scriptures — see BIBLE table 4 : a rule or principle of construction or procedure 5 : the science that deals with laws and their interpretation and application 6 : the profession of a lawyer 7 : a rule or principle stating something that always works in the same way under the same conditions

law·break·er \'lȯ-ˌbrā-kər\ *n* : a person who violates the law

law·ful \'lȯ-fəl\ *adj* 1 : permitted by law 2 : RIGHTFUL — **law·ful·ly** *adv*

law·giv·er \-ˌgi-vər\ *n* : LEGISLATOR

law·less \'lȯ-ləs\ *adj* 1 : having no laws 2 : UNRULY, DISORDERLY ⟨a ~ mob⟩ — **law·less·ly** *adv* — **law·less·ness** *n*

law·mak·er \-ˌmā-kər\ *n* : LEGISLATOR

law·man \'lȯ-mən\ *n* : a law enforcement official (as a sheriff or marshal)

¹lawn \'lȯn\ *n* : ground (as around a house) covered with mowed grass

²lawn *n* : a fine sheer linen or cotton fabric

lawn bowling *n* : a bowling game played on a green with wooden balls which are rolled at a jack

law·ren·ci·um \lȯ-'ren-sē-əm\ *n* : a short-lived radioactive element

law·suit \'lȯ-ˌsüt\ *n* : a suit in law

law·yer \'lȯ-yər\ *n* : one who conducts lawsuits for clients or advises as to legal rights and obligations in other matters — **law·yer·ly** *adv*

lax \'laks\ *adj* 1 : not strict ⟨~ discipline⟩ 2 : not tense or rigid ✦ *Synonyms* REMISS, NEGLIGENT, NEGLECTFUL, DELINQUENT, DERELICT — **lax·i·ty** \'lak-sə-tē\ *n* — **lax·ly** *adv* — **lax·ness** *n*

¹**lax·a·tive** \'lak-sə-tiv\ *adj* : relieving constipation

²**laxative** *n* : a usu. mild laxative drug

¹**lay** \'lā\ *vb* **laid** \'lād\; **lay·ing** **1** : to beat or strike down **2** : to put on or set down : PLACE **3** : to produce and deposit eggs **4** : SETTLE; *also* : ALLAY **5** : SPREAD **6** : PREPARE, CONTRIVE **7** : WAGER **8** : to impose esp. as a duty or burden **9** : to set in order or position **10** : to bring to a specified condition **11** : to put forward : SUBMIT

²**lay** *n* : the way in which something lies or is laid in relation to something else

³**lay** *past of* ¹LIE

⁴**lay** *n* **1** : a simple narrative poem **2** : SONG

⁵**lay** *adj* **1** : of or relating to the laity **2** : not of a particular profession; *also* : lacking extensive knowledge of a particular subject

lay·away \'lā-ə-,wā\ *n* : a purchasing agreement by which a retailer agrees to hold merchandise secured by a deposit until the price is paid in full

lay·er \'lā-ər\ *n* **1** : one that lays **2** : one thickness, course, or fold laid or lying over or under another

lay·ette \lā-'et\ *n* [F, fr. MF, dim. of *laye* box] : an outfit of clothing and equipment for a newborn infant

lay·man \'lā-mən\ *n* : a person who is a member of the laity

lay·off \'lā-,óf\ *n* **1** : a period of inactivity **2** : the act of laying off an employee

lay off *vb* **1** : to cease to employ (a worker) often temporarily **2** : to leave undisturbed **3** : to stop doing something

lay·out \'lā-,aút\ *n* : the final arrangement, plan, or design of something

lay·over \-,ō-vər\ *n* : STOPOVER

lay·per·son \-,pər-sən\ *n* : a member of the laity

lay·wom·an \'lā-,wù-mən\ *n* : a woman who is a member of the laity

la·zar \'la-zər, 'lā-\ *n* : LEPER

laze \'lāz\ *vb* **lazed; laz·ing** : to pass time in idleness or relaxation

la·zy \'lā-zē\ *adj* **la·zi·er; -est** **1** : disliking activity or exertion **2** : encouraging idleness ⟨a ~ day⟩ **3** : SLUGGISH **4** : DROOPY, LAX **5** : not rigorous or strict ⟨~ work habits⟩ — **la·zi·ly** \-zə-lē\ *adv* — **la·zi·ness** \-zē-nəs\ *n*

la·zy·bones \-,bōnz\ *n sing or pl* : a lazy person

lazy Su·san \,lā-zē-'süz-ᵊn\ *n* : a revolving tray used for serving food

lb *abbr* [L *libra*] pound

lc *abbr* lowercase

LC *abbr* Library of Congress

¹**LCD** \,el-(,)sē-'dē\ *n* [*liquid crystal display*] : a display (as of the time in a digital watch) that consists of segments of a liquid crystal whose reflectivity varies with the voltage applied to them

²**LCD** *abbr* least common denominator; lowest common denominator

LCDR *abbr* lieutenant commander

LCM *abbr* least common multiple; lowest common multiple

LCpl *abbr* lance corporal

LCS *abbr* League Championship Series

ld *abbr* **1** load **2** lord

LD *abbr* learning disabled; learning disability

LDC *abbr* less developed country

ldg *abbr* **1** landing **2** loading

LDL \,el-(,)dē-'el\ *n* [*low-density lipoprotein*] : a cholesterol-rich protein-poor lipoprotein of blood plasma correlated with increased probability of developing atherosclerosis

L–do·pa \'el-'dō-pə\ *n* : an isomer of dopa used esp. in the treatment of Parkinson's disease

LDS *abbr* Latter-day Saints

lea \'lē, 'lā\ *n* : PASTURE, MEADOW

leach \'lēch\ *vb* : to pass a liquid (as water) through to carry off the soluble components; *also* : to dissolve out by such means ⟨~ alkali from ashes⟩

¹**lead** \'lēd\ *vb* **led** \'led\; **lead·ing** **1** : to guide on a way **2** : LIVE ⟨~ a quiet life⟩ **3** : to direct the operations, activity, or performance of ⟨~ an orchestra⟩ **4** : to go at the head of : be first ⟨~ a parade⟩ **5** : to begin play with; *also* : BEGIN, OPEN **6** : to tend toward a definite result ⟨study ~ing to a degree⟩ — **lead·er** *n* — **lead·er·less** *adj* — **lead·er·ship** *n*

²**lead** \'lēd\ *n* **1** : a position at the front; *also* : a margin by which one leads **2** : the privilege of leading in cards; *also* : the card or suit led **3** : EXAMPLE **4** : one that leads **5** : a principal role (as in a play); *also* : one who plays such a role **6** : INDICATION, CLUE **7** : an insulated electrical conductor

³**lead** \'led\ *n* **1** : a heavy malleable bluish white chemical element **2** : an article made of lead; *esp* : a weight for sounding at sea **3** : a thin strip of metal used to separate lines of type in printing **4** : a thin stick of marking substance in or for a pencil

⁴**lead** \'led\ *vb* **1** : to cover, line, or weight with lead **2** : to fix (glass) in position with lead **3** : to treat or mix with lead or a lead compound

lead·en \'led-ᵊn\ *adj* **1** : made of lead; *also* : of the color of lead **2** : SLUGGISH, DULL

lead off *vb* : OPEN, BEGIN; *esp* : to bat first in an inning — **lead-off** \'lēd-,óf\ *n or adj*

¹**leaf** \'lēf\ *n, pl* **leaves** \'lēvz\ **1** : a usu. flat and green outgrowth of a plant stem that is a unit of foliage and functions esp. in photosynthesis; *also* : FOLIAGE **2** : something (as a page or a flat moving part) that is suggestive of a leaf — **leaf·less** *adj* — **leafy** *adj*

²**leaf** *vb* **1** : to produce leaves **2** : to turn the pages of a book

leaf·age \'lē-fij\ *n* : FOLIAGE

leafed \'lēft\ *adj* : LEAVED

leaf·hop·per \'lēf-,hä-pər\ *n* : any of a family of small leaping insects related to the cicadas that suck the juices of plants

leaf·let \'lē-flət\ *n* **1** : a division of a compound leaf **2** : PAMPHLET, FOLDER

leaf mold *n* : a compost or layer composed chiefly of decayed leaves

leaf·stalk \'lēf-,stók\ *n* : PETIOLE

¹**league** \'lēg\ *n* : a unit of distance equal to about three miles (five kilometers)

²**league** *n* **1** : an association or alliance (as of nations or sports teams) for a common purpose **2** : CLASS, CATEGORY — **league** *vb* — **leagu·er** \'lē-gər\ *n*

¹**leak** \'lēk\ *vb* **1** : to enter or escape through a leak **2** : to let a substance in or out through an opening **3** : to become or make known ⟨~ed the news⟩

²**leak** *n* **1** : a crack or hole that accidentally admits a fluid or light or lets it escape; *also* : something that secretly or accidentally permits the admission or escape of something else **2** : LEAKAGE — **leaky** *adj*

leak·age \'lē-kij\ *n* **1** : the act of leaking **2** : the thing or amount that leaks

¹**lean** \'lēn\ *vb* **1** : to bend from a vertical position : INCLINE **2** : to cast one's weight to one side for support **3** : to rely on for support **4** : to incline in opinion, taste, or desire — **lean** *n*

²**lean** *adj* **1** : lacking or deficient in flesh and esp. in fat ⟨~ meat⟩ **2** : lacking richness or productiveness ⟨~ profits⟩ **3** : low in fuel content — **lean·ness** *n*

leant \'lent\ *chiefly Brit past of* LEAN

lean-to \'lēn-,tü\ *n, pl* **lean-tos** \-,tüz\ : a wing or extension of a building having a roof of only one slope; *also* : a rough shed or shelter with a similar roof

¹**leap** \'lēp\ *vb* **leapt** \'lēpt, 'lept\ *or* **leaped; leap·ing** : to spring free from a surface or over an obstacle : JUMP

²**leap** *n* : JUMP

leap·frog \'lēp-,fróg, -,fräg\ *n* : a game in which a player bends down and is vaulted over by another — **leapfrog** *vb*

leap year *n* : a year containing 366 days with February 29 as the extra day

learn \'lərn\ *vb* **learned** \'lərnd, 'lərnt\; **learn·ing** **1** : to gain knowledge, understanding, or skill by study or experience; *also* : MEMORIZE **2** : to find out : ASCERTAIN — **learn·er** *n*

learn·ed \'lər-nəd\ *adj* : SCHOLARLY, ERUDITE — **learn·ed·ly** *adv* — **learn·ed·ness** *n*

learn·ing \'lər-nin\ *n* : KNOWLEDGE, ERUDITION

learning disability *n* : any of various conditions (as dyslexia) that interfere with a person's ability to learn and so result in impaired functioning (as in language) — **learning disabled** *adj*

learnt \'lərnt\ *chiefly Brit past and past part of* LEARN

¹**lease** \'lēs\ *n* : a contract transferring real estate for a term of years or at will usu. for a specified rent

²**lease** vb **leased; leas·ing** [AF lesser, lescher to leave, hand over, lease, fr. L laxare to loosen, fr. laxus slack] **1** : to grant by lease **2** : to hold under a lease ✦ **Synonyms** LET, CHARTER, HIRE, RENT

lease·hold \'lēs-ˌhōld\ n **1** : a tenure by lease **2** : land held by lease — **lease·hold·er** n

leash \'lēsh\ n [ME lees, leshe, fr. AF *lesche, lesse prob. fr. lesser to leave, let go] **1** : a line for leading or restraining an animal **2** : a state of restraint ⟨kept spending on a tight ∼⟩ — **leash** vb

¹**least** \'lēst\ adj **1** : lowest in importance or position **2** : smallest in size or degree **3** : SLIGHTEST

²**least** n : one that is least

³**least** adv : in the smallest or lowest degree

least common denominator n : the least common multiple of two or more denominators

least common multiple n : the smallest common multiple of two or more numbers

least·wise \'lēst-ˌwīz\ adv : at least

leath·er \'le-thər\ n : animal skin dressed for use — **leath·ern** \-thərn\ adj — **leath·ery** adj

leath·er·back \-ˌbak\ n : the largest existing sea turtle with a flexible leathery carapace

leath·er·neck \-ˌnek\ n : MARINE

¹**leave** \'lēv\ vb **left** \'left\; **leav·ing 1** : to allow or cause to remain behind **2** : to have as a remainder **3** : BEQUEATH **4** : to let stay without interference **5** : to go away : depart from **6** : GIVE UP, ABANDON

²**leave** n **1** : PERMISSION; also : authorized absence from duty **2** : DEPARTURE

³**leave** vb **leaved; leav·ing** : LEAF

leaved \'lēvd\ adj : having leaves

¹**leav·en** \'le-vən\ n **1** : a substance (as yeast) used to produce fermentation (as in dough) **2** : something that modifies or lightens

²**leaven** vb : to raise (dough) with a leaven; also : to permeate with a modifying or vivifying element ⟨lectures ∼ed with humor⟩

leav·en·ing n : LEAVEN

leaves pl of LEAF

leave–tak·ing \'lēv-ˌtā-kiŋ\ n : DEPARTURE, FAREWELL

leav·ings \'lē-viŋz\ n pl : REMNANT, RESIDUE

lech·ery \'le-chə-rē\ n : inordinate indulgence in sexual activity — **lech·er** \'le-chər\ n — **lech·er·ous** \'le-chə-rəs\ adj — **lech·er·ous·ly** adv — **lech·er·ous·ness** n

lec·i·thin \'le-sə-thən\ n : any of several waxy phosphorus-containing substances that are common in animals and plants, form colloidal solutions in water, and have emulsifying and wetting properties

lect abbr lecture; lecturer

lec·tern \'lek-tərn\ n : a stand to support a book for a standing reader

lec·tor \-tər\ n : one whose chief duty is to read the lessons in a church service

lec·ture \'lek-chər\ n **1** : a discourse given before an audience esp. for instruction **2** : REPRIMAND — **lec·ture** vb — **lec·tur·er** n — **lec·ture·ship** n

led past and past part of LEAD

LED \ˌel-(ˌ)ē-'dē\ n [light-emitting diode] : a semiconductor diode that emits light when a voltage is applied to it and is used esp. for electronic displays

le·der·ho·sen \'lā-dər-ˌhōz-ᵊn\ n pl : leather shorts often with suspenders worn esp. in Bavaria

ledge \'lej\ n [ME legge bar of a gate] **1** : a shelflike projection from a top or an edge **2** : REEF

led·ger \'le-jər\ n : a book containing accounts to which debits and credits are transferred in final form

lee \'lē\ n **1** : a protecting shelter **2** : the side (as of a ship) that is sheltered from the wind — **lee** adj

leech \'lēch\ n **1** : any of various bloodsucking segmented usu. freshwater worms that are related to the earthworms and have a sucker at each end **2** : a hanger-on who seeks gain

leek \'lēk\ n : an onionlike herb grown for its mildly pungent leaves and stalk

leer \'lir\ n : a suggestive, knowing, or malicious look — **leer** vb

leery \'lir-ē\ adj : SUSPICIOUS, WARY

lees \'lēz\ n pl : DREGS

¹**lee·ward** \'lē-wərd, 'lü-ərd\ n : the lee side

²**leeward** adj : situated away from the wind

lee·way \'lē-ˌwā\ n **1** : lateral movement of a ship when under way **2** : an allowable margin of freedom or variation

¹**left** \'left\ adj [ME, fr. OE, weak; fr. the left hand's being the weaker in most individuals] **1** : of, relating to, or being the side of the body in which the heart is mostly located; also : located nearer to this side than to the right **2** often cap : of, adhering to, or constituted by the political left — **left** adv

²**left** n **1** : the left hand; also : the side or part that is on or toward the left side **2** often cap : those professing political views marked by desire to reform the established order and usu. to give greater freedom to the common people — **left·ward** \-wərd\ adv or adj

³**left** past and past part of LEAVE

left–hand adj **1** : situated on the left **2** : LEFT-HANDED

left–hand·ed \'left-'han-dəd\ adj **1** : using the left hand habitually or more easily than the right **2** : designed for or done with the left hand **3** : INSINCERE, BACKHANDED ⟨a ∼ compliment⟩ **4** : COUNTERCLOCKWISE — **left-handed** adv — **left–hand·ed·ness** n — **left–hand·er** \-dər\ n

left·ism \'lef-ˌti-zəm\ n **1** : the principles and views of the left **2** : advocacy of the doctrines of the left — **left·ist** \-tist\ n or adj

left·over \'left-ˌō-vər\ n : something that remains unused or unconsumed

lefty \'lef-tē\ n, pl **left·ies 1** : a left-handed person **2** : an advocate of leftism

¹**leg** \'leg\ n **1** : a limb of an animal used esp. for supporting the body and in walking; also : the part of the vertebrate leg between knee and foot **2** : something resembling or analogous to an animal leg ⟨table ∼⟩ **3** : the part of an article of clothing that covers the leg **4** : a portion of a trip **5** pl : long-term appeal or interest ⟨a musical that has ∼s⟩ — **leg·ged** \'le-gəd\ adj — **leg·less** adj

²**leg** vb **legged; leg·ging** : to use the legs in walking or esp. in running

³**leg** abbr **1** legal **2** legislative; legislature

leg·a·cy \'le-gə-sē\ n, pl **-cies** : INHERITANCE; also : something that has come from a predecessor or the past

le·gal \'lē-gəl\ adj **1** : of or relating to law or lawyers **2** : LAWFUL; also : STATUTORY **3** : enforced in courts of law — **le·gal·i·ty** \li-'ga-lə-tē\ n — **le·gal·ize** \'lē-gə-ˌlīz\ vb — **le·gal·ly** adv

le·gal·ese \ˌlē-gə-'lēz\ n : the specialized language of the legal profession

le·gal·ism \'lē-gə-ˌli-zəm\ n **1** : strict, literal, or excessive conformity to the law or to a religious or moral code **2** : a legal term — **le·gal·is·tic** \ˌlē-gə-'lis-tik\ adj

le·gate \'le-gət\ n : an official representative

leg·a·tee \ˌle-gə-'tē\ n : a person to whom a legacy is bequeathed

le·ga·tion \li-'gā-shən\ n **1** : a diplomatic mission headed by a minister **2** : the official residence and office of a minister in a foreign country

le·ga·to \li-'gä-tō\ adv or adj [It, lit., tied] : in a smooth and connected manner (as of music)

leg·end \'le-jənd\ n [ME legende, fr. AF & ML; AF legende, fr. ML legenda, fr. L legere to read] **1** : a story coming down from the past; esp : one popularly accepted as historical though not verifiable **2** : an inscription on an object; also : CAPTION **3** : an explanatory list of the symbols on a map or chart

leg·end·ary \'le-jən-ˌder-ē\ adj **1** : of, relating to, or characteristic of a legend **2** : FAMOUS — **leg·en·dari·ly** \ˌder-ə-lē\ adv

leg·er·de·main \ˌle-jər-də-'mān\ n [ME, fr. MF leger de main light of hand] : SLEIGHT OF HAND

leg·ging or **leg·gin** \'le-gən, -gin\ n : a covering for the leg; also : TIGHTS

leg·gy \'le-gē\ adj **leg·gi·er; -est 1** : having unusually long legs **2** : having long and attractive legs **3** : SPINDLY — used of a plant

leg·horn \'leg-ˌhorn, 'le-gərn\ n **1** : a fine plaited straw; also : a hat made of this straw **2** : any of a Mediterranean breed of small hardy chickens

leg·i·ble \'le-jə-bəl\ adj : capable of being read : CLEAR — **leg·i·bil·i·ty** \ˌle-jə-'bi-lə-tē\ n — **leg·i·bly** \'le-jə-blē\ adv

¹**le·gion** \'lē-jən\ n **1** : a unit of the Roman army comprising 3000 to 6000 soldiers **2** : MULTITUDE **3** : an associa-

tion of ex-servicemen — **le·gion·ar·y** \-jə-ˌner-ē\ *n* — **le-gion·naire** \ˌlē-jə-'nar\ *n*
²**legion** *adj* : MANY, NUMEROUS
Legionnaires' disease *also* **Legionnaire's disease** \-'nerz-\ *n* : a lobar pneumonia caused by a bacterium
legis *abbr* legislation; legislative; legislature
leg·is·late \'le-jəs-ˌlāt\ *vb* **-lat·ed; -lat·ing** : to make or enact laws; *also* : to bring about by legislation — **leg·is·la·tor** \-ˌlā-tər\ *n*
leg·is·la·tion \ˌle-jəs-'lā-shən\ *n* 1 : the action of legislating 2 : laws made by a legislative body
leg·is·la·tive \'le-jəs-ˌlā-tiv\ *adj* 1 : having the power of legislating 2 : of or relating to a legislature or legislation
leg·is·la·ture \'le-jəs-ˌlā-chər\ *n* : an organized body of persons having the authority to make laws
le·git \li-'jit\ *adj, slang* : LEGITIMATE
¹**le·git·i·mate** \li-'ji-tə-mət\ *adj* 1 : lawfully begotten 2 : GENUINE 3 : LAWFUL 4 : conforming to recognized principles or accepted rules or standards — **le·git·i·ma·cy** \-mə-sē\ *n* — **le·git·i·mate·ly** *adv*
²**le·git·i·mate** \-ˌmāt\ *vb* : to make legitimate
le·git·i·mise *Brit var of* LEGITIMIZE
le·git·i·mize \li-'ji-tə-ˌmīz\ *vb* **-mized; -miz·ing** : LEGITIMATE
leg·man \'leg-ˌman\ *n* 1 : a reporter assigned usu. to gather information 2 : an assistant who gathers information and runs errands
le·gume \'le-ˌgyüm, li-'gyüm\ *n* [F] 1 : any of a large family of plants having fruits that are dry pods and split when ripe and including important food and forage plants (as beans and clover); *also* : the part (as seeds or pods) of a legume used as food 2 : the pod of a legume — **le·gu·mi·nous** \li-'gyü-mə-nəs\ *adj*

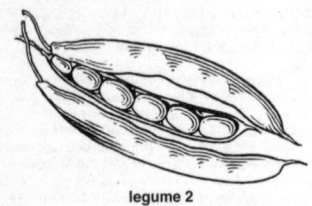

legume 2

¹**lei** \'lā, 'lā-ˌē\ *n* : a wreath or necklace usu. of flowers
²**lei** \'lā\ *pl of* LEU
lei·sure \'lē-zhər, 'le-, 'lā-\ *n* 1 : time free from work or duties 2 : EASE; *also* : CONVENIENCE ✦ **Synonyms** RELAXATION, REST, REPOSE — **lei·sure·ly** *adj or adv*
leit·mo·tif *also* **leit·mo·tiv** \'līt-mō-ˌtēf\ *n* [G *Leitmotiv*, fr. *leiten* to lead + *Motiv* motive] : a dominant recurring theme
lek \'lek\ *n, pl* **leks** *or* **le·ke** *or* **lekë** \'le-kə\ — see MONEY table
lem·ming \'le-miŋ\ *n* [Norw] : any of various short-tailed rodents found mostly in northern regions and noted for recurrent mass migrations
lem·on \'le-mən\ *n* 1 : an acid yellow usu. nearly oblong citrus fruit; *also* : a citrus tree that bears lemons 2 : something (as an automobile) unsatisfactory or defective — **lem·ony** *adj*
lem·on·ade \ˌle-mə-'nād\ *n* : a beverage of lemon juice, sugar, and water
lemon curd *n* : a custard made with lemon juice, butter, sugar, and eggs
lem·on·grass \'le-mən-ˌgras\ *n* : a tropical Asian grass grown for its lemon-scented foliage used as a seasoning
lem·pi·ra \lem-'pir-ə\ *n* — see MONEY table
le·mur \'lē-mər\ *n* : any of various arboreal primates largely of Madagascar that have large eyes, very soft woolly fur, and a long furry tail
Len·a·pe \'le-nə-pē, lə-'nä-pē\ *n, pl* **Lenape** *or* **Lenapes** : DELAWARE
lend \'lend\ *vb* **lent** \'lent\; **lend·ing** 1 : to give for temporary use on condition that the same or its equivalent be returned 2 : AFFORD, FURNISH 3 : ACCOMMODATE — **lend·er** *n*
lend–lease \-'lēs\ *n* : the transfer of goods and services to

an ally to aid in a common cause with payment made by a return of the items or their use in the cause or by a similar transfer of other goods and services
length \'leŋth\ *n* 1 : the longer or longest dimension of an object; *also* : a measured distance 2 : duration or extent in time or space 3 : the length of something taken as a unit of measure 4 : a single piece of a series of pieces that may be joined together ⟨a ～ of pipe⟩ — **at length** 1 : in full 2 : FINALLY
length·en \'leŋ-thən\ *vb* : to make or become longer ✦ **Synonyms** EXTEND, ELONGATE, PROLONG, PROTRACT
length·wise \'leŋth-ˌwīz\ *adv* : in the direction of the length — **lengthwise** *adj*
lengthy \'leŋ-thē\ *adj* **length·i·er; -est** 1 : protracted excessively 2 : EXTENDED, LONG ⟨a ～ journey⟩
le·nient \'lē-nē-ənt, -nyənt\ *adj* : of mild and tolerant disposition or effect ✦ **Synonyms** INDULGENT, FORBEARING, MERCIFUL, TOLERANT — **le·ni·en·cy** \'lē-nē-ən-sē, -nyən-sē\ *n* — **le·ni·ent·ly** *adv*
len·i·tive \'le-nə-tiv\ *adj* : alleviating pain or harshness
len·i·ty \'le-nə-tē\ *n* : LENIENCY
lens \'lenz\ *n* [L *lent-, lens* lentil; so called fr. the shape of a convex lens] 1 : a curved piece of glass or plastic used singly or combined in an optical instrument for forming an image; *also* : a device for focusing radiation other than light 2 : a transparent body in the eye that focuses light rays on receptors at the back of the eye
Lent \'lent\ *n* : a 40-day period of penitence and fasting observed from Ash Wednesday to Easter by many churches — **Lent·en** \'len-tᵊn\ *adj*
len·til \'len-tᵊl\ *n* : a Eurasian annual legume grown for its flat edible seeds and for fodder; *also* : its seed
Leo \'lē-ō\ *n* [L, lit., lion] 1 : a zodiacal constellation between Cancer and Virgo usu. pictured as a lion 2 : the 5th sign of the zodiac in astrology; *also* : one born under this sign
le·one \lē-'ōn\ *n, pl* **leones** *or* **leone** — see MONEY table
le·o·nine \'lē-ə-ˌnīn\ *adj* : of, relating to, or resembling a lion
leop·ard \'le-pərd\ *n* : a large usu. tawny and black-spotted cat of southern Asia and Africa
le·o·tard \'lē-ə-ˌtärd\ *n* : a close-fitting garment worn esp. by dancers and for exercise
lep·er \'le-pər\ *n* 1 : a person affected with leprosy 2 : OUTCAST
lep·re·chaun \'le-prə-ˌkän\ *n* : a mischievous elf of Irish folklore
lep·ro·sy \'le-prə-sē\ *n* : a chronic bacterial disease marked esp. if not treated by slow-growing swellings with deformity and loss of sensation of affected parts — **lep·rous** \-prəs\ *adj*
lep·tin \'lep-tən\ *n* : a hormone that is produced by fat-containing cells and plays a role in body weight regulation
lep·ton \lep-'tän\ *n, pl* **lep·ta** \-'tä\ : a former monetary unit equal to ¹/₁₀₀ drachma
les·bi·an \'lez-bē-ən\ *n* [fr. the reputed homosexual group associated with the poet Sappho of Lesbos] : a woman who is a homosexual — **lesbian** *adj* — **les·bi·an·ism** \-ə-ˌni-zəm\ *n*
lèse ma·jes·té *or* **lese maj·es·ty** \'läz-'ma-jə-stē, 'lez-, 'lēz-\ *n* [MF *lese majesté*, fr. L *laesa majestas*, lit., injured majesty] : an offense violating the dignity of a sovereign
le·sion \'lē-zhən\ *n* : an abnormal structural change in the body due to injury or disease; *esp* : one clearly marked off from healthy tissue around it
¹**less** \'les\ *adj, comparative of* ¹LITTLE 1 : FEWER ⟨～ than six⟩ 2 : of lower rank, degree, or importance 3 : SMALLER; *also* : more limited in quantity
²**less** *adv, comparative of* ²LITTLE : to a lesser extent or degree
³**less** *n, pl* **less** 1 : a smaller portion 2 : something of less importance
⁴**less** *prep* : diminished by : MINUS ⟨list price ～ the discount⟩
-less \ləs\ *adj suffix* 1 : destitute of : not having ⟨childless⟩ 2 : unable to be acted on or to act (in a specified way) ⟨dauntless⟩
les·see \le-'sē\ *n* : a tenant under a lease
less·en \'le-sᵊn\ *vb* : to make or become less ✦ **Synonyms** DECREASE, DIMINISH, DWINDLE, ABATE

less·er \'le-sər\ *adj, comparative of* ¹LITTLE : of less size, quality, or significance

les·son \'le-s°n\ *n* **1** : a passage from sacred writings read in a service of worship **2** : a reading or exercise to be studied by a pupil; *also* **3** : something learned **4** : a period of instruction **4** : an instructive example

les·sor \'le-,sȯr, le-'sȯr\ *n* : one who conveys property by a lease

lest \'lest\ *conj* : for fear that

¹let \'let\ *n* [ME *lette,* fr. *letten* to delay, hinder, fr. OE *lettan*] **1** : HINDRANCE, OBSTACLE **2** : a shot or point in racket games that does not count

²let *vb* **let; let·ting** [ME *leten,* fr. OE *lætan*] **1** : to cause to : MAKE ⟨∼ it be known⟩ **2** : RENT, LEASE; *also* : to assign esp. after bids **3** : ALLOW, PERMIT ⟨∼ me go⟩

-let *n suffix* **1** : small one ⟨book*let*⟩ **2** : article worn on ⟨wrist*let*⟩

let·down \'let-,daủn\ *n* **1** : DISAPPOINTMENT **2** : a slackening of effort

le·thal \'lē-thəl\ *adj* : DEADLY, FATAL — **le·thal·ly** *adv*

leth·ar·gy \'le-thər-jē\ *n* **1** : abnormal drowsiness **2** : the quality or state of being lazy or indifferent ♦ **Synonyms** LANGUOR, LASSITUDE, TORPOR — **le·thar·gic** \li-'thär-jik\ *adj*

let on *vb* **1** : REVEAL 1 **2** : PRETEND

let·ter \'le-tər\ *n* **1** : a symbol that stands for a speech sound and constitutes a unit of an alphabet **2** : a written or printed communication **3** *pl* : LITERATURE; *also* : LEARNING **4** : the literal meaning ⟨the ∼ of the law⟩ **5** : a single piece of type

²letter *vb* : to mark with letters : INSCRIBE — **let·ter·er** *n*

letter bomb *n* : an explosive device concealed in an envelope and mailed to the intended victim

let·ter-boxed \'le-tər-,bäkst\ *adj* : being a video recording formatted to display a frame size proportional to a standard theater screen

let·ter·head \'le-tər-,hed\ *n* : stationery with a printed or engraved heading; *also* : the heading itself

let·ter-per·fect \,le-tər-'pər-fikt\ *adj* : correct to the smallest detail

let·ter·press \'le-tər-,pres\ *n* : printing done directly by impressing the paper on an inked raised surface

letters of marque \-'märk\ : a license granted to a private person by a government to fit out an armed ship to capture enemy shipping

letters patent *n pl* : a written grant from a government to a person in a form readily open for inspection by all

let·tuce \'le-təs\ *n* [ME *letuse,* fr. AF, prob. fr. pl. of *letue* lettuce plant, fr. L *lactuca,* fr. *lac* milk; fr. its milky juice] : a garden composite plant with crisp leaves used esp. in salads

let·up \'let-,əp\ *n* : a lessening of effort

leu \'leủ\ *n, pl* **lei** \'lā\ — see MONEY table

leu·kae·mia *chiefly Brit var of* LEUKEMIA

leu·ke·mia \lü-'kē-mē-ə\ *n* : a malignant disease characterized by an abnormal increase in the number of white blood cells in the blood-forming tissues — **leu·ke·mic** \-mik\ *adj or n*

leu·ko·cyte \'lü-kə-,sīt\ *n* : WHITE BLOOD CELL

lev \'lef\ *n, pl* **le·va** \'le-və\ — see MONEY table

Lev *or* **Levit** *abbr* Leviticus

¹le·vee \'le-vē; lə-'vē, -'vā\ *n* [F *lever* act of arising] : a reception held by or for a person of distinction

²lev·ee \'le-vē\ *n* : an embankment to prevent or confine flooding; *also* : a river landing place

¹lev·el \'le-vəl\ *n* **1** : a device for establishing a horizontal line or plane **2** : horizontal condition **3** : a horizontal position, line, or surface often taken as an index of altitude; *also* : a flat area of ground **4** : height, position, rank, or size in a scale

²level *vb* **-eled** *or* **-elled; -el·ing** *or* **-el·ling** **1** : to make flat or level; *also* : to come to a level **2** : AIM, DIRECT **3** : EQUALIZE **4** : RAZE — **lev·el·er** *n*

³level *adj* **1** : having a flat even surface **2** : HORIZONTAL **3** : of the same height or rank; *also* : UNIFORM **4** : steady and cool in judgment — **lev·el·ly** *adv* — **lev·el·ness** *n*

lev·el·head·ed \,le-vəl-'he-dəd\ *adj* : having or showing sound judgment : SENSIBLE

le·ver \'le-vər, 'lē-\ *n* **1** : a bar used for prying or dislodging something; *also* : a means for achieving one's pur-

pose **2** : a rigid piece turning about an axis and used for transmitting and changing force and motion

le·ver·age \'le-vrij, 'lē-, -və-rij\ *n* : the action or mechanical effect of a lever

le·vi·a·than \li-'vī-ə-thən\ *n* **1** : a large sea animal **2** : something large or formidable

lev·i·tate \'le-və-,tāt\ *vb* **-tat·ed; -tat·ing** : to rise or cause to rise in the air in seeming defiance of gravitation — **lev·i·ta·tion** \,le-və-'tā-shən\ *n*

Le·vit·i·cus \li-'vi-tə-kəs\ *n* — see BIBLE table

lev·i·ty \'le-və-tē\ *n* : lack of seriousness ♦ **Synonyms** LIGHTNESS, FLIPPANCY, FRIVOLITY

levo·do·pa \,le-və-'dō-pə\ *n* : L-DOPA

¹levy \'le-vē\ *n, pl* **lev·ies** **1** : the imposition or collection of an assessment; *also* : an amount levied **2** : the enlistment or conscription of men for military service; *also* : troops raised by levy

²levy *vb* **lev·ied; levy·ing** **1** : to impose or collect by legal authority **2** : to enlist for military service **3** : WAGE ⟨∼ war⟩ **4** : to seize property

lewd \'lüd\ *adj* [ME *lewed* vulgar, fr. OE *lǣwede* lay, ignorant] : sexually unchaste; *also* : OBSCENE, VULGAR — **lewd·ly** *adv* — **lewd·ness** *n*

lex·i·cog·ra·phy \,lek-sə-'kä-grə-fē\ *n* **1** : the editing or making of a dictionary **2** : the principles and practices of dictionary making — **lex·i·cog·ra·pher** \-fər\ *n* — **lex·i·co·graph·i·cal** \-kō-'gra-fi-kəl\ *or* **lex·i·co·graph·ic** \-fik\ *adj*

lex·i·con \'lek-sə-,kän\ *n, pl* **lex·i·ca** \-si-kə\ *or* **lexicons** **1** : DICTIONARY **2** : the vocabulary of a language, speaker, or subject

lg *abbr* **1** large **2** long

LH *abbr* **1** left hand **2** lower half

li *abbr* link

Li *symbol* lithium

LI *abbr* Long Island

li·a·bil·i·ty \,lī-ə-'bi-lə-tē\ *n, pl* **-ties** **1** : the quality or state of being liable **2** *pl* : DEBTS **3** : DISADVANTAGE

li·a·ble \'lī-ə-bəl\ *adj* **1** : legally obligated : RESPONSIBLE **2** : LIKELY, APT ⟨∼ to fall⟩ **3** : SUSCEPTIBLE ⟨∼ to disease⟩

li·ai·son \'lē-ə-,zän, lē-'ā-\ *n* [F] **1** : a close bond : INTERRELATIONSHIP **2** : an illicit sexual relationship **3** : communication for mutual understanding (as between parts of an armed force); *also* : one that carries on a liaison

li·ar \'lī(-ə)r\ *n* : a person who lies

¹lib \'lib\ *n* : LIBERATION

²lib *abbr* **1** liberal **2** librarian; library

li·ba·tion \lī-'bā-shən\ *n* **1** : an act of pouring a liquid as a sacrifice (as to a god); *also* : the liquid poured **2** : DRINK

¹li·bel \'lī-bəl\ *n* [ME, written declaration, fr. AF, fr. L *libellus,* dim. of *liber* book] **1** : a spoken or written statement or a representation that gives an unjustly unfavorable impression of a person or thing **2** : the action or crime of publishing a libel — **li·bel·ous** *or* **li·bel·lous** \-bə-ləs\ *adj*

²libel *vb* **-beled** *or* **-belled; -bel·ing** *or* **-bel·ling** : to make or publish a libel — **li·bel·er** *n* — **li·bel·ist** *n*

¹lib·er·al \'li-brəl, -bə-rəl\ *adj* [ME, fr. AF, fr. L *liberalis* suitable for a freeman, generous, fr. *liber* free] **1** : of, relating to, or based on the liberal arts **2** : GENEROUS, BOUNTIFUL ⟨a ∼ serving⟩ **3** : not literal **4** : not narrow in opinion or judgment : TOLERANT; *also* : not orthodox **5** : not conservative — **lib·er·al·i·ty** \,li-bə-'ra-lə-tē\ *n* — **lib·er·al·i·za·tion** \,li-brə-lə-'zā-shən, -bə-rə-\ *n* — **lib·er·al·ize** \'li-brə-,līz, -bə-rə-\ *vb* — **lib·er·al·ly** *adv*

²liberal *n* : a person who holds liberal views

liberal arts *n pl* : the studies (as language, philosophy, history, literature, or abstract science) in a college or university intended to provide chiefly general knowledge and to develop the general intellectual capacities

lib·er·al·ism \'li-brə-,li-zəm, -bə-rə-\ *n* : liberal principles and theories

lib·er·ate \'li-bə-,rāt\ *vb* **-at·ed; -at·ing** **1** : to free from bondage or restraint; *also* : to raise to equal rights and status **2** : to free (as a gas) from combination — **lib·er·a·tion** \,li-bə-'rā-shən\ *n* — **lib·er·a·tor** \'li-bə-,rā-tər\ *n*

liberated *adj* : freed from or opposed to traditional social and sexual attitudes or roles ⟨a ∼ marriage⟩

lib·er·tar·i·an \,li-bər-'ter-ē-ən\ *n* **1** : an advocate of the doctrine of free will **2** : one who upholds the principles of unrestricted liberty

lib·er·tine \'li-bər-ˌtēn\ *n* : a person who leads a dissolute life

lib·er·ty \'li-bər-tē\ *n, pl* **-ties** **1** : FREEDOM **2** : an action going beyond normal limits; *esp* : FAMILIARITY **3** : a short leave from naval duty

li·bid·i·nous \lə-'bi-də-nəs\ *adj* **1** : LASCIVIOUS **2** : LIBIDINAL

li·bi·do \lə-'bē-dō\ *n, pl* **-dos** [NL, fr. L, desire, lust] **1** : psychic energy derived from basic biological urges **2** : sexual drive — **li·bid·i·nal** \lə-'bi-də-nəl\ *adj*

Li·bra \'lē-brə\ *n* [L, lit., scales] **1** : a zodiacal constellation between Virgo and Scorpio usu. pictured as a balance scale **2** : the 7th sign of the zodiac in astrology; *also* : one born under this sign

li·brar·i·an \lī-'brer-ē-ən\ *n* : a specialist in the management of a library

li·brary \'lī-ˌbrer-ē\ *n, pl* **-brar·ies** **1** : a place in which books and related materials are kept for use but not for sale **2** : a collection of books

li·bret·to \lə-'bre-tō\ *n, pl* **-tos** *or* **-ti** \-tē\ [It, dim. of *libro* book, fr. L *liber*] : the text esp. of an opera — **li·bret·tist** \-tist\ *n*

lice *pl of* LOUSE

li·cense *or* **li·cence** \'lī-s³ns\ *n* **1** : permission to act **2** : a permission granted by authority to engage in an activity **3** : a document, plate, or tag providing proof of a license **4** : freedom used irresponsibly — **license** *vb*

licensed practical nurse *n* : a specially trained person who is licensed (as by a state) to provide routine care for the sick

li·cens·ee \ˌlī-s³n-'sē\ *n* : a licensed person

licente *pl of* SENTE

li·cen·ti·ate \lī-'sen-chē-ət\ *n* : one licensed to practice a profession

li·cen·tious \lī-'sen-chəs\ *adj* : LEWD, LASCIVIOUS — **li·cen·tious·ly** *adv* — **li·cen·tious·ness** *n*

lichee *var of* LITCHI

li·chen \'lī-kən\ *n* : any of various complex plantlike organisms made up of an alga and a fungus growing as a unit on a solid surface — **li·chen·ous** *adj*

lic·it \'li-sət\ *adj* : LAWFUL

¹**lick** \'lik\ *vb* **1** : to draw the tongue over; *also* : to flicker over like a tongue **2** : THRASH; *also* : DEFEAT

²**lick** *n* **1** : a stroke of the tongue **2** : a small amount **3** : a hasty careless effort **4** : BLOW **5** : a natural deposit of salt that animals lick

lick·e·ty-split \ˌli-kə-tē-'split\ *adv* : at great speed

lick·spit·tle \'lik-ˌspi-t³l\ *n* : a fawning subordinate : TOADY

lic·o·rice \'li-kə-rish, -rəs\ *n* [ME, fr. AF *licoris*, fr. LL *liquiritia*, alter. of L *glycyrrhiza*, fr. Gk *glykyrrhiza*, fr. *glykys* sweet + *rhiza* root] **1** : the dried root of a European leguminous plant; *also* : an extract from it used esp. as a flavoring and in medicine **2** : a candy flavored with licorice **3** : a plant yielding licorice

lid \'lid\ *n* **1** : a movable cover **2** : EYELID **3** : something that confines or suppresses — **lid·ded** \'li-dəd\ *adj*

li·do \'lē-dō\ *n, pl* **lidos** : a fashionable beach resort

¹**lie** \'lī\ *vb* **lay** \'lā\; **lain** \'lān\; **ly·ing** \'lī-iŋ\ **1** : to be in, stay at rest in, or assume a horizontal position; *also* : to be in a helpless or defenseless state **2** : EXTEND ⟨our route *lay* to the west⟩ **3** : to occupy a certain relative position **4** : to have an effect esp. through mere presence

²**lie** *n* : the position in which something lies

³**lie** *vb* **lied; ly·ing** \'lī-iŋ\ : to tell a lie

⁴**lie** *n* : an untrue statement made with intent to deceive

lied \'lēt\ *n, pl* **lie·der** \'lē-dər\ [G] : a German song esp. of the 19th century

lie detector *n* : a polygraph for detecting physiological evidence of the tension that accompanies lying

lief \'lēv, 'lēf\ *adv* : GLADLY, WILLINGLY

¹**liege** \'lēj\ *adj* : LOYAL, FAITHFUL

²**liege** *n* **1** : VASSAL **2** : a feudal superior

lien \'lēn, 'lē-ən\ *n* : a legal claim on the property of another for the satisfaction of a debt or duty

lieu \'lü\ *n, archaic* : PLACE, STEAD — **in lieu of** : in the place of

lieut *abbr* lieutenant

lieu·ten·ant \lü-'te-nənt\ *n* [ME, fr. AF *lieu tenant*, fr. *liu,*

lieu place + *tenant* holding, fr. *tenir* to hold, fr. L *tenēre*] **1** : a representative of another in the performance of duty **2** : FIRST LIEUTENANT; *also* : SECOND LIEUTENANT **3** : a commissioned officer in the navy ranking next below a lieutenant commander — **lieu·ten·an·cy** \-nən-sē\ *n*

lieutenant colonel *n* : a commissioned officer (as in the army) ranking next below a colonel

lieutenant commander *n* : a commissioned officer in the navy ranking next below a commander

lieutenant general *n* : a commissioned officer (as in the army) ranking next below a general

lieutenant governor *n* : a deputy or subordinate governor

lieutenant junior grade *n, pl* **lieutenants junior grade** : a commissioned officer in the navy ranking next below a lieutenant

life \'līf\ *n, pl* **lives** \'līvz\ **1** : the quality that distinguishes a vital and functional being from a dead body or inanimate matter; *also* : a state of an organism characterized esp. by capacity for metabolism, growth, reaction to stimuli, and reproduction **2** : the physical and mental experiences of an individual **3** : BIOGRAPHY **4** : a specific phase or period ⟨adult ∼⟩ **5** : the period from birth to death; *also* : a sentence of imprisonment for the remainder of a person's life **6** : a way of living **7** : PERSON ⟨many *lives* were lost in the fire⟩ **8** : ANIMATION, SPIRIT ⟨danced without ∼⟩ **9** : living beings ⟨forest ∼⟩ **10** : animate activity ⟨signs of ∼⟩ **11** : one providing interest and vigor ⟨∼ of the party⟩ — **life·less** *adj* — **life·like** *adj*

life·blood \'līf-ˌbləd\ *n* : a basic source of strength and vitality

life·boat \-ˌbōt\ *n* : a sturdy boat designed for use in saving lives at sea

life·guard \-ˌgärd\ *n* : a usu. expert swimmer employed to safeguard bathers

life·line \-ˌlīn\ *n* **1** : a line to which persons may cling for safety **2** : something considered vital for survival

life·long \-ˌlȯŋ\ *adj* : continuing through life

life preserver *n* : a buoyant device designed to save a person from drowning

lif·er \'lī-fər\ *n* **1** : a person sentenced to life imprisonment **2** : a person who makes a career in the armed forces

life raft *n* : a raft for use by people forced into the water

life·sav·ing \'līf-ˌsā-viŋ\ *n* : the skill or practice of saving or protecting lives esp. of drowning persons — **life·sav·er** \-ˌsā-vər\ *n*

life science *n* : a branch of science (as biology, medicine, and sometimes anthropology or sociology) that deals with living organisms and life processes — usu. used in pl. — **life scientist** *n*

¹**life·style** \'līf-ˌstī(-ə)l\ *n* : a way of living

²**lifestyle** *adj* : associated with, reflecting, or promoting an enhanced or more desirable lifestyle

life·time \-ˌtīm\ *n* : the duration of an individual's existence

life·work \-'wərk\ *n* : the entire or principal work of one's lifetime; *also* : a work extending over a lifetime

life·world \-ˌwər(-ə)ld\ *n* : the total of an individual's physical surroundings and everyday experiences

LIFO *abbr* last in, first out

¹**lift** \'lift\ *vb* **1** : RAISE, ELEVATE; *also* : RISE, ASCEND **2** : to put an end to : STOP **3** : to pay off ⟨∼ a mortgage⟩ — **lift·er** *n*

²**lift** *n* **1** : LOAD **2** : the action or an instance of lifting **3** : HELP; *also* : a ride along one's way **4** : RISE, ADVANCE **5** *chiefly Brit* : ELEVATOR **6** : an elevation of the spirits **7** : the upward force that is developed by a moving airfoil and that opposes the pull of gravity

lift-off \-ˌȯf\ *n* : a vertical takeoff (as by a rocket)

lift truck *n* : a small truck for lifting and transporting loads

lig·a·ment \'li-gə-mənt\ *n* : a band of tough fibrous tissue that holds bones together or supports an organ in place

li·gate \'lī-ˌgāt\ *vb* **li·gat·ed; li·gat·ing** : to tie with a ligature — **li·ga·tion** \lī-'gā-shən\ *n*

lig·a·ture \'li-gə-ˌchur, -chər\ *n* **1** : something that binds or ties; *also* : a thread used in surgery esp. for tying blood vessels **2** : a printed or written character consisting of two or more letters or characters (as æ) united

¹**light** \'līt\ *n* **1** : something that makes vision possible : electromagnetic radiation visible to the human eye; *also* : the sensation aroused by stimulation of the visual sense

organs **2** : DAYLIGHT **3** : a source of light (as a candle) **4** : ENLIGHTENMENT; *also* : TRUTH **5** : public knowledge ⟨facts brought to ∼⟩ **6** : a particular aspect presented to view ⟨saw the matter in a different ∼⟩ **7** : WINDOW **8** *pl* : STANDARDS ⟨according to his ∼*s*⟩ **9** : CELEBRITY **10** : LIGHTHOUSE, BEACON; *also* : TRAFFIC LIGHT **11** : a flame for lighting something

²light *adj* **1** : having light : BRIGHT **2** : PALE 2 ⟨∼ blue⟩ — **light·ness** *n*

³light *vb* **lit** \'lit\ *or* **light·ed; light·ing** **1** : to make or become light **2** : to cause to burn : BURN **3** : to conduct with a light **4** : ILLUMINATE

⁴light *adj* **1** : not heavy ⟨∼ reading⟩ **3** : SCANTY ⟨∼ rain⟩ **4** : easily disturbed ⟨a ∼ sleeper⟩ **5** : GENTLE ⟨a ∼ blow⟩ **6** : easily endurable ⟨a ∼ cold⟩; *also* : requiring little effort ⟨∼ exercise⟩ **7** : SWIFT, NIMBLE **8** : FRIVOLOUS **9** : DIZZY **10** : made with lower calorie content or less of some ingredient than usual ⟨∼ salad dressing⟩ **11** : producing goods for direct consumption by the consumer ⟨∼ industry⟩ — **light·ly** *adv* — **light·ness** *n*

⁵light *adv* **1** : LIGHTLY **2** : with little baggage ⟨travel ∼⟩

⁶light *vb* **lit** \'lit\ *or* **light·ed; light·ing** **1** : SETTLE, ALIGHT **2** : to fall unexpectedly : HAPPEN

light bulb *n* **1** : a lamp in which an electrically heated filament emits light **2** : FLUORESCENT LAMP

light–emitting diode *n* : LED

¹light·en \'lī-t⁼n\ *vb* **1** : ILLUMINATE, BRIGHTEN **2** : to give out flashes of lightning

²lighten *vb* **1** : to relieve of a burden **2** : GLADDEN **3** : to become lighter

lighten up *vb* : to take things less seriously

¹ligh·ter \'lī-tər\ *n* : a barge used esp. in loading or unloading ships

²light·er \'lī-tər\ *n* : one that lights; *esp* : a device for lighting (as a fire or cigarette)

light·face \'līt-ˌfās\ *n* : a type having light thin lines — **light·faced** \-ˌfāst\ *adj*

light–head·ed \'līt-ˌhe-dəd\ *adj* **1** : feeling confused or dizzy **2** : lacking maturity or seriousness

light·heart·ed \-ˌhär-təd\ *adj* : free from worry — **light·heart·ed·ly** *adv* — **light·heart·ed·ness** *n*

light·house \-ˌhaùs\ *n* : a structure with a powerful light for guiding sailors

light meter *n* : a usu. hand-held device for indicating correct photographic exposure

¹light·ning \'līt-niŋ\ *n* : the flashing of light produced by a discharge of atmospheric electricity; *also* : the discharge itself

²lightning *adj* : extremely fast

lightning bug *n* : FIREFLY

lightning rod *n* : a grounded metallic rod set up on a structure to protect it from lightning

light out *vb* : to leave in a hurry

light-proof \'līt-ˌprüf\ *adj* : impenetrable by light

lights \'līts\ *n pl* : the lungs esp. of a slaughtered animal

light·ship \'līt-ˌship\ *n* : a ship with a powerful light moored at a place dangerous to navigation

light show *n* : a kaleidoscopic display (as of colored lights)

light·some \'līt-səm\ *adj* **1** : free from care **2** : NIMBLE

¹light·weight \'līt-ˌwāt\ *n* : one of less than average weight; *esp* : a boxer weighing not over 135 pounds

²lightweight *adj* **1** : INCONSEQUENTIAL **2** : of less than average weight

light–year \'līt-ˌyir\ *n* **1** : an astronomical unit of distance equal to the distance that light travels in one year in a vacuum or about 5.88 trillion miles (9.46 trillion kilometers) **2** : an extremely large measure of comparison ⟨saw it ∼*s* ago⟩

lig·nin \'lig-nən\ *n* : a substance related to cellulose that occurs in the woody cell walls of plants and in the cementing material between them

lig·nite \'lig-ˌnīt\ *n* : brownish black soft coal

¹like \'līk\ *vb* **liked; lik·ing** **1** : ENJOY ⟨∼*s* baseball⟩ **2** : WANT ⟨∼ a drink⟩ **3** : CHOOSE ⟨does as she ∼*s*⟩ — **lik·able** *or* **like·able** \'lī-kə-bəl\ *adj*

²like *n* : PREFERENCE

³like *adj* : SIMILAR ✦ **Synonyms** ALIKE, ANALOGOUS, COMPARABLE, PARALLEL, UNIFORM

⁴like *prep* **1** : similar or similarly to ⟨seems ∼ a dream⟩

2 : typical of **3** : comparable to **4** : as though there would be ⟨looks ∼ rain⟩ **5** : such as ⟨a subject ∼ physics⟩

⁵like *n* **1** : COUNTERPART **2** : one that is similar to another — **and the like** : ET CETERA

⁶like *conj* **1** : AS IF ⟨acted ∼ they were scared⟩ **2** : in the same way that ⟨do it ∼ mom said⟩

-like *adj comb form* : resembling or characteristic of ⟨la-dy*like*⟩ ⟨life*like*⟩

like·li·hood \'lī-klē-ˌhùd\ *n* : PROBABILITY

¹like·ly \'lī-klē\ *adj* **like·li·er; -est** **1** : very probable **2** : BELIEVABLE **3** : PROMISING ⟨a ∼ place to fish⟩

²likely *adv* : in all probability

lik·en \'lī-kən\ *vb* : COMPARE

like·ness \'līk-nəs\ *n* **1** : COPY, PORTRAIT **2** : SEMBLANCE **3** : RESEMBLANCE

like·wise \-ˌwīz\ *adv* **1** : in like manner **2** : in addition : ALSO

lik·ing \'lī-kiŋ\ *n* : favorable regard ⟨took a ∼ to the newcomer⟩; *also* : TASTE

li·lac \'lī-lək, -ˌlak, -ˌläk\ *n* [obs. F (now *lilas*), fr. Ar *līlak*, fr. Pers *nīlak* bluish, fr. *nīl* blue, fr. Skt *nīla* dark blue] **1** : a shrub related to the olive that produces large clusters of fragrant grayish pink, purple, or white flowers **2** : a moderate purple color

lil·an·ge·ni \ˌli-lən-ˈge-nē\ *n, pl* **em·a·lan·ge·ni** \ˌe-mə-lən-ˈge-nē\ — see MONEY table

lil·li·pu·tian \ˌli-lə-ˈpyü-shən\ *adj, often cap* **1** : SMALL, MINIATURE **2** : PETTY

lilt \'lilt\ *n* **1** : a cheerful lively song or tune **2** : a rhythmical swing or flow

lily \'li-lē\ *n, pl* **lil·ies** : any of a genus of tall bulbous herbs with leafy stems and usu. funnel-shaped flowers; *also* : any of various related plants

lily of the valley : a low perennial herb related to the lilies that produces a raceme of fragrant nodding bell-shaped white flowers

li·ma bean \'lī-mə-\ *n* : a bushy or tall-growing bean widely cultivated for its flat edible usu. pale green or whitish seeds; *also* : the seed

limb \'lim\ *n* **1** : one of the projecting paired appendages (as legs, arms, or wings) used by an animal esp. in moving or grasping **2** : a large branch of a tree : BOUGH — **limb·less** *adj*

¹lim·ber \'lim-bər\ *adj* **1** : FLEXIBLE, SUPPLE **2** : LITHE, NIMBLE

²limber *vb* : to make or become limber

lim·bic \'lim-bik\ *adj* : of, relating to, or being a group of structures of the brain (**limbic system**) concerned esp. with emotion and motivation

¹lim·bo \'lim-bō\ *n, pl* **limbos** [ME, fr. ML, abl. of *limbus* limbo, fr. L, border] **1** *often cap* : an abode of souls barred from heaven through no fault of their own **2** : a place or state of confinement, oblivion, or uncertainty

²limbo *n, pl* **limbos** : an acrobatic dance or contest that involves passing under a horizontal pole

Lim·burg·er \'lim-ˌbər-gər\ *n* : a pungent semisoft surface-ripened cheese

¹lime \'līm\ *n* : a caustic powdery white solid that consists of calcium and oxygen, is obtained from limestone or shells, and is used in making cement and in fertilizer — **lime** *vb* — **limy** \'lī-mē\ *adj*

²lime *n* : a small yellowish green citrus fruit with juicy acid pulp

lime·ade \ˌlīm-ˈād, 'lī-ˌmād\ *n* : a beverage of lime juice, sugar, and water

lime·light \'līm-ˌlīt\ *n* **1** : a device in which flame is directed against a cylinder of lime formerly used in the theater to cast a strong white light on the stage **2** : the center of public attention

lim·er·ick \'li-mə-rik\ *n* : a light or humorous poem of 5 lines

lime·stone \'līm-ˌstōn\ *n* : a rock that is formed by accumulation of organic remains (as shells), is used in building, and yields lime when burned

¹lim·it \'li-mət\ *n* **1** : something that restrains or confines; *also* : the utmost extent **2** : BOUNDARY; *also,* **lim·its** : BOUNDS **3** : a prescribed maximum or minimum **4** : a number whose value becomes arbitrarily close to that of a function as its independent variable approaches a given value — **lim·it·less** *adj* — **lim·it·less·ness** *n*

²**limit** *vb* **1** : to set limits to **2** : to reduce in quantity or extent — **lim·i·ta·tion** \ˌli-mə-ˈtā-shən\ *n*

lim·it·ed *adj* **1** : confined within limits **2** : offering faster service esp. by making fewer stops

limn \ˈlim\ *vb* **limned; limn·ing** \ˈli-miŋ, ˈlim-niŋ\ **1** : DRAW; *also* : PAINT **2** : DELINEATE **3** : DESCRIBE

limo \ˈli-(ˌ)mō\ *n, pl* **limos** : LIMOUSINE

li·mo·nite \ˈlī-mə-ˌnīt\ *n* : a ferric oxide that is a major ore of iron — **li·mo·nit·ic** \ˌlī-mə-ˈni-tik\ *adj*

lim·ou·sine \ˈli-mə-ˌzēn, ˌli-mə-ˈzēn\ *n* [F] **1** : a large luxurious often chauffeur-driven sedan **2** : a large vehicle for transporting passengers to and from an airport

¹**limp** \ˈlimp\ *vb* : to walk lamely; *also* : to proceed with difficulty

²**limp** *n* : a limping movement or gait

³**limp** *adj* **1** : having no defined shape; *also* : not stiff or rigid **2** : lacking in strength or firmness — **limp·ly** *adv* — **limp·ness** *n*

lim·pet \ˈlim-pət\ *n* : any of numerous gastropod sea mollusks with a conical shell that clings to rocks or timbers

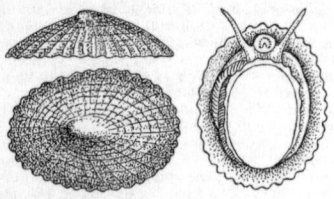

limpet: shell and bottom view

lim·pid \ˈlim-pəd\ *adj* : CLEAR, TRANSPARENT

lin *abbr* **1** lineal **2** linear

lin·age \ˈlī-nij\ *n* : the number of lines of written or printed matter

linch·pin \ˈlinch-ˌpin\ *n* : a locking pin inserted crosswise (as through the end of an axle)

lin·den \ˈlin-dən\ *n* : any of a genus of trees with large heart-shaped leaves and clustered yellowish flowers; *also* : the light white wood of a linden

¹**line** \ˈlīn\ *n* **1** : CORD, ROPE, WIRE; *also* : a length of material used in measuring and leveling **2** : pipes for conveying a fluid ⟨a gas ∼⟩ **3** : a horizontal row of written or printed characters; *also* : VERSE **4** : NOTE **5** : the words making up a part in a drama — usu. used in pl. **6** : something distinct, long, and narrow; *also* : ROUTE **7** : a state of agreement **8** : a course of conduct, action, or thought; *also* : OCCUPATION **9** : LIMIT **10** : an arrangement of persons or objects of one kind in an orderly series ⟨waiting in ∼⟩ **11** : a transportation system **12 a** : the football players who are stationed on the line of scrimmage **b** : a group of three players who play together as a unit in hockey **13** : a long narrow mark; *also* : EQUATOR **14** : a geometric element that is the path of a moving point **15** : CONTOUR **16** : a general plan ⟨thinking along these ∼s⟩ **17** : an indication based on insight or investigation

²**line** *vb* **lined; lin·ing** **1** : to mark with a line **2** : to place or form a line along **3** : ALIGN

³**line** *vb* **lined; lin·ing** : to cover the inner surface of

lin·eage \ˈli-nē-ij\ *n* : lineal descent from a common progenitor; *also* : FAMILY

lin·eal \ˈli-nē-əl\ *adj* **1** : LINEAR **2** : consisting of or being in a direct line of ancestry; *also* : HEREDITARY

lin·ea·ment \ˈli-nē-ə-mənt\ *n* : an outline, feature, or contour of a body and esp. of a face — usu. used in pl.

lin·ear \ˈli-nē-ər\ *adj* **1** : of, relating to, resembling, or having a graph that is a line and esp. a straight line : STRAIGHT **2** : composed of simply drawn lines with little attempt at pictorial representation ⟨∼ script⟩ **3** : being long and uniformly narrow

line·back·er \ˈlīn-ˌba-kər\ *n* : a defensive football player who lines up just behind the line of scrimmage

line drive *n* : a batted baseball hit in a flatter path than a fly ball

line–item veto *n* : the power of a government executive to veto specific items in an appropriations bill

line·man \ˈlīn-mən\ *n* **1** : a person who sets up or repairs communication or power lines **2** : a player in the line in football

lin·en \ˈli-nən\ *n* **1** : cloth made of flax; *also* : thread or yarn spun from flax **2** : clothing or household articles made of linen cloth or similar fabric

line of scrimmage : an imaginary line in football parallel to the goal lines and tangent to the nose of the ball laid on the ground before a play

¹**lin·er** \ˈlī-nər\ *n* : a ship or airplane of a regular transportation line

²**liner** *n* : one that lines or is used as a lining — **lin·er·less** *adj*

line score *n* : a score of a baseball game giving the runs, hits, and errors made by each team

lines·man \ˈlīnz-mən\ *n* **1** : LINEMAN 1 **2** : an official who assists a referee

line·up \ˈlī-ˌnəp\ *n* **1** : a list of players taking part in a game (as of baseball) **2** : a line of persons arranged esp. for identification by police

ling \ˈliŋ\ *n* : any of various fishes related to the cod

-ling *n suffix* **1** : one associated with ⟨nest*ling*⟩ **2** : young, small, or minor one ⟨duck*ling*⟩

lin·ger \ˈliŋ-gər\ *vb* : TARRY; *also* : PROCRASTINATE — **lin·ger·er** *n*

lin·ge·rie \ˌlän-jə-ˈrā, ˌlaⁿ-zhə-, -ˈrē\ *n* [F, fr. MF, fr. *linge* linen, fr. L *lineus* made of linen, fr. *linum* flax, linen] : women's intimate apparel

lin·go \ˈliŋ-gō\ *n, pl* **lingoes** : a usu. strange or incomprehensible language

lin·gua fran·ca \ˌliŋ-gwə-ˈfraŋ-kə\ *n, pl* **lingua francas** *or* **lin·guae fran·cae** \-ˌgwē-ˈfraŋ-ˌkē\ [It] **1** *often cap* : a common language consisting of Italian mixed with French, Spanish, Greek, and Arabic that was formerly spoken in Mediterranean ports **2** : a common or commercial tongue among speakers of different languages

lin·gual \ˈliŋ-gwəl\ *adj* : of, relating to, or produced by the tongue

lin·gui·ca \liŋ-ˈgwē-sə\ *n* : a spicy Portuguese sausage

lin·guist \ˈliŋ-gwist\ *n* **1** : a person skilled in languages **2** : a person who specializes in linguistics

lin·guis·tics \liŋ-ˈgwis-tiks\ *n* : the study of human speech including the units, nature, structure, and modification of language — **lin·guis·tic** \-tik\ *adj*

lin·i·ment \ˈli-nə-mənt\ *n* : a liquid preparation rubbed on the skin esp. to relieve pain

lin·ing \ˈlī-niŋ\ *n* : material used to line esp. an inner surface

link \ˈliŋk\ *n* **1** : a connecting structure; *esp* : a single ring of a chain **2** : BOND, TIE **3** : HYPERLINK — **link** *vb* — **link·er** *n*

link·age \ˈliŋ-kij\ *n* **1** : the manner or style of being united **2** : the quality or state of being linked **3** : a system of links

linking verb *n* : a word or expression (as a form of *be, become, feel,* or *seem*) that links a subject with its predicate

links \ˈliŋks\ *n pl* : a golf course

link·up \ˈliŋ-ˌkəp\ *n* **1** : MEETING **2** : something that serves as a linking device or factor

lin·net \ˈli-nət\ *n* : an Old World finch

li·no·leum \lə-ˈnō-lē-əm\ *n* [L *linum* flax + *oleum* oil] : a floor covering with a canvas back and a surface of hardened linseed oil and a filler

lin·seed \ˈlin-ˌsēd\ *n* : the seeds of flax yielding a yellowish oil (**linseed oil**) used esp. in paints and linoleum

lin·sey–wool·sey \ˌlin-zē-ˈwùl-zē\ *n* : a coarse sturdy fabric of wool and linen or cotton

lint \ˈlint\ *n* **1** : linen made into a soft fleecy substance **2** : fine ravels and short fibers of yarn or fabric **3** : the fibers that surround cotton seeds and form the cotton staple

lin·tel \ˈlin-tᵊl\ *n* : a horizontal piece across the top of an opening (as of a door) that carries the weight of the structure above it

linz·er torte \ˈlin-sər-, -zər-\ *n, often cap L* : a baked buttery torte made with chopped almonds, sugar, and spices and filled with jam or preserves

li·on \ˈlī-ən\ *n, pl* **lions** : a large heavily-built cat of Africa and southern Asia with a shaggy mane in the male

li·on·ess \ˈlī-ə-nəs\ *n* : a female lion

li·on·heart·ed \ˌlī-ən-ˈhär-təd\ *adj* : COURAGEOUS, BRAVE

li·on·ise *Brit var of* LIONIZE
li·on·ize \'lī-ə-ˌnīz\ *vb* **-ized; -iz·ing** : to treat as an object of great interest or importance — **li·on·i·za·tion** \ˌlī-ə-nə-'zā-shən\ *n*
lion's den *n* : a place or state of extreme disadvantage, antagonism, or hostility
lip \'lip\ *n* **1** : either of the two fleshy folds that surround the mouth; *also* : the margin of the human lip **2** : a part or projection suggesting a lip **3** : the edge of a hollow vessel or cavity — **lipped** \'lipt\ *adj*
li·pa \'lē-ˌpä, -pə\ *n, pl* **lipa** — see *kuna* at MONEY table
lip·id \'li-pəd\ *n* : any of various substances (as fats and waxes) that with proteins and carbohydrates make up the principal structural parts of living cells
lip–lock \'lip-ˌläk\ *n* : a long amorous kiss
li·po·pro·tein \ˌli-pō-'prō-ˌtēn, ˌlī-\ *n* : a protein that is a complex of protein and lipid
li·po·suc·tion \'li-pə-ˌsək-shən, 'lī-\ *n* : surgical removal of local fat deposits (as in the thighs) esp. for cosmetic purposes
lip·read·ing \'lip-ˌrē-diŋ\ *n* : the interpreting of a speaker's words by watching lip and facial movements without hearing the voice
lip service *n* : an avowal of allegiance that is not matched by action
lip·stick \'lip-ˌstik\ *n* : a waxy solid colored cosmetic in stick form for the lips — **lip·sticked** \-ˌstikt\ *adj*
liq *abbr* **1** liquid **2** liquor
liq·ue·fy *also* **liq·ui·fy** \'li-kwə-ˌfī\ *vb* **-fied; -fy·ing** : to make or become liquid — **liq·ue·fi·er** \-ˌfī(-ə)r\ *n*
li·queur \li-'kər\ *n* [F] : a distilled alcoholic liquor flavored with aromatic substances and usu. sweetened
¹liq·uid \'li-kwəd\ *adj* **1** : flowing freely like water **2** : neither solid nor gaseous **3** : shining and clear ⟨large ∼ eyes⟩ **4** : smooth and musical in tone; *also* : smooth and unconstrained in movement **5** : consisting of or capable of ready conversion into cash ⟨∼ assets⟩ — **li·quid·i·ty** \li-'kwi-də-tē\ *n*
²liquid *n* : a liquid substance
liq·ui·date \'li-kwə-ˌdāt\ *vb* **-dat·ed; -dat·ing** **1** : to settle the accounts and distribute the assets of (as a business) **2** : to pay off ⟨∼ a debt⟩ **3** : to get rid of; *esp* : KILL — **liq·ui·da·tion** \ˌli-kwə-'dā-shən\ *n*
liquid crystal *n* : an organic liquid that resembles a crystal in having ordered molecular arrays
liquid crystal display *n* : LCD
liquid measure *n* : a unit or series of units for measuring liquid capacity — see METRIC SYSTEM table,, WEIGHT table
li·quor \'li-kər\ *n* [ME *licour*, fr. AF, fr. L *liquor*, fr. *liquēre* to be fluid] : a liquid substance; *esp* : a distilled alcoholic beverage
li·quo·rice *chiefly Brit var of* LICORICE
li·ra \'lir-ə, 'lē-rə\ *n* **1** *pl* **li·re** \'lē-rā\ : the former basic monetary unit of Italy **2** : the basic monetary unit of Turkey — see MONEY table **3** *pl* **li·ri** \'lē-rē\ : the basic monetary unit of Malta — see MONEY table
lisente *pl of* SENTE
lisle \'lī(-ə)l\ *n* : a smooth tightly twisted thread usu. made of long-staple cotton
lisp \'lisp\ *vb* : to pronounce \s\ and \z\ imperfectly esp. by turning them into \th\ and \th\; *also* : to speak childishly — **lisp** *n* — **lisp·er** *n*
lis·some *also* **lis·som** \'li-səm\ *adj* **1** : easily flexed **2** : LITHE **2 3** : NIMBLE — **lis·some·ly** *adv*
¹list \'list\ *vb, archaic* : PLEASE; *also* : WISH
²list *vb, archaic* : LISTEN
³list *n* : a leaning to one side : TILT
⁴list *vb* : TILT
⁵list *n* **1** : a simple series of words or numerals; *also* : an official roster **2** : CATALOG, CHECKLIST
⁶list *vb* : to make a list of; *also* : to include on a list — **list·ee** \li-'stē\ *n*
lis·ten \'li-sᵊn\ *vb* **1** : to pay attention in order to hear **2** : HEED — **lis·ten·er** *n*
lis·ten·er·ship \'li-sᵊn-ər-ˌship\ *n* : the audience for a radio program or recording
list·ing \'lis-tiŋ\ *n* **1** : an act or instance of making or including in a list **2** : something that is listed
list·less \'list-ləs\ *adj* : SPIRITLESS, LANGUID ⟨a ∼ performance⟩ — **list·less·ly** *adv* — **list·less·ness** *n*

list price *n* : the price of an item as published in a catalog, price list, or advertisement before being discounted
lists \'lists\ *n pl* : an arena for combat (as jousting)
¹lit \'lit\ *past and past part of* LIGHT
²lit *abbr* **1** liter **2** literal; literally **3** literary **4** literature
lit·a·ny \'li-tə-nē\ *n, pl* **-nies** [ME *letanie*, fr. AF & LL; AF, fr. LL *litania*, fr. LGk *litaneia*, fr. Gk, entreaty, fr. *litanos* suppliant] **1** : a prayer consisting of a series of supplications and responses said alternately by a leader and a group **2** : a lengthy recitation ⟨a ∼ of complaints⟩
li·tas \'lē-ˌtäs\ *n, pl* **li·tai** \-ˌtī\ *or* **li·tu** \-ˌtü\ — see MONEY table
litchi *var of* LYCHEE
lite \'līt\ *adj* **1** : ⁴LIGHT 10 ⟨∼ beer⟩ **2** : lacking in substance or seriousness ⟨∼ news⟩
li·ter \'lē-tər\ *n* — see METRIC SYSTEM table
lit·er·al \'li-tə-rəl\ *adj* **1** : adhering to fact or to the ordinary or usual meaning (as of a word) **2** : UNADORNED; *also* : PROSAIC **3** : VERBATIM
lit·er·al·ism \-rə-ˌli-zəm\ *n* **1** : adherence to the explicit substance (as of an idea) **2** : fidelity to observable fact — **lit·er·al·ist** \-list\ *n* — **lit·er·al·is·tic** \ˌli-tə-rə-'lis-tik\ *adj*
lit·er·al·ly \'li-tə-rə-lē, 'li-trə-\ *adv* **1** : ACTUALLY ⟨was ∼ insane⟩ **2** : VIRTUALLY ⟨∼ poured out new ideas⟩
lit·er·ary \'li-tə-ˌrer-ē\ *adj* **1** : of or relating to literature **2** : WELL-READ
lit·er·ate \'li-trət, -tə-rət\ *adj* **1** : EDUCATED; *also* : able to read and write **2** : LITERARY; *also* : POLISHED, LUCID — **lit·er·a·cy** \'li-trə-sē, -tə-rə-\ *n* — **literate** *n*
li·te·ra·ti \ˌli-tə-'rä-tē\ *n pl* **1** : the educated class **2** : persons interested in literature or the arts
lit·er·a·ture \'li-trə-ˌchùr, -tə-rə-, -chər\ *n* **1** : the production of written works having excellence of form or expression and dealing with ideas of permanent interest **2** : the written works produced in a particular language, country, or age
lithe \'līth, 'līth\ *adj* **1** : SUPPLE **2** : characterized by effortless grace; *also* : athletically slim
lithe·some \'līth-səm, 'līth-\ *adj* : LISSOME
lith·i·um \'li-thē-əm\ *n* : a light silver-white metallic chemical element
li·thog·ra·phy \li-'thä-grə-fē\ *n* : the process of printing from a plane surface (as a smooth stone or metal plate) on which the image to be printed is ink-receptive and the blank area ink-repellent — **lith·o·graph** \'li-thə-ˌgraf\ *vb* — **lithograph** *n* — **li·thog·ra·pher** \li-'thä-grə-fər, 'li-thə-ˌgra-fər\ *n* — **lith·o·graph·ic** \ˌli-thə-'gra-fik\ *adj* — **lith·o·graph·i·cal·ly** \-fi-k(ə-)lē\ *adv*
li·thol·o·gy \li-'thä-lə-jē\ *n, pl* **-gies** : the study of rocks — **lith·o·log·ic** \ˌli-thə-'lä-jik\ *or* **lith·o·log·i·cal** \-ji-kəl\ *adj*
lith·o·sphere \'li-thə-ˌsfir\ *n* : the outer part of the solid earth
Lith·u·a·nian \ˌli-thə-'wā-nē-ən, -thyü-\ *n* **1** : a native or inhabitant of Lithuania **2** : the language of the Lithuanians — **Lithuanian** *adj*
lit·i·gant \'li-ti-gənt\ *n* : a party to a lawsuit — **litigant** *adj*
lit·i·gate \-ˌgāt\ *vb* **-gat·ed; -gat·ing** : to carry on a legal contest by judicial process; *also* : to contest at law — **lit·i·ga·tion** \ˌli-tə-'gā-shən\ *n*
li·ti·gious \lə-'ti-jəs\ *adj* **1** : CONTENTIOUS **2** : prone to engage in lawsuits **3** : of or relating to litigation — **li·ti·gious·ly** *adv* — **li·ti·gious·ness** *n*
lit·mus \'lit-məs\ *n* : a coloring matter from lichens that turns red in acid solutions and blue in alkaline
litmus test *n* : a test in which a single factor (as an attitude) is decisive
Litt D *or* **Lit D** *abbr* [ML *litterarum doctor*] : doctor of letters; doctor of literature
¹lit·ter \'li-tər\ *n* [ME, fr. AF *litere*, fr. *lit* bed, fr. L *lectus*] **1** : a covered and curtained couch with shafts that is used to carry a single passenger; *also* : a device (as a stretcher) for carrying a sick or injured person **2** : material used as bedding for animals; *also* : material used to absorb the urine and feces of animals **3** : the offspring of an animal at one birth **4** : RUBBISH
²litter *vb* **1** : to give birth to young **2** : to strew or mark with scattered objects
lit·ter·bug \'li-tər-ˌbəg\ *n* : one who litters a public area
¹lit·tle \'li-tᵊl\ *adj* **lit·tler** \'li-tᵊl-ər\ *or* **less** \'les\ *or* **less·er** \'le-sər\; **lit·tlest** \'li-tᵊl-əst\ *or* **least** \'lēst\ **1** : not big;

also : YOUNG **2** : not important **3** : PETTY 3 **4** : not much — **lit·tle·ness** *n*

²**little** *adv* **less** \'les\; **least** \'lēst\ **1** : SLIGHTLY; *also* : not at all **2** : INFREQUENTLY

³**little** *n* **1** : a small amount or quantity **2** : a short time or distance

Little Dipper *n* : the seven bright stars of Ursa Minor arranged in a form resembling a dipper

little finger *n* : PINKIE

little theater *n* : a small theater for low-cost dramatic productions designed for a limited audience

lit·to·ral \'li-tə-rəl; ˌli-tə-'ral\ *adj* : of, relating to, or growing on or near a shore esp. of the sea — **littoral** *n*

lit·ur·gy \'li-tər-jē\ *n, pl* **-gies** : a rite or body of rites prescribed for public worship — **li·tur·gi·cal** \lə-'tər-ji-kəl\ *adj* — **li·tur·gi·cal·ly** \-k(ə-)lē\ *adv* — **lit·ur·gist** \'li-tər-jist\ *n*

liv·able *also* **live·able** \'li-və-bəl\ *adj* **1** : suitable for living in or with ⟨a ~ house⟩ ⟨~wages⟩ **2** : ENDURABLE — **liv·a·bil·i·ty** \ˌli-və-'bi-lə-tē\ *n*

¹**live** \'liv\ *vb* **lived; liv·ing 1** : to be or continue alive ⟨*lived* 80 years⟩ **2** : SUBSIST **3** : RESIDE ⟨~s next door⟩ **4** : to conduct one's life **5** : to remain in human memory or record ⟨his legacy ~s⟩

²**live** \'līv\ *adj* **1** : having life ⟨~ worms⟩ **2** : ACTUAL ⟨a real ~ celebrity⟩ **3** : BURNING, GLOWING ⟨a ~ cigar⟩ **4** : connected to electric power ⟨a ~ wire⟩ **5** : UNEXPLODED ⟨a ~ bomb⟩ **6** : of continuing interest ⟨a ~ issue⟩ **7** : of or involving the actual presence of real people ⟨~ audience⟩; *also* : broadcast directly at the time of production **8** : being in play ⟨a ~ ball⟩

lived–in \'livd-ˌin\ *adj* : of or suggesting long-term human habitation or use

live down *vb* : to live so as to wipe out the memory or effects of

live in *vb* : to live in one's place of employment — used of a servant — **live–in** \'liv-ˌin\ *adj*

live·li·hood \'līv-lē-ˌhůd\ *n* : means of support or subsistence

live·long \'liv-ˌlȯn\ *adj* [ME *lef long*, fr. *lef* dear + *long* long] : WHOLE, ENTIRE ⟨the ~ day⟩

live·ly \'līv-lē\ *adj* **live·li·er; -est 1** : ANIMATED ⟨~ debate⟩ **2** : KEEN, VIVID ⟨~ interest⟩ **3** : showing activity or vigor ⟨a ~ manner⟩ **4** : quick to rebound ⟨a ~ ball⟩ **5** : full of life ♦ *Synonyms* VIVACIOUS, SPRIGHTLY, GAY, SPIRITED — **live·li·ness** *n* — **live·ly** *adv*

liv·en \'lī-vən\ *vb* : ENLIVEN

live oak *n* : any of several American evergreen oaks; *esp* : one of the southeastern U.S. that is often planted as a shade tree

¹**liv·er** \'li-vər\ *n* **1** : a large glandular organ of vertebrates that secretes bile and is a center of metabolic activity **2** : the liver of an animal (as a calf or chicken) eaten as food

²**liver** *n* : one that lives esp. in a specified way ⟨a fast ~⟩

liv·er·ish \'li-və-rish\ *adj* **1** : resembling liver esp. in color **2** : BILIOUS **3** : PEEVISH — **liv·er·ish·ness** *adj*

liver spots *n pl* : AGE SPOTS

liv·er·wort \'li-vər-ˌwərt\ *n* : any of a class of flowerless plants resembling the related mosses

liv·er·wurst \-ˌwərst, -ˌwůrst\ *n* [part trans. of G *Leberwurst*, fr. *Leber* liver + *Wurst* sausage] : a sausage consisting chiefly of liver

liv·ery \'li-və-rē\ *n, pl* **-er·ies 1** : a servant's uniform; *also* : distinctive dress **2** : the feeding, care, and stabling of horses for pay; *also* : an establishment (as a stable or business) keeping horses or vehicles for hire — **liv·er·ied** \-rēd\ *adj* — **liv·ery·man** \'li-və-rē-mən\ *n*

lives *pl of* LIFE

live·stock \'līv-ˌstäk\ *n* : farm animals kept for use and profit

live wire *n* : an alert, active, or aggressive person — **live–wire** *adj*

liv·id \'li-vəd\ *adj* [F *livide*, fr. L *lividus*, fr. *livēre* to be blue] **1** : discolored by bruising **2** : ASHEN, PALLID **3** : REDDISH **4** : ENRAGED — **li·vid·i·ty** \li-'vi-də-tē\ *n*

¹**liv·ing** \'li-viŋ\ *adj* **1** : having life **2** : NATURAL **3** : full of life and vigor; *also* : VIVID ⟨in ~ color⟩

²**living** *n* **1** : the condition of being alive **2** : LIVELIHOOD **3** : manner of life

living room *n* : a room in a residence used for the common social activities of the occupants

living wage *n* : a wage sufficient to provide an acceptable standard of living

living will *n* : a document requesting that the signer not be kept alive by artificial means unless there is a reasonable expectation of recovery

livre \'lēvrᵊ\ *n* : the pound of Lebanon

liz·ard \'li-zərd\ *n* : any of a group of 4-legged reptiles with long tapering tails

Lk *abbr* Luke

ll *abbr* lines

lla·ma \'lä-mə\ *n* [Sp, fr. Quechua] : any of a genus of wild or domesticated So. American mammals related to the camels but smaller and without a hump

lla·no \'lä-nō\ *n, pl* **llanos** : an open grassy plain esp. of Latin America

LLD *abbr* [NL *legum doctor*] doctor of laws

LNG *abbr* liquefied natural gas

¹**load** \'lōd\ *n* **1** : PACK; *also* : CARGO **2** : a mass of weight supported by something **3** : something that burdens the mind or spirits **4** : a large quantity — usu. used in pl. **5** : a standard, expected, or authorized burden

²**load** *vb* **1** : to put a load in or on; *also* : to receive a load **2** : to encumber with an obligation or something heavy or disheartening **3** : to increase the weight of by adding something **4** : to supply abundantly **5** : to put a charge in (as a firearm) **6** : to copy or transfer into a computer's memory esp. from an external source

load·ed *adj* **1** *slang* : HIGH 12 **2** : having a large amount of money **3** : equipped with an abundance of options ⟨a ~ car⟩

load-stone *var of* LODESTONE

¹**loaf** \'lōf\ *n, pl* **loaves** \'lōvz\ : a shaped or molded mass esp. of bread

²**loaf** *vb* : to spend time in idleness : LOUNGE

loaf·er \'lō-fər\ *n* **1** : one that loafs : IDLER **2** : a low step-in shoe

loam \'lōm, 'lüm\ *n* : SOIL; *esp* : a loose soil of mixed clay, sand, and silt — **loamy** *adj*

¹**loan** \'lōn\ *n* **1** : money lent at interest; *also* : something lent for the borrower's temporary use **2** : the grant of temporary use

²**loan** *vb* : LEND

loan shark *n* : a person who lends money at excessive rates of interest — **loan–shark·ing** \'lōn-ˌshär-kiŋ\ *n*

loan·word \'lōn-ˌwərd\ *n* : a word taken from another language and at least partly naturalized

loath *also* **loth** \'lōth, 'lȯth\ *or* **loathe** \'lōth, 'lȯth\ *adj* : RELUCTANT

loathe \'lōth\ *vb* **loathed; loath·ing** : to dislike greatly ♦ *Synonyms* ABOMINATE, ABHOR, DETEST, HATE

loath·ing \'lō-thiŋ\ *n* : extreme disgust

loath·some \'lōth-səm, 'lȯth-\ *adj* : exciting loathing : REPULSIVE

lob \'läb\ *vb* **lobbed; lob·bing 1** : to throw, hit, or propel something in a high arc **2** : to direct (as a question) so as to elicit a response — **lob** *n*

¹**lob·by** \'lä-bē\ *n, pl* **lobbies 1** : a corridor used esp. as a passageway or waiting room **2** : a group of persons engaged in lobbying

²**lobby** *vb* **lob·bied; lob·by·ing** : to try to influence public officials and esp. legislators — **lob·by·ist** *n*

lobe \'lōb\ *n* : a curved or rounded part esp. of a bodily organ — **lo·bar** \'lō-bər\ *adj* — **lobed** \'lōbd\ *adj*

lo·be·lia \lō-'bēl-yə\ *n* : any of a genus of plants often grown for their clusters of showy flowers

lo·bot·o·my \lō-'bä-tə-mē\ *n, pl* **-mies** : surgical severance of certain nerve fibers in the brain used esp. formerly to relieve some mental disorders

lob·ster \'läb-stər\ *n* [ME, fr. OE *loppestre*, fr. *loppe* spider] : any of a family of edible marine crustaceans with two large pincerlike claws and four other pairs of legs; *also* : SPINY LOBSTER

¹**lo·cal** \'lō-kəl\ *adj* **1** : of, relating to, or occupying a particular place **2** : serving a particular limited district; *also* : making all stops ⟨a ~ train⟩ **3** : affecting a small part of the body ⟨a ~ infection⟩ — **lo·cal·ly** *adv*

²**local** *n* : one that is local

local area network *n* : a network of personal computers in a small area (as an office)

lo·cale \lō-'kal\ *n* : a place that is the setting for a particular event

lo·cal·ise *Brit var of* LOCALIZE

lo·cal·i·ty \lō-'ka-lə-tē\ *n, pl* **-ties** : a particular spot, situation, or location

lo·cal·ize \'lō-kə-ˌlīz\ *vb* **-ized; -iz·ing** : to fix in or confine to a definite place or locality — **lo·cal·i·za·tion** \ˌlō-kə-lə-'zā-shən\ *n*

lo·cate \'lō-ˌkāt, lō-'kāt\ *vb* **lo·cat·ed; lo·cat·ing 1** : STATION, SETTLE **2** : to determine the site of **3** : to find or fix the place of in a sequence

lo·ca·tion \lō-'kā-shən\ *n* **1** : SITUATION, PLACE **2** : the process of locating **3** : a place outside a studio where a motion picture is filmed

loc cit *abbr* [L *loco citato*] in the place cited

loch \'läk, 'läḵ\ *n, Scot* : LAKE; *also* : a bay or arm of the sea esp. when nearly landlocked

¹lock \'läk\ *n* : a tuft, strand, or ringlet of hair; *also* : a cohering bunch (as of wool or flax)

²lock *n* **1** : a fastening in which a bolt is operated **2** : the mechanism of a firearm by which the charge is exploded **3** : an enclosure (as in a canal) used in raising or lowering boats from level to level **4** : AIR LOCK **5** : a wrestling hold

³lock *vb* **1** : to fasten the lock of; *also* : to make fast with a lock **2** : to confine or exclude by means of a lock **3** : INTERLOCK **4** : to make or become motionless by the interlocking of parts

lock·er \'lä-kər\ *n* **1** : a drawer, cupboard, or compartment for individual storage use **2** : an insulated compartment for storing frozen food

lock·et \'lä-kət\ *n* : a small usu. metal case for a memento worn suspended from a chain or necklace

lock·jaw \'läk-ˌjó\ *n* : a symptom of tetanus marked by spasms of the jaw muscles and inability to open the jaws; *also* : TETANUS

lock·nut \-ˌnət\ *n* **1** : a nut screwed tight on another to prevent it from slacking back **2** : a nut designed to lock itself when screwed tight

lock·out \-ˌaút\ *n* : the suspension of work by an employer during a labor dispute in order to make employees accept the terms being offered

lock·smith \-ˌsmith\ *n* : one who makes or repairs locks

lock·step \-ˌstep\ *n* : a mode of marching in step by a body of men moving in a very close single file

lock·up \-ˌəp\ *n* : JAIL

lo·co \'lō-kō\ *adj* [Sp] *slang* : CRAZY, FRENZIED

lo·co·mo·tion \ˌlō-kə-'mō-shən\ *n* **1** : the act or power of moving from place to place **2** : TRAVEL

¹lo·co·mo·tive \ˌlō-kə-'mō-tiv\ *adj* : of or relating to locomotion or a locomotive

²locomotive *n* : a self-propelled vehicle used to move railroad cars

lo·co·mo·tor \ˌlō-kə-'mō-tər\ *adj* : of or relating to locomotion or organs used in locomotion

lo·co·weed \'lō-kō-ˌwēd\ *n* : any of several leguminous plants of western No. America that are poisonous to livestock

lo·cus \'lō-kəs\ *n, pl* **lo·ci** \'lō-ˌsī\ [L] **1** : PLACE, LOCALITY **2** : the set of all points whose location is determined by stated conditions

lo·cust \'lō-kəst\ *n* **1** : a usu. destructive migratory grasshopper **2** : CICADA **3** : any of various leguminous trees; *also* : the wood of a locust

lo·cu·tion \lō-'kyü-shən\ *n* : a particular form of expression; *also* : PHRASEOLOGY

lode \'lōd\ *n* : ore deposit

lode·stone \-ˌstōn\ *n* : an iron-containing rock with magnetic properties

¹lodge \'läj\ *vb* **lodged; lodg·ing 1** : to provide quarters for; *also* : to settle in a place **2** : CONTAIN **3** : to come to a rest and remain ⟨*lodged* in his throat⟩ **4** : to deposit for safekeeping **5** : to vest (as authority) in an agent **6** : FILE ⟨~ a complaint⟩

²lodge *n* **1** : a house set apart for residence in a special season or by an employee on an estate; *also* : INN **2** : a den or lair esp. of gregarious animals **3** : the meeting place of a branch of a fraternal organization; *also* : the members of such a branch

lodg·er \'lä-jər\ *n* : a person who occupies a rented room in another's house

lodg·ing \'lä-jiŋ\ *n* **1** : DWELLING **2** : a room or suite of rooms in another's house rented as a dwelling place — usu. used in pl.

lodg·ment *or* **lodge·ment** \'läj-mənt\ *n* **1** : a lodging place **2** : the act or manner of lodging **3** : DEPOSIT

loess \'les, 'ləs\ *n* : a usu. yellowish brown loamy deposit believed to be chiefly deposited by the wind

lo–fi \'lō-ˌfī\ *n* : audio production of rough or unpolished sound quality — **lo–fi** *adj*

¹loft \'lóft\ *n* [ME, fr. OE, air, sky, fr. ON *lopt*] **1** : ATTIC **2** : GALLERY ⟨organ ~⟩ **3** : an upper floor (as in a warehouse or barn) esp. when not partitioned **4** : the thickness of a fabric or insulated material (as of a sleeping bag)

²loft *vb* : to strike or throw a ball so that it rises high in the air

lofty \'lóf-tē\ *adj* **loft·i·er; -est 1** : NOBLE; *also* : SUPERIOR ⟨~ ideals⟩ **2** : extremely proud **3** : HIGH, TALL — **loft·i·ly** \'lóf-tə-lē\ *adv* — **loft·i·ness** \-tē-nəs\ *n*

¹log \'lóg, 'läg\ *n* **1** : a bulky piece of a cut or fallen tree **2** : an apparatus for measuring a ship's speed **3** : the daily record of a ship's progress; *also* : a regularly kept record of performance or events ⟨a pilot's ~⟩ ⟨a runner's ~⟩

²log *vb* **logged; log·ging 1** : to cut (trees) for lumber; *also* : to clear (land) of trees in lumbering **2** : to enter in a log **3** : to sail a ship or fly an airplane for (an indicated distance or period of time) **4** : to have (an indicated record) to one's credit : ACHIEVE — **log·ger** \'lό-gər, 'lä-\ *n*

³log *n* : LOGARITHM

lo·gan·ber·ry \'lō-gən-ˌber-ē\ *n* : a red-fruited upright² growing dewberry; *also* : its berry

log·a·rithm \'lό-gə-ˌri-thəm, 'lä-\ *n* : the exponent that indicates the power to which a base is raised to produce a given number ⟨the ~ of 100 to base 10 is 2 since $10^2 = 100$⟩ — **log·a·rith·mic** \ˌlό-gə-'rith-mik, ˌlä-\ *adj*

loge \'lōzh\ *n* **1** : a small compartment; *also* : a box in a theater **2** : a small partitioned area; *also* : the forward section of a theater mezzanine **3** : a raised level of seats in a stadium

log·ger·head \'lό-gər-ˌhed, 'lä-\ *n* : a large sea turtle of subtropical and temperate waters — **at loggerheads** : in a state of quarrelsome disagreement

log·gia \'lō-jē-ə, 'lό-jä\ *n, pl* **loggias** \'lō-jē-əz, 'lό-jäz\ : a roofed open gallery

log·ic \'lä-jik\ *n* **1** : a science that deals with the rules and tests of sound thinking and proof by reasoning **2** : sound reasoning **3** : the arrangement of circuit elements for arithmetical computation in a computer — **log·i·cal** \-ji-kəl\ *adj* — **log·i·cal·ly** \-jik(ə-)lē\ *adv* — **lo·gi·cian** \lō-'ji-shən\ *n*

lo·gis·tics \lō-'jis-tiks\ *n sing or pl* : the procurement, maintenance, and transportation of matériel, facilities, and personnel — **lo·gis·tic** \-tik\ *or* **lo·gis·ti·cal** \-ti-kəl\ *adj*

log·jam \'lόg-ˌjam, 'läg-\ *n* **1** : a deadlocked jumble of logs in a watercourse **2** : DEADLOCK — **logjam** *vt*

logo \'lō-gō\ *n, pl* **log·os** \-gōz\ : an identifying symbol (as for advertising)

logo·type \'lό-gə-ˌtīp, 'lä-\ *n* : LOGO

log·roll·ing \-ˌrō-liŋ\ *n* : the trading of votes by legislators to secure favorable action on projects of individual interest

lo·gy \'lō-gē\ *also* **log·gy** \'lό-gē, 'lä-\ *adj* **lo·gi·er; -est** : deficient in vitality : SLUGGISH

loin \'lóin\ *n* [ME *loyne*, fr. AF *loigne*, fr. VL **lumbea*, fr. L *lumbus*] **1** : the part of the body on each side of the spinal column and between the hip and the lower ribs; *also* : a cut of meat from this part of an animal **2** *pl* : the pubic region; *also* : the organs of reproduction

loin·cloth \-ˌklóth\ *n* : a cloth worn about the loins often as the sole article of clothing in warm climates

loi·ter \'lói-tər\ *vb* **1** : LINGER **2** : to hang around idly : TARRY — **loi·ter·er** *n*
   ♦ **Synonyms** DAWDLE, DALLY, PROCRASTINATE, LAG, TARRY

loll \'läl\ *vb* **1** : DROOP, DANGLE **2** : LOUNGE

lol·la·pa·loo·za \ˌlä-lə-pə-'lü-zə\ *n* : something extraordinarily impressive or outstanding

lol·li·pop *or* **lol·ly·pop** \'lä-li-ˌpäp\ *n* : a lump of hard candy on a stick

lol·ly·gag \'lä-lē-ˌgag\ *vb* **-gagged; -gag·ging** : DAWDLE

Lond *abbr* London

lone \'lōn\ *adj* **1** : SOLITARY ⟨a ~ sentinel⟩ **2** : SOLE, ONLY ⟨the ~ theater in town⟩ **3** : ISOLATED ⟨a ~ tree⟩

lone·ly \ˈlōn-lē\ *adj* **lone·li·er; -est 1** : being without company **2** : UNFREQUENTED ⟨a ~ spot⟩ **3** : LONE-SOME — **lone·li·ness** *n*
lon·er \ˈlō-nər\ *n* : one that avoids others
lone·some \ˈlōn-səm\ *adj* **1** : sad from lack of companionship **2** : REMOTE; *also* : SOLITARY ⟨a ~ road⟩ — **lone·some·ly** *adv* — **lone·some·ness** *n*
¹**long** \ˈloŋ\ *adj* **lon·ger** \ˈloŋ-gər\; **lon·gest** \ˈloŋ-gəst\ **1** : extending for a considerable distance ⟨a ~ corridor⟩; *also* : TALL, ELONGATED ⟨~ legs⟩ **2** : having a specified length **3** : extending over a considerable time; *also* : TEDIOUS ⟨~ lectures⟩ **4** : containing many items in a series ⟨a ~ list⟩ **5** : being a syllable or speech sound of relatively great duration **6** : extending far into the future **7** : well furnished with something — used with *on*
²**long** *adv* : for or during a long time
³**long** *n* : a long period of time
⁴**long** *vb* **longed; long·ing** \ˈloŋ-iŋ\ : to feel a strong desire or wish ◆ **Synonyms** YEARN, HANKER, PINE, HUNGER, THIRST
⁵**long** *abbr* longitude
long·boat \ˈloŋ-ˌbōt\ *n* : a large boat usu. carried by a merchant sailing ship
long·bow \-ˌbō\ *n* : a wooden bow drawn by hand and used esp. by medieval English archers
lon·gev·i·ty \län-ˈje-və-tē\ *n* [LL *longaevitas*, fr. L *longaevus* long-lived, fr. *longus* long + *aevum* age] : a long duration of individual life; *also* : length of life
long·hair \ˈloŋ-ˌher\ *n* **1** : a lover of classical music **2** : HIPPIE **3** : a domestic cat having long outer fur — **long–haired** \-ˌherd\ *or* **long·hair** *adj*
long·hand \-ˌhand\ *n* : HANDWRITING
long·horn \-ˌhorn\ *n* : any of the cattle with long horns formerly common in the southwestern U.S.
long hundredweight *n, Brit* — see WEIGHT table
long·ing \ˈloŋ-iŋ\ *n* : a strong desire esp. for something unattainable — **long·ing·ly** *adv*
lon·gi·tude \ˈlän-jə-ˌtüd, -ˌtyüd\ *n* : angular distance expressed usu. in degrees east or west from the prime meridian through Greenwich, England
lon·gi·tu·di·nal \ˌlän-jə-ˈtü-dᵊn-əl, -ˈtyüd-\ *adj* **1** : extending lengthwise **2** : of or relating to length — **lon·gi·tu·di·nal·ly** *adv*
long–range \ˈloŋ-ˈrānj\ *adj* **1** : relating to or fit for long distances **2** : involving a long period of time
long·shore·man \ˈloŋ-ˌshȯr-mən\ *n* : a laborer at a wharf who loads and unloads cargo
long–suf·fer·ing \-ˈsə-friŋ, -fə-riŋ\ *adj* : patiently enduring lasting offense or hardship
long–term \ˈloŋ-ˈtərm\ *adj* **1** : extending over or involving a long period of time **2** : constituting a financial obligation based on a term usu. of more than 10 years ⟨~ bonds⟩
long·time \ˈloŋ-ˈtīm\ *adj* : of long duration ⟨~ friends⟩
long ton *n* — see WEIGHT table
lon·gueur \loⁿ-ˈgœr\ *n, pl* **longueurs** *same or* -ˈgœrz\ [F, lit., length] : a dull tedious portion (as of a book)
long–wind·ed \ˌloŋ-ˈwin-dəd\ *adj* : tediously long in speaking or writing
loo·fah \ˈlü-fə\ *n* : a sponge consisting of the fibrous skeleton of a gourd
¹**look** \ˈlük\ *vb* **1** : to exercise the power of vision : SEE ⟨~ what I won⟩ **2** : EXPECT **3** : to have an appearance that befits ⟨~*s* the part⟩ **4** : SEEM ⟨~*s* thin⟩ **5** : to direct one's attention : HEED ⟨~ at the sign⟩ **6** : POINT, FACE ⟨~*s* east⟩ **7** : to show a tendency — **look after** : to take care of — **look at 1** : CONSIDER ⟨*looking at* all possibilities⟩ **2** : CONFRONT, FACE ⟨*looking at* stiff fines⟩ — **look for** : EXPECT — **look forward** : to anticipate with pleasure ⟨*look forward* to summer⟩
²**look** *n* **1** : the action of looking : GLANCE **2** : EXPRESSION; *also* : physical appearance **3** : ASPECT
look down *vb* : to regard with contempt — used with *on* or *upon*
looking glass *n* : MIRROR
look·out \ˈlük-ˌaut\ *n* **1** : a person assigned to watch (as on a ship) **2** : a careful watch **3** : VIEW **4** : a matter of concern
look up *vb* **1** : IMPROVE ⟨business is *looking up*⟩ **2** : to search for in or as if in a reference work **3** : to seek out esp. for a brief visit

¹**loom** \ˈlüm\ *n* : a frame or machine for weaving together threads or yarns into cloth
²**loom** *vb* **1** : to come into sight in an unnaturally large, indistinct, or distorted form **2** : to appear in an impressively exaggerated form
loon \ˈlün\ *n* : any of several web-footed black-and-white fish-eating diving birds

loon

loo·ny *or* **loo·ney** \ˈlü-nē\ *adj* **loo·ni·er; -est** : CRAZY, FOOLISH
loony bin *n* : a psychiatric hospital
loop \ˈlüp\ *n* **1** : a fold or doubling of a line through which another line or hook can be passed; *also* : a loop-shaped figure or course ⟨a ~ in a river⟩ **2** : a circular airplane maneuver executed in the vertical plane **3** : a continuously repeated segment of film, music, or sound — **loop** *vb*
loop·er \ˈlü-pər\ *n* : any of numerous rather small hairless moth caterpillars that move with a looping motion
loop·hole \ˈlüp-ˌhōl\ *n* **1** : a small opening in a wall through which firearms may be discharged **2** : a means of escape; *esp* : an ambiguity or omission that allows one to evade the intent of a law or contract
loopy \ˈlü-pē\ *adj* **loop·i·er; -est 1** : having loops **2** : CRAZY, BIZARRE — **loop·i·ly** \-pə-lē\ *adv* — **loop·i·ness** \-pē-nəs\ *n*
¹**loose** \ˈlüs\ *adj* **loos·er; loos·est 1** : not rigidly fastened **2** : free from restraint or obligation **3** : not dense or compact in structure **4** : not chaste : LEWD **5** : SLACK **6** : not precise or exact — **loose·ly** *adv* — **loose·ness** *n*
²**loose** *vb* **loosed; loos·ing 1** : RELEASE **2** : UNTIE **3** : DETACH **4** : DISCHARGE **5** : RELAX, SLACKEN
³**loose** *adv* : LOOSELY
loos·en \ˈlü-sᵊn\ *vb* **1** : FREE **2** : to make or become loose **3** : to relax the severity of ⟨~ rules⟩
loot \ˈlüt\ *n* [Hindi & Urdu *lūṭ*; akin to Skt *luṇṭati* he plunders] : goods taken in war or by robbery : PLUNDER — **loot** *vb* — **loot·er** *n*
¹**lop** \ˈläp\ *vb* **lopped; lop·ping** : to cut branches or twigs from : TRIM; *also* : to cut off
²**lop** *vb* **lopped; lop·ping** : to hang downward; *also* : to flop or sway loosely
lope \ˈlōp\ *n* : an easy bounding gait — **lope** *vb*
lop-sid·ed \ˈläp-ˈsī-dəd\ *adj* **1** : leaning to one side **2** : UNSYMMETRICAL — **lop·sid·ed·ly** *adv* — **lop·sid·ed·ness** *n*
lo·qua·cious \lō-ˈkwā-shəs\ *adj* : excessively talkative — **lo·quac·i·ty** \-ˈkwa-sə-tē\ *n*
¹**lord** \ˈlȯrd\ *n* [ME *loverd, lord*, fr. OE *hlāford*, fr. *hlāf* loaf + *weard* keeper] **1** : one having power and authority over others; *esp* : a person from whom a feudal fee or estate is held **2** *cap* : GOD 1 **3** : a man of rank or high position; *esp* : a British nobleman **4** *pl, cap* : the upper house of the British parliament **5** : a person of great power in some field
²**lord** *vb* : to act like a lord; *esp* : to put on airs — usu. used with *it*
lord chancellor *n, pl* **lords chancellor** : a British officer of state who presides over the House of Lords, serves as head of the British judiciary, and is usu. a leading member of the cabinet
lord·ly \-lē\ *adj* **lord·li·er; -est 1** : DIGNIFIED; *also* : NOBLE **2** : HAUGHTY
lord·ship \-ˌship\ *n* **1** : the rank or dignity of a lord — used as a title **2** : the authority or territory of a lord
Lord's Supper *n* : COMMUNION

lore \'lōr\ *n* : KNOWLEDGE; *esp* : traditional knowledge or belief

lor·gnette \lȯrn-'yet\ *n* [F, fr. *lorgner* to take a sidelong look at, fr. MF, fr. *lorgne* squinting] : a pair of eyeglasses or opera glasses with a handle

lorn \'lȯrn\ *adj* : FORSAKEN, DESOLATE

lor·ry \'lȯr-ē\ *n, pl* **lorries** *chiefly Brit* : MOTORTRUCK

lose \'lüz\ *vb* **lost** \'lȯst\; **los·ing** \'lü-ziŋ\ **1** : DESTROY **2** : to miss from a customary place : MISLAY **3** : to suffer deprivation of **4** : to fail to use : WASTE ⟨no time to ∼⟩ **5** : to fail to win or obtain ⟨∼ the game⟩ **6** : to fail to keep or maintain ⟨∼ his balance⟩ **7** : to wander from ⟨∼ her way⟩ **8** : to get rid of ⟨should ∼ the beard⟩ — **los·er** *n* — **lose it 1** : to go crazy **2** : to fail to keep one's composure

loss \'lȯs\ *n* **1** : RUIN **2** : the harm resulting from losing **3** : something that is lost **4** *pl* : killed, wounded, or captured soldiers **5** : failure to win **6** : an amount by which the cost exceeds the selling price **7** : decrease in amount or degree

loss leader *n* : an article sold at a loss in order to draw customers

lost \'lȯst\ *adj* **1** : not used, won, or claimed **2** : no longer possessed or known **3** : ruined or destroyed physically or morally **4** : DENIED; *also* : HARDENED **5** : unable to find the way; *also* : HELPLESS **6** : ABSORBED, RAPT **7** : not appreciated or understood ⟨his jokes were ∼ on me⟩ **8** : made obscure : OVERLOOKED ⟨∼ in translation⟩ **9** : FUTILE ⟨a ∼ cause⟩

lot \'lät\ *n* **1** : an object used in deciding something by chance; *also* : the use of lots to decide something **2** : SHARE, PORTION; *also* : FORTUNE, FATE **3** : a plot of land **4** : a group of individuals : SET **5** : a considerable quantity

loth *var of* LOATH

lo·ti \'lō-tē\ *n, pl* **ma·lo·ti** \mə-'lō-tē\ — see MONEY table

lo·tion \'lō-shən\ *n* : a liquid preparation for cosmetic and external medicinal use

lot·tery \'lä-tə-rē\ *n, pl* **-ter·ies 1** : a drawing of lots in which prizes are given to the winning names or numbers **2** : a matter determined by chance

lo·tus \'lō-təs\ *n* **1** : a fruit held in Greek legend to cause dreamy contentment and forgetfulness **2** : any of various water lilies represented esp. in ancient Egyptian and Hindu art **3** : any of several leguminous forage plants

loud \'laůd\ *adj* **1** : marked by intensity or volume of sound **2** : CLAMOROUS, NOISY **3** : obtrusive or offensive in color or pattern ⟨a ∼ tie⟩ — **loud** *adv* — **loud·ly** *adv* — **loud·ness** *n*

loud-mouthed \-ˌmaůthd, -ˌmaůthd\ *adj* : given to loud offensive talk

loud·speak·er \-ˌspē-kər\ *n* : a device that changes electrical signals into sound

¹lounge \'laůnj\ *vb* **lounged; loung·ing** : to act or move lazily or listlessly

²lounge *n* **1** : a room with comfortable furniture; *also* : a room (as in a theater) with lounging, smoking, and toilet facilities **2** : a long couch

lour, loury *var of* LOWER, LOWERY

louse \'laůs\ *n, pl* **lice** \'līs\ **1** : any of various small wingless usu. flattened insects parasitic on warm-blooded animals **2** : a plant pest (as an aphid) **3** *pl* **lous·es** \'laů-səz\ : a contemptible person

lousy \'laů-zē\ *adj* **lous·i·er; -est 1** : infested with lice **2** : POOR, INFERIOR **3** : somewhat ill **4** : amply supplied ⟨∼ with money⟩ — **lous·i·ly** \-zə-lē\ *adv* — **lous·i·ness** \-zē-nəs\ *n*

lout \'laůt\ *n* : a stupid awkward fellow — **lout·ish** *adj* — **lout·ish·ly** *adv*

lou·ver *or* **lou·vre** \'lü-vər\ *n* **1** : an opening having parallel slanted slats to allow flow of air but to exclude rain or sun or to provide privacy; *also* : a slat in such an opening **2** : a device with movable slats for controlling the flow of air or light

¹love \'ləv\ *n* **1** : strong affection **2** : warm attachment ⟨∼ of the sea⟩ **3** : attraction based on sexual desire **4** : a beloved person **5** : unselfish loyal and benevolent concern for others **6** : a score of zero in tennis — **love·less** *adj*

²love *vb* **loved; lov·ing 1** : CHERISH **2** : to feel a passion, devotion, or tenderness for **3** : CARESS **4** : to take pleasure in ⟨∼s to play bridge⟩ — **lov·able** *also* **love·able** \'lə-və-bəl\ *adj* — **lov·er** *n*

love·bird \'ləv-ˌbərd\ *n* : any of various small usu. gray or green parrots that seem to show caring behavior for their mates

love·lorn \-ˌlȯrn\ *adj* : deprived of love or of a lover

love·ly \'ləv-lē\ *adj* **love·li·er; -est** : BEAUTIFUL — **love·li·ly** \'ləv-lə-lē\ *adv* — **love·li·ness** *n* — **lovely** *adv*

love·mak·ing \-ˌmā-kiŋ\ *n* **1** : COURTSHIP **2** : sexual activity; *esp* : COPULATION

love·sick \-ˌsik\ *adj* **1** : YEARNING **2** : expressing a lover's longing — **love·sick·ness** *n*

lov·ing \'lə-viŋ\ *adj* **1** : AFFECTIONATE **2** : PAINSTAKING — **lov·ing·ly** *adv*

¹low \'lō\ *vb* : MOO

²low *n* : MOO

³low \'lō\ *adj* **low·er** \'lō-ər\; **low·est** \'lō-əst\ **1** : not high or tall ⟨∼ wall⟩; *also* : DÉCOLLETÉ **2** : situated or passing below the normal level or surface ⟨∼ ground⟩; *also* : marking a nadir **3** : not loud ⟨∼ voice⟩ **4** : being near the equator **5** : humble in status **6** : WEAK; *also* : DEPRESSED **7** : STRICKEN, PROSTRATE **8** : less than usual in number, amount, or value; *also* : of lesser degree than average **9** : falling short of a standard **10** : UNFAVORABLE — **low** *adv* — **low·ness** *n*

⁴low *n* **1** : something that is low **2** : a region of low barometric pressure **3** : the arrangement of gears in an automobile transmission that gives the slowest speed and greatest power

low·ball \'lō-ˌbȯl\ *vb* : to give a deceptively low price, cost estimate, or offer to

low beam *n* : a vehicle headlight beam with short-range focus

low blow *n* : an unprincipled attack

low·brow \'lō-ˌbraů\ *adj* : having little taste or intellectual interest ⟨∼ humor⟩ — **lowbrow** *n*

low–density lipoprotein *n* : LDL

low·down \-ˌdaůn\ *n* : pertinent and esp. guarded information

low–down \-ˌdaůn\ *adj* **1** : MEAN, CONTEMPTIBLE **2** : deeply emotional

low–end \-ˌend\ *adj* : of, relating to, or being the lowest-priced merchandise in a manufacturer's line

¹low·er *also* **lour** \'laů(-ə)r\ *vb* **1** : FROWN **2** : to become dark, gloomy, and threatening — **lower** *also* **lour** *n*

²low·er \'lō-ər\ *adj* **1** : relatively low (as in rank) **2** : SOUTHERN ⟨the ∼ states⟩ **3** : less advanced in the scale of evolutionary development ⟨∼ animals⟩ **4** : situated beneath the earth's surface **5** : constituting the popular and more representative branch of a bicameral legislative body

³low·er \'lō-ər\ *vb* **1** : DROP; *also* : DIMINISH **2** : to let descend by its own weight; *also* : to reduce the height of **3** : to reduce in value, number, or amount **4** : DEGRADE; *also* : HUMBLE

low·er·case \ˌlō-ər-'kās\ *adj* : being a letter that belongs to or conforms to the series a, b, c, etc., rather than A, B, C, etc. — **lowercase** *n*

lower class *n* : a social class occupying a position below the middle class and having the lowest status in a society — **lower–class** \-'klas\ *adj*

low·er·most \'lō-ər-ˌmōst\ *adj* : LOWEST

low·ery *also* **loury** \'laů-(ə-)rē\ *adj* : GLOOMY, LOWERING

lowest common denominator *n* **1** : LEAST COMMON DENOMINATOR **2** : something designed to appeal to a low-brow audience; *also* : such an audience

lowest common multiple *n* : LEAST COMMON MULTIPLE

low–key \'lō-'kē\ *also* **low–keyed** \-'kēd\ *adj* : of low intensity : RESTRAINED

low·land \'lō-lənd, -ˌland\ *n* : low and usu. level country

low·lev·el \'lō-'le-vəl\ *adj* **1** : being of low importance or rank **2** : being or relating to nuclear waste of low concentration

low·life \'lō-ˌlīf\ *n, pl* **low·lifes** \-ˌlīfs\ *also* **low·lives** \-ˌlīvz\ : a person of low social status or moral character

low·ly \'lō-lē\ *adj* **low·li·er; -est 1** : HUMBLE, MEEK **2** : ranking low in some hierarchy — **low·li·ness** *n*

low–rise \'lō-'rīz\ *adj* **1** : having few stories and not equipped with elevators ⟨a ∼ building⟩ **2** : of, relating to, or characterized by low-rise buildings

low–slung \\'lō-ˌsləη\ *adj* : relatively low to the ground or floor ⟨a ~ building⟩ ⟨~ pants⟩
low–tech \\'lō-'tek\ *adj* : technologically simple or unsophisticated
¹lox \\'läks\ *n* : liquid oxygen
²lox *n, pl* **lox** *or* **lox·es** : salmon cured in brine and sometimes smoked
loy·al \\'lȯi(-ə)l\ *adj* [MF, fr. OF *leial, leel,* fr. L *legalis* legal] **1** : faithful in allegiance to one's government **2** : faithful esp. to a cause or ideal : CONSTANT — **loy·al·ly** \\'lȯi-ə-lē\ *adv* — **loy·al·ty** \\'lȯi(-ə)l-tē\ *n*
loy·al·ist \\'lȯi-ə-list\ *n* : one who is or remains loyal to a political party, government, or sovereign
loz·enge \\'lä-zənj\ *n* **1** : a diamond-shaped figure **2** : a small flat often medicated candy
LP *abbr* low pressure
LPG *abbr* liquefied petroleum gas
LPGA *abbr* Ladies Professional Golf Association
LPN \\'el-'pē-'en\ *n* : LICENSED PRACTICAL NURSE
Lr *symbol* Lawrencium
LSD \\'el-(ˌ)es-'dē\ *n* [G *Lysergsäure-Diäthylamid* lysergic acid diethylamide] : an illicit and highly potent hallucinogenic drug derived from ergot or produced synthetically
lt *abbr* light
Lt *abbr* lieutenant
LT *abbr* long ton
LTC *or* **Lt Col** *abbr* lieutenant colonel
Lt Comdr *abbr* lieutenant commander
ltd *abbr* limited
LTG *or* **Lt Gen** *abbr* lieutenant general
LTJG *abbr* lieutenant, junior grade
ltr *abbr* letter
Lu *symbol* lutetium
lu·au \\'lü-ˌau̇\ *n* : a Hawaiian feast
lub *abbr* lubricant; lubricating
lub·ber \\'lə-bər\ *n* **1** : LOUT **2** : an unskilled seaman — **lub·ber·ly** *adj*
lube \\'lüb\ *n* : LUBRICANT; *also* : an application of a lubricant
lu·bri·cant \\'lü-bri-kənt\ *n* : a material capable of reducing friction when applied between moving parts
lu·bri·cate \\'lü-brə-ˌkāt\ *vb* **-cat·ed; -cat·ing** : to apply a lubricant to — **lu·bri·ca·tion** \ˌlü-brə-'kā-shən\ *n* — **lu·bri·ca·tor** \\'lü-brə-ˌkā-tər\ *n*
lu·bri·cious \lü-'bri-shəs\ *or* **lu·bri·cous** \\'lü-bri-kəs\ *adj* **1** : SMOOTH, SLIPPERY **2** : LECHEROUS; *also* : SALACIOUS — **lu·bric·i·ty** \lü-'bri-sə-tē\ *n*
lu·cent \\'lü-sᵊnt\ *adj* **1** : LUMINOUS **2** : CLEAR, LUCID — **lu·cent·ly** *adv*
lu·cerne \lü-'sərn\ *n, chiefly Brit* : ALFALFA
lu·cid \\'lü-səd\ *adj* **1** : SHINING **2** : mentally sound **3** : easily understood — **lu·cid·i·ty** \lü-'si-də-tē\ *n* — **lu·cid·ly** *adv* — **lu·cid·ness** *n*
Lu·ci·fer \\'lü-sə-fər\ *n* [ME, the morning star, a fallen rebel archangel, the Devil, fr. OE, fr. L, the morning star, fr. *lucifer* light-bearing] : DEVIL, SATAN
¹luck \\'lək\ *n* **1** : CHANCE, FORTUNE **2** : good fortune — **luck·less** *adj*
²luck *vb* **1** : to prosper or succeed esp. through chance or good fortune — usu. used with *out* **2** : to come upon something desirable by chance — usu. used with *out, on, onto,* or *into*
luck·i·ly \\'lə-kə-lē\ *adv* **1** : in a lucky manner **2** : FORTUNATELY **2**
lucky \\'lə-kē\ *adj* **luck·i·er; -est** **1** : favored by luck : FORTUNATE **2** : FORTUITOUS **3** : seeming to bring good luck ⟨a ~ penny⟩ — **luck·i·ness** *n*
lu·cra·tive \\'lü-krə-tiv\ *adj* : PROFITABLE ⟨~ business deals⟩ — **lu·cra·tive·ly** *adv* — **lu·cra·tive·ness** *n*
lu·cre \\'lü-kər\ *n* [ME, fr. AF, fr. L *lucrum*] : PROFIT; *also* : MONEY
lu·cu·bra·tion \ˌlü-kyə-'brā-shən, -kə-\ *n* : laborious study : MEDITATION
Lud·dite \\'lə-ˌdīt\ *n* [perh. fr. Ned *Ludd,* 18th cent. Eng. workman who destroyed a knitting frame] : one who is opposed to technological change
lu·di·crous \\'lü-də-krəs\ *adj* : LAUGHABLE, RIDICULOUS — **lu·di·crous·ly** *adv* — **lu·di·crous·ness** *n*
luff \\'ləf\ *vb* : to turn the head of a ship toward the wind
¹lug \\'ləg\ *vb* **lugged; lug·ging** **1** : DRAG, PULL **2** : to carry laboriously

²lug *n* **1** : a projecting piece (as for fastening, support, or traction) **2** : a nut securing a wheel on an automobile
lug·gage \\'lə-gij\ *n* : containers (as suitcases) for carrying personal belongings : BAGGAGE
lu·gu·bri·ous \lu̇-'gü-brē-əs\ *adj* : mournful often to an exaggerated degree — **lu·gu·bri·ous·ly** *adv* — **lu·gu·bri·ous·ness** *n*
Luke \\'lük\ *n* — see BIBLE table
luke·warm \\'lük-'wȯrm\ *adj* **1** : moderately warm : TEPID **2** : not enthusiastic ⟨~ praise⟩ — **luke·warm·ly** *adv*
¹lull \\'ləl\ *vb* **1** : SOOTHE, CALM **2** : to cause to relax vigilance
²lull *n* **1** : a temporary calm (as during a storm) **2** : a temporary drop in activity ⟨a ~ in sales⟩
lul·la·by \\'lə-lə-ˌbī\ *n, pl* **-bies** : a song to lull children to sleep
lu·ma \ˌlü-'mä\ *n* — see *dram* at MONEY table
lum·ba·go \ˌləm-'bā-gō\ *n* : acute or chronic pain in the lower back
lum·bar \\'ləm-bər, -ˌbär\ *adj* : of, relating to, or constituting the loins or the vertebrae between the thoracic vertebrae and sacrum ⟨~ region⟩
¹lum·ber \\'ləm-bər\ *vb* : to move heavily or clumsily
²lumber *n* **1** : surplus or disused articles that are stored away **2** : timber or logs esp. when dressed for use
³lumber *vb* : to cut logs; *also* : to saw logs into lumber — **lum·ber·man** \-mən\ *n*
lum·ber·jack \-ˌjak\ *n* : LOGGER
lum·ber·yard \-ˌyärd\ *n* : a place where lumber is kept for sale
lu·mi·nary \\'lü-mə-ˌner-ē\ *n, pl* **-nar·ies** **1** : a very famous person **2** : a source of light; *esp* : a celestial body
lu·mi·nes·cence \ˌlü-mə-'ne-sᵊns\ *n* : the low-temperature emission of light (as by a chemical or physiological process); *also* : such light — **lu·mi·nes·cent** \-sᵊnt\ *adj*
lu·mi·nous \\'lü-mə-nəs\ *adj* **1** : emitting light; *also* : LIGHTED **2** : CLEAR, INTELLIGIBLE **3** : ILLUSTRIOUS — **lu·mi·nance** \-nəns\ *n* — **lu·mi·nos·i·ty** \ˌlü-mə-'nä-sə-tē\ *n* — **lu·mi·nous·ly** *adv*
lum·mox \\'lə-məks\ *n* : a clumsy person
¹lump \\'ləmp\ *n* **1** : a piece or mass of indefinite size and shape **2** : AGGREGATE, TOTALITY **3** : a usu. abnormal swelling — **lump·ish** *adj* — **lumpy** *adj*
²lump *vb* **1** : to heap together in a lump **2** : to form into lumps
³lump *adj* : not divided into parts ⟨a ~ sum⟩
lump·ec·to·my \ˌləm-'pek-tə-mē\ *n, pl* **-mies** : excision of a breast tumor
lu·na·cy \\'lü-nə-sē\ *n, pl* **-cies** **1** : INSANITY **2** : extreme folly
lu·nar \\'lü-nər\ *adj* : of or relating to the moon
lu·nate \\'lü-ˌnāt\ *adj* : shaped like a crescent
lu·na·tic \\'lü-nə-ˌtik\ *adj* [ME *lunatik,* fr. AF & LL; AF *lunatik,* fr. LL *lunaticus,* fr. L *luna* moon; fr. the belief that lunacy fluctuated with the phases of the moon] **1** : INSANE; *also* : used for insane persons **2** : extremely foolish — **lunatic** *n*
¹lunch \\'lənch\ *n* **1** : a light meal usu. eaten in the middle of the day **2** : the food prepared for a lunch
²lunch *vb* : to eat lunch
lun·cheon \\'lən-chən\ *n* : a usu. formal lunch
lun·cheon·ette \ˌlən-chə-'net\ *n* : a small restaurant serving light lunches
lunch·room \\'lənch-ˌrüm, -ˌru̇m\ *n* **1** : LUNCHEONETTE **2** : a room (as in a school) where lunches are sold and eaten or lunches brought from home may be eaten
lu·nette \lü-'net\ *n* : something shaped like a crescent
lung \\'ləη\ *n* **1** : one of the usu. paired baglike breathing organs in the chest of an air-breathing vertebrate **2** : a mechanical device to promote breathing and make it easier — **lunged** \\'ləηd\ *adj*
lunge \\'lənj\ *n* **1** : a sudden thrust or pass (as with a sword) **2** : a sudden forward stride or leap — **lunge** *vb*
lu·pine \\'lü-pən\ *n* : any of a genus of leguminous plants with long upright clusters of pealike flowers
lu·pus \\'lü-pəs\ *n* [ML, fr. L, wolf] : any of several diseases characterized by skin lesions; *esp* : SYSTEMIC LUPUS ERYTHEMATOSUS
lurch \\'lərch\ *n* : a sudden swaying or tipping movement — **lurch** *vb*

¹**lure** \'lu̇r\ *n* **1** : ENTICEMENT; *also* : APPEAL **2** : an artificial bait for catching fish

²**lure** *vb* **lured; lur·ing** : to draw on with a promise of pleasure or gain

lu·rid \'lu̇r-əd\ *adj* **1** : GRUESOME; *also* : SENSATIONAL **2** : wan and ghostly pale in appearance **3** : shining with the red glow of fire seen through smoke or cloud ✦ *Synonyms* GHASTLY, GRISLY, GRIM, HORRIBLE, MACABRE — **lu·rid·ly** *adv*

lurk \'lərk\ *vb* **1** : to move furtively : SNEAK **2** : to lie concealed

lus·cious \'lə-shəs\ *adj* **1** : having a pleasingly sweet taste or smell **2** : sensually appealing — **lus·cious·ly** *adv* — **lus·cious·ness** *n*

¹**lush** \'ləsh\ *adj* : having or covered with abundant growth ⟨~ pastures⟩

²**lush** *n* : a habitual heavy drinker

lust \'ləst\ *n* **1** : usu. intense or unbridled sexual desire : LASCIVIOUSNESS **2** : an intense longing ⟨a ~ to succeed⟩ — **lust** *vb* — **lust·ful** *adj*

lus·ter *or* **lus·tre** \'ləs-tər\ *n* **1** : a shine or sheen esp. from reflected light **2** : BRIGHTNESS, GLITTER **3** : GLORY, SPLENDOR — **lus·ter·less** *adj* — **lus·trous** \-trəs\ *adj*

lus·tral \'ləs-trəl\ *adj* : serving or intended to purify ⟨~ water⟩

lusty \'ləs-tē\ *adj* **lust·i·er; -est** : full of vitality : ROBUST — **lust·i·ly** \'ləs-tə-lē\ *adv* — **lust·i·ness** \-tē-nəs\ *n*

lute \'lüt\ *n* : a stringed musical instrument with a large pear-shaped body and a fretted fingerboard — **lu·te·nist** *or* **lu·ta·nist** \'lü-tə-nist\ *n*

lu·te·tium *also* **lu·te·cium** \lü-'tē-shē-əm, -shəm\ *n* : a metallic chemical element

Lu·ther·an \'lü-thə-rən\ *n* : a member of a Protestant denomination adhering to the doctrines of Martin Luther — **Lu·ther·an·ism** \-rə-,ni-zəm\ *n*

lux·u·ri·ant \,ləg-'zhu̇r-ē-ənt, ,lək-'shu̇r-\ *adj* **1** : yielding or growing abundantly : LUSH, PRODUCTIVE ⟨~ vegetation⟩ **2** : abundantly rich and varied; *also* : FLORID ⟨a ~ fabric⟩ ✦ *Synonyms* EXUBERANT, LAVISH, OPULENT, PRODIGAL, PROFUSE, RIOTOUS — **lux·u·ri·ance** \-ē-əns\ *n* — **lux·u·ri·ant·ly** *adv*

lux·u·ri·ate \-ē-,āt\ *vb* **-at·ed; -at·ing** **1** : to grow profusely **2** : REVEL

lux·u·ry \'lək-shə-rē, 'ləg-zhə-\ *n, pl* **-ries** **1** : great ease and comfort **2** : something adding to pleasure or comfort but not absolutely necessary — **lux·u·ri·ous** \,ləg-'zhu̇r-ē-əs, ,lək-'shu̇r-\ *adj* — **lux·u·ri·ous·ly** *adv*

lv *abbr* leave

lwei \lə-'wā\ *n, pl* **lwei** — see *kwanza* at MONEY table

LWV *abbr* League of Women Voters

¹**-ly** \lē\ *adj suffix* **1** : like in appearance, manner, or nature ⟨queen*ly*⟩ **2** : characterized by regular recurrence in (specified) units of time : every ⟨hour*ly*⟩ ⟨week*ly*⟩

²**-ly** *adv suffix* **1** : in a (specified) manner ⟨slow*ly*⟩ **2** : from a (specified) point of view ⟨grammatical*ly*⟩

ly·ce·um \lī-'sē-əm, 'lī-sē-\ *n* **1** : a hall for public lectures **2** : an association providing public lectures, concerts, and entertainments

ly·chee *or* **li·tchi** \'lē-chē, 'lī-\ *n* [Ch(Beijing) *lìzhī*] **1** : an oval fruit with a hard scaly outer covering, a small hard seed, and edible flesh **2** : an Asian tree bearing lychees

lye \'lī\ *n* : a corrosive alkaline substance used esp. in making soap

ly·ing \'lī-iŋ\ *adj* : UNTRUTHFUL, FALSE

ly·ing–in \,lī-iŋ-'in\ *n, pl* **lyings–in** *or* **lying–ins** : the state during and consequent to childbirth : CONFINEMENT

Lyme disease \'līm-\ *n* [*Lyme*, Connecticut, where it was first reported] : an acute inflammatory disease that is caused by a spirochete transmitted by ticks, is characterized usu. by chills and fever, and if left untreated may result in joint pain, arthritis, and cardiac and neurological disorders

lymph \'limf\ *n* : a usu. clear fluid consisting chiefly of blood plasma and white blood cells, circulating in thin-walled tubes (**lymphatic vessels**), and bathing the body tissues — **lym·phat·ic** \lim-'fa-tik\ *adj*

lymph·ade·nop·a·thy \,lim-,fa-də-'nä-pə-thē\ *n, pl* **-thies** : abnormal enlargement of the lymph nodes

lymph node *n* : any of the rounded masses of lymphoid tissue surrounded by a capsule of connective tissue

lym·pho·cyte \'lim-fə-,sīt\ *n* : any of the white blood cells arising from lymphoid tissue that are typically found in lymph and blood and that include the cellular mediators (as a B cell or a T cell) of immunity — **lym·pho·cyt·ic** \,lim-fə-'si-tik\ *adj*

lym·phoid \'lim-,fȯid\ *adj* **1** : of, relating to, or being tissue (as of the lymph nodes) containing lymphocytes **2** : of, relating to, or resembling lymph

lym·pho·ma \lim-'fō-mə\ *n, pl* **-mas** *also* **-ma·ta** \-mə-tə\ : a usu. malignant tumor of lymphoid tissue

lynch \'linch\ *vb* : to put to death by mob action without legal sanction or due process of law — **lynch·er** *n*

lynx \'liŋks\ *n, pl* **lynx** *or* **lynx·es** : any of several wildcats with a short tail, long legs, and usu. tufted ears

lyre \'lī(-ə)r\ *n* : a stringed musical instrument of the harp class having a U-shaped frame and used by the ancient Greeks

¹**lyr·ic** \'lir-ik\ *n* **1** : a lyric poem **2** *pl* : the words of a popular song — **lyr·i·cal** \-i-kəl\ *adj*

²**lyric** *adj* **1** : suitable for singing : MELODIC **2** : expressing direct and usu. intense personal emotion

ly·ser·gic acid di·eth·yl·am·ide \lə-'sər-jik . . . ,dī-,e-thə-'la-,mīd, lī-, -'la-məd\ *n* : LSD

LZ *abbr* landing zone

¹**m** \'em\ *n, pl* **m's** *or* **ms** \'emz\ *often cap* **1** : the 13th letter of the English alphabet **2** : one thousand in Roman numerals

²**m** *abbr, often cap* **1** Mach **2** male **3** married **4** masculine **5** medium **6** [L *meridies*] noon **7** meter **8** mile **9** [L *mille*] thousand **10** minute **11** month **12** moon

ma \'mä\ *n* : MOTHER

MA *abbr* **1** [ML *magister artium*] master of arts **2** Massachusetts **3** mental age

ma'am \'mam, *after* "*yes*" *often* əm\ *n* : MADAM

Mac *abbr* Machabees

Mac *or* **Macc** *abbr* Maccabees

ma·ca·bre \mə-'käb; 'kä-brə, -bər\ *adj* [F] **1** : having death as a subject **2** : GRUESOME **3** : HORRIBLE

mac·ad·am \mə-'ka-dəm\ *n* [John L. *McAdam* †1836 Brit. engineer] : a roadway or pavement of small closely packed broken stone — **mac·ad·am·ize** \-də-,mīz\ *vb*

mac·a·da·mia nut \,ma-kə-'dā-mē-ə-\ *n* : a hard-shelled richly-flavored nut of any of several Australian trees

ma·caque \mə-'kak, -'käk\ *n* : any of a genus of short-tailed chiefly Asian monkeys; *esp* : RHESUS MONKEY

mac·a·ro·ni \,ma-kə-'rō-nē\ *n* **1** : pasta made chiefly of wheat flour and shaped in the form of slender tubes **2** *pl* **-nis** *or* **-nies** : FOP, DANDY

mac·a·roon \,ma-kə-'rün\ *n* : a small cookie made chiefly of egg whites, sugar, and ground almonds or coconut

ma·caw \mə-'kȯ\ *n* : any of numerous parrots of Central and So. America

Mac·ca·bees \'ma-kə-,bēz\ *n* — see BIBLE table

¹**mace** \'mās\ *n* : a spice made from the fibrous coating of the nutmeg

²**mace** *n* **1** : a heavy often spiked club used as a weapon esp. in the Middle Ages **2** : an ornamental staff carried as a symbol of authority

mac·er·ate \'ma-sə-ˌrāt\ *vb* **-at·ed; -at·ing** **1** : to cause to waste away **2** : to soften by steeping or soaking so as to separate the parts — **mac·er·a·tion** \ˌma-sə-'rā-shən\ *n*

Mac·Guf·fin *or* **Mc·Guf·fin** \mə-'gə-fən\ *n* : an object, event, or character whose main purpose is to advance the plot of a motion picture

mach *abbr* machine; machinery; machinist

Mach \'mäk\ *n* : a speed expressed by a Mach number

Mach·a·bees \'ma-kə-ˌbēz\ *n* : MACCABEES

ma·chete \mə-'she-tē\ *n* : a large heavy knife used for cutting sugarcane and underbrush and as a weapon

Ma·chi·a·vel·lian \ˌma-kē-ə-'ve-lē-ən\ *adj* [Niccolò *Machiavelli*, †1527 Ital. political philosopher] : characterized by cunning, duplicity, and bad faith — **Ma·chi·a·vel·lian·ism** *n*

mach·i·na·tion \ˌma-kə-'nā-shən, ˌma-shə-\ *n* : an act of planning *esp.* to do harm; *esp* : PLOT — **mach·i·nate** \'ma-kə-ˌnāt, 'ma-shə-\ *vb*

¹ma·chine \mə-'shēn\ *n* **1** : CONVEYANCE, VEHICLE; *esp* : AUTOMOBILE **2** : a combination of mechanical parts that transmit forces, motion, and energy one to another **3** : an instrument (as a lever) for transmitting or modifying force or motion **4** : an electrical, electronic, or mechanical device for performing a task ⟨a sewing ∼⟩ **5** : a highly organized political group under the leadership of a boss or small clique

²machine *vb* **ma·chined; ma·chin·ing** : to shape or finish by machine-operated tools — **ma·chin·able** \-'shē-nə-bəl\ *adj*

machine gun *n* : an automatic gun capable of rapid continuous firing — **machine–gun** *vb* — **machine gunner** *n*

machine language *n* : the set of symbolic instruction codes used to represent operations and data in a machine (as a computer)

machine–readable *adj* : directly usable by a computer

ma·chin·ery \mə-'shē-nə-rē\ *n, pl* **-er·ies** **1** : MACHINES; *also* : the working parts of a machine **2** : the means by which something is done

ma·chin·ist \mə-'shē-nist\ *n* : a person who makes or works on machines

ma·chis·mo \mä-'chēz-(ˌ)mō, -'chiz-\ *n* : a strong or exaggerated pride in one's masculinity

Mach number \'mäk-\ *n* : a number representing the ratio of the speed of a body (as an aircraft) to the speed of sound in the surrounding atmosphere

ma·cho \'mä-chō\ *adj* [Sp, lit., male, fr. L *masculus*] : characterized by machismo

mack·er·el \'ma-kə-rəl\ *n, pl* **mackerel** *or* **mackerels** : a No. Atlantic food fish greenish above and silvery below

mack·i·naw \'ma-kə-ˌnó\ *n* : a short heavy plaid coat

mack·in·tosh *also* **mac·in·tosh** \'ma-kən-ˌtäsh\ *n* **1** *chiefly Brit* : RAINCOAT **2** : a lightweight waterproof fabric

mac·ra·mé *also* **mac·ra·me** \'ma-krə-ˌmā\ *n* [ultim. fr. Ar *miqrama* coverlet] : a coarse lace or fringe made by knotting threads or cords in a geometrical pattern

¹mac·ro \'ma-(ˌ)krō\ *adj* : very large; *also* : involving large quantities or being on a large scale

²macro *n, pl* **macros** : a single computer instruction that stands for a sequence of operations

mac·ro·bi·ot·ic \ˌma-krō-bī-'ä-tik, -bē-\ *adj* : relating to or being a very restricted diet (as one containing chiefly whole cereals or grains)

mac·ro·cosm \'ma-krə-ˌkä-zəm\ *n* : the great world : UNIVERSE

ma·cron \'mā-ˌkrän, 'ma-\ *n* : a mark ⁻ placed over a vowel (as in \mäk\) to show that the vowel is long

mac·ro·scop·ic \ˌma-krə-'skä-pik\ *adj* : visible to the naked eye — **mac·ro·scop·i·cal·ly** \-pi-k(ə-)lē\ *adv*

mac·u·la \'ma-kyə-lə\ *n, pl* **-lae** \-ˌlē, -ˌlī\ *also* **-las** : an anatomical spot distinguishable from surrounding tissues — **mac·u·lar** \-lər\ *adj*

mad \'mad\ *adj* **mad·der; mad·dest** **1** : disordered in mind : INSANE **2** : being rash and foolish **3** : FURIOUS, ENRAGED **4** : carried away by enthusiasm **5** : RABID **6** : marked by wild gaiety and merriment **7** : FRANTIC — **mad·ly** *adv* — **mad·ness** *n*

mad·am \'ma-dəm\ *n* **1** *pl* **mes·dames** \mā-'däm\ — used as a form of polite address to a woman **2** *pl* **mad·ams** : the female head of a house of prostitution

ma·dame \mə-'dam, *before a surname also* 'ma-dəm\ *n, pl*

mes·dames \mā-'däm\ : MISTRESS — used as a title equivalent to *Mrs.* for a married woman not of English-speaking nationality

mad·cap \'mad-ˌkap\ *adj* : WILD, RECKLESS ⟨a ∼ scheme⟩ — **madcap** *n*

mad cow disease *n* : a fatal encephalopathy of cattle that affects the nervous system causing the brain tissue to resemble a porous sponge

mad·den \'ma-dᵊn\ *vb* : to make mad — **mad·den·ing·ly** *adv*

mad·der \'ma-dər\ *n* : a Eurasian herb with yellow flowers and fleshy red roots; *also* : its root or a dye prepared from it

made *past and past part of* MAKE

Ma·dei·ra \mə-'dir-ə\ *n* : an amber-colored dessert wine

ma·de·moi·selle \ˌma-də-mə-'zel, -mwə-, mam-'zel\ *n, pl* **ma·de·moi·selles** \-'zelz\ *or* **mes·de·moi·selles** \ˌmā-də-me-'zel, -mwə-\ : an unmarried girl or woman — used as a title for an unmarried woman not of English-speaking nationality

made–to–measure *adj* : CUSTOM-MADE

made–up \'mād-'əp\ *adj* **1** : fancifully conceived or falsely devised **2** : marked by the use of makeup

mad·house \'mad-ˌhaús\ *n* **1** : a place for the detention and care of the insane **2** : a place of great uproar

mad·man \'mad-ˌman, -mən\ *n* : LUNATIC

Ma·don·na \mə-'dä-nə\ *n* : a representation (as a picture or statue) of the Virgin Mary

ma·dras \'ma-drəs; mə-'dras, -'dräs\ *n* [*Madras*, India] : a fine usu. cotton fabric with various designs (as plaid)

ma·dras·sa *or* **ma·dra·sa** \mə-'dra-sə, -'drä-\ *n* : a Muslim school, college, or university that is often part of a mosque

mad·ri·gal \'ma-dri-gəl\ *n* [It *madrigale*] **1** : a short lyrical poem in a strict poetic form **2** : an elaborate part-song esp. of the 16th and 17th centuries

mad·wom·an \'mad-ˌwù-mən\ *n* : a woman who is insane

mael·strom \'māl-strəm\ *n* **1** : a violent whirlpool **2** : TUMULT

mae·stro \'mī-strō\ *n, pl* **maestros** *or* **mae·stri** \-ˌstrē\ [It] : a master in an art; *esp* : an eminent composer, conductor, or teacher of music

Ma·fia \'mä-fē-ə\ *n* [It] : a secret criminal society of Sicily or Italy; *also* : a similar organization elsewhere

ma·fi·o·so \ˌmä-fē-'ō-(ˌ)sō\ *n, pl* **-si** \-(ˌ)sē\ : a member of the Mafia

¹mag \'mag\ *n* : MAGAZINE

²mag *abbr* **1** magnetism **2** magneto **3** magnitude

mag·a·zine \'ma-gə-ˌzēn\ *n* [MF, fr. Old Occitan, fr. Ar *makhāzin*, pl. of *makhzan* storehouse] **1** : a storehouse esp. for military supplies **2** : a place for keeping gunpowder in a fort or ship **3** : a publication usu. containing stories, articles, or poems and issued periodically **4** : a container in a gun for holding cartridges; *also* : a chamber (as on a camera) for film

ma·gen·ta \mə-'jen-tə\ *n* : a deep purplish red color

mag·got \'ma-gət\ *n* : the legless wormlike larva of a dipteran fly — **mag·goty** *adj*

ma·gi \'mā-ˌjī\ *n pl, often cap* : the three wise men from the East who paid homage to the infant Jesus

mag·ic \'ma-jik\ *n* **1** : the use of means (as charms or spells) believed to have supernatural power over natural forces **2** : an extraordinary power or influence seemingly from a supernatural force **3** : SLEIGHT OF HAND — **magic** *adj* — **mag·i·cal** \-ji-kəl\ *adj* — **mag·i·cal·ly** \-ji-k(ə-)lē\ *adv*

ma·gi·cian \mə-'ji-shən\ *n* : a person skilled in magic

mag·is·te·ri·al \ˌma-jə-'stir-ē-əl\ *adj* **1** : AUTHORITATIVE **2** : of or relating to a magistrate or a magistrate's office or duties

mag·is·tral \'ma-jə-strəl\ *adj* : AUTHORITATIVE

mag·is·trate \'ma-jə-ˌstrāt\ *n* : an official entrusted with administration of the laws — **mag·is·tra·cy** \-strə-sē\ *n*

mag·lev \'mag-lev\ *n* **1** : the use of magnetic fields to float an object above a solid surface **2** : a train using maglev technology

mag·ma \'mag-mə\ *n* : molten rock material within the earth — **mag·mat·ic** \mag-'ma-tik\ *adj*

mag·nan·i·mous \mag-'na-nə-məs\ *adj* **1** : showing or suggesting a lofty and courageous spirit **2** : NOBLE, GENEROUS — **mag·na·nim·i·ty** \ˌmag-nə-'ni-mə-tē\ *n* — **mag·nan·i·mous·ly** *adv* — **mag·nan·i·mous·ness** *n*

mag·nate \'mag-ˌnāt\ n : a person of rank, influence, or distinction

mag·ne·sia \mag-'nē-shə, -zhə\ n [NL, fr. *magnes carneus*, a white earth, lit., flesh magnet] : a light white oxide of magnesium used as a laxative

mag·ne·sium \mag-'nē-zē-əm, -zhəm\ n : a silver-white light malleable metallic chemical element

mag·net \'mag-nət\ n 1 : LODESTONE 2 : a body that is able to attract iron 3 : something that attracts

mag·net·ic \mag-'ne-tik\ adj 1 : having an unusual ability to attract ⟨a ~ leader⟩ 2 : of or relating to a magnet or magnetism 3 : magnetized or capable of being magnetized — **mag·net·i·cal·ly** \-ti-k(ə-)lē\ adv

magnetic disk n : DISK 3

magnetic levitation n : MAGLEV 1

magnetic north n : the northerly direction in the earth's magnetic field indicated by the north-seeking pole of a compass needle

magnetic resonance imaging n : a noninvasive diagnostic technique that produces computerized images of internal body tissues based on electromagnetically induced activity of atoms within the body

magnetic tape n : a ribbon coated with a magnetic material on which information (as sound) may be stored

mag·ne·tise *Brit var of* MAGNETIZE

mag·ne·tism \'mag-nə-ˌti-zəm\ n 1 : the power (as of a magnet) to attract iron 2 : the science that deals with magnetic phenomena 3 : an ability to attract or charm

mag·ne·tite \'mag-nə-ˌtīt\ n : a black mineral that is an important iron ore

mag·ne·tize \'mag-nə-ˌtīz\ vb **-tized; -tiz·ing** 1 : to induce magnetic properties in 2 : to attract like a magnet : CHARM — **mag·ne·tiz·able** adj — **mag·ne·ti·za·tion** \ˌmag-nə-tə-'zā-shən\ n — **mag·ne·tiz·er** n

mag·ne·to \mag-'nē-tō\ n, pl **-tos** : a generator used to produce sparks in an internal combustion engine

mag·ne·tom·e·ter \ˌmag-nə-'tä-mə-tər\ n : an instrument for measuring the strength of a magnetic field

mag·ne·to·sphere \mag-'nē-tə-ˌsfir, -'ne-\ n : a region around a celestial object (as the earth) in which charged particles are trapped by its magnetic field — **mag·ne·to·spher·ic** \-ˌnē-tə-'sfir-ik, -'sfer-\ adj

mag·ni·fi·ca·tion \ˌmag-nə-fə-'kā-shən\ n 1 : the act of magnifying 2 : the amount by which an optical lens or instrument magnifies

mag·nif·i·cent \mag-'ni-fə-sənt\ adj 1 : characterized by grandeur or beauty : SPLENDID 2 : EXALTED, NOBLE ✦ *Synonyms* IMPOSING, STATELY, GRAND, MAJESTIC — **mag·nif·i·cence** \-səns\ n — **mag·nif·i·cent·ly** adv

mag·nif·i·co \mag-'ni-fi-ˌkō\ n, pl **-coes** or **-cos** 1 : a nobleman of Venice 2 : a person of high position

mag·ni·fy \'mag-nə-ˌfī\ vb **-fied; -fy·ing** 1 : EXTOL, LAUD; *also* : to cause to be held in greater esteem 2 : INTENSIFY; *also* : EXAGGERATE 3 : to enlarge in fact or in appearance ⟨a microscope *magnifies* an object⟩ — **mag·ni·fi·er** \'mag-nə-ˌfī(-ə)r\ n

mag·nil·o·quent \mag-'ni-lə-kwənt\ adj : characterized by an exalted and often bombastic style or manner — **mag·nil·o·quence** \-kwəns\ n

mag·ni·tude \'mag-nə-ˌtüd, -tyüd\ n 1 : greatness of size or extent 2 : SIZE 3 : QUANTITY 4 : a number representing the brightness of a celestial body 5 : a number representing the intensity of an earthquake

mag·no·lia \mag-'nōl-yə\ n : any of a genus of usu. spring-flowering shrubs and trees with large often fragrant flowers

mag·num opus \'mag-nəm-'ō-pəs\ n [L] : the greatest achievement of an artist or writer

mag·pie \'mag-ˌpī\ n : any of various long-tailed often black-and-white birds related to the jays

Mag·yar \'mag-ˌyär, 'mäg-; 'mä-ˌjär\ n : a member of the dominant people of Hungary — **Magyar** adj

ma·ha·ra·ja or **ma·ha·ra·jah** \ˌmä-hə-'rä-jə\ n : a Hindu prince ranking above a raja

ma·ha·ra·ni or **ma·ha·ra·nee** \-'rä-nē\ n 1 : the wife of a maharaja 2 : a Hindu princess ranking above a rani

ma·ha·ri·shi \ˌmä-hə-'rē-shē\ n : a Hindu teacher of mystical knowledge

ma·hat·ma \mə-'hät-mə, -'hat-\ n [Skt *mahātman*, fr. *mahātman* great-souled, fr. *mahat* great + *ātman* soul] : a person revered for high-mindedness, wisdom, and selflessness

Ma·hi·can \mə-'hē-kən\ or **Mo·hi·can** \mō-, mə-\ n, pl **-can** or **-cans** : a member of an American Indian people of the upper Hudson River valley

ma·hog·a·ny \mə-'hä-gə-nē\ n, pl **-nies** : the reddish wood of any of various chiefly tropical trees that is used in furniture; *also* : a tree yielding this wood

ma·hout \mə-'haút\ n [Hindi & Urdu *mahāwat, mahāut*] : a keeper and driver of an elephant

maid \'mād\ n 1 : an unmarried girl or young woman 2 : MAIDSERVANT; *also* : a woman or girl employed to do domestic work

¹**maid·en** \'mā-dᵊn\ n : MAID 1 — **maid·en·ly** adj

²**maiden** adj 1 : UNMARRIED; *also* : VIRGIN 2 : of, relating to, or befitting a maiden 3 : FIRST ⟨a ship's ~ voyage⟩

maid·en·hair fern \-ˌher-\ n : any of a genus of ferns with delicate feathery fronds

maid·en·head \'mā-dᵊn-ˌhed\ n 1 : VIRGINITY 2 : HYMEN

maid·en·hood \-ˌhùd\ n : the condition or time of being a maiden

maid–in–waiting n, pl **maids–in–waiting** : a young woman appointed to attend a queen or princess

maid of honor : a bride's principal unmarried wedding attendant

maid·ser·vant \'mād-ˌsər-vənt\ n : a girl or woman who is a servant

¹**mail** \'māl\ n [ME *male* bag, fr. AF, of Gmc origin] 1 : material sent or carried in the postal system 2 : a nation's postal system — often used in pl. 3 : E-MAIL

²**mail** vb : to send by mail

³**mail** n [ME *maille* metal link, mail, fr. AF, fr. L *macula* spot, mesh] : armor made of metal links or plates

mail·box \'māl-ˌbäks\ n 1 : a public box for the collection of mail 2 : a private box for the delivery of mail

mail·man \-ˌman\ n : a man who delivers mail

maim \'mām\ vb : to mutilate, disfigure, or wound seriously

¹**main** \'mān\ n 1 : FORCE ⟨with might and ~⟩ 2 : MAINLAND; *also* : HIGH SEA 3 : the chief part 4 : a principal pipe, duct, or circuit of a utility system

²**main** adj 1 : CHIEF, PRINCIPAL ⟨the ~ idea⟩ 2 : fully exerted ⟨~ force⟩ 3 : expressing the chief predication in a complex sentence ⟨the ~ clause⟩ — **main·ly** adv

main·frame \'mān-ˌfrām\ n : a large fast computer

main·land \-ˌland, -lənd\ n : a continuous body of land constituting the chief part of a country or continent

main·line \-ˌlīn\ vb, slang : to inject a narcotic drug into a vein

main line n : a principal highway or railroad line

main·mast \'mān-ˌmast, -məst\ n : the principal mast on a sailing ship

main·sail \-ˌsāl, -səl\ n : the largest sail on the mainmast

main·spring \-ˌspriŋ\ n 1 : the chief spring in a mechanism (as of a watch) 2 : the chief motive, agent, or cause

main·stay \-ˌstā\ n 1 : a stay running from the head of the mainmast to the foot of the foremast 2 : a chief support

main·stream \-ˌstrēm\ n : a prevailing current or direction of activity or influence — **mainstream** adj

main·tain \mān-'tān\ vb [ME *mainteinen*, fr. AF *maintenir, mayntener*, fr. ML *manutenēre*, fr. L *manu tenēre* to hold in the hand] 1 : to keep in an existing state (as of repair) 2 : to sustain against opposition or danger 3 : to continue in : CARRY ON 4 : to provide for : SUPPORT 5 : ASSERT ⟨~ed his innocence⟩ — **main·tain·abil·i·ty** \-ˌtā-nə-'bi-lə-tē\ n — **main·tain·able** \-'tā-nə-bəl\ adj — **main·te·nance** \'mān-tə-nəns\ n

main·top \'mān-ˌtäp\ n : a platform at the head of the mainmast of a square-rigged ship

mai·son·ette \ˌmā-zə-'net\ n 1 : a small house 2 : an apartment often on two floors

mai tai \'mī-ˌtī\ n : a cocktail made with liquors and fruit juices

maî·tre d' \ˌmā-trə-'dē, ˌme-\ n, pl **maître d's** or **maitre d's** \-'dēz\ : MAÎTRE D'HÔTEL

maî·tre d'hô·tel \ˌmā-trə-dō-'tel, ˌme-\ n, pl **maîtres d'hôtel** *same*\ [F, lit., master of house] 1 : MAJORDOMO 2 : HEADWAITER

maize \'māz\ n : INDIAN CORN

Maj *abbr* major

maj·es·ty \'ma-jə-stē\ *n, pl* **-ties** **1** : sovereign power, authority, or dignity; *also* : the person of a sovereign — used as a title **2** : GRANDEUR, SPLENDOR — **ma·jes·tic** \mə-'jes-tik\ *adj* — **ma·jes·ti·cal·ly** \-ti-k(ə-)lē\ *adv*

Maj Gen *abbr* Major General

ma·jol·i·ca \mə-'jä-li-kə\ *also* **ma·iol·i·ca** \-'yä-\ *n* : any of several faiences; *esp* : an Italian tin-glazed pottery

¹ma·jor \'mā-jər\ *adj* **1** : greater in number, extent, or importance ⟨a ~ poet⟩ **2** : notable or conspicuous in effect or scope ⟨a ~ improvement⟩ **3** : SERIOUS ⟨a ~ illness⟩ **4** : having half steps between the 3d and 4th and the 7th and 8th degrees ⟨~ scale⟩; *also* : based on a major scale ⟨~ key⟩ ⟨~ chord⟩

²major *n* **1** : a commissioned officer (as in the army) ranking next below a lieutenant colonel **2** : an academic subject chosen as a field of specialization; *also* : a student specializing in such a field ⟨a history ~⟩

³major *vb* : to pursue an academic major

ma·jor·do·mo \mā-jər-'dō-mō\ *n, pl* **-mos** [Sp *mayordomo* or obs. It *maiordomo*, fr. ML *major domus*, lit., chief of the house] **1** : a head steward **2** : BUTLER

ma·jor·ette \mā-jə-'ret\ *n* : DRUM MAJORETTE

major general *n* : a commissioned officer (as in the army) ranking next below a lieutenant general

ma·jor·i·ty \mə-'jȯr-ə-tē\ *n, pl* **-ties** **1** : the age at which full civil rights are accorded; *also* : the status of one who has attained this age **2** : a number greater than half of a total; *also* : the excess of this greater number over the remainder **3** : the rank of a major

ma·jus·cule \'ma-jəs-ˌkyül, mə-'jəs-\ *n* : a large letter (as a capital)

Ma·kah \'mä-kä\ *n, pl* **Makah** *or* **Makahs** : a member of an American Indian people of the northwest coast of No. America

¹make \'māk\ *vb* **made** \'mād\; **mak·ing** **1** : to cause to exist, occur, or appear; *also* : DESTINE ⟨was *made* to be an actor⟩ **2** : FASHION ⟨~ a dress⟩; *also* : COMPOSE **3** : to formulate in the mind ⟨~ plans⟩ **4** : CONSTITUTE ⟨house *made* of stone⟩ **5** : to compute to be **6** : to set in order : PREPARE ⟨~ a bed⟩ **7** : to cause to be or become; *also* : APPOINT **8** : ENACT; *also* : EXECUTE ⟨~ a will⟩ **9** : CONCLUDE ⟨didn't know what to ~ of it⟩ **10** : CARRY OUT, PERFORM ⟨~ a gesture⟩ **11** : COMPEL **12** : to assure the success of ⟨will ~ us or break us⟩ **13** : to amount to in significance ⟨~s no difference⟩ **14** : to be capable of developing or being fashioned into **15** : REACH, ATTAIN; *also* : GAIN **16** : to start out : GO **17** : to have weight or effect ⟨courtesy ~s for safer driving⟩ **♦ Synonyms** FORM, SHAPE, FABRICATE, MANUFACTURE — **mak·er** *n* — **make believe** : PRETEND — **make do** : to manage with the means at hand — **make fun of** : RIDICULE, MOCK — **make good** **1** : INDEMNIFY ⟨*make good* the loss⟩; *also* : to carry out successfully ⟨*make* good his promise⟩ **2** : SUCCEED — **make way** **1** : to give room for passing, entering, or occupying **2** : to make progress

²make *n* **1** : the manner or style of construction; *also* : BRAND **3** **2** : MAKEUP **3** : the action of manufacturing — **on the make** : in search of wealth, social status, or sexual adventure

¹make–be·lieve \'māk-bə-ˌlēv\ *n* : a pretending that what is not real is real

²make–believe *adj* : IMAGINED, PRETENDED

make–do \-ˌdü\ *adj* : MAKESHIFT

make out *vb* **1** : to draw up in writing ⟨*make out* a list⟩ **2** : to find or grasp the meaning of ⟨can you *make* that *out*⟩ **3** : to represent as being **4** : to pretend to be true **5** : DISCERN ⟨*make out* a ship in the fog⟩ **6** : GET ALONG, FARE ⟨*make out* well in life⟩ **7** : to engage in amorous kissing and caressing

make over *vb* : REMAKE, REMODEL — **make·over** \'mā-ˌkō-vər\ *n*

make·shift \'māk-ˌshift\ *n* : a temporary expedient — **makeshift** *adj*

make·up \'mā-ˌkəp\ *n* **1** : the way in which something is put together; *also* : physical, mental, and moral constitution **2** : cosmetics esp. for the face; *also* : materials (as wigs and cosmetics) used in making up

make up *vb* **1** : FORM, COMPOSE **2** : to compensate for a deficiency **3** : SETTLE ⟨*made up* my mind⟩ **4** : INVENT,

IMPROVISE **5** : to become reconciled **6** : to put on makeup (as for a play)

make–work \'māk-ˌwərk\ *n* : BUSYWORK

mak·ings \'mā-kiŋz\ *n pl* : the material from which something is made

Mal *abbr* Malachi

Mal·a·chi \'ma-lə-ˌkī\ *n* — see BIBLE table

Mal·a·chi·as \ˌma-lə-'kī-əs\ *n* : MALACHI

mal·a·chite \'ma-lə-ˌkīt\ *n* : a green mineral that is a carbonate of copper used for making ornamental objects

mal·adapt·ed \ˌma-lə-'dap-təd\ *adj* : poorly suited to a particular use, purpose, or situation

mal·ad·just·ed \ˌma-lə-'jəs-təd\ *adj* : poorly or inadequately adjusted (as to one's environment) — **mal·ad·just·ment** \-'jəst-mənt\ *n*

mal·adroit \ˌma-lə-'drȯit\ *adj* : not adroit : INEPT

mal·a·dy \'ma-lə-dē\ *n, pl* **-dies** : a disease or disorder of body or mind

mal·aise \mə-'lāz, ma-\ *n* [F] : a hazy feeling of not being well

mal·a·mute \'ma-lə-ˌmyüt\ *n* : a dog often used to draw sleds esp. in northern No. America

mal·a·prop·ism \'ma-lə-ˌprä-ˌpi-zəm\ *n* : a usu. humorous misuse of a word

mal·ap·ro·pos \ˌma-ˌla-prə-'pō, ma-'la-prə-ˌpō\ *adv* : in an inappropriate or inopportune way — **malapropos** *adj*

ma·lar·ia \mə-'ler-ē-ə\ *n* [It, fr. *mala aria* bad air] : a disease marked by recurring chills and fever and caused by a protozoan parasite of the blood that is transmitted by anopheles mosquitoes — **ma·lar·i·al** \-əl\ *adj*

ma·lar·key \mə-'lär-kē\ *n* : insincere or foolish talk

mal·a·thi·on \ˌma-lə-'thī-ən, -ˌän\ *n* : an insecticide with a relatively low toxicity for mammals

Ma·lay \mə-'lā, 'mā-ˌlā\ *n* **1** : a member of a people of the Malay Peninsula and Archipelago **2** : the language of the Malays — **Malay** *adj* — **Ma·lay·an** \mə-'lā-ən, 'mā-ˌlā-\ *n or adj*

mal·con·tent \ˌmal-kən-'tent\ *adj* : marked by a dissatisfaction with the existing state of affairs : DISCONTENTED — **malcontent** *n*

mal de mer \ˌmal-də-'mer\ *n* [F] : SEASICKNESS

¹male \'māl\ *n* : a male individual

²male *adj* **1** : of, relating to, or being the sex that produces germ cells which fertilize the eggs of a female; *also* : STAMINATE **2** : MASCULINE — **male·ness** *n*

male·dic·tion \ˌma-lə-'dik-shən\ *n* : CURSE, EXECRATION

male·fac·tor \'ma-lə-ˌfak-tər\ *n* : EVILDOER; *esp* : one who commits an offense against the law — **male·fac·tion** \ˌma-lə-'fak-shən\ *n*

ma·lef·ic \mə-'le-fik\ *adj* **1** : BALEFUL **2** : MALICIOUS

ma·lef·i·cent \-fə-sənt\ *adj* : working or productive of harm or evil

ma·lev·o·lent \mə-'le-və-lənt\ *adj* : having, showing, or arising from ill will, spite, or hatred **♦ Synonyms** MALIGNANT, MALIGN, MALICIOUS, SPITEFUL — **ma·lev·o·lence** \-ləns\ *n*

mal·fea·sance \mal-'fē-zᵊns\ *n* : wrongful conduct esp. by a public official

mal·for·ma·tion \ˌmal-fȯr-'mā-shən\ *n* : irregular or faulty formation or structure; *also* : an instance of this — **mal·formed** \mal-'fȯrmd\ *adj*

mal·func·tion \mal-'fəŋk-shən\ *vb* : to fail to operate normally — **malfunction** *n*

mal·ice \'ma-ləs\ *n* : desire to cause injury or distress to another — **ma·li·cious** \mə-'li-shəs\ *adj* — **ma·li·cious·ly** *adv*

¹ma·lign \mə-'līn\ *adj* **1** : evil in nature, influence, or effect; *also* : MALIGNANT **2** : moved by ill will

²malign *vb* : to speak evil of : DEFAME

ma·lig·nant \mə-'lig-nənt\ *adj* **1** : INJURIOUS, MALIGN **2** : tending to produce death or deterioration ⟨a ~ tumor⟩ — **ma·lig·nan·cy** \-nən-sē\ *n* — **ma·lig·nant·ly** *adv* — **ma·lig·ni·ty** \-nə-tē\ *n*

ma·lin·ger \mə-'liŋ-gər\ *vb* [F *malingre* sickly] : to pretend illness so as to avoid duty — **ma·lin·ger·er** *n*

mal·i·son \'ma-lə-sən, -zən\ *n* : CURSE

mall \'mȯl, 'mal\ *n* **1** : a shaded walk : PROMENADE **2** : an urban shopping area featuring a variety of shops surrounding a concourse **3** : a usu. large enclosed suburban shopping area containing various shops

mal·lard \\'ma-lərd\\ *n, pl* **mallard** *or* **mallards** : a common wild duck that is the source of domestic ducks

mal·lea·ble \\'ma-lē-ə-bəl\\ *adj* **1** : capable of being extended or shaped by beating with a hammer or by the pressure of rollers **2** : ADAPTABLE, PLIABLE ✦ *Synonyms* PLASTIC, PLIANT, DUCTILE, SUPPLE — **mal·le·a·bil·i·ty** \\,ma-lē-ə-'bi-lə-tē\\ *n*

mal·let \\'ma-lət\\ *n* **1** : a tool with a large head for driving another tool or for striking a surface without marring it **2** : a long-handled hammerlike implement for striking a ball (as in croquet)

mal·le·us \\'ma-lē-əs\\ *n, pl* **mal·lei** \\-lē-,ī, -lē-,ē\\ [NL, fr. L, hammer] : the outermost of the three small bones of the mammalian middle ear

mal·low \\'ma-lō\\ *n* : any of a genus of herbs with lobed leaves, usu. showy flowers, and a disk-shaped fruit

malm·sey \\'mälm-zē\\ *n, often cap* : the sweetest variety of Madeira

mal·nour·ished \\mal-'nər-isht\\ *adj* : UNDERNOURISHED

mal·nu·tri·tion \\,mal-nü-'tri-shən, -nyü-\\ *n* : faulty and esp. inadequate nutrition

mal·oc·clu·sion \\,ma-lə-'klü-zhən\\ *n* : faulty coming together of teeth in biting

mal·odor·ous \\ma-'lō-də-rəs\\ *adj* : ill-smelling — **mal·odor·ous·ly** *adv* — **mal·odor·ous·ness** *n*

maloti *pl of* LOTI

mal·prac·tice \\mal-'prak-təs\\ *n* : a dereliction of professional duty or a failure of professional skill that results in injury, loss, or damage

malt \\'mólt\\ *n* **1** : grain and esp. barley steeped in water until it has sprouted and used in brewing and distilling **2** : liquor made with malt — **malty** *adj*

malted milk \\'mól-təd-\\ *n* : a powder prepared from dried milk and an extract from malt; *also* : a beverage of this powder in milk or other liquid

Mal·thu·sian \\mal-'thü-zhən, -'thyü-\\ *adj* : of or relating to a theory that population unless checked (as by war) tends to increase faster than its means of subsistence — **Malthusian** *n* — **Mal·thu·sian·ism** \\-zhə-,ni-zəm\\ *n*

malt·ose \\'mól-,tōs\\ *n* : a sugar formed esp. from starch by the action of enzymes

mal·treat \\mal-'trēt\\ *vb* : to treat cruelly or roughly : ABUSE — **mal·treat·ment** *n*

ma·ma *or* **mam·ma** \\'mä-mə\\ *n* : MOTHER

mam·bo \\'mäm-bō\\ *n, pl* **mambos** : a dance of Cuban origin related to the rumba — **mambo** *vb*

mam·mal \\'ma-məl\\ *n* [NL *Mammalia*, fr. LL, neut. pl. of *mammalis* of the breast, fr. L *mamma* breast] : any of a class of warm-blooded vertebrates that includes humans and all other animals which nourish their young with milk and have the skin more or less covered with hair — **mam·ma·li·an** \\mə-'mä-lē-ən, ma-\\ *adj or n*

mam·ma·ry \\'ma-mə-rē\\ *adj* : of, relating to, or being the glands (**mammary glands**) that in female mammals secrete milk

mam·mo·gram \\'ma-mə-,gram\\ *n* : an X-ray photograph of the breasts

mam·mog·ra·phy \\ma-'mä-grə-fē\\ *n* : X-ray examination of the breasts (as for early detection of cancer)

mam·mon \\'ma-mən\\ *n, often cap* : material wealth having a debasing influence

¹**mam·moth** \\'ma-məth\\ *n* : any of a genus of large hairy extinct elephants

²**mammoth** *adj* : of very great size : GIGANTIC ✦ *Synonyms* COLOSSAL, ENORMOUS, IMMENSE, VAST, ELEPHANTINE

¹**man** \\'man\\ *n, pl* **men** \\'men\\ **1** : a human being; *esp* : an adult male **2** : the human race : MANKIND **3** : one possessing in high degree the qualities considered distinctive of manhood **4** : an adult male servant or employee **5** : the individual who can fulfill one's requirements ⟨he's your ∼⟩ **6 a** : one of the pieces with which various games (as chess) are played **b** : one of the players on a team **7** *often cap* : white society or people

²**man** *vb* **manned; man·ning 1** : to supply with men ⟨∼ a fleet⟩ **2** : FORTIFY, BRACE

³**man** *abbr* manual

Man *abbr* Manitoba

man–about–town *n, pl* **men–about–town** : a worldly and socially active man

man·a·cle \\'ma-ni-kəl\\ *n* **1** : a shackle for the hand or wrist **2** : something used as a restraint

man·age \\'ma-nij\\ *vb* **man·aged; man·ag·ing 1** : HANDLE, CONTROL ⟨∼s her skis well⟩; *also* : to direct or carry on business or affairs **2** : to make and keep compliant **3** : to treat with care : HUSBAND **4** : to achieve one's purpose : CONTRIVE — **man·age·abil·i·ty** \\,ma-ni-jə-'bi-lə-tē\\ *n* — **man·age·able** \\'ma-ni-jə-bəl\\ *adj* — **man·age·able·ness** *n* — **man·age·ably** \\-blē\\ *adv*

managed care *n* : a health-care system that controls costs by limiting doctor's fees and by restricting the patient's choice of doctors

man·age·ment \\'ma-nij-mənt\\ *n* **1** : the act or art of managing **2** : judicious use of means to accomplish an end **3** : the group of those who manage or direct an enterprise

man·ag·er \\'ma-ni-jər\\ *n* : one that manages — **man·a·ge·ri·al** \\,ma-nə-'jir-ē-əl\\ *adj*

ma·ña·na \\mən-'yä-nə\\ *n* [Sp, lit., tomorrow] : an indefinite time in the future

ma·nat \\mä-'nät\\ *n, pl* **manat** *or* **manats** — see MONEY table

man–at–arms *n, pl* **men–at–arms** : SOLDIER; *esp* : one who is heavily armed and mounted

man·a·tee \\'ma-nə-,tē\\ *n* : any of a genus of chiefly tropical plant-eating aquatic mammals having a broad rounded tail

man·ci·ple \\'man-sə-pəl\\ *n* : a steward or purveyor esp. for a college or monastery

man·da·mus \\man-'dä-məs\\ *n* [L, we enjoin] : a writ issued by a superior court commanding that an official act or duty be performed

man·da·rin \\'man-də-rən\\ *n* **1** : a public official of high rank under the Chinese Empire **2** *cap* : the chief dialect group of China **3** : a yellow to reddish orange looseskinned citrus fruit; *also* : a tree that bears mandarins

man·date \\'man-,dāt\\ *n* **1** : an authoritative command **2** : an authorization to act given to a representative **3** : a commission granted by the League of Nations to a member nation for governing conquered territory; *also* : a territory so governed

man·da·to·ry \\'man-də-,tór-ē\\ *adj* **1** : containing or constituting a command : OBLIGATORY **2** : of or relating to a League of Nations mandate

man·di·ble \\'man-də-bəl\\ *n* **1** : JAW; *esp* : a lower jaw **2** : either segment of a bird's bill — **man·dib·u·lar** \\man-'di-byə-lər\\ *adj*

man·do·lin \\,man-də-'lin, 'man-də-lən\\ *n* : a stringed musical instrument with a pear-shaped body and a fretted neck

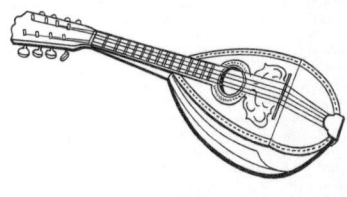

mandolin

man·drake \\'man-,drāk\\ *n* **1** : an Old World herb related to the nightshades or its large forked root formerly credited with magical properties **2** : MAYAPPLE

man·drel *also* **man·dril** \\'man-drəl\\ *n* **1** : an axle or spindle inserted into a hole in a piece of work to support it during machining **2** : a metal bar used as a core around which material may be cast, shaped, or molded

man·drill \\'man-drəl\\ *n* : a large baboon of western central Africa

mane \\'mān\\ *n* : long heavy hair growing about the neck of some mammals (as horses) — **maned** \\'mānd\\ *adj*

man-eat·er \\'man-,ē-tər\\ *n* : one (as a shark or cannibal) that has or is thought to have an appetite for human flesh — **man-eat·ing** *adj*

ma·nège \\ma-'nezh, mə-\\ *n* : the art of horsemanship or of training horses

ma·nes \'mä-ˌnās, 'mä-ˌnēz\ *n pl, often cap* : the spirits of the dead and gods of the lower world in ancient Roman belief

ma·neu·ver \mə-'nü-vər, -'nyü-\ *n* [F *manœuvre*, fr. OF *maneuvre* work done by hand, fr. ML *manuopera*, fr. *manu operare* to work by hand] **1** : a military or naval movement; *also* : an armed forces training exercise — often used in pl. **2** : a procedure involving expert physical movement **3** : an evasive movement or shift of tactics; *also* : an action taken to gain a tactical end — **maneuver** *vb* — **ma·neu·ver·abil·i·ty** \-ˌnü-və-rə-'bi-lə-tē, -ˌnyü-\ *n* — **ma·neu·ver·able** \-'nü-və-rə-bəl, -'nyü-\ *adj*

man Friday *n* : an efficient and devoted aide or employee

man·ful \'man-fəl\ *adj* : having or showing courage and resolution — **man·ful·ly** *adv*

man·ga·nese \'maŋ-gə-ˌnēz, -ˌnēs\ *n* : a metallic chemical element resembling iron but not magnetic

mange \'mānj\ *n* : any of several contagious itchy skin diseases esp. of domestic animals — **mangy** \'mān-jē\ *adj*

man·ger \'mān-jər\ *n* : a trough or open box for livestock feed or fodder

¹man·gle \'man-gəl\ *vb* **man·gled; man·gling 1** : to cut, bruise, or hack with repeated blows **2** : to spoil or injure esp. through ineptitude — **man·gler** *n*

²mangle *n* : a machine with heated rollers for ironing laundry

man·go \'maŋ-gō\ *n, pl* **mangoes** *also* **mangos** [Pg *manga*, prob. fr. Malayalam (Dravidian language of India) *māṅṅa*] : an edible juicy yellowish-red fruit borne by a tropical evergreen tree related to the sumacs; *also* : this tree

man·grove \'man-ˌgrōv\ *n* : any of a genus of tropical maritime trees that send out many prop roots and form dense thickets important in coastal land building

man·han·dle \'man-ˌhan-dªl\ *vb* : to handle roughly

man·hat·tan \man-'ha-tªn\ *n, often cap* : a cocktail made of whiskey and vermouth

man·hole \'man-ˌhōl\ *n* : a hole through which a person may go esp. to gain access to an underground or enclosed structure

man·hood \-ˌhud\ *n* **1** : the condition of being an adult male **2** : qualities associated with men : MANLINESS **3** : MEN ⟨the nation's ∼⟩

man–hour \-'au̇(-ə)r\ *n* : a unit of one hour's work by one person

man·hunt \-ˌhənt\ *n* : an organized hunt for a person and esp. for one charged with a crime

ma·nia \'mā-nē-ə, -nyə\ *n* **1** : excitement manifested by mental and physical hyperactivity, disorganized behavior, and elevated mood **2** : excessive enthusiasm

ma·ni·ac \'mā-nē-ˌak\ *n* : LUNATIC, MADMAN

ma·ni·a·cal \mə-'nī-ə-kəl\ *also* **ma·ni·ac** \'mā-nē-ak\ *adj* **1** : affected with or suggestive of madness **2** : FRANTIC ⟨a ∼ mob⟩

man·ic \'ma-nik\ *adj* : affected with, relating to, characterized by, or resulting from mania — **manic** *n* — **man·i·cal·ly** \-ni-k(ə-)lē\ *adv*

manic depression *n* : BIPOLAR DISORDER

man·ic–de·pres·sive \ˌma-nik-di-'pre-siv\ *adj* : characterized by or affected with either mania or depression or alternating episodes of mania and depression — **manic–depressive** *n*

¹man·i·cure \'ma-nə-ˌkyu̇r\ *n* **1** : MANICURIST **2** : a treatment for the care of the hands and nails

²manicure *vb* **-cured; -cur·ing 1** : to do manicure work on **2** : to trim closely and evenly

man·i·cur·ist \-ˌkyu̇r-ist\ *n* : a person who gives manicure treatments

¹man·i·fest \'ma-nə-ˌfest\ *adj* [ME, fr. AF or L; AF *manifeste*, fr. L *manifestus*, caught in the act, flagrant, obvious, perh. fr. *manus* hand + *-festus* (akin to L in*festus* hostile)] **1** : readily perceived by the senses and esp. by the sight **2** : easily understood : OBVIOUS — **man·i·fest·ly** *adv*

²manifest *vb* : to make evident or certain by showing or displaying ✦ *Synonyms* EVINCE, DEMONSTRATE, EXHIBIT

³manifest *n* : a list of passengers or an invoice of cargo for a ship or plane

man·i·fes·ta·tion \ˌma-nə-fə-'stā-shən\ *n* : DISPLAY, DEMONSTRATION

man·i·fes·to \ˌma-nə-'fes-tō\ *n, pl* **-tos** *or* **-toes** : a public declaration of intentions, motives, or views

¹man·i·fold \'ma-nə-ˌfōld\ *adj* **1** : marked by diversity or variety **2** : consisting of or operating many of one kind combined

²manifold *n* : a pipe fitting with several lateral outlets for connecting it with other pipes

³manifold *vb* **1** : MULTIPLY **2** : to make a number of copies of (as a letter)

man·i·kin *also* **man·ni·kin** \'ma-ni-kən\ *n* **1** : MANNEQUIN **2** : a little man : DWARF

Ma·nila hemp \mə-'ni-lə-\ *n* : a tough fiber from a Philippine plant related to the banana that is used for cordage

manila paper *n, often cap M* : a tough brownish paper made orig. from Manila hemp

man·i·oc \'ma-nē-ˌäk\ *n* : CASSAVA

ma·nip·u·late \mə-'ni-pyə-ˌlāt\ *vb* **-lat·ed; -lat·ing 1** : to treat or operate manually or mechanically esp. with skill **2** : to manage or use skillfully **3** : to influence esp. with intent to deceive — **ma·nip·u·la·tion** \mə-ni-pyə-'lā-shən\ *n* — **ma·nip·u·la·tive** \-'ni-pyə-ˌlā-tiv\ *adj* — **ma·nip·u·la·tor** \-ˌlā-tər\ *n*

ma·nip·u·la·tives \mə-'ni-pyə-ˌlā-tivz\ *n pl* : objects that a student is instructed to use in a way that teaches or reinforces a lesson

man·kind *n* **1** \'man-'kīnd\ : the human race **2** \-ˌkīnd\ : men as distinguished from women

¹man·ly \'man-lē\ *adv* : in a manly manner

²manly *adj* **man·li·er; -est** : having qualities appropriate to or generally associated with a man : BOLD, RESOLUTE — **man·li·ness** *n*

man–made \'man-'mād\ *adj* : made by humans rather than nature ⟨∼ systems⟩; *esp* : SYNTHETIC ⟨∼ fibers⟩

man·na \'ma-nə\ *n* **1** : food miraculously supplied to the Israelites in the wilderness **2** : something of value that comes unexpectedly : WINDFALL

manned \'mand\ *adj* : carrying or performed by a person ⟨∼ spaceflight⟩

man·ne·quin \'ma-ni-kən\ *n* **1** : a form representing the human figure used esp. for displaying clothes **2** : a person employed to model clothing

man·ner \'ma-nər\ *n* **1** : KIND, SORT ⟨what ∼ of man is he⟩ **2** : a way of acting or proceeding ⟨worked in a brisk ∼⟩; *also* : normal behavior ⟨spoke bluntly as was his ∼⟩ **3** : a method of artistic execution **4** *pl* : social conduct; *also* : BEARING **5** *pl* : BEHAVIOR ⟨taught the child good ∼⟩

man·nered \'ma-nərd\ *adj* **1** : having manners of a specified kind ⟨well-*mannered*⟩ **2** : having an artificial character ⟨a highly ∼ style⟩

man·ner·ism \'ma-nə-ˌri-zəm\ *n* **1** : ARTIFICIALITY, PRECIOSITY **2** : a peculiarity of action, bearing, or treatment ✦ *Synonyms* POSE, AIR, AFFECTATION

man·ner·ly \-nər-lē\ *adj* : showing good manners : POLITE — **man·ner·li·ness** *n* — **mannerly** *adv*

man·nish \'ma-nish\ *adj* **1** : resembling or suggesting a man rather than a woman **2** : generally associated with or characteristic of a man — **man·nish·ly** *adv* — **man·nish·ness** *n*

ma·no a ma·no \ˌmä-nō-ä-'mä-nō\ *adv or adj* : in direct competition or conflict

ma·noeu·vre \mə-'nü-vər, -'nyü-\ *chiefly Brit var of* MANEUVER

man–of–war \ˌman-əv-'wȯr\ *n, pl* **men–of–war** \ˌmen-\ : WARSHIP

ma·nom·e·ter \ma-'nä-mə-tər\ *n* : an instrument for measuring the pressure of gases and vapors — **mano·met·ric** \ˌma-nə-'me-trik\ *adj*

man·or \'ma-nər\ *n* **1** : the house or hall of an estate; *also* : a landed estate **2** : an English estate of a feudal lord — **ma·no·ri·al** \mə-'nȯr-ē-əl\ *adj* — **ma·no·ri·al·ism** \-ə-ˌli-zəm\ *n*

man power *n* **1** : power available from or supplied by the physical effort of human beings **2** *usu* **man·pow·er** : the total supply of persons available and fitted for service

man·qué \mäⁿ-'kā\ *adj* [F, fr. pp. of *manquer* to lack, fail] : short of or frustrated in the fulfillment of one's aspirations or talents ⟨a poet ∼⟩

man·sard \'man-ˌsärd, -sərd\ *n* : a roof having two slopes on all sides with the lower slope steeper than the upper one

manse \'mans\ *n* : the residence esp. of a Presbyterian minister

man·ser·vant \'man-ˌsər-vənt\ *n, pl* **men·ser·vants** \'men-ˌsər-vənts\ : a male servant
man·sion \'man-chən\ *n* : a large imposing residence; *also* : a separate apartment in a large structure
man–size \'man-ˌsīz\ *or* **man–sized** \-ˌsīzd\ *adj* : suitable for or requiring a man
man·slaugh·ter \-ˌslȯ-tər\ *n* : the unlawful killing of a human being without express or implied malice
man·ta \'man-tə\ *n* : a square piece of cloth or blanket used in southwestern U.S. and Latin America as a cloak or shawl
man·teau \man-'tō\ *n* : a loose cloak, coat, or robe
man·tel \'man-tᵊl\ *n* : a beam, stone, or arch serving as a lintel to support the masonry above a fireplace; *also* : a shelf above a fireplace
man·tel·piece \'man-tᵊl-ˌpēs\ *n* : the shelf of a mantel
man·til·la \man-'tē-yə, -'til-ə\ *n* : a light scarf worn over the head and shoulders esp. by Spanish and Latin-American women
man·tis \'man-təs\ *n, pl* **man·tis·es** *also* **man·tes** \-ˌtēz\ [NL, fr. Gk, lit., diviner, prophet] : any of a group of large usu. green insect-eating insects that hold their prey in forelimbs folded as if in prayer
man·tis·sa \man-'ti-sə\ *n* : the part of a logarithm to the right of the decimal point
¹**man·tle** \'man-tᵊl\ *n* **1** : a loose sleeveless garment worn over other clothes **2** : something that covers, enfolds, or envelops **3** : a lacy sheath that gives light by incandescence when placed over a flame **4** : the portion of the earth lying between the crust and the core **5** : MANTEL
²**mantle** *vb* **man·tled; man·tling 1** : to cover with a mantle **2** : BLUSH
man·tra \'man-trə\ *n* : a mystical formula of invocation or incantation (as in Hinduism)
¹**man·u·al** \'man-yə-wəl\ *adj* **1** : of, relating to, or involving the hands; *also* : worked by hand ⟨a ∼ pump⟩ **2** : requiring or using physical skill and energy — **man·u·al·ly** *adv*
²**manual** *n* **1** : a small book; *esp* : HANDBOOK **2** : the prescribed movements in the handling of a military item and esp. a weapon during a drill or ceremony ⟨the ∼ of arms⟩ **3** : a keyboard esp. of an organ
man·u·fac·to·ry \ˌman-yə-'fak-tə-rē\ *n* : FACTORY
¹**man·u·fac·ture** \ˌman-yə-'fak-chər\ *n* [MF, fr. ML *manufactura*, L *manu factus* made by hand] **1** : something made from raw materials **2** : the process of making wares by hand or by machinery; *also* : a productive industry using machinery
²**manufacture** *vb* **-tured; -tur·ing 1** : to make from raw materials by hand or by machinery; *also* : to engage in manufacture **2** : INVENT, FABRICATE; *also* : CREATE — **man·u·fac·tur·er** *n*
man·u·mit \ˌman-yə-'mit\ *vb* **-mit·ted; -mit·ting** : to free from slavery — **man·u·mis·sion** \-'mi-shən\ *n*
¹**ma·nure** \mə-'nu̇r, -'nyu̇r\ *vb* **ma·nured; ma·nur·ing** : to fertilize land with manure
²**manure** *n* : FERTILIZER; *esp* : refuse from stables and barnyards — **ma·nu·ri·al** \-'nu̇r-ē-əl, -'nyu̇r-\ *adj*
man·u·script \'man-yə-ˌskript\ *n* [L *manu scriptus* written by hand] **1** : a written or typewritten composition or document; *also* : a document submitted for publication **2** : writing as opposed to print
Manx \'maŋks\ *n pl* : the people of the Isle of Man — **Manx** *adj*
¹**many** \'me-nē\ *adj* **more** \'mȯr\; **most** \'mōst\ : consisting of or amounting to a large but indefinite number ⟨∼ years ago⟩
²**many** *pron* : a large number ⟨∼ are called⟩
³**many** *n* : a large but indefinite number ⟨a good ∼ of them⟩
many·fold \ˌme-nē-'fōld\ *adv* : by many times
many–sid·ed \-'sī-dəd\ *adj* **1** : having many sides or aspects **2** : VERSATILE
Mao·ism \'mau̇-ˌi-zəm\ *n* : the theory and practice of Communism developed in China chiefly by Mao Zedong — **Mao·ist** \'mau̇-ist\ *n or adj*
Mao·ri \'mau̇(-ə)r-ē\ *n, pl* **Maori** *or* **Maoris** : a member of a Polynesian people native to New Zealand
¹**map** \'map\ *n* [ML *mappa*, fr. L, napkin, towel] **1** : a representation usu. on a flat surface of the whole or part of an area **2** : a representation of the celestial sphere or part of it

²**map** *vb* **mapped; map·ping 1** : to make a map of **2** : to plan in detail ⟨∼ out a program⟩ — **map·pa·ble** \'ma-pə-bəl\ *adj* — **map·per** *n*
MAP *abbr* modified American plan
ma·ple \'mā-pəl\ *n* : any of a genus of trees or shrubs with 2-winged dry fruit and opposite leaves; *also* : the hard light-colored wood of a maple used esp. for floors and furniture
maple sugar *n* : sugar made by boiling maple syrup
maple syrup *n* : syrup made by concentrating the sap of maple trees and esp. the sugar maple
mar \'mär\ *vb* **marred; mar·ring** : to detract from the wholeness or perfection of : SPOIL ♦ **Synonyms** INJURE, HURT, HARM, DAMAGE, IMPAIR, BLEMISH
Mar *abbr* March
ma·ra·ca \mə-'rä-kə, -'ra-\ *n* [Pg *maracá*] : a rattle usu. made from a gourd and used as a percussion instrument
mar·a·schi·no \ˌmer-ə-'skē-nō-, -'shē-\ *n, often cap* : a cherry preserved in a sweet liqueur made from the juice of a bitter wild cherry
mar·a·thon \'mer-ə-ˌthän\ *n* [*Marathon*, Greece, site of a victory of Greeks over Persians in 490 B.C. the news of which was carried to Athens by a long-distance runner] **1** : a long-distance race esp. on foot **2** : an endurance contest
mar·a·thon·er \'mer-ə-ˌthä-nər\ *n* : a person who takes part in a marathon — **mar·a·thon·ing** *n*
ma·raud \mə-'rȯd\ *vb* : to roam about and raid in search of plunder : PILLAGE — **ma·raud·er** *n*
mar·ble \'mär-bəl\ *n* **1** : a limestone that can be polished and used in fine building work **2** : something resembling marble (as in coldness) **3** : a small ball (as of glass) used in various games; *also, pl* : a children's game played with these small balls — **marble** *adj*
mar·bling \-bə-liŋ, -bliŋ\ *n* : an intermixture of fat through the lean of a cut of meat
mar·cel \mär-'sel\ *n* : a deep soft wave made in the hair by the use of a heated curling iron — **marcel** *vb*
¹**march** \'märch\ *n* : a border region : FRONTIER
²**march** *vb* **1** : to move along in or as if in military formation **2** : to walk in a direct purposeful manner; *also* : PROGRESS, ADVANCE **3** : TRAVERSE ⟨∼ed 10 miles⟩ — **march·er** *n*
³**march** *n* **1** : the action of marching; *also* : the distance covered (as by a military unit) in a march **2** : a regular measured stride or rhythmic step used in marching **3** : forward movement **4** : a piece of music with marked rhythm suitable for marching to
March *n* [ME, fr. AF, fr. L *martius*, fr. *martius* of Mars, fr. *Mart-, Mars*, Roman god of war] : the 3d month of the year
mar·chio·ness \'mär-shə-nəs\ *n* **1** : the wife or widow of a marquess **2** : a woman holding the rank of a marquess in her own right
Mar·di Gras \'mär-dē-ˌgrä\ *n* [F, lit., fat Tuesday] : the Tuesday before Ash Wednesday often observed with parades and merrymaking
¹**mare** \'mer\ *n* : an adult female of the horse or a related mammal
²**ma·re** \'mär-(ˌ)ā\ *n, pl* **ma·ria** \'mär-ē-ə\ : any of several large dark areas on the surface of the moon or Mars
mar·ga·rine \'mär-jə-rən\ *n* : a food product made usu. from vegetable oils churned with skimmed milk and used as a substitute for butter
mar·ga·ri·ta \ˌmär-gə-'rē-tə\ *n* : a cocktail consisting of tequila, lime or lemon juice, and an orange-flavored liqueur
mar·gin \'mär-jən\ *n* **1** : the part of a page outside the main body of printed or written matter **2** : EDGE ⟨continental ∼⟩ **3** : a spare amount, measure, or degree allowed for use if needed **4** : measure or degree of difference ⟨a one-vote ∼⟩
mar·gin·al \-jə-nəl\ *adj* **1** : written or printed in the margin **2** : of, relating to, or situated at a margin or border **3** : close to the lower limit of quality or acceptability **4** : excluded from or existing outside the mainstream of society or a group — **mar·gin·al·ly** *adv*
mar·gi·na·lia \ˌmär-jə-'nā-lē-ə\ *n pl* : marginal notes or embellishments
mar·gin·al·ize \'mär-jə-nᵊl-ˌīz\ *vb* **-ized; -iz·ing** : to relegate to an unimportant position within a society or group

mar·grave \'mär-ˌgräv\ *n* : the military governor esp. of a medieval German border province

ma·ri·a·chi \ˌmär-ē-'ä-chē, ˌmer-\ *n* : a Mexican street band; *also* : a member of or the music of such a band

mari·gold \'mer-ə-ˌgōld\ *n* : any of a genus of tropical American herbs related to the daisies that are grown for their showy usu. yellow, orange, or maroon flower heads

mar·i·jua·na *also* **mar·i·hua·na** \ˌmer-ə-'wä-nə, -'hwä-\ *n* [MexSp *marihuana*] : the dried leaves and flowering tops of the female hemp plant smoked usu. illegally for their intoxicating effect; *also* : HEMP

ma·rim·ba \mə-'rim-bə\ *n* : a xylophone of southern Africa and Central America; *also* : a modern version of it

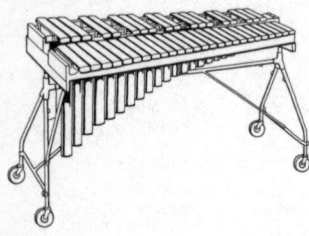

marimba

ma·ri·na \mə-'rē-nə\ *n* : a dock or basin providing secure moorings for pleasure boats

mar·i·na·ra \ˌmer-ə-'ner-ə\ *adj* [It (*alla*) *marinara*, lit., in sailor style] : made with tomatoes, onions, garlic, and spices; *also* : served with marinara sauce

mar·i·nade \ˌmer-ə-'nād\ *n* : a savory usu. acidic sauce in which meat, fish, or a vegetable is soaked to enrich its flavor or to tenderize it

mar·i·nate \'mer-ə-ˌnāt\ *vb* **-nat·ed; -nat·ing** : to steep (as meat or fish) in a marinade

¹ma·rine \mə-'rēn\ *adj* **1** : of or relating to the sea or its navigation or commerce **2** : of or relating to marines

²marine *n* **1** : the mercantile and naval shipping of a country **2** : any of a class of soldiers serving on shipboard or with a naval force

mar·i·ner \'mer-ə-nər\ *n* : SAILOR

mar·i·o·nette \ˌmer-ē-ə-'net\ *n* : a puppet moved by strings or by hand

mar·i·tal \'mer-ə-t²l\ *adj* : of or relating to marriage : CONJUGAL ◆ **Synonyms** MATRIMONIAL, CONNUBIAL, NUPTIAL

mar·i·time \'mer-ə-ˌtīm\ *adj* **1** : of, relating to, or bordering on the sea **2** : of or relating to navigation or commerce of the sea

mar·jo·ram \'mär-jə-rəm\ *n* : any of various fragrant mints often used as seasoning

¹mark \'märk\ *n* **1** : something (as a line or fixed object) designed to record position; *also* : the starting line or position in a track event **2** : TARGET; *also* : GOAL, OBJECT **3** : an object of abuse or ridicule **4** : the question under discussion **5** : NORM ⟨not up to the ∼⟩ **6** : a visible sign : INDICATION; *also* : CHARACTERISTIC **7** : a written or printed symbol **8** : GRADE **5** ⟨a ∼ of B+⟩ **9** : IMPORTANCE, DISTINCTION **10** : a lasting impression ⟨made his ∼ in the world⟩; *also* : a damaging impression left on a surface

²mark *vb* **1** : to set apart by a line or boundary **2** : to designate by a mark or make a mark on **3** : CHARACTERIZE ⟨the vehemence that ∼s his speeches⟩; *also* : SIGNALIZE ⟨this year ∼s our 50th anniversary⟩ **4** : to take notice of : OBSERVE — **mark·er** *n*

³mark *n* : DEUTSCHE MARK

Mark \'märk\ *n* — see BIBLE table

mark·down \'märk-ˌdaún\ *n* **1** : a lowering of price **2** : the amount by which an original price is reduced

mark down *vb* : to put a lower price on

marked \'märkt\ *adj* : NOTICEABLE — **mark·ed·ly** \'mär-kəd-lē\ *adv*

¹mar·ket \'mär-kət\ *n* **1** : a meeting together of people for trade by purchase and sale; *also* : a public place where such a meeting is held **2** : the rate or price offered for a

commodity or security **3** : the course of commercial activity by which the exchange of commodities is effected **4** : a geographical area of demand for commodities; *also* : extent of demand **5** : a retail establishment usu. of a specific kind

²market *vb* : to go to a market to buy or sell; *also* : SELL — **mar·ket·able** *adj*

mar·ket·place \'mär-kət-ˌplās\ *n* **1** : an open square in a town where markets are held **2** : the world of trade or economic activity

mark·ka \'mär-ˌkä\ *n*, *pl* **mark·kaa** \'mär-ˌkä\ *or* **markkas** \-ˌkäz\ : the basic monetary unit of Finland from 1917 to 2001

marks·man \'märks-mən\ *n* : a person skillful at hitting a target — **marks·man·ship** *n*

mark·up \'mär-ˌkəp\ *n* **1** : a raising of price **2** : an amount added to the cost price of an article to determine the selling price

mark up *vb* : to put a higher price on

markup language *n* : a system for marking the components and layout of a computer document

marl \'märl\ *n* : an earthy deposit rich in lime used esp. as fertilizer — **marly** \'mär-lē\ *adj*

mar·lin \'mär-lən\ *n* : any of several large oceanic sport fishes related to sailfishes

mar·line·spike *also* **mar·lin·spike** \'mär-lən-ˌspīk\ *n* : a pointed iron tool used to separate strands of rope or wire (as in splicing)

mar·ma·lade \'mär-mə-ˌlād\ *n* : a clear jelly holding in suspension pieces of fruit and fruit rind

mar·mo·re·al \mär-'mȯr-ē-əl\ *adj* : of, relating to, or suggestive of marble

mar·mo·set \'mär-mə-ˌset\ *n* : any of numerous small bushy-tailed monkeys of Central and So. America

mar·mot \'mär-mət\ *n* : any of a genus of stout short-legged burrowing No. American rodents

¹ma·roon \mə-'rün\ *vb* **1** : to put ashore (as on a desolate island) and leave to one's fate **2** : to leave in isolation and without hope of escape

²maroon *n* : a dark red color

¹mar·quee \mär-'kē\ *n* [modif. of F *marquise*, lit., marchioness] **1** : a large tent set up (as for an outdoor party) **2** : a usu. metal and glass canopy over an entrance (as of a theater) **3** : a sign over the entrance of a theater or arena advertising a performance

²marquee *adj* : having or being a great attraction : PREEMINENT ⟨∼ athletes⟩

mar·quess \'mär-kwəs\ *or* **mar·quis** \'mär-kwəs, mär-'kē\ *n* **1** : a nobleman of hereditary rank in Europe and Japan **2** : a member of the British peerage ranking below a duke and above an earl

mar·que·try \'mär-kə-trē\ *n* : inlaid work of wood, shell, or ivory (as on a table or cabinet)

mar·quise \mär-'kēz\ *n*, *pl* **mar·quises** *same as* -'kē-zəz\ : MARCHIONESS

mar·riage \'mer-ij\ *n* **1** : the state of being united to another person as a usu. contractual relationship according to law or custom **2** : a wedding ceremony and attendant festivities **3** : a close union ⟨a ∼ of light and shadow⟩ — **mar·riage·able** *adj*

married name *n* : a woman's surname acquired through marriage

mar·row \'mer-ō\ *n* : a soft vascular tissue that fills the cavities of most bones

mar·row·bone \'mer-ə-ˌbōn, 'mer-ō-\ *n* : a bone (as a shinbone) rich in marrow

mar·ry \'mer-ē\ *vb* **mar·ried; mar·ry·ing** **1** : to join in marriage **2** : to take as a spouse : WED **3** : to enter into a close union **4** : COMBINE, UNITE — **mar·ried** *adj or n*

Mars \'märz\ *n* : the planet 4th from the sun and conspicuous for its red color — see PLANET table

marsh \'märsh\ *n* : a tract of soft wet land — **marshy** *adj*

¹mar·shal \'mär-shəl\ *n* [ME, fr. AF *mareschal*, of Gmc origin; akin to OHG *marahscalc* marshal, fr. *marah* horse + *scalc* servant] **1** : a high official in a medieval household; *also* : a person in charge of the ceremonial aspects of a gathering **2** : a general officer of the highest military rank **3** : an administrative officer (as of a U.S. judicial district) having duties similar to a sheriff's **4** : the administrative head of a city police or fire department

²marshal *vb* **mar·shaled** *or* **mar·shalled; mar·shal·ing** *or*

mar·shal·ling 1 : to arrange in order, rank, or position 2 : to bring together 3 : to lead with ceremony : USHER

marsh gas *n* : METHANE

marsh·mal·low \'märsh-ˌme-lō, -ˌma-\ *n* : a light spongy confection made from corn syrup, sugar, albumen, and gelatin

marsh marigold *n* : a swamp herb related to the buttercups that has bright yellow flowers

mar·su·pi·al \mär-'sü-pē-əl\ *n* : any of an order of primitive mammals (as opossums, kangaroos, or wombats) that bear very immature young which are nourished in a pouch on the abdomen of the female — **marsupial** *adj*

mart \'märt\ *n* : MARKET

mar·ten \'mär-tᵊn\ *n, pl* **marten** *or* **martens** : a slender mammal that is larger than the related weasels and has soft gray or brown fur; *also* : this fur

mar·tial \'mär-shəl\ *adj* [L *martialis* of Mars, fr. *Mart-, Mars* Mars, Roman god of war] 1 : of, relating to, or suited for war or a warrior ⟨∼ music⟩ 2 : of or relating to an army or military life 3 : WARLIKE

martial law *n* 1 : the law applied in occupied territory by the occupying military forces 2 : the established law of a country administered by military forces in an emergency when civilian law enforcement agencies are unable to maintain public order and safety

mar·tian \'mär-shən\ *adj, often cap* : of or relating to the planet Mars or its hypothetical inhabitants — **martian** *n, often cap*

mar·tin \'mär-tᵊn\ *n* : any of several swallows and esp. one of No. America with purplish blue plumage

mar·ti·net \ˌmär-tə-'net\ *n* : a strict disciplinarian

mar·tin·gale \'mär-tᵊn-ˌgāl\ *n* : a strap connecting a horse's girth to the bit or reins so as to hold down its head

mar·ti·ni \mär-'tē-nē\ *n* : a cocktail made of gin or vodka and dry vermouth

¹**mar·tyr** \'mär-tər\ *n* [ME, fr. OE, fr. LL, fr. Gk *martyr-, martys* witness] 1 : a person who dies rather than renounce a religion; *also* : a person who makes a great sacrifice for the sake of principle 2 : a great or constant sufferer

²**martyr** *vb* 1 : to put to death for adhering to a belief 2 : TORTURE

mar·tyr·dom \'mär-tər-dəm\ *n* 1 : the suffering and death of a martyr 2 : TORTURE

¹**mar·vel** \'mär-vəl\ *n* 1 : one that causes wonder or astonishment 2 : intense surprise or interest

²**marvel** *vb* **mar·veled** *or* **mar·velled; mar·vel·ing** *or* **mar·vel·ling** 1 : to feel surprise, wonder, or amazed curiosity ⟨∼ed at the circus act⟩

mar·vel·ous *or* **mar·vel·lous** \'mär-və-ləs\ *adj* 1 : causing wonder 2 : of the highest kind or quality — **mar·vel·ous·ly** *adv* — **mar·vel·ous·ness** *n*

Marx·ism \'märk-ˌsi-zəm\ *n* : the political, economic, and social principles and policies advocated by Karl Marx — **Marx·ist** \-sist\ *n or adj*

mar·zi·pan \'märt-sə-ˌpän, -ˌpan; 'mär-zə-ˌpan\ *n* [G, fr. It *marzapane*] : a confection of almond paste, sugar, and egg whites

masc *abbr* masculine

mas·cara \ma-'sker-ə\ *n* : a cosmetic esp. for darkening the eyelashes

mas·car·po·ne \ˌmas-kär-'pō-nā\ *n* : an Italian cream cheese

mas·cot \'mas-ˌkät, -kət\ *n* [F *mascotte*, fr. Occitan *mascoto*, fr. *masco* witch, fr. ML *masca*] : a person, animal, or object adopted usu. by a group to bring good luck

¹**mas·cu·line** \'mas-kyə-lən\ *adj* 1 : MALE; *also* : MANLY 2 : of, relating to, or constituting the gender that includes most words or grammatical forms referring to males — **mas·cu·lin·i·ty** \ˌmas-kyə-'li-nə-tē\ *n*

²**masculine** *n* : a noun, pronoun, adjective, or inflectional form or class of the masculine gender; *also* : the masculine gender

¹**mash** \'mash\ *n* 1 : a mixture of ground feeds for livestock 2 : crushed malt or grain steeped in hot water to make wort 3 : a soft pulpy mass

²**mash** *vb* 1 : to reduce to a soft pulpy state 2 : CRUSH, SMASH ⟨∼ a finger⟩ — **mash·er** *n*

MASH *abbr* mobile army surgical hospital

¹**mask** \'mask\ *n* 1 : a cover for the face usu. for disguise or protection 2 : MASQUE 3 : a figure of a head worn on the stage in antiquity 4 : a copy of a face made by means of a mold ⟨death ∼⟩ 5 : something that conceals or disguises 6 : the face of an animal

²**mask** *vb* 1 : to conceal from view : DISGUISE 2 : to cover for protection

mask·er \'mas-kər\ *n* : a participant in a masquerade

mas·och·ism \'ma-sə-ˌki-zəm, 'ma-zə-\ *n* 1 : a sexual perversion characterized by pleasure in being subjected to pain or humiliation 2 : pleasure in being abused or dominated — **mas·och·ist** \-kist\ *n* — **mas·och·is·tic** \ˌma-sə-'kis-tik, ˌma-zə-\ *adj*

ma·son \'mā-sᵊn\ *n* 1 : a skilled worker who builds with stone, brick, or concrete 2 *cap* : FREEMASON

Ma·son·ic \mə-'sä-nik\ *adj* : of or relating to Freemasons or Freemasonry

ma·son·ry \'mā-sᵊn-rē\ *n, pl* **-ries** 1 : something constructed of materials used by masons 2 : the art, trade, or work of a mason 3 *cap* : FREEMASONRY

masque \'mask\ *n* 1 : MASQUERADE 2 : a short allegorical dramatic performance (as of the 17th century)

¹**mas·quer·ade** \ˌmas-kə-'rād\ *n* 1 : a social gathering of persons wearing masks; *also* : a costume for wear at such a gathering 2 : DISGUISE

²**masquerade** *vb* **-ad·ed; -ad·ing** 1 : to disguise oneself : POSE 2 : to take part in a masquerade — **mas·quer·ad·er** *n*

¹**mass** \'mas\ *n* 1 *cap* : a sequence of prayers and ceremonies forming the eucharistic service of the Roman Catholic Church 2 *often cap* : a celebration of the Eucharist 3 : a musical setting for parts of the Mass

²**mass** *n* 1 : a quantity or aggregate of matter usu. of considerable size 2 : EXPANSE, BULK; *also* : MASSIVENESS 3 : the principal part 4 : AGGREGATE, WHOLE 5 : the quantity of matter that a body possesses as measured by its inertia 6 : a large quantity, amount, or number 7 : the great body of people — usu. used in pl. — **massy** *adj*

³**mass** *vb* : to form or collect into a mass

Mass *abbr* Massachusetts

mas·sa·cre \'ma-si-kər\ *n* 1 : the killing of many persons under cruel or atrocious circumstances 2 : a wholesale slaughter — **massacre** *vb*

¹**mas·sage** \mə-'säzh, -'säj\ *n* : manipulation of tissues (as by rubbing and kneading) for therapeutic purposes

²**massage** *vb* **mas·saged; mas·sag·ing** 1 : to subject to massage 2 : to treat flatteringly; *also* : MANIPULATE, DOCTOR ⟨∼ data⟩

mas·seur \ma-'sər\ *n* : a man who practices massage

mas·seuse \-'sərz, -'süz\ *n* : a woman who practices massage

mas·sif \ma-'sēf\ *n* : a principal mountain mass

mas·sive \'ma-siv\ *adj* 1 : forming or consisting of a large mass 2 : large in structure, scope, or degree — **mas·sive·ly** *adv* — **mas·sive·ness** *n*

mass·less \'mas-ləs\ *adj* : having no mass ⟨∼ particles⟩

mass medium *n, pl* **mass media** : a medium of communication (as the newspapers or television) that is designed to reach the mass of the people

mass–pro·duce \ˌmas-prə-'düs, -'dyüs\ *vb* : to produce in quantity usu. by machinery — **mass production** *n*

¹**mast** \'mast\ *n* 1 : a long pole or spar rising from the keel or deck of a ship and supporting the yards, booms, and rigging 2 : a slender vertical structure — **mast·ed** \'mas-təd\ *adj*

²**mast** *n* : nuts (as acorns) accumulated on the forest floor and often serving as food for animals (as hogs)

mas·tec·to·my \ma-'stek-tə-mē\ *n, pl* **-mies** : surgical removal of the breast

¹**mas·ter** \'mas-tər\ *n* 1 : a male teacher; *also* : a person holding an academic degree higher than a bachelor's but lower than a doctor's 2 : one highly skilled (as in an art or profession) 3 : one having authority or control 4 : VICTOR, SUPERIOR 5 : the commander of a merchant ship 6 : a youth or boy too young to be called *mister* — used as a title 7 : an original from which copies are made

²**master** *vb* 1 : to become master of : OVERCOME 2 : to become skilled or proficient in 3 : to produce a master recording of (as a musical performance)

master chief petty officer *n* : a petty officer of the highest rank in the navy

mas·ter·ful \'mas-tər-fəl\ *adj* 1 : inclined and usu. competent to act as master **2** : having or reflecting the skill of a master ⟨∼ verse⟩ — **mas·ter·ful·ly** *adv* — **mas·ter·ful·ness** *n*

master gunnery sergeant *n* : a noncommissioned officer in the marine corps ranking above a master sergeant

master key *n* : a key designed to open several different locks

mas·ter·ly \'mas-tər-lē\ *adj* **1** : indicating thorough knowledge or superior skill ⟨∼ performance⟩ **2** : having the skill of a master ⟨a ∼ writer⟩ — **mas·ter·ly** *adv*

mas·ter·mind \-ˌmīnd\ *n* : a person who directs or provides creative intelligence for a project — **mastermind** *vb*

master of ceremonies : a person who acts as host at a formal event or a program of entertainment

mas·ter·piece \'mas-tər-ˌpēs\ *n* : a work done with extraordinary skill

master plan *n* : an overall plan

mas·ter's \'mas-tərz\ *n* : a master's degree

master sergeant *n* **1** : a noncommissioned officer in the army ranking next below a sergeant major **2** : a noncommissioned officer in the air force ranking next below a senior master sergeant **3** : a noncommissioned officer in the marine corps ranking next below a master gunnery sergeant

mas·ter·stroke \'mas-tər-ˌstrōk\ *n* : a masterly performance or move

mas·ter·work \-ˌwərk\ *n* : MASTERPIECE

mas·tery \'mas-tə-rē\ *n* **1** : DOMINION; *also* : SUPERIORITY **2** : possession or display of great skill or knowledge

mast·head \'mast-ˌhed\ *n* **1** : the top of a mast **2** : the printed matter in a newspaper or periodical giving the title and details of ownership and rates of subscription or advertising

mas·tic \'mas-tik\ *n* : a pasty material used as a coating or cement

mas·ti·cate \'mas-tə-ˌkāt\ *vb* **-cat·ed; -cat·ing** : CHEW — **mas·ti·ca·tion** \ˌmas-tə-'kā-shən\ *n*

mas·tiff \'mas-təf\ *n* : any of a breed of large smooth-coated dogs used esp. as guard dogs

mast·odon \'mas-tə-ˌdän\ *n* [NL, fr. Gk *mastos* breast + *odōn, odous* tooth] : any of numerous huge extinct mammals related to the mammoths

mas·toid \'mas-ˌtòid\ *n* : a bony prominence behind the ear — **mastoid** *adj*

mas·tur·ba·tion \ˌmas-tər-'bā-shən\ *n* : stimulation of the genital organs apart from sexual intercourse, usu. to orgasm, and esp. by use of one's own hand — **mas·tur·bate** \'mas-tər-ˌbāt\ *vb* — **mas·tur·ba·to·ry** \'mas-tər-bə-ˌtòr-ē\ *adj*

¹**mat** \'mat\ *n* **1** : a piece of coarse woven or plaited fabric **2** : something made up of many intertwined strands **3** : a large thick pad used as a surface for wrestling and gymnastics

²**mat** *vb* **mat·ted; mat·ting** **1** : to provide with a mat **2** : to form into a tangled mass ⟨dirt *matted* her hair⟩

³**mat** *vb* **mat·ted; mat·ting** **1** *also* **matte** or **matt** : to make (as a color) matte **2** : to provide (a picture) with a mat

⁴**mat** *var of* ²MATTE

⁵**mat** or **matt** or **matte** *n* : a border going around a picture between picture and frame or serving as the frame

mat·a·dor \'ma-tə-ˌdòr\ *n* [Sp, fr. *matar* to kill] : a bullfighter whose role is to kill the bull in a bullfight

¹**match** \'mach\ *n* **1** : a person or thing equal or similar to another; *also* : one able to cope with another : RIVAL **2** : a suitable pairing of persons or objects **3** : a contest or game between two or more individuals **4** : a marriage union; *also* : a prospective marriage partner — **match·less** *adj*

²**match** *vb* **1** : to meet as an antagonist; *also* : PIT ⟨∼ wits⟩ **2** : to provide with a worthy competitor; *also* : to set in comparison with **3** : MARRY **4** : to combine suitably or congenially ⟨∼ed the drapes with the rug⟩; *also* : ADAPT, SUIT **5** : to act in harmony ⟨his shoes and belt ∼⟩ **6** : to provide with a counterpart

³**match** *n* : a short slender piece of flammable material (as wood) tipped with a combustible mixture that ignites through friction

match·book \'mach-ˌbùk\ *n* : a small folder containing rows of paper matches

match·lock \-ˌläk\ *n* : a musket with a slow-burning cord lowered over a hole in the breech to ignite the charge

match·mak·er \-ˌmā-kər\ *n* : one who arranges a match and esp. a marriage

match·wood \-ˌwùd\ *n* : small pieces of wood

¹**mate** \'māt\ *vb* **mat·ed; mat·ing** : CHECKMATE — **mate** *n*

²**mate** *n* **1** : ASSOCIATE, COMPANION; *also* : HELPER **2** : a deck officer on a merchant ship ranking below the captain **3** : one of a pair; *esp* : either member of a married couple or a breeding pair of animals

³**mate** *vb* **mat·ed; mat·ing** **1** : to join or fit together **2** : to come or bring together as mates **3** : COPULATE

¹**ma·te·ri·al** \mə-'tir-ē-əl\ *adj* **1** : PHYSICAL ⟨∼ world⟩; *also* : BODILY ⟨∼ needs⟩ **2** : of or relating to matter rather than form ⟨∼ cause⟩; *also* : EMPIRICAL ⟨∼ knowledge⟩ **3** : highly important : SIGNIFICANT **4** : of a physical or worldly nature ⟨∼ progress⟩ — **ma·te·ri·al·ly** *adv*

²**material** *n* **1** : the elements or substance of which something is composed or made **2** : apparatus necessary for doing or making something

ma·te·ri·al·ise *Brit var of* MATERIALIZE

ma·te·ri·al·ism \mə-'tir-ē-ə-ˌli-zəm\ *n* **1** : a theory that everything can be explained as being or coming from matter **2** : a preoccupation with material rather than intellectual or spiritual things — **ma·te·ri·al·ist** \-list\ *n* or *adj* — **ma·te·ri·al·is·tic** \-ˌtir-ē-ə-'lis-tik\ *adj* — **ma·te·ri·al·is·ti·cal·ly** \-ti-k(ə-)lē\ *adv*

ma·te·ri·al·ize \mə-'tir-ē-ə-ˌlīz\ *vb* **-ized; -iz·ing** **1** : to give material form to; *also* : to assume bodily form **2** : to make an often unexpected appearance — **ma·te·ri·al·i·za·tion** \mə-ˌtir-ē-ə-lə-'zā-shən\ *n*

ma·té·ri·el or **ma·te·ri·el** \mə-ˌtir-ē-'el\ *n* [F *matériel*] : equipment, apparatus, and supplies used by an organization

ma·ter·nal \mə-'tər-nᵊl\ *adj* **1** : MOTHERLY **2** : related through or inherited or derived from a female parent — **ma·ter·nal·ly** *adv*

¹**ma·ter·ni·ty** \mə-'tər-nə-tē\ *n, pl* **-ties** **1** : the quality or state of being a mother; *also* : MOTHERLINESS **2** : a hospital facility for the care of women before and during childbirth and for newborn babies

²**maternity** *adj* **1** : designed for wear during pregnancy ⟨a ∼ dress⟩ **2** : effective for the period close to and including childbirth ⟨∼ leave⟩

¹**math** \'math\ *n* : MATHEMATICS

²**math** *abbr* mathematical; mathematician

math·e·mat·ics \ˌma-thə-'ma-tiks\ *n* : the science of numbers and their properties, operations, and relations and with shapes in space and their structure and measurement — **math·e·mat·i·cal** \-'ma-ti-kəl\ *adj* — **math·e·mat·i·cal·ly** \-ti-k(ə-)lē\ *adv* — **math·e·ma·ti·cian** \ˌma-thə-mə-'ti-shən\ *n*

mat·i·nee or **mat·i·née** \ˌma-tə-'nā\ *n* [F *matinée*, lit., morning, fr. OF, fr. *matin* morning, fr. L *matutinum*, fr. neut. of *matutinus* of the morning, fr. *Matuta*, goddess of morning] : a musical or dramatic performance in the daytime and esp. the afternoon

mat·ins \'ma-tᵊnz\ *n pl, often cap* **1** : special prayers said between midnight and 4 a.m. **2** : a morning service of liturgical prayer in Anglican churches

ma·tri·arch \'mā-trē-ˌärk\ *n* : a woman who rules or dominates a family, group, or state — **ma·tri·ar·chal** \ˌmā-trē-'är-kəl\ *adj* — **ma·tri·ar·chy** \'mā-trē-ˌär-kē\ *n*

ma·tri·cide \'ma-trə-ˌsīd, 'mā-\ *n* : the murder of a mother by her child — **ma·tri·cid·al** \ˌma-trə-'sī-dᵊl, ˌmā-\ *adj*

ma·tric·u·late \mə-'tri-kyə-ˌlāt\ *vb* **-lat·ed; -lat·ing** : to enroll as a member of a body and esp. of a college or university — **ma·tric·u·la·tion** \-ˌtri-kyə-'lā-shən\ *n*

mat·ri·mo·ny \'ma-trə-ˌmō-nē\ *n* [ME, fr. AF *matrimoignie*, fr. L *matrimonium*, fr. *mater* mother, matron] : MARRIAGE — **mat·ri·mo·nial** \ˌma-trə-'mō-nē-əl\ *adj* — **mat·ri·mo·nial·ly** *adv*

ma·trix \'mā-triks\ *n, pl* **ma·tri·ces** \'mā-trə-ˌsēz, 'ma-\ *or* **ma·trix·es** \'mā-trik-səz\ **1** : something within or from which something else originates, develops, or takes form **2** : a mold from which a relief surface (as a piece of type) is made

ma·tron \'mā-trən\ *n* **1** : a married woman usu. of dignified maturity or social distinction **2** : a woman supervisor (as in a school or police station) — **ma·tron·ly** *adj*

Matt *abbr* Matthew

¹**matte** or **matt** *var of* ³MAT

²**matte** *also* **matt** \'mat\ *adj* : not shiny : DULL
¹**mat·ter** \'ma-tər\ *n*   **1** : a subject of interest or concern   **2**
pl : events or circumstances of a particular situation   **3**
: the subject of a discourse or writing   **4** : TROUBLE, DIF-
FICULTY ⟨what's the ∼⟩   **5** : the substance of which a
physical object is composed   **6** : PUS   **7** : an indefinite
amount or quantity ⟨a ∼ of a few days⟩   **8** : something
written or printed   **9** : MAIL — **as a matter of fact** : AC-
TUALLY — **no matter** : without regard to ⟨will follow *no
matter* where you go⟩ — **no matter what** : regardless of
the consequences ⟨must win, *no matter what*⟩
²**matter** *vb* : to be of importance
mat·ter-of-fact \,ma-tə-rəv-'fakt\ *adj* : adhering to fact;
also : being plain, straightforward, or unemotional —
mat·ter-of-fact·ly *adv* — **mat·ter-of-fact·ness** *n*
Mat·thew \'ma-thyü\ *n* — see BIBLE table
mat·tins *often cap chiefly Brit var of* MATINS
mat·tock \'ma-tək\ *n* : a digging and grubbing tool with
features of an adze and an ax or pick
mat·tress \'ma-trəs\ *n*   **1** : a fabric case filled with resilient material used as or for a bed   **2** : an inflatable airtight sack for use as a mattress
mat·u·rate \'ma-chə-,rāt\ *vb* **-rat·ed; -rat·ing** : MATURE
mat·u·ra·tion \,ma-chə-'rā-shən\ *n*   **1** : the process of becoming mature   **2** : the emergence of personal and behavioral characteristics through growth processes —
mat·u·ra·tion·al \-shə-nəl\ *adj*
¹**ma·ture** \mə-'tuṙ, -'tyuṙ\ *adj* **ma·tur·er; -est**   **1** : based on
slow careful consideration   **2** : having attained a final or
desired state   **3** : of or relating to a condition of full development   **4** : suitable only for adults ⟨∼ content⟩   **5**
: due for payment — **ma·ture·ly** *adv*
²**mature** *vb* **ma·tured; ma·tur·ing** : to reach or bring to maturity or completion
ma·tu·ri·ty \mə-'tuṙ-ə-tē, -'tyuṙ-\ *n*   **1** : the quality or state
of being mature; *esp* : full development   **2** : the date when
a note becomes due for payment
ma·tu·ti·nal \,ma-chù-'tī-nᵊl; mə-'tü-tə-nəl, -'tyü-\ *adj* : of,
relating to, or occurring in the morning : EARLY
mat·zo *or* **mat·zoh** \'mät-sə\ *n, pl* **mat·zoth** \-,sōt, -,sōth,
-sōs\ *or* **mat·zos** *or* **mat·zohs** [Yiddish *matse,* fr. Heb
maṣṣāh] : unleavened bread eaten esp. at the Passover
maud·lin \'mȯd-lən\ *adj* [alter. of Mary *Magdalene;* fr. her
depiction as a weeping, penitent sinner]   **1** : drunk
enough to be silly   **2** : weakly and effusively sentimental
¹**maul** \'mȯl\ *n* : a heavy hammer often with a wooden head
used esp. for driving wedges
²**maul** *vb*   **1** : BEAT, BRUISE; *also* : MANGLE   **2** : to handle
roughly
maun·der \'mȯn-dər\ *vb*   **1** : to wander slowly and idly   **2**
: to speak indistinctly or disconnectedly
mau·so·le·um \,mȯ-sə-'lē-əm, ,mȯ-zə-\ *n, pl* **-leums** *or* **-lea**
\-'lē-ə\ [L, fr. Gk *mausōleion,* fr. *Mausōlos* Mausolus † *ab*
353 B.C. ruler of Caria whose tomb was one of the seven
wonders of the ancient world] : a large tomb; *esp* : a usu.
stone building for entombment of the dead above ground
mauve \'mōv, 'mȯv\ *n* : a moderate purple, violet, or lilac
color
ma·ven *also* **ma·vin** \'mā-vən\ *n* [Yiddish *meyvn,* fr. LHeb
mēbhîn] : EXPERT
mav·er·ick \'ma-vrik, -və-rik\ *n* [Samuel A. *Maverick* †
1870 Am. pioneer who did not brand his calves]   **1** : an
unbranded range animal   **2** : NONCONFORMIST
maw \'mȯ\ *n*   **1** : STOMACH; *also* : the crop of a bird   **2**
: the throat, gullet, or jaws esp. of a voracious animal
mawk·ish \'mȯ-kish\ *adj* : sickly sentimental — **mawk-
ish·ly** *adv* — **mawk·ish·ness** *n*
max *abbr* maximum
maxi \'mak-sē\ *n, pl* **max·is** : a long skirt, dress, or coat
maxi- *comb form*   **1** : extra long ⟨*maxi*-kilt⟩   **2** : extra
large ⟨*maxi*-problems⟩
max·il·la \mak-'si-lə\ *n, pl* **max·il·lae** \-'si-(,)lē\ *or* **maxil-
las** : JAW 1; *esp* : an upper jaw — **max·il·lary** \'mak-sə-
,ler-ē\ *adj*
max·im \'mak-səm\ *n* : a proverbial saying
max·i·mal \'mak-sə-məl\ *adj* : MAXIMUM — **max·i·mal·ly**
adv
max·i·mise *Brit var of* MAXIMIZE
max·i·mize \'mak-sə-,mīz\ *vb* **-mized; -miz·ing**   **1** : to increase to a maximum   **2** : to make the most of — **max·i-
mi·za·tion** \,mak-sə-mə-'zā-shən\ *n*

max·i·mum \'mak-sə-məm\ *n, pl* **-ma** \-mə\ *or* **-mums**   **1**
: the greatest quantity, value, or degree   **2** : an upper
limit allowed by authority   **3** : the largest of a set of numbers — **maximum** *adj*
max out *vb*   **1** : to push to or reach a limit or an extreme
2 : to use up all available credit on (a credit card)
may \'mā\ *verbal auxiliary, past* **might** \'mīt\ *pres sing & pl*
may   **1** : have permission or liberty to ⟨you ∼ go now⟩
2 : be in some degree likely to ⟨you ∼ be right⟩   **3** :
used as an auxiliary to express a wish, purpose, contingency, or concession ⟨∼ the best man win⟩
May \'mā\ *n* [ME, fr. OF *mai,* fr. L *Maius,* fr. *Maia,* Roman
goddess] : the 5th month of the year
Ma·ya \'mī-ə\ *n, pl* **Maya** *or* **Mayas** : a member of a group
of American Indian peoples of Yucatán, Guatemala, and
adjacent areas — **Ma·yan** \'mī-ən\ *n or adj*
may·ap·ple \'mā-,a-pəl\ *n* : a No. American woodland herb
related to the barberry that has a poisonous root, one or
two large leaves, and an edible egg-shaped yellow fruit
may·be \'mā-bē, 'me-\ *adv* : PERHAPS
May Day \'mā-,dā\ *n* : May 1 celebrated as a springtime
festival and in some countries as Labor Day
may·flow·er \'mā-,flau̇(-ə)r\ *n* : any of several spring
blooming herbs (as the trailing arbutus or an anemone)
may·fly \'mā-flī\ *n* : any of an order of insects with an
aquatic nymph and a short-lived fragile adult having
membranous wings

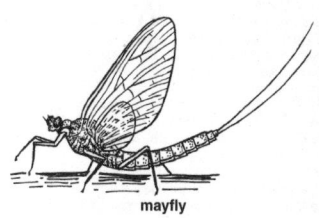

mayfly

may·hem \'mā-,hem, 'mā-əm\ *n*   **1** : willful and permanent crippling, mutilation, or disfigurement of a person
2 : needless or willful damage
may·on·naise \'mā-ə-,nāz\ *n* [F] : a dressing made of egg
yolks, vegetable oil, and vinegar or lemon juice
may·or \'mā-ər\ *n* : an official elected to act as chief executive or nominal head of a city or borough — **may·or·al**
\-əl\ *adj* — **may·or·al·ty** \-əl-tē\ *n*
may·pole \'mā-,pōl\ *n, often cap* : a tall flower-wreathed
pole forming a center for May Day sports and dances
maze \'māz\ *n* : a confusing intricate network of passages
— **mazy** *adj*
ma·zur·ka \mə-'zər-kə\ *n* : a Polish dance in moderate
triple measure
MB *abbr* Manitoba
MBA *abbr* master of business administration
mc *abbr* megacycle
¹**MC** *n* : MASTER OF CEREMONIES
²**MC** *abbr* member of Congress
Mc- \mək\ *mə before forms beginning with* k *or* g\ *prefix*
: used to indicate a convenient, low-quality version of a
specified thing ⟨*Mc*Book⟩
Mc·Coy \mə-'kȯi\ *n* : something that is neither imitation
nor substitute ⟨the real ∼⟩
McGuffin *var of* MACGUFFIN
MCPO *abbr* master chief petty officer
¹**Md** *abbr* Maryland
²**Md** *symbol* mendelevium
MD *abbr*   **1** [NL *medicinae doctor*] doctor of medicine   **2**
Maryland   **3** muscular dystrophy
MDMA \,em-,dē-,em-'ā\ *n* : ECSTASY 2
mdnt *abbr* midnight
mdse *abbr* merchandise
MDT *abbr* mountain daylight (saving) time
me \'mē\ *pron, objective case of* I
Me *abbr* Maine
ME *abbr*   **1** Maine   **2** mechanical engineer   **3** medical
examiner
¹**mead** \'mēd\ *n* : an alcoholic beverage brewed from water
and honey, malt, and yeast

²mead *n, archaic* : MEADOW

mead·ow \'me-dō\ *n* : land in or mainly in grass; *esp* : a tract of moist low-lying usu. level grassland — **mead·ow·land** \-,land\ *n* — **mead·owy** \'me-də-wē\ *adj*

mead·ow·lark \'me-dō-,lärk\ *n* : any of several American songbirds related to the orioles that are streaked brown above and in northernmost forms have a yellow breast marked with a black crescent

mead·ow·sweet \-,swēt\ *n* : a No. American native or naturalized spirea

mea·ger *or* **mea·gre** \'mē-gər\ *adj* **1** : THIN **2** : lacking richness, fertility, or strength; *also* : POOR ⟨a ~ income⟩ ♦ **Synonyms** SCANTY, SCANT, SPARE, SPARSE — **mea·ger·ly** *adv* — **mea·ger·ness** *n*

¹meal \'mēl\ *n* **1** : an act or the time of eating a portion of food **2** : the portion of food eaten at a meal

²meal *n* **1** : usu. coarsely ground seeds of a cereal **2** : a product resembling seed meal — **mealy** *adj*

meal·time \'mēl-,tīm\ *n* : the usual time at which a meal is served

mealy·bug \'mē-lē-,bəg\ *n* : any of a family of scale insects with a white cottony or waxy covering that are destructive pests esp. of fruit trees

mealy·mouthed \'mē-lē-,mau̇thd, -,mau̇tht\ *adj* : not plain and straightforward : DEVIOUS

¹mean \'mēn\ *vb* **meant** \'ment\; **mean·ing 1** : to have in the mind as a purpose **2** : to serve to convey, show, or indicate : SIGNIFY ⟨red ~s stop⟩ **3** : to have importance to the degree of ⟨~s the world to me⟩ **4** : to direct to a particular individual ⟨a gift *meant* for me⟩

²mean *adj* **1** : HUMBLE **2** : lacking acumen : DULL **3** : SHABBY, CONTEMPTIBLE ⟨no ~ feat⟩ **4** : IGNOBLE, BASE **5** : STINGY **6** : pettily selfish or malicious **7** : VEXATIOUS **8** : EXCELLENT ⟨throws a ~ slider⟩ — **mean·ly** *adv* — **mean·ness** *n*

³mean *adj* **1** : occupying a middle position (as in space, order, or time) **2** : being a mean : AVERAGE ⟨a ~ value⟩

⁴mean *n* **1** : a middle point between extremes **2** *pl* : something helpful in achieving a desired end **3** *pl* : material resources affording a secure life **4** : ARITHMETIC MEAN

¹me·an·der \mē-'an-dər\ *n* [L *maeander*, fr. Gk *maiandros*, fr. *Maiandros* (now *Menderes*), river in Asia Minor] **1** : a winding course **2** : a winding of a stream — **me·an·drous** \-drəs\ *adj*

²meander *vb* **1** : to follow a winding course **2** : to wander aimlessly or casually

mean·ing *n* **1** : the thing one intends to convey esp. by language; *also* : the thing that is thus conveyed **2** : AIM **3** : SIGNIFICANCE; *esp* : implication of a hidden significance **4** : CONNOTATION; *also* : DENOTATION — **mean·ing·ful** \-fəl\ *adj* — **mean·ing·ful·ly** *adv* — **mean·ing·less** *adj*

¹mean·time \'mēn-,tīm\ *n* : the intervening time

²meantime *adv* : MEANWHILE

¹mean·while \-,hwīl(-ə)l\ *n* : MEANTIME

²meanwhile *adv* **1** : during the intervening time **2** : at the same time

meas *abbr* measure

mea·sles \'mē-zəlz\ *n sing or pl* : an acute virus disease marked by fever and an eruption of distinct circular red spots

mea·sly \'mēz-lē, -zə-lē\ *adj* **mea·sli·er; -est** : contemptibly small or insignificant

¹mea·sure \'me-zhər, 'mā-\ *n* **1** : an adequate or moderate portion; *also* : a suitable limit **2** : the dimensions, capacity, or amount of something ascertained by measuring; *also* : an instrument for measuring **3** : a unit of measurement; *also* : a system of such units **4** : the act or process of measuring **5** : rhythmic structure or movement **6** : the part of a musical staff between two bars **7** : CRITERION **8** : a means to an end **9** : a legislative bill — **mea·sure·less** *adj*

²measure *vb* **mea·sured; mea·sur·ing 1** : to mark or fix in multiples of a specific unit ⟨~ off five centimeters⟩ **2** : to find out the size, extent, or amount of **3** : to bring into comparison or competition **4** : to serve as a means of measuring **5** : to have a specified measurement — **mea·sur·able** \'me-zhə-rə-bəl, 'mā-\ *adj* — **mea·sur·ably** \-blē\ *adv* — **mea·sur·er** *n*

mea·sure·ment \'me-zhər-mənt, 'mā-\ *n* **1** : the act or

process of measuring **2** : a figure, extent, or amount obtained by measuring

measure up *vb* **1** : to have necessary or fitting qualifications **2** : to equal esp. in ability

meat \'mēt\ *n* **1** : FOOD; *esp* : solid food as distinguished from drink **2** : animal and esp. mammal flesh considered as food **3** : the edible part inside a covering (as a shell or rind) — **meaty** *adj*

meat·ball \-,bȯl\ *n* : a small ball of chopped or ground meat

meat loaf *n* : a dish of ground meat seasoned and baked in the form of a loaf

mec·ca \'me-kə\ *n, often cap* [*Mecca,* Saudi Arabia, a destination of pilgrims in the Islamic world] : a center of a specified activity or interest ⟨a shopping ~⟩

mech *abbr* mechanical; mechanics

¹me·chan·ic \mi-'ka-nik\ *adj* : of or relating to manual work or skill

²mechanic *n* **1** : a manual worker **2** : MACHINIST; *esp* : one who repairs cars

me·chan·i·cal \mi-'ka-ni-kəl\ *adj* **1** : of or relating to machinery, to manual operations, or to mechanics **2** : done as if by a machine : AUTOMATIC ⟨a ~ response⟩ ♦ **Synonyms** INSTINCTIVE, IMPULSIVE, SPONTANEOUS — **me·chan·i·cal·ly** \-k(ə-)lē\ *adv*

mechanical drawing *n* : drawing done with the aid of instruments

me·chan·ics \mi-'ka-niks\ *n sing or pl* **1** : a branch of physics that deals with energy and forces and their effect on bodies **2** : the practical application of mechanics (as to the operation of machines) **3** : mechanical or functional details ⟨the ~ of the brain⟩

mech·a·nism \'me-kə-,ni-zəm\ *n* **1** : a piece of machinery; *also* : a process or technique for achieving a result **2** : mechanical operation or action **3** : the fundamental processes involved in or responsible for a natural phenomenon ⟨the visual ~⟩

mech·a·nis·tic \,me-kə-'nis-tik\ *adj* **1** : mechanically determined ⟨~ universe⟩ **2** : MECHANICAL — **mech·a·nis·ti·cal·ly** \-ti-k(ə-)lē\ *adv*

mech·a·nize \'me-kə-,nīz\ *vb* **-nized; -niz·ing 1** : to make mechanical **2** : to equip with machinery esp. in order to replace human or animal labor **3** : to equip with armed and armored motor vehicles — **mech·a·ni·za·tion** \,me-kə-nə-'zā-shən\ *n* — **mech·a·niz·er** *n*

¹med \'med\ *adj* : MEDICAL ⟨~ school⟩

²med *n* : MEDICINE **1** — usu. used in pl.

³med *abbr* **1** medical; medicine **2** medieval **3** medium

MEd *abbr* master of education

med·al \'me-dᵊl\ *n* [MF *medaille,* fr. OIt *medaglia* coin worth half a denarius, medal, fr. VL **medalis* half, alter. of LL *medialis* middle, fr. L *medius*] **1** : a small usu. metal object bearing a religious emblem or picture **2** : a piece of metal issued to commemorate a person or event or to award excellence or achievement

med·al·ist *or* **med·al·list** \'me-dᵊl-ist\ *n* **1** : a designer or maker of medals **2** : a recipient of a medal as an award

me·dal·lion \mə-'dal-yən\ *n* **1** : a large medal **2** : a tablet or panel bearing a portrait or an ornament

med·dle \'me-dᵊl\ *vb* **med·dled; med·dling** : to interfere without right or propriety — **med·dler** \'me-dᵊl-ər\ *n*

med·dle·some \'me-dᵊl-səm\ *adj* : inclined to meddle

med·e·vac *also* **med·i·vac** \'me-də-,vak\ *n* **1** : emergency evacuation of the sick or wounded **2** : a helicopter used for medevac

me·dia \'mē-dē-ə\ *n, pl* **me·di·as 1** : MEDIUM 4 **2** *sing or pl in constr* : MASS MEDIA

me·di·al \'mē-dē-əl\ *adj* : occurring in or extending toward the middle

¹me·di·an \'mē-dē-ən\ *n* **1** : a value in an ordered set of values below and above which there are an equal number of values **2** : MEDIAN STRIP

²median *adj* **1** : being in the middle or in an intermediate position **2** : relating to or constituting a statistical median

median strip *n* : a strip dividing a highway into lanes according to the direction of travel

me·di·ate \'mē-dē-,āt\ *vb* **-at·ed; -at·ing 1** : to act as an intermediary; *esp* : to work with opposing sides in order to resolve (as a dispute) or bring about (as a settlement) **2** : to bring about, influence, or transmit (as a physical process or effect) by acting as an intermediate or controlling agent or mechanism ◆ *Synonyms* INTERCEDE, INTERVENE, INTERPOSE, INTERFERE — **me·di·a·tion** \ˌmē-dē-ˈā-shən\ *n* — **me·di·a·tor** \ˈmē-dē-ˌā-tər\ *n*

med·ic \ˈme-dik\ *n* : one engaged in medical work; *esp* : CORPSMAN

med·i·ca·ble \ˈme-di-kə-bəl\ *adj* : CURABLE

Med·ic·aid \ˈme-di-ˌkād\ *n* : a program of financial assistance for medical care designed for those unable to afford regular medical service and financed jointly by the state and federal governments

med·i·cal \ˈme-di-kəl\ *adj* : of or relating to the science or practice of medicine or the treatment of disease — **med·i·cal·ly** \-k(ə-)lē\ *adv*

medical examiner *n* : a public officer who performs autopsies on bodies to find the cause of death

me·di·ca·ment \mi-ˈdi-kə-mənt, ˈme-di-kə-\ *n* : a substance used in therapy

Medi·care \ˈme-di-ˌker\ *n* : a government program of financial assistance for medical care esp. for the aged

med·i·cate \ˈme-də-ˌkāt\ *vb* **-cat·ed; -cat·ing** : to treat with medicine

med·i·ca·tion \ˌme-də-ˈkā-shən\ *n* **1** : the act or process of medicating **2** : MEDICINE 1

me·dic·i·nal \mə-ˈdi-sᵊn-əl\ *adj* : tending or used to cure disease or relieve pain — **me·dic·i·nal·ly** *adv*

med·i·cine \ˈme-də-sən\ *n* **1** : a substance or preparation used in treating disease **2** : a science and art dealing with the prevention, alleviation, and cure of disease

medicine ball *n* : a heavy stuffed leather ball used for conditioning exercises

medicine man *n* : a priestly healer or sorcerer esp. among the American Indians : SHAMAN

med·i·co \ˈme-di-ˌkō\ *n, pl* **-cos** : a medical practitioner or student

me·di·e·val *also* **me·di·ae·val** \ˌmē-dē-ˈē-vəl, ˌme-, mē-ˈdē-vəl\ *adj* **1** : of, relating to, or characteristic of the Middle Ages **2** : having a quality (as cruelty) associated with the Middle Ages **3** : extremely outmoded or antiquated — **me·di·e·val·ism** \-və-ˌli-zəm\ *n* — **me·di·e·val·ist** \-list\ *n*

me·di·o·cre \ˌmē-dē-ˈō-kər\ *adj* [MF, fr. L *mediocris*, fr. *medius* middle + *ocris* stony mountain] : of moderate or low quality : ORDINARY — **me·di·oc·ri·ty** \-ˈä-krə-tē\ *n*

med·i·tate \ˈme-də-ˌtāt\ *vb* **-tat·ed; -tat·ing 1** : to muse over : CONTEMPLATE, PONDER **2** : to engage in deep mental exercise directed toward a heightened level of spiritual awareness **3** : INTEND, PLAN — **med·i·ta·tion** \ˌme-də-ˈtā-shən\ *n* — **med·i·ta·tive** \ˈme-də-ˌtā-tiv\ *adj* — **med·i·ta·tive·ly** *adv*

Med·i·ter·ra·nean \ˌme-də-tə-ˈrā-nē-ən, -ˈrā-nyən\ *adj* : of or relating to the Mediterranean Sea or to the lands or people around it

¹me·di·um \ˈmē-dē-əm\ *n, pl* **mediums** *or* **me·dia** \-dē-ə\ [L] **1** : something in a middle position; *also* : a middle position or degree **2** : a means of effecting or conveying something **3** : a surrounding or enveloping substance **4** : a channel or system of communication, information, or entertainment **5** : a mode of artistic expression **6** : an individual held to be a channel of communication between the earthly world and a world of spirits **7** : a condition or environment in which something may function or flourish

²medium *adj* : intermediate in amount, quality, position, or degree

me·di·um·is·tic \ˌmē-dē-ə-ˈmis-tik\ *adj* : of, relating to, or being a spiritualistic medium

medivac *var of* MEDEVAC

med·ley \ˈmed-lē\ *n, pl* **medleys 1** : HODGEPODGE **2** : a musical composition made up esp. of a series of songs

me·dul·la \mə-ˈdə-lə\ *n, pl* **-las** *or* **-lae** \-(ˌ)lē, -ˌlī\ : an inner or deep anatomical part; *also* : the posterior part (**medulla ob·lon·ga·ta** \-ˌä-blón-ˈgä-tə\) of the vertebrate brain that is continuous with the spinal cord

meed \ˈmēd\ *n* : a fitting return

meek \ˈmēk\ *adj* **1** : enduring injury with patience and without resentment **2** : deficient in spirit and courage **3** : MODERATE — **meek·ly** *adv* — **meek·ness** *n*

meer·schaum \ˈmir-shəm, -ˌshóm\ *n* [G, fr. *Meer* sea + *Schaum* foam] : a tobacco pipe made of a light white clayey mineral

¹meet \ˈmēt\ *vb* **met** \ˈmet\; **meet·ing 1** : to come upon

: FIND **2** : JOIN, INTERSECT **3** : to appear to the perception of **4** : OPPOSE, FIGHT **5** : to join in conversation or discussion; *also* : ASSEMBLE **6** : to conform to **7** : to pay fully **8** : to cope with **9** : to provide for **10** : to be introduced to

²meet *n* : an assembling esp. for a hunt or for competitive sports

³meet *adj* : SUITABLE, PROPER

meet·ing \ˈmē-tiŋ\ *n* **1** : an act of coming together : ASSEMBLY **2** : JUNCTION, INTERSECTION

meet·ing·house \-ˌhaůs\ *n* : a building for public assembly and esp. for Protestant worship

meg \ˈmeg\ *n* : MEGABYTE

mega- *or* **meg-** *comb form* **1** : great : large ⟨*mega*hit⟩ **2** : million ⟨*mega*hertz⟩

mega·byte \ˈme-gə-ˌbīt\ *n* : 1024 kilobytes or 1,048,576 bytes; *also* : one million bytes

mega·cy·cle \-ˌsī-kəl\ *n* : MEGAHERTZ

mega·death \-ˌdeth\ *n* : one million deaths — used as a unit in reference to nuclear warfare

mega·hertz \ˈme-gə-ˌhərts, -ˌherts\ *n* : a unit of frequency equal to one million hertz

mega·lith \ˈme-gə-ˌlith\ *n* : a large stone used in prehistoric monuments — **mega·lith·ic** \ˌme-gə-ˈli-thik\ *adj*

meg·a·lo·ma·nia \ˌme-gə-lō-ˈmā-nē-ə, -nyə\ *n* : a mental disorder marked by feelings of personal omnipotence and grandeur — **meg·a·lo·ma·ni·ac** \-ˈmā-nē-ˌak\ *adj or n* — **meg·a·lo·ma·ni·a·cal** \-mə-ˈnī-ə-kəl\ *adj*

meg·a·lop·o·lis \ˌme-gə-ˈlä-pə-ləs\ *n* : a very large urban unit

mega·phone \ˈme-gə-ˌfōn\ *n* : a cone-shaped device used to intensify or direct the voice — **megaphone** *vb*

mega·pix·el \ˈme-gə-ˌpik-səl\ *n* : one million pixels

mega·plex \-ˌpleks\ *n* : a cineplex having usu. at least 16 movie theaters

mega·ton \-ˌtən\ *n* : an explosive force equivalent to that of one million tons of TNT

mega·vi·ta·min \-ˌvī-tə-mən\ *adj* : relating to or consisting of very large doses of vitamins — **mega·vi·ta·mins** *n pl*

mei·o·sis \mī-ˈō-səs\ *n* : a process of cell division in gamete-producing cells in which the number of chromosomes is reduced to one half — **mei·ot·ic** \mī-ˈä-tik\ *adj*

meit·ner·i·um \mīt-ˈnir-ē-əm, -ˈner-\ *n* : an artificially produced radioactive chemical element

mel·an·cho·lia \ˌme-lən-ˈkō-lē-ə\ *n* : a mental condition marked by extreme depression often with delusions

mel·an·chol·ic \ˌme-lən-ˈkä-lik\ *adj* **1** : DEPRESSED **2** : of or relating to melancholia

mel·an·choly \ˈme-lən-ˌkä-lē\ *n, pl* **-chol·ies** [ME *malencolie*, fr. AF, fr. LL *melancholia*, fr. Gk, fr. *melan-, melas* black + *cholē* bile; so called fr. the former belief that it was caused by an excess of black bile] : depression of spirits : DEJECTION — **melancholy** *adj*

Mel·a·ne·sian \ˌme-lə-ˈnē-zhən\ *n* : a member of the dominant native group of the Pacific island grouping of Melanesia — **Melanesian** *adj*

mé·lange \mā-ˈlä°zh, -ˈlänj\ *n* : a mixture esp. of incongruous elements

mel·a·nin \ˈme-lə-nən\ *n* : any of various dark brown pigments of animal or plant structures (as skin or hair)

mel·a·nism \ˈme-lə-ˌni-zəm\ *n* : an increased amount of black or nearly black pigmentation

mel·a·no·ma \ˌme-lə-ˈnō-mə\ *n, pl* **-mas** *also* **-ma·ta** \-mə-tə\ : a usu. malignant tumor containing dark pigment

¹meld \ˈmeld\ *vb* : to show or announce for a score in a card game

²meld *n* : a card or combination of cards that is or can be melded

me·lee \ˈmā-ˌlā, mā-ˈlā\ *n* [F *mêlée*] : a confused struggle ◆ *Synonyms* FRACAS, ROW, BRAWL, DONNYBROOK

me·lio·rate \ˈmēl-yə-ˌrāt, ˈmē-lē-ə-\ *vb* **-rat·ed; -rat·ing** : AMELIORATE — **me·lio·ra·tion** \ˌmēl-yə-ˈrā-shən, ˌmē-lē-ə-\ *n* — **me·lio·ra·tive** \ˈmēl-yə-ˌrā-tiv, ˈmē-lē-ə-\ *adj*

mel·lif·lu·ous \me-ˈli-flə-wəs, mə-\ *adj* [ME *mellyfluous*, fr. LL *melliflus*, fr. L *mel* honey + *fluere* to flow] : sweetly flowing — **mel·lif·lu·ous·ly** *adv* — **mel·lif·lu·ous·ness** *n*

¹mel·low \ˈme-lō\ *adj* **1** : soft and sweet because of ripeness; *also* : well aged and pleasingly mild (⟨∼ wine⟩ **2** : made gentle by age or experience **3** : being rich and full but not garish or strident (⟨∼ colors⟩ **4** : of soft loamy consistency (⟨∼ soil⟩ — **mel·low·ness** *n*

²**mellow** vb : to make or become mellow — often used with *out*

me·lo·di·ous \mə-'lō-dē-əs\ adj : pleasing to the ear — **me·lo·di·ous·ly** adv — **me·lo·di·ous·ness** n

melo·dra·ma \'me-lə-ˌdrä-mə, -ˌdra-\ n 1 : an extravagantly theatrical play in which action and plot predominate over characterization 2 : something having a sensational or theatrical quality — **melo·dra·mat·ic** \ˌme-lə-drə-'ma-tik\ adj — **melo·dra·mat·i·cal·ly** \-ti-k(ə-)lē\ adv — **melo·dra·ma·tist** \ˌme-lə-'dra-mə-tist, -'drä-\ n

mel·o·dy \'me-lə-dē\ n, pl **-dies** 1 : sweet or agreeable sound 2 : a particular succession of notes : TUNE, AIR — **me·lod·ic** \mə-'lä-dik\ adj — **me·lod·i·cal·ly** \-di-k(ə-)lē\ adv

mel·on \'me-lən\ n : any of various typically sweet fruits (as a muskmelon or watermelon) of the gourd family usu. eaten raw

¹**melt** \'melt\ vb 1 : to change from a solid to a liquid state usu. by heat 2 : DISSOLVE, DISINTEGRATE; also : to cause to disperse or disappear 3 : to make or become tender or gentle

²**melt** n : a melted substance

melt·down \'melt-ˌdaùn\ n 1 : the melting of the core of a nuclear reactor 2 : a collapse of something (as one's self-control)

melting pot n : a place where different races, cultures, or individuals assimilate into a cohesive whole

melt·wa·ter \-ˌwö-tər, -ˌwä-\ n : water derived from the melting of ice and snow

mem abbr 1 member 2 memoir 3 memorial

mem·ber \'mem-bər\ n 1 : a part (as an arm, leg, leaf, or branch) of an animal or plant 2 : one of the individuals composing a group 3 : a part of a whole ⟨∼s of a set⟩

mem·ber·ship \-ˌship\ n 1 : the state or status of being a member 2 : the body of members

mem·brane \'mem-ˌbrān\ n : a thin pliable layer esp. of animal or plant origin — **mem·bra·nous** \-brə-nəs\ adj

me·men·to \mə-'men-tō\ n, pl **-tos** or **-toes** [ME, fr. L, remember, imper. of *meminisse* to remember] : something that serves to warn or remind; also : SOUVENIR

memo \'me-mō\ n, pl **mem·os** : MEMORANDUM

mem·oir \'mem-ˌwär\ n 1 : MEMORANDUM 2 : AUTOBIOGRAPHY — usu. used in pl. 3 : an account of something noteworthy; also, pl : the record of the proceedings of a learned society

mem·o·ra·bil·ia \ˌme-mə-rə-'bi-lē-ə, -'bil-yə\ n pl [L] 1 : things worthy of remembrance 2 : things associated with a particular interest and that are usu. collected : MEMENTOS

mem·o·ra·ble \'me-mə-rə-bəl\ adj : worth remembering : NOTABLE — **mem·o·ra·bil·i·ty** \ˌme-mə-rə-'bi-lə-tē\ n — **mem·o·ra·ble·ness** n — **mem·o·ra·bly** \-blē\ adv

mem·o·ran·dum \ˌme-mə-'ran-dəm\ n, pl **-dums** or **-da** \-də\ 1 : an informal record; also : a written reminder 2 : an informal written note

¹**me·mo·ri·al** \mə-'mòr-ē-əl\ adj : serving to preserve remembrance

²**memorial** n 1 : something designed to keep remembrance alive; esp : MONUMENT 2 : a statement of facts often accompanied with a petition — **me·mo·ri·al·ize** vb

Memorial Day n : the last Monday in May or formerly May 30 observed as a legal holiday in honor of those who died in war

mem·o·rise Brit var of MEMORIZE

mem·o·rize \'me-mə-ˌrīz\ vb **-rized; -riz·ing** : to learn by heart — **mem·o·ri·za·tion** \ˌme-mə-rə-'zā-shən\ n — **mem·o·riz·er** n

mem·o·ry \'me-mə-rē\ n, pl **-ries** 1 : the power or process of remembering 2 : the store of things remembered 3 : COMMEMORATION 4 : something remembered 5 : the time within which past events are remembered 6 : a device (as in a computer) in which information can be stored; esp : RAM 7 : capacity for storing information ⟨512 megabytes of ∼⟩ ♦ Synonyms REMEMBRANCE, RECOLLECTION, REMINISCENCE

men pl of MAN

¹**men·ace** \'me-nəs\ n 1 : THREAT 2 : DANGER; also : NUISANCE

²**menace** vb **men·aced; men·ac·ing** 1 : THREATEN 2 : ENDANGER — **men·ac·ing·ly** adv

mé·nage \mā-'näzh\ n [F] : HOUSEHOLD

ménage à trois \-ä-'trwä\ n : an arrangement in which three persons share sexual relations esp. while living together

me·nag·er·ie \mə-'na-jə-rē\ n : a collection of wild animals esp. for exhibition

¹**mend** \'mend\ vb 1 : to improve in manners or morals 2 : to put into good shape : REPAIR 2 : to improve in or restore to health : HEAL — **mend·er** n

²**mend** n 1 : an act of mending 2 : a mended place

men·da·cious \men-'dā-shəs\ adj : given to deception or falsehood : UNTRUTHFUL ♦ Synonyms DISHONEST, DECEITFUL — **men·da·cious·ly** adv — **men·dac·i·ty** \-'da-sə-tē\ n

men·de·le·vi·um \ˌmen-də-'lē-vē-əm, -'lā-\ n : a radioactive metallic chemical element artificially produced

men·di·cant \'men-di-kənt\ n 1 : BEGGAR 2 often cap : FRIAR — **men·di·can·cy** \-kən-sē\ n — **mendicant** adj

men·folk \'men-ˌfōk\ or **men·folks** \-ˌfōks\ n pl 1 : men in general 2 : the men of a family or community

men·ha·den \men-'hā-dᵊn, mən-\ n, pl **-den** also **-dens** : a marine fish related to the herring that is abundant along the Atlantic coast of the U.S.

¹**me·nial** \'mē-nē-əl, -nyəl\ n : a domestic servant

²**menial** adj 1 : of or relating to servants 2 : HUMBLE, SERVILE ⟨answered in ∼ tones⟩ — **me·ni·al·ly** adv

men·in·gi·tis \ˌme-nən-'jī-təs\ n, pl **-git·i·des** \-'ji-tə-ˌdēz\ : inflammation of the membranes enclosing the brain and spinal cord; also : a usu. bacterial disease marked by this

me·ninx \'mē-niŋks, 'me-\ n, pl **me·nin·ges** \mə-'nin-(ˌ)jēz\ : any of the three membranes that envelop the brain and spinal cord — **men·in·ge·al** \ˌme-nən-'jē-əl\ adj

me·nis·cus \mə-'nis-kəs\ n, pl **me·nis·ci** \-'nis-ˌkī, -ˌkē\ also **me·nis·cus·es** 1 : CRESCENT 2 : the curved upper surface of a column of liquid

men·o·pause \'me-nə-ˌpöz\ n : the period of life when menstruation stops naturally — **men·o·paus·al** \ˌme-nə-'pö-zəl\ adj

me·no·rah \mə-'nòr-ə\ n [Heb *mĕnōrāh* candlestick] : a candelabrum that is used in Jewish worship

men·ses \'men-ˌsēz\ n sing or pl : the menstrual flow

menstrual cycle n : the complete cycle of physiological changes from the beginning of one menstrual period to the beginning of the next

men·stru·a·tion \ˌmen-strə-'wā-shən, men-'strā-\ n : a discharging of bloody matter at approximately monthly intervals from the uterus of breeding-age nonpregnant primate females; also : PERIOD 6 — **men·stru·al** \'men-strə-wəl\ adj — **men·stru·ate** \'men-strə-ˌwāt, -ˌstrāt\ vb

men·su·ra·ble \'men-sə-rə-bəl, '-chə-\ adj : MEASURABLE

men·su·ra·tion \ˌmen-sə-'rā-shən, ˌmen-chə-\ n : MEASUREMENT

-ment n suffix 1 : concrete result, object, or agent of a (specified) action ⟨embank*ment*⟩ ⟨entangle*ment*⟩ 2 : concrete means or instrument of a (specified) action ⟨entertain*ment*⟩ 3 : action : process ⟨encircle*ment*⟩ ⟨develop*ment*⟩ 4 : place of a (specified) action ⟨encamp*ment*⟩ 5 : state : condition ⟨amaze*ment*⟩

men·tal \'men-tᵊl\ adj 1 : of or relating to the mind 2 : of, relating to, or affected with a disorder of the mind ⟨∼ illness⟩ — **men·tal·ly** adv

mental age n : a measure of a child's mental development in terms of the number of years it takes an average child to reach the same level

mental deficiency n : MENTAL RETARDATION

men·tal·i·ty \men-'ta-lə-tē\ n, pl **-ties** 1 : mental power or capacity 2 : mode or way of thought

mental retardation n : subaverage intellectual ability present from infancy that is characterized by an IQ of 70 or less and problems in development, learning, and social adjustment — **mentally retarded** adj

men·tee \men-'tē\ n : PROTÉGÉ

men·thol \'men-ˌthòl, -ˌthōl\ n : an alcohol occurring esp. in mint oils that has the odor and cooling properties of peppermint — **men·tho·lat·ed** \-thə-ˌlā-təd\ adj

¹**men·tion** \'men-chən\ n 1 : a brief or casual reference 2 : a formal citation for outstanding achievement

²**mention** vb : to refer to : CITE 2 : to cite for superior achievement — **not to mention** : not even yet counting or considering

men·tor \'men-,tŏr, -tər\ *n* : a trusted counselor or guide; *also* : TUTOR, COACH — **mentor** *vb*

menu \'men-yū, 'mān-\ *n, pl* **menus** [F, fr. *menu* small, detailed, fr. OF, fr. L *minutus* minute (adj.)] **1** : a list of the dishes available (as in a restaurant) for a meal; *also* : the dishes served **2** : a list of offerings or options

me·ow \mē-'aù\ *vb* : to make the characteristic cry of a cat — **meow** *n*

mer *abbr* meridian

mer·can·tile \'mər-kən-,tēl, -,tī(-ə)l\ *adj* : of or relating to merchants or trading

¹mer·ce·nary \'mər-sə-,ner-ē\ *n, pl* **-nar·ies** : a person who serves merely for wages; *esp* : a soldier hired into foreign service

²mercenary *adj* **1** : serving merely for pay or gain **2** : hired for service in a foreign army

mer·cer \'mər-sər\ *n, Brit* : a dealer in usu. expensive fabrics

mer·cer·ise *Brit var of* MERCERIZE

mer·cer·ize \'mər-sə-,rīz\ *vb* **-ized; -iz·ing** : to treat cotton yarn or cloth with alkali so that it looks silky or takes a better dye

¹mer·chan·dise \'mər-chən-,dīz, -,dīs\ *n* : the commodities or goods that are bought and sold in business

²mer·chan·dise \-,dīz\ *vb* **-dised; -dis·ing** : to buy and sell in business : TRADE — **mer·chan·dis·er** *n*

mer·chant \'mər-chənt\ *n* **1** : a buyer and seller of commodities for profit **2** : STOREKEEPER

mer·chant·able \'mər-chən-tə-bəl\ *adj* : acceptable to buyers : MARKETABLE

mer·chant·man \'mər-chənt-mən\ *n* : a ship used in commerce

merchant marine *n* : the commercial ships of a nation

merchant ship *n* : MERCHANTMAN

mer·ci·ful·ly \'mər-si-fə-lē\ *adv* **1** : in a merciful manner **2** : FORTUNATELY 2 〈~ we didn't have to attend〉

mer·cu·ri·al \,mər-'kyùr-ē-əl\ *adj* **1** : unpredictably changeable **2** : MERCURIC — **mer·cu·ri·al·ly** *adv* — **mer·cu·ri·al·ness** *n*

mer·cu·ric \,mər-'kyùr-ik\ *adj* : of, relating to, or containing mercury

mercuric chloride *n* : a poisonous compound of mercury and chlorine used as an antiseptic and fungicide

mer·cu·ry \'mər-kyə-rē\ *n, pl* **-ries** **1** : a heavy silver-white liquid metallic chemical element used esp. in scientific instruments **2** *cap* : the planet nearest the sun — see PLANET table

mer·cy \'mər-sē\ *n, pl* **mercies** [ME, fr. AF *merci*, fr. ML *merced-, merces*, fr. L, price paid, wages, fr. *merc-, merx* merchandise] **1** : compassion shown to an offender; *also* : imprisonment rather than death for first-degree murder **2** : a blessing resulting from divine favor or compassion; *also* : a fortunate circumstance **3** : compassion shown to victims of misfortune — **mer·ci·ful** \-si-fəl\ *adj* — **mer·ci·less** \-si-ləs\ *adj* — **mer·ci·less·ly** *adv* — **mercy** *adj*

mercy killing *n* : EUTHANASIA

¹mere \'mir\ *n* : LAKE, POOL

²mere *adj, superlative* **mer·est** **1** : not diluted : PURE **2** : being nothing more than 〈a ~ child〉 — **mere·ly** *adv*

mer·e·tri·cious \,mer-ə-'tri-shəs\ *adj* [L *meretricius*, fr. *meretrix* prostitute, fr. *merēre* to earn] : tawdrily attractive 〈~ trinkets〉; *also* : SPECIOUS — **mer·e·tri·cious·ly** *adv* — **mer·e·tri·cious·ness** *n*

mer·gan·ser \(,)mər-'gan-sər\ *n* : any of various fish-eating wild ducks with a usu. crested head and a slender bill hooked at the end and serrated along the margins

merganser

merge \'mərj\ *vb* **merged; merg·ing** **1** : to blend gradually **2** : to combine, unite, or coalesce into one ✦ **Synonyms** MINGLE, AMALGAMATE, FUSE, INTERFUSE, INTERMINGLE

merg·er \'mər-jər\ *n* **1** : the act or process of merging **2** : absorption by a corporation of one or more others

me·rid·i·an \mə-'ri-dē-ən\ *n* [ME, fr. AF *meridien*, fr. *meridien* of noon, fr. L *meridianus*, fr. *meridies* noon, south, irreg. fr. *medius* mid + *dies* day] **1** : the highest point : CULMINATION **2** : any of the imaginary circles on the earth's surface passing through the north and south poles **3** : any of the pathways along which the body's vital energy flows according to the theory behind acupuncture — **meridian** *adj*

me·ringue \mə-'raŋ\ *n* [F] : a baked dessert topping of stiffly beaten egg whites and powdered sugar

me·ri·no \mə-'rē-nō\ *n, pl* **-nos** [Sp] **1** : any of a breed of sheep noted for fine soft wool **2** : a fine soft fabric or yarn of wool or wool and cotton

¹mer·it \'mer-ət\ *n* **1** : laudable or blameworthy traits or actions **2** : a praiseworthy quality; *also* : character or conduct deserving reward or honor **3** *pl* : the intrinsic nature of a legal case; *also* : legal significance

²merit *vb* : EARN, DESERVE

mer·i·toc·ra·cy \,mer-ə-'tä-krə-sē\ *n, pl* **-cies** : a system in which the talented are chosen and moved ahead based on their achievement; *also* : leadership by the talented

mer·i·to·ri·ous \,mer-ə-'tòr-ē-əs\ *adj* : deserving honor or esteem — **mer·i·to·ri·ous·ly** *adv* — **mer·i·to·ri·ous·ness** *n*

mer·lin \'mər-lən\ *n* : a small compact falcon of the northern hemisphere

mer·lot \mer-'lō, mər-\ *n* : a dry red wine made from a widely grown grape; *also* : the grape itself

mer·maid \'mər-,mād\ *n* : a legendary sea creature with a woman's upper body and a fish's tail

mer·man \-,man, -mən\ *n* : a legendary sea creature with a man's upper body and a fish's tail

mer·ri·ment \'mer-i-mənt\ *n* **1** : HILARITY **2** : FESTIVITY

mer·ry \'mer-ē\ *adj* **mer·ri·er; -est** **1** : full of gaiety or high spirits **2** : marked by festivity **3** : BRISK 〈a ~ pace〉 ✦ **Synonyms** BLITHE, JOCUND, JOVIAL, JOLLY, MIRTHFUL — **mer·ri·ly** \'mer-ə-lē\ *adv*

merry–go–round \'mer-ē-gō-,raùnd\ *n* **1** : a circular revolving platform with benches and figures of animals on which people sit for a ride **2** : a busy round of activities

mer·ry·mak·ing \'mer-ē-,mā-kiŋ\ *n* **1** : jovial or festive activity **2** : a festive occasion — **mer·ry·mak·er** \-,mā-kər\ *n*

me·sa \'mā-sə\ *n* [Sp, lit., table, fr. L *mensa*] : a flat-topped hill with steep sides

mes·cal \me-'skal, mə-\ *n* **1** : PEYOTE 2 **2** : a usu. colorless liquor distilled from the leaves of an agave; *also* : this agave

mes·ca·line \'mes-kə-lən, -,lēn\ *n* : a hallucinatory alkaloid from the peyote cactus

mes·clun \'mes-klən\ *n* : a mixture of young tender greens; *also* : a salad made with mesclun

mesdames *pl of* MADAM, *or of* MADAME, *or of* MRS.

mesdemoiselles *pl of* MADEMOISELLE

¹mesh \'mesh\ *n* **1** : one of the openings between the threads or cords of a net; *also* : one of the similar spaces in a network **2** : the fabric of a net **3** : NETWORK **4** : working contact (as of the teeth of gears) 〈in ~〉 — **meshed** \'mesht\ *adj*

²mesh *vb* **1** : to catch in or as if in a mesh **2** : to be in or come into mesh : ENGAGE **3** : to fit together properly

mesh·work \'mesh-,wərk\ *n* : NETWORK

me·si·al \'mē-zē-əl, -sē-\ *adj* : of, relating to, or being the surface of a tooth that is closest to the middle of the front of the jaw

mes·mer·ise *Brit var of* MESMERIZE

mes·mer·ize \'mez-mə-,rīz\ *vb* **-ized; -iz·ing** : HYPNOTIZE — **mes·mer·ic** \mez-'mer-ik\ *adj* — **mes·mer·ism** \'mez-mə-,ri-zəm\ *n*

Me·so·lith·ic \,me-zə-'li-thik\ *adj* : of, relating to, or being a transitional period of the Stone Age between the Paleolithic and the Neolithic periods

me·so·sphere \'me-zə-,sfir\ *n* : a layer of the atmosphere between the stratosphere and the thermosphere

Me·so·zo·ic \,me-zə-'zō-ik, ,mē-\ *adj* : of, relating to, or being the era of geologic history between the Paleozoic and the Cenozoic and extending from about 245 million years ago to about 65 million years ago — **Mesozoic** n

mes·quite \mə-ˈskēt, me-\ n : any of several spiny leguminous trees and shrubs chiefly of the southwestern U.S. with sugar-rich pods important as fodder; also : mesquite wood used esp. in grilling food

¹**mess** \ˈmes\ n [ME mes, fr. AF, fr. LL missus course at a meal, fr. missus, pp. of mittere to put, fr. L, to send] **1** : a quantity of food; also : enough food of a specified kind for a dish or meal ⟨a ~ of beans⟩ **2** : a group of persons who regularly eat together; also : a meal eaten by such a group **3** : a place where meals are regularly served to a group **4** : a confused, dirty, or offensive state — **messy** adj

²**mess** vb **1** : to supply with meals; also : to take meals with a mess **2** : to make dirty or untidy; also : BUNGLE **3** : INTERFERE, MEDDLE ⟨don't ~ with me⟩ **4** : PUTTER, TRIFLE

mes·sage \ˈme-sij\ n : a communication sent by one person to another

message board n : BULLETIN BOARD 2

messeigneurs pl of MONSEIGNEUR

mes·sen·ger \ˈme-sᵊn-jər\ n : one who carries a message or does an errand

messenger RNA n : an RNA that carries the code for a particular protein from DNA in the nucleus to a ribosome in the cytoplasm and acts as a template for the formation of that protein

Mes·si·ah \mə-ˈsī-ə\ n **1** : the expected king and deliverer of the Jews **2** : Jesus **3** not cap : a professed or accepted leader of a cause — **mes·si·an·ic** \ˌme-sē-ˈa-nik\ adj

messieurs pl of MONSIEUR

mess·mate \ˈmes-ˌmāt\ n : a member of a group who eat regularly together

Messrs. \ˈme-sərz\ pl of MR.

mes·ti·zo \me-ˈstē-zō\ n, pl **-zos** [Sp] : a person of mixed blood

¹**met** past and past part of MEET

²**met** abbr metropolitan

me·tab·o·lism \mə-ˈta-bə-ˌli-zəm\ n : the processes by which the substance of plants and animals incidental to life is built up and broken down; also : the processes by which a substance is handled in the living body ⟨the ~ of sugar⟩ — **met·a·bol·ic** \ˌme-tə-ˈbä-lik\ adj — **me·tab·o·lize** \mə-ˈta-bə-ˌlīz\ vb

me·tab·o·lite \-ˌlīt\ n **1** : a product of metabolism **2** : a substance essential to the metabolism of a particular organism or to a metabolic process

meta·car·pal \ˌme-tə-ˈkär-pəl\ n : any of usu. five more or less elongated bones of the part of the hand or forefoot between the wrist and the bones of the digits — **metacarpal** adj

meta·car·pus \-ˈkär-pəs\ n : the part of the hand or forefoot that contains the metacarpals

met·al \ˈme-tᵊl\ n **1** : any of various opaque, fusible, ductile, and typically lustrous substances that are good conductors of electricity and heat **2** : METTLE; also : the material out of which a person or thing is made — **me·tal·lic** \mə-ˈta-lik\ adj

met·al·lur·gy \ˈme-tᵊl-ˌər-jē\ n : the science and technology of metals — **met·al·lur·gi·cal** \ˌme-tᵊl-ˈər-ji-kəl\ adj — **met·al·lur·gist** \ˈme-tᵊl-ˌər-jist\ n

met·al·ware \ˈme-tᵊl-ˌwer\ n : metal utensils for household use

met·al·work \-ˌwərk\ n : work and esp. artistic work made of metal — **met·al·work·er** \-ˌwər-kər\ n — **met·al·work·ing** n

meta·mor·phism \ˌme-tə-ˈmȯr-ˌfi-zəm\ n : a change in the structure of rock; esp : a change to a more compact and more highly crystalline form produced by pressure, heat, and water — **meta·mor·phic** \-ˈmȯr-fik\ adj

meta·mor·pho·sis \ˌme-tə-ˈmȯr-fə-səs\ n, pl **-pho·ses** \-ˌsēz\ **1** : a change of physical form, structure, or substance esp. by supernatural means; also : a striking alteration (as in appearance or character) **2** : a fundamental change in form and often habits of an animal accompanying the transformation of a larva into an adult — **meta·mor·phose** \-ˌfōz, -ˌfōs\ vb

met·a·phor \ˈme-tə-ˌfȯr\ n : a figure of speech in which a word for one idea or thing is used in place of another to

suggest a likeness between them (as in "the ship plows the sea") — **met·a·phor·ic** \ˌme-tə-ˈfȯr-ik\ or **met·a·phor·i·cal** \ˌme-tə-ˈfȯr-i-kəl\ adj — **met·a·phor·i·cal·ly** \-i-k(ə-)lē\ adv

meta·phys·ics \ˌme-tə-ˈfi-ziks\ n [ML Metaphysica, title of Aristotle's treatise on the subject, fr. Gk (ta) meta (ta) physika, lit., the (works) after the physical (works); fr. its position in his collected works] : the philosophical study of the ultimate causes and underlying nature of things — **meta·phys·i·cal** \-ˈfi-zi-kəl\ adj — **meta·phy·si·cian** \-fə-ˈzi-shən\ n

me·tas·ta·sis \mə-ˈtas-tə-səs\ n, pl **-ta·ses** \-ˌsēz\ : the spread of a health-impairing agency (as cancer cells) from the initial or primary site of disease to another part of the body; also : a secondary growth of a malignant tumor — **me·tas·ta·size** \-tə-ˌsīz\ vb — **met·a·stat·ic** \ˌme-tə-ˈsta-tik\ adj

meta·tar·sal \ˌme-tə-ˈtär-səl\ n : any of the bones of the foot between the tarsus and the bones of the digits that in humans include five elongated bones — **metatarsal** adj

meta·tar·sus \-ˈtär-səs\ n : the part of the human foot or the hind foot in quadrupeds that contains the metatarsals

¹**mete** \ˈmēt\ vb **met·ed; met·ing** **1** archaic : MEASURE **2** : ALLOT — usu. used with out ⟨~ out punishment⟩

²**mete** n : BOUNDARY ⟨~s and bounds⟩

me·te·or \ˈmē-tē-ər, -ˌȯr\ n **1** : a small particle of matter in the solar system directly observable only by its glow from frictional heating on falling into the earth's atmosphere **2** : the streak of light produced by a meteor

me·te·or·ic \ˌmē-tē-ˈȯr-ik\ adj **1** : of, relating to, or resembling a meteor **2** : transiently brilliant ⟨a ~ career⟩ — **me·te·or·i·cal·ly** \-i-k(ə-)lē\ adv

me·te·or·ite \ˈmē-tē-ə-ˌrīt\ n : a meteor that reaches the surface of the earth

me·te·or·oid \ˈmē-tē-ə-ˌrȯid\ n : a small particle of matter in the solar system

me·te·o·rol·o·gy \ˌmē-tē-ə-ˈrä-lə-jē\ n : a science that deals with the atmosphere and its phenomena and esp. with weather forecasting — **me·te·o·ro·log·ic** \ˌmē-tē-ˌȯr-ə-ˈlä-jik\ or **me·te·o·ro·log·i·cal** \-ˈlä-ji-kəl\ adj — **me·te·o·rol·o·gist** \ˌmē-tē-ə-ˈrä-lə-jist\ n

¹**me·ter** \ˈmē-tər\ n : rhythm in verse or music

²**meter** n : the basic metric unit of length — see METRIC SYSTEM table

³**meter** n : a measuring and sometimes recording instrument

⁴**meter** vb **1** : to measure by means of a meter **2** : to print postal indicia on by means of a postage meter ⟨~ed mail⟩

meter–kilogram–second adj : of, relating to, or being a system of units based on the meter, the kilogram, and the second

meter maid n : a woman assigned to write tickets for parking violations

meth·a·done \ˈme-thə-ˌdōn\ also **meth·a·don** \-ˌdän\ n : a synthetic addictive narcotic drug used esp. as a substitute narcotic in the treatment of heroin addiction

meth·am·phet·amine \ˌme-tham-ˈfe-tə-ˌmēn, -thəm-, -mən\ n : a drug used medically in the form of its hydrochloride in the treatment of obesity and often illicitly as a stimulant

meth·ane \ˈme-ˌthān\ n : a colorless odorless flammable gas produced by decomposition of organic matter or from coal and used esp. as a fuel

meth·a·nol \ˈme-thə-ˌnȯl, -ˌnōl\ n : a volatile flammable poisonous liquid alcohol used esp. as a solvent and as an antifreeze

meth·aqua·lone \me-ˈtha-kwə-ˌlōn\ n : a sedative and hypnotic habit-forming drug that is not a barbiturate

meth·od \ˈme-thəd\ n [ME, prescribed treatment, fr. L methodus, fr. Gk methodos, fr. meta with + hodos way] **1** : a procedure or process for achieving an end **2** : orderly arrangement : PLAN ✦ Synonyms MODE, MANNER, WAY, FASHION, SYSTEM — **me·thod·i·cal** \mə-ˈthä-di-kəl\ adj — **me·thod·i·cal·ly** \-k(ə-)lē\ adv — **me·thod·i·cal·ness** n

meth·od·ise Brit var of METHODIZE

Meth·od·ist \ˈme-thə-dist\ n : a member of a Protestant denomination adhering to the doctrines of John Wesley — **Meth·od·ism** \-ˌdi-zəm\ n

meth·od·ize \ˈme-thə-ˌdīz\ vb **-ized; -iz·ing** : SYSTEMATIZE

meth·od·ol·o·gy \ˌme-thə-'dä-lə-jē\ *n, pl* **-gies** **1** : a body of methods and rules followed in a science or discipline **2** : the study of the principles or procedures of inquiry in a particular field
meth·yl \'me-thəl\ *n* : a chemical radical consisting of carbon and hydrogen
methyl alcohol *n* : METHANOL
meth·yl·mer·cury \ˌme-thəl-'mər-kyə-rē\ *n* : any of various toxic compounds of mercury that often occur as pollutants which accumulate in animals esp. at the top of a food chain
met·i·cal \'me-ti-kəl\ *n, pl* **met·i·cais** \-kī\ *also* **meticals** — see MONEY table
me·tic·u·lous \mə-'ti-kyə-ləs\ *adj* [L *meticulosus* fearful, fr. *metus* fear] : extremely careful in attending to details — **me·tic·u·lous·ly** *adv* — **me·tic·u·lous·ness** *n*
mé·tier \'me-ˌtyā, me-'tyā\ *n* : an area of activity in which one is expert or successful
me·tre \'mē-tər\ *chiefly Brit var of* METER
met·ric \'me-trik\ *adj* **1** : of or relating to measurement; *esp* : of or relating to the metric system **2** : METRICAL 1
met·ri·cal \'me-tri-kəl\ *adj* **1** : of, relating to, or composed in meter **2** : METRIC 1 — **met·ri·cal·ly** \-k(ə-)lē\ *adv*
met·ri·ca·tion \ˌme-tri-'kā-shən\ *n* : the act or process of converting into or expressing in the metric system
met·ri·cize \'me-trə-ˌsīz\ *vb* **-cized; -ciz·ing** : to change into or express in the metric system
metric system *n* : a decimal system of weights and measures based on the meter and on the kilogram
☞ the METRIC SYSTEM table is on page 310
metric ton — see METRIC SYSTEM table
¹me·tro \'me-trō\ *n, pl* **metros** : SUBWAY
²metro *adj* : of, relating to, or characteristic of a metropolis and sometimes including its suburbs
met·ro·nome \'me-trə-ˌnōm\ *n* : an instrument for marking exact time by a regularly repeated tick
me·trop·o·lis \mə-'trä-pə-ləs\ *n* [ME, fr. LL, fr. Gk *mētropolis*, fr. *mētēr* mother + *polis* city] : the chief or capital city of a country, state, or region — **met·ro·pol·i·tan** \ˌme-trə-'pä-lə-tən\ *adj*
met·tle \'me-t³l\ *n* **1** : SPIRIT, COURAGE **2** : quality of temperament
met·tle·some \'me-t³l-səm\ *adj* : full of mettle : COURAGEOUS
MeV *abbr* million electron volts
¹mew \'myü\ *vb* : MEOW — **mew** *n*
²mew *vb* : CONFINE
mews \'myüz\ *n sing or pl, chiefly Brit* : stables usu. with living quarters built around a court; *also* : a narrow street with dwellings converted from stables
Mex *abbr* Mexican; Mexico
mez·za·nine \'me-zə-ˌnēn, ˌme-zə-'\ *n* **1** : a low-ceilinged story between two main stories of a building **2** : the lowest balcony in a theater; *also* : the first few rows of such a balcony
mez·zo for·te \ˌmet-(ˌ)sō-'fȯr-ˌtā, ˌmed-(ˌ)zō-, -tē\ *adj or adv* [It] : moderately loud — used as a direction in music
mez·zo pia·no \-pē-'ä-(ˌ)nō\ *adj or adv* [It] : moderately soft — used as a direction in music
mez·zo-so·pra·no \-sə-'pra-nō, -'prä-\ *n* : a woman's voice having a range between that of the soprano and contralto; *also* : a singer having such a voice
MFA *abbr* master of fine arts
mfr *abbr* manufacture; manufacturer
mg *abbr* milligram
Mg *symbol* magnesium
MG *abbr* **1** machine gun **2** major general **3** military government
mgr *abbr* **1** manager **2** monseigneur **3** monsignor
mgt *or* **mgmt** *abbr* management
MGy Sgt *abbr* master gunnery sergeant
MHz *abbr* megahertz
mi *abbr* **1** mile; mileage **2** mill
MI *abbr* **1** Michigan **2** military intelligence
MIA \ˌem-(ˌ)ī-'ä\ *n* [*missing in action*] : a member of the armed forces whose whereabouts following a combat mission are unknown
Mi·ami \mī-'a-mē, -mə\ *n, pl* **Mi·ami** *or* **Mi·am·is** : a member of an American Indian people orig. of Wisconsin and Indiana

mi·as·ma \mī-'az-mə, mē-\ *n, pl* **-mas** *also* **-ma·ta** \-mə-tə\ **1** : a vapor from a swamp formerly believed to cause disease **2** : a harmful influence or atmosphere — **mi·as·mal** \-məl\ *adj* — **mi·as·mic** \-mik\ *adj*
mic \'mīk\ *n* : MICROPHONE
Mic *abbr* Micah
mi·ca \'mī-kə\ *n* [NL, fr. L, grain, crumb] : any of various mineral silicates readily separable into thin transparent sheets
Mi·cah \'mī-kə\ *n* — see BIBLE table
mice *pl of* MOUSE
Mich *abbr* Michigan
Mi·che·as \'mī-kē-əs, mī-'kē-əs\ *n* : MICAH
Mic·mac \'mik-ˌmak\ *n, pl* **Micmac** *or* **Micmacs** : a member of an American Indian people of eastern Canada
micr- *or* **micro-** *comb form* **1** : small : minute ⟨*micro*capsule⟩ **2** : one millionth part of a specified unit ⟨*micro*second⟩
¹mi·cro \'mī-krō\ *adj* **1** : very small; *esp* : MICROSCOPIC **2** : involving minute quantities or variations
²micro *n* : MICROCOMPUTER
mi·crobe \'mī-ˌkrōb\ *n* : MICROORGANISM; *esp* : one causing disease — **mi·cro·bi·al** \mī-'krō-bē-əl\ *adj*
mi·cro·bi·ol·o·gy \ˌmī-krō-bī-'ä-lə-jē\ *n* : a branch of biology dealing esp. with microscopic forms of life — **mi·cro·bi·o·log·i·cal** \-ˌbī-ə-'lä-ji-kəl\ *adj* — **mi·cro·bi·ol·o·gist** \-bī-'ä-lə-jist\ *n*
mi·cro·brew·ery \'mī-krō-ˌbrü-ə-rē\ *n* : a small brewery making specialty beer in limited quantities
mi·cro·burst \-ˌbərst\ *n* : a violent short-lived localized downdraft that creates extreme wind shears at low altitudes
mi·cro·cap·sule \'mī-krō-ˌkap-səl, -ˌsül\ *n* : a tiny capsule containing material (as a medicine) released when the capsule is broken, melted, or dissolved
mi·cro·chip \-ˌchip\ *n* : INTEGRATED CIRCUIT
mi·cro·cir·cuit \-ˌsər-kət\ *n* : a compact electronic circuit
mi·cro·com·put·er \-kəm-ˌpyü-tər\ *n* : a small computer that uses a microprocessor; *esp* : PERSONAL COMPUTER
mi·cro·cosm \'mī-krə-ˌkä-zəm\ *n* : an individual or community thought of as a miniature world or universe
mi·cro·elec·tron·ics \'mī-krō-i-ˌlek-'trä-niks\ *n* : a branch of electronics that deals with the miniaturization of electronic circuits and components — **mi·cro·elec·tron·ic** \-nik\ *adj*
mi·cro·en·cap·su·late \ˌmī-krō-in-'kap-sə-ˌlāt\ *vb* : to enclose (as a drug) in a microcapsule — **mi·cro·en·cap·su·la·tion** \-in-ˌkap-sə-'lā-shən\ *n*
mi·cro·fi·ber \'mī-krō-ˌfī-bər\ *n* : a fine usu. soft polyester fiber; *also* : fabric made from such fibers
mi·cro·fiche \'mī-krō-ˌfēsh, -ˌfish\ *n, pl* **-fiche** *or* **-fiches** *same or* -fē-shəz, -fi-\ : a sheet of microfilm containing rows of images of pages of printed matter
mi·cro·film \-ˌfilm\ *n* : a film bearing a photographic record (as of print) on a reduced scale — **microfilm** *vb*
mi·cro·graph \'mī-krə-ˌgraf\ *n* : a graphic reproduction of the image of an object formed by a microscope
mi·cro·man·age \ˌmī-krō-'ma-nij\ *vb* : to manage esp. with excessive control or attention to details — **mi·cro·man·age·ment** \-mənt\ *n* — **mi·cro·man·ag·er** \-ni-jər\ *n*
mi·cro·me·te·or·ite \ˌmī-krō-'mē-tē-ə-ˌrīt\ *n* : a very small particle in interplanetary space
mi·crom·e·ter \mī-'krä-mə-tər\ *n* : an instrument used with a telescope or microscope for measuring minute distances
mi·cro·min·ia·tur·i·za·tion \ˌmī-krō-ˌmi-nē-ə-ˌchùr-ə-'zā-shən, -ˌmi-ni-ˌchùr-, -char-\ *n* : the process of producing things in a very small size and esp. in a size smaller than one considered miniature — **mi·cro·min·ia·tur·ized** \-'mi-nē-ə-chə-ˌrīzd, -'mi-ni-chə-\ *adj*
mi·cron \'mī-ˌkrän\ *n* : one millionth of a meter
mi·cro·or·gan·ism \ˌmī-krō-'ȯr-gə-ˌni-zəm\ *n* : an organism (as a bacterium) too tiny to be seen by the unaided eye
mi·cro·phone \'mī-krə-ˌfōn\ *n* : an instrument for converting sound waves into variations of an electric current for transmitting or recording sound
mi·cro·pho·to·graph \ˌmī-krə-'fō-tə-ˌgraf\ *n* : PHOTOMICROGRAPH
mi·cro·pro·ces·sor \ˌmī-krō-'prä-ˌse-sər\ *n* : a computer processor contained on a microchip
mi·cro·scope \'mī-krə-ˌskōp\ *n* : an instrument for mak-

METRIC SYSTEM

LENGTH

UNIT (SYMBOL)	METRIC EQUIVALENT	U.S. EQUIVALENT
kilometer (km)	1,000 meters	0.62 mile
hectometer (hm)	100 meters	328.08 feet
dekameter (dam)	10 meters	32.81 feet
meter (m)	1 meter	39.37 inches
decimeter (dm)	0.1 meter	3.94 inches
centimeter (cm)	0.01 meter	0.39 inch
millimeter (mm)	0.001 meter	0.039 inch
micrometer (μm)	0.000001 meter	0.000039 inch

AREA

UNIT (SYMBOL)	METRIC EQUIVALENT	U.S. EQUIVALENT
square kilometer (sq km or km^2)	1,000,000 square meters	0.39 square miles
hectare (ha)	10,000 square meters	2.47 acres
are (a)	100 square meters	119.60 square yards
square centimeter (sq cm or cm^2)	0.0001 square meter	0.16 square inch

VOLUME

UNIT (SYMBOL)	METRIC EQUIVALENT	U.S. EQUIVALENT
cubic meter (m^3)		1.31 cubic yards
cubic decimeter (dm^3)	0.001 cubic meter	61.02 cubic inches
cubic centimeter (cu cm or cm^3 also cc)	0.000001 cubic meter	0.061 cubic inch

MASS AND WEIGHT

UNIT (SYMBOL)	METRIC EQUIVALENT	U.S. EQUIVALENT
metric ton (t)	1,000,000 grams	1.10 short tons
kilogram (kg)	1,000 grams	2.20 pounds
hectogram (hg)	100 grams	3.53 ounces
dekagram (dag)	10 grams	0.35 ounce
gram (g)		0.035 ounce
decigram (dg)	0.1 gram	1.54 grains
centigram (cg)	0.01 gram	0.15 grain
milligram (mg)	0.001 gram	0.015 grain
microgram (μg or mcg)	0.000001 gram	0.000015 grain

CAPACITY

UNIT (SYMBOL)	METRIC EQUIVALENT	U.S. EQUIVALENT		
		CUBIC	DRY	LIQUID
kiloliter (kl)	1,000 liters	1.31 cubic yards	28.38 bushels	264.17 gallons
hectoliter (hl)	100 liters	3.53 cubic feet	2.84 bushels	26.42 gallons
dekaliter (dal)	10 liters	0.35 cubic foot	1.14 pecks	2.64 gallons
liter (l)		61.02 cubic inches	0.91 quart	1.06 quarts
deciliter (dl)	0.1 liter	6.10 cubic inches	0.18 pint	0.21 pint
centiliter (cl)	0.01 liter	0.61 cubic inch		0.34 fluid ounce
milliliter (ml)	0.001 liter	0.061 cubic inch		0.27 fluid dram
microliter (μl)	0.000001 liter	0.000061 cubic inch		0.00027 fluid dram

For metric system equivalents of U.S. system units, see WEIGHTS AND MEASURES table.

ing magnified images of minute objects usu. using light —

mi·cros·co·py \mī-'kräs-kə-pē\ n

mi·cro·scop·ic \ˌmī-krə-'skä-pik\ *also* **mi·cro·scop·i·cal** \-pi-kəl\ *adj* **1** : of, relating to, or involving the use of the microscope **2** : too tiny to be seen without the use of a microscope : very small — **mi·cro·scop·i·cal·ly** \-pi-k(ə-)lē\ *adv*

mi·cro·sec·ond \'mī-krō-ˌse-kənd\ n : one millionth of a second

mi·cro·sur·gery \ˌmī-krō-'sər-jə-rē\ n : minute dissection or manipulation (as by a laser beam) of living structures or tissue — **mi·cro·sur·gi·cal** \-'sər-ji-kəl\ *adj*

mi·cro·tech·nol·o·gy \-tek-'nä-lə-jē\ n : technology on a small or microscopic scale

¹**mi·cro·wave** \'mī-krə-ˌwāv\ n **1** : a radio wave between one millimeter and one meter in wavelength **2** : MICROWAVE OVEN

²**microwave** *vb* : to heat or cook in a microwave oven — **mi·cro·wav·able** *or* **mi·cro·wave·able** \ˌmī-krə-'wā-və-bəl\ *adj*

microwave oven n : an oven in which food is cooked by the absorption of microwave energy by water molecules in the food

¹**mid** \'mid\ *adj* : MIDDLE

²**mid** *abbr* middle

mid·air \'mid-'er\ n : a point or region in the air well above the ground

mid·day \'mid-ˌdā, -'dā\ n : NOON

mid·den \'mi-dᵊn\ n : a refuse heap

¹**mid·dle** \'mi-dᵊl\ *adj* **1** : equally distant from the extremes : MEDIAL, CENTRAL **2** : being at neither extreme : INTERMEDIATE **3** *cap* : constituting an intermediate period

²**middle** n **1** : a middle part, point, or position **2** : WAIST

middle age n : the period of life from about 45 to about 64 — **mid·dle-aged** \ˌmi-dᵊl-'äjd\ *adj*

Middle Ages n pl : the period of European history from about A.D. 500 to about 1500

mid·dle·brow \'mi-dᵊl-ˌbrau̇\ n : a person who is moderately but not highly cultivated — **middlebrow** *adj*

middle class n : a social class holding a position between the upper class and the lower class — **middle-class** *adj*

middle ear n : a small membrane-lined cavity of the ear through which sound waves are transmitted by a chain of tiny bones

middle finger n : the midmost of the five digits of the hand

mid·dle·man \'mi-dᵊl-ˌman\ n : INTERMEDIARY; *esp* : one intermediate between the producer of goods and the retailer or consumer

middle-of-the-road *adj* : standing for or following a course of action midway between extremes; *esp* : being neither liberal nor conservative in politics — **mid·dle-of-the-road·er** \-'rō-dər\ n — **mid·dle-of-the-road·ism** \-'rō-ˌdi-zəm\ n

middle school n : a school usu. including grades 5 to 8 or 6 to 8

mid·dle·weight \'mi-dᵊl-ˌwāt\ n : one of average weight; *esp* : a boxer weighing not over 160 pounds

mid·dling \'mid-liŋ, -lən\ *adj* **1** : of middle, medium, or moderate size, degree, or quality **2** : MEDIOCRE

mid·dy \'mi-dē\ n, pl **middies** : MIDSHIPMAN

midge \'mij\ n : a very small fly : GNAT

midg·et \'mi-jət\ n **1** : something (as an animal) very small for its kind **2** *sometimes offensive* : a very small person

midi \'mi-dē\ n : a calf-length dress, coat, or skirt

MIDI \'mi-dē\ n [*musical instrument digital interface*] : a protocol for the transmission of digitally encoded music

mid·land \'mid-lənd, -ˌland\ n : the interior or central region of a country

mid·life \'mid-'līf\ n : MIDDLE AGE

midlife crisis n : a period of emotional turmoil in middle age characterized esp. by a strong desire for change

mid·most \-ˌmōst\ *adj* : being in or near the exact middle — **midmost** *adv*

mid·night \-ˌnīt\ n : 12 o'clock at night

mid-ocean ridge \'mid-'ō-shən-\ n : an elevation on an ocean floor at the boundary of diverging tectonic plates

mid·point \'mid-ˌpȯint, -'pȯint\ n : a point at or near the center or middle

mid·riff \'mi-ˌdrif\ n [ME *midrif*, fr. OE *midhrif*, fr. *midde*

mid + *hrif* belly] **1** : DIAPHRAGM 1 **2** : the mid-region of the human torso

mid·sec·tion \-ˌsek-shən\ n : a section midway between the extremes; *esp* : MIDRIFF 2

mid·ship·man \'mid-ˌship-mən, (ˌ)mid-'ship-\ n : a student in a naval academy

mid·ships \-ˌships\ *adv* : AMIDSHIPS

midst \'midst\ n **1** : the interior or central part or point **2** : a position of proximity to the members of a group ⟨in our ∼⟩ **3** : the condition of being surrounded or beset — **midst** *prep*

mid·stream \'mid-'strēm, -ˌstrēm\ n : the middle of a stream

mid·sum·mer \-'sə-mər, -ˌsə-\ n **1** : the middle of summer **2** : the summer solstice

mid·town \'mid-ˌtau̇n, -'tau̇n\ n : a central section of a city; *esp* : one situated between sections called *downtown* and *uptown* — **midtown** *adj*

¹**mid·way** \'mid-ˌwā, -'wā\ *adv* : in the middle of the way or distance

²**mid·way** \-ˌwā\ n : an avenue (as at a carnival) for concessions and amusements

mid·week \-ˌwēk\ n : the middle of the week — **mid·week·ly** \-ˌwē-klē, -'wē-\ *adj or adv*

mid·wife \'mid-ˌwīf\ n : a person who helps women in childbirth — **mid·wife·ry** \-ˌwi-fə-rē\ n

mid·win·ter \'mid-'win-tər, -ˌwin-\ n **1** : the winter solstice **2** : the middle of winter

mid·year \-ˌyir\ n **1** : the middle of a year **2** : a midyear examination — **midyear** *adj*

mien \'mēn\ n **1** : air or bearing esp. as expressive of mood or personality : DEMEANOR **2** : APPEARANCE, ASPECT ⟨dresses of formal ∼⟩

miff \'mif\ *vb* : to put into an ill humor

¹**might** \'mīt\ *verbal auxiliary, past of* MAY — used as an auxiliary to express permission or possibility in the past, a present condition contrary to fact, less probability or possibility than *may*, or as a polite alternative to *may*, *ought*, or *should*

²**might** n : the power, authority, or resources of an individual or a group

mighty \'mī-tē\ *adj* **might·i·er; -est 1** : very strong : POWERFUL **2** : GREAT, NOTABLE — **might·i·ly** \'mī-tə-lē\ — **might·i·ness** \-tē-nəs\ n — **mighty** *adv*

mi·gnon·ette \ˌmin-yə-'net\ n : an annual garden herb with spikes of tiny fragrant flowers

mi·graine \'mī-ˌgrān\ n [ME *mygreyn*, fr. MF *migraine*, fr. LL *hemicrania* pain in one side of the head, fr. Gk *hēmikrania*, fr. *hēmi-* half + *kranion* cranium] : a condition marked by recurrent severe headache and often nausea; *also* : an attack of migraine

mi·grant \'mī-grənt\ n : one that migrates; *esp* : a person who moves in order to find work (as picking crops) — **migrant** *adj*

mi·grate \'mī-ˌgrāt\ *vb* **mi·grat·ed; mi·grat·ing 1** : to move from one country or place to another **2** : to pass usu. periodically from one region or climate to another for feeding or breeding — **mi·gra·tion** \mī-'grā-shən\ n — **mi·gra·to·ry** \'mī-grə-ˌtȯr-ē\ *adj*

mi·ka·do \mə-'kä-dō\ n, pl **-dos** : an emperor of Japan

mike \'mīk\ n : MICROPHONE

¹**mil** \'mil\ n : a unit of length equal to ¹/₁₀₀₀ inch

²**mil** *abbr* military

milch \'milk, 'milch\ *adj* : giving milk ⟨∼ cow⟩

mild \'mī(-ə)ld\ *adj* **1** : gentle in nature or behavior **2** : moderate in action or effect **3** : TEMPERATE ⟨∼ weather⟩ ◆ ***Synonyms*** EASY, COMPLAISANT, AMIABLE, LENIENT — **mild·ly** *adv* — **mild·ness** n

mil·dew \'mil-ˌdü, -ˌdyü\ n : a superficial usu. whitish growth produced on organic matter and on plants by a fungus; *also* : a fungus producing this growth — **mildew** *vb*

mile \'mī(-ə)l\ n [ME, fr. OE *mīl*, fr. L *milia* miles, fr. *milia passuum*, lit., thousands of paces] **1** — see WEIGHT table **2** : NAUTICAL MILE

mile·age \'mī-lij\ n **1** : an allowance for traveling expenses at a certain rate per mile **2** : distance in miles traveled (as in a day) **3** : the amount of service yielded (as by a tire) expressed in terms of miles of travel **4** : the average number of miles a motor vehicle will travel on a gallon of gasoline

mile·post \'mī(-ə)l-ˌpōst\ *n* : a post indicating the distance in miles from a given point

mile·stone \-ˌstōn\ *n* **1** : a stone serving as a milepost **2** : a significant point in development

mi·lieu \mēl-'yər, -'yü, -'yœ̃\ *n, pl* **mi·lieus** *or* **mi·lieux** *same or* -'yərz, -'yüz, -'yœz\ [F] : ENVIRONMENT, SETTING

mil·i·tant \'mi-lə-tənt\ *adj* **1** : engaged in warfare **2** : aggressively active esp. in a cause — **mil·i·tance** \-təns\ *n* — **mil·i·tan·cy** \-tən-sē\ *n* — **militant** *n* — **mil·i·tant·ly** *adv*

mil·i·ta·rise *Brit var of* MILITARIZE

mil·i·ta·rism \'mi-lə-tə-ˌri-zəm\ *n* **1** : predominance of the military class or its ideals **2** : a policy of aggressive military preparedness — **mil·i·ta·rist** \-rist\ *n* — **mil·i·ta·ris·tic** \ˌmi-lə-tə-'ris-tik\ *adj*

mil·i·ta·rize \'mi-lə-tə-ˌrīz\ *vb* **-rized; -riz·ing** **1** : to equip with military forces and defenses **2** : to give a military character to

¹mil·i·tary \'mi-lə-ˌter-ē\ *adj* **1** : of or relating to soldiers, arms, war, or the army **2** : performed by armed forces; *also* : supported by armed force ◆ *Synonyms* MARTIAL, WARLIKE — **mil·i·tar·i·ly** \ˌmi-lə-'ter-ə-lē\ *adv*

²military *n, pl* **military** *also* **mil·i·tar·ies** **1** : the military, naval, and air forces of a nation **2** : military persons

military police *n* : a branch of an army that exercises guard and police functions

mil·i·tate \'mi-lə-ˌtāt\ *vb* **-tat·ed; -tat·ing** : to have weight or effect ⟨disagreements ∼ against an alliance⟩

mi·li·tia \mə-'li-shə\ *n* : a part of the organized armed forces of a country liable to call only in emergency — **mi·li·tia·man** \-mən\ *n*

¹milk \'milk\ *n* **1** : a nutritive usu. whitish fluid secreted by female mammals for feeding their young **2** : a milklike liquid (as a plant juice) — **milk·i·ness** \'mil-kē-nəs\ *n* — **milky** *adj*

²milk *vb* **1** : to draw off the milk of ⟨∼ a cow⟩ **2** : to draw something from as if by milking

milk·maid \'milk-ˌmād\ *n* : DAIRYMAID

milk·man \-ˌman, -mən\ *n* : a person who sells or delivers milk

milk of magnesia : a milk-white mixture of hydroxide of magnesium and water used as an antacid and laxative

milk shake *n* : a thoroughly blended drink made of milk, a flavoring syrup, and often ice cream

milk·sop \'milk-ˌsäp\ *n* : an unmanly man

milk·weed \-ˌwēd\ *n* : any of a genus of herbs with milky juice and clustered flowers

Milky Way *n* **1** : a broad irregular band of light that stretches across the sky and is caused by the light of a very great number of faint stars **2** : MILKY WAY GALAXY

Milky Way galaxy *n* : the galaxy of which the sun is a member and which includes the stars that create the light of the Milky Way

¹mill \'mil\ *n* **1** : a building with machinery for grinding grain into flour **2** : a machine used in processing (as by grinding, stamping, cutting, or finishing) raw material **3** : FACTORY

²mill *vb* **1** : to process in a mill **2** : to move in a circle or in an eddying mass

³mill *n* : one tenth of a cent

mill·age \'mi-lij\ *n* : a rate (as of taxation) expressed in mills

mil·len·ni·um \mə-'le-nē-əm\ *n, pl* **-nia** \-nē-ə\ *or* **-niums** **1** : a period of 1000 years; *also* : a 1000th anniversary or its celebration **2** : the 1000 years mentioned in Revelation 20 when holiness is to prevail and Christ is to reign on earth **3** : a period of great happiness or human perfection

mill·er \'mi-lər\ *n* **1** : one that operates a mill and esp. a flour mill **2** : any of various moths having powdery wings

mil·let \'mi-lət\ *n* : any of several small-seeded cereal and forage grasses cultivated for grain or hay; *also* : the grain of a millet

milli- *comb form* : one thousandth part of

mil·li·am·pere \ˌmi-lē-'am-ˌpir\ *n* : one thousandth of an ampere

mil·liard \'mil-ˌyärd, 'mi-lē-ˌärd\ *n, Brit* : a thousand millions

mil·li·bar \'mi-lə-ˌbär\ *n* : a unit of atmospheric pressure

mil·li·gram \-ˌgram\ *n* — see METRIC SYSTEM table

mil·li·li·ter \-ˌlē-tər\ *n* — see METRIC SYSTEM table

mil·lime \mə-'lēm\ *n* — see *dinar* at MONEY table

mil·li·me·ter \'mi-lə-ˌmē-tər\ *n* — see METRIC SYSTEM table

mil·li·ner \'mi-lə-nər\ *n* [irreg. fr. *Milan*, Italy; fr. the importation of women's finery from Italy in the 16th century] : a person who designs, makes, trims, or sells women's hats

mil·li·nery \'mi-lə-ˌner-ē\ *n* **1** : women's apparel for the head **2** : the business or work of a milliner

mill·ing \'mi-liŋ\ *n* : a corrugated edge on a coin

mil·lion \'mil-yən\ *n, pl* **millions** *or* **million** : a thousand thousands — **million** *adj* — **mil·lionth** \-yənth\ *adj or n*

mil·lion·aire \ˌmil-yə-'ner, 'mil-yə-ˌner\ *n* : one whose wealth is estimated at a million or more (as of dollars or pounds)

mil·li·pede \'mi-lə-ˌpēd\ *n* : any of a class of arthropods related to the centipedes and having a long segmented body with a hard covering, two pairs of legs on most segments, and no poison fangs

mil·li·sec·ond \-ˌse-kənd\ *n* : one thousandth of a second

mil·li·volt \-ˌvōlt\ *n* : one thousandth of a volt

mill·pond \'mil-ˌpänd\ *n* : a pond made by damming a stream to produce a fall of water for operating a mill

mill·race \-ˌrās\ *n* : a canal in which water flows to and from a mill wheel

mill·stone \-ˌstōn\ *n* : either of two round flat stones used for grinding grain

mill·stream \-ˌstrēm\ *n* : a stream whose flow is used to run a mill; *also* : the stream in a millrace

mill wheel *n* : a waterwheel that drives a mill

mill·wright \'mil-ˌrīt\ *n* : a person who builds mills or sets up or maintains their machinery

milt \'milt\ *n* : the sperm-containing fluid of a male fish

mime \'mīm\ *n* **1** : MIMIC **2** : PANTOMIME — **mime** *vb*

mim·eo·graph \'mi-mē-ə-ˌgraf\ *n* : a machine for making many copies by means of a stencil through which ink is pressed — **mimeograph** *vb*

mi·me·sis \mə-'mē-səs, mī-\ *n* : IMITATION, MIMICRY

mi·met·ic \-'me-tik\ *adj* **1** : IMITATIVE **2** : relating to, characterized by, or exhibiting mimicry

¹mim·ic \'mi-mik\ *n* : one that mimics

²mimic *vb* **mim·icked** \-mikt\; **mim·ick·ing** **1** : to imitate closely **2** : to ridicule by imitation **3** : to resemble by biological mimicry

mim·ic·ry \'mi-mi-krē\ *n, pl* **-ries** **1** : an instance of mimicking **2** : a superficial resemblance of one organism to another or to natural objects among which it lives that gives it an advantage (as protection from predation)

mi·mo·sa \mə-'mō-sə, mī-, -zə\ *n* : any of a genus of trees, shrubs, and herbs of the legume family that occur in warm regions and have ball-shaped heads of small white or pink flowers

min *abbr* **1** minim **2** minimum **3** mining **4** minister **5** minor **6** minute

min·a·ret \ˌmi-nə-'ret\ *n* [F, fr. Turk *minare*, fr. Ar *manāra* lighthouse] : a tall slender tower of a mosque from which a muezzin calls the faithful to prayer

mi·na·to·ry \'mi-nə-ˌtȯr-ē, 'mī-\ *adj* : THREATENING, MENACING

mince \'mins\ *vb* **minced; minc·ing** [ME, fr. AF *mincer*, fr. VL **minutiare*, fr. L *minutia* smallness, fr. *minutus* small, fr. pp. of *minuere* to lessen] **1** : to cut into very small pieces **2** : to restrain (words) within the bounds of decorum **3** : to walk in a prim affected manner

mince·meat \'mins-ˌmēt\ *n* : a finely chopped mixture esp. of raisins, apples, spices, and often meat used as a filling for a pie

¹mind \'mīnd\ *n* **1** : MEMORY **2** : the part of an individual that feels, perceives, thinks, wills, and esp. reasons **3** : INTENTION, DESIRE **4** : normal mental condition **5** : OPINION, VIEW **6** : MOOD **7** : mental qualities of a person or group **8** : intellectual ability **9** : ATTENTION ⟨pay him no ∼⟩

²mind *vb* **1** *chiefly dial* : REMEMBER **2** : to attend to closely **3** : HEED, OBEY **4** : to be concerned about; *also* : DISLIKE **5** : to be careful or cautious **6** : to take charge of **7** : to regard with attention

mind–bend·ing \'mīnd-ˌben-diŋ\ *adj* : MIND-BLOWING — **mind–bend·ing·ly** *adv*
mind–blow·ing \-ˌblō-iŋ\ *adj* : PSYCHEDELIC 1; *also* : MIND-BOGGLING — **mind·blow·er** \-ˌblō-ər\ *n* — **mind–blow·ing·ly** *adv*
mind–bog·gling \-ˌbä-gə-liŋ\ *adj* : mentally or emotionally exciting or overwhelming
mind·ed \'mīn-dəd\ *adj* 1 : INCLINED, DISPOSED 2 : having a mind of a specified kind or concerned with a specific thing — usu. used in combination ⟨narrow-*minded*⟩ ⟨health-*minded*⟩
mind·ful \'mīnd-fəl\ *adj* : bearing in mind : AWARE — **mind·ful·ly** *adv* — **mind·ful·ness** *n*
mind·less \-ləs\ *adj* 1 : marked by a lack of mind or consciousness; *esp* : marked by no use of the intellect 2 : not mindful : HEEDLESS — **mind·less·ly** *adv* — **mind·less·ness** *n*
¹**mine** \'mīn\ *pron* : that which belongs to me
²**mine** *n* 1 : an excavation in the earth from which minerals are taken; *also* : an ore deposit 2 : an underground passage beneath an enemy position 3 : an explosive device for destroying enemy personnel, vehicles, or ships 4 : a rich source of supply
³**mine** *vb* **mined; min·ing** 1 : to dig a mine 2 : UNDERMINE 3 : to get ore from the earth 4 : to place military mines in — **min·er** *n*
mine·field \'mīn-ˌfēld\ *n* 1 : an area set with mines 2 : something resembling a minefield esp. in having many dangers ⟨a political ∼⟩
mine·lay·er \-ˌlā-ər\ *n* : a naval vessel for laying underwater mines
min·er·al \'mi-nə-rəl\ *n* 1 : a crystalline substance (as diamond or quartz) of inorganic origin 2 : a naturally occurring substance (as coal, salt, or water) obtained usu. from the ground — **mineral** *adj*
min·er·al·ise *Brit var of* MINERALIZE
min·er·al·ize \'mi-nə-rə-ˌlīz\ *vb* **-ized; -iz·ing** 1 : to impregnate or supply with minerals 2 : to change into mineral form — **min·er·al·i·za·tion** \-rə-lə-'zā-shən\ *n*
min·er·al·o·gy \ˌmi-nə-'rä-lə-jē, -'ra-\ *n* : a science dealing with minerals — **min·er·al·og·i·cal** \ˌmi-nə-rə-'lä-ji-kəl\ *adj* — **min·er·al·o·gist** \ˌmi-nə-'rä-lə-jist, -'ra-\ *n*
mineral oil *n* : an oil of mineral origin; *esp* : a refined petroleum oil used as a laxative
mineral water *n* : water infused with mineral salts or gases
min·e·stro·ne \ˌmi-nə-'strō-nē, -'strön\ *n* [It, fr. *minestra*, fr. *minestrare* to serve, dish up, fr. L *ministrare*, fr. *minister* servant] : a rich thick vegetable soup
mine·sweep·er \'mīn-ˌswē-pər\ *n* : a warship for removing or neutralizing underwater mines
min·gle \'miŋ-gəl\ *vb* **min·gled; min·gling** 1 : to bring or combine together : MIX ⟨*mingling* odors⟩ 2 : ASSOCIATE; *also* : to move about socially ⟨*mingled* with the guests⟩
ming tree \'miŋ-\ *n* : a dwarfed usu. evergreen tree grown as bonsai; *also* : an artificial plant resembling this
mini \'mi-nē\ *n, pl* **min·is** : something small of its kind — **mini** *adj*
mini- *comb form* : smaller or briefer than usual, normal, or standard
min·ia·ture \'mi-nē-ə-ˌchùr, 'mi-ni-ˌchùr, -chər\ *n* [It *miniatura* art of illuminating a manuscript, fr. ML, fr. L *miniare* to color with red lead, fr. *minium* red lead] 1 : a copy on a much reduced scale; *also* : something small of its kind 2 : a small painting (as on ivory or metal) — **miniature** *adj* — **min·ia·tur·ist** \-ˌchùr-ist, -chər-\ *n*
min·ia·tur·ize \'mi-nē-ə-ˌchə-ˌrīz, 'mi-ni-\ *vb* **-ized; -iz·ing** : to design or construct in small size — **min·ia·tur·i·za·tion** \ˌmi-nē-ə-ˌchùr-ə-'zā-shən, ˌmi-ni-, -chər-\ *n*
mini·bar \'mi-nē-ˌbär\ *n* : a small refrigerator in a hotel room that is stocked with beverages and snacks
mini·bike \'mi-nē-ˌbīk\ *n* : a small one-passenger motorcycle
mini·bus \-ˌbəs\ *n* : a small bus or van
mini·com·put·er \-kəm-ˌpyü-tər\ *n* : a computer between a mainframe and a microcomputer in size and speed
mini·disc \'mi-nē-ˌdisk\ *n* : a miniature optical disk
min·im \'mi-nəm\ *n* — see WEIGHT table
min·i·mal \'mi-nə-məl\ *adj* 1 : relating to or being a min-

imum : LEAST 2 : of or relating to minimalism or minimal art — **min·i·mal·ly** *adv*
minimal art *n* : abstract art consisting primarily of simple geometric forms executed in an impersonal style — **minimal artist** *n*
min·i·mal·ism \'mi-nə-mə-ˌli-zəm\ *n* : MINIMAL ART; *also* : a style (as in music or literature) marked by extreme spareness or simplicity — **min·i·mal·ist** \-list\ *n*
mini·mart \'mi-nē-ˌmärt\ *n* : CONVENIENCE STORE
min·i·mise *Brit var of* MINIMIZE
min·i·mize \'mi-nə-ˌmīz\ *vb* **-mized; -miz·ing** 1 : to reduce or keep to a minimum 2 : to underestimate intentionally ⟨∼ the defects⟩ ✦ *Synonyms* DEPRECIATE, DECRY, DISPARAGE
min·i·mum \'mi-nə-məm\ *n, pl* **-ma** \-mə\ *or* **-mums** 1 : the least quantity assignable, admissible, or possible 2 : the least of a set of numbers 3 : the lowest degree or amount of variation (as of temperature) reached or recorded — **minimum** *adj*
min·ion \'min-yən\ *n* [MF *mignon* darling] 1 : a servile dependent, follower, or underling 2 : one highly favored 3 : a subordinate official
min·is·cule \'mi-nəs-ˌkyül\ *var of* MINUSCULE
mini·se·ries \'mi-nē-ˌsir-ēz\ *n* : a television story presented in sequential episodes
mini·skirt \-ˌskərt\ *n* : a skirt with the hemline several inches above the knee
¹**min·is·ter** \'mi-nə-stər\ *n* 1 : AGENT 2 : a member of the clergy esp. of a Protestant communion 3 : a high officer of state who heads a division of governmental activities 4 : a diplomatic representative to a foreign state — **min·is·te·ri·al** \ˌmi-nə-'stir-ē-əl\ *adj*
²**minister** *vb* 1 : to perform the functions of a minister of religion 2 : to give aid or service — **min·is·tra·tion** \ˌmi-nə-'strā-shən\ *n*
¹**min·is·trant** \'mi-nə-strənt\ *adj, archaic* : performing service as a minister
²**ministrant** *n* : one that ministers
min·is·try \'mi-nə-strē\ *n, pl* **-tries** 1 : MINISTRATION 2 : the office, duties, or functions of a minister; *also* : the period of service or office 3 : CLERGY 4 : AGENCY 5 *often cap* : the body of ministers governing a nation or state; *also* : a government department headed by a minister
mini·tow·er \'mi-nē-ˌtaù(-ə)r\ *n* : a computer tower of intermediate size
mini·van \'mi-nē-ˌvan\ *n* : a small van
mink \'miŋk\ *n, pl* **mink** *or* **minks** : either of two slender flesh-eating mammals resembling the related weasels; *also* : the soft lustrous typically dark brown fur of a mink

mink

min·ke whale \'miŋ-kə-\ *n* : a small grayish baleen whale with a whitish underside
Minn *abbr* Minnesota
min·ne·sing·er \'mi-ni-ˌsiŋ-ər, -ˌziŋ-\ *n* [G, fr. Middle High German, fr. *minne* love + *singer* singer] : any of a class of German lyric poets and musicians of the 12th to the 14th centuries
min·now \'mi-nō\ *n, pl* **minnows** *also* **minnow** : any of numerous small freshwater fishes
¹**mi·nor** \'mī-nər\ *adj* 1 : inferior in importance, size, or degree 2 : not having reached majority 3 : having the third, sixth, and sometimes the seventh degrees lowered by a half step ⟨∼ scale⟩; *also* : based on a minor scale ⟨∼ key⟩ 4 : not serious ⟨∼ illness⟩
²**minor** *n* 1 : a person who has not attained majority 2 : a subject of academic study chosen as a secondary field of specialization

3minor vb : to pursue an academic minor ⟨~ed in philosophy⟩

mi·nor·i·ty \mə-'nȯr-ə-tē, mī-\ n, pl **-ties** **1** : the period or state of being a minor **2** : the smaller in number of two groups; esp : a group having less than the number of votes necessary for control **3** : a part of a population differing from others (as in race); also : a member of a minority

mi·nox·i·dil \mə-'näk-sə-ˌdil\ n : a drug used orally to treat hypertension and topically in solution to promote hair regrowth in some forms of baldness

min·ster \'min-stər\ n : a large or important church

min·strel \'min-strəl\ n **1** : a medieval singer of verses; also : MUSICIAN, POET **2** : any of a group of performers usu. with blackened faces in a program of black American songs, jokes, and impersonations ⟨a ~ show⟩

min·strel·sy \-sē\ n : the singing and playing of a minstrel; also : a body of minstrels

1mint \'mint\ n **1** : any of a large family of aromatic square-stemmed herbs and shrubs; esp : one (as spearmint) that is fragrant and is the source of a flavoring oil **2** : a mint-flavored piece of candy — **minty** adj

2mint n **1** : a place where coins are made **2** : a vast sum ⟨worth a ~⟩

3mint vb **1** : to make (as coins) out of metal **2** : CREATE; also : to give a certain status to ⟨newly ~ed lawyers⟩ — **mint·age** \-ij\ n — **mint·er** n

4mint adj : unmarred as if fresh from a mint ⟨in ~ condition⟩

min·u·end \'min-yə-ˌwend\ n : a number from which another is to be subtracted

min·u·et \ˌmin-yə-'wet\ n : a slow graceful dance

1mi·nus \'mī-nəs\ prep **1** : diminished by : LESS ⟨seven ~ three equals four⟩ **2** : LACKING, WITHOUT ⟨~ his hat⟩

2minus n : a negative quantity or quality

3minus adj **1** : algebraically negative ⟨~ quantity⟩ **2** : having a negative quality

1mi·nus·cule \'mi-nəs-ˌkyül\ n : a lowercase letter

2minuscule also **min·is·cule** adj : very small

minus sign n : a sign – used in mathematics to indicate subtraction or a negative quantity

1min·ute \'mi-nət\ n **1** : the 60th part of an hour or of a degree : 60 seconds **2** : a short space of time **3** pl : the official record of the proceedings of a meeting

2mi·nute \mī-'nüt, mə-, -'nyüt\ adj **mi·nut·er; -est** **1** : very small **2** : of little importance : TRIFLING **3** : marked by close attention to details ✦ Synonyms DIMINUTIVE, TINY, MINIATURE, WEE — **mi·nute·ly** adv — **mi·nute·ness** n

min·ute·man \'mi-nət-ˌman\ n : a member of a group of armed men pledged to take the field at a minute's notice during and immediately before the American Revolution

mi·nu·tia \mə-'nü-shə, -'nyü-, -shē-ə\ n, pl **-ti·ae** \-shē-ˌē\ [L] : a minute or minor detail — usu. used in pl.

minx \'miŋks\ n : a pert girl

Mio·cene \'mī-ə-ˌsēn\ adj : of, relating to, or being the epoch of the Tertiary between the Oligocene and the Pliocene — **Miocene** n

mir·a·cle \'mir-i-kəl\ n **1** : an extraordinary event manifesting divine intervention in human affairs **2** : an unusual event, thing, or accomplishment : WONDER, MARVEL — **mi·rac·u·lous** \mə-'ra-kyə-ləs\ adj — **mi·rac·u·lous·ly** adv

miracle drug n : a usu. newly discovered drug that elicits a dramatic response in a patient's condition

mi·rage \mə-'räzh\ n **1** : an illusion that often appears as a pool of water or a mirror in which distant objects are seen inverted, is sometimes seen at sea, in the desert, or over a hot pavement, and results from atmospheric conditions **2** : something illusory and unattainable

1mire \'mī(-ə)r\ n **1** : heavy and often deep mud or slush — **miry** adj

2mire vb **mired; mir·ing** : to stick or sink in or as if in mire

mire·poix \mir-'pwä\ n, pl **mirepoix** : a mixture of diced vegetables and sometimes meats used in soups, stews, and sauces

1mir·ror \'mir-ər\ n **1** : a polished or smooth surface (as of glass) that forms images by reflection **2** : a true representation

2mirror vb **1** : to reflect in or as if in a mirror **2** : RESEMBLE

mirth \'mərth\ n : gladness or gaiety accompanied with laughter ✦ Synonyms GLEE, JOLLITY, HILARITY, MERRIMENT — **mirth·ful** \-fəl\ adj — **mirth·ful·ly** adv — **mirth·ful·ness** n — **mirth·less** adj

MIRV \'mərv\ n [multiple independently targeted reentry vehicle] : an ICBM with multiple warheads that have different targets — **MIRV** vb

mis·ad·ven·ture \ˌmi-səd-'ven-chər\ n : MISFORTUNE, MISHAP

mis·aligned \ˌmi-sə-'līnd\ adj : not properly aligned — **mis·align·ment** \-'līn-mənt\ n

mis·al·li·ance \ˌmi-sə-'lī-əns\ n : an improper or unsuitable marriage

mis·al·lo·ca·tion \ˌmi-ˌsa-lə-'kā-shən\ n : faulty or improper allocation

mis·an·dry \'mi-ˌsan-drē\ n : a hatred of men — **mis·an·drist** \-drist\ n or adj

mis·an·thrope \'mi-sⁿn-ˌthrōp\ n : one who hates humankind — **mis·an·throp·ic** \ˌmi-sⁿn-'thrä-pik\ adj — **mis·an·throp·i·cal·ly** \-pi-k(ə-)lē\ adv — **mis·an·thro·py** \mi-'san-thrə-pē\ n

mis·ap·ply \ˌmi-sə-'plī\ vb : to apply wrongly — **mis·ap·pli·ca·tion** \ˌmi-ˌsa-plə-'kā-shən\ n

mis·ap·pre·hend \ˌmi-ˌsa-pri-'hend\ vb : MISUNDERSTAND — **mis·ap·pre·hen·sion** \-'hen-chən\ n

mis·ap·pro·pri·ate \ˌmi-sə-'prō-prē-ˌāt\ vb : to appropriate wrongly (as by embezzlement) — **mis·ap·pro·pri·a·tion** \-ˌprō-prē-'ā-shən\ n

mis·be·got·ten \-bi-'gä-tⁿn\ adj : ILLEGITIMATE; also : ill-conceived

mis·be·have \ˌmis-bi-'hāv\ vb : to behave improperly — **mis·be·hav·er** n — **mis·be·hav·ior** \-'hā-vyər\ n

mis·be·liev·er \-bə-'lē-vər\ n : one who holds a false or unorthodox belief

mis·brand \mis-'brand\ vb : to brand falsely or in a misleading manner

misc abbr miscellaneous

mis·cal·cu·late \mis-'kal-kyə-ˌlāt\ vb : to calculate wrongly — **mis·cal·cu·la·tion** \ˌmis-ˌkal-kyə-'lā-shən\ n

mis·call \mis-'kȯl\ vb : MISNAME

mis·car·riage \-'ker-ij\ n **1** : failure in the administration of justice **2** : spontaneous expulsion of a fetus before it is capable of independent life

mis·car·ry \-'ker-ē\ vb **1** : to have a miscarriage of a fetus **2** : to go wrong; also : to be unsuccessful

mis·ce·ge·na·tion \mi-ˌse-jə-'nā-shən, ˌmi-si-jə-'nā-\ n [L miscēre to mix + genus race] : marriage, cohabitation, or sexual intercourse between persons of different races

mis·cel·la·neous \ˌmi-sə-'lā-nē-əs\ adj **1** : consisting of diverse things or members **2** : having various traits; also : dealing with or interested in diverse subjects — **mis·cel·la·neous·ly** adv — **mis·cel·la·neous·ness** n

mis·cel·la·ny \'mi-sə-ˌlā-nē\ n, pl **-nies** **1** : a collection of writings on various subjects **2** : HODGEPODGE

mis·chance \mis-'chans\ n : bad luck; also : MISHAP

mis·chief \'mis-chəf\ n [ME meschief, fr. AF, fr. meschever to come out badly, fr. mes- badly + chief head, end] **1** : injury caused by a particular agent **2** : a source of harm or irritation **3** : action that annoys; also : MISCHIEVOUSNESS

mis·chie·vous \'mis-chə-vəs\ adj **1** : HARMFUL, INJURIOUS **2** : causing annoyance or minor injury **3** : irresponsibly playful — **mis·chie·vous·ly** adv — **mis·chie·vous·ness** n

mis·ci·ble \'mi-sə-bəl\ adj : capable of being mixed

mis·com·mu·ni·ca·tion \ˌmis-kə-ˌmyü-nə-'kā-shən\ n : failure to communicate clearly

mis·con·ceive \ˌmis-kən-'sēv\ vb : to interpret incorrectly — **mis·con·cep·tion** \-'sep-shən\ n

mis·con·duct \mis-'kän-(ˌ)dəkt\ n **1** : MISMANAGEMENT **2** : intentional wrongdoing **3** : improper behavior; also : a penalty in a sport for improper behavior

mis·con·strue \ˌmis-kən-'strü\ vb : MISINTERPRET — **mis·con·struc·tion** \-'strək-shən\ n

mis·count \mis-'kau̇nt\ vb : to count incorrectly : MISCALCULATE

mis·cre·ant \'mis-krē-ənt\ n : one who behaves criminally or viciously — **miscreant** adj

mis·cue \mis-'kyü\ n : MISTAKE, ERROR — **miscue** vb

mis·deed \mis-'dēd\ n : a wrong deed

315 misdemeanor • mistral

mis·de·mean·or \ˌmis-di-'mē-nər\ *n* **1** : a crime less serious than a felony **2** : MISDEED
mis·di·rect \ˌmis-də-'rekt, -dī-\ *vb* : to give a wrong direction to — **mis·di·rec·tion** \-'rek-shən\ *n*
mis·do·ing \mis-'dü-iŋ\ *n* : WRONGDOING — **mis·do** \-'dü\ *vb* — **mis·do·er** \-'dü-ər\ *n*
mise–en–scène \ˌmē-ˌzänⁿ-'sen, -'sän\ *n, pl* **mise–en–scènes** *same or* -'senz, -'sänz\ [F] **1** : the arrangement of the scenery, property, and actors on a stage **2** : SETTING; *also* : ENVIRONMENT
mi·ser \'mī-zər\ *n* [L *miser* miserable] : a person who hoards and is stingy with money — **mi·ser·li·ness** \-lē-nəs\ *n* — **mi·ser·ly** *adj*
mis·er·a·ble \'mi-zə-rə-bəl, 'miz-rə-\ *adj* **1** : wretchedly deficient; *also* : causing extreme discomfort **2** : being in a state of distress **3** : SHAMEFUL — **mis·er·a·ble·ness** *n* — **mis·er·a·bly** \-blē\ *adv*
mis·ery \'mi-zə-rē\ *n, pl* **-er·ies** **1** : suffering and want caused by poverty or affliction **2** : a cause of suffering or discomfort **3** : emotional distress
mis·fea·sance \mis-'fē-zⁿns\ *n* : the performance of a lawful action in an illegal or improper manner
mis·file \-'fī(-ə)l\ *vb* : to file in the wrong place
mis·fire \-'fī(-ə)r\ *vb* **1** : to fail to fire **2** : to miss an intended effect — **misfire** *n*
mis·fit \'mis-ˌfit, *sense 1 also* mis-'fit\ *n* **1** : something that fits badly **2** : a person who is poorly adjusted to a situation or environment
mis·for·tune \mis-'fór-chən\ *n* **1** : bad luck **2** : an unfortunate condition or event
mis·giv·ing \-'gi-viŋ\ *n* : a feeling of doubt or suspicion esp. concerning a future event
mis·gov·ern \-'gə-vərn\ *vb* : to govern badly — **mis·gov·ern·ment** *n*
mis·guid·ance \mis-'gī-dⁿns\ *n* : faulty guidance — **mis·guide** \-'gīd\ *vb*
mis·guid·ed \-'gī-dəd\ *adj* : led or prompted by wrong or inappropriate motives or ideals — **mis·guid·ed·ly** *adv*
mis·han·dle \-'han-dᵒl\ *vb* **1** : MALTREAT **2** : to manage wrongly
mis·hap \'mis-ˌhap\ *n* : an unfortunate accident
mish·mash \'mish-ˌmash, -ˌmäsh\ *n* : HODGEPODGE, JUMBLE
mis·in·form \ˌmi-sⁿn-'fórm\ *vb* : to give false or misleading information to — **mis·in·for·ma·tion** \ˌmi-ˌsin-fər-'mā-shən\ *n*
mis·in·ter·pret \ˌmi-sⁿn-'tər-prət\ *vb* : to understand or explain wrongly — **mis·in·ter·pre·ta·tion** \-ˌtər-prə-'tā-shən\ *n*
mis·judge \mis-'jəj\ *vb* **1** : to estimate wrongly **2** : to have an unjust opinion of — **mis·judg·ment** \mis-'jəj-mənt\ *n*
mis·la·bel \-'lā-bəl\ *vb* : to label incorrectly or falsely ⟨was ~ed a liar⟩
mis·lay \mis-'lā\ *vb* **-laid** \-'lād\; **-lay·ing** : MISPLACE, LOSE ⟨*mislaid* his keys⟩
mis·lead \mis-'lēd\ *vb* **-led** \-'led\; **-lead·ing** : to lead in a wrong direction or into a mistaken action or belief — **mis·lead·ing·ly** *adv*
mis·like \-'līk\ *vb* : DISLIKE — **mis·like** *n*
mis·man·age \-'ma-nij\ *vb* : to manage badly — **mis·man·age·ment** *n*
mis·match \-'mach\ *vb* : to match unsuitably or badly — **mis·match** \-'mach, 'mis-ˌmach\ *n*
mis·name \-'nām\ *vb* : to name incorrectly : MISCALL
mis·no·mer \mis-'nō-mər\ *n* : a wrong or inappropriate name or designation
mi·so \'mē-sō\ *n* : a high-protein fermented food paste consisting chiefly of soybeans, salt, and usu. grain
mi·sog·y·ny \mə-'sä-jə-nē\ *n* [Gk *misogynia*, fr. *misein* to hate + *gynē* woman] : a hatred of women — **mi·sog·y·nist** \-nist\ *n or adj* — **mi·sog·y·nis·tic** \mə-ˌsä-jə-'nistik\ *adj*
mis·ori·ent \mis-'sór-ē-ˌent\ *vb* : to orient improperly or incorrectly — **mis·ori·en·ta·tion** \mi-ˌsór-ē-ən-'tā-shən\ *n*
mis·place \mis-'plās\ *vb* **1** : to put in a wrong or unremembered place **2** : to set on a wrong object ⟨~ trust⟩
mis·play \-'plā\ *n* : a wrong or unskillful play — **mis·play** \mis-'plā, 'mis-ˌplā\ *vb*

mis·print \'mis-ˌprint\ *n* : a mistake in printed matter — **mis·print** \mis-'print\ *vb*
mis·pro·nounce \ˌmis-prə-'naúns\ *vb* : to pronounce incorrectly — **mis·pro·nun·ci·a·tion** \-prə-ˌnən-sē-'ā-shən\ *n*
mis·quote \mis-'kwōt\ *vb* : to quote incorrectly — **mis·quo·ta·tion** \ˌmis-kwō-'tā-shən\ *n*
mis·read \-'rēd\ *vb* **-read** \-'red\; **-read·ing** \-'rē-diŋ\ : to read or interpret incorrectly ⟨~ her expression⟩
mis·rep·re·sent \ˌmis-ˌre-pri-'zent\ *vb* : to represent falsely or unfairly ⟨~the facts⟩ — **mis·rep·re·sen·ta·tion** \-ˌzen-'tā-shən\ *n*
¹mis·rule \mis-'rül\ *vb* : MISGOVERN
²misrule *n* **1** : MISGOVERNMENT **2** : DISORDER
¹miss \'mis\ *vb* **1** : to fail to hit, reach, or contact **2** : to feel the absence of **3** : to fail to obtain **4** : AVOID ⟨just ~ed hitting the other car⟩ **5** : OMIT **6** : to fail to understand ⟨~ the point⟩ **7** : to fail to perform or attend; *also* : MISFIRE
²miss *n* **1** : a failure to hit or to attain a result **2** : MISFIRE
³miss *n* **1** *cap* — used as a title prefixed to the name of an unmarried woman or girl **2** : a young unmarried woman or girl
Miss *abbr* Mississippi
mis·sal \'mi-səl\ *n* : a book containing all that is said or sung at mass during the entire year
mis·send \mis-'send\ *vb* : to send incorrectly (as to a wrong destination)
mis·shap·en \-'shā-pən\ *adj* : badly shaped : having an ugly shape
mis·sile \'mi-səl\ *n* [L, fr. neut. of *missilis* capable of being thrown, fr. *mittere* to let go, send] : an object (as a stone, bullet, or rocket) thrown or projected usu. so as to strike a target
miss·ing \'mi-siŋ\ *adj* : ABSENT; *also* : LOST ⟨~ in action⟩
mis·sion \'mi-shən\ *n* **1** : a group of missionaries; *also* : a place where missionaries work **2** : a group of envoys to a foreign country; *also* : a team of specialists or cultural leaders sent to a foreign country **3** : TASK, OBJECTIVE
¹mis·sion·ary \'mi-shə-ˌner-ē\ *adj* : of, relating to, or engaged in missions
²missionary *n, pl* **-ar·ies** : a person commissioned by a church to spread its faith or carry on humanitarian work
mis·sion·er \'mi-shə-nər\ *n* : MISSIONARY
Mis·sis·sip·pi·an \ˌmi-sə-'si-pē-ən\ *adj* **1** : of or relating to Mississippi, its people, or the Mississippi River **2** : of, relating to, or being the period of the Paleozoic era between the Devonian and the Pennsylvanian — **Mississippian** *n*
mis·sive \'mi-siv\ *n* : LETTER
mis·speak \mis-'spēk\ *vb* : to say imperfectly or incorrectly
mis·spell \-'spel\ *vb* : to spell incorrectly — **mis·spell·ing** \-'spe-liŋ\ *n*
mis·spend \-'spend\ *vb* **-spent** \-'spent\; **-spend·ing** : WASTE, SQUANDER ⟨my *misspent* youth⟩
mis·state \mis-'stāt\ *vb* : to state incorrectly — **mis·state·ment** *n*
mis·step \-'step\ *n* **1** : a wrong step **2** : MISTAKE, BLUNDER
mist \'mist\ *n* **1** : water in the form of particles suspended or falling in the air **2** : something that obscures understanding — **mist** *vb*
mis·tak·able \mə-'stā-kə-bəl\ *adj* : capable of being misunderstood or mistaken
¹mis·take \mə-'stāk\ *vb* **-took** \-'stúk\; **-tak·en** \-'stā-kən\; **-tak·ing** **1** : to blunder in the choice of **2** : MISINTERPRET **3** : to make a wrong judgment of the character or ability of **4** : to confuse with another — **mis·tak·en·ly** *adv* — **mis·tak·er** *n*
²mistake *n* **1** : a wrong judgment : MISUNDERSTANDING **2** : a wrong action or statement : ERROR
¹mis·ter \'mis-tər\ *n* **1** *cap* — used sometimes instead of *Mr.* **2** : SIR — used without a name in addressing a man
²mist·er \'mis-tər\ *n* : a device for spraying mist
mis·tle·toe \'mi-səl-ˌtō\ *n* : a European parasitic green shrub that grows on trees and has yellowish flowers and waxy white berries
mis·tral \'mis-trəl, mi-'sträl\ *n* [F, fr. Occitan, fr. *mistral*

masterful, fr. LL *magistralis* of a teacher, fr. L *magister* master] : a strong cold dry northerly wind of southern France

mis·treat \mis-'trēt\ *vb* : to treat badly : ABUSE — **mis·treat·ment** *n*

mis·tress \'mis-trəs\ *n* **1** : a woman who has power, authority, or ownership ⟨~ of the house⟩ **2** : something personified as female that rules or dominates ⟨when Rome was ~ of the world⟩ **3** : a woman other than his wife with whom a married man has sexual relations; *also, archaic* : SWEETHEART **4** — used archaically as a title prefixed to the name of a married or unmarried woman

mis·tri·al \'mis-,trī(-ə)l\ *n* : a trial that has no legal effect

¹**mistrust** \mis-'trəst\ *n* : a lack of confidence : DISTRUST — **mis·trust·ful** \-fəl\ *adj* — **mis·trust·ful·ly** *adv* — **mis·trust·ful·ness** *n*

²**mistrust** *vb* : to have no trust or confidence in : SUSPECT

misty \'mis-tē\ *adj* **mist·i·er; -est** **1** : obscured by or as if by mist : INDISTINCT **2** : TEARFUL — **mist·i·ly** \-tə-lē\ *adv* — **mist·i·ness** \-tē-nəs\ *n*

mis·un·der·stand \,mi-,sən-dər-'stand\ *vb* **-stood** \-'stůd\; **-stand·ing** **1** : to fail to understand **2** : to interpret incorrectly

mis·un·der·stand·ing \-'stan-diŋ\ *n* **1** : MISINTERPRETATION **2** : DISAGREEMENT, QUARREL

mis·us·age \mis-'yü-sij\ *n* **1** : bad treatment : ABUSE **2** : wrong or improper use

mis·use \mis-'yüz\ *vb* **1** : to use incorrectly **2** : ABUSE, MISTREAT — **mis·use** \-'yüs\ *n*

¹**mite** \'mīt\ *n* : any of numerous tiny arthropod animals related to the spiders that often live and feed on animals or plants

¹**mite** *n* **1** : a small coin or sum of money **2** : a small amount : BIT

¹**mi·ter** *or* **mi·tre** \'mī-tər\ *n* [ME *mitre*, fr. AF, fr. L *mitra* headband, turban, fr. Gk] **1** : a headdress worn by bishops and abbots **2** : MITER JOINT

²**miter** *or* **mitre** *vb* **mi·tered** *or* **mi·tred; mi·ter·ing** *or* **mi·tring** \'mī-tə-riŋ\ **1** : to match or fit together in a miter joint **2** : to bevel the ends of for making a miter joint

miter joint *n* : a usu. perpendicular joint made by fitting together two parts with the ends cut at an angle

miter joints

mit·i·gate \'mi-tə-,gāt\ *vb* **-gat·ed; -gat·ing** **1** : to make less harsh or hostile **2** : to make less severe or painful — **mit·i·ga·tion** \,mi-tə-'gā-shən\ *n* — **mit·i·ga·tive** \'mi-tə-,gā-tiv\ *adj*

mi·to·chon·dri·on \,mī-tə-'kän-drē-ən\ *n, pl* **-dria** \-drē-ə\ : any of various round or long cellular organelles that produce energy for the cell — **mi·to·chon·dri·al** \-drē-əl\ *adj*

mi·to·sis \mī-'tō-səs\ *n, pl* **-to·ses** \-,sēz\ : a process that takes place in the nucleus of a dividing cell and results in the formation of two new nuclei each of which has the same number of chromosomes as the parent nucleus; *also* : cell division in which mitosis occurs — **mi·tot·ic** \-'tä-tik\ *adj*

mitt \'mit\ *n* **1** : a baseball catcher's or first baseman's glove **2** *slang* : HAND

mit·ten \'mi-t⁰n\ *n* : a covering for the hand having a separate section for the thumb only — **mit·tened** \-t⁰nd\ *adj*

¹**mix** \'miks\ *vb* **1** : to combine into one mass **2** : ASSOCIATE **3** : to form by mingling components **4** : to produce (a recording) by electronically combining sounds from different sources **5** : HYBRIDIZE **6** : CONFUSE ⟨~es up the facts⟩ **7** : to become involved ✦ *Synonyms* BLEND, MERGE, COALESCE, AMALGAMATE, FUSE — **mix·able** *adj* — **mix it up** : to engage in a fight, contest, or dispute

²**mix** *n* : a product of mixing; *esp* : a commercially prepared mixture of food ingredients

mixed \'mikst\ *adj* **1** : combining features of more than one kind **2** : made up of or involving individuals or items of more than one kind **3** : including or accompanied by different or opposing elements ⟨a ~ blessing⟩ **4** : resulting from the crossing or breeding of individuals of different races or breeds ⟨a stallion of ~ blood⟩

mixed number *n* : a number (as 5²/₃) composed of an integer and a fraction

mixed–up \'mikst-'əp\ *adj* : CONFUSED

mix·er \'mik-sər\ *n* **1** : one that mixes; *esp* : a machine or device for mixing **2** : an event (as a dance) that encourages meeting and socializing **3** : a nonalcoholic beverage used in a cocktail

mixt *abbr* mixture

mix·ture \'miks-chər\ *n* **1** : the act or process of mixing; *also* : the state of being mixed **2** : a product of mixing

mix–up \'miks-,əp\ *n* **1** : an instance of confusion **2** : CONFLICT, FIGHT

miz·zen *also* **miz·en** \'mi-z⁰n\ *n* **1** : a fore-and-aft sail set on the mizzenmast **2** : MIZZENMAST — **mizzen** *also* **mizen** *adj*

miz·zen·mast \-,mast, -məst\ *n* : the mast aft or next aft of the mainmast

mk *abbr* **1** mark **2** markka

Mk *abbr* Mark

mks *abbr* meter-kilogram-second

mkt *abbr* market

mktg *abbr* marketing

ml *abbr* milliliter

Mlle *abbr* [F] mademoiselle

Mlles *abbr* [F] mesdemoiselles

mm *abbr* millimeter

MM *abbr* [F] messieurs

Mme *abbr* [F] madame

Mmes *abbr* [F] mesdames

Mn *symbol* manganese

MN *abbr* Minnesota

mne·mon·ic \nə-'mä-nik\ *adj* : assisting or designed to assist memory; *also* : of or relating to memory

mo *abbr* month

¹**Mo** *abbr* **1** Missouri **2** Monday

²**Mo** *symbol* molybdenum

MO *abbr* **1** mail order **2** medical officer **3** Missouri **4** modus operandi **5** money order

moan \'mōn\ *n* : a low prolonged sound indicative of pain or grief — **moan** *vb*

moat \'mōt\ *n* : a deep wide usu. water-filled trench around a castle

¹**mob** \'mäb\ *n* [L *mobile vulgus* vacillating crowd] **1** : MASSES, RABBLE **2** : a disorderly crowd **3** : a criminal gang

²**mob** *vb* **mobbed; mob·bing** **1** : to crowd about and attack or annoy ⟨*mobbed* by fans⟩ **2** : to crowd into or around ⟨shoppers *mobbed* the stores⟩

¹**mo·bile** \'mō-bəl, -,bī(-ə)l, -,bēl\ *adj* **1** : capable of moving or being moved **2** : changeable in appearance, mood, or purpose; *also* : ADAPTABLE **3** : having the opportunity for or undergoing a shift in social status **4** : using vehicles for transportation ⟨~ warfare⟩ **5** : CELLULAR 2 — **mo·bil·i·ty** \mō-'bi-lə-tē\ *n*

²**mo·bile** \'mō-,bēl\ *n* : a construction or sculpture (as of wire and sheet metal) with parts that can be set in motion by air currents; *also* : a similar structure suspended so that it is moved by a current of air

mobile home *n* : a trailer used as a permanent dwelling

mo·bi·lise *chiefly Brit var of* MOBILIZE

mo·bi·lize \'mō-bə-,līz\ *vb* **-lized; -liz·ing** **1** : to put into movement or circulation **2** : to assemble and make ready for action ⟨~ army reserves⟩ — **mo·bi·li·za·tion** \,mō-bə-lə-'zā-shən\ *n* — **mo·bi·liz·er** \'mō-bə-,lī-zər\ *n*

mob·ster \'mäb-stər\ *n* : a member of a criminal gang

moc·ca·sin \'mä-kə-sən\ *n* **1** : a soft leather heelless shoe **2** : WATER MOCCASIN

mo·cha \'mō-kə\ *n* [*Mocha*, port in Yemen] **1** : choice coffee grown in Arabia **2** : a mixture of coffee and chocolate or cocoa **3** : a dark chocolate-brown color

¹**mock** \'mäk, 'mök\ *vb* **1** : to treat with contempt or ridicule **2** : DELUDE **3** : DEFY **4** : to mimic in sport or derision — **mock·er** *n* — **mock·ery** \'mä-kə-rē, 'mó-\ *n* — **mock·ing·ly** *adv*

²**mock** *adj* : SIMULATED ⟨a ~ trial⟩

mock–he·ro·ic \ˌmäk-hi-'rō-ik, ˌmȯk-\ *adj* : ridiculing or burlesquing heroic style, character, or action ⟨a ~ poem⟩

mock·ing·bird \'mä-kiŋ-ˌbərd, 'mȯ-\ *n* : a grayish No. American songbird related to the catbirds and thrashers that mimics the calls of other birds

mock–up \'mä-ˌkəp, 'mȯ-\ *n* **1** : a full-sized structural model built for study, testing, or display ⟨a ~ of a car⟩ **2** : a working sample (as of a magazine) for review

¹**mod** \'mäd\ *adj* **1** : of, relating to, or being the style of the 1960s British youth culture **2** : HIP, TRENDY

²**mod** *abbr* **1** moderate **2** modern **3** modification; modified

mode \'mōd\ *n* **1** : a particular form or variety of something; *also* : STYLE **2** : a manner of doing something **3** : the most frequent value of a set of data — **mod·al** \'mōdᵊl\ *adj*

¹**mod·el** \'mä-dᵊl\ *n* **1** : structural design **2** : a miniature representation; *also* : a pattern of something to be made **3** : an example for imitation or emulation **4** : one who poses (as for an artist or to display clothes) **5** : TYPE, DESIGN ⟨a new car ~⟩

²**model** *vb* **mod·eled** *or* **mod·elled; mod·el·ing** *or* **mod·el·ling 1** : SHAPE, FASHION, CONSTRUCT ⟨~ed in clay⟩ **2** : to work as a fashion model

³**model** *adj* **1** : serving as or worthy of being a pattern ⟨a ~ student⟩ **2** : being a miniature representation of something ⟨a ~ airplane⟩

mo·dem \'mō-dəm, -ˌdem\ *n* : a device that converts signals from one device (as a computer) to a form compatible with another (as a telephone)

¹**mod·er·ate** \'mä-də-rət\ *adj* **1** : avoiding extremes; *also* : TEMPERATE **2** : AVERAGE; *also* : MEDIOCRE **3** : limited in scope or effect **4** : not expensive — **moderate** *n* — **mod·er·ate·ly** *adv* — **mod·er·ate·ness** *n*

²**mod·er·ate** \'mä-də-ˌrāt\ *vb* **-at·ed; -at·ing 1** : to lessen the intensity of : TEMPER **2** : to act as a moderator — **mod·er·a·tion** \ˌmä-də-'rā-shən\ *n*

mod·er·a·tor \'mä-də-ˌrā-tər\ *n* **1** : MEDIATOR **2** : one who presides over an assembly, meeting, or discussion

mod·ern \'mä-dərn\ *adj* [LL *modernus,* fr. L *modo* just now, fr. *modus* measure] : of, relating to, or characteristic of the present or the immediate past : CONTEMPORARY — **modern** *n* — **mo·der·ni·ty** \mə-'dər-nə-tē\ *n* — **mod·ern·ly** *adv* — **mod·ern·ness** *n*

mod·ern·ise, mod·ern·i·sa·tion *Brit var of* MODERNIZE, MODERNIZATION

mod·ern·ism \'mä-dər-ˌni-zəm\ *n* : a practice, movement, or belief peculiar to modern times

mod·ern·ize \'mä-dər-ˌnīz\ *vb* **-ized; -iz·ing** : to make or become modern — **mod·ern·i·za·tion** \ˌmä-dər-nə-'zā-shən\ *n* — **mod·ern·iz·er** *n*

mod·est \'mä-dəst\ *adj* **1** : having a moderate estimate of oneself; *also* : DIFFIDENT **2** : observing the proprieties of dress and behavior **3** : limited in size, amount, or scope ⟨a ~ income⟩ — **mod·est·ly** *adv* — **mod·es·ty** \-də-stē\ *n*

mod·i·cum \'mä-di-kəm\ *n* : a small amount

modif *abbr* modification

mod·i·fy \'mä-də-ˌfī\ *vb* **-fied; -fy·ing 1** : MODERATE **2** : to limit the meaning of esp. in a grammatical construction **3** : CHANGE, ALTER — **mod·i·fi·ca·tion** \ˌmä-də-fə-'kā-shən\ *n* — **mod·i·fi·er** \'mä-də-ˌfī-ər\ *n*

mod·ish \'mō-dish\ *adj* : FASHIONABLE, STYLISH — **mod·ish·ly** *adv* — **mod·ish·ness** *n*

mo·diste \mō-'dēst\ *n* : a maker of fashionable dresses and hats

mod·u·lar \'mä-jə-lər\ *adj* : constructed with standardized units

mod·u·lar·ized \'mä-jə-lə-ˌrīzd\ *adj* : containing or consisting of modules

mod·u·late \'mä-jə-ˌlāt\ *vb* **-lat·ed; -lat·ing 1** : to tune to a key or pitch **2** : to keep in proper measure or proportion : TEMPER **3** : to vary the amplitude or frequency of a carrier wave for the transmission of information (as in radio or television) — **mod·u·la·tion** \ˌmä-jə-'lā-shən\ *n* — **mod·u·la·tor** \'mä-jə-ˌlā-tər\ *n* — **mod·u·la·to·ry** \-lə-ˌtȯr-ē\ *adj*

mod·ule \'mä-jül\ *n* **1** : any in a series of standardized units for use together **2** : an assembly of wired electronic parts for use with other such assemblies **3** : an inde-

pendent unit that constitutes a part of the total structure of a space vehicle ⟨a propulsion ~⟩

mo·dus ope·ran·di \ˌmō-dəs-ˌä-pə-'ran-dē, -ˌdī\ *n, pl* **mo·di operandi** \ˌmō-ˌdē-, ˌmō-ˌdī-\ [NL] : a method of procedure

¹**mo·gul** \'mō-gəl, mō-'gəl\ *n* [fr. *Mogul,* member of a Muslim dynasty ruling northern India] : an important person : MAGNATE ⟨a media ~⟩

²**mogul** \'mō-gəl\ *n* : a bump in a ski run

mo·hair \'mō-ˌher\ *n* [modif. of obs. It *mocaiarro,* fr. Ar *mukhayyar,* lit., choice] : a fabric or yarn made wholly or in part from the long silky hair of the Angora goat; *also* : this goat hair

Mo·ham·med·an *also* **Mu·ham·mad·an** \mō-'ha-mə-dən, -'hä-, mü-\ *n* : MUSLIM — **Mo·ham·med·an·ism** *also* **Mu·ham·mad·an·ism** \-də-ˌni-zəm\ *n*

Mo·hawk \'mō-ˌhȯk\ *n, pl* **Mohawk** *or* **Mohawks 1** : a member of an American Indian people of the Mohawk River valley, New York; *also* : the language of the Mohawk people **2** : a hairstyle with a narrow strip of upright hair down the center and the sides shaved

Mo·he·gan \mō-'hē-gən, mə-\ *or* **Mo·hi·can** \-'hē-kən\ *n, pl* **Mohegan** *or* **Mohegans** *or* **Mohican** *or* **Mohicans** : a member of an American Indian people of southeastern Connecticut

mo·hel \'mō-(h)el, 'mȯi(-ə)l\ *n, pl* **mohels** *also* **mo·hal·im** \ˌmō-hä-'lēm\ *also* **mo·hel·im** \-(h)e-'lēm\ : a person who performs Jewish circumcisions

Mohican *var of* MAHICAN

moi·e·ty \'mȯi-ə-tē\ *n, pl* **-ties** : one of two equal or approximately equal parts

moil \'mȯi(-ə)l\ *vb* : to work hard : DRUDGE — **moil** *n* — **moil·er** *n*

moi·ré \mȯ-'rā, mwä-\ *or* **moire** *same or* 'mȯir, 'mwär\ *n* : a fabric (as silk) having a watered appearance

moist \'mȯist\ *adj* : slightly or moderately wet — **moist·ly** *adv* — **moist·ness** *n*

moist·en \'mȯi-sᵊn\ *vb* : to make or become moist — **moist·en·er** *n*

mois·ture \'mȯis-chər\ *n* : the small amount of liquid that causes dampness

mois·tur·ise *Brit var of* MOISTURIZE

mois·tur·ize \'mȯis-chə-ˌrīz\ *vb* **-ized; -iz·ing** : to add moisture to ⟨~ the skin⟩ — **mois·tur·iz·er** *n*

mol *abbr* molecular; molecule

mo·lar \'mō-lər\ *n* [ME *molares,* pl., fr. L *molaris,* fr. *mola* millstone] : any of the broad teeth adapted to grinding food and located in the back of the jaw — **molar** *adj*

mo·las·ses \mə-'la-səz\ *n* : the thick brown syrup that is separated from raw sugar in sugar manufacture

¹**mold** \'mōld\ *n* : crumbly soil rich in organic matter

²**mold** *n* **1** : distinctive nature or character **2** : the frame on or around which something is constructed **3** : a cavity in which something is shaped; *also* : an object so shaped **4** : MOLDING

³**mold** *vb* **1** : to shape in or as if in a mold **2** : to ornament with molding — **mold·er** *n*

⁴**mold** *n* : a surface growth of fungus esp. on damp or decaying matter; *also* : a fungus that produces mold — **mold·i·ness** \'mōl-dē-nəs\ *n* — **moldy** *adj*

⁵**mold** *vb* : to become moldy

mold·board \'mōld-ˌbȯrd\ *n* : a curved iron plate attached above the plowshare to lift and turn the soil

mold·er \'mōl-dər\ *vb* : to crumble into small pieces

mold·ing \'mōl-diŋ\ *n* **1** : an act or process of shaping in a mold; *also* : an object so shaped **2** : a decorative surface, plane, or curved strip

¹**mole** \'mōl\ *n* : a small often pigmented spot or protuberance on the skin

²**mole** *n* **1** : any of numerous small burrowing insect-eating mammals related to the shrews and hedgehogs **2** : a spy embedded within an organization

³**mole** *n* : a massive breakwater or jetty

molecular biology *n* : a branch of biology dealing with the ultimate physical and chemical organization of living matter and esp. with the molecular basis of inheritance and protein synthesis — **molecular biologist** *n*

molecular weight *n* : the mass of a molecule that is equal to the sum of the masses of all atoms contained in the molecule's formula

mol·e·cule \'mä-li-ˌkyül\ n : the smallest particle of matter that is the same chemically as the whole mass — **mo·lec·u·lar** \mə-'le-kyə-lər\ adj

mole·hill \'mōl-ˌhil\ n : a little ridge of earth thrown up by a mole

mole·skin \-ˌskin\ n **1** : the skin of the mole used as fur **2** : a heavy durable cotton fabric

mo·lest \mə-'lest\ vb **1** : ANNOY, DISTURB **2** : to make annoying sexual advances to; esp : to force physical and usu. sexual contact on — **mo·les·ta·tion** \ˌmō-ˌles-'tā-shən\ n — **mo·lest·er** n

moll \'mäl\ n : a gangster's girlfriend

mol·li·fy \'mä-lə-ˌfī\ vb **-fied; -fy·ing 1** : to soothe in temper : APPEASE **2** : SOFTEN **3** : to reduce in intensity : ASSUAGE — **mol·li·fi·ca·tion** \ˌmä-lə-fə-'kā-shən\ n

mol·lusk or **mol·lusc** \'mä-ləsk\ n : any of a large phylum of usu. shelled and aquatic invertebrate animals (as snails, clams, and squids) — **mol·lus·can** also **mol·lus·kan** \mə-'ləs-kən\ adj

¹mol·ly·cod·dle \'mä-lē-ˌkä-dᵊl\ n : a pampered man or boy
²mollycoddle vb **mol·ly·cod·dled; mol·ly·cod·dling** : PAMPER

Mo·lo·tov cocktail \'mä-lə-ˌtóf-, 'mò-\ n [Vyacheslav M. Molotov †1986 Soviet foreign minister] : a crude bomb made of a bottle filled usu. with gasoline and fitted with a wick (as a saturated rag) that is ignited just prior to hurling

¹molt \'mōlt\ vb : to shed hair, feathers, outer skin, or horns periodically with the cast-off parts being replaced by new growth — **molt·er** n
²molt n : the act or process of molting

mol·ten \'mōl-tᵊn\ adj **1** : fused or liquefied by heat **2** : GLOWING

mo·ly \'mō-lē\ n : a mythical herb with black root, white flowers, and magic powers

mo·lyb·de·num \mə-'lib-də-nəm\ n : a metallic chemical element used in strengthening and hardening steel

mom \'mäm, 'məm\ n : MOTHER

mom–and–pop adj : being a small owner-operated business

mo·ment \'mō-mənt\ n **1** : a minute portion of time : INSTANT **2** : a time of excellence ⟨he has his ∼s⟩ **3** : IMPORTANCE ♦ Synonyms CONSEQUENCE, SIGNIFICANCE, WEIGHT, IMPORT

mo·men·tari·ly \ˌmō-mən-'ter-ə-lē\ adv **1** : for a moment **2** archaic : INSTANTLY **3** : at any moment : SOON

mo·men·tary \'mō-mən-ˌter-ē\ adj **1** : continuing only a moment; also : EPHEMERAL **2** : recurring at every moment — **mo·men·tar·i·ness** \-ˌter-ē-nəs\ n

mo·men·tous \mō-'men-təs\ adj : very important — **mo·men·tous·ly** adv — **mo·men·tous·ness** n

mo·men·tum \mō-'men-təm\ n, pl **mo·men·ta** \-'men-tə\ or **momentums** : a property that a moving body has due to its mass and motion; also : IMPETUS

mom·my \'mä-mē, 'mə-\ n, pl **mom·mies** : MOTHER

Mon abbr Monday

mon·arch \'mä-nərk, -ˌnärk\ n **1** : a person who reigns over a kingdom or an empire **2** : one holding preeminent position or power **3** : MONARCH BUTTERFLY — **mo·nar·chi·cal** \mə-'när-ki-kəl\ also **mo·nar·chic** \-'när-kik\ adj

monarch butterfly n : a large orange and black migratory American butterfly whose larva feeds on milkweed

mon·ar·chist \'mä-nər-kist\ n : a believer in monarchical government — **mon·ar·chism** \-ˌki-zəm\ n

mon·ar·chy \'mä-nər-kē\ n, pl **-chies** : a nation or state governed by a monarch

mon·as·tery \'mä-nə-ˌster-ē\ n, pl **-ter·ies** : a house for persons under religious vows (as monks)

mo·nas·tic \mə-'nas-tik\ adj : of or relating to monasteries or to monks or nuns — **monastic** n — **mo·nas·ti·cal·ly** \-ti-k(ə-)lē\ adv — **mo·nas·ti·cism** \-tə-ˌsi-zəm\ n

mon·au·ral \mä-'nȯr-əl\ adj : MONOPHONIC — **mon·au·ral·ly** adv

Mon·day \'mən-dē, -ˌdā\ n : the second day of the week

mon·e·tary \'mä-nə-ˌter-ē, 'mə-\ adj : of or relating to money or to the mechanisms by which it is supplied and circulated in the economy

mon·ey \'mə-nē\ n, pl **moneys** or **mon·ies** \'mə-nēz\ **1** : something (as metal currency) accepted as a medium of exchange **2** : wealth reckoned in monetary terms **3** : the 1st, 2d, and 3d places in a horse or dog race

mon·eyed \'mə-nēd\ adj **1** : having money : WEALTHY **2** : consisting in or derived from money

mon·ey·lend·er \'mə-nē-ˌlen-dər\ n : one (as a bank or pawnbroker) whose business is lending money

money market n : the trade in short-term negotiable financial instruments

money of account : a denominator of value or basis of exchange used in keeping accounts

money order n : an order purchased at a post office, bank, or telegraph office directing another office to pay a sum of money to a party named on it

mon·ger \'məŋ-gər, 'mäŋ-\ n **1** : DEALER **2** : one who tries to stir up or spread something — usu. used in combination ⟨warmonger⟩

mon·go \'mäŋ-(ˌ)gō\ n, pl **mongo** — see tugrik at MONEY table

Mon·gol \'mäŋ-gəl, 'mäŋ-ˌgōl\ n : a member of any of several traditionally pastoral peoples of Mongolia — **Mongol** adj

Mon·go·lian \män-'gōl-yən, mäŋ-, -'gō-lē-ən\ n **1** : a native or inhabitant of Mongolia **2** : a member of the Mongoloid racial stock — **Mongolian** adj

Mon·gol·oid \'mäŋ-gə-ˌlȯid\ adj : of or relating to a major racial stock native to Asia that includes peoples of northern and eastern Asia, Malaysians, Eskimos, and often American Indians — **Mongoloid** n

mon·goose \'män-ˌgüs, 'mäŋ-\ n, pl **mon·goos·es** also **mon·geese** \-ˌgēs\ : any of a group of small agile Old World mammals that are related to the civet cats and feed chiefly on small animals and fruits

mon·grel \'mäŋ-grəl, 'məŋ-\ n : an offspring of parents of different breeds; esp : one of uncertain ancestry

mon·i·ker \'mä-ni-kər\ n : NAME, NICKNAME

mo·nism \'mō-ˌni-zəm, 'mä-\ n : a view that reality is basically one unitary organic whole — **mo·nist** \'mō-nist, 'mä-\ n

mo·ni·tion \mō-'ni-shən, mə-\ n : WARNING, CAUTION

¹mon·i·tor \'mä-nə-tər\ n **1** : a student appointed to assist a teacher **2** : one that monitors; esp : a video display screen (as for a computer)
²monitor vb : to watch, check, or observe for a special purpose

mon·i·to·ry \'mä-nə-ˌtȯr-ē\ adj : giving admonition : WARNING

¹monk \'məŋk\ n [ME, fr. OE munuc, fr. LL monachus, fr. LGk monachos, fr. Gk, adj., single, fr. monos single, alone] : a man belonging to a religious order and living in a monastery — **monk·ish** adj
²monk n : MONKEY

¹mon·key \'məŋ-kē\ n, pl **monkeys** : a nonhuman primate mammal; esp : one of the smaller, longer-tailed, and usu. more arboreal primates as contrasted with the apes
²monkey vb **mon·keyed; mon·key·ing 1** : FOOL, TRIFLE — often used with around **2** : TAMPER — usu. used with with

monkey bars n pl : a framework of bars on which children can play

mon·key·shine \'məŋ-kē-ˌshīn\ n : PRANK — usu. used in pl.

monkey wrench n : a wrench with one fixed and one adjustable jaw at right angles to a handle

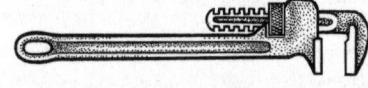

monkey wrench

monk·fish \'məŋk-ˌfish\ n : either of two marine bony fishes that have a large flattened head and are used for food

monks·hood \'məŋks-ˌhùd\ n : any of a genus of poisonous plants related to the buttercups; esp : a tall Eurasian herb with white or purplish flowers

¹mo·no \'mä-nō\ adj : MONOPHONIC
²mono n : INFECTIOUS MONONUCLEOSIS

mono·chro·mat·ic \ˌmä-nə-krō-'ma-tik\ adj **1** : having or consisting of one color **2** : consisting of radiation (as light) of a single wavelength

MONEY — WORLD CURRENCIES

NAME	SUBDIVISION	COUNTRY	NAME	SUBDIVISION	COUNTRY
afghani	100 puls	Afghanistan	dollar — see RINGGIT, below		
ariary	5 iraimbilanja	Madagascar	dong	100 xu	Vietnam
baht	100 satang	Thailand	dram	100 luma	Armenia
or tical			escudo	100 centavos	Cape Verde
balboa[1]	100 centesimos	Panama	euro[4]	100 cents	Austria,
birr	100 cents	Ethiopia		Belgium, Finland, France, Germany,	
bolivar	100 centimos	Venezuela		Greece, Ireland, Italy, Luxembourg,	
boliviano	100 centavos	Bolivia		Netherlands, Portugal, Spain	
cedi	100 pesewas	Ghana	florin — see GULDEN, below		
colón	100 centimos	Costa Rica	forint	100 fillers	Hungary
colón[1]	100 centavos	El Salvador	franc[5]	100 centimes	Benin,
córdoba	100 centavos	Nicaragua		Burkina Faso, Cameroon, Central	
dalasi	100 bututs	Gambia		African Republic, Chad, Republic	
denar	100 deni[2]	Republic of		of the Congo, Equatorial Guinea,	
		Macedonia		Gabon, Guinea-Bissau, Ivory Coast,	
dinar	100 centimes	Algeria		Mali, Niger, Senegal, Togo	
dinar	1000 fils	Bahrain	franc	100 centimes	Burundi
dinar	1000 fils	Iraq	franc	100 centimes	Comoros
dinar	1000 fils	Jordan	franc	100 centimes	Democratic
dinar	1000 fils	Kuwait		Republic of the Congo	
dinar	1000 dirhams	Libya	franc	100 centimes	Djibouti
dinar		Sudan	franc	100 centimes	Guinea
dinar	1000 millimes	Tunisia	franc	100 centimes[2]	Rwanda
dirham	100 centimes	Morocco	franc	100 centimes	Switzerland
dirham	100 fils	United Arab		*or* rappen	
		Emirates	gourde	100 centimes	Haiti
dobra	100 centimos	São Tomé and	guarani	100 centimos	Paraguay
		Príncipe	gulden	100 cents	Suriname
dollar[3]	100 cents	Antigua and	*or* florin		
	Barbuda, Dominica, Grenada,		hryvnia	100 kopiykas	Ukraine
	St. Kitts-Nevis, St. Lucia,		kina	100 toea	Papua New
	St. Vincent and the Grenadines				Guinea
dollar	100 cents	Australia	kip	100 at	Laos
dollar	100 cents	Bahamas	koruna	100 haleru	Czech
dollar	100 cents	Barbados			Republic
dollar	100 cents	Belize	koruna	100 haleru	Slovakia
dollar	100 cents	Bermuda	krona	100 aurar	Iceland
dollar	100 sen	Brunei		(*sing* eyrir)	
	or cents		krona	100 ore	Sweden
dollar	100 cents	Canada	krone	100 ore	Denmark
dollar	100 cents	Fiji	krone	100 ore	Norway
dollar	100 cents	Guyana	kroon	100 senti	Estonia
dollar	100 cents	Hong Kong		(*sing* sent)	
dollar	100 cents	Jamaica	kuna	100 lipa	Croatia
dollar	100 cents	Liberia	kwacha	100 tambala	Malawi
dollar	100 cents	Namibia	kwacha	100 ngwee	Zambia
dollar	100 cents	New Zealand	kwanza	100 lwei	Angola
dollar	100 cents	Singapore	kyat	100 pyas	Myanmar
dollar	100 cents	Solomon	lari	100 tetri	Republic of
		Islands			Georgia
dollar	100 cents	Taiwan	lats	100 santimi	Latvia
or yuan				(*sing* santims)	
dollar	100 cents	Trinidad and	lek	100 qindarka	Albania
		Tobago		(*sing* qintar)	
dollar	100 cents	United States	lempira	100 centavos	Honduras
dollar	100 cents	Zimbabwe	leone	100 cents	Sierra Leone

MONEY — WORLD CURRENCIES

NAME	SUBDIVISION	COUNTRY	NAME	SUBDIVISION	COUNTRY
leu	100 bani (*sing* ban)	Moldova	rial *also* riyal	100 fils	Yemen
leu	100 bani (*sing* ban)	Romania	rial — see RIYAL, below		
lev	100 stotinki	Bulgaria	riel	100 sen	Cambodia
lilangeni (*pl* emalangeni)	100 cents	Swaziland	ringgit *or* dollar	100 sen	Malaysia
lira *or* pound	100 cents	Malta	riyal	100 dirhams	Qatar
			riyal *also* rial	100 halala	Saudi Arabia
lira	100 kurus	Turkey	riyal — see RIAL, above		
litas	100 centai (*sing* centas)	Lithuania	rubel	100 kapeek (*sing* kapeyka)	Belarus
livre — see POUND, below			ruble	100 kopecks	Russia
loti	100 licente (*sing* sente)	Lesotho	rufiyaa	100 laari	Maldives
			rupee	100 paisa	India
manat	100 gopik	Azerbaijan	rupee	100 cents	Mauritius
manat	100 tennesi	Turkmenistan	rupee	100 paisa	Nepal
metical	100 centavos	Mozambique	rupee	100 paisa	Pakistan
naira	100 kobo	Nigeria	rupee	100 cents	Seychelles
nakfa	100 cents	Eritrea	rupee	100 cents	Sri Lanka
ngultrum	100 chetrums	Bhutan	rupiah	100 sen	Indonesia
ouguiya	5 khoums	Mauritania	shekel	100 agorot	Israel
pa'anga	100 seniti	Tonga	shilling	100 cents	Kenya
pataca	100 avos	Macao	shilling	100 cents	Somalia
peso	100 centavos	Argentina	shilling	100 cents	Tanzania
peso	100 centavos	Chile	shilling	100 cents	Uganda
peso	100 centavos	Colombia	sol	100 centimos	Peru
peso	100 centavos	Cuba	som	100 tyiyn	Kyrgyzstan
peso	100 centavos	Dominican Republic	som	100 tiyin	Uzbekistan
			somoni	100 dirams	Tajikistan
peso	100 centavos	Mexico	sucre[1]	100 centavos	Ecuador
peso *or* piso	100 sentimos *or* centavos	Philippines	taka	100 paisa *or* poisha	Bangladesh
peso	100 centesimos	Uruguay	tala	100 sene	Samoa
pound	100 cents	Cyprus	tenge	100 tyin	Kazakhstan
pound	100 piastres	Egypt	tical — see BAHT, above		
pound *or* livre	100 piastres	Lebanon	tolar	100 stotinov (*sing* stotin)	Slovenia
pound	100 piastres	Syria	tugrik	100 mongo	Mongolia
pound	100 pence (*sing* penny)	United Kingdom	vatu		Vanuatu
			won	100 chon	North Korea
pound — see LIRA, above			won	100 chon	South Korea
pula	100 thebe	Botswana			
quetzal	100 centavos	Guatemala	yen	100 sen[2]	Japan
rand	100 cents	South Africa	yuan	100 fen	China
real	100 centavos	Brazil	yuan — see DOLLAR, above		
rial	100 dinars	Iran	zloty	100 groszy	Poland
rial	1000 baiza	Oman			

[1] A monetary unit in name only; replaced by the U.S. dollar.
[2] Now a subdivision in name only.
[3] Dollars issued by the Eastern Caribbean Central Bank, established to promote economic cooperation among the member nations.
[4] Replaced the individual monetary units of participating European Union countries Jan. 1, 2002.
[5] Francs issued by the African Financial Community, established to promote economic cooperation among member nations.

mono·chrome \'mä-nə-ˌkrōm\ *adj* : involving or producing visual images in a single color or in varying tones of a single color 〈~ television〉

mon·o·cle \'mä-ni-kəl\ *n* : an eyeglass for one eye

mono·clo·nal \ˌmä-nə-'klō-nəl\ *adj* : produced by, being, or composed of cells derived from a single cell 〈~ antibodies〉

mono·cot·y·le·don \ˌmä-nə-ˌkät-tə-'lē-dᵉn\ *n* : any of a class or subclass of chiefly herbaceous seed plants having an embryo with a single cotyledon and usu. parallel-veined leaves

mon·o·dy \'mä-nə-dē\ *n*, *pl* **-dies** : ELEGY, DIRGE — **mo·nod·ic** \mə-'nä-dik\ *or* **mo·nod·i·cal** \-di-kəl\ *adj* — **mon·o·dist** \'mä-nə-dist\ *n*

mo·nog·a·my \mə-'nä-gə-mē\ *n* **1** : marriage with but one person at a time **2** : the practice of having a single mate during a period of time — **mo·nog·a·mist** \-mist\ *n* — **mo·nog·a·mous** \-məs\ *adj*

mono·gram \'mä-nə-ˌgram\ *n* : a sign of identity composed of the combined initials of a name — **monogram** *vb*

mono·graph \'mä-nə-ˌgraf\ *n* : a learned treatise on a small area of learning

mono·lin·gual \ˌmä-nə-'liŋ-gwəl\ *adj* : knowing or using only one language

mono·lith \'mä-nə-ˌlith\ *n* **1** : a single great stone often in the form of a monument or column **2** : something large and powerful that acts as a single unified force — **mono·lith·ic** \ˌmä-nə-'li-thik\ *adj*

mono·logue *also* **mono·log** \'mä-nə-ˌlȯg\ *n* **1** : a dramatic soliloquy; *also* : a long speech monopolizing conversation **2** : the routine of a stand-up comic — **mono·logu·ist** \-ˌlȯg-ist\ *or* **mo·no·lo·gist** \mə-'nä-lə-jist; 'mä-nə-ˌlȯ-gist\ *n*

mono·ma·nia \ˌmä-nə-'mä-nē-ə, -nyə\ *n* **1** : mental disorder limited in expression to one area of thought **2** : excessive concentration on a single object or idea — **mono·ma·ni·ac** \-nē-ˌak\ *n or adj*

mono·mer \'mä-nə-mər\ *n* : a simple chemical compound that can be polymerized

mono·nu·cle·o·sis \ˌmä-nō-ˌnü-klē-'ō-səs, -ˌnyü-\ *n* : INFECTIOUS MONONUCLEOSIS

mono·phon·ic \ˌmä-nə-'fä-nik\ *adj* : of or relating to sound recording or reproduction involving a single transmission path

mono·plane \'mä-nə-ˌplān\ *n* : an airplane with only one set of wings

mo·nop·o·ly \mə-'nä-pə-lē\ *n*, *pl* **-lies** [L *monopolium*, fr. Gk *monopōlion*, fr. *monos* alone, single + *pōlein* to sell] **1** : exclusive ownership (as through command of supply) **2** : a commodity controlled by one party **3** : one that has a monopoly — **mo·nop·o·list** \-list\ *n* — **mo·nop·o·lis·tic** \mə-ˌnä-pə-'lis-tik\ *adj* — **mo·nop·o·li·za·tion** \-lə-'zā-shən\ *n* — **mo·nop·o·lize** \mə-'nä-pə-ˌlīz\ *vb*

mono·rail \'mä-nə-ˌrāl\ *n* : a single rail serving as a track for a vehicle; *also* : a vehicle traveling on such a track

monorail

mono·so·di·um glu·ta·mate \ˌmä-nə-ˌsō-dē-əm-'glü-tə-ˌmāt\ *n* : a crystalline salt used to enhance the flavor of food

mono·syl·la·ble \'mä-nə-ˌsi-lə-bəl\ *n* : a word of one syllable — **mono·syl·lab·ic** \ˌmä-nə-sə-'la-bik\ *adj* — **mono·syl·lab·i·cal·ly** \-bi-k(ə-)lē\ *adv*

mono·the·ism \'mä-nə-(ˌ)thē-ˌi-zəm\ *n* : a doctrine or belief that there is only one deity — **mono·the·ist** \-ˌthē-ist\ *n* — **mono·the·is·tic** \-thē-'is-tik\ *adj*

mono·tone \'mä-nə-ˌtōn\ *n* : a succession of syllables, words, or sentences in one unvaried key or pitch

mo·not·o·nous \mə-'nä-tə-nəs\ *adj* **1** : uttered or sounded in one unvarying tone **2** : tediously uniform — **mo·not·o·nous·ly** *adv* — **mo·not·o·nous·ness** *n*

mo·not·o·ny \mə-'nä-tə-nē\ *n* : tedious sameness or uniformity

mono·un·sat·u·rat·ed \ˌmä-nō-ˌən-'sa-chə-ˌrā-təd\ *adj* : containing one double or triple bond per molecule — used esp. of an oil, fat, or fatty acid

mon·ox·ide \mə-'näk-ˌsīd\ *n* : an oxide containing one atom of oxygen in a molecule

mon·sei·gneur \ˌmōⁿ-ˌsān-'yər\ *n*, *pl* **mes·sei·gneurs** \ˌmā-ˌsān-'yər, -'yərz\ : a French dignitary — used as a title

mon·sieur \məs-'yər\ *n*, *pl* **mes·sieurs** *same or* -'yərz\ : a Frenchman of high rank or station — used as a title equivalent to *Mister*

mon·si·gnor \män-'sē-nyər\ *n*, *pl* **monsignors** *or* **mon·si·gno·ri** \ˌmän-ˌsēn-'yȯr-ē\ [It *monsignore*] : a Roman Catholic prelate — used as a title

mon·soon \män-'sün\ *n* [obs. Dutch *monssoen*, fr. Pg *monção*, fr. Ar *mawsim* time, season] **1** : a periodic wind esp. in the Indian Ocean and southern Asia **2** : the season of the southwest monsoon esp. in India **3** : rainfall associated with the monsoon

¹**mon·ster** \'män-stər\ *n* **1** : an abnormally developed plant or animal **2** : an animal of strange or terrifying shape; *also* : one unusually large of its kind **3** : an extremely ugly, wicked, or cruel person — **mon·stros·i·ty** \män-'strä-sə-tē\ *n* — **mon·strous** \'män-strəs\ *adj* — **mon·strous·ly** *adv*

²**monster** *adj* : very large : ENORMOUS

mon·strance \'män-strəns\ *n* : a vessel in which the consecrated Host is exposed for the adoration of the faithful

Mont *abbr* Montana

mon·tage \män-'täzh\ *n* [F] **1** : a composite photograph made by combining several separate pictures **2** : an artistic composition made up of several different kinds of elements **3** : a varied mixture : JUMBLE

month \'mənth\ *n*, *pl* **months** \'məns, 'mənths\ : one of the 12 parts into which the year is divided — **month·ly** *adv or adj or n*

month·long \'mənth-'lȯŋ\ *adj* : lasting a month

mon·u·ment \'män-yə-mənt\ *n* **1** : a lasting reminder; *esp* : a structure erected in remembrance of a person or event **2** : NATIONAL MONUMENT

mon·u·men·tal \ˌmän-yə-'men-tᵉl\ *adj* **1** : of or relating to a monument **2** : MASSIVE; *also* : OUTSTANDING 〈a ~ achievement〉 **3** : very great — **mon·u·men·tal·ly** *adv*

moo \'mü\ *vb* : to make the natural throat noise of a cow — **moo** *n*

¹**mood** \'müd\ *n* **1** : a conscious state of mind or predominant emotion : FEELING **2** : a prevailing attitude : DISPOSITION **3** : a distinctive atmosphere

²**mood** *n* : distinction of form of a verb to express whether its action or state is conceived as fact or in some other manner (as wish)

moody \'mü-dē\ *adj* **mood·i·er; -est** **1** : GLOOMY **2** : subject to moods : TEMPERAMENTAL — **mood·i·ly** \-də-lē\ *adv* — **mood·i·ness** \-dē-nəs\ *n*

¹**moon** \'mün\ *n* **1** : the earth's natural satellite **2** : SATELLITE 2

²**moon** *vb* : to engage in idle reverie

moon·beam \'mün-ˌbēm\ *n* : a ray of light from the moon

¹**moon·light** \-ˌlīt\ *n* : the light of the moon — **moon·lit** \-ˌlit\ *adj*

²**moonlight** *vb* **moon·light·ed; moon·light·ing** : to hold a second job in addition to a regular one — **moon·light·er** *n*

moon·roof \-ˌrüf, -ˌrúf\ *n* : a glass sunroof

moon·scape \-ˌskāp\ *n* : the surface of the moon as seen or as pictured

moon·shine \-ˌshīn\ *n* **1** : MOONLIGHT **2** : empty talk **3** : intoxicating liquor usu. illegally distilled

moon·stone \-ˌstōn\ *n* : a transparent or translucent feldspar of pearly luster used as a gem

moon·struck \-ˌstrək\ *adj* **1** : mentally unbalanced **2** : romantically sentimental **3** : lost in fantasy

¹**moor** \'mùr\ *n* **1** *chiefly Brit* : an expanse of open rolling infertile land **2** : a boggy area; *esp* : one that is peaty and dominated by grasses and sedges

²**moor** *vb* : to make fast with or as if with cables, lines, or anchors

Moor \'mùr\ *n* : one of the Arab and Berber conquerors of Spain — **Moor·ish** *adj*

moor·ing \'mùr-iŋ\ *n* **1** : a place where or an object to which a craft can be made fast **2** : an established practice or stabilizing influence — usu. used in pl.

moor·land \-lənd, -ˌland\ *n* : land consisting of moors

moose \'müs\ *n, pl* **moose** : a large heavy-antlered ruminant mammal related to the deer that has humped shoulders and long legs and inhabits northern forested areas

¹**moot** \'müt\ *vb* : to bring up for discussion; *also* : DEBATE

²**moot** *adj* **1** : open to question; *also* : DISPUTED **2** : having no practical significance

¹**mop** \'mäp\ *n* : an implement made of absorbent material fastened to a handle and used esp. for cleaning floors

²**mop** *vb* **mopped; mop·ping** : to use a mop on : clean with a mop

mope \'mōp\ *vb* **moped; mop·ing 1** : to become dull, dejected, or listless **2** : DAWDLE

mo·ped \'mō-ˌped\ *n* : a light low-powered motorbike that can be pedaled

mop·pet \'mä-pət\ *n* [obs. E *mop* fool, child] : CHILD

mo·raine \mə-'rān\ *n* : an accumulation of earth and stones left by a glacier

¹**mor·al** \'mòr-əl\ *adj* **1** : of or relating to principles of right and wrong behavior; *also* : conforming to a standard of right behavior; *also* : capable of right and wrong action **3** : probable but not proved ⟨a ∼ certainty⟩ **4** : perceptual or psychological rather than tangible or practical in nature or effect ⟨a ∼ victory⟩ ✦ **Synonyms** VIRTUOUS, RIGHTEOUS, NOBLE, ETHICAL, PRINCIPLED — **mor·al·ly** *adv*

²**moral** *n* **1** : the practical meaning (as of a story) **2** *pl* : moral practices or teachings

mo·rale \mə-'ral\ *n* **1** : MORALITY **2** : the mental and emotional attitudes of an individual to the tasks at hand; *also* : ESPRIT DE CORPS

mor·al·ise *Brit var of* MORALIZE

mor·al·ist \'mòr-ə-list\ *n* **1** : one who leads a moral life **2** : a thinker or writer concerned with morals **3** : one concerned with regulating the morals of others — **mor·al·is·tic** \ˌmòr-ə-'lis-tik\ *adj* — **mor·al·is·ti·cal·ly** \-ti-k(ə-)lē\ *adv*

mo·ral·i·ty \mə-'ra-lə-tē\ *n, pl* **-ties** : moral conduct : VIRTUE

mor·al·ize \'mòr-ə-ˌlīz\ *vb* **-ized; -iz·ing** : to make moral reflections — **mor·al·i·za·tion** \ˌmòr-ə-lə-'zā-shən\ *n* — **mor·al·iz·er** \'mòr-ə-ˌlī-zər\ *n*

mo·rass \mə-'ras\ *n* [D *moeras*, fr. OF *maresc*, of Gmc origin; akin to OE *mersc* marsh] : SWAMP; *also* : something that entangles, impedes, or confuses

mor·a·to·ri·um \ˌmòr-ə-'tòr-ē-əm\ *n, pl* **-ri·ums** *or* **-ria** \-ē-ə\ [ultim. fr. L *mora* delay] : a suspension of activity

mo·ray eel \mə-'rā-, 'mòr-ˌā-\ *n* : any of numerous often brightly colored biting eels of warm seas

mor·bid \'mòr-bəd\ *adj* **1** : of, relating to, or typical of disease; *also* : DISEASED, SICKLY **2** : characterized by gloomy or unwholesome ideas or feelings **3** : GRISLY, GRUESOME ⟨∼ details⟩ — **mor·bid·i·ty** \mòr-'bi-də-tē\ *n* — **mor·bid·ly** *adv* — **mor·bid·ness** *n*

mor·dant \'mòr-d⁽ᵊ⁾nt\ *adj* **1** : biting or caustic in manner or style **2** : BURNING, PUNGENT — **mor·dant·ly** *adv*

¹**more** \'mòr\ *adj* **1** : GREATER ⟨something ∼ than I expected⟩ **2** : ADDITIONAL

²**more** *adv* **1** : in addition **2** : to a greater or higher degree ⟨∼ evenly matched⟩

³**more** *n* **1** : a greater quantity, number, or amount ⟨the ∼ the merrier⟩ **2** : an additional amount ⟨costs a little ∼⟩

⁴**more** *pron* : additional persons or things or a greater amount

mo·rel \mə-'rel\ *n* : any of several pitted edible fungi

more·over \mòr-'ō-vər\ *adv* : in addition : FURTHER

mo·res \'mòr-ˌāz\ *n pl* [L, pl. of *mor-, mos* custom] **1** : the fixed morally binding customs of a group **2** : HABITS, MANNERS

Mor·gan \'mòr-gən\ *n* : any of an American breed of lightly built horses

morgue \'mòrg\ *n* : a place where the bodies of dead persons are kept until released for burial or autopsy

mor·i·bund \'mòr-ə-(ˌ)bənd\ *adj* : being in a dying condition

Mor·mon \'mòr-mən\ *n* : a member of the Church of Jesus Christ of Latter-day Saints — **Mor·mon·ism** \-mə-ˌni-zəm\ *n*

morn \'mòrn\ *n* : MORNING

morn·ing \'mòr-niŋ\ *n* **1** : the early part of the day; *esp* : the time from the sunrise to noon **2** : BEGINNING

morn·ing-after pill \ˌmòr-niŋ-'af-tər-\ *n* : a contraceptive drug taken up to usu. three days after sexual intercourse

morning glory *n* : any of various twining plants related to the sweet potato that have often showy bell-shaped or funnel-shaped flowers

morning sickness *n* : nausea and vomiting that typically occur in the morning esp. during early pregnancy

morning star *n* : a bright planet (as Venus) seen in the eastern sky before or at sunrise

mo·roc·co \mə-'rä-kō\ *n* : a fine leather made of goatskins tanned with sumac

mo·ron \'mòr-ˌän\ *n* **1** *usu. offensive* : a mildly mentally retarded person **2** : a very stupid person — **mo·ron·ic** \mə-'rä-nik\ *adj* — **mo·ron·i·cal·ly** \-ni-k(ə-)lē\ *adv*

mo·rose \mə-'rōs\ *adj* [L *morosus* hard to please, exacting, fr. *mor-, mos* custom, disposition] : having a sullen disposition; *also* : GLOOMY — **mo·rose·ly** *adv* — **mo·rose·ness** *n*

morph \'mòrf\ *vb* : to change the form or character of : TRANSFORM

mor·pheme \'mòr-ˌfēm\ *n* : a meaningful linguistic unit that contains no smaller meaningful parts — **mor·phe·mic** \mòr-'fē-mik\ *adj*

mor·phia \'mòr-fē-ə\ *n* : MORPHINE

mor·phine \'mòr-ˌfēn\ *n* [F, fr. Gk *Morpheus*, Greek god of dreams] : an addictive drug obtained from opium and used to ease pain or induce sleep

mor·phol·o·gy \mòr-'fä-lə-jē\ *n* **1** : a branch of biology dealing with the form and structure of organisms **2** : a study and description of word formation in a language — **mor·pho·log·i·cal** \ˌmòr-fə-'lä-ji-kəl\ *adj* — **mor·phol·o·gist** \mòr-'fä-lə-jist\ *n*

mor·ris \'mòr-əs\ *n* : a vigorous English dance traditionally performed by men wearing costumes and bells

mor·row \'mär-ō\ *n* : the next day

Morse code \'mòrs-\ *n* : either of two codes consisting of dots and dashes or long and short sounds used for transmitting messages

mor·sel \'mòr-səl\ *n* [ME, fr. AF, dim. of *mors* bite, fr. L *morsus*, fr. *mordēre* to bite] **1** : a small piece or quantity **2** : a tasty dish

mor·tal \'mòr-t⁽ᵊ⁾l\ *adj* **1** : causing death : FATAL; *also* : leading to eternal punishment ⟨∼ sin⟩ **2** : subject to death ⟨∼ man⟩ **3** : implacably hostile ⟨∼ foe⟩ **4** : very great : EXTREME ⟨∼ fear⟩ **5** : HUMAN ⟨∼ limitations⟩ — **mortal** *n* — **mor·tal·i·ty** \mòr-'ta-lə-tē\ *n* — **mor·tal·ly** \'mòr-t⁽ᵊ⁾l-ē\ *adv*

¹**mor·tar** \'mòr-tər\ *n* **1** : a strong bowl in which substances are pounded or crushed with a pestle **2** : a short-barreled cannon used to fire shells at high angles

²**mortar** *n* : a building material (as a mixture of lime and cement with sand and water) that is spread between bricks or stones to bind them together as it hardens — **mortar** *vb*

mor·tar·board \'mòr-tər-ˌbòrd\ *n* **1** : a square board for holding mortar **2** : an academic cap with a flat square top

mort·gage \'mòr-gij\ *n* [ME *morgage*, fr. AF *mortgage*, fr. *mort* dead + *gage* pledge] : a transfer of rights to a piece of property usu. as security for the payment of a loan or debt that becomes void when the debt is paid — **mortgage** *vb* — **mort·gag·ee** \ˌmòr-gi-'jē\ *n* — **mort·gag·or** \ˌmòr-gi-'jòr\ *n*

mor·ti·cian \mòr-'ti-shən\ *n* [L *mort-, mors* death + E *-ician* (as in *physician*)] : UNDERTAKER

mor·ti·fy \'mòr-tə-ˌfī\ *vb* **-fied; -fy·ing 1** : to subdue (as the body) esp. by abstinence or self-inflicted pain **2** : HUMILIATE **3** : to become necrotic or gangrenous — **mor·ti·fi·ca·tion** \ˌmòr-tə-fə-'kā-shən\ *n*

mor·tise *also* **mor·tice** \'mòr-təs\ *n* : a hole cut in a piece of wood into which another piece fits to form a joint

mor·tu·ary \'mȯr-chə-ˌwer-ē\ *n*, *pl* **-ar·ies** : a place in which dead bodies are kept until burial

mos *abbr* months

mo·sa·ic \mō-'zā-ik\ *n* : a surface decoration made by inlaying small pieces (as of colored glass or stone) to form figures or patterns; *also* : a design made in mosaic — **mosaic** *adj*

mo·sey \'mō-zē\ *vb* **mo·seyed; mo·sey·ing** : SAUNTER

mosh \'mäsh\ *vb* : to engage in rough uninhibited dancing near the stage at a rock concert

mosh pit *n* : an area in front of a stage where rough dancing takes place at a rock concert

Mos·lem \'mäz-ləm\ *var of* MUSLIM

mosque \'mäsk\ *n* : a building used for public worship by Muslims

mos·qui·to \mə-'skē-tō\ *n*, *pl* **-toes** *also* **-tos** : any of a family of dipteran flies the female of which sucks the blood of animals

mosquito net *n* : a net or screen for keeping out mosquitoes

moss \'mȯs\ *n* : any of a class of green plants that lack flowers but have small leafy stems and often grow in clumps — **mossy** *adj*

moss·back \'mȯs-ˌbak\ *n* : an extremely conservative person : FOGY

¹most \'mōst\ *adj* **1** : GREATEST ⟨the ~ ability⟩ **2** : the majority of ⟨~ people⟩

²most *adv* **1** : to the greatest or highest degree ⟨~ beautiful⟩ **2** : to a very great degree ⟨a ~ careful driver⟩

³most *n* : the greatest amount ⟨the ~ I can do⟩

⁴most *pron* : the greatest number or part ⟨~ became discouraged⟩

-most *adj suffix* : most ⟨inner*most*⟩ : most toward ⟨end*most*⟩

most·ly \'mōst-lē\ *adv* : MAINLY

mot \'mō\ *n*, *pl* **mots** *same or* 'mōz\ [F, word, saying, fr. LL *muttum* grunt] : a witty saying

mote \'mōt\ *n* : a small particle

mo·tel \mō-'tel\ *n* [blend of *motor* and *hotel*] : a hotel in which the rooms are accessible from the parking area

mo·tet \mō-'tet\ *n* : a choral work on a sacred text for several voices usu. without instrumental accompaniment

moth \'mȯth\ *n*, *pl* **moths** \'mȯthz, 'mȯths\ : any of various insects belonging to the same order as the butterflies but usu. night-flying and with a stouter body and smaller wings

moth·ball \'mȯth-ˌbȯl\ *n* **1** : a ball (as of naphthalene) used to keep moths out of clothing **2** *pl* : protective storage

¹moth·er \'mə-thər\ *n* **1** : a female parent **2** : the superior of a religious community of women **3** : SOURCE, ORIGIN ⟨*necessity* is the ~ of invention⟩ — **moth·er·hood** \-ˌhu̇d\ *n* — **moth·er·less** *adj* — **moth·er·li·ness** \-lē-nəs\ *n* — **moth·er·ly** *adj*

²mother *vb* : to give birth to; *also* : PRODUCE **2** : to care for or protect like a mother

moth·er·board \'mə-thər-ˌbȯrd\ *n* : the main circuit board esp. of a microcomputer

moth·er–in–law \'mə-thər-ən-ˌlȯ\ *n*, *pl* **mothers–in–law** \'mə-thərz-\ : the mother of one's spouse

moth·er·land \'mə-thər-ˌland\ *n* **1** : the land of origin of something **2** : the native land of one's ancestors

moth·er–of–pearl \ˌmə-thər-əv-'pərl\ *n* : the hard pearly matter forming the inner layer of a mollusk shell

mother ship *n* : a ship serving smaller craft

mo·tif \mō-'tēf\ *n* [F, motive, motif] : a dominant idea or central theme (as in a work of art)

mo·tile \'mōt-ᵊl, 'mō-ˌtī(-ə)l\ *adj* : capable of spontaneous movement — **mo·til·i·ty** \mō-'ti-lə-tē\ *n*

¹mo·tion \'mō-shən\ *n* **1** : an act, process, or instance of moving **2** : a proposal for action (as by a deliberative body) **3** *pl* : ACTIVITIES, MOVEMENTS — **mo·tion·less** *adj* — **mo·tion·less·ly** *adv* — **mo·tion·less·ness** *n*

²motion *vb* : to direct or signal by a movement

motion picture *n* : a series of pictures projected on a screen so rapidly that they produce a continuous picture in which persons and objects seem to move

motion sickness *n* : sickness induced by motion and characterized by nausea

mo·ti·vate \'mō-tə-ˌvāt\ *vb* **-vat·ed; -vat·ing** : to provide with a motive : IMPEL — **mo·ti·va·tion** \ˌmō-tə-'vā-shən\

n — **mo·ti·va·tion·al** \-shə-nəl\ *adj* — **mo·ti·va·tor** \'mō-tə-ˌvā-tər\ *n*

¹mo·tive \'mō-tiv, 2 *also* mō-'tēv\ *n* **1** : something (as a need or desire) that causes a person to act **2** : a recurrent theme in a musical composition **3** : MOTIF — **motive·less** *adj*

²mo·tive \'mō-tiv\ *adj* **1** : moving to action **2** : of or relating to motion

mot·ley \'mät-lē\ *adj* **1** : variegated in color **2** : made up of diverse often incongruous elements ✦ **Synonyms** HETEROGENEOUS, MISCELLANEOUS, ASSORTED, MIXED, VARIED

¹mo·tor \'mō-tər\ *n* [L, fr. *movēre* to move] **1** : one that imparts motion **2** : a machine that produces motion or power for doing work **3** : AUTOMOBILE

²motor *vb* : to travel or transport by automobile : DRIVE — **mo·tor·ist** *n*

mo·tor·bike \'mō-tər-ˌbīk\ *n* : a small lightweight motorcycle

mo·tor·boat \-ˌbōt\ *n* : a boat propelled by a motor

mo·tor·cade \-ˌkād\ *n* : a procession of motor vehicles

mo·tor·car \-ˌkär\ *n* : AUTOMOBILE

mo·tor·cy·cle \'mō-tər-ˌsī-kəl\ *n* : a 2-wheeled automotive vehicle — **mo·tor·cy·clist** \-k(ə-)list\ *n*

motor home *n* : a large motor vehicle equipped as living quarters

motor inn *n* : MOTEL

mo·tor·ise *Brit var of* MOTORIZE

mo·tor·ize \'mō-tə-ˌrīz\ *vb* **-ized; -iz·ing** **1** : to equip with a motor **2** : to equip with automobiles

mo·tor·man \'mō-tər-mən\ *n* : an operator of a motor-driven vehicle (as a streetcar or subway train)

motor scooter *n* : a low 2- or 3-wheeled automotive vehicle resembling a child's scooter but having a seat

mo·tor·truck \'mō-tər-ˌtrək\ *n* : an automotive truck

motor vehicle *n* : an automotive vehicle (as an automobile) not operated on rails

mot·tle \'mä-tᵊl\ *vb* **mot·tled; mot·tling** : to mark with spots of different color : BLOTCH

mot·to \'mä-tō\ *n*, *pl* **mottoes** *also* **mottos** [It, fr. LL *muttum* grunt, fr. L *muttire* to mutter] **1** : a sentence, phrase, or word inscribed on something to indicate its character or use **2** : a short expression of a guiding rule of conduct

moue \'mü\ *n* : a little grimace

mould *chiefly Brit var of* MOLD

moult *chiefly Brit var of* MOLT

mound \'mau̇nd\ *n* **1** : an artificial bank or hill of earth or stones **2** : KNOLL **3** : HEAP, PILE ⟨a ~ of work⟩

¹mount \'mau̇nt\ *n* : a high hill

²mount *vb* **1** : to increase in amount or extent; *also* : RISE, ASCEND **2** : to get up on something; *esp* : to seat oneself on (as a horse) for riding **3** : to put in position ⟨~ artillery⟩ **4** : to set on something that elevates **5** : to attach to a support **6** : to prepare esp. for examination or display — **mount·able** *adj* — **mount·er** *n*

³mount *n* **1** : FRAME, SUPPORT **2** : a means of conveyance; *esp* : SADDLE HORSE

moun·tain \'mau̇n-tᵊn\ *n* : a landmass higher than a hill — **moun·tain·ous** \-tə-nəs\ *adj* — **moun·tainy** \-tᵊn-ē\ *adj*

mountain ash *n* : any of various trees related to the roses that have pinnate leaves and red or orange-red fruits

mountain bike *n* : a bicycle with wide knobby tires, straight handlebars, and 18 or 21 gears that is designed to operate esp. over unpaved terrain

moun·tain·eer \ˌmau̇n-tə-'nir\ *n* **1** : a native or inhabitant of a mountainous region **2** : one who climbs mountains for sport

mountain goat *n* : a ruminant mammal of mountainous northwestern No. America that resembles a goat

mountain laurel *n* : a No. American evergreen shrub or small tree of the heath family with glossy leaves and clusters of rose-colored or white flowers

mountain lion *n* : COUGAR

moun·tain·side \'mau̇n-tᵊn-ˌsīd\ *n* : the side of a mountain

moun·tain·top \-ˌtäp\ *n* : the summit of a mountain

moun·te·bank \'mau̇n-ti-ˌbaŋk\ *n* [It *montimbanco*, fr. *montare* to mount + *in* in, on + *banco*, *banca* bench] : QUACK, CHARLATAN

Mount·ie \'mau̇n-tē\ *n* : a member of the Royal Canadian Mounted Police

mount·ing \'maún-tiŋ\ *n* : something that serves as a frame or support

mourn \'mōrn\ *vb* : to feel or express grief or sorrow — **mourn·er** *n*

mourn·ful \-fəl\ *adj* : expressing, feeling, or causing sorrow — **mourn·ful·ly** *adv* — **mourn·ful·ness** *n*

mourn·ing \'mōr-niŋ\ *n* **1** : an outward sign (as black clothes) of grief for a person's death **2** : a period of time during which signs of grief are shown

mouse \'maús\ *n, pl* **mice** \'mīs\ **1** : any of numerous small rodents with pointed snout, long body, and slender tail **2** : a small manual device that controls cursor movement on a computer display

mouse pad *n* : a thin flat pad on which a computer mouse is used

mous·er \'maú-sər\ *n* : a cat proficient at catching mice

mouse·trap \'maús-ˌtrap\ *n* **1** : a trap for catching mice **2** : a stratagem that lures one to defeat or destruction — **mousetrap** *vb*

mousse \'müs\ *n* [F, lit., froth, moss] **1** : a molded chilled dessert made with sweetened and flavored whipped cream or egg whites and gelatin **2** : a foamy preparation used in styling hair — **mousse** *vb*

moustache *var of* MUSTACHE

mousy *or* **mous·ey** \'maú-sē, -zē\ *adj* **mous·i·er; -est 1** : QUIET, STEALTHY **2** : TIMID **3** : grayish brown — **mous·i·ness** \'maú-sē-nəs, -zē-\ *n*

¹mouth \'maúth\ *n, pl* **mouths** \'maúthz, 'maúths\ **1** : the opening through which an animal takes in food; *also* : the cavity that encloses the tongue, lips, and teeth in the typical vertebrate **2** : something resembling a mouth (as in affording entrance) — **mouthed** \'maúthd, 'maútht\ *adj* — **mouth·ful** *n*

²mouth \'maúth\ *vb* **1** : SPEAK; *also* : DECLAIM **2** : to repeat without comprehension or sincerity **3** : to form soundlessly with the lips

mouth harp *n* : HARMONICA

mouth·part \'maúth-ˌpärt\ *n* : a structure or appendage near the mouth (as of an insect) esp. when adapted for eating

mouth·piece \-ˌpēs\ *n* **1** : a part (as of a musical instrument) that goes in the mouth or to which the mouth is applied **2** : SPOKESMAN

mouth-to-mouth *adj* : of, relating to, or being a method of artificial respiration in which air from a rescuer's mouth is forced into a victim's lungs

mouth·wash \-ˌwòsh, -ˌwäsh\ *n* : a usu. antiseptic liquid preparation for cleaning the mouth and teeth

mou·ton \'mü-ˌtän\ *n* : processed sheepskin that has been sheared or dyed to resemble beaver or seal

¹move \'müv\ *vb* **moved; mov·ing 1** : to change or cause to change position or posture **2** : to go or cause to go from one point to another; *also* : DEPART **3** : to take or cause to take action **4** : to show marked activity **5** : to stir the emotions **6** : to make a formal request, application, or appeal **7** : to change one's residence **8** : EVACUATE **2** — **mov·able** *or* **move·able** \'mü-və-bəl\ *adj*

²move *n* **1** : an act of moving **2** : a calculated step taken to gain an objective **3** : a change of location **4** : an agile action esp. in sports

move·ment \'müv-mənt\ *n* **1** : the act or process of moving : MOVE **2** : a series of organized activities working toward an objective **3** : the moving parts of a mechanism (as of a watch) **4** : RHYTHM **5** : a section of an extended musical composition **6** : an act of voiding the bowels; *also* : STOOL **4**

mov·er \'mü-vər\ *n* : one that moves; *esp* : one that moves the belongings of others from one location to another

mov·ie \'mü-vē\ *n* **1** : MOTION PICTURE **2** *pl* : a showing of a motion picture **3** *pl* : the motion-picture industry

¹mow \'maú\ *n* : the part of a barn where hay or straw is stored

²mow \'mō\ *vb* **mowed; mowed** *or* **mown** \'mōn\; **mow·ing 1** : to cut (as grass) with a scythe or machine **2** : to cut the standing herbage of ⟨~ the lawn⟩ — **mow·er** *n*

mox·ie \'mäk-sē\ *n* **1** : ENERGY, PEP **2** : COURAGE, DETERMINATION

moz·za·rel·la \ˌmät-sə-'re-lə\ *n* [It] : a moist white unsalted unripened mild cheese of a smooth rubbery texture

¹MP \'em-'pē\ *n* **1** : a member of the military police **2** : an elected member of a parliament

²MP *abbr* **1** melting point **2** metropolitan police

mpg *abbr* miles per gallon

mph *abbr* miles per hour

Mr. \'mis-tər\ *n, pl* **Messrs.** \'me-sərz\ — used as a conventional title of courtesy before a man's surname or his title of office

MRI *n* MAGNETIC RESONANCE IMAGING; *also* : the procedure in which magnetic resonance imaging is used

Mr. Right *n* : a man who would make the perfect husband

Mrs. \'mi-səz, -səs, *esp Southern* 'mi-zəz, -zəs\ *n, pl* **Mesdames** \mā-'däm, -'dam\ — used as a conventional title of courtesy before a married woman's surname

Ms. \'miz\ *n, pl* **Mss.** *or* **Mses.** \'mi-zez\ — used instead of *Miss* or *Mrs.*

MS *abbr* **1** manuscript **2** master of science **3** military science **4** Mississippi **5** motor ship **6** multiple sclerosis

msec *abbr* millisecond

msg *abbr* message

MSG *abbr* **1** master sergeant **2** monosodium glutamate

msgr *abbr* **1** monseigneur **2** monsignor

MSgt *abbr* master sergeant

MSS *abbr* manuscripts

MST *abbr* mountain standard time

mt *abbr* mount; mountain

¹Mt *abbr* Matthew

²Mt *symbol* meitnerium

MT *abbr* **1** metric ton **2** Montana **3** mountain time

mtg *abbr* **1** meeting **2** mortgage

mtge *abbr* mortgage

mu \'myü, 'mü\ *n* : the 12th letter of the Greek alphabet — M or μ

¹much \'məch\ *adj* **more** \'mòr\; **most** \'mōst\ : great in quantity, amount, extent, or degree ⟨~ money⟩

²much *adv* **more; most 1** : to a great degree or extent ⟨~ happier⟩ **2** : ALMOST, NEARLY ⟨looks ~ as he did before⟩

³much *n* **1** : a great quantity, amount, extent, or degree **2** : something considerable or impressive

mu·ci·lage \'myü-sə-lij\ *n* : a watery sticky solution (as of a gum) used esp. as an adhesive — **mu·ci·lag·i·nous** \ˌmyü-sə-'la-jə-nəs\ *adj*

muck \'mək\ *n* **1** : soft moist barnyard manure **2** : FILTH, DIRT **3** : a dark richly organic soil; *also* : MUD, MIRE — **mucky** *adj*

muck·rake \-ˌrāk\ *vb* : to expose publicly real or apparent misconduct of a prominent individual or business — **muck·rak·er** *n*

mu·cus \'myü-kəs\ *n* : a slimy slippery protective secretion of membranes (**mucous membranes**) lining some body cavities — **mu·cous** \-kəs\ *adj*

mud \'məd\ *n* : soft wet earth : MIRE

mud·dle \'mə-dᵊl\ *vb* **mud·dled; mud·dling 1** : to make muddy **2** : to confuse esp. with liquor **3** : to mix up or make a mess of **4** : to think or act in a confused way

mud·dle·head·ed \ˌmə-dᵊl-'he-dəd\ *adj* **1** : mentally confused **2** : INEPT

¹mud·dy \'mə-dē\ *adj* **mud·di·er; -est 1** : full of or covered with mud **2** : suggestive of mud **3** : CLOUDY, OBSCURE — **mud·di·ness** *n*

²muddy *vb* **mud·died; mud·dy·ing 1** : to soil or stain with or as if with mud **2** : to make cloudy or obscure **3** : CONFUSE

mud·flat \'məd-ˌflat\ *n* : a level tract alternately covered and left bare by the tide

mud·guard \'məd-ˌgärd\ *n* : a guard over or a flap behind a wheel of a vehicle to catch or deflect mud

mud·room \-ˌrüm, -ˌrûm\ *n* : a room in a house for removing dirty or wet footwear and clothing

mud·sling·er \-ˌsliŋ-ər\ *n* : one who uses invective esp. against a political opponent — **mud·sling·ing** \-ˌsliŋ-iŋ\ *n*

Muen·ster \'mən-stər, 'mün-, 'mùn-\ *n* : a semisoft bland cheese

mu·ez·zin \mü-'e-zᵊn, myü-\ *n* : a Muslim crier who calls the hour of daily prayer

¹muff \'məf\ *n* : a warm tubular covering for the hands

²muff *n* : a bungling performance; *esp* : a failure to hold a ball in attempting a catch — **muff** *vb*

muf·fin \'mə-fən\ *n* : a small soft cake baked in a cup-shaped container

muf·fle \'mə-fəl\ *vb* **muf·fled; muf·fling 1** : to wrap up so as to conceal or protect **2** : to wrap or pad with something to dull the sound of **3** : to keep down : SUPPRESS

muf·fler \'mə-flər\ *n* **1** : a scarf worn around the neck **2** : a device (as on a car's exhaust) to deaden noise

muf·ti \'məf-tē\ *n* : civilian clothes

¹mug \'məg\ *n* : a usu. metal or earthenware cylindrical drinking cup

²mug *vb* **mugged; mug·ging 1** : to pose or make faces esp. to attract attention or for a camera **2** : PHOTOGRAPH

³mug *vb* **mugged; mug·ging** : to assault usu. with intent to rob — **mug·ger** *n*

mug·gy \'mə-gē\ *adj* **mug·gi·er; -est** : being warm and humid — **mug·gi·ness** \-gē-nəs\ *n*

mug·wump \'məg-ˌwəmp\ *n* [obs. slang *mugwump* kingpin, fr. Massachusett (Algonquian language of New England) *mugquomp* war leader] : an independent in politics

Muhammadan, Muhammadanism *var of* MOHAMMEDAN, MOHAMMEDANISM

mu·ja·hid·een *or* **mu·ja·hed·in** \mü-ˌjä-hi-ˈdēn, -ˌjä-\ *n pl* [Ar *mujāhidīn*, pl. of *mujāhid*, lit., person who wages jihad] : Islamic guerrilla fighters esp. in the Middle East

muk·luk \'mək-ˌlək\ *n* **1** : an Eskimo boot of sealskin or reindeer skin **2** : a boot with a soft leather sole worn over several pairs of socks

mu·lat·to \mü-ˈla-tō, myü-, -ˈlä-\ *n, pl* **-toes** *or* **-tos** [Sp *mulato*, fr. *mulo* mule, fr. L *mulus*] : a first-generation offspring of a black person and a white person; *also* : a person of mixed white and black ancestry

mul·ber·ry \'məl-ˌber-ē\ *n* : any of a genus of trees with edible berrylike fruit and leaves used as food for silkworms; *also* : the fruit

mulch \'məlch\ *n* : a protective covering (as of straw or leaves) spread on the ground esp. to reduce evaporation or control weeds — **mulch** *vb*

¹mulct \'məlkt\ *n* : FINE, PENALTY

²mulct *vb* **1** : FINE **2** : CHEAT, DEFRAUD

¹mule \'myül\ *n* **1** : a hybrid offspring of a male donkey and a female horse **2** : a very stubborn person — **mul·ish** \'myü-lish\ *adj* — **mul·ish·ly** *adv* — **mu·lish·ness** *n*

²mule *n* : a slipper whose upper does not extend around the heel of the foot

mule deer *n* : a long-eared deer of western No. America

mu·le·teer \ˌmyü-lə-ˈtir\ *n* : one who drives mules

¹mull \'məl\ *vb* : PONDER, MEDITATE

²mull *vb* : to heat, sweeten, and flavor (as wine) with spices

mul·lein \'mə-lən\ *n* : a tall herb related to the snapdragons that has coarse woolly leaves and flowers in spikes

mul·let \'mə-lət\ *n, pl* **mullet** *or* **mullets** : any of a family of largely gray chiefly marine bony fishes including valuable food fishes

mul·li·gan stew \'mə-li-gən-\ *n* : a stew made from whatever ingredients are available

mul·li·ga·taw·ny \ˌmə-li-gə-ˈtȯ-nē\ *n* : a soup usu. of chicken stock seasoned with curry

mul·lion \'məl-yən\ *n* : a vertical strip separating windowpanes

multi- *comb form* **1** : many : multiple ⟨*multi*unit⟩ **2** : many times over ⟨*multi*millionaire⟩

mul·ti·col·ored \ˌməl-ti-ˈkə-lərd\ *adj* : having many colors

mul·ti·cul·tur·al \ˌməl-tē-ˈkəl-chə-rəl, -ˌtī-\ *adj* : of, relating to, reflecting, or adapted to diverse cultures ⟨a ∼ society⟩ — **mul·ti·cul·tur·al·ism** \-rə-ˌli-zəm\ *n* — **mul·ti·cul·tur·al·ist** \-rə-list\ *n or adj*

mul·ti·di·men·sion·al \-ti-də-ˈmen-chə-nəl, -ˌtī-, -dī-\ *adj* : of, relating to, or having many facets or dimensions ⟨a ∼ problem⟩ ⟨∼ space⟩

mul·ti·eth·nic \-ˈeth-nik\ *adj* : including, involving, or made up of people of various ethnic groups

mul·ti·fac·et·ed \-ˈfa-sə-təd\ *adj* : having many facets or aspects

mul·ti·fam·i·ly \-ˈfam-lē, -ˈfa-mə-\ *adj* : designed for use by several families

mul·ti·far·i·ous \ˌməl-tə-ˈfer-ē-əs\ *adj* : having great variety : DIVERSE — **mul·ti·far·i·ous·ness** *n*

mul·ti·form \'məl-ti-ˌfȯrm\ *adj* : having many forms or appearances — **mul·ti·for·mi·ty** \ˌməl-ti-ˈfȯr-mə-tē\ *n*

mul·ti·lat·er·al \ˌməl-ti-ˈla-tə-rəl, -ˌtī-, -ˈla-trəl\ *adj* : having many sides or participants ⟨∼ treaty⟩ — **mul·ti·lat·er·al·ism** \-ˈla-tə-rə-ˌli-zəm\ *n* — **mul·ti·lat·er·al·ly** *adv*

multilayered \-ˈlā-ərd, -ˈlerd\ *or* **multilayer** \-ˈlā-ər, ˈler\ *adj* : having or involving several distinct layers or levels

mul·ti·lev·el \-ˈle-vəl\ *adj* : having several levels

mul·ti·lin·gual \-ˈliŋ-gwəl\ *adj* : knowing or using several languages — **mul·ti·lin·gual·ism** \-gwə-ˌli-zəm\ *n*

¹mul·ti·me·dia \-ˈmē-dē-ə\ *adj* : using, involving, or encompassing several media ⟨a ∼ advertising campaign⟩

²multimedia *n sing or pl* **1** : the technique of using several media (as in art); *also* : something (as software) that uses or facilitates it

mul·ti·mil·lion·aire \ˌməl-ti-ˌmil-yə-ˈnar, -ˌtī-, -ˈmil-yə-ˌnar\ *n* : a person worth several million dollars

mul·ti·na·tion·al \-ˈna-shə-nəl\ *adj* **1** : of or relating to several nationalities **2** : relating to or involving several nations **3** : having divisions in several countries ⟨a ∼ corporation⟩ — **multinational** *n*

mul·ti·pack \'məl-tē-ˌpak\ *n* : a package of several individually packed items sold as a unit

¹mul·ti·ple \'məl-tə-pəl\ *adj* **1** : more than one; *also* : MANY ⟨∼ achievements⟩ **2** : VARIOUS

²multiple *n* : the product of a quantity by an integer ⟨35 is a ∼ of 7⟩

multiple–choice *adj* : having several answers given from which the correct one is to be chosen ⟨a ∼ question⟩

multiple personality disorder *n* : a neurosis in which the personality becomes separated into two or more parts each of which controls behavior part of the time

multiple sclerosis *n* : a disease marked by patches of hardened tissue in the brain or spinal cord and associated esp. with partial or complete paralysis and muscular tremor

mul·ti·plex \'məl-tə-ˌpleks\ *n* : CINEPLEX

mul·ti·pli·cand \ˌməl-tə-pli-ˈkand\ *n* : the number that is to be multiplied by another

mul·ti·pli·ca·tion \ˌməl-tə-plə-ˈkā-shən\ *n* **1** : INCREASE **2** : a short method of finding the result of adding a figure the number of times indicated by another figure

multiplication sign *n* **1** : TIMES SIGN **2** : a centered dot indicating multiplication

mul·ti·plic·i·ty \ˌməl-tə-ˈpli-sə-tē\ *n, pl* **-ties** : a great number or variety

mul·ti·pli·er \'məl-tə-ˌplī(-ə)r\ *n* : one that multiplies; *esp* : a number by which another number is multiplied

mul·ti·ply \'məl-tə-ˌplī\ *vb* **-plied; -ply·ing 1** : to increase in number (as by breeding) **2** : to find the product of by multiplication; *also* : to perform multiplication

mul·ti·pur·pose \ˌməl-ti-ˈpər-pəs, -ˌtī-\ *adj* : having or serving several purposes

mul·ti·ra·cial \-ˈrā-shəl\ *adj* : composed of, involving, or representing various races

mul·ti·sense \-ˌsens\ *adj* : having several meanings ⟨∼ words⟩

mul·ti·sto·ry \-ˌstȯr-ē\ *adj* : having several stories ⟨∼ buildings⟩

mul·ti·task·ing \'məl-tē-ˌtas-kiŋ, -ˌtī-\ *n* **1** : the concurrent performance of several jobs by a computer **2** : the performance of multiple tasks at one time — **mul·ti·task** \-ˌtask\ *vb* — **mul·ti·task·er** \-ˌtaskər\ *n*

mul·ti·tude \'məl-tə-ˌtüd, -ˌtyüd\ *n* : a great number — **mul·ti·tu·di·nous** \ˌməl-tə-ˈtü-dᵊn-əs, -ˈtyüd-\ *adj*

mul·ti·unit \ˌməl-ti-ˈyü-nət, -ˌtī-\ *adj* : having several units

mul·ti·vi·ta·min \-ˈvī-tə-mən\ *adj* : containing several vitamins and esp. all known to be essential to health — **multivitamin** *n*

¹mum \'məm\ *adj* : SILENT

²mum *chiefly Brit var of* MOM

³mum *n* : CHRYSANTHEMUM

mum·ble \'məm-bəl\ *vb* **mum·bled; mum·bling** : to speak in a low indistinct manner — **mumble** *n* — **mum·bler** *n* — **mum·bly** *adj*

mum·ble·ty–peg \'məm-bəl-tē-ˌpeg\ *also* **mumble–the–peg** \'məm-bəl-thə-\ *n* : a game in which the players try to flip a knife from various positions so that the blade will stick into the ground

mum·bo jum·bo \ˌməm-bō-ˈjəm-bō\ *n* **1** : a complicated ritual with elaborate trappings **2** : GIBBERISH, NONSENSE

mum·mer \'mə-mər\ *n* **1** : an actor esp. in a pantomime **2** : a person who goes merrymaking in disguise during festivals — **mum·mery** *n*

mum·my \'mə-mē\ *n, pl* **mummies** [ME *mummie* powdered parts of a mummified body used as a drug, fr. AF *mumie*, fr. ML *mumia*, fr. Ar *mūmiya* bitumen, mummy, fr. Per *mūm* wax] : a body embalmed for burial in the manner of the ancient Egyptians — **mum·mi·fi·ca·tion** \ˌmə-mi-fə-ˈkā-shən\ *n* — **mum·mi·fy** \ˈmə-mi-ˌfī\ *vb*

mumps \ˈməmps\ *n sing or pl* [fr. pl. of obs. *mump* grimace] : a virus disease marked by fever and swelling esp. of the salivary glands

mun *or* **munic** *abbr* municipal

munch \ˈmənch\ *vb* : to eat with a chewing action; *also* : to snack on

munch·ies \ˈmən-chēz\ *n pl* **1** : hunger pangs **2** : light snack foods

mun·dane \ˌmən-ˈdān, ˈmən-ˌdān\ *adj* **1** : of or relating to the world **2** : concerned with the practical details of everyday life — **mun·dane·ly** *adv*

mung bean \ˈmən-\ *n* : an erect bushy bean widely grown in warm regions for its edible seeds and as the chief source of bean sprouts; *also* : its seed

mu·nic·i·pal \myu̇-ˈni-sə-pəl\ *adj* **1** : of, relating to, or characteristic of a municipality **2** : restricted to one locality — **mu·nic·i·pal·ly** *adv*

mu·nic·i·pal·i·ty \myu̇-ˌni-sə-ˈpa-lə-tē\ *n, pl* **-ties** : an urban political unit with corporate status and usu. powers of self-government

mu·nif·i·cent \myu̇-ˈni-fə-sənt\ *adj* : liberal in giving : GENEROUS — **mu·nif·i·cence** \-səns\ *n*

mu·ni·tion \myu̇-ˈni-shən\ *n* : ARMAMENT, AMMUNITION

¹mu·ral \ˈmyu̇r-əl\ *adj* **1** : of or relating to a wall **2** : applied to and made part of a wall or ceiling surface

²mural *n* : a mural painting — **mu·ral·ist** *n*

¹mur·der \ˈmər-dər\ *n* **1** : the crime of unlawfully killing a person esp. with malice aforethought **2** : something unusually difficult or dangerous

²murder *vb* **1** : to commit a murder; *also* : to kill brutally **2** : to put an end to **3** : to spoil by performing poorly ⟨∼ a song⟩ — **mur·der·er** *n*

mur·der·ess \ˈmər-də-rəs\ *n* : a woman who murders

mur·der·ous \ˈmər-də-rəs\ *adj* **1** : having or appearing to have the purpose of murder **2** : marked by or causing murder or bloodshed ⟨∼ gunfire⟩ — **mur·der·ous·ly** *adv*

murk \ˈmərk\ *n* : DARKNESS, GLOOM — **murk·i·ly** \ˈmər-kə-lē\ *adv* — **murk·i·ness** \-kē-nəs\ *n* — **murky** *adj*

mur·mur \ˈmər-mər\ *n* **1** : a muttered complaint **2** : a low indistinct often continuous sound — **murmur** *vb* — **mur·mur·er** *n* — **mur·mur·ous** *adj*

mus *abbr* **1** museum **2** music; musical; musician

mus·ca·tel \ˌməs-kə-ˈtel\ *n* : a sweet fortified wine

¹mus·cle \ˈmə-səl\ *n* [ME, fr. L *musculus*, fr. dim. of *mus* mouse] **1** : a body tissue consisting of long cells that contract when stimulated and produce motion; *also* : an organ consisting of this tissue and functioning in moving a body part **2** : STRENGTH, BRAWN — **mus·cled** \ˈmə-səld\ *adj* — **mus·cu·lar** \ˈməs-kyə-lər\ *adj* — **mus·cu·lar·i·ty** \ˌməs-kyə-ˈlar-ə-tē\ *n*

²muscle *vb* **mus·cled; mus·cling** : to force one's way

mus·cle–bound \ˈmə-səl-ˌbau̇nd\ *adj* : having some of the muscles abnormally enlarged and lacking in elasticity (as from excessive exercise)

mus·cle·man \-ˌman\ *n* : a man with a muscular physique

muscular dystrophy *n* : any of a group of diseases characterized by progressive wasting of muscles

mus·cu·la·ture \ˈməs-kyə-lə-ˌchu̇r\ *n* : the muscles of the body or its parts

muscu·lo·skel·e·tal \ˌməs-kyə-lō-ˈske-lə-t³l\ *adj* : of, relating to, or involving both musculature and skeleton

¹muse \ˈmyu̇z\ *vb* **mused; mus·ing** [ME, fr. AF *muser* to gape, idle, muse, fr. OF *mus mouth of an animal, fr. ML *musus*] : to become absorbed in thought — **mus·ing·ly** *adv*

²muse *n* [fr. *Muse* any of the nine sister goddesses of learning and the arts in Greek myth, fr. ME, fr. MF, fr. L *Musa*, fr. Gk *Mousa*] : a source of inspiration

mu·se·um \myu̇-ˈzē-əm\ *n* : an institution devoted to the procurement, care, and display of objects of lasting interest or value

¹mush \ˈməsh\ *n* **1** : cornmeal boiled in water **2** : sentimental drivel

²mush *vb* : to travel esp. over snow with a sled drawn by dogs

¹mush·room \ˈməsh-ˌrüm, -ˌru̇m\ *n* : the fleshy usu.caplike spore-bearing organ of various fungi esp.when edible; *also* : such a fungus

²mushroom *vb* **1** : to spread out : EXPAND **2** : to collect wild mushrooms **3** : to grow rapidly

mushy \ˈmə-shē\ *adj* **mush·i·er; -est** **1** : soft like mush **2** : excessively sentimental

mu·sic \ˈmyü-zik\ *n* **1** : the science or art of combining tones into a composition having structure and continuity; *also* : vocal or instrumental sounds having rhythm, melody, or harmony **2** : an agreeable sound

¹mu·si·cal \ˈmyü-zi-kəl\ *adj* **1** : of or relating to music or musicians **2** : having the pleasing tonal qualities of music **3** : fond of or gifted in music — **mu·si·cal·ly** \-k(ə-)lē\ *adv*

²musical *n* : a film or theatrical production consisting of musical numbers and dialogue based on a unifying plot

mu·si·cale \ˌmyü-zi-ˈkal\ *n* : a usu. private social gathering featuring music

mu·si·cian \myü-ˈzi-shən\ *n* : a composer, conductor, or performer of music — **mu·si·cian·ly** *adj* — **mu·si·cian·ship** *n*

mu·si·col·o·gy \ˌmyü-zi-ˈkä-lə-jē\ *n* : the study of music as a field of knowledge or research — **mu·si·co·log·i·cal** \-kə-ˈlä-ji-kəl\ *adj* — **mu·si·col·o·gist** \-ˈkä-lə-jist\ *n*

musk \ˈməsk\ *n* : a substance obtained esp. from a small Asian deer (**musk deer**) and used as a perfume fixative — **musk·i·ness** \ˈməs-kē-nəs\ *n* — **musky** *adj*

mus·keg \ˈməs-ˌkeg\ *n* : BOG; *esp* : a mossy bog in northern No. America

mus·kel·lunge \ˈməs-kə-ˌlənj\ *n, pl* **muskellunge** : a large No. American pike that is a valuable sport fish

mus·ket \ˈməs-kət\ *n* [MF *mousquet*, fr. It *moschetto* small artillery piece, kind of small hawk, fr. dim. of *mosca* fly, fr. L *musca*] : a heavy large-caliber muzzle-loading shoulder firearm — **mus·ke·teer** \ˌməs-kə-ˈtir\ *n*

mus·ket·ry \ˈməs-kə-trē\ *n* **1** : MUSKETS **2** : MUSKETEERS **3** : musket fire

musk·mel·on \ˈməsk-ˌme-lən\ *n* : a small round to oval melon that has usu. a sweet edible green or orange flesh and a musky odor

musk ox *n* : a heavyset shaggy-coated wild ox of Greenland and the arctic tundra of northern No. America

musk·rat \ˈməs-ˌkrat\ *n, pl* **muskrat** *or* **muskrats** : a large No. American aquatic rodent with webbed feet and dark brown fur; *also* : its fur

Mus·lim \ˈməz-ləm\ *n* : an adherent of Islam — **Muslim** *adj*

mus·lin \ˈməz-lən\ *n* : a plain-woven sheer to coarse cotton fabric

¹muss \ˈməs\ *n* : a state of disorder — **muss·i·ly** \ˈmə-sə-lē\ *adv* — **muss·i·ness** \-sē-nəs\ *n* — **mussy** *adj*

²muss *vb* : to make untidy : DISARRANGE

mus·sel \ˈmə-səl\ *n* **1** : a dark edible saltwater bivalve mollusk **2** : any of various freshwater bivalve mollusks of the central U.S. having shells with a pearly lining

¹must \ˈməst\ *vb* — used as an auxiliary esp. to express a command, requirement, obligation, or necessity

²must *n* **1** : an imperative duty **2** : an indispensable item

mus·tache *also* **mous·tache** \ˈməs-ˌtash, (ˌ)məs-ˈtash\ *n* : the hair growing on the human upper lip — **mus·tached** *also* **mous·tached** \-ˌtasht, -ˈtasht\ *adj*

mus·tang \ˈməs-ˌtaŋ\ *n* [MexSp *mestengo*, fr. Sp, stray, fr. *mesteño* strayed, fr. *mesta* annual roundup of cattle that disposed of its strays, fr. ML *(animalia) mixta* mixed animals] : a small hardy naturalized horse of the western plains of America; *also* : BRONC

mus·tard \ˈməs-tərd\ *n* **1** : a pungent yellow powder of the seeds of an herb related to the cabbage and used as a condiment or in medicine **2** : a plant that yields mustard; *also* : a closely related plant — **mustardy** *adj*

mustard gas *n* : a poison gas used in warfare that has violent irritating and blistering effects

¹mus·ter \ˈməs-tər\ *n* **1** : an act of assembling (as for military inspection); *also* : critical examination **2** : an assembled group

²muster *vb* [ME *mustren* to show, muster, fr. AF *mustrer, monstrer*, fr. L *monstrare* to show, fr. *monstrum* evil omen, monster] **1** : CONVENE, ASSEMBLE; *also* : to call the roll of **2** : ACCUMULATE **3** : to call forth : ROUSE **4** : to amount to : COMPRISE

muster out *vb* : to discharge from military service

musty \ˈməs-tē\ *adj* **mus·ti·er; -est** : MOLDY, STALE; *also* : tasting or smelling of damp or decay — **must·i·ly** \-tə-lē\ *adv* — **must·i·ness** \-tē-nəs\ *n*

mu·ta·ble \'myü-tə-bəl\ *adj* **1** : prone to change : FICKLE **2** : capable of or liable to mutation : VARIABLE — **mu·ta·bil·i·ty** \ˌmyü-tə-'bi-lə-tē\ *n*

mu·tant \'myü-t³nt\ *adj* : of, relating to, or produced by mutation — **mu·tant** *n*

mu·tate \'myü-ˌtāt\ *vb* **mu·tat·ed; mu·tat·ing** : to undergo or cause to undergo mutation — **mu·ta·tive** \'myü-ˌtā-tiv, -tə-tiv\ *adj*

mu·ta·tion \myü-'tā-shən\ *n* **1** : CHANGE **2** : an inherited physical or biochemical change in genetic material; *also* : the process of producing a mutation **3** : an individual, strain, or trait resulting from mutation — **mu·ta·tion·al** *adj*

¹mute \'myüt\ *adj* **mut·er; mut·est** **1** : unable to speak **2** : SILENT — **mute·ly** *adv* — **mute·ness** *n*

²mute *n* **1** : a person who cannot or does not speak **2** : a device on a musical instrument that reduces, softens, or muffles the tone

³mute *vb* **mut·ed; mut·ing** : to muffle, reduce, or eliminate the sound of

mu·ti·late \'myü-tə-ˌlāt\ *vb* **-lat·ed; -lat·ing** **1** : to cut up or alter radically so as to make imperfect **2** : MAIM, CRIPPLE — **mu·ti·la·tion** \ˌmyü-tə-'lā-shən\ *n* — **mu·ti·la·tor** \'myü-tə-ˌlā-tər\ *n*

mu·ti·ny \'myü-tə-nē\ *n, pl* **-nies** : willful refusal to obey constituted authority; *esp* : revolt against a superior officer — **mu·ti·neer** \ˌmyü-tə-'nir\ *n* — **mu·ti·nous** \'myü-tə-nəs\ *adj* — **mu·ti·nous·ly** *adv* — **mutiny** *vb*

mutt \'mət\ *n* : MONGREL, CUR

mut·ter \'mə-tər\ *vb* **1** : to speak indistinctly or with a low voice and lips partly closed **2** : GRUMBLE — **mutter** *n*

mut·ton \'mə-t³n\ *n* [ME *motoun* mutton, sheep, fr. AF *mutun* ram, sheep, mutton] : the flesh of a mature sheep used for food — **mut·tony** *adj*

mut·ton-chops \'mə-t³n-ˌchäps\ *n pl* : whiskers on the side of the face that are narrow at the temple and broad and round by the lower jaws

mu·tu·al \'myü-chə-wəl\ *adj* **1** : given and received in equal amount 〈~ trust〉 **2** : having the same feelings one for the other 〈~ enemies〉 **3** : COMMON, JOINT 〈a ~ friend〉 — **mu·tu·al·ly** *adv*

mutual fund *n* : an investment company that invests money of its shareholders in a usu. diversified group of securities of other corporations

muu·muu \'mü-ˌmü\ *n* : a loose dress of Hawaiian origin

¹muz·zle \'mə-zəl\ *n* **1** : the nose and jaws of an animal; *also* : a covering for the muzzle to prevent biting or eating **2** : the mouth of a gun

²muzzle *vb* **muz·zled; muz·zling** **1** : to put a muzzle on **2** : to restrain from expression : GAG

mV *abbr* millivolt

MV *abbr* motor vessel

MVP *abbr* most valuable player

MW *abbr* megawatt

my \'mī\ *adj* **1** : of or relating to me or myself **2** — used interjectionally esp. to express surprise

my·col·o·gy \mī-'kä-lə-jē\ *n* : a branch of biology dealing with fungi — **my·co·log·i·cal** \ˌmī-kə-'lä-ji-kəl\ *adj* — **my·col·o·gist** \mī-'kä-lə-jist\ *n*

my·elo·ma \ˌmī-ə-'lō-mə\ *n, pl* **-mas** *or* **-ma·ta** \-mə-tə\ : a primary tumor of the bone marrow

my·nah *or* **my·na** \'mī-nə\ *n* : any of several Asian starlings; *esp* : a dark brown slightly crested bird sometimes taught to mimic speech

my·o·pia \mī-'ō-pē-ə\ *n* : a condition in which visual images come to a focus in front of the retina resulting esp. in defective vision of distant objects — **my·o·pic** \-'ō-pik, -'ä-\ *adj* — **my·o·pi·cal·ly** \-pi-k(ə-)lē\ *adv*

¹myr·i·ad \'mir-ē-əd\ *n* [Gk *myriad-, myrias,* fr. *myrioi* countless, ten thousand] : an indefinitely large number

²myriad *adj* : consisting of a very great but indefinite number

myr·mi·don \'mər-mə-ˌdän\ *n* : a loyal follower; *esp* : one who executes orders without protest or pity

myrrh \'mər\ *n* : a fragrant aromatic plant gum used in perfumes and formerly for incense

myr·tle \'mər-t³l\ *n* : an evergreen shrub of southern Europe with shiny leaves, fragrant flowers, and black berries; *also* : PERIWINKLE

my·self \mī-'self, mə-\ *pron* : I, ME — used reflexively, for emphasis, or in absolute constructions 〈I hurt ~〉 〈I ~ did it〉 〈~ busy, I sent him instead〉

mys·tery \'mis-tə-rē\ *n, pl* **-ter·ies** **1** : a religious truth known by revelation alone **2** : something not understood or beyond understanding **3** : enigmatic quality or character **4** : a work of fiction dealing with the solution of a mysterious crime — **mys·te·ri·ous** \mis-'tir-ē-əs\ *adj* — **mys·te·ri·ous·ly** *adv* — **mys·te·ri·ous·ness** *n*

¹mys·tic \'mis-tik\ *adj* **1** : of or relating to mystics or mysticism **2** : MYSTERIOUS; *also* : MYSTIFYING

²mystic *n* : a person who follows, advocates, or experiences mysticism

mys·ti·cal \'mis-ti-kəl\ *adj* **1** : SPIRITUAL, SYMBOLIC **2** : of or relating to an intimate knowledge of or direct communion with God (as through contemplation or visions)

mys·ti·cism \'mis-tə-ˌsi-zəm\ *n* : the belief that direct knowledge of God or ultimate reality is attainable through immediate intuition or insight

mys·ti·fy \'mis-tə-ˌfī\ *vb* **-fied; -fy·ing** **1** : to perplex the mind of **2** : to make mysterious — **mys·ti·fi·ca·tion** \ˌmis-tə-fə-'kā-shən\ *n*

mys·tique \mi-'stēk\ *n* [F] **1** : an air or attitude of mystery and reverence developing around something or someone **2** : the special esoteric skill essential in a calling or activity

myth \'mith\ *n* **1** : a usu. legendary narrative that presents part of the beliefs of a people or explains a practice or natural phenomenon **2** : an imaginary or unverifiable person or thing — **myth·i·cal** \'mi-thi-kəl\ *or* **myth·ic** \-thik\ *adj*

my·thol·o·gy \mi-'thä-lə-jē\ *n, pl* **-gies** : a body of myths and esp. of those dealing with the gods and heroes of a people — **myth·o·log·i·cal** \ˌmi-thə-'lä-ji-kəl\ *adj* — **my·thol·o·gist** \mi-'thä-lə-jist\ *n* — **my·thol·o·gize** \-ˌjīz\ *vb*

¹n \'en\ *n, pl* **n's** *or* **ns** \'enz\ *often cap* **1** : the 14th letter of the English alphabet **2** : an unspecified quantity

²n *abbr, often cap* **1** net **2** neuter **3** noon **4** normal **5** north; northern **6** note **7** noun **8** number

N *symbol* nitrogen

-n — see -EN

Na *symbol* [NL *natrium*] sodium

NA *abbr* **1** no account **2** North America **3** not applicable **4** not available

NAACP \ˌen-ˌdə-bəl-ˌā-ˌsē-'pē, ˌen-ˌā-ˌā-ˌsē-\ *abbr* National Association for the Advancement of Colored People

nab \'nab\ *vb* **nabbed; nab·bing** : SEIZE; *esp* : ARREST

NAB *abbr* New American Bible

na·bob \'nā-ˌbäb\ *n* [Hindi *navāb* & Urdu *nawāb*, provincial governor (in the Mogul empire), fr. Ar *nuwwāb*, pl. of *nā'ib* governor] : a person of great wealth or prominence

na·celle \nə-'sel\ *n* : an enclosure (as for an engine) on an aircraft

na·cho \'nä-chō\ *n, pl* **nachos** [AmerSp] : a tortilla chip topped with melted cheese and often additional savory toppings

na·cre \'nä-kər\ *n* : MOTHER-OF-PEARL — **na·cre·ous** \'nä-krē-əs\ *adj*

na·dir \\'nā-ˌdir, -dər\ *n* [ME, fr. MF, fr. Ar *naḍhīr* opposite] **1** : the point of the celestial sphere that is directly opposite the zenith and directly beneath the observer **2** : the lowest point

¹nag \\'nag\ *n* : HORSE; *esp* : an old or decrepit horse

²nag *vb* **nagged; nag·ging 1** : to find fault incessantly : COMPLAIN **2** : to irritate by constant scolding or urging **3** : to be a continuing source of annoyance ⟨a *nagging* backache⟩

³nag *n* : one who nags habitually

Nah *abbr* Nahum

Na·huatl \\'nä-ˌwä-t°l\ *n* : a group of American Indian languages of central and southern Mexico

Na·hum \\'nä-həm, -əm\ *n* — see BIBLE table

NAIA *abbr* National Association of Intercollegiate Athletes

na·iad \\'nā-əd, 'nī-, -ˌad\ *n, pl* **naiads** *or* **na·ia·des** \-ə-ˌdēz\ **1** : one of the nymphs in ancient mythology living in lakes, rivers, springs, and fountains **2** : an aquatic young of some insects (as a dragonfly)

¹na·if *or* **na·ïf** \nä-'ēf\ *adj* : NAIVE

²naïf *or* **naif** *n* : a naive person

¹nail \\'nāl\ *n* **1** : a horny sheath protecting the end of each finger and toe in humans and related primates **2** : a slender pointed fastener with a head designed to be pounded in

²nail *vb* : to fasten with or as if with a nail — **nail·er** *n*

nail down *vb* : to settle or establish clearly and unmistakably

nain·sook \\'nān-ˌsu̇k\ *n* : a soft lightweight muslin

nai·ra \\'nī-rə\ *n* — see MONEY table

na·ive *or* **na·ïve** \nä-'ēv\ *adj* **na·iv·er; -est** [F *naïve*, fem. of *naïf*, fr. OF, inborn, natural, fr. L *nativus* native] **1** : marked by unaffected simplicity : ARTLESS, INGENUOUS **2** : CREDULOUS ♦ *Synonyms* NATURAL, INNOCENT, SIMPLE, UNAFFECTED, UNSOPHISTICATED, UNSTUDIED — **na·ive·ly** *adv* — **na·ive·ness** *n*

na·ive·té *also* **na·ïve·te** *or* **na·ive·té** \ˌnä-ˌē-və-'tā, nä-'ē-və-ˌtā\ *n* **1** : a naive remark or action **2** : the quality or state of being naive

na·ked \\'nā-kəd\ *adj* **1** : having no clothes on : NUDE **2** : UNSHEATHED ⟨a ~ sword⟩ **3** : lacking a usual or natural covering (as of foliage or feathers) **4** : PLAIN, UNADORNED ⟨the ~ truth⟩ **5** : not aided by artificial means ⟨seen by the ~ eye⟩ — **na·ked·ly** *adv* — **na·ked·ness** *n*

nak·fa \\'näk-ˌfä\ *n, pl* **nakfa** — see MONEY table

nam·by–pam·by \ˌnam-bē-'pam-bē\ *adj* **1** : INSIPID **2** : WEAK, INDECISIVE ♦ *Synonyms* BLAND, FLAT, INANE, JEJUNE, VAPID, WISHY-WASHY

¹name \\'nām\ *n* **1** : a word or words by which a person or thing is known **2** : a disparaging epithet ⟨call him ~s⟩ **3** : REPUTATION; *esp* : distinguished reputation ⟨made a ~ for herself⟩ **4** : FAMILY, CLAN ⟨was a disgrace to their ~⟩ **5** : appearance as opposed to reality ⟨a friend in ~ only⟩

²name *vb* **named; nam·ing 1** : to give a name to : CALL **2** : to mention or identify by name **3** : NOMINATE, APPOINT **4** : to decide on : CHOOSE **5** : to mention explicitly : SPECIFY ⟨~ a price⟩ — **name·able** *adj*

³name *adj* **1** : of, relating to, or bearing a name ⟨~ tag⟩ **2** : having an established reputation ⟨~ brands⟩

name day *n* : the church feast day of the saint after whom one is named

name·less \\'nām-ləs\ *adj* **1** : having no name **2** : not marked with a name ⟨a ~ grave⟩ **3** : not known by name ⟨a ~ hero⟩ **4** : too distressing to be described ⟨~ fears⟩ — **name·less·ly** *adv*

name·ly \-lē\ *adv* : that is to say : AS ⟨the cat family, ~, lions, tigers, and similar animals⟩

name·plate \-ˌplāt\ *n* : a plate or plaque bearing a name (as of a resident)

name·sake \-ˌsāk\ *n* : one that has the same name as another; *esp* : one named after another

nan·keen \nan-'kēn\ *n* : a durable brownish yellow cotton fabric orig. woven by hand in China

nan·ny goat \\'na-nē-\ *n* : a female domestic goat

nano·me·ter \\'na-nə-ˌmē-tər\ *n* : one billionth of a meter

nano·scale \-ˌskāl\ *adj* : having dimensions measured in nanometers

nano·sec·ond \-ˌse-kənd\ *n* : one billionth of a second

nano·tech·nol·o·gy \ˌna-nō-tek-'nä-lə-jē\ *n* : the manipulation of materials on an atomic or molecular scale

nano·tube \\'na-nō-ˌtüb\ *n* : a microscope tube (as of carbon) whose diameter is measured in nanometers

¹nap \\'nap\ *vb* **napped; nap·ping 1** : to sleep briefly esp. during the day : DOZE **2** : to be off guard ⟨was caught *napping*⟩

²nap *n* : a short sleep esp. during the day

³nap *n* : a soft downy fibrous surface (as on yarn and cloth) — **nap·less** *adj* — **napped** \\'napt\ *adj*

na·palm \\'nā-ˌpälm, -ˌpäm\ *n* [*naphthalene + palm*itate, salt of a fatty acid] **1** : a thickener used in jelling gasoline (as for incendiary bombs) **2** : fuel jelled with napalm

nape \\'nāp, 'nap\ *n* : the back of the neck

na·pery \\'nā-pə-rē\ *n* : household linen esp. for the table

naph·tha \\'naf-thə, 'nap-\ *n* : any of various liquid hydrocarbon mixtures used chiefly as solvents

naph·tha·lene \-ˌlēn\ *n* : a crystalline substance used esp. in organic synthesis and as a moth repellent

nap·kin \\'nap-kən\ *n* **1** : a piece of material (as cloth) used at table to wipe the lips or fingers and protect the clothes **2** : a small cloth or towel

na·po·leon \nə-'pōl-yən, -'pō-lē-ən\ *n* : an oblong pastry with a filling of cream, custard, or jelly

Na·po·le·on·ic \nə-ˌpō-lē-'ä-nik\ *adj* : of, relating to, or characteristic of Napoleon I or his family

narc *also* **nark** \\'närk\ *n, slang* : a person (as a government agent) who investigates narcotics violations

nar·cis·sism \\'när-sə-ˌsi-zəm\ *n* [G *Narzissismus*, fr. *Narziss* Narcissus, beautiful youth of Greek mythology who fell in love with his own image] **1** : undue dwelling on one's own self or attainments **2** : love of or sexual desire for one's own body — **nar·cis·sist** \-sist\ *n or adj* — **nar·cis·sis·tic** \ˌnär-sə-'sis-tik\ *adj*

nar·cis·sus \när-'si-səs\ *n, pl* **nar·cis·si** \-ˌsī, -ˌsē\ *or* **nar·cis·sus·es** *or* **narcissus** : DAFFODIL; *esp* : one with short-tubed flowers usu. borne separately

nar·co·lep·sy \\'när-kə-ˌlep-sē\ *n, pl* **-sies** : a condition characterized by brief attacks of deep sleep — **nar·co·lep·tic** \ˌnär-kə-'lep-tik\ *adj or n*

nar·co·sis \när-'kō-səs\ *n, pl* **-co·ses** \-ˌsēz\ : a state of stupor, unconsciousness, or arrested activity produced by the influence of chemicals (as narcotics)

nar·co·ter·ror·ism \\'när-kō-'ter-ər-ˌi-zəm\ *n* : terrorism financed by profits from illegal drug trafficking

nar·cot·ic \när-'kä-tik\ *n* [ME *narkotik*, fr. MF *narcotique*, fr. *narcotique*, adj., fr. ML *narcoticus*, fr. Gk *narkōtikos*, fr. *narkoun* to benumb, fr. *narkē* numbness] **1** : a drug (as opium) that dulls the senses, relieves pain, and induces sleep **2** : an illegal drug (as marijuana or LSD) — **narcotic** *adj*

nar·co·tize \\'när-kə-ˌtīz\ *vb* **-tized; -tiz·ing 1** : to treat with or subject to a narcotic; *also* : to put into a state of narcosis **2** : to soothe to unconsciousness or unawareness

nard \\'närd\ *n* : a fragrant ointment of the ancients

na·res \\'ner-(ˌ)ēz\ *n pl* [L] : the pair of openings of the nose

Nar·ra·gan·sett \ˌna-rə-'gan-sət\ *n, pl* **-sett** *or* **-setts 1** : a member of an American Indian people of Rhode Island **2** : the Algonquian language of the Narragansett people

nar·rate \\'ner-ˌāt\ *vb* **nar·rat·ed; nar·rat·ing** : to recite the details of (as a story) : RELATE, TELL — **nar·ra·tion** \na-'rā-shən\ *n* — **nar·ra·tor** \\'ner-ˌā-tər\ *n*

nar·ra·tive \\'ner-ə-tiv\ *n* **1** : something that is narrated : STORY **2** : the art or practice of narrating

¹nar·row \\'ner-ō\ *adj* **1** : of slender or less than standard width **2** : limited in size or scope : RESTRICTED **3** : not liberal in views : PREJUDICED **4** : interpreted or interpreting strictly **5** : CLOSE ⟨won by a ~ margin⟩; *also* : barely successful ⟨a ~ escape⟩ — **nar·row·ly** *adv* — **nar·row·ness** *n*

²narrow *vb* : to lessen in width or extent

³narrow *n* : a narrow passage : STRAIT — usu. used in pl.

nar·row–mind·ed \ˌner-ō-'mīn-dəd\ *adj* : not liberal or broad-minded ♦ *Synonyms* ILLIBERAL, BIGOTED, HIDEBOUND, INTOLERANT

nar·whal \\'när-ˌhwäl, 'när-wəl\ *n* : an arctic sea mammal about 20 feet (6 meters) long that is related to the dolphins and in the male has a long twisted ivory tusk

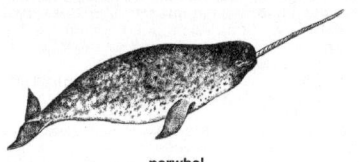

narwhal

NAS *abbr* naval air station

NASA \ˈna-sə\ *abbr* National Aeronautics and Space Administration

¹na·sal \ˈnā-zəl\ *n* 1 : a nasal part 2 : a nasal consonant or vowel

²nasal *adj* 1 : of or relating to the nose 2 : uttered through the nose — **na·sal·ly** *adv*

na·sal·ize \ˈnā-zə-ˌlīz\ *vb* **-ized; -iz·ing** : to make nasal or pronounce as a nasal sound — **na·sal·i·za·tion** \ˌnā-zə-lə-ˈzā-shən\ *n*

na·scent \ˈna-sᵊnt, ˈnā-\ *adj* : coming into existence : beginning to grow or develop — **na·scence** \-sᵊns\ *n*

nas·tur·tium \nə-ˈstər-shəm, na-\ *n* : either of two widely cultivated watery-stemmed herbs with showy spurred flowers and pungent edible seeds

nas·ty \ˈnas-tē\ *adj* **nas·ti·er; -est** 1 : FILTHY 2 : INDECENT, OBSCENE 3 : HARMFUL, DANGEROUS ⟨took a ~ fall⟩ 4 : DISAGREEABLE ⟨~ weather⟩ 5 : MEAN, ILL-NATURED ⟨a ~ temper⟩ 6 : DIFFICULT, VEXATIOUS ⟨a ~ problem⟩ 7 : UNFAIR, DIRTY ⟨a ~ trick⟩ — **nas·ti·ly** \ˈnas-tə-lē\ *adv* — **nas·ti·ness** \-tē-nəs\ *n*

nat *abbr* 1 national 2 native 3 natural

na·tal \ˈnā-tᵊl\ *adj* 1 : NATIVE 2 : of, relating to, or present at birth

na·ta·to·ri·um \ˌnā-tə-ˈtȯr-ē-əm, ˌna-\ *n* : a swimming pool esp. indoors

na·tion \ˈnā-shən\ *n* [ME *nacioun*, fr. AF *naciun* fr. L *nation-, natio* birth, race, nation, fr. *nasci* to be born] 1 : NATIONALITY 5; *also* : a politically organized nationality 2 : a community of people composed of one or more nationalities with its own territory and government 3 : the territory of a nation 4 : a federation of tribes (as of American Indians) — **na·tion·hood** *n*

¹na·tion·al \ˈna-shə-nəl\ *adj* 1 : of or relating to a nation 2 : comprising or characteristic of a nationality 3 : FEDERAL 3 — **na·tion·al·ly** *adv*

²national *n* 1 : one who owes allegiance to a nation 2 : a competition that is national in scope — usu. used in pl.

national guard *n* 1 : a military force serving as a national constabulary and defense force 2 *cap* : a militia force recruited by each state of the U.S., equipped by the federal government, and jointly maintained subject to the call of either — **national guardsman** *n, often cap*

na·tion·al·ise *chiefly Brit var of* NATIONALIZE

na·tion·al·ism \ˈna-shə-nə-ˌli-zəm\ *n* : devotion to national interests, unity, and independence

na·tion·al·ist \-list\ *n* 1 : an advocate of or believer in nationalism 2 : a member of a political party or group advocating national independence or strong national government — **nationalist** *adj* — **na·tion·al·is·tic** \ˌna-shə-nə-ˈlis-tik\ *adj*

na·tion·al·i·ty \ˌna-shə-ˈna-lə-tē\ *n, pl* **-ties** 1 : national character 2 : a legal relationship involving allegiance of an individual and protection on the part of the state 3 : membership in a particular nation 4 : political independence or existence as a separate nation 5 : a people having a common origin, tradition, and language and capable of forming a state 6 : an ethnic group within a larger unit (as a nation)

na·tion·al·ize \ˈna-shə-nə-ˌlīz\ *vb* **-ized; -iz·ing** 1 : to make national : make a nation of 2 : to remove from private ownership and place under government control — **na·tion·al·i·za·tion** \ˌna-shə-nə-lə-ˈzā-shən\ *n*

national monument *n* : a place of historic, scenic, or scientific interest set aside for preservation usu. by presidential proclamation

national park *n* : an area of special scenic, historical, or

scientific importance set aside and maintained by a national government esp. for recreation or study

national seashore *n* : a recreational area adjacent to a seacoast and maintained by the federal government

na·tion·wide \ˌnā-shən-ˈwīd\ *adj* : extending throughout a nation

¹na·tive \ˈnā-tiv\ *adj* 1 : INBORN, NATURAL ⟨~ talents⟩ 2 : born in a particular place or country 3 : belonging to a person because of the place or circumstances of birth ⟨her ~ language⟩ 4 : grown, produced, or originating in a particular place : INDIGENOUS 5 *cap* : NATIVE AMERICAN ♦ **Synonyms** ABORIGINAL, AUTOCHTHONOUS, ENDEMIC

²native *n* : one that is native; *esp* : a person who belongs to a particular country by birth

Native American *n* : a member of any of the aboriginal peoples of No. America and esp. the U.S.

na·tiv·ism \ˈnā-ti-ˌvi-zəm\ *n* 1 : a policy of favoring native inhabitants over immigrants 2 : the revival or perpetuation of a native culture esp. in opposition to acculturation

na·tiv·i·ty \nə-ˈti-və-tē, nā-\ *n, pl* **-ties** 1 : the process or circumstances of being born : BIRTH 2 *cap* : the birth of Christ

natl *abbr* national

NATO \ˈnā-(ˌ)tō\ *abbr* North Atlantic Treaty Organization

nat·ty \ˈna-tē\ *adj* **nat·ti·er; -est** : trimly neat and tidy : SMART — **nat·ti·ly** \-tə-lē\ *adv* — **nat·ti·ness** \-tē-nəs\ *n*

¹nat·u·ral \ˈna-chə-rəl\ *adj* 1 : determined by nature : INBORN, INNATE ⟨~ ability⟩ 2 : BORN ⟨a ~ fool⟩ 3 : ILLEGITIMATE ⟨a ~ child⟩ 4 : HUMAN 5 : of or relating to nature 6 : not artificial 7 : being simple and sincere : not affected 8 : LIFELIKE 9 : being neither sharp nor flat ♦ **Synonyms** INGENUOUS, NAIVE, UNSOPHISTICATED, ARTLESS, GUILELESS — **nat·u·ral·ness** *n*

²natural *n* 1 : IDIOT 2 : a character ♮ placed on a line or space of the musical staff to nullify the effect of a preceding sharp or flat 3 : one obviously suitable for a purpose 4 : AFRO

natural childbirth *n* : a system of managing childbirth in which the mother prepares to remain conscious and assist in delivery with little or no use of drugs

natural gas *n* : a combustible gaseous mixture of hydrocarbons coming from the earth's crust and used chiefly as a fuel and raw material

natural history *n* 1 : a treatise on some aspect of nature 2 : the study of natural objects esp. from an amateur or popular point of view

nat·u·ral·ise *Brit var of* NATURALIZE

nat·u·ral·ism \ˈna-chə-rə-ˌli-zəm\ *n* 1 : action or thought based only on natural desires and instincts 2 : a doctrine that denies a supernatural explanation of the origin or development of the universe and holds that scientific laws account for all of nature 3 : realism in art and literature — **nat·u·ral·is·tic** \ˌna-chə-rə-ˈlis-tik\ *adj*

nat·u·ral·ist \-list\ *n* 1 : one that advocates or practices naturalism 2 : a student of animals or plants esp. in the field

nat·u·ral·ize \-ˌlīz\ *vb* **-ized; -iz·ing** 1 : to confer the rights of a citizen on 2 : to become or cause to become established as if native ⟨new forage crops⟩ — **nat·u·ral·i·za·tion** \ˌna-chə-rə-lə-ˈzā-shən\ *n*

nat·u·ral·ly \ˈna-chə-rə-lē, ˈnach-rə-\ *adv* 1 : by nature : by natural character or ability 2 : as might be expected 3 : without artificial aid; *also* : without affectation 4 : REALISTICALLY

natural science *n* : a science (as physics, chemistry, or biology) that deals with matter, energy, and their interrelations and transformations or with objectively measurable phenomena — **natural scientist** *n*

natural selection *n* : the natural process that results in the survival of individuals or groups best adjusted to their environment

na·ture \ˈnā-chər\ *n* [ME, fr. MF, fr. L *natura*, fr. *natus*, pp. of *nasci* to be born] 1 : the inherent quality or basic constitution of a person or thing; *also* : DISPOSITION, TEMPERAMENT 2 : KIND, SORT 3 : the physical universe 4 : one's natural instincts or way of life ⟨quirks of human ~⟩; *also* : primitive state ⟨a return to ~⟩ 5 : natural scenery or environment ⟨beauties of ~⟩

¹naught *also* **nought** \ˈnȯt, ˈnät\ *pron* : NOTHING ⟨efforts came to ~⟩

²**naught** also **nought** n 1 : NOTHINGNESS, NONEXIS-TENCE 2 : the arithmetical symbol 0 : ZERO

naugh·ty \'nȯ-tē, 'nä-\ adj **naugh·ti·er; -est** 1 : guilty of disobedience or misbehavior 2 : lacking in taste or propriety — **naugh·ti·ly** \-tə-lē\ adv — **naugh·ti·ness** \-tē-nəs\ n

nau·sea \'nȯ-zē-ə, -sē-; 'nȯ-zhə, -shə\ n [L, seasickness, nausea, fr. Gk nautia, nausia, fr. nautēs sailor] 1 : sickness of the stomach with a desire to vomit 2 : extreme disgust

nau·se·ate \'nȯ-zē-ät, -sē-, -zhē-, -shē-\ vb **-at·ed; -at·ing** : to affect or become affected with nausea — **nau·se·at·ing·ly** adv

nau·seous \'nȯ-shəs, -zē-əs\ adj 1 : causing nausea or disgust 2 : affected with nausea or disgust

naut abbr nautical

nau·ti·cal \'nȯ-ti-kəl\ adj : of or relating to sailors, navigation, or ships — **nau·ti·cal·ly** \-k(ə-)lē\ adv

nautical mile n : a unit of distance equal to about 6080 feet (1852 meters)

nau·ti·lus \'nȯ-tə-l-əs\ n, pl **-lus·es** or **-li** \ˌlī, -lˌē\ : any of a genus of sea mollusks related to the octopuses but having a spiral chambered shell

nav abbr 1 naval 2 navigable; navigation

Na·va·jo also **Na·va·ho** \'na-və-ˌhō, 'nä-\ n, pl **-jo** or **-jos** also **-ho** or **-hos** : a member of an American Indian people of northern New Mexico and Arizona; also : their language

na·val \'nā-vəl\ adj : of, relating to, or possessing a navy

naval stores n pl : products (as pitch, turpentine, or rosin) obtained from resinous conifers (as pines)

nave \'nāv\ n [ML navis, fr. L, ship] : the central part of a church running lengthwise

na·vel \'nā-vəl\ n : a depression in the middle of the abdomen that marks the point of attachment of fetus and mother

navel–gaz·ing \'nā-vəl-ˈgā-ziŋ\ n : useless or excessive self-contemplation

navel orange n : a seedless orange having a pit at the blossom end where the fruit encloses a small secondary fruit

nav·i·ga·ble \'na-vi-gə-bəl\ adj 1 : capable of being navigated ⟨a ∼ river⟩ 2 : capable of being steered — **nav·i·ga·bil·i·ty** \ˌna-vi-gə-ˈbi-lə-tē\ n

nav·i·gate \'na-və-ˌgāt\ vb **-gat·ed; -gat·ing** 1 : to sail on or through ⟨∼ the Atlantic Ocean⟩ 2 : to steer or direct the course of a ship or aircraft 3 : MOVE; esp : WALK ⟨could hardly ∼⟩ — **nav·i·ga·tion** \ˌna-və-ˈgā-shən\ n — **nav·i·ga·tor** \'na-və-ˌgā-tər\ n

na·vy \'nā-vē\ n, pl **navies** 1 : FLEET; also : the warships belonging to a nation 2 often cap : a nation's organization for naval warfare

navy yard n : a yard where naval vessels are built or repaired

¹**nay** \'nā\ adv : NO

²**nay** n : a negative vote; also : a person casting such a vote

³**nay** conj : not merely this but also : not only so but ⟨he was happy, ∼, ecstatic⟩

nay·say·er \'nā-ˌsā-ər\ n : one who denies, refuses, or opposes something

Na·zi \'nät-sē, 'nat-\ n [G, fr. Nationalsozialist, lit., national socialist] : a member of a German fascist party controlling Germany from 1933 to 1945 under Adolf Hitler — **Nazi** adj — **Na·zism** \'nät-ˌsi-zəm, 'nat-\ also **Na·zi·ism** \-sē-ˌi-zəm\ n

Nb symbol niobium

NB abbr 1 New Brunswick 2 nota bene

NBA abbr 1 National Basketball Association 2 National Boxing Association

NBC abbr National Broadcasting Company

NBS abbr National Bureau of Standards

NC abbr 1 no charge 2 North Carolina

NCAA abbr National Collegiate Athletic Association

NCO \ˌen-ˌsē-ˈō\ n : NONCOMMISSIONED OFFICER

nd abbr no date

Nd symbol neodymium

ND abbr North Dakota

-nd symbol — used after the figure 2 to indicate the ordinal number second

N Dak abbr North Dakota

Ne symbol neon

NE abbr 1 Nebraska 2 New England 3 northeast

Ne·an·der·thal \nē-ˈan-dər-ˌthȯl, nā-ˈän-dər-ˌtäl\ n 1 or **Ne·an·der·tal** \-ˌtäl\ : an extinct Old World hominid that lived from about 30,000 to 200,000 years ago 2 : a person who resembles or suggests a caveman — **Neanderthal** or **Neandertal** adj

neap tide \'nēp-\ n : a tide of minimum range occurring at the first and third quarters of the moon

¹**near** \'nir\ adv 1 : at, within, or to a short distance or time 2 : ALMOST ⟨was ∼ dead⟩

²**near** prep : close to

³**near** adj 1 : closely related or associated; also : INTIMATE 2 : not far away; also : being the closer or left-hand member of a pair 3 : barely avoided ⟨a ∼ accident⟩ 4 : DIRECT, SHORT ⟨by the ∼est route⟩ 5 : STINGY 6 : not real but very like ⟨∼ silk⟩ — **near·ly** adv — **near·ness** n

⁴**near** vb : APPROACH

near beer n : any of various malt liquors low in alcohol

near·by \nir-ˈbī, 'nir-ˌbī\ adv or adj : close at hand

near·sight·ed \'nir-ˈsī-təd\ adj : able to see near things more clearly than distant ones : MYOPIC — **near·sight·ed·ly** adv — **near·sight·ed·ness** n

neat \'nēt\ adj [MF net, fr. L nitidus bright, neat, fr. nitēre to shine] 1 : being orderly and clean 2 : not mixed or diluted ⟨∼ brandy⟩ 3 : marked by tasteful simplicity 4 : PRECISE, SYSTEMATIC 5 : SKILLFUL, ADROIT 6 : FINE, ADMIRABLE ♦ *Synonyms* SHIPSHAPE, TIDY, TRIG, TRIM — **neat** adv — **neat·ly** adv — **neat·ness** n

neath \'nēth\ prep, dial : BENEATH

neat·nik \'nēt-nik\ n : a person who is compulsively neat

neb \'neb\ n 1 : the beak of a bird or tortoise; also : NOSE, SNOUT 2 : NIB

Neb or **Nebr** abbr Nebraska

NEB abbr New English Bible

neb·u·la \'ne-byə-lə\ n, pl **-lae** \-ˌlē, -ˌlī\ also **-las** [NL, fr. L, mist, cloud] 1 : any of numerous clouds of gas or dust in interstellar space 2 : GALAXY — **neb·u·lar** \-lər\ adj

neb·u·liz·er \'ne-byə-ˌlī-zər\ n : ATOMIZER

neb·u·lous \'ne-byə-ləs\ adj 1 : of or relating to a nebula 2 : HAZY, INDISTINCT

¹**nec·es·sary** \'ne-sə-ˌser-ē\ adj 1 : INEVITABLE, INESCAPABLE; also : CERTAIN 2 : PREDETERMINED 3 : COMPULSORY 4 : positively needed : INDISPENSABLE ♦ *Synonyms* IMPERATIVE, NECESSITOUS, ESSENTIAL — **nec·es·sar·i·ly** \ˌne-sə-ˈser-ə-lē\ adv

²**necessary** n, pl **-sar·ies** : an indispensable item

ne·ces·si·tate \ni-ˈse-sə-ˌtāt\ vb **-tat·ed; -tat·ing** : to make necessary

ne·ces·si·tous \ni-ˈse-sə-təs\ adj 1 : NEEDY, IMPOVERISHED 2 : URGENT 3 : NECESSARY ⟨∼ bargaining⟩

ne·ces·si·ty \ni-ˈse-sə-tē\ n, pl **-ties** 1 : conditions that cannot be changed 2 : WANT, POVERTY 3 : something that is necessary 4 : very great need

¹**neck** \'nek\ n 1 : the part of the body connecting the head and the trunk 2 : the part of a garment covering or near to the neck 3 : a relatively narrow part suggestive of a neck ⟨∼ of a bottle⟩ ⟨∼ of land⟩ : a narrow margin esp. of victory ⟨won by a ∼⟩ — **necked** \'nekt\ adj

²**neck** vb : to kiss and caress amorously

neck and neck adv or adj : very close (as in a race)

neck·er·chief \'ne-kər-chəf, -ˌchēf\ n, pl **-chiefs** \-chəfs, -ˌchēfs\ also **-chieves** \-ˌchēvz\ : a square of cloth worn folded about the neck like a scarf

neck·lace \'ne-kləs\ n : an ornament worn around the neck

neck·line \'nek-ˌlīn\ n : the outline of the neck opening of a garment

neck·tie \-ˌtī\ n : a strip of cloth worn around the neck and tied in front

ne·crol·o·gy \nə-ˈkrä-lə-jē\ n, pl **-gies** 1 : OBITUARY 2 : a list of the recently dead

nec·ro·man·cy \'ne-krə-ˌman-sē\ n 1 : the art or practice of conjuring up the spirits of the dead for purposes of magically revealing the future 2 : MAGIC, SORCERY — **nec·ro·man·cer** \-sər\ n

ne·crop·o·lis \nə-ˈkrä-pə-ləs, ne-\ n, pl **-lis·es** or **-les** \-ˌlēz\ or **-leis** \-ˌlās\ or **-li** \-ˌlī, -ˌlē\ [LL, fr. Gk nekropolis, fr. nekros dead body + polis city] : CEMETERY; esp : a large elaborate cemetery of an ancient city

nec·rop·sy \'ne-ˌkräp-sē\ n, pl **-sies** : AUTOPSY; esp : an autopsy performed on an animal

ne·cro·sis \nə-ˈkrō-səs, ne-\ n, pl **ne·cro·ses** \-ˌsēz\ : usu. local death of body tissue — **ne·crot·ic** \-ˈkrä-tik\ adj

nec·tar \'nek-tər\ n **1** : the drink of the Greek and Roman gods; *also* : any delicious drink **2** : a sweet plant secretion that is the raw material of honey

nec·tar·ine \ˌnek-tə-'rēn\ n : a smooth-skinned peach

née or **nee** \'nā\ adj [F, lit., born] — used to identify a woman by her maiden family name

¹need \'nēd\ n **1** : OBLIGATION ⟨no ∼ to hurry⟩ **2** : a lack of something requisite, desirable, or useful **3** : a condition requiring supply or relief ⟨when the ∼ arises⟩ **4** : POVERTY ✦ **Synonyms** NECESSITY, EXIGENCY

²need vb **1** : to be in want **2** : to have cause or occasion for : REQUIRE ⟨he ∼s advice⟩ **3** : to be under obligation or necessity ⟨we ∼ to know the truth⟩

need·ful \'nēd-fəl\ adj : NECESSARY, REQUISITE

¹nee·dle \'nē-d³l\ n **1** : a slender pointed usu. steel implement used in sewing **2** : a slender rod (as for knitting, controlling a small opening, or transmitting vibrations to or from a recording) ⟨a phonograph ∼⟩ **3** : a slender hollow instrument from which material is introduced into or withdrawn from the body **4** : a slender indicator on a dial **5** : a needle-shaped leaf (as of a pine)

²needle vb **nee·dled; nee·dling** : PROD, GOAD; *esp* : to incite to action by repeated gibes

nee·dle–nose pliers \'nē-d³l-ˌnōz-\ n pl : pliers with long slender jaws for grasping small or thin objects

nee·dle·point \'nē-d³l-ˌpöint\ n **1** : lace worked with a needle over a paper pattern **2** : embroidery done on canvas across counted threads — **needlepoint** adj

need·less \'nēd-ləs\ adj : UNNECESSARY ⟨∼ waste⟩ — **need·less·ly** adv — **need·less·ness** n

nee·dle·wom·an \'nē-d³l-ˌwù-mən\ n : a woman who does needlework; *esp* : SEAMSTRESS

nee·dle·work \-ˌwərk\ n : work done with a needle; *esp* : work (as embroidery) other than plain sewing

needs \'nēdz\ adv : of necessity : NECESSARILY ⟨must ∼ be recognized⟩

needy \'nē-dē\ adj **need·i·er; -est** : being in want : POVERTY-STRICKEN

ne'er \'ner\ adv : NEVER

ne'er–do–well \'ner-dù-ˌwel\ n : an idle worthless person — **ne'er–do–well** adj

ne·far·i·ous \ni-'fer-ē-əs\ adj [L nefarius, fr. nefas crime, fr. ne- not + fas right, divine law] : very wicked : EVIL ✦ **Synonyms** BAD, IMMORAL, INIQUITOUS, SINFUL, VICIOUS — **ne·far·i·ous·ly** adv

neg abbr negative

ne·gate \ni-'gāt\ vb **ne·gat·ed; ne·gat·ing 1** : to deny the existence or truth of **2** : to cause to be ineffective or invalid : NULLIFY

ne·ga·tion \ni-'gā-shən\ n **1** : the action or operation of negating or making negative **2** : a negative doctrine or statement

¹neg·a·tive \'ne-gə-tiv\ adj **1** : marked by denial, prohibition, or refusal ⟨a ∼ reply⟩ **2** : not positive or constructive; *esp* : not affirming the presence of what is sought or suspected to be present ⟨test results were ∼⟩ **3** : less than zero ⟨a ∼ number⟩ **4** : being, relating to, or charged with electricity of which the electron is the elementary unit **5** : having the light and dark parts opposite to what they were in the original photographic subject — **neg·a·tive·ly** adv — **neg·a·tive·ness** n — **neg·a·tiv·i·ty** \ˌne-gə-'ti-və-tē\ n

²negative n **1** : a negative word or statement **2** : a negative vote or reply; *also* : REFUSAL **3** : something that is the opposite or negation of something else **4** : a negative number **5** : the side that votes or argues for the opposition (as in a debate) **6** : a negative photographic image on transparent material

³negative vb **-tived; -tiv·ing 1** : to refuse to accept or approve **2** : to vote against **3** : DISPROVE

negative income tax n : a system of federal subsidy payments to families with incomes below a stipulated level

neg·a·tiv·ism \'ne-gə-ti-ˌvi-zəm\ n : an attitude of skepticism and denial of nearly everything affirmed or suggested by others

¹ne·glect \ni-'glekt\ vb [L neglectus, pp. of neglegere, neclegere, fr. nec- not + legere to gather] **1** : DISREGARD **2** : to leave undone or unattended to esp. through carelessness ✦ **Synonyms** OMIT, IGNORE, OVERLOOK, SLIGHT, FORGET, MISS

²neglect n **1** : an act or instance of neglecting something **2** : the condition of being neglected — **ne·glect·ful** adj

neg·li·gee also **neg·li·gé** \ˌne-glə-'zhā\ n : a woman's long flowing dressing gown

neg·li·gent \'ne-gli-jənt\ adj : marked by neglect ✦ **Synonyms** NEGLECTFUL, REMISS, DELINQUENT, DERELICT — **neg·li·gence** \-jəns\ n — **neg·li·gent·ly** adv

neg·li·gi·ble \'ne-gli-jə-bəl\ adj : so small as to be neglected or disregarded

ne·go·tiant \ni-'gō-shē-ənt\ n : NEGOTIATOR

ne·go·ti·ate \ni-'gō-shē-ˌāt\ vb **-at·ed; -at·ing** [L negotiari to carry on business, fr. negotium business, fr. neg- not + otium leisure] **1** : to confer with another so as to arrive at the settlement of some matter; *also* : to arrange for or bring about by such conferences ⟨∼ a treaty⟩ **2** : to transfer to another by delivery or endorsement in return for equivalent value ⟨∼ a check⟩ **3** : to get through, around, or over successfully ⟨∼ a turn⟩ — **ne·go·tia·ble** \-shə-bəl, -shē-ə-\ adj — **ne·go·ti·a·tion** \ni-ˌgō-sē-'ā-shən, -shē-\ n — **ne·go·ti·a·tor** \-'gō-shē-ˌā-tər\ n

ne·gri·tude \'ne-grə-ˌtüd, -ˌtyüd, 'nē-\ n : a consciousness of and pride in one's African heritage

Ne·gro \'nē-grō\ n, pl **Negroes** [Sp or Pg, fr. negro black] *sometimes offensive* : a member of the human race native to Africa and classified according to physical features (as dark skin pigmentation) — **Negro** adj, *sometimes offensive* — **Ne·groid** \'nē-ˌgröid\ n or adj, *often not cap, sometimes offensive*

Neh abbr Nehemiah

Ne·he·mi·ah \ˌnē-ə-'mī-ə\ n — see BIBLE table

neigh \'nā\ n : a loud prolonged cry of a horse — **neigh** vb

¹neigh·bor \'nā-bər\ n **1** : one living or located near another **2** : FELLOW MAN

²neighbor vb : to be next to or near to : border on

neigh·bor·hood \'nā-bər-ˌhùd\ n **1** : NEARNESS **2** : a place or region near : VICINITY; *also* : a number or amount near ⟨costs in the ∼ of $10⟩ **3** : the people living near one another **4** : a section lived in by neighbors and usu. having distinguishing characteristics

neigh·bor·ly \-lē\ adj : befitting congenial neighbors; *esp* : FRIENDLY ⟨a ∼ welcome⟩ — **neigh·bor·li·ness** n

neigh·bour chiefly Brit var of NEIGHBOR

¹nei·ther \'nē-thər, 'nī-\ conj **1** : not either ⟨∼ good nor bad⟩ **2** : NOR ⟨∼ did I⟩

²neither pron : neither one : not the one and not the other ⟨∼ of the two⟩

³neither adj : not either ⟨∼ hand⟩

nel·son \'nel-sən\ n : a wrestling hold in which one applies leverage against an opponent's arm, neck, and head

nem·a·tode \'ne-mə-ˌtōd\ n : any of a phylum of elongated cylindrical worms parasitic in animals or plants or free= living in soil or water

nem·e·sis \'ne-mə-səs\ n, pl **-e·ses** \-ˌsēz\ [L Nemesis, goddess of divine retribution, fr. Gk] **1** : one that inflicts retribution or vengeance **2** : a formidable and usu. victorious rival **3** : an act or effect of retribution; *also* : CURSE

neo·clas·sic \ˌnē-ō-'kla-sik\ or **neo·clas·si·cal** \-si-kəl\ adj : of or relating to a revival or adaptation of the classical style esp. in literature, art, or music

neo·co·lo·nial·ism \ˌnē-ō-kə-'lō-nē-ə-ˌli-zəm\ n : the economic and political policies by which a nation indirectly maintains or extends its influence over other areas or peoples — **neo·co·lo·nial** adj — **neo·co·lo·nial·ist** \-list\ n or adj

neo·con \'nē-ō-ˌkän\ n : NEOCONSERVATIVE

neo·con·ser·va·tive \ˌnē-ō-'sər-və-tiv\ n : a former liberal espousing political conservatism — **neo·con·ser·va·tism** \-və-ˌti-zəm\ n — **neoconservative** adj

neo·dym·i·um \ˌnē-ō-'di-mē-əm\ n : a silver-white to yellow metallic chemical element

neo–im·pres·sion·ism \ˌnē-ō-im-'pre-shə-ˌni-zəm\ n, often cap N&I : a late 19th century French art movement that attempted to make impressionism more precise and to apply its painting technique

Neo·lith·ic \ˌnē-ə-'li-thik\ adj : of or relating to the latest period of the Stone Age characterized by polished stone implements

ne·ol·o·gism \nē-'ä-lə-ˌji-zəm\ n : a new word or expression

ne·on \'nē-ˌän\ n [Gk, neut. of neos new] **1** : a gaseous colorless chemical element used in electric lamps **2** : a lamp in which a discharge through neon gives a reddish glow — **neon** adj

neo·na·tal \ˌnē-ō-ˈnā-tᵊl\ adj : of, relating to, or affecting the newborn ⟨a ∼ infection⟩ — **neo·na·tal·ly** adv

ne·o·nate \ˈnē-ə-ˌnāt\ n : a newborn child

neo·pa·gan \ˌnē-ō-ˈpā-gən\ n : a person who practices a contemporary form of paganism

neo·phyte \ˈnē-ə-ˌfīt\ n **1** : a new convert : PROSELYTE **2** : NOVICE **3** : BEGINNER ✦ **Synonyms** APPRENTICE, FRESHMAN, NEWCOMER, ROOKIE, TENDERFOOT, TYRO

neo·plasm \ˈnē-ə-ˌpla-zəm\ n : a new growth of tissue serving no useful purpose in the body : TUMOR — **neo·plas·tic** \ˌnē-ə-ˈplas-tik\ adj

neo·prene \ˈnē-ə-ˌprēn\ n : a synthetic rubber used esp. for special-purpose clothing (as wet suits)

neo·trop·i·cal \ˌnē-ō-ˈträ-pi-kəl\ adj, often cap : of or relating to a zoogeographic region of America that extends south from the central plateau of Mexico

ne·pen·the \nə-ˈpen-thē\ n **1** : a potion used by the ancients to dull pain and sorrow **2** : something capable of making one forget grief or suffering

neph·ew \ˈne-fyü, chiefly Brit -vyü\ n [ME nevew, fr. AF neveu, fr. LL nepot-, nepos, fr. L, grandson, descendant] : a son of one's brother, sister, brother-in-law, or sister-in-law

ne·phrit·ic \ni-ˈfri-tik\ adj **1** : RENAL **2** : of, relating to, or affected with nephritis

ne·phri·tis \ni-ˈfrī-təs\ n, pl **ne·phrit·i·des** \-ˈfri-tə-ˌdēz\ : kidney inflammation

ne plus ul·tra \ˌnē-ˌpləs-ˈəl-trə\ n [NL, (go) no more beyond] : the highest point capable of being attained

nep·o·tism \ˈne-pə-ˌti-zəm\ n [F népotisme, fr. It nepotismo, fr. nepote nephew, fr. LL nepot-, nepos] : favoritism shown to a relative (as in the granting of jobs)

Nep·tune \ˈnep-ˌtün, -ˌtyün\ n : the planet 8th in order from the sun — see PLANET table — **Nep·tu·ni·an** \nep-ˈtü-nē-ən, -ˈtyü-\ adj

nep·tu·ni·um \nep-ˈtü-nē-əm, -ˈtyü-\ n : a short-lived radioactive element

nerd \ˈnərd\ n : an unstylish or socially inept person; esp : one slavishly devoted to intellectual pursuits — **nerdy** adj

Ne·re·id \ˈnir-ē-əd\ n : a sea nymph in Greek mythology

¹nerve \ˈnərv\ n **1** : SINEW, TENDON ⟨strain every ∼⟩ **2** : any of the strands of nervous tissue that carry nerve impulses between the brain and spinal cord and every part of the body **3** : power of endurance or control : FORTITUDE; also : BOLDNESS, DARING **4** pl : NERVOUSNESS **5** : a vein of a leaf or insect wing — **nerved** \ˈnərvd\ adj — **nerve·less** adj

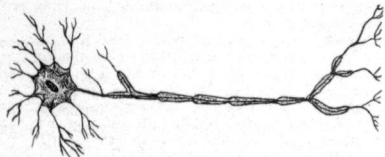

nerve 2: cell body at left and nerve ending at right

²nerve vb **nerved; nerv·ing** : to give strength or courage to

nerve cell n : NEURON; also : CELL BODY

nerve gas n : a chemical weapon damaging esp. to the nervous and respiratory systems

nerve impulse n : a physical and chemical change that moves along a process of a neuron after stimulation and carries a record of sensation or an instruction to act

nerve-rack·ing or **nerve–wrack·ing** \ˈnərv-ˌra-kiŋ\ adj : extremely trying on the nerves

ner·vous \ˈnər-vəs\ adj **1** : FORCIBLE, SPIRITED **2** : of, relating to, or made up of neurons or nerves **3** : easily excited or annoyed : JUMPY **4** : TIMID, APPREHENSIVE ⟨a ∼ smile⟩ **5** : UNEASY, UNSTEADY — **ner·vous·ly** adv — **ner·vous·ness** n

nervous breakdown n : an attack of mental or emotional disorder of sufficient severity to be incapacitating esp. when requiring hospitalization

nervous system n : a bodily system that in vertebrates is made up of the brain and spinal cord, nerves, ganglia, and parts of the sense organs and that receives and interprets stimuli and transmits nerve impulses

nervy \ˈnər-vē\ adj **nerv·i·er; -est** **1** : showing calm courage **2** : marked by impudence or presumption ⟨a ∼ salesperson⟩ **3** : EXCITABLE, NERVOUS ✦ **Synonyms** BOLD, CHEEKY, FORWARD, FRESH, IMPUDENT, SAUCY

-ness \nəs\ n suffix : state : condition : quality : degree ⟨good*ness*⟩

¹nest \ˈnest\ n **1** : the shelter prepared by a bird for its eggs and young **2** : a place where eggs (as of insects or fish) are laid and hatched **3** : a place of rest, retreat, or lodging **4** : DEN, HANGOUT ⟨a ∼ of thieves⟩ **5** : the occupants of a nest **6** : a series of objects (as bowls or tables) fitting inside or under one another

²nest vb **1** : to build or occupy a nest **2** : to fit compactly together or within one another

nest egg n : a fund of money accumulated as a reserve

nes·tle \ˈne-səl\ vb **nes·tled; nes·tling** **1** : to settle snugly or comfortably **2** : to press closely and affectionately : CUDDLE **3** : to settle, shelter, or house as if in a nest

nest·ling \ˈnest-liŋ\ n : a bird too young to leave its nest

¹net \ˈnet\ n **1** : a meshed fabric twisted, knotted, or woven together at regular intervals **2** : a device made all or partly of net and used esp. to catch birds, fish, or insects **3** : something made of net used esp. for protecting, confining, carrying, or dividing ⟨a tennis ∼⟩ **4** : SNARE, TRAP **5** often cap : INTERNET

²net vb **net·ted; net·ting** **1** : to cover or enclose with or as if with a net **2** : to catch in or as if in a net

³net adj : free from all charges or deductions ⟨∼ profit⟩ ⟨∼ weight⟩

⁴net vb **net·ted; net·ting** : to gain or produce as profit : CLEAR, YIELD ⟨his business netted $50,000 a year⟩

⁵net n : a net amount, profit, weight, or price

Neth abbr Netherlands

neth·er \ˈne-thər\ adj : situated down or below ⟨the ∼ regions of the earth⟩

neth·er·most \-ˌmōst\ adj : LOWEST

neth·er·world \-ˌwərld\ n **1** : the world of the dead **2** : UNDERWORLD

net·i·quette \ˈne-ti-kət, -ˌket\ n : etiquette governing communication on the Internet

nett Brit var of NET

net·ting n **1** : NETWORK **2** : the act or process of making a net or network

¹net·tle \ˈne-tᵊl\ n : any of a genus of coarse herbs with stinging hairs

²nettle vb **net·tled; net·tling** : PROVOKE, VEX, IRRITATE

net·tle·some \ˈne-tᵊl-səm\ adj : causing vexation : IRRITATING

net·work \ˈnet-ˌwərk\ n **1** : NET **2** : a system of elements (as lines or channels) that cross in the manner of the threads in a net **3** : a group or system of related or connected parts; esp : a chain of radio or television stations **4** : a system of computers that are connected (as by telephone wires)

net·work·ing \ˈnet-ˌwər-kiŋ\ n **1** : the exchange of information or services among individuals, groups, or institutions **2** : the cultivation of productive business relationships

neu·ral \ˈnur-əl, ˈnyur-\ adj : of, relating to, or involving a nerve or the nervous system ⟨∼ pathways⟩

neu·ral·gia \nu̇-ˈral-jə, nyu̇-\ n : acute pain that follows the course of a nerve — **neu·ral·gic** \-jik\ adj

neur·as·the·nia \ˌnu̇r-əs-ˈthē-nē-ə, ˌnyu̇r-\ n [NL, fr. Gk neuron nerve + asthenia weakness, fr. asthenēs weak, fr. a- not + sthenos strength] : a psychological disorder marked esp. by fatiguing easily, lack of motivation, feelings of inadequacy, and psychosomatic symptoms — **neur·as·then·ic** \-the-nik, -ˈthē-\ adj or n

neu·ri·tis \nu̇-ˈrī-təs, nyu̇-\ n, pl **-rit·i·des** \-ˈri-tə-ˌdēz\ or **-ri·tis·es** : inflammation of a nerve — **neu·rit·ic** \-ˈri-tik\ adj or n

neu·ro·bi·ol·o·gy \ˌnu̇r-ō-bī-ˈä-lə-jē\ n : a branch of biology that deals with the nervous system — **neu·ro·bi·o·log·i·cal** \-ˌbī-ə-ˈlä-ji-kəl\ adj — **neu·ro·bi·ol·o·gist** \-bī-ˈä-lə-jist\ n

neu·rol·o·gy \nu̇-ˈrä-lə-jē, nyu̇-\ n : the scientific study of the nervous system — **neu·ro·log·i·cal** \ˌnu̇r-ə-ˈlä-ji-kəl, ˌnyu̇r-\ or **neu·ro·log·ic** \-jik\ adj — **neu·ro·log·i·cal·ly** \-ji-k(ə-)lē\ adv — **neu·rol·o·gist** \nu̇-ˈrä-lə-jist, nyu̇-\ n

neu·ro·mus·cu·lar \ˌnür-ō-'məs-kyə-lər, ˌnyür-\ *adj* : of, relating to, or affecting nerves and muscles ⟨a ∼ disease⟩

neu·ron \'nü-ˌrän, 'nyü-\ *n* : a cell with specialized processes that is the fundamental functional unit of nervous tissue — **neu·ro·nal** \'nür-ə-nᵊl, 'nyür-\ *adj*

neu·rone \-ˌrōn\ *chiefly Brit var of* NEURON

neu·ro·sci·ence \ˌnür-ō-'sī-əns, ˌnyür-\ *n* : a branch of the life sciences that deals with the anatomy, physiology, biochemistry, or molecular biology of nerves and nervous tissue and esp. with their relation to behavior and learning — **neu·ro·sci·en·tist** \-ən-tist\ *n*

neu·ro·sis \nü-'rō-səs, nyü-\ *n, pl* **-ro·ses** \-ˌsēz\ : a mental and emotional disorder that is less serious than a psychosis, is not characterized by disturbance of the use of language, and is accompanied by various bodily and mental disturbances (as visceral symptoms, anxieties, or phobias)

neu·ro·sur·gery \ˌnür-ō-'sər-jə-rē, ˌnyür-\ *n* : surgery of nervous structures (as nerves, the brain, or the spinal cord) — **neu·ro·sur·geon** \-'sər-jən\ *n*

¹**neu·rot·ic** \nü-'rä-tik, nyü-\ *adj* : of, relating to, being, or affected with a neurosis — **neu·rot·i·cal·ly** \-ti-k(ə-)lē\ *adv*

²**neurotic** *n* : an emotionally unstable or neurotic person

neu·ro·trans·mit·ter \ˌnür-ō-trans-'mi-tər, ˌnyür-, -tranz-\ *n* : a substance (as acetylcholine) that transmits nerve impulses across a synapse

neut *abbr* neuter

¹**neu·ter** \'nü-tər, 'nyü-\ *adj* [ME *neutre*, fr. MF & L; MF *neutre*, fr. L *neuter*, lit., neither, fr. *ne-* not + *uter* which of two] **1** : of, relating to, or constituting the gender that includes most words or grammatical forms referring to things classed as neither masculine nor feminine **2** : lacking or having imperfectly developed sex organs

²**neuter** *n* **1** : a noun, pronoun, adjective, or inflectional form or class of the neuter gender; *also* : the neuter gender **2** : WORKER 2; *also* : a spayed or castrated animal

³**neuter** *vb* **1** : CASTRATE, SPAY **2** : to remove the force or effectiveness of

¹**neu·tral** \'nü-trəl, 'nyü-\ *n* **1** : one that is neutral **2** : a neutral color **3** : a position of disengagement (as of gears)

²**neutral** *adj* **1** : not favoring either side in a quarrel, contest, or war **2** : of or relating to a neutral state or power **3** : MIDDLING, INDIFFERENT **4** : having no hue : GRAY; *also* : not decided in color **5** : neither acid nor basic ⟨a ∼ solution⟩ **6** : not electrically charged

neu·tral·ise *Brit var of* NEUTRALIZE

neu·tral·ism \'nü-trə-ˌli-zəm, 'nyü-\ *n* : a policy or the advocacy of neutrality esp. in international affairs

neu·tral·i·ty \nü-'tra-lə-tē, nyü-\ *n* : the quality or state of being neutral; *esp* : refusal to take part in a war between other powers

neu·tral·ize \'nü-trə-ˌlīz, 'nyü-\ *vb* **-ized; -iz·ing** : to make neutral; *esp* : COUNTERACT — **neu·tral·i·za·tion** \ˌnü-trə-lə-'zā-shən, ˌnyü-\ *n*

neu·tri·no \nü-'trē-nō, nyü-\ *n, pl* **-nos** : an uncharged elementary particle held to be massless or very light

neu·tron \'nü-ˌträn, 'nyü-\ *n* : an uncharged atomic particle that is nearly equal in mass to the proton

neutron bomb *n* : a nuclear bomb designed to produce lethal neutrons but less blast and fire damage than other nuclear bombs

neutron star *n* : a dense celestial object that results from the collapse of a large star

Nev *abbr* Nevada

nev·er \'ne-vər\ *adv* **1** : not ever **2** : not in any degree, way, or condition

nev·er·more \ˌne-vər-'mór\ *adv* : never again

nev·er–nev·er land \ˌne-vər-'ne-vər-\ *n* : an ideal or imaginary place

nev·er·the·less \ˌne-vər-thə-'les\ *adv* : in spite of that : HOWEVER

ne·vus \'nē-vəs\ *n, pl* **ne·vi** \-ˌvī\ : a usu. pigmented area on the skin : MOLE

¹**new** \'nü, 'nyü\ *adj* **1** : not old : RECENT, MODERN **2** : recently discovered, recognized, or learned about ⟨∼ drugs⟩ **3** : UNFAMILIAR ⟨visit ∼ places⟩ **4** : different from the former **5** : not accustomed ⟨∼ to the work⟩ **6** : beginning as a repetition of a previous act or thing ⟨a ∼ year⟩ **7** : REFRESHED, REGENERATED ⟨rest made a ∼

man of him⟩ **8** : being in a position or place for the first time ⟨a ∼ member⟩ **9** *cap* : having been in use after medieval times : MODERN ⟨*New* Latin⟩ ♦ **Synonyms** NOVEL, NEWFANGLED, FRESH — **new·ish** *adj* — **new·ness** *n*

²**new** *adv* : NEWLY ⟨*new*-mown hay⟩

¹**new age** *adj, often cap N&A* **1** : of, relating to, or being New Age **2** : CONTEMPORARY, MODERN

²**new age** *n* **1** *cap* : a group of late 20th century social attitudes adapted from a variety of ancient and modern beliefs relating to spirituality, right living, and health **2** : a soft soothing form of instrumental music

new·bie \'nü-bē, 'nyü-\ *n* : a newcomer esp. to cyberspace

new blood *n* : persons accepted into a group or organization and expected to provide fresh ideas and vitality

¹**new·born** \-'bórn\ *adj* **1** : recently born **2** : born anew ⟨∼ hope⟩

²**newborn** *n, pl* **newborn** *or* **newborns** : a newborn individual

new·com·er \-ˌkə-mər\ *n* **1** : one recently arrived **2** : BEGINNER

New Deal *n* : the legislative and administrative program of President F. D. Roosevelt to promote economic recovery and social reform during the 1930s — **New Dealer** *n*

new·el \'nü-əl, 'nyü-\ *n* : a post about which the steps of a circular staircase wind; *also* : a post at the foot of a stairway or one at a landing

new·fan·gled \'nü-'faŋ-gəld, 'nyü-\ *adj* **1** : attracted to novelty **2** : of the newest style : NOVEL

new–fash·ioned \-'fa-shənd\ *adj* **1** : made in a new fashion or form **2** : UP-TO-DATE

new·found \-'faúnd\ *adj* : newly found

New Left *n* : a radical political movement originating in the 1960s

new·ly \'nü-lē, 'nyü-\ *adv* **1** : LATELY, RECENTLY ⟨a ∼ married couple⟩ **2** : ANEW, AFRESH ⟨∼ painted⟩

new·ly·wed \-ˌwed\ *n* : a person recently married

new moon *n* : the phase of the moon with its dark side toward the earth; *also* : the thin crescent moon seen for a few days after the new moon phase

news \'nüz, 'nyüz\ *n* **1** : a report of recent events : TIDINGS **2** : material reported in a newspaper or news periodical or on a newscast

news·boy \'nüz-ˌbói, 'nyüz-\ *n* : one who delivers or sells newspapers

news·cast \-ˌkast\ *n* : a radio or television broadcast of news — **news·cast·er** \-ˌkas-tər\ *n*

news·group \-ˌgrüp\ *n* : an Internet bulletin devoted to a certain topic

news·let·ter \'nüz-ˌle-tər, 'nyüz-\ *n* : a small newspaper containing news or information of interest chiefly to a special group

news·mag·a·zine \-ˌma-gə-ˌzēn\ *n* : a usu. weekly magazine devoted chiefly to summarizing and analyzing news

news·man \-mən, -ˌman\ *n* : a person who gathers, reports, or comments on the news : REPORTER

news·pa·per \-ˌpā-pər\ *n* : a paper that is published at regular intervals and contains news, articles of opinion, features, and advertising

news·pa·per·man \-ˌpā-pər-ˌman\ *n* : a person who owns or is employed by a newspaper

news·print \-ˌprint\ *n* : paper made chiefly from wood pulp and used mostly for newspapers

news·reel \-ˌrēl\ *n* : a short motion picture portraying current events

news·stand \-ˌstand\ *n* : a place where newspapers and periodicals are sold

news·week·ly \-ˌwēk-lē\ *n* : a weekly newspaper or newsmagazine

news·wire \-ˌwī(-ə)r\ *n* : WIRE SERVICE

news·wom·an \-ˌwù-mən\ *n* : a woman who is a reporter

news·wor·thy \-ˌwər-thē\ *adj* : sufficiently interesting to the general public to warrant reporting

newsy \'nü-zē, 'nyü-\ *adj* **news·i·er; -est** : filled with news; *esp* : TALKATIVE

newt \'nüt, 'nyüt\ *n* [ME, alter. (from misdivision of *an ewte*) of *ewt, ewete*, fr. OE *efete*] : any of various small chiefly aquatic salamanders

New Testament *n* : the second of the two chief divisions of the Christian Bible — see BIBLE table

new·ton \'nü-tᵊn, 'nyü-\ *n* : the unit of force in the metric system equal to the force required to impart an acceleration of one meter per second per second to a mass of one kilogram

new wave *n, often cap N&W* : the latest and esp. the most outrageous style — **new-wave** *adj*

New Year *n* **1** : NEW YEAR'S DAY; *also* : the first days of the year **2** : ROSH HASHANAH

New Year's Day *n* : January 1 observed as a legal holiday

¹**next** \'nekst\ *adj* : immediately preceding or following : NEAREST

²**next** *prep* : nearest or adjacent to

³**next** *adv* **1** : in the time, place, or order nearest or immediately succeeding **2** : on the first occasion to come

⁴**next** *n* : one that is next

nex·us \'nek-səs\ *n, pl* **nex·us·es** \-sə-səz\ *or* **nex·us** \-səs, -ˌsüs\ : CONNECTION, LINK

Nez Percé \'nez-'pərs\ *n* : a member of an American Indian people of Idaho, Washington, and Oregon; *also* : the language of the Nez Percé

NF *abbr* Newfoundland

NFC *abbr* National Football Conference

NFL *abbr* National Football League

Nfld *abbr* Newfoundland

NG *abbr* **1** National Guard **2** no good

ngul·trum \əŋ-'gül-trəm\ *n* — see MONEY table

ngwee \əŋ-'gwē\ *n, pl* **ngwee** — see *kwacha* at MONEY table

NH *abbr* New Hampshire

NHL *abbr* National Hockey League

Ni *symbol* nickel

ni·a·cin \'nī-ə-sən\ *n* : an organic acid of the vitamin B complex found widely in plants and animals and used esp. against pellagra

nib \'nib\ *n* : POINT; *esp* : a pen point

¹**nib·ble** \'ni-bəl\ *vb* **nib·bled; nib·bling** : to bite gently or bit by bit

²**nibble** *n* : a small or cautious bite

ni·cad \'nī-ˌkad\ *n* : a rechargeable dry cell that has a nickel cathode and a cadmium anode

nice \'nīs\ *adj* **nic·er; nic·est** [ME, foolish, wanton, fr. AF, silly, simple, fr. L *nescius* ignorant, fr. *nescire* to not know] **1** : FASTIDIOUS, DISCRIMINATING **2** : marked by delicate discrimination or treatment **3** : PLEASING, AGREEABLE ⟨had a ∼ time⟩; *also* : well-executed ⟨a ∼ shot⟩ **4** : WELL-BRED ⟨∼ people⟩ **5** : VIRTUOUS, RESPECTABLE ◆ *Synonyms* CHOOSY, FINICKY, PARTICULAR, PERSNICKETY, PICKY — **nice·ly** *adv* — **nice·ness** *n*

nice·nel·ly \'nīs-'ne-lē\ *adj, often cap 2d N* **1** : marked by euphemism **2** : PRUDISH — **nice nelly** *n, often cap 2d N* — **nice·nel·ly·ism** \-ˌi-zəm\ *n, often cap 2d N*

nice·ty \'nī-sə-tē\ *n, pl* **-ties** **1** : a dainty, delicate, or elegant thing ⟨enjoy the *niceties* of life⟩ **2** : a fine point or distinction ⟨*niceties* of workmanship⟩ **3** : EXACTNESS, PRECISION, ACCURACY

niche \'nich\ *n* [F] **1** : a recess in a wall esp. for a statue **2** : a place, employment, or activity for which a person or thing is best fitted **3** : the living space or role of an organism in an ecological community esp. with regard to food consumption

¹**nick** \'nik\ *n* **1** : a small notch, groove, or chip **2** : the final critical moment ⟨in the ∼ of time⟩

²**nick** *vb* : NOTCH, CHIP

nick·el \'ni-kəl\ *n* **1** : a hard silver-white metallic chemical element capable of a high polish and used in alloys **2** : the U.S. 5-cent piece made of copper and nickel; *also* : the Canadian 5-cent piece

nick·el·ode·on \ˌni-kə-'lō-dē-ən\ *n* **1** : an early movie theater to which admission cost five cents **2** : JUKEBOX

nick·er \'ni-kər\ *vb* : NEIGH, WHINNY — **nicker** *n*

nick·name \'nik-ˌnām\ *n* [ME *nekename* additional name, alter. (from misdivision of *an ekename*) of *ekename*, fr. *eke* also + *name*] **1** : a usu. descriptive name given instead of or in addition to the one belonging to a person, place, or thing **2** : a familiar form of a proper name — **nickname** *vb*

nic·o·tine \'ni-kə-ˌtēn\ *n* : a poisonous and addictive substance in tobacco that is used as an insecticide

nic·o·tin·ic acid \ˌni-kə-ˌtē-nik-, -'ti-\ *n* : NIACIN

niece \'nēs\ *n* : a daughter of one's brother, sister, brother-in-law, or sister-in-law

nif·ty \'nif-tē\ *adj* **nif·ti·er; -est** : very good : very attractive

nig·gard \'ni-gərd\ *n* : a stingy person : MISER — **nig·gard·li·ness** \-lē-nəs\ *n* — **nig·gard·ly** *adj or adv*

nig·gling \'ni-gə-liŋ\ *adj* **1** : PETTY **2** : bothersome in a petty way ◆ *Synonyms* INCONSEQUENTIAL, MEASLY, PICAYUNE, PIDDLING, TRIFLING, TRIVIAL

¹**nigh** \'nī\ *adv* **1** : near in place, time, or relationship **2** : NEARLY, ALMOST

²**nigh** *adj* : CLOSE, NEAR

³**nigh** *prep* : NEAR

night \'nīt\ *n* **1** : the period between dusk and dawn **2** : the darkness of night **3** : a period of misery or unhappiness **4** : NIGHTFALL — **night** *adj*

night blindness *n* : reduced visual capacity in faint light (as at night)

night·cap \'nīt-ˌkap\ *n* **1** : a cloth cap worn with nightclothes **2** : a usu. alcoholic drink taken at bedtime

night·clothes \-ˌklōthz, -ˌklōz\ *n pl* : garments worn in bed

night·club \-ˌkləb\ *n* : a place of entertainment open at night usu. serving food and liquor and providing music for dancing

night crawl·er \-ˌkrò-lər\ *n* : EARTHWORM; *esp* : a large earthworm found on the soil surface at night

night·dress \'nīt-ˌdres\ *n* : NIGHTGOWN

night·fall \-ˌfòl\ *n* : the coming of night

night·gown \-ˌgaủn\ *n* : a loose garment for wear in bed

night·hawk \-ˌhòk\ *n* : any of a genus of American birds related to and resembling the whip-poor-will

night·in·gale \'nī-t³n-ˌgāl, 'nī-tiŋ-\ *n* [ME, fr. OE *nihtegale*, fr. *niht* night + *galan* to sing] : any of several Old World thrushes noted for the sweet usu. nocturnal song of the male

night·life \'nīt-ˌlīf\ *n* : the activity of pleasure-seekers at night

night·ly \'nīt-lē\ *adj* **1** : happening, done, or produced by night or every night **2** : of or relating to the night or every night — **nightly** *adv*

night·mare \'nīt-ˌmer\ *n* **1** : a frightening dream **2** : a frightening or horrible experience — **nightmare** *adj* — **night·mar·ish** *adj*

night rider *n* : a member of a secret band who ride masked at night doing violence to punish or terrorize

night·shade \'nīt-ˌshād\ *n* : any of a large genus of herbs, shrubs, and trees that includes poisonous forms (as the belladonna), ornamentals (as the petunias), and important food plants (as the potato and eggplant)

night·shirt \-ˌshərt\ *n* : a nightgown resembling a shirt

night soil *n* : human feces used esp. for fertilizing the soil

night·stick \'nīt-ˌstik\ *n* : a police officer's club

night·time \-ˌtīm\ *n* : the time from dusk to dawn

night·walk·er \-ˌwò-kər\ *n* : a person who roves about at night esp. with criminal or immoral intent

ni·hil·ism \'nī-ə-ˌli-zəm, 'nē-hə-\ *n* **1** : a viewpoint that traditional values and beliefs are unfounded and that existence is senseless and useless **2** : ANARCHISM — **ni·hil·ist** \-list\ *n or adj* — **ni·hil·is·tic** \ˌnī-ə-'lis-tik, ˌnē-hə-\ *adj*

nil \'nil\ *n* : ZERO, NOTHING

nim·ble \'nim-bəl\ *adj* **nim·bler; nim·blest** [ME *nimel*, fr. OE *numol* holding much, fr. *niman* to take] **1** : quick and light in motion : AGILE ⟨a ∼ dancer⟩ **2** : quick in understanding and learning : CLEVER ⟨a ∼ mind⟩ ◆ *Synonyms* ACTIVE, BRISK, SPRIGHTLY, SPRY, ZIPPY — **nim·ble·ness** *n* — **nim·bly** \-blē\ *adv*

nim·bus \'nim-bəs\ *n, pl* **nim·bi** \-ˌbī, -bē\ *or* **nim·bus·es** **1** : a figure (as a disk) in an art work suggesting radiant light about the head of a divinity, saint, or sovereign **2** : a rain cloud; *also* : THUNDERHEAD

NIMBY \'nim-bē\ *n* [not in my backyard] : opposition to the placement of something undesirable (as a prison) in one's neighborhood

nim·rod \'nim-ˌräd\ *n* **1** : HUNTER **2** : IDIOT, JERK

nin·com·poop \'nin-kəm-ˌpüp\ *n* : FOOL, SIMPLETON

nine \'nīn\ *n* **1** : one more than eight **2** : the 9th in a set or series **3** : something having nine units; *esp* : a baseball team — **nine** *adj or pron* — **ninth** \'nīnth\ *adj or adv or n* — **to the nines 1** : to perfection **2** : in an elaborate manner ⟨dressed *to the nines*⟩

nine days' wonder *n* : something that creates a short-lived sensation

nine·pins \'nīn-ˌpinz\ *n* : a bowling game using nine pins arranged usu. in a diamond-shaped configuration

nine·teen \'nīn-'tēn\ *n* : one more than 18 — **nineteen** *adj or pron* — **nine·teenth** \-'tēnth\ *adj or n*
nine·ty \'nīn-tē\ *n, pl* **nineties** : nine times 10 — **nine·tieth** \-tē-əth\ *adj or n* — **ninety** *adj or pron*
nin·ja \'nin-jə, -(ˌ)jä\ *n, pl* **ninja** *or* **ninjas** [Jp] : a person trained in ancient Japanese martial arts and employed esp. for espionage and assassinations
nin·ny \'ni-nē\ *n, pl* **ninnies** : FOOL
ni·o·bi·um \nī-'ō-bē-əm\ *n* : a gray metallic chemical element used in alloys
¹**nip** \'nip\ *vb* **nipped; nip·ping** **1** : to catch hold of and squeeze tightly between two surfaces, edges, or points **2** : ³CLIP **3** : to destroy the growth, progress, or fulfillment of ⟨*nipped* in the bud⟩ **4** : to injure or make numb with cold : CHILL **5** : SNATCH, STEAL
²**nip** *n* **1** : a sharp stinging cold **2** : a biting or pungent flavor **3** : PINCH, BITE **4** : a small portion : BIT
³**nip** *n* : a small quantity of liquor : SIP
⁴**nip** *vb* **nipped; nip·ping** : to take liquor in nips : TIPPLE
nip and tuck *adj or adv* : so close that the lead shifts rapidly from one contestant to another
nip·per \'ni-pər\ *n* **1** : one that nips **2** *pl* : PINCERS **3** : CHILD; *esp* : a small boy
nip·ple \'ni-pəl\ *n* : the protuberance of a mammary gland through which milk is drawn off : TEAT; *also* : something resembling a nipple
nip·py \'ni-pē\ *adj* **nip·pi·er; -est** **1** : PUNGENT, SHARP **2** : CHILLY
nir·va·na \nər-'vä-nə\ *n, often cap* [Skt *nirvāṇa*, lit., act of extinguishing, fr. *nis-* out + *vāti* it blows] **1** : the final freeing of a soul from all that enslaves it; *esp* : the supreme happiness that according to Buddhism comes when all passion, hatred, and delusion die out and the soul is released from the necessity of further purification **2** : OBLIVION; *also* : PARADISE
ni·sei \nē-'sā, 'nē-ˌsā\ *n, pl* **nisei** *often cap* : a son or daughter of immigrant Japanese parents who is born and educated in America
ni·si \'nī-ˌsī\ *adj* [L, unless, fr. *ne-* not + *si* if] : taking effect at a specified time unless previously modified or voided ⟨a divorce decree ∼⟩
nit \'nit\ *n* **1** : the egg of a parasitic insect (as a louse); *also* : the young insect **2** : a minor shortcoming
nite *var of* NIGHT
ni·ter \'nī-tər\ *n* : POTASSIUM NITRATE
nit–pick·ing \'nit-ˌpi-kiŋ\ *n* : minute and usu. unjustified criticism — **nit-pick·er** *n*
¹**ni·trate** \'nī-ˌtrāt, -trət\ *n* **1** : a salt or ester of nitric acid **2** : sodium nitrate or potassium nitrate used as a fertilizer
²**ni·trate** \-ˌtrāt\ *vb* **ni·trat·ed; ni·trat·ing** : to treat or combine with nitric acid or a nitrate — **ni·tra·tion** \nī-'trā-shən\ *n*
ni·tre *chiefly Brit var of* NITER
ni·tric acid \'nī-trik-\ *n* : a corrosive liquid acid used esp. in making dyes, explosives, and fertilizers
ni·tri·fi·ca·tion \ˌnī-trə-fə-'kā-shən\ *n* : the oxidation (as by bacteria) of ammonium salts to nitrites and then to nitrates — **ni·tri·fy·ing** \'nī-trə-fī-iŋ\ *adj*
ni·trite \'nī-ˌtrīt\ *n* : a salt of nitrous acid
ni·tro \'nī-trō\ *n, pl* **nitros** : any of various nitrated products; *esp* : NITROGLYCERIN
ni·tro·gen \'nī-trə-jən\ *n* : a tasteless odorless gaseous chemical element constituting 78 percent of the atmosphere by volume — **ni·trog·e·nous** \nī-'trä-jə-nəs\ *adj*
nitrogen narcosis *n* : a state of euphoria and confusion caused by nitrogen forced into a diver's bloodstream from atmospheric air under pressure
ni·tro·glyc·er·in *or* **ni·tro·glyc·er·ine** \ˌnī-trə-'gli-sə-rən\ *n* : an oily explosive liquid used to make dynamite and in medicine to dilate blood vessels
ni·trous acid \'nī-trəs-\ *n* : an unstable nitrogen-containing acid known only in solution or in the form of its salts
nitrous oxide *n* : a colorless gas used esp. as an anesthetic in dentistry
nit·ty–grit·ty \'ni-tē-ˌgri-tē, ˌni-tē-'gri-tē\ *n* : what is essential and basic : specific practical details
nit·wit \'nit-ˌwit\ *n* : a scatterbrained or stupid person
¹**nix** \'niks\ *n* : NOTHING
²**nix** *vb* : VETO, REJECT
³**nix** *adv* : NO
NJ *abbr* New Jersey

NL *abbr* National League
NLRB *abbr* National Labor Relations Board
NM *abbr* **1** nautical mile **2** New Mexico
N Mex *abbr* New Mexico
NMI *abbr* no middle initial
NNE *abbr* north-northeast
NNW *abbr* north-northwest
¹**no** \'nō\ *adv* **1** — used to express the negative of an alternative ⟨shall we continue or ∼⟩ **2** : in no respect or degree ⟨he is ∼ better than the others⟩ **3** : not so ⟨∼, I'm not ready⟩ **4** — used with an adjective to imply a meaning opposite to the positive statement ⟨in ∼ uncertain terms⟩ **5** — used to introduce a more emphatic or explicit statement ⟨has the right, ∼, the duty to continue⟩ **6** — used as an interjection to express surprise or doubt ⟨∼—you don't say⟩ **7** — used in combination with a verb to form a compound adjective ⟨*no*-bake pie⟩ **8** : in negation ⟨shook his head ∼⟩
²**no** *adj* **1** : not any; *also* : hardly any **2** : not a ⟨she's ∼ expert⟩
³**no** \'nō\ *n, pl* **noes** *or* **nos** \'nōz\ **1** : REFUSAL, DENIAL ⟨got a ∼ in reply⟩ **2** : a negative vote or decision; *also, pl* : persons voting in the negative
⁴**no** *abbr* **1** north; northern **2** [L *numero*, abl. of *numerus*] number
¹**No** *var of* NOH
²**No** *symbol* nobelium
No·bel·ist \nō-'be-list\ *n* : a winner of a Nobel prize
no·bel·i·um \nō-'be-lē-əm\ *n* : a radioactive metallic chemical element produced artificially
Nobel prize \nō-'bel-, 'nō-ˌbel-\ *n* : any of various annual prizes (as in peace, literature, or medicine) established by the will of Alfred Nobel for the encouragement of persons who work for the interests of humanity
no·bil·i·ty \nō-'bi-lə-tē\ *n* **1** : the quality or state of being noble **2** : nobles considered as forming a class
¹**no·ble** \'nō-bəl\ *adj* **no·bler; no·blest** [ME, fr. AF, fr. L *nobilis* well known, noble, fr. *noscere* to come to know] **1** : ILLUSTRIOUS; *also* : FAMOUS, NOTABLE **2** : of high birth, rank, or station : ARISTOCRATIC **3** : EXCELLENT **4** : STATELY, IMPOSING ⟨a ∼ edifice⟩ **5** : of a superior nature ◆ **Synonyms** AUGUST, BARONIAL, GRAND, GRANDIOSE, MAGNIFICENT, MAJESTIC — **no·ble·ness** *n* — **no·bly** \-blē\ *adv*
²**no·ble** *n* : a person of noble rank or birth
noble gas *n* : any of a group of rare gases that include helium, neon, argon, krypton, xenon, and usu. radon and that exhibit great stability and extremely low reaction rates
no·ble·man \'nō-bəl-mən\ *n* : a member of the nobility : PEER
no·blesse oblige \nō-ˌbles-ə-'blēzh\ *n* [F, lit., nobility obligates] : the obligation of honorable, generous, and responsible behavior associated with high rank or birth
no·ble·wom·an \'nō-bəl-ˌwú-mən\ *n* : a woman of noble rank : PEERESS
¹**no·body** \'nō-ˌbä-dē, -bə-\ *pron* : no person
²**nobody** *n, pl* **no·bod·ies** : a person of no influence or importance
no–brain·er \'nō-'brā-nər\ *n* : something that requires a minimum of thought
noc·tur·nal \näk-'tər-n°l\ *adj* **1** : of, relating to, or occurring in the night **2** : active at night ⟨a ∼ bird⟩
noc·turne \'näk-ˌtərn\ *n* : a work of art dealing with night; *esp* : a dreamy pensive composition for the piano
noc·u·ous \'nä-kyə-wəs\ *adj* : HARMFUL — **noc·u·ous·ly** *adv*
nod \'näd\ *vb* **nod·ded; nod·ding** **1** : to bend the head downward or forward (as in bowing, going to sleep, or giving assent) **2** : to move up and down ⟨tulips *nodding* in the breeze⟩ **3** : to show by a nod of the head ⟨∼ agreement⟩ **4** : to make a slip or error in a moment of abstraction — **nod** *n*
nod·dle \'nä-d°l\ *n* : HEAD
nod·dy \'nä-dē\ *n, pl* **noddies** **1** : FOOL **2** : a stout-bodied tropical tern
node \'nōd\ *n* : a thickened, swollen, or differentiated area (as of tissue); *esp* : the part of a stem from which a leaf arises — **nod·al** \-°l\ *adj*
nod·ule \'nä-jül\ *n* : a small lump or swelling — **nod·u·lar** \'nä-jə-lər\ *adj*

no·el \nō-ˈel\ n [F noël Christmas, carol, fr. OF Nael (Deu), Noel Christmas, fr. L natalis birthday] **1** : a Christmas carol **2** cap : the Christmas season

noes pl of NO

no–fault \ˈnō-ˈfȯlt\ adj **1** : of, relating to, or being a motor vehicle insurance plan under which someone involved in an accident is compensated usu. up to a stipulated limit for actual losses by that person's own insurance company regardless of who is responsible **2** : of, relating to, or being a divorce law under which neither party is held responsible for the breakup of the marriage

nog·gin \ˈnä-gən\ n **1** : a small mug or cup; also : a small quantity of drink **2** : a person's head

no–good \ˈnō-ˈgu̇d\ adj : having no worth, virtue, use, or chance of success — **no–good** \ˈnō-ˌgu̇d\ n

Noh also **No** \ˈnō\ n, pl **Noh** also **No** : classic Japanese dance-drama having a heroic theme, a chorus, and highly stylized action, costuming, and scenery

no–hit·ter \(ˌ)nō-ˈhi-tər\ n : a baseball game or part of a game in which a pitcher allows no base hits

no·how \ˈnō-ˌhau̇\ adv : in no manner

¹**noise** \ˈnȯiz\ n [ME, fr. AF, disturbance, noise, fr. L nausea nausea] **1** : loud, confused, or senseless shouting or outcry **2** : SOUND; esp : one that lacks agreeable musical quality or is noticeably unpleasant **3** : unwanted electronic signal or disturbance — **noise·less** adj — **noise·less·ly** adv

²**noise** vb **noised; nois·ing** : to spread by rumor or report ⟨the story was noised abroad⟩

noise·mak·er \ˈnȯiz-ˌmā-kər\ n : one that makes noise; esp : a device used to make noise at parties

noise pollution n : annoying or harmful noise in an environment

noi·some \ˈnȯi-səm\ adj **1** : HARMFUL, UNWHOLESOME **2** : offensive to the senses (as smell) : DISGUSTING ⟨~ habits⟩ ♦ **Synonyms** INSALUBRIOUS, NOXIOUS, SICKLY, UNHEALTHFUL, UNHEALTHY

noisy \ˈnȯi-zē\ adj **nois·i·er; -est** **1** : making loud noises **2** : full of noises : LOUD — **nois·i·ly** \-zə-lē\ adv — **nois·i·ness** \-zē-nəs\ n

nol·le pro·se·qui \ˌnä-lē-ˈprä-sə-ˌkwī\ n [L, to be unwilling to pursue] : an entry on the record of a legal action that the prosecutor or plaintiff will proceed no further in an action or suit or in some aspect of it

no·lo con·ten·de·re \ˌnō-lō-kən-ˈten-də-rē\ n [L, I do not wish to contend] : a plea in a criminal prosecution that subjects the defendant to conviction but does not admit guilt or preclude denying the charges in another proceeding

nol–pros \ˈnäl-ˈpräs\ vb **nol–prossed; nol–pros·sing** : to discontinue by entering a nolle prosequi

nom abbr nominative

no·mad \ˈnō-ˌmad\ n **1** : a member of a people who have no fixed residence but move from place to place **2** : an individual who roams about aimlessly — **nomad** adj — **no·mad·ic** \nō-ˈma-dik\ adj

no–man's–land \ˈnō-ˌmanz-ˌland\ n **1** : an area of unowned, unclaimed, or uninhabited land **2** : an unoccupied area between opposing troops

nom de guerre \ˌnäm-di-ˈger\ n, pl **noms de guerre** \same or ˌnämz-\ [F, lit., war name] : PSEUDONYM

nom de plume \-ˈplüm\ n, pl **noms de plume** \same or ˌnämz-\ [F, pen name; prob. coined in E] : PEN NAME

no·men·cla·ture \ˈnō-mən-ˌklā-chər\ n **1** : NAME, DESIGNATION **2** : a system of terms used in a science or art

nom·i·nal \ˈnä-mə-nᵊl\ adj **1** : being something in name or form only ⟨~ head of a party⟩ **2** : TRIFLING ⟨a ~ price⟩ — **nom·i·nal·ly** adv

nom·i·nate \ˈnä-mə-ˌnāt\ vb **-nat·ed; -nat·ing** : to choose as a candidate for election, appointment, or honor ♦ **Synonyms** APPOINT, DESIGNATE, NAME, TAP — **nom·i·na·tion** \ˌnä-mə-ˈnā-shən\ n

nom·i·na·tive \ˈnä-mə-nə-tiv\ adj : of, relating to, or constituting a grammatical case marking typically the subject of a verb — **nominative** n

nom·i·nee \ˌnä-mə-ˈnē\ n : a person nominated for an office, duty, or position

non- \(ˈ)nän or ˌnän before stressed syllables; ˌnän elsewhere\ prefix **1** : not : reverse of : absence of **2** : having no importance

nonabrasive	noninterference
nonabsorbent	nonintoxicant
nonacademic	nonintoxicating
nonacceptance	noninvasive
nonacid	nonionizing
nonactivated	nonirritating
nonadaptive	nonlegal
nonaddictive	nonlethal
nonadhesive	nonlife
nonadjacent	nonlinear
nonadjustable	nonliterary
nonaggression	nonliving
nonalcoholic	nonlogical
nonappearance	nonmagnetic
nonaromatic	nonmalignant
nonathletic	nonmaterial
nonattendance	nonmember
nonbeliever	nonmembership
nonbelligerent	nonmigratory
nonbreakable	nonmilitary
noncancerous	nonmoral
noncandidate	nonmotile
noncellular	nonmoving
nonclerical	nonnegotiable
noncoital	nonobservance
noncombat	nonoccurrence
noncombative	nonofficial
noncombustible	nonoily
noncommercial	nonorthodox
noncommunist	nonparallel
noncompeting	nonparasitic
noncompetitive	nonparticipant
noncompliance	nonparticipating
noncomplying	nonpathogenic
nonconducting	nonpaying
nonconflicting	nonpayment
nonconformance	nonperformance
nonconforming	nonperishable
nonconstructive	nonphysical
noncontagious	nonpoisonous
noncontinuous	nonpolar
noncorroding	nonpolitical
noncorrosive	nonporous
noncritical	nonpregnant
noncrystalline	nonproductive
nondeductible	nonprofessional
nondelivery	nonprotein
nondemocratic	nonradioactive
nondenominational	nonrandom
nondepartmental	nonreactive
nondestructive	nonreciprocal
nondevelopment	nonrecognition
nondiscrimination	nonrecurrent
nondiscriminatory	nonrecurring
nondistinctive	nonrefillable
nondurable	nonreligious
noneconomic	nonrenewable
noneducational	nonresidential
nonelastic	nonrestricted
nonelection	nonreturnable
nonelective	nonreversible
nonelectric	nonrigid
nonelectrical	nonruminant
nonemotional	nonsalable
nonenforcement	nonscientific
nonethical	nonscientist
non-euclidean	nonseasonal
nonexclusive	nonsectarian
nonexempt	nonsegregated
nonexistence	nonselective
nonexistent	non-self-governing
nonexplosive	nonsexist
nonfarm	nonsexual
nonfatal	nonshrinkable
nonfattening	nonsinkable
nonfederated	nonsmoker
nonferrous	nonsmoking
nonfiction	nonsocial
nonfictional	nonspeaking
nonfilamentous	nonspecialist
nonfilterable	nonspecific
nonflammable	nonsteroidal
nonflowering	nonsuccess
nonfood	nonsurgical
nonfreezing	nontaxable
nonfulfillment	nonteaching
nonfunctional	nontechnical
nongraded	nontemporal
nonhereditary	nontenured
nonhomogeneous	nontheistic
nonhomologous	nonthreatening
nonhuman	nontoxic
nonidentical	nontraditional
nonimportation	nontransferable
nonindustrial	nontypical
noninfectious	nonuniform
noninflammable	nonvascular
nonintellectual	nonvenomous
nonintercourse	nonverbal

nonviable
nonvisual
nonvocal
nonvolatile
nonvoter

nonvoting
nonworker
nonworking
nonzero

non·age \'nä-nij, 'nō-\ *n* **1** : legal minority **2** : a period of youth **3** : IMMATURITY

no·na·ge·nar·i·an \ˌnō-nə-jə-'ner-ē-ən, ˌnä-\ *n* : a person whose age is in the nineties

non·aligned \ˌnän-ə-'līnd\ *adj* : not allied with other nations

no—name \'nō-ˌnām\ *adj* : not having a readily recognizable name ⟨~ brands⟩

non·book \'nän-ˌbŭk\ *n* : a book of little literary merit that is often a compilation (as of pictures or speeches)

¹**nonce** \'näns\ *n* : the one, particular, or present occasion or purpose ⟨for the ~⟩

²**nonce** *adj* : occurring, used, or made only once or for a special occasion ⟨a ~ word⟩

non·cha·lant \ˌnän-shə-'länt\ *adj* [F, fr. OF, fr. prp. of *nonchaloir* to disregard, fr. *non-* not + *chaloir* to concern, fr. L *calēre* to be warm] : giving an effect of unconcern or indifference ✦ **Synonyms** COLLECTED, COMPOSED, COOL, IMPERTURBABLE, UNFLAPPABLE, UNRUFFLED — **non·cha·lance** \-'läns\ *n* — **non·cha·lant·ly** *adv*

non·com \'nän-ˌkäm\ *n* : NONCOMMISSIONED OFFICER

non·com·ba·tant \ˌnän-kəm-'ba-tᵊnt, nän-'käm-bə-tənt\ *n* : a member (as a chaplain) of the armed forces whose duties do not include fighting; *also* : CIVILIAN — **noncombatant** *adj*

non·com·mis·sioned officer \ˌnän-kə-'mi-shənd-\ *n* : a subordinate officer in the armed forces appointed from enlisted personnel

non·com·mit·tal \ˌnän-kə-'mi-tᵊl\ *adj* : indicating neither consent nor dissent ⟨a ~ reply⟩

non com·pos men·tis \ˌnän-ˌkäm-pəs-'men-təs\ *adj* : not of sound mind

non·con·duc·tor \ˌnän-kən-'dək-tər\ *n* : a substance that is a very poor conductor of heat, electricity, or sound

non·con·form·ist \-kən-'fŏr-mist\ *n* **1** *often cap* : a person who does not conform to an established church and esp. the Church of England **2** : a person who does not conform to a generally accepted pattern of thought or action ✦ **Synonyms** DISSENTER, DISSIDENT, HERETIC, SCHISMATIC, SECTARY, SEPARATIST — **non·con·for·mi·ty** \-'fŏr-mə-tē\ *n*

non·co·op·er·a·tion \ˌnän-kō-ˌä-pə-'rā-shən\ *n* : failure or refusal to cooperate; *esp* : refusal through civil disobedience of a people to cooperate with the government of a country

non·cred·it \(ˌ)nän-'kre-dət\ *adj* : not offering credit toward a degree

non·cus·to·di·al \ˌnän-kə-'stō-dē-əl\ *adj* : of or being a parent who does not have legal custody of a child

non·dairy \'nän-'der-ē\ *adj* : containing no milk or milk products

non·de·script \ˌnän-di-'skript\ *adj* **1** : not belonging to any particular class or kind **2** : lacking distinctive qualities ⟨a ~ building⟩

non·drink·er \-'driŋ-kər\ *n* : a person who abstains from alcohol

¹**none** \'nən\ *pron* **1** : not any ⟨~ of them went⟩ **2** : not one ⟨~ of the family⟩ **3** : not any such thing or person ⟨half a loaf is better than ~⟩

²**none** *adj, archaic* : not any : NO

³**none** *adv* : by no means : not at all ⟨he got there ~ too soon⟩

non·en·ti·ty \ˌnän-'en-tə-tē\ *n* **1** : something that does not exist or exists only in the imagination **2** : one of no consequence or significance ✦ **Synonyms** NOBODY, NOTHING, WHIPPERSNAPPER

nones \'nōnz\ *n sing or pl* : the 7th day of March, May, July, or October or the 5th day of any other month in the ancient Roman calendar

non·es·sen·tial \ˌnän-i-'sen-shəl\ *adj* **1** : not essential **2** : being a substance synthesized by the body in sufficient quantity to satisfy dietary needs

none·such \'nən-ˌsəch\ *n* : one without an equal — **nonesuch** *adj*

none·the·less \ˌnən-thə-'les\ *adv* : NEVERTHELESS

non·event \'nän-i-ˌvent\ *n* **1** : an event that fails to take

place or to satisfy expectations **2** : a highly promoted event of little intrinsic interest

non·fat \-'fat\ *adj* : lacking fat solids : having fat solids removed ⟨~ milk⟩

non·gono·coc·cal \ˌnän-ˌgä-nə-'kä-kəl\ *adj* : not caused by a gonococcus

non·he·ro \'nän-'hē-rō\ *n* : ANTIHERO

non—Hodg·kin's lymphoma \'nän-'häj-kənz-\ *n* : any of numerous malignant lymphomas not classified as Hodgkin's disease

non·in·ter·ven·tion \ˌnän-ˌin-tər-'ven-chən\ *n* : refusal or failure to intervene (as in the affairs of other countries)

non·is·sue \'nän-'i-shü\ *n* : an issue of little importance or concern

non·met·al \'nän-'me-tᵊl\ *n* : a chemical element (as carbon) that lacks the characteristics of a metal — **non·me·tal·lic** \ˌnän-mə-'ta-lik\ *adj*

non·neg·a·tive \-'ne-gə-tiv\ *adj* : not negative : being either positive or zero

non·nu·cle·ar \'nän-'nü-klē-ər\ *adj* **1** : not nuclear **2** : not having, using, or involving nuclear weapons

non·ob·jec·tive \ˌnän-əb-'jek-tiv\ *adj* **1** : not objective **2** : representing no natural or actual object, figure, or scene ⟨~ art⟩

¹**non·pa·reil** \-pə-'rel\ *adj* : having no equal : PEERLESS

²**nonpareil** *n* **1** : an individual of unequaled excellence : PARAGON **2** : a small flat disk of chocolate covered with white sugar pellets

non·par·ti·san \'nän-'pär-tə-zən\ *adj* : not partisan; *esp* : not influenced by political party spirit or interests

non·per·son \-'pər-sᵊn\ *n* **1** : UNPERSON **2** : a person having no social or legal status

non·plus \'nän-'pləs\ *vb* -**plussed** *also* -**plused** \-'pləst\; -**plus·sing** *also* -**plus·ing** : PUZZLE, PERPLEX

non·pre·scrip·tion \ˌnän-pri-'skrip-shən\ *adj* : available for sale legally without a doctor's prescription

non·prof·it \'nän-'prä-fət\ *adj* : not conducted or maintained for the purpose of making a profit ⟨a ~ organization⟩

non·pro·lif·er·a·tion \ˌnän-prə-ˌli-fə-'rā-shən\ *adj* : providing for the stoppage of proliferation (as of nuclear arms) ⟨a ~ treaty⟩

non·read·er \'nän-'rē-dər\ *n* : one who does not read or has difficulty reading

non·rep·re·sen·ta·tion·al \ˌnän-ˌre-pri-ˌzen-'tā-shə-nəl\ *adj* : NONOBJECTIVE 2

non·res·i·dent \'nän-'re-zə-dənt\ *adj* : not living in a particular place — **non·res·i·dence** \-dəns\ *n* — **nonresident** *n*

non·re·sis·tance \ˌnän-ri-'zis-təns\ *n* : the principles or practice of passive submission to authority even when unjust or oppressive

non·re·stric·tive \-ri-'strik-tiv\ *adj* **1** : not serving or tending to restrict **2** : not limiting the reference of the word or phrase modified ⟨a ~ clause⟩

non·sched·uled \'nän-'ske-jüld\ *adj* : licensed to carry passengers or freight by air without a regular schedule

non·sense \'nän-ˌsens, -səns\ *n* **1** : foolish or meaningless words or actions **2** : things of no importance or value — **non·sen·si·cal** \nän-'sen-si-kəl\ *adj* — **non·sen·si·cal·ly** \-k(ə-)lē\ *adv*

non se·qui·tur \'nän-'se-kwə-tər\ *n* [L, it does not follow] : an inference that does not follow from the premises

non·skid \'nän-'skid\ *adj* : designed to prevent skidding

non·slip \-'slip\ *adj* : designed to prevent slipping

non·stan·dard \ˌnän-'stan-dərd\ *adj* **1** : not standard **2** : not conforming to the usage characteristic of educated native speakers of a language

non·start·er \'nän-'stär-tər\ *n* **1** : one that does not start **2** : one that is not productive or effective

non·stick \-'stik\ *adj* : allowing easy removal of cooked food particles

¹**non·stop** \-'stäp\ *adj* : done or made without a stop — **nonstop** *adv*

²**nonstop** *n* : a nonstop airplane flight

non·sup·port \ˌnän-sə-'pŏrt\ *n* : failure to support; *esp* : failure on the part of one under obligation to provide maintenance

non·threat·en·ing \-'thret-niŋ, -'thre-tᵊn-iŋ\ *adj* : not likely to cause danger or anxiety ⟨a ~ illness⟩ ⟨a ~ environment⟩

non·U \'nän-'yü\ *adj* : not characteristic of the upper classes

non·union \-'yü-nyən\ *adj* **1** : not belonging to a trade union ⟨∼ carpenters⟩ **2** : not recognizing or favoring trade unions or their members ⟨∼ employers⟩

non·us·er \-'yü-zər\ *n* : one who does not make use of something (as drugs)

non·vi·o·lence \'nän-'vī-ə-ləns\ *n* **1** : abstention from violence as a matter of principle **2** : avoidance of violence **3** : nonviolent political demonstrations — **non·vi·o·lent** \-lənt\ *adj*

non·white \,nän-'hwīt, -'wīt\ *n* : a person whose features and esp. skin color are different from those of peoples of northwestern Europe — **nonwhite** *adj*

non·wo·ven \'nän-'wō-vən\ *adj* : made of fibers held together by interlocking or bonding (as by chemical or thermal means) — **nonwoven** *n*

noo·dle \'nü-dᵊl\ *n* [G *Nudel*] : a food paste made usu. with egg and shaped typically in ribbon form

nook \'núk\ *n* **1** : an interior angle or corner formed usu. by two walls ⟨a chimney ∼⟩ **2** : a sheltered or hidden place ⟨searched every ∼ and cranny⟩ **3** : a usu. recessed section of a larger room ⟨a breakfast ∼⟩

noon \'nün\ *n* : the middle of the day : 12 o'clock in the daytime — **noon** *adj*

noon·day \'nün-,dā\ *n* : NOON, MIDDAY

no one *pron* : NOBODY

noon·tide \'nün-,tīd\ *n* : NOON

noon·time \-,tīm\ *n* : NOON

noose \'nüs\ *n* : a loop with a slipknot that binds closer the more it is drawn

nope \'nōp\ *adv* : NO

nor \'nōr\ *conj* : and not ⟨not for you ∼ for me⟩ — used esp. to introduce and negate the second member and each later member of a series of items preceded by *neither* ⟨neither here ∼ there⟩

Nor·dic \'nōr-dik\ *adj* **1** : of or relating to the Germanic peoples of northern Europe and esp. of Scandinavia **2** : of or relating to competitive ski events involving cross-country skiing, ski jumping, or biathlon — **Nordic** *n*

nor·epi·neph·rine \'nōr-,e-pə-'ne-frən\ *n* : a nitrogen-containing neurotransmitter in parts of the sympathetic and central nervous systems

norm \'nōrm\ *n* [L *norma*, lit., carpenter's square] **1** : an authoritative standard or model; *esp* : a set standard of development or achievement usu. derived from the average or median achievement of a large group ♦ *Synonyms* AVERAGE, MEAN, MEDIAN, PAR

¹nor·mal \'nōr-məl\ *adj* **1** : REGULAR, STANDARD, NATURAL **2** : of average intelligence; *also* : sound in mind and body — **nor·mal·cy** \-sē\ *n* — **nor·mal·i·ty** \nōr-'ma-lə-tē\ *n* — **nor·mal·ly** *adv*

²normal *n* **1** : one that is normal **2** : the usual condition, level, or quantity

nor·mal·ise *Brit var of* NORMALIZE

nor·mal·ize \'nōr-mə-,līz\ *vb* **-ized; -iz·ing** : to make or restore to normal — **nor·mal·i·za·tion** \,nōr-mə-lə-'zā-shən\ *n*

Nor·man \'nōr-mən\ *n* **1** : a native or inhabitant of Normandy **2** : one of the 10th century Scandinavian conquerors of Normandy **3** : one of the Norman-French conquerors of England in 1066 — **Norman** *adj*

nor·ma·tive \'nōr-mə-tiv\ *adj* : of, relating to, or determining norms — **nor·ma·tive·ly** *adv* — **nor·ma·tive·ness** *n*

Norse \'nōrs\ *n, pl* **Norse** **1** : NORWEGIAN; *also* : any of the western Scandinavian dialects or languages **2** *pl* : SCANDINAVIANS; *also* : NORWEGIANS

Norse·man \-mən\ *n* : any of the ancient Scandinavians

¹north \'nōrth\ *adv* : to, toward, or in the north

²north *adj* **1** : situated toward or at the north **2** : coming from the north

³north *n* **1** : the direction to the left of one facing east **2** : the compass point directly opposite to south **3** *cap* : regions or countries north of a specified or implied point — **north·er·ly** \'nōr-thər-lē\ *adv or adj* — **north·ern** \-thərn\ *adj* — **North·ern·er** \-thər-nər\ *n* — **north·ern·most** \-thərn-,mōst\ *adj* — **north·ward** \'nōrth-wərd\ *adv or adj* — **north·wards** \-wərdz\ *adv*

north·east \nòrth-'ēst\ *n* **1** : the general direction be-

tween north and east **2** : the compass point midway between north and east **3** *cap* : regions or countries northeast of a specified or implied point — **northeast** *adj or adv* — **north·east·er·ly** \-'thē-stər-lē\ *adv or adj* — **north·east·ern** \-stərn\ *adj*

north·east·er \-'ēs-tər\ *n* **1** : a strong northeast wind **2** : a storm with northeast winds

north·er \'nòr-thər\ *n* **1** : a strong north wind **2** : a storm with north winds

northern lights *n pl* : AURORA BOREALIS

north pole *n, often cap N&P* : the northernmost point of the earth

North Star *n* : the star toward which the northern end of the earth's axis points

north·west \nòrth-'west\ *n* **1** : the general direction between north and west **2** : the compass point midway between north and west **3** *cap* : regions or countries northwest of a specified or implied point — **northwest** *adj or adv* — **north·west·er·ly** \-'we-stər-lē\ *adv or adj* — **north·west·ern** \-'we-stərn\ *adj*

Norw *abbr* Norway; Norwegian

Nor·we·gian \nòr-'wē-jən\ *n* **1** : a native or inhabitant of Norway **2** : the language of Norway — **Norwegian** *adj*

nos *abbr* numbers

¹nose \'nōz\ *n* **1** : the part of the face or head containing the nostrils and covering the front of the nasal cavity **2** : the sense of smell **3** : something (as a point, edge, or projecting front part) that resembles a nose ⟨the ∼ of a plane⟩ — **nosed** \'nōzd\ *adj* — **on the nose** : on target : ACCURATELY — **under one's nose** : extremely near : in one's presence

²nose *vb* **nosed; nos·ing** **1** : to detect by or as if by smell : SCENT **2** : to push or move with the nose **3** : to touch or rub with the nose : NUZZLE **4** : PRY **5** : to move ahead slowly ⟨the ship *nosed* into her berth⟩

nose·bleed \'nōz-,blēd\ *n* : a bleeding from the nose

nose cone *n* : a protective cone constituting the forward end of an aerospace vehicle

nose·dive \'nōz-,dīv\ *n* **1** : a downward nose-first plunge (as of an airplane) **2** : a sudden extreme drop (as in prices)

nose·gay \'nōz-,gā\ *n* : a small bunch of flowers : POSY

nose out *vb* **1** : to discover often by prying **2** : to defeat by a narrow margin

nose·piece \-,pēs\ *n* **1** : a fitting at the lower end of a microscope tube to which the objectives are attached **2** : the bridge of a pair of eyeglasses

no–show \'nō-'shō\ *n* : a person who does not show up for an event as expected

nos·tal·gia \nä-'stal-jə\ *n* [NL, fr. Gk *nostos* return home + *algos* pain, grief] **1** : HOMESICKNESS **2** : a wistful yearning for something past or irrecoverable — **nos·tal·gic** \-jik\ *adj* — **nos·tal·gist** \-jist\ *n*

nos·tril \'näs-trəl\ *n* [ME *nosethirl*, fr. OE *nosthyrl*, fr. *nosu* nose + *thyrel* hole] **1** : either of the nares usu. with the adjoining nasal wall and passage **2** : either fleshy lateral wall of the nose

nos·trum \'näs-trəm\ *n* [L, neut. of *noster* our, ours, fr. *nos* we] : a questionable medicine or remedy

nosy *or* **nos·ey** \'nō-zē\ *adj* **nos·i·er; -est** : INQUISITIVE, PRYING

not \'nät\ *adv* **1** — used to make negative a group of words or a word ⟨the boys are ∼ here⟩ **2** — used to stand for the negative of a preceding group of words ⟨sometimes hard to see and sometimes ∼⟩

no·ta be·ne \,nō-tə-'be-nē, -'be-\ [L, mark well] — used to call attention to something important

no·ta·bil·i·ty \,nō-tə-'bi-lə-tē\ *n, pl* **-ties** **1** : the quality or state of being notable **2** : NOTABLE

¹no·ta·ble \'nō-tə-bəl\ *adj* **1** : NOTEWORTHY, REMARKABLE ⟨a ∼ achievement⟩ **2** : DISTINGUISHED, PROMINENT ⟨two ∼ politicians made speeches⟩

²notable *n* : a person of note ♦ *Synonyms* BIGWIG, EMINENCE, NABOB, PERSONAGE, SOMEBODY, VIP

no·ta·bly \'nō-tə-blē\ *adv* **1** : in a notable manner **2** : ESPECIALLY, PARTICULARLY

no·tar·i·al \nō-'ter-ē-əl\ *adj* : of, relating to, or done by a notary public

no·ta·rize \'nō-tə-,rīz\ *vb* **-rized; -riz·ing** : to acknowledge or make legally authentic as a notary public

no·ta·ry public \'nō-tə-rē-\ *n, pl* **notaries public** *or* **notary publics** : a public official who attests or certifies writings (as deeds) to make them legally authentic

no·ta·tion \nō-'tā-shən\ *n* **1** : ANNOTATION, NOTE **2** : the act, process, or method of representing data by marks, signs, figures, or characters; *also* : a system of symbols (as letters, numerals, or musical notes) used in such notation

¹**notch** \'näch\ *n* **1** : a V-shaped hollow in an edge or surface **2** : a narrow pass between two mountains

²**notch** *vb* **1** : to cut or make notches in **2** : to score or record by or as if by cutting a series of notches 〈~ed 20 points for the team〉

notch·back \'näch-ˌbak\ *n* : an automobile with a trunk whose lid forms a distinct deck

¹**note** \'nōt\ *vb* **not·ed; not·ing** **1** : to notice or observe with care; *also* : to record or preserve in writing **2** : to make special mention of : REMARK

²**note** *n* **1** : a musical sound **2** : a cry, call, or sound esp. of a bird **3** : a special tone in a person's words or voice 〈a ~ of fear〉 **4** : a character in music used to indicate duration of a tone by its shape and pitch by its position on the staff **5** : a characteristic feature : MOOD, QUALITY 〈a ~ of optimism〉 **6** : MEMORANDUM **7** : a brief and informal record; *also* : a written or printed comment or explanation **8** : a written promise to pay a debt **9** : a piece of paper money **10** : a short informal letter **11** : a formal diplomatic or official communication **12** : DISTINCTION, REPUTATION 〈an artist of ~〉 **13** : OBSERVATION, NOTICE, HEED 〈take ~ of the time〉

note·book \'nōt-ˌbúk\ *n* **1** : a book for notes or memoranda **2** : a portable microcomputer smaller than a laptop computer

not·ed \'nō-təd\ *adj* : well known by reputation : EMINENT, CELEBRATED

note·wor·thy \'nōt-ˌwər-thē\ *adj* : worthy of note : REMARKABLE

¹**noth·ing** \'nə-thiŋ\ *pron* **1** : no thing 〈leaves ~ to the imagination〉 **2** : no part **3** : one of no interest, value, or importance 〈she's ~ to me〉 **4** : a light playful remark 〈sweet ~s〉

²**nothing** *adv* : not at all : in no degree

³**nothing** *n* **1** : something that does not exist **2** : ZERO **3** : a person or thing of little or no value or importance

⁴**nothing** *adj* : of no account : WORTHLESS

noth·ing·ness \'nə-thiŋ-nəs\ *n* **1** : the quality or state of being nothing **2** : NONEXISTENCE; *also* : utter insignificance **3** : something insignificant or valueless

¹**no·tice** \'nō-təs\ *n* **1** : WARNING, ANNOUNCEMENT **2** : notification of the termination of an agreement or contract at a specified time **3** : ATTENTION, HEED 〈bring the matter to my ~〉 **4** : a written or printed announcement **5** : a short critical account or examination (as of a play) : REVIEW

²**notice** *vb* **no·ticed; no·tic·ing** **1** : to make mention of : remark on : NOTE **2** : to take notice of : OBSERVE, MARK

no·tice·able \'nō-tə-sə-bəl\ *adj* **1** : worthy of notice **2** : likely to be noticed — **no·tice·ably** \-blē\ *adv*

no·ti·fy \'nō-tə-ˌfī\ *vb* **-fied; -fy·ing** **1** : to give notice of : report the occurrence of **2** : to give notice to — **no·ti·fi·ca·tion** \ˌnō-tə-fə-'kā-shən\ *n*

no·tion \'nō-shən\ *n* **1** : IDEA, CONCEPTION 〈have a ~ of what he means〉 **2** : a belief held : OPINION, VIEW **3** : WHIM, FANCY 〈a sudden ~ to go〉 **4** *pl* : small useful articles (as pins, needles, or thread)

no·tion·al \'nō-shə-nəl\ *adj* **1** : existing in the mind only : IMAGINARY, UNREAL **2** : given to foolish or fanciful moods or ideas : WHIMSICAL

no·to·ri·ous \nō-'tȯr-ē-əs\ *adj* : generally known and talked of; *esp* : widely and unfavorably known — **no·to·ri·ety** \ˌnō-tə-'rī-ə-tē\ *n* — **no·to·ri·ous·ly** \nō-'tȯr-ē-əs-lē\ *adv*

¹**not·with·stand·ing** \ˌnät-with-'stan-diŋ, -with-\ *prep* : in spite of

²**notwithstanding** *adv* : NEVERTHELESS

³**notwithstanding** *conj* : ALTHOUGH

nou·gat \'nü-gət\ *n* [F, fr. Occitan, fr. Old Occitan, *nogat*, fr. *noga* nut, ultim. fr. L *nuc-, nux*] : a confection of nuts or fruit pieces in a sugar paste

nought *var of* NAUGHT

noun \'naún\ *n* : a word that is the name of a subject of discourse (as a person or place)

nour·ish \'nər-ish\ *vb* : to promote the growth or development of

nour·ish·ing *adj* : giving nourishment

nour·ish·ment \'nər-ish-mənt\ *n* **1** : FOOD, NUTRIENT **2** : the action or process of nourishing

nou·veau riche \ˌnü-ˌvō-'rēsh\ *n, pl* **nou·veaux riches** *same*\ [F] : a person newly rich : PARVENU

Nov *abbr* November

no·va \'nō-və\ *n, pl* **novas** *or* **no·vae** \-(ˌ)vē, -ˌvī\ [NL, fem. of L *novus* new] : a star that suddenly increases greatly in brightness and then within a few months or years grows dim again

¹**nov·el** \'nä-vəl\ *adj* **1** : having no precedent : NEW **2** : STRANGE, UNUSUAL

²**novel** *n* : a long invented prose narrative dealing with human experience through a connected sequence of events — **nov·el·ist** \-və-list\ *n*

nov·el·ette \ˌnä-və-'let\ *n* : a brief novel or long short story

nov·el·ize \'nä-və-ˌlīz\ *vb* **-ized; -iz·ing** : to convert into the form of a novel — **nov·el·i·za·tion** \ˌnä-və-lə-'zā-shən\ *n*

no·vel·la \nō-'ve-lə\ *n, pl* **novellas** *or* **no·vel·le** \-'ve-lē\ : NOVELETTE

nov·el·ty \'nä-vəl-tē\ *n, pl* **-ties** **1** : something new or unusual **2** : NEWNESS **3** : a small manufactured article intended mainly for personal or household adornment — usu. used in pl.

No·vem·ber \nō-'vem-bər\ *n* [ME *Novembre*, fr. AF, fr. L *November* ninth month of the early Roman calendar, fr. *novem* nine] : the 11th month of the year

no·ve·na \nō-'vē-nə\ *n* : a Roman Catholic nine-day period of prayer

nov·ice \'nä-vəs\ *n* **1** : a new member of a religious order who is preparing to take the vows of religion **2** : one who is inexperienced or untrained

no·vi·tiate \nō-'vi-shət\ *n* **1** : the period or state of being a novice **2** : a house where novices are trained **3** : NOVICE

¹**now** \'naú\ *adv* **1** : at the present time or moment **2** : in the time immediately before the present **3** : IMMEDIATELY, FORTHWITH **4** — used with the sense of present time weakened or lost (as to express command, introduce an important point, or indicate a transition) 〈~ hear this〉 **5** : SOMETIMES 〈~ one and ~ another〉 **6** : under the present circumstances **7** : at the time referred to **8** : by this time

²**now** *conj* : in view of the fact 〈~ that you're here, we'll start〉

³**now** *n* : the present time or moment : PRESENT

⁴**now** *adj* **1** : of or relating to the present time 〈the ~ president〉 **2** : excitingly new 〈~ clothes〉; *also* : constantly aware of what is new 〈~ people〉

NOW *abbr* **1** National Organization for Women **2** negotiable order of withdrawal

now·a·days \'naú-ə-ˌdāz\ *adv* : at the present time

no·way \'nō-ˌwā\ *or* **no·ways** \-ˌwāz\ *adv* : NOWISE

no·where \-ˌhwer\ *adv* **1** : not anywhere **2** : not at all — usu. used with *near* 〈~ near enough〉 — **nowhere** *n*

no·wise \'nō-ˌwīz\ *adv* : in no way

nox·ious \'näk-shəs\ *adj* : harmful esp. to health or morals

noz·zle \'nä-zəl\ *n* : a short tube constricted in the middle or at one end and used (as on a hose) to speed up or direct a flow of fluid

np *abbr* **1** no pagination **2** no place (of publication)

Np *symbol* neptunium

NP *abbr* notary public

NR *abbr* not rated

NRA *abbr* National Rifle Association

NS *abbr* **1** not specified **2** Nova Scotia

NSA *abbr* National Security Agency

NSC *abbr* National Security Council

NSF *abbr* **1** National Science Foundation **2** not sufficient funds

NSW *abbr* New South Wales

NT *abbr* **1** New Testament **2** Northern Territory **3** Northwest Territories

nth \'enth\ *adj* **1** : numbered with an unspecified or indefinitely large ordinal number 〈for the ~ time〉 **2** : EXTREME, UTMOST 〈to the ~ degree〉

NTP *abbr* normal temperature and pressure

nt wt *or* **n wt** *abbr* net weight

nu \'nü, 'nyü\ *n* : the 13th letter of the Greek alphabet — N or *v*

NU *abbr* name unknown

nu·ance \'nü-,äns, 'nyü-, nü-'äns, nyü-\ *n* [F] : a shade of difference : a delicate variation (as in tone or meaning)

nub \'nəb\ *n* 1 : KNOB, LUMP 2 : GIST, POINT (the ~ of the story)

nub·bin \'nə-bən\ *n* 1 : something (as an ear of Indian corn) that is small for its kind, stunted, undeveloped, or imperfect 2 : a small projecting bit

nu·bile \'nü-,bīl(-ə)l, 'nyü-, -bəl\ *adj* 1 : of marriageable condition or age 2 : sexually attractive (~ young women)

nu·cle·ar \'nü-klē-ər, 'nyü-\ *adj* 1 : of, relating to, or constituting a nucleus 2 : of, relating to, or using the atomic nucleus or energy derived from it 3 : of, relating to, or being a weapon whose destructive power results from an uncontrolled nuclear reaction

nu·cle·ate \'nü-klē-,āt, 'nyü-\ *vb* -at·ed; -at·ing : to form, act as, or have a nucleus — nu·cle·ation \,nü-klē-'ā-shən, ,nyü-\ *n*

nu·cle·ic acid \nü-'klē-ik-, nyü-, -'klā-\ *n* : any of various complex organic acids (as DNA or RNA) found esp. in cell nuclei

nu·cle·o·tide \'nü-klē-ə-,tīd, 'nyü-\ *n* : any of several compounds that are the basic structural units of nucleic acids

nu·cle·us \'nü-klē-əs, 'nyü-\ *n, pl* nu·clei \-klē-,ī\ *also* nu·cle·us·es [NL, fr. L, kernel, dim. of *nuc-, nux* nut] 1 : a central mass or part about which matter gathers or is collected : CORE 2 : a cell part that is characteristic of all living things except viruses, bacteria, and certain algae, that is necessary for heredity and for making proteins, that contains the chromosomes with their genes, and that is enclosed in a membrane 3 : a mass of gray matter or group of cell bodies of neurons in the central nervous system 4 : the central part of an atom that comprises nearly all of the atomic mass 5 : a basic or essential part

¹nude \'nüd, 'nyüd\ *adj* nud·er; nud·est 1 : BARE, NAKED, UNCLOTHED 2 : featuring or catering to naked people (a ~ beach) — nu·di·ty \'nü-də-tē, 'nyü-\ *n*

²nude *n* 1 : a nude human figure esp. as depicted in art 2 : the condition of being nude (in the ~)

nudge \'nəj\ *vb* nudged; nudg·ing : to touch or push gently (as with the elbow) usu. in order to seek attention — nudge *n*

nud·ism \'nü-,di-zəm, 'nyü-\ *n* : the practice of going nude esp. in mixed groups at specially secluded places — nud·ist \-dist\ *n*

nu·ga·to·ry \'nü-gə-,tòr-ē\ *adj* 1 : INCONSEQUENTIAL, WORTHLESS 2 : having no force : INEFFECTUAL

nug·get \'nə-gət\ *n* 1 : a lump of precious metal (as gold) 2 : TIDBIT

nui·sance \'nü-s°ns, 'nyü-\ *n* : an annoying or troublesome person or thing

nuisance tax *n* : an excise tax collected in small amounts directly from the consumer

¹nuke \'nük, 'nyük\ *n* 1 : a nuclear weapon 2 : a nuclear power plant

²nuke *vb* nuked; nuk·ing 1 : to attack with nuclear weapons 2 : MICROWAVE

null \'nəl\ *adj* 1 : having no legal or binding force : INVALID, VOID 2 : amounting to nothing 3 : INSIGNIFICANT — nul·li·ty \'nə-lə-tē\ *n*

null and void *adj* : having no force, binding power, or validity

nul·li·fy \'nə-lə-,fī\ *vb* -fied; -fy·ing : to make null or valueless; *also* : ANNUL — nul·li·fi·ca·tion \,nə-lə-fə-'kā-shən\ *n*

num *abbr* numeral

Num *abbr* Numbers

numb \'nəm\ *adj* : lacking sensation or emotion : BENUMBED — numb *vb* — numb·ly *adv* — numb·ness *n*

¹num·ber \'nəm-bər\ *n* 1 : the total of individuals or units taken together 2 : an indefinite total (a small ~ of tickets remain unsold) 3 : an ascertainable total (the sands of the desert are without ~) 4 : a distinction of word form to denote reference to one or more than one 5 : a unit belonging to a mathematical system and subject to its laws; *also, pl* : ARITHMETIC 6 : a symbol used to represent a mathematical number; *also* : such a number used to identify or designate (a phone ~) 7 : one in a

series of musical or theatrical performances 8 : an act of transforming or impairing (tripped and did a ~ on her knee)

²number *vb* 1 : COUNT, ENUMERATE 2 : to include with or be one of a group 3 : to restrict to a small or definite number 4 : to assign a number to 5 : to comprise in number : TOTAL

num·ber·less \-ləs\ *adj* : INNUMERABLE, COUNTLESS

Numbers *n* — see BIBLE table

numb·ing \'nə-miŋ\ *adj* : tending to make numb (a ~ lecture) (a ~ realization)

numbskull *var of* NUMSKULL

nu·mer·a·cy \'nü-mə-rə-sē, 'nyü-\ *n* : the capacity for quantitative thought or expression

nu·mer·al \'nü-mə-rəl, 'nyü-\ *n* : a conventional symbol representing a number — numeral *adj*

nu·mer·ate \'nü-mə-,rāt, 'nyü-\ *vb* -at·ed; -at·ing : ENUMERATE

nu·mer·a·tor \-,rā-tər\ *n* : the part of a fraction above the line

nu·mer·ic \nü-'mer-ik, nyü-\ *adj* : NUMERICAL; *esp* : denoting a number or a system of numbers

nu·mer·i·cal \-'mer-i-kəl\ *adj* 1 : of or relating to numbers 2 : expressed in or involving numbers — nu·mer·i·cal·ly \-k(ə-)lē\ *adv*

nu·mer·ol·o·gy \,nü-mə-'rä-lə-jē, ,nyü-\ *n* : the study of the occult significance of numbers — nu·mer·ol·o·gist \-jist\ *n*

nu·mer·ous \'nü-mə-rəs, 'nyü-\ *adj* : consisting of, including, or relating to a great number : MANY

nu·mis·mat·ics \,nü-məz-'ma-tiks, ,nyü-\ *n* : the study of collection of monetary objects — nu·mis·mat·ic \-tik\ *adj* — nu·mis·ma·tist \nü-'miz-mə-tist, nyü-\ *n*

num·skull *also* numb·skull \'nəm-,skəl\ *n* : a stupid person : DUNCE

nun \'nən\ *n* : a woman belonging to a religious order; *esp* : one under solemn vows of poverty, chastity, and obedience

nun·cio \'nən-sē-,ō, 'nùn-\ *n, pl* -ci·os [It, fr. L *nuntius* messenger] : a permanent high-ranking papal representative to a civil government

nun·nery \'nə-nə-rē\ *n, pl* -ner·ies : a convent of nuns

¹nup·tial \'nəp-shəl\ *adj* : of or relating to marriage or a wedding

²nuptial *n* : MARRIAGE, WEDDING — usu. used in pl.

¹nurse \'nərs\ *n* [ME *norice, nurse,* fr. AF *nurice,* fr. LL *nutricia,* fr. L, fem. of *nutricius* nourishing] 1 : a girl or woman employed to take care of children 2 : a person trained to care for sick people

²nurse *vb* nursed; nurs·ing 1 : SUCKLE 2 : to take charge of and watch over 3 : TEND (~ an invalid) 4 : to treat with special care (~ a headache) 5 : to hold in one's mind or consideration (~ a grudge) 6 : to act or serve as a nurse

nurse·maid \'nərs-,mād\ *n* : NURSE 1

nurse-prac·ti·tion·er \-prak-'ti-shə-nər\ *n* : a registered nurse who is qualified to assume some of the duties formerly assumed only by a physician

nurs·ery \'nər-s(ə-)rē\ *n, pl* -er·ies 1 : a room for children 2 : a place where children are temporarily cared for in their parents' absence 3 : a place where young plants are grown usu. for transplanting

nurs·ery·man \-mən\ *n* : a man who keeps or works in a plant nursery

nursery school *n* : a school for children under kindergarten age

nursing home *n* : a private establishment providing care for persons (as the aged or the chronically ill) who are unable to care for themselves

nurs·ling \'nərs-liŋ\ *n* 1 : one that is solicitously cared for 2 : a nursing child

¹nur·ture \'nər-chər\ *n* 1 : TRAINING, UPBRINGING; *also* : the influences that modify the expression of an individual's heredity 2 : FOOD, NOURISHMENT

²nurture *vb* nur·tured; nur·tur·ing 1 : to care for : FEED, NOURISH 2 : EDUCATE, TRAIN 3 : FOSTER

nut \'nət\ *n* 1 : a dry fruit or seed with a hard shell and a firm inner kernel; *also* : its kernel 2 : a metal block with a hole through it that is fastened to a bolt or screw by means of a screw thread within the hole 3 : the ridge on the upper end of the fingerboard in a stringed musical in-

NUMBER TABLE

CARDINAL NUMBERS[1]

NAME[2]	SYMBOL Arabic	Roman[3]
zero *or* naught *or* cipher	0	
one	1	I
two	2	II
three	3	III
four	4	IV
five	5	V
six	6	VI
seven	7	VII
eight	8	VIII
nine	9	IX
ten	10	X
eleven	11	XI
twelve	12	XII
thirteen	13	XIII
fourteen	14	XIV
fifteen	15	XV
sixteen	16	XVI
seventeen	17	XVII
eighteen	18	XVIII
nineteen	19	XIX
twenty	20	XX
twenty-one	21	XXI
twenty-two	22	XXII
twenty-three	23	XXIII
twenty-four	24	XXIV
twenty-five	25	XXV
twenty-six	26	XVI
twenty-seven	27	XVII
twenty-eight	28	XVIII
twenty-nine	29	XXIX
thirty	30	XXX
thirty-one	31	XXXI
thirty-two *etc*	32	XXXII
forty	40	XL
forty-one	41	XLI
forty-two *etc*	42	XLII
fifty	50	L
sixty	60	LX
seventy	70	LXX
eighty	80	LXXX
ninety	90	XC
one hundred	100	C
one hundred and one	101	CI
one hundred and two *etc*	102	CII
two hundred	200	CC
three hundred	300	CCC
four hundred	400	CD
five hundred	500	D
six hundred	600	DC
seven hundred	700	DCC
eight hundred	800	DCCC
nine hundred	900	CM
one thousand	1,000	M
two thousand *etc*	2,000	MM
five thousand	5,000	$\bar{\text{V}}$
ten thousand	10,000	$\bar{\text{X}}$
one hundred thousand	100,000	$\bar{\text{C}}$
one million	1,000,000	$\bar{\text{M}}$

ORDINAL NUMBERS[4]

NAME[5]	SYMBOL[6]
first	1st
second	2d *or* 2nd
third	3d *or* 3rd
fourth	4th
fifth	5th
sixth	6th
seventh	7th
eighth	8th
ninth	9th
tenth	10th
eleventh	11th
twelfth	12th
thirteenth	13th
fourteenth	14th
fifteenth	15th
sixteenth	16th
seventeenth	17th
eighteenth	18th
nineteenth	19th
twentieth	20th
twenty-first	21st
twenty-second	22d *or* 22nd
twenty-third	23d *or* 23rd
twenty-fourth	24th
twenty-fifth	25th
twenty-sixth	26th
twenty-seventh	27th
twenty-eighth	28th
twenty-ninth	29th
thirtieth	30th
thirty-first	31st
thirty-second *etc*	32d *or* 32nd
fortieth	40th
forty-first	41st
forty-second *etc*	42d *or* 42nd
fifty	50th
sixty	60th
seventieth	70th
eightieth	80th
ninetieth	90th
one hundredth	100th
one hundred and first	101st
one hundred and second *etc*	102d *or* 102nd
two hundredth	200th
three hundredth	300th
four hundredth	400th
five hundredth	500th
six hundredth	600th
seven hundredth	700th
eight hundredth	800th
nine hundredth	900th
one thousandth	1,000th
two thousandth *etc*	2,000th
five thousandth	5,000th
ten thousandth	10,000th
hundred thousandth *or* one hundred thousandth	100,000th
millionth *or* one millionth	1,000,000th

[1] The cardinal numbers are used in simple counting or in answer to "how many?" The words for these numbers may be used as nouns (he counted to *twelve*), as pronouns (*twelve* were found), or as adjectives (*twelve* girls).

[2] In formal contexts the numbers one to one hundred and in less formal contexts the numbers one to nine are commonly written out in words, while larger numbers are given in numerals. In nearly all contexts a number occurring at the beginning of a sentence is usually written out. Except in very formal contexts numerals are invariably used for dates. Arabic numbers from 1,000 to 9,999 are often written without commas or spaces (1000, 9999). Year numbers are always written without commas (1783).

[3] The Roman numerals are written either in capitals or in lowercase letters.

[4] The ordinal numbers are used to show the order of succession in which such items as names, objects, and periods of time are considered (the *twelfth* month; the *fourth* row of seats; the *18th* century).

[5] Each of the terms for the ordinal numbers excepting *first* and *second* is used in designating one of a number of parts into which a whole may be divided (a *fourth*; a *sixth*; a *tenth*) and as the denominator in fractions designating the number of such parts constituting a certain portion of a whole *one fourth*; *three fifths*). When used as nouns the fractions are usually written as two words, although they are regularly hyphenated as adjectives (a *two-thirds* majority). When fractions are written in numerals, the cardinal symbols are used ($\frac{1}{4}$, $\frac{3}{5}$, $\frac{5}{6}$).

[6] The Arabic symbols for the cardinal numbers may be read as ordinals in certain contexts (January 1 = January first; 2 Samuel = Second Samuel). The Roman numerals are sometimes read as ordinals (Henry IV = Henry the Fourth); sometimes they are written with the ordinal suffixes (XIXth Dynasty).

strument over which the strings pass 4 : a foolish, eccentric, or crazy person 5 : ENTHUSIAST
nut·crack·er \'nət-ˌkra-kər\ n : an instrument for cracking
nuts
nut·hatch \-ˌhach\ n : any of various small tree-climbing
chiefly insect-eating birds

nuthatch

nut·meg \-ˌmeg, -ˌmäg\ n [ME notemuge, ultim. fr. Old Occitan noz muscada, lit., musky nut] : a spice made by
grinding the nutlike aromatic seed of a tropical tree; also
: the seed or tree
nu·tria \'nü-trē-ə, 'nyü-\ n [Sp] 1 : the durable usu. light
brown fur of a nutria 2 : a large So. American aquatic
rodent with webbed hind feet
¹nu·tri·ent \'nü-trē-ənt, 'nyü-\ adj : NOURISHING
²nutrient n : a nutritive substance or ingredient
nu·tri·ment \-trə-mənt\ n : NUTRIENT
nu·tri·tion \nu̇-'tri-shən, nyu̇-\ n : the act or process of
nourishing; esp : the processes by which an individual
takes in and utilizes food material — nu·tri·tion·al \-shə-
nəl\ adj — nu·tri·tion·al·ly adv — nu·tri·tion·ist \-shə-
nist\ n — nu·tri·tive \'nü-trə-tiv, 'nyü-\ adj
nu·tri·tious \-shəs\ adj : NOURISHING — nu·tri·tious·ly
adv
nuts \'nəts\ adj 1 : ENTHUSIASTIC, KEEN 2 : CRAZY, DE-
MENTED
nut·shell \'nət-ˌshel\ n : the shell of a nut — in a nutshell
: in a few words ⟨that's the story in a nutshell⟩
nut·ty \'nə-tē\ adj nut·ti·er; -est 1 : containing or suggesting nuts ⟨a ~ flavor⟩ 2 : mentally unbalanced
nuz·zle \'nə-zəl\ vb nuz·zled; nuz·zling 1 : to root
around, push, or touch with or as if with the nose 2
: NESTLE, SNUGGLE
NV abbr Nevada
NW abbr northwest
NWT abbr Northwest Territories
NY abbr New York
NYC abbr New York City
ny·lon \'nī-ˌlän\ n 1 : any of numerous strong tough elastic synthetic materials used esp. in textiles and plastics 2
pl : stockings made of nylon
nymph \'nimf\ n 1 : any of the lesser goddesses in ancient
mythology represented as maidens living in the mountains, forests, meadows, and waters 2 : GIRL 3 : an immature insect resembling the adult but smaller, less differentiated, and usu. lacking developed wings
nym·pho·ma·nia \ˌnim-fə-'mā-nē-ə, -nyə\ n : excessive
sexual desire by a female — nym·pho·ma·ni·ac \-nē-ˌak\
n or adj
NZ abbr New Zealand

¹o \'ō\ n, pl o's or os \'ōz\ often cap 1 : the 15th letter of
the English alphabet 2 : ZERO
²o abbr, often cap 1 ocean 2 Ohio 3 ohm
¹O var of OH
²O symbol oxygen
o/a abbr on or about
oaf \'ōf\ n : a stupid or awkward person — oaf·ish adj
oak \'ōk\ n, pl oaks or oak : any of a genus of trees or
shrubs related to the beech and chestnut and bearing a
rounded thin-shelled nut surrounded at the base by a
hardened cup; also : the usu. tough hard durable wood of
an oak — oak·en \'ō-kən\ adj
oa·kum \'ō-kəm\ n [ME okum, fr. OE ācumba flax fiber,
from a- out + -cumba (akin to OE camb comb)] : loosely
twisted hemp or jute fiber impregnated with tar and used
esp. in caulking ships
oar \'ȯr\ n : a long pole with a broad blade at one end used
for propelling or steering a boat
oar·lock \'ȯr-ˌläk\ n : a U-shaped device for holding an oar
in place
oars·man \'ȯrz-mən\ n : one who rows esp. in a racing
crew
OAS abbr Organization of American States
oa·sis \ō-'ā-səs\ n, pl oa·ses \-ˌsēz\ : a fertile or green area
in an arid region
oat \'ōt\ n : a cereal grass widely grown for its edible seed;
also : this seed — oat·en \'ō-tᵊn\ adj
oat·cake \'ōt-ˌkāk\ n : a thin flat oatmeal cake
oath \'ōth\ n, pl oaths \'ōthz, 'ōths\ 1 : a solemn appeal
to God to witness to the truth of a statement or the sacredness of a promise 2 : an irreverent or careless use of
a sacred name
oat·meal \'ōt-ˌmēl\ n 1 : ground or rolled oats 2 : porridge made from ground or rolled oats
Ob or Obad abbr Obadiah
Oba·di·ah \ˌō-bə-'dī-ə\ n — see BIBLE table
ob·bli·ga·to \ˌä-blə-'gä-tō\ n, pl -tos also -ti \-'gä-tē\ [It]
: an accompanying part usu. played by a solo instrument

ob·du·rate \'äb-də-rət, -dyə-\ adj : stubbornly resistant
: UNYIELDING ♦ Synonyms INFLEXIBLE, ADAMANT,
RIGID, UNCOMPROMISING — ob·du·ra·cy \-rə-sē\ n
obe·di·ent \ō-'bē-dē-ənt\ adj : submissive to the restraint
or command of authority ♦ Synonyms DOCILE,
TRACTABLE, AMENABLE, BIDDABLE — obe·di·ence
\-əns\ n — obe·di·ent·ly adv
obei·sance \ō-'bē-səns, -'bā-\ n 1 : a bow made to show
respect or submission 2 : DEFERENCE, HOMAGE ⟨makes
~ to her mentors⟩
obe·lisk \'ä-bə-ˌlisk\ n [MF obelisque, fr. L obeliscus, fr.
Gk obeliskos, fr. dim. of obelos spit, pointed pillar] : a
4-sided pillar that tapers toward the top and ends in a
pyramid
obese \ō-'bēs\ adj [L obesus, fr. ob- against + esus, pp. of
edere to eat] : having excessive body fat ♦ Synonyms
CORPULENT, FLESHY, GROSS, OVERWEIGHT, PORTLY,
STOUT — obe·si·ty \-'bē-sə-tē\ n
obey \ō-'bā\ vb obeyed; obey·ing 1 : to follow the commands or guidance of : behave obediently 2 : to comply
with ⟨~ orders⟩ ♦ Synonyms CONFORM, KEEP, MIND,
OBSERVE
ob·fus·cate \'äb-fə-ˌskāt\ vb -cat·ed; -cat·ing 1 : to make
dark or obscure 2 : CONFUSE — ob·fus·ca·tion \ˌäb-fəs-
'kā-shən\ n
OB–GYN abbr obstetrician gynecologist; obstetrics gynecology
obi \'ō-bē\ n [Jp] : a broad sash worn esp. with a Japanese
kimono
obit \ō-'bit, 'ō-bət\ n : OBITUARY
obi·ter dic·tum \ˌō-bə-tər-'dik-təm\ n, pl obiter dic·ta \-tə\
[LL, lit., something said in passing] : an incidental remark
or observation
obit·u·ary \ə-'bi-chə-ˌwer-ē\ n, pl -ar·ies : a notice of a
person's death usu. with a short biographical account
obj abbr object; objective
¹ob·ject \'äb-jikt\ n 1 : something that may be seen or felt;
also : something that may be perceived or examined men-

tally **2** : something that arouses an emotional response (as of affection or pity) **3** : AIM, PURPOSE ⟨the ∼ is to raise money⟩ **4** : a word or word group denoting that on or toward which the action of a verb is directed; *also* : a noun or noun equivalent in a prepositional phrase

²ob·ject \əb-'jekt\ *vb* **1** : to offer in opposition **2** : to oppose something; *also* : DISAPPROVE ✦ **Synonyms** PROTEST, REMONSTRATE, EXPOSTULATE — **ob·jec·tor** \-'jek-tər\ *n*

object code *n* : a computer program after translation from source code

ob·jec·ti·fy \əb-'jek-tə-ˌfī\ *vb* **-fied; -fy·ing** : to make objective

ob·jec·tion \əb-'jek-shən\ *n* **1** : the act of objecting **2** : a reason for or a feeling of disapproval

ob·jec·tion·able \əb-'jek-shə-nə-bəl\ *adj* : UNDESIRABLE, OFFENSIVE — **ob·jec·tion·ably** \-blē\ *adv*

¹ob·jec·tive \əb-'jek-tiv\ *adj* **1** : of or relating to an object or end **2** : existing outside and independent of the mind **3** : of, relating to, or constituting a grammatical case marking typically the object of a verb or preposition **4** : treating or dealing with facts without distortion by personal feelings or prejudices — **ob·jec·tive·ly** *adv* — **ob·jec·tive·ness** *n* — **ob·jec·tiv·i·ty** \ˌäb-jek-'ti-və-tē\ *n*

²objective *n* **1** : the lens (as in a microscope) nearest the object and forming an image of it **2** : an aim, goal, or end of action

ob·jet d'art \ˌȯb-ˌzhä-'där\ *n, pl* **ob·jets d'art** *same*\ [F] **1** : an article of artistic worth **2** : CURIO ✦ **Synonyms** KNICKKNACK, BAUBLE, BIBELOT, GEWGAW, NOVELTY, TRINKET

ob·jet trou·vé \ˌȯb-ˌzhä-trü-'vä\ *n, pl* **objets trouvés** *same*\ [F, lit., found object] : a found natural or discarded object (as a piece of driftwood or an old bathtub) held to have aesthetic value

ob·jur·ga·tion \ˌäb-jər-'gā-shən\ *n* : a harsh rebuke — **ob·jur·gate** \'äb-jər-ˌgāt\ *vb*

obl *abbr* **1** oblique **2** oblong

ob·late \ä-'blāt\ *adj* : flattened or depressed at the poles ⟨an ∼ spheroid⟩

ob·la·tion \ə-'blā-shən\ *n* : a religious offering

ob·li·gate \'ä-blə-ˌgāt\ *vb* **-gat·ed; -gat·ing** : to bind legally or morally

ob·li·ga·tion \ˌä-blə-'gā-shən\ *n* **1** : an act of obligating oneself to a course of action **2** : something (as a promise or a contract) that binds one to a course of action **3** : INDEBTEDNESS; *also* : LIABILITY **4** : DUTY — **oblig·a·to·ry** \ə-'bli-gə-ˌtȯr-ē\ *adj*

oblige \ə-'blīj\ *vb* **obliged; oblig·ing** [ME, fr. AF *obliger*, fr. L *obligare*, lit., to bind to, fr. *ob-* toward + *ligare* to bind] **1** : FORCE, COMPEL ⟨the soldiers were *obliged* to retreat⟩ **2** : to bind by a favor; *also* : to do a favor for or do something as a favor

oblig·ing *adj* : willing to do favors — **oblig·ing·ly** *adv*

oblique \ō-'blēk\ *adj* **1** : neither perpendicular nor parallel : SLANTING **2** : not straightforward : INDIRECT — **oblique·ly** *adv* — **oblique·ness** *n* — **obliq·ui·ty** \-'bli-kwə-tē\ *n*

oblique case *n* : a grammatical case other than the nominative or vocative

oblit·er·ate \ə-'bli-tə-ˌrāt\ *vb* **-at·ed; -at·ing** [L *oblitterare*, fr. *ob* in the way of + *littera* letter] **1** : to remove from recognition or memory **2** : to make undecipherable by wiping out or covering over **3** : CANCEL — **oblit·er·a·tion** \-ˌbli-tə-'rā-shən\ *n*

obliv·i·on \ə-'bli-vē-ən\ *n* **1** : the condition of being oblivious **2** : the condition or state of being forgotten

obliv·i·ous \ə-'bli-ve-əs\ *adj* **1** : lacking memory or mindful attention **2** : UNAWARE ⟨∼ of the risks⟩ — **obliv·i·ous·ly** *adv* — **obliv·i·ous·ness** *n*

ob·long \'ä-ˌblȯŋ\ *adj* : deviating from a square, circular, or spherical form by elongation in one dimension — **oblong** *n*

ob·lo·quy \'ä-blə-kwē\ *n, pl* **-quies** **1** : strongly condemnatory utterance or language **2** : bad repute : DISGRACE ✦ **Synonyms** DISHONOR, SHAME, INFAMY, DISREPUTE, IGNOMINY

ob·nox·ious \äb-'näk-shəs\ *adj* : REPUGNANT, OFFENSIVE — **ob·nox·ious·ly** *adv* — **ob·nox·ious·ness** *n*

oboe \'ō-bō\ *n* [It, fr. F *hautbois*, fr. *haut* high + *bois* wood] : a woodwind instrument with a slender conical tube and a double reed mouthpiece — **obo·ist** \'ō-ˌbō-ist\ *n*

ob·scene \äb-'sēn\ *adj* **1** : REPULSIVE **2** : deeply offensive to morality or decency; *esp* : designed to incite to lust or depravity ✦ **Synonyms** GROSS, VULGAR, COARSE, CRUDE, INDECENT — **ob·scene·ly** *adv* — **ob·scen·i·ty** \-'se-nə-tē\ *n*

ob·scu·ran·tism \äb-'skyùr-ən-ˌti-zəm, ˌäb-skyù-'ran-\ *n* **1** : opposition to the spread of **2** : deliberate vagueness or abstruseness — **ob·scu·ran·tist** \-tist\ *n or adj*

¹ob·scure \äb-'skyùr\ *adj* **1** : DIM, GLOOMY **2** : not readily understood : VAGUE **3** : REMOTE; *also* : HUMBLE ✦ **Synonyms** DARK, DUSKY, MURKY, TENEBROUS — **ob·scure·ly** *adv* — **ob·scu·ri·ty** \-'skyùr-ə-tē\ *n*

²obscure *vb* **ob·scured; ob·scur·ing** **1** : to make dark, dim, or indistinct **2** : to conceal or hide by or as if by covering

ob·se·qui·ous \əb-'sē-kwē-əs\ *adj* : humbly or excessively attentive (as to a person in authority) : FAWNING, SYCOPHANTIC ✦ **Synonyms** MENIAL, SERVILE, SLAVISH, SUBSERVIENT — **ob·se·qui·ous·ly** *adv* — **ob·se·qui·ous·ness** *n*

ob·se·quy \'äb-sə-kwē\ *n, pl* **-quies** : a funeral or burial rite — usu. used in pl.

ob·serv·able \əb-'zər-və-bəl\ *adj* **1** : NOTEWORTHY **2** : capable of being observed — **ob·serv·abil·i·ty** \-'bi-lə-tē\ *n*

ob·ser·vance \əb-'zər-vəns\ *n* **1** : a customary practice or ceremony **2** : an act or instance of following a custom, rule, or law **3** : OBSERVATION

ob·ser·vant \-vənt\ *adj* **1** : WATCHFUL ⟨∼ spectators⟩ **2** : KEEN, PERCEPTIVE **3** : MINDFUL ⟨∼ of the amenities⟩

¹ob·ser·va·tion \ˌäb-sər-'vä-shən, -zər-\ *n* **1** : an act or instance of observing **2** : the gathering of information (as for scientific studies) by noting facts or occurrences **3** : a conclusion drawn from observing; *also* : REMARK, STATEMENT **4** : the fact of being observed — **ob·ser·va·tion·al** \-shə-nəl\ *adj*

²observation *adj* : designed for use in viewing or in making observations

ob·ser·va·to·ry \əb-'zər-və-ˌtȯr-ē\ *n, pl* **-ries** : a place or institution equipped for observation of natural phenomena (as in astronomy)

ob·serve \əb-'zərv\ *vb* **ob·served; ob·serv·ing** **1** : to conform one's action or practice to **2** : CELEBRATE **3** : to make a scientific observation of **4** : to see or sense esp. through careful attention **5** : to come to realize esp. through consideration of noted facts **6** : REMARK — **ob·serv·er** *n*

ob·sess \əb-'ses\ *vb* : to preoccupy intensely or abnormally

ob·ses·sion \äb-'se-shən\ *n* : a persistent disturbing preoccupation with an idea or feeling; *also* : an emotion or idea causing such a preoccupation — **ob·ses·sive** \-'se-siv\ *adj or n* — **ob·ses·sive·ly** *adv*

obsessive–compulsive *adj* : relating to, characterized by, or affected with recurring obsessions and compulsions esp. as symptoms of a neurotic state

ob·sid·i·an \əb-'si-dē-ən\ *n* : a dark natural glass formed by the cooling of molten lava

ob·so·les·cent \ˌäb-sə-'le-sᵊnt\ *adj* : going out of use : becoming obsolete — **ob·so·les·cence** \-sᵊns\ *n*

ob·so·lete \ˌäb-sə-'lēt, 'äb-sə-ˌlēt\ *adj* : no longer in use; *also* : OLD-FASHIONED ⟨an ∼ technology⟩ ✦ **Synonyms** EXTINCT, OUTWORN, PASSÉ, SUPERSEDED

ob·sta·cle \'äb-sti-kəl\ *n* : something that stands in the way or opposes

ob·stet·rics \əb-'ste-triks\ *n sing or pl* : a branch of medicine that deals with birth and with its antecedents and sequels — **ob·stet·ric** \-trik\ *or* **ob·stet·ri·cal** \-tri-kəl\ *adj* — **ob·ste·tri·cian** \ˌäb-stə-'tri-shən\ *n*

ob·sti·nate \'äb-stə-nət\ *adj* : fixed and unyielding (as in an opinion or course) despite reason or persuasion : STUBBORN — **ob·sti·na·cy** \-nə-sē\ *n* — **ob·sti·nate·ly** *adv*

ob·strep·er·ous \äb-'stre-pə-rəs\ *adj* **1** : uncontrollably noisy **2** : stubbornly resistant to control : UNRULY — **ob·strep·er·ous·ness** *n*

ob·struct \əb-'strəkt\ *vb* **1** : to block by an obstacle **2** : to impede the passage, action, or operation of **3** : to cut off from sight — **ob·struc·tive** \-'strək-tiv\ *adj* — **ob·struc·tor** \-tər\ *n*

ob·struc·tion \əb-'strək-shən\ *n* **1** : an act of obstructing : the state of being obstructed **2** : something that obstructs : HINDRANCE

ob·struc·tion·ist \-shə-nist\ *n* : a person who hinders progress or business esp. in a legislative body — **ob·struc·tion·ism** \-shə-,ni-zəm\ *n*

ob·tain \əb-'tān\ *vb* **1** : to gain or attain usu. by planning or effort **2** : to be generally recognized or established ◆ **Synonyms** PROCURE, SECURE, WIN, EARN, ACQUIRE — **ob·tain·able** *adj*

ob·trude \əb-'trüd\ *vb* **ob·trud·ed; ob·trud·ing** **1** : to thrust out **2** : to thrust forward without warrant or request **3** : INTRUDE — **ob·tru·sion** \-'trü-zhən\ *n* — **ob·tru·sive** \-'trü-siv\ *adj* — **ob·tru·sive·ly** *adv* — **ob·tru·sive·ness** *n*

ob·tuse \äb-'tüs, -'tyüs\ *adj* **ob·tus·er; -est** **1** : exceeding 90 degrees but less than 180 degrees ⟨∼ angle⟩ **2** : not pointed or acute : BLUNT **3** : not sharp or quick of wit — **ob·tuse·ly** *adv* — **ob·tuse·ness** *n*

obv *abbr* obverse

¹ob·verse \äb-'vərs, 'äb-,vərs\ *adj* **1** : facing the observer or opponent **2** : being a counterpart or complement — **ob·verse·ly** *adv*

²ob·verse \'äb-,vərs, äb-'vərs\ *n* **1** : the side (as of a coin) bearing the principal design and lettering **2** : a front or principal surface **3** : a counterpart having the opposite orientation or force

ob·vi·ate \'äb-vē-,āt\ *vb* **-at·ed; -at·ing** : to anticipate and prevent (as a situation) or make unnecessary (as an action) ◆ **Synonyms** PREVENT, AVERT, FORESTALL, FORFEND, PRECLUDE — **ob·vi·a·tion** \,äb-vē-'ā-shən\ *n*

ob·vi·ous \'äb-vē-əs\ *adj* [L *obvius,* fr. *obviam* in the way, fr. *ob-* in the way of + *viam,* acc. of *via* way] : easily found, seen, or understood : PLAIN ◆ **Synonyms** EVIDENT, MANIFEST, PATENT, CLEAR — **ob·vi·ous·ly** *adv* — **ob·vi·ous·ness** *n*

OC *abbr* officer candidate

oc·a·ri·na \,ä-kə-'rē-nə\ *n* [It] : a wind instrument typically having an oval body with finger holes and a projecting mouthpiece

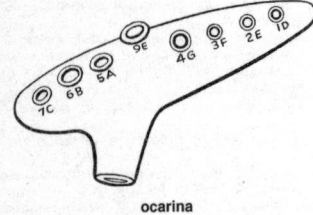

ocarina

occas *abbr* occasionally

¹oc·ca·sion \ə-'kā-zhən\ *n* **1** : a favorable opportunity **2** : a direct or indirect cause **3** : the time of an event **4** : EXIGENCY **5** *pl* : AFFAIRS, BUSINESS **6** : a special event : CELEBRATION

²occasion *vb* : BRING ABOUT, CAUSE

oc·ca·sion·al \ə-'kā-zhə-nəl\ *adj* **1** : happening or met with now and then ⟨∼ visits⟩ **2** : used or designed for a special occasion ⟨∼ verse⟩ ◆ **Synonyms** INFREQUENT, RARE, SPORADIC — **oc·ca·sion·al·ly** *adv*

oc·ci·den·tal \,äk-sə-'den-tʳl\ *adj, often cap* [fr. *Occident* West, fr. ME, fr. AF, fr. L *occident-, occidens,* fr. prp. of *occidere* to fall, set (of the sun)] : WESTERN — **Occidental** *n*

Oc·ci·tan \'äk-sə-,tan\ *n* [F, fr. ML *occitanus,* fr. Old Occitan *oc* yes (contrasted with OF *oil* yes)] : a Romance language spoken in southern France

oc·clude \ə-'klüd\ *vb* **oc·clud·ed; oc·clud·ing** **1** : OBSTRUCT ⟨an *occluded* artery⟩ **2** : to come together with opposing surfaces in contact — used of teeth — **oc·clu·sion** \-'klü-zhən\ *n* — **oc·clu·sive** \-'klü-siv\ *adj*

¹oc·cult \ə-'kəlt\ *adj* **1** : not revealed : SECRET **2** : ABSTRUSE, MYSTERIOUS **3** : of or relating to supernatural agencies, their effects, or knowledge of them — **oc·cult·ism** \-'kəl-,ti-zəm\ *n* — **oc·cult·ist** \-tist\ *n*

²occult *n* : occult matters — used with *the*

oc·cu·pan·cy \'ä-kyə-pən-sē\ *n, pl* **-cies** **1** : the act of occupying : the state of being occupied **2** : an occupied building or part of a building

oc·cu·pant \-pənt\ *n* : one who occupies something; *esp* : RESIDENT

oc·cu·pa·tion \,ä-kyə-'pā-shən\ *n* **1** : an activity in which one engages; *esp* : VOCATION **2** : the taking possession of property; *also* : the taking possession of an area by a foreign military force — **oc·cu·pa·tion·al** \-shə-nəl\ *adj* — **oc·cu·pa·tion·al·ly** *adv*

occupational therapy *n* : therapy by means of activity; *esp* : creative activity prescribed for its effect in promoting recovery or rehabilitation — **occupational therapist** *n*

oc·cu·py \'ä-kyə-,pī\ *vb* **-pied; -py·ing** **1** : to engage the attention or energies of **2** : to fill up (an extent in space or time) **3** : to take or hold possession of **4** : to reside in as owner or tenant — **oc·cu·pi·er** *n*

oc·cur \ə-'kər\ *vb* **-curred; -cur·ring** [L *occurrere,* fr. *ob-* in the way + *currere* to run] **1** : to be found or met with : APPEAR **2** : HAPPEN **3** : to come to mind

oc·cur·rence \ə-'kər-əns\ *n* **1** : something that takes place **2** : the action or process of occurring

ocean \'ō-shən\ *n* **1** : the whole body of salt water that covers nearly three fourths of the surface of the earth **2** : any of the large bodies of water into which the great ocean is divided — **oce·an·ic** \,ō-shē-'a-nik\ *adj*

ocean·ar·i·um \,ō-shə-'nar-ē-əm\ *n, pl* **-iums** *or* **-ia** \-ē-ə\ : a large marine aquarium

ocean·front \'ō-shən-,frənt\ *n* : a shore area on the ocean

ocean·go·ing \-,gō-iŋ\ *adj* : of, relating to, or suitable for travel on the ocean

ocean·og·ra·phy \,ō-shə-'nä-grə-fē\ *n* : a science dealing with the ocean and its phenomena — **ocean·og·ra·pher** \-fər\ *n* — **ocean·o·graph·ic** \-nə-'gra-fik\ *adj*

oce·lot \'ä-sə-,lät, 'ō-\ *n* : a medium-sized American wildcat ranging southward from Texas to northern Argentina and having a tawny yellow or gray coat with black markings

ocher *or* **ochre** \'ō-kər\ *n* : an earthy usu. red or yellow iron ore used as a pigment; *also* : the color esp. of yellow ocher

o'·clock \ə-'kläk\ *adv* : according to the clock

OCR *abbr* optical character reader; optical character recognition

OCS *abbr* officer candidate school

oct *abbr* octavo

Oct *abbr* October

oc·ta·gon \'äk-tə-,gän\ *n* : a polygon of eight angles and eight sides — **oc·tag·o·nal** \äk-'ta-gən-ʳl\ *adj*

oc·tane \'äk-,tān\ *n* : OCTANE NUMBER

octane number *n* : a number used to measure the antiknock properties of gasoline that increases as the likelihood of knocking decreases

oc·tave \'äk-tiv\ *n* **1** : a musical interval embracing eight degrees; *also* : a tone or note at this interval or the whole series of notes, tones, or keys within this interval **2** : a group of eight

oc·ta·vo \äk-'tā-vō, -'tä-\ *n, pl* **-vos** **1** : the size of a piece of paper cut eight from a sheet **2** : a book printed on octavo pages

oc·tet \äk-'tet\ *n* **1** : a musical composition for eight voices or eight instruments; *also* : the performers of such a composition **2** : a group or set of eight

Oc·to·ber \äk-'tō-bər\ *n* [ME *Octobre,* fr. OE *October,* fr. L, eighth month of the early Roman calendar, fr. *octo* eight] : the 10th month of the year

oc·to·ge·nar·i·an \,äk-tə-jə-'ner-ē-ən\ *n* : a person whose age is in the eighties

oc·to·pus \'äk-tə-pəs\ *n, pl* **-pus·es** *or* **-pi** \-,pī\ : any of various sea mollusks with eight long muscular arms furnished with suckers

oc·to·syl·lab·ic \,äk-tə-sə-'la-bik\ *adj* : composed of verses having eight syllables — **octosyllabic** *n*

¹oc·u·lar \'ä-kyə-lər\ *adj* **1** : VISUAL **2** : of or relating to the eye or the eyesight

²ocular *n* : EYEPIECE

oc·u·list \'ä-kyə-list\ *n* **1** : OPHTHALMOLOGIST **2** : OPTOMETRIST

¹OD \'ō-'dē\ *n* : an overdose of a drug and esp. a narcotic

²OD *vb* **OD'd** *or* **ODed; OD'ing; OD's** : to become ill or die from an OD

³OD *abbr* **1** doctor of optometry **2** [L *oculus dexter*] right eye **3** officer of the day **4** olive drab **5** overdraft **6** overdrawn

odd \'äd\ *adj* [ME *odde*, fr. ON *oddi* point of land, triangle, odd number] **1** : being only one of a pair or set ⟨an ∼ shoe⟩ **2** : somewhat more than the number mentioned ⟨forty ∼ years ago⟩ **3** : being an integer (as 1, 3, or 5) not divisible by two without leaving a remainder **4** : additional to what is usual ⟨∼ jobs⟩ **5** : STRANGE ⟨an ∼ way of behaving⟩ — **odd·ness** *n*

odd·ball \'äd-₁bôl\ *n* : one that is eccentric — **oddball** *adj*

odd·i·ty \'ä-də-tē\ *n*, *pl* **-ties** **1** : one that is odd **2** : the quality or state of being odd

odd·ly \'äd-lē\ *adv* **1** : in an odd manner **2** : as is odd

odd·ment \'äd-mənt\ *n* : something left over : REMNANT

odds \'ädz\ *n pl* **1** : a difference by which one thing is favored over another **2** : DISAGREEMENT — usu. used with *at* **3** : the ratio between the amount to be paid for a winning bet and the amount of the bet ⟨the horse went off at ∼ of 6–1⟩

odds and ends *n pl* : miscellaneous things or matters

odds–on \'ädz-'ôn, -'än\ *adj* : having a better than even chance to win

ode \'ōd\ *n* : a lyric poem that expresses a noble feeling with dignity

odi·ous \'ō-dē-əs\ *adj* : arousing or deserving hatred or repugnance — **odi·ous·ly** *adv* — **odi·ous·ness** *n*

odi·um \'ō-dē-əm\ *n* **1** : merited loathing : HATRED **2** : DISGRACE

odom·e·ter \ō-'dä-mə-tər\ *n* [F *odomètre*, fr. Gk *hodometron*, fr. *hodos* way, road + *metron* measure] : an instrument for measuring distance traveled (as by a vehicle)

odor \'ō-dər\ *n* **1** : the quality of something that stimulates the sense of smell; *also* : a sensation resulting from such stimulation **2** : REPUTE, ESTIMATION — **odored** \'ō-dərd\ *adj* — **odor·less** *adj* — **odor·ous** *adj*

odor·if·er·ous \₁ō-də-'ri-fə-rəs \ *adj* : having or yielding an odor

odour *chiefly Brit var of* ODOR

od·ys·sey \'ä-də-sē\ *n*, *pl* **-seys** [the *Odyssey*, epic poem attributed to Homer recounting the long wanderings of Odysseus] : a long wandering marked usu. by many changes of fortune

oe·cu·men·i·cal *esp Brit* ₁ē-\ *chiefly Brit var of* ECUMENICAL

OED *abbr* Oxford English Dictionary

oe·de·ma *chiefly Brit var of* EDEMA

oe·di·pal \'e-də-pəl, 'ē-\ *adj, often cap* : of, relating to, or resulting from the Oedipus complex

Oe·di·pus complex \-pəs-\ *n* : the positive sexual feelings of a child toward the parent of the opposite sex and hostile or jealous feelings toward the parent of the same sex that may be a source of adult personality disorder when unresolved

OEO *abbr* Office of Economic Opportunity

o'er \'ôr\ *adv or prep* : OVER

OES *abbr* Order of the Eastern Star

oe·soph·a·gus *chiefly Brit var of* ESOPHAGUS

oeu·vre \'ər-vrə, 'œvr³\ *n*, *pl* **oeuvres** *same*\ : a substantial body of work constituting the lifework of a writer, an artist, or a composer

of \'əv, 'äv\ *prep* **1** : FROM ⟨a man ∼ the West⟩ **2** : having as a significant physical or character element ⟨a man ∼ noble birth⟩ ⟨a woman ∼ ability⟩ **3** : owing to ⟨died ∼ flu⟩ **4** : BY ⟨the plays ∼ Shakespeare⟩ **5** : having as component parts or material, contents, or members ⟨a house ∼ brick⟩ ⟨a glass ∼ water⟩ ⟨a pack ∼ fools⟩ **6** : belonging to or included by ⟨the front ∼ the house⟩ ⟨a time ∼ life⟩ ⟨one ∼ you⟩ ⟨the best ∼ its kind⟩ ⟨the son ∼ a doctor⟩ **7** : ABOUT ⟨tales ∼ the West⟩ **8** : connected with : OVER ⟨the queen ∼ England⟩ **9** : that is : signified as ⟨the city ∼ Rome⟩ **10** — used to indicate apposition of the words it joins ⟨that fool ∼ a husband⟩ **11** : as concerns : FOR ⟨love ∼ nature⟩ **12** — used to indicate the application of an adjective ⟨fond ∼ candy⟩ **13** : BEFORE ⟨quarter ∼ ten⟩

OF *abbr* outfield

¹off \'ôf\ *adv* **1** : from a place or position ⟨drove ∼ in a new car⟩; *also* : ASIDE ⟨turned ∼ into a side road⟩ **2** : at a distance in time or space ⟨stood ∼ a few yards⟩ ⟨several years ∼⟩ **3** : so as to be unattached or removed ⟨the lid blew ∼⟩ **4** : to a state of discontinuance, exhaustion, or completion ⟨shut the radio ∼⟩ **5** : away from regular work ⟨took time ∼ for lunch⟩

²off *prep* **1** : away from ⟨just ∼ the highway⟩ ⟨take it ∼ the table⟩ **2** : to seaward of ⟨two miles ∼ the coast⟩ **3** : FROM ⟨borrowed a dollar ∼ me⟩ **4** : at the expense of ⟨lives ∼ his parents⟩ **5** : not now engaged in ⟨∼ duty⟩ **6** : abstaining from ⟨∼ liquor⟩ **7** : below the usual level of ⟨∼ his game⟩

³off *adj* **1** : more removed or distant **2** : started on the way **3** : not operating **4** : not correct **5** : REMOTE, SLIGHT ⟨an ∼ chance⟩ **6** : INFERIOR ⟨∼ grade of oil⟩ **7** : provided for ⟨well ∼⟩

⁴off *abbr* office; officer; official

of·fal \'ô-fəl\ *n* [ME, fr. *of* off + *fall* fall] : the waste or by-product of a process; *esp* : the viscera and trimmings of a butchered animal removed in dressing

off and on *adv* : INTERMITTENTLY ⟨rained *off and on*⟩

¹off·beat \'ôf-₁bēt\ *n* : the unaccented part of a musical measure

²offbeat *adj* : ECCENTRIC, UNCONVENTIONAL ⟨an ∼ style⟩

off–col·or \'ôf-'kə-lər\ *or* **off–col·ored** \-lərd\ *adj* **1** : not having the right or standard color **2** : of doubtful propriety : verging on indecency ⟨∼ stories⟩

of·fend \ə-'fend\ *vb* **1** : SIN, TRANSGRESS **2** : to cause discomfort or pain : HURT **3** : to cause dislike or vexation : ANNOY ♦ **Synonyms** AFFRONT, INSULT, OUTRAGE — **of·fend·er** *n*

of·fense *or* **of·fence** \ə-'fens, *esp for 2 & 3* 'ä-₁fens\ *n* **1** : something that outrages the senses **2** : ATTACK, ASSAULT **3** : the offensive team or members of a team playing offensive positions **4** : DISPLEASURE **5** : SIN, MISDEED **6** : an infraction of law : CRIME

¹of·fen·sive \ə-'fen-siv *esp for 1 & 2* 'ä-₁fen-\ *adj* **1** : AGGRESSIVE **2** : of or relating to an attempt to score in a game; *also* : of or relating to a team in possession of the ball or puck **3** : OBNOXIOUS ⟨an ∼ odor⟩ **4** : INSULTING ⟨∼ remarks⟩ — **of·fen·sive·ly** *adv* — **of·fen·sive·ness** *n*

²offensive *n* : ATTACK

¹of·fer \'ô-fər\ *vb* **of·fered; of·fer·ing** **1** : SACRIFICE **2** : to present for acceptance : TENDER; *also* : to propose as payment **3** : PROPOSE, SUGGEST; *also* : to declare one's readiness **4** : to try or begin to exert ⟨∼ resistance⟩ **5** : to place on sale — **of·fer·ing** *n*

²offer *n* **1** : PROPOSAL **2** : BID **3** : TRY

of·fer·to·ry \'ô-fər-₁tôr-ē\ *n*, *pl* **-ries** : the presentation of offerings at a church service; *also* : the musical accompaniment during it

off–gas·sing \'ôf-₁ga-siŋ\ *n* : the emission of esp. noxious gases (as from a building material)

off–hand \'ôf-'hand\ *adv or adj* : without previous thought or preparation

off–hour \-₁aü(-ə)r\ *n* : a period of time other than a rush hour; *also* : a period of time other than business hours

of·fice \'ô-fəs\ *n* **1** : a special duty or position; *esp* : a position of authority in government ⟨run for ∼⟩ **2** : a prescribed form or service of worship; *also* : RITE **3** : an assigned or assumed duty or role **4** : a place where a business is transacted or a service is supplied

of·fice·hold·er \'ô-fəs-₁hōl-dər\ *n* : one holding a public office

of·fi·cer \'ô-fə-sər\ *n* **1** : one charged with the enforcement of law **2** : one who holds an office of trust or authority **3** : a person who holds a position of authority or command in the armed forces; *esp* : COMMISSIONED OFFICER

¹of·fi·cial \ə-'fi-shəl\ *n* : OFFICER 2

²official *adj* **1** : of or relating to an office or to officers **2** : AUTHORIZED, AUTHORITATIVE ⟨∼ statement⟩ **3** : befitting or characteristic of a person in office — **of·fi·cial·ly** *adv*

of·fi·cial·dom \ə-'fi-shəl-dəm\ *n* : officials as a class

of·fi·cial·ism \ə-'fi-shə-₁li-zəm\ *n* : lack of flexibility and initiative combined with excessive adherence to regulations

of·fi·ci·ant \ə-'fi-shē-ənt\ *n* : one (as a priest) who officiates at a religious rite

of·fi·ci·ate \ə-'fi-shē-₁āt\ *vb* **-at·ed; -at·ing** **1** : to perform a ceremony, function, or duty **2** : to act in an official capacity

of·fi·cious \ə-'fi-shəs\ *adj* : volunteering one's services where they are neither asked for nor needed — **of·fi·cious·ly** *adv* — **of·fi·cious·ness** *n*

off·ing \'ȯ-fiŋ\ *n* : the near or foreseeable future

off–line \'ȯf-'līn\ *adj or adv* : not connected to or controlled directly by a computer

off of *prep* : OFF

off·print \'ȯf-ˌprint\ *n* : a separately printed excerpt (as from a magazine)

off–road \-'rōd\ *adj* : of, relating to, or being a vehicle designed for use away from public roads — **off–road·er** \-'rō-dər\ *n*

off–sea·son \-ˌsē-z³n\ *n* : a time of suspended or reduced activity

¹**off·set** \-ˌset\ *n* **1** : a sharp bend (as in a pipe) by which one part is turned aside out of line **2** : a printing process in which an inked impression is first made on a rubber= blanketed cylinder and then transferred to the paper

²**off·set** *vb* **off·set; off·set·ting 1** : to place over against : BALANCE **2** : to compensate for **3** : to form an offset in (∼ a wall)

off·shoot \'ȯf-ˌshüt\ *n* **1** : a collateral or derived branch, descendant, or member **2** : a branch of a main stem (as of a plant)

¹**off·shore** \'ȯf-'shȯr\ *adv* **1** : at a distance from the shore **2** : outside the country : ABROAD

²**off·shore** \'ȯf-ˌshȯr\ *adj* **1** : moving away from the shore **2** : situated off the shore but within waters under a country's control

off·side \-'sīd\ *adv or adj* : illegally in advance of the ball or puck

off·spring \-ˌspriŋ\ *n, pl* **offspring** *also* **offsprings** : PROGENY, YOUNG

off·stage \'ȯf-'stāj, -ˌstāj\ *adv or adj* **1** : off or away from the stage **2** : out of the public view ⟨deals made ∼⟩

off–the–record *adj* : given or made in confidence and not for publication

off–the–shelf *adj* : available as a stock item : not specially designed or made

off–the–wall *adj* : highly unusual : BIZARRE

off·track \'ȯf-'trak\ *adv or adj* : away from a racetrack

off–white \'ȯf-'hwīt\ *n* : a yellowish or grayish white color

off year *n* **1** : a year in which no major election is held **2** : a year of diminished activity or production

oft \'ȯft\ *adv* : OFTEN

of·ten \'ȯ-fən\ *adv* : many times : FREQUENTLY

of·ten·times \-ˌtīmz\ *or* **oft·times** \'ȯf-ˌtīmz, 'ȯft-\ *adv* : OFTEN

ogle \'ō-gəl\ *vb* **ogled; ogling** : to look at in a flirtatious way — **ogle** *n* — **ogler** *n*

ogre \'ō-gər\ *n* **1** : a monster of fairy tales and folklore that eats people **2** : a dreaded person or object

ogress \'ō-grəs\ *n* : a female ogre

oh *also* **O** \'ō\ *interj* **1** — used to express an emotion or in response to physical stimuli **2** — used in direct address

OH *abbr* Ohio

ohm \'ōm\ *n* : a unit of electrical resistance equal to the resistance of a circuit in which a potential difference of one volt produces a current of one ampere — **ohm·ic** \'ō-mik\ *adj*

ohm·me·ter \'ōm-ˌmē-tər\ *n* : an instrument for indicating resistance in ohms directly

¹**oil** \'ȯi(-ə)l\ *n* [ME *oile*, fr. AF, fr. L *oleum* olive oil, fr. Gk *elaion*, fr. *elaia* olive] **1** : any of numerous fatty or greasy liquid substances obtained from plants, animals, or minerals and used for fuel, food, medicines, and manufacturing **2** : PETROLEUM **3** : artists' colors made with oil; *also* : a painting in such colors — **oil·i·ness** \'ȯi-lē-nəs\ *n* — **oily** \'ȯi-lē\ *adj*

²**oil** *vb* : to put oil in or on — **oil·er** *n*

oil·cloth \'ȯi(-ə)l-ˌklȯth\ *n* : cloth treated with oil or paint and used for table and shelf coverings

oil pan *n* : the lower section of a crankcase used as an oil reservoir

oil shale *n* : a rock (as shale) from which oil can be recovered

oil·skin \'ȯi(-ə)l-ˌskin\ *n* **1** : an oiled waterproof cloth **2** : an oilskin raincoat **3** *pl* : an oilskin coat and pants

oink \'ȯiŋk\ *n* : the natural noise of a hog — **oink** *vb*

oint·ment \'ȯint-mənt\ *n* : a salve for use on the skin

OJ *abbr* orange juice

Ojib·wa *or* **Ojib·way** *or* **Ojibwe** \ō-'jib-ˌwä\ *n, pl* **Ojibwa** *or* **Ojibwas** *or* **Ojibway** *or* **Ojibways** *or* **Ojibwe** *or* **Ojibwes 1** : a member of an American Indian people of the region around Lake Superior and westward **2** : the Algonquian language of the Ojibwa people

OJT *abbr* on-the-job training

¹**OK** *or* **okay** \ō-'kā\ *adv or adj* : all right

²**OK** *or* **okay** *vb* **OK'd** *or* **okayed; OK'·ing** *or* **okay·ing** : APPROVE, AUTHORIZE — **OK** *or* **okay** *n*

³**OK** *abbr* Oklahoma

Okla *abbr* Oklahoma

okra \'ō-krə\ *n* : a tall annual plant related to the mallows that has edible green pods; *also* : these pods

¹**old** \'ōld\ *adj* **1** : ANCIENT; *also* : of long standing **2** *cap* : belonging to an early period ⟨*Old* Irish⟩ **3** : having existed for a specified period of time **4** : of or relating to a past era **5** : advanced in years **6** : showing the effects of age or use **7** : no longer in use — **old·ish** \'ōl-dish\ *adj*

²**old** *n* : old or earlier time ⟨days of ∼⟩

old·en \'ōl-dən\ *adj* : of or relating to a bygone era

¹**old–fash·ioned** \'ōld-'fa-shənd\ *adj* **1** : OUT-OF-DATE, ANTIQUATED **2** : CONSERVATIVE

²**old–fashioned** *n* : a cocktail usu. made with whiskey, bitters, sugar, a twist of lemon peel, and water or soda water

old–growth \'ōld-'grōth\ *adj* : of, relating to, or being a forest with large old trees, numerous snags and woody debris, and a multilayered canopy

old guard *n, often cap O&G* : the conservative members of an organization

old hat *adj* **1** : OLD-FASHIONED **2** : STALE, TRITE

old·ie \'ōl-dē\ *n* : something old; *esp* : a popular song from the past

old–line \'ōld-'līn\ *adj* **1** : ORIGINAL, ESTABLISHED ⟨an ∼ business⟩ **2** : adhering to old policies or practices

old maid *n* **1** : SPINSTER **2** : a prim fussy person — **old–maid·ish** \'ōld-'mā-dish\ *adj*

old man *n* **1** : HUSBAND **2** : FATHER

old–school *adj* : adhering to traditional policies or practices

old·ster \'ōld-stər\ *n* : an old or elderly person

Old Testament *n* : the first of the two chief divisions of the Christian Bible — see BIBLE table

old–time \'ōld-'tīm\ *adj* **1** : of, relating to, or characteristic of an earlier period **2** : of long standing

old–tim·er \-'tī-mər\ *n* : VETERAN; *also* : OLDSTER

old–world \-'wərld\ *adj* : having old-fashioned charm

ole·ag·i·nous \ˌō-lē-'a-jə-nəs\ *adj* : OILY

ole·an·der \'ō-lē-ˌan-dər\ *n* : a poisonous evergreen shrub often grown for its fragrant white to red flowers

oleo \'ō-lē-ˌō\ *n, pl* **ole·os** : MARGARINE

oleo·mar·ga·rine \ˌō-lē-ō-'mär-jə-rən\ *n* : MARGARINE

ol·fac·to·ry \äl-'fak-tə-rē, ōl-\ *adj* : of or relating to the sense of smell

oli·gar·chy \'ä-lə-ˌgär-kē, 'ō-\ *n, pl* **-chies 1** : a government in which power is in the hands of a few **2** : a state having an oligarchy; *also* : the group holding power in such a state — **oli·garch** \-ˌgärk\ *n* — **oli·gar·chic** \ˌä-lə-'gär-kik, ˌō-\ *or* **oli·gar·chi·cal** \-ki-kəl\ *adj*

Oli·go·cene \'ä-li-gə-ˌsēn, ə-'li-gə-ˌsēn\ *adj* : of, relating to, or being the epoch of the Tertiary between the Eocene and the Miocene — **Oligocene** *n*

olio \'ō-lē-ˌō\ *n, pl* **oli·os** : HODGEPODGE, MEDLEY

ol·ive \'ä-liv\ *n* **1** : an Old World evergreen tree grown in warm regions for its fruit that is a food and the source of an edible oil (**olive oil**) **2** : a dull yellowish green color

olive drab *n* **1** : a grayish olive color **2** : an olive drab wool or cotton fabric; *also* : a uniform of this fabric

ol·iv·ine \'ä-lə-ˌvēn\ *n* : a usu. greenish mineral that is a complex silicate of magnesium and iron

Olym·pic Games \ō-'lim-pik-\ *n pl* : a modified revival of an ancient Greek festival consisting of international athletic contests that are held at separate winter and summer gatherings at four-year intervals

om \'ōm\ *n* : a mantra consisting of the sound "om" used in contemplating ultimate reality

Oma·ha \'ō-mə-ˌhä, -ˌhȯ\ *n, pl* **-ha** *or* **-has** : a member of an American Indian people of northeastern Nebraska

om·buds·man \'äm-ˌbudz-mən, äm-'budz-\ *n, pl* **-men** \-mən\ **1** : a government official appointed to investigate

complaints made by individuals against abuses or capricious acts of public officials **2** : one that investigates reported complaints (as from students or consumers)
ome·ga \ō-'mā-gə\ *n* : the 24th and last letter of the Greek alphabet — Ω or ω
om·elet *or* **om·elette** \'äm-lət, 'ä-mə-\ *n* [F *omelette*, alter. of MF *amelette, alemette*, alter. of *alemelle* thin plate, ultim. fr. L *lamella*, dim. of *lamina*] : eggs beaten with milk or water, cooked without stirring until set, and folded over
omen \'ō-mən\ *n* : an event or phenomenon believed to be a sign or warning of a future occurrence
om·i·cron \'ä-mə-ˌkrän, 'ō-\ *n* : the 15th letter of the Greek alphabet — O or ο
om·i·nous \'ä-mə-nəs\ *adj* : foretelling evil : THREATENING — **om·i·nous·ly** *adv* — **om·i·nous·ness** *n*
omis·si·ble \ō-'mi-sə-bəl\ *adj* : that may be omitted
omis·sion \ō-'mi-shən\ *n* **1** : something neglected or left undone **2** : the act of omitting : the state of being omitted
omit \ō-'mit\ *vb* **omit·ted; omit·ting** **1** : to leave out or leave unmentioned **2** : to leave undone : FAIL
¹om·ni·bus \'äm-ni-(ˌ)bəs\ *n* : BUS
²omnibus *adj* : of, relating to, or providing for many things at once ⟨an ~ bill⟩
om·nip·o·tent \äm-'ni-pə-tənt\ *adj* **1** *often cap* : ALMIGHTY 1 **2** : having unlimited authority or influence — **om·nip·o·tence** \-əns\ *n* — **om·nip·o·tent·ly** *adv*
om·ni·pres·ent \ˌäm-ni-'pre-zᵊnt\ *adj* : present in all places at all times — **om·ni·pres·ence** \-zᵊns\ *n*
om·ni·scient \äm-'ni-shənt\ *adj* : having infinite awareness, understanding, and insight — **om·ni·science** \-shəns\ *n* — **om·ni·scient·ly** *adv*
om·ni·um–gath·er·um \ˌäm-nē-əm-'ga-thə-rəm\ *n, pl* **omnium–gatherums** : a miscellaneous collection
om·niv·o·rous \äm-'ni-və-rəs\ *adj* **1** : feeding on both animal and vegetable substances **2** : AVID ⟨an ~ reader⟩ — **om·ni·vore** \'äm-ni-ˌvȯr\ *n* — **om·niv·o·rous·ly** *adv*
¹on \'ȯn, 'än\ *prep* **1** : in or to a position over and in contact with ⟨jumped ~ his horse⟩ **2** : touching the surface of ⟨shadows ~ the wall⟩ **3** : AT, TO ⟨~ the right were the mountains⟩ **4** : IN, ABOARD ⟨went ~ the train⟩ **5** : during or at the time of ⟨came ~ Monday⟩ ⟨every hour ~ the hour⟩ **6** : through the agency of ⟨was cut ~ a tin can⟩ **7** : in a state or process of ⟨~ fire⟩ ⟨~ the wane⟩ **8** : connected with as a member or participant ⟨~ a committee⟩ ⟨~ tour⟩ **9** — used to indicate a basis, source, or standard of computation ⟨has it ~ good authority⟩ ⟨10 cents ~ the dollar⟩ **10** : with regard to ⟨a monopoly ~ wheat⟩ **11** : at or toward as an object ⟨crept up ~ her⟩ **12** : ABOUT, CONCERNING ⟨a book ~ minerals⟩
²on *adv* **1** : in or into a position of contact with or attachment to a surface **2** : FORWARD **3** : into operation
³on *adj* : being in operation or in progress
ON *abbr* Ontario
¹once \'wəns\ *adv* [ME *ones*, fr. genitive of *on* one] **1** : one time only **2** : at any one time ⟨didn't ~ thank me⟩ **3** : FORMERLY ⟨was ~ young⟩ **4** : by one degree of relationship ⟨first cousin ~ removed⟩
²once *n* : one single time — **at once** **1** : at the same time **2** : IMMEDIATELY
³once *adj* : FORMER ⟨a ~ successful actor⟩
⁴once *conj* : AS SOON AS ⟨~ we're finished, we can leave⟩
once–over \'wəns-ˌō-vər\ *n* : a swift examination or survey
on·co·gene \'äŋ-kō-ˌjēn\ *n* : a gene having the potential to cause a normal cell to become cancerous
on·col·o·gy \än-'kä-lə-jē\ *n* : the study of tumors — **on·co·log·i·cal** \ˌäŋ-kə-'lä-ji-kəl\ *also* **on·co·log·ic** \-jik\ *adj* — **on·col·o·gist** \än-'kä-lə-jist\ *n*
on·com·ing \'ȯn-ˌkə-miŋ, 'än-\ *adj* : APPROACHING ⟨~ traffic⟩
¹one \'wən\ *adj* **1** : being a single unit or thing ⟨~ person went⟩ **2** : being one in particular ⟨early ~ morning⟩ **3** : being the same in kind or quality ⟨members of ~ race⟩; *also* : UNITED **4** : being not specified or fixed ⟨~ day soon⟩
²one *n* **1** : the number denoting a single unit **2** : the 1st in a set or series **3** : a single person or thing — **one·ness** \'wən-nəs\ *n*
³one *pron* **1** : a certain indefinitely indicated person or

thing ⟨saw ~ of his friends⟩ **2** : a person in general ⟨~ never knows⟩ **3** — used in place of a first-person pronoun
Onei·da \ō-'nī-də\ *n, pl* **Oneida** *or* **Oneidas** : a member of an American Indian people orig. of New York
one–man band *n* **1** : a musician who plays several instruments during a solo performance **2** : a person who alone undertakes or is responsible for several tasks
oner·ous \'ä-nə-rəs, 'ō-\ *adj* : imposing or constituting a burden : TROUBLESOME ✦ **Synonyms** OPPRESSIVE, EXACTING, BURDENSOME, WEIGHTY
one·self \(ˌ)wən-'self\ *also* **one's self** *pron* : one's own self — usu. used reflexively or for emphasis
one–sid·ed \'wən-'sī-dəd\ *adj* **1** : having or occurring on one side only; *also* : having one side prominent or more developed **2** : PARTIAL ⟨a ~ interpretation⟩
one·time \'wən-ˌtīm\ *adj* : FORMER ⟨a ~ actor⟩
one–to–one \ˌwən-tə-'wən\ *adj* : pairing each element of a set uniquely with an element of another set
one up *adj* : being in a position of advantage ⟨was *one up* on the others⟩
one–way *adj* : moving, allowing movement, or functioning in only one direction ⟨~ streets⟩
on·go·ing \'ȯn-ˌgō-iŋ, 'än-\ *adj* : continuously moving forward
on·ion \'ən-yən\ *n* : the pungent edible bulb of a widely cultivated plant related to the lilies; *also* : this plant
on·ion·skin \-ˌskin\ *n* : a thin strong translucent paper of very light weight
on·line \'ȯn-'līn, 'än-\ *adj or adv* : connected to, served by, or available through a computer network (as the Internet); *also* done while online ⟨~shopping⟩ — **online** *adv*
on·look·er \'ȯn-ˌlu̇-kər, 'än-\ *n* : SPECTATOR
¹on·ly \'ōn-lē\ *adj* **1** : unquestionably the best **2** : SOLE ⟨the ~ one left⟩
²only *adv* **1** : MERELY, JUST ⟨~ $2⟩ **2** : SOLELY ⟨known ~ to me⟩ **3** : at the very least ⟨was ~ too true⟩ **4** : as a final result ⟨will ~ make you sick⟩
³only *conj* : except that
on·o·mato·poe·ia \ˌä-nə-ˌmä-tə-'pē-ə\ *n* [LL, fr. Gk *onomatopoiia*, fr. *onoma* name + *poiein* to make] **1** : formation of words in imitation of natural sounds (as *buzz* or *hiss*) **2** : the use of words whose sound suggests the sense — **on·o·mato·poe·ic** \-'pē-ik\ *or* **on·o·mato·po·et·ic** \-pō-'e-tik\ *adj* — **on·o·mato·poe·i·cal·ly** \-'pē-ə-k(ə-)lē\ *or* **on·o·mato·po·et·i·cal·ly** \-pō-'e-ti-k(ə-)lē\ *adv*
On·on·da·ga \ˌä-nən-'dȯ-gə, -'dä-, -'dä-\ *n, pl* **-ga** *or* **-gas** : a member of an American Indian people of New York and Canada
on·rush \'ȯn-ˌrəsh, 'än-\ *n* : a rushing onward — **on·rushing** *adj*
on–screen \'ȯn-'skrēn, 'än-\ *adv or adj* : on a computer or television screen
on·set \-ˌset\ *n* **1** : ATTACK **2** : BEGINNING ⟨the ~ of winter⟩
on·shore \-ˌshȯr\ *adj* **1** : moving toward the shore **2** : situated on or near the shore — **on·shore** \-'shȯr\ *adv*
on·slaught \'ȯn-ˌslȯt, 'än-\ *n* : a fierce attack; *also* : something resembling such an attack ⟨an ~ of questions⟩
Ont *abbr* Ontario
on·to \'ȯn-tü, 'än-\ *prep* : to a position or point on
onus \'ō-nəs\ *n* **1** : BURDEN **2** : OBLIGATION **3** : BLAME
¹on·ward \'ȯn-wərd, 'än-\ *also* **on·wards** \-wərdz\ *adv* : FORWARD ⟨kept moving ~⟩
²onward *adj* : directed or moving onward : FORWARD
on·yx \'ä-niks\ *n* [ME *oniche, onyx*, fr. AF & L; AF, fr. L *onyx*, fr. Gk, lit., claw, nail] : a translucent chalcedony in parallel layers of different colors
oo·dles \'ü-dᵊlz\ *n pl* : a great quantity
oo·lite \'ō-ə-ˌlīt\ *n* : a rock consisting of small round grains cemented together — **oo·lit·ic** \ˌō-ə-'li-tik\ *adj*
¹ooze \'üz\ *n* [ME *wose*, fr. OE *wāse* mire] **1** : a soft deposit (as of mud) on the bottom of a body of water **2** : soft wet ground : MUD — **oozy** \'ü-zē\ *adj*
²ooze *vb* **oozed; ooz·ing** **1** : to flow or leak out slowly or imperceptibly **2** : EXUDE ⟨~ confidence⟩
³ooze *n* : something that oozes
op *abbr* **1** operation; operative; operator **2** opportunity **3** opus
OP *abbr* **1** observation post **2** out of print
opac·i·ty \ō-'pa-sə-tē\ *n, pl* **-ties** **1** : obscurity of mean-

ing   **2** : mental dullness   **3** : the quality or state of being opaque   **4** : an opaque spot in a normally transparent structure

opal \'ō-pəl\ *n* : a mineral with iridescent colors that is used as a gem

opal·es·cent \ˌō-pə-'le-sᵊnt\ *adj* : IRIDESCENT — **opal·es·cence** \-sᵊns\ *n*

opaque \ō-'pāk\ *adj*   **1** : blocking the passage of radiant energy and esp. light   **2** : not easily understood; *also* : OBTUSE — **opaque·ly** *adv* — **opaque·ness** *n*

op art \'äp-\ *n* : OPTICAL ART — **op artist** *n*

op cit *abbr* [L *opere citato*] in the work cited

ope \'ōp\ *vb* **oped; op·ing** *archaic* : OPEN

OPEC *abbr* Organization of Petroleum Exporting Countries

op–ed \'äp-'ed\ *n, often cap O&E* : a page of special features usu. opposite the editorial page of a newspaper

¹**open** \'ō-pən\ *adj* **open·er; open·est**   **1** : not shut or shut up ⟨an ~ door⟩   **2** : not secret or hidden; *also* : FRANK   **3** : not enclosed or covered ⟨an ~ fire⟩; *also* : not protected   **4** : free to be entered or used ⟨an ~ tournament⟩   **5** : easy to get through or see ⟨~ country⟩   **6** : spread out : EXTENDED   **7** : not decided ⟨an ~ question⟩   **8** : readily accessible and cooperative; *also* : GENEROUS   **9** : having openings, interruptions, or spaces ⟨an ~ mesh⟩; *also* : having components separated by a space in writing and printing ⟨the name *Spanish moss* is an ~ compound⟩   **10** : ready to operate ⟨stores are ~⟩   **11** : free from restraints or controls ⟨~ season⟩ — **open·ly** *adv* — **open·ness** *n*

²**open** \'ō-pən\ *vb* **opened; open·ing**   **1** : to change or move from a shut position; *also* : to make open by clearing away obstacles   **2** : to make accessible   **3** : to make openings in   **4** : to make or become functional ⟨~ a store⟩   **5** : REVEAL; *also* : ENLIGHTEN   **6** : BEGIN ⟨~ talks⟩ — **open·er** *n*

³**open** *n*   **1** : OUTDOORS   **2** : a contest or tournament open to all

open–air *adj* : OUTDOOR ⟨~ theaters⟩

open arms *n pl* : an eager or warm welcome

open–faced \-'fāst\ *also* **open–face** \-'fās\ *adj* : served without a covering layer of bread ⟨an ~ sandwich⟩

open·hand·ed \ˌō-pən-'han-dəd\ *adj* : GENEROUS — **open·hand·ed·ly** *adv*

open–heart *adj* : of, relating to, or performed on a heart temporarily relieved of circulatory function and laid open for repair of defects or damage

open–hearth *adj* : of, relating to, or being a process of making steel in a furnace that reflects the heat from the roof onto the material

opening *n*   **1** : an act or instance of making or becoming open   **2** : BEGINNING   **3** : something that is open   **4** : OCCASION; *also* : an opportunity for employment

open mike *n* : an event in which amateurs may perform

open–mind·ed \ˌō-pən-'mīn-dəd\ *adj* : free from rigidly fixed preconceptions — **open–mind·ed·ness** *n*

open sentence *n* : a statement (as in mathematics) containing at least one blank or unknown so that when the blank is filled or a quantity substituted for the unknown the statement becomes a complete statement that is either true or false

open shop *n* : an establishment having members and nonmembers of a labor union on the payroll

open·work \'ō-pən-ˌwərk\ *n* : work so made as to show openings through its substance ⟨a railing of wrought-iron ~⟩ — **open–worked** \-ˌwərkt\ *adj*

¹**opera** *pl of* OPUS

²**op·era** \'ä-prə, -pə-rə\ *n* : a drama set to music — **op·er·at·ic** \ˌä-pə-'ra-tik\ *adj*

op·er·a·ble \'ä-pə-rə-bəl\ *adj*   **1** : fit, possible, or desirable to use   **2** : likely to result in a favorable outcome upon surgical treatment

opera glasses *n pl* : small binoculars for use in a theater

op·er·ate \'ä-pə-ˌrāt\ *vb* **-at·ed; -at·ing**   **1** : to perform work : FUNCTION   **2** : to produce an effect   **3** : to put or keep in operation   **4** : to perform or subject to an operation — **op·er·a·tor** \-ˌrā-tər\ *n*

operating system *n* : software that controls the operation of a computer

op·er·a·tion \ˌä-pə-'rā-shən\ *n*   **1** : a doing or performing of a practical work   **2** : an exertion of power or influence;

also : method or manner of functioning   **3** : a surgical procedure   **4** : a process of deriving one mathematical expression from others according to a rule   **5** : a military action or mission   **6** : a usu. small business — **op·er·a·tion·al** \-shə-nəl\ *adj*

¹**op·er·a·tive** \'ä-pə-rə-tiv, -ˌrā-\ *adj*   **1** : producing an appropriate effect; *also* : most significant or essential   **2** : OPERATING ⟨an ~ force⟩   **3** : having to do with physical operations; *also* : WORKING ⟨an ~ craftsman⟩   **4** : based on or consisting of an operation ⟨~ dentistry⟩

²**operative** *n*   **1** : OPERATOR; *esp* : a secret agent   **2** : a person who works toward achieving the objectives of a larger interest

op·er·et·ta \ˌä-pə-'re-tə\ *n* [It, dim. of *opera* opera] : a light musical-dramatic work with a romantic plot, spoken dialogue, and dancing scenes

oph·thal·mic \äf-'thal-mik, äp-\ *adj* [Gk *ophthalmikos*, fr. *ophthalmos* eye] : of, relating to, or located near the eye

oph·thal·mol·o·gy \ˌäf-ˌthal-'mä-lə-jē, ˌäp-\ *n* : a branch of medicine dealing with the structure, functions, and diseases of the eye — **oph·thal·mol·o·gist** \-jist\ *n*

oph·thal·mo·scope \äf-'thal-mə-ˌskōp, äp-\ *n* : an instrument for use in viewing the interior of the eye and esp. the retina

opi·ate \'ō-pē-ət, -pē-ˌāt\ *n* : a preparation or derivative of opium; *also* : a narcotic or a substance with similar activity — **opiate** *adj*

opine \ō-'pīn\ *vb* **opined; opin·ing** : to express an opinion : STATE

opin·ion \ə-'pin-yən\ *n*   **1** : JUDGMENT   **2** : a belief stronger than impression and less strong than positive knowledge   **3** : a formal statement by an expert after careful study

opin·ion·at·ed \ə-'pin-yə-ˌnā-təd\ *adj* : obstinately adhering to personal opinions

opi·um \'ō-pē-əm\ *n* [ME, fr. L, fr. Gk *opion*, fr. dim. of *opos* sap] : an addictive narcotic drug that is the dried latex of an Eurasian poppy

opos·sum \ə-'pä-səm\ *n, pl* **opossums** *also* **opossum** : an omnivorous tree-dwelling No. American marsupial that is active chiefly at night and has a pointed snout and a prehensile tail

opossum

opp *abbr* opposite

op·po·nent \ə-'pō-nənt\ *n* : one that opposes : ADVERSARY

op·por·tune \ˌä-pər-'tün, -'tyün\ *adj* [ME, fr. MF *opportun*, fr. L *opportunus*, fr. *ob-* toward + *portus* port, harbor] : SUITABLE ⟨an ~ moment⟩ — **op·por·tune·ly** *adv*

op·por·tun·ism \ˌä-pər-'tü-ˌni-zəm, -'tyü-\ *n* : a taking advantage of opportunities or circumstances esp. with little regard for principles or ultimate consequences — **op·por·tun·ist** \-nist\ *n* — **op·por·tu·nis·tic** \-tü-'nis-tik, -tyü-\ *adj*

op·por·tu·ni·ty \ˌä-pər-'tü-nə-tē, -'tyü-\ *n, pl* **-ties**   **1** : a favorable combination of circumstances, time, and place   **2** : a chance for advancement

op·pose \ə-'pōz\ *vb* **op·posed; op·pos·ing**   **1** : to place opposite or against something (as to provide resistance or contrast)   **2** : to strive against : RESIST — **op·po·si·tion** \ˌä-pə-'zi-shən\ *n*

¹**op·po·site** \'ä-pə-zət\ *adj*   **1** : set over against something that is at the other end or side   **2** : OPPOSED, HOSTILE; *also* : CONTRARY   **3** : contrarily turned or moving   **4** : being the other of a matching or contrasting pair ⟨the ~ sex⟩ — **op·po·site·ly** *adv* — **op·po·site·ness** *n*

²**op·po·site** *n* : one that is opposed or contrary
³**op·po·site** *adv* : on or to an opposite side
⁴**op·po·site** *prep* : across from and usu. facing ⟨the house ∼ ours⟩

op·press \ə-'pres\ *vb* **1** : to crush by abuse of power or authority **2** : to weigh down : BURDEN ♦ *Synonyms* AGGRIEVE, WRONG, PERSECUTE — **op·pres·sive** \-'pre-siv\ *adj* — **op·pres·sive·ly** *adv* — **op·pres·sor** \-'pre-sər\ *n*

op·pres·sion \ə-'pre-shən\ *n* **1** : unjust or cruel exercise of power or authority **2** : DEPRESSION

op·pro·bri·ous \ə-'prō-brē-əs\ *adj* : expressing or deserving opprobrium — **op·pro·bri·ous·ly** *adv*

op·pro·bri·um \-brē-əm\ *n* **1** : something that brings disgrace **2** : public disgrace or ill fame

¹**opt** \'äpt\ *vb* : to make a choice; *esp* : to decide in favor of something

²**opt** *abbr* **1** optical; optician; optics **2** option; optional

op·tic \'äp-tik\ *adj* : of or relating to vision or the eye

op·ti·cal \'äp-ti-kəl\ *adj* **1** : relating to optics **2** : OPTIC **3** : of, relating to, or using light

optical art *n* : nonobjective art characterized by the use of geometric patterns often for an illusory effect

optical disk *n* : a disk on which information has been recorded digitally and which is read using a laser

optical fiber *n* : a single fiber-optic strand

op·ti·cian \äp-'ti-shən\ *n* **1** : a maker of or dealer in optical items and instruments **2** : a person who makes or orders eyeglasses and contact lenses to prescription and sells them

op·tics \'äp-tiks\ *n* : a science that deals with the nature and properties of light

op·ti·mal \'äp-tə-məl\ *adj* : most desirable or satisfactory — **op·ti·mal·ly** *adv*

op·ti·mism \'äp-tə-,mi-zəm\ *n* [F *optimisme*, fr. L *optimum*, n., best, fr. neut. of *optimus* best] **1** : a doctrine that this world is the best possible world **2** : an inclination to anticipate the best possible outcome of actions

op·ti·mize \'äp-tə-,mīz\ *vb* **-mized; -miz·ing** : to make as perfect, effective, or functional as possible — **op·ti·mi·za·tion** \,äp-tə-mə-'zā-shən\ *n*

op·ti·mum \'äp-tə-məm\ *n, pl* **-ma** \-mə\ *also* **-mums** [L] : the amount or degree of something most favorable to an end; *also* : greatest degree attained under implied or specified conditions

op·tion \'äp-shən\ *n* **1** : the power or right to choose **2** : a right to buy or sell something at a specified price during a specified period **3** : something offered for choice — **op·tion·al** \-shə-nəl\ *adj*

op·tom·e·try \äp-'tä-mə-trē\ *n* : the health-care profession concerned esp. with examining the eyes for defects of vision and with prescribing corrective lenses or eye exercises — **op·to·met·ric** \,äp-tə-'me-trik\ *adj* — **op·tom·e·trist** \äp-'tä-mə-trist\ *n*

opt out *vb* : to choose not to participate

op·u·lence \'ä-pyə-ləns\ *n* **1** : WEALTH **2** : ABUNDANCE

op·u·lent \'ä-pyə-lənt\ *adj* **1** : WEALTHY **2** : richly abundant — **op·u·lent·ly** *adv*

opus \'ō-pəs\ *n, pl* **opera** \'ō-pə-rə, 'ä-\ *also* **opus·es** \'ō-pə-səz\ : WORK; *esp* : a musical composition

or \'ȯr\ *conj* — used as a function word to indicate an alternative ⟨sink ∼ swim⟩

OR *abbr* **1** operating room **2** Oregon

-or *n suffix* : one that does a (specified) thing ⟨calculator⟩

or·a·cle \'ȯr-ə-kəl\ *n* **1** : one held to give divinely inspired answers or revelations **2** : an authoritative or wise utterance; *also* : a person of great authority or wisdom — **orac·u·lar** \ȯ-'ra-kyə-lər\ *adj*

¹**oral** \'ȯr-əl\ *adj* **1** : SPOKEN ⟨an ∼ report⟩ **2** : of, given through, or involving the mouth ⟨an ∼ vaccine⟩ **3** : of, relating to, or characterized by the first stage of psychosexual development in psychoanalytic theory in which libidinal gratification is derived from intake (as of food), by sucking, and later by biting **4** : relating to or characterized by personality traits of passive dependency and aggressiveness — **oral·ly** *adv*

²**oral** *n* : an oral examination — usu. used in pl.

oral sex *n* : oral stimulation of the genitals : CUNNILINGUS, FELLATIO

orang \ə-'raŋ\ *n* : ORANGUTAN

or·ange \'är-inj, 'ȯr-\ *n* **1** : a juicy citrus fruit with red-

dish yellow rind; *also* : an evergreen tree with fragrant white flowers that bears this fruit **2** : a color between red and yellow — **or·ang·ey** *or* **or·angy** \'är-in-jē, 'ȯr-\ *adj*

or·ange·ade \,är-in-'jād, ,ȯr-\ *n* : a beverage of orange juice, sugar, and water

orange hawkweed *n* : a weedy herb related to the daisies with bright orange-red flower heads

or·ange·ry \'är-inj-rē, 'ȯr-\ *n, pl* **-ries** : a protected place (as a greenhouse) for raising oranges in cool climates

orang·utan \ə-'raŋ-ə-,taŋ, -,tan\ *n* [Bazaar Malay (Malay-based pidgin), fr. Malay *orang* man + *hutan* forest] : a large reddish brown tree-living anthropoid ape of Borneo and Sumatra

orate \ȯ-'rāt\ *vb* **orat·ed; orat·ing** : to speak in a declamatory manner

ora·tion \ə-'rā-shən\ *n* : an elaborate discourse delivered in a formal and dignified manner

or·a·tor \'ȯr-ə-tər\ *n* : one noted for skill and power as a public speaker

or·a·tor·i·cal \,ȯr-ə-'tȯr-i-kəl\ *adj* : of, relating to, or characteristic of an orator or oratory — **or·a·tor·i·cal·ly** \-'tȯr-i-k(ə-)lē\ *adv*

or·a·to·rio \,ȯr-ə-'tȯr-ē-,ō\ *n, pl* **-rios** : a lengthy choral work usu. on a scriptural subject

¹**or·a·to·ry** \'ȯr-ə-,tȯr-ē\ *n, pl* **-ries** : a private or institutional chapel

²**oratory** *n* : the art of speaking eloquently and effectively in public ♦ *Synonyms* RHETORIC, ELOCUTION

orb \'ȯrb\ *n* : a spherical body; *also* : EYE

¹**or·bit** \'ȯr-bət\ *n* [L *orbita*, lit., path, rut] **1** : a path described by one body in its revolution about another **2** : range or sphere of activity — **or·bit·al** \-bə-t³l\ *adj*

²**orbit** *vb* **1** : CIRCLE **2** : to send up and make revolve in an orbit ⟨∼ a satellite⟩ — **or·bit·er** *n*

or·ca \'ȯr-kə\ *n* : KILLER WHALE

orch *abbr* orchestra

or·chard \'ȯr-chərd\ *n* [ME, fr. OE *ortgeard*, fr. *ort*- (fr. L *hortus* garden) + *geard* yard] : a place where fruit trees, sugar maples, or nut trees are grown; *also* : the trees of such a place — **or·chard·ist** \-chər-dist\ *n*

or·ches·tra \'ȯr-kə-strə\ *n* **1** : the front section of seats on the main floor of a theater **2** : a group of instrumentalists organized to perform ensemble music — **or·ches·tral** \ȯr-'kes-trəl\ *adj* — **or·ches·tral·ly** *adv*

or·ches·trate \'ȯr-kə-,strāt\ *vb* **-trat·ed; -trat·ing** **1** : to compose or arrange for an orchestra **2** : to arrange so as to achieve a desired effect — **or·ches·tra·tion** \,ȯr-kə-'strā-shən\ *n*

or·chid \'ȯr-kəd\ *n* : any of a large family of plants having often showy flowers with three petals of which the middle one is enlarged into a lip; *also* : a flower of an orchid

ord *abbr* **1** order **2** ordnance

or·dain \ȯr-'dān\ *vb* **1** : to admit to the ministry or priesthood by the ritual of a church **2** : DECREE, ENACT; *also* : DESTINE — **or·dain·ment** *n*

or·deal \ȯr-'dēl, 'ȯr-,dēl\ *n* : a severe trial or experience

¹**or·der** \'ȯr-dər\ *vb* **1** : ARRANGE, REGULATE **2** : COMMAND **3** : to place an order

²**order** *n* **1** : a group of people formally united; *also* : a badge or medal of such a group **2** : any of the several grades of the Christian ministry; *also, pl* : ORDINATION **3** : a rank, class, or special group of persons or things **4** : a category of biological classification ranking above the family and below the class **5** : ARRANGEMENT, SEQUENCE; *also* : the prevailing state of things **6** : a customary mode of procedure; *also* : the rule of law or proper authority **7** : a specific rule, regulation, or authoritative direction **8** : a style of building; *also* : an architectural column forming the unit of a style **9** : condition esp. with regard to repair **10** : a direction to pay money or to buy or sell goods; *also* : goods bought or sold — **in order** : APPROPRIATE, DESIRABLE ⟨apologies are *in order*⟩ — **in order to** : for the purpose of

¹**or·der·ly** \'ȯr-dər-lē\ *adj* **1** : arranged according to some order; *also* : NEAT, TIDY **2** : well behaved ⟨an ∼ crowd⟩ ♦ *Synonyms* METHODICAL, SYSTEMATIC, REGULAR — **or·der·li·ness** *n*

²**orderly** *n, pl* **-lies** **1** : a soldier who attends a superior officer **2** : a hospital attendant who does general work

or·di·nal \'ȯrd-³n-əl\ *adj* : indicating order or rank (as sixth) in a series

ordinal number *n* : a number (as first, second, or third) that designates the place of an item in an ordered sequence — compare CARDINAL NUMBER

or·di·nance \'ȯr-də-nəns\ *n* : an authoritative decree or law; *esp* : a municipal regulation

or·di·nary \'ȯr-də-ˌner-ē\ *adj* **1** : to be expected : USUAL **2** : of common quality, rank, or ability ⟨∼ kids⟩; *also* : POOR, INFERIOR ⟨∼ wine⟩ ♦ **Synonyms** CUSTOMARY, ROUTINE, NORMAL, EVERYDAY — **or·di·nar·i·ly** \ˌȯr-də-ner-ə-lē\ *adv* — **or·di·nar·i·ness** \'ȯr-dən-ˌner-ē-nəs\ *n*

or·di·nate \'ȯr-də-nət, -ˌnāt\ *n* : the vertical coordinate of a point in a plane coordinate system obtained by measuring parallel to the y-axis

or·di·na·tion \ˌȯr-də-'nā-shən\ *n* : the act or ceremony by which a person is ordained

ord·nance \'ȯrd-nəns\ *n* **1** : military supplies **2** : CANNON, ARTILLERY

Or·do·vi·cian \ˌȯr-də-'vi-shən\ *adj* : of, relating to, or being the period of the Paleozoic era between the Cambrian and the Silurian — **Ordovician** *n*

or·dure \'ȯr-jər\ *n* : EXCREMENT

¹ore \'ȯr\ *n* : a naturally occurring mineral mined to obtain a substance that it contains

²ore \'ər-ə\ *n, pl* **ore** — see *krona, krone* at MONEY table

Ore *or* **Oreg** *abbr* Oregon

oreg·a·no \ə-'re-gə-ˌnō\ *n* : a bushy perennial mint used as a seasoning and a source of oil

org *abbr* organization; organized

or·gan \'ȯr-gən\ *n* **1** : a musical instrument having sets of pipes sounded by compressed air and controlled by keyboards; *also* : an electronic keyboard instrument that approximates the sounds of the pipe organ by electronic devices **2** : a differentiated animal or plant structure (as a heart or a leaf) made up of cells and tissues and performing some bodily function **3** : a group that performs a specialized function ⟨the various ∼s of government⟩ **4** : PERIODICAL

or·gan·dy *also* **or·gan·die** \'ȯr-gən-dē\ *n, pl* **-dies** [F *organdi*] : a fine transparent muslin with a stiff finish

or·gan·elle \ˌȯr-gə-'nel\ *n* : a specialized cell part that resembles an organ in having a special function

or·gan·ic \ȯr-'ga-nik\ *adj* **1** : of, relating to, or arising in a bodily organ **2** : of, relating to, or derived from living things **3** : of, relating to, or containing carbon compounds **4** : of or relating to a branch of chemistry dealing with carbon compounds **5** : involving, producing, or dealing in foods produced without the use of laboratory-made fertilizers, growth substances, antibiotics, or pesticides ⟨∼ farming⟩ **6** : ORGANIZED ⟨an ∼ whole⟩ — **or·gan·i·cal·ly** \-ni-k(ə-)lē\ *adv*

or·ga·ni·sa·tion, or·ga·nise *Brit var of* ORGANIZATION, ORGANIZE

or·gan·ism \'ȯr-gə-ˌni-zəm\ *n* : an individual living thing (as a person, animal, or plant) — **or·gan·is·mic** \ˌȯr-gə-'niz-mik\ *adj*

or·gan·ist \'ȯr-gə-nist\ *n* : a person who plays an organ

or·ga·ni·za·tion \ˌȯr-gə-nə-'zā-shən\ *n* **1** : the act or process of organizing or of being organized; *also* : the condition or manner of being organized **2** : ASSOCIATION, SOCIETY **3** : an administrative structure (as a business or a political party) — **or·ga·ni·za·tion·al** \-shə-nəl\ *adj*

or·ga·nize \'ȯr-gə-ˌnīz\ *vb* **-nized; -niz·ing 1** : to develop an organic structure **2** : to form into a complete and functioning whole **3** : to set up an administrative structure for **4** : to arrange by systematic planning and united effort **5** : to join in a union; *also* : UNIONIZE ♦ **Synonyms** INSTITUTE, FOUND, ESTABLISH, CONSTITUTE — **or·ga·niz·er** *n*

or·gano·chlo·rine \ȯr-ˌga-nə-'klȯr-ˌēn\ *adj* : of, relating to, or being a chlorinated hydrocarbon pesticide (as DDT) — **organochlorine** *n*

or·gano·phos·phate \-'fäs-ˌfāt\ *n* : an organophosphorus pesticide — **organophosphate** *adj*

or·gano·phos·pho·rus \-'fäs-fə-rəs\ *also* **or·gano·phos·pho·rous** \-fäs-'fȯr-əs\ *adj* : of, relating to, or being a phosphorus-containing organic pesticide (as malathion)

or·gan·za \ȯr-'gan-zə\ *n* : a sheer dress fabric resembling organdy and usu. made of silk, rayon, or nylon

or·gasm \'ȯr-ˌga-zəm\ *n* : the climax of sexual excitement — **or·gas·mic** \ȯr-'gaz-mik\ *adj*

or·gi·as·tic \ˌȯr-jē-'as-tik\ *adj* : of, relating to, or marked by orgies

or·gu·lous \'ȯr-gyə-ləs, -gə-\ *adj* : PROUD

or·gy \'ȯr-jē\ *n, pl* **orgies** : a gathering marked by unrestrained indulgence (as in sexual activity, alcohol, or drugs)

ori·el \'ȯr-ē-əl\ *n* : a window built out from a wall and usu. supported by a bracket

ori·ent \'ȯr-ē-ˌent\ *vb* **1** : to set in a definite position esp. in relation to the points of the compass **2** : to acquaint with an existing situation or environment **3** : to direct toward the interests of a particular group

Orient *n* **1** : EAST **3**; *esp* : the countries of eastern Asia

ori·en·tal \ˌȯr-ē-'en-t°l\ *adj, often cap* [fr. *Orient* East, fr. ME, fr. AF, fr. L *orient-, oriens*, fr. prp. of *oriri* to rise] : of or situated in Asia

ori·en·tate \ˌȯr-ē-ən-ˌtāt\ *vb* **-tat·ed; -tat·ing 1** : ORIENT **2** : to face east

ori·en·ta·tion \ˌȯr-ē-ən-tā-shən\ *n* **1** : the act or state of being oriented **2** : a person's identity based on sexual tendencies

or·i·fice \'ȯr-ə-fəs\ *n* : OPENING, MOUTH

ori·flamme \'ȯr-ə-ˌflam\ *n* : a brightly colored banner used as a standard or ensign in battle

orig *abbr* original; originally

ori·ga·mi \ˌȯr-ə-'gä-mē\ *n* : the Japanese art or process of paper folding

or·i·gin \'ȯr-ə-jən\ *n* **1** : ANCESTRY **2** : rise, beginning, or derivation from a source; *also* : CAUSE **3** : the intersection of coordinate axes

¹orig·i·nal \ə-'ri-jə-nəl\ *n* : something from which a copy, reproduction, or translation is made : PROTOTYPE

²original *adj* **1** : FIRST, INITIAL **2** : not copied from something else : FRESH **3** : INVENTIVE — **orig·i·nal·i·ty** \-ˌri-jə-'na-lə-tē\ *n* — **orig·i·nal·ly** \-'ri-jə-n°l-ē\ *adv*

orig·i·nate \ə-'ri-jə-ˌnāt\ *vb* **-nat·ed; -nat·ing 1** : to give rise to : INITIATE **2** : to come into existence : BEGIN — **orig·i·na·tor** \-ˌnā-tər\ *n*

ori·ole \'ȯr-ē-ˌōl\ *n* : any of various New World birds of which the males are usu. black and yellow or black and orange

or·i·son \'ȯr-ə-sən\ *n* : PRAYER

or·mo·lu \'ȯr-mə-ˌlü\ *n* : a golden or gilded brass used for decorative purposes

¹or·na·ment \'ȯr-nə-mənt\ *n* : something that lends grace or beauty — **or·na·men·tal** \ˌȯr-nə-'men-t°l\ *adj*

²or·na·ment \-ˌment\ *vb* : to provide with ornament : ADORN — **or·na·men·ta·tion** \ˌȯr-nə-mən-'tā-shən\ *n*

or·nate \ȯr-'nāt\ *adj* : elaborately decorated ⟨an ∼ mantel⟩ — **or·nate·ly** *adv* — **or·nate·ness** *n*

or·nery \'ȯr-nə-rē, 'ä-nə-\ *adj* : having an irritable disposition

or·ni·thol·o·gy \ˌȯr-nə-'thä-lə-jē\ *n, pl* **-gies** : a branch of zoology dealing with birds — **or·ni·tho·log·i·cal** \-thə-'lä-ji-kəl\ *adj* — **or·ni·thol·o·gist** \-'thä-lə-jist\ *n*

oro·tund \'ȯr-ə-ˌtənd\ *adj* **1** : SONOROUS ⟨an ∼ voice⟩ **2** : POMPOUS ⟨an ∼ speech⟩ — **oro·tun·di·ty** \ˌȯr-ə-'tən-di-tē\ *n*

or·phan \'ȯr-fən\ *n* : a child deprived by death of one or usu. both parents — **orphan** *vb*

or·phan·age \'ȯr-fə-nij\ *n* : an institution for the care of orphans

or·tho·don·tia \ˌȯr-thə-'dän-chə, -chē-ə\ *n* : ORTHODONTICS

or·tho·don·tics \ˌȯr-thə-'dän-tiks\ *n* : a branch of dentistry concerned with the correction of faults in the arrangement and placing of the teeth — **or·tho·don·tic** \-tik\ *adj* — **or·tho·don·tist** \-'dän-tist\ *n*

or·tho·dox \'ȯr-thə-ˌdäks\ *adj* [MF or LL; MF *orthodoxe*, fr. LL *orthodoxus*, fr. LGk *orthodoxos*, fr. Gk *orthos* right + *doxa* opinion] **1** : conforming to established doctrine esp. in religion **2** : CONVENTIONAL **3** *cap* : of or relating to a Christian church originating in the church of the Eastern Roman Empire — **or·tho·doxy** \-ˌdäk-sē\ *n*

or·thog·ra·phy \ȯr-'thä-grə-fē\ *n* : SPELLING — **or·tho·graph·ic** \ˌȯr-thə-'gra-fik\ *adj*

or·tho·pe·dics *also* **or·tho·pae·dics** \ˌȯr-thə-'pē-diks\ *n sing or pl* : a branch of medicine concerned with the correction or prevention of skeletal injuries or disorders — **or·tho·pe·dic** \-dik\ *also* **or·tho·pae·dic** *adj* — **or·tho·pe·dist** \-dist\ *n*

-ory *adj suffix* **1** : of, relating to, or characterized by ⟨anticipat*ory*⟩ **2** : serving for, producing, or maintaining ⟨illus*ory*⟩

Os *symbol* osmium

OS *abbr* **1** [L *oculus sinister*] left eye **2** ordinary seaman **3** out of stock

Osage \ō-ˈsāj\ *n, pl* **Osag·es** *or* **Osage** : a member of an American Indian people orig. of Missouri

os·cil·late \ˈä-sə-ˌlāt\ *vb* **-lat·ed; -lat·ing 1** : to swing backward and forward like a pendulum **2** : to move or travel back and forth between two points **3** : VARY, FLUCTUATE — **os·cil·la·tion** \ˌä-sə-ˈlā-shən\ *n* — **os·cil·la·tor** \ˈä-sə-ˌlā-tər\ *n* — **os·cil·la·to·ry** \ˈä-sə-lə-ˌtȯr-ē\ *adj*

os·cil·lo·scope \ä-ˈsi-lə-ˌskōp\ *n* : an instrument in which variations in current or voltage appear as a visible wave form on a fluorescent screen

os·cu·late \ˈäs-kyə-ˌlāt\ *vb* **-lat·ed; -lat·ing** : KISS — **os·cu·la·tion** \ˌäs-kyə-ˈlā-shən\ *n* — **os·cu·la·to·ry** \ˈäs-kyə-lə-ˌtōr-ē\ *adj*

Osee \ˈō-ˌzē, ō-ˈzā-ə\ *n* : HOSEA

OSHA \ˈō-shə\ *abbr* Occupational Safety and Health Administration

osier \ˈō-zhər\ *n* : any of various willows with pliable twigs used esp. in making baskets and furniture; *also* : a twig from an osier

os·mi·um \ˈäz-mē-əm\ *n* : a very heavy hard brittle metallic chemical element used esp. as a catalyst and in alloys

os·mo·sis \äz-ˈmō-səs, äs-\ *n* : movement of a solvent through a semipermeable membrane into a solution of higher concentration that tends to equalize the concentrations of the solutions on either side of the membrane — **os·mot·ic** \-ˈmä-tik\ *adj*

os·prey \ˈäs-prē, -ˌprā\ *n, pl* **ospreys** : a large dark brown and white fish-eating hawk

os·si·fy \ˈä-sə-ˌfī\ *vb* **-fied; -fy·ing** : to make or become hardened or set in one's ways — **os·si·fi·ca·tion** \ˌä-sə-fə-ˈkā-shən\ *n*

os·su·ary \ˈä-shə-ˌwer-ē, -syə-\ *n, pl* **-ar·ies** : a depository for the bones of the dead

os·ten·si·ble \ä-ˈsten-sə-bəl\ *adj* : shown outwardly : PROFESSED, APPARENT — **os·ten·si·bly** \-blē\ *adv*

os·ten·ta·tion \ˌäs-tən-ˈtā-shən\ *n* : pretentious or excessive display — **os·ten·ta·tious** \-shəs\ *adj* — **os·ten·ta·tious·ly** *adv*

os·te·o·ar·thri·tis \ˌäs-tē-ō-är-ˈthrī-təs\ *n* : arthritis marked by degeneration of the cartilage and bone of joints

os·te·o·path \ˈäs-tē-ə-ˌpath\ *n* : a practitioner of osteopathy

os·te·op·a·thy \ˌäs-tē-ˈä-pə-thē\ *n* : a system of treating diseases emphasizing manipulation (as of joints) but not excluding other agencies (as the use of medicine and surgery) — **os·te·o·path·ic** \ˌäs-tē-ə-ˈpa-thik\ *adj*

os·te·o·po·ro·sis \ˌäs-tē-ō-pə-ˈrō-səs\ *n, pl* **-ro·ses** \-ˌsēz\ : a condition affecting esp. older women and characterized by fragile and porous bones

os·tra·cise *Brit var of* OSTRACIZE

os·tra·cize \ˈäs-trə-ˌsīz\ *vb* **-cized; -ciz·ing** [Gk *ostrakizein* to banish by voting with potsherds, fr. *ostrakon* shell, potsherd] : to exclude from a group by common consent — **os·tra·cism** \-ˌsi-zəm\ *n*

os·trich \ˈäs-trich, ˈȯs-\ *n* : a very large swift-footed flightless bird of Africa

Os·we·go tea \ä-ˈswē-gō-\ *n* : a No. American mint with showy scarlet flowers

OT *abbr* **1** occupational therapy **2** Old Testament **3** overtime

¹oth·er \ˈə-thər\ *adj* **1** : being the one left; *also* : being the ones distinct from those first mentioned **2** : ALTERNATE ⟨every ~ day⟩ **3** : DIFFERENT **4** : ADDITIONAL **5** : recently past ⟨the ~ night⟩

²other *pron* **1** : remaining one or ones **2** : a different or additional one ⟨something or ~⟩

oth·er·wise \ˈə-thər-ˌwīz\ *adv* **1** : in a different way **2** : in different circumstances **3** : in other respects **4** : if not **5** : NOT — **otherwise** *adj*

oth·er·world \-ˌwərld\ *n* : a world beyond death or beyond present reality

oth·er·world·ly \ˌə-thər-ˈwərld-lē\ *adj* : not worldly : concerned with spiritual, intellectual, or imaginative matters

oti·ose \ˈō-shē-ˌōs, ˈō-tē-\ *adj* **1** : FUTILE **2** : IDLE **3** : USELESS ⟨~ details⟩

oto·lar·yn·gol·o·gy \ˌō-tō-ˌla-rən-ˈgä-lə-jē\ *n* : a medical specialty concerned esp. with the ear, nose, and throat — **oto·lar·yn·gol·o·gist** \-jist\ *n*

oto·rhi·no·lar·yn·gol·o·gy \ˌō-tō-ˌrī-nō-ˌla-rən-ˈgä-lə-jē\ *n* : OTOLARYNGOLOGY — **oto·rhi·no·lar·yn·gol·o·gist** \-jist\ *n*

OTS *abbr* officers' training school

Ot·ta·wa \ˈä-tə-wə, -ˌwä, -ˌwȯ\ *n, pl* **Ottawas** *or* **Ottawa** : a member of an American Indian people of Michigan and southern Ontario

ot·ter \ˈä-tər\ *n, pl* **otters** *also* **otter** : any of various webfooted fish-eating mammals with dark brown fur that are related to the weasels; *also* : the fur

otter

ot·to·man \ˈä-tə-mən\ *n* : an upholstered seat or couch usu. without a back; *also* : an overstuffed footstool

ou·bli·ette \ˌü-blē-ˈet\ *n* [F, fr. MF, fr. *oublier* to forget, ultim. fr. L *oblivisci*] : a dungeon with an opening at the top

ought \ˈȯt\ *verbal auxiliary* — used to express moral obligation, advisability, natural expectation, or logical consequence

ou·gui·ya \ü-ˈgwē-ə, -ˈgē-\ *n, pl* **ouguiya** — see MONEY table

ounce \ˈaůns\ *n* [ME, fr. AF *unce*, fr. L *uncia* twelfth part, ounce, fr. *unus* one] **1** : a unit of avoirdupois, troy, and apothecaries' weight — see WEIGHT table **2** : FLUID OUNCE

our \är, ˈaů(-ə)r\ *adj* : of or relating to us or ourselves

ours \ˈaů(-ə)z, ˈärz\ *pron* : that which belongs to us

our·selves \är-ˈselvz, aů(-ə)r-\ *pron* : our own selves — used reflexively, for emphasis, or in absolute constructions ⟨we pleased ~⟩ ⟨we'll do it ~⟩ ⟨we were tourists ~⟩

-ous *adj suffix* : full of : abounding in : having : possessing the qualities of ⟨clamor*ous*⟩ ⟨poison*ous*⟩

oust \ˈaůst\ *vb* : to eject from or deprive of property or position : EXPEL ♦ **Synonyms** EVICT, DISMISS, BANISH, DEPORT

oust·er \ˈaůs-tər\ *n* : EXPULSION

¹out \ˈaůt\ *adv* **1** : in a direction away from the inside or center **2** : beyond control **3** : to extinction, exhaustion, or completion **4** : in or into the open **5** : so as to retire a batter or base runner; *also* : so as to be retired

²out *vb* : to become known ⟨the truth will ~⟩

³out *prep* **1** : out through ⟨looked ~ the window⟩ **2** : outward on or along ⟨drive ~ the river road⟩

⁴out *adj* **1** : situated outside or at a distance **2** : not in : ABSENT; *also* : not being in power **3** : removed from play as a batter or base runner **4** : not being in vogue or fashion : not up-to-date **5** : attempting a particular activity ⟨won his first time ~⟩

⁵out *n* **1** : one who is out of office **2** : the retiring of a batter or base runner

out·age \ˈaů-tij\ *n* : a period or instance of interruption esp. of electricity

out–and–out *adj* : COMPLETE, THOROUGHGOING ⟨an ~ fraud⟩

out·bid \ˌaůt-ˈbid\ *vb* : to make a higher bid than

¹out·board \ˈaůt-ˌbȯrd\ *adj* **1** : situated outboard **2** : having or using an outboard motor

²outboard *adv* **1** : outside a ship's hull : away from the long axis of a ship **2** : in a position closer to the wing tip of an airplane

outboard motor *n* : a small internal combustion engine with propeller attached for mounting at the stern of a small boat

out·bound \ˈaůt-ˌbaůnd\ *adj* : outward bound ⟨~ traffic⟩

out·break \-ˌbrāk\ *n* 1 : a sudden increase in activity, incidence, or numbers 2 : INSURRECTION, REVOLT

out·build·ing \-ˌbil-diŋ\ *n* : a building separate from but accessory to a main house

out·burst \-ˌbərst\ *n* : ERUPTION; *esp* : a violent expression of feeling

out·cast \-ˌkast\ *n* : one that is cast out by society

out·class \aut-ˈklas\ *vb* : SURPASS

out·come \ˈau̇t-ˌkəm\ *n* : a final consequence : RESULT

out·crop \-ˌkräp\ *n* : a coming out of bedrock to the surface of the ground; *also* : the part of a rock formation that thus appears — **outcrop** *vb*

out·cry \-ˌkrī\ *n* : a loud cry : CLAMOR

out·dat·ed \au̇t-ˈdā-təd\ *adj* : OUTMODED

out·dis·tance \-ˈdis-təns\ *vb* : to go far ahead of (as in a race) : OUTSTRIP

out·do \-ˈdü\ *vb* **-did** \-ˈdid\; **-done** \-ˈdən\; **-do·ing; -does** \-ˈdəz\ : to go beyond in action or performance

out·door \ˈau̇t-ˌdȯr, -ˈdȯr\ *also* **out·doors** \-ˌdȯrz, -ˈdȯrz\ *adj* 1 : of or relating to the outdoors 2 : performed outdoors 3 : not enclosed (as by a roof)

¹out·doors \ˈau̇t-ˌdȯrz, -ˈdȯrz\ *adv* : in or into the open air

²outdoors *n* 1 : the open air 2 : the world away from human habitation — **out·doorsy** \ˌau̇t-ˈdȯr-zē\ *adj*

out·draw \au̇t-ˈdrȯ\ *vb* **-drew** \-ˈdrü\; **-drawn** \-ˈdrȯn\; **-draw·ing** 1 : to attract a larger audience than 2 : to draw a handgun more quickly than

out·er \ˈau̇-tər\ *adj* 1 : EXTERNAL 2 : situated farther out; *also* : being away from a center

outer ear *n* : the outer visible portion of the ear that collects and directs sound waves toward the eardrum

out·er·most \-ˌmōst\ *adj* : farthest out

outer space *n* : SPACE 5

out·er·wear \ˈau̇-tər-ˌwer\ *n* 1 : clothing for outdoor wear 2 : outer clothing as opposed to underwear

out·face \au̇t-ˈfās\ *vb* 1 : to cause to waver or submit 2 : DEFY

out·field \ˈau̇t-ˌfēld\ *n* : the part of a baseball field beyond the infield and within the foul lines; *also* : players in the outfield — **out·field·er** \-ˌfēl-dər\ *n*

out·fight \au̇t-ˈfīt\ *vb* : to surpass in fighting : DEFEAT

¹out·fit \ˈau̇t-ˌfit\ *n* 1 : the equipment or apparel for a special purpose or occasion 2 : GROUP

²outfit *vb* **out·fit·ted; out·fit·ting** : EQUIP — **out·fit·ter** *n*

out·flank \au̇t-ˈflaŋk\ *vb* : to get around the flank of (an opposing force)

out·flow \ˈau̇t-ˌflō\ *n* 1 : a flowing out 2 : something that flows out

out·fox \au̇t-ˈfäks\ *vb* : OUTWIT

out·go \ˈau̇t-ˌgō\ *n, pl* **outgoes** : EXPENDITURES, OUTLAY

out·go·ing \-ˌgō-iŋ\ *adj* 1 : going out (⁓ tide) 2 : retiring from a place or position 3 : FRIENDLY

out·grow \au̇t-ˈgrō\ *vb* **-grew** \-ˈgrü\; **-grown** \-ˈgrōn\; **-grow·ing** 1 : to grow faster than 2 : to grow too large for

out·growth \ˈau̇t-ˌgrōth\ *n* : a product of growing out : OFFSHOOT; *also* : CONSEQUENCE, RESULT

out·guess \au̇t-ˈges\ *vb* : OUTWIT

out·gun \-ˈgən\ *vb* : to surpass in firepower

out·house \ˈau̇t-ˌhau̇s\ *n* : OUTBUILDING; *esp* : an outdoor toilet

out·ing \ˈau̇-tiŋ\ *n* : a brief stay or trip in the open

out·land·ish \au̇t-ˈlan-dish\ *adj* 1 : of foreign appearance or manner; *also* : BIZARRE 2 : remote from civilization — **out·land·ish·ly** *adv*

out·last \-ˈlast\ *vb* : to last longer than

¹out·law \ˈau̇t-ˌlȯ\ *n* 1 : a person excluded from the protection of the law 2 : a lawless person

²outlaw *vb* 1 : to deprive of the protection of the law 2 : to make illegal — **out·law·ry** \ˈau̇t-ˌlȯr-ē\ *n*

out·lay \ˈau̇t-ˌlā\ *n* 1 : the act of spending 2 : EXPENDITURE

out·let \ˈau̇t-ˌlet, -lət\ *n* 1 : EXIT, VENT 2 : a means of release (as for an emotion) 3 : a medium for usu. public expression : a media organization 4 : a market for a commodity 5 : a receptacle for the plug of an electrical device

¹out·line \ˈau̇t-ˌlīn\ *n* 1 : a line marking the outer limits of an object or figure 2 : a drawing in which only contours are marked 3 : SUMMARY, SYNOPSIS 4 : PLAN

²outline *vb* 1 : to draw the outline of 2 : to indicate the chief features or parts of

out·live \au̇t-ˈliv\ *vb* : to live longer than

out·look \ˈau̇t-ˌlu̇k\ *n* 1 : a place offering a view; *also* : VIEW 2 : STANDPOINT 3 : the prospect for the future

out·ly·ing \ˈau̇t-ˌlī-iŋ\ *adj* : distant from a center or main body

out·ma·neu·ver \ˌau̇t-mə-ˈnü-vər, -ˈnyü-\ *vb* : to defeat by more skillful maneuvering

out·mod·ed \au̇t-ˈmō-dəd\ *adj* 1 : no longer in style 2 : no longer acceptable or current

out·num·ber \-ˈnəm-bər\ *vb* : to exceed in number

out of *prep* 1 : out from within or behind ⟨walk *out of* the room⟩ ⟨look *out of* the window⟩ 2 : from a state of ⟨wake up *out of* a deep sleep⟩ 3 : beyond the limits of ⟨*out of* sight⟩ 4 : BECAUSE OF ⟨asked *out of* curiosity⟩ 5 : FROM, WITH ⟨built it *out of* scrap⟩ 6 : in or into a state of loss or not having ⟨cheated him *out of* $5000⟩ ⟨we're *out of* matches⟩ 7 : from among ⟨one *out of* four⟩ — **out of it** : SQUARE, OLD-FASHIONED

out-of-bounds *adv or adj* : outside the prescribed boundaries or limits

out-of-date *adj* : no longer in fashion or in use : OUTMODED

out-of-door *or* out-of-doors *adj* : OUTDOOR

out-of-the-way *adj* 1 : UNUSUAL 2 : being off the beaten track

out·pa·tient \ˈau̇t-ˌpā-shənt\ *n* : a patient who visits a hospital or clinic for diagnosis or treatment without staying overnight

out·per·form \ˌau̇t-pər-ˈfȯrm\ *vb* : to perform better than

out·play \au̇t-ˈplā\ *vb* : to play more skillfully than

out·point \-ˈpȯint\ *vb* : to win more points than

out·post \ˈau̇t-ˌpōst\ *n* 1 : a security detachment dispatched by a main body of troops to protect it from enemy surprise; *also* : a military base established (as by treaty) in a foreign country 2 : an outlying or frontier settlement

out·pour·ing \-ˌpȯr-iŋ\ *n* : something that pours out or is poured out

out·pull \au̇t-ˈpu̇l\ *vb* : OUTDRAW 1

¹out·put \ˈau̇t-ˌpu̇t\ *n* 1 : the amount produced (as by a machine or factory) : PRODUCTION 2 : the information produced by a computer

²output *vb* **out·put·ted** *or* **output; out·put·ting** : to produce as output

¹out·rage \ˈau̇t-ˌrāj\ *n* [ME, fr. AF *utrage, outrage* insult, excess, fr. *utre, outre* beyond, fr. L *ultra*] 1 : a violent or shameful act 2 : INJURY, INSULT 3 : the anger or resentment aroused by injury or insult

²outrage *vb* **out·raged; out·rag·ing** 1 : RAPE 2 : to subject to violent injury or gross insult 3 : to arouse to extreme resentment

out·ra·geous \au̇t-ˈrā-jəs\ *adj* : extremely offensive, insulting, or shameful : SHOCKING — **out·ra·geous·ly** *adv*

out·rank \-ˈraŋk\ *vb* : to rank higher than

ou·tré \ü-ˈtrā\ *adj* [F] : violating convention or propriety : BIZARRE

¹out·reach \au̇t-ˈrēch\ *vb* 1 : to surpass in reach 2 : to get the better of by trickery

²out·reach \ˈau̇t-ˌrēch\ *n* 1 : the act of reaching out 2 : the extent of reach 3 : the extending of services beyond usual limits

out·rid·er \ˈau̇t-ˌrī-dər\ *n* : a mounted attendant

out·rig·ger \-ˌri-gər\ *n* 1 : a frame attached to the side of a boat to prevent capsizing 2 : a craft equipped with an outrigger

¹out·right \au̇t-ˈrīt\ *adv* 1 : COMPLETELY 2 : INSTANTANEOUSLY

²out·right \ˈau̇t-ˌrīt\ *adj* 1 : being exactly what is stated ⟨an ⁓ lie⟩ 2 : given or made without reservation or encumbrance ⟨an ⁓ sale⟩

out·run \au̇t-ˈrən\ *vb* **-ran** \-ˈran\; **-run; -run·ning** : to run faster than; *also* : EXCEED

out·sell \-ˈsel\ *vb* **-sold** \-ˈsōld\; **-sell·ing** : to exceed in sales

out·set \ˈau̇t-ˌset\ *n* : BEGINNING, START

out·shine \au̇t-ˈshīn\ *vb* **-shone** \-ˈshōn\ *or* **-shined; -shin·ing** 1 : to shine brighter than 2 : SURPASS

¹out·side \au̇t-ˈsīd, ˈau̇t-ˌsīd\ *n* 1 : a place or region beyond an enclosure or boundary 2 : EXTERIOR 3 : the utmost limit or extent

²outside *adj* 1 : OUTER 2 : coming from without ⟨⁓ in-

fluences⟩ **3** : being apart from one's regular duties ⟨∼ activities⟩ **4** : REMOTE ⟨an ∼ chance⟩
³outside *adv* : on or to the outside
⁴outside *prep* **1** : on or to the outside of **2** : beyond the limits of **3** : EXCEPT
outside of *prep* **1** : OUTSIDE **2** : BESIDES
out·sid·er \aut-'sī-dər\ *n* : a person who does not belong to a group
out·size \'aut-ˌsīz\ *also* **out·sized** \-ˌsīzd\ *adj* : unusually large : extravagant in size or degree
out·skirts \-ˌskərts\ *n pl* : the outlying parts (as of a city) : BORDERS
out·smart \aut-'smärt\ *vb* : OUTWIT
out·source \'aut-ˌsórs\ *vb* **-sourced; -sourcing** : to obtain (goods or services) from an outside supplier
out·spend \-'spend\ *vb* **1** : to exceed the limits of in spending ⟨∼s his income⟩ **2** : to spend more than
out·spo·ken \aut-'spō-kən\ *adj* : direct and open in speech or expression — **out·spo·ken·ly** *adv* — **out·spo·ken·ness** *n*
out·spread \-'spred\ *vb* **-spread; -spread·ing** : to spread out
out·stand·ing \-'stan-diŋ\ *adj* **1** : PROJECTING **2** : UNPAID; *also* : UNRESOLVED ⟨∼ warrants⟩ **3** : publicly issued and sold **4** : CONSPICUOUS; *also* : DISTINGUISHED — **out·stand·ing·ly** *adv*
out·stay \-'stā\ *vb* **1** : OVERSTAY **2** : to surpass in endurance
out·stretch \ˌaut-'strech\ *vb* : to stretch out : EXTEND
out·strip \-'strip\ *vb* **1** : to go faster than **2** : EXCEL, SURPASS
out·take \'aut-ˌtāk\ *n* : something taken out; *esp* : a take that is not used in an edited version of a film or videotape
out·vote \-'vōt\ *vb* : to defeat by a majority of votes
¹out·ward \'aut-wərd\ *adj* **1** : moving or directed toward the outside **2** : showing outwardly
²outward *or* **out·wards** \-wərdz\ *adv* : toward the outside
out·ward·ly \-wərd-lē\ *adv* : on the outside : EXTERNALLY
out·wear \aut-'wer\ *vb* **-wore** \-'wór\; **-worn** \-'wórn\; **-wear·ing** : to wear longer than : OUTLAST
out·weigh \-'wā\ *vb* : to exceed in weight, value, or importance
out·wit \-'wit\ *vb* : to get the better of by superior cleverness
¹out·work \-'wərk\ *vb* : to outdo in working
²out·work \'aut-ˌwərk\ *n* : a minor defensive position outside a fortified area
out·worn \aut-'wórn\ *adj* : OUTMODED
ou·zo \'ü-(ˌ)zō\ *n* : a colorless anise-flavored unsweetened Greek liqueur
ova *pl of* OVUM
oval \'ō-vəl\ *adj* [ML *ovalis*, fr. LL, of an egg, fr. L *ovum* egg] : egg-shaped; *also* : broadly elliptical — **oval** *n*
ova·ry \'ō-və-rē\ *n, pl* **-ries** **1** : one of the usu. paired female reproductive organs producing eggs and in vertebrates sex hormones **2** : the part of a flower in which seeds are produced — **ovar·i·an** \ō-'ver-ē-ən\ *adj*
ovate \'ō-ˌvāt\ *adj* : egg-shaped
ova·tion \ō-'vā-shən\ *n* [L *ovation-, ovatio*, fr. *ovare* to exult] : an enthusiastic popular tribute
ov·en \'ə-vən\ *n* : a chamber (as in a stove) for baking, heating, or drying
oven·bird \-ˌbərd\ *n* : a large olive-green American warbler that builds its dome-shaped nest on the ground
¹over \'ō-vər\ *adv* **1** : across a barrier or intervening space **2** : across the brim ⟨boil ∼⟩ **3** : so as to bring the underside up **4** : out of a vertical position **5** : beyond some quantity, limit, or norm **6** : ABOVE **7** : at an end **8** : THROUGH ⟨read it ∼⟩; *also* : THOROUGHLY **9** : AGAIN ⟨do it ∼⟩
²over *prep* **1** : above in position, authority, or scope ⟨towered ∼ her⟩ ⟨obeyed those ∼ him⟩ **2** : more than ⟨cost ∼ $100⟩ **3** : ON, UPON ⟨a cape ∼ her shoulders⟩ **4** : along the length of ⟨∼ the road⟩ **5** : through the medium of : ON ⟨spoke ∼ TV⟩ **6** : all through ⟨showed me ∼ the house⟩ **7** : on or to the other side or beyond ⟨jump ∼ a ditch⟩ **8** : DURING ⟨∼ the past 25 years⟩ **9** : on account of ⟨trouble ∼ money⟩
³over *adj* **1** : UPPER, HIGHER **2** : REMAINING **3** : ENDED
over- *prefix* **1** : so as to exceed or surpass **2** : excessive; excessively

overabundance
overabundant
overachiever
overactive
overaggressive
overambitious
overanxious
overbid
overbold
overbuild
overburden
overbuy
overcapacity
overcapitalize
overcareful
overcautious
overcompensation
overconfidence
overconfident
overconscientious
overcook
overcritical
overcrowd
overdecorated
overdependence
overdetermined
overdevelop
overdress
overeager
overeat
overeducated
overemphasis
overemphasize
overenthusiastic
overestimate
overexcite
overexcited
overexert
overexertion
overextend
overfatigued
overfeed
overfill
overgeneralization
overgeneralize

overgenerous
overgraze
overhasty
overheat
overindulge
overindulgence
overindulgent
overlarge
overlearn
overload
overlong
overmodest
overnice
overoptimism
overoptimistic
overpay
overpraise
overproduce
overproduction
overprotect
overprotective
overrate
overreact
overreaction
overrefinement
overrepresented
overripe
oversensitive
oversensitiveness
oversimple
oversimplification
oversimplify
overspecialization
overspecialize
overspend
overstimulation
overstock
oversubtle
oversupply
overtax
overtired
overtrain
overuse
overvalue
overzealous

over·act \ˌō-vər-'akt\ *vb* : to exaggerate in acting
¹over·age \ō-vər-'āj\ *adj* **1** : too old to be useful **2** : older than is normal for one's position, function, or grade
²over·age \'ō-və-rij\ *n* : SURPLUS
over·all \ˌō-vər-'ól\ *adj* : including everything ⟨∼ expenses⟩
over·alls \'ō-vər-ˌólz\ *n pl* : pants of strong material usu. with a piece extending up to cover the chest
over·arm \-ˌärm\ *adj* : done with the arm raised above the shoulder
over·awe \ˌō-vər-'ó\ *vb* : to restrain or subdue by awe
over·bal·ance \-'ba-ləns\ *vb* **1** : OUTWEIGH **2** : to cause to lose balance
over·bear·ing \-'ber-iŋ\ *adj* : ARROGANT, DOMINEERING
over·bite \'ō-vər-ˌbīt\ *n* : the projection of the upper front teeth over the lower
over·blown \-'blōn\ *adj* **1** : PORTLY **2** : INFLATED, PRETENTIOUS
over·board \'ō-vər-ˌbórd\ *adv* **1** : over the side of a ship into the water **2** : to extremes of enthusiasm
¹over·cast \'ō-vər-ˌkast\ *adj* : clouded over : GLOOMY
²overcast *n* : COVERING; *esp* : a covering of clouds
over·charge \ˌō-vər-'chärj\ *vb* **1** : to charge too much **2** : to fill or load too full — **over·charge** \'ō-vər-ˌchärj\ *n*
over·coat \'ō-vər-ˌkōt\ *n* : a warm coat worn over indoor clothing
over·come \ˌō-vər-'kəm\ *vb* **-came** \-'kām\; **-come; -coming** **1** : CONQUER **2** : to make helpless or exhausted
over·do \ˌō-vər-'dü\ *vb* **-did** \-'did\; **-done** \-'dən\; **-doing; -does** \-'dəz\ **1** : to do too much; *also* : to tire oneself **2** : EXAGGERATE **3** : to cook too long
over·dose \'ō-vər-ˌdōs\ *n* : too great a dose (as of medicine); *also* : a lethal or toxic amount (as of a drug) — **over·dose** \ˌō-vər-'dōs\ *vb*
over·draft \'ō-vər-ˌdraft\ *n* : an overdrawing of a bank account; *also* : the sum overdrawn
over·draw \ˌō-vər-'dró\ *vb* **-drew** \-'drü\; **-drawn** \-'drón\; **-draw·ing** **1** : to draw checks on a bank account for more than the balance **2** : EXAGGERATE
over·drive \'ō-vər-ˌdrīv\ *n* : an automotive transmission gear that transmits to the driveshaft a speed greater than the engine speed
over·dub \ˌō-vər-'dəb\ *vb* : to transfer (recorded sound)

onto an earlier recording for a combined effect — **over-dub** \'ō-vər-ˌdəb\ n

over·due \-'dü, -'dyü\ adj **1** : unpaid when due ⟨an ~ bill⟩; also : not appearing or presented on time ⟨an ~ train⟩ **2** : more than ready

over·ex·pose \ˌō-vər-ik-'spōz\ vb : to expose (as film) for more time than is needed — **over·ex·po·sure** \-'spō-zhər\ n

¹**over·flow** \-'flō\ vb **1** : INUNDATE; also : to pour forth in a flood **2** : to flow over the brim or top of

²**over·flow** \'ō-vər-ˌflō\ n **1** : FLOOD; also : SURPLUS **2** : an outlet for surplus liquid

over·fly \ˌō-vər-'flī\ vb **-flew** \-'flü\; **-flown** \-'flōn\; **-fly·ing** : to fly over in an aircraft or spacecraft — **over·flight** \'ō-vər-ˌflīt\ n

over·grow \ˌō-vər-'grō\ vb **-grew** \-'grü\; **-grown** \-'grōn\; **-grow·ing 1** : to grow over so as to cover **2** : OUTGROW **3** : to grow excessively — **over·growth** \'ō-vər-ˌgrōth\ n

over·hand \'ō-vər-ˌhand\ adj : made with the hand brought down from above — **overhand** adv — **over·hand·ed** \-ˌhan-dəd\ adv or adj

¹**over·hang** \'ō-vər-ˌhaŋ, ˌō-vər-'haŋ\ vb **-hung** \-ˌhəŋ, -'həŋ\; **-hang·ing 1** : to project over : jut out **2** : to hang over threateningly

²**over·hang** \'ō-vər-ˌhaŋ\ n : a part (as of a roof) that overhangs

over·haul \ˌō-vər-'hȯl\ vb **1** : to examine thoroughly and make necessary repairs and adjustments **2** : OVERTAKE

¹**over·head** \ˌō-vər-'hed\ adv : ALOFT

²**over·head** \'ō-vər-ˌhed\ adj : operating or lying above ⟨~ door⟩

³**over·head** \'ō-vər-ˌhed\ n : business expenses not chargeable to a particular part of the work

over·hear \ˌō-vər-'hir\ vb **-heard** \-'hərd\; **-hear·ing** : to hear without the speaker's knowledge or intention

over·joyed \ˌō-vər-'jȯid\ adj : filled with great joy

over·kill \'ō-vər-ˌkil\ n **1** : destructive capacity greatly exceeding that required for a target **2** : a large excess

over·land \'ō-vər-ˌland, -lənd\ adv or adj : by, on, or across land

over·lap \ˌō-vər-'lap\ vb **1** : to lap over **2** : to have something in common — **over·lap** \'ō-vər-ˌlap\ n

over·lay \ˌō-vər-'lā\ vb **-laid** \-'lād\; **-lay·ing** : to lay or spread over or across — **over·lay** \'ō-vər-ˌlā\ n

over·leap \ˌō-vər-'lēp\ vb **-leaped** or **-leapt** \-'lēpt, -'lept\; **-leap·ing 1** : to leap over or across **2** : to defeat (oneself) by going too far

over·lie \ˌō-vər-'lī\ vb **-lay** \-'lā\; **-lain** \-'lān\; **-ly·ing** : to lie over or upon

¹**over·look** \ˌō-vər-'lük\ vb **1** : INSPECT **2** : to look down on from above **3** : to fail to see **4** : IGNORE; also : EXCUSE **5** : SUPERINTEND

²**over·look** \'ō-vər-ˌlük\ n : a place from which to look upon a scene below

over·lord \-ˌlȯrd\ n : a lord who has supremacy over other lords

over·ly \'ō-vər-lē\ adv : EXCESSIVELY

over·match \ˌō-vər-'mach\ vb : to be more than a match for : DEFEAT

over·much \-'məch\ adj or adv : too much

¹**over·night** \-'nīt\ adv **1** : on or during the night **2** : SUDDENLY ⟨became famous ~⟩

²**overnight** adj : of, lasting, or staying the night ⟨~ guests⟩

over·pass \'ō-vər-ˌpas\ n **1** : a crossing (as of two highways) at different levels by means of a bridge **2** : the upper level of an overpass

over·play \ˌō-vər-'plā\ vb **1** : EXAGGERATE; also : OVER-EMPHASIZE **2** : to rely too much on the strength of

over·pop·u·la·tion \ˌō-vər-ˌpä-pyə-'lā-shən\ n : the condition of having a population so dense as to cause a decline in population or in living conditions — **over·pop·u·lat·ed** \-'pä-pyə-ˌlā-təd\ adj

over·pow·er \-'pau̇(-ə)r\ vb : to overcome by superior force

over·price \ˌō-vər-'prīs\ vb : to price too high

over·print \-'print\ vb : to print over with something additional — **over·print** \'ō-vər-ˌprint\ n

over·qual·i·fied \-'kwä-lə-ˌfīd\ adj : having more education, training, or experience than a job calls for

over·reach \ˌō-vər-'rēch\ vb : to defeat (oneself) by too great an effort

over·ride \-'rīd\ vb **-rode** \-'rōd\; **-rid·den** \-'ri-d²n\; **-rid·ing 1** : to ride over or across **2** : to prevail over; also : to set aside ⟨~ a veto⟩

over·rule \-'rül\ vb **1** : to prevail over **2** : to rule against **3** : to set aside

¹**over·run** \-'rən\ vb **-ran** \-'ran\; **-run; -run·ning 1** : to defeat and occupy the positions of **2** : OVERSPREAD; also : INFEST **3** : to go beyond **4** : to flow over

²**over·run** \'ō-vər-ˌrən\ n **1** : an act or instance of overrunning; esp : an exceeding of estimated costs **2** : the amount by which something overruns

over·sea \ˌō-vər-'sē, 'ō-vər-ˌsē\ adj or adv : OVERSEAS

over·seas \ˌō-vər-'sēz, -ˌsēz\ adv or adj : beyond or across the sea : ABROAD

over·see \ˌō-vər-'sē\ vb **-saw** \-'sȯ\; **-seen** \-'sēn\; **-see·ing 1** : OVERLOOK **2** : INSPECT; also : SUPERVISE — **over·seer** \'ō-vər-ˌsir\ n

over·sell \ˌō-vər-'sel\ vb **-sold; -sell·ing** : to sell too much to or too much of

over·sexed \ˌō-vər-'sekst\ adj : exhibiting excessive sexual drive or interest

over·shad·ow \-'sha-dō\ vb **1** : to cast a shadow over **2** : to exceed in importance

over·shoe \'ō-vər-ˌshü\ n : a protective outer shoe; esp : GALOSH

over·shoot \ˌō-vər-'shüt\ vb **-shot** \-'shät\; **-shoot·ing 1** : to pass swiftly beyond **2** : to shoot over or beyond

over·sight \'ō-vər-ˌsīt\ n **1** : SUPERVISION **2** : an inadvertent omission or error

over·size \ˌō-vər-'sīz\ or **over·sized** \-'sīzd\ adj : of more than ordinary size

over·sleep \ˌō-vər-'slēp\ vb **-slept** \-'slept\; **-sleep·ing** : to sleep beyond the time for waking

over·spread \-'spred\ vb **-spread; -spread·ing** : to spread over or above

over·state \-'stāt\ vb : EXAGGERATE — **over·state·ment** n

over·stay \-'stā\ vb : to stay beyond the time or limits of

over·step \-'step\ vb : EXCEED

over·sub·scribe \-səb-'skrīb\ vb : to subscribe for more of than is available, asked for, or offered for sale

overt \ō-'vərt, 'ō-ˌvərt\ adj [ME, fr. AF, fr. pp. of ovrir to open] : not secret — **overt·ly** adv

over·take \ˌō-vər-'tāk\ vb **-took** \-'tük\; **-tak·en** \-'tā-kən\; **-tak·ing** : to catch up with; also : to catch up with and pass by ⟨~ the lead runner⟩

over–the–counter adj : sold lawfully without a prescription ⟨~ drugs⟩

over–the–hill adj **1** : past one's prime **2** : advanced in age

over–the–top adj **1** : extremely flamboyant or outrageous ⟨an ~ performance⟩

over·throw \ˌō-vər-'thrō\ vb **-threw** \-'thrü\; **-thrown** \-'thrōn\; **-throw·ing 1** : UPSET **2** : to bring down : DEFEAT ⟨~ a government⟩ **3** : to throw over or past — **over·throw** \'ō-vər-ˌthrō\ n

over·time \'ō-vər-ˌtīm\ n : time beyond a set limit; esp : working time in excess of a standard day or week — **overtime** adv

over·tone \-ˌtōn\ n **1** : one of the higher tones in a complex musical tone **2** : IMPLICATION, SUGGESTION

over·trick \'ō-vər-ˌtrik\ n : a card trick won in excess of the number bid

over·ture \'ō-vər-ˌchu̇r, -chər\ n [ME, lit., opening, fr. AF, fr. VL *opertura, alter. of L apertura] **1** : an opening offer **2** : an orchestral introduction to a musical dramatic work

over·turn \ˌō-vər-'tərn\ vb **1** : to turn over : UPSET ⟨~ a vase⟩ **2** : INVALIDATE ⟨~ a court ruling⟩

over·view \'ō-vər-ˌvyü\ n : a general survey : SUMMARY

over·ween·ing \ˌō-vər-'wē-niŋ\ adj **1** : ARROGANT **2** : IMMODERATE

over·weight \'ō-vər-ˌwāt\ n **1** : weight above what is required or allowed **2** : bodily weight greater than normal — **overweight** adj

over·whelm \ˌō-vər-'hwelm\ vb **1** : OVERTHROW **2** : SUBMERGE **3** : to overcome completely

over·whelm·ing adj : EXTREME, GREAT ⟨~ joy⟩ — **over·whelm·ing·ly** adv

over·win·ter \-'win-tər\ vb : to survive or pass the winter

over·work \-'wərk\ vb **1** : to work or cause to work too hard or long **2** : to use too much — **overwork** n

over·wrought \ˌō-vər-ˈrȯt\ *adj* **1** : extremely excited **2** : elaborated to excess

ovi·duct \ˈō-və-ˌdəkt\ *n* : a tube that serves for the passage of eggs from an ovary

ovip·a·rous \ō-ˈvi-pə-rəs\ *adj* : reproducing by eggs that hatch outside the parent's body

ovoid \ˈō-ˌvȯid\ *or* **ovoi·dal** \ō-ˈvȯi-dᵊl\ *adj* : egg-shaped : OVAL

ovu·la·tion \ˌäv-yə-ˈlā-shən, ˌōv-\ *n* : the discharge of a mature egg from the ovary — **ovu·late** \ˈäv-yə-ˌlāt, ˈōv-\ *vb*

ovule \ˈäv-yül, ˈōv-\ *n* : any of the bodies in a plant ovary that after fertilization become seeds

ovum \ˈō-vəm\ *n, pl* **ova** \-və\ : EGG 2

ow \ˈau̇\ *interj* — used esp. to express sudden pain

owe \ˈō\ *vb* **owed; ow·ing** **1** : to be under obligation to pay or render **2** : to be indebted to or for; *also* : to be in debt

owing to *prep* : BECAUSE OF

owl \ˈau̇(-ə)l\ *n* : any of an order of chiefly nocturnal birds of prey with a large head and eyes and strong talons — **owl·ish** *adj* — **owl·ish·ly** *adv*

owl·et \ˈau̇-lət\ *n* : a young or small owl

¹own \ˈōn\ *adj* : belonging to oneself — used as an intensive after a possessive adjective ⟨her ~ car⟩

²own *vb* **1** : to have or hold as property **2** : to have power or mastery over **3** : ACKNOWLEDGE; *also* : CONFESS — **own·er** *n* — **own·er·ship** *n*

³own *pron* : one or ones belonging to oneself — **on one's own** : for or by oneself : left to one's own resources

ox \ˈäks\ *n, pl* **ox·en** \ˈäk-sən\ *also* **ox** : any of the large domestic bovine mammals kept for milk, draft, and meat; *esp* : an adult castrated male ox

ox·blood \ˈäks-ˌbləd\ *n* : a moderate reddish brown

ox·bow \-ˌbō\ *n* **1** : a U-shaped collar worn by a draft ox **2** : a U-shaped bend in a river — **oxbow** *adj*

ox·ford \ˈäks-fərd\ *n* : a low shoe laced or tied over the instep

ox·i·dant \ˈäk-sə-dənt\ *n* : OXIDIZING AGENT — **oxidant** *adj*

ox·i·da·tion \ˌäk-sə-ˈdā-shən\ *n* : the act or process of oxidizing; *also* : the condition of being oxidized — **ox·i·da·tive** \ˈäk-sə-ˌdā-tiv\ *adj*

ox·ide \ˈäk-ˌsīd\ *n* : a compound of oxygen with another element or group

ox·i·dize \ˈäk-sə-ˌdīz\ *vb* **-dized; -diz·ing** : to combine with oxygen ⟨iron rusts because it is *oxidized* by exposure to the air⟩ — **ox·i·diz·er** *n*

oxidizing agent *n* : a substance (as oxygen or nitric acid) that oxidizes by taking up electrons

ox·y·gen \ˈäk-si-jən\ *n* [F *oxygène*, fr. Gk *oxys* acidic, lit., sharp + *-genēs* giving rise to; so called because it was once thought to be an essential element of all acids] : a colorless odorless gaseous chemical element that is found in the air, is essential to life, and is involved in combustion

ox·y·gen·ate \ˈäk-si-jə-ˌnāt\ *vb* **-at·ed; -at·ing** : to impregnate, combine, or supply with oxygen — **ox·y·gen·a·tion** \ˌäk-si-jə-ˈnā-shən\ *n*

oxygen mask *n* : a device worn over the nose and mouth through which oxygen is supplied

oxygen tent *n* : a canopy which can be placed over a bedridden person and within which a flow of oxygen can be maintained

ox·y·mo·ron \ˌäk-sē-ˈmȯr-ˌän\ *n* : a combination of contradictory words (as *cruel kindness*) — **ox·y·mo·ron·ic** \-mə-ˈrä-nik\ *adj*

oys·ter \ˈȯi-stər\ *n* : any of various marine mollusks with an irregular 2-valved shell that include commercially important edible shellfish and pearl producers — **oys·ter·ing** *n* — **oys·ter·man** \-mən\ *n*

oz *abbr* [obs. It *onza* (now *oncia*)] ounce; ounces

ozone \ˈō-ˌzōn\ *n* **1** : a bluish gaseous reactive form of oxygen that is formed naturally in the atmosphere and is used for disinfecting, deodorizing, and bleaching **2** : pure and refreshing air

ozone layer *n* : an atmospheric layer at heights of about 25 miles (40 kilometers) with high ozone content which blocks most solar ultraviolet radiation

¹p \ˈpē\ *n, pl* **p's** *or* **ps** \ˈpēz\ *often cap* : the 16th letter of the English alphabet

²p *abbr, often cap* **1** page **2** participle **3** past **4** pawn **5** pence; penny **6** per **7** petite **8** pint **9** pressure **10** purl

P *symbol* phosphorus

pa \ˈpä, ˈpȯ\ *n* : FATHER

¹Pa *abbr* **1** pascal **2** Pennsylvania

²Pa *symbol* protactinium

¹PA \ˌ(ˌ)pē-ˈä\ *n* : PHYSICIAN'S ASSISTANT

²PA *abbr* **1** Pennsylvania **2** per annum **3** power of attorney **4** press agent **5** private account **6** professional association **7** public address **8** purchasing agent

pa·'an·ga \pä-ˈäŋ-gə\ *n* — see MONEY table

pab·u·lum \ˈpa-byə-ləm\ *n* [L, food, fodder] : usu. soft digestible food

Pac *abbr* Pacific

PAC *abbr* political action committee

¹pace \ˈpās\ *n* **1** : rate of movement or progress (as in walking or working) **2** : a step in walking; *also* : a measure of length based on such a step **3** : GAIT; *esp* : a horse's gait in which the legs on the same side move together

²pace *vb* **paced; pac·ing** **1** : to go or cover at a pace or with slow steps **2** : to measure off by paces **3** : to set or regulate the pace of

³pace \ˈpä-sē, ˈpä-ˌkä, -ˌchä\ *prep* : contrary to the opinion of

pace·mak·er \ˈpās-ˌmā-kər\ *n* **1** : one that sets the pace for another **2** : a body part (as of the heart) that serves to establish and maintain a rhythmic activity **3** : an electrical device for stimulating or steadying the heartbeat

pac·er \ˈpā-sər\ *n* **1** : a horse that paces **2** : PACEMAKER

pachy·derm \ˈpa-ki-ˌdərm\ *n* [F *pachyderme*, fr. Gk *pachydermos* thick-skinned, fr. *pachys* thick + *derma* skin] : any of various thick-skinned hoofed mammals (as an elephant)

pachy·san·dra \ˌpa-ki-ˈsan-drə\ *n* : any of a genus of low perennial evergreen plants used as a ground cover

pa·cif·ic \pə-ˈsi-fik\ *adj* **1** : tending to lessen conflict **2** : CALM, PEACEFUL

pac·i·fi·er \ˈpa-sə-ˌfī(-ə)r\ *n* : one that pacifies; *esp* : a device for a baby to chew or suck on

pac·i·fism \ˈpa-sə-ˌfi-zəm\ *n* : opposition to war or violence as a means of settling disputes — **pac·i·fist** \-fist\ *n or adj* — **pac·i·fis·tic** \ˌpa-sə-ˈfis-tik\ *adj*

pac·i·fy \ˈpa-sə-ˌfī\ *vb* **-fied; -fy·ing** **1** : to allay anger or agitation in : SOOTHE **2** : SETTLE; *also* : SUBDUE — **pac·i·fi·ca·tion** \ˌpa-sə-fə-ˈkā-shən\ *n*

¹pack \ˈpak\ *n* **1** : a compact bundle; *also* : a flexible container for carrying a bundle esp. on the back **2** : a large amount : HEAP **3** : a set of playing cards **4** : a group or band of people or animals **5** : wet absorbent material for application to the body

²pack *vb* **1** : to stow goods in for transportation **2** : to fill in or surround so as to prevent passage of air, steam, or water **3** : to put into a protective container **4** : to load with a pack ⟨~ a mule⟩ **5** : to crowd in **6** : to make into a pack **7** : to cause to go without ceremony ⟨~ them off to school⟩ **8** : WEAR, CARRY ⟨~ a gun⟩

³pack *vb* : to make up fraudulently so as to secure a desired result ⟨∼ a jury⟩

¹pack·age \'pa-kij\ *n* 1 : BUNDLE, PARCEL 2 : a group of related things offered as a whole

²package *vb* **pack·aged; pack·ag·ing** : to make into or enclose in a package

package deal *n* : an offer containing several items all or none of which must be accepted

package store *n* : a store that sells alcoholic beverages in sealed containers for consumption off the premises

pack·er \'pa-kər\ *n* : one that packs; *esp* : a wholesale food dealer

pack·et \'pa-kət\ *n* 1 : a small bundle or package 2 : a passenger boat carrying mail and cargo on a regular schedule

pack·horse \'pak-ˌhòrs\ *n* : a horse used to carry goods or supplies

pack·ing \'pa-kin\ *n* : material used to pack something

pack·ing·house \-ˌhaùs\ *n* : an establishment for processing and packing food and esp. meat and its by-products

pack rat *n* 1 : a bushy-tailed rodent of western No. America that hoards food and miscellaneous objects; *also* : any of several rodents of similar habit 2 : a person who collects or saves many esp. unneeded items

pack·sad·dle \'pak-ˌsa-dᵊl\ *n* : a saddle for supporting loads on the back of an animal

pack·thread \-ˌthred\ *n* : strong thread for tying

pact \'pakt\ *n* : AGREEMENT, TREATY

¹pad \'pad\ *n* 1 : a cushioning part or thing : CUSHION 2 : the cushioned underside of the foot or toes of some mammals 3 : the floating leaf of a water plant 4 : a writing tablet 5 : LAUNCHPAD 6 : living quarters; *also* : BED

²pad *vb* **pad·ded; pad·ding** 1 : to furnish with a pad or padding 2 : to expand with needless or fraudulent matter

pad·ding *n* : the material with which something is padded

¹pad·dle \'pa-dᵊl\ *vb* **pad·dled; pad·dling** : to move the hands and feet about in shallow water

²paddle *n* 1 : an implement with a flat blade used in propelling and steering a small craft (as a canoe) 2 : an implement used for stirring, mixing, or beating 3 : a broad board on the outer rim of a waterwheel or a paddle wheel

³paddle *vb* **pad·dled; pad·dling** 1 : to move on or through water by or as if by using a paddle 2 : to beat or stir with a paddle

paddle wheel *n* : a wheel with paddles around its outer edge used to move a boat

paddle wheeler *n* : a steam-driven vessel propelled by a paddle wheel

paddle wheeler

pad·dock \'pa-dək\ *n* 1 : a usu. enclosed area for pasturing or exercising animals; *esp* : one where racehorses are saddled and paraded before a race 2 : an area at a racecourse where racing cars are parked

pad·dy \'pa-dē\ *n, pl* **paddies** : wet land where rice is grown

paddy wagon *n* : an enclosed motortruck for carrying prisoners

pad·lock \'pad-ˌläk\ *n* : a removable lock with a curved piece that snaps into a catch — **padlock** *vb*

pa·dre \'pä-drā\ *n* [Sp or It or Pg, lit., father, fr. L *pater*] 1 : PRIEST 2 : a military chaplain

pad thai \'päd-'tī\ *n, often cap T* : a Thai dish of rice noodles stir-fried with additional ingredients

pae·an \'pē-ən\ *n* : an exultant song of praise or thanksgiving

pae·di·at·ric, pae·di·a·tri·cian, pae·di·at·rics *chiefly Brit var of* PEDIATRIC, PEDIATRICIAN, PEDIATRICS

pa·el·la \pä-'e-lə; -'äl-yə, -'ā-yə\ *n* : a saffron-flavored dish of rice, meat, seafood, and vegetables

pa·gan \'pā-gən\ *n* [ME, fr. LL *paganus*, fr. L, civilian, country dweller, fr. *pagus* country district] : HEATHEN — **pagan** *adj* — **pa·gan·ism** \-gə-ˌni-zəm\ *n*

¹page \'pāj\ *n* : ATTENDANT; *esp* : one employed to deliver messages

²page *vb* **paged; pag·ing** 1 : to summon by repeatedly calling out the name of 2 : to send a message to via a pager

³page *n* 1 : a single leaf (as of a book); *also* : a single side of such a leaf 2 : the information at a single World Wide Web address

⁴page *vb* **paged; pag·ing** : to mark or number the pages of

pag·eant \'pa-jənt\ *n* [ME *pagyn, padgeant*, lit., scene of a play, fr. AF *pagine, pagent*, fr. ML *pagina*, perh. fr. L, page] : an elaborate spectacle, show, or procession esp. with tableaux or floats — **pag·eant·ry** \-jən-trē\ *n*

page·boy \'pāj-ˌbòi\ *n* [¹*page*] : an often shoulder-length hairdo with the ends of the hair turned smoothly under

pag·er \'pā-jər\ *n* : one that pages; *esp* : a small radio receiver that alerts its user to incoming messages

pag·i·nate \'pa-jə-ˌnāt\ *vb* **-nat·ed; -nat·ing** : ⁴PAGE

pag·i·na·tion \ˌpa-jə-'nā-shən\ *n* 1 : the paging of written or printed matter 2 : the number and arrangement of pages (as of a book)

pa·go·da \pə-'gō-də\ *n* : a tower with roofs curving upward at the division of each of several stories

paid *past and past part of* PAY

pail \'pāl\ *n* : a usu. cylindrical vessel with a handle — **pail·ful** \-ˌfùl\ *n*

¹pain \'pān\ *n* 1 : PUNISHMENT, PENALTY 2 : suffering or distress of body or mind; *also* : a basic bodily sensation marked by discomfort (as throbbing or aching) 3 *pl* : great care 4 : one that irks or annoys — **pain·ful** \-fəl\ *adj* — **pain·ful·ly** *adv* — **pain·less** *adj* — **pain·less·ly** *adv*

²pain *vb* : to cause or experience pain

pain·kill·er \'pān-ˌki-lər\ *n* : something (as a drug) that relieves pain — **pain·kill·ing** *adj*

pains·tak·ing \'pān-ˌstā-kin\ *adj* : taking pains : showing care — **painstaking** *n* — **pains·tak·ing·ly** *adv*

¹paint \'pānt\ *vb* 1 : to apply color, pigment, or paint to 2 : to produce or portray in lines or colors on a surface; *also* : to practice the art of painting 3 : to decorate with colors 4 : to use cosmetics 5 : to describe vividly 6 : SWAB — **paint·er** *n*

²paint *n* 1 : something produced by painting 2 : MAKEUP 3 : a mixture of a pigment and a liquid that forms a thin adherent coating when spread on a surface; *also* : the dry pigment used in making this mixture 4 : an applied coating of paint

paint·ball \'pānt-ˌbòl\ *n* : a game in which two teams try to capture each other's flag using guns that shoot paint-filled pellets

paint·brush \'pānt-ˌbrəsh\ *n* : a brush for applying paint

painted lady *n* : a migratory butterfly with wings mottled in brown, orange, black, and white

painting *n* 1 : a work (as a picture) produced by painting 2 : the art or occupation of painting

¹pair \'per\ *n, pl* **pairs** *also* **pair** [ME *paire*, fr. AF, fr. L *paria* equal things, fr. neut. pl. of *par* equal] 1 : two things of a kind designed for use together 2 : something made up of two corresponding pieces ⟨a ∼ of pants⟩ 3 : a set of two people or animals

²pair *vb* 1 : to arrange in pairs 2 : to form a pair : MATCH 3 : to become associated with another

pai·sa \pi-'sä\ *n, pl* **paisa** *or* **pai·se** \-'sā\ — see *rupee, taka* at MONEY table

pais·ley \'pāz-lē\ *adj, often cap* : decorated with colorful curved abstract figures ⟨a ∼ shawl⟩

Pai·ute \'pī-ˌüt, -ˌyüt\ *n* : a member of an American Indian people orig. of Utah, Arizona, Nevada, and California

pa·ja·mas \pə-'jä-məz, -'ja-\ *n pl* : a loose suit for sleeping or lounging

pal \'pal\ *n* : a close friend

pal·ace \'pa-ləs\ *n* [ME *palais*, fr. AF, fr. L *palatium*, fr. *Palatium*, the Palatine Hill in Rome where the emperors' residences were built] 1 : the official residence of a chief of state 2 : MANSION

pal·a·din \'pa-lə-dən\ *n* **1** : a trusted military leader (as for a medieval prince) **2** : a leading champion of a cause

pa·laes·tra \pə-'les-trə\ *n, pl* **-trae** \-(ˌ)trē\ : a school in ancient Greece or Rome for sports (as wrestling)

pa·lan·quin \ˌpa-lən-'kēn\ *n* : an enclosed couch for one person borne on the shoulders of men by means of poles

pal·at·able \'pa-lə-tə-bəl\ *adj* : agreeable to the taste ✦ **Synonyms** APPETIZING, SAVORY, TASTY, TOOTHSOME

pal·a·tal \'pa-lə-tᵊl\ *adj* **1** : of or relating to the palate **2** : pronounced with some part of the tongue near or touching the hard palate ⟨the \y\ in *yeast* and the \sh\ in *she* are ∼ sounds⟩

pal·a·tal·ize \'pa-lə-tə-ˌlīz\ *vb* **-ized; -iz·ing** : to pronounce as or change into a palatal sound — **pal·a·tal·i·za·tion** \ˌpa-lə-tə-lə-'zā-shən\ *n*

pal·ate \'pa-lət\ *n* **1** : the roof of the mouth separating the mouth from the nasal cavity **2** : TASTE

pa·la·tial \pə-'lā-shəl\ *adj* **1** : of, relating to, or being a palace **2** : MAGNIFICENT

pa·lat·i·nate \pə-'la-tə-nət\ *n* : the territory of a palatine

¹pal·a·tine \'pa-lə-ˌtīn\ *adj* **1** : possessing royal privileges; *also* : of or relating to a palatine or a palatinate **2** : of or relating to a palace : PALATIAL

²palatine *n* **1** : a feudal lord having sovereign power within his domains **2** : a high officer of an imperial palace

pa·la·ver \pə-'la-vər, -'lä-\ *n* [Pg *palavra* word, speech, fr. LL *parabola* parable, speech] **1** : a long parley **2** : idle talk — **palaver** *vb*

¹pale \'pāl\ *n* **1** : a stake or picket of a fence **2** : an enclosed place; *also* : a district or territory within certain bounds or under a particular jurisdiction **3** : LIMITS, BOUNDS ⟨conduct beyond the ∼⟩

²pale *vb* **paled; pal·ing** : to enclose with or as if with pales : FENCE

³pale *adj* **pal·er; pal·est** **1** : deficient in color or intensity : WAN ⟨a ∼ face⟩ **2** : lacking in brightness : DIM ⟨a ∼ star⟩ **3** : not dark or intense in hue ⟨a ∼ blue⟩ — **paleness** *n*

⁴pale *vb* **paled; pal·ing** : to make or become pale

pale ale *n* : a medium-colored very dry ale

pale·face \'pāl-ˌfās\ *n* : a white person

Pa·leo·cene \'pā-lē-ə-ˌsēn\ *adj* : of, relating to, or being the earliest epoch of the Tertiary — **Paleocene** *n*

pa·leo·con·ser·va·tive \ˌpā-lē-ō-kən-'sər-və-tiv\ *n* : a conservative espousing traditional principles and policies

pa·le·og·ra·phy \ˌpā-lē-'ä-grə-fē\ *n* [NL *palaeographia*, fr. Gk *palaios* ancient + *graphein* to write] : the study of ancient writings and inscriptions — **pa·le·og·ra·pher** *n*

Pa·leo·lith·ic \ˌpā-lē-ə-'li-thik\ *adj* : of or relating to the earliest period of the Stone Age characterized by rough or chipped stone implements

pa·le·on·tol·o·gy \ˌpā-lē-ˌän-'tä-lə-jē\ *n* : a science dealing with the life of past geologic periods as known from fossil remains — **pa·le·on·to·log·i·cal** \-ˌän-tə-'lä-ji-kəl\ *adj* — **pa·le·on·tol·o·gist** \-ˌän-'tä-lə-jist, -ən-\ *n*

Pa·leo·zo·ic \ˌpā-lē-ə-'zō-ik\ *adj* : of, relating to, or being the era of geologic history extending from about 570 million years ago to about 245 million years ago — **Paleozoic** *n*

pal·ette \'pa-lət\ *n* : a thin often oval board that a painter holds and mixes colors on; *also* : the colors on a palette

pal·frey \'pȯl-frē\ *n, pl* **palfreys** *archaic* : a saddle horse that is not a warhorse; *esp* : one suitable for a woman

pa·limp·sest \'pa-ləmp-ˌsest\ *n* [L *palimpsestus*, fr. Gk *palimpsēstos* scraped again] : writing material (as a parchment) used after the erasure of earlier writing

pal·in·drome \'pa-lən-ˌdrōm\ *n* : a word, verse, or sentence (as "Able was I ere I saw Elba") or a number (as 1881) that reads the same backward or forward

pal·ing \'pā-liŋ\ *n* **1** : a fence of pales **2** : material for pales **3** : PALE, PICKET

pal·i·sade \ˌpa-lə-'sād\ *n* **1** : a high fence of stakes esp. for defense **2** : a line of steep cliffs

¹pall \'pȯl\ *vb* **1** : to lose in interest or attraction **2** : SATIATE, CLOY

²pall *n* **1** : a heavy cloth draped over a coffin **2** : something that produces a gloomy atmosphere

pal·la·di·um \pə-'lā-dē-əm\ *n* : a silver-white metallic chemical element used esp. as a catalyst and in alloys

pall·bear·er \'pȯl-ˌber-ər\ *n* : a person who attends the coffin at a funeral

¹pal·let \'pa-lət\ *n* : a small, hard, or makeshift bed

²pallet *n* : a portable platform for transporting and storing materials

pal·li·ate \'pa-lē-ˌāt\ *vb* **-at·ed; -at·ing** **1** : to ease (as a disease) without curing **2** : to cover by excuses and apologies — **pal·li·a·tion** \ˌpa-lē-'ā-shən\ *n* — **pal·li·a·tive** \'pa-lē-ˌā-tiv\ *adj or n*

pal·lid \'pa-ləd\ *adj* : PALE, WAN

pal·lor \'pa-lər\ *n* : PALENESS

¹palm \'päm, 'pälm\ *n* [ME, fr. OE, fr. L *palma* palm of the hand, palm tree; fr. the resemblance of the tree's leaves to the outstretched hand] **1** : any of a family of mostly tropical trees, shrubs, or vines usu. with a tall unbranched stem topped by a crown of large leaves **2** : a symbol of victory; *also* : VICTORY

²palm *n* : the underpart of the hand between the fingers and the wrist

³palm *vb* **1** : to conceal in or with the hand ⟨∼ a card⟩ **2** : to impose by fraud

palm·ate \'pal-ˌmāt, 'päl-\ *also* **palm·mat·ed** \-ˌmā-təd\ *adj* : resembling a hand with the fingers spread

palm·met·to \pal-'me-tō\ *n, pl* **-tos** *or* **-toes** : any of several usu. small palms with fan-shaped leaves

palm·ist·ry \'päl-mə-strē, 'päl-\ *n* : the practice of reading a person's character or future from the markings on the palms — **palm·ist** \'pä-mist, 'päl-\ *n*

Palm Sunday *n* : the Sunday preceding Easter and commemorating Christ's triumphal entry into Jerusalem

palm·top \'päm-ˌtäp, 'pälm-\ *n* : a portable computer small enough to hold in the hand

palmy \'pä-mē, 'päl-\ *adj* **palm·i·er; -est** **1** : abounding in or bearing palms **2** : FLOURISHING, PROSPEROUS

pal·o·mi·no \ˌpa-lə-'mē-nō\ *n, pl* **-nos** [AmerSp, fr. Sp, like a dove, fr. L *palumbinus*, fr. *palumbes*, a species of dove] : a horse with a pale cream to golden coat and cream or white mane and tail

pal·pa·ble \'pal-pə-bəl\ *adj* **1** : capable of being touched or felt : TANGIBLE **2** : OBVIOUS, PLAIN ✦ **Synonyms** PERCEPTIBLE, SENSIBLE, APPRECIABLE, TANGIBLE, DETECTABLE — **pal·pa·bly** \-blē\ *adv*

pal·pate \'pal-ˌpāt\ *vb* **pal·pat·ed; pal·pat·ing** : to examine by touch esp. medically — **pal·pa·tion** \pal-'pā-shən\ *n*

pal·pi·tate \'pal-pə-ˌtāt\ *vb* **-tat·ed; -tat·ing** : to beat rapidly and strongly : THROB — **pal·pi·ta·tion** \ˌpal-pə-'tā-shən\ *n*

pal·sy \'pȯl-zē\ *n, pl* **palsies** **1** : PARALYSIS **2** : a condition marked by tremor — **pal·sied** \-zēd\ *adj*

pal·ter \'pȯl-tər\ *vb* **pal·tered; pal·ter·ing** **1** : to act insincerely : EQUIVOCATE **2** : HAGGLE

pal·try \'pȯl-trē\ *adj* **pal·tri·er; -est** **1** : TRASHY ⟨a ∼ pamphlet⟩ **2** : MEAN, DESPICABLE ⟨a ∼ trick⟩ **3** : TRIVIAL ⟨∼ excuses⟩ **4** : MEAGER, MEASLY ⟨a ∼ sum⟩

pam *abbr* pamphlet

pam·pas \'pam-pəz, 'päm-, -pəs\ *n pl* : wide grassy So. American plains

pam·per \'pam-pər\ *vb* : to treat with excessive attention : INDULGE ✦ **Synonyms** CODDLE, HUMOR, BABY, SPOIL

pam·phlet \'pam-flət\ *n* [ME *pamflet* unbound booklet, fr. *Pamphilus seu De Amore* Pamphilus or On Love, popular Latin love poem of the 12th cent.] : an unbound printed publication

pam·phle·teer \ˌpam-flə-'tir\ *n* : a writer of pamphlets attacking something or urging a cause

¹pan \'pan\ *n* **1** : a usu. broad, shallow, and open container for domestic use; *also* : something resembling such a container **2** : a basin or depression in land **3** : HARDPAN

²pan *vb* **panned; pan·ning** **1** : to wash earth or gravel in a pan in searching for gold **2** : to criticize severely

Pan *abbr* Panama

pan·a·cea \ˌpa-nə-'sē-ə\ *n* : a remedy for all ills or difficulties : CURE-ALL

pa·nache \pə-'nash, -'näsh\ *n* [MF *pennache*, ultim. fr. LL *pinnaculum* small wing] **1** : an ornamental tuft (as of feathers) esp. on a helmet **2** : dash or flamboyance in style and action

pan·a·ma \'pa-nə-ˌmä, -ˌmȯ\ *n, often cap* : a handmade hat braided from strips of the leaves from a tropical American tree

pan·a·tela \ˌpa-nə-'te-lə\ *n* : a long slender cigar with straight sides pan·cake \'pan-ˌkāk\ *n* : a flat cake made of thin batter and fried on both sides

pan·chro·mat·ic \ˌpan-krō-'ma-tik\ *adj* : sensitive to all colors of visible light ⟨~ film⟩

pan·cre·as \'paŋ-krē-əs, 'pan-\ *n* : a large compound gland of vertebrates that produces insulin and discharges enzymes into the intestine — pan·cre·at·ic \ˌpaŋ-krē-'a-tik, ˌpan-\ *adj*

pan·da \'pan-də\ *n* 1 : a long-tailed reddish brown Himalayan mammal related to and resembling the racoon 2 : a large black-and-white mammal of China usu. classified with the bears

pan·dem·ic \pan-'de-mik\ *n* : a widespread outbreak of disease — pandemic *adj*

pan·de·mo·ni·um \ˌpan-də-'mō-nē-əm\ *n* : a wild uproar : TUMULT

¹pan·der \'pan-dər\ *vb* : to act as a pander

²pander *n* 1 : a go-between in love intrigues; *also* : PIMP 2 : a person who caters to or exploits others' desires or weaknesses

P & I *abbr* principal and interest

P & L *abbr* profit and loss

Pan·do·ra's box \pan-'dȯr-əz-\ *n* : a prolific source of troubles

pan·dow·dy \pan-'daù-dē\ *n, pl* -dies : a deep-dish apple dessert spiced, sweetened, and covered with a crust

pane \'pān\ *n* : a sheet of glass (as in a door or window)

pan·e·gy·ric \ˌpa-nə-'jir-ik\ *n* : a eulogistic oration or writing — pan·e·gyr·ist \-'jir-ist\ *n*

¹pan·el \'pa-nᵊl\ *n* [ME, piece of cloth, jury list on a piece of parchment, fr. AF, fr. VL *pannellus*, dim. of L *pannus* cloth, rag] 1 : a list of persons appointed for special duty ⟨a jury ~⟩; *also* : a group of people taking part in a discussion or quiz program 2 : a section of something (as a wall or door) often sunk below the level of the frame; *also* : a flat piece of construction material 3 : a flat piece of wood on which a picture is painted 4 : a mount for controls or dials

²panel *vb* -eled *or* -elled; -el·ing *or* -el·ling : to decorate with panels

paneling *n* : decorative panels

pan·el·ist \'pa-nᵊl-ist\ *n* : a member of a discussion or quiz panel

panel truck *n* : a small motortruck with a fully enclosed body

pang \'paŋ\ *n* : a sudden sharp spasm (as of pain) or attack (as of remorse)

¹pan·han·dle \'pan-ˌhan-dᵊl\ *n* : a narrow projection of a larger territory (as a state) ⟨the Texas ~⟩

²panhandle *vb* -dled; -dling : to ask for money on the street — pan·han·dler *n*

¹pan·ic \'pa-nik\ *n* : a sudden overpowering fright; *also* : extreme anxiety ⟨a ~ disorder⟩ ⟨~ attacks⟩ ♦ *Synonyms* TERROR, CONSTERNATION, DISMAY, ALARM, DREAD, FEAR — pan·icky \-ni-kē\ *adj*

²panic *vb* pan·icked \-nikt\; pan·ick·ing : to affect or be affected with panic

pan·i·cle \'pa-ni-kəl\ *n* : a branched flower cluster (as of a lilac) in which each branch from the main stem has one or more flowers

pan·jan·drum \pan-'jan-drəm\ *n, pl* -drums *also* -dra \-drə\ : a powerful personage or pretentious official

pan·nier *also* pan·ier \'pan-yər\ *n* : a large basket esp. for bearing on the back

pan·o·ply \'pa-nə-plē\ *n, pl* -plies 1 : a full suit of armor 2 : a protective covering 3 : an impressive array

pan·ora·ma \ˌpa-nə-'ra-mə, -'rä-\ *n* 1 : a picture unrolled before one's eyes 2 : a complete view in every direction — pan·oram·ic \-'ra-mik\ *adj*

pan out *vb* : TURN OUT; *esp* : SUCCEED

pan·sy \'pan-zē\ *n, pl* pansies [ME *pancy, pensee*, fr. MF *pensée*, fr. *pensée* thought, fr. *penser* to think, fr. L *pensare* to ponder] : a low-growing garden herb related to the violet; *also* : its showy flower

¹pant \'pant\ *vb* [ME, fr. AF *panteiser*, fr. VL *phantasiare* to have hallucinations, fr. Gk *phantasioun*, fr. *phantasia* appearance, imagination] 1 : to breathe in a labored manner 2 : YEARN 3 : THROB

²pant *n* : a panting breath or sound

³pant *n* 1 : an outer garment covering each leg separately

and usu. extending from the waist to the ankle — usu. used in pl. 2 *pl* : PANTIE

pan·ta·loons \ˌpan-tə-'lünz\ *n pl* 1 : close-fitting pants of the 19th century usu. having straps passing under the instep 2 : loose-fitting usu. shorter than ankle-length trousers

pan·the·ism \'pan-thē-ˌi-zəm\ *n* : a doctrine that equates God with the forces and laws of the universe — pan·the·ist \-ist\ *n* — pan·the·is·tic \ˌpan-thē-'is-tik\ *adj*

pan·the·on \'pan-thē-ˌän, -ən\ *n* 1 : a temple dedicated to all the gods; *also* : the gods of a people 2 : a group of illustrious people

pan·ther \'pan-thər\ *n, pl* panthers *also* panther 1 : LEOPARD; *esp* : a black one 2 : COUGAR 3 : JAGUAR

pant·ie *or* panty \'pan-tē\ *n, pl* pant·ies : a woman's or child's short underpants — usu. used in pl.

pan·to·mime \'pan-tə-ˌmīm\ *n* 1 : a play in which the actors use no words 2 : expression of something by bodily or facial movements only — pantomime *vb* — pan·to·mim·ic \ˌpan-tə-'mi-mik\ *adj*

pan·try \'pan-trē\ *n, pl* pantries : a storage room for food or dishes

pant·suit \'pant-ˌsüt\ *n* : a woman's outfit consisting usu. of a long jacket and pants of the same material

panty hose *n pl* : a one-piece undergarment for women consisting of hosiery combined with a pantie

panty·waist \'pan-tē-ˌwāst\ *n* : SISSY

pap \'pap\ *n* : soft food for infants or invalids

pa·pa \'pä-pə\ *n* : FATHER

pa·pa·cy \'pā-pə-sē\ *n, pl* -cies 1 : the office of pope 2 : a succession of popes 3 : the term of a pope's reign 4 *cap* : the system of government of the Roman Catholic Church

pa·pa·in \pə-'pā-ən, -'pī-ən\ *n* : an enzyme in papaya juice used esp. as a meat tenderizer and in medicine

pa·pal \'pā-pəl\ *adj* : of or relating to the pope or to the Roman Catholic Church

papaw *var of* PAWPAW

pa·pa·ya \pə-'pī-ə\ *n* : a tropical American tree with large yellow black-seeded edible fruit; *also* : its fruit

pa·per \'pā-pər\ *n* [ME *papir*, fr. AF, fr. L *papyrus* papyrus, paper, fr. Gk *papyros* papyrus] 1 : a pliable substance made usu. of vegetable matter and used to write or print on, to wrap things in, or to cover walls; *also* : a single sheet of this substance 2 : a printed or written document 3 : NEWSPAPER 4 : WALLPAPER — paper *adj or vb* — pa·pery \'pā-pə-rē\ *adj*

pa·per·back \-ˌbak\ *n* : a paper-covered book

pa·per·board \-ˌbȯrd\ *n* : CARDBOARD

pa·per·hang·er \'pā-pər-ˌhaŋ-ər\ *n* : one that applies wallpaper — pa·per·hang·ing *n*

pa·per·weight \-ˌwāt\ *n* : an object used to hold down loose papers by its weight

pa·pier–mâ·ché \ˌpā-pər-mə-'shā, ˌpa-ˌpyā-mə-, -ma-\ *n* [F, lit., chewed paper] : a molding material of wastepaper and additives (as glue) — papier–mâché *adj*

pa·pil·la \pə-'pi-lə\ *n, pl* -lae \-ˌlē, -ˌlī\ [L, nipple] : a small projecting bodily part (as one of the nubs on the surface of the tongue) that resembles a tiny nipple in form — pap·il·lary \'pa-pə-ˌler-ē, pə-'pi-lə-rē\ *adj*

pa·poose \pa-'püs, pə-\ *n* [Narragansett *papoòs*] : a young child of No. American Indian parents

pa·pri·ka \pə-'prē-kə, pa-\ *n* [Hung] : a mild red spice made from the fruit of various cultivated sweet peppers

Pap smear \'pap-\ *n* : a method for the early detection of cancer esp. of the uterine cervix

Pap test *n* : PAP SMEAR

pap·ule \'pa-pyül\ *n* : a small solid usu. conical elevation of the skin — pap·u·lar \-pyə-lər\ *adj*

pa·py·rus \pə-'pī-rəs\ *n, pl* -ri \-ˌrē, -ˌrī\ *or* -rus·es 1 : a tall grassy sedge of the Nile valley 2 : paper made from papyrus pith

¹par \'pär\ *n* 1 : a stated value (as of a security) 2 : a common level : EQUALITY 3 : an accepted standard or normal condition 4 : the score standard set for each hole of a golf course — par *adj*

²par *abbr* 1 paragraph 2 parallel 3 parish

par·a·ble \'pa-rə-bəl\ *n* : a simple story told to illustrate a moral truth

pa·rab·o·la \pə-'ra-bə-lə\ *n* : a plane curve formed by a point moving so that its distance from a fixed point is equal to its distance from a fixed line — **par·a·bol·ic** \,par-ə-'bä-lik\ *adj*

para·chute \'pa-rə-,shüt\ *n* [F, fr. *para-* (as in *parasol*) + *chute* fall] : a device for slowing the descent of a person or object through the air that consists of a usu. hemispherical canopy beneath which the person or object is suspended — **parachute** *vb* — **para·chut·ist** \-'shü-tist\ *n*

parachute pants *n pl* : baggy casual pants of lightweight fabric

¹**pa·rade** \pə-'rād\ *n* 1 : a pompous display : EXHIBITION 2 : MARCH, PROCESSION; *esp* : a ceremonial formation and march 3 : a place for strolling

²**parade** *vb* **pa·rad·ed; pa·rad·ing** 1 : to march in a parade 2 : PROMENADE 3 : SHOW OFF ⟨*paraded* her knowledge⟩ 4 : MASQUERADE

par·a·digm \'pa-rə-,dīm, -,dim\ *n* 1 : MODEL, PATTERN 2 : a systematic inflection of a verb or noun showing a complete conjugation or declension — **par·a·dig·mat·ic** \,pa-rə-dig-'ma-tik\ *adj*

par·a·dise \'pa-rə-,dīs, -,dīz\ *n* [ME *paradis*, fr. AF, fr. LL *paradisus*, fr. Gk *paradeisos*, lit., enclosed park, of Iranian origin] 1 : HEAVEN 2 : a place or state of bliss

par·a·di·si·a·cal \,pa-rə-də-'sī-ə-kəl\ or **par·a·dis·i·ac** \-'di-zē-,ak, -sē-\ *adj* : of, relating to, or resembling paradise

par·a·dox \'pa-rə-,däks\ *n* : a statement that seems contrary to common sense and yet is perhaps true — **par·a·dox·i·cal** \,pa-rə-'däk-si-kəl\ *adj* — **par·a·dox·i·cal·ly** \-k(ə-)lē\ *adv*

par·af·fin \'pa-rə-fən\ *n* : a waxy substance used esp. for making candles and sealing foods

para·glid·ing \'pa-rə-,glī-diŋ\ *n* : the sport of soaring from a slope or cliff using a modified parachute

par·a·gon \'pa-rə-,gän, -gən\ *n* : a model of perfection : PATTERN

¹**para·graph** \'pa-rə-,graf\ *n* : a subdivision of a written composition that deals with one point or gives the words of one speaker; *also* : a character (as ¶) marking the beginning of a paragraph

²**paragraph** *vb* : to divide into paragraphs

par·a·keet \'pa-rə-,kēt\ *n* : any of numerous usu. small slender parrots with a long graduated tail

para·le·gal \,pa-rə-'lē-gəl\ *adj* : of, relating to, or being a paraprofessional who assists a lawyer — **paralegal** *n*

Par·a·li·pom·e·non \,pa-rə-lə-'pä-mə-,nän\ *n* : CHRONICLES

par·al·lax \'pa-rə-,laks\ *n* : the difference in apparent direction of an object as seen from two different points

¹**par·al·lel** \'pa-rə-,lel\ *adj* [L *parallelus*, fr. Gk *parallēlos*, fr. *para* beside + *allos* of one another, fr. *allos . . . allos* one . . . another, fr. *allos* other] 1 : lying or moving in the same direction but always the same distance apart 2 : similar in essential parts — **par·al·lel·ism** \-,le-,li-zəm\ *n*

²**parallel** *n* 1 : a parallel line, curve, or surface 2 : one of the imaginary circles on the earth's surface that parallel the equator and mark the latitude 3 : something essentially similar to another 4 : SIMILARITY, LIKENESS

³**parallel** *vb* 1 : COMPARE 2 : to correspond to 3 : to extend in a parallel direction with

par·al·lel·o·gram \,pa-rə-'le-lə-,gram\ *n* : a 4-sided geometric figure with opposite sides equal and parallel

par·a·lyse *Brit var of* PARALYZE

pa·ral·y·sis \pə-'ra-lə-səs\ *n, pl* **-y·ses** \-,sēz\ : complete or partial loss of function esp. when involving the motion or sensation in a part of the body — **par·a·lyt·ic** \,pa-rə-'li-tik\ *adj or n*

par·a·lyze \'pa-rə-,līz\ *vb* **-lyzed; -lyz·ing** 1 : to affect with paralysis 2 : to make powerless or inactive — **par·a·lyz·ing·ly** *adv*

par·a·me·cium \,pa-rə-'mē-shəm, -shē-əm, -sē-əm\ *n, pl* **-cia** \-shə, -shē-ə, -sē-ə\ *also* **-ciums** : any of a genus of slipper-shaped protozoans that move by cilia

para·med·ic \,pa-rə-'me-dik\ *also* **para·med·i·cal** \-di-kəl\ *n* 1 : a person who assists a physician in a paramedical capacity 2 : a specially trained medical technician licensed to provide a wide range of emergency services before or during transportation to a hospital

para·med·i·cal \,pa-rə-'me-di-kəl\ *also* **para·med·ic** \-'me-dik\ *adj* : concerned with supplementing the work of trained medical professionals

pa·ram·e·ter \pə-'ra-mə-tər\ *n* 1 : a quantity whose value characterizes a statistical population or a member of a

system (as a family of curves) 2 : a physical property whose value determines the characteristics or behavior of a system 3 : a characteristic element : FACTOR — **para·met·ric** \,pa-rə-'me-trik\ *adj*

para·mil·i·tary \,pa-rə-'mi-lə-,ter-ē\ *adj* : formed on a military pattern esp. as an auxiliary military force

par·a·mount \'pa-rə-,maunt\ *adj* : superior to all others : SUPREME ♦ *Synonyms* PREPONDERANT, PREDOMINANT, DOMINANT, CHIEF, SOVEREIGN

par·amour \'pa-rə-,mur\ *n* : an illicit lover

para·noia \,pa-rə-'nói-ə\ *n* : a psychosis marked by delusions and irrational suspicion usu. without hallucinations — **par·a·noid** \'pa-rə-,nóid\ *adj or n*

para·nor·mal \,pa-rə-'nór-məl\ *adj* : not scientifically explainable : SUPERNATURAL

par·a·pet \'pa-rə-pət, -,pet\ *n* 1 : a protecting rampart 2 : a low wall or railing (as at the edge of a bridge)

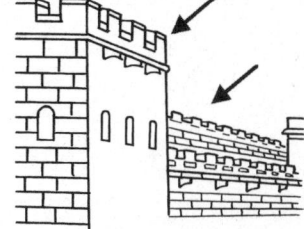

parapet 1

par·a·pher·na·lia \,pa-rə-fə-'nāl-yə, -,fər-\ *n sing or pl* 1 : personal belongings 2 : EQUIPMENT, APPARATUS

para·phrase \'pa-rə-,frāz\ *n* : a restatement of a text giving the meaning in different words — **paraphrase** *vb*

para·ple·gia \,pa-rə-'plē-jə, -jē-ə\ *n* : paralysis of the lower trunk and legs — **para·ple·gic** \-jik\ *adj or n*

para·pro·fes·sion·al \-prə-'fe-shə-nəl\ *n* : a trained aide who assists a professional — **paraprofessional** *adj*

para·psy·chol·o·gy \,pa-rə-sī-'kä-lə-jē\ *n* : a field of study concerned with investigating paranormal psychological phenomena (as extrasensory perception) — **para·psy·chol·o·gist** \-jist\ *n*

par·a·site \'pa-rə-,sīt\ *n* [MF, fr. L *parasitus*, fr. Gk *parasitos*, fr. *para-* beside + *sitos* grain, food] 1 : a plant or animal living in, with, or on another organism usu. to its harm 2 : one depending on another and not making adequate return — **par·a·sit·ic** \,pa-rə-'si-tik\ *adj* — **par·a·sit·ism** \'pa-rə-sə-,ti-zəm, -,sī-,ti-\ *n* — **par·a·sit·ize** \-sə-,tīz\ *vb*

par·a·si·tol·o·gy \,pa-rə-sə-'tä-lə-jē\ *n* : a branch of biology dealing with parasites and parasitism esp. among animals — **par·a·si·tol·o·gist** \-jist\ *n*

para·sol \'pa-rə-,sól\ *n* [F, fr. It *parasole*, fr. *parare* to shield + *sole* sun, fr. L *sol*] : a lightweight umbrella used as a shield against the sun

para·sym·pa·thet·ic nervous system \,pa-rə-,sim-pə-'the-tik-\ *n* : the part of the autonomic nervous system that tends to induce secretion, to increase the tone and contractility of smooth muscle, and to slow heart rate

para·thi·on \,pa-rə-'thī-ən, -,än\ *n* : an extremely toxic insecticide

para·thy·roid \-'thī-,róid\ *n* : PARATHYROID GLAND — **parathyroid** *adj*

parathyroid gland *n* : any of usu. four small endocrine glands adjacent to or embedded in the thyroid gland that produce a hormone (**parathyroid hormone**) concerned with calcium and phosphorus metabolism

para·tran·sit \,pa-rə-'tran-sət, -zət\ *n* : transportation service that provides individualized rules without fixed routes or timetables

para·troop·er \'pa-rə-,trü-pər\ *n* : a member of the paratroops

para·troops \-,trüps\ *n pl* : troops trained to parachute from an airplane

para·ty·phoid \,pa-rə-'tī-,fóid\ *n* : a bacterial food poisoning resembling typhoid fever

par·boil \'pär-ˌbȯi(-ə)l\ *vb* : to boil briefly

¹**par·cel** \'pär-səl\ *n* 1 : a tract or plot of land 2 : COLLECTION, LOT ⟨the story was a ∼ of lies⟩ 3 : a wrapped bundle : PACKAGE

²**parcel** *vb* **-celed** *or* **-celled; -cel·ing** *or* **-cel·ling** : to divide into portions

parcel post *n* 1 : a mail service handling parcels 2 : packages handled by parcel post

parch \'pärch\ *vb* 1 : to toast under dry heat 2 : to shrivel with heat

parch·ment \'pärch-mənt\ *n* : the skin of an animal prepared for writing on; *also* : a writing on such material

pard \'pärd\ *n* : LEOPARD

¹**par·don** \'pär-dᵊn\ *n* : excuse of an offense without penalty; *esp* : an official release from legal punishment

²**pardon** *vb* : to free from penalty : EXCUSE, FORGIVE — **par·don·able** \'pär-dᵊn-ə-bəl\ *adj*

par·don·er \'pär-dᵊn-ər\ *n* 1 : a medieval preacher delegated to raise money for religious works by soliciting offerings and granting indulgences 2 : one that pardons

pare \'per\ *vb* **pared; par·ing** 1 : to trim off an outside part (as the skin or rind) of 2 : to reduce as if by paring ⟨∼ expenses⟩ — **par·er** *n*

par·e·gor·ic \ˌper-ə-'gȯr-ik\ *n* : an alcoholic preparation of opium and camphor used esp. to relieve pain

par·ent \'per-ənt\ *n* 1 : one that begets or brings forth offspring : FATHER, MOTHER 2 : one who brings up and cares for another 3 : SOURCE, ORIGIN — **par·ent·age** \-ən-tij\ *n* — **pa·ren·tal** \pə-'ren-tᵊl\ *adj* — **par·ent·hood** *n*

pa·ren·the·sis \pə-'ren-thə-səs\ *n, pl* **-the·ses** \-ˌsēz\ 1 : a word, phrase, or sentence inserted in a passage to explain or modify the thought 2 : one of a pair of punctuation marks ( ) used to enclose parenthetic matter — **par·en·thet·ic** \ˌper-ən-'the-tik\ *or* **par·en·thet·i·cal** \-ti-kəl\ *adj* — **par·en·thet·i·cal·ly** \-k(ə-)lē\ *adv*

pa·ren·the·size \pə-'ren-thə-ˌsīz\ *vb* **-sized; -siz·ing** : to make a parenthesis of

par·ent·ing \'per-ən-tiŋ\ *n* : the raising of a child by its parents

pa·re·sis \pə-'rē-səs, 'pa-rə-\ *n, pl* **pa·re·ses** \-ˌsēz\ : a usu. incomplete paralysis; *also* : insanity caused by syphilitic alteration of the brain that leads to dementia and paralysis

par ex·cel·lence \ˌpär-ˌek-sə-'läⁿs\ *adj* [F, lit., by excellence] : being the best of a kind : PREEMINENT

par·fait \pär-'fā\ *n* [F, lit., something perfect] : a cold dessert made of layers of fruit, syrup, ice cream, and whipped cream

pa·ri·ah \pə-'rī-ə\ *n* : OUTCAST

pa·ri·etal \pə-'rī-ə-tᵊl\ *adj* 1 : of, relating to, or forming the walls of an anatomical structure 2 : of or relating to college living or its regulation

pari–mu·tu·el \ˌper-i-'myü-chə-wəl\ *n* : a betting system in which winners share the total stakes minus a percentage for the management

paring *n* : a pared-off piece

pa·ri pas·su \ˌpä-ri-'pä-sü\ *adv or adj* [L, with equal step] : at an equal rate or pace

par·ish \'per-ish\ *n* 1 : a church district in the care of one pastor; *also* : the residents of such an area 2 : a local church community 3 : a civil division of the state of Louisiana : COUNTY

pa·rish·io·ner \pə-'ri-shə-nər\ *n* : a member or resident of a parish

par·i·ty \'per-ə-tē\ *n, pl* **-ties** : EQUALITY, EQUIVALENCE

¹**park** \'pärk\ *n* 1 : a tract of ground kept as a game preserve or recreation area 2 : a place where vehicles (as automobiles) are parked 3 : an enclosed stadium used esp. for ball games

²**park** *vb* 1 : to leave a vehicle temporarily (as in a parking lot or garage) 2 : to set and leave temporarily

par·ka \'pär-kə\ *n* : a very warm jacket with a hood

Par·kin·son's disease \'pär-kən-sənz-\ *n* : a chronic progressive neurological disease chiefly of later life marked esp. by tremor and weakness of resting muscles and by a shuffling gait

Parkinson's Law *n* : an observation in office organization: work expands so as to fill the time available for its completion

park·way \'pärk-ˌwā\ *n* : a broad landscaped thoroughfare

par·lance \'pär-ləns\ *n* 1 : SPEECH 2 : manner of speaking ⟨military ∼⟩

¹**par·lay** \'pär-ˌlā, -lē\ *vb* : to increase or change into something of much greater value

²**parlay** *n* : a series of bets in which the original stake plus its winnings are risked on successive wagers

par·ley \'pär-lē\ *n, pl* **parleys** : a conference usu. over matters in dispute : DISCUSSION — **parley** *vb*

par·lia·ment \'pär-lə-mənt\ *n* [ME, fr. AF *parlement*, fr. *parler* to speak, fr. ML *parabolare*, fr. LL *parabola* speech, parable] 1 : a formal governmental conference 2 *cap* : an assembly that constitutes the supreme legislative body of a country (as the United Kingdom) — **par·lia·men·ta·ry** \ˌpär-lə-'men-tə-rē\ *adj*

par·lia·men·tar·i·an \ˌpär-lə-ˌmen-'ter-ē-ən\ *n* 1 *often cap* : an adherent of the parliament during the English Civil War 2 : an expert in parliamentary procedure

par·lor \'pär-lər\ *n* 1 : a room for conversation or the reception of guests 2 : a place of business ⟨beauty ∼⟩

par·lour \'pär-lər\ *chiefly Brit var of* PARLOR

par·lous \'pär-ləs\ *adj* : full of danger or risk : PRECARIOUS — **par·lous·ly** *adv*

Par·me·san \'pär-mə-ˌzän, -ˌzhän, -ˌzan\ *n* : a hard dry cheese with a sharp flavor

par·mi·gia·na \ˌpär-mi-'jä-nə, ˌpär-mi-'zhän\ *or* **par·mi·gia·no** \-'jä-(ˌ)nō\ *adj* : made or covered with Parmesan cheese ⟨veal ∼⟩

pa·ro·chi·al \pə-'rō-kē-əl\ *adj* 1 : of or relating to a church parish 2 : limited in scope : NARROW, PROVINCIAL — **pa·ro·chi·al·ism** \-ə-ˌli-zəm\ *n*

parochial school *n* : a school maintained by a religious body

par·o·dy \'per-ə-dē\ *n, pl* **-dies** [L *parodia*, fr. Gk *parōidia*, fr. *para-* beside + *aidein* to sing] : a humorous or satirical imitation — **parody** *vb*

pa·role \pə-'rōl\ *n* : a conditional release of a prisoner whose sentence has not expired — **parole** *vb* — **pa·rol·ee** \-ˌrō-'lē, -'rō-ˌlē\ *n*

par·ox·ysm \'pa-rək-ˌsi-zəm, pə-'räk-\ *n* : a sudden sharp attack (as of pain or coughing) : CONVULSION — **par·ox·ys·mal** \ˌpa-rək-'siz-məl, pə-ˌräk-\ *adj*

par·quet \'pär-ˌkā, pär-'kā\ *n* [F] 1 : a flooring of parquetry 2 : the lower floor of a theater; *esp* : the forward part of the orchestra

par·que·try \'pär-kə-trē\ *n, pl* **-tries** : fine woodwork inlaid in patterns

par·ri·cide \'pa-rə-ˌsīd\ *n* 1 : one that murders a parent or a close relative 2 : the act of a parricide

par·rot \'per-ət\ *n* : any of numerous bright-colored tropical birds that have a stout hooked bill

parrot fever *n* : PSITTACOSIS

par·ry \'per-ē\ *vb* **par·ried; par·ry·ing** 1 : to ward off a weapon or blow 2 : to evade esp. by an adroit answer — **parry** *n*

parse \'pärs *also* 'pärz\ *vb* **parsed; pars·ing** : to give a grammatical description of a word or a group of words

par·sec \'pär-ˌsek\ *n* : a unit of measure for interstellar space equal to 3.26 light-years

par·si·mo·ny \'pär-sə-ˌmō-nē\ *n* : extreme or excessive frugality — **par·si·mo·ni·ous** \ˌpär-sə-'mō-nē-əs\ *adj* — **par·si·mo·ni·ous·ly** *adv*

pars·ley \'pär-slē\ *n* : a garden plant related to the carrot that has finely divided leaves used as a seasoning or garnish; *also* : the leaves

pars·nip \'pär-snəp\ *n* : a garden plant related to the carrot that has a long edible usu. whitish root which is cooked as a vegetable; *also* : the root

par·son \'pär-sᵊn\ *n* [ME *persone*, fr. AF, fr. ML *persona*, lit., person, fr. L] : MINISTER 2, PASTOR

par·son·age \'pär-sə-nij\ *n* : a house provided by a church for its pastor

¹**part** \'pärt\ *n* 1 : a division or portion of a whole 2 : the melody or score for a particular voice or instrument 3 : a spare piece for a machine 4 : DUTY, FUNCTION 5 : one of the sides in a dispute 6 : ROLE; *also* : an actor's lines in a play 7 *pl* : TALENTS, ABILITY ⟨a man of many ∼s⟩ 8 : the line where one's hair divides (as in combing)

²**part** *vb* 1 : to take leave of someone 2 : to divide or break into parts : SEPARATE 3 : to go away : DEPART; *also* : DIE 4 : to give up possession ⟨∼ed with her jewels⟩ 5 : APPORTION, SHARE

³part *abbr* **1** participial; participle **2** particular

par·take \pär-'tāk\ *vb* **-took** \-'tùk\; **-tak·en** \-'tā-kən\; **-tak·ing 1** : to have a share or part **2** : to take a portion (as of food) — **par·tak·er** *n*

par·terre \pär-'ter\ *n* [F, fr. MF, fr. *par terre* on the ground] **1** : an ornamental garden with paths between the flower beds **2** : the part of a theater floor behind the orchestra

par·the·no·gen·e·sis \ˌpär-thə-nō-'je-nə-səs\ *n* [NL, fr. Gk *parthenos* virgin + L *genesis* genesis] : development of a new individual from an unfertilized usu. female sex cell — **par·the·no·ge·net·ic** \-jə-'ne-tik\ *adj*

par·tial \'pär-shəl\ *adj* **1** : not total or general : affecting a part only **2** : favoring one party over the other : BIASED **3** : markedly fond — used with *to* — **par·tial·i·ty** \ˌpär-shē-'a-lə-tē\ *n* — **par·tial·ly** *adv*

par·tic·i·pate \pär-'ti-sə-ˌpāt\ *vb* **-pat·ed; -pat·ing 1** : to take part in something ⟨∼ in a game⟩ **2** : SHARE — **par·tic·i·pant** \-pənt\ *adj or n* — **par·tic·i·pa·tion** \-ˌti-sə-'pā-shən\ *n* — **par·tic·i·pa·tor** \-'ti-sə-ˌpā-tər\ *n* — **par·tic·i·pa·to·ry** \-'ti-sə-pə-ˌtȯr-ē\ *adj*

par·ti·ci·ple \'pär-tə-ˌsi-pəl\ *n* : a word having the characteristics of both verb and adjective — **par·ti·cip·i·al** \ˌpär-tə-'si-pē-əl\ *adj*

par·ti·cle \'pär-ti-kəl\ *n* **1** : a very small bit of matter **2** : a unit of speech (as an article, preposition, or conjunction) expressing some general aspect of meaning or some connective or limiting relation

par·ti·cle·board \-ˌbȯrd\ *n* : a board made of very small pieces of wood bonded together

par·ti–col·or \ˌpär-tē-'kə-lər\ *or* **par·ti–col·ored** \-lərd\ *adj* : showing different colors or tints; *esp* : having one main color broken by patches of one or more other colors

¹par·tic·u·lar \pər-'ti-kyə-lər\ *adj* **1** : of or relating to a specific person or thing ⟨the laws of a ∼ state⟩ **2** : DISTINCTIVE, SPECIAL ⟨the ∼ point of his talk⟩ **3** : SEPARATE, INDIVIDUAL ⟨each ∼ hair⟩ **4** : attentive to details : PRECISE **5** : hard to please : EXACTING — **par·tic·u·lar·i·ty** \-ˌti-kyə-'lar-ə-tē\ *n* — **par·tic·u·lar·ly** *adv*

²particular *n* : an individual fact or detail

par·tic·u·lar·ise *Brit var of* PARTICULARIZE

par·tic·u·lar·ize \pər-'ti-kyə-lə-ˌrīz\ *vb* **-ized; -iz·ing 1** : to state in detail : SPECIFY **2** : to go into details

par·tic·u·late \pər-'ti-kyə-lət, pär-, -ˌlāt\ *adj* : relating to or existing as minute separate particles — **particulate** *n*

¹part·ing *n* : a place or point of separation or divergence

²parting *adj* : given, taken, or done at parting ⟨a ∼ kiss⟩

par·ti·san *also* **par·ti·zan** \'pär-tə-zən, -sən\ *n* **1** : one that takes the part of another : ADHERENT **2** : GUERRILLA — **partisan** *adj* — **par·ti·san·ship** *n*

par·tite \'pär-ˌtīt\ *adj* : divided into a usu. specified number of parts

par·ti·tion \pär-'ti-shən\ *n* **1** : DIVISION **2** : something that divides or separates; *esp* : an interior dividing wall — **partition** *vb*

par·ti·tive \'pär-tə-tiv\ *adj* : of, relating to, or denoting a part

part·ly \'pärt-lē\ *adv* : in part : in some measure or degree

part·ner \'pärt-nər\ *n* **1** : ASSOCIATE, COLLEAGUE **2** : either of two persons who dance together **3** : one who plays on the same team with another **4** : SPOUSE **5** : one of two or more persons contractually associated as joint principals in a business — **part·ner·ship** *n*

part of speech : a class of words (as nouns or verbs) distinguished according to the kind of idea denoted and the function performed in a sentence

par·tridge \'pär-trij\ *n, pl* **partridge** *or* **par·tridg·es** : any of various stout-bodied Old World game birds

part–song \'pärt-ˌsȯŋ\ *n* : a song with two or more voice parts

part–time \-'tīm\ *adj or adv* : involving or working less than a full or regular schedule — **part–tim·er** \-ˌtī-mər\ *n*

par·tu·ri·tion \ˌpär-tə-'ri-shən, ˌpär-chə-, ˌpär-tyù-\ *n* : CHILDBIRTH

part·way \'pärt-'wā\ *adv* : to some extent : PARTLY

par·ty \'pär-tē\ *n, pl* **parties 1** : a person or group taking one side of a question; *esp* : a group of persons organized for the purpose of directing the policies of a government **2** : a person or group concerned in an action or affair : PARTICIPANT **3** : a group of persons detailed for a common task **4** : a social gathering

party animal *n* : a person known for frequent attendance at parties

par·ty·go·er \'pär-tē-ˌgō-ər\ *n* : a person who attends a party or who attends parties frequently

par·ve·nu \'pär-və-ˌnü, -ˌnyü\ *n* [F, fr. pp. of *parvenir* to arrive, fr. L *pervenire*, fr. *per* through + *venire* to come] : one who has recently or suddenly risen to wealth or power but has not yet secured the social position associated with it

pas \'pä\ *n, pl* **pas** *same or* 'päz\ : a dance step or combination of steps

pas·cal \pas-'kal\ *n* : a unit of pressure in the metric system equal to one newton per square meter

pas·chal \'pas-kəl\ *adj* : of, relating to, appropriate for, or used during Passover or Easter ceremonies

pa·sha \'pä-shə, 'pa-; pə-'shä\ *n* : a man (as formerly a governor in Turkey) of high rank

pash·mi·na \ˌpəsh-'mē-nə\ *n* : a fine wool from the undercoat of domestic Himalayan goats; *also* : a shawl made from this wool

¹pass \'pas\ *vb* **1** : MOVE, PROCEED **2** : to go away; *also* : DIE **3** : to move past, beyond, or over **4** : to allow to elapse : SPEND **5** : to go or make way through **6** : to go or allow to go unchallenged **7** : to undergo transfer **8** : to render a legal judgment **9** : OCCUR **10** : to secure the approval of (as a legislature) **11** : to go or cause to go through an inspection, test, or course of study successfully **12** : to be regarded **13** : CIRCULATE ⟨∼ a note⟩ **14** : VOID **15** : to transfer the ball or puck to another player **16** : to decline to bid or bet on one's hand in a card game **17** : to give a base on balls to **18** : to let something go by without accepting ⟨∼ed on his offer⟩ — **pass·er** *n*

²pass *n* : a gap in a mountain range

³pass *n* **1** : the act or an instance of passing **2** : REALIZATION, ACCOMPLISHMENT **3** : a state of affairs **4** : a written authorization to leave, enter, or move about freely **5** : a transfer of a ball or puck from one player to another **6** : BASE ON BALLS **7** : EFFORT, TRY **8** : a sexually inviting gesture or approach

⁴pass *abbr* **1** passenger **2** passive

pass·able \'pa-sə-bəl\ *adj* **1** : capable of being passed or traveled on **2** : just good enough : TOLERABLE — **pass·ably** \-blē\ *adv*

pas·sage \'pa-sij\ *n* **1** : a means (as a road or corridor) of passing **2** : the action or process of passing **3** : a voyage esp. by sea or air **4** : a right or permission to pass **5** : ENACTMENT **6** : a usu. brief portion or section (as of a book)

pas·sage·way \-ˌwā\ *n* : a way that allows passage

pass·book \'pas-ˌbùk\ *n* : BANKBOOK

pas·sé \pa-'sā\ *adj* **1** : past one's prime **2** : not up-to-date : OUTMODED

pas·sel \'pa-səl\ *n* : a large number

pas·sen·ger \'pa-sⁿn-jər\ *n* : a traveler in a public or private conveyance

pass·er·by \'pa-sər-ˌbī\ *n, pl* **pass·ers·by** : one who passes by

pas·ser·ine \'pa-sə-ˌrīn\ *adj* : of or relating to the large order of birds comprising singing birds that perch

pas·sim \'pa-səm\ *adv* [L, fr. *passus* scattered, fr. pp. of *pandere* to spread] : here and there : THROUGHOUT

pass·ing *n* : the act of one that passes or causes to pass; *esp* : DEATH

pas·sion \'pa-shən\ *n* **1** *often cap* : the sufferings of Christ between the night of the Last Supper and his death **2** : strong feeling; *also, pl* : the emotions as distinguished from reason **3** : RAGE, ANGER **4** : LOVE; *also* : an object of affection or enthusiasm **5** : sexual desire — **pas·sion·ate** \'pa-shə-nət\ *adj* — **pas·sion·ate·ly** *adv* — **pas·sion·less** *adj*

pas·sion·flow·er \'pa-shən-ˌflaù-(ə)r\ *n* [fr. the fancied resemblance of parts of the flower to the instruments of Christ's crucifixion] : any of a genus of chiefly tropical woody climbing vines or erect herbs with showy flowers and pulpy often edible berries (passion fruit)

pas·sive \'pa-siv\ *adj* **1** : not active : acted upon **2** : asserting that the grammatical subject is subjected to or affected by the action represented by the verb ⟨∼ voice⟩ **3** : making use of the sun's heat usu. without the aid of mechanical devices **4** : SUBMISSIVE, PATIENT — **passive** *n* — **pas·sive·ly** *adv* — **pas·siv·i·ty** \pa-'si-və-tē\ *n*

pas·sive–ma·trix \-'mā-triks\ *adj* : of, relating to, or being on LCD in which pixels are controlled in groups
pass·key \'pas-ˌkē\ *n* : a key for opening two or more locks
pass out *vb* : to lose consciousness
Pass·over \'pas-ˌō-vər\ *n* [fr. the exemption of the Israelites from the slaughter of the firstborn in Egypt (Exod 12:23–27)] : a Jewish holiday celebrated in March or April in commemoration of the Hebrews' liberation from slavery in Egypt
pass·port \'pas-ˌpȯrt\ *n* : an official document issued by a country upon request to a citizen requesting protection during travel abroad
pass up *vb* : DECLINE, REJECT
pass·word \'pas-ˌwərd\ *n* 1 : a word or phrase that must be spoken by a person before being allowed to pass a guard 2 : a sequence of characters required for access to a computer system
¹**past** \'past\ *adj* 1 : AGO ⟨10 years ~⟩ 2 : just gone or elapsed ⟨the ~ month⟩ 3 : having existed or taken place in a period before the present : BYGONE 4 : of, relating to, or constituting a verb tense that expresses time gone by
²**past** *prep or adv* : BEYOND
³**past** *n* 1 : time gone by 2 : something that happened or was done in a former time 3 : the past tense; *also* : a verb form in it 4 : a secret past life
pas·ta \'päs-tə\ *n* [It] 1 : a paste in processed form (as macaroni) or in the form of fresh dough (as ravioli) 2 : a dish of cooked pasta
¹**paste** \'pāst\ *n* [ME, fr. AF, fr. LL *pasta* dough, paste] 1 : DOUGH 2 : a smooth food product made by evaporation or grinding ⟨tomato ~⟩ 3 : a shaped dough (as spaghetti or ravioli) 4 : a preparation (as of flour and water) for sticking things together 5 : a brilliant glass used for artificial gems
²**paste** *vb* **past·ed; past·ing** : to cause to adhere by paste : STICK
paste·board \'pāst-ˌbȯrd\ *n* : CARDBOARD
¹**pas·tel** \pas-'tel\ *n* 1 : a paste made of powdered pigment; *also* : a crayon of such paste 2 : a drawing in pastel 3 : a pale or light color
²**pastel** *adj* 1 : of or relating to a pastel 2 : pale in color
pas·tern \'pas-tərn\ *n* : the part of a horse's foot extending from the fetlock to the top of the hoof
pas·teur·i·za·tion \ˌpas-chə-rə-'zā-shən, ˌpas-tə-\ *n* : partial sterilization of a substance (as milk) by heat or radiation — **pas·teur·ize** \'pas-chə-ˌrīz, 'pas-tə-\ *vb* — **pas·teur·iz·er** *n*
pas·tiche \pas-'tēsh\ *n* : a composition (as in literature or music) made up of selections from different works
pas·tille \pas-'tēl\ *n* : LOZENGE 2
pas·time \'pas-ˌtīm\ *n* : DIVERSION; *esp* : something that serves to make time pass agreeably
pas·tor \'pas-tər\ *n* [ME *pastour*, fr. AF, fr. L *pastor*, herdsman, fr. *pascere* to feed, pasture, nurture] : a minister or priest serving a local church or parish — **pas·tor·ate** \-tə-rət\ *n*
¹**pas·to·ral** \'pas-tə-rəl\ *adj* 1 : of or relating to shepherds or rural life 2 : of or relating to spiritual guidance esp. of a congregation 3 : of or relating to the pastor of a church
²**pastoral** *n* : a literary work dealing with shepherds or rural life
pas·to·rale \ˌpas-tə-'räl, -'ral\ *n* [It] : a musical composition having a pastoral theme
past participle *n* : a participle that typically expresses completed action, that is one of the principal parts of the verb, and that is used in the formation of perfect tenses in the active voice and of all tenses in the passive voice
pas·tra·mi \pə-'strä-mē\ *n* [Yiddish *pastrame*] : a highly seasoned smoked beef prepared esp. from shoulder cuts
pas·try \'pā-strē\ *n, pl* **pastries** : sweet baked goods made of dough or with a crust made of enriched dough
pas·tur·age \'pas-chə-rij\ *n* : PASTURE
¹**pas·ture** \'pas-chər\ *n* 1 : plants (as grass) for the feeding esp. of grazing livestock 2 : land or a plot of land used for grazing
²**pasture** *vb* **pas·tured; pas·tur·ing** 1 : GRAZE 2 : to use as pasture

pasty \'pā-stē\ *adj* **past·i·er; -est** : resembling paste; *esp* : pallid and unhealthy in appearance
¹**pat** \'pat\ *n* 1 : a light tap esp. with the hand or a flat instrument; *also* : the sound made by it 2 : something (as butter) shaped into a small flat usu. square individual portion
²**pat** *adv* : in a pat manner : PERFECTLY
³**pat** *vb* **pat·ted; pat·ting** 1 : to strike lightly with a flat instrument 2 : to flatten, smooth, or put into place or shape with a pat 3 : to tap gently or lovingly with the hand
⁴**pat** *adj* 1 : exactly suited to the occasion : APT 2 : memorized exactly 3 : UNYIELDING ⟨stood ~ on the issue⟩
PAT *abbr* point after touchdown
pa·ta·ca \pə-'tä-kə\ *n* — see MONEY table
¹**patch** \'pach\ *n* 1 : a piece used to cover a torn or worn place; *also* : one worn on a garment as an ornament or insignia 2 : a small area distinct from that about it 3 : a shield worn over the socket of an injured or missing eye
²**patch** *vb* 1 : to mend or cover with a patch 2 : to make of fragments 3 : to repair usu. in hasty fashion
patch·ou·li \'pa-chə-lē, pə-'chü-lē\ *n* : a heavy perfume made from the fragrant essential oil of an Asian mint; *also* : the plant itself
patch test *n* : a test for allergic sensitivity made by applying to the unbroken skin small pads soaked with the allergen to be tested
patch·work \'pach-ˌwərk\ *n* : something made of pieces of different materials, shapes, or colors
patchy \'pa-chē\ *adj* **patch·i·er; -est** : marked by or consisting of patches; *also* : irregular in appearance or quality — **patch·i·ness** \-chē-nəs\ *n*
pate \'pāt\ *n* : HEAD; *esp* : the crown of the head
pâ·té *also* **pate** \pä-'tā\ *n* [F] 1 : a meat or fish pie or patty 2 : a spread of finely chopped or pureed seasoned meat
pa·tel·la \pə-'te-lə\ *n, pl* **-lae** \-'te-(ˌ)lē, -ˌlī\ *or* **-las** [L] : KNEECAP — **pa·tel·lar** \-'te-lər\ *adj*
pat·en \'pa-tⁿn\ *n* 1 : PLATE; *esp* : one of precious metal for the eucharistic bread 2 : a thin disk
¹**pat·ent** \/ 1 & 4 are 'pa-tⁿnt, *Brit also* 'pā-, 2 & 3 are 'pa-tⁿnt, 'pā-\ *adj* 1 : open to public inspection — used chiefly in the phrase *letters patent* 2 : free from obstruction 3 : EVIDENT, OBVIOUS 4 : protected by a patent ♦ **Synonyms** MANIFEST, DISTINCT, APPARENT, PALPABLE, PLAIN, CLEAR — **pat·ent·ly** *adv*
²**pat·ent** \'pa-tⁿnt, *Brit also* 'pā-\ *n* 1 : an official document conferring a right or privilege 2 : a document securing to an inventor for a term of years exclusive right to his or her invention 3 : something patented
³**pat·ent** *vb* : to secure by patent
pat·en·tee \ˌpa-tⁿn-'tē, *Brit also* ˌpā-\ *n* : one to whom a grant is made or a privilege secured by patent
patent medicine \'pa-tⁿnt-\ *n* : a packaged nonprescription drug protected by a trademark; *also* : any proprietary drug
pa·ter·fa·mil·i·as \ˌpā-tər-fə-'mi-lē-əs\ *n, pl* **pa·tres·fa·mil·i·as** \ˌpā-ˌtrēz-\ [L] : the father of a family : the male head of a household
pa·ter·nal \pə-'tər-nⁿl\ *adj* 1 : FATHERLY 2 : related through or inherited or derived from a father — **pa·ter·nal·ly** *adv*
pa·ter·nal·ism \-nə-ˌli-zəm\ *n* : a system under which an authority treats those under its control paternally (as by regulating their conduct and supplying their needs)
¹**pa·ter·ni·ty** \pə-'tər-nə-tē\ *n* 1 : FATHERHOOD 2 : descent from a father
²**paternity** *adj* 1 : granted to a father ⟨~ leave⟩ 2 of or relating to the determination of paternity ⟨a ~ suit⟩
¹**path** \'path, 'päth\ *n, pl* **paths** \'pathz, 'paths, 'päthz, 'päths\ 1 : a trodden way 2 : ROUTE, COURSE — **path·less** *adj*
²**path** *or* **pathol** *abbr* pathology
path·break·ing \'path-ˌbrā-kiŋ\ *adj* : TRAILBLAZING
pa·thet·ic \pə-'the-tik\ *adj* 1 : evoking tenderness, pity, or sorrow 2 : pitifully inadequate ⟨a ~ performance⟩ ♦ **Synonyms** PITIFUL, PITEOUS, PITIABLE, POOR — **pa·thet·i·cal·ly** \-ti-k(ə-)lē\ *adv*
path·find·er \'path-ˌfīn-dər, 'päth-\ *n* : one that discovers a way; *esp* : one that explores untraveled regions to mark out a new route

patho·gen \'pa-thə-jən\ *n* : a specific agent (as a bacterium) causing disease — **patho·gen·ic** \ˌpa-thə-'je-nik\ *adj* — **patho·ge·nic·i·ty** \-jə-'ni-sə-tē\ *n*

pa·thog·ra·phy \pə-'thä-grə-fē\ *n* : biography focusing on a person's flaws and misfortunes

pa·thol·o·gy \pə-'thä-lə-jē\ *n, pl* **-gies** 1 : the study of the essential nature of disease 2 : the abnormality of structure and function characteristic of a disease 3 : deviation giving rise to social ills — **path·o·log·i·cal** \ˌpa-thə-'lä-ji-kəl\ *adj* — **pa·thol·o·gist** \pə-'thä-lə-jist\ *n*

pa·thos \'pā-ˌthäs, -ˌthōs\ *n* : an element in experience or artistic representation evoking pity or compassion

path·way \'path-ˌwā, 'pàth-\ *n* : PATH

pa·tience \'pā-shəns\ *n* 1 : the capacity, habit, or fact of being patient 2 *chiefly Brit* : SOLITAIRE 2

¹**pa·tient** \'pā-shənt\ *adj* 1 : bearing pain or trials without complaint 2 : showing self-control : CALM 3 : STEADFAST, PERSEVERING — **pa·tient·ly** *adv*

²**patient** *n* : one under medical care

pa·ti·na \'pa-tə-nə, pə-'tē-\ *n, pl* **pa·ti·nas** \-nəz\ *or* **pa·ti·nae** \'pa-tə-ˌnē, -ˌnī\ 1 : a green film formed on copper and bronze by exposure to moist air 2 : a superficial covering or exterior

pa·tio \'pa-tē-ˌō, 'pä-\ *n, pl* **pa·ti·os** 1 : COURTYARD 2 : an often paved area near a dwelling used esp. for outdoor dining

pa·tois \'pa-ˌtwä\ *n, pl* **pa·tois** \-ˌtwäz\ [F] 1 : a dialect other than the standard dialect; *esp* : uneducated or provincial speech 2 : JARGON 2

pa·tri·arch \'pā-trē-ˌärk\ *n* 1 : a man revered as father or founder (as of a tribe) 2 : a venerable old man 3 : an ecclesiastical dignitary (as the bishop of an Eastern Orthodox see) — **pa·tri·ar·chal** \ˌpā-trē-'är-kəl\ *adj* — **pa·tri·arch·ate** \'pā-trē-ˌär-kət, -ˌkät\ *n* — **pa·tri·ar·chy** \-ˌär-kē\ *n*

pa·tri·cian \pə-'tri-shən\ *n* : a person of high birth : ARISTOCRAT — **patrician** *adj*

pat·ri·cide \'pa-trə-ˌsīd\ *n* 1 : one who murders his or her own father 2 : the murder of one's own father

pat·ri·mo·ny \'pa-trə-ˌmō-nē\ *n* : something (as an estate) inherited or derived esp. from one's father : HERITAGE — **pat·ri·mo·ni·al** \ˌpa-trə-'mō-nē-əl\ *adj*

pa·tri·ot \'pā-trē-ət, -ˌät\ *n* [MF *patriote* compatriot, fr. LL *patriota*, fr. Gk *patriōtēs*, fr. *patria* lineage, fr. *patr-, patēr* father] : one who loves his or her country — **pa·tri·ot·ic** \ˌpā-trē-'ä-tik\ *adj* — **pa·tri·ot·i·cal·ly** \-ti-k(ə-)lē\ *adv* — **pa·tri·o·tism** \'pā-trē-ə-ˌti-zəm\ *n*

pa·tris·tic \pə-'tris-tik\ *adj* : of or relating to the church fathers or their writings

¹**pa·trol** \pə-'trōl\ *n* : the action of going the rounds (as of an area) for observation or the maintenance of security; *also* : a person or group performing such an action

²**patrol** *vb* **pa·trolled; pa·trol·ling** : to carry out a patrol

pa·trol·man \pə-'trōl-mən\ *n* : a police officer assigned to a beat

patrol wagon *n* : PADDY WAGON

pa·tron \'pā-trən\ *n* [ME, fr. AF, fr. ML & L; ML *patronus* patron saint, patron of a benefice, pattern, fr. L, defender, fr. *patr-, pater* father] 1 : a person chosen or named as special protector 2 : a wealthy or influential supporter ⟨~ of poets⟩; *also* : BENEFACTOR 3 : a regular client or customer ⟨diner ~s⟩

pa·tron·age \'pa-trə-nij, 'pā-\ *n* 1 : the support or influence of a patron 2 : the trade of customers 3 : control of appointment to government jobs

pa·tron·ess \'pā-trə-nəs\ *n* : a woman who is a patron

pa·tron·ise *Brit var of* PATRONIZE

pa·tron·ize \'pā-trə-ˌnīz, 'pa-\ *vb* **-ized; -iz·ing** 1 : to be a customer of 2 : to treat condescendingly, haughtily, or coolly

pat·ro·nym·ic \ˌpa-trə-'ni-mik\ *n* : a name derived from the name of one's father or a paternal ancestor usu. by the addition of an affix

pa·troon \pə-'trün\ *n* : the proprietor of a manorial estate esp. in New York under Dutch rule

pat·sy \'pat-sē\ *n, pl* **pat·sies** : a person who is easily duped or victimized

¹**pat·ter** \'pa-tər\ *vb* : to talk glibly or mechanically ♦ **Synonyms** CHATTER, PRATE, CHAT, PRATTLE, BABBLE

²**patter** *n* 1 : a specialized lingo 2 : extremely rapid talk ⟨a comedian's ~⟩

³**patter** *vb* : to strike, pat, or tap rapidly

⁴**patter** *n* : a quick succession of taps or pats ⟨the ~ of rain⟩

¹**pat·tern** \'pa-tərn\ *n* [ME *patron*, fr. AF, fr. ML *patronus*, fr. L, defender, fr. *patr-, pater* father] 1 : an ideal model 2 : something used as a model for making things ⟨a dressmaker's ~⟩ 3 : SAMPLE 4 : an artistic design 5 : CONFIGURATION 6 : a sample of a person's behaviors or characteristics ⟨a ~ of violence⟩

²**pattern** *vb* : to form according to a pattern

pat·ty *also* **pat·tie** \'pa-tē\ *n, pl* **patties** 1 : a little pie 2 : a small flat cake esp. of chopped food

pau·ci·ty \'pò-sə-tē\ *n* : smallness of number or quantity

paunch \'pònch\ *n* : a usu. large belly : POTBELLY — **paunchy** *adj*

pau·per \'pò-pər\ *n* : a person without means of support except from charity — **pau·per·ism** \-pə-ˌri-zəm\ *n* — **pau·per·ize** \-pə-ˌrīz\ *vb*

¹**pause** \'pòz\ *n* 1 : a temporary stop; *also* : a period of inaction 2 : a brief suspension of the voice 3 : a sign ⌒ or above or below a musical note or rest to show it is to be prolonged 4 : a reason for pausing 5 : a function of an electronic device that pauses a recording

²**pause** *vb* **paused; paus·ing** : to stop, rest, or linger for a time

pave \'pāv\ *vb* **paved; pav·ing** : to cover (as a road) with hard material in order to smooth or firm the surface

pave·ment \'pāv-mənt\ *n* 1 : a paved surface 2 : the material with which something is paved

pa·vil·ion \pə-'vil-yən\ *n* [ME *pavilloun, pavillioun*, fr. AF, fr. L *papilion-, papilio* butterfly] 1 : a large tent 2 : a usu. open structure (as in a park) used for entertainment or shelter

pav·ing \'pā-viŋ\ *n* : PAVEMENT

¹**paw** \'pò\ *n* : the foot of a quadruped (as a dog or lion) having claws

²**paw** *vb* 1 : to touch or strike with a paw; *also* : to scrape with a hoof 2 : to feel or handle clumsily or rudely 3 : to flail about or grab for with the hands

pawl \'pòl\ *n* : a pivoted tongue or sliding bolt designed to fall into notches on another machine part to permit motion in one direction only

¹**pawn** \'pòn\ *n* [ME *pown*, fr. AF *peoun, paun*, fr. ML *pedon-, pedo* foot soldier, fr. LL, one with broad feet, fr. L *ped-, pes* foot] 1 : a chess piece of the least value 2 : one used for the purposes of another

²**pawn** *n* 1 : something deposited as security for a loan; *also* : HOSTAGE 2 : the state of being pledged

³**pawn** *vb* : to deposit as a pledge

pawn·bro·ker \'pòn-ˌbrō-kər\ *n* : one who lends money on goods pledged

Paw·nee \pò-'nē\ *n, pl* **Pawnee** *or* **Pawnees** : a member of an American Indian people orig. of Kansas and Nebraska

pawn·shop \'pòn-ˌshäp\ *n* : a pawnbroker's place of business

paw·paw *also* **pa·paw** 1 \pə-'pò\ : PAPAYA 2 \'pä-ˌpò, 'pò-\ : a No. American tree with green-skinned edible fruit; *also* : its fruit

¹**pay** \'pā\ *vb* **paid** \'pād\ *also in sense 7* **payed; pay·ing** [ME, fr. AF *paier*, fr. L *pacare* to pacify, fr. *pac-, pax* peace] 1 : to make due return to for goods or services 2 : to discharge indebtedness for : SETTLE ⟨~ a bill⟩ 3 : to give in forfeit ⟨~ the penalty⟩ 4 : REQUITE 5 : to give, offer, or make freely or as fitting ⟨~ attention⟩ 6 : to be profitable to : RETURN 7 : to make slack and allow to run out ⟨~ out a rope⟩ — **pay·able** *adj* — **pay·ee** \pā-'ē\ *n* — **pay·er** *n*

²**pay** *n* 1 : something paid; *esp* : WAGES 2 : the status of being paid by an employer : EMPLOY

³**pay** *adj* 1 : containing something valuable (as gold) ⟨~ dirt⟩ 2 : equipped to receive a fee for use ⟨~ telephone⟩ 3 : requiring payment

pay·back \'pā-ˌbak\ *n* 1 : a return on an investment equal to the original capital outlay 2 : something given in return, compensation, or retaliation

pay·check \'pā-ˌchek\ *n* 1 : a check in payment of wages or salary 2 : WAGES, SALARY

pay·load \-ˌlōd\ *n* : the load carried by a vehicle in addition to what is necessary for its operation; *also* : the weight of such a load

pay·mas·ter \-₁mas-tər\ *n* : one who distributes the payroll
pay·ment \'pā-mənt\ *n* **1** : the act of paying **2** : something paid
pay·off \-₁òf\ *n* **1** : PROFIT, REWARD; *also* : RETRIBUTION **2** : the climax of an incident or enterprise ⟨the ~ of a story⟩
pay–per–view *n* : a cable television service by which customers can order access to a single airing of a TV feature
pay·roll \-₁rōl\ *n* : a list of persons entitled to receive pay; *also* : the money to pay those on such a list
payt *abbr* payment
pay up *vb* : to pay what is due; *also* : to pay in full
Pb *symbol* [L *plumbum*] lead
PBS *abbr* Public Broadcasting Service
PBX \₁pē-(₁)bē-'eks\ *n* [*private branch exchange*] : a private telephone switchboard
¹PC \₁pē-'sē\ *n, pl* **PCs** *or* **PC's** [*personal computer*] : MICROCOMPUTER
²PC *abbr* **1** Peace Corps **2** percent; percentage **3** politically correct **4** postcard **5** [L *post cibum*] after meals **6** professional corporation
PCB \₁pē-₁sē-'bē\ *n* : POLYCHLORINATED BIPHENYL
PCP \₁pē-₁sē-'pē\ *n* : PHENCYCLIDINE
pct *abbr* percent; percentage
pd *abbr* paid
Pd *symbol* palladium
PD *abbr* **1** per diem **2** police department **3** potential difference
PDA \₁pē-₁dē-'ā\ *n* [*personal digital assistant*] : a small microprocessor device for storing and organizing personal information
PDQ \₁pē-₁dē-'kyü\ *adv, often not cap* [abbr. of *pretty damned quick*] : IMMEDIATELY
PDT *abbr* Pacific daylight (saving) time
PE *abbr* **1** physical education **2** printer's error **3** professional engineer
pea \'pē\ *n, pl* **peas** *also* **pease** \'pēz\ **1** : the round edible protein-rich seed borne in the pod of a widely grown leguminous vine; *also* : this vine **2** : any of various plants resembling or related to the pea
peace \'pēs\ *n* **1** : a state of calm and quiet; *esp* : public security under law **2** : freedom from disturbing thoughts or emotions **3** : a state of concord (as between persons or governments); *also* : an agreement to end hostilities — **peace·able** \'pē-sə-bəl\ *adj* — **peace·ably** \-blē\ *adv* — **peace·ful** *adj* — **peace·ful·ly** *adv*
peace·keep·ing \'pēs-₁kē-piŋ\ *n* : the preserving of peace; *esp* : international enforcement and supervision of a truce — **peace·keep·er** *n*
peace·mak·er \-₁mā-kər\ *n* : one who settles an argument or stops a fight
peace·time \-₁tīm\ *n* : a time when a nation is not at war
peach \'pēch\ *n* [ME *peche*, fr. AF *pesche, peche*, fr. LL *persica*, fr. L (*malum*) *Persicum*, lit., Persian fruit] : a sweet juicy fuzzy-skinned fruit of a small usu. pink-flowered tree related to the cherry and plums; *also* : this tree — **peachy** *adj*
pea·cock \'pē-₁käk\ *n* [ME *pecok*, fr. *pe-* (fr. OE *pēa* peafowl, fr. L *pavo* peacock) + *cok* cock] : the male peafowl that can spread its long tail feathers to make a colorful display
pea·fowl \-₁faú(-ə)l\ *n* : either of two large domesticated Asian pheasants
pea·hen \-₁hen\ *n* : the female peafowl
¹peak \'pēk\ *n* **1** : a pointed or projecting part **2** : the top of a hill or mountain; *also* : MOUNTAIN **3** : the front projecting part of a cap **4** : the narrow part of a ship's bow or stern **5** : the highest level or greatest degree — **peak** *adj*
²peak *vb* : to bring to or reach a maximum
peak·ed \'pē-kəd\ *adj* : THIN, SICKLY
¹peal \'pēl\ *n* **1** : the loud ringing of bells **2** : a set of tuned bells **3** : a loud sound or succession of sounds
²peal *vb* : to give out peals : RESOUND
pea·nut \'pē-(₁)nət\ *n* **1** : an annual herb related to the pea but having pods that ripen underground; *also* : this pod or one of the edible seeds it bears **2** *pl* : a very small amount **3** : a pellet of polystyrene foam
pear \'per\ *n* : the fleshy fruit of a tree related to the apple; *also* : this tree

pearl \'pərl\ *n* **1** : a small hard often lustrous body formed within the shell of some mollusks and used as a gem **2** : one that is choice or precious ⟨~s of wisdom⟩ **3** : a slightly bluish medium gray color — **pearly** \'pər-lē\ *adj*
peas·ant \'pe-zᵊnt\ *n* **1** : any of a class of small landowners or laborers tilling the soil **2** : a usu. uneducated person of low social status — **peas·ant·ry** \-zᵊn-trē\ *n*
pea·shoot·er \'pē-₁shü-tər\ *n* : a toy blowgun for shooting peas
peat \'pēt\ *n* : a dark substance formed by partial decay of plants (as mosses) in water — **peaty** *adj*
peat moss *n* : SPHAGNUM
¹peb·ble \'pe-bəl\ *n* : a small usu. round stone — **peb·bly** \-b(ə-)lē\ *adj*
²pebble *vb* **peb·bled; peb·bling** : to produce a rough surface texture in ⟨~ leather⟩
pec \'pek\ *n* : PECTORAL MUSCLE
pe·can \pi-'kän, -'kan; 'pē-₁kan\ *n* : the smooth thin-shelled edible nut of a large American hickory; *also* : this tree
pec·ca·dil·lo \₁pe-kə-'di-lō\ *n, pl* **-loes** *or* **-los** : a slight offense
pec·ca·ry \'pe-kə-rē\ *n, pl* **-ries** : any of several American chiefly tropical mammals resembling but smaller than the related pigs
pec·ca·vi \pe-'kä-₁vē\ *n* [L, I have sinned, fr. *peccare* to sin] : an acknowledgment of sin
¹peck \'pek\ *n* — see WEIGHT table
²peck *vb* **1** : to strike or pierce with or as if with the bill **2** : to make (as a hole) by pecking **3** : to pick up with or as if with the bill
³peck *n* **1** : an impression made by pecking **2** : a quick sharp stroke
pecking order *also* **peck order** *n* : a basic pattern of social organization within a flock of poultry in which each bird pecks another lower in the scale without being pecked in return and submits to pecking by one of higher rank; *also* : a social hierarchy
pec·tin \'pek-tən\ *n* : any of various water-soluble plant substances that cause fruit jellies to set — **pec·tic** \-tik\ *adj*
pec·to·ral \'pek-tə-rəl\ *adj* : of or relating to the breast or chest
pectoral muscle *n* : either of two muscles on each side of the body which connect the front walls of the chest with the bones of the upper arm and shoulder
pe·cu·liar \pi-'kyül-yər\ *adj* [ME *peculier*, fr. L *peculiaris* of private property, special, fr. *peculium* private property, fr. *pecus* cattle] **1** : belonging exclusively to one person or group **2** : CHARACTERISTIC, DISTINCTIVE **3** : QUEER, ODD ♦ **Synonyms** IDIOSYNCRATIC, ECCENTRIC, SINGULAR, STRANGE, WEIRD — **pe·cu·liar·i·ty** \-₁kyül-'ya-rə-tē, -₁kyü-lē-'a-\ *n* — **pe·cu·liar·ly** *adv*
pe·cu·ni·ary \pi-'kyü-nē-₁er-ē\ *adj* : of or relating to money : MONETARY
ped·a·gogue *also* **ped·a·gog** \'pe-də-₁gäg\ *n* : TEACHER, SCHOOLMASTER
ped·a·go·gy \'pe-də-₁gō-jē, -₁gä-\ *n* : the art or profession of teaching; *esp* : EDUCATION **2** — **ped·a·gog·ic** \₁pe-də-'gä-jik, -'gō-\ *or* **ped·a·gog·i·cal** \-ji-kəl\ *adj*
¹ped·al \'pe-dᵊl\ *n* : a lever worked by the foot
²pedal *adj* : of or relating to the foot
³pedal *vb* **ped·aled** *also* **ped·alled; ped·al·ing** *also* **ped·al·ling** **1** : to use or work a pedal (as of a piano or bicycle) **2** : to ride a bicycle
ped·ant \'pe-dᵊnt\ *n* **1** : a person who makes a show of knowledge **2** : a formal uninspired teacher — **pe·dan·tic** \pi-'dan-tik\ *adj* — **ped·ant·ry** \'pe-dᵊn-trē\ *n*
ped·dle \'pe-dᵊl\ *vb* **ped·dled; ped·dling** : to sell or offer for sale from place to place — **ped·dler** *also* **ped·lar** \'ped-lər\ *n*
ped·er·ast \'pe-də-₁rast\ *n* [Gk *paiderastēs*, lit., lover of boys] : one who practices anal intercourse esp. with a boy — **ped·er·as·ty** \'pe-də-₁ras-tē\ *n*
ped·es·tal \'pe-dəs-tᵊl\ *n* **1** : the support or foot of something (as a column, statue, or vase) that is upright **2** : a position of high regard
¹pe·des·tri·an \pə-'des-trē-ən\ *adj* **1** : ORDINARY **2** : going on foot
²pedestrian *n* : WALKER

pe·di·at·rics \ˌpē-dē-'a-triks\ *n* : a branch of medicine dealing with the development, care, and diseases of children — **pe·di·at·ric** \-trik\ *adj* — **pe·di·a·tri·cian** \ˌpē-dē-ə-'tri-shən\ *n*

pedi·cab \'pe-di-ˌkab\ *n* : a pedal-driven tricycle with seats for a driver and two passengers

ped·i·cure \'pe-di-ˌkyür\ *n* : care of the feet, toes, and nails; *also* : a single treatment of these parts — **ped·i·cur·ist** \-ˌkyür-ist\ *n*

ped·i·gree \'pe-də-ˌgrē\ *n* [ME *pedegru*, fr. AF *pé de grue*, lit., crane's foot; fr. the shape made by the lines of a genealogical chart] **1** : a record of a line of ancestors **2** : an ancestral line — **ped·i·greed** \-grēd\ *adj*

ped·i·ment \'pe-də-mənt\ *n* : a low triangular gablelike decoration (as over a door or window) on a building

pe·dom·e·ter \pi-'dä-mə-tər\ *n* : an instrument that measures the distance one walks

pe·do·phile \'pe-də-ˌfī(-ə)l, 'pē-\ *n* : one affected with pedophilia

pe·do·phil·ia \ˌpe-də-'fi-lē-ə, ˌpē-\ *n* : sexual perversion in which children are the preferred sexual object

pe·dun·cle \'pē-ˌdəŋ-kəl\ *n* : a narrow supporting stalk

peek \'pēk\ *vb* **1** : to look furtively **2** : to peer from a place of concealment **3** : GLANCE — **peek** *n*

¹peel \'pēl\ *vb* [ME *pelen*, fr. AF *peler*, fr. L *pilare* to remove the hair from, fr. *pilus* hair] **1** : to strip the skin, bark, or rind from **2** : to strip off (as a coat); *also* : to come off **3** : to lose the skin, bark, or rind

²peel *n* : a skin or rind esp. of a fruit

peel·ing \'pē-liŋ\ *n* : a peeled-off piece or strip (as of skin or rind)

peen \'pēn\ *n* : the usu. hemispherical or wedge-shaped end of the head of a hammer opposite the face

¹peep \'pēp\ *vb* : to utter a feeble shrill sound or the slightest sound

²peep *n* : a feeble shrill sound

³peep *vb* **1** : to look slyly esp. through an aperture : PEEK **2** : to begin to emerge **3** : to look at : WATCH — **peep·er** *n*

⁴peep *n* **1** : a first faint appearance **2** : a brief or furtive look

peep·hole \'pēp-ˌhōl\ *n* : a hole to peep through

¹peer \'pir\ *n* **1** : one of equal standing with another : EQUAL **2** : NOBLE — **peer·age** \-ij\ *n*

²peer *vb* **1** : to look intently or curiously **2** : to come slightly into view

peer·ess \'pir-əs\ *n* : a woman who is a peer

peer·less \'pir-ləs\ *adj* : having no equal : MATCHLESS ♦ *Synonyms* SUPREME, UNEQUALED, UNPARALLELED, INCOMPARABLE

¹peeve \'pēv\ *vb* **peeved**; **peev·ing** : to make resentful : ANNOY

²peeve *n* **1** : a feeling or mood of resentment **2** : a particular grievance

pee·vish \'pē-vish\ *adj* : querulous in temperament : FRETFUL ♦ *Synonyms* IRRITABLE, PETULANT, HUFFY — **pee·vish·ly** *adv* — **pee·vish·ness** *n*

pee·wee \'pē-(ˌ)wē\ *n* **1** : one that is diminutive or tiny **2** : a level of sports usu. for young children — **peewee** *adj*

¹peg \'peg\ *n* **1** : a small pointed piece (as of wood) used to pin down or fasten things or to fit into holes **2** : a projecting piece used as a support or boundary marker **3** : SUPPORT, PRETEXT **4** : STEP, DEGREE **5** : THROW

²peg *vb* **pegged**; **peg·ging** **1** : to put a peg into : fasten, pin down, or attach with or as if with pegs **2** : to work hard and steadily : PLUG **3** : HUSTLE **4** : to mark by pegs **5** : to hold (as prices) at a set level or rate **6** : IDENTIFY ⟨was *pegged* as an intellectual⟩ **7** : THROW

PEI *abbr* Prince Edward Island

pei·gnoir \pān-'wär, pen-\ *n* [F, lit., garment worn while combing the hair, fr. MF, fr. *peigner* to comb the hair, fr. L *pectinare*, fr. *pectin-, pecten* comb] : NEGLIGEE

¹pe·jo·ra·tive \pi-'jȯr-ə-tiv\ *n* : a pejorative word or phrase

²pejorative *adj* : having negative connotations : DISPARAGING — **pe·jo·ra·tive·ly** *adv*

peke \'pēk\ *n, often cap* : PEKINGESE

Pe·king·ese *or* **Pe·kin·ese** \ˌpē-kə-'nēz, -'nēs; -kiŋ-'ēz, -'ēs\ *n, pl* **Pekingese** *or* **Pekinese** : any of a breed of Chinese origin of small short-legged long-haired dogs

pe·koe \'pē-(ˌ)kō\ *n* : a black tea made from young tea leaves

pel·age \'pe-lij\ *n* : the hairy covering of a mammal

pe·lag·ic \pə-'la-jik\ *adj* : OCEANIC

pelf \'pelf\ *n* : MONEY, RICHES

pel·i·can \'pe-li-kən\ *n* : any of a genus of large web-footed birds having a pouched lower bill used to scoop in fish

pel·la·gra \pə-'la-grə, -'lä-\ *n* : a disease caused by a diet with too little niacin and protein and marked by a skin rash, disease of the digestive system, and mental disturbances

pel·let \'pe-lət\ *n* **1** : a little ball (as of medicine) **2** : BULLET — **pel·let·al** \-lə-təl\ *adj* — **pel·let·ize** \-ˌtīz\ *vb*

pell–mell \ˌpel-'mel\ *adv* **1** : in mingled confusion ⟨papers strewn ∼ on the desk⟩ **2** : HEADLONG ⟨ran ∼ for the door⟩

pel·lu·cid \pə-'lü-səd\ *adj* : extremely clear : LIMPID, TRANSPARENT ⟨a ∼ stream⟩ ♦ *Synonyms* TRANSLUCENT, LUCID, LUCENT

pe·lo·ton \ˌpe-lə-'tän\ *n* : the main body of riders in a bicycle race

¹pelt \'pelt\ *n* : a skin esp. of a fur-bearing animal

²pelt *vb* : to strike with a succession of blows or missiles

pel·vis \'pel-vəs\ *n, pl* **pel·vis·es** \-və-səz\ *or* **pel·ves** \-ˌvēz\ : a basin-shaped part of the vertebrate skeleton consisting of the large bone of each hip and the nearby bones of the spine — **pel·vic** \-vik\ *adj*

pem·mi·can *also* **pem·i·can** \'pe-mi-kən\ *n* : dried meat pounded fine and mixed with melted fat

¹pen \'pen\ *vb* **penned**; **pen·ning** : to shut in or as if in a pen

²pen *n* **1** : a small enclosure for animals **2** : a small place of confinement or storage

³pen *n* **1** : an implement for writing or drawing with ink or a similar fluid **2** : a writing instrument regarded as a means of expression **3** : STYLUS 3

⁴pen *vb* **penned**; **pen·ning** : WRITE

⁵pen *n* : PENITENTIARY

⁶pen *abbr* peninsula

PEN *abbr* International Association of Poets, Playwrights, Editors, Essayists and Novelists

pe·nal \'pē-nᵊl\ *adj* : of or relating to punishment

pe·nal·ise *Brit var of* PENALIZE

pe·nal·ize \'pē-nə-ˌlīz, 'pe-\ *vb* **-ized**; **-iz·ing** : to put a penalty on

pen·al·ty \'pe-nᵊl-tē\ *n, pl* **-ties** **1** : punishment for crime or offense **2** : something forfeited when a person fails to do something agreed to **3** : disadvantage, loss, or hardship (as to a competitor) due to some action

pen·ance \'pe-nəns\ *n* **1** : an act performed to show sorrow or repentance for sin **2** : a sacrament (as in the Roman Catholic Church) consisting of confession, absolution, and a penance directed by the confessor

pence \'pens\ *pl of* PENNY

pen·chant \'pen-chənt\ *n* [F, fr. prp. of *pencher* to incline, fr. VL *pendicare*, fr. L *pendere* to weigh] : a strong inclination : LIKING ♦ *Synonyms* LEANING, PROPENSITY, PREDILECTION, PREDISPOSITION

¹pen·cil \'pen-səl\ *n* : a writing or drawing tool consisting of or containing a slender cylinder of a solid marking substance

²pencil *vb* **-ciled** *or* **-cilled**; **-cil·ing** *or* **-cil·ling** **1** : to draw or write with a pencil **2** : to plan or designate tentatively ⟨∼ed in the appointment⟩

pen·dant *also* **pen·dent** \'pen-dənt\ *n* : a hanging ornament (as on a necklace)

pen·dent *or* **pen·dant** \'pen-dənt\ *adj* : SUSPENDED, OVERHANGING

Pekingese

¹**pend·ing** \'pen-diŋ\ *prep* **1** : DURING **2** : while awaiting ⟨~ approval⟩

²**pending** *adj* **1** : not yet decided ⟨a ~ application⟩ **2** : IMMINENT

pen·du·lous \'pen-jə-ləs, -də-\ *adj* : hanging loosely : DROOPING

pen·du·lum \-ləm\ *n* : a body that swings freely from a fixed point

pe·ne·plain *also* **pe·ne·plane** \'pē-ni-ˌplān\ *n* : a large almost flat land surface shaped by erosion

pen·e·trate \'pe-nə-ˌtrāt\ *vb* **-trat·ed; -trat·ing** **1** : to enter into : PIERCE **2** : PERMEATE **3** : to see into : UNDERSTAND **4** : to affect deeply — **pen·e·tra·ble** \-trə-bəl\ *adj* — **pen·e·tra·tion** \ˌpe-nə-'trā-shən\ *n* — **pen·e·tra·tive** \'pe-nə-ˌtrā-tiv\ *adj*

penetrating *adj* **1** : having the power of entering, piercing, or pervading ⟨a ~ shriek⟩ ⟨a ~ odor⟩ **2** : ACUTE, DISCERNING ⟨a ~ look⟩

pen·guin \'pen-gwən, 'peŋ-\ *n* : any of various erect short-legged flightless seabirds of the southern hemisphere

pen·i·cil·lin \ˌpe-nə-'si-lən\ *n* : any of several antibiotics produced by molds or synthetically and used against various bacteria

pen·in·su·la \pə-'nin-sə-lə\ *n* [L *paeninsula*, fr. *paene* almost + *insula* island] : a long narrow portion of land extending out into the water — **pen·in·su·lar** \-lər\ *adj*

pe·nis \'pē-nəs\ *n, pl* **pe·nis·es** *also* **penes** \-ˌnēz\ : a male organ of copulation that in the human male also functions as the channel by which urine leaves the body

¹**pen·i·tent** \'pe-nə-tənt\ *adj* : feeling sorrow for sins or offenses : REPENTANT — **pen·i·tence** \-təns\ *n* — **pen·i·ten·tial** \ˌpe-nə-'ten-chəl\ *adj*

²**penitent** *n* : a penitent person

¹**pen·i·ten·tia·ry** \ˌpe-nə-'ten-chə-rē\ *n, pl* **-ries** : a state or federal prison

²**penitentiary** *adj* : of, relating to, or incurring confinement in a penitentiary

pen·knife \'pen-ˌnīf\ *n* : a small pocketknife

pen·light *also* **pen·lite** \-ˌlīt\ *n* : a small flashlight resembling a fountain pen in size or shape

pen·man \'pen-mən\ *n* **1** : COPYIST **2** : one skilled in penmanship **3** : AUTHOR

pen·man·ship \-ˌship\ *n* : the art or practice of writing with the pen

Penn *or* **Penna** *abbr* Pennsylvania

pen name *n* : an author's pseudonym

pen·nant \'pe-nənt\ *n* **1** : a tapering flag used esp. for signaling **2** : a flag symbolic of championship

pen·ne \'pe-nā\ *n* : short diagonally cut tubular pasta

pen·ni \'pe-nē\ *n, pl* **pen·nia** \-nē-ə\ *or* **pen·nis** \-nēz\ : a former monetary unit equal to ¹⁄₁₀₀ markka

pen·non \'pe-nən\ *n* **1** : a long narrow ribbonlike flag borne on a lance **2** : WING

Penn·syl·va·nian \ˌpen-səl-'vā-nyən\ *adj* **1** : of or relating to Pennsylvania or its people **2** : of, relating to, or being the period of the Paleozoic era between the Mississippian and the Permian — **Pennsylvanian** *n*

pen·ny \'pe-nē\ *n, pl* **pennies** \-nēz\ *or* **pence** \'pens\ **1** *pl usu* **pence** : a British monetary unit formerly equal to ¹⁄₁₂ shilling but now equal to ¹⁄₁₀₀ pound; *also* : a coin of this value — see *pound* at MONEY table **2** *pl* **pennies** : a cent of the U.S. or Canada **3** : a former monetary unit equal to ¹⁄₁₀₀ Irish pound — **pen·ni·less** \'pe-ni-ləs\ *adj*

pen·ny-pinch·ing \'pe-nē-ˌpin-chin\ *n* : PARSIMONY — **pen·ny-pinch·er** *n* — **penny-pinching** *adj*

pen·ny·weight \-ˌwāt\ *n* — see WEIGHT table

pen·ny-wise \-ˌwīz\ *adj* : wise or prudent only in small matters

pe·nol·o·gy \pi-'nä-lə-jē\ *n* : a branch of criminology dealing with prisons and the treatment of offenders

¹**pen·sion** \'pen-chən\ *n* : a fixed sum paid regularly esp. to a person retired from service

²**pension** *vb* : to pay a pension to — **pen·sion·er** *n*

pen·sive \'pen-siv\ *adj* : musingly, dreamily, or sadly thoughtful **♦ Synonyms** REFLECTIVE, SPECULATIVE, CONTEMPLATIVE, MEDITATIVE — **pen·sive·ly** *adv*

pen·stock \'pen-ˌstäk\ *n* **1** : a sluice or gate for regulating a flow **2** : a pipe for carrying water

pent \'pent\ *adj* : shut up : CONFINED

pen·ta·gon \'pen-tə-ˌgän\ *n* : a polygon of five angles and five sides — **pen·tag·o·nal** \pen-'ta-gə-n³l\ *adj*

pen·tam·e·ter \pen-'ta-mə-tər\ *n* : a line of verse containing five metrical feet

pen·tath·lon \pen-'tath-lən\ *n* : a composite athletic contest consisting of five events

Pen·te·cost \'pen-ti-ˌkȯst\ *n* : the 7th Sunday after Easter observed as a church festival commemorating the descent of the Holy Spirit on the apostles — **Pen·te·cos·tal** \ˌpen-ti-'käs-t³l\ *adj*

Pentecostal *n* : a member of a Christian religious body that stresses expressive worship, evangelism, and spiritual gifts — **Pen·te·cos·tal·ism** \ˌpen-ti-'käs-tə-ˌli-zəm \

pent·house \'pent-ˌhaùs\ *n* [alter. of ME *pentis*, fr. AF *apentiz*, fr. *apent*, pp. of *apendre* to attach, hang against] **1** : a shed or sloping roof attached to a wall or building **2** : an apartment built on the roof of a building

pen·ul·ti·mate \pi-'nəl-tə-mət\ *adj* : next to the last ⟨~ syllable⟩

pen·um·bra \pə-'nəm-brə\ *n, pl* **-brae** \-ˌ(ˌ)brē\ *or* **-bras** **1** : the partial shadow surrounding a complete shadow (as in an eclipse) **2** : something that covers or obscures ⟨a ~ of secrecy⟩

pe·nu·ri·ous \pə-'nùr-ē-əs, -'nyùr-\ *adj* **1** : marked by penury **2** : MISERLY **♦ Synonyms** STINGY, CLOSE, TIGHTFISTED, PARSIMONIOUS

pen·u·ry \'pe-nyə-rē\ *n* **1** : extreme poverty **2** : extreme frugality

pe·on \'pē-ˌän, -ən\ *n, pl* **peons** *or* **pe·o·nes** \pā-'ō-nēz\ **1** : a member of the landless laboring class in Spanish America **2** : one bound to service for payment of a debt — **pe·on·age** \-ə-nij\ *n*

pe·o·ny \'pē-ə-nē\ *n, pl* **-nies** : any of a genus of chiefly Eurasian plants with large often double red, pink, or white flowers; *also* : the flower

¹**peo·ple** \'pē-pəl\ *n, pl* **people** [ME *peple*, fr. AF *peple, peuple*, fr. L *populus*] **1** : human beings making up a group or linked by a common characteristic or interest **2** *pl* : human beings — often used in compounds instead of *persons* ⟨sales*people*⟩ *or* attributively ⟨~ skills⟩ **3** *pl* : the mass of persons in a community : POPULACE; *also* : ELECTORATE ⟨the ~'s choice⟩ **4** *pl* **peoples** : a body of persons (as a tribe, nation, or race) united by a common culture, sense of kinship, or political organization

²**people** *vb* **peo·pled; peo·pling** : to supply or fill with or as if with people

¹**pep** \'pep\ *n* : brisk energy or initiative — **pep·py** *adj*

²**pep** *vb* **pepped; pep·ping** : to put pep into : STIMULATE

¹**pep·per** \'pe-pər\ *n* **1** : either of two pungent condiments from the berry (**pep·per·corn** \-ˌkȯrn\) of an Indian climbing plant : BLACK PEPPER, WHITE PEPPER; *also* : this plant **2** : a plant related to the tomato and widely grown for its hot or mild sweet fruit; *also* : this fruit

²**pepper** *vb* **pep·pered; pep·per·ing** **1** : to shower with missiles or rapid blows **2** : to sprinkle or season with or as if with pepper **3** : to deliver something in rapid succession ⟨~ed him with questions⟩

pep·per·mint \-ˌmint, -mənt\ *n* : a pungent aromatic mint; *also* : candy flavored with its oil

pep·per·o·ni \ˌpe-pə-'rō-nē\ *n* : a highly seasoned beef and pork sausage

pepper spray *n* : a temporarily disabling aerosol that causes irritation and blinding of the eyes and inflammation of the nose, throat, and skin

pep·pery \'pe-pə-rē\ *adj* **1** : having the qualities of pepper : PUNGENT, HOT **2** : having a hot temper **3** : FIERY

pep·sin \'pep-sən\ *n* : an enzyme of the stomach that promotes digestion by breaking down proteins; *also* : a preparation of this used medicinally

pep·tic \'pep-tik\ *adj* [L *pepticus*, fr. Gk *peptikos*, fr. *peptos* cooked, *peptein* to cook, digest] **1** : relating to or promoting digestion **2** : caused by digestive juices ⟨a ~ ulcer⟩

pep·tide \'pep-ˌtīd\ *n* : any of various organic compounds composed of two or more amino acids bonded together

Pe·quot \'pē-ˌkwät\ *n* : a member of an American Indian people of eastern Connecticut

¹**per** \'pər\ *prep* **1** : by means of **2** : to or for each **3** : ACCORDING TO

²**per** *adv* : for each : APIECE

³**per** *abbr* **1** period **2** person

¹**per·ad·ven·ture** \'pər-əd-ˌven-chər\ *adv, archaic* : PERHAPS

²**per·ad·ven·ture** *n* **1** : DOUBT **2** : CHANCE **4**

per·am·bu·late \pə-'ram-byə-ˌlāt\ *vb* **-lat·ed; -lat·ing** : to travel over esp. on foot — **per·am·bu·la·tion** \-ˌram-byə-'lā-shən\ *n*

per·am·bu·la·tor \pə-'ram-byə-ˌlā-tər\ *n, chiefly Brit* : a baby carriage

per an·num \(ˌ)pər-'a-nəm\ *adv* [ML] : in or for each year : ANNUALLY

per·cale \(ˌ)pər-'kāl, 'pər-ˌ; (ˌ)pər-'kal\ *n* : a fine woven cotton cloth

per cap·i·ta \(ˌ)pər-'ka-pə-tə\ *adv or adj* [ML, by heads] : by or for each person

per·ceive \pər-'sēv\ *vb* **per·ceived; per·ceiv·ing** **1** : to attain awareness : REALIZE **2** : to become aware of through the senses — **per·ceiv·able** *adj*

¹**per·cent** \pər-'sent\ *adv* [*per* + L *centum* hundred] : in each hundred

²**percent** *n, pl* **percent** *or* **percents** **1** : one part in a hundred : HUNDREDTH **2** : PERCENTAGE

per·cent·age \pər-'sen-tij\ *n* **1** : a part of a whole expressed in hundredths **2** : the result obtained by multiplying a number by a percent **3** : ADVANTAGE, PROFIT **4** : PROBABILITY; *also* : favorable odds

percentage point *n* : one hundredth of a whole ⟨rates rose one *percentage point* from 6.5 to 7.5 percent⟩

per·cen·tile \pər-'sen-ˌtī(-ə)l\ *n* : a value on a scale of one hundred indicating the standing of a score or grade in terms of the percentage of scores or grades falling with or below it

per·cept \'pər-ˌsept\ *n* : an impression of an object obtained by use of the senses

per·cep·ti·ble \pər-'sep-tə-bəl\ *adj* : capable of being perceived ⟨a barely ∼ light⟩ — **per·cep·ti·bly** \-blē\ *adv*

per·cep·tion \pər-'sep-shən\ *n* **1** : an act or result of perceiving **2** : awareness of one's environment through physical sensation **3** : ability to understand : INSIGHT, COMPREHENSION ♦ *Synonyms* PENETRATION, DISCERNMENT, DISCRIMINATION

per·cep·tive \pər-'sep-tiv\ *adj* : capable of or exhibiting keen perception : OBSERVANT — **per·cep·tive·ly** *adv*

per·cep·tu·al \pər-'sep-chə-wəl\ *adj* : of, relating to, or involving sensory stimulus as opposed to abstract concept — **per·cep·tu·al·ly** *adv*

¹**perch** \'pərch\ *n* **1** : a roost for a bird **2** : a high station or vantage point

²**perch** *vb* : ROOST

³**perch** *n, pl* **perch** *or* **perch·es** : either of two small freshwater bony fishes used for food; *also* : any of various fishes resembling or related to these

per·chance \pər-'chans\ *adv* : PERHAPS

per·cip·i·ent \pər-'si-pē-ənt\ *adj* : capable of or characterized by perception — **per·cip·i·ence** \-əns\ *n*

per·co·late \'pər-kə-ˌlāt\ *vb* **-lat·ed; -lat·ing** **1** : to trickle or filter through a permeable substance **2** : to filter hot water through to extract the essence ⟨∼ coffee⟩ — **per·co·la·tor** \-ˌlā-tər\ *n*

per con·tra \(ˌ)pər-'kän-trə\ *adv* [It, by the opposite side (of the ledger)] **1** : on the contrary **2** : by way of contrast

per·cus·sion \pər-'kə-shən\ *n* **1** : a sharp blow : IMPACT; *esp* : a blow upon a cap (**percussion cap**) designed to explode the charge in a firearm **2** : the beating or striking of a musical instrument; *also* : instruments sounded by striking, shaking, or scraping

per di·em \pər-'dē-əm, -'dī-\ *adv* [ML] : by the day — **per diem** *adj or n*

per·di·tion \pər-'di-shən\ *n* **1** : eternal damnation **2** : HELL

per·du·ra·ble \(ˌ)pər-'dúr-ə-bəl, -'dyúr-\ *adj* : very durable — **per·du·ra·bil·i·ty** \-ˌdúr-ə-'bi-lə-tē, -ˌdyúr-\ *n*

per·e·gri·na·tion \ˌper-ə-grə-'nā-shən\ *n* : a traveling about esp. on foot

per·e·grine falcon \'per-ə-grən, -ˌgrēn\ *n* : a swift nearly cosmopolitan falcon that often nests in cities and is often used in falconry

pe·remp·to·ry \pə-'remp-tə-rē\ *adj* **1** : barring a right of action or delay **2** : expressive of urgency or command : IMPERATIVE **3** : marked by arrogant self-assurance ♦ *Synonyms* IMPERIOUS, MASTERFUL, DOMINEERING, MAGISTERIAL — **pe·remp·to·ri·ly** \-tə-rə-lē\ *adv*

¹**per·en·ni·al** \pə-'re-nē-əl\ *adj* **1** : present at all seasons of

the year ⟨∼ streams⟩ **2** : continuing to live from year to year ⟨∼ plants⟩ **3** : recurring regularly : PERMANENT ⟨∼ problems⟩ ♦ *Synonyms* LASTING, PERPETUAL, ENDURING, EVERLASTING — **pe·ren·ni·al·ly** *adv*

²**perennial** *n* : a perennial plant

perf *abbr* **1** perfect **2** perforated

¹**per·fect** \'pər-fikt\ *adj* **1** : being without fault or defect **2** : EXACT, PRECISE **3** : COMPLETE **4** : relating to or being a verb tense that expresses an action or state completed at the time of speaking or at a time spoken of — **per·fect·ly** *adv* — **per·fect·ness** *n*

²**per·fect** \'pər-'fekt\ *vb* : to make perfect

³**per·fect** \'pər-fikt\ *n* : the perfect tense; *also* : a verb form in it

per·fect·ible \pər-'fek-tə-bəl, 'pər-fik-\ *adj* : capable of improvement or perfection — **per·fect·ibil·i·ty** \pər-ˌfek-tə-'bi-lə-tē, ˌpər-fik-\ *n*

per·fec·tion \pər-'fek-shən\ *n* **1** : the quality or state of being perfect **2** : the highest degree of excellence **3** : the act or process of perfecting

per·fec·tion·ist \-shə-nist\ *n* : a person who will not accept or be content with anything less than perfection

per·fec·to \pər-'fek-tō\ *n, pl* **-tos** : a cigar that is thick in the middle and tapers almost to a point at each end

per·fi·dy \'pər-fə-dē\ *n, pl* **-dies** [L *perfidia*, fr. *perfidus* faithless, fr. *per-* detrimental to + *fides* faith] : violation of faith or loyalty : TREACHERY — **per·fid·i·ous** \pər-'fi-dē-əs\ *adj* — **per·fid·i·ous·ly** *adv*

per·fo·rate \'pər-fə-ˌrāt\ *vb* **-rat·ed; -rat·ing** : to bore through : PIERCE; *esp* : to make a line of holes in to facilitate separation — **per·fo·ra·tion** \ˌpər-fə-'rā-shən\ *n*

per·force \pər-'förs\ *adv* : of necessity ⟨we attended ∼⟩

per·form \pər-'förm\ *vb* **1** : FULFILL **2** : CARRY OUT, DO **3** : FUNCTION **4** : to do in a set manner **5** : to give a performance — **per·form·er** *n*

per·for·mance \pər-'för-məns\ *n* **1** : the act or process of performing **2** : DEED, FEAT **3** : a public presentation

¹**per·fume** \pər-'fyüm, 'pər-ˌfyüm\ *n* **1** : a usu. pleasant odor : FRAGRANCE **2** : a preparation used for scenting

²**per·fume** \pər-'fyüm, 'pər-ˌfyüm\ *vb* **per·fumed; per·fum·ing** : SCENT

per·fum·ery \pər-'fyü-mə-rē\ *n, pl* **-er·ies** **1** : the art or process of making perfume **2** : PERFUMES **3** : an establishment where perfumes are made

per·func·to·ry \pər-'fəŋk-tə-rē\ *adj* : done merely as a duty — **per·func·to·ri·ly** *adv*

per·go·la \'pər-gə-lə\ *n* [It] : a structure consisting of posts supporting an open roof in the form of a trellis

perh *abbr* perhaps

per·haps \pər-'haps\ *adv* : possibly but not certainly

per·i·gee \'per-ə-ˌjē\ *n* [MF, fr. NL *perigeum*, fr. Gk *perigeion*, fr. *peri* around, near + *gē* earth] : the point at which an orbiting object is nearest the body (as the earth) being orbited

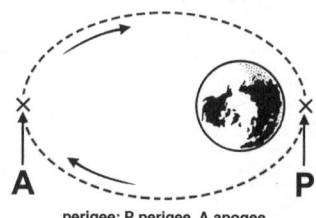

perigee: P perigee, A apogee

peri·he·lion \ˌper-ə-'hēl-yən\ *n, pl* **-he·lia** \-'hēl-yə\ : the point in the path of a celestial body (as a planet) that is nearest to the sun

per·il \'per-əl\ *n* : DANGER; *also* : a source of danger : RISK — **per·il·ous** *adj* — **per·il·ous·ly** *adv*

pe·rim·e·ter \pə-'ri-mə-tər\ *n* **1** : the boundary of a closed plane figure; *also* : its length **2** : a line bounding or protecting an area

peri·na·tal \ˌper-ə-'nā-t°l\ *adj* : occurring in, concerned with, or being in the period around the time of birth ⟨∼ care⟩

¹**pe·ri·od** \'pir-ē-əd\ *n* [ultim. fr. Gk *periodos* circuit, period,

of time, rhetorical period, fr. *peri* around + *hodos* way] **1** : SENTENCE; *also* : the full pause closing the utterance of a sentence **2** : END, STOP **3** : a punctuation mark . used esp. to mark the end of a declarative sentence or an abbreviation **4** : an extent of time; *esp* : one regarded as a stage or division in a process or development **5** : a portion of time in which a recurring phenomenon completes one cycle and is ready to begin again **6** : a single cyclic occurrence of menstruation

²**period** *adj* : of or relating to a particular historical period ⟨~ furniture⟩

pe·ri·od·ic \ˌpir-ē-ˈä-dik\ *adj* **1** : occurring at regular intervals of time **2** : happening repeatedly **3** : of or relating to a sentence that has no trailing elements following full grammatical statement of the essential idea

¹**pe·ri·od·i·cal** \ˌpir-ē-ˈä-di-kəl\ *adj* **1** : PERIODIC **2** : published at regular intervals **3** : of or relating to a periodical — **pe·ri·od·i·cal·ly** \-k(ə-)lē\ *adv*

²**periodical** *n* : a periodical publication

periodic table *n* : an arrangement of chemical elements based on their atomic structure and on their properties

peri·odon·tal \ˌper-ē-ō-ˈdän-tᵊl\ *adj* **1** : surrounding a tooth **2** : of or affecting periodontal tissues or regions

per·i·pa·tet·ic \ˌper-ə-pə-ˈte-tik\ *adj* : performed or performing while moving about : ITINERANT

pe·riph·er·al \pə-ˈri-fər-əl\ *n* : a device connected to a computer to provide communication or auxiliary functions

peripheral nervous system *n* : the part of the nervous system that is outside the central nervous system and comprises the spinal nerves, the cranial nerves except the one supplying the retina, and the autonomic nervous system

pe·riph·ery \pə-ˈri-fə-rē\ *n, pl* **-er·ies** **1** : the boundary of a rounded figure **2** : outward bounds : border area — **pe·riph·er·al** \-fə-rəl\ *adj*

pe·riph·ra·sis \pə-ˈri-frə-səs\ *n, pl* **-ra·ses** \-ˌsēz\ : CIRCUMLOCUTION

peri·scope \ˈper-ə-ˌskōp\ *n* : a tubular optical instrument enabling an observer to see an otherwise blocked field of view

per·ish \ˈper-ish\ *vb* : to become destroyed or ruined : cease to exist

per·ish·able \ˈper-i-shə-bəl\ *adj* : easily spoiled ⟨~ foods⟩ — **perishable** *n*

peri·stal·sis \ˌper-ə-ˈstȯl-səs, -ˈstal-\ *n, pl* **-stal·ses** : waves of contraction passing along the walls of a hollow muscular organ (as the intestine) and forcing its contents onward — **per·i·stal·tic** \-ˈstȯl-tik, -ˈstal-\ *adj*

peri·style \ˈper-ə-ˌstīl\ *n* : a row of columns surrounding a building or court

peri·to·ne·um \ˌper-ə-tə-ˈnē-əm\ *n, pl* **-ne·ums** *or* **-nea** : the smooth transparent serous membrane that lines the cavity of the abdomen — **peri·to·ne·al** \-ˈnē-əl\ *adj*

peri·to·ni·tis \ˌper-ə-tə-ˈnī-təs\ *n* : inflammation of the peritoneum

peri·wig \ˈper-i-ˌwig\ *n* : WIG

¹**per·i·win·kle** \ˈper-i-ˌwiŋ-kəl\ *n* : a usu. blue-flowered creeping plant cultivated as a ground cover

²**periwinkle** *n* : any of various small edible seashore snails

per·ju·ry \ˈpər-jə-rē\ *n* : the voluntary violation of an oath to tell the truth : lying under oath — **per·jure** \ˈpər-jər\ *vb* — **per·jur·er** *n*

¹**perk** \ˈpərk\ *vb* **1** : to thrust (as the head) up impudently or jauntily **2** : to regain vigor or spirit **3** : to make trim or brisk : FRESHEN — **perky** *adj*

²**perk** *vb* : PERCOLATE

³**perk** *n* : PERQUISITE — usu. used in pl.

per·lite \ˈpər-ˌlīt\ *n* : volcanic glass that when expanded by heat forms a lightweight material used esp. in concrete and plaster and for potting plants

¹**perm** \ˈpərm\ *n* : PERMANENT

²**perm** *vb* : to give (hair) a permanent

³**perm** *abbr* permanent

per·ma·frost \ˈpər-mə-ˌfrȯst\ *n* : a permanently frozen layer below the surface in frigid regions of a planet

¹**per·ma·nent** \ˈpər-mə-nənt\ *adj* : LASTING, STABLE — **per·ma·nence** \-nəns\ *n* — **per·ma·nen·cy** \-nən-sē\ *n* — **per·ma·nent·ly** *adv*

²**permanent** *n* : a long-lasting hair wave or straightening

permanent press *n* : the process of treating fabrics with

chemicals (as resin) and heat for setting the shape and for aiding wrinkle resistance

per·me·able \ˈpər-mē-ə-bəl\ *adj* : having small openings that permit liquids or gases to seep through — **per·me·a·bil·i·ty** \ˌpər-mē-ə-ˈbi-lə-tē\ *n*

per·me·ate \ˈpər-mē-ˌāt\ *vb* **-at·ed; -at·ing** **1** : PERVADE **2** : to seep through the pores of : PENETRATE — **per·me·ation** \ˌpər-mē-ˈā-shən\ *n*

Perm·ian \ˈpər-mē-ən\ *adj* : of, relating to, or being the latest period of the Paleozoic era — **Permian** *n*

per·mis·si·ble \pər-ˈmi-sə-bəl\ *adj* : that may be permitted : ALLOWABLE

per·mis·sion \pər-ˈmi-shən\ *n* : formal consent : AUTHORIZATION

per·mis·sive \pər-ˈmi-siv\ *adj* : granting permission; *esp* : INDULGENT — **per·mis·sive·ly** *adv* — **per·mis·sive·ness** *n*

¹**per·mit** \pər-ˈmit\ *vb* **per·mit·ted; per·mit·ting** **1** : to consent to : ALLOW **2** : to make possible

²**per·mit** \ˈpər-ˌmit, pər-ˈmit\ *n* : a written permission : LICENSE

per·mu·ta·tion \ˌpər-myü-ˈtā-shən\ *n* **1** : a major or fundamental change **2** : the act or process of changing the order of an ordered set of objects ✦ *Synonyms* INNOVATION, MUTATION, VICISSITUDE

per·ni·cious \pər-ˈni-shəs\ *adj* [ME, fr. AF, fr. L *perniciosus*, fr. *pernicies* destruction, fr. *per-* through + *nec-, nex* violent death] : very destructive or injurious — **per·ni·cious·ly** *adv*

per·ora·tion \ˈper-ə-ˌrā-shən, ˈpər-\ *n* : the concluding part of a speech

¹**per·ox·ide** \pə-ˈräk-ˌsīd\ *n* : an oxide containing a large proportion of oxygen; *esp* : HYDROGEN PEROXIDE

²**peroxide** *vb* **-id·ed; -id·ing** : to bleach with hydrogen peroxide

perp *abbr* **1** perpendicular **2** perpetrator

per·pen·dic·u·lar \ˌpər-pən-ˈdi-kyə-lər\ *adj* **1** : standing at right angles to the plane of the horizon **2** : forming a right angle with each other or with a given line or plane — **perpendicular** *n* — **per·pen·dic·u·lar·i·ty** \-ˌdi-kyə-ˈla-rə-tē\ *n* — **per·pen·dic·u·lar·ly** *adv*

per·pe·trate \ˈpər-pə-ˌtrāt\ *vb* **-trat·ed; -trat·ing** : to carry out (as a crime) : COMMIT — **per·pe·tra·tion** \ˌpər-pə-ˈtrā-shən\ *n* — **per·pe·tra·tor** \ˈpər-pə-ˌtrā-tər\ *n*

per·pet·u·al \pər-ˈpe-chə-wəl\ *adj* **1** : continuing forever : EVERLASTING **2** : occurring continually : CONSTANT ⟨~ annoyance⟩ ✦ *Synonyms* CEASELESS, UNCEASING, CONTINUAL, CONTINUOUS, INCESSANT, UNREMITTING — **per·pet·u·al·ly** *adv*

per·pet·u·ate \pər-ˈpe-chə-ˌwāt\ *vb* **-at·ed; -at·ing** : to make perpetual : cause to last indefinitely — **per·pet·u·a·tion** \-ˌpe-chə-ˈwā-shən\ *n*

per·pe·tu·i·ty \ˌpər-pə-ˈtü-ə-tē, -ˈtyü-\ *n, pl* **-ties** : ETERNITY **1 2** : the quality or state of being perpetual

per·plex \pər-ˈpleks\ *vb* : to disturb mentally; *esp* : CONFUSE — **per·plex·i·ty** \-ˈplek-sə-tē\ *n*

per·plexed \-ˈplekst\ *adj* **1** : filled with uncertainty : PUZZLED **2** : full of difficulty : COMPLICATED — **per·plexed·ly** \-ˈplek-səd-lē\ *adv*

per·qui·site \ˈpər-kwə-zət\ *n* : a privilege or profit beyond regular pay

pers *abbr* person; personal

¹**per se** \(ˌ)pər-ˈsā\ *adv* [L] : by, of, or in itself : as such

²**per se** *adj* : being such inherently, clearly, or as a matter of law

per·se·cute \ˈpər-si-ˌkyüt\ *vb* **-cut·ed; -cut·ing** : to pursue in such a way as to injure or afflict : HARASS; *esp* : to cause to suffer because of belief — **per·se·cu·tion** \ˌpər-si-ˈkyü-shən\ *n* — **per·se·cu·tor** \ˈpər-si-ˌkyü-tər\ *n*

per·se·vere \ˌpər-sə-ˈvir\ *vb* **-vered; -ver·ing** : to persist (as in an undertaking) in spite of difficulties — **per·se·ver·ance** \-ˈvir-əns\ *n*

Per·sian \ˈpər-zhən\ *n* **1** : a native or inhabitant of ancient Persia **2** : a member of one of the peoples of modern Iran **3** : the language of the Persians

Persian cat *n* : any of a breed of stocky round-headed domestic cats that have a long silky coat

Persian lamb *n* : a pelt with very silky tightly curled fur that is obtained from newborn lambs which are older than those yielding broadtail

per·si·flage \ˈpər-si-ˌfläzh, ˈper-\ *n* [F, fr. *persifler* to ban-

PERIODIC TABLE

This is the common long form of the table, with atomic numbers given along with the symbols. Roman numerals and letters heading the vertical columns indicate the groups. (There are differences of opinion regarding the letter designations, but those given here are probably the most generally used. International standards favor numbering the groups 1-18 from left to right using Arabic numerals, but the designations shown below remain quite common.) Horizontal rows represent the periods, with two series removed from the two very long periods and represented below the main table.

IA[1]	IIA[2]	IIIB	IVB	VB	VIB	VIIB	VIII			IB	IIB	IIIA	IVA	VA	VIA	VIIA[3]	VIIIA[4]
1 H																1 H	2 He
3 Li	4 Be											5 B	6 C	7 N	8 O	9 F	10 Ne
11 Na	12 Mg											13 Al	14 Si	15 P	16 S	17 Cl	18 Ar
19 K	20 Ca	21 Sc	22 Ti	23 V	24 Cr	25 Mn	26 Fe	27 Co	28 Ni	29 Cu	30 Zn	31 Ga	32 Ge	33 As	34 Se	35 Br	36 Kr
37 Rb	38 Sr	39 Y	40 Zr	41 Nb	42 Mo	43 Tc	44 Ru	45 Rh	46 Pd	47 Ag	48 Cd	49 In	50 Sn	51 Sb	52 Te	53 I	54 Xe
55 Cs	56 Ba	57 *La	72 Hf	73 Ta	74 W	75 Re	76 Os	77 Ir	78 Pt	79 Au	80 Hg	81 Tl	82 Pb	83 Bi	84 Po	85 At	86 Rn
87 Fr	88 Ra	89 #Ac	104 Rf	105 Db	106 Sg	107 Bh	108 Hs	109 Mt	110 Ds								

*LANTHANIDE SERIES	58 Ce	59 Pr	60 Nd	61 Pm	62 Sm	63 Eu	64 Gd	65 Tb	66 Dy	67 Ho	68 Er	69 Tm	70 Yb	71 Lu
#ACTINIDE SERIES	90 Th	91 Pa	92 U	93 Np	94 Pu	95 Am	96 Cm	97 Bk	98 Cf	99 Es	100 Fm	101 Md	102 No	103 Lr

[1] Group IA (excluding hydrogen) comprises the alkali metals.
[2] Group IIA comprises the alkaline earth metals.
[3] Group VIIA (excluding hydrogen) comprises the halogens.
[4] Group VIIIA (also called group Zero) comprises the noble gases.

ter, fr. *per-* thoroughly + *siffler* to whistle, hiss, boo, ultim. fr. L *sibilare*] : lightly jesting or mocking talk

per·sim·mon \pər-'si-mən\ *n* : either of two trees related to the ebony; *also* : the edible usu. orange or red plumlike fruit of a persimmon

per·sist \pər-'sist, -'zist\ *vb* **1** : to go on resolutely or stubbornly in spite of difficulties **2** : to continue to exist — **per·sis·tence** \-'sis-təns, -'zis-\ *n* — **per·sis·ten·cy** \-tən-sē\ *n* — **per·sis·tent** \-tənt\ *adj* — **per·sis·tent·ly** *adv*

per·snick·e·ty \pər-'sni-kə-tē\ *adj* : fussy about small details

per·son \'pər-sən\ *n* [ME, fr. AF *persone*, fr. L *persona* actor's mask, character in a play, person, prob. fr. Etruscan *phersu* mask, fr. Gk *prosōpa*, pl. of *prosōpon* face, mask] **1** : a human being : INDIVIDUAL — used in combination esp. by those who prefer to avoid *man* in compounds applicable to both sexes 〈chair*person*〉 **2** : one of the three modes of being in the Godhead as understood by Trinitarians **3** : the body of a human being **4** : the individual personality of a human being : SELF **5** : reference of a segment of discourse to the speaker, to one spoken to, or to one spoken of esp. as indicated by certain pronouns

per·so·na \pər-'sō-nə\ *n, pl* **-nae** \-nē\ *or* **-nas** : the personality that a person projects in public

per·son·able \'pər-sə-nə-bəl\ *adj* : pleasant in person : ATTRACTIVE

per·son·age \'pər-sə-nij\ *n* : a person of rank, note, or distinction

¹per·son·al \'pər-sə-nəl\ *adj* **1** : of, relating to, or affecting a person : PRIVATE 〈~ correspondence〉 **2** : done in person 〈a ~ inquiry〉 **3** : relating to the person or body 〈~ injuries〉 **4** : relating to an individual esp. in an offensive way 〈resented such ~ remarks〉 **5** : of or relating to temporary or movable property as distinguished from real estate **6** : denoting grammatical person **7** : intended for use by one person

²personal *n* **1** : a short newspaper paragraph relating to a person or group or to personal matters **2** : a short personal or private communication in the classified ads section of a newspaper

personal computer *n* : a computer with a microprocessor designed for an individual user to run esp. commercial software

personal digital assistant *n* : PDA

per·son·al·ise *Brit var of* PERSONALIZE

per·son·al·i·ty \,pər-sə-'na-lə-tē\ *n, pl* **-ties** **1** : an offensively personal remark 〈indulges in *personalities*〉 **2** : the collection of emotional and behavioral traits that characterize a person **3** : distinction of personal and social traits **4** : a well-known person 〈a TV ~〉 ✦ **Synonyms** INDIVIDUALITY, TEMPERAMENT, DISPOSITION, MAKEUP

per·son·al·ize \'pər-sə-nə-,līz\ *vb* **-ized; -iz·ing 1** : to make personal or individual; *esp* : to mark as belonging to a particular person

per·son·al·ly \-nə-lē\ *adv* **1** : in person **2** : as a person **3** : as far as oneself is concerned 〈~, I don't want to go〉

per·son·al·ty \'pər-sə-nəl-tē\ *n, pl* **-ties** : personal property

per·so·na non gra·ta \pər-'sō-nə-,nän-'gra-tə, -'grä-\ *adj* [L] : being personally unacceptable or unwelcome

per·son·ate \'pər-sə-,nāt\ *vb* **-at·ed; -at·ing** : IMPERSONATE, REPRESENT

per·son·i·fy \pər-'sä-nə-,fī\ *vb* **-fied; -fy·ing 1** : to think of or represent as a person **2** : to be the embodiment of : INCARNATE 〈~ the law〉 — **per·son·i·fi·ca·tion** \-,sä-nə-fə-'kā-shən\ *n*

per·son·nel \,pər-sə-'nel\ *n* : a body of persons employed

per·spec·tive \pər-'spek-tiv\ *n* **1** : the science of painting and drawing so that objects represented have apparent depth and distance **2** : the aspect in which a subject or its parts are mentally viewed; *esp* : a view of things (as objects or events) in their true relationship or relative importance

per·spi·ca·cious \,pər-spə-'kā-shəs\ *adj* : having or showing keen understanding or discernment — **per·spi·cac·i·ty** \-'ka-sə-tē\ *n*

per·spic·u·ous \pər-'spi-kyə-wəs\ *adj* : plain to the understanding — **per·spi·cu·i·ty** \,pər-spə-'kyü-ə-tē\ *n*

per·spire \pər-'spī(-ə)r\ *vb* **per·spired; per·spir·ing** : SWEAT — **per·spi·ra·tion** \,pər-spə-'rā-shən\ *n*

per·suade \pər-'swäd\ *vb* **per·suad·ed; per·suad·ing** : to win over to a belief or course of action by argument or entreaty — **per·sua·sive** \-'swä-siv, -ziv\ *adj* — **per·sua·sive·ly** *adv* — **per·sua·sive·ness** *n*

per·sua·sion \pər-'swä-zhən\ *n* **1** : the act or process of persuading **2** : a system of religious beliefs; *also* : a group holding such beliefs

pert \'pərt\ *adj* [ME, evident, attractive, saucy, short for *apert* evident, fr. AF, fr. L *apertus* open, fr. pp. of *aperire* to open] **1** : saucily free and forward : IMPUDENT **2** : stylishly trim : JAUNTY **3** : LIVELY

per·tain \pər-'tān\ *vb* **1** : to belong to as a part, quality, or function 〈duties ~*ing* to the office〉 **2** : to have reference : RELATE 〈books ~*ing* to birds〉

per·ti·na·cious \,pər-tə-'nā-shəs\ *adj* **1** : holding resolutely to an opinion or purpose **2** : obstinately persistent 〈a ~ bill collector〉 ✦ **Synonyms** DOGGED, MULISH, HEADSTRONG, PERVERSE — **per·ti·nac·i·ty** \-'na-sə-tē\ *n*

per·ti·nent \'pər-tə-nənt\ *adj* : relating to the matter under consideration ✦ **Synonyms** RELEVANT, GERMANE, APPLICABLE, APROPOS — **per·ti·nence** \-əns\ *n*

per·turb \pər-'tərb\ *vb* **1** : to disturb greatly esp. in mind : UPSET — **per·tur·ba·tion** \,pər-tər-'bä-shən\ *n*

per·tus·sis \pər-'tə-səs\ *n* : WHOOPING COUGH

pe·ruke \pə-'rük\ *n* : WIG

pe·ruse \pə-'rüz\ *vb* **pe·rused; pe·rus·ing 1** : READ; *esp* : to read over attentively or leisurely — **pe·rus·al** \-'rü-zəl\ *n*

per·vade \pər-'vād\ *vb* **per·vad·ed; per·vad·ing** : to spread through every part of : PERMEATE, PENETRATE — **per·va·sive** \-'vä-siv, -ziv\ *adj*

per·verse \pər-'vərs\ *adj* **1** : turned away from what is right or good : CORRUPT **2** : obstinate in opposing what is reasonable or accepted **3** : marked by perversion — **per·verse·ly** *adv* — **per·verse·ness** *n* — **per·ver·si·ty** \-'vər-sə-tē\ *n*

per·ver·sion \pər-'vər-zhən\ *n* **1** : the action of perverting : the condition of being perverted **2** : a perverted form of something; *esp* : aberrant sexual behavior

¹per·vert \pər-'vərt\ *vb* **1** : to lead astray : CORRUPT 〈~ the young〉 **2** : to divert to a wrong purpose : MISAPPLY 〈~ evidence〉 ✦ **Synonyms** DEPRAVE, DEBASE, DEBAUCH, DEMORALIZE — **per·ver·ter** *n*

²per·vert \'pər-,vərt\ *n* : one that is perverted; *esp* : one given to sexual perversion

pe·se·ta \pə-'sā-tə\ *n* : the former basic monetary unit of Spain

pe·se·wa \pə-'sā-wə\ *n* — see *cedi* at MONEY table

pes·ky \'pes-kē\ *adj* **pes·ki·er; -est** : causing annoyance : TROUBLESOME

pe·so \'pā-sō\ *n, pl* **pesos** — see MONEY table

pes·si·mism \'pe-sə-,mi-zəm\ *n* [F *pessimisme*, fr. L *pessimus* worst] : an inclination to take the least favorable view (as of events) or to expect the worst — **pes·si·mist** \-mist\ *n* — **pes·si·mis·tic** \,pe-sə-'mis-tik\ *adj*

pest \'pest\ *n* **1** : a destructive epidemic disease : PLAGUE **2** : a plant or animal detrimental to humans **3** : one that pesters : NUISANCE — **pesty** *adj*

pes·ter \'pes-tər\ *vb* : to harass with petty irritations : ANNOY

pes·ti·cide \'pes-tə-,sīd\ *n* : an agent used to destroy pests

pes·tif·er·ous \pes-'ti-fə-rəs\ *adj* **1** : PESTILENT **2** : ANNOYING

pes·ti·lence \'pes-tə-ləns\ *n* : a destructive infectious swiftly spreading disease; *esp* : BUBONIC PLAGUE

pes·ti·lent \-lənt\ *adj* **1** : dangerous to life : DEADLY **2** : PERNICIOUS, HARMFUL **3** : TROUBLESOME **4** : INFECTIOUS, CONTAGIOUS

pes·ti·len·tial \,pes-tə-'len-chəl\ *adj* **1** : causing or tending to cause pestilence : DEADLY **2** : morally harmful

pes·tle \'pes-əl, 'pes-t^əl\ *n* : an implement for grinding substances in a mortar — **pestle** *vb*

¹pet \'pet\ *n* **1** : FAVORITE, DARLING **2** : a domesticated animal kept for pleasure rather than utility

²pet *adj* **1** : kept or treated as a pet 〈~ dog〉 **2** : expressing fondness 〈~ name〉 **3** : particularly liked or favored

³pet *vb* **pet·ted; pet·ting 1** : to stroke gently or lovingly **2** : to make a pet of : PAMPER **3** : to engage in amorous kissing and caressing

⁴pet *n* : a fit of peevishness, sulkiness, or anger — **pet·tish** *adj*

Pet *abbr* Peter

pet·al \'pe-t^əl\ *n* : one of the modified leaves of a flower's corolla

pe·tard \pə-'tärd, -'tär\ *n* : a case containing an explosive to break down a door or gate or breach a wall

pe·ter \'pē-tər\ *vb* : to diminish gradually and come to an end ⟨his energy ~*ed* out⟩

Pe·ter \'pē-tər\ *n* — see BIBLE table

pet·i·ole \'pe-tē-ˌōl\ *n* : a slender stem that supports a leaf

pe·tite \pə-'tēt\ *adj* [F] : small and trim of figure ⟨a ~ woman⟩ — **petite** *n*

pe·tit four \ˌpe-tē-'fȯr\ *n, pl* **petits fours** *or* **petit fours** \-'fȯrz\ [F, lit., small oven] : a small cake cut from pound or sponge cake and frosted

¹pe·ti·tion \pə-'ti-shən\ *n* : an earnest request : ENTREATY; *esp* : a formal written request made to an authority

²petition *vb* : to make a request to or for — **pe·ti·tion·er** *n*

pe·trel \'pe-trəl\ *n* : any of numerous seabirds that fly far from land

pe·tri dish \'pē-trē-\ *n* **1** : a small shallow dish used esp. for growing bacteria **2** : something fosterng development or innovation

pet·ri·fy \'pe-trə-ˌfī\ *vb* **-fied; -fy·ing 1** : to convert (organic matter) into stone or stony material **2** : to make rigid or inactive (as from fear or awe) — **pet·ri·fac·tion** \ˌpe-trə-'fak-shən\ *n*

pet·ro·chem·i·cal \ˌpe-trō-'ke-mi-kəl\ *n* : a chemical isolated or derived from petroleum or natural gas — **pet·ro·chem·is·try** \-'ke-mə-strē\ *n*

pet·rol \'pe-trəl\ *n, chiefly Brit* : GASOLINE

pet·ro·la·tum \ˌpe-trə-'lā-təm\ *n* : PETROLEUM JELLY

pe·tro·leum \pə-'trō-lē-əm\ *n* [ML, fr. Gk *petra* rock + L *oleum* oil] : an oily flammable liquid obtained from wells drilled in the ground and refined into gasoline, fuel oils, and other products

petroleum jelly *n* : a tasteless, odorless, and oily or greasy substance from petroleum that is used esp. in ointments and dressings

¹pet·ti·coat \'pe-tē-ˌkōt\ *n* **1** : a skirt worn under a dress **2** : an outer skirt

²petticoat *adj* : of, relating to, or exercised by women : FEMALE

pet·ti·fog·ger \'pe-tē-ˌfȯ-gər, -ˌfä-\ *n* **1** : a lawyer whose methods are petty, underhanded, or disreputable **2** : one given to quibbling over trifles — **pet·ti·fog·ging** \-giŋ\ *adj or n*

pet·ty \'pe-tē\ *adj* **pet·ti·er; -est** [ME *pety* small, minor, alter. of *petit*, fr. AF, small] **1** : having secondary rank : MINOR ⟨~ prince⟩ **2** : of little importance : TRIFLING ⟨~ faults⟩ **3** : marked by narrowness or meanness — **pet·ti·ly** \'pe-tə-lē\ *adv* — **pet·ti·ness** \-tē-nəs\ *n*

petty officer *n* : a subordinate officer in the navy or coast guard appointed from among the enlisted men

petty officer first class *n* : a petty officer ranking below a chief petty officer

petty officer second class *n* : a petty officer ranking below a petty officer first class

petty officer third class *n* : a petty officer ranking below a petty officer second class

pet·u·lant \'pe-chə-lənt\ *adj* : marked by capricious ill humor ✦ **Synonyms** IRRITABLE, PEEVISH, FRETFUL, FRACTIOUS, QUERULOUS — **pet·u·lance** \-ləns\ *n* — **pet·u·lant·ly** *adv*

pe·tu·nia \pi-'tün-yə, -'tyün-\ *n* : any of a genus of tropical So. American herbs related to the potato and having bright funnel-shaped flowers

pew \'pyü\ *n* [ME *pewe*, fr. MF *puie* balustrade, fr. L *podia*, pl. of *podium* parapet, podium, fr. Gk *podion* base, dim. of *pod-, pous* foot] : any of the benches with backs fixed in rows in a church

pe·wee \'pē-(ˌ)wē\ *n* : any of various small American flycatchers

pew·ter \'pyü-tər\ *n* **1** : an alloy of tin used esp. for household utensils **2** : a bluish gray color — **pewter** *adj* — **pew·ter·er** *n*

pey·o·te \pā-'ō-tē\ *also* **pey·otl** \-'ō-t^əl\ *n* **1** : a hallucinogenic drug derived from the peyote cactus and containing mescaline **2** : a small cactus of the southwestern U.S. and Mexico

pf *abbr* **1** pfennig **2** preferred

PFC *or* **Pfc** *abbr* private first class

pfd *abbr* preferred

pfen·nig \'fe-nig\ *n, pl* **pfennig** *also* **pfennigs** *or* **pfen·ni·ge** \'fe-ni-gə\ : a former monetary unit equal to ¹⁄₁₀₀ deutsche mark

pg *abbr* page

PG *abbr* postgraduate

PGA *abbr* Professional Golfers' Association

pH \(ˌ)pē-'āch\ *n* : a value used to express acidity and alkalinity; *also* : the condition represented by such a value

PH *abbr* **1** pinch hit **2** public health

pha·eton \'fā-ə-t^ən\ *n* [F *phaéton*, fr. *Phaéton*, fr. Gk *Phaethōn*, son of the sun god who persuaded his father to let him drive the chariot of the sun but who lost control of the horses with disastrous consequences] **1** : a light 4-wheeled horse-drawn vehicle **2** : an open automobile with two cross seats

phage \'fāj\ *n* : BACTERIOPHAGE

pha·lanx \'fā-ˌlaŋks\ *n, pl* **pha·lanx·es** *or* **pha·lan·ges** \fə-'lan-ˌjēz\ **1** : a group or body (as of troops) in compact formation **2** *pl* **phalanges** : one of the digital bones of the hand or foot of a vertebrate

phal·a·rope \'fa-lə-ˌrōp\ *n, pl* **-ropes** *also* **-rope** : any of a genus of small shorebirds related to sandpipers

phal·lus \'fa-ləs\ *n, pl* **phal·li** \'fa-ˌlī\ *or* **phal·lus·es** : PENIS; *also* : a symbolic representation of the penis — **phal·lic** \'fa-lik\ *adj* **1** : of, relating to, or resembling a phallus **2** : relating to or being the stage of psychosexual development in psychoanalytic theory during which children become interested in their own sexual organs

Phan·er·o·zo·ic \ˌfa-nə-rə-'zō-ik\ *adj* : of, relating to, or being an eon of geologic history comprising the Paleozoic, Mesozoic, and Cenozoic

phan·tasm \'fan-ˌta-zəm\ *n* : a product of the imagination : ILLUSION — **phan·tas·mal** \ˌfan-'taz-məl\ *adj*

phan·tas·ma·go·ria \fan-ˌtaz-mə-'gȯr-ē-ə\ *n* : a constantly shifting complex succession of things seen or imagined; *also* : a scene that constantly changes or fluctuates

phantasy *var of* FANTASY

phan·tom \'fan-təm\ *n* **1** : something (as a specter) that is apparent to sense but has no substantial existence **2** : a mere show : SHADOW — **phantom** *adj*

pha·raoh \'fer-ō, 'fā-rō\ *n, often cap* : a ruler of ancient Egypt

phar·i·sa·ical \ˌfa-rə-'sā-ə-kəl\ *adj* : hypocritically self-righteous

phar·i·see \'fa-rə-ˌsē\ *n* **1** *cap* : a member of an ancient Jewish sect noted for strict observance of rites and ceremonies of the traditional law **2** : a self-righteous or hypocritical person — **phar·i·sa·ic** \ˌfa-rə-'sā-ik\ *adj*

pharm *abbr* pharmaceutical; pharmacist; pharmacy

phar·ma·ceu·ti·cal \ˌfär-mə-'sü-ti-kəl\ *adj* : of, relating to, or engaged in pharmacy or the manufacture and sale of medicinal drugs — **pharmaceutical** *n*

phar·ma·col·o·gy \ˌfär-mə-'kä-lə-jē\ *n* **1** : the science of drugs esp. as related to medicinal uses **2** : the reactions and properties of one or more drugs — **phar·ma·co·log·i·cal** \-kə-'lä-ji-kəl\ *also* **phar·ma·co·log·ic** \-kə-'lä-jik\ *adj* — **phar·ma·col·o·gist** \-'kä-lə-jist\ *n*

phar·ma·co·poe·ia *also* **phar·ma·co·pe·ia** \-kə-'pē-ə\ *n* **1** : a book describing drugs and medicinal preparations **2** : a stock of drugs

phar·ma·cy \'fär-mə-sē\ *n, pl* **-cies 1** : the art, practice, or profession of preparing and dispensing medicinal drugs **2** : DRUGSTORE — **phar·ma·cist** \-sist\ *n*

phar·ynx \'fa-riŋks\ *n, pl* **pha·ryn·ges** \fə-'rin-ˌjēz\ *also* **phar·ynx·es** : the muscular tubular passage extending from the back of the nasal cavity and mouth to the esophagus — **pha·ryn·ge·al** \fə-'rin-jəl, ˌfa-rən-'jē-əl\ *adj*

phase \'fāz\ *n* **1** : a particular appearance in a recurring series of changes ⟨~*s* of the moon⟩ **2** : a stage or interval in a process or cycle ⟨first ~ of an experiment⟩ **3** : an aspect or part under consideration — **pha·sic** \'fā-zik\ *adj*

phase down *vb* : to reduce the size or amount of by phases

phase in *vb* : to introduce in stages

phase-out \'fāz-ˌaut\ *n* : a gradual stopping of operations or production

phase out *vb* : to stop production or use of in stages

PhD *abbr* [L *philosophiae doctor*] doctor of philosophy

pheas·ant \'fe-z³nt\ *n, pl* **pheasant** *or* **pheasants** : any of numerous long-tailed brilliantly colored game birds related to the domestic chicken

pheasant

phen·cy·cli·dine \,fen-'sī-klə-,dēn\ *n* : a drug used esp. as a veterinary anesthetic and sometimes illicitly as a hallucinogenic drug

phe·no·bar·bi·tal \,fē-nō-'bär-bə-,tól\ *n* : a crystalline drug used as a hypnotic and sedative

phe·nol \'fē-,nól\ *n* : a corrosive poisonous acidic compound present in coal and wood tars and used in solution as a disinfectant

phe·nom·e·non \fi-'nä-mə-,nän, -nən\ *n, pl* **-na** \-nə\ *or* **-nons** [LL *phaenomenon,* fr. Gk *phainomenon,* fr. neut. of *phainomenos,* prp. of *phainesthai* to appear] **1** *pl* **-na** : an observable fact or event **2** : an outward sign of the working of a law of nature **3** *pl* **-nons** : an extraordinary person or thing : PRODIGY — **phe·nom·e·nal** \-'nä-mə-n³l\ *adj* — **phe·nom·e·non·al·ly** *adv*

pher·o·mone \'fer-ə-,mōn\ *n* : a chemical substance that is usu. produced by an animal and serves to stimulate a behavioral response in other individuals of the same species — **pher·o·mon·al** \,fer-ə-'mō-n³l\ *adj*

phi \'fī\ *n* : the 21st letter of the Greek alphabet — Φ *or* φ

phi·al \'fī(-ə)l\ *n* : VIAL

Phil *abbr* Philippians

phi·lan·der \fə-'lan-dər\ *vb* : to have casual or illicit sexual relations with many women — **phi·lan·der·er** *n*

phi·lan·thro·py \fə-'lan-thrə-pē\ *n, pl* **-pies** **1** : goodwill toward all people; *esp* : effort to promote human welfare **2** : a charitable act or gift; *also* : an organization that distributes or is supported by donated funds — **phil·an·throp·ic** \,fi-lən-'thrä-pik\ *adj* — **phil·an·throp·i·cal·ly** \-pi-k(ə-)lē\ *adv* — **phi·lan·thro·pist** \fə-'lan-thrə-pist\ *n*

phi·lat·e·ly \fə-'la-tə-lē\ *n* : the collection and study of postage and imprinted stamps — **phil·a·tel·ic** \,fi-lə-'te-lik\ *adj* — **phi·lat·e·list** \fə-'la-tə-list\ *n*

Phi·le·mon \fə-'lē-mən, fī-\ *n* — see BIBLE table

Phi·lip·pi·ans \fə-'li-pē-ənz\ *n* — see BIBLE table

phi·lip·pic \fə-'li-pik\ *n* : TIRADE

phi·lis·tine \'fi-lə-,stēn; fə-'lis-tən\ *n, often cap* [*Philistine,* inhabitant of ancient Philistia (Palestine)] : a person who is smugly insensitive or indifferent to intellectual or artistic values — **philistine** *adj, often cap*

Phil·lips \'fi-ləps\ *adj* : of, relating to, or being a screw having a head with a cross slot or its corresponding screwdriver

philo·den·dron \,fi-lə-'den-drən\ *n, pl* **-drons** *also* **-dra** \-drə\ [NL, fr. Gk, neut. of *philodendros* loving trees, fr. *philos* dear, friendly + *dendron* tree] : any of various plants of the arum family grown for their showy foliage

phi·lol·o·gy \fə-'lä-lə-jē\ *n* **1** : the study of literature and relevant fields **2** : LINGUISTICS; *esp* : historical and comparative linguistics — **phil·o·log·i·cal** \,fi-lə-'lä-ji-kəl\ *adj* — **phi·lol·o·gist** \fə-'lä-lə-jist\ *n*

philos *abbr* philosopher; philosophy

phi·los·o·pher \fə-'lä-sə-fər\ *n* **1** : a reflective thinker : SCHOLAR **2** : a student of or specialist in philosophy **3** : a person whose philosophical perspective makes it possible to meet trouble calmly

phi·los·o·phise *Brit var of* PHILOSOPHIZE

phi·los·o·phize \fə-'lä-sə-,fīz\ *vb* **-phized; -phiz·ing** **1** : to reason like a philosopher : THEORIZE **2** : to expound a philosophy esp. superficially

phi·los·o·phy \fə-'lä-sə-fē\ *n, pl* **-phies** **1** : sciences and liberal arts exclusive of medicine, law, and theology ⟨doc-

tor of ∼⟩ **2** : a critical study of fundamental beliefs and the grounds for them **3** : a system of philosophical concepts ⟨Aristotelian ∼⟩ **4** : a basic theory concerning a particular subject or sphere of activity **5** : the sum of the ideas and convictions of an individual or group ⟨her ∼ of life⟩ **6** : calmness of temper and judgment — **phil·o·soph·i·cal** \-fi-kəl\ *also* **phil·o·soph·ic** \,fi-lə-'sä-fik\ *adj* — **phil·o·soph·i·cal·ly** \-k(ə-)lē\ *adv*

phil·ter \'fil-tər\ *n* **1** : a magic potion **2** : a potion, drug, or charm held to arouse sexual passion

phil·tre *chiefly Brit var of* PHILTER

phle·bi·tis \fli-'bī-təs\ *n* : inflammation of a vein

phle·bot·o·my \fli-'bä-tə-mē\ *n, pl* **-mies** : the opening of a vein esp. for removing or releasing blood

phlegm \'flem\ *n* [ME *fleume,* fr. AF, fr. LL *phlegma,* fr. Gk, flame, inflammation, phlegm, fr. *phlegein* to burn] : thick mucus secreted in abnormal quantity esp. in the nose and throat

phleg·mat·ic \fleg-'ma-tik\ *adj* : having or showing a slow and stolid temperament ♦ *Synonyms* IMPASSIVE, APATHETIC, STOIC

phlo·em \'flō-,em\ *n* : a vascular plant tissue external to the xylem that carries dissolved food material and functions in support and storage

phlox \'fläks\ *n, pl* **phlox** *or* **phlox·es** : any of a genus of American herbs that have tall stalks with showy spreading terminal clusters of flowers

pho·bia \'fō-bē-ə\ *n* : an irrational persistent fear or dread — **pho·bic** \'fō-bik\ *adj*

phoe·be \'fē-(,)bē\ *n* : a flycatcher of the eastern U.S. that has a slight crest and is grayish brown above and yellowish white below

phoe·nix \'fē-niks\ *n* : a legendary bird held to live for centuries and then to burn itself to death and rise fresh and young from its ashes

¹phone \'fōn\ *n* **1** : TELEPHONE **2** : EARPHONE

²phone *vb* **phoned; phon·ing** : TELEPHONE

phone card *n* : a prepaid card used in paying for telephone calls

pho·neme \'fō-,nēm\ *n* : one of the elementary units of speech that distinguish one utterance from another — **pho·ne·mic** \fō-'nē-mik\ *adj*

pho·net·ics \fə-'ne-tiks\ *n* : the study and systematic classification of the sounds made in spoken utterance — **pho·net·ic** \-tik\ *adj* — **pho·ne·ti·cian** \,fō-nə-'ti-shən\ *n*

pho·nic \'fä-nik\ *adj* **1** : of, relating to, or producing sound **2** : of or relating to the sounds of speech or to phonics — **pho·ni·cal·ly** \-ni-k(ə-)lē\ *adv*

pho·nics \'fä-niks\ *n* : a method of teaching people to read and pronounce words by learning the phonetic value of letters, letter groups, and esp. syllables

pho·no·graph \'fō-nə-,graf\ *n* : an instrument for reproducing sounds by means of the vibration of a needle following a spiral groove on a revolving disc

pho·nol·o·gy \fə-'nä-lə-jē\ *n* : a study and description of the sound changes in a language — **pho·no·log·i·cal** \,fō-nə-'lä-ji-kəl\ *adj* — **pho·nol·o·gist** \fə-'nä-lə-jist\ *n*

pho·ny *also* **pho·ney** \'fō-nē\ *adj* **pho·ni·er; -est** : marked by empty pretension : FAKE — **phony** *n*

phos·phate \'fäs-,fāt\ *n* : a salt of a phosphoric acid — **phos·phat·ic** \fäs-'fa-tik\ *adj*

phos·phor \'fäs-fər\ *n* : a phosphorescent substance

phos·pho·res·cence \,fäs-fə-'re-s³ns\ *n* **1** : luminescence caused by the absorption of radiations (as light or electrons) and continuing after these radiations stop **2** : an enduring luminescence without sensible heat — **phos·pho·res·cent** \-s³nt\ *adj* — **phos·pho·res·cent·ly** *adv*

phosphoric acid \fäs-'fór-ik-, -'fär-\ *n* : any of several oxygen-containing acids of phosphorus

phos·pho·rus *also* **phos·pho·rous** \'fäs-fə-rəs\ *n* [NL, fr. Gk *phōsphoros* light-bearing, fr. *phōs* light + *pherein* to carry, bring] : a nonmetallic chemical element that has characteristics similar to nitrogen and occurs widely esp. as phosphates — **phos·pho·ric** \fäs-'fór-ik, -'fär-\ *adj* — **phos·pho·rous** \'fäs-fə-rəs; fäs-'fór-əs\ *adj*

phot- *or* **photo-** *comb form* **1** : light ⟨*photography*⟩ **2** : photograph : photographic ⟨*photo*engraving⟩ **3** : photoelectric ⟨*photocell*⟩

pho·to \'fō-tō\ *n, pl* **photos** : PHOTOGRAPH — **photo** *vb or adj*

pho·to·cell \'fō-tə-,sel\ *n* : PHOTOELECTRIC CELL

pho·to·chem·i·cal \ˌfō-tō-'ke-mi-kəl\ *adj* : of, relating to, or resulting from the chemical action of radiant energy

pho·to·com·pose \-kəm-'pōz\ *vb* : to compose reading matter for reproduction by means of characters photographed on film — **pho·to·com·po·si·tion** \-ˌkäm-pə-'zi-shən\ *n*

pho·to·copy \'fō-tə-ˌkä-pē\ *n* : a photographic reproduction of graphic matter — **photocopy** *vb*

pho·to·elec·tric \ˌfō-tō-i-'lek-trik\ *adj* : relating to an electrical effect due to the interaction of light with matter — **pho·to·elec·tri·cal·ly** \-tri-k(ə-)lē\ *adv*

photoelectric cell *n* : a device whose electrical properties are modified by the action of light

pho·to·en·grave \ˌfō-tō-in-'grāv\ *vb* : to make a photoengraving of

pho·to·en·grav·ing *n* : a process by which an etched printing plate is made from a photograph or drawing; *also* : a print made from such a plate

photo finish *n* : a race finish so close that a photograph of the finish is used to determine the winner

pho·tog \fə-'täg\ *n* : PHOTOGRAPHER

pho·to·ge·nic \ˌfō-tə-'je-nik\ *adj* : eminently suitable esp. aesthetically for being photographed

pho·to·graph \'fō-tə-ˌgraf\ *n* : a picture taken by photography — **photograph** *vb* — **pho·tog·ra·pher** \fə-'tä-grə-fər\ *n*

pho·tog·ra·phy \fə-'tä-grə-fē\ *n* : the art or process of producing images on a sensitive surface (as film or a CCD chip by the action of light — **pho·to·graph·ic** \ˌfō-tə-'gra-fik\ *adj* — **pho·to·graph·i·cal·ly** \-fi-k(ə-)lē\ *adv*

pho·to·gra·vure \ˌfō-tə-grə-'vyu̇r\ *n* : a process for making prints from an intaglio plate prepared by photographic methods

pho·to·li·thog·ra·phy \ˌfō-tō-li-'thä-grə-fē\ *n* : the process of photographically transferring a pattern to a surface for etching (as in making an integrated circuit)

pho·tom·e·ter \fō-'tä-mə-tər\ *n* : an instrument for measuring the intensity of light — **pho·to·met·ric** \ˌfō-tə-'me-trik\ *adj* — **pho·tom·e·try** \fō-'tä-mə-trē\ *n*

pho·to·mi·cro·graph \ˌfō-tə-'mī-krə-ˌgraf\ *n* : a photograph of a microscope image — **pho·to·mi·crog·ra·phy** \-mī-'krä-grə-fē\ *n*

pho·ton \'fō-ˌtän\ *n* : a quantum of electromagnetic radiation

photo op *n* : a situation or event that lends itself to the taking of pictures which favor the individuals photographed

pho·to·play \'fō-tō-ˌplā\ *n* : MOTION PICTURE

pho·to·sen·si·tive \ˌfō-tə-'sen-sə-tiv\ *adj* : sensitive or sensitized to the action of radiant energy

pho·to·sphere \'fō-tə-ˌsfir\ *n* : the luminous surface of a star — **pho·to·spher·ic** \ˌfō-tə-'sfir-ik, -'sfer-\ *adj*

pho·to·syn·the·sis \ˌfō-tō-'sin-thə-səs\ *n* : the process by which chlorophyll-containing plants make carbohydrates from water and from carbon dioxide in the air in the presence of light — **pho·to·syn·the·size** \-ˌsīz\ *vb* — **pho·to·syn·thet·ic** \-sin-'the-tik\ *adj*

phr *abbr* phrase

¹phrase \'frāz\ *n* 1 : a brief expression 2 : a group of two or more grammatically related words that form a sense unit expressing a thought

²phrase *vb* phrased; phras·ing : to express in words

phrase·ol·o·gy \ˌfrä-zē-'ä-lə-jē\ *n, pl* -gies : a manner of phrasing : STYLE

phras·ing *n* : style of expression

phre·net·ic *archaic var of* FRENETIC

phren·ic \'fre-nik\ *adj* : of or relating to the diaphragm ⟨∼ nerves⟩

phre·nol·o·gy \fri-'nä-lə-jē\ *n* : the study of the conformation of the skull based on the belief that it indicates mental faculties and character traits

phy·lac·tery \fə-'lak-tə-rē\ *n, pl* -ter·ies 1 : one of two small square leather boxes containing slips inscribed with scripture passages and traditionally worn on the left arm and forehead by Jewish men during morning weekday prayers 2 : AMULET

phy·lum \'fī-ləm\ *n, pl* **phy·la** \-lə\ [NL, fr. Gk *phylon* tribe, race] : a major category in biological classification esp. of animals that ranks above the class and below the kingdom; *also* : a group (as of people) apparently of common origin

phys *abbr* 1 physical 2 physics

¹phys·ic \'fi-zik\ *n* 1 : the profession of medicine 2 : MEDICINE; *esp* : PURGATIVE

²physic *vb* **phys·icked; phys·ick·ing** : PURGE 2

¹phys·i·cal \'fi-zi-kəl\ *adj* 1 : of or relating to nature or the laws of nature 2 : material as opposed to mental or spiritual 3 : of, relating to, or produced by the forces and operations of physics 4 : of or relating to the body — **phys·i·cal·ly** \-k(ə-)lē\ *adv*

²physical *n* : PHYSICAL EXAMINATION

physical education *n* : instruction in the development and care of the body ranging from simple calisthenics to training in hygiene, gymnastics, and the performance and management of athletic games

physical examination *n* : an examination of the bodily functions and condition of an individual

phys·i·cal·ize \'fi-zi-kə-ˌlīz\ *vb* **-ized; -iz·ing** : to give physical form or expression to

physical science *n* : any of the sciences (as physics and astronomy) that deal primarily with nonliving materials — **physical scientist** *n*

physical therapy *n* : the treatment of disease by physical and mechanical means (as massage, exercise, water, or heat) — **physical therapist** *n*

phy·si·cian \fə-'zi-shən\ *n* : a doctor of medicine

physician's assistant *n* : a person certified to provide basic medical care usu. under a licensed physician's supervision

phys·i·cist \'fi-zə-sist\ *n* : a scientist who specializes in physics

phys·ics \'fi-ziks\ *n* [L *physica*, pl., natural sciences, fr. Gk *physika*, fr. *physis* growth, nature, fr. *phyein* to bring forth] 1 : the science of matter and energy and their interactions 2 : the physical properties and composition of something

phys·i·og·no·my \ˌfi-zē-'äg-nə-mē\ *n, pl* -mies : facial appearance esp. as a reflection of inner character

phys·i·og·ra·phy \ˌfi-zē-'ä-grə-fē\ *n* : geography dealing with physical features of the earth — **phys·io·graph·ic** \ˌfi-zē-ō-'gra-fik\ *adj*

phys·i·ol·o·gy \ˌfi-zē-'ä-lə-jē\ *n* 1 : a branch of biology dealing with the functions and functioning of living matter and organisms 2 : functional processes in an organism or any of its parts — **phys·i·o·log·i·cal** \-zē-ə-'lä-ji-kəl\ *or* **phys·i·o·log·ic** \-jik\ *adj* — **phys·i·o·log·i·cal·ly** \-ji-k(ə-)lē\ *adv* — **phys·i·ol·o·gist** \-zē-'ä-lə-jist\ *n*

phys·io·ther·a·py \ˌfi-zē-ō-'ther-ə-pē\ *n* : PHYSICAL THERAPY — **phys·io·ther·a·pist** \-pist\ *n*

phy·sique \fə-'zēk\ *n* : the build of a person's body : bodily constitution

phy·to·chem·i·cal \ˌfī-tō-'ke-mi-kəl\ *n* : a chemical compound occurring naturally in plants

phy·to·plank·ton \'fī-tō-ˌplaŋk-tən\ *n* : plant life of the plankton

pi \'pī\ *n, pl* **pis** \'pīz\ 1 : the 16th letter of the Greek alphabet — Π or π 2 : the symbol π denoting the ratio of the circumference of a circle to its diameter; *also* : the ratio itself equal to approximately 3.1416

PI *abbr* private investigator

pi·a·nis·si·mo \pē-ə-'ni-sə-ˌmō\ *adv or adj* : very softly — used as a direction in music

pi·a·nist \pē-'a-nist, 'pē-ə-\ *n* : a person who plays the piano

¹pi·a·no \pē-'ä-nō\ *adv or adj* : SOFTLY — used as a direction in music

²piano \pē-'a-nō\ *n, pl* **pianos** [It, short for *pianoforte*, fr. *gravicembalo col piano e forte*, lit., harpsichord with soft and loud; fr. the fact that its tones could be varied in loudness] : a musical instrument having steel strings sounded by felt-covered hammers operated from a keyboard

pi·ano·forte \pē-ˌa-nō-'fȯr-ˌtā, -tē; pē-'a-nə-ˌfȯrt\ *n* : PIANO

pi·as·tre *also* **pi·as·ter** \pē-'as-tər\ *n* : see *pound* at MONEY table

pi·az·za \pē-'a-zə, *esp for 1* -'at-sə\ *n, pl* **piazzas** *or* **pi·az·ze** \-'at-(ˌ)sā, -'ät-\ [It, fr. L *platea* broad street] 1 : an open square esp. in an Italian town 2 : a long hall with an arched roof 3 *dial* : VERANDA, PORCH

pi·broch \'pē-ˌbräk\ *n* : a set of variations for the bagpipe

pic \'pik\ *n, pl* **pics** *or* **pix** \'piks\ 1 : PHOTOGRAPH 2 : MOTION PICTURE

pi·ca \'pī-kə\ *n* : a typewriter type with 10 characters to the inch

pi·ca·resque \pi-kə-'resk, pē-\ *adj* : of or relating to rogues ⟨~ fiction⟩

pic·a·yune \pi-kē-'yün\ *adj* : of little value : TRIVIAL; *also* : PETTY

pic·ca·lil·li \pi-kə-'li-lē\ *n* : a relish of chopped vegetables and spices

pic·co·lo \'pi-kə-lō\ *n, pl* **-los** [It, short for *piccolo flauto* small flute] : a small shrill flute pitched an octave higher than the ordinary flute

pice \'pīs\ *n, pl* **pice** : PAISA

¹pick \'pik\ *vb* **1** : to pierce or break up with a pointed instrument **2** : to remove bit by bit; *also* : to remove covering matter from **3** : to gather by plucking ⟨~ apples⟩ **4** : CULL, SELECT **5** : ROB ⟨~ a pocket⟩ **6** : PROVOKE ⟨~ a quarrel⟩ **7** : to dig into or pull lightly at **8** : to pluck with fingers or a pick **9** : to loosen or pull apart with a sharp point ⟨~ wool⟩ **10** : to unlock with a wire **11** : to eat sparingly — **pick·er** *n* — **pick on** : to single out for criticism, teasing, or bullying

²pick *n* **1** : the act or privilege of choosing **2** : the best or choicest one **3** : the part of a crop gathered at one time

³pick *n* **1** : a heavy wooden-handled tool pointed at one or both ends **2** : a pointed implement used for picking **3** : a small thin piece (as of plastic) used to pluck the strings of a stringed instrument

pick·a·back \'pi-gē-bak, 'pi-kə-\ *var of* PIGGYBACK

pick·ax \'pik-aks\ *n* : ³PICK 1

pick·er·el \'pi-kə-rəl\ *n, pl* **pickerel** *or* **pickerels** : either of two bony fishes related to the pikes; *also* : WALLEYE 2

pickerel

pick·er·el·weed \-wēd\ *n* : a No. American shallow-water herb that bears spikes of purplish blue flowers

¹pick·et \'pi-kət\ *n* **1** : a pointed stake (as for a fence) **2** : a detached body of soldiers on outpost duty; *also* : SENTINEL **3** : a person posted by a labor union where workers are on strike; *also* : a person posted for a protest

²picket *vb* **1** : to guard with pickets **2** : TETHER ⟨~ a horse⟩ **3** : to post pickets at ⟨~ a factory⟩ **4** : to serve as a picket

pick·ings \'pi-kiŋz, -kənz\ *n pl* **1** : gleanable or eatable fragments : SCRAPS **2** : yield for effort expended : RETURN

pick·le \'pi-kəl\ *n* **1** : a brine or vinegar solution for preserving foods; *also* : a food (as a cucumber) preserved in a pickle **2** : a difficult situation : PLIGHT — **pickle** *vb*

pick·lock \'pik-läk\ *n* **1** : BURGLAR, THIEF **2** : a tool for picking locks

pick·pock·et \'pik-pä-kət\ *n* : one who steals from pockets

¹pick·up \'pik-əp\ *n* **1** : a hitchhiker who is given a ride **2** : a temporary chance acquaintance **3** : a picking up **4** : revival of business activity **5** : ACCELERATION **6** : the conversion of mechanical movements into electrical impulses in the reproduction of sound; *also* : a device for making such conversion **7** : a light truck having an enclosed cab and an open body with low sides and a tailgate **8** : a pickup game **9** : a player acquired from another team

²pickup *adj* : using or comprising local or available personnel ⟨a ~ game⟩

pick up *vb* **1** : to take hold of and lift **2** : IMPROVE **3** : to put in order

picky \'pi-kē\ *adj* **pick·i·er; -est** : FUSSY, FINICKY ⟨a ~ eater⟩

¹pic·nic \'pik-nik\ *n* : an outing with food usu. provided by members of the group and eaten in the open

²picnic *vb* **pic·nicked; pic·nick·ing** : to go on a picnic : eat in picnic fashion

pi·cot \'pē-kō\ *n* : one of a series of small loops forming an edging on ribbon or lace

pic·to·ri·al \pik-'tór-ē-əl\ *adj* : of, relating to, or consisting of pictures

¹pic·ture \'pik-chər\ *n* **1** : a representation made by painting, drawing, or photography **2** : a vivid description in words **3** : IMAGE, COPY ⟨was the ~ of his father⟩ **4** : a transitory visual image (as on a TV screen) **5** : MOTION PICTURE **6** : SITUATION ⟨a bleak economic ~⟩

²picture *vb* **pic·tured; pic·tur·ing** **1** : to paint or draw a picture of **2** : to describe vividly in words **3** : to form a mental image of

pic·tur·esque \pik-chə-'resk\ *adj* **1** : resembling a picture ⟨a ~ landscape⟩ **2** : CHARMING, QUAINT ⟨a ~ character⟩ **3** : GRAPHIC 3, VIVID ⟨a ~ account⟩ — **pic·tur·esque·ness** *n*

picture tube *n* : a cathode-ray tube on which the picture appears in a television

pid·dle \'pi-dᵊl\ *vb* **pid·dled; pid·dling** : to act or work idly : DAWDLE

pid·dling \'pi-dᵊl-ən, -iŋ\ *adj* : TRIVIAL, PALTRY ⟨spent a ~ sum⟩

pid·dly \'pid-lē\ *adj* : TRIVIAL, PIDDLING

pid·gin \'pi-jən\ *n* [fr. *pidgin English*, fr. Chinese Pidgin English *pidgin* business] : a simplified speech used for communication between people with different languages

pie \'pī\ *n* : a dish consisting of a pastry crust and a filling (as of fruit or meat)

¹pie·bald \'pī-bòld\ *adj* : of different colors; *esp* : blotched with white and black ⟨a ~ horse⟩

²piebald *n* : a piebald animal

¹piece \'pēs\ *n* **1** : a part of a whole : FRAGMENT, PORTION **2** : one of a group, set, or mass ⟨~s of flatware⟩; *also* : a single item ⟨a ~ of news⟩ **3** : a movable object used in a board game **4** : a length, weight, or size in which something is made or sold **5** : a product (as an essay) of creative work **6** : FIREARM **7** : COIN

²piece *vb* **pieced; piec·ing** **1** : to repair or complete by adding pieces : PATCH **2** : to join into a whole

pièce de ré·sis·tance \pē-es-də-rā-zē-'stäns\ *n, pl* **pièces de ré·sis·tance** *same*\ [F] **1** : the chief dish of a meal **2** : an outstanding item

piece·meal \'pēs-mēl\ *adv or adj* : one piece at a time : GRADUALLY

piece·work \-wərk\ *n* : work done and paid for by the piece — **piece·work·er** *n*

pie chart *n* : a circular chart that shows quantities or frequencies by parts of a circle shaped like pieces of pie

pied \'pīd\ *adj* : of two or more colors in blotches : VARIEGATED

pied-à-terre \pē-ā-ə-də-'ter\ *n, pl* **pieds-à-terre** *same*\ [F, lit., foot to the ground] : a temporary or second lodging

pier \'pir\ *n* **1** : a support for a bridge span **2** : a structure built out into the water for use as a landing place or a promenade or to protect or form a harbor **3** : an upright supporting part (as a pillar) of a building or structure

pierce \'pirs\ *vb* **pierced; pierc·ing** **1** : to enter or thrust into sharply or painfully : STAB **2** : to make a hole in or through : PERFORATE ⟨*pierced* ears⟩ **3** : to force or make a way into or through : PENETRATE **4** : to see through : DISCERN — **pierc·er** *n*

piercing *n* : a piece of jewelry attached to pierced flesh

pies *pl of* PI, *or of* PIE

pi·ety \'pī-ə-tē\ *n, pl* **pi·et·ies** **1** : fidelity to natural obligations (as to parents) **2** : dutifulness in religion : DEVOUTNESS **3** : a pious act

pif·fle \'pi-fəl\ *n* : trifling talk or action

pig \'pig\ *n* **1** : SWINE; *esp* : a young domesticated swine **2** : PORK **3** : a dirty, gluttonous, or repulsive person **4** : a crude casting of metal (as iron)

pi·geon \'pi-jən\ *n* : any of numerous stout-bodied short-legged birds with smooth thick plumage

¹pi·geon·hole \'pi-jən-hōl\ *n* : a small open compartment (as in a desk) for keeping letters or documents

²pigeonhole *vb* **1** : to place in or as if in a pigeonhole : FILE **2** : to lay aside **3** : to assign to a usu. restrictive category

pi·geon-toed \-tōd\ *adj* : having the toes and forefoot turned inward

pig·gish \'pi-gish\ *adj* **1** : GREEDY **2** : STUBBORN

pig·gy·back \'pi-gē-bak\ *also* **pick·a·back** \'pi-gē-, 'pi-kə-\

adv or adj **1** : up on the back and shoulders **2** : on a railroad flatcar
pig·head·ed \'pig-'he-dəd\ *adj* : OBSTINATE, STUBBORN
pig latin *n, often cap L* : a jargon that is made by systematic alteration of English
pig·let \'pi-glət\ *n* : a small usu. young swine
pig·ment \'pig-mənt\ *n* **1** : coloring matter **2** : a powder mixed with a liquid to give color (as in paints) — **pigment·ed** \-mən-təd\ *adj*
pig·men·ta·tion \ˌpig-mən-'tā-shən\ *n* : coloration with or deposition of pigment; *esp* : an excessive deposition of bodily pigment
pigmy *var of* PYGMY
pig·nut \'pig-ˌnət\ *n* : the bitter nut of any of several hickory trees; *also* : any of these trees
pig·pen \-ˌpen\ *n* **1** : a pen for pigs **2** : a dirty place
pig·skin \-ˌskin\ *n* **1** : the skin of a swine or leather made of it **2** : FOOTBALL 2
pig·sty \-ˌstī\ *n* : PIGPEN
pig·tail \-ˌtāl\ *n* : a tight braid of hair
pi·ka \'pē-kə, 'pī-\ *n* : any of various small short-eared mammals related to the rabbits and occurring in rocky uplands of Asia and western No. America
¹pike \'pīk\ *n* : a sharp point or spike
²pike *n, pl* **pike** *or* **pikes** : a large slender long-snouted freshwater bony fish valued for food; *also* : any of various related fishes
³pike *n* : a long wooden shaft with a pointed steel head formerly used as a foot soldier's weapon
⁴pike *n* : TURNPIKE
pik·er \'pī-kər\ *n* **1** : one who does things in a small way or on a small scale **2** : TIGHTWAD, CHEAPSKATE
pike·staff \'pīk-ˌstaf\ *n* : the staff of a foot soldier's pike
pi·laf *also* **pi·laff** \pi-'läf, 'pē-ˌläf\ *or* **pi·lau** \pi-'lō, -'lȯ, 'pē-lō, -lȯ\ *n* : a dish made of seasoned rice often with meat
pi·las·ter \pi-'las-tər, 'pī-ˌlas-tər\ *n* : an architectural support that looks like a rectangular column and projects slightly from a wall
pil·chard \'pil-chərd\ *n* : a small European marine fish related to the herrings and often packed as a sardine
¹pile \'pī(-ə)l\ *n* : a long slender column (as of wood or steel) driven into the ground to support a vertical load
²pile *n* **1** : a quantity of things heaped together **2** : PYRE **3** : a great number or quantity : LOT
³pile *vb* **piled; pil·ing** **1** : to lay in a pile : STACK **2** : to heap up : ACCUMULATE **3** : to press forward in a mass : CROWD
⁴pile *n* : a velvety surface of fine short hairs or threads (as on cloth) — **piled** \'pī(-ə)ld\ *adj* — **pile·less** *adj*
piles \'pī(-ə)lz\ *n pl* : HEMORRHOIDS
pil·fer \'pil-fər\ *vb* : to steal in small quantities
pil·grim \'pil-grəm\ *n* [ME, fr. AF *pelerin, pilegrin,* fr. LL *pelegrinus,* alter. of L *peregrinus* foreigner, fr. *peregrinus* foreign, fr. *peregri* abroad, fr. *per* through + *ager* land] **1** : one who journeys in foreign lands : WAYFARER **2** : one who travels to a shrine or holy place as an act of devotion **3** *cap* : one of the English settlers founding Plymouth colony in 1620
pil·grim·age \-grə-mij\ *n* : a journey of a pilgrim esp. to a shrine or holy place
pil·ing \'pī-liŋ\ *n* : a structure of piles
pill \'pil\ *n* **1** : a small rounded mass usu. of medicine that is swallowed whole **2** : a disagreeable or tiresome person **3** *often cap* : an oral contraceptive — usu. used with *the*
pil·lage \'pi-lij\ *vb* **pil·laged; pil·lag·ing** : to take booty : LOOT, PLUNDER — **pillage** *n* — **pil·lag·er** *n*
pil·lar \'pi-lər\ *n* **1** : a strong upright support (as for a roof) **2** : a column or shaft standing alone esp. as a monument **3** : an integral or upstanding member or part **4** : a fundamental tenet ⟨the five ~s of Islam⟩ — **pil·lared** \-lərd\ *adj*
pill·box \'pil-ˌbäks\ *n* **1** : a shallow round box for pills **2** : a low concrete emplacement esp. for machine guns
pil·lion \'pil-yən\ *n* **1** : a pad or cushion placed behind a saddle for an extra rider **2** *chiefly Brit* : a motorcycle or bicycle saddle for a passenger
¹pil·lo·ry \'pi-lə-rē\ *n, pl* **-ries** : a wooden frame for public punishment having holes in which the head and hands can be locked
²pillory *vb* **-ried; -ry·ing** **1** : to set in a pillory **2** : to expose to public scorn

¹pil·low \'pi-lō\ *n* : a case filled with springy material (as feathers) and used to support the head of a resting person
²pillow *vb* **1** : to rest or place on or as if on a pillow; *also* : to serve as a pillow for
pil·low·case \-ˌkās\ *n* : a removable covering for a pillow
¹pi·lot \'pī-lət\ *n* **1** : HELMSMAN, STEERSMAN **2** : a person qualified and licensed to take ships into and out of a port **3** : GUIDE, LEADER **4** : one that flies an aircraft or spacecraft **5** : a television show filmed or taped as a sample of a proposed series — **pi·lot·less** *adj*
²pilot *vb* : CONDUCT, GUIDE; *esp* : to act as pilot of
³pilot *adj* : serving as a guiding or activating device or as a testing or trial unit ⟨a ~ light⟩ ⟨a ~ factory⟩
pi·lot·house \'pī-lət-ˌhaus\ *n* : a shelter on the upper deck of a ship for the steering gear and the helmsman
pilot whale *n* : either of two mostly black medium-sized whales
pil·sner *also* **pil·sen·er** \'pilz-nər, 'pil-zə-\ *n* [G, lit., of Pilsen (Plzeň), city in the Czech Republic] **1** : a light beer with a strong flavor of hops **2** : a tall slender footed glass for beer
pi·men·to \pə-'men-tō\ *n, pl* **pimentos** *or* **pimento** [Sp *pimienta* allspice, pepper, fr. LL *pigmenta,* pl. of *pigmentum* plant juice, fr. L, pigment] **1** : ALLSPICE **2** : PIMIENTO
pi·mien·to \pə-'men-tō\ *n, pl* **-tos** : any of various mild red sweet pepper fruits used esp. to stuff olives and to make paprika
pimp \'pimp\ *n* : a man who solicits clients for a prostitute — **pimp** *vb*
pim·per·nel \'pim-pər-ˌnel, -nəl\ *n* : any of a genus of herbs related to the primroses
pim·ple \'pim-pəl\ *n* : a small inflamed swelling on the skin often containing pus — **pim·ply** \-p(ə-)lē\ *adj*
¹pin \'pin\ *n* **1** : a piece of wood or metal used esp. for fastening things together or as a support by which one thing may be suspended from another; *esp* : a small pointed piece of wire with a head used for fastening clothes or attaching papers **2** : an ornament or emblem fastened to clothing with a pin **3** : one of the pieces constituting the target (as in bowling); *also* : the staff of the flag marking a hole on a golf course **4** : LEG
²pin *vb* **pinned; pin·ning** **1** : to fasten, join, or secure with a pin **2** : to hold fast or immobile **3** : ATTACH, HANG ⟨*pinned* their hopes on one man⟩ **4** : to assign the blame for ⟨~ a crime on someone⟩ **5** : to define clearly : ESTABLISH ⟨~ down an idea⟩
PIN *abbr* personal identification number
pi·ña co·la·da \ˌpēn-yə-kō-'lä-də, ˌpē-nə-\ *n* [Sp, lit., strained pineapple] : a tall drink made of rum, cream of coconut, and pineapple juice mixed with ice
pin·afore \'pi-nə-ˌfȯr\ *n* : a sleeveless dress or apron fastened at the back
pin·ball machine \'pin-ˌbȯl-\ *n* : an amusement device in which a ball is maneuvered along a slanted surface among a series of targets for points
pince–nez \ˌpaⁿs-'nā\ *n, pl* **pince–nez** ⟨*same or* -'nāz⟩ [F, fr. *pincer* to pinch + *nez* nose] : eyeglasses clipped to the nose by a spring
pin·cer \'pin-sər\ *n* **1** *pl* : a gripping instrument with two handles and two grasping jaws **2** : a claw (as of a lobster) resembling pincers
¹pinch \'pinch\ *vb* [ME, fr. AF *pincher, pincer,* fr. VL *pinctiare, punctiare,* fr. L *punctum* puncture] **1** : to squeeze between the finger and thumb or between the jaws of an instrument **2** : to compress painfully **3** : CONTRACT, SHRIVEL **4** : to be miserly; *also* : to subject to strict economy **5** : to confine or limit narrowly **6** : STEAL **7** : ARREST
²pinch *n* **1** : a critical point : EMERGENCY **2** : painful effect **3** : an act of pinching **4** : a very small quantity **5** : ARREST
³pinch *adj* : SUBSTITUTE ⟨a ~ runner⟩
pinch–hit \ˌpinch-'hit\ *vb* **1** : to bat in the place of another player esp. when a hit is particularly needed **2** : to act or serve in place of another — **pinch hit** *n* — **pinch hit·ter** *n*
pin curl *n* : a curl made usu. by dampening a strand of hair, coiling it, and securing it by a hairpin or clip
pin·cush·ion \'pin-ˌku̇-shən\ *n* : a cushion for pins not in use

¹pine \'pīn\ *n* : any of a genus of evergreen cone-bearing trees; *also* : the light durable resinous wood of a pine

²pine *vb* **pined; pin·ing** **1** : to lose vigor or health through distress **2** : to long for something intensely

pi·ne·al \'pī-nē-əl, pī-'nē-əl\ *n* : PINEAL GLAND — **pineal** *adj*

pineal gland *n* : a small usu. conical appendage of the brain of all vertebrates with a cranium that functions primarily as an endocrine organ

pine·ap·ple \'pīn-ˌa-pəl\ *n* : a tropical plant bearing a large edible juicy fruit; *also* : its fruit

pin·feath·er \'pin-ˌfe-thər\ *n* : a new feather just coming through the skin

ping \'piŋ\ *n* **1** : a sharp sound like that of a bullet striking **2** : engine knock

pin·hole \'pin-ˌhōl\ *n* : a small hole made by, for, or as if by a pin

¹pin·ion \'pin-yən\ *n* : the end section of a bird's wing; *also* : WING

²pinion *vb* : to restrain by binding the arms; *also* : SHACKLE

³pinion *n* : a gear with a small number of teeth designed to mesh with a larger wheel or rack

¹pink \'piŋk\ *n* **1** : any of a genus of plants with narrow leaves often grown for their showy flowers **2** : the highest degree : HEIGHT ⟨the ∼ of condition⟩

²pink *n* : a light tint of red

³pink *adj* **1** : of the color pink **2** : holding socialistic views — **pink·ish** *adj*

⁴pink *vb* **1** : to perforate in an ornamental pattern **2** : PIERCE, STAB **3** : to cut a saw-toothed edge on

pink·eye \'piŋk-ˌī\ *n* : an acute contagious eye inflammation

pin·kie *or* **pin·ky** \'piŋ-kē\ *n, pl* **pinkies** : the smallest finger of the hand

pin·nace \'pi-nəs\ *n* **1** : a light sailing ship **2** : a ship's boat

pin·na·cle \'pi-ni-kəl\ *n* [ME *pinacle*, fr. AF, fr. LL *pinnaculum* small wing, gable, fr. L *pinna* wing, battlement] **1** : a turret ending in a small spire **2** : a lofty peak **3** : ACME

pin·nate \'pi-ˌnāt\ *adj* : resembling a feather esp. in having similar parts arranged on each side of an axis ⟨a ∼ leaf⟩ — **pin·nate·ly** *adv*

pi·noch·le \'pē-ˌnə-kəl\ *n* : a card game played with a 48-card deck

pi·ñon *or* **pin·yon** \'pin-ˌyōn, -ˌyän\ *n, pl* **pi·ñons** *or* **pin·yons** *or* **pi·ño·nes** \pin-'yō-nēz\ [AmerSp *piñón*] : any of various small pines of western No. America with edible seeds; *also* : the edible seed of a piñon

pin·point \'pin-ˌpȯint\ *vb* : to locate, hit, or aim with great precision

pin·prick \-ˌprik\ *n* **1** : a small puncture made by or as if by a pin **2** : a petty irritation or annoyance

pins and needles *n pl* : a pricking tingling sensation in a limb growing numb or recovering from numbness — **on pins and needles** : in a nervous or jumpy state of anticipation

pin·stripe \'pin-ˌstrīp\ *n* : a narrow stripe on a fabric; *also* : a suit with such stripes — **pin–striped** \-ˌstrīpt\ *adj*

pint \'pīnt\ *n* — see WEIGHT table

pin·to \'pin-ˌtō\ *n, pl* **pintos** *also* **pintoes** : a spotted horse or pony

pinto bean *n* : a spotted seed produced by a kind of kidney bean and used for food

pin·up \'pin-ˌəp\ *adj* : suitable or designed for hanging on a wall; *also* : suited (as by beauty) to be the subject of a pinup photograph

pin·wheel \-ˌhwēl, -ˌwēl\ *n* **1** : a fireworks device in the form of a revolving wheel of colored fire **2** : a toy consisting of lightweight vanes that revolve at the end of a stick

pin·worm \-ˌwərm\ *n* : a nematode worm parasitic in the human intestine

pin·yin \'pin-'yin\ *n, often cap* : a system for writing Chinese ideograms by using Roman letters to represent the sounds

¹pi·o·neer \ˌpī-ə-'nir\ *n* **1** : one that originates or helps open up a new line of thought or activity **2** : an early settler in a territory

²pioneer *vb* **1** : to act as a pioneer **2** : to open or prepare for others to follow; *also* : SETTLE

pi·ous \'pī-əs\ *adj* **1** : marked by reverence for deity : DEVOUT **2** : excessively or affectedly religious **3** : SACRED, DEVOTIONAL **4** : showing loyal reverence for a person or thing : DUTIFUL **5** : marked by sham or hypocrisy — **pi·ous·ly** *adv*

¹pip \'pip\ *n* : one of the dots used on dice and dominoes to indicate numerical value

²pip *n* : a small fruit seed (as of an apple)

¹pipe \'pīp\ *n* **1** : a tubular musical instrument played by forcing air through it **2** : BAGPIPE **3** : a tube designed to conduct something (as water, steam, or oil) **4** : a device for smoking having a tube with a bowl at one end and a mouthpiece at the other **5** : a means of transmission (as of computer data)

²pipe *vb* **piped; pip·ing** **1** : to play on a pipe **2** : to speak in a high or shrill voice **3** : to convey by or as if by pipes — **pip·er** *n*

pipe down *vb* : to stop talking or making noise

pipe dream *n* : an illusory or fantastic hope

pipe·line \'pīp-ˌlīn\ *n* **1** : a line of pipe with pumps, valves, and control devices for conveying fluids **2** : a channel for information **3** : PIPE 5

pi·pette *or* **pi·pet** \pī-'pet\ *n* : a device for measuring and transferring small volumes of liquid

pipe up *vb* : to speak loudly and distinctly; *also* : to express an opinion freely

pip·ing \'pī-piŋ\ *n* **1** : the music of pipes **2** : a narrow fold of material used to decorate edges or seams

piping hot *adj* : very hot

pip·pin \'pi-pən\ *n* : a crisp tart usu. yellowish apple

pip–squeak \'pip-ˌskwēk\ *n* : one that is small or insignificant

pi·quant \'pē-kənt\ *adj* **1** : pleasantly savory : PUNGENT **2** : engagingly provocative; *also* : having a lively charm — **pi·quan·cy** \-kən-sē\ *n*

¹pique \'pēk\ *n* [F] : a passing feeling of wounded vanity : RESENTMENT

²pique *vb* **piqued; piqu·ing** **1** : IRRITATE 1 **2** : to arouse by a provocation or challenge : GOAD

pi·qué *or* **pi·que** \pi-'kā\ *n* : a durable ribbed clothing fabric

pi·quet \pi-'kā\ *n* : a 2-handed card game played with 32 cards

pi·ra·cy \'pī-rə-sē\ *n, pl* **-cies** **1** : robbery on the high seas; *also* : an act resembling such robbery **2** : the unauthorized use of another's production or invention

pi·ra·nha \pə-'rä-nə, -'rän-yə\ *n* [Pg, fr. Tupi (So. American Indian language) *pir{atildeac}a*, fr. *pir´* fish + *{atildeac}a* tooth] : any of various usu. small So. American fishes with sharp teeth that include some known to attack humans and large animals

pi·rate \'pī-rət\ *n* [ME, fr. MF or L; MF, fr. L *pirata*, fr. Gk *peiratēs*, fr. *peiran* to attempt, test] : one who commits piracy — **pirate** *vb* — **pi·rat·i·cal** \pə-'ra-ti-kəl, pī-\ *adj*

pir·ou·ette \ˌpir-ə-'wet\ *n* [F] : a rapid whirling about of the body; *esp* : a full turn on the toe or ball of one foot in ballet — **pirouette** *vb*

pis *pl of* PI

pis·ca·to·ri·al \ˌpis-kə-'tȯr-ē-əl\ *adj* : of or relating to fishing

Pi·sces \'pī-sēz\ *n* [ME, fr. L, lit., fishes] **1** : a zodiacal constellation between Aquarius and Aries usu. pictured as a fish **2** : the 12th sign of the zodiac in astrology; *also* : one born under this sign

pis·mire \'pis-ˌmī(-ə)r\ *n* : ANT

pi·so \'pē-(ˌ)sō\ *n* : the peso of the Philippines

pis·ta·chio \pə-'sta-shē-ˌō, -'stä-\ *n, pl* **-chios** : the greenish edible seed of a small Asian tree related to the sumacs; *also* : the tree

pis·til \'pist-ʲl\ *n* : the female reproductive organ in a flower — **pis·til·late** \'pis-tə-ˌlāt\ *adj*

pis·tol \'pis-tʲl\ *n* : a handgun whose chamber is integral with the barrel

pis·tol–whip \-ˌhwip\ *vb* : to beat with a pistol

pis·ton \'pis-tən\ *n* : a sliding piece that receives and transmits motion and that usu. consists of a short cylinder inside a large cylinder

¹pit \'pit\ *n* **1** : a hole, shaft, or cavity in the ground **2** : an often sunken area designed for a particular use; *also* : an enclosed place (as for cockfights) **3** : HELL; *also, pl* : WORST ⟨it's the ∼s⟩ **4** : a natural hollow or indentation in a surface **5** : a small indented mark or scar (as from disease or corrosion) **6** : an area beside a racecourse where cars are fueled and repaired during a race

²pit *vb* **pit·ted; pit·ting 1** : to form pits in or become marred with pits **2** : to match for fighting

³pit *n* : the stony seed of some fruits (as the cherry, peach, and date)

⁴pit *vb* **pit·ted; pit·ting** : to remove the pit from

pi·ta \'pē-tə\ *n* [ModGk] : a thin flat bread

pit–a–pat \ˌpi-ti-'pat\ *n* : PITTER-PATTER — **pit–a–pat** *adv or adj*

pit bull *n* : a powerful compact short-haired dog developed for fighting

¹pitch \'pich\ *n* **1** : a dark sticky substance left over esp. from distilling tar or petroleum **2** : resin from various conifers — **pitchy** *adj*

²pitch *vb* **1** : to erect and fix firmly in place ⟨∼ a tent⟩ **2** : THROW, FLING **3** : to deliver a baseball to a batter **4** : to toss (as coins) toward a mark **5** : to set at a particular level ⟨∼ the voice low⟩ **6** : to fall headlong **7** : to have the front end (as of a ship) alternately plunge and rise **8** : to incline downward : SLOPE

³pitch *n* **1** : the action or a manner of pitching **2** : degree of slope ⟨∼ of a roof⟩ **3** : the relative level of some quality or state ⟨a high ∼ of excitement⟩ **4** : highness or lowness of sound; *also* : a standard frequency for tuning instruments **5** : a presentation delivered to sell or promote something **6** : the delivery of a baseball to a batter; *also* : the baseball delivered

pitch·blende \'pich-ˌblend\ *n* : a dark mineral that is the chief source of uranium

¹pitch·er \'pi-chər\ *n* : a container for liquids that usu. has a lip and a handle

²pitcher *n* : one that pitches esp. in a baseball game

pitcher plant *n* : any of various plants with leaves modified to resemble pitchers in which insects are trapped and digested

pitch·fork \'pich-ˌfȯrk\ *n* : a long-handled fork used esp. in pitching hay

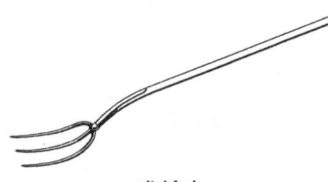

pitchfork

pitch in *vb* **1** : to begin to work **2** : to contribute to a common effort

pitch·man \'pich-mən\ *n* : SALESMAN; *esp* : one who sells merchandise on the streets or from a concession

pitch–per·fect \'pich-'pər-fikt\ *adj* : having just the right tone or style ⟨a ∼ translation⟩

pit·e·ous \'pi-tē-əs\ *adj* : arousing pity : PITIFUL — **pit·e·ous·ly** *adv*

pit·fall \'pit-ˌfȯl\ *n* **1** : TRAP, SNARE; *esp* : a covered pit used for capturing animals **2** : a hidden danger or difficulty

pith \'pith\ *n* **1** : loose spongy tissue esp. in the center of the stem of vascular plants **2** : the essential part : CORE

pithy \'pi-thē\ *adj* **pith·i·er; -est 1** : consisting of or filled with pith **2** : having substance and point : CONCISE

piti·able \'pi-tē-ə-bəl\ *adj* : PITIFUL

piti·ful \'pi-ti-fəl\ *adj* **1** : arousing or deserving pity ⟨a ∼ sight⟩ **2** : lamentably inadequate : MEAGER — **piti·ful·ly** *adv*

piti·less \'pi-ti-ləs\ *adj* : devoid of pity : HARSH, CRUEL — **pit·i·less·ly** *adv*

pi·ton \'pē-ˌtän\ *n* [F] : a spike, wedge, or peg that can be driven into a rock or ice surface as a support

pit·tance \'pi-t³ns\ *n* : a small portion, amount, or allowance

pit·ted \'pi-təd\ *adj* : marked with pits

pit·ter–pat·ter \'pi-tər-ˌpa-tər, 'pi-tē-\ *n* : a rapid succession of light taps or sounds — **pitter–patter** \ˌpi-tər-'pa-tər, ˌpi-tē-\ *adv or adj* — **pitter–patter** *same as adv*\ *vb*

pi·tu·i·tary \pə-'tü-ə-ˌter-ē, -'tyü-\ *n, pl* **-itar·ies** : PITUITARY GLAND — **pituitary** *adj*

pituitary gland *n* : a small oval endocrine gland located at the base of the brain that produces various hormones that affect most basic bodily functions (as growth and reproduction)

pit viper *n* : any of various mostly New World venomous snakes with a sensory pit on each side of the head and hollow perforated fangs

¹pity \'pi-tē\ *n, pl* **pit·ies** [ME *pite*, fr. AF *pité*, fr. L *pietas* piety, pity, fr. *pius* pious] **1** : sympathetic sorrow : COMPASSION **2** : something to be regretted

²pity *vb* **pit·ied; pity·ing** : to feel pity for

¹piv·ot \'pi-vət\ *n* : a fixed pin on which something turns — **pivot** *adj*

²pivot *vb* : to turn on or as if on a pivot

piv·ot·al \'pi-və-t³l\ *adj* **1** : of or relating to a pivot **2** : vitally important : CRITICAL

pix *pl of* PIC

pix·el \'pik-səl, -ˌsel\ *n* **1** : any of the small elements that together make up an image (as on a television screen) **2** : any of the detecting elements of a charge-coupled device used as an optical sensor

pix·ie *also* pixy \'pik-sē\ *n, pl* **pix·ies** : FAIRY; *esp* : a mischievous sprite

piz·za \'pēt-sə\ *n* [It] : an open pie made of rolled bread dough spread with a spiced mixture (as of tomatoes, cheese, and ground meat) and baked

piz·zazz *or* pi·zazz \pə-'zaz\ *n* **1** : GLAMOUR **2** : VITALITY

piz·ze·ria \ˌpēt-sə-'rē-ə\ *n* : an establishment where pizzas are made and sold

piz·zi·ca·to \ˌpit-si-'kä-tō\ *adv or adj* [It] : by means of plucking instead of bowing — used as a direction in music

pj's \'pē-ˌjāz\ *n pl* : PAJAMAS

pk *abbr* **1** park **2** peak **3** peck **4** pike

pkg *abbr* package

pkt *abbr* **1** packet **2** pocket

pkwy *abbr* parkway

pl *abbr* **1** place **2** plate **3** plural

¹plac·ard \'pla-kərd, -ˌkärd\ *n* : a notice posted in a public place : POSTER

²plac·ard \-ˌkärd, -kərd\ *vb* **1** : to cover with or as if with placards **2** : to announce by or as if by posting

pla·cate \'plā-ˌkāt, 'pla-\ *vb* **pla·cat·ed; pla·cat·ing** : to soothe esp. by concessions : APPEASE — **pla·ca·ble** \'plakə-bəl, 'plā-\ *adj*

¹place \'plās\ *n* [ME, fr. AF, open space, fr. L *platea* broad street, fr. Gk *plateia* (*hodos*), fr. fem. of *platys* broad, flat] **1** : SPACE, ROOM **2** : an indefinite region : AREA **3** : a building or locality used for a special purpose **4** : a center of population **5** : a particular part of a surface : SPOT **6** : relative position in a scale or sequence; *also* : position at the end of a competition ⟨last ∼⟩ **7** : ACCOMMODATION; *esp* : SEAT **8** : the position of a figure within a numeral ⟨12 is a two ∼ number⟩ **9** : JOB; *esp* : public office **10** : a public square **11** : 2d place at the finish (as of a horse race) — **in place of** : INSTEAD OF — **out of place** : not in the proper location : INAPPROPRIATE

²place *vb* **placed; plac·ing 1** : to put in a particular place : SET **2** : to distribute in an orderly manner : ARRANGE **3** : IDENTIFY **4** : to give an order for ⟨∼ a bet⟩ **5** : to earn a given spot in a competition; *esp* : to come in 2d

pla·ce·bo \plə-'sē-bō\ *n, pl* **-bos** [L, I shall please] : an inert medication used for its psychological effect or for purposes of comparison in an experiment

place·hold·er \'plās-ˌhōl-dər\ *n* : a symbol in a mathematical or logical expression that may be replaced by the name of any element of a set

place·kick \-ˌkik\ *n* : the kicking of a ball placed or held on the ground — **placekick** *vb* — **place·kick·er** *n*

place·ment \'plās-mənt\ *n* : an act or instance of placing

place–name \-ˌnām\ *n* : the name of a geographical locality

pla·cen·ta \plə-'sen-tə\ *n, pl* **-tas** *or* **-tae** \-(ˌ)tē\ [NL, fr. L, flat cake] : the organ in most mammals by which the fetus is joined to the maternal uterus and is nourished — **pla·cen·tal** \-'sen-t³l\ *adj or n*

plac·er \'pla-sər\ *n* : a deposit of sand or gravel containing particles of valuable mineral (as gold)

plac·id \'pla-səd\ *adj* : UNDISTURBED, PEACEFUL ♦ *Syno-*

nyms TRANQUIL, SERENE, CALM — **pla·cid·i·ty** \pla-'si-də-tē\ n — **plac·id·ly** adv

plack·et \'pla-kət\ n : a slit in a garment

pla·gia·rise *Brit var of* PLAGIARIZE

pla·gia·rize \'plā-jə-ˌrīz\ vb **-rized; -riz·ing** : to present the ideas or words of another as one's own — **pla·gia·rism** \-ˌri-zəm\ n — **pla·gia·rist** \-rist\ n

¹**plague** \'plāg\ n **1** : a disastrous evil or influx; *also* : NUISANCE **2** : PESTILENCE; *esp* : a destructive contagious bacterial disease (as bubonic plague)

²**plague** vb **plagued; plagu·ing 1** : to afflict with or as if with disease or disaster **2** : TEASE, TORMENT, HARASS

plaid \'plad\ n [ScGael *plaide*] **1** : a rectangular length of tartan worn esp. over the left shoulder as part of the Scottish national costume **2** : a twilled woolen fabric with a tartan pattern **3** : a pattern of unevenly spaced repeated stripes crossing at right angles — **plaid** adj

¹**plain** \'plān\ n : an extensive area of level or rolling treeless country

²**plain** adj **1** : lacking ornament ⟨a ~ dress⟩ **2** : free of extraneous matter **3** : OPEN, UNOBSTRUCTED ⟨~ view⟩ **4** : EVIDENT, OBVIOUS **5** : easily understood : CLEAR **6** : CANDID, BLUNT **7** : SIMPLE, UNCOMPLICATED ⟨~ cooking⟩ **8** : lacking beauty or ugliness — **plain·ly** adv — **plain·ness** n

plain-clothes·man \'plān-'klōthz-mən, -'klōz-, -ˌman\ n : a police officer who wears civilian clothes instead of a uniform while on duty : DETECTIVE

plain-spo·ken \-'spō-kən\ adj : FRANK

plaint \'plānt\ n **1** : LAMENTATION, WAIL **2** : PROTEST, COMPLAINT

plain·tiff \'plān-təf\ n : the complaining party in a lawsuit

plain·tive \'plān-tiv\ adj : expressive of suffering or woe : MELANCHOLY ⟨a ~ sigh⟩ — **plain·tive·ly** adv

plait \'plāt, 'plat\ n **1** : PLEAT **2** : a braid esp. of hair or straw — **plait** vb

¹**plan** \'plan\ n **1** : a drawing or diagram showing the parts or details of something **2** : a method for accomplishing an objective; *also* : GOAL, AIM

²**plan** vb **planned; plan·ning 1** : to form a plan of ⟨~ a new city⟩ **2** : INTEND ⟨planned to go⟩ — **plan·ner** n

¹**plane** \'plān\ vb **planed; plan·ing** : to smooth or level off with or as if with a plane — **plan·er** n

²**plane** n : PLANE TREE

³**plane** n : a tool for smoothing or shaping a wood surface

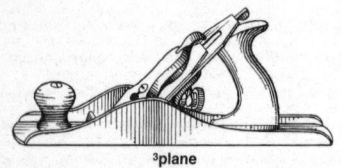

³**plane**

⁴**plane** n **1** : a level or flat surface **2** : a level of existence, consciousness, or development **3** : AIRPLANE

⁵**plane** adj **1** : FLAT, LEVEL **2** : dealing with flat surfaces or figures ⟨~ geometry⟩

plane·load \'plān-ˌlōd\ n : a load that fills an airplane

plan·et \'pla-nət\ n [ME *planete*, fr. AF, fr. LL *planeta*, fr. Gk *planēt-, planēs*, lit., wanderer, fr. *planasthai* to wander] : any of the large bodies in the solar system that revolve around the sun — **plan·e·tary** \-nə-ˌter-ē\ adj

plan·e·tar·i·um \ˌpla-nə-'ter-ē-əm\ n, pl **-i·ums** or **-ia** \-ē-ə\ : a building or room housing a device to project images of celestial bodies

plan·e·tes·i·mal \ˌpla-nə-'tes-ə-məl\ n : any of numerous small solid celestial bodies which may have existed during the formation of the solar system

plan·e·toid \'pla-nə-ˌtȯid\ n : a body resembling a planet; *esp* : ASTEROID

plane tree n : any of a genus of trees (as a sycamore) with large lobed leaves and globe-shaped fruit

plan·gent \'plan-jənt\ adj **1** : having a loud reverberating sound ⟨a ~ roar⟩ **2** : having an expressive esp. plaintive quality ⟨~ lyrics⟩ — **plan·gen·cy** \-jən-sē\ n

¹**plank** \'plaŋk\ n **1** : a heavy thick board **2** : an article in the platform of a political party

²**plank** vb **1** : to cover with planks **2** : to set or lay down forcibly **3** : to cook and serve on a board

plank·ing \'plaŋ-kiŋ\ n : a quantity or covering of planks

plank·ton \'plaŋk-tən\ n [G, fr. Gk, neut. of *planktos* drifting] : the passively floating or weakly swimming animal and plant life of a body of water — **plank·ton·ic** \plaŋk-'tä-nik\ adj

¹**plant** \'plant\ vb **1** : to set in the ground to grow **2** : ESTABLISH, SETTLE **3** : to stock or provide with something **4** : to place firmly or forcibly **5** : to hide or arrange with intent to deceive

²**plant** n **1** : any of a kingdom of living things that usu. have no locomotor ability or obvious sense organs and have cellulose cell walls and usu. capacity for indefinite growth **2** : the land, buildings, and machinery used in carrying on a trade or business

¹**plan·tain** \'plan-tⁿn\ n [ME, fr. AF, fr. L *plantagin-, plantago*, fr. *planta* sole of the foot; fr. its broad leaves] : any of a genus of weedy herbs with spikes of tiny greenish flowers

²**plantain** n [Sp *plántano, plátano* plane tree, banana tree, fr. ML *plantanus* plane tree, alter. of L *platanus*] : a banana plant with starchy greenish fruit that is eaten cooked; *also* : its fruit

plan·tar \'plan-tər, -ˌtär\ adj : of or relating to the sole of the foot

plan·ta·tion \plan-'tā-shən\ n **1** : a large group of plants and esp. trees under cultivation **2** : an agricultural estate usu. worked by resident laborers

plant·er \'plan-tər\ n **1** : one that plants or sows; *esp* : an owner or operator of a plantation **2** : a container for plants

plant louse n : APHID

plaque \'plak\ n [F] **1** : an ornamental brooch **2** : a flat thin piece (as of metal) used for decoration; *also* : a commemorative tablet **3** : a bacteria-containing film on a tooth

plash \'plash\ n : SPLASH — **plash** vb

plas·ma \'plaz-mə\ n **1** : the fluid part of blood, lymph, or milk **2** : a gas composed of ionized particles **3** : a display (as a television screen) in which cells of plasma emit

PLANETS

NAME	SYMBOL	MEAN DISTANCE FROM THE SUN		PERIOD OF REVOLUTION IN DAYS OR YEARS	EQUATORIAL DIAMETER	
		million miles	million kilometers		miles	kilometers
Mercury	☿	35.99	57.91	87.97 d.	3,033	4,879
Venus	♀	67.25	108.21	224.70 d.	7,522	12,104
Earth	♁	92.98	149.60	365.26 d.	7,928	12,756
Mars	♂	141.67	227.94	686.99 d.	4,222	6,794
Jupiter	♃	483.78	778.41	11.86 y.	88,865	142,984
Saturn	♄	886.72	1,426.73	29.47 y.	74,914	120,536
Uranus	♅	1,784.32	2,870.97	84.02 y.	31,770	51,118
Neptune	♆	2,795.68	4,498.25	164.79 y.	30,782	49,528
Pluto	♇	3,670.84	5,906.38	247.92 y.	1,485	2,390

light upon receiving an electric current — **plas·mat·ic** \plaz-'ma-tik\ *adj*

¹plas·ter \'plas-tər\ *n* **1** : a dressing consisting of a backing spread with an often medicated substance that clings to the skin ⟨adhesive ∼⟩ **2** : a paste that hardens as it dries and is used for coating walls and ceilings

²plaster *vb* : to cover with or as if with plaster — **plas·ter·er** *n*

plas·ter·board \'plas-tər-,bȯrd\ *n* : DRYWALL

plaster of par·is \-'pa-rəs\ *often cap 2d P* : a white powder made from gypsum and used as a quick-setting paste with water for casts and molds

¹plas·tic \'plas-tik\ *adj* [L *plasticus* of molding, fr. Gk *plastikos*, fr. *plassein* to mold, form] **1** : capable of being molded ⟨∼ clay⟩ **2** : characterized by or using modeling ⟨∼ arts⟩ **3** : made or consisting of a plastic ✦ *Synonyms* PLIABLE, PLIANT, DUCTILE, MALLEABLE, ADAPTABLE — **plas·tic·i·ty** \plas-'ti-sə-tē\ *n*

²plastic *n* : a plastic substance; *esp* : a synthetic or processed material that can be formed into rigid objects or into films or filaments

plastic surgery *n* : surgery to repair, restore, or improve lost, injured, defective, or misshapen body parts — **plastic surgeon** *n*

¹plat \'plat\ *n* **1** : a small plot of ground **2** : a plan of a piece of land with actual or proposed features (as lots)

²plat *vb* **plat·ted; plat·ting** : to make a plat of

¹plate \'plāt\ *n* **1** : a flat thin piece of material **2** : domestic hollowware made of or plated with gold, silver, or base metals **3** : DISH **4** : HOME PLATE **5** : the molded metal or plastic cast of a page of type to be printed from **6** : a sheet of glass or plastic coated with a chemical sensitive to light and used in photography **7** : the part of a denture that fits to the mouth; *also* : DENTURE **8** : something printed from an engraving **9** : a huge mobile segment of the earth's crust

²plate *vb* **plat·ed; plat·ing** **1** : to overlay with metal (as gold or silver) **2** : to make a printing plate of

pla·teau \pla-'tō\ *n, pl* **plateaus** *or* **pla·teaux** \-'tōz\ [F] : a large level area of high land

plate glass *n* : rolled, ground, and polished sheet glass

plate·let \'plāt-lət\ *n* : a minute flattened body; *esp.* : a minute colorless disklike body of mammalian blood that assists in blood clotting

plat·en \'pla-t⁹n\ *n* **1** : a flat plate; *esp* : one that exerts or receives pressure (as in a printing press) **2** : the roller of a typewriter or printer

plate tectonics *n* **1** : a theory in geology that the lithosphere is divided into plates at the boundaries of which much of earth's seismic activity occurs **2** : the process and dynamics of tectonic plate movement — **plate–tectonic** *adj*

plat·form \'plat-,fȯrm\ *n* **1** : a raised flooring or stage for speakers, performers, or workers **2** : a declaration of the principles on which a group of persons (as a political party) stands **3** : OPERATING SYSTEM

plat·ing \'plā-tiŋ\ *n* : a coating of metal plates or plate ⟨the ∼ of a ship⟩

plat·i·num \'pla-tə-nəm\ *n* : a heavy grayish white metallic chemical element

plat·i·tude \'pla-tə-,tüd, -,tyüd\ *n* : a flat or trite remark — **plat·i·tu·di·nous** \-'tü-də-nəs, -'tyü-\ *adj*

pla·ton·ic love \plə-'tä-nik-, plā-\ *n, often cap P* : a close relationship between two persons without sexual desire

pla·toon \plə-'tün\ *n* [F *peloton* small detachment, lit., |ball, fr. *pelote* little ball] **1** : a subdivision of a company² size military unit consisting of two or more squads or sections **2** : a group of football players trained either for offense or for defense and sent into the game as a body

platoon sergeant *n* : a noncommissioned officer in the army ranking below a first sergeant

plat·ter \'pla-tər\ *n* **1** : a large serving plate **2** : a phonograph record

platy \'pla-tē\ *n, pl* **platy** *or* **platys** *or* **plat·ies** : either of two small stocky usu. brilliantly colored bony-fishes often kept in tropical aquariums

platy·pus \'pla-ti-pəs\ *n, pl* **platy·pus·es** *also* **platy·pi** \-,pī\ [NL, fr. Gk *platypous* flat-footed, fr. *platys* broad, flat + *pous* foot] : a small aquatic egg-laying marsupial mammal of Australia with webbed feet and a fleshy bill like a duck's

plau·dit \'plȯ-dət\ *n* : an act of applause

plau·si·ble \'plȯ-zə-bəl\ *adj* [L *plausibilis* worthy of applause, fr. *plausus*, pp. of *plaudere* to applaud] : seemingly worthy of belief — **plau·si·bil·i·ty** \,plȯ-zə-'bi-lə-tē\ *n* — **plau·si·bly** \'plȯ-zə-blē\ *adv*

¹play \'plā\ *n* **1** : brisk handling of something (as a weapon) **2** : the course of a game; *also* : a particular act or maneuver in a game **3** : recreational activity; *esp* : the spontaneous activity of children **4** : JEST ⟨said in ∼⟩ **5** : the act or an instance of punning **6** : GAMBLING **7** : OPERATION ⟨bring extra force into ∼⟩ **8** : a brisk or light movement **9** : free motion (as of part of a machine) **10** : scope for action **11** : PUBLICITY **12** : an effort to arouse liking ⟨made a ∼ for her⟩ **13** : a stage representation of a drama; *also* : a dramatic composition **14** : a function of an electronic device that causes a recording to play — **play·ful** \-fəl\ *adj* — **play·ful·ly** *adv* — **play·ful·ness** *n* — **in play** : in condition or position to be played

²play *vb* **1** : to engage in recreation : FROLIC **2** : to handle or behave lightly or absentmindedly **3** : to make a pun ⟨∼ on words⟩ **4** : to take advantage ⟨∼ on fears⟩ **5** : to move or operate in a brisk or irregular manner ⟨a flashlight ∼ed over the wall⟩ **6** : to perform music ⟨∼ on a violin⟩; *also* : to perform (music) on an instrument ⟨∼ a waltz⟩ **7** : to perform music upon ⟨∼ the piano⟩; *also* : to sound in performance ⟨the organ is ∼ing⟩ **8** : to cause to emit sounds ⟨∼ a radio⟩; *also* : to cause to reproduce recorded material ⟨∼ a DVD⟩ **9** : to act in a dramatic medium; *also* : to act in the character of ⟨∼ the hero⟩ **10** : GAMBLE **11** : to produce a specified impression in performance ⟨∼s like a comedy⟩ **12** : to behave in a specified way ⟨∼ safe⟩; *also* : COOPERATE ⟨∼ along with him⟩ **13** : to deal with; *also* : EMPHASIZE ⟨∼ up her good qualities⟩ **14** : to perform for amusement ⟨∼ a trick⟩ **15** : WREAK **16** : to use as an esp. political strategy **17** : to contend with in a game; *also* : to fill (a certain position) on a team **18** : to make wagers on ⟨∼ the races⟩ **19** : WIELD, PLY **20** : to keep in action — **play·er** *n*

play·act·ing \'plā-,ak-tiŋ\ *n* **1** : performance in theatrical productions **2** : insincere or artificial behavior

play·back \-,bak\ *n* : an act of reproducing recorded sound or pictures — **play back** *vb*

play·bill \-,bil\ *n* : a poster advertising the performance of a play

play·book \-,bùk\ *n* **1** : a notebook containing diagrammed football plays **2** : a stock of usual tactics or methods

play·boy \-,bȯi\ *n* : a man whose chief interest is the pursuit of pleasure

play·date \-,dāt\ *n* : a usu. prearranged play session for small children

play·go·er \-,gō-ər\ *n* : a person who frequently attends plays

play·ground \-,graùnd\ *n* : an area used for games and play esp. by children

play·house \-,haùs\ *n* **1** : THEATER **2** : a small house for children to play in

playing card *n* : any of a set of 24 to 78 cards marked to show its rank and suit and used to play a game of cards

play·let \'plā-lət\ *n* : a short play

play·mate \-,māt\ *n* : a companion in play

play–off \-,ȯf\ *n* : a contest or series of contests to break a tie or determine a championship

play out *vb* : DEVELOP, UNFOLD ⟨see how things *play out*⟩

play·pen \-,pen\ *n* : a portable enclosure in which a young child may play

play·suit \-,süt\ *n* : a sports and play outfit for women and children

play·thing \-,thiŋ\ *n* : TOY

play·wright \-,rīt\ *n* : a writer of plays

pla·za \'pla-zə, 'plä-\ *n* [Sp, fr. L *platea* broad street] **1** : a public square in a city or town **2** : a shopping center

PLC *abbr, Brit* public limited company

plea \'plē\ *n* **1** : a defendant's answer in law to a charge or indictment **2** : something alleged as an excuse **3** : ENTREATY, APPEAL

plead \'plēd\ *vb* **plead·ed** *or* **pled** \'pled\; **plead·ing** **1** : to argue before a court or authority ⟨∼ a case⟩ **2** : to answer to a charge or indictment ⟨∼ guilty⟩ **3** : to argue for or against something ⟨~ for acquittal⟩ **4** : to appeal earnestly ⟨~s for help⟩ **5** : to offer as a plea (as in defense) ⟨~ed illness⟩ — **plead·er** *n*

pleas·ant \'ple-zᵊnt\ *adj* **1** : giving pleasure : AGREEABLE ⟨a ~ experience⟩ **2** : marked by pleasing behavior or appearance ⟨a ~ person⟩ — **pleas·ant·ly** *adv* — **pleas·ant·ness** *n*

pleas·ant·ry \-zᵊn-trē\ *n, pl* **-ries** : a pleasant and casual act or speech

¹**please** \'plēz\ *vb* **pleased; pleas·ing 1** : to give pleasure or satisfaction to **2** : LIKE ⟨do as you ~⟩ **3** : to be the will or pleasure of ⟨may it ~ his Majesty⟩

²**please** *adv* — used as a function word to express politeness or emphasis in a request ⟨~ come in⟩

pleasing *adj* : giving pleasure — **pleas·ing·ly** *adv*

plea·sur·able \'ple-zhə-rə-bəl\ *adj* : PLEASANT, GRATIFYING — **plea·sur·ably** \-blē\ *adv*

plea·sure \'ple-zhər\ *n* **1** : DESIRE, INCLINATION ⟨await your ~⟩ **2** : a state of gratification : ENJOYMENT **3** : a source of delight or joy

¹**pleat** \'plēt\ *vb* **1** : FOLD; *esp* : to arrange in pleats **2** : BRAID

²**pleat** *n* : a fold (as in cloth) made by doubling material over on itself

plebe \'plēb\ *n* : a freshman at a military or naval academy

¹**ple·be·ian** \pli-'bē-ən\ *n* **1** : a member of the Roman plebs **2** : one of the common people

²**plebeian** *adj* **1** : of or relating to plebeians **2** : COMMON, VULGAR

pleb·i·scite \'ple-bə-ˌsīt, -sət\ *n* : a vote of the people (as of a country) on a proposal submitted to them

plebs \'plebz\ *n, pl* **ple·bes** \'plē-bēz\ **1** : the general populace **2** : the common people of ancient Rome

plec·trum \'plek-trəm\ *n, pl* **plec·tra** \-trə\ *or* **plec·trums** [L] : ³PICK 3

¹**pledge** \'plej\ *n* [ME *plegge* security, fr. AF *plege*, fr. LL *plebium*, fr. *plebere* to pledge, prob. of Gmc origin] **1** : something given as security for the performance of an act **2** : the state of being held as a security or guaranty **3** : TOAST 3 **4** : PROMISE, VOW

²**pledge** *vb* **pledged; pledg·ing 1** : to deposit as a pledge **2** : TOAST **3** : to bind by a pledge : PLIGHT **4** : PROMISE

Pleis·to·cene \'plī-stə-ˌsēn\ *adj* : of, relating to, or being the earlier epoch of the Quaternary — **Pleistocene** *n*

ple·na·ry \'plē-nə-rē, 'ple-\ *adj* **1** : FULL ⟨~ power⟩ **2** : including all entitled to attend ⟨~ session⟩

pleni·po·ten·tia·ry \ˌple-nə-pə-'ten-chə-rē, -'ten-chē-ˌer-ē\ *n, pl* **-ries** : a diplomatic agent having full authority — **plenipotentiary** *adj*

plen·i·tude \'ple-nə-ˌtüd, -ˌtyüd\ *n* **1** : COMPLETENESS **2** : ABUNDANCE

plen·te·ous \'plen-tē-əs\ *adj* **1** : FRUITFUL **2** : existing in plenty

plen·ti·ful \'plen-ti-fəl\ *adj* **1** : containing or yielding plenty **2** : ABUNDANT — **plen·ti·ful·ly** *adv*

plen·ty \'plen-tē\ *n* : a more than adequate number or amount

ple·num \'ple-nəm, 'plē-\ *n, pl* **-nums** *or* **-na** \-nə\ : a general assembly of all members esp. of a legislative body

pleth·o·ra \'ple-thə-rə\ *n* : an excessive quantity or fullness; *also* : PROFUSION

pleu·ri·sy \'plur-ə-sē\ *n* : inflammation of the membrane that lines the chest and covers the lungs

plex·us \'plek-səs\ *n, pl* **plex·us·es** \-sə-səz\ : an interlacing network esp. of blood vessels or nerves

pli·able \'plī-ə-bəl\ *adj* **1** : FLEXIBLE **2** : yielding easily to others ♦ *Synonyms* PLASTIC, PLIANT, DUCTILE, MALLEABLE, ADAPTABLE — **pli·abil·i·ty** \ˌplī-ə-'bi-lə-tē\ *n*

pli·ant \'plī-ənt\ *adj* **1** : FLEXIBLE **2** : easily influenced : PLIABLE — **pli·an·cy** \-ən-sē\ *n*

pli·ers \'plī-ərz\ *n pl* : small pincers for bending or cutting wire or handling small objects

¹**plight** \'plīt\ *vb* : to put or give in pledge : ENGAGE

²**plight** *n* : an unfortunate, difficult, or precarious situation

plinth \'plinth\ *n* : the lowest part of the base of an architectural column

Plio·cene \'plī-ə-ˌsēn\ *adj* : of, relating to, or being the latest epoch of the Tertiary — **Pliocene** *n*

PLO *abbr* Palestine Liberation Organization

plod \'pläd\ *vb* **plod·ded; plod·ding 1** : to walk heavily

or slowly : TRUDGE **2** : to work laboriously and monotonously : DRUDGE — **plod·der** *n* — **plod·ding·ly** *adv*

plonk *var of* PLUNK

plop \'pläp\ *vb* **plopped; plop·ping 1** : to fall or move with a sound like that of something dropping into water **2** : to set, drop, or throw heavily or hastily ⟨*plopped* down on the couch⟩ ⟨~ down $20⟩ — **plop** *n*

¹**plot** \'plät\ *n* **1** : a small area of ground **2** : a ground plan (as of an area) **3** : the main story (as of a book or movie) **4** : a secret scheme : INTRIGUE

²**plot** *vb* **plot·ted; plot·ting 1** : to make a plot or plan of **2** : to mark on or as if on a chart **3** : to plan or contrive esp. secretly — **plot·ter** *n*

plo·ver \'plə-vər, 'plō-\ *n, pl* **plover** *or* **plovers** [ME, fr. AF, fr. VL *pluviarius*, fr. L *pluvia* rain] : any of a family of shorebirds that differ from the sandpipers in having shorter stouter bills

¹**plow** *or* **plough** \'plau̇\ *n* **1** : an implement used to cut, lift, turn over, and partly break up soil **2** : a device (as a snowplow) operating like a plow

²**plow** *or* **plough** *vb* **1** : to open, break up, or work with a plow **2** : to move through like a plow ⟨a ship ~*ing* the waves⟩ **3** : to proceed laboriously — **plow·able** *adj* — **plow·er** *n*

plow·boy \'plau̇-ˌbȯi\ *n* : a boy who leads the horse drawing a plow

plow·man \-mən, -ˌman\ *n* **1** : a man who guides a plow **2** : a farm laborer

plow·share \-ˌsher\ *n* : a part of a plow that cuts the earth

ploy \'plȯi\ *n* : a tactic intended to embarrass or frustrate an opponent

¹**pluck** \'plək\ *vb* **1** : to pull off or out : PICK; *also* : to pull something from **2** : to play (an instrument) by pulling the strings **3** : TUG, TWITCH

²**pluck** *n* **1** : an act or instance of plucking **2** : SPIRIT, COURAGE

plucky \'plə-kē\ *adj* **pluck·i·er; -est** : COURAGEOUS, SPIRITED

¹**plug** \'pləg\ *n* **1** : STOPPER; *also* : an obstructing mass **2** : a cake of tobacco **3** : a poor or worn-out horse **4** : SPARK PLUG **5** : a lure with several hooks used in fishing **6** : a device on the end of a cord for making an electrical connection **7** : a piece of favorable publicity

²**plug** *vb* **plugged; plug·ging 1** : to stop, make tight, or secure by inserting a plug **2** : HIT, SHOOT **3** : to publicize insistently **4** : PLOD, DRUDGE

plug and play *n* : a computer feature enabling the operating system to automatically detect and configure peripherals — **plug-and-play** *adj*

plugged–in \'pləgd-'in\ *adj* : technologically or socially informed and connected

plug–in \'pləg-ˌin\ *n* : a small piece of software that supplements a larger program

plum \'pləm\ *n* [ME, fr. OE *plūme*, modif. of L *prunum* plum, fr. Gk *proumnon*] **1** : a smooth-skinned juicy fruit borne by trees related to the peach and cherry; *also* : a tree bearing plums **2** : a raisin when used in desserts (as puddings) **3** : something excellent; *esp* : something desirable given in return for a favor

plum·age \'plü-mij\ *n* : the feathers of a bird — **plum·aged** \-mijd\ *adj*

¹**plumb** \'pləm\ *n* : a weight on the end of a line (**plumb line**) used esp. by builders to show vertical direction

²**plumb** *adv* **1** : VERTICALLY **2** : COMPLETELY **3** : EXACTLY; *also* : IMMEDIATELY

³**plumb** *vb* : to sound, adjust, or test with a plumb ⟨~ the depth of a well⟩

⁴**plumb** *adj* **1** : VERTICAL **2** : COMPLETE

plumb·er \'plə-mər\ *n* : a worker who fits or repairs pipes and fixtures

plumb·ing \'plə-miŋ\ *n* : a system of pipes in a building for supplying and carrying off water

¹**plume** \'plüm\ *n* : FEATHER; *esp* : a large, conspicuous, or showy feather — **plumed** \'plümd\ *adj* — **plumy** \'plü-mē\ *adj*

²**plume** *vb* **plumed; plum·ing 1** : to provide or deck with feathers **2** : to indulge (oneself) in pride

¹**plum·met** \'plə-mət\ *n* : PLUMB; *also* : PLUMB LINE

²**plummet** *vb* : to drop or plunge straight down

¹**plump** \'pləmp\ *vb* **1** : to drop or fall suddenly or heavily **2** : to favor something strongly ⟨~*ing* for change⟩

²**plump** *n* : a sudden heavy fall or blow; *also* : the sound made by it
³**plump** *adv* **1** : straight down; *also* : straight ahead **2** : UNQUALIFIEDLY ⟨came out ~ for free trade⟩
⁴**plump** *adj* : having a full rounded usu. pleasing form
✦ *Synonyms* FLESHY, STOUT, ROLY-POLY, ROTUND — **plump·ness** *n*
¹**plun·der** \'plən-dər\ *vb* : to take the goods of by force or wrongfully : PILLAGE — **plun·der·er** *n*
²**plunder** *n* : something taken by force or theft : LOOT
¹**plunge** \'plənj\ *vb* **plunged; plung·ing 1** : IMMERSE, SUBMERGE **2** : to enter or cause to enter a state or course of action suddenly or violently ⟨~ into war⟩ **3** : to cast oneself into or as if into water **4** : to gamble heavily and recklessly **5** : to descend suddenly
²**plunge** *n* : a sudden dive, leap, or rush
plung·er \'plən-jər\ *n* **1** : one that plunges **2** : a sliding piece driven by or against fluid pressure : PISTON **3** : a rubber cup on a handle pushed against an opening to free a waste outlet of an obstruction
plunk \'pləŋk\ *or* **plonk** \'pläŋk, 'plóŋk\ *vb* **1** : to make or cause to make a hollow metallic sound **2** : to drop heavily or suddenly — **plunk** *n*
plu·per·fect \(ˌ)plü-'pər-fikt\ *adj* [ME *pluperfyth*, modif. of LL *plusquamperfectus*, lit., more than perfect] : of, relating to, or constituting a verb tense that denotes an action or state as completed at or before a past time spoken of — **pluperfect** *n*
plu·ral \'plúr-əl\ *adj* [ME, fr. AF & L; AF *plurel*, fr. L *pluralis*, fr. *plur-, plus* more] : of, relating to, or constituting a word form used to denote more than one — **plural** *n*
plu·ral·i·ty \plù-'ra-lə-tē\ *n, pl* **-ties 1** : the state of being plural **2** : an excess of votes over those cast for an opposing candidate **3** : the greatest number of votes cast when not a majority
plu·ral·ize \'plúr-ə-ˌlīz\ *vb* **-ized; -iz·ing** : to make plural or express in the plural form — **plu·ral·i·za·tion** \ˌplùr-ə-lə-'zā-shən\ *n*
¹**plus** \'pləs\ *adj* [L, more] **1** : mathematically positive **2** : having or being in addition to what is anticipated **3** : falling high in a specified range ⟨a grade of B ~⟩
²**plus** *n, pl* **plus·es** \'plə-səz\ *also* **plus·ses 1** : a sign + (**plus sign**) used in mathematics to indicate addition or a positive quantity **2** : an added quantity; *also* : a positive quality **3** : SURPLUS
³**plus** *prep* **1** : increased by : with the addition of ⟨3 ~ 4⟩ **2** : BESIDES
⁴**plus** *conj* : AND ⟨soup ~ salad and bread⟩
¹**plush** \'pləsh\ *n* : a fabric with a pile longer and less dense than velvet pile — **plushy** *adj*
²**plush** *adj* : notably luxurious — **plush·ly** *adv* — **plush·ness** *n*
plus/minus sign *n* : the sign ± used to indicate a quantity taking on both a positive value and its negative or to indicate a plus or minus quantity
plus or minus *adj* : indicating a quantity whose positive and negative values bracket a range of values ⟨*plus or minus* 3 inches⟩
Plu·to \'plü-tō\ *n* : the planet farthest from the sun — see PLANET table
plu·toc·ra·cy \plü-'tä-krə-sē\ *n, pl* **-cies 1** : government by the wealthy **2** : a controlling class of the wealthy — **plu·to·crat** \'plü-tə-ˌkrat\ *n* — **plu·to·crat·ic** \ˌplü-tə-'kra-tik\ *adj*
plu·to·ni·um \plü-'tō-nē-əm\ *n* : a radioactive chemical element formed by the decay of neptunium
plu·vi·al \'plü-vē-əl\ *adj* **1** : of or relating to rain **2** : characterized by abundant rain
¹**ply** \'plī\ *vb* **plied; ply·ing 1** : to use, practice, or work diligently ⟨~ a trade⟩ **2** : to keep supplying something to ⟨*plied* them with liquor⟩ **3** : to go or travel regularly esp. by sea
²**ply** *n, pl* **plies** : one of the folds, thicknesses, or strands of which something (as plywood or yarn) is made
³**ply** *vb* **plied; ply·ing** : to twist together ⟨~ yarns⟩
ply·wood \'plī-ˌwùd\ *n* : material made of thin sheets of wood glued and pressed together
pm *abbr* premium
Pm *symbol* promethium
PM *abbr* **1** paymaster **2** police magistrate **3** postmaster **4** post meridiem — often not cap. and often punctu-

ated **5** postmortem **6** prime minister **7** provost marshal
pmk *abbr* postmark
PMS \ˌpē-ˌem-'es\ *n* : PREMENSTRUAL SYNDROME
pmt *abbr* payment
pneu·mat·ic \nù-'ma-tik, nyù-\ *adj* **1** : of, relating to, or using air or wind **2** : moved by air pressure **3** : filled with compressed air — **pneu·mat·i·cal·ly** \-ti-k(ə-)lē\ *adv*
pneu·mo·coc·cus \ˌnü-mə-'kä-kəs, ˌnyü-\ *n, pl* **-coc·ci** \-'käk-ˌsī, -ˌsē; -'käk-ˌkī, -ˌkē\ : a bacterium that causes pneumonia — **pneu·mo·coc·cal** \-'kä-kəl\ *adj*
pneu·mo·co·ni·o·sis \ˌnü-mō-ˌkō-nē-'ō-səs, ˌnyü-\ *n* : a disease of the lungs caused by habitual inhalation of irritant mineral or metallic particles
pneu·mo·nia \nù-'mō-nyə, nyù-\ *n* : an inflammatory disease of the lungs
Po *symbol* polonium
PO *abbr* **1** petty officer **2** post office
¹**poach** \'pōch\ *vb* [ME *pocchen*, fr. MF *pocher*, fr. OF *poché* poached, lit., bagged, fr. *poche* bag, pouch, of Gmc origin] : to cook (as an egg or fish) in simmering liquid
²**poach** *vb* : to hunt or fish unlawfully — **poach·er** *n*
POB *abbr* post office box
po·bla·no \pō-'blä-nō\ *n, pl* **-nos** : a heart-shaped usu. mild chili pepper esp. when fresh and dark green
po'·boy \'pō-ˌbói\ *also* **poor boy** *n* : SUBMARINE **2**
pock \'päk\ *n* : a small swelling on the skin (as in smallpox); *also* : a spot suggesting this
¹**pock·et** \'pä-kət\ *n* **1** : a small bag open at the top or side inserted in a garment **2** : supply of money : MEANS **3** : RECEPTACLE, CONTAINER **4** : a small isolated area or group **5** : a small body of ore — **pock·et·ful** *n*
²**pocket** *vb* **1** : to put in or as if in a pocket **2** : STEAL ⟨~ed the profits⟩
³**pocket** *adj* **1** : small enough to fit in a pocket; *also* : SMALL, MINIATURE ⟨a ~ park⟩ **2** : carried in or paid from one's own pocket
¹**pock·et·book** \-ˌbùk\ *n* **1** : PURSE; *also* : HANDBAG **2** : financial resources
²**pocketbook** *adj* : relating to money
pocket gopher *n* : GOPHER **2**
pock·et·knife \'pä-kət-ˌnīf\ *n* : a knife with a folding blade to be carried in the pocket
pocket veto *n* : an indirect veto of a legislative bill by an executive through retention of the bill unsigned until after adjournment of the legislature
pock·mark \'päk-ˌmärk\ *n* : a pit or scar caused by smallpox or acne — **pock·marked** \-ˌmärkt\ *adj*
po·co \'pō-kō, 'pò-\ *adv* [It, little, fr. L *paucus*] : SOMEWHAT — used to qualify a direction in music ⟨~ allegro⟩
po·co a po·co \ˌpō-kō-ä-'pō-kō, ˌpò-kō-ä-'pò-\ *adv* : little by little : GRADUALLY — used as a direction in music
pod \'päd\ *n* **1** : a dry fruit (as of a pea) that splits open when ripe **2** : an external streamlined compartment (as for a jet engine) on an airplane **3** : a compartment (as for personnel, a power unit, or an instrument) on a ship or craft
POD *abbr* pay on delivery
po·di·a·try \pə-'dī-ə-trē, pō-\ *n* : the medical care and treatment of the human foot — **po·di·at·ric** \ˌpō-dē-'a-trik\ *adj* — **po·di·a·trist** \pə-'dī-ə-trist, pō-\ *n*
po·di·um \'pō-dē-əm\ *n, pl* **podiums** *or* **po·dia** \-dē-ə\ **1** : a dais esp. for an orchestral conductor **2** : LECTERN
POE *abbr* port of entry
po·em \'pō-əm\ *n* : a composition in verse
po·esy \'pō-ə-zē\ *n* : POETRY
po·et \'pō-ət\ *n* [ME, fr. AF *poete*, fr. L *poeta*, fr. Gk *poiētēs* maker, poet, fr. *poiein* to make] : a writer of poetry; *also* : a creative artist of great sensitivity
po·et·as·ter \'pō-ə-ˌtas-tər\ *n* : an inferior poet
po·et·ess \'pō-ə-təs\ *n* : a girl or woman who is a poet
poetic justice *n* : an outcome in which vice is punished and virtue rewarded usu. in a manner peculiarly or ironically appropriate
po·et·ry \'pō-ə-trē\ *n* **1** : metrical writing **2** : POEMS — **po·et·ic** \pō-'e-tik\ *or* **po·et·i·cal** \-ti-kəl\ *adj*
po·grom \'pō-grəm, pō-'gräm\ *n* [Yiddish, fr. Russ, lit., devastation] : an organized massacre of helpless people and esp. of Jews
poi \'pói\ *n, pl* **poi** *or* **pois** : a Hawaiian food of taro root

cooked, pounded, and kneaded to a paste and often allowed to ferment

poi·gnant \'pȯi-nyənt\ *adj* **1** : painfully affecting the feelings ⟨~ grief⟩ **2** : deeply moving ⟨~ scene⟩ — **poignan·cy** \-nyən-sē\ *n*

poin·ci·ana \ˌpȯin-sē-'a-nə\ *n* : any of several ornamental tropical leguminous trees or shrubs with bright orange or red flowers

poin·set·tia \pȯin-'se-tē-ə\ *n* : a showy tropical American spurge with usu. scarlet bracts that suggest petals and surround small yellow flowers

¹**point** \'pȯint\ *n* **1** : an individual detail; *also* : the most important essential **2** : PURPOSE ⟨no ~ in continuing⟩ **3** : a geometric element that has position but no size **4** : a particular place : LOCALITY **5** : a particular stage or degree **6** : a sharp end : TIP **7** : a projecting piece of land **8** : a punctuation mark; *esp* : PERIOD **9** : DECIMAL POINT **10** : one of the divisions of the compass **11** : a unit of counting (as in a game score) — **point·less** *adj* — **pointy** \'pȯin-tē\ *adj* — **beside the point** : IRRELEVANT — **to the point** : RELEVANT, PERTINENT ⟨her remark was *to the point*⟩

²**point** *vb* **1** : to furnish with a point : SHARPEN **2** : PUNCTUATE **3** : to separate (a decimal fraction) from an integer by a decimal point — usu. used with *off* **4** : to indicate the position of esp. by extending a finger **5** : to direct attention to ⟨~ out an error⟩ **6** : AIM, DIRECT **7** : to lie extended, aimed, or turned in a particular direction : FACE, LOOK

point–and–click *adj* : relating to or being a computer interface that allows the activation of a file by selection with a pointing device (as a mouse)

point–and–shoot *adj* : having or using preset or automatically adjusted controls ⟨a ~ camera⟩

point–blank \'pȯint-'blaŋk\ *adj* **1** : so close to the target that a missile fired will travel in a straight line to the mark **2** : DIRECT, BLUNT ⟨a ~ refusal⟩ — **point–blank** *adv*

point·ed \'pȯin-təd\ *adj* **1** : having a point **2** : being to the point : DIRECT **3** : aimed at a particular person or group; *also* : CONSPICUOUS, MARKED ⟨~ indifference⟩ — **point·ed·ly** *adv*

point·er \'pȯin-tər\ *n* **1** : one that points out : INDICATOR **2** : a large short-haired hunting dog **3** : HINT, TIP ⟨gave me some ~s on how to play⟩

poin·til·lism \'pwan-tē-ˌyi-zəm, 'pȯin-tə-ˌli-zəm\ *n* [F *pointillisme*, fr. *pointiller* to stipple, fr. *point* spot, point] : the theory or practice in painting of applying small strokes or dots of color to a surface so that from a distance they blend together — **poin·til·list** \ˌpwan-tē-'yēst, 'pȯin-tə-list\ *n or adj*

point man *n* : a principal spokesman or advocate

point of no return *n* : a critical point at which turning back or reversal is not possible

point of view *n* : a position from which something is considered or evaluated

point spread *n* : the number of points by which a favorite is expected to defeat an underdog

¹**poise** \'pȯiz\ *vb* **poised; pois·ing** : BALANCE

²**poise** *n* **1** : BALANCE **2** : self-possessed calmness; *also* : a particular way of carrying oneself

poi·sha \'pȯi-shə\ *n, pl* **poisha** : the paisa of Bangladesh

¹**poi·son** \'pȯi-zᵊn\ *n* [ME, fr. AF *poisun* drink, potion, poison, fr. L *potion-, potio* drink] : a substance that through its chemical action can injure or kill — **poi·son·ous** \-zᵊn-əs\ *adj*

²**poison** *vb* **1** : to injure or kill with poison **2** : to treat or taint with poison **3** : to affect destructively : CORRUPT ⟨~ed her mind⟩ — **poi·son·er** *n*

poison hemlock *n* : a large branching poisonous herb with finely divided leaves and white flowers that is related to the carrot

poison ivy *n* **1** : a usu. climbing plant related to the sumacs that has leaves composed of three shiny leaflets and produces an irritating oil causing a usu. intensely itching skin rash; *also* : any of several related plants **2** : a skin rash caused by poison ivy

poison oak *n* : any of several shrubby plants closely related to poison ivy and having similar properties

poison sumac *n* : a No. American swamp shrub with pin-

nate leaves, greenish flowers, greenish white berries, and irritating properties

¹**poke** \'pōk\ *n, chiefly Southern & Midland* : BAG, SACK

²**poke** *vb* **poked; pok·ing 1** : PROD; *also* : to stir up by prodding **2** : to make a prodding or jabbing movement esp. repeatedly **3** : HIT, PUNCH **4** : to thrust forward obtrusively **5** : RUMMAGE ⟨*poking* around the attic⟩ **6** : MEDDLE, PRY **7** : DAWDLE — **poke fun at** : RIDICULE, MOCK

³**poke** *n* : a quick thrust; *also* : PUNCH

¹**pok·er** \'pō-kər\ *n* : a metal rod for stirring a fire

²**pok·er** \'pō-kər\ *n* : any of several card games in which the player with the highest hand at the end of the betting wins

poke·weed \'pōk-ˌwēd\ *n* : a coarse American perennial herb with clusters of white flowers and dark purple juicy berries

poky *or* **pok·ey** \'pō-kē\ *adj* **pok·i·er; -est 1** : small and cramped **2** : SHABBY, DULL **3** : annoyingly slow

pol \'päl\ *n* : POLITICIAN

po·lar \'pō-lər\ *adj* **1** : of or relating to a geographical pole **2** : of or relating to a pole (as of a magnet)

polar bear *n* : a large creamy-white bear that inhabits arctic regions

Po·lar·is \pə-'ler-əs\ *n* : NORTH STAR

po·lar·ise *Brit var of* POLARIZE

po·lar·i·ty \pō-'ler-ə-tē\ *n, pl* **-ties** : the condition of having poles and esp. magnetic or electrical poles

po·lar·i·za·tion \ˌpō-lə-rə-'zā-shən\ *n* **1** : the action of polarizing : the state of being polarized **2** : concentration about opposing extremes

po·lar·ize \'pō-lə-ˌrīz\ *vb* **-ized; -iz·ing 1** : to cause (light waves) to vibrate in a definite way **2** : to give physical polarity to **3** : to break up into opposing groups

pol·der \'pōl-dər, 'päl-\ *n* [D] : a tract of low land reclaimed from the sea

¹**pole** \'pōl\ *n* : a long slender piece of wood or metal ⟨telephone ~⟩

²**pole** *vb* **poled; pol·ing** : to impel or push with a pole

³**pole** *n* **1** : either end of an axis esp. of the earth **2** : either of the terminals of an electric device (as a battery or generator) **3** : one of two or more regions in a magnetized body at which the magnetism is concentrated — **pole·ward** \'pōl-wərd\ *adj or adv*

¹**pole·ax** \'pōl-ˌaks\ *n* : a battle-ax with a short handle

²**poleax** *vb* : to attack or fell with or as if with a poleax

pole·cat \'pōl-ˌkat\ *n, pl* **polecats** *or* **polecat 1** : a European carnivorous mammal of which the ferret is considered a domesticated variety **2** : SKUNK

polecat 1

po·lem·ic \pə-'le-mik\ *n* : the art or practice of disputation — usu. used in pl. — **po·lem·i·cal** \-mi-kəl\ *also* **po·lem·ic** \-mik\ *adj* — **po·lem·i·cist** \-sist\ *n*

pole·star \'pōl-ˌstär\ *n* **1** : NORTH STAR **2** : a directing principle : GUIDE

pole vault *n* : a field contest in which each contestant uses a pole to vault for height over a crossbar — **pole–vault** *vb* — **pole–vault·er** *n*

¹**po·lice** \pə-'lēs\ *vb* **po·liced; po·lic·ing 1** : to control, regulate, or keep in order esp. by use of police ⟨~ a highway⟩ **2** : to make clean and put in order

²**police** *n, pl* **police** [F, government, fr. OF, fr. LL *politia*, fr. Gk *politeia*, fr. *politēs* citizen, fr. *polis* city, state] **1** : the department of government that keeps public order and safety and enforces the laws; *also* : the members of this department **2** : a private organization resembling a police force; *also* : its members **3** : military personnel detailed to clean and put in order

po·lice·man \-mən\ *n* : POLICE OFFICER

police officer *n* : a member of a police force

police state *n* : a state characterized by repressive, arbitrary, totalitarian rule by means of secret police

po·lice·wom·an \pə-'lēs-ˌwu̇-mən\ *n* : a woman who is a police officer

¹**pol·i·cy** \'pä-lə-sē\ *n, pl* **-cies** : a definite course or method of action selected to guide and determine present and future decisions

²**policy** *n, pl* **-cies** : a writing whereby a contract of insurance is made

pol·i·cy·hold·er \'pä-lə-sē-ˌhōl-dər\ *n* : one granted an insurance policy

po·lio \'pō-lē-ˌō\ *n* : POLIOMYELITIS — **polio** *adj*

po·lio·my·eli·tis \-ˌmī-ə-'lī-təs\ *n* : an acute virus disease marked by inflammation of the gray matter of the spinal cord leading usu. to paralysis

¹**pol·ish** \'pä-lish\ *vb* **1** : to make smooth and glossy usu. by rubbing **2** : to refine or improve in manners, condition, or style

²**polish** *n* **1** : a smooth glossy surface : LUSTER **2** : REFINEMENT, CULTURE **3** : the action or process of polishing **4** : a preparation used to produce a gloss

Pol·ish \'pō-lish\ *n* : the Slavic language of the Poles — **Polish** *adj*

polit *abbr* political; politician

po·lit·bu·ro \'pä-lət-ˌbyu̇r-ō, 'pō-, pə-'lit-\ *n* [Russ *politbyuro*] : the principal policy-making committee of a Communist party

po·lite \pə-'līt\ *adj* **po·lit·er; -est 1** : REFINED, CULTIVATED ⟨~ society⟩ **2** : marked by correct social conduct : COURTEOUS; *also* : CONSIDERATE, TACTFUL — **po·lite·ly** *adv* — **po·lite·ness** *n*

po·li·tesse \ˌpä-li-'tes\ *n* [F] : formal politeness

pol·i·tic \'pä-lə-ˌtik\ *adj* **1** : wise in promoting a policy ⟨a ~ statesman⟩ **2** : shrewdly tactful ⟨a ~ move⟩

po·lit·i·cal \pə-'li-ti-kəl\ *adj* **1** : of or relating to government or politics **2** : involving or charged or concerned with acts against a government or a political system ⟨~ prisoners⟩ — **po·lit·i·cal·ly** \-k(ə-)lē\ *adv*

politically correct *adj* : conforming to a belief that language and practices which could offend sensibilities (as in matters of sex or race) should be eliminated — **political correctness** *n*

pol·i·ti·cian \ˌpä-lə-'ti-shən\ *n* : a person actively engaged in government or politics

pol·i·tick \'pä-lə-ˌtik\ *vb* : to engage in political discussion or activity

pol·i·ti·co \pə-'li-ti-ˌkō\ *n, pl* **-cos** *also* **-coes** : POLITICIAN

pol·i·tics \'pä-lə-ˌtiks\ *n sing or pl* **1** : the art or science of government, of guiding or influencing governmental policy, or of winning and holding control over a government **2** : political affairs or business; *esp* : competition between groups or individuals for power and leadership **3** : political opinions

pol·i·ty \'pä-lə-tē\ *n, pl* **-ties** : a politically organized unit; *also* : the form or constitution of such a unit

pol·ka \'pōl-kə, 'pō-kə\ *n* [Czech, fr. *Polka* Polish woman, fem. of *Polák* Pole] : a lively couple dance of Bohemian origin; *also* : music for this dance — **polka** *vb*

pol·ka dot \'pō-kə-ˌdät\ *n* : a dot in a pattern of regularly distributed dots — **polka–dot** *or* **polka–dot·ted** \-ˌdä-təd\ *adj*

¹**poll** \'pōl\ *n* **1** : HEAD **2** : the casting and recording of votes; *also* : the total vote cast **3** : the place where votes are cast — usu. used in pl. **4** : a questioning of persons to obtain information or opinions to be analyzed

²**poll** *vb* **1** : to cut off or shorten a growth or part of : CLIP, SHEAR **2** : to receive and record the votes of **3** : to receive (as votes) in an election **4** : to question in a poll

pol·lack *or* **pol·lock** \'pä-lək\ *n, pl* **pollack** *or* **pollock** : an important No. Atlantic food fish that is related to the cods; *also* : a related food fish of the No. Pacific

pol·len \'pä-lən\ *n* [NL, fr. L, fine flour] : a mass of male spores of a seed plant usu. appearing as a yellow dust

pol·li·na·tion \ˌpä-lə-'nā-shən\ *n* : the carrying of pollen to the female part of a plant to fertilize the seed — **pol·li·nate** \'pä-lə-ˌnāt\ *vb* — **pol·li·na·tor** \-ˌnā-tər\ *n*

poll·ster \'pōl-stər\ *n* : one that conducts a poll or compiles data obtained by a poll

poll tax *n* : a tax of a fixed amount per person levied on adults and often linked to the right to vote

pol·lute \pə-'lüt\ *vb* **pol·lut·ed; pol·lut·ing** : to make impure; *esp* : to contaminate (an environment) esp. with man-made waste — **pol·lut·ant** \-'lü-tⁿt\ *n* — **pol·lut·er** *n* — **pol·lu·tion** \-'lü-shən\ *n*

pol·ly·wog *or* **pol·li·wog** \'pä-lē-ˌwäg\ *n* : TADPOLE

po·lo \'pō-lō\ *n* [Balti (Tibetan language of northern Kashmir), ball] : a game played by two teams on horseback using long-handled mallets to drive a wooden ball

po·lo·ni·um \pə-'lō-nē-əm\ *n* : a radioactive metallic chemical element

pol·ter·geist \'pōl-tər-ˌgīst\ *n* [G, fr. *poltern* to knock + *Geist* spirit] : a noisy usu. mischievous ghost held to be responsible for unexplained noises

pol·troon \päl-'trün\ *n* : COWARD

poly- *comb form* [Gk, fr. *polys* many] **1** : many : several ⟨*poly*syllabic⟩ **2** : polymeric ⟨*poly*ester⟩

poly·chlo·ri·nat·ed bi·phe·nyl \ˌpä-li-'klōr-ə-ˌnā-təd-ˌbī-'fen-³l, -'fēn-\ *n* : any of several industrial compounds that are toxic environmental pollutants

poly·clin·ic \ˌpä-li-'kli-nik\ *n* : a clinic or hospital treating diseases of many sorts

poly·es·ter \'pä-lē-ˌes-tər\ *n* : a polymer composed of ester groups used esp. in making fibers or plastics; *also* : a product (as fabric) composed of polyester

poly·eth·yl·ene \ˌpä-lē-'e-thə-ˌlēn\ *n* : a lightweight plastic resistant to chemicals and moisture and used chiefly in packaging

po·lyg·a·my \pə-'li-gə-mē\ *n* : the practice of having more than one wife or husband at one time — **po·lyg·a·mist** \-mist\ *n* — **po·lyg·a·mous** \-məs\ *adj*

poly·glot \'pä-li-ˌglät\ *adj* **1** : speaking or writing several languages **2** : containing or made up of several languages — **polyglot** *n*

poly·gon \'pä-li-ˌgän\ *n* : a closed plane figure bounded by straight lines — **po·lyg·o·nal** \pə-'li-gə-n³l\ *adj*

poly·graph \'pä-li-ˌgraf\ *n* : an instrument (as a lie detector) for recording variations of several bodily functions (as blood pressure) simultaneously — **po·lyg·ra·pher** \pə-'li-grə-fər, 'pä-li-ˌgra-fər\ *n*

poly·he·dron \ˌpä-li-'hē-drən\ *n* : a solid formed by plane faces that are polygons — **poly·he·dral** \-drəl\ *adj*

poly·math \'pä-li-ˌmath\ *n* : a person of encyclopedic learning

poly·mer \'pä-lə-mər\ *n* : a chemical compound formed by union of small molecules and usu. consisting of repeating structural units — **poly·mer·ic** \ˌpä-lə-'mer-ik\ *adj*

po·lym·er·i·za·tion \pə-ˌli-mə-rə-'zā-shən\ *n* : a chemical reaction in which two or more small molecules combine to form polymers — **po·lym·er·ize** \pə-'li-mə-ˌrīz\ *vb*

Poly·ne·sian \ˌpä-lə-'nē-zhən\ *n* **1** : a member of any of the indigenous peoples of Polynesia **2** : a group of Austronesian languages spoken in Polynesia — **Polynesian** *adj*

poly·no·mi·al \ˌpä-lə-'nō-mē-əl\ *n* : an algebraic expression having one or more terms each of which consists of a constant multiplied by one or more variables raised to a nonnegative integral power — **polynomial** *adj*

pol·yp \'pä-ləp\ *n* **1** : an invertebrate animal (as a coral) that is a coelenterate having a hollow cylindrical body closed at one end **2** : a growth projecting from a mucous membrane (as of the colon or vocal cords)

po·lyph·o·ny \pə-'li-fə-nē\ *n* : music consisting of two or more melodically independent but harmonizing voice parts — **poly·phon·ic** \ˌpä-li-'fä-nik\ *adj*

poly·pro·pyl·ene \ˌpä-lē-'prō-pə-ˌlēn\ *n* : any of various polymer plastics or fibers

poly·sty·rene \ˌpä-li-'stī-ˌrēn\ *n* : a rigid transparent nonconducting thermoplastic used esp. in molded products and foams

poly·syl·lab·ic \-sə-'la-bik\ *adj* **1** : having more than three syllables **2** : characterized by polysyllabic words

poly·syl·la·ble \'pä-li-ˌsi-lə-bəl\ *n* : a polysyllabic word

poly·tech·nic \ˌpä-li-'tek-nik\ *adj* : of, relating to, or instructing in many technical arts or applied sciences

poly·the·ism \'pä-li-thē-ˌi-zəm\ *n* : belief in or worship of many gods — **poly·the·ist** \-ˌthē-ist\ *adj or n* — **poly·the·is·tic** \ˌpä-li-thē-'is-tik\ *adj*

poly·un·sat·u·rat·ed \ˌpä-lē-ˌən-'sa-chə-ˌrā-təd\ *adj* : having many double or triple bonds in a molecule — used esp. of an oil or fatty acid

poly·ure·thane \ˌpä-lē-ˈyúr-ə-ˌthān\ *n* : any of various polymers used esp. in foams and in resins (as for coatings)

poly·vi·nyl \ˌpä-li-ˈvī-nᵊl\ *adj* : of, relating to, or being a polymerized vinyl compound, resin, or plastic — often used in combination

pome·gran·ate \ˈpä-mə-ˌgra-nət\ *n* [ME *poumgrenet,* fr. AF *pome garnette,* lit., seedy fruit] : a many-seeded reddish fruit that has an edible crimson pulp and is borne by a tropical Asian tree; *also* : the tree

¹pom·mel \ˈpə-məl, ˈpä-\ *n* **1** : the knob on the hilt of a sword **2** : the knoblike bulge at the front and top of a saddlebow

²pom·mel \ˈpə-məl\ *vb* **-meled** *or* **-melled; -mel·ing** *or* **-mel·ling** : PUMMEL

pomp \ˈpämp\ *n* **1** : brilliant display : SPLENDOR **2** : OSTENTATION

pom·pa·dour \ˈpäm-pə-ˌdòr\ *n* : a style of dressing the hair high over the forehead

pom·pa·no \ˈpäm-pə-ˌnō, ˈpəm-\ *n, pl* **-no** *or* **-nos** : a narrow silvery fish of coastal waters of the western Atlantic

pom-pom \ˈpäm-ˌpäm\ *n* **1** : an ornamental ball or tuft used on a cap or costume **2** : a fluffy ball flourished by cheerleaders

pom·pon \ˈpäm-ˌpän\ *n* **1** : POM-POM **2** : a chrysanthemum or dahlia with small rounded flower heads

pomp·ous \ˈpäm-pəs\ *adj* **1** : suggestive of pomp; *esp* : OSTENTATIOUS **2** : pretentiously dignified **3** : excessively elevated or ornate ✦ *Synonyms* ARROGANT, MAGISTERIAL, SELF-IMPORTANT — **pom·pos·i·ty** \päm-ˈpä-sə-tē\ *n* — **pomp·ous·ly** *adv*

pon·cho \ˈpän-chō\ *n, pl* **ponchos** [AmerSp, fr. Mapuche (American Indian language of Chile)] **1** : a blanket with a slit in the middle for the head so that it can be worn as a garment **2** : a waterproof garment resembling a poncho

pond \ˈpänd\ *n* : a small body of water

pon·der \ˈpän-dər\ *vb* **pon·dered; pon·der·ing** **1** : to weigh in the mind **2** : to consider carefully

pon·der·o·sa pine \ˈpän-də-ˌrō-sə-, -zə-\ *n* : a tall pine of western No. America with long needles; *also* : its strong reddish wood

pon·der·ous \ˈpän-də-rəs\ *adj* **1** : of very great weight **2** : UNWIELDY, CLUMSY ⟨a ~ weapon⟩ **3** : oppressively dull ⟨a ~ speech⟩ ✦ *Synonyms* CUMBROUS, CUMBERSOME, WEIGHTY

pone \ˈpōn\ *n, Southern & Midland* : an oval-shaped cornmeal cake; *also* : corn bread in the form of pones

pon·iard \ˈpän-yərd\ *n* : DAGGER

pon·tiff \ˈpän-təf\ *n* : POPE — **pon·tif·i·cal** \pän-ˈti-fi-kəl\ *adj*

¹pon·tif·i·cate \pän-ˈti-fi-kət, -fə-ˌkāt\ *n* : the state, office, or term of office of a pontiff

²pon·tif·i·cate \pän-ˈti-fə-ˌkāt\ *vb* **-cat·ed; -cat·ing** : to deliver dogmatic opinions

pon·toon \pän-ˈtün\ *n* **1** : a flat-bottomed boat **2** : a boat or float used in building a floating temporary bridge **3** : a float of a seaplane

po·ny \ˈpō-nē\ *n, pl* **ponies** : a small horse

po·ny·tail \-ˌtāl\ *n* : a style of arranging hair to resemble the tail of a pony

pooch \ˈpüch\ *n* : DOG

poo·dle \ˈpü-dᵊl\ *n* [G *Pudel,* short for *Pudelhund,* fr. *pudeln* to splash + *Hund* dog] : any of a breed of active intelligent dogs with a dense curly solid-colored coat

pooh–pooh \ˈpü-ˈpü\ *also* **pooh** \ˈpü\ *vb* **1** : to express contempt or impatience **2** : DERIDE, SCORN ⟨~ed my idea⟩

¹pool \ˈpül\ *n* **1** : a small deep body of usu. fresh water **2** : a small body of standing liquid **3** : SWIMMING POOL

²pool *vb* : to form a pool

³pool *n* **1** : all the money bet on the result of a particular event **2** : any of several games of billiards played on a table having six pockets **3** : the amount contributed by the participants in a joint venture **4** : a combination between competing firms for mutual profit **5** : a readily available supply

⁴pool *vb* : to combine (as resources) in a common fund or effort

¹poop \ˈpüp\ *n* : an enclosed superstructure at the stern of a ship

²poop *n, slang* : INFORMATION

poop deck *n* : a partial deck above a ship's main afterdeck

poor \ˈpúr\ *adj* **1** : lacking material possessions ⟨~ people⟩ **2** : less than adequate : MEAGER ⟨a ~ crop⟩ **3** : arousing pity ⟨you ~ thing⟩ **4** : inferior in quality or value **5** : UNPRODUCTIVE, BARREN ⟨~ soil⟩ **6** : fairly unsatisfactory ⟨~ prospects⟩; *also* : UNFAVORABLE ⟨~ opinion⟩ — **poor·ly** *adv*

poor boy *var of* PO'BOY

poor·house \ˈpúr-ˌhaùs\ *n* : a publicly supported home for needy or dependent persons

poor–mouth \-ˌmaúth, -ˌmaúth\ *vb* : to plead poverty as a defense or excuse

¹pop \ˈpäp\ *vb* **popped; pop·ping** **1** : to go, come, enter, or issue forth suddenly or quickly ⟨~ into bed⟩ **2** : to put or thrust suddenly ⟨~ questions⟩ **3** : to burst or cause to burst with a sharp sound; *also* : to make a sharp sound **4** : to protrude from the sockets **5** : SHOOT **6** : to hit a pop-up

²pop *n* **1** : a sharp explosive sound **2** : SHOT **3** : SODA POP

³pop *n* : FATHER

⁴pop *adj* **1** : POPULAR ⟨~ music⟩ **2** : of or relating to pop music ⟨~ singer⟩ **3** : of or relating to the popular culture disseminated through the mass media ⟨~ psychology⟩ **4** : of, relating to, or imitating pop art ⟨~ painter⟩

⁵pop *n* : pop music or culture; *also* : POP ART

⁶pop *abbr* population

pop art *n, often cap P&A* : art in which commonplace objects (as comic strips or soup cans) are used as subject matter — **pop artist** *n*

¹pop·corn \ˈpäp-ˌkórn\ *n* : an Indian corn whose kernels burst open into a white starchy mass when heated; *also* : the burst kernels

²popcorn *adj* : having widespread appeal but little artistic merit

pope \ˈpōp\ *n, often cap* : the head of the Roman Catholic Church

pop–eyed \ˈpäp-ˌīd\ *adj* : having eyes that bulge (as from disease)

pop fly *n* : POP-UP

pop·gun \ˈpäp-ˌgən\ *n* : a toy gun for shooting pellets with compressed air

pop·in·jay \ˈpä-pən-ˌjā\ *n* [ME *papejay* parrot, fr. MF *papegai, papejai,* fr. Ar *babghā'*] : a strutting supercilious person

pop·lar \ˈpä-plər\ *n* **1** : any of a genus of slender quick-growing trees (as a cottonwood) related to the willows **2** : the wood of a poplar

pop·lin \ˈpä-plən\ *n* : a strong plain-woven fabric with crosswise ribs

pop·over \ˈpäp-ˌō-vər\ *n* : a hollow muffin made from a thin batter rich in egg

pop·per \ˈpä-pər\ *n* : a utensil for popping corn

pop·py \ˈpä-pē\ *n, pl* **poppies** : any of a genus of herbs with showy flowers including one that yields opium

pop·py·cock \-ˌkäk\ *n* : empty talk or writing : NONSENSE

pop·u·lace \ˈpä-pyə-ləs\ *n* **1** : the common people **2** : POPULATION

pop·u·lar \ˈpä-pyə-lər\ *adj* **1** : of or relating to the general public ⟨~ government⟩ **2** : suited to the tastes of the general public ⟨~ style⟩ **3** : INEXPENSIVE ⟨~ rates⟩ **4** : frequently encountered or widely accepted ⟨~ notion⟩ **5** : commonly liked or approved ⟨a ~ teacher⟩ — **pop·u·lar·i·ty** \ˌpä-pyə-ˈla-rə-tē\ *n* — **pop·u·lar·ize** \ˈpä-pyə-lə-ˌrīz\ *vb* — **pop·u·lar·ly** *adv*

pop·u·late \ˈpä-pyə-ˌlāt\ *vb* **-lat·ed; -lat·ing** **1** : to have a place in : INHABIT **2** : PEOPLE

pop·u·la·tion \ˌpä-pyə-ˈlā-shən\ *n* **1** : the people or number of people in an area **2** : the organisms inhabiting a particular locality **3** : a group of individuals or items from which samples are taken for statistical measurement

population explosion *n* : a pyramiding of numbers of a biological population; *esp* : the recent great increase in human numbers resulting from increased survival and exponential population growth

pop·u·list \ˈpä-pyə-list\ *n* : a believer in or advocate of the rights, wisdom, or virtues of the common people — **pop·u·lism** \-ˌli-zəm\ *n*

pop·u·lous \ˈpä-pyə-ləs\ *adj* **1** : densely populated; *also* : having a large population **2** : CROWDED — **pop·u·lous·ness** *n*

¹**pop–up** \'päp-,əp\ n : a short high fly in baseball

²**pop–up** adj : of, relating to, or having a component or device that pops up

por·ce·lain \'pòr-sə-lən\ n : a fine-grained translucent ceramic ware

porch \'pòrch\ n : a covered entrance usu. with a separate roof

por·cine \'pòr-,sīn\ adj : of, relating to, or suggesting swine

por·ci·ni \pòr-'chē-nē\ n, pl **porcini** [It] : a large edible brownish mushroom

por·ci·no \pòr-'chē-nō\ n, pl **-ni** : PORCINI

por·cu·pine \'pòr-kyə-,pīn\ n [ME porke despyne, fr. MF porc espin, fr. It porcospino, fr. L porcus pig + spina spine, prickle] : any of various mammals having stiff sharp spines mingled with their hair

¹**pore** \'pòr\ vb **pored; por·ing** 1 : to read studiously or attentively ⟨~ over a book⟩ 2 : PONDER, REFLECT

²**pore** n : a tiny hole or space (as in the skin or soil) — **pored** \'pòrd\ adj

pork \'pòrk\ n : the flesh of swine dressed for use as food

pork barrel n : government projects or appropriations yielding rich patronage benefits

pork·er \'pòr-kər\ n : HOG; esp : a young pig suitable for use as fresh pork

por·nog·ra·phy \pòr-'nä-grə-fē\ n : the depiction of erotic behavior intended to cause sexual excitement — **por·no·graph·ic** \,pòr-nə-'gra-fik\ adj

po·rous \'pòr-əs\ adj 1 : full of pores 2 : permeable to fluids : ABSORPTIVE — **po·ros·i·ty** \pə-'rä-sə-tē\ n

por·phy·ry \'pòr-fə-rē\ n, pl **-ries** : a rock consisting of feldspar crystals embedded in a compact fine-grained base material — **por·phy·rit·ic** \,pòr-fə-'ri-tik\ adj

por·poise \'pòr-pəs\ n [ME porpoys, fr. AF porpeis, fr. ML porcopiscis, fr. L porcus pig + piscis fish] : any of a family of small gregarious blunt-snouted whales with spadelike teeth; also : DOLPHIN 1

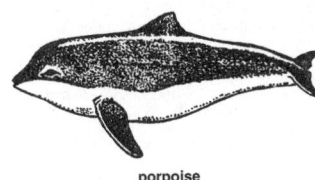

porpoise

por·ridge \'pòr-ij\ n : a soft food made by boiling meal of grains or legumes in milk or water

por·rin·ger \'pòr-ən-jər\ n : a low one-handled metal bowl or cup

¹**port** \'pòrt\ n 1 : HARBOR 2 : a city with a harbor 3 : AIRPORT

²**port** n 1 : an inlet or outlet (as in an engine) for a fluid 2 : PORTHOLE 3 : JACK 7

³**port** vb : to turn or put a helm to the left

⁴**port** n : the left side of a ship or airplane looking forward — **port** adj

⁵**port** n : a sweet fortified wine

portabella or **portabello** var of PORTOBELLO

por·ta·bil·i·ty \,pòr-tə-'bil-ə-tē\ n, pl **-ties** 1 : the quality or state of being portable 2 : the ability to transfer benefits from one pension fund to another when a worker changes jobs

por·ta·ble \'pòr-tə-bəl\ adj : capable of being carried — **portable** n

¹**por·tage** \'pòr-tij, pòr-'täzh\ n [ME, fr. AF, fr. porter to carry] : the carrying of boats and goods overland between navigable bodies of water; also : a route for such carrying

²**portage** vb **por·taged; por·tag·ing** : to carry gear over a portage

por·tal \'pòr-t³l\ n : DOOR, ENTRANCE; esp : a grand or imposing one

portal–to–portal adj : of or relating to the time spent by a worker in traveling from the entrance to an employer's property to the worker's actual job site (as in a mine)

port·cul·lis \pòrt-'kə-ləs\ n : a grating at the gateway of a castle or fortress that can be let down to stop entrance

porte co·chere \,pòrt-kō-'sher\ n [F porte cochère, lit., coach door] : a roofed structure extending from the entrance of a building over an adjacent driveway and sheltering those getting in or out of vehicles

por·tend \pòr-'tend\ vb 1 : to give a sign or warning of beforehand 2 : INDICATE, SIGNIFY ♦ **Synonyms** AUGUR, PROGNOSTICATE, FORETELL, PREDICT, FORECAST, PROPHESY

por·tent \'pòr-,tent\ n 1 : something that foreshadows a coming event : OMEN 2 : MARVEL, PRODIGY

por·ten·tous \pòr-'ten-təs\ adj 1 : of, relating to, or constituting a portent 2 : PRODIGIOUS 3 : self-consciously solemn : POMPOUS

¹**por·ter** \'pòr-tər\ n, chiefly Brit : DOORKEEPER

²**porter** n 1 : a person who carries burdens; esp : one employed (as at a terminal) to carry baggage 2 : an attendant in a railroad car 3 : a dark heavy ale

por·ter·house \'pòr-tər-,haus\ n : a choice beefsteak with a large tenderloin

port·fo·lio \pòrt-'fō-lē-,ō\ n, pl **-li·os** 1 : a portable case for papers or drawings 2 : the office and functions of a minister of state 3 : the securities held by an investor

port·hole \'pòrt-,hōl\ n : an opening (as a window) in the side of a ship or aircraft

por·ti·co \'pòr-ti-,kō\ n, pl **-coes** or **-cos** [It] : a row of columns supporting a roof around or at the entrance of a building

¹**por·tion** \'pòr-shən\ n 1 : one's part or share ⟨a ~ of food⟩ 2 : DOWRY 3 : an individual's lot 4 : a part of a whole ⟨a ~ of the sky⟩

²**portion** vb 1 : to divide into portions 2 : to allot to as a portion

portland cement \'pòrt-lənd-\ n : a cement made by calcining and grinding a mixture of clay and limestone

port·ly \'pòrt-lē\ adj **port·li·er; -est** : somewhat stout

port·man·teau \pòrt-'man-,tō\ n, pl **-teaus** or **-teaux** \-,tōz\ [MF portemanteau, fr. porter to carry + manteau mantle, fr. L mantellum] : a large traveling bag

por·to·bel·lo \,pòr-tə-'be-lō\ also **por·ta·bel·la** \-lə\ or **por·ta·bel·lo** \-lō\ n, pl **-los** also **-las** : a large dark mature mushroom noted for its meaty texture

port of call : an intermediate port where ships customarily stop for supplies, repairs, or transshipment of cargo

port of entry 1 : a place where foreign goods may be cleared through a customhouse 2 : a place where an alien may enter a country

por·trait \'pòr-trət, -,trāt\ n : a picture (as a painting or photograph) of a person usu. showing the face — **por·trait·ist** \-trə-tist\ n

por·trai·ture \'pòr-trə-,chùr\ n : the practice or art of making portraits

por·tray \pòr-'trā\ vb 1 : to make a picture of : DEPICT 2 : to describe in words 3 : to play the role of — **por·tray·al** n

Por·tu·guese \'pòr-chə-,gēz, -,gēs; ,pòr-chə-'gēz, -'gēs\ n, pl **Portuguese** 1 : a native or inhabitant of Portugal 2 : the language of Portugal and Brazil — **Portuguese** adj

Portuguese man–of–war n : any of several large colonial marine invertebrate animals related to the jellyfishes and having a large sac by which the colony floats at the surface

por·tu·laca \,pòr-chə-'la-kə\ n : any of a genus of succulent herbs cultivated for their showy flowers

pos abbr 1 position 2 positive

¹**pose** \'pōz\ vb **posed; pos·ing** 1 : to assume or cause to assume a posture usu. for artistic purposes 2 : to set forth : PROPOSE ⟨~ a question⟩ 3 : to affect an attitude or character

²**pose** n 1 : a sustained posture; esp : one assumed by a model 2 : an attitude assumed for effect : PRETENSE

¹**pos·er** \'pō-zər\ n : a puzzling question

²**poser** n : a person who poses

po·seur \pō-'zər\ n [F, lit., poser] : an affected or insincere person

posh \'päsh\ adj : FASHIONABLE ⟨a ~ restaurant⟩

pos·it \'pä-zət\ vb : to assume the existence of : POSTULATE

po·si·tion \pə-'zi-shən\ n 1 : an arranging in order 2 : the stand taken on a question 3 : the point or area occupied by something : SITUATION 4 : a certain arrangement of bodily parts ⟨exercise in a sitting ~⟩ 5 : RANK,

STATUS **6** : EMPLOYMENT, JOB — **position** *vb* — **po·si·tion·al** \-'shə-nəl\ *adj*

¹**pos·i·tive** \'pä-zə-tiv\ *adj* **1** : expressed definitely ⟨her answer was a ∼ *no*⟩ **2** : CONFIDENT, CERTAIN ⟨∼ it was my book⟩ **3** : of, relating to, or constituting the degree of grammatical comparison that denotes no increase in quality, quantity, or relation **4** : not fictitious : REAL **5** : active and effective in function ⟨∼ leadership⟩ **6** : having the light and shade as existing in the original subject ⟨a ∼ photograph⟩ **7** : numerically greater than zero ⟨a ∼ number⟩ **8** : being, relating to, or charged with electricity of which the proton is the elementary unit **9** : AFFIRMATIVE ⟨a ∼ response⟩ **10** : FAVORABLE; *also* : marked by optimism — **pos·i·tive·ly** *adv* — **pos·i·tive·ness** *n*

²**positive** *n* **1** : the positive degree or a positive form in a language **2** : a positive photograph

pos·i·tron \'pä-zə-ˌträn\ *n* : a positively charged particle having the same mass and magnitude of charge as the electron

po·so·le *or* **po·zo·le** \pō-'sō-lā\ *n* : a thick Mexican soup made with pork, hominy, garlic, and chili

poss *abbr* possessive

pos·se \'pä-sē\ *n* [ML *posse comitatus*, lit., power or authority of the county] **1** : a body of persons organized to assist a sheriff in an emergency **2** : a body of attendants or followers

pos·sess \pə-'zes\ *vb* **1** : to have as property : OWN **2** : to have as an attribute, knowledge, or skill **3** : to enter into and control firmly ⟨∼*ed* by a devil⟩ — **pos·ses·sor** \-'ze-sər\ *n*

pos·ses·sion \-'ze-shən\ *n* **1** : control or occupancy of property **2** : OWNERSHIP **3** : something owned : PROPERTY **4** : domination by something (as an evil spirit, a passion, or an idea) **5** : SELF-CONTROL

pos·ses·sive \pə-'ze-siv\ *adj* **1** : of, relating to, or constituting a grammatical case denoting ownership **2** : showing the desire to possess ⟨a ∼ nature⟩ — **possessive** *n* — **pos·ses·sive·ness** *n*

pos·si·ble \'pä-sə-bəl\ *adj* **1** : being within the limits of ability, capacity, or realization **2** : being something that may or may not occur ⟨∼ dangers⟩ **3** : able or fitted to become ⟨a ∼ site for a bridge⟩ — **pos·si·bil·i·ty** \ˌpä-sə-'bi-lə-tē\ *n* — **pos·si·bly** \'pä-sə-blē\ *adv*

pos·sum \'pä-səm\ *n* : OPOSSUM

¹**post** \'pōst\ *n* **1** : an upright piece of timber or metal serving esp. as a support : PILLAR **2** : a pole or stake set up as a mark or indicator

²**post** *vb* **1** : to affix to a usual place (as a wall) for public notices **2** : to publish or announce by or as if by a public notice ⟨∼ grades⟩ **3** : to forbid (property) to trespassers by putting up a notice **4** : SCORE 4 **5** : to publish in an online forum

³**post** *n* **1** *obs* : COURIER **2** *chiefly Brit* : ¹MAIL; *also* : POST OFFICE **3** : something that is published online

⁴**post** *vb* **1** : to ride or travel with haste : HURRY **2** : MAIL ⟨∼ a letter⟩ **3** : to enter in a ledger **4** : INFORM ⟨kept him ∼*ed* on new developments⟩

⁵**post** *n* **1** : the place at which a soldier is stationed; *esp* : a sentry's beat or station **2** : a station or task to which a person is assigned **3** : the place at which a body of troops is stationed : CAMP **4** : OFFICE, POSITION **5** : a trading settlement or station

⁶**post** *vb* **1** : to station in a given place **2** : to put up (as bond)

post·age \'pōs-tij\ *n* : the fee for postal service; *also* : stamps representing this fee

post·al \'pōs-tᵊl\ *adj* : of or relating to the mails or the post office

postal card *n* : POSTCARD

postal service *n* : a government agency or department handling the transmission of mail

¹**post·card** \'pōst-ˌkärd\ *n* : a card on which a message may be written for mailing without an envelope

²**postcard** *adj* : PICTURESQUE

post chaise *n* : a 4-wheeled closed carriage for two to four persons

post·con·sum·er \ˌpōst-kən-'sü-mər\ *adj* **1** : discarded by a consumer **2** : having been used and recycled for reuse in another product

post·date \ˌpōst-'dāt\ *vb* : to date with a date later than that of execution ⟨∼ a check⟩

post·doc·tor·al \-'däk-tə-rəl\ *also* **post·doc·tor·ate** \-tə-rət\ *adj* : of, relating to, or engaged in advanced academic or professional work beyond a doctor's degree

post·er \'pō-stər\ *n* : a bill or placard for posting often in a public place

¹**pos·te·ri·or** \pō-'stir-ē-ər, pä-\ *adj* **1** : later in time **2** : situated behind

²**pos·te·ri·or** \pä-'stir-ē-ər, pō-\ *n* : the hinder bodily parts; *esp* : BUTTOCKS

pos·ter·i·ty \pä-'ster-ə-tē\ *n* **1** : the descendants from one ancestor **2** : all future generations

pos·tern \'pōs-tərn, 'päs-\ *n* **1** : a back door or gate **2** : a private or side entrance

post exchange *n* : a store at a military post that sells to military personnel and authorized civilians

post·grad \'pōst-ˌgrad\ *adj* : POSTGRADUATE

post·grad·u·ate \(ˌ)pōst-'gra-jə-wət\ *adj* : of or relating to studies beyond the bachelor's degree — **postgraduate** *n*

post·haste \'pōst-'hāst\ *adv* : with all possible speed

post·hole \-ˌhōl\ *n* : a hole for a post and esp. a fence post

post·hu·mous \'päs-chə-məs\ *adj* [L *posthumus*, alter. of *postumus* last-born, posthumous, fr. superl. of *posterus* coming after] **1** : born after the death of the father **2** : published after the death of the author — **post·hu·mous·ly** *adv*

post·hyp·not·ic \ˌpōst-hip-'nä-tik\ *adj* : of, relating to, or characteristic of the period following a hypnotic trance

pos·til·ion *or* **pos·til·lion** \pō-'stil-yən\ *n* : a rider on the left-hand horse of a pair drawing a coach

Post·im·pres·sion·ism \ˌpōst-im-'pre-shə-ˌni-zəm\ *n* : a late 19th century French theory or practice of art that stresses variously volume, picture structure, or expressionism

post·lude \'pōst-ˌlüd\ *n* : an organ solo played at the end of a church service

post·man \-mən, -ˌman\ *n* : MAILMAN

post·mark \-ˌmärk\ *n* : an official postal marking on a piece of mail; *esp* : the mark canceling the postage stamp — **postmark** *vb*

post·mas·ter \-ˌmas-tər\ *n* : a person who has charge of a post office

postmaster general *n*, *pl* **postmasters general** : an official in charge of a national postal service

post·men·o·paus·al \ˌpōst-ˌme-nə-'pȯ-zəl\ *adj* **1** : having undergone menopause **2** : occurring or administered after menopause

post me·ri·di·em \ˌpōst-mə-'ri-dē-əm\ *adj* [L] : being after noon

post·mis·tress \'pōst-ˌmis-trəs\ *n* : a woman in charge of a post office

post·mod·ern \ˌpōst-'mä-dərn\ *adj* : of, relating to, or being any of various movements in reaction to modernism

¹**post·mor·tem** \ˌpōst-'mȯr-təm\ *adj* [L *post mortem* after death] **1** : done, occurring, or collected after death **2** : following the event

²**postmortem** *n* **1** : AUTOPSY **2** : an analysis or discussion of an event after it is over

post·na·sal drip \'pōst-ˌnā-zəl-\ *n* : flow of mucous secretion from the posterior part of the nasal cavity onto the wall of the pharynx

post·na·tal \(ˌ)pōst-'nā-tᵊl\ *adj* : occurring or being after birth; *esp* : of or relating to a newborn infant

post office *n* **1** : POSTAL SERVICE **2** : a local branch of a post office department

post·op·er·a·tive \(ˌ)pōst-'ä-prə-tiv, -pə-ˌrā-\ *adj* : following or having undergone a surgical operation ⟨∼ care⟩

post·paid \'pōst-'pād\ *adj* : having the postage paid by the sender and not chargeable to the receiver

post·par·tum \(ˌ)pōst-'pär-təm\ *adj* [NL *post partum* after birth] : following parturition — **postpartum** *adv*

post·pone \pōst-'pōn\ *vb* **post·poned; post·pon·ing** : to put off to a later time — **post·pone·ment** *n*

post road *n* : a road over which mail is carried

post·script \'pōst-ˌskript\ *n* : a note added esp. to a completed letter

post time *n* : the designated time for the start of a horse race

post–traumatic *adj* : occurring after or as a result of trauma ⟨∼ stress⟩

pos·tu·lant \'päs-chə-lənt\ *n* : a probationary candidate for membership in a religious order

¹**pos·tu·late** \\'päs-chə-ˌlāt\\ *vb* **-lat·ed; -lat·ing** : to assume as true

²**pos·tu·late** \\'päs-chə-lət, -ˌlāt\\ *n* : a proposition taken for granted as true esp. as a basis for a chain of reasoning

¹**pos·ture** \\'päs-chər\\ *n* **1** : the position or bearing of the body or one of its parts **2** : STATE, CONDITION **3** : ATTITUDE ⟨a ∼ of arrogance⟩

²**posture** *vb* **pos·tured; pos·tur·ing** : to strike a pose esp. for effect

post·war \\'pōst-'wȯr\\ *adj* : occurring or existing after a war

po·sy \\'pō-zē\\ *n, pl* **posies** **1** : a brief sentiment : MOTTO **2** : a bunch of flowers; *also* : FLOWER

¹**pot** \\'pät\\ *n* **1** : a rounded container used chiefly for domestic purposes **2** : the total of the bets at stake at one time **3** : RUIN ⟨go to ∼⟩ — **pot·ful** *n*

²**pot** *vb* **pot·ted; pot·ting** **1** : to preserve or place in a pot **2** : SHOOT

³**pot** *n* : MARIJUANA

po·ta·ble \\'pō-tə-bəl\\ *adj* : suitable for drinking — **po·ta·bil·i·ty** \\ˌpō-tə-'bi-lə-tē\\ *n*

po·tage \\pȯ-'täzh\\ *n* : a thick soup

pot·ash \\'pät-ˌash\\ *n* [sing. of *pot ashes*] : potassium or any of its various compounds esp. as used in agriculture

po·tas·si·um \\pə-'ta-sē-əm\\ *n* : a silver-white soft metallic chemical element that occurs abundantly in nature

potassium bromide *n* : a crystalline salt used as a sedative and in photography

potassium carbonate *n* : a white salt used in making glass and soap

potassium nitrate *n* : a soluble salt used in making gunpowder, as a fertilizer, and in medicine

po·ta·tion \\pō-'tā-shən\\ *n* : a usu. alcoholic drink; *also* : the act of drinking

po·ta·to \\pə-'tā-tō\\ *n, pl* **-toes** : the edible starchy tuber of a plant related to the tomato; *also* : this plant

potato beetle *n* : COLORADO POTATO BEETLE

potato bug *n* : COLORADO POTATO BEETLE

potbellied pig *n* : any of an Asian breed of small pigs having a straight tail, potbelly, and black, white, or black and white coat

pot·bel·ly \\'pät-ˌbe-lē\\ *n* : a protruding abdomen — **pot·bel·lied** \\-lēd\\ *adj*

pot·boil·er \\-ˌbȯi-lər\\ *n* : a usu. inferior work of art or literature produced chiefly for profit

po·tent \\'pō-tᵊnt\\ *adj* **1** : having authority or influence : POWERFUL **2** : chemically or medicinally effective **3** : able to copulate — used esp. of the male ✦ *Synonyms* FORCEFUL, FORCIBLE, MIGHTY, PUISSANT — **po·ten·cy** \\-tᵊn-sē\\ *n*

po·ten·tate \\'pō-tᵊn-ˌtāt\\ *n* : one who wields controlling power : RULER

¹**po·ten·tial** \\pə-'ten-chəl\\ *adj* : existing in possibility : capable of becoming actual ⟨a ∼ champion⟩ ✦ *Synonyms* DORMANT, LATENT, QUIESCENT — **po·ten·ti·al·i·ty** \\pə-ˌten-chē-'a-lə-tē\\ *n* — **po·ten·tial·ly** \\-'ten-chə-lē\\ *adv*

²**potential** *n* **1** : something that can develop or become actual ⟨a ∼ for violence⟩ **2** : the work required to move a unit positive charge from infinity to a point in question; *also* : POTENTIAL DIFFERENCE

potential difference *n* : the difference in potential between two points that represents the work involved in the transfer of a unit quantity of electricity from one point to the other

potential energy *n* : the energy an object has because of its position or nature or the arrangement of its parts

po·ten·ti·ate \\pə-'ten-chē-ˌāt\\ *vb* **-at·ed; -at·ing** : to make potent; *esp* : to augment the activity of (as a drug) synergistically — **po·ten·ti·a·tion** \\-ˌten-chē-'ā-shən\\ *n*

pot·head \\'pät-ˌhed\\ *n* : a person who frequently smokes marijuana

poth·er \\'pä-thər\\ *n* : a noisy disturbance; *also* : FUSS

pot·herb \\'pät-ˌərb, -ˌhərb\\ *n* : an herb whose leaves or stems are boiled for greens or used to season food

pot·hole \\'pät-ˌhōl\\ *n* : a large pit or hole (as in a road surface)

pot·hook \\-ˌhu̇k\\ *n* : an S-shaped hook for hanging pots and kettles over an open fire

po·tion \\'pō-shən\\ *n* : a mixture of liquids (as liquor or medicine)

pot·luck \\'pät-'lək\\ *n* : the regular meal available to a guest for whom no special preparations have been made

pot·pie \\-'pī\\ *n* : pastry-covered meat and vegetables cooked in a deep dish

pot·pour·ri \\ˌpō-pu̇-'rē\\ *n* [F *pot pourri*, lit., rotten pot] **1** : a mixture of flowers, herbs, and spices used for scent **2** : a miscellaneous collection

pot·sherd \\'pät-ˌshərd\\ *n* : a pottery fragment

pot·shot \\-ˌshät\\ *n* **1** : a shot taken from ambush or at a random or easy target **2** : a critical remark made in a random or sporadic manner

pot sticker *n* : a crescent-shaped dumpling that is steamed and fried

pot·tage \\'pä-tij\\ *n* : a thick soup of vegetables and often meat

¹**pot·ter** \\'pä-tər\\ *n* : one that makes pottery

²**potter** *vb* : PUTTER

pot·tery \\'pä-tə-rē\\ *n, pl* **-ter·ies** **1** : a place where earthen pots and dishes are made **2** : the art of the potter **3** : dishes, pots, and vases made from clay

pot·ty-mouthed \\'pä-tē-ˌmau̇thd, -ˌmau̇tht\\ *adj* : given to the use of vulgar language

¹**pouch** \\'pau̇ch\\ *n* [ME *pouche*, fr. AF, of Gmc origin; akin to OE *pocca* bag] **1** : a small bag (as for tobacco) carried on the person **2** : a bag for storing or transporting goods ⟨mail ∼⟩ ⟨diplomatic ∼⟩ **3** : an anatomical sac; *esp* : one for carrying the young on the abdomen of a female marsupial (as a kangaroo)

²**pouch** *vb* : to put or form into or as if into a pouch

poult \\'pōlt\\ *n* : a young fowl; *esp* : a young turkey

poul·ter·er \\'pōl-tər-ər\\ *n* : one that deals in poultry

poul·tice \\'pōl-təs\\ *n* : a soft usu. heated and medicated mass spread on cloth and applied to a sore or injury — **poultice** *vb*

poul·try \\'pōl-trē\\ *n* : domesticated birds kept for eggs or meat — **poul·try·man** \\-mən\\ *n*

pounce \\'pau̇ns\\ *vb* **pounced; pounc·ing** : to spring or swoop upon and seize something

¹**pound** \\'pau̇nd\\ *n, pl* **pounds** *also* **pound** **1** : a unit of avoirdupois, troy, and apothecaries' weight — see WEIGHT table **2** — see MONEY table **3** : the former basic monetary unit of Ireland

²**pound** *n* : a public enclosure where stray animals are kept

³**pound** *vb* **1** : to crush to a powder or pulp by beating **2** : to strike or beat heavily or repeatedly **3** : DRILL 1 **4** : to move or move along heavily

pound·age \\'pau̇n-dij\\ *n* : POUNDS; *also* : weight in pounds

pound cake *n* : a rich cake made with a large proportion of eggs and shortening

pound-fool·ish \\'pau̇nd-'fu̇-lish\\ *adj* : imprudent in dealing with large sums or large matters

pour \\'pȯr\\ *vb* **1** : to flow or cause to flow in a stream or flood **2** : to rain hard **3** : to supply freely and copiously

pour·boire \\pu̇r-'bwär\\ *n* [F, fr. *pour boire* for drinking] : TIP, GRATUITY

pout \\'pau̇t\\ *vb* **1** : to show displeasure by thrusting out the lips; *also* : to look sullen — **pout** *n*

pov·er·ty \\'pä-vər-tē\\ *n* [ME *poverte*, fr. AF *poverté*, fr. L *paupertat-*, *paupertas*, fr. *pauper* poor] **1** : lack of money or material possessions : WANT **2** : poor quality (as of soil)

poverty line *n* : a level of personal or family income below which one is classified as poor according to government standards

pov·er·ty–strick·en \\'pä-vər-tē-ˌstri-kən\\ *adj* : very poor : DESTITUTE

POW \\ˌpē-(ˌ)ō-'də-bəl-(ˌ)yü\\ *n* : PRISONER OF WAR

¹**pow·der** \\'pau̇-dər\\ *vb* **1** : to sprinkle or cover with or as if with powder **2** : to reduce to powder

²**powder** *n* [ME *poudre*, fr. AF *pudre, podre*, fr. L *pulver-, pulvis* dust] **1** : dry material made up of fine particles; *also* : a usu. medicinal or cosmetic preparation in this form **2** : a solid explosive (as gunpowder) — **pow·dery** *adj*

powder room *n* : a rest room for women

¹**pow·er** \\'pau̇(-ə)r\\ *n* **1** : the ability to act or produce an effect **2** : a position of ascendancy over others : AUTHORITY **3** : one that has control or authority; *esp* : a sovereign state **4** : physical might; *also* : mental or moral vigor **5** : the number of times as indicated by an exponent a num-

ber is to be multiplied by itself ⟨5 to the third ∼ is 125⟩; *also* : the product itself ⟨8 is a ∼ of 2⟩ **6** : force or energy used to do work; *also* : the time rate at which work is done or energy transferred **7** : MAGNIFICATION 2 — **pow·er·ful** \-fəl\ *adj* — **pow·er·ful·ly** *adv* — **pow·er·less** *adj*

²**power** *vb* : to supply with power and esp. motive power

³**power** *adj* **1** : operated mechanically or electrically rather than manually **2** : of, relating to, or utilizing strength

pow·er·boat \-ˌbōt\ *n* : MOTORBOAT

pow·er·house \ˈpaȯ(-ə)r-ˌhaȯs\ *n* **1** : POWER PLANT 1 **2** : one having great drive, energy, or ability

power plant *n* **1** : a building in which electric power is generated **2** : an engine and related parts supplying the motive power of a self-propelled vehicle

pow·wow \ˈpaȯ-ˌwaȯ\ *n* **1** : a No. American Indian ceremony (as for victory in war) **2** : a meeting for discussion : CONFERENCE

pox \ˈpäks\ *n, pl* **pox** *or* **pox·es** : any of various diseases (as smallpox or syphilis) marked by a rash on the skin

pozole *var of* POSOLE

pp *abbr* **1** pages **2** pianissimo

PP *abbr* **1** parcel post **2** past participle **3** postpaid **4** prepaid

ppd *abbr* **1** postpaid **2** prepaid

PPO \ˌpē-ˌpē-ˈō\ *n, pl* **PPOs** [*preferred provider organization*] : a health-care organization that gives economic incentives to enrolled individuals who use certain health-care providers

PPS *abbr* [L *post postscriptum*] an additional postscript

ppt *abbr* precipitate

PQ *abbr* Province of Quebec

pr *abbr* **1** pair **2** price

Pr *symbol* praseodymium

¹**PR** *or* **p.r.** \ˈpē-ˈär\ *n* : PUBLIC RELATIONS

²**PR** *abbr* **1** payroll **2** public relations **3** Puerto Rico

prac·ti·ca·ble \ˈprak-ti-kə-bəl\ *adj* : capable of being put into practice, done, or accomplished — **prac·ti·ca·bil·i·ty** \ˌprak-ti-kə-ˈbi-lə-tē\ *n*

prac·ti·cal \ˈprak-ti-kəl\ *adj* **1** : of, relating to, or shown in practice ⟨∼ questions⟩ **2** : VIRTUAL ⟨∼ control⟩ **3** : capable of being put to use ⟨a ∼ knowledge of French⟩ **4** : inclined to action as opposed to speculation ⟨a ∼ person⟩ **5** : qualified by practice ⟨a good ∼ mechanic⟩ — **prac·ti·cal·i·ty** \ˌprak-ti-ˈka-lə-tē\ *n* — **prac·ti·cal·ly** \-k(ə-)lē\ *adv*

practical joke *n* : a prank intended to trick or embarrass someone or cause physical discomfort

practical nurse *n* : a professional nurse without all of the qualifications of a registered nurse; *esp* : LICENSED PRACTICAL NURSE

¹**prac·tice** *also* **prac·tise** \ˈprak-təs\ *vb* **prac·ticed** *also* **prac·tised; prac·tic·ing** *also* **prac·tis·ing** **1** : CARRY OUT, APPLY ⟨∼ what you preach⟩ **2** : to perform or work at repeatedly so as to become proficient ⟨∼ tennis strokes⟩ **3** : to do or perform customarily ⟨∼ politeness⟩ **4** : to be professionally engaged in ⟨∼ law⟩

²**practice** *also* **practise** *n* **1** : actual performance or application **2** : customary action : HABIT **3** : systematic exercise for proficiency **4** : the exercise of a profession; *also* : a professional business

prac·ti·tion·er \prak-ˈti-shə-nər\ *n* : one who practices a profession

prae·tor \ˈprē-tər\ *n* : an ancient Roman magistrate ranking below a consul — **prae·to·ri·an** \prē-ˈtȯr-ē-ən\ *adj*

prag·mat·ic \prag-ˈma-tik\ *also* **prag·mat·i·cal** \-ti-kəl\ *adj* **1** : of or relating to practical affairs **2** : concerned with the practical consequences of actions or beliefs — **pragmatic** *n* — **prag·mat·i·cal·ly** \-ti-k(ə-)lē\ *adv*

prag·ma·tism \ˈprag-mə-ˌti-zəm\ *n* : a practical approach to problems and affairs

prai·rie \ˈprer-ē\ *n* [F, fr. OF *praierie*, fr. VL *prataria, fr. L *pratum* meadow] : a broad tract of level or rolling grassland

prairie dog *n* : an American burrowing black-tailed rodent related to the squirrels and living in colonies

prairie schooner *n* : a covered wagon used by pioneers in cross-country travel

praise \ˈprāz\ *vb* **praised; prais·ing** **1** : to express approval of : COMMEND **2** : to glorify (a divinity or a saint) esp. in song — **praise** *n*

praise·wor·thy \-ˌwər-thē\ *adj* : LAUDABLE ⟨a ∼ effort⟩

pra·line \ˈprä-ˌlēn, ˈprā-\ *n* [F] : a confection of nuts and sugar

pram \ˈpram\ *n, chiefly Brit* : PERAMBULATOR

prance \ˈprans\ *vb* **pranced; pranc·ing** **1** : to spring from the hind legs ⟨a *prancing* horse⟩ **2** : SWAGGER; *also* : CAPER — **prance** *n* — **pranc·er** *n*

prank \ˈpraŋk\ *n* : a playful or mildly mischievous act : TRICK

prank·ster \ˈpraŋk-stər\ *n* : a person who plays pranks

pra·seo·dym·i·um \ˌprā-zē-ō-ˈdi-mē-əm\ *n* : a yellowish white metallic chemical element

prate \ˈprāt\ *vb* **prat·ed; prat·ing** : to talk long and idly : chatter foolishly

prat·fall \ˈprat-ˌfȯl\ *n* **1** : a fall on the buttocks **2** : a humiliating blunder

¹**prat·tle** \ˈpra-tᵊl\ *vb* **prat·tled; prat·tling** : PRATE, BABBLE

²**prattle** *n* : trifling or childish talk

prawn \ˈprȯn\ *n* : any of various edible shrimplike crustaceans; *also* : SHRIMP 1

pray \ˈprā\ *vb* **1** : ENTREAT, IMPLORE **2** : to ask earnestly for something **3** : to address God or a god esp. with supplication

prayer \ˈprer\ *n* **1** : a supplication or expression addressed to God or a god; *also* : a set order of words used in praying **2** : an earnest request or wish **3** : the act or practice of praying to God or a god **4** : a religious service consisting chiefly of prayers — often used in pl. **5** : something prayed for **6** : a slight chance

prayer book *n* : a book containing prayers and often directions for worship

prayer·ful \ˈprer-fəl\ *adj* **1** : DEVOUT **2** : EARNEST — **prayer·ful·ly** *adv*

praying mantis *n* : MANTIS

PRC *abbr* People's Republic of China

preach \ˈprēch\ *vb* **1** : to deliver a sermon **2** : to set forth in a sermon **3** : to advocate earnestly — **preach·er** *n* — **preach·ment** *n*

pre·ad·o·les·cence \ˌprē-ˌa-də-ˈle-sᵊns\ *n* : the period of human development just preceding adolescence — **pre·ad·o·les·cent** \-sᵊnt\ *adj or n*

pre·am·ble \ˈprē-ˌam-bəl\ *n* [ME, fr. MF *preambule*, fr. ML *preambulum*, fr. LL, neut. of *praeambulus* walking in front of, fr. L *prae* in front of + *ambulare* to walk] : an introductory part ⟨the ∼ to a constitution⟩

pre·ar·range \ˌprē-ə-ˈrānj\ *vb* : to arrange beforehand — **pre·ar·range·ment** *n*

pre·as·sign \ˌprē-ə-ˈsīn\ *vb* : to assign beforehand

Pre·cam·bri·an \ˈprē-ˈkam-brē-ən, -ˈkäm-\ *adj* : of, relating to, or being the era that is earliest in geologic history and is characterized esp. by the appearance of single-celled organisms — **Precambrian** *n*

pre·can·cel \(ˌ)prē-ˈkan-səl\ *vb* : to cancel (a postage stamp) in advance of use — **precancel** *n* — **pre·can·cel·la·tion** \ˌprē-ˌkan-sə-ˈlā-shən\ *n*

pre·can·cer·ous \(ˌ)prē-ˈkan-sə-rəs\ *adj* : likely to become cancerous

pre·car·i·ous \pri-ˈker-ē-əs\ *adj* : dependent on uncertain conditions : dangerously insecure : UNSTABLE ⟨a ∼ foothold⟩ ⟨∼ prosperity⟩ ♦ **Synonyms** DELICATE, SENSITIVE, TICKLISH, TOUCHY, TRICKY — **pre·car·i·ous·ly** *adv* — **pre·car·i·ous·ness** *n*

pre·cau·tion \pri-ˈkȯ-shən\ *n* : a measure taken beforehand to prevent harm or secure good — **pre·cau·tion·ary** \-shə-ˌner-ē\ *adj*

pre·cede \pri-ˈsēd\ *vb* **pre·ced·ed; pre·ced·ing** : to be, go, or come ahead or in front of (as in rank or time)

pre·ce·dence \ˈpre-sə-dəns, pri-ˈsēd-ᵊns\ *n* **1** : the act or fact of preceding **2** : consideration based on order of importance : PRIORITY

¹**pre·ce·dent** \pri-ˈsēd-ᵊnt, ˈpre-sə-dənt\ *adj* : prior in time, order, or significance

²**prec·e·dent** \ˈpre-sə-dənt\ *n* : something said or done that may serve to authorize or justify further words or acts of the same or a similar kind

pre·ced·ing \pri-ˈsēd-iŋ\ *adj* : that precedes ♦ **Synonyms** ANTECEDENT, FOREGOING, PRIOR, FORMER, ANTERIOR

pre·cen·tor \pri-ˈsen-tər\ *n* : a leader of the singing of a choir or congregation

pre·cept \ˈprē-ˌsept\ *n* : a command or principle intended as a general rule of action or conduct

pre·cep·tor \pri-'sep-tər, 'prē-ˌsep-\ *n* : TUTOR

pre·ces·sion \prē-'se-shən\ *n* : a slow gyration of the rotation axis of a spinning body (as the earth) — **pre·cess** \prē-'ses\ *vb* — **pre·ces·sion·al** \-'se-shə-nəl\ *adj*

pre·cinct \'prē-ˌsiŋkt\ *n* **1** : an administrative subdivision (as of a city) : DISTRICT ⟨police ∼⟩ ⟨electoral ∼⟩ **2** : an enclosure bounded by the limits of a building or place — often used in pl. **3** *pl* : ENVIRONS

pre·ci·os·i·ty \ˌpre-shē-'ä-sə-tē\ *n, pl* **-ties** : fastidious refinement

pre·cious \'pre-shəs\ *adj* **1** : of great value ⟨∼ jewels⟩ **2** : greatly cherished : DEAR ⟨∼ memories⟩ **3** : AFFECTED ⟨∼ language⟩

prec·i·pice \'pre-sə-pəs\ *n* : a steep cliff

pre·cip·i·tan·cy \pri-'si-pə-tən-sē\ *n* : undue hastiness or suddenness

¹pre·cip·i·tate \pri-'si-pə-ˌtāt\ *vb* **-tat·ed; -tat·ing** [L *praecipitare,* fr. *praecipit-, praeceps* headlong, fr. *prae* in front of + *caput* head] **1** : to throw violently **2** : to throw down **3** : to cause to happen quickly or abruptly ⟨∼ a quarrel⟩ **4** : to cause to separate from solution or suspension **5** : to fall as rain, snow, or hail ✦ *Synonyms* SPEED, ACCELERATE, QUICKEN, HASTEN, HURRY

²pre·cip·i·tate \pri-'si-pə-tət, -ˌtāt\ *n* : the solid matter that separates from a solution or suspension

³pre·cip·i·tate \pri-'si-pə-tət\ *adj* **1** : showing extreme or unwise haste : RASH **2** : falling with steep descent; *also* : PRECIPITOUS — **pre·cip·i·tate·ly** *adv* — **pre·cip·i·tate·ness** *n*

pre·cip·i·ta·tion \pri-ˌsi-pə-'tā-shən\ *n* **1** : rash haste **2** : the process of precipitating or forming a precipitate **3** : water that falls to earth esp. as rain or snow; *also* : the quantity of this water

pre·cip·i·tous \pri-'si-pə-təs\ *adj* **1** : PRECIPITATE **2** : having the character of a precipice : very steep ⟨a ∼ slope⟩; *also* : containing precipices ⟨∼ trails⟩ — **pre·cip·i·tous·ly** *adv*

pré·cis \prā-'sē\ *n, pl* **pré·cis** \-'sēz\ [F] : a concise summary of essentials

pre·cise \pri-'sīs\ *adj* **1** : exactly defined or stated : DEFINITE **2** : highly accurate : EXACT **3** : conforming strictly to a standard : SCRUPULOUS — **pre·cise·ly** *adv* — **pre·cise·ness** *n*

pre·ci·sion \pri-'si-zhən\ *n* : the quality or state of being precise

pre·clude \pri-'klüd\ *vb* **pre·clud·ed; pre·clud·ing** : to make impossible : BAR, PREVENT

pre·co·cious \pri-'kō-shəs\ *adj* [L *praecoc-, praecox,* lit., ripening early, fr. *prae-* ahead + *coquere* to cook] : early in development and esp. in mental development — **pre·co·cious·ly** *adv* — **pre·coc·i·ty** \pri-'kä-sə-tē\ *n*

pre·con·ceive \ˌprē-kən-'sēv\ *vb* : to form an opinion of beforehand — **pre·con·cep·tion** \-'sep-shən\ *n*

pre·con·di·tion \-'di-shən\ *vb* : to put in proper or desired condition or frame of mind in advance

pre·cook \ˌprē-'kuk\ *vb* : to cook partially or entirely before final cooking or reheating

pre·cur·sor \pri-'kər-sər\ *n* : one that precedes and indicates the approach of another : FORERUNNER

pred *abbr* predicate

pre·da·ceous *or* **pre·da·cious** \pri-'dā-shəs\ *adj* : living by preying on others : PREDATORY

pre·date \'prē-ˌdāt\ *vb* : ANTEDATE

pre·da·tion \pri-'dā-shən\ *n* **1** : the act of preying or plundering **2** : a mode of life in which food is primarily obtained by killing and consuming animals

pred·a·tor \'pre-də-tər\ *n* : an animal that lives by predation

pred·a·to·ry \'pre-də-ˌtȯr-ē\ *adj* **1** : of or relating to plunder ⟨∼ warfare⟩ **2** : disposed to exploit others **3** : preying upon other animals

pre·dawn \('ˌ)prē-'dȯn\ *adj* : of or relating to the time just before dawn

pre·de·cease \ˌprē-di-'sēs\ *vb* **-ceased; -ceas·ing** : to die before another person

pre·de·ces·sor \'pre-də-ˌse-sər, 'prē-\ *n* : a previous holder of a position to which another has succeeded

pre·des·ig·nate \(ˌ)prē-'de-zig-ˌnāt\ *vb* : to designate beforehand

pre·des·ti·na·tion \ˌprē-ˌdes-tə-'nā-shən\ *n* : the act of foreordaining to an earthly lot or eternal destiny by divine decree; *also* : the state of being so foreordained — **pre·des·ti·nate** \prē-'des-tə-ˌnāt\ *vb*

pre·des·tine \prē-'des-tən\ *vb* : to settle beforehand : FOREORDAIN

pre·de·ter·mine \ˌprē-di-'tər-mən\ *vb* : to determine beforehand

pred·i·ca·ble \'pre-di-kə-bəl\ *adj* : capable of being predicated or affirmed

pre·dic·a·ment \pri-'di-kə-mənt\ *n* : a difficult or trying situation ✦ *Synonyms* DILEMMA, PICKLE, QUAGMIRE, JAM

¹pred·i·cate \'pre-di-kət\ *n* : the part of a sentence or clause that expresses what is said of the subject

²pred·i·cate \'pre-də-ˌkāt\ *vb* **-cat·ed; -cat·ing 1** : AFFIRM **2** : to assert to be a quality or attribute **3** : FOUND, BASE — usu. used with *on* — **pred·i·ca·tion** \ˌpre-də-'kā-shən\ *n*

pre·dict \pri-'dikt\ *vb* : to declare in advance — **pre·dict·abil·i·ty** \-ˌdik-tə-'bi-lə-tē\ *n* — **pre·dict·able** \-'dik-tə-bəl\ *adj* — **pre·dict·ably** \-blē\ *adv* — **pre·dic·tion** \-'dik-shən\ *n*

pre·di·gest \ˌprē-dī-'jest\ *vb* : to simplify for easy use; *also* : to subject to artificial or natural partial digestion

pre·di·lec·tion \ˌpre-də-'lek-shən, ˌprē-\ *n* : an established preference for something

pre·dis·pose \ˌprē-di-'spōz\ *vb* : to incline in advance : make susceptible — **pre·dis·po·si·tion** \ˌprē-ˌdis-pə-'zi-shən\ *n*

pre·dom·i·nant \pri-'dä-mə-nənt\ *adj* : greater in importance, strength, influence, or authority — **pre·dom·i·nance** \-nəns\ *n*

pre·dom·i·nant·ly \-nənt-lē\ *adv* : for the most part : MAINLY

pre·dom·i·nate \pri-'dä-mə-ˌnāt\ *vb* : to be superior esp. in power or numbers : PREVAIL

pre·dom·i·nate·ly \pri-'dä-mə-nət-lē\ *adv* : PREDOMINANTLY

pree·mie \'prē-mē\ *n* : a premature baby

pre·em·i·nent \prē-'e-mə-nənt\ *adj* : having highest rank : OUTSTANDING — **pre·em·i·nence** \-nəns\ *n* — **pre·em·i·nent·ly** *adv*

pre·empt \prē-'empt\ *vb* **1** : to settle upon (public land) with the right to purchase before others; *also* : to take by such right **2** : to seize upon before someone else can **3** : to take the place of ✦ *Synonyms* USURP, CONFISCATE, APPROPRIATE, EXPROPRIATE — **pre·emp·tion** \-'emp-shən\ *n*

pre·emp·tive \prē-'emp-tiv\ *adj* : marked by the seizing of the initiative : initiated by oneself ⟨∼ attack⟩

preen \'prēn\ *vb* [ME *prenen,* alter. of *proynen, prunen,* fr. AF *puroindre, proindre,* fr. *pur-* thoroughly + *oindre* to anoint, rub, fr. L *unguere*] **1** : to groom with the bill — used of a bird **2** : to dress or smooth up : PRIMP **3** : to pride (oneself) for achievement

pre·ex·ist \ˌprē-ig-'zist\ *vb* : to exist before — **pre·ex·is·tence** \-'zis-təns\ *n* — **pre·ex·is·tent** \-tənt\ *adj*

pref *abbr* **1** preface **2** preference **3** preferred **4** prefix

¹pre·fab \(ˌ)prē-'fab, 'prē-ˌfab\ *adj* : produced by prefabrication

²prefab *n* : a prefabricated structure

pre·fab·ri·cate \(ˌ)prē-'fa-brə-ˌkāt\ *vb* : to manufacture the parts of (a structure) beforehand for later assembly — **pre·fab·ri·ca·tion** \ˌprē-ˌfa-bri-'kā-shən\ *n*

¹pref·ace \'pre-fəs\ *n* : the introductory remarks of a speaker or writer — **pref·a·to·ry** \'pre-fə-ˌtȯr-ē\ *adj*

²preface *vb* **pref·aced; pref·ac·ing** : to introduce with a preface

pre·fect \'prē-ˌfekt\ *n* **1** : a high official; *esp* : a chief officer or magistrate **2** : a student monitor

pre·fec·ture \'prē-ˌfek-chər\ *n* : the office, term, or residence of a prefect

pre·fer \pri-'fər\ *vb* **pre·ferred; pre·fer·ring 1** : PROMOTE **2** : to like better **3** : to bring (as a charge) against a person — **pref·er·a·ble** \'pre-fə-rə-bəl\ *adj* — **pref·er·a·bly** \-blē\ *adv*

pref·er·ence \'pre-frəns, -fə-rəns\ *n* **1** : a special liking for one thing over another **2** : CHOICE, SELECTION — **pref·er·en·tial** \ˌpre-fə-'ren-chəl\ *adj*

pre·fer·ment \pri-'fər-mənt\ *n* : PROMOTION, ADVANCEMENT

preferred provider organization *n* : PPO

pre·fig·ure \prē-'fi-gyər\ *vb* **1** : FORESHADOW **2** : to imagine beforehand

¹pre·fix \'prē-,fiks, prē-'fiks\ *vb* : to place before ⟨~ a title to a name⟩

²pre·fix \'prē-,fiks\ *n* : an affix occurring at the beginning of a word

pre·flight \,prē-'flīt\ *adj* : preparing for or preliminary to flight

pre·form \(,)prē-'form, 'prē-,form\ *vb* : to form or shape beforehand

preg·na·ble \'preg-nə-bəl\ *adj* : vulnerable to capture ⟨a ~ fort⟩

preg·nant \'preg-nənt\ *adj* **1** : containing unborn offspring within the body **2** : rich in significance : MEANINGFUL — **preg·nan·cy** \-nən-sē\ *n*

pre·heat \prē-'hēt\ *vb* : to heat beforehand; *esp* : to heat (an oven) to a designated temperature before using

pre·hen·sile \prē-'hen-səl, -,sīl\ *adj* : adapted for grasping esp. by wrapping around ⟨a monkey with a ~ tail⟩

pre·his·tor·ic \prē-his-'tor-ik\ *also* **pre·his·tor·i·cal** \-i-kəl\ *adj* : of, relating to, or existing in the period before written history began

pre·judge \(,)prē-'jəj\ *vb* : to judge before full hearing or examination

¹prej·u·dice \'pre-jə-dəs\ *n* **1** : DAMAGE; *esp* : detriment to one's rights or claims **2** : an opinion made without adequate basis — **prej·u·di·cial** \,pre-jə-'di-shəl\ *adj*

²prejudice *vb* **-diced; -dic·ing 1** : to damage by a judgment or action esp. at law **2** : to cause to have prejudice

pre·kin·der·gar·ten \-(')prē-'kin-dər-,gär-tᵊn\ *n* **1** : NURSERY SCHOOL **2** : a class or program preceding kindergarten

prel·ate \'pre-lət\ *n* : an ecclesiastic (as a bishop) of high rank — **prel·a·cy** \-lə-sē\ *n*

pre·launch \'prē-,lonch\ *adj* : preparing for or preliminary to launch

pre·lim \'prē-,lim, pri-'lim\ *n or adj* : PRELIMINARY

¹pre·lim·i·nary \pri-'li-mə-,ner-ē\ *n, pl* **-nar·ies** : something that precedes or introduces the main business or event

²preliminary *adj* : preceding the main discourse or business

pre·lude \'prel-,yüd; 'prē-,lüd, 'prā-\ *n* **1** : an introductory performance or event **2** : a musical section or movement introducing the main theme; *also* : an organ solo played at the beginning of a church service

pre·mar·i·tal \(,)prē-'mer-ə-tᵊl\ *adj* : existing or occurring before marriage

pre·ma·ture \prē-mə-'tùr, -'tyùr, -'chùr\ *adj* : happening, coming, born, or done before the usual or proper time — **pre·ma·ture·ly** *adv*

¹pre·med \'prē-'med\ *n* : a premedical student or course of study

²premed *adj* : PREMEDICAL

pre·med·i·cal \(,)prē-'me-di-kəl\ *adj* : preceding and preparing for the professional study of medicine

pre·med·i·tate \pri-'me-də-,tāt\ *vb* : to consider and plan beforehand — **pre·med·i·ta·tion** \-,me-də-'tā-shən\ *n*

pre·men·o·paus·al \(,)prē-,me-nə-'po-zəl\ *adj* : of, relating to, or being in the period preceding menopause

pre·men·stru·al \(,)prē-'men-strə-wəl\ *adj* : of, relating to, or occurring in the period just before menstruation

premenstrual syndrome *n* : a varying group of symptoms manifested by some women prior to menstruation

premie *var of* PREEMIE

¹pre·mier \pri-'mir, -'myir, 'prē-mē-ər\ *adj* [ME *primer, primier*, fr. AF, first, chief, fr. L *primarius* of the first rank] : first in rank or importance : CHIEF; *also* : first in time : EARLIEST

²premier *n* : PRIME MINISTER — **pre·mier·ship** *n*

¹pre·miere \pri-'myer, -'mir\ *n* : a first performance

²premiere *also* **pre·mier** *same as* ¹PREMIERE\ *vb* **pre·miered; pre·mier·ing** : to give or receive a first public performance

¹prem·ise \'pre-məs\ *n* **1** : a statement of fact or a supposition made or implied as a basis of argument **2** *pl* : a piece of land with the structures on it; *also* : the place of business of an enterprise

²premise *vb* **prem·ised; prem·is·ing** : to base on certain assumptions

pre·mi·um \'prē-mē-əm\ *n* [L *praemium* booty, profit, reward, fr. *prae* before + *emere* to take, buy] **1** : REWARD,

PRIZE **2** : a sum over and above the stated value **3** : something paid over and above a fixed wage or price **4** : something given with a purchase **5** : the sum paid for a contract of insurance **6** : an unusually high value

pre·mix \prē-'miks\ *vb* : to mix before use

pre·mo·lar \(,)prē-'mō-lər\ *adj* : situated in front of or preceding the molar teeth; *esp* : being or relating to those teeth of a mammal in front of the true molars and behind the canines — **premolar** *n*

pre·mo·ni·tion \prē-mə-'ni-shən, ,pre-\ *n* **1** : previous warning **2** : PRESENTIMENT — **pre·mon·i·to·ry** \pri-'mä-nə-,tór-ē\ *adj*

pre·na·tal \'prē-'nā-tᵊl\ *adj* : occurring, existing, or taking place before birth

pre·nup·tial \prē-'nəp-shəl\ *adj* : made or occurring before marriage

prenuptial agreement *n* : an agreement between a man and woman before marrying in which they give up future rights to each other's property in the event of divorce or death

pre·oc·cu·pa·tion \prē-,ä-kyə-'pā-shən\ *n* : complete absorption of the mind or interests; *also* : something that causes such absorption

pre·oc·cu·pied \prē-'ä-kyə-,pīd\ *adj* **1** : lost in thought; *also* : absorbed in some preoccupation **2** : already occupied ♦ **Synonyms** ABSTRACTED, ABSENT, ABSENTMINDED

pre·oc·cu·py \-,pī\ *vb* **1** : to occupy the attention of beforehand **2** : to take possession of before another

pre·op·er·a·tive \(,)prē-'ä-prə-tiv, -pə-,rā-\ *adj* : occurring before a surgical operation

pre·or·dain \prē-ór-'dān\ *vb* : FOREORDAIN

pre–owned \(,)prē-'ōnd\ *adj* : SECONDHAND ⟨~ vehicles⟩

prep *abbr* **1** preparatory **2** preposition

pre·pack·age \(,)prē-'pa-kij\ *vb* : to package (as food) before offering for sale to the customer

preparatory school *n* **1** : a usu. private school preparing students primarily for college **2** *Brit* : a private elementary school preparing students primarily for British public schools

pre·pare \pri-'per\ *vb* **pre·pared; pre·par·ing 1** : to make or get ready ⟨~ dinner⟩ ⟨~ a student for college⟩ **2** : to get ready beforehand **3** : to put together : COMPOUND ⟨~ a prescription⟩ — **prep·a·ra·tion** \,pre-pə-'rā-shən\ *n* — **pre·pa·ra·to·ry** \pri-'per-ə-,tór-ē\ *adj*

pre·pared·ness \pri-'per-əd-nəs\ *n* : a state of adequate preparation

pre·pay \(,)prē-'pā\ *vb* **-paid** \-'pād\; **-pay·ing** : to pay or pay the charge on in advance

pre·pon·der·ant \pri-'pän-də-rənt\ *adj* : having greater weight, force, influence, or frequency — **pre·pon·der·ance** \-rəns\ *n* — **pre·pon·der·ant·ly** *adv*

pre·pon·der·ate \pri-'pän-də-,rāt\ *vb* **-at·ed; -at·ing** [L *praeponderare*, fr. *prae-* ahead + *ponder-, pondus* weight] : to exceed in weight, force, influence, or frequency : PREDOMINATE

prep·o·si·tion \,pre-pə-'zi-shən\ *n* : a word that combines with a noun or pronoun to form a phrase — **prep·o·si·tion·al** \-'zi-shə-nəl\ *adj*

pre·pos·sess \,prē-pə-'zes\ *vb* **1** : to cause to be preoccupied **2** : to influence beforehand esp. favorably

pre·pos·sess·ing *adj* : tending to create a favorable impression ⟨a ~ manner⟩

pre·pos·ses·sion \-'ze-shən\ *n* **1** : PREJUDICE **2** : an exclusive concern with one idea or object

pre·pos·ter·ous \pri-'päs-tə-rəs\ *adj* : contrary to nature or reason : ABSURD

prep·py *or* **prep·pie** \'pre-pē\ *n, pl* **preppies 1** : a student at or a graduate of a preparatory school **2** : a person deemed to dress or behave like a preppy

pre·puce \'prē-,pyüs\ *n* : FORESKIN

pre·quel \'prē-kwəl\ *n* : a literary or dramatic work whose story precedes that of an earlier work

pre·re·cord·ed \(,)prē-ri-'kór-dəd\ *adj* : recorded for later broadcast or play

pre·req·ui·site \(,)prē-'re-kwə-zət\ *n* : something required beforehand or for the end in view — **prerequisite** *adj*

pre·rog·a·tive \pri-'rä-gə-tiv\ *n* : an exclusive or special right, power, or privilege

pres *abbr* **1** present **2** president

¹pres·age \'pre-sij\ *n* [ME, fr. L *praesagium*, fr. *praesagus* having a foreboding, fr. *prae* before + *sagus* prophetic] **1** : something that foreshadows a future event : OMEN **2** : FOREBODING

²**pre·sage** \'prez-sij, pri-'sāj\ *vb* **pre·saged; pre·sag·ing** **1** : to give an omen or warning of : FORESHADOW **2** : FORETELL, PREDICT

pres·by·o·pia \,prez-bē-'ō-pē-ə\ *n* : a visual condition in which loss of elasticity of the lens of the eye causes defective accommodation and inability to focus sharply for near vision — **pres·by·o·pic** \-'ō-pik, -'ä-\ *adj or n*

pres·by·ter \'prez-bə-tər\ *n* [LL, elder, priest, fr. Gk *presbyteros*, compar. of *presbys* elder, old man] **1** : PRIEST, MINISTER **2** : an elder in a Presbyterian church

¹**Pres·by·te·ri·an** \,prez-bə-'tir-ē-ən\ *n* : a member of a Presbyterian church

²**Presbyterian** *adj* **1** *often not cap* : characterized by a graded system of representative ecclesiastical bodies (as presbyteries) exercising legislative and judicial powers **2** : of or relating to a group of Protestant Christian bodies that are presbyterian in government — **Pres·by·te·ri·an·ism** \-ə,ni-zəm\ *n*

pres·by·tery \'prez-bə-,ter-ē\ *n, pl* **-ter·ies** **1** : the part of a church reserved for the officiating clergy **2** : a ruling body in Presbyterian churches consisting of the ministers and representative elders of a district

¹**pre·school** \'prē-,skül\ *adj* : of or relating to the period in a child's life from infancy to the age of five or six — **pre·school·er** \-,skü-lər\ *n*

²**preschool** *n* : NURSERY SCHOOL

pre·science \'pre-shəns, 'prē-\ *n* : foreknowledge of events; *also* : FORESIGHT — **pre·scient** \-shənt, -shē-ənt\ *adj*

pre·scribe \pri-'skrīb\ *vb* **pre·scribed; pre·scrib·ing** **1** : to lay down as a guide or rule of action **2** : to direct the use of (as a medicine) as a remedy

pre·scrip·tion \pri-'skrip-shən\ *n* **1** : the action of prescribing rules or directions **2** : a written direction for the preparation and use of a medicine; *also* : a medicine prescribed

pre·scrip·tive \pri-'skrip-tiv\ *adj* **1** : serving to prescribe ⟨~ rules⟩ **2** : acquired by, based on, or determined by prescription or by custom

pres·ence \'pre-z³ns\ *n* **1** : the fact or condition of being present **2** : the space immediately around a person **3** : one that is present **4** : the bearing of a person; *esp* : stately bearing

¹**pres·ent** \'pre-z³nt\ *n* : something presented : GIFT

²**pre·sent** \pri-'zent\ *vb* **1** : to bring into the presence or acquaintance of : INTRODUCE **2** : to bring before the public ⟨~ a play⟩ **3** : to make a gift to **4** : to give formally **5** : to lay (as a charge) before a court for inquiry **6** : to aim or direct (as a weapon) so as to face in a particular direction — **pre·sent·able** *adj* — **pre·sen·ta·tion** \,prē-,zen-'tā-shən, ,pre-z³n-\ *n* — **pre·sent·ment** \pri-'zent-mənt\ *n*

³**pres·ent** \'pre-z³nt\ *adj* **1** : now existing or in progress ⟨~ conditions⟩ **2** : being in view or at hand ⟨~ at the meeting⟩ **3** : under consideration ⟨the ~ problem⟩ **4** : of, relating to, or constituting a verb tense that expresses present time or the time of speaking

⁴**pres·ent** \'pre-z³nt\ *n* **1** *pl* : the present legal document **2** : the present tense; *also* : a verb form in it **3** : the present time

pres·ent–day \'pre-z³nt-'dā\ *adj* : now existing or occurring : CURRENT

pre·sen·ti·ment \pri-'zen-tə-mənt\ *n* : a feeling that something is about to happen : PREMONITION

pres·ent·ly \'pre-z³nt-lē\ *adv* **1** : SOON ⟨~ they arrived⟩ **2** : NOW ⟨~ busy⟩

present participle *n* : a participle that typically expresses present action and that in English is formed with the suffix *-ing* and is used in the formation of the progressive tenses

¹**pre·serve** \pri-'zərv\ *vb* **pre·served; pre·serv·ing** **1** : to keep safe : GUARD, PROTECT **2** : to keep from decaying; *esp* : to process food (as by canning or pickling) to prevent spoilage **3** : MAINTAIN ⟨~ silence⟩ — **pres·er·va·tion** \,pre-zər-'vā-shən\ *n* — **pre·ser·va·tive** \pri-'zər-və-tiv\ *adj or n* — **pre·serv·er** *n*

²**preserve** *n* **1** : preserved fruit — often used in pl. **2** : an area for the protection of natural resources (as animals)

pre·set \'prē-,set\ *vb* **-set; -set·ting** : to set beforehand — **preset** *n*

pre·shrink \prē-'shriŋk\ *vb* **-shrank** \-'shraŋk\; **-shrunk** \-'shrəŋk\ : to shrink (as a fabric) before making into a garment

pre·side \pri-'zīd\ *vb* **pre·sid·ed; pre·sid·ing** [L *praesidēre* to guard, preside over, fr. *prae* in front of + *sedēre* to sit] **1** : to exercise guidance or control **2** : to occupy the place of authority; *esp* : to act as chairman

pres·i·dent \'pre-zə-dənt\ *n* **1** : one chosen to preside ⟨~ of the assembly⟩ **2** : the chief officer of an organization (as a corporation or society) **3** : an elected official serving as both chief of state and chief political executive; *also* : a chief of state often with only minimal political powers — **pres·i·den·cy** \-dən-sē\ *n* — **pres·i·den·tial** \,pre-zə-'den-chəl\ *adj*

pre·si·dio \pri-'sē-dē-,ō, -'si-\ *n, pl* **-di·os** [Sp] : a military post or fortified settlement in an area currently or orig. under Spanish control

pre·sid·i·um \pri-'si-dē-əm\ *n, pl* **-ia** \-dē-ə\ *or* **-iums** [Russ *prezidium*, fr. L *praesidium* garrison] : a permanent executive committee that acts for a larger body in a Communist country

¹**pre·soak** \(,)prē-'sōk\ *vb* : to soak beforehand

²**pre·soak** \'prē-,sōk\ *n* **1** : an instance of presoaking **2** : a preparation used in presoaking clothes

pre·sort \(,)prē-'sòrt\ *vb* : to sort (mail) by zip code usu. before delivery to a post office

¹**press** \'pres\ *n* **1** : a crowded condition : THRONG **2** : a machine for exerting pressure **3** : CLOSET, CUPBOARD **4** : PRESSURE **5** : the properly creased condition of a freshly pressed garment **6** : PRINTING PRESS; *also* : the act or the process of printing **7** : a printing or publishing establishment **8** : the media (as newspapers and magazines) of public news and comment; *also* : persons (as reporters) employed in these media **9** : comment in newspapers and periodicals

²**press** *vb* **1** : to bear down upon : push steadily against **2** : ASSAIL, COMPEL **3** : to squeeze out the juice or contents of ⟨~ grapes⟩ **4** : to squeeze to a desired density, shape, or smoothness; *esp* : IRON **5** : to try hard to persuade : URGE **6** : to follow through : PROSECUTE **7** : CROWD **8** : to force one's way **9** : to require haste or speed in action — **press·er** *n*

press agent *n* : an agent employed to establish and maintain good public relations through publicity

press·ing *adj* : URGENT ⟨a ~ need⟩

press·man \'pres-mən, -,man\ *n* : the operator of a press and esp. a printing press

press·room \-,rüm, -,rùm\ *n* **1** : a room in a printing plant containing the printing presses **2** : a room for the use of reporters

¹**pres·sure** \'pre-shər\ *n* **1** : the burden of physical or mental distress **2** : the action of pressing; *esp* : the application of force to something by something else in direct contact with it **3** : the force exerted over a surface divided by its area **4** : the stress or urgency of matters demanding attention

²**pressure** *vb* **pres·sured; pres·sur·ing** : to apply pressure to

pressure group *n* : a group that seeks to influence governmental policy but not to elect candidates to office

pressure suit *n* : an inflatable suit for high-altitude flight or spaceflight to protect the body from low pressure

pres·sur·ise *Brit var of* PRESSURIZE

pres·sur·ize \'pre-shə-,rīz\ *vb* **-ized; -iz·ing** **1** : to maintain higher pressure within than without; *esp* : to maintain normal atmospheric pressure within (as an airplane cabin) during high-altitude flight or spaceflight **2** : to apply pressure to **3** : to design to withstand pressure — **pres·sur·i·za·tion** \,pre-shə-rə-'zā-shən\ *n*

pres·ti·dig·i·ta·tion \,pres-tə-,di-jə-'tā-shən\ *n* : SLEIGHT OF HAND

pres·tige \pres-'tēzh, -'tēj\ *n* [F, fr. MF, conjuror's trick, illusion, fr. LL *praestigium*, fr. L *praestigiae*, pl., conjuror's tricks, fr. *praestringere* to graze, blunt, constrict, fr. *prae-* in front of + *stringere* to bind tight] : standing or estimation in the eyes of people : REPUTATION ◆ *Synonyms* INFLUENCE, AUTHORITY, WEIGHT, CACHET

pres·ti·gious \-'ti-jəs, -'tē-\ *adj*

¹**pres·to** \'pres-tō\ *interj* [It, quick, quickly] — used to indicate the sudden appearance or occurrence of something

²**presto** *adv or adj* **1** : suddenly as if by magic : IMMEDIATELY **2** : at a rapid tempo — used as a direction in music

pre·stress \(ˌ)prē-'stres\ *vb* : to introduce internal stresses into (as a structural beam) to counteract later load stresses

pre·sum·ably \pri-'zü-mə-blē\ *adv* : by reasonable assumption

pre·sume \pri-'züm\ *vb* **pre·sumed; pre·sum·ing 1** : to take upon oneself without leave or warrant : DARE **2** : to take for granted : ASSUME **3** : to act or behave with undue boldness — **pre·sum·able** \-'zü-mə-bəl\ *adj*

pre·sump·tion \pri-'zəmp-shən\ *n* **1** : presumptuous attitude or conduct : AUDACITY **2** : an attitude or belief dictated by probability; *also* : the grounds lending probability to a belief — **pre·sump·tive** \-tiv\ *adj*

pre·sump·tu·ous \pri-'zəmp-chə-wəs\ *adj* : overstepping due bounds : taking liberties — **pre·sump·tu·ous·ly** *adv*

pre·sup·pose \ˌprē-sə-'pōz\ *vb* **1** : to suppose beforehand **2** : to require beforehand as a necessary condition — **pre·sup·po·si·tion** \(ˌ)prē-ˌsə-pə-'zi-shən\ *n*

pre·teen \'prē-'tēn\ *n* : a boy or girl not yet 13 years old — **preteen** *adj*

pre·tend \pri-'tend\ *vb* **1** : PROFESS ⟨doesn't ~ to be scientific⟩ **2** : FEIGN ⟨~ to be angry⟩ **3** : to lay claim ⟨~ to a throne⟩ — **pre·tend·er** *n*

pre·tense *or* **pre·tence** \'prē-ˌtens, pri-'tens\ *n* **1** : CLAIM; *esp* : one not supported by fact **2** : mere display : SHOW **3** : an attempt to attain a certain condition ⟨made a ~ at discipline⟩ **4** : false show : PRETEXT — **pre·ten·sion** \pri-'ten-chən\ *n*

pre·ten·tious \pri-'ten-chəs\ *adj* **1** : making or possessing usu. unjustified claims (as to excellence) ⟨a ~ literary style⟩ **2** : making demands on one's ability or means : AMBITIOUS ⟨too ~ an undertaking⟩ — **pre·ten·tious·ly** *adv* — **pre·ten·tious·ness** *n*

pret·er·it *or* **pret·er·ite** \'pre-tə-rət\ *n* : a verb form expressing action in the past

pre·term \(ˌ)prē-'tərm, 'prē-ˌ\ *adj* : of, relating to, being, or brought forth by premature birth ⟨a ~ infant⟩

pre·ter·nat·u·ral \ˌprē-tər-'na-chə-rəl\ *adj* **1** : exceeding what is natural **2** : inexplicable by ordinary means — **pre·ter·nat·u·ral·ly** *adv*

pre·text \'prē-ˌtekst\ *n* : a purpose stated or assumed to cloak the real intention or state of affairs

pret·ti·fy \'pri-ti-ˌfī\ *vb* **-fied; -fy·ing** : to make pretty — **pret·ti·fi·ca·tion** \ˌpri-ti-fə-'kā-shən\ *n*

pret·ty \'pri-tē\ *adj* **pret·ti·er; -est** [ME *praty, prety,* fr. OE *prættig* tricky, fr. *prætt* trick] **1** : pleasing by delicacy or grace : having conventionally accepted elements of beauty ⟨~ flowers⟩ **2** : MISERABLE, TERRIBLE ⟨a ~ state of affairs⟩ **3** : moderately large ⟨a ~ profit⟩ **4** : PLEASANT — usu. used in negative constructions ⟨the truth was not so ~⟩ ♦ **Synonyms** COMELY, FAIR, BEAUTIFUL, ATTRACTIVE, LOVELY — **pret·ti·ly** \-tə-lē\ *adv* — **pret·ti·ness** \-tē-nəs\ *n*

²**pretty** *adv* : in some degree : MODERATELY; *also* : QUITE, MAINLY

³**pretty** *vb* **pret·tied; pret·ty·ing** : to make pretty — usu. used with *up*

pretty boy *n* : a man who is notably good-looking

pret·zel \'pret-səl\ *n* [G *Brezel,* ultim. fr. L *brachiatus* having branches like arms, fr. *brachium* arm] : a brittle or chewy glazed usu. salted slender bread often shaped like a loose knot

prev *abbr* previous; previously

pre·vail \pri-'vāl\ *vb* **1** : to win mastery : TRIUMPH **2** : to be or become effective : SUCCEED **3** : to urge successfully ⟨~*ed* upon her to sing⟩ **4** : to be frequent : PREDOMINATE — **pre·vail·ing·ly** *adv*

prev·a·lent \'pre-və-lənt\ *adj* : generally or widely existent : WIDESPREAD — **prev·a·lence** \-ləns\ *n*

pre·var·i·cate \pri-'ver-ə-ˌkāt\ *vb* **-cat·ed; -cat·ing** [L *praevoricari* to act in collusion, lit., to straddle, fr. *prae* in front of + *varicare* to straddle, fr. *varus* bowlegged] : to deviate from the truth : EQUIVOCATE — **pre·var·i·ca·tion** \-ˌver-ə-'kā-shən\ *n* — **pre·var·i·ca·tor** \-'ver-ə-ˌkā-tər\ *n*

pre·vent \pri-'vent\ *vb* **1** : to keep from happening or existing ⟨steps to ~ war⟩ **2** : to hold back : HINDER, STOP

⟨~ us from going⟩ — **pre·vent·able** *also* **pre·vent·ible** \-'ven-tə-bəl\ *adj* — **pre·ven·tion** \-'ven-chən\ *n* — **pre·ven·tive** \-'ven-tiv\ *adj or n* — **pre·ven·ta·tive** \-'ven-tə-tiv\ *adj or n*

pre·ver·bal \ˌprē-'vər-bəl\ *adj* : having not yet acquired the faculty of speech

¹**pre·view** \'prē-ˌvyü\ *vb* : to see or discuss beforehand; *esp* : to view or show in advance of public presentation

²**preview** *n* **1** : FORETASTE **2** : an advance showing or viewing **3** *also* **pre·vue** \-ˌvyü\ : a showing of snatches from a motion picture advertised for future appearance

pre·vi·ous \'prē-vē-əs\ *adj* : going before : EARLIER, FORMER ♦ **Synonyms** FOREGOING, PRIOR, PRECEDING, ANTECEDENT — **pre·vi·ous·ly** *adv*

pre·vi·sion \prē-'vi-zhən\ *n* **1** : FORESIGHT, PRESCIENCE **2** : FORECAST, PREDICTION

pre·war \'prē-'wȯr\ *adj* : occurring or existing before a war

¹**prey** \'prā\ *n, pl* **prey** *also* **preys 1** : an animal taken for food by a predator; *also* : VICTIM **2** : the act or habit of preying

²**prey** *vb* **1** : to raid for booty **2** : to seize and devour prey **3** : to have a harmful or wearing effect

prf *abbr* proof

¹**price** \'prīs\ *n* **1** *archaic* : VALUE **2** : the amount of money paid or asked for the sale of a specified thing; *also* : the cost at which something is obtained

²**price** *vb* **priced; pric·ing 1** : to set a price on **2** : to ask the price of **3** : to drive by raising prices ⟨*priced* themselves out of the market⟩

price-fix·ing \'prīs-ˌfik-siŋ\ *n* : the setting of prices artificially (as by producers or government)

price·less \-ləs\ *adj* : having a value beyond any price : INVALUABLE ♦ **Synonyms** PRECIOUS, COSTLY, EXPENSIVE

price support *n* : artificial maintenance of prices of a commodity at a level usu. fixed through government action

price war *n* : a period of commercial competition in which prices are repeatedly cut by the competitors

pric·ey *also* **pricy** \'prī-sē\ *adj* **pric·i·er; -est** : EXPENSIVE

¹**prick** \'prik\ *n* **1** : a mark or small wound made by a pointed instrument **2** : something sharp or pointed **3** : an instance of pricking; *also* : a sensation of being pricked

²**prick** *vb* **1** : to pierce slightly with a sharp point; *also* : to have or cause a pricking sensation **2** : to affect with anguish or remorse ⟨~*s* his conscience⟩ **3** : to outline with punctures ⟨~ out a pattern⟩ **4** : to stand or cause to stand erect ⟨the dog's ears ~*ed* up at the sound⟩ ♦ **Synonyms** PUNCH, PUNCTURE, PERFORATE, BORE, DRILL

prick·er \'pri-kər\ *n* : BRIAR; *also* : THORN

¹**prick·le** \'pri-kəl\ *n* **1** : a small sharp process (as on a plant) **2** : a slight stinging pain — **prick·ly** \'pri-klē\ *adj*

²**prickle** *vb* **prick·led; prick·ling 1** : to prick lightly **2** : TINGLE

prickly heat *n* : a red cutaneous eruption with intense itching and tingling caused by inflammation around the ducts of the sweat glands

prickly pear *n* : any of numerous cacti with usu. yellow flowers and prickly flat or rounded joints; *also* : the sweet pulpy pear-shaped edible fruit of various prickly pears

¹**pride** \'prīd\ *n* **1** : CONCEIT **2** : justifiable self-respect **3** : elation over an act or possession **4** : haughty behavior : DISDAIN **5** : ostentatious display — **pride·ful** *adj*

²**pride** *vb* **prid·ed; prid·ing** : to indulge (as oneself) in pride

priest \'prēst\ *n* [ME *preist,* fr. OE *prēost,* ultim. fr. LL *presbyter* elder, priest, fr. Gk *presbyteros,* fr. compar. of *presbys* old man, elder] : a person having authority to perform the sacred rites of a religion; *esp* : a member of the Anglican, Eastern, or Roman Catholic clergy ranking below a bishop and above a deacon — **priest·hood** *n* — **priest·li·ness** *n* — **priest·ly** *adj*

priest·ess \'prēs-təs\ *n* : a woman authorized to perform the sacred rites of a religion

prig \'prig\ *n* : one who irritates by rigid or pointed observance of proprieties — **prig·gish** \'pri-gish\ *adj* — **prig·gish·ly** *adv*

¹**prim** \'prim\ *adj* **prim·mer; prim·mest** : stiffly formal and precise — **prim·ly** *adv* — **prim·ness** *n*

²**prim** *abbr* **1** primary **2** primitive

pri·ma·cy \'prī-mə-sē\ *n* **1** : the state of being first (as in rank) **2** : the office, rank, or character of an ecclesiastical primate

pri·ma don·na \ˌprī-mə-ˈdä-nə\ *n, pl* **prima donnas** [It, lit., first lady] **1** : a principal female singer (as in an opera company) **2** : a vain undisciplined usu. uncooperative person

pri·ma fa·cie \ˈprī-mə-ˈfā-shə, -sē, -shē\ *adj or adv* [L, at first view] **1** : based on immediate impression : APPARENT **2** : SELF-EVIDENT

pri·mal \ˈprī-məl\ *adj* **1** : ORIGINAL, PRIMITIVE **2** : first in importance

pri·mar·i·ly \prī-ˈmer-ə-lē\ *adv* **1** : FUNDAMENTALLY **2** : ORIGINALLY

¹pri·ma·ry \ˈprī-ˌmer-ē, -mə-rē\ *adj* **1** : first in order of time or development; *also* : present at the start **2** : of first rank or importance; *also* : FUNDAMENTAL **3** : not derived from or dependent on something else ⟨~ sources⟩

²primary *n, pl* **-ries** : a preliminary election in which voters nominate or express a preference among candidates usu. of their own party

primary care *n* : health care provided by a medical professional with whom a patient has initial contact

primary color *n* : any of a set of colors from which all other colors may be derived

primary school *n* **1** : a school usu. including grades 1-3 and sometimes kindergarten **2** : ELEMENTARY SCHOOL

pri·mate \ˈprī-ˌmāt *or esp for 1* -mət\ *n* **1** *often cap* : the highest-ranking bishop of a province or nation **2** : any of an order of mammals including humans, apes, and monkeys

¹prime \ˈprīm\ *n* **1** : the earliest stage of something; *esp* : SPRINGTIME **2** : the most active, thriving, or successful stage or period (as of one's life) **3** : the best individual; *also* : the best part of something **4** : any integer other than 0, +1, or −1 that is not divisible without remainder by any integer except +1, −1, and plus or minus itself; *esp* : any such integer that is positive

²prime *adj* **1** : standing first (as in time, rank, significance, or quality) ⟨~ requisite⟩ **2** : of, relating to, or being a number that is prime

³prime *vb* **primed; prim·ing** **1** : FILL, LOAD **2** : to lay a preparatory coating upon (as in painting) **3** : to put in working condition **4** : to instruct beforehand : COACH

prime meridian *n* : the meridian of 0° longitude which runs through Greenwich, England, and from which other longitudes are reckoned east and west

prime minister *n* **1** : the chief minister of a ruler or state **2** : the chief executive of a parliamentary government

¹prim·er \ˈpri-mər\ *n* [ME, layperson's prayer book, fr. AF, fr. ML *primarium*, fr. LL, neut. of *primarius* primary] **1** : a small book for teaching children to read **2** : a small introductory book on a subject **3** : a short informative piece of writing

²prim·er \ˈprī-mər\ *n* : one that primes **2** : a device for igniting an explosive **3** : material for priming a surface

prime rate *n* : an interest rate announced by a bank to be the lowest available to its most credit-worthy customers

prime time *n* **1** : the time period when the television or radio audience is largest; *also* : television shows aired in prime time **2** : the choicest or busiest time

pri·me·val \prī-ˈmē-vəl\ *adj* : of or relating to the earliest ages : PRIMITIVE

¹prim·i·tive \ˈpri-mə-tiv\ *adj* **1** : ORIGINAL, PRIMARY **2** : of, relating to, or characteristic of an early stage of development or evolution **3** : ELEMENTAL, NATURAL **4** : of, relating to, or produced by a tribal people or culture **5** : SELF-TAUGHT; *also* : produced by a self-taught artist — **prim·i·tive·ly** *adv* — **prim·i·tive·ness** *n* — **prim·i·tiv·i·ty** \ˌpri-mə-ˈti-və-tē\ *n*

²primitive *n* **1** : something primitive **2** : a primitive artist **3** : a member of a primitive people

prim·i·tiv·ism \ˈpri-mə-ti-ˌvi-zəm\ *n* **1** : primitive practices or procedures; *also* : a primitive quality or state **2** : belief in the superiority of a simple way of life close to nature **3** : the style of art of primitive peoples or primitive artists

pri·mo·gen·i·tor \ˌprī-mō-ˈje-nə-tər\ *n* : ANCESTOR, FOREFATHER

pri·mo·gen·i·ture \-ˈje-nə-ˌchùr\ *n* **1** : the state of being the firstborn of a family **2** : an exclusive right of inheritance belonging to the eldest son

pri·mor·di·al \prī-ˈmȯr-dē-əl\ *adj* : first created or developed : existing in its original state : PRIMEVAL

primp \ˈprimp\ *vb* : to dress in a careful or finicky manner

prim·rose \ˈprim-ˌrōz\ *n* : any of a genus of perennial herbs with large leaves arranged at the base of the stem and clusters of showy flowers

prin *abbr* **1** principal **2** principle

prince \ˈprins\ *n* [ME, fr. AF, fr. L *princeps* leader, initiator, fr. *primus* first + *capere* to take] **1** : MONARCH, KING **2** : a male member of a royal family; *esp* : a son of the monarch **3** : a person of high standing (as in a class) — **prince·dom** \-dəm\ *n* — **prince·ly** *adj*

prince·ling \-liŋ\ *n* : a petty prince

prin·cess \ˈprin-səs, -ˌses\ *n* **1** : a female member of a royal family **2** : the consort of a prince

¹prin·ci·pal \ˈprin-sə-pəl\ *adj* : most important — **prin·ci·pal·ly** *adv*

²principal *n* **1** : a leading person (as in a play) **2** : the chief officer of an educational institution **3** : the person from whom an agent's authority derives **4** : a capital sum earning interest or used as a fund

prin·ci·pal·i·ty \ˌprin-sə-ˈpa-lə-tē\ *n, pl* **-ties** : the position, territory, or jurisdiction of a prince

principal parts *n pl* : the inflected forms of a verb

prin·ci·ple \ˈprin-sə-pəl\ *n* **1** : a general or fundamental law, doctrine, or assumption **2** : a rule or code of conduct; *also* : devotion to such a code **3** : the laws or facts of nature underlying the working of an artificial device **4** : a primary source : ORIGIN; *also* : an underlying faculty or endowment **5** : the active part (as of a drug)

prin·ci·pled \-pəld\ *adj* : exhibiting, based on, or characterized by principle ⟨high-*principled*⟩

prink \ˈpriŋk\ *vb* : PRIMP

¹print \ˈprint\ *n* [ME *prente*, fr. AF, fr. *preint, prient*, pp. of *priendre* to press, fr. L. *premere*] **1** : a mark made by pressure **2** : something stamped with an impression **3** : printed state or form **4** : printed matter **5** : a copy made by printing **6** : cloth with a pattern applied by printing

²print *vb* **1** : to stamp (as a mark) in or on something **2** : to produce impressions of (as from type) **3** : to write in letters like those of printer's type **4** : to make a (positive picture) from a photographic negative

print·able \ˈprin-tə-bəl\ *adj* **1** : capable of being printed or of being printed from **2** : worthy or fit to be published

print·er \ˈprin-tər\ *n* : one that prints; *esp* : a device that produces printout

print·ing *n* **1** : reproduction in printed form **2** : the art, practice, or business of a printer **3** : IMPRESSION 5

printing press *n* : a machine that produces printed copies

print·out \ˈprint-ˌaùt\ *n* : a printed output produced by a computer — **print out** *vb*

¹pri·or \ˈpr(ī)-ər\ *n* : the superior ranking next to the abbot or abbess of a religious house

²prior *adj* **1** : earlier in time or order **2** : taking precedence logically or in importance — **pri·or·i·ty** \prī-ˈȯr-ə-tē\ *n*

pri·or·ess \ˈprī-ə-rəs\ *n* : a nun corresponding in rank to a prior

pri·or·i·tize \prī-ˈȯr-ə-ˌtīz, ˈprī-ə-rə-ˌtīz\ *vb* **-tized; -tiz·ing** : to list or rate in order of priority

prior to *prep* : in advance of : BEFORE

pri·o·ry \ˈprī-ə-rē\ *n, pl* **-ries** : a religious house under a prior or prioress

prise *chiefly Brit var of* ⁵PRIZE

prism \ˈpri-zəm\ *n* [LL *prisma*, fr. Gk, lit., something sawed, fr. *priein* to saw] **1** : a solid whose sides are parallelograms and whose ends are parallel and alike in shape and size **2** : a usu. 3-sided transparent object that refracts light so that it breaks up into rainbow colors — **pris·mat·ic** \priz-ˈma-tik\ *adj*

pris·on \ˈpri-zᵊn\ *n* : a place or state of confinement esp. for criminals

pris·on·er \ˈpri-zᵊn-ər\ *n* : a person deprived of liberty; *esp* : one on trial or in prison

prisoner of war : a person captured in war

pris·sy \ˈpri-sē\ *adj* **pris·si·er; -est** : being overly prim and precise : PRIGGISH — **pris·si·ness** \-sē-nəs\ *n*

pris·tine \ˈpris-ˌtēn, pris-ˈtēn\ *adj* **1** : PRIMITIVE **2** : having the purity of its original state : UNSPOILED

prith·ee \'pri-<u>th</u>ē\ *interj, archaic* — used to express a wish or request

pri·va·cy \'prī-və-sē\ *n, pl* **-cies** 1 : the quality or state of being apart from others 2 : SECRECY

¹**pri·vate** \'prī-vət\ *adj* 1 : belonging to or intended for a particular individual or group ⟨~ property⟩ 2 : restricted to the individual : PERSONAL ⟨~ opinion⟩ 3 : carried on by the individual independently ⟨~ study⟩ 4 : not holding public office ⟨a ~ citizen⟩ 5 : withdrawn from company or observation ⟨a ~ place⟩ 6 : not known publicly ⟨~ dealings⟩ — **pri·vate·ly** *adv*

²**private** *n* : an enlisted man of the lowest rank in the marine corps or of one of the two lowest ranks in the army — **in private** : not openly or in public

pri·va·teer \ˌprī-və-'tir\ *n* : an armed private ship licensed to attack enemy shipping; *also* : a sailor on such a ship

private first class *n* : an enlisted man ranking next below a corporal in the army and next below a lance corporal in the marine corps

pri·va·tion \prī-'vā-shən\ *n* 1 : DEPRIVATION 1 2 : the state of being deprived; *esp* : lack of what is needed for existence

priv·et \'pri-vət\ *n* : a nearly evergreen shrub related to the olive and widely used for hedges

privet: branch and hedge

¹**priv·i·lege** \'priv-lij, 'pri-və-\ *n* [ME, fr. AF, fr. L *privilegium* law for or against a private person, fr. *privus* private + *leg-, lex* law] : a right or immunity granted as an advantage or favor esp. to some and not others

²**privilege** *vb* **-leged; -leg·ing** 1 : to grant a privilege to 2 : to accord a higher value to : FAVOR

privileged *adj* 1 : having or enjoying one or more privileges ⟨~ classes⟩ 2 : not subject to disclosure in a court of law ⟨a ~ communication⟩

¹**privy** \'pri-vē\ *adj* 1 : PERSONAL, PRIVATE 2 : SECRET 3 : admitted as one sharing in a secret ⟨~ to the conspiracy⟩ — **priv·i·ly** \'pri-və-lē\ *adv*

²**privy** *n, pl* **priv·ies** : TOILET; *esp* : OUTHOUSE

¹**prize** \'prīz\ *n* 1 : something offered or striven for in competition or in contests of chance 2 : something exceptionally desirable

²**prize** *adj* 1 : awarded or worthy of a prize ⟨a ~ essay⟩; *also* : awarded as a prize ⟨a ~ medal⟩ 2 : OUTSTANDING

³**prize** *vb* **prized; priz·ing** : to value highly : ESTEEM ⟨a prized possession⟩

⁴**prize** *n* : property (as a ship) lawfully captured in time of war

⁵**prize** *vb* **prized; priz·ing** : PRY

prize·fight \'prīz-ˌfīt\ *n* : a professional boxing match — **prize·fight·er** *n* — **prize·fight·ing** *n*

prize·win·ner \-ˌwi-nər\ *n* : a winner of a prize — **prize·win·ning** *adj*

¹**pro** \'prō\ *n, pl* **pros** : a favorable argument, person, or position

²**pro** *adv* : in favor of : FOR

³**pro** *n or adj* : PROFESSIONAL

PRO *abbr* public relations officer

pro·ac·tive \prō-'ak-tiv\ *adj* : acting in anticipation of future problems or needs — **pro·ac·tive·ly** *adv*

pro–am \'prō-'am\ *adj* : involving professionals competing alongside or against amateurs ⟨a ~ tournament⟩ — **pro–am** *n*

prob *abbr* 1 probable; probably 2 problem

prob·a·bil·i·ty \ˌprä-bə-'bi-lə-tē\ *n, pl* **-ties** 1 : the quality or state of being probable 2 : something probable 3 : a measure of how often a particular event will occur if something (as tossing a coin) is done repeatedly which results in any of a number of possible events

prob·a·ble \'prä-bə-bəl\ *adj* 1 : apparently or presumably true ⟨a ~ hypothesis⟩ 2 : likely to be or become true or real ⟨a ~ result⟩ — **prob·a·bly** \-bə-blē\ *adv*

¹**pro·bate** \'prō-ˌbāt\ *n* : the judicial determination of the validity of a will

²**pro·bate** *vb* **pro·bat·ed; pro·bat·ing** : to establish (a will) by probate as genuine and valid

pro·ba·tion \prō-'bā-shən\ *n* 1 : subjection of an individual to a period of testing and trial to ascertain fitness (as for a job) 2 : the action of giving a convicted offender freedom during good behavior under the supervision of a probation officer — **pro·ba·tion·ary** \-shə-ˌner-ē\ *adj*

pro·ba·tion·er \-shə-nər\ *n* 1 : a person (as a newly admitted student nurse) whose fitness is being tested during a trial period 2 : a convicted offender on probation

pro·ba·tive \'prō-bə-tiv\ *adj* 1 : serving to test or try 2 : serving to prove

¹**probe** \'prōb\ *n* 1 : a slender instrument for examining a cavity (as a wound) 2 : an information-gathering device sent into outer space 3 : a penetrating investigation ♦ **Synonyms** INQUIRY, INQUEST, RESEARCH, INQUISITION

²**probe** *vb* **probed; prob·ing** 1 : to examine with a probe 2 : to investigate thoroughly

pro·bi·ty \'prō-bə-tē\ *n* : UPRIGHTNESS, HONESTY

prob·lem \'prä-bləm\ *n* 1 : a question raised for consideration or solution 2 : an intricate unsettled question 3 : a source of perplexity or vexation — **problem** *adj*

prob·lem·at·ic \ˌprä-blə-'ma-tik\ *also* **prob·lem·at·i·cal** \-ti-kəl\ *adj* 1 : difficult to solve or decide : PUZZLING 2 : DUBIOUS, QUESTIONABLE

pro·bos·cis \prə-'bä-səs, -'bäs-kəs\ *n, pl* **-bos·cis·es** *also* **-bos·ci·des** \-'bä-sə-ˌdēz\ [L, fr. Gk *proboskis*, fr. *pro-* before + *boskein* to feed] : a long flexible snout (as the trunk of an elephant)

proc *abbr* proceedings

pro·caine \'prō-ˌkān\ *n* : a drug used esp. as a local anesthetic

pro·ce·dure \prə-'sē-jər\ *n* 1 : a particular way of doing something ⟨democratic ~⟩ 2 : a series of steps followed in a regular order ⟨a surgical ~⟩ — **pro·ce·dur·al** \-'sē-jə-rəl\ *adj*

pro·ceed \prō-'sēd\ *vb* 1 : to come forth : ISSUE 2 : to go on in an orderly way; *also* : CONTINUE 3 : to begin and carry on an action 4 : to take legal action 5 : to go forward : ADVANCE

pro·ceed·ing *n* 1 : PROCEDURE 2 *pl* : DOINGS 3 *pl* : legal action 4 : TRANSACTION 5 *pl* : an official record of things said or done

pro·ceeds \'prō-ˌsēdz\ *n pl* : the total amount or the profit arising from a business deal : RETURN

¹**pro·cess** \'prä-ˌses, 'prō-\ *n, pl* **pro·cess·es** \-ˌse-səz, -sə-səz, -sə-ˌsēz\ 1 : PROGRESS, ADVANCE 2 : something going on : PROCEEDING 3 : a natural phenomenon marked by gradual changes that lead toward a particular result ⟨the ~ of growth⟩ 4 : a series of actions or operations directed toward a particular result ⟨a manufacturing ~⟩ 5 : legal action 6 : a mandate issued by a court; *esp* : SUMMONS 7 : a projecting part of an organism or organic structure

²**process** *vb* : to subject to a special process

pro·ces·sion \prə-'se-shən\ *n* : a group of individuals moving along in an orderly often ceremonial way

pro·ces·sion·al \-'se-shə-nəl\ *n* 1 : music for a procession 2 : a ceremonial procession

pro·ces·sor \'prä-ˌse-sər, 'prō-\ *n* 1 : one that processes 2 : CPU

pro–choice \(ˌ)prō-'chȯis\ *adj* : favoring the legalization of abortion

pro·claim \prō-'klām\ *vb* : to make known publicly : DECLARE

proc·la·ma·tion \ˌprä-klə-'mā-shən\ *n* : an official public announcement

pro·cliv·i·ty \prō-'kli-və-tē\ *n, pl* **-ties** : an inherent inclination esp. toward something objectionable

pro·con·sul \-'kän-səl\ *n* 1 : a governor or military commander of an ancient Roman province 2 : an adminis-

trator in a modern colony or occupied area — **pro·con·su·lar** \-sə-lər\ *adj*
pro·cras·ti·nate \prə-'kras-tə-ˌnāt, prō-\ *vb* **-nat·ed; -nat·ing** [L *procrastinare*, fr. *pro-* forward + *crastinus* of tomorrow, fr. *cras* tomorrow] **:** to put off usu. habitually doing something that should be done ✦ *Synonyms* DAWDLE, DELAY — **pro·cras·ti·na·tion** \-ˌkras-tə-'nā-shən\ *n* — **pro·cras·ti·na·tor** \-'kras-tə-ˌnā-tər\ *n*
pro·cre·ate \'prō-krē-ˌāt\ *vb* **-at·ed; -at·ing :** to beget or bring forth offspring ✦ *Synonyms* REPRODUCE, BREED, GENERATE, PROPAGATE — **pro·cre·ation** \ˌprō-krē-'ā-shən\ *n* — **pro·cre·ative** \'prō-krē-ˌā-tiv\ *adj* — **pro·cre·ator** \-ˌā-tər\ *n*
pro·crus·te·an \prə-'krəs-tē-ən\ *adj, often cap* [fr. *Procrustes*, villain of Greek mythology who made victims fit his bed by stretching them or cutting off their legs] **:** marked by arbitrary often ruthless disregard of individual differences or special circumstances
proc·tor \'präk-tər\ *n* **:** one appointed to supervise students (as at an examination) — **proctor** *vb* — **proc·to·ri·al** \präk-'tȯr-ē-əl\ *adj*
proc·u·ra·tor \'prä-kyə-ˌrā-tər\ *n* **:** a Roman provincial administrator
pro·cure \prə-'kyu̇r\ *vb* **pro·cured; pro·cur·ing** **1 :** to get possession of **:** OBTAIN **2 :** to make women available for promiscuous sexual intercourse **3 :** ACHIEVE ✦ *Synonyms* SECURE, ACQUIRE, GAIN, WIN, EARN — **pro·cur·able** \-'kyu̇r-ə-bəl\ *adj* — **pro·cure·ment** *n* — **pro·cur·er** *n*
¹prod \'präd\ *vb* **prod·ded; prod·ding** **1 :** to thrust a pointed instrument into **:** GOAD **2 :** INCITE, STIR — **prod** *n*
²prod *abbr* product; production
prod·i·gal \'pri-di-gəl\ *adj* **1 :** recklessly extravagant; *also* **:** LUXURIANT **2 :** WASTEFUL, LAVISH ✦ *Synonyms* PROFUSE, LUSH, OPULENT — **prodigal** *n* — **prod·i·gal·i·ty** \ˌprä-də-'ga-lə-tē\ *n*
pro·di·gious \prə-'di-jəs\ *adj* **1 :** exciting wonder **2 :** extraordinary in size or degree **:** ENORMOUS ✦ *Synonyms* MONSTROUS, TREMENDOUS, STUPENDOUS, MONUMENTAL — **pro·di·gious·ly** *adv*
prod·i·gy \'prä-də-jē\ *n, pl* **-gies** **1 :** something extraordinary **:** WONDER **2 :** a highly talented child
¹pro·duce \prə-'düs, -'dyüs\ *vb* **pro·duced; pro·duc·ing** **1 :** to present to view **:** EXHIBIT **2 :** to give birth or rise to **:** YIELD **3 :** EXTEND, PROLONG **4 :** to give being or form to **:** BRING ABOUT, MAKE; *esp* **:** MANUFACTURE **5 :** to sponsor or oversee the making of **6 :** to cause to accrue ⟨~ a profit⟩ — **pro·duc·er** *n*
²pro·duce \'prä-(ˌ)düs, 'prō- *also* -(ˌ)dyüs\ *n* **:** PRODUCT 2; *also* **:** agricultural products and esp. fresh fruits and vegetables
prod·uct \'prä-(ˌ)dəkt\ *n* **1 :** the number resulting from multiplication **2 :** something produced
pro·duc·tion \prə-'dək-shən\ *n* **1 :** something produced **:** PRODUCT **2 :** the act or process of producing — **pro·duc·tive** \-'dək-tiv\ *adj* — **pro·duc·tive·ness** *n* — **pro·duc·tiv·i·ty** \(ˌ)prō-ˌdək-'ti-və-tē, ˌprä-(ˌ)dək-\ *n*
product placement *n* **:** the inclusion of a product in a television program or film as a means of advertising
pro·em \'prō-ˌem\ *n* **1 :** preliminary comment **:** PREFACE **2 :** PRELUDE
¹prof \'präf\ *n* **:** PROFESSOR
²prof *abbr* professional
¹pro·fane \prō-'fān\ *vb* **pro·faned; pro·fan·ing** **1 :** to treat (something sacred) with irreverence or contempt **2 :** to debase by an unworthy use — **prof·a·na·tion** \ˌprä-fə-'nā-shən\ *n*
²profane *adj* [ME *prophane*, fr. MF, fr. L *profanus*, fr. *pro-* before + *fanum* temple] **1 :** not concerned with religion **:** SECULAR **2 :** not holy because unconsecrated, impure, or defiled **3 :** serving to debase what is holy **:** IRREVERENT **4 :** OBSCENE, VULGAR — **pro·fane·ly** *adv* — **pro·fane·ness** *n*
pro·fan·i·ty \prō-'fa-nə-tē\ *n, pl* **-ties** **1 :** the quality or state of being profane **2 :** the use of profane language **3 :** profane language
pro·fess \prə-'fes\ *vb* **1 :** to declare or admit openly **:** AFFIRM **2 :** to declare in words only **:** PRETEND **3 :** to confess one's faith in **4 :** to practice or claim to be versed in (a calling or occupation) — **pro·fess·ed·ly** \-'fe-səd-lē\ *adv*

pro·fes·sion \prə-'fe-shən\ *n* **1 :** an open declaration or avowal of a belief or opinion **2 :** a calling requiring specialized knowledge and often long academic preparation **3 :** the whole body of persons engaged in a calling
¹pro·fes·sion·al \prə-'fe-shə-nəl\ *adj* **1 :** of, relating to, or characteristic of a profession **2 :** engaged in one of the professions **3 :** participating for gain in an activity often engaged in by amateurs — **pro·fes·sion·al·ly** *adv*
²professional *n* **:** one that engages in an activity professionally
pro·fes·sion·al·ism \-nə-ˌli-zəm\ *n* **1 :** the conduct, aims, or qualities that characterize or mark a profession or a professional person **2 :** the following of a profession (as athletics) for gain or livelihood
pro·fes·sion·al·ize \-nə-ˌlīz\ *vb* **-ized; -iz·ing :** to give a professional nature to
pro·fes·sor \prə-'fe-sər\ *n* **:** a teacher at a university or college; *esp* **:** a faculty member of the highest academic rank — **pro·fes·so·ri·al** \ˌprō-fə-'sȯr-ē-əl, ˌprä-\ *adj* — **pro·fes·sor·ship** *n*
prof·fer \'prä-fər\ *vb* **prof·fered; prof·fer·ing :** to present for acceptance **:** OFFER — **proffer** *n*
pro·fi·cient \prə-'fi-shənt\ *adj* **:** well advanced in an art, occupation, or branch of knowledge ✦ *Synonyms* ADEPT, SKILLFUL, EXPERT, MASTERFUL, MASTERLY — **pro·fi·cien·cy** \-shən-sē\ *n* — **proficient** *n* — **pro·fi·cient·ly** *adv*
¹pro·file \'prō-ˌfī(-ə)l\ *n* [It *profilo*, fr. *profilare* to draw in outline, fr. *pro-* forward (fr. L) + *filare* to spin, fr. LL, fr. L *filum* thread] **1 :** a representation of something in outline; *esp* **:** a human head seen in side view **2 :** a concise biographical sketch **3 :** degree or level of public exposure ⟨keep a low ~⟩
²profile *vb* **pro·filed; pro·fil·ing :** to write or draw a profile of
profiling *n* **:** the act of suspecting or targeting a person solely on the basis of observed characteristics or behavior ⟨racial ~⟩
¹prof·it \'prä-fət\ *n* **1 :** a valuable return **:** GAIN **2 :** the excess of the selling price of goods over their cost — **prof·it·less** *adj*
²profit *vb* **1 :** to be of use **:** BENEFIT **2 :** to derive benefit **:** GAIN — **prof·it·able** \'prä-fə-tə-bəl\ *adj* — **prof·it·ably** \-blē\ *adv*
prof·i·teer \ˌprä-fə-'tir\ *n* **:** one who makes what is considered an unreasonable profit — **profiteer** *vb*
prof·li·gate \'prä-fli-gət, -flə-ˌgāt\ *adj* **1 :** completely given up to dissipation and licentiousness **2 :** wildly extravagant — **prof·li·ga·cy** \-gə-sē\ *n* — **profligate** *n* — **prof·li·gate·ly** *adv*
pro for·ma \(ˌ)prō-'fȯr-mə\ *adj* **:** done or existing as a matter of form
pro·found \prə-'fau̇nd, prō-\ *adj* **1 :** marked by intellectual depth or insight ⟨a ~ thought⟩ **2 :** coming from or reaching to a depth ⟨a ~ sigh⟩ **3 :** deeply felt **:** INTENSE ⟨~ sympathy⟩ — **pro·found·ly** *adv* — **pro·fun·di·ty** \-'fən-də-tē\ *n*
pro·fuse \prə-'fyüs, prō-\ *adj* **:** pouring forth liberally **:** ABUNDANT ⟨~ bleeding⟩ ✦ *Synonyms* LAVISH, PRODIGAL, LUXURIANT, EXUBERANT — **pro·fuse·ly** *adv* — **pro·fu·sion** \-'fyü-zhən\ *n*
prog *abbr* program
pro·gen·i·tor \prō-'je-nə-tər\ *n* **1 :** a direct ancestor **:** FOREFATHER **2 :** ORIGINATOR, PRECURSOR
prog·e·ny \'prä-jə-nē\ *n, pl* **-nies** **:** OFFSPRING, CHILDREN, DESCENDANTS
pro·ges·ter·one \prō-'jes-tə-ˌrōn\ *n* **:** a female hormone that causes the uterus to undergo changes so as to provide a suitable environment for a fertilized egg
prog·na·thous \'präg-nə-thəs\ *adj* **:** having the lower jaw projecting beyond the upper part of the face
prog·no·sis \präg-'nō-səs\ *n, pl* **-no·ses** \-ˌsēz\ **1 :** the prospect of recovery from disease **2 :** FORECAST
¹prog·nos·tic \präg-'näs-tik\ *n* **1 :** PORTENT **2 :** PROPHECY
²prognostic *adj* **:** of, relating to, or serving as ground for prognostication or a prognosis
prog·nos·ti·cate \präg-'näs-tə-ˌkāt\ *vb* **-cat·ed; -cat·ing :** to foretell from signs or symptoms — **prog·nos·ti·ca·tion** \-ˌnäs-tə-'kā-shən\ *n* — **prog·nos·ti·ca·tor** \-'näs-tə-ˌkā-tər\ *n*

program • pronged

396

¹pro·gram \'prō-ˌgram, -grəm\ *n* [F *programme* agenda, public notice, fr. Gk *programma*, fr. *prographein* to write in advance, fr. *pro-* before + *graphein* to write] **1** : a brief outline of the order to be pursued or the subjects included (as in a public entertainment); *also* : PERFORMANCE **2** : a plan of procedure esp. toward a goal **3** : coded instructions for a computer — **pro·gram·mat·ic** \ˌprō-grə-'ma-tik\ *adj*

²program *also* **programme** *vb* **-grammed** *or* **-gramed; -gram·ming** *or* **-gram·ing** **1** : to arrange or furnish a program of or for **2** : to enter in a program **3** : to provide (as a computer) with a program — **pro·gram·ma·bil·i·ty** \(ˌ)prō-ˌgra-mə-'bi-lə-tē\ *n* — **pro·gram·ma·ble** \'prō-ˌgra-mə-bəl\ *adj* — **pro·gram·mer** *also* **pro·gram·er** \'prō-ˌgra-mər, -grə-\ *n*

programme *chiefly Brit var of* PROGRAM

programmed instruction *n* : instruction through information given in small steps with each requiring a correct response by the learner before going on to the next step

pro·gram·ming *also* **pro·gram·ing** *n* **1** : the planning, scheduling, or performing of a program **2** : the process of instructing or learning by means of an instruction program **3** : the process of preparing an instruction program

¹prog·ress \'prä-grəs, -ˌgres\ *n* **1** : a forward movement : ADVANCE **2** : a gradual betterment

²pro·gress \prə-'gres\ *vb* **1** : to move forward : PROCEED **2** : to develop to a more advanced stage : IMPROVE

pro·gres·sion \prə-'gre-shən\ *n* **1** : an act of progressing : ADVANCE **2** : a continuous and connected series

¹pro·gres·sive \prə-'gre-siv\ *adj* **1** : of, relating to, or characterized by progress ⟨a ∼ city⟩ **2** : moving forward or onward : ADVANCING **3** : increasing in extent or severity ⟨a ∼ disease⟩ **4** *often cap* : of or relating to political Progressives **5** : of, relating to, or constituting a verb form that expresses action in progress at the time of speaking or a time spoken of — **pro·gres·sive·ly** *adv*

²progressive *n* **1** : one that is progressive **2** : a person believing in moderate political change and social improvement by government action; *esp, cap* : a member of a Progressive Party in the U.S.

pro·hib·it \prō-'hi-bət\ *vb* **1** : to forbid by authority **2** : to prevent from doing something

pro·hi·bi·tion \ˌprō-ə-'bi-shən\ *n* **1** : the act of prohibiting **2** : the forbidding by law of the sale or manufacture of alcoholic beverages — **pro·hi·bi·tion·ist** \-'bi-shə-nist\ *n* — **pro·hib·i·tive** \prō-'hi-bə-tiv\ *adj* — **pro·hib·i·tive·ly** *adv* — **pro·hib·i·to·ry** \-'hi-bə-ˌtòr-ē\ *adj*

¹proj·ect \'prä-ˌjekt, -jikt\ *n* **1** : a specific plan or design : SCHEME **2** : a planned undertaking ⟨a research ∼⟩

²pro·ject \prə-'jekt\ *vb* **1** : to devise in the mind : DESIGN **2** : to throw forward **3** : PROTRUDE **4** : to cause (light or shadow) to fall into space or (an image) to fall on a surface ⟨∼ a beam of light⟩ **5** : to attribute (a thought, feeling, or personal characteristic) to a person, group, or object **6** : to display outwardly — **pro·jec·tion** \-'jek-shən\ *n*

pro·jec·tile \prə-'jek-t³l, -'jek-tī(-ə)l\ *n* **1** : a body hurled or projected by external force; *esp* : a missile for a firearm **2** : a self-propelling weapon

pro·jec·tion·ist \prə-'jek-shə-nist\ *n* : one that operates a motion-picture projector or television equipment

pro·jec·tor \-'jek-tər\ *n* : one that projects; *esp* : a device for projecting pictures on a screen

pro·lapse \prō-'laps, 'prō-ˌ\ *n* : the falling down or slipping of a body part from its usual position

pro·le·gom·e·non \ˌprō-li-'gä-mə-ˌnän, -nən\ *n, pl* **-e·na** \-nə\ : prefatory remarks

pro·le·tar·i·an \ˌprō-lə-'ter-ē-ən\ *n* [L *proletarius* belonging to the lowest class of citizens, fr. *proles* progeny, fr. *proforth* + *-oles* (akin to *alere* to nourish)] : a member of the proletariat — **proletarian** *adj*

pro·le·tar·i·at \-ē-ət\ *n* : the laboring class; *esp* : industrial workers who sell their labor to live

pro–life \(ˌ)prō-'līf\ *n* : ANTIABORTION

pro·lif·er·ate \prə-'li-fə-ˌrāt\ *vb* **-at·ed; -at·ing** : to grow or increase by rapid production of new units (as cells, offspring, or nuclear weapons) — **pro·lif·er·a·tion** \-ˌli-fə-'rā-shən\ *n*

pro·lif·ic \prə-'li-fik\ *adj* **1** : producing young or fruit

abundantly **2** : marked by abundant inventiveness or productivity ⟨a ∼ writer⟩ — **pro·lif·i·cal·ly** \-fi-k(ə-)lē\ *adv*

pro·lix \prō-'liks, 'prō-ˌliks\ *adj* : VERBOSE ♦ **Synonyms** WORDY, DIFFUSE, REDUNDANT — **pro·lix·i·ty** \prō-'lik-sə-tē\ *n*

pro·logue *also* **pro·log** \'prō-ˌlòg, -ˌläg\ *n* : PREFACE ⟨∼ of a play⟩

pro·long \prə-'lòŋ\ *vb* **1** : to lengthen in time : CONTINUE ⟨∼ a meeting⟩ **2** : to lengthen in extent or range ♦ **Synonyms** PROTRACT, EXTEND, ELONGATE, STRETCH — **pro·lon·ga·tion** \ˌprō-ˌlòŋ-'gä-shən\ *n*

prom \'präm\ *n* : a formal dance given by a high school or college class

¹prom·e·nade \ˌprä-mə-'nād, -'näd\ *vb* **-nad·ed; -nad·ing** **1** : to take a promenade **2** : to walk about in or on

²promenade *n* [F, fr. *promener* to take for a walk, fr. MF, alter. of OF *pourmener*, fr. *pour-* completely (fr. L *pro-*) + *mener* to lead, fr. LL *minare* to drive, fr. L *minari* to threaten] **1** : a place for strolling **2** : a leisurely walk for pleasure or display **3** : an opening grand march at a formal ball

pro·me·thi·um \prə-'mē-thē-əm\ *n* : a metallic chemical element obtained from uranium or neodymium

prom·i·nence \'prä-mə-nəns\ *n* **1** : something prominent **2** : the quality, state, or fact of being prominent or conspicuous **3** : a mass of cloudlike gas that arises from the sun's chromosphere

prom·i·nent \-nənt\ *adj* **1** : jutting out : PROJECTING **2** : readily noticeable : CONSPICUOUS **3** : DISTINGUISHED, EMINENT ♦ **Synonyms** REMARKABLE, OUTSTANDING, STRIKING, SALIENT — **prom·i·nent·ly** *adv*

pro·mis·cu·ous \prə-'mis-kyə-wəs\ *adj* **1** : consisting of various sorts and kinds : MIXED **2** : not restricted to one class or person **3** : having a number of sexual partners ♦ **Synonyms** MISCELLANEOUS, ASSORTED, HETEROGENEOUS, MOTLEY, VARIED — **pro·mis·cu·i·ty** \ˌprä-mis-'kyü-ə-tē, ˌprō-ˌmis-\ *n* — **pro·mis·cu·ous·ly** *adv* — **pro·mis·cu·ous·ness** *n*

¹prom·ise \'prä-məs\ *n* **1** : a pledge to do or not to do something specified **2** : ground for expectation of success or improvement **3** : something promised

²promise *vb* **prom·ised; prom·is·ing** **1** : to engage to do, bring about, or provide ⟨∼ help⟩ **2** : to suggest beforehand ⟨dark clouds ∼ rain⟩ **3** : to give ground for expectation ⟨it ∼s to be a good game⟩

promising *adj* : likely to succeed or yield good results ⟨a ∼ new medicine⟩ — **prom·is·ing·ly** *adv*

prom·is·so·ry \'prä-mə-ˌsòr-ē\ *adj* : containing a promise

prom·on·to·ry \'prä-mən-ˌtòr-ē\ *n, pl* **-ries** : a point of land jutting into the sea : HEADLAND

pro·mote \prə-'mōt\ *vb* **pro·mot·ed; pro·mot·ing** **1** : to advance in station, rank, or honor **2** : to contribute to the growth or prosperity of : FURTHER **3** : LAUNCH — **pro·mo·tion** \-'mō-shən\ *n* — **pro·mo·tion·al** \-shə-nəl\ *adj*

pro·mot·er \-'mō-tər\ *n* : one that promotes; *esp* : one that assumes the financial responsibilities of a sports event ⟨a boxing ∼⟩

¹prompt \'prämpt\ *vb* **1** : INCITE **2** : to assist (one acting or reciting) by suggesting the next words **3** : INSPIRE, URGE — **prompt·er** *n*

²prompt *adj* **1** : being ready and quick to act; *also* : PUNCTUAL **2** : performed readily or immediately ⟨∼ service⟩ — **prompt·ly** *adv* — **prompt·ness** *n*

prompt·book \-ˌbùk\ *n* : a copy of a play with directions for performance used by a theater prompter

promp·ti·tude \'prämp-tə-ˌtüd, -ˌtyüd\ *n* : the quality or habit of being prompt : PROMPTNESS

pro·mul·gate \'prä-məl-ˌgāt; prō-'məl-\ *vb* **-gat·ed; -gat·ing** : to make known or put into force by open declaration — **prom·ul·ga·tion** \ˌprä-məl-'gä-shən, ˌprō-(ˌ)məl-\ *n*

pron *abbr* **1** pronoun **2** pronounced **3** pronunciation

prone \'prōn\ *adj* **1** : having a tendency or inclination : DISPOSED **2** : lying face downward; *also* : lying flat or prostrate ♦ **Synonyms** SUBJECT, EXPOSED, OPEN, LIABLE, SUSCEPTIBLE — **prone·ness** *n*

prong \'pròŋ\ *n* : one of the sharp points of a fork : TINE; *also* : a slender projecting part (as of an antler) — **pronged** \'pròŋd\ *adj*

prong·horn \'pròŋ-ˌhòrn\ *n, pl* **pronghorn** *or* **pronghorns** : a swift horned ruminant mammal chiefly of grasslands of western No. America that resembles an antelope

pro·noun \'prō-ˌnaùn\ *n* : a word used as a substitute for a noun

pro·nounce \prə-'naùns\ *vb* **pro·nounced; pro·nounc·ing** **1** : to utter officially or as an opinion ⟨~ sentence⟩ **2** : to employ the organs of speech in order to produce ⟨~ a word⟩; *esp* : to say or speak correctly ⟨she can't ~ his name⟩ — **pro·nounce·able** *adj* — **pro·nun·ci·a·tion** \-ˌnən-sē-'ā-shən\ *n*

pro·nounced *adj* : strongly marked : DECIDED ⟨a ~ dislike⟩

pro·nounce·ment \prə-'naùns-mənt\ *n* : a formal declaration of opinion; *also* : ANNOUNCEMENT

pron·to \'prän-ˌtō\ *adv* [Sp, fr. L *promptus* prompt] : QUICKLY

pro·nu·clear \'prō-'nü-klē-ər, -'nyü-\ *adj* : supporting the use of nuclear-powered electric generating stations

pro·nun·ci·a·men·to \prō-ˌnən-sē-ə-'men-tō\ *n, pl* **-tos** *or* **-toes** : PROCLAMATION, MANIFESTO

¹**proof** \'prüf\ *n* [ME *prof, prove*, alter. of *preve*, fr. AF *preove*, fr. LL *proba*, fr. L *probare* to test, prove, fr. *probus* good, honest] **1** : the evidence that compels acceptance by the mind of a truth or fact **2** : a process or operation that establishes validity or truth : TEST **3** : a trial impression (as from type) **4** : a trial print from a photographic negative **5** : alcoholic content (as of a beverage) indicated by a number that is twice the percent by volume of alcohol present ⟨whiskey of 90 ~ is 45% alcohol⟩

²**proof** *adj* **1** : successful in resisting or repelling ⟨~ against tampering⟩ ⟨water*proof*⟩ **2** : of standard strength or quality or alcoholic content

proof·read \-ˌrēd\ *vb* : to read and mark corrections in — **proof·read·er** *n*

¹**prop** \'präp\ *n* : something that props

²**prop** *vb* **propped; prop·ping** **1** : to support by placing something under or against **2** : SUSTAIN, STRENGTHEN

³**prop** *n* : PROPERTY 4

⁴**prop** *n* : PROPELLER

⁵**prop** *abbr* **1** property **2** proposition **3** proprietor

pro·pa·gan·da \ˌprä-pə-'gan-də, ˌprō-\ *n* [NL, fr. *Congregatio de propaganda fide* Congregation for propagating the faith, organization established by Pope Gregory XVI] : the spreading of ideas or information to further or damage a cause; *also* : ideas or allegations spread for such a purpose — **pro·pa·gan·dist** \-dist\ *n*

pro·pa·gan·dize \-ˌdīz\ *vb* **-dized; -diz·ing** : to subject to or carry on propaganda

prop·a·gate \'prä-pə-ˌgāt\ *vb* **-gat·ed; -gat·ing** **1** : to reproduce or cause to reproduce biologically : MULTIPLY **2** : to cause to spread — **prop·a·ga·tion** \ˌprä-pə-'gā-shən\ *n*

pro·pane \'prō-ˌpān\ *n* : a heavy flammable gas found in petroleum and natural gas and used esp. as a fuel

pro·pel \prə-'pel\ *vb* **pro·pelled; pro·pel·ling** : to drive forward or onward ✦ *Synonyms* PUSH, SHOVE, THRUST

pro·pel·lant *also* **pro·pel·lent** \-'pe-lənt\ *n* : something (as a fuel) that propels — **propellant** *also* **propellent** *adj*

pro·pel·ler \prə-'pe-lər\ *n* : a device consisting of a hub fitted with blades that is used to propel a vehicle (as a motorboat or an airplane)

pro·pen·si·ty \prə-'pen-sə-tē\ *n, pl* **-ties** : an often intense natural inclination or preference

¹**prop·er** \'prä-pər\ *adj* **1** : referring to one individual only ⟨~ noun⟩ **2** : belonging characteristically to a species or individual : PECULIAR **3** : very satisfactory : EXCELLENT **4** : strictly limited to a specified thing ⟨the city ~⟩ **5** : CORRECT ⟨the ~ way to proceed⟩ **6** : strictly decorous : GENTEEL **7** : marked by suitability or rightness ⟨~ punishment⟩ ✦ *Synonyms* MEET, APPROPRIATE, FITTING, SEEMLY — **prop·er·ly** *adv*

²**proper** *n* : the parts of the Mass that vary according to the liturgical calendar

prop·er·tied \'prä-pər-tēd\ *adj* : owning property and esp. much property

prop·er·ty \'prä-pər-tē\ *n, pl* **-ties** **1** : a quality peculiar to an individual or thing **2** : something owned; *esp* : a piece of real estate **3** : OWNERSHIP **4** : an article or object

used in a play or motion picture other than painted scenery and actor's costumes

proph·e·cy *also* **proph·e·sy** \'prä-fə-sē\ *n, pl* **-cies** *also* **-sies** **1** : an inspired utterance of a prophet **2** : PREDICTION

proph·e·sy \-ˌsī\ *vb* **-sied; -sy·ing** **1** : to speak or utter by divine inspiration **2** : PREDICT — **proph·e·si·er** *n*

proph·et \'prä-fət\ *n* [ME *prophete*, fr. AF, fr. L *propheta*, fr. Gk *prophētēs*, fr. *pro* for + *phanai* to speak] **1** : one who utters divinely inspired revelations **2** : one who foretells future events

proph·et·ess \'prä-fə-təs\ *n* : a woman who is a prophet

pro·phet·ic \prə-'fe-tik\ *or* **pro·phet·i·cal** \-ti-kəl\ *adj* : of, relating to, or characteristic of a prophet or prophecy — **pro·phet·i·cal·ly** \-ti-k(ə-)lē\ *adv*

Proph·ets \'prä-fəts\ *n pl* — see BIBLE table

¹**pro·phy·lac·tic** \ˌprō-fə-'lak-tik, ˌprä-\ *adj* **1** : preventing or guarding from the spread or occurrence of disease or infection **2** : PREVENTIVE

²**prophylactic** *n* : something prophylactic; *esp* : a device (as a condom) for preventing venereal infection or conception

pro·phy·lax·is \-'lak-səs\ *n, pl* **-lax·es** \-'lak-ˌsēz\ : measures designed to preserve health and prevent the spread of disease

pro·pin·qui·ty \prə-'piŋ-kwə-tē\ *n* **1** : KINSHIP **2** : nearness in place or time : PROXIMITY

pro·pi·ti·ate \prō-'pi-shē-ˌāt\ *vb* **-at·ed; -at·ing** : to gain or regain the favor of : APPEASE — **pro·pi·ti·a·tion** \-ˌpi-shē-'ā-shən\ *n* — **pro·pi·tia·to·ry** \-'pi-shē-ə-ˌtór-ē\ *adj*

pro·pi·tious \prə-'pi-shəs\ *adj* **1** : favorably disposed ⟨~ deities⟩ **2** : being of good omen ⟨~ circumstances⟩

prop·man \'präp-ˌman\ *n* : one who is in charge of stage properties

pro·po·nent \prə-'pō-nənt\ *n* : one who argues in favor of something

¹**pro·por·tion** \prə-'pór-shən\ *n* **1** : BALANCE, SYMMETRY **2** : SHARE, QUOTA **3** : the relation of one part to another or to the whole with respect to magnitude, quantity, or degree : RATIO **4** : SIZE, DEGREE — **in proportion** : PROPORTIONAL

²**proportion** *vb* **-tioned; -tion·ing** **1** : to adjust (a part or thing) in size relative to other parts or things **2** : to make the parts of harmonious

pro·por·tion·al \prə-'pór-shə-nəl\ *adj* : corresponding in size, degree, or intensity; *also* : having the same or a constant ratio — **pro·por·tion·al·ly** *adv*

pro·por·tion·ate \prə-'pór-shə-nət\ *adj* : PROPORTIONAL — **pro·por·tion·ate·ly** *adv*

pro·pose \prə-'pōz\ *vb* **pro·posed; pro·pos·ing** **1** : PLAN, INTEND ⟨~s to buy a house⟩ **2** : to make an offer of marriage **3** : to offer for consideration : SUGGEST ⟨~ a policy⟩ — **pro·pos·al** \-'pō-zəl\ *n* — **pro·pos·er** *n*

¹**prop·o·si·tion** \ˌprä-pə-'zi-shən\ *n* **1** : something proposed for consideration : PROPOSAL **2** : a request for sexual intercourse **3** : a statement of something to be discussed, proved, or explained **4** : SITUATION, AFFAIR ⟨a tough ~⟩ — **prop·o·si·tion·al** \-'zi-shə-nəl\ *adj*

²**proposition** *vb* **-tioned; -tion·ing** : to make a proposal to; *esp* : to suggest sexual intercourse to

pro·pound \prə-'paùnd\ *vb* : to set forth for consideration ⟨~ a doctrine⟩

pro·pri·e·tary \prə-'prī-ə-ˌter-ē\ *adj* **1** : of, relating to, or characteristic of a proprietor ⟨~ rights⟩ **2** : made and sold by one with the sole right to do so ⟨~ medicines⟩ ⟨~ software⟩

pro·pri·e·tor \prə-'prī-ə-tər\ *n* : OWNER — **pro·pri·e·tor·ship** *n*

pro·pri·e·tress \-'prī-ə-trəs\ *n* : a woman who is a proprietor

pro·pri·e·ty \prə-'prī-ə-tē\ *n, pl* **-ties** **1** : the standard of what is socially acceptable in conduct or speech **2** *pl* : the customs of polite society

props \'präps\ *n sing or pl* **1** *slang* : DUE 1 ⟨gave him his ~⟩ **2** *slang* : RESPECT 2 ⟨earned the ~ of his peers⟩ **3** *slang* : ACKNOWLEDGMENT ⟨deserves ~ for the effort⟩

pro·pul·sion \prə-'pəl-shən\ *n* **1** : the action or process of propelling **2** : something that propels — **pro·pul·sive** \-siv\ *adj*

pro ra·ta \(ˌ)prō-'rä-tə, -'rä-\ *adv* : in proportion to the share of each : PROPORTIONATELY

pro·rate \(ˌ)prō-ˈrāt\ *vb* **pro·rat·ed; pro·rat·ing** : to divide, distribute, or assess proportionately

pro·rogue \prə-ˈrōg\ *vb* **pro·rogued; pro·rogu·ing** : to suspend or end a session of (a legislative body) — **pro·ro·ga·tion** \ˌprō-rō-ˈgā-shən\ *n*

pros *pl of* PRO

pro·sa·ic \prō-ˈzā-ik\ *adj* : lacking imagination or excitement : DULL

pro·sce·ni·um \prō-ˈsē-nē-əm\ *n* **1** : the part of a stage in front of the curtain **2** : the wall containing the arch that frames the stage

pro·scribe \prō-ˈskrīb\ *vb* **pro·scribed; pro·scrib·ing** **1** : OUTLAW **2** : to condemn or forbid as harmful — **pro·scrip·tion** \-ˈskrip-shən\ *n*

prose \ˈprōz\ *n* [ME, fr. AF, fr. L *prosa*, fr. fem. of *prorsus, prosus*, straightforward, being in prose, alter. of *proversus*, pp. of *provertere* to turn forward] : the ordinary language people use in speaking or writing

pros·e·cute \ˈprä-si-ˌkyüt\ *vb* **-cut·ed; -cut·ing** **1** : to follow to the end ⟨~ an investigation⟩ **2** : to seek legal punishment of ⟨~ a forger⟩ — **pros·e·cu·tion** \ˌprä-si-ˈkyü-shən\ *n* — **pros·e·cu·tor** \ˈprä-si-ˌkyü-tər\ *n* — **pros·e·cu·to·ri·al** \ˌprä-si-kyü-ˈtòr-ē-əl\ *adj*

¹pros·e·lyte \ˈprä-sə-ˌlīt\ *n* : a new convert to a religion, belief, or party — **pros·e·ly·tism** \-ˌlī-ˌti-zəm\ *n*

²proselyte *vb* **-lyt·ed; -lyt·ing** : PROSELYTIZE

pros·e·ly·tise *Brit var of* PROSELYTIZE

pros·e·ly·tize \ˈprä-sə-lə-ˌtīz\ *vb* **-tized; -tiz·ing** **1** : to induce someone to convert to one's faith **2** : to recruit someone to join one's party, institution, or cause

pros·o·dy \ˈprä-sə-dē, -zə-\ *n, pl* **-dies** : the study of versification and esp. of metrical structure — **pro·sod·ic** \prə-ˈsä-dik\ *adj*

¹pros·pect \ˈprä-ˌspekt\ *n* **1** : an extensive view; *also* : OUTLOOK **2** : the act of looking forward **3** : a mental vision of something to come **4** : something that is awaited or expected : POSSIBILITY **5** : a potential buyer or customer; *also* : a likely candidate (as for a job) — **pro·spec·tive** \prə-ˈspek-tiv, ˈprä-ˌspek-\ *adj* — **pro·spec·tive·ly** *adv*

²pros·pect \ˈprä-ˌspekt\ *vb* : to explore esp. for mineral deposits — **pros·pec·tor** \-ˌspek-tər, prä-ˈspek-\ *n*

pro·spec·tus \prə-ˈspek-təs\ *n* : a preliminary statement that describes an enterprise and is distributed to prospective buyers or participants

pros·per \ˈpräs-pər\ *vb* **pros·pered; pros·per·ing** : SUCCEED; *esp* : to achieve economic success

pros·per·i·ty \präs-ˈper-ə-tē\ *n* : thriving condition : SUCCESS; *esp* : economic well-being

pros·per·ous \ˈpräs-pə-rəs\ *adj* **1** : FAVORABLE ⟨~ winds⟩ **2** : marked by success or economic well-being ⟨a ~ business⟩

pros·ta·glan·din \ˌpräs-tə-ˈglan-dən\ *n* : any of various oxygenated unsaturated fatty acids of animals that perform a variety of hormonelike actions

pros·tate \ˈpräs-ˌtāt\ *n* [NL *prostata*, fr. Gk *prostatēs*, fr. *proïstanai* to put in front] : PROSTATE GLAND — **pros·tat·ic** \prä-ˈsta-tik\ *adj*

prostate gland *n* : a glandular body about the base of the male urethra that produces a secretion which is a major part of the fluid ejaculated during an orgasm

pros·ta·ti·tis \ˌpräs-tə-ˈtī-təs\ *n* : inflammation of the prostate gland

pros·the·sis \präs-ˈthē-səs, ˈpräs-thə-\ *n, pl* **-the·ses** \-ˌsēz\ : an artificial replacement for a missing body part — **pros·thet·ic** \präs-ˈthe-tik\ *adj*

pros·thet·ics \-ˈthe-tiks\ *n pl* : the surgical or dental specialty concerned with the design, construction, and fitting of prostheses

¹pros·ti·tute \ˈpräs-tə-ˌtüt, -ˌtyüt\ *vb* **-tut·ed; -tut·ing** **1** : to offer indiscriminately for sexual activity esp. for money **2** : to devote to corrupt or unworthy purposes — **pros·ti·tu·tion** \ˌpräs-tə-ˈtü-shən, -ˈtyü-\ *n*

²prostitute *n* : one who engages in sexual activities for money

¹pros·trate \ˈprä-ˌstrāt\ *adj* **1** : stretched out with face on the ground in adoration or submission **2** : lying flat **3** : completely overcome ⟨~ with a cold⟩

²prostrate *vb* **pros·trat·ed; pros·trat·ing** **1** : to throw or put into a prostrate position **2** : to reduce to a weak or powerless condition — **pros·tra·tion** \prä-ˈstrā-shən\ *n*

prosy \ˈprō-zē\ *adj* **pros·i·er; -est** **1** : PROSAIC, ORDINARY **2** : TEDIOUS

Prot *abbr* Protestant

prot·ac·tin·i·um \ˌprō-ˌtak-ˈti-nē-əm\ *n* : a metallic radioactive chemical element of relatively short life

pro·tag·o·nist \prō-ˈta-gə-nist\ *n* **1** : the principal character in a drama or story **2** : a leader or supporter of a cause

pro·te·an \ˈprō-tē-ən\ *adj* : able to assume different shapes or roles

pro·tect \prə-ˈtekt\ *vb* : to shield from injury : GUARD

pro·tec·tion \prə-ˈtek-shən\ *n* **1** : the act of protecting : the state of being protected **2** : one that protects ⟨wear a helmet as a ~⟩ **3** : the supervision or support of one that is smaller and weaker **4** : the freeing of producers from foreign competition in their home market by high duties on foreign competitive goods — **pro·tec·tive** \-ˈtek-tiv\ *adj*

pro·tec·tion·ist \-shə-nist\ *n* : an advocate of government economic protection for domestic producers through restrictions on foreign competitors — **pro·tec·tion·ism** \-shə-ˌni-zəm\ *n*

pro·tec·tor \prə-ˈtek-tər\ *n* **1** : one that protects : GUARDIAN **2** : a device used to prevent injury : GUARD **3** : REGENT 1

pro·tec·tor·ate \-tə-rət\ *n* **1** : government by a protector **2** : the relationship of superior authority assumed by one state over a dependent one; *also* : the dependent political unit in such a relationship

pro·té·gé \ˈprō-tə-ˌzhā\ *n* [F] : one who is protected, trained, or guided by an influential person

pro·tein \ˈprō-ˌtēn\ *n* [F *protéine*, fr. LGk *prōteios* primary, fr. Gk *prōtos* first] : any of various complex nitrogen-containing substances that consist of chains of amino acids, are present in all living cells, and are an essential part of the human diet

pro tem \prō-ˈtem\ *adv* : PRO TEMPORE

pro tem·po·re \prō-ˈtem-pə-rē\ *adv* [L] : for the time being

Pro·te·ro·zo·ic \ˌprä-tə-rə-ˈzō-ik, ˌprō-\ *adj* : of, relating to, or being the eon of geologic history between the Archean and the Phanerozoic — **Proterozoic** *n*

¹pro·test \ˈprō-ˌtest\ *n* **1** : the act of protesting; *esp* : an organized public demonstration of disapproval **2** : a complaint or objection against an idea, an act, or a course of action

²pro·test \prō-ˈtest\ *vb* **1** : to assert positively : make solemn declaration of ⟨~*s* his innocence⟩ **2** : to object strongly : make a protest against ⟨~ a ruling⟩ — **pro·tes·ta·tion** \ˌprä-təs-ˈtā-shən\ *n* — **pro·test·er** *or* **pro·tes·tor** \-tər\ *n*

Prot·es·tant \ˈprä-təs-tənt, *3 also* prə-ˈtes-\ *n* **1** : a member or adherent of one of the Christian churches deriving from the Reformation **2** : a Christian not of a Catholic or Orthodox church **3** *not cap* : one who makes a protest — **Prot·es·tant·ism** \ˈprä-təs-tən-ˌti-zəm\ *n*

pro·tha·la·mi·on \ˌprō-thə-ˈlā-mē-ən\ *or* **pro·tha·la·mi·um** \-mē-əm\ *n, pl* **-mia** \-mē-ə\ : a song in celebration of a marriage

pro·to·col \ˈprō-tə-ˌkòl\ *n* [MF *prothocole*, fr. ML *protocollum*, fr. LGk *prōtokollon* first sheet of a papyrus roll bearing data of manufacture, fr. Gk *prōtos* first + *kollan* to glue together, fr. *kolla* glue] **1** : an original draft or record **2** : a preliminary memorandum of diplomatic negotiation **3** : a code of diplomatic or military etiquette **4** : a set of conventions for formatting data in an electronic communications system

pro·ton \ˈprō-ˌtän\ *n* [Gk *prōton*, neut. of *prōtos* first] : a positively charged atomic particle present in all atomic nuclei — **pro·ton·ic** \-ˈtä-nik\ *adj*

pro·to·plasm \ˈprō-tə-ˌpla-zəm\ *n* : the complex colloidal largely protein substance of living plant and animal cells — **pro·to·plas·mic** \ˌprō-tə-ˈplaz-mik\ *adj*

pro·to·type \ˈprō-tə-ˌtīp\ *n* : an original model : ARCHETYPE

pro·to·zo·an \ˌprō-tə-ˈzō-ən\ *n* : any of a phylum or subkingdom of unicellular lower invertebrate animals that include some pathogenic parasites of humans and domestic animals — **protozoan** *adj*

pro·tract \prō-ˈtrakt\ *vb* : to prolong in time or space
◆ Synonyms EXTEND, LENGTHEN, ELONGATE, STRETCH

pro·trac·tor \-'trak-tər\ *n* : an instrument for drawing and measuring angles

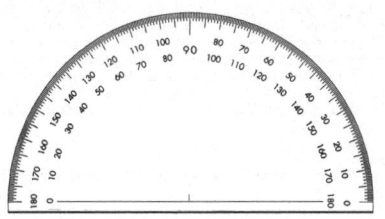

protractor

pro·trude \prō-'trüd\ *vb* **pro·trud·ed; pro·trud·ing** : to stick out or cause to stick out : jut out — **pro·tru·sion** \-'trü-zhən\ *n*

pro·tu·ber·ance \prō-'tü-bə-rəns, -'tyü-\ *n* : something that protrudes

pro·tu·ber·ant \-rənt\ *adj* : extending beyond the surrounding surface in a bulge

proud \'praud\ *adj* **1** : having or showing excessive self-esteem : HAUGHTY **2** : highly pleased : EXULTANT **3** : having proper self-respect ⟨too ∼ to beg⟩ **4** : GLORIOUS ⟨a ∼ occasion⟩ **5** : SPIRITED ⟨a ∼ steed⟩ ✦ *Synonyms* ARROGANT, INSOLENT, OVERBEARING, DISDAINFUL — **proud·ly** *adv*

prov *abbr* **1** province; provincial **2** provisional

Prov *abbr* Proverbs

prove \'prüv\ *vb* **proved; proved** *or* **prov·en** \'prü-vən\; **prov·ing** **1** : to test by experiment or by a standard **2** : to establish the truth of by argument or evidence **3** : to show to be correct, valid, or genuine **4** : to turn out esp. after trial or test ⟨the car *proved* to be a good choice⟩ — **prov·able** \'prü-və-bəl\ *adj*

prov·e·nance \'prä-və-nəns\ *n* : ORIGIN, SOURCE

Pro·ven·çal \ˌprō-ˌvän-'säl, ˌprä-vən-\ *n* **1** : a native or inhabitant of Provence **2** : OCCITAN — **Provençal** *adj*

prov·en·der \'prä-vən-dər\ *n* **1** : dry food for domestic animals : FEED **2** : FOOD, VICTUALS

pro·ve·nience \prə-'vē-nyəns\ *n* : ORIGIN, SOURCE

prov·erb \'prä-ˌvərb\ *n* : a pithy popular saying : ADAGE

pro·ver·bi·al \prə-'vər-bē-əl\ *adj* **1** : of, relating to, or resembling a proverb **2** : commonly spoken of

Proverbs *n* — see BIBLE table

pro·vide \prə-'vīd\ *vb* **pro·vid·ed; pro·vid·ing** [ME, fr. L *providēre*, lit., to see ahead, fr. *pro-* forward + *vidēre* to see] **1** : to take measures beforehand ⟨∼ against inflation⟩ **2** : to make a proviso or stipulation **3** : to supply what is needed ⟨∼ for a family⟩ **4** : EQUIP **5** : to supply for use : YIELD — **pro·vid·er** *n*

pro·vid·ed *conj* : on condition that : IF

prov·i·dence \'prä-və-dəns\ *n* **1** *often cap* : divine guidance or care **2** *cap* : GOD **1 3** : the quality or state of being provident

prov·i·dent \-dənt\ *adj* **1** : making provision for the future : PRUDENT **2** : FRUGAL — **prov·i·dent·ly** *adv*

prov·i·den·tial \ˌprä-və-'den-chəl\ *adj* **1** : of, relating to, or determined by Providence **2** : OPPORTUNE, LUCKY

providing *conj* : PROVIDED

prov·ince \'prä-vəns\ *n* **1** : an administrative district or division of a country **2** *pl* : all of a country except the metropolises **3** : proper business or scope : SPHERE

pro·vin·cial \prə-'vin-chəl\ *adj* **1** : of or relating to a province **2** : limited in outlook : NARROW ⟨∼ ideas⟩ — **pro·vin·cial·ism** \-chə-ˌli-zəm\ *n*

proving ground *n* : a place for scientific experimentation or testing

¹pro·vi·sion \prə-'vi-zhən\ *n* **1** : the act or process of providing; *also* : a measure taken beforehand **2** : a stock of needed supplies; *esp* : a stock of food — usu. used in pl. **3** : PROVISO

²provision *vb* : to supply with provisions

pro·vi·sion·al \-'vi-zhə-nəl\ *adj* : provided for a temporary need : CONDITIONAL — **pro·vi·sion·al·ly** *adv*

pro·vi·so \prə-'vī-zō\ *n*, *pl* **-sos** *also* **-soes** [ME, fr. ML *proviso quod* provided that] : an article or clause that introduces a condition : STIPULATION

pro·vo·ca·teur \prō-ˌvä-kə-'tər\ *n* : one who provokes

prov·o·ca·tion \ˌprä-və-'kā-shən\ *n* **1** : the act of provoking **2** : something that provokes

pro·voc·a·tive \prə-'vä-kə-tiv\ *adj* : serving to provoke or excite

pro·voke \prə-'vōk\ *vb* **pro·voked; pro·vok·ing** **1** : to incite to anger : INCENSE **2** : to call forth : EVOKE ⟨a remark that *provoked* laughter⟩ **3** : to stir up on purpose ⟨∼ an argument⟩ ✦ *Synonyms* IRRITATE, EXASPERATE, AGGRAVATE, INFLAME, RILE, PIQUE — **pro·vok·er** *n*

pro·vo·lo·ne \ˌprō-və-'lō-nē\ *n* : a usu. firm pliant often smoked Italian cheese

pro·vost \'prō-ˌvōst, 'prä-vəst\ *n* : a high official : DIGNITARY; *esp* : a high-ranking university administrative officer

pro·vost mar·shal \'prō-ˌvō-'mär-shəl\ *n* : an officer who supervises the military police of a command

prow \'prau\ *n* : the bow of a ship

prow·ess \'prau-əs\ *n* **1** : military valor and skill **2** : extraordinary ability

prowl \'praul\ *vb* : to roam about stealthily — **prowl** *n* — **prowl·er** *n*

prox·i·mal \'präk-sə-məl\ *adj* **1** : next to or nearest the point of attachment or origin; *esp* : located toward the center of the body **2** : of, relating to, or being the mesial and distal surfaces of a tooth — **prox·i·mal·ly** *adv*

prox·i·mate \'präk-sə-mət\ *adj* **1** : DIRECT ⟨the ∼ cause⟩ **2** : very near

prox·im·i·ty \präk-'si-mə-tē\ *n* : NEARNESS

prox·i·mo \'präk-sə-ˌmō\ *adj* [L *proximo mense* in the next month] : of or occurring in the next month after the present

proxy \'präk-sē\ *n*, *pl* **prox·ies** [ME *proxi, procucie*, alter. of *procuracie*, fr. AF, fr. ML *procuratia*, alter. of L *procuratio* appointment of another as an agent, fr. *procurare* to take care of] : the authority or power to act for another; *also* : a document giving such authorization — **proxy** *adj*

prude \'prüd\ *n* : a person who shows or affects extreme modesty — **prud·ery** \'prü-də-rē\ *n* — **prud·ish** *adj* — **prud·ish·ly** *adv*

pru·dent \'prü-dᵊnt\ *adj* **1** : shrewd in the management of practical affairs **2** : CAUTIOUS, DISCREET **3** : PROVIDENT, FRUGAL ✦ *Synonyms* JUDICIOUS, FORESIGHTED, SENSIBLE, SANE — **pru·dence** \-ᵊns\ *n* — **pru·den·tial** \prü-'den-chəl\ *adj* — **pru·dent·ly** *adv*

¹prune \'prün\ *n* : a dried plum

²prune *vb* **pruned; prun·ing** : to cut off unwanted parts (as of a tree)

pru·ri·ent \'prur-ē-ənt\ *adj* : LASCIVIOUS; *also* : exciting to lasciviousness — **pru·ri·ence** \-ē-əns\ *n*

¹pry \'prī\ *vb* **pried; pry·ing** : to look closely or inquisitively; *esp* : SNOOP

²pry *vb* **pried; pry·ing** **1** : to raise, move, or pull apart with a pry or lever **2** : to detach or open with difficulty

³pry *n* : a tool for prying

Ps *or* **Psa** *abbr* Psalms

PS *abbr* **1** [L *postscriptum*] postscript **2** public school

PSA *abbr* public service announcement

psalm \'säm, 'sälm\ *n*, *often cap* [ME, fr. OE *psealm*, fr. LL *psalmus*, fr. Gk *psalmos*, lit., twanging of a harp, fr. *psallein* to pluck, play a stringed instrument] : a sacred song or poem; *esp* : one of the hymns collected in the Book of Psalms — **psalm·ist** *n*

psalm·o·dy \'sä-mə-dē, 'säl-\ *n* : the singing of psalms in worship

Psalms *n* — see BIBLE table

Psal·ter \'sȯl-tər\ *n* : the Book of Psalms; *also* : a collection of the Psalms arranged for devotional use

pseud *abbr* pseudonym; pseudonymous

pseu·do \'sü-dō\ *adj* : SPURIOUS, SHAM

pseu·do·nym \'sü-də-ˌnim\ *n* : a fictitious name — **pseu·don·y·mous** \sü-'dä-nə-məs\ *adj*

pseu·do·sci·ence \ˌsü-dō-'sī-əns\ *n* : a system of theories, assumptions, and methods erroneously regarded as scientific — **pseu·do·sci·en·tif·ic** \-ˌsī-ən-'ti-fik\ *adj*

PSG *abbr* platoon sergeant

¹psi \'sī, 'psī\ *n* : the 23d letter of the Greek alphabet — Ψ or ψ

²psi *abbr* pounds per square inch

psit·ta·co·sis \ˌsi-tə-'kō-səs\ *n* : an infectious disease of birds marked by diarrhea and wasting and transmissible to humans

pso·ri·a·sis \sə-ʹrī-ə-səs\ *n* : a chronic skin disease characterized by red patches covered with white scales

PST *abbr* Pacific standard time

¹**psych** *or* **psyche** \ʹsīk\ *vb* **psyched; psych·ing** 1 : OUTWIT, OUTGUESS; *also* : to analyze beforehand 2 : INTIMIDATE; *also* : to prepare oneself psychologically ⟨get *psyched* up for the game⟩

²**psych** *abbr* psychology

psy·che \ʹsī-kē\ *n* : SOUL, PERSONALITY; *also* : MIND

psy·che·del·ic \ˌsī-kə-ʹde-lik\ *adj* 1 : of, relating to, or causing abnormal psychic effects ⟨~ drugs⟩ 2 : relating to the taking of psychedelic drugs ⟨~ experience⟩ 3 : imitating, suggestive of, or reproducing the effects of psychedelic drugs ⟨~ art⟩ ⟨~ colors⟩ — **psychedelic** *n* — **psy·che·del·i·cal·ly** \-li-k(ə-)lē\ *adv*

psy·chi·a·try \sə-ʹkī-ə-trē, sī-\ *n* [prob. fr. F *psychiatrie*, fr. *psychiatre* psychiatrist, fr. Gk *psychē* breath, soul + *iatros* physician] : a branch of medicine dealing with mental, emotional, and behavioral disorders — **psy·chi·at·ric** \ˌsī-kē-ʹa-trik\ *adj* — **psy·chi·a·trist** \sə-ʹkī-ə-trist, sī-\ *n*

¹**psy·chic** \ʹsī-kik\ *also* **psy·chi·cal** \-ki-kəl\ *adj* 1 : of or relating to the psyche 2 : lying outside the sphere of physical science 3 : sensitive to nonphysical or supernatural forces — **psy·chi·cal·ly** \-k(ə-)lē\ *adv*

²**psychic** *n* : a person apparently sensitive to nonphysical forces; *also* : MEDIUM 6

psy·cho \ʹsī-kō\ *n, pl* **psychos** : a mentally disturbed person — **psycho** *adj*

psy·cho·ac·tive \ˌsī-kō-ʹak-tiv\ *adj* : affecting the mind or behavior

psy·cho·anal·y·sis \ˌsī-kō-ə-ʹna-lə-səs\ *n* : a method of dealing with psychic disorders by having the patient talk freely about personal experiences and esp. about early childhood and dreams — **psy·cho·an·a·lyst** \-ʹa-nə-list\ *n* — **psy·cho·an·a·lyt·ic** \-ˌa-nə-ʹli-tik\ *adj* — **psy·cho·an·a·lyze** \-ʹa-nə-ˌlīz\ *vb*

psy·cho·bab·ble \ʹsī-kō-ˌba-bəl\ *n* : psychological jargon esp. when used in a trite or simplistic manner

psy·cho·dra·ma \ˌsī-kə-ʹdrä-mə, -ʹdra-\ *n* 1 : an extemporized dramatization designed to afford catharsis for one or more of the participants from whose life the plot is taken 2 : a dramatic event or story with psychological overtones

psy·cho·gen·ic \-ʹje-nik\ *adj* : originating in the mind or in mental or emotional conflict

psy·cho·graph·ics \ˌsī-kə-ʹgra-fiks\ *n sing or pl* : market research or statistics classifying population groups according to psychological variables

psychol *abbr* psychologist; psychology

psy·chol·o·gy \sī-ʹkä-lə-jē\ *n, pl* **-gies** 1 : the science of mind and behavior 2 : the mental and behavioral characteristics of an individual or group — **psy·cho·log·i·cal** \ˌsī-kə-ʹlä-ji-kəl\ *adj* — **psy·cho·log·i·cal·ly** \-ji-k(ə-)lē\ *adv* — **psy·chol·o·gist** \sī-ʹkä-lə-jist\ *n*

psy·cho·path \ʹsī-kō-ˌpath\ *n* : a mentally ill or unstable person; *esp* : a person who engages in antisocial behavior and exhibits a pervasive disregard for the rights, feelings, and safety of others — **psy·cho·path·ic** \ˌsī-kə-ʹpa-thik\ *adj*

psy·cho·sex·u·al \ˌsī-kō-ʹsek-shə-wəl\ *adj* 1 : of or relating to the mental, emotional, and behavioral aspects of sexual development 2 : of or relating to the physiological psychology of sex

psy·cho·sis \sī-ʹkō-səs\ *n, pl* **-cho·ses** \-ˌsēz\ : a serious mental illness (as schizophrenia) marked by loss of or greatly lessened ability to test whether what one is thinking and feeling about the real world is really true

psy·cho·so·cial \ˌsī-kō-ʹsō-shəl\ *adj* 1 : involving both psychological and social aspects 2 : relating social conditions to mental health

psy·cho·so·mat·ic \ˌsī-kō-sə-ʹma-tik\ *adj* : of, relating to, involving, or concerned with bodily symptoms caused by mental or emotional disturbance

psy·cho·ther·a·py \ˌsī-kō-ʹther-ə-pē\ *n* : treatment of mental or emotional disorder or of related bodily ills by psychological means — **psy·cho·ther·a·pist** \-pist\ *n*

psy·chot·ic \sī-ʹkä-tik\ *adj* : of or relating to psychosis ⟨~ behavior⟩ ⟨a ~ patient⟩ — **psychotic** *n*

psy·cho·tro·pic \ˌsī-kə-ʹtrō-pik\ *adj* : acting on the mind ⟨~ drugs⟩

pt *abbr* 1 part 2 payment 3 pint 4 point 5 port

Pt *symbol* platinum

PT *abbr* 1 Pacific time 2 part-time 3 physical therapy 4 physical training

PTA *abbr* Parent-Teacher Association

ptar·mi·gan \ʹtär-mi-gən\ *n, pl* **-gan** *or* **-gans** : any of various grouses of northern regions with completely feathered feet

PT boat \ˌ(ˌ)pē-ʹtē-\ *n* [*patrol torpedo*] : a small fast patrol craft usu. armed with torpedos

pte *abbr, Brit* private

ptg *abbr* printing

PTO *abbr* 1 Parent-Teacher Organization 2 please turn over

pto·maine \ʹtō-ˌmān\ *n* : any of various chemical substances formed by bacteria in decaying matter (as meat) and including a few poisonous ones

Pu *symbol* plutonium

¹**pub** \ʹpəb\ *n* 1 *chiefly Brit* : PUBLIC HOUSE 2 2 : TAVERN

²**pub** *abbr* 1 public 2 publication 3 published; publisher; publishing

pu·ber·ty \ʹpyü-bər-tē\ *n* : the condition of being or period of becoming first capable of reproducing sexually — **pu·ber·tal** \-bər-t°l\ *adj*

pu·bes \ʹpyü-bēz\ *n, pl* **pubes** [NL, fr. L, manhood, body hair, pubic region] 1 : the hair that appears upon the lower middle region of the abdomen at puberty 2 : the pubic region

pu·bes·cence \pyü-ʹbe-s°ns\ *n* 1 : the quality or state of being pubescent 2 : a pubescent covering or surface

pu·bes·cent \-s°nt\ *adj* 1 : arriving at or having reached puberty 2 : covered with fine soft short hairs

pu·bic \ʹpyü-bik\ *adj* : of, relating to, or situated near the pubes or the pubis

pu·bis \ʹpyü-bəs\ *n, pl* **pu·bes** \-bēz\ : the ventral and anterior of the three principal bones composing either half of the pelvis

publ *abbr* 1 publication 2 published; publisher

¹**pub·lic** \ʹpə-blik\ *adj* 1 : exposed to general view ⟨the story became ~⟩ 2 : of, relating to, or affecting the people as a whole ⟨~ opinion⟩ 3 : CIVIC, GOVERNMENTAL ⟨~ expenditures⟩ 4 : of, relating to, or serving the community ⟨~ officials⟩ 5 : not private : SOCIAL ⟨~ morality⟩ 6 : open to all ⟨~ library⟩ 7 : well known : PROMINENT ⟨~ figures⟩ 8 : supported by public funds and private contributions rather than by income from commercials — **pub·lic·ly** *adv*

²**public** *n* 1 : the people as a whole : POPULACE 2 : a group of people having common interests

pub·li·can \ʹpə-bli-kən\ *n* 1 : a Jewish tax collector for the ancient Romans 2 *chiefly Brit* : the licensee of a pub

pub·li·ca·tion \ˌpə-blə-ʹkā-shən\ *n* 1 : the act or process of publishing 2 : a published work

public house *n* 1 : INN 2 *chiefly Brit* : a licensed saloon or bar

pub·li·cise *Brit var of* PUBLICIZE

pub·li·cist \ʹpə-blə-sist\ *n* : one that publicizes; *esp* : PRESS AGENT

pub·lic·i·ty \(ˌ)pə-ʹbli-sə-tē\ *n* 1 : information with news value issued to gain public attention or support 2 : public attention or acclaim

pub·li·cize \ʹpə-blə-ˌsīz\ *vb* **-cized; -ciz·ing** : to bring to public attention : ADVERTISE

pub·lic–key \ˌpə-blik-ʹkē\ *n* : the publicly shared element of a code usable only to encode messages

public relations *n sing or pl* : the business of fostering public goodwill toward a person, firm, or institution; *also* : the degree of goodwill and understanding achieved

public school *n* 1 : an endowed secondary boarding school in Great Britain offering a classical curriculum and preparation for the universities or public service 2 : a free tax-supported school controlled by a local governmental authority

public–spirited *adj* : motivated by devotion to the general or national welfare

public works *n pl* : works (as schools or highways) constructed with public funds for public use

pub·lish \ʹpə-blish\ *vb* 1 : to make generally known 2 : to produce or release literature, information, musical scores or sometimes recordings, or art for sale to the public — **pub·lish·er** *n*

¹**puck** \'pək\ *n* : a mischievous sprite — **puck·ish** *adj* — **puck·ish·ly** *adv*

²**puck** *n* : a disk used in ice hockey

¹**puck·er** \'pə-kər\ *vb* : to contract into folds or wrinkles

²**pucker** *n* : FOLD, WRINKLE

pud·ding \'pu̇-diŋ\ *n* : a soft, spongy, or thick creamy dessert

pud·dle \'pə-dᵊl\ *n* : a very small pool of usu. dirty or muddy water

pu·den·dum \pyu̇-'den-dəm\ *n, pl* **-da** \-də\ [NL, fr. L *pudēre* to be ashamed] : the human external genital organs esp. of a woman

pudgy \'pə-jē\ *adj* **pudg·i·er; -est** : being short and plump : CHUBBY

pueb·lo \'pwe-blō, pü-'e-\ *n, pl* **-los** [Sp, village, lit., people, fr. L *populus*] **1** : an American Indian village of Arizona or New Mexico that consists of flat-roofed stone or adobe houses joined in groups sometimes several stories high **2** *cap* : a member of a group of American Indian peoples of the southwestern U.S.

pu·er·ile \'pyu̇-ə-rəl\ *adj* : CHILDISH, SILLY ⟨~ remarks⟩ — **pu·er·il·i·ty** \ˌpyu̇-ə-'ri-lə-tē\ *n*

pu·er·per·al \pyu̇-'ər-pə-rəl\ *adj* : of, relating to, or occurring during childbirth or the period immediately following ⟨~ infection⟩ ⟨~ depression⟩

puerperal fever *n* : an abnormal condition that results from infection of the placental site following childbirth or abortion

¹**puff** \'pəf\ *vb* **1** : to blow in short gusts **2** : PANT **3** : to emit small whiffs or clouds **4** : BLUSTER, BRAG **5** : INFLATE, SWELL **6** : to make proud or conceited **7** : to praise extravagantly

²**puff** *n* **1** : a short discharge (as of air or smoke); *also* : a slight explosive sound accompanying it **2** : a light fluffy pastry **3** : a soft swelling **4** : a fluffy mass; *also* : a small pad for applying cosmetic powder **5** : a laudatory notice or review — **puffy** *adj*

³**puff** *adj* : of, relating to, or designed for promotion or flattery ⟨~ articles on the new TV series⟩

puff·ball \'pəf-ˌbȯl\ *n* : any of various globe-shaped and often edible fungi

puf·fin \'pə-fən\ *n* : any of several seabirds having a short neck and a deep grooved parti-colored bill

¹**pug** \'pəg\ *n* **1** : any of a breed of small stocky short-haired dogs with a wrinkled face **2** : a close coil of hair

²**pug** *n* : ¹BOXER

pu·gi·lism \'pyü-jə-ˌli-zəm\ *n* : BOXING — **pu·gi·list** \-list\ *n* — **pu·gi·lis·tic** \ˌpyü-jə-'lis-tik\ *adj*

pug·na·cious \ˌpəg-'nā-shəs\ *adj* : having a quarrelsome or combative nature ♦ *Synonyms* BELLIGERENT, BELLICOSE, CONTENTIOUS, TRUCULENT — **pug·nac·i·ty** \-'na-sə-tē\ *n*

puis·sance \'pwi-səns, 'pyü-ə-\ *n* : POWER, STRENGTH — **puis·sant** \-sənt\ *adj*

puke \'pyük\ *vb* **puked; puk·ing** : VOMIT — **puke** *n*

puk·ka \'pə-kə\ *adj* [Hindi *pakkā* cooked, ripe, solid, fr. Skt *pakva*] : GENUINE, AUTHENTIC; *also* : FIRST-CLASS, COMPLETE

pul \'pül\ *n, pl* **puls** \'pülz\ *or* **pul** — see *afghani* at MONEY table

pu·la \'pü-lə, 'pyü-\ *n, pl* **pula** — see MONEY table

pul·chri·tude \'pəl-krə-ˌtüd, -ˌtyüd\ *n* : BEAUTY — **pul·chri·tu·di·nous** \ˌpəl-krə-'tü-dᵊn-əs, -'tyü-\ *adj*

pule \'pyül\ *vb* **puled; pul·ing** : WHINE, WHIMPER

¹**pull** \'pül\ *vb* **1** : to exert force so as to draw (something) toward the force; *also* : MOVE ⟨~ out of a driveway⟩ **2** : PLUCK; *also* : EXTRACT ⟨~ a tooth⟩ **3** : STRETCH, STRAIN ⟨~ a tendon⟩ **4** : to draw apart : TEAR **5** : to make (as a proof) by printing **6** : REMOVE ⟨~ed the pitcher in the third inning⟩ **7** : DRAW ⟨~ a gun⟩ **8** : to carry out esp. with daring ⟨~ a robbery⟩ **9** : PERPETRATE, COMMIT **10** : ATTRACT **11** : to express strong sympathy — **pull·er** *n*

²**pull** *n* **1** : the act or an instance of pulling **2** : the effort expended in moving **3** : ADVANTAGE ⟨had the ~ of a respected family name⟩; *esp* : special influence **4** : a device for pulling something or for operating by pulling **5** : a force that attracts or compels **6** : an injury from abnormal straining or stretching ⟨a muscle ~⟩

pull·back \'pül-ˌbak\ *n* : an orderly withdrawal of troops

pull–down *adj* : appearing below a selected item (as a menu title) on a computer display ⟨a ~ menu⟩

pul·let \'pu̇-lət\ *n* : a young hen esp. of the domestic chicken when less than a year old

pul·ley \'pu̇-lē\ *n, pl* **pulleys** : a wheel used to transmit power by means of a belt, rope, or chain; *esp* : one with a grooved rim that forms part of a tackle for hoisting or for changing the direction of a force

Pull·man \'pu̇l-mən\ *n* : a railroad passenger car with comfortable furnishings esp. for night travel

pull off *vb* : to accomplish successfully

pull·out \'pu̇l-ˌau̇t\ *n* : PULLBACK

pull·over \'pu̇l-ˌō-vər\ *adj* : put on by being pulled over the head ⟨~ sweater⟩ — **pull·over** *n*

pull–up \'pu̇l-ˌəp\ *n* : CHIN-UP

pull up *vb* : to bring or come to an often abrupt halt : STOP

pul·mo·nary \'pu̇l-mə-ˌner-ē, 'pəl-\ *adj* : of, relating to, or carried on by the lungs ⟨the ~ circulation⟩

pulp \'pəlp\ *n* **1** : the soft juicy or fleshy part of a fruit or vegetable **2** : a soft moist mass **3** : the soft sensitive tissue that fills the central cavity of a tooth **4** : a material (as from wood) used in making paper **5** : a magazine using cheap paper and often dealing with sensational material — **pulpy** *adj*

pul·pit \'pu̇l-ˌpit\ *n* : a raised platform or high reading desk used in preaching or conducting a worship service

pulp·wood \'pəlp-ˌwu̇d\ *n* : wood used in making pulp for paper

pul·sar \'pəl-ˌsär\ *n* : a celestial source of pulsating electromagnetic radiation (as radio waves)

pul·sate \'pəl-ˌsāt\ *vb* **pul·sat·ed; pul·sat·ing** : to expand and contract rhythmically : BEAT — **pul·sa·tion** \ˌpəl-'sā-shən\ *n*

pulse \'pəls\ *n* **1** : the regular throbbing in the arteries caused by the contractions of the heart **2** : rhythmical beating, vibrating, or sounding **3** : a brief change in electrical current or voltage — **pulse** *vb*

pul·ver·ise *Brit var of* PULVERIZE

pul·ver·ize \'pəl-və-ˌrīz\ *vb* **-ized; -iz·ing** **1** : to reduce (as by crushing or grinding) or be reduced to very small particles **2** : DEMOLISH

pu·ma \'pü-mə, 'pyü-\ *n, pl* **pumas** *also* **puma** [Sp, fr. Quechua] : COUGAR

pum·ice \'pə-məs\ *n* : a light porous volcanic glass used esp. for smoothing and polishing

pum·mel \'pə-məl\ *vb* **-meled** *also* **-melled; -mel·ing** *also* **-mel·ling** : POUND, BEAT

¹**pump** \'pəmp\ *n* : a device for raising, transferring, or compressing fluids esp. by suction or pressure

²**pump** *vb* **1** : to raise (as water) with a pump **2** : to draw fluid from with a pump; *also* : to fill by means of a pump ⟨~ up a tire⟩ **3** : to force or propel in the manner of a pump — **pump·er** *n*

³**pump** *n* : a low shoe that grips the foot chiefly at the toe and heel

pumped \'pəmpt\ *adj* : filled with energetic excitement and enthusiasm

pum·per·nick·el \'pəm-pər-ˌni-kəl\ *n* : a dark rye bread

pump·kin \'pəmp-kən, 'pəŋ-kən\ *n* : the large usu. orange fruit of a vine of the gourd family that is widely used as food; *also* : this vine

pun \'pən\ *n* : the humorous use of a word in a way that suggests two or more interpretations — **pun** *vb*

¹**punch** \'pənch\ *n* : a tool for piercing, stamping, cutting, or forming

²**punch** *vb* **1** : PROD, POKE; *also* : DRIVE, HERD ⟨~ing cattle⟩ **2** : to strike with the fist **3** : to emboss, perforate, or make with a punch **4** : to operate, produce, or enter (as data) by or as if by punching — **punch·er** *n*

³**punch** *n* **1** : a quick blow with or as if with the fist **2** : effective energy or forcefulness

⁴**punch** *n* [perh. fr. Hindi *pāc* five, fr. Skt *pañca;* fr. the number of ingredients] : a drink usu. composed of wine or alcoholic liquor and nonalcoholic beverages; *also* : a drink composed of nonalcoholic beverages

punch card *n* : a card with holes punched in particular positions to represent data

punch–drunk \'pənch-ˌdrəŋk\ *adj* **1** : suffering from brain injury resulting from repeated head blows received in boxing **2** : DAZED, CONFUSED

pun·cheon \'pən-chən\ *n* : a large cask

punch line *n* : the sentence or phrase in a joke that makes the point

punch list *n* : a list of tasks to be completed at the end of a project

punchy \'pən-chē\ *adj* **punch·i·er; -est** **1** : having punch : FORCEFUL **2** : DAZED, CONFUSED **3** : VIVID, VIBRANT ⟨∼ graphics⟩

punc·til·io \ˌpəŋk-'ti-lē-ˌō\ *n, pl* **-i·os** **1** : a nice detail of conduct in a ceremony or in observance of a code **2** : careful observance of forms (as in social conduct)

punc·til·i·ous \ˌpəŋk-'ti-lē-əs\ *adj* : marked by precise accordance with codes or conventions ✦ *Synonyms* METICULOUS, SCRUPULOUS, CAREFUL, PUNCTUAL

punc·tu·al \'pəŋk-chə-wəl\ *adj* : being on time : PROMPT — **punc·tu·al·i·ty** \ˌpəŋk-chə-'wa-lə-tē\ *n* — **punc·tu·al·ly** *adv*

punc·tu·ate \'pəŋk-chə-ˌwāt\ *vb* **-at·ed; -at·ing** **1** : to mark or divide (written matter) with punctuation marks **2** : to break into at intervals **3** : EMPHASIZE

punc·tu·a·tion \ˌpəŋk-chə-'wā-shən\ *n* : the act, practice, or system of inserting standardized marks in written matter to clarify the meaning and separate structural units

¹punc·ture \'pəŋk-chər\ *n* **1** : an act of puncturing **2** : a small hole or wound made by puncturing

²puncture *vb* **punc·tured; punc·tur·ing** **1** : to make a hole in : PIERCE **2** : to make useless as if by a puncture

pun·dit \'pən-dət\ *n* [Hindi *paṇḍit*, fr. Skt *paṇḍita*, fr. *paṇḍita* learned] **1** : a learned person : TEACHER **2** : AUTHORITY, CRITIC

pun·dit·oc·ra·cy \ˌpən-dət-'ä-krə-sē\ *n, pl* **-cies** : a group of powerful and influential political commentators

pun·gent \'pən-jənt\ *adj* **1** : having a sharp incisive quality : CAUSTIC ⟨a ∼ editorial⟩ **2** : causing a sharp, intense, or irritating sensation (as of taste or smell); *esp* : ACRID ⟨a ∼ odor⟩ — **pun·gen·cy** \-jən-sē\ *n* — **pun·gent·ly** *adv*

pun·ish \'pə-nish\ *vb* **1** : to impose a penalty on for a fault or crime ⟨∼ an offender⟩ **2** : to inflict a penalty for ⟨∼ treason with death⟩ **3** : to inflict injury on : HURT ✦ *Synonyms* CHASTISE, CASTIGATE, CHASTEN, DISCIPLINE, CORRECT — **pun·ish·able** *adj*

pun·ish·ment *n* **1** : retributive suffering, pain, or loss : PENALTY **2** : rough treatment

pu·ni·tive \'pyü-nə-tiv\ *adj* : inflicting, involving, or aiming at punishment

¹punk \'pəŋk\ *n* **1** : a young inexperienced person **2** : a petty hoodlum

²punk *adj* : very poor : INFERIOR

³punk *n* : dry crumbly wood useful for tinder; *also* : a substance made from fungi for use as tinder

pun·ster \'pən-stər\ *n* : one who is given to punning

¹punt \'pənt\ *n* : a long narrow flat-bottomed boat with square ends

¹punt

²punt *vb* : to propel (as a punt) with a pole

³punt *vb* : to kick a football or soccer ball dropped from the hands before it touches the ground

⁴punt *n* : the act or an instance of punting a ball

pu·ny \'pyü-nē\ *adj* **pu·ni·er; -est** [AF *puisné* younger, weakly, lit., born afterward, fr. *puis* afterward (fr. L *post*) + *né* born, fr. L *natus*] : slight in power, size, or importance : WEAK

pup \'pəp\ *n* : a young dog; *also* : one of the young of some other animals

pu·pa \'pyü-pə\ *n, pl* **pu·pae** \-ˌ(ˌ)pē\ *or* **pupas** [NL, fr. L *pupa* doll] : a form of some insects (as a bee, moth, or beetle) between the larva and the adult that usu. has a protective covering (as a cocoon) — **pu·pal** \-pəl\ *adj*

¹pu·pil \'pyü-pəl\ *n* **1** : a child or young person in school or in the charge of a tutor **2** : DISCIPLE

²pupil *n* : the dark central opening of the iris of the eye

pup·pet \'pə-pət\ *n* [ME *popet* youth, doll, fr. MF *poupette*, ultim. fr. L *pupa* doll] **1** : a small figure of a person or animal moved by hand or by strings or wires **2** : DOLL **3** : one whose acts are controlled by an outside force or influence

pup·pe·teer \ˌpə-pə-'tir\ *n* : one who manipulates puppets

pup·py \'pə-pē\ *n, pl* **puppies** : a young domestic dog

pu·pu \'pü-ˌpü\ *n* : an Asian dish consisting of a variety of foods

pur·blind \'pər-ˌblīnd\ *adj* **1** : partly blind **2** : lacking in insight : OBTUSE

¹pur·chase \'pər-chəs\ *vb* **pur·chased; pur·chas·ing** : to obtain by paying money or its equivalent : BUY — **pur·chas·able** \-chə-sə-bəl\ *adj* — **pur·chas·er** *n*

²purchase *n* **1** : an act or instance of purchasing **2** : something purchased **3** : a secure hold or grasp; *also* : advantageous leverage

pur·dah \'pər-də\ *n* **1** : seclusion of women from public observation among Muslims and some Hindus esp. in India; *also* : a state of seclusion

pure \'pyür\ *adj* **pur·er; pur·est** **1** : unmixed with any other matter : free from taint ⟨∼ gold⟩ ⟨∼ water⟩ **2** : SHEER, ABSOLUTE ⟨∼ nonsense⟩ **3** : ABSTRACT, THEORETICAL ⟨∼ mathematics⟩ **4** : free from what vitiates, weakens, or pollutes ⟨speaks a ∼ French⟩ **5** : free from moral fault : INNOCENT **6** : CHASTE, CONTINENT — **pure·ly** *adv*

pure-blood·ed \-ˌblə-dəd\ *or* **pure–blood** \-ˌbləd\ *adj* : FULL-BLOODED — **pure·blood** *n*

pure·bred \-'bred\ *adj* : bred from members of a recognized breed, strain, or kind without crossbreeding over many generations — **pure·bred** \-ˌbred\ *n*

¹pu·ree \pyu̇-'rā, -'rē\ *n* [F *purée*, fr. MF, fr. fem. of *puré*, pp. of *purer* to purify, strain, fr. L *purare* to purify] : a paste or thick liquid suspension usu. made from finely ground cooked food; *also* : a thick soup made of puréed vegetables

²puree *vb* **pu·reed; pu·ree·ing** : to make a puree of

pur·ga·tion \ˌpər-'gā-shən\ *n* : the act or result of purging

¹pur·ga·tive \'pər-gə-tiv\ *adj* : purging or tending to purge

²purgative *n* : a strong laxative : CATHARTIC

pur·ga·to·ry \'pər-gə-ˌtȯr-ē\ *n, pl* **-ries** **1** : an intermediate state after death for expiatory purification **2** : a place or state of temporary punishment — **pur·ga·tor·i·al** \ˌpər-gə-'tȯr-ē-əl\ *adj*

¹purge \'pərj\ *vb* **purged; purg·ing** **1** : to cleanse or purify esp. from sin **2** : to have or cause strong and usu. repeated emptying of the bowels **3** : to get rid of ⟨the leaders had been *purged*⟩

²purge *n* **1** : something that purges; *esp* : PURGATIVE **2** : an act or result of purging; *esp* : a ridding of persons regarded as treacherous or disloyal

pu·ri·fy \'pyür-ə-ˌfī\ *vb* **-fied; -fy·ing** : to make or become pure — **pu·ri·fi·ca·tion** \ˌpyür-ə-fə-'kā-shən\ *n* — **pu·ri·fi·ca·to·ry** \pyu̇-'ri-fi-kə-ˌtȯr-ē\ *adj* — **pu·ri·fi·er** *n*

Pu·rim \'pu̇r-(ˌ)im\ *n* : a Jewish holiday celebrated in February or March in commemoration of the deliverance of the Jews from the massacre plotted by Haman

pu·rine \'pyu̇r-ˌēn\ *n* : any of a group of bases including several (as adenine or guanine) that are constituents of DNA or RNA

pur·ism \'pyu̇r-ˌi-zəm\ *n* : rigid adherence to or insistence on purity or nicety esp. in use of words — **pur·ist** \-ist\ *n* — **pu·ris·tic** \pyu̇-'ris-tik\ *adj*

pu·ri·tan \'pyu̇r-ə-tən\ *n* **1** *cap* : a member of a 16th and 17th century Protestant group in England and New England opposing the ceremonies and government of the Church of England **2** : one who practices or preaches a stricter or professedly purer moral code than that which prevails — **pu·ri·tan·i·cal** \ˌpyu̇r-ə-'ta-ni-kəl\ *adj* — **pu·ri·tan·i·cal·ly** *adv*

pu·ri·ty \'pyu̇r-ə-tē\ *n* : the quality or state of being pure

¹purl \'pərl\ *n* : a stitch in knitting

²purl *vb* : to knit in purl stitch

³**purl** *n* : a gentle murmur or movement (as of purling water)

⁴**purl** *vb* **1** : EDDY, SWIRL **2** : to make a soft murmuring sound

pur·lieu \'pər-lü, 'pərl-yü\ *n* **1** : an outlying district : SUBURB **2** *pl* : ENVIRONS

pur·loin \(,)pər-'lȯin, 'pər-,lȯin\ *vb* : STEAL, FILCH

¹**pur·ple** \'pər-pəl\ *adj* **pur·pler; pur·plest 1** : of the color purple **2** : highly rhetorical ⟨a ~ passage⟩ **3** : PROFANE ⟨~ language⟩ — **pur·plish** *adj*

²**purple** *n* **1** : a bluish red color **2** : a purple robe emblematic esp. of regal rank or authority

¹**pur·port** \'pər-,pȯrt\ *n* [ME, fr. AF, content, tenor, fr. *purporter* to carry, mean, purport, fr. *pur-* thoroughly + *porter* to carry] : meaning conveyed or implied; *also* : GIST

²**pur·port** \(,)pər-'pȯrt\ *vb* : to convey or profess outwardly as the meaning or intention : CLAIM — **pur·port·ed·ly** \-'pȯr-təd-lē\ *adv*

¹**pur·pose** \'pər-pəs\ *n* **1** : an object or result aimed at : INTENTION **2** : RESOLUTION, DETERMINATION — **pur·pose·ful** \-fəl\ *adj* — **pur·pose·ful·ly** *adv* — **pur·pose·less** *adj* — **pur·pose·ly** *adv*

²**purpose** *vb* **pur·posed; pur·pos·ing** : to propose as an aim to oneself

purr \'pər\ *n* : a low murmur typical of a contented cat — **purr** *vb*

¹**purse** \'pərs\ *n* **1** : a receptacle (as a pouch) to carry money and often other small objects in **2** : RESOURCES **3** : a sum of money offered as a prize or present

²**purse** *vb* **pursed; purs·ing** : PUCKER

purs·er \'pər-sər\ *n* : an official on a ship who keeps accounts and attends to the comfort of passengers

purs·lane \'pər-slən, -,slān\ *n* : a fleshy-leaved weedy trailing plant with tiny yellow flowers that is sometimes used in salads

pur·su·ance \pər-'sü-əns\ *n* : the act of carrying out or into effect

pur·su·ant to \-'sü-ənt-\ *prep* : in carrying out : ACCORDING TO

pur·sue \pər-'sü\ *vb* **pur·sued; pur·su·ing 1** : to follow in order to overtake or overcome : CHASE **2** : to seek to accomplish ⟨~ a goal⟩ **3** : to proceed along ⟨~ a course⟩ **4** : to engage in ⟨~ a career⟩ — **pur·su·er** *n*

pur·suit \pər-'süt\ *n* **1** : the act of pursuing **2** : OCCUPATION, BUSINESS

pu·ru·lent \'pyur-ə-lənt, -yə-\ *adj* : containing or accompanied by pus ⟨a ~ discharge⟩ — **pu·ru·lence** \-ləns\ *n*

pur·vey \(,)pər-'vā\ *vb* **pur·veyed; pur·vey·ing** : to supply (as provisions) usu. as a business — **pur·vey·ance** \-əns\ *n* — **pur·vey·or** \-ər\ *n*

pur·view \'pər-,vyü\ *n* **1** : the range or limit esp. of authority, responsibility, or intention **2** : range of vision, understanding, or cognizance

pus \'pəs\ *n* : thick yellowish white fluid matter (as in a boil) formed at a place of inflammation and infection (as an abscess) and containing germs, white blood cells, and tissue debris

¹**push** \'push\ *vb* [ME *possen, pusshen,* prob. fr. OF *pousser* to exert pressure, fr. L *pulsare,* fr. *pellere* to drive, strike] **1** : to press against with force in order to drive or impel **2** : to thrust forward, downward, or outward **3** : to urge on : press forward **4** : to cause to increase ⟨~ prices to record levels⟩ **5** : to urge or press the advancement, adoption, or practice of; *esp* : to make aggressive efforts to sell **6** : to engage in the illicit sale of narcotics

²**push** *n* **1** : a vigorous effort : DRIVE **2** : an act of pushing : SHOVE **3** : vigorous enterprise : ENERGY

push–button *adj* **1** : operated or done by means of push buttons **2** : using or dependent on complex and more or less automatic mechanisms ⟨~ warfare⟩

push button *n* : a small button or knob that when pushed operates something esp. by closing an electric circuit

push·cart \'push-,kärt\ *n* : a cart or barrow pushed by hand

push·er \'pu-shər\ *n* : one that pushes; *esp* : one that pushes illegal drugs

push·over \-,ō-vər\ *n* **1** : something easily accomplished **2** : an opponent easy to defeat **3** : SUCKER

push–up \-,əp\ *n* : a conditioning exercise performed in a prone position by raising and lowering the body while keeping the

back straight and supporting the body on the hands and toes

pushy \'pu-shē\ *adj* **push·i·er; -est** : aggressive often to an objectionable degree

pu·sil·lan·i·mous \,pyü-sə-'la-nə-məs\ *adj* [LL *pusillanimis,* fr. L *pusillus* very small (dim. of *pusus* boy) + *animus* spirit] : contemptibly timid : COWARDLY — **pu·sil·la·nim·i·ty** \,pyü-sə-lə-'ni-mə-tē\ *n*

¹**puss** \'pus\ *n* : CAT

²**puss** *n, slang* : FACE

¹**pussy** \'pu-sē\ *n, pl* **puss·ies** : CAT

²**pus·sy** \'pə-sē\ *adj* **pus·si·er; -est** : full of or resembling pus

pussy·cat \'pu-sē-,kat\ *n* : CAT

pussy·foot \-,fut\ *vb* **1** : to tread or move warily or stealthily **2** : to refrain from committing oneself

pussy willow \'pu-sē-\ *n* : a willow having large silky catkins

pus·tule \'pəs-chül\ *n* : a pus-filled pimple

put \'put\ *vb* **put; put·ting 1** : to bring into a specified position : PLACE ⟨~ the book on the table⟩ **2** : SEND, THRUST **3** : to throw with an upward pushing motion ⟨~ the shot⟩ **4** : to bring into a specified state ⟨~ the plan into effect⟩ **5** : SUBJECT ⟨~ traitors to death⟩ **6** : IMPOSE **7** : to set before one for decision ⟨~ the question⟩ **8** : EXPRESS, STATE ⟨~ my feelings into words⟩ **9** : TRANSLATE, ADAPT **10** : APPLY, ASSIGN ⟨~ them to work⟩ **11** : ESTIMATE ⟨~ the number at 20⟩ **12** : ATTACH, ATTRIBUTE ⟨~ a high value on it⟩ **13** : to take a specified course ⟨the ship ~ out to sea⟩

pu·ta·tive \'pyü-tə-tiv\ *adj* **1** : commonly accepted **2** : assumed to exist or to have existed

put–down \'put-,daun\ *n* : a belittling remark

put in *vb* **1** : to come in with : INTERPOSE ⟨*put in* a good word for me⟩ **2** : to spend time at some occupation or job ⟨*put in* eight hours at the office⟩

put off *vb* : POSTPONE, DELAY ⟨*put off* my visit⟩

¹**put–on** \'put-,ȯn, -,än\ *adj* : PRETENDED, ASSUMED

²**put–on** *n* **1** : a deliberate act of misleading someone **2** : PARODY, SPOOF

put·out \'put-,aut\ *n* : the retiring of a base runner or batter in baseball

put out *vb* **1** : EXTINGUISH **2** : ANNOY; *also* : INCONVENIENCE **3** : to cause to be out (as in baseball)

pu·tre·fy \'pyü-trə-,fī\ *vb* **-fied; -fy·ing** : to make or become putrid : ROT — **pu·tre·fac·tion** \,pyü-trə-'fak-shən\ *n* — **pu·tre·fac·tive** \-tiv\ *adj*

pu·tres·cent \pyü-'tre-sᵊnt\ *adj* : becoming putrid : ROTTING — **pu·tres·cence** \-sᵊns\ *n*

pu·trid \'pyü-trəd\ *adj* **1** : ROTTEN, DECAYED ⟨~ meat⟩ **2** : VILE, CORRUPT — **pu·trid·i·ty** \pyü-'tri-də-tē\ *n*

putsch \'puch\ *n* [G] : a secretly plotted and suddenly executed attempt to overthrow a government

putt \'pət\ *n* : a golf stroke made on the green to cause the ball to roll into the hole — **putt** *vb*

put·ta·nes·ca \,pü-tä-'nes-kä\ *adj* : served with or being a pungent tomato sauce

put·tee \,pə-'tē, 'pə-tē\ *n* [Hindi *paṭṭī* strip of cloth] **1** : a cloth strip wrapped around the lower leg **2** : a leather legging

¹**put·ter** \'pu-tər\ *n* : one that puts

²**putt·er** \'pə-tər\ *n* **1** : a golf club used in putting **2** : one that putts

³**put·ter** \'pə-tər\ *vb* **1** : to move or act aimlessly or idly **2** : TINKER

put·ty \'pə-tē\ *n, pl* **putties** [F *potée* potter's glaze, lit., potful, fr. OF, fr. *pot* pot] **1** : a doughlike cement used esp. to fasten glass in sashes **2** : one who is easily manipulated — **putty** *vb*

put up *vb* **1** : SHEATHE **2** : to prepare so as to preserve for later use **3** : to offer for public sale ⟨*put* the house *up* for auction⟩ **4** : ACCOMMODATE, LODGE ⟨*put* us *up* for the night⟩ **5** : BUILD **6** : to engage in ⟨*put up* a struggle⟩ **7** : CONTRIBUTE, PAY — **put up with** : TOLERATE **2**

¹**puz·zle** \'pə-zəl\ *vb* **puz·zled; puz·zling 1** : to bewilder mentally : PERPLEX **2** : to solve with difficulty or ingenuity ⟨~ out a riddle⟩ **3** : to be in a quandary ⟨~ over what to do⟩ **4** : to attempt a solution of a puzzle ⟨~ over a person's words⟩ ◆ *Synonyms* MYSTIFY, BEWILDER, NONPLUS, CONFOUND — **puz·zle·ment** *n* — **puz·zler** *n*

²**puzzle** *n* 1 : something that puzzles 2 : a question, problem, or contrivance designed for testing ingenuity
PVC *abbr* polyvinyl chloride
pvt *abbr* private
PW *abbr* prisoner of war
pwt *abbr* pennyweight
PX *abbr* post exchange
pya \pē-'ä\ *n* — see *kyat* at MONEY table
pyg·my *also* **pig·my** \'pig-mē\ *n, pl* **pygmies** *also* **pigmies** [ME *pigmei*, fr. L *pygmaeus* of a pygmy, dwarfish, fr. Gk *pygmaios*, fr. *pygmē* fist, measure of length] 1 *cap* : any of a small people of equatorial Africa 2 : an unusually small person; *also* : an insignificant or unimpressive person — **pygmy** *adj*
py·ja·mas \pə-'jä-məz\ *chiefly Brit var of* PAJAMAS
py·lon \'pī-,län, -lən\ *n* 1 : a usu. massive gateway; *esp* : an Egyptian one flanked by flat-topped pyramids 2 : a tower that supports wires over a long span 3 : a post or tower marking the course in an airplane race
py·or·rhea \,pī-ə-'rē-ə\ *n* : an inflammation with pus of the sockets of the teeth
¹**pyr·a·mid** \'pir-ə-,mid\ *n* 1 : a massive structure with a square base and four triangular faces meeting at a point 2 : a geometrical solid having a polygon for its base and three or more triangles for its sides that meet at a point to form the top — **py·ra·mi·dal** \pə-'ra-mə-d°l, ,pir-ə-'mid-\ *adj*
²**pyramid** *vb* 1 : to build up in the form of a pyramid : heap up 2 : to increase rapidly on a broadening base
pyramid scheme *n* : a usu. illegal operation in which participants pay to join and profit from payments made by subsequent participants

pyre \'pī(-ə)r\ *n* : a combustible heap for burning a dead body as a funeral rite
py·re·thrum \pī-'rē-thrəm\ *n* : an insecticide made from the dried heads of any of several Old World chrysanthemums
py·rim·i·dine \pī-'ri-mə-,dēn\ *n* : any of a group of bases including several (as cytosine, thymine, or uracil) that are constituents of DNA or RNA
py·rite \'pī-,rīt\ *n* : a mineral containing sulfur and iron that is brass-yellow in color
py·rol·y·sis \pī-'rä-lə-səs\ *n* : chemical change caused by the action of heat
py·ro·ma·nia \,pī-rō-'mā-nē-ə\ *n* : an irresistible impulse to start fires — **py·ro·ma·ni·ac** \-nē-,ak\ *n*
py·ro·tech·nics \,pī-rə-'tek-niks\ *n pl* 1 : a display of fireworks 2 : a spectacular display (as of extreme virtuosity) — **py·ro·tech·nic** \-nik\ *also* **py·ro·tech·ni·cal** \-ni-kəl\ *adj*
Pyr·rhic \'pir-ik\ *adj* : achieved at excessive cost ⟨a ~ victory⟩; *also* : costly to the point of outweighing expected benefits
Py·thag·o·re·an theorem \pī-,tha-gə-'rē-ən-\ *n* : a theorem in geometry: the square of the length of the hypotenuse of a right triangle equals the sum of the squares of the lengths of the other two sides
py·thon \'pī-,thän, -thən\ *n* [L, monstrous serpent killed by the god Apollo, fr. Gk *Pythōn*] : a large snake (as a boa) that squeezes and suffocates its prey; *esp* : any of the large Old World snakes that include the largest snakes living at the present time
pyx \'piks\ *n* : a small case used to carry the Eucharist to the sick

Q

¹**q** \'kyü\ *n, pl* **q's** *or* **qs** \'kyüz\ *often cap* : the 17th letter of the English alphabet
²**q** *abbr, often cap* 1 quart 2 quarto 3 queen 4 query 5 question
QB *abbr* quarterback
QED *abbr* [L *quod erat demonstrandum*] which was to be demonstrated
qin·tar \kin-'tär\ *n, pl* **qin·dar·ka** \kin-'där-kə\ — see *lek* at MONEY table
qi·vi·ut \'kē-vē-,üt\ *n* [Inuit] : the wool of the undercoat of the musk ox
Qld *abbr* Queensland
QM *abbr* quartermaster
QMC *abbr* quartermaster corps
QMG *abbr* quartermaster general
qq v *abbr* [L *quae vide*] which (*pl*) see
qr *abbr* quarter
Q rating *n* [quotient] : a scale measuring popularity based on dividing an assessment of familiarity or recognition by an assessment of favorable opinion; *also* : position on such a scale
qt *abbr* 1 quantity 2 quart
q.t. \,kyü-'tē\ *n, often cap* Q&T : QUIET — usu. used in the phrase *on the q.t.*
qto *abbr* quarto
qty *abbr* quantity
qu *or* **ques** *abbr* question
¹**quack** \'kwak\ *vb* : to make the characteristic cry of a duck
²**quack** *n* : a sound made by quacking
³**quack** *n* 1 : CHARLATAN 2 : a pretender to medical skill
  ✦ **Synonyms** FAKER, IMPOSTOR, MOUNTEBANK — **quack** *adj* — **quack·ery** \'kwa-kə-rē\ *n* — **quack·ish** *adj*
¹**quad** \'kwäd\ *n* : QUADRANGLE
²**quad** *n* 1 : QUADRUPLET 2 : a ski lift that accommodates four people
³**quad** *abbr* quadrant
quad·ran·gle \'kwä-,draŋ-gəl\ *n* 1 : QUADRILATERAL 2

: a 4-sided courtyard or enclosure — **quad·ran·gu·lar** \kwä-'draŋ-gyə-lər\ *adj*
quad·rant \'kwä-drənt\ *n* 1 : one quarter of a circle : an arc of 90° 2 : any of the four quarters into which something is divided by two lines intersecting each other at right angles
qua·drat·ic \kwä-'dra-tik\ *adj* : having or being a term in which the variable (as *x*) is squared but containing no term in which the variable is raised to a higher power than a square ⟨a ~ equation⟩ — **quadratic** *n*
qua·dren·ni·al \kwä-'dre-nē-əl\ *adj* 1 : consisting of or lasting for four years 2 : occurring every four years
qua·dren·ni·um \-nē-əm\ *n, pl* **-ni·ums** *or* **-nia** \-nē-ə\ : a period of four years
quad·ri·ceps \'kwä-drə-,seps\ *n* : a muscle of the front of the thigh that is divided into four parts
¹**quad·ri·lat·er·al** \,kwä-drə-'la-tə-rəl\ *n* : a polygon of four sides

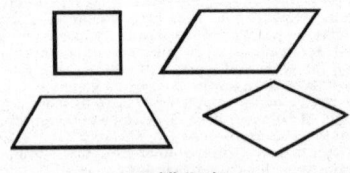

quadrilaterals

²**quadrilateral** *adj* : having four sides
qua·drille \kwä-'dril, kə-\ *n* : a square dance made up of five or six figures in various rhythms
quad·ri·par·tite \,kwä-drə-'pär-,tīt\ *adj* 1 : consisting of four parts 2 : shared by four parties or persons
quad·ri·ple·gia \,kwä-drə-'plē-jə, -jē-ə\ *n* : paralysis of both arms and both legs — **quad·ri·ple·gic** \-jik\ *adj or n*

qua·driv·i·um \kwä-ʹdri-vē-əm\ *n* : the four liberal arts of arithmetic, music, geometry, and astronomy in a medieval university

quad·ru·ped \ʹkwä-drə-ˌped\ *n* : an animal having four feet — **qua·dru·pe·dal** \kwä-ʹdrü-pə-dᵊl, ˌkwä-drə-ʹpe-\ *adj*

¹qua·dru·ple \kwä-ʹdrü-pəl, -ʹdrə-; ʹkwä-drə-\ *vb* **qua·dru·pled; qua·dru·pling** : to make or become four times as great or as many

²quadruple *adj* : FOURFOLD

qua·dru·plet \kwä-ʹdrə-plət, -ʹdrü-; ʹkwä-drə-\ *n* **1** : a combination of four of a kind **2** : one of four offspring born at one birth

¹qua·dru·pli·cate \kwä-ʹdrü-pli-kət\ *adj* **1** : repeated four times **2** : FOURTH

²qua·dru·pli·cate \-plə-ˌkāt\ *vb* **-cat·ed; -cat·ing 1** : QUADRUPLE **2** : to prepare in quadruplicate — **qua·dru·pli·ca·tion** \-ˌdrü-plə-ʹkā-shən\ *n*

³qua·dru·pli·cate \-ʹdrü-pli-kət\ *n* **1** : four copies all alike ⟨typed in ∼⟩ **2** : one of four like things

quaff \ʹkwäf, ʹkwaf\ *vb* : to drink deeply or repeatedly — **quaff** *n*

quag·mire \ʹkwag-ˌmī(-ə)r, ʹkwäg-\ *n* **1** : soft miry land that yields under the foot **2** : PREDICAMENT

qua·hog \ʹkō-ˌhòg, ʹkwò-, ʹkwō-, -ˌhäg\ *n* [modif. of Narragansett *poquaûhock*] : a round thick-shelled edible clam of the U.S.

quai \ʹkā\ *n* : QUAY

¹quail \ʹkwāl\ *n, pl* **quail** *or* **quails** [ME *quaile*, fr. AF, fr. ML *quaccula*, of imit. origin] : any of numerous small short-winged plump game birds (as a bobwhite) related to the domestic chicken

²quail *vb* [ME, to grow feeble, fr. MD *quelen*] : to lose heart : COWER ♦ **Synonyms** RECOIL, SHRINK, FLINCH, WINCE, BLANCH

quaint \ʹkwānt\ *adj* : unusual or different in character or appearance; *esp* : pleasingly old-fashioned or unfamiliar ♦ **Synonyms** ODD, QUEER, CURIOUS, STRANGE — **quaint·ly** *adv* — **quaint·ness** *n*

¹quake \ʹkwāk\ *vb* **quaked; quak·ing 1** : to shake usu. from shock or instability **2** : to tremble usu. from cold or fear

²quake *n* : a shaking or trembling; *esp* : EARTHQUAKE

Quak·er \ʹkwä-kər\ *n* : FRIEND 5

qual *abbr* quality

qual·i·fi·ca·tion \ˌkwä-lə-fə-ʹkā-shən\ *n* **1** : LIMITATION, MODIFICATION ⟨her statement stands without ∼⟩ **2** : a special skill that fits a person for some work or position **3** : REQUIREMENT ⟨a ∼ for membership⟩

qual·i·fied \ʹkwä-lə-ˌfīd\ *adj* **1** : fitted for a given purpose or job **2** : limited in some way ⟨∼ approval⟩

qual·i·fi·er \ʹkwä-lə-ˌfī(-ə)r\ *n* **1** : one that satisfies requirements **2** : a word or word group that limits the meaning of another word or word group

qual·i·fy \ʹkwä-lə-ˌfī\ *vb* **-fied; -fy·ing 1** : to reduce from a general to a particular form : MODIFY **2** : to make less harsh **3** : to limit the meaning of (as a noun) **4** : to fit by skill or training for some purpose **5** : to give or have a legal right to do something **6** : to demonstrate the necessary ability ⟨∼ for the finals⟩ ♦ **Synonyms** MODERATE, TEMPER

qual·i·ta·tive \ʹkwä-lə-ˌtā-tiv\ *adj* : of, relating to, or involving quality — **qual·i·ta·tive·ly** *adv*

¹qual·i·ty \ʹkwä-lə-tē\ *n, pl* **-ties 1** : peculiar and essential character : NATURE **2** : degree of excellence **3** : high social status **4** : a distinguishing attribute

²quality *adj* : being of high quality

qualm \ʹkwäm, ʹkwälm\ *n* **1** : a sudden attack (as of nausea) **2** : a sudden feeling of doubt, fear, or uneasiness esp. in not following one's conscience or better judgment

qualm·ish \ʹkwä-mish, ʹkwäl-\ *adj* **1** : feeling qualms : NAUSEATED **2** : overly scrupulous : SQUEAMISH **3** : of, relating to, or producing qualms

quan·da·ry \ʹkwän-drē\ *n, pl* **-ries** : a state of perplexity or doubt

quan·ti·fy \ʹkwän-tə-ˌfī\ *vb* **-fied; -fy·ing** : to determine, express, or measure the quantity of — **quan·ti·fi·able** \ˌkwän-tə-ʹfī-ə-bəl\ *adj*

quan·ti·ta·tive \ʹkwän-tə-ˌtā-tiv\ *adj* : of, relating to, or involving quantity — **quan·ti·ta·tive·ly** *adv*

quan·ti·ty \ʹkwän-tə-tē\ *n, pl* **-ties 1** : AMOUNT, NUMBER **2** : a considerable amount

quan·tize \ʹkwän-ˌtīz\ *vb* **quan·tized; quan·tiz·ing** : to subdivide (as energy) into small units

¹quan·tum \ʹkwän-təm\ *n, pl* **quan·ta** \-tə\ [L, neut. of *quantus* how much] **1** : QUANTITY, AMOUNT **2** : an elemental unit of energy

²quantum *adj* **1** : LARGE, SIGNIFICANT **2** : relating to or employing the principles of quantum mechanics

quantum mechanics *n sing or pl* : a theory of matter based on the concept of possession of wave properties by elementary particles — **quantum mechanical** *adj* — **quantum mechanically** *adv*

quantum theory *n* **1** : a theory in physics based on the idea that radiant energy (as light) is composed of small separate packets of energy **2** : QUANTUM MECHANICS

quar *abbr* quarterly

quar·an·tine \ʹkwòr-ən-ˌtēn\ *n* [modif. of It *quarantena*, lit., period of forty days, fr. *quaranta* forty, fr. L *quadraginta*] **1** : a period during which a ship suspected of carrying contagious disease is forbidden contact with the shore **2** : a restraint on the movements of persons or goods to prevent the spread of pests or disease **3** : a place or period of quarantine **4** : a state of enforced isolation — **quarantine** *vb*

quark \ʹkwórk, ʹkwärk\ *n* : a hypothetical elementary particle that carries a fractional charge and is held to be a constituent of heavier particles (as protons and neutrons)

¹quar·rel \ʹkwór-əl\ *n* **1** : a ground of dispute **2** : a verbal clash : CONFLICT — **quar·rel·some** \-səm\ *adj*

²quarrel *vb* **-reled** *or* **-relled; -rel·ing** *or* **-rel·ling 1** : to find fault **2** : to dispute angrily : WRANGLE

¹quar·ry \ʹkwór-ē\ *n, pl* **quarries** [ME *querre* entrails of game given to the hounds, fr. AF *cureie*, *quereie*, fr. *quir*, *cuir* skin, hide (on which the entrails were placed), fr. L *corium*] **1** : game hunted with hawks **2** : PREY

²quarry *n, pl* **quarries** [ME *quarey*, alter. of *quarrere*, fr. AF, fr. VL **quadraria*, fr. LL *quadrus* hewn (lit., squared) stone, fr. L *quadrum* square] : an open excavation usu. for obtaining building stone or limestone — **quarry** *vb*

quart \ʹkwórt\ *n* — see WEIGHT table

¹quar·ter \ʹkwór-tər\ *n* **1** : one of four equal parts **2** : a fourth of a dollar; *also* : a coin of this value **3** : a district of a city **4** *pl* : LODGINGS ⟨moved into new ∼s⟩ **5** : MERCY, CLEMENCY ⟨gave no ∼⟩ **6** : a fourth part of the moon's period

²quarter *vb* **1** : to divide into four equal parts **2** : to provide with shelter

¹quar·ter·back \-ˌbak\ *n* : a football player who calls the signals and directs the offensive play for the team

²quarterback *vb* **1** : to direct the offensive play of a football team **2** : LEAD, BOSS

quar·ter·deck \-ˌdek\ *n* : the stern area of a ship's upper deck

quarter horse *n* : any of a breed of compact muscular saddle horses characterized by great endurance and by high speed for short distances

¹quar·ter·ly \ʹkwór-tər-lē\ *adv* : at 3-month intervals

²quarterly *adj* : occurring, issued, or payable at 3-month intervals

³quarterly *n, pl* **-lies** : a periodical published four times a year

quar·ter·mas·ter \-ˌmas-tər\ *n* **1** : a petty officer who attends to a ship's helm, binnacle, and signals **2** : an army officer who provides clothing and subsistence for troops

quar·ter·staff \-ˌstaf\ *n, pl* **-staves** \-ˌstavz, -ˌstävz\ : a long stout staff formerly used as a weapon

quar·tet *also* **quar·tette** \kwór-ʹtet\ *n* **1** : a musical composition for four instruments or voices **2** : a group of four and esp. of four musicians

quar·to \ʹkwór-tō\ *n, pl* **quartos 1** : the size of a piece of paper cut four from a sheet **2** : a book printed on quarto pages

quartz \ʹkwórts\ *n* : a common often transparent crystalline mineral that is a form of silica

quartz·ite \ʹkwórt-ˌsīt\ *n* : a compact granular rock composed of quartz and derived from sandstone

qua·sar \ʹkwā-ˌzär, -ˌsär\ *n* : any of a class of extremely distant starlike celestial objects

¹quash \ʹkwäsh, ʹkwòsh\ *vb* **1** : to suppress or extinguish summarily and completely : QUELL

²quash *vb* : to nullify by judicial action

qua·si \'kwā-ˌzī, -ˌsī; 'kwä-zē, -sē\ *adj* : being in some sense or degree ⟨a ~ corporation⟩

quasi- *comb form* [L, as if, as it were, approximately, fr. *quam* as + *si* if] : in some sense or degree ⟨*quasi*-historical⟩

qua·si·gov·ern·men·tal \-gə-vərn-'men-t°l\ *adj* : supported by the government but managed privately

Qua·ter·na·ry \'kwä-tər-ˌner-ē, kwə-'tər-nə-rē\ *adj* : of, relating to, or being the geologic period from the end of the Tertiary to the present — **Quaternary** *n*

qua·train \'kwä-ˌtrān\ *n* : a unit of four lines of verse

qua·tre·foil \'ka-tər-ˌfȯi(-ə)l, 'ka-trə-\ *n* : a stylized figure often of a flower with four petals

qua·ver \'kwä-vər\ *vb* **1** : TREMBLE, SHAKE **2** : TRILL **3** : to speak in tremulous tones ✦ *Synonyms* SHUDDER, QUAKE, TWITTER, QUIVER, SHIVER — **quaver** *n*

quay \'kē, 'kwä, 'kā\ *n* : WHARF

Que *abbr* Quebec

quean \'kwēn\ *n* : PROSTITUTE

quea·sy \'kwē-zē\ *adj* **quea·si·er; -est** : NAUSEATED — **quea·si·ly** \-zə-lē\ *adv* — **quea·si·ness** \-zē-nəs\ *n*

Que·chua \'ke-chə-wə, 'kech-wə\ *n* : a family of languages spoken in Peru and adjacent countries of the So. American Andes

queen \'kwēn\ *n* [ME *quene*, fr. OE *cwēn* woman, wife, queen] **1** : the wife or widow of a king **2** : a female monarch **3** : a woman notable for rank, power, or attractiveness **4** : the most powerful piece in the game of chess **5** : a playing card bearing the figure of a queen **6** : a fertile female of a social insect (as a bee or termite) — **queen·ly** *adj*

Queen Anne's lace \-'anz-\ *n* : a widely naturalized Eurasian herb from which the cultivated carrot originated

queen consort *n, pl* **queens consort** : the wife of a reigning king

queen mother *n* : a dowager queen who is mother of the reigning sovereign

queen–size *adj* : having dimensions of approximately 60 inches by 80 inches ⟨a ~ bed⟩; *also* : of a size that fits a queen-size bed

¹queer \'kwir\ *adj* **1** : COUNTERFEIT ⟨~ money⟩ **2** : differing from the usual or normal : PECULIAR, STRANGE **3** *often disparaging* : HOMOSEXUAL; *also, sometimes offensive* : of, relating to, or used by homosexuals ✦ *Synonyms* WEIRD, BIZARRE, ECCENTRIC, CURIOUS — **queer** *n* — **queer·ly** *adv* — **queer·ness** *n*

²queer *vb* : to spoil the effect of : DISRUPT ⟨~ed our plans⟩

queer theory *n* : an approach to literary and cultural study that rejects traditional categories of gender and sexuality

quell \'kwel\ *vb* **1** : to put an end to by force ⟨~ a riot⟩ **2** : CALM, PACIFY ⟨~ fears⟩

quench \'kwench\ *vb* **1** : PUT OUT, EXTINGUISH **2** : SUBDUE **3** : SLAKE, SATISFY ⟨~ed his thirst⟩ — **quench·able** *adj* — **quench·er** *n* — **quench·less** *adj*

quer·u·lous \'kwer-ə-ləs, -yə-\ *adj* **1** : constantly complaining **2** : FRETFUL, WHINING ⟨a ~ voice⟩ ✦ *Synonyms* PETULANT, PETTISH, IRRITABLE, PEEVISH, HUFFY — **quer·u·lous·ly** *adv* — **quer·u·lous·ness** *n*

que·ry \'kwir-ē, 'kwer-\ *n, pl* **queries** : QUESTION — **query** *vb*

que·sa·dil·la \ˌkā-sə-'dē-ə\ *n* : a tortilla filled with a savory mixture, folded, and usu. fried

quest \'kwest\ *n* : SEARCH ⟨in ~ of game⟩ — **quest** *vb*

¹ques·tion \'kwes-chən\ *n* **1** : an interrogative expression **2** : a subject for debate; *also* : a proposition to be voted on **3** : INQUIRY **4** : DISPUTE ⟨true beyond ~⟩

²question *vb* **1** : to ask questions **2** : DOUBT, DISPUTE ⟨~ed the verdict⟩ **3** : to subject to analysis : EXAMINE ✦ *Synonyms* INTERROGATE, QUIZ, QUERY — **question·er** *n*

ques·tion·able \'kwes-chə-nə-bəl\ *adj* **1** : not certain or exact : DOUBTFUL **2** : not believed to be true, sound, or moral ✦ *Synonyms* DUBIOUS, PROBLEMATICAL, MOOT, DEBATABLE — **ques·tion·ably** \-blē\ *adv*

question mark *n* : a punctuation mark ? used esp. at the end of a sentence to indicate a direct question

ques·tion·naire \ˌkwes-chə-'ner\ *n* : a set of questions for obtaining information

quet·zal \ket-'säl, -'sal\ *n, pl* **quetzals** *or* **quet·za·les** \-'sä-

lās, -'sa-\ **1** : a Central American bird with brilliant plumage **2** *pl* **quetzales** — see MONEY table

¹queue \'kyü\ *n* [F, lit., tail, fr. OF *cue, coe,* fr. L *cauda, coda*] **1** : a braid of hair usu. worn hanging at the back of the head **2** : a waiting line (as of persons)

²queue *vb* **queued; queu·ing** *or* **queue·ing** : to line up in a queue

quib·ble \'kwi-bəl\ *n* **1** : an evasion of or shifting from the point at issue **2** : a minor objection or criticism — **quibble** *vb* — **quib·bler** *n*

¹quick \'kwik\ *adj* **1** : LIVING **2** : RAPID, SPEEDY ⟨~ steps⟩ **3** : prompt to understand, think, or perceive : ALERT **4** : easily aroused ⟨a ~ temper⟩ **5** : turning or bending sharply ⟨a ~ turn in the road⟩ ✦ *Synonyms* FLEET, FAST, HASTY, EXPEDITIOUS — **quick** *adv* — **quick·ly** *adv* — **quick·ness** *n*

²quick *n* **1** : a sensitive area of living flesh **2** : a vital part : HEART

quick bread *n* : a bread made with a leavening agent that permits immediate baking of the dough or batter

quick·en \'kwi-kən\ *vb* **1** : to come to life : REVIVE **2** : AROUSE, STIMULATE ⟨curiosity ~ed my interest⟩ **3** : to increase in speed : HASTEN **4** : to show vitality (as by growing or moving) ✦ *Synonyms* ANIMATE, ENLIVEN, LIVEN, VIVIFY

quick–freeze \'kwik-'frēz\ *vb* **-froze** \-'frōz\; **-fro·zen** \-'frō-z°n\; **-freez·ing** : to freeze (food) for preservation so rapidly that the natural juices and flavor are not lost

quick·ie \'kwi-kē\ *n* : something hurriedly done or made

quick·lime \'kwik-ˌlīm\ *n* : ¹LIME

quick·sand \-ˌsand\ *n* : a deep mass of loose sand mixed with water

quick·sil·ver \-ˌsil-vər\ *n* : MERCURY 1

quick·step \-ˌstep\ *n* : a spirited march tune or dance

quick–wit·ted \'kwik-'wi-təd\ *adj* : mentally alert ✦ *Synonyms* CLEVER, BRIGHT, SMART, INTELLIGENT

quid \'kwid\ *n* : a lump of something chewable ⟨a ~ of tobacco⟩

quid pro quo \ˌkwid-ˌprō-'kwō\ *n* [NL, something for something] : something given or received for something else

qui·es·cent \kwī-'e-s°nt\ *adj* : being at rest : QUIET ✦ *Synonyms* LATENT, DORMANT, POTENTIAL — **qui·es·cence** \-s°ns\ *n*

¹qui·et \'kwī-ət\ *n* : REPOSE

²quiet *adj* **1** : marked by little motion or activity : CALM **2** : GENTLE, MILD ⟨a ~ disposition⟩ **3** : enjoyed in peace and relaxation ⟨a ~ cup of tea⟩ **4** : free from noise or uproar **5** : not showy : MODEST ⟨~ clothes⟩ **6** : SECLUDED ⟨a ~ nook⟩ — **quiet** *adv* — **qui·et·ly** *adv* — **qui·et·ness** *n*

³quiet *vb* **1** : CALM, PACIFY **2** : to become quiet — usu. used with *down*

qui·etude \'kwī-ə-ˌtüd, -ˌtyüd\ *n* : QUIETNESS, REPOSE

qui·etus \kwī-'ē-təs\ *n* [ME *quietus est,* fr. ML, he is quit, formula of discharge from obligation] **1** : final settlement (as of a debt) **2** : DEATH

quill \'kwil\ *n* **1** : a large stiff feather; *also* : the hollow tubular part of a feather **2** : one of the hollow sharp spines of a hedgehog or porcupine **3** : a pen made from a feather

¹quilt \'kwilt\ *n* : a padded bed coverlet

²quilt *vb* **1** : to fill, pad, or line like a quilt **2** : to stitch or sew in layers with padding in between **3** : to make quilts

quince \'kwins\ *n* : a hard yellow applelike fruit; *also* : a tree related to the roses that bears this fruit

qui·nine \'kwī-ˌnīn\ *n* : a bitter white drug obtained from cinchona bark and used esp. in treating malaria

qui·noa \'kēn-ˌwä, kē-'nō-ə\ *n* [Sp, fr. Quechua *kinua*] : the starchy seeds of an annual herb related to spinach which are used as food and ground into flour; *also* : this herb

quint \'kwint\ *n* : QUINTUPLET

quin·tal \'kwin-t°l, 'kan-\ *n* : HUNDREDWEIGHT

quin·tes·sence \kwin-'te-s°ns\ *n* **1** : the purest essence of something **2** : the most typical example — **quin·tes·sen·tial** \ˌkwin-tə-'sen-chəl\ *adj* — **quin·tes·sen·tial·ly** *adv*

quin·tet \kwin-'tet\ *n* **1** : a musical composition for five instruments or voices **2** : a group of five and esp. of five musicians

¹quin·tu·ple \kwin-'tü-pəl, -'tyü-, -'tə-\ *adj* **1** : having five units or members **2** : being five times as great or as many — **quintuple** *n*

²quintuple *vb* **quin·tu·pled; quin·tu·pling** : to make or become five times as great or as many

quin·tu·plet \kwin-'tə-plət, -'tü-, -'tyü-\ *n* **1** : a group of five of a kind **2** : one of five offspring born at one birth

¹quin·tu·pli·cate \kwin-'tü-pli-kət, -'tyü-\ *adj* **1** : repeated five times **2** : FIFTH ⟨file the ~ copy⟩

²quintuplicate *n* **1** : one of five like things **2** : five copies all alike ⟨typed in ~⟩

³quin·tu·pli·cate \-plə-ˌkāt\ *vb* **-cat·ed; -cat·ing** **1** : QUINTUPLE **2** : to provide in quintuplicate

¹quip \'kwip\ *n* : a clever remark : GIBE

²quip *vb* **quipped; quip·ping** **1** : to make quips : GIBE **2** : to jest or gibe at

quire \'kwī(-ə)r\ *n* : a set of 24 or sometimes 25 sheets of paper of the same size and quality

quirk \'kwərk\ *n* : a peculiarity of action or behavior — **quirky** *adj*

quirt \'kwərt\ *n* : a riding whip with a short handle and a rawhide lash

quis·ling \'kwiz-liŋ\ *n* [Vidkun *Quisling* †1945 Norw. politician who collaborated with the Nazis] : one who helps the invaders of one's own country

quit \'kwit\ *vb* **quit** *also* **quit·ted; quit·ting** **1** : CONDUCT, BEHAVE ⟨~ themselves well⟩ **2** : to depart from : LEAVE; *also* : to bring to an end **3** : to give up for good ⟨~ smoking⟩ ⟨~ my job⟩ **♦ Synonyms** ACQUIT, COMPORT, DEPORT, DEMEAN — **quit·ter** *n*

quite \'kwīt\ *adv* **1** : COMPLETELY, WHOLLY ⟨not ~ finished⟩ **2** : to an extreme : POSITIVELY **3** : to a considerable extent : RATHER

quits \'kwits\ *adj* : even or equal with another

quit·tance \'kwi-tᵊns\ *n* : REQUITAL

¹quiv·er \'kwi-vər\ *n* : a case for carrying arrows

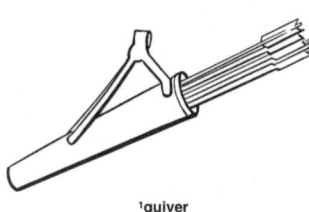

¹quiver

²quiver *vb* **quiv·ered; quiv·er·ing** : to shake with a slight trembling motion **♦ Synonyms** SHIVER, SHUDDER, QUAVER, QUAKE, TREMBLE — **quiv·er·ing·ly** *adv*

³quiver *n* : the act or action of quivering : TREMOR

qui vive \kē-'vēv\ *n* [F *qui-vive,* fr. *qui vive?* long live who?, challenge of a French sentry] : ALERT ⟨on the *qui vive* for prowlers⟩

quix·ot·ic \kwik-'sä-tik\ *adj* [fr. Don *Quixote,* hero of the novel *Don Quixote de la Mancha* by Cervantes] : foolishly impractical esp. in the pursuit of ideals — **quix·ot·i·cal·ly** \-ti-kə-lē\ *adv*

¹quiz \'kwiz\ *n, pl* **quiz·zes** **1** : an eccentric person **2** : PRACTICAL JOKE **3** : a short oral or written test

²quiz *vb* **quizzed; quiz·zing** **1** : MOCK **2** : to look at inquisitively **3** : to question closely **♦ Synonyms** ASK, INTERROGATE, QUERY

quiz·zi·cal \'kwi-zi-kəl\ *adj* **1** : comically quaint **2** : mildly teasing or mocking **3** : expressive of puzzlement, curiosity, or disbelief

quoit \'kwät, 'kwȯit, 'kȯit\ *n* **1** : a flattened ring of iron or circle of rope used in a throwing game **2** *pl* : a game in which quoits are thrown at an upright pin in an attempt to ring the pin

quon·dam \'kwän-dəm, -ˌdam\ *adj* [L, at one time, formerly, fr. *quom, cum* when] : FORMER ⟨a ~ friend⟩

quo·rum \'kwȯr-əm\ *n* : the number of members required to be present for business to be legally transacted

quot *abbr* quotation

quo·ta \'kwō-tə\ *n* : a proportional part esp. when assigned : SHARE

quot·able \'kwō-tə-bəl\ *adj* : fit for or worth quoting — **quot·abil·i·ty** \-'bi-lə-tē\ *n*

quo·ta·tion \kwō-'tā-shən\ *n* **1** : the act or process of quoting **2** : the price currently bid or offered for something **3** : something that is quoted

quotation mark *n* : one of a pair of punctuation marks " " or ' ' used esp. to indicate the beginning and end of a quotation in which exact phraseology is directly cited

quote \'kwōt\ *vb* **quot·ed; quot·ing** [ML *quotare* to mark the number of, number references, fr. L *quotus* of what number or quantity, fr. *quot* how many, (as) many as] **1** : to speak or write a passage from another usu. with acknowledgment; *also* : to repeat a passage in substantiation or illustration **2** : to state the market price of a commodity, stock, or bond **3** : to inform a hearer or reader that matter following is quoted — **quote** *n*

quoth \'kwōth\ *vb past* [ME, past of *quethen* to say, fr. OE *cwethan*] *archaic* : SAID — usu. used in the 1st and 3d persons with the subject following

quo·tid·i·an \kwō-'ti-dē-ən\ *adj* **1** : DAILY **2** : COMMONPLACE, ORDINARY ⟨~ concerns⟩

quo·tient \'kwō-shənt\ *n* : the number obtained by dividing one number by another

qv *abbr* [L *quod vide*] which see

qy *abbr* query

R

¹r \'är\ *n, pl* **r's** *or* **rs** \'ärz\ *often cap* : the 18th letter of the English alphabet

²r *abbr, often cap* **1** rabbi **2** radius **3** rare **4** Republican **5** rerun **6** resistance **7** right **8** river **9** roentgen **10** rook **11** run

Ra *symbol* radium

RA *abbr* **1** regular army **2** Royal Academy

¹rab·bet \'ra-bət\ *n* : a groove in the edge or face of a surface (as a board) esp. to receive another piece

²rabbet *vb* : to cut a rabbet in; *also* : to join by means of a rabbet

rab·bi \'ra-ˌbī\ *n* [ME, fr. OE, fr. LL, fr. Gk *rhabbi,* fr. Heb *rabbī* my master, fr. *rabh* master + *-ī* my] **1** : MASTER, TEACHER — used by Jews as a term of address **2** : a Jew trained and ordained for professional religious leadership — **rab·bin·ic** \rə-'bi-nik\ *or* **rab·bin·i·cal** \-ni-kəl\ *adj*

rab·bin·ate \'ra-bə-nət, -ˌnāt\ *n* **1** : the office of a rabbi **2** : the whole body of rabbis

rab·bit \'ra-bət\ *n, pl* **rabbit** *or* **rabbits** : any of various long-eared short-tailed burrowing mammals distinguished from the related hares by being blind, furless, and helpless at birth; *also* : the pelt of a rabbit

rabbit ears *n pl* : an indoor V-shaped television antenna

rab·ble \'ra-bəl\ *n* **1** : MOB **2** : the lowest class of people

rab·ble-rous·er \'ra-bəl-ˌraü-zər\ *n* : one that stirs up (as to hatred or violence) the masses of people

ra·bid \'ra-bəd\ *adj* **1** : VIOLENT, FURIOUS **2** : being fanatical or extreme **3** : affected with rabies — **ra·bid·ly** *adv*

ra·bies \'rā-bēz\ *n, pl* **rabies** [NL, fr. L, madness] : an acute deadly virus disease of the nervous system transmitted by the bite of an affected animal

rac·coon \ra-'kün\ *n, pl* **raccoon** *or* **raccoons** : a gray No. American chiefly tree-dwelling mammal with a black mask, a bushy ringed tail, and nocturnal habits; *also* : its pelt

¹**race** \'rās\ *n* **1** : a strong current of running water; *also* : its channel **2** : an onward course (as of time or life) **3** : a contest of speed **4** : a contest for a desired end (as election to office)

²**race** *vb* **raced; rac·ing** **1** : to run in a race **2** : to run swiftly : RUSH **3** : to engage in a race with **4** : to drive or ride at high speed — **rac·er** *n*

³**race** *n* **1** : a family, tribe, people, or nation of the same stock **2** : a group of individuals within a biological species able to breed together **3** : a category of humankind that shares certain distinctive physical traits — **ra·cial** \'rā-shəl\ *adj* — **ra·cial·ly** *adv*

race·course \'rās-ˌkórs\ *n* : a course for racing

race·horse \-ˌhórs\ *n* : a horse bred or kept for racing

ra·ceme \rā-'sēm\ *n* [L *racemus* bunch of grapes] : a flower cluster with flowers borne along a stem and blooming from the base toward the tip — **rac·e·mose** \'ra-sə-ˌmōs\ *adj*

race·track \'rās-ˌtrak\ *n* : a usu. oval course on which races are run

race·way \-ˌwā\ *n* **1** : a channel for a current of water **2** : RACECOURSE

ra·cial·ism \'rā-shə-ˌli-zəm\ *n* : a theory that race determines human traits and capacities; *also* : RACISM — **ra·cial·ist** \-list\ *n* — **ra·cial·is·tic** \ˌrā-shə-'lis-tik\ *adj*

ra·cial·ize \'rā-shə-ˌlīz\ *vb* **-ized; -iz·ing** : to give a racial character to

racing form *n* : a paper giving data about racehorses for use by bettors

rac·ism \'rā-ˌsi-zəm\ *n* : a belief that some races are by nature superior to others; *also* : discrimination based on such belief — **rac·ist** \-sist\ *n*

¹**rack** \'rak\ *n* **1** : an instrument of torture on which a body is stretched **2** : a framework on or in which something may be placed (as for display or storage) **3** : a bar with teeth on one side to mesh with a pinion or worm gear

rack 3: with pinion gear

²**rack** *vb* **1** : to torture on or as if on a rack **2** : to stretch or strain by force **3** : TORMENT **4** : to place on or in a rack

¹**rack·et** *or* **rac·quet** \'ra-kət\ *n* [MF *raquette*, ultim. fr. ML *rasceta* wrist, carpus, fr. Ar *rusgh* wrist] : a light bat made of netting stretched in an oval open frame having a handle and used for striking a ball or shuttlecock

²**racket** *n* **1** : confused noise : DIN **2** : a fraudulent or dishonest scheme or activity

³**racket** *vb* : to make a racket

rack·e·teer \ˌra-kə-'tir\ *n* : a person who obtains money by an illegal enterprise usu. involving intimidation — **rack·e·teer·ing** *n*

rack up *vb* : ACHIEVE, GAIN ⟨*racked up* their 10th victory⟩

ra·con·teur \ˌra-ˌkän-'tər\ *n* : one good at telling anecdotes

rac·quet·ball \'ra-kət-ˌbòl\ *n* : a game similar to handball that is played on a 4-walled court with a short-handled racket

racy \'rā-sē\ *adj* **rac·i·er; -est** **1** : full of zest **2** : PUNGENT, SPICY **3** : RISQUÉ, SUGGESTIVE ⟨~ jokes⟩ — **rac·i·ly** \'rā-sə-lē\ *adv* — **rac·i·ness** \-sē-nəs\ *n*

rad *abbr* **1** radical **2** radio **3** radius

ra·dar \'rā-ˌdär\ *n* [*radio detecting and ranging*] : a device that emits radio waves for detecting and locating an object by the reflection of the radio waves and that may use this reflection to determine the object's direction and speed

radar gun *n* : a handheld device that uses radar to measure the speed of a moving object

ra·dar·scope \'rā-ˌdär-ˌskōp\ *n* : a visual display for a radar receiver

¹**ra·di·al** \'rā-dē-əl\ *adj* : arranged or having parts arranged like rays around a common center ⟨the ~ form of a starfish⟩ — **ra·di·al·ly** *adv*

²**radial** *n* : a pneumatic tire with cords laid perpendicular to the center line

radial engine *n* : an internal combustion engine with cylinders arranged radially like the spokes of a wheel

ra·di·an \'rā-dē-ən\ *n* : a unit of measure for angles that is equal to approximately 57.3 degrees

ra·di·ant \'rā-dē-ənt\ *adj* **1** : SHINING, GLOWING **2** : beaming with happiness **3** : transmitted by radiation
✦ **Synonyms** BRILLIANT, BRIGHT, LUMINOUS, LUSTROUS — **ra·di·ance** \-əns\ *n* — **ra·di·ant·ly** *adv*

radiant energy *n* : energy traveling as electromagnetic waves

ra·di·ate \'rā-dē-ˌāt\ *vb* **-at·ed; -at·ing** **1** : to send out rays : SHINE, GLOW **2** : to issue in or as if in rays ⟨light ~*s*⟩ **3** : to spread around as from a center

ra·di·a·tion \ˌrā-dē-'ā-shən\ *n* **1** : the action or process of radiating **2** : the process of emitting radiant energy in the form of waves or particles; *also* : something (as an X-ray beam) that is radiated

radiation sickness *n* : sickness that results from exposure to radiation and is commonly marked by fatigue, nausea, vomiting, loss of teeth and hair, and in more severe cases by damage to blood-forming tissue

radiation therapy *n* : RADIOTHERAPY

ra·di·a·tor \'rā-dē-ˌā-tər\ *n* : any of various devices (as a set of pipes or tubes) for transferring heat from a fluid within to an area or object outside

¹**rad·i·cal** \'ra-di-kəl\ *adj* [ME, fr. LL *radicalis*, fr. L *radic-, radix* root] **1** : FUNDAMENTAL, EXTREME, THOROUGHGOING **2** : of or relating to radicals in politics — **rad·i·cal·ism** \-kə-ˌli-zəm\ *n* — **rad·i·cal·ly** *adv*

²**radical** *n* **1** : a person who favors rapid and sweeping changes in laws and methods of government **2** FREE RADICAL; *also* : a group of atoms considered as a unit in certain reactions or as a subunit of a larger molecule **3** : a mathematical expression indicating a root by means of a radical sign; *also* : RADICAL SIGN

rad·i·cal·ise *Brit var of* RADICALIZE

rad·i·cal·ize \-kə-ˌlīz\ *vb* **-ized; -iz·ing** : to make radical esp. in politics — **rad·i·cal·i·za·tion** \ˌra-di-kə-lə-'zā-shən\ *n*

radical sign *n* : the sign √ placed before a mathematical expression to indicate that its root is to be taken

ra·dic·chio \ra-'di-kē-ō\ *n, pl* **-chios** : a chicory with reddish variegated leaves

radii *pl of* RADIUS

¹**ra·dio** \'rā-dē-ˌō\ *n, pl* **ra·di·os** **1** : the wireless transmission or reception of signals using electromagnetic waves **2** : a radio receiving set **3** : the radio broadcasting industry — **radio** *adj*

²**radio** *vb* : to communicate or send a message to by radio

ra·dio·ac·tiv·i·ty \ˌrā-dē-ō-ˌak-'ti-və-tē\ *n* : the property that some elements or isotopes have of spontaneously emitting energetic particles by the disintegration of their atomic nuclei — **ra·dio·ac·tive** \-'ak-tiv\ *adj*

radio astronomy *n* : astronomy dealing with radio waves received from outside the earth's atmosphere

ra·dio·car·bon \ˌrā-dē-ō-'kär-bən\ *n* : CARBON 14

radio frequency *n* : an electromagnetic wave frequency intermediate between audio frequencies and infrared frequencies used esp. for communication and radar signals

ra·dio·gram \'rā-dē-ō-ˌgram\ *n* : a message transmitted by radio

ra·dio·graph \-ˌgraf\ *n* : a photograph made by some form of radiation other than light; *esp* : an X-ray photograph — **radiograph** *vb* — **ra·dio·graph·ic** \ˌrā-dē-ō-'gra-fik\ *adj* — **ra·dio·graph·i·cal·ly** \-fi-k(ə-)lē\ *adv* — **ra·di·og·ra·phy** \ˌrā-dē-'ä-grə-fē\ *n*

ra·dio·iso·tope \ˌrā-dē-ō-'ī-sə-ˌtōp\ *n* : a radioactive isotope

ra·di·ol·o·gy \ˌrā-dē-'ä-lə-jē\ *n* : the use of radiant energy (as X-rays and radium radiations) in medicine — **ra·di·ol·o·gist** \-jist\ *n*

ra·dio·man \'rā-dē-ō-ˌman\ *n* : a radio operator or technician

ra·di·om·e·ter \ˌrā-dē-'ä-mə-tər\ *n* : an instrument for measuring the intensity of radiant energy — **ra·dio·met·ric** \ˌrā-dē-ō-'me-trik\ *adj* — **ra·di·om·e·try** \-mə-trē\ *n*

ra·dio·phone \'rā-dē-ə-ˌfōn\ *n* : RADIOTELEPHONE

ra·dio·sonde \'rā-dē-ō-ˌsänd\ *n* : a small radio transmitter carried aloft (as by balloon) and used to transmit meteorological data

ra·dio·tele·phone \ˌrā-dē-ō-'te-lə-ˌfōn\ *n* : a telephone that uses radio waves wholly or partly instead of connecting wires — **ra·dio·te·le·pho·ny** \-tə-'le-fə-nē, -'te-lə-ˌfō-nē\ *n*

radio telescope *n* : a radio receiver-antenna combination used for observation in radio astronomy

ra·dio·ther·a·py \ˌrā-dē-ō-'ther-ə-pē\ *n* : the treatment of disease by means of radiation (as X-rays) — **ra·dio·ther·a·pist** \-pist\ *n*

rad·ish \'ra-dish\ *n* [ME, alter. of OE rædic, fr. L radic-, radix root, radish] : a pungent fleshy root usu. eaten raw; *also* : a plant related to the mustards that produces this root

ra·di·um \'rā-dē-əm\ *n* [NL, fr. L radius ray] : a very radioactive metallic chemical element that is used in the treatment of cancer

ra·di·us \'rā-dē-əs\ *n, pl* **ra·dii** \-ē-ˌī\ *also* **ra·di·us·es** **1** : a straight line extending from the center of a circle or a sphere to the circumference or surface; *also* : the length of a radius **2** : the bone on the thumb side of the human forearm **3** : a circular area defined by the length of its radius ♦ *Synonyms* RANGE, REACH, SCOPE, COMPASS

RADM *abbr* rear admiral

ra·don \'rā-ˌdän\ *n* : a heavy radioactive gaseous chemical element

RAF *abbr* Royal Air Force

raf·fia \'ra-fē-ə\ *n* : fiber used esp. for making baskets and hats that is obtained from the stalks of the leaves of a tropical African palm (**raffia palm**)

raff·ish \'ra-fish\ *adj* : jaunty or sporty esp. in a flashy or vulgar manner — **raff·ish·ly** *adv* — **raff·ish·ness** *n*

¹raf·fle \'ra-fəl\ *vb* **raf·fled; raf·fling** : to dispose of by a raffle

²raffle *n* : a lottery in which the prize is won by one of a number of persons buying chances

¹raft \'raft\ *n* **1** : a number of logs or timbers fastened together to form a float **2** : a flat structure for support or transportation on water

²raft *vb* **1** : to travel or transport by raft **2** : to make into a raft

³raft *n* : a large amount or number

raf·ter \'raf-tər\ *n* : any of the parallel beams that support a roof

¹rag \'rag\ *n* **1** : a waste piece of cloth **2** : a sleazy newspaper

²rag *n* : a composition in ragtime

ra·ga \'rä-gə\ *n* **1** : a traditional melodic pattern or mode in Indian music **2** : an improvisation based on a raga

rag·a·muf·fin \'ra-gə-ˌmə-fən\ *n* [ME Ragamuffyn, name for a ragged, oafish person] : a ragged dirty person; *esp* : a poorly clothed often dirty child

¹rage \'rāj\ *n* **1** : violent and uncontrolled anger **2** : VOGUE, FASHION

²rage *vb* **raged; rag·ing** **1** : to be furiously angry : RAVE **2** : to continue out of control ⟨the fire *raged*⟩

rag·ged \'ra-gəd\ *adj* **1** : TORN, TATTERED ⟨a ~ dress⟩; *also* : wearing tattered clothes **2** : done in an uneven way ⟨a ~ performance⟩ — **rag·ged·ly** *adv* — **rag·ged·ness** *n*

rag·lan \'ra-glən\ *n* : an overcoat with sleeves (**raglan sleeves**) sewn in with seams slanting from neck to underarm

ra·gout \ra-'gü\ *n* [F ragoût, fr. ragoûter to revive the taste, fr. MF ragouster, fr. re- + a- to (fr. L ad-) + goust taste, fr. L gustus] : a highly seasoned meat stew with vegetables

rag·pick·er \'rag-ˌpi-kər\ *n* : one who collects rags and refuse for a living

rag·time \-ˌtīm\ *n* : music in which there is more or less continuous syncopation in the melody

rag·top \'rag-ˌtäp\ *n* : CONVERTIBLE

rag·weed \-ˌwēd\ *n* : any of several chiefly No. American weedy composite herbs with allergenic pollen

¹raid \'rād\ *n* : a sudden usu. surprise attack or invasion : FORAY

²raid *vb* : to make a raid on — **raid·er** *n*

¹rail \'rāl\ *n* [ME raile, fr. AF raille, reille bar, rule, fr. L regula straightedge, rule, fr. regere to keep straight, direct] **1** : a bar extending from one support to another as a guard or barrier **2** : a bar of steel forming a track for wheeled vehicles **3** : RAILROAD

²rail *vb* : to provide with a railing

³rail *n, pl* **rail** *or* **rails** : any of numerous small wading birds often hunted as game birds

⁴rail *vb* [ME, fr. MF railler to mock, prob. fr. OF reillier to growl, mutter, fr. VL *ragulare to bray, fr. LL ragere to neigh] : to complain angrily : SCOLD, REVILE — **rail·er** *n*

rail·ing \'rā-liŋ\ *n* : a barrier of rails

rail·lery \'rā-lə-rē\ *n, pl* **-ler·ies** : good-natured ridicule : BANTER

¹rail·road \'rāl-ˌrōd\ *n* : a permanent road with rails fixed to ties providing a track for cars; *also* : such a road and its assets constituting a property

²railroad *vb* **1** : to put through (as a law) too hastily **2** : to convict hastily or with insufficient or improper evidence **3** : to send by rail **4** : to work on a railroad — **rail·road·er** *n* — **rail·road·ing** *n*

rail·way \-ˌwā\ *n* : RAILROAD

rai·ment \'rā-mənt\ *n* : CLOTHING

¹rain \'rān\ *n* **1** : water falling in drops from the clouds **2** : a shower of objects ⟨a ~ of bullets⟩ — **rainy** *adj*

²rain *vb* **1** : to send down rain **2** : to fall as or like rain **3** : to pour down

¹rain·bow \-ˌbō\ *n* : an arc or circle of colors formed by the refraction and reflection of the sun's rays in rain, spray, or mist

²rainbow *adj* **1** : having many colors **2** : of, relating to, or made up of people of different races or cultural backgrounds

rainbow trout *n* : a large stout-bodied fish of western No. America closely related to the salmons of the Pacific and usu. having red or pink stripes with black dots along its sides

rain check *n* **1** : a ticket stub good for a later performance when the scheduled one is rained out **2** : an assurance of a deferred extension of an offer

rain·coat \'rān-ˌkōt\ *n* : a waterproof or water-repellent coat

rain date *n* : an alternative date for an event postponed due to rain

rain·drop \-ˌdräp\ *n* : a drop of rain

rain·fall \-ˌfȯl\ *n* **1** : amount of precipitation measured by depth **2** : a fall of rain

rain forest *n* : a tropical woodland having an annual rainfall of at least 100 inches (254 centimeters) and marked by lofty broad-leaved evergreen trees forming a continuous canopy

rain·mak·ing \'rān-ˌmā-kiŋ\ *n* : the action or process of producing or attempting to produce rain by artificial means — **rain·mak·er** *n*

rain out *vb* : to interrupt or prevent by rain

rain·storm \'rān-ˌstȯrm\ *n* : a storm of or with rain

rain·wa·ter \-ˌwȯ-tər, -ˌwä-\ *n* : water fallen as rain

¹raise \'rāz\ *vb* **raised; rais·ing** **1** : to cause or help to rise : LIFT ⟨~ a window⟩ **2** : AWAKEN, AROUSE ⟨enough to ~ the dead⟩ **3** : BUILD, ERECT ⟨~ a monument⟩ **4** : PROMOTE ⟨was *raised* to captain⟩ **5** : END ⟨~ a siege⟩ **6** : COLLECT ⟨~ money⟩ **7** : BREED, GROW ⟨~ cattle⟩ ⟨~ corn⟩; *also* : BRING UP ⟨~ a family⟩ **8** : PROVOKE ⟨~ a laugh⟩ **9** : to bring to notice ⟨~ an objection⟩ **10** : INCREASE ⟨~ prices⟩; *also* : to bet more than **11** : to make light and spongy ⟨~ dough⟩ **12** : to multiply a quantity by itself a specified number of times ⟨~ 2 to the third power⟩ **13** : to cause to form ⟨~ a blister⟩ ♦ *Synonyms* LIFT, HOIST, BOOST, ELEVATE — **rais·er** *n* —

raise the bar : to set a higher standard

²raise *n* : an increase in amount (as of a bid or bet); *also* : an increase in pay

rai·sin \'rā-zⁿn\ *n* [ME, fr. AF, grape, raisin, fr. L racemus cluster of grapes or berries] : a grape dried for food

rai·son d'être \ˌrā-ˌzōⁿ-'detrⁿ\ *n, pl* **rai·sons d'être** \-ˌzōⁿz-\ : reason or justification for existence

ra·ja *or* **ra·jah** \'rä-jə\ *n* [Hindi rājā, fr. Skt rājan king] : an Indian prince

¹rake \'rāk\ *n* : a long-handled garden tool having a crossbar with prongs

²rake *vb* **raked; rak·ing** **1** : to gather, loosen, or smooth with or as if with a rake **2** : to sweep the length of (as a trench or ship) with gunfire

³rake *n* : inclination from either perpendicular or horizontal : SLANT

⁴rake *n* : a dissolute man : LIBERTINE

rake–off \'rāk-ˌȯf\ *n* : a percentage or cut taken

¹**rak·ish** \'rā-kish\ *adj* : DISSOLUTE — **rak·ish·ly** *adv* — **rak·ish·ness** *n*

²**rakish** *adj* 1 : having a trim appearance indicative of speed ⟨a ~ sloop⟩ 2 : JAUNTY, SPORTY ⟨~ clothes⟩ — **rak·ish·ly** *adv* — **rak·ish·ness** *n*

¹**ral·ly** \'ra-lē\ *vb* **ral·lied; ral·ly·ing** 1 : to bring together for a common purpose; *also* : to bring back to order ⟨a leader ~ing his forces⟩ 2 : to arouse to activity or from depression or weakness 3 : to make a comeback ♦ **Synonyms** STIR, ROUSE, AWAKEN, WAKEN, KINDLE

²**rally** *n, pl* **rallies** 1 : an act of rallying 2 : a mass meeting to arouse enthusiasm 3 : a competitive automobile event run over public roads

³**rally** *vb* **ral·lied; ral·ly·ing** : BANTER

rallying cry *n* : WAR CRY 2

¹**ram** \'ram\ *n* 1 : a male sheep 2 : BATTERING RAM

²**ram** *vb* **rammed; ram·ming** 1 : to force or drive in or through 2 : CRAM, CROWD 3 : to strike against violently

RAM \'ram\ *n* : a computer memory that provides the main internal storage for programs and data

¹**ram·ble** \'ram-bəl\ *vb* **ram·bled; ram·bling** : to go about aimlessly : ROAM, WANDER

²**ramble** *n* : a leisurely excursion; *esp* : an aimless walk

ram·bler \'ram-blər\ *n* 1 : a person who rambles 2 : any of various climbing roses with large clusters of small often double flowers

ram·bunc·tious \ram-'bəŋk-shəs\ *adj* : UNRULY

ra·mie \'rā-mē, 'ra-\ *n* : a strong lustrous bast fiber from an Asian nettle

ram·i·fi·ca·tion \ˌra-mə-fə-'kā-shən\ *n* 1 : the act or process of branching 2 : CONSEQUENCE, OUTGROWTH ⟨the ~s of the decision⟩

ram·i·fy \'ra-mə-ˌfī\ *vb* **-fied; -fy·ing** : to branch out

ramp \'ramp\ *n* : a sloping passage or roadway connecting different levels

¹**ram·page** \'ram-ˌpāj, (ˌ)ram-'pāj\ *vb* **ram·paged; ram·pag·ing** : to rush about wildly

²**ram·page** \'ram-ˌpāj\ *n* : a course of violent or riotous action or behavior — **ram·pa·geous** \ram-'pā-jəs\ *adj*

ram·pant \'ram-pənt\ *adj* : unchecked in growth or spread : RIFE ⟨fear was ~ in the town⟩ — **ram·pan·cy** \-pən-sē\ *n* — **ram·pant·ly** *adv*

ram·part \'ram-ˌpärt\ *n* 1 : a protective barrier 2 : a broad embankment raised as a fortification

¹**ram·rod** \'ram-ˌräd\ *n* 1 : a rod used to ram a charge into a muzzle-loading gun 2 : a cleaning rod for small arms 3 : BOSS, OVERSEER

²**ramrod** *adj* : marked by rigidity or severity

³**ramrod** *vb* : to direct, supervise, and control

ram·shack·le \'ram-ˌsha-kəl\ *adj* : RICKETY, TUMBLE-DOWN

ran *past of* RUN

¹**ranch** \'ranch\ *n* [MexSp *rancho* small ranch, fr. Sp, camp, hut & Sp dial., small farm, fr. Old Spanish *ranchear* (se) to take up quarters, fr. MF (se) *ranger* to take up a position, fr. *ranger* to set in a row] 1 : an establishment for the raising and grazing of livestock (as cattle, sheep, or horses) 2 : a large farm devoted to a specialty 3 : RANCH HOUSE 2

²**ranch** *vb* : to live or work on a ranch — **ranch·er** *n*

ranch house *n* 1 : the main house on a ranch 2 : a one-story house typically with a low-pitched roof

ran·cho \'ran-chō, 'rän-\ *n, pl* **ranchos** : RANCH 1

ran·cid \'ran-səd\ *adj* 1 : having a rank smell or taste 2 : OFFENSIVE 3 — **ran·cid·i·ty** \ran-'si-də-tē\ *n*

ran·cor \'ran-kər\ *n* : bitter deep-seated ill will ♦ **Synonyms** ANTAGONISM, ANIMOSITY, ANTIPATHY, ENMITY, HOSTILITY — **ran·cor·ous** *adj*

ran·cour *Brit var of* RANCOR

rand \'rand, 'ränd, 'ränt\ *n, pl* **rand** — see MONEY table

R & B *abbr* rhythm and blues

R & D *abbr* research and development

ran·dom \'ran-dəm\ *adj* 1 : CHANCE, HAPHAZARD — **ran·dom·ly** *adv* — **ran·dom·ness** *n*

random–access *adj* : allowing access to stored data in any order the user desires

random–access memory *n* : RAM

ran·dom·ize \'ran-də-ˌmīz\ *vb* **-ized; -iz·ing** : to select, assign, or arrange in a random way — **ran·dom·i·za·tion** \ˌran-də-mə-'zā-shən\ *n*

R & R *abbr* rest and recreation; rest and recuperation

rang *past of* RING

¹**range** \'rānj\ *n* 1 : a series of things in a row 2 : a cooking stove having an oven and a flat top with burners 3 : open land where animals (as livestock) may roam and graze 4 : the region throughout which an organism occurs 5 : the act of ranging about 6 : the distance a weapon will shoot or is to be shot 7 : a place where shooting is practiced 8 : the space or extent included, covered, or used : SCOPE 9 : a variation within limits ♦ **Synonyms** REACH, COMPASS, RADIUS, CIRCLE

²**range** *vb* **ranged; rang·ing** [ME, fr. AF *renger*, fr. *renc, reng* line, place, row, of Gmc origin] 1 : to set in a row or in proper order 2 : to set in place among others of the same kind 3 : to roam over or through : EXPLORE 4 : to roam at large or freely 5 : to correspond in direction or line 6 : to vary within limits 7 : to find the range of an object by instrument (as radar)

rang·er \'rān-jər\ *n* 1 : FOREST RANGER 2 : a member of a body of troops who range over a region 3 : an expert in close-range fighting and raiding tactics

rangy \'rān-jē\ *adj* **rang·i·er; -est** : being long-limbed and slender — **rang·i·ness** \'rān-jē-nəs\ *n*

ra·ni *or* **ra·nee** \rä-'nē, 'rä-ˌnē\ *n* : a raja's wife

¹**rank** \'raŋk\ *adj* 1 : strong and vigorous and usu. coarse in growth 2 : unpleasantly strong-smelling — **rank·ly** *adv* — **rank·ness** *n*

²**rank** *n* 1 : ROW ⟨~s of houses⟩ 2 : a line of soldiers ranged side by side 3 *pl* : the body of enlisted personnel ⟨rose from the ~s⟩ 4 : position in a group 5 : superior position 6 : a grade of official standing (as in an army) 7 : an orderly arrangement 8 : CLASS, DIVISION — usu. used in pl.

³**rank** *vb* 1 : to arrange in lines or in regular formation 2 : RATE 3 : to rate above (as in official standing) 4 : to take or have a relative position

rank and file *n* : the general membership of a body as contrasted with its leaders

rank·ing \'ran-kiŋ\ *adj* 1 : having a high position : of the highest rank 2 : being next to the chairman in seniority

ran·kle \'raŋ-kəl\ *vb* **ran·kled; ran·kling** [ME *ranclen* to fester, fr. AF *rancler*, fr. OF *draoncler, raoncler*, fr. *draoncle, raoncle* festering sore, fr. ML *dracunculus*, fr. L, dim. of *draco* serpent] : to cause anger, irritation, or bitterness

ran·sack \'ran-ˌsak\ *vb* : to search thoroughly; *esp* : to search through and rob

¹**ran·som** \'ran-səm\ *n* [ME *ransoun*, fr. OF *rançun*, fr. L *redemption-, redemptio* act of buying back, fr. *redimere* to buy back, redeem] 1 : something paid or demanded for the freedom of a captive 2 : the act of ransoming

²**ransom** *vb* : to free from captivity or punishment by paying a price — **ran·som·er** *n*

rant \'rant\ *vb* 1 : to talk loudly and wildly 2 : to scold violently — **rant·er** *n* — **rant·ing·ly** *adv*

¹**rap** \'rap\ *n* 1 : a sharp blow 2 : a sharp rebuke 3 : a negative often undeserved reputation ⟨a bum ~⟩ 4 : responsibility for or consequences of an action ⟨take the ~⟩

²**rap** *vb* **rapped; rap·ping** 1 : to strike sharply : KNOCK 2 : to utter sharply 3 : to criticize sharply

³**rap** *vb* **rapped; rap·ping** 1 : to talk freely and frankly 2 : to perform rap music — **rap·per** *n*

⁴**rap** *n* 1 : TALK, CONVERSATION 2 : a rhythmic chanting of usu. rhymed couplets to a musical accompaniment; *also* : a piece so performed

ra·pa·cious \rə-'pā-shəs\ *adj* 1 : excessively greedy or covetous 2 : living on prey 3 : RAVENOUS 2 ⟨a ~ appetite⟩ — **ra·pa·cious·ly** *adv* — **ra·pa·cious·ness** *n* — **ra·pac·i·ty** \-'pa-sə-tē\ *n*

¹**rape** \'rāp\ *n* : an Old World herb related to the mustards that is grown as a forage crop and for its seeds (**rapeseed** \-ˌsēd\)

²**rape** *vb* **raped; rap·ing** : to commit rape on — **rap·er** *n* — **rap·ist** \'rā-pist\ *n*

³**rape** *n* 1 : a carrying away by force 2 : unlawful sexual activity and usu. sexual intercourse carried out forcibly or under threat of injury

¹**rap·id** \'ra-pəd\ *adj* [L *rapidus* strong-flowing, rapid, fr. *rapere* to seize, carry away] : very fast : SWIFT ♦ **Synonyms** FLEET, QUICK, SPEEDY — **ra·pid·i·ty** \rə-'pi-də-tē\ *n* — **rap·id·ly** *adv*

²**rapid** *n* : a place in a stream where the current flows very fast usu. over obstructions — usu. used in pl.

rapid eye movement *n* : rapid conjugate movement of the eyes associated with REM sleep

rapid transit *n* : fast passenger transportation (as by subway) in cities

¹**ra·pi·er** \'rā-pē-ər\ *n* : a straight 2-edged sword with a narrow pointed blade

rapier

wheel having slanted teeth into which a pawl drops so as to allow motion in only one direction

ratchet

²**rapier** *adj* : extremely sharp or keen ⟨∼ wit⟩

rap·ine \'ra-pən, -,pīn\ *n* : PILLAGE, PLUNDER

rap·pel \ra-'pel, ra-\ *vb* -**pelled**; -**pel·ling** : to descend (as from a cliff) by sliding down a rope

rap·pen \'rä-pən\ *n, pl* **rappen** : the centime of Switzerland

rap·port \ra-'pór\ *n* : RELATION; *esp* : relation characterized by harmony

rap·proche·ment \,ra-,prōsh-'mäⁿ, ra-'prōsh-,mäⁿ\ *n* : the establishment of or a state of having cordial relations

rap·scal·lion \rap-'skal-yən\ *n* : RASCAL, SCAMP

rapt \'rapt\ *adj* 1 : carried away with emotion 2 : ABSORBED, ENGROSSED ⟨listened with ∼ attention⟩ — **rapt·ly** \'rapt-lē\ *adv* — **rapt·ness** *n*

rap·tor \'rap-tər, -,tór\ *n* 1 : BIRD OF PREY 2 : a usu. small-to-medium-sized predatory dinosaur

rap·ture \'rap-chər\ *n* : spiritual or emotional ecstasy — **rap·tur·ous** \-chə-rəs\ *adj* — **rap·tur·ous·ly** *adv*

rapture of the deep : NITROGEN NARCOSIS

ra·ra avis \,rer-ə-'ā-vəs, ,rär-ə-'ä-wəs\ *n, pl* **ra·ra avis·es** \-'ä-və-səz\ *or* **ra·rae aves** \,rär-,ī-'ä-,wās\ [L, rare bird] : a rare person or thing : RARITY

¹**rare** \'rar\ *adj* **rar·er**; **rar·est** 1 : not thick or dense : THIN ⟨∼ air⟩ 2 : unusually fine : EXCELLENT, SPLENDID 3 : seldom met with — **rare·ly** *adv* — **rare·ness** *n* — **rar·i·ty** \'rar-ə-tē\ *n*

²**rare** *adj* **rar·er**; **rar·est** : cooked so that the inside is still red ⟨∼ beef⟩

rare·bit \'rer-bət\ *n* : WELSH RABBIT

rar·efac·tion \,rer-ə-'fak-shən\ *n* 1 : the action or process of rarefying 2 : the state of being rarefied

rar·e·fy *also* **rar·i·fy** \'rer-ə-,fī\ *vb* -**fied**; -**fy·ing** : to make or become rare, thin, or less dense

rar·ing \'rer-ən, -iŋ\ *adj* : full of enthusiasm or eagerness ⟨∼ to go⟩

ras·cal \'ras-kəl\ *n* [ME *rascaile* foot soldiers, commoners, worthless person, fr. AF *rascaille*, fr. OF dial. *rasquer* to scrape, clean off, ultim. fr. L *radere* to scrape, shave] 1 : a mean or dishonest person 2 : a mischievous person — **ras·cal·i·ty** \ras-'ka-lə-tē\ *n* — **ras·cal·ly** \'ras-kə-lē\ *adj*

¹**rash** \'rash\ *adj* : having or showing little regard for consequences : too hasty in decision, action, or speech : RECKLESS ✦ *Synonyms* DARING, FOOLHARDY, ADVENTUROUS, VENTURESOME — **rash·ly** *adv* — **rash·ness** *n*

²**rash** *n* : an eruption on the body

rash·er \'ra-shər\ *n* : a thin slice of bacon or ham broiled or fried; *also* : a portion consisting of several such slices

¹**rasp** \'rasp\ *vb* 1 : to rub with or as if with a rough file 2 : to grate harshly on (as one's nerves) 3 : to speak in a grating tone

²**rasp** *n* : a coarse file with cutting points instead of ridges

rasp·ber·ry \'raz-,ber-ē, -bə-rē\ *n* 1 : any of various edible usu. black or red berries produced by some brambles; *also* : such a bramble 2 : a sound of contempt made by protruding the tongue through the lips and expelling air forcibly

rat \'rat\ *n* 1 : any of numerous rodents larger than the related mice 2 : a contemptible person; *esp* : one that betrays friends or associates

²**rat** *vb* **rat·ted**; **rat·ting** 1 : to betray or inform on one's associates 2 : to hunt or catch rats

rat cheese *n* : CHEDDAR

ratch·et \'ra-chət\ *n* : a device that consists of a bar or

¹**rate** \'rāt\ *vb* **rat·ed**; **rat·ing** : to scold violently

²**rate** *n* 1 : quantity, amount, or degree measured by some standard 2 : an amount (as of payment) measured by its relation to some other amount (as of time) 3 : a charge, payment, or price fixed according to a ratio, scale, or standard ⟨tax ∼⟩ 4 : RANK, CLASS

³**rate** *vb* **rat·ed**; **rat·ing** 1 : ESTIMATE 2 : CONSIDER, REGARD ⟨*rated* as a good pianist⟩ 3 : to settle the relative rank or class of 4 : to be classed : RANK 5 : to have a right to : DESERVE 6 : to be of consequence — **rat·er** *n*

rath·er \'ra-thər, 'rä-, 'rə-\ *adv* [ME, fr. OE *hrathor*, compar. of *hrathe* quickly] 1 : more properly 2 : PREFERABLY ⟨I'd ∼ not go⟩ 3 : more correctly speaking 4 : to the contrary : INSTEAD 5 : SOMEWHAT ⟨∼ warm⟩

rather than *prep* : INSTEAD OF

raths·kel·ler \'rät-,ske-lər, 'rat-\ *n* [obs. G (now *Ratskeller*), city-hall basement restaurant, fr. *Rat* council + *Keller* cellar] : a usu. basement tavern or restaurant

rat·i·fy \'ra-tə-,fī\ *vb* -**fied**; -**fy·ing** : to approve and accept formally — **rat·i·fi·ca·tion** \,ra-tə-fə-'kā-shən\ *n*

rat·ing \'rā-tiŋ\ *n* 1 : a classification according to grade : RANK 2 *Brit* : a naval enlisted man 3 : an estimate of the credit standing and business responsibility of a person or firm

ra·tio \'rā-shō, -shē-ō\ *n, pl* **ra·tios** 1 : the indicated quotient of two numbers or mathematical expressions 2 : the relationship in number, quantity, or degree between two or more things

ra·ti·o·ci·na·tion \,ra-tē-,ō-sə-'nā-shən, -,ä-\ *n* : exact thinking : REASONING — **ra·ti·o·ci·nate** \-'ō-sə-,nāt, -'ä-\ *vb* — **ra·ti·o·ci·na·tive** \-'ō-sə-,nā-tiv, -'ä-\ *adj* — **ra·ti·o·ci·na·tor** \-'ō-sə-,nā-tər, -'ä-sə-\ *n*

¹**ra·tion** \'ra-shən, 'rā-\ *n* 1 : a food allowance for one day 2 : FOOD, PROVISIONS, DIET — usu. used in pl. 3 : SHARE, ALLOTMENT

²**ration** *vb* 1 : to supply with or allot as rations 2 : to use or allot sparingly ✦ *Synonyms* APPORTION, PORTION, PRORATE, PARCEL

¹**ra·tio·nal** \'ra-shə-nəl\ *adj* 1 : having reason or understanding 2 : of or relating to reason 3 : relating to, consisting of, or being one or more rational numbers — **ra·tio·nal·ly** *adv*

²**rational** *n* : RATIONAL NUMBER

ra·tio·nale \,ra-shə-'nal\ *n* 1 : an explanation of principles controlling belief or practice 2 : an underlying reason

ra·tio·nal·ise *Brit var of* RATIONALIZE

ra·tio·nal·ism \'ra-shə-nə-,li-zəm\ *n* : the practice of guiding one's actions and opinions solely by what seems reasonable — **ra·tio·nal·ist** \-list\ *n* — **rationalist** *or* **ra·tio·nal·is·tic** \,ra-shə-nə-'lis-tik\ *adj* — **ra·tio·nal·is·ti·cal·ly** \-ti-k(ə-)lē\ *adv*

ra·tio·nal·i·ty \,ra-shə-'na-lə-tē\ *n, pl* -**ties** : the quality or state of being rational

ra·tio·nal·ize \'ra-shə-nə-,līz\ *vb* -**ized**; -**iz·ing** 1 : to make (something irrational) appear rational or reasonable 2 : to provide a natural explanation of (as a myth) 3 : to justify (as one's behavior or weaknesses) esp. to oneself 4 : to find plausible but untrue reasons for conduct — **ra·tio·nal·i·za·tion** \,ra-shə-nə-lə-'zā-shən\ *n*

rational number *n* : a number that can be expressed as an integer or the quotient of an integer divided by a nonzero integer

rat race *n* : strenuous, tiresome, and usu. competitive activity or rush

rat·tan \ra-'tan, rə-\ *n* : a cane or switch made from one of the long stems of an Asian climbing palm; *also* : this palm

rat·ter \'ra-tər\ *n* : a rat-catching dog or cat

¹rat·tle \'ra-t°l\ *vb* **rat·tled; rat·tling** **1** : to make or cause to make a series of clattering sounds **2** : to move with a clattering sound **3** : to say or do in a brisk lively fashion ⟨~ off the answers⟩ **4** : CONFUSE, UPSET ⟨~ a witness⟩

²rattle *n* **1** : a toy that produces a rattle when shaken **2** : a series of clattering and knocking sounds **3** : a rattling organ at the end of a rattlesnake's tail

rat·tler \'rat-lər\ *n* : RATTLESNAKE

rat·tle·snake \'ra-t°l-,snāk\ *n* : any of various American pit vipers with a rattle at the end of the tail

rat·tle·trap \'ra-t°l-,trap\ *n* : something (as an old car) rickety and full of rattles

rat·tling \'rat-lin\ *adj* **1** : LIVELY, BRISK ⟨moved at a ~ pace⟩ **2** : FIRST-RATE, SPLENDID

rat·trap \'rat-,trap\ *n* **1** : a trap for rats **2** : a dilapidated building

rat·ty \'ra-tē\ *adj* **rat·ti·er; -est** **1** : infested with rats **2** : of, relating to, or suggestive of rats **3** : SHABBY ⟨a ~ old coat⟩

rau·cous \'ro-kəs\ *adj* **1** : HARSH, HOARSE, STRIDENT ⟨~ voices⟩ **2** : boisterously disorderly — **rau·cous·ly** *adv* — **rau·cous·ness** *n*

raun·chy \'ron-chē, 'rän-\ *adj* **raun·chi·er; -est** **1** : SLOVENLY, DIRTY **2** : OBSCENE, SMUTTY ⟨~ jokes⟩ — **raun·chi·ness** \-chē-nəs\ *n*

¹rav·age \'ra-vij\ *n* [F] : an act or result of ravaging : DEVASTATION

²ravage *vb* **rav·aged; rav·ag·ing** : to lay waste : DEVASTATE — **rav·ag·er** *n*

¹rave \'rāv\ *vb* **raved; rav·ing** **1** : to talk wildly in or as if in delirium : STORM, RAGE **2** : to talk with extreme enthusiasm — **rav·er** *n*

²rave *n* **1** : an act or instance of raving **2** : an extravagantly favorable criticism

¹rav·el \'ra-vəl\ *vb* **-eled** *or* **-elled; -el·ing** *or* **-el·ling** **1** : UNRAVEL, UNTWIST **2** : TANGLE, CONFUSE

²ravel *n* **1** : something tangled **2** : something raveled out; *esp* : a loose thread

¹ra·ven \'rā-vən\ *n* : a large black bird related to the crow

²raven *adj* : black and glossy like a raven's feathers

³rav·en \'ra-vən\ *vb* **1** : to devour greedily **2** : DESPOIL, PLUNDER **3** : PREY

rav·en·ous \'ra-və-nəs\ *adj* **1** : RAPACIOUS, VORACIOUS ⟨~ wolves⟩ **2** : eager for food : very hungry — **rav·en·ous·ly** *adv* — **rav·en·ous·ness** *n*

ra·vine \rə-'vēn\ *n* : a small narrow steep-sided valley larger than a gully

rav·i·o·li \,ra-vē-'ō-lē\ *n, pl* **ravioli** *also* **raviolis** [It, fr. It dial., pl. of *raviolo*, lit., little turnip, dim. of *rava* turnip, fr. L *rapa*] : small cases of dough with a savory filling (as of meat or cheese)

rav·ish \'ra-vish\ *vb* **1** : to seize and take away by violence **2** : to overcome with emotion and esp. with joy or delight **3** : RAPE — **rav·ish·er** *n* — **rav·ish·ment** *n*

¹raw \'ro\ *adj* **raw·er** \'ro-ər\; **raw·est** \'ro-əst\ **1** : not cooked **2** : changed little from the original form : not processed ⟨~ materials⟩ **3** : having the surface abraded or irritated ⟨a ~ sore⟩ **4** : not trained or experienced ⟨~ recruits⟩ **5** : VULGAR, COARSE ⟨~ language⟩ **6** : disagreeably cold and damp ⟨a ~ day⟩ **7** : UNFAIR ⟨~ deal⟩ — **raw·ness** *n*

²raw *n* : a raw place or state — **in the raw** : NAKED

raw·boned \'ro-,bōnd\ *adj* : LEAN, GAUNT; *also* : having a heavy frame that seems to have little flesh

raw·hide \'ro-,hīd\ *n* : the untanned skin of cattle; *also* : a whip made of this

¹ray \'rā\ *n* : any of an order of large flat cartilaginous fishes that have the eyes on the upper surface and the hind end of the body slender and taillike

²ray *n* [ME, fr. AF *rai*, fr. L *radius* rod, ray] **1** : any of the lines of light that appear to radiate from a bright object **2** : a thin beam of radiant energy (as light) **3** : light from a beam **4** : a thin line like a beam of light **5** : an animal or plant structure resembling a ray **6** : a tiny bit : PARTICLE ⟨a ~ of hope⟩

ray·on \'rā-,än\ *n* : a fiber made from cellulose; *also* : a yarn, thread, or fabric made from such fibers

raze \'rāz\ *vb* **razed; raz·ing** **1** : to scrape, cut, or shave off **2** : to destroy to the ground : DEMOLISH

ra·zor \'rā-zər\ *n* : a sharp cutting instrument used to shave off hair

ra·zor–backed \'rā-zər-,bakt\ *or* **ra·zor·back** \-,bak\ *adj* : having a sharp narrow back ⟨a ~ horse⟩

razor clam *n* : any of a family of marine bivalve mollusks having a long narrow curved thin shell

razor wire *n* : coiled wire fitted with sharp edges and used as an obstacle or barrier

¹razz \'raz\ *n* : RASPBERRY 2

²razz *vb* : RIDICULE, TEASE ⟨fans ~ed visiting players⟩

Rb *symbol* rubidium

RBC *abbr* red blood cells

RBI \,är-(,)bē-'ī, 'ri-bē\ *n, pl* **RBIs** *or* **RBI** [run batted in] : a run in baseball that is driven in by a batter

RC *abbr* **1** Red Cross **2** Roman Catholic

RCAF *abbr* Royal Canadian Air Force

RCMP *abbr* Royal Canadian Mounted Police

RCN *abbr* Royal Canadian Navy

rct *abbr* recruit

rd *abbr* **1** road **2** rod **3** round

RD *abbr* rural delivery

-rd *symbol* — used after the figure 3 to indicate the ordinal number third

RDA *abbr* recommended daily allowance; recommended dietary allowance

re \'rā, 'rē\ *prep* : with regard to

Re *symbol* rhenium

re- \rē, ,rē, 'rē\ *prefix* **1** : again : for a second time **2** : anew : in a new or different form **3** : back : backward

reabsorb
reacquire
reactivate
reactivation
readdress
readjust
readjustment
readmission
readmit
reaffirm
reaffirmation
realign
realignment
reallocate
reallocation
reanalysis
reanalyze
reanimate
reanimation
reannex
reannexation
reappear
reappearance
reapplication
reapply
reappoint
reappointment
reapportion
reapportionment
reappraisal
reappraise
rearm
rearmament
rearouse
rearrange
rearrangement
rearrest
reascend
reassemble
reassembly
reassert
reassess
reassessment
reassign
reassignment
reassume
reattach
reattachment
reattain

reattempt
reauthorization
reauthorize
reawaken
rebaptism
rebaptize
rebid
rebind
reboil
rebroadcast
reburial
rebury
recalculate
recalculation
rechannel
recharge
rechargeable
recharter
recheck
rechristen
reclassification
reclassify
recoin
recolonization
recolonize
recolor
recombine
recommence
recommission
recommit
recompile
recompose
recomputation
recompute
reconceive
reconcentrate
reconception
recondensation
recondense
reconfirm
reconfirmation
reconnect
reconquer
reconquest
reconsecrate
reconsecration
recontact
recontaminate
recontamination

reconvene
reconvert
recook
recopy
recross
recrystallize
recut
redecorate
redecoration
rededicate
rededication
redefine
redefinition
redeposit
redesign
redetermination
redetermine
redevelop
redevelopment
redirect
rediscount
rediscover
rediscovery
redissolve
redistill
redistillation
redraft
redraw
reecho
reedit
reelect
reelection
reemerge
reemergence
reemphasis
reemphasize
reemploy
reemployment
reenact
reenactment
reenergize
reenlist
reenlistment
reenter
reequip
reestablish
reestablishment
reevaluate
reevaluation
reexamination
reexamine
reexport
refashion
refight
refigure
refinish
refit
refix
refloat
refold
reforge
reformulate
reformulation
refortify
refound
refreeze
refuel
refurnish
regain
regather
regild
regive
regrade
regrind
regrow
regrowth
rehandle
rehear
reheat
rehouse
reimpose

reimposition
reincorporate
reinsert
reinsertion
reintegrate
reinterpret
reinterpretation
reintroduce
reintroduction
reinvention
reinvest
reinvestment
reinvigorate
reinvigoration
reissue
rejudge
rekindle
reknit
relaunch
relearn
relight
reline
reload
remanufacture
remap
remarriage
remarry
rematch
remelt
remigration
remold
rename
renegotiate
renegotiation
renominate
renomination
renumber
reoccupy
reoccur
reopen
reorder
reorganization
reorganize
reorient
reorientation
repack
repaint
repass
repeople
rephotograph
rephrase
replant
repopulate
reprice
reprocess
reprogram
republication
republish
repurchase
reradiate
reread
rereading
rerecord
reroute
reschedule
rescore
rescreen
reseal
reseed
resell
reset
resettle
resettlement
resew
reshow
resocialization
resow
respell
restaff
restart
restate

restatement
restock
restrengthen
restructure
restudy
restuff
restyle
resubmit
resummon
resupply
resurface
resurvey
resynthesis
resynthesize
retaste
retell
retest
retool
retrain

retransmission
retransmit
retrial
reunification
reunify
reunite
reusable
reuse
revaluate
revaluation
revalue
revisit
rewarm
rewash
reweave
rewed
reweigh
rewire
rezone

¹reach \'rēch\ *vb* **1** : to stretch out **2** : to touch or attempt to touch or seize **3** : to extend to **4** : to communicate with **5** : to arrive at ✦ **Synonyms** GAIN, REALIZE, ACHIEVE, ATTAIN — **reach·able** *adj* — **reach·er** *n*

²reach *n* **1** : an unbroken stretch of a river **2** : the act of reaching **3** : a reachable distance; *also* : ability to reach **4** : a range of knowledge or comprehension

re·act \rē-'akt\ *vb* **1** : to exert a return or counteracting influence **2** : to have or show a reaction **3** : to act in opposition to a force or influence **4** : to move or tend in a reverse direction **5** : to undergo chemical reaction

re·ac·tant \rē-'ak-tənt\ *n* : a chemically reacting substance

re·ac·tion \rē-'ak-shən\ *n* **1** : the act or process of reacting **2** : a counter tendency; *esp* : a tendency toward a former esp. outmoded political or social order or policy **3** : bodily, mental, or emotional response to a stimulus **4** : chemical change **5** : a process involving change in atomic nuclei

re·ac·tion·ary \rē-'ak-shə-ner-ē\ *adj* : relating to, marked by, or favoring esp. political reaction — **reactionary** *n*

re·ac·tive \rē-'ak-tiv\ *adj* : reacting or tending to react

re·ac·tor \rē-'ak-tər\ *n* **1** : one that reacts **2** : a device for the controlled release of nuclear energy

¹read \'rēd\ *vb* read \'red\; **read·ing** [ME *reden* to advise, interpret, read, fr. OE *rǣdan*] **1** : to understand language by interpreting written symbols for speech sounds **2** : to utter aloud written or printed words **3** : to learn by observing ⟨~ nature's signs⟩ **4** : to study by a course of reading ⟨~*s* law⟩ **5** : to discover the meaning of ⟨~ the clues⟩ **6** : to recognize or interpret as if by reading **7** : to attribute (a meaning) to something ⟨~ guilt in his manner⟩ **8** : INDICATE ⟨thermometer ~*s* 10°⟩ **9** : to consist in phrasing or meaning ⟨the two versions ~ differently⟩ — **read·abil·i·ty** \rē-də-'bi-lə-tē\ *n* — **read·able** \'rē-də-bəl\ *adj* — **read·ably** \-blē\ *adv* — **read·er** *n*

²read \'red\ *adj* : informed by reading ⟨widely ~⟩

read·er·ship \'rē-dər-ship\ *n* : the mass or a particular group of readers

read·ing *n* **1** : something read or for reading **2** : a particular version **3** : data indicated by an instrument ⟨thermometer ~⟩ **4** : a particular interpretation (as of a law) **5** : a particular performance (as of a musical work) **6** : an indication of a certain state of affairs

read–only memory *n* : ROM

read·out \'rēd-,aut\ *n* **1** : the process of removing information from an automatic device (as a computer) and displaying it in an understandable form; *also* : the information removed from such a device **2** : an electronic device that presents information in visual form

read out *vb* **1** : to read aloud **2** : to expel from an organization

¹ready \'re-dē\ *adj* **read·i·er; -est** **1** : prepared for use or action **2** : likely to do something indicated; *also* : willingly disposed : INCLINED **3** : spontaneously prompt ⟨her ~ wit⟩ **4** : immediately available ⟨~ cash⟩ — **read·i·ly** \'re-də-lē\ *adv* — **read·i·ness** \-dē-nəs\ *n* — **at the ready** : ready for immediate use

²ready *vb* **read·ied; ready·ing** : to make ready : PREPARE

ready–made \,re-dē-'mād\ *adj* : already made up for general sale : not specially made — **ready–made** *n*

ready room *n* : a room in which pilots are briefed and await orders

re·agent \rē-'ā-jənt\ *n* : a substance that takes part in or brings about a particular chemical reaction

¹**re·al** \'rēl\ *adj* [ME, real, relating to things (in law), fr. AF, fr. ML & LL; ML *realis* relating to things (in law), fr. LL, real, fr. L *res* thing, fact] **1** : of or relating to fixed or immovable things (as land) ⟨~ property⟩ **2** : not artificial : GENUINE; *also* : not imaginary — **re·al·ness** *n* — **for real** **1** : in earnest **2** : GENUINE ⟨the threat was *for real*⟩

²**real** *adv* : VERY ⟨had a ~ good time⟩

³**re·al** \rā-'äl\ *n* — see MONEY table

real estate *n* : property in buildings and land

re·al·ism \'rē-ə-ˌli-zəm\ *n* **1** : the disposition to face facts and to deal with them practically **2** : true and faithful portrayal of nature and of people in art or literature — **re·al·ist** \-list\ *adj or n* — **re·al·is·tic** \ˌrē-ə-'lis-tik\ *adj* — **re·al·is·ti·cal·ly** \-ti-k(ə-)lē\ *adv*

re·al·i·ty \rē-'a-lə-tē\ *n, pl* **-ties** **1** : the quality or state of being real **2** : something real **3** : the totality of real things and events

re·al·ize \'rē-ə-ˌlīz\ *vb* **-ized; -iz·ing** **1** : to make actual : ACCOMPLISH **2** : to convert into money ⟨~ assets⟩ **3** : OBTAIN, GAIN ⟨~ a profit⟩ **4** : to be aware of : UNDERSTAND — **re·al·iz·able** *adj* — **re·al·i·za·tion** \ˌrē-ə-lə-'zā-shən\ *n*

re·al·ly \'rē-lē, 'ri-\ *adv* : in truth : in fact : ACTUALLY

realm \'relm\ *n* **1** : KINGDOM **2** : SPHERE, DOMAIN ⟨within the ~ of possibility⟩

real number *n* : a number that has no imaginary part ⟨the set of all *real numbers* comprises the rationals and the irrationals⟩

re·al·po·li·tik \rā-'äl-ˌpō-li-ˌtēk\ *n, often cap* [G] : politics based on practical and material factors rather than on theoretical or ethical objectives

real time *n* : the actual time during which something takes place — **real–time** *adj*

re·al·ty \'rēl-tē\ *n* : REAL ESTATE

¹**ream** \'rēm\ *n* [ME *reme*, fr. AF, ultim. fr. Ar *rizmah*, lit., bundle] : a quantity of paper that is variously 480, 500, or 516 sheets

²**ream** *vb* : to enlarge, shape, or clear with a reamer

ream·er \'rē-mər\ *n* : a tool with cutting edges that is used to enlarge or shape a hole

reap \'rēp\ *vb* **1** : to cut or clear with a scythe, sickle, or machine **2** : to gather by or as if by cutting : HARVEST ⟨~ a reward⟩ — **reap·er** *n*

¹**rear** \'rir\ *vb* **1** : to erect by building **2** : to set or raise upright **3** : to breed and raise for use or market ⟨~ livestock⟩ **4** : BRING UP, FOSTER **5** : to lift or rise up; *esp* : to rise on the hind legs

²**rear** *n* **1** : the unit (as of an army) or area farthest from the enemy **2** : BACK; *also* : the position at the back of something

³**rear** *adj* : being at the back

rear admiral *n* : a commissioned officer in the navy or coast guard ranking next below a vice admiral

¹**rear·ward** \'rir-wərd\ *adj* **1** : being at or toward the rear **2** : directed toward the rear ⟨a ~ glance⟩

²**rear·ward** *also* **rear·wards** \-wərdz\ *adv* : at or toward the rear ⟨looking ~⟩

reas *abbr* reasonable

¹**rea·son** \'rē-zᵊn\ *n* [ME *resoun*, fr. AF *raisun*, fr. L *ration-, ratio* reason, computation] **1** : a statement offered in explanation or justification **2** : GROUND, CAUSE **3** : the power to think : INTELLECT **4** : a sane or sound mind **5** : due exercise of the faculty of logical thought

²**reason** *vb* **1** : to talk with another to cause a change of mind **2** : to use the faculty of reason : THINK **3** : to discover or formulate by the use of reason — **rea·son·er** *n* — **rea·son·ing** *n*

rea·son·able \'rē-zᵊn-ə-bəl\ *adj* **1** : being within the bounds of reason : not extreme **2** : INEXPENSIVE **3** : able to reason : RATIONAL — **rea·son·able·ness** *n* — **rea·son·ably** \-blē\ *adv*

re·as·sure \ˌrē-ə-'shùr\ *vb* **1** : to assure again **2** : to restore confidence to : free from fear — **re·as·sur·ance** \-'shùr-əns\ *n* — **re·as·sur·ing·ly** *adv*

¹**re·bate** \'rē-ˌbāt\ *vb* **re·bat·ed; re·bat·ing** : to make or give a rebate

²**rebate** *n* : a return of part of a payment ♦ *Synonyms* DEDUCTION, ABATEMENT, DISCOUNT

¹**reb·el** \'re-bəl\ *adj* [ME, fr. AF fr. L *rebellis*, fr. *re-* + *bellum* war] : of or relating to rebels

²**rebel** *n* : one that rebels against authority

³**re·bel** \ri-'bel\ *vb* **re·belled; re·bel·ling** **1** : to resist the authority of one's government **2** : to act in or show disobedience **3** : to feel or exhibit anger or revulsion

re·bel·lion \ri-'bel-yən\ *n* : resistance to authority; *esp* : defiance against a government through uprising or revolt

re·bel·lious \-yəs\ *adj* **1** : given to or engaged in rebellion **2** : inclined to resist authority — **re·bel·lious·ly** *adv* — **re·bel·lious·ness** *n*

re·birth \ˌrē-'bərth\ *n* **1** : a new or second birth **2** : RENAISSANCE, REVIVAL

re·born \-'bòrn\ *adj* : born again : REGENERATED, REVIVED

¹**re·bound** \ˌrē-'baund, 'rē-ˌbaund\ *vb* **1** : to spring back on or as if on impact with another body **2** : to recover from a setback or frustration

²**re·bound** \'rē-ˌbaund\ *n* **1** : the action of rebounding **2** : a rebounding ball **3** : a reaction to setback or frustration

re·buff \ri-'bəf\ *vb* : to reject or criticize sharply : SNUB — **rebuff** *n*

re·build \(ˌ)rē-'bild\ *vb* **-built** \-'bilt\; **-build·ing** **1** : REPAIR, RECONSTRUCT; *also* : REMODEL **2** : to build again

¹**re·buke** \ri-'byük\ *vb* **re·buked; re·buk·ing** : to reprimand sharply : REPROVE

²**rebuke** *n* : a sharp reprimand

re·bus \'rē-bəs\ *n* [L, by things, abl. pl. of *res* thing] : a representation of syllables or words by means of pictures; *also* : a riddle composed of such pictures

rebus

re·but \ri-'bət\ *vb* **re·but·ted; re·but·ting** : to refute esp. formally (as in debate) by evidence and arguments ♦ *Synonyms* DISPROVE, CONTROVERT, CONFUTE — **re·but·ter** *n*

re·but·tal \ri-'bə-tᵊl\ *n* : the act of rebutting

rec *abbr* **1** receipt **2** record; recording **3** recreation

re·cal·ci·trant \ri-'kal-sə-trənt\ *adj* [LL *recalcitrant-, recalcitrans*, prp. of *recalcitrare* to be stubbornly disobedient, fr. L, to kick back, fr. *re-* back, again + *calcitrare* to kick, fr. *calc-, calx* heel] **1** : stubbornly resisting authority **2** : resistant to handling or treatment ♦ *Synonyms* REFRACTORY, HEADSTRONG, WILLFUL, UNRULY, UNGOVERNABLE — **re·cal·ci·trance** \-trəns\ *n*

¹**re·call** \ri-'kòl\ *vb* **1** : REVOKE, CANCEL **2** : to call back **3** : REMEMBER, RECOLLECT ⟨~*ed* their last meeting⟩

²**re·call** \ri-'kòl, 'rē-ˌkòl\ *n* **1** : a summons to return **2** : the procedure of removing an official by popular vote **3** : remembrance of things learned or experienced **4** : the act of revoking **5** : a call by a manufacturer for the return of a product that may be defective or contaminated

re·cant \ri-'kant\ *vb* : to take back (something one has said) publicly : make an open confession of error — **re·can·ta·tion** \ˌrē-ˌkan-'tā-shən\ *n*

¹**re·cap** \'rē-ˌkap, rē-'kap\ *vb* **re·capped; re·cap·ping** : RECAPITULATE — **re·cap** \'rē-ˌkap\ *n*

²**recap** *vb* **re·capped; re·cap·ping** : RETREAD — **re·cap** \'rē-ˌkap\ *n*

re·ca·pit·u·late \ˌrē-kə-'pi-chə-ˌlāt\ *vb* **-lat·ed; -lat·ing** : to restate briefly : SUMMARIZE — **re·ca·pit·u·la·tion** \-ˌpi-chə-'lā-shən\ *n*

re·cap·ture \(ˌ)rē-'kap-chər\ *vb* **1** : to capture again **2** : to experience again ⟨~ happy times⟩

re·cast \(ˌ)rē-'kast\ *vb* **1** : to cast again **2** : REVISE, REMODEL ⟨~ a sentence⟩

recd *abbr* received

re·cede \ri-'sēd\ *vb* **re·ced·ed; re·ced·ing** **1** : to move back or away ⟨a *receding* hairline⟩ **2** : to slant backward **3** : DIMINISH, CONTRACT ⟨a *receding* deficit⟩

¹re·ceipt \ri-'sēt\ *n* **1** : RECIPE **2** : the act of receiving **3** : something received — usu. used in pl. **4** : a written acknowledgment of something received

²receipt *vb* **1** : to give a receipt for **2** : to mark as paid

re·ceiv·able \ri-'sē-və-bəl\ *adj* **1** : capable of being received; *esp* : acceptable as legal ⟨∼ certificates⟩ **2** : subject to call for payment ⟨notes ∼⟩

re·ceive \ri-'sēv\ *vb* **re·ceived; re·ceiv·ing** **1** : to take in or accept (as something sent or paid) : come into possession of : GET **2** : CONTAIN, HOLD **3** : to permit to enter : GREET, WELCOME **4** : to be at home to visitors **5** : to accept as true or authoritative **6** : to be the subject of : UNDERGO, EXPERIENCE ⟨∼ a shock⟩ **7** : to change incoming radio waves into sounds or pictures

re·ceiv·er \ri-'sē-vər\ *n* **1** : one that receives **2** : a person legally appointed to receive and have charge of property or money involved in a lawsuit **3** : a device for converting electromagnetic waves or signals into audio or visual form ⟨telephone ∼⟩

re·ceiv·er·ship \-,ship\ *n* **1** : the office or function of a receiver **2** : the condition of being in the hands of a receiver

re·cen·cy \'rē-s²n-sē\ *n* : RECENTNESS

re·cent \'rē-s²nt\ *adj* **1** : of the present time or time just past ⟨∼ history⟩ **2** : having lately come into existence : NEW, FRESH **3** *cap* : HOLOCENE — **re·cent·ly** *adv* — **re·cent·ness** *n*

re·cep·ta·cle \ri-'sep-ti-kəl\ *n* **1** : something used to receive and hold something else : CONTAINER **2** : the enlarged end of a flower stalk upon which the parts of the flower grow **3** : an electrical fitting that contains the live parts of a circuit

re·cep·tion \ri-'sep-shən\ *n* **1** : the act of receiving **2** : a social gathering at which guests are formally welcomed

re·cep·tion·ist \ri-'sep-shə-nist\ *n* : a person employed to greet callers

re·cep·tive \ri-'sep-tiv\ *adj* : able or inclined to receive; *esp* : open and responsive to ideas, impressions, or suggestions — **re·cep·tive·ly** *adv* — **re·cep·tive·ness** *n* — **re·cep·tiv·i·ty** \,rē-,sep-'ti-və-tē\ *n*

re·cep·tor \ri-'sep-tər\ *n* **1** : one that receives stimuli : SENSE ORGAN **2** : a chemical group or molecule in the outer cell membrane or in the cell interior that has an affinity for a specific chemical group, molecule, or virus

¹re·cess \'rē-,ses, ri-'ses\ *n* **1** : a secret or secluded place **2** : an indentation in a line or surface (as an alcove in a room) **3** : a suspension of business or procedure for rest or relaxation

²recess *vb* **1** : to put into a recess **2** : to make a recess in **3** : to interrupt for a recess **4** : to take a recess

re·ces·sion \ri-'se-shən\ *n* **1** : the act of receding : WITHDRAWAL **2** : a departing procession (as at the end of a church service) **3** : a period of reduced economic activity

re·ces·sion·al \ri-'se-shə-nəl\ *n* **1** : a hymn or musical piece at the conclusion of a service or program **2** : RECESSION 2

¹re·ces·sive \ri-'se-siv\ *adj* **1** : tending to recede **2** : producing or being a bodily characteristic that is masked or not expressed when a contrasting dominant gene or trait is present ⟨∼ genes⟩ ⟨∼ traits⟩

²recessive *n* : a recessive characteristic or gene; *also* : an individual that has one or more recessive characteristics

re·cher·ché \rə-,sher-'shā, -'sher-,shā\ *adj* [F] **1** : CHOICE, RARE **2** : excessively refined

re·cid·i·vism \ri-'si-də-,vi-zəm\ *n* : a tendency to relapse into a previous condition; *esp* : relapse into criminal behavior — **re·cid·i·vist** \-vist\ *n*

rec·i·pe \'re-sə-(,)pē\ *n* [L, take, imperative of *recipere* to take, receive, fr. *re-* back + *capere* to take] **1** : a set of instructions for making something from various ingredients **2** : a method of procedure : FORMULA

re·cip·i·ent \ri-'si-pē-ənt\ *n* : one that receives

¹re·cip·ro·cal \ri-'si-prə-kəl\ *adj* **1** : inversely related **2** : MUTUAL, SHARED **3** : serving to reciprocate **4** : mutually corresponding — **re·cip·ro·cal·ly** *adv*

²reciprocal *n* **1** : something in a reciprocal relationship to another **2** : one of a pair of numbers (as ⅔ and ⅜) whose product is one

re·cip·ro·cate \-,kāt\ *vb* **-cat·ed; -cat·ing** **1** : to move backward and forward alternately **2** : to give and take mutually **3** : to make a return for something done or given — **re·cip·ro·ca·tion** \-,si-prə-'kā-shən\ *n*

rec·i·proc·i·ty \,re-sə-'prä-sə-tē\ *n, pl* **-ties** **1** : the quality or state of being reciprocal **2** : mutual exchange of privileges (as trade advantages between countries)

re·cit·al \ri-'sī-t²l\ *n* **1** : an act or instance of reciting : ACCOUNT **2** : a public reading or recitation ⟨a poetry ∼⟩ **3** : a concert given by a musician, dancer, or dance troupe **4** : a public exhibition of skill given by music or dance pupils — **re·cit·al·ist** \-t²l-ist\ *n*

rec·i·ta·tion \,re-sə-'tā-shən\ *n* **1** : RECITING, RECITAL **2** : delivery before an audience usu. of something memorized **3** : a classroom exercise in which pupils answer questions on a lesson they have studied

re·cite \ri-'sīt\ *vb* **re·cit·ed; re·cit·ing** **1** : to repeat verbatim (as something memorized) **2** : to recount in some detail : RELATE **3** : to reply to a teacher's questions on a lesson — **re·cit·er** *n*

reck·less \'re-kləs\ *adj* : lacking caution ⟨a ∼ driver⟩ ♦ **Synonyms** HASTY, BRASH, HOTHEADED, THOUGHTLESS — **reck·less·ly** *adv* — **reck·less·ness** *n*

reck·on \'re-kən\ *vb* **1** : COUNT, CALCULATE, COMPUTE **2** : CONSIDER, REGARD **3** *chiefly dial* : THINK, SUPPOSE, GUESS

reck·on·ing *n* **1** : an act or instance of reckoning **2** : a settling of accounts ⟨day of ∼⟩

re·claim \ri-'klām\ *vb* **1** : to recall from wrong conduct : REFORM **2** : to change from an undesirable to a desired condition ⟨∼ marshy land⟩ **3** : to obtain from a waste product or by-product ⟨∼ed plastic⟩ **4** : to demand or obtain the return of — **re·claim·able** *adj* — **rec·la·ma·tion** \,re-klə-'mā-shən\ *n*

re·cline \ri-'klīn\ *vb* **re·clined; re·clin·ing** **1** : to lean or incline backward **2** : to lie down : REST

re·clin·er \ri-'klī-nər\ *n* : a chair with an adjustable back and footrest

re·cluse \'re-,klüs, ri-'klüs\ *n* : a person who leads a secluded or solitary life : HERMIT — **re·clu·sive** \ri-'klü-siv\ *adj*

rec·og·nise *chiefly Brit var of* RECOGNIZE

rec·og·ni·tion \,re-kəg-'ni-shən\ *n* **1** : the act of recognizing : the state of being recognized : ACKNOWLEDGMENT **2** : special notice or attention

re·cog·ni·zance \ri-'käg-nə-zəns\ *n* : a promise recorded before a court or magistrate to do something (as to appear in court or to keep the peace) usu. under penalty of a money forfeiture

rec·og·nize \'re-kəg-,nīz\ *vb* **-nized; -niz·ing** **1** : to acknowledge (as a speaker in a meeting) as one entitled to be heard at the time **2** : to acknowledge the existence or the independence of (a country or government) **3** : to take notice of **4** : to acknowledge with appreciation **5** : to acknowledge acquaintance with **6** : to identify as previously known **7** : to perceive clearly : REALIZE — **rec·og·niz·able** \'re-kəg-,nī-zə-bəl\ *adj* — **rec·og·niz·ably** \-blē\ *adv*

¹re·coil \ri-'kȯi(-ə)l\ *vb* [ME *reculen, recoilen,* fr. AF *reculer, reculir,* fr. *re-* back + *cul* backside, fr. L *culus*] **1** : to draw back : RETREAT **2** : to spring back to or as if to a starting point ♦ **Synonyms** SHRINK, FLINCH, WINCE, QUAIL, BLENCH

²re·coil \'rē-,kȯi(-ə)l, ri-'kȯil\ *n* : the action of recoiling (as by a gun or spring)

re·coil·less \-,kȯi(-ə)l-ləs, -'kȯi(-ə)l-\ *adj* : venting expanding propellant gas before recoil is produced ⟨∼ gun⟩

rec·ol·lect \,re-kə-'lekt\ *vb* : to recall to mind : REMEMBER ♦ **Synonyms** RECALL, REMIND, REMINISCE, BETHINK

rec·ol·lec·tion \,re-kə-'lek-shən\ *n* **1** : the act or power of recollecting **2** : something recollected

re·com·bi·nant \(,)rē-'käm-bə-nənt\ *adj* **1** : relating to genetic recombination **2** : containing or produced by recombinant DNA ⟨∼ vaccines⟩

recombinant DNA *n* : genetically engineered DNA prepared in vitro by joining together DNA usu. from more than one species of organism

re·com·bi·na·tion \,rē-,käm-bə-'nā-shən\ *n* : the formation of new combinations of genes

rec·om·mend \,re-kə-'mend\ *vb* **1** : to present as deserving of acceptance or trial **2** : to give in charge : COMMIT

3 : to make acceptable 4 : ADVISE, COUNSEL — **rec·om·mend·able** \-'men-də-bəl\ *adj*

rec·om·men·da·tion \ˌre-kə-mən-'dā-shən\ *n* 1 : the act of recommending 2 : something recommended 3 : something that recommends

¹**rec·om·pense** \'re-kəm-ˌpens\ *vb* **-pensed; -pens·ing** 1 : to give compensation to : pay for 2 : to return in kind : REQUITE ♦ **Synonyms** REIMBURSE, INDEMNIFY, REPAY, COMPENSATE

²**recompense** *n* : COMPENSATION

rec·on·cile \'re-kən-ˌsī(-ə)l\ *vb* **-ciled; -cil·ing** 1 : to cause to be friendly or harmonious again 2 : ADJUST, SETTLE ⟨~ differences⟩ 3 : to bring to submission or acceptance ♦ **Synonyms** CONFORM, ACCOMMODATE, HARMONIZE, COORDINATE — **rec·on·cil·able** *adj* — **rec·on·cile·ment** *n* — **rec·on·cil·er** *n*

rec·on·cil·i·a·tion \ˌre-kən-ˌsi-lē-'ā-shən\ *n* 1 : the action of reconciling 2 : the Roman Catholic sacrament of penance

re·con·dite \'re-kən-ˌdīt\ *adj* 1 : hard to understand : PROFOUND, ABSTRUSE 2 : little known : OBSCURE

re·con·di·tion \ˌrē-kən-'di-shən\ *vb* 1 : to restore to good condition (as by replacing parts) 2 : to condition anew

re·con·nais·sance \ri-'kä-nə-zəns, -səns\ *n* [F, lit., recognition] : a preliminary survey of an area; *esp* : an exploratory military survey of enemy territory

re·con·noi·ter *or* **re·con·noi·tre** \ˌrē-kə-'nói-tər, ˌre-\ *vb* **-noi·tered** *or* **-noi·tred; -noi·ter·ing** *or* **-noi·tring** 1 : to make a reconnaissance of : engage in reconnaissance

re·con·sid·er \ˌrē-kən-'si-dər\ *vb* : to consider again with a view to changing or reversing — **re·con·sid·er·a·tion** \-ˌsi-də-'rā-shən\ *n*

re·con·sti·tute \ˌrē-'kän-stə-ˌtüt, -ˌtyüt\ *vb* : to restore to a former condition by adding water ⟨~ powdered milk⟩

re·con·struct \ˌrē-kən-'strəkt\ *vb* : to construct again : REBUILD

re·con·struc·tion \ˌrē-kən-'strək-shən\ *n* 1 : the action of reconstructing : the state of being reconstructed 2 *often cap* : the reorganization and reestablishment of the seceded states in the Union after the American Civil War 3 : something reconstructed

¹**re·cord** \ri-'kòrd\ *vb* [ME, lit., to recall, fr. AF *recorder*, fr. L *recordari*, fr. *re-* back, again + *cord-, cors* heart] 1 : to set down in writing 2 : to register permanently 3 : INDICATE, READ 4 : to give evidence of 5 : to cause (as sound or visual images) to be registered (as on a disc or a magnetic tape) in a form that permits reproduction

²**rec·ord** \'re-kərd\ *n* 1 : the act of being recorded 2 : a written account of proceedings 3 : known facts about a person; *also* : a collection of items of information (as in a database) treated as a unit 4 : an attested top performance 5 : something on which sound or visual images have been recorded

³**re·cord** \ri-'kòrd\ *n* : a function of an electronic device that causes it to record

re·cord·er \ri-'kòr-dər\ *n* 1 : a judge in some city courts 2 : one who records transactions officially 3 : a recording device 4 : a wind instrument with a whistle mouthpiece and eight fingerholes

re·cord·ing *n* : RECORD 5

re·cord·ist \ri-'kòr-dist\ *n* : one who records sound esp. on film

¹**re·count** \ri-'kaùnt\ *vb* : to relate in detail : TELL ♦ **Synonyms** RECITE, REHEARSE, NARRATE, DESCRIBE, STATE, REPORT

²**re·count** \'rē-ˌkaùnt, (ˌ)rē-'kaùnt\ *vb* : to count again

³**re·count** \'rē-ˌkaùnt, (ˌ)rē-'kaùnt\ *n* : a second or fresh count

re·coup \ri-'küp\ *vb* : to get an equivalent or compensation for : make up for something lost

re·course \'rē-ˌkòrs, ri-'kòrs\ *n* 1 : a turning to someone or something for assistance or protection 2 : a source of aid : RESORT

re·cov·er \ri-'kə-vər\ *vb* ·1 : to get back again : REGAIN, RETRIEVE 2 : to regain normal health, poise, or status 3 : to make up for : RECOUP ⟨~ed all his losses⟩ 4 : RECLAIM ⟨~ land from the sea⟩ 5 : to obtain a legal judgment in one's favor — **re·cov·er·able** *adj* — **re·cov·ery** \-'kə-və-rē\ *n*

re-cov·er \ˌrē-'kə-vər\ *vb* : to cover again

recovering *adj* : being in the process of overcoming a shortcoming or problem ⟨a ~ alcoholic⟩

re·cov·ery \ri-'kə-və-rē\ *n* 1 : an act or instance of recovering; *esp* : an economic upturn 2 : the process of combating a disorder or problem

¹**re·cre·ant** \'re-krē-ənt\ *adj* [ME, fr. AF, fr. prp. of (*se*) *recreire* to give up, yield, fr. ML (*se*) *recredere* to resign oneself (to a judgment), fr. L *re-* back +*credere* to believe] 1 : COWARDLY 2 : UNFAITHFUL

²**recreant** *n* 1 : COWARD 2 : DESERTER

rec·re·ate \'re-krē-ˌāt\ *vb* **-at·ed; -at·ing** 1 : to give new life or freshness to 2 : to take recreation — **rec·re·ative** \-ˌā-tiv\ *adj*

re-cre·ate \ˌrē-krē-'āt\ *vb* : to create again — **re-cre·ation** \-'ā-shən\ *n* — **re-cre·ative** \-'ā-tiv\ *adj*

rec·re·ation \ˌre-krē-'ā-shən\ *n* : a refreshing of strength or spirits after work; *also* : a means of refreshment ♦ **Synonyms** DIVERSION, ENTERTAINMENT, AMUSEMENT — **rec·re·ation·al** \-shə-nəl\ *adj*

recreational vehicle *n* : a vehicle designed for recreational use (as camping)

re·crim·i·na·tion \ri-ˌkri-mə-'nā-shən\ *n* : a retaliatory accusation — **re·crim·i·nate** \-'kri-mə-nāt\ *vb* — **re·crim·i·na·tory** \-'kri-mə-nə-ˌtòr-ē\ *adj*

re·cru·des·cence \ˌrē-krü-'de-sᵊns\ *n* : a renewal or breaking out again esp. of something unhealthful or dangerous

¹**re·cruit** \ri-'krüt\ *vb* 1 : to form or strengthen with new members ⟨~ an army⟩ 2 : to enlist as a member of an armed service 3 : to secure the services of 4 : to seek to enroll 5 : to restore or increase in health or vigor ⟨resting to ~ his strength⟩ — **re·cruit·er** *n* — **re·cruit·ment** *n*

²**recruit** *n* [F *recrute, recrue* fresh growth, new levy of soldiers, fr. MF, fr. *recroistre* to grow up again, fr. L *recrescere*] : a newcomer to an activity or field; *esp* : a newly enlisted member of the armed forces

rec·tal \'rek-tᵊl\ *adj* : of or relating to the rectum — **rec·tal·ly** *adv*

rect·an·gle \'rek-ˌtan-gəl\ *n* : a 4-sided figure with four right angles; *esp* : one with adjacent sides of unequal length — **rect·an·gu·lar** \rek-'tan-gyə-lər\ *adj*

rec·ti·fi·er \'rek-tə-ˌfī(-ə)r\ *n* : one that rectifies; *esp* : a device for converting alternating current into direct current

rec·ti·fy \'rek-tə-ˌfī\ *vb* **-fied; -fy·ing** : to make or set right : CORRECT ♦ **Synonyms** EMEND, AMEND, MEND, RIGHT — **rec·ti·fi·ca·tion** \ˌrek-tə-fə-'kä-shən\ *n*

rec·ti·lin·ear \ˌrek-tə-'li-nē-ər\ *adj* 1 : moving in a straight line ⟨~ motion⟩ 2 : characterized by straight lines

rec·ti·tude \'rek-tə-ˌtüd, -ˌtyüd\ *n* 1 : moral integrity 2 : correctness of procedure ♦ **Synonyms** VIRTUE, GOODNESS, MORALITY, PROBITY

rec·to \'rek-tō\ *n, pl* **rectos** : a right-hand page

rec·tor \'rek-tər\ *n* 1 : a priest or minister in charge of a parish 2 : the head of a university or school — **rec·to·ri·al** \rek-'tòr-ē-əl\ *adj*

rec·to·ry \'rek-tə-rē\ *n, pl* **-ries** : the residence of a rector or a parish priest

rec·tum \'rek-təm\ *n, pl* **rectums** *or* **rec·ta** \-tə\ [ME, fr. ML, fr. *rectum intestinum*, lit., straight intestine] : the last part of the intestine joining the colon and anus

re·cum·bent \ri-'kəm-bənt\ *adj* : lying down : RECLINING

re·cu·per·ate \ri-'kü-pə-ˌrāt-, -'kyü-\ *vb* **-at·ed; -at·ing** : to get back (as health or strength) : RECOVER — **re·cu·per·a·tion** \-ˌkü-pə-'rā-shən, -ˌkyü-\ *n* — **re·cu·per·a·tive** \-'kü-pə-ˌrā-tiv, -'kyü-\ *adj*

re·cur \ri-'kər\ *vb* **re·curred; re·cur·ring** 1 : to go or come back in thought or discussion 2 : to occur or appear again esp. after an interval : occur time after time ⟨*recurring* headaches⟩ — **re·cur·rence** \-'kər-əns\ *n* — **re·cur·rent** \-ənt\ *adj*

re·cy·cle \rē-'sī-kəl\ *vb* 1 : to pass again through a cycle of changes or treatment 2 : to process (as liquid body waste, glass, or cans) in order to regain materials for human use — **re·cy·cla·bil·i·ty** \-ˌsī-klə-'bil-ə-tē\ *n* — **re·cy·cla·ble** \-k(ə)lə-bəl\ *adj* — **recycle** *n*

¹**red** \'red\ *adj* **red·der; red·dest** 1 : of the color red 2 : endorsing radical social or political change esp. by force 3 *often cap* : of or relating to the former U.S.S.R. or its allies — **red·ly** *adv* — **red·ness** *n*

²**red** *n* 1 : the color of blood or of the ruby 2 : a revolu-

tionary in politics **3** *cap* : COMMUNIST **4** : the condition of showing a loss ⟨in the ∼⟩

re·dact \ri-'dakt\ *vb* **1** : to put in writing : FRAME **2** : EDIT — **re·dac·tor** \-'dak-tər\ *n*

re·dac·tion \-'dak-shən\ *n* **1** : an act or instance of redacting **2** : EDITION

red alga *n* : any of a group of reddish usu. marine algae

red blood cell *n* : any of the hemoglobin-containing cells that carry oxygen from the lungs to the tissues and are responsible for the red color of vertebrate blood

red·breast \'red-ˌbrest\ *n* : ROBIN

red–carpet *adj* : marked by ceremonial courtesy

red cedar *n* : an American juniper with scalelike leaves and fragrant close-grained red wood; *also* : its wood

red clover *n* : a European clover that has globe-shaped heads of reddish flowers and is widely cultivated for hay and forage

red·coat \'red-ˌkōt\ *n* : a British soldier esp. during the Revolutionary War

red·den \'red-ᵈn\ *vb* : to make or become red or reddish : FLUSH, BLUSH

red·dish \'re-dish\ *adj* : tinged with red — **red·dish·ness** *n*

red dwarf *n* : a star with lower temperature and less mass than the sun

re·deem \ri-'dēm\ *vb* [ME *redemen*, fr. AF *rdemer*, modif. of L *redimere*, fr. *re-*, *red-* back, again + *emere* to take, buy] **1** : to recover (property) by discharging an obligation **2** : to ransom, free, or rescue by paying a price **3** : to free from the consequences of sin **4** : to remove the obligation of by payment ⟨the government ∼s savings bonds⟩; *also* : to convert into something of value **5** : to make good (a promise) by performing : FULFILL **6** : to atone for — **re·deem·able** *adj* — **re·deem·er** *n*

re·demp·tion \ri-'demp-shən\ *n* : the act of redeeming : the state of being redeemed — **re·demp·tive** \-tiv\ *adj* — **re·demp·to·ry** \-tə-rē\ *adj*

re·de·ploy \ˌrē-di-'plói\ *vb* **1** : to transfer from one area or activity to another **2** : to relocate men or equipment — **re·de·ploy·ment** *n*

red–eye \'red-ˌī\ *n* **1** : cheap whiskey **2** : a late night or overnight flight

red·fish \'red-ˌfish\ *n* : any of various reddish marine fishes of the Atlantic including some used for food

red fox *n* : a fox with orange-red to reddish brown fur

red giant *n* : a very large star with a relatively low surface temperature

red–hand·ed \'red-'han-dəd\ *adv or adj* : in the act of committing a misdeed

red·head \-ˌhed\ *n* : a person having red hair — **red·head·ed** \-ˌhe-dəd\ *adj*

red herring *n* : a diversion intended to distract attention from the real issue

red–hot \'red-'hät\ *adj* **1** : extremely hot; *esp* : glowing with heat **2** : EXCITED, FURIOUS **3** : very new ⟨∼ news⟩

re·dial \'rē-ˌdī(-ə)l\ *n* : a telephone function that automatically repeats the dialing of the last number called — **redial** *vb*

re·dis·trib·ute \ˌrē-də-'stri-byüt\ *vb* **1** : to alter the distribution of **2** : to spread to other areas — **re·dis·tri·bu·tion** \-(ˌ)rē-ˌdis-trə-'byü-shən\ *n*

re·dis·trict \ˌrē-'dis-(ˌ)trikt\ *vb* : to organize into new territorial and esp. political divisions

red–let·ter \'red-ˌle-tər\ *adj* : of special significance : MEMORABLE

red–light *adj* : having many houses of prostitution ⟨a ∼district⟩

re·do \(ˌ)rē-'dü\ *vb* : to do over or again; *esp* : REDECORATE

red oak *n* : any of various No. American oaks with leaves usu. having spiny-tipped lobes and acorns that take two years to mature; *also* : the wood of a red oak

red·o·lent \'re-də-lənt\ *adj* **1** : FRAGRANT, AROMATIC **2** : having a specified fragrance ⟨a room ∼ of cooked cabbage⟩ **3** : REMINISCENT, SUGGESTIVE — **red·o·lence** \-ləns\ *n* — **red·o·lent·ly** *adv*

re·dou·ble \(ˌ)rē-'də-bəl\ *vb* : to make twice as great or in amount; *also* : INTENSIFY

re·doubt \ri-'daút\ *n* [F *redoute*, fr. It *ridotto*, fr. ML *reductus* secret place, fr. L, withdrawn, fr. *reducere* to lead

back, fr. *re-* back + *ducere* to lead] : a small usu. temporary fortification

re·doubt·able \ri-'daú-tə-bəl\ *adj* [ME *redoutable*, fr. AF, fr. *reduter* to dread, fr. *re-* back, again + *duter* to doubt] : arousing dread or fear : FORMIDABLE

re·dound \ri-'daúnd\ *vb* **1** : to have an effect **2** : to become added or transferred : ACCRUE

red pepper *n* **1** : CAYENNE PEPPER **2** : a mature red hot pepper or sweet pepper

¹re·dress \ri-'dres\ *vb* **1** : to set right : REMEDY **2** : COMPENSATE **3** : to remove the cause of (a grievance) **4** : AVENGE

²re·dress *n* **1** : relief from distress **2** : means or possibility of seeking a remedy **3** : compensation for loss or injury **4** : an act or instance of redressing

red·shift \'red-'shift\ *n* : displacement of the spectrum of a heavenly body toward longer wavelength; *also* : a measure of this displacement

red snapper *n* : any of various reddish fishes including several food fishes

red spider *n* : SPIDER MITE

red squirrel *n* : a common No. American squirrel with the upper parts chiefly red

red–tailed hawk \'red-ˌtāld-\ *n* : a rodent-eating No. American hawk with a rather short tyically reddish tail

red tape *n* [fr. the red tape formerly used to bind legal documents in England] : official routine or procedure marked by excessive complexity which results in delay or inaction

red tide *n* : seawater discolored by the presence of large numbers of dinoflagellates which produce a toxin that renders infected shellfish poisonous

re·duce \ri-'düs, -'dyüs\ *vb* **re·duced; re·duc·ing 1** : LESSEN **2** : to bring to a specified state or condition ⟨*reduced* them to tears⟩ **3** : to put in a lower rank or grade **4** : CONQUER ⟨∼ a fort⟩ **5** : to bring into a certain order or classification **6** : to correct (as a fracture) by restoration of displaced parts **7** : to lessen one's weight ✦ **Synonyms** DECREASE, DIMINISH, ABATE, DWINDLE, RECEDE — **re·duc·er** *n* — **re·duc·ible** \-'dü-sə-bəl, -'dyü-\ *adj*

re·duc·tion \ri-'dək-shən\ *n* **1** : the act of reducing : the state of being reduced **2** : something made by reducing **3** : the amount taken off in reducing something

re·dun·dan·cy \ri-'dən-dən-sē\ *n, pl* **-cies 1** : the quality or state of being redundant : SUPERFLUITY **2** : something redundant or in excess **3** : the use of surplus words

re·dun·dant \-dənt\ *adj* **1** : exceeding what is needed or normal : SUPERFLUOUS; *esp* : using more words than necessary **2** : marked by repetition — **re·dun·dant·ly** *adv*

red–winged blackbird \'red-ˌwiŋd-\ *n* : a No. American blackbird of which the adult male is black with a patch of bright scarlet on the wings

red·wood \'red-ˌwúd\ *n* : a tall coniferous timber tree esp. of coastal California; *also* : its durable wood

reed \'rēd\ *n* **1** : any of various tall slender grasses of wet areas; *also* : a stem or growth of reed **2** : a musical instrument made from the hollow stem of a reed **3** : an elastic tongue of cane, wood, or metal by which tones are produced in organ pipes and certain other wind instruments — **reedy** *adj*

re·ed·u·cate \ˌrē-'e-jə-ˌkāt\ *vb* : to train again; *esp* : to rehabilitate through education — **re·ed·u·ca·tion** *n*

¹reef \'rēf\ *n* **1** : a part of a sail taken in or let out in regulating the sail's size **2** : reduction in sail area by reefing

²reef *vb* : to reduce the area of a sail by rolling or folding part of it

³reef *n* : a ridge of rocks, sand or coral at or near the surface of the water

reef·er \'rē-fər\ *n* : a marijuana cigarette

¹reek \'rēk\ *n* : a strong or disagreeable fume or odor

²reek *vb* **1** : to give off or become permeated with a strong or offensive odor **2** : to give a strong impression of some constituent quality ⟨an excuse that ∼ed of falsehood⟩ — **reek·er** *n* — **reeky** \'rē-kē\ *adj*

¹reel \'rēl\ *n* : a revolvable device on which something flexible (as film or tape) is wound; *also* : a quantity of something wound on such a device

²reel *vb* **1** : to wind on or as if on a reel **2** : to pull or draw (as a fish) by reeling a line — **reel·able** *adj* — **reel·er** *n*

³**reel** *vb* **1** : WHIRL; *also* : to be giddy **2** : to waver or fall back (as from a blow) **3** : to walk or move unsteadily

⁴**reel** *n* : a reeling motion

⁵**reel** *n* : a lively Scottish dance or its music

reel off *vb* **1** : to tell or recite rapidly and easily ⟨*reeled off the right answers*⟩ **2** : to achieve usu. consecutively ⟨*reeled off six straight wins*⟩

re·en·try \rē-'en-trē\ *n* **1** : a second or new entry **2** : the action of reentering the earth's atmosphere from space

reeve \'rēv\ *vb* **rove** \'rōv\ *or* **reeved; reev·ing** : to pass (as a rope) through a hole in a block or cleat

¹**ref** \'ref\ *n* : REFEREE 2

²**ref** *abbr* **1** reference **2** referred **3** reformed **4** refunding

re·fec·tion \ri-'fek-shən\ *n* **1** : refreshment esp. after hunger or fatigue **2** : food and drink together : REPAST

re·fec·to·ry \ri-'fek-tə-rē\ *n, pl* **-ries** : a dining hall (as in a monastery or college)

re·fer \ri-'fər\ *vb* **re·ferred; re·fer·ring** [ME *referren*, fr. AF *referer, referir,* fr. L *referre* to bring back, report, refer, fr. *re-* back + *ferre* to carry] **1** : to assign to a certain source, cause, or relationship **2** : to direct or send to some person or place (as for information or help) **3** : to submit to someone else for consideration or action **4** : to have recourse (as for information or aid) **5** : to have connection : RELATE **6** : to direct attention : speak of : MENTION, ALLUDE ✦ **Synonyms** RECUR, REPAIR, RESORT, APPLY, GO, TURN — **re·fer·able** \'re-fə-rə-bəl, ri-'fər-ə-\ *adj*

¹**ref·er·ee** \₁re-fə-'rē\ *n* **1** : a person to whom an issue esp. in law is referred for investigation or settlement **2** : an umpire in certain games

²**referee** *vb* **-eed; -ee·ing** : to act as referee

ref·er·ence \'re-frəns, -fə-rəns\ *n* **1** : the act of referring **2** : RELATION, RESPECT **3** : ALLUSION, MENTION **4** : something that refers a reader to another passage or book **5** : consultation esp. for obtaining information ⟨books for ∼⟩ **6** : a person of whom inquiries as to character or ability can be made **7** : a written recommendation of a person for employment

ref·er·en·dum \₁re-fə-'ren-dəm\ *n, pl* **-da** \-də\ *or* **-dums** : the submitting of legislative measures to the voters for approval or rejection; *also* : a vote on a measure so submitted

ref·er·ent \'re-frənt, -fə-rənt\ *n* : one that refers or is referred to; *esp* : the thing a word stands for — **referent** *adj*

re·fer·ral \ri-'fər-əl\ *n* **1** : the act or an instance of referring **2** : one that is referred

¹**re·fill** \rē-'fil\ *vb* : to fill again : REPLENISH — **re·fill·able** *adj*

²**re·fill** \'rē-₁fil\ *n* : a new or fresh supply of something

re·fi·nance \₁rē-fə-'nans, (₁)rē-'fī-nans\ *vb* : to renew or reorganize the financing of

re·fine \ri-'fīn\ *vb* **re·fined; re·fin·ing** **1** : to free from impurities or waste matter **2** : IMPROVE, PERFECT **3** : to free or become free of what is coarse or uncouth **4** : to make improvements by introducing subtle changes — **re·fin·er** *n*

re·fined \ri-'fīnd\ *adj* **1** : freed from impurities **2** : CULTURED, CULTIVATED **3** : SUBTLE

re·fine·ment \ri-'fīn-mənt\ *n* **1** : the action of refining **2** : the quality or state of being refined **3** : a refined feature or method; *also* : something intended to improve or perfect

re·fin·ery \ri-'fī-nə-rē\ *n, pl* **-er·ies** : a building and equipment for refining metals, oil, or sugar

re·flect \ri-'flekt\ *vb* [ME, fr. L *reflectere* to bend back, fr. *re-* back + *flectere* to bend] **1** : to bend or cast back (as light, heat, or sound) **2** : to give back a likeness or image of as a mirror does **3** : to bring as a result ⟨∼*ed* credit on him⟩ **4** : to make apparent : SHOW ⟨figures that ∼ economic growth⟩ **5** : to cast reproach or blame ⟨their bad conduct ∼*ed* on their training⟩ **6** : PONDER, MEDITATE — **re·flec·tion** \-'flek-shən\ *n* — **re·flec·tive** \-tiv\ *adj* — **re·flec·tiv·i·ty** \(₁)rē-₁flek-'ti-və-tē\ *n*

re·flec·tor \ri-'flek-tər\ *n* : one that reflects; *esp* : a polished surface for reflecting radiation (as light)

¹**re·flex** \'rē-₁fleks\ *n* **1** : an automatic and usu. inborn response to a stimulus not involving higher mental centers **2** *pl* : the power of acting or responding with enough speed ⟨an athlete with great ∼*es*⟩

²**reflex** *adj* **1** : bent or directed back **2** : of, relating to, or produced by a reflex ⟨a ∼ action⟩ — **re·flex·ly** *adv*

¹**re·flex·ive** \ri-'flek-siv\ *adj* : of or relating to an action directed back upon the doer or the grammatical subject ⟨a ∼ verb⟩ ⟨the ∼ pronoun *himself*⟩ — **re·flex·ive·ly** *adv* — **re·flex·ive·ness** *n*

²**reflexive** *n* : a reflexive verb or pronoun

re·flex·ol·o·gy \₁rē-₁flek-'sä-lə-jē\ *n* : massage in which pressure is applied to specific points on the hands or feet

re·flux \'rē-₁fləks\ *n* : a flowing back

re·fo·cus \(₁)rē-'fō-kəs\ *vb* **1** : to focus again **2** : to change the emphasis or direction of ⟨∼*ed* her life⟩

re·for·es·ta·tion \₁rē-₁fȯr-ə-'stā-shən\ *n* : the action of renewing forest cover by planting seeds or young trees — **re·for·est** \rē-'fȯr-əst\ *vb*

¹**re·form** \ri-'fȯrm\ *vb* **1** : to make better or improve by removal of faults **2** : to correct or improve one's own character or habits ✦ **Synonyms** CORRECT, RECTIFY, EMEND, REMEDY, REDRESS, REVISE — **re·form·able** *adj* — **re·for·ma·tive** \-'fȯr-mə-tiv\ *adj*

²**reform** *n* : improvement or correction of what is corrupt or defective

re–form \₁rē-'fȯrm\ *vb* : to form again

ref·or·ma·tion \₁re-fər-'mā-shən\ *n* **1** : the act of reforming : the state of being reformed **2** *cap* : a 16th century religious movement marked by the establishment of the Protestant churches

re·for·ma·to·ry \ri-'fȯr-mə-₁tȯr-ē\ *adj* : aiming at or tending toward reformation : REFORMATIVE

²**reformatory** *n, pl* **-ries** : a penal institution for reforming esp. young or first offenders

re·form·er \ri-'fȯr-mər\ *n* **1** : one that works for or urges reform **2** *cap* : a leader of the Protestant Reformation

refr *abbr* refraction

re·fract \ri-'frakt\ *vb* [L *refractus,* pp. of *refringere* to break open, break up, fr. *re-* back + *frangere* to break] : to subject to refraction

re·frac·tion \ri-'frak-shən\ *n* : the bending of a ray (as of light) when it passes obliquely from one medium into another in which its speed is different — **re·frac·tive** \-tiv\ *adj*

refractive index *n* : the ratio of the speed of radiation in one medium to that in another medium

re·frac·to·ry \ri-'frak-tə-rē\ *adj* **1** : OBSTINATE, STUBBORN, UNMANAGEABLE **2** : capable of enduring high temperature ⟨∼ bricks⟩ ✦ **Synonyms** RECALCITRANT, INTRACTABLE, UNGOVERNABLE, UNRULY, HEADSTRONG, WILLFUL — **re·frac·to·ri·ness** \ri-'frak-tə-rē-nəs\ *n* — **refractory** *n*

¹**re·frain** \ri-'frān\ *vb* : to hold oneself back : FORBEAR — **re·frain·ment** *n*

²**refrain** *n* : a phrase or verse recurring regularly in a poem or song

re·fresh \ri-'fresh\ *vb* **1** : to make or become fresh or fresher **2** : to revive by or as if by renewal of supplies ⟨∼ one's memory⟩ **3** : to freshen up **4** : to supply or take refreshment **5** : to update or renew esp. by sending a new signal ⟨∼ the Web page⟩ ✦ **Synonyms** RESTORE, REJUVENATE, RENOVATE, REFURBISH — **re·fresh·er** *n* — **re·fresh·ing·ly** *adv*

re·fresh·ment \-mənt\ *n* **1** : the act of refreshing : the state of being refreshed **2** : something that refreshes **3** *pl* : a light meal; *also* : assorted light foods

re·fried beans \'rē-₁frīd-\ *n pl* : beans cooked with seasonings, fried, then mashed and fried again

refrig *abbr* refrigerating; refrigeration

re·frig·er·ate \ri-'fri-jə-₁rāt\ *vb* **-at·ed; -at·ing** : to make cool; *esp* : to chill or freeze (food) for preservation — **re·frig·er·ant** \-jə-rənt\ *adj or n* — **re·frig·er·a·tion** \-₁fri-jə-'rā-shən\ *n* — **re·frig·er·a·tor** \-'fri-jə-₁rā-tər\ *n*

ref·uge \'re-₁fyüj\ *n* **1** : shelter or protection from danger or distress **2** : a place that provides protection

ref·u·gee \₁re-fyu-'jē\ *n* : one who flees for safety esp. to a foreign country

re·ful·gence \ri-'fu̇l-jəns, -'fəl-\ *n* : a radiant or resplendent quality or state — **re·ful·gent** \-jənt\ *adj*

¹**re·fund** \ri-'fənd, 'rē-₁fənd\ *vb* : to give or put back (money) : REPAY — **re·fund·able** *adj*

²**re·fund** \'rē-₁fənd\ *n* **1** : the act of refunding **2** : a sum refunded

re·fur·bish \ri-'fər-bish\ *vb* : to brighten or freshen up : RENOVATE

¹**re·fuse** \ri-'fyüz\ *vb* **re·fused; re·fus·ing** **1** : to decline to accept : REJECT **2** : to decline to do, give, or grant : DENY — **re·fus·al** \-'fyü-zəl\ *n*

²**ref·use** \'re-,fyüs, -,fyüz\ *n* : rejected or worthless matter : RUBBISH, TRASH

re·fute \ri-'fyüt\ *vb* **re·fut·ed; re·fut·ing** [L *refutare* to check, suppress, refute] : to prove to be false by argument or evidence — **ref·u·ta·tion** \,re-fyù-'tā-shən\ *n* — **re·fut·er** *n*

¹**reg** \'reg\ *n* : REGULATION

²**reg** *abbr* **1** region **2** register; registered; registration **3** regular

re·gal \'rē-gəl\ *adj* **1** : of, relating to, or befitting a king : ROYAL **2** : STATELY, SPLENDID — **re·gal·ly** *adv*

re·gale \ri-'gāl\ *vb* **re·galed; re·gal·ing** **1** : to entertain richly or agreeably **2** : to give pleasure or amusement to ⟨*regaled* us with stories⟩ ◆ *Synonyms* GRATIFY, DELIGHT, PLEASE, REJOICE, GLADDEN

re·ga·lia \ri-'gāl-yə\ *n pl* **1** : the emblems, symbols, or paraphernalia of royalty (as the crown and scepter) **2** : the insignia of an office or order **3** : special costume : FINERY

¹**re·gard** \ri-'gärd\ *n* **1** : CONSIDERATION, HEED; *also* : CARE, CONCERN **2** : GAZE, GLANCE, LOOK **3** : RESPECT, ESTEEM ⟨held in high ∼⟩ **4** *pl* : friendly greetings implying respect and esteem **5** : an aspect to be considered : PARTICULAR — **re·gard·ful** *adj* — **re·gard·less** *adj*

²**regard** *vb* **1** : to think of : CONSIDER **2** : to pay attention to **3** : to show respect for : HEED ⟨∼s *his elders*⟩ **4** : to hold in high esteem : care for **5** : to look at : gaze upon ⟨∼*ed* the landscape⟩ **6** *archaic* : to relate to

re·gard·ing *prep* : CONCERNING

regardless of \ri-'gärd-ləs-\ *prep* : in spite of

re·gat·ta \ri-'gä-tə, -'ga-\ *n* : a boat race or a series of boat races

re·gen·cy \'rē-jən-sē\ *n, pl* **-cies** **1** : the office or government of a regent or body of regents **2** : a body of regents **3** : the period during which a regent governs

re·gen·er·a·cy \ri-'je-nə-rə-sē\ *n* : the state of being regenerated

¹**re·gen·er·ate** \ri-'je-nə-rət\ *adj* **1** : formed or created again **2** : spiritually reborn or converted

²**re·gen·er·ate** \ri-'je-nə-,rāt\ *vb* **1** : to subject to spiritual renewal **2** : to reform completely **3** : to replace (a body part) by a new growth of tissue **4** : to give new life to : REVIVE — **re·gen·er·a·tion** \-je-nə-'rā-shən\ *n* — **re·gen·er·a·tive** \-'je-nə-,rā-tiv\ *adj* — **re·gen·er·a·tor** \-,rā-tər\ *n*

re·gent \'rē-jənt\ *n* **1** : a person who rules during the childhood, absence, or incapacity of the sovereign **2** : a member of a governing board (as of a state university) — **regent** *adj*

reg·gae \'re-,gä\ *n* : popular music of Jamaican origin that combines native styles with elements of rock and soul music

reg·i·cide \'re-jə-,sīd\ *n* **1** : one who murders a king **2** : murder of a king

re·gime *also* **ré·gime** \rā-'zhēm, ri-\ *n* **1** : REGIMEN **2** : a form or system of government **3** : a government in power; *also* : a period of rule

reg·i·men \'re-jə-mən\ *n* [ME, fr. ML, position of authority, direction, set of rules, fr. L, steering, control, fr. *regere* to direct] **1** : a systematic course of treatment or training ⟨a strict dietary ∼⟩ **2** : GOVERNMENT

¹**reg·i·ment** \'re-jə-mənt\ *n* : a military unit consisting usu. of a number of battalions — **reg·i·men·tal** \,re-jə-'mentəl\ *adj*

²**reg·i·ment** \'re-jə-,ment\ *vb* : to organize rigidly esp. for regulation or central control; *also* : to subject to order or uniformity — **reg·i·men·ta·tion** \,re-jə-mən-'tā-shən\ *n*

reg·i·men·tals \,re-jə-'men-təlz\ *n pl* **1** : a regimental uniform **2** : military dress

re·gion \'rē-jən\ *n* [ME, fr. AF *regiun*, fr. L *region-, regio* line, direction, area, fr. *regere* to rule] : an often indefinitely defined part or area

re·gion·al \'rē-jə-nəl\ *adj* **1** : affecting a particular region : LOCALIZED **2** : of, relating to, characteristic of, or serving a region — **re·gion·al·ly** *adv*

¹**reg·is·ter** \'re-jə-stər\ *n* **1** : a record of items or details; *also* : a book or system for keeping such a record **2** : the range of a voice or instrument **3** : a device to regulate ventilation or heating **4** : an automatic device recording a number or quantity **5** : CASH REGISTER

²**register** *vb* **-tered; -ter·ing** **1** : to enter in a register (as in a list of guests) **2** : to record automatically **3** : to secure special care for (mail matter) by paying additional postage **4** : to convey an impression of : EXPRESS **5** : to make or adjust so as to correspond exactly

registered nurse *n* : a graduate trained nurse who has been licensed to practice by a state authority after passing qualifying examinations

reg·is·trant \'re-jə-strənt\ *n* : one that registers or is registered

reg·is·trar \'re-jə-,strär\ *n* : an official recorder or keeper of records (as at an educational institution)

reg·is·tra·tion \,re-jə-'strā-shən\ *n* **1** : the act of registering **2** : an entry in a register **3** : the number of persons registered : ENROLLMENT **4** : a document certifying an act of registering

reg·is·try \'re-jə-strē\ *n, pl* **-tries** **1** : ENROLLMENT, REGISTRATION **2** : a place of registration **3** : an official record book or an entry in one

reg·nant \'reg-nənt\ *adj* **1** : REIGNING **2** : DOMINANT **3** : of common or widespread occurrence

¹**re·gress** \'rē-,gres\ *n* **1** : an act or the privilege of going or coming back **2** : RETROGRESSION

²**re·gress** \ri-'gres\ *vb* : to go or cause to go back or to a lower level — **re·gres·sive** *adj* — **re·gres·sor** \-'gre-sər\ *n*

re·gres·sion \ri-'gre-shən\ *n* : the act or an instance of regressing; *esp* : reversion to an earlier mental or behavioral level

¹**re·gret** \ri-'gret\ *vb* **re·gret·ted; re·gret·ting** **1** : to mourn the loss or death of **2** : to be very sorry for **3** : to experience regret — **re·gret·ta·ble** \-'gre-tə-bəl\ *adj* — **re·gret·ter** *n*

²**regret** *n* **1** : sorrow caused by something beyond one's power to remedy **2** : an expression of sorrow **3** *pl* : a note politely declining an invitation — **re·gret·ful** \-fəl\ *adj* — **re·gret·ful·ly** *adv*

re·gret·ta·bly \-'gre-tə-blē\ *adv* **1** : to a regrettable extent **2** : it is to be regretted

re·group \(,)rē-'grüp\ *vb* : to form into a new grouping

regt *abbr* regiment

¹**reg·u·lar** \'re-gyə-lər\ *adj* [ME *reguler*, fr. AF, fr. LL *regularis* regular, fr. L, of a bar, fr. *regula* rule, straightedge, fr. *regere* to keep straight, direct] **1** : belonging to a religious order **2** : made, built, or arranged according to a rule, standard, or type; *also* : even or symmetrical in form or structure **3** : ORDERLY, METHODICAL ⟨∼ habits⟩; *also* : not varying : STEADY ⟨a ∼ pace⟩ **4** : made, selected, or conducted according to rule or custom **5** : properly qualified ⟨not a ∼ lawyer⟩ **6** : conforming to the normal or usual manner or inflection **7** : of, relating to, or constituting the permanent standing military force of a state — **reg·u·lar·i·ty** \,re-gyə-'la-rə-tē\ *n* — **reg·u·lar·ize** \'re-gyə-lə-,rīz\ *vb* — **reg·u·lar·ly** *adv*

²**regular** *n* **1** : one that is regular (as in attendance) **2** : a member of the regular clergy **3** : a soldier in a regular army **4** : a player on an athletic team who is usu. in the starting lineup

reg·u·late \'re-gyə-,lāt\ *vb* **-lat·ed; -lat·ing** **1** : to govern or direct according to rule : CONTROL **2** : to bring under the control of law or authority **3** : to put in good order **4** : to fix or adjust the time, amount, degree, or rate of — **reg·u·la·tive** \-,lā-tiv\ *adj* — **reg·u·la·tor** \-,lā-tər\ *n* — **reg·u·la·to·ry** \-lə-,tòr-ē\ *adj*

reg·u·la·tion \,re-gyə-'lā-shən\ *n* **1** : the act of regulating : the state of being regulated **2** : a rule dealing with details of procedure **3** : an order issued by an executive authority of a government and having the force of law

re·gur·gi·tate \rē-'gər-jə-,tāt\ *vb* **-tat·ed; -tat·ing** [ML *regurgitare*, fr. L *re-* re- + LL *gurgitare* to engulf, fr. L *gurgit-, gurges* whirlpool] : to throw or be thrown back, up, or out ⟨∼ food⟩ — **re·gur·gi·ta·tion** \-,gər-jə-'tā-shən\ *n*

re·hab \'rē-,hab\ *n* **1** : REHABILITATION **2** : a rehabilitated building — **rehab** *vb*

re·ha·bil·i·tate \,rē-hə-'bi-lə-,tāt, ,rē-ə-\ *vb* **-tat·ed; -tat·ing** **1** : to restore to a former capacity, rank, or right

: REINSTATE 2 : to restore to good condition or health — **re·ha·bil·i·ta·tion** \-,bi-lə-'tā-shən\ n — **re·ha·bil·i·ta·tive** \-,tā-tiv\ adj

re·hash \,rē-'hash\ vb : to present again in another form without real change or improvement — **rehash** n

re·hear·ing \,rē-'hir-iŋ\ n : a second or new hearing by the same tribunal

re·hears·al \ri-'hər-səl\ n 1 : something told again : RECITAL 2 : a private performance or practice session preparatory to a public appearance

re·hearse \ri-'hərs\ vb **re·hearsed; re·hears·ing** 1 : to say again : REPEAT 2 : to recount in order : ENUMERATE; also : RELATE 1 3 : to give a rehearsal of 4 : to train by rehearsal 5 : to engage in a rehearsal — **re·hears·er** n

¹**reign** \'rān\ n 1 : the authority or rule of a sovereign 2 : the time during which a sovereign rules

²**reign** vb 1 : to rule as a sovereign 2 : to be predominant or prevalent

re·im·burse \,rē-əm-'bərs\ vb **-bursed; -burs·ing** [re- re- + obs. E imburse to put in the pocket, pay, fr. ML imbursare to put into a purse, fr. L in- in + ML bursa purse, fr. LL, hide of an ox, fr. Gk byrsa] : to pay back : make restitution : REPAY ♦ **Synonyms** INDEMNIFY, RECOMPENSE, REQUITE, COMPENSATE — **re·im·burs·able** adj — **re·im·burse·ment** n

¹**rein** \'rān\ n 1 : a strap fastened to a bit by which a rider or driver controls an animal 2 : a restraining influence : CHECK 3 : controlling or guiding power 4 : complete freedom — usu. used in the phrase give rein to

²**rein** vb : to check or direct by reins

re·in·car·na·tion \,rē-(,)in-(,)kär-'nā-shən\ n : rebirth of the soul in a new body — **re·in·car·nate** \,rē-in-'kär-,nāt\ vb

rein·deer \'rān-,dir\ n [ME reindere, fr. ON hreinn reindeer + ME deer animal, deer] : CARIBOU — used esp. for one of the Old World

reindeer moss n : a gray, erect, tufted, and much-branched edible lichen of northern regions that is an important food of reindeer

re·in·fec·tion \,rē-in-'fek-shən\ n : infection following another infection of the same type

re·in·force \,rē-ən-'fórs\ vb 1 : to strengthen with additional forces ⟨∼ our troops⟩ 2 : to strengthen with new force, aid, material, or support — **re·in·force·ment** n — **re·in·forc·er** n

re·in·scribe \,rē-ən-'skrīb\ vb : to reestablish or rename in a new and esp. stronger form or context

re·in·state \,rē-in-'stāt\ vb **-stat·ed; -stat·ing** : to restore to a former position, condition, or capacity — **re·in·state·ment** n

re·in·vent \,rē-in-'vent\ vb 1 : to make as if for the first time something already invented ⟨∼ the wheel⟩ 2 : to remake completely

re·it·er·ate \rē-'i-tə-,rāt\ vb **-at·ed; -at·ing** : to state or do over again or repeatedly — **re·it·er·a·tion** \-,i-tə-'rā-shən\ n

¹**re·ject** \ri-'jekt\ vb 1 : to refuse to accept, consider, use, or submit to 2 : to refuse to hear, receive, or admit : REPEL 3 : to rebuff or withhold love from 4 : to throw out esp. as useless or unsatisfactory 5 : to subject (a transplanted tissue) to an attack by immune system components of the recipient organism — **re·jec·tion** \-'jek-shən\ n

²**re·ject** \'rē-jekt\ n : a rejected person or thing

re·joice \ri-'jóis\ vb **re·joiced; re·joic·ing** 1 : to give joy to : GLADDEN 2 : to feel joy or great delight — **re·joic·er** n

re·join \(,)rē-'jóin for 1, ri- for 2\ vb 1 : to join again 2 : to say in answer (as to a plaintiff's plea in court) : REPLY

re·join·der \ri-'join-dər\ n : REPLY; esp : an answer to a reply

re·ju·ve·nate \ri-'jü-və-,nāt\ vb **-nat·ed; -nat·ing** : to make young or youthful again : give new vigor to ♦ **Synonyms** RENEW, REFRESH, RENOVATE, RESTORE — **re·ju·ve·na·tion** \-,jü-və-'nā-shən\ n

rel abbr 1 relating; relative 2 religion; religious

¹**re·lapse** \ri-'laps, 'rē-,laps\ n [ME, fr. ML relapsus, fr. L relabi to slide back] 1 : the act or process of backsliding or worsening 2 : a recurrence of illness after a period of improvement

²**re·lapse** \ri-'laps\ vb **re·lapsed; re·laps·ing** : to slip or fall back into a former worse state (as of illness)

re·late \ri-'lāt\ vb **re·lat·ed; re·lat·ing** 1 : to give an account of : TELL, NARRATE 2 : to show or establish logical or causal connection between 3 : to have relationship or connection 4 : to have or establish relationship ⟨the way a child ∼s to a teacher⟩ 5 : to respond favorably — **re·lat·able** adj — **re·lat·er** or **re·la·tor** \-'lā-tər\ n

re·lat·ed adj 1 : connected by some understood relationship 2 : connected through membership in the same family — **re·lat·ed·ness** n

re·la·tion \ri-'lā-shən\ n 1 : NARRATION, ACCOUNT 2 : CONNECTION, RELATIONSHIP 3 : connection by blood or marriage : KINSHIP; also : RELATIVE 4 : REFERENCE, RESPECT ⟨in ∼ to⟩ 5 : the state of being mutually interested or involved (as in social or commercial matters) 6 pl : DEALINGS, AFFAIRS ⟨foreign ∼s⟩ 7 pl : SEXUAL INTERCOURSE — **re·la·tion·al** \-shə-nəl\ adj

re·la·tion·ship \-,ship\ n : the state of being related or interrelated

¹**rel·a·tive** \'re-lə-tiv\ n 1 : a word referring grammatically to an antecedent 2 : a thing having a relation to or a dependence upon another thing 3 : a person connected with another by blood or marriage

²**relative** adj 1 : introducing a subordinate clause qualifying an expressed or implied antecedent ⟨∼ pronoun⟩; also : introduced by such a connective ⟨∼ clause⟩ 2 : PERTINENT, RELEVANT ⟨matters ∼ to world peace⟩ 3 : not absolute or independent : COMPARATIVE 4 : expressed as the ratio of the specified quantity to the total magnitude or to the mean of all quantities involved ♦ **Synonyms** DEPENDENT, CONTINGENT, CONDITIONAL — **rel·a·tive·ly** adv — **rel·a·tive·ness** n

relative humidity n : the ratio of the amount of water vapor actually present in the air to the greatest amount possible at the same temperature

rel·a·tiv·is·tic \,re-lə-ti-'vis-tik\ adj 1 : of, relating to, or characterized by relativity 2 : moving at a velocity that is a significant fraction of the speed of light so that effects predicted by the theory of relativity become evident ⟨a ∼ electron⟩ — **rel·a·tiv·is·ti·cal·ly** \-ti-k(ə-)lē\ adv

rel·a·tiv·i·ty \,re-lə-'ti-və-tē\ n, pl **-ties** 1 : the quality or state of being relative 2 : a theory in physics that considers mass and energy to be equivalent and that predicts changes in mass, dimension, and time which are related to speed but are noticeable esp. at speeds approaching that of light; also : an extension of the theory to include gravitation and related acceleration phenomena

re·lax \ri-'laks\ vb 1 : to make or become less firm, tense, or rigid 2 : to make less severe or strict 3 : to seek rest or recreation — **re·lax·er** n

¹**re·lax·ant** \ri-'lak-sənt\ adj : of, relating to, or producing relaxation

²**relaxant** n : a relaxing agent; esp : a drug that induces muscular relaxation

re·lax·ation \,rē-,lak-'sā-shən\ n 1 : the act of relaxing or state of being relaxed : a lessening of tension 2 : DIVERSION, RECREATION

¹**re·lay** \'rē-,lā\ n [ME, set of fresh hounds, fr. MF relayen to release fresh hounds, take a fresh horse, fr. MF relaier, fr. re- again + laier to let go, leave] 1 : a fresh supply (as of horses or men) arranged beforehand to relieve others 2 : a race between teams in which each team member covers a specified part of a course 3 : an electromagnetic device in which the opening or closing of one circuit activates another device (as a switch in another circuit) 4 : the act of passing along by stages

²**re·lay** \'rē-,lā, ri-'lā\ vb **re·layed; re·lay·ing** 1 : to place in or provide with relays 2 : to pass along by relays 3 : to control or operate by a relay

³**re·lay** \(,)rē-'lā\ vb **-laid** \-'lād\; **-lay·ing** : to lay again

¹**re·lease** \ri-'lēs\ vb **re·leased; re·leas·ing** 1 : to set free from confinement or restraint; also : DISMISS ⟨released from her job⟩ 2 : to relieve from something that oppresses, confines, or burdens 3 : RELINQUISH ⟨∼ a claim⟩ 4 : to permit publication, performance, exhibition, or sale of; also : to make available to the public ♦ **Synonyms** EMANCIPATE, DISCHARGE, FREE, LIBERATE

²**release** n 1 : relief or deliverance from sorrow, suffering, or trouble 2 : discharge from an obligation or responsi-

bility **3** : an act of setting free : the state of being freed **4** : a document effecting a legal release **5** : a releasing for performance or publication; *also* : the matter released (as to the press) **6** : a device for holding or releasing a mechanism as required

rel·e·gate \'re-lə-ˌgāt\ *vb* **-gat·ed; -gat·ing** **1** : to send into exile : BANISH **2** : to remove or dismiss to some less prominent position **3** : to assign to a particular class or sphere **4** : to submit to someone or something for appropriate action : DELEGATE ✦ *Synonyms* COMMIT, ENTRUST, CONSIGN, COMMEND — **rel·e·ga·tion** \ˌre-lə-'gā-shən\ *n*

re·lent \ri-'lent\ *vb* **1** : to become less stern, severe, or harsh **2** : SLACKEN

re·lent·less \-ləs\ *adj* : showing or promising no abatement of severity, intensity, or pace ⟨~ pressure⟩ — **re·lent·less·ly** *adv* — **re·lent·less·ness** *n*

rel·e·vance \'re-lə-vəns\ *n* : relation to the matter at hand; *also* : practical and esp. social applicability

rel·e·van·cy \-vən-sē\ *n* : RELEVANCE

rel·e·vant \'re-lə-vənt\ *adj* : bearing on the matter at hand : PERTINENT ✦ *Synonyms* GERMANE, MATERIAL, APPLICABLE, APROPOS — **rel·e·vant·ly** *adv*

re·li·able \ri-'lī-ə-bəl\ *adj* : fit to be trusted or relied on : DEPENDABLE, TRUSTWORTHY — **re·li·abil·i·ty** \-ˌlī-ə-'bi-lə-tē\ *n* — **re·li·able·ness** *n* — **re·li·ably** \-'lī-ə-blē\ *adv*

re·li·ance \ri-'lī-əns\ *n* **1** : the act of relying **2** : the state of being reliant **3** : one relied on

re·li·ant \ri-'lī-ənt\ *adj* : having reliance on someone or something : DEPENDENT

rel·ic \'re-lik\ *n* **1** : an object venerated because of its association with a saint or martyr **2** : SOUVENIR, MEMENTO **3** *pl* : REMAINS, RUINS **4** : a remaining trace : VESTIGE

rel·ict \'re-likt\ *n* : WIDOW

re·lief \ri-'lēf\ *n* **1** : removal or lightening of something oppressive, painful, or distressing **2** : WELFARE 2 **3** : military assistance to an endangered post or force **4** : release from a post or from performance of a duty; *also* : one that takes the place of another on duty **5** : legal remedy or redress **6** : projection of figures or ornaments from the background (as in sculpture) **7** : the state of being distinguished by contrast **8** : the elevations of a land surface

relief pitcher *n* : a baseball pitcher who takes over for another during a game

re·lieve \ri-'lēv\ *vb* **re·lieved; re·liev·ing** **1** : to free partly or wholly from a burden or from distress **2** : to bring about the removal or alleviation of : MITIGATE **3** : to release from a post or duty; *also* : to take the place of **4** : to break the monotony of **5** : to discharge the bladder or bowels of (oneself) ✦ *Synonyms* ALLEVIATE, LIGHTEN, ASSUAGE, ALLAY — **re·liev·er** *n*

relig *abbr* religion

re·li·gion \ri-'li-jən\ *n* **1** : the service and worship of God or the supernatural **2** : devotion to a religious faith **3** : a personal set or institutionalized system of religious beliefs, attitudes, and practices **4** : a cause, principle, or belief held to with faith and ardor — **re·li·gion·ist** *n*

¹re·li·gious \ri-'li-jəs\ *adj* **1** : relating or devoted to an acknowledged ultimate reality or deity **2** : of or relating to religious beliefs or observances **3** : scrupulously and conscientiously faithful **4** : FERVENT, ZEALOUS — **re·li·gious·ly** *adv*

²religious *n, pl* **religious** : a member of a religious order under monastic vows

re·lin·quish \ri-'liŋ-kwish, -'lin-\ *vb* **1** : to withdraw or retreat from : ABANDON, QUIT **2** : GIVE UP ⟨~ a title⟩ **3** : to let go of : RELEASE ✦ *Synonyms* YIELD, LEAVE, RESIGN, SURRENDER, CEDE, WAIVE — **re·lin·quish·ment** *n*

rel·i·quary \'re-lə-ˌkwer-ē\ *n, pl* **-quar·ies** : a container for religious relics

¹rel·ish \'re-lish\ *n* [ME *reles* taste, fr. OF, something left behind, release, fr. *relessier* to relax, release, fr. L *relaxare*] **1** : characteristic flavor : SAVOR **2** : keen enjoyment or delight in something : GUSTO **3** : APPETITE, INCLINATION ⟨has no ~ for sports⟩ **4** : a highly seasoned sauce (as of pickles) eaten with other food to add flavor

²relish *vb* **1** : to add relish to **2** : to take pleasure in : ENJOY **3** : to eat with pleasure — **rel·ish·able** *adj*

re·live \(ˌ)rē-'liv\ *vb* : to live again or over again; *esp* : to experience again in the imagination

re·lo·cate \(ˌ)rē-'lō-ˌkāt, ˌrē-lō-'kāt\ *vb* **1** : to locate again **2** : to move to a new location — **re·lo·ca·tion** \ˌrē-lō-'kā-shən\ *n*

re·luc·tant \ri-'lək-tənt\ *adj* : feeling or showing aversion, hesitation or unwillingness ⟨~ to get involved⟩ ✦ *Synonyms* DISINCLINED, INDISPOSED, HESITANT, LOATH, AVERSE — **re·luc·tance** \-təns\ *n* — **re·luc·tant·ly** *adv*

re·ly \ri-'lī\ *vb* **re·lied; re·ly·ing** [ME *relien* to rally, fr. AF *relier* to rally, rally, fr. L *religare* to tie out of the way, fr. *re-* back + *ligare* to tie] : to place faith or confidence : DEPEND

REM \'rem\ *n* : RAPID EYE MOVEMENT

re·main \ri-'mān\ *vb* **1** : to be left after others have been removed, subtracted, or destroyed **2** : to be something yet to be shown, done, or treated ⟨it ~s to be seen⟩ **3** : to stay after others have gone **4** : to continue unchanged

re·main·der \ri-'mān-dər\ *n* **1** : that which is left over : a remaining group, part, or trace **2** : the number left after a subtraction **3** : the number that is left over from the dividend after division and that is less than the divisor **4** : a book sold at a reduced price by the publisher after sales have slowed ✦ *Synonyms* LEAVINGS, REST, BALANCE, REMNANT, RESIDUE

re·mains \-'mānz\ *n pl* **1** : a remaining part or trace ⟨the ~ of a meal⟩ **2** : a dead body

¹re·make \(ˌ)rē-'māk\ *vb* **-made** \-'mād\; **-mak·ing** : to make anew or in a different form

²re·make \'rē-ˌmāk\ *n* : one that is remade; *esp* : a new version of a motion picture

re·mand \ri-'mand\ *vb* : to order back; *esp* : to return to custody pending trial or for further detention

¹re·mark \ri-'märk\ *n* **1** : the act of remarking : OBSERVATION, NOTICE **2** : a passing observation or comment

²remark *vb* **1** : to take notice of : OBSERVE **2** : to express as an observation or comment : SAY

re·mark·able \ri-'mär-kə-bəl\ *adj* : worthy of being or likely to be noticed : UNUSUAL, EXTRAORDINARY, NOTEWORTHY — **re·mark·able·ness** *n*

re·mark·ably \ri-'mär-kə-blē\ *adv* **1** : in a remarkable manner **2** : as is remarkable ⟨~, no one was hurt⟩

re·me·di·a·ble \ri-'mē-dē-ə-bəl\ *adj* : capable of being remedied

re·me·di·al \ri-'mē-dē-əl\ *adj* : intended to remedy or improve

¹rem·e·dy \'re-mə-dē\ *n, pl* **-dies** [ME *remedie*, fr. AF, fr. L *remedium*, fr. *re-* back, again + *mederi* to heal] **1** : a medicine or treatment that cures or relieves a disease or condition **2** : something that corrects or counteracts an evil or compensates for a loss

²remedy *vb* **-died; -dy·ing** : to provide or serve as a remedy for

re·mem·ber \ri-'mem-bər\ *vb* **-bered; -ber·ing** **1** : to bring to mind or think of again : RECOLLECT **2** : to keep from forgetting : keep in mind **3** : to convey greetings from **4** : COMMEMORATE

re·mem·brance \-brəns\ *n* **1** : an act of remembering : RECOLLECTION **2** : the ability to remember : MEMORY **3** : the period over which one's memory extends **4** : a memory of a person, thing, or event **5** : something that serves to bring to mind : REMINDER **6** : a greeting or gift recalling or expressing friendship or affection

re·mind \ri-'mīnd\ *vb* : to put in mind of something : cause to remember — **re·mind·er** *n*

rem·i·nisce \ˌre-mə-'nis\ *vb* **-nisced; -nisc·ing** : to indulge in reminiscence

rem·i·nis·cence \-'ni-s³ns\ *n* **1** : a recalling or telling of a past experience **2** : an account of a memorable experience

rem·i·nis·cent \-s³nt\ *adj* **1** : of or relating to reminiscence **2** : marked by or given to reminiscence **3** : serving to remind : SUGGESTIVE — **rem·i·nis·cent·ly** *adv*

re·miss \ri-'mis\ *adj* **1** : negligent or careless in the performance of work or duty **2** : showing neglect or inattention ✦ *Synonyms* LAX, NEGLECTFUL, DELINQUENT, DERELICT — **re·miss·ness** *n*

re·mis·sion \ri-'mi-shən\ *n* **1** : the act or process of remitting **2** : a state or period during which something is remitted

re·mit \ri-'mit\ vb **re·mit·ted; re·mit·ting** 1 : FORGIVE, PARDON ⟨~ sins⟩ 2 : to give or gain relief from (as pain) 3 : to refer for consideration, report, or decision 4 : to refrain from exacting or enforcing (as a penalty) 5 : to send (money) in payment of a bill

re·mit·tal \ri-'mi-t³l\ n : REMISSION

re·mit·tance \ri-'mi-t³ns\ n 1 : a sum of money remitted 2 : transmittal of money (as to a distant place)

rem·nant \'rem-nənt\ n 1 : a usu. small part or trace remaining 2 : an unsold or unused end of a fabric that is sold by the yard

re·mod·el \rē-'mä-d³l\ vb : to alter the structure of : MAKE OVER

re·mon·strance \ri-'män-strəns\ n : an act or instance of remonstrating

re·mon·strant \-strənt\ adj : vigorously objecting or opposing — **remonstrant** n — **re·mon·strant·ly** adv

re·mon·strate \ri-'män-ˌstrāt\ vb **-strat·ed; -strat·ing** : to plead in opposition to something : speak in protest or reproof ✦ **Synonyms** EXPOSTULATE, OBJECT, PROTEST — **re·mon·stra·tion** \ri-ˌmän-'strā-shən, ˌre-mən-\ n — **re·mon·stra·tor** \ri-'män-ˌstrā-tər\ n

rem·o·ra \'re-mə-rə\ n : any of a family of marine bony fishes with sucking organs on the head by which they cling esp. to other fishes

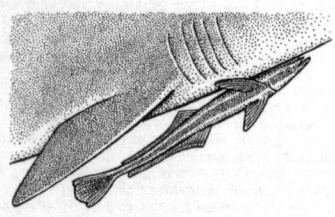

remora: on a shark

re·morse \ri-'mȯrs\ n [ME, fr. AF remors, fr. ML remorsus, fr. LL, act of biting again, fr. L remordēre to bite again, fr. re- again + mordēre to bite] : a gnawing distress arising from a sense of guilt for past wrongs ✦ **Synonyms** PENITENCE, REPENTANCE, CONTRITION — **remorse·ful** adj

re·morse·less \-ləs\ adj 1 : MERCILESS 2 : PERSISTENT, RELENTLESS

¹**re·mote** \ri-'mōt\ adj **re·mot·er; -est** 1 : far off in place or time : not near 2 : not closely related : DISTANT 3 : located out of the way : SECLUDED 4 : acting, acted on, or controlled indirectly or from a distance 5 : small in degree : SLIGHT ⟨a ~ chance⟩ 6 : distant in manner — **re·mote·ly** adv — **re·mote·ness** n

²**remote** n 1 : a radio or television program or a portion of a program originating outside the studio 2 : REMOTE CONTROL 2

remote control n 1 : control (as by radio signal) of operation from a point at some distance removed 2 : a device or mechanism for controlling something from a distance

¹**re·mount** \(ˌ)rē-'maȯnt\ vb 1 : to mount again 2 : to furnish remounts to

²**re·mount** \'rē-ˌmaȯnt\ n : a fresh horse to replace one no longer available

¹**re·move** \ri-'müv\ vb **re·moved; re·mov·ing** 1 : to move from one place to another : TRANSFER 2 : to move by lifting or taking off or away 3 : DISMISS, DISCHARGE 4 : to get rid of : ELIMINATE ⟨~ a fire hazard⟩ 5 : to change one's residence or location 6 : to go away : DEPART 7 : to be capable of being removed — **re·mov·able** adj — **re·mov·al** \-'mü-vəl\ n — **re·mov·er** n

²**remove** n 1 : a transfer from one location to another : MOVE 2 : a degree or stage of separation

REM sleep n : a state of sleep that recurs cyclically several times during normal sleep and is associated with rapid eye movements and dreaming

re·mu·ner·ate \ri-'myü-nə-ˌrāt\ vb **-at·ed; -at·ing** : to pay an equivalent for or to : RECOMPENSE — **re·mu·ner·a·tor** \-ˌrā-tər\ n

re·mu·ner·a·tion \ri-ˌmyü-nə-'rā-shən\ n : COMPENSATION, PAYMENT

re·mu·ner·a·tive \ri-'myü-nə-rə-tiv, -ˌrā-\ adj : serving to remunerate : GAINFUL

re·nais·sance \ˌre-nə-'säns, -'zäns\ n 1 cap : the cultural revival and beginnings of modern science in Europe in the 14th-17th centuries; also : the period of the Renaissance 2 often cap : a movement or period of vigorous artistic and intellectual activity 3 : REBIRTH, REVIVAL

re·nal \'rē-n³l\ adj : of, relating to, or located in or near the kidneys

re·na·scence \ri-'na-s³ns, -'nä-\ n, often cap : RENAISSANCE

rend \'rend\ vb **rent** \'rent\; **rend·ing** 1 : to remove by violence : WREST 2 : to tear forcibly apart : SPLIT

ren·der \'ren-dər\ vb 1 : to extract (as lard) by heating 2 : to give to another; also : YIELD 3 : to give in return 4 : to do (a service) for another ⟨~ aid⟩ 5 : to cause to be or become : MAKE 6 : to reproduce or represent by artistic or verbal means 7 : TRANSLATE ⟨~ into English⟩

¹**ren·dez·vous** \'rän-di-ˌvü, -dā-\ n, pl **ren·dez·vous** \-ˌvüz\ [MF, fr. rendez vous present yourselves] 1 : a place appointed for a meeting; also : a meeting at an appointed place 2 : a place of popular resort 3 : the process of bringing two spacecraft together

²**rendezvous** vb **-voused** \-ˌvüd\; **-vous·ing** \-ˌvü-iŋ\; **-vouses** \-ˌvüz\ : to come or bring together at a rendezvous

ren·di·tion \ren-'di-shən\ n : an act or a result of rendering ⟨first ~ of the work into English⟩

ren·e·gade \'re-ni-ˌgād\ n [Sp renegado, fr. ML renegatus, fr. pp. of renegare to deny, fr. L re- re- + negare to deny] : a deserter from one faith, cause, principle, or party for another

re·nege \ri-'neg\ vb **re·neged; re·neg·ing** 1 : to go back on a promise or commitment 2 : to fail to follow suit when able in a card game in violation of the rules — **re·neg·er** n

re·new \ri-'nü, -'nyü\ vb 1 : to make or become new, fresh, or strong again 2 : to restore to existence : RECREATE, REVIVE 3 : to make or do again : REPEAT ⟨~ a complaint⟩ 4 : to begin again : RESUME ⟨~ed efforts⟩ 5 : REPLACE ⟨~ the lining of a coat⟩ 6 : to grant or obtain an extension of or on ⟨~ a lease⟩ ⟨~ a subscription⟩ — **re·new·er** n

re·new·able \ri-'nü-ə-bəl, -'nyü-\ adj 1 : capable of being renewed 2 : capable of being replaced by natural ecological cycles or sound management procedures ⟨~ resources⟩

re·new·al \ri-'nü-əl, -'nyü-\ n 1 : the act of renewing : the state of being renewed 2 : something renewed

ren·net \'re-nət\ n 1 : the contents of the stomach of an unweaned animal (as a calf) or the lining membrane of the stomach used for curdling milk 2 : rennin or a substitute used to curdle milk

ren·nin \'re-nən\ n : a stomach enzyme that coagulates casein and is used commercially to curdle milk in the making of cheese

re·nounce \ri-'naȯns\ vb **re·nounced; re·nounc·ing** 1 : to give up, refuse, or resign usu. by formal declaration 2 : to refuse further to follow, obey, or recognize : REPUDIATE — **re·nounce·ment** n

ren·o·vate \'re-nə-ˌvāt\ vb **-vat·ed; -vat·ing** : to make like new again : put in good condition : REPAIR 2 : to restore to vigor or activity — **ren·o·va·tion** \ˌre-nə-'vā-shən\ n — **ren·o·va·tor** \'re-nə-ˌvā-tər\ n

re·nown \ri-'naȯn\ n : a state of being widely acclaimed and honored : FAME, CELEBRITY ✦ **Synonyms** HONOR, GLORY, REPUTATION, REPUTE — **re·nowned** \-'naȯnd\ adj

¹**rent** \'rent\ n 1 : money or the amount of money paid or due at intervals for the use of another's property 2 : property rented or for rent

²**rent** vb 1 : to give possession and use of in return for rent 2 : to take and hold under an agreement to pay rent 3 : to be for rent ⟨~s for $100 a month⟩ — **rent·er** n

³**rent** n 1 : a tear made by or as if by rending 2 : a split in a party or organized group : SCHISM

rent·al \'ren-təl\ n 1 : an amount paid or collected as rent 2 : something that is rented 3 : an act of renting

²**rent·al** *adj* : of or relating to rent

re·nun·ci·a·tion \ri-ˌnən-sē-ˈā-shən\ *n* : the act of renouncing : REPUDIATION

¹**rep** \ˈrep\ *n* : REPRESENTATIVE ⟨sales ∼*s*⟩

²**rep** *abbr* 1 repair 2 repeat 3 report; reporter 4 republic

Rep *abbr* Republican

re·pack·age \(ˌ)rē-ˈpa-kij\ *vb* : to package again or anew; *esp* : to put into a more attractive form

¹**re·pair** \ri-ˈper\ *vb* [ME, fr. AF *repairer* to go back, return, fr. LL *repatriare* to go home again, fr. L *re-* back + *patria* native country] : to make one's way : GO ⟨∼*ed* to the drawing room⟩

²**repair** *vb* [ME, fr. AF *reparer*, fr. L *reparare*, fr. *re-* back + *parare* to prepare] 1 : to restore to good condition : FIX 2 : to restore to a healthy state 3 : REMEDY ⟨∼ a wrong⟩ — **re·pair·er** *n* — **re·pair·man** \-ˌman\ *n*

³**repair** *n* 1 : a result of repairing 2 : an act of repairing 3 : condition with respect to need of repairing ⟨in bad ∼⟩

rep·a·ra·tion \ˌre-pə-ˈrā-shən\ *n* 1 : the act of making amends for a wrong 2 : amends made for a wrong; *esp* : money paid by a defeated nation in compensation for damages caused during hostilities — usu. used in pl.

✦ **Synonyms** REDRESS, RESTITUTION, INDEMNITY

re·par·a·tive \ri-ˈpa-rə-tiv\ *adj* 1 : of, relating to, or effecting repairs 2 : serving to make amends

rep·ar·tee \ˌre-pər-ˈtē\ *n* 1 : a witty reply 2 : a succession of clever replies; *also* : skill in making such replies

re·past \ri-ˈpast, ˈrē-ˌpast\ *n* : a supply of food and drink served as a meal

re·pa·tri·ate \rē-ˈpā-trē-ˌāt\ *vb* -**at·ed**; -**at·ing** : to send or bring back to the country of origin or citizenship ⟨∼ prisoners of war⟩ — **re·pa·tri·ate** \-trē-ət, -trē-ˌāt\ *n* — **re·pa·tri·a·tion** \-ˌpā-trē-ˈā-shən\ *n*

re·pay \rē-ˈpā\ *vb* -**paid** \-ˈpād\; -**pay·ing** 1 : to pay back : REFUND 2 : to give or do in return or requital 3 : to make a return payment to : RECOMPENSE, REQUITE ✦ **Synonyms** REMUNERATE, COMPENSATE, REIMBURSE, INDEMNIFY — **re·pay·able** *adj* — **re·pay·ment** *n*

re·peal \ri-ˈpēl\ *vb* [ME *repelen*, fr. AF *repeler*, lit., to call back, fr. *re-* back + *apeler* to appeal, call] : to annul by authoritative and esp. legislative action — **repeal** *n* — **re·peal·er** *n*

¹**re·peat** \ri-ˈpēt\ *vb* 1 : to say again 2 : to do again 3 : to say over from memory — **re·peat·able** *adj* — **re·peat·er** *n*

²**re·peat** \ri-ˈpēt, ˈrē-ˌpēt\ *n* 1 : the act of repeating 2 : something repeated or to be repeated (as a radio or television program)

³**re·peat** \ri-ˈpēt\ *adj* : of, relating to, or being one that repeats an offense, achievement, or action

re·peat·ed \ri-ˈpē-təd\ *adj* : done or recurring again and again : FREQUENT — **re·peat·ed·ly** *adv*

re·pel \ri-ˈpel\ *vb* **re·pelled**; **re·pel·ling** 1 : to drive away : REPULSE 2 : to fight against : RESIST 3 : to turn away : REJECT 4 : to cause aversion in : DISGUST

¹**re·pel·lent** *also* **re·pel·lant** \ri-ˈpe-lənt\ *adj* 1 : tending to drive away ⟨a mosquito-*repellent* spray⟩ 2 : causing disgust

²**repellent** *also* **repellant** *n* : something that repels; *esp* : a substance that repels insects

re·pent \ri-ˈpent\ *vb* 1 : to turn from sin and resolve to reform one's life 2 : to feel sorry for (something done) : REGRET — **re·pen·tance** \ri-ˈpen-tᵊns\ *n* — **re·pen·tant** \-tᵊnt\ *adj*

re·per·cus·sion \ˌrē-pər-ˈkə-shən, ˌre-\ *n* 1 : REVERBERATION 2 : a reciprocal action or effect 3 : a widespread, indirect, or unforeseen effect of something done or said

rep·er·toire \ˈre-pər-ˌtwär\ *n* [F] 1 : a list of plays, operas, pieces, or parts which a company or performer is prepared to present 2 : a list of the skills or devices possessed by a person or needed in a person's occupation

rep·er·to·ry \ˈre-pər-ˌtȯr-ē\ *n, pl* -**ries** 1 : REPOSITORY 2 : REPERTOIRE 3 : a company that presents its repertoire in the course of one season at one theater

rep·e·ti·tion \ˌre-pə-ˈti-shən\ *n* 1 : the act or an instance of repeating 2 : the fact of being repeated

rep·e·ti·tious \-ˈti-shəs\ *adj* : marked by repetition; *esp* : tediously repeating — **rep·e·ti·tious·ly** *adv* — **rep·e·ti·tious·ness** *n*

re·pet·i·tive \ri-ˈpe-ti-tiv\ *adj* : REPETITIOUS — **re·pet·i·tive·ly** *adv* — **re·pet·i·tive·ness** *n*

re·pine \ri-ˈpīn\ *vb* **re·pined**; **re·pin·ing** 1 : to feel or express discontent or dejection 2 : to long for something

repl *abbr* replace; replacement

re·place \ri-ˈplās\ *vb* 1 : to restore to a former place or position 2 : to take the place of : SUPPLANT 3 : to put something new in the place of — **re·place·able** *adj* — **re·plac·er** *n*

re·place·ment \ri-ˈplās-mənt\ *n* 1 : the act of replacing : the state of being replaced 2 : one that replaces another esp. in a job or function

¹**re·play** \(ˌ)rē-ˈplā\ *vb* : to play again or over

²**re·play** \ˈrē-ˌplā\ *n* 1 : an act or instance of replaying 2 : the playing of a tape (as a videotape)

re·plen·ish \ri-ˈple-nish\ *vb* : to fill or build up again : stock or supply anew — **re·plen·ish·ment** *n*

re·plete \ri-ˈplēt\ *adj* 1 : fully provided ⟨a kit ∼ with instructions⟩ 2 : FULL; *esp* : full of food — **re·plete·ness** *n* — **re·ple·tion** \ri-ˈplē-shən\ *n*

rep·li·ca \ˈre-pli-kə\ *n* [It, repetition, fr. *replicare* to repeat, fr. LL, fr. L, to fold back, fr. *re-* back + *plicare* to fold] 1 : an exact reproduction (as of a painting) executed by the original artist 2 : a copy exact in all details : DUPLICATE

¹**rep·li·cate** \ˈre-plə-ˌkāt\ *vb* -**cat·ed**; -**cat·ing** : DUPLICATE, REPEAT

²**rep·li·cate** \-pli-kət\ *n* : one of several identical experiments or procedures

rep·li·ca·tion \ˌre-plə-ˈkā-shən\ *n* 1 : ANSWER, REPLY 2 : precise copying or reproduction; *also* : an act or process of this ⟨∼ of DNA⟩

¹**re·ply** \ri-ˈplī\ *vb* **re·plied**; **re·ply·ing** : to say or do in answer : RESPOND

²**reply** *n, pl* **replies** : ANSWER, RESPONSE

repo \ˈrē̞pō\ *adj* : of, relating to, or being in the business of repossessing property (as a car)

¹**re·port** \ri-ˈpȯrt\ *n* [ME, fr. AF, fr. *reporter* to bring back, report, fr. L *reportare*, fr. *re-* back + *portare* to carry] 1 : common talk : RUMOR 2 : FAME, REPUTATION ⟨a person of good ∼⟩ 3 : a usu. detailed account or statement 4 : an explosive noise

²**report** *vb* 1 : to give an account of : RELATE, TELL 2 : to serve as carrier of (a message) 3 : to prepare or present (as an account of an event) for a newspaper or a broadcast 4 : to make a charge of misconduct against 5 : to present oneself (as for work) 6 : to make known to the authorities ⟨∼ a fire⟩ 7 : to return or present (as a matter referred to a committee) with conclusions and recommendations 8 : to work as a subordinate ⟨∼*s* to the vice president⟩ — **re·port·able** *adj*

re·port·age \ri-ˈpȯr-tij, *esp for 2* ˌre-pər-ˈtäzh, ˌre-ˌpȯr-ˈ\ *n* [F] 1 : the act or process of reporting news 2 : writing intended to give an account of observed or documented events

report card *n* : a periodic report on a student's grades

re·port·ed·ly \ri-ˈpȯr-təd-lē\ *adv* : according to report

re·port·er \ri-ˈpȯr-tər\ *n* : one that reports; *esp* : a person who gathers and reports news for a news medium — **re·por·to·ri·al** \ˌre-pər-ˈtȯr-ē-əl\ *adj*

¹**re·pose** \ri-ˈpōz\ *vb* **re·posed**; **re·pos·ing** 1 : to lay at rest 2 : to lie at rest 3 : to lie dead 4 : to take a rest 5 : to rest for support : LIE

²**repose** *n* 1 : a state of resting (as after exertion); *esp* : SLEEP 2 : eternal or heavenly rest 3 : CALM, PEACE ⟨the ∼ of the bayous⟩ 4 : cessation or absence of activity, movement, or animation 5 : composure of manner : POISE — **re·pose·ful** *adj*

³**repose** *vb* **re·posed**; **re·pos·ing** 1 : to place (as trust) in someone or something 2 : to place for control, management, or use

re·pos·i·to·ry \ri-ˈpä-zə-ˌtȯr-ē\ *n, pl* -**ries** 1 : a place where something is deposited or stored 2 : a person to whom something is entrusted

re·pos·sess \ˌrē-pə-ˈzes\ *vb* 1 : to regain possession of 2 : to take possession of in default of the payment of installments due — **re·pos·ses·sion** \-ˈze-shən\ *n*

rep·re·hend \ˌre-pri-ˈhend\ *vb* : to express disapproval of : CENSURE ✦ **Synonyms** CRITICIZE, CONDEMN, DENOUNCE, BLAME, PAN — **rep·re·hen·sion** \-ˈhen-chən\ *n*

rep·re·hen·si·ble \-ˈhen-sə-bəl\ *adj* : deserving blame or censure : CULPABLE — **rep·re·hen·si·bly** \-blē\ *adv*

rep·re·sent \,re-pri-'zent\ *vb* **1** : to present a picture or a likeness of : PORTRAY, DEPICT **2** : to serve as a sign or symbol of **3** : to act the role of **4** : to stand in the place of : act or speak for; *also* : to manage the legal and business affairs of **5** : to be a member or example of : TYPIFY **6** : to serve as an elected representative of **7** : to describe as having a specified quality or character **8** : to state with the purpose of affecting judgment or action

rep·re·sen·ta·tion \,re-pri-,zen-'tā-shən\ *n* **1** : the act of representing **2** : one (as a picture or image) that represents something else **3** : the state of being represented in a legislative body; *also* : the body of persons representing a constituency **4** : a usu. formal statement made to effect a change

¹**rep·re·sen·ta·tive** \,re-pri-'zen-tə-tiv\ *adj* **1** : serving to represent **2** : standing or acting for another **3** : founded on the principle of representation : carried on by elected representatives ⟨∼ government⟩ — **rep·re·sen·ta·tive·ly** *adv* — **rep·re·sen·ta·tive·ness** *n*

²**representative** *n* **1** : one that represents another; *esp* : one representing a district in a legislative body usu. as a member of a lower house **2** : a typical example of a group, class, or quality

re·press \ri-'pres\ *vb* **1** : CURB, SUBDUE **2** : RESTRAIN, SUPPRESS **3** : to exclude from consciousness — **re·pres·sion** \-'presh-ən\ *n* — **re·pres·sive** \-'pres-siv\ *adj*

¹**re·prieve** \ri-'prēv\ *vb* **re·prieved; re·priev·ing 1** : to delay the punishment or execution of **2** : to give temporary relief to

²**reprieve** *n* **1** : the act of reprieving : the state of being reprieved **2** : a formal temporary suspension of a sentence esp. of death **3** : a temporary respite

¹**rep·ri·mand** \'re-prə-,mand\ *n* : a severe or formal reproof

²**reprimand** *vb* : to reprove severely or formally

¹**re·print** \(,)rē-'print\ *vb* : to print again

²**re·print** \'rē-,print\ *n* : a reproduction of printed matter

re·pri·sal \ri-'prī-zəl\ *n* : an act in retaliation for something done by another

re·prise \ri-'prēz\ *n* : a recurrence, renewal, or resumption of an action; *also* : a musical repetition

¹**re·proach** \ri-'prōch\ *n* **1** : an expression of disapproval **2** : DISGRACE, DISCREDIT **3** : the act of reproaching : REBUKE **4** : a cause or occasion of blame or disgrace — **re·proach·ful** \-fəl\ *adj* — **re·proach·ful·ly** *adv* — **re·proach·ful·ness** *n*

²**reproach** *vb* **1** : CENSURE, REBUKE **2** : to cast discredit on ✦ *Synonyms* CHIDE, ADMONISH, REPROVE, REPRIMAND — **re·proach·able** *adj*

rep·ro·bate \'re-prə-,bāt\ *n* **1** : a person foreordained to damnation **2** : a thoroughly bad person : SCOUNDREL — **reprobate** *adj*

rep·ro·ba·tion \,re-prə-'bā-shən\ *n* : strong disapproval : CONDEMNATION

re·pro·duce \,rē-prə-'düs, -'dyüs\ *vb* **1** : to produce again or anew **2** : to produce offspring — **re·pro·duc·ible** \-'dü-sə-bəl, -'dyü-\ *adj* — **re·pro·duc·tion** \-'dək-shən\ *n* — **re·pro·duc·tive** \-'dək-tiv\ *adj*

re·proof \ri-'prüf\ *n* : blame or censure for a fault

re·prove \ri-'prüv\ *vb* **re·proved; re·prov·ing 1** : to administer a rebuke to **2** : to express disapproval of ✦ *Synonyms* REPRIMAND, ADMONISH, REPROACH, CHIDE — **re·prov·er** *n*

rept *abbr* report

rep·tile \'rep-tī(-ə)l, -tᵊl\ *n* [ME *reptil*, fr. MF or LL; MF *reptile*, fr. LL *reptile*, fr. L *repere* to crawl] : any of a large class of air-breathing scaly vertebrates including snakes, lizards, alligators, turtles, and extinct related forms (as dinosaurs) — **rep·til·i·an** \rep-'ti-lē-ən\ *adj or n*

re·pub·lic \ri-'pə-blik\ *n* [F *république*, fr. MF *republique*, fr. L *respublica*, fr. *res* thing, wealth + *publica*, fem. of *publicus* public] **1** : a government having a chief of state who is not a monarch and is usu. a president; *also* : a nation or other political unit having such a government **2** : a government in which supreme power is held by the citizens entitled to vote and is exercised by elected officers and representatives governing according to law; *also* : a nation or other political unit having such a form of government **3** : a constituent political and territorial unit of the former nations of Czechoslovakia, the U.S.S.R., or Yugoslavia

¹**re·pub·li·can** \-bli-kən\ *n* **1** : one that favors or supports a republican form of government **2** *cap* : a member of a republican party and esp. of the Republican party of the U.S.

²**republican** *adj* **1** : of, relating to, or resembling a republic **2** : favoring or supporting a republic **3** *cap* : of, relating to, or constituting one of the two major political parties in the U.S. evolving in the mid-19th century — **re·pub·li·can·ism** *n, often cap*

re·pu·di·ate \ri-'pyü-dē-,āt\ *vb* **-at·ed; -at·ing** [L *repudiare* to cast off, divorce, fr. *repudium* rejection of a prospective spouse, divorce] **1** : to cast off : DISOWN **2** : to refuse to have anything to do with : refuse to acknowledge, accept, or pay ⟨∼ a charge⟩ ⟨∼ a debt⟩ ✦ *Synonyms* SPURN, REJECT, DECLINE — **re·pu·di·a·tion** \-,pyü-dē-'ā-shən\ *n* — **re·pu·di·a·tor** \-'pyü-dē-,ā-tər\ *n*

re·pug·nance \ri-'pəg-nəns\ *n* **1** : the quality or fact of being contradictory or inconsistent **2** : strong dislike, distaste, or antagonism

re·pug·nant \-nənt\ *adj* **1** : marked by repugnance **2** : contrary to a person's tastes or principles : exciting distaste or aversion ✦ *Synonyms* REPELLENT, ABHORRENT, DISTASTEFUL, OBNOXIOUS, REVOLTING, LOATHSOME — **re·pug·nant·ly** *adv*

¹**re·pulse** \ri-'pəls\ *vb* **re·pulsed; re·puls·ing 1** : to drive or beat back : REPEL **2** : to repel by discourtesy or denial : REBUFF **3** : to cause a feeling of repulsion in : DISGUST

²**repulse** *n* **1** : REBUFF, REJECTION **2** : the action of repelling an attacker : the fact of being repelled

re·pul·sion \ri-'pəl-shən\ *n* **1** : the action of repulsing : the state of being repulsed **2** : the force with which bodies, particles, or like forces repel one another **3** : a feeling of aversion

re·pul·sive \-siv\ *adj* **1** : serving or tending to repel or reject **2** : arousing aversion or disgust ✦ *Synonyms* REPUGNANT, REVOLTING, LOATHSOME, NOISOME — **re·pul·sive·ly** *adv* — **re·pul·sive·ness** *n*

re·pur·pose \(,)rē-'pər-pəs\ *vb* : to give a new purpose or use to

rep·u·ta·ble \'re-pyə-tə-bəl\ *adj* : having a good reputation : ESTIMABLE — **rep·u·ta·bly** \-blē\ *adv*

rep·u·ta·tion \,re-pyù-'tā-shən\ *n* **1** : overall quality or character as seen or judged by people in general **2** : place in public esteem or regard

¹**re·pute** \ri-'pyüt\ *vb* **re·put·ed; re·put·ing** : BELIEVE, CONSIDER ⟨*reputed* to be a millionaire⟩

²**repute** *n* **1** : REPUTATION ⟨knew her by ∼⟩ **2** : the state of being favorably known or spoken of

re·put·ed \ri-'pyü-təd\ *adj* **1** : REPUTABLE **2** : according to reputation : SUPPOSED — **re·put·ed·ly** *adv*

req *abbr* **1** request **2** require; required **3** requisition

¹**re·quest** \ri-'kwest\ *n* **1** : an act or instance of asking for something **2** : a thing asked for **3** : the condition of being asked for ⟨available on ∼⟩

²**request** *vb* **1** : to make a request to or of **2** : to ask for — **re·quest·er** *or* **re·quest·or** *n*

re·qui·em \'re-kwē-əm, 'rā-\ *n* [ME, fr. L (first word of the requiem mass), acc. of *requies* rest, fr. *quies* quiet, rest] **1** : a mass for a dead person; *also* : a musical setting for this **2** : a musical service or hymn in honor of the dead

re·quire \ri-'kwī(-ə)r\ *vb* **re·quired; re·quir·ing 1** : to demand as necessary or essential **2** : COMMAND, ORDER ⟨the law ∼s that everyone pay the tax⟩

re·quire·ment \-mənt\ *n* **1** : something (as a condition or quality) required ⟨entrance ∼s⟩ **2** : NECESSITY ⟨production was sufficient to satisfy military ∼s⟩

req·ui·site \'re-kwə-zət\ *adj* : REQUIRED, NECESSARY — **requisite** *n*

req·ui·si·tion \,re-kwə-'zi-shən\ *n* **1** : formal application or demand (as for supplies) **2** : the state of being in demand or use — **requisition** *vb*

re·quite \ri-'kwīt\ *vb* **re·quit·ed; re·quit·ing 1** : to make return for : REPAY **2** : to make retaliation for : AVENGE **3** : to make return to — **re·quit·al** \-'kwī-tᵊl\ *n*

rere·dos \'rer-ə-,däs\ *n* : a usu. ornamental wood or stone screen or partition wall behind an altar

re·run \'rē-,rən, (,)rē-'rən\ *n* : the act or an instance of running again or anew; *esp* : a showing of a motion picture or television program after its first run — **re·run** \(,)rē-'rən\ *vb*

res *abbr* **1** research **2** reservation; reserve **3** reservoir **4** residence; resident **5** resolution

re·sale \\'rē-ˌsāl, (ˌ)rē-'sāl\ *n* : the act of selling again usu. to a new party — **re·sal·able** \(ˌ)rē-'sā-lə-bəl\ *adj*

re·scind \ri-'sind\ *vb* : REPEAL, CANCEL, ANNUL — **re·scis·sion** \-'si-zhən\ *n*

re·script \'rē-ˌskript\ *n* : an official or authoritative order or decree

res·cue \'res-kyü\ *vb* **res·cued; res·cu·ing** [ME *rescouen, rescuen,* fr. AF *rescure,* fr. *re-* back, again + *escure* to shake off, fr. L *excutere*] : to free from danger, harm, or confinement — **rescue** *n* — **res·cu·er** *n*

re·search \ri-'sərch, 'rē-ˌsorch\ *n* **1** : careful or diligent search **2** : studious inquiry or examination aimed at the discovery and interpretation of new knowledge **3** : the collecting of information about a particular subject — **research** *vb* — **re·search·er** *n*

re·sec·tion \ri-'sek-shən\ *n* : the surgical removal of part of an organ or structure

re·sem·blance \ri-'zem-bləns\ *n* : the quality or state of resembling

re·sem·ble \ri-'zem-bəl\ *vb* **-bled; -bling** : to be like or similar to

re·sent \ri-'zent\ *vb* : to feel or exhibit annoyance or indignation at — **re·sent·ful** \-fəl\ *adj* — **re·sent·ful·ly** *adv* — **re·sent·ment** *n*

re·ser·pine \ri-'sər-ˌpēn, -pən\ *n* : a drug used in treating high blood pressure and nervous tension

res·er·va·tion \ˌre-zər-'vā-shən\ *n* **1** : an act of reserving **2** : something (as a room in a hotel) arranged for in advance **3** : something reserved; *esp* : a tract of public land set aside for special use **4** : a limiting condition

¹re·serve \ri-'zərv\ *vb* **re·served; re·serv·ing 1** : to store for future or special use **2** : to hold back for oneself **3** : to set aside or arrange to have set aside or held for special use

²reserve *n* **1** : something reserved : STOCK, STORE **2** : a military force withheld from action for later use — usu. used in pl. **3** : the military forces of a country not part of the regular services; *also* : RESERVIST **4** : a tract set apart : RESERVATION **5** : an act of reserving **6** : restraint or caution in one's words or bearing **7** : money or its equivalent kept in hand or set apart to meet liabilities

re·served \ri-'zərvd\ *adj* **1** : restrained in words and actions **2** : set aside for future or special use — **re·serv·ed·ly** \-'zər-vəd-lē\ *adv* — **re·serv·ed·ness** \-vəd-nəs\ *n*

re·serv·ist \ri-'zər-vist\ *n* : a member of a military reserve

res·er·voir \'re-zə-ˌvwär, -zər-, -ˌvwȯr\ *n* [F] : a place where something is kept in store; *esp* : an artificial lake where water is collected and kept for use

re·shuf·fle \ri-'shə-fəl\ *vb* **1** : to shuffle again **2** : to reorganize usu. by redistribution of existing elements — **reshuffle** *n*

re·side \ri-'zīd\ *vb* **re·sid·ed; re·sid·ing 1** : to make one's home : DWELL **2** : to be present as a quality or vested as a right

res·i·dence \'re-zə-dəns\ *n* **1** : the act or fact of residing in a place as a dweller or in discharge of a duty or an obligation **2** : the place where one actually lives **3** : a building used as a home : DWELLING **4** : the period of living in a place

res·i·den·cy \'re-zə-dən-sē\ *n, pl* **-cies 1** : the residence of or the territory under a diplomatic resident **2** : a period of advanced training in a medical specialty

¹res·i·dent \-dənt\ *adj* **1** : RESIDING **2** : being in residence **3** : not migratory

²resident *n* **1** : one who resides in a place **2** : a diplomatic representative with governing powers (as in a protectorate) **3** : a physician serving a residency

res·i·den·tial \ˌre-zə-'den-chəl\ *adj* **1** : used as a residence or by residents **2** : occupied by or restricted to residences — **res·i·den·tial·ly** *adv*

¹re·sid·u·al \ri-'zi-jə-wəl\ *n* **1** : a residual product or substance **2** : a payment (as to an actor or writer) for each rerun after an initial showing (as of a taped TV show)

²residual *adj* : being a residue or remainder

re·sid·u·ary \ri-'zi-jə-ˌwer-ē\ *adj* : of, relating to, or constituting a residue esp. of an estate

res·i·due \'re-zə-ˌdü, -ˌdyü\ *n* : a part remaining after another part has been taken away : REMAINDER

re·sid·u·um \ri-'zi-jə-wəm\ *n, pl* **re·sid·ua** \-jə-wə\ [L] **1**

: something remaining or residual after certain deductions are made **2** : a residual product

re·sign \ri-'zīn\ *vb* [ME, fr. AF *resigner,* fr. L *resignare,* lit., to unseal, cancel, fr. *signare* to sign, seal] **1** : to give up deliberately (as one's position) esp. by a formal act **2** : to give (oneself) over (as to grief or despair) without resistance — **re·sign·ed·ly** \-'zī-nəd-lē\ *adv*

re–sign \(ˌ)rē-'sīn\ *vb* : to sign again

res·ig·na·tion \ˌre-zig-'nā-shən\ *n* **1** : an act or instance of resigning; *also* : a formal notification of such an act **2** : the quality or state of being resigned

re·sil·ience \ri-'zil-yəns\ *n* **1** : the ability of a body to regain its original size and shape after being compressed, bent, or stretched **2** : an ability to recover from or adjust easily to change or misfortune

re·sil·ien·cy \-yən-sē\ *n* : RESILIENCE

re·sil·ient \-yənt\ *adj* : marked by resilience

res·in \'re-z'n\ *n* : any of various substances obtained from the gum or sap of some trees and used esp. in varnishes, plastics, and medicine; *also* : a comparable synthetic product — **res·in·ous** *adj*

¹re·sist \ri-'zist\ *vb* **1** : to fight against : OPPOSE ⟨~ aggression⟩ **2** : to withstand the force or effect of ⟨~ed temptation⟩ ⟨~ disease⟩ **♦ Synonyms** COMBAT, REPEL — **re·sist·ible** \-'zis-tə-bəl\ *adj* — **re·sist·less** *adj*

²resist *n* : something (as a coating) that resists or prevents a particular action

re·sis·tance \ri-'zis-təns\ *n* **1** : the act or an instance of resisting : OPPOSITION **2** : the power or capacity to resist; *esp* : the inherent ability of an organism to resist harmful influences (as disease or infection) **3** : the opposition offered by a body to the passage through it of a steady electric current

re·sis·tant \-tənt\ *adj* : giving, capable of, or exhibiting resistance

re·sis·tor \ri-'zis-tər\ *n* : a device used to provide resistance to the flow of an electric current in a circuit

res·o·lute \'re-zə-ˌlüt\ *adj* : firmly determined in purpose : RESOLVED ⟨a ~ leader⟩ **♦ Synonyms** STEADFAST, STAUNCH, FAITHFUL, TRUE, LOYAL — **res·o·lute·ly** *adv* — **res·o·lute·ness** *n*

res·o·lu·tion \ˌre-zə-'lü-shən\ *n* **1** : the act or process of resolving **2** : the action of solving; *also* : SOLUTION **3** : the quality of being resolute : FIRMNESS, DETERMINATION **4** : a formal statement expressing the opinion, will, or intent of a body of persons **5** : a measure of the sharpness of an image or of the fineness with which a device can produce or record such an image

¹re·solve \ri-'zälv\ *vb* **re·solved; re·solv·ing 1** : to break up into constituent parts : ANALYZE **2** : to distinguish between or make visible adjacent parts of **3** : to find an answer to : SOLVE ⟨~ a dispute⟩ **4** : DETERMINE, DECIDE **5** : to make or pass a formal resolution — **re·solv·able** *adj*

²resolve *n* **1** : fixity of purpose **2** : something resolved

res·o·nance \'re-zə-nəns\ *n* **1** : the quality or state of being resonant **2** : a reinforcement of sound in a vibrating body caused by waves from another body vibrating at nearly the same rate

res·o·nant \-nənt\ *adj* **1** : continuing to sound : RESOUNDING **2** : relating to or exhibiting resonance **3** : intensified and enriched by or as if by resonance — **res·o·nant·ly** *adv*

res·o·nate \-ˌnāt\ *vb* **-nat·ed; -nat·ing 1** : to produce or exhibit resonance **2** : REVERBERATE, RESOUND **3** : to relate harmoniously ⟨~ with voters⟩

res·o·na·tor \-ˌnā-tər\ *n* : something that resounds or exhibits resonance

re·sorp·tion \rē-'sȯrp-shən, -'zȯrp-\ *n* : the action or process of breaking down and assimilating something (as a tooth or an embryo)

¹re·sort \ri-'zȯrt\ *n* [ME, return, source of aid, fr. AF, fr. *resortir* to rebound, resort, fr. *sortir* to go out, leave] **1** : one looked to for help : REFUGE **2** : RECOURSE **3** : frequent or general visiting ⟨place of ~⟩ **4** : a frequently visited place : HAUNT **5** : a place providing recreation esp. to vacationers

²resort *vb* **1** : to go often or habitually **2** : to have recourse ⟨~ed to violence⟩

re·sound \ri-'zaůnd\ *vb* **1** : to become filled with sound : REVERBERATE, RING **2** : to sound loudly

re·sound·ing *adj* **1** : RESONATING, RESONANT **2** : impressively sonorous ⟨∼ name⟩ **3** : EMPHATIC, UNEQUIVOCAL ⟨a ∼ success⟩ — **re·sound·ing·ly** *adv*

re·source \'rē-ˌsȯrs, ri-'sȯrs\ *n* [F *ressource,* fr. OF *ressourse* relief, resource, fr. *resourdre* to relieve, lit., to rise again, fr. L *resurgere,* fr. *re-* again + *surgere* to rise] **1** : a source of supply or support — usu. used in pl. **2** : a natural feature or phenomenon that enhances the quality of human life **3** *pl* : available funds **4** : a possibility of relief or recovery **5** : a means of spending leisure time **6** : ability to meet and handle situations — **re·source·ful** \ri-'sȯrs-fəl\ *adj* — **re·source·ful·ness** *n*

¹re·spect \ri-'spekt\ *n* **1** : relation to something usu. specified : REGARD ⟨in ∼ to⟩ **2** : high or special regard : ESTEEM **3** *pl* : an expression of respect or deference **4** : DETAIL, PARTICULAR — **re·spect·ful** \-fəl\ *adj* — **re·spect·ful·ly** *adv* — **re·spect·ful·ness** *n*

²respect *vb* **1** : to consider deserving of high regard : ESTEEM **2** : to refrain from interfering with ⟨∼ another's privacy⟩ **3** : to have reference to : CONCERN — **re·spect·er** *n*

re·spect·able \ri-'spek-tə-bəl\ *adj* **1** : worthy of respect : ESTIMABLE **2** : decent or correct in conduct : PROPER **3** : fair in size, quantity, or quality ⟨a ∼ score⟩ : MODERATE, TOLERABLE **4** : fit to be seen : PRESENTABLE — **re·spect·a·bil·i·ty** \-ˌspek-tə-'bi-lə-tē\ *n* — **re·spect·ably** \-'spek-tə-blē\ *adv*

re·spect·ing *prep* : with regard to

re·spec·tive \-tiv\ *adj* : PARTICULAR, SEPARATE ⟨returned to their ∼ homes⟩

re·spec·tive·ly \-lē\ *adv* **1** : as relating to each **2** : each in the order given

res·pi·ra·tion \ˌres-pə-'rā-shən\ *n* **1** : an act or the process of breathing **2** : the physical and chemical processes (as breathing and oxidation) by which a living thing obtains oxygen and eliminates waste gases (as carbon dioxide) — **re·spi·ra·to·ry** \'res-pə-rə-ˌtȯr-ē, ri-'spī-rə-\ *adj* — **re·spire** \ri-'spī(-ə)r\ *vb*

res·pi·ra·tor \'res-pə-ˌrā-tər\ *n* **1** : a device covering the mouth and nose esp. to prevent inhaling harmful vapors **2** : a device for artificial respiration

re·spite \'res-pət\ *n* [ME *respit,* fr. AF, fr. ML *respectus,* fr. L, act of looking back] **1** : a temporary delay **2** : an interval of rest or relief

re·splen·dent \ri-'splen-dənt\ *adj* : shining brilliantly : gloriously bright : SPLENDID — **re·splen·dence** \-dəns\ *n* — **re·splen·dent·ly** *adv*

re·spond \ri-'spänd\ *vb* **1** : ANSWER, REPLY **2** : REACT ⟨∼ed to a call for help⟩ **3** : to show favorable reaction ⟨∼ to medication⟩ — **re·spond·er** *n*

re·spon·dent \ri-'spän-dənt\ *n* : one who responds; *esp* : one who answers in various legal proceedings — **respondent** *adj*

re·sponse \ri-'späns\ *n* **1** : an act of responding **2** : something constituting a reply or a reaction

re·spon·si·bil·i·ty \ri-ˌspän-sə-'bi-lə-tē\ *n, pl* **-ties** **1** : the quality or state of being responsible **2** : something for which one is responsible

re·spon·si·ble \ri-'spän-sə-bəl\ *adj* **1** : liable to be called upon to answer for one's acts or decisions : ANSWERABLE **2** : able to fulfill one's obligations : RELIABLE, TRUSTWORTHY **3** : able to choose for oneself between right and wrong **4** : involving accountability or important duties ⟨∼ position⟩ — **re·spon·si·ble·ness** *n* — **re·spon·si·bly** \-blē\ *adv*

re·spon·sive \-siv\ *adj* **1** : RESPONDING **2** : quick to respond : SENSITIVE **3** : using responses ⟨∼ readings⟩ — **re·spon·sive·ly** *adv* — **re·spon·sive·ness** *n*

¹rest \'rest\ *n* **1** : REPOSE, SLEEP **2** : freedom from work or activity **3** : a state of motionlessness or inactivity **4** : a place of shelter or lodging **5** : a silence in music equivalent in duration to a note of the same value; *also* : a character indicating this **6** : something used as a support — **rest·ful** \-fəl\ *adj* — **rest·ful·ly** *adv*

¹rest 5: symbols for five kinds

²rest *vb* **1** : to get rest by lying down; *esp* : SLEEP **2** : to cease from action or motion **3** : to give rest to : set at rest **4** : to sit or lie fixed or supported **5** : to place on or against a support **6** : to remain based or founded **7** : to cause to be firmly fixed : GROUND **8** : to remain for action : DEPEND

³rest *n* : something left over

res·tau·rant \'res-trənt, -tə-ˌränt\ *n* [F, fr. prp. of *restaurer* to restore, fr. L *restaurare*] : a public eating place

res·tau·ra·teur \ˌres-tə-rə-'tər\ *also* **res·tau·ran·teur** \-ˌrän-\ *n* : the operator or proprietor of a restaurant

rest home *n* : an establishment that gives care for the aged or convalescent

res·ti·tu·tion \ˌres-tə-'tü-shən, -'tyü-\ *n* : the act of restoring : the state of being restored; *esp* : restoration of something to its rightful owner ♦ *Synonyms* AMENDS, REDRESS, REPARATION, INDEMNITY, COMPENSATION

res·tive \'res-tiv\ *adj* [ME *restyf,* fr. AF *restif,* fr. *rester* to stop, resist, remain, fr. L *restare,* fr. *re-* back + *stare* to stand] **1** : BALKY **2** : UNEASY, FIDGETY ♦ *Synonyms* RESTLESS, IMPATIENT, NERVOUS — **res·tive·ly** *adv* — **res·tive·ness** *n*

rest·less \'rest-ləs\ *adj* **1** : lacking or denying rest ⟨a ∼ night⟩ **2** : never resting or settled : always moving ⟨the ∼ sea⟩ **3** : marked by or showing unrest esp. of mind ⟨∼ pacing back and forth⟩ ♦ *Synonyms* RESTIVE, IMPATIENT, NERVOUS, FIDGETY — **rest·less·ly** *adv* — **rest·less·ness** *n*

re·stor·able \ri-'stȯr-ə-bəl\ *adj* : fit for restoring or reclaiming

res·to·ra·tion \ˌres-tə-'rā-shən\ *n* **1** : an act of restoring : the state of being restored **2** : something (as a building) that has been restored

re·stor·ative \ri-'stȯr-ə-tiv\ *n* : something that restores esp. to consciousness or health — **restorative** *adj*

re·store \ri-'stȯr\ *vb* **re·stored; re·stor·ing** **1** : to give back : RETURN **2** : to put back into use or service **3** : to put or bring back into a former or original state **4** : to put again in possession of something — **re·stor·er** *n*

re·strain \ri-'strān\ *vb* **1** : to prevent from doing something **2** : to limit, restrict, or keep under control : CURB **3** : to place under restraint or arrest — **re·strain·able** *adj* — **re·strain·er** *n*

re·strained \ri-'strānd\ *adj* : marked by restraint : DISCIPLINED — **re·strain·ed·ly** \-'strā-nəd-lē\ *adv*

restraining order *n* : a legal order directing one person to stay away from another

re·straint \ri-'strānt\ *n* **1** : an act of restraining : the state of being restrained **2** : a restraining force, agency, or device **3** : deprivation or limitation of liberty : CONFINEMENT **4** : control over one's feelings : RESERVE

re·strict \ri-'strikt\ *vb* **1** : to confine within bounds : LIMIT **2** : to place under restriction as to use — **re·stric·tive** *adj* — **re·stric·tive·ly** *adv*

re·stric·tion \ri-'strik-shən\ *n* **1** : something (as a law or rule) that restricts **2** : an act of restricting : the state of being restricted

rest room *n* : a room or suite of rooms that includes sinks and toilets

¹re·sult \ri-'zəlt\ *vb* [ME, fr. ML *resultare,* fr. L, to rebound, fr. *re-* re- + *saltare* to leap] : to come about as an effect or consequence ⟨an injury ∼ing from a fall⟩ — **re·sul·tant** \-'zəl-tᵊnt\ *adj or n*

²result *n* **1** : something that results : EFFECT, CONSEQUENCE **2** : beneficial or discernible effect **3** : something obtained by calculation or investigation

re·sume \ri-'züm\ *vb* **re·sumed; re·sum·ing** **1** : to take or assume again **2** : to return to or begin again after interruption **3** : to take back to oneself — **re·sump·tion** \-'zəmp-shən\ *n*

ré·su·mé *or* **re·su·me** *or* **re·su·mé** \'re-zə-ˌmā, ˌre-zə-'mā\ *n* [F *résumé*] **1** : SUMMARY; *esp* : a short account of one's career and qualifications usu. prepared by a job applicant **2** : a set of accomplishments ⟨a musical ∼⟩

re·sur·gence \ri-'sər-jəns\ *n* : a rising again into life, activity, or prominence — **re·sur·gent** \-jənt\ *adj*

res·ur·rect \ˌre-zə-'rekt\ *vb* **1** : to raise from the dead **2** : to bring to attention or use again

res·ur·rec·tion \ˌre-zə-'rek-shən\ *n* **1** *cap* : the rising of Christ from the dead **2** *often cap* : the rising to life of all human dead before the final judgment **3** : REVIVAL

re·sus·ci·tate \ri-'sə-sə-ˌtāt\ *vb* **-tat·ed; -tat·ing** : to revive from apparent death or unconsciousness; *also* : REVITALIZE — **re·sus·ci·ta·tion** \ri-ˌsə-sə-'tā-shən, ˌrē-\ *n* — **re·sus·ci·ta·tor** \ri-'sə-sə-ˌtā-tər\ *n*

ret *abbr* retired

¹**re·tail** \'rē-ˌtāl, *esp for 2 also* ri-'tāl\ *vb* **1** : to sell in small quantities directly to the ultimate consumer **2** : to tell in detail or to one person after another — **re·tail·er** *n*

²**re·tail** \'rē-ˌtāl\ *n* : the sale of goods in small amounts to ultimate consumers — **retail** *adj or adv*

re·tain \ri-'tān\ *vb* **1** : to hold in possession or use **2** : to engage (as a lawyer) by paying a fee in advance **3** : to keep in a fixed place or position ✦ *Synonyms* DETAIN, WITHHOLD, RESERVE

¹**re·tain·er** \ri-'tā-nər\ *n* **1** : one that retains **2** : a servant in a wealthy household; *also* : EMPLOYEE **3** : a device that holds something (as teeth) in place

²**retainer** *n* : a fee paid to secure services (as of a lawyer)

¹**re·take** \(ˌ)rē-'tāk\ *vb* **-took** \-'tùk\; **-tak·en** \-'tā-kən\; **-tak·ing** **1** : to take or seize again **2** : to photograph again

²**re·take** \'rē-ˌtāk\ *n* : a second photographing of a motion⁼picture scene

re·tal·i·ate \ri-'ta-lē-ˌāt\ *vb* **-at·ed; -at·ing** : to return like for like; *esp* : to get revenge — **re·tal·i·a·tion** \-ˌta-lē-'ā-shən\ *n* — **re·tal·ia·to·ry** \-'tal-yə-ˌtòr-ē\ *adj*

re·tard \ri-'tärd\ *vb* : to hold back : delay the progress of ✦ *Synonyms* SLOW, SLACKEN, DETAIN — **re·tar·da·tion** \ˌrē-ˌtär-'dā-shən, ri-\ *n* — **re·tard·er** *n*

re·tar·dant \ri-'tär-d³nt\ *adj* : serving or tending to retard — **retardant** *n*

re·tard·ed *adj, sometimes offensive* : slow or limited in intellectual, emotional, or academic progress

retch \'rech\ *vb* : to try to vomit; *also* : VOMIT

re·ten·tion \ri-'ten-chən\ *n* **1** : the act of retaining : the state of being retained **2** : the power of retaining esp. in the mind : RETENTIVENESS

re·ten·tive \-'ten-tiv\ *adj* : having the power of retaining; *esp* : retaining knowledge easily — **re·ten·tive·ness** *n*

re·think \(ˌ)rē-'thiŋk\ *vb* **-thought** \-'thòt\; **-think·ing** : to think about again : RECONSIDER

ret·i·cent \'re-tə-sənt\ *adj* **1** : tending not to talk or give out information **2** : RELUCTANT ✦ *Synonyms* RESERVED, TACITURN, CLOSEMOUTHED — **ret·i·cence** \-səns\ *n* — **ret·i·cent·ly** *adv*

ret·i·na \'re-tə-nə\ *n, pl* **retinas** *or* **ret·i·nae** \-ˌnē\ : the sensory membrane lining the eye that receives the image formed by the lens — **ret·i·nal** \'re-tə-nəl\ *adj*

ret·i·nue \'re-tə-ˌnü, -ˌnyü\ *n* : the body of attendants or followers of a distinguished person

re·tire \ri-'tī(-ə)r\ *vb* **re·tired; re·tir·ing** **1** : RETREAT **2** : to withdraw esp. for privacy **3** : to withdraw from one's occupation or position : conclude one's career **4** : to withdraw from use or service **5** : to go to bed **6** : to cause to be out in baseball — **re·tire·ment** *n*

re·tired \ri-'tī(-ə)rd\ *adj* **1** : SECLUDED, QUIET **2** : withdrawn from active duty or from one's career

re·tir·ee \ri-ˌtī-'rē\ *n* : a person who has retired from a career

re·tir·ing *adj* : SHY, RESERVED

re·tool \(ˌ)rē-'tül\ *vb* **1** : to reequip with tools **2** : to modify with usu. minor improvements ⟨~ed the team for next year⟩

¹**re·tort** \ri-'tòrt\ *vb* [L *retortus*, pp. of *retorquēre*, lit., to twist back, hurl back, fr. *re-* back + *torquēre* to twist] **1** : to say in reply : answer back usu. sharply **2** : to answer (an argument) by a counter argument **3** : RETALIATE

²**retort** *n* : a quick, witty, or cutting reply

³**re·tort** \ri-'tòrt, 'rē-ˌtòrt\ *n* [MF *retorte*, fr. ML *retorta*, fr. L, fem. of *retortus*, pp. of *retorquēre* to twist back; fr. its shape] : a vessel in which substances are distilled or broken up by heat

re·touch \(ˌ)rē-'təch\ *vb* : TOUCH UP; *esp* : to change (as a photographic negative) in order to produce a more desirable appearance

re·trace \(ˌ)rē-'trās\ *vb* : to go over again or in a reverse direction ⟨*retraced* his steps⟩

re·tract \ri-'trakt\ *vb* **1** : to draw back or in **2** : to withdraw (as a charge or promise) : DISAVOW — **re·tract·able** *adj* — **re·trac·tion** \-'trak-shən\ *n*

re·trac·tile \ri-'trak-t³l, -ˌtrak-ˌtī(-ə)l\ *adj* : capable of being drawn back or in ⟨~ claws⟩

¹**re·tread** \(ˌ)rē-'tred\ *vb* **re·tread·ed; re·tread·ing** : to put a new tread on (a worn tire)

²**re·tread** \'rē-ˌtred\ *n* **1** : a retreaded tire **2** : one pressed into service again; *also* : REMAKE

¹**re·treat** \ri-'trēt\ *n* **1** : an act of withdrawing esp. from something dangerous, difficult, or disagreeable **2** : a military signal for withdrawal; *also* : a military flag-lowering ceremony **3** : a place of privacy or safety : REFUGE **4** : a group withdrawal for prayer, meditation, or study

²**retreat** *vb* **1** : to make a retreat : WITHDRAW **2** : to slope backward

re·trench \ri-'trench\ *vb* [obs. F *retrencher* (now *retrancher*), fr. MF *retrenchier*, fr. *re-* + *trenchier* to cut] **1** : to cut down or pare away : REDUCE, CURTAIL **2** : to cut down expenses : ECONOMIZE — **re·trench·ment** *n*

ret·ri·bu·tion \ˌre-trə-'byü-shən\ *n* : something administered or exacted in recompense; *esp* : PUNISHMENT ✦ *Synonyms* REPRISAL, VENGEANCE, REVENGE, RETALIATION — **re·trib·u·tive** \ri-'tri-byə-tiv\ *adj* — **re·trib·u·to·ry** \-byə-ˌtòr-ē\ *adj*

re·trieve \ri-'trēv\ *vb* **re·trieved; re·triev·ing** **1** : to search about for and bring in (killed or wounded game) **2** : RECOVER, RESTORE — **re·triev·able** *adj* — **re·triev·al** \-'trē-vəl\ *n*

re·triev·er \ri-'trē-vər\ *n* : one that retrieves; *esp* : a dog of any of several breeds used esp. for retrieving game

ret·ro \'re-trō\ *adj* : relating to or being the styles and fashions of the past ⟨~ clothing⟩

ret·ro·ac·tive \ˌre-trō-'ak-tiv\ *adj* : made effective as of a date prior to enactment ⟨a ~ pay raise⟩ — **ret·ro·ac·tive·ly** *adv*

ret·ro·fit \'re-trō-ˌfit, ˌre-trō-'fit\ *vb* **1** : to furnish (as an aircraft) with newly available equipment **2** : to adapt to a new purpose or need : MODIFY — **ret·ro·fit** \'re-trō-ˌfit\ *n*

¹**ret·ro·grade** \'re-trə-ˌgrād\ *adj* **1** : moving or tending backward **2** : tending toward or resulting in a worse condition

²**retrograde** *vb* **1** : RETREAT **2** : DETERIORATE, DEGENERATE

ret·ro·gres·sion \ˌre-trə-'gre-shən\ *n* : return to a former and less complex level of development or organization — **ret·ro·gress** \ˌre-trə-'gres\ *vb* — **ret·ro·gres·sive** \ˌre-trə-'gre-siv\ *adj*

ret·ro·rock·et \'re-trō-ˌrä-kət\ *n* : an auxiliary rocket engine (as on a spacecraft) used to slow forward motion

ret·ro·spect \'re-trə-ˌspekt\ *n* : a review of past events — **ret·ro·spec·tion** \ˌre-trə-'spek-shən\ *n*

ret·ro·spec·tive \ˌre-trə-'spek-tiv\ *n* **1** : a comprehensive examination of an artist's work over many years **2** : REVIEW **4** ⟨a war ~⟩ — **retrospective** *adj* — **ret·ro·spec·tive·ly** *adv*

ret·ro·vi·rus \'re-trō-ˌvī-rəs\ *n* : any of a group of RNA⁼ containing viruses (as HIV) that make DNA using RNA instead of the reverse — **re·tro·vi·ral** \-rəl\ *adj*

¹**re·turn** \ri-'tərn\ *vb* **1** : to go or come back **2** : to pass, give, or send back to an earlier possessor **3** : to put back to or in a former place or state **4** : REPLY, ANSWER **5** : to report esp. officially **6** : to elect to office **7** : to bring in (as profit) : YIELD **8** : to give or perform in return ⟨~ a favor⟩ — **re·turn·er** *n*

²**return** *n* **1** : an act of coming or going back to or from a former place or state **2** : RECURRENCE **3** : a report of the results of balloting **4** : a formal statement of taxable income **5** : the profit from labor, investment, or business : YIELD **6** : the act of returning something **7** : something that returns or is returned; *also* : a means for conveying something (as water) back to its starting point **8** : something given in repayment or reciprocation; *also* : ANSWER, RETORT **9** : an answering play — **return** *adj*

¹**re·turn·able** \ri-'tər-nə-bəl\ *adj* : capable of being returned (as for reuse); *also* : permitted to be returned

²**returnable** *n* : a returnable beverage container

re·turn·ee \ri-ˌtər-'nē\ *n* : one who returns

re·union \rē-'yün-yən\ *n* **1** : an act of reuniting : the state of being reunited **2** : a meeting of persons after separation

¹**rev** \'rev\ *n* : a revolution of a motor

²**rev** *vb* **revved; rev·ving** **1** : to increase the revolutions per minute of (a motor) **2** : STIMULATE, EXCITE

³**rev** *abbr* **1** revenue **2** reverse **3** review; reviewed **4** revised; revision **5** revolution

Rev *abbr* **1** Revelation **2** Reverend
re·vamp \(ˌ)rē-ˈvamp\ *vb* : RECONSTRUCT, REVISE; *also* : RENOVATE
re·vanche \rə-ˈväⁿsh\ *n* [F] : REVENGE; *esp* : a usu. political policy designed to recover lost territory or status
re·veal \ri-ˈvēl\ *vb* **1** : to make known **2** : to show plainly : open up to view
rev·eil·le \ˈre-və-lē\ *n* [modif. of F *réveillez*, imper. pl. of *réveiller* to awaken, fr. MF *eveiller* to awaken, fr. (assumed) VL *exvigilare*, fr. L *vigilare* to keep watch, stay awake] : a military signal sounded at about sunrise
¹**rev·el** \ˈre-vəl\ *vb* -eled *or* -elled; -el·ing *or* -el·ling **1** : to take part in a revel **2** : to take great pleasure or satisfaction \\<~ed in the quiet> — **rev·el·er** *or* **rev·el·ler** *n* — **rev·el·ry** \-vəl-rē\ *n*
²**revel** *n* : a usu. wild party or celebration
rev·e·la·tion \ˌre-və-ˈlā-shən\ *n* **1** : an act of revealing **2** : something revealed; *esp* : an enlightening or astonishing disclosure
Revelation *n* — see BIBLE table
¹**re·venge** \ri-ˈvenj\ *vb* **re·venged; re·veng·ing** : to inflict harm or injury in return for (a wrong) : AVENGE — **re·veng·er** *n*
²**revenge** *n* **1** : a desire for revenge **2** : an act or instance of retaliation to get even **3** : an opportunity for getting satisfaction ♦ *Synonyms* VENGEANCE, RETRIBUTION, REPRISAL — **re·venge·ful** *adj*
rev·e·nue \ˈre-və-ˌnü, -ˌnyü\ *n* [ME, return, revenue, fr. AF, fr. *revenir* to return, fr. L *revenire*, fr. *re-* back + *venire* to come] **1** : investment income **2** : money collected by a government (as through taxes)
rev·e·nu·er \ˈre-və-ˌnü-ər, -ˌnyü-\ *n* : a revenue officer or boat
re·verb \ri-ˈvərb, ˈrē-ˌvərb\ *n* : an electronically produced echo effect in recorded music; *also* : a device for producing reverb
re·ver·ber·ate \ri-ˈvər-bə-ˌrāt\ *vb* -at·ed; -at·ing **1** : REFLECT \\<~ light or heat> **2** : to resound in or as if in a series of echoes — **re·ver·ber·a·tion** \-ˌvər-bə-ˈrā-shən\ *n*
re·vere \ri-ˈvir\ *vb* **re·vered; re·ver·ing** : to show honor and devotion to : VENERATE \\<a teacher *revered* by students> ♦ *Synonyms* REVERENCE, WORSHIP, ADORE
¹**rev·er·ence** \ˈre-vrəns, -və-rəns\ *n* **1** : honor or respect felt or shown **2** : a gesture (as a bow or curtsy) of respect
²**reverence** *vb* -enced; -enc·ing : to regard or treat with reverence
¹**rev·er·end** \ˈre-vrənd, -və-rənd\ *adj* **1** : worthy of reverence : REVERED **2** : being a member of the clergy — used as a title
²**reverend** *n* : a member of the clergy
rev·er·ent \ˈre-vrənt, -və-rənt\ *adj* : expressing reverence — **rev·er·ent·ly** *adv*
rev·er·en·tial \ˌre-və-ˈren-chəl\ *adj* : REVERENT
rev·er·ie *also* **rev·ery** \ˈre-və-rē\ *n, pl* -er·ies [F *rêverie*, fr. MF, delirium, fr. *resver, rever* to wander, be delirious] **1** : DAYDREAM **2** : the state of being lost in thought
re·ver·sal \ri-ˈvər-səl\ *n* : an act or process of reversing
¹**re·verse** \ri-ˈvərs\ *adj* **1** : opposite to a previous or normal condition \\<in ~ order> **2** : acting or working in a manner opposite the usual **3** : bringing about reverse movement \\<~ gear> — **re·verse·ly** *adv*
²**reverse** *vb* **re·versed; re·vers·ing** **1** : to turn upside down or completely about in position or direction **2** : to set aside or change (as a legal decision) **3** : to change to the contrary \\<~ a policy> **4** : to go or cause to go in the opposite direction **5** : to put (as a car) in reverse — **re·vers·ible** \-ˈvər-sə-bəl\ *adj*
³**reverse** *n* **1** : something contrary to something else : OPPOSITE **2** : an act or instance of reversing; *esp* : a change for the worse **3** : the back side of something (as a coin or card) **4** : a gear that reverses something
reverse engineer *vb* : to disassemble or analyze in detail in order to discover concepts involved in manufacture — **reverse engineering** *n*
re·ver·sion \ri-ˈvər-zhən\ *n* **1** : the right of succession or future possession (as to a title or property) **2** : return toward some former or ancestral condition; *also* : a product of this — **re·ver·sion·ary** \-zhə-ˌner-ē\ *adj*
re·vert \ri-ˈvərt\ *vb* **1** : to come or go back \\<~ed to sav-

agery> **2** : to return to a proprietor or his or her heirs **3** : to return to an ancestral type
¹**re·view** \ri-ˈvyü\ *n* **1** : an act of revising **2** : a formal military inspection **3** : a general survey **4** : INSPECTION, EXAMINATION; *esp* : REEXAMINATION **5** : a critical evaluation (as of a book) **6** : a magazine devoted to reviews and essays **7** : a renewed study of previously studied material **8** : REVUE
²**re·view** \ri-ˈvyü, *1 also* ˈrē-\ *vb* **1** : to examine or study again; *esp* : to reexamine judicially **2** : to hold a review of \\<~ troops> **3** : to write a critical examination of \\<~ a novel> **4** : to look back over \\<~ed her accomplishments> **5** : to study material again
re·view·er \ri-ˈvyü-ər\ *n* : one that reviews; *esp* : a writer of critical reviews
re·vile \ri-ˈvī(-ə)l\ *vb* **re·viled; re·vil·ing** : to abuse verbally : rail at ♦ *Synonyms* VITUPERATE, BERATE, RATE, UPBRAID, SCOLD — **re·vile·ment** *n* — **re·vil·er** *n*
re·vise \ri-ˈvīz\ *vb* **re·vised; re·vis·ing** **1** : to look over something written in order to correct or improve \\<~ an essay> **2** : to make a new version of \\<~ an almanac> — **re·vis·able** *adj* — **revise** *n* — **re·vis·er** *or* **re·vi·sor** \-ˈvī-zər\ *n* — **re·vi·sion** \-ˈvi-zhən\ *n*
re·vi·tal·ise *Brit var of* REVITALIZE
re·vi·tal·ize \ˌrē-ˈvīt-tə-ˌlīz\ *vb* -ized; -iz·ing : to give new life or vigor to \\<~ the shopping district> — **re·vi·tal·i·za·tion** \(ˌ)rē-ˌvīt-tə-lə-ˈzā-shən\ *n*
re·viv·al \ri-ˈvī-vəl\ *n* **1** : an act of reviving : the state of being revived **2** : a new publication or presentation (as of a book or play) **3** : an evangelistic meeting or series of meetings
re·vive \ri-ˈvīv\ *vb* **re·vived; re·viv·ing** **1** : to bring back to life, consciousness, or activity : make or become fresh or strong again **2** : to bring back into use — **re·viv·er** *n*
re·viv·i·fy \ri-ˈvi-və-ˌfī\ *vb* : REVIVE — **re·viv·i·fi·ca·tion** \-ˌvi-və-fə-ˈkā-shən\ *n*
re·vo·ca·ble \ˈre-və-kə-bəl *also* ri-ˈvō-kə-bəl\ *adj* : capable of being revoked
re·vo·ca·tion \ˌre-və-ˈkā-shən\ *n* : an act or instance of revoking
re·voke \ri-ˈvōk\ *vb* **re·voked; re·vok·ing** **1** : to annul by recalling or taking back : REPEAL, RESCIND \\<~ a license> **2** : RENEGE **2** — **re·vok·er** *n*
¹**re·volt** \ri-ˈvōlt\ *vb* [MF *revolter*, fr. It *rivoltare* to overthrow, fr. VL **revolvitare*, fr. L *revolvere* to revolve, roll back] **1** : to throw off allegiance to a ruler or government : REBEL **2** : to experience disgust or shock **3** : to turn or cause to turn away with disgust or abhorrence — **re·volt·er** *n*
²**revolt** *n* : REBELLION, INSURRECTION
re·volt·ing *adj* : extremely offensive \\<a ~ odor> — **re·volt·ing·ly** *adv*
rev·o·lu·tion \ˌre-və-ˈlü-shən\ *n* **1** : the action by a heavenly body of going round in an orbit **2** : ROTATION **3** : a sudden, radical, or complete change; *esp* : the overthrow or renunciation of one ruler or government and substitution of another by the governed
¹**rev·o·lu·tion·ary** \-shə-ˌner-ē\ *adj* **1** : of or relating to revolution **2** : tending to or promoting revolution **3** : constituting or bringing about a major change
²**revolutionary** *n, pl* -ar·ies : one who takes part in a revolution or who advocates revolutionary doctrines
rev·o·lu·tion·ise *Brit var of* REVOLUTIONIZE
rev·o·lu·tion·ist \ˌre-və-ˈlü-shə-nist\ *n* : REVOLUTIONARY — **revolutionist** *adj*
rev·o·lu·tion·ize \-ˌnīz\ *vb* -ized; -iz·ing : to change fundamentally or completely \\<~ an industry> — **rev·o·lu·tion·iz·er** *n*
re·volve \ri-ˈvälv\ *vb* **re·volved; re·volv·ing** **1** : to turn over in the mind : reflect upon : PONDER **2** : to move in an orbit; *also* : ROTATE **3** : to have a specified focus \\<the debate *revolved* around taxes> — **re·volv·able** *adj*
re·volv·er \ri-ˈväl-vər\ *n* : a pistol with a revolving cylinder of several chambers
re·vue \ri-ˈvyü\ *n* : a theatrical production consisting typically of brief often satirical sketches and songs
re·vul·sion \ri-ˈvəl-shən\ *n* **1** : a strong sudden reaction or change of feeling **2** : a feeling of complete distaste or repugnance
revved *past and past part of* REV
revving *pres part of* REV

¹re·ward \ri-'word\ *vb* **1** : to give a reward to or for **2** : RECOMPENSE

²reward *n* **1** : something given in return for good or evil done or received or for some service or attainment **2** : a stimulus that is administered to an organism after a response and that increases the probability of occurrence of the response ✦ *Synonyms* PREMIUM, PRIZE, AWARD

¹re·wind \(,)rē-'wīnd\ *vb* **-wound; -wind·ing** **1** : to wind again **2** : to reverse the winding of (as film)

²re·wind \'rē-,wīnd\ *n* **1** : something that rewinds **2** : an act of rewinding **3** : a function of an electronic device that reverses a recording to a previous portion

re·work \(,)rē-'wərk\ *vb* **1** : REVISE **2** : to reprocess for further use

¹re·write \(,)rē-'rīt\ *vb* **-wrote; -writ·ten; -writ·ing** : to make a revision of : REVISE

²re·write \'rē-,rīt\ *n* : an instance or a piece of rewriting

RF *abbr* radio frequency

RFD *abbr* rural free delivery

Rh *symbol* rhodium

RH *abbr* right hand

rhap·so·dy \'rap-sə-dē\ *n, pl* **-dies** [L *rhapsodia* portion of an epic poem adapted for recitation, fr. Gk *rhapsōidia* recitation of selections from epic poetry, ultim. fr. *rhaptein* to sew, stitch together + *aidein* to sing] **1** : an expression of extravagant praise or ecstasy **2** : a musical of irregular form — **rhap·sod·ic** \rap-'sä-dik\ *adj* — **rhap·sod·i·cal·ly** \-di-k(ə-)lē\ *adv* — **rhap·so·dize** \'rap-sə-,dīz\ *vb*

rhea \'rē-ə\ *n* : either of two large flightless 3-toed So. American birds that resemble but are smaller than the African ostrich

rhe·ni·um \'rē-nē-əm\ *n* : a rare heavy metallic chemical element

rheo·stat \'rē-ə-,stat\ *n* : a resistor for regulating an electric current by means of variable resistances — **rheo·stat·ic** \,rē-ə-'sta-tik\ *adj*

rhe·sus monkey \'rē-səs-\ *n* : a pale brown Asian monkey often used in medical research

rhet·o·ric \'re-tə-rik\ *n* [ME *rethorik*, fr. AF *rethorique*, fr. L *rhetorica*, fr. Gk *rhētorikē*, lit., art of oratory, fr. *rhētōr* public speaker, fr. *eirein* to speak] : the art of speaking or writing effectively — **rhet·o·ri·cian** \,re-tə-'ri-shən\ *n*

rhe·tor·i·cal \ri-'tór-i-kəl\ *adj* **1** : of or relating to rhetoric **2** : asked merely for effect with no answer expected ⟨a ~ question⟩

rheum \'rüm\ *n* : a watery discharge from the mucous membranes esp. of the eyes or nose — **rheumy** *adj*

rheu·mat·ic fever \rü-'ma-tik-\ *n* : an acute disease chiefly of children and young adults that is characterized by fever, by inflammation and pain in and around the joints, and by inflammation of the membranes surrounding the heart and the heart valves

rheu·ma·tism \'rü-mə-,ti-zəm, 'rü-\ *n* **1** : any of various conditions marked by stiffness, pain, or swelling in muscles or joints **2** : RHEUMATOID ARTHRITIS — **rheu·mat·ic** \rü-'ma-tik\ *adj*

rheu·ma·toid arthritis \-,tóid-\ *n* : a usu. chronic progressive autoimmune disease characterized by inflammation and swelling of joint structures

rheu·ma·tol·o·gy \,rü-mə-'tä-lə-jē, ,rü-\ *n* : a medical science dealing with rheumatic diseases — **rheu·ma·tol·o·gist** \-jist\ *n*

Rh factor \,är-'āch-\ *n* [*rhe*sus monkey (in which it was first detected)] : any of one or more inherited substances in red blood cells that may cause dangerous reactions in some infants or in transfusions

rhine·stone \'rīn-,stōn\ *n* : a colorless imitation stone of high luster made of glass, paste, or gem quartz

rhi·no \'rī-nō\ *n, pl* **rhinos** *also* **rhino** : RHINOCEROS

rhi·noc·er·os \rī-'nä-sə-rəs\ *n, pl* **-noc·er·os·es** *also* **-noc·er·os** *or* **-noc·eri** \-'nä-sə-,rī\ [ME *rinoceros*, fr. AF, fr. L *rhinoceros*, fr. Gk *rhinokerōs*, fr. *rhin-, rhis* nose + *keras* horn] : any of a family of large thick-skinned mammals of Africa and Asia with one or two upright horns of keratin on the snout and three toes on each foot

rhi·zome \'rī-,zōm\ *n* : a fleshy, rootlike, and usu. horizontal underground plant stem that forms shoots above and roots below — **rhi·zom·a·tous** \rī-'zä-mə-təs\ *adj*

Rh−neg·a·tive \,är-,āch-'ne-gə-tiv\ *adj* : lacking Rh factors in the red blood cells

rho \'rō\ *n* : the 17th letter of the Greek alphabet — P or ρ

rho·di·um \'rō-dē-əm\ *n* : a rare hard ductile metallic chemical element

rho·do·den·dron \,rō-də-'den-drən\ *n* : any of a genus of shrubs or trees of the heath family with clusters of large bright flowers

rhom·boid \'räm-,bóid\ *n* : a parallelogram with unequal adjacent sides and angles that are not right angles — **rhomboid** *or* **rhom·boi·dal** \räm-'bói-d³l\ *adj*

rhom·bus \'räm-bəs\ *n, pl* **rhom·bus·es** *or* **rhom·bi** \-,bī\ : a parallelogram having all four sides equal

Rh−pos·i·tive \,är-,āch-'pä-zə-tiv\ *adj* : containing one or more Rh factors in the red blood cells

rhu·barb \'rü-,bärb\ *n* [ME *rubarbe*, fr. AF *reubarbe*, fr. ML *reubarbarum*, alter. of *rha barbarum*, lit., barbarian rhubarb] : a garden plant related to the buckwheat having leaves with thick juicy edible pink and red stems

¹rhyme *also* rime \'rīm\ *n* **1** : a composition in verse that rhymes; *also* : POETRY **2** : correspondence in terminal sounds (as of two lines of verse)

²rhyme *also* rime *vb* **rhymed** *also* **rimed; rhym·ing** *also* **rim·ing** **1** : to make rhymes; *also* : to write poetry **2** : to have rhymes : be in rhyme

rhythm \'ri-thəm\ *n* **1** : regular rise and fall in the flow of sound in speech **2** : a movement or activity in which some action or element recurs regularly — **rhyth·mic** \'rith-mik\ *or* **rhyth·mi·cal** \-mi-kəl\ *adj* — **rhyth·mi·cal·ly** \-k(ə-)lē\ *adv*

rhythm and blues *n* : popular music based on blues and black folk music

rhythm method *n* : birth control by refraining from sexual intercourse during the time when ovulation is most likely to occur

RI *abbr* Rhode Island

ri·al \rē-'ól, -'äl\ *n* — see MONEY table

¹rib \'rib\ *n* **1** : any of the series of curved bones of the chest of most vertebrates that are joined to the backbone in pairs and help to support the body wall and protect the organs inside **2** : something resembling a rib in shape or function **3** : an elongated ridge (as in fabric)

²rib *vb* **ribbed; rib·bing** **1** : to furnish or strengthen with ribs **2** : to knit so as to form ridges

³rib *vb* **ribbed; rib·bing** : to poke fun at : TEASE — **rib·ber** *n*

rib·ald \'ri-bəld\ *adj* : coarse or indecent esp. in language ⟨~ jokes⟩ — **rib·ald·ry** \-bəl-drē\ *n*

rib·and \'ri-bənd\ *n* : RIBBON

rib·bon \'ri-bən\ *n* **1** : a narrow fabric typically of silk or velvet used for trimming and for badges **2** : a strip of inked cloth (as in a typewriter) **3** : TATTER, SHRED ⟨torn to ~s⟩

ri·bo·fla·vin \,rī-bə-'flā-vən, 'rī-bə-,flā-vən\ *n* : a growth-promoting vitamin of the vitamin B complex occurring esp. in milk and liver

ri·bo·nu·cle·ic acid \,rī-bō-nü-,klē-ik-, -nyü-, -,klā-\ *n* : RNA

ri·bose \'rī-,bōs\ *n* : a sugar with five carbon atoms and five oxygen atoms in each molecule that is part of RNA

ri·bo·some \'rī-bə-,sōm\ *n* : any of the RNA-rich cytoplasmic granules in a cell that are sites of protein synthesis — **ri·bo·som·al** \,rī-bə-'sō-məl\ *adj*

rice \'rīs\ *n* : the starchy seeds of an annual grass that are cooked and used for food; *also* : this widely cultivated grass of warm wet areas

rich \'rich\ *adj* **1** : possessing or controlling great wealth : WEALTHY **2** : COSTLY, VALUABLE **3** : deep and pleasing in color or tone **4** : ABUNDANT **5** : containing much sugar, fat, or seasoning; *also* : high in combustible content **6** : FRUITFUL, FERTILE — **rich·ly** *adv* — **rich·ness** *n*

rhinoceros

rich·es \\'ri-chəz\\ *n pl* [ME, sing. or pl., fr. *richesse* wealth, fr. AF *richesce*, fr. *riche* rich] : things that make one rich : WEALTH

Rich·ter scale \\'rik-tər-\\ *n* : a scale for expressing the magnitude of a seismic disturbance (as an earthquake) in terms of the energy dissipated in it

rick \\'rik\\ *n* : a large stack (as of hay) in the open air

rick·ets \\'ri-kəts\\ *n* : a childhood deficiency disease marked esp. by soft deformed bones and caused by lack of vitamin D

rick·ett·sia \\ri-'ket-sē-ə\\ *n, pl* **-si·as** *or* **-si·ae** \\-sē-,ē\\ : any of a group of usu. rod-shaped bacteria that cause various diseases (as typhus)

rick·ety \\'ri-kə-tē\\ *adj* **1** : affected with rickets **2** : SHAKY; *also* : in unsound physical condition ⟨~ stairs⟩

rick·shaw *also* **rick·sha** \\'rik-,shò\\ *n* : a small covered 2-wheeled carriage pulled by one person and used orig. in Japan

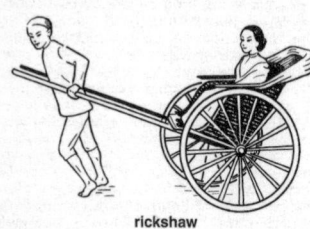

rickshaw

¹ric·o·chet \\'ri-kə-,shā, *Brit also* -,shet\\ *n* [F] : a bouncing off at an angle (as of a bullet off a wall); *also* : an object that ricochets

²ricochet *vb* **-cheted** \\-,shād\\ *also* **-chet·ted** \\-,she-təd\\; **-chet·ing** \\-,shā-iŋ\\ *or* **-chet·ting** \\-,she-tiŋ\\ : to bounce or skip with or as if with a glancing rebound

ri·cot·ta \\ri-'kä-tə, -'kò-\\ *n* : a white unripened whey cheese of Italy that resembles cottage cheese

rid \\'rid\\ *vb* **rid** *also* **rid·ded**; **rid·ding** : to make free : CLEAR, RELIEVE — **rid·dance** \\'ri-dᵊns\\ *n*

rid·den \\'ri-dᵊn\\ *adj* **1** : harassed, oppressed, or obsessed by ⟨debt-*ridden*⟩ **2** : excessively full of or supplied with ⟨slum-*ridden*⟩

¹rid·dle \\'ri-dᵊl\\ *n* : a puzzling question to be solved or answered by guessing

²riddle *vb* **rid·dled**; **rid·dling** **1** : EXPLAIN, SOLVE **2** : to speak in riddles

³riddle *n* : a coarse sieve

⁴riddle *vb* **rid·dled**; **rid·dling** **1** : to sift with a riddle **2** : to pierce with many holes **3** : PERMEATE

¹ride \\'rīd\\ *vb* **rode** \\'rōd\\; **rid·den** \\'ri-dᵊn\\; **rid·ing** **1** : to go on an animal's back or in a conveyance (as a boat, car, or airplane); *also* : to sit on and control so as to be carried along ⟨~ a bicycle⟩ **2** : to float or move on water ⟨~ at anchor⟩; *also* : to move like a floating object **3** : to bear along : CARRY ⟨*rode* her on their shoulders⟩ **4** : to travel over a surface ⟨the car ~s well⟩ **5** : to proceed over on horseback **6** : to torment by nagging or teasing

²ride *n* **1** : an act of riding; *esp* : a trip on horseback or by vehicle **2** : a way (as a road or path) suitable for riding **3** : a mechanical device (as a merry-go-round) for riding on **4** : a means of transportation

rid·er \\'rī-dər\\ *n* **1** : one that rides **2** : an addition to a document often attached on a separate piece of paper **3** : a clause dealing with an unrelated matter attached to a legislative bill during passage — **rid·er·less** *adj*

¹ridge \\'rij\\ *n* [ME *rigge*, fr. OE *hrycg*] **1** : an elevated body part or structure **2** : a range of hills **3** : a raised line or strip **4** : the line made where two sloping surfaces (as of a roof) meet — **ridgy** *adj*

²ridge *vb* **ridged**; **ridg·ing** **1** : to form into a ridge **2** : to extend in ridges

¹rid·i·cule \\'ri-də-,kyül\\ *n* : the act of ridiculing : DERISION, MOCKERY

²ridicule *vb* **-culed**; **-cul·ing** : to laugh at or make fun of mockingly or contemptuously ⟨was *ridiculed* by his peers⟩ ✦ *Synonyms* DERIDE, TAUNT, TWIT, MOCK

ri·dic·u·lous \\rə-'di-kyə-ləs\\ *adj* : arousing or deserving ridicule : ABSURD, PREPOSTEROUS ✦ *Synonyms* LAUGHABLE, LUDICROUS, FARCICAL, RISIBLE — **ri·dic·u·lous·ly** *adv* — **ri·dic·u·lous·ness** *n*

ri·el \\rē-'el\\ *n* — see MONEY table

Ries·ling \\'rēz-liŋ, 'rēs-\\ *n* : a sweet to very dry white wine made from a single variety of grape orig. grown in Germany

RIF *abbr* reduction in force

rife \\'rīf\\ *adj* : WIDESPREAD, PREVALENT, ABOUNDING — **rife·ly** *adv*

¹riff \\'rif\\ *n* : a repeated phrase in jazz typically supporting a solo improvisation; *also* : a piece based on such a phrase **2** : a usu. witty or improvised remark or outpouring **3** : a distinct variation : TAKE — **riff** *vb*

riff·raff \\'rif-,raf\\ *n* [ME *riffe raffe*, fr. *rif and raf* every single one, fr. AF *rif et raf* altogether] **1** : RABBLE **2** : REFUSE, RUBBISH

¹ri·fle \\'rī-fəl\\ *vb* **ri·fled**; **ri·fling** : to ransack esp. with the intent to steal — **ri·fler** *n*

²rifle *vb* **ri·fled**; **ri·fling** : to cut spiral grooves into the bore of ⟨*rifled* pipe⟩ — **rifling** *n*

³rifle *n* **1** : a shoulder weapon with a rifled bore **2** *pl* : soldiers armed with rifles — **ri·fle·man** \\-fəl-mən\\ *n*

rift \\'rift\\ *n* **1** : CLEFT, FISSURE **2** : FAULT 6 **3** : ESTRANGEMENT, SEPARATION ⟨a ~ between spouses⟩ — **rift** *vb*

¹rig \\'rig\\ *vb* **rigged**; **rig·ging** **1** : to fit out (as a ship) with rigging **2** : CLOTHE, DRESS **3** : EQUIP **4** : to set up esp. as a makeshift ⟨~ up a shelter⟩

²rig *n* **1** : the distinctive shape, number, and arrangement of sails and masts of a ship **2** : a carriage with its horse **3** : CLOTHING, DRESS **4** : EQUIPMENT

³rig *vb* **rigged**; **rig·ging** **1** : to manipulate or control esp. by deceptive or dishonest means **2** : to fix in advance for a desired result — **rig·ger** *n*

rig·ging \\'ri-giŋ, -gən\\ *n* **1** : the ropes and chains that hold and move masts, sails, and spars of a ship **2** : a network (as in theater scenery) used for support and manipulation

¹right \\'rīt\\ *adj* **1** : RIGHTEOUS, UPRIGHT **2** : JUST, PROPER **3** : conforming to truth or fact : CORRECT **4** : APPROPRIATE, SUITABLE **5** : STRAIGHT ⟨a ~ line⟩ **6** : GENUINE, REAL **7** : of, relating to, or being the side of the body which is away from the side on which the heart is mostly located **8** : located nearer to the right hand; *esp* : being on the right when facing in the same direction as the observer **9** : made to be placed or worn outward ⟨~ side of a rug⟩ **10** : NORMAL, SOUND ⟨not in her ~ mind⟩ ✦ *Synonyms* CORRECT, ACCURATE, EXACT, PRECISE, NICE — **right·ness** *n*

²right *n* **1** : qualities that constitute what is correct, just, proper, or honorable **2** : something (as a power or privilege) to which one has a just or lawful claim **3** : just action or decision : the cause of justice **4** : the side or part that is on or toward the right side **5** *cap* : political conservatives **6** *often cap* : a conservative position — **right·ward** \\-wərd\\ *adj or adv*

³right *adv* **1** : according to what is right ⟨live ~⟩ **2** : EXACTLY, PRECISELY ⟨~ here and now⟩ **3** : DIRECTLY ⟨went ~ home⟩ **4** : according to fact or truth ⟨guess ~⟩ **5** : all the way : COMPLETELY ⟨~ to the end⟩ **6** : IMMEDIATELY ⟨~ after lunch⟩ **7** : QUITE, VERY ⟨~ nice weather⟩ **8** : on or to the right ⟨looked ~ and left⟩

⁴right *vb* **1** : to relieve from wrong **2** : to adjust or restore to a proper state or position **3** : to bring or restore to an upright position **4** : to become upright — **right·er** *n*

right angle *n* : an angle whose measure is 90° : an angle whose sides are perpendicular to each other — **right-angled** \\'rīt-'aŋ-gəld\\ *or* **right–an·gle** \\-gəl\\ *adj*

right circular cone *n* — see CONE 2

righ·teous \\'rī-chəs\\ *adj* : acting or being in accordance with what is just, honorable, and free from guilt or wrong : UPRIGHT ✦ *Synonyms* VIRTUOUS, NOBLE, MORAL, ETHICAL — **righ·teous·ly** *adv* — **righ·teous·ness** *n*

right·ful \\'rīt-fəl\\ *adj* **1** : JUST; *also* : FITTING **2** : having or held by a legally just claim — **right·ful·ly** *adv* — **right·ful·ness** *n*

right–hand \'rīt-ˌhand\ *adj* **1** : situated on the right **2** : RIGHT-HANDED **3** : chiefly relied on ⟨his ~ man⟩
right–hand·ed \-'han-dəd\ *adj* **1** : using the right hand habitually or better than the left **2** : designed for or done with the right hand **3** : CLOCKWISE ⟨a ~ twist⟩ — **right–handed** *adv* — **right–hand·ed·ly** *adv* — **right–hand·ed·ness** *n*
right·ly \'rīt-lē\ *adv* **1** : FAIRLY, JUSTLY **2** : PROPERLY **3** : CORRECTLY, EXACTLY
right–of–way *n, pl* **rights–of–way** **1** : a legal right of passage over another person's ground **2** : the area over which a right-of-way exists **3** : the land on which a public road is built **4** : the land occupied by a railroad **5** : the land used by a public utility **6** : the right of traffic to take precedence over other traffic
right on *interj* — used to express agreement or give encouragement
right–to–life *adj* : ANTIABORTION — **right–to–lifer** *n*
right triangle *n* : a triangle having one right angle
right whale *n* : any of a family of large baleen whales having a very large head on a stocky body
rig·id \'ri-jəd\ *adj* **1** : lacking flexibility **2** : strictly observed ♦ **Synonyms** SEVERE, STERN, RIGOROUS, STRINGENT — **ri·gid·i·ty** \rə-'ji-də-tē\ *n* — **rig·id·ly** *adv*
rig·ma·role \'ri-gə-mə-ˌrōl\ *n* [alter. of obs. *ragman roll* long list, catalog] **1** : confused or senseless talk **2** : a complex and ritualistic procedure
rig·or \'ri-gər\ *n* **1** : the quality of being inflexible or unyielding : STRICTNESS **2** : HARSHNESS, SEVERITY **3** : a tremor caused by a chill **4** : strict precision : EXACTNESS — **rig·or·ous** *adj* — **rig·or·ous·ly** *adv*
rig·or mor·tis \ri-gər-'mȯr-təs\ *n* [NL, stiffness of death] : temporary rigidity of muscles occurring after death
rig·our *chiefly Brit var of* RIGOR
rile \'rī(-ə)l\ *vb* **riled; ril·ing** **1** : to make angry **2** : ROIL 1
rill \'ril\ *n* : a very small brook
¹rim \'rim\ *n* **1** : the outer part of a wheel **2** : an outer edge esp. of something curved : BORDER, MARGIN
²rim *vb* **rimmed; rim·ming** **1** : to serve as a rim for : BORDER **2** : to run around the rim of
¹rime \'rīm\ *n* : FROST 2 — **rimy** \'rī-mē\ *adj*
²rime *var of* RHYME
rind \'rīnd\ *n* : a usu. hard or tough outer layer ⟨lemon ~⟩
¹ring \'riŋ\ *n* **1** : a circular band worn as an ornament or token or used for holding or fastening ⟨wedding ~⟩ ⟨key ~⟩ **2** : something circular in shape ⟨smoke ~⟩ **3** : a place for contest or display ⟨boxing ~⟩; *also* : PRIZEFIGHTING **4** : ANNUAL RING **5** : a group of people who work together for selfish or dishonest purposes — **ringed** *adj* — **ring·like** \'riŋ-ˌlīk\ *adj*
²ring *vb* **ringed; ring·ing** \'riŋ-iŋ\ **1** : ENCIRCLE **2** : to throw a ring over (a mark) in a game (as quoits) **3** : to move in a ring or spirally
³ring *vb* **rang** \'raŋ\; **rung** \'rəŋ\; **ring·ing** \'riŋ-iŋ\ **1** : to sound resonantly when struck; *also* : to feel as if filled with such sound **2** : to cause to make a clear metallic sound by striking **3** : to announce or call by or as if by striking a bell ⟨~ an alarm⟩ **4** : to repeat loudly and persistently **5** : to summon esp. by a bell ⟨~ for the butler⟩ — **ring a bell** : to arouse a response ⟨that name *rings a bell*⟩
⁴ring *n* **1** : a set of bells **2** : the clear resonant sound of vibrating metal **3** : resonant tone : SONORITY **4** : a sound or character expressive of a particular quality **5** : an act or instance of ringing; *esp* : a telephone call
¹ring·er \'riŋ-ər\ *n* **1** : one that sounds by ringing **2** : one that enters a competition under false representations **3** : one that closely resembles another
²ringer *n* : one that encircles or puts a ring around
ring finger *n* : the third finger of the left hand counting the index finger as the first
ring·git \'riŋ-git\ *n* — see MONEY table
ring·lead·er \'riŋ-ˌlē-dər\ *n* : a leader esp. of a group of troublemakers
ring·let \-lət\ *n* : a long curl
ring·mas·ter \-ˌmas-tər\ *n* : one in charge of performances in a circus ring
ring up *vb* **1** : to total and record esp. by means of a cash register **2** : ACHIEVE ⟨*rang up* many triumphs⟩
ring·worm \'riŋ-ˌwərm\ *n* : any of several contagious skin

diseases caused by fungi and marked by ring-shaped discolored patches
rink \'riŋk\ *n* : a level extent of ice marked off for skating or various games; *also* : a similar surface (as of wood) marked off or enclosed for a sport or game ⟨roller-skating ~⟩
¹rinse \'rins\ *vb* **rinsed; rins·ing** [ME *rincen*, AF *rincer*, alter. of OF *recincier*, fr. VL **recentiare*, fr. L *recent-, recens* fresh, recent] **1** : to wash lightly or in water only **2** : to cleanse (as of soap) with clear water **3** : to treat (hair) with a rinse — **rins·er** *n*
²rinse *n* **1** : an act of rinsing **2** : a liquid used for rinsing **3** : a solution that temporarily tints hair
ri·ot \'rī-ət\ *n* **1** *archaic* : disorderly behavior **2** : disturbance of the public peace; *esp* : a violent public disorder **3** : random or disorderly profusion ⟨a ~ of color⟩ **4** : one that is wildly amusing ⟨the comedy is a ~⟩ — **riot** *vb* — **ri·ot·er** *n* — **ri·ot·ous** *adj*
¹rip \'rip\ *vb* **ripped; rip·ping** **1** : to cut or tear open **2** : to saw or split (wood) with the grain **3** : CRITICIZE, DISPARAGE — **rip·per** *n*
²rip *n* : a rent made by ripping
RIP *abbr* [L *requiescat in pace*] may he rest in peace, may she rest in peace; [L *requiescant in pace*] may they rest in peace
ri·par·i·an \rə-'per-ē-ən\ *adj* : of or relating to the bank of a stream, river, or lake ⟨~ trees⟩
rip cord *n* : a cord that is pulled to release a parachute out of its container
ripe \'rīp\ *adj* **rip·er; rip·est** **1** : fully grown and developed : MATURE ⟨~ fruit⟩ **2** : fully prepared : READY ⟨slaves ~ for a revolt⟩ — **ripe·ly** *adv* — **ripe·ness** *n*
rip·en \'rī-pən\ *vb* **rip·ened; rip·en·ing** **1** : to grow or make ripe **2** : to bring to completeness or perfection; *also* : to age or cure (cheese) to develop characteristic flavor, odor, body, texture, and color
rip–off \'rip-ˌȯf\ *n* **1** : an act of stealing : THEFT **2** : a cheap imitation — **rip off** *vb*
ri·poste \ri-'pōst\ *n* [F, modif. of It *risposta*, lit., answer] **1** : a fencer's return thrust after a parry **2** : a retaliatory maneuver or response; *esp* : a quick retort — **riposte** *vb*
ripped \'ript\ *adj* : having high muscle definition
rip·ple \'ri-pəl\ *vb* **rip·pled; rip·pling** **1** : to become lightly ruffled on the surface **2** : to make a sound like that of rippling water — **ripple** *n*
rip·saw \'rip-ˌsȯ\ *n* : a coarse-toothed saw used to cut wood in the direction of the grain
rip·stop \-ˌstäp\ *adj* : being a fabric woven in such a way that small tears do not spread ⟨~ nylon⟩ — **ripstop** *n*
¹rise \'rīz\ *vb* **rose** \'rōz\; **ris·en** \'riz-ᵊn\; **ris·ing** **1** : to get up from sitting, kneeling, or lying **2** : to get up from sleep or from one's bed **3** : to return from death **4** : to take up arms **5** : to end a session : ADJOURN **6** : to appear above the horizon **7** : to move upward : ASCEND **8** : to extend above other objects **9** : to attain a higher level or rank **10** : to increase in quantity, intensity, or pitch **11** : to come into being : HAPPEN, BEGIN, ORIGINATE
²rise *n* **1** : a spot higher than surrounding ground **2** : an upward slope **3** : an act of rising : a state of being risen **4** : BEGINNING, ORIGIN **5** : the elevation of one point above another **6** : an increase in amount, number, or volume **7** : an angry reaction
ris·er \'rī-zər\ *n* **1** : one that rises **2** : the upright part between stair treads
ris·i·bil·i·ty \ˌri-zə-'bi-lə-tē\ *n, pl* **-ties** : the ability or inclination to laugh — often used in pl.
ris·i·ble \'ri-zə-bəl\ *adj* **1** : able or inclined to laugh **2** : arousing laughter; *esp* : amusingly ridiculous
¹risk \'risk\ *n* **1** : exposure to possible loss or injury : DANGER, PERIL **2** : the chance that an investment will lose value — **risk·i·ness** \'ris-kē-nəs\ *n* — **risky** *adj*
²risk *vb* **1** : to expose to danger ⟨~ed his life⟩ **2** : to incur the danger of
ri·sot·to \ri-'sȯ-tō, -'zȯ-\ *n, pl* **-tos** : rice cooked usu. in meat or seafood stock and seasoned
ris·qué \ris-'kā\ *adj* [F] : verging on impropriety or indecency ⟨~ jokes⟩
ri·tard \ri-'tärd\ *adv or adj* : with a gradual slackening in tempo — used as a direction in music
rite \'rīt\ *n* **1** : a set form for conducting a ceremony **2** : the liturgy of a church **3** : a ceremonial act or action

rit·u·al \'ri-chǝ-wǝl\ *n* **1** : the established form esp. for a religious ceremony **2** : a system of rites **3** : a ceremonial act or action **4** : an act or series of acts regularly repeated in a precise manner — **ritual** *adj* — **rit·u·al·ism** \-wǝ-,li-zǝm\ *n* — **rit·u·al·is·tic** \,ri-chǝ-wǝ-'lis-tik\ *adj* — **rit·u·al·is·ti·cal·ly** \-ti-k(ǝ-)lē\ *adv* — **rit·u·al·ly** *adv*

ritzy \'rit-sē\ *adj* **ritz·i·er; -est** : showily elegant : POSH

riv *abbr* river

¹ri·val \'rī-vǝl\ *n* [MF or L; MF, fr. L *rivalis* one using the same stream as another, rival in love, fr. *rivalis* of a stream, fr. *rivus* stream] **1** : one of two or more trying to get what only one can have **2** : one striving for competitive advantage **3** : one that equals another esp. in desired qualities : MATCH, PEER

²rival *adj* : COMPETING

³rival *vb* **-valed** *or* **-valled; -val·ing** *or* **-val·ling** **1** : to be in competition with **2** : to try to equal or excel **3** : to have qualities that approach or equal another's

ri·val·ry \'rī-vǝl-rē\ *n, pl* **-ries** : COMPETITION

rive \'rīv\ *vb* **rived** \'rīvd\; **riv·en** \'ri-vǝn\ *also* **rived; riv·ing** **1** : SPLIT, REND **2** : SHATTER ⟨nations *riven* by war⟩

riv·er \'ri-vǝr\ *n* **1** : a natural stream larger than a brook **2** : a large stream or flow

riv·er·bank \-,baŋk\ *n* : the bank of a river

riv·er·bed \-,bed\ *n* : the channel occupied by a river

riv·er·boat \-,bōt\ *n* : a boat for use on a river

riv·er·front \-,frǝnt\ *n* : the land or area along a river

riv·er·side \-,sīd\ *n* : the side or bank of a river

¹riv·et \'ri-vǝt\ *n* : a metal bolt with a head at one end used to join parts by being put through holes in them and then being flattened on the plain end to make another head

²rivet *vb* : to fasten with or as if with a rivet — **riv·et·er** *n*

riv·u·let \'ri-vyǝ-lǝt, -vǝ-\ *n* : a small stream

ri·yal *also* **ri·al** \rē-'äl, -'al\ *n* — see MONEY table

rm *abbr* room

Rn *symbol* radon

¹RN \,är-'en\ *n* : REGISTERED NURSE

²RN *abbr* Royal Navy

RNA \,är-(,)en-'ä\ *n* : any of various nucleic acids (as messenger RNA) that are found esp. in the cytoplasm of cells, have ribose as the 5-carbon sugar, and are associated with the control of cellular chemical activities

rnd *abbr* round

¹roach \'rōch\ *n, pl* **roach** *also* **roach·es** : any of various bony fishes related to the carp; *also* : any of several sunfishes

²roach *n* **1** : COCKROACH **2** : the butt of a marijuana cigarette

road \'rōd\ *n* [ME *rode,* fr. OE *rād* ride, journey] **1** : ROADSTEAD — often used in pl. **2** : an open way for vehicles, persons, and animals : HIGHWAY **3** : a way to a conclusion or end ⟨the ~ to success⟩ **4** : a series of scheduled visits (as games or performances) in several locations or the travel necessary to make these visits ⟨the team is on the ~⟩

road·bed \'rōd-,bed\ *n* **1** : the foundation of a road or railroad **2** : the part of the surface of a road on which vehicles travel

road·block \-,bläk\ *n* **1** : a barricade on the road ⟨a police ~⟩ **2** : an obstruction to progress

road·ie \'rō-dē\ *n* : a person who works for traveling entertainers

road·kill \'rōd-,kil\ *n* **1** : the remains of an animal that has been killed on a road by a motor vehicle **2** : one that falls victim to intense competition ⟨political ~⟩

road·run·ner \-,rǝ-nǝr\ *n* : a largely terrestrial bird of the southwestern U.S. and Mexico that is a speedy runner

road·side \'rōd-,sīd\ *n* : the strip of land along a road — **roadside** *adj*

road·stead \-,sted\ *n* : an anchorage for ships usu. less sheltered than a harbor

road·ster \'rōd-stǝr\ *n* **1** : a driving horse **2** : an open automobile that seats two often with a storage compartment or rumble seat in the rear

road·way \-,wā\ *n* : ROAD; *esp* : ROADBED

road·work \-,wǝrk\ *n* **1** : work done in constructing or repairing roads **2** : conditioning for an athletic contest (as a boxing match) consisting mainly of long runs

roam \'rōm\ *vb* **1** : WANDER, ROVE **2** : to range or wander over or about **3** : to use a cell phone outside one's local calling area

¹roan \'rōn\ *adj* : of dark color (as black, red, or brown) sprinkled with white ⟨a ~ horse⟩

²roan *n* : an animal (as a horse) with a roan coat; *also* : its color

¹roar \'rȯr\ *vb* **1** : to utter a full loud prolonged sound **2** : to make a loud confused sound (as of wind or waves) — **roar·er** *n*

²roar *n* : a sound of roaring

¹roast \'rōst\ *vb* **1** : to cook by exposure to dry heat or an open flame **2** : to criticize severely or kiddingly

²roast *n* **1** : a piece of meat suitable for roasting **2** : an outing at which food is roasted ⟨corn ~⟩ **3** : severe criticism or kidding

³roast *adj* : ROASTED

roast·er \'rō-stǝr\ *n* **1** : one that roasts **2** : a device for roasting **3** : something (as a young chicken) fit for roasting

rob \'räb\ *vb* **robbed; rob·bing** **1** : to steal from **2** : to deprive of something due or expected **3** : to commit robbery — **rob·ber** *n*

robber fly *n* : any of a family of predaceous flies resembling bumblebees

rob·bery \'rä-bǝ-rē\ *n, pl* **-ber·ies** : the act or practice of robbing; *esp* : theft of something from a person by use of violence or threat

¹robe \'rōb\ *n* **1** : a long flowing outer garment; *esp* : one used for ceremonial occasions **2** : a wrap or covering for the lower body (as for sitting outdoors)

²robe *vb* **robed; rob·ing** **1** : to clothe with or as if with a robe **2** : DRESS

rob·in \'rä-bǝn\ *n* **1** : a small chiefly European thrush with a somewhat orange face and breast **2** : a large No. American thrush with a grayish back, a streaked throat, and a chiefly dull reddish breast

ro·bot \'rō-,bät, -bǝt\ *n* [Czech, fr. *robota* compulsory labor] **1** : a machine that looks and acts like a human being **2** : an efficient but insensitive person **3** : a device that automatically performs esp. repetitive tasks **4** : something guided by automatic controls — **ro·bot·ic** \rō-'bä-tik\ *adj*

ro·bot·ics \rō-'bä-tiks\ *n* : technology dealing with the design, construction, and operation of robots

ro·bust \rō-'bǝst, 'rō-(,)bǝst\ *adj* [L *robustus* oaken, strong, fr. *robur* oak, strength] **1** : strong and vigorously healthy **2** : capable of performing without failure under a wide range of conditions ⟨~ software⟩ — **ro·bust·ly** *adv* — **ro·bust·ness** *n*

ROC *abbr* Republic of China (Taiwan)

¹rock \'räk\ *vb* **1** : to move back and forth in or as if in a cradle **2** : to sway or cause to sway back and forth **3** : to arouse to excitement (as with rock music) ⟨~ed the crowd⟩ **4** *slang* : to be extremely enjoyable or effective ⟨this car ~s⟩

²rock *n* **1** : a rocking movement **2** : popular music usu. played on electric instruments and characterized by a strong beat and much repetition

³rock *n* **1** : a mass of stony material; *also* : broken pieces of stone **2** : solid mineral deposits **3** : something like a rock in firmness **4** : GEM; *esp* : DIAMOND — **rock** *adj* — **rock·like** *adj* — **rocky** *adj* — **on the rocks** **1** : in a state of ruin ⟨a marriage *on the rocks*⟩ **2** : on ice cubes ⟨bourbon *on the rocks*⟩

rock and roll *n* : ²ROCK 2

roadrunner

rock·bound \'räk-ˌbau̇nd\ *adj* : fringed or covered with rocks
rock·er \'rä-kər\ *n* **1** : one of the curved pieces on which something (as a chair or cradle) rocks **2** : a chair that rocks on rockers **3** : a device that works with a rocking motion **4** : a rock performer, song, or enthusiast
¹**rock·et** \'rä-kət\ *n* [It *rocchetta*, lit., small distaff] **1** : a firework that is propelled through the air by the discharge of gases produced by a burning substance **2** : a jet engine that operates on the same principle as a firework rocket but carries the oxygen needed for burning its fuel **3** : a rocket-propelled bomb or missile
²**rocket** *vb* **1** : to convey by means of a rocket **2** : to rise abruptly and rapidly
rock·et·ry \'rä-kə-trē\ *n* : the study or use of rockets
rocket ship *n* : a rocket-propelled spacecraft
rock·fall \'räk-ˌfȯl\ *n* : a mass of falling or fallen rocks
rock·fish \-ˌfish\ *n* : any of various bony fishes that live among rocks or on rocky bottoms
rock salt *n* : common salt in rocklike masses or large crystals
Rocky Mountain sheep *n* : BIGHORN
ro·co·co \rə-'kō-kō\ *adj* [F, irreg. fr. *rocaille* style of ornament, lit., stone debris] : of or relating to an artistic style esp. of the 18th century marked by fanciful curved forms and elaborate ornamentation — **rococo** *n*
rod \'räd\ *n* **1** : a straight slender stick **2** : a stick or bundle of twigs used in punishing a person; *also* : PUNISHMENT **3** : a staff borne to show rank **4** — see WEIGHT table **5** : any of the rod-shaped receptor cells of the retina that are sensitive to faint light **6** *slang* : HANDGUN
rode *past of* RIDE
ro·dent \'rō-d°nt\ *n* [ultim. fr. L *rodent-, rodens*, prp. of *rodere* to gnaw] : any of an order of relatively small mammals (as mice, squirrels, and beavers) with sharp front teeth used for gnawing
ro·deo \'rō-dē-ˌō, rə-'dā-ō\ *n, pl* **ro·de·os** [Sp, fr. *rodear* to surround, fr. *rueda* wheel, fr. L *rota*] **1** : ROUNDUP 1 **2** : a public performance featuring cowboy skills (as riding and roping)
¹**roe** \'rō\ *n, pl* **roe** *or* **roes** : DOE
²**roe** *n* : the eggs of a fish esp. while bound together in a mass
roe·buck \'rō-ˌbək\ *n, pl* **roebuck** *or* **roebucks** : a male roe deer
roe deer *n* : either of two small nimble European or Asian deers
roent·gen \'rent-gən, 'rənt-, -jən\ *n* : the international unit of measurement for X-rays and gamma rays
rog·er \'rä-jər\ *interj* — used esp. in radio and signaling to indicate that a message has been received and understood
¹**rogue** \'rōg\ *n* **1** : a dishonest person : SCOUNDREL **2** : a mischievous person : SCAMP — **rogu·ery** \'rō-gə-rē\ *n* — **rogu·ish** *adj* — **rogu·ish·ly** *adv* — **rogu·ish·ness** *n*
²**rogue** *adj* **1** : CORRUPT, DISHONEST ⟨~ cops⟩ **2** : of or being a nation whose leaders defy international law or norms
roil \'rȯi(-ə)l, *for 2 also* 'rī(-ə)l\ *vb* **1** : to make cloudy or muddy by stirring up **2** : RILE 1 — **roily** \'rȯi-lē\ *adj*
rois·ter \'rȯi-stər\ *vb* **rois·tered; rois·ter·ing** : to engage in noisy revelry : CAROUSE — **rois·ter·er** *n* — **rois·ter·ous** \-stə-rəs\ *adj*
ROK *abbr* Republic of Korea (South Korea)
role *also* **rôle** \'rōl\ *n* **1** : an assigned or assumed character; *also* : a part played (as by an actor) **2** : FUNCTION
role model *n* : a person whose behavior in a particular role is imitated by others
¹**roll** \'rōl\ *n* [ME *rolle* scroll, fr. AF, fr. ML *rolla*, alter. of *rotula*, fr. L, dim. of *rota* wheel] **1** : a document containing an official record **2** : an official list of names **3** : something (as a bun) that is rolled up or rounded as if rolled **4** : something that rolls : ROLLER
²**roll** *vb* **1** : to move by turning over and over ⟨~ dice⟩ ⟨~ed her eyes⟩ **2** : to press with a roller ⟨~ dough⟩ **3** : to move on wheels **4** : to sound with a full reverberating tone **5** : to make a continuous beating sound (as on a drum) **6** : to utter with a trill **7** : to move onward as if by completing a revolution ⟨years ~ed by⟩ **8** : to flow or seem to flow in a continuous stream or with a rising and falling motion ⟨the river ~ed on⟩ **9** : to swing or sway from side to side **10** : to shape or become shaped in

rounded form ⟨~ up the paper⟩ **11** : to move by or as if by turning a crank ⟨~down the window⟩
³**roll** *n* **1** : a sound produced by rapid strokes on a drum **2** : a heavy reverberating sound **3** : a rolling movement or action **4** : a swaying movement (as of a ship) **5** : a somersault made in contact with the ground
roll·back \'rōl-ˌbak\ *n* : the act or an instance of rolling back
roll back *vb* **1** : to reduce (as a commodity price) on a national scale **2** : to cause to withdraw : push back
roll bar *n* : an overhead metal bar on an automobile designed to protect riders in case the automobile overturns
roll call *n* : the act or an instance of calling off a list of names (as of soldiers); *also* : a time for a roll call
roll·er \'rō-lər\ *n* **1** : a revolving cylinder used for moving, pressing, shaping, applying, or smoothing something **2** : a rod on which something is rolled up **3** : a long heavy ocean wave
roll·er coast·er \'rō-lər-ˌkō-stər\ *n* : an amusement ride consisting of an elevated railway having sharp curves and steep slopes
roller skate *n* : a skate with wheels instead of a runner — **roller–skate** *vb* — **roller skater** *n*
rol·lick \'rä-lik\ *vb* : ROMP, FROLIC
rol·lick·ing *adj* : full of fun and good spirits ⟨a ~ good time⟩
roly–poly \ˌrō-lē-'pō-lē\ *adj* : ROTUND
Rom *abbr* **1** Roman **2** Romance **3** Romania; Romanian **4** Romans
ROM \'räm\ *n* : a computer memory that contains special-purpose information (as a program) which cannot be altered
ro·maine \rō-'mān\ *n* [F, lit., Roman] : a garden lettuce with a tall loose head of long crisp leaves
¹**Ro·man** \'rō-mən\ *n* **1** : a native or resident of Rome **2** *not cap* : roman letters or type
²**Roman** *adj* **1** : of or relating to Rome or the Romans and esp. the ancient Romans **2** *not cap* : relating to type in which the letters are upright **3** : of or relating to the Roman Catholic Church
Roman candle *n* : a cylindrical firework that discharges balls of fire
Roman Catholic *adj* : of, relating to, or being a Christian church led by the pope and having a liturgy centered in the Mass — **Roman Catholicism** *n*
¹**ro·mance** \rō-'mans, 'rō-ˌmans\ *n* [ME *romauns*, fr. AF *romanz*, something written in French, tale in verse, fr. ML *Romanice* in a vernacular language, ultim. fr. L *Romanus* Roman] **1** : a medieval tale of knightly adventure **2** : a prose narrative dealing with heroic or mysterious events set in a remote time or place **3** : a love story **4** : a romantic attachment or episode between lovers — **ro·manc·er** *n*
²**romance** *vb* **ro·manced; ro·manc·ing** **1** : to exaggerate or invent detail or incident **2** : to have romantic fancies **3** : to carry on a romantic episode with
Ro·mance \rō-'mans, 'rō-ˌmans\ *adj* : of or relating to any of several languages developed from Latin
Ro·ma·nian \ru̇-'mā-nē-ən, rō-, -nyən\ *also* **Ru·ma·nian** \ru̇-\ *n* **1** : a native or inhabitant of Romania **2** : the language of the Romanians
Roman numeral *n* : a numeral in a system of notation that is based on the ancient Roman system
Ro·ma·no \rō-'mä-nō\ *n* : a hard Italian cheese that is sharper than Parmesan
Ro·mans \'rō-mənz\ *n* — see BIBLE table
¹**ro·man·tic** \rō-'man-tik\ *adj* **1** : IMAGINARY **2** : VISIONARY **3** : having an imaginative or emotional appeal **4** : of, relating to, or having the characteristics of romanticism — **ro·man·ti·cal·ly** \-ti-k(ə-)lē\ *adv*
²**romantic** *n* : a romantic person; *esp* : a romantic writer, composer, or artist
ro·man·ti·cism \rō-'man-tə-ˌsi-zəm\ *n, often cap* : a literary movement (as in early 19th century England) marked esp. by emphasis on the imagination and the emotions and by the use of autobiographical material — **ro·man·ti·cist** \-sist\ *n, often cap*
ro·man·ti·cize \-'man-tə-ˌsīz\ *vb* **-cized; -ciz·ing** **1** : to make romantic **2** : to have romantic ideas
romp \'rämp\ *vb* **1** : to play actively and noisily **2** : to win a contest easily — **romp** *n*

romp·er \'räm-pər\ *n* **1** : one that romps **2** : a jumpsuit usu. for infants — usu. used in pl.

rood \'rüd\ *n* : CROSS, CRUCIFIX

¹roof \'rüf, 'rüf\ *n, pl* **roofs** \'rüfs, 'rüfs; 'rüvz, 'rüvz\ **1** : the upper covering part of a building **2** : something suggesting a roof of a building — **roofed** \'rüft, 'rüft\ *adj* — **roof·ing** *n* — **roof·less** *adj* — **through the roof** : to an extremely high level ⟨prices went *through the roof*⟩

²roof *vb* : to cover with a roof

roof·top \-,täp\ *n* : a roof esp. of a house

¹rook \'rük\ *n* : a common Old World bird resembling the related crow

²rook *vb* : CHEAT, SWINDLE

³rook *n* : a chess piece that can move parallel to the sides of the board across any number of unoccupied squares

rook·ery \'rü-kə-rē\ *n, pl* **-er·ies** : a breeding ground or haunt of gregarious birds or mammals; *also* : a colony of such birds or mammals

rook·ie \'rü-kē\ *n* : BEGINNER, RECRUIT; *esp* : a first-year player in a professional sport

¹room \'rüm, 'rüm\ *n* **1** : an extent of space occupied by or sufficient or available for something **2** : a partitioned part of a building : CHAMBER; *also* : the people in a room **3** : OPPORTUNITY, CHANCE ⟨∼ to develop his talents⟩ — **room·ful** *n* — **roomy** *adj*

²room *vb* : to occupy or share lodgings : LODGE — **room·er** *n*

room·ette \rü-'met, rü-\ *n* : a small private room on a railroad sleeping car

room·mate \'rüm-,māt, 'rüm-\ *n* : one of two or more persons sharing the same room or dwelling

¹roost \'rüst\ *n* : a support on which or a place where birds perch

²roost *vb* : to settle on or as if on a roost

roost·er \'rüs-tər, 'rüs-\ *n* : an adult male domestic chicken : COCK

¹root \'rüt, 'rüt\ *n* **1** : the leafless usu. underground part of a seed plant that functions in absorption, aeration, and storage or as a means of anchorage; *also* : an underground plant part esp. when fleshy and edible **2** : something (as the basal part of a tooth or hair) resembling a root **3** : SOURCE, ORIGIN; *esp* : ANCESTRY — usu. used in pl. **4** : the essential core : HEART ⟨get to the ∼ of the matter⟩ **5** : a number that when taken as a factor an indicated number of times gives a specified number **6** : the lower part — **root·less** *adj* — **root·like** *adj*

²root *vb* **1** : to form roots **2** : to fix or become fixed by or as if by roots : ESTABLISH **3** : UPROOT

³root *vb* **1** : to turn up or dig with the snout ⟨pigs ∼*ing*⟩ **2** : to poke or dig around (as in search of something)

⁴root \'rüt\ *vb* **1** : to applaud or encourage noisily : CHEER **2** : to wish success or lend support to — **root·er** *n*

root beer *n* : a sweetened carbonated beverage flavored with extracts of roots and herbs

root canal *n* : a dental operation to save a tooth by removing the pulp in the root of the tooth and filling the cavity with a protective substance

root·let \'rüt-lət, 'rüt-\ *n* : a small root

root·stock \-,stäk\ *n* : an underground part of a plant that resembles a rhizome

¹rope \'rōp\ *n* **1** : a large strong cord made of strands of fiber **2** : a hangman's noose **3** : a thick string (as of pearls) made by twisting or braiding

²rope *vb* **roped; rop·ing** **1** : to bind, tie, or fasten together with a rope **2** : to separate or divide by means of a rope **3** : LASSO

Ror·schach test \'rór-,shäk-\ *n* : a psychological test in which a subject interprets ink-blot designs in terms that reveal intellectual and emotional factors

ro·sa·ry \'rō-zə-rē\ *n, pl* **-ries** **1** *often cap* : a Roman Catholic devotion consisting of meditation on sacred mysteries during recitation of Hail Marys **2** : a string of beads used in praying

¹rose *past of* RISE

²rose \'rōz\ *n* **1** : any of a genus of usu. prickly often climbing shrubs with divided leaves and bright often fragrant flowers; *also* : one of these flowers **2** : something resembling a rose in form **3** : a moderate purplish red color — **rose** *adj*

ro·sé \rō-'zā\ *n* [F] : a light pink wine

ro·se·ate \'rō-zē-ət, -zē-,āt\ *adj* **1** : resembling a rose esp. in color **2** : OPTIMISTIC ⟨a ∼ view of the future⟩

rose·bud \'rōz-,bəd\ *n* : the flower of a rose when it is at most partly open

rose·bush \-,bush\ *n* : a shrubby rose

rose·mary \'rōz-,mer-ē\ *n, pl* **-mar·ies** [ME *rosmarine*, fr. AF *rosmarin*, fr. L *rosmarinus*, fr. *ros* dew + *marinus* of the sea, fr. *mare* sea] : a fragrant shrubby Mediterranean mint; *also* : its leaves used as a seasoning

ro·sette \rō-'zet\ *n* [F] **1** : a usu. small badge or ornament of ribbon gathered in the shape of a rose **2** : a circular ornament filled with representations of leaves

rose wa·ter \'rōz-,wò-tər, -,wä-\ *n* : a watery solution of the fragrant constituents of the rose used as a perfume

rose·wood \-,wud\ *n* : any of various tropical trees with dark red wood streaked with black; *also* : this wood

Rosh Ha·sha·nah \,räsh-hə-'shä-nə, ,rōsh-, -'shō-\ *n* [Heb *rōsh hashshānāh*, lit., beginning of the year] : the Jewish New Year observed as a religious holiday in September or October

ros·in \'rä-z²n\ *n* : a brittle resin obtained esp. from pine trees and used esp. in varnishes and on violin bows

ros·ter \'räs-tər\ *n* **1** : a list of personnel; *also* : the persons listed on a roster **2** : an itemized list

ros·trum \'räs-trəm\ *n, pl* **rostrums** *or* **ros·tra** \-trə\ [L *Rostra*, pl., a platform for speakers in the Roman Forum decorated with the beaks of captured ships, fr. pl. of *rostrum* beak, ship's beak, fr. *rodere* to gnaw] : a stage or platform for public speaking

rosy \'rō-zē\ *adj* **ros·i·er; -est** **1** : of the color rose **2** : HOPEFUL, PROMISING ⟨a ∼ outlook⟩ — **ros·i·ly** \'rō-zə-lē\ *adv* — **ros·i·ness** \-zē-nəs\ *n*

¹rot \'rät\ *vb* **rot·ted; rot·ting** : to undergo decomposition : DECAY

²rot *n* **1** : DECAY **2** : any of various diseases of plants or animals in which tissue breaks down **3** : NONSENSE

¹ro·ta·ry \'rō-tə-rē\ *adj* **1** : turning on an axis like a wheel **2** : having a rotating part ⟨a ∼ telephone⟩

²rotary *n, pl* **-ries** **1** : a rotary machine **2** : a one-way circular road junction

ro·tate \'rō-,tāt\ *vb* **ro·tat·ed; ro·tat·ing** **1** : to turn or cause to turn about an axis or a center : REVOLVE **2** : to alternate in a series ✦ **Synonyms** TURN, CIRCLE, SPIN, WHIRL, TWIRL — **ro·ta·tion** \rō-'tā-shən\ *n* — **ro·ta·tor** \'rō-,tā-tər\ *n* — **ro·ta·to·ry** \'rō-tə-,tór-ē\ *adj*

ROTC *abbr* Reserve Officers' Training Corps

rote \'rōt\ *n* **1** : repetition from memory often without attention to meaning ⟨learn by ∼⟩ **2** : mechanical or unthinking routine or repetition — **rote** *adj*

ro·tis·ser·ie \rō-'ti-sə-rē\ *n* [F] **1** : a restaurant specializing in broiled and barbecued meats **2** : an appliance fitted with a spit on which food is rotated before or over a source of heat

ro·to·gra·vure \,rō-tə-grə-'vyúr\ *n* : PHOTOGRAVURE

ro·tor \'rō-tər\ *n* **1** : a part that rotates; *esp* : the rotating part of an electrical machine **2** : a system of rotating horizontal blades for supporting a helicopter

ro·to·till·er \'rō-tō-,ti-lər\ *n* : an engine-powered machine with rotating blades used to lift and turn over soil

rot·ten \'rä-t²n\ *adj* **1** : having rotted **2** : CORRUPT **3** : extremely unpleasant or inferior — **rot·ten·ness** *n*

rot·ten·stone \'rä-t²n-,stōn\ *n* : a decomposed siliceous limestone used for polishing

rott·wei·ler \'rät-,wī-lər\ *n, often cap* : any of a breed of tall powerful black-and-tan short-haired dogs

ro·tund \rō-'tənd\ *adj* : rounded out ✦ **Synonyms** PLUMP, CHUBBY, PORTLY, STOUT — **ro·tun·di·ty** \-'tən-də-tē\ *n*

ro·tun·da \rō-'tən-də\ *n* **1** : a round building; *esp* : one covered by a dome **2** : a large round room

rouble *var of* RUBLE

roué \rü-'ā\ *n* [F, lit., broken on the wheel, fr. pp. of *rouer* to break on the wheel, fr. ML *rotare*, fr. L, to rotate; fr. the feeling that such a person deserves this punishment] : a man devoted to a life of sensual pleasure : RAKE

rouge \'rüzh, 'rüj\ *n* [F, lit., red] : a cosmetic used to give a red color to cheeks and lips — **rouge** *vb*

¹rough \'rəf\ *adj* **rough·er; rough·est** **1** : uneven in surface : not smooth **2** : SHAGGY **3** : not calm : TURBULENT, TEMPESTUOUS **4** : marked by harshness or violence **5** : DIFFICULT, TRYING **6** : coarse or rugged in character or appearance **7** : marked by lack of refinement **8** : CRUDE, UNFINISHED **9** : done or made hastily or tentatively — **rough·ly** *adv* — **rough·ness** *n*

²**rough** *n* **1** : uneven ground covered with high grass esp. along a golf fairway **2** : a crude, unfinished, or preliminary state; *also* : something in such a state **3** : ROWDY, TOUGH

³**rough** *vb* **1** : ROUGHEN **2** : MANHANDLE **3** : to make or shape roughly esp. in a preliminary way — **rough·er** *n*

rough·age \'rə-fij\ *n* : FIBER 2; *also* : food containing much indigestible material acting as fiber

rough–and–ready \,rə-fən-'re-dē\ *adj* : rude or unpolished in nature, method, or manner but effective in action or use ⟨a ∼ solution⟩

rough–and–tum·ble \-'təm-bəl\ *n* : rough unrestrained fighting or struggling — **rough–and–tumble** *adj*

rough·en \'rə-fən\ *vb* **rough·ened; rough·en·ing** : to make or become rough

rough–hewn \'rəf-'hyün\ *adj* **1** : being rough and unfinished ⟨∼ beams⟩ **2** : lacking smooth manners or social grace — **rough–hew** \-'hyü\ *vb*

rough·house \'rəf-,haus\ *vb* **rough·housed; rough·hous·ing** : to participate in rough noisy behavior — **rough·house** *n*

rough·neck \'rəf-,nek\ *n* **1** : ROWDY, TOUGH **2** : a worker on a crew drilling oil wells

rough·shod \'rəf-,shäd\ *adv* : in a roughly forceful manner ⟨rode ∼ over the opposition⟩

rou·lette \rü-'let\ *n* [F, lit., small wheel] **1** : a gambling game in which a whirling wheel is used **2** : a wheel or disk with teeth around the outside

¹**round** \'raund\ *adj* **1** : having every part of the surface or circumference the same distance from the center **2** : CYLINDRICAL **3** : COMPLETE, FULL **4** : approximately correct; *esp* : exact only to a specific decimal or place ⟨∼ numbers⟩ **5** : liberal or ample in size or amount **6** : BLUNT, OUTSPOKEN **7** : moving in or forming a circle **8** : having curves rather than angles — **round·ish** *adj* — **round·ness** *n*

²**round** *prep or adv* : AROUND

³**round** *n* **1** : something round (as a circle, globe, or ring) **2** : a curved or rounded part (as a rung of a ladder) **3** : an indirect path or course; *also* : a regularly covered route (as of a security guard) **4** : a series or cycle of recurring actions or events **5** : one shot fired by a soldier or a gun; *also* : ammunition for one shot **6** : a period of time or a unit of play in a game or contest **7** : a cut of meat (as beef) esp. between the rump and the lower leg — **in the round** **1** : FREESTANDING **2** : with a center stage surrounded by an audience ⟨theater *in the round*⟩

⁴**round** *vb* **1** : to make or become round **2** : to go or pass around or part way around **3** : COMPLETE, FINISH **4** : to become plump or shapely **5** : to express as a round number — often used with *off* **6** : to follow a winding course : BEND

¹**round·about** \'raun-də-,baut\ *adj* : INDIRECT, CIRCUITOUS

²**roundabout** *n, Brit* : MERRY-GO-ROUND

roun·de·lay \'raun-də-,lā\ *n* **1** : a simple song with a refrain **2** : a poem with a recurring refrain

round·house \'raund-,haus\ *n* **1** : a circular building for housing and repairing locomotives **2** : a blow with the hand made with a wide swing — **roundhouse** *adj*

round·ly \'raund-lē\ *adv* **1** : in a complete manner; *also* : WIDELY **2** : in a blunt way **3** : with vigor

round–rob·in \'round-,rä-bən\ *n* : a tournament in which each contestant meets every other contestant in turn

round–shoul·dered \-,shōl-dərd\ *adj* : having the shoulders stooping or rounded

round–trip *n* : a trip to a place and back

round–up \'raund-,əp\ *n* **1** : the gathering together of cattle on the range by riding around them and driving them in; *also* : the ranch hands and horses engaged in a roundup **2** : a gathering in of scattered persons or things : SUMMARY ⟨news ∼⟩ — **round up** *vb*

round·worm \-,wərm\ *n* : NEMATODE

rouse \'rauz\ *vb* **roused; rous·ing** **1** : to excite to activity : stir up **2** : to wake from sleep — **rous·er** *n*

roust·about \'raus-tə-,baut\ *n* **1** : one who does heavy unskilled labor (as on a dock or in an oil field) **2** : a laborer at a circus **3** : a person with no established home or occupation

¹**rout** \'raut\ *n* **1** : MOB 1, 2 **2** : DISTURBANCE **3** : a fashionable gathering

²**rout** *vb* **1** : RUMMAGE **2** : to gouge out **3** : to expel by force

³**rout** *n* **1** : a state of wild confusion or disorderly retreat **2** : a disastrous defeat

⁴**rout** *vb* **1** : to put to flight **2** : to defeat decisively

¹**route** \'rüt, 'raut\ *n* [ME, fr. AF *rute*, fr. VL **rupta* (*via*), lit., broken way] **1** : a traveled way **2** : CHANNEL **3** : a line of travel

²**route** *vb* **rout·ed; rout·ing** : to send by a selected route : DIRECT

route·man \-mən, -,man\ *n* : a person who sells and makes deliveries on an assigned route

rout·er \'rau-tər\ *n* : a machine with a revolving spindle and cutter for shaping a surface (as of wood)

rou·tine \rü-'tēn\ *n* [F, fr. MF, fr. *route* traveled way] **1** : a regular course of procedure **2** : an often repeated speech or formula **3** : a part fully worked out ⟨a comedy ∼⟩ **4** : a set of computer instructions that will perform a certain task — **routine** *adj* — **rou·tine·ly** *adv* — **rou·tin·ize** \-'tē-,nīz\ *vb*

¹**rove** \'rōv\ *vb* **roved; rov·ing** : to wander over or through — **rov·er** *n*

²**rove** *past and past part of* REEVE

¹**row** \'rō\ *vb* **1** : to propel a boat with oars **2** : to transport in a rowboat **3** : to pull an oar in a crew — **row·er** \'rō-ər\ *vb*

²**row** *n* : an act or instance of rowing

³**row** *n* **1** : a number of objects in an orderly sequence **2** : WAY, STREET

⁴**row** \'rau\ *n* : a noisy quarrel

⁵**row** \'rau\ *vb* : to engage in a row

row·boat \'rō-,bōt\ *n* : a small boat designed to be rowed

row·dy \'rau-dē\ *adj* **row·di·er; -est** : coarse or boisterous in behavior : ROUGH — **row·di·ness** \'rau-dē-nəs\ *n* — **rowdy** *n* — **row·dy·ish** *adj* — **row·dy·ism** *n*

row·el \'rau(-ə)l\ *n* : a small pointed wheel on a rider's spur — **rowel** *vb*

¹**roy·al** \'ròi(-ə)l\ *adj* [ME *roial*, fr. AF *real, roial*, fr. L *regalis*, fr. *reg-, rex* king] **1** : of or relating to a sovereign : REGAL **2** : fit for a king or queen ⟨a ∼ welcome⟩ — **roy·al·ly** *adv*

²**royal** *n* : a person of royal blood

royal flush *n* : a straight flush having an ace as the highest card

roy·al·ist \'ròi-ə-list\ *n* : an adherent of a king or of monarchical government

roy·al·ty \'ròi-əl-tē\ *n, pl* **-ties** **1** : the state of being royal **2** : royal persons **3** : a share of a product or profit (as of a mine or oil well) claimed by the owner for allowing another person to use the property **4** : a payment made to an author or composer for each copy of a work sold or to an inventor for each article sold under a patent

RP *abbr* **1** relief pitcher **2** Republic of the Philippines

rpm *abbr* revolutions per minute

rps *abbr* revolutions per second

rpt *abbr* **1** repeat **2** report

RR *abbr* **1** railroad **2** rural route

RS *abbr* **1** recording secretary **2** revised statutes **3** Royal Society

RSV *abbr* Revised Standard Version

RSVP *abbr* [F *répondez s'il vous plaît*] please reply

rt *abbr* **1** right **2** route

RT *abbr* round-trip

rte *abbr* route

Ru *symbol* ruthenium

¹**rub** \'rəb\ *vb* **rubbed; rub·bing** **1** : to use pressure and friction on a body or object **2** : to fret or chafe with friction **3** : to scour, polish, erase, or smear by pressure and friction

²**rub** *n* **1** : DIFFICULTY, OBSTRUCTION **2** : something grating to the feelings

¹**rub·ber** \'rə-bər\ *n* **1** : one that rubs **2** : ERASER **3** : a flexible waterproof elastic substance made from the milky juice of various tropical plants or made synthetically; *also* : something made of this material **4** : CONDOM — **rubber** *adj* — **rub·ber·ize** \'rə-bə-,rīz\ *vb* — **rub·bery** *adj*

²**rubber** *n* **1** : a contest that consists of an odd number of games and is won by the side that takes a majority **2** : an extra game played to decide a tie

¹**rub·ber·neck** \-ˌnek\ *n* **1** : an idly or overly inquisitive person **2** : a person on a guided tour

²**rubberneck** *vb* : to look about, stare, or listen with excessive curiosity ⟨∼*ing* drivers⟩ — **rub·ber·neck·er** *n*

rub·bish \'rə-bish\ *n* **1** : useless waste or rejected matter : TRASH **2** : something worthless or nonsensical

rub·ble \'rə-bəl\ *n* : broken fragments esp. of a destroyed building

ru·bel·la \rü-'be-lə\ *n* : GERMAN MEASLES

ru·bi·cund \'rü-bi-(ˌ)kənd\ *adj* : RED, RUDDY

ru·bid·i·um \rü-'bi-dē-əm\ *n* : a soft silvery metallic chemical element

ru·ble *also* **rou·ble** \'rü-bəl\ *n* — see MONEY table

ru·bric \'rü-brik\ *n* [ME *rubrike* red ocher, heading in red letters of part of a book, fr. AF, fr. L *rubrica*, fr. *ruber* red] **1** : HEADING, TITLE; *also* : CLASS, CATEGORY **2** : a rule esp. for the conduct of a religious service

ru·by \'rü-bē\ *n, pl* **rubies** : a clear red precious stone — **ruby** *adj*

ru·by–throat·ed hummingbird \'rü-bē-ˌthrō-təd-\ *n* : a bright green and whitish hummingbird of eastern No. America with a red throat in the male

ruck·us \'rə-kəs\ *n* : ROW, DISTURBANCE

rud·der \'rə-dər\ *n* : a movable flat piece attached at the rear of a ship or aircraft for steering

rud·dy \'rə-dē\ *adj* **rud·di·er; -est** : REDDISH; *esp* : of a healthy reddish complexion — **rud·di·ness** \'rə-dē-nəs\ *n*

rude \'rüd\ *adj* **rud·er; rud·est** **1** : roughly made : CRUDE **2** : UNDEVELOPED, PRIMITIVE **3** : IMPOLITE **4** : UNSKILLED — **rude·ly** *adv* — **rude·ness** *n*

ru·di·ment \'rü-də-mənt\ *n* **1** : an elementary principle or basic skill — usu. used in pl. ⟨the ∼*s* of mathematics⟩ **2** : something not fully developed — usu. used in pl. ⟨the ∼*s* of a plan⟩ — **ru·di·men·ta·ry** \ˌrü-də-'men-tə-rē\ *adj*

¹**rue** \'rü\ *n* : REGRET, SORROW — **rue·ful** \-fəl\ *adj* — **rue·ful·ly** *adv* — **rue·ful·ness** *n*

²**rue** *vb* **rued; ru·ing** : to feel regret, remorse, or penitence for

³**rue** *n* : a European strong-scented woody herb with bitter-tasting leaves

ruff \'rəf\ *n* **1** : a large round pleated collar worn about 1600 **2** : a fringe of long hair or feathers around the neck of an animal — **ruffed** \'rəft\ *adj*

ruf·fi·an \'rə-fē-ən\ *n* : a brutal person — **ruf·fi·an·ly** *adj*

¹**ruf·fle** \'rə-fəl\ *vb* **ruf·fled; ruf·fling** **1** : to roughen the surface of **2** : IRRITATE, VEX **3** : to erect (as hair or feathers) in or like a ruff **4** : to flip through (as pages) **5** : to draw into or provide with plaits or folds

²**ruffle** *n* **1** : a strip of fabric gathered or pleated on one edge **2** : RUFF **2 3** : RIPPLE — **ruf·fly** \'rə-fə-lē, -flē\ *adj*

ru·fi·yaa \'rü-fē-ˌyä\ *n, pl* **rufiyaa** — see MONEY table

RU–486 \'är-ˌyü-ˌfȯr-ˌā-tē-'siks\ *n* : a drug taken orally to induce abortion esp. early in pregnancy

rug \'rəg\ *n* **1** : a covering for the legs, lap, and feet **2** : a piece of heavy fabric usu. with a nap or pile used as a floor covering

rug·by \'rəg-bē\ *n, often cap* [*Rugby* School, Rugby, England, where it was first played] : a football game in which play is continuous and interference and forward passing are not permitted

rug·ged \'rə-gəd\ *adj* **1** : having a rough uneven surface **2** : TURBULENT, STORMY **3** : HARSH, STERN **4** : ROBUST, STURDY — **rug·ged·ize** \'rə-gə-ˌdīz\ *vb* — **rug·ged·ly** *adv* — **rug·ged·ness** *n*

¹**ru·in** \'rü-ən\ *n* **1** : complete collapse or destruction **2** : the remains of something destroyed — usu. used in pl. **3** : a cause of destruction **4** : the action of destroying

²**ruin** *vb* **1** : DESTROY **2** : to damage beyond repair **3** : BANKRUPT

ru·in·ation \ˌrü-ə-'nā-shən\ *n* : RUIN, DESTRUCTION

ru·in·ous \'rü-ə-nəs\ *adj* **1** : RUINED, DILAPIDATED **2** : causing ruin — **ru·in·ous·ly** *adv*

¹**rule** \'rül\ *n* [ME *reule*, fr. AF, fr. L *regula* straightedge, rule, fr. *regere* to keep straight, direct] **1** : a guide or principle for governing action : REGULATION **2** : the usual way of doing something **3** : the exercise of authority or control : GOVERNMENT **4** : RULER 2

²**rule** *vb* **ruled; rul·ing** **1** : CONTROL; *also* : GOVERN **2** : to be supreme or outstanding in **3** : to give or state as a considered decision **4** : to mark on paper with or as if with a ruler **5** *slang* : to be extremely cool or popular

rul·er \'rü-lər\ *n* **1** : SOVEREIGN **2** : a straight strip of material (as wood or metal) marked off in units and used for measuring or as a straightedge

rum \'rəm\ *n* **1** : an alcoholic liquor made from sugarcane products (as molasses) **2** : alcoholic liquor

Ru·ma·nian *var of* ROMANIAN

rum·ba \'rəm-bə, 'rùm-\ *n* : a dance of Cuban origin marked by strong rhythmic movements

¹**rum·ble** \'rəm-bəl\ *vb* **rum·bled; rum·bling** : to make a low heavy rolling sound; *also* : to move along with such a sound — **rum·bler** *n*

²**rumble** *n* **1** : a low heavy rolling sound **2** : a street fight esp. among gangs

rumble seat *n* : a folding seat in the back of an automobile that is not covered by the top

rum·bling \'rəm-bliŋ\ *n* **1** : RUMBLE **2** : widespread talk or complaints — usu. used in pl.

ru·men \'rü-mən\ *n, pl* **ru·mi·na** \-mə-nə\ *or* **rumens** : the large first compartment of the stomach of a ruminant (as a cow)

¹**ru·mi·nant** \'rü-mə-nənt\ *n* : a ruminant mammal

²**ruminant** *adj* **1** : chewing the cud; *also* : of or relating to a group of hoofed mammals (as cattle, deer, and camels) that chew the cud and have a complex 3- or 4-chambered stomach **2** : MEDITATIVE

ru·mi·nate \'rü-mə-ˌnāt\ *vb* **-nat·ed; -nat·ing** [L *ruminari* to chew the cud, muse upon, fr. *rumin-, rumen* first stomach chamber of a ruminant] **1** : MEDITATE, MUSE **2** : to chew the cud — **ru·mi·na·tion** \ˌrü-mə-'nā-shən\ *n*

¹**rum·mage** \'rə-mij\ *vb* **rum·maged; rum·mag·ing** : to search thoroughly — **rum·mag·er** *n*

²**rummage** *n* **1** : a miscellaneous collection **2** : an act of rummaging

rum·my \'rə-mē\ *n* : any of several card games for two or more players

ru·mor \'rü-mər\ *n* **1** : common talk **2** : a statement or report current but not authenticated — **rumor** *vb*

ru·mour *chiefly Brit var of* RUMOR

rump \'rəmp\ *n* **1** : the rear part of an animal; *also* : a cut of meat (as beef) behind the upper sirloin **2** : a small or inferior remnant (as of a group)

rum·ple \'rəm-pəl\ *vb* **rum·pled; rum·pling** : TOUSLE, MUSS, WRINKLE — **rumple** *n* — **rum·ply** \'rəm-pə-lē\ *adj*

rum·pus \'rəm-pəs\ *n* : DISTURBANCE, RUCKUS

rumpus room *n* : a room usu. in the basement of a home that is used for games, parties, and recreation

¹**run** \'rən\ *vb* **ran** \'ran\; **run; run·ning** **1** : to go faster than a walk **2** : to take to flight : FLEE **3** : to go without restraint ⟨let chickens ∼ loose⟩ **4** : to go rapidly or hurriedly : HASTEN, RUSH **5** : to make a quick or casual trip or visit **6** : to contend in a race; *esp* : to enter an election ⟨∼ for mayor⟩ **7** : to put forward as a candidate for office **8** : to move on or as if on wheels : pass or slide freely **9** : to go back and forth : PLY **10** : to move in large numbers esp. to a spawning ground ⟨shad are *running*⟩ **11** : FUNCTION, OPERATE ⟨∼*s* on gasoline⟩ ⟨software that ∼*s* on her computer⟩ **12** : to continue in force ⟨two years to ∼⟩ **13** : to flow rapidly or under pressure : MELT, FUSE, DISSOLVE; *also* : DISCHARGE **7** ⟨my nose is *running*⟩ **14** : to tend to produce or to recur ⟨family ∼*s* to blonds⟩ ⟨stubbornness ∼*s* in the family⟩ **15** : to take a certain direction **16** : to be worded or written **17** : to be current ⟨rumors *running* wild⟩ **18** : to cause to produce a flow ⟨*ran* the faucet⟩ **19** : TRACE ⟨∼ down a rumor⟩ **20** : to perform or bring about by running **21** : to cause to pass ⟨∼ a wire from the antenna⟩ **22** : to cause to collide **23** : SMUGGLE **24** : MANAGE, CONDUCT, OPERATE ⟨∼ a business⟩ **25** : INCUR ⟨∼ a risk⟩ **26** : to permit to accumulate before settling ⟨∼ up a bill⟩ **27** : PRINT, PUBLISH ⟨∼ a news story⟩

²**run** *n* **1** : an act or the action of running **2** : a migration of fish; *also* : the migrating fish **3** : a score in baseball **4** : BROOK, CREEK **5** : a continuous series esp. of similar things **6** : persistent heavy demands from depositors, creditors, or customers **7** : the quantity of work turned out in a continuous operation; *also* : a period of operation (as of a machine or plant) **8** : the usual or normal kind ⟨the ordinary ∼ of students⟩ **9** : the distance covered in continuous travel or sailing **10** : a regular course or trip **11** : freedom of movement in a place or area ⟨has the ∼ of the house⟩ **12** : an enclosure for animals **13** : an in-

clined course (as for skiing)   **14** : a lengthwise ravel (as in a stocking) — **run·less** *adj*

run·about \\'rə-nə-ˌbau̇t\\ *n* : a light wagon, automobile, or motorboat

run·a·gate \\'rə-nə-ˌgāt\\ *n*   **1** : VAGABOND   **2** : FUGITIVE

run·around \\'rə-nə-ˌrau̇nd\\ *n* : evasive or delaying action esp. in response to a request

¹**run·away** \\'rə-nə-ˌwā\\ *n*   **1** : one that runs away : FUGITIVE   **2** : the act of running away out of control; *also* : something (as a horse) that is running out of control

²**runaway** *adj*   **1** : FUGITIVE   **2** : won by a long lead; *also* : extremely successful   **3** : subject to uncontrolled changes ⟨∼ inflation⟩   **4** : operating out of control ⟨a ∼ locomotive⟩

run·down \\'rən-ˌdau̇n\\ *n* : an item-by-item report or review : SUMMARY

run–down \\'rən-'dau̇n\\ *adj*   **1** : EXHAUSTED, WORN-OUT ⟨that ∼ feeling⟩   **2** : being in poor repair ⟨a ∼ farm⟩

run down *vb*   **1** : to collide with and knock down   **2** : to chase until exhausted or captured   **3** : to find by search   **4** : DISPARAGE   **5** : to cease to operate for lack of motive power   **6** : to decline in physical condition

rune \\'rün\\ *n*   **1** : any of the characters of any of several alphabets formerly used by the Germanic peoples   **2** : MYSTERY, MAGIC   **3** : a poem esp. in Finnish or Old Norse — **ru·nic** \\'rü-nik\\ *adj*

rune 1

¹**rung** *past part of* RING

²**rung** \\'rəŋ\\ *n*   **1** : a rounded crosspiece between the legs of a chair   **2** : one of the crosspieces of a ladder

run–in \\'rən-ˌin\\ *n*   **1** : ALTERCATION, QUARREL   **2** : something run in

run in *vb*   **1** : to insert as additional matter   **2** : to arrest esp. for a minor offense   **3** : to pay a casual visit

run·nel \\'rə-nᵊl\\ *n* : BROOK, STREAMLET

run·ner \\'rə-nər\\ *n*   **1** : one that runs   **2** : BASE RUNNER   **3** : BALLCARRIER   **4** : a thin piece or part on which something (as a sled or an ice skate) slides   **5** : the support of a drawer or a sliding door   **6** : a horizontal branch from the base of a plant that produces new plants   **7** : a plant producing runners   **8** : a long narrow carpet   **9** : a narrow decorative cloth cover for a table or dresser top

run·ner–up \\'rə-nər-ˌəp\\ *n, pl* **runners–up** *also* **runner–ups** : the competitor in a contest who finishes second

¹**run·ning** *adj*   **1** : FLOWING   **2** : FLUID, RUNNY   **3** : CONTINUOUS, INCESSANT   **4** : measured in a straight line ⟨cost per ∼ foot⟩   **5** : of or relating to an act of running   **6** : made or trained for running ⟨∼ horse⟩ ⟨∼ shoes⟩

²**running** *adv* : in succession

running light *n* : any of the lights carried by a vehicle (as a ship) at night

run·ny \\'rə-nē\\ *adj* : having a tendency to run ⟨a ∼ dough⟩ ⟨a ∼ nose⟩

run–off \\'rən-ˌȯf\\ *n* : a final contest (as an election) to decide a previous indecisive contest

run–of–the–mill *adj* : not outstanding : AVERAGE

run on *vb*   **1** : to talk at length   **2** : to continue (matter in type) without a break or a new paragraph   **3** : to place or add (as an entry in a dictionary) at the end of a paragraphed item — **run–on** \\'rən-ˌȯn, -ˌän\\ *n*

run out *vb* : to use up or exhaust a supply ⟨*ran out of* gas⟩

runt \\'rənt\\ *n* : an unusually small person or animal : DWARF — **runty** *adj*

run·way \\'rən-ˌwā\\ *n*   **1** : a beaten path made by animals; *also* : a passage for animals   **2** : a paved strip of ground for the landing and takeoff of aircraft   **3** : a narrow plat-

form from a stage into an auditorium   **4** : a support (as a track) on which something runs

ru·pee \\rü-'pē, 'rü-ˌpē\\ *n* — see MONEY table

ru·pi·ah \\rü-'pē-ə\\ *n, pl* **rupiah** *or* **rupiahs** — see MONEY table

¹**rup·ture** \\'rəp-chər\\ *n* : a breaking or tearing apart; *also* : HERNIA

²**rupture** *vb* **rup·tured; rup·tur·ing** : to cause or undergo rupture

ru·ral \\'ru̇r-əl\\ *adj* : of or relating to the country, country people, or agriculture

ruse \\'rüs, 'rüz\\ *n* : a wily subterfuge : TRICK, ARTIFICE

¹**rush** \\'rəsh\\ *n* : any of various often tufted and hollow-stemmed grasslike marsh plants — **rushy** *adj*

²**rush** *vb* [ME *russhen*, fr. AF *reuser, ruser, russher* to drive back, repulse, fr. L *recusare* to oppose]   **1** : to move forward or act with too great haste or eagerness or without preparation   **2** : to perform in a short time or at high speed   **3** : ATTACK, CHARGE   **4** : to advance a football by running — **rush·er** *n*

³**rush** *n*   **1** : a violent forward motion   **2** : unusual demand or activity   **3** : a crowding of people to one place   **4** : a running play in football   **5** : a sudden feeling of pleasure

⁴**rush** *adj* : requiring or marked by special speed or urgency ⟨∼ orders⟩

rush hour *n* : a time when the amount of traffic or business is at a peak

rusk \\'rəsk\\ *n* : a sweet or plain bread baked, sliced, and baked again until dry and crisp

rus·set \\'rə-sət\\ *n*   **1** : a coarse reddish brown cloth   **2** : a reddish brown   **3** : a baking potato — **russet** *adj*

Rus·sian \\'rə-shən\\ *n*   **1** : a native or inhabitant of Russia   **2** : a Slavic language of the Russian people — **Russian** *adj*

rust \\'rəst\\ *n*   **1** : a reddish coating formed on iron when it is exposed to usu. moist air   **2** : any of numerous plant diseases characterized by usu. reddish spots; *also* : a fungus causing rust   **3** : a strong reddish brown — **rust** *vb* — **rusty** *adj*

¹**rus·tic** \\'rəs-tik\\ *adj* : of, relating to, or suitable for the country or country people — **rus·ti·cal·ly** \\-ti-k(ə-)lē\\ *adv* — **rus·tic·i·ty** \\ˌrəs-'ti-sə-tē\\ *n*

²**rustic** *n* : a rustic person

rus·ti·cate \\'rəs-ti-ˌkāt\\ *vb* **-cat·ed; -cat·ing** : to go into or reside in the country — **rus·ti·ca·tion** \\ˌrəs-ti-'kā-shən\\ *n*

¹**rus·tle** \\'rə-səl\\ *vb* **rus·tled; rus·tling**   **1** : to make or cause a rustle   **2** : to cause to rustle ⟨∼ a newspaper⟩   **3** : to act or move with energy or speed; *also* : to procure in this way   **4** : to forage food   **5** : to steal cattle from the range — **rus·tler** *n*

²**rustle** *n* : a quick series of small sounds ⟨∼ of leaves⟩

¹**rut** \\'rət\\ *n* : state or period of sexual excitement esp. in male deer — **rut** *vb*

²**rut** *n*   **1** : a track worn by wheels or by habitual passage of something   **2** : a usual or fixed routine

ru·ta·ba·ga \\ˌrü-tə-'bā-gə, ˌrü-\\ *n* : a turnip with a large yellowish root

Ruth \\'rüth\\ *n* — see BIBLE table

ru·the·ni·um \\rü-'thē-nē-əm\\ *n* : a rare hard metallic chemical element

ruth·er·ford·ium \\ˌrə-thər-'fȯr-dē-əm\\ *n* : an artifically produced radioactive chemical element

ruth·less \\'rüth-ləs\\ *adj* [fr. *ruth* compassion, pity, fr. ME *ruthe*, fr. *ruen* to rue, fr. OE *hrēowan*] : having no pity : MERCILESS, CRUEL ⟨a ∼ tyrant⟩ — **ruth·less·ly** *adv* — **ruth·less·ness** *n*

¹**RV** \\ˌär-'vē\\ *n* : RECREATIONAL VEHICLE

²**RV** *abbr* Revised Version

R–value \\'är-ˌval-yü\\ *n* : a measure of resistance to the flow of heat through a substance (as insulation)

RW *abbr*   **1** right worshipful   **2** right worthy

rwy *or* **ry** *abbr* railway

-ry *n suffix* : -ERY ⟨bigotry⟩

rye \\'rī\\ *n*   **1** : a hardy annual grass grown for grain or as a cover crop; *also* : its seed   **2** : a whiskey distilled from a rye mash

S

¹**s** \'es\ *n, pl* **s's** *or* **ss** \'e-səz\ *often cap* : the 19th letter of the English alphabet

²**s** *abbr, often cap* **1** saint **2** second **3** senate **4** series **5** shilling **6** singular **7** small **8** son **9** south; southern

¹**-s** \s *after sounds* f, k, k, p, t, th; əz *after sounds* ch, j, s, sh, z, zh; z *after other sounds*\ *n pl suffix* — used to form the plural of most nouns that do not end in *s, z, sh,* or *ch* or *y* following a consonant ⟨head*s*⟩ ⟨book*s*⟩ ⟨boy*s*⟩ ⟨belief*s*⟩, to form the plural of proper nouns that end in *y* following a consonant ⟨Mary*s*⟩, and with or without a preceding apostrophe to form the plural of abbreviations, numbers, letters, and symbols used as nouns ⟨MC*s*⟩ ⟨4*s*⟩ ⟨#*s*⟩ ⟨B's⟩

²**-s** *adv suffix* — used to form adverbs denoting usual or repeated action or state ⟨work*s* nights⟩

³**-s** *vb suffix* — used to form the third person singular present of most verbs that do not end in *s, z, sh,* or *ch* or *y* following a consonant ⟨fall*s*⟩ ⟨take*s*⟩ ⟨play*s*⟩

S *symbol* sulfur

SA *abbr* **1** Salvation Army **2** seaman apprentice **3** sex appeal **4** [L *sine anno* without year] without date **5** South Africa **6** South America **7** subject to approval

Saami *var of* SAMI

Sab·bath \'sa-bəth\ *n* [ME *sabat,* fr. AF & OE, fr. L *sabbatum,* fr. Gk *sabbaton,* fr. Heb *shabbāth,* lit., rest] **1** : the 7th day of the week observed as a day of worship by Jews and some Christians **2** : Sunday observed among Christians as a day of worship

sab·bat·i·cal \sə-'ba-ti-kəl\ *n* : a leave often with pay granted (as to a college professor) usu. every 7th year for rest, travel, or research

sa·ber *or* **sa·bre** \'sā-bər\ *n* [F *sabre*] : a cavalry sword with a curved blade and thick back

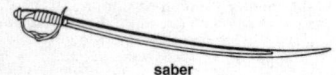

saber

saber saw *n* : a portable electric saw with a pointed reciprocating blade; *esp* : JIGSAW

sa·ble \'sā-bəl\ *n, pl* **sables** **1** : the color black **2** *pl* : mourning garments **3** : a dark brown mammal chiefly of northern Asia related to the weasels; *also* : its fur or pelt

¹**sab·o·tage** \'sa-bə-ˌtäzh\ *n* [F] **1** : deliberate destruction of an employer's property or hindering of production by workers **2** : destructive or hampering action by enemy agents or sympathizers in time of war

²**sabotage** *vb* **-taged; -tag·ing** : to practice sabotage on : WRECK

sab·o·teur \ˌsa-bə-'tər\ *n* : a person who practices sabotage

sac \'sak\ *n* : a pouch in an animal or plant often containing a fluid

SAC *abbr* Strategic Air Command

sac·cha·rin \'sa-kə-rən\ *n* : a white crystalline compound used as an artificial calorie-free sweetener

sac·cha·rine \'sa-kə-rən\ *adj* : nauseatingly sweet ⟨∼ poetry⟩

sac·er·do·tal \ˌsa-sər-'dō-t³l, -kər-\ *adj* : PRIESTLY

sac·er·do·tal·ism \-t³-ˌli-zəm\ *n* : a religious belief emphasizing the powers of priests as essential mediators between God and man

sa·chem \'sā-chəm\ *n* [Narragansett *sâchim*] : a No. American Indian chief

sa·chet \sa-'shā\ *n* [MF, fr. OF, dim. of *sac* bag] : a small bag filled with perfumed powder for scenting clothes

¹**sack** \'sak\ *n* **1** : a usu. rectangular-shaped bag (as of paper or burlap) **2** : a loose jacket or short coat

²**sack** *vb* : DISMISS, FIRE

³**sack** *n* [modif. of MF *sec* dry, fr. L *siccus*] : a white wine popular in England in the 16th and 17th centuries

⁴**sack** *vb* : to plunder a captured town

sack·cloth \-ˌklóth\ *n* : a rough garment worn as a sign of penitence

sac·ra·ment \'sa-krə-mənt\ *n* **1** : a formal religious act or rite; *esp* : one (as baptism or the Eucharist) held to have been instituted by Christ **2** : the elements of the Eucharist — **sac·ra·men·tal** \ˌsa-krə-'men-t³l\ *adj*

sa·cred \'sā-krəd\ *adj* **1** : set apart for the service or worship of deity **2** : devoted exclusively to one service or use **3** : worthy of veneration or reverence **4** : of or relating to religion : RELIGIOUS ✦ *Synonyms* BLESSED, DIVINE, HALLOWED, HOLY, SANCTIFIED — **sa·cred·ly** *adv* — **sa·cred·ness** *n*

sacred cow *n* : one that is often unreasonably immune from criticism

¹**sac·ri·fice** \'sa-krə-ˌfīs\ *n* **1** : the offering of something precious to deity **2** : something offered in sacrifice **3** : LOSS, DEPRIVATION **4** : a bunt allowing a base runner to advance while the batter is put out; *also* : a fly ball allowing a runner to score after the catch — **sac·ri·fi·cial** \ˌsa-krə-'fi-shəl\ *adj* — **sac·ri·fi·cial·ly** *adv*

²**sac·ri·fice** *vb* **-ficed; -fic·ing** **1** : to offer up or kill as a sacrifice **2** : to accept the loss or destruction of for an end, cause, or ideal **3** : to make a sacrifice in baseball

sac·ri·lege \'sa-krə-lij\ *n* [ME, fr. AF, fr. L *sacrilegium,* fr. *sacrilegus* one who robs sacred property fr. *sacr-, sacer* sacred + *legere* to gather, steal] **1** : violation of something consecrated to God **2** : gross irreverence toward a hallowed person, place, or thing — **sac·ri·le·gious** \ˌsa-krə-'li-jəs, -'lē-\ *adj* — **sac·ri·le·gious·ly** *adv*

sac·ris·tan \'sa-krə-stən\ *n* **1** : a church officer in charge of the sacristy **2** : SEXTON

sac·ris·ty \'sa-krə-stē\ *n, pl* **-ties** : VESTRY

sac·ro·il·i·ac \ˌsa-krō-'i-lē-ˌak\ *n* : the joint between the upper part of the hipbone and the sacrum

sac·ro·sanct \'sa-krō-ˌsaŋkt\ *adj* : SACRED, INVIOLABLE

sa·crum \'sa-krəm, 'sā-\ *n, pl* **sa·cra** \'sa-krə, 'sā-\ : the part of the vertebral column that is directly connected with or forms a part of the pelvis and in humans consists of five fused vertebrae

sad \'sad\ *adj* **sad·der; sad·dest** **1** : GRIEVING, MOURNFUL, DOWNCAST **2** : causing sorrow **3** : DULL, SOMBER — **sad·ly** *adv* — **sad·ness** *n*

sad·den \'sa-d³n\ *vb* : to make sad

¹**sad·dle** \'sa-d³l\ *n* : a usu. padded leather-covered seat (as for a rider on horseback)

²**saddle** *vb* **sad·dled; sad·dling** **1** : to put a saddle on **2** : OPPRESS, BURDEN

sad·dle·bow \'sa-d³l-ˌbō\ *n* : the arch in the front of a saddle

saddle horse *n* : a horse suited for or trained for riding

Sad·du·cee \'sa-jə-ˌsē, 'sa-dyə-\ *n* : a member of an ancient Jewish sect consisting of a ruling class of priests and rejecting certain doctrines — **Sad·du·ce·an** \ˌsa-jə-'sē-ən, ˌsa-dyə-\ *adj*

sad·iron \'sa-ˌdi-ərn\ *n* : a flatiron with a removable handle

sa·dism \'sā-ˌdi-zəm, 'sa-\ *n* : a sexual perversion in which gratification is obtained by inflicting physical or mental pain on others — **sa·dist** \'sā-dist, 'sa-\ *n* — **sa·dis·tic** \sə-'dis-tik\ *adj* — **sa·dis·ti·cal·ly** \-ti-k(ə-)lē\ *adv*

sa·do·mas·och·ism \ˌsā-(ˌ)dō-'ma-sə-ˌki-zəm, ˌsa-, -'ma-zə-\ *n* : the derivation of pleasure from the infliction of physical or mental pain either on others or on oneself — **sa·do·mas·och·is·tic** \-ˌma-sə-'kis-tik, -ˌma-zə-\ *adj*

SAE *abbr* **1** self-addressed envelope **2** Society of Automotive Engineers **3** stamped addressed envelope

sa·fa·ri \sə-'fär-ē\ *n* [Swahili, trip, fr. Ar *safarī* of a trip] **1** : a hunting expedition esp. in eastern Africa **2** : JOURNEY, TRIP

¹**safe** \'sāf\ *adj* **saf·er; saf·est** **1** : free from harm or risk **2** : affording safety; *also* : secure from danger or loss **3** : RELIABLE — **safe·ly** *adv*

²**safe** *n* : a container for keeping articles (as valuables) safe

safe–con·duct \-'kän-(,)dəkt\ *n* : a pass permitting a person to go through enemy lines

¹**safe·guard** \-,gärd\ *n* : a measure or device for preventing accident

²**safeguard** *vb* : to provide a safeguard for : PROTECT

safe·keep·ing \'sāf-'kē-piŋ\ *n* : a keeping or being kept in safety

safer sex *n* : SAFE SEX

safe sex *n* : sexual activity and esp. sexual intercourse in which various measures (as the use of latex condoms) are taken to avoid disease (as AIDS) transmitted by sexual contact

safe·ty \'sāf-tē\ *n, pl* **safeties** **1** : freedom from danger : SECURITY **2** : a protective device **3** : a football play in which the ball is downed by the offensive team behind its own goal line **4** : a defensive football back in the deepest position — **safety** *adj*

safety glass *n* : shatter-resistant material formed of two sheets of glass with a sheet of clear plastic between them

safety match *n* : a match that ignites only when struck on a special surface

saf·flow·er \'sa-,flau̇(-ə)r\ *n* : a widely grown Old World herb related to the daisies that has large orange or red flower heads yielding a dyestuff and seeds rich in edible oil

saf·fron \'sa-frən\ *n* : a deep orange powder from the flower of a crocus used to color and flavor foods

sag \'sag\ *vb* **sagged; sag·ging** **1** : to droop or settle from or as if from pressure **2** : to lose firmness or vigor — **sag** *n*

sa·ga \'sä-gə\ *n* [ON] : a narrative of heroic deeds; *esp* : one recorded in Iceland in the 12th and 13th centuries

sa·ga·cious \sə-'gā-shəs\ *adj* : of keen mind : SHREWD — **sa·gac·i·ty** \-'ga-sə-tē\ *n*

sag·a·more \'sa-gə-,mȯr\ *n* : a subordinate No. American Indian chief

¹**sage** \'sāj\ *adj* [ME, fr. AF, fr. VL *sapius*, fr. L *sapere* to taste, have good taste, be wise] : WISE, PRUDENT — **sage·ly** *adv*

²**sage** *n* : one who is distinguished for wisdom

³**sage** *n* [ME, fr. AF *sage, salge*, fr. L *salvia*, fr. *salvus* healthy; fr. its use as a medicinal herb] **1** : a perennial mint with aromatic leaves used in flavoring; *also* : its leaves **2** : SAGEBRUSH **3** : a light grayish green

sage·brush \'sāj-,brəsh\ *n* : any of several low shrubby No. American composite plants; *esp* : one of the western U.S. with a sagelike odor

Sag·it·tar·i·us \,sa-jə-'ter-ē-əs\ *n* [L, lit., archer] **1** : a zodiacal constellation between Scorpio and Capricorn usu. pictured as a centaur archer **2** : the 9th sign of the zodiac in astrology; *also* : one born under this sign

sa·go \'sā-gō\ *n, pl* **sagos** : a dry granulated starch esp. from the pith of various tropical palms (**sago palm**)

sa·gua·ro \sə-'wär-ə, -'gwär-, -ō\ *n, pl* **-ros** [MexSp] : a tall columnar usu. sparsely-branched cactus of dry areas of the southwestern U.S. and Mexico that may attain a height of up to 50 feet (16 meters)

said *past and past part of* SAY

¹**sail** \'sāl\ *n* **1** : a piece of fabric by means of which the wind is used to propel a ship **2** : a sailing ship **3** : something resembling a sail **4** : a trip on a sailboat

²**sail** *vb* **1** : to travel on a sailing ship **2** : to pass over in a ship **3** : to manage or direct the course of a ship **4** : to move with ease, grace, or nonchalance

sail·board \'sāl-,bȯrd\ *n* : a modified surfboard having a mast and sailed by a standing person

sail·boat \-,bōt\ *n* : a boat propelled primarily by sail

sail·cloth \-,klȯth\ *n* : a heavy canvas used for sails, tents, or upholstery

sail·fish \-,fish\ *n* : any of a genus of large marine bony fishes with a large dorsal fin that are related to marlins

sail·ing *n* : the sport of handling or riding in a sailboat

sail·or \'sā-lər\ *n* : one that sails; *esp* : a member of a ship's crew

sail·plane \'sāl-,plān\ *n* : a glider designed to rise in an upward air current

saint \'sānt, *before a name* (,)sānt *or* sənt\ *n* **1** : one officially recognized as preeminent for holiness **2** : one of the spirits of the departed in heaven **3** : a holy or godly person — **saint·ed** \-'sān-təd\ *adj* — **saint·hood** \-,hu̇d\ *n*

Saint Ber·nard \-bər-'närd\ *n* : any of a Swiss alpine breed of tall powerful working dogs used esp. formerly in aiding lost travelers

Saint–John's–wort \'sānt-'jänz-,wərt, -,wȯrt\ *n* **1** : any of a genus of herbs and shrubs with showy yellow flowers **2** : the dried aerial parts of a Saint-John's-wort used esp. in herbal remedies

saint·ly \'sānt-lē\ *adj* : relating to, resembling, or befitting a saint — **saint·li·ness** \-lē-nəs\ *n*

Saint Val·en·tine's Day \-'va-lən-,tīnz-\ *n* : VALENTINE'S DAY

¹**sake** \'sāk\ *n* **1** : END, PURPOSE **2** : personal or social welfare, safety, or well-being

²**sa·ke** *or* **sa·ki** \'sä-kē\ *n* : a Japanese alcoholic beverage of fermented rice

sa·laam \sə-'läm\ *n* [Ar *salām*, lit., peace] **1** : a salutation or ceremonial greeting in the East **2** : an obeisance performed by bowing very low and placing the right palm on the forehead — **salaam** *vb*

sa·la·cious \sə-'lā-shəs\ *adj* **1** : arousing sexual desire or imagination **2** : LUSTFUL — **sa·la·cious·ly** *adv* — **sa·la·cious·ness** *n*

sal·ad \'sa-ləd\ *n* : a cold dish (as of lettuce, vegetables, fish, eggs, or fruit) served with dressing

sal·a·man·der \'sa-lə-,man-dər\ *n* : any of numerous amphibians that look like lizards but have scaleless usu. smooth moist skin

sa·la·mi \sə-'lä-mē\ *n* [It] : a highly seasoned sausage of pork and beef

sal·a·ry \'sa-lə-rē\ *n, pl* **-ries** [ME *salarie*, fr. AF, fr. L *salarium* pension, salary, fr. neut. of *salarius* of salt, fr. *sal* salt] : payment made at regular intervals for services

sale \'sāl\ *n* **1** : transfer of ownership of property from one person to another in return for money **2** : ready market : DEMAND **3** : AUCTION **4** : a selling of goods at bargain prices — **sal·able** *or* **sale·able** \'sā-lə-bəl\ *adj*

sales·girl \'sālz-,gərl\ *n* : SALESWOMAN

sales·man \-mən\ *n* : a person who sells in a store or to outside customers — **sales·man·ship** *n*

sales·per·son \-,pər-sən\ *n* : a salesman or saleswoman

sales·wom·an \-,wu̇-mən\ *n* : a woman who sells merchandise

sal·i·cyl·ic acid \,sa-lə-'si-lik-\ *n* : a crystalline organic acid used in making aspirin and other medicinal preparations (as skin lotions)

¹**sa·lient** \'sāl-yənt, 'sā-lē-ənt\ *adj* : jutting forward beyond a line; *also* : PROMINENT ♦ **Synonyms** CONSPICUOUS, STRIKING, NOTICEABLE

²**salient** *n* : a projecting part in a line of defense

¹**sa·line** \'sā-,lēn, -,līn\ *adj* : consisting of or containing salt : SALTY — **sa·lin·i·ty** \sā-'li-nə-tē, sə-\ *n*

²**saline** *n* **1** : a metallic salt esp. with a purgative action **2** : a saline solution

sa·li·va \sə-'lī-və\ *n* : a liquid secreted into the mouth that helps digestion — **sal·i·vary** \'sa-lə-,ver-ē\ *adj*

sal·i·vate \'sa-lə-,vāt\ *vb* **-vat·ed; -vat·ing** : to produce saliva esp. in excess — **sal·i·va·tion** \,sa-lə-'vā-shən\ *n*

sal·low \'sa-lō\ *adj* : of a yellowish sickly color ⟨a ~ face⟩

sal·ly \'sa-lē\ *n, pl* **sallies** **1** : a rushing attack on besiegers by troops of a besieged place **2** : a witty remark or retort **3** : a brief excursion — **sally** *vb*

salm·on \'sa-mən\ *n, pl* **salmon** *also* **salmons** **1** : any of several bony fishes with pinkish flesh that are used for food and are related to the trouts **2** : a strong yellowish pink color

sal·mo·nel·la \,sal-mə-'ne-lə\ *n, pl* **-nel·lae** \-'ne-(,)lē, -,lī\ *or* **-nella** *or* **-nellas** : any of a genus of rod-shaped bacteria that cause various illnesses (as food poisoning)

sa·lon \sə-'län, 'sa-,län, sa-'lōⁿ\ *n* [F] : an elegant drawing room; *also* : a fashionable shop ⟨beauty ~⟩

sa·loon \sə-'lün\ *n* **1** : a large public cabin on a ship **2** : a place where liquors are sold and drunk : BARROOM **3** *Brit* : SEDAN 2

sal·sa \'sȯl-sə, 'säl-\ *n* : a spicy sauce of tomatoes, onions, and hot peppers

¹**salt** \'sȯlt\ *n* **1** : a white crystalline substance that consists of sodium and chlorine and is used in seasoning foods **2**

: a saltlike cathartic substance (as Epsom salts) **3** : a compound formed usu. by action of an acid on metal **4** : SAILOR — **salt·i·ness** \'sȯl-tē-nəs\ n — **salty** \'sȯl-tē\ adj

²**salt** vb : to preserve, season, or feed with salt

³**salt** adj : preserved or treated with salt; also : SALTY

SALT abbr Strategic Arms Limitation Talks

salt away vb : to lay away safely : SAVE

salt-box \'sȯlt-ˌbäks\ n : a frame dwelling with two stories in front and one behind and a long sloping roof

salt·cel·lar \-ˌse-lər\ n : a small container for holding salt at the table

sal·tine \sȯl-'tēn\ n : a thin crisp cracker sprinkled with salt

salt lick n : LICK 5

salt·pe·ter \'sȯlt-'pē-tər\ n [ME salt petre, alter. of salpetre, fr. ML sal petrae, lit., salt of the rock] **1** : POTASSIUM NITRATE **2** : SODIUM NITRATE

salt·wa·ter \-ˌwȯ-tər, -ˌwä-\ adj : of, relating to, or living in salt water

sa·lu·bri·ous \sə-'lü-brē-əs\ adj : favorable to health ⟨a ∼ climate⟩

sal·u·tary \'sal-yə-ˌter-ē\ adj : health-giving; also : BENEFICIAL ⟨∼ effects⟩

sal·u·ta·tion \ˌsal-yə-'tā-shən\ n : an expression of greeting, goodwill, or courtesy usu. by word or gesture

sa·lu·ta·to·ri·an \sə-ˌlü-tə-'tȯr-ē-ən\ n : the student having the 2d highest rank in a graduating class who delivers the salutatory address

sa·lu·ta·to·ry \sə-'lü-tə-ˌtȯr-ē\ adj : relating to or being the welcoming oration delivered at an academic commencement

¹**sa·lute** \sə-'lüt\ vb **sa·lut·ed; sa·lut·ing** **1** : GREET **2** : to honor by special ceremonies **3** : to show respect to (a superior officer) by a formal position of hand, rifle, or sword

²**salute** n **1** : GREETING **2** : the formal position assumed in saluting a superior

¹**sal·vage** \'sal-vij\ n **1** : money paid for saving a ship, its cargo, or passengers when the ship is wrecked or in danger **2** : the saving of a ship **3** : the saving of possessions in danger of being lost **4** : things saved from loss or destruction (as by a wreck or fire)

²**salvage** vb **sal·vaged; sal·vag·ing** : to rescue from destruction

sal·va·tion \sal-'vā-shən\ n **1** : the saving of a person from sin or its consequences esp. in the life after death **2** : the saving from danger, difficulty, or evil **3** : something that saves

¹**salve** \'sav, 'säv\ n **1** : a medicinal substance applied to the skin **2** : a soothing influence

²**salve** vb **salved; salv·ing** : EASE, SOOTHE

sal·ver \'sal-vər\ n [F salve, fr. Sp salva sampling of food to detect poison, tray, fr. salvar to save, sample food to detect poison, fr. LL salvare to save, fr. L salvus safe] : a small serving tray

sal·vo \'sal-vō\ n, pl **salvos** or **salvoes** : a simultaneous discharge of guns

Sam or **Saml** abbr Samuel

SAM \'sam, ˌes-ˌā-'em\ n [surface-to-air missile] : a guided missile for use against aircraft by ground units

Sa·mar·i·tan \sə-'mer-ə-tən\ n **1** : a native or inhabitant of Samaria **2** : a person who is generous in helping those in distress

sa·mar·i·um \sə-'mer-ē-əm\ n : a silvery-white lustrous rare metallic chemical element

¹**same** \'sām\ adj **1** : being the one referred to : not different **2** : SIMILAR — **same·ness** n

²**same** pron : the same one or ones

³**same** adv : in the same manner

Sa·mi also **Saa·mi** \'sä-mē\ n, pl **Sami** or **Samis** also **Saami** or **Saamis** : a member of a people of northern Scandinavia, Finland, and the Kola Peninsula of Russia

Sa·mo·an \sə-'mō-ən\ n : a native or inhabitant of Samoa — **Samoan** adj

sa·mo·sa \sə-'mō-sə\ n : a small triangular pastry filled with spiced meat or vegetables and fried

sam·o·var \'sa-mə-ˌvär\ n [Russ, fr. samo- self + varit' to boil] : an urn with a spigot at the base used esp. in Russia to boil water for tea

sam·pan \'sam-ˌpan\ n : a flat-bottomed skiff of eastern Asia usu. propelled by two short oars

¹**sam·ple** \'sam-pəl\ n : a representative piece, item, or set of individuals that shows the quality or nature of the whole from which it was taken : EXAMPLE, SPECIMEN

²**sample** vb **sam·pled; sam·pling** : to judge the quality of by a sample

sam·pler \'sam-plər\ n : a piece of needlework; esp : one testing skill in embroidery

Sam·u·el \'sam-yə-wəl\ n — see BIBLE table

sam·u·rai \'sa-mə-ˌrī, 'sam-yə-\ n, pl **samurai** : a military retainer of a Japanese feudal lord who adhered to strict principles of honor and duty

san·a·to·ri·um \ˌsa-nə-'tȯr-ē-əm\ n, pl **-ri·ums** or **-ria** \-ē-ə\ **1** : a health resort **2** : an establishment for the care esp. of convalescents or the chronically ill

sanc·ti·fy \'saŋk-tə-ˌfī\ vb **-fied; -fy·ing** **1** : to make holy : CONSECRATE **2** : to free from sin — **sanc·ti·fi·ca·tion** \ˌsaŋk-tə-fə-'kā-shən\ n

sanc·ti·mo·nious \ˌsaŋk-tə-'mō-nē-əs\ adj : hypocritically pious — **sanc·ti·mo·nious·ly** adv

¹**sanc·tion** \'saŋk-shən\ n **1** : authoritative approval **2** : a measure (as a threat or fine) designed to enforce a law or standard ⟨economic ∼s⟩

²**sanction** vb : to give approval to : RATIFY ♦ **Synonyms** ENDORSE, ACCREDIT, CERTIFY, APPROVE

sanc·ti·ty \'saŋk-tə-tē\ n, pl **-ties** **1** : GODLINESS **2** : SACREDNESS

sanc·tu·ary \'saŋk-chə-ˌwer-ē\ n, pl **-ar·ies** **1** : a consecrated place (as the part of a church in which the altar is placed) **2** : a place of refuge ⟨bird ∼⟩

sanc·tum \'saŋk-təm\ n, pl **sanctums** also **sanc·ta** \-tə\ : a private office or study : DEN ⟨an editor's ∼⟩

¹**sand** \'sand\ n : loose particles of hard broken rock — **sandy** adj

²**sand** vb **1** : to cover or fill with sand **2** : to scour, smooth, or polish with an abrasive (as sandpaper) — **sand·er** n

san·dal \'san-dᵊl\ n : a shoe consisting of a sole strapped to the foot; also : a low or open slipper or rubber overshoe

san·dal·wood \-ˌwu̇d\ n : the fragrant yellowish heartwood of a parasitic tree of southern Asia that is much used in ornamental carving and cabinetwork; also : the tree

sand·bag \'sand-ˌbag\ n : a bag filled with sand and used in fortifications, as ballast, or as a weapon

sand·bank \-ˌbaŋk\ n : a deposit of sand (as in a bar or shoal)

sand·bar \-ˌbär\ n : a ridge of sand formed in water by tides or currents

sand·blast \-ˌblast\ vb : to treat with a stream of sand blown (as for cleaning stone) by compressed air — **sand·blast·er** n

sand dollar n : any of numerous flat circular sea urchins living chiefly on sandy bottoms in shallow water

S & H abbr shipping and handling

sand·hog \'sand-ˌhȯg, -ˌhäg\ n : a laborer who builds underwater tunnels

sand·lot \-ˌlät\ n : a vacant lot esp. when used for the unorganized sports of children — **sand·lot** adj — **sand·lot·ter** n

sand·man \-ˌman\ n : the genie of folklore who makes children sleepy

sand·pa·per \-ˌpā-pər\ n : paper with abrasive (as sand) glued on one side used in smoothing and polishing surfaces — **sandpaper** vb

sand·pip·er \-ˌpī-pər\ n : any of various shorebirds with a soft-tipped bill longer than that of the related plovers

sand·stone \-ˌstōn\ n : rock made of sand united by a natural cement

sand·storm \-ˌstȯrm\ n : a windstorm that drives clouds of sand

sand trap n : a hazard on a golf course consisting of a hollow containing sand

¹**sand·wich** \'sand-(ˌ)wich\ n [after John Montagu, 4th Earl of Sandwich †1792 Eng. diplomat] **1** : two or more slices of bread with a layer (as of meat or cheese) spread between them **2** : something resembling a sandwich

²**sandwich** vb : to squeeze or crowd in

sane \'sān\ adj **san·er; san·est** : mentally sound and healthy; also : SENSIBLE, RATIONAL — **sane·ly** adv

sang past of SING

sang·froid \'sä⁽ⁿ⁾-'frwä\ n [F sang-froid, lit., cold blood]

: self-possession or an imperturbable state esp. under strain

san·gui·nary \'saŋ-gwə-ˌner-ē\ *adj* : BLOODY ⟨~ battle⟩

san·guine \'saŋ-gwən\ *adj* **1** : RUDDY **2** : CHEERFUL, HOPEFUL

sanit *abbr* sanitary; sanitation

san·i·tar·i·an \ˌsa-nə-'ter-ē-ən\ *n* : a specialist in sanitation and public health

san·i·tar·i·um \ˌsa-nə-'ter-ē-əm\ *n, pl* **-i·ums** *or* **-ia** \-ē-ə\ : SANATORIUM

san·i·tary \'sa-nə-ˌter-ē\ *adj* **1** : of or relating to health : HYGIENIC **2** : free from filth or infective matter

sanitary napkin *n* : a disposable absorbent pad used to absorb uterine flow (as during menstruation)

san·i·ta·tion \ˌsa-nə-'tā-shən\ *n* : the act or process of making sanitary; *also* : protection of health by maintenance of sanitary conditions

san·i·tize \'sa-nə-ˌtīz\ *vb* **-tized; -tiz·ing** **1** : to make sanitary **2** : to make more acceptable by removing unpleasant features

san·i·ty \'sa-nə-tē\ *n* : soundness of mind

sank *past of* SINK

sans \'sanz\ *prep* : WITHOUT

San·skrit \'san-ˌskrit\ *n* : an ancient language that is the classical language of India and of Hinduism — **Sanskrit** *adj*

San·ta Ana \ˌsan-tə-'a-nə\ *n* [*Santa Ana* Mountains in southern Calif.] : a hot dry wind from the north, northeast, or east in southern California

san·tims \'sän-ˌtims\ *n, pl* **san·ti·mi** \-ti-mē\ — see *lats* at MONEY table

¹sap \'sap\ *n* **1** : a vital fluid; *esp* : a watery fluid that circulates through a vascular plant **2** : a foolish gullible person — **sap·less** *adj*

²sap *vb* **sapped; sap·ping** **1** : UNDERMINE **2** : to weaken gradually

sap·id \'sa-pəd\ *adj* : FLAVORFUL

sa·pi·ent \'sā-pē-ənt, 'sa-\ *adj* : WISE, DISCERNING — **sa·pi·ence** \-əns\ *n*

sap·ling \'sa-pliŋ\ *n* : a young tree

sap·phire \'sa-ˌfī(-ə)r\ *n* : a hard transparent usu. rich blue gem

sap·py \'sa-pē\ *adj* **sap·pi·er; -est** **1** : full of sap **2** : overly sentimental **3** : SILLY, FOOLISH

sap·ro·phyte \'sa-prə-ˌfīt\ *n* : a living thing and esp. a plant living on dead or decaying organic matter — **sap·ro·phyt·ic** \ˌsa-prə-'fi-tik\ *adj*

sap·suck·er \'sap-ˌsə-kər\ *n* : any of a genus of No. American woodpeckers

sap·wood \-ˌwùd\ *n* : the younger active and usu. lighter and softer outer layer of wood (as of a tree trunk)

sar·casm \'sär-ˌka-zəm\ *n* **1** : a cutting or contemptuous remark **2** : ironic criticism or reproach — **sar·cas·tic** \sär-'kas-tik\ *adj* — **sar·cas·ti·cal·ly** \-ti-k(ə-)lē\ *adv*

sar·co·ma \sär-'kō-mə\ *n, pl* **-mas** *also* **-ma·ta** \-mə-tə\ : a malignant tumor esp. of connective tissue, bone, cartilage, or striated muscle

sar·coph·a·gus \sär-'kä-fə-gəs\ *n, pl* **-gi** \-ˌgī, -ˌjī\ *also* **-gus·es** [L *sarcophagus* (*lapis*) limestone used for coffins, fr. Gk (*lithos*) *sarkophagos*, lit., flesh-eating stone, fr. *sark-, sarx* flesh + *phagein* to eat] : a large stone coffin

sar·dine \sär-'dēn\ *n, pl* **sardines** *also* **sardine** : a young or small fish preserved for use as food

sar·don·ic \sär-'dä-nik\ *adj* : disdainfully or skeptically humorous : derisively mocking ♦ **Synonyms** IRONIC, SATIRIC, SARCASTIC — **sar·don·i·cal·ly** \-ni-k(ə-)lē\ *adv*

sa·ri *also* **sa·ree** \'sär-ē\ *n* [Hindi *sāṛī*] : a garment worn by women in southern Asia that consists of a long cloth draped around the body and head or shoulder

sa·rin \'sär-ən, zä-'rēn\ *n* : an extremely toxic chemical weapon used as a lethal nerve gas

sa·rong \sə-'ròŋ, -'räŋ\ *n* : a loose garment wrapped around the body and worn by men and women of the Malay Archipelago and the Pacific islands

sar·sa·pa·ril·la \ˌsas-pə-'ri-lə, ˌsärs-\ *n* **1** : the dried roots of a tropical American smilax used esp. for flavoring; *also* : the plant **2** : a sweetened carbonated beverage flavored with sassafras and an oil from a birch

sar·to·ri·al \sär-'tòr-ē-əl\ *adj* : of or relating to a tailor or tailored clothes — **sar·to·ri·al·ly** *adv*

SASE *abbr* self-addressed stamped envelope

¹sash \'sash\ *n* : a broad band worn around the waist or over the shoulder

²sash *n, pl* **sash** *also* **sash·es** : a frame for panes of glass in a door or window; *also* : the movable part of a window

sa·shay \sa-'shā\ *vb* **1** : WALK, GLIDE, GO **2** : to strut or move about in an ostentatious manner **3** : to proceed in a diagonal or sideways manner

Sask *abbr* Saskatchewan

Sas·quatch \'sas-ˌkwach, -ˌkwäch\ *n* [Halkomelem (American Indian language of British Columbia) *sésq̓əc*] : a large hairy humanlike creature reported to exist in the northwestern U.S. and western Canada

sas·sa·fras \'sa-sə-ˌfras\ *n* [Sp *sasafrás*] : an aromatic No. American tree related to the laurel; *also* : its carcinogenic dried root bark

sassy \'sa-sē\ *adj* **sass·i·er; -est** : SAUCY

¹sat *past and past part of* SIT

²sat *abbr* **1** satellite **2** saturated

Sat *abbr* Saturday

Sa·tan \'sā-tᵊn\ *n* : DEVIL

sa·tang \sə-'täŋ\ *n, pl* **satang** *or* **satangs** — see *baht* at MONEY table

sa·tan·ic \sə-'ta-nik, sā-\ *adj* **1** : of or characteristic of Satan **2** : extremely malicious or wicked — **sa·tan·i·cal·ly** \-ni-k(ə-)lē\ *adv*

satch·el \'sa-chəl\ *n* : SUITCASE

sate \'sāt\ *vb* **sat·ed; sat·ing** : to satisfy to the full; *also* : SURFEIT, GLUT

sa·teen \sa-'tēn, sə-\ *n* : a cotton cloth finished to resemble satin

sat·el·lite \'sa-tə-ˌlīt\ *n* [MF, fr. L *satelles* attendant] **1** : an obsequious follower of a distinguished person : TOADY **2** : a celestial body that orbits a larger body **3** : a manufactured object that orbits a celestial body

satellite dish *n* : a microwave dish for receiving esp. television transmissions from an orbiting satellite

sa·ti·ate \'sā-shē-ˌāt\ *vb* **-at·ed; -at·ing** : to satisfy fully or to excess

sa·ti·ety \sə-'tī-ə-tē\ *n* : fullness to the point of excess

sat·in \'sa-tᵊn\ *n* : a fabric (as of silk) with a glossy surface — **sat·iny** *adj*

sat·in·wood \'sa-tᵊn-ˌwùd*n* : a hard yellowish brown wood of satiny luster; *also* : a tree yielding this wood

sat·ire \'sa-ˌtī(-ə)r\ *n* : biting wit, irony, or sarcasm used to expose vice or folly; *also* : a literary work having these qualities — **sa·tir·ic** \sə-'tir-ik\ *or* **sa·tir·i·cal** \-i-kəl\ *adj* — **sa·tir·i·cal·ly** *adv* — **sat·i·rist** \'sa-tə-rist\ *n* — **sat·i·rize** \-tə-ˌrīz\ *vb*

sat·is·fac·tion \ˌsa-təs-'fak-shən\ *n* **1** : payment through penance or punishment incurred by sin **2** : CONTENTMENT, GRATIFICATION **3** : reparation for an insult **4** : settlement of a claim

sat·is·fac·to·ry \-'fak-tə-rē\ *adj* : giving satisfaction : ADEQUATE — **sat·is·fac·to·ri·ly** \-'fak-tə-rə-lē\ *adv*

sat·is·fy \'sa-təs-ˌfī\ *vb* **-fied; -fy·ing** **1** : to answer or discharge (a claim) in full **2** : to make happy : GRATIFY **3** : to pay what is due to **4** : CONVINCE **5** : to meet the requirements of — **sat·is·fy·ing·ly** *adv*

sa·trap \'sā-ˌtrap, 'sa-\ *n* [ME, fr. L *satrapes*, fr. Gk *satrapēs*, fr. OPers *khshathrapāvan*, lit., protector of the dominion] : a petty prince : a subordinate ruler

sat·u·rate \'sa-chə-ˌrāt\ *vb* **-rat·ed; -rat·ing** **1** : to soak thoroughly **2** : to treat or charge with something to the point where no more can be absorbed, dissolved, or retained — **sat·u·ra·ble** \'sa-chə-rə-bəl\ *adj* — **sat·u·ra·tion** \ˌsa-chə-'rā-shən\ *n*

saturated *adj* **1** : full of moisture **2** : having no double or triple bonds between carbon atoms ⟨~ fats⟩

Sat·ur·day \'sa-tər-dē, -ˌdā\ *n* : the 7th day of the week

Saturday night special *n* : a cheap easily concealed handgun

Sat·urn \'sa-tərn\ *n* : the planet 6th in order from the sun — see PLANET table

sat·ur·nine \'sa-tər-ˌnīn\ *adj* : SULLEN, SARDONIC

sa·tyr \'sā-tər\ *n* **1** *often cap* : a woodland deity in Greek mythology having certain characteristics of a horse or goat **2** : a lecherous man

¹sauce \'sòs, *3 usu* 'sas\ *n* **1** : a fluid dressing or topping for food **2** : stewed fruit **3** : IMPUDENCE

²sauce \'sòs, *2 usu* 'säs\ *vb* **sauced; sauc·ing** **1** : to put sauce on; *also* : to add zest to **2** : to be impudent to

sauce·pan \'sȯs-ˌpan\ *n* : a small deep cooking pan with a handle

sau·cer \'sȯ-sər\ *n* : a rounded shallow dish for use under a cup

saucy \'sä-sē, 'sȯ-\ *adj* **sauc·i·er; -est** : IMPUDENT, PERT — **sauc·i·ly** \-sə-lē\ *adv* — **sauc·i·ness** \-sē-nəs\ *n*

Sau·di \'saú-dē, 'sȯ-; sä-'ü-dē\ *n* : SAUDI ARABIAN — **Saudi** *adj*

Saudi Arabian *n* : a native or inhabitant of Saudi Arabia — **Saudi Arabian** *adj*

sau·er·kraut \'saú-(ə)r-ˌkraút\ *n* [G, fr. *sauer* sour + *Kraut* greens] : finely cut cabbage fermented in brine

Sauk \'sȯk\ *or* **Sac** \'sak, 'sȯk\ *n, pl* **Sauk** *or* **Sauks** *or* **Sac** *or* **Sacs** : a member of an American Indian people formerly living in what is now Wisconsin

sau·na \'sȯ-nə, 'saú-nə\ *n* **1** : a Finnish steam bath in which the steam is provided by water thrown on hot stones **2** : a dry heat bath; *also* : a room or cabinet used for such a bath

saun·ter \'sȯn-tər, 'sän-\ *vb* : STROLL

sau·ro·pod \'sȯr-ə-ˌpäd\ *n* : any of a suborder of plant-eating dinosaurs (as a brontosaurus) with a long neck and tail and a small head — **sauropod** *adj*

sau·sage \'sȯ-sij\ *n* [ME *sausige*, fr. AF *sauseche*, fr. LL *salsicia*, fr. L *salsus* salted] : minced and highly seasoned meat (as pork) usu. enclosed in a tubular casing

S Aust *abbr* South Australia

sau·té \sȯ-'tā, sō-\ *vb* **sau·téed** *or* **sau·téd; sau·té·ing** [F] : to fry lightly in a little fat — **sauté** *n*

sau·terne \sō-'tərn, sȯ-\ *n, often cap* : a usu. semisweet American white wine

¹sav·age \'sa-vij\ *adj* [ME, fr. AF *salvage, savage,* LL *salvaticus,* alter. of L *silvaticus* of the woods, wild, fr. *silva* forest] **1** : WILD, UNTAMED **2** : UNCIVILIZED, BARBAROUS **3** : CRUEL, FIERCE — **sav·age·ly** *adv* — **sav·age·ness** *n* — **sav·age·ry** \-rē\ *n*

²savage *n* **1** : a member of a primitive human society **2** : a rude, unmannerly, or brutal person

sa·van·na *or* **sa·van·nah** \sə-'va-nə\ *n* [Sp *zavana*] : grassland containing scattered trees

sa·vant \sa-'vänt, sə-, 'sa-vənt\ *n* : a learned person : SCHOLAR

¹save \'sāv\ *vb* **saved; sav·ing** **1** : to redeem from sin **2** : to rescue from danger **3** : to preserve or guard from destruction or loss; *also* : to store (data) in a computer or on a storage device **4** : to put aside as a store or reserve — **sav·er** *n*

²save *n* : a play that prevents an opponent from scoring or winning

³save *prep* : EXCEPT

⁴save *conj* : BUT

savings and loan association *n* : a cooperative association that holds savings of members in the form of dividend-bearing shares and that invests chiefly in mortgage loans

savings bank *n* : a bank that holds funds of individual depositors in interest-bearing accounts and makes long-term investments (as mortgage loans)

savings bond *n* : a registered U.S. bond issued in denominations of $50 to $10,000

sav·ior *or* **sav·iour** \'sāv-yər\ *n* **1** : one who saves **2** *cap* : Jesus Christ

sa·voir faire \ˌsav-ˌwär-'fer\ *n* [F *savoir-faire,* lit., knowing how to do] : sureness in social behavior

¹sa·vor *also* **sa·vour** \'sā-vər\ *n* **1** : the taste and odor of something **2** : a special flavor or quality — **sa·vory** *adj*

²savor *also* **savour** *vb* **1** : to have a specified taste, smell, or quality **2** : to taste with pleasure

sa·vo·ry \'sā-və-rē\ *n, pl* **-ries** : either of two aromatic mints used in cooking

¹sav·vy \'sa-vē\ *vb* **sav·vied; sav·vy·ing** : UNDERSTAND, COMPREHEND

²savvy *n* : practical know-how ⟨political ∼⟩ — **savvy** *adj*

¹saw *past of* SEE

²saw \'sȯ\ *n* : a cutting tool with a blade having a line of teeth along its edge

³saw *vb* **sawed** \'sȯd\; **sawed** *or* **sawn** \'sȯn\; **saw·ing** : to cut or shape with or as if with a saw

⁴saw *n* : a common saying : MAXIM

saw·dust \'sȯ-(ˌ)dəst\ *n* : fine particles made by a saw in cutting

saw·fly \-ˌflī\ *n* : any of numerous insects belonging to the same order as bees and wasps and including many whose larvae are plant-feeding pests

saw·horse \-ˌhȯrs\ *n* : a rack on which wood is rested while being sawed by hand

saw·mill \-ˌmil\ *n* : a mill for sawing logs

saw palmetto *n* **1** : any of several shrubby palms with spiny-toothed petioles **2** : the fruit of a saw palmetto used esp. in herbal remedies

saw·yer \'sȯ-yər\ *n* : a person who saws timber

sax \'saks\ *n* : SAXOPHONE

sax·i·frage \'sak-sə-frij, -ˌfrāj\ *n* [ME, fr. AF, fr. LL *saxifraga,* fr. L, fem. of *saxifragus,* breaking rocks] : any of a genus of plants with showy flowers and usu. with leaves growing in tufts close to the ground

sax·o·phone \'sak-sə-ˌfōn\ *n* : a musical instrument having a conical metal tube with a reed mouthpiece and finger keys — **sax·o·phon·ist** \-ˌfō-nist\ *n*

¹say \'sā\ *vb* **said** \'sed\; **say·ing; says** \'sez\ **1** : to express in words ⟨∼ what you mean⟩ **2** : to state as opinion or belief **3** : PRONOUNCE; *also* : RECITE, REPEAT ⟨∼ your prayers⟩ **4** : INDICATE ⟨the clock ∼s noon⟩

²say *n, pl* **says** \'sāz\ **1** : an expression of opinion **2** : power of decision

say·ing *n* : a commonly repeated statement

say-so \'sā-(ˌ)sō\ *n* : an esp. authoritative assertion or decision; *also* : the right to decide

sb *abbr* substantive

Sb *symbol* [L *stibium*] antimony

SB *abbr* [NL *scientiae baccalaureus*] bachelor of science

SBA *abbr* Small Business Administration

sc *abbr* **1** scene **2** science

Sc *symbol* scandium

SC *abbr* **1** South Carolina **2** supreme court

¹scab \'skab\ *n* **1** : scabies of domestic animals **2** : a crust of hardened blood forming over a wound **3** : a worker who replaces a striker or works under conditions not authorized by a union **4** : any of various bacterial or fungus plant diseases marked by crusted spots on stems or leaves — **scab·by** *adj*

²scab *vb* **scabbed; scab·bing** **1** : to become covered with a scab **2** : to work as a scab

scab·bard \'ska-bərd\ *n* : a sheath for the blade of a weapon (as a sword)

sca·bies \'skā-bēz\ *n* [L] : contagious itch or mange caused by mites living as parasites under the skin

sca·brous \'ska-brəs, 'skā-\ *adj* **1** : DIFFICULT, KNOTTY **2** : rough to the touch : SCALY, SCURFY ⟨a ∼ leaf⟩ **3** : dealing with suggestive, indecent, or scandalous themes; *also* : SQUALID

scad \'skad\ *n* : a large number or quantity — usu. used in pl.

scaf·fold \'ska-fəld, -ˌfōld\ *n* **1** : a raised platform for workers to sit or stand on **2** : a platform on which a criminal is executed (as by hanging)

scaf·fold·ing *n* : a system of scaffolds; *also* : materials for scaffolds

scal·a·wag *or* **scal·ly·wag** \'ska-li-ˌwag\ *n* : RASCAL

¹scald \'skȯld\ *vb* **1** : to burn with or as if with hot liquid or steam **2** : to heat to just below the boiling point

²scald *n* : a burn caused by scalding

¹scale \'skāl\ *n* **1** : either pan of a balance **2** : BALANCE — usu. used in pl. **3** : a weighing instrument

²scale *vb* **scaled; scal·ing** : WEIGH

³scale *n* **1** : one of the small thin plates that cover the body esp. of a fish or reptile **2** : a thin plate or flake **3** : a thin coating, layer, or incrustation **4** : SCALE INSECT — **scaled** \'skāld\ *adj* — **scale·less** \'skāl-ləs\ *adj* — **scaly** *adj*

⁴scale *vb* **scaled; scal·ing** : to strip of scales

⁵scale *n* [ME, fr. LL *scala* ladder, staircase, fr. L *scalae,* pl., stairs, rungs, ladder] **1** : something divided into regular spaces as a help in drawing or measuring **2** : a graduated series **3** : the size of a sample (as a model) in proportion to the size of the actual thing **4** : a standard of estimation or judgment **5** : a series of musical tones going up or down in pitch according to a specified scheme

⁶scale *vb* **scaled; scal·ing** **1** : to climb by or as if by a ladder **2** : to arrange in a graded series

scale insect *n* : any of numerous small insects with wingless scale-covered females that are related to aphids and feed on and are often pests of plants

scale·pan \'skāl-,pan\ *n* : ¹SCALE 1

scal·lion \'skal-yən\ *n* [ultim. fr. L *ascalonia* (*caepa*) onion of Ascalon (seaport in Palestine)] : an onion without an enlarged bulb

¹**scal·lop** \'skä-ləp, 'ska-\ *n* 1 : any of numerous marine bivalve mollusks with radially ridged shells; *also* : a large edible muscle of this mollusk 2 : one of a continuous series of rounded projections forming an edge

²**scallop** *vb* 1 : to bake in a casserole ⟨~ed potatoes⟩ 2 : to shape, cut, or finish in scallops ⟨~ed edges⟩

¹**scalp** \'skalp\ *n* : the part of the skin and flesh of the head usu. covered with hair

²**scalp** *vb* 1 : to remove the scalp from 2 : to resell at greatly increased prices ⟨~ tickets⟩ — **scalp·er** *n*

scal·pel \'skal-pəl\ *n* : a small straight knife with a thin blade used esp. in surgery

scam \'skam\ *n* : a fraudulent or deceptive act or operation

scamp \'skamp\ *n* : RASCAL

scam·per \'skam-pər\ *vb* : to run nimbly and playfully — **scamper** *n*

scam·pi \'skam-pē\ *n, pl* **scampi** [It] : a usu. large shrimp; *also* : large shrimp prepared with a garlic-flavored sauce

¹**scan** \'skan\ *vb* **scanned; scan·ning** 1 : to read (verses) so as to show metrical structure 2 : to examine closely 3 : to input or examine systematically in order to obtain data esp. for display or storage 4 : to make a scan of (as the human body) — **scan·ner** *n*

²**scan** *n* 1 : the act or process of scanning 2 : a picture of the distribution of radioactive material in something; *also* : an image of a bodily part produced (as by computer) by combining radiographic data obtained from several angles or sections

Scand *abbr* Scandinavia

scan·dal \'skan-dᵊl\ *n* [ME, fr. LL *scandalum* stumbling block, offense, fr. Gk *skandalon*] 1 : DISGRACE, DISHONOR 2 : malicious gossip : SLANDER — **scan·dal·ize** *vb* — **scan·dal·ous** *adj* — **scan·dal·ous·ly** *adv*

scan·dal·mon·ger \-,məŋ-gər, -,mäŋ-\ *n* : a person who circulates scandal

Scan·di·na·vian \,skan-də-'nā-vē-ən\ *n* : a native or inhabitant of Scandinavia — **Scandinavian** *adj*

scan·di·um \'skan-dē-əm\ *n* : a silvery-white metallic chemical element

scan·ner \'ska-nər\ *n* 1 : a radio receiver that sequentially scans a range of frequencies for a signal 2 : a device that scans an image or document esp. for use or storage on a computer

¹**scant** \'skant\ *adj* 1 : barely sufficient 2 : having scarcely enough ♦ **Synonyms** SCANTY, SKIMPY, MEAGER, SPARSE, EXIGUOUS

²**scant** *vb* 1 : SKIMP 2 : STINT

scant·ling \'skant-liŋ\ *n* : a small piece of lumber (as an upright in a house)

scanty \'skan-tē\ *adj* **scant·i·er; -est** : barely sufficient : SCANT — **scant·i·ly** \'skan-tə-lē\ *adv* — **scant·i·ness** \-tē-nəs\ *n*

scape·goat \'skāp-,gōt\ *n* : one that bears the blame for others

scape·grace \-,grās\ *n* [*scape* (escape)] : an incorrigible rascal

scap·u·la \'ska-pyə-lə\ *n, pl* **-lae** \-,lē\ *or* **-las** [L] : SHOULDER BLADE

scap·u·lar \-lər\ *n* : a pair of small cloth squares worn on the breast and back under the clothing esp. for religious purposes

scar \'skär\ *n* : a mark left after injured tissue has healed — **scar** *vb*

scar·ab \'ska-rəb\ *n* [MF *scarabee*, fr. L *scarabaeus*] : any of a family of large stout beetles; *also* : an ornament (as a gem) representing such a beetle

scarce \'skers\ *adj* **scarc·er; scarc·est** 1 : deficient in quantity or number : not plentiful 2 : intentionally absent ⟨made himself ~ at inspection time⟩ — **scar·ci·ty** \'sker-sə-tē\ *n*

scarce·ly \-lē\ *adv* 1 : BARELY 2 : almost not 3 : very probably not

¹**scare** \'sker\ *vb* **scared; scar·ing** : FRIGHTEN, STARTLE

²**scare** *n* : FRIGHT — **scary** *adj*

scare·crow \'sker-,krō\ *n* : a crude figure set up to scare birds away from crops

¹**scarf** \'skärf\ *n, pl* **scarves** \'skärvz\ *or* **scarfs** 1 : a broad band (as of cloth) worn about the shoulders, around the neck, over the head, or about the waist 2 : a long narrow cloth cover for a table or dresser top

²**scarf** *vb* [alter. of earlier *scoff* eat greedily] : to eat greedily

scar·i·fy \'sker-ə-,fī\ *vb* **-fied; -fy·ing** 1 : to make scratches or small cuts in ⟨~ skin for vaccination⟩ ⟨~ seeds to help them germinate⟩ 2 : to lacerate the feelings of 3 : to break up and loosen the surface of (as a road) — **scar·i·fi·ca·tion** \,skar-ə-fə-'kā-shən\ *n*

scar·let \'skär-lət\ *n* : a bright red color — **scarlet** *adj*

scarlet fever *n* : an acute contagious disease marked by fever, sore throat, and red rash and caused by certain streptococci

scarp \'skärp\ *n* : a line of cliffs produced by faulting or erosion

scath·ing \'skā-thiŋ\ *adj* : bitterly severe ⟨a ~ condemnation⟩

scat·o·log·i·cal \,ska-tə-'lä-ji-kəl\ *adj* : concerned with obscene matters

scat·ter \'ska-tər\ *vb* 1 : to distribute or strew about irregularly 2 : DISPERSE

scat·ter·brain \'ska-tər-,brān\ *n* : a silly careless person — **scat·ter·brained** \-,brānd\ *adj*

scav·enge \'ska-vənj\ *vb* **scav·enged; scav·eng·ing** : to work or function as a scavenger

scav·en·ger \'ska-vən-jər\ *n* [alter. of earlier *scavager*, fr. AF *scawageour* collector of scavage (duty imposed on nonresident street merchants), fr. *skawage* scavage, fr. MF dial. (Flanders) *escauver* to inspect, fr. MD *scouwen*] : a person or animal that collects, eats, or disposes of refuse or waste

sce·nar·io \sə-'ner-ē-,ō\ *n, pl* **-i·os** : the plot or outline of a dramatic work; *also* : an account of a possible action

scene \'sēn\ *n* [MF, stage, fr. L *scena, scaena* stage, scene, prob. fr. Etruscan, fr. Gk *skēnē* temporary shelter, tent, building forming the background for a dramatic performance, stage] 1 : a division of one act of a play 2 : a single situation or sequence in a play or motion picture 3 : a stage setting 4 : VIEW, PROSPECT 5 : the place of an occurrence or action 6 : a display of strong feeling and esp. anger 7 : a sphere of activity ⟨the fashion ~⟩ — **sce·nic** \'sē-nik\ *adj*

scen·ery \'sē-nə-rē\ *n, pl* **-er·ies** 1 : the painted scenes or hangings and accessories used on a theater stage 2 : a picturesque view or landscape

¹**scent** \'sent\ *n* 1 : ODOR, SMELL 2 : sense of smell 3 : course of pursuit : TRACK 4 : PERFUME 2 — **scent·ed** \'sen-təd\ *adj* — **scent·less** *adj*

²**scent** *vb* 1 : SMELL 2 : to imbue or fill with odor

scep·ter \'sep-tər\ *n* : a staff borne by a sovereign as an emblem of authority

sceptic *var of* SKEPTIC

scep·tre *Brit var of* SCEPTER

sch *abbr* school

¹**sched·ule** \'ske-jül, *esp Brit* 'she-dyül\ *n* 1 : a list of items or details 2 : TIMETABLE

²**schedule** *vb* **sched·uled; sched·ul·ing** 1 : to appoint, assign, or designate for a fixed time 2 : to make a schedule of; *also* : to enter on a schedule

sche·ma \'skē-mə\ *n, pl* **sche·ma·ta** \-mə-tə\ *also* **schemas** : a diagrammatic presentation or plan : OUTLINE

sche·mat·ic \ski-'ma-tik\ *adj* : of or relating to a scheme or diagram : DIAGRAMMATIC — **schematic** *n* — **sche·mat·i·cal·ly** \-ti-k(ə-)lē\ *adv*

¹**scheme** \'skēm\ *n* 1 : a plan for doing something; *esp* : a crafty plot 2 : a systematic design ⟨a color ~⟩

²**scheme** *vb* **schemed; schem·ing** : to form a plot : INTRIGUE — **schem·er** *n*

schil·ling \'shi-liŋ\ *n* — see MONEY table

schism \'si-zəm, 'ski-\ *n* 1 : DIVISION, SPLIT; *also* : DISCORD, DISSENSION 2 : a formal division in or separation from a religious body

schis·mat·ic \siz-'ma-tik, ski-\ *n* : one who creates or takes part in schism — **schismatic** *adj*

schist \'shist\ *n* : a metamorphic crystalline rock

schizo·phre·nia \,skit-sə-'frē-nē-ə\ *n* [NL, fr. Gk *schizein* to split + *phrēn* diaphragm, mind] : a psychotic mental illness that is characterized by a distorted view of the real world, by a greatly reduced ability to carry out one's daily tasks, and by abnormal ways of thinking, feeling, perceiving, and behaving — **schiz·oid** \'skit-ˌsȯid\ *adj or n* — **schizo·phren·ic** \ˌskit-sə-'fre-nik\ *adj or n*

schle·miel *also* **shle·miel** \shlə-'mēl\ *n* : an unlucky bungler : CHUMP

schlep *or* **schlepp** \'shlep\ *vb* [Yiddish *shlepn*] **1** : DRAG, HAUL **2** : to move slowly or awkwardly

schlock \'shläk\ *or* **schlocky** \'shlä-kē\ *adj* : of low quality or value — **schlock** *n*

schlub *also* **shlub** \'shləb\ *n* [Yiddish *zhlob, zhlub* yokel, boor] *slang* : a stupid, ineffectual, or unattractive person

schmaltz *also* **schmalz** \'shmȯlts, 'shmälts\ *n* [Yiddish *shmalts*, lit., rendered fat] : sentimental or florid music or art — **schmaltzy** *adj*

schmooze *or* **shmooze** \'shmüz\ *vb* : to chat informally esp. to gain favor — **schmooze** *n*

schnapps \'shnaps\ *n, pl* **schnapps** : a liquor (as gin) of high alcoholic content

schnau·zer \'shnau̇-zər, 'shnau̇t-sər\ *n* [G, fr. *Schnauze* snout] : a dog of any of three breeds that are characterized by a wiry coat, long head, pointed ears, heavy eyebrows, and long hair on the muzzle

schol·ar \'skä-lər\ *n* **1** : STUDENT, PUPIL **2** : a learned person : SAVANT — **schol·ar·ly** *adj*

schol·ar·ship \-ˌship\ *n* **1** : the qualities or learning of a scholar **2** : money awarded to a student to help pay for further education

scho·las·tic \skə-'las-tik\ *adj* : of or relating to schools, scholars, or scholarship

¹school \'skül\ *n* **1** : an institution for teaching and learning; *also* : the pupils in attendance **2** : a body of persons of like opinions or beliefs ⟨the radical ∼⟩

²school *vb* : TEACH, TRAIN, DRILL

³school *n* : a large number of one kind of water animal swimming and feeding together

school·boy \-ˌbȯi\ *n* : a boy attending school

school·fel·low \-ˌfe-lō\ *n* : SCHOOLMATE

school·girl \-ˌgərl\ *n* : a girl attending school

school·house \-ˌhau̇s\ *n* : a building used as a school

school·marm \-ˌmärm\ *or* **school·ma'am** \-ˌmäm, -ˌmam\ *n* **1** : a woman who is a schoolteacher **2** : a person who exhibits characteristics popularly attributed to schoolteachers

school·mas·ter \-ˌmas-tər\ *n* : a man who is a schoolteacher

school·mate \-ˌmāt\ *n* : a school companion

school·mis·tress \-ˌmis-trəs\ *n* : a woman who is a schoolteacher

school·room \-ˌrüm, -ˌru̇m\ *n* : CLASSROOM

school·teach·er \-ˌtē-chər\ *n* : one who teaches in a school

schoo·ner \'skü-nər\ *n* : a fore-and-aft rigged sailing ship

schtick *var of* SHTICK

schuss \'shu̇s, 'shüs\ *vb* [G *Schuss*, n., lit., shot] : to ski down a slope at high speed — **schuss** *n*

sci *abbr* science; scientific

sci·at·i·ca \sī-'a-ti-kə\ *n* : pain in the region of the hips or along the course of the nerve at the back of the thigh

sci·ence \'sī-əns\ *n* [ME, fr. AF, fr. L *scientia*, fr. *scient-, sciens* having knowledge, fr. prp. of *scire* to know] **1** : an area of knowledge that is an object of study; *esp* : NATURAL SCIENCE **2** : knowledge covering general truths or the operation of general laws especially as obtained and tested through the scientific method — **sci·en·tif·ic** \ˌsī-ən-'ti-fik\ *adj* — **sci·en·tif·i·cal·ly** \-fi-k(ə-)lē\ *adv* — **sci·en·tist** \'sī-ən-tist\ *n*

science fiction *n* : fiction dealing principally with the impact of actual or imagined science on society or individuals

scientific method *n* : the rules and methods for the pursuit of knowledge involving the finding and stating of a problem, the collection of facts through observation and experiment, and the making and testing of ideas that need to be proven right or wrong

scim·i·tar \'si-mə-tər\ *n* : a curved sword used chiefly by Arabs and Turks

scin·til·la \sin-'ti-lə\ *n* : SPARK, TRACE

scin·til·late \'sin-tə-ˌlāt\ *vb* **-lat·ed; -lat·ing** : SPARKLE, GLEAM — **scin·til·la·tion** \ˌsin-tə-'lā-shən\ *n*

sci·on \'sī-ən\ *n* **1** : a shoot of a plant joined to a stock in grafting **2** : DESCENDANT

scis·sors \'si-zərz\ *n pl* : a cutting instrument like shears but usu. smaller

scissors kick *n* : a swimming kick in which the legs move like scissors

sclero·der·ma \ˌskler-ə-'dər-mə\ *n* : a chronic disease characterized by the usu. progressive hardening and thickening of the skin

scle·ro·sis \sklə-'rō-səs\ *n* : abnormal hardening of tissue (as of an artery); *also* : a disease characterized by this — **scle·rot·ic** \-'rä-tik\ *adj*

scoff \'skäf\ *vb* : MOCK, JEER — **scoff·er** *n*

scoff·law \-ˌlȯ\ *n* : a contemptuous law violator

¹scold \'skōld\ *n* : a person who scolds

²scold *vb* : to censure severely or angrily

sconce \'skäns\ *n* : a candlestick or an electric light fixture fastened to a wall

scone \'skōn, 'skän\ *n* : a biscuit (as of oatmeal) baked on a griddle

¹scoop \'sküp\ *n* **1** : a large shovel; *also* : a utensil with a shovellike or rounded end **2** : the amount contained by a scoop **3** : an act of scooping **4** : information of immediate interest

²scoop *vb* **1** : to take out or up or empty with or as if with a scoop **2** : to make hollow **3** : to report a news item in advance of

scoot \'sküt\ *vb* : to move swiftly

scoot·er \'skü-tər\ *n* **1** : a child's vehicle consisting of a narrow board mounted between two wheels tandem with an upright steering handle attached to the front wheel **2** : MOTOR SCOOTER

¹scope \'skōp\ *n* [It *scopo* purpose, goal, fr. Gk *skopos*] **1** : space or opportunity for action or thought **2** : extent covered : RANGE

²scope *n* : an instrument (as a microscope or telescope) for viewing

scorch \'skȯrch\ *vb* : to burn the surface of; *also* : to dry or shrivel with heat ⟨∼ed lawns⟩

¹score \'skȯr\ *n, pl* **scores 1** *or pl* **score** : TWENTY **2** : CUT, SCRATCH, SLASH **3** : a record of points made (as in a game) **4** : DEBT **5** : REASON, GROUND **6** : the music of a composition or arrangement with different parts indicated **7** : success in obtaining something (as drugs) esp. illegally

²score *vb* **scored; scor·ing 1** : RECORD **2** : to keep score in a game **3** : to mark with lines, grooves, scratches, or notches **4** : to gain or tally in or as if in a game ⟨*scored* a point⟩ **5** : to assign a grade or score to ⟨∼ the tests⟩ **6** : to compose a score for **7** : SUCCEED **8** : ACQUIRE ⟨*scored* tickets to the game⟩ — **score·less** *adj* — **scor·er** *n*

¹scorn \'skȯrn\ *n* : an emotion involving both anger and disgust : CONTEMPT — **scorn·ful** \-fəl\ *adj* — **scorn·ful·ly** *adv*

²scorn *vb* : to hold in contempt : DISDAIN — **scorn·er** *n*

Scor·pio \'skȯr-pē-ˌō\ *n* [L, lit., scorpion] **1** : a zodiacal constellation between Libra and Sagittarius usu. pictured as a scorpion **2** : the 8th sign of the zodiac in astrology; *also* : one born under this sign

scor·pi·on \'skȯr-pē-ən\ *n* : any of an order of arthropods related to the spiders that have a poisonous stinger at the tip of a long jointed tail

¹Scot \'skät\ *n* : a native or inhabitant of Scotland

²Scot *abbr* Scotland; Scottish

Scotch \'skäch\ *n* **1** : SCOTS **2** **Scotch** *pl* : the people of Scotland **3** : a whiskey distilled in Scotland esp. from malted barley — **Scotch** *adj* — **Scotch·man** \-mən\ *n* — **Scotch·wom·an** \-ˌwu̇-mən\ *n*

Scotch bonnet *n* : a small roundish very hot chili pepper esp. of the Caribbean

Scotch pine *n* : a pine that is naturalized in the U.S. from northern Europe and Asia and is a valuable timber tree

Scotch terrier *n* : SCOTTISH TERRIER

scot-free \'skät-'frē\ *adj* : free from obligation, harm, or penalty

Scots \'skäts\ *n* : the English language of Scotland

Scots·man \'skäts-mən\ *n* : SCOT

Scots·wom·an \-ˌwu̇-mən\ *n* : a woman who is a Scot

Scot·tie \'skä-tē\ *n* : SCOTTISH TERRIER

Scot·tish \'skä-tish\ *adj* : of, relating to, or characteristic of Scotland, Scots, or the Scots
Scottish terrier *n* : any of an old Scottish breed of terrier with short legs, a long head with small erect ears, a broad deep chest, and a thick rough coat
scoun·drel \'skaùn-drəl\ *n* : a disreputable person : VILLAIN
¹scour \'skaù(-ə)r\ *vb* **1** : to rub (as with a gritty substance) in order to clean **2** : to cleanse by or as if by rubbing
²scour *vb* **1** : to move rapidly through : RUSH **2** : to examine thoroughly
¹scourge \'skərj\ *n* **1** : LASH, WHIP **2** : PUNISHMENT; *also* : a cause of affliction (as a plague)
²scourge *vb* scourged; scourg·ing **1** : LASH, FLOG **2** : to punish severely
¹scout \'skaùt\ *vb* [ME, fr. AF *escuter* to listen, fr. L *auscultare*] **1** : to look around : RECONNOITER **2** : to inspect or observe to get information
²scout *n* **1** : a person sent out to get information; *also* : a soldier, airplane, or ship sent out to reconnoiter **2** : BOY SCOUT **3** : GIRL SCOUT — **scout·mas·ter** \-ˌmas-tər\ *n*
³scout *vb* : SCORN, SCOFF
scow \'skaù\ *n* : a large flat-bottomed boat with square ends
scowl \'skaù(-ə)l\ *vb* : to make a frowning expression of displeasure — **scowl** *n*
SCPO *abbr* senior chief petty officer
scrab·ble \'skra-bəl\ *vb* scrab·bled; scrab·bling **1** : SCRAPE, SCRATCH **2** : CLAMBER, SCRAMBLE **3** : to work hard and long **4** : SCRIBBLE — **scrabble** *n* — **scrab·bler** *n*
scrag·gly \'skra-glē\ *adj* : IRREGULAR; *also* : RAGGED, UNKEMPT 〈a ~ beard〉
scram \'skram\ *vb* scrammed; scram·ming : to go away at once
scram·ble \'skram-bəl\ *vb* scram·bled; scram·bling **1** : to clamber clumsily around **2** : to struggle for or as if for possession of something **3** : to spread irregularly **4** : to mix together **5** : to cook (eggs) by stirring during frying — **scramble** *n*
¹scrap \'skrap\ *n* **1** : FRAGMENT, PIECE **2** : discarded material : REFUSE
²scrap *vb* scrapped; scrap·ping **1** : to make into scrap 〈~ a battleship〉 **2** : to get rid of as useless 〈*scrapped* the plans〉
³scrap *n* : FIGHT
⁴scrap *vb* scrapped; scrap·ping : FIGHT, QUARREL — **scrap·per** *n*
scrap·book \'skrap-ˌbùk\ *n* : a blank book in which mementos are kept
¹scrape \'skrāp\ *vb* scraped; scrap·ing **1** : to remove by drawing a knife over; *also* : to clean or smooth by rubbing off the covering **2** : to damage or injure the surface of by contact with something rough **3** : to draw across a surface with a grating sound **4** : to get together (money) by strict economy **5** : to get along with difficulty 〈barely *scraping* by on her income〉 — **scrap·er** *n*
²scrape *n* **1** : the act or effect of scraping **2** : a bow accompanied by a drawing back of the foot **3** : an unpleasant predicament
scra·pie \'skrā-pē\ *n* : a usu. fatal degenerative disease of the brain esp. of sheep that is related to mad cow disease
¹scrap·py \'skra-pē\ *adj* scrap·pi·er; -est : DISCONNECTED, FRAGMENTARY
²scrappy *adj* scrap·pi·er; -est **1** : QUARRELSOME **2** : having an aggressive and determined spirit 〈a ~ competitor〉
¹scratch \'skrach\ *vb* **1** : to scrape, dig, or rub with or as if with claws or nails 〈a dog ~*ing* at the door〉 〈~*ed* my arm〉 **2** : SCRAPE **3** 〈~*ed* his nails across the blackboard〉 **3** : SCRAPE **4** : to cancel or erase by or as if by drawing a line through **4** **5** : to withdraw from a contest — **scratchy** *adj* — **scratch one's head** : to become confused or perplexed
²scratch *n* **1** : a mark or injury made by or as if by scratching; *also* : a sound so made **2** : the starting line in a race — **from scratch** : with no steps completed or ingredients prepared ahead of time 〈built from ~〉
³scratch *adj* **1** : made or done by chance 〈a ~ hit〉 **2** : made as or used for a trial attempt 〈~ paper〉

scrawl \'skròl\ *vb* : to write hastily and carelessly — **scrawl** *n*
scraw·ny \'skrò-nē\ *adj* scraw·ni·er; -est : very thin : SKINNY
¹scream \'skrēm\ *vb* : to cry out loudly and shrilly
²scream *n* : a loud shrill cry
scream·ing \'skrē-miŋ\ *adj* : so striking as to attract notice as if by screaming 〈~ headlines〉
screech \'skrēch\ *vb* : SHRIEK — **screech** *n* — **screechy** \'skrē-chē\ *adj*
screech·ing \'skrē-chiŋ\ *adj* : ABRUPT 〈came to a ~ halt〉
¹screen \'skrēn\ *n* **1** : a device or partition used to hide, restrain, protect, or decorate 〈a window ~〉; *also* : something that shelters, protects, or conceals **2** : a sieve or perforated material for separating finer from coarser parts (as of sand) **3** : a surface on which an image is made to appear (as in television); *also* : the information displayed on a computer screen at one time **4** : the motion-picture industry
²screen *vb* **1** : to shield with or as if with a screen **2** : to separate with a screen; *also* : to select or categorize methodically 〈~ contestants〉 **3** : to present (as a motion picture) on the screen
screen·ing \'skrē-niŋ\ *n* **1** : metal or plastic mesh (as for window screens) **2** : a showing of a motion picture
screen saver *n* : a computer program that displays something (as images) on the screen of a computer that is on but not in use
¹screw \'skrü\ *n* [ME, fr. MF *escroe* female screw, nut, fr. ML *scrofa*, fr. L, sow] **1** : a machine consisting of a solid cylinder with a spiral groove around it and a corresponding hollow cylinder into which it fits **2** : a naillike metal piece with a spiral groove and a head with a slot that is inserted into material by rotating and is used to fasten pieces of solid material together **3** : PROPELLER
²screw *vb* **1** : to fasten or close by means of a screw **2** : to operate or adjust by means of a screw **3** : to move or cause to move spirally; *also* : to close or set in position by such an action
screw·ball \'skrü-ˌból\ *n* **1** : a baseball pitch breaking in a direction opposite to a curve **2** : a whimsical, eccentric, or crazy person
screw·driv·er \-ˌdrī-vər\ *n* **1** : a tool for turning screws **2** : a drink made of vodka and orange juice
screw·worm \'skrü-ˌwərm\ *n* : an American blowfly of warm regions whose larva matures in wounds or sores of mammals and may cause disease or death; *esp* : its larva
screwy \'skrü-ē\ *adj* screw·i·er; -est **1** : crazily absurd, eccentric, or unusual **2** : CRAZY, INSANE
scrib·ble \'skri-bəl\ *vb* scrib·bled; scrib·bling : to write hastily or carelessly — **scribble** *n* — **scrib·bler** *n*
scribe \'skrīb\ *n* **1** : a scholar of Jewish law in New Testament times **2** : a person whose business is the copying of writing **3** : JOURNALIST
scrim \'skrim\ *n* : a light loosely woven cotton or linen cloth
scrim·mage \'skri-mij\ *n* : the play between two football teams beginning with the snap of the ball; *also* : practice play between two teams — **scrimmage** *vb*
scrimp \'skrimp\ *vb* : to economize greatly 〈~ and save〉
scrim·shaw \'skrim-ˌshò\ *n* : carved or engraved articles made orig. by American whalers usu. from baleen or whale ivory — **scrimshaw** *vb*
scrip \'skrip\ *n* **1** : a certificate showing its holder is entitled to something (as stock or land) **2** : paper money issued for temporary use in an emergency
¹script \'skript\ *n* **1** : written matter (as lines for a play or broadcast) **2** : HANDWRITING
²script *abbr* scripture
scrip·ture \'skrip-chər\ *n* **1** *cap* : the books of the Bible — often used in pl. **2** : the sacred writings of a religion — **scrip·tur·al** \'skrip-chə-rəl\ *adj* — **scrip·tur·al·ly** *adv*
scriv·en·er \'skri-və-nər\ *n* : SCRIBE, COPYIST, WRITER
scrod \'skräd\ *n* [prob. fr. Brit. dial. (Cornwall) *scrawed*, pp. of *scraw, scrawl* to split, salt, and dry (young fish)] : a young fish (as a cod or haddock); *esp* : one split and boned for cooking
scrof·u·la \'skrò-fyə-lə\ *n* : tuberculosis of lymph nodes esp. in the neck
¹scroll \'skrōl\ *n* : a roll of paper or parchment for writing

a document; *also* : a spiral or coiled ornamental form suggesting a loosely or partly rolled scroll

²**scroll** *vb* : to move or cause to move text or graphics up, down, or across a display screen

scroll saw *n* **1** : FRETSAW **2** : a machine saw with a narrow vertically reciprocating blade for cutting curved lines or openwork

scro·tum \'skrō-təm\ *n, pl* **scro·ta** \-tə\ *or* **scrotums** [L] : a pouch that in most male mammals contains the testes

scrounge \'skraůnj\ *vb* **scrounged; scroung·ing** : to collect by or as if by foraging

¹**scrub** \'skrəb\ *n* **1** : a thick growth of stunted trees or shrubs; *also* : an area of land covered with scrub **2** : an inferior domestic animal **3** : a person of insignificant size or standing **4** : a player not on the first team — **scrub** *adj* — **scrub·by** *adj*

²**scrub** *vb* **scrubbed; scrub·bing 1** : to clean or wash by rubbing ⟨~ clothes⟩ ⟨~ out a spot⟩ **2** : CANCEL

³**scrub** *n* **1** : an act or instance of scrubbing ⟨gave the clothes a good ~⟩ **2** *pl* : loose-fitting clothing worn by hospital staff ⟨surgical ~s⟩

scrub·ber \'skrə-bər\ *n* : one that scrubs; *esp* : an apparatus for removing impurities esp. from gases

scruff \'skrəf\ *n* : the loose skin of the back of the neck : NAPE

scruffy \'skrə-fē\ *adj* **scruff·i·er; -est** : UNKEMPT, SLOVENLY

scrump·tious \'skrəmp-shəs\ *adj* : DELIGHTFUL, EXCELLENT; *esp* : DELICIOUS — **scrump·tious·ly** *adv*

scrunch·ie *or* **scrunchy** \'skrən-chē, 'skrůn-\ *n* : a fabric-covered elastic for the hair

¹**scru·ple** \'skrü-pəl\ *n* [ME *scrupil, scriple*, fr. AF *scruble*, fr. L *scrupulus*, dim. of *scrupus* source of uneasiness, lit., sharp stone] **1** : a point of conscience or honor **2** : hesitation due to ethical considerations

²**scruple** *vb* **scru·pled; scru·pling** : to be reluctant on grounds of conscience : HESITATE

scru·pu·lous \'skrü-pyə-ləs\ *adj* **1** : having moral integrity **2** : PAINSTAKING — **scru·pu·lous·ly** *adv* — **scru·pu·lous·ness** *n*

scru·ti·nise *Brit var of* SCRUTINIZE

scru·ti·nize \'skrü-tə-ˌnīz\ *vb* **-nized; -niz·ing** : to examine closely

scru·ti·ny \'skrü-tə-nē\ *n, pl* **-nies** [L *scrutinium*, fr. *scrutari* to search, examine, prob. fr. *scruta* trash] : a careful looking over ♦ **Synonyms** INSPECTION, EXAMINATION, ANALYSIS

scu·ba \'skü-bə\ *n* [*self-contained underwater breathing apparatus*] : an apparatus for breathing while swimming underwater

scuba diver *n* : one who swims underwater with the aid of scuba gear

¹**scud** \'skəd\ *vb* **scud·ded; scud·ding** : to move speedily

²**scud** *n* : light clouds driven by the wind

¹**scuff** \'skəf\ *vb* **1** : to scrape the feet while walking : SHUFFLE **2** : to scratch or become scratched or worn away

²**scuff** *n* **1** : a mark or injury caused by scuffing **2** : a flat-soled slipper without heel strap

scuf·fle \'skə-fəl\ *vb* **scuf·fled; scuf·fling 1** : to struggle confusedly at close quarters **2** : to shuffle one's feet — **scuffle** *n*

¹**scull** \'skəl\ *n* **1** : an oar for use in sculling; *also* : one of a pair of short oars for a single oarsman **2** : a racing shell propelled by one or two persons using sculls

²**scull** *vb* : to propel (a boat) by an oar over the stern

scul·lery \'skə-lə-rē\ *n, pl* **-ler·ies** [ME *squilerie, sculerie* department of household in charge of dishes, fr. AF *esquilerie*, fr. *escuele* bowl, fr. L *scutella* drinking bowl] : a small room near the kitchen used for cleaning dishes, cooking utensils, and vegetables

scul·lion \'skəl-yən\ *n* : a kitchen helper

sculpt \'skəlpt\ *vb* : CARVE, SCULPTURE

sculp·tor \'skəlp-tər\ *n* : a person who produces works of sculpture

¹**sculp·ture** \'skəlp-chər\ *n* : the act, process, or art of carving or molding material (as stone, wood, or plastic); *also* : work produced this way — **sculp·tur·al** \'skəlp-chə-rəl\ *adj*

²**sculpture** *vb* **sculp·tured; sculp·tur·ing** : to form or alter as or as if a work of sculpture

scum \'skəm\ *n* **1** : a slimy or filmy covering on the surface of a liquid **2** : waste matter **3** : RABBLE

scup·per \'skə-pər\ *n* [ME *skopper-*, perh. fr. AF **escopoir*, fr. *escopir* to spit out] : an opening in the side of a ship through which water on deck is drained overboard

scurf \'skərf\ *n* : thin dry scales of skin (as dandruff); *also* : a scaly deposit or covering — **scurfy** \'skər-fē\ *adj*

scur·ri·lous \'skər-ə-ləs\ *adj* : coarsely jesting : OBSCENE, VULGAR

scur·ry \'skər-ē\ *vb* **scur·ried; scur·ry·ing** : SCAMPER

¹**scur·vy** \'skər-vē\ *n* : a disease caused by a lack of vitamin C and characterized by spongy gums, loosened teeth, and bleeding under the skin

²**scurvy** *adj* : MEAN, CONTEMPTIBLE — **scur·vi·ly** \'skər-və-lē\ *adv*

scutch·eon \'skə-chən\ *n* : ESCUTCHEON

¹**scut·tle** \'skə-t³l\ *n* : a pail for carrying coal

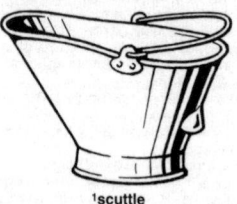

¹**scuttle**

²**scuttle** *n* : a small opening with a lid esp. in the deck, side, or bottom of a ship

³**scuttle** *vb* **scut·tled; scut·tling** : to cut a hole in the deck, side, or bottom of (a ship) in order to sink

⁴**scuttle** *vb* **scut·tled; scut·tling** : SCURRY, SCAMPER

scut·tle·butt \'skə-t³l-ˌbət\ *n* : GOSSIP

scythe \'sīth\ *n* : an implement for mowing (as grass or grain) by hand — **scythe** *vb*

SD *abbr* **1** South Dakota **2** special delivery

S Dak *abbr* South Dakota

SDI *abbr* Strategic Defense Initiative

Se *symbol* selenium

SE *abbr* southeast

sea \'sē\ *n* **1** : a large body of salt water **2** : OCEAN **3** : rough water; *also* : a large wave **4** : something likened to the sea esp. in vastness — **sea** *adj* — **at sea** : LOST, BEWILDERED

sea anemone *n* : any of numerous coelenterate polyps whose form, bright and varied colors, and cluster of tentacles superficially resemble a flower

sea·bird \'sē-ˌbərd\ *n* : a bird (as a gull) frequenting the open ocean

sea·board \-ˌbórd\ *n* : SEACOAST; *also* : the land bordering a coast

sea·borg·i·um \sē-'bór-gē-əm\ *n* : a short-lived radioactive chemical element produced artificially

sea·coast \-ˌkōst\ *n* : the shore of the sea

sea·far·er \-ˌfer-ər\ *n* : SEAMAN 1

sea·far·ing \-ˌfer-iŋ\ *n* : the use of the sea for travel or transportation — **seafaring** *adj*

sea·food \-ˌfüd\ *n* : edible marine fish and shellfish

sea·go·ing \-ˌgō-iŋ\ *adj* : OCEANGOING

sea·gull \-ˌgəl\ *n* : GULL

sea horse *n* : any of a genus of small marine fishes with the head and forepart of the body sharply flexed like the head and neck of a horse

¹**seal** \'sēl\ *n, pl* **seals** *also* **seal** [ME *sele*, fr. OE *seolh*] **1** : any of numerous large carnivorous sea mammals occurring chiefly in cold regions and having limbs adapted for swimming **2** : the pelt of a seal

²**seal** *vb* : to hunt seals

³**seal** *n* [ME *sele, seel*, fr. AF *seal, sel*, fr. L *sigillum*, fr. dim. of *signum* sign, seal] **1** : GUARANTEE, PLEDGE **2** : a device having a raised design that can be stamped on clay or wax; *also* : the impression made by stamping with such a device **3** : something that seals or closes up ⟨safety ~⟩

⁴**seal** *vb* **1** : to affix a seal to; *also* : AUTHENTICATE **2** : to fasten with or as if with a seal to prevent tampering **3** : to close or make secure against access, leakage, or passage **4** : to determine irrevocably ⟨~ed his fate⟩

sea–lane \'sē-ˌlān\ *n* : an established sea route

seal·ant \'sē-lənt\ *n* : a sealing agent

seal·er \'sē-lər\ *n* : a coat applied to prevent subsequent coats of paint or varnish from sinking in

sea level *n* : the level of the surface of the sea esp. at its mean midway between mean high and low water

sea·lift \'sē-ˌlift\ *n* : transport of military personnel and equipment by ship

sea lion *n* : any of several large Pacific seals with small external ears

seal·skin \'sēl-ˌskin\ *n* 1 : ¹SEAL 2 2 : a garment of sealskin

¹seam \'sēm\ *n* 1 : the line of junction of two edges and esp. of edges of fabric sewn together 2 : a layer of mineral matter 3 : WRINKLE

²seam *vb* 1 : to join by or as if by sewing 2 : WRINKLE, FURROW

sea·man \'sē-mən\ *n* 1 : one who assists in the handling of ships : MARINER 2 : an enlisted man in the navy ranking next below a petty officer third class

seaman apprentice *n* : an enlisted man in the navy ranking next below a seaman

seaman recruit *n* : an enlisted man of the lowest rank in the navy

sea·man·ship \'sē-mən-ˌship\ *n* : the art or skill of handling a ship

seam·less \'sēm-ləs\ *adj* : having no flaws or interruptions ⟨a ~ transition⟩ — seam·less·ly *adv*

sea·mount \'sē-ˌmau̇nt\ *n* : an underwater mountain

seam·stress \'sēm-strəs\ *n* : a woman who does sewing

seamy \'sē-mē\ *adj* seam·i·er; -est 1 : UNPLEASANT 2 : DEGRADED, SORDID ⟨the ~ part of town⟩

sé·ance \'sā-ˌäns\ *n* [F] : a meeting to receive communications from spirits

sea·plane \'sē-ˌplān\ *n* : an airplane that can take off from and land on water

sea·port \'sē-ˌpȯrt\ *n* : a port for oceangoing ships

sear \'sir\ *vb* 1 : WITHER 2 : to cook, burn, or scorch esp. on the surface; *also* : BRAND — sear *n*

¹search \'sərch\ *vb* [ME *cerchen*, fr. AF *cercher* to travel about, investigate, search, fr. LL *circare* to go about, fr. L *circum* round about] 1 : to look through in trying to find something 2 : SEEK 3 : PROBE — search·er *n*

²search *n* : the act of searching

search engine *n* : computer software or a Web site used to search data (as text or other Web sites) for specified information

search·light \-ˌlīt\ *n* : an apparatus for projecting a powerful beam of light; *also* : the light projected

sear·ing \'sir-iŋ\ *adj* : very sharp, harsh or intense ⟨~ pain⟩ ⟨a ~ review⟩

sea scallop *n* : a large scallop of the Atlantic coast of No. America that is harvested for food

sea·scape \'sē-ˌskāp\ *n* 1 : a view of the sea 2 : a picture representing a scene at or of the sea

sea·shell \'sē-ˌshel\ *n* : the shell of a marine animal and esp. a mollusk

sea·shore \-ˌshȯr\ *n* : the shore of a sea

sea·sick \'sē-ˌsik\ *adj* : nauseated by or as if by the motion of a ship — sea·sick·ness *n*

sea·side \'sē-ˌsīd\ *n* : SEASHORE

¹sea·son \'sē-zən\ *n* [ME *sesoun*, fr. AF *seison* natural season, appropriate time, fr. L *sation-, satio* action of sowing, fr. *serere* to sow] 1 : one of the divisions of the year (as spring or summer) 2 : a period of the year associated with a particular activity, event, or holiday ⟨the Easter ~⟩ ⟨hunting ~⟩ — sea·son·al \-zə-nəl\ *adj* — sea·son·al·ly *adv*

²season *vb* 1 : to make pleasant to the taste by use of salt, pepper, or spices 2 : to make (as by aging or drying) suitable for use 3 : to accustom or habituate to something (as hardship) ✦ *Synonyms* HARDEN, INURE, ACCLIMATE, TOUGHEN — sea·son·er *n*

sea·son·able \'sē-zə-nə-bəl\ *adj* : occurring at a good or proper time ✦ *Synonyms* TIMELY, PROPITIOUS, OPPORTUNE — sea·son·ably \-blē\ *adv*

seasonal affective disorder *n* : depression that recurs as the days grow shorter during the fall and winter

sea·son·ing *n* : something that seasons : CONDIMENT

¹seat \'sēt\ *n* 1 : a chair, bench, or stool for sitting on 2 : a place which serves as a capital or center

²seat *vb* 1 : to place in or on a seat 2 : to provide seats for

seat belt *n* : straps designed to hold a person in a seat

SEATO \'sē-ˌtō\ *abbr* Southeast Asia Treaty Organization

seat–of–the–pants *adj* : employing or based on personal experience, judgment, and effort rather than technological aids ⟨~ navigation⟩

sea turtle *n* : any of two families of marine turtles that have the feet modified into paddles

sea urchin *n* : any of numerous spiny marine echinoderms having thin brittle globular shells

sea·wall \'sē-ˌwȯl\ *n* : an embankment to protect the shore from erosion

¹sea·ward \'sē-wərd\ *n* : the direction or side away from land and toward the open sea

²seaward *also* sea·wards \-wərdz\ *adv* : toward the sea

³seaward *adj* 1 : directed or situated toward the sea 2 : coming from the sea

sea·wa·ter \'sē-ˌwȯ-tər, -ˌwä-\ *n* : water in or from the sea

sea·way \-ˌwā\ *n* : an inland waterway that admits ocean shipping

sea·weed \-ˌwēd\ *n* : a marine alga (as a kelp); *also* : a mass of marine algae

sea·wor·thy \-ˌwər-thē\ *adj* : fit for a sea voyage ⟨a ~ ship⟩

se·ba·ceous \si-'bā-shəs\ *adj* : of, relating to, or secreting fatty material

sec *abbr* 1 second; secondary 2 secretary 3 section 4 [L *secundum*] according to

SEC *abbr* Securities and Exchange Commission

se·cede \si-'sēd\ *vb* se·ced·ed; se·ced·ing : to withdraw from an organized body and esp. from a political body

se·ces·sion \si-'se-shən\ *n* : the act of seceding — se·ces·sion·ist *n*

se·clude \si-'klüd\ *vb* se·clud·ed; se·clud·ing : to keep or shut away from others

se·clu·sion \si-'klü-zhən\ *n* : the act of secluding : the state of being secluded — se·clu·sive \-siv\ *adj*

¹sec·ond \'se-kənd\ *adj* [ME, fr. AF *secund*, fr. L *secundus* second, following, favorable, fr. *sequi* to follow] 1 : being number two in a countable series 2 : next after the first 3 : ALTERNATE ⟨every ~ year⟩ — second *or* sec·ond·ly *adv*

²second *n* 1 : one that is second 2 : one who assists another (as in a duel) 3 : an inferior or flawed article (as of) 4 : the second forward gear in a motor vehicle

³second *n* [ME *secounde*, fr. ML *secunda*, fr. L, fem. of *secundus* second; fr. its being the second division of a unit into 60 parts, as a minute is the first] 1 : the 60th part of a minute of time or angular measure 2 : an instant of time

⁴second *vb* 1 : to encourage or give support to 2 : to act as a second to 3 : to support (a motion) by adding one's voice to that of a proposer

¹sec·ond·ary \'se-kən-ˌder-ē\ *adj* 1 : second in rank, value, or occurrence : LESSER 2 : belonging to a second or later stage of development 3 : coming after the primary or elementary ⟨~ schools⟩ ✦ *Synonyms* SUBORDINATE, COLLATERAL, DEPENDENT

²secondary *n, pl* -ar·ies : the defensive backfield of a football team

secondary sex characteristic *n* : a physical characteristic that appears in members of one sex at puberty or in seasonal breeders at breeding season and is not directly concerned with reproduction

second fiddle *n* : one that plays a supporting or subservient role

sec·ond–guess \ˌse-kənd-'ges\ *vb* 1 : to think out other strategies or explanations for after the event 2 : to seek to anticipate or predict

sec·ond·hand \-'hand\ *adj* 1 : not original 2 : not new : USED ⟨~ clothes⟩ 3 : dealing in used goods

secondhand smoke *n* : tobacco smoke that is exhaled by smokers or is given off by burning tobacco and is inhaled by persons nearby

second lieutenant *n* : a commissioned officer (as in the army) ranking next below a first lieutenant

sec·ond–rate \ˌse-kənd-'rāt\ *adj* : INFERIOR

sec·ond–string \'se-kənd-'striŋ\ *adj* : being a substitute (as on a team)

se·cre·cy \'sē-krə-sē\ *n, pl* -cies 1 : the habit or practice of being secretive **2** : the condition of being hidden or concealed

¹se·cret \'sē-krət\ *adj* **1** : HIDDEN, CONCEALED ⟨a ∼ staircase⟩ **2** : COVERT, STEALTHY; *also* : engaged in detecting or spying ⟨a ∼ agent⟩ **3** : kept from general knowledge — **se·cret·ly** *adv*

²secret *n* **1** : MYSTERY **2** : something kept from the knowledge of others

sec·re·tar·i·at \ˌse-krə-'ter-ē-ət\ *n* **1** : the office of a secretary **2** : the secretarial staff in an office **3** : the administrative department of a governmental organization ⟨the UN ∼⟩

sec·re·tary \'se-krə-ˌter-ē\ *n, pl* **-tar·ies 1** : a person employed to handle records, correspondence, and routine work for another person **2** : an officer of a corporation or business who is in charge of correspondence and records **3** : an official at the head of a department of government **4** : a writing desk — **sec·re·tari·al** \ˌse-krə-'ter-ē-əl\ *adj* — **sec·re·tary·ship** \'se-krə-ˌter-ē-ˌship\ *n*

¹se·crete \si-'krēt\ *vb* **se·cret·ed; se·cret·ing** : to form and give off (a secretion)

²se·crete \si-'krēt, 'sē-krət\ *vb* **se·cret·ed; se·cret·ing** : HIDE, CONCEAL

se·cre·tion \si-'krē-shən\ *n* **1** : the process of secreting something **2** : a product of glandular activity; *esp* : one (as a hormone) useful in the organism **3** : the act of hiding something — **se·cre·to·ry** \'sē-krə-ˌtȯr-ē\ *adj*

se·cre·tive \'sē-krə-tiv, si-'krē-\ *adj* : tending to keep secrets or to act secretly — **se·cre·tive·ly** *adv* — **se·cre·tive·ness** *n*

¹sect \'sekt\ *n* **1** : a dissenting religious body **2** : a religious denomination **3** : a group adhering to a distinctive doctrine or to a leader

²sect *abbr* section; sectional

¹sec·tar·i·an \sek-'ter-ē-ən\ *adj* **1** : of or relating to a sect or sectarian **2** : limited in character or scope — **sec·tar·i·an·ism** *n*

²sectarian *n* **1** : an adherent of a sect **2** : a narrow or bigoted person

sec·ta·ry \'sek-tə-rē\ *n, pl* **-ries** : a member of a sect

¹sec·tion \'sek-shən\ *n* **1** : a part cut off or separated **2** : a distinct part **3** : the appearance that a thing has or would have if cut straight through

²section *vb* **1** : to separate or become separated into sections **2** : to represent in sections

sec·tion·al \'sek-shə-nəl\ *adj* **1** : of, relating to, or characteristic of a section **2** : local or regional rather than general in character **3** : divided into sections — **sec·tion·al·ism** *n*

sec·tor \'sek-tər\ *n* **1** : a part of a circle between two radii **2** : an area assigned to a military leader to defend **3** : a subdivision of society

sec·u·lar \'se-kyə-lər\ *adj* **1** : not sacred or ecclesiastical **2** : not bound by monastic vows ⟨a ∼ priest⟩

sec·u·lar·ise *Brit var of* SECULARIZE

sec·u·lar·ism \'se-kyə-lə-ˌri-zəm\ *n* : indifference to or exclusion of religion — **sec·u·lar·ist** \-rist\ *n* — **secularist** *also* **sec·u·lar·is·tic** \ˌse-kyə-lə-'ris-tik\ *adj*

sec·u·lar·ize \'se-kyə-lə-ˌrīz\ *vb* **-ized; -iz·ing 1** : to make secular **2** : to transfer from ecclesiastical to civil or lay use, possession, or control — **sec·u·lar·i·za·tion** \ˌse-kyə-lə-rə-'zā-shən\ *n* — **sec·u·lar·iz·er** \'se-kyə-lə-ˌrī-zər\ *n*

¹se·cure \si-'kyùr\ *adj* **se·cur·er; -est** [L *securus* safe, secure, fr. *se* without + *cura* care] **1** : easy in mind : free from fear **2** : free from danger or risk of loss : SAFE **3** : CERTAIN, SURE — **se·cure·ly** *adv*

²secure *vb* **se·cured; se·cur·ing 1** : to make safe : GUARD **2** : to assure payment of by giving a pledge or collateral **3** : to fasten safely ⟨∼ a door⟩ **4** : GET, ACQUIRE

se·cu·ri·ty \si-'kyùr-ə-tē\ *n, pl* **-ties 1** : SAFETY **2** : freedom from worry **3** : something given as pledge of payment ⟨a ∼ deposit⟩ **4** *pl* : bond or stock certificates **5** : PROTECTION

secy *abbr* secretary

se·dan \si-'dan\ *n* **1** : a covered chair borne on poles by two men **2** : an automobile seating four or more people and usu. having a permanent top

¹se·date \si-'dāt\ *adj* : quiet and dignified in behavior ◆ *Synonyms* STAID, SOBER, SERIOUS, SOLEMN — **se·date·ly** *adv*

²sedate *vb* **se·dat·ed; se·dat·ing** : to dose with sedatives — **se·da·tion** \si-'dā-shən\ *n*

¹sed·a·tive \'se-də-tiv\ *adj* : serving or tending to relieve tension

²sedative *n* : a sedative drug

sed·en·tary \'se-d°n-ˌter-ē\ *adj* : characterized by or requiring much sitting

sedge \'sej\ *n* : any of a family of plants esp. of marshy areas that differ from the related grasses esp. in having solid stems — **sedgy** \'se-jē\ *adj*

sed·i·ment \'se-də-mənt\ *n* **1** : the material that settles to the bottom of a liquid **2** : material (as stones and sand) deposited by water, wind, or a glacier — **sed·i·men·ta·ry** \ˌse-də-'men-tə-rē\ *adj* — **sed·i·men·ta·tion** \-mən-'tā-shən, -ˌmen-\ *n*

se·di·tion \si-'di-shən\ *n* : the causing of discontent, insurrection, or resistance against a government — **se·di·tious** \-shəs\ *adj*

se·duce \si-'düs, -'dyüs\ *vb* **se·duced; se·duc·ing 1** : to persuade to disobedience or disloyalty **2** : to lead astray **3** : to entice to sexual intercourse ◆ *Synonyms* TEMPT, ENTICE, INVEIGLE, LURE — **se·duc·er** *n* — **se·duc·tion** \-'dək-shən\ *n* — **se·duc·tive** \-tiv\ *adj*

sed·u·lous \'se-jə-ləs\ *adj* [L *sedulus*, fr. *sedulo* sincerely, diligently, fr. *se* without + *dolus* guile] : DILIGENT, PAINSTAKING

¹see \'sē\ *vb* **saw** \'sȯ\; **seen** \'sēn\; **see·ing 1** : to perceive by the eye; *also* : to have the power of sight **2** : EXPERIENCE **3** : UNDERSTAND **4** : to make sure ⟨∼ that order is kept⟩ **5** : to meet with **6** : to keep company with esp. in dating **7** : ACCOMPANY, ESCORT ⟨∼ the guests to the door⟩ ◆ *Synonyms* BEHOLD, DESCRY, ESPY, VIEW, OBSERVE, NOTE, DISCERN — **see red** : to become very angry — **see the light** : to realize an obscured truth

²see *n* : the authority or jurisdiction of a bishop

¹seed \'sēd\ *n, pl* **seed** *or* **seeds 1** : the grains of plants used for sowing **2** : a ripened ovule of a flowering plant that may develop into a new plant; *also* : a plant structure (as a spore or small dry fruit) capable of producing a new plant **3** : DESCENDANTS **4** : SOURCE, ORIGIN **5** : a competitor seeded in a tournament — **seed·less** *adj* — **go to seed** *or* **run to seed 1** : to develop seed **2** : DECAY, DETERIORATE

²seed *vb* **1** : SOW, PLANT ⟨∼ land with grass⟩ **2** : to bear or shed seeds **3** : to remove seeds from **4** : to rank or schedule (contestants) in a tournament — **seed·er** *n*

seed·bed \-ˌbed\ *n* : soil or a bed of soil prepared for planting seed

seed·ling \'sēd-liŋ\ *n* **1** : a young plant grown from seed **2** : a young tree before it becomes a sapling

seed·time \'sēd-ˌtīm\ *n* : the season for sowing

seedy \'sē-dē\ *adj* **seed·i·er; -est 1** : containing or full of seeds **2** : SHABBY

seek \'sēk\ *vb* **sought** \'sȯt\; **seek·ing 1** : to search for **2** : to try to reach or obtain **3** : ATTEMPT — **seek·er** *n*

seem \'sēm\ *vb* **1** : to appear to the observation or understanding **2** : to give the impression of being : APPEAR

seem·ing *adj* : outwardly apparent — **seem·ing·ly** *adv*

seem·ly \'sēm-lē\ *adj* **seem·li·er; -est 1** : conventionally proper **2** : FIT

seep \'sēp\ *vb* : to flow or pass slowly through fine pores or cracks — **seep·age** \'sē-pij\ *n*

seer \'sir\ *n* : a person who foresees or predicts events : PROPHET

seer·suck·er \'sir-ˌsə-kər\ *n* [Hindi *śīrsakar*, fr. Pers *shīr-o-shakar*, lit., milk and sugar] : a light fabric of linen, cotton, or rayon usu. striped and slightly puckered

see·saw \'sē-ˌsȯ\ *n* **1** : a contest in which each side assumes then relinquishes the lead **2** : a children's sport of riding up and down on the ends of a plank supported in the middle; *also* : the plank so used — **seesaw** *vb*

seethe \'sēth\ *vb* **seethed; seeth·ing** [archaic *seethe* boil] : to become violently agitated ⟨∼ with jealousy⟩

seg·ment \'seg-mənt\ *n* **1** : a part cut off from a geometrical figure (as a circle) by one or more points, lines, or planes **2** : a division of a thing : SECTION — **seg·men·tal** \seg-'men-t°l\ *adj* — **seg·men·ta·tion** \ˌseg-mən-'tā-shən\ *n* — **seg·ment·ed** \'seg-ˌmen-təd\ *adj*

seg·re·gate \'se-gri-ˌgāt\ *vb* **-gat·ed; -gat·ing** [L *segregare*, fr. *se-* apart + *greg-, grex* herd, flock] : to cut off from others; *esp* : to separate esp. by races or ethnic groups — **seg·re·ga·tion** \ₛse-gri-'gā-shən\ *n*

seg·re·ga·tion·ist \ₛse-gri-'gā-shə-nist\ *n* : one who believes in or practices the segregation of races

sei·gneur \sān-'yər\ *n, often cap* [MF, fr. ML *senior*, fr. L, adj., elder] : a feudal lord

¹**seine** \'sān\ *n* : a large weighted fishing net

²**seine** *vb* **seined; sein·ing** : to fish or catch with a seine — **sein·er** *n*

seis·mic \'sīz-mik, 'sīs-\ *adj* : of, relating to, resembling, or caused by an earthquake — **seis·mi·cal·ly** \-mi-k(ə-)lē\ *adv* — **seis·mic·i·ty** \sīz-'mi-sə-tē, sīs-\ *n*

seis·mo·gram \'sīz-mə-ₓgram, 'sīs-\ *n* : the record of an earth tremor made by a seismograph

seis·mo·graph \-ₓgraf\ *n* : an apparatus to measure and record seismic vibrations — **seis·mo·graph·ic** \ₓsīz-mə-'gra-fik, ₓsīs-\ *adj* — **seis·mog·ra·phy** \sīz-'mä-grə-fē, sīs-\ *n*

seis·mol·o·gy \sīz-'mä-lə-jē, sīs-\ *n* : a science that deals with earthquakes — **seis·mo·log·i·cal** \ₓsīz-mə-'lä-ji-kəl, ₓsīs-\ *adj* — **seis·mol·o·gist** \sīz-'mä-lə-jist, sīs-\ *n*

seis·mom·e·ter \sīz-'mä-mə-tər, sīs-\ *n* : a seismograph measuring the actual movement of the ground

seize \'sēz\ *vb* **seized; seiz·ing** 1 : to lay hold of or take possession of by force 2 : ARREST 3 : UNDERSTAND 4 : to attack or overwhelm physically : AFFLICT ✦ *Synonyms* TAKE, GRASP, CLUTCH, SNATCH, GRAB

sei·zure \'sē-zhər\ *n* 1 : the act of seizing : the state of being seized 2 : a sudden attack (as of disease)

sel *abbr* select; selected; selection

sel·dom \'sel-dəm\ *adv* : not often : RARELY

¹**se·lect** \sə-'lekt\ *adj* 1 : CHOSEN, PICKED; *also* : CHOICE 2 : judicious or restrictive in choice : DISCRIMINATING

²**select** *vb* : to choose from a number or group : pick out

se·lec·tion \sə-'lek-shən\ *n* 1 : the act or process of selecting 2 : something selected : CHOICE 3 : a natural or artificial process that tends to favor the survival and reproduction of individuals with certain traits but not those with others

se·lec·tive \sə-'lek-tiv\ *adj* : of or relating to selection : selecting or tending to select ⟨∼ shoppers⟩

selective service *n* : a system for calling men up for military service : DRAFT

se·lect·man \si-'lekt-ₓman, -mən\ *n* : one of a board of officials elected in towns of most New England states to administer town affairs

se·le·ni·um \sə-'lē-nē-əm\ *n* : a photosensitive chemical element

self \'self\ *n, pl* **selves** \'selvz\ 1 : the essential person distinct from all other persons in identity 2 : a particular side of a person's character 3 : personal interest : SELFISHNESS

self- *comb form* 1 : oneself : itself 2 : of oneself or itself 3 : by oneself or itself; *also* : automatic 4 : to, for, or toward oneself

self-abasement	self-confident
self-absorbed	self-congratulation
self-absorption	self-congratulatory
self-acceptance	self-constituted
self-accusation	self-contempt
self-acting	self-contradiction
self-addressed	self-contradictory
self-adjusting	self-control
self-administer	self-correcting
self-advancement	self-created
self-aggrandizement	self-criticism
self-aggrandizing	self-cultivation
self-analysis	self-deceit
self-anointed	self-deception
self-appointed	self-defeating
self-appraisal	self-definition
self-asserting	self-delusion
self-assertion	self-denial
self-assertive	self-denying
self-assurance	self-deprecating
self-assured	self-deprecation
self-awareness	self-depreciation
self-betrayal	self-described
self-cleaning	self-despair
self-closing	self-destruct
self-complacent	self-destruction
self-conceit	self-destructive
self-concern	self-determination
self-condemned	self-directed
self-confessed	self-discipline
self-confidence	self-distrust

self-doubt	self-portrait
self-educated	self-possessed
self-employed	self-possession
self-employment	self-preservation
self-enhancement	self-proclaimed
self-esteem	self-professed
self-examination	self-promotion
self-explaining	self-propelled
self-explanatory	self-propelling
self-expression	self-protection
self-forgetful	self-realization
self-giving	self-referential
self-governing	self-regard
self-government	self-reliance
self-hate	self-reliant
self-hypnosis	self-renewing
self-image	self-reproach
self-importance	self-respect
self-important	self-respecting
self-imposed	self-restraint
self-improvement	self-revelation
self-incrimination	self-rule
self-induced	self-sacrifice
self-indulgence	self-sacrificing
self-indulgent	self-satisfaction
self-inflicted	self-satisfied
self-instruction	self-service
self-interest	self-serving
self-knowledge	self-starting
self-limiting	self-styled
self-love	self-sufficiency
self-lubricating	self-sufficient
self-luminous	self-supporting
self-operating	self-sustaining
self-perception	self-taught
self-perpetuating	self-torment
self-pity	self-winding
	self-worth

self–cen·tered \'self-'sen-tərd\ *adj* : concerned only with one's own self — **self–cen·tered·ness** *n*

self–com·posed \ₓself-kəm-'pōzd\ *adj* : having control over one's emotions

self–con·scious \'self-'kän-chəs\ *adj* : uncomfortably conscious of oneself as an object of observation by others — **self–con·scious·ly** *adv* — **self–con·scious·ness** *n*

self–con·tained \ₓself-kən-'tānd\ *adj* 1 : complete in itself 2 : showing self-control; *also* : reserved in manner

self–de·fense \'self-di-'fens\ *n* 1 : a plea of justification for the use of force or homicide 2 : the act of defending oneself, one's property, or a close relative

self–ef·fac·ing \-ə-'fā-siŋ\ *adj* : RETIRING, SHY

self–ev·i·dent \ₓself-'e-və-dənt\ *adj* : evident without proof or reasoning

self–fer·til·i·za·tion \ₓself-ₓfər-tə-lə-'zā-shən\ *n* : fertilization of a plant or animal by its own pollen or sperm

self–ful·fill·ing \ₓself-fül-'fi-liŋ\ *adj* : becoming real or true by virtue of having been predicted or expected ⟨a ∼ prophecy⟩

self–help \'self-'help\ *n* : the process of bettering oneself or coping with one's problems without the aid of others — **self–help** *adj*

self·ish \'sel-fish\ *adj* : concerned with one's own welfare excessively or without regard for others — **self·ish·ly** *adv* — **self·ish·ness** *n*

self·less \'self-ləs\ *adj* : UNSELFISH — **self·less·ness** *n*

self–made \'self-'mād\ *adj* : having achieved success or prominence by one's own efforts ⟨a ∼ man⟩

self–pol·li·na·tion \ₓself-ₓpä-lə-'nā-shən\ *n* : pollination of a flower by its own pollen or sometimes by pollen from another flower on the same plant

self–reg·u·lat·ing \'self-'re-gyə-ₓlā-tiŋ\ *adj* : AUTOMATIC

self–righ·teous \-'rī-chəs\ *adj* : strongly convinced of one's own righteousness — **self–righ·teous·ly** *adv*

self–same \'self-ₓsām\ *adj* : precisely the same : IDENTICAL

self–seal·ing \'self-'sē-liŋ\ *adj* : capable of sealing itself (as after puncture)

self–seek·ing \'self-'sē-kiŋ\ *adj* : seeking only to further one's own interests — **self–seeking** *n*

self–start·er \-'stär-tər\ *n* : a person who has initiative

self–will \'self-'wil\ *n* : OBSTINACY

sell \'sel\ *vb* **sold** \'sōld\; **sell·ing** 1 : to transfer (property) in return for money or something else of value 2 : to deal in as a business 3 : to be sold ⟨cars are ∼*ing* well⟩ — **sell·er** *n*

sell out *vb* 1 : to dispose of entirely by sale; *esp* : to sell one's business 2 : BETRAY — **sell·out** \'sel-ₓaút\ *n*

selt·zer \'selt-sər\ *n* [modif. of G *Selterser (Wasser)* water of Selters, fr. Nieder *Selters*, Germany] : artificially carbonated water

sel·vage *or* **sel·vedge** \'sel-vij\ *n* : the edge of a woven fabric so formed as to prevent raveling

selves *pl of* SELF

sem *abbr* 1 semicolon 2 seminar 3 seminary

se·man·tic \si-'man-tik\ *also* **se·man·ti·cal** \-ti-kəl\ *adj* : of or relating to meaning in language

se·man·tics \si-'man-tiks\ *n sing or pl* : the study of meanings in language

sema·phore \'se-mə-ˌför\ *n* 1 : a visual signaling apparatus with movable arms 2 : signaling by hand-held flags

sem·blance \'sem-bləns\ *n* 1 : outward appearance 2 : IMAGE, LIKENESS

se·men \'sē-mən\ *n* [NL, fr. L, seed] : a sticky whitish fluid of the male reproductive tract that contains the sperm

se·mes·ter \sə-'mes-tər\ *n* [G, fr. L *semestris* half-yearly, fr. *sex* six + *mensis* month] 1 : half a year 2 : one of the two terms into which many colleges divide the school year

semi- \'se-mi, -ˌmī\ *prefix* 1 : precisely half of 2 : half in quantity or value; *also* : half of or occurring halfway through a specified period 3 : partly : incompletely 4 : partial : incomplete 5 : having some of the characteristics of

semiannual	semiofficial
semiarid	semipermanent
semicentennial	semipolitical
semicircle	semiprecious
semicircular	semiprivate
semicivilized	semiprofessional
semiclassical	semireligious
semiconscious	semiretired
semidarkness	semiskilled
semidivine	semisoft
semiformal	semisolid
semigloss	semisweet
semi–independent	semitransparent
semiliquid	semiweekly
semiliterate	semiyearly
semimonthly	

semi \'se-ˌmī\ *n, pl* **sem·is** : SEMITRAILER

semi·au·to·mat·ic \ˌse-mē-ˌo-tə-'ma-tik\ *adj, of a firearm* : able to fire repeatedly but requiring release and another press of the trigger for each successive shot

semi·co·lon \'se-mi-ˌkō-lən\ *n* : a punctuation mark; used esp. to separate major sentence elements

semi·con·duc·tor \ˌse-mi-kən-'dək-tər\ *n* : a substance whose electrical conductivity is between that of a conductor and an insulator — **semi·con·duct·ing** *adj*

¹**semi·fi·nal** \ˌse-mi-'fī-nºl\ *adj* : being next to the last in an elimination tournament

²**semi·fi·nal** \'se-mi-ˌfī-nºl\ *n* : a semifinal round or match — **semi·fi·nal·ist** \-ist\ *n*

semi·lu·nar \-'lü-nər\ *adj* : LUNATE

sem·i·nal \'se-mə-nºl\ *adj* 1 : of, relating to, or consisting of seed or semen 2 : containing or contributing the seeds of later development : CREATIVE, ORIGINAL — **sem·i·nal·ly** *adv*

sem·i·nar \'se-mə-ˌnär\ *n* 1 : a course of study pursued by a group of advanced students doing original research under a professor 2 : CONFERENCE

sem·i·nary \'se-mə-ˌner-ē\ *n, pl* **-nar·ies** [ME, seedbed, nursery, fr. L *seminarium*, fr. *semen* seed] : an educational institution; *esp* : one that gives theological training — **sem·i·nar·i·an** \ˌse-mə-'ner-ē-ən\ *n*

Sem·i·nole \'se-mə-ˌnōl\ *n, pl* **Semi·noles** *or* **Seminole** : a member of an American Indian people of Florida

semi·per·me·able \ˌse-mi-'pər-mē-ə-bəl\ *adj* : partially but not freely or wholly permeable; *esp* : permeable to some usu. small molecules but not to other usu. larger particles ⟨a ~ membrane⟩ — **semi·per·me·abil·i·ty** \-ˌpər-mē-ə-'bi-lə-tē\ *n*

Sem·ite \'se-ˌmīt\ *n* : a member of any of a group of peoples (as the Hebrews or Arabs) of southwestern Asia — **Se·mit·ic** \sə-'mi-tik\ *adj*

semi·trail·er \'se-mi-ˌtrā-lər, -ˌmī-\ *n* : a freight trailer that when attached is supported at its forward end by the truck tractor; *also* : a semitrailer with attached tractor

sem·o·li·na \ˌse-mə-'lē-nə\ *n* : the purified hard grains produced from the milling of wheat and used esp. for pasta

sempstress *var of* SEAMSTRESS

¹**sen** \'sen\ *n, pl* **sen** — see *yen* at MONEY table

²**sen** *n, pl* **sen** — see *dollar, ringgit, rupiah* at MONEY table

³**sen** *n, pl* **sen** — see *riel* at MONEY table

⁴**sen** *abbr* 1 senate; senator 2 senior

sen·ate \'se-nət\ *n* : the second of two chambers of a legislature

sen·a·tor \'se-nə-tər\ *n* : a member of a senate — **sen·a·to·ri·al** \ˌse-nə-'tór-ē-əl\ *adj*

send \'send\ *vb* **sent** \'sent\; **send·ing** 1 : to cause to go 2 : EMIT 3 : to propel or drive esp. with force 4 : to put or bring into a certain condition ⟨*sent* them into a rage⟩ 5 : to convey or transmit by an agent — **send·er** *n*

send–off \'send-ˌóf\ *n* : a demonstration of goodwill and enthusiasm at the start of a new venture (as a trip)

send–up \'send-ˌəp\ *n* : PARODY, TAKEOFF

se·ne \'sā-(ˌ)nä\ *n, pl* **sene** — see *tala* at MONEY table

Sen·e·ca \'se-ni-kə\ *n, pl* **Seneca** *or* **Senecas** : a member of an American Indian people of western New York

Sen·e·ga·lese \ˌse-ni-gə-'lēz, -'lēs\ *n, pl* **Senegalese** : a native or inhabitant of Senegal — **Senegalese** *adj*

se·nes·cence \si-'ne-sºns\ *n* : the state of being old; *also* : the process of becoming old — **se·nes·cent** \-ºnt\ *adj*

se·nile \'sē-ˌnī(-ə)l, 'se-\ *adj* : OLD, AGED; *esp* : exhibiting a loss of cognitive abilities associated with old age — **se·nil·i·ty** \si-'ni-lə-tē\ *n*

¹**se·nior** \'sē-nyər\ *n* 1 : a person older or of higher rank than another 2 : a member of the graduating class of a high school or college

²**senior** *adj* [ME, fr. L, older, elder, compar. of *senex* old] 1 : ELDER 2 : more advanced in dignity or rank 3 : belonging to the final year of a school or college course

senior chief petty officer *n* : a petty officer in the navy or coast guard ranking next below a master chief petty officer

senior citizen *n* : an elderly person; *esp* : one who has retired

senior high school *n* : a school usu. including grades 10 to 12

se·nior·i·ty \sēn-'yór-ə-tē\ *n* 1 : the quality or state of being senior 2 : a privileged status owing to length of continuous service

senior master sergeant *n* : a noncommissioned officer in the air force ranking next below a chief master sergeant

sen·i·ti \'se-nə-tē\ *n, pl* **seniti** — see *pa'anga* at MONEY table

sen·na \'se-nə\ *n* 1 : CASSIA 2; *esp* : one used medicinally 2 : the dried leaflets or pods of a cassia used as a purgative

sen·sa·tion \sen-'sā-shən\ *n* 1 : awareness (as of noise or heat) or a mental process (as seeing or hearing) due to stimulation of a sense organ; *also* : an indefinite bodily feeling 2 : a condition of excitement; *also* : the thing that causes this condition

sen·sa·tion·al \-shə-nəl\ *adj* 1 : of or relating to sensation or the senses 2 : arousing an intense and usu. superficial interest or emotional reaction — **sen·sa·tion·al·ly** *adv*

sen·sa·tion·al·ise *Brit var of* SENSATIONALIZE

sen·sa·tion·al·ism \-nə-ˌli-zəm\ *n* : the use or effect of sensational subject matter or treatment — **sen·sa·tion·al·ist** \-nə-list\ *adj or n* — **sen·sa·tion·al·is·tic** \-ˌsā-shə-nə-'lis-tik\ *adj*

sen·sa·tion·al·ize \-nə-ˌlīz\ *vb* **-ized; -iz·ing** : to present in a sensational manner

¹**sense** \'sens\ *n* 1 : semantic content : MEANING 2 : the faculty of perceiving by means of sense organs; *also* : a bodily function or mechanism (as sight, hearing, or smell) involving the action and effect of a stimulus on a sense organ 3 : SENSATION, AWARENESS 4 : INTELLIGENCE, JUDGMENT 5 : OPINION ⟨the ~ of the meeting⟩ — **sense·less** *adj* — **sense·less·ly** *adv* — **sense·less·ness** *n*

²**sense** *vb* **sensed; sens·ing** 1 : to be or become aware of ⟨~ danger⟩; *also* : to perceive by the senses 2 : to detect (as radiation) automatically

sense organ *n* : a bodily structure (as an eye or ear) that receives stimuli (as heat or light) which excite neurons to send information to the brain

sen·si·bil·i·ty \ˌsen-sə-'bi-lə-tē\ *n, pl* **-ties** : delicacy of feeling : SENSITIVITY

sen·si·ble \'sen-sə-bəl\ *adj* 1 : capable of being perceived by the senses or the mind; *also* : capable of receiving sense impressions 2 : AWARE, CONSCIOUS 3 : REASONABLE, RATIONAL — **sen·si·bly** \-blē\ *adv*

sen·si·tive \'sen-sə-tiv\ *adj* 1 : subject to excitation by or responsive to stimuli **2** : having power of feeling **3** : of such a nature as to be easily affected **4** : TOUCHY ⟨a ~ issue⟩ — **sen·si·tive·ly** adv — **sen·si·tive·ness** n — **sen·si·tiv·i·ty** \ˌsen-sə-'ti-və-tē\ n

sensitive plant n : any of several mimosas with leaves that fold or droop when touched

sen·si·tize \'sen-sə-ˌtīz\ vb **-tized; -tiz·ing** : to make or become sensitive or hypersensitive — **sen·si·ti·za·tion** \ˌsen-sə-tə-'zā-shən\ n

sen·sor \'sen-ˌsȯr, -sər\ n : a device that responds to a physical stimulus

sen·so·ry \'sen-sə-rē\ adj **1** : of or relating to sensation or the senses **2** : AFFERENT

sen·su·al \'sen-shə-wəl\ adj **1** : relating to gratification of the senses **2** : devoted to the pleasures of the senses — **sen·su·al·ist** n — **sen·su·al·i·ty** \ˌsen-shə-'wa-lə-tē\ n — **sen·su·al·ly** adv

sen·su·ous \'sen-shə-wəs\ adj **1** : relating to the senses or to things that can be perceived by the senses **2** : VOLUPTUOUS — **sen·su·ous·ly** adv — **sen·su·ous·ness** n

¹sent past and past part of SEND

²sent \'sent\ n, pl **sen·ti** \'sen-tē\ — see kroon at MONEY table

sen·te \'sen-tē\ n, pl **li·cen·te** or **li·sen·te** \li-'sen-tē\ — see loti at MONEY table

¹sen·tence \'sen-tᵊns, -tᵊnz\ n [ME, fr. AF, fr. L sententia, lit., feeling, opinion, fr. sentire to feel] **1** : the punishment set by a court **2** : a grammatically self-contained speech unit that expresses an assertion, a question, a command, a wish, or an exclamation

²sentence vb **sen·tenced; sen·tenc·ing** : to impose a sentence on

sen·ten·tious \sen-'ten-chəs\ adj : using wise sayings or proverbs; also : using pompous language — **sen·ten·tious·ly** adv — **sen·ten·tious·ness** n

sen·tient \'sen-chənt, -chē-ənt\ adj : capable of feeling : having perception

sen·ti·ment \'sen-tə-mənt\ n **1** : FEELING; also : thought and judgment influenced by feeling : emotional attitude **2** : OPINION, NOTION

sen·ti·men·tal \ˌsen-tə-'men-tᵊl\ adj **1** : influenced by tender feelings **2** : affecting the emotions ✦ Synonyms BATHETIC, MAUDLIN, MAWKISH, MUSHY — **sen·ti·men·tal·ism** n — **sen·ti·men·tal·ist** n — **sen·ti·men·tal·i·ty** \-ˌmen-'ta-lə-tē, -mən-\ n — **sen·ti·men·tal·ly** adv

sen·ti·men·tal·ise Brit var of SENTIMENTALIZE

sen·ti·men·tal·ize \-'men-tə-ˌlīz\ vb **-ized; -iz·ing 1** : to indulge in sentiment **2** : to look upon or imbue with sentiment — **sen·ti·men·tal·i·za·tion** \-ˌmen-tə-lə-'zā-shən\ n

sen·ti·mo \sen-'tē-(ˌ)mō\ n, pl **-mos** — see peso at MONEY table

sen·ti·nel \'sen-tᵊn-əl\ n [MF sentinelle, fr. It sentinella, fr. sentina vigilance, fr. sentire to perceive, fr. L] : SENTRY

sen·try \'sen-trē\ n, pl **sentries** : a guard at a point of passage

sep abbr separate, separated

Sep abbr September

SEP abbr simplified employee pension

se·pal \'sē-pəl, 'se-\ n : one of the modified leaves comprising a flower calyx

sep·a·ra·ble \'se-pə-rə-bəl\ adj : capable of being separated — **sep·a·ra·bil·i·ty** \ˌse-pə-rə-'bi-lə-tē\

¹sep·a·rate \'se-pə-ˌrāt\ vb **-rat·ed; -rat·ing 1** : to set or keep apart : DISCONNECT, SEVER **2** : to keep apart by something intervening **3** : to cease to be together : PART

²sep·a·rate \'se-prət, -pə-rət\ adj **1** : not connected **2** : divided from each other **3** : SINGLE, PARTICULAR ⟨the ~ pieces of the puzzle⟩ — **sep·a·rate·ly** adv

³sep·a·rate \'se-prət, -pə-rət\ n : an article of dress designed to be worn interchangeably with others to form various combinations

sep·a·ra·tion \ˌse-pə-'rā-shən\ n **1** : the act or process of separating : the state of being separated **2** : a point, line, means, or area of division **3** : a formal separating of a married couple by agreement but without divorce

sep·a·rat·ist \'se-prə-tist, 'se-pə-ˌrā-\ n : an advocate of separation (as from a political body) — **sep·a·rat·ism** \'se-prə-ˌti-zəm\ n

sep·a·ra·tive \'se-pə-ˌrā-tiv, 'se-prə-tiv\ adj : tending toward, causing, or expressing separation

sep·a·ra·tor \'se-pə-ˌrā-tər\ n : one that separates; esp : a device for separating cream from milk

se·pia \'sē-pē-ə\ n : a brownish gray to dark brown color

sep·sis \'sep-səs\ n, pl **sep·ses** \'sep-ˌsēz\ : a toxic condition due to spread of bacteria or their toxic products in the body

Sept abbr September

Sep·tem·ber \sep-'tem-bər\ n [ME Septembre, fr. AF & OE, both fr. L September (seventh month), fr. septem seven] : the 9th month of the year having 30 days

sep·tic \'sep-tik\ adj **1** : PUTREFACTIVE **2** : relating to or involving sepsis **3** : of, relating to, or used for sewage treatment and disposal

sep·ti·ce·mia \ˌsep-tə-'sē-mē-ə\ n : BLOOD POISONING

septic tank n : a tank in which sewage is disintegrated by bacteria

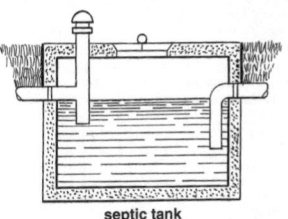

septic tank

sep·tu·a·ge·nar·i·an \ˌsep-ˌtü-ə-jə-'ner-ē-ən, -ˌtyü-\ n : a person whose age is in the seventies — **septuagenarian** adj

Sep·tu·a·gint \sep-'tü-ə-jənt, -'tyü-\ n : a Greek version of the Old Testament prepared in the 3d and 2d centuries B.C. by Jewish scholars

sep·tum \'sep-təm\ n, pl **sep·ta** \-tə\ : a dividing wall or membrane esp. between bodily spaces or masses of soft tissue

se·pul·chral \sə-'pəl-krəl\ adj **1** : relating to burial or the grave **2** : GLOOMY

¹sep·ul·chre or **sep·ul·cher** \'se-pəl-kər\ n : a burial vault : TOMB

²sepulchre or **sepulcher** vb **-chred** or **-chered; -chring** or **-cher·ing** : BURY, ENTOMB

sep·ul·ture \'se-pəl-ˌchùr\ n **1** : BURIAL **2** : SEPULCHRE

se·quel \'sē-kwəl\ n **1** : logical consequence **2** : a literary or cinematic work continuing a story begun in a preceding one

¹se·quence \'sē-kwəns\ n **1** : SERIES **2** : chronological order of events **3** : RESULT, SEQUEL ✦ Synonyms SUCCESSION, CHAIN, PROGRESSION, TRAIN — **se·quen·tial** \si-'kwen-chəl\ adj — **se·quen·tial·ly** adv

²sequence vb **se·quenced; se·quenc·ing 1** : to arrange in a sequence **2** : to determine the sequence of chemical constituents in ⟨~ DNA⟩

se·quent \'sē-kwənt\ adj **1** : SUCCEEDING, CONSECUTIVE **2** : RESULTANT

se·ques·ter \si-'kwes-tər\ vb : to set apart : SEGREGATE ⟨~ a jury⟩

se·ques·trate \'sē-kwəs-ˌtrāt, si-'kwes-\ vb **-trat·ed; -trat·ing** : SEQUESTER — **se·ques·tra·tion** \ˌsē-kwəs-'trā-shən, ˌse-\ n

se·quin \'sē-kwən\ n **1** : an old gold coin of Turkey and Italy **2** : a small metal or plastic plate used for ornamentation esp. on clothing — **se·quined** or **se·quinned** \-kwənd\ adj

se·quoia \si-'kwȯi-ə\ n : either of two huge California coniferous trees

ser abbr **1** serial **2** series **3** service

sera pl of SERUM

se·ra·glio \sə-'ral-yō\ n, pl **-glios** [It serraglio] : HAREM

se·ra·pe \sə-'rä-pē\ n : a colorful woolen shawl worn over the shoulders esp. by Mexican men

ser·aph \'ser-əf\ n, pl **ser·a·phim** \-ə-ˌfim, -ˌfēm\ or **ser·aphs** : one of the 6-winged angels standing in the presence of God

ser·a·phim \'ser-ə-ˌfim, -ˌfēm\ n pl **1** : the highest order of angels **2** sing, pl **seraphim** : SERAPH — **se·raph·ic** \sə-'ra-fik\ adj

Ser·bi·an \'sər-bē-ən\ *n* **1** : SERB **2** : a south Slavic language spoken by the Serbian people — **Serbian** *adj*

Ser·bo-Cro·a·tian \,sər-(,)bō-krō-'ā-shən\ *n* : the Serbian and Croatian languages together with the Slavic speech of Bosnia, Herzegovina, and Montenegro taken as a single language with regional variants

sere \'sir\ *adj* : DRY, WITHERED

¹ser·e·nade \,ser-ə-'nād\ *n* [F, fr. It serenata, fr. sereno clear, calm (of weather) fr. L serenus] : music sung or played as a compliment esp. outdoors at night for a woman being courted

²serenade *vb* **-nad·ed; -nad·ing** : to entertain with or perform a serenade

ser·en·dip·i·ty \,ser-ən-'dip-ə-tē\ *n* [fr. its possession by the heroes of the Persian fairy tale *The Three Princes of Serendip*] : the gift of finding valuable or agreeable things not sought for — **ser·en·dip·i·tous** \-təs\ *adj* — **ser·en·dip·i·tous·ly** *adv*

se·rene \sə-'rēn\ *adj* **1** : CLEAR ⟨~ skies⟩ **2** : QUIET, CALM ♦ *Synonyms* TRANQUIL, PEACEFUL, PLACID — **se·rene·ly** *adv* — **se·ren·i·ty** \sə-'re-nə-tē\ *n*

serf \'sərf\ *n* : a member of a servile class bound to the land and subject to the will of the landowner — **serf·dom** \-dəm\ *n*

serge \'sərj\ *n* : a twilled woolen cloth

ser·geant \'sär-jənt\ *n* [ME, servant, attendant, sergeant, fr. AF *sergant, serjant,* fr. L *servient-, serviens,* prp. of *servire* to serve] **1** : a noncommissioned officer (as in the army) ranking next below a staff sergeant **2** : an officer in a police force

sergeant at arms : an officer of an organization who preserves order and executes commands

sergeant first class *n* : a noncommissioned officer in the army ranking next below a master sergeant

sergeant major *n, pl* **sergeants major** *or* **sergeant majors 1** : a noncommissioned officer in the army or marine corps serving as chief administrative assistant in a headquarters **2** : a noncommissioned officer in the marine corps ranking above a first sergeant

¹se·ri·al \'sir-ē-əl\ *adj* **1** : appearing in parts that follow regularly ⟨a ~ story⟩ **2** : performing a series of similar acts over a period of time ⟨a ~ killer⟩; *also* : occurring in such a series — **se·ri·al·ly** *adv*

²serial *n* : a serial story or other writing — **se·ri·al·ist** \-ə-list\ *n*

se·ries \'sir-ēz\ *n, pl* **series** : a number of things or events arranged in order and connected by being alike in some way ♦ *Synonyms* SUCCESSION, PROGRESSION, SEQUENCE, CHAIN, TRAIN, STRING

seri·graph \'ser-ə-,graf\ *n* : an original silk-screen print — **se·rig·ra·pher** \sə-'ri-grə-fər\ *n* — **se·rig·ra·phy** \-fē\ *n*

se·ri·ous \'sir-ē-əs\ *adj* **1** : thoughtful or subdued in appearance or manner : SOBER **2** : requiring much thought or work **3** : EARNEST, DEVOTED **4** : DANGEROUS, HARMFUL **5** : excessive or impressive in quantity or degree ⟨making ~ money⟩ ♦ *Synonyms* GRAVE, SEDATE, STAID — **se·ri·ous·ly** *adv* — **se·ri·ous·ness** *n*

ser·mon \'sər-mən\ *n* [ME, fr. AF *sermun,* fr. ML *sermon, sermo,* fr. L, speech, conversation, fr. *serere* to link together] **1** : a religious discourse esp. as part of a worship service **2** : a lecture on conduct or duty

ser·mon·ize \'sər-mə-,nīz\ *vb* **-ized; -iz·ing 1** : to compose or deliver a sermon **2** : to preach to or on at length

se·rol·o·gy \sə-'rä-lə-jē\ *n* : a science dealing with serums and esp. their reactions and properties — **se·ro·log·i·cal** \,sir-ə-'lä-ji-kəl\ *or* **se·ro·log·ic** \-jik\ *adj* — **se·ro·log·i·cal·ly** \-ji-k(ə-)lē\ *adv*

se·ro·to·nin \,sir-ə-'tō-nən, ,ser-\ *n* : a neurotransmitter that is a powerful vasoconstrictor

se·rous \'sir-əs\ *adj* : of, relating to, resembling, or producing serum; *esp* : of thin watery constitution

ser·pent \'sər-pənt\ *n* : SNAKE

¹ser·pen·tine \'sər-pən-,tēn, -,tīn\ *adj* **1** : SLY, CRAFTY **2** : WINDING, TURNING

²ser·pen·tine \-,tēn\ *n* : a dull-green mineral having a mottled appearance

ser·rate \'ser-,āt\ *adj* : having a saw-toothed edge ⟨a ~ leaf⟩

ser·ried \'ser-ēd\ *adj* : crowded together

se·rum \'sir-əm\ *n, pl* **serums** *or* **se·ra** \-ə\ [L, whey, wheylike fluid] : the clear yellowish antibody-containing fluid that can be separated from blood when it clots; *also* : a preparation of animal serum containing specific antibodies and used to prevent or cure disease

serv *abbr* service

ser·vant \'sər-vənt\ *n* : one that serves others; *esp* : a person employed for domestic or personal work

¹serve \'sərv\ *vb* **served; serv·ing 1** : to work as a servant **2** : to render obedience and worship to (God) **3** : to comply with the commands or demands of **4** : to work through or perform a term of service (as in the army) **5** : PUT IN ⟨served five years in jail⟩ **6** : to be of use : ANSWER ⟨pine boughs served for a bed⟩ **7** : BENEFIT **8** : to prove adequate or satisfactory for ⟨a pie that ~s eight people⟩ **9** : to make ready and pass out ⟨~ drinks⟩ **10** : to furnish or supply with something ⟨one power company serving the whole state⟩ **11** : to wait on ⟨~ a customer⟩ **12** : to treat or act toward in a specified way **13** : to put the ball in play (as in tennis)

²serve *n* : the act of serving a ball (as in tennis)

ser·ver \'sər-vər\ *n* **1** : one that serves **2** : a computer in a network that is used to provide services (as access to files) to other computers in the network

¹ser·vice \'sər-vəs\ *n* **1** : the occupation of a servant **2** : HELP, BENEFIT **3** : a meeting for worship; *also* : a form followed in worship or in a ceremony ⟨burial ~⟩ **4** : the act, fact, or means of serving **5** : performance of official or professional duties **6** : SERVE **7** : a set of dishes or silverware **8** : a branch of public employment; *also* : the persons in it ⟨civil ~⟩ **9** : military or naval duty

²service *vb* **ser·viced; ser·vic·ing** : to do maintenance or repair work on or for

ser·vice·able \'sər-və-sə-bəl\ *adj* : prepared for service : USEFUL, USABLE

ser·vice·man \'sər-vəs-,man, -mən\ *n* **1** : a man who is a member of the armed forces **2** : a man employed to repair or maintain equipment

service mark *n* : a mark or device used to identify a service (as transportation or insurance) offered to customers

service station *n* : GAS STATION

ser·vice·wom·an \'sər-vəs-,wu̇-mən\ *n* : a woman who is a member of the armed forces

ser·vile \'sər-vəl, -,vī(-ə)l\ *adj* **1** : befitting a slave or servant **2** : behaving like a slave : SUBMISSIVE — **ser·vile·ly** *adv* — **ser·vil·i·ty** \sər-'vi-lə-tē\ *n*

serv·ing \'sər-viŋ\ *n* : HELPING

ser·vi·tor \'sər-və-tər\ *n* : a male servant

ser·vi·tude \'sər-və-,tüd, -,tyüd\ *n* : SLAVERY, BONDAGE

ser·vo \'sər-vō\ *n, pl* **servos 1** : SERVOMOTOR **2** : SERVOMECHANISM

ser·vo·mech·a·nism \'sər-vō-,me-kə-,ni-zəm\ *n* : a device for automatically correcting the performance of a mechanism

ser·vo·mo·tor \-,mō-tər\ *n* : a mechanism that supplements a primary control

ses·a·me \'se-sə-mē\ *n* : a widely cultivated annual herb of warm regions; *also* : its seeds that yield an edible oil (**sesame oil**) and are used in flavoring

ses·qui·cen·ten·ni·al \,ses-kwi-sen-'te-nē-əl\ *n* [L sesqui- one and a half, half again] : a 150th anniversary or its celebration — **sesquicentennial** *adj*

ses·qui·pe·da·lian \,ses-kwə-pə-'dāl-yən\ *adj* **1** : having many syllables : LONG **2** : using long words

ses·sile \'se-sī(-ə)l, -səl\ *adj* : permanently attached and not free to move about

ses·sion \'se-shən\ *n* **1** : a meeting or series of meetings of a body (as a court or legislature) for the transaction of business **2** : a meeting or period devoted to a particular activity

¹set \'set\ *vb* **set; set·ting 1** : to cause to sit **2** : PLACE **3** : ARRANGE, ADJUST **4** : to cause to be or do **5** : SETTLE, DECREE **6** : to fix in a frame **7** : to fix at a certain amount **8** : WAGER, STAKE **9** : to make or become fast or rigid **10** : to adapt (as words) to something (as music) **11** : to become fixed or firm or solid **12** : to be suitable : FIT **13** : BROOD **14** : to have a certain direction **15** : to pass below the horizon **16** : to defeat in bridge — **set about** : to begin to do — **set forth** : to begin a trip — **set off 1** : to start out on a course or a trip **2** : to cause to explode — **set out** : to begin a trip or undertaking — **set sail** : to begin a voyage — **set upon** : to attack usu. with violence

²**set** *n* **1** : a setting or a being set **2** : DIRECTION, COURSE; *also* : TENDENCY **3** : FORM, BUILD **4** : the fit of something (as a coat) **5** : an artificial setting for the scene of a play or motion picture **6** : a group of tennis games in which one side wins at least six **7** : a group of persons or things of the same kind or having a common characteristic usu. classed together **8** : a collection of things and esp. of mathematical elements (as numbers or points) **9** : an electronic apparatus ⟨a television ∼⟩

³**set** *adj* **1** : DELIBERATE, INTENT **2** : fixed by authority or custom **3** : RIGID **4** : PERSISTENT

set·back \'set-ˌbak\ *n* : a temporary defeat : REVERSE

set back *vb* **1** : HINDER, DELAY; *also* : REVERSE **2** : COST

set piece 1 : a composition (as in literature or music) executed in fixed or ideal form often with brilliant effect **2** : a scene, depiction, speech, or event obviously designed to have an imposing effect

set·screw \'set-ˌskrü\ *n* : a screw screwed through one part tightly upon or into another part to prevent relative movement

set·tee \se-'tē\ *n* : a bench or sofa with a back and arms

set·ter \'se-tər\ *n* : a large long-coated hunting dog

set·ting \'se-tiŋ\ *n* **1** : the frame in which a gem is set **2** : the time, place, and circumstances in which something occurs or develops; *also* : SCENERY **3** : music written for a text (as of a poem) **4** : the eggs that a fowl sits on for hatching at one time

set·tle \'se-tᵊl\ *vb* **set·tled; set·tling** [ME *settlen* to seat, bring to rest, come to rest, fr. OE *setlan*, fr. *setl* seat] **1** : to place so as to stay **2** : to establish in residence; *also* : COLONIZE **3** : to make compact **4** : QUIET, CALM **5** : to establish or secure permanently **6** : to direct one's efforts **7** : to fix by agreement **8** : to give legally **9** : ADJUST, ARRANGE **10** : DECIDE, DETERMINE **11** : to make a final disposition of ⟨∼ an account⟩ **12** : to come to rest **13** : to reach an agreement on **14** : to sink gradually to a lower level **15** : to become clear by depositing sediment — **set·tler** *n*

set·tle·ment \'se-tᵊl-mənt\ *n* **1** : the act or process of settling **2** : BESTOWAL ⟨a marriage ∼⟩ **3** : payment or adjustment of an account **4** : COLONY **5** : a small village **6** : an institution providing various community services esp. to large city populations **7** : adjustment of doubts and differences

set-to \'set-ˌtü\ *n, pl* **set-tos** : FIGHT

set·up \'set-ˌəp\ *n* **1** : the manner or act of arranging **2** : glass, ice, and nonalcoholic beverage for mixing served to patrons who supply their own liquor **3** : something (as a plot) that has been constructed or contrived; *also* : FRAME-UP

set up *vb* **1** : to place in position; *also* : ASSEMBLE **2** : CAUSE **3** : FOUND, ESTABLISH **4** : FRAME **5**

sev·en \'se-vən\ *n* **1** : one more than six **2** : the 7th in a set or series **3** : something having seven units — **seven** *adj or pron* — **sev·enth** \-vənth\ *adj or adv or n*

sev·en·teen \ˌse-vən-'tēn\ *n* : one more than 16 — **seventeen** *adj or pron* — **sev·en·teenth** \-'tēnth\ *adj or n*

seventeen–year locust *n* : a cicada of the U.S. that has in the North a life of 17 years and in the South of 13 years of which most is spent underground as a nymph and only a few weeks as a winged adult

sev·en·ty \'se-vən-tē\ *n, pl* **-ties** : seven times 10 — **sev·en·ti·eth** \-tē-əth\ *adj or n* — **seventy** *adj or pron*

sev·er \'se-vər\ *vb* **sev·ered; sev·er·ing** : DIVIDE; *esp* : to separate by or as if by cutting — **sev·er·ance** \'sev-rəns, 'se-və-\ *n*

sev·er·al \'sev-rəl, 'se-və-\ *adj* [ME, fr. AF, fr. ML *separalis*, fr. L *separ* separate, fr. *separare* to separate] **1** : INDIVIDUAL, DISTINCT ⟨federal union of the ∼ states⟩ **2** : consisting of an indefinite number but yet not very many — **sev·er·al·ly** *adv*

severance pay *n* : extra pay given an employee on termination of employment

se·vere \sə-'vir\ *adj* **se·ver·er; -est 1** : marked by strictness or sternness : AUSTERE **2** : strict in discipline **3** : causing distress and esp. physical discomfort or pain ⟨∼ weather⟩ ⟨a ∼ wound⟩ **4** : hard to endure ⟨∼ trials⟩ **5** : SERIOUS ⟨∼ depression⟩ ♦ **Synonyms** STERN, ASCETIC, ASTRINGENT — **se·vere·ly** *adv* — **se·ver·i·ty** \-'ver-ə-tē\ *n*

sew \'sō\ *vb* **sewed; sewn** \'sōn\ *or* **sewed; sew·ing 1** : to unite or fasten by stitches **2** : to engage in sewing

sew·age \'sü-ij\ *n* : waste materials carried off by sewers

¹**sew·er** \'sō-ər\ *n* : one that sews

²**sew·er** \'sü-ər\ *n* : an artificial pipe or channel to carry off waste matter

sew·er·age \'sü-ə-rij\ *n* **1** : a system of sewers **2** : SEWAGE

sew·ing *n* **1** : the activity of one who sews **2** : material that has been or is to be sewed

sex \'seks\ *n* **1** : either of the two major forms that occur in many living things and are designated male or female according to their role in reproduction; *also* : the qualities by which these sexes are differentiated and which directly or indirectly function in reproduction involving two parents **2** : sexual activity or behavior; *also* : SEXUAL INTERCOURSE — **sexed** \'sekst\ *adj* — **sex·less** *adj*

sex·a·ge·nar·i·an \ˌsek-sə-jə-'ner-ē-ən\ *n* : a person whose age is in the sixties — **sexagenarian** *adj*

sex appeal : personal appeal or physical attractiveness esp. for members of the opposite sex

sex cell *n* : an egg cell or sperm cell

sex chromosome *n* : one of usu. a pair of chromosomes that are usu. similar in one sex but different in the other sex and are concerned with the inheritance of sex

sex hormone *n* : a steroid hormone (as estrogen or testosterone) that is produced esp. by the gonads or adrenal cortex and chiefly affects the growth or function of the reproductive organs

sex·ism \'sek-ˌsi-zəm\ *n* : prejudice or discrimination based on sex; *esp* : discrimination against women — **sex·ist** \'sek-sist\ *adj or n*

sex·ol·o·gy \sek-'sä-lə-jē\ *n* : the study of sex or of the interactions of the sexes — **sex·ol·o·gist** \-jist\ *n*

sex·pot \'seks-ˌpät\ *n* : a conspicuously sexy woman

sex symbol *n* : a usu. renowned person (as an entertainer) noted and admired for conspicuous attractiveness

sex·tant \'sek-stənt\ *n* [NL *sextant-, sextans* sixth part of a circle, fr. L, sixth part, fr. *sextus* sixth] : a navigational instrument for determining latitude

sex·tet \sek-'stet\ *n* **1** : a musical composition for six voices or instruments; *also* : the performers of such a composition **2** : a group or set of six

sex·ton \'sek-stən\ *n* : one who takes care of church property

sex·u·al \'sek-shə-wəl\ *adj* : of, relating to, or involving sex or the sexes ⟨a ∼ spore⟩ ⟨∼ relations⟩ — **sex·u·al·i·ty** \ˌsek-shə-'wa-lə-tē\ *n* — **sex·u·al·ly** \'sek-shə-wə-lē\ *adv*

sexual intercourse *n* **1** : intercourse between a male and a female in which the penis is inserted into the vagina **2** : intercourse between individuals involving genital contact other than insertion of the penis into the vagina

sexually transmitted disease *n* : a disease (as syphilis, gonorrhea, AIDS, or the genital form of herpes simplex) that is caused by a microorganism or virus usu. or often transmitted by direct sexual contact

sexual relations *n pl* : SEXUAL INTERCOURSE

sexy \'sek-sē\ *adj* **sex·i·er; -est** : sexually suggestive or stimulating : EROTIC — **sex·i·ly** \-sə-lē\ *adv* — **sex·i·ness** \-sē-nəs\ *n*

SF *abbr* **1** sacrifice fly **2** science fiction **3** square feet

SFC *abbr* sergeant first class

Sg *symbol* seaborgium

SG *abbr* **1** sergeant **2** solicitor general **3** surgeon general

sgd *abbr* signed

Sgt *abbr* sergeant

Sgt Maj *abbr* sergeant major

sh *abbr* share

shab·by \'sha-bē\ *adj* **shab·bi·er; -est 1** : dressed in worn clothes **2** : threadbare and faded from wear **3** : DESPICABLE, MEAN; *also* : UNFAIR ⟨∼ treatment⟩ — **shab·bi·ly** \'sha-bə-lē\ *adv* — **shab·bi·ness** \-bē-nəs\ *n*

shack \'shak\ *n* : HUT, SHANTY

¹**shack·le** \'sha-kəl\ *n* **1** : something (as a manacle or fetter) that confines the legs or arms **2** : a check on free action made as if by fetters **3** : a device for making something fast or secure

²**shackle** *vb* **shack·led; shack·ling** : to bind or fasten with shackles

shad \'shad\ *n, pl* **shad** : any of several sea fishes related to the herrings that swim up rivers to spawn and include some important food fishes

¹**shade** \'shād\ *n* **1** : partial obscurity **2** : space sheltered from the light esp. of the sun **3** : PHANTOM **4** : something that shelters from or intercepts light or heat; *also, pl* : SUNGLASSES **5** : a dark color or a variety of a color **6** : a small difference

²**shade** *vb* **shad·ed; shad·ing 1** : to shelter from light and heat **2** : DARKEN, OBSCURE **3** : to mark with degrees of light or color **4** : to show slight differences esp. in color or meaning

shad·ing *n* : the color and lines representing darkness or shadow in a drawing or painting

¹**shad·ow** \'sha-dō\ *n* **1** : partial darkness in a space from which light rays are cut off **2** : SHELTER **3** : shade cast upon a surface by something intercepting rays from a light ⟨the ∼ of a tree⟩ **4** : PHANTOM **5** : a shaded portion of a picture **6** : a small portion or degree : TRACE ⟨a ∼ of doubt⟩ **7** : a source of gloom or unhappiness — **shad·owy** *adj*

²**shadow** *vb* **1** : to cast a shadow on **2** : to represent faintly or vaguely **3** : to follow and watch closely : TRAIL

shad·ow·box \'sha-dō-ˌbäks\ *vb* : to box with an imaginary opponent esp. for training

shady \'shā-dē\ *adj* **shad·i·er; -est 1** : affording shade **2** : of questionable honesty or reputation

¹**shaft** \'shaft\ *n, pl* **shafts 1** : the long handle of a spear or lance **2** : SPEAR, LANCE **3** *or pl* **shaves** \'shavz\ : POLE; *esp* : one of two poles between which a horse is hitched to pull a vehicle **4** : something (as a column) long and slender **5** : a bar to support a rotating piece or to transmit power by rotation **6** : an inclined opening in the ground (as for finding or mining ore) **7** : a vertical opening (as for an elevator) through the floors of a building **8** : harsh or unfair treatment — usu. used with *the*

²**shaft** *vb* **1** : to fit with a shaft **2** : to treat unfairly or harshly

shag \'shag\ *n* : a shaggy tangled mass or covering (as of wool) : long coarse or matted fiber, nap, or pile

shag·gy \'sha-gē\ *adj* **shag·gi·er; -est 1** : rough with or as if with long hair or wool **2** : tangled or rough in surface

shah \'shä, 'shò\ *n, often cap* : a sovereign of Iran

Shak *abbr* Shakespeare

¹**shake** \'shāk\ *vb* **shook** \'shùk\; **shak·en** \'shā-kən\; **shak·ing 1** : to move or cause to move jerkily or irregularly **2** : BRANDISH, WAVE ⟨*shaking* his fist⟩ **3** : to disturb emotionally ⟨*shaken* by her death⟩ **4** : WEAKEN ⟨*shook* his faith⟩ **5** : to bring or come into a certain position, condition, or arrangement by or as if by moving jerkily **6** : to clasp (hands) in greeting or as a sign of goodwill or agreement ✦ *Synonyms* TREMBLE, QUAKE, QUAVER, SHIVER, QUIVER — **shak·able** *or* **shake·able** \'shā-kə-bəl\ *adj*

²**shake** *n* **1** : the act or a result of shaking **2** : DEAL, TREATMENT ⟨a fair ∼⟩

shake·down \'shāk-ˌdaùn\ *n* **1** : an improvised bed **2** : EXTORTION **3** : a process or period of adjustment **4** : a test (as of a new ship or airplane) under operating conditions

shake down *vb* **1** : to take up temporary quarters **2** : to occupy a makeshift bed **3** : to become accustomed esp. to new surroundings or duties **4** : to settle down **5** : to give a shakedown test to **6** : to obtain money from in a deceitful or illegal manner **7** : to bring about a reduction of

shak·er \'shā-kər\ *n* **1** : one that shakes ⟨pepper ∼⟩ **2** *cap* : a member of a religious sect founded in England in 1747

Shake·spear·ean *or* **Shake·spear·ian** \shāk-'spir-ē-ən\ *adj* : of, relating to, or having the characteristics of Shakespeare or his writings

shake-up \'shāk-ˌəp\ *n* : an extensive often drastic reorganization

shaky \'shā-kē\ *adj* **shak·i·er; -est** : UNSOUND, WEAK — **shak·i·ly** \'shā-kə-lē\ *adv* — **shak·i·ness** \-kē-nəs\ *n*

shale \'shāl\ *n* : a finely layered rock formed from clay, mud, or silt

shall \shəl, 'shal\ *vb, past* **should** \shəd, 'shùd\ *pres sing & pl* **shall** — used as an auxiliary to express a command, what seems inevitable or likely in the future, simple futurity, or determination

shal·lop \'sha-ləp\ *n* : a light open boat

shal·lot \shə-'lät, 'sha-lət\ *n* [modif. of F *échalote*] **1** : a small clustered bulb that is used in seasoning and is produced by a perennial herb belonging to a subspecies of the onion; *also* : this herb **2** : GREEN ONION

¹**shal·low** \'sha-lō\ *adj* **1** : not deep **2** : not intellectually profound

²**shallow** *n* : a shallow place in a body of water — usu. used in pl.

¹**sham** \'sham\ *n* **1** : an ornamental covering for a pillow **2** : COUNTERFEIT, IMITATION **3** : a person who shams

²**sham** *vb* **shammed; sham·ming 1** : FEIGN, PRETEND — **sham·mer** *n*

³**sham** *adj* : not genuine : FALSE, FEIGNED

sha·man \'shä-mən, 'shā-\ *n* [ultim. fr. Evenki (a language of Siberia) *šamán*] : a priest or priestess who uses magic to cure the sick, to divine the hidden, and to control events

sham·ble \'sham-bəl\ *vb* **sham·bled; sham·bling** : to shuffle along — **sham·ble** *n*

sham·bles \'sham-bəlz\ *n* **1** : a scene of great slaughter **2** : a scene or state of great destruction or disorder; *also* : MESS

¹**shame** \'shām\ *n* **1** : a painful sense of having done something wrong, improper, or immodest **2** : DISGRACE, DISHONOR **3** : a cause of feeling shame **4** : something to be regretted ⟨it's a ∼ you'll miss the party⟩ — **shame·ful** \-fəl\ *adj* — **shame·ful·ly** *adv* — **shame·less** *adj* — **shame·less·ly** *adv*

²**shame** *vb* **shamed; sham·ing 1** : DISGRACE **2** : to make ashamed

shame·faced \'shām-ˌfāst\ *adj* : ASHAMED, ABASHED — **shame·fac·ed·ly** \-ˌfā-səd-lē, -ˌfāst-lē\ *adv*

¹**sham·poo** \sham-'pü\ *vb* [Hindi *cāpo*, imper. of *cāpnā* to press, shampoo] : to wash (as the hair) with soap and water or with a special preparation; *also* : to clean (as a rug) similarly

²**shampoo** *n, pl* **shampoos 1** : the act or an instance of shampooing **2** : a preparation for use in shampooing

sham·rock \'sham-ˌräk\ *n* [Ir *seamróg*, dim. of *seamar* clover] : a plant of folk legend with leaves composed of three leaflets that is associated with St. Patrick and Ireland

shang·hai \shaŋ-'hī\ *vb* **shang·haied; shang·hai·ing** [*Shanghai*, China] : to force aboard a ship for service as a sailor; *also* : to force into an undesirable position

Shan·gri-la \ˌshaŋ-gri-'lä\ *n* [*Shangri-La*, imaginary land depicted in the novel *Lost Horizon* (1933) by James Hilton] : a remote idyllic hideaway

shank \'shaŋk\ *n* **1** : the part of the leg between the knee and the human ankle or a corresponding part of a quadruped **2** : a cut of meat from the leg **3** : the narrow part of the sole of a shoe beneath the instep **4** : the part of a tool or instrument (as a key or anchor) connecting the functioning part with a part by which it is held or moved

shan·tung \shan-'təŋ\ *n* : a fabric in plain weave having a slightly irregular surface

shan·ty \'shan-tē\ *n, pl* **shanties** [prob. fr. CanF *chantier* lumber camp, hut, fr. F, builder's yard, ways, support for barrels, fr. OF, support, fr. L *cantherius* rafter, trellis] : a small roughly built shelter or dwelling

¹**shape** \'shāp\ *vb* **shaped; shap·ing 1** : to form esp. in a particular shape **2** : DESIGN **3** : ADAPT, ADJUST **4** : REGULATE ✦ *Synonyms* MAKE, FASHION, FABRICATE, MANUFACTURE, FRAME, MOLD

²**shape** *n* **1** : APPEARANCE **2** : surface configuration : FORM **3** : bodily contour apart from the head and face : FIGURE **4** : PHANTOM **5** : CONDITION — **shaped** *adj*

shape·less \'shā-pləs\ *adj* **1** : having no definite shape **2** : not shapely — **shape·less·ly** *adv* — **shape·less·ness** *n*

shape·ly \'shā-plē\ *adj* **shape·li·er; -est** : having a pleasing shape — **shape·li·ness** *n*

shape-shift·er \'shāp-ˌshif-tər\ *n* : one that seems able to change form or identity at will

shard \'shärd\ *also* **sherd** \'shərd\ *n* : a broken piece : FRAGMENT

¹**share** \'sher\ *n* : PLOWSHARE

²**share** *n* **1** : a portion belonging to one person or group **2** : any of the equal interests into which the capital stock of a corporation is divided

³**share** *vb* **shared; shar·ing 1** : APPORTION **2** : to use or enjoy with others **3** : PARTICIPATE — **shar·er** *n*

share·crop·per \-ˌkrä-pər\ *n* : a farmer who works another's land in return for a share of the crop — **share·crop** *vb*

share·hold·er \-ˌhōl-dər\ *n* : STOCKHOLDER

share·ware \'sher-ˌwer\ *n* : software available for usu. limited trial use at little or no cost but that can be upgraded for a fee

¹**shark** \'shärk\ *n* : any of various active, usu. predatory, and mostly large marine cartilaginous fishes

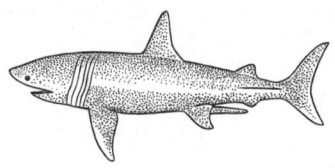

¹**shark**

²**shark** *n* : a greedy crafty person

shark·skin \-ˌskin\ *n* 1 : the hide of a shark or leather made from it 2 : a fabric woven from strands of many fine threads and having a sleek appearance and silky feel

¹**sharp** \'shärp\ *adj* 1 : having a thin cutting edge or fine point : not dull or blunt 2 : COLD, NIPPING ⟨a ∼ wind⟩ 3 : keen in intellect, perception, or attention 4 : BRISK, ENERGETIC 5 : IRRITABLE ⟨a ∼ temper⟩ 6 : causing intense distress ⟨a ∼ pain⟩ 7 : HARSH, CUTTING ⟨a ∼ rebuke⟩ 8 : affecting the senses as if cutting or piercing ⟨a ∼ sound⟩ ⟨a ∼ smell⟩ 9 : not smooth or rounded ⟨∼ features⟩ 10 : involving an abrupt or extreme change ⟨a ∼ turn⟩ 11 : CLEAR, DISTINCT ⟨mountains in ∼ relief⟩; *also* : easy to perceive ⟨a ∼ contrast⟩ 12 : higher than the true pitch; *also* : raised by a half step 13 : STYLISH ⟨a ∼ dresser⟩ ✦ *Synonyms* KEEN, ACUTE, QUICK-WITTED, PENETRATIVE — **sharp·ly** *adv* — **sharp·ness** *n*

²**sharp** *adv* 1 : in a sharp manner 2 : EXACTLY, PRECISELY ⟨left at 8 ∼⟩

³**sharp** *n* 1 : a sharp edge or point 2 : a character ♯ which indicates that a specified note is to be raised by a half step; *also* : the resulting note 3 : SHARPER

⁴**sharp** *vb* : to raise in pitch by a half step

shar·pei \ˌshä-ˈpā, ˌshär-\ *n, pl* **shar·peis** *often cap S&P* [Chin (Guangdong dial.) *sà* sand + *péi* fur] : any of a Chinese breed of dogs that have loose wrinkled skin esp. when young

sharp·en \'shär-pən\ *vb* : to make or become sharp — **sharp·en·er** *n*

sharp·er \'shär-pər\ *n* : SWINDLER; *esp* : a cheating gambler

sharp·ie *or* **sharpy** \'shär-pē\ *n, pl* **sharp·ies** 1 : SHARPER 2 : a person who is exceptionally keen or alert

sharp·shoot·er \'shärp-ˌshü-tər\ *n* : a proficient marksman — **sharp·shoot·ing** *n*

shat·ter \'sha-tər\ *vb* : to dash or burst into fragments — **shat·ter·proof** \'sha-tər-ˌprüf\ *adj*

¹**shave** \'shāv\ *vb* **shaved; shaved** *or* **shav·en** \'shā-vən\; **shav·ing** 1 : to slice in thin pieces 2 : to make bare or smooth by cutting the hair from 3 : to cut or pare off by the sliding movement of a razor 4 : to skim along or near the surface of

²**shave** *n* 1 : any of various tools for cutting thin slices 2 : an act or process of shaving

shav·er \'shā-vər\ *n* 1 : an electric razor 2 : BOY, YOUNGSTER

shaves *pl of* SHAFT

shaving *n* 1 : the act of one that shaves 2 : something shaved off

shawl \'shȯl\ *n* : a square or oblong piece of fabric used esp. by women as a loose covering for the head or shoulders

Shaw·nee \shȯ-'nē, shä-\ *n, pl* **Shawnee** *or* **Shawnees** : a member of an American Indian people orig. of the central Ohio valley; *also* : their language

shd *abbr* should

she \'shē\ *pron* : that female one ⟨who is ∼⟩; *also* : that one regarded as feminine ⟨∼'s a fine ship⟩

sheaf \'shēf\ *n, pl* **sheaves** \'shēvz\ 1 : a bundle of stalks and ears of grain 2 : a group of things bound together

¹**shear** \'shir\ *vb* **sheared; sheared** *or* **shorn** \'shȯrn\; **shear·ing** 1 : to cut the hair or wool from : CLIP, TRIM 2 : to deprive by or as if by cutting 3 : to cut or break sharply

²**shear** *n* 1 : any of various cutting tools that consist of two blades fastened together so that the edges slide one by the other — usu. used in pl. 2 *chiefly Brit* : the act, an instance, or the result of shearing 3 : an action or stress caused by applied forces that causes two parts of a body to slide on each other

shear·wa·ter \'shir-ˌwȯ-tər, -ˌwä-\ *n* : any of several seabirds related to the petrels that often skim along waves in flight

sheath \'shēth\ *n, pl* **sheaths** \'shēthz, 'shēths\ 1 : a case for a blade (as of a knife); *also* : an anatomical covering suggesting such a case 2 : a close-fitting dress usu. worn without a belt

sheathe \'shēth\ *also* **sheath** \'shēth\ *vb* **sheathed; sheath·ing** 1 : to put into a sheath 2 : to cover with something that guards or protects

sheath·ing \'shē-thiŋ, -thiŋ\ *n* : material used to sheathe something; *esp* : the first covering of boards or of waterproof material on the outside wall of a frame house or on a timber roof

sheave \'shiv, 'shēv\ *n* : a grooved wheel or pulley (as on a pulley block)

she-bang \shi-'baŋ\ *n* : everything involved in what is under consideration ⟨sold the whole ∼⟩

¹**shed** \'shed\ *vb* **shed; shed·ding** 1 : to cause to flow from a cut or wound ⟨∼ blood⟩ 2 : to pour down in drops ⟨∼ tears⟩ 3 : to give out (as light) : DIFFUSE 4 : to throw off (as a natural covering) : DISCARD ⟨∼ skin⟩

²**shed** *n* : a slight structure built for shelter or storage

sheen \'shēn\ *n* : a subdued luster

sheep \'shēp\ *n, pl* **sheep** 1 : any of various cud-chewing mammals that are stockier than the related goats and lack a beard in the male; *esp* : one raised for meat or for its wool or skin 2 : a timid or defenseless person 3 : SHEEPSKIN

sheep·dog \'shēp-ˌdȯg\ *n* : a dog used to tend, drive, or guard sheep

sheep·fold \'shēp-ˌfōld\ *n* : a pen or shelter for sheep

sheep·herd·er \-ˌhər-dər\ *n* : a worker in charge of sheep esp. on open range — **sheep·herd·ing** *n*

sheep·ish \'shē-pish\ *adj* : BASHFUL, TIMID; *esp* : embarrassed by consciousness of a fault — **sheep·ish·ly** *adv*

sheep·skin \'shēp-ˌskin\ *n* 1 : the hide of a sheep or leather prepared from it; *also* : PARCHMENT 2 : DIPLOMA

¹**sheer** \'shir\ *vb* : to turn from a course

²**sheer** *adj* 1 : very thin or transparent 2 : UNQUALIFIED ⟨∼ folly⟩ 3 : very steep ✦ *Synonyms* PURE, SIMPLE, ABSOLUTE, UNADULTERATED, UNMITIGATED — **sheer** *adv*

¹**sheet** \'shēt\ *n* 1 : a broad piece of cloth (as for a bed); *also* : SAIL 2 : a single piece of paper 3 : a broad flat surface ⟨a ∼ of ice⟩ 4 : something broad and long and relatively thin

²**sheet** *n* : a rope used to trim a sail

sheet·ing \'shē-tiŋ\ *n* : material in the form of sheets or suitable for forming into sheets

sheikh *or* **sheik** \'shēk, 'shāk\ *n* : an Arab chief — **sheikh·dom** *or* **sheik·dom** \-dəm\ *n*

shek·el \'she-kəl\ *n* — see MONEY table

shelf \'shelf\ *n, pl* **shelves** \'shelvz\ 1 : a thin flat usu. long and narrow structure fastened horizontally (as on a wall) above the floor to hold things 2 : something (as a sandbar) that suggests a shelf

shelf life *n* : the period of storage time during which a material will remain useful

¹**shell** \'shel\ *n* 1 : a hard or tough often thin outer covering of an animal (as a beetle, turtle, or mollusk) or of an egg or a seed or fruit (as a nut); *also* : something that resembles a shell ⟨a pastry ∼⟩ 2 : a light narrow racing boat propelled by oarsmen 3 : a case holding an explosive and designed to be fired from a cannon; *also* : a case holding the charge of powder and shot or bullet for small arms 4 : a plain usu. sleeveless blouse or sweater — **shelled** \'sheld\ *adj* — **shell·like** \'she-lē\ *adj*

²**shell** *vb* 1 : to remove from a shell or husk 2 : BOMBARD — **shell·er** *n*

¹**shel·lac** \shə-'lak\ *n* 1 : a purified lac 2 : lac dissolved in alcohol and used as a wood filler or finish

²**shellac** *vb* **shel·lacked; shel·lack·ing** **1** : to coat or treat with shellac **2** : to defeat decisively
shellacking *n* : a sound drubbing
shell bean *n* : a bean grown esp. for its edible seeds; *also* : its edible seed
shell·fish \-ˌfish\ *n* : an invertebrate water animal (as an oyster or lobster) with a shell
shell out *vb* : PAY
shell shock *n* : COMBAT FATIGUE — **shell–shocked** \ˈshel-ˌshäkt\ *adj*
¹**shel·ter** \ˈshel-tər\ *n* : something that gives protection : REFUGE
²**shelter** *vb* **shel·tered; shel·ter·ing** : to give protection or refuge to
shelve \ˈshelv\ *vb* **shelved; shelv·ing** **1** : to slope gradually **2** : to store on shelves **3** : to dismiss from service or use **4** : to put aside : DEFER ⟨∼ a proposal⟩
shelv·ing \ˈshel-viŋ\ *n* : material for shelves; *also* : SHELVES
she·nan·i·gan \shə-ˈna-ni-gən\ *n* **1** : an underhand trick **2** : questionable conduct — usu. used in pl. **3** : high-spirited or mischievous activity — usu. used in pl.
¹**shep·herd** \ˈshe-pərd\ *n* **1** : one who tends sheep **2** : GERMAN SHEPHERD
²**shepherd** *vb* : to tend as or in the manner of a shepherd
shep·herd·ess \ˈshe-pər-dəs\ *n* : a woman who tends sheep
shepherd's pie *n* : a meat pie with a mashed potato crust
sheqel *n, pl* **sheqalim** *var of* SHEKEL
sher·bet \ˈshər-bət\ *n* [Turk *şerbet*, fr. Pers *sharbat*, fr. Ar *sharba* drink] **1** : a drink of sweetened diluted fruit juice **2** *also* **sher·bert** \-bərt\ : a frozen dessert of fruit juices, sugar, milk or water, and egg whites or gelatin
sherd *var of* SHARD
sher·iff \ˈsher-əf\ *n* [ME *shirreve*, fr. OE *scīrgerēfa*, lit., shire reeve (local official)] : a county officer charged with the execution of the law and the preservation of order
sher·ry \ˈsher-ē\ *n, pl* **sherries** [alter. of earlier *sherris* (taken as pl.), fr. *Xeres* (now *Jerez*), Spain] : a fortified wine with a nutty flavor
Shet·land pony \ˈshet-lənd-\ *n* : any of a breed of small stocky hardy ponies
shew \ˈshō\ *Brit var of* SHOW
shi·at·su *also* **shi·at·zu** \shē-ˈät-sü\ *n* : a form of acupressure originating in Japan
shib·bo·leth \ˈshi-bə-ləth\ *n* [Heb *shibbōleth* stream; fr. the use of this word as a test to distinguish the men of Gilead from members of the tribe of Ephraim (Judges 12:5, 6)] **1** : CATCHPHRASE **2** : language that is a criterion for distinguishing members of a group
¹**shield** \ˈshēld\ *n* **1** : a broad piece of defensive armor carried on the arm **2** : something that protects or hides **3** : a police officer's badge
²**shield** *vb* : to protect or hide with a shield ✦ **Synonyms** PROTECT, GUARD, SAFEGUARD
shier *comparative of* SHY
shiest *superlative of* SHY
¹**shift** \ˈshift\ *vb* **1** : EXCHANGE, REPLACE **2** : to change place, position, or direction : MOVE; *also* : to change gears **3** : GET BY, MANAGE
²**shift** *n* **1** : SCHEME, TRICK **2** : a woman's slip or loose-fitting dress **3** : a change in direction, emphasis, or attitude **4** : a group working together alternating with other groups **5** : TRANSFER **6** : GEARSHIFT
shift·less \ˈshift-ləs\ *adj* : LAZY, INEFFICIENT — **shift·less·ness** *n*
shifty \ˈshif-tē\ *adj* **shift·i·er; -est** **1** : TRICKY; *also* : ELUSIVE **2** : indicative of a tricky nature ⟨∼ eyes⟩
shih tzu \ˈshēd-ˈzü, ˈshēt-ˈsü\ *n, pl* **shih tzus** *also* **shih tzu** *often cap* S&T [Chin (Beijing) *shīzi* (*gǒu*,) fr. *shīzi* lion + *gǒu* dog] : any of a breed of small short-legged dogs of Chinese origin that have a short muzzle and a long dense coat
shii·ta·ke \shē-ˈtä-kē\ *n* [Jp] : a dark Asian mushroom widely cultivated for its edible cap
shill \ˈshil\ *n* : one who acts as a decoy (as for a pitchman) — **shill** *vb*
shil·le·lagh *also* **shil·la·lah** \shə-ˈlā-lē\ *n* [*Shillelagh*, town in Ireland] : CUDGEL, CLUB
shil·ling \ˈshi-liŋ\ *n* : a former basic monetary unit of Austria

shilly–shally \ˈshi-lē-ˌsha-lē\ *vb* **shilly–shall·ied; shilly–shally·ing** **1** : to show hesitation or lack of decisiveness **2** : to waste time
shim \ˈshim\ *n* : a thin often tapered piece of wood, metal, or stone used (as in leveling) to fill in space
shim·mer \ˈshi-mər\ *vb* : to shine waveringly or tremulously : GLIMMER ✦ **Synonyms** FLASH, GLEAM, GLINT, SPARKLE, GLITTER — **shimmer** *n* — **shim·mery** *adj*
shim·my \ˈshi-mē\ *n, pl* **shimmies** : an abnormal vibration esp. in the front wheels of a motor vehicle — **shimmy** *vb*
¹**shin** \ˈshin\ *n* : the front part of the leg below the knee
²**shin** *vb* **shinned; shin·ning** : to climb (as a pole) by gripping alternately with arms or hands or legs
shin·bone \ˈshin-ˌbōn\ *n* : TIBIA
¹**shine** \ˈshīn\ *vb* **shone** \ˈshōn\ *or* **shined; shin·ing** **1** : to give or cause to give light **2** : GLEAM, GLITTER **3** : to be eminent, conspicuous, or distinguished ⟨gave her a chance to ∼⟩ **4** : POLISH ⟨∼ your shoes⟩
²**shine** *n* **1** : BRIGHTNESS, RADIANCE **2** : LUSTER, BRILLIANCE **3** : fair weather : SUNSHINE ⟨rain or ∼⟩ **4** : LIKING, FANCY ⟨took a ∼ to them⟩ **5** : a polish given to shoes
shin·er \ˈshī-nər\ *n* **1** : a silvery fish; *esp* : any of numerous small freshwater American fishes related to the carp **2** : BLACK EYE
¹**shin·gle** \ˈshiŋ-gəl\ *n* **1** : a small thin piece of building material used in overlapping rows for covering a roof or outside wall **2** : a small sign
²**shingle** *vb* **shin·gled; shin·gling** : to cover with shingles
³**shingle** *n* : a beach strewn with gravel; *also* : coarse gravel (as on a beach)
shin·gles \ˈshiŋ-gəlz\ *n* : an acute inflammation of the spinal and cranial nerves caused by reactivation of the chicken pox virus and associated with eruptions and pain along the course of the affected nerves
shin·ny \ˈshi-nē\ *vb* **shin·nied; shin·ny·ing** : SHIN
shin splints *n sing or pl* : a condition marked by pain and sometimes tenderness and swelling in the shin caused by repeated small injuries to muscles and associated tissue esp. from running
Shin·to \ˈshin-ˌtō\ *n* : the indigenous religion of Japan consisting esp. in reverence of the spirits of natural forces and imperial ancestors — **Shin·to·ism** *n* — **Shin·to·ist** *n or adj*
shiny \ˈshī-nē\ *adj* **shin·i·er; -est** : BRIGHT, RADIANT; *also* : POLISHED
¹**ship** \ˈship\ *n* **1** : a large oceangoing boat **2** : a ship's officers and crew **3** : AIRSHIP, AIRCRAFT, SPACECRAFT
²**ship** *vb* **shipped; ship·ping** **1** : to put or receive on board a ship for transportation **2** : to have transported by a carrier **3** : to take or draw into a boat ⟨∼ oars⟩ ⟨∼ water⟩ **4** : to engage to serve on a ship — **ship·per** *n*
-ship \ˌship\ *n suffix* **1** : state : condition : quality ⟨friendship⟩ **2** : office : dignity : profession ⟨lordship⟩ ⟨clerkship⟩ **3** : art : skill ⟨horsemanship⟩ **4** : something showing, exhibiting, or embodying a quality or state ⟨township⟩ **5** : one entitled to a (specified) rank, title, or appellation ⟨his Lordship⟩ **6** : the body of persons engaged in a specified activity ⟨readership⟩
ship·board \ˈship-ˌbȯrd\ *n* : SHIP
ship·build·er \-ˌbil-dər\ *n* : one who designs or builds ships
ship·fit·ter \-ˌfi-tər\ *n* **1** : one who constructs ships **2** : a naval enlisted man who works as a plumber
ship·mate \-ˌmāt\ *n* : a fellow sailor
ship·ment \-mənt\ *n* : the process of shipping; *also* : the goods shipped
shipping *n* **1** : SHIPS; *esp* : ships in one port or belonging to one country **2** : transportation of goods
ship·shape \ˈship-ˌshāp\ *adj* : TRIM, TIDY ⟨kept the garage ∼⟩
ship·worm \-ˌwərm\ *n* : any of various wormlike marine clams that bore a shell used for burrowing in wood and damage wooden ships and wharves
¹**ship·wreck** \-ˌrek\ *n* **1** : a wrecked ship **2** : destruction or loss of a ship **3** : total loss or failure : RUIN
²**shipwreck** *vb* : to cause or meet disaster at sea through destruction or foundering
ship·wright \ˈship-ˌrīt\ *n* : a carpenter skilled in ship construction and repair
ship·yard \-ˌyärd\ *n* : a place where ships are built or repaired

shire \'shī(-ə)r, *in place-name compounds* ˌshir, shər\ *n* : a county in Great Britain
shirk \'shərk\ *vb* : to avoid performing (duty or work) — **shirk·er** *n*
shirr \'shər\ *vb* **1** : to make shirring in **2** : to bake (eggs removed from the shell) until set
shirr·ing \'shər-iŋ\ *n* : a decorative gathering in cloth made by drawing up parallel lines of stitches
shirt \'shərt\ *n* **1** : a loose cloth garment usu. having a collar, sleeves, a front opening, and a tail long enough to be tucked inside pants or a skirt **2** : UNDERSHIRT — **shirt·less** *adj*
shirt·ing \'shər-tiŋ\ *n* : cloth suitable for making shirts
shish ke·bab \'shish-kə-ˌbäb\ *n* [Turk *şiş kebabı,* fr. *şiş* spit + *kebap* roast meat] : kebab cooked on skewers
shiv \'shiv\ *n, slang* : KNIFE
¹shiv·er \'shi-vər\ *vb* : TREMBLE, QUIVER **♦ Synonyms** SHUDDER, QUAVER, SHAKE, QUAKE
²shiver *n* : an instance of shivering — **shiv·ery** *adj*
shlemiel *var of* SCHLEMIEL
shlub *var of* SCHLUB
shmooze *var of* SCHMOOZE
Sho·ah \'shō-ə, -ˌä\ *n* : HOLOCAUST 2
¹shoal \'shōl\ *n* **1** : SHALLOW **2** : a sandbank or bar creating a shallow
²shoal *n* : a large group (as of fish)
shoat \'shōt\ *n* : a weaned young pig
¹shock \'shäk\ *n* : a pile of sheaves of grain or cornstalks set up in a field
²shock *n* [MF *choc,* fr. *choquer* to strike against] **1** : a sharp impact or violent shake or jar **2** : a sudden violent mental or emotional disturbance **3** : a state of bodily collapse that is often marked by a drop in blood pressure and volume and that is caused esp. by crushing wounds, blood loss, or burns **4** : the effect of a charge of electricity passing through the body **5** : SHOCK ABSORBER — **shock·proof** \-ˌprüf\ *adj*
³shock *vb* **1** : to strike with surprise, horror, or disgust **2** : to subject to the action of an electrical discharge
⁴shock *n* : a thick bushy mass (as of hair)
shock absorber *n* : any of several devices for absorbing the energy of sudden shocks in machinery
shock·er \'shä-kər\ *n* : one that shocks; *esp* : a sensational work of fiction or drama
shock·ing \'shä-kiŋ\ *adj* : extremely startling and offensive — **shock·ing·ly** *adv*
shock therapy *n* : the treatment of mental disorder by induction of coma or convulsions by drugs or electricity
shock wave *n* : a wave formed by the sudden violent compression of the medium through which it travels
¹shod·dy \'shä-dē\ *n* **1** : wool reclaimed from old rags; *also* : a fabric made from it **2** : inferior or imitation material
²shoddy *adj* **shod·di·er; -est** **1** : made of shoddy **2** : poorly done or made — **shod·di·ly** \'shä-də-lē\ *adv* — **shod·di·ness** \-dē-nəs\ *n*
¹shoe \'shü\ *n* **1** : a covering for the human foot **2** : HORSESHOE **3** : the part of a brake that presses on the wheel
²shoe *vb* **shod** \'shäd\ *also* **shoed** \'shüd\; **shoe·ing** : to put a shoe or shoes on
shoe·horn \-ˌhȯrn\ *n* : a curved implement (as of horn or plastic) used in putting on a shoe
shoe·lace \'shü-ˌlās\ *n* : a lace or string for fastening a shoe
shoe·mak·er \-ˌmā-kər\ *n* : one who makes or repairs shoes
shoe·string \-ˌstriŋ\ *n* **1** : SHOELACE **2** : a small sum of money
sho·gun \'shō-gən\ *n* [Jp *shōgun* general] : any of a line of military governors ruling Japan until the revolution of 1867–68 — **sho·gun·ate** \'shō-gə-nət, -ˌnät\ *n*
shone *past and past part of* SHINE
shook *past of* SHAKE
shook–up \(ˌ)shu̇k-'əp\ *adj* : nervously upset : AGITATED
¹shoot \'shüt\ *vb* **shot** \'shät\; **shoot·ing** **1** : to drive (as an arrow or bullet) forward quickly or forcibly **2** : to hit, kill, or wound with a missile **3** : to cause a missile to be driven forth or forth from ⟨~ a gun⟩ **4** : to send forth (as a ray of light) **5** : to thrust forward or out **6** : to pass rapidly along ⟨~ the rapids⟩ **7** : PHOTOGRAPH,

FILM **8** : to move swiftly : DART **9** : to grow by or as if by sending out shoots; *also* : MATURE, DEVELOP — **shoot·er** *n*
²shoot *n* **1** : a plant stem with its leaves and branches esp. when not yet mature **2** : an act of shooting **3** : a shooting match
shooting iron *n* : FIREARM
shooting star *n* : METEOR 2
shoot up *vb* : to inject a narcotic into a vein
¹shop \'shäp\ *n* [ME *shoppe,* fr. OE *sceoppa* booth] **1** : a place where things are made or worked on : FACTORY, MILL **2** : a retail store ⟨dress ~⟩
²shop *vb* **shopped; shop·ping** : to visit stores for purchasing or examining goods — **shop·per** *n*
shop·keep·er \'shäp-ˌkē-pər\ *n* : a retail merchant
shop·lift \-ˌlift\ *vb* : to steal goods on display from a store — **shop·lift·er** *n*
shop·talk \-ˌtȯk\ *n* : talk about one's business or special interests
shop·worn \-ˌwȯrn\ *adj* : soiled or frayed from much handling in a store
¹shore \'shȯr\ *n* : land along the edge of a body of water — **shore·less** *adj*
²shore *vb* **shored; shor·ing** : to give support to : BRACE
³shore *n* : ¹PROP
shore·bird \-ˌbərd\ *n* : any of a suborder of birds (as the plovers and sandpipers) found mostly along the seashore
shore patrol *n* : a branch of a navy that exercises guard and police functions
shor·ing \'shȯr-iŋ\ *n* : a group of things that shore something up
shorn *past part of* SHEAR
¹short \'shȯrt\ *adj* **1** : not long or tall **2** : not great in distance **3** : brief in time **4** : not coming up to standard or to an expected amount **5** : CURT, ABRUPT **6** : insufficiently supplied ⟨~ of cash⟩ **7** : made with shortening : FLAKY **8** : consisting of or relating to a sale of securities or commodities that the seller does not possess or has not contracted for at the time of the sale ⟨~ sale⟩ — **short·ness** *n*
²short *adv* **1** : ABRUPTLY, CURTLY **2** : at some point before a goal aimed at
³short *n* **1** : something shorter than normal or standard **2** *pl* : drawers or pants of less than knee length **3** : SHORT CIRCUIT
⁴short *vb* : SHORT-CIRCUIT
short·age \'shȯr-tij\ *n* : LACK, DEFICIT
short·cake \'shȯrt-ˌkāk\ *n* : a dessert consisting of short biscuit spread with sweetened fruit
short·change \-'chānj\ *vb* : to cheat esp. by giving less than the correct amount of change
short circuit *n* : a connection made between points in an electric circuit where current is not intended to flow — **short–circuit** *vb*
short·com·ing \'shȯrt-ˌkə-miŋ\ *n* : FAULT 1, FLAW
short·cut \-ˌkət\ *n* **1** : a route more direct than that usu. taken **2** : a quicker way of doing something
short·en \'shȯr-tᵊn\ *vb* : to make or become short **♦ Synonyms** CURTAIL, ABBREVIATE, ABRIDGE, RETRENCH
short·en·ing \'shȯrt-tᵊn-iŋ\ *n* : a substance (as lard or butter) that makes pastry tender and flaky
short·hand \'shȯrt-ˌhand\ *n* : a method of writing rapidly by using symbols and abbreviations for letters, words, or phrases : STENOGRAPHY
short·hand·ed \ˌshȯrt-'han-dəd\ *adj* : short of the needed number of people
short·horn \'shȯrt-ˌhȯrn\ *n, often cap* : any of a breed of red, roan, or white cattle of English origin
short hundredweight *n* — see WEIGHT table
short–lived \'shȯrt-'līvd, -'livd\ *adj* : of short life or duration
short·ly \'shȯrt-lē\ *adv* **1** : in a few words **2** : in a short time : SOON
short–or·der \'shȯrt-ˌȯr-dər\ *adj* : preparing or serving food that can be quickly cooked
short shrift *n* **1** : a brief respite from death **2** : little consideration
short·sight·ed \'shȯrt-ˌsī-təd\ *adj* **1** : lacking foresight **2** : NEARSIGHTED — **short·sight·ed·ness** *n*
short·stop \-ˌstäp\ *n* : a baseball player defending the area between second and third base

short story *n* : a short work of fiction usu. dealing with a few characters and a single event

short–tem·pered \ˌshȯrt-ˈtem-pərd\ *adj* : having a quick temper

short–term \ˈshȯrt-ˌtərm\ *adj* **1** : occurring over or involving a relatively short period of time **2** : of or relating to a financial transaction based on a term usu. of less than a year

short ton *n* — see WEIGHT table

short·wave \ˈshȯrt-ˌwāv\ *n* : a radio wave with a wavelength between 10 and 100 meters

Sho·sho·ne *or* **Sho·sho·ni** \shə-ˈshō-nē\ *n, pl* **Shoshones** *or* **Shoshoni** : a member of an American Indian people orig. ranging through California, Idaho, Nevada, Utah, and Wyoming

¹**shot** \ˈshät\ *n* **1** : an act of shooting **2** : a stroke or throw in some games **3** : something that is shot : MISSILE, PROJECTILE; *esp* : small pellets forming a charge for a shotgun **4** : a metal sphere that is thrown for distance in the shot put **5** : RANGE, REACH **6** : MARKSMAN **7** : a single photographic exposure **8** : a single sequence of a motion picture or a television program made by one camera **9** : an injection (as of medicine) into the body **10** : a small serving of undiluted liquor or other beverage

²**shot** *past and past part of* SHOOT

shot·gun \ˈshät-ˌgən\ *n* : a gun with a smooth bore used to fire shot at short range

shot put *n* : a field event in which a shot is heaved for distance

should \ˈshu̇d, shəd\ *past of* SHALL — used as an auxiliary to express condition, obligation or propriety, probability, or futurity from a point of view in the past

¹**shoul·der** \ˈshōl-dər\ *n* **1** : the part of the body of a person or animal where the arm or foreleg joins the body **2** : either edge of a roadway **3** : a rounded or sloping part (as of a bottle) where the neck joins the body

²**shoulder** *vb* **1** : to push or thrust with the shoulder **2** : to bear on the shoulder **3** : to take the responsibility of

shoulder belt *n* : an automobile safety belt worn across the torso and over the shoulder

shoulder blade *n* : a flat triangular bone at the back of each shoulder

shout \ˈshau̇t\ *vb* : to utter a sudden loud cry — **shout** *n*

shove \ˈshəv\ *vb* **shoved; shov·ing** : to push along, aside, or away — **shove** *n*

¹**shov·el** \ˈshə-vəl\ *n* **1** : a broad long-handled scoop used to lift and throw material **2** : the amount a shovel will hold — **shov·el·ful** \ˈshə-vəl-ˌfu̇l\ *n*

²**shovel** *vb* **-eled** *or* **-elled; -el·ing** *or* **-el·ling** **1** : to take up and throw with a shovel **2** : to dig or clean out with a shovel

¹**show** \ˈshō\ *vb* **showed** \ˈshōd\; **shown** \ˈshōn\ *or* **showed; show·ing** **1** : to cause or permit to be seen : EXHIBIT ⟨~ anger⟩ **2** : CONFER, BESTOW ⟨~ mercy⟩ **3** : REVEAL, DISCLOSE ⟨~ed courage in battle⟩ **4** : INSTRUCT ⟨~ me how⟩ **5** : PROVE ⟨~s he was guilty⟩ **6** : APPEAR **7** : to be noticeable **8** : to be third in a horse race

²**show** *n* **1** : a demonstrative display **2** : outward appearance ⟨a ~ of resistance⟩ **3** : SPECTACLE **4** : a theatrical presentation **5** : a radio or television program **6** : third place in a horse race

¹**show·case** \ˈshō-ˌkās\ *n* : a cabinet for displaying items (as in a store)

²**showcase** *vb* **show·cased; show·cas·ing** : EXHIBIT

show·down \ˈshō-ˌdau̇n\ *n* : a decisive confrontation or contest; *esp* : the showing of poker hands to determine the winner of a pot

¹**show·er** \ˈshau̇(-ə)r\ *n* **1** : a brief fall of rain **2** : a party given by friends who bring gifts **3** : a bath in which water is showered on the person; *also* : a facility (as a stall) for such a bath — **show·ery** *adj*

²**shower** *vb* **1** : to rain or fall in a shower **2** : to bathe in a shower

show·man \ˈshō-mən\ *n* : a notably spectacular, dramatic, or effective performer — **show·man·ship** *n*

show–off \ˈshō-ˌȯf\ *n* : one that seeks to attract attention by conspicuous behavior

show off *vb* **1** : to display proudly **2** : to act as a show-off

show·piece \ˈshō-ˌpēs\ *n* : an outstanding example used for exhibition

show·place \-ˌplās\ *n* : an estate or building that is a showpiece

show up *vb* : ARRIVE

showy \ˈshō-ē\ *adj* **show·i·er; -est** : superficially impressive or striking ⟨a ~ orchid⟩ — **show·i·ly** \ˈshō-ə-lē\ *adv* — **show·i·ness** \-ē-nəs\ *n*

shpt *abbr* shipment

shrap·nel \ˈshrap-nəl\ *n, pl* **shrapnel** [Henry *Shrapnel* †1842 Eng. artillery officer] : bomb, mine, or shell fragments

¹**shred** \ˈshred\ *n* : a narrow strip cut or torn off : a small fragment

²**shred** *vb* **shred·ded; shred·ding** : to cut or tear into shreds

shrew \ˈshrü\ *n* **1** : any of a family of very small mammals with short velvety fur that are related to the moles **2** : a scolding woman

shrewd \ˈshrüd\ *adj* : CLEVER, ASTUTE — **shrewd·ly** *adv* — **shrewd·ness** *n*

shrew·ish \ˈshrü-ish\ *adj* : having an irritable disposition : ILL-TEMPERED — **shrew·ish·ly** *adv* — **shrew·ish·ness** *n*

shriek \ˈshrēk\ *n* : a shrill cry : SCREAM, YELL — **shriek** *vb*

shrift \ˈshrift\ *n, archaic* : the act of shriving : CONFESSION

shrike \ˈshrīk\ *n* : any of numerous usu. largely grayish or brownish birds that often impale their usu. insect prey upon thorns before devouring it

¹**shrill** \ˈshril\ *vb* : to make a high-pitched piercing sound

²**shrill** *adj* : high-pitched : PIERCING ⟨~ whistle⟩ — **shril·ly** *adv*

shrimp \ˈshrimp\ *n, pl* **shrimps** *or* **shrimp** **1** : any of various small marine crustaceans related to the lobsters **2** : a small or puny person

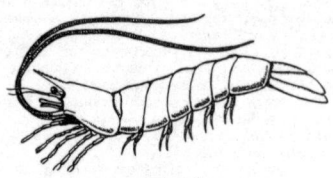

shrimp 1

shrine \ˈshrīn\ *n* [ME, receptacle for the relics of a saint, fr. OE *scrīn*, fr. L *scrinium* case, chest] **1** : the tomb of a saint; *also* : a place where devotion is paid to a saint or deity **2** : a place or object hallowed by its associations

¹**shrink** \ˈshriŋk\ *vb* **shrank** \ˈshraŋk\ *or* **shrunk** \ˈshrəŋk\; **shrunk** *or* **shrunk·en** \ˈshrəŋ-kən\; **shrink·ing** **1** : to draw back or away **2** : to become smaller or more compact **3** : to lessen in value ✦ *Synonyms* CONTRACT, CONSTRICT, COMPRESS, CONDENSE — **shrink·able** *adj*

²**shrink** *n* : a clinical psychiatrist or psychologist

shrink·age \ˈshriŋ-kij\ *n* **1** : the act of shrinking **2** : the amount lost by shrinkage

shrive \ˈshrīv\ *vb* **shrived** *or* **shrove** \ˈshrōv\; **shriv·en** \ˈshri-vən\ *or* **shrived** [ME, fr. OE *scrīfan* to prescribe, allot, shrive, fr. L *scribere* to write] : to administer the sacrament of reconciliation to

shriv·el \ˈshri-vəl\ *vb* **-eled** *or* **-elled; -el·ing** *or* **-el·ling** : to shrink and draw into wrinkles : DWINDLE

¹**shroud** \ˈshrau̇d\ *n* **1** : something that covers or screens **2** : a cloth placed over a dead body **3** : any of the ropes leading from the masthead of a ship to the side to support the mast

²**shroud** *vb* : to veil or screen from view

shrub \ˈshrəb\ *n* : a low usu. several-stemmed woody plant — **shrub·by** *adj*

shrub·bery \ˈshrə-bə-rē\ *n, pl* **-ber·ies** : a planting or growth of shrubs

shrug \ˈshrəg\ *vb* **shrugged; shrug·ging** : to hunch (the shoulders) up to express aloofness, indifference, or uncertainty — **shrug** *n*

shrug off *vb* **1** : to brush aside : MINIMIZE **2** : to shake off **3** : to remove (a garment) by wriggling out

shtick *also* **schtick** *or* **shtik** \ˈshtik\ *n* [Yiddish *shtik* pranks, lit., piece] **1** : a usu. comic or repetitious performance or routine **2** : one's special trait, interest, or activity

¹shuck \'shək\ *n* : SHELL, HUSK

²shuck *vb* : to strip of shucks

shud·der \'shə-dər\ *vb* : TREMBLE, QUAKE — **shudder** *n*

shuf·fle \'shə-fəl\ *vb* **shuf·fled; shuf·fling 1** : to mix in a disorderly mass **2** : to rearrange the order of (cards in a pack) by mixing two parts of the pack together **3** : to shift from place to place **4** : to move with a sliding or dragging gait **5** : to dance in a slow lagging manner — **shuffle** *n*

shuf·fle·board \'shə-fəl-ˌbórd\ *n* : a game in which players use long-handled cues to shove disks into scoring areas marked on a smooth surface

shun \'shən\ *vb* **shunned; shun·ning** : to avoid deliberately or habitually ✦ *Synonyms* EVADE, ELUDE, ESCAPE, DUCK

¹shunt \'shənt\ *vb* [ME, to turn away] : to turn off to one side; *esp* : to switch (a train) from one track to another

²shunt 1 : a method or device for turning or thrusting aside **2** : a conductor joining two points in an electrical circuit forming an alternate path through which a portion of the current may pass

shut \'shət\ *vb* **shut; shut·ting 1** : CLOSE **2** : to forbid entrance into **3** : to lock up **4** : to fold together ⟨∼ a penknife⟩ **5** : to cease or suspend activity ⟨∼ down an assembly line⟩

shut·down \-ˌdaún\ *n* : a temporary cessation of activity (as in a factory)

shut–in \'shət-ˌin\ *n* : a person confined to home, a room, or bed because of illness or incapacity

shut·out \'shət-ˌaút\ *n* : a game or contest in which one side fails to score

shut out *vb* **1** : EXCLUDE **2** : to prevent (an opponent) from scoring in a game or contest

shut·ter \'shə-tər\ *n* **1** : a movable cover for a door or window : BLIND **2** : the part of a camera that opens and closes to allow light to enter

shut·ter·bug \'shə-tər-ˌbəg\ *n* : a photography enthusiast

¹shut·tle \'shə-t°l\ *n* **1** : an instrument used in weaving for passing the horizontal threads between the vertical threads **2** : a vehicle traveling back and forth over a short route ⟨a ∼ bus⟩ **3** : SPACE SHUTTLE

²shuttle *vb* **shut·tled; shut·tling** : to move back and forth frequently

shut·tle·cock \'shə-t°l-ˌkäk\ *n* : a light conical object (as of cork or plastic) used in badminton

shut up *vb* : to cease or cause to cease talking

¹shy \'shī\ *adj* **shi·er** *or* **shy·er** \'shī-ər\; **shi·est** *or* **shy·est** \'shī-əst\ **1** : easily frightened : TIMID **2** : WARY **3** : BASHFUL **4** : DEFICIENT, LACKING — **shy·ly** *adv* — **shy·ness** *n*

²shy *vb* **shied; shy·ing 1** : to show a dislike : RECOIL **2** : to start suddenly aside through fright ⟨the horse *shied*⟩

shy·ster \'shīs-tər\ *n* : an unscrupulous lawyer or politician

Si *symbol* silicon

SI *abbr* [F *Système International d'Unités*] International System of Units

Si·a·mese \ˌsī-ə-ˈmēz, -ˈmēs\ *n, pl* **Sia·mese** : THAI — **Siamese** *adj*

Siamese cat *n* : any of a breed of slender blue-eyed short-haired domestic cats of Asian origin

Siamese twin *n* [fr. Chang †1874 and Eng †1874 twins born in Siam with bodies united] : one of a pair of twins with bodies joined together at birth

Siberian husky *n* : any of a breed of thick-coated compact dogs orig. developed in Siberia to pull sleds

¹sib·i·lant \'si-bə-lənt\ *adj* : having, containing, or producing the sound of or a sound resembling that of the *s* or the *sh* in *sash* — **sib·i·lant·ly** *adv*

²sibilant *n* : a sibilant speech sound (as English \s\, \z\, \sh\, \zh\, \ch (=tsh)\, or \j (=dzh)\)

sib·ling \'si-blin\ *n* : a brother or sister considered irrespective of sex; *also* : one of two or more offspring having one common parent

sib·yl \'si-bəl\ *n, often cap* : PROPHETESS — **sib·yl·line** \-bə-ˌlīn, -ˌlēn\ *adj*

sic \'sik, 'sēk\ *adv* : intentionally so written — used after a printed word or passage to indicate that it exactly reproduces an original ⟨said he seed [∼] it all⟩

sick \'sik\ *adj* **1** : not in good health : ILL; *also* : of, relating to, or intended for use in sickness ⟨∼ pay⟩ **2** : NAUSEATED **3** : DISGUSTED **4** : PINING **5** : mentally or emotionally unsound **6** : MACABRE, SADISTIC ⟨∼ jokes⟩ — **sick·ly** *adj*

sick·bed \'sik-ˌbed\ *n* : a bed on which one lies sick

sick·en \'si-kən\ *vb* : to make or become sick — **sick·en·ing·ly** *adv*

sick·le \'si-kəl\ *n* : a cutting tool consisting of a curved metal blade with a short handle

sickle–cell anemia *n* : an inherited anemia in which red blood cells tend to become crescent-shaped and clog small blood vessels and which occurs esp. in individuals of African, Mediterranean, or southwest Asian ancestry

sick·ness \'sik-nəs\ *n* **1** : ill health; *also* : a specific disease **2** : NAUSEA

side \'sīd\ *n* **1** : the right or left part of the trunk of a body **2** : a place away from a central point or line **3** : a border of an object; *esp* : one of the longer borders as contrasted with an end **4** : an outer surface of an object **5** : a position regarded as opposite to another **6** : a body of contestants — **side** *adj* — **on the side** : in addition to the main portion

side·arm \-ˌärm\ *adj* : made with a sideways sweep of the arm ⟨a ∼ pitch⟩ — **sidearm** *adv*

side arm *n* : a weapon worn at the side or in the belt

side·bar \'sīd-ˌbär\ *n* : a short news story accompanying a major story and presenting related information

side·board \-ˌbórd\ *n* : a piece of dining-room furniture for holding articles of table service

side·burns \-ˌbərnz\ *n pl* : whiskers on the side of the face in front of the ears

side by side *adv* **1** : beside one another **2** : in the same place, time, or circumstance — **side–by–side** *adj*

side·car \-ˌkär\ *n* : a one-wheeled passenger car attached to the side of a motorcycle

side effect *n* : a secondary or esp. adverse effect (as of a drug)

side·kick \'sīd-ˌkik\ *n* : PAL, PARTNER

side·line \'sīd-ˌlīn\ *n* **1** : an activity pursued in addition to one's regular occupation **2** : the space immediately outside the lines of an athletic field or court **3** : a sphere of little or no participation — usu. used in pl.

¹side·long \'sīd-ˌlón\ *adv* : in the direction of or along the side : OBLIQUELY

²sidelong *adj* : directed to one side ⟨∼ look⟩

side·man \'sīd-ˌman\ *n* : a member of a jazz or swing orchestra

side·piece \-ˌpēs\ *n* : a piece forming or contained in the side of something

si·de·re·al \sī-ˈdir-ē-əl, sə-\ *adj* [L *sidereus*, fr. *sider-*, *sidus* star, constellation] **1** : of or relating to the stars **2** : measured by the apparent motion of the stars

side·sad·dle \'sīd-ˌsa-d°l\ *n* : a saddle for women on which the rider sits with both legs on the same side of the horse — **sidesaddle** *adv*

side·show \'sīd-ˌshō\ *n* **1** : a minor show offered in addition to a main exhibition (as of a circus) **2** : an incidental diversion

side·step \-ˌstep\ *vb* **1** : to step aside **2** : AVOID, EVADE

side·stroke \-ˌstrōk\ *n* : a swimming stroke which is executed on the side and in which the arms are swept backward and downward and the legs do a scissors kick

side·swipe \-ˌswīp\ *vb* : to strike with a glancing blow along the side — **sideswipe** *n*

¹side·track \-ˌtrak\ *n* : SIDING 1

²sidetrack *vb* **1** : to switch from a main railroad line to a siding **2** : to turn aside from a purpose

side·walk \'sīd-ˌwók\ *n* : a paved walk at the side of a road or street

side·wall \-ˌwól\ *n* **1** : a wall forming the side of something **2** : the side of an automobile tire

side·ways \-ˌwāz\ *adv or adj* **1** : from the side **2** : with one side to the front **3** : to, toward, or at one side

side·wind·er \-ˌwīn-dər\ *n* : a small pale-colored desert rattlesnake of the southwestern U.S.

sid·ing \'sī-din\ *n* **1** : a short railroad track connected with the main track **2** : material (as boards) covering the outside of frame buildings

si·dle \'sī-d°l\ *vb* **si·dled; si·dling** : to move sideways or with one side foremost

SIDS *abbr* sudden infant death syndrome

siege \'sēj\ *n* **1** : the placing of an army around or before a fortified place to force its surrender **2** : a persistent attack (as of illness)

sie·mens \'sē-mənz, 'zē-\ *n* : a unit of conductance equivalent to one ampere per volt

si·er·ra \sē-'er-ə\ *n* [Sp, lit., saw, fr. L *serra*] : a range of mountains esp. with jagged peaks

si·es·ta \sē-'es-tə\ *n* [Sp, fr. L *sexta (hora)* noon, lit., sixth hour] : a midday rest or nap

sieve \'siv\ *n* : a utensil with meshes or holes to separate finer particles from coarser or solids from liquids

sift \'sift\ *vb* **1** : to pass through a sieve **2** : to separate with or as if with a sieve **3** : to examine carefully **4** : to scatter by or as if by passing through a sieve — **sift·er** *n*

sig *abbr* signature

SIG *abbr* special interest group

sigh \'sī\ *vb* **1** : to let out a deep audible breath (as in weariness or sorrow) **2** : GRIEVE, YEARN — **sigh** *n*

¹sight \'sīt\ *n* **1** : something seen or worth seeing **2** : the process or power of seeing; *esp* : the sense of which the eye is the receptor and by which qualities of appearance (as position, shape, and color) are perceived **3** : INSPECTION **4** : a device (as a small bead on a gun barrel) that aids the eye in aiming **5** : VIEW, GLIMPSE **6** : the range of vision — **sight·less** *adj*

²sight *vb* **1** : to get sight of **2** : to aim by means of a sight

sight·ed \'sī-təd\ *adj* : having sight

sight·ly \-lē\ *adj* : pleasing to the sight

sight·see·ing \'sīt-,sē-iŋ\ *adj* : engaged in or used for seeing sights of interest — **sight·seer** \-,sē-ər\ *n*

sig·ma \'sig-mə\ *n* : the 18th letter of the Greek alphabet — Σ or σ or ς

¹sign \'sīn\ *n* **1** : a gesture expressing a command, wish, or thought **2** : SYMBOL **3** : a notice publicly displayed for advertising purposes or for giving direction or warning **4** : OMEN, PORTENT **5** : TRACE, VESTIGE

²sign *vb* **1** : to mark with a sign **2** : to represent by a sign **3** : to make a sign or signal **4** : to write one's name on in token of assent or obligation **5** : to assign legally **6** : to use sign language — **sign·er** *n*

¹sig·nal \'sig-nəl\ *n* **1** : a sign agreed on as the start of some joint action **2** : a sign giving warning or notice of something **3** : the message, sound, or image transmitted in electronic communication (as radio)

²signal *vb* **-naled** *or* **-nalled; -nal·ing** *or* **-nal·ling** **1** : to notify by a signal **2** : to communicate by signals

³signal *adj* : DISTINGUISHED ⟨a ~ honor⟩ — **sig·nal·ly** *adv*

sig·nal·ize \'sig-nə-,līz\ *vb* **-ized; -iz·ing** : to point out or make conspicuous — **sig·nal·i·za·tion** \,sig-nə-lə-'zā-shən\ *n*

sig·nal·man \'sig-nəl-mən, -,man\ *n* : a person who signals or works with signals

sig·na·to·ry \'sig-nə-,tōr-ē\ *n, pl* **-ries** : a person or government that signs jointly with others — **signatory** *adj*

sig·na·ture \'sig-nə-,chùr\ *n* **1** : the name of a person written by himself or herself **2** : the sign placed after the clef to indicate the key or the meter of a piece of music

sign·board \'sīn-,bȯrd\ *n* : a board bearing a sign or notice

sig·net \'sig-nət\ *n* : a small intaglio seal (as in a ring)

sig·nif·i·cance \sig-'ni-fi-kəns\ *n* **1** : something signified : MEANING **2** : SUGGESTIVENESS **3** : CONSEQUENCE, IMPORTANCE

sig·nif·i·cant \-kənt\ *adj* **1** : having meaning; *esp* : having a hidden or special meaning **2** : having or likely to have considerable influence or effect : IMPORTANT — **sig·nif·i·cant·ly** *adv*

sig·ni·fy \'sig-nə-,fī\ *vb* **-fied; -fy·ing** **1** : to show by a sign **2** : MEAN, IMPORT **3** : to have significance — **sig·ni·fi·ca·tion** \,sig-nə-fə-'kā-shən\ *n*

sign in *vb* : to make a record of arrival (as by signing a register)

sign language *n* : a formal system of hand gestures used for communication (as by the deaf)

sign off *vb* : to announce the end (as of a program or broadcast)

sign of the cross : a gesture of the hand forming a cross (as to invoke divine blessing)

sign on *vb* **1** : ENLIST **2** : to announce the start of broadcasting for the day

sign out *vb* : to make a record of departure (as by signing a register)

sign·post \'sīn-,pōst\ *n* : a post bearing a sign

sign up *vb* : to sign one's name in order to obtain, do, or join something

Sikh \'sēk\ *n* : an adherent of a religion of India marked by rejection of caste — **Sikh·ism** *n*

si·lage \'sī-lij\ *n* : fodder fermented (as in a silo) to produce a rich moist animal feed

¹si·lence \'sī-ləns\ *n* **1** : the state of being silent **2** : STILLNESS **3** : SECRECY

²silence *vb* **si·lenced; si·lenc·ing** **1** : to reduce to silence **2** : to cause to cease hostile firing or criticism

si·lenc·er \'sī-lən-sər\ *n* : a device for muffling the noise of a gunshot

si·lent \'sī-lənt\ *adj* **1** : not speaking : MUTE; *also* : TACITURN **2** : STILL, QUIET **3** : performed or borne without utterance ♦ **Synonyms** RETICENT, RESERVED, CLOSEMOUTHED, CLOSE — **si·lent·ly** *adv*

¹sil·hou·ette \,si-lə-'wet\ *n* [F] **1** : a representation of the outlines of an object filled in with black or some other uniform color **2** : OUTLINE ⟨~ of a ship⟩

²silhouette *vb* **-ett·ed; -ett·ing** : to represent by a silhouette; *also* : to show against a light background

sil·i·ca \'si-li-kə\ *n* : a mineral that consists of silicon and oxygen

sil·i·cate \'si-lə-,kāt, 'si-li-kət\ *n* : a chemical salt that consists of a metal combined with silicon and oxygen

si·li·ceous *also* **si·li·cious** \sə-'li-shəs\ *adj* : of, relating to, or containing silica or a silicate

sil·i·con \'si-li-kən, 'si-lə-,kän\ *n* : a nonmetallic chemical element that occurs in combination as the most abundant element next to oxygen in the earth's crust and is used esp. in alloys and semiconductors

sil·i·cone \'si-lə-,kōn\ *n* : an organic silicon compound used esp. for lubricants and varnishes

sil·i·co·sis \,si-lə-'kō-səs\ *n* : a lung disease caused by prolonged inhaling of silica dusts

silk \'silk\ *n* **1** : a fine strong lustrous protein fiber produced by insect larvae usu. for their cocoons; *esp* : one from moth larvae (**silk·worms** \-,wərmz\) used for cloth **2** : thread or cloth made from silk — **silk·en** \'sil-kən\ *adj* — **silky** *adj*

silk screen *n* : a stencil process in which coloring matter is forced through the meshes of a prepared silk or organdy screen; *also* : a print made by this process — **silk–screen** *vb*

sill \'sil\ *n* : a heavy crosspiece (as of wood or stone) that forms the bottom member of a window frame or a doorway; *also* : a horizontal supporting piece at the base of a structure

sil·ly \'si-lē\ *adj* **sil·li·er; -est** [ME *sely, silly* happy, innocent, pitiable, feeble, fr. OE *sǣlig*, fr. *sǣl* happiness] **1** : FOOLISH, ABSURD **2** : TACKY — **sil·li·ness** *n*

si·lo \'sī-lō\ *n, pl* **silos** [Sp] **1** : a trench, pit, or esp. a tall cylinder for making and storing silage **2** : an underground structure for housing a guided missile

¹silt \'silt\ *n* **1** : fine earth; *esp* : particles of such soil floating in rivers, ponds, or lakes **2** : a deposit (as by a river) of silt — **silty** *adj*

²silt *vb* : to obstruct or cover with silt — **silt·ation** \sil-'tā-shən\ *n*

Si·lu·ri·an \sī-'lùr-ē-ən\ *adj* : of, relating to, or being the period of the Paleozoic era between the Ordovician and the Devonian marked by the appearance of the first land plants — **Silurian** *n*

¹sil·ver \'sil-vər\ *n* **1** : a white ductile metallic chemical element that takes a high polish and is a better conductor of heat and electricity than any other substance **2** : coin made of silver **3** : FLATWARE **4** : a grayish white color — **sil·very** *adj*

²silver *adj* **1** : relating to, made of, or coated with silver **2** : SILVERY

³silver *vb* **sil·vered; sil·ver·ing** : to coat with or as if with silver — **sil·ver·er** *n*

silver bromide *n* : a light-sensitive compound used esp. in photography

sil·ver·fish \'sil-vər-,fish\ *n* : any of various small wingless insects found in houses and sometimes injurious esp. to sized paper and starched clothes

silver iodide *n* : a light-sensitive compound used in photography, rainmaking, and medicine
silver maple *n* : a No. American maple with deeply cut leaves that are green above and silvery white below
silver nitrate *n* : a soluble compound used in photography and as an antiseptic
sil·ver·ware \'sil-vər-,wer\ *n* : FLATWARE
sim *abbr* simulation; simulator
sim·i·an \'si-mē-ən\ *n* : MONKEY, APE — **simian** *adj*
simian immunodeficiency virus *n* : SIV
sim·i·lar \'si-mə-lər\ *adj* : marked by correspondence or resemblance ✦ *Synonyms* ALIKE, AKIN, COMPARABLE, PARALLEL — **sim·i·lar·i·ty** \,si-mə-'ler-ə-tē\ *n* — **sim·i·lar·ly** *adv*
sim·i·le \'si-mə-(,)lē\ *n* [ME, fr. L, likeness, comparison, fr. neut. of *similis* like, similar] : a figure of speech in which two dissimilar things are compared by the use of *like* or *as* (as in "cheeks like roses")
si·mil·i·tude \sə-'mi-lə-,tüd, -,tyüd\ *n* : LIKENESS, RESEMBLANCE
sim·mer \'si-mər\ *vb* **sim·mered; sim·mer·ing** **1** : to stew at or just below the boiling point **2** : to be on the point of bursting out with violence or emotional disturbance — **simmer** *n*
simmer down *vb* : to become calm or peaceful
si·mo·nize \'sī-mə-,nīz\ *vb* **-nized; -niz·ing** : to polish with or as if with wax
si·mo·ny \'sī-mə-nē, 'si-\ *n* [ME *symonie*, fr. AF *simonie*, fr. LL *simonia*, fr. *Simon* Magus sorcerer of Samaria in Acts 8:9–24] : the buying or selling of a church office
sim·pa·ti·co \sim-'pä-ti-,kō, -'pa-\ *adj* : CONGENIAL, LIKABLE
sim·per \'sim-pər\ *vb* : to smile in a silly manner — **simper** *n*
sim·ple \'sim-pəl\ *adj* **sim·pler** \-pə-lər\; **sim·plest** \-pə-ləst\ [ME, fr. AF, plain, uncomplicated, artless, fr. L *simplus, simplex*, lit., single; L *simplus* fr. *sim-* one + *-plus* multiplied by; L *simplex* fr. *sim-* + *-plex* -fold] **1** : free from dishonesty or vanity : INNOCENT **2** : free from ostentation **3** : of humble origin or modest position **4** : STUPID **5** : not complex : PLAIN ⟨a ~ melody⟩ ⟨~ directions⟩ **6** : lacking education, experience, or intelligence **7** : developing from a single ovary ⟨a ~ fruit⟩ ✦ *Synonyms* EASY, FACILE, LIGHT, EFFORTLESS — **sim·ple·ness** *n* — **sim·ply** *adv*
simple interest *n* : interest paid or computed on the original principal only of a loan or on the amount of an account
sim·ple·ton \'sim-pəl-tən\ *n* : FOOL
sim·plic·i·ty \sim-'pli-sə-tē\ *n, pl* **-ties** **1** : lack of complication : CLEARNESS **2** : CANDOR, ARTLESSNESS **3** : plainness in manners or way of life **4** : SILLINESS, FOLLY
sim·pli·fy \'sim-plə-,fī\ *vb* **-fied; -fy·ing** : to make less complex — **sim·pli·fi·ca·tion** \,sim-plə-fə-'kā-shən\ *n*
sim·plis·tic \sim-'plis-tik\ *adj* : excessively simple : tending to overlook complexities ⟨a ~ solution⟩
sim·u·late \'sim-yə-,lāt\ *vb* **-lat·ed; -lat·ing** : to give or create the effect or appearance of : IMITATE; *also* : to make a simulation of — **sim·u·la·tor** \'sim-yə-,lā-tər\ *n*
sim·u·la·tion \,sim-yə-'lā-shən\ *n* **1** : the act or process of simulating **2** : an object that is not genuine **3** : the imitation by one system or process of the way in which another system or process works
si·mul·ta·ne·ous \,sī-məl-'tā-nē-əs, ,si-\ *adj* : occurring or operating at the same time — **si·mul·ta·ne·ous·ly** *adv* — **si·mul·ta·ne·ous·ness** *n*
¹sin \'sin\ *n* **1** : an offense esp. against God **2** : FAULT **3** : a weakened state of human nature in which the self is estranged from God — **sin·less** *adj*
²sin *vb* **sinned; sin·ning** : to commit a sin — **sin·ner** *n*
³sin *abbr* sine
¹since \'sins\ *adv* **1** : from a past time until now **2** : backward in time : AGO **3** : after a time in the past
²since *conj* **1** : from the time when **2** : seeing that : BECAUSE
³since *prep* **1** : in the period after ⟨changes made ~ the war⟩ **2** : continuously from ⟨has been here ~ 1980⟩
sin·cere \sin-'sir\ *adj* **sin·cer·er; sin·cer·est** **1** : free from hypocrisy : HONEST **2** : GENUINE, REAL — **sin·cere·ly** *adv* — **sin·cer·i·ty** \-'ser-ə-tē\ *n*

sine \'sīn\ *n* [ML *sinus*, fr. L, curve] : the trigonometric function that is the ratio between the side opposite an acute angle in a right triangle and the hypotenuse
si·ne·cure \'sī-ni-,kyúr, 'si-\ *n* : a paying job that requires little or no work
si·ne die \,sī-ni-'dī-,ē, ,si-nā-'dē-,ā\ *adv* [L, without day] : INDEFINITELY ⟨the meeting adjourned *sine die*⟩
si·ne qua non \,si-ni-,kwä-'nän, -'nōn\ *n, pl* **sine qua nons** *also* **sine qui·bus non** \-,kwi-(,)bús-\ [LL, without which not] : something indispensable or essential
sin·ew \'sin-yü\ *n* **1** : TENDON **2** : physical strength — **sin·ewy** *adj*
sin·ful \'sin-fəl\ *adj* : marked by or full of sin : WICKED — **sin·ful·ly** *adv* — **sin·ful·ness** *n*
¹sing \'siŋ\ *vb* **sang** \'saŋ\ *or* **sung** \'səŋ\; **sung; sing·ing** **1** : to produce musical tones with the voice; *also* : to utter with musical tones **2** : to make a prolonged shrill sound ⟨locusts ~*ing*⟩ **3** : to produce harmonious sustained sounds ⟨birds ~*ing*⟩ **4** : CHANT, INTONE **5** : to write poetry; *also* : to celebrate in song or verse **6** : to give information or evidence — **sing·er** *n*
²sing *abbr* singular
singe \'sinj\ *vb* **singed; singe·ing** : to scorch lightly the outside of; *esp* : to remove the hair or down from usu. by passing over a flame
¹sin·gle \'siŋ-gəl\ *adj* **1** : UNMARRIED **2** : being alone : being the only one **3** : having only one feature or part **4** : made for one person ✦ *Synonyms* SOLE, UNIQUE, LONE, SOLITARY, SEPARATE, PARTICULAR — **sin·gle·ness** *n* — **sin·gly** *adv*
²single *n* **1** : a separate person or thing; *also* : an unmarried person **2** : a hit in baseball that enables the batter to reach first base **3** *pl* : a tennis match with one player on each side
³single *vb* **sin·gled; sin·gling** **1** : to select (one) from a group **2** : to hit a single
single bond *n* : a chemical bond in which one pair of electrons is shared by two atoms in a molecule
single-lens reflex *n* : a camera having a single lens that forms an image which is reflected to the viewfinder or recorded on film
sin·gle-mind·ed \,siŋ-gəl-'mīn-dəd\ *adj* : having one driving purpose or resolve — **sin·gle-mind·ed·ly** *adv* — **sin·gle-mind·ed·ness** *n*
sing·song \'siŋ-,sȯŋ\ *n* **1** : verse with marked and regular rhythm and rhyme **2** : a voice delivery marked by monotonous rhythm — **sing·songy** \-,sȯŋ-ē\ *adj*
sin·gu·lar \'siŋ-gyə-lər\ *adj* **1** : of, relating to, or constituting a word form denoting one person, thing, or instance **2** : OUTSTANDING, EXCEPTIONAL **3** : of unusual quality **4** : ODD, PECULIAR — **singular** *n* — **sin·gu·lar·i·ty** \,siŋ-gyə-'lar-ə-tē\ *n* — **sin·gu·lar·ly** *adv*
sin·is·ter \'si-nəs-tər\ *adj* [ME *sinistre*, fr. AF *senestre* on the left, fr. L *sinister* on the left side, inauspicious] **1** : singularly evil or productive of evil : accompanied by or leading to disaster ✦ *Synonyms* BALEFUL, MALIGN, MALEFIC, MALEFICENT — **sin·is·ter·ly** *adv*
¹sink \'siŋk\ *vb* **sank** \'saŋk\ *or* **sunk** \'səŋk\; **sunk; sink·ing** **1** : SUBMERGE **2** : to descend lower and lower **3** : to grow less in volume or height **4** : to slope downward **5** : to penetrate downward **6** : to fail in health or strength **7** : LAPSE, DEGENERATE **8** : to cause (a ship) to descend to the bottom **9** : to make (a hole or shaft) by digging, boring, or cutting **10** : INVEST — **sink·able** *adj*
²sink *n* **1** : DRAIN, SEWER **2** : a basin connected with a drain **3** : an extensive depression in the land surface
sink·er \'siŋ-kər\ *n* : a weight for sinking a fishing line or net
sink·hole \'siŋk-,hōl\ *n* : a hollow place in which drainage collects
si·nol·o·gy \sī-'nä-lə-jē\ *n, often cap* : the study of the Chinese and esp. their language, history, and culture — **si·no·log·i·cal** \,sī-nə-'lä-ji-kəl\ *adj, often cap* — **si·nol·o·gist** \sī-'nä-lə-jist\ *n, often cap*
sin tax *n* : a tax on substances or activities considered sinful or harmful
sin·u·ous \'sin-yə-wəs\ *adj* : bending in and out : WINDING — **sin·u·os·i·ty** \,sin-yə-'wä-sə-tē\ *n* — **sin·u·ous·ly** *adv*
si·nus \'sī-nəs\ *n* [ME, fr. ML, fr. L, curve, hollow] **1** : any of several cavities of the skull usu. connecting with

the nostrils **2** : a space forming a channel (as for the passage of blood)

si·nus·itis \ˌsī-nə-'sī-təs\ *n* : inflammation of a sinus of the skull

Sioux \'sü\ *n, pl* **Sioux** *same or* 'süz\ [AmerF, short for *Nadouessioux*, fr. Ojibwa *na·towe·ssiw-*, prob. fr. Algonquian **a·towe·*- speak another language] : DAKOTA

sip \'sip\ *vb* **sipped; sip·ping** : to drink in small quantities — **sip** *n*

¹**si·phon** *also* **sy·phon** \'sī-fən\ *n* **1** : a bent tube through which a liquid can be transferred by means of air pressure up and over the edge of one container and into another container placed at a lower level **2** *usu* **sy·phon** : a bottle that ejects soda water through a tube when a valve is opened

²**siphon** *also* **sypon** *vb* **si·phoned** *also* **sy·phoned; si·phon·ing** *also* **sy·phon·ing** : to draw off by means of a siphon

sir \'sər\ *n* [ME *sir, sire*, fr. AF, lord, feudal superior, fr. VL **seior*, alter. of L *senior*, compar. of *senex* old, old man] **1** : a man of rank or position — used as a title before the given name of a knight or baronet **2** — used as a usu. respectful form of address

Si·rach \'sī-rak, sə-'räk\ *n* — see BIBLE table

¹**sire** \'sī(-ə)r\ *n* **1** : FATHER; *also, archaic* : FOREFATHER **2** *archaic* : LORD — used as a form of address and a title **3** : the male parent of an animal (as a horse or dog)

²**sire** *vb* **sired; sir·ing** : BEGET

si·ren \'sī-rən\ *n* **1** : a seductive or alluring woman **2** : an electrically operated device for producing a loud shrill warning signal — **siren** *adj*

sir·loin \'sər-ˌlȯin\ *n* [alter. of earlier *surloin*, modif. of MF *surlonge*, fr. *sur* over (fr. L *super*) + *longe* loin] : a cut of beef taken from the part in front of the round

sirup *var of* SYRUP

si·sal \'sī-səl, -zəl\ *n* : a strong cordage fiber from an agave; *also* : this agave

sis·sy \'si-sē\ *n, pl* **sissies** : an effeminate boy or man; *also* : a timid or cowardly person

sis·ter \'sis-tər\ *n* **1** : a female having one or both parents in common with another individual **2** : a member of a religious order of women : NUN **3** *chiefly Brit* : NURSE **4 a** : a girl or woman regarded as a comrade **b** : a girl or woman who shares with another a common national or racial origin — **sis·ter·ly** *adj*

sis·ter·hood \-ˌhu̇d\ *n* **1** : the state of being a sister **2** : a community or society of sisters **3** : the solidarity of women based on shared conditions

sis·ter–in–law \'sis-tə-rən-ˌlȯ\ *n, pl* **sisters–in–law** : the sister of one's spouse; *also* : the wife of one's brother

sit \'sit\ *vb* **sat** \'sat\; **sit·ting 1** : to rest upon the buttocks or haunches **2** : ROOST, PERCH **3** : to occupy a seat **4** : to hold a session **5** : to cover eggs for hatching : BROOD **6** : to pose for a portrait **7** : to remain quiet or inactive **8** : FIT **9** : to cause (oneself) to be seated **10** : to place in position **11** : to keep one's seat on ⟨~ a horse⟩ **12** : BABYSIT — **sit·ter** *n*

si·tar \si-'tär\ *n* [Hindi & Urdu *sitār*] : an Indian lute with a long neck and a varying number of strings

sit.com \'sit-ˌkäm\ *n* : SITUATION COMEDY

site \'sīt\ *n* **1** : LOCATION **2** : WEB SITE

sit–in \'sit-ˌin\ *n* : an act of sitting in the seats or on the floor of an establishment as a means of organized protest

sit·u·at·ed \'si-chə-ˌwā-təd\ *adj* : LOCATED, PLACED

sit·u·a·tion \ˌsi-chə-'wā-shən\ *n* **1** : LOCATION, SITE **2** : JOB **3** : CONDITION, CIRCUMSTANCES — **sit·u·a·tion·al** \-shə-nəl\ *adj*

situation comedy *n* : a radio or television comedy series that involves a continuing cast of characters in a succession of episodes

sit–up \'sit-ˌəp\ *n* : an exercise performed from a supine position by raising the torso to a sitting position and returning to the original position without lifting the feet

SIV \ˌes-ˌī-'vē\ *n* [*simian immunodeficiency virus*] : a retrovirus related to HIV that causes a disease in monkeys similar to AIDS

six \'siks\ *n* **1** : one more than five **2** : the 6th in a set or series **3** : something having six units — **six** *adj or pron* — **sixth** \'siksth\ *adj or adv or n*

six–gun \'siks-ˌgən\ *n* : a 6-chambered revolver

six–pack \-ˌpak\ *n* : six bottles or cans (as of beer) packaged and purchased together; *also* : the contents of a six-pack

six·pence \-pəns, *US also* -ˌpens\ *n* : the sum of six pence; *also* : an English silver coin of this value

six–shoot·er \'siks-ˌshü-tər\ *n* : SIX-GUN

six·teen \ˌsiks-'tēn\ *n* : one more than 15 — **sixteen** *adj or pron* — **six·teenth** \-'tēnth\ *adj or n*

six·ty \'siks-tē\ *n, pl* **sixties** : six times 10 — **six·ti·eth** \'siks-tē-əth\ *adj or n* — **sixty** *adj or pron*

siz·able *or* **size·able** \'sī-zə-bəl\ *adj* : quite large — **siz·ably** \-blē\ *adv*

¹**size** \'sīz\ *n* [ME *sise* assize, judgment, quantity, fr. AF, short for *assise* assize] : physical extent or bulk : DIMENSIONS; *also* : considerable proportions — **sized** \'sīzd\ *adj*

²**size** *vb* **sized; siz·ing 1** : to grade or classify according to size **2** : to form a judgment of ⟨~ up the situation⟩

³**size** *n* : a gluey material used for filling the pores in paper, plaster, or textiles — **siz·ing** *n*

⁴**size** *vb* **sized; siz·ing** : to cover, stiffen, or glaze with size

siz·zle \'si-zəl\ *vb* **siz·zled; siz·zling** : to fry or shrivel up with a hissing sound — **sizzle** *n*

SJ *abbr* Society of Jesus

SK *abbr* Saskatchewan

ska \'skä\ *n* : popular music of Jamaican origin combining traditional Caribbean rhythms and jazz

¹**skate** \'skāt\ *n, pl* **skates** *also* **skate** : any of a family of rays with thick broad winglike fins

²**skate** *n* **1** : a metal frame and runner attached to a shoe and used for gliding over ice **2** : ROLLER SKATE; *esp* : IN-LINE SKATE — **skate** *vb* — **skat·er** *n*

skate·board \'skāt-ˌbȯrd\ *n* : a short board mounted on small wheels — **skateboard** *vb* — **skate·board·er** *n*

skeet \'skēt\ *n* : trapshooting in which clay targets are thrown in such a way that their angle of flight simulates that of a flushed game bird

skein \'skān\ *n* : a loosely twisted quantity of yarn or thread wound on a reel

skel·e·ton \'ske-lə-t⁹n\ *n* **1** : a usu. bony supporting framework of an animal body **2** : a bare minimum **3** : FRAMEWORK — **skel·e·tal** \-lə-t⁹l\ *adj*

skep·tic \'skep-tik\ *n* **1** : one who believes in skepticism **2** : a person disposed to skepticism esp. regarding religion — **skep·ti·cal** \-ti-kəl\ *adj* — **skep·ti·cal·ly** \-k(ə-)lē\ *adv*

skep·ti·cism \'skep-tə-ˌsi-zəm\ *n* **1** : a doubting state of mind **2** : a doctrine that certainty of knowledge cannot be attained **3** : doubt concerning religion

sketch \'skech\ *n* [D *schets*, fr. It. *schizzo*, lit., splash] **1** : a rough drawing or outline **2** : a short or light literary composition (as a story or essay); *also* : a short comedy piece — **sketch** *vb* — **sketchy** *adj*

¹**skew** \'skyü\ *vb* : TWIST, SWERVE

²**skew** *n* : SLANT

skew·er \'skyü-ər\ *n* : a long pin for holding small pieces of meat and vegetables for broiling — **skewer** *vb*

¹**ski** \'skē\ *n, pl* **skis** [Norw, fr. ON *skīth* stick of wood, ski] : one of a pair of long strips (as of wood, metal, or plastic) curving upward in front that are used for gliding over snow or water

²**ski** *vb* **skied** \'skēd\; **ski·ing** : to glide on skis — **ski·able** \'skē-ə-bəl\ *adj* — **ski·er** *n*

¹**skid** \'skid\ *n* **1** : a plank for supporting something above the ground **2** : a device placed under a wheel to prevent turning **3** : a timber or rail over or on which something is slid or rolled **4** : the act of skidding **5** : a runner on the landing gear of an aircraft **6** : ²PALLET

²**skid** *vb* **skid·ded; skid·ding 1** : to slide without rotating ⟨a *skidding* wheel⟩ **2** : to slide sideways on the road ⟨the car *skidded* on ice⟩ **3** : SLIDE, SLIP

skid row *n* : a district of cheap saloons frequented by vagrants and alcoholics

skiff \'skif\ *n* : a small boat

ski jump *n* : a jump made by a person wearing skis; *also* : a course or track prepared for such jumping — **ski jump** *vb* — **ski jumper** *n*

skil·ful *chiefly Brit var of* SKILLFUL

ski lift *n* : a mechanical device (as a chairlift) for carrying skiers up a long slope

skill \'skil\ *n* **1** : ability to use one's knowledge effectively in doing something **2** : developed or acquired ability ♦ **Synonyms** ART, CRAFT, CUNNING, DEXTERITY, EXPERTISE, KNOW-HOW — **skilled** \'skild\ *adj*

skil·let \'ski-lət\ *n* : a frying pan

skill·ful \'skil-fəl\ *adj* **1** : having or displaying skill : EX-
PERT **2** : accomplished with skill — **skill·ful·ly** *adv* —
skill·ful·ness *n*

¹**skim** \'skim\ *vb* **skimmed; skim·ming 1** : to take off
from the top of a liquid; *also* : to remove (scum or cream)
from ⟨~ milk⟩ **2** : to read rapidly and superficially **3**
: to pass swiftly over — **skim·mer** *n*

²**skim** *adj* : having the cream removed

skimp \'skimp\ *vb* : to give insufficient attention, effort, or
funds; *also* : to save by skimping

skimpy \'skim-pē\ *adj* **skimp·i·er; -est** : deficient in supply or execution — **skimp·i·ly** \-pə-lē\ *adv*

¹**skin** \'skin\ *n* **1** : the outer limiting layer of an animal
body; *also* : the usu. thin tough tissue of which this is
made **2** : an outer or surface layer (as a rind or peel) —
skin·less *adj* — **skinned** *adj*

²**skin** *vb* **skinned; skin·ning** : to free from skin : remove
the skin of

³**skin** *adj* : devoted to showing nudes ⟨~ magazines⟩

skin diving *n* : the sport of swimming under water with a
face mask and flippers and esp. without a portable
breathing device — **skin–dive** *vb* — **skin diver** *n*

skin·flint \'skin-ˌflint\ *n* : a very stingy person

skin graft *n* : a piece of skin surgically removed from one
area to replace skin in another area — **skin grafting** *n*

skin·head \'skin-ˌhed\ *n* : a person whose hair is cut very
short

¹**skin·ny** \'skin-nē\ *adj* **skin·ni·er; -est 1** : resembling skin
2 : very thin

²**skinny** *n* : inside information

skin·ny–dip \'skin-nē-ˌdip\ *vb* : to swim in the nude —
skin·ny–dip·per \-ˌdi-pər\ *n*

skin·tight \'skin-ˈtīt\ *adj* : closely fitted to the figure ⟨~
pants⟩

¹**skip** \'skip\ *vb* **skipped; skip·ping 1** : to move with leaps
and bounds **2** : to leap lightly over **3** : to pass from
point to point (as in reading) disregarding what is in between **4** : to pass over without notice or mention

²**skip** *n* : a light bouncing step; *also* : a gait of alternate hops
and steps

skip·jack \'skip-ˌjak\ *n* : a small sailboat with vertical sides
and a bottom similar to a flat V

skip·per \'ski-pər\ *n* [ME, fr. MD *schipper*, fr. *schip* ship]
: the master of a ship; *also* : the manager of a baseball
team — **skipper** *vb*

skir·mish \'skər-mish\ *n* : a minor engagement in war; *also*
: a minor dispute or contest — **skirmish** *vb*

¹**skirt** \'skərt\ *n* : a free-hanging garment or part of a garment extending from the waist down

²**skirt** *vb* **1** : to pass around the outer edge of **2** : BOR-
DER **3** : EVADE

skit \'skit\ *n* : a brief dramatic sketch

ski tow *n* : SKI LIFT

skit·ter \'ski-tər\ *vb* : to glide or skip lightly or quickly
: skim along a surface

skit·tish \'ski-tish\ *adj* **1** : CAPRICIOUS **2** : easily frightened ⟨a ~ horse⟩; *also* : WARY

ski·wear \'skē-ˌwer\ *n* : clothing suitable for wear while
skiing

skosh \'skōsh\ *n* [Jp *sukoshi*] : a small amount : BIT

skul·dug·gery *or* **skull·dug·gery** \ˌskəl-ˈdə-gə-rē\ *n, pl*
-ger·ies : underhanded or unscrupulous behavior

skulk \'skəlk\ *vb* : to move furtively : SNEAK, LURK —
skulk·er *n*

skull \'skəl\ *n* : the skeleton of the head of a vertebrate
that protects the brain and supports the jaws

skull and crossbones *n, pl* **skulls and crossbones** : a
depiction of a human skull over crossbones usu. indicating a danger

skull·cap \'skəl-ˌkap\ *n* : a close-fitting brimless cap

¹**skunk** \'skəŋk\ *n, pl* **skunks** *also* **skunk 1** : any of various black-and-white New World mammals related to the
weasels that can forcibly eject an ill-smelling fluid when
startled **2** : a contemptible person

²**skunk** *vb* : to defeat decisively; *esp* : to prevent entirely
from scoring in a game

skunk cabbage *n* : either of two No. American perennial
herbs related to the arums that occur in shaded wet to
swampy areas and have a fetid odor suggestive of a
skunk

sky \'skī\ *n, pl* **skies** [ME, sky, cloud, fr. ON *skȳ* cloud] **1**
: the upper air **2** : HEAVEN — **sky·ey** \'skī-ē\ *adj*

sky·cap \-ˌkap\ *n* : a person employed to carry luggage at
an airport

sky·div·ing \-ˌdī-viŋ\ *n* : the sport of jumping from an airplane and executing various body maneuvers before
opening a parachute — **skydiver** *n*

sky·jack \-ˌjak\ *vb* : to commandeer an airplane in flight
by threat of violence — **sky·jack·er** *n* — **sky·jack·ing** *n*

¹**sky·lark** \-ˌlärk\ *n* : a European lark noted for singing during flight

²**sky·lark** *vb* : FROLIC, SPORT

sky·light \'skī-ˌlīt\ *n* : a window in a roof or ceiling — **sky-
light·ed** \-ˌlī-təd\ *adj*

sky·line \-ˌlīn\ *n* **1** : HORIZON **2** : an outline (as of buildings) against the sky

¹**sky·rock·et** \-ˌrä-kət\ *n* : ROCKET 1

²**skyrocket** *vb* : ROCKET 2

sky·scrap·er \-ˌskrā-pər\ *n* : a very tall building

sky·surf·ing \-ˌsər-fiŋ\ *n* : skydiving with a short modified
surfboard attached to the feet — **sky·surf·er** \-fər\ *n*

sky·walk \-ˌwȯk\ *n* : an aerial walkway connecting two
buildings

sky·ward \-wərd\ *adv* : toward the sky

sky·writ·ing \-ˌrī-tiŋ\ *n* : writing in the sky formed by
smoke emitted from an airplane — **sky·writ·er** *n*

sl *abbr* **1** slightly **2** slip **3** slow

slab \'slab\ *n* : a thick flat piece or slice

¹**slack** \'slak\ *adj* **1** : CARELESS, NEGLIGENT **2** : SLUG-
GISH, LISTLESS **3** : not taut : LOOSE **4** : not busy or ac-
tive ♦ *Synonyms* LAX, REMISS, NEGLECTFUL, DELIN-
QUENT, DERELICT — **slack·ly** *adv* — **slack·ness** *n*

²**slack** *vb* **1** : to make or become slack : LOOSEN, RELAX
2 : SLAKE 2

³**slack** *n* **1** : cessation of movement or flow : LETUP **2** : a
part that hangs loose without strain ⟨~ of a rope⟩ **3**
: pants esp. for casual wear — usu. used in pl.

slack·en \'sla-kən\ *vb* : to make or become slack

slack·er \'sla-kər\ *n* **1** : one that shirks work or evades
military duty **2** : a young person perceived to be disaf-
fected, apathetic, cynical, or lacking ambition

slag \'slag\ *n* : the waste left after the melting of ores and
the separation of metal from them

slain *past part of* SLAY

slake \'slāk, *for 2 also* 'slak\ *vb* **slaked; slak·ing 1** : to relieve or satisfy with or as if with refreshing drink ⟨~
thirst⟩ **2** : to cause (lime) to crumble by mixture with
water

sla·lom \'slä-ləm\ *n* [Norw *slalam*, lit., sloping track] : skiing in a zigzag course between obstacles

¹**slam** \'slam\ *n* : the winning of every trick or of all tricks
but one in bridge

²**slam** *n* **1** : a heavy jarring impact : BANG **2** : harsh criticism **3** : a poetry competition

³**slam** *vb* **slammed; slam·ming 1** : to shut violently and
noisily **2** : to throw or strike with a loud impact **3** : to
criticize harshly

slam·mer \'sla-mər\ *n* : JAIL, PRISON

¹**slan·der** \'slan-dər\ *vb* : to utter slander against : DEFAME
— **slan·der·er** *n*

²**slander** *n* [ME *sclaundre, slaundre*, fr. AF *esclandre*, alter.
of *escandle*, fr. LL *scandalum* stumbling block, offense]
: a false report maliciously uttered and tending to injure
the reputation of a person — **slan·der·ous** *adj*

slang \'slaŋ\ *n* : an informal nonstandard vocabulary composed typically of invented words, arbitrarily changed
words, and extravagant figures of speech — **slangy** *adj*

skunk 1

¹**slant** \'slant\ *n* **1** : a sloping direction, line, or plane **2** : a particular or personal viewpoint — **slant** *adj* — **slantwise** \-ˌwīz\ *adv or adj*

²**slant** *vb* **1** : SLOPE **2** : to interpret or present in accordance with a special viewpoint or bias ✦ *Synonyms* INCLINE, LEAN, LIST, TILT, HEEL — **slant·ing·ly** *adv*

slap \'slap\ *vb* **slapped; slap·ping 1** : to strike sharply with the open hand **2** : REBUFF, INSULT — **slap** *n*

slap-stick \-ˌstik\ *n* : comedy stressing horseplay

¹**slash** \'slash\ *vb* **1** : to cut with sweeping strokes **2** : to cut slits in (a garment) **3** : to reduce sharply — **slash·er** \'sla-shər\ *n*

²**slash** *n* **1** : GASH **2** : an ornamental slit in a garment **3** : a mark / used to denote "or" (as in *and/or*), "and or" (as in *straggler/deserter*), or "per" (as in *feet/second*)

slat \'slat\ *n* : a thin narrow flat strip

¹**slate** \'slāt\ *n* **1** : a dense fine-grained rock that splits into thin layers **2** : a roofing tile or a writing tablet made from this rock **3** : a written or unwritten record ⟨start with a clean ∼⟩ **4** : a list of candidates for election

²**slate** *vb* **slat·ed; slat·ing 1** : to cover with slate **2** : to designate for action or appointment

slath·er \'sla-thər\ *vb* : to spread with or on thickly or lavishly

slat·tern \'sla-tərn\ *n* : a slovenly woman — **slat·tern·ly** *adj*

¹**slaugh·ter** \'slȯ-tər\ *n* **1** : the butchering of livestock for market **2** : great destruction of lives esp. in battle

²**slaughter** *vb* **1** : to kill (animals) for food : BUTCHER **2** : to kill in large numbers or in a bloody way : MASSACRE

slaugh·ter·house \-ˌhau̇s\ *n* : an establishment where animals are butchered

Slav \'släv, 'slav\ *n* : a person speaking a Slavic language

¹**slave** \'slāv\ *n* [ME *sclave*, fr. AF or ML; AF *esclave*, fr. ML *sclavus*, fr. *Sclavus* Slav; fr. the enslavement of Slavs in central Europe in the Middle Ages] **1** : a person held in servitude as property **2** : a device (as the printer of a computer) that is directly responsive to another — **slave** *adj*

²**slave** *vb* **slaved; slav·ing** : to work like a slave : DRUDGE

¹**sla·ver** \'sla-vər, 'slā-\ *n* : SLOBBER — **slaver** *vb*

²**slav·er** \'slā-vər\ *n* : a ship or a person engaged in transporting slaves

slav·ery \'slāv-rē, 'slā-və-\ *n* **1** : wearisome drudgery **2** : the condition of being a slave **3** : the practice of owning slaves ✦ *Synonyms* SERVITUDE, BONDAGE, ENSLAVEMENT

¹**Slav·ic** \'sla-vik, 'slä-\ *n* : a branch of the Indo-European language family including various languages (as Russian or Polish) of eastern Europe

²**Slavic** *adj* : of or relating to the Slavs or their languages

slav·ish \'slā-vish\ *adj* **1** : SERVILE **2** : obeying or imitating with no freedom of judgment or choice — **slav·ish·ly** *adv*

slaw \'slȯ\ *n* : COLESLAW

slay \'slā\ *vb* **slew** \'slü\; **slain** \'slān\; **slay·ing** : KILL — **slay·er** *n*

SLBM *abbr* submarine-launched ballistic missile

sleaze \'slēz\ *n* : a sleazy quality, appearance, or behavior

slea·zy \'slē-zē\ *adj* **slea·zi·er; -est 1** : FLIMSY, SHODDY **2** : marked by low character or quality

¹**sled** \'sled\ *n* : a vehicle usu. on runners adapted esp. for sliding on snow

²**sled** *vb* **sled·ded, sled·ding** : to ride or carry on a sled

¹**sledge** \'slej\ *n* : SLEDGEHAMMER

²**sledge** *n* : a strong heavy sled

sledge·ham·mer \'slej-ˌha-mər\ *n* : a large heavy hammer wielded with both hands — **sledgehammer** *adj or vb*

¹**sleek** \'slēk\ *vb* **1** : to make smooth or glossy **2** : to gloss over

²**sleek** *adj* **1** : having a smooth well-groomed look **2** : trim and graceful in design ⟨a ∼ car⟩

¹**sleep** \'slēp\ *n* **1** : the natural periodic suspension of consciousness during which bodily powers are restored **2** : a state (as death or coma) suggesting sleep — **sleep·less** *adj* — **sleep·less·ness** *n*

²**sleep** *vb* **slept** \'slept\; **sleep·ing 1** : to rest or be in a state of sleep; *also* : to spend in sleep **2** : to have sexual intercourse — usu. used with *with* **3** : to provide sleeping space for

sleep·er \'slē-pər\ *n* **1** : one that sleeps **2** : a horizontal beam to support something on or near ground level **3**

: SLEEPING CAR **4** : someone or something unpromising or unnoticed that suddenly attains prominence or value

sleeping bag *n* : a warmly lined bag for sleeping esp. outdoors

sleeping car *n* : a railroad car with berths for sleeping

sleeping pill *n* : a drug in tablet or capsule form taken to induce sleep

sleeping sickness *n* : a serious disease of tropical Africa that is marked by fever, lethargy, confusion, and sleep disturbances and is caused by protozoans transmitted by the tsetse fly

sleep-over \'slēp-ˌō-vər\ *n* : an overnight stay (as at another's home)

sleep·walk·er \'slēp-ˌwȯ-kər\ *n* : one that walks while or as if while asleep — **sleep·walk** \-ˌwȯk\ *vb*

sleepy \'slē-pē\ *adj* **sleep·i·er; -est 1** : ready for sleep **2** : quietly inactive — **sleep·i·ly** \'slē-pə-lē\ *adv* — **sleep·i·ness** \-pē-nəs\ *n*

sleet \'slēt\ *n* : frozen or partly frozen rain — **sleet** *vb* — **sleety** *adj*

sleeve \'slēv\ *n* **1** : a part of a garment covering an arm **2** : a tubular part designed to fit over another part — **sleeved** *adj* — **sleeve·less** *adj*

¹**sleigh** \'slā\ *n* : an open usu. horse-drawn vehicle on runners for use on snow or ice

²**sleigh** *vb* : to drive or travel in a sleigh

sleight \'slīt\ *n* **1** : TRICK **2** : DEXTERITY

sleight of hand : a trick requiring skillful manual manipulation

slen·der \'slen-dər\ *adj* **1** : SLIM, THIN **2** : WEAK, SLIGHT **3** : MEAGER, INADEQUATE

slen·der·ize \-də-ˌrīz\ *vb* **-ized; -iz·ing** : to make slender

sleuth \'slüth\ *n* [short for *sleuthhound* bloodhound, fr. ME (Sc) *sleuth hund*, fr. ME *sleuth, slouth, sloth* track of an animal or person, fr. ON *slōth*] : DETECTIVE

¹**slew** \'slü\ *past of* SLAY

²**slew** *vb* : TURN, VEER, SKID

¹**slice** \'slīs\ *vb* **sliced; slic·ing 1** : to cut a slice from; *also* : to cut into slices **2** : to hit (a ball) so that a slice results

²**slice** *n* **1** : a thin flat piece cut from something **2** : a flight of a ball (as in golf) that curves in the direction of the dominant hand of the player hitting it

¹**slick** \'slik\ *vb* : to make smooth or sleek

²**slick** *adj* **1** : very smooth : SLIPPERY **2** : CLEVER, SMART ⟨a ∼ salesperson⟩

³**slick** *n* **1** : a smooth patch of water covered with a film of oil **2** : a popular magazine printed on coated paper

slick·er \'sli-kər\ *n* **1** : a long loose raincoat **2** : a sly tricky person **3** : a city dweller esp. of natty appearance or sophisticated mannerisms

¹**slide** \'slīd\ *vb* **slid** \'slid\; **slid·ing** \'slī-diŋ\ **1** : to move smoothly along a surface **2** : to fall by a loss of support **3** : to pass unobtrusively **4** : to move or pass smoothly; *also* : to pass unnoticed ⟨let it ∼ by⟩ **5** : to fall or dive toward a base in baseball

²**slide** *n* **1** : an act or instance of sliding **2** : something (as a cover or fastener) that operates by sliding **3** : a fall of a mass of earth or snow down a hillside **4** : a surface on which something slides **5** : a glass plate on which a specimen is mounted for examination under a microscope **6** : a small transparent photograph that can be projected on a screen

slid·er \'slī-dər\ *n* **1** : one that slides **2** : a baseball pitch that looks like a fastball but curves slightly

slide rule *n* : a manual device for calculation consisting of a ruler and a movable middle piece graduated with logarithmic scales

slier *comparative of* SLY

sliest *superlative of* SLY

¹**slight** \'slīt\ *adj* **1** : SLENDER; *also* : FRAIL **2** : UNIMPORTANT **3** : small of its kind or in amount ⟨a ∼ odor⟩ — **slight·ly** *adv*

²**slight** *vb* **1** : to treat as unimportant **2** : to ignore discourteously **3** : to perform or attend to carelessly

³**slight** *n* : a humiliating discourtesy

¹**slim** \'slim\ *adj* **slim·mer; slim·mest** [D, bad, inferior, fr. MD, *slimp* crooked, bad] **1** : SLENDER, SLIGHT, THIN **2** : SMALL, SLIGHT ⟨a ∼ chance⟩

²**slim** *vb* **slimmed; slim·ming** : to make or become slender

slime \'slīm\ *n* **1** : sticky mud **2** : a slippery substance (as on the skin of a slug or catfish) — **slimy** *adj*

¹**sling** \'sliŋ\ *vb* **slung** \'sləŋ\; **sling·ing** **1** : to throw forcibly : FLING **2** : to hurl with or as if with a sling

²**sling** *n* **1** : a short strap with strings attached for hurling stones or shot **2** : something (as a rope or chain) used to hoist, lower, support, or carry; *esp* : a bandage hanging from the neck to support an arm or hand

sling·shot \'sliŋ-ˌshät\ *n* : a forked stick with elastic bands for shooting small stones or shot

slink \'sliŋk\ *vb* **slunk** \'sləŋk\ *also* **slinked** \'sliŋkt\; **slink·ing** **1** : to move stealthily or furtively **2** : to move sinuously — **slinky** *adj*

¹**slip** \'slip\ *vb* **slipped; slip·ping** **1** : to escape quietly or secretly **2** : to slide along or cause to slide along smoothly **3** : to make a mistake **4** : to pass unnoticed or undone **5** : to fall off from a standard or level

²**slip** *n* **1** : a ramp for repairing ships **2** : a ship's berth between two piers **3** : secret or hurried departure, escape, or evasion **4** : BLUNDER **5** : a sudden mishap **6** : a woman's one-piece garment worn under a dress **7** : PILLOWCASE

³**slip** *n* **1** : a shoot or twig from a plant for planting or grafting **2** : a long narrow strip; *esp* : one of paper used for a record ⟨deposit ∼⟩

⁴**slip** *vb* **slipped; slip·ping** : to take slips from (a plant)

slip·knot \'slip-ˌnät\ *n* : a knot that slips along the rope around which it is made

slipped disk *n* : a protrusion of one of the disks of cartilage between vertebrae with pressure on spinal nerves resulting esp. in low back pain

slip·per \'sli-pər\ *n* : a light low shoe that may be easily slipped on and off

slip·pery \'sli-pə-rē\ *adj* **slip·per·i·er; -est** **1** : icy, wet, smooth, or greasy enough to cause one to fall or lose one's hold **2** : not to be trusted : TRICKY — **slip·per·i·ness** *n*

slip·shod \'slip-'shäd\ *adj* : SLOVENLY, CARELESS ⟨∼ work⟩

slip·stream \'slip-ˌstrēm\ *n* : a stream (as of air) driven aft by a propeller

slip-up \'slip-ˌəp\ *n* **1** : MISTAKE **2** : ACCIDENT

¹**slit** \'slit\ *vb* **slit; slit·ting** **1** : SLASH **2** : to cut off or away

²**slit** *n* : a long narrow cut or opening

slith·er \'sli-thər\ *vb* : to slip or glide along like a snake — **slith·ery** *adj*

sliv·er \'sli-vər\ *n* : SPLINTER

slob \'släb\ *n* : a slovenly or boorish person

slob·ber \'slä-bər\ *vb* **slob·bered; slob·ber·ing** : to dribble saliva — **slobber** *n*

sloe \'slō\ *n* : the fruit of the blackthorn

slog \'släg\ *vb* **slogged; slog·ging** **1** : to hit hard : BEAT **2** : to work hard and steadily

slo·gan \'slō-gən\ *n* [alter. of earlier *slogorn*, fr. ScGael *sluagh-ghairm*, fr. *sluagh* army, host + *gairm* cry] : a word or phrase expressing the spirit or aim of a party, group, or cause

slo–mo \'slō-ˌmō\ *n* : SLOW MOTION — **slo–mo** *adj*

sloop \'slüp\ *n* [D *sloep*] : a single-masted sailboat with a jib and a fore-and-aft mainsail

¹**slop** \'släp\ *n* **1** : thin tasteless drink or liquid food — usu. used in pl. **2** : food waste for animal feed : SWILL **3** : excreted body waste — usu. used in pl.

²**slop** *vb* **slopped; slop·ping** **1** : SPILL **2** : to feed with slop ⟨∼ hogs⟩

¹**slope** \'slōp\ *vb* **sloped; slop·ing** : SLANT, INCLINE

²**slope** *n* **1** : upward or downward slant or degree of slant **2** : ground that forms an incline **3** : the part of a landmass draining into a particular ocean

slop·py \'slä-pē\ *adj* **slop·pi·er; -est** **1** : MUDDY, SLUSHY **2** : SLOVENLY, MESSY

sloppy joe \-'jō\ *n* : ground beef cooked in a thick spicy sauce and usu. served on a bun

slosh \'släsh\ *vb* **1** : to flounder through or splash about in or with water, mud, or slush **2** : to move with a splashing motion

slot \'slät\ *n* **1** : a long narrow opening or groove **2** : a position in a sequence

slot car *n* : an electric toy racing car that runs on a grooved track

sloth \'slōth\ *n, pl* **sloths** \'slōths, 'slòthz\ **1** : LAZINESS, INDOLENCE **2** : any of several slow-moving plant-eating arboreal mammals of So. and Central America — **slothful** *adj*

slot machine *n* **1** : a machine whose operation is begun by dropping a coin into a slot **2** : a coin-operated gambling machine that pays off according to the matching of symbols on wheels spun by a handle

¹**slouch** \'slaüch\ *n* **1** : a lazy or incompetent person **2** : a loose or drooping gait or posture

²**slouch** *vb* : to walk, stand, or sit with a slouch : SLUMP

¹**slough** \'slü, 2 *usu* 'slaü\ *n* **1** : a wet and marshy or muddy place (as a swamp) **2** : a discouraged state of mind

²**slough** \'sləf\ *also* **sluff** *n* : something that has been or may be shed or cast off

³**slough** \'sləf\ *also* **sluff** *vb* : to cast off

Slo·vak \'slō-ˌväk, -ˌvak\ *n* **1** : a member of a Slavic people of Slovakia **2** : the language of the Slovaks — **Slovak** *adj* — **Slo·va·ki·an** \slō-'vä-kē-ən, -'va-\ *adj or n*

slov·en \'slə-vən\ *n* [ME *sloveyn* slut, rascal, perh. fr. MD *slof* negligent] : an untidy person

Slo·vene \'slō-ˌvēn\ *n* **1** : a member of a Slavic people living largely in Slovenia **2** : the language of the Slovenes — **Slovene** *adj* — **Slo·ve·nian** \slō-'vē-nē-ən\ *adj or n*

slov·en·ly \'slə-vən-lē\ *adj* **1** : untidy in dress or person **2** : lazily or carelessly done : SLIPSHOD

¹**slow** \'slō\ *adj* **1** : SLUGGISH; *also* : dull in mind : STUPID **2** : moving, flowing, or proceeding at less than the usual speed **3** : taking more than the usual time **4** : registering behind the correct time **5** : not lively : BORING

✦ **Synonyms** DILATORY, LAGGARD, DELIBERATE, LEISURELY — **slow** *adv* — **slow·ly** *adv* — **slow·ness** *n*

²**slow** *vb* **1** : to make slow : hold back **2** : to go slower

slow motion *n* : motion-picture action photographed so as to appear much slower than normal — **slow–motion** *adj*

SLR *abbr* single-lens reflex

sludge \'sləj\ *n* : a slushy mass : OOZE; *esp* : solid matter produced by sewage treatment processes

slue *var of* ²SLEW

¹**slug** \'sləg\ *n* **1** : a small mass of metal; *esp* : BULLET **2** : a metal disk for use (as in a slot machine) in place of a coin **3** : any of numerous wormlike mollusks related to the snails **4** : a quantity of liquor drunk

²**slug** *vb* **slugged; slug·ging** : to strike forcibly and heavily — **slug·ger** *n*

slug·gard \'slə-gərd\ *n* : a lazy person

slug·gish \'slə-gish\ *adj* **1** : SLOTHFUL, LAZY **2** : slow in movement or flow **3** : STAGNANT, DULL — **slug·gish·ly** *adv* — **slug·gish·ness** *n*

¹**sluice** \'slüs\ *n* [ME *sluse, scluse*, fr. AF *escluse*, fr. LL *exclusa*, fr. L, fem. of *exclusus*, pp. of *excludere* to shut out, exclude] : an artificial passage for water with a gate for controlling the flow; *also* : the gate so used **2** : a channel that carries off surplus water **3** : an inclined trough or flume for washing ore or floating logs

²**sluice** *vb* **sluiced; sluic·ing** **1** : to draw off through a sluice **2** : to wash with running water : FLUSH

¹**slum** \'sləm\ *n* : a thickly populated area marked by poverty and dirty or deteriorated houses — **slum·my** \'slə-mē\ *adj*

²**slum** *vb* **slummed; slum·ming** : to visit slums esp. out of curiosity; *also* : to go somewhere or do something that might be considered beneath one's station

¹**slum·ber** \'sləm-bər\ *vb* **slum·bered; slum·ber·ing** **1** : DOZE; *also* : SLEEP **2** : to be in a sluggish or torpid state

²**slumber** *n* : SLEEP

slum·ber·ous \'sləm-bə-rəs\ *or* **slum·brous** \-brəs\ *adj* **1** : SLUMBERING, SLEEPY **2** : PEACEFUL, INACTIVE

slum·lord \'sləm-ˌlòrd\ *n* : a landlord who receives unusually large profits from substandard properties

slump \'sləmp\ *vb* **1** : to sink down suddenly : COLLAPSE **2** : SLOUCH **3** : to decline sharply — **slump** *n*

slung *past and past part of* SLING

slunk *past and past part of* SLINK

¹**slur** \'slər\ *n* : a slighting remark : ASPERSION — **slur** *vb*

²**slur** *vb* **slurred; slur·ring** **1** : to slide or slip over without due mention or emphasis **2** : to perform two or more successive notes of different pitch in a smooth or connected way

³**slur** *n* : a curved line connecting notes to be slurred; *also* : a group of slurred notes

slurp \'slərp\ *vb* : to eat or drink noisily — **slurp** *n*

slur·ry \'slər-ē\ *n, pl* **slur·ries** : a watery mixture of insoluble matter

slush \\'sləsh\ *n* **1** : partly melted or watery snow **2** : soft mud — **slushy** *adj*

slush fund *n* : an unregulated fund often for illicit purposes

slut \\'slət\ *n* **1** : a slovenly woman **2** : a promiscuous woman — **slut·tish** *adj*

sly \\'slī\ *adj* **sly·er** *also* **sli·er** \\'slī-ər\; **sly·est** *also* **sli·est** \\'slī-əst\ **1** : CRAFTY, CUNNING **2** : SECRETIVE, FURTIVE **3** : ROGUISH ✦ *Synonyms* TRICKY, WILY, ARTFUL, FOXY, GUILEFUL — **sly·ly** *also* **sli·ly** *adv* — **sly·ness** *n*

sm *abbr* small

Sm *symbol* samarium

SM *abbr* **1** master of science **2** sergeant major **3** service mark **4** stage manager

SMA *abbr* sergeant major of the army

¹smack \\'smak\ *n* : characteristic flavor; *also* : a slight trace

²smack *vb* **1** : to have a taste **2** : to have a trace or suggestion 〈~s of treason〉

³smack *vb* **1** : to move (the lips) so as to make a sharp noise **2** : to kiss or slap with a loud noise

⁴smack *n* **1** : a sharp noise made by the lips **2** : a loud kiss or slap

⁵smack *adv* : squarely and sharply

⁶smack *n* : a sailing ship used in fishing

⁷smack *n, slang* : HEROIN

SMaj *abbr* sergeant major

¹small \\'smól\ *adj* **1** : little in size or amount **2** : operating on a limited scale **3** : little or close to zero (as in number or value) **4** : made up of little things **5** : TRIFLING, UNIMPORTANT **6** : MEAN, PETTY ✦ *Synonyms* DIMINUTIVE, PETITE, WEE, TINY, MINUTE — **small·ish** *adj* — **small·ness** *n*

²small *n* : a small part or product 〈the ~ of the back〉

small·pox \\'smól-ˌpäks\ *n* : a contagious virus disease of humans formerly common but now eradicated

small talk *n* : light or casual conversation

small–time \\'smól-ˈtīm\ *adj* : insignificant in performance and standing : MINOR — **small–timer** *n*

smarmy \\'smär-mē\ *adj* **smarm·i·er; -est** : marked by a smug, ingratiating, or false earnestness

¹smart \\'smärt\ *adj* **1** : making one smart 〈a ~ blow〉 **2** : mentally quick : BRIGHT **3** : WITTY, CLEVER **4** : STYLISH **5** : being a guided missile **6** : containing a microprocessor for limited computing capability 〈~ terminal〉 ✦ *Synonyms* KNOWING, QUICK-WITTED, INTELLIGENT, BRAINY, SHARP — **smart·ly** *adv* — **smart·ness** *n*

²smart *vb* **1** : to cause or feel a stinging pain **2** : to feel or endure distress — **smart** *n*

smart al·eck \\'smärt-ˌa-lik\ *n* : a person given to obnoxious cleverness

smart card *n* : a small plastic card that has a built-in microprocessor to store and handle data

smart·en \\'smär-tᵊn\ *vb* : to make smart or smarter — usu. used with *up*

¹smash \\'smash\ *n* **1** : a smashing blow **2** : a hard, overhand stroke in tennis **3** : the act or sound of smashing **4** : collision of vehicles : CRASH **5** : COLLAPSE, RUIN; *esp* : BANKRUPTCY **6** : a striking success : HIT — **smash** *adj*

²smash *vb* **1** : to break or be broken into pieces **2** : to move forward with force and shattering effect **3** : to destroy utterly : WRECK

smat·ter·ing \\'sma-tə-riŋ\ *n* **1** : superficial knowledge **2** : a small scattered number or amount

¹smear \\'smir\ *n* **1** : a spot left by an oily or sticky substance **2** : material smeared on a surface (as of a microscope slide)

²smear *vb* **1** : to overspread esp. with something oily or sticky **2** : SMUDGE, SOIL **3** : to injure by slander or insults

¹smell \\'smel\ *vb* **smelled** \\'smeld\ *or* **smelt** \\'smelt\; **smell·ing** **1** : to perceive the odor of by sense organs of the nose; *also* : to detect or seek with or as if with these organs **2** : to have or give off an odor

²smell *n* **1** : ODOR, SCENT **2** : the process or power of perceiving odor; *also* : the sense by which one perceives odor **3** : an act of smelling — **smelly** *adj*

smelling salts *n pl* : an aromatic preparation used as a stimulant and restorative (as to relieve faintness)

¹smelt \\'smelt\ *n, pl* **smelts** *or* **smelt** : any of a family of small food fishes of coastal or fresh waters that are related to the trouts and salmons

²smelt *vb* : to melt or fuse (ore) in order to separate the metal; *also* : REFINE

smelt·er \\'smel-tər\ *n* **1** : one that smelts **2** : an establishment for smelting

smid·gen *also* **smid·geon** *or* **smid·gin** \\'smi-jən\ *n* : a small amount : BIT

smi·lax \\'smī-ˌlaks\ *n* **1** : any of various mostly climbing and prickly plants related to the lilies **2** : an ornamental plant related to the asparagus

¹smile \\'smī(-ə)l\ *vb* **smiled; smil·ing** **1** : to look with a smile **2** : to be favorable **3** : to express by a smile

²smile *n* : a change of facial expression to express amusement, pleasure, or affection — **smile·less** \\'smī(-ə)l-ləs\ *adj*

smil·ey \\'smī-lē\ *adj* : exhibiting a smile : frequently smiling

smirch \\'smərch\ *vb* **1** : to make dirty or stained **2** : to bring disgrace on — **smirch** *n*

smirk \\'smərk\ *vb* : to smile in an affected or smug manner : SIMPER — **smirk** *n*

smite \\'smīt\ *vb* **smote** \\'smōt\; **smit·ten** \\'smi-tᵊn\ *or* **smote; smit·ing** \\'smī-tiŋ\ **1** : to strike heavily; *also* : to kill by striking **2** : to affect as if by a heavy blow

smith \\'smith\ *n* : a worker in metals; *esp* : BLACKSMITH

smith·er·eens \ˌsmi-thə-ˈrēnz\ *n pl* [perh. fr. Ir *smidiríní*] : FRAGMENTS, BITS

smithy \\'smi-thē\ *n, pl* **smith·ies** **1** : a smith's workshop **2** : BLACKSMITH

¹smock \\'smäk\ *n* : a loose garment worn over other clothes as a protection

²smock *vb* : to gather (cloth) in regularly spaced tucks — **smock·ing** *n*

smog \\'smäg, 'smóg\ *n* [blend of *smoke* and *fog*] : a thick haze caused by the action of sunlight on air polluted by smoke and automobile exhaust fumes — **smog·gy** *adj*

¹smoke \\'smōk\ *n* **1** : the gas from burning material (as coal, wood, or tobacco) in which are suspended particles of soot **2** : a mass or column of smoke **3** : something (as a cigarette) to smoke; *also* : the act of smoking — **smoke·less** *adj* — **smoky** *adj*

²smoke *vb* **smoked; smok·ing** **1** : to emit smoke **2** : to inhale and exhale the fumes of burning tobacco; *also* : to use in smoking 〈~ a pipe〉 **3** : to stupefy or drive away by smoke **4** : to discolor with smoke **5** : to cure (as meat) with smoke — **smok·er** *n*

smoke detector *n* : an alarm that sounds automatically when it detects smoke

smoke jumper *n* : a forest firefighter who parachutes to locations otherwise difficult to reach

smoke screen *n* **1** : a screen of smoke to hinder enemy observation **2** : something designed to obscure, confuse, or mislead

smoke·stack \\'smōk-ˌstak\ *n* : a pipe or funnel through which smoke and gases are discharged

smol·der *or* **smoul·der** \\'smōl-dər\ *vb* **smol·dered** *or* **smoul·dered; smol·der·ing** *or* **smoul·der·ing** **1** : to burn and smoke without flame **2** : to burn inwardly — **smolder** *n*

smooch \\'smüch\ *vb* : KISS, PET — **smooch** *n*

¹smooth \\'smüth\ *adj* **1** : not rough or uneven **2** : not jarring or jolting **3** : BLAND, MILD **4** : fluent in speech and agreeable in manner — **smooth·ly** *adv* — **smooth·ness** *n*

²smooth *vb* **1** : to make smooth **2** : to free from trouble or difficulty

smooth muscle *n* : muscle with no cross striations that is typical of visceral organs (as the stomach and bladder) and is not under voluntary control

smoothy *or* **smooth·ie** \\'smü-thē\ *n, pl* **smooth·ies** **1** : an artfully suave person **2** *smoothie* : a creamy beverage of fruit blended with juice, milk, or yogurt

s'more \\'smór\ *n* : a dessert of marshmallow and pieces of chocolate sandwiched between graham crackers

smor·gas·bord \\'smór-gəs-ˌbórd\ *n* [Sw *smörgåsbord*, fr. *smörgås* open sandwich + *bord* table] : a luncheon or supper buffet consisting of many foods

smote *past and past part of* SMITE

¹smoth·er \\'smə-thər\ *n* **1** : thick stifling smoke **2** : a dense cloud (as of fog or dust) **3** : a confused multitude of things

²**smother** *vb* **smoth·ered; smoth·er·ing** **1** : to be overcome by or die from lack of air **2** : to kill by depriving of air **3** : SUPPRESS **4** : to cover thickly

SMSgt *abbr* senior master sergeant

¹**smudge** \'sməj\ *vb* **smudged; smudg·ing** : to soil or blur by rubbing or smearing

²**smudge** *n* : a dirty or blurred spot — **smudgy** *adj*

smug \'sməg\ *adj* **smug·ger; smug·gest** : conscious of one's virtue and importance : SELF-SATISFIED — **smug·ly** *adv* — **smug·ness** *n*

smug·gle \'smə-gəl\ *vb* **smug·gled; smug·gling** **1** : to import or export secretly, illegally, or without paying the duties required by law **2** : to convey secretly — **smuggler** \'smə-glər\ *n*

smut \'smət\ *n* **1** : something (as soot) that smudges; *also* : SMUDGE, SPOT **2** : any of various destructive diseases of plants caused by fungi; *also* : a fungus causing smut **3** : indecent language or matter — **smut·ty** *adj*

smutch \'sməch\ *n* : SMUDGE

Sn *symbol* [LL *stannum*] tin

SN *abbr* seaman

snack \'snak\ *n* : a light meal : BITE — **snack** *vb*

snaf·fle \'sna-fəl\ *n* : a simple jointed bit for a horse's bridle

¹**snag** \'snag\ *n* **1** : a stump or piece of a tree esp. when under water **2** : an unexpected difficulty ✦ **Synonyms** OBSTACLE, OBSTRUCTION, IMPEDIMENT, BAR

²**snag** *vb* **snagged; snag·ging** **1** : to become caught on or as if on a snag **2** : to seize quickly : SNATCH

snail \'snāl\ *n* : any of numerous small gastropod mollusks with a spiral shell into which they can withdraw

snail mail *n* **1** : mail delivered by a postal system **2** : MAIL **2**

snake \'snāk\ *n* **1** : any of numerous long-bodied limbless reptiles **2** : a treacherous person **3** : something that resembles a snake — **snake·like** \-,līk\ *adj* — **snaky** *adj*

snake·bite \-,bīt\ *n* : the bite of a snake and esp. a venomous snake

¹**snap** \'snap\ *vb* **snapped; snap·ping** **1** : to grasp or slash at something with the teeth **2** : to get or buy quickly **3** : to utter sharp or angry words **4** : to break suddenly with a sharp sound **5** : to give a sharp cracking noise **6** : to throw with a quick motion **7** : FLASH ⟨her eyes *snapped*⟩ **8** : to put a football into play — **snap·per** *n* — **snap·pish** *adj*

²**snap** *n* **1** : the act or sound of snapping **2** : something very easy to do : CINCH **3** : a short period of cold weather **4** : a catch or fastening that closes with a click **5** : a thin brittle cookie **6** : ENERGY, VIM; *also* : smartness of movement **7** : the putting of the ball into play in football

snap bean *n* : a bean grown primarily for its long pods that are cooked as a vegetable when young and tender

snap·drag·on \'snap-,dra-gən\ *n* : any of a genus of herbs with long spikes of showy flowers

snapping turtle *n* : either of two large American turtles with powerful jaws and a strong musky odor

snap·py \'sna-pē\ *adj* **1** : quickly made or done **2** : marked by vigor **3** : STYLISH

snap·shot \'snap-,shät\ *n* : a photograph taken usu. with an inexpensive hand-held camera

snare \'sner\ *n* : a trap often consisting of a noose for catching birds or mammals — **snare** *vb*

¹**snarl** \'snärl\ *vb* : to cause to become knotted and intertwined

²**snarl** *n* : TANGLE — **snarly** \'snär-lē\ *adj*

³**snarl** *vb* : to growl angrily or threateningly

⁴**snarl** *n* : an angry ill-tempered growl

¹**snatch** \'snach\ *vb* **1** : to try to grasp something suddenly **2** : to seize or take away suddenly ✦ **Synonyms** CLUTCH, SEIZE, GRAB, NAB

²**snatch** *n* **1** : a short period **2** : an act of snatching **3** : something brief or fragmentary ⟨∼*es* of song⟩

¹**sneak** \'snēk\ *vb* **sneaked** \'snēkt\ *or* **snuck** \'snək\; **sneak·ing** : to move, act, or take in a furtive manner — **sneak·ing·ly** *adv*

²**sneak** *n* **1** : one who acts in a furtive or shifty manner **2** : a stealthy or furtive move or escape — **sneak·i·ly** \'snē-kə-lē\ *adv* — **sneaky** *adj*

sneak·er \'snē-kər\ *n* : a sports shoe with a pliable rubber sole

sneer \'snir\ *vb* : to show scorn or contempt by curling the lip or by a jeering tone — **sneer** *n*

sneeze \'snēz\ *vb* **sneezed; sneez·ing** [ME *snesen*, alter. of *fnesen*, fr. OE *fnēosan*] : to force the breath out suddenly and violently as a reflex act — **sneeze** *n*

SNF *abbr* skilled nursing facility

snick·er \'sni-kər\ *n* : a partly suppressed laugh — **snicker** *vb*

snide \'snīd\ *adj* **1** : MEAN, LOW ⟨a ∼ trick⟩ **2** : slyly disparaging ⟨a ∼ remark⟩ — **snide·ly** *adv* — **snide·ness** *n*

sniff \'snif\ *vb* **1** : to draw air audibly up the nose esp. for smelling **2** : to show disdain or scorn **3** : to detect by or as if by smelling — **sniff** *n*

snif·fle \'sni-fəl\ *n* **1** *pl* : a head cold marked by nasal discharge **2** : SNUFFLE — **sniffle** *vb*

¹**snip** \'snip\ *n* **1** : a fragment snipped off **2** : a simple stroke of the scissors or shears

²**snip** *vb* **snipped; snip·ping** : to cut off by bits : CLIP; *also* : to remove by cutting off

¹**snipe** \'snīp\ *n, pl* **snipes** *or* **snipe** : any of several long-billed game birds esp. of marshy areas that belong to the same family as the sandpipers

²**snipe** *vb* **sniped; snip·ing** : to shoot at an exposed enemy from a concealed position — **snip·er** *n*

snip·py \'sni-pē\ *adj* **snip·pi·er; -est** : CURT, SNAPPISH — **snip·pi·ly** \-pə-lē\ *adv*

snips \'snips\ *n pl* : hand shears used esp. for cutting sheet metal ⟨tin ∼⟩

snitch \'snich\ *vb* **1** : INFORM, TATTLE **2** : PILFER, SNATCH — **snitch** *n*

sniv·el \'sni-vəl\ *vb* **-eled** *or* **-elled; -el·ing** *or* **-el·ling** **1** : to have a running nose; *also* : SNUFFLE **2** : to whine in a snuffling manner — **snivel** *n*

snob \'snäb\ *n* : one who seeks association with persons of higher social position and looks down on those considered inferior — **snob·bish** *adj* — **snob·bish·ly** *adv* — **snob·bish·ness** *n* — **snob·by** \'snä-bē\ *adj*

snob·bery \'snä-bə-rē\ *n, pl* **-ber·ies** : snobbish conduct

¹**snoop** \'snüp\ *vb* [D *snoepen* to buy or eat on the sly] : to pry in a furtive or meddlesome way

²**snoop** *n* : a prying meddlesome person

snoopy \'snü-pē\ *adj* **snoop·i·er; -est** : given to snooping

snooty \'snü-tē\ *adj* **snoot·i·er; -est** : DISDAINFUL, SNOBBISH — **snoot·i·ly** \'snü-tə-lē\ *adv*

snooze \'snüz\ *vb* **snoozed; snooz·ing** : to take a nap : DOZE — **snooze** *n*

snore \'snȯr\ *vb* **snored; snor·ing** : to breathe with a rough hoarse noise while sleeping — **snore** *n*

snor·kel \'snȯr-kəl\ *n* [G *Schnorchel*] : a tube projecting above the water used by swimmers for breathing with the face under water — **snorkel** *vb*

snort \'snȯrt\ *vb* **1** : to force air violently and noisily through the nose ⟨his horse ∼*ed*⟩ **2** : to inhale (a drug) through the nostrils — **snort** *n*

snot \'snät\ *n* : nasal mucus

snot·ty \'snä-tē\ *adj* **snot·ti·er; -est** **1** : soiled with snot **2** : meanly contemptible

snout \'snaůt\ *n* **1** : a long projecting muzzle (as of a pig) **2** : a usu. large or grotesque nose

¹**snow** \'snō\ *n* **1** : crystals of ice formed from water vapor in the air **2** : a descent or shower of snow crystals

²**snow** *vb* **1** : to fall or cause to fall in or as snow **2** : to cover or shut in with or as if with snow

¹**snow·ball** \'snō-,bȯl\ *n* : a round mass of snow pressed into shape in the hand for throwing

²**snowball** *vb* **1** : to throw snowballs at **2** : to increase or expand at a rapidly accelerating rate

snow·bank \-,baŋk\ *n* : a mound or slope of snow

snow·belt \-,belt\ *n, often cap* : a region that receives an appreciable amount of annual snowfall

snow·blow·er \-,blō-ər\ *n* : a machine in which a rotating spiral blade picks up and propels snow aside

snow·board \-,bȯrd\ *n* : a board like a wide ski ridden in a surfing position downhill over snow

snow·drift \-,drift\ *n* : a bank of drifted snow

snow·drop \-,dräp\ *n* : a plant with narrow leaves and a nodding white flower that blooms early in the spring

snow·fall \-,fȯl\ *n* : a fall of snow

snow fence *n* : a fence across the path of prevailing winds to protect something (as a road) from drifting snow

snow·field \'snō-ˌfēld\ *n* : a mass of perennial snow at the head of a glacier

snow·mo·bile \'snō-mō-ˌbēl\ *n* : any of various automotive vehicles for travel on snow — **snow·mo·bil·er** \-ˌbē-lər\ *n* — **snow·mo·bil·ing** \-liŋ\ *n*

snow pea *n* : a cultivated pea with flat edible pods

snow·plow \'snō-ˌplaů\ *n* 1 : a device for clearing away snow 2 : a skiing maneuver in which the heels of both skis are slid outward for slowing down or stopping

¹**snow·shoe** \-ˌshü\ *n* : a lightweight platform for the foot designed to enable a person to walk on soft snow without sinking

²**snowshoe** *vb* **snow·shoed; snow·shoe·ing** : to travel on snowshoes

snow·storm \-ˌstȯrm\ *n* : a storm of falling snow

snow thrower *n* : SNOWBLOWER

snowy \'snō-ē\ *adj* **snow·i·er; -est** 1 : marked by snow 2 : white as snow

snowy egret *n* : a white American egret with a slender black bill

snub \'snǝb\ *vb* **snubbed; snub·bing** : to treat with disdain : SLIGHT — **snub** *n*

snub–nosed \'snǝb-ˌnōzd\ *adj* : having a nose slightly turned up at the end

snuck *past and past part of* SNEAK

¹**snuff** \'snǝf\ *vb* 1 : to pinch off the charred end of (a candle) 2 : to put out (a candle) — **snuff·er** *n*

²**snuff** *vb* 1 : to draw forcibly into or through the nose 2 : SMELL

³**snuff** *n* : SNIFF

⁴**snuff** *n* : pulverized tobacco

snuf·fle \'snǝ-fǝl\ *vb* **snuf·fled; snuf·fling** 1 : to snuff or sniff audibly and repeatedly 2 : to breathe with a sniffing sound — **snuf·fle** *n*

snug \'snǝg\ *adj* **snug·ger; snug·gest** 1 : fitting closely and comfortably 2 : CONCEALED — **snug·ly** *adv* — **snug·ness** *n*

snug·gle \'snǝ-gǝl\ *vb* **snug·gled; snug·gling** : to curl up or draw close comfortably : NESTLE

¹**so** \'sō\ *adv* 1 : in the manner indicated 2 : in the same way ⟨he's hungry and ∼ am I⟩ 3 : THUS 4 : FINALLY 5 : to an indicated or great extent ⟨I'm ∼ bored⟩ 6 : THEREFORE

²**so** *conj* : for that reason ⟨he wanted it, ∼ he took it⟩

³**so** *pron* 1 : the same ⟨became chairman and remained ∼⟩ 2 : approximately that ⟨a dozen or ∼⟩

⁴**so** *abbr* south; southern

SO *abbr* strikeout

¹**soak** \'sōk\ *vb* 1 : to remain in a liquid 2 : WET, SATURATE 3 : to draw in by or as if by absorption ⟨∼ up the sunshine⟩ ✦ *Synonyms* DRENCH, STEEP, IMPREGNATE

²**soak** *n* 1 : the act of soaking 2 : the liquid in which something is soaked 3 : DRUNKARD

soap \'sōp\ *n* : a cleansing substance made usu. by action of alkali on fat — **soap** *vb* — **soapy** *adj*

soap·box \'sōp-ˌbäks\ *n* : an improvised platform used for delivering informal speeches

soap opera *n* [fr. its sponsorship by soap manufacturers] : a radio or television daytime serial drama

soap·stone \'sōp-ˌstōn\ *n* : a soft talc-containing stone with a soapy feel

soar \'sȯr\ *vb* : to fly upward or at a height on or as if on wings

sob \'säb\ *vb* **sobbed; sob·bing** : to weep with convulsive heavings of the chest or contractions of the throat — **sob** *n*

so·ba \'sō-bǝ\ *n* [Jp] : a Japanese noodle made from buckwheat flour

so·ber \'sō-bǝr\ *adj* **so·ber·er** \-bǝr-ǝr\; **so·ber·est** \-bǝ-rǝst\ 1 : temperate in the use of liquor 2 : not drunk 3 : serious or grave in mood or disposition 4 : having a quiet tone or color ✦ *Synonyms* SOLEMN, EARNEST, STAID, SEDATE — **so·ber·ly** *adv* — **so·ber·ness** *n*

so·bri·ety \sǝ-'brī-ǝ-tē\ *n* : the quality or state of being sober

so·bri·quet \'sō-bri-ˌkā, -ˌket\ *n* [F] : NICKNAME

soc *abbr* 1 social; society 2 sociology

so·ca \'sō-kǝ, -kä\ *n* : soul music blended with calypso

so–called \'sō-'kȯld\ *adj* : commonly but often inaccurately so termed

soc·cer \'sä-kǝr\ *n* [by shortening & alter. fr. *association*

football] : a game played on a field by two teams with a round inflated ball that is kicked or hit with any body part other than the hands or arms

¹**so·cia·ble** \'sō-shǝ-bǝl\ *adj* 1 : liking companionship : FRIENDLY 2 : characterized by pleasant social relations ✦ *Synonyms* GRACIOUS, CORDIAL, AFFABLE, GENIAL — **so·cia·bil·i·ty** \ˌsō-shǝ-'bi-lǝ-tē\ *n* — **so·cia·bly** \'sō-shǝ-blē\ *adv*

²**sociable** *n* : SOCIAL

¹**so·cial** \'sō-shǝl\ *adj* 1 : marked by pleasant companionship with one's friends 2 : naturally living and breeding in organized communities ⟨∼ insects⟩ 3 : of or relating to human society ⟨∼ institutions⟩ 4 : of, relating to, or based on rank in a particular society ⟨∼ circles⟩; *also* : of or relating to fashionable society — **so·cial·ly** *adv*

²**social** *n* : a social gathering

so·cial·ise *Brit var of* SOCIALIZE

so·cial·ism \'sō-shǝ-ˌli-zǝm\ *n* : any of various social systems based on shared or government ownership and administration of the means of production and distribution of goods — **so·cial·ist** \'sō-shǝ-list\ *n or adj* — **so·cial·is·tic** \ˌsō-shǝ-'lis-tik\ *adj*

so·cial·ite \'sō-shǝ-ˌlīt\ *n* : a person prominent in fashionable society

so·cial·ize \'sō-shǝ-ˌlīz\ *vb* **-ized; -iz·ing** 1 : to regulate according to the theory and practice of socialism 2 : to adapt to social needs or uses 3 : to participate actively in a social gathering — **so·cial·i·za·tion** \ˌsō-shǝ-lǝ-'zā-shǝn\ *n*

social science *n* : a science (as economics or political science) dealing with a particular aspect of human society — **social scientist** *n*

social work *n* : services, activities, or methods providing social services esp. to the economically or socially disadvantaged — **social worker** *n*

so·ci·e·ty \sǝ-'sī-ǝ-tē\ *n, pl* **-ties** [MF *societé*, fr. L *societat-, societas*, fr. *socius* companion] 1 : COMPANIONSHIP 2 : a voluntary association of persons for common ends 3 : a part of a community bound together by common interests and standards; *esp* : the group or set of fashionable people

so·cio·eco·nom·ic \ˌsō-sē-ō-ˌe-kǝ-'nä-mik, ˌsō-shē-, -ˌē-kǝ-\ *adj* : of, relating to, or involving both social and economic factors

sociol *abbr* sociologist; sociology

so·ci·ol·o·gy \ˌsō-sē-'ä-lǝ-jē, ˌsō-shē-\ *n* : the science of society, social institutions, and social relationships — **so·cio·log·i·cal** \ˌsō-sē-ǝ-'lä-ji-kǝl, ˌsō-shē-\ *adj* — **so·ci·ol·o·gist** \-'ä-lǝ-jist\ *n*

so·cio·path \'sō-sē-ǝ-ˌpath, 'sō-sh(ē-)ǝ-\ *n* : a person exhibiting antisocial behavior : PSYCHOPATH — **so·cio·path·ic** \ˌsō-sē-ǝ-'pa-thik, ˌsō-sh(ē-)ǝ-\ *adj*

¹**sock** \'säk\ *n, pl* **socks** *or* **sox** \'säks\ : a stocking with a short leg

²**sock** *vb* : to hit, strike, or apply forcefully

³**sock** *n* : a vigorous blow : PUNCH

sock·et \'sä-kǝt\ *n* : an opening or hollow that forms a holder for something

socket wrench *n* : a wrench usu. in the form of a bar and removable socket made to fit a bolt or nut

socket wrench

sock·eye salmon \'säk-ˌī-\ *n* : a commercially important Pacific salmon

¹**sod** \'säd\ *n* : TURF 1

²**sod** *vb* **sod·ded; sod·ding** : to cover with sod

so·da \'sō-dǝ\ *n* 1 : SODIUM CARBONATE 2 : SODIUM BICARBONATE 3 : SODIUM 4 : SODA WATER 5 : SODA POP 6 : a sweet drink of soda water, flavoring, and often ice cream

soda pop *n* : a carbonated, sweetened, and flavored soft drink

soda water *n* : a beverage of water charged with carbon dioxide

sod·den \'sä-d⁰n\ *adj* 1 : lacking spirit : DULLED 2

: SOAKED, DRENCHED **3** : heavy or doughy from being improperly cooked ⟨~ biscuits⟩

so·di·um \'sō-dē-əm\ *n* : a soft waxy silver white metallic chemical element occurring in nature in combined form (as in salt)

sodium bicarbonate *n* : a white weakly alkaline salt used esp. in baking powders, fire extinguishers, and medicine

sodium carbonate *n* : a carbonate of sodium used esp. in washing and bleaching textiles

sodium chloride *n* : SALT 1

sodium fluoride *n* : a salt used chiefly in tiny amounts (as in fluoridation) to prevent tooth decay

sodium hydroxide *n* : a white brittle caustic substance used in making soap and rayon and in bleaching

sodium nitrate *n* : a crystalline salt used as a fertilizer and in curing meat

sodium thiosulfate *n* : a hygroscopic crystalline salt used as a photographic fixing agent

sod·omy \'sä-də-mē\ *n* : anal or oral sexual intercourse with a member of the same or opposite sex; *also* : sexual intercourse with an animal — **sod·om·ize** \'sä-də-ˌmīz\ *vb*

so·ev·er \sō-'e-vər\ *adv* **1** : in any degree or manner ⟨how bad ~⟩ **2** : at all : of any kind ⟨any help ~⟩

so·fa \'sō-fə\ *n* [earlier, raised carpeted floor, fr. It *sofà*, fr. Turk *sofa*, fr. Ar *ṣuffa* carpet, divan] : a couch usu. with upholstered back and arms

soft \'sȯft\ *adj* **1** : not hard or rough : NONVIOLENT **2** : RESTFUL, GENTLE, SOOTHING **3** : emotionally susceptible **4** : not prepared to endure hardship **5** : not containing certain salts that prevent lathering ⟨~ water⟩ **6** : occurring at such a speed as to avoid destructive impact ⟨~ landing of a spacecraft on the moon⟩ **7** : BIODEGRADABLE ⟨a ~ pesticide⟩ **8** : not alcoholic ⟨~ drinks⟩ **9** : less detrimental than a hard narcotic ⟨~ drugs⟩ — **soft·ly** *adv* — **soft·ness** *n*

soft·ball \'sȯft-ˌbȯl\ *n* : a game similar to baseball played with a ball larger and softer than a baseball; *also* : the ball used in this game

soft·bound \-ˌbaůnd\ *adj* : not bound in hard covers ⟨~ books⟩

soft coal *n* : BITUMINOUS COAL

soft·en \'sȯ-fən\ *vb* : to make or become soft — **soft·en·er** *n*

soft palate *n* : the fold at the back of the hard palate that partially separates the mouth from the pharynx

soft·ware \'sȯft-ˌwer\ *n* : the entire set of programs, procedures, and related documentation associated with a system; *esp* : computer programs

soft·wood \-ˌwůd\ *n* **1** : the wood of a coniferous tree as compared to that of a broad-leaved deciduous tree **2** : a tree yielding softwood — **softwood** *adj*

sog·gy \'sä-gē\ *adj* **sog·gi·er; -est** : heavy with water or moisture — **sog·gi·ly** \'sä-gə-lē\ *adv* — **sog·gi·ness** \-gē-nəs\ *n*

soi·gné *or* **soi·gnée** \swän-'yā\ *adj* : elegantly maintained; *esp* : WELL-GROOMED

¹soil \'sȯi(-ə)l\ *vb* **1** : CORRUPT, POLLUTE **2** : to make or become dirty **3** : STAIN, DISGRACE ⟨~*ed* his reputation⟩

²soil *n* **1** : STAIN, DEFILEMENT **2** : EXCREMENT, WASTE

³soil *n* **1** : firm land **2** : EARTH **3** : the upper layer of earth in which plants grow **3** : COUNTRY, REGION

soi·ree *or* **soi·rée** \swä-'rā\ *n* [F *soirée* evening period, evening party, fr. MF, fr. *soir* evening, fr. L *sero* at a late hour] : an evening party

so·journ \'sō-ˌjərn, sō-'jərn\ *vb* : to dwell in a place temporarily — **so·journ** *n* — **so·journ·er** *n*

¹sol \'säl, 'sȯl\ *n* — see MONEY table

²sol *n* : a fluid colloidal system

³sol *abbr* **1** solicitor **2** soluble **3** solution

Sol \'säl\ *n* : SUN

¹sol·ace \'sä-ləs\ *n* : COMFORT

²solace *vb* **so·laced; so·lac·ing** : to give solace to : CONSOLE

so·lar \'sō-lər\ *adj* **1** : of, derived from, or relating to the sun **2** : measured by the earth's course in relation to the sun ⟨the ~ year⟩ **3** : operated by or using the sun's light or heat ⟨~ energy⟩

solar cell *n* : a photoelectric cell used as a power source

solar collector *n* : a device for the absorption of solar radiation for the heating of water or buildings or the production of electricity

solar flare *n* : a sudden temporary outburst of energy from a small area of the sun's surface

so·lar·i·um \sō-'ler-ē-əm\ *n, pl* **-ia** \-ē-ə\ *also* **-i·ums** : a room exposed to the sun; *esp* : a room (as in a hospital) for exposure of the body to sunshine

solar mass *n* : a unit of mass equal to the mass of the sun or about 2×10^{30} kilograms

solar plexus *n* : the general area of the stomach below the sternum

solar system *n* : the sun together with the group of celestial bodies that revolve around it

solar wind *n* : plasma continuously ejected from the sun's surface

sold *past and past part of* SELL

sol·der \'sä-dər, 'sȯ-\ *n* : a metallic alloy used when melted to mend or join metallic surfaces — **solder** *vb*

soldering iron *n* : a metal device for applying heat in soldering

¹sol·dier \'sōl-jər\ *n* [ME *soudeour*, fr. AF, mercenary, fr. *soudee* shilling's worth, wage, fr. *sou, soud* shilling, fr. LL *solidus* a Roman coin, fr. L, solid] : a person in military service; *esp* : an enlisted man or woman — **sol·dier·ly** *adj or adv*

²soldier *vb* **sol·diered; sol·dier·ing** **1** : to serve as a soldier **2** : to pretend to work while actually doing nothing

soldier of fortune *n* : ADVENTURER 2

sol·diery \'sōl-jə-rē\ *n* : a body of soldiers

¹sole \'sōl\ *n* : any of various flatfishes including some used for food

²sole *n* **1** : the undersurface of the foot **2** : the bottom of a shoe

³sole *vb* **soled; sol·ing** : to furnish (a shoe) with a sole

⁴sole *adj* : SINGLE, ONLY ⟨the ~ survivor⟩ — **sole·ly** \'sōl-lē\ *adv*

so·le·cism \'sä-lə-ˌsi-zəm, 'sō-\ *n* **1** : a mistake in grammar **2** : a breach of etiquette

sol·emn \'sä-ləm\ *adj* **1** : marked by or observed with full religious ceremony ⟨a ~ oath⟩ **2** : FORMAL, CEREMONIOUS **3** : highly serious : GRAVE ⟨a ~ gathering⟩ **4** : SOMBER, GLOOMY ⟨a ~ city⟩ — **so·lem·ni·ty** \sə-'lem-nə-tē\ *n* — **sol·emn·ly** \'sä-ləm-lē\ *adv*

sol·em·nize \'sä-ləm-ˌnīz\ *vb* **-nized; -niz·ing** **1** : to observe or honor with solemnity **2** : to celebrate (a marriage) with religious rites — **sol·em·ni·za·tion** \ˌsä-ləm-nə-'zā-shən\ *n*

so·le·noid \'sō-lə-ˌnȯid, 'sä-\ *n* : a coil of wire usu. in cylindrical form when carrying a current acts like a magnet

so·lic·it \sə-'li-sət\ *vb* **1** : ENTREAT, BEG **2** : to approach with a request or plea **3** : TEMPT, LURE **4** : to try to obtain by request ⟨~ donations⟩ — **so·lic·i·ta·tion** \-ˌli-sə-'tā-shən\ *n*

so·lic·i·tor \sə-'li-sə-tər\ *n* **1** : one that solicits **2** : LAWYER; *esp* : a legal official of a city or state

so·lic·i·tous \sə-'li-sə-təs\ *adj* **1** : WORRIED, CONCERNED **2** : EAGER, WILLING ✦ *Synonyms* AVID, IMPATIENT, KEEN, ANXIOUS — **so·lic·i·tous·ly** *adv*

so·lic·i·tude \sə-'li-sə-ˌtüd, -ˌtyüd\ *n* : CONCERN, ANXIETY

¹sol·id \'sä-ləd\ *adj* **1** : not hollow; *also* : written as one word without a hyphen ⟨a ~ compound⟩ **2** : having, involving, or dealing with three dimensions or with solids ⟨~ geometry⟩ **3** : not loose or spongy : COMPACT ⟨a ~ mass of rock⟩; *also* : neither gaseous nor liquid : HARD, RIGID ⟨~ ice⟩ **4** : of good substantial quality or kind ⟨~ comfort⟩ **5** : thoroughly dependable : RELIABLE ⟨a ~ citizen⟩; *also* : serious in purpose or character ⟨~ reading⟩ **6** : UNANIMOUS, UNITED ⟨~ for pay increases⟩ **7** : of one substance or character — **solid** *adv* — **sol·id·i·ly** \sə-'li-də-tē\ *adv* — **sol·id·ly** *adv* — **sol·id·ness** *n*

²solid *n* **1** : a geometrical figure (as a cube or sphere) having three dimensions **2** : a solid substance

sol·i·dar·i·ty \ˌsä-lə-'der-ə-tē\ *n* : unity based on shared interests, objectives, or standards

so·lid·i·fy \sə-'li-də-ˌfī\ *vb* **-fied; -fy·ing** : to make or become solid — **so·lid·i·fi·ca·tion** \-ˌli-də-fə-'kā-shən\ *n*

solid–state *adj* **1** : relating to the structure and properties of solid material **2** : using semiconductor devices rather than vacuum tubes

so·lil·o·quize \sə-'li-lə-ˌkwīz\ *vb* **-quized; -quiz·ing** : to talk to oneself : utter a soliloquy

so·lil·o·quy \sə-'li-lə-kwē\ *n, pl* **-quies** [LL *soliloquium*, fr.

solitaire • soprano

L *solus* alone + *loqui* to speak] **1** : the act of talking to oneself **2** : a dramatic monologue that represents unspoken reflections by a character

sol·i·taire \'säl-ə-ˌter\ *n* **1** : a single gem (as a diamond) set alone **2** : a card game for one person

sol·i·tary \'säl-ə-ˌter-ē\ *adj* **1** : being or living apart from others **2** : LONELY, SECLUDED **3** : SOLE, ONLY

sol·i·tude \'säl-ə-ˌtüd, -ˌtyüd\ *n* **1** : the state of being alone : SECLUSION **2** : a lonely place

soln *abbr* solution

¹**so·lo** \'sō-lō\ *n, pl* **solos** [It, fr. *solo* alone, fr. L *solus*] **1** : a piece of music for a single voice or instrument with or without accompaniment **2** : an action in which there is only one performer — **solo** *adj or vb* — **so·lo·ist** *n*

²**solo** *adv* : without a companion : ALONE

so·lon \'sō-lən\ *n* **1** : a wise and skillful lawgiver **2** : a member of a legislative body

sol·stice \'säl-stəs, 'sōl-\ *n* [ME, fr. L *solstitium*, fr. *sol* sun + *-stit-*, *-stes* standing] : the time of the year when the sun is farthest north of the equator (**summer solstice**) about June 22 or farthest south (**winter solstice**) about Dec. 22 — **sol·sti·tial** \säl-'sti-shəl, sōl-\ *adj*

sol·u·ble \'säl-yə-bəl\ *adj* **1** : capable of being dissolved in or as if in a liquid **2** : capable of being solved or explained — **sol·u·bil·i·ty** \ˌsäl-yə-'bi-lə-tē\ *n*

sol·ute \'säl-ˌyüt\ *n* : a dissolved substance

so·lu·tion \sə-'lü-shən\ *n* **1** : an action or process of solving a problem; *also* : an answer to a problem **2** : an act or the process by which one substance is homogeneously mixed with another usu. liquid substance; *also* : a mixture thus formed

solve \'sälv\ *vb* **solved; solv·ing** : to find the answer to or a solution for — **solv·able** *adj*

sol·ven·cy \'säl-vən-sē\ *n* : the condition of being solvent

¹**sol·vent** \-vənt\ *adj* **1** : able or sufficient to pay all legal debts **2** : dissolving or able to dissolve

²**solvent** *n* : a usu. liquid substance capable of dissolving or dispersing one or more other substances

som \'sōm\ *n, pl* **som** — see MONEY table

so·mat·ic \sō-'ma-tik\ *adj* : of, relating to, or affecting the body in contrast to the mind or the sex cells and their precursors

som·ber *or* **som·bre** \'säm-bər\ *adj* **1** : DARK, GLOOMY **2** : GRAVE, MELANCHOLY — **som·ber·ly** *adv*

som·bre·ro \səm-'brer-ō\ *n, pl* **-ros** [Sp, fr. *sombra* shade] : a broad-brimmed felt hat worn esp. in the Southwest and in Mexico

¹**some** \'səm\ *adj* **1** : one unspecified ⟨~ man called⟩ **2** : an unspecified or indefinite number of ⟨~ berries are ripe⟩ **3** : at least a few or a little ⟨~ years ago⟩

²**some** *pron* : a certain number or amount ⟨~ of the berries are ripe⟩ ⟨~ of it is missing⟩

¹**-some** \səm\ *adj suffix* : characterized by a (specified) thing, quality, state, or action ⟨awe*some*⟩ ⟨burden*some*⟩

²**-some** *n suffix* : a group of (so many) members and esp. persons ⟨four*some*⟩

¹**some·body** \'səm-ˌbä-dē, -bə-\ *pron* : some person

²**somebody** *n* : a person of importance

some·day \'səm-ˌdā\ *adv* : at some future time

some·how \-ˌhau̇\ *adv* : by some means

some·one \-(ˌ)wən\ *pron* : some person

som·er·sault *also* **sum·mer·sault** \'sə-mər-ˌsȯlt\ *n* [MF *sombresaut* leap, ultim. fr. L *super* over + *saltus* leap, fr. *salire* to jump] : a leap or roll in which a person turns heels over head — **somersault** *vb*

som·er·set \-ˌset\ *n or vb* : SOMERSAULT

some·thing \'səm-thiŋ\ *pron* : some undetermined or unspecified thing

some·time \-ˌtīm\ *adv* **1** : at a future time **2** : at an unknown or unnamed time

some·times \-ˌtīmz\ *adv* : OCCASIONALLY

¹**some·what** \-ˌhwät, -ˌhwət\ *pron* : SOMETHING

²**somewhat** *adv* : in some degree

some·where \-ˌhwer\ *adv* : in, at, or to an unknown or unnamed place

som·nam·bu·lism \säm-'nam-byə-ˌli-zəm\ *n* : performance of motor acts (as walking) during sleep; *also* : an abnormal condition of sleep characterized by this — **som·nam·bu·list** \-list\ *n*

som·no·lent \'säm-nə-lənt\ *adj* : SLEEPY, DROWSY — **som·no·lence** \-ləns\ *n*

so·mo·ni \ˌsō-mō-'nē\ *n* — see MONEY table

son \'sən\ *n* **1** : a male offspring or descendant **2** *cap* : Jesus Christ **3** : a person deriving from a particular source (as a country, race, or school)

so·nar \'sō-ˌnär\ *n* [*sound navigation ranging*] : a method or device for detecting and locating submerged objects (as submarines) by sound waves

so·na·ta \sə-'nä-tə\ *n* [It] : an instrumental composition with three or four movements differing in rhythm and mood but related in key

son·a·ti·na \ˌsä-nə-'tē-nə\ *n* [It, dim. of *sonata*] : a short usu. simplified sonata

song \'sȯŋ\ *n* **1** : vocal music; *also* : a short composition of words and music **2** : poetic composition **3** : a distinctive or characteristic sound (as of a bird) **4** : a small amount ⟨sold for a ~⟩

song·bird \'sȯŋ-ˌbərd\ *n* : a bird that utters a series of musical tones

Song of Sol·o·mon \-'sä-lə-mən\ — see BIBLE table

Song of Songs — see BIBLE table

song·ster \'sȯŋ-stər\ *n* : one that sings

song·stress \-strəs\ *n* : a girl or woman who is a singer

son·ic \'sä-nik\ *adj* : of or relating to sound waves or the speed of sound

sonic boom *n* : an explosive sound produced by an aircraft traveling at supersonic speed

son–in–law \'sən-ən-ˌlȯ\ *n, pl* **sons–in–law** : the husband of one's daughter

son·net \'sä-nət\ *n* : a poem of 14 lines usu. in iambic pentameter with a definite rhyme scheme

son of a gun *n* : an offensive or disagreeable person

so·no·rous \sə-'nȯr-əs, 'sä-nə-rəs\ *adj* **1** : giving out sound when struck **2** : loud, deep, or rich in sound : RESONANT **3** : high-sounding : IMPRESSIVE — **so·nor·i·ty** \sə-'nȯr-ə-tē\ *n*

soon \'sün\ *adv* **1** : before long **2** : PROMPTLY, QUICKLY **3** *archaic* : EARLY **4** : WILLINGLY, READILY

soot \'su̇t, 'sət, 'süt\ *n* : a fine black powder consisting chiefly of carbon that is formed when something burns and that colors smoke — **sooty** *adj*

sooth \'süth\ *n, archaic* : TRUTH

soothe \'sü<u>th</u>\ *vb* **soothed; sooth·ing** **1** : to please by flattery or attention **2** : RELIEVE, ALLEVIATE ⟨~ a burn⟩ **3** : to calm down : COMFORT ⟨~ a child⟩ — **sooth·er** *n* — **sooth·ing·ly** *adv*

sooth·say·er \'süth-ˌsā-ər\ *n* : one who foretells events — **sooth·say·ing** *n*

¹**sop** \'säp\ *n* : a conciliatory bribe, gift, or concession

²**sop** *vb* **sopped; sop·ping** **1** : to steep or dip in or as if in a liquid **2** : to wet thoroughly : SOAK; *also* : to mop up (a liquid)

SOP *abbr* standard operating procedure; standing operating procedure

soph *abbr* sophomore

soph·ism \'sä-ˌfi-zəm\ *n* **1** : an argument correct in form but embodying a subtle fallacy **2** : SOPHISTRY

soph·ist \'sä-fist\ *n* : PHILOSOPHER; *esp* : a captious or fallacious reasoner

so·phis·tic \sä-'fis-tik, sə-\ *or* **so·phis·ti·cal** \-ti-kəl\ *adj* : of or characteristic of sophists or sophistry ♦ **Synonyms** FALLACIOUS, ILLOGICAL, UNREASONABLE, SPECIOUS

so·phis·ti·cat·ed \sə-'fis-tə-ˌkā-təd\ *adj* **1** : COMPLEX ⟨~ instruments⟩ **2** : made worldly-wise by wide experience **3** : intellectually appealing ⟨a ~ novel⟩ — **so·phis·ti·ca·tion** \-ˌfis-tə-'kā-shən\ *n*

soph·ist·ry \'sä-fə-strē\ *n* : subtly deceptive reasoning or argument

soph·o·more \'säf-ˌmȯr, 'sä-fə-\ *n* : a student in the second year of high school or college

soph·o·mor·ic \ˌsäf-'mȯr-ik, ˌsä-fə-\ *adj* **1** : being overconfident of knowledge but poorly informed and immature ⟨~ reasoning⟩ **2** : of, relating to, or characteristic of a sophomore ⟨~ humor⟩

So·pho·ni·as \ˌsä-fə-'nī-əs, ˌsō-\ *n* : ZEPHANIAH

sop·o·rif·ic \ˌsä-pə-'ri-fik\ *adj* **1** : causing sleep or drowsiness **2** : LETHARGIC

so·pra·no \sə-'pra-nō, -'prä-\ *n, pl* **-nos** [It, fr. *sopra* above, fr. L *supra*] **1** : the highest singing voice; *also* : a singer with this voice **2** : the highest part in a 4-part chorus — **soprano** *adj*

sor·bet \sȯr-ˈbā\ *n* : a usu. fruit-flavored ice served for dessert or between courses as a palate refresher

sor·cery \ˈsȯr-sə-rē\ *n* [ME *sorcerie*, fr. AF, fr. *sorcer* sorcerer, fr. ML *sortiarius*, fr. L *sort-, sors* chance, lot] : the use of magic : WITCHCRAFT — **sor·cer·er** \-rər\ *n* — **sor·cer·ess** \-rəs\ *n*

sor·did \ˈsȯr-dəd\ *adj* **1** : marked by baseness or grossness : VILE **2** : DIRTY, SQUALID — **sor·did·ly** *adv* — **sor·did·ness** *n*

¹sore \ˈsȯr\ *adj* **sor·er; sor·est 1** : causing pain or distress ⟨a ∼ bruise⟩ **2** : painfully sensitive ⟨∼ muscles⟩ **3** : SEVERE, INTENSE **4** : IRRITATED, ANGRY — **sore·ly** *adv* — **sore·ness** *n*

²sore *n* **1** : a sore spot on the body; *esp* : one (as an ulcer) with the tissues broken and usu. infected **2** : a source of pain or vexation

sore·head \ˈsȯr-ˌhed\ *n* : a person easily angered or discontented

sore throat *n* : painful throat due to inflammation of the fauces and pharynx

sor·ghum \ˈsȯr-gəm\ *n* : a tall variable Old World tropical grass grown widely for its edible seed, for forage, or for its sweet juice which yields a syrup

so·ror·i·ty \sə-ˈrȯr-ə-tē\ *n, pl* **-ties** [ML *sororitas* sisterhood, fr. L *soror* sister] : a club or organization usu. of female students for social purposes

¹sor·rel \ˈsȯr-əl\ *n* : a brownish orange to light brown color; *also* : a sorrel-colored animal (as a horse)

²sorrel *n* : any of various herbs having a sour juice

sor·row \ˈsär-ō\ *n* **1** : deep distress, sadness, or regret; *also* : resultant unhappy or unpleasant state **2** : a cause of grief or sadness **3** : a display of grief or sadness — **sorrow** *vb* — **sor·row·ful** \-fəl\ *adj* — **sor·row·ful·ly** \-f(ə-)lē\ *adv*

sor·ry \ˈsär-ē\ *adj* **sor·ri·er; -est 1** : feeling sorrow, regret, or penitence ⟨∼ for yelling at her⟩ **2** : MOURNFUL, SAD **3** : causing sorrow, pity, or scorn : PITIFUL ⟨a ∼ lot of ragamuffins⟩

¹sort \ˈsȯrt\ *n* **1** : a group of persons or things that have similar characteristics : CLASS **2** : QUALITY, NATURE **3** : an instance of sorting — **all sorts of** : many different — **out of sorts 1** : somewhat ill **2** : GROUCHY, IRRITABLE

²sort *vb* **1** : to put in a certain place according to kind, class, or nature **2** : to be in accord : AGREE **3** : SEARCH ⟨∼ through this mess⟩ — **sort·er** *n*

sor·tie \ˈsȯr-tē, sȯr-ˈtē\ *n* **1** : a sudden issuing of troops from a defensive position against the enemy **2** : one mission or attack by one airplane

sort of *adv* : to a moderate degree

SOS \ˌes-(ˌ)ō-ˈes\ *n* : a call or request for help or rescue

so–so \ˈsō-ˈsō\ *adv or adj* : PASSABLY

sot \ˈsät\ *n* : a habitual drunkard — **sot·tish** *adj* — **sot·tish·ly** *adv*

souf·flé \sü-ˈflā\ *n* [F, fr. *soufflé*, pp. of *souffler* to blow, puff up, fr. OF *sufler*, fr. L *sufflare*, fr. *sub-* up + *flare* to blow] : a spongy dish made light in baking by stiffly beaten egg whites

sough \ˈsau̇, ˈsəft\ *vb* : to make a moaning or sighing sound — **sough** *n*

sought *past and past part of* SEEK

¹soul \ˈsōl\ *n* **1** : the immaterial essence of an individual life **2** : the spiritual principle embodied in human beings or the universe **3** : an active or essential part **4** : the moral and emotional nature of human beings **5** : spiritual or moral force **6** : PERSON ⟨a kindly ∼⟩ **7** : a strong, positive feeling (as of intense sensitivity and emotional fervor) conveyed esp. by black American performers; *also* : NEGRITUDE **8** : SOUL MUSIC — **souled** \ˈsōld\ *adj* — **soul·less** \ˈsōl-ləs\ *adj*

²soul *adj* **1** : of, relating to, or characteristic of black Americans or their culture ⟨∼ food⟩ **2** : designed for or controlled by blacks ⟨∼ radio stations⟩

soul brother *n* : a black male

soul·ful \ˈsōl-fəl\ *adj* : full of or expressing deep feeling ⟨a ∼ ballad⟩ — **soul·ful·ly** *adv*

soul music *n* : music that is closely related to rhythm and blues and characterized by intensity of feeling

¹sound \ˈsau̇nd\ *adj* **1** : not diseased or sickly **2** : free from flaw or defect ⟨a ∼ structure⟩ **3** : FIRM, STRONG **4** : free from error or fallacy : RIGHT ⟨∼ logic⟩ **5** : LEGAL, VALID **6** : THOROUGH **7** : UNDISTURBED ⟨∼

sleep⟩ **8** : showing good judgment — **sound·ly** *adv* — **sound·ness** *n*

²sound *n* **1** : the sensation of hearing; *also* : mechanical energy transmitted by longitudinal pressure waves **(sound waves)** (as in air) that is the stimulus to hearing **2** : something heard : NOISE, TONE; *also* : hearing distance : EARSHOT **3** : a musical style — **sound·less** *adj* — **sound·less·ly** *adv* — **sound·proof** \-ˌprüf\ *adj or vb*

³sound *vb* **1** : to make or cause to make a sound **2** : to order or proclaim by a sound ⟨∼ the alarm⟩ **3** : to convey a certain impression : SEEM ⟨that ∼s like fun⟩ **4** : to examine the condition of by causing to give out sounds — **sound·able** \ˈsau̇n-də-bəl\ *adj*

⁴sound *n* : a long passage of water wider than a strait often connecting two larger bodies of water

⁵sound *vb* **1** : to measure the depth of (water) esp. by a weighted line dropped from the surface : FATHOM **2** : PROBE **3** : to dive down suddenly ⟨the hooked fish ∼ed⟩ — **sound·ing** *n*

sound bite *n* : a brief recorded statement broadcast esp. on a news program — **sound–bite** *adj*

sound card *n* : a circuit board in a computer system designed to produce or reproduce sound

sound·er \ˈsau̇n-dər\ *n* : one that sounds; *esp* : a device for making soundings

sound·stage \ˈsau̇nd-ˌstāj\ *n* : the part of a motion-picture studio in which a production is filmed

sound·track \ˈsau̇nd(d)-ˌtrak\ *n* : music recorded to accompany a film or videotape

soup \ˈsüp\ *n* **1** : a liquid food with stock as its base and often containing pieces of solid food **2** : something having the consistency of soup **3** : an unfortunate predicament ⟨in the ∼⟩

soup·çon \süp-ˈsōⁿ\ *n* [F, lit., suspicion] : a little bit : ¹TRACE 2

soup up *vb* : to increase the power of — **souped–up** \ˈsüpt-ˈəp\ *adj*

soupy \ˈsü-pē\ *adj* **soup·i·er; -est 1** : having the consistency of soup **2** : densely foggy or cloudy

¹sour \ˈsau̇(-ə)r\ *adj* **1** : having an acid or tart taste ⟨∼ as vinegar⟩ **2** : SPOILED, PUTRID ⟨a ∼ odor⟩ **3** : UNPLEASANT, DISAGREEABLE ⟨∼ disposition⟩ — **sour·ish** *adj* — **sour·ly** *adv* — **sour·ness** *n*

²sour *vb* : to become or make sour

source \ˈsȯrs\ *n* **1** : ORIGIN, BEGINNING **2** : a supplier of information **3** : the beginning of a stream of water

source code *n* : a computer program in its original programming language and before translation (as by a compiler)

¹souse \ˈsau̇s\ *vb* **soused; sous·ing 1** : PICKLE **2** : to plunge into a liquid **3** : DRENCH **4** : to make drunk

²souse *n* **1** : something (as pigs' feet) steeped in pickle **2** : a soaking in liquid **3** : DRUNKARD

¹south \ˈsau̇th\ *adv* : to or toward the south; *also* : into a state of decline

²south *adj* **1** : situated toward or at the south **2** : coming from the south

³south *n* **1** : the direction to the right of one facing east **2** : the compass point directly opposite to north **3** *cap* : regions or countries south of a specified or implied point; *esp* : the southeastern part of the U.S. — **south·er·ly** \ˈsə-thər-lē\ *adv or adj* — **south·ern** \ˈsə-thərn\ *adj* — **South·ern·er** *n* — **south·ern·most** \-ˌmōst\ *adj* — **south·ward** \ˈsau̇th-wərd\ *adv or adj* — **south·wards** \-wərdz\ *adv*

south·east \sau̇-ˈthēst, *naut* sau̇-ˈēst\ *n* **1** : the general direction between south and east **2** : the compass point midway between south and east **3** *cap* : regions or countries southeast of a specified or implied point — **southeast** *adj or adv* — **south·east·er·ly** *adv or adj* — **south·east·ern** \-ˈēs-tərn\ *adj*

south·paw \ˈsau̇th-ˌpȯ\ *n* : a left-handed person; *esp* : a left-handed baseball pitcher — **southpaw** *adj*

south pole *n, often cap S&P* : the southernmost point of the earth

south·west \sau̇th-ˈwest, *naut* sau̇-ˈwest\ *n* **1** : the general direction between south and west **2** : the compass point midway between south and west **3** *cap* : regions or countries southwest of a specified or implied point — **southwest** *adj or adv* — **south·west·er·ly** *adv or adj* — **south·west·ern** \-ˈwes-tərn\ *adj*

sou·ve·nir \ˌsü-və-ˈnir\ *n* [F] : something serving as a reminder

sou'·west·er \saú-ˈwes-tər\ *n* : a long waterproof coat worn at sea in stormy weather; *also* : a waterproof hat

¹sov·er·eign \ˈsä-vrən, -və-rən\ *n* **1** : one possessing the supreme power and authority in a state **2** : a gold coin of the United Kingdom

²sovereign *adj* **1** : EXCELLENT, FINE **2** : supreme in power or authority **3** : CHIEF, HIGHEST **4** : having independent authority♦ **Synonyms** DOMINANT, PREDOMINANT, PARAMOUNT, PREPONDERANT

sov·er·eign·ty \-tē\ *n, pl* **-ties 1** : supremacy in rule or power **2** : power to govern without external control **3** : the supreme political power in a state

so·vi·et \ˈsō-vē-ˌet, ˈsä-, -ət\ *n* **1** : an elected governmental council in a Communist country **2** *pl, cap* : the people and esp. the leaders of the U.S.S.R. — **soviet** *adj, often cap* — **so·vi·et·ize** *vb, often cap*

¹sow \ˈsaú\ *n* : an adult female swine

²sow \ˈsō\ *vb* **sowed; sown** \ˈsōn\ *or* **sowed; sow·ing 1** : to plant seed for growing esp. by scattering **2** : to strew with seed **3** : to scatter abroad — **sow·er** \ˈsō-ər\ *n*

sow bug \ˈsaú-\ *n* : WOOD LOUSE

sox *pl of* SOCK

soy \ˈsói\ *n* : a sauce made from soybeans fermented in brine

soy·bean \ˈsói-ˌbēn\ *n* : an Asian legume widely grown for forage and for its edible seeds that yield a valuable oil (**soybean oil**); *also* : its seed

sp *abbr* **1** special **2** species **3** specimen **4** spelling **5** spirit

Sp *abbr* Spain

SP *abbr* **1** shore patrol; shore patrolman **2** shore police **3** specialist

spa \ˈspä\ *n* [*Spa*, watering place in Belgium] **1** : a mineral spring; *also* : a resort with mineral springs **2** : a health and fitness facility **3** : a hot tub with a whirlpool device

¹space \ˈspās\ *n* **1** : a period of time **2** : some small measurable distance, area, or volume **3** : the limitless area in which all things exist and move **4** : an empty place **5** : the region beyond the earth's atmosphere **6** : a definite place (as a seat on a train or ship) **7** : the distance from others that a person needs for comfort

²space *vb* **spaced; spac·ing** : to place at intervals — **spac·er** *n*

space·age \ˈspās-ˌāj\ *adj* : of or relating to the age of space exploration

space·craft \-ˌkraft\ *n* : a vehicle for travel beyond the earth's atmosphere

space·flight \-ˌflīt\ *n* : flight beyond the earth's atmosphere

space heater *n* : a usu. portable device for heating a relatively small area

space·man \ˈspās-ˌman, -mən\ *n* : one who travels outside the earth's atmosphere

space out *vb* : to become distracted or inattentive

space·ship \-ˌship\ *n* : a vehicle used for space travel

space shuttle *n* : a reusable spacecraft designed to transport people and cargo between earth and space

space station *n* : a large artificial satellite serving as a base (as for scientific observation)

space suit *n* : a suit equipped to make life in space possible for its wearer

space walk *n* : a period of activity outside a spacecraft by an astronaut in space — **space·walk** \ˈspās-ˌwók\ *vb* — **space·walk·er** *n*

spa·cious \ˈspā-shəs\ *adj* : very large in extent : ROOMY ♦ **Synonyms** COMMODIOUS, CAPACIOUS, AMPLE — **spa·cious·ly** *adv* — **spa·cious·ness** *n*

¹spade \ˈspād\ *n* : a shovel with a blade for digging — **spade·ful** *n*

²spade *vb* **spad·ed; spad·ing** : to dig with a spade — **spad·er** *n*

³spade *n* : any of a suit of playing cards marked with a black figure resembling an inverted heart with a short stem at the bottom

spa·dix \ˈspā-diks\ *n, pl* **spa·di·ces** \ˈspā-də-ˌsēz\ : a floral spike with a fleshy or succulent axis usu. enclosed in a spathe

spa·ghet·ti \spə-ˈge-tē\ *n* [It, fr. pl. of *spaghetto*, dim. of *spago* cord, string] : pasta made in thin solid strings

spam \ˈspam\ *n* : unsolicited usu. commercial e-mail sent to a large number of addresses — **spam** *vb*

¹span \ˈspan\ *n* **1** : an English unit of length equal to nine inches (about 23 centimeters) **2** : a limited portion of time **3** : the spread (as of an arch) from one support to another

²span *vb* **spanned; span·ning 1** : MEASURE **2** : to extend across

³span *n* : a pair of animals (as mules) driven together

Span *abbr* Spanish

span·dex \ˈspan-ˌdeks\ *n* : any of various elastic synthetic textile fibers

span·gle \ˈspaŋ-gəl\ *n* : a small disk of shining metal or plastic used esp. on a dress for ornament — **spangle** *vb*

Span·glish \ˈspaŋ-glish\ *n* : Spanish with many English words included; *also* : a combination of Spanish and English

Span·iard \ˈspan-yərd\ *n* : a native or inhabitant of Spain

span·iel \ˈspan-yəl\ *n* [ME *spaynel, spaniell*, fr. AF *espainnel*, alter. of *espaignol*, Spaniard] : a dog of any of several breeds of mostly small and short-legged dogs usu. with long wavy hair and large drooping ears

Span·ish \ˈspa-nish\ *n* **1** : the chief language of Spain and of the countries colonized by the Spanish **2 Spanish** *pl* : the people of Spain — **Spanish** *adj*

Spanish American *n* : a resident of the U.S. whose native language is Spanish; *also* : a native or inhabitant of one of the countries of America in which Spanish is the national language — **Spanish–American** *adj*

Spanish fly *n* : a toxic preparation of dried green European beetles that causes the skin to blister and is thought to be an aphrodisiac

Spanish moss *n* : a plant related to the pineapple that grows in pendent tufts of grayish green filaments on trees from the southern U.S. to Argentina

Spanish onion *n* : a large mild-flavored onion

spank \ˈspaŋk\ *vb* : to hit on the buttocks with the open hand — **spank** *n*

spank·ing \ˈspaŋ-kiŋ\ *adj* : BRISK, LIVELY ⟨~ breeze⟩ — **spanking** *adv*

¹spar \ˈspär\ *n* : a rounded wood or metal piece (as a mast, yard, boom, or gaff) for supporting sail rigging

²spar *vb* **sparred; spar·ring** : to box for practice without serious hitting; *also* : SKIRMISH, WRANGLE

¹spare \ˈsper\ *vb* **spared; spar·ing 1** : to refrain from punishing or injuring : show mercy to **2** : to exempt from something **3** : to get along without **4** : to use frugally or rarely

²spare *adj* **spar·er; spar·est 1** : held in reserve **2** : SUPERFLUOUS **3** : not liberal or profuse **4** : LEAN, THIN **5** : SCANTY ♦ **Synonyms** MEAGER, SPARSE, SKIMPY, EXIGUOUS, SCANT — **spare·ness** *n*

³spare *n* **1** : a duplicate kept in reserve; *esp* : a spare tire **2** : the knocking down of all the bowling pins with the first two balls

sparing *adj* : SAVING, FRUGAL ♦ **Synonyms** THRIFTY, ECONOMICAL, PROVIDENT — **spar·ing·ly** *adv*

¹spark \ˈspärk\ *n* **1** : a small particle of a burning substance or a hot glowing particle struck from a mass (as by steel on flint) **2** : a short bright flash of electricity between two points **3** : SPARKLE **4** : a particle capable of being kindled or developed : GERM

²spark *vb* **1** : to emit or produce sparks **2** : to stir to activity : INCITE

³spark *vb* : WOO, COURT

¹spar·kle \ˈspär-kəl\ *vb* **spar·kled; spar·kling 1** : FLASH, GLEAM **2** : to perform brilliantly **3** : EFFERVESCE — **spar·kler** *n*

²sparkle *n* **1** : GLEAM **2** : ANIMATION

spark plug *n* : a device that produces a spark to ignite the fuel mixture in an engine cylinder

spark plug

spar·row \'spa-rō\ *n* : any of several small dull-colored singing birds

sparse \'spärs\ *adj* **spars·er; spars·est** : thinly scattered : SCANTY ◆ *Synonyms* MEAGER, SPARE, SKIMPY, EXIGUOUS, SCANT — **sparse·ly** *adv* — **sparse·ness** *n*

¹**Spar·tan** \'spär-tᵊn\ *n* **1** : a native or inhabitant of ancient Sparta **2** : a person of great courage and self-discipline

²**Spartan** *adj* **1** : of or relating to Sparta or Spartans **2** *often not cap* : marked by simplicity, frugality, or avoidance of luxury and comfort ⟨a ∼ room⟩

spasm \'spa-zəm\ *n* **1** : an involuntary and abnormal muscular contraction **2** : a sudden, violent, and temporary effort, emotion, or sensation — **spas·mod·ic** \spaz-'mä-dik\ *adj* — **spas·mod·i·cal·ly** \-di-k(ə-)lē\ *adv*

spas·tic \'spas-tik\ *adj* : of, relating to, marked by, or affected with muscular spasm ⟨∼ paralysis⟩ — **spastic** *n*

¹**spat** \'spat\ *past and past part of* SPIT

²**spat** *n, pl* **spat** *or* **spats** : a young bivalve mollusk (as an oyster)

³**spat** *n* : a gaiter covering instep and ankle

⁴**spat** *n* : a brief petty quarrel : DISPUTE

⁵**spat** *vb* **spat·ted; spat·ting** : to quarrel briefly

spate \'spāt\ *n* : a sudden outburst

spathe \'spāth\ *n* : a sheathing bract or pair of bracts enclosing an inflorescence (as of the calla lily) and esp. a spadix on the same axis

spa·tial \'spā-shəl\ *adj* : of or relating to space or to the facility to perceive objects in space — **spa·tial·ly** *adv*

spat·ter \'spa-tər\ *vb* **1** : to splash with drops of liquid **2** : to sprinkle around — **spatter** *n*

spat·u·la \'spa-chə-lə\ *n* : a flexible knifelike implement for scooping, spreading, or mixing soft substances

spav·in \'spa-vən\ *n* : a bony enlargement of the hock of a horse — **spav·ined** \-vənd\ *adj*

¹**spawn** \'spȯn\ *vb* [ME, fr. AF *espandre* to spread out, shed, scatter, spawn, fr. L *expandere*, fr. *ex-* out + *pandere* to spread] **1** : to produce eggs or offspring esp. in large numbers **2** : GENERATE ⟨∼ed much protest⟩ — **spawn·er** *n*

²**spawn** *n* **1** : the eggs of water animals (as fishes or oysters) that lay many small eggs **2** : offspring esp. when produced in great numbers

spay \'spā\ *vb* **spayed; spay·ing** : to remove the ovaries of (a female animal)

SPCA *abbr* Society for the Prevention of Cruelty to Animals

SPCC *abbr* Society for the Prevention of Cruelty to Children

speak \'spēk\ *vb* **spoke** \'spōk\; **spo·ken** \'spō-kən\; **speak·ing 1** : to utter words **2** : to express orally **3** : to mention in speech or writing **4** : to address an audience **5** : to use or be able to use (a language) in talking — **to speak of** : worthy of mention ⟨no progress *to speak of*⟩

speak·easy \'spēk-ˌē-zē\ *n, pl* **-eas·ies** : an illicit drinking place

speak·er \'spē-kər\ *n* **1** : one that speaks **2** : the presiding officer of a deliberative assembly **3** : LOUDSPEAKER

¹**spear** \'spir\ *n* **1** : a long-shafted weapon with a sharp point for thrusting or throwing **2** : a sharp-pointed instrument with barbs used in spearing fish — **spear·man** \-mən\ *n*

²**spear** *vb* : to strike or pierce with or as if with a spear — **spear·er** *n*

³**spear** *n* : a usu. young blade, shoot, or sprout (as of asparagus)

spear·head \-ˌhed\ *n* : a leading force, element, or influence — **spearhead** *vb*

spear·mint \-ˌmint\ *n* : a common highly aromatic garden mint

¹**spec** *abbr* **1** special **2** specifically

²**spec** \'spek\ *n* : SPECIFICATION 2 — usu. used in pl.

spe·cial \'spe-shəl\ *adj* **1** : UNCOMMON, NOTEWORTHY **2** : particularly favored **3** : INDIVIDUAL, UNIQUE **4** : EXTRA, ADDITIONAL **5** : confined to or designed for a definite field of action, purpose, or occasion — **special** *n*

special delivery *n* : delivery of mail by messenger for an extra fee

special effects *n pl* : visual or sound effects introduced into a motion picture, video recording, or taped television production

Special Forces *n pl* : a branch of the army composed of soldiers specially trained in guerrilla warfare

spe·cial·ise *Brit var of* SPECIALIZE

spe·cial·ist \'spe-shə-list\ *n* **1** : a person who specializes in a particular branch of learning or activity **2** : any of four enlisted ranks in the army corresponding to the grades of corporal through sergeant first class

spe·cial·ize \'spe-shə-ˌlīz\ *vb* **-ized; -iz·ing** : to concentrate one's efforts in a special activity or field; *also* : to change in an adaptive manner — **spe·cial·i·za·tion** \ˌspe-shə-lə-'zā-shən\ *n*

spe·cial·ly \'spe-shə-lē\ *adv* **1** : in a special manner **2** : for a special purpose : in particular

spe·cial·ty \'spe-shəl-tē\ *n, pl* **-ties 1** : a particular quality or detail **2** : a product of a special kind or of special excellence **3** : a skill or discipline in which one specializes

spe·cie \'spē-shē, -shē\ *n* : money in coin

spe·cies \'spē-shēz, -sēz\ *n, pl* **spe·cies** [ME, fr. L, appearance, kind, species, fr. *specere* to look] **1** : SORT, KIND **2** : a category of biological classification ranking just below the genus or subgenus and comprising closely related organisms potentially able to breed with one another

specif *abbr* specific; specifically

¹**spe·cif·ic** \spi-'si-fik\ *adj* **1** : having a unique effect or influence or reacting in only one way or with only one thing ⟨∼ antibodies⟩ ⟨∼ enzymes⟩ **2** : DEFINITE, EXACT ⟨a ∼ agreement⟩ **3** : of, relating to, or constituting a species — **spe·cif·i·cal·ly** \-fi-k(ə-)lē\ *adv* — **spec·i·fic·i·ty** \ˌspe-sə-'fi-sə-tē\ *n*

²**specific** *n* : something specific : DETAIL, PARTICULAR — usu. used in pl.

spec·i·fi·ca·tion \ˌspe-sə-fə-'kā-shən\ *n* **1** : the act or process of specifying **2** : a description of work to be done and materials to be used (as in building) — usu. used in pl.

specific gravity *n* : the ratio of the density of a substance to the density of some substance (as water) taken as a standard when both densities are obtained by weighing in air

spec·i·fy \'spe-sə-ˌfī\ *vb* **-fied; -fy·ing** : to mention or name explicitly

spec·i·men \'spe-sə-mən\ *n* : an item or part typical of a group or whole

spe·cious \'spē-shəs\ *adj* : seeming to be genuine, correct, or beautiful but not really so ⟨∼ reasoning⟩

speck \'spek\ *n* **1** : a small spot or blemish **2** : a small particle — **speck** *vb*

speck·le \'spe-kəl\ *n* : a little speck — **speckle** *vb*

specs \'speks\ *n pl* : GLASSES

spec·ta·cle \'spek-ti-kəl\ *n* **1** : an unusual or impressive public display **2** *pl* : GLASSES — **spec·ta·cled** \-kəld\ *adj*

spec·tac·u·lar \spek-'ta-kyə-lər\ *adj* : exciting to see : SENSATIONAL

spec·ta·tor \'spek-ˌtā-tər\ *n* : a person who looks on (as at a sports event) ◆ *Synonyms* OBSERVER, WITNESS, BYSTANDER, ONLOOKER, EYEWITNESS

spec·ter *or* **spec·tre** \'spek-tər\ *n* : a visible disembodied spirit : GHOST

spec·tral \'spek-trəl\ *adj* **1** : of, relating to, or resembling a specter **2** : of, relating to, or made by a spectrum

spec·tro·gram \'spek-trə-ˌgram\ *n* : a photograph, image, or diagram of a spectrum

spec·tro·graph \-ˌgraf\ *n* : an instrument for dispersing radiation into a spectrum and recording or mapping the spectrum — **spec·tro·graph·ic** \ˌspek-trə-'gra-fik\ *adj* — **spec·tro·graph·i·cal·ly** \-fi-k(ə-)lē\ *adv*

spec·trom·e·ter \spek-'trä-mə-tər\ *n* : an instrument for measuring spectra — **spec·tro·met·ric** \ˌspek-trə-'me-trik\ *adj* — **spec·trom·e·try** \spek-'trä-mə-trē\ *n*

spec·tro·scope \'spek-trə-ˌskōp\ *n* : an instrument that produces spectra esp. of visible electromagnetic radiation — **spec·tro·scop·ic** \ˌspek-trə-'skä-pik\ *adj* — **spec·tro·scop·i·cal·ly** \-pi-k(ə-)lē\ *adv* — **spec·tros·co·pist** \spek-'trä-skə-pist\ *n* — **spec·tros·co·py** \-pē\ *n*

spec·trum \'spek-trəm\ *n, pl* **spec·tra** \-trə\ *or* **spectrums** [NL, fr. L, appearance, fr. *specere* to look] **1** : a series of colors formed when a beam of white light is dispersed (as by a prism) so that its parts are arranged in the order of their wavelengths **2** : a series of radiations arranged in regular order **3** : a continuous sequence or range ⟨a wide ∼ of political opinions⟩

spec·u·late \'spe-kyə-ˌlāt\ *vb* **-lat·ed; -lat·ing** [L *speculari* to spy out, examine, fr. *specula* lookout post, fr. *specere* to look, look at] **1** : to think or wonder about a subject **2** : to take a business risk in hope of gain ✦ *Synonyms* REASON, THINK, DELIBERATE, COGITATE — **spec·u·la·tion** \ˌspe-kyə-'lā-shən\ *n* — **spec·u·la·tive** \'spe-kyə-ˌlā-tiv\ *adj* — **spec·u·la·tive·ly** *adv* — **spec·u·la·tor** \-ˌlā-tər\ *n*

speech \'spēch\ *n* **1** : the act of speaking **2** : TALK, CONVERSATION **3** : a public talk or lecture **4** : LANGUAGE, DIALECT **5** : an individual manner of speaking **6** : the power of speaking — **speech·less** *adj*

¹**speed** \'spēd\ *n* **1** *archaic* : SUCCESS **2** : SWIFTNESS, RAPIDITY **3** : rate of motion or performance **4** : a transmission gear (as of a bicycle) **5** : METHAMPHETAMINE; *also* : a related drug ✦ *Synonyms* HASTE, HURRY, DISPATCH, CELERITY — **speed·i·ly** \'spē-də-lē\ *adv* — **speedy** *adj*

²**speed** *vb* **sped** \'spēd\ *or* **speed·ed; speed·ing 1** *archaic* : PROSPER; *also* : GET ALONG, FARE **2** : to go fast; *esp* : to go at an excessive or illegal speed **3** : to cause to go faster — **speed·er** *n*

speed·boat \-ˌbōt\ *n* : a fast motorboat

speed bump *n* : a low raised ridge across a roadway (as in a parking lot) to limit vehicle speed

speed of light : a fundamental physical constant that is the speed of electromagnetic radiation propagation in a vacuum and has the value of 299,792,458 meters per second

speed·om·e·ter \spi-'dä-mə-tər\ *n* : an instrument for indicating speed

speed·up \'spēd-ˌəp\ *n* : ACCELERATION

speed·way \-ˌwā\ *n* : a racecourse for motor vehicles

speed·well \'spēd-ˌwel\ *n* : VERONICA

¹**spell** \'spel\ *vb* **spelled** \'speld, 'spelt\; **spell·ing** [ME, to signify, read by spelling out, fr. AF *espeleir*, of Gmc origin] **1** : to name, write, or print in order the letters of a word **2** : MEAN ⟨another drought may ∼ famine⟩

²**spell** *n* [ME, talk, tale, fr. OE] **1** : a magic formula : INCANTATION **2** : a controlling influence

³**spell** *n* **1** : one's turn at work or duty **2** : a stretch of a specified kind of weather **3** : a period of bodily or mental distress or disorder : ATTACK

⁴**spell** *vb* **spelled** \'speld\; **spell·ing** : to take the place of for a time in work or duty : RELIEVE

spell·bind·er \-ˌbīn-dər\ *n* : a speaker of compelling eloquence; *also* : one that compels attention

spell·bound \-ˌbaùnd\ *adj* : held by or as if by a spell : FASCINATED

spell–check·er \'spel-ˌche-kər\ *n* : a computer program that identifies possible misspellings in a block of text — **spell–check** \-ˌchek\ *vb*

spell·er \'spe-lər\ *n* **1** : one who spells words **2** : a book with exercises for teaching spelling

spelt \'spelt\ *chiefly Brit past and past part of* ¹SPELL

spe·lunk·er \spi-'ləŋ-kər, 'spē-ˌləŋ-kər\ *n* [L *spelunca* cave, fr. Gk *spēlynx*] : one who makes a hobby of exploring caves — **spe·lunk·ing** *n*

spend \'spend\ *vb* **spent** \'spent\; **spend·ing 1** : to pay out : EXPEND **2** : WEAR OUT, EXHAUST; *also* : to consume wastefully **3** : to cause or permit to elapse : PASS — **spend·er** *n*

spend·thrift \'spend-ˌthrift\ *n* : one who spends wastefully or recklessly

spent \'spent\ *adj* : drained of energy

sperm \'spərm\ *n, pl* **sperm** *or* **sperms 1** : SEMEN **2** : a male gamete

sper·ma·to·zo·on \(ˌ)spər-ˌma-tə-'zō-ˌän, -'zō-ən\ *n, pl* **-zoa** \-'zō-ə\ : a motile male gamete of an animal usu. with a rounded or elongated head and a long posterior flagellum

sperm cell *n* : SPERM 2

sper·mi·cide \'spər-mə-ˌsīd\ *n* : a preparation or substance used to kill sperm — **sper·mi·cid·al** \ˌspər-mə-'sī-dəl\ *adj*

sperm whale *n* : a large whale with a massive square-shaped head containing a fluid-filled cavity

spew \'spyü\ *vb* : VOMIT

SPF *abbr* sun protection factor

sp gr *abbr* specific gravity

sphag·num \'sfag-nəm\ *n* : any of a genus of atypical mosses that grow in wet acid areas where their remains become compacted with other plant debris to form peat; *also* : a mass of these mosses

sphere \'sfir\ *n* [ME *spere* globe, celestial sphere, fr. AF *espere*, fr. L *sphaera*, fr. Gk *sphaira*, lit., ball] **1** : a globe-shaped body : BALL **2** : a celestial body **3** : a solid figure so shaped that every point on its surface is an equal distance from the center **4** : range of action or influence — **spher·i·cal** \'sfir-i-kəl, 'sfer-\ *adj* — **spher·i·cal·ly** \-i-k(ə-)lē\ *adv*

spher·oid \'sfir-ˌòid, 'sfer-\ *n* : a figure similar to a sphere but not perfectly round — **sphe·roi·dal** \sfir-'òi-dəl\ *adj*

sphinc·ter \'sfiŋk-tər\ *n* : a muscular ring that closes a bodily opening

sphinx \'sfiŋks\ *n, pl* **sphinx·es** *or* **sphin·ges** \'sfin-jēz\ **1** : a winged monster in Greek mythology having a woman's head and a lion's body and noted for killing anyone unable to answer its riddle **2** : an enigmatic or mysterious person **3** : an ancient Egyptian image having the body of a lion and the head of a man, ram, or hawk

spice \'spīs\ *n* **1** : any of various aromatic plant products (as pepper or nutmeg) used to season or flavor foods **2** : something that adds interest and relish — **spice** *vb* — **spicy** *adj*

spick–and–span *or* **spic–and–span** \ˌspik-ənd-'span\ *adj* : quite new; *also* : spotlessly clean

spic·ule \'spi-kyül\ *n* : a slender pointed body esp. of calcium or silica ⟨sponge ∼s⟩

spi·der \'spī-dər\ *n* **1** : any of an order of arachnids that have a 2-part body, eight legs, and two or more pairs of abdominal organs for spinning threads of silk used esp. in making webs for catching prey **2** : a cast-iron frying pan — **spi·dery** *adj*

spider mite *n* : any of various small web-spinning mites that feed on and are pests of plants

spider plant *n* : a houseplant of the lily family having long green leaves usu. striped with white and producing tufts of small plants on long hanging stems

spi·der·web \'spī-dər-ˌweb\ *n* : the web spun by a spider

spiel \'spēl\ *vb* : to talk in a fast, smooth, and usu. colorful manner — **spiel** *n*

spig·ot \'spi-gət, -kət\ *n* : FAUCET

¹**spike** \'spīk\ *n* **1** : a very large nail **2** : any of various pointed projections (as on the sole of a shoe to prevent slipping) — **spiky** *adj*

²**spike** *vb* **spiked; spik·ing 1** : to fasten with spikes **2** : to put an end to : QUASH ⟨∼ a rumor⟩ **3** : to pierce with or impale on a spike **4** : to add alcoholic liquor to (a drink)

³**spike** *n* **1** : an ear of grain **2** : a long cluster of usu. stemless flowers

¹**spill** \'spil\ *vb* **spilled** \'spild, 'spilt\ *also* **spilt** \'spilt\; **spill·ing 1** : to cause or allow to fall, flow, or run out esp. unintentionally **2** : to cause (blood) to be lost by wounding **3** : to run out or over with resulting loss or waste **4** : to let out : DIVULGE — **spill·able** *adj*

²**spill** *n* **1** : an act of spilling; *also* : a fall from a horse or vehicle or an erect position **2** : something spilled

spill·way \-ˌwā\ *n* : a passage for surplus water to run over or around an obstruction (as a dam)

¹**spin** \'spin\ *vb* **spun** \'spən\; **spin·ning 1** : to draw out (fiber) and twist into thread; *also* : to form (thread) by such means **2** : to form thread by extruding a sticky quickly hardening fluid; *also* : to construct from such thread ⟨spiders ∼ their webs⟩ **3** : to produce slowly and by degrees ⟨∼ a story⟩ **4** : TWIRL **5** : WHIRL, REEL ⟨my head is *spinning*⟩ **6** : to move rapidly along **7** : to present (as information) with a particular spin — **spin·ner** *n*

²**spin** *n* **1** : a rapid rotating motion **2** : an excursion in a wheeled vehicle **3** : a particular point of view, emphasis, or interpretation

spi·na bi·fi·da \ˌspī-nə-'bi-fə-də\ *n* : a birth defect in which the spinal column has a fissure

sperm whale

spin·ach \'spi-nich\ *n* : a dark green herb grown for its edible leaves

spi·nal \'spī-n°l\ *adj* : of or relating to the backbone or spinal cord — **spi·nal·ly** *adv*

spinal column *n* : BACKBONE 1

spinal cord *n* : the thick cord of nervous tissue that extends from the brain along the back in the cavity of the backbone and carries nerve impulses to and from the brain

spinal nerve *n* : any of the paired nerves which arise from the spinal cord and pass to various parts of the body and of which there are normally 31 pairs in human beings

spin control *n* : the act or practice of attempting to manipulate the way an event is interpreted

spin·dle \'spin-d°l\ *n* 1 : a round tapering stick or rod by which fibers are twisted in spinning 2 : a turned part of a piece of furniture ⟨the ∼s of a chair⟩ 3 : a slender pin or rod which turns or on which something else turns

spin·dling \'spind-liŋ\ *adj* : SPINDLY

spin·dly \'spind-lē\ *adj* : being long or tall and thin and usu. weak

spin·drift \'spin-ˌdrift\ *n* : spray blown from waves

spine \'spīn\ *n* 1 : BACKBONE 2 : a stiff sharp process esp. on a plant or animal 3 : the part of a book where the pages are attached — **spiny** *adj*

spi·nel \spə-'nel\ *n* : a hard crystalline mineral of variable color used as a gem

spine·less \'spīn-ləs\ *adj* 1 : having no spines, thorns, or prickles 2 : lacking a backbone 3 : lacking courage or determination

spin·et \'spin-nət\ *n* 1 : an early harpsichord having a single keyboard and only one string for each note 2 : a small upright piano

spin·na·ker \'spi-ni-kər\ *n* : a large triangular sail set on a long light pole

spinning jen·ny \-'je-nē\ *n* : an early multiple-spindle machine for spinning wool or cotton

spinning wheel *n* : a small machine for spinning thread or yarn in which a large wheel drives a single spindle

spin-off \'spin-ˌȯf\ *n* 1 : a usu. useful by-product 2 : something (as a TV show) derived from an earlier work — **spin off** *vb*

spin·ster \'spin-stər\ *n* : an unmarried woman past the common age for marrying — **spin·ster·hood** \-ˌhu̇d\ *n*

spiny lobster *n* : any of several edible crustaceans differing from the related lobsters in lacking the large front claws and in having a spiny carapace

¹**spi·ral** \'spī-rəl\ *adj* : winding or coiling around a center or axis and usu. getting closer to or farther away from it — **spi·ral·ly** *adv*

²**spiral** *n* 1 : something that has a spiral form; *also* : a single turn in a spiral object 2 : a continuously spreading and accelerating increase or decrease

³**spiral** *vb* **-raled** *or* **-ralled; -ral·ing** *or* **-ral·ling** 1 : to move and esp. to rise or fall in a spiral course 2 : to form into a spiral

spi·rant \'spī-rənt\ *n* : a consonant (as \f\, \s\, \sh\) uttered with decided friction of the breath against some part of the oral passage — **spirant** *adj*

spire \'spī(-ə)r\ *n* 1 : a slender tapering stalk (as of grass) 2 : a pointed tip (as of an antler) 3 : STEEPLE — **spiry** *adj*

spi·rea *or* **spi·raea** \spī-'rē-ə\ *n* : any of a genus of shrubs related to the roses with dense clusters of small usu. white or pink flowers

¹**spir·it** \'spir-ət\ *n* [ME, fr. AF or L; AF, fr. L *spiritus*, lit., breath, fr. *spirare* to blow, breathe] 1 : a life-giving force; *also* : the animating principle : SOUL 2 *cap* : HOLY SPIRIT 3 : SPECTER, GHOST 4 : PERSON ⟨a bold ∼⟩ 5 : DISPOSITION, MOOD ⟨in good ∼s⟩ 6 : VIVACITY, ARDOR 7 : essential or real meaning : INTENT 8 : distilled alcoholic liquor 9 : LOYALTY ⟨school ∼⟩ — **spir·it·less** *adj*

²**spirit** *vb* : to carry off secretly or mysteriously

spir·it·ed \'spir-ə-təd\ *adj* : full of energy, animation, or courage

¹**spir·i·tu·al** \'spir-i-chəl, -chə-wəl\ *adj* 1 : of, relating to, consisting of, or affecting the spirit : INCORPOREAL 2 : of or relating to sacred matters 3 : ecclesiastical rather than lay or temporal — **spir·i·tu·al·i·ty** \ˌspir-i-chə-'wa-lə-tē\ *n* — **spir·i·tu·al·ize** \'spir-i-chə-ˌlīz, -chə-wə-\ *vb* — **spir·i·tu·al·ly** *adv*

²**spiritual** *n* : a religious song originating among blacks of the southern U.S.

spir·i·tu·al·ism \'spir-i-chə-ˌli-zəm, -chə-wə-\ *n* : a belief that spirits of the dead communicate with the living usu. through a medium — **spir·i·tu·al·ist** \-list\ *n, often cap* — **spir·i·tu·al·is·tic** \ˌspir-i-chə-'lis-tik, -chə-wə-\ *adj*

spir·i·tu·ous \'spir-i-chəs, -chə-wəs; 'spir-ə-təs\ *adj* : containing alcohol

spi·ro·chete *also* **spi·ro·chaete** \'spī-rə-ˌkēt\ *n* : any of an order of spirally undulating bacteria including those causing syphilis and Lyme disease

spirt *var of* SPURT

¹**spit** \'spit\ *n* 1 : a thin pointed rod for holding meat over a fire 2 : a point of land that runs out into the water

²**spit** *vb* **spit·ted; spit·ting** : to pierce with or as if with a spit

³**spit** *vb* **spit** *or* **spat** \'spat\; **spit·ting** 1 : to eject (saliva) from the mouth 2 : to express by or as if by spitting 3 : to rain or snow lightly

⁴**spit** *n* 1 : SALIVA 2 : perfect likeness ⟨∼ and image of his father⟩

spit·ball \'spit-ˌbȯl\ *n* 1 : paper chewed and rolled into a ball to be thrown as a missile 2 : a baseball pitch delivered after the ball has been moistened with saliva or sweat

¹**spite** \'spīt\ *n* : ill will with a wish to annoy, anger, or frustrate : petty malice ◆ *Synonyms* MALIGNITY, SPLEEN, GRUDGE, MALEVOLENCE — **spite·ful** \-fəl\ *adj* — **spite·ful·ly** *adv* — **spite·ful·ness** *n* — **in spite of** : in defiance or contempt of : NOTWITHSTANDING

²**spite** *vb* **spit·ed; spit·ing** : to treat maliciously : ANNOY, OFFEND

spit·tle \'spi-t°l\ *n* : SALIVA

spit·tle·bug \-ˌbəg\ *n* : any of a family of leaping insects with froth-secreting larvae that are related to aphids

spit·toon \spi-'tün\ *n* : a receptacle for spit

splash \'splash\ *vb* 1 : to dash a liquid about 2 : to scatter a liquid on : SPATTER 3 : to fall or strike with a splashing noise ◆ *Synonyms* SPRINKLE, BESPATTER, DOUSE, SPLATTER — **splash** *n*

splash·down \'splash-ˌdau̇n\ *n* : the landing of a manned spacecraft in the ocean — **splash down** *vb*

splashy \'spla-shē\ *adj* **splash·i·er; -est** : conspicuously showy : OSTENTATIOUS

¹**splat·ter** \'spla-tər\ *vb* : SPATTER — **splatter** *n*

²**splatter** *adj* : extremely gory or violent ⟨a ∼ movie⟩

¹**splay** \'splā\ *vb* : to spread outward or apart — **splay** *n*

²**splay** *adj* 1 : spread out : turned outward 2 : AWKWARD, CLUMSY

spleen \'splēn\ *n* 1 : a vascular organ located near the stomach in most vertebrates that is concerned esp. with the filtration and storage of blood, destruction of red blood cells, and production of lymphocytes 2 : SPITE, MALICE ◆ *Synonyms* MALIGNITY, GRUDGE, MALEVOLENCE, ILL WILL, SPITEFULNESS

splen·did \'splen-dəd\ *adj* [L *splendidus*, fr. *splendēre* to shine] 1 : SHINING, BRILLIANT 2 : SHOWY, GORGEOUS 3 : ILLUSTRIOUS 4 : EXCELLENT ⟨a ∼ opportunity⟩ ◆ *Synonyms* RESPLENDENT, GLORIOUS, SUBLIME, SUPERB — **splen·did·ly** *adv*

splen·dor \'splen-dər\ *n* 1 : BRILLIANCE ⟨the ∼ of the sun⟩ 2 : POMP, MAGNIFICENCE

splen·dour \'splen-dər\ *chiefly Brit var of* SPLENDOR

sple·net·ic \spli-'ne-tik\ *adj* : marked by bad temper or spite

splen·ic \'sple-nik\ *adj* : of, relating to, or located in the spleen

splice \'splīs\ *vb* **spliced; splic·ing** 1 : to unite (as two ropes) by weaving the strands together 2 : to unite (as two lengths of film) by connecting the ends together — **splice** *n*

splint \'splint\ *n* 1 : a thin strip of wood interwoven with others to make something (as a basket) 2 : material or a device used to protect and keep in place an injured body part (as a broken arm)

¹**splin·ter** \'splin-tər\ *n* : a thin piece of something split off lengthwise : SLIVER

²**splinter** *vb* : to split into splinters

split \'split\ *vb* **split; split·ting** 1 : to divide lengthwise or along a grain or seam 2 : to burst or break in pieces 3 : to divide into parts or sections 4 : LEAVE ⟨∼ the party⟩ ◆ *Synonyms* REND, CLEAVE, RIP, TEAR — **split** *n*

split-lev·el \'split-'le-vəl\ *n* : a house divided so that the floor in one part is about halfway between two floors in the other

split personality *n* : SCHIZOPHRENIA; *also* : MULTIPLE PERSONALITY DISORDER

split–second \'split-'se-kənd\ *adj* 1 : occurring in a very brief time 2 : extremely precise ⟨∼ timing⟩

split·ting *adj* : causing a piercing sensation ⟨a ∼ headache⟩

splotch \'spläch\ *n* : BLOTCH

splurge \'splərj\ *vb* **splurged; splurg·ing** : to spend more than usual esp. on oneself — **splurge** *n*

splut·ter \'splə-tər\ *n* : SPUTTER — **splutter** *vb*

¹spoil \'spȯi(-ə)l\ *n* : PLUNDER ⟨∼s of war⟩

²spoil *vb* **spoiled** \'spȯi(-ə)ld, 'spȯi(-ə)lt\ *or* **spoilt** \'spȯi(-ə)lt\; **spoil·ing** 1 : ROB, PILLAGE 2 : to damage seriously : RUIN 3 : to impair the quality or effect of 4 : to damage the disposition of by pampering; *also* : INDULGE, CODDLE 5 : DECAY, ROT 6 : to have an eager desire ⟨∼ing for a fight⟩ ◆ **Synonyms** INJURE, HARM, HURT, MAR — **spoil·age** \'spȯi-lij\ *n*

spoil·er \'spȯi-lər\ *n* 1 : one that spoils 2 : a device (as on an airplane or automobile) used to disrupt airflow and decrease lift

spoil·sport \'spȯi(-ə)l-ˌspȯrt\ *n* : one who spoils the fun of others

¹spoke \'spōk\ *past & archaic past part of* SPEAK

²spoke *n* : any of the rods extending from the hub of a wheel to the rim

spo·ken \'spō-kən\ *past part of* SPEAK

spokes·man \'spōks-mən\ *n* : a person who speaks as the representative of another or others

spokes·mod·el \-ˌmä-d³l\ *n* : a model who is a spokesman or spokeswoman

spokes·per·son \-ˌpər-sən\ *n* : SPOKESMAN

spokes·wom·an \-ˌwu̇-mən\ *n* : a woman who speaks as the representative of another or others

spo·li·a·tion \ˌspō-lē-'ā-shən\ *n* : the act of plundering : the state of being plundered

¹sponge \'spənj\ *n* 1 : an elastic porous water-absorbing mass of fibers that forms the skeleton of various primitive sea animals; *also* : any of a phylum of chiefly marine sea animals that are the source of natural sponges 2 : a spongelike or porous mass or material — **spongy** \'spən-jē\ *adj*

²sponge *vb* **sponged; spong·ing** 1 : to bathe or wipe with a sponge 2 : to live at another's expense 3 : to gather sponges — **spong·er** *n*

sponge cake *n* : a light cake made without shortening

sponge rubber *n* : a cellular rubber resembling natural sponge

spon·sor \'spän-sər\ *n* [LL, fr. L, guarantor, surety, fr. *spondēre* to promise] 1 : one who takes the responsibility for some other person or thing : SURETY 2 : GODPARENT 3 : a business firm that pays the cost of a radio or television program usu. in return for advertising time during its course — **sponsor** *vb* — **spon·sor·ship** *n*

spon·ta·ne·ous \spän-'tā-nē-əs\ *adj* [LL *spontaneus*, fr. L *sponte* of one's free will, voluntarily] 1 : done or produced freely or naturally 2 : acting or taking place without external force or cause ◆ **Synonyms** IMPULSIVE, INSTINCTIVE, AUTOMATIC, UNPREMEDITATED — **spon·ta·ne·ity** \ˌspän-tə-'nē-ə-tē, -'nā-\ *n* — **spon·ta·ne·ous·ly** *adv*

spontaneous combustion *n* : a bursting into flame of material through heat produced within itself by chemical action (as oxidation)

spoof \'spüf\ *vb* 1 : DECEIVE, HOAX 2 : to make good-naturedly fun of — **spoof** *n*

¹spook \'spük\ *n* 1 : GHOST, APPARITION 2 : SPY 2 — **spooky** *adj*

²spook *vb* : FRIGHTEN

¹spool \'spül\ *n* : a cylinder on which flexible material (as thread) is wound

²spool *vb* 1 : to wind on a spool 2 : to regulate data flow by means of a spooler

spool·er \'spü-lər\ *n* : a computer program or routine for regulating data flow

spoon \'spün\ *n* [ME, fr. OE *spōn* splinter, chip] 1 : an eating or cooking implement consisting of a small shallow bowl with a handle 2 : a metal piece used on a fishing line as a lure — **spoon** *vb* — **spoon·ful** *n*

spoon·bill \'spün-ˌbil\ *n* : any of several wading birds related to the ibises that have a bill with a broad flat tip

spoon–feed \-ˌfēd\ *vb* **-fed** \-ˌfed\; **-feed·ing** : to feed by means of a spoon

spoor \'spu̇r, 'spȯr\ *n, pl* **spoor** *or* **spoors** : a track, a trail, a scent, or droppings esp. of a wild animal

spo·rad·ic \spə-'ra-dik\ *adj* : occurring now and then ⟨∼ outbreaks of disease⟩ ◆ **Synonyms** OCCASIONAL, RARE, SCARCE, INFREQUENT, UNCOMMON — **spo·rad·i·cal·ly** \-di-k(ə-)lē\ *adv*

spore \'spȯr\ *n* : a primitive usu. one-celled often environmentally resistant dormant or reproductive body produced by plants, fungi, and some microorganisms

¹sport \'spȯrt\ *vb* [ME, to divert, amuse, short for *disporten*, fr. AF *desporter*, to carry away, comfort, entertain, fr. *des-* (fr. L *dis-* apart) + *porter* to carry, fr. L *portare*] 1 : to amuse oneself : FROLIC 2 : SHOW OFF 1 ⟨∼ing new shoes⟩ — **sport·ive** *adj*

²sport *n* 1 : a source of diversion : PASTIME 2 : physical activity engaged in for pleasure 3 : JEST 4 : MOCKERY ⟨make ∼ of his efforts⟩ 5 : BUTT, LAUGHINGSTOCK 6 : one who accepts results cheerfully whether favorable or not 7 : an individual exhibiting marked deviation from its normal type esp. as a result of mutation ◆ **Synonyms** PLAY, FROLIC, FUN, RECREATION — **sporty** *adj*

³sport *or* **sports** *adj* : of, relating to, or suitable for sport or casual wear ⟨∼ coats⟩

sport fish *n* : a fish noted for the sport it affords anglers

sports·cast \'spȯrts-ˌkast\ *n* : a broadcast dealing with sports events — **sports·cast·er** \-ˌkas-tər\ *n*

sports·man \'spȯrts-mən\ *n* 1 : a person who engages in sports (as in hunting or fishing) 2 : one who plays fairly and wins or loses gracefully — **sports·man·like** \-ˌlīk\ *adj* — **sports·man·ship** *n*

sports medicine *n* : a field of medicine dealing with the prevention and treatment of sports-related injuries

sports·wom·an \-ˌwu̇-mən\ *n* : a woman who engages in sports

sports·writ·er \-ˌrī-tər\ *n* : one who writes about sports esp. for a newspaper — **sports·writ·ing** *n*

sport–utility vehicle \'spȯrt-yü-'ti-lə-tē-\ *n* : SUV

¹spot \'spät\ *n* 1 : STAIN, BLEMISH 2 : a small part different (as in color) from the main part 3 : LOCATION, SITE — **spot·less** *adj* — **spot·less·ly** *adv* — **on the spot** 1 : at the place of action 2 : in difficulty or danger

²spot *vb* **spot·ted; spot·ting** 1 : to mark or disfigure with spots 2 : to pick out : RECOGNIZE, IDENTIFY

³spot *adj* 1 : being, done, or originating on the spot ⟨a ∼ broadcast⟩ 2 : paid upon delivery 3 : made at random or at a few key points ⟨a ∼ check⟩

spot–check \'spät-ˌchek\ *vb* : to make a spot check of

spot·light \-ˌlīt\ *n* 1 : a circle of brilliant light projected upon a particular area, person, or object (as on a stage); *also* : the device that produces this light 2 : public notice — **spotlight** *vb*

spot–on \'spät-'än\ *adj* : exactly correct ⟨a ∼ forecast⟩

spotted owl *n* : a rare large dark brown dark-eyed owl of humid old growth forests and thickly wooded canyons from British Columbia to southern California and central Mexico

spot·ter \'spä-tər\ *n* 1 : one that keeps watch : OBSERVER 2 : one that removes spots

spot·ty \'spä-tē\ *adj* **spot·ti·er; -est** : uneven in quality; *also* : sparsely distributed ⟨∼ attendance⟩

spou·sal \'spau̇-zəl, -səl\ *n* : MARRIAGE 2, WEDDING — usu. used in pl.

spouse \'spau̇s\ *n* : one's husband or wife — **spou·sal** \'spau̇-zəl, -səl\ *adj*

¹spout \'spau̇t\ *vb* 1 : to eject or issue forth forcibly and freely ⟨wells ∼ing oil⟩ 2 : to speak pompously

²spout *n* 1 : a pipe or hole through which liquid spouts 2 : a jet of liquid; *esp* : WATERSPOUT 2

spp *abbr, pl* species

¹sprain \'sprān\ *n* : a sudden or severe twisting of a joint with stretching or tearing of ligaments; *also* : a sprained condition

²sprain *vb* : to subject to sprain

sprat \'sprat\ *n* 1 : a small European fish related to the herring; *also* : SARDINE

sprawl \'sprȯl\ *vb* 1 : to lie or sit with limbs spread out awkwardly 2 : to spread out irregularly — **sprawl** *n*

¹**spray** \'sprā\ *n* : a usu. flowering branch; *also* : a decorative arrangement of flowers and foliage

²**spray** *n* **1** : liquid flying in small drops like water blown from a wave **2** : a jet of fine vapor (as from an atomizer) **3** : an instrument (as an atomizer) for scattering fine liquid

³**spray** *vb* **1** : to discharge spray on or into **2** : to scatter or let fall in a spray — **spray·er** *n*

spray can *n* : a pressurized container from which aerosols are sprayed

spray gun *n* : a device for spraying liquids (as paint or insecticide)

¹**spread** \'spred\ *vb* **spread**; **spread·ing 1** : to scatter over a surface **2** : to flatten out : open out **3** : to distribute over a period of time or among many persons **4** : to cover something with ⟨~ rugs on the floor⟩ **5** : to prepare for a meal ⟨~ a table⟩ **6** : to pass on from person to person **7** : to stretch, force, or push apart — **spread·er** *n*

²**spread** *n* **1** : the act or process of spreading **2** : EXPANSE, EXTENT **3** : a prominent display in a periodical **4** : a food to be spread on bread or crackers **5** : a cloth cover for a bed **6** : distance between two points : GAP

spread·sheet \'spred-,shēt\ *n* : an accounting program for a computer

spree \'sprē\ *n* : an unrestrained outburst ⟨buying ~⟩; *also* : a drinking bout

sprig \'sprig\ *n* : a small shoot or twig

spright·ly \'sprīt-lē\ *adj* **spright·li·er; -est** : LIVELY, SPIRITED ⟨a ~ musical⟩ ✦ *Synonyms* ANIMATED, VIVACIOUS, GAY — **spright·li·ness** *n*

¹**spring** \'spriŋ\ *vb* **sprang** \'spraŋ\ *or* **sprung** \'sprəŋ\; **sprung; spring·ing 1** : to move suddenly upward or forward **2** : to grow quickly ⟨weeds *sprang* up overnight⟩ **3** : to come from by birth or descent **4** : to move quickly by elastic force **5** : WARP **6** : to develop (a leak) through the seams **7** : to cause to close suddenly ⟨~ a trap⟩ **8** : to make known suddenly ⟨~ a surprise⟩ **9** : to make lame : STRAIN

²**spring** *n* **1** : a source of supply; *esp* : an issuing of water from the ground **2** : SOURCE, ORIGIN; *also* : MOTIVE **3** : the season between winter and summer **4** : an elastic body or device that recovers its original shape when it is released after being distorted **5** : the act or an instance of leaping up or forward **6** : RESILIENCE — **springy** *adj*

spring·board \'spriŋ-,bȯrd\ *n* : a springy board used in jumping or vaulting or for diving

spring fever *n* : a lazy or restless feeling often associated with the onset of spring

spring tide *n* : a tide of greater-than-average range that occurs at each new moon and full moon

spring·time \'spriŋ-,tīm\ *n* : the season of spring

¹**sprin·kle** \'spriŋ-kəl\ *vb* **sprin·kled; sprin·kling** : to scatter in small drops or particles — **sprin·kler** *n*

²**sprinkle** *n* : a light rainfall

sprin·kling *n* : SMATTERING

¹**sprint** \'sprint\ *vb* : to run at top speed esp. for a short distance — **sprint·er** *n*

²**sprint** *n* **1** : a short run at top speed **2** : a short-distance race

sprite \'sprīt\ *n* **1** : GHOST, SPIRIT **2** : ELF, FAIRY

spritz *vb* : to make a spray

sprock·et \'sprä-kət\ *n* : a toothed wheel whose teeth engage the links of a chain

sprocket

¹**sprout** \'spraút\ *vb* : to send out new growth ⟨~*ing* seeds⟩

²**sprout** *n* : a usu. young and growing plant shoot (as from a seed)

¹**spruce** \'sprüs\ *vb* **spruced; spruc·ing** : to make or become spruce

²**spruce** *adj* **spruc·er; spruc·est** : neat and smart in appearance ✦ *Synonyms* STYLISH, FASHIONABLE, MODISH, DAPPER, NATTY

³**spruce** *n, pl* **spruc·es** *also* **spruce** : any of a genus of evergreen pyramid-shaped trees related to the pines and having soft light wood; *also* : the wood of a spruce

sprung *past and past part of* SPRING

spry \'sprī\ *adj* **spri·er** *or* **spry·er** \'sprī-ər\; **spri·est** *or* **spry·est** \'sprī-əst\ : NIMBLE, ACTIVE ⟨a ~ 75-year-old⟩ ✦ *Synonyms* AGILE, BRISK, LIVELY, SPRIGHTLY

spud \'spəd\ *n* **1** : a sharp narrow spade **2** : POTATO

spume \'spyüm\ *n* : frothy matter on liquids : FOAM — **spumy** \'spyü-mē\ *adj*

spu·mo·ni *also* **spu·mo·ne** \spù-'mō-nē\ *n* [It *spumone*, fr. *spuma* foam] : ice cream in layers of different colors, flavors, and textures often with candied fruits and nuts

spun *past and past part of* SPIN

spun glass *n* : FIBERGLASS

spunk \'spəŋk\ *n* [fr. *spunk* tinder, fr. ScGael *spong* sponge, tinder, fr. Middle Irish *spongc*, fr. L *spongia* sponge] : PLUCK, COURAGE — **spunky** *adj*

¹**spur** \'spər\ *n* **1** : a pointed device fastened to a rider's boot and used to urge on a horse **2** : something that urges to action **3** : a stiff sharp spine (as on the leg of a cock); *also* : a hollow projecting appendage of a flower (as a columbine) **4** : a ridge extending sideways from a mountain **5** : a branch of railroad track extending from the main line ✦ *Synonyms* GOAD, MOTIVE, IMPULSE, INCENTIVE, INDUCEMENT — **spurred** \'spərd\ *adj* — **on the spur of the moment** : on hasty impulse

²**spur** *vb* **spurred; spur·ring 1** : to urge a horse on with spurs **2** : INCITE

spurge \'spərj\ *n* : any of a family of herbs and woody plants with a bitter milky juice

spu·ri·ous \'spyúr-ē-əs\ *adj* [LL *spurius* false, fr. L, *spurius*, n., son of an unknown father] : not genuine : FALSE ⟨~ eminence⟩

spurn \'spərn\ *vb* **1** : to kick away or trample on **2** : to reject with disdain

¹**spurt** \'spərt\ *vb* : to gush out : SPOUT

²**spurt** *n* : a sudden gushing or spouting

³**spurt** *n* **1** : a sudden brief burst of effort, speed, or development **2** : a sharp increase of activity ⟨~ in sales⟩

⁴**spurt** *vb* : to make a spurt

sput·ter \'spə-tər\ *vb* **1** : to spit small scattered particles : SPLUTTER **2** : to utter words hastily or explosively in excitement or confusion **3** : to make small popping sounds — **sputter** *n*

spu·tum \'spyü-təm\ *n, pl* **spu·ta** \-tə\ [L] : material (as phlegm) that is spit out or coughed up esp. during illness

¹**spy** \'spī\ *vb* **spied; spy·ing 1** : to watch or search for information secretly : act as a spy **2** : to get a momentary or quick glimpse of : SEE

²**spy** *n, pl* **spies 1** : one who secretly watches others **2** : a secret agent who tries to get information for one country in the territory of an enemy

spy·glass \'spī-,glas\ *n* : a small telescope

sq *abbr* **1** squadron **2** square

squab \'skwäb\ *n, pl* **squabs** *or* **squab** : a young bird and esp. a pigeon

squab·ble \'skwä-bəl\ *n* : a noisy altercation : WRANGLE ✦ *Synonyms* QUARREL, SPAT, ROW, TIFF — **squabble** *vb*

squad \'skwäd\ *n* **1** : a small organized group of military personnel **2** : a small group engaged in a common effort

squad car *n* : a police car connected by two-way radio with headquarters

squad·ron \'skwä-drən\ *n* : any of several units of military organization

squal·id \'skwä-ləd\ *adj* **1** : filthy or degraded through neglect or poverty **2** : SORDID, DEBASED ⟨a ~ political ploy⟩ ✦ *Synonyms* NASTY, FOUL, DIRTY, GRUBBY

squall \'skwȯl\ *n* : a sudden violent gust of wind often with rain or snow — **squally** *adj*

squa·lor \'skwä-lər\ *n* : the quality or state of being squalid

squa·mous cell \'skwä-məs-\ *n* : a scalelike cell of the outer layers of the skin from which a type of carcinoma arises

squan·der \'skwän-dər\ *vb* : to spend wastefully or foolishly

¹**square** \'skwer\ *n* **1** : an instrument used to lay out or

test right angles   **2** : a rectangle with all four sides equal   **3** : something square   **4** : the product of a number multiplied by itself   **5** : an area bounded by four streets   **6** : an open area in a city where streets meet   **7** : a highly conventional person

²**square** *adj* **squar·er; squar·est**   **1** : having four equal sides and four right angles   **2** : forming a right angle ⟨cut a ∼ corner⟩   **3** : multiplied by itself : SQUARED ⟨x² is the symbol for x ∼⟩   **4** : being a unit of square measure equal to a square each side of which measures one unit ⟨a ∼ foot⟩   **5** : being of a specified length in each of two dimensions ⟨an area 10 feet ∼⟩   **6** : exactly adjusted   **7** : JUST, FAIR ⟨a ∼ deal⟩   **8** : leaving no balance ⟨make accounts ∼⟩   **9** : SUBSTANTIAL ⟨a ∼ meal⟩   **10** : highly conservative or conventional — **square·ly** *adv*

³**square** *vb* **squared; squar·ing**   **1** : to form with four equal sides and right angles or with flat surfaces ⟨∼ a timber⟩   **2** : to multiply (a number) by itself   **3** : CONFORM, AGREE   **4** : BALANCE, SETTLE ⟨∼ an account⟩

square dance *n* : a dance for four couples arranged to form a square

square measure *n* : a unit or system of units for measuring area — see METRIC SYSTEM table, WEIGHT table

square–rigged \'skwer-'rigd\ *adj* : having the chief sails extended on yards that are fastened to the masts horizontally and at their center

square–rig·ger \-ˌri-gər\ *n* : a square-rigged craft

square root *n* : either of the two numbers whose squares are equal to a given number ⟨the *square root* of 9 is +3 or −3⟩

¹**squash** \'skwäsh, 'skwȯsh\ *vb*   **1** : to beat or press into a pulp or flat mass : QUASH, SUPPRESS ⟨∼ a revolt⟩

²**squash** *n*   **1** : the impact of something soft and heavy; *also* : the sound of such impact   **2** : a crushed mass   **3** : a game played on a 4-wall court with a racket and rubber ball

³**squash** *n, pl* **squash·es** *or* **squash** : any of various fruits of plants of the gourd family that are used esp. as vegetables; *also* : a plant and esp. a vine bearing squashes

squash racquets *n* : SQUASH 3

¹**squat** \'skwät\ *vb* **squat·ted; squat·ting** [ME *squatten* to crush, crouch in hiding, fr. MF (dial. of Picardy) *esquatir, escuater*, fr. OF *es- ex- + quatir* to hide, fr. VL *coactire to squeeze, alter. of L *coactare* to compel, fr. *cogere* to compel]   **1** : to sit down upon the hams or heels   **2** : to settle on land without right or title; *also* : to settle on public land with a view to acquiring title — **squat·ter** *n*

²**squat** *adj* **squat·ter; squat·test** : low to the ground; *also* : short and thick in stature ◆ *Synonyms* THICKSET, STOCKY, HEAVYSET, STUBBY

³**squat** *n* : the act or posture of squatting

squawk \'skwȯk\ *n* : a harsh loud cry; *also* : a noisy protest — **squawk** *vb*

squeak \'skwēk\ *vb*   **1** : to utter or speak in a weak shrill tone   **2** : to make a thin high-pitched sound — **squeak** *n* — **squeaky** *adj*

¹**squeal** \'skwēl\ *vb*   **1** : to make a shrill sound or cry   **2** : to betray a secret or turn informer   **3** : COMPLAIN, PROTEST

²**squeal** *n* : a shrill sharp cry or noise

squea·mish \'skwē-mish\ *adj*   **1** : easily nauseated; *also* : NAUSEATED   **2** : easily disgusted ◆ *Synonyms* FUSSY, NICE, DAINTY, FASTIDIOUS, PERSNICKETY — **squea·mish·ness** *n*

squee·gee \'skwē-jē\ *n* : a blade set crosswise on a handle and used for spreading or wiping liquid on, across, or off a surface — **squeegee** *vb*

¹**squeeze** \'skwēz\ *vb* **squeezed; squeez·ing**   **1** : to exert pressure on the opposite sides or parts of   **2** : to obtain by pressure ⟨∼ juice from a lemon⟩   **3** : to force, thrust, or cause to pass by pressure — **squeez·er** *n*

²**squeeze** *n*   **1** : an act of squeezing   **2** : a quantity squeezed out

squeeze bottle *n* : a flexible plastic bottle that dispenses its contents when it is squeezed

squelch \'skwelch\ *vb*   **1** : to suppress completely : CRUSH ⟨∼ resistance⟩   **2** : to move in soft mud — **squelch** *n*

squib \'skwib\ *n* : a brief witty writing or speech

squid \'skwid\ *n, pl* **squid** *or* **squids** : any of an order of long-bodied sea mollusks having eight short arms and two longer tentacles and usu. a slender internal shell

squint \'skwint\ *vb*   **1** : to look or aim obliquely   **2** : to look or peer with the eyes partly closed   **3** : to be cross=eyed — **squint** *n or adj*

¹**squire** \'skwī(-ə)r\ *n* [ME *squier*, fr. AF *esquier*, fr. LL *scutarius*, fr. L *scutum* shield]   **1** : an armor-bearer of a knight   **2** : a man gallantly devoted to a lady   **3** : a member of the British gentry ranking below a knight and above a gentleman; *also* : a prominent landowner   **4** : a local magistrate

²**squire** *vb* **squired; squir·ing** : to attend as a squire or escort

squirm \'skwərm\ *vb* : to twist about like a worm : WRIGGLE

¹**squir·rel** \'skwər-əl\ *n, pl* **squirrels** *also* **squirrel** [ME *squirel*, fr. AF *escurel, esquirel*, fr. VL **scuriolus*, dim. of **scurius*, alter. of L *sciurus*, fr. Gk *skiouros*, prob. fr. *skia* shadow + *oura* tail] : any of various rodents usu. with a long bushy tail and strong hind legs; *also* : the fur of a squirrel

²**squirrel** *vb* **-reled** *or* **-relled; -rel·ing** *or* **-rel·ling** : to store up for future use

¹**squirt** \'skwərt\ *vb* : to eject liquid in a thin spurt

²**squirt** *n*   **1** : an instrument (as a syringe) for squirting   **2** : a small forcible jet of liquid

¹**Sr** *abbr*   **1** senior   **2** sister

²**Sr** *symbol* strontium

SR *abbr* seaman recruit

¹**SRO** \ˌes-(ˌ)är-'ō\ *n* [*single-room occupancy*] : a house or apartment building in which low-income tenants live in single rooms

²**SRO** *abbr* standing room only

SS *abbr*   **1** saints   **2** Social Security   **3** steamship   **4** sworn statement

SSA *abbr* Social Security Administration

SSE *abbr* south-southeast

SSG *or* **SSgt** staff sergeant

SSI *abbr* supplemental security income

SSM *abbr* staff sergeant major

SSN *abbr* Social Security Number

ssp *abbr* subspecies

SSR *abbr* Soviet Socialist Republic

SSS *abbr* Selective Service System

SST \ˌes-(ˌ)es-'tē\ *n* [*supersonic transport*] : a supersonic passenger airplane

SSW *abbr* south-southwest

st *abbr*   **1** stanza   **2** state   **3** stitch   **4** stone   **5** street

St *abbr* saint

ST *abbr*   **1** short ton   **2** standard time

¹**-st** — see -EST

²**-st** *symbol* — used after the figure 1 to indicate the ordinal number first

sta *abbr* station; stationary

¹**stab** \'stab\ *n*   **1** : a wound produced by a pointed weapon   **2** : a quick thrust   **3** : a brief attempt

²**stab** *vb* **stabbed; stab·bing** : to pierce or wound with or as if with a pointed weapon; *also* : THRUST, DRIVE

sta·bile \'stā-ˌbēl\ *n* : an abstract sculpture or construction similar to a mobile but made to be stationary

sta·bi·lize \'stā-bə-ˌlīz\ *vb* **-lized; -liz·ing**   **1** : to make stable   **2** : to hold steady ⟨∼ prices⟩ — **sta·bi·li·za·tion** \ˌstā-bə-lə-'zā-shən\ *n* — **sta·bi·liz·er** \'stā-bə-ˌlī-zər\ *n*

¹**sta·ble** \'stā-bəl\ *n* : a building in which domestic animals are sheltered and fed — **sta·ble·man** \-mən, -ˌman\ *n*

²**stable** *vb* **sta·bled; sta·bling** : to put or keep in a stable

³**stable** *adj* **sta·bler;; sta·blest**   **1** : firmly established; *also* : mentally and emotionally healthy   **2** : steady in purpose : CONSTANT   **3** : DURABLE, ENDURING ⟨∼ civilizations⟩   **4** : resistant to chemical or physical change ◆ *Synonyms* LASTING, PERMANENT, PERPETUAL, PERDURABLE — **sta·bil·i·ty** \stə-'bi-lə-tē\ *n*

stac·ca·to \stə-'kä-tō\ *adj or adv* [It] : cut short so as not to sound connected ⟨∼ notes⟩

¹**stack** \'stak\ *n*   **1** : a large pile (as of hay or grain)   **2** : an orderly pile (as of poker chips)   **3** : a large quantity   **4** : a vertical pipe : SMOKESTACK   **5** : a rack with shelves for storing books

²**stack** *vb*   **1** : to pile up   **2** : to arrange (cards) secretly for cheating

stack up *vb* : MEASURE UP ⟨how do they *stack up* against the competition?⟩

sta·di·um \'stā-dē-əm\ *n, pl* **-dia** \-dē-ə\ *or* **-di·ums** : a structure with tiers of seats for spectators built around a field for sports events

¹staff \'staf\ *n, pl* staffs \'stafs, 'stavz\ *or* staves \'stavz, 'stāvz\ **1** : a pole, stick, rod, or bar used for supporting, for measuring, or as a symbol of authority; *also* : CLUB, CUDGEL **2** : something that sustains ⟨bread is the ∼ of life⟩ **3** : the five horizontal lines on which music is written **4** : a body of assistants to an executive **5** : a group of officers holding no command but having duties concerned with planning and managing

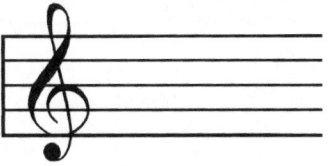

staff 3

²staff *vb* : to supply with a staff or with workers

staff•er \'sta-fər\ *n* : a member of a staff (as of a newspaper)

staff sergeant *n* : a noncommissioned officer ranking in the army next below a sergeant first class, in the air force next below a technical sergeant, and in the marine corps next below a gunnery sergeant

¹stag \'stag\ *n, pl* stags *or* stag : an adult male of various large deer

²stag *adj* : restricted to or intended for men ⟨a ∼ party⟩ ⟨∼ movies⟩

³stag *adv* : unaccompanied by a date

¹stage \'stāj\ *n* [ME, fr. AF *estage* abode, story of a building, stage, fr. VL *staticum*, fr. L *stare* to stand] **1** : a raised platform on which an orator may speak or a play may be presented **2** : the acting profession : THEATER **3** : the scene of a notable action or event **4** : a station or resting place on a traveled road **5** : STAGECOACH **6** : a degree of advance in an undertaking, process, or development **7** : a propulsion unit in a rocket — stagy \'stā-jē\ *adj*

²stage *vb* staged; stag•ing : to produce or perform on or as if on a stage — stage•able *adj*

stage•coach \'stāj-ˌkōch\ *n* : a horse-drawn coach that runs regularly between stations

stage manager *n* : one who supervises the physical aspects of a stage production

stag•fla•tion \ˌstag-'flā-shən\ *n* : inflation with stagnant economic activity and high unemployment

¹stag•ger \'sta-gər\ *vb* **1** : to reel from side to side : TOTTER **2** : to begin to doubt : WAVER **3** : to cause to reel or waver **4** : to arrange in overlapping or alternating positions or times ⟨∼ working hours⟩ **5** : ASTONISH — stag•ger•ing•ly *adv*

²stagger *n* **1** *sing or pl* : an abnormal condition of domestic animals associated with damage to the central nervous system and marked by lack of coordination and a reeling unsteady gait **2** : a reeling or unsteady gait or stance

stag•ing \'stā-jiŋ\ *n* **1** : SCAFFOLDING **2** : the assembling of troops and matériel in transit in a particular place

staging post *n* : STOPOVER 2

stag•nant \'stag-nənt\ *adj* **1** : not flowing : MOTIONLESS ⟨∼ water in a pond⟩ **2** : DULL, INACTIVE ⟨∼ business⟩

stag•nate \'stag-ˌnāt\ *vb* stag•nat•ed; stag•nat•ing : to be or become stagnant — stag•na•tion \stag-'nā-shən\ *n*

staid \'stād\ *adj* : SOBER, SEDATE **✦ Synonyms** GRAVE, SERIOUS, EARNEST

¹stain \'stān\ *vb* **1** : DISCOLOR, SOIL **2** : TAINT, CORRUPT **3** : DISGRACE **4** : to color (as wood, paper, or cloth) by processes affecting the material itself

²stain *n* **1** : a small soiled or discolored area **2** : a taint of guilt : STIGMA **3** : a preparation (as a dye or pigment) used in staining — stain•less *adj*

stainless steel *n* : steel alloyed with chromium that is highly resistant to stain, rust, and corrosion

stair \'ster\ *n* **1** : a series of steps or flights of steps for passing from one level to another — often used in pl. **2** : one step of a stairway

stair•case \-ˌkās\ *n* : a flight of steps with their supporting framework, casing, and balusters

stair•way \-ˌwā\ *n* : one or more flights of stairs with connecting landings

stair•well \-ˌwel\ *n* : a vertical shaft in which stairs are located

¹stake \'stāk\ *n* **1** : a pointed piece of material (as of wood) driven into the ground as a marker or a support **2** : a post to which a person is bound for death by burning; *also* : execution by burning at the stake **3** : something that is staked for gain or loss **4** : the prize in a contest

²stake *vb* staked; stak•ing **1** : to mark the limits of by or as if by stakes **2** : to tie to a stake **3** : to support or secure with stakes **4** : BET, WAGER

stake•out \'stāk-ˌaut\ *n* : a surveillance by police (as of a suspected criminal)

sta•lac•tite \stə-'lak-ˌtīt\ *n* [NL *stalactites*, fr. Gk *stalaktos* dripping, fr. *stalassein* to let drip] : an icicle-shaped deposit hanging from the roof or sides of a cavern

sta•lag•mite \stə-'lag-ˌmīt\ *n* [NL *stalagmites*, fr. Gk *stalagma* drop *or stalagmos* dripping, fr. *stalassein* to let drip] : a deposit resembling an inverted stalactite rising from the floor of a cavern

stale \'stāl\ *adj* stal•er; stal•est **1** : having lost good taste and quality from age ⟨∼ bread⟩ **2** : used or heard so often as to be dull ⟨∼ news⟩ **3** : not as strong or effective as before ⟨∼ from lack of practice⟩ — stale•ness *n*

stale•mate \'stāl-ˌmāt\ *n* : a drawn contest : DEADLOCK — stalemate *vb*

¹stalk \'stök\ *n* : a plant stem; *also* : any slender usu. upright supporting or connecting part — stalked \'stökt\ *adj*

²stalk *vb* **1** : to pursue (game) stealthily **2** : to walk stiffly or haughtily

¹stall \'stöl\ *n* **1** : a compartment in a stable or barn for one animal **2** : a booth or counter where articles may be displayed for sale **3** : a seat in a church choir; *also* : a church pew **4** *chiefly Brit* : a front orchestra seat in a theater

²stall *vb* : to bring or come to a standstill unintentionally ⟨∼ an engine⟩

³stall *n* : the condition of an airfoil or aircraft in which lift is lost and the airfoil or aircraft tends to drop

⁴stall *n* [alter. of *stale* lure] : a ruse to deceive or delay

⁵stall *vb* : to hold off, divert, or delay by evasion or deception

stal•lion \'stal-yən\ *n* : a male horse

stal•wart \'stöl-wərt\ *adj* : STOUT, STRONG; *also* : BRAVE, VALIANT

sta•men \'stā-mən\ *n* : an organ of a flower that produces pollen

stam•i•na \'sta-mə-nə\ *n* [L, pl. of *stamen* warp, thread of life spun by the Fates] : VIGOR, ENDURANCE

sta•mi•nate \'stā-mə-nət, 'sta-mə-, -ˌnāt\ *adj* **1** : having or producing stamens **2** : having stamens but no pistils

stam•mer \'sta-mər\ *vb* : to hesitate or stumble in speaking — stammer *n* — stam•mer•er *n*

¹stamp \'stamp; *for 2 also* 'stämp *or* 'stömp\ *vb* **1** : to pound or crush with a heavy instrument **2** : to strike or beat with the bottom of the foot **3** : IMPRESS, IMPRINT ⟨∼ "paid" on the bill⟩ **4** : to cut out or indent with a stamp or die **5** : to attach a postage stamp to

²stamp *n* **1** : a device or instrument for stamping **2** : the mark made by stamping; *also* : a distinctive mark or quality **3** : the act of stamping **4** : a stamped or printed paper affixed to show that a charge has been paid ⟨postage ∼⟩ ⟨tax ∼⟩

¹stam•pede \stam-'pēd\ *n* : a wild headlong rush or flight esp. of frightened animals

²stampede *vb* stam•ped•ed; stam•ped•ing **1** : to flee or cause to flee in panic **2** : to act or cause to act together suddenly and heedlessly

stance \'stans\ *n* : a way of standing

¹stanch \'stönch, 'stänch, 'stanch\ *or* staunch \'stönch, 'stänch\ *vb* : to check the flowing of (as blood); *also* : to cease flowing or bleeding

²stanch *var of* ²STAUNCH

stan•chion \'stan-chən\ *n* : an upright bar, post, or support

¹stand \'stand\ *vb* stood \'stud\; stand•ing **1** : to take or be at rest in an upright or firm position **2** : to assume a

specified position **3** : to remain stationary or unchanged **4** : to be steadfast **5** : to act in resistance ⟨∼ against a foe⟩ **6** : to maintain a relative position or rank **7** : to gather slowly and remain ⟨tears *stood* in her eyes⟩ **8** : to set upright **9** : ENDURE, TOLERATE ⟨I won't ∼ for that⟩ **10** : to submit to ⟨∼ trial⟩ — **stand pat** : to oppose or resist change

²**stand** *n* **1** : an act of standing, staying, or resisting **2** : a stop made to give a performance **3** : POSITION, VIEWPOINT **4** : a place taken by a witness to testify in court **5** *pl* : tiered seats for spectators **6** : a raised platform (as for speakers) **7** : a structure for a small retail business **8** : a structure for supporting or holding something upright ⟨music ∼⟩ **9** : a group of plants growing in a continuous area

stand-alone \'stan-də-ˌlōn\ *adj* : SELF-CONTAINED; *esp* : capable of operation independent of a computer system

¹**stan·dard** \'stan-dərd\ *n* **1** : a figure adopted as an emblem by a people **2** : the personal flag of a ruler; *also* : FLAG **3** : something set up as a rule for measuring or as a model to be followed **4** : an upright support ⟨lamp ∼⟩

²**standard** *adj* **1** : used as or meeting a standard established by law or custom **2** : regularly and widely used ⟨a ∼ practice⟩ **3** : well established by usage in speech or writing

stan·dard–bear·er \-ˌber-ər\ *n* : the leader of a cause

standard deviation *n* : a measure of dispersion in a set of data

stan·dard·ise *Brit var of* STANDARDIZE

stan·dard–is·sue \'stan-dərd-'i-shü\ *adj* : STANDARD, TYPICAL ⟨a ∼ blue suit⟩

stan·dard·ize \'stan-dər-ˌdīz\ *vb* **-ized; -iz·ing** : to make standard or uniform — **stan·dard·i·za·tion** \ˌstan-dər-də-'zā-shən\ *n*

standard of living : the necessities, comforts, and luxuries that a person or group is accustomed to

standard time *n* : the time established by law or by general usage over a region or country

¹**stand·by** \'stand-ˌbī\ *n, pl* **stand·bys** \-ˌbīz\ **1** : one that can be relied on **2** : a substitute in reserve — **on standby** : ready or available for immediate action or use

²**standby** *adj* **1** : ready for use **2** : relating to airline travel in which the passenger must wait for an available unreserved seat — **standby** *adv*

stand–in \'stan-ˌdin\ *n* **1** : someone employed to occupy an actor's place while lights and camera are readied **2** : SUBSTITUTE

¹**stand·ing** \'stan-diŋ\ *adj* **1** : ERECT ⟨∼ timber⟩ **2** : not flowing : STAGNANT **3** : remaining at the same level or amount for an indefinite period ⟨∼ offer⟩ **4** : PERMANENT ⟨a ∼ army⟩ **5** : done from a standing position ⟨a ∼ jump⟩

²**standing** *n* **1** : length of service; *also* : relative position in society or in a profession : RANK **2** : DURATION ⟨a custom of long ∼⟩

stand·off \'stan-ˌdóf\ *n* : TIE, DRAW

stand·off·ish \stan-'dó-fish\ *adj* : somewhat cold and reserved

stand·out \'stan-ˌdaút\ *n* : something conspicuously excellent

stand·pipe \'stand-ˌpīp\ *n* : a high vertical pipe or reservoir for water used to produce a uniform pressure

stand·point \-ˌpóint\ *n* : a position from which objects or principles are judged

stand·still \-ˌstil\ *n* : a state of rest

stand–up \'stan-ˌdəp\ *adj* : done or performing in a standing position ⟨a ∼ comic⟩ ⟨∼ comedy⟩

stank *past of* STINK

stan·za \'stan-zə\ *n* [It] : a group of lines forming a division of a poem

sta·pes \'stā-ˌpēz\ *n, pl* **stapes** *or* **sta·pe·des** \'stā-pə-ˌdēz\ : the innermost bone of the middle ear of mammals

staph \'staf\ *n* : STAPHYLOCOCCUS

staph·y·lo·coc·cus \ˌsta-fə-lō-'kä-kəs\ *n, pl* **-coc·ci** \-'kä-ˌkī, -'käk-ˌsī\ : any of a genus of spherical bacteria including some pathogens of skin and mucous membranes — **staph·y·lo·coc·cal** \-'kä-kəl\ *adj*

¹**sta·ple** \'stā-pəl\ *n* : a U-shaped piece of metal or wire with sharp points to be driven into a surface or through thin layers (as paper) for attaching or holding together — **staple** *vb* — **sta·pler** *n*

²**staple** *n* **1** : a chief commodity or product **2** : a chief part of something ⟨a ∼ of their diet⟩ **3** : unmanufactured or raw material **4** : a textile fiber suitable for spinning into yarn

³**staple** *adj* **1** : regularly produced in large quantities **2** : PRINCIPAL, MAIN ⟨the ∼ crop⟩

¹**star** \'stär\ *n* **1** : a celestial body that appears as a fixed point of light; *esp* : such a body that is gaseous, self-luminous, and of great mass **2** : a planet or configuration of planets that is held in astrology to influence one's fortune — usu. used in pl. **3** *obs* : DESTINY **4** : a conventional figure representing a star; *esp* : ASTERISK **5** : an actor or actress playing the leading role **6** : a brilliant performer — **star·dom** \'stär-dəm\ *n* — **star·less** *adj* — **star·like** *adj* — **star·ry** *adj*

²**star** *vb* **starred; star·ring 1** : to adorn with stars **2** : to mark with an asterisk **3** : to play the leading role

star anise *n* : the small brown star-shaped fruit of an Asian tree used as a spice esp. in Chinese cooking

star·board \'stär-bərd\ *n* [ME *sterbord,* fr. OE *stēorbord,* fr. *stēor-* steering oar + *bord* ship's side] : the right side of a ship or airplane looking forward — **starboard** *adj*

star·burst \'stär-bərst\ *n* : a pattern that resembles diverging rays of light

¹**starch** \'stärch\ *vb* : to stiffen with or as if with starch

²**starch** *n* : a complex carbohydrate that is stored in plants, is an important foodstuff, and is used in adhesives and sizes, in laundering, and in pharmacy — **starchy** *adj*

stare \'ster\ *vb* **stared; star·ing** : to look fixedly with wide-open eyes — **stare** *n* — **star·er** *n*

star·fish \'stär-ˌfish\ *n* : any of a class of echinoderms that have usu. five arms arranged around a central disk and feed largely on mollusks

star fruit *n* : CARAMBOLA 1

¹**stark** \'stärk\ *adj* **1** : rigid as if in death; *also* : STRICT **2** *archaic* : STRONG, ROBUST **3** : SHEER, UTTER ⟨∼ nonsense⟩ **4** : BARREN, DESOLATE ⟨∼ landscape⟩; *also* : UNADORNED ⟨∼ realism⟩ **5** : sharply delineated — **stark·ly** *adv*

²**stark** *adv* : WHOLLY, ABSOLUTELY ⟨∼ naked⟩

star·light \'stär-ˌlīt\ *n* : the light given by the stars

star·ling \'stär-liŋ\ *n* : a dark brown or in summer glossy greenish black European bird related to the crows that is naturalized nearly worldwide and often considered a pest

¹**start** \'stärt\ *vb* **1** : to give an involuntary twitch or jerk (as from surprise) **2** : BEGIN, COMMENCE **3** : to set going ⟨∼ an engine⟩ **4** : to enter or cause to enter a game or contest; *also* : to be in the starting lineup — **start·er** *n*

²**start** *n* **1** : a sudden involuntary motion : LEAP **2** : a spasmodic and brief effort or action **3** : BEGINNING; *also* : the place of beginning

start·er \'stär-tər\ *adj* : being an item acquired with the expectation that a more elaborate one will be acquired in the future ⟨a ∼ home⟩

star·tle \'stär-t⁹l\ *vb* **star·tled; star·tling** : to frighten or surprise suddenly : cause to start

star·tling *adj* : causing sudden fear, surprise, or anxiety — **star·tling·ly** *adv*

starve \'stärv\ *vb* **starved; starv·ing** [ME *sterven* to die, fr. OE *steorfan*] **1** : to die or cause to die from hunger **2** : to suffer extreme hunger or deprivation ⟨*starving* for affection⟩ **3** : to subdue by famine — **star·va·tion** \stär-'vā-shən\ *n*

starve·ling \'stärv-liŋ\ *n* : one that is thin from lack of nourishment

stash \'stash\ *vb* : to store in a secret place for future use — **stash** *n*

sta·sis \'stā-səs, 'sta-\ *n, pl* **sta·ses** \'stā-ˌsēz, 'sta-\ **1** : a stoppage or slowing of the normal flow of a bodily fluid (as blood) **2** : a state of static balance : STAGNATION

¹**stat** \'stat\ *adv* [L *statim*] : without delay : IMMEDIATELY

²**stat** *abbr* statute

¹**state** \'stāt\ *n* [ME *stat,* fr. AF & L; AF *estat,* fr. L *status,* fr. *stare* to stand] **1** : mode or condition of being ⟨the four ∼s of matter⟩ **2** : condition of mind **3** : social position **4** : a body of people occupying a territory and organized under one government; *also* : the government of such a body of people **5** : one of the constituent units of a nation having a federal government — **state·hood** \-ˌhùd\ *n*

²**state** *vb* **stat·ed; stat·ing 1** : to set by regulation or authority **2** : to express in words

state·craft \'stāt-ˌkraft\ *n* : the art of conducting state affairs

state·house \-ˌhaùs\ *n* : the building in which a state legislature meets

state·ly \'stāt-lē\ *adj* **state·li·er; -est** **1** : having lofty dignity **2** : HAUGHTY **2** : IMPRESSIVE, MAJESTIC ⟨∼ homes⟩ ♦ *Synonyms* MAGNIFICENT, IMPOSING, AUGUST — **state·li·ness** *n*

state·ment \'stāt-mənt\ *n* **1** : the act or result of presenting in words **2** : a summary of a financial account

state·room \'stāt-ˌrüm, -ˌrùm\ *n* : a private room on a ship or railroad car

state·side \'stāt-ˌsīd\ *adj* : of or relating to the U.S. as regarded from outside its continental limits — **stateside** *adv*

states·man \'stāts-mən\ *n* : a person engaged in fixing the policies and conducting the affairs of a government; *esp* : one wise and skilled in such matters — **states·man·like** *adj* — **states·man·ship** *n*

¹**stat·ic** \'sta-tik\ *adj* **1** : acting by mere weight without motion ⟨∼ pressure⟩ **2** : relating to bodies at rest or forces in equilibrium **3** : showing little change **4** : not moving : not active **5** : of or relating to stationary charges of electricity **6** : of, relating to, or caused by radio static

²**static** *n* : noise produced in a radio or television receiver by atmospheric or other electrical disturbances

stat·in \'sta-tᵊn\ *n* : any of a group of drugs that inhibit the synthesis of cholesterol

¹**sta·tion** \'stā-shən\ *n* **1** : the place where a person or thing stands or is assigned to remain **2** : a regular stopping place on a transportation route : DEPOT **3** : a place where a fleet is assigned for duty **4** : a stock farm or ranch esp. in Australia or New Zealand **5** : social standing **6** : a complete assemblage of radio or television equipment for sending or receiving

²**station** *vb* : to assign to a station

sta·tio·nary \'stā-shə-ˌner-ē\ *adj* **1** : fixed in a station, course, or mode **2** : unchanging in condition ⟨a ∼ population⟩

stationary front *n* : the boundary between two air masses neither of which is advancing

station break *n* : a pause in a radio or television broadcast to announce the identity of the network or station

sta·tio·ner \'stā-shə-nər\ *n* : one that sells stationery

sta·tio·nery \'stā-shə-ˌner-ē\ *n* : materials (as paper, pens, or ink) for writing; *esp* : letter paper with envelopes

station wagon *n* : an automobile having a long interior, one or more folding or removable rear seats, and usu. a door at the rear

sta·tis·tic \stə-'tis-tik\ *n* **1** : a single term or datum in a collection of statistics **2** : a quantity (as the mean) that is computed from a sample

sta·tis·tics \-tiks\ *n sing or pl* [G *Statistik* study of political facts and figures, fr. NL *statisticus* of politics, fr. L *status* state] : a branch of mathematics dealing with the collection, analysis, and interpretation of masses of numerical data; *also* : a collection of such numerical data — **sta·tis·ti·cal** \-ti-kəl\ *adj* — **sta·tis·ti·cal·ly** \-ti-k(ə-)lē\ *adv* — **stat·is·ti·cian** \ˌsta-tə-'sti-shən\ *n*

stat·u·ary \'sta-chə-ˌwer-ē\ *n, pl* **-ar·ies** **1** : the art of making statues **2** : STATUES

stat·ue \'sta-chü\ *n* : a likeness (as of a person or animal) sculptured, modeled, or cast in a solid substance

stat·u·esque \ˌsta-chə-'wesk\ *adj* : tall and shapely

stat·u·ette \'sta-chə-'wet\ *n* : a small statue

stat·ure \'sta-chər\ *n* **1** : natural height (as of a person) **2** : quality or status gained (as by achievement)

sta·tus \'stā-təs, 'sta-\ *n* **1** : the condition of a person in the eyes of others or of the law **2** : state or condition with respect to circumstances

sta·tus quo \-'kwō\ *n* [L, state in which] : the existing state of affairs

stat·ute \'sta-chüt\ *n* : a law enacted by a legislative body

stat·u·to·ry \'sta-chə-ˌtór-ē\ *adj* : imposed by statute : LAWFUL

statutory rape *n* : sexual intercourse with a person who is below the statutory age of consent

¹**staunch** *var of* STANCH

²**staunch** \'stónch, 'stänch\ *adj* **1** : WATERTIGHT ⟨a ∼ ship⟩ **2** : FIRM, STRONG; *also* : STEADFAST, LOYAL

♦ *Synonyms* RESOLUTE, CONSTANT, TRUE, FAITHFUL — **staunch·ly** *adv*

¹**stave** \'stāv\ *n* **1** : CUDGEL, STAFF **2** : any of several narrow strips of wood placed edge to edge to make something (as a barrel) **3** : STANZA

²**stave** *vb* **staved** *or* **stove** \'stōv\; **stav·ing** **1** : to break in the staves of; *also* : to break a hole in **2** : to drive or thrust away

staves *pl of* STAFF

¹**stay** \'stā\ *n* **1** : a strong rope or wire used to support a mast **2** : ¹GUY

²**stay** *vb* **stayed** \'stād\ *also* **staid** \'stād\; **stay·ing** **1** : PAUSE, WAIT **2** : REMAIN **3** : to stand firm **4** : LIVE, DWELL **5** : DELAY, POSTPONE **6** : to last out (as a race) **7** : STOP, CHECK **8** : to satisfy (as hunger) for a time ♦ *Synonyms* REMAIN, ABIDE, LINGER, TARRY

³**stay** *n* **1** : STOP, HALT **2** : a residence or sojourn in a place

⁴**stay** *n* **1** : PROP, SUPPORT **2** : CORSET — usu. used in pl.

⁵**stay** *vb* : to hold up : PROP

staying power *n* : STAMINA

stbd *abbr* starboard

std *abbr* standard

STD \ˌes-(ˌ)tē-'dē\ *n* : SEXUALLY TRANSMITTED DISEASE

Ste *abbr* [F *sainte*] saint (female)

stead \'sted\ *n* **1** : ADVANTAGE ⟨stood him in good ∼⟩ **2** : the place or function ordinarily occupied or carried out by another ⟨acted in her brother's ∼⟩

stead·fast \'sted-ˌfast\ *adj* **1** : firmly fixed in place **2** : not subject to change **3** : firm in belief, determination, or adherence : LOYAL ♦ *Synonyms* RESOLUTE, TRUE, FAITHFUL, STAUNCH — **stead·fast·ly** *adv* — **stead·fast·ness** *n*

¹**steady** \'ste-dē\ *adj* **steadi·er; -est** **1** : direct or sure in movement; *also* : CALM **2** : FIRM, FIXED ⟨held the pole ∼⟩ **3** : STABLE ⟨∼ prices⟩ **4** : not easily disturbed **5** : RELIABLE ⟨∼ friends⟩ **6** : temperate in character or demeanor ♦ *Synonyms* UNIFORM, EVEN — **steadi·ly** \-də-lē\ *adv* — **steadi·ness** \-dē-nəs\ *n* — **steady** *adv*

²**steady** *vb* **stead·ied; steady·ing** : to make or become steady

steak \'stāk\ *n* : a slice of meat and esp. beef; *also* : a slice of a large fish

¹**steal** \'stēl\ *vb* **stole** \'stōl\; **sto·len** \'stō-lən\; **steal·ing** **1** : to take and carry away without right or permission **2** : to come or go secretly or gradually **3** : to get for oneself slyly or by skill and daring ⟨∼ a kiss⟩ ⟨∼ the ball in basketball⟩ **4** : to gain or attempt to gain a base in baseball by running without the aid of a hit or an error ♦ *Synonyms* PILFER, FILCH, PURLOIN, SWIPE

²**steal** *n* **1** : an act of stealing **2** : BARGAIN

¹**stealth** \'stelth\ *n* **1** : secret or unobtrusive procedure **2** : an aircraft design intended to produce a weak radar return

²**stealth** *adj* : STEALTHY ⟨a ∼ campaign⟩

stealthy \'stel-thē\ *adj* **stealth·i·er; -est** : done by stealth : FURTIVE, SLY ♦ *Synonyms* SECRET, COVERT, CLANDESTINE, SURREPTITIOUS, UNDERHANDED — **stealth·i·ly** \'stel-thə-lē\ *adv*

¹**steam** \'stēm\ *n* **1** : the vapor into which water is changed when heated to the boiling point **2** : water vapor when compressed so that it supplies heat and power **3** : POWER, FORCE, ENERGY — **steamy** *adj*

²**steam** *vb* **1** : to pass off as vapor **2** : to emit vapor **3** : to move by or as if by the agency of steam — **steam·er** *n*

steam·boat \'stēm-ˌbōt\ *n* : a boat driven by steam

steam engine *n* : a reciprocating engine having a piston driven by steam

steam·fit·ter \'stēm-ˌfi-tər\ *n* : a worker who puts in or repairs equipment (as steam pipes) for heating, ventilating, or refrigerating systems

steam·roll·er \-ˌrō-lər\ *n* : a machine for compacting roads or pavements — **steam·roll·er** *also* **steam·roll** \-ˌrōl\ *vb*

steam·ship \-ˌship\ *n* : a ship driven by steam

steed \'stēd\ *n* : HORSE

¹**steel** \'stēl\ *n* **1** : iron treated with intense heat and mixed with carbon to make it hard and tough **2** : an article made of steel **3** : a quality (as hardness of mind) that suggests steel — **steel** *adj* — **steely** *adj*

²**steel** *vb* : to fill with courage or determination

steel wool n : long fine steel shavings used esp. for cleaning and polishing

¹**steep** \'stēp\ adj 1 : having a very sharp slope : PRECIPITOUS 2 : too high ⟨~ prices⟩ — **steep·ly** adv — **steepness** n

²**steep** n : a steep slope

³**steep** vb 1 : to soak in a liquid; esp : to extract the essence of by soaking ⟨~ tea⟩ 2 : SATURATE ⟨~ed in learning⟩

stee·ple \'stē-pəl\ n : a tall tapering structure built on top of a church tower; also : a church tower

stee·ple·chase \-,chās\ n [fr. the use of church steeples as landmarks to guide the riders] : a horse race across country; also : a race over a course obstructed by hurdles

¹**steer** \'stir\ n : a male bovine animal castrated before sexual maturity and usu. raised for beef

²**steer** vb 1 : to direct the course of (as by a rudder or wheel) 2 : GUIDE, CONTROL 3 : to pursue a course of action 4 : to be subject to guidance or direction — **steers·man** \'stirz-mən\ n

steer·age \'stir-ij\ n 1 : DIRECTION, GUIDANCE 2 : a section in a passenger ship for passengers paying the lowest fares

stego·sau·rus \,ste-gə-'sȯr-əs\ n : any of a genus of plant-eating armored dinosaurs with a series of bony plates along the backbone

stein \'stīn\ n : an earthenware mug

stel·lar \'ste-lər\ adj : of or relating to stars : resembling a star

¹**stem** \'stem\ n 1 : the main stalk of a plant; also : a plant part that supports another part (as a leaf or fruit) 2 : the bow of a ship 3 : a line of ancestry : STOCK 4 : that part of an inflected word which remains unchanged throughout a given inflection 5 : something resembling the stem of a plant — **stem·less** adj — **stemmed** \'stemd\ adj

²**stem** vb **stemmed; stem·ming** : to have a specified source : DERIVE

³**stem** vb **stemmed; stem·ming** : to make headway against ⟨~ the tide⟩

⁴**stem** vb **stemmed; stem·ming** : to stop or check by or as if by damming

stem cell n : an undifferentiated cell that may give rise to many different types of cell

stench \'stench\ n : STINK

sten·cil \'sten-səl\ n [prob. ultim. fr. ME stanseld brightly ornamented, fr. AF estencelé spangled, pp. of estenceler to sparkle, fr. estencele spark, fr. VL *stincilla, alter. of L scintilla] : an impervious material (as metal or paper) perforated with lettering or a design through which a substance (as ink or paint) is applied to a surface to be printed — **stencil** vb

ste·nog·ra·phy \stə-'nä-grə-fē\ n : the art or process of writing in shorthand — **ste·nog·ra·pher** \-fər\ n — **steno·graph·ic** \,ste-nə-'gra-fik\ adj

ste·no·sis \stə-'nō-səs\ n, pl **-no·ses** \-,sēz\ : a narrowing of a bodily passage or orifice

stent \'stent\ n : a short narrow tube inserted into an anatomical vessel esp. to keep a passage open

sten·to·ri·an \sten-'tȯr-ē-ən\ adj : extremely loud ⟨~ tones⟩

¹**step** \'step\ n 1 : a rest for the foot in ascending or descending : STAIR 2 : an advance made by raising one foot and putting it down elsewhere 3 : manner of walking 4 : a small space or distance 5 : a degree, rank, or plane in a series 6 : a sequential measure leading to a result

²**step** vb **stepped; step·ping** 1 : to advance or recede by steps 2 : to go on foot : WALK 3 : to move along briskly 4 : to press down with the foot 5 : to measure by steps 6 : to construct or arrange in or as if in steps

step aerobics n sing or pl : aerobics that involves repeatedly stepping on and off a raised platform

step aside vb : STEP DOWN 1

step·broth·er \'step-,brə-thər\ n : the son of one's stepparent by a former marriage

step·child \-,chī(-ə)ld\ n : a child of one's husband or wife by a former marriage

step·daugh·ter \-,dȯ-tər\ n : a daughter of one's wife or husband by a former marriage

step down vb 1 : to give up a position : RETIRE, RESIGN 2 : to lower (a voltage) by means of a transformer

step·fa·ther \-,fä-thər\ n : the husband of one's mother when distinct from one's natural or legal father

step·lad·der \'step-,la-dər\ n : a light portable set of steps in a hinged frame

step·moth·er \-,mə-thər\ n : the wife of one's father when distinct from one's natural or legal mother

step·par·ent \-,per-ənt\ n : a person who is a stepfather or stepmother

steppe \'step\ [Russ step'] : dry level grass-covered treeless land in regions of wide temperature range esp. in southeastern Europe and Asia

step·sis·ter \'step-,sis-tər\ n : the daughter of one's stepparent by a former marriage

step·son \-,sən\ n : a son of one's wife or husband by a former marriage

step up vb 1 : to increase (a voltage) by means of a transformer 2 : INCREASE, ACCELERATE 3 : to come forward — **step–up** \'step-,əp\ n

ster abbr sterling

ste·reo \'ster-ē-,ō, 'stir-\ n, pl **ste·re·os** 1 : stereophonic reproduction 2 : a stereophonic sound system — **stereo** adj

ste·reo·phon·ic \,ster-ē-ə-'fä-nik, ,stir-\ adj : of or relating to sound reproduction designed to create the effect of listening to the original — **ste·reo·phon·i·cal·ly** \-'fä-ni-k(ə-)lē\ adv

ster·e·o·scope \'ster-ē-ə-,skōp, 'stir-\ n [Gk stereos solid + -skopion means for viewing] : an optical instrument that blends two slightly different pictures of the same subject to give the effect of depth

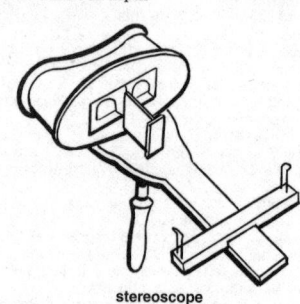

stereoscope

ste·reo·scop·ic \,ster-ē-ə-'skä-pik, ,stir-\ adj 1 : of or relating to the stereoscope 2 : characterized by the seeing of objects in three dimensions ⟨~ vision⟩ — **ste·reo·scop·i·cal·ly** \-'skä-pi-k(ə-)lē\ adv — **ste·re·os·co·py** \,ster-ē-'äs-kə-pē, ,stir-\ n

ste·reo·type \'ster-ē-ə-,tīp, 'stir-\ n 1 : a metal printing plate cast from a mold made from set type 2 : something agreeing with a pattern; esp : an idea that many people have about a thing or a group and that may often be untrue or only partly true — **stereotype** vb — **ste·reo·typ·i·cal** \,ster-ē-ə-'ti-pi-kəl\ adj — **ste·reo·typ·i·cal·ly** \-pi-k(ə-)lē\ adv

ste·reo·typed \-,tīpt\ adj : lacking originality or individuality ♦ **Synonyms** TRITE, CLICHÉD, COMMONPLACE, HACKNEYED, STALE, THREADBARE

ster·ile \'ster-əl\ adj 1 : unable to bear fruit, crops, or offspring 2 : free from living things and esp. germs — **ste·ril·i·ty** \stə-'ri-lə-tē\ n

ster·il·ize \'ster-ə-,līz\ vb **-ized; -iz·ing** : to make sterile; esp : to free from germs — **ster·il·i·za·tion** \,ster-ə-lə-'zā-shən\ n — **ster·il·iz·er** \'ster-ə-,lī-zər\ n

¹**ster·ling** \'stər-lin\ n 1 : British money 2 : sterling silver

²**sterling** adj 1 : of, relating to, or calculated in terms of British sterling 2 : having a fixed standard of purity represented by an alloy of 925 parts of silver with 75 parts of copper 3 : made of sterling silver 4 : EXCELLENT ⟨a ~ record of achievement⟩

¹**stern** \'stərn\ adj 1 : SEVERE, AUSTERE ⟨~ taskmasters⟩ 2 : STOUT, STURDY ⟨~ resolve⟩ — **stern·ly** adv — **stern·ness** n

²**stern** n : the rear end of a boat

ster·num \'stər-nəm\ n, pl **sternums** or **ster·na** \-nə\ : a long flat bone or cartilage at the center front of the chest connecting the ribs of the two sides

ste·roid \'stir-ˌóid, 'ster-\ n : any of various compounds including numerous hormones (as anabolic steroids) and sugar derivatives — **steroid** or **ste·roi·dal** \stə-'rói-dᵊl\ adj

stetho·scope \'ste-thə-ˌskōp\ n : an instrument used to detect and listen to sounds produced in the body

ste·ve·dore \'stē-və-ˌdór\ n [Sp estibador, fr. estibar to pack, fr. L stipare to press together] : one who works at loading and unloading ships

¹**stew** \'stü, 'styü\ n 1 : a dish of stewed meat and vegetables served in gravy 2 : a state of agitation, worry, or resentment

²**stew** vb 1 : to boil slowly : SIMMER 2 : to be in a state of agitation, worry, or resentment

stew·ard \'stü-ərd, 'styü-\ n [ME, fr. OE stīweard, fr. stī, stig hall, sty + weard ward] 1 : one employed on a large estate to manage domestic concerns 2 : one who supervises the provision and distribution of food (as on a ship); also : an employee on a ship or airplane who serves passengers 3 : one actively concerned with the direction of the affairs of an organization — **stew·ard·ship** n

stew·ard·ess \'stü-ər-dəs, 'styü-\ n : a woman who is a steward esp. on an airplane

stg abbr sterling

¹**stick** \'stik\ n 1 : a cut or broken branch or twig; also : a long slender piece of wood 2 : ROD, STAFF 3 : something resembling a stick 4 : a dull uninteresting person 5 pl : remote usu. rural areas

²**stick** vb stuck \'stək\; **stick·ing** 1 : STAB, PRICK 2 : IMPALE 3 : ATTACH, FASTEN 4 : to thrust or project in some direction or manner 5 : to be unable to proceed or move freely 6 : to hold fast by or as if by gluing : ADHERE 7 : to hold to something firmly or closely : CLING 8 : to become jammed or blocked

stick·er \'sti-kər\ n : one that sticks (as a bur) or causes sticking (as glue); esp : an adhesive label

sticker shock n : astonishment and dismay on being informed of a product's unexpectedly high price

stick insect n : any of various usu. wingless insects with a long round body resembling a stick

stick·ler \'sti-klər, -kə-lər\ n : one who insists on exactness or completeness

stick shift n : a manually operated automobile gearshift usu. mounted on the floor

stick–to–it·ive·ness \stik-'tü-ə-tiv-nəs\ n : dogged perseverance : TENACITY

stick up vb : to rob at gunpoint — **stick-up** \'stik-ˌəp\ n

sticky \'sti-kē\ adj **stick·i·er; -est** 1 : ADHESIVE 2 : VISCOUS, GLUEY 3 : tending to stick ⟨∼ valve⟩ 4 : DIFFICULT

¹**stiff** \'stif\ adj 1 : not pliant : RIGID 2 : not limber ⟨∼ joints⟩; also : TENSE, TAUT 3 : not flowing or working easily ⟨∼ paste⟩ 4 : not natural and easy : FORMAL 5 : STRONG, FORCEFUL ⟨∼ breeze⟩ 6 : HARSH, SEVERE ⟨a ∼ penalty⟩ ◆ **Synonyms** INFLEXIBLE, INELASTIC — **stiff·ly** adv — **stiff·ness** n

²**stiff** vb : to refuse to pay or tip

stiff–arm \'stif-ˌärm\ vb : to treat with disdain or neglect ⟨∼ed her advice⟩

stiff·en \'sti-fən\ vb : to make or become stiff — **stiff·en·er** n

stiff–necked \'stif-'nekt\ adj : STUBBORN, HAUGHTY

sti·fle \'stī-fəl\ vb **sti·fled; sti·fling** 1 : to kill by depriving of or die from lack of oxygen or air : SMOTHER 2 : to keep in check by effort : SUPPRESS ⟨∼ a sneeze⟩ — **sti·fling·ly** adv

stig·ma \'stig-mə\ n, pl **stig·ma·ta** \stig-'mä-tə, 'stig-mə-tə\ or **stigmas** [L] 1 : a mark of disgrace or discredit 2 stigmata pl : bodily marks resembling the wounds of the crucified Jesus 3 : the upper part of the pistil of a flower that receives the pollen in fertilization — **stig·mat·ic** \stig-'ma-tik\ adj

stig·ma·tize \'stig-mə-ˌtīz\ vb **-tized; -tiz·ing** 1 : to mark with a stigma 2 : to characterize as disgraceful

stile \'stī(-ə)l\ n : steps used for crossing a fence or wall

sti·let·to \stə-'le-tō\ n, pl **-tos** or **-toes** [It, dim. of stilo stylus, dagger] : a slender dagger

¹**still** \'stil\ adj 1 : MOTIONLESS 2 : making no sound : SILENT — **still·ness** n

²**still** vb : to make or become still

³**still** adv 1 : without motion ⟨sit ∼⟩ 2 : up to and during

this or that time 3 : in spite of that : NEVERTHELESS 4 : EVEN ⟨ran ∼ faster⟩ 5 : YET ⟨has ∼ to be recognized⟩

⁴**still** n 1 : STILLNESS, SILENCE 2 : a static photograph esp. from a motion picture

⁵**still** n 1 : DISTILLERY 2 : apparatus used in distillation

still-birth \'stil-ˌbərth\ n : the birth of a dead fetus

still-born \-'bórn\ adj : born dead

still life n, pl **still lifes** : a picture of inanimate objects

stilt \'stilt\ n : one of a pair of poles for walking with each having a step or loop for the foot to elevate the wearer above the ground; also : a polelike support of a structure above ground or water level

stilt·ed \'stil-təd\ adj : not easy and natural ⟨∼ language⟩

Stil·ton \'stil-tᵊn\ n : a blue cheese of English origin

stim·u·lant \'sti-myə-lənt\ n 1 : an agent (as a drug) that temporarily increases the activity of an organism or any of its parts 2 : STIMULUS 3 : an alcoholic beverage — **stimulant** adj

stim·u·late \-ˌlāt\ vb **-lat·ed; -lat·ing** : to make active or more active : ANIMATE, AROUSE ◆ **Synonyms** EXCITE, PROVOKE, MOTIVATE, QUICKEN — **stim·u·la·tion** \ˌsti-myə-'lā-shən\ n — **stim·u·la·tive** \'sti-myə-ˌlā-tiv\ adj — **stim·u·la·tor** \-ˌlā-tər\ n — **stim·u·la·to·ry** \-lə-ˌtór-ē\ adj

stim·u·lus \'sti-myə-ləs\ n, pl **-li** \-ˌlī\ [L] 1 : something that moves to activity 2 : an agent that directly influences the activity of a living organism or one of its parts

¹**sting** \'stiŋ\ vb stung \'stəŋ\; **sting·ing** 1 : to prick painfully esp. with a sharp or poisonous process 2 : to cause to suffer acutely — **sting·er** n

²**sting** n 1 : an act of stinging; also : a resultant wound, sore, or pain 2 : a pointed often venom-bearing organ (as of a bee) : STINGER 3 : an elaborate confidence game; esp : one worked by undercover police to trap criminals

sting·ray \'stiŋ-ˌrā\ n : any of numerous rays with sharp stinging spines on a whiplike tail

stin·gy \'stin-jē\ adj **stin·gi·er; -est** : not generous : giving or spending as little as possible — **stin·gi·ness** n

stink \'stiŋk\ vb stank \'staŋk\ or stunk \'stəŋk\; stunk; **stink·ing** : to give forth a strong and offensive smell; also : to be extremely bad in quality or repute — **stink** n — **stink·er** n

stink·bug \'stiŋk-ˌbəg\ n : any of various true bugs that emit a disagreeable odor

¹**stint** \'stint\ vb 1 : to be sparing or frugal 2 : to cut short in amount

²**stint** n 1 : an assigned amount of work 2 : RESTRAINT, LIMITATION 3 : a period of time spent at a particular activity

sti·pend \'stī-ˌpend, -pənd\ n [ME, alter. of stipendy, fr. L stipendium, fr. stips gift + pendere to weigh, pay] : a fixed sum of money paid periodically for services or to defray expenses

stip·ple \'sti-pəl\ vb **stip·pled; stip·pling** 1 : to engrave by means of dots and light strokes 2 : to apply (as paint or ink) with small short touches — **stipple** n

stip·u·late \'sti-pyə-ˌlāt\ vb **-lat·ed; -lat·ing** : to make an agreement; esp : to make a special demand for something as a condition in an agreement — **stip·u·la·tion** \ˌsti-pyə-'lā-shən\ n

¹**stir** \'stər\ vb stirred; **stir·ring** 1 : to move slightly 2 : AROUSE, EXCITE 3 : to mix, dissolve, or make by continued circular movement ⟨∼ eggs into cake batter⟩ 4 : to move to activity (as by pushing, beating, or prodding)

²**stir** n 1 : a state of agitation or activity 2 : an act of stirring

stir–fry \'stər-ˌfrī\ vb : to fry quickly over high heat while stirring continuously — **stir–fry** n

¹**stir·ring** \'stər-iŋ\ adj 1 : ACTIVE, BUSTLING 2 : ROUSING, INSPIRING ⟨a ∼ speech⟩

²**stirring** n : a beginning of activity ⟨the first ∼s of revolution⟩

stir·rup \'stər-əp\ n [ME stirop, fr. OE stigrāp, lit., mounting rope] 1 : a light frame hung from a saddle to support the rider's foot 2 : STAPES

¹**stitch** \'stich\ n 1 : a sudden sharp pain esp. in the side 2 : one of the series of loops formed by or over a needle in sewing

²**stitch** vb 1 : to fasten or join with stitches 2 : to decorate with stitches 3 : SEW

stk abbr stock

stoat \'stōt\ *n, pl* **stoats** *also* **stoat** : the common Old and New World ermine esp. in its brown summer coat

¹stock \'stäk\ *n* **1** *archaic* : a block of wood **2** : a stupid person **3** : a wooden part of a thing serving as its support, frame, or handle **4** *pl* : a device for publicly punishing offenders consisting of a wooden frame with holes in which the feet and hands can be locked **5** : the original from which others derive; *also* : a group having a common origin : FAMILY **6** : LIVESTOCK **7** : a supply of goods **8** : the ownership element in a corporation divided to give the owners an interest and usu. voting power **9** : a company of actors playing at a particular theater and presenting a series of plays **10** : liquid in which meat, fish, or vegetables have been simmered that is used as a basis for soup, gravy, or sauce

²stock *vb* : to provide with stock

³stock *adj* : kept regularly for sale or use; *also* : commonly used : STANDARD

stock·ade \stä-'kād\ *n* [Sp *estacada*, fr. *estaca* stake, pale, of Gmc origin] : an enclosure (as of posts and stakes) for defense or confinement

stock·bro·ker \-ˌbrō-kər\ *n* : one who executes orders to buy and sell securities

stock car *n* : a racing car that is similar to a regular car

stock exchange *n* : a place where the buying and selling of securities is conducted

stock·hold·er \'stäk-ˌhōl-dər\ *n* : one who owns corporate stock

stock·i·nette *or* **stock·i·net** \ˌstäk-kə-'net\ *n* : an elastic knitted fabric used esp. for infants' wear and bandages

stock·ing \'stä-kiŋ\ *n* : a close-fitting knitted covering for the foot and leg

stock market *n* **1** : STOCK EXCHANGE **2** : a market for stocks

stock·pile \'stäk-ˌpī(-ə)l\ *n* : a reserve supply of something essential — **stockpile** *vb*

stocky \'stä-kē\ *adj* **stock·i·er; -est** : being short and relatively thick : STURDY ✦ *Synonyms* THICKSET, SQUAT, HEAVYSET, STUBBY

stock·yard \'stäk-ˌyärd\ *n* : a yard for stock; *esp* : one for livestock about to be slaughtered or shipped

stodgy \'stä-jē\ *adj* **stodg·i·er; -est** **1** : thick in texture : HEAVY ⟨∼ bread⟩ **2** : not interesting : DULL ⟨a ∼ accountant⟩ **3** : extremely old-fashioned

¹sto·ic \'stō-ik\ *n* [ME, fr. L *stoicus*, fr. Gk *stōïkos*, lit., of the portico, fr. *Stoa* (*Poikilē*) the Painted Portico, portico at Athens where the philosopher Zeno taught] : one who suffers without complaining

²stoic *or* sto·i·cal \-i-kəl\ *adj* : not affected by passion or feeling; *esp* : showing indifference to pain ✦ *Synonyms* IMPASSIVE, PHLEGMATIC, APATHETIC, STOLID — **sto·ical·ly** \-i-k(ə-)lē\ *adv* — **sto·icism** \'stō-ə-ˌsi-zəm\ *n*

stoke \'stōk\ *vb* **stoked; stok·ing** **1** : to stir up a fire **2** : to tend and supply fuel to a furnace — **stok·er** *n*

STOL *abbr* short takeoff and landing

¹stole *past of* STEAL

²stole \'stōl\ *n* **1** : a long narrow band worn round the neck by some members of the clergy **2** : a long wide scarf or similar covering worn by women

stolen *past part of* STEAL

stol·id \'stä-ləd\ *adj* : not easily aroused or excited : showing little or no emotion ✦ *Synonyms* PHLEGMATIC, APATHETIC, IMPASSIVE, STOIC — **sto·lid·i·ty** \stä-'li-də-tē\ *n* — **stol·id·ly** *adv*

sto·lon \'stō-lən, -ˌlän\ *n* : RUNNER 6

¹stom·ach \'stə-mək\ *n* **1** : a saclike digestive organ of a vertebrate into which food goes from the mouth by way of the throat and which opens below into the intestine **2** : a cavity in an invertebrate animal that is analogous to a stomach **3** : ABDOMEN **4** : desire for food caused by hunger : APPETITE **5** : INCLINATION, DESIRE ⟨had no ∼ for an argument⟩

²stomach *vb* : to bear without open resentment : put up with

stom·ach·ache \-ˌāk\ *n* : pain in or in the region of the stomach

stom·ach·er \'stə-mi-kər, -chər\ *n* : the front of a bodice often appearing between the laces of an outer garment (as in 16th century costume)

stomp \'stämp, 'stȯmp\ *vb* : STAMP — **stomp** *n*

stone \'stōn\ *n* **1** : hardened earth or mineral matter : ROCK **2** : a small piece of rock **3** : a precious stone : GEM **4** : CALCULUS 3 **5** : a hard stony seed (as of a date) or one (as of a plum) with a stony covering **6** *pl usu* **stone** : a British unit of weight equal to 14 pounds — **stony** *also* **ston·ey** \'stō-nē\ *adj*

²stone *vb* **stoned; ston·ing** **1** : to pelt or kill with stones **2** : to remove the stones of (a fruit)

Stone Age *n* : the first known period of prehistoric human culture characterized by the use of stone tools

stoned \'stōnd\ *adj* **1** : DRUNK **2** : being under the influence of a drug

stone·wall \'stōn-ˌwȯl\ *vb* : to refuse to comply or cooperate with

stone·washed \'stōn-ˌwȯsht, -ˌwäsht\ *adj* : having been washed with stones during manufacture to create a softer fabric ⟨∼ jeans⟩

stood *past and past part of* STAND

stooge \'stüj\ *n* **1** : a person who plays a subordinate or compliant role to a principal **2** : STRAIGHT MAN

stool \'stül\ *n* **1** : a seat usu. without back or arms **2** : FOOTSTOOL **3** : a seat used while urinating or defecating **4** : a discharge of fecal matter

stool pigeon *n* : DECOY, INFORMER

¹stoop \'stüp\ *vb* **1** : to bend forward and downward **2** : CONDESCEND **3** : to lower oneself morally

²stoop *n* **1** : an act of bending forward **2** : a bent position of head and shoulders

³stoop *n* [D *stoep*] : a porch, platform, or entrance stairway at a house door

stop \'stäp\ *vb* **stopped; stop·ping** **1** : to close (an opening) by filling or covering closely **2** : BLOCK, HALT **3** : to cease to go on **4** : to bring activity or operation to an end **5** : STAY, TARRY ✦ *Synonyms* QUIT, DISCONTINUE, DESIST, CEASE

²stop *n* **1** : END, CESSATION **2** : a set of organ pipes of one tone quality; *also* : a control knob for such a set **3** : OBSTRUCTION **4** : PLUG, STOPPER **5** : an act of stopping : CHECK **6** : a delay in a journey : STAY **7** : a place for stopping **8** *chiefly Brit* : any of several punctuation marks **9** : a function of an electronic device that stops a recording

stop–ac·tion \'stäp-'ak-shən\ *n* : STOP-MOTION

stop·gap \'stäp-ˌgap\ *n* : something that serves as a temporary expedient

stop·light \-ˌlīt\ *n* : TRAFFIC LIGHT

stop–mo·tion \'stäp-'mō-shən\ *n* : a filming technique in which successive positions of objects are photographed to produce the appearance of movement

stop·over \'stäp-ˌō-vər\ *n* **1** : a stop at an intermediate point in one's journey **2** : a stopping place on a journey

stop·page \'stä-pij\ *n* : the act of stopping : the state of being stopped

stop·per \'stä-pər\ *n* : something (as a cork) for sealing an opening

stop·watch \'stäp-ˌwäch\ *n* : a watch that can be started or stopped at will for exact timing

stor·age \'stȯr-ij\ *n* **1** : space for storing; *also* : cost of storing **2** : MEMORY 6 **3** : the act of storing; *esp* : the safekeeping of goods (as in a warehouse)

storage battery *n* : a group of connected rechargeable electrochemical cells used to provide electric current

¹store \'stȯr\ *vb* **stored; stor·ing** **1** : to place or leave in a safe location for preservation or future use **2** : to provide esp. for a future need

²store *n* **1** : something accumulated and kept for future use **2** : a large or ample quantity **3** : STOREHOUSE **4** : a retail business establishment

store·house \-ˌhau̇s\ *n* : a building for storing goods or supplies; *also* : an abundant source or supply

store·keep·er \-ˌkē-pər\ *n* : one who operates a retail store

store·room \-ˌrüm, -ˌru̇m\ *n* : a room for storing goods or supplies

sto·ried \'stȯr-ēd\ *adj* : celebrated in story or history

stork \'stȯrk\ *n* : any of various large stout-billed Old World wading birds related to the herons and ibises

¹storm \'stȯrm\ *n* **1** : a heavy fall of rain, snow, or hail with high wind **2** : a violent outbreak or disturbance **3** : a mass attack on a defended position — **storm·i·ly** \'stȯr-mə-lē\ *adv* — **storm·i·ness** \-mē-nəs\ *n* — **stormy** *adj*

²storm *vb* **1** : to blow with violence; *also* : to rain, snow, or

hail heavily **2** : to make a mass attack against **3** : to be violently angry : RAGE **4** : to rush along furiously

¹sto·ry \'stȯr-ē\ *n, pl* **stories 1** : NARRATIVE, ACCOUNT **2** : REPORT, STATEMENT **3** : ANECDOTE **4** : SHORT STORY **5** : LIE, FALSEHOOD **6** : a news article or broadcast ♦ *Synonyms* UNTRUTH, TALE, CANARD

²story *also* **sto·rey** \'stȯr-ē\ *n, pl* **stories** *also* **storeys** : a floor of a building or the space between two adjacent floor levels

sto·ry·tell·er \-ˌte-lər\ *n* : a teller of stories

sto·tin \stō-'tēn\ *n, pl* **sto·ti·nov** \stō-'tē-ˌnȯv\ — see *tolar* at MONEY table

sto·tin·ka \stō-'tiŋ-kə\ *n, pl* **-tin·ki** \-kē\ — see *lev* at MONEY table

¹stout \'staut\ *adj* **1** : BRAVE **2** : FIRM ⟨a ∼ refusal⟩ **3** : STURDY **4** : STAUNCH, ENDURING ⟨∼ loyalty⟩ **5** : SOLID **6** : FORCEFUL, VIOLENT ⟨a ∼ attack⟩ ⟨a ∼ wind⟩ **7** : BULKY, THICKSET ♦ *Synonyms* FLESHY, FAT, PORTLY, CORPULENT, OBESE, PLUMP — **stout·ly** *adv* — **stout·ness** *n*

²stout *n* : a dark heavy ale

¹stove \'stōv\ *n* : an apparatus that burns fuel or uses electricity to provide heat (as for cooking or heating)

²stove *past and past part of* STAVE

stow \'stō\ *vb* **1** : HIDE, STORE **2** : to pack in a compact mass

stow·away \'stō-ə-ˌwā\ *n* : one who hides on a vehicle to ride free

STP *abbr* standard temperature and pressure

strad·dle \'stra-dᵊl\ *vb* **strad·dled; strad·dling 1** : to stand, sit, or walk with legs spread apart **2** : to favor or seem to favor two apparently opposite sides — **straddle** *n*

strafe \'strāf\ *vb* **strafed; straf·ing** [G *Gott strafe England* may God punish England, propaganda slogan during World War I] : to fire upon with machine guns from a low-flying airplane

strag·gle \'stra-gəl\ *vb* **strag·gled; strag·gling 1** : to wander from the direct course : ROVE, STRAY **2** : to become separated from others of the same kind — **strag·gler** *n* — **strag·gly** \'stra-g(ə-)lē\ *adj*

¹straight \'strāt\ *adj* **1** : free from curves, bends, angles, or irregularities **2** : not wandering from the main point or proper course ⟨∼ thinking⟩ **3** : HONEST ⟨a ∼ answer⟩ **4** : having the elements in correct order **5** : UNMIXED, UNDILUTED ⟨∼ whiskey⟩ **6** : CONVENTIONAL, SQUARE **7** : HETEROSEXUAL

²straight *adv* : in a straight manner

³straight *n* **1** : a straight line, course, or arrangement **2** : the part of a racetrack between the last turn and the finish **3** : a sequence of five cards in a poker hand

straight–arm \'strāt-ˌärm\ *n* : an act of warding off a person with the arm fully extended — **straight–arm** *vb*

straight·away \'strā-tə-ˌwā\ *n* : a straight stretch (as at a racetrack)

straight·edge \'strāt-ˌej\ *n* : a piece of material with a straight edge for testing straight lines and surfaces or for cutting along or drawing straight lines

straight·en \'strā-tᵊn\ *vb* : to make or become straight

straight flush *n* : a poker hand containing five cards of the same suit in sequence

straight·for·ward \strāt-'fȯr-wərd\ *adj* **1** : FRANK, CANDID, HONEST ⟨a ∼ account⟩ **2** : proceeding in a straight course or manner

straight man *n* : an entertainer who feeds lines to a comedian who replies with usu. humorous quips

straight shooter *n* : a thoroughly upright straightforward person

straight·way \'strāt-'wā, -ˌwā\ *adv* : IMMEDIATELY ⟨get ∼ to work⟩

¹strain \'strān\ *n* [ME *streen* progeny, lineage, fr. OE *strēon* gain, acquisition] **1** : LINEAGE, ANCESTRY **2** : a group (as of people or plants) of presumed common ancestry **3** : an inherited or inherent character or quality ⟨a ∼ of madness in the family⟩ **4** : STREAK, TRACE ⟨a ∼ of fanaticism⟩ **5** : MELODY **6** : the general style or tone

²strain *vb* [ME, fr. AF *estreindre*, fr. L *stringere* to bind or draw tight, press together] **1** : to draw taut **2** : to exert to the utmost **3** : to strive violently **4** : to injure by improper or excessive use **5** : to filter or remove by filtering **6** : to stretch beyond a proper limit — **strain·er** *n*

³strain *n* **1** : excessive tension or exertion (as of body or mind) **2** : bodily injury from excessive tension, effort, or use; *esp* : one in which muscles or ligaments are unduly stretched usu. from a wrench or twist **3** : deformation of a material body under the action of applied forces

¹strait \'strāt\ *adj* [ME, fr. AF *estreit*, fr. L *strictus* strait, strict, fr. pp. of *stringere*] **1** *archaic* : STRICT **2** *archaic* : NARROW **3** *archaic* : CONSTRICTED **4** : DIFFICULT, STRAITENED

²strait *n* **1** : a narrow channel connecting two bodies of water **2** *pl* : DISTRESS

strait·en \'strā-tᵊn\ *vb* **1** : to hem in : CONFINE **2** : to make distressing or difficult

strait·jack·et *also* **straight·jack·et** \'strāt-ˌja-kət\ *n* : a cover or garment of strong material (as canvas) used to bind the body and esp. the arms closely in restraining a violent prisoner or patient — **straitjacket** *vb*

strait·laced *or* **straight·laced** \-'lāst\ *adj* : strict in manners, morals, or opinion

¹strand \'strand\ *n* : SHORE, BEACH

²strand *vb* **1** : to run, drift, or drive upon the shore ⟨∼ed ship⟩ **2** : to place or leave in a helpless position

³strand *n* **1** : one of the fibers twisted or plaited together into a cord, rope, or cable; *also* : a cord, rope, or cable made up of such fibers **2** : a twisted or plaited ropelike mass ⟨a ∼ of pearls⟩ — **strand·ed** \'stran-dəd\ *adj*

¹strange \'strānj\ *adj* **strang·er; strang·est** [ME, fr. AF *estrange*, fr. L *extraneus*, lit., external, fr. *extra* outside] **1** : of external origin, kind, or character **2** : NEW, UNFAMILIAR ⟨moved to a ∼ neighborhood⟩ **3** : DISTANT **6 4** : UNACCUSTOMED, INEXPERIENCED ⟨she was ∼ to his ways⟩ ♦ *Synonyms* SINGULAR, PECULIAR, ECCENTRIC, ERRATIC, ODD, QUEER, QUAINT, CURIOUS — **strange·ly** *adv* — **strange·ness** *n*

²strange *n* : a quark with a charge of $-\frac{1}{3}$ and a measured energy of approximately 150 million electron volts

strang·er \'strān-jər\ *n* **1** : FOREIGNER **2** : INTRUDER **3** : a person with whom one is unacquainted

stran·gle \'straŋ-gəl\ *vb* **stran·gled; stran·gling 1** : to choke to death : THROTTLE **2** : STIFLE, SUPPRESS ⟨repression ∼s free speech⟩ — **stran·gler** *n*

strangler fig *n* : any of several figs that begin life atop a host tree and then send down roots that surround it

stran·gu·late \'straŋ-gyə-ˌlāt\ *vb* **-lat·ed; -lat·ing 1** : STRANGLE, CONSTRICT **2** : to become so constricted as to stop circulation

stran·gu·la·tion \ˌstraŋ-gyə-'lā-shən\ *n* : the act or process of strangling or strangulating; *also* : the state of being strangled or strangulated

¹strap \'strap\ *n* : a narrow strip of flexible material used esp. for fastening, holding together, or wrapping

²strap *vb* **strapped; strap·ping 1** : to secure with a strap **2** : BIND, CONSTRICT **3** : to flog with a strap **4** : STROP

strap·less \-ləs\ *adj* : having no straps; *esp* : having no shoulder straps

¹strapping *adj* : LARGE, STRONG, HUSKY

²strapping *n* : material for a strap

strat·a·gem \'stra-tə-jəm, -ˌjem\ *n* **1** : a trick to deceive or outwit the enemy; *also* : a deceptive scheme **2** : skill in deception

strat·e·gy \'stra-tə-jē\ *n, pl* **-gies** [Gk *stratēgia* generalship, fr. *stratēgos* general, fr. *stratos* camp, army + *agein* to lead] **1** : the science and art of military command aimed at meeting the enemy under conditions advantageous to one's own force **2** : a careful plan or method esp. for achieving an end — **stra·te·gic** \strə-'tē-jik\ *adj* — **strat·e·gist** \'stra-tə-jist\ *n*

strat·i·fy \'stra-tə-ˌfī\ *vb* **-fied; -fy·ing** : to form or arrange in layers — **strat·i·fi·ca·tion** \ˌstra-tə-fə-'kā-shən\ *n*

stra·tig·ra·phy \strə-'ti-grə-fē\ *n* : geology that deals with rock strata — **strati·graph·ic** \ˌstra-tə-'gra-fik\ *adj*

strato·sphere \'stra-tə-ˌsfir\ *n* : the part of the earth's atmosphere between about 7 miles (11 kilometers) and 31 miles (50 kilometers) above the earth — **strato·spher·ic** \ˌstra-tə-'sfir-ik, -'sfer-\ *adj*

stra·tum \'strā-təm, 'stra-\ *n, pl* **stra·ta** \'strā-tə, 'stra-\ [NL, fr. L *stratus*, bed, fr. neut. of *stratus*, pp. of *sternere* to spread out] **1** : a bed, layer, or sheetlike mass (as of one kind of rock lying between layers of other kinds of rock) **2** : a level of culture; *also* : a group of people representing one stage in cultural development

¹**straw** \'strȯ\ n 1 : stalks of grain after threshing; *also* : a single coarse dry stem (as of a grass) 2 : a thing of small worth : TRIFLE 3 : a tube (as of paper or plastic) for sucking up a beverage

²**straw** adj 1 : made of straw 2 : having no real force or validity ⟨a ~ vote⟩

straw·ber·ry \'strȯ-ˌber-ē, -bə-rē\ n : an edible juicy usu. red pulpy fruit of any of several low herbs with white flowers and long slender runners; *also* : one of these herbs

straw boss n : a foreman of a small group of workers

straw·flow·er \'strȯ-ˌflau̇(-ə)r\ n : any of several plants whose flowers can be dried with little loss of form or color

¹**stray** \'strā\ n 1 : a domestic animal wandering at large or lost 2 : WAIF

²**stray** vb 1 : to wander or roam without purpose 2 : DEVIATE

³**stray** adj 1 : having strayed : separated from the group or the main body 2 : occurring at random ⟨~ remarks⟩

¹**streak** \'strēk\ n 1 : a line or mark of a different color or texture from its background 2 : a narrow band of light; *also* : a lightning bolt 3 : a slight admixture : TRACE 4 : a brief run (as of luck); *also* : an unbroken series

²**streak** vb 1 : to form streaks in or on 2 : to move very swiftly

¹**stream** \'strēm\ n 1 : a body of water (as a river) flowing on the earth; *also* : any body of flowing fluid (as water or gas) 2 : a continuous procession ⟨a ~ of traffic⟩

²**stream** vb 1 : to flow in or as if in a stream 2 : to pour out streams of liquid 3 : to trail out in length 4 : to move forward in a steady stream

stream·bed \'strēm-ˌbed\ n : the channel occupied by a stream

stream·er \'strē-mər\ n 1 : a long narrow ribbonlike flag 2 : a long ribbon on a dress or hat 3 : a newspaper headline that runs across the entire sheet 4 pl : AURORA

stream·ing \'strē-miŋ\ adj : relating to or being the transfer of data (as music) in a continuous stream esp. for immediate processing or playback

stream·let \'strēm-lət\ n : a small stream

stream·lined \-ˌlīnd\ adj 1 : made with contours to reduce resistance to motion through water or air 2 : SIMPLIFIED 3 : MODERNIZED — **stream·line** vb

street \'strēt\ n [ME strete, fr. OE strǣt, fr. LL strata paved road, fr. L, fem. of stratus, pp. of sternere to spread out] 1 : a thoroughfare esp. in a city, town, or village 2 : the occupants of the houses on a street

street·car \-ˌkär\ n : a passenger vehicle running on rails on city streets

streetcar

street fighter n : a tough belligerent person

street hockey n : a game resembling ice hockey played on a hard surface with hockey sticks and a small ball

street railway n : a company operating streetcars or buses

street·walk·er \'strēt-ˌwȯ-kər\ n : PROSTITUTE

strength \'streŋth\ n 1 : the quality or state of being strong : ability to do or endure : POWER 2 : TOUGHNESS, SOLIDITY 3 : power to resist attack 4 : INTENSITY 5 : force as measured in numbers ⟨the ~ of an army⟩

strength·en \'streŋ-thən\ vb : to make or become stronger — **strength·en·er** n

stren·u·ous \'stren-yə-wəs\ adj 1 : VIGOROUS, ENERGETIC 2 : requiring energy or stamina — **stren·u·ous·ly** adv

strep \'strep\ n : STREPTOCOCCUS

strep throat n : an inflammatory sore throat caused by streptococci and marked by fever, prostration, and toxemia

strep·to·coc·cus \ˌstrep-tə-'kä-kəs\ n, pl **-coc·ci** \-'kä-ˌkī, -'käk-ˌsī, -'kä-ˌkē, -'käk-ˌsē\ : any of various spherical bacteria that usu. grow in chains and include some causing serious diseases — **strep·to·coc·cal** \-kəl\ adj

strep·to·my·cin \-'mī-sᵊn\ n : an antibiotic produced by soil bacteria and used esp. in treating tuberculosis

¹**stress** \'stres\ n 1 : PRESSURE, STRAIN; *esp* : a force that tends to distort a body 2 : a factor that induces bodily or mental tension; *also* : a state induced by such a stress 3 : EMPHASIS 4 : relative prominence of sound 5 : ACCENT; *also* : any syllable carrying the accent — **stress·ful** \'stres-fəl\ adj

²**stress** vb 1 : to put pressure or strain on 2 : to put emphasis on : ACCENT

¹**stretch** \'strech\ vb 1 : to spread or reach out : EXTEND ⟨~ed out her arm⟩ 2 : to draw out in length or breadth : EXPAND 3 : to make tense : STRAIN 4 : EXAGGERATE 5 : to become extended without breaking ⟨rubber ~es easily⟩ — **stretchy** \'stre-chē\ adj

²**stretch** n 1 : an act of extending or drawing out beyond ordinary or normal limits 2 : a continuous extent in length, area, or time 3 : the extent to which something may be stretched 4 : either of the straight sides of a racecourse

³**stretch** adj : easily stretched ⟨~ pants⟩

¹**stretch·er** \'stre-chər\ n 1 : one that stretches 2 : a device for carrying a sick, injured, or dead person

²**stretcher** vb : to carry or transport on a stretcher

stretch marks n pl : striae on the skin (as of the abdomen) due to excessive stretching and rupture of elastic fibers (as from pregnancy)

strew \'strü\ vb **strewed**; **strewed** or **strewn** \'strün\; **strew·ing** 1 : to spread by scattering 2 : to cover by or as if by scattering something over or on 3 : DISSEMINATE

stria \'strī-ə\ n, pl **stri·ae** \'strī-ˌē\ 1 : STRIATION 3 2 : a stripe or line (as in the skin)

stri·at·ed muscle \'strī-ˌā-təd-\ n : muscle tissue made up of long thin cells with many nuclei and alternate light and dark stripes that includes esp. the muscle of the heart and muscle that moves the vertebrate skeleton and is mostly under voluntary control

stri·a·tion \strī-'ā-shən\ n 1 : the state of being marked with stripes or lines 2 : arrangement of striations or striae 3 : a minute groove, scratch, or channel esp. when one of a parallel series

strick·en \'stri-kən\ adj 1 : afflicted by or as if by disease, misfortune, or sorrow 2 : WOUNDED

strict \'strikt\ adj 1 : allowing no evasion or escape : RIGOROUS ⟨~ discipline⟩ 2 : ACCURATE, PRECISE ⟨the ~ sense of the word⟩ ♦ **Synonyms** STRINGENT, RIGID — **strict·ly** adv — **strict·ness** n

stric·ture \'strik-chər\ n 1 : an abnormal narrowing of a bodily passage; *also* : the narrowed part 2 : hostile criticism : a critical remark

¹**stride** \'strīd\ vb **strode** \'strōd\; **strid·den** \'stri-dᵊn\; **strid·ing** : to walk or run with long regular steps — **strid·er** n

²**stride** n 1 : a long step 2 : a stage of progress 3 : manner of striding : GAIT

stri·dent \'strī-dᵊnt\ adj : harsh sounding : GRATING, SHRILL

strife \'strīf\ n : CONFLICT, FIGHT, STRUGGLE ♦ **Synonyms** DISCORD, CONTENTION, DISSENSION

¹**strike** \'strīk\ vb **struck** \'strək\; **struck** also **strick·en** \'stri-kən\; **strik·ing** 1 : to take a course : GO ⟨struck off through the brush⟩ 2 : to touch or hit sharply; *also* : to deliver a blow 3 : to produce by or as if by a blow ⟨struck terror in the foe⟩ 4 : to lower (as a flag or sail) 5 : to collide with; *also* : to injure or destroy by collision 6 : DELETE, CANCEL 7 : to produce by impressing ⟨struck a medal⟩; *also* : COIN ⟨~ a new cent⟩ 8 : to cause to sound ⟨~ a bell⟩ 9 : to afflict suddenly : lay low ⟨stricken with a high fever⟩ 10 : to appear to; *also* : to appear to as remarkable : IMPRESS 11 : to reach by reckoning ⟨~ an average⟩ 12 : to stop work in order to obtain a change in conditions of employment 13 : to cause (a match) to ignite by rubbing 14 : to come upon ⟨~ gold⟩ 15 : TAKE ON, ASSUME ⟨~ a pose⟩ — **strik·er** n

²**strike** *n* 1 : an act or instance of striking 2 : a sudden discovery of rich ore or oil deposits 3 : a pitched baseball that is swung at but not hit 4 : the knocking down of all the bowling pins with the 1st ball 5 : a military attack

strike·break·er \-ˌbrā-kər\ *n* : a person hired to replace a striking worker

strike·out \-ˌaút\ *n* : an out in baseball as a result of a batter's being charged with three strikes

strike out *vb* 1 : to enter upon a course of action 2 : to start out vigorously 3 : to make an out in baseball by a strikeout

strike·slip \'strīk-ˌslip\ *n* : a fault about which movement is predominantly horizontal

strike up *vb* 1 : to begin or cause to begin to sing or play 2 : BEGIN ⟨~ a conversation⟩

strike zone *n* : the area over home plate through which a pitched baseball must pass to be called a strike

striking *adj* : attracting attention : very noticeable ♦ **Synonyms** ARRESTING, SALIENT, CONSPICUOUS, OUTSTANDING, REMARKABLE, PROMINENT — **strik·ing·ly** *adv*

¹**string** \'striŋ\ *n* 1 : a line usu. composed of twisted threads 2 : a series of things arranged as if strung on a cord 3 : a plant fiber (as a leaf vein) 4 *pl* : the stringed instruments of an orchestra ♦ **Synonyms** SUCCESSION, PROGRESSION, SEQUENCE, CHAIN, TRAIN

²**string** *vb* **strung** \'strəŋ\; **string·ing** 1 : to provide with strings ⟨~ a racket⟩ 2 : to make tense 3 : to thread on or as if on a string ⟨~ pearls⟩ 4 : to hang, tie, or fasten by a string 5 : to take the strings out of ⟨~ beans⟩ 6 : to extend like a string

string bean *n* : a bean of one of the older varieties of kidney bean that have stringy fibers on the lines of separation of the pods; *also* : SNAP BEAN

string bikini *n* : a scanty bikini

string cheese *n* : cheese that can be pulled apart in narrow strips

stringed \'striŋd\ *adj* 1 : having strings ⟨~ instruments⟩ 2 : produced by strings

strin·gen·cy \'strin-jən-sē\ *n* 1 : STRICTNESS, SEVERITY 2 : SCARCITY ⟨~ of money⟩ — **strin·gent** \-jənt\ *adj*

string·er \'striŋ-ər\ *n* 1 : a long horizontal member in a framed structure or a bridge 2 : a news correspondent paid by the amount of copy

stringy \'striŋ-ē\ *adj* **string·i·er; -est** 1 : resembling string esp. in tough, fibrous, or disordered quality ⟨~ meat⟩ ⟨~ hair⟩ 2 : lean and sinewy in build

¹**strip** \'strip\ *vb* **stripped** \'stript\ *also* **stript; strip·ping** 1 : to take the covering or clothing from 2 : to take off one's clothes 3 : to pull or tear off 4 : to make bare or clear (as by cutting or grazing) 5 : PLUNDER, PILLAGE ♦ **Synonyms** DIVEST, DENUDE, DEPRIVE, DISMANTLE — **strip·per** *n*

²**strip** *n* 1 : a long narrow flat piece 2 : AIRSTRIP

¹**stripe** \'strīp\ *vb* **striped** \'strīpt\; **strip·ing** : to make stripes on

²**stripe** *n* 1 : a line or long narrow division having a different color from the background 2 : a strip of braid (as on a sleeve) indicating military rank or length of service 3 : TYPE, CHARACTER — **striped** \'strīpt, 'strī-pəd\ *adj*

striped bass *n* : a large black-striped marine bony fish that occurs along the Atlantic and Pacific coasts of the U.S. and is an excellent food and sport fish

strip·ling \'stri-pliŋ\ *n* : YOUTH, LAD

strip mall *n* : a long building or group of buildings housing several retail stores or service establishments

strip mine *n* : a mine that is worked from the earth's surface by the stripping of the topsoil — **strip·mine** *vb*

strip·tease \'strip-ˌtēz\ *n* : a burlesque act in which a performer removes clothing piece by piece — **strip·teas·er** *n*

strive \'strīv\ *vb* **strove** \'strōv\ *also* **strived** \'strīvd\; **striv·en** \'stri-vən\ *or* **strived; striv·ing** 1 : to make effort : labor hard 2 : to struggle in opposition : CONTEND ♦ **Synonyms** ENDEAVOR, ATTEMPT, TRY, ASSAY

strobe \'strōb\ *n* 1 : STROBOSCOPE 2 : a device for high-speed intermittent illumination (as in photography)

stro·bo·scope \'strō-bə-ˌskōp\ *n* : an instrument for studying rapid motion by means of a rapidly flashing light

strode *past of* STRIDE

¹**stroke** \'strōk\ *vb* **stroked; strok·ing** 1 : to rub gently 2 : to flatter in a manner designed to persuade

²**stroke** *n* 1 : the act of striking : BLOW, KNOCK 2 : a sudden action or process producing an impact ⟨~ of lightning⟩; *also* : an unexpected result 3 : sudden weakening or loss of consciousness or the power to move or feel caused by rupture or obstruction (as by a clot) of a blood vessel of the brain 4 : one of a series of movements against air or water to get through or over it ⟨the ~ of a bird's wing⟩ 5 : a rower who sets the pace for a crew 6 : a vigorous effort 7 : the sound of striking (as of a clock) 8 : a single movement with or as if with a tool or implement (as a pen)

stroll \'strōl\ *vb* : to walk in a leisurely or idle manner — **stroll** *n* — **stroll·er** *n*

strong \'strȯŋ\ *adj* **stron·ger** \'strȯŋ-gər\; **stron·gest** \'strȯŋ-gəst\ 1 : POWERFUL, VIGOROUS 2 : HEALTHY, ROBUST 3 : of a specified number ⟨an army 10 thousand ~⟩ 4 : not mild or weak 5 : VIOLENT ⟨~ wind⟩ 6 : ZEALOUS ⟨a ~ supporter⟩ 7 : not easily broken 8 : FIRM, SOLID ⟨~ beliefs⟩ ♦ **Synonyms** STOUT, STURDY, STALWART, TOUGH — **strong·ly** *adv*

strong–arm \'strȯŋ-ˌärm\ *adj* : having or using undue force ⟨~ operatives⟩

strong force *n* : the physical force responsible for binding together nucleons in the atomic nucleus

strong·hold \-ˌhold\ *n* : a fortified place : FORTRESS

strong·man \-ˌman\ *n* : one who leads or controls by force of will and character or by military strength

stron·tium \'strän-chē-əm, 'strän-tē-əm\ *n* : a soft malleable metallic chemical element

¹**strop** \'sträp\ *n* : STRAP; *esp* : one for sharpening a razor

²**strop** *vb* **stropped; strop·ping** : to sharpen a razor on a strop

stro·phe \'strō-fē\ *n* [Gk *strophē*, lit., act of turning] : a division of a poem — **stroph·ic** \'strä-fik\ *adj*

strove *past of* STRIVE

struck *past and past part of* STRIKE

¹**struc·ture** \'strək-chər\ *n* [ME, fr. L *structura*, fr. *structus*, pp. of *struere* to heap up, build] 1 : the action of building : CONSTRUCTION 2 : something built (as a house or a dam); *also* : something made up of interdependent parts in a definite pattern of organization 3 : arrangement or relationship of elements (as particles, parts, or organs) in a substance, body, or system — **struc·tur·al** *adj*

²**structure** *vb* **struc·tured; struc·tur·ing** : to make into a structure

stru·del \'strüd-ᵊl, 'shtrü-\ *n* [G, lit., whirlpool] : a pastry made of a thin sheet of dough rolled up with filling and baked ⟨apple ~⟩

¹**strug·gle** \'strə-gəl\ *vb* **strug·gled; strug·gling** 1 : to make strenuous efforts against opposition : STRIVE 2 : to proceed with difficulty or with great effort ♦ **Synonyms** ENDEAVOR, ATTEMPT, TRY, ASSAY

²**struggle** *n* 1 : CONTEST, STRIFE 2 : a violent effort or exertion

strum \'strəm\ *vb* **strummed; strum·ming** : to play on a stringed instrument by brushing the strings with the fingers ⟨~ a guitar⟩

strum·pet \'strəm-pət\ *n* : PROSTITUTE

strung \'strəŋ\ *past and past part of* STRING

¹**strut** \'strət\ *vb* **strut·ted; strut·ting** : to walk with an affectedly proud gait

²**strut** *n* 1 : a bar or rod for resisting lengthwise pressure 2 : a haughty or pompous gait

strych·nine \'strik-ˌnīn, -nən, -ˌnēn\ *n* : a bitter poisonous plant alkaloid used as a poison (as for rats) and medicinally as a stimulant of the central nervous system

¹**stub** \'stəb\ *n* 1 : STUMP 2 : a short blunt end 3 : a small part of each leaf (as of a checkbook) kept as a memorandum of the items on the detached part

²**stub** *vb* **stubbed; stub·bing** : to strike (as one's toe) against something

stub·ble \'stə-bəl\ *n* 1 : the cut stem ends of herbs and esp. grasses left in the soil after harvest 2 : a rough surface or growth resembling stubble — **stub·bly** \-b(ə-)lē\ *adj*

stub·born \'stə-bərn\ *adj* 1 : FIRM, DETERMINED 2 : done or continued in a willful, unreasonable, or persistent manner 3 : not easily controlled or remedied ⟨a ~ cold⟩ — **stub·born·ly** *adv* — **stub·born·ness** *n*

stub·by \'stə-bē\ *adj* : short, blunt, and thick like a stub

stuc·co \'stə-kō\ *n, pl* **stuccos** *or* **stuccoes** [It] : plaster for coating exterior walls — **stuc·coed** \'stə-kōd\ *adj*

stuck *past and past part of* STICK

stuck-up \'stək-'əp\ *adj* : CONCEITED

¹stud \'stəd\ *n* : a male animal and esp. a horse (**stud·horse** \-ˌhȯrs\) kept for breeding

²stud *n* **1** : one of the smaller uprights in a building to which the wall materials are fastened **2** : a removable device like a button used as a fastener or ornament ⟨shirt ~s⟩ **3** : a projecting nail, pin, or rod

³stud *vb* **stud·ded; stud·ding 1** : to supply with or adorn with studs **2** : DOT ⟨the sky was *studded* with stars⟩

⁴stud *abbr* student

stud·book \'stəd-ˌbu̇k\ *n* : an official record of the pedigree of purebred animals (as horses or dogs)

studding *n* : the studs in a building or wall

stu·dent \'stü-d⁰nt, 'styü-\ *n* : SCHOLAR, PUPIL; *esp* : one who attends a school

stud·ied \'stə-dēd\ *adj* : INTENTIONAL ⟨a ~ insult⟩ ♦ **Synonyms** DELIBERATE, CONSIDERED, PREMEDITATED, DESIGNED

stu·dio \'stü-dē-ˌō, 'styü-\ *n, pl* **-dios 1** : a place where an artist works; *also* : a place for the study of an art **2** : a place where motion pictures are made **3** : a place equipped for the transmission of radio or television programs

stu·di·ous \'stü-dē-əs, 'styü-\ *adj* : devoted to study — **stu·di·ous·ly** *adv*

¹study \'stə-dē\ *n, pl* **stud·ies 1** : the use of the mind to gain knowledge **2** : the act or process of learning about something **3** : careful examination **4** : INTENT, PURPOSE **5** : a branch of learning **6** : a room esp. for reading and writing

²study *vb* **stud·ied; study·ing 1** : to engage in study or the study of **2** : to consider attentively or in detail ♦ **Synonyms** CONSIDER, CONTEMPLATE, WEIGH

¹stuff \'stəf\ *n* [ME, fr. AF *estuffes* goods, fr. *estuffer* to fill in (with rubble), furnish, equip, of Gmc origin] **1** : personal property **2** : raw material **3** : a finished textile fabric; *esp* : a worsted fabric **4** : writing, talk, or ideas of little or transitory worth **5** : an unspecified material substance or aggregate of matter **6** : fundamental material **7** : special knowledge or capability

²stuff *vb* **1** : to fill by packing things in : CRAM **2** : to eat greedily : GORGE **3** : to prepare (as meat) by filling with a stuffing **4** : to fill (as a cushion) with a soft material **5** : to stop up : PLUG

stuffed shirt \'stəft-\ *n* : a smug, conceited, and usu. pompous and inflexibly conservative person

stuff·ing *n* : material used to fill tightly; *esp* : a mixture of bread crumbs and spices used to stuff food

stuffy \'stə-fē\ *adj* **stuff·i·er; -est 1** : STODGY **2** : lacking fresh air : CLOSE; *also* : blocked up ⟨a ~ nose⟩

stul·ti·fy \'stəl-tə-ˌfī\ *vb* **-fied; -fy·ing 1** : to cause to appear foolish or stupid **2** : to impair, invalidate, or make ineffective **3** : to have a dulling effect on — **stul·ti·fi·ca·tion** \ˌstəl-tə-fə-'kā-shən\ *n*

stum·ble \'stəm-bəl\ *vb* **stum·bled; stum·bling 1** : to blunder morally **2** : to trip in walking or running **3** : to walk unsteadily; *also* : to speak or act in a blundering or clumsy manner **4** : to happen by chance — **stumble** *n*

stumbling block *n* : an obstacle to belief, understanding, or progress

¹stump \'stəmp\ *n* **1** : the base of a bodily part (as a leg or tooth) left after the rest is removed **2** : the part of a plant and esp. a tree remaining with the root after the trunk is cut off **3** : a place or occasion for political public speaking — **stumpy** *adj*

²stump *vb* **1** : BAFFLE, PERPLEX **2** : to clear (land) of stumps **3** : to tour (a region) making political speeches **4** : to walk clumsily and heavily

stun \'stən\ *vb* **stunned; stun·ning 1** : to make senseless or dizzy by or as if by a blow **2** : BEWILDER, STUPEFY ⟨*stunned* by the news⟩

stung *past and past part of* STING

stunk *past and past part of* STINK

stun·ning *adj* **1** : causing astonishment or disbelief **2** : strikingly beautiful — **stun·ning·ly** *adv*

¹stunt \'stənt\ *vb* : to hinder the normal growth or progress of

²stunt *n* : an unusual or spectacular feat

stu·pe·fy \'stü-pə-ˌfī, 'styü-\ *vb* **-fied; -fy·ing 1** : to make stupid, groggy, or insensible **2** : ASTONISH — **stu·pe·fac·tion** \ˌstü-pə-'fak-shən, ˌstyü-\ *n*

stu·pen·dous \stu̇-'pen-dəs, styu̇-\ *adj* : causing astonishment esp. because of great size or height ♦ **Synonyms** TREMENDOUS, PRODIGIOUS, MONUMENTAL, MONSTROUS — **stu·pen·dous·ly** *adv*

stu·pid \'stü-pəd, 'styü-\ *adj* [MF *stupide*, fr. L *stupidus*, fr. *stupēre* to be numb, be astonished] **1** : very dull in mind **2** : showing or resulting from dullness of mind — **stu·pid·i·ty** \stü-'pi-də-tē, styü-\ *n* — **stu·pid·ly** *adv*

stu·por \'stü-pər, 'styü-\ *n* **1** : a condition of greatly dulled or completely suspended sense or feeling **2** : a state of extreme apathy or torpor often following stress or shock — **stu·por·ous** *adj*

stur·dy \'stər-dē\ *adj* **stur·di·er; -est** [ME, brave, stubborn, fr. AF *esturdi* stunned, fr. pp. of *esturdir* to stun, fr. VL **exturdire*, fr. L *ex-* + VL **turdus* simpleton, fr. L *turdus* thrush] **1** : STRONG, ROBUST **2** : RESOLUTE, UNYIELDING ♦ **Synonyms** STOUT, STALWART, TOUGH, TENACIOUS — **stur·di·ly** \-də-lē\ *adv* — **stur·di·ness** \-dē-nəs\ *n*

stur·geon \'stər-jən\ *n* : any of a family of large bony fishes including some whose roe are made into caviar

stut·ter \'stə-tər\ *vb* : to speak with involuntary disruption or blocking of sounds — **stutter** *n* — **stut·ter·er** *n*

stutter step *n* : a move made by a runner (as in football) done to fake a defender out of position

¹sty \'stī\ *n, pl* **sties** : PIGPEN

²sty *or* **stye** *n, pl* **sties** *or* **styes** : an inflamed swelling of a skin gland on the edge of an eyelid

¹style \'stī(-ə)l\ *n* **1** : mode of address : TITLE **2** : a way of speaking or writing; *esp* : one characteristic of an individual, period, school, or nation ⟨ornate ~⟩ **3** : manner or method of acting, making, or performing; *also* : a distinctive or characteristic manner **4** : a slender pointed instrument or process; *esp* : STYLUS **5** : a fashionable manner or mode **6** : overall excellence, skill, or grace in performance, manner, or appearance **7** : the custom followed in spelling, capitalization, punctuation, and typography — **sty·lis·tic** \stī-'lis-tik\ *adj*

²style *vb* **styled; styl·ing 1** : NAME, DESIGNATE **2** : to make or design in accord with a prevailing mode

styling *n* : the way in which something is styled

styl·ise *Brit var of* STYLIZE

styl·ish \'stī-lish\ *adj* : conforming to current fashion ♦ **Synonyms** MODISH, SMART, CHIC — **styl·ish·ly** *adv* — **styl·ish·ness** *n*

styl·ist \'stī-list\ *n* **1** : one (as a writer) noted for a distinctive style **2** : a developer or designer of styles

styl·ize \'stī-ˌlīz, 'stī-ə-\ *vb* **styl·ized; styl·iz·ing** : to conform to a style; *esp* : to represent or design according to a pattern or style rather than according to nature or tradition — **styl·i·za·tion** \ˌstī-lə-'zā-shən\ *n*

sty·lus \'stī-ləs\ *n, pl* **sty·li** \'stī-ˌlī\ *also* **sty·lus·es** \'stī-lə-səz\ [L *stylus, stilus* spike, stylus] **1** : a pointed implement used by the ancients for writing on wax **2** : a phonograph needle **3** : a pen-shaped pointing device for entering data into a computer

sty·mie \'stī-mē\ *vb* **sty·mied; sty·mie·ing** : BLOCK, FRUSTRATE ⟨managed to ~ opposition⟩

styp·tic \'stip-tik\ *adj* : tending to check bleeding — **styptic** *n*

suave \'swäv\ *adj* [F, fr. MF, pleasant, sweet, fr. L *suavis*] : persuasively pleasing : smoothly agreeable ♦ **Synonyms** URBANE, SMOOTH, BLAND — **suave·ly** *adv* — **sua·vi·ty** \'swä-və-tē\ *n*

¹sub \'səb\ *n* : SUBSTITUTE — **sub** *vb*

²sub *n* : SUBMARINE

³sub *abbr* **1** subtract **2** suburb

sub- \'səb\ *prefix* **1** : under : beneath **2** : subordinate : secondary **3** : subordinate portion of : subdivision of **4** : with repetition of a process described in a simple verb so as to form, stress, or deal with subordinate parts or relations **5** : somewhat **6** : falling nearly in the category of : bordering on

subacute	subatmospheric
subagency	subaverage
subagent	subbasement
subaqueous	subcategory
subarctic	subcellular
subarea	subchapter

subclass
subclassify
subcommittee
subcontract
subcontractor
subculture
subcutaneous
subdiscipline
subentry
subfamily
subfield
subfreezing
subgenre
subgenus
subgroup
subhead
subheading
subhuman
subkingdom
sublethal
subliterate
subminimal
subminimum
suboptimal
suborder
subparagraph

subparallel
subphylum
subplot
subpopulation
subproblem
subprofessional
subprogram
subregion
subroutine
subsection
subsense
subsoil
substage
substation
subsystem
subteen
subthreshold
subtopic
subtotal
subtreasury
subtype
subunit
subvariety
subvisible
subzero

sub·al·pine \ˌsəb-ˈal-ˌpīn\ *adj* **1** : of or relating to the region about the foot and lower slopes of the Alps **2** : of, relating to, or inhabiting high upland slopes esp. just below the timberline

sub·al·tern \sə-ˈbȯl-tərn\ *n* : SUBORDINATE; *esp* : a junior officer (as in the British army)

sub·as·sem·bly \ˌsəb-ə-ˈsem-blē\ *n* : an assembled unit to be incorporated with other units in a finished product

sub·atom·ic \ˌsəb-ə-ˈtä-mik\ *adj* : of or relating to the inside of the atom or to particles smaller than atoms

sub·clin·i·cal \ˌsəb-ˈkli-nə-kəl\ *adj* : not detectable by the usual clinical tests ⟨a ∼ infection⟩

sub·com·pact \ˈsəb-ˈkäm-ˌpakt\ *n* : an automobile smaller than a compact

¹sub·con·scious \ˌsəb-ˈkän-chəs, ˈsəb-\ *adj* : existing in the mind without entering conscious awareness — **sub·con·scious·ly** *adv* — **sub·con·scious·ness** *n*

²subconscious *n* : mental activities just below the threshold of consciousness

sub·con·ti·nent \ˈsəb-ˈkän-tə-nənt\ *n* : a major subdivision of a continent — **sub·con·ti·nen·tal** \ˌsəb-ˌkän-tə-ˈnen-tᵊl\ *adj*

sub·di·vide \ˌsəb-də-ˈvīd, ˈsəb-də-ˌvīd\ *vb* : to divide the parts of into more parts; *esp* : to divide (a tract of land) into building lots — **sub·di·vi·sion** \-ˈvi-zhən, -ˌvi-\ *n*

sub·duc·tion \səb-ˈdək-shən\ *n* : the descent of the edge of one crustal plate beneath the edge of an adjacent plate

sub·due \səb-ˈdü, -ˈdyü\ *vb* **sub·dued; sub·du·ing** **1** : to bring into subjection : VANQUISH **2** : to bring under control : CURB **3** : to reduce the intensity of

subj *abbr* **1** subject **2** subjunctive

¹sub·ject \ˈsəb-jikt\ *n* [ME *suget, subget*, fr. AF, fr. L *subjectus* one under authority & *subjectum* subject of a proposition, fr. *subicere* to subject, lit., to throw under, fr. *sub-* under + *jacere* to throw] **1** : a person under the authority of another **2** : a person subject to a sovereign **3** : an individual that is studied or experimented on **4** : the person or thing discussed or treated : TOPIC, THEME **5** : a word or word group denoting that of which something is predicated

²subject *adj* **1** : being under the power or rule of another **2** : LIABLE, EXPOSED ⟨∼ to floods⟩ **3** : dependent on some act or condition ⟨appointment ∼ to senate approval⟩ ✦ *Synonyms* SUBORDINATE, SECONDARY, TRIBUTARY, COLLATERAL, DEPENDENT

³sub·ject \səb-ˈjekt\ *vb* **1** : to bring under control : CONQUER **2** : to make liable **3** : to cause to undergo or endure — **sub·jec·tion** \-ˈjek-shən\ *n*

sub·jec·tive \(ˌ)səb-ˈjek-tiv\ *adj* **1** : of, relating to, or constituting a subject **2** : of, relating to, or arising within one's self or mind in contrast to what is outside : PERSONAL ⟨∼ judgments⟩ ⟨a ∼ sensation⟩ — **sub·jec·tive·ly** *adv* — **sub·jec·tiv·i·ty** \-jek-ˈti-və-tē\ *n*

subject matter *n* : matter presented for consideration, discussion, or study

sub·join \(ˌ)səb-ˈjȯin\ *vb* : APPEND ⟨∼ed a statement of expenses to her report⟩

sub ju·di·ce \(ˌ)sùb-ˈyü-di-ˌkā, ˈsəb-ˈjü-də-(ˌ)sē\ *adv* [L] : before a judge or court : not yet legally decided

sub·ju·gate \ˈsəb-ji-ˌgāt\ *vb* **-gat·ed; -gat·ing** : CONQUER, SUBDUE; *also* : ENSLAVE ✦ *Synonyms* REDUCE, OVERCOME, OVERTHROW, VANQUISH, DEFEAT, BEAT — **sub·ju·ga·tion** \ˌsəb-ji-ˈgā-shən\ *n*

sub·junc·tive \səb-ˈjəŋk-tiv\ *adj* : of, relating to, or constituting a verb form that represents an act or state as contingent or possible or viewed emotionally (as with desire) ⟨the ∼ mood⟩ — **subjunctive** *n*

sub·lease \ˈsəb-ˈlēs, -ˌlēs\ *n* : a lease by a lessee of part or all of leased premises to another person with the original lessee retaining some right under the original lease — **sublease** *vb*

¹sub·let \ˈsəb-ˈlet\ *vb* **-let; -let·ting** : to let all or a part of (a leased property) to another; *also* : to rent (a property) from a lessee

²sublet \-ˌlet\ *n* : property and esp. housing obtained by or available through a sublease

sub·li·mate \ˈsə-blə-ˌmāt\ *vb* **-mat·ed; -mat·ing** **1** : SUBLIME **2** : to direct the expression of (as a desire or impulse) from a primitive to a more socially and culturally acceptable form — **sub·li·ma·tion** \ˌsə-blə-ˈmā-shən\ *n*

¹sub·lime \sə-ˈblīm\ *vb* **sub·limed; sub·lim·ing** : to pass or cause to pass directly from the solid to the vapor state

²sublime *adj* **1** : EXALTED, NOBLE **2** : having awe-inspiring beauty or grandeur ✦ *Synonyms* GLORIOUS, SPLENDID, SUPERB, RESPLENDENT, GORGEOUS — **sub·lime·ly** *adv* — **sub·lim·i·ty** \-ˈbli-mə-tē\ *n*

sub·lim·i·nal \(ˌ)səb-ˈli-mə-nᵊl, ˈsəb-\ *adj* [*sub-* + L *limin-, limen* threshold] **1** : inadequate to produce a sensation or mental awareness ⟨∼ stimuli⟩ **2** : existing or functioning below the threshold of consciousness ⟨the ∼ mind⟩ ⟨∼ advertising⟩

sub·ma·chine gun \ˌsəb-mə-ˈshēn-ˌgən\ *n* : an automatic firearm fired from the shoulder or hip

¹sub·ma·rine \ˈsəb-mə-ˌrēn, ˌsəb-mə-ˈrēn\ *adj* : UNDERWATER; *esp* : UNDERSEA

²submarine *n* **1** : a naval vessel designed to operate underwater **2** : a large sandwich made from a long split roll with any of a variety of fillings

sub·merge \səb-ˈmərj\ *vb* **sub·merged; sub·merg·ing** **1** : to put or plunge under the surface of water **2** : INUNDATE — **sub·mer·gence** \-ˈmər-jəns\ *n*

sub·merse \səb-ˈmərs\ *vb* **sub·mersed; sub·mers·ing** : SUBMERGE — **sub·mer·sion** \-ˈmər-zhən\ *n*

¹sub·mers·ible \səb-ˈmər-sə-bəl\ *adj* : capable of being submerged

²submersible *n* : something that is submersible; *esp* : a small underwater craft used for deep-sea research

sub·mi·cro·sco·pic \ˌsəb-ˌmī-krə-ˈskä-pik\ *adj* : too small to be seen in an ordinary light microscope

sub·min·ia·ture \ˌsəb-ˈmi-nē-ə-ˌchùr, ˈsəb-, -ˈmi-ni-ˌchùr, -chər\ *adj* : very small

sub·mit \səb-ˈmit\ *vb* **sub·mit·ted; sub·mit·ting** **1** : to commit to the discretion or decision of another or of others **2** : YIELD, SURRENDER **3** : to put forward as an opinion — **sub·mis·sion** \-ˈmi-shən\ *n* — **sub·mis·sive** \-ˈmi-siv\ *adj*

sub·nor·mal \ˌsəb-ˈnȯr-məl\ *adj* : falling below what is normal; *also* : having less of something and esp. intelligence than is normal — **sub·nor·mal·i·ty** \ˌsəb-nȯr-ˈma-lə-tē\ *n*

sub·or·bit·al \ˌsəb-ˈȯr-bə-tᵊl, ˈsəb-\ *adj* : being or involving less than one orbit

¹sub·or·di·nate \sə-ˈbȯr-də-nət\ *adj* **1** : of lower class or rank ⟨a ∼ officer⟩ **2** : INFERIOR **3** : submissive to authority **4** : subordinated to other elements in a sentence : DEPENDENT ⟨∼ clause⟩ ✦ *Synonyms* SECONDARY, SUBJECT, TRIBUTARY, COLLATERAL

²subordinate *n* : one that is subordinate

³sub·or·di·nate \sə-ˈbȯr-də-ˌnāt\ *vb* **-nat·ed; -nat·ing** **1** : SUBDUE **2** : to place in a lower rank or class — **sub·or·di·na·tion** \-ˌbȯr-də-ˈnā-shən\ *n*

sub·orn \sə-ˈbȯrn\ *vb* **1** : to induce secretly to do an unlawful thing **2** : to induce to commit perjury — **sub·or·na·tion** \ˌsə-ˌbȯr-ˈnā-shən\ *n*

¹sub·poe·na \sə-ˈpē-nə\ *n* [ME *suppena*, fr. L *sub poena* under penalty] : a writ commanding the person named in it to attend court under penalty for failure to do so

²subpoena vb **-naed; -na·ing** : to summon with a subpoena

sub–Sa·ha·ran \ˌsəb-sə-'her-ən\ adj : of, relating to, or being the part of Africa south of the Sahara

sub·scribe \səb-'skrīb\ vb **sub·scribed; sub·scrib·ing 1** : to sign one's name to a document **2** : to give consent by or as if by signing one's name **3** : to promise to contribute by signing one's name with the amount promised **4** : to place an order by signing **5** : to receive a periodical or service regularly on order **6** : FAVOR, APPROVE ✦ **Synonyms** AGREE, ACQUIESCE, ASSENT, ACCEDE — **sub·scrib·er** n

sub·script \'səb-ˌskript\ n : a symbol (as a letter or number) immediately below or below and to the right or left of another written character — **subscript** adj

sub·scrip·tion \səb-'skrip-shən\ n **1** : the act of subscribing : SIGNATURE **2** : a purchase by signed order

sub·se·quent \'səb-si-kwənt, -sə-ˌkwent\ adj : following after : SUCCEEDING ⟨∼ events⟩ — **sub·se·quent·ly** adv

sub·ser·vi·ence \səb-'sər-vē-əns\ n **1** : a subordinate place or condition **2** : SERVILITY — **sub·ser·vi·en·cy** \-ən-sē\ n — **sub·ser·vi·ent** \-ənt\ adj

sub·set \'səb-ˌset\ n : a set each of whose elements is an element of an inclusive set

sub·side \səb-'sīd\ vb **sub·sid·ed; sub·sid·ing** [L subsidere, fr. sub- under + sidere to sit down, sink] **1** : to settle to the bottom of a liquid **2** : to tend downward : DESCEND **3** : SINK, SUBMERGE ⟨subsided into a chair⟩ **4** : to become quiet and tranquil ✦ **Synonyms** ABATE, WANE, MODERATE, SLACKEN — **sub·sid·ence** \səb-'sīd°ns, 'səb-sə-dəns\ n

¹sub·sid·iary \səb-'si-dē-ˌer-ē\ adj **1** : furnishing aid or support **2** : of secondary importance **3** : of or relating to a subsidy ✦ **Synonyms** AUXILIARY, CONTRIBUTORY, SUBSERVIENT, ACCESSORY

²subsidiary n, pl **-iar·ies** : one that is subsidiary; esp : a company controlled by another

sub·si·dise Brit var of SUBSIDIZE

sub·si·dize \'səb-sə-ˌdīz\ vb **-dized; -diz·ing** : to aid or furnish with a subsidy

sub·si·dy \'səb-sə-dē\ n, pl **-dies** [ME, subsidie, fr. AF, fr. L subsidium reserve troops, support, assistance, fr. sub- near + sedēre to sit] : a gift of public money to a private person or company or to another government

sub·sist \səb-'sist\ vb **1** : EXIST, PERSIST **2** : to have the means (as food and clothing) of maintaining life; esp : to nourish oneself

sub·sis·tence \səb-'sis-təns\ n **1** : EXISTENCE **2** : means of subsisting : the minimum (as of food and clothing) necessary to support life

sub·son·ic \ˌsəb-'sä-nik, 'səb-\ adj : being or relating to a speed less than that of sound; also : moving at such a speed

sub·species \'səb-ˌspē-shēz, -ˌsēz\ n : a subdivision of a species; esp : a category in biological classification ranking just below a species that designates a geographic population genetically distinct from other such populations and potentially able to breed with them where its range overlaps theirs

sub·stance \'səb-stəns\ n **1** : essential nature : ESSENCE ⟨divine ∼⟩; also : the fundamental or essential part or quality ⟨the ∼ of the speech⟩ **2** : physical material from which something is made or which has discrete existence; also : matter of particular or definite chemical constitution **3** : something (as drugs or alcohol) deemed harmful and usu. subject to legal restriction ⟨∼ abuse⟩ **4** : material possessions : PROPERTY, WEALTH

sub·stan·dard \ˌsəb-'stan-dərd\ adj : falling short of a standard or norm

sub·stan·tial \səb-'stan-chəl\ adj **1** : existing as or in substance : MATERIAL; also : not illusory : REAL **2** : IMPORTANT, ESSENTIAL ⟨a ∼ difference in the stories⟩ **3** : NOURISHING, SATISFYING ⟨∼ meal⟩ **4** : having means : WELL-TO-DO **5** : CONSIDERABLE ⟨∼ profit⟩ **6** : STRONG, FIRM — **sub·stan·tial·ly** adv

sub·stan·ti·ate \səb-'stan-chē-ˌāt\ vb **-at·ed; -at·ing 1** : to give substance or body to **2** : VERIFY, PROVE ⟨∼ a charge⟩ — **sub·stan·ti·a·tion** \-ˌstan-chē-'ā-shən\ n

sub·stan·tive \'səb-stən-tiv\ n : NOUN; also : a word or phrase used as a noun

¹sub·sti·tute \'səb-stə-ˌtüt, -ˌtyüt\ n : a person or thing replacing another — **substitute** adj

²substitute vb **-tut·ed; -tut·ing 1** : to put or use in the place of another **2** : to serve as a substitute — **sub·sti·tu·tion** \ˌsəb-stə-'tü-shən, -'tyü-\ n

sub·strate \'səb-ˌstrāt\ n **1** : the base on which a plant or animal lives **2** : a substance acted upon (as by an enzyme)

sub·stra·tum \'səb-ˌstrā-təm, -ˌstra-\ n, pl **-stra·ta** \-tə\ : the layer or structure (as subsoil) lying underneath

sub·struc·ture \'səb-ˌstrək-chər\ n : FOUNDATION, GROUNDWORK

sub·sume \səb-'süm\ vb **sub·sumed; sub·sum·ing** : to include or place within something larger or more comprehensive

sub·sur·face \'səb-ˌsər-fəs\ n : earth material near the surface of the ground — **subsurface** adj

sub·ter·fuge \'səb-tər-ˌfyüj\ n : a trick or device used in order to conceal, escape, or evade ✦ **Synonyms** FRAUD, DECEPTION, TRICKERY

sub·ter·ra·nean \ˌsəb-tə-'rā-nē-ən\ adj **1** : lying or being underground **2** : SECRET, HIDDEN ⟨a ∼ network of criminals⟩

sub·tile \'sə-t°l\ adj **sub·til·er** \'sə-t°l-ər\; **sub·til·est** \'sə-t°l-əst\ : SUBTLE ⟨a ∼ aroma⟩

sub·ti·tle \'səb-ˌtī-t°l\ n **1** : a secondary or explanatory title (as of a book) **2** : printed matter projected on a motion-picture screen during or between the scenes

sub·tle \'sə-t°l\ adj **sub·tler** \'sə-t°l-ər\; **sub·tlest** \'sə-t°l-əst\ **1** : hardly noticeable ⟨∼ differences⟩ **2** : SHREWD, PERCEPTIVE ⟨a ∼ mind⟩ **3** : CLEVER, SLY ⟨a ∼ rogue⟩ — **sub·tle·ty** \-tē\ n — **sub·tly** \'sə-t°l-ē\ adv

sub·tract \səb-'trakt\ vb : to take away (as one part or number) from another; also : to perform the operation of deducting one number from another — **sub·trac·tion** \-'trak-shən\ n

sub·tra·hend \'səb-trə-ˌhend\ n : a number that is to be subtracted from another

sub·trop·i·cal \ˌsəb-'trä-pi-kəl, 'səb-\ also **sub·trop·ic** \-pik\ adj : of, relating to, or being regions bordering on the tropical zone ⟨a ∼ environment⟩ — **sub·trop·ics** \-piks\ n pl

sub·urb \'sə-ˌbərb\ n **1** : an outlying part of a city; also : a small community adjacent to a city **2** pl : a residential area adjacent to a city — **sub·ur·ban** \sə-'bər-bən\ adj or n — **sub·ur·ban·ite** \sə-'bər-bə-ˌnīt\ n

sub·ur·bia \sə-'bər-bē-ə\ n **1** : SUBURBS **2** : suburban people or customs

sub·ven·tion \səb-'ven-chən\ n : SUBSIDY, ENDOWMENT

sub·vert \səb-'vərt\ vb **1** : OVERTHROW, RUIN **2** : CORRUPT — **sub·ver·sion** \-'vər-zhən\ n — **sub·ver·sive** \-'vər-siv\ adj

sub·way \'səb-ˌwā\ n : an underground way; esp : an underground electric railway

sub·woof·er \'səb-ˌwü-fər\ n : a loudspeaker responsive only to the lowest acoustic frequencies

suc·ceed \sək-'sēd\ vb **1** : to follow next in order or next after another; esp : to inherit sovereignty, rank, title, or property **2** : to attain a desired object or end : be successful

suc·cess \sək-'ses\ n **1** : favorable or desired outcome **2** : the gaining of wealth and fame **3** : one that succeeds — **suc·cess·ful** \-fəl\ adj — **suc·cess·ful·ly** adv

suc·ces·sion \sək-'se-shən\ n **1** : the order, act, or right of succeeding to a property, title, or throne **2** : the act or process of following in order **3** : a series of persons or things that follow one after another ✦ **Synonyms** PROGRESSION, SEQUENCE, CHAIN, TRAIN, STRING

suc·ces·sive \sək-'se-siv\ adj : following in order : CONSECUTIVE — **suc·ces·sive·ly** adv

suc·ces·sor \sək-'se-sər\ n : one that succeeds (as to a throne, title, estate, or office)

suc·cinct \(ˌ)sək-'siŋkt, sə-'siŋkt\ adj : BRIEF, CONCISE ⟨a ∼ description⟩ ✦ **Synonyms** TERSE, LACONIC, SUMMARY, CURT, SHORT — **suc·cinct·ly** adv — **suc·cinct·ness** n

suc·cor \'sə-kər\ n [ME socour, sucurs (taken as pl.), fr. AF sucur, sucors, fr. ML succursus, fr. L succurrere to run to the rescue, bring aid] : AID, HELP, RELIEF — **succor** n

suc·co·tash \'sə-kə-ˌtash\ n [Narragansett msíckquatash boiled corn kernels] : beans and corn kernels cooked together

suc·cour chiefly Brit var of SUCCOR

¹suc·cu·lent \'sə-kyə-lənt\ adj : full of juice : JUICY; also : having fleshy tissues that conserve moisture ⟨∼ plants⟩ — **suc·cu·lence** \-ləns\ n

²**succulent** *n* : a succulent plant (as a cactus or an aloe)

suc·cumb \sə-'kəm\ *vb* **1** : to yield to superior strength or force or overpowering appeal or desire **2** : DIE ♦ *Synonyms* SUBMIT, CAPITULATE, RELENT, DEFER

¹**such** \'səch, 'sich\ *adj* **1** : of this or that kind **2** : having a quality just specified or to be specified

²**such** *pron* **1** : such a one or ones ⟨he's a star, and acted as ∼⟩ **2** : that or those similar or related thereto ⟨boards and nails and ∼⟩

³**such** *adv* : to that degree : so

such·like \'səch-,līk\ *adj* : SIMILAR

¹**suck** \'sək\ *vb* **1** : to draw in liquid and esp. mother's milk with the mouth **2** : to draw liquid from by action of the mouth ⟨∼ an orange⟩ **3** : to take in or up or remove by or as if by suction **4** *slang* : to be objectionable

²**suck** *n* **1** : a sucking movement or force **2** : the act of sucking

suck·er \'sə-kər\ *n* **1** : one that sucks **2** : a part of an animal's body used for sucking or for clinging **3** : any of numerous freshwater fishes with thick soft lips for sucking in food **4** : a shoot from the roots or lower part of a plant **5** : a person easily deceived **6** — used as a generalized term of reference ⟨see if you can get that ∼ working again⟩

suck·le \'sə-kəl\ *vb* **suck·led; suck·ling** : to give or draw milk from the breast or udder; *also* : NURTURE

suck·ling \'sə-kliŋ\ *n* : a young unweaned mammal

suck–up \'sək-,əp\ *n* : a person who seeks to gain favor by flattery ⟨a ∼ to the teacher⟩

su·cre \'sü-(,)krā\ *n* — see MONEY table

su·crose \'sü-,krōs, -,krōz\ *n* : a sweet sugar obtained commercially esp. from sugarcane or sugar beets

suc·tion \'sək-shən\ *n* **1** : the act of sucking **2** : the act or process of drawing something (as liquid or dust) into a space (as in a vacuum cleaner or a pump) by partially exhausting the air in the space — **suc·tion·al** \-shə-nəl\ *adj*

suction cup *n* : a cup-shaped device in which a partial vacuum is produced when applied to a surface

sud·den \'sə-dᵊn\ *adj* [ME *sodain*, fr. AF *sudain*, fr. L *subitaneus*, fr. *subitus* sudden, fr. pp. of *subire* to come up] **1** : happening or coming unexpectedly ⟨∼ shower⟩; *also* : changing angle or character all at once ⟨∼ turn⟩ ⟨∼ descent⟩ **2** : HASTY, RASH ⟨∼ decision⟩ **3** : made or brought about in a short time : PROMPT ⟨∼ cure⟩ ♦ *Synonyms* PRECIPITATE, HEADLONG, IMPETUOUS — **sud·den·ly** *adv* — **sud·den·ness** *n*

sudden infant death syndrome *n* : death due to unknown causes of an apparently healthy infant usu. before one year of age and esp. during sleep

suds \'sədz\ *n pl* : soapy water esp. when frothy — **sudsy** \'səd-zē\ *adj*

sue \'sü\ *vb* **sued; su·ing** [ME *sewen, siuen* to follow, strive for, petition, fr. AF *sivre, siure*, fr. VL **sequere*, fr. L *sequi* to follow] **1** : PETITION, SOLICIT **2** : to seek justice or right by bringing legal action

suede *also* **suède** \'swād\ *n* [F *gants de Suède* Swedish gloves] **1** : leather with a napped surface **2** : a fabric with a suedelike nap

su·et \'sü-ət\ *n* : the hard fat from beef and mutton that yields tallow

suff *abbr* **1** sufficient **2** suffix

suf·fer \'sə-fər\ *vb* **suf·fered; suf·fer·ing** **1** : to feel or endure pain **2** : EXPERIENCE, UNDERGO ⟨∼ a defeat⟩ **3** : to bear loss, damage, or injury **4** : ALLOW, PERMIT ♦ *Synonyms* ENDURE, ABIDE, TOLERATE, STAND, BROOK, STOMACH — **suf·fer·able** \'sə-fə-rə-bəl\ *adj* — **suf·fer·er** *n*

suf·fer·ance \'sə-frəns, -fə-rəns\ *n* **1** : consent or approval implied by lack of interference or resistance **2** : ENDURANCE, PATIENCE

suf·fer·ing \'sə-friŋ, -fə-riŋ\ *n* : PAIN, MISERY, HARDSHIP

suf·fice \sə-'fīs\ *vb* **suf·ficed; suf·fic·ing** **1** : to satisfy a need : be sufficient **2** : to be capable or competent

suf·fi·cien·cy \sə-'fi-shən-sē\ *n* **1** : a sufficient quantity to meet one's needs **2** : ADEQUACY

suf·fi·cient \sə-'fi-shənt\ *adj* : adequate to accomplish a purpose or meet a need — **suf·fi·cient·ly** *adv*

¹**suf·fix** \'sə-,fiks\ *n* : an affix occurring at the end of a word

²**suf·fix** \'sə-fiks, (,)sə-'fiks\ *vb* : to attach as a suffix — **suf·fix·ation** \,sə-,fik-'sā-shən\ *n*

suf·fo·cate \'sə-fə-,kāt\ *vb* **-cat·ed; -cat·ing** : STIFLE,

SMOTHER, CHOKE — **suf·fo·cat·ing·ly** *adv* — **suf·fo·ca·tion** \,sə-fə-'kā-shən\ *n*

suf·fra·gan \'sə-fri-gən\ *n* : an assistant bishop; *esp* : one not having the right of succession — **suffragan** *adj*

suf·frage \'sə-frij\ *n* [L *suffragium*] **1** : VOTE **2** : the right to vote : FRANCHISE

suf·frag·ette \,sə-fri-'jet\ *n* : a woman who advocates suffrage for women

suf·frag·ist \'sə-fri-jist\ *n* : one who advocates extension of the suffrage esp. to women

suf·fuse \sə-'fyüz\ *vb* **suf·fused; suf·fus·ing** : to spread over or through in the manner of a fluid or light ♦ *Synonyms* INFUSE, IMBUE, INGRAIN, STEEP — **suf·fu·sion** \-'fyü-zhən\ *n*

¹**sug·ar** \'shù-gər\ *n* **1** : a sweet substance that is colorless or white when pure and is chiefly sucrose from sugarcane or sugar beets **2** : a water-soluble compound (as glucose) similar to sucrose — **sug·ary** *adj*

²**sugar** *vb* **sug·ared; sug·ar·ing** **1** : to mix, cover, or sprinkle with sugar **2** : SWEETEN ⟨∼ advice with flattery⟩ **3** : to form sugar ⟨a syrup that ∼s⟩ **4** : GRANULATE

sugar beet *n* : a large beet with a white root from which sugar is made

sug·ar·cane \'shù-gər-,kān\ *n* : a tall grass widely grown in warm regions for the sugar in its stalks

sugar daddy *n* **1** : a well-to-do usu. older man who supports or spends lavishly on a mistress or girlfriend **2** : a generous benefactor of a cause

sugar maple *n* : a maple with a sweet sap; *esp* : one of eastern No. America with sap that is the chief source of maple syrup and maple sugar

sugar pea *n* : SNOW PEA

sug·ar·plum \'shù-gər-,pləm\ *n* : a small ball of candy

sug·gest \səg-'jest, sə-\ *vb* **1** : to put (as a thought, plan, or desire) into a person's mind **2** : to remind or evoke by association of ideas ♦ *Synonyms* IMPLY, HINT, INTIMATE, INSINUATE, CONNOTE

sug·gest·ible \səg-'jes-tə-bəl, sə-\ *adj* : easily influenced by suggestion

sug·ges·tion \-'jes-chən\ *n* **1** : an act or instance of suggesting; *also* : something suggested **2** : a slight indication ⟨a ∼ of garlic⟩

sug·ges·tive \-'jes-tiv\ *adj* : tending to suggest something; *esp* : suggesting something improper or indecent — **sug·ges·tive·ly** *adv* — **sug·ges·tive·ness** *n*

¹**sui·cide** \'sü-ə-,sīd\ *n* **1** : the act of killing oneself purposely **2** : one that commits or attempts suicide — **sui·cid·al** \,sü-ə-'sī-dᵊl\ *adj*

²**suicide** *adj* : being or performing a deliberate act resulting in the voluntary death of the person who does it ⟨a ∼ mission⟩ ⟨a ∼ bomber⟩

sui ge·ner·is \,sü-,ī-'je-nə-rəs, ,sü-ē-\ *adj* [L, of its own kind] : being in a class by itself : UNIQUE

¹**suit** \'süt\ *n* **1** : an action in court to recover a right or claim **2** : an act of suing or entreating; *esp* : COURTSHIP **3** : a number of things used together ⟨∼ of clothes⟩ **4** : all the playing cards in a pack bearing the same symbol

²**suit** *vb* **1** : to be appropriate or fitting **2** : to be becoming to **3** : to meet the needs or desires of : PLEASE

suit·able \'sü-tə-bəl\ *adj* : FITTING, PROPER, APPROPRIATE ⟨∼ dress⟩ ♦ *Synonyms* FIT, MEET, APT, HAPPY — **suit·abil·i·ty** \,sü-tə-'bi-lə-tē\ *n* — **suit·able·ness** \'sü-tə-bəl-nəs\ *n* — **suit·ably** \-tə-blē\ *adv*

suit·case \'süt-,kās\ *n* : a portable case designed to hold a traveler's clothing and personal articles

suite \'swēt, *for 4 also* 'süt\ *n* **1** : RETINUE **2** : a group of rooms occupied as a unit **3** : a modern instrumental composition in several movements of different character; *also* : a long orchestral concert arrangement in suite form of material drawn from a longer work **4** : a set of matched furniture for a room

suit·ing \'sü-tiŋ\ *n* : fabric for suits of clothing

suit·or \'sü-tər\ *n* **1** : one who sues or petitions **2** : one who courts a woman or seeks to marry her

su·ki·ya·ki \skē-'yä-kē, ,sù-kē-'yä-\ *n* : thin slices of meat, tofu, and vegetables cooked in soy sauce and sugar

sul·fa drug \'səl-fə-\ *n* : any of various synthetic organic bacteria-inhibiting drugs

sul·fate \'səl-,fāt\ *n* : a salt or ester of sulfuric acid

sul·fide \'səl-'fīd\ *n* : a compound of sulfur

sul·fur *also* **sul·phur** \'səl-fər\ *n* : a nonmetallic chemical element used esp. in the chemical and paper industries and in vulcanizing rubber

sulfur di·ox·ide \-dī-'äk-sīd\ *n* : a heavy pungent toxic gas that is used esp. in bleaching, as a preservative, and as a refrigerant, and is a major air pollutant

sul·fu·ric \ˌsəl-'fyu̇r-ik\ *adj* : of, relating to, or containing sulfur

sulfuric acid *or* **sul·phu·ric acid** \ˌsəl-'fyu̇r-ik-\ *n* : a heavy corrosive oily strong acid

sul·fu·rous *also* **sul·phu·rous** \'səl-fə-rəs, -fyə-, *also esp for 1* ˌsəl-'fyu̇r-əs\ *adj* **1** : of, relating to, or containing sulfur **2** : of or relating to brimstone or the fire of hell : INFERNAL **3** : FIERY, INFLAMED ⟨~ sermons⟩

¹sulk \'səlk\ *vb* : to be or become moodily silent or irritable

²sulk *n* : a sulky mood or spell

¹sulky \'səl-kē\ *adj* **sulk·i·er; -est** : inclined to sulk : MOROSE, MOODY ♦ **Synonyms** SURLY, GLUM, SULLEN, GLOOMY — **sulk·i·ly** \'səl-kə-lē\ *adv* — **sulk·i·ness** \-kē-nəs\ *n*

²sulky *n, pl* **sulkies** : a light 2-wheeled horse-drawn vehicle with a seat for the driver and usu. no body

sul·len \'sə-lən\ *adj* **1** : gloomily silent : MOROSE **2** : DISMAL, GLOOMY ⟨a ~ sky⟩ ♦ **Synonyms** GLUM, SURLY, DOUR, SATURNINE — **sul·len·ly** *adv* — **sul·len·ness** *n*

sul·ly \'sə-lē\ *vb* **sul·lied; sul·ly·ing** : SOIL, SMIRCH, DEFILE

sul·tan \'səl-t³n\ *n* : a sovereign esp. of a Muslim state — **sul·tan·ate** \-ˌāt\ *n*

sul·ta·na \ˌsəl-'ta-nə\ *n* **1** : a female member of a sultan's family **2** : a pale seedless grape; *also* : a raisin of this grape

sul·try \'səl-trē\ *adj* **sul·tri·er; -est** [obs. E *sulter* to swelter, alter. of E *swelter*] : very hot and moist : SWELTERING; *also* : exciting sexual desire

¹sum \'səm\ *n* [ME *summe*, fr. AF *sume, somme*, fr. L *summa*, fr. fem. of *summus* highest] **1** : a quantity of money **2** : the whole amount **3** : GIST ⟨the ~ of an argument⟩ **4** : the result obtained by adding numbers **5** : a problem in arithmetic

²sum *vb* **summed; sum·ming** : to find the sum of by adding or counting

su·mac *also* **su·mach** \'sü-ˌmak, 'shü-\ *n* : any of a genus of trees, shrubs, and woody vines having spikes or loose clusters of red or whitish berries

sum·ma·rise *Brit var of* SUMMARIZE

sum·ma·rize \'sə-mə-ˌrīz\ *vb* **-rized; -riz·ing** : to tell in a summary

¹sum·ma·ry \'sə-mə-rē\ *adj* **1** : covering the main points briefly : CONCISE **2** : done without delay or formality ⟨~ punishment⟩ ♦ **Synonyms** TERSE, SUCCINCT, LACONIC — **sum·mar·i·ly** \(ˌ)sə-'mer-ə-lē, 'sə-mə-rə-lē\ *adv*

²summary *n, pl* **-ries** : a concise statement of the main points

sum·ma·tion \(ˌ)sə-'mā-shən\ *n* : a summing up; *esp* : a speech in court summing up the arguments in a case

sum·mer \'sə-mər\ *n* : the season of the year in a region in which the sun shines most directly : the warmest period of the year — **sum·mery** *adj*

sum·mer·house \'sə-mər-ˌhau̇s\ *n* : a covered structure in a garden or park to provide a shady retreat

summersault *var of* SOMERSAULT

summer squash *n* : any of various squashes (as zucchini) used as a vegetable while immature

sum·mit \'sə-mət\ *n* **1** : the highest point **2** : a conference of highest-level officials ⟨an economic ~⟩

sum·mon \'sə-mən\ *vb* [ME *somnen, somonen*, fr. AF *somondre*, fr. VL *summonere*, alter. of L *summonēre* to remind secretly] **1** : to call to a meeting : CONVOKE **2** : to send for; *also* : to order to appear in court **3** : to evoke esp. by an act of the will ⟨~ up courage⟩ — **sum·mon·er** *n*

sum·mons \'sə-mənz\ *n, pl* **sum·mons·es 1** : an authoritative call to appear at a designated place or to attend to a duty **2** : a warning or citation to appear in court at a specified time to answer charges

sump·tu·ous \'səmp-shə-wəs, -shü-\ *adj* : LAVISH, LUXURIOUS ⟨a ~ banquet⟩ ⟨a ~ residence⟩

sum up *vb* : SUMMARIZE

¹sun \'sən\ *n* **1** : the shining celestial body around which the earth and other planets revolve and from which they

receive light and heat **2** : a celestial body like the sun **3** : SUNSHINE — **sun·less** *adj* — **sun·ny** *adj*

²sun *vb* **sunned; sun·ning 1** : to expose to or as if to the rays of the sun **2** : to sun oneself

Sun *abbr* Sunday

sun·bath \'sən-ˌbath, -ˌbäth\ *n* : an exposure to sunlight or a sunlamp — **sun·bathe** \-ˌbāth\ *vb*

sun·beam \-ˌbēm\ *n* : a ray of sunlight

sun·block \'sən-ˌbläk\ *n* : a preparation used on the skin to prevent sunburn (as by blocking ultraviolet radiation)

sun·bon·net \-ˌbä-nət\ *n* : a bonnet with a wide brim to shield the face and neck from the sun

¹sun·burn \-ˌbərn\ *vb* **-burned** \-ˌbərnd\ *or* **-burnt** \-ˌbərnt\; **-burn·ing** : to cause or become affected with sunburn

²sunburn *n* : a skin inflammation caused by overexposure to ultraviolet radiation esp. from sunshine

sun·dae \'sən-(ˌ)dā, -dē\ *n* : ice cream served with topping

Sun·day \'sən-ˌdā, -dē\ *n* : the 1st day of the week : the Christian Sabbath

sun·der \'sən-dər\ *vb* : to force apart ♦ **Synonyms** SEVER, PART, DISJOIN, DISUNITE

sun·di·al \'sən-ˌdī(-ə)l\ *n* : a device for showing the time of day from the shadow cast on a plate by an object with a straight edge

sundial

sun·down \-ˌdau̇n\ *n* : SUNSET 2

sun·dries \'sən-drēz\ *n pl* : various small articles or items

sun·dry \'sən-drē\ *adj* : SEVERAL, DIVERS, VARIOUS ⟨for ~ reasons⟩

sun·fish \'sən-ˌfish\ *n* **1** : a large marine fish with a deep flattened body **2** : any of numerous often brightly colored No. American freshwater fishes related to the perches and usu. having the body flattened from side to side

sun·flow·er \-ˌflau̇(-ə)r\ *n* : any of a genus of tall New World plants related to the daisies and often grown for the oil-rich seeds of their yellow-petaled dark-centered flower heads

sung *past and past part of* SING

sun·glasses \'sən-ˌgla-səz\ *n pl* : glasses to protect the eyes from the sun

sunk *past and past part of* SINK

sunk·en \'səŋ-kən\ *adj* **1** : SUBMERGED ⟨~ ships⟩ **2** : fallen in : HOLLOW ⟨~ cheeks⟩ **3** : lying in a depression ⟨~ garden⟩; *also* : constructed below the general floor level ⟨a ~ living room⟩

sun·lamp \'sən-ˌlamp\ *n* : an electric lamp designed to emit radiation of wavelengths from ultraviolet to infrared

sun·light \-ˌlīt\ *n* : SUNSHINE

sun·lit \-ˌlit\ *adj* : lighted by or as if by the sun

sun protection factor *n* : a number that is the factor by which the time required for unprotected skin to become sunburned is increased when a sunscreen is used

sun·rise \-ˌrīz\ *n* **1** : the apparent rising of the sun above the horizon **2** : the time at which the sun rises

sun·roof \-ˌrüf, -ˌru̇f\ *n* : a panel in an automobile roof that can be opened

sun·screen \-ˌskrēn\ *n* : a preparation on the skin to prevent sunburn (as by absorbing ultraviolet radiation)

sun·set \-ˌset\ *n* **1** : the apparent descent of the sun below the horizon **2** : the time at which the sun sets

sun·shade \-ˌshād\ *n* : something (as a parasol or awning) used as a protection from the sun's rays

sun·shine \-ˌshīn\ *n* : the direct light of the sun — **sun·shiny** *adj*

sun·spot \-ˌspät\ *n* : any of the dark spots that appear at times on the sun's surface

sun·stroke \-₁strōk\ *n* : heatstroke caused by direct exposure to the sun

sun·tan \-₁tan\ *n* : a browning of the skin from exposure to the sun's rays

sun·up \-₁əp\ *n* : SUNRISE 2

¹**sup** \'səp\ *vb* **supped; sup·ping** : to take or drink in swallows or gulps

²**sup** *n* : a mouthful esp. of liquor or broth; *also* : a small quantity of liquid

³**sup** *vb* **supped; sup·ping 1** : to eat the evening meal **2** : to make one's supper ⟨*supped* on roast beef⟩

⁴**sup** *abbr* **1** superior **2** supplement; supplementary **3** supply **4** supra

¹**su·per** \'sü-pər\ *adj* **1** : very fine : EXCELLENT **2** : EXTREME, EXCESSIVE ⟨~ secrecy⟩

²**super** *n* : SUPERINTENDENT

super- \₁sü-pər\ *prefix* **1** : over and above : higher in quantity, quality, or degree than : more than **2** : in addition : extra **3** : exceeding a norm **4** : in excessive degree or intensity **5** : surpassing all or most others of its kind **6** : situated above, on, or at the top of **7** : next above or higher **8** : more inclusive than **9** : superior in status or position

superabsorbent	superpatriotism
superachiever	superpremium
superagency	superrich
superblock	supersalesman
superbomb	supersecret
supercity	supersize
superclean	supersized
superexpensive	supersmart
superfast	supersophisticated
superfine	superspy
superheat	superstar
superheavy	superstate
superhero	superstore
superhuman	superstratum
superhumanly	superstrength
superindividual	superstrong
superliner	supersubtle
superman	supersystem
supernormal	supertanker
superpatriot	superthin
superpatriotic	superwoman

su·per·abun·dant \₁sü-pər-ə-'bən-dənt\ *adj* : more than ample — **su·per·abun·dance** \-dəns\ *n*

su·per·an·nu·ate \₁sü-pər-'an-yə-₁wāt\ *vb* **-at·ed; -at·ing 1** : to make out-of-date **2** : to retire and pension because of age or infirmity — **su·per·an·nu·at·ed** *adj*

su·perb \su-'pərb\ *adj* [L *superbus* excellent, proud, fr. *super* above] : marked to the highest degree by excellence, brilliance, or competence ◆ *Synonyms* RESPLENDENT, GLORIOUS, GORGEOUS, SUBLIME — **su·perb·ly** *adv*

su·per·charg·er \'sü-pər-₁chär-jər\ *n* : a device for increasing the amount of air supplied to an internal combustion engine

su·per·cil·ious \₁sü-pər-'si-lē-əs\ *adj* [L *supercilium* eyebrow, haughtiness] : haughtily contemptuous ◆ *Synonyms* DISDAINFUL, OVERBEARING, ARROGANT, LORDLY, SUPERIOR

su·per·com·pu·ter \'sü-pər-kəm-₁pyü-tər\ *n* : a large very fast mainframe

su·per·con·duc·tiv·i·ty \₁sü-pər-₁kän-₁dək-'ti-və-tē\ *n* : a complete disappearance of electrical resistance in a substance esp. at very low temperatures — **su·per·con·duc·tive** \-kən-'dək-tiv\ *adj* — **su·per·con·duc·tor** \-'dək-tər\ *n*

su·per·con·ti·nent \'sü-pər-₁kän-tə-nənt\ *n* : a former large continent from which other continents are held to have broken off and drifted away

su·per·ego \₁sü-pər-'ē-gō\ *n* : the one of the three divisions of the psyche in psychoanalytic theory that functions to reward and punish through a system of moral attitudes, conscience, and a sense of guilt

su·per·fi·cial \₁sü-pər-'fi-shəl\ *adj* **1** : of or relating to the surface or appearance only **2** : not thorough : SHALLOW — **su·per·fi·ci·al·i·ty** \-₁fi-shē-'a-lə-tē\ *n* — **su·per·fi·cial·ly** *adv*

su·per·flu·ous \su-'pər-flə-wəs\ *adj* : exceeding what is sufficient or necessary : SURPLUS ◆ *Synonyms* EXTRA, SPARE, SUPERNUMERARY — **su·per·flu·i·ty** \₁sü-pər-'flü-ə-tē\ *n*

su·per·high·way \₁sü-pər-'hī-₁wā\ *n* : a broad highway designed for high-speed traffic

su·per·im·pose \-im-'pōz\ *vb* : to lay (one thing) over or above something else

su·per·in·tend \₁sü-pə-rin-'tend\ *vb* : to have or exercise the charge and oversight of : DIRECT — **su·per·in·ten·dence** \-'ten-dəns\ *n* — **su·per·in·ten·den·cy** \-dən-sē\ *n* — **su·per·in·ten·dent** \-dənt\ *n*

¹**su·pe·ri·or** \su̇-'pir-ē-ər\ *adj* **1** : situated higher up, over, or near the top; *also* : higher in rank or numbers **2** : of greater value or importance **3** : courageously indifferent (as to pain or misfortune) **4** : better than most others of its kind **5** : ARROGANT, HAUGHTY — **su·pe·ri·or·i·ty** \-₁pir-ē-'ȯr-ə-tē\ *n*

²**superior** *n* **1** : one who is above another in rank, office, or station; *esp* : the head of a religious house or order **2** : one higher in quality or merit

¹**su·per·la·tive** \su̇-'pər-lə-tiv\ *adj* **1** : of, relating to, or constituting the degree of grammatical comparison that denotes an extreme or unsurpassed level or extent **2** : surpassing others : SUPREME ◆ *Synonyms* PEERLESS, INCOMPARABLE, SUPERB — **su·per·la·tive·ly** *adv*

²**superlative** *n* **1** : the superlative degree or a superlative form in a language **2** : the utmost degree : ACME

su·per·mar·ket \'sü-pər-₁mär-kət\ *n* : a self-service retail market selling foods and household merchandise

su·per·mod·el \'sü-pər-₁mä-dᵊl\ *n* : a famous and successful fashion model

su·per·mom \'sü-pər-₁mäm\ *n* : an exemplary mother; *also* : a woman who performs the duties of housekeeping and raising children while also having a full-time job

su·per·nal \su̇-'pər-nᵊl\ *adj* **1** : being or coming from on high **2** : of heavenly or spiritual character

su·per·nat·u·ral \₁sü-pər-'na-chə-rəl\ *adj* : of or relating to phenomena beyond or outside of nature; *esp* : relating to or attributed to a divinity, ghost, or devil — **su·per·nat·u·ral·ly** *adv*

su·per·no·va \₁sü-pər-'nō-və\ *n* : the explosion of a very large star

¹**su·per·nu·mer·ary** \-'nü-mə-₁rer-ē, -'nyü-\ *adj* : exceeding the usual or required number : EXTRA ◆ *Synonyms* SURPLUS, SUPERFLUOUS, SPARE

²**supernumerary** *n, pl* **-ar·ies** : an extra person or thing; *esp* : an actor hired for a nonspeaking part

su·per·pose \₁sü-pər-'pōz\ *vb* **-posed; -pos·ing** : SUPERIMPOSE — **su·per·po·si·tion** \-pə-'zi-shən\ *n*

su·per·pow·er \'sü-pər-₁paú(-ə)r\ *n* **1** : excessive or superior power **2** : one of a few politically and militarily dominant nations

su·per·sat·u·rat·ed \-'sa-chə-₁rā-təd\ *adj* : containing an amount of a substance greater than that required for saturation

su·per·scribe \'sü-pər-₁skrīb, ₁sü-pər-'skrīb\ *vb* **-scribed; -scrib·ing** : to write on the top or outside : ADDRESS — **su·per·scrip·tion** \₁sü-pər-'skrip-shən\ *n*

su·per·script \'sü-pər-₁skript\ *n* : a symbol (as a numeral or letter) written immediately above or above and to one side of another character

su·per·sede \₁sü-pər-'sēd\ *vb* **-sed·ed; -sed·ing** [ME (Sc) *superceden* to defer, fr. MF *superceder*, fr. L *supersedēre* to be superior to, refrain from, fr. *super-* above + *sedēre* to sit] : to take the place of : REPLACE

su·per·son·ic \-'sä-nik\ *adj* **1** : ULTRASONIC **2** : being or relating to speeds from one to five times the speed of sound; *also* : capable of moving at such a speed ⟨a ~ airplane⟩

su·per·sti·tion \₁sü-pər-'sti-shən\ *n* **1** : beliefs or practices resulting from ignorance, fear of the unknown, or trust in magic or chance **2** : an unreasoning fear of nature, the unknown, or God resulting from superstition — **su·per·sti·tious** \-shəs\ *adj*

su·per·struc·ture \'sü-pər-₁strək-chər\ *n* : something built on a base or as a vertical extension

su·per·ti·tle \'sü-pər-₁tī-tᵊl\ *n* : a translation of foreign-language dialogue displayed above a screen or performance

su·per·vene \₁sü-pər-'vēn\ *vb* **-vened; -ven·ing** : to occur as something additional or unexpected

su·per·vise \'sü-pər-₁vīz\ *vb* **-vised; -vis·ing** : OVERSEE, SUPERINTEND — **su·per·vi·sion** \₁sü-pər-'vi-zhən\ *n* — **su·per·vi·sor** \'sü-pər-₁vī-zər\ *n* — **su·per·vi·so·ry** \₁sü-pər-'vī-zə-rē\ *adj*

su·pine \sü-'pīn\ *adj* **1** : lying on the back or with the face upward **2** : LETHARGIC, SLUGGISH; *also* : ABJECT ✦ *Synonyms* INACTIVE, INERT, PASSIVE, IDLE

supp *or* **suppl** *abbr* supplement; supplementary

sup·per \'sə-pər\ *n* : the evening meal esp. when dinner is taken at midday — **sup·per·time** \-,tīm\ *n*

sup·plant \sə-'plant\ *vb* **1** : to take the place of (another) esp. by force or trickery **2** : REPLACE

sup·ple \'sə-pəl\ *adj* **sup·pler; sup·plest** **1** : COMPLIANT, ADAPTABLE ⟨a ~ soprano⟩ **2** : capable of bending without breaking or creasing : LIMBER ✦ *Synonyms* RESILIENT, ELASTIC, FLEXIBLE

¹sup·ple·ment \'sə-plə-mənt\ *n* **1** : something that supplies a want or makes an addition **2** : DIETARY SUPPLEMENT **3** : a continuation (as of a book) containing corrections or additional material — **sup·ple·men·tal** \,sə-plə-'men-t°l\ *adj* — **sup·ple·men·ta·ry** \-'men-tə-rē\ *adj*

²sup·ple·ment \'sə-plə-,ment\ *vb* : to fill up the deficiencies of : add to — **sup·ple·men·ta·tion** \,sə-plə-,men-'tā-shən, -mən-\ *n*

sup·pli·ant \'sə-plē-ənt\ *n* : one who supplicates : PETITIONER, PLEADER

sup·pli·cant \'sə-pli-kənt\ *n* : SUPPLIANT

sup·pli·cate \'sə-plə-,kāt\ *vb* **-cat·ed; -cat·ing** **1** : to make a humble entreaty; *esp* : to pray to God **2** : to ask earnestly and humbly : BESEECH ✦ *Synonyms* IMPLORE, BEG, ENTREAT, PLEAD — **sup·pli·ca·tion** \,sə-plə-'kā-shən\ *n*

¹sup·ply \sə-'plī\ *vb* **sup·plied; sup·ply·ing** [ME *supplien*, to complete, compensate for, fr. MF *soupplier* fr. L *supplēre* to fill up, supplement, supply, fr. *sub-* under, up to + *plēre* to fill] **1** : to add as a supplement **2** : to satisfy the needs of **3** : FURNISH, PROVIDE — **sup·pli·er** *n*

²supply *n, pl* **supplies** **1** : the quantity or amount (as of a commodity) needed or available; *also* : PROVISIONS, STORES — usu. used in pl. **2** : the act or process of filling a want or need : PROVISION **3** : the quantities of goods or services offered for sale at a particular time or at one price

sup·ply–side \sə-'plī-,sīd\ *adj* : of, relating to, or being an economic theory that recommends the reduction of tax rates to expand economic activity

¹sup·port \sə-'pört\ *vb* **1** : BEAR, TOLERATE **2** : to take sides with : BACK, ASSIST **3** : to provide with food, clothing, and shelter **4** : to hold up or serve as a foundation for ✦ *Synonyms* UPHOLD, ADVOCATE, CHAMPION — **sup·port·able** *adj* — **sup·port·er** *n* — **sup·port·ive** \-'pȯr-tiv\ *adj*

²support *n* **1** : the act of supporting : the state of being supported **2** : one that supports : PROP, BASE

support group *n* : a group of people with common experiences and concerns who provide emotional and moral support for one another

sup·pose \sə-'pōz\ *vb* **sup·posed; sup·pos·ing** **1** : to assume to be true (as for the sake of argument) **2** : EXPECT ⟨I am *supposed* to go⟩ **3** : to think probable — **sup·pos·al** *n*

sup·posed \sə-'pōzd, -'pō-zəd\ *adj* : BELIEVED; *also* : mistakenly believed — **sup·pos·ed·ly** \-'pō-zəd-lē, -'pōzd-lē\ *adv*

sup·pos·ing *conj* : if by way of hypothesis : on the assumption that ⟨~ I did agree with you⟩

sup·po·si·tion \,sə-pə-'zi-shən\ *n* **1** : something that is supposed : HYPOTHESIS **2** : the act of supposing

sup·pos·i·to·ry \sə-'pä-zə-,tȯr-ē\ *n, pl* **-ries** [ME *suppositorie*, fr. AF, fr. ML *suppositorium*, fr. LL, neut. of *suppositorius* placed beneath] : a small easily melted mass of usu. medicated material for insertion (as into the rectum)

sup·press \sə-'pres\ *vb* **1** : to put down by authority or force : SUBDUE ⟨~ a revolt⟩ **2** : to keep from being known; *also* : to stop the publication or circulation of **3** : to hold back : REPRESS ⟨~ anger⟩ ⟨~ a cough⟩ — **sup·press·ible** \-'pre-sə-bəl\ *adj* — **sup·pres·sion** \-'pre-shən\ *n* — **sup·pres·sor** \-'pre-sər\ *n*

sup·pres·sant \sə-'pre-s°nt\ *n* : an agent (as a drug) suppressing rather than eliminating something ⟨a cough ~⟩

sup·pu·rate \'sə-pyə-,rāt\ *vb* **-rat·ed; -rat·ing** : to form or give off pus — **sup·pu·ra·tion** \,sə-pyə-'rā-shən\ *n*

su·pra \'sü-prə, -,prä\ *adv* : earlier in this writing : ABOVE

su·pra·na·tion·al \,sü-prə-'na-shə-nəl, -,prä-\ *adj* : going beyond national boundaries, authority, or interests ⟨~ organizations⟩

su·prem·a·cist \sü-'pre-mə-sist\ *n* : an advocate of group supremacy

su·prem·a·cy \sü-'pre-mə-sē\ *n, pl* **-cies** : supreme rank, power, or authority

su·preme \sü-'prēm\ *adj* [L *supremus*, superl. of *superus* upper, fr. *super* over, above] **1** : highest in rank or authority **2** : highest in degree or quality ⟨~ among poets⟩ **3** : ULTIMATE ⟨the ~ sacrifice⟩ ✦ *Synonyms* SUPERLATIVE, SURPASSING, PEERLESS, INCOMPARABLE — **su·preme·ly** *adv* — **su·preme·ness** *n*

Supreme Being *n* : GOD 1

supt *abbr* superintendent

sur·cease \'sər-,sēs\ *n* : CESSATION, RESPITE

¹sur·charge \'sər-,chärj\ *vb* **1** : to fill to excess : OVERLOAD **2** : to apply a surcharge to (postage stamps)

²surcharge *n* **1** : an extra fee or cost **2** : an excessive load or burden **3** : something officially printed on a postage stamp esp. to change its value

sur·cin·gle \'sər-,siŋ-gəl\ *n* : a band put around a horse's body to make something (as a saddle) fast

¹sure \'shu̇r\ *adj* **sur·er; sur·est** [ME, *seur, sure*, fr. AF *seur*, fr. L *securus* secure] **1** : firmly established **2** : TRUSTWORTHY, RELIABLE ⟨a ~ friend⟩ **3** : CONFIDENT ⟨I'm ~ I'm right⟩ **4** : not to be disputed : UNDOUBTED **5** : bound to happen **6** : careful to remember or attend to something ⟨be ~ to lock the door⟩ ✦ *Synonyms* CERTAIN, COCKSURE, POSITIVE — **sure·ness** *n*

²sure *adv* : SURELY

sure·fire \'shu̇r-'fī(-ə)r\ *adj* : certain to get results : DEPENDABLE

sure·ly \'shu̇r-lē\ *adv* **1** : in a sure manner **2** : without doubt **3** : INDEED, REALLY ⟨~, you don't believe that⟩

sure·ty \'shu̇r-ə-tē\ *n, pl* **-ties** **1** : SURENESS, CERTAINTY **2** : something that makes sure : GUARANTEE **3** : one who is a guarantor for another person

¹surf \'sərf\ *n* : waves that break upon the shore; *also* : the sound or foam of breaking waves

²surf *vb* **1** : to ride the surf (as on a surfboard) **2** : to scan the offerings of (as television or the Internet) for something of interest — **surf·er** *n* — **surf·ing** *n*

¹sur·face \'sər-fəs\ *n* **1** : the outside of an object or body **2** : outward aspect or appearance — **surface** *adj*

²surface *vb* **sur·faced; sur·fac·ing** **1** : to give a surface to : make smooth **2** : to rise to the surface

surf·board \'sərf-,bȯrd\ *n* : a buoyant board used in surfing

¹sur·feit \'sər-fət\ *n* **1** : EXCESS, SUPERABUNDANCE **2** : excessive indulgence (as in food or drink) **3** : disgust caused by excess

²surfeit *vb* : to feed, supply, or indulge to the point of surfeit : CLOY

surg *abbr* surgeon; surgery; surgical

¹surge \'sərj\ *vb* **surged; surg·ing** **1** : to rise and fall actively : TOSS **2** : to move in waves **3** : to rise suddenly to an excessive or abnormal value

²surge *n* **1** : a sweeping onward like a wave of the sea ⟨a ~ of emotion⟩ **2** : a large billow **3** : a transient sudden increase of current or voltage in an electrical circuit

sur·geon \'sər-jən\ *n* : a physician who specializes in surgery

sur·gery \'sər-jə-rē\ *n, pl* **-ger·ies** [ME *surgerie*, fr. AF *cirurgerie, surgerie*, fr. L *chirurgia*, fr. Gk *cheirourgia*, fr. *cheirourgos* surgeon, fr. *cheirourgos* doing by hand, fr. *cheir* hand + *ergon* work] **1** : a branch of medicine concerned with the correction of physical defects, the cure of injuries, and the treatment of disease esp. by operations **2** : a room or area where surgery is performed **3** : the work done by a surgeon

sur·gi·cal \'sər-ji-kəl\ *adj* : of, relating to, or associated with surgeons or surgery — **sur·gi·cal·ly** \-k(ə-)lē\ *adv*

sur·ly \'sər-lē\ *adj* **sur·li·er; -est** [alter. of ME *serreli* lordly, imperious, prob. fr. *sire, ser* sire] : having a rude unfriendly disposition ✦ *Synonyms* MOROSE, GLUM, SULLEN, SULKY, GLOOMY — **sur·li·ness** \-lē-nəs\ *n*

sur·mise \sər-'mīz\ *vb* **sur·mised; sur·mis·ing** : to form a notion of from scanty evidence ✦ *Synonyms* CONJECTURE, PRESUME, SUPPOSE — **surmise** *n*

sur·mount \sər-'mau̇nt\ *vb* **1** : to prevail over : OVERCOME **2** : to get to or lie at the top of

sur·name \'sər-ˌnām\ *n* **1** : NICKNAME **2** : the name borne in common by members of a family

sur·pass \sər-'pas\ *vb* **1** : to be superior to in quality, degree, or performance : EXCEL **2** : to go beyond the reach or powers of ♦ *Synonyms* TRANSCEND, OUTDO, OUTSTRIP, EXCEED — **sur·pass·ing·ly** *adv*

sur·plice \'sər-pləs\ *n* : a loose white outer vestment usu. of knee length

sur·plus \'sər-(ˌ)pləs\ *n* **1** : quantity left over : EXCESS **2** : the excess of assets over liabilities ♦ *Synonyms* SUPERFLUITY, OVERABUNDANCE, SURFEIT

¹sur·prise \sər-'prīz\ *n* **1** : an attack made without warning **2** : a taking unawares **3** : something that surprises **4** : AMAZEMENT, ASTONISHMENT

²surprise *vb* **sur·prised; sur·pris·ing 1** : to come upon and attack unexpectedly **2** : to take unawares **3** : AMAZE ⟨his conduct *surprised* me⟩ **4** : to cause astonishment or surprise ⟨her success didn't ∼⟩ ♦ *Synonyms* ASTONISH, ASTOUND, DUMBFOUND — **sur·pris·ing** *adj*

sur·pris·ing·ly \-'prī-ziŋ-lē\ *adv* **1** : in a surprising manner or degree **2** : it is surprising that ⟨∼, voter turnout was high⟩

sur·re·al \sə-'rē-əl, -'rēl\ *adj* **1** : having the intense irrational reality of a dream **2** : of or relating to surrealism — **sur·re·al·ly** *adv*

sur·re·al·ism \sə-'rē-ə-ˌli-zəm\ *n* : art, literature, or theater characterized by fantastic or incongruous imagery or effects produced by unnatural juxtapositions and combinations — **sur·re·al·ist** \-list\ *n or adj* — **sur·re·al·is·tic** \sə-ˌrē-ə-'lis-tik\ *adj* — **sur·re·al·is·ti·cal·ly** \-ti-k(ə-)lē\ *adv*

¹sur·ren·der \sə-'ren-dər\ *vb* **1** : to yield to the power of another : give up under compulsion **2** : RELINQUISH

²surrender *n* : the act of giving up or yielding oneself or the possession of something to another

sur·rep·ti·tious \ˌsər-əp-'ti-shəs\ *adj* : done, made, or acquired by stealth : CLANDESTINE ♦ *Synonyms* UNDERHAND, COVERT, FURTIVE — **sur·rep·ti·tious·ly** *adv*

sur·rey \'sər-ē\ *n, pl* **surreys** : a 2-seated horse-drawn carriage

surrey

sur·ro·ga·cy \'sər-ə-gə-sē\ *n* : SURROGATE MOTHERHOOD

sur·ro·gate \'sər-ə-ˌgāt, -gət\ *n* **1** : DEPUTY, SUBSTITUTE **2** : a law officer in some states with authority in the probate of wills, the settlement of estates, and the appointment of guardians **3** : SURROGATE MOTHER

surrogate mother *n* : a woman who becomes pregnant (as by surgical implantation of a fertilized egg) in order to carry the fetus for another woman — **surrogate motherhood** *n*

sur·round \sə-'raund\ *vb* **1** : to enclose on all sides : ENCIRCLE **2** : to enclose so as to cut off retreat or escape

sur·round·ings \sə-'raun-diŋz\ *n pl* : conditions by which one is surrounded

surround sound *n* : sound reproduction that uses three or more transmission channels

sur·tax \'sər-ˌtaks\ *n* : an additional tax over and above a normal tax

sur·tout \(ˌ)sər-'tü\ *n* [F, fr. *sur* over + *tout* all] : a man's long close-fitting overcoat

surv *abbr* survey; surveying; surveyor

sur·veil·lance \sər-'vā-ləns\ *n* [F] : close watch; *also* : SUPERVISION

¹sur·vey \sər-'vā\ *vb* **sur·veyed; sur·vey·ing** [ME, fr. AF *surveer* to look over, fr. *sur-* over + *veer* to see, fr. L *vidēre*] **1** : to look over and examine closely **2** : to find and represent the contours, measurements, and position of a part of the earth's surface (as a tract of land) **3** : to view or study something as a whole ♦ *Synonyms* SCRUTINIZE, EXAMINE, INSPECT, STUDY — **sur·vey·or** \-ər\ *n*

²sur·vey \'sər-ˌvā\ *n, pl* **surveys** : the act or an instance of surveying; *also* : something that is surveyed

sur·viv·al·ism \sər-'vī-və-ˌli-zəm\ *n* : an attitude, policy, or practice based on the primacy of survival as a value — **sur·viv·al·ist** \-və-list\ *n or adj*

sur·vive \sər-'vīv\ *vb* **sur·vived; sur·viv·ing 1** : to remain alive or existent **2** : OUTLIVE, OUTLAST — **sur·vi·vor** \-'vī-vər\ *n*

sus·cep·ti·ble \sə-'sep-tə-bəl\ *adj* **1** : of such a nature as to permit ⟨words ∼ of being misunderstood⟩ **2** : having little resistance to a stimulus or agency ⟨∼ to colds⟩ **3** : IMPRESSIONABLE, RESPONSIVE ⟨a ∼ mind⟩ ♦ *Synonyms* SENSITIVE, SUBJECT, EXPOSED, PRONE, LIABLE, OPEN — **sus·cep·ti·bil·i·ty** \-ˌsep-tə-'bi-lə-tē\ *n*

su·shi \'sü-shē\ *n* [Jp] : cold rice formed into various shapes and garnished esp. with bits of raw fish or seafood

¹sus·pect \'səs-ˌpekt, sə-'spekt\ *adj* : regarded with suspicion; *also* : QUESTIONABLE

²sus·pect \'səs-ˌpekt\ *n* : one who is suspected (as of a crime)

³sus·pect \sə-'spekt\ *vb* **1** : to have doubts of : MISTRUST **2** : to imagine to be guilty without proof **3** : SURMISE

sus·pend \sə-'spend\ *vb* **1** : to bar temporarily from a privilege, office, or function **2** : to stop temporarily : make inactive for a time **3** : to withhold (judgment) for a time **4** : HANG; *esp* : to hang so as to be free except at one point **5** : to put or hold in suspension **6** : to keep from falling or sinking by some invisible support

sus·pend·er \sə-'spen-dər\ *n* : one of two supporting straps which pass over the shoulders and to which the pants are fastened

sus·pense \sə-'spens\ *n* **1** : SUSPENSION **2** : mental uncertainty : ANXIETY **3** : excitement as to an outcome — **sus·pense·ful** *adj*

sus·pen·sion \sə-'spen-chən\ *n* **1** : the act of suspending : the state or period of being suspended **2** : the state of a substance when its particles are mixed with but undissolved in a fluid or solid; *also* : a substance in this state **3** : something suspended **4** : the system of devices supporting the upper part of a vehicle on the axles

sus·pen·so·ry \sə-'spen-sə-rē\ *adj* **1** : SUSPENDED; *also* : fitted or serving to suspend something **2** : temporarily leaving undetermined

sus·pi·cion \sə-'spi-shən\ *n* **1** : the act or an instance of suspecting something wrong without proof **2** : TRACE, SOUPÇON ⟨a ∼ of garlic⟩ ♦ *Synonyms* MISTRUST, UNCERTAINTY, DOUBT, SKEPTICISM

sus·pi·cious \sə-'spi-shəs\ *adj* **1** : open to or arousing suspicion **2** : inclined to suspect **3** : showing suspicion — **sus·pi·cious·ly** *adv*

sus·tain \sə-'stān\ *vb* **1** : to provide with nourishment **2** : to keep going : PROLONG ⟨∼ed effort⟩ **3** : to hold up : PROP **4** : to hold up under : ENDURE **5** : SUFFER ⟨∼ a broken arm⟩ **6** : to support as true, legal, or valid **7** : PROVE, CORROBORATE — **sus·tain·able** \səs-'tā-nə-bəl\ *adj*

sus·te·nance \'səs-tə-nəns\ *n* **1** : FOOD, NOURISHMENT **2** : a supplying with the necessities of life **3** : something that sustains or supports

su·ture \'sü-chər\ *n* **1** : material or a stitch for sewing a wound together **2** : a seam or line along which two things or parts are joined by or as if by sewing

SUV \ˌes-ˌyü-'vē\ *n* [sport-*u*tility *v*ehicle] : a vehicle similar to a station wagon but built on a light-truck chassis

su·zer·ain \'sü-zə-rən, -ˌrān\ *n* [F] **1** : a feudal lord **2** : a nation that has political control over the foreign relations of another nation — **su·zer·ain·ty** \-tē\ *n*

svc *or* **svce** *abbr* service

svelte \'sfelt\ *adj* **svelt·er; svelt·est** [F, fr. It *svelto*, fr. pp. of *svellere* to pluck out, modif. of L *evellere*, fr. *e-* out + *vellere* to pluck] : SLENDER, LITHE

svgs *abbr* savings

SW *abbr* **1** shortwave **2** southwest

¹swab \'swäb\ *n* **1** : MOP **2** : a wad of absorbent material esp. for applying medicine or for cleaning; *also* : a sample taken with a swab **3** : SAILOR

²swab *vb* **swabbed; swab·bing** : to use a swab on : MOP

swad·dle \'swä-dᵊl\ *vb* **swad·dled; swad·dling 1** : to bind (an infant) in bands of cloth **2** : to wrap up : SWATHE

swaddling clothes *n pl* : bands of cloth wrapped around an infant

swag \'swag\ *n* : stolen goods : LOOT

swag·ger \'swa-gər\ *vb* **1** : to walk with a conceited swing or strut **2** : BOAST, BRAG — **swagger** *n*

Swa·hi·li \swä-'hē-lē\ *n* : a language that is a trade and governmental language over much of eastern Africa and the Congo region

swain \'swān\ *n* [ME *swein* boy, servant, fr. ON *sveinn*] **1** : RUSTIC; *esp* : SHEPHERD **2** : ADMIRER, SUITOR

SWAK *abbr* sealed with a kiss

¹**swal·low** \'swä-lō\ *n* : any of numerous small long-winged migratory birds that often have a deeply forked tail

²**swallow** *vb* **1** : to take into the stomach through the throat **2** : to envelop or take in as if by swallowing **3** : to accept or believe without question, protest, or anger

³**swallow** *n* **1** : an act of swallowing **2** : an amount that can be swallowed at one time

swal·low·tail \'swä-lō-ˌtāl\ *n* **1** : a deeply forked and tapering tail like that of a swallow **2** : TAILCOAT **3** : any of various large butterflies with the border of each hind wing usu. drawn out into a process resembling a tail — **swal·low–tailed** \-ˌtāld\ *adj*

swam *past of* SWIM

swa·mi \'swä-mē\ *n* [Hindi *svāmī*, fr. Skt *svāmin* owner, lord] : a Hindu ascetic or religious teacher

¹**swamp** \'swämp\ *n* : a spongy wetland — **swamp** *adj* — **swampy** *adj*

²**swamp** *vb* **1** : to fill or become filled with or as if with water **2** : OVERWHELM **3**

swamp·land \-ˌland\ *n* : SWAMP

swan \'swän\ *n, pl* **swans** *also* **swan** : any of various heavy-bodied long-necked mostly pure white swimming birds related to the geese

¹**swank** \'swaŋk\ *or* **swanky** \'swaŋ-kē\ *adj* **swank·er** *or* **swank·i·er; -est** : showily smart and dashing; *also* : fashionably elegant

²**swank** *n* **1** : PRETENTIOUSNESS **2** : ELEGANCE

swans–down \'swänz-ˌdaún\ *n* **1** : the very soft down of a swan used esp. for trimming **2** : a soft thick cotton flannel

swan song *n* : a farewell appearance, act, or pronouncement

swap \'swäp\ *vb* **swapped; swap·ping** : TRADE, EXCHANGE — **swap** *n*

sward \'swórd\ *n* : the grassy surface of land

¹**swarm** \'swórm\ *n* **1** : a great number of honeybees leaving together from a hive with a queen to start a new colony; *also* : a hive of bees **2** : a large crowd

²**swarm** *vb* **1** : to form in a swarm and depart from a hive **2** : to throng together : gather in great numbers

swart \'swórt\ *adj* : SWARTHY

swar·thy \'swór-thē, -thē\ *adj* **swar·thi·er; -est** : dark in color or complexion : dark-skinned

swash \'swäsh\ *vb* : to move about with a splashing sound — **swash** *n*

swash·buck·ler \-ˌbə-klər\ *n* : a swaggering or daring soldier or adventurer — **swash·buck·ling** *adj*

swas·ti·ka \'swäs-ti-kə\ *n* [Skt *svastika*, fr. *svasti* well-being, fr. *su-* well + *as-* to be] : a symbol or ornament in the form of a cross with the ends of the arms bent at right angles

swat \'swät\ *vb* **swat·ted; swat·ting** : to hit sharply ⟨~ a fly⟩ ⟨~ a ball⟩ — **swat** *n* — **swat·ter** *n*

SWAT *abbr* Special Weapons and Tactics

swatch \'swäch\ *n* : a sample piece (as of fabric) or a collection of samples

swath \'swäth, 'swóth\ *or* **swathe** \'swäth, 'swóth, 'swäth\ *n* [ME, fr. OE *swæth* footstep, trace] **1** : a row of cut grass or grain **2** : the sweep of a scythe or mowing machine or the path cut in mowing

swathe \'swäth, 'swóth, 'swäth\ *vb* **swathed; swath·ing** : to bind or wrap with or as if with a bandage

¹**sway** \'swā\ *n* **1** : a gentle swinging from side to side **2** : controlling influence or power : DOMINION

²**sway** *vb* **1** : to swing gently from side to side **2** : RULE, GOVERN **3** : to cause to sway from side to side **4** : BEND, SWERVE; *also* : INFLUENCE ♦ *Synonyms* OSCILLATE, FLUCTUATE, VIBRATE, WAVER

sway·backed \'swā-ˌbakt\ *also* **sway·back** \-ˌbak\ *adj* : having an abnormally sagging back ⟨a ~ mare⟩ — **swayback** *n*

swear \'swer\ *vb* **swore** \'swór\; **sworn** \'swórn\; **swear·ing 1** : to make a solemn statement or promise under oath **2** : to assert or promise emphatically or earnestly **3** : to administer an oath to **4** : to bind by or as if by an oath **5** : to use profane or obscene language — **swear·er** *n*

swear in *vb* : to induct into office by administration of an oath

sweat \'swet\ *vb* **sweat** *or* **sweat·ed; sweat·ing 1** : to excrete salty moisture from glands of the skin : PERSPIRE **2** : to form drops of moisture on the surface **3** : to work so that one sweats : TOIL **4** : to cause to sweat **5** : to draw out or get rid of by or as if by sweating **6** : to make a person overwork — **sweat** *n* — **sweaty** *adj*

sweat·er \'swe-tər\ *n* **1** : one that sweats **2** : a knitted or crocheted jacket or pullover

sweat·shirt \'swet-ˌshərt\ *n* : a loose collarless pullover or jacket usu. of heavy cotton jersey

sweat·shop \'swet-ˌshäp\ *n* : a shop or factory in which workers are employed for long hours at low wages and under unhealthy conditions

Swed *abbr* Sweden

swede \'swēd\ *n* **1** *cap* : a native or inhabitant of Sweden **2** *chiefly Brit* : RUTABAGA

Swed·ish \'swē-dish\ *n* **1** : the language of Sweden **2** **Swedish** *pl* : the people of Sweden — **Swedish** *adj*

¹**sweep** \'swēp\ *vb* **swept** \'swept\; **sweep·ing 1** : to remove or clean by or as if by brushing **2** : to destroy completely; *also* : to remove or take with a single swift movement **3** : to remove from sight or consideration **4** : to move over with speed and force ⟨the tide *swept* over the shore⟩ **5** : to win an overwhelming victory in; *also* : to win all the games or contests of **6** : to move or extend in a wide curve — **sweep·er** *n*

²**sweep** *n* **1** : something (as a long oar) that operates with a sweeping motion **2** : a clearing off or away **3** : a winning of all the contests or prizes in a competition **4** : a sweeping movement **5** : CURVE, BEND **6** : RANGE, SCOPE

sweeping *adj* : EXTENSIVE ⟨~ reforms⟩; *also* : indiscriminately inclusive ⟨~ generalities⟩

sweep·ings \'swē-piŋz\ *n pl* : things collected by sweeping

sweep–sec·ond hand \'swēp-ˌse-kənd-\ *n* : a hand marking seconds on a timepiece

sweep·stakes \'swēp-ˌstāks\ *also* **sweep·stake** \-ˌstāk\ *n, pl* **sweepstakes 1** : a race or contest in which the entire prize may go to the winner **2** : any of various lotteries

¹**sweet** \'swēt\ *adj* **1** : being or causing the one of the four basic taste sensations that is caused esp. by table sugar and is identified esp. by the taste buds at the front of the tongue; *also* : pleasing to the taste **2** : AGREEABLE ⟨how ~ it is⟩ **3** : pleasing to a sense other than taste ⟨a ~ smell⟩ ⟨~ music⟩ **4** : not stale or spoiled : WHOLESOME ⟨~ milk⟩ **5** : not salted ⟨~ butter⟩ — **sweet·ish** *adj* — **sweet·ly** *adv* — **sweet·ness** *n*

²**sweet** *n* **1** : something sweet : CANDY **2** : DARLING

sweet·bread \'swēt-ˌbred\ *n* : the pancreas or thymus of an animal (as a calf or lamb) used for food

sweet·bri·ar *or* **sweet·bri·er** \-ˌbrī-ər\ *n* : a thorny Old World rose with fragrant white to deep pink flowers

sweet clover *n* : any of a genus of erect legumes widely grown for soil improvement or hay

sweet corn *n* : an Indian corn with wrinkled translucent kernels that are rich in sugar

sweet·en \'swē-tᵊn\ *vb* **sweet·ened; sweet·en·ing** : to make sweet — **sweet·en·er** *n* — **sweet·en·ing** *n*

sweet·heart \'swēt-ˌhärt\ *n* : one who is loved

sweet·meat \-ˌmēt\ *n* : CANDY 1

sweet pea *n* : a garden plant of the legume family with climbing stems and fragrant flowers of many colors; *also* : its flower

sweet pepper *n* : any of various large mild thick-walled fruits of a pepper; *also* : a plant bearing sweet peppers

sweet potato *n* : a tropical vine related to the morning glory; *also* : its large sweet edible root

sweet–talk \'swēt-ˌtók\ *vb* : FLATTER, COAX — **sweet talk** *n*

sweet tooth *n* : a craving or fondness for sweet food

sweet wil·liam \⸲swēt-ʼwil-yəm\ *n, often cap W* : a widely cultivated Old World pink with small white to deep red or purple flowers often showily spotted, banded, or mottled

¹**swell** \ʼswel\ *vb* **swelled; swelled** *or* **swol·len** \ʼswō-lən\; **swell·ing 1** : to grow big or make bigger **2** : to expand or distend abnormally or excessively ⟨a *swollen* joint⟩; *also* : BULGE **3** : to fill or be filled with emotion (as pride) ♦ *Synonyms* EXPAND, AMPLIFY, DISTEND, INFLATE, DILATE — **swell·ing** *n*

²**swell** *n* **1** : a long crestless wave or series of waves in the open sea **2** : the condition of being protuberant **3** : a person dressed in the height of fashion; *also* : a person of high social position

³**swell** *adj* **1** : STYLISH; *also* : socially prominent **2** : EXCELLENT

swelled head *n* : an exaggerated opinion of oneself : SELF= CONCEIT

swel·ter \ʼswel-tər\ *vb* [ME *sweltren,* fr. *swelten* to die, be overcome by heat, fr. OE *sweltan* to die] **1** : to be faint or oppressed with the heat **2** : to become exceedingly hot — **swel·ter·ing** \-tə-riŋ\ *adj*

swept *past and past part of* SWEEP

swerve \ʼswərv\ *vb* **swerved; swerv·ing** : to move abruptly aside from a straight line or course — **swerve** *n*

¹**swift** \ʼswift\ *adj* **1** : moving or capable of moving with great speed **2** : occurring suddenly **3** : READY, ALERT — **swift·ly** *adv* — **swift·ness** *n*

²**swift** *n* : any of numerous small insect-eating birds with long narrow wings

swig \ʼswig\ *vb* **swigged; swig·ging** : to drink in long drafts — **swig** *n*

¹**swill** \ʼswil\ *vb* **1** : to swallow greedily : GUZZLE **2** : to feed (as hogs) on swill

²**swill** *n* **1** : food for animals composed of edible refuse mixed with liquid **2** : GARBAGE

¹**swim** \ʼswim\ *vb* **swam** \ʼswam\; **swum** \ʼswəm\; **swim·ming 1** : to propel oneself along in water by natural means (as by hands and legs, by tail, or by fins) **2** : to glide smoothly along **3** : FLOAT **4** : to be covered with or as if with a liquid **5** : to be dizzy ⟨his head *swam*⟩ **6** : to cross or go over by swimming — **swim·mer** *n*

²**swim** *n* **1** : an act of swimming **2** : the main current of activity ⟨in the ∼⟩

swim·ming *n* : the action, art, or sport of swimming and diving

swimming pool *n* : a tank (as of concrete or plastic) designed for swimming

swim·suit \ʼswim-⸲süt\ *n* : a suit for swimming or bathing

swim·wear \ʼswim-⸲wer\ *n* : clothing for wear while swimming or bathing

swin·dle \ʼswin-dᵊl\ *vb* **swin·dled; swin·dling** [fr. *swindler,* fr. G *Schwindler* giddy person, fr. *schwindeln* to be dizzy] : CHEAT, DEFRAUD — **swindle** *n* — **swin·dler** *n*

swine \ʼswīn\ *n, pl* **swine 1** : any of a family of stout short-legged hoofed mammals with bristly skin and a long flexible snout; *esp* : one widely raised as a meat animal **2** : a contemptible person — **swin·ish** *adj*

¹**swing** \ʼswiŋ\ *vb* **swung** \ʼswəŋ\; **swing·ing 1** : to move or cause to move rapidly in an arc **2** : to sway or cause to sway back and forth **3** : to hang so as to move freely back and forth or in a curve **4** : to be executed by hanging **5** : to move or turn on a hinge or pivot **6** : to manage or handle successfully **7** : to march or walk with free swaying movements **8** : to have a steady pulsing rhythm; *also* : to play swing music **9** : to be lively and up-to-date; *also* : to engage frequently in sex ♦ *Synonyms* WIELD, MANIPULATE, PLY, MANEUVER — **swing·er** *n* — **swing·ing** *adj*

²**swing** *n* **1** : the act of swinging **2** : a swinging blow, movement, or rhythm **3** : the distance through which something swings : FLUCTUATION **4** : progression of an activity or process ⟨in full ∼⟩ **5** : a seat suspended by a rope or chain for swinging back and forth for pleasure **6** : jazz music played esp. by a large band and marked by a steady lively rhythm, simple harmony, and a basic melody often submerged in improvisation

³**swing** *adj* **1** : of or relating to musical swing **2** : that may swing decisively either way (as on an issue) ⟨∼ voters⟩

¹**swipe** \ʼswīp\ *n* : a strong sweeping blow

²**swipe** *vb* **swiped; swip·ing 1** : to strike or wipe with a

sweeping motion **2** : PILFER, SNATCH **3** : to slide (a card having a magnetic code) through a reading device

swirl \ʼswərl\ *vb* : to move or cause to move with a whirling motion — **swirl** *n* — **swirly** \ʼswər-lē\ *adj*

swish \ʼswish\ *n* **1** : a prolonged hissing sound **2** : a light sweeping or brushing sound — **swish** *vb*

Swiss \ʼswis\ *n, pl* **Swiss** : a native or inhabitant of Switzerland **2** : a hard cheese with large holes — **Swiss** *adj*

Swiss chard *n* : a beet having large leaves and succulent stalks often cooked as a vegetable

¹**switch** \ʼswich\ *n* **1** : a slender flexible whip, rod, or twig **2** : a blow with a switch **3** : a shift from one thing to another; *also* : change from the usual **4** : a device for adjusting the rails of a track so that a locomotive or train may be turned from one track to another; *also* : a railroad siding **5** : a device for making, breaking, or changing the connections in an electrical circuit **6** : a heavy strand of hair often used in addition to a person's own hair for some coiffures

²**switch** *vb* **1** : to punish or urge on with a switch **2** : WHISK ⟨a cow ∼*ing* her tail⟩ **3** : to shift or turn by operating a switch **4** : CHANGE, EXCHANGE

switch·back \ʼswich-⸲bak\ *n* : a zigzag road, trail, or section of railroad tracks for climbing a steep hill

switch·blade \-⸲blād\ *n* : a pocket-knife with a spring-operated blade

switch·board \-⸲bōrd\ *n* : a panel for controlling the operation of a number of electric circuits; *esp* : one used to make and break telephone connections

switch–hit·ter \-ʼhi-tər\ *n* : a baseball player who bats either right-handed or left-handed — **switch–hit** \-ʼhit\ *vb*

switch·man \ʼswich-mən\ *n* : one who attends a railroad switch

Switz *abbr* Switzerland

¹**swiv·el** \ʼswi-vəl\ *n* : a device joining two parts so that one or both can turn freely

²**swivel** *vb* **-eled** *or* **-elled; -el·ing** *or* **-el·ling** : to swing or turn on or as if on a swivel

swiv·et \ʼswi-vət\ *n* : an agitated state

swiz·zle stick \ʼswi-zəl-\ *n* : a stick used to stir mixed drinks

swollen *past part of* SWELL

swoon \ʼswün\ *vb* : FAINT — **swoon** *n*

swoop \ʼswüp\ *vb* : to move with a sweep ⟨the eagle ∼*ed* down on its prey⟩ — **swoop** *n*

swoopy \ʼswü-pē\ *adj* : having lines that extend in a wide curve ⟨a ∼ silhouette⟩

swop *chiefly Brit var of* SWAP

sword \ʼsȯrd\ *n* **1** : a weapon with a long blade for cutting or thrusting **2** : the use of force

sword·fish \-⸲fish\ *n* : a very large ocean fish used for food that has the upper jaw prolonged into a long swordlike beak

swordfish

sword·play \-⸲plā\ *n* : the art or skill of wielding a sword

swords·man \ʼsȯrdz-mən\ *n* : one skilled in swordplay; *esp* : FENCER

sword·tail \ʼsȯrd-⸲tāl\ *n* : a small brightly marked Central American fish often kept in aquariums

swore *past of* SWEAR

sworn *past part of* SWEAR

swum *past part of* SWIM

swung *past and past part of* SWING

syb·a·rite \ʼsi-bə-⸲rīt\ *n* : a lover of luxury : VOLUPTUARY — **syb·a·rit·ic** \⸲si-bə-ʼri-tik\ *adj*

syc·a·more \ʼsi-kə-⸲mȯr\ *n* : a large spreading tree chiefly of the eastern and central U.S. that has light brown flaky bark and small round fruits hanging on long stalks

sy·co·phant \ʼsi-kə-fənt\ *n* : a servile flatterer — **sy·co·phan·cy** \ʼsi-kə-fən-sē\ *n* — **sy·co·phan·tic** \⸲si-kə-ʼfan-tik\ *adj*

syl *or* **syll** *abbr* syllable
syl·lab·i·ca·tion \sə-ˌla-bə-'kā-shən\ *n* : the division of words into syllables
syl·lab·i·fy \sə-'la-bə-ˌfī\ *vb* **-fied; -fy·ing** : to form or divide into syllables — **syl·lab·i·fi·ca·tion** \-ˌla-bə-fə-'kā-shən\ *n*
syl·la·ble \'si-lə-bəl\ *n* [ME, fr. AF *sillabe*, *silable*, fr. L *syllaba*, fr. Gk *syllabē*, fr. *syllambanein* to gather together, fr. *syn-* with + *lambanein* to take] : a unit of spoken language consisting of an uninterrupted utterance and forming either a whole word (as *cat*) or a commonly recognized division of a word (as *syl* in *syl-la-ble*); *also* : one or more letters representing such a unit — **syl·lab·ic** \sə-'la-bik\ *adj*
syl·la·bus \'si-lə-bəs\ *n, pl* **-bi** \-ˌbī\ *or* **-bus·es** : a summary containing the heads or main topics of a speech, book, or course of study
syl·lo·gism \'si-lə-ji-zəm\ *n* : a logical scheme of a formal argument consisting of a major and a minor premise and a conclusion which must logically be true if the premises are true — **syl·lo·gis·tic** \ˌsi-lə-'jis-tik\ *adj*
sylph \'silf\ *n* **1** : an imaginary being inhabiting the air **2** : a slender graceful woman
syl·van \'sil-vən\ *adj* **1** : living or located in a wooded area; *also* : of, relating to, or characteristic of forest **2** : abounding in woods or trees
sym *abbr* **1** symbol **2** symmetrical
sym·bi·o·sis \ˌsim-ˌbī-'ō-səs, -bē-\ *n, pl* **-o·ses** \-ˌsēz\ : the living together in close association of two dissimilar organisms esp. when mutually beneficial — **sym·bi·ot·ic** \-'ä-tik\ *adj*
sym·bol \'sim-bəl\ *n* **1** : something that stands for something else; *esp* : something concrete that represents or suggests another thing that cannot in itself be pictured ⟨the lion is a ∼ of bravery⟩ **2** : a letter, character, or sign used in writing or printing to represent operations, quantities, elements, sounds, or other ideas — **sym·bol·ic** \sim-'bä-lik\ *also* **sym·bol·i·cal** \-li-kəl\ *adj* — **sym·bol·i·cal·ly** \-k(ə-)lē\ *adv*
sym·bol·ise *Brit var of* SYMBOLIZE
sym·bol·ism \'sim-bə-ˌli-zəm\ *n* : representation of abstract or intangible things by means of symbols
sym·bol·ize \'sim-bə-ˌlīz\ *vb* **-ized; -iz·ing 1** : to serve as a symbol of **2** : to represent by symbols — **sym·bol·i·za·tion** \ˌsim-bə-lə-'zā-shən\ *n*
sym·me·try \'si-mə-trē\ *n, pl* **-tries 1** : an arrangement marked by regularity and balanced proportions **2** : correspondence in size, shape, and position of parts that are on opposite sides of a dividing line or center — **sym·met·ri·cal** \sə-'me-tri-kəl\ *or* **sym·met·ric** \sə-'me-trik\ *adj* — **sym·met·ri·cal·ly** \-k(ə-)lē\ *adv*
sympathetic nervous system *n* : the part of the autonomic nervous system that is concerned esp. with the body's repsonse to stress and that tends to decrease the tone and contractility of smooth muscle and increase blood pressure and the activity of the heart
sym·pa·thise *chiefly Brit var of* SYMPATHIZE
sym·pa·thize \'sim-pə-ˌthīz\ *vb* **-thized; -thiz·ing** : to feel or show sympathy — **sym·pa·thiz·er** *n*
sym·pa·thy \'sim-pə-thē\ *n, pl* **-thies 1** : a relationship between persons or things wherein whatever affects one similarly affects the other **2** : harmony of interests and aims **3** : FAVOR, SUPPORT **4** : the capacity for entering into and sharing the feelings or interests of another; *also* : COMPASSION, PITY **5** : an expression of sorrow for another's loss, grief, or misfortune — **sym·pa·thet·ic** \ˌsim-pə-'the-tik\ *adj* — **sym·pa·thet·i·cal·ly** \-ti-k(ə-)lē\ *adv*
sym·pho·ny \'sim-fə-nē\ *n, pl* **-nies 1** : harmony of sounds **2** : a large and complex composition for a full orchestra **3** : a large orchestra of a kind that plays symphonies — **sym·phon·ic** \sim-'fä-nik\ *adj*
sym·po·sium \sim-'pō-zē-əm\ *n, pl* **-sia** \-zē-ə\ *or* **-siums** : a conference at which a particular topic is discussed by various speakers; *also* : a collection of opinions about a subject
symp·tom \'simp-təm\ *n* [LL *symptoma*, fr. Gk *symptōma* happening, attribute, symptom, fr. *sympiptein* to happen, fr. *syn-* with + *piptein* to fall] **1** : something that indicates the presence of disease or abnormality; *esp* : something (as a headache) that can be sensed only by the individual affected **2** : SIGN, INDICATION ⟨∼s of inner turmoil⟩ — **symp·tom·at·ic** \ˌsimp-tə-'ma-tik\ *adj*

syn *abbr* synonym; synonymous; synonymy
syn·a·gogue *also* **syn·a·gog** \'si-nə-ˌgäg\ *n* [ME *synagoge*, fr. AF, fr. LL *synagoga*, fr. Gk *synagōgē* assembly, synagogue, fr. *synagein* to bring together] **1** : a Jewish congregation **2** : the house of worship of a Jewish congregation
syn·apse \'si-ˌnaps, sə-'naps\ *n* : the point at which a nervous impulse passes from one neuron to another — **syn·ap·tic** \sə-'nap-tik\ *adj*
¹sync *also* **synch** \'siŋk\ *vb* **synced** *also* **synched** \'siŋkt\; **sync·ing** *also* **synch·ing** \'siŋ-kiŋ\ : SYNCHRONIZE
²sync *also* **synch** *n* : SYNCHRONIZATION, SYNCHRONISM — **sync** *adj*
syn·chro·ni·sa·tion, syn·chro·nise *Brit var of* SYNCHRONIZATION, SYNCHRONIZE
syn·chro·nize \'siŋ-krə-ˌnīz, 'sin-\ *vb* **-nized; -niz·ing 1** : to occur or cause to occur at the same instant **2** : to represent, arrange, or tabulate according to dates or time **3** : to cause to agree in time **4** : to make synchronous in operation — **syn·chro·nism** \-ˌni-zəm\ *n* — **syn·chro·ni·za·tion** \ˌsiŋ-krə-nə-'zā-shən, ˌsin-\ *n* — **syn·chro·niz·er** *n*
syn·chro·nous \'siŋ-krə-nəs, 'sin-\ *adj* **1** : happening at the same time : CONCURRENT **2** : working, moving, or occurring together at the same rate and at the proper time
syn·co·pa·tion \ˌsiŋ-kə-'pā-shən, ˌsin-\ *n* : a shifting of the regular musical accent : occurrence of accented notes on the weak beat — **syn·co·pate** \'siŋ-kə-ˌpāt, 'sin-\ *vb*
syn·co·pe \'siŋ-kə-(ˌ)pē, 'sin-\ *n* : the loss of one or more sounds or letters in the interior of a word (as in *fo'c'sle* for *forecastle*)
¹syn·di·cate \'sin-di-kət\ *n* **1** : a group of persons who combine to carry out a financial or industrial undertaking **2** : a loose association of racketeers **3** : a business concern that sells materials for publication in many newspapers and periodicals at the same time
²syn·di·cate \-də-ˌkāt\ *vb* **-cat·ed; -cat·ing 1** : to combine into or manage as a syndicate **2** : to publish through a syndicate — **syn·di·ca·tion** \ˌsin-də-'kā-shən\ *n*
syn·drome \'sin-ˌdrōm\ *n* : a group of signs and symptoms that occur together and characterize a particular abnormality or condition
syn·er·gism \'sin-ər-ˌji-zəm\ *n* : interaction of discrete agencies (as industrial firms), agents (as drugs), or conditions such that the total effect is greater than the sum of the individual effects — **syn·er·gist** \-jist\ *n* — **syn·er·gis·tic** \ˌsi-nər-'jis-tik\ *adj* — **syn·er·gis·ti·cal·ly** \-ti-k(ə-)lē\ *adv*
syn·er·gy \'si-nər-jē\ *n, pl* **-gies** : SYNERGISM
syn·fuel \'sin-ˌfyül\ *n* [*synthetic*] : a fuel derived esp. from a fossil fuel
syn·od \'si-nəd\ *n* : COUNCIL, ASSEMBLY; *esp* : a religious governing body — **syn·od·al** \-nə-dᵊl, -ˌnä-dᵊl\ *adj* — **syn·od·ic** \si-'nä-dik\ *or* **syn·od·i·cal** \-di-kəl\ *adj*
syn·onym \'si-nə-ˌnim\ *n* : one of two or more words in the same language which have the same or very nearly the same meaning — **syn·on·y·mous** \sə-'nä-nə-məs\ *adj* — **syn·on·y·mous·ly** *adv* — **syn·on·y·my** \-mē\ *n*
syn·op·sis \sə-'näp-səs\ *n, pl* **-op·ses** \-ˌsēz\ : a condensed statement or outline (as of a treatise) : ABSTRACT
syn·op·tic \sə-'näp-tik\ *also* **syn·op·ti·cal** \-ti-kəl\ *adj* : characterized by or affording a comprehensive view
syn·tax \'sin-ˌtaks\ *n* : the way in which words are put together to form phrases, clauses, or sentences — **syn·tac·tic** \sin-'tak-tik\ *or* **syn·tac·ti·cal** \-ti-kəl\ *adj*
syn·the·sis \'sin-thə-səs\ *n, pl* **-the·ses** \-ˌsēz\ : the combination of parts or elements into a whole; *esp* : the production of a substance by union of chemically simpler substances — **syn·the·size** \-ˌsīz\ *vb* — **syn·the·siz·er** *n*
syn·thet·ic \sin-'the-tik\ *adj* : produced artificially esp. by chemical means; *also* : not genuine — **synthetic** *n* — **syn·thet·i·cal·ly** \-ti-k(ə-)lē\ *adv*
syph·i·lis \'si-fə-ləs\ *n* [NL, fr. *Syphilus*, hero of the poem *Syphilis sive Morbus Gallicus* (*Syphilis or the French disease*) (1530) by Girolamo Fracastoro †1553 Ital. physician] : an infectious usu. venereal disease caused by a spirochete — **syph·i·lit·ic** \ˌsi-fə-'li-tik\ *adj or n*
syphon *var of* SIPHON
Sy·rah \sē-'rä\ *n* : a red wine
¹sy·ringe \sə-'rinj\ *n* : a device used esp. for injecting liquids into or withdrawing them from the body

²**syringe** *vb* **sy·ringed; sy·ring·ing** : to flush or cleanse with or as if with a syringe
syr·up \'sər-əp, 'sir-əp\ *n* **1** : a thick sticky solution of sugar and water often flavored or medicated **2** : the concentrated juice of a fruit or plant — **syr·upy** *adj*
syst *abbr* system
sys·tem \'sis-təm\ *n* **1** : a group of units so combined as to form a whole and to operate in unison **2** : the body as a functioning whole; *also* : a group of bodily organs (as the nervous system) that together carry on some vital function **3** : a definite scheme or method of procedure or classification **4** : regular method or order — **sys·tem·at·ic** \,sis-tə-'ma-tik\ — **sys·tem·at·i·cal·ly** \-ti-k(ə-)lē\ *adv*
sys·tem·a·tise *Brit var of* SYSTEMATIZE
sys·tem·a·tize \'sis-tə-mə-,tīz\ *vb* **-tized; -tiz·ing** : to make into a system : arrange methodically
¹**sys·tem·ic** \sis-'te-mik\ *adj* **1** : of, relating to, or affecting the whole body ⟨∼ disease⟩ **2** : of, relating to, or being a pesticide that when absorbed into the sap or bloodstream makes the entire plant or animal toxic to a pest (as an insect or fungus)
²**systemic** *n* : a systemic pesticide
systemic lupus erythematosus *n* : a systemic disease esp. of women characterized by fever, skin rash, and arthritis, often by anemia, by small hemorrhages of the skin and mucous membranes, and in serious cases by involvement of internal organs
sys·tem·ize \'sis-tə-,mīz\ *vb* **-ized; -iz·ing** : SYSTEMATIZE
systems analyst *n* : a person who studies a procedure or business to determine its goals or purposes and to discover the best ways to accomplish them — **systems analysis** *n*
sys·to·le \'sis-tə-(,)lē\ *n* : a rhythmically recurrent contraction of the heart — **sys·tol·ic** \sis-'tä-lik\ *adj*

¹**t** \'tē\ *n, pl* **t's** *or* **ts** \'tēz\ *often cap* : the 20th letter of the English alphabet
²**t** *abbr, often cap* **1** tablespoon **2** teaspoon **3** temperature **4** ton **5** transitive **6** troy **7** true
T *abbr* **1** toddler **2** T-shirt
Ta *symbol* tantalum
TA *abbr* teaching assistant
¹**tab** \'tab\ *n* **1** : a short projecting flap, loop, or tag; *also* : a small insert or addition **2** : close surveillance : WATCH ⟨keep ∼s on him⟩ **3** : BILL, CHECK **4** : a key on a keyboard esp. for putting data in columns
²**tab** *vb* **tabbed; tab·bing** : DESIGNATE
tab·by \'ta-bē\ *n, pl* **tabbies** : a usu. striped or mottled domestic cat; *also* : a female domestic cat
tab·er·na·cle \'ta-bər-,na-kəl\ *n* [ME, fr. AF, fr. LL *tabernaculum*, fr. L, tent, fr. *taberna* hut] **1** *often cap* : a tent sanctuary used by the Israelites during the Exodus **2** : a receptacle for the consecrated elements of the Eucharist **3** : a house of worship
¹**ta·ble** \'tā-bəl\ *n* **1** : TABLET 1 **2** : a piece of furniture consisting of a smooth flat top fixed on legs **3** : a supply of food : BOARD, FARE **4** : a group of people assembled at or as if at a table **5** : an orderly arrangement of data usu. in rows and columns **6** : a short list ⟨∼ of contents⟩ — **ta·ble·top** \-,täp\ *n*
²**table** *vb* **ta·bled; ta·bling** **1** *Brit* : to place on the agenda **2** : to remove (a parliamentary motion) from consideration indefinitely
tab·leau \'ta-,blō\ *n, pl* **tab·leaux** \-,blōz\ *also* **tableaus** \-,blōz\ *also* **tableaus** [F] : a scene or event usu. presented on a stage by silent and motionless costumed participants
ta·ble·cloth \'tā-bəl-,klöth\ *n* : a covering spread over a dining table before the table is set
ta·ble d'hôte \,tä-bəl-'dōt\ *n* [F, lit., host's table] : a complete meal of several courses offered at a fixed price
ta·ble·land \'tā-bəl-,land\ *n* : PLATEAU
ta·ble·spoon \-,spün\ *n* **1** : a large spoon used esp. for serving **2** : a unit of measure equal to ½ fluid ounce (15 milliliters)
ta·ble·spoon·ful \-,fül\ *n, pl* **-spoonfuls** \-,fülz\ *also* **-spoons·ful** \-,spünz-fül\ : TABLESPOON 2
tab·let \'ta-blət\ *n* **1** : a flat slab suited for or bearing an inscription **2** : a collection of sheets of paper glued together at one edge **3** : a compressed or molded block of material; *esp* : a usu. disk-shaped medicated mass
table tennis *n* : a game resembling tennis played on a tabletop with wooden paddles and a small hollow plastic ball
ta·ble·ware \'tā-bəl-,wer\ *n* : utensils (as of china or silver) for table use
¹**tab·loid** \'ta-,blóid\ *adj* : condensed into small scope
²**tabloid** *n* : a newspaper marked by small pages, condensation of the news, and usu. many photographs

¹**ta·boo** *also* **ta·bu** \ta-'bü, ta-\ *adj* [Tongan (a Polynesian language) *tabu*] : prohibited by a taboo
²**taboo** *also* **tabu** *n, pl* **taboos** *also* **tabus** **1** : a prohibition against touching, saying, or doing something for fear of immediate harm from a supernatural force **2** : a prohibition imposed by social custom
ta·bor *also* **ta·bour** \'tā-bər\ *n* : a small drum used to accompany a pipe or fife played by the same person
tab·u·lar \'ta-byə-lər\ *adj* **1** : having a flat surface **2** : arranged in a table; *esp* : set up in rows and columns **3** : computed by means of a table
tab·u·late \'ta-byə-,lāt\ *vb* **-lat·ed; -lat·ing** : to put into tabular form — **tab·u·la·tion** \,ta-byə-'lā-shən\ *n* — **tab·u·la·tor** \'ta-byə-,lā-tər\ *n*
TAC *abbr* Tactical Air Command
tach \'tak\ *n* : TACHOMETER
ta·chom·e·ter \ta-'kä-mə-tər, tə-\ *n* [ultim. fr. Gk *tachos* speed] : a device to indicate speed of rotation
tachy·car·dia \,ta-ki-'kär-dē-ə\ *n* : relatively rapid heart action
tachy·on \'ta-kē-,än\ *n* : a hypothetical particle held to travel faster than light
tac·it \'ta-sət\ *adj* [F or L; F *tacite*, fr. L *tacitus* silent, fr. *tacēre* to be silent] **1** : expressed without words or speech **2** : implied or indicated but not actually expressed ⟨∼ consent⟩ — **tac·it·ly** *adv* — **tac·it·ness** *n*
tac·i·turn \'ta-sə-,tərn\ *adj* : disinclined to talk ♦ *Synonyms* UNCOMMUNICATIVE, RESERVED, RETICENT, CLOSEMOUTHED — **tac·i·tur·ni·ty** \,ta-sə-'tər-nə-tē\ *n*
¹**tack** \'tak\ *vb* **1** : to fasten with tacks; *also* : to add on **2** : to change the direction of (a sailing ship) from one tack to another **3** : to follow a zigzag course
²**tack** *n* **1** : a small sharp nail with a broad flat head **2** : the direction toward the wind that a ship is sailing ⟨starboard ∼⟩; *also* : the run of a ship on one tack **3** : a change of course from one tack to another **4** : a zigzag course **5** : a course of action
³**tack** *n* : gear for harnessing a horse
¹**tack·le** \'ta-kəl, *naut often* 'tā-\ *n* **1** : GEAR, APPARATUS, EQUIPMENT **2** : the rigging of a ship **3** : an arrangement of ropes and pulleys for hoisting or pulling heavy objects **4** : the act or an instance of tackling; *also* : a football lineman playing between guard and end
²**tackle** *vb* **tack·led; tack·ling** **1** : to attach and secure with or as if with tackle **2** : to seize, grapple with, or throw down with the intention of subduing or stopping **3** : to set about dealing with ⟨∼ a problem⟩ — **tack·ler** *n*
¹**tacky** \'ta-kē\ *adj* **tack·i·er; -est** : sticky to the touch
²**tacky** *adj* **tack·i·er; -est** **1** : SHABBY, SEEDY **2** : marked by lack of style or good taste; *also* : cheaply showy ⟨a ∼ publicity stunt⟩ ⟨a ∼ outfit⟩
ta·co \'tä-kō\ *n, pl* **tacos** \-kōz\ [MexSp] : a usu. fried tortilla rolled up with or folded over a filling

tact \'takt\ *n* [F, sense of touch, fr. L *tactus*, fr. *tangere* to touch] : a keen sense of what to do or say to keep good relations with others — **tact·ful** \-fəl\ *adj* — **tact·ful·ly** *adv* — **tact·less** *adj* — **tact·less·ly** *adv*

tac·tic \'tak-tik\ *n* : a planned action for accomplishing an end

tac·tics \'tak-tiks\ *n sing or pl* **1** : the science of maneuvering forces in combat **2** : the skill of using available means to accomplish an end — **tac·ti·cal** \-ti-kəl\ *adj* — **tac·ti·cian** \tak-'ti-shən\ *n*

tac·tile \'takt-ᵊl, 'tak-ᵊtī(-ə)l\ *adj* : of, relating to, or perceptible through the sense of touch

tad·pole \'tad-ˌpōl\ *n* [ME *taddepol*, fr. *tode* toad + *polle* head] : an aquatic larva of a frog or toad that has a tail and gills

tadpole: in stages

tae kwon do \'tī-'kwän-'dō\ *n* : a Korean martial art of self-defense

taf·fe·ta \'ta-fə-tə\ *n* : a crisp lustrous fabric (as of silk or rayon)

taff·rail \'taf-ˌrāl, -rəl\ *n* : the rail around a ship's stern

taf·fy \'ta-fē\ *n, pl* **taffies** : a candy usu. of molasses or brown sugar stretched until porous and light-colored

¹tag \'tag\ *n* **1** : a metal or plastic binding on an end of a shoelace **2** : a piece of hanging or attached material **3** : a hackneyed quotation or saying **4** : a descriptive or identifying epithet

²tag *vb* **tagged; tag·ging** **1** : to provide or mark with or as if with a tag; *esp* : IDENTIFY **2** : to attach as an addition **3** : to follow closely and persistently ⟨~s along everywhere we go⟩ **4** : to hold responsible for something

³tag *n* : a game in which one player chases others and tries to touch one of them

⁴tag *vb* **tagged; tag·ging** **1** : to touch in or as if in a game of tag **2** : SELECT

TAG *abbr* the adjutant general

tag sale *n* : GARAGE SALE

Ta·hi·tian \tə-'hē-shən\ *n* **1** : a native or inhabitant of Tahiti **2** : the Polynesian language of the Tahitians — **Tahitian** *adj*

tai·ga \'tī-gə\ *n* [Russ *taĭga*] : a moist coniferous subarctic forest extending south from the tundra

¹tail \'tāl\ *n* **1** : the rear end or a process extending from the rear end of an animal **2** : something resembling an animal's tail **3** *pl* : full evening dress for men **4** : the back, last, lower, or inferior part of something; *esp* : the reverse of a coin — usu. used in pl. ⟨~s, I win⟩ **5** : one who follows or keeps watch on someone — **tailed** \'tāld\ *adj* — **tail·less** \'tāl-ləs\ *adj*

²tail *vb* : FOLLOW; *esp* : to follow for the purpose of surveillance

tail·coat \-'kōt\ *n* : a coat with tails; *esp* : a man's full-dress coat with two long tapering skirts at the back

¹tail·gate \-ˌgāt\ *n* : a board or gate at the back end of a vehicle that can be let down (as for loading)

²tailgate *vb* **tail·gat·ed; tail·gat·ing** **1** : to drive dangerously close behind another vehicle **2** : to hold a tailgate picnic

³tailgate *adj* : relating to or being a picnic set up on a tailgate

tail·light \-ˌlīt\ *n* : a usu. red warning light mounted at the rear of a vehicle

¹tai·lor \'tā-lər\ *n* [ME *taillour*, fr. AF *taillur*, fr. *tailler* to cut, fr. LL *taliare*, fr. L *talea* twig, cutting] : a person whose occupation is making or altering garments

²tailor *vb* **1** : to make or fashion as the work of a tailor **2** : to make or adapt to suit a special purpose

tail·pipe \'tāl-ˌpīp\ *n* : an outlet by which engine exhaust gases are expelled from a vehicle (as an automobile)

tail·spin \'tāl-ˌspin\ *n* : a rapid descent or downward spiral

tail·wind \'tāl-ˌwind\ *n* : a wind blowing in the same general direction as a course of movement (as of an aircraft)

¹taint \'tānt\ *vb* **1** : CORRUPT, CONTAMINATE **2** : to affect or become affected with something bad (as putrefaction)

²taint *n* : a contaminating mark or influence

ta·ka \'tä-kə\ *n* — see MONEY table

¹take \'tāk\ *vb* **took** \'tuk\; **tak·en** \'tā-kən\; **tak·ing** [ME, fr. OE *tacan*, fr. ON *taka*] **1** : to get into one's hands or possession : GRASP, SEIZE **2** : CAPTURE; *also* : DEFEAT **3** : to obtain or secure for use **4** : to catch or attack through the effect of a sudden force or influence ⟨*taken* ill⟩ **5** : CAPTIVATE, DELIGHT **6** : to bring into a relation ⟨~ a wife⟩ **7** : REMOVE, SUBTRACT ⟨~ three from eight⟩ **8** : to pick out : CHOOSE **9** : ASSUME, UNDERTAKE **10** : RECEIVE, ACCEPT **11** : to use for transportation ⟨~ a bus⟩ **12** : to become impregnated with : ABSORB ⟨~s a dye⟩ **13** : to receive into one's body (as by swallowing) ⟨~ a pill⟩ **14** : ENDURE, UNDERGO ⟨~ a cut in pay⟩ **15** : to lead, carry, or cause to go along to another place **16** : NEED, REQUIRE ⟨~s a size nine shoe⟩ **17** : to obtain as the result of a special procedure ⟨~ a snapshot⟩ **18** : to undertake and do, make, or perform ⟨~ a walk⟩ **19** : to take effect : ACT, OPERATE ♦ **Synonyms** GRAB, CLUTCH, SNATCH, SEIZE, NAB, GRAPPLE — **tak·er** *n* — **take advantage of** **1** : to profit by **2** : EXPLOIT — **take after** : RESEMBLE — **take care** : to be careful — **take care of** : to attend to — **take effect** : to become operative — **take exception** : OBJECT — **take for** : to suppose to be; *esp* : to mistake for — **take place** : HAPPEN — **take to** **1** : to go to **2** : to apply or devote oneself to **3** : to conceive a liking for

²take *n* **1** : the number or quantity taken; *also* : PROCEEDS, RECEIPTS **2** : an act or the action of taking **3** : a television or movie scene filmed or taped at one time; *also* : a sound recording made at one time **4** : a distinct or personal point of view

take·off \'tāk-ˌȯf\ *n* **1** : IMITATION; *esp* : PARODY **2** : an act or instance of taking off

take off *vb* **1** : REMOVE **2** : DEDUCT **3** : to set out : go away **4** : to begin flight

take on *vb* **1** : to begin to perform or deal with; *also* : to contend with as an opponent **2** : ENGAGE, HIRE **3** : to assume or acquire as or as if one's own **4** : to make an unusual show of one's feelings esp. of grief or anger

take over *vb* : to assume control or possession of or responsibility for — **take·over** \'tāk-ˌō-vər\ *n*

take up *vb* **1** : PICK UP **2** : to begin to occupy (land) **3** : to absorb or incorporate into itself ⟨plants *taking up* nutrients⟩ **4** : to begin to engage in ⟨*took up* jogging⟩ **5** : to make tighter or shorter ⟨*take up* the slack⟩

tak·ings \'tā-kiŋz\ *n pl, chiefly Brit* : receipts esp. of money

ta·la \'tä-lə\ *n, pl* **tala** — see MONEY table

talc \'talk\ *n* : a soft mineral with a soapy feel used esp. in making a soothing powder (**tal·cum powder** \'tal-kəm-\) for the skin

tale \'tāl\ *n* **1** : a relation of a series of events **2** : a report of a confidential matter **3** : idle talk; *esp* : harmful gossip **4** : a usu. imaginative narrative **5** : FALSEHOOD **6** : COUNT, TALLY

tal·ent \'ta-lənt\ *n* **1** : an ancient unit of weight and value **2** : the natural endowments of a person **3** : a special often creative or artistic aptitude **4** : mental power : ABILITY **5** : a person of talent ♦ **Synonyms** GENIUS, GIFT, FACULTY, APTITUDE, KNACK — **tal·ent·ed** *adj*

ta·ler \'tä-lər\ *n* : any of numerous silver coins issued by German states from the 15th to the 19th centuries

tales·man \'tālz-mən\ *n* : a person summoned for jury duty

tal·is·man \'ta-ləs-mən, -ləz-\ *n, pl* **-mans** [F *talisman* or Sp *talismán* or It *talismano*, fr. Ar *ṭilsam*, fr. MGk *telesma*, fr. Gk, consecration, fr. *telein* to initiate into the mysteries, complete, fr. *telos* end] : an object thought to act as a charm

¹talk \'tȯk\ *vb* **1** : to express in speech : utter words : SPEAK **2** : DISCUSS ⟨~ business⟩ **3** : to influence or cause by talking ⟨~ed him into going⟩ **4** : to use (a language) for communicating **5** : CONVERSE **6** : to reveal confidential information; *also* : GOSSIP **7** : to give a talk

: LECTURE — **talk·er** *n* — **talk back** : to answer impertinently

²**talk** *n*   **1** : the act of talking   **2** : a way of speaking   **3** : a formal discussion   **4** : REPORT, RUMOR   **5** : the topic of comment or gossip ⟨the ~ of the town⟩   **6** : an informal address or lecture

talk·ative \'tȯ-kə-tiv\ *adj* : given to talking ✦ *Synonyms* LOQUACIOUS, CHATTY, GABBY, GARRULOUS — **talk·ative·ly** *adv* — **talk·ative·ness** *n*

talk·ing–to \'tȯ-kiŋ-ˌtü\ *n* : REPRIMAND, REPROOF

talk radio *n* : radio programming consisting of call-in shows

tall \'tȯl\ *adj*   **1** : high in stature; *also* : of a specified height ⟨six feet ~⟩   **2** : LARGE, FORMIDABLE ⟨a ~ order⟩   **3** : UNBELIEVABLE, IMPROBABLE ⟨a ~ story⟩ — **tall·ness** *n*

tal·low \'ta-lō\ *n* : a hard white fat rendered usu. from cattle or sheep tissues and used esp. in candles

¹**tal·ly** \'ta-lē\ *n*, *pl* **tallies**   **1** : a device for visibly recording or accounting esp. business transactions   **2** : a recorded account   **3** : a corresponding part; *also* : CORRESPONDENCE

²**tally** *vb* **tal·lied; tal·ly·ing**   **1** : to mark on or as if on a tally   **2** : to make a count of : RECKON; *also* : SCORE   **3** : CORRESPOND, MATCH ✦ *Synonyms* SQUARE, ACCORD, HARMONIZE, CONFORM, JIBE

tal·ly·ho \ˌta-lē-'hō\ *n*, *pl* **-hos** : a call of a huntsman at sight of the fox

Tal·mud \'täl-ˌmu̇d, 'tal-məd\ *n* [Late Heb *talmūdh*, lit., instruction] : the authoritative body of Jewish tradition — **Tal·mu·dic** \tal-'mü-dik, -'myü-, -'mə-; täl-'mù-\ *adj* — **Tal·mud·ist** \'täl-ˌmù-dist, 'tal-mə-\ *n*

tal·on \'ta-lən\ *n* : the claw of an animal and esp. of a bird of prey

ta·lus \'tā-ləs, 'ta-\ *n* : rock debris at the base of a cliff

tam \'tam\ *n* : TAM-O'-SHANTER

ta·ma·le \tə-'mä-lē\ *n* [MexSp *tamales*, pl. of *tamal* tamale, fr. Nahuatl *tamalli* steamed cornmeal dough] : ground meat seasoned with chili, rolled in cornmeal dough, wrapped in corn husks, and steamed

tam·a·rack \'ta-mə-ˌrak\ *n* : a larch of northern No. America; *also* : its hard resinous wood

tam·a·rin \'ta-mə-rən\ *n* : any of several small So. American monkeys related to the marmosets

tam·a·rind \'ta-mə-rənd, -ˌrind\ *n* [Sp & Pg *tamarindo*, fr. Ar *tamr hindī*, lit., Indian date] : a tropical tree of the legume family with hard yellowish wood and feathery leaves; *also* : its acid fruit

tam·ba·la \täm-'bä-lə\ *n*, *pl* **-la** *or* **-las** — see *kwacha* at MONEY table

tam·bou·rine \ˌtam-bə-'rēn\ *n* : a small shallow drum with loose disks at the sides played by shaking or striking with the hand

¹**tame** \'tām\ *adj* **tam·er; tam·est**   **1** : reduced from a state of native wildness esp. so as to be useful to humans : DOMESTICATED   **2** : made docile : SUBDUED   **3** : lacking spirit or interest : INSIPID ✦ *Synonyms* SUBMISSIVE, DOMESTIC, DOMESTICATED — **tame·ly** *adv* — **tame·ness** *n*

²**tame** *vb* **tamed; tam·ing**   **1** : to make or become tame; *also* : to subject (land) to cultivation   **2** : HUMBLE, SUBDUE — **tam·able** *or* **tame·able** \'tā-mə-bəl\ *adj* — **tame·less** *adj* — **tam·er** *n*

tam-o'-shan·ter \'ta-mə-ˌshan-tər\ *n* [fr. poem *Tam o' Shanter* (1790) by Robert Burns †1796 Scot. poet] : a Scottish woolen cap with a wide flat circular crown and usu. a pom-pom in the center

ta·mox·i·fen \tə-'mäk-sə-ˌfen\ *n* : a drug used esp. to treat breast cancer

tamp \'tamp\ *vb* : to drive down or in by a series of light blows

tam·per \'tam-pər\ *vb*   **1** : to carry on underhand negotiations (as by bribery) ⟨~ with a witness⟩   **2** : to interfere so as to weaken or change for the worse ⟨~ with a document⟩   **3** : to try foolish or dangerous experiments

tam·pon \'tam-ˌpän\ *n* [F, lit., plug] : a plug (as of cotton) introduced into a body cavity usu. to absorb secretions (as from menstruation) or to arrest bleeding

¹**tan** \'tan\ *vb* **tanned; tan·ning**   **1** : to change (hide) into leather esp. by soaking in a liquid containing tannin   **2** : to make or become brown (as by exposure to the sun)   **3** : WHIP, THRASH

²**tan** *n*   **1** : a brown skin color induced by sun or weather   **2** : a light yellowish brown color

³**tan** *abbr* tangent

tan·a·ger \'ta-ni-jər\ *n* : any of numerous American birds that are often brightly colored

tan·bark \'tan-ˌbärk\ *n* : bark (as of oak or sumac) that is rich in tannin and used in tanning

¹**tan·dem** \'tan-dəm\ *n* [L, at last, at length (taken to mean "lengthwise"), fr. *tam* so]   **1** : a 2-seated carriage with horses hitched tandem; *also* : its team   **2** : a bicycle for two persons sitting one behind the other — **in tandem** : in a tandem arrangement

²**tandem** *adv* : one behind another

³**tandem** *adj*   **1** : consisting of things arranged one behind the other   **2** : working in conjunction with each other

tang \'taŋ\ *n*   **1** : a part in a tool that connects the blade with the handle   **2** : a sharp distinctive flavor; *also* : a pungent odor — **tangy** *adj*

¹**tan·gent** \'tan-jənt\ *adj* [L *tangent-, tangens*, prp. of *tangere* to touch] : TOUCHING; *esp* : touching a circle or sphere at only one point

²**tangent** *n*   **1** : the trigonometric function that is the ratio between the side opposite and the side adjacent to an acute angle in a right triangle   **2** : a tangent line, curve, or surface   **3** : an abrupt change of course

tan·gen·tial \tan-'jen-chəl\ *adj*   **1** : TANGENT   **2** : touching lightly : INCIDENTAL ⟨~ involvement⟩ — **tan·gen·tial·ly** *adv*

tan·ger·ine \'tan-jə-ˌrēn, ˌtan-jə-'rēn\ *n* : a deep orange loose-skinned citrus fruit; *also* : a tree that bears tangerines

¹**tan·gi·ble** \'tan-jə-bəl\ *adj*   **1** : perceptible esp. by the sense of touch : PALPABLE   **2** : substantially real : MATERIAL ⟨~ rewards⟩   **3** : capable of being appraised ⟨~ assets⟩ ✦ *Synonyms* APPRECIABLE, PERCEPTIBLE, SENSIBLE, DISCERNIBLE — **tan·gi·bil·i·ty** \ˌtan-jə-'bi-lə-tē\ *n*

²**tangible** *n* : something tangible; *esp* : a tangible asset

¹**tan·gle** \'tan-gəl\ *vb* **tan·gled; tan·gling**   **1** : to involve so as to hamper or embarrass; *also* : ENTRAP   **2** : to unite or knit together in intricate confusion : ENTANGLE

²**tangle** *n*   **1** : a tangled twisted mass   **2** : a confusedly complicated state : MUDDLE

tan·go \'taŋ-gō\ *n*, *pl* **tangos** : a dance of Latin-American origin — **tango** *vb*

tank \'taŋk\ *n*   **1** : a large artificial receptacle for liquids   **2** : a heavily armed and armored combat vehicle that moves on tracks — **tank·ful** *n*

tan·kard \'taŋ-kərd\ *n* : a tall one-handled drinking vessel

tank·er \'taŋ-kər\ *n* : a vehicle equipped for transporting a liquid

tank top *n* : a sleeveless collarless pullover shirt with shoulder straps

tank town *n* : a small town

tan·ner \'ta-nər\ *n* : one that tans hides

tan·nery \'ta-nə-rē\ *n*, *pl* **-ner·ies** : a place where tanning is carried on

tan·nic acid \'ta-nik-\ *n* : TANNIN

tan·nin \'ta-nən\ *n* : any of various plant substances used esp. in tanning and dyeing, in inks, and as astringents

tan·sy \'tan-zē\ *n*, *pl* **tansies** : a common weedy herb related to the daisies with an aromatic odor and bitter-tasting finely divided leaves

tan·ta·lise *Brit var of* TANTALIZE

tan·ta·lize \'tan-tə-ˌlīz\ *vb* **-lized; -liz·ing** [fr. *Tantalus*, king of Greek myth punished in Hades by having to stand up to his chin in water that receded as he bent to drink] : to tease or torment by presenting something desirable but keeping it out of reach — **tan·ta·liz·er** *n* — **tan·ta·liz·ing·ly** *adv*

tan·ta·lum \'tan-tə-ləm\ *n* : a gray-white ductile metallic chemical element

tan·ta·mount \'tan-tə-ˌmau̇nt\ *adj* : equivalent in value or meaning ⟨a relationship ~ to marriage⟩

tan·trum \'tan-trəm\ *n* : a fit of bad temper

Tao·ism \'tau̇-ˌi-zəm, 'dau̇-\ *n* : a Chinese mystical philosophy; *also* : a religion developed from Taoist philosophy and Buddhism — **Tao·ist** \-ist\ *adj or n*

¹**tap** \'tap\ *n*   **1** : FAUCET, COCK   **2** : liquor drawn through a tap   **3** : the removing of fluid from a container or cavity by tapping   **4** : a tool for forming an internal screw

thread **5** : a point in an electric circuit where a connection may be made

²tap *vb* **tapped; tap·ping 1** : to release or cause to flow by piercing or by drawing a plug from a container or cavity **2** : to pierce so as to let out or draw off a fluid **3** : to draw from ⟨~ resources⟩ **4** : to cut in on (as a telephone signal) to get information **5** : to form an internal screw thread in by means of a tap **6** : to connect (as a gas or water main) with a local supply — **tap·per** *n*

³tap *vb* **tapped; tap·ping 1** : to rap lightly **2** : to bring about by repeated light blows **3** : SELECT; *esp* : to elect to membership

⁴tap *n* **1** : a light blow or stroke; *also* : its sound **2** : a small metal plate for the sole or heel of a shoe

ta·pa \'tä-pə, 'tä-\ *n* [Sp, lit., cover, lid] : an hors d'oeuvre served with drinks esp. in Spanish bars — usu. used in pl.

¹tape \'tāp\ *n* **1** : a narrow flexible band or strip (as of woven fabric) **2** : MAGNETIC TAPE; *also* : CASSETTE

²tape *vb* **taped; tap·ing 1** : to fasten or support with tape **2** : to record on magnetic tape

tape deck *n* : a device used to play back cassette tapes that usu. has to be connected to an audio system

tape measure *n* : a tape marked off in units (as inches) for measuring

¹ta·per \'tä-pər\ *n* **1** : a slender wax candle; *also* : a long waxed wick **2** : a gradual lessening of thickness or width in a long object

²taper *vb* **ta·pered; ta·per·ing 1** : to make or become gradually smaller toward one end **2** : to diminish gradually

tape-re·cord \ˌtāp-ri-'kȯrd\ *vb* : to make a recording of on magnetic tape — **tape recorder** *n* — **tape recording** *n*

tap·es·try \'ta-pə-strē\ *n, pl* **-tries** : a heavy reversible textile that has designs or pictures woven into it and is used esp. as a wall hanging

tape·worm \'tāp-ˌwərm\ *n* : any of a class of long flat segmented worms parasitic esp. in vertebrate intestines

tap·i·o·ca \ˌta-pē-'ō-kə\ *n* : a usu. granular preparation of cassava starch used esp. in puddings; *also* : a dish (as pudding) that contains tapioca

ta·pir \'tā-pər\ *n, pl* **tapirs** *also* **tapir** [Pg *tapir, tapira*, fr. Tupinambà (American Indian language of Brazil) *tapiʔíra*] : any of a genus of large herbivorous hoofed mammals of tropical America and southeastern Asia

tap·pet \'ta-pət\ *n* : a lever or projection moved by some other piece (as a cam) or intended to move something else

tap·room \'tap-ˌrüm, -ˌrùm\ *n* : BARROOM

tap·root \-ˌrüt, -ˌrùt\ *n* : a large main root growing straight down and giving off small side roots

taps \'taps\ *n sing or pl* : the last bugle call at night blown as a signal that lights are to be put out; *also* : a similar call blown at military funerals and memorial services

tap·ster \'tap-stər\ *n* : BARTENDER

¹tar \'tär\ *n* **1** : a thick dark sticky liquid distilled from organic material (as wood or coal) **2** : SAILOR, SEAMAN

²tar *vb* **tarred; tar·ring** : to cover or smear with or as if with tar

tar·an·tel·la \ˌtar-ən-'te-lə\ *n* : a lively folk dance of southern Italy in 6/8 time

ta·ran·tu·la \tə-'ran-chə-lə, -tə-lə\ *n, pl* **tarantulas** *also* **ta·ran·tu·lae** \-'ran-chə-ˌlē, -tə-ˌlē\ : any of a family of large hairy American spiders with a sharp bite that is not very poisonous to human beings

tar·dy \'tär-dē\ *adj* **tar·di·er; -est 1** : moving slowly : SLUGGISH **2** : LATE ♦ *Synonyms* BEHINDHAND, OVERDUE, BELATED — **tar·di·ly** \-də-lē\ *adv* — **tar·di·ness** \-dē-nəs\ *n*

¹tare \'ter\ *n* : a weed of grain fields

²tare *n* : a deduction from the gross weight of a substance and its container made in allowance for the weight of the container — **tare** *vb*

¹tar·get \'tär-gət\ *n* [ME, fr. MF *targette*, dim. of *targe* light shield, of Gmc origin] **1** : a mark to shoot at **2** : an object of ridicule or criticism **3** : a goal to be achieved

²target *vb* : to make a target of

tar·iff \'ta-rəf\ *n* [It *tariffa*, fr. Ar *taʕrīf* notification] **1** : a schedule of duties imposed by a government esp. on imported goods; *also* : a duty or rate of duty imposed in such a schedule **2** : a schedule of rates or charges

tar·mac \'tär-ˌmak\ *n* : a surface paved with crushed stone covered with tar

tarn \'tärn\ *n* : a small mountain lake

tar·nish \'tär-nish\ *vb* : to make or become dull or discolored — **tarnish** *n*

ta·ro \'tär-ō, 'ter-\ *n, pl* **taros** : a large-leaved tropical plant related to the arums that is grown for its edible starchy corms; *also* : its corms

tar·ot \'ter-ō, 'ta-rō\ *n* : one of a set of usu. 78 playing cards used esp. for fortune-telling

tar·pau·lin \tär-'pȯ-lən, 'tär-pə-\ *n* : a piece of material (as durable plastic) used for protecting exposed objects

tar·pon \'tär-pən\ *n, pl* **tarpon** *or* **tarpons** : a large silvery bony fish often caught for sport in the warm coastal waters of the Atlantic esp. off Florida

tar·ra·gon \'ter-ə-gän\ *n* [MF *targon*, ultim. fr. Ar *ṭarkhūn*] : a small widely cultivated perennial wormwood with aromatic leaves used as a seasoning; *also* : its leaves

¹tar·ry \'ta-rē\ *vb* **tar·ried; tar·ry·ing 1** : to be tardy : DELAY; *esp* : to be slow in leaving **2** : to stay in or at a place : SOJOURN ♦ *Synonyms* REMAIN, WAIT, LINGER, ABIDE

²tar·ry \'tär-ē\ *adj* : of, resembling, or smeared with tar

tar sand *n* : sand or sandstone that is naturally soaked with the heavy sticky portions of petroleum

tar·sus \'tär-səs\ *n, pl* **tar·si** \-ˌsī\ [NL] : the part of a vertebrate foot between the metatarsus and the leg; *also* : the small bones that support this part — **tar·sal** \-səl\ *adj or n*

¹tart \'tärt\ *adj* **1** : agreeably sharp to the taste : PUNGENT **2** : BITING, CAUSTIC — **tart·ly** *adv* — **tart·ness** *n*

²tart *n* **1** : a small pie or pastry shell containing jelly, custard, or fruit **2** : PROSTITUTE

tar·tan \'tärt-ᵊn\ *n* : a plaid textile design of Scottish origin usu. distinctively patterned to designate a particular clan

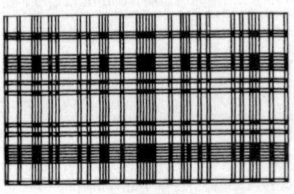

tartan

tar·tar \'tär-tər\ *n* **1** : a substance in the juice of grapes deposited (as in wine casks) as a reddish crust or sediment **2** : a crust on the teeth formed from plaque hardened by calcium salts

tar·tar sauce *or* **tar·tare sauce** \'tär-tər-\ *n* : mayonnaise with chopped pickles, olives, or capers

¹task \'task\ *n* [ME *taske*, fr. MF dial. *tasque*, fr. ML *tasca* tax or service imposed by a feudal superior, fr. *taxare* to tax] : a piece of assigned work ♦ *Synonyms* JOB, DUTY, CHORE, STINT, ASSIGNMENT

²task *vb* : to oppress with great labor

task force *n* : a temporary grouping to accomplish a particular objective

task·mas·ter \'task-ˌmas-tər\ *n* : one that imposes a task or burdens another with labor

¹tas·sel \'ta-səl, 'tä-\ *n* **1** : a hanging ornament made of a bunch of cords of even length fastened at one end **2** : something suggesting a tassel; *esp* : a male flower cluster of Indian corn

²tassel *vb* **-seled** *or* **-selled; -sel·ing** *or* **-sel·ling** : to adorn with or put forth tassels

¹taste \'tāst\ *vb* **tast·ed; tast·ing 1** : EXPERIENCE, UNDERGO **2** : to try or determine the flavor of by taking a bit into the mouth **3** : to eat or drink esp. in small quantities : SAMPLE **4** : to have a specific flavor

²taste *n* **1** : a small amount tasted **2** : BIT; *esp* : a sample of experience **3** : the special sense that perceives and identifies sweet, sour, bitter, or salty qualities and is mediated by taste buds on the tongue **4** : a quality perceptible to the sense of taste; *also* : the sensation obtained from a substance in the mouth : FLAVOR **5** : individual preference **6** : critical judgment, discernment, or appreciation; *also* : aesthetic quality ♦ *Synonyms* TANG, RELISH, FLAVOR, SAVOR — **taste·ful** \-fəl\ *adj* — **taste·ful·ly** *adv* — **taste·less** *adj* — **taste·less·ly** *adv* — **tast·er** *n*

taste bud *n* : a sense organ mediating the sensation of taste

tasty \'tā-stē\ *adj* **tast·i·er; -est** : pleasing to the taste : SAVORY ✦ *Synonyms* PALATABLE, APPETIZING, TOOTHSOME, FLAVORSOME — **tast·i·ness** \'tā-stē-nəs\ *n*

tat \'tat\ *vb* **tat·ted; tat·ting** : to work at or make by tatting

¹tat·ter \'ta-tər\ *vb* : to make or become ragged

²tatter *n* **1** : a part torn and left hanging **2** *pl* : tattered clothing

tat·ter·de·ma·lion \,ta-tər-di-'māl-yən\ *n* : one that is ragged or disreputable

tat·ter·sall \'ta-tər-,sȯl, -səl\ *n* : a pattern of colored lines forming squares on solid background; *also* : a fabric in a tattersall pattern

tat·ting \'ta-tiŋ\ *n* : a delicate handmade lace formed usu. by looping and knotting with a single thread and a small shuttle; *also* : the act or process of making such lace

tat·tle \'tat-ᵊl\ *vb* **tat·tled; tat·tling 1** : CHATTER, PRATE **2** : to tell secrets; *also* : to inform against another — **tat·tler** *n*

tat·tle·tale \'tat-ᵊl-,tāl\ *n* : one that tattles : INFORMER

¹tat·too \ta-'tü\ *n, pl* **tattoos** [alter. of earlier *taptoo*, fr. D *taptoe*, fr. the phrase *tap toe!* taps shut!] **1** : a call sounded before taps as notice to go to quarters **2** : a rapid rhythmic rapping

²tattoo *vb* : to mark (the skin) with tattoos

³tattoo *n, pl* **tattoos** [Tahitian *tatau*] : an indelible figure fixed upon the body esp. by insertion of pigment under the skin

tau \'taú, 'tȯ\ *n* : the 19th letter of the Greek alphabet — T or τ

taught *past and past part of* TEACH

¹taunt \'tȯnt\ *n* : a sarcastic challenge or insult

²taunt *vb* : to reproach or challenge in a mocking manner : jeer at ✦ *Synonyms* MOCK, DERIDE, RIDICULE, TWIT — **taunt·er** *n*

taupe \'tōp\ *n* : a brownish gray

Tau·rus \'tȯr-əs\ *n* [L, lit., bull] **1** : a zodiacal constellation between Aries and Gemini usu. pictured as a bull **2** : the 2d sign of the zodiac in astrology; *also* : one born under this sign

taut \'tȯt\ *adj* **1** : tightly drawn : not slack **2** : extremely nervous : TENSE **3** : TRIM, TIDY ⟨a ~ ship⟩ — **taut·ly** *adv* — **taut·ness** *n*

tau·tol·o·gy \tȯ-'tä-lə-jē\ *n, pl* **-gies** : needless repetition of an idea, statement, or word; *also* : an instance of such repetition — **tau·to·log·i·cal** \,tȯt-ᵊl-ä-ji-kəl\ *adj* — **tau·to·log·i·cal·ly** \-ji-k(ə-)lē\ *adv* — **tau·tol·o·gous** \tȯ-'tä-lə-gəs\ *adj* — **tau·tol·o·gous·ly** *adv*

tav·ern \'ta-vərn\ *n* [ME *taverne*, fr. AF, fr. L *taberna* hut, shop] **1** : an establishment where alcoholic liquors are sold to be drunk on the premises **2** : INN

taw \'tȯ\ *n* **1** : a marble used as a shooter **2** : the line from which players shoot at marbles

taw·dry \'tȯ-drē\ *adj* **taw·dri·er; -est** [*tawdry lace* a tie of lace for the neck, fr. *St. Audrey* (St. Etheldreda) †680 queen of Northumbria] : cheap and gaudy in appearance and quality ✦ *Synonyms* GARISH, FLASHY, CHINTZY, MERETRICIOUS — **taw·dri·ly** *adv*

taw·ny \'tȯ-nē\ *adj* **taw·ni·er; -est** : of a brownish orange color

¹tax \'taks\ *vb* **1** : to levy a tax on **2** : CHARGE, ACCUSE **3** : to put under pressure — **tax·able** \'tak-sə-bəl\ *adj* — **tax·a·tion** \tak-'sä-shən\ *n*

²tax *n* **1** : a charge usu. of money imposed by authority on persons or property for public purposes **2** : a heavy charge : STRAIN

¹taxi \'tak-sē\ *n, pl* **tax·is** \-sēz\ *also* **tax·ies** : TAXICAB; *also* : a similarly operated boat or aircraft

²taxi *vb* **tax·ied; taxi·ing** *or* **taxy·ing; tax·is** *or* **tax·ies 1** : to move along the ground or on the water under an aircraft's own power when starting or after a landing **2** : to go by taxicab

taxi·cab \'tak-sē-,kab\ *n* : an automobile that carries passengers for a fare usu. based on the distance traveled

taxi·der·my \'tak-sə-,dər-mē\ *n* : the skill or occupation of preparing, stuffing, and mounting skins of animals — **taxi·der·mist** \-mist\ *n*

tax·on \'tak-,sän\ *n, pl* **taxa** \-sə\; *also* **taxons** : a taxonomic group or entity

tax·on·o·my \tak-'sä-nə-mē\ *n* : classification esp. of animals or plants according to natural relationships — **tax·o·nom·ic** \,tak-sə-'nä-mik\ *adj* — **tax·on·o·mist** \tak-'sä-nə-mist\ *n*

tax·pay·er \'taks-,pā-ər\ *n* : one who pays or is liable for a tax — **tax·pay·ing** *adj*

Tay–Sachs disease \'tā-'saks-\ *n* : a hereditary disorder caused by the absence of an enzyme needed to break down fatty material, marked by buildup of lipids in nervous tissue, and causing death in childhood

tb *abbr* tablespoon; tablespoonful

Tb *symbol* terbium

TB \,tē-'bē\ *n* : TUBERCULOSIS

TBA *abbr, often not cap* to be announced

T–bar \'tē-,bär\ *n* : a ski lift with a series of T-shaped bars

tbs *or* **tbsp** *abbr* tablespoon; tablespoonful

Tc *symbol* technetium

TC *abbr* teachers college

T cell *n* : any of several lymphocytes (as a helper T cell) specialized esp. for activity in and control of immunity and the immune response

TCP/IP \,tē-(,)sē-pē-,ī-'pē\ *n* [*transmission control protocol/Internet protocol*] : a set of communications protocols used over networks and esp. the Internet

TD *abbr* **1** touchdown **2** Treasury Department

TDD *abbr* telecommunications device for the deaf

TDY *abbr* temporary duty

Te *symbol* tellurium

tea \'tē\ *n* [Chin (dialect of Fujian province) *dé*] **1** : the cured leaves and leaf buds of a shrub grown chiefly in China, Japan, India, and Sri Lanka; *also* : this shrub **2** : a drink made by steeping tea in boiling water **3** : refreshments usu. including tea served in late afternoon; *also* : a reception at which tea is served

teach \'tēch\ *vb* **taught** \'tȯt\; **teach·ing 1** : to cause to know something : act as a teacher **2** : to show how ⟨~ a child to swim⟩ **3** : to make to know the disagreeable consequences of an action **4** : to guide the studies of **5** : to impart the knowledge of ⟨~ algebra⟩ — **teach·able** *adj* — **teach·er** *n*

teach·ing *n* **1** : the act, practice, or profession of a teacher **2** : something taught; *esp* : DOCTRINE

tea·cup \'tē-,kəp\ *n* : a small cup used with a saucer for hot beverages

teak \'tēk\ *n* : the hard durable yellowish brown wood of a tall tropical Asian timber tree related to the vervains; *also* : this tree

tea·ket·tle \'tē-,ket-ᵊl\ *n* : a covered kettle with a handle and spout for boiling water

teal \'tēl\ *n, pl* **teal** *or* **teals 1** : any of various small short-necked wild ducks **2** : a dark greenish blue color

¹team \'tēm\ *n* [ME *teme*, fr. OE *tēam* offspring, lineage, group of draft animals] **1** : two or more draft animals harnessed to the same vehicle or implement **2** : a number of persons associated in work or activity; *esp* : a group on one side in a match

²team *adj* : of or performed by a team; *also* : marked by devotion to teamwork ⟨a ~ player⟩

³team *vb* **1** : to haul with or drive a team **2** : to form a team : join forces

team·mate \-,māt\ *n* : a fellow member of a team

team·ster \'tēm-stər\ *n* : one who drives a team or truck

team·work \-,wərk\ *n* : the work or activity of a number of persons acting in close association as members of a unit

tea·pot \'tē-,pät\ *n* : a vessel with a spout for brewing and serving tea

¹tear \'tir\ *n* : a drop of the salty liquid that moistens the eye and inner side of the eyelids; *also, pl* : an act of weeping or grieving — **tear·ful** \-fəl\ *adj* — **tear·ful·ly** *adv* — **teary** \'tir-ē\ *adj*

²tear \'tir\ *vb* : to fill with or shed tears ⟨eyes ~ing in the wind⟩

³tear \'ter\ *vb* **tore** \'tȯr\; **torn** \'tȯrn\; **tear·ing 1** : to separate parts of or pull apart by force : REND **2** : LACERATE **3** : to disrupt by the pull of contrary forces **4** : to remove by force : WRENCH **5** : to move or act with violence, haste, or force ✦ *Synonyms* RIP, SPLIT, CLEAVE, REND

⁴tear \'ter\ *n* **1** : the act of tearing **2** : a hole or flaw made by tearing : RENT

tear gas \'tir-\ *n* : a substance that on dispersion in the atmosphere blinds the eyes with tears — **tear gas** *vb*

tear·jerk·er \'tir-,jər-kər\ *n* : an extravagantly pathetic story, song, play, movie, or broadcast

¹**tease** \'tēz\ *vb* **teased; teas·ing 1** : to disentangle and lay parallel by combing or carding ⟨~ wool⟩ **2** : to scratch the surface of (cloth) so as to raise a nap **3** : to annoy persistently esp. in fun by goading, coaxing, or tantalizing **4** : to comb (hair) by taking a strand and pushing the short hairs toward the scalp with the comb ♦ **Synonyms** HARASS, WORRY, PESTER, ANNOY

²**tease** *n* **1** : the act of teasing or state of being teased **2** : one that teases

tea·sel \'tē-zəl\ *n* : a prickly herb or its flower head covered with stiff hooked bracts and used to raise the nap on cloth; *also* : an artificial device used for this purpose

tea·spoon \'tē-,spün\ *n* **1** : a small spoon suitable for stirring beverages **2** : a unit of measure equal to ⅙ fluid ounce (5 milliliters)

tea·spoon·ful \-,fül\ *n, pl* **-spoonfuls** *also* **-spoons·ful** \-,spünz-,fül\ : TEASPOON 2

teat \'tit, 'tēt\ *n* : the protuberance through which milk is drawn from an udder or breast

tech *abbr* **1** technical; technically; technician **2** technological; technology

tech·ne·tium \tek-'nē-shē-əm\ *n* : a radioactive metallic chemical element

tech·nic \'tek-nik, tek-'nēk\ *n* : TECHNIQUE 1

tech·ni·cal \'tek-ni-kəl\ *adj* [Gk *technikos* of art, skillful, fr. *technē* art, craft, skill] **1** : having special knowledge esp. of a mechanical or scientific subject ⟨~ experts⟩ **2** : of or relating to a particular and esp. a practical or scientific subject ⟨~ training⟩ **3** : according to a strict interpretation of the rules **4** : of or relating to technique — **tech·ni·cal·ly** \-k(ə-)lē\ *adv*

tech·ni·cal·i·ty \,tek-nə-'ka-lə-tē\ *n, pl* **-ties 1** : a detail meaningful only to a specialist **2** : the quality or state of being technical

technical sergeant *n* : a noncommissioned officer in the air force ranking next below a master sergeant

tech·ni·cian \tek-'ni-shən\ *n* : a person who has acquired the technique of a specialized skill or subject

tech·nique \tek-'nēk\ *n* [F] **1** : the manner in which technical details are treated or basic physical movements are used **2** : technical methods

tech·no \'tek-nō\ *n* : dance music featuring a fast beat and electronically created sounds usu. without vocals

tech·noc·ra·cy \tek-'nä-krə-sē\ *n* : management of society by technical experts — **tech·no·crat** \'tek-nə-,krat\ *n* — **tech·no·crat·ic** \,tek-nə-'kra-tik\ *adj*

tech·nol·o·gy \tek-'nä-lə-jē\ *n, pl* **-gies** : ENGINEERING; *also* : a manner of accomplishing a task using technical methods or knowledge — **tech·no·log·i·cal** \,tek-nə-'lä-ji-kəl\ *adj*

tec·ton·ics \tek-'tä-niks\ *n sing or pl* **1** : geological structural features **2** : geology dealing esp. with the faulting and folding of a planet or moon — **tec·ton·ic** \-nik\ *adj*

ted·dy bear \'te-dē-,ber\ *n* [*Teddy* Roosevelt; fr. a cartoon depicting the president sparing the life of a bear cub while hunting] : a stuffed toy bear

te·dious \'tē-dē-əs\ *adj* : tiresome because of length or dullness ♦ **Synonyms** BORING, TIRING, IRKSOME — **te·dious·ly** *adv* — **te·dious·ness** *n*

te·di·um \'tē-dē-əm\ *n* : TEDIOUSNESS; *also* : BOREDOM

¹**tee** \'tē\ *n* : a small mound or peg on which a golf ball is placed to be hit at the beginning of play on a hole; *also* : the area from which the ball is hit to begin play

²**tee** *vb* **teed; tee·ing** : to place (a ball) on a tee

teem \'tēm\ *vb* : to become filled to overflowing : ABOUND ♦ **Synonyms** SWARM, CRAWL, FLOW

teen *adj* : TEENAGE

teen·age \'tē-,nāj\ *or* **teen·aged** \-,nājd\ *adj* : of, being, or relating to people in their teens — **teen·ag·er** \-,nā-jər\ *n*

teens \'tēnz\ *n pl* : the numbers 13 to 19 inclusive; *esp* : the years 13 to 19 in a person's life

tee·ny \'tē-nē\ *adj* **tee·ni·er; -est** : TINY

teepee *var of* TEPEE

tee shirt *var of* T-SHIRT

tee·ter \'tē-tər\ *vb* **1** : to move unsteadily **2** : SEESAW — **teeter** *n*

teeth *pl of* TOOTH

teethe \'tēth\ *vb* **teethed; teeth·ing** : to experience the rising of one's teeth through the gums : to grow teeth

teething *n* : growth of the first set of teeth through the gums with its accompanying phenomena

tee·to·tal·er *or* **tee·to·tal·ler** \'tē-'tōt-ᵊl-ər\ *n* : a person who practices complete abstinence from alcoholic drinks — **tee·to·tal** \'tē-'tōt-ᵊl, -,tō-\ *adj* — **tee·to·tal·ism** \-ᵊl-,i-zəm\ *n*

TEFL *abbr* teaching English as a foreign language

Te·ja·no \tā-'hä-(,)nō\ *n, pl* **-nos** [Mex Sp, fr. *Tejas* Texas] : a Texan of Hispanic descent

tek·tite \'tek-,tīt\ *n* : a glassy body of probably meteoric origin

tel *abbr* **1** telegram **2** telegraph **3** telephone

tele·cast \'te-li-,kast\ *vb* **-cast** *also* **-cast·ed; -cast·ing** : to broadcast by television — **telecast** *n* — **tele·cast·er** *n*

tel·e·com \'te-li-,käm\ *n* : TELECOMMUNICATION; *also* : the telecommunications industry

tele·com·mu·ni·ca·tion \,te-li-kə-,myü-nə-'kā-shən\ *n* : communication at a distance (as by telephone or radio)

tele·com·mute \'te-li-kə-,myüt\ *vb* : to work at home by the use of an electronic linkup with a central office

tele·con·fer·ence \'te-li-,kän-fə-rəns\ *n* : a conference among people remote from one another held using telecommunications — **tele·con·fer·enc·ing** *n*

teleg *abbr* telegraphy

tele·gen·ic \,te-lə-'je-nik, -'jē-\ *adj* : markedly attractive to television viewers

tele·gram \'te-lə-,gram\ *n* : a message sent by telegraph

¹**tele·graph** \-,graf\ *n* : an electric apparatus or system for sending messages by a code over wires — **tele·graph·ic** \,te-lə-'gra-fik\ *adj*

²**telegraph** *vb* : to send or communicate by or as if by telegraph — **te·leg·ra·pher** \tə-'le-grə-fər\ *n*

te·leg·ra·phy \tə-'le-grə-fē\ *n* : the use or operation of a telegraph apparatus or system

tele·mar·ket·ing \,te-lə-'mär-kə-tiŋ\ *n* : the marketing of goods or services by telephone — **tele·mar·ket·er** \-tər\ *n*

tele·med·i·cine \,te-lə-'me-də-sən\ *n* : the practice of medicine using two-way voice and visual communication

te·lem·e·try \tə-'le-mə-trē\ *n* : the transmission esp. by radio of measurements made by automatic instruments to a distant station — **tele·me·ter** \'te-lə-,mē-tər\ *n*

te·lep·a·thy \tə-'le-pə-thē\ *n* : apparent communication from one mind to another by extrasensory means — **tele·path·ic** \,te-lə-'pa-thik\ *adj* — **tele·path·i·cal·ly** \-thi-k(ə-)lē\ *adv*

¹**tele·phone** \'te-lə-,fōn\ *n* : an instrument for sending and receiving sounds over long distances by electricity

²**telephone** *vb* **-phoned; -phon·ing 1** : to send or communicate by telephone **2** : to speak to (a person) by telephone — **tele·phon·er** *n*

te·le·pho·ny \tə-'le-fə-nē, 'te-lə-,fō-\ *n* : use or operation of an apparatus for transmission of sounds as electrical signals between distant points — **tel·e·phon·ic** \,te-lə-'fä-nik\ *adj*

tele·pho·to \,te-lə-'fō-tō\ *adj* : being a camera lens giving a large image of a distant object — **tele·pho·tog·ra·phy** \-fə-'tä-grə-fē\ *n*

tele·play \'te-li-,plā\ *n* : a story prepared for television production

tele·print·er \'te-lə-,prin-tər\ *n* : TELETYPEWRITER

tele·prompt·er \'te-lə-,prämp-tər\ *n* : a device for displaying prepared text to a speaker or performer

¹**tele·scope** \'te-lə-,skōp\ *n* **1** : a cylindrical instrument equipped with lenses or mirrors for viewing distant objects **2** : RADIO TELESCOPE

²**telescope** *vb* **-scoped; -scop·ing 1** : to slide or pass or cause to slide or pass one within another like the sections of a collapsible hand telescope **2** : COMPRESS, CONDENSE

tele·scop·ic \,te-lə-'skä-pik\ *adj* **1** : of or relating to a telescope **2** : seen only by a telescope **3** : able to discern objects at a distance **4** : having parts that telescope — **tele·scop·i·cal·ly** \-pi-k(ə-)lē\ *adv*

tele·text \'te-lə-,tekst\ *n* : a system for broadcasting text over a television signal and displaying it on a decoder-equipped television

tele·thon \'te-lə-,thän\ *n* : a long television program usu. to solicit funds for a charity

tele·type·writ·er \,te-lə-'tīp-,rī-tər\ *n* : a printing device resembling a typewriter used to send and receive signals over telephone lines

tele·vise \'te-lə-ˌvīz\ *vb* -vised; -vis·ing : to broadcast by television

tele·vi·sion \'te-lə-ˌvi-zhən\ *n* [F *télévision,* fr. Gk *tēle* far, at a distance + F *vision* vision] : a system for transmitting images and sound by converting them into electrical or radio waves which are converted back into images and sound by a receiver; *also* : a television receiving set

tell \'tel\ *vb* **told** \'tōld\; **tell·ing 1** : COUNT, ENUMERATE **2** : to relate in detail : NARRATE ⟨*told* us what happened⟩ **3** : SAY, UTTER **4** : to make known : REVEAL **5** : to report to : INFORM ⟨*tell* me her name⟩ **6** : ORDER, DIRECT **7** : to find out by observing ⟨can ∼ the difference⟩ **8** : to have a marked effect **9** : to serve as evidence ✦ *Synonyms* DISCLOSE, DISCOVER, BETRAY

tell·er \'te-lər\ *n* **1** : one that relates : NARRATOR **2** : one that counts **3** : a bank employee handling money received or paid out

tell·ing \'te-liŋ\ *adj* : producing a marked effect : EFFECTIVE ⟨∼ evidence⟩ ✦ *Synonyms* COGENT, CONVINCING, SOUND

tell off *vb* : REPRIMAND, SCOLD

tell·tale \'tel-ˌtāl\ *n* **1** : INFORMER, TATTLETALE **2** : something that serves to disclose : INDICATION — **telltale** *adj*

tel·lu·ri·um \tə-'lùr-ē-əm\ *n* : a chemical element used esp. in alloys

tel·net \'tel-ˌnet\ *n* : a telecommunications protocol for accessing and using a remote computer via a local computer — **telnet** *vb*

tem·blor \'tem-blər\ *n* [Sp, lit., trembling] : EARTHQUAKE

te·mer·i·ty \tə-'mer-ə-tē\ *n, pl* **-ties** : rash or presumptuous daring : BOLDNESS ✦ *Synonyms* AUDACITY, EFFRONTERY, GALL, NERVE, CHEEK

¹temp \ *n* **1** : TEMPERATURE **2** : a temporary worker

²temp *abbr* temporary

¹tem·per \'tem-pər\ *vb* **1** : to dilute or soften by the addition of something else ⟨∼ justice with mercy⟩ **2** : to bring (as steel) to a desired hardness by reheating and cooling **3** : to toughen (glass) by gradual heating and cooling **4** : TOUGHEN **5** : TUNE

²temper *n* **1** : characteristic tone : TENDENCY **2** : the hardness or toughness of a substance ⟨the ∼ of a knife blade⟩ **3** : a characteristic frame of mind : DISPOSITION **4** : calmness of mind : COMPOSURE **5** : state of feeling or frame of mind at a particular time **6** : heat of mind or emotion ✦ *Synonyms* TEMPERAMENT, CHARACTER, PERSONALITY, MAKEUP — **tem·pered** \'tem-pərd\ *adj*

tem·pera \'tem-pə-rə\ *n* [It] : a painting process using an albuminous or colloidal medium as a vehicle; *also* : a painting done in tempera

tem·per·a·ment \'tem-prə-mənt, -pər-mənt\ *n* **1** : characteristic or habitual inclination or mode of emotional response : DISPOSITION ⟨nervous ∼⟩ **2** : excessive sensitiveness or irritability ✦ *Synonyms* CHARACTER, PERSONALITY, NATURE, MAKEUP — **tem·per·a·men·tal** \ˌtem-prə-'ment-ᵊl, -pər-'ment-\ *adj*

tem·per·ance \'tem-prəns, -pə-rəns\ *n* : habitual moderation in the indulgence of the appetites or passions; *esp* : moderation in or abstinence from the use of alcoholic beverages

tem·per·ate \'tem-prət, -pə-rət\ *adj* **1** : not extreme or excessive : MILD **2** : moderate in indulgence of appetite or desire **3** : moderate in the use of alcoholic beverages **4** : having a moderate climate ✦ *Synonyms* SOBER, CONTINENT, ABSTEMIOUS

temperate zone *n, often cap T&Z* : the region between the Tropic of Cancer and the arctic circle or between the Tropic of Capricorn and the antarctic circle

tem·per·a·ture \'tem-pər-ˌchùr, -prə-ˌchùr, -chər\ *n* **1** : degree of hotness or coldness of something (as air, water, or the body) as shown by a thermometer **2** : FEVER 1

tem·pest \'tem-pəst\ *n* [ME *tempeste,* fr. AF, ultim. fr. L *tempestas* season, weather, storm, fr. *tempus* time] : a violent storm

tempest in a teapot : a great commotion over an unimportant matter

tem·pes·tu·ous \tem-'pes-chə-wəs\ *adj* : of, involving, or resembling a tempest : STORMY — **tem·pes·tu·ous·ly** *adv* — **tem·pes·tu·ous·ness** *n*

tem·plate \'tem-plət\ *n* : a gauge, mold, or pattern that functions as a guide to the form or structure of something being made

¹tem·ple \'tem-pəl\ *n* **1** : a building reserved for religious practice **2** : a place devoted to a special or exalted purpose ⟨a ∼of cuisine⟩

²temple *n* : the flattened space on each side of the forehead esp. of humans

tem·po \'tem-pō\ *n, pl* **tem·pi** \-(ˌ)pē\ *or* **tempos** [It, lit., time] **1** : the rate of speed of a musical piece or passage **2** : rate of motion or activity : PACE

¹tem·po·ral \'tem-pə-rəl\ *adj* **1** : of, relating to, or limited by time ⟨∼ and spatial bounds⟩ **2** : of or relating to earthly life or secular concerns ⟨∼ power⟩

²temporal *adj* : of or relating to the temples or the sides of the skull

¹tem·po·rary \'tem-pə-ˌrer-ē\ *adj* : lasting for a time only : TRANSITORY ✦ *Synonyms* TRANSIENT, EPHEMERAL, MOMENTARY, IMPERMANENT — **tem·po·rar·i·ly** \ˌtem-pə-'rer-ə-lē\ *adv*

²temporary *n, pl* **-rar·ies** : one serving for a limited time

tem·po·rise *Brit var of* TEMPORIZE

tem·po·rize \'tem-pə-ˌrīz\ *vb* **-rized; -riz·ing 1** : to adapt one's actions to the time or the dominant opinion : COMPROMISE **2** : to draw out matters so as to gain time — **tem·po·riz·er** *n*

tempt \'tempt\ *vb* **1** : to entice to do wrong by promise of pleasure or gain **2** : PROVOKE ⟨∼ fate⟩ **3** : to risk the dangers of **4** : to induce to do something : INCITE ✦ *Synonyms* INVEIGLE, DECOY, SEDUCE, LURE — **tempt·er** *n* — **tempt·ing·ly** *adv*

temp·ta·tion \temp-'tā-shən\ *n* **1** : the act of tempting : the state of being tempted **2** : something that tempts

tempt·ress \'temp-trəs\ *n* : a woman who tempts

ten \'ten\ *n* **1** : one more than nine **2** : the 10th in a set or series **3** : something having 10 units — **ten** *adj or pron* — **tenth** \'tenth\ *adj or adv or n*

ten·a·ble \'te-nə-bəl\ *adj* : capable of being held, maintained, or defended — **ten·a·bil·i·ty** \ˌte-nə-'bi-lə-tē\ *n*

te·na·cious \tə-'nā-shəs\ *adj* **1** : not easily pulled apart : COHESIVE, TOUGH ⟨a ∼ metal⟩ **2** : holding fast ⟨∼ of his rights⟩ **3** : RETENTIVE ⟨a ∼ memory⟩ — **te·na·cious·ly** *adv* — **te·nac·i·ty** \tə-'na-sə-tē\ *n*

ten·an·cy \'te-nən-sē\ *n, pl* **-cies** : the temporary possession or occupancy of something (as a house) that belongs to another; *also* : the period of a tenant's occupancy

ten·ant \'te-nənt\ *n* **1** : one who rents or leases (as a house) from a landlord **2** : DWELLER, OCCUPANT — **tenant** *vb* — **ten·ant·less** *adj*

tenant farmer *n* : a farmer who works land owned by another and pays rent either in cash or in shares of produce

ten·ant·ry \'te-nən-trē\ *n, pl* **-ries** : the body of tenants esp. on an estate

Ten Commandments *n pl* : the commandments of God given to Moses on Mount Sinai

¹tend \'tend\ *vb* **1** : to apply oneself ⟨∼ to your affairs⟩ **2** : to take care of ⟨∼ a plant⟩ **3** : to manage the operations of ⟨∼ a machine⟩

²tend *vb* **1** : to move or develop one's course in a particular direction **2** : to show an inclination or tendency

ten·den·cy \'ten-dən-sē\ *n, pl* **-cies 1** : DRIFT, TREND **2** : a proneness to or readiness for a particular kind of thought or action : PROPENSITY ✦ *Synonyms* BENT, LEANING, DISPOSITION, INCLINATION

ten·den·tious \ten-'den-chəs\ *adj* : marked by a tendency in favor of a particular point of view : BIASED — **ten·den·tious·ly** *adv* — **ten·den·tious·ness** *n*

¹ten·der \'ten-dər\ *adj* [ME, fr. AF *tendre,* fr. L *tener*] **1** : having a soft texture : easily broken, chewed, or cut **2** : physically weak : DELICATE; *also* : IMMATURE **3** : expressing or responsive to love or sympathy : LOVING, COMPASSIONATE **4** : SENSITIVE, TOUCHY ⟨a ∼ ego⟩ ✦ *Synonyms* SYMPATHETIC, WARM, WARMHEARTED — **ten·der·ly** *adv* — **ten·der·ness** *n*

²tender *n* [AF *tendre,* fr. *tendre,* v., to stretch, hold out, offer, fr. L *tendere* to stretch, direct] **1** : an offer or proposal made for acceptance; *esp* : an offer of a bid for a contract **2** : something (as money) that may be offered in payment

³tender *vb* : to present for acceptance

⁴tend·er \'ten-dər\ *n* **1** : one that tends or takes care **2** : a boat carrying passengers and freight to a larger ship **3** : a car attached to a steam locomotive for carrying fuel and water

⁵tender *n* [prob. short for *tenderloin*] : a strip of meat (as chicken) often breaded

ten·der·foot \'ten-dər-ˌfu̇t\ *n, pl* **-feet** \-ˌfēt\ *also* **-foots** \-ˌfu̇ts\ **1** : one not hardened to frontier or rough outdoor life **2** : an inexperienced beginner

ten·der·heart·ed \ˌten-dər-'här-təd\ *adj* : easily moved to love, pity, or sorrow

ten·der·ize \'ten-də-ˌrīz\ *vb* **-ized; -iz·ing** : to make (meat) tender — **ten·der·iz·er** \'ten-də-ˌrī-zər\ *n*

ten·der·loin \'ten-dər-ˌlȯin\ *n* **1** : a tender strip of beef or pork from near the backbone **2** : a district of a city largely devoted to vice

ten·di·ni·tis *or* **ten·don·itis** \ˌten-də-'nī-təs\ *n* : inflammation of a tendon

ten·don \'ten-dən\ *n* : a tough cord of dense white fibrous tissue uniting a muscle with another part (as a bone) — **ten·di·nous** \-də-nəs\ *adj*

ten·dril \'ten-drəl\ *n* : a slender coiling organ by which some climbing plants attach themselves to a support

ten·e·brous \'te-nə-brəs\ *adj* : shut off from the light : GLOOMY, OBSCURE

ten·e·ment \'te-nə-mənt\ *n* **1** : a house used as a dwelling **2** : a building divided into apartments for rent to families; *esp* : one meeting only minimum standards of safety and comfort **3** : APARTMENT, FLAT

te·net \'te-nət\ *n* [L, he holds, fr. *tenēre* to hold] : one of the principles or doctrines held in common by members of a group (as a church or profession) ♦ **Synonyms** DOCTRINE, DOGMA, BELIEF

ten·fold \'ten-ˌfōld, -'fōld\ *adj* : being 10 times as great or as many — **ten·fold** \-'fōld\ *adv*

ten–gallon hat *n* : a wide-brimmed hat with a large soft crown

Tenn *abbr* Tennessee

ten·nis \'te-nəs\ *n* : a game played with a ball and racket on a court divided by a net

ten·on \'te-nən\ *n* : a projecting part in a piece of material (as wood) for insertion into a mortise to make a joint

ten·or \'te-nər\ *n* **1** : the general drift of something spoken or written **2** : the highest natural adult male voice; *also* : a singer having this voice **3** : a continuing in a course, movement, or activity (the ~ of my life)

tenpenny nail *n* : a nail three inches (about 7.6 centimeters) long

ten·pin \'ten-ˌpin\ *n* : a bottle-shaped bowling pin set in groups of 10 and bowled at in a game (**tenpins**)

¹tense \'tens\ *n* [ME *tens* time, tense, fr. AF, fr. L *tempus*] : distinction of form of a verb to indicate the time of the action or state

²tense *adj* **tens·er; tens·est** [L *tensus*, fr. pp. of *tendere* to stretch] **1** : stretched tight : TAUT **2** : feeling or showing nervous tension (a ~ smile) ♦ **Synonyms** STIFF, RIGID, INFLEXIBLE — **tense·ly** *adv* — **tense·ness** *n* — **ten·si·ty** \'ten-sə-tē\ *n*

³tense *vb* **tensed; tens·ing** : to make or become tense

ten·sile \'ten-səl, -ˌsī(-ə)l\ *adj* : of or relating to tension (~ strength)

ten·sion \'ten-chən\ *n* **1** : the act of straining or stretching; *also* : the condition of being strained or stretched **2** : a state of mental unrest often with signs of bodily stress **3** : a state of latent hostility or opposition

ten–speed \'ten-ˌspēd\ *n* : a bicycle with a derailleur having 10 possible combinations of gears

¹tent \'tent\ *n* **1** : a collapsible shelter of material stretched and supported by poles **2** : a canopy placed over the head and shoulders to retain vapors or oxygen given for medical reasons

²tent *vb* **1** : to lodge in tents **2** : to cover with or as if with a tent

ten·ta·cle \'ten-ti-kəl\ *n* : any of various long flexible projections about the head or mouth (as of an insect, mollusk, or fish) — **ten·ta·cled** \-kəld\ *adj* — **ten·tac·u·lar** \ten-'ta-kyə-lər\ *adj*

ten·ta·tive \'ten-tə-tiv\ *adj* **1** : not fully worked out or developed (~ plans) **2** : HESITANT, UNCERTAIN (a ~ smile) — **ten·ta·tive·ly** *adv* — **ten·ta·tive·ness** *n*

ten·u·ous \'ten-yə-wəs\ *adj* **1** : not dense : RARE (a ~ fluid) **2** : not thick : SLENDER (a ~ rope) **3** : having lit-

tle substance : FLIMSY, WEAK (~ influences) **4** : lacking stability : SHAKY (~ reasoning) — **te·nu·i·ty** \te-'nü-ə-tē, tə-, -'nyü-\ *n* — **ten·u·ous·ly** *adv* — **ten·u·ous·ness** *n*

ten·ure \'ten-yər\ *n* : the act, right, manner, or period of holding something (as a landed property, an office, or a position)

ten·ured \'ten-yərd\ *adj* : having tenure (~ faculty members)

te·o·sin·te \ˌtā-ō-'sin-tē\ *n* : a tall annual grass of Mexico that is closely related to Indian corn

te·pee *or* **tee·pee** \'tē-(ˌ)pē\ *n* [Dakota *t-ípi*, fr. *t-i-* to dwell] : an American Indian conical tent usu. of skins

tep·id \'te-pəd\ *adj* **1** : moderately warm : LUKEWARM **2** : HALFHEARTED

te·qui·la \tə-'kē-lə, tā-\ *n* : a Mexican liquor distilled from an agave's sap

ter *abbr* **1** terrace **2** territory

tera·byte \'ter-ə-ˌbīt\ *n* [*tera-* trillion (10¹²), fr. Gk *terat-, teras* monster] : 1024 gigabytes; *also* : one trillion bytes

ter·bi·um \'tər-bē-əm\ *n* : a metallic chemical element

ter·cen·te·na·ry \ˌtər-ˌsen-'te-nə-rē, tər-'sen-tə-ˌner-ē\ *n, pl* **-ries** : a 300th anniversary or its celebration — **tercentenary** *adj*

ter·cen·ten·ni·al \ˌtər-ˌsen-'te-nē-əl\ *adj or n* : TERCENTENARY

te·re·do \tə-'rē-dō, -'rā-\ *n, pl* **-dos** [L] : SHIPWORM

ter·i·ya·ki \ˌter-ē-'yä-kē\ *n* [Jp] : a Japanese dish of meat or fish soaked in a soy marinade and cooked

¹term \'tərm\ *n* **1** : END, TERMINATION **2** : DURATION; *esp* : a period of time fixed esp. by law or custom **3** : a mathematical expression connected with another by a plus or minus sign; *also* : an element (as a numerator) of a fraction or proportion **4** : a word or expression that has a precise meaning in some uses or is limited to a particular subject or field **5** *pl* : PROVISIONS, CONDITIONS (~s of a contract) **6** *pl* : mutual relationship (on good ~s) **7** : AGREEMENT, CONCORD **8** : a state of acceptance (come to ~s with his grief)

²term *vb* : to apply a term to : CALL

ter·ma·gant \'tər-mə-gənt\ *n* : an overbearing or nagging woman : SHREW

¹ter·mi·nal \'tər-mə-nªl\ *adj* **1** : of, relating to, or forming an end, limit, or terminus **2** : FATAL 2 (~ cancer); *also* : being in or relating to the final stages of a fatal disease (a ~ patient) ♦ **Synonyms** FINAL, CONCLUDING, LAST, LATEST — **ter·mi·nal·ly** *adv*

²terminal *n* **1** : EXTREMITY, END **2** : a device at the end of a wire or on electrical equipment for making a connection **3** : either end of a transportation line (as a railroad) with its offices and freight and passenger stations; *also* : a freight or passenger station **4** : a device (as in a computer system) for data entry and display

ter·mi·nate \'tər-mə-ˌnāt\ *vb* **-nat·ed; -nat·ing** : to bring or come to an end ♦ **Synonyms** CONCLUDE, FINISH, COMPLETE — **ter·mi·na·ble** \-nə-bəl\ *adj* — **ter·mi·na·tion** \ˌtər-mə-'nā-shən\ *n* — **ter·mi·na·tor** \'tər-mə-ˌnā-tər\ *n*

ter·mi·nol·o·gy \ˌtər-mə-'nä-lə-jē\ *n, pl* **-gies** : the technical or special terms used in a business, art, science, or special subject

ter·mi·nus \'tər-mə-nəs\ *n, pl* **-ni** \-ˌnī\ *or* **-nus·es** [L] **1** : final goal : END **2** : either end of a transportation line or travel route; *also* : the station or city at such a place

ter·mite \'tər-ˌmīt\ *n* : any of numerous pale soft-bodied social insects that feed on wood

tern \'tərn\ *n* : any of various chiefly marine birds with narrow wings and often a forked tail

ter·na·ry \'tər-nə-rē\ *adj* **1** : of, relating to, or proceeding by threes **2** : having three elements or parts

terr *abbr* territory

¹ter·race \'ter-əs\ *n* **1** : a flat roof or open platform **2** : a level area next to a building **3** : an embankment with level top **4** : a bank or ridge on a slope to conserve moisture and soil **5** : a row of houses on raised land; *also* : a street with such a row of houses **6** : a strip of park in the middle of a street

²terrace *vb* **ter·raced; ter·rac·ing** : to form into a terrace or supply with terraces

ter·ra–cot·ta \ˌter-ə-'kä-tə\ *n* [It *terra cotta*, lit., baked earth] : a reddish brown earthenware

terra fir·ma \-'fər-mə\ *n* [NL] : solid ground

ter·rain \tə-ˈrān\ *n* : the surface features of an area of land ⟨a rough ∼⟩
ter·ra in·cog·ni·ta \ˈter-ə-ˌin-ˌkäg-ˈnē-tə\ *n, pl* **ter·rae in·cog·ni·tae** \ˈter-ˌī-ˌin-ˌkäg-ˈnē-tī\ [L] : an unexplored area or field of knowledge
ter·ra·pin \ˈter-ə-pən\ *n* : any of various turtles of fresh or brackish water

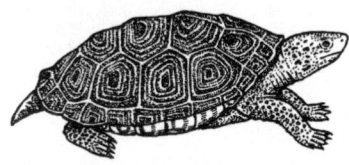

terrapin

ter·rar·i·um \tə-ˈrer-ē-əm\ *n, pl* **-ia** \-ē-ə\ *or* **-i·ums** : a usu. transparent enclosure for keeping or raising plants or small animals indoors
ter·res·tri·al \tə-ˈres-trē-əl\ *adj* **1** : of or relating to the earth or its inhabitants **2** : living or growing on land ⟨∼ plants⟩ ✦ **Synonyms** MUNDANE, EARTHLY, WORLDLY
ter·ri·ble \ˈter-ə-bəl\ *adj* **1** : exciting terror : FEARFUL, DREADFUL ⟨∼ weapons⟩ **2** : hard to bear : DISTRESSING ⟨a ∼ situation⟩ **3** : extreme in degree : INTENSE ⟨∼ heat⟩ **4** : of very poor quality : AWFUL ⟨a ∼ play⟩ ✦ **Synonyms** FRIGHTFUL, HORRIBLE, SHOCKING, APPALLING — **ter·ri·bly** \-blē\ *adv*
ter·ri·er \ˈter-ē-ər\ *n* [ME *terryer, terrer,* fr. AF (*chen*) *terrer,* lit., earth dog, fr. *terre* earth, fr. L *terra*] : any of various usu. small energetic dogs orig. used by hunters to drive small game animals from their holes
ter·rif·ic \tə-ˈri-fik\ *adj* **1** : exciting terror **2** : EXTRAORDINARY, ASTOUNDING ⟨∼ speed⟩ **3** : MAGNIFICENT ⟨makes ∼ chili⟩
ter·ri·fy \ˈter-ə-ˌfī\ *vb* **-fied; -fy·ing** : to fill with terror : FRIGHTEN ✦ **Synonyms** SCARE, TERRORIZE, STARTLE, ALARM — **ter·ri·fy·ing·ly** *adv*
ter·ri·to·ri·al·i·ty \ˌterə,tòrē'alətē\ *n* : persistent attachment to a specific territory
ter·ri·to·ry \ˈter-ə-ˌtòr-ē\ *n, pl* **-ries** **1** : a geographic area belonging to or under the jurisdiction of a governmental authority **2** : a part of the U.S. not included within any state but organized with a separate legislature **3** : REGION, DISTRICT; *also* : a region in which one feels at home **4** : a field of knowledge or interest **5** : an assigned area **6** : an area occupied and defended by one or a group of animals — **ter·ri·to·ri·al** \ˌter-ə-ˈtòr-ē-əl\ *adj* — **go with the territory** *or* **come with the territory** : to accompany a situation naturally
ter·ror \ˈter-ər\ *n* **1** : a state of intense fear : FRIGHT **2** : one that inspires fear **3** : violent or destructive acts committed to intimidate a people or government ✦ **Synonyms** PANIC, CONSTERNATION, DREAD, ALARM, DISMAY, HORROR, TREPIDATION
ter·ror·ism \ˈter-ər-ˌi-zəm\ *n* : the systematic use of terror esp. as a means of coercion — **ter·ror·ist** \-ist\ *adj or n*
ter·ror·ize \ˈter-ər-ˌīz\ *vb* **-ized; -iz·ing** **1** : to fill with terror : SCARE **2** : to coerce by threat or violence ✦ **Synonyms** TERRIFY, FRIGHTEN, ALARM, STARTLE
ter·ry \ˈter-ē\ *n, pl* **terries** : an absorbent fabric with a loose pile of uncut loops
terse \ˈtərs\ *adj* **ters·er; ters·est** [L *tersus* clean, neat, fr. pp. of *tergēre* to wipe off] : effectively brief : CONCISE — **terse·ly** *adv* — **terse·ness** *n*
ter·tia·ry \ˈtər-shē-ˌer-ē\ *adj* **1** : of third rank, importance, or value **2** *cap* : of, relating to, or being the earlier period of the Cenozoic era **3** : occurring in or being the third stage
Tertiary *n* : the Tertiary period
TESL *abbr* teaching English as a second language
TESOL *abbr* Teachers of English to Speakers of Other Languages
¹test \ˈtest\ *n* [ME, vessel in which metals were assayed, potsherd, fr. AF, pot, fr. L *testum* earthen vessel] **1** : a critical examination or evaluation : TRIAL **2** : a means or result of testing

²test *vb* **1** : to put to test : TRY, EXAMINE **2** : to undergo or score on tests
³test *adj* : relating to or used in testing ⟨a ∼ group⟩
tes·ta·ment \ˈtes-tə-mənt\ *n* **1** *cap* : either of two main divisions of the Bible **2** : EVIDENCE, WITNESS **3** : CREED **4** : the legal instructions for the disposition of one's property after death : WILL — **tes·ta·men·ta·ry** \ˌtes-tə-ˈmen-tə-rē\ *adj*
tes·tate \ˈtes-ˌtāt, -tət\ *adj* : having left a valid will
tes·ta·tor \ˈtes-ˌtā-tər, tes-ˈtā-\ *n* : a person who dies leaving a valid will
tes·ta·trix \tes-ˈtā-triks\ *n* : a woman who is a testator
¹tes·ter \ˈtēs-tər, ˈtes-\ *n* : a canopy over a bed, pulpit, or altar
²test·er \ˈtes-tər\ *n* : one that tests
tes·ti·cle \ˈtes-ti-kəl\ *n* : TESTIS; *esp* : one of a mammal usu. with its enclosing structures — **tes·tic·u·lar** *adj*
tes·ti·fy \ˈtes-tə-ˌfī\ *vb* **-fied; -fy·ing** **1** : to make a statement based on personal knowledge or belief : bear witness **2** : to serve as evidence or proof
tes·ti·mo·ni·al \ˌtes-tə-ˈmō-nē-əl\ *n* **1** : a statement testifying to benefits received; *also* : a character reference **2** : an expression of appreciation : TRIBUTE — **testimonial** *adj*
tes·ti·mo·ny \ˈtes-tə-ˌmō-nē\ *n, pl* **-nies** **1** : evidence based on observation or knowledge **2** : an outward sign : SYMBOL **3** : a solemn declaration made by a witness under oath esp. in a court ✦ **Synonyms** EVIDENCE, CONFIRMATION, PROOF, TESTAMENT
tes·tis \ˈtes-təs\ *n, pl* **tes·tes** \ˈtes-ˌtēz\ [L, witness, testis] : a typically paired male reproductive gland that produces sperm and testosterone and that in most mammals is contained within the scrotum at sexual maturity
tes·tos·ter·one \te-ˈstäs-tə-ˌrōn\ *n* : a male sex hormone causing development of the male reproductive system and secondary sex characteristics
test–tube *adj* **1** : IN VITRO ⟨∼ experiments⟩ **2** : produced by in vitro fertilization ⟨∼ babies⟩
test tube *n* : a glass tube closed at one end and used esp. in chemistry and biology
tes·ty \ˈtes-tē\ *adj* **tes·ti·er; -est** [ME *testif,* fr. AF, headstrong, fr. *teste* head, fr. LL *testa* skull, fr. L, shell] : easily annoyed; *also* : marked by ill humor
tet·a·nus \ˈte-tə-nəs\ *n* : an infectious disease caused by bacterial poisons and marked by muscle stiffness and spasms esp. of the jaws — **tet·a·nal** \-əl\ *adj*
tetchy \ˈte-chē\ *adj* **tetchi·er, -est** : irritably or peevishly sensitive
¹tête-à-tête \ˈtāt-ə-ˌtāt\ *n* [F, lit., head to head] : a private conversation between two persons
²tête-à-tête \ˈtāt-ə-ˈtāt\ *adv* : in private
³tête-à-tête \ˈtāt-ə-ˌtāt\ *adj* : being face-to-face : PRIVATE
¹teth·er \ˈte-thər\ *n* **1** : something (as a rope) by which an animal is fastened **2** : the limit of one's strength or resources
²tether *vb* : to fasten or restrain by or as if by a tether
tet·ra·eth·yl lead \ˌte-trə-ˈe-thəl-\ *n* : a heavy oily poisonous liquid used esp. formerly as an antiknock agent in gasoline
tet·ra·he·dron \-ˈhē-drən\ *n, pl* **-drons** *or* **-dra** \-drə\ : a polyhedron that has four faces — **tet·ra·he·dral** \-drəl\ *adj*
tet·ra·hy·dro·can·nab·i·nol \-ˌhī-drə-kə-ˈna-bə-ˌnòl, -ˌnōl\ *n* : THC
te·tram·e·ter \te-ˈtra-mə-tər\ *n* : a line of verse consisting of four metrical feet
Teu·ton·ic \tü-ˈtä-nik, tyü-\ *adj* : GERMANIC
Tex *abbr* Texas
Tex–Mex \ˈteks-ˈmeks\ *adj* : characteristic of Mexican-American culture and esp. that of southern Texas
text \ˈtekst\ *n* **1** : the actual words of an author's work **2** : the main body of printed or written matter on a page **3** : a scriptural passage chosen as the subject esp. of a sermon **4** : THEME, TOPIC **5** : TEXTBOOK — **tex·tu·al** \ˈteks-chə-wəl\ *adj*
text·book \ˈtekst-ˌbúk\ *n* : a book used in the study of a subject
tex·tile \ˈtek-ˌstī(-ə)l, ˈteks-təl\ *n* : CLOTH; *esp* : a woven or knit cloth
tex·ture \ˈteks-chər\ *n* **1** : the visual or tactile surface characteristics and appearance of something ⟨a coarse

~-> **2** : essential part **3** : basic scheme or structure : FABRIC **4** : overall structure — **tex·tur·al** \-chə-rəl\ adj

TGIF abbr thank God it's Friday

¹Th abbr Thursday

²Th symbol thorium

¹-th — see ¹-ETH

²-th or **-eth** adj suffix — used in forming ordinal numbers ⟨hundred*th*⟩

³-th n suffix **1** : act or process **2** : state or condition ⟨dear*th*⟩

Thai \'tī\ n, pl **Thai** or **Thais 1** : a native or inhabitant of Thailand **2** : the official language of Thailand — **Thai** adj

thal·a·mus \'tha-lə-məs\ n, pl **-mi** \-ˌmī\ [NL] : a subdivision of the thalamus that serves as a relay station to and from the cerebral cortex and functions in arousal and the integration of sensory information — **tha·lam·ic** \thə-'la-mik\ adj

thal·as·se·mia \ˌtha-lə-'sē-mē-ə\ n : any of a group of inherited disorders of hemoglobin synthesis

tha·las·so·ther·a·py \thə-ˌla-sō-'ther-ə-pē\ n [Gk *thalassa* sea] : the use of seawater or sea products (as seaweed) for the benefit of health or beauty

thal·li·um \'tha-lē-əm\ n : a poisonous metallic chemical element

¹than \'thən, 'than\ conj **1** — used after a comparative adjective or adverb to introduce the second part of a comparison expressing inequality ⟨older ~ I am⟩ **2** — used after *other* or a word of similar meaning to express a difference of kind, manner, or identity ⟨adults other ~ parents⟩

²than prep : in comparison with ⟨older ~ me⟩

thane \'thān\ n **1** : a free retainer of an Anglo-Saxon lord **2** : a Scottish feudal lord

thank \'thaŋk\ vb : to express gratitude to ⟨~ed them for the present⟩

thank·ful \'thaŋk-fəl\ adj **1** : conscious of benefit received **2** : expressive of thanks **3** : GLAD — **thank·ful·ness** n

thank·ful·ly \-fə-lē\ adv **1** : in a thankful manner **2** : as makes one thankful

thank·less \'thaŋ-kləs\ adj **1** : UNAPPRECIATED **2** : UNGRATEFUL

thanks \'thaŋks\ n pl : an expression of gratitude

thanks·giv·ing \thaŋks-'gi-viŋ\ n **1** : the act of giving thanks **2** : a prayer expressing gratitude **3** cap : the 4th Thursday in November observed as a legal holiday for giving thanks for divine goodness

¹that \'that, thət\ pron, pl **those** \'thōz\ **1** : the one indicated, mentioned, or understood ⟨~ is my house⟩ **2** : the one farther away or first mentioned ⟨this is an elm, ~'s a maple⟩ **3** : what has been indicated or mentioned ⟨after ~, we left⟩ **4** : the one or ones : IT, THEY ⟨*those* who wish to leave may do so⟩

²that \thət, 'that\ conj **1** : the following, namely ⟨he said ~ he would⟩; *also* : which is, namely ⟨there's a chance ~ it may fail⟩ **2** : to this end or purpose ⟨shouted ~ all might hear⟩ **3** : as to result in the following, namely ⟨so heavy ~ it can't be moved⟩ **4** : for this reason, namely ⟨BECAUSE ⟨we're glad ~ you came⟩

³that adj, pl **those 1** : being the one mentioned, indicated, or understood ⟨~ boy⟩ ⟨*those* people⟩ **2** : being the one farther away or less immediately under discussion ⟨this chair or ~ one⟩

⁴that \thət, 'that\ pron **1** : WHO, WHOM, WHICH ⟨the man ~ saw you⟩ ⟨the man ~ you saw⟩ ⟨the money ~ was spent⟩ **2** : in, on, or at which ⟨the way ~ he drives⟩ ⟨the day ~ it rained⟩

⁵that \'that\ adv : to such an extent or degree ⟨I like it, but not ~ much⟩

¹thatch \'thach\ vb : to cover with or as if with thatch — **thatch·er** n

²thatch n **1** : plant material (as straw) for use as roofing **2** : a mat of grass clippings accumulated next to the soil on a lawn **3** : a covering of or as if of thatch ⟨a ~ of white hair⟩

thaw \'thȯ\ vb **1** : to melt or cause to melt **2** : to become so warm as to melt ice or snow **3** : to abandon aloofness or hostility — **thaw** n

THC \ˌtē-(ˌ)āch-'sē\ n [*tetra*hydrocannabinol] : a physio-

logically active chemical from hemp plant resin that is the chief intoxicant in marijuana

¹the \thə, before vowel sounds usu thē\ definite article **1** : that in particular **2** — used before adjectives functioning as nouns ⟨a word to ~ wise⟩

²the adv **1** : to what extent ⟨~ sooner, the better⟩ **2** : to that extent ⟨the sooner, ~ better⟩

theat abbr theater; theatrical

the·ater or **the·atre** \'thē-ə-tər\ n [ME *theatre*, fr. MF, fr. L *theatrum*, fr. Gk *theatron*, fr. *theasthai* to view, fr. *thea* act of seeing] **1** : a building or area for dramatic performances; *also* : a building or area for showing motion pictures **2** : a place of enactment of significant events ⟨~ of war⟩ **3** : a place (as a lecture room) resembling a theater **4** : dramatic literature or performance

theater–in–the–round n : a theater with the stage in the center of the auditorium

the·at·ri·cal \thē-'a-tri-kəl\ also **the·at·ric** \-trik\ adj **1** : of or relating to the theater **2** : marked by artificiality of emotion : HISTRIONIC **3** : marked by extravagant display : SHOWY

the·at·ri·cals \-kəlz\ n pl : the performance of plays

the·at·rics \thē-'a-triks\ n pl **1** : THEATRICALS **2** : staged or contrived effects

the·be \'thā-bā\ n, pl **thebe** — see *pula* at MONEY table

thee \'thē\ pron, archaic objective case of THOU

theft \'theft\ n : the act of stealing

thegn \'thān\ n : THANE 1

their \thər, 'ther\ adj : of or relating to them or themselves

theirs \'therz\ pron : their one : their ones

the·ism \'thē-ˌi-zəm\ n : belief in the existence of a god or gods — **the·ist** \-ist\ n or adj — **the·is·tic** \thē-'is-tik\ adj

them \thəm, 'them\ pron, objective case of THEY

theme \'thēm\ n **1** : a subject or topic of discourse or of artistic representation **2** : a written exercise : COMPOSITION **3** : a melodic subject of a musical composition or movement — **the·mat·ic** \thi-'ma-tik\ adj

them·selves \thəm-'selvz, them-\ pron pl : THEY, THEM — used reflexively, for emphasis, or in absolute constructions ⟨they govern ~⟩ ⟨they ~ came⟩ ⟨~ busy, they sent me⟩

¹then \'then\ adv **1** : at that time **2** : soon after that : NEXT **3** : in addition : BESIDES **4** : in that case **5** : CONSEQUENTLY

²then n : that time ⟨since ~⟩

³then adj : existing or acting at that time ⟨the ~ attorney general⟩

thence \'thens, 'thens\ adv **1** : from that place **2** archaic : THENCEFORTH **3** : from that fact : THEREFROM

thence·forth \-ˌfȯrth\ adv : from that time forward : THEREAFTER

thence·for·ward \thens-'fȯr-wərd, thens-\ also **thence·for·wards** \-wərdz\ adv : onward from that place or time

the·oc·ra·cy \thē-'ä-krə-sē\ n, pl **-cies 1** : government by officials regarded as divinely inspired **2** : a state governed by a theocracy — **the·o·crat·ic** \ˌthē-ə-'kra-tik\ adj

theol abbr theological; theology

the·ol·o·gy \thē-'ä-lə-jē\ n, pl **-gies 1** : the study of religious faith, practice, and experience; *esp* : the study of God and of God's relation to the world **2** : a theory or system of theology — **the·o·lo·gian** \ˌthē-ə-'lō-jən\ n — **the·o·log·i·cal** \-'lä-ji-kəl\ adj

the·o·rem \'thē-ə-rəm, 'thir-əm\ n **1** : a statement esp. in mathematics that has been or is to be proved **2** : an idea accepted or proposed as a demonstrable truth : PROPOSITION

the·o·ret·i·cal \ˌthē-ə-'re-ti-kəl\ also **the·o·ret·ic** \-tik\ adj **1** : relating to or having the character of theory **2** : existing only in theory : HYPOTHETICAL — **the·o·ret·i·cal·ly** \-ti-k(ə-)lē\ adv

the·o·rise Brit var of THEORIZE

the·o·rize \'thē-ə-ˌrīz\ vb **-rized; -riz·ing** : to form a theory : SPECULATE — **the·o·rist** \-rist\ n

the·o·ry \'thē-ə-rē, 'thir-ē\ n, pl **-ries 1** : abstract thought **2** : the general principles of a subject **3** : a plausible or scientifically acceptable general principle offered to explain observed facts **4** : HYPOTHESIS, CONJECTURE

theory of games : GAME THEORY

the·os·o·phy \thē-'ä-sə-fē\ n : belief about God and the world held to be based on mystical insight — **theo·soph·i·cal** \ˌthē-ə-'sä-fi-kəl\ *adj* — **the·os·o·phist** \thē-'ä-sə-fist\ *n*

ther·a·peu·tic \ˌther-ə-'pyü-tik\ *adj* [Gk *therapeutikos*, fr. *therapeuein* to attend, treat, fr. *theraps* attendant] : of, relating to, or dealing with healing and esp. with remedies for diseases — **ther·a·peu·ti·cal·ly** \-ti-k(ə-)lē\ *adv*

ther·a·peu·tics \ˌther-ə-'pyü-tiks\ *n* : a branch of medical or dental science dealing with the use of remedies

ther·a·py \'ther-ə-pē\ *n, pl* **-pies** : treatment of bodily, mental, or behavioral disorders — **ther·a·pist** \-pist\ *n*

¹**there** \'ther\ *adv* **1** : in or at that place — often used interjectionally **2** : to or into that place : THITHER **3** : in that matter or respect

²**there** \'ther, thər\ *pron* — used as a function word to introduce a sentence or clause \<~'s a pen here\>

³**there** \'ther\ *n* **1** : that place \<get away from ~\> **2** : that point \<you take it from ~\>

there·abouts \ˌther-ə-'baüts, 'ther-ə-ˌbaüts\ *or* **there·about** \-'baüt, -ˌbaüt\ *adv* **1** : near that place or time **2** : near that number, degree, or quantity

there·af·ter \thr-'af-tər\ *adv* : after that : AFTERWARD

there·at \-'at\ *adv* **1** : at that place **2** : at that occurrence : on that account

there·by \ther-'bī, 'ther-ˌbī\ *adv* **1** : by that : by that means **2** : connected with or with reference to that

there·for \ther-'fōr\ *adv* : for or in return for that

there·fore \'ther-ˌfōr\ *adv* : for that reason : CONSEQUENTLY

there·from \ther-'frəm\ *adv* : from that or it

there·in \ther-'in\ *adv* **1** : in or into that place, time, or thing **2** : in that respect

there·of \-'əv, -'äv\ *adv* **1** : of that or it **2** : from that : THEREFROM

there·on \-'òn, -'än\ *adv* **1** : on that **2** *archaic* : THEREUPON 3

there·to \ther-'tü\ *adv* : to that

there·un·to \ther-'ən-(ˌ)tü, ˌther-ən-'tü\ *adv, archaic* : THERETO

there·upon \'ther-ə-ˌpòn, -ˌpän; ˌther-ə-'pòn, -'pän\ *adv* **1** : on that matter **2** : THEREFORE **3** : immediately after that : at once

there·with \ther-'with -with\ *adv* **1** : with that **2** *archaic* : THEREUPON, FORTHWITH

there·with·al \'ther-wi-ˌthól, -ˌthól\ *adv* **1** *archaic* : BESIDES **2** : THEREWITH

therm *abbr* thermometer

ther·mal \'thər-məl\ *adj* **1** : of, relating to, or caused by heat **2** : designed to prevent the loss of body heat \<~ underwear\> — **ther·mal·ly** *adv*

thermal pollution *n* : the discharge of heated liquid (as waste water from a factory) into natural waters at a temperature harmful to the environment

therm·is·tor \'thər-ˌmis-tər\ *n* : an electrical resistor whose resistance varies sharply with temperature

ther·mo·cline \'thər-mə-ˌklīn\ *n* : the region in a thermally stratified body of water that separates warmer surface water from cold deep water

ther·mo·cou·ple \'thər-mə-ˌkə-pəl\ *n* : a device for measuring temperature by measuring the temperature-dependent potential difference created at the junction of two dissimilar metals

ther·dy·nam·ics \ˌthər-mə-dī-'na-miks\ *n* : physics that deals with the mechanical action or relations of heat — **ther·mo·dy·nam·ic** \-mik\ *adj* — **ther·mo·dy·nam·i·cal·ly** \-mi-k(ə-)lē\ *adv*

ther·mom·e·ter \thər-'mä-mə-tər\ *n* [F *thermomètre*, fr. Gk *thermē* heat + *metron* measure] : an instrument for measuring temperature typically by the rise or fall of a liquid (as mercury) in a thin glass tube — **ther·mo·met·ric** \ˌthər-mə-'me-trik\ *adj* — **ther·mo·met·ri·cal·ly** \-tri-k(ə-)lē\ *adv*

ther·mo·nu·cle·ar \ˌthər-mō-'nü-klē-ər, -'nyü-\ *adj* **1** : of or relating to changes in the nucleus of atoms of low atomic weight (as hydrogen) that require a very high temperature (as in the hydrogen bomb) **2** : utilizing or relating to a thermonuclear bomb \<~ war\>

ther·mo·plas·tic \ˌthər-mə-'plas-tik\ *adj* : capable of softening when heated and of hardening again when cooled \<~ resins\> — **thermoplastic** *n*

ther·mos \'thər-məs\ *n* : a cylindrical container with a

vacuum between an inner and an outer wall used to keep liquids hot or cold

ther·mo·sphere \'thər-mə-ˌsfir\ *n* : the part of the earth's atmosphere that lies above the mesosphere and that is characterized by steadily increasing temperature with height

ther·mo·stat \'thər-mə-ˌstat\ *n* : a device that automatically controls temperature — **ther·mo·stat·ic** \ˌthər-mə-'sta-tik\ *adj* — **ther·mo·stat·i·cal·ly** \-ti-k(ə-)lē\ *adv*

the·sau·rus \thi-'sòr-əs\ *n, pl* **-sau·ri** \-'sòr-ˌī\ *or* **-sau·rus·es** \-'sòr-ə-səz\ [NL, fr. L, treasure, collection, fr. Gk *thēsauros*] : a book of words and their synonyms — **the·sau·ral** \-'sòr-əl\ *adj*

these *pl of* THIS

the·sis \'thē-səs\ *n, pl* **the·ses** \'thē-ˌsēz\ **1** : a proposition that a person advances and offers to maintain by argument **2** : an essay embodying results of original research; *esp* : one written for an academic degree

¹**thes·pi·an** \'thes-pē-ən\ *adj, often cap* [fr. *Thespis*, 6th cent. B.C. Greek poet and reputed originator of tragedy] : relating to the drama : DRAMATIC

²**thespian** *n* : ACTOR

Thess *abbr* Thessalonians

Thes·sa·lo·nians \ˌthe-sə-'lō-nyənz, -nē-ənz\ *n* — see BIBLE table

the·ta \'thā-tə\ *n* : the 8th letter of the Greek alphabet — Θ or θ

thew \'thü, 'thyü\ *n* : MUSCLE, SINEW — usu. used in pl.

they \'thā\ *pron* **1** : those individuals under discussion : the ones previously mentioned or referred to **2** : unspecified persons : PEOPLE

thi·a·mine \'thī-ə-mən, -ˌmēn\ *also* **thi·a·min** \-mən\ *n* : a vitamin of the vitamin B complex essential to normal metabolism and nerve function

¹**thick** \'thik\ *adj* **1** : having relatively great depth or extent from one surface to its opposite \<a ~ plank\>; *also* : heavily built : THICKSET **2** : densely massed : CROWDED; *also* : FREQUENT, NUMEROUS **3** : dense or viscous in consistency \<~ syrup\> **4** : marked by haze, fog, or mist \<~ weather\> **5** : measuring in thickness \<one meter ~\> **6** : imperfectly articulated : INDISTINCT \<~ speech\> **7** : STUPID, OBTUSE **8** : associated on close terms : INTIMATE **9** : EXCESSIVE ♦ **Synonyms** COMPACT, CLOSE, TIGHT — **thick·ly** *adv*

²**thick** *n* **1** : the most crowded or active part **2** : the part of greatest thickness

thick and thin *n* : every difficulty and obstacle \<was loyal through *thick and thin*\>

thick·en \'thi-kən\ *vb* : to make or become thick — **thick·en·er** *n*

thick·et \'thi-kət\ *n* : a dense growth of bushes or small trees

thick·ness \-nəs\ *n* **1** : the smallest of three dimensions \<length, width, and ~\> **2** : the quality or state of being thick **3** : LAYER, SHEET \<a single ~ of canvas\>

thick·set \'thik-'set\ *adj* **1** : closely placed or planted **2** : having a thick body : BURLY

thick–skinned \-'skind\ *adj* **1** : having a thick skin **2** : not easily bothered by criticism or insult

thief \'thēf\ *n, pl* **thieves** \'thēvz\ : one that steals esp. secretly

thieve \'thēv\ *vb* **thieved; thiev·ing** : STEAL, ROB ♦ **Synonyms** FILCH, PILFER, PURLOIN, SWIPE

thiev·ery \'thē-və-rē\ *n, pl* **-er·ies** : the act of stealing : THEFT

thigh \'thī\ *n* : the part of the vertebrate hind or lower limb between the knee and the hip

thigh·bone \'thī-ˌbōn\ *n* : FEMUR

thim·ble \'thim-bəl\ *n* : a cap or guard worn on the finger to push the needle in sewing — **thim·ble·ful** *n*

¹**thin** \'thin\ *adj* **thin·ner; thin·nest 1** : having little extent from one surface through to its opposite : not thick : SLENDER **2** : not closely set or placed : SPARSE \<~ hair\> **3** : not dense or not dense enough : more fluid or rarefied than normal \<~ air\> \<~ syrup\> **4** : lacking substance, fullness, or strength \<~ broth\> **5** : FLIMSY \<a ~ excuse\> — **thin·ly** *adv* — **thin·ness** *n*

²**thin** *vb* **thinned; thin·ning** : to make or become thin

thine \'thīn\ *pron, archaic* : one or the ones belonging to thee

thing \'thiŋ\ *n* **1** : a matter of concern : AFFAIR \<~s to do⟩ **2** *pl* : state of affairs ⟨∼*s* are improving⟩ **3** : EVENT, CIRCUMSTANCE ⟨the crime was a terrible ∼⟩ **4** : DEED, ACT ⟨expected great ∼*s* of him⟩ **5** : a distinct entity : OBJECT **6** : an inanimate object distinguished from a living being **7** *pl* : POSSESSIONS, EFFECTS **8** : an article of clothing **9** : DETAIL, POINT ⟨checks every little ∼⟩ **10** : IDEA, NOTION ⟨says the first ∼ he thinks of⟩ **11** : something one likes to do : SPECIALTY ⟨doing her ∼⟩

think \'think\ *vb* **thought** \'thȯt\; **think·ing** **1** : to form or have in the mind **2** : to have an opinion : BELIEVE **3** : to reflect on : PONDER **4** : to call to mind : REMEMBER **5** : REASON **6** : to form a mental picture of : IMAGINE **7** : to devise by thinking ⟨*thought* up a plan to escape⟩ ◆ *Synonyms* CONCEIVE, FANCY, REALIZE, ENVISAGE — **think·er** *n*

think tank *n* : an institute, corporation, or group organized for interdisciplinary research (as in technological or social problems)

thin·ner \'thi-nər\ *n* : a volatile liquid (as turpentine) used to thin paint

thin–skinned \'thin-'skind\ *adj* **1** : having a thin skin or rind **2** : extremely sensitive to criticism or insult

¹**third** \'thərd\ *adj* : next after the second — **third** *or* **third·ly** *adv*

²**third** *n* **1** : one of three equal parts of something **2** : one that is number three in a countable series **3** : the 3d forward gear in an automotive vehicle

third degree *n* : the subjection of a prisoner to mental or physical torture to force a confession

third dimension *n* **1** : thickness, depth, or apparent thickness or depth that confers solidity on an object **2** : a quality that confers reality — **third–dimensional** *adj*

third world *n, often cap T&W* : the aggregate of the underdeveloped nations of the world

¹**thirst** \'thərst\ *n* **1** : a feeling of dryness in the mouth and throat associated with a desire to drink; *also* : a bodily condition producing this **2** : an ardent desire : CRAVING ⟨a ∼ for knowledge⟩ — **thirsty** *adj*

²**thirst** *vb* **1** : to need drink : suffer thirst **2** : to have a strong desire : CRAVE

thir·teen \,thər-'tēn\ *n* : one more than 12 — **thirteen** *adj or pron* — **thir·teenth** \-'tēnth\ *adj or n*

thir·ty \'thər-tē\ *n, pl* **thirties** : three times 10 — **thir·ti·eth** \-tē-əth\ *adj or n* — **thirty** *adj or pron*

¹**this** \'this\ *pron, pl* **these** \'thēz\ **1** : the one close or closest in time or space ⟨∼ is your book⟩ **2** : what is in the present or under immediate observation or discussion ⟨∼ is a mess⟩; *also* : what is happening or being done now ⟨after ∼ we'll leave⟩

²**this** *adj, pl* **these** **1** : being the one near, present, just mentioned, or more immediately under observation ⟨∼ book⟩ **2** : constituting the immediate past or future ⟨friends all *these* years⟩

³**this** *adv* : to such an extent or degree ⟨didn't expect to wait ∼ long⟩

this·tle \'thi-səl\ *n* : any of various tall prickly composite plants with often showy heads of tightly packed tubular flowers

this·tle·down \-,daủn\ *n* : the down from the ripe flower head of a thistle

¹**thith·er** \'thi-thər\ *adv* : to that place

²**thither** *adj* : being on the farther side

thith·er·ward \-wərd\ *adv* : toward that place : THITHER

thong \'thȯŋ\ *n* **1** : a strip esp. of leather or hide **2** : a sandal held on the foot by a thong between the toes **3** : a narrow strip of swimwear or underwear that passes between the thighs

tho·rax \'thȯr-,aks\ *n, pl* **tho·rax·es** *or* **tho·ra·ces** \'thȯr-ə-,sēz\ **1** : the part of the body of a mammal between the neck and the abdomen; *also* : its cavity containing the heart and lungs **2** : the middle of the three main divisions of the body of an insect — **tho·rac·ic** \thə-'ra-sik\ *adj*

tho·ri·um \'thȯr-ē-əm\ *n* : a radioactive metallic chemical element

thorn \'thȯrn\ *n* **1** : a woody plant bearing sharp processes **2** : a sharp rigid plant process that is usu. a modified leafless branch **3** : something that causes distress — **thorny** *adj*

thor·ough \'thər-ō\ *adj* **1** : COMPLETE, EXHAUSTIVE ⟨a ∼ search⟩ **2** : very careful : PAINSTAKING ⟨a ∼ schol-

ar⟩ **3** : having full mastery — **thor·ough·ly** *adv* — **thor·ough·ness** *n*

¹**thor·ough·bred** \'thər-ə-,bred\ *adj* **1** : bred from the best blood through a long line **2** *cap* : of or relating to the Thoroughbred breed of horses **3** : marked by high-spirited grace

²**thoroughbred** *n* **1** *cap* : any of an English breed of light speedy horses kept chiefly for racing **2** : one (as a pedigreed animal) of excellent quality

thor·ough·fare \-,far\ *n* : a public road or street

thor·ough·go·ing \,thər-ə-'gō-iŋ\ *adj* : marked by thoroughness or zeal

thorp \'thȯrp\ *n, archaic* : VILLAGE

those *pl of* THAT

¹**thou** \'thaủ\ *pron, archaic* : the person addressed

²**thou** \'thaủ\ *n, pl* **thou** : a thousand of something (as dollars)

¹**though** \'thō\ *conj* **1** : despite the fact that ⟨∼ the odds are hopeless, they fight on⟩ **2** : granting that ⟨∼ it may look bad, still, all is not lost⟩

²**though** *adv* : HOWEVER, NEVERTHELESS ⟨not for long, ∼⟩

¹**thought** \'thȯt\ *past and past part of* THINK

²**thought** *n* **1** : the process of thinking **2** : serious consideration : REGARD **3** : reasoning power **4** : the power to imagine : CONCEPTION **5** : IDEA, NOTION **6** : OPINION, BELIEF ⟨spoke his ∼*s* freely⟩

thought·ful \'thȯt-fəl\ *adj* **1** : absorbed in thought **2** : marked by careful thinking ⟨a ∼ essay⟩ **3** : considerate of others ⟨a ∼ host⟩ — **thought·ful·ly** *adv* — **thought·ful·ness** *n*

thought·less \-ləs\ *adj* **1** : insufficiently alert : CARELESS ⟨a ∼ worker⟩ **2** : RECKLESS ⟨a ∼ act⟩ **3** : lacking concern for others : INCONSIDERATE ⟨∼ remarks⟩ — **thought·less·ly** *adv* — **thought·less·ness** *n*

thou·sand \'thaủz-ᵊnd\ *n, pl* **thousands** *or* **thousand** : 10 times 100 — **thousand** *adj* — **thou·sandth** \-ᵊnth\ *adj or n*

thousands place *n* : the place four to the left of the decimal point in an Arabic number

thrall \'thrȯl\ *n* **1** : SLAVE, BONDMAN **2** : a state of servitude — **thrall·dom** *or* **thral·dom** \'thrȯl-dəm\ *n*

¹**thrash** \'thrash\ *vb* **1** : THRESH 1 **2** : BEAT, WHIP; *also* : DEFEAT **3** : to move about violently **4** : to go over again and again ⟨∼ over the matter⟩; *also* : to hammer out ⟨∼ out a plan⟩

²**thrash** *n* : rock music that is extremely fast and loud

¹**thrash·er** \'thra-shər\ *n* : one that thrashes or threshes

²**thrasher** *n* : any of various long-tailed American songbirds related to the mockingbird

¹**thread** \'thred\ *n* **1** : a thin continuous strand of spun and twisted textile fibers **2** : something resembling a textile thread **3** : the ridge or groove that winds around a screw **4** : a line of reasoning or train of thought **5** : a continuing element **6** : a tenuous or feeble support

²**thread** *vb* **1** : to pass a thread through the eye of (a needle) **2** : to pass (as film) through something **3** : to make one's way through or between **4** : to put together on a thread ⟨∼ beads⟩ **5** : to form a screw thread on or in

thread·bare \-,ber\ *adj* **1** : having the nap worn off so that the thread shows : SHABBY **2** : TRITE

thready \'thre-dē\ *adj* **1** : consisting of or bearing fibers of filaments ⟨a ∼ bark⟩ **2** : lacking in fullness, body, or vigor ⟨a ∼ voice⟩

threat \'thret\ *n* **1** : an expression of intent to do harm **2** : one that threatens

threat·en \'thre-tᵊn\ *vb* **1** : to utter threats against **2** : to give signs or warning of : PORTEND **3** : to hang over as a threat : MENACE **4** : to cause to feel insecure or anxious — **threat·en·ing·ly** *adv*

threat·ened \-tᵊnd\ *adj* : having an uncertain chance of continued survival; *esp* : likely to become an endangered species

three \'thrē\ *n* **1** : one more than two **2** : the 3d in a set or series **3** : something having three units — **three** *adj or pron*

3–D \'thrē-'dē\ *n* : a three-dimensional form or picture

three–dimensional *adj* **1** : relating to or having three dimensions **2** : giving the illusion of varying distances ⟨a ∼ picture⟩

three·fold \'thrē-,fōld, -'fōld\ *adj* **1** : having three parts

: TRIPLE   **2** : being three times as great or as many —
three·fold \-'fōld\ *adv*
three·pence \'thre-pəns, 'thri-, 'thrə-, *US also* 'thrē-pens\
n   **1** *pl* **threepence** *or* **three·penc·es** : a coin worth
three pennies   **2** : the sum of three British pennies
three·score \'thrē-'skȯr\ *adj* : being three times twenty
: SIXTY
three·some \'thrē-səm\ *n* : a group of three persons or
things
thren·o·dy \'thre-nə-dē\ *n*, *pl* **-dies** : a song of lamentation
: ELEGY
thresh \'thresh, 'thrash\ *vb*   **1** : to separate (as grain from
straw) mechanically   **2** : THRASH — **thresh·er** *n*
thresh·old \'thresh-,hōld\ *n*   **1** : the sill of a door   **2** : a
point or place of beginning or entering : OUTSET   **3** : a
point at which a physiological or psychological effect begins to be produced
threw *past of* THROW
thrice \'thrīs\ *adv*   **1** : three times   **2** : in a threefold manner or degree
thrift \'thrift\ *n* [ME, fr. ON, prosperity, fr. *thrīfask* to
thrive] : careful management esp. of money : FRUGALITY
— **thrift·i·ly** \'thrif-tə-lē\ *adv* — **thrift·less** *adj* — **thrifty**
adj
thrill \'thril\ *vb* [ME *thirlen, thrillen* to pierce, fr. OE *thyr-
lian*, fr. *thyrel* hole, fr. *thurh* through]   **1** : to have or
cause to have sudden sharp feeling of excitement; *also*
: TINGLE, SHIVER   **2** : TREMBLE, VIBRATE — **thrill** *n* —
thrill·er *n* — **thrill·ing·ly** *adv*
thrips \'thrips\ *n*, *pl* **thrips** : any of an order of minute
sucking insects including many plant-feeding pests
thrive \'thrīv\ *vb* **thrived** *or* **throve** \'thrōv\; **thrived** *also*
thriv·en \'thri-vən\; **thriv·ing**   **1** : to grow luxuriantly
: FLOURISH   **2** : to gain in wealth or possessions : PROSPER
throat \'thrōt\ *n* : the part of the neck in front of the spinal
column; *also* : the passage through it to the stomach and
lungs — **throat·ed** *adj*
throaty \'thrō-tē\ *adj* **throat·i·er; -est**   **1** : uttered or produced from low in the throat ⟨a ~ voice⟩   **2** : heavy,
thick, or deep as if from the throat ⟨~ notes of a horn⟩
— **throat·i·ly** \-tə-lē\ *adv* — **throat·i·ness** \-tē-nəs\ *n*
¹throb \'thräb\ *vb* **throbbed; throb·bing** : to pulsate or
pound esp. with abnormal force or rapidity : BEAT, VI-
BRATE
²throb *n* : BEAT, PULSE
throe \'thrō\ *n*   **1** : PANG, SPASM ⟨death ~s⟩   **2** *pl* : a
hard or painful struggle
throm·bo·lyt·ic \,thräm-bə-'li-tik\ *adj* : destroying or
breaking up a thrombus — **thrombolytic** *n*
throm·bo·sis \thräm-'bō-səs\ *n*, *pl* **-bo·ses** \-,sēz\ : the
formation or presence of a clot in a blood vessel —
throm·bot·ic \-'bä-tik\ *adj*
throm·bus \'thräm-bəs\ *n*, *pl* **throm·bi** \-,bī\ [NL, fr. Gk
thrombos lump, clot] : a clot of blood formed within a
blood vessel and remaining attached to its place of origin
throne \'thrōn\ *n*   **1** : the chair or seat of a sovereign or
high dignitary   **2** : royal power : SOVEREIGNTY
¹throng \'thröŋ\ *n*   **1** : MULTITUDE   **2** : a crowding together of many persons
²throng *vb* **thronged; throng·ing** : CROWD
¹throt·tle \'thrä-t²l\ *vb* **throt·tled; throt·tling** [ME *throtlen*,
fr. *throte* throat]   **1** : CHOKE, STRANGLE   **2** : SUPPRESS
⟨policies that ~ creativity⟩   **3** : to reduce the speed of
(an engine) by closing the throttle — **throt·tler** *n*
²throttle *n* : a valve regulating the flow of steam or fuel to
an engine; *also* : the lever controlling this valve
¹through \'thrü\ *prep*   **1** : into at one side and out at the
other side of ⟨go ~ the door⟩   **2** : by way of ⟨entered ~
a skylight⟩   **3** : in the midst of ⟨a path ~ the trees⟩   **4** : by
means of ⟨succeeded ~ hard work⟩   **5** : over the whole of
⟨rumors swept ~ the office⟩   **6** : during the whole of ⟨~
the night⟩   **7** : to and including ⟨Monday ~ Friday⟩
²through *adv*   **1** : from one end or side to the other   **2**
: from beginning to end : to completion ⟨see it ~⟩   **3** : to
the core : THOROUGHLY ⟨he was wet ~⟩   **4** : into the
open : OUT ⟨break ~⟩
³through *adj*   **1** : permitting free passage ⟨a ~ street⟩   **2**
: going from point of origin to destination without change
or transfer ⟨a ~ train⟩   **3** : coming from or going to
points outside a local area ⟨~ traffic⟩   **4** : FINISHED ⟨~
with the job⟩

¹through·out \thrü-'aut\ *adv*   **1** : EVERYWHERE   **2** : from
beginning to end
²throughout *prep*   **1** : in or to every part of   **2** : during the
whole period of
through·put \'thrü-,put\ *n* : OUTPUT, PRODUCTION ⟨the
~ of a computer⟩
throve *past of* THRIVE
¹throw \'thrō\ *vb* **threw** \'thrü\; **thrown** \'thrōn\; **throw·ing**
[ME, to cause to twist, throw, fr. OE *thrāwan* to cause to
twist]   **1** : to propel through the air esp. with a forward
motion of the hand and arm ⟨~ a ball⟩   **2** : to cause to
fall or fall off   **3** : to put suddenly in a certain position or
condition ⟨~ into panic⟩   **4** : to put on or take off hastily ⟨~ on a coat⟩   **5** : to lose intentionally ⟨~ a game⟩   **6**
: to move (a lever) so as to connect or disconnect parts of
something (as a clutch)   **7** : to put (an automobile) into a
different gear   **8** : to act as host for ⟨~ a party⟩   ✦ *Synonyms* TOSS, FLING, PITCH, SLING — **throw·er** *n*
²throw *n*   **1** : an act of throwing, hurling, or flinging; *also*
: CAST   **2** : the distance a missile may be thrown   **3** : a
light coverlet   **4** : a woman's scarf or light wrap
¹throw·away \'thrō-ə-,wā\ *n* : something that is or is designed to be thrown away esp. after one use
²throwaway *adj* : overly wasteful ⟨a ~ society⟩
throw·back \-,bak\ *n* : reversion to an earlier type or
phase; *also* : an instance or product of this
throw up *vb*   **1** : to build hurriedly   **2** : VOMIT
thrum \'thrəm\ *vb* **thrummed; thrum·ming** : to play or
pluck a stringed instrument idly : STRUM
thrush \'thrəsh\ *n* : any of numerous small or medium=
sized songbirds that are mostly of a plain color often with
spotted underparts
¹thrust \'thrəst\ *vb* **thrust; thrust·ing**   **1** : to push or drive
with force : SHOVE   **2** : STAB, PIERCE   **3** : INTERJECT   **4**
: to press the acceptance of upon someone
²thrust *n*   **1** : a lunge with a pointed weapon   **2** : ATTACK
3 : the pressure of one part of a construction against another (as of an arch against an abutment)   **4** : the force
produced by a propeller or jet or rocket engine that
drives a vehicle (as an aircraft) forward   **5** : a violent
push : SHOVE   **6** : prominent or essential element
thrust·er *also* **thrust·or** \'thrəs-tər\ *n* : one that thrusts; *esp*
: a rocket engine
thru·way \'thrü-,wā\ *n* : EXPRESSWAY
¹thud \'thəd\ *n*   **1** : ⁴BLOW   **2** : a dull sound
²thud *vb* **thud·ded; thud·ding** : to move or strike so as to
make a thud
thug \'thəg\ *n* [Hindi & Urdu *thag*, lit., thief] : a brutal ruffian or assassin — **thug·gish** *adj*
thu·li·um \'thü-lē-əm, 'thyü-\ *n* : a rare metallic chemical
element
¹thumb \'thəm\ *n*   **1** : the short thick first digit of the
human hand or a corresponding digit of a lower animal
2 : the part of a glove or mitten that covers the thumb
²thumb *vb*   **1** : to leaf through (pages) with the thumb   **2**
: to wear or soil with the thumb by frequent handling   **3**
: to request or obtain (a ride) in a passing automobile by
signaling with the thumb
¹thumb·nail \'thəm-,nāl\ *n* : the nail of the thumb
²thumbnail *adj* : BRIEF, CONCISE ⟨a ~ description⟩ ⟨a ~
picture⟩
thumb·print \-,print\ *n* : an impression made by the thumb
thumb·screw \-,skrü\ *n*   **1** : a device of torture for squeezing the thumb   **2** : a screw with a head that may be
turned by the thumb and forefinger
thumb·tack \-,tak\ *n* : a tack with a broad flat head for
pressing with one's thumb into a board or wall
¹thump \'thəmp\ *vb*   **1** : to strike with or as if with something thick or heavy so as to cause a dull sound   **2**
: POUND
²thump *n*   **1** : a blow with or as if with something blunt or
heavy; *also* : the sound made by such a blow
¹thun·der \'thən-dər\ *n*   **1** : the sound following a flash of
lightning; *also* : a noise like such a sound   **2** : a loud utterance or threat
²thunder *vb*   **1** : to produce thunder   **2** : ROAR, SHOUT
thun·der·bolt \-,bōlt\ *n* : a flash of lightning with its accompanying thunder
thun·der·clap \-,klap\ *n* : a crash of thunder
thun·der·cloud \-,klaud\ *n* : a cloud charged with electricity and producing lightning and thunder

thun·der·head \-ˌhed\ *n* : a large cumulus or cumulonimbus cloud often appearing before a thunderstorm

thun·der·ous \'thən-də-rəs\ *adj* : producing thunder; *also* : making a noise like thunder — **thun·der·ous·ly** *adv*

thun·der·show·er \'thən-dər-ˌshaů-(ə)r\ *n* : a shower accompanied by thunder and lightning

thun·der·storm \-ˌstȯrm\ *n* : a storm accompanied by thunder and lightning

thun·der·struck \-ˌstrək\ *adj* : stunned as if struck by a thunderbolt

Thurs *or* **Thu** *abbr* Thursday

Thurs·day \'thərz-ˌdā, -dē\ *n* [ME, fr. OE *thursdæg*, fr. ON *thōrsdagr*, lit., day of Thor (Norse god)] : the 5th day of the week

thus \'thəs\ *adv* **1** : in this or that manner **2** : to this degree or extent : SO **3** : because of this or that : HENCE

¹thwack \'thwak\ *vb* : to strike with or as if with something flat or heavy

²thwack *n* : a heavy blow : WHACK

¹thwart \'thwȯrt\ *vb* **1** : FOIL, BAFFLE **2** : BLOCK, DEFEAT
✦ **Synonyms** BALK, OUTWIT, FRUSTRATE

²thwart \'thwȯrt, *naut often* 'thȯrt\ *adv* : ATHWART

³thwart *adj* : situated or placed across something else

⁴thwart *n* : a seat extending across a boat

thy \'thī\ *adj, archaic* : of, relating to, or done by or to thee or thyself

thyme \'tīm, 'thīm\ *n* [ME, fr. AF *time*, fr. L *thymum*, fr. Gk *thymon*, prob. fr. *thyein* to make a burnt offering, sacrifice] : a garden mint with small aromatic leaves used esp. in seasoning; *also* : its leaves so used

thy·mine \'thī-ˌmēn\ *n* : a pyrimidine base that is one of the four bases coding genetic information in the molecular chain of DNA

thy·mus \'thī-məs\ *n, pl* **thy·mus·es** : a glandular organ of the neck region that is composed largely of lymphoid tissue, functions esp. in the development of the immune system, and tends to atrophy in the adult

thy·ris·tor \thī-'ris-tər\ *n* : a semiconductor device that acts as a switch, rectifier, or voltage regulator

thy·roid \'thī-ˌrȯid\ *adj* [NL *thyroides*, fr. Gk *thyreoeidēs* shield-shaped, thyroid, fr. *thyreos* shield shaped like a door, fr. *thyra* door] : a large 2-lobed endocrine gland that lies at the base of the neck and produces several iodine-containing hormones that affect growth, development, and metabolism — **thyroid** *also* **thy·roi·dal** \thī-'rȯi-dᵊl\ *adj*

thy·rox·ine *or* **thy·rox·in** \thī-'räk-ˌsēn, -sən\ *n* : an iodine-containing hormone that is produced by the thyroid gland, increases metabolic rate, and is used to treat thyroid disorders

thy·self \thī-'self\ *pron, archaic* : YOURSELF

Ti *symbol* titanium

ti·ara \tē-'er-ə, -'är-\ *n* **1** : a 3-tiered crown worn by the pope **2** : a decorative headband or semicircle for formal wear by women

Ti·bet·an \tə-'bet-ᵊn\ *n* **1** : the language of the Tibetan people **2** : a native or inhabitant of Tibet — **Tibetan** *adj*

tib·ia \'ti-bē-ə\ *n, pl* **-i·ae** \-bē-ˌē\ *also* **-i·as** [L] : the inner of the two bones of the vertebrate hind or lower limb between the knee and the ankle

tic \'tik\ *n* : a local and habitual twitching of muscles esp. of the face

ti·cal \ti-'käl, 'ti-kəl\ *n, pl* **ticals** *or* **tical** : BAHT

¹tick \'tik\ *n* : any of a large group of small bloodsucking arachnids

²tick *n* : the fabric case of a mattress or pillow; *also* : a mattress consisting of a tick and its filling

³tick *n* **1** : a light rhythmic audible tap or beat **2** : a small mark used to draw attention to or check something

⁴tick *vb* **1** : to make the sound of a tick or series of ticks **2** : to mark, count, or announce by or as if by ticking beats **3** : to mark or check with a tick **4** : to function as an operating mechanism : RUN

⁵tick *n, chiefly Brit* : CREDIT; *also* : a credit account

tick·er \'ti-kər\ *n* **1** : something (as a watch) that ticks **2** : a telegraph instrument that prints information (as stock prices) on paper tape **3** *slang* : HEART

ticker tape *n* : the paper ribbon on which a telegraphic ticker prints

¹tick·et \'ti-kət\ *n* [MF *etiquet, estiquette* notice attached to something, fr. MF dial. *estiquier* to attach, fr. MD *steken* to stick] **1** : CERTIFICATE, LICENSE, PERMIT; *esp* : a certificate or token showing that a fare or admission fee has been paid **2** : TAG, LABEL **3** : SLATE **4** : a summons issued to a traffic offender

²ticket *vb* **1** : to attach a ticket to **2** : to furnish or serve with a ticket

tick·ing \'ti-kiŋ\ *n* : a strong fabric used in upholstering and as a mattress covering

tick·le \'ti-kəl\ *vb* **tick·led; tick·ling** **1** : to excite or stir up agreeably : PLEASE, AMUSE **2** : to have a tingling sensation **3** : to touch (as a body part) lightly so as to cause uneasiness, laughter, or spasmodic movements — **tickle** *n* — **tick·ler** *n*

tick·lish \-kə-lish\ *adj* **1** : OVERSENSITIVE, TOUCHY **2** : UNSTABLE ⟨a ∼ foothold⟩ **3** : requiring delicate handling ⟨∼ subject⟩ **4** : sensitive to tickling — **tick·lish·ly** *adv* — **tick·lish·ness** *n*

tidal wave *n* **1** : an unusually high sea wave that sometimes follows an earthquake **2** : an unusual rise of water alongshore due to strong winds

tid·bit \'tid-ˌbit\ *n* : a choice morsel

¹tide \'tīd\ *n* [ME, time, fr. OE *tīd*] **1** : the alternate rising and falling of the surface of the ocean **2** : something that fluctuates like the tides of the sea — **tid·al** \'tī-dᵊl\ *adj*

²tide *vb* **tid·ed; tid·ing** : to carry through or help along as if by the tide ⟨a loan to ∼ us over⟩

tide·land \'tīd-ˌland, -lənd\ *n* **1** : land overflowed during flood tide **2** : land under the ocean within a nation's territorial waters — often used in pl.

tide·wa·ter \-ˌwȯ-tər, -ˌwä-\ *n* **1** : water overflowing land at flood tide **2** : low-lying coastal land

tid·ings \'tī-diŋz\ *n pl* : NEWS, MESSAGE

¹ti·dy \'tī-dē\ *adj* **ti·di·er; -est** **1** : well ordered and cared for : NEAT **2** : LARGE, SUBSTANTIAL ⟨a ∼ sum⟩ — **ti·di·ness** \'tī-dē-nəs\ *n*

²tidy *vb* **ti·died; ti·dy·ing** **1** : to put in order **2** : to make things tidy

³tidy *n, pl* **tidies** : a decorated covering used to protect the back or arms of a chair from wear or soil

¹tie \'tī\ *n* **1** : a line, ribbon, or cord used for fastening, uniting, or closing **2** : a structural element (as a beam or rod) holding two pieces together **3** : one of the cross supports to which railroad rails are fastened **4** : a connecting link : BOND ⟨family ∼s⟩ **5** : an equality in number (as of votes or scores); *also* : an undecided or deadlocked contest **6** : NECKTIE

²tie *vb* **tied; ty·ing** *or* **tie·ing** **1** : to fasten, attach, or close by means of a tie **2** : to bring together firmly : UNITE **3** : to form a knot or bow in ⟨∼ a scarf⟩ **4** : to restrain from freedom of action : CONSTRAIN **5** : to make or have an equal score with

tie·back \'tī-ˌbak\ *n* : a decorative strip for draping a curtain to the side of a window

tie–dye·ing \'tī-ˌdī-iŋ\ *n* : a method of producing patterns in textiles by tying parts of the fabric so that they will not absorb the dye — **tie–dyed** \-ˌdīd\ *adj*

tie–in \'tī-ˌin\ *n* : CONNECTION

tier \'tir\ *n* : ROW, LAYER; *esp* : one of two or more rows arranged one above another — **tiered** \'tird\ *adj*

tie–rod \'tī-ˌräd\ *n* : a rod used as a connecting member or brace

tie–up \-ˌəp\ *n* **1** : a slowing or stopping of traffic or business **2** : CONNECTION

tiff \'tif\ *n* : a petty quarrel — **tiff** *vb*

Tif·fa·ny \'ti-fə-nē\ *adj* : made of pieces of stained glass ⟨a ∼ lamp⟩

ti·ger \'tī-gər\ *n* : a very large tawny black-striped Asian cat — **ti·ger·ish** *adj*

tiger

¹**tight** \'tīt\ *adj* **1** : so close in structure as to prevent passage of a liquid or gas **2** : strongly fixed or held : SECURE **3** : TAUT **4** : fitting usu. too closely ⟨∼ shoes⟩ **5** : set close together : COMPACT ⟨a ∼ formation⟩ **6** : DIFFICULT, TRYING ⟨get in a ∼ spot⟩ **7** : STINGY, MISERLY **8** : evenly contested : CLOSE **9** : INTOXICATED **10** : low in supply : hard to get ⟨money is ∼⟩ — **tight·ly** *adv* — **tight·ness** *n*

²**tight** *adv* **1** : TIGHTLY, FIRMLY **2** : SOUNDLY ⟨sleep ∼⟩

tight·en \'tī-t³n\ *vb* : to make or become tight

tight·fist·ed \'tīt-'fis-təd\ *adj* : STINGY

tight·rope \-,rōp\ *n* : a taut rope or wire for acrobats to perform on

tights \'tīts\ *n pl* : skintight garments covering the body esp. below the waist; *also, Brit* : PANTY HOSE

tight·wad \'tīt-,wäd\ *n* : a stingy person

ti·gress \'tī-grəs\ *n* : a female tiger

ti·la·pia \tə-'lä-pē-ə, -'lā-\ *n, pl* **tilapia** *also* **ti·la·pi·as** : any of numerous chiefly African freshwater fishes widely raised for food

til·de \'til-də\ *n* [Sp, fr. ML *titulus* tittle] : a mark ˜ placed esp. over the letter *n* (as in Spanish *señor* sir) to denote the sound \n˄\ or over vowels (as in Portuguese *irmã* sister) to indicate nasal quality

¹**tile** \'tī(-ə)l\ *n* **1** : a flat or curved piece of fired clay, stone, or concrete used for roofs, floors, or walls; *also* : a pipe of earthenware or concrete used for a drain **2** : a thin piece (as of linoleum) used for covering walls or floors — **til·ing** \'tī-liŋ\ *n*

²**tile** *vb* **tiled; til·ing** : to cover with tiles — **til·er** *n*

¹**till** \'til\ *prep or conj* : UNTIL

²**till** *vb* : to work by plowing, sowing, and raising crops : CULTIVATE — **till·able** *adj*

³**till** *n* : DRAWER; *esp* : a money drawer in a store or bank

till·age \'ti-lij\ *n* **1** : the work of tilling land **2** : cultivated land

¹**til·ler** \'ti-lər\ *n* [OE *telgor, telgra* twig, shoot] : a sprout or stalk esp. from the base or lower part of a plant

²**til·ler** \'ti-lər\ *n* : one that tills

³**til·ler** \'ti-lər\ *n* [ME *tiler* stock of a crossbow, tiller, fr. AF *teiler* stock of a crossbow] : a lever used for turning a boat's rudder from side to side

¹**tilt** \'tilt\ *n* **1** : a contest in which two combatants charging usu. with lances try to unhorse each other : JOUST; *also* : a tournament of tilts **2** : a verbal contest : DISPUTE **3** : a sloping surface : SLANT

²**tilt** *vb* **1** : to move or shift so as to incline : TIP **2** : to engage in or as if in combat with lances : JOUST, ATTACK

tilth \'tilth\ *n* **1** : TILLAGE 2 **2** : the state of a soil esp. in relation to the suitability of its particle size and structure for growing crops

Tim *abbr* Timothy

tim·ber \'tim-bər\ *n* [ME, fr. OE, building, wood] **1** : growing trees or their wood — often used interjectionally to warn of a falling tree **2** : wood for use in making something **3** : a usu. large squared or dressed piece of wood

tim·bered \'tim-bərd\ *adj* : having walls framed by exposed timbers

tim·ber·land \'tim-bər-,land\ *n* : wooded land

tim·ber·line \'tim-bər-,līn\ *n* : the upper limit of tree growth in mountains or high latitudes

timber rattlesnake *n* : a widely distributed rattlesnake of the eastern U.S.

timber wolf *n* : GRAY WOLF

tim·bre *also* **tim·ber** \'tam-bər, 'tim-\ *n* [F, fr. MF, bell struck by a hammer, fr. OF, drum, fr. MGk *tymbanon* kettledrum, fr. Gk *tympanon*] : the distinctive quality given to a sound by its overtones

tim·brel \'tim-brəl\ *n* : a small hand drum or tambourine

¹**time** \'tīm\ *n* **1** : a period during which an action, process, or condition exists or continues ⟨gone a long ∼⟩ **2** : LEISURE ⟨found ∼ to read⟩ **3** : a point or period when something occurs : OCCASION ⟨the last ∼ we met⟩ **4** : a set or customary moment or hour for something to occur ⟨arrived on ∼⟩ **5** : AGE, ERA **6** : state of affairs : CONDITIONS ⟨hard ∼s⟩ **7** : a rate of speed : TEMPO **8** : a moment, hour, day, or year as indicated by a clock or calendar ⟨what ∼ is it⟩ **9** : a system of reckoning time ⟨solar ∼⟩ **10** : one of a series of recurring instances; *also, pl* : added or accumulated quantities or examples

⟨five ∼s greater⟩ **11** : a person's experience during a particular period ⟨had a good ∼⟩ **12** : the hours or days of one's work; *also* : an hourly pay rate ⟨straight ∼⟩ **13** : TIME-OUT 1

²**time** *vb* **timed; tim·ing** **1** : to arrange or set the time of : SCHEDULE ⟨∼s his calls conveniently⟩ **2** : to set the tempo or duration of ⟨∼ a performance⟩ **3** : to cause to keep time with **4** : to determine or record the time, duration, or rate of ⟨∼ a sprinter⟩ — **tim·er** *n*

time bomb *n* **1** : a bomb so made as to explode at a predetermined time **2** : something with a potentially dangerous delayed reaction

time clock *n* : a clock that records the time workers arrive and depart

time frame *n* : a period of time esp. with respect to some action or project

time–hon·ored \'tīm-,ä-nərd\ *adj* : honored because of age or long usage

time·keep·er \-,kē-pər\ *n* **1** : a clerk who keeps records of the time worked by employees **2** : one appointed to mark and announce the time in an athletic game or contest

time·less \-ləs\ *adj* **1** : ETERNAL **2** : not limited or affected by time ⟨∼ works of art⟩ — **time·less·ly** *adv* — **time·less·ness** *n*

time·ly \-lē\ *adj* **time·li·er; -est** **1** : coming early or at the right time ⟨a ∼ decision⟩ ∼ payment⟩ **2** : appropriate to the time ⟨a ∼ book⟩ — **time·li·ness** *n*

time–out \'tīm-'aút\ *n* **1** : a brief suspension of activity esp. in an athletic game **2** : a quiet period used esp. as a disciplinary measure for a child

time·piece \-,pēs\ *n* : a device (as a clock) to show the passage of time

times \'tīmz\ *prep* : multiplied by ⟨2 ∼ 2 is 4⟩

time–shar·ing \'tīm-,sher-iŋ\ *n* **1** : simultaneous use of a computer by many users **2** *or* **time–share** \-,sher\ : joint ownership or rental of a vacation lodging by several persons with each taking turns using the place

times sign *n* : the symbol × used to indicate multiplication

time·ta·ble \'tīm-,tā-bəl\ *n* **1** : a table of the departure and arrival times (as of trains) **2** : a schedule showing a planned order or sequence

time warp *n* : an anomaly, discontinuity, or suspension held to occur in the progress of time

time·worn \-,wȯrn\ *adj* **1** : worn by time **2** : HACKNEYED, STALE ⟨a ∼ joke⟩

tim·id \'ti-məd\ *adj* : lacking in courage or self-confidence : FEARFUL — **ti·mid·i·ty** \tə-'mi-də-tē\ *n* — **tim·id·ly** *adv*

tim·o·rous \'ti-mə-rəs\ *adj* : of a timid disposition : AFRAID — **tim·o·rous·ly** *adv* — **tim·o·rous·ness** *n*

tim·o·thy \'ti-mə-thē\ *n* : a perennial grass with long cylindrical spikes widely grown for hay in the U.S.

Tim·o·thy \'ti-mə-thē\ *n* — see BIBLE table

tim·pa·ni \'tim-pə-nē\ *n sing or pl* [It] : a set of kettledrums played by one performer in an orchestra — **tim·pa·nist** \-nist\ *n*

¹**tin** \'tin\ *n* **1** : a soft white metallic chemical element malleable at ordinary temperatures that is used esp. in solders and alloys **2** : a container (as a can) made of metal (as tinplate)

²**tin** *vb* **tinned; tin·ning** **1** : to cover or plate with tin **2** : to pack in tins

TIN *abbr* taxpayer identification number

tinct \'tiŋkt\ *n* : TINCTURE, TINGE

¹**tinc·ture** \'tiŋk-chər\ *n* **1** *archaic* : a substance that colors **2** : a slight admixture : TRACE **3** : an alcoholic solution of a medicinal substance ✦ *Synonyms* TOUCH, SUGGESTION, SUSPICION, TINGE

²**tincture** *vb* **tinc·tured; tinc·tur·ing** **1** : COLOR, TINGE **2** : AFFECT

tin·der \'tin-dər\ *n* **1** : a very flammable substance used as kindling **2** : something serving to incite or inflame

tin·der·box \'tin-dər-,bäks\ *n* **1** : a metal box for holding tinder and usu. flint and steel for striking a spark **2** : a highly flammable object or place

tine \'tīn\ *n* : a slender pointed part (as of a fork or an antler) : PRONG

tin·foil \'tin-,fȯi(-ə)l\ *n* : a thin metal sheeting usu. of aluminum or tin–lead alloy

¹**tinge** \'tinj\ *vb* **tinged; tinge·ing** *or* **ting·ing** **1** : to color

slightly : TINT **2** : to affect or modify esp. with a slight odor or taste

²**tinge** *n* : a slight coloring, flavor, or quality : TRACE ✦ *Synonyms* TOUCH, SUGGESTION, SUSPICION, TINCTURE, SOUPÇON

tin·gle \'tiŋ-gəl\ *vb* **tin·gled; tin·gling 1** : to feel a prickling or thrilling sensation **2** : TINKLE — **tingle** *n*

¹**tin·ker** \'tiŋ-kər\ *n* **1** : a usu. itinerant mender of household utensils **2** : an unskillful mender : BUNGLER

²**tinker** *vb* : to repair or adjust something in an unskillful or experimental manner — **tin·ker·er** *n*

¹**tin·kle** \'tiŋ-kəl\ *vb* **tin·kled; tin·kling** : to make or cause to make a tinkle

²**tinkle** *n* : a series of short high ringing or clinking sounds

tin·ni·tus \'ti-nə-təs, tə-'nī-təs\ *n* : a sensation of noise (as ringing or roaring) in the ears

tin·ny \'ti-nē\ *adj* **tin·ni·er; -est 1** : abounding in or yielding tin **2** : resembling tin; *also* : LIGHT, CHEAP **3** : thin in tone ⟨a ∼ voice⟩ — **tin·ni·ly** \-nə-lē\ *adv* — **tin·ni·ness** \-nē-nəs\ *n*

tin·plate \'tin-'plāt\ *n* : thin sheet iron or steel coated with tin — **tin–plate** *vb*

tin·sel \'tin-səl\ *n* [ME *tyneseyle* cloth interwoven with metallic thread, prob. fr. AF *tencelé*, pp. of *tenceler, estenceler* to sparkle] **1** : threads, strips, or sheets of metal, paper, or plastic used to produce a glittering appearance **2** : something superficially attractive but of little worth

tin·smith \'tin-ˌsmith\ *n* : one that works with sheet metal (as tinplate)

¹**tint** \'tint\ *n* **1** : a slight or pale coloration : HUE **2** : any of various shades of a color

²**tint** *vb* : to impart a tint to : COLOR

tin·tin·nab·u·la·tion \ˌtin-tə-ˌna-byə-'lā-shən\ *n* **1** : the ringing of bells **2** : a tingling sound as if of bells

tin·ware \'tin-ˌwer\ *n* : articles and esp. utensils made of tinplate

ti·ny \'tī-nē\ *adj* **ti·ni·er; -est** : very small : MINUTE ✦ *Synonyms* MINIATURE, DIMINUTIVE, WEE, LILLIPUTIAN

¹**tip** \'tip\ *vb* **tipped; tip·ping 1** : OVERTURN, UPSET **2** : LEAN, SLANT; *also* : to raise and tilt forward ⟨*tipped* his hat⟩

²**tip** *n* : the act or an instance of tipping

³**tip** *vb* **tipped; tip·ping 1** : to furnish with a tip **2** : to cover or adorn the tip of

⁴**tip** *n* **1** : the usu. pointed end of something **2** : a small piece or part serving as an end, cap, or point

⁵**tip** *n* : a light touch or blow

⁶**tip** *vb* **tipped; tip·ping** : to strike lightly : TAP

⁷**tip** *n* : a piece of advice or expert or confidential information : HINT

⁸**tip** *vb* **tipped; tip·ping** : to impart a piece of information about or to

⁹**tip** *vb* **tipped; tip·ping** : to give a gratuity to — **tip·per** *n*

¹⁰**tip** *n* : a gift or small sum given for a service performed or anticipated

tip–off \'tip-ˌof\ *n* : WARNING, TIP

tip·pet \'ti-pət\ *n* : a long scarf or shoulder cape

tip·ple \'ti-pəl\ *vb* **tip·pled; tip·pling** : to drink intoxicating liquor esp. habitually or excessively — **tipple** *n* — **tip·pler** *n*

tip·ster \'tip-stər\ *n* : a person who gives or sells tips esp. for gambling

tip·sy \'tip-sē\ *adj* **tip·si·er; -est** : unsteady or foolish from the effects of alcohol — **tip·si·ly** \-sə-lē\ *adv* — **tip·si·ness** \-sē-nəs\ *n*

¹**tip·toe** \'tip-ˌtō\ *n* : the position of being balanced on the balls of the feet and toes with the heels raised; *also* : the ends of the toes

²**tiptoe** *adv or adj* : on or as if on tiptoe

³**tiptoe** *vb* **tip·toed; tip·toe·ing** : to walk or proceed on or as if on tiptoe ⟨∼ around the issue⟩

¹**tip–top** \'tip-'täp\ *n* : the highest point

²**tip–top** *adj* : EXCELLENT, FIRST-RATE

ti·rade \'tī-ˌrād\ *n* [F, shot, tirade, fr. MF, fr. It *tirata*, fr. *tirare* to draw, shoot] : a prolonged speech of abuse or condemnation

tir·a·mi·su \ˌtir-ə-'mē-sü, -mē-'sü\ *n* [It *tiramisù*] : a dessert made with ladyfingers, mascarpone, and espresso

¹**tire** \'tī(-ə)r\ *vb* **tired; tir·ing 1** : to make or become weary : FATIGUE **2** : to wear out the patience of : BORE

²**tire** *n* **1** : a metal hoop that forms the tread of a wheel **2**

: a rubber cushion usu. containing compressed air that encircles a wheel (as of a bike)

tired *adj* **1** : WEARY, FATIGUED **2** : HACKNEYED — **tired·ness** *n*

tire·less \'tī(-ə)r-ləs\ *adj* : not tiring : UNTIRING, INDEFATIGABLE — **tire·less·ly** *adv* — **tire·less·ness** *n*

tire·some \-səm\ *adj* : tending to bore : WEARISOME, TEDIOUS — **tire·some·ly** *adv* — **tire·some·ness** *n*

ti·ro *chiefly Brit var of* TYRO

tis·sue \'ti-shü\ *n* [ME *tysshewe, tyssew*, a rich fabric, fr. AF, fr. *tistre* to weave, fr. L *texere*] **1** : a fine lightweight often sheer fabric **2** : NETWORK, WEB ⟨a ∼ of lies⟩ **3** : a soft absorbent paper **4** : a mass or layer of cells forming a basic structural material of an animal or plant

¹**tit** \'tit\ *n* : TEAT

²**tit** *n* : any of various small plump Old World songbirds related to the titmice

Tit *abbr* Titus

ti·tan \'tī-t⁽ə⁾n\ *n* **1** *cap* : one of a family of giants overthrown by the gods in Greek mythology **2** : one gigantic in size or power

ti·tan·ic \tī-'ta-nik\ *adj* : enormous in size, force, or power ✦ *Synonyms* IMMENSE, GIGANTIC, GIANT, COLOSSAL, MAMMOTH

ti·ta·ni·um \tī-'tā-nē-əm\ *n* : a gray light strong metallic chemical element used esp. in alloys

titbit *var of* TIDBIT

tithe \'tīth\ *n* [ME, fr. OE *teogotha* tenth] : a 10th part paid or given esp. for the support of a church — **tithe** *vb* — **tith·er** *n*

tit·il·late \'ti-t⁽ə⁾l-ˌāt\ *vb* **-lat·ed; -lat·ing 1** : to excite pleasurably **2** : TICKLE **3** — **tit·il·la·tion** \ˌti-t⁽ə⁾l-'ā-shən\ *n*

tit·i·vate *or* **tit·ti·vate** \'ti-tə-ˌvāt\ *vb* **-vat·ed; -vat·ing** : to dress up : spruce up — **tit·i·va·tion** \ˌti-tə-'vā-shən\ *n*

ti·tle \'tī-t⁽ə⁾l\ *n* **1** : CLAIM, RIGHT; *esp* : a legal right to the ownership of property **2** : the distinguishing name of a written, filmed, or musical production or a work of art **3** : an appellation of honor, rank, or office **4** : CHAMPIONSHIP ✦ *Synonyms* DESIGNATION, DENOMINATION, APPELLATION

ti·tled \'tī-t⁽ə⁾ld\ *adj* : having a title esp. of nobility

title page *n* : a page of a book bearing the title and usu. the names of the author and publisher

tit·mouse \'tit-ˌmaůs\ *n, pl* **tit·mice** \-ˌmīs\ : any of several small long-tailed No. American songbirds related to the chickadees

ti·tra·tion \tī-'trā-shən\ *n* : a process of finding the concentration of a solution (as of an acid) by adding small portions of a second solution of known concentration (as of a base) to a fixed amount of the first until an expected change (as in color) occurs

tit·ter \'ti-tər\ *vb* : to laugh in an affected or in a nervous or half-suppressed manner : GIGGLE — **titter** *n*

tit·tle \'ti-t⁽ə⁾l\ *n* : a tiny part

tit·tle–tat·tle \'ti-t⁽ə⁾l-ˌta-t⁽ə⁾l\ *n* : idle talk : GOSSIP — **tittle–tattle** *vb*

tit·u·lar \'ti-chə-lər\ *adj* **1** : existing in title only : NOMINAL ⟨∼ ruler⟩ **2** : of, relating to, or bearing a title ⟨∼ role⟩

Ti·tus \'tī-təs\ *n* — see BIBLE table

tiz·zy \'ti-zē\ *n, pl* **tizzies** : a highly excited and distracted state of mind

tk *abbr* **1** tank **2** truck

TKO \ˌtē-ˌkā-'ō\ *n* [*technical k*nockout] : the termination of a boxing match when a boxer is declared unable to continue the fight

tkt *abbr* ticket

Tl *symbol* thallium

TLC *abbr* tender loving care

T lymphocyte *n* : T CELL

Tm *symbol* thulium

TM *abbr* trademark

T–man \'tē-ˌman\ *n* : a special agent of the U.S. Treasury Department

tn *abbr* **1** ton **2** town

TN *abbr* Tennessee

tng *abbr* training

tnpk *abbr* turnpike

TNT \ˌtē-(ˌ)en-'tē\ *n* : a flammable toxic compound used as a high explosive and in chemical synthesis

¹**to** \tə, 'tü\ *prep* **1** : in the direction of and reaching ⟨drove

~ town〉 2 : in the direction of : TOWARD 3 : ON, AGAINST 〈apply salve ~ a burn〉 4 : as far as 〈can pay up ~ a dollar〉 5 : so as to become or bring about 〈beaten ~ death〉 〈broken ~ pieces〉 6 : BEFORE 〈it's five minutes ~ six〉 7 : UNTIL 〈from May ~ December〉 8 : fitting or being a part of : FOR 〈key ~ the lock〉 9 : with the accompaniment of 〈sing ~ the music〉 10 : in relation or comparison with 〈similar ~ that one〉 〈won 10 ~ 6〉 11 : in accordance with 〈add salt ~ taste〉 12 : within the range of 〈~ my knowledge〉 13 : contained, occurring, or included in 〈two pints ~ a quart〉 14 : as regards 〈agreeable ~ everyone〉 15 : affecting as the receiver or beneficiary 〈whispered ~ her〉 〈gave it ~ me〉 16 : for no one except 〈a room ~ myself〉 17 : into the action of 〈we got ~ talking〉 18 — used for marking the following verb as an infinitive 〈wants ~ go〉 and often used by itself at the end of a clause in place of an infinitive suggested by the preceding context 〈goes to town whenever he wants ~〉 〈can leave if you'd like ~〉
²to \'tü\ adv 1 : in a direction toward 〈run ~ and fro〉 2 : into contact esp. with the frame of a door 〈the door slammed ~〉 3 : to the matter in hand 〈fell ~ and ate heartily〉 4 : to a state of consciousness or awareness 〈came ~ hours after the accident〉
TO abbr turn over
toad \'tōd\ n : any of numerous tailless leaping amphibians differing typically from the related frogs in having a shorter stockier build, rough dry warty skin, and less aquatic habits
toad·stool \-ˌstül\ n : MUSHROOM; esp : one that is poisonous or inedible
toady \'tō-dē\ n, pl toad·ies : a person who flatters in the hope of gaining favors : SYCOPHANT — toady vb
to–and–fro \ˌtü-ən-'frō\ adj : forward and backward — to–and–fro n
¹toast \'tōst\ vb 1 : to warm thoroughly 2 : to make (as bread) crisp, hot, and brown by heat 3 : to become toasted
²toast n 1 : sliced toasted bread 2 : someone or something in whose honor persons drink 3 : an act of drinking in honor of a toast
³toast vb : to propose or drink to as a toast
toast·er \'tōs-stər\ n : an electrical appliance for toasting
toaster oven n : a portable electrical appliance that bakes, broils, and toasts
toast·mas·ter \'tōst-ˌmas-tər\ n : a person who presides at a banquet and introduces the after-dinner speakers
toast·mis·tress \-ˌmis-trəs\ n : a woman who acts as toastmaster
toasty \'tō-stē\ adj toast·i·er; -est : pleasantly warm
Tob abbr Tobit
to·bac·co \tə-'ba-kō\ n, pl -cos [Sp tabaco] 1 : a tall broad-leaved herb related to the potato; also : its leaves prepared for smoking or chewing or as snuff 2 : manufactured tobacco products; also : smoking as a practice
to·bac·co·nist \tə-'ba-kə-nist\ n : a dealer in tobacco
To·bi·as \tō-'bī-əs\ n : TOBIT
To·bit \'tō-bət\ n — see BIBLE table
¹to·bog·gan \tə-'bä-gən\ n : a long flat-bottomed light sled made of thin boards curved up at one end

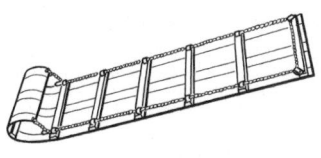

toboggan

²toboggan vb 1 : to coast on or as if on a toboggan 2 : to decline suddenly (as in value) — to·bog·gan·er n
toc·sin \'täk-sən\ n 1 : an alarm bell 2 : a warning signal
¹to·day \tə-'dā\ adv 1 : on or for this day 2 : at the present time
²today n : the present day, time, or age

tod·dle \'täd-ᵊl\ vb tod·dled; tod·dling : to walk with short tottering steps in the manner of a young child — toddle n — tod·dler n
tod·dy \'tä-dē\ n, pl toddies [Hindi & Urdu tāṛī juice of a palm, fr. tāṛ a palm, fr. Skt tāla] : a drink made of liquor, sugar, spices, and hot water
to–do \tə-'dü\ n, pl to–dos \-'düz\ : BUSTLE, STIR, FUSS
¹toe \'tō\ n 1 : one of the jointed parts of the front end of the vertebrate foot 2 : the front part of a foot or hoof
²toe vb toed; toe·ing : to touch, reach, or drive with the toes
toea \'tȯi-ə\ n — see kina at MONEY table
toe·hold \'tō-ˌhōld\ n 1 : a place of support for the toes 2 : a slight footing
toe·nail \'tō-ˌnāl\ n : a nail of a toe
tof·fee or tof·fy \'tȯ-fē, 'tȯ-\ n, pl toffees or toffies : candy of brittle but tender texture made by boiling sugar and butter together
to·fu \'tō-(ˌ)fü\ n [Jp tōfu] : a soft white food product made from soybeans
tog \'täg, 'tȯg\ vb togged; tog·ging : to put togs on : DRESS
to·ga \'tō-gə\ n : the loose outer garment worn in public by citizens of ancient Rome — to·gaed \-gəd\ adj
¹to·geth·er \tə-'ge-thər\ adv 1 : in or into one place or group 2 : in or into contact or association 〈mix ~〉 3 : at one time : SIMULTANEOUSLY 〈talk and work ~〉 4 : in succession 〈for days ~〉 5 : in or into harmony or coherence 〈get ~ on a plan〉 6 : as a group : JOINTLY — to·geth·er·ness n
²together adj : composed in mind or manner
together with prep : in addition to : in association with
tog·gery \'tä-gə-rē, 'tȯ-\ n : CLOTHING
tog·gle \'tä-gəl\ vb : to switch between two options esp. of an electronic device
toggle switch n : an electric switch operated by pushing a projecting lever through a small arc
togs \'tägz, 'tȯgz\ n pl : CLOTHING; esp : clothes for a specified use 〈riding ~〉
¹toil \'tȯi(-ə)l\ n 1 : laborious effort 2 : long fatiguing labor : DRUDGERY — toil·ful \-fəl\ adj — toil·some adj
²toil vb [ME, to argue, struggle, fr. AF toiller to make dirty, fight, wrangle, fr. L tudiculare to crush, grind, fr. tudicula machine for crushing olives, dim. of tudes hammer] 1 : to work hard and long 2 : to proceed with great effort : PLOD — toil·er n
³toil n [ME toile cloth, net, fr. OF teile, fr. L tela cloth on a loom] : NET, TRAP — usu. used in pl. 〈caught in the ~s of the law〉
toi·let \'tȯi-lət\ n 1 : the act or process of dressing and grooming oneself 2 : BATHROOM 3 : a fixture for use in urinating and defecating; esp : one consisting essentially of a water-flushed bowl and seat — toilet vb
toi·let·ry \'tȯi-lə-trē\ n, pl -ries : an article or preparation used in cleaning or grooming oneself — usu. used in pl.
toi·lette \twä-'let\ n 1 : TOILET 1 2 : formal attire; also : a particular costume
toilet training n : the process of training a child to control bladder and bowel movements and to use the toilet — toilet train vb
toil·worn \'tȯi(-ə)l-ˌwȯrn\ adj : showing the effects of toil
To·kay \tō-'kā\ n : naturally sweet wine from Hungary
toke \'tōk\ n, slang : a puff on a marijuana cigarette or pipe
¹to·ken \'tō-kən\ n 1 : an outward sign 2 : SYMBOL, EMBLEM 3 : SOUVENIR, KEEPSAKE 4 : a small part representing the whole 5 : a piece resembling a coin issued as money or for use by a particular group on specified terms
²token adj 1 : done or given as a token esp. in partial fulfillment of an obligation 2 : representing only a symbolic effort : MINIMAL, PERFUNCTORY
to·ken·ism \'tō-kə-ˌni-zəm\ n : the policy or practice of making only a symbolic effort (as to desegregate)
told past and past part of TELL
tole \'tōl\ n : sheet metal and esp. tinplate for use in domestic and ornamental wares
tol·er·a·ble \'tä-lə-rə-bəl\ adj 1 : capable of being borne or endured 2 : moderately good : PASSABLE — tol·er·a·bly \-blē\ adv
tol·er·ance \'tä-lə-rəns\ n 1 : the act or practice of tolerating; esp : sympathy or indulgence for beliefs or prac-

tices differing from one's own **2** : the allowable deviation from a standard (as of size) **3** : the body's capacity to become less responsive over time to something (as a drug used repeatedly) — **tol·er·ant** *adj* — **tol·er·ant·ly** *adv*
tol·er·ate \'tä-lə-ˌrāt\ *vb* **-at·ed; -at·ing 1** : to exhibit physiological tolerance for (as a drug) **2** : to allow to be or to be done without hindrance ♦ *Synonyms* ABIDE, BEAR, SUFFER, STAND, BROOK — **tol·er·a·tion** \ˌtä-lə-'rā-shən\ *n*
¹**toll** \'tōl\ *n* **1** : a tax paid for a privilege (as for passing over a bridge) **2** : a charge for a service (as for a long-distance telephone call) **3** : the cost in life, health, loss, or suffering
²**toll** *vb* **1** : to cause the slow regular sounding of (a bell) esp. by pulling a rope **2** : to give signal of : SOUND **3** : to sound with slow measured strokes **4** : to announce by tolling
³**toll** *n* : the sound of a tolling bell
toll·booth \'tōl-ˌbüth\ *n* : a booth where tolls are paid
toll·gate \-ˌgāt\ *n* : a point where vehicles stop to pay a toll
toll·house \-ˌhaus\ *n* : a house or booth where tolls are paid
tol·u·ene \'täl-yə-ˌwēn\ *n* : a liquid hydrocarbon used esp. as a solvent
tom \'täm\ *n* : the male of various animals (as a cat or turkey)
¹**tom·a·hawk** \'tä-mə-ˌhòk\ *n* : a light ax used as a missile and as a hand weapon esp. by No. American Indians
²**tomahawk** *vb* : to strike or kill with a tomahawk
to·ma·til·lo \ˌtō-mə-'tē-(ˌ)yō\ *n, pl* **-los** : a small round usu. pale green edible fruit of a Mexican herb related to the tomato; *also* : this herb
to·ma·to \tə-'mā-tō, -'mä-\ *n, pl* **-toes** [alter. of earlier *tomate*, fr. Sp, fr. Nahuatl *tomatl*] : a usu. large, rounded, and red or yellow pulpy edible berry of a widely grown tropical herb related to the potato; *also* : this herb
tomb \'tüm\ *n* **1** : a place of burial : GRAVE **2** : a house, chamber, or vault for the dead — **tomb** *vb*
tom·boy \'täm-ˌbòi\ *n* : a girl who behaves in a manner usu. considered boyish — **tom·boy·ish** *adj*
tomb·stone \'tüm-ˌstōn\ *n* : a stone marking a grave
tom·cat \'täm-ˌkat\ *n* : a male domestic cat
Tom Col·lins \'täm-'kä-lənz\ *n* : a tall iced drink with a base of gin
tome \'tōm\ *n* : BOOK; *esp* : a large or weighty one
tom·fool·ery \täm-'fü-lə-rē\ *n* : playful or foolish behavior
tom·my gun \'tä-mē-ˌgən\ *n* : SUBMACHINE GUN — **tommy–gun** *vb*
to·mog·ra·phy \tō-'mä-grə-fē\ *n* : a method of producing a three-dimensional image of the internal structures of a solid object (as the human body or the earth) — **to·mo·graph·ic** \ˌtō-mə-'gra-fik\ *adj*
to·mor·row \tə-'mär-ō\ *adv* : on or for the day after today — **tomorrow** *n*
tom–tom \'täm-ˌtäm\ *n* : a small-headed drum beaten with the hands
ton \'tən\ *n, pl* **tons** *also* **ton 1** — see WEIGHT table **2** : a unit equal to the volume of a long ton weight of seawater used in reckoning the displacement of ships and equal to 35 cubic feet
to·nal·i·ty \tō-'na-lə-tē\ *n, pl* **-ties** : tonal quality
¹**tone** \'tōn\ *n* [ME, fr. L *tonus* tension, tone, fr. Gk *tonos*, lit., act of stretching; fr. the dependence of the pitch of a musical string on its tension] **1** : vocal or musical sound; *esp* : sound quality **2** : a sound of definite pitch **3** : WHOLE STEP **4** : accent or inflection expressive of an emotion **5** : the pitch of a word often used to express differences of meaning **6** : style or manner of expression **7** : color quality; *also* : SHADE, TINT **8** : the effect in painting of light and shade together with color **9** : healthy and vigorous condition of a living body or bodily part; *also* : the state of partial contraction characteristic of normal muscle **10** : general character, quality, or trend ♦ *Synonyms* ATMOSPHERE, FEELING, MOOD, VEIN — **ton·al** \'tōn-ᵊl\ *adj*
²**tone** *vb* **toned; ton·ing 1** : to give a particular intonation or inflection to **2** : to impart tone to **3** : SOFTEN, MELLOW **4** : to harmonize in color : BLEND
tone·arm *n* : the movable part of a record player that carries the pickup and the needle
toney *var of* TONY

tong \'täŋ, 'tòŋ\ *n* : a Chinese secret society in the U.S.
tongs \'täŋz, 'tòŋz\ *n pl* : a grasping device consisting of two pieces joined at one end by a pivot or hinged like scissors — **tong** *vb*
¹**tongue** \'təŋ\ *n* **1** : a fleshy movable process of the floor of the mouth used in tasting and in taking and swallowing food and in humans as a speech organ **2** : the flesh of a tongue (as of the ox) used as food **3** : the power of communication **4** : LANGUAGE 1 **5** : manner or quality of utterance; *also* : intended meaning **6** : ecstatic usu. unintelligible utterance accompanying religious excitation — usu. used in pl. **7** : something resembling an animal's tongue esp. in being elongated and fastened at one end only — **tongued** \'təŋd\ *adj* — **tongue·less** *adj*
²**tongue** *vb* **tongued; tongu·ing 1** : to touch or lick with the tongue **2** : to articulate notes on a wind instrument
tongue–in–cheek *adj* : characterized by insincerity, irony, or whimsical exaggeration — **tongue in cheek** *adv*
tongue–lash \'təŋ-ˌlash\ *vb* : CHIDE, REPROVE — **tongue–lash·ing** \-iŋ\ *n*
tongue–tied \-ˌtīd\ *adj* : unable or disinclined to speak clearly or freely (as from shyness or a tongue impairment)
tongue twister *n* : an utterance that is difficult to articulate because of a succession of similar consonants
¹**ton·ic** \'tä-nik\ *adj* **1** : of, relating to, or producing a healthy physical or mental condition : INVIGORATING **2** : relating to or based on the 1st tone of a scale — **to·nic·i·ty** \tō-'ni-sə-tē\ *n*
²**tonic** *n* **1** : the 1st degree of a musical scale **2** : something that invigorates, restores, or refreshes
tonic water *n* : a carbonated beverage flavored with a bit of quinine, lemon, and lime
¹**to·night** \tə-'nīt\ *adv* : on this present night or the coming night
²**tonight** *n* : the present or the coming night
ton·nage \'tə-nij\ *n* **1** : a duty on ships based on tons carried **2** : ships in terms of the number of tons registered or carried **3** : total weight in tons shipped, carried, or mined
ton·sil \'tän-səl\ *n* : either of a pair of oval masses of lymphoid tissue that lie one on each side of the throat at the back of the mouth
ton·sil·lec·to·my \ˌtän-sə-'lek-tə-mē\ *n, pl* **-mies** : the surgical removal of the tonsils
ton·sil·li·tis \-'lī-təs\ *n* : inflammation of the tonsils
ton·so·ri·al \tän-'sòr-ē-əl\ *adj* : of or relating to a barber or a barber's work
ton·sure \'tän-chər\ *n* [ME, fr. AF, ML *tonsura*, fr. L, act of shearing, fr. *tonsus*, pp. of *tondēre* to shear] **1** : the rite of admission to the clerical state by the clipping or shaving of the head **2** : the shaven crown or patch worn by clerics (as monks) — **tonsure** *vb*
tony *also* **ton·ey** \'tō-nē\ *adj* **ton·i·er; -est** : marked by an aristocratic manner or style
too \'tü\ *adv* **1** : in addition : ALSO **2** : EXCESSIVELY **3** : to such a degree as to be regrettable **4** : VERY ⟨didn't seem ~ interested⟩
took *past of* TAKE
¹**tool** \'tül\ *n* **1** : a hand instrument that aids in accomplishing a task **2** : the cutting or shaping part in a machine; *also* : a machine for shaping metal in any way **3** : something used in doing a job ⟨a scholar's books are his ~s⟩; *also* : a means to an end **4** : a person used by another : DUPE **5** *pl* : natural ability
²**tool** *vb* **1** : to shape, form, or finish with a tool; *esp* : to letter or decorate (as a book cover) by means of hand tools **2** : to equip a plant or industry with machines and tools for production **3** : DRIVE, RIDE ⟨~ing along at 60 miles per hour⟩
tool bar *n* : a strip of icons on a computer display providing quick access to the pictured functions
¹**toot** \'tüt\ *vb* **1** : to sound or cause to sound in short blasts **2** : to blow an instrument (as a horn) — **toot·er** *n*
²**toot** *n* : a short blast (as on a horn)
tooth \'tüth\ *n, pl* **teeth** \'tēth\ **1** : one of the hard bony structures borne esp. on the jaws of vertebrates and used for seizing and chewing food and as weapons; *also* : a hard sharp structure esp. around the mouth of an invertebrate **2** : something resembling an animal's tooth **3** : any of the projections on the edge of a wheel that fits

into corresponding projections on another wheel **4** *pl* : effective means of enforcement — **toothed** \'tütht\ *adj* — **tooth·less** *adj*

tooth·ache \'tüth-ˌāk\ *n* : pain in or about a tooth

tooth·brush \-ˌbrəsh\ *n* : a brush for cleaning the teeth

tooth·paste \-ˌpāst\ *n* : a paste for cleaning the teeth

tooth·pick \-ˌpik\ *n* : a pointed instrument for removing food particles caught between the teeth

tooth powder *n* : a powder for cleaning the teeth

tooth·some \'tüth-səm\ *adj* **1** : AGREEABLE, ATTRACTIVE **2** : pleasing to the taste : DELICIOUS ◆ *Synonyms* PALATABLE, APPETIZING, SAVORY, TASTY

toothy \'tü-thē\ *adj* **tooth·i·er; -est** : having or showing prominent teeth

¹**top** \'täp\ *n* **1** : the highest part, point, or level of something **2** : the part of a plant with edible roots lying above the ground ⟨beet ∼*s*⟩ **3** : the upper end, edge, or surface ⟨the ∼ of a page⟩ **4** : an upper piece, lid, or covering **5** : the highest degree, pitch, or rank **6** : a quark with a charge of +⅔ and a measured energy of approximately 175 billion electron volts

²**top** *vb* **topped; top·ping** **1** : to remove or trim the top of : PRUNE ⟨∼ a tree⟩ **2** : to cover with a top or on the top : CROWN, CAP **3** : to be superior to : EXCEL, SURPASS **4** : to go over the top of **5** : to strike (a ball) above the center **6** : to make an end or conclusion ⟨∼ off a meal with coffee⟩

³**top** *adj* **1** : of, relating to, or being at the top : HIGHEST **2** : CHIEF

⁴**top** *n* : a toy that has a tapering point on which it is made to spin

to·paz \'tō-ˌpaz\ *n* : a hard silicate of aluminum; *esp* : a yellow transparent topaz used as a gem

top·coat \'täp-ˌkōt\ *n* **1** : a lightweight overcoat **2** : a protective coating (as of paint)

top dollar *n* : the highest amount being paid for a commodity or service

top–dress \-ˌdres\ *vb* : to apply material to (as land) without working it in; *esp* : to scatter fertilizer over

top-dress·ing \-ˌdre-siŋ\ *n* : a material used to top-dress soil

top–end \'täp-ˈend\ *adj* : TOPFLIGHT

top·flight \'täp-ˈflīt\ *adj* : of, relating to, or being the highest level of excellence or rank — **top flight** *n*

top hat *n* : a tall-crowned hat usu. of beaver or silk

top–heavy \'täp-ˌhe-vē\ *adj* : having the top part too heavy for the lower part

to·pi·ary \'tō-pē-ˌer-ē\ *n, pl* **-ar·ies** : the art of training and trimming trees or shrubs with decorative shapes — **topiary** *adj*

top·ic \'tä-pik\ *n* **1** : a heading in an outlined argument **2** : the subject of a discourse or a section of it : THEME

top·i·cal \-pi-kəl\ *adj* **1** : of, relating to, or arranged by topics ⟨a ∼ outline⟩ **2** : relating to current or local events **3** : designed to be applied to or to work on a part (as of the body) — **top·i·cal·ly** \-k(ə-)lē\ *adv*

top·knot \'täp-ˌnät\ *n* **1** : an ornament (as a knot of ribbons) forming a headdress **2** : a crest of feathers or tuft of hair on the top of the head

top·less \-ləs\ *adj* **1** : wearing no clothing on the upper body **2** : featuring topless waitresses or entertainers

top·mast \'täp-ˌmast, -məst\ *n* : the 2d mast above a ship's deck

top·most \'täp-ˌmōst\ *adj* : highest of all : UPPERMOST

top–notch \-ˈnäch\ *adj* : of the highest quality : FIRST= RATE

top–of–the–line *adj* : being or belonging to the highest or most expensive class

to·pog·ra·phy \tə-ˈpä-grə-fē\ *n* **1** : the art of showing in detail on a map or chart the physical features of a place or region **2** : the outline of the form of a place showing its relief and the position of features (as rivers, roads, or cities) — **to·pog·ra·pher** \-fər\ *n* — **top·o·graph·ic** \ˌtä-pə-ˈgra-fik\ *or* **top·o·graph·i·cal** \-fi-kəl\ *adj*

topping *n* : a food served on top of another to make it look or taste better

top·ple \'tä-pəl\ *vb* **top·pled; top·pling** **1** : to fall from or as if from being top-heavy **2** : to push over : OVERTURN; *also* : OVERTHROW

¹**tops** \'täps\ *adj* : topmost in quality or importance ⟨∼ in his field⟩

²**tops** *adv* : at the very most

top·sail \'täp-ˌsāl, -səl\ *also* **top·s'l** \-səl\ *n* : the sail next above the lowest sail on a mast in a square-rigged ship

top secret *adj* : demanding complete secrecy among those concerned

top·side \'täp-ˈsīd\ *adv or adj* **1** : to or on the top or surface **2** : on deck

top·sides \-ˈsīdz\ *n pl* : the top portion of the outer surface of a ship on each side above the waterline

top·soil \'täp-ˌsȯi(-ə)l\ *n* : surface soil usu. including the organic layer in which plants have most of their roots

top·sy–tur·vy \ˌtäp-sē-ˈtər-vē\ *adv* **1** : in utter confusion **2** : UPSIDE DOWN — **topsy–turvy** *adj*

toque \'tōk\ *n* : a woman's small hat without a brim

tor \'tȯr\ *n* : a high craggy hill

To·rah \'tȯr-ə\ *n* **1** : a scroll of the first five books of the Old Testament used in a synagogue; *also* : these five books **2** : the body of divine knowledge and law found in the Jewish scriptures and tradition

¹**torch** \'tȯrch\ *n* **1** : a flaming light made of something that burns brightly and usu. carried in the hand **2** : something that resembles a torch in giving light, heat, or guidance **3** : a portable burner for producing a hot flame **4** *chiefly Brit* : FLASHLIGHT

²**torch** *vb* : to set fire to

torch·bear·er \'tȯrch-ˌber-ər\ *n* **1** : a person who carries a torch **2** : one in the forefront (as of a political campaign)

torch·light \-ˌlīt\ *n* : light given by torches

torch song *n* : a popular sentimental song of unrequited love

to·re *past of* TEAR

to·re·ador \'tȯr-ē-ə-ˌdȯr\ *n* : BULLFIGHTER

to·re·ro \tə-ˈrer-ō\ *n, pl* **-ros** [Sp] : BULLFIGHTER

¹**tor·ment** \'tȯr-ˌment\ *n* **1** : extreme pain or anguish of body or mind **2** : a source of vexation or pain

²**tor·ment** \tȯr-ˈment\ *vb* **1** : to cause severe suffering of body or mind to **2** : DISTORT, TWIST ◆ *Synonyms* RACK, AFFLICT, TRY, TORTURE — **tor·men·tor** \-ˈmen-tər\ *n*

torn *past part of* TEAR

tor·na·do \tȯr-ˈnā-dō\ *n, pl* **-does** *or* **-dos** [modif of Sp *tronada* thunderstorm, fr. *tronar* to thunder, fr. L *tonare*] : a violent destructive whirling wind accompanied by a funnel-shaped cloud that moves over a narrow path

¹**tor·pe·do** \tȯr-ˈpē-dō\ *n, pl* **-does** : a thin cylindrical self= propelled underwater weapon

²**torpedo** *vb* **tor·pe·doed; tor·pe·do·ing** **1** : to hit or destroy with or as if with a torpedo

torpedo boat *n* : a small very fast boat for firing torpedoes

tor·pid \'tȯr-pəd\ *adj* **1** : having lost motion or the power of exertion : DORMANT **2** : SLUGGISH **3** : lacking vigor — **tor·pid·i·ty** \tȯr-ˈpi-də-tē\ *n*

tor·por \'tȯr-pər\ *n* **1** : DULLNESS, APATHY **2** : extreme sluggishness : STAGNATION ◆ *Synonyms* STUPOR, LETHARGY, LANGUOR, LASSITUDE

¹**torque** \'tȯrk\ *n* : a force that produces or tends to produce rotation or torsion

²**torque** *vb* **torqued; torqu·ing** : to impart torque to : cause to twist (as about an axis)

tor·rent \'tȯr-ənt\ *n* [F, fr. L *torrent-, torrens*, fr. *torrent-, torrens* burning, seething, rushing, fr. prp. of *torrēre* to parch, burn] **1** : a tumultuous outburst **2** : a rushing stream (as of water)

tor·ren·tial \tȯ-ˈren-chəl\ *adj* : relating to or resembling a torrent ⟨∼ rains⟩

tor·rid \'tȯr-əd\ *adj* **1** : parched with heat esp. of the sun : HOT **2** : ARDENT

torrid zone *n* : the region of the earth between the Tropic of Cancer and the Tropic of Capricorn

tor·sion \'tȯr-shən\ *n* **1** : a wrenching by which one part of a body is under pressure to turn against a longitudinal axis while the other part is held fast or is under pressure to turn in the opposite direction **2** : a twisting of a bodily organ or part on its own axis — **tor·sion·al** \'tȯr-shə-nəl\ *adj* — **tor·sion·al·ly** *adv*

tor·so \'tȯr-sō\ *n, pl* **torsos** *or* **tor·si** \'tȯr-ˌsē\ [It, lit., stalk] : the trunk of the human body

tort \'tȯrt\ *n* : a wrongful act which does not involve a breach of contract and for which the injured party can recover damages in a civil action

tor·ti·lla \tȯr-ˈtē-ə\ *n* : a round thin cake of unleavened cornmeal or wheat flour bread

tor·toise \'tȯr-təs\ *n* : TURTLE; *esp* : any of a family of land turtles

tor·toise·shell \-ˌshel\ *n* : the mottled horny substance of the shell of some turtles used in inlaying and in making various ornamental articles — **tortoiseshell** *adj*

tor·to·ni \tȯr-'tō-nē\ *n* : rich ice cream often made with minced almonds and chopped cherries and flavored with rum

tor·tu·ous \'tȯr-chə-wəs\ *adj* **1** : marked by twists or turns : WINDING **2** : DEVIOUS, TRICKY

¹**tor·ture** \'tȯr-chər\ *n* **1** : anguish of body or mind **2** : the infliction of severe pain esp. to punish or coerce — **tor·tur·ous** \'tȯrch-rəs, 'tȯr-chə-\ *adj*

²**torture** *vb* **tor·tured; tor·tur·ing 1** : to cause intense suffering to : TORMENT **2** : to punish or coerce by inflicting severe pain **3** : TWIST, DISTORT ◆ *Synonyms* RACK, HARROW, AFFLICT, TRY — **tor·tur·er** *n*

To·ry \'tȯr-ē\ *n, pl* **Tories 1** : a member of a chiefly 18th century British party upholding the established church and the traditional political structure **2** : an American supporter of the British during the American Revolution **3** *often not cap* : an extreme conservative — **Tory** *adj*

¹**toss** \'tȯs, 'täs\ *vb* **1** : to fling to and fro or up and down **2** : to throw with a quick light motion; *also* : BANDY **3** : to fling or lift with a sudden motion ⟨~ed her head angrily⟩ **4** : to move restlessly or turbulently ⟨~es on the waves⟩ **5** : to twist and turn repeatedly **6** : FLOUNCE **7** : to accomplish readily ⟨~ off an article⟩ **8** : to decide an issue by flipping a coin

²**toss** *n* : an act or instance of tossing; *esp* : TOSS-UP 1

toss–up \-ˌəp\ *n* **1** : a deciding by flipping a coin **2** : an even chance **3** : something that offers no clear basis for choice

¹**tot** \'tät\ *n* **1** : a small child **2** : a small drink of alcoholic liquor : SHOT

²**tot** *vb* **tot·ted; tot·ting** : to add up

³**tot** *abbr* total

¹**to·tal** \'tō-t³l\ *adj* **1** : making up a whole : ENTIRE ⟨~ amount⟩ **2** : COMPLETE, UTTER ⟨a ~ failure⟩ ⟨a ~ stranger⟩ **3** : involving a complete and unified effort esp. to achieve a desired effect — **to·tal·ly** *adv*

²**total** *n* **1** : SUM **4 2** : the entire amount ◆ *Synonyms* AGGREGATE, WHOLE, GROSS, TOTALITY

³**total** *vb* **to·taled** or **to·talled; to·tal·ing** or **to·tal·ling 1** : to add up : COMPUTE **2** : to amount to : NUMBER **3** : to make a total wreck of (a car)

to·tal·i·tar·i·an \tō-ˌta-lə-'ter-ē-ən\ *adj* : of, relating to, or advocating a political regime based on subordination of the individual to the state and strict control of all aspects of life esp. by coercive measures — **totalitarian** *n* — **to·tal·i·tar·i·an·ism** \-ē-ə-ˌni-zəm\ *n*

to·tal·i·ty \tō-'ta-lə-tē\ *n, pl* **-ties 1** : an aggregate amount : SUM, WHOLE **2** : ENTIRETY, WHOLENESS

to·tal·iza·tor or **to·tal·isa·tor** \'tō-t³l-ə-ˌzā-tər\ *n* : a machine for registering and indicating the number of bets and the odds on a horse or dog race

¹**tote** \'tōt\ *vb* **tot·ed; tot·ing** : CARRY

²**tote** *vb* **tot·ed; tot·ing** : ADD, TOTAL — usu. used with *up*

to·tem \'tō-təm\ *n* [Ojibwa *oto·te·man* his totem] : an object (as an animal or plant) serving as the emblem of a family or clan and often as a reminder of its ancestry; *also* : something usu. carved or painted to represent such an object

totem pole *n* : a pole that is carved with a series of totems and is erected before the houses of some northwest American Indians

tot·ter \'tä-tər\ *vb* **1** : to tremble or rock as if about to fall : SWAY **2** : to move unsteadily : STAGGER

tou·can \'tü-ˌkan\ *n* [F, fr. Pg *tucano*, fr. Tupinambá (American Indian language of Brazil) *tukána*] : any of a family of chiefly fruit-eating birds of tropical America with brilliant coloring and a very large bill

¹**touch** \'təch\ *vb* **1** : to bring a bodily part (as the hand) into contact with so as to feel **2** : to be or cause to be in contact **3** : to strike or push lightly esp. with the hand or foot **4** : DISTURB, HARM **5** : to make use of ⟨never ~es alcohol⟩ **6** : to induce to give or lend **7** : to get to : REACH **8** : to refer to in passing : MENTION **9** : to affect the interest of : CONCERN **10** : to leave a mark on; *also* : BLEMISH **11** : to move to sympathetic feeling **12** : to come close : VERGE **13** : to have a bearing : RELATE

14 : to make a usu. brief or incidental stop in port ◆ *Synonyms* AFFECT, INFLUENCE, IMPRESS, STRIKE, SWAY

²**touch** *n* **1** : a light stroke or tap **2** : the act or fact of touching or being touched **3** : the sense by which pressure or traction on the skin or mucous membrane is perceived; *also* : a particular sensation conveyed by this sense **4** : mental or moral sensitiveness : TACT **5** : a small quantity : HINT ⟨a ~ of spring in the air⟩ **6** : a manner of striking or touching esp. the keys of a keyboard instrument **7** : an improving detail ⟨add a few ~es to the painting⟩ **8** : distinctive manner or skill ⟨the ~ of a master⟩ **9** : the state of being in contact ⟨keep in ~⟩ ◆ *Synonyms* SUGGESTION, SUSPICION, TINCTURE, TINGE

touch·down \'təch-ˌdaùn\ *n* : the act of scoring six points in American football by being lawfully in possession of the ball on, above, or behind an opponent's goal line

tou·ché \tü-'shā\ *interj* [F] — used to acknowledge a hit in fencing or the success of an argument, an accusation, or a witty point

touch football *n* : football in which touching is substituted for tackling

touch·ing \'tə-chiŋ\ *adj* : capable of stirring emotions ◆ *Synonyms* MOVING, IMPRESSIVE, POIGNANT, AFFECTING

touch off *vb* **1** : to describe with precision **2** : to start by or as if by touching with fire

touch·stone \'təch-ˌstōn\ *n* : a test or criterion of genuineness or quality ◆ *Synonyms* STANDARD, GAUGE, BENCHMARK, YARDSTICK

touch–tone \'təch-'tōn\ *adj* : of, relating to, or being a telephone having push buttons that produce tones corresponding to numbers

touch up *vb* : to improve or perfect by small additional strokes or alterations — **touch–up** \'təch-ˌəp\ *n*

touchy \'tə-chē\ *adj* **touch·i·er; -est 1** : easily offended : PEEVISH **2** : calling for tact in treatment ⟨a ~ subject⟩ ◆ *Synonyms* IRASCIBLE, CRANKY, CROSS, TETCHY, TESTY

¹**tough** \'təf\ *adj* **1** : strong or firm in texture but flexible and not brittle **2** : not easily chewed **3** : characterized by severity and determination ⟨a ~ policy⟩ **4** : capable of enduring strain or hardship : ROBUST **5** : hard to influence : STUBBORN **6** : difficult to accomplish, resolve, or cope with ⟨a ~ problem⟩ **7** : ROWDYISH ◆ *Synonyms* TENACIOUS, STOUT, STURDY, STALWART — **tough·ly** *adv* — **tough·ness** *n*

²**tough** *n* : a tough person : ROWDY

tough·en \'tə-fən\ *vb* **tough·ened; tough·en·ing** : to make or become tough

tou·pee \tü-'pā\ *n* [F *toupet* forelock] : a small wig for a bald spot

¹**tour** \'tùr, *1 is also* 'taù(-ə)r\ *n* **1** : one's turn : SHIFT **2** : a journey in which one returns to the starting point

²**tour** *vb* : to make a tour

tour de force \ˌtùr-də-'fȯrs\ *n, pl* **tours de force** *same*\ [F] : a feat or display of strength, skill, or ingenuity

Tou·rette's syndrome \tù-'rets-\ *n* : a familial neurological disorder marked by recurrent involuntary tics and vocal sounds

tour·ism \'tùr-ˌi-zəm\ *n* **1** : the practice of traveling for recreation **2** : promotion of touring **3** : accommodation of tourists — **tour·ist** \-ist\ *n*

tourist class *n* : economy accommodations (as on a ship)

tour·ma·line \'tùr-mə-lən, -ˌlēn\ *n* : a mineral that when transparent is valued as a gem

tour·na·ment \'tùr-nə-mənt, 'tȯr-\ *n* **1** : a medieval sport in which mounted armored knights contended with blunted lances or swords **2** : a championship series of games or athletic contests

tour·ney \-nē\ *n, pl* **tourneys** : TOURNAMENT

tour·ni·quet \'tùr-ni-kət, 'tȯr-\ *n* : a device (as a tight bandage) to check bleeding or blood flow

tou·sle \'taù-zəl\ *vb* **tou·sled; tou·sling** : to disorder by rough handling : DISHEVEL, MUSS

tout \'taùt, *2 is also* 'tüt\ *vb* **1** : to give a tip or solicit bets on a racehorse **2** : to praise or publicize loudly — **tout** *n*

¹**tow** \'tō\ *vb* : to draw or pull along behind

²**tow** *n* **1** : an act of towing or condition of being towed **2** : something (as a barge) that is towed

³**tow** *n* : short or broken fiber (as of flax or hemp) used esp. for yarn, twine, or stuffing

to·ward \'tórd, 'tō-ərd, tə-'wórd\ *or* **to·wards** \'tórdz, 'tō-ərdz, tə-'wórdz\ *prep* **1** : in the direction of ⟨heading ∼ the river⟩ **2** : along a course leading to ⟨efforts ∼ reconciliation⟩ **3** : in regard to ⟨tolerance ∼ minorities⟩ **4** : so as to face ⟨turn the chair ∼ the window⟩ **5** : close upon ⟨it was getting along ∼ sundown⟩ **6** : for part payment of ⟨here's $100 ∼ your tuition⟩

tow·boat \'tō-,bōt\ *n* : TUGBOAT

tow·el \'taù(-ə)l\ *n* : an absorbent cloth or paper for wiping or drying

tow·el·ing *or* **tow·el·ling** *n* : a cotton or linen fabric for making towels

¹tow·er \'taù(-ə)r\ *n* **1** : a tall structure either isolated or built upon a larger structure ⟨an observation ∼⟩ **2** : a towering citadel **3** : a personal computer case that stands in an upright position — **tow·ered** *adj*

²tower *vb* : to reach or rise to a great height

tow·er·ing \'taù(-ə)r-iŋ\ *adj* **1** : LOFTY ⟨∼ pines⟩ **2** : reaching high intensity ⟨a ∼ rage⟩ **3** : EXCESSIVE ⟨∼ ambition⟩

tow·head \'tō-,hed\ *n* : a person having whitish blond hair — **tow·head·ed** \-,he-dəd\ *adj*

to·whee \'tō-,hē, 'tō-(,)ē, tō-'hē\ *n* : a common finch of eastern No. America having the male black, white, and reddish; *also* : any of several closely related finches

to wit *adv* : NAMELY

town \'taùn\ *n* **1** : a compactly settled area usu. larger than a village but smaller than a city **2** : CITY **3** : the inhabitants of a town **4** : a New England territorial and political unit usu. containing both rural and urban areas; *also* : a New England community in which matters of local government are decided by a general assembly (**town meeting**) of qualified voters

town house *n* **1** : the city residence of a person having a country home **2** : a single-family house of two or sometimes three stories connected to another house by a common wall

town·ie *or* **towny** \'taù-nē\ *n, pl* **townies** : a permanent resident of a town as distinguished from a member of another group

towns·folk \'taùnz-,fōk\ *n pl* : TOWNSPEOPLE

town·ship \'taùn-,ship\ *n* **1** : TOWN 4 **2** : a unit of local government in some states **3** : an unorganized subdivision of a county **4** : a division of territory in surveys of U.S. public land containing 36 square miles **5** : an area in the Republic of South Africa segregated for occupation by persons of non-European descent

towns·man \'taùnz-mən\ *n* **1** : a native or resident of a town or city **2** : a fellow citizen of a town

towns·peo·ple \-,pē-pəl\ *n pl* **1** : the inhabitants of a town or city **2** : town-bred persons

towns·wom·an \-,wù-mən\ *n* **1** : a woman who is a native or resident of a town or city **2** : a woman who is a fellow citizen of a town

tow·path \'tō-,path, -,päth\ *n* : a path (as along a canal) traveled esp. by draft animals towing boats

tow truck *n* : a truck equipped for towing vehicles

tox·emia \täk-'sē-mē-ə\ *n* : a bodily disorder associated with the presence of toxic substances in the blood

tox·ic \'täk-sik\ *adj* [LL *toxicus*, fr. L *toxicum* poison, fr. Gk *toxikon* arrow poison, fr. neut. of *toxikos* of a bow, fr. *toxon* bow, arrow] : of, relating to, or caused by poison or a toxin : POISONOUS — **tox·ic·i·ty** \täk-'si-sə-tē\ *n*

tox·i·col·o·gy \,täk-si-'kä-lə-jē\ *n* : a science that deals with poisons and esp. with problems of their use and control — **tox·i·co·log·i·cal** \-kə-'lä-ji-kəl\ *also* **tox·i·co·log·ic** \-kə-'lä-jik\ *adj* — **tox·i·col·o·gist** \-'kä-lə-jist\ *n*

toxic shock syndrome *n* : an acute disease associated with the presence of a bacterium that is characterized by fever, diarrhea, nausea, diffuse erythema, and shock and occurs esp. in menstruating females using tampons

tox·in \'täk-sən\ *n* : a poisonous substance produced by metabolic activities of a living organism that is usu. unstable, very toxic when introduced into the tissues, and usu. capable of inducing antibodies

¹toy \'tói\ *n* **1** : something trifling **2** : a small ornament : BAUBLE **3** : something for a child to play with

²toy *vb* **1** : to deal with something lightly : TRIFLE **2** : FLIRT **3** : to amuse oneself as if with a plaything

³toy *adj* **1** : DIMINUTIVE ⟨a ∼ dog⟩ **2** : designed for use as a toy

tp *abbr* **1** title page **2** township

tpk *or* **tpke** *abbr* turnpike

tr *abbr* **1** translated; translation; translator **2** transpose **3** troop

¹trace \'trās\ *n* **1** : a mark (as a footprint or track) left by something that has passed **2** : a minute or barely detectable amount

²trace *vb* **traced; trac·ing** **1** : to mark out : SKETCH **2** : to form (as letters) carefully **3** : to copy (a drawing) by marking lines on transparent paper laid over the drawing to be copied **4** : to follow the trail of : track down **5** : to study out and follow the development of — **trace·able** *adj*

³trace *n* : either of two lines of a harness for fastening a draft animal to a vehicle

trac·er \'trā-sər\ *n* **1** : one that traces **2** : ammunition containing a chemical to mark the flight of projectiles by a trail of smoke or light

trac·ery \'trā-sə-rē\ *n, pl* **-er·ies** : ornamental work having a design with branching or interlacing lines

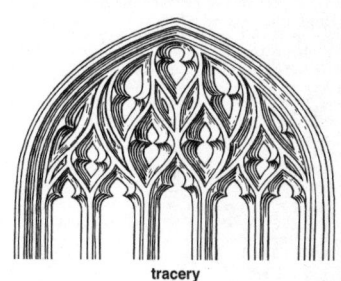

tracery

tra·chea \'trā-kē-ə\ *n, pl* **-che·ae** \-kē-,ē\ *also* **-che·as** *or* **-chea** : the main tube by which air passes from the larynx to the lungs of vertebrates — **tra·che·al** \-kē-əl\ *adj*

tra·che·ot·o·my \,trā-kē-'ä-tə-mē\ *n, pl* **-mies** : the surgical operation of cutting into the trachea esp. through the skin

tracing *n* **1** : the act of one that traces **2** : something that is traced **3** : a graphic record made by an instrument for measuring vibrations or pulsations

¹track \'trak\ *n* **1** : a mark left in passing **2** : PATH, ROUTE, TRAIL **3** : a course laid out for racing; *also* : track-and-field sports **4** : one of a series of paths along which material (as music) is recorded (as on a compact disc or magnetic tape) **5** : the course along which something moves; *esp* : a way made by two parallel lines of metal rails **6** : awareness of a fact or progression ⟨lost ∼ of time⟩ **7** : either of two endless metal belts on which a vehicle (as a bulldozer) travels

²track *vb* **1** : to follow the tracks or traces of : TRAIL **2** : to observe the moving path of (as a missile) **3** : to make tracks on **4** : to carry (as mud) on the feet and deposit — **track·er** *n*

track·age \'tra-kij\ *n* : lines of railway track

track–and–field *adj* : of or relating to athletic contests held on a running track or on the adjacent field

¹tract \'trakt\ *n* **1** : an area without precise boundaries ⟨huge ∼s of land⟩ **2** : a defined area of land **3** : a system of body parts or organs that act together to perform some function ⟨the digestive ∼⟩

²tract *n* : a pamphlet of political or religious propaganda

trac·ta·ble \'trak-tə-bəl\ *adj* : easily controlled : DOCILE ✦ *Synonyms* AMENABLE, OBEDIENT, BIDDABLE

tract house *n* : any of many similar houses built on a tract of land

trac·tion \'trak-shən\ *n* **1** : the act of drawing : the state of being drawn **2** : the drawing of a vehicle by motive power; *also* : the particular form of motive power used **3** : the adhesive friction of a body on a surface on which it moves **4** : a pulling force applied to a skeletal structure (as a broken bone) by means of a special device; *also* : a state of tension created by such a pulling force ⟨a leg in ∼⟩ — **trac·tion·al** \-shə-nəl\ *adj* — **trac·tive** \'trak-tiv\ *adj*

trac·tor \'trak-tər\ *n* **1** : an automotive vehicle used esp. for drawing farm equipment **2** : a truck for hauling a trailer

¹trade \'trād\ *n* **1** : one's regular business or work : OCCUPATION **2** : an occupation requiring manual or mechanical skill **3** : the persons engaged in a business or industry **4** : the business of buying and selling or bartering commodities **5** : an act of trading : TRANSACTION

²trade *vb* **trad·ed; trad·ing** **1** : to give in exchange for another commodity : BARTER **2** : to engage in the exchange, purchase, or sale of goods **3** : to deal regularly as a customer — **trade on** : EXPLOIT ⟨*trades on* his family name⟩

trade-in \'trād-,in\ *n* : an item of merchandise traded in

trade in *vb* : to turn in as part payment for a purchase

¹trade·mark \'trād-,märk\ *n* : a device (as a word or mark) that points distinctly to the origin or ownership of merchandise to which it is applied and that is legally reserved for the exclusive use of the owner; *also* : something that identifies a person or thing

²trademark *vb* : to secure the trademark rights for

trade name *n* : a name that is given by a manufacturer or merchant to a product to distinguish it as made or sold by him and that may be used and protected as a trademark

trad·er \'trā-dər\ *n* **1** : a person whose business is buying or selling **2** : a ship engaged in trade

trades·man \'trādz-mən\ *n* **1** : one who runs a retail store : SHOPKEEPER **2** : CRAFTSMAN

trades·peo·ple \-,pē-pəl\ *n pl* : people engaged in trade

trade union *n* : LABOR UNION

trade wind *n* : a wind blowing almost constantly in one direction

trading stamp *n* : a printed stamp given as a premium to a retail customer that when accumulated may be redeemed for merchandise

tra·di·tion \trə-'di-shən\ *n* **1** : an inherited, established, or customary pattern of thought or action **2** : the handing down of beliefs and customs by word of mouth or by example without written instruction; *also* : a belief or custom thus handed down — **tra·di·tion·al** \-,di-shə-nəl\ *adj* — **tra·di·tion·al·ly** *adv*

tra·duce \trə-'düs, -'dyüs\ *vb* **tra·duced; tra·duc·ing** : to lower the reputation of : DEFAME, SLANDER ♦ *Synonyms* MALIGN, LIBEL, CALUMNIATE — **tra·duc·er** *n*

¹traf·fic \'tra-fik\ *n* **1** : the business of bartering or buying and selling **2** : communication or dealings between individuals or groups **3** : the movement (as of vehicles) along a route; *also* : the vehicles, people, ships, or planes moving along a route **4** : the passengers or cargo carried by a transportation system

²traffic *vb* **traf·ficked; traf·fick·ing** **1** : to carry on business dealings **2** : DEAL, TRADE — **traf·fick·er** *n*

traffic circle *n* : ROTARY 2

traffic light *n* : a visual signal (as a system of lights) for controlling traffic

tra·ge·di·an \trə-'jē-dē-ən\ *n* **1** : a writer of tragedies **2** : an actor who plays tragic roles

tra·ge·di·enne \trə-,jē-dē-'en\ *n* [F] : an actress who plays tragic roles

trag·e·dy \'tra-jə-dē\ *n, pl* **-dies** [ME *tragedie*, fr. MF, fr. L *tragoedia*, fr. Gk *tragōidia*, fr. *tragos* goat + *aeidein* to sing] **1** : a serious drama with a sorrowful or disastrous conclusion **2** : a disastrous event : CALAMITY; *also* : MISFORTUNE **3** : tragic quality or element ⟨the ~ of life⟩

trag·ic \'tra-jik\ *also* **trag·i·cal** \-ji-kəl\ *adj* **1** : of, relating to, or expressive of tragedy **2** : appropriate to tragedy **3** : LAMENTABLE, UNFORTUNATE — **trag·i·cal·ly** \-ji-k(ə-)lē\ *adv*

¹trail \'trāl\ *vb* **1** : to hang down so as to drag along or sweep the ground **2** : to draw or drag along behind **3** : to extend over a surface in a straggling manner **4** : to lag behind **5** : to follow the track of : PURSUE **6** : DWINDLE ⟨her voice ~ed off⟩

²trail *n* **1** : something that trails or is trailed ⟨a ~ of smoke⟩ **2** : a trace or mark left by something that has passed or been drawn along : SCENT, TRACK ⟨a ~ of blood⟩ **3** : a beaten path; *also* : a marked path through woods

trail bike *n* : a small motorcycle for off-road use

trail·blaz·er \-,blā-zər\ *n* : PATHFINDER, PIONEER — **trail·blaz·ing** *adj or n*

trail·er \'trā-lər\ *n* **1** : one that trails; *esp* : a creeping plant (as an ivy) **2** : a vehicle that is hauled by another (as a tractor) **3** : a vehicle equipped to serve wherever parked as a dwelling or place of business **4** : PREVIEW 2

trailer park *n* : a site equipped to accommodate mobile homes

trailing arbutus *n* : a creeping spring-flowering plant of the heath family with fragrant pink or white flowers

¹train \'trān\ *n* [ME, fr. AF, fr. *trainer* to draw, drag] **1** : a part of a gown that trails behind the wearer **2** : RETINUE **3** : a moving file of persons, vehicles, or animals **4** : a connected series ⟨a ~ of thought⟩ **5** : AFTERMATH **6** : a connected line of railroad cars usu. hauled by a locomotive ♦ *Synonyms* SUCCESSION, SEQUENCE, PROCESSION, CHAIN

²train *vb* [ME, to trail, drag; train, fr. AF *trainer*] **1** : to cause to grow as desired ⟨~ a vine on a trellis⟩ **2** : to form by instruction, discipline, or drill **3** : to make or become prepared (as by exercise) for a test of skill **4** : to aim or point at an object ⟨~ guns on a fort⟩ ♦ *Synonyms* DISCIPLINE, SCHOOL, EDUCATE, INSTRUCT — **train·er** *n*

train·ee \trā-'nē\ *n* : one who is being trained esp. for a job

train·ing \'trā-niŋ\ *n* **1** : the act, process, or method of one who trains **2** : the skill, knowledge, or experience gained by one who trains

train·man \-mən\ *n* : a member of a train crew

traipse \'trāps\ *vb* **traipsed; traips·ing** : TRAMP, WALK ⟨~ the countryside⟩

trait \'trāt\ *n* **1** : a distinguishing quality (as of personality) **2** : an inherited characteristic

trai·tor \'trā-tər\ *n* [ME *traytour*, fr. AF *traitre*, fr. L *traditor*, fr. *tradere* to hand over, deliver, betray, fr. *trans-* across + *dare* to give] **1** : one who betrays another's trust or is false to an obligation **2** : one who commits treason — **trai·tor·ous** *adj*

tra·jec·to·ry \trə-'jek-tə-rē\ *n, pl* **-ries** : the curve that a body (as a planet in its orbit) describes in space

tram \'tram\ *n* **1** : a boxlike car running on rails (as in a mine) **2** *chiefly Brit* : STREETCAR **3** : an overhead cable car

¹tram·mel \'tra-məl\ *n* [ME *tramayle*, a kind of net, fr. MF *tramail*, fr. LL *tremaculum*, fr. L *tres* three + *macula* mesh, spot] : something impeding activity, progress, or freedom — usu. used in pl.

²trammel *vb* **-meled** *or* **-melled; -mel·ing** *or* **-mel·ling** **1** : to catch and hold in or as if in a net **2** : HAMPER ♦ *Synonyms* CLOG, FETTER, SHACKLE, HOBBLE

¹tramp \'tramp, *1 & 3 are also* 'trämp, 'trömp\ *vb* **1** : to walk, tread, or step heavily **2** : to walk about or through; *also* : HIKE **3** : to tread on forcibly and repeatedly

²tramp \'tramp, *5 is also* 'trämp, 'trömp\ *n* **1** : a begging or thieving vagrant **2** : a foot traveler **3** : an immoral woman; *esp* : PROSTITUTE **4** : a walking trip : HIKE **5** : the succession of sounds made by the beating of feet on a road **6** : a ship that does not follow a regular course but takes cargo to any port — **trampy** \'tram-pē\ *adj*

tram·ple \'tram-pəl\ *vb* **tram·pled; tram·pling** **1** : to tread heavily so as to bruise, crush, or injure **2** : to inflict injury or destruction **3** : to press down or crush by or as if by treading — **trample** *n* — **tram·pler** *n*

tram·po·line \,tram-pə-'lēn, 'tram-pə-,lēn\ *n* [It *trampolino* springboard] : a resilient sheet or web (as of nylon) supported by springs in a metal frame and used as a springboard in tumbling — **tram·po·lin·ist** \-'lē-nist, -,lē-\ *n*

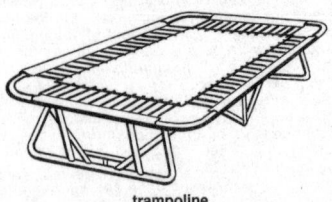

trampoline

trance \'trans\ *n* [ME, fr. AF *transe*, death, coma, rapture, fr. *transir* to depart, die, fr. L *transire* to cross, pass by, fr. *trans-* across + *ire* to go] **1** : STUPOR, DAZE **2** : a sleeplike

state of altered consciousness (as of deep hypnosis) **3** : a state of very deep absorption — **trance·like** \-ˌlīk\ *adj*
tran·quil \'traŋ-kwəl, 'tran-\ *adj* : free from agitation or disturbance : QUIET ♦ *Synonyms* SERENE, PLACID, PEACEFUL — **tran·quil·li·ty** *or* **tran·quil·i·ty** \tran-'kwi-lə-tē, traŋ-\ *n* — **tran·quil·ly** *adv*
tran·quil·ize *also* **tran·quil·lize** \'traŋ-kwə-ˌlīz, 'tran-\ *vb* **-ized** *also* **-lized; -iz·ing** *also* **-liz·ing** : to make or become tranquil; *esp* : to relieve of mental tension and anxiety by means of drugs
tran·quil·iz·er *also* **tran·quil·liz·er** \-ˌlī-zər\ *n* : a drug used to relieve mental disturbance (as tension and anxiety)
trans *abbr* **1** transaction **2** transitive **3** translated; translation; translator **4** transmission **5** transportation **6** transverse
trans·act \tran-'zakt, -'sakt\ *vb* : CARRY OUT, PERFORM; *also* : CONDUCT
trans·ac·tion \-'zak-shən, -'sak-\ *n* **1** : something transacted; *esp* : a business deal **2** : an act or process of transacting **3** *pl* : the records of the proceedings of a society or organization — **trans·ac·tion·al** \-shnəl, -shə-nᵊl\ *adj*
trans·at·lan·tic \ˌtrans-ət-'lan-tik, ˌtranz-\ *adj* : crossing or extending across or situated beyond the Atlantic Ocean ⟨a ~ flight⟩
trans·ax·le \trans-'ak-səl\ *n* : a unit combining the transmission and differential gear of a front-wheel-drive automobile
trans·ceiv·er \tran-'sē-vər\ *n* : a radio transmitter-receiver that uses many of the same components for both transmission and reception
tran·scend \tran-'send\ *vb* **1** : to rise above the limits of **2** : SURPASS ♦ *Synonyms* EXCEED, OUTDO, OUTSHINE, OUTSTRIP
tran·scen·dent \-'sen-dənt\ *adj* **1** : exceeding usual limits : SURPASSING **2** : transcending material existence ♦ *Synonyms* SUPERLATIVE, SUPREME, PEERLESS, INCOMPARABLE
tran·scen·den·tal \ˌtran-ˌsen-'den-tᵊl, -sən-\ *adj* **1** : TRANSCENDENT **2** **2** : of, relating to, or characteristic of transcendentalism; *also* : ABSTRUSE
tran·scen·den·tal·ism \-tə-ˌli-zəm\ *n* : a philosophy holding that ultimate reality is unknowable or asserting the primacy of the spiritual over the material and empirical — **tran·scen·den·tal·ist** \-tə-list\ *adj or n*
trans·con·ti·nen·tal \ˌtrans-ˌkän-tə-'nent-ᵊl\ *adj* : extending or going across a continent ⟨a ~ railroad⟩
tran·scribe \trans-'krīb\ *vb* **tran·scribed; tran·scrib·ing** **1** : to write a copy of **2** : to make a copy of (dictated or recorded matter) in longhand or on a typewriter **3** : to represent (speech sounds) by means of phonetic symbols; *also* : to make a musical transcription of
tran·script \'tran-ˌskript\ *n* **1** : a written, printed, or typed copy **2** : an official copy esp. of a student's educational record
tran·scrip·tion \tran-'skrip-shən\ *n* **1** : an act or process of transcribing **2** : COPY, TRANSCRIPT **3** : an arrangement of a musical composition for some instrument or voice other than the original **4** : the process of constructing a messenger RNA molecule using a DNA molecule as a template
tran·scrip·tion·ist \-shə-nist\ *n* : one that transcribes; *esp* : a typist who transcribes medical reports
trans·der·mal \trans-'dər-məl, 'tranz-\ *adj* : relating to, being, or supplying a medication in a form for absorption through the skin ⟨~ nicotine patch⟩
trans·duc·er \trans-'dü-sər, tranz-, -'dyü-\ *n* : a device that is actuated by power from one system and supplies power usu. in another form to a second system
tran·sept \'tran-ˌsept\ *n* : the part of a cruciform church that crosses at right angles to the greatest length; *also* : either of the projecting ends
trans fat \'tran(t)s-, 'tranz-\ *n* : a fat containing unsaturated fatty acids (**trans-fatty acids**) that have been linked to an increase in blood cholesterol
¹**trans·fer** \trans-'fər, 'trans-ˌfər\ *vb* **trans·ferred; trans·fer·ring** **1** : to pass or cause to pass from one person, place, or situation to another : MOVE, TRANSMIT **2** : to make over the possession of another to : CONVEY **3** : to print or copy from one surface to another by contact **4** : to change from one vehicle or transportation line to another — **trans·fer·able** \trans-'fər-ə-bəl\ *adj* — **trans·fer·al** \-əl\ *n*

²**trans·fer** \'trans-ˌfər\ *n* **1** : conveyance of right, title, or interest in property from one person to another **2** : an act or process of transferring **3** : one that transfers or is transferred **4** : a ticket entitling a passenger to continue a trip on another route
trans·fer·ence \trans-'fər-əns\ *n* : an act, process, or instance of transferring
trans·fig·ure \trans-'fi-gyər\ *vb* **-ured; -ur·ing** **1** : to change the form or appearance of **2** : EXALT, GLORIFY — **trans·fig·u·ra·tion** \ˌtrans-ˌfi-gyə-'rä-shən, -gə-\ *n*
trans·fix \trans-'fiks\ *vb* **1** : to pierce through with or as if with a pointed weapon **2** : to hold motionless by or as if by piercing ⟨stood ~ed by her gaze⟩
trans·form \trans-'fȯrm\ *vb* : to change in structure, appearance, or character ♦ *Synonyms* TRANSMUTE, TRANSFIGURE, TRANSMOGRIFY — **trans·for·ma·tion** \ˌtrans-fər-'mä-shən\ *n* — **trans·for·ma·tive** \trans-'fȯr-mə-tiv\ *adj*
trans·form·er \trans-'fȯr-mər\ *n* : one that transforms; *esp* : a device for converting variations of current in one circuit into variations of voltage and current in another circuit
trans·fuse \trans-'fyüz\ *vb* **trans·fused; trans·fus·ing** **1** : to cause to pass from one to another **2** : to diffuse into or through **3** : to transfer (as blood) into a vein or an artery of a person or animal — **trans·fu·sion** \-'fyü-zhən\ *n*
trans·gen·der \tranz-'jen-dər\ *adj* : having physical or behavioral characteristics transcending traditional gender boundaries
trans·gen·ic \tran(t)s-'je-nik\ *adj* : being or used to produce an organism or cell with genes introduced from another species of organism ⟨~ crops⟩
trans·gress \trans-'gres, tranz-\ *vb* [ME, fr. MF *transgresser*, fr. L *transgressus*, pp. of *transgredi* to step beyond or across, fr. *trans-* across + *gradi* to step] **1** : to go beyond the limits set by ⟨~ the divine law⟩ **2** : to go beyond : EXCEED **3** : SIN — **trans·gres·sion** \-'gre-shən\ *n* — **trans·gres·sor** \-'gre-sər\ *n*
¹**tran·sient** \'tran-shənt; -sē-ənt, -shē-, -zē-\ *adj* **1** : not lasting long : SHORT-LIVED ⟨~ opinions⟩ **2** : passing through a place with only a brief stay ⟨~visitors⟩ ♦ *Synonyms* TRANSITORY, PASSING, MOMENTARY, FLEETING — **tran·sient·ly** *adv*
²**transient** *n* : one that is transient; *esp* : a transient guest
tran·sis·tor \tran-'zis-tər, -'sis-\ *n* [*transfer* + *resistor*; fr. its transferring an electrical signal across a resistor] **1** : a small electronic semiconductor device used in electronic equipment **2** : a radio having transistors
tran·sis·tor·ized \-tə-ˌrīzd\ *adj* : having or using transistors
tran·sit \'tran-sət, -zət\ *n* **1** : a passing through, across, or over : PASSAGE **2** : conveyance of persons or things from one place to another **3** : usu. local transportation esp. of people by public conveyance **4** : a surveyor's instrument for measuring angles
tran·si·tion \tran-'si-shən, -'zi-\ *n* : passage from one state, place, stage, or subject to another : CHANGE — **tran·si·tion·al** \-'si-shə-nəl, 'zi-\ *adj*
tran·si·tive \'tran-sə-tiv, -zə-\ *adj* **1** : having or containing an object required to complete the meaning **2** : TRANSITIONAL — **tran·si·tive·ly** *adv* — **tran·si·tive·ness** *n* — **tran·si·tiv·i·ty** \ˌtran-sə-'ti-və-tē, -zə-\ *n*
tran·si·to·ry \'tran-sə-ˌtȯr-ē, -zə-\ *adj* : of brief duration : SHORT-LIVED, TEMPORARY ♦ *Synonyms* TRANSIENT, PASSING, MOMENTARY, FLEETING
transl *abbr* translated; translation
trans·late \trans-'lāt, tranz-\ *vb* **trans·lat·ed; trans·lat·ing** **1** : to change from one place, state, or form to another **2** : to convey to heaven without death **3** : to turn into one's own or another language — **trans·lat·able** *adj* — **trans·la·tor** \-'lā-tər\ *n*
trans·la·tion \tran(t)s-'lā-shən, tranz-\ *n* **1** : an act, process, or instance of translating **2** : the process of forming a protein molecule from information in messenger RNA — **trans·la·tion·al** \-shnəl, -shə-nᵊl\ *adj*
trans·lit·er·ate \trans-'li-tə-ˌrāt, tranz-\ *vb* **-at·ed; -at·ing** : to represent or spell in the characters of another alphabet — **trans·lit·er·a·tion** \ˌtrans-ˌli-tə-'rä-shən, ˌtranz-\ *n*
trans·lu·cent \trans-'lü-sᵊnt, tranz-\ *adj* : not transparent but clear enough to allow light to pass through — **trans·lu·cence** \-s³ns\ *n* — **trans·lu·cen·cy** \-s³n-sē\ *n* — **trans·lu·cent·ly** *adv*

trans·mi·grate \-'mī-,grāt\ *vb* : to pass at death from one body or being to another — **trans·mi·gra·tion** \,trans-mī-'grā-shən, ,tranz-\ *n* — **trans·mi·gra·to·ry** \trans-'mī-grə-,tōr-ē\ *adj*

trans·mis·sion \-'mi-shən\ *n* **1** : an act or process of transmitting **2** : the passage of radio waves between transmitting stations and receiving stations **3** : the gears by which power is transmitted from the engine of an automobile to the axle that propels the vehicle **4** : something transmitted

trans·mit \-'mit\ *vb* **trans·mit·ted; trans·mit·ting 1** : to transfer from one person or place to another : FORWARD **2** : to pass on by or as if by inheritance **3** : to cause or allow to spread abroad or to another ⟨∼ a disease⟩ **4** : to cause (as light, electricity, or force) to pass through space or a medium **5** : to send out (radio or television signals) ♦ **Synonyms** CONVEY, COMMUNICATE, IMPART — **trans·mis·si·ble** \-'mi-sə-bəl\ *adj* — **trans·mit·ta·ble** \-'mi-tə-bəl\ *adj* — **trans·mit·tal** \-'mit-ᵊl\ *n*

trans·mit·ter \-'mi-tər\ *n* : one that transmits; *esp* : an apparatus for transmitting telegraph, radio, or television signals

trans·mog·ri·fy \trans-'mä-grə-,fī, tranz-\ *vb* **-fied; -fy·ing** : to change or alter often with grotesque or humorous effect — **trans·mog·ri·fi·ca·tion** \-,mä-grə-fə-'kā-shən\ *n*

trans·mute \-'myüt\ *vb* **trans·muted; trans·mut·ing** : to change or alter in form, appearance, or nature ♦ **Synonyms** TRANSFORM, CONVERT, TRANSFIGURE, METAMORPHOSE — **trans·mu·ta·tion** \,trans-myü-'tā-shən, ,tranz-\ *n*

trans·na·tion·al \-'na-shə-nəl\ *adj* : extending beyond national boundaries

trans·oce·an·ic \,trans-,ō-shē-'a-nik, ,tranz-\ *adj* **1** : lying or dwelling beyond the ocean **2** : crossing or extending across the ocean

tran·som \'tran-səm\ *n* **1** : a piece (as a crossbar in the frame of a window or door) that lies crosswise in a structure **2** : a window above an opening (as a door) built on and often hinged to a horizontal crossbar

tran·son·ic *also* **trans·son·ic** \trans-'sä-nik\ *adj* : being or relating to speeds near that of sound in air or about 741 miles (1185 kilometers) per hour

trans·pa·cif·ic \,trans-pə-'si-fik\ *adj* : crossing, extending across, or situated beyond the Pacific Ocean

trans·par·ent \trans-'per-ənt\ *adj* **1** : clear enough to be seen through **2** : SHEER, DIAPHANOUS ⟨a ∼ fabric⟩ **3** : readily understood : CLEAR; *also* : easily detected ⟨a ∼ lie⟩ ♦ **Synonyms** LUCID, TRANSLUCENT, LUCENT — **trans·par·en·cy** \-ən-sē\ *n* — **trans·par·ent·ly** *adv*

tran·spire \trans-'pī(-ə)r\ *vb* **trans·pired; tran·spir·ing** [MF *transpirer*, fr. ML *transpirare*, fr. *trans-* across + *spirare* to breathe] **1** : to pass or give off (as water vapor) through pores or a membrane **2** : to become known **3** : to take place : HAPPEN — **tran·spi·ra·tion** \,trans-pə-'rā-shən\ *n*

¹trans·plant \trans-'plant\ *vb* **1** : to dig up and plant elsewhere **2** : to remove from one place and settle or introduce elsewhere : TRANSPORT **3** : to transfer (an organ or tissue) from one part or individual to another — **trans·plan·ta·tion** \,trans-,plan-'tā-shən\ *n*

²trans·plant \'trans-,plant\ *n* **1** : a person or thing transplanted **2** : the act or process of transplanting

trans·po·lar \trans-'pō-lər\ *adj* : going or extending across either of the polar regions

transponder \tran-'spän-dər\ *n* [*trans*mitter + re*sponder*] : a radio or radar set that upon receiving a certain signal emits a radio signal and that is used to locate and identify objects and in satellites to relay communications signals

¹trans·port \trans-'pōrt\ *vb* **1** : to convey from one place to another : CARRY **2** : to carry away by strong emotion : ENRAPTURE **3** : to send to a penal colony overseas ♦ **Synonyms** BEAR, FERRY — **trans·por·ta·tion** \,trans-pər-'tā-shən\ *n* — **trans·port·er** *n*

²trans·port \'trans-,pōrt\ *n* **1** : an act of transporting **2** : strong or intensely pleasurable emotion ⟨∼s of joy⟩ **3** : a ship used in transporting troops or supplies; *also* : a vehicle (as a truck or plane) used to transport persons or goods

trans·pose \trans-'pōz\ *vb* **trans·posed; trans·pos·ing 1** : to change the position or sequence of ⟨∼ the letters

in a word⟩ **2** : to write or perform (a musical composition) in a different key — **trans·po·si·tion** \,trans-pə-'zi-shən\ *n*

trans·sex·u·al \(,)trans-'sek-shə-wəl\ *n* : a person who psychologically identifies with the opposite sex and may seek to live as a member of this sex esp. by undergoing surgery to modify the external sex organs

trans·ship \tran-'ship, trans-\ *vb* : to transfer for further transportation from one ship or conveyance to another — **trans·ship·ment** *n*

tran·sub·stan·ti·a·tion \,tran-səb-,stan-chē-'ā-shən\ *n* : the change in the eucharistic elements from the substance of bread and wine to the substance of the body of Christ with only the appearances of bread and wine remaining

trans·verse \trans-'vərs, tranz-\ *adj* : lying across : set crosswise — **transverse** \'trans-,vərs, 'tranz-\ *n* — **trans·verse·ly** *adv*

trans·ves·tite \trans-'ves-,tīt, tranz-\ *n* : a person who adopts the dress and often the behavior of the opposite sex — **transvestite** *adj* — **trans·ves·tism** \-,ti-zəm\ *n*

¹trap \'trap\ *n* **1** : a device for catching animals **2** : something by which one is caught unawares; *also* : a situation from which escape is difficult or impossible **3** : a machine for throwing clay pigeons into the air; *also* : SAND TRAP **4** : a light one-horse carriage on springs **5** : a device to allow some one thing to pass through while keeping other things out ⟨a ∼ in a drainpipe⟩ **6** *pl* : a group of percussion instruments (as in a dance orchestra)

²trap *vb* **trapped; trap·ping 1** : to catch in or as if in a trap; *also* : CONFINE **2** : to provide or set (a place) with traps **3** : to set traps for animals esp. as a business ♦ **Synonyms** SNARE, ENTRAP, ENSNARE, BAG, LURE, DECOY — **trap·per** *n*

trap·door \'trap-'dòr\ *n* : a lifting or sliding door covering an opening in a floor or roof

tra·peze \tra-'pēz\ *n* : a gymnastic apparatus consisting of a horizontal bar suspended by two parallel ropes

trap·e·zoid \'tra-pə-,zóid\ *n* [NL *trapezoïdes*, fr. Gk *trapezoeidēs* trapezoidal, fr. *trapeza* table, fr. *tra-* four + *peza* foot] : a 4-sided polygon with exactly two sides parallel — **trap·e·zoi·dal** \,tra-pə-'zóid-ᵊl\ *adj*

trap·pings \'tra-piŋz\ *n pl* **1** : CAPARISON 1 **2** : outward decoration or dress; *also* : outward sign ⟨∼ of success⟩

traps \'traps\ *n pl* : personal belongings : LUGGAGE

trap·shoot·ing \'trap-,shü-tiŋ\ *n* : shooting at clay pigeons sprung from a trap into the air away from the shooter

¹trash \'trash\ *n* **1** : something of little worth : RUBBISH **2** : empty or disparaging talk **3** : a worthless person; *also* : such persons as a group : RIFFRAFF — **trashy** *adj*

²trash *vb* **1** : to dispose of : DISCARD ⟨∼ed the plans⟩ **2** : VANDALIZE, DESTROY **3** : ATTACK **4** : SPOIL, RUIN **5** : to criticize or disparage harshly

trau·ma \'traù-mə, 'trò-\ *n, pl* **traumas** *also* **trau·ma·ta** \-mə-tə\ [Gk, wound] : a bodily or mental injury usu. caused by an external agent; *also* : a cause of trauma — **trau·mat·ic** \trə-'ma-tik, trò-, traù-\ *adj*

trau·ma·tize \-,tīz\ *vb* **-tized; -tiz·ing** : to inflict trauma upon

¹tra·vail \trə-'vāl, 'tra-,vāl\ *n* **1** : painful work or exertion : TOIL **2** : AGONY, TORMENT **3** : CHILDBIRTH, LABOR

²travail *vb* : to labor hard : TOIL

¹trav·el \'tra-vəl\ *vb* **-eled** *or* **-elled; -el·ing** *or* **-el·ling** [ME *travailen* to torment, labor, journey, fr. AF *travailler* strive, fr. VL **trepaliare* to torture, fr. LL *trepalium* instrument of torture] **1** : to go on or as if on a trip or tour : JOURNEY **2** : to move as if by traveling ⟨news ∼s fast⟩ **3** : ASSOCIATE **4** : to go from place to place as a sales representative **5** : to move from point to point ⟨light waves ∼ very fast⟩ **6** : to journey over or through ⟨∼ing the highways⟩ **7** : to take excessive steps while holding a basketball — **trav·el·er** *or* **trav·el·ler** *n*

²travel *n* **1** : the act of traveling : PASSAGE **2** : JOURNEY, TRIP — often used in pl. **3** : the number traveling : TRAFFIC **4** : the motion of a piece of machinery and esp. when to and fro

traveler's check *n* : a check paid for in advance that is signed when bought and signed again when cashed

traveling bag *n* : SUITCASE

trav·el·ogue *or* **trav·el·og** \'tra-və-,lóg, -,läg\ *n* : a usu. illustrated lecture on travel

¹**tra·verse** \'tra-vərs\ *n* : something that crosses or lies across

²**tra·verse** \trə-'vərs, tra-'vərs *or* 'tra-vərs\ *vb* **tra·versed; tra·vers·ing 1** : to go or travel across or over **2** : to move or pass along or through **3** : to extend over **4** : SWIVEL

³**tra·verse** \'tra-ˌvərs\ *adj* : TRANSVERSE

trav·er·tine \'tra-vər-ˌtēn, -tən\ *n* : a crystalline mineral formed by deposition from spring waters

¹**trav·es·ty** \'tra-və-stē\ *vb* **-tied; -ty·ing** : to make a travesty of

²**travesty** *n, pl* **-ties** [obs. E *travesty* disguised, parodied, fr. F *travesti*, pp. of *travestir* to disguise, fr. It *travestire*, fr. *tra-* across (fr. L *trans-*) + *vestire* to dress] : an imitation that makes crude fun of something; *also* : an inferior imitation

¹**trawl** \'trȯl\ *vb* : to fish or catch with a trawl — **trawl·er** *n*

²**trawl** *n* **1** : a large conical net dragged along the sea bottom in fishing **2** : a long heavy fishing line equipped with many hooks in series

tray \'trā\ *n* : an open receptacle with flat bottom and low rim for holding, carrying, or exhibiting articles

treach·er·ous \'tre-chə-rəs\ *adj* **1** : characterized by treachery **2** : UNTRUSTWORTHY, UNRELIABLE **3** : providing insecure footing or support ⟨a ∼ slope⟩ ♦ **Synonyms** TRAITOROUS, FAITHLESS, FALSE, DISLOYAL — **treach·er·ous·ly** *adv*

treach·ery \'tre-chə-rē\ *n, pl* **-er·ies** : violation of allegiance or trust

trea·cle \'trē-kəl\ *n* [ME *triacle* a medicinal compound, fr. AF, fr. L *theriaca*, fr. Gk *thēriakē* antidote against a poisonous bite, fr. *thērion* wild animal] *chiefly Brit* : MOLASSES — **trea·cly** \-k(ə-)lē\ *adj*

¹**tread** \'tred\ *vb* **trod** \'träd\; **trod·den** \'trä-dᵊn\ *or* **trod; tread·ing 1** : to step or walk on or over **2** : to move on foot : WALK; *also* : DANCE **3** : to beat or press with the feet — **tread water** : to stay afloat and upright in water by sustaining a walking motion

²**tread** *n* **1** : a mark made by or as if by treading **2** : the manner or sound of stepping **3** : the part of a wheel that makes contact with a road **4** : the horizontal part of a step

trea·dle \'tre-dᵊl\ *n* : a lever device pressed by the foot to drive a machine — **treadle** *vb*

tread·mill \'tred-ˌmil\ *n* **1** : a mill worked by persons who tread on steps around the edge of a wheel or by animals that walk on an endless belt **2** : a device with an endless belt on which a person walks or runs in place **3** : a wearisome routine

treas *abbr* treasurer; treasury

trea·son \'trē-zᵊn\ *n* : the offense of attempting to overthrow the government of one's country or of assisting its enemies in war — **trea·son·able** \-zᵊn-ə-bəl\ *adj* — **trea·son·ous** \-ᵊn-əs\ *adj*

¹**trea·sure** \'tre-zhər, 'trā-\ *n* [ME *tresor*, fr. AF, fr. L *thesaurus*, fr. Gk *thēsauros*] **1** : wealth stored up or held in reserve **2** : something of great value

²**treasure** *vb* **trea·sured; trea·sur·ing 1** : HOARD **2** : to keep as precious : CHERISH ♦ **Synonyms** PRIZE, VALUE, APPRECIATE, ESTEEM

trea·sur·er \'tre-zhə-rər, 'trā-\ *n* : an officer of a club, business, or government who has charge of money taken in and paid out

treasure trove \-ˌtrōv\ *n* **1** : treasure of unknown ownership found buried or hidden **2** : a valuable discovery

trea·sury \'tre-zhə-rē, 'trā-\ *n, pl* **-sur·ies 1** : a place in which stores of wealth are kept **2** : the place where collected funds are stored and paid out **3** *cap* : a governmental department in charge of finances

¹**treat** \'trēt\ *vb* **1** : NEGOTIATE **2** : to deal with esp. in writing; *also* : HANDLE **3** : to pay for the food or entertainment of **4** : to behave or act toward ⟨∼ them well⟩ **5** : to regard in a specified manner ⟨∼ as inferiors⟩ **6** : to give medical or surgical care to **7** : to subject to some action ⟨∼ soil with lime⟩

²**treat** *n* **1** : an entertainment given free to those invited; *also* : food, drink, or entertainment provided at another's expense **2** : a source of joy or amusement

trea·tise \'trē-təs\ *n* : a systematic written exposition or argument

treat·ment \'trēt-mənt\ *n* : the act or manner or an instance of treating someone or something; *also* : a substance or method used in treating

trea·ty \'trē-tē\ *n, pl* **treaties** : an agreement made by negotiation or diplomacy esp. between two or more states or governments

¹**tre·ble** \'tre-bəl\ *n* **1** : the highest of the four voice parts in vocal music : SOPRANO **2** : a high-pitched or shrill voice or sound **3** : the upper half of the musical pitch range

²**treble** *adj* **1** : triple in number or amount **2** : relating to or having the range of a musical treble **3** : high-pitched : SHRILL — **tre·bly** *adv*

³**treble** *vb* **tre·bled; tre·bling** : to make or become three times the size, amount, or number

¹**tree** \'trē\ *n* **1** : a woody perennial plant usu. with a single main stem and a head of branches and leaves at the top **2** : a piece of wood adapted to a particular use ⟨a shoe ∼⟩ **3** : something resembling a tree ⟨a genealogical ∼⟩ — **tree·less** *adj*

²**tree** *vb* **treed; tree·ing** : to drive to or up a tree ⟨∼ a raccoon⟩

tree farm *n* : an area of forest land managed to ensure continuous commercial production

tree frog *n* : any of numerous usu. tree-dwelling amphibians with adhesive disks on the toes

tree line *n* : TIMBERLINE

tree of heaven : a Chinese ailanthus widely grown as an ornamental tree

tree surgery *n* : operative treatment of diseased trees esp. for control of decay — **tree surgeon** *n*

tre·foil \'trē-ˌfȯi(-ə)l, 'tre-\ *n* **1** : an herb (as a clover) with leaves that have three leaflets **2** : a decorative design with three leaflike parts

¹**trek** \'trek\ *vb* **trekked; trek·king 1** *chiefly southern Africa* : to travel or migrate by ox wagon **2** : to make one's way arduously

²**trek** *n* **1** *chiefly southern Africa* : a migration esp. of settlers by ox wagon **2** : a slow or difficult journey

trel·lis \'tre-ləs\ *n* [ME *trelis*, fr. AF *treleis*, fr. OF *treille* arbor, fr. L *trichila* summerhouse] : a frame of latticework used esp. to support climbing plants

²**trellis** *vb* : to provide with a trellis; *esp* : to train (as a vine) on a trellis

trem·a·tode \'tre-mə-ˌtōd\ *n* : any of a class of parasitic worms

¹**trem·ble** \'trem-bəl\ *vb* **trem·bled; trem·bling 1** : to shake involuntarily (as with fear or cold) : SHIVER **2** : to move, sound, pass, or come to pass as if shaken or tremulous **3** : to be affected with fear or doubt

²**tremble** *n* : a spell of shaking or quivering

tre·men·dous \tri-'men-dəs\ *adj* **1** : causing dread, awe, or terror : TERRIFYING **2** : unusually large, powerful, great, or excellent ♦ **Synonyms** STUPENDOUS, MONUMENTAL, MONSTROUS — **tre·men·dous·ly** *adv*

trem·o·lo \'tre-mə-ˌlō\ *n, pl* **-los** [It] : a rapid fluttering of a tone or alternating tones

trem·or \'tre-mər\ *n* **1** : a trembling or shaking esp. from weakness, emotional stress, or disease **2** : a quivering motion of the earth (as during an earthquake)

trem·u·lous \'trem-yə-ləs\ *adj* **1** : marked by trembling or tremors : QUIVERING **2** : TIMOROUS, TIMID — **trem·u·lous·ly** *adv*

¹**trench** \'trench\ *n* [ME *trenche* track cut through a wood, fr. AF, act of cutting, fr. *trencher* to cut, prob. fr. VL **trinicare* to cut in three, fr. L *trini* three each] **1** : a long narrow cut in the ground : DITCH; *esp* : a ditch protected by banks of earth and used to shelter soldiers **2** *pl* : a place or situation likened to warfare conducted from trenches **3** : a long narrow steep-sided depression in the ocean floor

²**trench** *vb* **1** : to cut or dig trenches in **2** : to protect (troops) with trenches **3** : to come close : VERGE

tren·chant \'tren-chənt\ *adj* **1** : vigorously effective; *also* : CAUSTIC **2** : sharply perceptive : KEEN **3** : CLEAR-CUT, DISTINCT

tren·cher \'tren-chər\ *n* : a wooden platter for serving food

tren·cher·man \'tren-chər-mən\ *n* : a hearty eater

trench foot *n* : a painful foot disorder resembling frostbite and resulting from exposure to cold and wet

trench mouth *n* : a progressive painful bacterial infection of the mouth and adjacent parts marked by ulceration, bleeding gums, and foul breath

¹trend \'trend\ *vb* **1** : to have or take a general direction : TEND **2** : to show a tendency : INCLINE

²trend *n* **1** : a general direction taken (as by a stream or mountain range) **2** : a prevailing tendency : DRIFT **3** : a current style or preference : VOGUE

trendy \'tren-dē\ *adj* **trend·i·er; -est** : very fashionable; *also* : marked by superficial or faddish appeal or taste

trep·i·da·tion \ˌtre-pə-'dā-shən\ *n* : nervous agitation : APPREHENSION ✦ **Synonyms** HORROR, TERROR, PANIC, CONSTERNATION, DREAD, FRIGHT, DISMAY

¹tres·pass \'tres-pəs, -ˌpas\ *n* **1** : SIN, OFFENSE **2** : unlawful entry on someone else's land ✦ **Synonyms** TRANSGRESSION, VIOLATION, INFRACTION, INFRINGEMENT

²trespass *vb* **1** : to commit an offense : ERR, SIN **2** : INTRUDE, ENCROACH; *esp* : to enter unlawfully upon the land of another — **tres·pass·er** *n*

tress \'tres\ *n* : a long lock of hair — usu. used in pl.

tres·tle *also* **tres·sel** \'tre-səl\ *n* **1** : a supporting framework consisting usu. of a horizontal piece with spreading legs at each end **2** : a braced framework of timbers, piles, or steel for carrying a road or railroad over a depression

T. rex \'tē-'reks\ *n* : TYRANNOSAUR

trey \'trā\ *n, pl* **treys** : a card or the side of a die with three spots

tri·ad \'trī-ˌad, -əd\ *n* : a union or group of three usu. closely related persons or things

tri·age \trē-'äzh, 'trē-ˌäzh\ *n* [F, sorting] : the sorting of and allocation of treatment to patients and esp. battle or disaster victims according to a system of priorities designed to maximize the number of survivors

tri·al \'trī-əl\ *n* **1** : the action or process of trying or putting to the proof : TEST **2** : the hearing and judgment of a matter in issue before a competent tribunal **3** : a source of vexation or annoyance **4** : an experiment to test quality, value, or usefulness **5** : EFFORT, ATTEMPT ✦ **Synonyms** CROSS, ORDEAL, TRIBULATION, AFFLICTION — **trial** *adj*

tri·an·gle \'trī-ˌaŋ-gəl\ *n* **1** : a polygon that has three sides **2** : something shaped like a triangle — **tri·an·gu·lar** \trī-'aŋ-gyə-lər\ *adj* — **tri·an·gu·lar·ly** *adv*

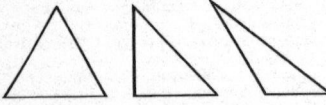

triangle 1: three kinds

tri·an·gu·la·tion \(ˌ)trī-ˌaŋ-gyə-'lā-shən\ *n* : a method using trigonometry to find the location of a point using bearings from two fixed points a known distance apart — **tri·an·gu·late** \trī-'aŋ-gyə-ˌlāt\ *vb*

Tri·as·sic \trī-'a-sik\ *adj* : of, relating to, or being the earliest period of the Mesozoic era marked by the first appearance of the dinosaurs — **Triassic** *n*

tri·ath·lon \trī-'ath-lən, -ˌlän\ *n* : an athletic contest consisting of three phases (as swimming, bicycling, and running)

trib *abbr* tributary

tribe \'trīb\ *n* **1** : a social group comprising numerous families, clans, or generations **2** : a group of persons having a common character, occupation, or interest **3** : a group of related plants or animals ⟨the cat ∼⟩ — **trib·al** \'trī-bəl\ *adj*

tribes·man \'trībz-mən\ *n* : a member of a tribe

trib·u·la·tion \ˌtri-byə-'lā-shən\ *n* [ME *tribulacion*, fr. AF, fr. L *tribulatio*, fr. *tribulare* to press, oppress, fr. *tribulum* drag used in threshing] : distress or suffering resulting from oppression or persecution; *also* : a trying experience ✦ **Synonyms** TRIAL, AFFLICTION, CROSS, ORDEAL

tri·bu·nal \trī-'byün-ᵊl, tri-\ *n* **1** : the seat of a judge **2** : a court of justice **3** : something that decides or determines ⟨the ∼ of public opinion⟩

tri·bune \'tri-ˌbyün, tri-'byün\ *n* **1** : an official in ancient Rome with the function of protecting the interests of ple-

beian citizens from the patricians **2** : a defender of the people

¹trib·u·tary \'tri-byə-ˌter-ē\ *adj* **1** : paying tribute : SUBJECT **2** : flowing into a larger stream or a lake ✦ **Synonyms** SUBORDINATE, SECONDARY, DEPENDENT

²tributary *n, pl* **-tar·ies** **1** : a ruler or state that pays tribute **2** : a tributary stream

trib·ute \'tri-(ˌ)byüt, -byət\ *n* **1** : a payment by one ruler or nation to another as an act of submission or price of protection **2** : a usu. excessive tax, rental, or levy exacted by a sovereign or superior **3** : a gift or service showing respect, gratitude, or affection; *also* : PRAISE ✦ **Synonyms** EULOGY, CITATION, ENCOMIUM, PANEGYRIC

trice \'trīs\ *n* : INSTANT, MOMENT

tri·ceps \'trī-ˌseps\ *n, pl* **triceps** : a large muscle along the back of the upper arm that is attached at its upper end by three main parts and acts to extend the forearm at the elbow joint

tri·cer·a·tops \(ˌ)trī-'ser-ə-ˌtäps\ *n, pl* **-tops** *also* **-tops·es** [NL, fr. Gk *tri-* three + *kerat-, keras* horn + *ōps* face] : any of a genus of large plant-eating Cretaceous dinosaurs with three horns, a bony crest on the neck, and hoofed toes

tri·chi·na \'trī-'kī-nə\ *n, pl* **-nae** \-(ˌ)nē\ *also* **-nas** : a small slender nematode worm that in the larval state is parasitic in the striated muscles of flesh-eating mammals (as humans)

trich·i·no·sis \ˌtri-kə-'nō-səs\ *n* : infestation with or disease caused by trichinae and marked esp. by muscular pain, fever, and swelling

¹trick \'trik\ *n* **1** : a crafty procedure meant to deceive **2** : a mischievous action : PRANK **3** : a childish action **4** : a deceptive or ingenious feat designed to puzzle or amuse **5** : PECULIARITY, MANNERISM **6** : a quick or artful way of getting a result : KNACK ⟨∼s of the trade⟩ **7** : the cards played in one round of a card game **8** : a tour of duty : SHIFT ✦ **Synonyms** RUSE, MANEUVER, ARTIFICE, WILE, FEINT

²trick *vb* **1** : to deceive by cunning or artifice : CHEAT **2** : to dress ornately

trick·ery \'tri-kə-rē\ *n* : deception by tricks and stratagems

trick·le \'tri-kəl\ *vb* **trick·led; trick·ling** **1** : to run or fall in drops **2** : to flow in a thin gentle stream — **trickle** *n*

trick·ster \'trik-stər\ *n* : one who tricks or cheats

tricky \'tri-kē\ *adj* **trick·i·er, -est** **1** : inclined to trickery **2** : requiring skill or caution ⟨a ∼ situation to handle⟩ **3** : UNRELIABLE ⟨a ∼ lock⟩

tri·col·or \'trī-ˌkə-lər\ *n* : a flag of three colors ⟨the French ∼⟩

tri·cy·cle \'trī-(ˌ)si-kəl\ *n* : a 3-wheeled vehicle usu. propelled by pedals

tri·dent \'trī-dᵊnt\ *n* [L *trident-, tridens,* fr. *tri-* three + *dent-, dens* tooth] : a 3-pronged spear

tried \'trīd\ *adj* **1** : found trustworthy through testing **2** : subjected to trials

tri·en·ni·al \trī-'e-nē-əl\ *adj* **1** : occurring or being done every three years **2** : lasting for three years — **triennial** *n*

tri·fle \'trī-fəl\ *n* **1** : something of little value or importance **2** : a dessert of cake soaked with liqueur and served with toppings (as fruit or cream)

²trifle *vb* **tri·fled; tri·fling** **1** : to talk in a jesting or mocking manner **2** : to treat someone or something as unimportant **3** : DALLY, FLIRT **4** : to handle idly : TOY — **tri·fler** *n*

tri·fling \'trī-fliŋ\ *adj* **1** : FRIVOLOUS **2** : TRIVIAL, INSIGNIFICANT ✦ **Synonyms** PETTY, PALTRY, MEASLY, INCONSEQUENTIAL

tri·fo·cals \trī-'fō-kəlz\ *n pl* : eyeglasses with lenses having one part for close focus, one for intermediate focus, and one for distant focus

tri·fo·li·ate \trī-'fō-lē-ət\ *adj* : having three leaves or leaflets

trig \'trig\ *adj* : stylishly trim : SMART

²trig *n* : TRIGONOMETRY

¹trig·ger \'tri-gər\ *n* [alter. of earlier *tricker,* fr. D *trekker,* fr. MD *trecker* one that pulls, fr. *trecken* to pull] : a movable lever that activates a device when it is squeezed; *esp* : the part of a firearm lock moved by the finger to fire a gun — **trigger** *adj* — **trig·gered** *adj*

²trigger *vb* **1** : to fire by pulling a trigger **2** : to initiate, actuate, or set off as if by a trigger ⟨remarks that ∼ed a fight⟩

tri·glyc·er·ide \trī-'gli-sə-ˌrīd\ *n* : any of a group of lipids that are formed from glycerol and fatty acids and are widespread in animal tissue

trig·o·nom·e·try \ˌtri-gə-'nä-mə-trē\ *n* : the branch of mathematics dealing with the properties of triangles and esp. with finding unknown angles or sides given the size or length of some angles or sides — **trig·o·no·met·ric** \-nə-'me-trik\ *also* **trig·o·no·met·ri·cal** \-tri-kəl\ *adj*

trike \'trīk\ *n* : TRICYCLE

¹**trill** \'tril\ *n* **1** : the alternation of two musical tones a scale degree apart **2** : WARBLE **3** : the rapid vibration of one speech organ against another (as of the tip of the tongue against the teeth)

²**trill** *vb* : to utter as or with a trill

tril·lion \'tril-yən\ *n* **1** : a thousand billions **2** *Brit* : a million billions — **trillion** *adj* — **tril·lionth** \-yənth\ *adj or n*

tril·li·um \'tri-lē-əm\ *n* : any of a genus of spring-blooming herbs that are related to the lilies and have an erect stem bearing a whorl of three leaves and a solitary flower

tril·o·gy \'tri-lə-jē\ *n, pl* **-gies** : a series of three dramas or literary or musical compositions that are closely related and develop one theme

¹**trim** \'trim\ *vb* **trimmed; trim·ming** [OE *trymian, trymman* to strengthen, arrange, fr. *trum* strong, firm] **1** : to put ornaments on : ADORN **2** : to defeat esp. resoundingly **3** : to make trim, neat, regular, or less bulky by or as if by cutting ⟨∼ a beard⟩ ⟨∼ a budget⟩ **4** : to cause (a boat) to assume a desired position in the water by arrangement of the load; *also* : to adjust (as a submarine or airplane) esp. for horizontal motion **5** : to adjust (a sail) to a desired position **6** : to change one's views for safety or expediency — **trim·ly** *adv* — **trim·mer** *n* — **trim·ness** *n*

²**trim** *adj* **trim·mer; trim·mest** : showing neatness, good order, or compactness ⟨a ∼ figure⟩ ✦ **Synonyms** TIDY, TRIG, SMART, SPRUCE, SHIPSHAPE

³**trim** *n* **1** : good condition : FITNESS **2** : material used for ornament or trimming; *esp* : the woodwork in the finish of a house esp. around doors and windows **3** : the position of a ship or boat esp. with reference to the horizontal; *also* : the relation between the plane of a sail and the direction of a ship **4** : the position of an airplane at which it will continue in level flight with no adjustments to the controls **5** : something that is trimmed off

tri·ma·ran \'trī-mə-ˌran, ˌtrī-mə-'ran\ *n* : a sailboat with three hulls

tri·mes·ter \trī-'mes-tər, 'trī-ˌmes-tər\ *n* **1** : a period of three or about three months (as in pregnancy) **2** : one of three terms into which an academic year is sometimes divided

trim·e·ter \'tri-mə-tər\ *n* : a line of verse consisting of three metrical feet

trim·ming \'tri-miŋ\ *n* **1** : DEFEAT **2** : the action of one that trims **3** : something that trims, ornaments, or completes

tri·month·ly \trī-'mənth-lē\ *adj* : occurring every three months

trine \'trīn\ *adj* : THREEFOLD, TRIPLE

Trin·i·da·di·an \ˌtri-nə-'dä-dē-ən, -'da-\ *n* : a native or inhabitant of the island of Trinidad — **Trinidadian** *adj*

Trin·i·tar·i·an \ˌtri-nə-'ter-ē-ən\ *n* : a believer in the doctrine of the Trinity — **Trin·i·tar·i·an·ism** \-ē-ə-ˌni-zəm\ *n*

Trin·i·ty \'tri-nə-tē\ *n* **1** : the unity of Father, Son, and Holy Spirit as three persons in one Godhead **2** *not cap* : TRIAD

trin·ket \'triŋ-kət\ *n* **1** : a small ornament (as a jewel or ring) **2** : TRIFLE 1

trio \'trē-ō\ *n, pl* **tri·os** **1** : a musical composition for three voices or three instruments **2** : the performers of a trio **3** : a group or set of three

¹**trip** \'trip\ *vb* **tripped; trip·ping** **1** : to move with light quick steps **2** : to catch the foot against something so as to stumble or cause to stumble **3** : to make a mistake : SLIP; *also* : to detect in a misstep : EXPOSE **4** : to release (as a spring or switch) by moving a catch; *also* : ACTIVATE ⟨∼ an alarm⟩ **5** : to get high on a usu. hallucinatory drug

²**trip** *n* **1** : JOURNEY, VOYAGE **2** : a quick light step **3** : a false step : STUMBLE; *also* : ERROR **4** : the action of tripping **5** : a device for tripping **5** : an intense experience; *esp* : one triggered by a hallucinatory drug **6** : absorption in an attitude or state of mind ⟨an ego ∼⟩

tri·par·tite \trī-'pär-ˌtīt\ *adj* **1** : divided into three parts **2** : having three corresponding parts or copies **3** : made between three parties ⟨a ∼ treaty⟩

tripe \'trīp\ *n* **1** : stomach tissue esp. of a ruminant (as an ox) used as food **2** : something poor, worthless, or offensive : TRASH

¹**tri·ple** \'tri-pəl\ *vb* **tri·pled; tri·pling** **1** : to make or become three times as great or as many **2** : to hit a triple

²**triple** *n* **1** : a triple quantity **2** : a group of three **3** : a hit in baseball that lets the batter reach third base

³**triple** *adj* **1** : being three times as great or as many **2** : having three units or members **3** : repeated three times

triple bond *n* : a chemical bond in which three pairs of electrons are shared by two atoms in a molecule

triple point *n* : the condition of temperature and pressure under which the gaseous, liquid, and solid forms of a substance can exist in equilibrium

trip·let \'tri-plət\ *n* **1** : a unit of three lines of verse **2** : a group of three of a kind **3** : one of three offspring born at one birth

tri·plex \'tri-ˌpleks, 'trī-\ *adj* : THREEFOLD, TRIPLE

¹**trip·li·cate** \'tri-pli-kət\ *adj* : made in three identical copies

²**trip·li·cate** \-plə-ˌkāt\ *vb* **-cat·ed; -cat·ing** **1** : TRIPLE **2** : to provide three copies of ⟨∼ a document⟩

³**trip·li·cate** \-pli-kət\ *n* : three copies all alike — used with *in* ⟨typed in ∼⟩

tri·ply \'tri-plē, 'tri-pə-lē\ *adv* : in a triple degree, amount, or manner

tri·pod \'trī-ˌpäd\ *n* : something (as a caldron, stool, or camera stand) that rests on three legs — **tripod** *or* **tri·po·dal** \'trī-pəd-ᵊl, 'tri-ˌpäd-\ *adj*

trip·tych \'trip-tik\ *n* : a picture or carving in three panels side by side

tri·reme \'trī-ˌrēm\ *n* : an ancient galley having three banks of oars

tri·sect \'trī-ˌsekt, trī-'sekt\ *vb* : to divide into three usu. equal parts — **tri·sec·tion** \'trī-ˌsek-shən\ *n*

trite \'trīt\ *adj* **trit·er; trit·est** [L *tritus,* fr. pp. of *terere* to rub, wear away] : used so commonly that the novelty is worn off : STALE ✦ **Synonyms** HACKNEYED, STEREOTYPED, COMMONPLACE, CLICHÉD

tri·ti·um \'tri-tē-əm, 'tri-shē-\ *n* : a radioactive form of hydrogen with one proton and two neutrons in its nucleus and three times the mass of ordinary hydrogen

tri·ton \'trī-tᵊn\ *n* : any of various large marine gastropod mollusks with a heavy elongated conical shell; *also* : the shell of a triton

trit·u·rate \'tri-chə-ˌrāt\ *vb* **-rat·ed; -rat·ing** : to rub or grind to a fine powder

¹**tri·umph** \'trī-əmf\ *n* **1** : the joy or exultation of victory or success **2** : VICTORY, CONQUEST — **tri·um·phal** \trī-'əm-fəl\ *adj*

²**triumph** *vb* **1** : to obtain victory : PREVAIL **2** : to celebrate victory or success exultantly — **tri·um·phant** \trī-'əm-fənt\ *adj* — **tri·um·phant·ly** *adv*

tri·um·vir \trī-'əm-vər\ *n, pl* **-virs** *also* **-vi·ri** \-və-ˌrī\ : a member of a triumvirate

tri·um·vi·rate \-və-rət\ *n* : a ruling body of three persons

tri·une \'trī-ˌün, -ˌyün\ *adj* : being three in one ⟨the ∼ God⟩

triv·et \'tri-vət\ *n* **1** : a 3-legged stand : TRIPOD **2** : a usu. metal stand with short feet for use under a hot dish

triv·ia \'tri-vē-ə\ *n sing or pl* : unimportant matters : obscure facts or details ⟨movie ∼⟩

triv·i·al \'tri-vē-əl\ *adj* [L *trivialis* found everywhere, commonplace, fr. *trivium* crossroads, fr. *tri-* three + *via* way] : of little importance — **triv·i·al·i·ty** \ˌtri-vē-'a-lə-tē\ *n*

triv·i·um \'tri-vē-əm\ *n, pl* **triv·ia** \-vē-ə\ : the three liberal arts of grammar, rhetoric, and logic in a medieval university

tri·week·ly \trī-'wē-klē\ *adj* **1** : occurring or appearing three times a week **2** : occurring or appearing every three weeks — **triweekly** *adv*

tro·che \'trō-kē\ *n* **1** : LOZENGE 2

tro·chee \'trō-(ˌ)kē\ *n* : a metrical foot of one accented syllable followed by one unaccented syllable — **tro·cha·ic** \trō-'kā-ik\ *adj*

trod *past and past part of* TREAD

trodden *past part of* TREAD

troi·ka \'trȯi-kə\ *n* [Russ *troĭka,* fr. *troe* three] : a group of three; *esp* : an administrative or ruling body of three

¹troll \'trōl\ *vb* 1 : to sing the parts of (a song) in succession 2 : to fish by trailing a lure or baited hook from a moving boat 3 : to sing or play jovially

²troll *n* : a lure used in trolling; *also* : the line with its lure

³troll *n* : a dwarf or giant in Scandinavian folklore inhabiting caves or hills

trol·ley *also* trol·ly \'trä-lē\ *n, pl* trolleys *also* trollies 1 : a device (as a grooved wheel on the end of a pole) to carry current from a wire to an electrically driven vehicle 2 : a streetcar powered electrically by overhead wires 3 : a wheeled carriage running on an overhead rail or track

trol·ley·bus \'trä-lē-,bəs\ *n* : a bus powered electrically by overhead wires

trolley car *n* : TROLLEY 2

trol·lop \'trä-ləp\ *n* : a disreputable woman; *esp* : one who engages in sex promiscuously

trom·bone \träm-'bōn, 'träm-,bōn\ *n* [It, fr. *tromba* trumpet] : a brass wind instrument that consists of a long metal tube with two turns and a flaring end and that usu. has a movable slide to vary the pitch — trom·bon·ist \-'bō-nist, -,bō-\ *n*

tromp \'trämp, 'trómp\ *vb* 1 : TRAMP, MARCH 2 : to stamp with the foot 3 : to defeat decisively

trompe l'oeil \(,)trómp-'lə-ē, trōⁿp-'lœi\ *n* [F *trompe-l'oeil*, lit., deceives the eye] : a style of painting in which objects are depicted with photographic detail

¹troop \'trüp\ *n* 1 : a cavalry unit corresponding to an infantry company 2 *pl* : armed forces : SOLDIERS 3 : a collection of people, animals, or things 4 : a unit of Girl Scouts or Boy Scouts under an adult leader

²troop *vb* : to move or gather in crowds

troop·er \'trü-pər\ *n* 1 : an enlisted cavalryman; *also* : a cavalry horse 2 : a mounted or a state police officer

troop·ship \'trüp-,ship\ *n* : a ship or aircraft for carrying troops

trope \'trōp\ *n* : a word or expression used in a figurative sense

tro·phic \'trō-fik\ *adj* : of or relating to nutrition

tro·phy \'trō-fē\ *n, pl* trophies : something gained or given in conquest or victory esp. when preserved or mounted as a memorial

trop·ic \'trä-pik\ *n* [ME *tropik*, fr. L *tropicus* of the solstice, fr. Gk *tropikos*, fr. *tropē* turn] 1 : either of the two parallels of latitude approximately 23½ degrees north (Tropic of Can·cer) or south (Tropic of Cap·ri·corn) of the equator where the sun is directly overhead when it reaches its most northerly or southerly point in the sky 2 *pl, often cap* : the region lying between the tropics — trop·i·cal \-pi-kəl\ *or* tropic *adj*

tro·pism \'trō-,pi-zəm\ *n* : an automatic movement by an organism in response to a source of stimulation; *also* : a reflex reaction involving this

tro·po·sphere \'trō-pə-,sfir, 'trä-\ *n* : the part of the atmosphere between the earth's surface and the stratosphere in which most weather changes occur — tro·po·spher·ic \,trō-pə-'sfir-ik, ,trä-, -'sfer-\ *adj*

¹trot \'trät\ *n* 1 : a moderately fast gait of a 4-footed animal (as a horse) in which the legs move in diagonal pairs 2 : a human jogging gait between a walk and a run

²trot *vb* trot·ted; trot·ting 1 : to ride, drive, or go at a trot 2 : to proceed briskly : HURRY — trot·ter *n*

troth \'träth, 'tróth, 'trōth\ *n* 1 : pledged faithfulness 2 : one's pledged word; *also* : BETROTHAL

trou·ba·dour \'trü-bə-,dór\ *n* [F, fr. Old Occitan *trobador*, fr. *trobar* to compose] : any of a class of poet-musicians flourishing esp. in southern France and northern Italy during the 11th, 12th, and 13th centuries

¹trou·ble \'trə-bəl\ *vb* trou·bled; trou·bling 1 : to agitate mentally or spiritually : DISTURB, WORRY 2 : to produce physical disorder in : AFFLICT 3 : to put to inconvenience 4 : RUFFLE ⟨~ the waters⟩ 5 : to make an effort ✦ Synonyms DISTRESS, AIL, UPSET — trou·ble·some *adj* — trou·ble·some·ly *adv* — trou·blous \-bə-ləs\ *adj*

²trouble *n* 1 : the quality or state of being troubled esp. mentally 2 : an instance of distress or annoyance 3 : DISEASE, AILMENT ⟨heart ~⟩ 4 : EXERTION, PAINS ⟨took the ~ to phone⟩ 5 : a cause of disturbance or distress

trou·ble·mak·er \-,mā-kər\ *n* : a person who causes trouble

trou·ble·shoot·er \-,shü-tər\ *n* 1 : a worker employed to locate trouble and make repairs in equipment 2 : an expert in resolving disputes or problems — trou·ble·shoot *vb*

trough \'tróf, 'tróth\ *n, pl* troughs \'trófs, 'tróvz; 'tróths, 'tróthz\ 1 : a long shallow open boxlike container esp. for water or feed for livestock 2 : a gutter along the eaves of a house 3 : a long channel or depression (as between waves or hills) 4 : an elongated area of low barometric pressure

trounce \'trauns\ *vb* trounced; trounc·ing 1 : to thrash or punish severely 2 : to defeat decisively

troupe \'trüp\ *n* : COMPANY; *esp* : a group of performers on the stage — troup·er *n*

trou·sers \'trau-zərz\ *n pl* [alter. of earlier *trouse*, fr. Sc-Gael *triubhas*] : PANTS — trouser *adj*

trous·seau \'trü-sō, trü-'sō\ *n, pl* trous·seaux \-sōz, -'sōz\ *or* trous·seaus [F] : the personal outfit of a bride

trout \'traut\ *n, pl* trout *also* trouts [ME, fr. OE *trūht*, fr. LL *tructa*, a fish with sharp teeth, fr. Gk *trōktēs*, lit., gnawer] : any of various mostly freshwater food and game fishes usu. smaller than the related salmons

trout

trow \'trō\ *vb, archaic* : THINK, SUPPOSE

trow·el \'trau(-ə)l\ *n* 1 : a hand tool used for spreading, shaping, or smoothing loose or plastic material (as mortar or plaster) 2 : a scoop-shaped tool used in gardening — trowel *vb*

troy \'trói\ *adj* : expressed in troy weight ⟨~ ounce⟩

troy weight *n* : a system of weights based on a pound of 12 ounces and an ounce of 480 grains (31 grams) — see WEIGHT table

tru·ant \'trü-ənt\ *n* [ME, vagabond, idler, fr. AF, of Celt origin] : a student who stays out of school without permission — tru·an·cy \-ən-sē\ *n* — truant *adj*

truce \'trüs\ *n* 1 : ARMISTICE 2 : a respite esp. from something unpleasant

¹truck \'trək\ *vb* 1 : EXCHANGE, BARTER 2 : to have dealings : TRAFFIC

²truck *n* 1 : BARTER 2 : DEALINGS 3 : small goods or merchandise; *esp* : vegetables grown for market

³truck *n* 1 : a wheeled vehicle (as a strong heavy automobile) designed for carrying heavy articles or hauling a trailer 2 : a swiveling frame with springs and one or more pairs of wheels used to carry and guide one end of a locomotive or railroad car

⁴truck *vb* 1 : to transport on a truck 2 : to be employed in driving a truck — truck·er *n*

truck farm *n* : a farm growing vegetables for market — truck farmer *n*

truck·le \'trə-kəl\ *vb* truck·led; truck·ling : to yield slavishly to the will of another : SUBMIT ✦ Synonyms FAWN, TOADY, CRINGE, COWER

truc·u·lent \'trə-kyə-lənt\ *adj* 1 : feeling or showing ferocity : SAVAGE 2 : aggressively self-assertive : BELLIGERENT — truc·u·lence \-ləns\ *n* — truc·u·len·cy \-lən-sē\ *n* — truc·u·lent·ly *adv*

trudge \'trəj\ *vb* trudged; trudg·ing : to walk or march steadily and usu. laboriously

¹true \'trü\ *adj* tru·er; tru·est 1 : STEADFAST, LOYAL 2 : agreeing with facts or reality ⟨a ~ description⟩ 3 : CONSISTENT ⟨~ to expectations⟩ 4 : properly so called ⟨~ love⟩ 5 : RIGHTFUL ⟨~ and lawful king⟩ 6 : conformable to a standard or pattern; *also* : placed or formed accurately ✦ Synonyms CONSTANT, STAUNCH, RESOLUTE, STEADFAST

²**true** *adv* **1** : TRUTHFULLY **2** : ACCURATELY ⟨the bullet flew straight and ∼⟩; *also* : without variation from type ⟨breed ∼⟩

³**true** *n* **1** : TRUTH, REALITY — usu. used with *the* **2** : the state of being accurate (as in alignment) ⟨out of ∼⟩

⁴**true** *vb* **trued; true·ing** *also* **tru·ing** : to bring or restore to a desired precision

true–blue *adj* : marked by unswerving loyalty

true bug *n* : BUG 2

true·heart·ed \'trü-'här-təd\ *adj* : FAITHFUL, LOYAL ⟨a ∼ soldier⟩

truf·fle \'trə-fəl, 'trü-\ *n* **1** : the dark or light edible spore-bearing organ of any of several European fungi that grow underground; *also* : one of these fungi **2** : a candy made of chocolate, butter, and sugar shaped into balls and coated with cocoa

tru·ism \'trü-ˌi-zəm\ *n* : an undoubted or self-evident truth ✦ **Synonyms** COMMONPLACE, PLATITUDE, CLICHÉ

tru·ly \'trü-lē\ *adv* **1** : in all sincerity **2** : in agreement with fact **3** : ACCURATELY **4** : in a proper or suitable manner

¹**trump** \'trəmp\ *n* : TRUMPET

²**trump** *n* : a card of a designated suit any of whose cards will win over a card that is not of this suit; *also* : the suit itself — often used in pl.

³**trump** *vb* : to take with a trump

trumped–up \'trəmpt-'əp\ *adj* : fraudulently concocted : SPURIOUS

trum·pery \'trəm-pə-rē\ *n* **1** : NONSENSE **2** : trivial articles : JUNK

¹**trum·pet** \'trəm-pət\ *n* **1** : a wind instrument consisting of a long curved metal tube flaring at one end and with a cup-shaped mouthpiece at the other **2** : something that resembles a trumpet or its tonal quality **3** : a funnel-shaped instrument for collecting, directing, or intensifying sound

²**trumpet** *vb* **1** : to blow a trumpet **2** : to proclaim on or as if on a trumpet ⟨∼ the news⟩ — **trum·pet·er** *n*

¹**trun·cate** \'trəŋ-ˌkāt, 'trən-\ *adj* : having the end square or blunt

²**truncate** *vb* **trun·cat·ed; trun·cat·ing** : to shorten by or as if by cutting : LOP — **trun·ca·tion** \ˌtrəŋ-'kā-shən\ *n*

trun·cheon \'trən-chən\ *n* : a police officer's billy club

trun·dle \'trən-dᵊl\ *vb* **trun·dled; trun·dling** : to roll along : WHEEL

trundle bed *n* : a low bed that can be stored under a higher bed

trunk \'trəŋk\ *n* **1** : the main stem of a tree **2** : the body of a person or animal apart from the head and limbs **3** : the main or central part of something **4** : a box or chest used to hold usu. clothes or personal effects (as of a traveler); *also* : the enclosed luggage space in the rear of an automobile **5** : the long muscular nose of an elephant **6** *pl* : men's shorts worn chiefly for sports ⟨swimming ∼s⟩ **7** : a usu. major channel or passage

trunk line *n* : a transportation system handling long-distance through traffic

¹**truss** \'trəs\ *vb* **1** : to secure tightly : BIND **2** : to arrange for cooking by binding close the wings or legs of (a fowl) **3** : to support, strengthen, or stiffen by or as if by a truss

²**truss** *n* **1** : a collection of structural parts (as beams) forming a rigid framework (as in bridge or building construction) **2** : a device worn to reduce a hernia by pressure

¹**trust** \'trəst\ *n* **1** : assured reliance on the character, strength, or truth of someone or something **2** : a basis of reliance, faith, or hope **3** : confident hope **4** : financial credit **5** : a property interest held by one person for the benefit of another **6** : a combination of firms formed by a legal agreement; *esp* : one that reduces competition **7** : something entrusted to one to be cared for in the interest of another **8** : CARE, CUSTODY ✦ **Synonyms** CONFIDENCE, DEPENDENCE, FAITH, RELIANCE

²**trust** *vb* **1** : to place confidence in : DEPEND **2** : to be confident : HOPE **3** : ENTRUST **4** : to permit to stay or go or to do something without fear or misgiving **5** : to rely on or on the truth of : BELIEVE **6** : to extend credit to

trust·ee \ˌtrəs-'tē\ *n* **1** : a person to whom property is legally committed in trust **2** : a country charged with the supervision of a trust territory

trust·ee·ship \ˌtrəs-'tē-ˌship\ *n* **1** : the office or function

of a trustee **2** : supervisory control by one or more nations over a trust territory

trust·ful \'trəst-fəl\ *adj* : full of trust : CONFIDING — **trust·ful·ly** *adv* — **trust·ful·ness** *n*

trust territory *n* : a non-self-governing territory placed under a supervisory authority by the Trusteeship Council of the United Nations

trust·wor·thy \-ˌwər-thē\ *adj* : worthy of confidence : DEPENDABLE ✦ **Synonyms** TRUSTY, TRIED, RELIABLE — **trust·wor·thi·ness** *n*

¹**trusty** \'trəs-tē\ *adj* **trust·i·er; -est** : TRUSTWORTHY, DEPENDABLE ⟨a ∼ friend⟩

²**trusty** \'trəs-tē, ˌtrəs-'tē\ *n, pl* **trust·ies** : a trusted person; *esp* : a convict considered trustworthy and allowed special privileges

truth \'trüth\ *n, pl* **truths** \'trüthz, 'trüths\ **1** : TRUTHFULNESS, HONESTY **2** : the real state of things : FACT **3** : the body of real events or facts : ACTUALITY **4** : a true or accepted statement or proposition ⟨the ∼s of science⟩ **5** : agreement with fact or reality : CORRECTNESS ✦ **Synonyms** VERACITY, VERITY

truth·ful \'trüth-fəl\ *adj* : telling or disposed to tell the truth — **truth·ful·ly** *adv* — **truth·ful·ness** *n*

truth serum *n* : a drug held to induce a subject under questioning to talk freely

¹**try** \'trī\ *vb* **tried; try·ing** [ME *trien*, fr. AF *trier* to select, sort, examine, prob. fr. LL *tritare* to grind] **1** : to examine or investigate judicially **2** : to conduct the trial of **3** : to put to test or trial **4** : to subject to strain, affliction, or annoyance **5** : to extract or clarify (as lard) by melting **6** : to make an effort to do something : ATTEMPT, ENDEAVOR ✦ **Synonyms** ESSAY, ASSAY, STRIVE, STRUGGLE

²**try** *n, pl* **tries** : an experimental trial

try·ing *adj* : severely straining the powers of endurance

try on *vb* : to put on (a garment) to test the fit and looks

try out *vb* : to participate in competition esp. for a position on an athletic team or a part in a play — **try·out** \'trī-ˌaůt\ *n*

tryp·to·phan \'trip-tə-ˌfan\ *n* : a crystalline essential amino acid that is widely distributed in proteins

tryst \'trist\ *n* .**1** : an agreement (as between lovers) to meet **2** : an appointed meeting or meeting place — **tryst** *vb* — **tryst·er** *n*

tsar *var of* CZAR

tsarina *var of* CZARINA

tset·se fly \'tset-sē-, 'tsēt-, 'tet-, 'tēt-, 'set-, 'sēt-\ *n* : any of several sub-Saharan African dipteran flies including the vector of sleeping sickness

TSgt *abbr* technical sergeant

T–shirt \'tē-ˌshərt\ *n* : a collarless short-sleeved or sleeveless cotton undershirt; *also* : an outer shirt of similar design — **T–shirt·ed** \-ˌshər-təd\ *adj*

tsk \a *click; often read as* 'tisk\ *interj* — used to express disapproval

tsp *abbr* teaspoon; teaspoonful

T square *n* : a ruler with a crosspiece at one end for making parallel lines

tsu·na·mi \sů-'nä-mē, tsů-\ *n* [Jp] : a tidal wave caused esp. by an underwater earthquake or volcanic eruption

TT *abbr* Trust Territories

TTY *abbr* teletypewriter

Tu *abbr* Tuesday

tub \'təb\ *n* **1** : a wide low bucketlike vessel **2** : BATHTUB; *also* : BATH **3** : the amount that a tub will hold

tu·ba \'tü-bə, 'tyü-\ *n* : a large low-pitched brass wind instrument

tub·al \'tü-bəl, 'tyü-\ *adj* : of, relating to, or involving a tube and esp. a fallopian tube ⟨∼ infection⟩

tube \'tüb, 'tyüb\ *n* **1** : any of various usu. cylindrical structures or devices; *esp* : one to convey fluids **2** : a slender hollow anatomical part (as a fallopian tube) functioning as a channel in a plant or animal body : DUCT **3** : a soft round container from which a paste is squeezed **4** : a tunnel for vehicular or rail travel **5** : INNER TUBE **6** : ELECTRON TUBE **7** : TELEVISION — **tubed** \'tübd, 'tyübd\ *adj* — **tube·less** *adj* — **tube·like** \'tüb-ˌlīk, 'tyüb-\ *adj*

tu·ber \'tü-bər, 'tyü-\ *n* : a short fleshy usu. underground stem (as of a potato plant) bearing minute scalelike leaves each with a bud at its base

tu·ber·cle \'tü-bər-kəl, 'tyü-\ *n* **1** : a small knobby prominence or outgrowth esp. on an animal or plant **2** : a small abnormal lump in an organ or on the skin; *esp* : one caused by tuberculosis

tubercle bacillus *n* : a bacterium that is the cause of tuberculosis

tu·ber·cu·lar \tù-'bər-kyə-lər, tyù-\ *adj* **1** : TUBERCULOUS **2** : of, resembling, or being a tubercle

tu·ber·cu·lin \tù-'bər-kyə-lən, tyù-\ *n* : a sterile liquid extracted from the tubercle bacillus and used in the diagnosis of tuberculosis in children and cattle

tu·ber·cu·lo·sis \tù-ˌbər-kyə-'lō-səs, tyù-\ *n, pl* **-lo·ses** \-ˌsēz\ : a communicable bacterial disease that affects esp. the lungs and is typically marked by fever, cough, difficulty in breathing, and formation of tubercles — **tu·ber·cu·lous** \-'bər-kyə-ləs\ *adj*

tube·rose \tüb-ˌrōz, tyüb-\ *n* : a bulbous herb related to the agaves and often grown for its spike of fragrant waxy-white flowers

tu·ber·ous \tü-bə-rəs, tyü-\ *adj* : of, resembling, or being a tuber

tub·ing \tü-biŋ, tyü-\ *n* **1** : material in the form of a tube; *also* : a length of tube **2** : a series or system of tubes

tu·bu·lar \tü-byə-lər, tyü-\ *adj* : having the form of or consisting of a tube; *also* : made with tubes

tu·bule \tü-byül, tyü-\ *n* : a small tube

¹**tuck** \tək\ *vb* **1** : to pull up into a fold ⟨~ed up her skirt⟩ **2** : to make tucks in **3** : to put into a snug often concealing place ⟨~ a book under the arm⟩ **4** : to secure in place by pushing the edges under ⟨~ in a blanket⟩ **5** : to cover by tucking in bedclothes

²**tuck** *n* **1** : a fold stitched into cloth to shorten, decorate, or control fullness **2** : a cosmetic surgical operation for the removal of excess skin or fat ⟨a tummy ~⟩

tuck·er \tə-kər\ *vb* **tuck·ered; tuck·er·ing** : EXHAUST, FATIGUE ⟨was ~ed out after a long day's work⟩

Tues *or* **Tue** *abbr* Tuesday

Tues·day \tüz-dē, tyüz-, -dā\ *n* : the 3d day of the week

tu·fa \tü-fə, tyü-\ *n* : a porous rock (as travertine) formed as a deposit from springs or streams

tuff \təf\ *n* : a rock composed of volcanic detritus

¹**tuft** \təft\ *n* **1** : a small cluster of long flexible outgrowths (as hairs); *also* : a bunch of soft fluffy threads cut off short and used as ornament **2** : CLUMP, CLUSTER — **tuft·ed** *adj*

²**tuft** *vb* **1** : to provide or adorn with a tuft **2** : to make (as a mattress) firm by stitching at intervals and sewing on tufts — **tuft·er** *n*

¹**tug** \təg\ *vb* **tugged; tug·ging 1** : to pull hard **2** : to struggle in opposition : CONTEND **3** : to move by pulling hard : HAUL **4** : to tow with a tugboat

²**tug** *n* **1** : a harness trace **2** : an act of tugging : PULL **3** : a straining effort **4** : a struggle between opposing people or forces **5** : TUGBOAT

tug·boat \-ˌbōt\ *n* : a strongly built boat used for towing or pushing

tug–of–war \ˌtəg-əv-'wòr\ *n, pl* **tugs–of–war 1** : a struggle for supremacy **2** : an athletic contest in which two teams pull against each other at opposite ends of a rope

tu·grik *or* **tu·ghrik** \tü-grik\ *n* — see MONEY table

tu·ition \tù-'i-shən, tyü-\ *n* : money paid for instruction ⟨college ~⟩

tu·la·re·mia \ˌtü-lə-'rē-mē-ə, ˌtyü-\ *n* : an infectious bacterial disease esp. of wild rabbits, rodents, humans, and some domestic animals that in humans is marked by symptoms (as fever) similar to those of influenza

tu·lip \tü-ləp, tyü-\ *n* [NL *tulipa*, fr. Turk *tülbent* turban] : any of a genus of Eurasian bulbous herbs related to the lilies and grown for their large showy erect cup-shaped flowers; *also* : a flower or bulb of a tulip

tulip tree *n* : a tall No. American timber tree that is related to the magnolias and has greenish tulip-shaped flowers and soft white wood

tulle \tül\ *n* : a sheer often stiffened silk, rayon, or nylon net ⟨a veil of ~⟩

¹**tum·ble** \təm-bəl\ *vb* **tum·bled; tum·bling** [ME, fr. *tumben* to dance, fr. OE *tumbian*] **1** : to fall or cause to fall suddenly and helplessly **2** : to fall into ruin **3** : to perform gymnastic feats of rolling and turning **4** : to roll over and over : TOSS **5** : to issue forth hurriedly and confusedly **6** : to come to understand **7** : to throw together in a confused mass

²**tumble** *n* **1** : a disorderly state **2** : an act or instance of tumbling

tum·ble·down \ˈtəm-bəl-ˈdaún\ *adj* : DILAPIDATED, RAMSHACKLE

tum·bler \təm-blər\ *n* **1** : one that tumbles; *esp* : ACROBAT **2** : a drinking glass without foot or stem **3** : a movable obstruction in a lock that must be adjusted to a particular position (as by a key) before the bolt can be thrown

tum·ble·weed \təm-bəl-ˌwēd\ *n* : a plant that breaks away from its roots in autumn and is driven about by the wind

tum·brel *or* **tum·bril** \təm-brəl\ *n* **1** : CART **2** : a vehicle carrying condemned persons (as during the French Revolution) to a place of execution

tu·mid \tü-məd, tyü-\ *adj* **1** : SWOLLEN, DISTENDED **2** : BOMBASTIC, TURGID

tum·my \tə-mē\ *n, pl* **tummies** : BELLY, ABDOMEN, STOMACH

tu·mor \tü-mər, tyü-\ *n* : an abnormal and functionless new growth of tissue that arises from uncontrolled cellular proliferation — **tu·mor·ous** *adj*

tu·mour *chiefly Brit var of* TUMOR

tu·mult \tü-ˌməlt, tyü-\ *n* **1** : UPROAR **2** : violent agitation of mind or feelings

tu·mul·tu·ous \tù-'məl-chə-wəs, tyù-, -chəs\ *adj* **1** : marked by tumult **2** : tending to incite a tumult **3** : marked by violent upheaval

tun \tən\ *n* : a large cask

tu·na \tü-nə, tyü-\ *n, pl* **tuna** *or* **tunas** : any of several mostly large marine fishes related to the mackerels and caught for food and sport; *also* : the flesh of a tuna

tun·able \tü-nə-bəl, tyü-\ *adj* : capable of being tuned — **tun·abil·i·ty** \ˌtü-nə-'bi-lə-tē, ˌtyü-\ *n*

tun·dra \tən-drə\ *n* [Russ] : a treeless plain of arctic and subarctic regions

¹**tune** \tün, tyün\ *n* **1** : a succession of pleasing musical tones : MELODY **2** : correct musical pitch **3** : harmonious relationship : AGREEMENT ⟨in ~ with the times⟩ **4** : general attitude ⟨changed his ~⟩ **5** : AMOUNT, EXTENT ⟨in debt to the ~ of millions⟩

²**tune** *vb* **tuned; tun·ing 1** : to adjust in musical pitch **2** : to bring or come into harmony : ATTUNE **3** : to put in good working order **4** : to adjust a radio or television receiver so as to receive a broadcast **5** : to adjust the frequency of the output of (a device) to a chosen frequency — **tun·er** *n*

tune·ful \-fəl\ *adj* : MELODIOUS, MUSICAL ⟨a ~ ballad⟩ — **tune·ful·ly** *adv* — **tune·ful·ness** *n*

tune·less \-ləs\ *adj* **1** : UNMELODIOUS **2** : not producing music — **tune·less·ly** *adv*

tune–up \tün-ˌəp, 'tyün-\ *n* : an adjustment to ensure efficient functioning ⟨an engine ~⟩

tung·sten \təŋ-stən\ *n* [Sw, fr. *tung* heavy + *sten* stone] : a gray-white hard heavy ductile metallic chemical element used esp. in carbide materials, electrical components, and alloys

tu·nic \tü-nik, tyü-\ *n* **1** : a usu. knee-length belted garment worn by ancient Greeks and Romans **2** : a hip-length or longer blouse or jacket

tuning fork *n* : a 2-pronged metal implement that gives a fixed tone when struck and is useful for tuning musical instruments

¹**tun·nel** \tə-nᵊl\ *n* : an enclosed passage (as a tube or conduit); *esp* : one underground (as in a mine)

²**tunnel** *vb* **-neled** *or* **-nelled; -nel·ing** *or* **-nel·ling** : to make a tunnel through or under — **tun·nel·er** \tən-lər, tə-nᵊl-ər\ *n*

tun·ny \tə-nē\ *n, pl* **tunnies** *also* **tunny** : TUNA

tuque \tük, tyük\ *n* [CanF] : a warm knitted cone-shaped cap

tur·ban \tər-bən\ *n* **1** : a headdress worn esp. by Muslims and made of a cap around which is wound a long cloth **2** : a headdress resembling a turban; *esp* : a woman's close-fitting hat without a brim

tur·bid \tər-bəd\ *adj* [L *turbidus* confused, turbid, fr. *turba* confusion, crowd] **1** : cloudy or discolored by suspended particles ⟨a ~ stream⟩ **2** : CONFUSED, MUDDLED — **tur·bid·i·ty** \ˌtər-'bi-də-tē\ *n*

tur·bine \tər-bən, -ˌbīn\ *n* [F, fr. L *turbin-, turbo* top, whirlwind, whirl] : an engine whose central driveshaft is fitted with curved vanes spun by the pressure of water, steam, or gas

tur·bo·fan \'tər-bō-,fan\ *n* : a jet engine having a fan driven by a turbine for supplying air for combustion

tur·bo·jet \-,jet\ *n* : an airplane powered by a jet engine **(turbojet engine)** having a turbine-driven air compressor supplying compressed air to the combustion chamber

tur·bo·prop \-,präp\ *n* : an airplane powered by a jet engine **(turboprop engine)** having a turbine-driven propeller

tur·bot \'tər-bət\ *n, pl* **turbot** *also* **turbots** : a European flatfish that is a popular food fish; *also* : any of several similar flatfishes

tur·bu·lence \'tər-byə-ləns\ *n* : the quality or state of being turbulent

tur·bu·lent \-lənt\ *adj* **1** : causing violence or disturbance **2** : marked by agitation or tumult : TEMPESTUOUS ⟨a ~ marriage⟩ — **tur·bu·lent·ly** *adv*

tu·reen \tə-'rēn, tyu̇-\ *n* [F *terrine*, fr. MF, fr. fem. of *terrin* of earth] : a deep bowl from which foods (as soup) are served at table

¹turf \'tərf\ *n, pl* **turfs** \'tərfs\ *also* **turves** \'tərvz\ **1** : the upper layer of soil bound by grass and roots into a close mat; *also* : a piece of this **2** : an artificial substitute for turf (as on a playing field) **3** : a piece of peat dried for fuel **4** : a track or course for horse racing; *also* : horse racing as a sport or business

²turf *vb* : to cover with turf

tur·gid \'tər-jəd\ *adj* **1** : being in a swollen state **2** : excessively embellished in style or language : BOMBASTIC — **tur·gid·i·ty** \,tər-'ji-də-tē\ *n*

tur·key \'tər-kē\ *n, pl* **turkeys** [*Turkey*, country in western Asia and southeastern Europe; fr. confusion with the guinea fowl, supposed to be imported from Turkish territory] : a large No. American bird related to the domestic chicken and widely raised for food

turkey buzzard *n* : TURKEY VULTURE

turkey vulture *n* : an American vulture with a red head and whitish bill

Turk·ish \'tər-kish\ *n* : the language of Turkey — **Turkish** *adj*

tur·mer·ic \'tər-mə-rik\ *n* : a spice or dyestuff obtained from the large aromatic deep-yellow rhizome of an Indian perennial herb related to the ginger; *also* : this herb

tur·moil \'tər-,mȯi(-ə)l\ *n* : an extremely confused or agitated condition

¹turn \'tərn\ *vb* **1** : to move or cause to move around an axis or center : ROTATE, REVOLVE ⟨~ a wheel⟩ **2** : to effect a desired end by turning something ⟨~ the oven on⟩ **3** : WRENCH ⟨~ an ankle⟩ **4** : to change or cause to change position by moving through an arc of a circle ⟨~ed her chair to the fire⟩ **5** : to cause to move around a center so as to show another side of ⟨~ a page⟩ **6** : to revolve mentally : PONDER **7** : to become dizzy : REEL **8** : to reverse the sides or surfaces of ⟨~ a pancake⟩ **9** : UPSET, DISORDER ⟨things were ~ed topsy-turvy⟩ **10** : to set in another step. contrary direction **11** : to change one's course or direction **12** : to go around ⟨~ a corner⟩ **13** : BECOME ⟨my hair ~ed gray⟩ ⟨~ed twenty-one⟩ **14** : to direct toward or away from something; *also* : DEVOTE, APPLY **15** : to have recourse **16** : to become or make hostile **17** : to cause to become of a specified nature or appearance ⟨~s the leaves yellow⟩ **18** : to make or become spoiled : SOUR **19** : to pass from one state to another ⟨water ~s to ice⟩ **20** : CONVERT, TRANSFORM **21** : TRANSLATE, PARAPHRASE **22** : to give a rounded form to; *esp* : to shape by means of a lathe **23** : to gain by passing in trade ⟨~ a quick profit⟩ — **turn·able** \'tər-nə-bəl\ *adj* — **turn color 1** : BLUSH **2** : to become pale — **turn loose** : to set free

²turn *n* **1** : a turning about a center or axis : REVOLUTION, ROTATION **2** : the action or an act of giving or taking a different direction ⟨make a left ~⟩ **3** : a change of course or tendency ⟨a ~ for the better⟩ **4** : a place at which something turns : BEND, CURVE **5** : a short walk or trip round about ⟨take a ~ around the block⟩ **6** : an act affecting another ⟨did him a good ~⟩ **7** : time, place, or opportunity accorded in a scheduled order ⟨waited his ~ in line⟩ **8** : a period of duty : SHIFT **9** : a short act esp. in a variety show **10** : a special purpose or requirement ⟨the job serves his ~⟩ **11** : a skillful fashioning ⟨neat ~ of phrase⟩ **12** : a single round (as of rope passed around an object) **13** : natural or special apti-

tude **14** : a usu. sudden and brief disorder of body or spirits; *esp* : a spell of nervous shock or faintness

turn·about \'tərn-ə-,bȧu̇t\ *n* **1** : a reversal of direction, trend, or policy **2** : RETALIATION

turn·buck·le \'tərn-,bə-kəl\ *n* : a link with a screw thread at one or both ends for tightening a rod or stay

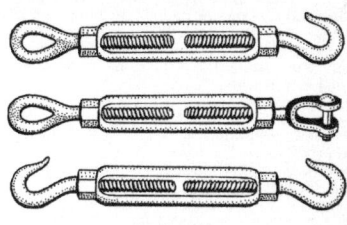

turnbuckles

turn·coat \-,kōt\ *n* : one who switches to an opposing side or party : TRAITOR

turn down *vb* : to decline to accept : REJECT — **turn·down** \'tərn-,dȧu̇n\ *n*

turn·er \'tər-nər\ *n* **1** : one that turns or is used for turning **2** : one that forms articles with a lathe

turn·ery \'tər-nə-rē\ *n, pl* **-er·ies** : the work, products, or shop of a turner

turn in *vb* **1** : to deliver up **2** : to inform on **3** : to acquit oneself of ⟨*turn in* a good job⟩ **4** : to go to bed

turn·ing \'tər-niṅ\ *n* **1** : the act or course of one that turns **2** : a place of a change of direction

tur·nip \'tər-nəp\ *n* **1** : a garden herb related to the cabbage with a thick edible usu. white root **2** : RUTABAGA **3** : the root of a turnip

turn·key \'tərn-,kē\ *n, pl* **turnkeys** : one who has charge of a prison's keys

turn·off \'tərn-,ȯf\ *n* : a place for turning off esp. from an expressway

turn off *vb* **1** : to deviate from a straight course or a main road **2** : to stop the functioning or flow of **3** : to cause to lose interest; *also* : to evoke a negative feeling in

turn on *vb* **1** : to cause to flow, function, or operate **2** : to get high or cause to get high as a result of using a drug (as marijuana) **3** : EXCITE, STIMULATE

turn·out \'tərn-,ȧu̇t\ *n* **1** : an act of turning out **2** : the number of people who participate or attend an event **3** : a widened place in a highway for vehicles to pass or park **4** : manner of dress **5** : net yield : OUTPUT

turn out *vb* **1** : EXPEL, EVICT **2** : PRODUCE **3** : to cause to stop functioning by turning a switch **4** : to come forth and assemble **5** : to get out of bed **6** : to prove to be in the end

¹turn·over \'tərn-,ō-vər\ *n* **1** : UPSET **2** : SHIFT, REVERSAL **3** : a filled pastry made by turning half of the crust over the other half **4** : the volume of business done **5** : movement (as of goods or people) into, through, and out of a place **6** : the number of persons hired within a period to replace those leaving or dropped **7** : an instance of a team's losing possession of the ball esp. through error

²turnover *adj* : capable of being turned over

turn over *vb* : TRANSFER ⟨*turn* the job *over* to her⟩

turn·pike \'tərn-,pīk\ *n* [ME *turnepike* revolving frame bearing spikes and serving as a barrier, fr. *turnen* to turn + *pike*] **1** : TOLLGATE; *also* : an expressway on which tolls are charged **2** : a main road

turn·stile \-,stī(-ə)l\ *n* : a post with arms pivoted on the top set in a passageway so that persons can pass through only on foot one by one

turn·ta·ble \-,tā-bəl\ *n* : a circular platform that revolves (as for turning a locomotive or a phonograph record)

turn to *vb* : to apply oneself to work

turn up *vb* **1** : to come to light or bring to light : DISCOVER, APPEAR **2** : to raise or increase by or as if by turning a control **3** : to arrive at an appointed time or place **4** : to happen unexpectedly

tur·pen·tine \'tər-pən-,tīn\ *n* **1** : a mixture of oil and resin obtained from various cone-bearing trees (as pines) **2**

: an oil distilled from turpentine or pine wood and used as a solvent and paint thinner

tur·pi·tude \'tər-pə-ˌtüd, -ˌtyüd\ *n* : inherent baseness : DEPRAVITY

tur·quoise *also* **tur·quois** \'tər-ˌkȯiz, -ˌkwȯiz\ *n* [ME *turkeys*, fr. AF *turkeise*, fr. fem. of *turkeis* Turkish, fr. *Turc* Turk] **1** : a blue, bluish green, or greenish gray mineral that is valued as a gem **2** : a light greenish blue color

tur·ret \'tər-ət\ *n* **1** : a little ornamental tower often at a corner of a building **2** : a low usu. revolving structure (as on a tank or warship) in which one or more guns are mounted — **tur·ret·ed** \'tər-ə-təd\ *adj*

¹tur·tle \'tər-t³l\ *n, archaic* : TURTLEDOVE

²turtle *n, pl* **turtles** *also* **turtle** : any of an order of hornybeaked land, freshwater, or sea reptiles with the trunk enclosed in a bony shell

tur·tle·dove \'tər-t³l-ˌdəv\ *n* : any of several small pigeons noted for plaintive cooing

tur·tle·neck \-ˌnek\ *n* : a high close-fitting turnover collar (as on a sweater); *also* : a sweater or shirt with a turtleneck — **tur·tle·necked** \-ˌnekt\ *adj*

turves *pl of* TURF

Tus·ca·ro·ra \ˌtəs-kə-'rȯr-ə\ *n, pl* **Tuscarora** *or* **Tuscaroras** : a member of an American Indian people of No. Carolina and later of New York and Ontario

tusk \'təsk\ *n* : a long enlarged protruding tooth (as of an elephant, walrus, or boar) used esp. to dig up food or as a weapon — **tusked** \'təskt\ *adj*

tusk·er \'təs-kər\ *n* : an animal with tusks; *esp* : a male elephant with two normally developed tusks

¹tus·sle \'tə-səl\ *n* **1** : a physical struggle : SCUFFLE **2** : an intense argument, controversy, or struggle

²tussle *vb* **tus·sled; tus·sling** : to struggle roughly

tus·sock \'tə-sək\ *n* : a dense tuft esp. of grass or sedge; *also* : a hummock in a marsh or bog bound together by roots — **tus·socky** *adj*

tu·te·lage \'tü-t³l-ij, 'tyü-\ *n* **1** : an act of guarding or protecting **2** : the state of being under a guardian or tutor **3** : instruction esp. of an individual

tu·te·lary \'tü-tə-ˌler-ē, 'tyü-\ *adj* : acting as a guardian ⟨~ deity⟩

¹tu·tor \'tü-tər, 'tyü-\ *n* **1** : a person charged with the instruction and guidance of another **2** : a private teacher

²tutor *vb* **1** : to have the guardianship of **2** : to teach or guide individually : COACH ⟨~ed her in Latin⟩ **3** : to receive instruction esp. privately

tu·to·ri·al \tü-'tȯr-ē-əl, tyü-\ *n* : a class conducted by a tutor for one student or a small number of students

tut·ti \'tü-tē, 'tü-, -tē\ *adj or adv* [It, pl. of *tutto* all] : with all voices and instruments playing together — used as a direction in music

tut·ti-frut·ti \ˌtü-ti-'frü-tē, ˌtü-\ *n* [It, lit., all fruits] : a confection or ice cream containing chopped usu. candied fruits

tu·tu \'tü-(ˌ)tü\ *n* [F] : a short projecting skirt worn by a ballerina

tux·e·do \ˌtək-'sē-dō\ *n, pl* **-dos** *or* **-does** [*Tuxedo* Park, N.Y.] **1** : a usu. black or blackish blue jacket **2** : a semiformal evening suit for men

TV \'tē-'vē\ *n* : TELEVISION

TVA *abbr* Tennessee Valley Authority

TV dinner *n* : a frozen packaged dinner that needs only heating before serving

twad·dle \'twä-d³l\ *n* : silly idle talk : DRIVEL — **twaddle** *vb*

twain \'twān\ *n* **1** : TWO **2** : PAIR

¹twang \'twaŋ\ *n* **1** : a harsh quick ringing sound like that of a plucked bowstring **2** : nasal speech or resonance **3** : the characteristic speech of a region

²twang *vb* **twanged; twang·ing** **1** : to sound or cause to sound with a twang **2** : to speak with a nasal twang

tweak \'twēk\ *vb* **1** : to pinch and pull with a sudden jerk and twitch **2** : to make small adjustments to — **tweak** *n*

tweed \'twēd\ *n* **1** : a rough woolen fabric made usu. in twill weaves **2** *pl* : tweed clothing; *esp* : a tweed suit

tweedy \'twē-dē\ *adj* **tweed·i·er; -est** **1** : of or resembling tweed **2** : given to wearing tweeds **3** : suggestive of the outdoors in taste or habits

tween \'twēn\ *prep* : BETWEEN

tweet \'twēt\ *n* : a chirping note — **tweet** *vb*

tweet·er \'twē-tər\ *n* : a small loudspeaker that reproduces sounds of high pitch

twee·zers \'twē-zərz\ *n pl* [obs. E *tweeze*, n., case for small implements, short for obs. E *etweese*, fr. pl. of obs. E *etwee*, fr. F *étui*] : a small pincerlike implement usu. held between the thumb and index finger and used for grasping something

twelve \'twelv\ *n* **1** : one more than 11 **2** : the 12th in a set or series **3** : something having 12 units — **twelfth** \'twelfth\ *adj or n* — **twelve** *adj or pron*

twelve·month \-ˌmənth\ *n* : YEAR

12-step \'twelv-ˌstep\ *adj* : of, relating to, or being a program designed esp. to help someone overcome a problem (as an addiction) by following 12 tenets

twen·ty \'twen-tē\ *n, pl* **twenties** : two times 10 — **twen·ti·eth** \-tē-əth\ *adj or n* — **twenty** *adj or pron*

twenty-twenty *or* **20/20** \ˌtwen-tē-'twen-tē\ *adj* : characterized by a visual capacity for seeing detail that is normal for the human eye ⟨~ vision⟩

twice \'twīs\ *adv* **1** : on two occasions **2** : two times ⟨~ two is four⟩

¹twid·dle \'twi-d³l\ *vb* **twid·dled; twid·dling** **1** : to be busy with trifles; *also* : to play idly with something **2** : to rotate lightly or idly

²twiddle *n* : TURN, TWIST

twig \'twig\ *n* : a small branch — **twig·gy** *adj*

twi·light \'twī-ˌlīt\ *n* **1** : the light from the sky between full night and sunrise or between sunset and full night **2** : a state of imperfect clarity **3** : a period of decline

twilight zone *n* **1** : an area just beyond ordinary legal or ethical limits **2** : TWILIGHT **2 3** : a world of fantasy or unreality

twill \'twil\ *n* [ME *twyll*, fr. OE *twilic* having a double thread, part trans. of L *bilic-, bilix*, fr. *bi-* two + *licium* thread] **1** : a fabric with a twill weave **2** : a textile weave that gives an appearance of diagonal lines

twilled \'twild\ *adj* : made with a twill weave

¹twin \'twin\ *n* **1** : either of two offspring produced at a birth **2** : one of two persons or things closely related to or resembling each other

²twin *vb* **twinned; twin·ning** **1** : to be coupled with another **2** : to bring forth twins

³twin *adj* **1** : born with one other or as a pair at one birth ⟨~ brother⟩ ⟨~ girls⟩ **2** : made up of two similar or related members or parts **3** : being one of a pair ⟨~ city⟩

¹twine \'twīn\ *n* **1** : a strong thread of two or three strands twisted together **2** : an act of entwining or interlacing — **twiny** *adj*

²twine *vb* **twined; twin·ing** **1** : to twist together; *also* : to form by twisting **2** : INTERLACE, WEAVE **3** : to coil about a support **4** : to stretch or move in a sinuous manner — **twin·er** *n*

¹twinge \'twinj\ *vb* **twinged; twing·ing** *or* **twinge·ing** : to affect with or feel a sharp sudden pain

²twinge *n* : a sudden sharp stab (as of pain or distress)

twin·kle \'twiŋ-kəl\ *vb* **twin·kled; twin·kling** **1** : to shine or cause to shine with a flickering or sparkling light **2** : to appear bright with merriment **3** : to flutter or flit rapidly — **twin·kler** *n*

²twinkle *n* **1** : a wink of the eyelids; *also* : the duration of a wink **2** : an intermittent radiance **3** : a rapid flashing motion — **twin·kly** \'twiŋ-klē\ *adj*

twin·kling \'twiŋ-kliŋ\ *n* : the time required for a wink : INSTANT

¹twirl \'twərl\ *vb* **1** : to turn or cause to turn rapidly ⟨~ a baton⟩ ♦ **Synonyms** REVOLVE, ROTATE, CIRCLE, SPIN, SWIRL, PIROUETTE — **twirl·er** *n*

²twirl *n* **1** : an act of twirling **2** : COIL, WHORL — **twirly** \'twər-lē\ *adj*

¹twist \'twist\ *vb* **1** : to unite by winding one thread or strand round another **2** : WREATHE, TWINE **3** : to turn so as to hurt : SPRAIN ⟨~ed my ankle⟩ **4** : to twirl into spiral shape **5** : to subject (as a shaft) to torsion **6** : to turn from the true form or meaning **7** : to pull off or break by torsion **8** : to follow a winding course **9** : to turn around

²twist *n* **1** : something formed by twisting or winding **2** : an act of twisting : the state of being twisted **3** : a spiral turn or curve; *also* : SPIN **4** : a turning aside **5** : ECCENTRICITY **6** : a distortion of meaning **7** : an unexpected turn or development **8** : DEVICE, TRICK **9** : a variant approach or method

twist·er \'twis-tər\ *n* **1** : one that twists; *esp* : a ball with a forward and spinning motion **2** : TORNADO; *also* : WATERSPOUT 2

¹twit \'twit\ *n* : FOOL

²twit *vb* **twit·ted; twit·ting** : to ridicule as a fault; *also* : TAUNT ♦ *Synonyms* DERIDE, MOCK, RAZZ

¹twitch \'twich\ *vb* **1** : to move or pull with a sudden motion : JERK **2** : to move jerkily : QUIVER **3** : to have a twitch

²twitch *n* **1** : an act or movement of twitching **2** : a brief spasmodic contraction of muscle fibers

¹twit·ter \'twi-tər\ *vb* **1** : to make a succession of chirping noises **2** : to talk in a chattering fashion **3** : to tremble with agitation : FLUTTER

²twitter *n* **1** : a slight agitation of the nerves **2** : a small tremulous intermittent noise (as made by a swallow) **3** : a light chattering

twixt \'twikst\ *prep* : BETWEEN ⟨∼ the two extremes⟩

two \'tü\ *n, pl* **twos** **1** : one more than one **2** : the second in a set or series **3** : something having two units — **two** *adj or pron*

two cents *n* **1** *or* **two cents' worth** : an opinion offered on a topic under discussion : COUPLE **2** : a sum or object of very small value

two–faced \'tü-'fāst\ *adj* **1** : DOUBLE-DEALING, FALSE **2** : having two faces

two–fold \'tü-,fōld, -'fōld\ *adj* **1** : having two units or members **2** : being twice as much or as many — **twofold** \-'fōld\ *adv*

2,4–D \,tü-,fōr-'dē\ *n* : an irritant compound used esp. as a weed killer

2,4,5–T \-,fiv-'tē\ *n* : an irritant compound used esp. as an herbicide and defoliant

two·pence \'tə-pəns, *US also* 'tü-,pens\ *n* : the sum of two pence

two·pen·ny \'tə-pə-nē, *US also* 'tü-,pe-nē\ *adj* : of the value of or costing twopence

two–ply \'tü-'plī\ *adj* **1** : woven as a double cloth **2** : consisting of two strands or thicknesses

two·some \'tü-səm\ *n* **1** : a group of two persons or things : COUPLE **2** : a golf match between two players

two–step \'tü-,step\ *n* : a ballroom dance performed with a sliding step in march or polka time; *also* : a piece of music for this dance — **two–step** *vb*

two–time \'tü-,tīm\ *vb* : to betray (a spouse or lover) by secret lovemaking with another — **two–tim·er** *n*

two–way *adj* : involving two elements or allowing movement or use in two directions or manners

2WD *abbr* two-wheel drive

twp *abbr* township

TWX *abbr* teletypewriter exchange

TX *abbr* Texas

ty·coon \tī-'kün\ *n* [Jp *taikun* feudal lord] **1** : a masterful leader (as in politics) **2** : a powerful businessman or industrialist

tyin \'tēn\ *n, pl* **tyin** — see *tenge* at MONEY table

tying *pres part of* TIE

ty·iyn \tē-'en\ *n, pl* **tyiyn** — see *som* at MONEY table

tyke \'tīk\ *n* : a small child

tym·pan·ic membrane \tim-'pa-nik-\ *n* : EARDRUM

tym·pa·num \'tim-pə-nəm\ *n, pl* **-na** \-nə\ *also* **-nums** : EARDRUM; *also* : MIDDLE EAR — **tym·pan·ic** \tim-'pa-nik\ *adj*

¹type \'tīp\ *n* [ME, fr. LL *typus*, fr. L & Gk; L *typus* image, fr. Gk *typos* blow, impression, model, fr. *typtein* to strike, beat] **1** : a person, thing, or event that foreshadows another to come : TOKEN, SYMBOL **2** : MODEL, EXAMPLE **3** : a distinctive stamp, mark, or sign : EMBLEM **4** : rectangular blocks usu. of metal each having a face so shaped as to produce a character when printed **5** : the letters or characters printed from or as if from type **6** : general character or form common to a number of individuals and setting them off as a distinguishable class ⟨horses of draft ∼⟩ **7** : a class, kind, or group set apart by common characteristics ⟨a seedless ∼ of orange⟩; *also* : something distinguishable as a variety ⟨reactions of this ∼⟩ ♦ *Synonyms* SORT, NATURE, CHARACTER, DESCRIPTION

²type *vb* **typed; typ·ing** **1** : to represent beforehand as a

type **2** : to produce a copy of; *also* : REPRESENT, TYPIFY **3** : to write with a typewriter or computer keyboard **4** : to identify as belonging to a type : TYPECAST

type A *adj* : relating to, having, or being a personality marked esp. by impatience and aggressiveness

type·cast \-,kast\ *vb* **-cast; -cast·ing** **1** : to cast (an actor) in a part calling for characteristics possessed by the actor **2** : to cast repeatedly in the same type of role

type·face \-,fās\ *n* : all type of a single design

type 1 diabetes \'tīp-'wən-\ *n* : a form of diabetes mellitus usu. developing before adulthood and marked by severe insulin deficiency

type·script \'tīp-,skript\ *n* : typewritten matter

type·set \-,set\ *vb* **-set; -set·ting** : to set in type : COMPOSE — **type·set·ter** *n*

type 2 diabetes \-'tü-\ *n* : a form of diabetes mellitus developing esp. in adults and usu. in obese individuals and marked by excess sugar in the blood

type·write \-,rīt\ *vb* **-wrote** \-,rōt\; **-writ·ten** \-,ri-tᵊn\ : TYPE 3

type·writ·er \-,rī-tər\ *n* **1** : a machine for writing in characters similar to those produced by printers' type by means of types striking a ribbon to transfer ink or carbon impressions onto paper **2** : TYPIST

type·writ·ing \-,rī-tiŋ\ *n* : the use of a typewriter ⟨teach ∼⟩; *also* : writing produced with a typewriter

¹ty·phoid \'tī-,fóid, tī-'fóid\ *adj* : of, relating to, or being a communicable bacterial disease (**typhoid fever**) marked by fever, diarrhea, prostration, and intestinal inflammation

²typhoid *n* : TYPHOID FEVER

ty·phoon \tī-'fün\ *n* : a hurricane occurring esp. in the region of the Philippines or the China sea

ty·phus \'tī-fəs\ *n* : a severe infectious disease transmitted esp. by body lice, caused by a rickettsia, and marked by high fever, stupor and delirium, intense headache, and a dark red rash

typ·i·cal \'ti-pi-kəl\ *adj* **1** : being or having the nature of a type **2** : exhibiting the essential characteristics of a group **3** : conforming to a type — **typ·i·cal·i·ty** \,ti-pə-'ka-lə-tē\ *n* — **typ·i·cal·ness** *n*

typ·i·cal·ly \-pi-k(ə-)lē\ *adv* **1** : in a typical manner **2** : in typical circumstances

typ·i·fy \'ti-pə-,fī\ *vb* **-fied; -fy·ing** **1** : to represent by an image, form, model, or resemblance **2** : to embody the essential or common characteristics of

typ·ist \'tī-pist\ *n* : a person who types esp. as a job

ty·po \'tī-pō\ *n, pl* **typos** : an error (as of spelling) in typed or typeset material

ty·pog·ra·pher \tī-'pä-grə-fər\ *n* : one who designs or arranges printing

ty·pog·ra·phy \tī-'pä-grə-fē\ *n* : the art of printing only; *also* : the style, arrangement, or appearance of printed matter — **ty·po·graph·ic** \,tī-pə-'gra-fik\ *or* **ty·po·graph·i·cal** \-fi-kəl\ *adj* — **ty·po·graph·i·cal·ly** *adv*

ty·ran·ni·cal \tə-'ra-ni-kəl, tī-\ *also* **ty·ran·nic** \-nik\ *adj* : of or relating to a tyrant : DESPOTIC ♦ *Synonyms* ARBITRARY, ABSOLUTE, AUTOCRATIC — **ty·ran·ni·cal·ly** \-ni-k(ə-)lē\ *adv*

tyr·an·nise *Brit var of* TYRANNIZE

tyr·an·nize \'tir-ə-,nīz\ *vb* **-nized; -niz·ing** : to act as a tyrant : rule with unjust severity — **tyr·an·niz·er** *n*

ty·ran·no·saur \tə-'ra-nə-,sór\ *n* : a massive American flesh-eating dinosaur of the Cretaceous that had small forelegs and walked on its hind legs

ty·ran·no·sau·rus \tə-,ra-nə-'sór-əs\ *n* : TYRANNOSAUR

tyr·an·nous \'tir-ə-nəs\ *adj* : unjustly severe — **tyr·an·nous·ly** *adv*

tyr·an·ny \'tir-ə-nē\ *n, pl* **-nies** **1** : oppressive power **2** : the rule or authority of a tyrant : government in which absolute power is vested in a single ruler **3** : a tyrannical act

ty·rant \'tī-rənt\ *n* **1** : an absolute ruler : DESPOT **2** : a ruler who governs oppressively or brutally **3** : one who uses authority or power harshly

tyre *chiefly Brit var of* ²TIRE

ty·ro \'tī-rō\ *n, pl* **tyros** [ML, fr. L *tiro* young soldier, tyro] : a beginner in learning : NOVICE

tzar, tzarist *var of* CZAR, CZARIST

¹u \'yü\ *n, pl* u's *or* us \'yüz\ *often cap* : the 21st letter of the English alphabet

²u *abbr, often cap* unit

¹U \'yü\ *adj* : characteristic of the upper classes

²U *abbr* 1 [abbr. of *Union of Orthodox Hebrew Congregations*] kosher certification — often enclosed in a circle 2 university 3 unsatisfactory

³U *symbol* uranium

UAE *abbr* United Arab Emirates

UAR *abbr* United Arab Republic

UAW *abbr* United Automobile Workers

ubiq·ui·tous \yü-'bi-kwə-təs\ *adj* : existing or being everywhere at the same time : OMNIPRESENT — ubiq·ui·tous·ly *adv* — ubiq·ui·ty \-kwə-tē\ *n*

U–boat \'yü-ˌbōt\ *n* [trans. of G *U-boot*, short for *Unterseeboot*, lit., undersea boat] : a German submarine

UC *abbr* uppercase

ud·der \'ə-dər\ *n* : an organ (as of a cow) consisting of two or more milk glands enclosed in a large hanging sac and each provided with a nipple

UFO \ˌyü-(ˌ)ef-'ō\ *n, pl* UFO's *or* UFOs \-'ōz\ : an unidentified flying object; *esp* : FLYING SAUCER

ug·ly \'ə-glē\ *adj* ug·li·er; -est [ME, fr. ON *uggligr*, fr. *uggr* fear] 1 : FRIGHTFUL, DIRE 2 : offensive to the sight : HIDEOUS 3 : offensive or unpleasant to any sense 4 : morally objectionable : REPULSIVE 5 : likely to cause inconvenience or discomfort 6 : SURLY, QUARRELSOME ⟨an ~ disposition⟩ — ug·li·ness \-glē-nəs\ *n*

UHF *abbr* ultrahigh frequency

UK *abbr* United Kingdom

ukase \yü-'kās, -'kāz\ *n* [F & Russ; F, fr. Russ *ukaz*, fr. *ukazat'* to show, order] : an edict esp. of a Russian emperor or government

uku·le·le *also* uke·le·le \ˌyü-kə-'lā-lē\ *n* [Hawaiian *'ukulele*, fr. *'uku* flea + *lele* jumping] : a small usu. 4-stringed guitar popularized in Hawaii

ul·cer \'əl-sər\ *n* 1 : an open eroded sore of skin or mucous membrane often discharging pus 2 : something that festers and corrupts like an open sore — ul·cer·ous *adj*

ul·cer·ate \'əl-sə-ˌrāt\ *vb* -at·ed; -at·ing : to become affected with an ulcer — ul·cer·a·tive \'əl-sə-ˌrā-tiv\ *adj*

ul·cer·a·tion \ˌəl-sə-'rā-shən\ *n* 1 : the process of forming or state of having an ulcer 2 : ULCER 1

ul·na \'əl-nə\ *n* : the bone on the little-finger side of the human forearm; *also* : a corresponding bone of the forelimb of vertebrates above fishes

ul·ster \'əl-stər\ *n* : a long loose overcoat

ult *abbr* 1 ultimate 2 ultimo

ul·te·ri·or \ˌəl-'tir-ē-ər\ *adj* 1 : lying farther away : more remote 2 : situated beyond or on the farther side 3 : going beyond what is openly said or shown : HIDDEN ⟨~ motives⟩

¹ul·ti·mate \'əl-tə-mət\ *adj* 1 : most remote in space or time : FARTHEST 2 : last in a progression : FINAL 3 : the best or most extreme of its kind 4 : arrived at as the last resort 5 : FUNDAMENTAL, ABSOLUTE, SUPREME ⟨~ reality⟩ 6 : incapable of further analysis or division : ELEMENTAL 7 : MAXIMUM ♦ *Synonyms* CONCLUDING, EVENTUAL, LATEST, TERMINAL — ul·ti·mate·ly *adv*

²ultimate *n* : something ultimate

ul·ti·ma·tum \ˌəl-tə-'mā-təm, -'mä-\ *n, pl* -tums *or* -ta \-tə\ : a final condition or demand whose rejection will bring about a resort to forceful action

ul·ti·mo \'əl-tə-ˌmō\ *adj* [L *ultimo mense* in the last month] : of or occurring in the month preceding the present

¹ul·tra \'əl-trə\ *adj* : going beyond others or beyond due limits : EXTREME

²ultra *n* : EXTREMIST

ul·tra·con·ser·va·tive \-kən-'sər-və-tiv\ *adj* : extremely conservative

ul·tra·high frequency \-'hī-\ *n* : a radio frequency between 300 and 3000 megahertz

¹ul·tra·light \'əl-trə-ˌlīt\ *adj* : extremely light esp. in weight

²ultralight *n* : a very light recreational aircraft typically carrying only one person

ul·tra·ma·rine \ˌəl-trə-mə-'rēn\ *n* 1 : a deep blue pigment 2 : a very bright deep blue color

ul·tra·mi·cro·scop·ic \ˌəl-mī-krə-'skä-pik\ *adj* : too small to be seen with an ordinary microscope

ul·tra·mod·ern \-'mä-dərn\ *adj* : extremely or excessively modern in idea, style, or tendency

ul·tra·mon·tane \-'män-ˌtān, -ˌmän-'tān\ *adj* 1 : of or relating to countries or peoples beyond the mountains (as the Alps) 2 : favoring greater or absolute supremacy of papal over national or diocesan authority in the Roman Catholic Church — ultramontane *n, often cap* — ul·tra·mon·tan·ism \-'män-tə-ˌni-zəm\ *n*

ul·tra·pure \-'pyu̇r\ *adj* : of the utmost purity

ul·tra·short \-'sho̍rt\ *adj* 1 : having a wavelength below 10 meters 2 : very short in duration

ul·tra·son·ic \ˌəl-trə-'sä-nik\ *adj* : having a frequency too high to be heard by the human ear — ul·tra·son·i·cal·ly \-ni-k(ə-)lē\ *adv*

ul·tra·son·ics \-'sä-niks\ *n sing or pl* 1 : ultrasonic vibrations 2 : the science of ultrasonic phenomena

ul·tra·sound \-ˌsau̇nd\ *n* 1 : ultrasonic vibrations 2 : the diagnostic or therapeutic use of ultrasound and esp. a technique involving the formation of a two-dimensional image of internal body structures 3 : a diagnostic examination using ultrasound

ul·tra·vi·o·let \-'vī-ə-lət\ *adj* : having a wavelength shorter than those of visible light and longer than those of X-rays ⟨~ radiation⟩; *also* : producing or employing ultraviolet radiation — ultraviolet *n*

ul·tra vi·res \'əl-trə-'vī-rēz\ *adv or adj* [NL, lit., beyond power] : beyond the scope of legal power or authority

ul·u·late \'əl-yə-ˌlāt\ *vb* -lat·ed; -lat·ing : HOWL, WAIL

uma·mi \ü-'mä-mē\ *n* [Jp, flavor] : a meaty or savory taste sensation produced esp. by monosodium glutamate

um·bel \'əm-bəl\ *n* : a flat-topped or rounded flower cluster in which the individual flower stalks all arise near one point on the main stem

um·ber \'əm-bər\ *n* : a brown earthy substance valued as a pigment either in its raw state or burnt — umber *adj*

umbilical cord *n* : a cord containing blood vessels that connects the navel of a fetus with the placenta of its mother

um·bi·li·cus \ˌəm-'bi-li-kəs, ˌəm-bə-'lī-\ *n, pl* um·bi·li·ci \ˌəm-'bi-lə-ˌkī; ˌəm-bə-'lī-ˌkī, -ˌsī\ *or* um·bi·li·cus·es : NAVEL — um·bil·i·cal \ˌəm-'bi-li-kəl\ *adj*

um·bra \'əm-brə\ *n, pl* umbras *or* um·brae \-(ˌ)brē, -ˌbrī\ 1 : SHADE, SHADOW 2 : the conical part of the shadow of a celestial body from which the sun's light is completely blocked

um·brage \'əm-brij\ *n* 1 : SHADE; *also* : FOLIAGE 2 : RESENTMENT, OFFENSE ⟨take ~ at a remark⟩

um·brel·la \ˌəm-'bre-lə\ *n* 1 : a collapsible shade for protection against weather consisting of fabric stretched over hinged ribs radiating from a center pole 2 : something that provides protection 3 : something that covers a range of elements

umi·ak \'ü-mē-ˌak\ *n* : an open Eskimo boat made of a wooden frame covered with skins

ump \'əmp\ *n* : UMPIRE

um·pire \'əm-ˌpī(-ə)r\ *n* [ME *oumpere*, alter. of *noumpere* (the phrase *a noumpere* being understood as *an oumpere*), fr. AF *nounpier* single, odd, fr. *non* not + *per* equal, fr. L *par*] 1 : one having authority to decide finally a controversy or question between parties 2 : an official in a sport who rules on plays — umpire *vb*

ump·teen \'əmp-ˌtēn\ *adj* : very many : indefinitely numerous — ump·teenth \-ˌtēnth\ *adj*

UN *abbr* United Nations

un- \ˌən, ˈən\ *prefix* **1** : not : IN-, NON- **2** : opposite of : contrary to

unabashed
unabated
unabsorbed
unabsorbent
unacademic
unaccented
unacceptable
unacclimatized
unaccommodating
unaccredited
unacknowledged
unacquainted
unadapted
unadjusted
unadorned
unadventurous
unadvertised
unaesthetic
unaffiliated
unafraid
unaggressive
unaided
unalike
unaltered
unambiguous
unambiguously
unambitious
unanchored
unannounced
unanswerable
unanswered
unanticipated
unapologetic
unapparent
unappealing
unappeased
unappetizing
unappreciated
unappreciative
unapproachable
unappropriated
unapproved
unarguable
unarguably
unarmored
unartistic
unashamed
unasked
unassertive
unassisted
unathletic
unattainable
unattended
unattested
unattractive
unauthentic
unauthorized
unavailable
unavowed
unawakened
unbaked
unbaptized
unbeloved
unbleached
unblemished
unblinking
unbound
unbranched
unbranded
unbreakable
unbridgeable
unbruised
unbrushed
unbudging
unburied
unburned
uncanceled
uncanonical
uncap
uncapitalized
uncared{ndash}for
uncataloged
uncaught
uncensored
uncensured
unchallenged
unchangeable
unchanged
unchanging
unchaperoned
uncharacteristic
unchaste
unchastely

unchasteness
unchastity
unchecked
unchivalrous
unchristened
unclad
unclaimed
unclassified
uncleaned
unclear
uncleared
unclouded
uncluttered
uncoated
uncollected
uncolored
uncombed
uncombined
uncomely
uncomic
uncommercial
uncompensated
uncomplaining
uncompleted
uncomplicated
uncomplimentary
uncompounded
uncomprehending
unconcealed
unconfined
unconfirmed
unconformable
uncongenial
unconnected
unconquered
unconsecrated
unconsidered
unconsolidated
unconstrained
unconsumed
unconsummated
uncontaminated
uncontested
uncontrolled
uncontroversial
unconverted
unconvincing
uncooked
uncooperative
uncoordinated
uncorrected
uncorroborated
uncountable
uncreative
uncredited
uncropped
uncrowded
uncrowned
uncrystallized
uncultivated
uncultured
uncured
uncurious
uncurtained
uncustomary
undamaged
undamped
undated
undecided
undecipherable
undeclared
undecorated
undefeated
undefended
undefiled
undefinable
undefined
undemanding
undemocratic
undenominational
undependable
undeserved
undeserving
undesired
undetected
undetermined
undeterred
undeveloped
undifferentiated
undigested
undignified
undiluted
undiminished

undimmed
undiplomatic
undirected
undisciplined
undisclosed
undiscovered
undiscriminating
undisguised
undismayed
undisputed
undissolved
undistinguished
undistributed
undisturbed
undivided
undogmatic
undomesticated
undone
undoubled
undramatic
undraped
undreamed
undressed
undrinkable
undulled
undutiful
undyed
uneager
uneatable
uneaten
uneconomic
uneconomical
unedifying
unedited
uneducated
unembarrassed
unemotional
unemphatic
unenclosed
unencumbered
unendurable
unenforceable
unenforced
unenlightened
unenterprising
unenthusiastic
unenviable
unequipped
unessential
unethical
unexamined
unexcelled
unexceptional
unexcited
unexciting
unexpired
unexplained
unexploded
unexplored
unexposed
unexpressed
unexpurgated
unfading
unfaltering
unfashionable
unfashionably
unfathomable
unfavorable
unfavorably
unfeasible
unfeminine
unfenced
unfermented
unfertilized
unfilled
unfiltered
unfitted
unflagging
unflattering
unflavored
unfocused
unfolded
unforced
unforeseeable
unforeseen
unforgivable
unforgiving
unformulated
unfortified
unframed
unfree
unfulfilled
unfunded
unfunny
unfurnished

unfussy
ungentle
ungentlemanly
ungerminated
unglamorous
unglazed
ungoverned
ungraceful
ungracefully
ungraded
ungrammatical
unground
ungrudging
unguided
unhackneyed
unhampered
unhardened
unharmed
unharvested
unhatched
unhealed
unhealthful
unheated
unheeded
unhelpful
unheralded
unheroic
unhesitating
unhindered
unhistorical
unhonored
unhoused
unhurried
unhurt
unhygienic
unidentifiable
unidentified
unidiomatic
unimaginable
unimaginative
unimpaired
unimpassioned
unimpeded
unimportant
unimposing
unimpressed
unimpressive
unimproved
unincorporated
uninfected
uninfluenced
uninformative
uninformed
uninhabitable
uninhabited
uninitiated
uninjured
uninspired
uninstructed
uninstructive
uninsured
unintelligent
unintelligible
unintelligibly
unintended
unintentional
unintentionally
uninteresting
uninterrupted
uninvited
uninviting
unjointed
unjustifiable
unjustified
unkept
unknowable
unknowledgeable
unlabeled
unladylike
unlamented
unleavened
unlicensed
unlighted
unlikable
unlimited
unlined
unlit
unliterary
unlivable
unlovable
unloved
unloving
unmade
unmalicious
unmanageable

unmanned
unmapped
unmarked
unmarketable
unmarred
unmarried
unmasculine
unmatched
unmeant
unmeasurable
unmeasured
unmelodious
unmentioned
unmerited
unmilitary
unmilled
unmixed
unmodified
unmolested
unmotivated
unmounted
unmovable
unmoved
unmusical
unnameable
unnamed
unnecessary
unneeded
unnewsworthy
unnoticeable
unnoticed
unobjectionable
unobservant
unobserved
unobstructed
unobtainable
unofficial
unofficially
unopened
unopposed
unoriginal
unorthodox
unorthodoxy
unostentatious
unowned
unpaged
unpaid
unpainted
unpaired
unpalatable
unpardonable
unpasteurized
unpatriotic
unpaved
unpeeled
unperceived
unperceptive
unperformed
unpersuaded
unpersuasive
unperturbed
unplanned
unplanted
unpleasing
unplowed
unpoetic
unpolished
unpolitical
unpolluted
unposed
unpractical
unpredictability
unpredictable
unprejudiced
unpremeditated
unprepared
unpreparedness
unprepossessing
unpressed
unpretending
unpretty
unprivileged
unprocessed
unproductive
unprofessed
unprofessional
unprogrammed
unprogressive
unpromising
unprompted
unpronounceable
unpropitious
unproven
unprovided
unprovoked

unpublished
unpunished
unquenchable
unquestioned
unraised
unrated
unratified
unreachable
unreadable
unready
unrealistic
unrealized
unrecognizable
unrecognized
unrecorded
unrecoverable
unredeemable
unrefined
unreflecting
unreflective
unregistered
unregulated
unrehearsed
unrelated
unreliable
unrelieved
unremarkable
unremembered
unremovable
unrepentant
unreported
unrepresentative
unrepresented
unrepressed
unresistant
unresisting
unresolved
unresponsive
unresponsiveness
unrestful
unrestricted
unreturnable
unrewarding
unrhymed
unrhythmic
unripened
unromantic
unromantically
unsafe
unsaid
unsalable
unsalted
unsanctioned
unsanitary
unsatisfactory
unsatisfied
unscented
unscheduled
unscholarly
unsealed
unseasoned
unseaworthy
unsegmented
unself—conscious
unself—consciously
unsensational
unsentimental
unserious
unserviceable
unsexual
unshaded
unshakable
unshaken
unshapely
unshaven
unshorn
unsifted
unsigned
unsinkable
unsmiling
unsociable
unsoiled
unsold
unsoldierly
unsolicited
unsolvable
unsolved
unsorted
unspecified
unspectacular
unspent
unspiritual
unspoiled
unspoken
unsportsmanlike

unstained
unstated
unsterile
unstructured
unstylish
unsubdued
unsubstantiated
unsubtle
unsuccessful
unsuccessfully
unsuitable
unsuited
unsullied
unsupervised
unsupportable
unsupported
unsure
unsurpassed
unsurprising
unsurprisingly
unsuspected
unsuspecting
unsuspicious
unsweetened
unsymmetrical
unsympathetic
unsystematic
untactful
untainted
untalented
untamed
untanned
untapped
untarnished
untaxed
unteachable
untenable
untenanted
untended
untested
unthrifty
untidy
untilled
untitled

untraceable
untraditional
untrained
untrammeled
untranslatable
untranslated
untraveled
untraversed
untreated
untrimmed
untrod
untrodden
untroubled
untrustworthy
untruthful
untypical
unusable
unvaried
unvarying
unventilated
unverifiable
unverified
unversed
unvisited
unwanted
unwarranted
unwary
unwashed
unwavering
unweaned
unwearable
unwearied
unweathered
unwed
unwelcome
unwilling
unwillingly
unwillingness
unwomanly
unworkable
unworn
unworried
unwounded
unwoven

un·able \\ˌən-ˈā-bəl\\ *adj* **1** : not able **2** : UNQUALIFIED, INCOMPETENT

un·abridged \\ˌən-ə-ˈbrijd\\ *adj* **1** : not abridged ⟨an ~ edition of Shakespeare⟩ **2** : complete of its class : not based on one larger ⟨an ~ dictionary⟩

un·ac·com·pa·nied \\ˌən-ə-ˈkəm-pə-nēd\\ *adj* : not accompanied; *esp* : being without instrumental accompaniment

un·ac·count·able \\ˌən-ə-ˈkaün-tə-bəl\\ *adj* **1** : not to be accounted for : INEXPLICABLE **2** : not responsible — **un·ac·count·ably** \\-blē\\ *adv*

un·ac·count·ed \\-ˈkaün-təd\\ *adj* : not accounted ⟨the loss was ~ for⟩

un·ac·cus·tomed \\ˌən-ə-ˈkəs-təmd\\ *adj* **1** : not customary : not usual or common **2** : not accustomed or habituated ⟨~ to noise⟩

un·adul·ter·at·ed \\ˌən-ə-ˈdəl-tə-ˌrā-təd\\ *adj* : PURE, UNMIXED ✦ *Synonyms* ABSOLUTE, SHEER, SIMPLE, UNALLOYED, UNDILUTED, UNMITIGATED

un·af·fect·ed \\ˌən-ə-ˈfek-təd\\ *adj* **1** : not influenced or changed mentally, physically, or chemically **2** : free from affectation : NATURAL, GENUINE — **un·af·fect·ed·ly** *adv*

un·alien·able \\-ˈāl-yə-nə-bəl, -ˈā-lē-ə-\\ *adj* : INALIENABLE

un·aligned \\ˌən-ə-ˈlīnd\\ *adj* : not associated with any one of competing international blocs ⟨~ nations⟩

un·al·loyed \\ˌən-ə-ˈlȯid\\ *adj* : UNMIXED, UNQUALIFIED, PURE ⟨~ happiness⟩

un·al·ter·able \\ˌən-ˈȯl-tə-rə-bəl\\ *adj* : not capable of being altered or changed — **un·al·ter·ably** \\-blē\\ *adv*

un–Amer·i·can \\ˌən-ə-ˈmer-ə-kən\\ *adj* : not characteristic of or consistent with American customs or principles

unan·i·mous \\yu̇-ˈna-nə-məs\\ *adj* [L *unanimus*, fr. *unus* one + *animus* mind] **1** : being of one mind : AGREEING **2** : formed with or indicating the agreement of all — **una·nim·i·ty** \\ˌyü-nə-ˈni-mə-tē\\ *n* — **unan·i·mous·ly** *adv*

un·arm \\ˌən-ˈärm\\ *vb* : DISARM

un·armed \\-ˈärmd\\ *adj* : not armed or armored ⟨~ civilians⟩

un·as·sail·able \\ˌən-ə-ˈsā-lə-bəl\\ *adj* : not liable to doubt, attack, or question ⟨an ~ argument⟩

un·as·sum·ing \\ˌən-ə-ˈsü-miŋ\\ *adj* : MODEST ⟨an ~ librarian⟩ ⟨an ~ manner⟩ ⟨an ~ neighborhood⟩ ✦ *Synonyms* HUMBLE, LOWLY, MEEK

un·at·tached \ˌən-ə-'tacht\ *adj* 1 : not married or engaged 2 : not joined or united

un·avail·ing \ˌən-ə-'vā-liŋ\ *adj* : being of no avail — **un·avail·ing·ly** *adv*

un·avoid·able \ˌən-ə-'vói-də-bəl\ *adj* : not avoidable : INEVITABLE ✦ **Synonyms** CERTAIN, INELUCTABLE, INESCAPABLE, NECESSARY — **un·avoid·ably** \-blē\ *adv*

¹**un·aware** \ˌən-ə-'wer\ *adv* : UNAWARES

²**unaware** *adj* : not aware : IGNORANT — **un·aware·ness** *n*

un·awares \-'werz\ *adv* 1 : without knowing : UNINTENTIONALLY 2 : without warning : by surprise ⟨taken ∼⟩

un·bal·anced \ˌən-'ba-lənst\ *adj* 1 : not in a state of balance 2 : mentally disordered 3 : not adjusted so as to make credits equal to debits

un·bar \-'bär\ *vb* : UNBOLT, OPEN

un·bear·able \ˌən-'ber-ə-bəl\ *adj* : greater than can be borne ⟨∼ pain⟩ ✦ **Synonyms** INSUFFERABLE, INSUPPORTABLE, INTOLERABLE, UNENDURABLE, UNSUPPORTABLE — **un·bear·ably** \-blē\ *adv*

un·beat·able \-'bē-tə-bəl\ *adj* : not capable of being defeated ✦ **Synonyms** INDOMITABLE, INVINCIBLE, INVULNERABLE, UNCONQUERABLE

un·beat·en \-'bē-tᵊn\ *adj* 1 : not pounded, beaten, or whipped 2 : UNTRODDEN 3 : UNDEFEATED

un·be·com·ing \ˌən-bi-'kə-miŋ\ *adj* : not becoming : UNSUITABLE, IMPROPER ✦ **Synonyms** INDECOROUS, INDECENT, INDELICATE, UNSEEMLY — **un·be·com·ing·ly** *adv*

un·be·knownst \ˌən-bi-'nōnst\ *also* **un·be·known** \-'nōn\ *adj* : happening or existing without one's knowledge

un·be·lief \ˌən-bə-'lēf\ *n* : the withholding or absence of belief : DOUBT — **un·be·liev·ing** \-'lē-viŋ\ *adj*

un·be·liev·able \-'lē-və-bəl\ *adj* : too improbable for belief; *also* : of such a superlative degree as to be hard to believe ⟨an ∼ catch for a touchdown⟩ ✦ **Synonyms** INCONCEIVABLE, UNIMAGINABLE, UNTHINKABLE — **un·be·liev·ably** \-blē\ *adv*

un·be·liev·er \-'lē-vər\ *n* 1 : INFIDEL 2 : DOUBTER

un·bend \-'bend\ *vb* **-bent** \-'bent\; **-bend·ing** 1 : to free from being bent : make or become straight 2 : UNTIE 3 : to make or become less stiff or more affable : RELAX

un·bend·ing *adj* : formal and distant in manner : INFLEXIBLE

un·bi·ased \ˌən-'bī-əst\ *adj* : free from bias; *esp* : UNPREJUDICED ⟨an ∼ opinion⟩ ✦ **Synonyms** DISINTERESTED, DISPASSIONATE, IMPARTIAL, NONDISCRIMINATORY, NONPARTISAN, OBJECTIVE, UNCOLORED

un·bid·den \-'bi-dᵊn\ *also* **un·bid** \-'bid\ *adj* : not bidden : UNASKED

un·bind \-'bīnd\ *vb* **-bound** \-'baùnd\; **-bind·ing** 1 : to remove bindings from : UNTIE 2 : RELEASE

un·blessed *also* **un·blest** \ˌən-'blest\ *adj* 1 : not blessed 2 : EVIL

un·block \-'bläk\ *vb* : to free from being blocked

un·blush·ing \-'blə-shiŋ\ *adj* 1 : not blushing 2 : SHAMELESS ⟨∼ greed⟩ — **un·blush·ing·ly** *adv*

un·bod·ied \-'bä-dēd\ *adj* 1 : having no body; *also* : DISEMBODIED 2 : FORMLESS

un·bolt \ˌən-'bōlt\ *vb* : to open or unfasten by withdrawing a bolt

un·bolt·ed \-'bōl-təd\ *adj* : not fastened by bolts

un·born \-'bórn\ *adj* : not yet born

un·bos·om \-'bù-zəm, -'bü-\ *vb* 1 : DISCLOSE, REVEAL 2 : to disclose the thoughts or feelings of oneself

un·bound·ed \-'baùn-dəd\ *adj* : having no bounds or limits ⟨∼ enthusiasm⟩ ✦ **Synonyms** BOUNDLESS, ENDLESS, IMMEASURABLE, LIMITLESS, MEASURELESS, UNLIMITED

un·bowed \ˌən-'baùd\ *adj* 1 : not bowed down 2 : UNSUBDUED

un·bri·dled \-'brī-dᵊld\ *adj* 1 : UNRESTRAINED ⟨∼ enthusiasm⟩ 2 : not confined by a bridle

un·bro·ken \-'brō-kən\ *adj* 1 : not damaged 2 : not subdued or tamed 3 : not interrupted : CONTINUOUS

un·buck·le \-'bə-kəl\ *vb* : to loose the buckle of : UNFASTEN ⟨∼ a belt⟩

un·bur·den \-'bər-dᵊn\ *vb* 1 : to free or relieve from a burden 2 : to relieve oneself of (as cares or worries)

un·but·ton \-'bə-tᵊn\ *vb* : to unfasten the buttons of ⟨∼ your coat⟩

un·called-for \ˌən-'kóld-ˌfór\ *adj* : not called for, needed, or wanted

un·can·ny \-'ka-nē\ *adj* 1 : GHOSTLY, MYSTERIOUS, EERIE 2 : suggesting superhuman or supernatural powers ✦ **Synonyms** SPOOKY, UNEARTHLY, WEIRD — **un·can·ni·ly** \-'ka-nə-lē\ *adv*

un·ceas·ing \-'sē-siŋ\ *adj* : never ceasing ✦ **Synonyms** CEASELESS, CONTINUOUS, ENDLESS, INTERMINABLE, UNENDING, UNREMITTING — **un·ceas·ing·ly** *adv*

un·cer·e·mo·ni·ous \ˌən-ˌser-ə-'mō-nē-əs\ *adj* : acting without or lacking ordinary courtesy : ABRUPT — **un·cer·e·mo·ni·ous·ly** *adv*

un·cer·tain \ˌən-'sər-tᵊn\ *adj* 1 : not determined or fixed ⟨an ∼ quantity⟩ 2 : subject to chance or change : not dependable ⟨∼ weather⟩ 3 : not definitely known 4 : not sure ⟨∼ of the truth⟩ — **un·cer·tain·ly** *adv*

un·cer·tain·ty \-tᵊn-tē\ *n* 1 : lack of certainty : DOUBT 2 : something that is uncertain ✦ **Synonyms** CONCERN, DOUBT, DUBIETY, INCERTITUDE, SKEPTICISM, SUSPICION

un·chain \ˌən-'chān\ *vb* : to free by or as if by removing a chain

un·charged \ˌən-'chärjd\ *adj* : having no electrical charge

un·char·i·ta·ble \-'cha-rə-tə-bəl\ *adj* : not charitable; *esp* : severe in judging others — **un·char·i·ta·ble·ness** *n* — **un·char·i·ta·bly** \-blē\ *adv*

un·chart·ed \-'chär-təd\ *adj* 1 : not recorded on a map, chart, or plan 2 : UNKNOWN ⟨discussion moving into ∼ territory⟩

un·chris·tian \-'kris-chən\ *adj* 1 : not of the Christian faith 2 : contrary to the Christian spirit

un·churched \-'chərcht\ *adj* : not belonging to or connected with a church

un·cial \'ən-shəl, -chəl; 'ən-sē-əl\ *adj* : relating to or written in a form of script with rounded letters used esp. in early Greek and Latin manuscripts — **uncial** *n*

un·cir·cu·lat·ed \ˌən-'sər-kyə-ˌlā-təd\ *adj* : issued for use as money but kept out of circulation

un·cir·cum·cised \ˌən-'sər-kəm-ˌsīzd\ *adj* 1 : not circumcised 2 : HEATHEN

un·civ·il \ˌən-'si-vəl\ *adj* 1 : not civilized : BARBAROUS 2 : DISCOURTEOUS, ILL-MANNERED, IMPOLITE ⟨∼ remarks⟩

un·civ·i·lized \-'si-və-ˌlīzd\ *adj* 1 : not civilized : BARBAROUS 2 : remote from civilization : WILD

un·clasp \-'klasp\ *vb* : to open by or as if by loosing the clasp

un·cle \'əŋ-kəl\ *n* [ME, fr. AF, fr. L *avunculus* mother's brother] 1 : the brother of one's father or mother 2 : the husband of one's aunt

un·clean \ˌən-'klēn\ *adj* 1 : morally or spiritually impure 2 : prohibited by ritual law for use or contact 3 : DIRTY, SOILED — **un·clean·li·ness** \-lē-nəs\ *n* — **un·clean·ly** *adj* — **un·clean·ness** *n*

un·clench \-'klench\ *vb* : to open from a clenched position : RELAX

Uncle Tom \-'täm\ *n* [fr. *Uncle Tom*, faithful slave in Harriet Beecher Stowe's novel *Uncle Tom's Cabin* (1851-52)] : a black who is eager to win the approval of whites

un·cloak \ˌən-'klōk\ *vb* 1 : to remove a cloak or cover from 2 : UNMASK, REVEAL ⟨∼ an impostor⟩

un·clog \-'kläg\ *vb* : to remove an obstruction from

un·close \-'klōz\ *vb* : OPEN — **un·closed** \-'klōzd\ *adj*

un·clothe \-'klōth\ *vb* : to strip of clothes or a covering — **un·clothed** \-'klōthd\ *adj*

un·coil \ˌən-'kói(-ə)l\ *vb* : to release or become released from a coiled state

un·com·fort·able \ˌən-'kəmf-tə-bəl, -'kəm-fər-tə-\ *adj* 1 : causing discomfort 2 : feeling discomfort — **un·com·fort·ably** \-blē\ *adv*

un·com·mit·ted \ˌən-kə-'mi-təd\ *adj* : not committed; *esp* : not pledged to a particular belief, allegiance, or program ⟨∼ voters⟩

un·com·mon \ˌən-'kä-mən\ *adj* 1 : not ordinarily encountered : UNUSUAL, RARE 2 : REMARKABLE, EXCEPTIONAL ⟨a soldier of ∼ courage⟩ ✦ **Synonyms** EXTRAORDINARY, PHENOMENAL, SINGULAR, UNIQUE — **un·com·mon·ly** *adv*

un·com·mu·ni·ca·tive \ˌən-kə-'myü-nə-ˌkā-tiv, -ni-kə-\ *adj* : not inclined to talk or impart information : RESERVED ✦ **Synonyms** CLOSEMOUTHED, RETICENT, SILENT, TACITURN

un·com·pro·mis·ing \ˌən-'käm-prə-ˌmī-ziŋ\ *adj* : not making or accepting a compromise : UNYIELDING ✦ **Syno-**

nyms ADAMANT, INFLEXIBLE, OBDURATE, RIGID, UN-BENDING

un·con·cern \ˌən-kən-ˈsərn\ *n* 1 : lack of care or interest : INDIFFERENCE 2 : freedom from excessive concern

un·con·cerned \-ˈsərnd\ *adj* 1 : not having any part or interest 2 : not anxious or upset : free of worry ✦ *Synonyms* ALOOF, DETACHED, INCURIOUS, REMOTE, UNCURIOUS, UNINTERESTED — **un·con·cern·ed·ly** \-ˈsər-nəd-lē\ *adv*

un·con·di·tion·al \ˌən-kən-ˈdi-shə-nəl\ *adj* : not limited in any way ⟨∼ surrender⟩ — **un·con·di·tion·al·ly** *adv*

un·con·di·tioned \-ˈdi-shənd\ *adj* 1 : not subject to conditions 2 : not acquired or learned : NATURAL ⟨∼ responses⟩ 3 : producing an unconditioned response ⟨∼ stimuli⟩

un·con·quer·able \ˌən-ˈkäŋ-kə-rə-bəl\ *adj* : incapable of being conquered or overcome : INDOMITABLE

un·con·scio·na·ble \-ˈkän-shə-nə-bəl\ *adj* 1 : not guided or controlled by conscience 2 : not in accordance with what is right or just ⟨∼ sales practices⟩ ✦ *Synonyms* UNREASONABLE, UNDUE, UNJUSTIFIABLE, UNWARRANTABLE, UNWARRANTED — **un·con·scio·na·bly** \-blē\ *adv*

¹un·con·scious \ˌən-ˈkän-chəs, -shəs\ *adj* 1 : not knowing or perceiving : not aware 2 : not done consciously or on purpose 3 : having lost consciousness 4 : of or relating to the unconscious — **un·con·scious·ly** *adv* — **un·con·scious·ness** *n*

²unconscious *n* : the part of one's mental life of which one is not ordinarily aware but which is often a powerful force in influencing behavior

un·con·sti·tu·tion·al \ˌən-ˌkän-stə-ˈtü-shə-nəl, -ˈtyü-\ *adj* : not according to or consistent with the constitution of a state or society — **un·con·sti·tu·tion·al·i·ty** \-ˌtü-shə-ˈna-lə-tē, -ˌtyü-\ *n* — **un·con·sti·tu·tion·al·ly** \-ˈtü-shə-nə-lē, -ˈtyü-\ *adv*

un·con·trol·la·ble \ˌən-kən-ˈtrō-lə-bəl\ *adj* : incapable of being controlled : UNGOVERNABLE — **un·con·trol·la·bly** \-blē\ *adv*

un·con·ven·tion·al \-ˈven-chə-nəl\ *adj* : not conventional : being out of the ordinary — **un·con·ven·tion·al·i·ty** \-ˌven-chə-ˈna-lə-tē\ *n* — **un·con·ven·tion·al·ly** \-ˈven-chə-nə-lē\ *adv*

un·cork \ˌən-ˈkórk\ *vb* 1 : to draw a cork from 2 : to release from a sealed or pent-up state; *also* : to let go

un·count·ed \-ˈkaún-təd\ *adj* 1 : not counted 2 : INNUMERABLE

un·cou·ple \-ˈkə-pəl\ *vb* : DISCONNECT ⟨∼ railroad cars⟩

un·couth \-ˈküth\ *adj* [ME, unfamiliar, fr. OE *uncūth*, fr. *un-* + *cūth* known] 1 : strange, awkward, and clumsy in shape or appearance 2 : vulgar in conduct or speech : RUDE ✦ *Synonyms* DISCOURTEOUS, ILL-MANNERED, IMPOLITE, UNGRACIOUS, UNMANNERED, UNMANNERLY

un·cov·er \-ˈkə-vər\ *vb* 1 : to make known : DISCLOSE, REVEAL 2 : to expose to view by removing some covering 3 : to take the cover from 4 : to remove the hat from; *also* : to take off the hat as a token of respect — **uncovered** *adj*

un·crit·i·cal \ˌən-ˈkri-ti-kəl\ *adj* 1 : not critical : lacking in discrimination 2 : showing lack or improper use of critical standards or procedures — **un·crit·i·cal·ly** \-k(ə-)lē\ *adv*

un·cross \-ˈkrós\ *vb* : to change from a crossed position ⟨∼ed his legs⟩

unc·tion \ˈəŋk-shən\ *n* 1 : the act of anointing as a rite of consecration or healing 2 : exaggerated or insincere earnestness of language or manner

unc·tu·ous \ˈəŋk-chə-wəs\ *adj* [ME, fr. MF or ML; MF *unctueus*, fr. ML *unctuosus*, fr. L *unctus* act of anointing, fr. *unguere* to anoint] 1 : FATTY, OILY 2 : insincerely smooth in speech and manner — **unc·tu·ous·ly** *adv*

un·curl \ˌən-ˈkərl\ *vb* : to make or become straightened out from a curled or coiled position

un·cut \ˌən-ˈkət\ *adj* 1 : not cut down or into 2 : not shaped by cutting ⟨an ∼ diamond⟩ 3 : not having the folds of the leaves slit ⟨an ∼ book⟩ 4 : not abridged or curtailed ⟨the ∼ version of the film⟩ 5 : not diluted ⟨∼ heroin⟩

un·daunt·ed \-ˈdón-təd\ *adj* : not daunted : not discouraged or dismayed ✦ *Synonyms* BOLD, BRAVE, DAUNTLESS, FEARLESS, INTREPID, VALIANT — **un·daunt·ed·ly** *adv*

un·de·ceive \ˌən-di-ˈsēv\ *vb* : to free from deception, illusion, or error

un·de·mon·stra·tive \ˌən-di-ˈmän-strə-tiv\ *adj* : restrained in expression of feeling : RESERVED

un·de·ni·able \ˌən-di-ˈnī-ə-bəl\ *adj* 1 : plainly true : INCONTESTABLE 2 : unquestionably excellent or genuine ✦ *Synonyms* INCONTROVERTIBLE, INDISPUTABLE, INDUBITABLE, UNQUESTIONABLE — **un·de·ni·ably** \-blē\ *adv*

¹un·der \ˈən-dər\ *adv* 1 : in or into a position below or beneath something 2 : below some quantity, level, or limit ⟨$10 or ∼⟩ 3 : in or into a condition of subjection, subordination, or unconsciousness ⟨the ether put him ∼⟩

²un·der \ˌən-dər, ˈən-\ *prep* 1 : lower than and overhung, surmounted, or sheltered by ⟨∼ a tree⟩ 2 : subject to the authority or guidance of ⟨served ∼ him⟩ ⟨was ∼ contract⟩ 3 : subject to the action or effect of ⟨∼ the influence of alcohol⟩ 4 : within the division or grouping of ⟨items ∼ this heading⟩ 5 : less or lower than (as in size, amount, or rank) ⟨earns ∼ $5000⟩

³under \ˈən-dər\ *adj* 1 : lying below, beneath, or on the ventral side 2 : facing or protruding downward 3 : SUBORDINATE 4 : lower than usual, proper, or desired in amount, quality, or degree

un·der·achiev·er \ˌən-dər-ə-ˈchē-vər\ *n* : one (as a student) who performs below an expected level of proficiency

un·der·act \-ˈakt\ *vb* : to perform feebly or with restraint

un·der·ac·tive \-ˈak-tiv\ *adj* : characterized by abnormally low activity ⟨an ∼ thyroid gland⟩ — **un·der·ac·tiv·i·ty** \-ˌak-ˈti-və-tē\ *n*

un·der·age \-ˈāj\ *adj* : of less than mature or legal age

un·der·arm \-ˈärm\ *adj* 1 : UNDERHAND 2 ⟨an ∼ throw⟩ 2 : placed under or on the underside of the arms ⟨∼ seams⟩ — **underarm** *adv or n*

un·der·bel·ly \ˈən-dər-ˌbe-lē\ *n* 1 : a vulnerable area 2 : the underside of a body or mass

un·der·bid \ˌən-dər-ˈbid\ *vb* **-bid; -bid·ding** 1 : to bid less than another 2 : to bid too low

un·der·body \ˈən-dər-ˌbä-dē\ *n* : the lower parts of the body of a vehicle

un·der·bred \ˌən-dər-ˈbred\ *adj* : marked by lack of good breeding

un·der·brush \ˈən-dər-ˌbrəsh\ *n* : shrubs, bushes, or small trees growing beneath large trees

un·der·car·riage \-ˌka-rij\ *n* 1 : a supporting framework or underside (as of an automobile) 2 : the landing gear of an airplane

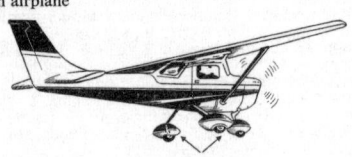

undercarriage 2

un·der·charge \ˌən-dər-ˈchärj\ *vb* : to charge (as a person) too little — **undercharge** \ˈən-dər-ˌchärj\ *n*

un·der·class \ˈən-dər-ˌklas\ *n* : LOWER CLASS

un·der·class·man \ˌən-dər-ˈklas-mən\ *n* : a member of the freshman or sophomore class

un·der·clothes \ˈən-dər-ˌklōthz\ *n pl* : UNDERWEAR

un·der·cloth·ing \-ˌklō-thiŋ\ *n* : UNDERWEAR

un·der·coat \-ˌkōt\ *n* 1 : a coat worn under another 2 : a growth of short hair or fur partly concealed by the longer and usu. coarser hairs of a mammal 3 : a coat of paint under another

un·der·coat·ing \-ˌkō-tiŋ\ *n* : a special waterproof coating applied to the underside of a vehicle

un·der·cov·er \ˌən-dər-ˈkə-vər\ *adj* : acting or executed in secret; *esp* : employed or engaged in secret investigation ⟨an ∼ agent⟩

un·der·croft \ˈən-dər-ˌkróft\ *n* [ME, fr. *under* + *crofte* crypt, fr. MD, fr. ML *crupta*, fr. L *crypta*] : a vaulted chamber under a church

un·der·cur·rent \-ˌkər-ənt\ *n* 1 : a current below the surface 2 : a hidden tendency of feeling or opinion ⟨an ∼ of dread⟩

un·der·cut \,ən-dər-'kət\ *vb* **-cut; -cut·ting** **1** : to cut away the underpart of **2** : to offer to sell or to work at a lower rate than **3** : to strike (the ball) obliquely downward so as to give a backward spin or elevation to the shot — **un·der·cut** \'ən-dər-ˌkət\ *n*

un·der·de·vel·oped \ˌən-dər-di-'ve-ləpt\ *adj* **1** : not normally or adequately developed ⟨∼ muscles⟩ **2** : having a relatively low level of economic development ⟨the ∼ nations⟩

un·der·dog \'ən-dər-ˌdȯg\ *n* : the loser or predicted loser in a struggle

un·der·done \ˌən-dər-'dən\ *adj* : not thoroughly done or cooked : RARE

un·der·draw·ers \'ən-dər-ˌdrȯrz, -ˌdrȯ-ərz\ *n pl* : UNDERPANTS

un·der·draw·ing \'ən-dər-ˌdrȯ-iŋ\ *n* : a preliminary sketch made prior to painting

un·der·em·pha·size \ˌən-dər-'em-fə-ˌsīz\ *vb* : to emphasize inadequately — **un·der·em·pha·sis** \-səs\ *n*

un·der·em·ployed \-im-'plȯid\ *adj* : having less than fulltime or adequate employment

un·der·es·ti·mate \-'es-tə-ˌmāt\ *vb* : to set too low a value on

un·der·ex·pose \-ik-'spōz\ *vb* : to expose (a photographic plate or film) for less time than is needed — **un·der·ex·po·sure** \-'spō-zhər\ *n*

un·der·feed \ˌən-dər-'fēd\ *vb* **-fed** \-'fed\; **-feed·ing** : to feed with too little food

un·der·foot \-'fut\ *adv* **1** : under the feet ⟨flowers trampled ∼⟩ **2** : close about one's feet : in the way

un·der·fur \'ən-dər-ˌfər\ *n* : an undercoat of fur esp. when thick and soft

un·der·gar·ment \-ˌgär-mənt\ *n* : a garment to be worn under another

un·der·gird \ˌən-dər-'gərd\ *vb* : to brace up : STRENGTHEN

un·der·go \ˌən-dər-'gō\ *vb* **-went** \-'went\; **-gone** \-'gȯn, -'gän\; **-go·ing** **1** : to submit to : ENDURE **2** : to go through : EXPERIENCE ⟨∼ a change⟩

un·der·grad \'ən-dər-ˌgrad\ *n* : UNDERGRADUATE

un·der·grad·u·ate \ˌən-dər-'gra-jə-wət, -jə-ˌwāt\ *n* : a student at a university or college who has not received a first degree

¹un·der·ground \ˌən-dər-'graund\ *adv* **1** : beneath the surface of the earth **2** : in or into hiding or secret operation

²un·der·ground \'ən-dər-ˌgraund\ *n* **1** : a space under the surface of the ground; *esp* : SUBWAY **2** : a secret political movement or group; *esp* : an organized body working in secret to overthrow a government or an occupying power **3** : an avant-garde group or movement that operates outside the establishment

³underground \'ən-dər-ˌgraund\ *adj* **1** : being, growing, operating, or located below the surface of the ground ⟨∼ stems⟩ **2** : conducted by secret means **3** : produced or published by the underground ⟨∼ publications⟩; *also* : of or relating to the avant-garde underground

un·der·growth \'ən-dər-ˌgrōth\ *n* : low growth (as of herbs and shrubs) on the floor of a forest

¹un·der·hand \'ən-dər-ˌhand\ *adv* **1** : in an underhanded or secret manner **2** : with an underhand motion

²underhand *adj* **1** : UNDERHANDED **2** : made with the hand kept below the level of the shoulder ⟨an ∼ pitch⟩

¹un·der·hand·ed \ˌən-dər-'han-dəd\ *adv* : UNDERHAND

²underhanded *adj* : marked by secrecy and deception — **un·der·hand·ed·ly** *adv* — **un·der·hand·ed·ness** *n*

un·der·lie \-'lī\ *vb* **-lay** \-'lā\; **-lain** \-'lān\; **-ly·ing** \-'lī-iŋ\ **1** : to lie or be situated under **2** : to be at the basis of : form the foundation of : SUPPORT

un·der·line \'ən-dər-ˌlīn\ *vb* **1** : to draw a line under **2** : EMPHASIZE, STRESS — **underline** *n*

un·der·ling \'ən-dər-liŋ\ *n* : SUBORDINATE, INFERIOR

un·der·lip \ˌən-dər-'lip\ *n* : the lower lip

un·der·ly·ing \ˌən-dər-ˌlī-iŋ\ *adj* **1** : lying under or below **2** : FUNDAMENTAL, BASIC ⟨∼ principles⟩

un·der·mine \-'mīn\ *vb* **1** : to excavate beneath **2** : to weaken or wear away secretly or gradually

un·der·most \'ən-dər-ˌmōst\ *adj* : lowest in relative position — **undermost** *adv*

¹un·der·neath \ˌən-dər-'nēth\ *prep* **1** : directly under **2** : under subjection to

²underneath *adv* **1** : below a surface or object : BENEATH **2** : on the lower side

un·der·nour·ished \ˌən-dər-'nər-isht\ *adj* : supplied with insufficient nourishment — **un·der·nour·ish·ment** \-'nər-ish-mənt\ *n*

un·der·pants \'ən-dər-ˌpants\ *n pl* : a usu. short undergarment for the lower trunk : DRAWERS

un·der·part \-ˌpärt\ *n* : a part lying on the lower side (as of a bird or mammal)

un·der·pass \-ˌpas\ *n* : a crossing of a highway and another way (as a road) at different levels; *also* : the lower level

un·der·pay \ˌən-dər-'pā\ *vb* : to pay less than what is normal or required

un·der·pin·ning \'ən-dər-ˌpi-niŋ\ *n* : the material and construction (as a foundation) used for support of a structure — **un·der·pin** \ˌən-dər-'pin\ *vb*

un·der·play \ˌən-dər-'plā\ *vb* : to treat or handle with restraint; *esp* : to play a role with subdued force

un·der·pop·u·lat·ed \ˌən-dər-'pä-pyə-ˌlā-təd\ *adj* : having a lower than normal or desirable density of population

un·der·priv·i·leged \-'priv-lijd, -'pri-və-lijd\ *adj* : having fewer esp. economic and social privileges than others

un·der·pro·duc·tion \ˌən-dər-prə-'dək-shən\ *n* : the production of less than enough to satisfy the demand or of less than the usual supply

un·der·rate \-'rāt\ *vb* : to rate or value too low

un·der·rep·re·sent·ed \-ˌre-pri-'zen-təd\ *adj* : inadequately represented

un·der·score \'ən-dər-ˌskȯr\ *vb* **1** : to draw a line under : UNDERLINE **2** : EMPHASIZE — **underscore** *n*

¹un·der·sea \ˌən-dər-'sē\ *adj* : being, carried on, or used beneath the surface of the sea

²undersea *or* **un·der·seas** \-'sēz\ *adv* : beneath the surface of the sea

un·der·sec·re·tary \ˌən-dər-'se-krə-ˌter-ē\ *n* : a secretary immediately subordinate to a principal secretary ⟨∼ of state⟩

un·der·sell \-'sel\ *vb* **-sold** \-'sōld\; **-sell·ing** : to sell articles cheaper than

un·der·sexed \-'sekst\ *adj* : deficient in sexual desire

un·der·shirt \'ən-dər-ˌshərt\ *n* : a collarless undergarment with or without sleeves

un·der·shoot \ˌən-dər-'shüt\ *vb* **-shot** \-'shät\; **-shoot·ing** **1** : to shoot short of or below (a target) **2** : to fall short of (a runway) in landing an airplane

un·der·shorts \'ən-dər-ˌshȯrts\ *n pl* : underpants for men or boys

un·der·shot \'ən-dər-ˌshät\ *adj* **1** : moved by water passing beneath ⟨an ∼ waterwheel⟩ **2** : having the lower front teeth projecting beyond the upper when the mouth is closed

un·der·side \'ən-dər-ˌsīd, ˌən-dər-'sīd\ *n* : the side or surface lying underneath

un·der·signed \'ən-dər-ˌsīnd\ *n, pl* **undersigned** : one whose name is signed at the end of a document

un·der·sized \ˌən-dər-'sīzd\ *also* **un·der·size** \-'sīz\ *adj* : of a size less than is common, proper, or normal

un·der·skirt \'ən-dər-ˌskərt\ *n* : a skirt worn under an outer skirt; *esp* : PETTICOAT

un·der·staffed \ˌən-dər-'staft\ *adj* : inadequately staffed

un·der·stand \ˌən-dər-'stand\ *vb* **-stood** \-'stud\; **-stand·ing** **1** : to grasp the meaning of : COMPREHEND **2** : to have thorough or technical acquaintance with or expertness in ⟨∼ finance⟩ **3** : to have reason to believe ⟨I ∼ you are leaving tomorrow⟩ **4** : INTERPRET ⟨we ∼ this to be a refusal⟩ **5** : to have a sympathetic attitude **6** : to accept as settled ⟨it is *understood* that he will pay the expenses⟩ — **un·der·stand·able** \-'stan-də-bəl\ *adj*

un·der·stand·ably \-blē\ *adv* : as can be easily understood

¹un·der·stand·ing \ˌən-dər-'stan-diŋ\ *n* **1** : knowledge and ability to judge : INTELLIGENCE ⟨a person of ∼⟩ **2** : agreement of opinion or feeling **3** : a mutual agreement informally or tacitly entered into

²understanding *adj* : endowed with understanding : TOLERANT, SYMPATHETIC

un·der·state \ˌən-dər-'stāt\ *vb* **1** : to represent as less than is the case **2** : to state with restraint esp. for effect — **un·der·state·ment** *n*

un·der·stood \ˌən-dər-'stud\ *adj* **1** : agreed upon **2** : IMPLICIT

un·der·sto·ry \'ən-dər-ˌstȯr-ē\ *n* : the vegetative layer between the top layer of a forest and the ground cover

un·der·study \'ən-dər-ˌstə-dē\ *n* : one who is prepared to act another's part or take over another's duties — **under-study** \'ən-dər-ˌstə-dē, ˌən-dər-'stə-dē\ vb

un·der·sur·face \'ən-dər-ˌsər-fəs\ n : UNDERSIDE

un·der·take \ˌən-dər-'tāk\ vb **-took** \-'tůk\; **-tak·en** \-'tā-kən\; **-tak·ing** **1** : to take upon oneself : set about ⟨~ a task⟩ **2** : to put oneself under obligation **3** : GUARANTEE, PROMISE

un·der·tak·er \'ən-dər-ˌtā-kər\ n : one whose business is to prepare the dead for burial and to arrange and manage funerals

un·der·tak·ing \'ən-dər-ˌtā-kiŋ, ˌən-dər-'tā-kiŋ; 2 is 'ən-dər-ˌtā-kiŋ only\ n **1** : the act of one who undertakes or engages in any project **2** : the business of an undertaker **3** : something undertaken **4** : PROMISE, GUARANTEE

under–the–counter adj : UNLAWFUL, ILLICIT ⟨~ sale of drugs⟩

un·der·tone \'ən-dər-ˌtōn\ n **1** : a low or subdued tone or utterance **2** : a subdued color (as seen through and modifying another color)

un·der·tow \-ˌtō\ n : the current beneath the surface that flows seaward when waves are breaking upon the shore

un·der·val·ue \ˌən-dər-'val-yü\ vb **1** : to value or estimate below the real worth **2** : to esteem lightly

un·der·wa·ter \ˌən-dər-'wò-tər, -'wä-\ adj : lying, growing, worn, or operating below the surface of the water — **un·der·wa·ter** adv

under way \-'wā\ adv **1** : into motion from a standstill **2** : in progress

un·der·wear \'ən-dər-ˌwer\ n : clothing or a garment worn next to the skin and under other clothing

un·der·weight \ˌən-dər-'wāt\ adj : weighing below what is normal, average, or necessary — **underweight** n

un·der·wire \'ən-dər-ˌwī(-ə)r\ n : a wire running through the bottom of a brassiere to aid in support

un·der·world \'ən-dər-ˌwərld\ n **1** : the place of departed souls : HADES **2** : the side of the world opposite to one **3** : the world of organized crime

un·der·write \'ən-dər-ˌrīt, ˌən-dər-'rīt\ vb **-wrote** \-ˌrōt, -'rōt\; **-writ·ten** \-ˌri-tⁿn, -'ri-tⁿn\; **-writ·ing** **1** : to write under or at the end of something else **2** : to set one's name to an insurance policy and thereby become answerable for a designated loss or damage **3** : to subscribe to : agree to **4** : to guarantee financial support of — **un·der·writ·er** n

un·de·sign·ing \ˌən-di-'zī-niŋ\ adj : having no artful, ulterior, or fraudulent purpose : SINCERE

un·de·sir·able \-'zī-rə-bəl\ adj : not desirable — **undesirable** n

un·de·vi·at·ing \ˌən-'dē-vē-ˌā-tiŋ\ adj : keeping a true course

un·dies \'ən-dēz\ n pl : UNDERWEAR; esp : women's underwear

un·do \ˌən-'dü\ vb **-did** \-'did\; **-done** \-'dən\; **-do·ing** **1** : to make or become unfastened or loosened : OPEN **2** : to make null or as if not done : REVERSE **3** : to bring to ruin; also : UPSET

un·doc·u·ment·ed \ˌən-'dä-kyə-ˌmen-təd\ adj **1** : not supported by documentary evidence **2** : lacking documents required for legal immigration

un·do·ing n : a cause of ruin

un·doubt·ed \-'daů-təd\ adj : not doubted or called into question : CERTAIN — **un·doubt·ed·ly** adv

¹un·dress \ˌən-'dres\ vb : to remove the clothes or covering of : STRIP, DISROBE

²undress n **1** : informal dress; esp : a loose robe or dressing gown **2** : ordinary dress **3** : NUDITY

un·due \-'dü, -'dyü\ adj **1** : not due **2** : exceeding or violating propriety or fitness : EXCESSIVE ⟨~ force⟩

un·du·lant \'ən-jə-lənt, 'ən-də-, -dyə-\ adj : rising and falling in waves

undulant fever n : a human disease caused by bacteria from infected domestic animals or their products and marked by intermittent fever, chills, headache, weakness, and weight loss

un·du·late \-ˌlāt\ vb **-lat·ed**; **-lat·ing** [LL undula small wave, fr. L unda wave] **1** : to have a wavelike motion or appearance **2** : to rise and fall in pitch or volume

un·du·la·tion \ˌən-jə-'lā-shən, ˌən-də-, -dyə-\ n **1** : wavy or wavelike motion **2** : pulsation of sound **3** : a wavy appearance or outline — **un·du·la·to·ry** \'ən-jə-lə-ˌtór-ē, 'ən-də-, -dyə-\ adj

un·du·ly \ˌən-'dü-lē, 'ən-, -'dyü-\ adv : in an undue manner : EXCESSIVELY

un·dy·ing \-'dī-iŋ\ adj : not dying : IMMORTAL, PERPETUAL

un·earned \-'ərnd\ adj : not earned by labor, service, or skill ⟨~ income⟩

un·earth \ˌən-'ərth\ vb **1** : to dig up out of or as if out of the earth ⟨~ buried treasure⟩ **2** : to bring to light : DISCOVER ⟨~ a secret⟩

un·earth·ly \-lē\ adj **1** : not of or belonging to the earth **2** : SUPERNATURAL, WEIRD; also : ABSURD

un·easy \ˌən-'ē-zē\ adj **1** : AWKWARD, EMBARRASSED ⟨~ among strangers⟩ **2** : disturbed by pain or worry; also : RESTLESS **3** : UNSTABLE ⟨an ~ truce⟩ — **un·eas·i·ly** \-'ē-zə-lē\ adv — **un·eas·i·ness** \-'ē-zē-nəs\ n

un·em·ployed \ˌən-im-'plòid\ adj : not being used; also : having no job

un·em·ploy·ment \-'plòi-mənt\ n **1** : lack of employment **2** : money paid at regular intervals (as by a government agency) to an unemployed person

un·end·ing \ˌən-'en-diŋ\ adj : having no ending : ENDLESS

un·equal \ˌən-'ē-kwəl\ adj **1** : not alike (as in size, amount, number, or value) **2** : not uniform : VARIABLE **3** : badly balanced or matched **4** : INADEQUATE, INSUFFICIENT ⟨~ to the task⟩ — **un·equal·ly** adv

un·equaled or **un·equalled** \-kwəld\ adj : not equaled : UNPARALLELED ⟨an artist of ~ talent⟩

un·equiv·o·cal \ˌən-i-'kwi-və-kəl\ adj : leaving no doubt : CLEAR — **un·equiv·o·cal·ly** adv

un·err·ing \ˌən-'er-iŋ, ˌən-'ər-\ adj : making no errors : CERTAIN, UNFAILING ⟨~ accuracy⟩ — **un·err·ing·ly** adv

UNES·CO \yü-'nes-kō\ abbr United Nations Educational, Scientific, and Cultural Organization

un·even \ˌən-'ē-vən\ adj **1** : ODD **3** **2** : not even : not level or smooth : RUGGED, RAGGED **3** : IRREGULAR; also : varying in quality — **un·even·ly** adv — **un·even·ness** n

un·event·ful \ˌən-i-'vent-fəl\ adj : lacking interesting or noteworthy incidents — **un·event·ful·ly** adv

un·evolved \ˌən-i-'välvd\ adj : not fully developed ⟨an ~ wine⟩ **2** : lacking cultural refinement

un·ex·am·pled \ˌən-ig-'zam-pəld\ adj : UNPRECEDENTED, UNPARALLELED ⟨fought with ~ passion⟩

un·ex·cep·tion·able \ˌən-ik-'sep-shə-nə-bəl\ adj : not open to exception or objection : beyond reproach

un·ex·pect·ed \ˌən-ik-'spek-təd\ adj : not expected : UNFORESEEN — **un·ex·pect·ed·ly** adv

un·fail·ing \ˌən-'fā-liŋ\ adj **1** : not failing, flagging, or waning : CONSTANT **2** : INEXHAUSTIBLE ⟨a subject of ~ interest⟩ **3** : INFALLIBLE, SURE ⟨an ~ test⟩ — **un·fail·ing·ly** adv

un·fair \-'fer\ adj **1** : marked by injustice, partiality, or deception : UNJUST **2** : not equitable in business dealings — **un·fair·ly** adv — **un·fair·ness** n

un·faith·ful \ˌən-'fāth-fəl\ adj **1** : not observant of vows, allegiance, or duty : DISLOYAL **2** : INACCURATE, UNTRUSTWORTHY ⟨an ~ copy of a document⟩ — **un·faith·ful·ly** adv — **un·faith·ful·ness** n

un·fa·mil·iar \ˌən-fə-'mil-yər\ adj **1** : not well-known : STRANGE ⟨an ~ place⟩ **2** : not well acquainted ⟨~ with the subject⟩ — **un·fa·mil·iar·i·ty** \-ˌmi-lē-'er-, -'yer-\ n

un·fas·ten \ˌən-'fa-sⁿn\ vb : to make or become loose : UNDO, DETACH

un·feel·ing \ˌən-'fē-liŋ\ adj **1** : lacking feeling : INSENSATE **2** : HARDHEARTED, CRUEL — **un·feel·ing·ly** adv

un·feigned \-'fānd\ adj : not feigned : not hypocritical : GENUINE

un·fet·ter \-'fe-tər\ vb **1** : to free from fetters **2** : LIBERATE

un·fil·ial \ˌən-'fi-lē-əl, -'fil-yəl\ adj : not observing the obligations of a child to a parent : UNDUTIFUL

un·fin·ished \ˌən-'fi-nisht\ adj **1** : not brought to an end **2** : being in a rough or unpolished state

¹un·fit \-'fit\ adj : not fit or suitable; esp : physically or mentally unsound — **un·fit·ness** n

²unfit vb : to make unfit : DISQUALIFY

un·fix \-'fiks\ vb **1** : to loosen from a fastening : DETACH **2** : UNSETTLE

un·flap·pa·ble \-'fla-pə-bəl\ adj : not easily upset or panicked — **un·flap·pa·bly** adv

un·fledged \-'flejd\ adj : not feathered or ready for flight; also : IMMATURE, CALLOW

un·flinch·ing \-'flin-chiŋ\ adj : not flinching or shrinking : STEADFAST — **un·flinch·ing·ly** adv

un·fold \-'fōld\ *vb* **1** : to open the folds of : open up **2** : to lay open to view : DISCLOSE **3** : BLOSSOM, DEVELOP

un·for·get·ta·ble \ˌən-fər-'ge-tə-bəl\ *adj* : incapable of being forgotten — **un·for·get·ta·bly** \-blē\ *adv*

un·formed \-'fȯrmd\ *adj* : not regularly formed or ordered : UNDEVELOPED

un·for·tu·nate \-'fȯr-chə-nət\ *adj* **1** : not fortunate : UNLUCKY **2** : attended with misfortune **3** : UNSUITABLE ⟨an ~ choice of words⟩ — **unfortunate** *n*

un·for·tu·nate·ly \-nət-lē\ *adv* **1** : in an unfortunate manner **2** : it is unfortunate

un·found·ed \ˌən-'faůn-dəd\ *adj* : lacking a sound basis : GROUNDLESS

un·freeze \-'frēz\ *vb* **-froze** \-'frōz\; **-fro·zen** \-'frō-z°n\; **-freez·ing** **1** : to cause to thaw **2** : to remove from a freeze ⟨~ prices⟩

un·fre·quent·ed \ˌən-frē-'kwen-təd; ˌən-'frē-kwən-\ *adj* : seldom visited or traveled over

un·friend·ly \ˌən-'frend-lē\ *adj* **1** : not friendly or kind : HOSTILE **2** : UNFAVORABLE ⟨~ to new business⟩ — **un·friend·li·ness** \-lē-nəs\ *n*

un·frock \-'fräk\ *vb* : DEFROCK

un·fruit·ful \-'früt-fəl\ *adj* **1** : not producing fruit or offspring : BARREN **2** : yielding no valuable result : UNPROFITABLE — **un·fruit·ful·ness** *n*

un·furl \-'fərl\ *vb* : to loose from a furled state : UNFOLD

un·gain·ly \-'gān-lē\ *adj* [*un-* + obs. *gainly* proper, becoming, fr. *gain* direct, handy, fr. ME *geyn*, fr. OE *gēn*, fr. ON *gegn* against] : CLUMSY, AWKWARD — **un·gain·li·ness** \-lē-nəs\ *n*

un·gen·er·ous \ˌən-'je-nə-rəs\ *adj* : not generous or liberal : STINGY

un·glued \ˌən-'glüd\ *adj* : UPSET, DISORDERED

un·god·ly \ˌən-'gäd-lē, -'gȯd-\ *adj* **1** : IMPIOUS, IRRELIGIOUS **2** : SINFUL, WICKED **3** : OUTRAGEOUS ⟨an ~ hour⟩ — **un·god·li·ness** \-lē-nəs\ *n*

un·gov·ern·able \-'gə-vər-nə-bəl\ *adj* : not capable of being governed, guided, or restrained : UNRULY

un·gra·cious \-'grā-shəs\ *adj* **1** : not courteous : RUDE **2** : not pleasing : DISAGREEABLE ⟨an ~ task⟩

un·grate·ful \ˌən-'grāt-fəl\ *adj* **1** : not thankful for favors **2** : DISAGREEABLE, THANKLESS — **un·grate·ful·ly** *adv* — **un·grate·ful·ness** *n*

un·guard·ed \-'gär-dəd\ *adj* **1** : UNPROTECTED **2** : DIRECT, INCAUTIOUS ⟨~ remarks⟩

un·guent \'əŋ-gwənt, 'ən-\ *n* : a soothing or healing salve : OINTMENT

¹un·gu·late \'əŋ-gyə-lət, 'ən-, -ˌlāt\ *adj* [LL *ungulatus*, fr. L *ungula* hoof, fr. *unguis* nail, hoof] : having hoofs

²ungulate *n* : a hoofed mammal (as a cow, horse, or rhinoceros)

un·hal·lowed \ˌən-'ha-lōd\ *adj* **1** : not consecrated : UNHOLY **2** : IMPIOUS, PROFANE **3** : contrary to accepted standards : IMMORAL

un·hand \ˌən-'hand\ *vb* : to remove the hand from : let go

un·hand·some \-'han-səm\ *adj* **1** : not beautiful or handsome : HOMELY **2** : UNBECOMING **3** : DISCOURTEOUS, RUDE

un·handy \-'han-dē\ *adj* : INCONVENIENT; *also* : AWKWARD

un·hap·py \-'ha-pē\ *adj* **1** : UNLUCKY, UNFORTUNATE ⟨an ~ coincidence⟩ **2** : SAD, MISERABLE **3** : INAPPROPRIATE ⟨an ~ choice⟩ — **un·hap·pi·ly** \-'ha-pə-lē\ *adv* — **un·hap·pi·ness** \-pē-nəs\ *n*

un·har·ness \-'här-nəs\ *vb* : to remove the harness from (as a horse)

un·healthy \-'hel-thē\ *adj* **1** : not conducive to health : UNWHOLESOME **2** : SICKLY, DISEASED

un·heard \-'hərd\ *adj* **1** : not heard **2** : not granted a hearing

unheard–of *adj* : previously unknown; *esp* : UNPRECEDENTED ⟨moving at ~ speeds⟩

un·hinge \ˌən-'hinj\ *vb* **1** : to make unstable esp. mentally **2** : to take from the hinges

un·hitch \-'hich\ *vb* : UNFASTEN, LOOSE

un·ho·ly \-'hō-lē\ *adj* **1** : not holy : PROFANE, WICKED **2** : very unpleasant ⟨an ~ mess⟩ — **un·ho·li·ness** \-lē-nəs\ *n*

un·hook \-'hůk\ *vb* : to loose from a hook

un·horse \-'hȯrs\ *vb* : to dislodge from or as if from a horse

uni·cam·er·al \ˌyü-ni-'ka-mə-rəl\ *adj* : having a single legislative house or chamber

UNI·CEF \'yü-nə-ˌsef\ *abbr* [United Nations International Children's Emergency Fund, its former name] United Nations Children's Fund

uni·cel·lu·lar \ˌyü-ni-'sel-yə-lər\ *adj* : having or consisting of a single cell

uni·corn \'yü-nə-ˌkȯrn\ *n* [ME *unicorne*, fr. AF, fr. LL *unicornis*, fr. L, having one horn, fr. *unus* one + *cornu* horn] : a mythical animal with one horn in the middle of the forehead

uni·cy·cle \'yü-ni-ˌsī-kəl\ *n* : a vehicle that has a single wheel and is usu. propelled by pedals

uni·di·rec·tion·al \ˌyü-ni-də-'rek-shə-nəl, -dī-\ *adj* : having, moving in, or responsive in a single direction

uni·fi·ca·tion \ˌyü-nə-fə-'kā-shən\ *n* : the act, process, or result of unifying : the state of being unified

¹uni·form \'yü-nə-ˌfȯrm\ *adj* **1** : not varying ⟨~ procedures⟩ **2** : of the same form with others — **uni·form·ly** *adv*

²uniform *vb* : to clothe with a uniform

³uniform *n* : distinctive dress worn by members of a particular group (as an army or a police force)

uni·for·mi·ty \ˌyü-nə-'fȯr-mə-tē\ *n, pl* **-ties** : the state of being uniform

uni·fy \'yü-nə-ˌfī\ *vb* **-fied; -fy·ing** : to make into a coherent whole : UNITE

uni·lat·er·al \ˌyü-ni-'la-tə-rəl\ *adj* : of, having, affecting, or done by one side only — **uni·lat·er·al·ly** *adv*

un·im·peach·able \ˌən-im-'pē-chə-bəl\ *adj* : not liable to accusation : IRREPROACHABLE ⟨an ~ reputation⟩

un·in·hib·it·ed \ˌən-in-'hi-bə-təd\ *adj* : free from inhibition; *also* : boisterously informal — **un·in·hib·it·ed·ly** *adv*

un·in·stall \ˌən-in-'stȯl\ *vb* : to remove (software) from a computer system

un·in·tel·li·gent \-'te-lə-jənt\ *adj* : lacking intelligence

un·in·tel·li·gi·ble \-jə-bəl\ *adj* : not intelligible : OBSCURE — **un·in·tel·li·gi·bly** \-blē\ *adv*

un·in·ter·est·ed \ˌən-'in-trəs-təd, -tə-rəs-, -tə-ˌres-\ *adj* : not interested : not having the mind or feelings engaged or aroused

un·in·ter·rupt·ed \ˌən-ˌin-tə-'rəp-təd\ *adj* : not interrupted : CONTINUOUS

union \'yün-yən\ *n* **1** : an act or instance of uniting two or more things into one : the state of being united : COMBINATION, JUNCTION **2** : a uniting in marriage **3** : something formed by a combining of parts or members; *esp* : a confederation of independent individuals (as nations or persons) for some common purpose **4** : an organization of workers (as a labor union or a trade union) formed to advance its members' interests esp. in respect to wages and working conditions **5** : a device emblematic of union used on or as a national flag; *also* : the upper inner corner of a flag **6** : a device for connecting parts (as of a machine); *esp* : a coupling for pipes

unionise *Brit var of* UNIONIZE

union·ism \'yün-yə-ˌni-zəm\ *n* **1** : the principle or policy of forming or adhering to a union; *esp, cap* : adherence to the policy of a firm federal union before or during the U.S. Civil War **2** : the principles or system of trade unions — **union·ist** *n*

union·ize \'yün-yə-ˌnīz\ *vb* **-ized; -iz·ing** : to form into or cause to join a labor union — **union·i·za·tion** \ˌyün-yə-nə-'zā-shən\ *n*

union jack *n* **1** : a flag consisting of the part of a national flag that signifies union **2** *cap U&J* : the national flag of the United Kingdom

unique \yu̇-'nēk\ *adj* **1** : being the only one of its kind : SINGLE, SOLE **2** : very unusual : NOTABLE — **unique·ly** *adv* — **unique·ness** *n*

uni·sex \'yü-nə-ˌseks\ *adj* : not distinguishable as male or female; *also* : suitable or designed for both males and females — **unisex** *n*

uni·sex·u·al \ˌyü-nə-'sek-shə-wəl\ *adj* **1** : having only male or only female sex organs **2** : UNISEX

uni·son \'yü-nə-sən, -zən\ *n* [ME *unisoun*, fr. MF *unisson*, fr. ML *unisonus* having the same sound, fr. L *unus* one + *sonus* sound] **1** : sameness or identity in musical pitch **2** : the condition of being tuned or sounded at the same pitch or in octaves ⟨sing in ~⟩ **3** : harmonious agreement or union : ACCORD

unit \'yü-nət\ *n* **1** : the smallest whole number greater than zero : ONE **2** : a definite amount or quantity used as a standard of measurement **3** : a single thing, person, or group that is a constituent of a whole; *also* : a part of a military establishment that has a prescribed organization — **unit** *adj*

Uni·tar·i·an \ˌyü-nə-'ter-ē-ən\ *n* : a member of a religious denomination stressing individual freedom of belief — **Uni·tar·i·an·ism** *n*

uni·tary \'yü-nə-ˌter-ē\ *adj* **1** : of or relating to a unit **2** : not divided — **uni·tar·i·ly** \ˌyü-nə-'ter-ə-lē\ *adv*

unite \yu̇-'nīt\ *vb* **unit·ed; unit·ing** **1** : to put or join together so as to make one : COMBINE, COALESCE **2** : to join by a legal or moral bond; *also* : to join in interest or fellowship **3** : AMALGAMATE, CONSOLIDATE **4** : to act in concert

unit·ed \yu̇-'nī-təd\ *adj* **1** : made one : COMBINED **2** : relating to or produced by joint action **3** : being in agreement : HARMONIOUS

unit·ize \'yü-nə-ˌtīz\ *vb* **-ized; -iz·ing** **1** : to form or convert into a unit **2** : to divide into units

uni·ty \'yü-nə-tē\ *n, pl* **-ties** **1** : the quality or state of being or being made one : ONENESS **2** : a definite quantity or combination of quantities taken as one or for which 1 is made to stand in calculation **3** : CONCORD, ACCORD, HARMONY **4** : continuity without change ⟨~ of purpose⟩ **5** : reference of all the parts of a literary or artistic composition to a single main idea **6** : totality of related parts ♦ **Synonyms** SOLIDARITY, UNION, INTEGRITY

univ *abbr* **1** universal **2** university

uni·valve \'yü-ni-ˌvalv\ *n* : a mollusk having a shell with only one piece; *esp* : GASTROPOD — **univalve** *adj*

uni·ver·sal \ˌyü-nə-'vər-səl\ *adj* **1** : including, covering, or affecting the whole without limit or exception : available or applying to everyone ⟨~ privileges⟩ ⟨a ~ rule⟩ **2** : present or occurring everywhere **3** : used or for use among all ⟨a ~ language⟩ **4** : adaptable for various purposes ⟨a ~ remote control⟩ — **uni·ver·sal·ly** *adv*

uni·ver·sal·i·ty \-vər-'sa-lə-tē\ *n* : the quality or state of being universal

uni·ver·sal·ize \'yü-vər-sə-ˌlīz\ *vb* **-ized; -iz·ing** : to make universal : GENERALIZE — **uni·ver·sal·i·za·tion** \-ˌvər-sə-lə-'zā-shən\ *n*

universal joint *n* : a shaft coupling for transmitting rotation from one shaft to another not in a straight line with it

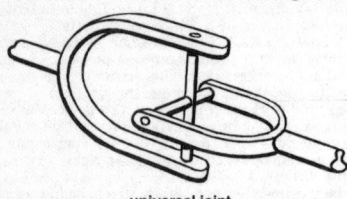

universal joint

Universal Product Code *n* : a combination of a bar code and numbers by which a scanner can identify a product and usu. assign a price

uni·verse \'yü-nə-ˌvərs\ *n* [ME, fr. L *universum*, fr. neut. of *universus* entire, whole, fr. *unus* one + *versus* turned toward, fr. pp. of *vertere* to turn] : the whole body of things observed or assumed : COSMOS

uni·ver·si·ty \ˌyü-nə-'vər-sə-tē\ *n, pl* **-ties** : an institution of higher learning authorized to confer degrees in various special fields (as theology, law, and medicine) as well as in the arts and sciences generally

un·just \ˌən-'jəst\ *adj* : characterized by injustice — **un·just·ly** *adv*

un·kempt \-'kempt\ *adj* **1** : lacking order or neatness; *also* : ROUGH, UNPOLISHED **2** : not combed : DISHEVELED

un·kind \-'kīnd\ *adj* : not kind or sympathetic ⟨an ~ remark⟩ — **un·kind·ly** *adv* — **un·kind·ness** *n*

un·kind·ly \-'kīnd-lē\ *adj* : UNKIND — **un·kind·li·ness** *n*

un·know·ing \ˌən-'nō-iŋ\ *adj* : not knowing — **un·know·ing·ly** *adv*

un·known \-'nōn\ *adj* : not known or not well-known — **unknown** *n*

un·lace \ˌən-'lās\ *vb* : to loose by undoing a lace

un·lade \-'lād\ *vb* **-lad·ed; -lad·ed** *or* **-lad·en** \-'lā-d°n\; **-lad·ing** : to take the load or cargo from : UNLOAD

un·latch \-'lach\ *vb* **1** : to open or loose by lifting the latch **2** : to become loosed or opened

un·law·ful \ˌən-'lȯ-fəl\ *adj* **1** : not lawful : ILLEGAL **2** : ILLEGITIMATE — **un·law·ful·ly** *adv*

un·lead·ed \-'le-dəd\ *adj* : not treated or mixed with lead or lead compounds

un·learn \-'lərn\ *vb* : to put out of one's knowledge or memory; *also* : to discard the habit of

un·learned \-'lər-nəd *for 1;* -'lərnd *for 2*\ *adj* **1** : UNEDUCATED, ILLITERATE **2** : not gained by study or training

un·leash \-'lēsh\ *vb* : to free from or as if from a leash : let loose

un·less \ən-'les, 'ən-ˌles\ *conj* : except on condition that ⟨won't go ~ you do⟩

un·let·tered \ˌən-'le-tərd\ *adj* : not educated : ILLITERATE

¹un·like \-'līk\ *adj* **1** : not like : DISSIMILAR, DIFFERENT **2** : UNEQUAL — **un·like·ness** *n*

²unlike *prep* **1** : different from ⟨she's quite ~ her sister⟩ **2** : unusual for ⟨it's ~ you to be late⟩ **3** : differently from ⟨behaves ~ his brother⟩

un·like·li·hood \ˌən-'lī-klē-ˌhu̇d\ *n* : IMPROBABILITY

un·like·ly \-'lī-klē\ *adj* **1** : not likely : IMPROBABLE **2** : likely to fail

un·lim·ber \ˌən-'lim-bər\ *vb* : to get ready for action

un·list·ed \ˌən-'lis-təd\ *adj* **1** : not appearing on a list; *esp* : not appearing in a telephone book **2** : not listed on a stock exchange

un·load \-'lōd\ *vb* **1** : to take away or off : REMOVE ⟨~ cargo from a hold⟩; *also* : to get rid of **2** : to take a load from ⟨~ the ship⟩; *also* : to relieve or set free : UNBURDEN ⟨~ one's mind of worries⟩ **3** : to draw the charge from ⟨~ed the gun⟩ **4** : to sell in volume

un·lock \-'läk\ *vb* **1** : to open or unfasten through release of a lock **2** : RELEASE ⟨~ a flood of emotions⟩ **3** : DISCLOSE, REVEAL ⟨~ nature's secrets⟩

un·looked-for \-'lu̇kt-fȯr\ *adj* : UNEXPECTED

un·loose \ˌən-'lüs\ *vb* **1** : to relax the strain of : set free; *also* : UNTIE

un·loos·en \-'lü-s°n\ *vb* : UNLOOSE

un·love·ly \-'ləv-lē\ *adj* : having no charm or appeal : not amiable

un·luck·i·ly \-'lə-kə-lē\ *adv* : UNFORTUNATELY

un·lucky \-'lə-kē\ *adj* **1** : UNFORTUNATE, ILL-FATED **2** : likely to bring misfortune : INAUSPICIOUS **3** : REGRETTABLE

un·man \ˌən-'man\ *vb* **1** : to deprive of manly courage **2** : CASTRATE

un·man·ly \-'man-lē\ *adj* : not manly : COWARDLY; *also* : EFFEMINATE

un·man·ner·ly \-'ma-nər-lē\ *adj* : RUDE, IMPOLITE — **unmannerly** *adv*

un·mask \ˌən-'mask\ *vb* **1** : to strip of a mask or a disguise : EXPOSE **2** : to remove one's mask

un·mean·ing \-'mē-niŋ\ *adj* : having no meaning : SENSELESS

un·me·di·at·ed \ˌən-'mē-dē-ˌā-təd\ *adj* : not mediated : not communicated or transformed by an intervening agency

un·meet \-'mēt\ *adj* : not meet or fit : UNSUITABLE, IMPROPER

un·men·tion·able \-'men-chə-nə-bəl\ *adj* : not fit or proper to be talked about ⟨an ~ topic⟩

un·mer·ci·ful \-'mər-si-fəl\ *adj* : not merciful : CRUEL, MERCILESS — **un·mer·ci·ful·ly** *adv*

un·mind·ful \-'mīnd-fəl\ *adj* : not mindful : CARELESS, UNAWARE

un·mis·tak·able \ˌən-mə-'stā-kə-bəl\ *adj* : not capable of being mistaken or misunderstood : CLEAR, OBVIOUS — **un·mis·tak·ably** \-blē\ *adv*

un·mit·i·gat·ed \ˌən-'mi-tə-ˌgā-təd\ *adj* : not softened or lessened **2** : ABSOLUTE, DOWNRIGHT ⟨an ~ liar⟩

un·moor \-'mu̇r\ *vb* : to loose from or as if from moorings

un·mor·al \-'mȯr-əl\ *adj* : having no moral perception or quality : AMORAL — **un·mo·ral·i·ty** \ˌən-mə-'ra-lə-tē\ *n*

un·muz·zle \-'mə-zəl\ *vb* : to remove a muzzle from

un·nat·u·ral \ˌən-'na-chə-rəl\ *adj* : contrary to or acting contrary to nature or natural instincts; *also* : ABNORMAL — **un·nat·u·ral·ly** *adv* — **un·nat·u·ral·ness** *n*

un·nec·es·sar·i·ly \ˌən-ˌne-sə-ˈser-ə-lē\ *adv* **1** : not by necessity **2** : to an unnecessary degree ⟨~ harsh⟩

un·nerve \ˌən-ˈnərv\ *vb* : to deprive of courage, strength, or steadiness; *also* : UPSET

un·num·bered \ˌən-ˈnəm-bərd\ *adj* : not numbered or counted : INNUMERABLE

un·ob·tru·sive \ˌən-əb-ˈtrü-siv\ *adj* : not obtrusive or forward : not bold : INCONSPICUOUS — **un·ob·tru·sive·ly** *adv*

un·oc·cu·pied \ˌən-ˈä-kyə-ˌpīd\ *adj* **1** : not busy : UNEMPLOYED **2** : not occupied : EMPTY, VACANT

un·or·ga·nized \-ˈȯr-gə-ˌnīzd\ *adj* **1** : not formed or brought into an integrated or ordered whole **2** : not organized into unions ⟨~ labor⟩

un·pack \ˌən-ˈpak\ *vb* **1** : to separate and remove things packed **2** : to open and remove the contents of

un·par·al·leled \ˌən-ˈpa-rə-ˌleld\ *adj* : having no parallel; *esp* : having no equal or match

un·par·lia·men·ta·ry \ˌən-ˌpär-lə-ˈmen-tə-rē\ *adj* : contrary to parliamentary practice

un·peg \ˌən-ˈpeg\ *vb* **1** : to remove a peg from **2** : to unfasten by or as if by removing a peg

un·per·son \ˈən-ˌpər-sᵒn, -ˌpər-\ *n* : a person who usu. for political or ideological reasons is removed from recognition or consideration

un·pile \ˌən-ˈp(-ə)l\ *vb* : to take or disentangle from a pile

un·pin \-ˈpin\ *vb* : to remove a pin from : UNFASTEN

un·pleas·ant \-ˈple-zᵒnt\ *adj* : not pleasant : DISAGREEABLE — **un·pleas·ant·ly** *adv* — **un·pleas·ant·ness** *n*

un·plug \ˌən-ˈpləg\ *vb* **1** : UNCLOG **2** : to remove (a plug) from a receptacle; *also* : to disconnect from an electric circuit by removing a plug

un·plumbed \-ˈpləmd\ *adj* **1** : not tested or measured with a plumb line **2** : not thoroughly explored

un·pop·u·lar \ˌən-ˈpä-pyə-lər\ *adj* : not popular : looked upon or received unfavorably — **un·pop·u·lar·i·ty** \ˌən-ˌpä-pyə-ˈla-rə-tē\ *n*

un·prec·e·dent·ed \ˌən-ˈpre-sə-ˌden-təd\ *adj* : having no precedent : NOVEL

un·pre·ten·tious \ˌən-pri-ˈten-chəs\ *adj* : not pretentious : MODEST

un·prin·ci·pled \ˌən-ˈprin-sə-pəld\ *adj* : lacking sound or honorable principles : UNSCRUPULOUS

un·print·able \-ˈprin-tə-bəl\ *adj* : unfit or too offensive to be printed ⟨~ remarks⟩

un·prof·it·able \ˌən-ˈprä-fə-tə-bəl\ *adj* : not profitable : USELESS, VAIN

un·pro·tect·ed \ˌən-prə-ˈtek-təd\ *adj* **1** : lacking protection **2** : performed without measures to prevent pregnancy or sexually transmitted disease ⟨~ sex⟩

un·qual·i·fied \ˌən-ˈkwä-lə-ˌfīd\ *adj* **1** : not having requisite qualifications **2** : not modified or restricted by reservations : COMPLETE — **un·qual·i·fied·ly** \-ˌfī-əd-lē\ *adv*

un·ques·tion·able \-ˈkwes-chə-nə-bəl\ *adj* : not questionable : INDISPUTABLE — **un·ques·tion·ably** \-blē\ *adv*

un·ques·tion·ing \-chə-niŋ\ *adj* : not questioning : accepting without examination or hesitation — **un·ques·tion·ing·ly** *adv*

un·qui·et \-ˈkwī-ət\ *adj* **1** : not quiet : AGITATED, DISTURBED **2** : physically, emotionally, or mentally restless : UNEASY

un·quote \ˈən-ˌkwōt\ *n* — used orally to indicate the end of a direct quotation

un·rav·el \ˌən-ˈra-vəl\ *vb* **1** : to separate the threads of **2** : SOLVE ⟨~ a mystery⟩ **3** : to become unraveled

un·read \-ˈred\ *adj* **1** : not read; *also* : left unexamined **2** : lacking the benefits or the experience of reading

un·re·al \-ˈrēl\ *adj* : lacking in reality, substance, or genuineness — **un·re·al·i·ty** \ˌən-rē-ˈa-lə-tē\ *n*

un·rea·son·able \-ˈrē-zᵒn-ə-bəl\ *adj* **1** : not governed by or acting according to reason; *also* : not conformable to reason : ABSURD **2** : exceeding the bounds of reason or moderation — **un·rea·son·able·ness** *n* — **un·rea·son·ably** *adv*

un·rea·soned \-ˈrē-zᵒnd\ *adj* : not based on reason or reasoning ⟨~ fears⟩

un·rea·son·ing \-ˈrē-zᵒn-iŋ\ *adj* : not using or showing the use of reason as a guide or control

un·re·con·struct·ed \ˌən-ˌrē-kən-ˈstrək-təd\ *adj* : not reconciled to some political, economic, or social change; *esp*

: holding stubbornly to a particular belief, view, place, or style

un·reel \ˌən-ˈrēl\ *vb* **1** : to unwind from or as if from a reel **2** : to perform successfully

un·re·gen·er·ate \ˌən-ri-ˈje-nə-rət\ *adj* : not regenerated or reformed

un·re·lent·ing \-ˈlen-tiŋ\ *adj* **1** : not yielding in determination : STERN ⟨~ leader⟩ **2** : not letting up or weakening in vigor or pace : CONSTANT — **un·re·lent·ing·ly** *adv*

un·re·mit·ting \-ˈmi-tiŋ\ *adj* : CONSTANT, INCESSANT ⟨~ pain⟩ — **un·re·mit·ting·ly** *adv*

un·re·quit·ed \ˌən-ri-ˈkwī-təd\ *adj* : not requited : not reciprocated or returned in kind ⟨~ love⟩

un·re·served \-ˈzərvd\ *adj* **1** : not limited or partial ⟨~ enthusiasm⟩ **2** : not cautious or reticent : FRANK, OPEN **3** : not set aside for special use — **un·re·serv·ed·ly** \-ˈzər-vəd-lē\ *adv*

un·rest \ˌən-ˈrest\ *n* : a disturbed or uneasy state : TURMOIL

un·re·strained \ˌən-ri-ˈstrānd\ *adj* **1** : IMMODERATE, UNCONTROLLED ⟨~ anger⟩ **2** : SPONTANEOUS

un·re·straint \-ri-ˈstränt\ *n* : lack of restraint

un·rid·dle \ˌən-ˈri-dᵒl\ *vb* : to find the explanation of : SOLVE

un·righ·teous \-ˈrī-chəs\ *adj* **1** : SINFUL, WICKED **2** : UNJUST — **un·righ·teous·ness** *n*

un·ripe \-ˈrīp\ *adj* : not ripe : IMMATURE

un·ri·valed *or* **un·ri·valled** \ˌən-ˈrī-vəld\ *adj* : having no rival : SUPREME

un·robe \-ˈrōb\ *vb* : DISROBE, UNDRESS

un·roll \-ˈrōl\ *vb* **1** : to unwind a roll of : open out **2** : DISPLAY, DISCLOSE **3** : to become unrolled or spread out

un·roof \-ˈrüf, -ˈrúf\ *vb* : to strip off the roof or covering of

un·ruf·fled \ˌən-ˈrə-fəld\ *adj* **1** : not agitated or upset **2** : not ruffled : SMOOTH ⟨~ water⟩

un·ruly \-ˈrü-lē\ *adj* [ME *unreuly*, fr. *un-* + *reuly* disciplined, fr. *reule* rule, fr. AF, fr. L *regula* straightedge, rule, fr. *regere* to direct] : not submissive to rule or restraint : TURBULENT ⟨~ passions⟩ — **un·rul·i·ness** \-ˈrü-lē-nəs\ *n*

un·sad·dle \ˌən-ˈsa-dᵒl\ *vb* **1** : to remove the saddle from a horse **2** : UNHORSE

un·sat·u·rat·ed \-ˈsa-chə-ˌrā-təd\ *adj* **1** : capable of absorbing or dissolving more of something **2** : containing double or triple bonds between carbon atoms ⟨~ fat⟩ — **un·sat·u·rate** \-rət\ *n*

un·saved \ˌən-ˈsāvd\ *adj* : not saved; *esp* : not rescued from eternal punishment

un·sa·vory \-ˈsā-və-rē\ *adj* **1** : TASTELESS **2** : unpleasant to taste or smell **3** : morally offensive ⟨~ characters⟩

un·say \-ˈsā\ *vb* **-said** \-ˈsed\; **-say·ing** : to take back (something said) : RETRACT, WITHDRAW

un·scathed \-ˈskāthd\ *adj* : wholly unharmed : not injured

un·schooled \-ˈsküld\ *adj* : not schooled : UNTAUGHT, UNTRAINED

un·sci·en·tif·ic \ˌən-ˌsī-ən-ˈti-fik\ *adj* : not scientific : not in accord with the principles and methods of science

un·scram·ble \ˌən-ˈskram-bəl\ *vb* **1** : RESOLVE, CLARIFY **2** : to restore (as a radio message) to intelligible form

un·screw \-ˈskrü\ *vb* **1** : to draw the screws from **2** : to loosen by turning

un·scru·pu·lous \-ˈskrü-pyə-ləs\ *adj* : not scrupulous : UNPRINCIPLED — **un·scru·pu·lous·ly** *adv* — **un·scru·pu·lous·ness** *n*

un·seal \-ˈsēl\ *vb* : to break or remove the seal of : OPEN

un·search·able \-ˈsər-chə-bəl\ *adj* : not capable of being searched or explored ⟨~ forests⟩

un·sea·son·able \-ˈsē-zᵒn-ə-bəl\ *adj* : not seasonable : happening or coming at the wrong time : UNTIMELY — **un·sea·son·ably** \-blē\ *adv*

un·seat \-ˈsēt\ *vb* **1** : to throw from one's seat esp. on horseback **2** : to remove from political office

un·seem·ly \-ˈsēm-lē\ *adj* : not in keeping with established standards of good form or taste; *also* : not suitable — **un·seem·li·ness** *n*

un·seen \ˌən-ˈsēn\ *adj* : not seen : INVISIBLE ⟨~ dangers⟩

un·seg·re·gat·ed \-ˈse-gri-ˌgā-təd\ *adj* : not segregated; *esp* : free from racial segregation

un·self·ish \-ˈsel-fish\ *adj* : not selfish : GENEROUS — **un·self·ish·ly** *adv* — **un·self·ish·ness** *n*

un·set·tle \ˌən-ˈse-tᵒl\ *vb* : to move or loosen from a settled position : DISPLACE, DISTURB

un·set·tled \-'se-t³ld\ *adj* **1** : not settled : not fixed (as in position or character) **2** : not calm : DISTURBED **3** : not decided in mind : UNRESOLVED **4** : not paid ⟨∼ accounts⟩ **5** : not occupied by settlers

un·shack·le \-'sha-kəl\ *vb* : to free from shackles

un·shaped \-'shāpt\ *adj* : not shaped; *esp* : not being in finished, final, or perfect form ⟨∼ ideas⟩ ⟨∼ timber⟩

un·sheathe \ˌən-'shēth\ *vb* : to draw from or as if from a sheath

un·ship \-'ship\ *vb* **1** : to remove from a ship **2** : to remove or become removed from position ⟨∼ an oar⟩

un·shod \ˌən-'shäd\ *adj* : not wearing or provided with shoes

un·sight·ly \ˌən-'sīt-lē\ *adj* : unpleasant to the sight : UGLY ⟨an ∼ mess⟩

un·skilled \-'skild\ *adj* **1** : not skilled; *esp* : not skilled in a specified branch of work **2** : not requiring skill

un·skill·ful \-'skil-fəl\ *adj* : lacking in skill or proficiency — **un·skill·ful·ly** *adv*

un·sling \-'sliŋ\ *vb* **-slung** \-'sləŋ\; **-sling·ing** : to remove from being slung

un·snap \-'snap\ *vb* : to loosen or free by or as if by undoing a snap

un·snarl \-'snärl\ *vb* : to remove snarls from : UNTANGLE

un·so·phis·ti·cat·ed \ˌən-sə-'fis-tə-ˌkā-təd\ *adj* **1** : not worldly-wise : lacking sophistication **2** : SIMPLE

un·sought \ˌən-'sot\ *adj* : not sought : not searched for or asked for : not obtained by effort ⟨∼ honors⟩

un·sound \-'saúnd\ *adj* **1** : not healthy or whole; *also* : not mentally normal ⟨of ∼ mind⟩ **2** : not valid **3** : not firmly made or fixed ⟨structurally ∼⟩ — **un·sound·ly** *adv* — **un·sound·ness** *n*

un·spar·ing \-'sper-iŋ\ *adj* **1** : HARD, RUTHLESS ⟨∼ criticism⟩ **2** : not frugal : LIBERAL, PROFUSE ⟨∼ generosity⟩

un·speak·able \-'spē-kə-bəl\ *adj* **1** : impossible to express in words **2** : extremely bad ⟨∼ offenses⟩ — **un·speak·ably** \-blē\ *adv*

un·spool \ˌən-'spül\ *vb* **1** : to unwind from a spool **2** : to present artfully ⟨∼ a new film⟩

un·spot·ted \-'spä-təd\ *adj* : not spotted or stained; *esp* : free from moral stain

un·sprung \-'sprəŋ\ *adj* : not sprung; *esp* : not equipped with springs

un·sta·ble \-'stā-bəl\ *adj* **1** : not stable **2** : FICKLE, VACILLATING; *also* : lacking effective emotional control **3** : readily changing (as by decomposing) in chemical or physical composition or in biological activity ⟨an ∼ atomic nucleus⟩

un·steady \ˌən-'ste-dē\ *adj* : not steady : UNSTABLE — **un·stead·i·ly** \-'ste-də-lē\ *adv* — **un·stead·i·ness** \-'ste-dē-nəs\ *n*

un·stint·ing \-'stin-tiŋ\ *adj* **1** : not restricting or holding back **2** : giving or being given freely or generously ⟨∼ praise⟩

un·stop \-'stäp\ *vb* **1** : UNCLOG **2** : to remove a stopper from

un·stop·pa·ble \ˌən-'stä-pə-bəl\ *adj* : incapable of being stopped

un·strap \-'strap\ *vb* : to remove or loose a strap from

un·stressed \ˌən-'strest\ *adj* : not stressed; *esp* : not bearing a stress or accent ⟨∼ syllables⟩

un·strung \-'strəŋ\ *adj* **1** : having the strings loose or detached **2** : made weak, disordered, or unstable

un·stud·ied \-'stə-dēd\ *adj* **1** : not acquired by study **2** : NATURAL, UNFORCED ⟨moved with ∼ grace⟩

un·sub·stan·tial \ˌən-səb-'stan-chəl\ *adj* : INSUBSTANTIAL

un·sung \ˌən-'səŋ\ *adj* **1** : not sung **2** : not celebrated in song or verse ⟨∼ heroes⟩

un·swerv·ing \ˌən-'swər-viŋ\ *adj* **1** : not swerving or turning aside **2** : STEADY

un·tan·gle \-'taŋ-gəl\ *vb* **1** : DISENTANGLE **2** : to straighten out : RESOLVE ⟨∼ a problem⟩

un·taught \-'tot\ *adj* **1** : not instructed or taught : IGNORANT **2** : NATURAL, SPONTANEOUS ⟨∼ kindness⟩

un·think·able \-'thiŋ-kə-bəl\ *adj* : not to be thought of or considered as possible ⟨∼ cruelty⟩

un·think·ing \ˌən-'thiŋ-kiŋ\ *adj* : not thinking; *esp* : THOUGHTLESS, HEEDLESS — **un·think·ing·ly** *adv*

un·thought \ˌən-'thot\ *adj* : not anticipated : UNEXPECTED — often used with *of* ⟨*unthought*-of development⟩

un·tie \-'tī\ *vb* **-tied**; **-ty·ing** *or* **-tie·ing** **1** : to free from

something that ties, fastens, or restrains : UNBIND **2** : DISENTANGLE, RESOLVE **3** : to become loosened or unbound

¹un·til \ˌən-'til\ *prep* : up to the time of ⟨worked ∼ 5 o'clock⟩

²until *conj* **1** : up to the time that ⟨wait ∼ he calls⟩ **2** : to the point or degree that ⟨ran ∼ she was breathless⟩

¹un·time·ly \ˌən-'tīm-lē\ *adv* : at an inopportune time : UNSEASONABLY; *also* : PREMATURELY

²untimely *adj* : PREMATURE ⟨∼ death⟩; *also* : INOPPORTUNE, UNSEASONABLE

un·tir·ing \ˌən-'tī-riŋ\ *adj* : not becoming tired : INDEFATIGABLE ⟨an ∼ worker⟩ — **un·tir·ing·ly** *adv*

un·to \'ən-tü\ *prep* : TO

un·told \ˌən-'tōld\ *adj* **1** : too great or numerous to count **2** : not told : not revealed

¹un·touch·able \ˌən-'tə-chə-bəl\ *adj* : forbidden to the touch

²untouchable *n* : a member of the lowest social class in India having in traditional Hindu belief the quality of defiling by contact a member of a higher caste

un·touched \ˌən-'təcht\ *adj* **1** : not subjected to touching **2** : not described or dealt with **3** : not tasted **4** : being in a primeval state or condition **5** : UNAFFECTED ⟨∼ by scandals⟩

un·to·ward \ˌən-'tord, -'tō-ərd; ˌən-tə-'word\ *adj* **1** : difficult to manage : STUBBORN, WILLFUL ⟨an ∼ child⟩ **2** : INCONVENIENT, TROUBLESOME ⟨an ∼ encounter⟩

un·tried \ˌən-'trīd\ *adj* : not tested or proved by experience or trial; *also* : not tried in court

un·true \-'trü\ *adj* **1** : not faithful : DISLOYAL **2** : not according with a standard of correctness **3** : FALSE

un·truth \ˌən-'trüth, 'ən-ˌtrüth\ *n* **1** : lack of truthfulness **2** : FALSEHOOD

un·tune \-'tün, -'tyün\ *vb* **1** : to put out of tune **2** : DISARRANGE, DISCOMPOSE

un·tu·tored \-'tü-tərd, -'tyü-\ *adj* : UNTAUGHT, UNLEARNED, IGNORANT

un·twine \-'twīn\ *vb* : UNWIND, DISENTANGLE

un·twist \ˌən-'twist\ *vb* **1** : to separate the twisted parts of : UNTWINE **2** : to become untwined

un·used \-'yüst, -'yüzd *for 1; -*'yüzd *for 2*\ *adj* **1** : UNACCUSTOMED ⟨∼ to such treatment⟩ **2** : not used

un·usu·al \-'yü-zhə-wəl\ *adj* : not usual : UNCOMMON, RARE — **un·usu·al·ly** *adv*

un·ut·ter·able \ˌən-'ə-tə-rə-bəl\ *adj* : being beyond the powers of description : INEXPRESSIBLE ⟨∼ shame⟩ — **un·ut·ter·ably** \-blē\ *adv*

un·var·nished \-'vär-nisht\ *adj* **1** : not varnished **2** : not embellished : PLAIN ⟨the ∼ truth⟩

un·veil \ˌən-'vāl\ *vb* **1** : to remove a veil or covering from : DISCLOSE **2** : to remove a veil : reveal oneself

un·voiced \-'voist\ *adj* **1** : not verbally expressed : UNSPOKEN **2** : VOICELESS 2

un·war·rant·able \-'wor-ən-tə-bəl\ *adj* : not justifiable : INEXCUSABLE — **un·war·rant·ably** \-blē\ *adv*

un·weave \-'wēv\ *vb* **-wove** \-'wōv\; **-wo·ven** \-'wō-vən\; **-weav·ing** : DISENTANGLE, RAVEL

un·well \ˌən-'wel\ *adj* : SICK, AILING

un·whole·some \-'hōl-səm\ *adj* **1** : harmful to physical, mental, or moral well-being ⟨∼ food⟩ **2** : CORRUPT, UNSOUND ⟨∼ deals⟩; *also* : offensive to the senses : LOATHSOME ⟨an ∼ stench⟩

un·wieldy \-'wēl-dē\ *adj* : not easily managed, handled, or used (as because of bulk, weight, or complexity) : AWKWARD ⟨an ∼ tool⟩

un·wind \-'wīnd\ *vb* **-wound** \-'waúnd\; **-wind·ing** **1** : to undo something that is wound : loose from coils **2** : to become unwound : be capable of being unwound **3** : RELAX

un·wise \ˌən-'wīz\ *adj* : not wise : FOOLISH — **un·wise·ly** *adv*

un·wit·ting \-'wi-tiŋ\ *adj* **1** : not knowing : UNAWARE **2** : not intended : INADVERTENT ⟨∼ mistake⟩ — **un·wit·ting·ly** *adv*

un·wont·ed \-'won-təd, -'wōn-\ *adj* **1** : RARE, UNUSUAL **2** : not accustomed by experience — **un·wont·ed·ly** *adv*

un·world·ly \-'wərld-lē\ *adj* **1** : not of this world; *esp* : SPIRITUAL **2** : NAIVE **3** : not swayed by worldly considerations — **un·world·li·ness** \-lē-nəs\ *n*

un·wor·thy \ˌən-'wər-thē\ *adj* **1** : BASE, DISHONORABLE **2** : not meritorious : not worthy : UNDESERVING **3** : not

deserved : UNMERITED ⟨∼ treatment⟩ — un·wor·thi·ly \-t͟hə-lē\ adv — un·wor·thi·ness \-t͟hē-nəs\ n
un·wrap \-'rap\ vb : to remove the wrapping from : DIS-CLOSE
un·writ·ten \-'ri-t³n\ adj 1 : not in writing : ORAL, TRADI-TIONAL ⟨an ∼ law⟩ 2 : containing no writing : BLANK
un·yield·ing \ˌən-'yēl-diŋ\ adj 1 : characterized by lack of softness or flexibility 2 : characterized by firmness or obduracy
un·yoke \-'yōk\ vb : to remove a yoke from; also : SEPA-RATE, DISCONNECT
un·zip \-'zip\ vb : to zip open : open by means of a zipper
¹up \'əp\ adv 1 : in or to a higher position or level; esp : away from the center of the earth 2 : from beneath a surface (as ground or water) 3 : from below the hori-zon 4 : in or into an upright position; esp : out of bed 5 : with greater intensity ⟨speak ∼⟩ 6 : to or at a greater rate or amount ⟨prices went ∼⟩ 7 : in or into a better or more advanced state or a state of greater intensity or ac-tivity ⟨stir ∼ a fire⟩ 8 : into existence, evidence, or knowledge ⟨the missing book turned ∼⟩ 9 : into con-sideration ⟨brought the matter ∼⟩ 10 : to or at bat 11 : into possession or custody ⟨gave himself ∼⟩ 12 : EN-TIRELY, COMPLETELY ⟨eat it ∼⟩ 13 — used for em-phasis ⟨clean ∼ a room⟩ 14 : ASIDE, BY ⟨lay ∼ sup-plies⟩ 15 : so as to arrive or approach ⟨ran ∼ the path⟩ 16 : in a direction opposite to down 17 : in or into parts ⟨tear ∼ paper⟩ 18 : to a stop ⟨pull ∼ at the curb⟩ 19 : for each side ⟨the score was 15 ∼⟩
²up adj 1 : risen above the horizon ⟨the sun is ∼⟩ 2 : being out of bed ⟨∼ by 6 o'clock⟩ 3 : relatively high ⟨prices are ∼⟩ 4 : RAISED, LIFTED ⟨windows are ∼⟩ 5 : BUILT, CONSTRUCTED ⟨the house is ∼⟩ 6 : grown above a surface ⟨the corn is ∼⟩ 7 : moving, inclining, or directed upward 8 : marked by agitation, excitement, or activity 9 : READY; esp : highly prepared 10 : going on : taking place ⟨find out what is ∼⟩ 11 : EXPIRED, ENDED ⟨the time is ∼⟩ 12 : extensively aware or in-formed ⟨∼ on the news⟩ 13 : being ahead or in advance of an opponent ⟨one hole ∼ in a match⟩ 14 : presented for or being under consideration ⟨∼ for promotion⟩ 15 : charged before a court ⟨∼ for robbery⟩
³up prep 1 : to, toward, or at a higher point of ⟨∼ a lad-der⟩ 2 : to or toward the source of ⟨∼ the river⟩ 3 : to or toward the northern part of ⟨∼ the coast⟩ 4 : to or toward the interior of ⟨traveling ∼ the country⟩ 5 : ALONG ⟨walk ∼ the street⟩
⁴up n 1 : an upward course or slope 2 : a period or state of prosperity or success ⟨he had his ∼s and downs⟩ 3 : a quark with a charge of +⅔ that is one of the constituents of the proton and neutron
⁵up vb upped \'əpt\ or in 2 up; upped; up·ping; ups or in 2 up 1 : to rise from a lying or sitting position 2 : to act abruptly or surprisingly ⟨she upped and left home⟩ 3 : to move or cause to move upward ⟨upped the prices⟩
Upa·ni·shad \ü-'pän-i-ˌshäd\ n : one of a set of Vedic philosophical treatises
¹up·beat \'əp-ˌbēt\ n : an unaccented beat in a musical measure; esp : the last beat of the measure
²upbeat adj : OPTIMISTIC, CHEERFUL
up·braid \ˌəp-'brād\ vb : to criticize, reproach, or scold se-verely
up·bring·ing \'əp-ˌbriŋ-iŋ\ n : the process of bringing up and training
UPC abbr Universal Product Code
up·chuck \'əp-ˌchək\ vb : VOMIT
up·com·ing \'əp-ˌkə-miŋ\ adj : FORTHCOMING, AP-PROACHING ⟨the ∼ election⟩
up·coun·try \'əp-ˌkən-trē\ adj : of or relating to the interi-or of a country or a region — up·country \'əp-'kən-\ adv
up·date \ˌəp-'dāt\ vb : to bring up to date — update \'əp-ˌdāt\ n
up·draft \'əp-ˌdraft, -ˌdräft\ n : an upward movement of gas (as air)
up·end \ˌəp-'end\ vb : to set, stand, or rise on end; also : OVERTURN
up·front \'əp-ˌfrənt, ˌəp-'frənt\ adj 1 : HONEST, CANDID ⟨an ∼ answer⟩ 2 : ADVANCE ⟨∼ payment⟩
up front adv : in advance ⟨paid up front⟩
¹up·grade \'əp-ˌgrād\ n 1 : an upward grade or slope 2 : INCREASE, RISE

²up·grade \'əp-ˌgrād, ˌəp-'grād\ vb 1 : to raise to a higher grade or position; esp : to advance to a job requiring a higher level of skill 2 : to improve or replace (as soft-ware or a device) for increased usefulness
up·growth \'əp-ˌgrōth\ n : the process of growing upward : DEVELOPMENT; also : a product or result of this
up·heav·al \ˌəp-'hē-vəl\ n 1 : the action or an instance of uplifting esp. of part of the earth's crust 2 : a violent ag-itation or change
¹up·hill \'əp-'hil\ adv : upward on a hill or incline; also : against difficulties
²up·hill \-ˌhil\ adj 1 : situated on elevated ground 2 : AS-CENDING 3 : DIFFICULT, LABORIOUS ⟨an ∼ struggle⟩
up·hold \ˌəp-'hōld\ vb -held \-'held\; -hold·ing 1 : to give support to 2 : to support against an opponent 3 : to keep elevated — up·hold·er n
up·hol·ster \ˌəp-'hōl-stər\ vb : to furnish with or as if with upholstery — up·hol·ster·er n
up·hol·stery \-stə-rē\ n, pl -ster·ies [ME upholdester up-holsterer, fr. upholden to uphold, fr. up + holden to hold] : materials (as fabrics, padding, and springs) used to make a soft covering esp. for a seat
UPI abbr United Press International
up·keep \'əp-ˌkēp\ n : the act or cost of keeping up or maintaining; also : the state of being maintained
up·land \'əp-lənd, -ˌland\ n : high land esp. at some dis-tance from the sea — upland adj
¹up·lift \ˌəp-'lift\ vb 1 : to lift or raise up : ELEVATE 2 : to improve the condition of esp. morally, socially, or intel-lectually
²up·lift \'əp-ˌlift\ n 1 : a lifting up; esp : an upheaval of the earth's surface 2 : moral or social improvement ⟨spiritu-al ∼⟩; also : a movement to make such improvement
up·mar·ket \ˌəp-'mär-kət\ adj : appealing to wealthy con-sumers
up·most \'əp-ˌmōst\ adj : UPPERMOST
up·on \ə-'pȯn, -'pän\ prep : ON
¹up·per \'ə-pər\ adj 1 : higher in physical position, rank, or order ⟨∼ management⟩ 2 : constituting the smaller and more restricted branch of a bicameral legislature 3 cap : being a later part or formation of a specific geolog-ical period 4 : being toward the interior ⟨the ∼ Ama-zon⟩ 5 : NORTHERN ⟨∼ Minnesota⟩
²upper n : one that is upper; esp : the parts of a shoe or boot above the sole
up·per·case \ˌə-pər-'kās\ adj : CAPITAL 1 — uppercase n
upper class n : a social class occupying a position above the middle class and having the highest status in a society — upper-class adj
up·per·class·man \ˌə-pər-'klas-mən\ n : a junior or senior in a college or high school
upper crust n : the highest social class or group; esp : the highest circle of the upper class
up·per·cut \'ə-pər-ˌkət\ n : a short swinging punch deliv-ered (as in boxing) in an upward direction usu. with a bent arm
upper hand n : MASTERY, ADVANTAGE
up·per·most \'ə-pər-ˌmōst\ adv : in or into the highest or most prominent position — uppermost adj
up·pish \'ə-pish\ adj : UPPITY
up·pi·ty \'ə-pə-tē\ adj : ARROGANT, PRESUMPTUOUS
up·raise \ˌəp-'rāz\ vb : to lift up : ELEVATE
¹up·right \'əp-ˌrīt\ adj 1 : PERPENDICULAR, VERTICAL 2 : erect in carriage or posture 3 : morally correct : JUST — upright adv — up·right·ly adv — up·right·ness n
²upright n 1 : the state of being upright : a vertical posi-tion 2 : something that stands upright
upright piano n : a piano whose strings run vertically

upright piano

up·ris·ing \'əp-ˌrī-ziŋ\ *n* : INSURRECTION, REVOLT, REBELLION

up·riv·er \'əp-'ri-vər\ *adv or adj* : toward or at a point nearer the source of a river

up·roar \'əp-ˌrór\ *n* [D *oproer*, fr. MD, fr. *op* up + *roer* motion] : a state of commotion, excitement, or violent disturbance

up·roar·i·ous \ˌəp-'ror-ē-əs\ *adj* 1 : marked by uproar 2 : extremely funny — **up·roar·i·ous·ly** *adv*

up·root \ˌəp-'rüt, -'rüt\ *vb* 1 : to remove by or as if by pulling up by the roots 2 : DISPLACE 1 ⟨families were ∼*ed*⟩

¹**up·set** \ˌəp-'set\ *vb* **-set; -set·ting** 1 : to force or be forced out of the usual upright, level, or proper position 2 : to disturb emotionally : WORRY; *also* : to make somewhat ill 3 : UNSETTLE, DISARRANGE 4 : to defeat unexpectedly

²**up·set** \'əp-ˌset\ *n* 1 : an upsetting or being upset; *esp* : a minor illness 2 : a derangement of plans or ideas 3 : an unexpected defeat

³**up·set** \(ˌ)əp-'set\ *adj* : emotionally disturbed or agitated

up·shot \'əp-ˌshät\ *n* : the final result

¹**up·side** \'əp-ˌsīd\ *n* 1 : the upper side 2 : a positive aspect 3 : PROMISE ⟨rookies with much ∼⟩

²**up·side** \ˌəp-'sīd\ *prep* : up on or against the side of ⟨knocked him ∼ the head⟩

up·side down \ˌəp-ˌsīd-'daún\ *adv* 1 : with the upper and the lower parts reversed in position 2 : in or into confusion or disorder — **upside–down** *adj*

up·si·lon \'üp-sə-ˌlän, 'yüp-, 'əp-\ *n* : the 20th letter of the Greek alphabet — Y or υ

¹**up·stage** \'əp-'stāj\ *adv or adj* : toward or at the rear of a theatrical stage

²**up·stage** \ˌəp-'stāj\ *vb* : to draw attention away from (as an actor)

¹**up·stairs** \ˌəp-'sterz\ *adv* 1 : up the stairs : to or on a higher floor 2 : to or at a higher position

²**up·stairs** \'əp-'sterz\ *adj* : situated above the stairs esp. on an upper floor ⟨∼ bedroom⟩

³**up·stairs** \'əp-'sterz, 'əp-ˌsterz\ *n sing or pl* : the part of a building above the ground floor

up·stand·ing \ˌəp-'stan-diŋ, 'əp-\ *adj* 1 : ERECT 1 : STRAIGHTFORWARD, HONEST

¹**up·start** \əp-'stärt\ *vb* : to jump up suddenly

²**up·start** \'əp-ˌstärt\ *n* : one that has risen suddenly; *esp* : one that claims more personal importance than is warranted — **up·start** \-'stärt\ *adj*

up·state \'əp-'stāt\ *adj* : of, relating to, or characteristic of a part of a state away from a large city and esp. to the north — **upstate** *adv* — **upstate** *n*

up·stream \'əp-'strēm\ *adv* : at or toward the source of a stream — **upstream** *adj*

up·stroke \'əp-ˌstrōk\ *n* : an upward stroke (as of a pen)

up·surge \-ˌsərj\ *n* : a rapid or sudden rise ⟨an ∼ in interest⟩

up·swept \'əp-ˌswept\ *adj* : swept upward ⟨∼ hairdo⟩

up·swing \'əp-ˌswiŋ\ *n* : an upward swing; *esp* : a marked increase or rise (as in activity)

up·take \'əp-ˌtāk\ *n* 1 : UNDERSTANDING, COMPREHENSION ⟨quick on the ∼⟩ 2 : an act or instance of absorbing and incorporating esp. into a living organism, tissue, or cell

up·thrust \'əp-ˌthrəst\ *n* : an upward thrust (as of the earth's crust) — **upthrust** *vb*

up·tight \'əp-'tīt\ *adj* 1 : TENSE, NERVOUS, UNEASY; *also* : ANGRY, INDIGNANT 2 : rigidly conventional

up–to–date *adj* 1 : extending up to the present time 2 : abreast of the times : MODERN — **up–to–date·ness** *n*

up·town \'əp-ˌtaún\ *n* : the upper part of a town or city; *esp* : the residential district — **up·town** \'əp-'taún\ *adj or adv*

¹**up·turn** \'əp-ˌtərn, ˌəp-'tərn\ *vb* 1 : to turn (as earth) up or over 2 : to turn or direct upward

²**up·turn** \'əp-ˌtərn\ *n* : an upward turn esp. toward better conditions or higher prices

¹**up·ward** \'əp-wərd\ *or* **up·wards** \-wərdz\ *adv* 1 : in a direction from lower to higher 2 : toward a higher or better condition 3 : toward a greater amount or higher number, degree, or rate

²**upward** *adj* : directed or moving toward or situated in a higher place or level : ASCENDING — **up·ward·ly** *adv*

upwards of *also* **upward of** *adv* : more than : in excess of ⟨they cost *upwards of* $25 each⟩

up·well \ˌəp-'wel\ *vb* : to move or flow upward

up·well·ing \-'we-liŋ\ *n* : a rising or an appearance of rising to the surface and flowing outward; *esp* : the movement of deep cold usu. nutrient-rich ocean water to the surface

up·wind \'əp-'wind\ *adv or adj* : in the direction from which the wind is blowing

ura·cil \'yúr-ə-ˌsil\ *n* : a pyrimidine base that is one of the four bases coding genetic information in the molecular chain of RNA

ura·ni·um \yú-'rā-nē-əm\ *n* : a silvery heavy radioactive metallic chemical element used as a source of atomic energy

Ura·nus \'yúr-ə-nəs, yú-'rā-\ *n* [LL, the sky personified as a god, fr. Gk *Ouranos*, fr. *ouranos* sky, heaven] : the planet 7th in order from the sun — see PLANET table

ur·ban \'ər-bən\ *adj* : of, relating to, characteristic of, or constituting a city

ur·bane \ˌər-'bān\ *adj* [L *urbanus* urban, urbane, fr. *urbs* city] : very polite and polished in manner : SUAVE

ur·ban·ite \'ər-bə-ˌnīt\ *n* : a person who lives in a city

ur·ban·i·ty \ˌər-'ba-nə-tē\ *n, pl* **-ties** : the quality or state of being urbane

ur·ban·ize \'ər-bə-ˌnīz\ *vb* **-ized; -iz·ing** : to cause to take on urban characteristics — **ur·ban·i·za·tion** \ˌər-bə-nə-'zā-shən\ *n*

ur·chin \'ər-chən\ *n* [ME, hedgehog, fr. AF *heriçun, hirechoun*, ultim. fr. L *ericius*] : a pert or mischievous youngster

Ur·du \'úr-dü, 'ər-\ *n* [Hindi & Urdu *urdū*, fr. Pers *zabān-e-urdū-e-muallā* language of the Exalted Comp (the imperial bazaar in Delhi)] : an Indo-Aryan language that is the official language of Pakistan and that is widely used by Muslims in urban areas of India

urea \yú-'rē-ə\ *n* : a soluble nitrogenous compound that is the chief solid constituent of mammalian urine

ure·mia \yú-'rē-mē-ə\ *n* : accumulation in the blood of materials normally passed off in the urine resulting in a poisoned condition — **ure·mic** \-mik\ *adj*

ure·ter \'yúr-ə-tər\ *n* : a duct that carries the urine from a kidney to the bladder

ure·thra \yú-'rē-thrə\ *n, pl* **-thras** *or* **-thrae** \-(ˌ)thrē\ : the canal that in most mammals carries off the urine from the bladder and in the male also serves to carry semen from the body — **ure·thral** \-thrəl\ *adj*

ure·thri·tis \ˌyúr-i-'thrī-təs\ *n* : inflammation of the urethra

¹**urge** \'ərj\ *vb* **urged; urg·ing** 1 : to present, advocate, or demand earnestly 2 : to try to persuade or sway ⟨∼ a guest to stay⟩ 3 : to serve as a motive or reason for 4 : to impress or impel to some course or activity ⟨the dog *urged* the sheep onward⟩

²**urge** *n* 1 : the act or process of urging 2 : a force or impulse that urges or drives

ur·gent \'ər-jənt\ *adj* 1 : calling for immediate attention : PRESSING 2 : urging insistently — **ur·gen·cy** \-jən-sē\ *n* — **ur·gent·ly** *adv*

uric \'yúr-ik\ *adj* : of, relating to, or found in urine

uric acid *n* : a nearly insoluble acid that is the chief nitrogenous excretory product of birds but is present in only small amounts in mammalian urine

uri·nal \'yúr-ə-nᵊl\ *n* 1 : a receptacle for urine 2 : a place for urinating

uri·nal·y·sis \ˌyúr-ə-'na-lə-səs\ *n* : chemical analysis of urine

uri·nary \'yúr-ə-ˌner-ē\ *adj* 1 : relating to, occurring in, or being organs for the formation and discharge of urine 2 : of, relating to, or for urine

urinary bladder *n* : a membranous sac in many vertebrates that serves for the temporary retention of urine and discharges by the urethra

uri·nate \'yúr-ə-ˌnāt\ *vb* **-nat·ed; -nat·ing** : to release or give off urine — **uri·na·tion** \ˌyúr-ə-'nā-shən\ *n*

urine \'yúr-ən\ *n* : a waste material from the kidneys that is usu. a yellowish watery liquid in mammals but is semisolid in birds and reptiles

URL \ˌyü-(ˌ)är-'el, 'ər-(ˌ)əl\ *n* [*uniform* (or *universal*) *resource locator*] : a series of usu. alphanumeric characters that specifies the storage location of a resource on the Internet

urn \'ərn\ *n* **1** : a vessel that typically has the form of a vase on a pedestal and often is used to hold the ashes of the dead **2** : a closed vessel usu. with a spout for serving a hot beverage

uro·gen·i·tal \,yu̇r-ō-'je-nə-t³l\ *adj* : of, relating to, or being the excretory and reproductive organs or functions

urol·o·gy \yu̇-'rä-lə-jē\ *n* : a branch of medical science dealing with the urinary or urogenital tract and its disorders — **uro·log·i·cal** \,yu̇r-ə-'lä-ji-kəl\ *also* **uro·log·ic** \-jik\ *adj* — **urol·o·gist** \yu̇-'rä-lə-jist\ *n*

Ur·sa Ma·jor \,ər-sə-'mā-jər\ *n* [L, lit., greater bear] : the northern constellation that contains the stars which form the Big Dipper

Ursa Mi·nor \-'mī-nər\ *n* [L, lit., lesser bear] : the constellation including the north pole of the heavens and the stars that form the Little Dipper with the North Star at the tip of the handle

ur·sine \'ər-ˌsīn\ *adj* : of, relating to, or resembling a bear

ur·ti·car·ia \,ər-tə-'ker-ē-ə\ *n* [NL, fr. L *urtica* nettle] : HIVES

us \'əs\ *pron, objective case of* WE

US *abbr* United States

USA *abbr* **1** United States Army **2** United States of America

us·able *also* **use·able** \'yü-zə-bəl\ *adj* : suitable or fit for use — **us·abil·i·ty** \,yü-zə-'bi-lə-tē\ *n*

USAF *abbr* United States Air Force

us·age \'yü-sij, -zij\ *n* **1** : habitual or customary practice or procedure **2** : the way in which words and phrases are actually used **3** : the action or mode of using **4** : manner of treating

USB \,yü-(,)es-'bē\ *n* [*universal serial bus*] : a standardized computer interface for attaching peripherals

USCG *abbr* United States Coast Guard

USDA *abbr* United States Department of Agriculture

¹use \'yüs\ *n* **1** : the act or practice of using or employing something : EMPLOYMENT, APPLICATION **2** : the fact or state of being used **3** : the way of using **4** : USAGE, CUSTOM **5** : the privilege or benefit of using something **6** : the ability or power to use something (as a limb) **7** : the legal enjoyment of property that consists in its employment, occupation, or exercise; *also* : the benefit or profit esp. from property held in trust **8** : USEFULNESS, UTILITY; *also* : the end served : OBJECT, FUNCTION **9** : something useful or beneficial ⟨it's no ~ arguing⟩ **10** : the occasion or need to employ ⟨he had no more ~ for it⟩ **11** : ESTEEM, LIKING ⟨had no ~ for modern art⟩

²use \'yüz\ *vb* **used** \'yüzd\; *"used to" usu* \'yüs-tə\; **us·ing** **1** : to put into action or service : EMPLOY **2** : to consume or take (as drugs) regularly **3** : UTILIZE ⟨~ tact⟩; *also* : MANIPULATE ⟨*used* his friends to get ahead⟩ **4** : to expend or consume by putting to use **5** : to behave toward : TREAT ⟨*used* the horse cruelly⟩ **6** : to benefit from ⟨house could ~ a coat of paint⟩ **7** — used in the past with *to* to indicate a former practice, fact, or state ⟨we *used* to work harder⟩ — **us·er** *n*

used \'yüzd\ *adj* **1** : having been used by another : SECONDHAND ⟨~ cars⟩ **2** : ACCUSTOMED, HABITUATED ⟨~ to the heat⟩

use·ful \'yüs-fəl\ *adj* : capable of being put to use : ADVANTAGEOUS; *esp* : serviceable for a beneficial end — **use·ful·ly** *adv* — **use·ful·ness** *n*

use·less \-ləs\ *adj* : having or being of no use : WORTHLESS, INEFFECTUAL — **use·less·ly** *adv* — **use·less·ness** *n*

USES *abbr* United States Employment Service

use up *vb* : to consume completely

¹ush·er \'ə-shər\ *n* [ME *ussher*, fr. AF *ussier, usscher*, fr. VL **ustiarius* doorkeeper, fr. L *ostium, ustium* door, mouth of a river] **1** : an officer who walks before a person of rank **2** : one who escorts people to their seats (as in a church or theater)

²usher *vb* **1** : to conduct to a place **2** : to precede as an usher, forerunner, or harbinger **3** : INAUGURATE, INTRODUCE ⟨~ in a new era⟩

ush·er·ette \,ə-shə-'ret\ *n* : a girl or woman who is an usher (as in a theater)

USIA *abbr* United States Information Agency

USMC *abbr* United States Marine Corps

USN *abbr* United States Navy

USO *abbr* United Service Organizations

USP *abbr* United States Pharmacopeia

USPS *abbr* United States Postal Service

USS *abbr* United States ship

USSR *abbr* Union of Soviet Socialist Republics

usu *abbr* usual; usually

usu·al \'yü-zhə-wəl\ *adj* **1** : accordant with usage, custom, or habit : NORMAL **2** : commonly or ordinarily used **3** : ORDINARY ✦ *Synonyms* CUSTOMARY, HABITUAL, ACCUSTOMED, ROUTINE — **usu·al·ly** \'yü-zhə-wə-lē, 'yü-zhə-lē\ *adv*

usu·fruct \'yü-zə-ˌfrəkt\ *n* [L *ususfructus*, fr. *usus et fructus* use and enjoyment] : the legal right to use and enjoy the benefits and profits of something belonging to another

usu·rer \'yü-zhər-ər\ *n* : one that lends money esp. at an exorbitant rate

usu·ri·ous \yu̇-'zhu̇r-ē-əs\ *adj* : practicing, involving, or constituting usury ⟨a ~ rate of interest⟩

usurp \yu̇-'sərp, -'zərp\ *vb* [ME, fr. AF *usorper*, fr. L *usurpare*, to take possession of without legal claim, fr. *usu* (abl. of *usus* use) + *rapere* to seize] : to seize and hold by force or without right ⟨~ a throne⟩ — **usur·pa·tion** \,yü-sər-'pā-shən, -zər-\ *n* — **usurp·er** \yü-'sər-pər, -'zər-\ *n*

usu·ry \'yü-zhə-rē\ *n, pl* **-ries** **1** : the lending of money with an interest charge for its use **2** : an excessive rate or amount of interest charged; *esp* : interest above an established legal rate

UT *abbr* Utah

Ute \'yüt\ *n, pl* **Ute** *or* **Utes** : a member of an American Indian people orig. ranging through Utah, Colorado, Arizona, and New Mexico

uten·sil \yu̇-'ten-səl\ *n* [ME, vessels for domestic use, fr. MF *utensile*, fr. L *utensilia*, fr. neut. pl. of *utensilis* useful, fr. *uti* to use] **1** : an instrument or vessel used in a household and esp. a kitchen **2** : a useful tool

uter·us \'yü-tə-rəs\ *n, pl* **uter·us·es** *or* **uteri** \'yü-tə-ˌrī\ : the muscular organ of a female mammal in which the young develop before birth — **uter·ine** \-ˌrīn, -rən\ *adj*

utile \'yüt-³l, 'yü-ˌtī(-ə)l\ *adj* : USEFUL

uti·lise *Brit var of* UTILIZE

¹util·i·tar·i·an \yu̇-ˌti-lə-'ter-ē-ən\ *n* : a person who believes in utilitarianism

²utilitarian *adj* **1** : of or relating to utilitarianism **2** : of or relating to utility : aiming at usefulness rather than beauty; *also* : serving a useful purpose

util·i·tar·i·an·ism \yu̇-ˌti-lə-'ter-ē-ə-ˌni-zəm\ *n* : a theory that the greatest good for the greatest number should be the main consideration in making a choice of actions

¹util·i·ty \yü-'ti-lə-tē\ *n, pl* **-ties** **1** : USEFULNESS **2** : something useful or designed for use **3** : a business organization performing a public service and subject to special governmental regulation **4** : a public service or a commodity (as electricity or water) provided by a public utility; *also* : equipment to provide such or a similar service

²utility *adj* **1** : capable of serving esp. as a substitute in various uses or positions ⟨a ~ outfielder⟩ ⟨a ~ cord⟩ **2** : being of a usable but poor quality ⟨~ beef⟩

utility knife *n* : a knife designed for general use; *esp* : one with a retractable blade

uti·lize \'yü-tə-ˌlīz\ *vb* **-lized; -liz·ing** : to make use of : turn to profitable account or use — **uti·li·za·tion** \,yü-tə-lə-'zā-shən\ *n*

ut·most \'ət-ˌmōst\ *adj* **1** : situated at the farthest or most distant point : EXTREME **2** : of the greatest or highest degree, quantity, number, or amount — **utmost** *n*

uto·pia \yu̇-'tō-pē-ə\ *n* [*Utopia*, imaginary island described in Sir Thomas More's *Utopia*, fr. Gk *ou* not, no + *topos* place] **1** *often cap* : a place of ideal perfection esp. in laws, government, and social conditions **2** : an impractical scheme for social improvement

¹uto·pi·an \-pē-ən\ *adj, often cap* **1** : of, relating to, or resembling a utopia **2** : proposing ideal social and political schemes that are impractical **3** : VISIONARY

²utopian *n* **1** : a believer in the perfectibility of human society **2** : one who proposes or advocates utopian schemes

¹ut·ter \'ə-tər\ *adj* [ME, remote, fr. OE *ūtera* outer, compar. adj. fr. *ūt* out, adv.] : ABSOLUTE, TOTAL ⟨~ ruin⟩ — **ut·ter·ly** *adv*

²utter *vb* [ME *uttren*, fr. *utter* outside, adv., fr. OE *ūtor*,

compar. of *ūt* out] **1** : to send forth as a sound : express in usu. spoken words : PRONOUNCE, SPEAK **2** : to put (as currency) into circulation — **ut·ter·er** *n*
ut·ter·ance \'ə-tə-rəns\ *n* **1** : something uttered; *esp* : an oral or written statement **2** : the action of uttering with the voice : SPEECH **3** : power, style, or manner of speaking
ut·ter·most \'ə-tər-ˌmōst\ *adj* : EXTREME, UTMOST ⟨the ～ parts of the earth⟩ — **uttermost** *n*

¹**v** \'vē\ *n, pl* **v's** *or* **vs** \'vēz\ *often cap* **1** : the 22d letter of the English alphabet **2** : five in Roman numerals
²**v** *abbr, often cap* **1** vector **2** velocity **3** verb **4** verse **5** versus **6** very **7** victory **8** vide **9** voice **10** voltage **11** volume **12** vowel
V *symbol* **1** vanadium **2** volt
Va *abbr* Virginia
VA *abbr* **1** Veterans Administration **2** vice admiral **3** Virginia
va·can·cy \'vā-kən-sē\ *n, pl* **-cies** **1** : a vacating esp. of an office, position, or piece of property **2** : a vacant office, position, or tenancy; *also* : the period during which it stands vacant **3** : empty space : VOID **4** : the state of being vacant
va·cant \'vā-kənt\ *adj* **1** : not occupied ⟨～ seat⟩ ⟨～ room⟩ **2** : EMPTY ⟨～ space⟩ **3** : free from business or care ⟨a few ～ hours⟩ **4** : devoid of thought, reflection, or expression ⟨a ～ smile⟩ — **va·cant·ly** *adv*
va·cate \'vā-ˌkāt\ *vb* **va·cat·ed; va·cat·ing** **1** : to make void : ANNUL **2** : to make vacant (as an office or house); *also* : to give up the occupancy of
¹**va·ca·tion** \vā-'kā-shən, və-\ *n* : a period of rest from work : HOLIDAY
²**vacation** *vb* : to take or spend a vacation — **va·ca·tion·er** *n*
va·ca·tion·ist \-shə-nist\ *n* : a person taking a vacation
va·ca·tion·land \-shən-ˌland\ *n* : an area with recreational attractions and facilities for vacationists
vac·ci·nate \'vak-sə-ˌnāt\ *vb* **-nat·ed; -nat·ing** : to administer a vaccine to usu. by injection
vac·ci·na·tion \ˌvak-sə-'nā-shən\ *n* **1** : the act of vaccinating **2** : the scar left by vaccinating
vac·cine \vak-'sēn, 'vak-ˌsēn\ *n* [F *vaccin,* fr. *vaccine* cowpox, fr. NL *vaccina* (in *variolae vaccinae* cowpox), fr. L, fem. of *vaccinus* of or from cows, fr. *vacca* cow] : a preparation of material (as of killed or weakened viruses or bacteria) used in vaccinating to produce or increase immunity to a disease
vac·cin·ia \vak-'si-nē-ə\ *n* : COWPOX
vac·il·late \'va-sə-ˌlāt\ *vb* **-lat·ed; -lat·ing** **1** : SWAY, TOTTER; *also* : FLUCTUATE **2** : to incline first to one course or opinion and then to another : WAVER — **vac·il·la·tion** \ˌva-sə-'lā-shən\ *n*
va·cu·ity \va-'kyü-ə-tē\ *n, pl* **-ities** **1** : an empty space **2** : the state, fact, or quality of being vacuous **3** : something that is vacuous
vac·u·ole \'va-kyə-ˌwōl\ *n* : a usu. fluid-filled cavity esp. in the cytoplasm of an individual cell — **vac·u·o·lar** \ˌva-kyə-'wō-lər, -ˌlär\ *adj*
vac·u·ous \'va-kyə-wəs\ *adj* **1** : EMPTY, VACANT, BLANK **2** : DULL, STUPID, INANE ⟨～ movies⟩ — **vac·u·ous·ly** *adv* — **vac·u·ous·ness** *n*
¹**vac·u·um** \'va-(ˌ)kyüm, -kyəm\ *n, pl* **vacuums** *or* **vac·ua** \-kyə-wə\ [L, fr. neut. of *vacuus* empty] **1** : a space entirely empty of matter **2** : a space from which most of the air has been removed (as by a pump) **3** : VOID, GAP **4** : VACUUM CLEANER — **vacuum** *adj*
²**vacuum** *vb* : to use a vacuum device (as a vacuum cleaner) on ⟨～ the den⟩
vacuum bottle *n* : THERMOS

vacuum cleaner *n* : a household appliance for cleaning (as floors or rugs) by suction
vacuum-packed *adj* : having much of the air removed before being hermetically sealed ⟨～ fish⟩
vacuum tube *n* : an electron tube from which most of the air has been removed
va·de me·cum \ˌvā-dē-'mē-kəm, ˌvä-dē-'mā-\ *n, pl* **vade mecums** [L, go with me] : something (as a handbook or manual) regularly carried about
VADM *abbr* vice admiral
¹**vag·a·bond** \'va-gə-ˌbänd\ *adj* **1** : WANDERING, HOMELESS **2** : of, characteristic of, or leading the life of a vagrant or tramp **3** : leading an unsettled or irresponsible life
²**vagabond** *n* : one leading a vagabond life; *esp* : VAGRANT, TRAMP
va·gar·i·ous \vā-'ger-ē-əs\ *adj* : marked by vagaries : CAPRICIOUS ⟨～ leadership⟩ — **va·gar·i·ous·ly** *adv*
va·ga·ry \'vā-gə-rē, və-'ger-ē\ *n, pl* **-ries** : an odd or eccentric idea or action : WHIM, CAPRICE
va·gi·na \və-'jī-nə\ *n, pl* **-nae** \-(ˌ)nē\ *or* **-nas** [L, lit., sheath] : a canal that leads from the uterus to the external opening of the female sex organs — **vag·i·nal** \'va-jə-nᵊl\ *adj* — **vag·i·nal·ly** \-nᵊl-ē\ *adv*
vag·i·ni·tis \ˌva-jə-'nī-təs\ *n* : inflammation of the vagina
va·gran·cy \'vā-grən-sē\ *n, pl* **-cies** **1** : the quality or state of being vagrant; *also* : a vagrant act or notion **2** : the offense of being a vagrant
¹**va·grant** \'vā-grənt\ *n* : a person who has no job and wanders from place to place
²**vagrant** *adj* **1** : of, relating to, or characteristic of a vagrant **2** : following no fixed course : RANDOM, CAPRICIOUS ⟨～ thoughts⟩ — **va·grant·ly** *adv*
vague \'vāg\ *adj* **vagu·er; vagu·est** [MF, fr. L *vagus,* lit., wandering] **1** : not clear, definite, or distinct ⟨a ～ plan⟩ ⟨～ silhouettes⟩ **2** : not clearly felt or analyzed ⟨a ～ unrest⟩ ♦ **Synonyms** OBSCURE, DARK, ENIGMATIC, AMBIGUOUS, EQUIVOCAL — **vague·ly** *adv* — **vague·ness** *n*
vain \'vān\ *adj* [ME, fr. AF, empty, futile, fr. L *vanus*] **1** : of no real value **2** : IDLE, WORTHLESS **2** : FUTILE, UNSUCCESSFUL **3** : proud of one's looks or abilities ♦ **Synonyms** CONCEITED, NARCISSISTIC, VAINGLORIOUS — **vain·ly** *adv* — **in vain 1** : without success ⟨her efforts were *in vain*⟩ **2** : in a blasphemous manner ⟨took the Lord's name *in vain*⟩
vain·glo·ri·ous \ˌvān-'glȯr-ē-əs\ *adj* : marked by vainglory : BOASTFUL
vain·glo·ry \'vān-ˌglȯr-ē\ *n* **1** : excessive or ostentatious pride esp. in one's own achievements **2** : vain display : VANITY
val *abbr* value; valued
va·lance \'va-ləns, 'vā-\ *n* **1** : drapery hanging from an edge (as of an altar, table, or bed) **2** : a drapery or a decorative frame across the top of a window
vale \'vāl\ *n* : VALLEY, DALE
vale·dic·tion \ˌva-lə-'dik-shən\ *n* [L *valedicere* to say farewell, fr. *vale* farewell + *dicere* to say] : an act or utterance of leave-taking : FAREWELL
vale·dic·to·ri·an \-ˌdik-'tȯr-ē-ən\ *n* : the student usu. of the highest rank in a graduating class who delivers the valedictory address at commencement

U–turn \'yü-ˌtərn\ *n* : a turn resembling the letter U; *esp* : a 180-degree turn made by a vehicle in a road
UV *abbr* ultraviolet
uvu·la \'yü-vyə-lə\ *n, pl* **-las** *or* **-lae** \-ˌlē, -ˌlī\ : the fleshy lobe hanging at the back of the roof of the mouth — **uvu·lar** \-lər\ *adj*
UW *abbr* underwriter
ux·o·ri·ous \ˌək-'sȯr-ē-əs, ˌəg-'zȯr-\ *adj* : excessively devoted or submissive to a wife

vale·dic·to·ry \-'dik-tə-rē\ adj : bidding farewell : delivered as a valediction ⟨a ∼ address⟩ — **valedictory** n

va·lence \'vā-ləns\ n [LL valentia power, capacity, fr. L valēre to be strong] : the combining power of an atom as shown by the number of its electrons that are lost, gained, or shared in the formation of chemical bonds

Va·len·ci·ennes \və-,len-sē-'en, ,va-lən-sē-, -'enz\ n : a fine handmade lace

val·en·tine \'va-lən-,tīn\ n : a sweetheart chosen or complimented on Valentine's Day; also : a gift or greeting given on this day

Valentine's Day also Valentine Day n : February 14 observed in honor of St. Valentine and as a time for exchanging valentines

¹va·let \'va-lət, -(,)lā; va-'lā\ n 1 : a male servant who takes care of a man's clothes and performs personal services 2 : an attendant in a hotel or restaurant who performs personal services (as parking cars) for customers

²valet vb : to serve as a valet

val·e·tu·di·nar·i·an \,va-lə-,tü-d-ə-'ner-ē-ən, -,tyü-\ n : a person of a weak or sickly constitution; esp : one whose chief concern is his or her ill health — **val·e·tu·di·nar·i·an·ism** \-ē-ə,ni-zəm\ n

val·iant \'val-yənt\ adj : having or showing valor : BRAVE, HEROIC ✦ Synonyms VALOROUS, DOUGHTY, COURAGEOUS, BOLD, AUDACIOUS, DAUNTLESS, UNDAUNTED, INTREPID — **val·iant·ly** adv

val·id \'va-ləd\ adj 1 : having legal force ⟨a ∼ contract⟩ 2 : founded on truth or fact : capable of being justified or defended : SOUND ⟨a ∼ argument⟩ ⟨∼ reasons⟩ — **va·lid·i·ty** \və-'li-də-tē\ n — **val·id·ly** adv

val·i·date \'va-lə-,dāt\ vb -dat·ed; -dat·ing 1 : to make legally valid 2 : to confirm the validity of 3 : VERIFY — **val·i·da·tion** \,va-lə-'dā-shən\ n

va·lise \və-'lēs\ n [F] : SUITCASE

val·ley \'va-lē\ n, pl valleys : a long depression between ranges of hills or mountains

val·or \'va-lər\ n [ME valour, worth, worthiness, bravery, fr. AF fr. ML valor, fr. L valēre to be strong] : personal bravery ✦ Synonyms HEROISM, PROWESS, GALLANTRY — **val·or·ous** \'va-lə-rəs\ adj

val·o·ri·za·tion \,va-lə-rə-'zā-shən\ n : the support of commodity prices by any of various forms of government subsidy — **val·o·rize** \'va-lə-,rīz\ vb

val·our chiefly Brit var of VALOR

¹valu·able \'val-yə-bəl, -yə-wə-bəl\ adj 1 : having money value 2 : having great money value 3 : of great use or service ✦ Synonyms INVALUABLE, PRICELESS, COSTLY, EXPENSIVE, DEAR, PRECIOUS

²valuable n : a usu. personal possession of considerable value ⟨their ∼s were stolen⟩

val·u·ate \'val-yə-,wāt\ vb -at·ed; -at·ing : to place a value on : APPRAISE — **val·u·a·tor** \-,wā-tər\ n

val·u·a·tion \,val-yə-'wā-shən\ n 1 : the act or process of valuing; esp : appraisal of property 2 : the estimated or determined market value of a thing

¹val·ue \'val-yü\ n 1 : a fair return or equivalent in money, goods, or services for something exchanged 2 : the monetary worth of a thing; also : relative worth, utility, or importance ⟨nothing of ∼ to say⟩ 3 : an assigned or computed numerical quantity ⟨the ∼ of x in an equation⟩ 4 : relative lightness or darkness of a color : LUMINOSITY 5 : the relative length of a tone or note 6 : something (as a principle or ideal) intrinsically valuable or desirable ⟨human rather than material ∼s⟩ — **val·ue·less** adj

²value vb val·ued; valu·ing 1 : to estimate the monetary worth of : APPRAISE 2 : to rate in usefulness, importance, or general worth 3 : to consider or rate highly : PRIZE, ESTEEM ⟨valued your opinions⟩ — **val·u·er** n

val·ue–add·ed tax n : an incremental excise tax that is levied on the value added at each stage of the processing of a raw material or the production and distribution of a commodity

valve \'valv\ n 1 : a structure (as in a vein) that temporarily closes a passage or that permits movement in one direction only 2 : a device by which the flow of a fluid material may be regulated by a movable part; also : the movable part of such a device 3 : a device in a brass wind instrument for quickly varying the tube length in order to change the fundamental tone by some definite interval 4 : one of the separate usu. hinged pieces of

which the shell of some animals and esp. bivalve mollusks consists 5 : one of the pieces into which a ripe seed capsule or pod separates — **valved** \'valvd\ adj — **valve·less** adj

val·vu·lar \'val-vyə-lər\ adj : of, relating to, or affecting a valve esp. of the heart ⟨∼ heart disease⟩

va·moose \va-'müs, va-\ vb va·moosed; va·moos·ing [Sp vamos let us go] : to leave or go away quickly

¹vamp n 1 : the part of a boot or shoe upper covering esp. the front part of the foot 2 : a short introductory musical passage often repeated

²vamp \'vamp\ vb 1 : to provide with a new vamp 2 : to patch up with a new part 3 : INVENT, IMPROVISE ⟨∼ up an excuse⟩

³vamp n : a woman who uses her charm or wiles to seduce and exploit men

⁴vamp vb : to practice seductive wiles on : to act like a vamp

vam·pire \'vam-,pī(-ə)r\ n [F, fr. G Vampir, fr. Serbian vampir] 1 : a night-wandering bloodsucking ghost 2 : a person who preys on other people; esp : a woman who exploits and ruins her lover 3 : VAMPIRE BAT

vampire bat n : any of various bats of Central and South America that feed on the blood of animals; also : any of several other bats that do not feed on blood but are sometimes reputed to do so

¹van \'van\ n : VANGUARD

²van n : a usu. enclosed wagon or motortruck for moving goods or animals; also : a versatile enclosed box-like motor vehicle

va·na·di·um \və-'nā-dē-əm\ n : a soft grayish ductile metallic chemical element used esp. to form alloys

Van Al·len belt \van-'a-lən-\ n : a belt of intense radiation in the magnetosphere composed of charged particles trapped by earth's magnetic field

van·co·my·cin \,van-kə-'mī-sᵊn\ n : an antibiotic used esp. against staphylococci

van·dal \'van-dᵊl\ n 1 cap : a member of a Germanic people who sacked Rome in A.D. 455 2 : a person who willfully mars or destroys property

van·dal·ism \'van-də-,li-zəm\ n : willful or malicious destruction or defacement of public or private property

van·dal·ize \-,līz\ vb -ized; -iz·ing : to subject to vandalism : DAMAGE

Van·dyke \van-'dīk\ n : a trim pointed beard

vane \'vān\ n [ME, fr. OE fana banner] 1 : a movable device attached to a high object for showing wind direction 2 : a thin flat or curved object that is rotated about an axis by a flow of fluid or that rotates to cause a fluid to flow or that redirects a flow of fluid ⟨the ∼s of a windmill⟩ 3 : a feather fastened near the back end of an arrow for stability in flight

van·guard \'van-,gärd\ n 1 : the troops moving at the front of an army 2 : the forefront of an action or movement

va·nil·la \və-'ni-lə\ n [NL, genus name, fr. Sp vainilla vanilla (plant and fruit), dim. of vaina sheath, fr. L vagina] : a flavoring extract made synthetically or obtained from the long beanlike pods (vanilla beans) of a tropical American climbing orchid; also : this orchid

van·ish \'va-nish\ vb : to pass from sight or existence : disappear completely — **van·ish·er** n

van·i·ty \'va-nə-tē\ n, pl -ties 1 : something that is vain, empty, or useless 2 : the quality or fact of being useless or futile : FUTILITY 3 : undue pride in oneself or one's appearance : CONCEIT 4 : a small case for cosmetics : COMPACT

vanity plate n : an automobile license plate bearing distinctive letters or numbers designated by the owner

van·quish \'van-kwish, 'van-\ vb 1 : to overcome in battle or in a contest 2 : to gain mastery over (as an emotion)

van·tage \'van-tij\ n 1 : superiority in a contest 2 : a position giving a strategic advantage or a commanding perspective

va·pid \'va-pəd, 'vā-\ adj : lacking spirit, liveliness, or zest : FLAT, INSIPID ⟨∼ gossip⟩ — **va·pid·i·ty** \va-'pi-də-tē\ n — **vap·id·ly** adv — **vap·id·ness** n

va·por \'vā-pər\ n 1 : fine separated particles (as fog or smoke) floating in the air and clouding it 2 : a substance in the gaseous state; *esp* : one that is liquid under ordinary conditions **3** : something insubstantial or fleeting **4** *pl* : a depressed or hysterical nervous condition

va·por·ing \'vā-pə-riŋ\ *n* : an idle, boastful, or high-flown expression or speech — usu. used in pl.

va·por·ise *Brit var of* VAPORIZE

va·por·ize \'vā-pə-ˌrīz\ *vb* **-ized; -iz·ing 1** : to convert into vapor **2** : to destroy as if by converting to vapor ⟨*vaporized* enemy tanks⟩ — **va·por·i·za·tion** \ˌvā-pə-rə-'zā-shən\ *n*

va·por·iz·er \-ˌrī-zər\ *n* : a device that vaporizes something (as a medicated liquid)

vapor lock *n* : an interruption of flow of a fluid (as fuel in an engine) caused by the formation of vapor in the feeding system

va·por·ous \'vā-pə-rəs\ *adj* **1** : full of vapors : FOGGY, MISTY **2** : UNSUBSTANTIAL, VAGUE ⟨∼ speculations⟩ — **va·por·ous·ly** *adv* — **va·por·ous·ness** *n*

va·pory \'vā-pə-rē\ *adj* : MISTY

va·pour *chiefly Brit var of* VAPOR

va·que·ro \vä-'ker-ō\ *n, pl* **-ros** [Sp, fr. *vaca* cow, fr. L *vacca*] : a ranch hand : COWBOY

var *abbr* **1** variable **2** variant; variation **3** variety **4** various

¹**var·i·able** \'ver-ē-ə-bəl\ *adj* **1** : able or apt to vary : CHANGEABLE **2** : FICKLE **3** : not true to type : ABERRANT ⟨a ∼ wheat⟩ — **var·i·abil·i·ty** \ˌver-ē-ə-'bi-lə-tē, ˌvar-\ *n* — **var·i·ably** \-blē\ *adv·*

²**variable** *n* **1** : a quantity that may take on any of a set of values; *also* : a mathematical symbol representing a variable **2** : something that is variable

var·i·ance \'ver-ē-əns\ *n* **1** : variation or a degree of variation : DEVIATION **2** : DISAGREEMENT, DISPUTE **3** : a license to do something contrary to the usual rule ⟨a zoning ∼⟩ **4** : the square of the standard deviation ♦ *Synonyms* DISCORD, CONTENTION, DISSENSION, STRIFE, CONFLICT

¹**var·i·ant** \'ver-ē-ənt\ *adj* **1** : differing from others of its kind or class **2** : varying usu. slightly from the standard or type

²**variant** *n* **1** : one that exhibits variation from a type or norm **2** : one of two or more different spellings or pronunciations of a word

var·i·a·tion \ˌver-ē-'ā-shən\ *n* **1** : the act, process, or an instance of varying : a change in form, position, or condition : MODIFICATION, ALTERATION **2** : extent of change or difference : divergence in the characteristics of an organism from those typical or usual for its group; *also* : one exhibiting such variation **4** : repetition of a musical theme with modifications in rhythm, tune, harmony, or key

vari·col·ored \'ver-i-ˌkə-lərd\ *adj* : having various colors : VARIEGATED

var·i·cose \'va-rə-ˌkōs\ *adj* : abnormally swollen and dilated ⟨∼ veins⟩ — **var·i·cos·i·ty** \ˌva-rə-'kä-sə-tē\ *n*

var·ied \'ver-ēd\ *adj* **1** : having many forms or types : DIVERSE **2** : VARIEGATED — **var·ied·ly** *adv*

var·ie·gat·ed \'ver-ē-ə-ˌgā-təd\ *adj* **1** : having patches, stripes, or marks of different colors ⟨∼ flowers⟩ **2** : VARIED 1 — **var·ie·gate** \-ˌgāt\ *vb* — **var·ie·ga·tion** \ˌver-ē-ə-'gā-shən\ *n*

¹**va·ri·etal** \və-'rī-ə-t³l\ *adj* : of or relating to a variety; *esp* : of, relating to, or producing a varietal

²**varietal** *n* : a wine bearing the name of the principal grape from which it is made

va·ri·ety \və-'rī-ə-tē\ *n, pl* **-et·ies 1** : the state of being varied or various : DIVERSITY **2** : a collection of different things : ASSORTMENT **3** : something varying from others of the same general kind **4** : any of various groups of plants or animals within a species distinguished by characteristics insufficient to separate species : SUBSPECIES **5** : entertainment such as is given in a stage presentation comprising a series of performances (as songs, dances, or acrobatic acts)

var·i·o·rum \ˌver-ē-'ōr-əm\ *n* : an edition or text of a work containing notes by various persons or variant readings of the text

var·i·ous \'ver-ē-əs\ *adj* **1** : VARICOLORED **2** : of differing kinds : MULTIFARIOUS **3** : UNLIKE ⟨animals as ∼ as the jaguar and the sloth⟩ **4** : having a number of different aspects **5** : NUMEROUS, MANY **6** : INDIVIDUAL, SEP-

ARATE ♦ *Synonyms* DIVERGENT, DISPARATE, DIFFERENT, DISSIMILAR, DIVERSE, UNALIKE — **var·i·ous·ly** *adv*

var·let \'vär-lət\ *n* **1** : ATTENDANT **2** : SCOUNDREL, KNAVE

var·mint \'vär-mənt\ *n* [alter. of *vermin*] **1** : an animal considered a pest; *esp* : one classed as vermin and unprotected by game law **2** : a contemptible person : RASCAL

¹**var·nish** \'vär-nish\ *n* **1** : a liquid preparation that is applied to a surface and dries into a hard glossy coating; *also* : the glaze of this coating **2** : something suggesting varnish by its gloss **3** : outside show : deceptive or superficial appearance

²**varnish** *vb* **1** : to cover with varnish **2** : to cover or conceal with something that gives a fair appearance : GLOSS

var·si·ty \'vär-sə-tē\ *n, pl* **-ties** [by shortening & alter. fr. *university*] **1** *Brit* : UNIVERSITY **2** : the principal team representing a college, school, or club

vary \'ver-ē\ *vb* **var·ied; vary·ing 1** : ALTER, CHANGE **2** : to make or be of different kinds : introduce or have variety : DIVERSIFY, DIFFER **3** : DEVIATE, SWERVE **4** : to change in bodily structure or function away from what is usual for members of a group

vas·cu·lar \'vas-kyə-lər\ *adj* [NL *vascularis*, fr. L *vasculum* small vessel, dim. of *vas* vase, vessel] : of or relating to a channel or system of channels for the conveyance of a body fluid (as blood or sap); *also* : supplied with or containing such vessels and esp. blood vessels ⟨the ∼ system⟩

vascular plant *n* : a plant having a specialized system for carrying fluids that includes xylem and phloem

vas def·er·ens \'vas-'de-fə-rənz\ *n, pl* **va·sa def·er·en·tia** \'vā-zə-ˌde-fə-'ren-shē-ə\ : a sperm-carrying duct of the testis

vase \'vās, 'vāz\ *n* : a usu. round vessel of greater depth than width used chiefly for ornament or for flowers

va·sec·to·my \və-'sek-tə-mē, vā-'zek-\ *n, pl* **-mies** : surgical excision of all or part of the vas deferens usu. to induce sterility

va·so·con·stric·tion \ˌvā-zō-kən-'strik-shən\ *n* : narrowing of the interior diameter of blood vessels

va·so·con·stric·tor \-tər\ *n* : an agent (as a nerve fiber or a drug) that initiates or induces vasoconstriction

vas·sal \'va-səl\ *n* **1** : a person under the protection of a feudal lord to whom he owes homage and loyalty : a feudal tenant **2** : one occupying a dependent or subordinate position — **vassal** *adj*

vas·sal·age \-sə-lij\ *n* **1** : the state of being a vassal **2** : the homage and loyalty due from a vassal **3** : SERVITUDE, SUBJECTION

¹**vast** \'vast\ *adj* : very great in size, amount, degree, intensity, or esp. extent ⟨∼ plains⟩ ⟨∼ knowledge⟩ ♦ *Synonyms* ENORMOUS, HUGE, GIGANTIC, COLOSSAL, MAMMOTH — **vast·ly** *adv* — **vast·ness** *n*

²**vast** *n* : a great expanse : IMMENSITY

vasty \'vas-tē\ *adj* **1** : VAST, IMMENSE

vat \'vat\ *n* : a large vessel (as a tub or barrel) esp. for holding liquids in manufacturing processes

VAT *abbr* value-added tax

vat·ic \'va-tik\ *adj* : PROPHETIC, ORACULAR

Vat·i·can \'va-ti-kən\ *n* **1** : the papal headquarters in Rome **2** : the papal government

va·tu \'vä-ˌtü\ *n, pl* **vatu** — see MONEY table

vaude·ville \'vōd-vəl, 'väd-, 'vōd-, -ˌvil\ *n* [F, fr. MF, satirical song, alter. of *vaudevire*, fr. *vau-de-Vire* valley of Vire, town in northwest France where such songs were composed] : a stage entertainment consisting of unrelated acts (as of acrobats, comedians, dancers, or singers)

¹**vault** \'vȯlt\ *n* **1** : an arched masonry structure usu. forming a ceiling or roof; *also* : something (as the sky) resembling a vault **2** : a room or space covered by a vault esp. when underground **3** : a room or compartment for the safekeeping of valuables **4** : a burial chamber; *also* : a usu. metal or concrete case in which a casket is enclosed at burial — **vaulty** *adj*

²**vault** *vb* : to form or cover with a vault

³**vault** *vb* : to leap vigorously esp. by aid of the hands or a pole — **vault·er** *n*

⁴**vault** *n* : an act of vaulting : LEAP

vault·ed \'vȯl-təd\ *adj* **1** : built in the form of a vault : ARCHED **2** : covered with a vault

vault·ing \'vȯ-tiŋ\ *adj* : reaching for the heights ⟨~ ambition⟩

vaunt \'vȯnt\ *vb* [ME, fr. AF *vanter*, fr. LL *vanitare*, ultim. fr. L *vanus* vain] : BRAG, BOAST — **vaunt** *n*

vaunt·ed \'vȯn-təd\ *adj* : much praised or boasted of

vb *abbr* verb; verbal

V-chip \'vē-ˌchip\ *n* : a computer chip in a television set used to block based on content the viewing of certain programs

VCR \ˌvē-(ˌ)sē-'är\ *n* [*videocassette recorder*] : a device that records and plays back videotapes

VD *abbr* venereal disease

VDT *abbr* video display terminal

veal \'vēl\ *n* : the flesh of a young calf

vec·tor \'vek-tər\ *n* **1** : a quantity that has magnitude and direction **2** : an organism (as a fly or tick) that transmits a pathogen

Ve·da \'vā-də\ *n* [Skt, lit., knowledge] : any of a class of Hindu sacred writings — **Ve·dic** \'vā-dik\ *adj*

Ve·dan·ta \vā-'dän-tə, və-, -'dan-\ *n* : an orthodox Hindu philosophy based on the Upanishads

vee·jay \'vē-ˌjā\ *n* : an announcer of a program featuring music videos

veep \'vēp\ *n* : VICE PRESIDENT

veer \'vir\ *vb* : to shift from one direction or course to another ♦ **Synonyms** TURN, AVERT, DEFLECT, DIVERT — **veer** *n*

veg·an \'vē-gən, 'vä-; 'vē-jən, -ˌjan\ *n* : a strict vegetarian who consumes no animal food or dairy products — **veg·an·ism** \'vē-gə-ˌni-zəm, 'vä-, 've-\ *n*

¹veg·e·ta·ble \'vej-tə-bəl, 've-jə-\ *adj* [ME, fr. ML *vegetabilis* vegetative, fr. *vegetare* to grow, fr. L, to animate, fr. *vegetus* lively, fr. *vegēre* to enliven] **1** : of, relating to, or growing like plants ⟨the ~ kingdom⟩ **2** : made from, obtained from, or containing plants or plant products ⟨~ oils⟩ **3** : suggesting that of a plant (as in inertness) ⟨a ~ existence⟩

²vegetable *n* **1** : PLANT 1 **2** : a usu. herbaceous plant grown for an edible part that is usu. eaten as part of a meal; *also* : such an edible part

veg·e·tal \'ve-jə-tᵊl\ *adj* **1** : VEGETABLE **2** : VEGETATIVE

veg·e·tar·i·an \ˌve-jə-'ter-ē-ən\ *n* : one that believes in or practices living on a diet of vegetables, fruits, grains, nuts, and sometimes animal products (such as milk and cheese) — **vegetarian** *adj* — **veg·e·tar·i·an·ism** \-ē-ə-ˌni-zəm\ *n*

veg·e·tate \'ve-jə-ˌtāt\ *vb* **-tat·ed; -tat·ing** : to live or grow in the manner of a plant; *esp* : to lead a dull inert life

veg·e·ta·tion \ˌve-jə-'tā-shən\ *n* **1** : the act or process of vegetating; *also* : inert existence **2** : plant life or cover (as of an area) — **veg·e·ta·tion·al** \-shə-nəl\ *adj*

veg·e·ta·tive \'ve-jə-ˌtā-tiv\ *adj* **1** : of or relating to nutrition and growth esp. as contrasted with reproduction **2** : of, relating to, or composed of vegetation **3** : VEGETABLE 3

veg out \'vej-\ *vb* **vegged out; vegging out** [short for *vegetate*] : to spend time idly or passively

ve·he·ment \'vē-ə-mənt\ *adj* **1** : marked by great force or energy **2** : marked by strong feeling or expression : PASSIONATE, FERVID — **ve·he·mence** \-məns\ *n* — **ve·he·ment·ly** *adv*

ve·hi·cle \'vē-ə-kəl, 'vē-ˌhi-\ *n* **1** : a medium by which a thing is applied or administered ⟨linseed oil is a ~ for pigments⟩ **2** : a medium through or by means of which something is conveyed or expressed **3** : a means of transporting persons or goods ♦ **Synonyms** INSTRUMENT, AGENT, AGENCY, ORGAN, CHANNEL — **ve·hic·u·lar** \vē-'hi-kyə-lər\ *adj*

¹veil \'vāl\ *n* **1** : a piece of often sheer or diaphanous material used to screen or curtain something or to cover the head or face **2** : the life of a nun ⟨take the ~⟩ **3** : something that hides or obscures like a veil ⟨a ~ of secrecy⟩

²veil *vb* : to cover with or as if with a veil : wear a veil

¹vein \'vān\ *n* **1** : a fissure in rock filled with mineral matter; *also* : a bed of useful mineral matter **2** : any of the tubular branching vessels that carry blood from the capillaries toward the heart **3** : any of the bundles of vascular vessels forming the framework of a leaf **4** : any of the thickened ribs that stiffen the wings of an insect **5** : something (as a wavy variegation in marble) suggesting veins **6** : a distinctive style of expression **7** : a distinctive element or quality : STRAIN **8** : MOOD, HUMOR — **veined** \'vānd\ *adj*

²vein *vb* : to pattern with or as if with veins — **vein·ing** *n*

vel *abbr* velocity

ve·lar \'vē-lər\ *adj* : of or relating to a velum esp. that of the soft palate

veld *or* **veldt** \'velt, 'felt\ *n* [Afrikaans *veld*, fr. D, field] : an open grassland esp. in southern Africa usu. with scattered shrubs or trees

vel·lum \'ve-ləm\ *n* [ME *velym*, fr. AF *velim*, *veeslin*, fr. **veelin*, adj., of a calf, fr. *veel* calf] **1** : a fine-grained lambskin, kidskin, or calfskin prepared for writing on or for binding books **2** : a strong cream-colored paper — **vellum** *adj*

ve·loc·i·pede \və-'lä-sə-ˌpēd\ *n* : an early bicycle

ve·loc·i·rap·tor \və-'lä-sə-ˌrap-tər\ *n* : any of a genus of agile flesh-eating bipedal dinosaurs of the Cretaceous having a sickle-shaped claw on each foot

ve·loc·i·ty \və-'lä-sə-tē\ *n, pl* **-ties** : quickness of motion : SPEED ⟨the ~ of light⟩

ve·lour *or* **ve·lours** \və-'lu̇r\ *n, pl* **velours** \-'lu̇rz\ : any of various textile fabrics with pile like that of velvet

ve·lum \'vē-ləm\ *n, pl* **ve·la** \-lə\ : a membranous body part (as the soft palate) resembling a veil

vel·vet \'vel-vət\ *n* [ME *veluet, velvet*, fr. AF, fr. *velu* shaggy, ultim. fr. L *villus* shaggy hair] **1** : a fabric having a short soft dense warp pile **2** : something resembling or suggesting velvet (as in softness or luster) **3** : the soft skin covering the growing antlers of deer — **velvet** *adj* — **velvety** *adj*

vel·ve·teen \ˌvel-və-'tēn\ *n* **1** : a fabric woven usu. of cotton in imitation of velvet **2** *pl* : clothes made of velveteen

Ven *abbr* venerable

ve·nal \'vē-nᵊl\ *adj* : capable of being bought or bribed : MERCENARY, CORRUPT — **ve·nal·i·ty** \vi-'na-lə-tē\ *n* — **ve·nal·ly** \'vē-nᵊl-ē\ *adv*

ve·na·tion \vi-'nā-shən, vē-\ *n* : an arrangement or system of veins ⟨the ~ of the hand⟩ ⟨leaf ~⟩

vend \'vend\ *vb* : SELL; *esp* : to sell as a hawker or peddler — **vend·ible** *adj*

vend·ee \ven-'dē\ *n* : one to whom a thing is sold : BUYER

ven·det·ta \ven-'de-tə\ *n* : a feud marked by acts of revenge

vending machine *n* : a coin-operated machine for selling merchandise

ven·dor \'ven-dər, *for 1 also* ven-'dȯr\ *n* **1** : one that vends : SELLER **2** : VENDING MACHINE

¹ve·neer \və-'nir\ *n* [G *Furnier*, fr. *furnieren* to veneer, fr. F *fournir* to furnish] **1** : a thin usu. superficial layer of material ⟨brick ~⟩; *esp* : a thin layer of fine wood glued over a cheaper wood **2** : superficial display : GLOSS

²veneer *vb* : to overlay with a veneer

ven·er·a·ble \'ve-nə-rə-bəl\ *adj* **1** : deserving to be venerated — often used as a religious title **2** : made sacred by association

ven·er·ate \'ve-nə-ˌrāt\ *vb* **-at·ed; -at·ing** : to regard with reverential respect ♦ **Synonyms** ADORE, REVERE, REVERENCE, WORSHIP — **ven·er·a·tion** \ˌve-nə-'rā-shən\ *n*

ve·ne·re·al \və-'nir-ē-əl\ *adj* : of or relating to sexual intercourse or to diseases transmitted by it ⟨a ~ infection⟩

venereal disease *n* : a contagious disease (as gonorrhea or syphilis) usu. acquired by having sexual intercourse with someone who already has it

ve·ne·tian blind \və-'nē-shən-\ *n* : a blind having thin horizontal parallel slats that can be adjusted to admit a desired amount of light

ven·geance \'ven-jəns\ *n* : punishment inflicted in retaliation for an injury or offense : REVENGE

venge·ful \'venj-fəl\ *adj* : filled with a desire for revenge : VINDICTIVE — **venge·ful·ly** *adv*

ve·nial \'vē-nē-əl\ *adj* : capable of being forgiven : EXCUSABLE ⟨~ sin⟩

ve·ni·re \və-'nī-rē\ *n* : a panel from which a jury is drawn

ve·ni·re fa·ci·as \-'fā-shē-əs\ *n* [ME, ML, you should cause to come] : a writ summoning persons to appear in court to serve as jurors

ve·ni·re·man \və-'nī-rē-mən, -'nir-ē-\ *n* : a member of a venire

ve·ni·son \'ve-nə-sən, -zən\ *n, pl* **venisons** *also* **venison** [ME, fr. AF *veneisun* game, venison, fr. L *venatio*, fr. *venari* to hunt, pursue] : the edible flesh of a deer

ven·om \'ve-nəm\ *n* [ME *venim*, fr. AF, ultim. fr. L *ve-nenum* magic charm, drug, poison] **1** : poisonous material secreted by some animals (as snakes, spiders, or bees) and transmitted usu. by biting or stinging **2** : ILL WILL, MALEVOLENCE

ven·om·ous \'ve-nə-məs\ *adj* **1** : full of venom : POISONOUS **2** : SPITEFUL, MALEVOLENT **3** : secreting and using venom ⟨∼ snakes⟩ — **ven·om·ous·ly** *adv*

ve·nous \'vē-nəs\ *adj* **1** : of, relating to, or full of veins **2** : being purplish red oxygen-deficient blood rich in carbon dioxide that is present in most veins

¹vent \'vent\ *vb* **1** : to provide with a vent **2** : to serve as a vent for **3** : EXPEL, DISCHARGE **4** : to relieve oneself by vigorous or emotional expression

²vent *n* **1** : an opportunity or way of escape or passage : OUTLET **2** : an opening for the escape of a gas or liquid or for the relief of pressure

³vent *n* : a slit in a garment esp. in the lower part of a seam (as of a jacket or skirt)

ven·ti·late \'ven-tə-ˌlāt\ *vb* **-lat·ed; -lat·ing 1** : to discuss freely and openly ⟨∼ a question⟩ **2** : to give vent to ⟨∼ one's grievances⟩ **3** : to cause fresh air to circulate through (as a room or mine) so as to replace foul air **4** : to provide with a vent or outlet ♦ *Synonyms* EXPRESS, VENT, AIR, UTTER, VOICE, BROACH — **ven·ti·la·tor** \-lā-tər\ *n*

ven·ti·la·tion \ˌven-tə-'lā-shən\ *n* **1** : the act or process of ventilating **2** : circulation of air (as in a room) **3** : a system or means of providing fresh air

ven·tral \'ven-trəl\ *adj* **1** : of or relating to the belly : ABDOMINAL **2** : of, relating to, or located on or near the surface of the body that in humans is the front but in most other animals is the lower surface — **ven·tral·ly** *adv*

ven·tri·cle \'ven-tri-kəl\ *n* **1** : a chamber of the heart that receives blood from the atrium of the same side and pumps it into the arteries **2** : any of the communicating cavities of the brain that are continuous with the central canal of the spinal cord — **ven·tric·u·lar** \ven-'tri-kyə-lər\ *adj*

ven·tril·o·quism \ven-'tri-lə-ˌkwi-zəm\ *n* [LL *ventriloquus* ventriloquist, fr. L *venter* belly + *loqui* to speak; fr. the belief that the voice is produced from the ventriloquist's stomach] : the production of the voice in such a manner that the sound appears to come from a source other than the speaker — **ven·tril·o·quist** \-kwist\ *n*

ven·tril·o·quy \-kwē\ *n* : VENTRILOQUISM

¹ven·ture \'ven-chər\ *vb* **ven·tured; ven·tur·ing 1** : to expose to hazard : RISK **2** : to undertake the risks of : BRAVE **3** : to offer at the risk of rebuff, rejection, or censure ⟨∼ an opinion⟩ **4** : to proceed despite danger : DARE

²venture *n* **1** : an undertaking involving chance or risk; *esp* : a speculative business enterprise **2** : something risked in a speculative venture : STAKE

ven·ture·some \'ven-chər-səm\ *adj* **1** : involving risk : DANGEROUS, HAZARDOUS **2** : inclined to venture : BOLD, DARING ♦ *Synonyms* ADVENTUROUS, VENTUROUS, RASH, RECKLESS, FOOLHARDY — **ven·ture·some·ly** *adv* — **ven·ture·some·ness** *n*

ven·tur·ous \'ven-chə-rəs\ *adj* : VENTURESOME — **ven·tur·ous·ly** *adv* — **ven·tur·ous·ness** *n*

ven·ue \'ven-yü\ *n* [AF, alter. of *vinné, visné*, lit., neighborhood, neighbors, ultim. fr. L *vicinitas* vicinity] **1** : the place from which the jury is taken and where the trial is held **2** : the place in which the alleged events from which a legal action arises took place **3** : a place where events are held ⟨music ∼s⟩

Ve·nus \'vē-nəs\ *n* : the planet 2d in order from the sun — see PLANET table

Ve·nu·sian \vi-'nü-zhən, -'nyü-\ *adj* : of or relating to the planet Venus

Venus fly·trap *or* **Ve·nus's–fly·trap** \'vē-nə-səz-'flī-ˌtrap\ *n* : an insect-eating plant of the Carolina coast that has the leaf tip modified into an insect trap

ve·ra·cious \və-'rā-shəs\ *adj* **1** : TRUTHFUL, HONEST **2** : TRUE, ACCURATE ⟨∼ report⟩ — **ve·ra·cious·ly** *adv*

ve·rac·i·ty \və-'ra-sə-tē\ *n, pl* **-ties 1** : devotion to truth : TRUTHFULNESS **2** : conformity with fact : ACCURACY **3** : something true

ve·ran·da *or* **ve·ran·dah** \və-'ran-də\ *n* : a long open usu. roofed porch

veranda

verb \'vərb\ *n* : a word that is the grammatical center of a predicate and expresses an act, occurrence, or mode of being

¹ver·bal \'vər-bəl\ *adj* **1** : of, relating to, or consisting of words; *esp* : having to do with words rather than with the ideas to be conveyed **2** : expressed in usu. spoken words : not written : ORAL ⟨a ∼ contract⟩ **3** : of, relating to, or formed from a verb **4** : LITERAL, VERBATIM — **ver·bal·ly** *adv*

²verbal *n* : a word that combines characteristics of a verb with those of a noun or adjective

verbal auxiliary *n* : an auxiliary verb

ver·bal·ize \'vər-bə-ˌlīz\ *vb* **-ized; -iz·ing 1** : to speak or write in wordy or empty fashion **2** : to express something in words : describe verbally **3** : to convert into a verb — **ver·bal·i·za·tion** \ˌvər-bə-lə-'zā-shən\ *n*

verbal noun *n* : a noun derived directly from a verb or verb stem and in some uses having the sense and constructions of a verb

ver·ba·tim \(ˌ)vər-'bā-təm\ *adv or adj* : in the same words : word for word

ver·be·na \(ˌ)vər-'bē-nə\ *n* : VERVAIN; *esp* : any of several garden vervains of hybrid origin with showy spikes of bright often fragrant flowers

ver·biage \'vər-bē-ij, -bij\ *n* **1** : superfluity of words usu. of little or obscure content **2** : DICTION, WORDING

ver·bose \(ˌ)vər-'bōs\ *adj* : using more words than are needed : WORDY ♦ *Synonyms* PROLIX, DIFFUSE, REDUNDANT, WINDY — **ver·bos·i·ty** \-'bä-sə-tē\ *n*

ver·bo·ten \vər-'bō-t³n, fər-\ *adj* [G] : forbidden usu. by dictate

ver·dant \'vər-d³nt\ *adj* : green with growing plants — **ver·dant·ly** *adv*

ver·dict \'vər-(ˌ)dikt\ *n* [ME *verdit, verdict*, fr. AF *verdit*, fr. *veir* true (fr. L *verus*) + *dit* saying, dictum, fr. L *dictum*, fr. *dicere* to say] **1** : the finding or decision of a jury **2** : DECISION, JUDGMENT

ver·di·gris \'vər-də-ˌgrēs, -ˌgris\ *n* : a green or bluish deposit that forms on copper, brass, or bronze surfaces

ver·dure \'vər-jər\ *n* : the greenness of growing vegetation; *also* : such vegetation

¹verge \'vərj\ *n* [[ME, rod, measuring rod, margin, fr. AF, rod, area of jurisdiction, fr. L *virga* twig, rod, line] **1** : a staff carried as an emblem of authority or office **2** : something that borders or bounds : EDGE, MARGIN **3** : BRINK, THRESHOLD ⟨on the ∼ of collapse⟩

²verge *vb* **verged; verg·ing 1** : to be contiguous **2** : to be on the verge

³verge *vb* **verged; verg·ing 1** : to move or extend in some direction or toward some condition : INCLINE **2** : to be in transition or change

verg·er \'vər-jər\ *n* **1** *chiefly Brit* : an attendant who carries a verge (as before a bishop) **2** : SEXTON

ve·rid·i·cal \və-'ri-di-kəl\ *adj* **1** : TRUTHFUL **2** : not illusory : GENUINE

ver·i·fy \'ver-ə-ˌfī\ *vb* **-fied; -fy·ing 1** : to confirm in law by oath **2** : to establish the truth, accuracy, or reality of ⟨∼ the claim⟩ ♦ *Synonyms* AUTHENTICATE, CORROBORATE, SUBSTANTIATE, VALIDATE — **ver·i·fi·able** *adj* — **ver·i·fi·ca·tion** \ˌver-ə-fə-'kā-shən\ *n*

ver·i·ly \'ver-ə-lē\ *adv* **1** : in very truth : CERTAINLY **2** : TRULY, CONFIDENTLY

veri·si·mil·i·tude \ˌver-ə-sə-'mi-lə-ˌtüd, -ˌtyüd\ *n* : the quality or state of appearing to be true or real

ver·i·ta·ble \'ver-ə-tə-bəl\ *adj* : ACTUAL, GENUINE, TRUE — **ver·i·ta·bly** *adv*

ver·i·ty \'ver-ə-tē\ *n, pl* **-ties** 1 : the quality or state of being true or real : TRUTH, REALITY 2 : something (as a statement) that is true 3 : HONESTY, VERACITY

ver·meil *n* [MF] 1 \'vər-məl, -ˌmāl\ : VERMILION 2 \ver-'mā\ : gilded silver

ver·mi·cel·li \ˌvər-mə-'che-lē, -'se-\ *n* [It, fr. pl. of *vermicello*, dim. of *verme* worm] : a pasta made in thinner strings than spaghetti

ver·mic·u·lite \vər-'mi-kyə-ˌlīt\ *n* : any of various lightweight water-absorbent minerals derived from mica

ver·mi·form appendix \'vər-mə-ˌform-\ *n* : APPENDIX 2

ver·mil·ion *also* **ver·mil·lion** \vər-'mil-yən\ *n* : a bright reddish orange color; *also* : any of various red pigments

ver·min \'vər-mən\ *n, pl* **vermin** 1 : small common harmful or objectionable animals (as lice or mice) that are difficult to get rid of 2 : birds and mammals that prey on game — **ver·min·ous** *adj*

ver·mouth \vər-'müth\ *n* [F *vermout*, fr. G *Wermut* wormwood] : a dry or sweet wine flavored with herbs and often used in mixed drinks

¹ver·nac·u·lar \vər-'na-kyə-lər\ *adj* [L *vernaculus* native, fr. *verna* slave born in the master's house, native] 1 : of, relating to, or being a language or dialect native to a region or country rather than a literary, cultured, or foreign language 2 : of, relating to, or being the normal spoken form of a language 3 : applied to a plant or animal in common speech as distinguished from biological nomenclature ⟨∼ names⟩

²vernacular *n* 1 : a vernacular language 2 : the mode of expression of a group or class 3 : a vernacular name of a plant or animal

ver·nal \'vər-nᵊl\ *adj* : of, relating to, or occurring in the spring

ver·ni·er \'vər-nē-ər\ *n* : a short scale made to slide along the divisions of a graduated instrument to indicate parts of divisions

ve·ron·i·ca \və-'rä-ni-kə\ *n* : any of a genus of herbs related to the snapdragons that have small usu. bluish flowers

ver·sa·tile \'vər-sə-tᵊl\ *adj* : turning with ease from one thing or position to another; *esp* : having many aptitudes — **ver·sa·til·i·ty** \ˌvər-sə-'ti-lə-tē\ *n*

¹verse \'vərs\ *n* 1 : a line of poetry; *also* : STANZA 2 : metrical writing distinguished from poetry esp. by its lower level of intensity 3 : POETRY 4 : POEM 5 : one of the short divisions of a chapter in the Bible

²verse *vb* **versed; vers·ing** : to familiarize by experience, study, or practice ⟨well *versed* in the theater⟩

ver·si·cle \'vər-si-kəl\ *n* : a verse or sentence said or sung by a leader in public worship and followed by a response from the people

ver·si·fi·ca·tion \ˌvər-sə-fə-'kā-shən\ *n* 1 : the making of verses 2 : metrical structure

ver·si·fy \'vər-sə-ˌfī\ *vb* **-fied; -fy·ing** 1 : to write verse 2 : to turn into verse — **ver·si·fi·er** \-ˌfī-ər\ *n*

ver·sion \'vər-zhən\ *n* 1 : TRANSLATION; *esp* : a translation of the Bible 2 : an account or description from a particular point of view esp. as contrasted with another 3 : a form or variant of a type or original

vers li·bre \ˌver-'lēbrᵊ\ *n, pl* **vers li·bres** *same*\ [F] : FREE VERSE

ver·so \'vər-sō\ *n, pl* **versos** : a left-hand page

ver·sus \'vər-səs\ *prep* 1 : AGAINST 1 ⟨the champion ∼ the challenger⟩ 2 : in contrast or as an alternative to ⟨free trade ∼ protection⟩

vert *abbr* vertical

ver·te·bra \'vər-tə-brə\ *n, pl* **-brae** \-ˌbrā, -(ˌ)brē\ *or* **-bras** [L] : one of the segments of bone or cartilage making up the backbone

ver·te·bral \(ˌ)vər-'tē-brəl, 'vər-tə-\ *adj* : of, relating to, or made up of vertebrae : SPINAL

vertebral column *n* : BACKBONE 1

¹ver·te·brate \'vər-tə-brət, -ˌbrāt\ *adj* 1 : having a backbone 2 : of or relating to the vertebrates

²vertebrate *n* : any of a large group of animals (as mammals, birds, reptiles, amphibians, or fishes) that have a backbone or in some primitive forms (as a lamprey) a flexible rod of cells and that have a tubular nervous system arranged along the back and divided into a brain and spinal cord

ver·tex \'vər-ˌteks\ *n, pl* **ver·ti·ces** \'vər-tə-ˌsēz\ *also* **ver·tex·es** [ME, top of the head, fr. L *vertex, vortex* whirl, whirlpool, top of the head, summit, fr. *vertere* to turn] 1 : the point opposite to and farthest from the base of a geometrical figure 2 : the point where the sides of an angle or three or more edges of a polyhedron (as a cube) meet 3 : the highest point : TOP, SUMMIT

ver·ti·cal \'vər-ti-kəl\ *adj* 1 : of, relating to, or located at the vertex : directly overhead 2 : rising perpendicularly from a level surface : UPRIGHT — **vertical** *n* — **ver·ti·cal·i·ty** \ˌvər-tə-'ka-lə-tē\ *n* — **ver·ti·cal·ly** \-k(ə-)lē\ *adv*

ver·tig·i·nous \(ˌ)vər-'ti-jə-nəs\ *adj* : marked by, affected with, or tending to cause dizziness

ver·ti·go \'vər-ti-ˌgō\ *n, pl* **-goes** *or* **-gos** : DIZZINESS, GIDDINESS

vertu *var of* VIRTU

ver·vain \'vər-ˌvān\ *n* : any of a genus of chiefly American herbs or low woody plants with often showy heads or spikes of tubular flowers

verve \'vərv\ *n* : liveliness of imagination; *also* : VIVACITY

¹very \'ver-ē\ *adj* **veri·er; -est** [ME *verray, verry,* fr. AF *verai,* ultim. fr. L *verax* truthful, fr. *verus* true] 1 : EXACT, PRECISE ⟨the ∼ heart of the city⟩ 2 : exactly suitable ⟨the ∼ tool for the job⟩ 3 : ABSOLUTE, UTTER ⟨the *veriest* nonsense⟩ 4 — used as an intensive esp. to emphasize identity ⟨before my ∼ eyes⟩ 5 : MERE, BARE ⟨the ∼ idea scared him⟩ 6 : SELFSAME, IDENTICAL ⟨the ∼ man I saw⟩

²very *adv* 1 : in actual fact : TRULY 2 : to a high degree : EXTREMELY

very high frequency *n* : a radio frequency of between 30 and 300 megahertz

ves·i·cant \'ve-si-kənt\ *n* : an agent that causes blistering — **vesicant** *adj*

ves·i·cle \'ve-si-kəl\ *n* : a membranous and usu. fluid-filled cavity in a plant or animal; *also* : BLISTER — **ve·sic·u·lar** \və-'si-kyə-lər\ *adj*

¹ves·per \'ves-pər\ *n* 1 *cap archaic* : EVENING STAR 2 : a vesper bell 3 *archaic* : EVENING, EVENTIDE

²vesper *adj* : of or relating to vespers or the evening

ves·pers \-pərz\ *n pl, often cap* : a late afternoon or evening worship service

ves·sel \'ve-səl\ *n* 1 : a container (as a barrel, bottle, bowl, or cup) for holding something 2 : a person held to be the recipient of a quality (as grace) 3 : a craft bigger than a rowboat 4 : a tube in which a body fluid (as blood or sap) is contained and circulated

¹vest \'vest\ *vb* 1 : to place or give into the possession or discretion of some person or authority 2 : to grant or endow with a particular authority, right, or property 3 : to become legally vested 4 : to clothe with or as if with a garment; *esp* : to garb in ecclesiastical vestments

²vest *n* 1 : a sleeveless garment for the upper body usu. worn over a shirt 2 *chiefly Brit* : a man's sleeveless undershirt 3 : a front piece of a dress resembling the front of a vest

¹ves·tal \'ves-tᵊl\ *adj* : CHASTE

²vestal *n* : VESTAL VIRGIN

vestal virgin *n* 1 : a virgin consecrated to the Roman goddess Vesta and to the service of watching the sacred fire perpetually kept burning on her altar 2 : a chaste woman

vest·ed \'ves-təd\ *adj* : fully and unconditionally guaranteed as a legal right, benefit, or privilege

vested interest *n* : an interest (as in an existing political, economic, or social arrangement) to which the holder has a strong commitment; *also* : one (as a corporation) having a vested interest

ves·ti·bule \'ves-tə-ˌbyül\ *n* 1 : a passage or room between the outer door and the interior of a building 2 : any of various bodily cavities forming or suggesting an entrance to some other cavity or space — **ves·tib·u·lar** \ve-'sti-byə-lər\ *adj*

ves·tige \'ves-tij\ *n* [F, fr. L *vestigium* footprint, track, vestige] : a trace or visible sign left by something lost or vanished; *also* : a minute remaining amount — **ves·ti·gial** \ve-'sti-jē-əl, -jəl\ *adj* — **ves·ti·gial·ly** *adv*

vest·ing \'ves-tiŋ\ *n* : the conveying to an employee of inalienable rights to share in a pension fund; *also* : the right so conveyed

vest·ment \'vest-mənt\ *n* 1 : an outer garment; *esp* : a ceremonial or official robe **2** *pl* : CLOTHING, GARB **3** : a garment or insignia worn by a cleric when officiating or assisting at a religious service

vest–pocket *adj* : very small ⟨a ~ park⟩

ves·try \'ves-trē\ *n, pl* **vestries 1** : a room in a church for vestments, altar linens, and sacred vessels **2** : a room used for church meetings and classes **3** : a body administering the temporal affairs of an Episcopal parish

ves·try·man \-mən\ *n* : a member of a vestry

ves·ture \'ves-chər\ *n* **1** : a covering garment **2** : CLOTHING, APPAREL

¹**vet** \'vet\ *n* : VETERINARIAN

²**vet** *adj or n* : VETERAN

³**vet** *vb* : to evaluate for appraisal or acceptance ⟨~ a manuscript⟩

vetch \'vech\ *n* : any of a genus of twining leguminous herbs including some grown for fodder and green manure

vet·er·an \'ve-trən, -tə-rən\ *n* [L *veteranus*, fr. *veteranus* old, of long experience, fr. *veter-, vetus* old] **1** : an old soldier of long service **2** : a former member of the armed forces **3** : a person of long experience usu. in an occupation or skill — **veteran** *adj*

Veterans Day *n* : November 11 observed as a legal holiday in commemoration of the end of hostilities in 1918 and 1945

vet·er·i·nar·i·an \₁ve-trə-'ner-ē-ən, ₁ve-tə-rə-\ *n* : one qualified and authorized to practice veterinary medicine

¹**vet·er·i·nary** \'ve-trə-₁ner-ē, 've-tə-rə-\ *adj* : of, relating to, or being the medical care of animals and esp. domestic animals

²**veterinary** *n, pl* **-nar·ies** : VETERINARIAN

¹**ve·to** \'vē-tō\ *n, pl* **vetoes** [L, I forbid] **1** : an authoritative prohibition **2** : a power of one part of a government to forbid the carrying out of projects attempted by another part; *esp* : a power vested in a chief executive to prevent the carrying out of measures adopted by a legislature **3** : the exercise of the power of veto

²**veto** *vb* **1** : FORBID, PROHIBIT **2** : to refuse assent to (a legislative bill) so as to prevent enactment or cause reconsideration — **ve·to·er** *n*

vex \'veks\ *vb* **vexed** *also* **vext; vex·ing 1** : to bring trouble, distress, or agitation to **2** : to annoy continually with little irritations

vex·a·tion \vek-'sā-shən\ *n* **1** : the act of vexing **2** : the quality or state of being vexed : IRRITATION **3** : a cause of trouble or annoyance

vex·a·tious \-shəs\ *adj* **1** : causing vexation : ANNOYING **2** : full of distress or annoyance : TROUBLED — **vex·a·tious·ly** *adv* — **vex·a·tious·ness** *n*

vexed \'vekst\ *adj* : fully debated or discussed ⟨a ~ question⟩

VF *abbr* **1** video frequency **2** visual field

VFD *abbr* volunteer fire department

VFW *abbr* Veterans of Foreign Wars

VG *abbr* **1** very good **2** vicar-general

VHF *abbr* very high frequency

VI *abbr* Virgin Islands

via \'vī-ə, 'vē-ə\ *prep* **1** : by way of **2** : by means of

vi·a·ble \'vī-ə-bəl\ *adj* **1** : capable of living; *esp* : sufficiently developed as to be capable of surviving outside the mother's womb ⟨a ~ fetus⟩ **2** : capable of growing and developing ⟨~ seeds⟩ **3** : capable of being put into practice : WORKABLE **4** : having a reasonable chance of succeeding ⟨a ~ candidate⟩ — **vi·a·bil·i·ty** \₁vī-ə-'bi-lə-tē\ *n* — **vi·a·bly** \'vī-ə-blē\ *adv*

via·duct \'vī-ə-₁dəkt\ *n* : a long elevated roadway usu. consisting of a series of short spans supported on arches, piers, or columns

vi·al \'vī-əl\ *n* : a small vessel for liquids

vi·and \'vī-ənd\ *n* : an article of food

vi·at·i·cum \vī-'a-ti-kəm, vē-\ *n, pl* **-cums** *or* **-ca** \-kə\ **1** : the Christian Eucharist given to a person in danger of death **2** : an allowance esp. in money for traveling needs and expenses

vibes \'vībz\ *n pl* **1** : VIBRAPHONE **2** : VIBRATIONS

vi·brant \'vī-brənt\ *adj* **1** : VIBRATING, PULSATING **2** : pulsating with vigor or activity ⟨a ~ personality⟩ **3** : readily set in vibration : RESPONSIVE **4** : sounding from vibration **5** : BRIGHT ⟨~ colors⟩ — **vi·bran·cy** \-brən-sē\ *n*

vi·bra·phone \'vī-brə-₁fōn\ *n* : a percussion instrument

like the xylophone but with metal bars and motor-driven resonators

vi·brate \'vī-₁brāt\ *vb* **vi·brat·ed; vi·brat·ing 1** : OSCILLATE **2** : to set in vibration **3** : to be in vibration **4** : WAVER, FLUCTUATE **5** : to respond sympathetically : THRILL

vi·bra·tion \vī-'brā-shən\ *n* **1** : a rapid to-and-fro motion of the particles of an elastic body or medium (as a stretched cord) that produces sound **2** : an act of vibrating : a state of being vibrated : OSCILLATION **3** : a trembling motion **4** : VACILLATION **5** : a feeling or impression that someone or something gives off — usu. used in pl. ⟨good ~s⟩ — **vi·bra·tion·al** \-shə-nəl\ *adj*

vi·bra·to \vi-'brä-tō\ *n, pl* **-tos** [It] : a slightly tremulous effect imparted to vocal or instrumental music

vi·bra·tor \'vī-₁brā-tər\ *n* : one that vibrates or causes vibration; *esp* : a vibrating electrical device used in massage or for sexual stimulation

vi·bra·to·ry \'vī-brə-₁tȯr-ē\ *adj* : consisting of, capable of, or causing vibration

vi·bur·num \vī-'bər-nəm\ *n* : any of a genus of widely distributed shrubs or small trees related to the honeysuckle and bearing small usu. white flowers in broad clusters

vic *abbr* vicinity

Vic *abbr* Victoria

vic·ar \'vi-kər\ *n* **1** : an administrative deputy **2** : a minister in charge of a church who serves under the authority of another minister — **vi·car·i·ate** \vī-'ker-ē-ət\ *n*

vic·ar·age \'vi-kə-rij\ *n* : a vicar's home

vicar–general *n, pl* **vicars–general** : an administrative deputy (as of a Roman Catholic or Anglican bishop)

vi·car·i·ous \vī-'ker-ē-əs\ *adj* [L *vicarius*, fr. *vicis* change, alternation, stead] **1** : acting for another **2** : done or suffered by one person on behalf of another or others ⟨a ~ sacrifice⟩ **3** : sharing in someone else's experience through the use of the imagination or sympathetic feelings — **vi·car·i·ous·ly** *adv* — **vi·car·i·ous·ness** *n*

¹**vice** \'vīs\ *n* **1** : DEPRAVITY, WICKEDNESS **2** : a moral fault or failing **3** : a habitual usu. trivial fault **4** : an undesirable behavior pattern in a domestic animal

²**vice** *chiefly Brit var of* VISE

³**vi·ce** \'vī-sē\ *prep* : in the place of; *also* : rather than

vice admiral *n* : a commissioned officer in the navy or coast guard ranking above a rear admiral

vice-ge·rent \'vīs-'jir-ənt\ *n* : an administrative deputy of a king or magistrate — **vice-ge·ren·cy** \-ən-sē\ *n*

vi·cen·ni·al \vī-'se-nē-əl\ *adj* : occurring once every 20 years

vice presidency *n* : the office of vice president

vice president *n* **1** : an officer ranking next to a president and usu. empowered to act for the president during an absence or disability **2** : any of several of a president's deputies

vice-re·gal \'vīs-'rē-gəl\ *adj* : of or relating to a viceroy

vice·roy \'vīs-₁rȯi\ *n* : the governor of a country or province who rules as representative of the sovereign — **vice·roy·al·ty** \-əl-tē\ *n*

vice ver·sa \₁vī-si-'vər-sə, 'vīs-'vər-\ *adv* : with the order reversed

vi·chys·soise \₁vi-shē-'swäz, ₁vē-\ *n* [F] : a soup made esp. from leeks or onions and potatoes, cream, and chicken stock and usu. served cold

vic·i·nage \'vi-sə-nij\ *n* : a neighboring or surrounding district : VICINITY

vi·cin·i·ty \və-'si-nə-tē\ *n, pl* **-ties** [MF *vicinité,* fr. L *vicinitas,* fr. *vicinus* neighboring, fr. *vicus* row of houses, village] **1** : NEARNESS, PROXIMITY **2** : a surrounding area : NEIGHBORHOOD

vi·cious \'vi-shəs\ *adj* **1** : having the quality of vice **2** : WICKED, DEPRAVED **3** : DEFECTIVE, FAULTY; *also* : INVALID **3** : IMPURE, FOUL **4** : having a savage disposition; *also* : marked by violence or ferocity **5** : MALICIOUS, SPITEFUL ⟨~ gossip⟩ **6** : worsened by internal causes that augment each other ⟨~ wage-price spiral⟩ — **vi·cious·ly** *adv* — **vi·cious·ness** *n*

vi·cis·si·tude \və-'si-sə-₁tüd, vī-, -₁tyüd\ *n* : an irregular, unexpected, or surprising change

vic·tim \'vik-təm\ *n* **1** : a living being offered as a sacrifice in a religious rite **2** : an individual injured or killed (as by disease or accident) **3** : a person cheated, fooled, or injured ⟨a ~ of circumstances⟩

vic·tim·ise \'vik-tə-ˌmīz\ *Brit var of* VICTIMIZE
vic·tim·ize \'vik-tə-ˌmīz\ *vb* -ized; -iz·ing : to make a victim of — vic·tim·i·za·tion \ˌvik-tə-mə-'zā-shən\ *n* — vic·tim·iz·er \'vik-tə-ˌmī-zər\ *n*
vic·tim·less \'vik-təm-ləs\ *adj* : having no victim ⟨considered gambling to be a ∼ crime⟩
vic·tor \'vik-tər\ *n* : WINNER, CONQUEROR
vic·to·ria \vik-'tȯr-ē-ə\ *n* : a low 4-wheeled carriage with a folding top and a raised driver's seat in front

victoria

¹Vic·to·ri·an \vik-'tȯr-ē-ən\ *adj* 1 : of or relating to the reign of Queen Victoria of England or the art, letters, or tastes of her time 2 : typical of the standards, attitudes, or conduct of the age of Victoria esp. when considered prudish or narrow
²Victorian *n* 1 : a person and esp. an author of the Victorian period 2 : a typically large ornate house built during Queen Victoria's reign
vic·to·ri·ous \vik-'tȯr-ē-əs\ *adj* 1 : having won a victory 2 : of, relating to, or characteristic of victory ⟨∼ exuberance⟩ — vic·to·ri·ous·ly *adv*
vic·to·ry \'vik-tə-rē\ *n, pl* -ries 1 : the overcoming of an enemy or an antagonist 2 : achievement of mastery or success in a struggle or endeavor
¹vict·ual \'vi-t⁹l\ *n* [ME *vitaille, victuayle*, fr. AF, fr. LL *victualia*, pl., provisions, food, fr. neut. pl. of *victualis* of nourishment, fr. L *victus* nourishment, way of living, fr. *vivere* to live] 1 : food fit for humans 2 *pl* : food supplies
²victual *vb* -ualed *or* -ualled; -ual·ing *or* -ual·ling 1 : to supply with food 2 : to store up provisions
vict·ual·ler *or* vict·ual·er \'vi-t⁹l-ər\ *n* : one that supplies provisions (as to an army or a ship)
vi·cu·ña *or* vi·cu·na \vi-'kün-yə, vī-; vī-'kü-nə, -'kyü-\ *n* 1 : a So. American wild mammal related to the llama and alpaca; *also* : its wool 2 : a soft fabric woven from the wool of the vicuña; *also* : a sheep's wool imitation of this
vi·de \'vī-dē, 'vē-ˌdā\ *vb imper* [L] : SEE — used to direct a reader to another item
vi·de·li·cet \və-'de-lə-ˌset, vī-; vi-'dā-li-ˌket\ *adv* [ME, fr. L, fr. *vidēre* to see + *licet* it is permitted] : that is to say : NAMELY
¹vid·eo \'vi-dē-ˌō\ *n* 1 : TELEVISION 2 : VIDEOTAPE; *also* : a recording similar to a videotape but stored in digital form 3 : a videotaped performance ⟨music ∼s⟩
²video *adj* 1 : relating to or used in transmission or reception of the television image 2 : relating to or being images on a television screen or computer display ⟨a ∼ terminal⟩
video camera *n* : a camera that records visual images and usu. sound; *esp* : CAMCORDER
vid·eo·cas·sette \ˌvi-dē-ō-kə-'set\ *n* 1 : a case containing videotape for use with a VCR 2 : a recording (as of a movie) on a videocassette
videocassette recorder *n* : VCR
vid·eo·disc *or* vid·eo·disk \'vi-dē-ō-ˌdisk\ *n* 1 : OPTICAL DISK 2 : a recording (as of a movie) on a videodisc
video game *n* : an electronic game played on a video screen
vid·e·o·gen·ic \ˌvi-dē-ō-'je-nik\ *adj* : TELEGENIC
vid·eo·phone \'vid-ē-ō-ˌfōn\ *n* : a telephone for transmitting both audio and video signals
¹vid·eo·tape \'vid-ē-ō-ˌtāp\ *n* : a recording of visual images and sound made on magnetic tape; *also* : the magnetic tape used for such a recording
²videotape *vb* : to make a videotape of
videotape recorder *n* : a device for recording and playing back videotapes
vie \'vī\ *vb* vied; vy·ing \'vī-iŋ\ : to compete for superiority : CONTEND — vi·er \'vī-ər\ *n*

Viet·cong \vē-'et-'käŋ, ˌvē-ət-, -'kȯŋ\ *n, pl* Vietcong : a guerrilla member of the Vietnamese communist movement
¹view \'vyü\ *n* 1 : the act of seeing or examining : INSPECTION; *also* : SURVEY 2 : a way of looking at or regarding something 3 : ESTIMATE, JUDGMENT ⟨stated his ∼s⟩ 4 : a sight (as of a landscape) regarded for its pictorial quality 5 : extent or range of vision ⟨within ∼⟩ 6 : OBJECT, PURPOSE ⟨done with a ∼ to promotion⟩ 7 : a picture of a scene
²view *vb* 1 : to look at attentively : EXAMINE 2 : SEE, WATCH ⟨∼ a film⟩ 3 : to examine mentally : CONSIDER — view·er *n*
view·er·ship \'vyü-ər-ˌship\ *n* : a television audience esp. with respect to size or makeup
view·find·er \'vyü-ˌfīn-dər\ *n* : a device on a camera for showing the view to be included in the picture
view·point \-ˌpȯint\ *n* : POINT OF VIEW, STANDPOINT
vi·ges·i·mal \vī-'je-sə-məl\ *adj* : based on the number 20
vig·il \'vi-jəl\ *n* 1 : a religious observance formerly held on the night before a religious feast 2 : the day before a religious feast observed as a day of spiritual preparation 3 : evening or nocturnal devotions or prayers — usu. used in pl. 4 : an act or a time of keeping awake when sleep is customary; *esp* : WATCH 1
vigilance committee *n* : a committee of vigilantes
vig·i·lant \'vi-jə-lənt\ *adj* : alertly watchful esp. to avoid danger — vig·i·lance \-ləns\ *n* — vig·i·lant·ly *adv*
vig·i·lan·te \ˌvi-jə-'lan-tē\ *n* : a member of a volunteer committee organized to suppress and punish crime summarily (as when the processes of law are viewed as inadequate); *also* : a self-appointed doer of justice — vig·i·lan·tism \-'lan-ˌti-zəm\ *n*
¹vi·gnette \vin-'yet\ *n* [F, fr. MF *vignete*, fr. dim. of *vigne* vine] 1 : a small decorative design 2 : a picture (as an engraving or a photograph) that shades off gradually into the surrounding ground 3 : a short descriptive literary sketch
²vignette *vb* vi·gnett·ed; vi·gnett·ing 1 : to finish (as a photograph) like a vignette 2 : to describe briefly
vig·or \'vi-gər\ *n* 1 : active strength or energy of body or mind 2 : INTENSITY, FORCE ⟨the ∼ of their quarrel⟩
vig·or·ous \'vi-gə-rəs\ *adj* 1 : having vigor : ROBUST 2 : done with force and energy — vig·or·ous·ly *adv* — vig·or·ous·ness *n*
vig·our *chiefly Brit var of* VIGOR
Vi·king \'vī-kiŋ\ *n* [ON *víkingr*] : any of the pirate Norsemen who raided or invaded the coasts of Europe in the 8th to 10th centuries
vile \'vī(-ə)l\ *adj* vil·er; vil·est 1 : morally despicable 2 : physically repulsive : FOUL 3 : of little worth 4 : DEGRADING, IGNOMINIOUS 5 : utterly bad or contemptible ⟨∼ weather⟩ — vile·ly \'vī(-ə)l-lē\ *adv* — vile·ness *n*
vil·i·fy \'vi-lə-ˌfī\ *vb* -fied; -fy·ing : to blacken the character of with abusive language : DEFAME ✦ *Synonyms* MALIGN, CALUMNIATE, SLANDER, LIBEL, TRADUCE — vil·i·fi·ca·tion \ˌvi-lə-fə-'kā-shən\ *n* — vil·i·fi·er \'vi-lə-ˌfī-ər\ *n*
vil·la \'vi-lə\ *n* 1 : a country estate 2 : the rural or suburban residence of a wealthy person
vil·lage \'vi-lij\ *n* [ME, fr. AF *vilage*, fr. *vile* manorial estate, farmstead, fr. L *villa*] 1 : a settlement usu. larger than a hamlet and smaller than a town 2 : an incorporated minor municipality 3 : the people of a village
vil·lag·er \'vi-li-jər\ *n* : an inhabitant of a village
vil·lain \'vi-lən\ *n* 1 : VILLEIN 2 : an evil person : SCOUNDREL
vil·lain·ess \-lə-nəs\ *n* : a woman who is a villain
vil·lain·ous \-lə-nəs\ *adj* 1 : befitting a villain : WICKED, EVIL 2 : highly objectionable : DETESTABLE ✦ *Synonyms* VICIOUS, INIQUITOUS, NEFARIOUS, INFAMOUS, CORRUPT, DEGENERATE — vil·lain·ous·ly *adv* — vil·lain·ous·ness *n*
vil·lainy \-lə-nē\ *n, pl* -lain·ies 1 : villainous conduct; *also* : a villainous act 2 : villainous character or nature
vil·lein \'vi-lən, -ˌlān\ *n* 1 : a free villager of Anglo-Saxon times 2 : an unfree peasant having the status of a slave to a feudal lord
vil·len·age \'vil-ə-nij\ *n* 1 : the holding of land at the will of a feudal lord 2 : the status of a villein
vil·lous \'vi-ləs\ *adj* : covered with fine hairs or villi
vil·lus \'vi-ləs\ *n, pl* vil·li \-ˌlī, -(ˌ)lē\ : a slender usu. vascu-

lar process; *esp* : one of the tiny projections of the mucous membrane of the small intestine that function in the absorption of food

vim \\'vim\\ *n* : robust energy and enthusiasm : VITALITY

VIN *abbr* vehicle identification number

vin·ai·grette \\,vi-ni-'gret\\ *n* [F] : a sauce made typically of oil, vinegar, and seasonings

vin·ci·ble \\'vin-sə-bəl\\ *adj* : capable of being overcome or subdued

vin·di·cate \\'vin-də-,kāt\\ *vb* -cat·ed; -cat·ing **1** : AVENGE **2** : EXONERATE, ABSOLVE **3** : CONFIRM, SUBSTANTIATE **4** : to provide defense for : JUSTIFY **5** : to maintain a right to : ASSERT — **vin·di·ca·tor** \\-,kā-tər\\ *n*

vin·di·ca·tion \\,vin-də-'kā-shən\\ *n* : the act of vindicating or the state of being vindicated; *esp* : justification against denial or censure : DEFENSE

vin·dic·tive \\vin-'dik-tiv\\ *adj* **1** : disposed to revenge **2** : intended for or involving revenge **3** : VICIOUS, SPITEFUL — **vin·dic·tive·ly** *adv* — **vin·dic·tive·ness** *n*

vine \\'vīn\\ *n* [ME, fr. AF *vigne*, fr. L *vinea* vine, vineyard, fr. fem. of *vineus* of wine, fr. *vinum* wine] **1** : GRAPE **2** **2** : a plant whose stem requires support and which climbs (as by tendrils) or trails along the ground; *also* : the stem of such a plant

vin·e·gar \\'vi-ni-gər\\ *n* [ME *vinegre*, fr. AF *vin egre*, lit., sour wine] : a sour liquid obtained by fermentation (as of cider, wine, or malt) and used to flavor or preserve foods

vin·e·gary \\-gə-rē\\ *adj* **1** : resembling vinegar : SOUR **2** : disagreeable in manner or disposition : CRABBED

vine·yard \\'vin-yərd\\ *n* **1** : a field of grapevines esp. to produce grapes for wine production **2** : a sphere of activity : field of endeavor

vi·nous \\'vī-nəs\\ *adj* **1** : of, relating to, or made with wine ⟨~ medications⟩ **2** : showing the effects of the use of wine ⟨~ bloodshot eyes⟩

¹vin·tage \\'vin-tij\\ *n* **1** : a season's yield of grapes or wine **2** : WINE; *esp* : a usu. superior wine which comes from a single year **3** : the act or period of gathering grapes or making wine **4** : a period of origin ⟨clothes of 1890 ~⟩

²vintage *adj* **1** : of, relating to, or produced in a particular vintage **2** : of old, recognized, and enduring interest, importance, or quality : CLASSIC ⟨~ cars⟩ **3** : of the best and most characteristic — used with a proper noun

vint·ner \\'vint-nər\\ *n* : a dealer in wines

vi·nyl \\'vī-nᵊl\\ *n* **1** : a chemical derived from ethylene by the removal of one hydrogen atom **2** : a polymer of a vinyl compound or a product (as a textile fiber) made from one

vinyl chloride *n* : a flammable gaseous carcinogenic compound used esp. to make vinyl resins

vi·ol \\'vī-əl\\ *n* : a bowed stringed instrument chiefly of the 16th and 17th centuries having a fretted neck and usu. six strings

¹vi·o·la \\vī-'ō-lə, 'vī-ə-lə\\ *n* : VIOLET **1**; *esp* : any of various hybrid garden plants with white, yellow, purple, or variously colored flowers that resemble but are smaller than those of the related pansies

²vi·o·la \\vē-'ō-lə\\ *n* : an instrument of the violin family slightly larger and tuned lower than a violin — **vi·o·list** \\-list\\ *n*

vi·o·la·ble \\'vī-ə-lə-bəl\\ *adj* : capable of being violated

vi·o·late \\'vī-ə-,lāt\\ *vb* -lat·ed; -lat·ing **1** : BREAK, DISREGARD ⟨~ a law⟩ ⟨~ a frontier⟩ **2** : RAPE **3** : PROFANE, DESECRATE **4** : INTERRUPT, DISTURB ⟨violated his privacy⟩ — **vi·o·la·tor** \\-,lā-tər\\ *n*

vi·o·la·tion \\,vī-ə-'lā-shən\\ *n* : an act or instance of violating : the state of being violated ♦ *Synonyms* BREACH, INFRACTION, TRESPASS, INFRINGEMENT, TRANSGRESSION

vi·o·lence \\'vī-ləns, 'vī-ə-\\ *n* **1** : exertion of physical force so as to injure or abuse **2** : injury by or as if by infringement or profanation **3** : intense or furious often destructive action or force **4** : vehement feeling or expression : INTENSITY **5** : jarring quality : DISCORDANCE ♦ *Synonyms* COMPULSION, COERCION, DURESS, CONSTRAINT

vi·o·lent \\-lənt\\ *adj* **1** : marked by extreme force or sudden intense activity **2** : caused by or showing strong feeling ⟨~ words⟩ **3** : EXTREME, INTENSE ⟨~ pain⟩ ⟨~ colors⟩ **4** : emotionally agitated to the point of loss of self-control **5** : caused by force : not natural ⟨~ death⟩ — **vi·o·lent·ly** *adv*

vi·o·let \\'vī-ə-lət\\ *n* **1** : any of a genus of herbs or small shrubs usu. with heart-shaped leaves and both aerial and underground flowers; *esp* : one with small usu. solid-colored flowers **2** : a reddish blue color

vi·o·lin \\,vī-ə-'lin\\ *n* : a bowed stringed instrument with four strings that has a shallow body, a fingerboard without frets, and a curved bridge — **vi·o·lin·ist** \\-'li-nist\\ *n*

vi·o·lon·cel·lo \\,vī-ə-lən-'che-lō\\ *n* [It] : CELLO — **vi·o·lon·cel·list** \\-list\\ *n*

VIP \\,vē-,ī-'pē\\ *n*, *pl* **VIPs** \\-'pēz\\ [*very important person*] : a person of great influence or prestige; *esp* : a high official with special privileges

vi·per \\'vī-pər\\ *n* **1** : a common stout-bodied Eurasian venomous snake having a bite only rarely fatal to humans; *also* : any snake (as a pit viper) of the same family as the viper **2** : any venomous or reputedly venomous snake **3** : a vicious or treacherous person — **vi·per·ine** \\-pə-,rīn\\ *adj*

vi·ra·go \\və-'rä-gō, -'rā-\\ *n*, *pl* **-goes** *or* **-gos** [ME, fr. L, strong or heroic woman, fr. *vir* man] **1** : a loud overbearing woman **2** : a woman of great strength and courage

vi·ral \\'vī-rəl\\ *adj* : of, relating to, or caused by a virus ⟨a ~ infection⟩ — **vi·ral·ly** *adv*

vir·eo \\'vir-ē-,ō\\ *n*, *pl* **-e·os** [L, a small bird, fr. *virēre* to be green] : any of various small insect-eating American songbirds mostly olive green and grayish in color

¹vir·gin \\'vər-jən\\ *n* **1** : an unmarried woman devoted to religion **2** : an unmarried girl or woman **3** *cap* : the mother of Jesus **4** : a person who has not had sexual intercourse

²virgin *adj* **1** : free from stain : PURE, SPOTLESS **2** : CHASTE **3** : befitting a virgin : MODEST **4** : FRESH, UNSPOILED; *esp* : not altered by human activity ⟨~ forest⟩ **5** : INITIAL, FIRST

¹vir·gin·al \\'vər-jə-nᵊl\\ *adj* : of, relating to, or characteristic of a virgin or virginity — **vir·gin·al·ly** *adv*

²virginal *n* : a small rectangular spinet without legs popular in the 16th and 17th centuries

Vir·gin·ia creeper \\vər-'jin-yə-\\ *n* : a No. American vine related to the grapes that has leaves with five leaflets and bluish-black berries

Virginia reel *n* : an American country-dance

vir·gin·i·ty \\vər-'ji-nə-tē\\ *n*, *pl* **-ties** **1** : the quality or state of being virgin; *esp* : MAIDENHOOD **2** : the unmarried life : CELIBACY

Vir·go \\'vər-,gō\\ *n* [L, lit., virgin] **1** : a zodiacal constellation between Leo and Libra usu. pictured as a young woman **2** : the 6th sign of the zodiac in astrology; *also* : one born under this sign

vir·gule \\'vər-gyül\\ *n* : ²SLASH **3**

vir·i·des·cent \\,vir-ə-'de-sᵊnt\\ *adj* : slightly green : GREENISH

vir·ile \\'vir-əl\\ *adj* **1** : having the nature, powers, or qualities of a man **2** : MASCULINE, MALE **3** : MASTERFUL, FORCEFUL — **vi·ril·i·ty** \\və-'ri-lə-tē\\ *n*

vi·ri·on \\'vī-rē-,än, 'vir-ē-\\ *n* : a complete virus particle consisting of an RNA or DNA core with a protein coat

vi·rol·o·gy \\vī-'rä-lə-jē\\ *n* : a branch of science that deals with viruses and viral diseases — **vi·rol·o·gist** \\-jist\\ *n*

vir·tu \\,vər-'tü, ,vir-\\ *or* **ver·tu** \\,vər-, ,ver-\\ *n* [It *virtù*, lit., virtue] **1** : a love of or taste for objects of art **2** : objects of art (as curios and antiques)

vir·tu·al \\'vər-chə-wəl\\ *adj* : being in essence or in effect though not formally recognized or admitted ⟨a ~ dictator⟩ **2** : being on or simulated on a computer or computer network

vir·tu·al·ly \\'vər-chə-wə-lē\\ *adv* **1** : almost entirely : NEARLY **2** : for all practical purposes ⟨~ unknown⟩

virtual reality *n* : an artificial environment that is experienced through sensory stimuli (as sights and sounds) provided by an interactive computer program; *also* : the technology used to create or access a virtual reality

vir·tue \\'vər-chü\\ *n* [ME *vertu*, fr. AF, fr. L *virtus* strength, manliness, virtue, fr. *vir* man] **1** : conformity to a standard of right : MORALITY **2** : a particular moral excellence **3** : manly strength or courage : VALOR **4** : a commendable quality : MERIT **5** : active power to accomplish a given effect : POTENCY, EFFICACY **6** : chastity esp. in a woman

vir·tu·os·i·ty \\,vər-chə-'wä-sə-tē\\ *n*, *pl* **-ties** : great technical skill in the practice of a fine art

vir·tu·o·so \ˌvər-chə-ˈwō-sō, -zō\ *n, pl* **-sos** *or* **-si** \-sē, -zē\ [It] **1** : one skilled in or having a taste for the fine arts **2** : one who excels in the technique of an art; *esp* : a highly skilled musical performer ✦ *Synonyms* EXPERT, ADEPT, ARTIST, DOYEN, MASTER — **virtuoso** *adj*
vir·tu·ous \ˈvər-chə-wəs\ *adj* **1** : having or showing virtue and esp. moral virtue **2** : CHASTE — **vir·tu·ous·ly** *adv*
vir·u·lent \ˈvir-ə-lənt, ˈvir-yə-\ *adj* **1** : highly infectious ⟨a ∼ germ⟩; *also* : marked by a rapid, severe, and often deadly course ⟨a ∼ disease⟩ **2** : extremely poisonous or venomous : NOXIOUS **3** : full of malice : MALIGNANT — **vir·u·lence** \-ləns\ *n* — **vir·u·lent·ly** *adv*
vi·rus \ˈvī-rəs\ *n, pl* **vi·rus·es** [L, venom, poisonous emanation] **1** : any of a large group of submicroscopic infectious agents that have an outside coat of protein around a core of RNA or DNA, that can grow and multiply only in living cells, and that cause important diseases in human beings, lower animals, and plants; *also* : a disease caused by a virus **2** : something (as a corrupting influence) that poisons the mind or spirit **3** : a computer program that is usu. hidden within another program and that reproduces itself and inserts the copies into other programs and usu. performs a malicious action (as destroying data)
vis *abbr* **1** visibility **2** visual
¹vi·sa \ˈvē-zə, -sə\ *n* [F] **1** : an endorsement by the proper authorities on a passport to show that it has been examined and the bearer may proceed **2** : a signature by a superior official signifying approval of a document
²visa *vb* **vi·saed** \-zəd, -səd\; **vi·sa·ing** \-zə-iŋ, -sə-\ : to give a visa to (a passport)
vis·age \ˈvi-zij\ *n* : the face or countenance of a person or sometimes an animal; *also* : LOOK, APPEARANCE
¹vis-à-vis \ˌvēz-ə-ˈvē, ˌvēs-\ *prep* [F, lit., face-to-face] **1** : face-to-face with : OPPOSITE **2** : in relation to **3** : as compared with
²vis-à-vis *n, pl* **vis-à-vis** *same or* -ˈvēz\ **1** : one that is face-to-face with another **2** : ESCORT **3** : COUNTERPART **4** : TÊTE-À-TÊTE
³vis-à-vis *adv* : in company : TOGETHER
viscera *pl of* VISCUS
vis·cer·al \ˈvi-sə-rəl\ *adj* **1** : felt in or as if in the viscera **2** : not intellectual : INSTINCTIVE **3** : of or relating to the viscera — **vis·cer·al·ly** *adv*
vis·cid \ˈvi-səd\ *adj* : VISCOUS — **vis·cid·i·ty** \vi-ˈsi-də-tē\ *n*
vis·cos·i·ty \vis-ˈkä-sə-tē\ *n, pl* **-ties** : the quality of being viscous; *esp* : the property of resistance to flow in a fluid
vis·count \ˈvī-ˌkaunt\ *n* : a member of the British peerage ranking below an earl and above a baron
vis·count·ess \-ˌkaun-təs\ *n* **1** : the wife or widow of a viscount **2** : a woman who holds the rank of viscount in her own right
vis·cous \ˈvis-kəs\ *adj* [ME *viscouse*, fr. AF *viscos*, fr. LL *viscosus* full of birdlime, viscous, fr. L *viscum* mistletoe, birdlime] **1** : having the sticky consistency of glue **2** : having or characterized by viscosity
vis·cus \ˈvis-kəs\ *n, pl* **vis·cera** \ˈvi-sə-rə\ : an internal organ of the body; *esp* : one (as the heart or liver) located in the cavity of the trunk
vise \ˈvīs\ *n* [ME *vys, vice* screw, fr. AF *vyz*, fr. L *vitis* vine] : a tool with two jaws for holding work that typically close by a screw or lever

vise

vis·i·bil·i·ty \ˌvi-zə-ˈbi-lə-tē\ *n, pl* **-ties** **1** : the quality, condition, or degree of being visible **2** : the degree of clearness of the atmosphere
vis·i·ble \ˈvi-zə-bəl\ *adj* : capable of being seen ⟨∼ stars⟩;

also : MANIFEST, APPARENT ⟨has no ∼ means of support⟩ — **vis·i·bly** \-blē\ *adv*
¹vi·sion \ˈvi-zhən\ *n* **1** : something seen otherwise than by ordinary sight (as in a dream or trance) **2** : a vivid picture created by the imagination **3** : the act or power of imagination **4** : unusual wisdom in foreseeing what is going to happen **5** : the act or power of seeing : SIGHT **6** : something seen; *esp* : a lovely sight
²vision *vb* : IMAGINE, ENVISION
¹vi·sion·ary \ˈvi-zhə-ˌner-ē\ *adj* **1** : of the nature of a vision : ILLUSORY, UNREAL **2** : not practical : UTOPIAN **3** : seeing or likely to see visions : given to dreaming or imagining ✦ *Synonyms* IMAGINARY, FANTASTIC, CHIMERICAL, QUIXOTIC
²visionary *n, pl* **-ar·ies** **1** : one whose ideas or projects are impractical : DREAMER **2** : one who sees visions
¹vis·it \ˈvi-zət\ *vb* **1** : to go to see in order to comfort or help **2** : to call on either as an act of courtesy or friendship **3** : to dwell for a time as a guest **4** : to come to or upon as a reward, affliction, or punishment **5** : INFLICT ⟨∼ed his wrath upon them⟩ **6** : to make a visit or regular or frequent visits **7** : CHAT, CONVERSE ⟨enjoys ∼*ing* with the neighbors⟩ — **vis·it·able** *adj*
²visit *n* **1** : a short stay : CALL **2** : a brief residence as a guest **3** : a journey to and stay at a place **4** : a formal or professional call (as by a doctor)
vis·i·tant \ˈvi-zə-tənt\ *n* : VISITOR
vis·i·ta·tion \ˌvi-zə-ˈtā-shən\ *n* **1** : VISIT; *esp* : an official visit **2** : a special dispensation of divine favor or wrath; *also* : a severe trial
visiting nurse *n* : a nurse employed to visit sick persons or perform public health services in a community
vis·i·tor \ˈvi-zə-tər\ *n* : one that visits
vi·sor \ˈvī-zər\ *n* **1** : the front piece of a helmet; *esp* : a movable upper piece **2** : VIZARD **3** : a projecting part (as on a cap) to shade the eyes — **vi·sored** \-zərd\ *adj*
vis·ta \ˈvis-tə\ *n* **1** : a distant view through or along an avenue or opening **2** : an extensive mental view over a series of years or events
VISTA *abbr* Volunteers in Service to America
¹vi·su·al \ˈvi-zhə-wəl\ *adj* **1** : of, relating to, or used in vision ⟨∼ organs⟩ **2** : perceived by vision ⟨a ∼ impression⟩ **3** : VISIBLE ⟨∼ objects⟩ **4** : done by sight only ⟨∼ navigation⟩ **5** : of or relating to instruction by means of sight ⟨∼ aids⟩ — **vi·su·al·ly** *adv*
²visual *n* : something (as a graphic) that appeals to the sight and is used for illustration, demonstration, or promotion — usu. used in pl.
vi·su·al·ize \ˈvi-zhə-wə-ˌlīz\ *vb* **-ized; -iz·ing** : to make visible; *esp* : to form a mental image of — **vi·su·al·i·za·tion** \ˌvi-zhə-wə-lə-ˈzā-shən\ *n* — **vi·su·al·iz·er** *n*
vi·ta \ˈvē-tə, ˈvī-\ *n, pl* **vi·tae** \ˈvē-ˌtī, ˈvī-tē\ [L, lit., life] : a brief autobiographical sketch
vi·tal \ˈvī-t³l\ *adj* **1** : concerned with or necessary to the maintenance of life **2** : full of life and vigor : ANIMATED **3** : of, relating to, or characteristic of life or living beings **4** : FATAL, MORTAL ⟨a ∼ wound⟩ **5** : FUNDAMENTAL, INDISPENSABLE — **vi·tal·ly** *adv*
vi·tal·i·ty \vī-ˈta-lə-tē\ *n, pl* **-ties** **1** : the property distinguishing the living from the nonliving **2** : mental and physical vigor **3** : enduring quality **4** : ANIMATION, LIVELINESS
vi·tal·ize \ˈvī-tə-ˌlīz\ *vb* **-ized; -iz·ing** : to impart life or vigor to : ANIMATE — **vi·tal·i·za·tion** \ˌvī-tə-lə-ˈzā-shən\ *n*
vi·tals \ˈvī-t³lz\ *n pl* **1** : vital organs (as the heart and brain) **2** : essential parts
vital signs *n pl* : the pulse rate, respiratory rate, body temperature, and often blood pressure of a person
vital statistics *n pl* : statistics dealing with births, deaths, marriages, health, and disease
vi·ta·min \ˈvī-tə-mən\ *n* : any of various organic substances that are essential in tiny amounts to the nutrition of most animals and some plants and are mostly obtained from foods
vitamin A *n* : any of several vitamins (as from egg yolk or fish-liver oils) required esp. for good vision
vitamin B *n* **1** : VITAMIN B COMPLEX **2** *or* **vitamin B₁** : THIAMINE
vitamin B complex *n* : a group of vitamins that are found widely in foods and are essential for normal function of certain enzymes and for growth

vitamin B₆ \-'bē-'siks\ *n* : any of several compounds that are considered essential to vertebrate nutrition

vitamin B₁₂ \-'bē-'twelv\ *n* : a complex cobalt-containing compound that occurs esp. in liver and is essential to normal blood formation, neural function, and growth; *also* : any of several compounds of similar action

vitamin C *n* : a vitamin found esp. in fruits and vegetables that is needed by the body to prevent scurvy

vitamin D *n* : any or all of several vitamins that are needed for normal bone and tooth structure and are found esp. in fish-liver oils, egg yolk, and milk or are produced by the body in response to ultraviolet light

vitamin E *n* : any of various oily fat-soluble liquid vitamins whose absence in the body is associated with such ailments as infertility, the breakdown of muscles, and vascular problems and which are found esp. in leaves and in seed germ oils

vitamin K *n* : any of several vitamins needed for blood to clot properly

vi·ti·ate \'vi-shē-,āt\ *vb* **-at·ed; -at·ing** **1** : CONTAMINATE, POLLUTE; *also* : DEBASE, PERVERT **2** : to make legally ineffective : INVALIDATE ⟨∼ a contract⟩ — **vi·ti·a·tion** \,vi-shē-'ā-shən\ *n* — **vi·ti·a·tor** \'vi-shē-,ā-tər\ *n*

vi·ti·cul·ture \'vi-tə-,kəl-chər\ *n* : the growing of grapes — **vi·ti·cul·tur·al** \,vi-tə-'kəl-chə-rəl\ *adj* — **vi·ti·cul·tur·ist** \-rist\ *n*

vit·re·ous \'vi-trē-əs\ *adj* **1** : of, relating to, or resembling glass : GLASSY ⟨∼ rocks⟩ **2** : of, relating to, or being the clear colorless transparent jelly (**vitreous humor**) behind the lens in the eyeball

vit·ri·ol \'vi-trē-əl\ *n* : something resembling acid in being caustic, corrosive, or biting — **vit·ri·ol·ic** \,vi-trē-'ä-lik\ *adj*

vit·tles \'vi-t°lz\ *n pl* : VICTUALS

vi·tu·per·ate \vī-'tü-pə-,rāt, və-, -'tyü-\ *vb* **-at·ed; -at·ing** : to abuse in words : SCOLD ♦ *Synonyms* REVILE, BERATE, RATE, UPBRAID, RAIL, LASH — **vi·tu·per·a·tive** \-'tü-pə-rə-tiv, -'tyü-, -,rā-\ *adj* — **vi·tu·per·a·tive·ly** *adv* — **vi·tu·per·a·tion** \(,)vī-tü-pə-'rā-shən, və-, -tyü-\ *n* : lengthy harsh criticism or abuse

vi·va \'vē-və\ *interj* [It & Sp, long live] — used to express goodwill or approval

vi·va·ce \vē-'vä-chā\ *adv or adj* [It] : in a brisk spirited manner — used as a direction in music

vi·va·cious \və-'vā-shəs, vī-\ *adj* : lively in temper, conduct, or spirit : SPRIGHTLY — **vi·va·cious·ly** *adv* — **vi·va·cious·ness** *n*

vi·vac·i·ty \-'va-sə-tē\ *n* : the quality or state of being vivacious

vi·va vo·ce \,vī-və-'vō-sē, ,vē-və-'vō-,chā\ *adj* [ML, with the living voice] : expressed or conducted by word of mouth : ORAL — **viva voce** *adv*

viv·id \'vi-vəd\ *adj* **1** : BRILLIANT, INTENSE ⟨a ∼ red⟩ **2** : having the appearance of vigorous life **3** : producing a strong impression on the senses; *esp* : producing distinct mental pictures ⟨a ∼ description⟩ — **viv·id·ly** *adv* — **viv·id·ness** *n*

viv·i·fy \'vi-və-,fī\ *vb* **-fied; -fy·ing** **1** : to put life into : ANIMATE **2** : to make vivid — **viv·i·fi·ca·tion** \,vi-və-fə-'kā-shən\ *n* — **viv·i·fi·er** *n*

vi·vip·a·rous \vī-'vi-pə-rəs, və-\ *adj* : producing living young from within the body rather than from eggs — **vi·vi·par·i·ty** \,vī-və-'pa-rə-tē, ,vi-\ *n*

viv·i·sec·tion \,vi-və-'sek-shən, 'vi-və-,sek-\ *n* : the cutting of or operation on a living animal; *also* : animal experimentation esp. if causing distress to the subject

vix·en \'vik-sən\ *n* **1** : an ill-tempered scolding woman **2** : a female fox

viz *abbr* videlicet

viz·ard \'vi-zərd\ *n* : a mask for disguise or protection

vi·zier \və-'zir\ *n* : a high executive officer of many Muslim countries

VJ *abbr* veejay

VOA *abbr* Voice of America

voc *abbr* **1** vocational **2** vocative

vocab *abbr* vocabulary

vo·ca·ble \'vō-kə-bəl\ *n* : TERM, NAME; *esp* : a word that can be stood with regard to its meaning

vo·cab·u·lary \vō-'ka-byə-,ler-ē\ *n, pl* **-lar·ies** **1** : a list or collection of words usu. alphabetically arranged and defined or explained : LEXICON **2** : a stock of words in a

language used by a class or individual or in relation to a subject

vocabulary entry *n* : a word (as the noun *book*), hyphened or open compound (as the verb *cross-refer* or the noun *boric acid*), word element (as the affix *-an*), abbreviation (as *agt*), verbalized symbol (as *Na*), or term (as *master of ceremonies*) entered alphabetically in a dictionary for the purpose of definition or identification or expressly included as an inflected form (as the noun *mice* or the verb *saw*) or as a derived form (as the noun *godlessness* or the adverb *globally*) or related phrase (as *in spite of*) run on at its base word and usu. set in a type (as boldface) readily distinguishable from that of the lightface running text which defines, explains, or identifies the entry

¹vo·cal \'vō-kəl\ *adj* **1** : uttered by the voice : ORAL **2** : relating to, composed or arranged for, or sung by the human voice ⟨∼ music⟩ **3** : given to expressing oneself freely or insistently : OUTSPOKEN **4** : of or relating to the voice

²vocal *n* **1** : a vocal sound **2** : a vocal composition or its performance

vocal cords *n pl* : either of two pairs of elastic folds of mucous membrane that project into the cavity of the larynx and function in the production of vocal sounds

vo·cal·ic \vō-'ka-lik\ *adj* : of, relating to, or functioning as a vowel

vo·cal·ise *Brit var of* VOCALIZE

vo·cal·ist \'vō-kə-list\ *n* : SINGER

vo·cal·ize \-,līz\ *vb* **-ized; -iz·ing** **1** : to give vocal expression to : UTTER; *esp* : SING **2** : to make voiced rather than voiceless — **vo·cal·iz·er** *n*

vo·ca·tion \vō-'kā-shən\ *n* **1** : a summons or strong inclination to a particular state or course of action ⟨religious ∼⟩ **2** : regular employment : OCCUPATION, PROFESSION — **vo·ca·tion·al** \-shə-nəl\ *adj*

vo·ca·tion·al·ism \-shə-nə-,li-zəm\ *n* : emphasis on vocational training in education

voc·a·tive \'vä-kə-tiv\ *adj* : of, relating to, or constituting a grammatical case marking the one addressed — **vocative** *n*

vo·cif·er·ate \vō-'si-fə-,rāt\ *vb* **-at·ed; -at·ing** [L *vociferari*, fr. *voc-*, *vox* voice + *ferre* to bear] : to cry out loudly : CLAMOR, SHOUT — **vo·cif·er·a·tion** \-,si-fə-'rā-shən\ *n*

vo·cif·er·ous \vō-'si-fə-rəs\ *adj* : making or given to loud outcry — **vo·cif·er·ous·ly** *adv* — **vo·cif·er·ous·ness** *n*

vod·ka \'väd-kə\ *n* [Russ, fr. *voda* water] : a colorless liquor distilled from a mash (as of rye or wheat)

vogue \'vōg\ *n* [MF, action of rowing, course, fashion, fr. *voguer* to sail, fr. OF, fr. OIt *vogare* to row] **1** : popular acceptance or favor : POPULARITY **2** : a period of popularity **3** : one that is in fashion at a particular time ♦ *Synonyms* MODE, FAD, RAGE, CRAZE, TREND, FASHION

vogu·ish \'vō-gish\ *adj* **1** : FASHIONABLE, SMART **2** : suddenly or temporarily popular

¹voice \'vȯis\ *n* **1** : sound produced through the mouth by vertebrates and esp. by human beings (as in speaking or singing) **2** : musical sound produced by the vocal cords : the power to produce such sound; *also* : one of the melodic parts in a vocal or instrumental composition **3** : the vocal organs as a means of tone production ⟨train the ∼⟩ **4** : sound produced by vibration of the vocal cords as heard in vowels and some consonants **5** : the power of speaking **6** : a sound suggesting a voice ⟨the ∼ of the sea⟩ **7** : an instrument or medium of expression **8** : a choice, opinion, or wish openly expressed; *also* : right of expression **9** : distinction of form of a verb to indicate the relation of the subject to the action expressed by the verb

²voice *vb* **voiced; voic·ing** : to give voice or expression to : UTTER ⟨∼ a complaint⟩ ♦ *Synonyms* EXPRESS, VENT, AIR, VENTILATE

voice box *n* : LARYNX

voiced \'vȯist\ *adj* **1** : having a voice ⟨soft-*voiced*⟩ **2** : uttered with voice ⟨a ∼ consonant⟩ — **voiced·ness** \'vȯist-nəs, 'vȯi-səd-nəs\ *n*

voice·less \'vȯis-ləs\ *adj* **1** : having no voice **2** : not pronounced with voice — **voice·less·ly** *adv* — **voice·less·ness** *n*

voice mail *n* : an electronic communication system in which spoken messages are recorded for later playback to the intended recipient; *also* : such a message

voice–over *n* : the voice in a film or television program of a person who is heard but not seen or not seen talking

voice·print \\'vȯis-ˌprint\ *n* : an individually distinctive pattern of voice characteristics that is spectrographically produced

¹void \\'vȯid\ *adj* **1** : UNOCCUPIED, VACANT ⟨a ∼ bishopric⟩ **2** : containing nothing : EMPTY **3** : LACKING, DEVOID ⟨proposals ∼ of sense⟩ **4** : VAIN, USELESS **5** : of no legal force or effect : NULL

²void *n* **1** : empty space : EMPTINESS, VACUUM **2** : a feeling of want or hollowness

³void *vb* **1** : to make or leave empty; *also* : VACATE, LEAVE **2** : DISCHARGE, EMIT ⟨∼ urine⟩ **3** : to render void : ANNUL, NULLIFY ⟨∼ a contract⟩ — **void·able** *adj* — **void·er** *n*

voi·là \vwä-'lä\ *interj* [F] — used to call attention or to express satisfaction or approval

voile \\'vȯi(-ə)l\ *n* : a sheer fabric used for women's clothing and curtains

vol *abbr* **1** volume **2** volunteer

vol·a·tile \\'vä-lə-t³l\ *adj* **1** : readily becoming a vapor at a relatively low temperature ⟨a ∼ liquid⟩ **2** : tending to erupt into violence **3** : likely to change suddenly — **vol·a·til·i·ty** \ˌvä-lə-'ti-lə-tē\ *n* — **vol·a·til·ize** \'vä-lə-tə-ˌlīz\ *vb*

vol·ca·nic \väl-'ka-nik\ *adj* **1** : of, relating to, or produced by a volcano **2** : explosively violent ⟨∼ emotions⟩

vol·ca·nism \\'väl-kə-ˌni-zəm\ *n* : volcanic action or activity

vol·ca·no \väl-'kā-nō\ *n, pl* **-noes** *or* **-nos** [It or Sp; It *vulcano*, fr. Sp *vulcán*, ultim fr. L *Volcanus*, Roman god of fire and metalworking] : an opening in the crust of the earth, a planet, or a moon from which molten rock and steam issue; *also* : a hill or mountain composed of the ejected material

vol·ca·nol·o·gy \ˌväl-kə-'nä-lə-jē\ *n* : a branch of geology that deals with volcanic phenomena — **vol·ca·nol·o·gist** \-kə-'nä-lə-jist\ *n*

vole \\'vōl\ *n* : any of various small rodents that are closely related to the lemmings and muskrats

vole

vo·li·tion \vō-'li-shən\ *n* **1** : the act or the power of making a choice or decision : WILL **2** : a choice or decision made — **vo·li·tion·al** \-'li-shə-nəl\ *adj*

¹vol·ley \\'vä-lē\ *n, pl* **volleys 1** : a flight of missiles (as arrows) **2** : simultaneous discharge of a number of missile weapons **3** : an act of volleying **4** : a burst of many things at once ⟨a ∼ of angry letters⟩

²volley *vb* **vol·leyed; vol·ley·ing 1** : to discharge or become discharged in or as if in a volley **2** : to hit an object of play (as a ball) in the air before it touches the ground

vol·ley·ball \-ˌbȯl\ *n* : a game played by volleying an inflated ball over a net; *also* : the ball used in this game

volt \\'vōlt\ *n* : the meter-kilogram-second unit of electrical potential difference and electromotive force equal to the difference in potential between two points in a wire carrying a constant current of one ampere when the power dissipated between the points is equal to one watt

volt·age \\'vōl-tij\ *n* : potential difference measured in volts

vol·ta·ic \väl-'tā-ik, vōl-\ *adj* : of, relating to, or producing direct electric current by chemical action

volte–face \ˌvȯlt-'fäs, ˌvȯl-tə-\ *n* : a reversal in policy : ABOUT-FACE

volt·me·ter \\'vōlt-ˌmē-tər\ *n* : an instrument for measuring in volts the difference in potential between different points of an electrical circuit

vol·u·ble \\'väl-yə-bəl\ *adj* : fluent and smooth in speech

: GLIB ♦ **Synonyms** GARRULOUS, LOQUACIOUS, TALKATIVE — **vol·u·bil·i·ty** \ˌväl-yə-'bi-lə-tē\ *n* — **vol·u·bly** \\'väl-yə-blē\ *adv*

vol·ume \\'väl-yəm, -(ˌ)yüm\ *n* [ME, fr. AF, fr. L *volumen* roll, scroll, fr. *volvere* to roll] **1** : a series of printed sheets bound typically in book form; *also* : an arbitrary number of issues of a periodical **2** : space occupied as measured by cubic units ⟨the ∼ of a cylinder⟩ **3** : sufficient matter to fill a book ⟨her glance spoke ∼s⟩ **4** : AMOUNT ⟨increasing ∼ of business⟩ **5** : the degree of loudness of a sound ♦ **Synonyms** BODY, BULK, MASS

vo·lu·mi·nous \və-'lü-mə-nəs\ *adj* : having or marked by great volume or bulk : LARGE — **vo·lu·mi·nous·ly** *adv* — **vo·lu·mi·nous·ness** *n*

¹vol·un·tary \\'vä-lən-ˌter-ē\ *adj* **1** : done, made, or given freely and without compulsion ⟨a ∼ sacrifice⟩ **2** : done on purpose : INTENTIONAL ⟨∼ manslaughter⟩ **3** : of, relating to, or regulated by the will ⟨∼ behavior⟩ **4** : having power of free choice **5** : provided or supported by voluntary action ⟨a ∼ organization⟩ ♦ **Synonyms** DELIBERATE, WILLFUL, WILLING, WITTING — **vol·un·tar·i·ly** \ˌvä-lən-'ter-ə-lē\ *adv*

²voluntary *n, pl* **-tar·ies** : an organ solo played in a religious service

voluntary muscle *n* : muscle (as most striated muscle) under voluntary control

¹vol·un·teer \ˌvä-lən-'tir\ *n* **1** : a person who voluntarily undertakes a service or duty **2** : a plant growing spontaneously esp. from seeds lost from a previous crop

²volunteer *vb* **1** : to offer or give voluntarily **2** : to offer oneself as a volunteer

vo·lup·tu·ary \və-'ləp-chə-ˌwer-ē\ *n, pl* **-ar·ies** : a person whose chief interest in life is the indulgence of sensual appetites

vo·lup·tu·ous \-chə-wəs\ *adj* **1** : giving sensual gratification **2** : given to or spent in enjoyment of luxury or pleasure ♦ **Synonyms** LUXURIOUS, EPICUREAN, SENSUOUS — **vo·lup·tu·ous·ly** *adv* — **vo·lup·tu·ous·ness** *n*

vo·lute \və-'lüt\ *n* : a spiral or scroll-shaped decoration

¹vom·it \\'vä-mət\ *n* : an act or instance of throwing up the contents of the stomach through the mouth; *also* : the matter thrown up

²vomit *vb* **1** : to throw up the contents of the stomach through the mouth **2** : to belch forth : GUSH

voo·doo \\'vü-dü\ *n, pl* **voodoos 1** : a religion that is derived from African polytheism and is practiced chiefly in Haiti **2** : a person who deals in spells and necromancy; *also* : ¹SPELL 1 **3** : a charm used in voodoo — **voodoo** *adj*

voo·doo·ism \-ˌi-zəm\ *n* **1** : VOODOO 1 **2** : the practice of witchcraft

vo·ra·cious \vȯ-'rā-shəs, və-\ *adj* **1** : having a huge appetite : RAVENOUS **2** : very eager ⟨a ∼ reader⟩ ♦ **Synonyms** GLUTTONOUS, RAVENING, RAPACIOUS — **vo·ra·cious·ly** *adv* — **vo·ra·cious·ness** *n* — **vo·rac·i·ty** \-'ra-sə-tē\ *n*

vor·tex \\'vȯr-ˌteks\ *n, pl* **vor·ti·ces** \'vȯr-tə-ˌsēz\ *also* **vor·tex·es** \'vȯr-ˌtek-səz\ : WHIRLPOOL; *also* : something resembling a whirlpool

vo·ta·ry \\'vō-tə-rē\ *n, pl* **-ries 1** : ENTHUSIAST, DEVOTEE; *also* : a devoted adherent or admirer **2** : a devout or zealous worshiper

¹vote \\'vōt\ *n* [ME (Sc), fr. L *votum* vow, wish, fr. *vovēre* to vow] **1** : a choice or opinion of a person or body of persons expressed usu. by a ballot, spoken word, or raised hand; *also* : the ballot, word, or gesture used to express a choice or opinion **2** : the decision reached by voting **3** : the right of suffrage **4** : a group of voters with some common characteristics ⟨the big city ∼⟩ — **vote·less** *adj*

²vote *vb* **vot·ed; vot·ing 1** : to cast a vote **2** : to elect, decide, pass, defeat, grant, or make legal by a vote **3** : to declare by general agreement **4** : to offer as a suggestion : PROPOSE **5** : to cause to vote esp. in a given way — **vot·er** *n*

vo·tive \\'vō-tiv\ *adj* : consisting of or expressing a vow, wish, or desire

vou *abbr* voucher

vouch \\'vauch\ *vb* **1** : PROVE, SUBSTANTIATE **2** : to verify by examining documentary evidence **3** : to give a guarantee **4** : to supply supporting evidence or testimony; *also* : to give personal assurance

vouch·er \'vaù-chər\ *n* **1** : an act of vouching **2** : one that vouches for another **3** : a documentary record of a business transaction **4** : a written affidavit or authorization **5** : a form indicating a credit against future purchases or expenditures

vouch·safe \vaùch-'sāf\ *vb* **vouch·safed; vouch·saf·ing** : to grant or give as or as if a privilege or a special favor

¹**vow** \'vaù\ *n* : a solemn promise or statement; *esp* : one by which a person is bound to an act, service, or condition ⟨marriage ∼*s*⟩

²**vow** *vb* **1** : to make a vow or as a vow **2** : to bind or commit by a vow — **vow·er** *n*

vow·el \'vaù-(ə)l\ *n* **1** : a speech sound produced without obstruction or friction in the mouth **2** : a letter representing such a sound

vox po·pu·li \'väks-'pä-pyə-ˌlī\ *n* [L, voice of the people] : popular sentiment

¹**voy·age** \'vòi-ij\ *n* [ME, *viage, veyage,* fr. AF *veiage,* fr. LL *viaticum,* fr. L, traveling money, fr. neut. of *viaticus* of a journey, fr. *via* way] : a journey esp. by water from one place or country to another

²**voyage** *vb* **voy·aged; voy·ag·ing** : to take or make a voyage — **voy·ag·er** *n*

voya·geur \ˌvòi-ə-'zhər, ˌvwä-yä-\ *n* [CanF] : a person employed by a fur company to transport goods to and from remote stations esp. in the Canadian Northwest

voy·eur \vwä-'yər, vòi-'ər\ *n* **1** : one who obtains sexual pleasure from viewing esp. covertly the nudity or sexual activity of others **2** : an observer of the sordid — **voy·eur·ism** \-ˌi-zəm\ *n* — **voy·eur·is·tic** \ˌvwä-(ˌ)yər-'is-tik, ˌvòi-ər-\ *adj*

VP *abbr* **1** verb phrase **2** vice president

vs *abbr* **1** verse **2** versus

vss *abbr* **1** verses **2** versions

V/STOL *abbr* vertical or short takeoff and landing

Vt *or* **VT** *abbr* Vermont

VTOL *abbr* vertical takeoff and landing

VTR *abbr* videotape recorder

vul·ca·nize \'vəl-kə-ˌnīz\ *vb* **-nized; -niz·ing** : to treat rub-

ber or rubberlike material chemically to give useful properties (as elasticity and strength)

Vulg *abbr* Vulgate

vul·gar \'vəl-gər\ *adj* [ME, fr. L *vulgaris* of the mob, vulgar, fr. *vulgus* mob, common people] **1** : VERNACULAR ⟨the ∼ tongue⟩ **2** : of or relating to the common people : GENERAL, COMMON **3** : lacking cultivation or refinement : BOORISH; *also* : offensive to good taste or refined feelings ✦ **Synonyms** GROSS, OBSCENE, RIBALD, DIRTY, INDECENT, PROFANE — **vul·gar·ly** *adv*

vul·gar·i·an \ˌvəl-'ger-ē-ən\ *n* : a vulgar person

vul·gar·ism \'vəl-gə-ˌri-zəm\ *n* **1** : VULGARITY **2** : a word or expression originated or used chiefly by illiterate persons **3** : a coarse expression : OBSCENITY

vul·gar·i·ty \ˌvəl-'ga-rə-tē\ *n, pl* **-ties 1** : something vulgar **2** : the quality or state of being vulgar

vul·gar·ize \'vəl-gə-ˌrīz\ *vb* **-ized; -iz·ing** : to make vulgar — **vul·gar·i·za·tion** \ˌvəl-gə-rə-'zā-shən\ *n* — **vul·gar·iz·er** \'vəl-gə-ˌrī-zər\ *n*

Vul·gate \'vəl-ˌgāt\ *n* [ML *vulgata,* fr. LL *vulgata editio* edition in general circulation] : a Latin version of the Bible used by the Roman Catholic Church

vul·ner·a·ble \'vəl-nə-rə-bəl\ *adj* **1** : capable of being wounded : susceptible to wounds **2** : open to attack **3** : liable to increased penalties in contract bridge — **vul·ner·a·bil·i·ty** \ˌvəl-nə-rə-'bi-lə-tē\ *n* — **vul·ner·a·bly** \'vəl-nə-rə-blē\ *adv*

vul·pine \'vəl-ˌpīn\ *adj* : of, relating to, or resembling a fox esp. in cunning ⟨∼ charms⟩

vul·ture \'vəl-chər\ *n* **1** : any of various large birds (as a turkey vulture) related to the hawks, eagles, and falcons but having weaker claws and the head usu. naked and living chiefly on carrion **2** : a rapacious person

vul·va \'vəl-və\ *n, pl* **vul·vae** \-ˌvē\ [ME, fr. ML, fr. L *volva, vulva* womb, female genitals] : the external parts of the female genital organs — **vul·val** \'vəl-vəl\ *or* **vul·var** \-vər, -ˌvär\ *adj*

vv *abbr* **1** verses **2** vice versa

VX \'vē-'eks\ *n* : an extremely toxic chemical weapon

vying *pres part of* VIE

¹**w** \'də-bəl-(ˌ)yü\ *n, pl* **w's** *or* **ws** *often cap* : the 23d letter of the English alphabet

²**w** *abbr, often cap* **1** water **2** watt **3** week **4** weight **5** west; western **6** wide; width **7** wife **8** with

W *symbol* [G *Wolfram*] tungsten

WA *abbr* **1** Washington **2** Western Australia

wacky \'wa-kē\ *adj* **wack·i·er; -est** : ECCENTRIC, CRAZY

¹**wad** \'wäd\ *n* **1** : a little mass, bundle, or tuft ⟨∼*s* of clay⟩ **2** : a soft mass of usu. light fibrous material **3** : a pliable plug (as of felt) used to retain a powder charge (as in a cartridge) **4** : a considerable amount (as of money) **5** : a roll of paper money

²**wad** *vb* **wad·ded; wad·ding 1** : to push a wad into ⟨∼ a gun⟩ **2** : to form into a wad **3** : to hold in by a wad ⟨∼ a bullet in a gun⟩ **4** : to stuff or line with a wad : PAD

wad·ding \'wä-diŋ\ *n* **1** : WADS; *also* : material for making wads **2** : a soft mass or sheet of short loose fibers used for stuffing or padding

wad·dle \'wä-dᵊl\ *vb* **wad·dled; wad·dling** : to walk with short steps swaying from side to side like a duck — **wad·dle** *n*

wade \'wäd\ *vb* **wad·ed; wad·ing 1** : to step in or through a medium (as water) more resistant than air **2** : to move or go with difficulty or labor and often with determination ⟨∼ through a dull book⟩ — **wad·able** *or* **wade·able** \'wä-də-bəl\ *adj* — **wade in** *n*

wad·er \'wä-dər\ *n* **1** : one that wades **2** : SHOREBIRD; *also* : WADING BIRD **3** *pl* : a waterproof garment consisting of pants with attached boots for wading

wa·di \'wä-dē\ *n* [Ar *wādī*] : a streambed of southwest Asia and northern Africa that is dry except in the rainy season

wading bird *n* : any of an order of long-legged birds (as sandpipers, cranes, or herons) that wade in water in search of food

wa·fer \'wä-fər\ *n* **1** : a thin crisp cake or cracker **2** : a thin round piece of unleavened bread used in the Eucharist **3** : something (as a piece of candy) that resembles a wafer

¹**waf·fle** \'wä-fəl\ *n* : a soft but crisped cake of batter cooked in a special hinged metal utensil (**waffle iron**)

²**waffle** *vb* **waf·fled; waf·fling** \-f(ə)liŋ\ : to speak or write in a vague or evasive manner

¹**waft** \'wäft, 'waft\ *vb* : to cause to move or go lightly by or as if by the impulse of wind or waves

²**waft** *n* **1** : a slight breeze : PUFF **2** : the act of waving

¹**wag** \'wag\ *vb* **wagged; wag·ging 1** : to sway or swing shortly from side to side or to-and-fro ⟨the dog *wagged* his tail⟩ **2** : to move in chatter or gossip ⟨scandal caused tongues to ∼⟩

²**wag** *n* : an act of wagging : a wagging movement

³**wag** *n* : WIT, JOKER

¹**wage** \'wāj\ *n* **1** : payment for labor or services usu. according to contract **2** *pl* : RECOMPENSE, REWARD

²**wage** *vb* **waged; wag·ing 1** : to engage in : CARRY ON ⟨∼ a war⟩ **2** : to be in process of being waged

¹**wa·ger** \'wā-jər\ *n* **1** : BET, STAKE **2** : something on which bets are laid : GAMBLE

²**wager** *vb* : BET — **wa·ger·er** *n*

wag·gery \'wa-gə-rē\ *n, pl* **-ger·ies** **1** : mischievous merriment : PLEASANTRY **2** : JEST, TRICK
wag·gish \'wa-gish\ *adj* **1** : resembling or characteristic of a wag : MISCHIEVOUS **2** : SPORTIVE, HUMOROUS
wag·gle \'wa-gəl\ *vb* **wag·gled; wag·gling** : to move backward and forward or from side to side : WAG — **waggle** *n*
wag·gon *chiefly Brit var of* WAGON
wag·on \'wa-gən\ *n* **1** : a 4-wheeled vehicle; *esp* : one drawn by animals and used for freight or merchandise **2** : PADDY WAGON **3** : a child's 4-wheeled cart **4** : STATION WAGON

wagon 1

wag·on·er \'wa-gə-nər\ *n* : the driver of a wagon
wag·on·ette \ˌwa-gə-'net\ *n* : a light wagon with two facing seats along the sides behind a cross seat in front
wa·gon–lit \vä-gō^ⁿ-'lē\ *n, pl* **wagons–lits** *or* **wagon–lits** *same or* -'lē\ [F, fr. *wagon* railroad car + *lit* bed] : a railroad sleeping car
wagon train *n* : a column of wagons traveling overland
wag·tail \'wag-ˌtāl\ *n* : any of various slender-bodied mostly Old World birds with a long tail that jerks up and down
wa·hi·ne \wä-'hē-nē, -ˌnä\ *n* **1** : a Polynesian woman **2** : a female surfer
wa·hoo \'wä-ˌhü\ *n, pl* **wahoos** : a large vigorous food and sport fish related to the mackerel and found in warm seas
waif \'wāf\ *n* **1** : something found without an owner and esp. by chance **2** : a stray person or animal; *esp* : a homeless child
wail \'wāl\ *vb* **1** : LAMENT, WEEP **2** : to make a sound suggestive of a mournful cry **3** : COMPLAIN — **wail** *n*
wail·ful \-fəl\ *adj* : SORROWFUL, MOURNFUL ✦ *Synonyms* MELANCHOLY, DOLEFUL, LUGUBRIOUS, LAMENTABLE, PLAINTIVE, WOEFUL — **wail·ful·ly** *adv*
wain \'wān\ *n* : a large heavy farm wagon
wain·scot \'wän-skət, -ˌskōt, -ˌskät\ *n* **1** : a usu. paneled wooden lining of an interior wall of a room **2** : the lower part of an interior wall when finished differently from the rest — **wainscot** *vb*
wain·scot·ing *or* **wain·scot·ting** \-ˌskō-tiŋ, -ˌskä-, -skə-\ *n* : material for a wainscot; *also* : WAINSCOT
waist \'wāst\ *n* **1** : the narrowed part of the body between the chest and hips **2** : a part resembling the human waist esp. in narrowness or central position 〈the ~ of a ship〉 **3** : a garment or part of a garment (as a blouse or bodice) for the upper part of the body
waist·band \-ˌband\ *n* : a band (as on pants or a skirt) that fits around the waist
waist·coat \'wes-kət, 'wāst-ˌkōt\ *n, chiefly Brit* : VEST 1
waist·line \'wāst-ˌlīn\ *n* **1** : a line around the waist at its narrowest part; *also* : the length of this **2** : the line at which the bodice and skirt of a dress meet
¹wait \'wāt\ *vb* **1** : to remain inactive in readiness or expectation : AWAIT 〈~ for orders〉 **2** : to delay serving (a meal) **3** : to act as attendant or servant 〈~ on customers〉 **4** : to attend as a waiter : SERVE 〈~ tables〉 〈~ at a banquet〉 **5** : to be ready
²wait *n* **1** : a position of concealment usu. with intent to attack or surprise 〈lie in ~〉 **2** : an act or period of waiting
wait·er \'wā-tər\ *n* **1** : one that waits on another; *esp* : a person who waits tables **2** : TRAY
waiting game *n* : a strategy in which one or more participants withhold action in the hope of an opportunity for more effective action later
waiting room *n* : a room (as at a doctor's office) for the use of persons who are waiting
wait·per·son \'wāt-ˌpər-sən\ *n* : a waiter or waitress
wait·ress \'wā-trəs\ *n* : a woman who waits tables
waive \'wāv\ *vb* **waived; waiv·ing** [ME *weiven* to decline, reject, give up, fr. AF *waiver, gaiver,* fr. *waif* lost, stray] **1** : to give up claim to 〈*waived* his right to a trial〉 **2** : POSTPONE

waiv·er \'wā-vər\ *n* : the act of waiving right, claim, or privilege; *also* : a document containing a declaration of such an act
¹wake \'wāk\ *vb* **woke** \'wōk\ *also* **waked** \'wākt\; **wo·ken** \'wō-kən\ *also* **waked** *or* **woke; wak·ing** **1** : to be or remain awake; *esp* : to keep watch (as over a corpse) **2** : AWAKE, AWAKEN 〈the baby *woke* up early〉
²wake *n* **1** : the state of being awake **2** : a watch held over the body of a dead person prior to burial
³wake *n* : the track left by a ship in the water; *also* : a track left behind
wake·board \'wāk-ˌbórd\ *n* : a short board with foot bindings on which a rider is towed by a motorboat across its wake — **wake·board·er** *n* — **wake·board·ing** *n*
wake·ful \'wāk-fəl\ *adj* : not sleeping or able to sleep : SLEEPLESS, ALERT — **wake·ful·ness** *n*
wak·en \'wā-kən\ *vb* : WAKE
wake–rob·in \'wāk-ˌrä-bən\ *n* : TRILLIUM
wak·ing \'wā-kiŋ\ *adj* : passed in a conscious or alert state 〈every ~ hour〉
wale \'wāl\ *n* : a ridge esp. on cloth; *also* : the texture esp. of a fabric
¹walk \'wók\ *vb* [partly fr. ME *walken,* fr. OE *wealcan* to roll, toss and partly fr. ME *walkien,* fr. OE *wealcian* to roll up, muffle up] **1** : to move or cause to move on foot usu. at a natural unhurried gait 〈~ to town〉 〈~ a horse〉 **2** : to pass over, through, or along by walking 〈~ the streets〉 **3** : to perform or accomplish by walking 〈~ guard〉 **4** : to follow a course of action or way of life 〈~ humbly in the sight of God〉 **5** : WALK OUT **6** : to receive a base on balls; *also* : to give a base on balls to — **walk·er** *n*
²walk *n* **1** : a going on foot 〈go for a ~〉 **2** : a place, path, or course for walking **3** : distance to be walked 〈a quarter-mile ~ from here〉 **4** : manner of living : CONDUCT, BEHAVIOR **5** : social or economic status 〈various ~s of life〉 **6** : manner of walking : GAIT; *esp* : a slow 4-beat gait of a horse **7** : BASE ON BALLS
walk·away \'wó-kə-ˌwä\ *n* : an easily won contest
walk·ie-talk·ie \ˌwó-kē-'tó-kē\ *n* : a small portable radio transmitting and receiving set
¹walk–in \'wók-ˌin\ *adj* : large enough to be walked into 〈a ~ refrigerator〉
²walk–in *n* **1** : an easy election victory **2** : one that walks in
walking papers *n pl* : DISMISSAL, DISCHARGE
walking stick *n* **1** : a stick used in walking **2** : STICK INSECT; *esp* : one of the U.S. and Canada
walk–on \'wók-ˌòn, -ˌän\ *n* : a small part in a dramatic production
walk–out \-ˌaút\ *n* **1** : a labor strike **2** : the action of leaving a meeting or organization as an expression of disapproval
walk out *vb* **1** : to leave suddenly often as an expression of disapproval **2** : to go on strike
walk–over \-ˌō-vər\ *n* : a one-sided contest : an easy victory
walk–up \'wók-ˌəp\ *n* : a building or apartment house without an elevator — **walk–up** *adj*
walk·way \-ˌwä\ *n* : a passage for walking
¹wall \'wól\ *n* [ME, fr. OE *weall,* fr. L *vallum* rampart, fr. *vallus* stake, palisade] **1** : a structure (as of stone or brick) intended for defense or security or for enclosing something **2** : one of the upright enclosing parts of a building or room **3** : the inside surface of a cavity or container 〈the ~ of a boiler〉 **4** : something like a wall in appearance, function, or effect 〈a tariff ~〉 — **walled** \'wóld\ *adj*
²wall *vb* **1** : to provide, separate, or surround with or as if with a wall 〈~ in a garden〉 **2** : to close (an opening) with or as if with a wall 〈~ up a door〉
wal·la·by \'wä-lə-bē\ *n, pl* **wallabies** *also* **wallaby** : any of various small or medium-sized kangaroos
wall·board \'wól-ˌbórd\ *n* : a structural material (as of wood pulp or plaster) made in large sheets and used for sheathing interior walls and ceilings
wal·let \'wä-lət\ *n* **1** : a bag or sack for carrying things on a journey **2** : a pocketbook with compartments (as for personal papers and usu. unfolded money) : BILLFOLD
wall·eye \'wól-ˌī\ *n* **1** : an eye with a whitish iris or an opaque white cornea **2** : a large vigorous No. American

food and sport fish related to the perches — **wall·eyed** \-ˌlīd\ *adj*

wall·flow·er \'wȯl-ˌflau̇(-ə)r\ *n* **1** : any of several Old World herbs related to the mustards; *esp* : one with showy fragrant flowers **2** : a person who usu. from shyness or unpopularity remains alone (as at a dance)

Wal·loon \wä-'lün\ *n* : a member of a people of southern and southeastern Belgium and adjacent parts of France — **Walloon** *adj*

¹**wal·lop** \'wä-ləp\ *vb* **1** : to beat soundly : TROUNCE **2** : to hit hard : SOCK ♦ **Synonyms** BATTER, BEAT, LAMBASTE, POUND, PUMMEL, THRASH

²**wallop** *n* **1** : a powerful blow or impact **2** : the ability to hit hard **3** : emotional, sensory, or psychological force : IMPACT ⟨a story with a ∼⟩

wal·lop·ing \'wä-lə-piṅ\ *adj* **1** : LARGE, WHOPPING **2** : exceptionally fine or impressive

¹**wal·low** \'wä-lō\ *vb* **1** : to roll oneself about sluggishly in or as if in deep mud ⟨hogs ∼*ing* in the mire⟩ **2** : to indulge oneself excessively ⟨∼ in luxury⟩ **3** : to become or remain helpless ⟨∼ in ignorance⟩ ♦ **Synonyms** BASK, INDULGE, LUXURIATE, REVEL, WELTER

²**wallow** *n* : a muddy or dust-filled area where animals wallow

wall·pa·per \'wȯl-ˌpā-pər\ *n* : decorative paper for the walls of a room — **wallpaper** *vb*

wall–to–wall *adj* **1** : covering the entire floor ⟨*wall-to-wall* carpeting⟩ **2** : covering or filling one entire space or time ⟨crowds of *wall-to-wall* people⟩

wal·nut \'wȯl-(ˌ)nət\ *n* [ME *walnot*, fr. OE *wealhhnutu*, lit., foreign nut, fr. *Wealh* Welshman, foreigner + *hnutu* nut] **1** : a nut with a furrowed usu. rough shell and an adherent husk from any of a genus of trees related to the hickories; *esp* : the large edible nut of a Eurasian tree **2** : a tree that bears walnuts **3** : the usu. reddish to dark brown wood of a walnut used esp. in cabinetwork and veneers

wal·rus \'wȯl-rəs, 'wäl-\ *n, pl* **walrus** *or* **wal·rus·es** : a large mammal of arctic waters that is related to the seals and has long ivory tusks

walrus

¹**waltz** \'wȯlts\ *n* [G *Walzer*, fr. *walzen* to roll, dance] **1** : a gliding dance done to music having three beats to the measure **2** : music for or suitable for waltzing

²**waltz** *vb* **1** : to dance a waltz **2** : to move or advance easily, successfully, or conspicuously ⟨he ∼*ed* off with the championship⟩ — **waltz·er** *n*

wam·ble \'wäm-bəl\ *vb* **wam·bled; wam·bling** : to progress unsteadily or with a lurching shambling gait

Wam·pa·no·ag \ˌwäm-pə-'nō-(ˌ)ag; ˌwȯm-\ *n, pl* **Wampanoag** *or* **Wampanoags** [Narragansett, lit., easterners] : a member of an American Indian people of parts of Rhode Island and Massachusetts

wam·pum \'wäm-pəm\ *n* [short for *wampumpeag*, fr. Massachuset (an Algonquian Indian language) *wampompeag*, fr. *wampan* white + *api* string + *-ag*, pl. suffix] **1** : beads made of shells strung in strands, belts, or sashes and used by No. American Indians as money and ornaments **2** *slang* : MONEY

wan \'wän\ *adj* **wan·ner; wan·nest 1** : SICKLY, PALLID; *also* : FEEBLE **2** : DIM, FAINT **3** : LANGUID ⟨a ∼ smile⟩ ♦ **Synonyms** ASHEN, BLANCHED, DOUGHY, LIVID, PALE, WAXEN — **wan·ly** *adv* — **wan·ness** *n*

wand \'wänd\ *n* **1** : a slender staff carried in a procession **2** : the staff of a fairy, diviner, or magician

wan·der \'wän-dər\ *vb* **1** : to move about aimlessly or without a fixed course or goal : RAMBLE **2** : to go astray in conduct or thought; *esp* : to become delirious ♦ **Synonyms** GAD, GALLIVANT, MEANDER, RANGE, ROAM, ROVE — **wan·der·er** *n*

wandering Jew *n* : either of two trailing or creeping plants cultivated for their showy and often white-striped foliage

wan·der·lust \'wän-dər-ˌləst\ *n* : strong longing for or impulse toward wandering

¹**wane** \'wän\ *vb* **waned; wan·ing 1** : to grow gradually smaller or less ⟨the full moon ∼*s* to new⟩ ⟨his strength *waned*⟩ **2** : to lose power, prosperity, or influence **3** : to draw near an end ⟨summer is *waning*⟩ ♦ **Synonyms** ABATE, EBB, MODERATE, RELENT, SLACKEN, SUBSIDE

²**wane** *n* : a waning (as in size or power); *also* : a period in which something is waning

wan·gle \'waṅ-gəl\ *vb* **wan·gled; wan·gling 1** : to obtain by sly or devious means; *also* : to use trickery or questionable means to achieve an end **2** : MANIPULATE; *also* : FINAGLE

wan·na·be *also* **wan·na·bee** \'wä-nə-ˌbē\ *n* : a person who wants or aspires to be someone or something else or who tries to look or act like someone else

¹**want** \'wȯnt, 'wänt\ *vb* **1** : to fail to possess : LACK ⟨they ∼ the necessities of life⟩ **2** : to feel or suffer the need of **3** : NEED, REQUIRE ⟨the house ∼*s* painting⟩ **4** : to desire earnestly : WISH

²**want** *n* **1** : a lack of a required or usual amount : SHORTAGE **2** : dire need : DESTITUTION **3** : something wanted : DESIRE **4** : personal defect : FAULT

¹**want·ing** \'wȯn-tiṅ, 'wän-\ *adj* **1** : not present or in evidence : ABSENT **2** : falling below standards or expectations **3** : lacking in ability or capacity : DEFICIENT ⟨∼ in common sense⟩

²**wanting** *prep* **1** : LESS, MINUS ⟨a month ∼ two days⟩ **2** : WITHOUT ⟨a book ∼ a cover⟩

¹**wan·ton** \'wȯn-tᵊn, 'wän-\ *adj* [ME, undisciplined, fr. *wan*-deficient, wrong + *towen*, pp. of *teen* to draw, train, discipline] **1** : UNCHASTE, LEWD, LUSTFUL; *also* : SENSUAL **2** : having no regard for justice or for other persons' feelings, rights, or safety : MERCILESS, INHUMANE ⟨∼ cruelty⟩ **3** : having no just cause ⟨a ∼ attack⟩ — **wan·ton·ly** *adv* — **wan·ton·ness** *n*

²**wanton** *n* : a wanton individual; *esp* : a lewd or immoral person

³**wanton** *vb* **1** : to be wanton : act wantonly **2** : to pass or waste wantonly

wa·pi·ti \'wä-pə-tē\ *n, pl* **wapiti** *or* **wapitis** : ELK 2

¹**war** \'wȯr\ *n* **1** : a state or period of usu. open and declared armed fighting between states or nations **2** : the art or science of warfare **3** : a state of hostility, conflict, or antagonism **4** : a struggle between opposing forces or for a particular end ⟨∼ against disease⟩ — **war·less** \-ləs\ *adj*

²**war** *vb* **warred; war·ring** : to engage in warfare : be in conflict

³**war** *abbr* warrant

¹**war·ble** \'wȯr-bəl\ *n* **1** : a melodious succession of low pleasing sounds **2** : a musical trill

²**warble** *vb* **war·bled; war·bling 1** : to sing or utter in a trilling manner or with variations **2** : to express by or as if by warbling

³**warble** *n* : a swelling under the skin esp. of the back of cattle, horses, and wild mammals caused by the maggot of a fly (**warble fly**); *also* : its maggot

war·bler \'wȯr-blər\ *n* **1** : SONGSTER **2** : any of various small slender-billed chiefly Old World songbirds related to the thrushes and noted for their singing **3** : any of numerous small bright-colored insect-eating American birds with a usu. weak and unmusical song

war·bon·net \'wȯr-ˌbä-nət\ *n* : a feathered American Indian ceremonial headdress

war crime *n* : a crime (genocide) committed during or in connection with war

war cry *n* **1** : a cry used by fighters in war **2** : a slogan used esp. to rally people to a cause

¹**ward** \'wȯrd\ *n* **1** : a guarding or being under guard or guardianship; *esp* : CUSTODY **2** : a body of guards **3** : a division of a prison **4** : a division in a hospital **5** : a division of a city for electoral or administrative purposes **6** : a person (as a child) under the protection of a guardian or a law court **7** : a person or body of persons under the protection or tutelage of a government **8** : a means of defense : PROTECTION

²**ward** *vb* : to turn aside : DEFLECT — usu. used with *off* ⟨∼ off a blow⟩

¹**-ward** *also* **-wards** *adj suffix* **1** : that moves, tends, faces,

or is directed toward ⟨wind*ward*⟩ **2** : that occurs or is situated in the direction of ⟨sea*ward*⟩

²-ward *or* **-wards** *adv suffix*   **1** : in a (specified) direction ⟨up*wards*⟩ ⟨after*ward*⟩   **2** : toward a (specified) point, position, or area ⟨sky*ward*⟩

war dance *n* : a dance performed (as by American Indians) before going to war or in celebration of victory

war·den \'wȯr-dᵊn\ *n*   **1** : GUARDIAN, KEEPER   **2** : the governor of a town, district, or fortress   **3** : an official charged with special supervisory or enforcement duties ⟨game ∼⟩ ⟨air raid ∼⟩   **4** : an official in charge of the operation of a prison   **5** : one of two ranking lay officers of an Episcopal parish   **6** : any of various British college officials

ward·er \'wȯr-dər\ *n* : WATCHMAN, WARDEN

ward heel·er \-,hē-lər\ *n* : a local worker for a political boss

ward·robe \'wȯr-,drōb\ *n* [ME *warderobe*, fr. AF *warderobe, garderobe,* fr. *warder, garder* to guard + *robe* robe]   **1** : a room or closet where clothes are kept; *also* : CLOTHES-PRESS   **2** : a collection of wearing apparel ⟨his summer ∼⟩

ward·room \-,drüm, -,drŭm\ *n* : the dining area for officers aboard a warship

ward·ship \'wȯrd-,ship\ *n*   **1** : GUARDIANSHIP   **2** : the state of being under care of a guardian

ware \'wer\ *n*   **1** : manufactured articles or products of art or craft : GOODS ⟨glass*ware*⟩   **2** : an article of merchandise ⟨a peddler hawking his ∼*s*⟩   **3** : items (as dishes) of fired clay : POTTERY

ware·house \-,haús\ *n* : a place for the storage of merchandise or commodities : STOREHOUSE — **warehouse** *vb* — **ware·house·man** \-mən\ *n* — **ware·hous·er** \-,haú-zər, -sər\ *n*

ware·room \'wer-,rüm, -,rŭm\ *n* : a room in which goods are exhibited for sale

war·fare \'wȯr-,fer\ *n*   **1** : military operations between enemies : WAR; *also* : an activity undertaken by one country to weaken or destroy another ⟨economic ∼⟩   **2** : STRUGGLE, CONFLICT

war·fa·rin \'wȯr-fə-rən\ *n* : an anticoagulant compound used as a rodent poison and in medicine

war·head \'wȯr-,hed\ *n* : the section of a missile containing the charge

war·horse \-,hȯrs\ *n*   **1** : a horse for use in war   **2** : a veteran soldier or public person (as a politician)   **3** : a musical composition that is often performed

war·like \-,līk\ *adj*   **1** : fond of war ⟨∼ peoples⟩   **2** : of, relating to, or useful in war : MILITARY, MARTIAL ⟨∼ supplies⟩   **3** : befitting or characteristic of war or of soldiers ⟨∼ attitudes⟩

war·lock \-,läk\ *n* [ME *warloghe*, fr. OE *wǣrloga* one that breaks faith, the Devil, fr. *wǣr* faith, troth + *-loga* (fr. *lēogan* to lie)] : SORCERER, WIZARD

war·lord \-,lȯrd\ *n*   **1** : a high military leader   **2** : a military commander exercising local civil power by force ⟨former Chinese ∼*s*⟩

¹warm \'wȯrm\ *adj*   **1** : having or giving out heat to a moderate or adequate degree ⟨∼ milk⟩ ⟨a ∼ stove⟩   **2** : serving to retain heat ⟨∼ clothes⟩   **3** : feeling or inducing sensations of heat ⟨∼ from exercise⟩ ⟨a ∼ climb⟩   **4** : showing or marked by strong feeling : ARDENT ⟨∼ support⟩   **5** : marked by tense excitement or hot anger ⟨a ∼ campaign⟩   **6** : giving a pleasant impression of warmth, cheerfulness, or friendliness ⟨∼ colors⟩ ⟨a ∼ tone of voice⟩   **7** : marked by or tending toward injury, distress, or pain ⟨made things ∼ for the enemy⟩   **8** : newly made : FRESH ⟨a ∼ scent⟩   **9** : near to a goal ⟨getting ∼ in a search⟩ — **warm·ly** *adv*

²warm *vb*   **1** : to make or become warm   **2** : to give a feeling of warmth or vitality to   **3** : to experience feelings of affection or pleasure ⟨she ∼*ed* to her guest⟩   **4** : to reheat for eating ⟨∼*ed* over the roast⟩   **5** : to make ready for operation or performance by preliminary exercise or operation ⟨∼ up the motor⟩   **6** : to become increasingly ardent, interested, or competent ⟨the speaker ∼*ed* to his topic⟩ — **warm·er** *n*

warm–blood·ed \-'blə-dəd\ *adj* : able to maintain a relatively high and constant body temperature relatively independent of that of the surroundings

warmed–over \'wȯrmd-'ō-vər\ *adj*   **1** : REHEATED ⟨∼ cabbage⟩   **2** : not fresh or new ⟨∼ ideas⟩

warm front *n* : an advancing edge of a warm air mass

warm-heart·ed \'wȯrm-'här-təd\ *adj* : marked by warmth of feeling : CORDIAL — **warm·heart·ed·ness** *n*

warming pan *n* : a long-handled covered pan filled with live coals and formerly used to warm a bed

war·mon·ger \'wȯr-,məŋ-gər, -,mäŋ-\ *n* : one who urges or attempts to stir up war — **war·mon·ger·ing** \-g(ə-)riŋ\ *n*

warmth \'wȯrmth\ *n*   **1** : the quality or state of being warm   **2** : ZEAL, ARDOR, FERVOR

warm up *vb* : to engage in exercise or practice esp. before entering a game or contest — **warm–up** \'wȯrm-,əp\ *n*

warn \'wȯrn\ *vb*   **1** : to put on guard : CAUTION; *also* : ADMONISH, COUNSEL   **2** : to notify esp. in advance : INFORM   **3** : to order to go or keep away

¹warn·ing \'wȯr-niŋ\ *n*   **1** : the act of warning : the state of being warned   **2** : something that warns or serves to warn ⟨a tornado ∼⟩

²warning *adj* : serving as an alarm, signal, summons, or admonition ⟨a ∼ bell⟩ — **warn·ing·ly** *adv*

¹warp \'wȯrp\ *n*   **1** : the lengthwise threads on a loom or in a woven fabric   **2** : a twist out of a true plane or straight line ⟨a ∼ in a board⟩

²warp *vb* [ME, fr. OE *weorpan* to throw]   **1** : to turn or twist out of shape; *also* : to become so twisted   **2** : to lead astray : PERVERT; *also* : FALSIFY, DISTORT

war paint *n* : paint put on the face and body by American Indians as a sign of going to war

war·path \'wȯr-,path, -,päth\ *n* : the course taken by a party of American Indians going on a hostile expedition — **on the warpath** : ready to fight or argue

war·plane \-,plān\ *n* : a military airplane; *esp* : one armed for combat

warp speed *n* : the highest possible speed

¹war·rant \'wȯr-ənt, 'wär-\ *n*   **1** : AUTHORIZATION; *also* : JUSTIFICATION, GROUND   **2** : evidence (as a document) of authorization; *esp* : a legal writ authorizing an officer to take action (as in making an arrest, seizure, or search)   **3** : a certificate of appointment issued to an officer of lower rank than a commissioned officer

²warrant *vb*   **1** : to guarantee security or immunity to : SECURE   **2** : to declare or maintain positively ⟨I ∼ this is so⟩   **3** : to assure (a person) of the truth of what is said   **4** : to guarantee to be as it appears or as it is represented ⟨∼ goods as of the first quality⟩   **5** : SANCTION, AUTHORIZE   **6** : to give proof of : ATTEST; *also* : GUARANTEE   **7** : JUSTIFY ⟨his need ∼*s* the expenditure⟩

warrant officer *n*   **1** : an officer in the armed forces ranking next below a commissioned officer   **2** : a commissioned officer ranking below an ensign in the navy or coast guard and below a second lieutenant in the marine corps

war·ran·ty \'wȯr-ən-tē, 'wär-\ *n, pl* **-ties** : an expressed or implied statement that some situation or thing is as it appears to be or is represented to be; *esp* : a usu. written guarantee of the integrity of a product and of the maker's responsibility for the repair or replacement of defective parts

war·ren \'wȯr-ən, 'wär-\ *n*   **1** : an area where rabbits breed; *also* : a structure where rabbits are bred or kept   **2** : a crowded tenement or district

war·rior \'wȯr-yər; 'wȯr-ē-ər, 'wär-\ *n* : a man engaged or experienced in warfare

war·ship \'wȯr-,ship\ *n* : a naval vessel

wart \'wȯrt\ *n*   **1** : a small usu. horny projecting growth on the skin; *esp* : one caused by a virus   **2** : a protuberance resembling a wart (as on a plant) — **warty** *adj*

wart·hog \'wȯrt-,hȯg, -,häg\ *n* : a wild African hog that has large tusks and in the male two pairs of rough warty protuberances below the eyes

warthog

war·time \'wȯr-ˌtīm\ *n* : a period during which a war is in progress

wary \'wer-ē\ *adj* **war·i·er; -est** : very cautious; *esp* : careful in guarding against danger or deception — **war·i·ly** \'wer-ə-lē\ *adv* — **war·i·ness** \'wer-ē-nəs\ *n*

was *past 1st & 3d sing of* BE

wa·sa·bi \'wä-sə-bē; wä-'sä-\ *n* [Jp] : a condiment prepared from the ground greenish root of an Asian herb and similar in flavor and use to horseradish; *also* : the herb or its root

¹wash \'wȯsh, 'wäsh\ *vb* **1** : to clean with water and usu. soap or detergent ⟨∼ clothes⟩ ⟨∼ your hands⟩ **2** : to wet thoroughly : DRENCH **3** : to flow along the border of ⟨waves ∼ the shore⟩ **4** : to pour or flow in a stream or current **5** : to move or remove by or as if by the action of water **6** : to cover or daub lightly with a liquid (as whitewash) **7** : to run water over (as gravel or ore) in order to separate valuable matter from refuse ⟨∼ sand for gold⟩ **8** : to undergo laundering ⟨a dress that doesn't ∼ well⟩ **9** : to stand a test ⟨that story will not ∼⟩ **10** : to be worn away by water

²wash *n* **1** : the act or process or an instance of washing or being washed **2** : articles to be washed or being washed **3** : a thin coat of paint (as watercolor) **4** : the flow or action of a mass of water (as a wave) **5** : worthless esp. liquid waste : REFUSE, SWILL **6** : erosion by waves (as of the sea) **7** : a disturbance in a fluid (as water or the air) caused by the passage of a wing or propeller **8** *West* : the dry bed of a stream

³wash *adj* : WASHABLE

Wash *abbr* Washington

wash·able \'wȯ-shə-bəl, 'wä-\ *adj* : capable of being washed without damage — **wash·abil·i·ty** \ˌwȯ-shə-'bi-lə-tē, ˌwä-\ *n*

wash–and–wear *adj* : of, relating to, or being a fabric or garment that needs little or no ironing after washing

wash·ba·sin \'wȯsh-ˌbā-sᵊn, 'wäsh-\ *n* : WASHBOWL

wash·board \-ˌbȯrd\ *n* : a grooved board to scrub clothes on

wash·bowl \-ˌbōl\ *n* : a large bowl for water for washing hands and face

wash·cloth \-ˌklȯth\ *n* : a cloth used for washing one's face and body

washed–out \'wȯsht-'aút, 'wäsht-\ *adj* **1** : faded in color **2** : EXHAUSTED ⟨felt ∼ after working all night⟩

washed–up \-'əp\ *adj* : no longer successful, popular, skillful, or needed

wash·er \'wȯ-shər, 'wä-\ *n* **1** : a ring or perforated plate used around a bolt or screw to ensure tightness or relieve friction **2** : one that washes; *esp* : a machine for washing

wash·er·wom·an \-ˌwù-mən\ *n* : a woman whose occupation is washing clothes

wash·ing \'wȯ-shiŋ, 'wä-\ *n* **1** : material obtained by washing **2** : articles washed or to be washed

washing soda *n* : SODIUM CARBONATE

Wash·ing·ton's Birthday \'wȯ-shiŋ-tənz-, 'wä-\ *n* : the 3d Monday in February observed as a legal holiday

wash·out \'wȯsh-ˌaút, 'wäsh-\ *n* **1** : the washing away of earth (as from a road); *also* : a place where earth is washed away **2** : a complete failure

wash·room \-ˌrüm, -ˌrúm\ *n* : BATHROOM

wash·stand \-ˌstand\ *n* **1** : a stand holding articles needed for washing face and hands **2** : LAVATORY 1

wash·tub \-ˌtəb\ *n* : a tub for washing or soaking clothes

wash·wom·an \'wȯsh-ˌwù-mən, 'wäsh-\ *n* : WASHER-WOMAN

washy \'wȯ-shē, 'wä-\ *adj* **wash·i·er; -est** **1** : WEAK, WATERY **2** : PALLID **3** : lacking in vigor, individuality, or definiteness

wasp \'wäsp, 'wȯsp\ *n* : any of numerous social or solitary winged insects related to the bees and ants with biting mouthparts and in females and workers an often formidable sting

WASP *or* **Wasp** *n* [*white Anglo-Saxon Protestant*] : an American of northern European and esp. British ancestry and of Protestant background

wasp·ish \'wäs-pish, 'wȯs-\ *adj* **1** : SNAPPISH, IRRITABLE **2** : resembling a wasp in form; *esp* : slightly built ✦ **Synonyms** FRACTIOUS, FRETFUL, HUFFY, PEEVISH, PETULANT, QUERULOUS

wasp waist *n* : a very slender waist

¹was·sail \'wä-səl, wä-'säl\ *n* [ME *wæs hæil, washayl,* fr. ON *ves heill* be well] **1** : an early English toast to someone's health **2** : a hot drink made with wine, beer, or cider, spices, sugar, and usu. baked apples and traditionally served at Christmas **3** : riotous drinking : REVELRY

²wassail *vb* **1** : CAROUSE **2** : to drink to the health of — **was·sail·er** *n*

Was·ser·mann test \'wä-sər-mən-, 'vä-\ *n* : a blood test for the detection of syphilis

wast·age \'wā-stij\ *n* : WASTE 3

¹waste \'wāst\ *n* **1** : a sparsely settled or barren region : DESERT; *also* : uncultivated land **2** : the act or an instance of wasting : the state of being wasted **3** : gradual loss or decrease by use, wear, or decay **4** : material left over, rejected, or thrown away; *also* : an unwanted by-product of a manufacturing or chemical process **5** : refuse (as garbage) that accumulates about habitations **6** : material (as feces) produced but not used by a living organism — **waste·ful** \-fəl\ *adj* — **waste·ful·ly** *adv* — **waste·ful·ness** *n*

²waste *vb* **wast·ed; wast·ing** **1** : DEVASTATE **2** : to wear away or diminish gradually : CONSUME **3** : to spend or use carelessly or uselessly : SQUANDER **4** : to lose or cause to lose weight, strength, or energy ⟨*wasting* away from fever⟩ **5** : to become diminished in bulk or substance : DWINDLE ✦ **Synonyms** DEPREDATE, DESOLATE, DESPOIL, RAVAGE, SPOIL, STRIP — **wast·er** *n*

³waste *adj* **1** : being wild and uninhabited : BARREN, DESOLATE; *also* : UNCULTIVATED **2** : being in a ruined condition **3** : discarded as worthless after being used ⟨∼ water⟩ **4** : excreted from or stored in inert form in a living organism as a by-product of vital activity ⟨∼ matter from birds⟩

waste·bas·ket \'wāst-ˌbas-kət\ *n* : a receptacle for refuse

waste·land \-ˌland, -lənd\ *n* : land that is barren or unfit for cultivation

waste·pa·per \-'pā-pər\ *n* : paper thrown away as used, not needed, or not fit for use

wast·rel \'wā-strəl\ *n* : a person who wastes resources : SPENDTHRIFT

¹watch \'wäch, 'wȯch\ *vb* **1** : to be or stay awake intentionally : keep vigil ⟨∼*ed* by the patient's bedside⟩ ⟨∼ and pray⟩ **2** : to be on the lookout for danger : be on one's guard **3** : to keep guard ⟨∼ outside the door⟩ **4** : OBSERVE ⟨∼ a game⟩ **5** : to keep in view so as to prevent harm or warn of danger ⟨∼ a brush fire carefully⟩ **6** : to keep oneself informed about ⟨∼ his progress⟩ **7** : to lie in wait for esp. so as to take advantage of ⟨∼*ed* her opportunity⟩ — **watch·er** *n*

²watch *n* **1** : the act of keeping awake to guard, protect, or attend; *also* : a state of alert and continuous attention **2** : a public weather alert ⟨a winter storm ∼⟩ **3** : close observation **4** : LOOKOUT, WATCHMAN, GUARD **5** : a period during which a part of a ship's crew is on duty; *also* : the part of a crew on duty during a watch **6** : a portable timepiece carried on the person

watch·band \'wäch-ˌband, 'wȯch-\ *n* : the bracelet or strap of a wristwatch

watch·dog \-ˌdȯg\ *n* **1** : a dog kept to guard property **2** : one that guards or protects

watch·ful \-fəl\ *adj* : steadily attentive and alert esp. to danger : VIGILANT — **watch·ful·ly** *adv* — **watch·ful·ness** *n*

watch·mak·er \-ˌmā-kər\ *n* : a person who makes or repairs watches — **watch·mak·ing** \-ˌmā-kiŋ\ *n*

watch·man \-mən\ *n* : a person assigned to watch : GUARD

watch night *n* : a devotional service lasting until after midnight esp. on New Year's Eve

watch·tow·er \'wäch-ˌtaú-(ə)r, 'wȯch-\ *n* : a tower for a lookout

watch·word \-ˌwərd\ *n* **1** : a secret word used as a signal or sign of recognition **2** : a word or motto used as a slogan or rallying cry

¹wa·ter \'wȯ-tər, 'wä-\ *n* **1** : the liquid that descends as rain and forms rivers, lakes, and seas **2** : a natural mineral water — usu. used in pl. **3** *pl* : the water occupying or flowing in a particular bed; *also* : a band of seawater bordering on and under the control of a country **4** : any of various liquids containing or resembling water; *esp* : a watery fluid (as tears, urine, or sap) formed or circulating in a living organism **5** : a specified degree of thoroughness or completeness ⟨a scoundrel of the first ∼⟩

²**water** *vb* **1** : to supply with or get or take water ⟨~ horses⟩ ⟨the ship ~ed at each port⟩ **2** : to treat (as cloth) so as to give a lustrous appearance in wavy lines **3** : to dilute by or as if by adding water to **4** : to form or secrete water or watery matter ⟨her eyes ~ed⟩ ⟨my mouth ~ed⟩
water bed *n* : a bed whose mattress is a watertight bag filled with water
wa·ter·borne \-ˌbȯrn\ *adj* : supported, carried, or transmitted by water
water buffalo *n* : a common oxlike often domesticated Asian bovine
water chestnut *n* : a whitish crunchy vegetable used esp. in Chinese cooking that is the peeled tuber of a widely cultivated Asian sedge; *also* : the tuber or the sedge itself
water closet *n* : a compartment or room with a toilet bowl : BATHROOM; *also* : a toilet bowl along with its accessories
wa·ter·col·or \ˈwȯ-tər-ˌkə-lər, ˈwä-\ *n* **1** : a paint whose liquid part is water **2** : the art of painting with watercolors **3** : a picture made with watercolors
wa·ter·course \-ˌkȯrs\ *n* : a stream of water; *also* : the bed of a stream
wa·ter·craft \-ˌkraft\ *n* : a craft for water transport : SHIP, BOAT
wa·ter·cress \-ˌkres\ *n* : an aquatic perennial Eurasian cress that is naturalized in the U.S. and has edible leaves used esp. in salads
wa·ter·fall \-ˌfȯl\ *n* : a very steep descent of the water of a stream
wa·ter·fowl \ˈwȯ-tər-ˌfau̇(-ə)l, ˈwä-\ *n, pl* **-fowl** *also* **-fowls** : a bird that frequents water; *esp* : a swimming bird (as a duck) hunted as game
wa·ter·front \-ˌfrənt\ *n* : land or a section of a town fronting or abutting on a body of water
water gap *n* : a pass in a mountain ridge through which a stream runs
water glass *n* : a drinking glass
water hyacinth *n* : a showy floating aquatic plant of tropical America that often clogs waterways (as in the southern U.S.)
watering hole *n* : a place (as a bar) where people gather socially
watering place *n* : a resort that features mineral springs or bathing
water lily *n* : any of various aquatic plants with floating roundish and showy solitary flowers
wa·ter·line \ˈwȯ-tər-ˌlīn, ˈwä-\ *n* : a line that marks the level of the surface of water on something (as a ship or the shore)
wa·ter·logged \-ˌlȯgd, -ˌlägd\ *adj* : so filled or soaked with water as to be heavy or unmanageable ⟨a ~ boat⟩
wa·ter·loo \ˌwȯ-tər-ˈlü, ˌwä-\ *n, pl* **-loos** [*Waterloo*, Belgium, scene of Napoleon's defeat in 1815] : a decisive or final defeat or setback
¹**wa·ter·mark** \ˈwȯ-tər-ˌmärk, ˈwä-\ *n* **1** : a mark indicating height to which water has risen **2** : a marking in paper visible when the paper is held up to the light
²**watermark** *vb* : to mark (paper) with a watermark
wa·ter·mel·on \-ˌme-lən\ *n* : a large roundish or oblong fruit with sweet juicy usu. red pulp; *also* : a widely grown African vine related to the squashes that produces watermelons
water moccasin *n* : a venomous pit viper chiefly of the southeastern U.S. that is related to the copperhead
water ou·zel \-ˈü-zəl\ *n* : DIPPER 1
water park *n* : an amusement park with a pool and wetted slides
water pill *n* : DIURETIC
water pipe *n* : a pipe for smoking that has a long flexible tube whereby the smoke is cooled by passing through water
water pistol *n* : a toy pistol for squirting a jet of liquid
water polo *n* : a team game played in a swimming pool with a ball resembling a soccer ball
wa·ter·pow·er \ˈwȯ-tər-ˌpau̇(-ə)r, ˈwä-\ *n* : the power of moving water used to run machinery
¹**wa·ter·proof** \ˈwȯ-tər-ˌprüf, ˈwä-\ *adj* : not letting water through; *esp* : covered or treated with a material to prevent permeation by water — **wa·ter·proof·ing** *n*
²**waterproof** *n* **1** : a waterproof fabric **2** *chiefly Brit* : RAINCOAT

³**waterproof** *vb* : to make waterproof
wa·ter–re·pel·lent \ˌwȯ-tər-ri-ˈpe-lənt, ˌwä-\ *adj* : treated with a finish that is resistant to water penetration
wa·ter–re·sis·tant \-ri-ˈzis-tənt\ *adj* : WATER-REPELLENT
wa·ter·shed \ˈwȯ-tər-ˌshed, ˈwä-\ *n* **1** : a dividing ridge between two drainage areas **2** : the region or area drained by a particular body of water
wa·ter·side \-ˌsīd\ *n* : the land bordering a body of water
water ski *n* : a ski used on water when the wearer is towed — **wa·ter–ski** *vb* — **wa·ter–ski·er** \-ˌskē-ər\ *n*
water snake *n* : any of various snakes found in or near freshwater and feeding largely on aquatic animals
wa·ter·spout \ˈwȯ-tər-ˌspau̇t, ˈwä-\ *n* **1** : a pipe for carrying water from a roof **2** : a funnel-shaped cloud extending from a cloud down to a spray torn up by whirling winds from an ocean or lake
water strider *n* : any of various long-legged bugs that move about swiftly on the surface of water
water table *n* : the upper limit of the portion of the ground wholly saturated with water
wa·ter·tight \ˌwȯ-tər-ˈtīt, ˌwä-\ *adj* **1** : constructed so as to keep water out **2** : allowing no possibility for doubt or uncertainty ⟨a ~ case against the accused⟩
wa·ter·way \ˈwȯ-tər-ˌwā, ˈwä-\ *n* : a navigable body of water
wa·ter·wheel \-ˌhwēl, -ˌwēl\ *n* : a wheel made to turn by water flowing against it
water wings *n pl* : an air-filled device to give support to a person's body esp. when learning to swim
wa·ter·works \ˈwȯ-tər-ˌwərks, ˈwä-\ *n pl* : a system for supplying water (as to a city)
wa·tery \ˈwȯ-tə-rē, ˈwä-\ *adj* **1** : containing, full of, or giving out water ⟨~ clouds⟩ **2** : being like water : THIN, WEAK ⟨~ lemonade⟩; *also* : being soft and soggy ⟨~ turnips⟩
WATS \ˈwäts\ *abbr* Wide-Area Telecommunications Service
watt \ˈwät\ *n* [James *Watt* †1819 Scottish engineer and inventor] : the metric unit of power equal to the work done at the rate of one joule per second or to the power produced by a current of one ampere across a potential difference of one volt
watt·age \ˈwä-tij\ *n* : amount of power expressed in watts
wat·tle \ˈwä-t³l\ *n* **1** : a framework of rods with flexible branches or reeds interlaced used esp. formerly in building; *also* : material for this framework **2** : a naked fleshy process hanging usu. from the head or neck (as of a bird) — **wat·tled** \-t³ld\ *adj*
W Aust *abbr* Western Australia
¹**wave** \ˈwāv\ *vb* **waved; wav·ing 1** : FLUTTER ⟨flags *waving* in the breeze⟩ **2** : to motion with the hands or with something held in them in signal or salute **3** : to become moved or brandished to-and-fro; *also* : BRANDISH, FLOURISH ⟨~ a sword⟩ **4** : to move before the wind with a wavelike motion ⟨fields of *waving* grain⟩ **5** : to curve up and down like a wave : UNDULATE
²**wave** *n* **1** : a moving ridge or swell on the surface of water **2** : a wavelike formation or shape ⟨a ~ in the hair⟩ **3** : the action or process of making wavy or curly **4** : a waving motion; *esp* : a signal made by waving something **5** : FLOW, GUSH ⟨a ~ of anger swept over her⟩ **6** : a peak of activity ⟨a ~ of selling⟩ **7** : a disturbance that transfers energy progressively from point to point in a medium ⟨light travels in ~s⟩ ⟨a sound ~⟩ **8** : a period of hot or cold weather — **wave·like** *adj*
wave·length \ˈwāv-ˌleŋth\ *n* **1** : the distance in the line of advance of a wave from any one point (as a crest) to the next corresponding point **2** : a line of thought that reveals a common understanding
wave·let \-lət\ *n* : a little wave : RIPPLE
wa·ver \ˈwā-vər\ *vb* **1** : to fluctuate in opinion, allegiance, or direction **2** : REEL, TOTTER; *also* : QUIVER, FLICKER ⟨~*ing* flames⟩ **3** : FALTER **4** : to give an unsteady sound : QUAVER ◆ *Synonyms* FALTER, HESITATE, SHILLY-SHALLY, VACILLATE — **waver** *n* — **wa·ver·er** *n* — **wa·ver·ing·ly** *adv*
wavy \ˈwā-vē\ *adj* **wav·i·er; -est** : having waves : moving in waves
¹**wax** \ˈwaks\ *n* **1** : a yellowish plastic substance secreted by bees for constructing the honeycomb **2** : any of various substances like beeswax

wax • weasels

564

²**wax** *vb* : to treat or rub with wax — **wax·er** *n*
³**wax** *vb* **1** : to increase in size, numbers, strength, volume, or duration **2** : to increase in apparent size ⟨the moon ∼*es* toward the full⟩ **3** : to take on a quality or state : BECOME ⟨∼*ed* indignant⟩ ⟨the party ∼*ed* merry⟩
wax bean *n* : a kidney bean with pods that turn creamy yellow to bright yellow when mature enough to use as snap beans
wax·en \'wak-sən\ *adj* **1** : made of or covered with wax **2** : resembling wax (as in color or consistency)
wax museum *n* : a place where wax effigies are exhibited
wax myrtle *n* : any of a genus of shrubs or trees with aromatic leaves; *esp* : an evergreen shrub or small tree of the eastern U.S. that produces small hard berries with a thick coating of bluish-white wax used for candles
wax·wing \'waks-ˌwiŋ\ *n* : any of a genus of chiefly brown to gray singing birds with a showy crest and red waxy material on the tips of some wing feathers
wax·work \-ˌwərk\ *n* **1** : an effigy usu. of a person in wax **2** *pl* : an exhibition of wax figures
waxy \'wak-sē\ *adj* **wax·i·er; -est** **1** : made of or full of wax **2** : WAXEN 2
way \'wā\ *n* **1** : a thoroughfare for travel or passage : ROAD, PATH, STREET **2** : ROUTE ⟨knew the ∼ home⟩ **3** : a course of action ⟨chose the easy ∼⟩; *also* : opportunity, capability, or fact of doing as one pleases ⟨always had your own ∼⟩ **4** : a possible course : POSSIBILITY ⟨no two ∼s about it⟩ **5** : METHOD, MODE ⟨this ∼ of thinking⟩ ⟨a new ∼ of painting⟩ **6** : FEATURE, RESPECT ⟨a good worker in many ∼s⟩ **7** : the usual or characteristic state of affairs ⟨as is the ∼ with old people⟩; *also* : individual characteristic or peculiarity ⟨used to her ∼s⟩ **8** : DISTANCE ⟨a short ∼ from here⟩ ⟨a long ∼ from success⟩ **9** : progress along a course ⟨working my ∼ through college⟩ **10** : something having direction : LOCALITY ⟨out our ∼⟩ **11** : STATE, CONDITION ⟨the ∼ things are⟩ **12** *pl* : an inclined structure upon which a ship is built or is supported in launching **13** : CATEGORY, KIND ⟨get what you need in the ∼ of supplies⟩ **14** : motion or speed of a boat through the water — **by the way** : by way of interjection or digression — **by way of** **1** : for the purpose of ⟨*by way of* illustration⟩ **2** : by the route through : VIA — **out of the way** **1** : WRONG, IMPROPER **2** : SECLUDED, REMOTE
way·bill \'wā-ˌbil\ *n* : a paper that accompanies a freight shipment and gives details of goods, route, and charges
way·far·er \'wā-ˌfer-ər\ *n* : a traveler esp. on foot — **way·far·ing** \-ˌfer-iŋ\ *adj*
way·lay \'wā-ˌlā\ *vb* **-laid** \-ˌlād\; **-lay·ing** : to lie in wait for or attack from ambush
way–out \'wā-'aút\ *adj* : FAR-OUT
-ways *adv suffix* : in (such) a way, course, direction, or manner ⟨sideways⟩
ways and means *n pl* : methods and resources esp. for raising revenues needed by a state; *also* : a legislative committee concerned with this function
way·side \'wā-ˌsīd\ *n* : the side of or land adjacent to a road or path
way station *n* : an intermediate station on a line of travel (as a railroad)
way·ward \'wā-wərd\ *adj* [ME, short for *awayward* turned away, fr. *away*, adv. + *-ward* directed toward] **1** : following one's own capricious or wanton inclinations ⟨∼ children⟩ **2** : UNPREDICTABLE, IRREGULAR ⟨a ∼ act⟩
WBC *abbr* white blood cells
WC *abbr* **1** water closet **2** without charge
WCTU *abbr* Women's Christian Temperance Union
we \'wē\ *pron* **1** — used of a group that includes the speaker or writer **2** — used for the singular *I* by a monarch, editor, or writer
weak \'wēk\ *adj* **1** : lacking strength or vigor : FEEBLE **2** : not able to sustain or resist much weight, pressure, or strain **3** : deficient in vigor of mind or character; *also* : resulting from or indicative of such deficiency ⟨a ∼ policy⟩ ⟨a ∼ will⟩ **4** : not supported by truth or logic ⟨a ∼ argument⟩ **5** : lacking skill or proficiency; *also* : indicative of a lack of skill or aptitude **6** : lacking vigor of expression or effect **7** : of less than usual strength ⟨∼ tea⟩ **8** : not having or exerting authority ⟨∼ government⟩; *also* : INEFFECTIVE, IMPOTENT ⟨∼ measures to control crime⟩ **9** : of, relating to, or consti-

tuting a verb or verb conjugation that forms the past tense and past participle by adding *-ed* or *-d* or *-t* — **weak·ly** *adv*
weak·en \'wē-kən\ *vb* : to make or become weak ♦ **Synonyms** ENFEEBLE, DEBILITATE, UNDERMINE, SAP, CRIPPLE, DISABLE
weak·fish \'wēk-ˌfish\ *n* [obs. D *weekvis*, fr. D *week* soft + *vis* fish] : a common marine fish of the Atlantic coast of the U.S. caught for food and sport; *also* : any of several related food fishes
weak force *n* : the physical force responsible for particle decay processes in radioactivity
weak–kneed \'wēk-'nēd\ *adj* : lacking willpower or resolution
weak·ling \'wē-kliŋ\ *n* : a person who is physically, mentally, or morally weak
weak·ly \'wē-klē\ *adj* : FEEBLE, WEAK
weak·ness \'wēk-nəs\ *n* **1** : the quality or state of being weak; *also* : an instance or period of being weak ⟨in a moment of ∼ he agreed to go⟩ **2** : FAULT, DEFECT **3** : an object of special desire or fondness ⟨chocolate is her ∼⟩
¹**weal** \'wēl\ *n* : WELL-BEING, PROSPERITY
²**weal** *n* : WELT
weald \'wēld\ *n* [The *Weald*, wooded district in England, fr. ME *Weeld*, fr. OE *weald* forest] **1** : FOREST **2** : WOLD
wealth \'welth\ *n* [ME *welthe* welfare, prosperity, fr. *wele* weal] **1** : abundance of possessions or resources : AFFLUENCE, RICHES **2** : abundant supply : PROFUSION ⟨a ∼ of detail⟩ **3** : all property that has a money or an exchange value; *also* : all objects or resources that have economic value ♦ **Synonyms** FORTUNE, PROPERTY, SUBSTANCE, WORTH
wealthy \'wel-thē\ *adj* **wealth·i·er; -est** : having wealth : RICH
wean \'wēn\ *vb* **1** : to accustom (a young mammal) to take food by means other than nursing **2** : to free from a source of dependence; *also* : to free from a usu. unwholesome habit or interest
weap·on \'we-pən\ *n* **1** : something (as a gun, knife, or club) used to injure, defeat, or destroy **2** : a means of contending against another — **weap·on·less** \-ləs\ *adj*
weap·on·ry \-rē\ *n* : WEAPONS
¹**wear** \'wear\ *vb* **wore** \'wór\; **worn** \'wórn\; **wear·ing** **1** : to use as an article of clothing or adornment ⟨∼ a coat⟩ ⟨∼s earrings⟩; *also* : to carry on the person ⟨∼ a gun⟩ **2** : EXHIBIT, PRESENT ⟨∼ a smile⟩ **3** : to impair, diminish, or decay by use or by scraping or rubbing ⟨clothes *worn* to shreds⟩; *also* : to produce gradually by friction, rubbing, or wasting away ⟨∼ a hole in the rug⟩ **4** : to exhaust or lessen the strength of : WEARY, FATIGUE ⟨*worn* by care and toil⟩ **5** : to endure use : last under use or the passage of time ⟨this cloth ∼s well⟩ **6** : to diminish or fail with the passage of time ⟨the day ∼s on⟩ ⟨the effect of the drug *wore* off⟩ **7** : to grow or become by attrition, use, or age ⟨the coin was *worn* thin⟩ — **wear·able** \'wer-ə-bəl\ *adj* — **wear·er** *n*
²**wear** *n* **1** : the act of wearing : the state of being worn ⟨clothes for everyday ∼⟩ **2** : clothing usu. of a particular kind or for a special occasion or use ⟨children's ∼⟩ **3** : wearing or lasting quality ⟨the coat still has lots of ∼ in it⟩ **4** : the result of wearing or use : impairment due to use ⟨the suit shows ∼⟩
wear and tear *n* : the loss, injury, or stress to which something is subjected in the course of use; *esp* : normal depreciation
wear down *vb* : to weary and overcome by persistent resistance or pressure
wea·ri·some \'wir-ē-səm\ *adj* : causing weariness : TIRESOME — **wea·ri·some·ly** *adv* — **wea·ri·some·ness** *n*
wear out *vb* **1** : TIRE **2** : to make or become useless by wear
¹**wea·ry** \'wir-ē\ *adj* **wea·ri·er; -est** **1** : worn out in strength, energy, or freshness **2** : expressing or characteristic of weariness ⟨a ∼ sigh⟩ **3** : having one's patience, tolerance, or pleasure exhausted ⟨∼ of war⟩ — **wea·ri·ly** \'wir-ə-lē\ *adv* — **wea·ri·ness** \-ē-nəs\ *n*
²**weary** *vb* **wea·ried; wea·ry·ing** : to become or make weary : TIRE
¹**wea·sel** \'wē-zəl\ *n, pl* **weasels** : any of various small slen-

der flesh-eating mammals related to the minks — **wea-sel·ly** *also* **wea·sely** \'wēz-lē, 'wē-zə-lē\ *adj*

²**weasel** *vb* **wea·seled; wea·sel·ing** 1 : to use weasel words : EQUIVOCATE 2 : to escape from or evade a situation or obligation — often used with *out* **weasel word** *n* [fr. the weasel's reputed habit of sucking the contents out of an egg while leaving the shell intact] : a word used to avoid a direct or forthright statement or position

¹**weath·er** \'we-thər\ 1 : the state of the atmosphere with respect to heat or cold, wetness or dryness, calm or storm, clearness or cloudiness 2 : a particular and esp. a disagreeable atmospheric state : RAIN, STORM

²**weather** *vb* 1 : to expose to or endure the action of weather; *also* : to alter (as in color or texture) by such exposure 2 : to bear up against successfully ⟨~ a storm⟩ ⟨~ troubles⟩

³**weather** *adj* : WINDWARD

weath·er–beat·en \'we-thər-ˌbē-tᵊn\ *adj* : worn or damaged by exposure to the weather; *also* : toughened or tanned by the weather ⟨~ face⟩

weath·er·cock \-ˌkäk\ *n* : a weather vane shaped like a rooster

weath·er·ing \'we-thə-riŋ\ *n* : the action of the weather in altering the color, texture, composition, or form of exposed objects; *also* : alteration thus effected

weath·er·ize \'we-thə-ˌrīz\ *vb* **-ized; -iz·ing** : to make (as a house) better protected against winter weather (as by adding insulation)

weath·er·man \-ˌman\ *n* : one who reports and forecasts the weather : METEOROLOGIST

weath·er·per·son \-ˌpər-sən\ *n* : a person who reports and forecasts the weather : METEOROLOGIST

weath·er·proof \'we-thər-ˌprüf\ *adj* : able to withstand exposure to weather — **weatherproof** *vb*

weath·er·strip·ping \'we-thər-ˌstri-piŋ\ *n* : material used to seal a door or window at the edges — **weath·er·strip** *vb* — **weather strip** *n*

weather vane *n* : VANE 1

weath·er·worn \'we-thər-ˌwȯrn\ *adj* : worn by exposure to the weather

¹**weave** \'wēv\ *vb* **wove** \'wōv\ *or* **weaved; wo·ven** \'wō-vən\ *or* **weaved; weav·ing** 1 : to form by interlacing strands of material; *esp* : to make on a loom by interlacing warp and filling threads ⟨~ cloth⟩ 2 : to interlace (as threads) into a fabric and esp. cloth 3 : SPIN 2 4 : to make as if by weaving together parts 5 : to insert as a part : work in 6 : to move in a winding or zigzag course esp. to avoid obstacles ⟨we *wove* our way through the crowd⟩ — **weav·er** *n*

²**weave** *n* : something woven; *also* : a pattern or method of weaving ⟨a loose ~⟩

¹**web** \'web\ *n* 1 : a fabric on a loom or coming from a loom 2 : COBWEB; *also* : SNARE, ENTANGLEMENT ⟨caught in a ~ of deceit⟩ 3 : an animal or plant membrane; *esp* : one uniting the toes (as in many birds) 4 : NETWORK ⟨a ~ of highways⟩ 5 : the series of barbs on each side of the shaft of a feather 6 : WORLD WIDE WEB — **webbed** \'webd\ *adj*

²**web** *vb* **webbed; web·bing** 1 : to make a web 2 : to cover or provide with webs or a network 3 : ENTANGLE, ENSNARE

web·bing \'we-biŋ\ *n* : a strong closely woven tape designed for bearing weight and used esp. for straps, harness, or upholstery

web·cam \'web-ˌkam\ *n* : a camera used in transmitting live images over the World Wide Web

web·cast \'web-ˌkast\ *n* : a transmission of sound and images via the World Wide Web — **webcast** *vb*

web–foot·ed \'web-'fu̇-tad\ *adj* : having webbed feet

web·mas·ter \'web-ˌmas-tər\ *n, often cap* : a person responsible for the creation or maintenance of a Web site

Web site *n* : a group of World Wide Web pages made available online (as by an individual or business)

wed \'wed\ *vb* **wed·ded** *also* **wed; wed·ding** 1 : to take, give, enter into, or join in marriage : MARRY 2 : to unite firmly

Wed *abbr* Wednesday

wed·ding \'we-diŋ\ *n* 1 : a marriage ceremony usu. with accompanying festivities : NUPTIALS 2 : a joining in

close association 3 : a wedding anniversary or its celebration

¹**wedge** \'wej\ *n* 1 : a piece of wood or metal that tapers to a thin edge and is used to split logs or rocks or to raise heavy weights 2 : something (as an action or policy) that serves to open up a way for a breach, change, or intrusion 3 : a wedge-shaped object or part ⟨a ~ of pie⟩

²**wedge** *vb* **wedged; wedg·ing** 1 : to hold firm by or as if by driving in a wedge 2 : to force (something) into a narrow space

wed·lock \'wed-ˌläk\ *n* [ME *wedlok*, fr. OE *wedlāc* marriage bond, fr. *wedd* pledge + *-lāc*, suffix denoting activity] : the state of being married : MARRIAGE, MATRIMONY

Wednes·day \'wenz-(ˌ)dā-dē\ *n* [ME, fr. OE *wōdensdæg*, lit., day of Woden (supreme god of the pagan Anglo-Saxons)] : the 4th day of the week

wee \'wē\ *adj* [ME (Sc) *we*, fr. *we*, n., little bit, fr. OE *wǣge* weight] 1 : very small : TINY 2 : very early ⟨~ hours of the morning⟩

¹**weed** \'wēd\ *n* 1 : a plant that tends to grow thickly where it is not wanted and to choke out more desirable plants 2 : MARIJUANA

²**weed** *vb* 1 : to clear of or remove weeds or something harmful, inferior, or superfluous ⟨~ a garden⟩ 2 : to get rid of ⟨~ out the troublemakers⟩ — **weed·er** *n*

³**weed** *n* : mourning clothes — usu. used in pl. ⟨widow's ~s⟩

weedy \'wē-dē\ *adj* 1 : full of weeds 2 : resembling a weed esp. in vigor of growth or spread 3 : noticeably lean and scrawny : LANKY

week \'wēk\ *n* 1 : seven successive days; *esp* : a calendar period of seven days beginning with Sunday and ending with Saturday 2 : the working or school days of the calendar week

week·day \'wēk-ˌdā\ *n* : a day of the week except Sunday or sometimes except Saturday and Sunday

¹**week·end** \-ˌend\ *n* : the period between the close of one working or business or school week and the beginning of the next

²**weekend** *vb* : to spend the weekend

¹**week·ly** \'wē-klē\ *adj* 1 : occurring, appearing, or done every week 2 : computed in terms of one week ⟨~ rental rates⟩ — **weekly** *adv*

²**weekly** *n, pl* **weeklies** : a weekly publication

ween \'wēn\ *vb, archaic* : SUPPOSE 3

wee·ny \'wē-nē\ *also* **ween·sy** \'wēn-sē\ *adj* : exceptionally small

weep \'wēp\ *vb* **wept** \'wept\; **weep·ing** 1 : to express emotion and esp. sorrow by shedding tears : BEWAIL, CRY 2 : to give off fluid slowly : OOZE — **weep·er** *n*

weeping *adj* 1 : TEARFUL ⟨~ gratitude⟩ 2 : having slender drooping branches

weeping willow *n* : a willow with slender drooping branches

weepy \'wē-pē\ *adj* : inclined to weep

wee·vil \'wē-vəl\ *n* : any of a large group of beetles having a long head usu. curved into a snout and including many whose larvae are destructive plant-feeding pests — **wee·vily** *or* **wee·vil·ly** \'wē-və-lē\ *adj*

weft \'weft\ *n* 1 : a filling thread or yarn in weaving 2 : WEB, FABRIC; *also* : something woven

¹**weigh** \'wā\ *vb* [ME *weyen*, fr. OE *wegan* to move, carry, weigh] 1 : to find the heaviness of 2 : to have weight or a specified weight 3 : to consider carefully : PONDER 4 : to merit consideration as important : COUNT ⟨evidence ~*ing* against him⟩ 5 : to raise before sailing ⟨~ anchor⟩ 6 : to press down with or as if with a heavy weight

²**weigh** *n* [alter. of *way*] : WAY — used in the phrase *under weigh*

¹**weight** \'wāt\ *n* 1 : the amount that something weighs; *also* : the standard amount that something should weigh 2 : a quantity or object weighing a usu. specified amount 3 : a unit (as a pound or kilogram) of weight or mass; *also* : a system of such units 4 : a heavy object for holding or pressing something down; *also* : a heavy object for throwing or lifting in an athletic contest 5 : a mental or emotional burden 6 : IMPORTANCE; *also* : INFLUENCE ⟨threw his ~ around⟩ 7 : overpowering force 8 : relative thickness (as of a textile) ⟨*summer-weight* clothes⟩

◆ **Synonyms** SIGNIFICANCE, MOMENT, CONSEQUENCE, IMPORT, AUTHORITY, PRESTIGE, CREDIT

☞ the U.S. WEIGHTS AND MEASURES table is on page 566

U.S. WEIGHTS AND MEASURES

LENGTH

UNIT (SYMBOL)	U.S. EQUIVALENT	METRIC EQUIVALENT
mile (mi)	5280 feet, 1760 yards	1.609 kilometers
rod (rd)	5.50 yards, 16.5 feet	5.029 meters
yard (yd)	3 feet, 36 inches	0.9144 meter
foot (ft *or* ')	12 inches	30.48 centimeters
inch (in *or* ")	0.083 foot, 0.028 yard	2.54 centimeters

AREA

UNIT (SYMBOL)	U.S. EQUIVALENT	METRIC EQUIVALENT
square mile (sq mi *or* mi²)	640 acres	2.590 square kilometers
acre (ac)	4840 square yards, 43,560 square feet	4047 square meters,
square rod (sq rd *or* rd²)	30.25 square yards	25.293 square meters
square yard (sq yd *or* yd²)	9 square feet	0.836 square meter
square foot (sq ft *or* ft²)	144 square inches	0.093 square meter
square inch (sq in *or* in²)	0.0069 square foot	6.452 square centimeter

VOLUME

UNIT (SYMBOL)	U.S. EQUIVALENT	METRIC EQUIVALENT
cubic yard (cu yd *or* yd³)	27 cubic feet	0.765 cubic meter
cubic foot (cu ft *or* ft³)	1728 cubic inches	0.028 cubic meter
cubic inch (cu in *or* in³)	0.00058 cubic foot	16.387 cubic centimeter

WEIGHT—AVOIRDUPOIS

UNIT (SYMBOL)	U.S. EQUIVALENT	METRIC EQUIVALENT
ton		
short ton	2000 pounds	0.907 metric ton
long ton	2240 pounds	1.016 metric tons
hundredweight (cwt)		
short hundredweight	100 pounds	45.359 kilograms
long hundredweight	112 pounds	50.802 kilograms
pound (lb *also* #)	16 ounces	0.454 kilogram
ounce (oz)	16 drams, 437.5 grains	28.350 grams
dram (dr)	27.344 grains	1.772 grams
grain (gr)	0.037 dram	0.0648 gram

CAPACITY

UNIT (SYMBOL)	U.S. EQUIVALENT	METRIC EQUIVALENT
	LIQUID MEASURE	
gallon (gal)	4 quarts	3.785 liters
quart (qt)	2 pints	0.946 liter
pint (pt)	4 gills	473.176 milliliters
gill (gi)	4 fluid ounces	118.294 milliliters
fluid ounce (fl oz *or* f℥)	8 fluid drams	29.573 milliliters
fluid dram (fl dr *or* f℥)	60 minims	3.697 milliliters
minim (min *or* ♏)	1/60 fluid dram	0.061610 milliliter
	DRY MEASURE	
bushel (bu)	4 pecks	35.239 liters
peck (pk)	8 quarts	8.810 liters
quart (qt)	2 pints	1.101 liters
pint (pt)	½ quart	0.551 liter

²weight *vb* **1** : to oppress with a burden ⟨~ed down with cares⟩ **2** : to load with or as if with a weight

weight·less \'wāt-ləs\ *adj* : having little weight : lacking apparent gravitational pull — **weight·less·ly** *adv* — **weight·less·ness** *n*

weighty \'wā-tē\ *adj* **weight·i·er; -est 1** : of much importance or consequence : MOMENTOUS, SERIOUS ⟨~ problems⟩ **2** : SOLEMN ⟨a ~ manner⟩ **3** : HEAVY **4** : POWERFUL, TELLING ⟨~ arguments⟩

weiner *var of* WIENER

weir \'wer, 'wir\ *n* **1** : a fence set in a waterway for catching fish **2** : a dam in a stream to raise the water level or divert its flow

weird \'wird\ *adj* [ME *wird, werd* fate, destiny, fr. OE *wyrd*] **1** : MAGICAL **2** : ODD, UNUSUAL **✦ Synonyms** EERIE, UNCANNY, SPOOKY — **weird·ly** *adv* — **weird·ness** *n*

weirdo \'wir-(,)dō\ *n, pl* **weird·os** : a person who is extraordinarily strange or eccentric

Welch *var of* WELSH

¹wel·come \'wel-kəm\ *vb* **wel·comed; wel·com·ing 1** : to greet cordially or courteously **2** : to accept, meet, or face with pleasure ⟨he ~s criticism⟩

²welcome *adj* **1** : received gladly into one's presence ⟨a ~ visitor⟩ **2** : giving pleasure : PLEASING ⟨~ news⟩ **3** : willingly permitted or admitted ⟨all are ~ to use the books⟩ **4** — used in the phrase "You're welcome" as a reply to an expression of thanks

³welcome *n* **1** : a cordial greeting or reception **2** : the state of being welcome ⟨overstayed their ~⟩

¹weld \'weld\ *vb* **1** : to unite (metal or plastic parts) either by heating and allowing the parts to flow together or by hammering or pressing together **2** : to unite closely or intimately ⟨~ed together in friendship⟩ — **weld·er** *n*

²weld *n* **1** : a welded joint **2** : union by welding

wel·fare \'wel-,fer\ *n* **1** : the state of doing well esp. in respect to happiness, well-being, or prosperity **2** : aid in the form of money or necessities for those in need; *also* : the agency through which the aid is given

welfare state *n* : a nation or state that assumes primary responsibility for the individual and social welfare of its citizens

wel·kin \'wel-kən\ *n* : SKY; *also* : AIR

¹well \'wel\ *n* **1** : a spring with its pool : FOUNTAIN; *also* : a source of supply ⟨a ~ of information⟩ **2** : a hole sunk in the earth to obtain a natural deposit (as of water, oil, or gas) **3** : an open space (as for a staircase) extending vertically through floors of a structure **4** : something suggesting a well

²well *vb* : to rise up and flow out

³well *adv* **bet·ter** \'be-tər\; **best** \'best\ **1** : in a good or proper manner : RIGHTLY; *also* : EXCELLENTLY, SKILLFULLY **2** : SATISFACTORILY, FORTUNATELY ⟨the party turned out ~⟩ **3** : ABUNDANTLY ⟨eat ~⟩ **4** : with reason or courtesy ⟨I cannot ~ refuse⟩ **5** : COMPLETELY, FULLY, QUITE ⟨~ worth the price⟩ ⟨*well*-hidden⟩ **6** : INTIMATELY, CLOSELY ⟨I know him ~⟩ **7** : CONSIDERABLY, FAR ⟨~ over a million⟩ ⟨~ ahead⟩ **8** : without trouble or difficulty ⟨we could ~ have gone⟩ **9** : EXACTLY, DEFINITELY ⟨remember it ~⟩

⁴well *adj* **1** : PROSPEROUS; *also* : being in satisfactory condition or circumstances **2** : SATISFACTORY, PLEASING ⟨all is ~⟩ **3** : ADVISABLE, DESIRABLE ⟨it is not ~ to anger him⟩ **4** : free or recovered from ill health : HEALTHY **5** : FORTUNATE ⟨it is ~ that this has happened⟩

well–ad·just·ed \,wel-ə-'jəs-təd\ *adj* : WELL-BALANCED 2

well–ad·vised \-əd-'vīzd\ *adj* **1** : PRUDENT ⟨~ restraint⟩ **2** : resulting from, based on, or showing careful deliberation or wise counsel ⟨~ plans⟩

well–ap·point·ed \-ə-'pȯin-təd\ *adj* : properly fitted out ⟨a ~ house⟩

well–ba·lanced \'wel-'ba-lənst\ *adj* **1** : nicely or evenly balanced or arranged **2** : emotionally or psychologically untroubled

well–be·ing \-'bē-iŋ\ *n* : the state of being happy, healthy, or prosperous

well–born \-'bȯrn\ *adj* : born of noble or wealthy lineage

well–bred \-'bred\ *adj* : having or indicating good breeding : REFINED

well–de·fined \-di-'fīnd\ *adj* : having clearly distinguishable limits or boundaries

well–dis·posed \-di-'spōzd\ *adj* : disposed to be friendly, favorable, or sympathetic

well–done \'wel-'dən\ *adj* **1** : rightly or properly performed **2** : cooked thoroughly

well–en·dowed \'wel-in-'daud\ *adj* **1** : having plenty of money or property **2** : having large breasts

well–fa·vored \-'fā-vərd\ *adj* : GOOD-LOOKING, HANDSOME ⟨a ~ face⟩

well–fixed \-'fikst\ *adj* : WELL-HEELED

well–found·ed \-'faun-dəd\ *adj* : based on good reasons

well–groomed \-'grümd, -'grumd\ *adj* : neatly dressed or cared for

well–ground·ed \-'graun-dəd\ *adj* **1** : having a firm foundation **2** : WELL-FOUNDED

well·head \-,hed\ *n* **1** : the source of a spring or a stream **2** : principal source **3** : the top of or a structure built over a well

well–heeled \-'hēld\ *adj* : financially well-off

well–known \-'nōn\ *adj* : fully or widely known

well–mean·ing \-'mē-niŋ\ *adj* : having or based on good intentions

well·ness \-nəs\ *n* : good health esp. as an actively sought goal ⟨~ clinics⟩ ⟨lifestyles that promote ~⟩

well–nigh \-'nī\ *adv* : ALMOST, NEARLY ⟨~ impossible⟩

well–off \-'ȯf\ *adj* : being in good condition or circumstances; *esp* : WELL-TO-DO

well–or·dered \-'ȯr-dərd\ *adj* : having an orderly procedure or arrangement

well–placed \-'plāst\ *adj* : appropriately or advantageously directed or positioned

well–read \-'red\ *adj* : well informed through reading

well–round·ed \-'raun-dəd\ *adj* **1** : broadly trained, educated, and experienced **2** : COMPREHENSIVE ⟨a ~ program of activities⟩

well–spo·ken \'wel-'spō-kən\ *adj* **1** : speaking well and esp. courteously **2** : spoken with propriety ⟨~ words⟩

well·spring \-,spriŋ\ *n* : a source of continuous supply

well–timed \-'tīmd\ *adj* : TIMELY ⟨a ~ announcement⟩

well–to–do \,wel-tə-'dü\ *adj* : having more than adequate financial resources : PROSPEROUS

well–turned \'wel-'tərnd\ *adj* **1** : pleasingly shaped ⟨a ~ ankle⟩ **2** : pleasingly expressed ⟨a ~ phrase⟩

well–wish·er \'wel-,wi-shər\ *n* : an admiring supporter or fan — **well–wish·ing** *adj or n*

welsh \'welsh, 'welch\ *vb* **1** : to avoid payment **2** : to break one's word ⟨~ed on his promises⟩

Welsh \'welsh\ *also* **Welch** \'welch\ *n* [ME *walisch, welisch,* adj., Welsh, fr. OE *wælisc* foreign, British, Welsh, fr. *Wealh* foreigner, Briton, Welshman] **1 Welsh** *pl* : the people of Wales **2** : the Celtic language of Wales — **Welsh** *adj* — **Welsh·man** \-mən\ *n*

Welsh cor·gi \-'kȯr-gē\ *n* [W *corgi,* fr. *cor* dwarf + *ci* dog] : a short-legged long-backed dog with foxy head of either of two breeds of Welsh origin

Welsh rabbit *n* : melted often seasoned cheese served over toast or crackers

Welsh rare·bit \-'rer-bət\ *n* : WELSH RABBIT

¹welt \'welt\ *n* **1** : the narrow strip of leather between a shoe upper and sole to which other parts are stitched **2** : a doubled edge, strip, insert, or seam for ornament or reinforcement **3** : a ridge or lump raised on the skin usu. by a blow; *also* : a heavy blow

²welt *vb* **1** : to furnish with a welt **2** : to hit hard

¹wel·ter \'wel-tər\ *vb* **1** : WRITHE, TOSS; *also* : WALLOW **2** : to rise and fall or toss about in or with waves **3** : to become deeply sunk, soaked, or involved **4** : to be in turmoil

²welter *n* **1** : TURMOIL **2** : a chaotic mass or jumble

wel·ter·weight \'wel-tər-,wāt\ *n* : a boxer weighing more than 135 but not over 147 pounds

wen \'wen\ *n* : an abnormal growth or a cyst protruding from a surface esp. of the skin

wench \'wench\ *n* [ME *wenche,* short for *wenchel* child, fr. OE *wencel*] **1** : a young woman **2** : a female servant

wend \'wend\ *vb* : to direct one's course : proceed on ⟨one's way⟩

went *past of* GO

wept *past and past part of* WEEP

were *past 2d sing, past pl, or past subjunctive of* BE

were·wolf \'wer-,wulf, 'wir-, 'wər-\ *n, pl* **were·wolves** \-,wulvz\ [ME, fr. OE *werwulf,* fr. *wer* man + *wulf* wolf] : a person transformed into a wolf or capable of assuming a wolf's form

wes·kit \'wes-kət\ *n* : VEST 1

¹west \'west\ *adv* : to or toward the west

²west *adj* **1** : situated toward or at the west **2** : coming from the west

³west *n* **1** : the general direction of sunset **2** : the compass point directly opposite to east **3** *cap* : regions or countries west of a specified or implied point **4** *cap* : Europe and the Americas — **west·er·ly** \'wes-tər-lē\ *adv or adj* — **west·ward** *adv or adj* — **west·wards** *adv*

¹west·ern \'wes-tərn\ *adj* **1** : lying toward or coming from the west **2** *cap* : of, relating to, or characteristic of a region conventionally designated West **3** *cap* : of or relating to the Roman Catholic or Protestant segment of Christianity — **West·ern·er** *n*

²western *n, often cap* : a novel, story, film, or radio or television show about life in the western U.S. during the latter half of the 19th century

west·ern·ize \'wes-tər-ˌnīz\ *vb* **-ized; -iz·ing** : to give western characteristics to — **west·ern·i·za·tion** \ˌwes-tər-nə-'zā-shən\ *n*

West Nile virus \-'nī(-ə)l-\ *n* [*West Nile* province of Uganda] : a virus that is transmitted to humans by mosquitoes and causes an illness marked by fever, headache, muscle ache, and sometimes encephalitis or meningitis; *also* : this illness

¹wet \'wet\ *adj* **wet·ter; wet·test** **1** : consisting of or covered or soaked with liquid (as water) **2** : RAINY ⟨~ days⟩ **3** : not dry ⟨~ paint⟩ **4** : permitting or advocating the manufacture and sale of alcoholic beverages ⟨a ~ town⟩ ⟨a ~ candidate⟩ ♦ **Synonyms** DAMP, DANK, MOIST, HUMID — **wet·ly** *adv* — **wet·ness** *n*

²wet *n* **1** : WATER; *also* : WETNESS, MOISTURE **2** : rainy weather : RAIN **3** : an advocate of a wet liquor policy

³wet *vb* **wet** *or* **wet·ted; wet·ting** : to make or become wet

wet blanket *n* : one that quenches or dampens enthusiasm or pleasure

weth·er \'we-thər\ *n* : a castrated male sheep or goat

wet·land \'wet-ˌland, -lənd\ *n* : land or areas (as swamps) containing much soil moisture — usu. used in pl.

wet nurse *n* : a woman who cares for and suckles children not her own

wet suit *n* : a rubber suit for swimmers that acts to retain body heat by keeping a layer of water against the body as insulation

wh *abbr* **1** which **2** white

¹whack \'hwak\ *vb* **1** : to strike with a smart or resounding blow **2** : to cut with or as if with a whack

²whack *n* **1** : a smart or resounding blow; *also* : the sound of such a blow **2** : PORTION, SHARE ⟨must each pay our ~⟩ **3** : CONDITION, STATE ⟨the machine is out of ~⟩ **4** : an opportunity or attempt to do something : CHANCE **5** : a single action or occasion ⟨made three pies at a ~⟩

¹whale \'hwāl\ *n, pl* **whales** **1** *or pl* **whale** : CETACEAN; *esp* : one (as a sperm whale or killer whale) of large size **2** : a person or thing impressive in size or quality ⟨a ~ of a story⟩

²whale *vb* **whaled; whal·ing** : to fish or hunt for whales

³whale *vb* **whaled; whal·ing** **1** : THRASH **2** : to strike or hit vigorously

whale·boat \-ˌbōt\ *n* : a long narrow rowboat originally used by whalers

whale·bone \-ˌbōn\ *n* : BALEEN

whal·er \'hwā-lər\ *n* **1** : a person or ship that hunts whales **2** : WHALEBOAT

whale shark *n* : a shark of warm waters that is the largest known fish

wham·my \'hwa-mē\ *n, pl* **wham·mies** : JINX, HEX

wharf \'hwȯrf\ *n, pl* **wharves** \'hwȯrvz\ *also* **wharfs** : a structure alongside which ships lie to load and unload

¹what \'hwät, 'hwət\ *pron* **1** — used to inquire about the identity or nature of a being, an object, or some matter or situation ⟨~ is he, a salesman⟩ ⟨~'s that⟩ ⟨~ happened⟩ **2** : that which ⟨I know ~ you want⟩ **3** : WHATEVER 1 ⟨take ~ you want⟩

²what *adv* **1** : in what respect : HOW ⟨~ does he care⟩ **2** — used with *with* to introduce a prepositional phrase that expresses cause ⟨kept busy ~ with school and work⟩

³what *adj* **1** — used to inquire about the identity or nature of a person, object, or matter ⟨~ books do you

read⟩ **2** : how remarkable or surprising ⟨~ an idea⟩ **3** : WHATEVER

¹what·ev·er \hwät-'e-vər, hwət-\ *pron* **1** : anything or everything that ⟨does ~ he wants to⟩ **2** : no matter what ⟨~ you do, don't cheat⟩ **3** : WHAT 1 — used as an intensive ⟨~ do you mean⟩

²whatever *adj* : of any kind at all ⟨no food ~⟩

³whatever *adv* : in any case : whatever the case may be — often used to suggest the unimportance of an issue or choice ⟨see a movie, watch TV, —~⟩

¹what·not \'hwät-ˌnät, 'hwət-\ *pron* : any of various other things that might also be mentioned ⟨needles, pins, and ~⟩

²whatnot *n* : a light open set of shelves for small ornaments

what·so·ev·er \ˌhwät-sō-'e-vər, ˌhwət-\ *pron or adj* : WHATEVER

wheal \'hwēl\ *n* : a rapidly formed flat slightly raised itching or burning patch on the skin; *also* : WELT

wheat \'hwēt\ *n* : a cereal grain that yields a fine white flour used chiefly in breads, baked goods, and pastas; *also* : any of several widely grown grasses yielding wheat — **wheat·en** *adj*

wheat germ *n* : the vitamin-rich wheat embryo separated in milling

whee·dle \'hwē-dᵊl\ *vb* **whee·dled; whee·dling** **1** : to entice by flattery **2** : to gain or get by wheedling

¹wheel \'hwēl\ *n* **1** : a disk or circular frame that turns on a central axis **2** : a device whose main part is a wheel **3** : something resembling a wheel in shape or motion **4** : a curving or circular movement **5** : machinery that imparts motion : moving power ⟨the ~s of government⟩ **6** : a person of importance **7** *pl, slang* : AUTOMOBILE — **wheeled** \'hwēld\ *adj* — **wheel·less** *adj*

²wheel *vb* **1** : ROTATE, REVOLVE **2** : to change direction as if turning on a pivot **3** : to convey or move on wheels or in a vehicle

wheel·bar·row \-ˌber-ō\ *n* : a vehicle with handles and usu. one wheel for carrying small loads

wheel·base \-ˌbās\ *n* : the distance in inches between the front and rear axles of an automotive vehicle

wheel·chair \-ˌcher\ *n* : a chair mounted on wheels esp. for the use of disabled persons

wheel·er \'hwē-lər\ *n* **1** : one that wheels **2** : WHEELHORSE **3** : something that has wheels — used in combination ⟨a side-*wheeler*⟩

wheel·er–deal·er \ˌhwē-lər-'dē-lər\ *n* : a shrewd operator esp. in business or politics

wheel·horse \'hwēl-ˌhȯrs\ *n* **1** : a horse in a position nearest the front wheels of a wagon **2** : a steady and effective worker esp. in a political body

wheel·house \-ˌhau̇s\ *n* : PILOTHOUSE

wheel–thrown \'hwēl-ˌthrōn\ *adj* : made on a potter's wheel

wheel·wright \-ˌrīt\ *n* : a maker and repairer of wheels and wheeled vehicles

¹wheeze \'hwēz\ *vb* **wheezed; wheez·ing** : to breathe with difficulty usu. with a whistling sound

²wheeze *n* **1** : a sound of wheezing **2** : an often repeated and well-known joke **3** : a trite saying

wheezy \'hwē-zē\ *adj* **wheez·i·er; -est** **1** : inclined to wheeze **2** : having a wheezing sound — **wheez·i·ly** \-zə-lē\ *adv* — **wheez·i·ness** \-zē-nəs\ *n*

whelk \'hwelk\ *n* : a large sea snail; *esp* : one much used as food in Europe

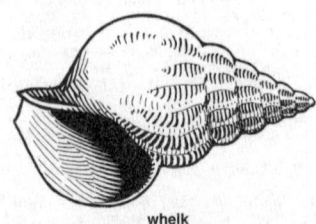

whelk

whelm \'hwelm\ *vb* : to overcome or engulf completely : OVERWHELM

¹**whelp** \'hwelp\ *n* : any of the young of various carnivorous mammals (as a dog)

²**whelp** *vb* : to give birth to (whelps); *also* : bring forth young

¹**when** \'hwen\ *adv* **1** : at what time ⟨~ will you return⟩ **2** : at or during which time ⟨a time ~ things were better⟩

²**when** *conj* **1** : at or during the time that ⟨leave ~ I do⟩ **2** : every time that ⟨they all clapped ~ he sang⟩ **3** : in the event that : IF ⟨disqualified ~ you cheat⟩ **4** : ALTHOUGH ⟨quit politics ~ he might have had a great career in it⟩

³**when** *pron* : what or which time ⟨since ~ have you been the boss⟩

⁴**when** *n* : the time of a happening

whence \'hwens\ *adv or conj* : from what place, source, or cause

when·ev·er \hwe-'ne-vər, hwə-\ *conj or adv* : at whatever time

when·so·ev·er \'hwen-sō-₁e-vər\ *conj* : at any or every time that

¹**where** \'hwer\ *adv* **1** : at, in, or to what place ⟨~ is it⟩ ⟨~ will we go⟩ **2** : at, in, or to what situation, position, direction, circumstances, or respect ⟨~ does this road lead⟩

²**where** *conj* **1** : at, in, or to what place ⟨knows ~ the house is⟩ **2** : at, in, or to what situation, position, direction, circumstances, or respect ⟨shows ~ the road leads⟩ **3** : WHEREVER ⟨goes ~ she likes⟩ **4** : at, in, or to which place ⟨the town ~ we live⟩ **5** : at, in, or to the place at, in, or to which ⟨stay ~ you are⟩ **6** : in a case, situation, or respect in which ⟨outstanding ~ endurance is called for⟩

³**where** *n* : PLACE, LOCATION ⟨the ~ and how of the accident⟩

¹**where·abouts** \-ə-₁baùts\ *also* **where·about** \-₁baùt\ *adv* : about where : near what place ⟨~ does he live⟩

²**whereabouts** *n sing or pl* : the place where a person or thing is ⟨his present ~ are unknown⟩

where·as \hwer-'az\ *conj* **1** : while on the contrary; *also* : ALTHOUGH **2** : in view of the fact that : SINCE

where·at \-'at\ *conj* **1** : at or toward which **2** : in consequence of which : WHEREUPON

where·by \-'bī\ *conj* : by, through, or in accordance with which ⟨the means ~ we achieved our goals⟩

¹**where·fore** \'hwer-₁fòr\ *adv* **1** : for what reason or purpose : WHY **2** : THEREFORE

²**wherefore** *n* : an answer or statement giving an explanation : REASON

¹**where·in** \hwer-'in\ *adv* : in what : in what respect ⟨~ was I wrong⟩

²**wherein** *conj* **1** : in which : WHERE ⟨the city ~ we live⟩ **2** : during which **3** : in what way : HOW ⟨showed me ~ I was wrong⟩

where·of \-'əv, -'äv\ *conj* **1** : of what ⟨knows ~ he speaks⟩ **2** : of which or whom ⟨books ~ the best are lost⟩

where·on \-'òn, -'än\ *conj* : on which ⟨the base ~ it rests⟩

where·so·ev·er \'hwer-sō-₁e-vər\ *conj* : WHEREVER

where·to \'hwer-₁tü\ *conj* : to which

where·up·on \'hwer-ə-₁pòn, -₁pän\ *conj* **1** : on which **2** : closely following and in consequence of which

¹**wher·ev·er** \hwer-'e-vər\ *adv* : where in the world ⟨~ did he get that tie⟩

²**wherever** *conj* **1** : at, in, or to whatever place ⟨thrives ~ he goes⟩ **2** : in any circumstance in which

where·with \'hwer-₁with, -₁with\ *conj* : with or by means of which ⟨lack the tools ~ to repair the damage⟩

where·with·al \'hwer-wi-₁thòl, -₁thòl\ *n* : MEANS, RESOURCES; *esp* : MONEY

wher·ry \'hwer-ē\ *n, pl* **wherries** : a long light rowboat sharp at both ends

whet \'hwet\ *vb* **whet·ted; whet·ting** **1** : to sharpen by rubbing on or with something abrasive (as a whetstone) **2** : to make keen : STIMULATE ⟨~ the appetite⟩

wheth·er \'hwe-thər\ *conj* **1** : if it is or was true that ⟨ask ~ he is going⟩ **2** : if it is or was better ⟨uncertain ~ to go or stay⟩ **3** : whichever is or was the case, namely that ⟨~ we succeed or fail, we must try⟩ **4** : EITHER ⟨turned out well ~ by accident or design⟩

whet·stone \'hwet-₁stōn\ *n* : a stone for sharpening blades

whey \'hwā\ *n* : the watery part of milk that separates after the milk sours and thickens

¹**which** \'hwich\ *adj* **1** : being what one or ones out of a group ⟨~ shirt should I wear⟩ **2** : WHICHEVER

²**which** *pron* **1** : which one or ones ⟨~ is yours⟩ ⟨~ are his⟩ ⟨it's in May or June, I'm not sure ~⟩ **2** : WHICHEVER ⟨we have all kinds; take ~ you like⟩ **3** — used to introduce a relative clause and to serve as a substitute therein for the noun modified by the clause ⟨the money ~ is coming to me⟩

¹**which·ev·er** \hwich-'e-vər\ *adj* : no matter which ⟨~ way you go⟩

²**whichever** *pron* : whatever one or ones

which·so·ev·er \₁hwich-sō-'e-vər\ *pron or adj, archaic* : WHICHEVER

whick·er \'hwi-kər\ *vb* : NEIGH, WHINNY — **whicker** *n*

¹**whiff** \'hwif\ *n* **1** : a quick puff or slight gust (as of air) **2** : an inhalation of odor, gas, or smoke **3** : a slight trace ⟨a ~ of scandal⟩ **4** : STRIKEOUT

²**whiff** *vb* **1** : to expel, puff out, or blow away in or as if in whiffs **2** : to inhale an odor **3** : STRIKE OUT 3

Whig \'hwig\ *n* [short for *Whiggamore*, member of a Scottish group that marched to Edinburgh in 1648 to oppose the court party] **1** : a member or supporter of a British political group of the late 17th through early 19th centuries seeking to limit royal authority and increase parliamentary power **2** : an American favoring independence from Great Britain during the American Revolution **3** : a member or supporter of an American political party formed about 1834 to oppose the Democrats

¹**while** \'hwī(-ə)l\ *n* **1** : a period of time ⟨stay a ~⟩ **2** : the time and effort used : TROUBLE ⟨worth your ~⟩

²**while** *conj* **1** : during the time that ⟨she called ~ you were out⟩ **2** : AS LONG AS ⟨~ there's life there's hope⟩ **3** : ALTHOUGH ⟨~ he's respected, he's not liked⟩

³**while** *vb* **whiled; whil·ing** : to cause to pass esp. pleasantly ⟨~ away an hour⟩

¹**whi·lom** \'hwī-ləm\ *adv* [ME, lit., at times, fr. OE *hwīlum*, dat. pl. of *hwīl* time, while] *archaic* : FORMERLY

²**whilom** *adj* : FORMER ⟨his ~ friends⟩

whilst \'hwīlst\ *conj, chiefly Brit* : WHILE

whim \'hwim\ *n* : a sudden wish, desire, or change of mind

whim·per \'hwim-pər\ *vb* : to make a low whining plaintive or broken sound — **whimper** *n*

whim·si·cal \'hwim-zi-kəl\ *adj* **1** : full of whims : CAPRICIOUS **2** : resulting from or characterized by whim or caprice : ERRATIC — **whim·si·cal·i·ty** \₁hwim-zə-'ka-lə-tē\ *n* — **whim·si·cal·ly** \'hwim-zi-k(ə-)lē\ *adv*

whim·sy *also* **whim·sey** \'hwim-zē\ *n, pl* **whimsies** *also* **whimseys** **1** : WHIM, CAPRICE **2** : a fanciful or fantastic device, object, or creation esp. in writing or art

whine \'hwīn\ *vb* **whined; whin·ing** [ME, fr. OE *hwīnan* to whiz] **1** : to utter a usu. high-pitched plaintive or distressed cry; *also* : to make a sound similar to such a cry **2** : to complain with or as if with a whine — **whine** *n* — **whin·er** *n* — **whiny** *also* **whin·ey** \'hwī-nē\ *adj*

¹**whin·ny** \'hwi-nē\ *vb* **whin·nied; whin·ny·ing** : to neigh usu. in a low or gentle manner

²**whinny** *n, pl* **whinnies** : NEIGH

¹**whip** \'hwip\ *vb* **whipped; whip·ping** **1** : to move, snatch, or jerk quickly or forcefully ⟨~ out a gun⟩ **2** : to strike with a slender lithe implement (as a lash) esp. as a punishment; *also* : SPANK **3** : to drive or urge on by or as if by using a whip **4** : to bind or wrap (as a rope or rod) with cord in order to protect and strengthen; *also* : to wind or wrap around something **5** : DEFEAT **6** : to stir up : INCITE ⟨~ up enthusiasm⟩ **7** : to produce in a hurry ⟨~ up a meal⟩ **8** : to beat (as eggs or cream) into a froth **9** : to proceed nimbly or briskly; *also* : to flap about forcefully ⟨flags *whipping* in the wind⟩ — **whip·per** *n* — **whip into shape** : to bring forcefully to a desired state or condition

²**whip** *n* **1** : a flexible instrument used for whipping **2** : a stroke or cut with or as if with a whip **3** : a dessert made by whipping a portion of the ingredients ⟨prune ~⟩ **4** : a person who handles a whip **5** : a member of a legislative body appointed by a party to enforce party discipline **6** : a whipping or thrashing motion

whip·cord \-₁kòrd\ *n* **1** : a thin tough braided cord **2** : a strong cloth with fine diagonal cords or ribs

whip hand *n* : positive control : ADVANTAGE

whip·lash \'hwip-₁lash\ *n* **1** : the lash of a whip **2** : injury resulting from a sudden sharp movement of the neck and head (as of a person in a vehicle that is struck from the rear)

whip·per·snap·per \'hwi-pər-ˌsna-pər\ *n* : a small, insignificant, or presumptuous person

whip·pet \'hwi-pət\ *n* : any of a breed of small swift slender dogs that are used for racing

whipping boy *n* : SCAPEGOAT

whip-poor-will \'hwi-pər-ˌwil\ *n* : an American insect-eating bird with dull variegated plumage whose call at nightfall and just before dawn is suggestive of its name

whip·saw \'hwip-ˌsò\ *vb* : to beset with two or more adverse conditions or situations at once

¹**whir** *also* **whirr** \'hwər\ *vb* **whirred; whir·ring** : to move, fly, or revolve with a whir

²**whir** *also* **whirr** *n* : a continuous fluttering or vibratory sound made by something in rapid motion

¹**whirl** \'hwərl\ *vb* **1** : to move or drive in a circle or curve esp. with force or speed **2** : to turn or cause to turn rapidly in circles **3** : to turn abruptly : WHEEL **4** : to move or go quickly **5** : to become dizzy or giddy : REEL

²**whirl** *n* **1** : a rapid rotating or circling movement; *also* : something whirling **2** : COMMOTION, BUSTLE ⟨the social ∼⟩ **3** : a state of mental confusion **4** : TRY ⟨gave it a ∼⟩

whirl·i·gig \'hwər-li-ˌgig\ *n* [ME *whirlegigg*, fr. *whirlen* to whirl + *gigg* top] **1** : a child's toy having a whirling motion **2** : something that continuously whirls or changes

whirl·pool \'hwərl-ˌpül\ *n* : water moving rapidly in a circle so as to produce a depression in the center into which floating objects may be drawn

whirl·wind \-ˌwind\ *n* **1** : a small whirling windstorm **2** : a confused rush **3** : a violent or destructive force

whirly·bird \'hwər-lē-ˌbərd\ *n* : HELICOPTER

¹**whish** \'hwish\ *vb* : to move with a whish or swishing sound

²**whish** *n* : a rushing sound : SWISH

¹**whisk** \'hwisk\ *n* **1** : a quick light sweeping or brushing motion **2** : a usu. wire kitchen implement for beating food by hand **3** : WHISK BROOM

²**whisk** *vb* **1** : to move nimbly and quickly **2** : to move or convey briskly ⟨∼ed the children off to bed⟩ **3** : to beat or whip lightly ⟨∼ eggs⟩ **4** : to brush or wipe off lightly ⟨∼ a coat⟩

whisk broom *n* : a small broom with a short handle used esp. as a clothes brush

whis·ker \'hwis-kər\ *n* **1** : one hair of the beard **2** *pl* : the part of the beard that grows on the sides of the face or on the chin **3** : one of the long bristles or hairs growing near the mouth of an animal (as a cat or mouse) — **whis·kered** \-kərd\ *adj*

whis·key *or* **whis·ky** \'hwis-kē\ *n*, *pl* **whiskeys** *or* **whiskies** [Ir *uisce beatha* & ScGael *uisge beatha*, lit., water of life] : a liquor distilled from fermented wort (as that obtained from rye, corn, or barley mash)

¹**whis·per** \'hwis-pər\ *vb* **1** : to speak very low or under the breath; *also* : to tell or utter by whispering ⟨∼ a secret⟩ **2** : to make a low rustling sound — **whis·per·er** \-pər-ər\ *n*

²**whisper** *n* **1** : something communicated by or as if by whispering : HINT, RUMOR **2** : an act or instance of whispering

whist \'hwist\ *n* : a card game played by four players in two partnerships with a deck of 52 cards

¹**whis·tle** \'hwi-səl\ *n* **1** : a device by which a shrill sound is produced ⟨steam ∼⟩ ⟨tin ∼⟩ **2** : a shrill clear sound made by forcing breath out or air in through the puckered lips **3** : the sound or signal produced by a whistle or as if by whistling **4** : the shrill clear note of an animal (as a bird)

²**whistle** *vb* **whis·tled; whis·tling** **1** : to utter a shrill clear sound by blowing or drawing air through the puckered lips **2** : to utter a shrill note or call resembling a whistle **3** : to make a shrill clear sound esp. by rapid movements ⟨the wind *whistled*⟩ **4** : to blow or sound a whistle **5** : to signal or call by a whistle **6** : to produce, utter, or express by whistling ⟨∼ a tune⟩ — **whis·tler** *n*

whis·tle–blow·er \'hwi-səl-ˌblō-ər\ *n* : INFORMER

whis·tle–stop \-ˌstäp\ *n* : a brief personal appearance by a political candidate orig. on the rear platform of a touring train

whit \'hwit\ *n* [prob. alter. of ME *wiht, wight* creature, thing, fr. OE *wiht*] : the smallest part or particle : BIT

¹**white** \'hwīt\ *adj* **whit·er; whit·est** **1** : free from color **2** : of the color of new snow or milk; *esp* : of the color white **3** : light or pallid in color ⟨lips ∼ with fear⟩ **4** : SILVERY; *also* : made of silver **5** : of, relating to, or being a member of a group or race characterized by light-colored skin **6** : free from spot or blemish : PURE, INNOCENT **7** : BLANK 2 ⟨∼ space in printed matter⟩ **8** : not intended to cause harm ⟨a ∼ lie⟩ **9** : wearing white ⟨∼ friars⟩ **10** : marked by snow ⟨∼ Christmas⟩ **11** : consisting of a wide range of frequencies ⟨∼ light⟩ — **whiteness** \-nəs\ *n* — **whit·ish** \'hwī-tish\ *adj*

²**white** *n* **1** : the color of maximal lightness that characterizes objects which both reflect and transmit light : the opposite of black **2** : a white or light-colored part or thing ⟨the ∼ of an egg⟩; *also, pl* : white garments **3** : the light-colored pieces in a 2-player board game; *also* : the person by whom these are played **4** : one that is or approaches the color white **5** : a person of a light-skinned race

white ant *n* : TERMITE

white blood cell *n* : any of the colorless blood cells (as lymphocytes) that do not contain hemoglobin but do have a nucleus

white–bread \'hwīt-'bred\ *adj* : being, typical of, or having qualities (as blandness) associated with the white middle class

white·cap \'hwīt-ˌkap\ *n* : a wave crest breaking into white foam

white chocolate *n* : a whitish confection chiefly of cocoa butter, milk, and sugar

white–col·lar \'hwīt-'kä-lər\ *adj* : of, relating to, or constituting the class of salaried workers whose duties do not require the wearing of work clothes or protective clothing

white dwarf *n* : a small very dense whitish star of low luminosity

white elephant *n* **1** : an Indian elephant of a pale color that is sometimes venerated in India, Sri Lanka, Thailand, and Myanmar **2** : something requiring much care and expense and giving little profit or enjoyment

white feather *n* [fr. the superstition that a white feather in the plumage of a gamecock is a mark of a poor fighter] : a mark or symbol of cowardice

white·fish \'hwīt-ˌfish\ *n* : any of various freshwater food fishes related to the salmons and trouts

white flag *n* : a flag of pure white used to signify truce or surrender

white gold *n* : a pale alloy of gold resembling platinum in appearance

white goods *n pl* : white fabrics or articles (as sheets or towels) typically made of cotton or linen

White·hall \'hwīt-ˌhòl\ *n* : the British government

white hat *n* **1** : an admirable and honorable person **2** : a mark or symbol of goodness

white·head \-ˌhed\ *n* : a small whitish lump in the skin due to retention of secretion in an oil gland duct

white heat *n* : a temperature higher than red heat at which a body becomes brightly incandescent

white–hot *adj* **1** : being at or radiating white heat **2** : FERVID ⟨∼ enthusiasm⟩

White House \-ˌhaùs\ *n* **1** : a residence of the president of the U.S. **2** : the executive department of the U.S. government

white lead *n* : a heavy white poisonous carbonate of lead used esp. formerly as a pigment in exterior paints

white matter *n* : whitish nerve tissue esp. of the brain and spinal cord that consists largely of neuron processes enclosed in a fatty material and that typically lies under the cortical gray matter

whit·en \'hwī-tᵊn\ *vb* : to make or become white ♦ *Synonyms* BLANCH, BLEACH — **whit·en·er** *n*

white oak *n* : any of various oaks with acorns that take one year to mature; *also* : its hard durable wood

white pepper *n* : a spice that consists of the berry of a pepper plant ground after removal of its black husk

white pine *n* : a tall-growing pine of eastern No. America with needles in clusters of five; *also* : its wood

white sale *n* : a sale on white goods

white shark *n* : GREAT WHITE SHARK

white slave *n* : a woman or girl held unwillingly for purposes of prostitution — **white slavery** *n*

white·tail \'hwīt-ˌtāl\ *n* : WHITE-TAILED DEER

white–tailed deer *n* : a No. American deer with a rather long tail white on the underside and the males of which have forward-arching antlers

white–tie \-'tī\ *adj* : characterized by or requiring formal evening clothes consisting of usu. white tie and tailcoat for men and a formal gown for women

white·wall \'hwit-,wól\ *n* : an automobile tire having a white band on the sidewall

¹white·wash \-,wòsh, -,wäsh\ *vb* 1 : to whiten with whitewash 2 : to clear of a charge of wrongdoing by offering excuses, hiding facts, or conducting a perfunctory investigation 3 : SHUT OUT 2

²whitewash *n* 1 : a liquid mixture (as of lime and water) for whitening a surface 2 : a clearing of wrongdoing by whitewashing

white water *n* : frothy water (as in breakers, rapids, or falls)

white·wood \-,wùd\ *n* : any of various trees and esp. a tulip tree having light-colored wood; *also* : such wood

¹whith·er \'hwi-<u>th</u>ər\ *adv* 1 : to what place 2 : to what situation, position, degree, or end ⟨~ will this drive him⟩

²whither *conj* 1 : to the place at, in, or to which; *also* : to which place 2 : to whatever place

whith·er·so·ev·er \,hwi-<u>th</u>ər-sō-'e-vər\ *conj* : to whatever place

¹whit·ing \'hwī-tiŋ\ *n, pl* **whiting** *also* **whit·ings** : any of several usu. light or silvery food fishes (as a hake) found mostly near seacoasts

²whiting *n* : calcium carbonate in powdered form used esp. as a pigment and in putty

whit·low \'hwit-,lō\ *n* : a deep inflammation of a finger or toe with pus formation

Whit·sun·day \'hwit-'sən-dē, -sən-,dā\ *n* [ME *Whitsonday*, fr. OE *hwīta sunnandæg*, lit., white Sunday; prob. fr. the custom of wearing white robes by those newly baptized at this season] : PENTECOST

whit·tle \'hwi-t²l\ *vb* **whit·tled; whit·tling** 1 : to pare or cut off chips from the surface of (wood) with a knife; *also* : to cut or shape by such paring 2 : to reduce as if by paring down ⟨~ down expenses⟩

¹whiz *or* **whizz** \'hwiz\ *vb* **whizzed; whiz·zing** : to hum, whir, or hiss like a speeding object (as an arrow or ball) passing through air

²whiz *or* **whizz** *n, pl* **whiz·zes** : a hissing, buzzing, or whizzing sound

³whiz *n, pl* **whiz·zes** : WIZARD 2

who \'hü\ *pron* 1 : what or which person or persons ⟨~ did it⟩ ⟨~ is he⟩ ⟨~ are they⟩ 2 : the person or persons that ⟨knows ~ did it⟩ 3 — used to introduce a relative clause and to serve as a substitute therein for the substantive modified by the clause ⟨the person ~ lives there is rich⟩

WHO *abbr* World Health Organization

whoa \'wō, 'hwō, 'hō\ *vb imper* 1 — a command to an animal to stand still 2 : cease or slow a course of action or a line of thought

who·dun·it *also* **who·dun·nit** \hü-'də-nət\ *n* : a detective or mystery story

who·ev·er \hü-'e-vər\ *pron* : whatever person : no matter who

¹whole \'hōl\ *adj* [ME *hool* healthy, unhurt, entire, fr. OE *hāl*] 1 : being in healthy or sound condition : free from defect or damage 2 : having all its proper parts or elements ⟨~ milk⟩ 3 : constituting the total sum of : ENTIRE ⟨owns the ~ island⟩ 4 : each or all of the ⟨the ~ family⟩ 5 : not scattered or divided : CONCENTRATED ⟨gave me his ~ attention⟩ 6 : seemingly complete or total ⟨the ~ idea is to help, not hinder⟩ ◆ **Synonyms** PERFECT, INTACT, SOUND — **whole·ness** *n*

²whole *n* 1 : a complete amount or sum 2 : something whole or entire — **on the whole** 1 : in view of all the circumstances or conditions 2 : in general

³whole *adv* : COMPLETELY, WHOLLY, ENTIRELY ⟨a ~ new term⟩

whole food *n* : a food eaten in its natural state with little or no artificial additives

whole·heart·ed \'hōl-'här-təd\ *adj* : undivided in purpose, enthusiasm, will, or commitment

whole hog *adv* : to the fullest extent : COMPLETELY ⟨accepted the proposals *whole hog*⟩

whole note *n* : a musical note equal to one measure of four beats

whole number *n* : any of the set of nonnegative integers; *also* : INTEGER

¹whole·sale \'hōl-,sāl\ *n* : the sale of goods in quantity usu. for resale by a retail merchant

²wholesale *adj* 1 : performed on a large scale without discrimination ⟨~ slaughter⟩ 2 : of, relating to, or engaged in wholesaling — **wholesale** *adv*

³wholesale *vb* **whole·saled; whole·sal·ing** : to sell at wholesale — **whole·sal·er** *n*

whole·some \'hōl-səm\ *adj* 1 : promoting mental, spiritual, or bodily health or well-being ⟨a ~ environment⟩ 2 : sound in body, mind, or morals : HEALTHY 3 : PRUDENT ⟨~ respect for the law⟩ — **whole·some·ness** *n*

whole step *n* : a musical interval comprising two half steps (as C–D or F♯–G♯)

whole wheat *adj* : made of ground entire wheat kernels

whol·ly \'hōl-lē\ *adv* 1 : COMPLETELY, TOTALLY 2 : SOLELY, EXCLUSIVELY

whom \'hüm\ *pron, objective case of* WHO

whom·ev·er \hü-'me-vər\ *pron, objective case of* WHOEVER

whom·so·ev·er \,hüm-sō-'e-vər\ *pron, objective case of* WHOSOEVER

¹whoop \'hwüp, 'hwùp, 'hüp, 'hùp\ *vb* 1 : to shout or call loudly and vigorously 2 : to make the characteristic whoop of whooping cough 3 : to go or pass with a loud noise 4 : to utter or express with a whoop; *also* : to urge, drive, or cheer with a whoop

²whoop *n* 1 : a whooping sound or utterance : SHOUT, HOOT 2 : a crowing intake of breath after a fit of coughing in whooping cough

¹whoop·ee \'hwü-(,)pē, 'hwü-\ *interj* — used to express exuberance

²whoopee *n* 1 : boisterous fun 2 : sexual play — usu. used with *make*

whooping cough *n* : an infectious bacterial disease esp. of children marked by convulsive coughing fits often followed by a shrill gasping intake of breath

whooping crane *n* : a large white nearly extinct No. American crane noted for its loud whooping call

whoop·la \'hwüp-,lä, 'hwüp-\ *n* 1 : HOOPLA 2 : boisterous merrymaking

whop·per \'hwä-pər\ *n* : something unusually large or extreme of its kind; *esp* : a monstrous lie

whop·ping \'hwä-piŋ\ *adj* : extremely large ⟨a ~ increase⟩

whore \'hòr\ *n* : PROSTITUTE

whorl \'hwòrl, 'hwərl\ *n* 1 : a group of parts (as leaves or petals) encircling an axis and esp. a plant stem 2 : something that whirls or coils around a center : COIL, SPIRAL 3 : one of the turns of a snail shell

whorled \'hwòrld, 'hwərld\ *adj* : having or arranged in whorls

¹whose \'hüz\ *adj* : of or relating to whom or which esp. as possessor or possessors, agent or agents, or object or objects of an action ⟨asked ~ bag it was⟩

²whose *pron* : whose one or ones ⟨~ is this car⟩ ⟨~ are those books⟩

who·so \'hü-,sō\ *pron* : WHOEVER

who·so·ev·er \,hü-sō-'e-vər\ *pron* : WHOEVER

whs *or* **whse** *abbr* warehouse

whsle *abbr* wholesale

¹why \'hwī\ *adv* : for what reason, cause, or purpose ⟨~ did you do it?⟩

²why *conj* 1 : the cause, reason, or purpose for which ⟨that is ~ you did it⟩ 2 : for which : on account of which ⟨knows the reason ~ you did it⟩

³why *n, pl* **whys** : REASON, CAUSE ⟨the ~s of racial prejudice⟩

⁴why \'wī, 'hwī\ *interj* — used to express surprise, hesitation, approval, disapproval, or impatience ⟨~, here's what I was looking for⟩

WI *abbr* 1 West Indies 2 Wisconsin

WIA *abbr* wounded in action

Wic·ca \'wi-kə\ *n* [prob. fr. OE *wicca* wizard] : a religion that affirms the existence of supernatural power (as magic) and of deities who inhere in nature and that ritually observes seasonal and life cycles

wick \'wik\ *n* : a loosely bound bundle of soft fibers that draws up oil, tallow, or wax to be burned in a candle, oil lamp, or stove

wick·ed \'wi-kəd\ *adj* 1 : morally bad : EVIL, SINFUL 2

: FIERCE, VICIOUS **3** : ROGUISH ⟨a ∼ glance⟩ **4** : REPUGNANT, VILE ⟨a ∼ odor⟩ **5** : HARMFUL, DANGEROUS ⟨a ∼ attack⟩ **6** : impressively excellent ⟨throws a ∼ fastball⟩ — **wick·ed·ly** *adv* — **wick·ed·ness** *n*

wick·er \'wi-kər\ *n* **1** : a small pliant branch (as an osier or a withe) **2** : WICKERWORK — **wicker** *adj*

wick·er·work \-,wərk\ *n* : work made of osiers, twigs, or rods : BASKETRY

wick·et \'wi-kət\ *n* **1** : a small gate or door; *esp* : one forming a part of or placed near a larger one **2** : a window-like opening usu. with a grille or grate (as at a ticket office) **3** : a set of three upright rods topped by two crosspieces bowled at in cricket **4** : an arch or hoop in croquet

wick·i·up \'wi-kē-,əp\ *n* : a hut used by nomadic Indians of the western and southwestern U.S. with a usu. oval base and a rough frame covered with reed mats, grass, or brushwood

wid *abbr* widow, widower

¹wide \'wīd\ *adj* **wid·er; wid·est** **1** : covering a vast area **2** : measured across or at right angles to the length **3** : not narrow : BROAD; *also* : ROOMY **4** : opened to full width ⟨eyes ∼ with wonder⟩ **5** : not limited : EXTENSIVE ⟨∼ experience⟩ **6** : far from the goal, mark, or truth ⟨was ∼ of the truth⟩ — **wide·ly** *adv*

²wide *adv* **wid·er; wid·est** **1** : over a great distance or extent : WIDELY ⟨searched far and ∼⟩ **2** : over a specified distance, area, or extent **3** : so as to leave a wide space between ⟨∼ apart⟩ **4** : so as to clear by a considerable distance ⟨ran ∼ around left end⟩ **5** : COMPLETELY, FULLY ⟨opened her eyes ∼⟩

wide area network *n* : a computer network (as the Internet) over a large area (as a country or the globe) for sharing resources or exchanging data

wide–awake \,wīd-ə-'wāk\ *adj* : fully awake; *also* : KNOWING, ALERT

wide–body \'wīd-,bä-dē\ *n* : a large jet aircraft having a wide cabin

wide–eyed \'wīd-'īd\ *adj* **1** : having the eyes wide open esp. with wonder or astonishment **2** : NAIVE

wide–mouthed \-'maùthd, -'maùtht\ *adj* **1** : having one's mouth opened wide (as in awe) **2** : having a wide mouth ⟨∼ jars⟩

wid·en \'wī-dᵊn\ *vb* : to increase in width, scope, or extent

wide·spread \'wīd-'spred\ *adj* **1** : widely scattered or prevalent **2** : widely extended or spread out ⟨∼ wings⟩

widgeon *var of* WIGEON

¹wid·ow \'wi-dō\ *n* : a woman who has lost her husband by death and has not married again — **wid·ow·hood** *n*

²widow *vb* : to cause to become a widow or widower

wid·ow·er \'wi-də-wər\ *n* : a man who has lost his wife by death and has not married again

width \'width\ *n* **1** : a distance from side to side : the measurement taken at right angles to the length : BREADTH **2** : largeness of extent or scope; *also* : FULLNESS **3** : a measured and cut piece of material ⟨a ∼ of calico⟩

wield \'wēld\ *vb* **1** : to use or handle esp. effectively ⟨∼ a broom⟩ **2** : to exert authority by means of : EMPLOY ⟨∼ influence⟩ — **wield·er** *n*

wie·ner *also* **wei·ner** \'wē-nər\ *n* [short for *wienerwurst*, fr. G, lit., Vienna sausage] : FRANKFURTER

wife \'wīf\ *n, pl* **wives** \'wīvz\ **1** *dial* : WOMAN **2** : a woman acting in a specified capacity — used in combination ⟨fish*wife*⟩ **3** : a female partner in a marriage — **wife·hood** *n* — **wife·less** *adj* — **wife·ly** *adj*

wig \'wig\ *n* [short for *periwig*, modif. of MF *perruque*, fr. It *parrucca, perrucca* hair, wig] : a manufactured covering of natural or synthetic hair for the head; *also* : TOUPEE

wi·geon *or* **wid·geon** \'wi-jən\ *n, pl* **wigeon** *or* **wigeons** *or* **widgeon** *or* **widgeons** : any of several medium-sized freshwater ducks

wig·gle \'wi-gəl\ *vb* **wig·gled; wig·gling** **1** : to move to and fro with quick jerky or shaking movements : JIGGLE **2** : WRIGGLE — **wiggle** *n*

wig·gler \'wi-glər, -gə-lər\ *n* **1** : a larva or pupa of a mosquito **2** : one that wiggles

wig·gly \'wi-glē, -gə-lē\ *adj* **1** : tending to wiggle ⟨a ∼ worm⟩ **2** : WAVY ⟨∼ lines⟩

wight \'wīt\ *n* : a living being : CREATURE

wig·let \'wi-glət\ *n* : a small wig used esp. to enhance a hairstyle

¹wig·wag \'wig-,wag\ *vb* **1** : to signal by or as if by a flag or light waved according to a code **2** : to make or cause to make a signal (as with the hand or arm)

²wigwag *n* : the art or practice of wigwagging

wig·wam \'wig-,wäm\ *n* : a hut of the Indians of the eastern U.S. having typically an arched framework of poles overlaid with bark, rush mats, or hides

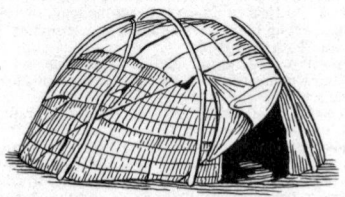

wigwam

¹wild \'wī(-ə)ld\ *adj* **1** : living in a state of nature and not ordinarily tamed ⟨∼ ducks⟩ **2** : growing or produced without human aid or care ⟨∼ honey⟩ ⟨∼ plants⟩ **3** : WASTE, DESOLATE ⟨∼ country⟩ **4** : UNCONTROLLED, UNRESTRAINED, UNRULY ⟨∼ passions⟩ ⟨a ∼ young stallion⟩ **5** : TURBULENT, STORMY ⟨a ∼ night⟩ **6** : EXTRAVAGANT, FANTASTIC, CRAZY ⟨∼ ideas⟩ **7** : indicative of strong passion, desire, or emotion ⟨a ∼ stare⟩ **8** : UNCIVILIZED, SAVAGE **9** : deviating from the natural or expected course : ERRATIC ⟨a ∼ throw⟩ **10** : able to represent any playing card designated by the holder ⟨deuces ∼⟩ — **wild·ly** *adv* — **wild·ness** *n*

²wild *adv* **1** : WILDLY **2** : without regulation or control ⟨running ∼⟩

³wild *n* **1** : WILDERNESS **2** : a natural or undomesticated state or existence

wild boar *n* : an Old World wild hog from which most domestic swine have been derived

wild card *n* **1** : an unknown or unpredictable factor **2** : one picked to fill a leftover play-off or tournament position **3** *usu* **wild·card** : a symbol (as ? or *) used in a keyword search to represent the presence of unspecified characters

wild carrot *n* : QUEEN ANNE'S LACE

¹wild·cat \'wī(-ə)ld-,kat\ *n, pl* **wildcats** **1** : any of various small or medium-sized cats (as a lynx or ocelot) **2** : a quick-tempered hard-fighting person

²wildcat *adj* **1** : not sound or safe ⟨∼ schemes⟩ **2** : initiated by a group of workers without formal union approval ⟨∼ strike⟩

³wildcat *vb* **wild·cat·ted; wild·cat·ting** : to drill an oil or gas well in a region not known to be productive

wil·de·beest \'wil-də-,bēst\ *n, pl* **wildebeests** *also* **wildebeest** [Afrikaans *wildebees*, fr. *wilde* wild + *bees* ox] : either of two large African antelopes with an oxlike head and horns and a horselike mane and tail

wil·der·ness \'wil-dər-nəs\ *n* [ME, fr. *wildern* wild, fr. OE *wilddēoren* of wild beasts] : an uncultivated and uninhabited region

wild·fire \'wī(-ə)ld-,fī(-ə)r\ *n* : an uncontrollable fire — **like wildfire** : very rapidly

wild·flow·er \-,flaù(-ə)r\ *n* : the flower of a wild or uncultivated plant or the plant bearing it

wild·fowl \-,faù(-ə)l\ *n* : a bird and esp. a waterfowl hunted as game

wild–goose chase *n* : the pursuit of something unattainable

wild·life \'wī(-ə)ld-,līf\ *n* : nonhuman living things and esp. wild animals living in their natural environment

wild oat *n* **1** : any of several Old World wild grasses **2** *pl* : offenses and indiscretions attributed to youthful exuberance — usu. used in the phrase *sow one's wild oats*

wild rice *n* : a No. American aquatic grass; *also* : its edible seed

wild type *n* : a gene or trait that is typical of a natural population of organisms in contrast to that of mutant forms; *also* : an organism with such a gene or trait

wild·wood \'wī(-ə)ld-,wùd\ *n* : a wood unaltered or unfrequented by humans

¹**wile** \'wī(-ə)l\ *n* **1** : a trick or stratagem intended to ensnare or deceive; *also* : a playful trick **2** : TRICKERY, GUILE

²**wile** *vb* **wiled; wil·ing** : LURE, ENTICE

¹**will** \'wil\ *vb, past* **would** \'wu̇d\ *pres sing & pl* **will** **1** : WISH, DESIRE ⟨call it what you ∼⟩ **2** — used as an auxiliary verb to express (1) desire, willingness, or in negative constructions refusal ⟨∼ you have another⟩ ⟨he won't do it⟩, (2) customary or habitual action ⟨∼ get angry over nothing⟩, (3) simple futurity ⟨tomorrow we ∼ go shopping⟩, (4) capability or sufficiency ⟨the back seat ∼ hold three⟩, (5) determination or willfulness ⟨I ∼ go despite them⟩, (6) probability ⟨that ∼ be the mailman⟩, (7) inevitability ⟨accidents ∼ happen⟩, or (8) a command ⟨you ∼ do as I say⟩

²**will** *n* **1** : wish or desire often combined with determination ⟨the ∼ to win⟩ **2** : something desired; *esp* : a choice or determination of one having authority or power **3** : the act, process, or experience of willing : VOLITION **4** : the mental powers manifested as wishing, choosing, desiring, or intending **5** : a disposition to act according to principles or ends **6** : power of controlling one's own actions or emotions ⟨a leader of iron ∼⟩ **7** : a legal document in which a person declares to whom his or her possessions are to go after death

³**will** *vb* **1** : to dispose of by or as if by a will : BEQUEATH **2** : to determine by an act of choice; *also* : DECREE, ORDAIN **3** : INTEND, PURPOSE; *also* : CHOOSE

will·ful *or* **wil·ful** \'wil-fəl\ *adj* **1** : governed by will without regard to reason : OBSTINATE **2** : INTENTIONAL ⟨∼ murder⟩ — **will·ful·ly** *adv*

wil·lies \'wi-lēz\ *n pl* : a fit of nervousness : JITTERS — used with *the*

will·ing \'wi-liŋ\ *adj* **1** : inclined or favorably disposed in mind : READY ⟨∼ to go⟩ **2** : prompt to act or respond ⟨∼ workers⟩ **3** : done, borne, or accepted voluntarily or without reluctance **4** : of or relating to the will : VOLITIONAL — **will·ing·ly** *adv* — **will·ing·ness** *n*

wil·li·waw \'wi-lē-ˌwȯ\ *n* : a sudden violent gust of cold land air common along mountainous coasts of high latitudes

will—o'—the—wisp \ˌwil-ə-thə-'wisp\ *n* **1** : a light that appears at night over marshy grounds **2** : a misleading or elusive goal or hope

wil·low \'wi-lō\ *n* **1** : any of a genus of quick-growing shrubs and trees with tough pliable shoots **2** : an object made of willow wood

wil·low·ware \-ˌwer\ *n* : dinnerware that is usu. blue and white and that is decorated with a story-telling design featuring a large willow tree by a little bridge

wil·lowy \'wi-lə-wē\ *adj; also* : gracefully tall and slender

will·pow·er \'wil-ˌpau̇-(ə)r\ *n* : energetic determination : RESOLUTENESS

wil·ly—nil·ly \ˌwi-lē-'ni-lē\ *adv or adj* [alter. of *will I nill I or will ye nill ye or will he nill he; nill* fr. archaic *nill* to be unwilling, fr. ME *nilen,* fr. OE *nyllan,* fr. *ne* not + *wyllan* to wish] : without regard for one's choice : by compulsion ⟨they rushed us along ∼⟩

¹**wilt** \'wilt\ *vb* **1** : to lose or cause to lose freshness and become limp esp. from lack of water : DROOP **2** : to grow weak or faint : LANGUISH

²**wilt** *n* : any of various plant disorders marked by wilting and often shriveling

wily \'wī-lē\ *adj* **wil·i·er; -est** : full of guile : TRICKY — **wil·i·ness** \-lē-nəs\ *n*

wimp \'wimp\ *n* : a weak, cowardly, or ineffectual person — **wimpy** \'wim-pē\ *adj*

¹**wim·ple** \'wim-pəl\ *n* : a cloth covering worn over the head and around the neck and chin by women esp. in the late medieval period and by some nuns

²**wimple** *vb* **wim·pled; wim·pling** **1** : to cover with or as if with a wimple **2** : to ripple or cause to ripple

¹**win** \'win\ *vb* **won** \'wən\; **win·ning** [ME *winnen,* fr. OE *winnan* to struggle] **1** : to get possession of esp. by effort : GAIN; *also* : to obtain by work : EARN **2** : to gain in or as if in battle or contest; *also* : to be the victor in ⟨won the war⟩ **3** : to solicit and gain the favor of; *esp* : to induce to accept oneself in marriage

²**win** *n* : VICTORY; *esp* : 1st place at the finish (as of a horse race)

wince \'wins\ *vb* **winced; winc·ing** : to shrink back involuntarily (as from pain) : FLINCH — **wince** *n*

winch \'winch\ *n* : a machine that has a drum on which is wound a rope or cable for hauling or hoisting — **winch** *vb*

¹**wind** \'wind\ *n* **1** : a movement of the air **2** : a prevailing force or influence : TENDENCY, TREND **3** : BREATH ⟨he had the ∼ knocked out of him⟩ **4** : gas produced in the stomach or intestines **5** : something insubstantial; *esp* : idle words **6** : air carrying a scent (as of game) **7** : INTIMATION ⟨they got ∼ of our plans⟩ **8** : WIND INSTRUMENTS; *also, pl* : players of wind instruments

²**wind** *vb* **1** : to get a scent of ⟨the dogs ∼ed the game⟩ **2** : to cause to be out of breath ⟨he was ∼ed from the climb⟩ **3** : to allow (as a horse) to rest so as to recover breath

³**wind** \'wīnd, 'wind\ *vb* **wind·ed** \'wīn-dəd, 'win-\ *or* **wound** \'wau̇nd\; **wind·ing** : to sound by blowing ⟨∼ a horn⟩

⁴**wind** \'wīnd\ *vb* **wound** \'wau̇nd\ *also* **wind·ed; wind·ing** **1** : ENTANGLE, INVOLVE **2** : to introduce stealthily : INSINUATE **3** : to encircle or cover with something pliable : WRAP, COIL, TWINE ⟨∼ a bobbin⟩ **4** : to hoist or haul by a rope or chain and a winch **5** : to tighten the spring of; *also* : CRANK **6** : to raise to a high level (as of excitement) **7** : to cause to move in a curving line or path **8** : to have a curving course or shape ⟨a river ∼ing through the valley⟩ **9** : to move or lie so as to encircle

⁵**wind** \'wīnd\ *n* : COIL, TURN

wind·age \'win-dij\ *n* : the influence of the wind in deflecting the course of a projectile through the air; *also* : the amount of such deflection

wind·bag \'wind-ˌbag\ *n* : an overly talkative person

wind·blown \-ˌblōn\ *adj* : blown by the wind; *also* : having the appearance of being blown by the wind

wind·break \-ˌbrāk\ *n* : a growth of trees or shrubs serving to break the force of the wind; *also* : a shelter from the wind

wind·burned \-ˌbərnd\ *adj* : irritated and inflamed by exposure to the wind — **wind·burn** \-ˌbərn\ *n*

wind·chill \-ˌchil\ *n* : a still-air temperature that would have the same cooling effect on exposed human skin as a given combination of temperature and wind speed

windchill factor *n* : WINDCHILL

wind down *vb* **1** : to draw toward an end **2** : RELAX, UNWIND

wind·er \'wīn-dər\ *n* : one that winds

wind·fall \'wind-ˌfȯl\ *n* **1** : something (as a tree or fruit) blown down by the wind **2** : an unexpected or sudden gift, gain, or advantage

wind·flow·er \-ˌflau̇-(ə)r\ *n* : ANEMONE

¹**wind·ing** \'wīn-diŋ\ *n* : material (as wire) wound or coiled about an object

²**winding** *adj* **1** : having a pronounced curve or spiral ⟨∼ stairs⟩ **2** : having a course that winds ⟨a ∼ road⟩

wind·ing—sheet \-ˌshēt\ *n* : SHROUD

wind instrument *n* : a musical instrument (as a flute or horn) sounded by wind esp. by the breath

wind·jam·mer \'wind-ˌja-mər\ *n* : a sailing ship; *also* : one of its crew

wind·lass \'wind-ləs\ *n* [ME *wyndlas,* alter. of *wyndase,* OF *guindas, windas,* fr. ON *vindáss,* fr. *vinda* to wind + *áss* pole] : a winch used esp. on ships for hoisting or hauling

wind·mill \'wind-ˌmil\ *n* : a mill or machine worked by the wind turning sails or vanes that radiate from a central shaft

win·dow \'win-dō\ *n* [ME *windowe,* fr. ON *vindauga,* fr. *vindr* wind + *auga* eye] **1** : an opening in the wall of a building to let in light and air; *also* : the framework with fittings that closes such an opening **2** : WINDOWPANE **3** : an opening resembling or suggesting that of a window in a building **4** : an interval of time during which certain conditions or an opportunity exists **5** : a rectangular box appearing on a computer screen on which information (as files or program output) is displayed — **win·dow·less** *adj*

window box *n* : a box for growing plants in or by a window

window dressing *n* **1** : display of merchandise in a store window **2** : a showing made to create a deceptively favorable impression

win·dow·pane \'win-dō-ˌpān\ *n* : a pane in a window
win·dow–shop \-ˌshäp\ *vb* : to look at the displays in store windows without going inside the stores to make purchases — **win·dow–shop·per** *n*
win·dow·sill \-ˌsil\ *n* : the horizontal member at the bottom of a window
wind·pipe \'wind-ˌpīp\ *n* : TRACHEA
wind·proof \-'prüf\ *adj* : impervious to wind ⟨a ~ jacket⟩
wind·row \'wind-ˌrō\ *n* **1** : hay raked up into a row to dry **2** : a row of something (as dry leaves) swept up by or as if by the wind
wind shear *n* : a radical shift in wind speed and direction that occurs over a very short distance
wind·shield \'wind-ˌshēld\ *n* : a transparent screen (as of glass) in front of the occupants of a vehicle
wind sock *n* : an open-ended truncated cloth cone mounted in an elevated position to indicate wind direction
wind·storm \-ˌstorm\ *n* : a storm with high wind and little or no rain
wind·surf·ing \-ˌsər-fiŋ\ *n* : the sport or activity of riding a sailboard — **wind·surf** \-ˌsərf\ *vb* — **wind·surf·er** *n*
wind·swept \'wind-ˌswept\ *adj* : swept by or as if by wind ⟨~ plains⟩
wind tunnel *n* : an enclosed passage through which air is blown to investigate air flow around an object
wind·up \'wīn-ˌdəp\ *n* **1** : CONCLUSION, FINISH **2** : a series of regular and distinctive motions made by a pitcher preliminary to delivering a pitch
wind up *vb* **1** : to bring or come to a conclusion : END **2** : to put in order for the purpose of bringing to an end **3** : to arrive in a place, situation, or condition at the end or as a result of a course of action ⟨*wound up* as paupers⟩ **4** : to make a pitching windup
¹wind·ward \'win-dwərd\ *n* : the side or direction from which the wind is blowing
²windward *adj* : being in or facing the direction from which the wind is blowing
windy \'win-dē\ *adj* **wind·i·er; -est** **1** : having wind : exposed to winds ⟨a ~ day⟩ ⟨a ~ prairie⟩ **2** : STORMY : FLATULENT **4** : indulging in or characterized by useless talk : VERBOSE
¹wine \'wīn\ *n* [ME *win*, fr. OE *wīn*, ultim. fr. L *vinum*] **1** : fermented grape juice used as a beverage **2** : the usu. fermented juice of a plant product (as fruit) used as a beverage ⟨rice ~⟩
²wine *vb* **wined; win·ing** : to treat to or drink wine
wine cellar *n* : a room for storing wines; *also* : a stock of wines
wine·grow·er \-ˌgrō-ər\ *n* : one that cultivates a vineyard and makes wine
wine·press \-ˌpres\ *n* : a vat in which juice is pressed from grapes
win·ery \'wī-nə-rē, 'wīn-rē\ *n, pl* **-eries** : a wine-making establishment
¹wing \'wiŋ\ *n* **1** : one of the movable feathered or membranous paired appendages by means of which a bird, bat, or insect flies **2** : something suggesting a wing; *esp* : an airfoil that develops the lift which supports an aircraft in flight **3** : a plant or animal appendage or part likened to a wing **4** : a turned-back or extended edge on an article of clothing **5** : a means of flight or rapid progress **6** : the act or manner of flying : FLIGHT **7** *pl* : the area at the side of the stage out of sight **8** : one of the positions or players on either side of a center position or line **9** : either of two opposing groups within an organization : FACTION **10** : a unit in military aviation consisting of two or more squadrons — **wing·less** *adj* — **wing·like** \-ˌlīk\ *adj* — **on the wing** : in flight : FLYING — **under one's wing** : in one's charge or care
²wing *vb* **1** : to fit with wings; *also* : to enable to fly easily **2** : to pass through in flight : FLY ⟨~ the air⟩ ⟨swallows ~*ing* southward⟩ **3** : to let fly : DISPATCH **4** : to wound in the wing ⟨~ a bird⟩; *also* : to wound without killing **5** : to perform without preparation : IMPROVISE ⟨~*ing* it⟩
wing·ding \'wiŋ-ˌdiŋ\ *n* : a wild, lively, or lavish party
winged \'wiŋd, 'wiŋ-əd, *in compounds* 'wiŋd\ *adj* **1** : having wings esp. of a specified character **2** : soaring with or as if with wings : ELEVATED **3** : SWIFT, RAPID
wing nut *n* : a nut with winglike extensions that can be gripped with the thumb and finger

wing·span \'wiŋ-ˌspan\ *n* : the distance between the tips of a pair of wings
wing·spread \-ˌspred\ *n* : the spread of the wings; *esp* : the distance between the tips of the fully extended wings of a winged animal
¹wink \'wiŋk\ *vb* **1** : to close and open one eye quickly as a signal or hint **2** : to close and open the eyes quickly : BLINK **3** : to avoid seeing or noticing something ⟨~ at a traffic violation⟩ **4** : TWINKLE, FLICKER — **wink·er** \'wiŋ-kər\ *n*
²wink *n* **1** : a brief period of sleep : NAP **2** : an act of winking; *esp* : a hint or sign given by winking **3** : INSTANT ⟨dries in a ~⟩
win·ner \'wi-nər\ *n* : one that wins
¹win·ning \'wi-niŋ\ *n* **1** : VICTORY **2** : something won; *esp* : money won at gambling ⟨large ~s⟩
²winning *adj* **1** : successful esp. in competition **2** : ATTRACTIVE, CHARMING
win·now \'wi-nō\ *vb* **1** : to remove (as chaff) by a current of air; *also* : to free (as grain) from waste in this manner **2** : to sort or separate as if by winnowing
wino \'wī-nō\ *n, pl* **win·os** : one who is addicted to drinking wine
win·some \'win-səm\ *adj* [ME *winsum*, fr. OE *wynsum*, fr. *wynn* joy] **1** : generally pleasing and engaging **2** : CHEERFUL, GAY — **win·some·ly** *adv* — **win·some·ness** *n*
¹win·ter \'win-tər\ *n* : the season of the year in any region in which the noonday sun shines most obliquely : the coldest period of the year
²winter *vb* **1** : to pass the winter ⟨~*ed* in Florida⟩ **2** : to feed or find food during the winter ⟨~*ed* on hay⟩
³winter *adj* : sown in autumn for harvesting in the following spring or summer ⟨~ wheat⟩
win·ter·green \'win-tər-ˌgrēn\ *n* **1** : a low evergreen plant of the heath family with white bell-shaped flowers and spicy red berries **2** : an aromatic oil or its flavor from the wintergreen
win·ter·ize \'win-tə-ˌrīz\ *vb* **-ized; -iz·ing** : to make ready for winter
win·ter–kill \'win-tər-ˌkil\ *vb* : to kill or die by exposure to winter weather
winter squash *n* : any of various hard-shelled squashes that keep well in storage
win·ter·tide \-ˌtīd\ *n* : WINTER
win·ter·time \-ˌtīm\ *n* : WINTER
win·try \'win-trē\ *also* **win·tery** \'win-tə-rē\ *adj* **win·tri·er; -est** **1** : of, relating to, or characteristic of winter ⟨~ weather⟩ **2** : CHILLING, CHEERLESS ⟨a ~ welcome⟩
¹wipe \'wīp\ *vb* **wiped; wip·ing** **1** : to clean or dry by rubbing ⟨~ dishes⟩ **2** : to remove by or as if by rubbing ⟨~ away tears⟩ **3** : to erase completely : OBLITERATE **4** : to pass or draw over a surface ⟨*wiped* his hand across his face⟩ — **wip·er** *n*
²wipe *n* **1** : an act or instance of wiping; *also* : BLOW, STRIKE, SWIPE **2** : something used for wiping
wipe out *vb* : to destroy completely
¹wire \'wī(-ə)r\ *n* **1** : metal in the form of a thread or slender rod; *also* : a thread or rod of metal **2** : hidden or secret influences controlling the action of a person or organization — usu. used in pl. ⟨pull ~s⟩ **3** : a line of wire for conducting electric current **4** : a telegraph or telephone wire or system **5** : TELEGRAM, CABLEGRAM **6** : the finish line of a race
²wire *vb* **wired; wir·ing** **1** : to provide or equip with wire ⟨~ a house⟩ **2** : to bind, string, or mount with wire **3** : to send or send word to by telegraph
wired *adj* **1** : furnished with wires **2** : connected to the Internet **3** : feverishly excited
wire·hair \'wī(-ə)r-ˌher\ *n* : a wirehaired dog or cat
wire·haired \-'herd\ *adj* : having a stiff wiry outer coat of hair
¹wire·less \-ləs\ *adj* **1** : having no wire or wires **2** : RADIO **3** : of or relating to data communications using radio waves
²wireless *n* **1** : telecommunication involving signals transmitted by radio waves; *also* : the technology used in radio telecommunication **2** *chiefly Brit* : RADIO
wire–pull·er \-ˌpu̇-lər\ *n* : one who uses secret or underhanded means to influence the acts of a person or organization — **wire–pull·ing** *n*

wire service *n* : a news agency that sends out syndicated news copy to subscribers by wire or satellite

wire·tap \-₁tap\ *n* : the act or an instance of tapping a telephone or telegraph wire to get information; *also* : an electrical connection used for such tapping — **wiretap** *vb* — **wire·tap·per** \-₁ta-pər\ *n*

wire·worm \-₁wərm\ *n* : any of various slender hard-coated beetle larvae esp. destructive to plant roots

wir·ing \'wī(-ə)r-iŋ\ *n* : a system of wires

wiry \'wī(-ə)r-ē\ *adj* **wir·i·er** \'wī-rē-ər\; **-est** **1** : made of or resembling wire **2** : slender yet strong and sinewy — **wir·i·ness** \'wī-rē-nəs\ *n*

Wis *or* **Wisc** *abbr* Wisconsin

Wisd *abbr* Wisdom

wis·dom \'wiz-dəm\ *n* [ME, fr. OE *wīsdom*, fr. *wīs* wise] **1** : accumulated philosophic or scientific learning : KNOWLEDGE; *also* : INSIGHT **2** : good sense : JUDGMENT **3** : a wise attitude or course of action

Wisdom *n* — see BIBLE table

Wisdom of Sol·o·mon \-'sä-lə-mən\ — see BIBLE table

wisdom tooth *n* : the last tooth of the full set on each side of the upper and lower jaws of humans

¹wise \'wīz\ *n* : WAY, MANNER, FASHION ⟨in no ∼⟩ ⟨in this ∼⟩

²wise *adj* **wis·er; wis·est** **1** : having wisdom : SAGE **2** : having or showing good sense or good judgment **3** : aware of what is going on : KNOWING ⟨got ∼ to his secrets⟩; *also* : CRAFTY, SHREWD **4** : possessing inside information **5** : INSOLENT, FRESH ⟨a ∼ retort⟩ — **wise·ly** *adv*

-wise \-₁wīz\ *adv comb form* : in the manner or direction of ⟨slant*wise*⟩

wise·acre \'wīz-₁ā-kər\ *n* [MD *wijssegger* soothsayer] : SMART ALECK

¹wise·crack \'wīz-₁krak\ *n* : a clever, smart, or flippant remark

²wisecrack *vb* : to make a wisecrack

wise guy *n* : SMART ALECK

¹wish \'wish\ *vb* **1** : to have a desire : long for ⟨∼ you were here⟩ ⟨∼ for a puppy⟩ **2** : to form or express a wish concerning ⟨∼ed him a happy birthday⟩ **3** : BID ⟨he ∼ed me good morning⟩ **4** : to request by expressing a desire ⟨I ∼ you to go now⟩

²wish *n* **1** : an act or instance of wishing or desire : WANT; *also* : GOAL **2** : an expressed will or desire

wish·bone \-₁bōn\ *n* : a forked bone in front of the breastbone in most birds

wish·ful \'wish-fəl\ *adj* **1** : expressive of a wish; *also* : having a wish **2** : according with wishes rather than fact ⟨∼ thinking⟩

wishy–washy \'wi-shē-₁wò-shē, -₁wä-\ *adj* : WEAK, INSIPID; *also* : morally feeble

wisp \'wisp\ *n* **1** : a small handful (as of hay or straw) **2** : a thin strand, strip, or fragment ⟨a ∼ of hair⟩; *also* : a thready streak ⟨a ∼ of smoke⟩ **3** : something frail, slight, or fleeting ⟨a ∼ of a smile⟩ — **wispy** *adj*

wis·te·ria \wis-'tir-ē-ə\ *also* **wis·tar·ia** \-'tir-ē-ə *also* -'ter-\ *n* : any of a genus of chiefly Asian mostly woody vines related to the peas and widely grown for their long showy clusters of blue, white, purple, or rose flowers

wist·ful \'wist-fəl\ *adj* : feeling or showing a timid desire — **wist·ful·ly** *adv* — **wist·ful·ness** *n*

wit \'wit\ *n* **1** : reasoning power : INTELLIGENCE **2** : mental soundness : SANITY — usu. used in pl. **3** : RESOURCEFULNESS, INGENUITY; *esp* : quickness and cleverness·in handling words and ideas **4** : a talent for making clever remarks; *also* : a person noted for making witty remarks — **wit·ted** \'wi-təd\ *adj* — **at one's wit's end** : at a loss for a means of solving a problem

¹witch \'wich\ *n* **1** : a person believed to have magic power; *esp* : SORCERESS **2** : an ugly old woman : HAG **3** : a charming or alluring girl or woman

²witch *vb* : BEWITCH

witch·craft \'wich-₁kraft\ *n* : the power or practices of a witch : SORCERY

witch doctor *n* : a person in a primitive society who uses magic to treat sickness and to fight off evil spirits

witch·ery \'wi-chə-rē\ *n, pl* **-er·ies** **1** : SORCERY **2** : FASCINATION, CHARM

witch·grass \'wich-₁gras\ *n* : any of several grasses that are weeds in cultivated areas

witch ha·zel \'wich-₁hā-zəl\ *n* **1** : a shrub of eastern No. America bearing small yellow flowers in the fall **2** : a soothing alcoholic lotion made from witch hazel bark

witch–hunt \'wich-₁hənt\ *n* **1** : a searching out and persecution of persons accused of witchcraft **2** : the searching out and deliberate harassment esp. of political opponents

witch·ing \'wi-chiŋ\ *adj* : of, relating to, or suitable for sorcery or supernatural occurrences

with \'with, 'with\ *prep* **1** : AGAINST ⟨a fight ∼ his brother⟩ **2** : FROM ⟨parting ∼ friends⟩ **3** : in mutual relation to ⟨talk ∼ a friend⟩ **4** : in the company of ⟨went there ∼ her⟩ **5** : AS REGARDS, TOWARD ⟨is patient ∼ children⟩ **6** : compared to ⟨on equal terms ∼ another⟩ **7** : in support of ⟨I'm ∼ you all the way⟩ **8** : in the presence of : CONTAINING ⟨tea ∼ sugar⟩ **9** : in the opinion of : as judged by ⟨their arguments had weight ∼ her⟩ **10** : BECAUSE OF, THROUGH ⟨pale ∼ anger⟩; *also* : by means of ⟨hit him ∼ a club⟩ **11** : in a manner indicating ⟨work ∼ a will⟩ **12** : GIVEN, GRANTED ⟨∼ your permission I'll leave⟩ **13** : HAVING ⟨came ∼ good news⟩ ⟨stood there ∼ his mouth open⟩ **14** : characterized by ⟨boys ∼ good morals⟩ **15** : at the time of : right after ⟨∼ that we left⟩ **16** : DESPITE ⟨∼ all her cleverness, she failed⟩ **17** : in the direction of ⟨swim ∼ the tide⟩

with·al \wi-'thòl, -'thól\ *adv* **1** : together with this : BESIDES **2** : on the other hand : NEVERTHELESS

with·draw \with-'drò, with-\ *vb* **-drew** \-'drü\; **-drawn** \-'dròn\; **-draw·ing** \-'dró-iŋ\ **1** : to take back or away **2** : REMOVE **2** : to call back (as from consideration); *also* : RETRACT **3** : to go away : RETREAT, LEAVE **4** : to terminate one's participation in or use of something

with·draw·al \-'dró-əl\ *n* **1** : an act or instance of withdrawing **2** : the discontinuance of the use or administration of a drug and esp. an addicting drug; *also* : the period following such discontinuance marked by often painful physiological and psychological symptoms **3** : a pathological retreat from the real world (as in some schizophrenic states)

with·drawn \with-'dròn\ *adj* **1** : ISOLATED, SECLUDED **2** : socially detached and unresponsive

withe \'with\ *n* : a slender flexible twig or branch

with·er \'wi-thər\ *vb* **1** : to shrivel from or as if from loss of bodily moisture and esp. sap **2** : to lose or cause to lose vitality, force, or freshness ⟨their enthusiasm ∼ed⟩ **3** : to cause to feel shriveled ⟨∼ed him with a glance⟩

with·ers \'wi-thərz\ *n pl* : the ridge between the shoulder bones of a horse; *also* : the corresponding part in other 4-footed animals

with·hold \with-'hōld, with-\ *vb* **-held** \-'held\; **-hold·ing** **1** : to hold back : RESTRAIN; *also* : RETAIN **2** : to refrain from granting, giving, or allowing ⟨∼ permission⟩ ⟨∼ names⟩

withholding tax *n* : a tax on income withheld at the source

¹with·in \wi-'thin, -'thin-\ *adv* **1** : in or into the interior : INSIDE **2** : inside oneself : INWARDLY

²within *prep* **1** : inside the limits or influence of ⟨∼ call⟩ **2** : in the limits or compass of ⟨∼ a mile⟩ **3** : in or to the inner part of ⟨∼ the room⟩

with·it \'wi-thət, -thət\ *adj* : socially or culturally up-to-date

¹with·out \wi-'thaùt, -'thaùt\ *prep* **1** : OUTSIDE **2** : LACKING ⟨∼ hope⟩; *also* : not accompanied by or showing ⟨spoke ∼ thinking⟩

²without *adv* **1** : on the outside : EXTERNALLY **2** : with something lacking or absent ⟨has learned to do ∼⟩

with·stand \with-'stand, with-\ *vb* **-stood** \-'stùd\; **-standing** : to stand against : RESIST; *esp* : to oppose (as an attack) successfully

wit·less \'wit-ləs\ *adj* : lacking wit or understanding : FOOLISH — **wit·less·ly** *adv* — **wit·less·ness** *n*

¹wit·ness \'wit-nəs\ *n* [ME *witnesse*, fr. OE *witnes* knowledge, testimony, witness, fr. *wit* mind, intelligence] **1** : TESTIMONY ⟨bear ∼ to the fact⟩ **2** : one that gives evidence; *esp* : one who testifies in a cause or before a court **3** : one present at a transaction so as to be able to testify that it has taken place **4** : one who has personal knowledge or experience of something **5** : something serving as evidence or proof : SIGN

²witness *vb* **1** : to bear witness : TESTIFY **2** : to act as legal witness of **3** : to furnish proof of : BETOKEN **4** : to be a witness of **5** : to be the scene of ⟨this region has ~ed many wars⟩

wit·ti·cism \'wi-tə-ˌsi-zəm\ n : a witty saying or phrase

wit·ting \'wi-tiŋ\ adj : done knowingly : INTENTIONAL — **wit·ting·ly** adv

wit·ty \'wi-tē\ adj **wit·ti·er; -est** : marked by or full of wit : AMUSING ⟨a ~ writer⟩ ⟨a ~ remark⟩ ◆ **Synonyms** HUMOROUS, FACETIOUS, JOCULAR, JOCOSE — **wit·ti·ly** \-tə-lē\ adv — **wit·ti·ness** \-tē-nəs\ n

wive \'wiv\ vb **wived; wiv·ing** : to take a wife

wives pl of WIFE

wiz·ard \'wi-zərd\ n [ME wysard wise man, fr. wys wise] **1** : MAGICIAN, SORCERER **2** : a very clever or skillful person ⟨a ~ at chess⟩

wiz·ard·ry \'wi-zər-drē\ n, pl **-ries 1** : magic skill : SORCERY **2** : great skill or cleverness in an activity

wiz·en \'wi-zᵊn, 'wē-\ vb : to become or cause to become dry, shrunken, or wrinkled ⟨a face ~ed by age⟩

wk abbr **1** week **2** work

WL abbr wavelength

wmk abbr watermark

WNW abbr west-northwest

WO abbr warrant officer

w/o abbr without

woad \'wōd\ n : a European herb related to the mustards; also : a blue dyestuff made from its leaves

wob·ble \'wä-bəl\ vb **wob·bled; wob·bling 1** : to move or cause to move with an irregular rocking or side-to-side motion **2** : TREMBLE, QUAVER **3** : WAVER, VACILLATE — **wobble** n — **wob·bly** \-bə-lē\ adj

woe \'wō\ n **1** : deep suffering from misfortune, affliction, or grief **2** : TROUBLE, MISFORTUNE ⟨economic ~s⟩

woe·be·gone \'wō-bi-ˌgȯn\ adj : exhibiting woe, sorrow, or misery; also : being in a sorry condition

woe·ful also **wo·ful** \'wō-fəl\ adj **1** : full of woe : AFFLICTED **2** : involving, bringing, or relating to woe ⟨~ stories⟩ **3** : DEPLORABLE ⟨~ test scores⟩ — **woe·ful·ly** adv

wok \'wäk\ n [Chin (Guangzhou & Hong Kong dial.) wohk] : a bowl-shaped cooking utensil used esp. in stir= frying

woke past and past part of WAKE

woken past part of WAKE

wold \'wōld\ n : an upland plain or stretch of rolling land without woods

¹wolf \'wu̇lf\ n, pl **wolves** \'wu̇lvz\ **1** : any of several large erect-eared bushy-tailed doglike predatory mammals that live and hunt in packs; esp : GRAY WOLF **2** : a fierce or destructive person — **wolf·ish** adj — **wolf in sheep's clothing** : one who hides a hostile intention with a friendly manner

²wolf vb : to eat greedily : DEVOUR

wolf·hound \-ˌhau̇nd\ n : any of several large dogs orig. used in hunting wolves

wol·fram \'wu̇l-frəm\ n : TUNGSTEN

wol·ver·ine \ˌwu̇l-və-'rēn\ n, pl **wolverines** also **wolverine** : a dark shaggy-coated flesh-eating mammal of northern forests and associated tundra that is related to the weasels

wom·an \'wu̇-mən\ n, pl **wom·en** \'wi-mən\ [ME, fr. OE wīfman, fr. wīf woman, wife + man human being, man] **1** : an adult female person **2** : WOMANKIND **3** : feminine nature : WOMANLINESS **4** : a female servant or attendant

wom·an·hood \'wu̇-mən-ˌhu̇d\ n **1** : the state of being a woman : the distinguishing qualities of a woman or of womankind **2** : WOMEN, WOMANKIND

wom·an·ish \'wu̇-mə-nish\ adj **1** : associated with or characteristic of women rather than men **2** : suggestive of a weak character : EFFEMINATE

wom·an·ize \'wu̇-mə-ˌnīz\ vb : to pursue casual sexual relationships with numerous women — **wom·an·iz·er** n

wom·an·kind \'wu̇-mən-ˌkīnd\ n : the females of the human race : WOMEN

wom·an·like \-ˌlīk\ adj : WOMANLY

wom·an·ly \-lē\ adj : having qualities characteristic of a woman — **wom·an·li·ness** \-lē-nəs\ n

woman suffrage n : possession and exercise of suffrage by women

womb \'wüm\ n **1** : UTERUS **2** : a place where something is generated

wom·bat \'wäm-ˌbat\ n : any of several stocky burrowing Australian marsupials that resemble small bears

wom·en·folk \'wi-mən-ˌfōk\ also **wom·en·folks** \-ˌfōks\ n pl : WOMEN

¹won \'wən\ past and past part of WIN

²won \'wȯn\ n, pl **won** — see MONEY table

¹won·der \'wən-dər\ n **1** : a cause of astonishment or surprise : MARVEL; also : MIRACLE **2** : the quality of exciting wonder ⟨the charm and ~ of the scene⟩ **3** : a feeling (as of awed uncertainty or uncertainty) aroused by something extraordinary or affecting

²wonder vb **1** : to feel surprise or amazement **2** : to feel curiosity or doubt ⟨~ about the future⟩

wonder drug n : MIRACLE DRUG

won·der·ful \'wən-dər-fəl\ adj **1** : exciting wonder : MARVELOUS, ASTONISHING **2** : unusually good : ADMIRABLE ⟨did a ~ job⟩ — **won·der·ful·ly** \-f(ə-)lē\ adv — **won·der·ful·ness** n

won·der·land \-ˌland, -lənd\ n **1** : an imaginary place of delicate beauty or magical charm **2** : a place that excites admiration or wonder ⟨a scenic ~⟩

won·der·ment \-mənt\ n **1** : ASTONISHMENT, SURPRISE **2** : a cause of or occasion for wonder **3** : curiosity about something

won·drous \'wən-drəs\ adj : WONDERFUL, MARVELOUS ⟨a ~ feat⟩ — **won·drous·ly** adv — **won·drous·ness** n

wonk \'wäŋk, 'wȯŋk\ n : one who works in a specialized usu. intellectual field ⟨computer ~⟩

¹wont \'wȯnt, 'wōnt\ adj [ME woned, wont, fr. pp. of wonen to dwell, be used to, fr. OE wunian] **1** : ACCUSTOMED, USED ⟨as we are ~ to do⟩ **2** : INCLINED, APT

²wont n : CUSTOM, USAGE, HABIT ⟨according to her ~⟩

won't \'wōnt\ : will not

wont·ed \'wȯn-təd, 'wōn-\ adj : ACCUSTOMED, CUSTOMARY ⟨his ~ courtesy⟩

woo \'wü\ vb **1** : to try to gain the love of : COURT **2** : to SOLICIT, ENTREAT **3** : to try to gain or bring about ⟨~ public favor⟩ — **woo·er** n

¹wood \'wu̇d\ n **1** : a dense growth of trees usu. larger than a grove and smaller than a forest — often used in pl. **2** : a hard fibrous substance that is basically xylem and forms the bulk of trees and shrubs beneath the bark; also : this material fit or prepared for some use (as burning or building) **3** : something made of wood

²wood adj **1** : WOODEN **2** : suitable for holding, cutting, or working with wood **3** or **woods** \'wu̇dz\ : living or growing in woods

³wood vb **1** : to supply or load with wood esp. for fuel **2** : to cover with a growth of trees

wood alcohol n : METHANOL

wood·bine \'wu̇d-ˌbīn\ n : any of several honeysuckles; also : VIRGINIA CREEPER

wood·block \-ˌbläk\ n : WOODCUT

wood·chop·per \-ˌchä-pər\ n : one engaged esp. in chopping down trees

wood·chuck \-ˌchək\ n : a thickset grizzled marmot of Alaska, Canada, and the northeastern U.S.

wood·cock \'wu̇d-ˌkäk\ n, pl **woodcocks** : a brown eastern No. American game bird with a short neck and long bill that is related to the snipe; also : a related and similar Old World bird

wood·craft \-ˌkraft\ n **1** : skill and practice in matters relating to the woods and esp. in how to take care of oneself in them **2** : skill in shaping or constructing articles from wood

wood·cut \-ˌkət\ n **1** : a relief printing surface engraved on a block of wood **2** : a print from a woodcut

wood·cut·ter \-ˌkə-tər\ n : a person who cuts wood

wood duck n : a showy crested American duck of which the male has iridescent multicolored plumage

wood·ed \'wu̇-dəd\ adj : covered with woods or trees ⟨~ slopes⟩

wood·en \'wu̇-dᵊn\ adj **1** : made of wood **2** : lacking flexibility : awkwardly stiff — **wood·en·ly** adv — **wood·en·ness** n

wood·en·ware \'wu̇-dᵊn-ˌwer\ n : articles made of wood for domestic use

wood·land \'wu̇d-lənd, -ˌland\ n : land covered with trees : FOREST — **woodland** adj

wood·lot \'wu̇d-ˌlät\ n : a restricted area of woodland usu. privately kept to meet fuel and timber needs

wood louse n : any of various small flat crustaceans that live esp. in ground litter and under stones and bark

wood·man \\'wu̇d-mən\\ *n* : WOODSMAN

wood·note \\-ˌnōt\\ *n* : verbal expression that is natural and artless

wood nymph *n* : a nymph living in the woods

wood·peck·er \\'wu̇d-ˌpe-kər\\ *n* : any of numerous usu. brightly marked climbing birds with stiff spiny tail feathers and a chisellike bill used to drill into trees for insects

wood·pile \\-ˌpī(-ə)l\\ *n* : a pile of wood and esp. firewood

wood rat *n* : PACK RAT

wood·shed \\-ˌshed\\ *n* : a shed for storing wood and esp. firewood

woods·man \\'wu̇dz-mən\\ *n* : a person who frequents or works in the woods; *esp* : one skilled in woodcraft

woodsy \\'wu̇d-zē\\ *adj* **woods·i·er; -est** : relating to or suggestive of woods ⟨a ～ odor⟩

wood·wind \\'wu̇d-ˌwind\\ *n* : one of a group of wind instruments including flutes, clarinets, oboes, bassoons, and sometimes saxophones

wood·work \\-ˌwərk\\ *n* : work made of wood; *esp* : interior fittings (as moldings or stairways) of wood

woody \\'wu̇-dē\\ *adj* **wood·i·er; -est** **1** : abounding or overgrown with woods ⟨a ～ trail⟩ **2** : of or containing wood or wood fibers ⟨～ plants⟩ **3** : characteristic or suggestive of wood — **wood·i·ness** \\'wu̇-dē-nəs\\ *n*

woof \\'wu̇f\\ *n* [alter. of ME *oof*, fr. OE *ōwef*, fr. *ō-* (fr. *on* on) + *wefan* to weave] **1** : WEFT 1 **2** : a woven fabric; *also* : its texture

woof·er \\'wu̇-fər\\ *n* : a loudspeaker that reproduces sounds of low pitch

wool \\'wu̇l\\ *n* **1** : the soft wavy or curly hair of some mammals and esp. the domestic sheep; *also* : something (as a textile or garment) made of wool **2** : material that resembles a mass of wool — **wooled** \\'wu̇ld\\ *adj*

¹wool·en *or* **wool·len** \\'wu̇-lən\\ *adj* **1** : made of wool **2** : of or relating to the manufacture or sale of woolen products ⟨～ mills⟩

²woolen *or* **woollen** *n* **1** : a fabric made of wool **2** : garments of woolen fabric — usu. used in pl.

wool·gath·er·ing \\-ˌga-thə-riŋ\\ *n* : idle daydreaming

¹wool·ly *also* **wooly** \\'wu̇-lē\\ *adj* **wool·li·er; -est** **1** : of, relating to, or bearing wool **2** : consisting of or resembling wool **3** : mentally confused ⟨～ thinking⟩ **4** : marked by a lack of order or restraint ⟨the wild and ～ West⟩

²wool·ly *also* **wool·ie** *or* **wooly** \\'wu̇-lē\\ *n, pl* **wool·lies** : a garment made from wool; *esp* : underclothing of knitted wool — usu. used in pl.

woolly adel·gid \\-ə-'del-jəd\\ *n* : either of two aphids accidentally introduced into No. America where they are serious pests of firs and hemlocks

woolly bear *n* : any of numerous very hairy moth caterpillars

woolly mammoth *n* : a heavy-coated mammoth formerly inhabiting colder parts of the northern hemisphere

woo·zy \\'wü-zē\\ *adj* **woo·zi·er; -est** **1** : BEFUDDLED **2** : somewhat dizzy, nauseated, or weak **3** : somewhat indistinct or unfocused : FUZZY — **woo·zi·ness** \\'wü-zē-nəs\\ *n*

¹word \\'wərd\\ *n* **1** : something that is said; *esp* : a brief remark **2** : a speech sound or series of speech sounds that communicates a meaning; *also* : a graphic representation of such a sound or series of sounds **3** : ORDER, COMMAND **4** *often cap* : the 2d person of the Trinity; *also* : GOSPEL **5** : NEWS, INFORMATION **6** : PROMISE **7** *pl* : QUARREL, DISPUTE **8** : a verbal signal : PASSWORD — **word·less** *adj*

²word *vb* : to express in words : PHRASE

word·age \\'wər-dij\\ *n* **1** : WORDS **2** : number of words **3** : WORDING

word·book \\'wərd-ˌbu̇k\\ *n* : VOCABULARY, DICTIONARY

word·ing \\'wər-diŋ\\ *n* : verbal expression : PHRASEOLOGY

word of mouth : oral communication

word·play \\'wərd-ˌplā\\ *n* : playful use of words

word processing *n* : the production of typewritten documents with automated and manu. computerized text-editing equipment — **word process** *vb*

word processor *n* : a keyboard-operated terminal for use in word processing; *also* : software to perform word processing

wordy \\'wər-dē\\ *adj* **word·i·er; -est** : using many words : VERBOSE ✦ *Synonyms* PROLIX, DIFFUSE, REDUNDANT — **word·i·ness** \\-dē-nəs\\ *n*

wore *past of* WEAR

¹work \\'wərk\\ *n* **1** : TOIL, LABOR; *also* : EMPLOYMENT ⟨out of ～⟩ **2** : TASK, JOB ⟨have ～ to do⟩ **3** : the energy used when a force is applied over a given distance **4** : DEED, ACHIEVEMENT **5** : a fortified structure **6** *pl* : engineering structures **7** *pl* : a place where industrial labor is done : PLANT, FACTORY **8** *pl* : the moving parts of a mechanism **9** : something produced by mental effort or physical labor; *esp* : an artistic production (as a book or needlework) **10** : WORKMANSHIP ⟨careless ～⟩ **11** : material in the process of manufacture **12** *pl* : everything possessed, available, or belonging ⟨the whole ～s went overboard⟩; *also* : drastic treatment ⟨gave him the ～s⟩ ✦ *Synonyms* OCCUPATION, EMPLOYMENT, BUSINESS, PURSUIT, CALLING — **in the works** : in process of preparation

²work *adj* **1** : used for work ⟨～ elephants⟩ **2** : suitable or styled for wear while working ⟨～ clothes⟩

³work *vb* **worked** \\'wərkt\\ *or* **wrought** \\'rȯt\\; **work·ing** **1** : to bring to pass : EFFECT **2** : to fashion or create a useful or desired product through labor or exertion **3** : to prepare for use (as by kneading) **4** : to bring into a desired form by a manufacturing process ⟨～ cold steel⟩ **5** : to set or keep in operation : OPERATE ⟨a pump ～ed by hand⟩ **6** : to solve by reasoning or calculation ⟨～ out a problem⟩ **7** : to cause to toil or labor ⟨～ed the men hard⟩; *also* : to make use of ⟨～ a mine⟩ **8** : to pay for with labor or service ⟨～ off a debt⟩ **9** : to bring or get into some position or condition by stages ⟨the stream ～ed itself clear⟩ ⟨the knot ～ed loose⟩ **10** : CONTRIVE, ARRANGE ⟨～ it so you can leave early⟩ **11** : to practice trickery or cajolery on ⟨～ed the management for a free ticket⟩ **12** : EXCITE, PROVOKE ⟨～ed himself into a rage⟩ **13** : to exert oneself physically or mentally; *esp* : to perform work regularly for wages **14** : to function according to plan or design **15** : to produce a desired effect : SUCCEED ⟨the plan ～ed⟩ **16** : to make way slowly and with difficulty ⟨he ～ed forward through the crowd⟩ **17** : to permit of being worked ⟨this wood ～s easily⟩ **18** : to be in restless motion; *also* : FERMENT 1 — **work on** **1** : AFFECT **2** : to try to influence or persuade — **work upon** : to have effect upon : operate on : INFLUENCE

work·able \\'wər-kə-bəl\\ *adj* **1** : capable of being worked ⟨～ clay⟩ **2** : PRACTICABLE, FEASIBLE — **work·able·ness** *n*

work·a·day \\'wər-kə-ˌdā\\ *adj* **1** : relating to or suited for working days **2** : PROSAIC, ORDINARY ⟨～ chores⟩

work·a·hol·ic \\ˌwər-kə-'hȯ-lik, -'hä-\\ *n* : a compulsive worker

work·bench \\-ˌbench\\ *n* : a bench on which work esp. of mechanics, machinists, and carpenters is performed

work·book \\-ˌbu̇k\\ *n* **1** : a worker's manual **2** : a student's book of problems to be answered directly on the pages

work·day \\'wərk-ˌdā\\ *n* **1** : a day on which work is done as distinguished from a day off **2** : the period of time in a day when work is performed

work·er \\'wər-kər\\ *n* **1** : one that works; *esp* : a person who works for wages **2** : any of the sexually undeveloped individuals of a colony of social insects (as bees, ants, or termites) that perform the work of the community

workers' compensation *n* : a system of insurance that reimburses an employer for damages paid to an employee who was injured while working

work ethic *n* : belief in work as a moral good

work farm *n* : a farm on which persons guilty of minor law violations are confined

work·horse \\'wərk-ˌhȯrs\\ *n* **1** : a horse used for hard work **2** : a person who does most of the work of a group task **3** : something that is useful, durable, or dependable

work·house \\-ˌhau̇s\\ *n* **1** *Brit* : POORHOUSE **2** : a house of correction for persons guilty of minor law violations

¹work·ing \\'wər-kiŋ\\ *n* **1** : manner of functioning — usu. used in pl. **2** *pl* : an excavation made in mining or tunneling

²working *adj* **1** : engaged in work ⟨a ～ journalist⟩ **2** : adequate to allow work to be done ⟨a ～ majority⟩ ⟨a ～ knowledge of French⟩ **3** : adopted or assumed to help further work or activity ⟨a ～ draft⟩ **4** : spent at work ⟨～ life⟩

work·ing·man \\'wər-kiŋ-ˌman\\ *n* : WORKER 1

work·man \'wərk-mən\ *n* **1** : WORKER 1 **2** : ARTISAN, CRAFTSMAN

work·man·like \-,līk\ *adj* : worthy of a good workman : SKILLFUL

work·man·ship \-,ship\ *n* : the art or skill of a workman : CRAFTSMANSHIP; *also* : the quality of a piece of work ⟨a vase of exquisite ∼⟩

work·out \'wərk-,aut\ *n* **1** : a practice or exercise to test or improve one's fitness, ability, or performance **2** : a test or trial to determine ability or capacity or suitability

work out *vb* **1** : to bring about esp. by resolving difficulties **2** : DEVELOP, ELABORATE **3** : to prove effective, practicable, or suitable ⟨our plan didn't *work out*⟩ **4** : to amount to a total or calculated figure — used with *at* **5** : to engage in a workout

work·place \'wərk-,plās\ *n* : a place (as an office) where work is done

work·room \'wərk-,rüm, -,rum\ *n* : a room used for work

work·shop \-,shäp\ *n* **1** : a shop where manufacturing or handicrafts are carried on **2** : a seminar emphasizing exchange of ideas and practical methods

work·sta·tion \-,stā-shən\ *n* : an area with equipment for the performance of a specialized task; *also* : a personal computer usu. connected to a computer network

world \'wərld\ *n* [ME, fr. OE *woruld* human existence, this world, age, fr. a prehistoric compound whose first constituent is represented by OE *wer* man and whose second constituent is akin to OE *eald* old] **1** : the earth with its inhabitants and all things upon it **2** : people in general : MANKIND **3** : human affairs ⟨withdraw from the ∼⟩ **4** : UNIVERSE, CREATION **5** : a state of existence : scene of life and action ⟨the ∼ of the future⟩ **6** : a distinctive class of persons or their sphere of interest ⟨the musical ∼⟩ **7** : a part or section of the earth or its inhabitants by itself **8** : a great number or quantity ⟨a ∼ of troubles⟩ **9** : a celestial body

world–beat·er \-,bē-tər\ *n* : one that excels all others of its kind : CHAMPION

world-class *adj* : of the highest caliber in the world ⟨a ∼ athlete⟩

world·ling \-lin\ *n* : a person absorbed in the concerns of the present world

world·ly \-lē\ *adj* **1** : of, relating to, or devoted to this world and its pursuits rather than to religion or spiritual affairs **2** : WORLDLY-WISE, SOPHISTICATED — **world·li·ness** \-lē-nəs\ *n*

world·ly–wise \-,wīz\ *adj* : possessing a practical and often shrewd understanding of human affairs

world·wide \'wərld-'wīd\ *adj* : extended throughout the entire world — **worldwide** *adv*

World Wide Web *n* : a part of the Internet usu. accessed through a browser and containing files connected by hyperlinks

¹**worm** \'wərm\ *n* **1** : any of various small long usu. naked and soft-bodied round or flat invertebrate animals (as an earthworm, nematode, tapeworm, or maggot) **2** : a human being who is an object of contempt, loathing, or pity : WRETCH **3** : something that inwardly torments or devours **4** *pl* : infestation with or disease caused by parasitic worms **5** : a spiral or wormlike thing (as the thread of a screw) — **worm·like** \-,līk\ *adj* — **wormy** *adj*

²**worm** *vb* **1** : to move or cause to move or proceed slowly and deviously **2** : to insinuate or introduce (oneself) by devious or subtle means **3** : to obtain or extract by artful or insidious pleading, asking, or persuading ⟨∼ed the truth out of him⟩ **4** : to treat (an animal) with a drug to destroy or expel parasitic worms

worm–eat·en \'wərm-,ē-t⁰n\ *adj* : eaten or burrowed by worms

worm gear *n* : a mechanical linkage consisting of a short rotating screw whose threads mesh with the teeth of a gear wheel

worm·hole \'wərm-,hōl\ *n* : a hole or passage burrowed by a worm

worm·wood \-,wud\ *n* **1** : any of a genus of aromatic woody plants (as a sagebrush; *esp* : one of Europe used in absinthe **2** : something bitter or grievous : BITTERNESS

worn *past part of* WEAR

worn–out \'wōrn-'aut\ *adj* : exhausted or used up by or as if by wear

wor·ri·some \'wər-ē-səm\ *adj* **1** : causing distress or worry ⟨∼ news⟩ **2** : inclined to worry or fret ⟨a ∼ mother⟩

¹**wor·ry** \'wər-ē\ *vb* **wor·ried; wor·ry·ing 1** : to shake and mangle with the teeth ⟨a terrier ∼ing a rat⟩ **2** : to make anxious or upset ⟨her poor health *worries* me⟩ **3** : to feel or express great care or anxiety : FRET ⟨∼ing about his health⟩ — **wor·ri·er** *n*

²**worry** *n, pl* **worries 1** : ANXIETY **2** : a cause of anxiety : TROUBLE

wor·ry·wart \'wər-ē-,wort\ *n* : one who is inclined to worry unduly

¹**worse** \'wərs\ *adj, comparative of* BAD, *or of* ILL **1** : bad or evil in a greater degree : less good **2** : more unfavorable, unpleasant, or painful; *also* : SICKER

²**worse** *n* **1** : one that is worse **2** : a greater degree of ill or badness ⟨a turn for the ∼⟩

³**worse** *adv, comparative of* BAD, *or of* ILL : in a worse manner : to a worse extent or degree

wors·en \'wər-s⁰n\ *vb* : to make or become worse ⟨the rash ∼ed⟩

¹**wor·ship** \'wər-shəp\ *n* [ME *worshipe* worthiness, respect, reverence paid to a divine being, fr. OE *weorthscipe* worthiness, respect, fr. *weorth* worthy, worth + *-scipe* -ship, suffix denoting quality or condition] **1** *chiefly Brit* : a person of importance — used as a title for officials **2** : reverence toward a divine being or supernatural power; *also* : the expression of such reverence **3** : extravagant respect or admiration for or devotion ⟨∼ of the dollar⟩

²**worship** *vb* **-shipped** *also* **-shiped; -ship·ping** *also* **-ship·ing 1** : to honor or reverence as a divine being or supernatural power **2** : IDOLIZE ⟨∼s his brother⟩ **3** : to perform or take part in worship — **wor·ship·er** *or* **wor·ship·per** *n*

wor·ship·ful \'wər-shəp-fəl\ *adj* **1** *archaic* : NOTABLE, DISTINGUISHED **2** *chiefly Brit* — used as a title for various persons or groups of rank or distinction **3** : VENERATING, WORSHIPING

¹**worst** \'wərst\ *adj, superlative of* BAD, *or of* ILL **1** : most bad, evil, ill, or corrupt ⟨the ∼ criminals⟩ **2** : most unfavorable, unpleasant, or painful ⟨the ∼ scenario⟩; *also* : most unsuitable, faulty, or unattractive **3** : least skillful or efficient ⟨her ∼ students⟩

²**worst** *adv, superlative of* ILL, *or of* BAD, *or* BADLY **1** : to the extreme degree of badness or inferiority ⟨the ∼ dressed person⟩ : in the worst manner **2** : MOST ⟨those who need help ∼⟩

³**worst** *n* : one that is worst

⁴**worst** *vb* : DEFEAT

wor·sted \'wus-təd, 'wər-stəd\ *n* [ME, fr. *Worsted* (now *Worstead*), England] **1** : a smooth compact yarn from long wool fibers; *also* : a fabric made from such yarn

wort \'wərt, 'wort\ *n* : a sweet liquid drained from mash and fermented to form beer and whiskey

¹**worth** \'wərth\ *n* **1** : monetary value; *also* : the equivalent of a specified amount or figure ⟨$5 ∼ of gas⟩ **2** : the value of something measured by its qualities **3** : MERIT, EXCELLENCE

²**worth** *prep* **1** : equal in value to; *also* : having possessions or income equal to **2** : deserving of ⟨well ∼ the effort⟩

worth·less \'wərth-ləs\ *adj* **1** : lacking worth : VALUELESS; *also* : USELESS **2** : LOW, DESPICABLE — **worth·less·ness** *n*

worth·while \'wərth-'hwī(-ə)l\ *adj* : being worth the time or effort spent

¹**wor·thy** \'wər-thē\ *adj* **wor·thi·er; -est 1** : having worth or value : ESTIMABLE ⟨a ∼ cause⟩ **2** : HONORABLE, MERITORIOUS ⟨my ∼ opponent⟩ **3** : having sufficient

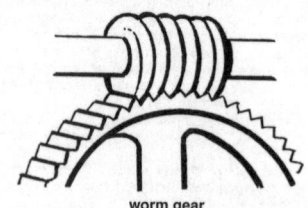

worm gear

worth ⟨∼ of the honor⟩ — **wor·thi·ly** \'wər-<u>th</u>ə-lē\ *adv* — **wor·thi·ness** \-<u>th</u>ē-nəs\ *n*

²**worthy** *n, pl* **worthies** : a worthy person

would \'wu̇d\ *past of* WILL **1** *archaic* : wish for : WANT **2** : strongly desire : WISH ⟨I ∼ I were young again⟩ **3** — used as an auxiliary to express (1) preference ⟨∼ rather run than fight⟩, (2) wish, desire, or intent ⟨those who ∼ forbid gambling⟩, (3) habitual action ⟨we ∼ meet often for lunch⟩, (4) a contingency or possibility ⟨if he were coming, he ∼ be here by now⟩, (5) probability ⟨∼ have won if he hadn't tripped⟩, or (6) a request ⟨∼ you help us⟩ **4** : COULD **5** : SHOULD

would–be \'wu̇d-'bē\ *adj* : desiring or pretending to be ⟨a ∼ artist⟩

¹**wound** \'wünd\ *n* **1** : an injury involving cutting or breaking of bodily tissue (as by violence, accident, or surgery) **2** : an injury or hurt to feelings or reputation

²**wound** *vb* : to inflict a wound to or in

³**wound** \'wau̇nd\ *past and past part of* WIND

wove *past of* WEAVE

woven *past part of* WEAVE

¹**wow** \'wau̇\ *n* : a striking success : HIT

²**wow** *vb* : to arouse enthusiastic approval ⟨∼ed the critics⟩

WP *abbr* word processing; word processor

WPM *abbr* words per minute

wpn *abbr* weapon

wrack \'rak\ *n* [ME, fr. OE *wræc* misery, punishment, something driven by the sea] : violent or total destruction

wraith \'rāth\ *n, pl* **wraiths** \'rāths, 'rā<u>th</u>z\ **1** : GHOST, SPECTER **2** : an insubstantial appearance : SHADOW

¹**wran·gle** \'raŋ-gəl\ *vb* **wran·gled; wran·gling** **1** : to quarrel angrily or peevishly : BICKER **2** : ARGUE **3** : to obtain by persistent arguing **4** : to herd and care for (livestock) on the range — **wran·gler** *n*

²**wrangle** *n* : an angry, noisy, or prolonged dispute; *also* : CONTROVERSY

¹**wrap** \'rap\ *vb* **wrapped; wrap·ping** **1** : to cover esp. by winding or folding **2** : to envelop and secure for transportation or storage **3** : to enclose wholly : ENFOLD **4** : to coil, fold, draw, or twine about something **5** : SURROUND, ENGROSS ⟨*wrapped* in mystery⟩ **6** : INVOLVE, ENGROSS ⟨*wrapped* up in a hobby⟩ **7** : to complete filming or recording

²**wrap** *n* **1** : WRAPPER, WRAPPING **2** : an article of clothing that may be wrapped around a person **3** *pl* : SECRECY ⟨kept under ∼s⟩ **4** : completion of filming or recording

wrap·around \'ra-pə-ˌrau̇nd\ *n* : a garment (as a dress) adjusted to the figure by wrapping around

wrap·per \'ra-pər\ *n* **1** : that in which something is wrapped **2** : one that wraps **3** : an article of clothing worn wrapped around the body

wrap·ping \'ra-piŋ\ *n* : something used to wrap an object : WRAPPER

wrap–up \'rap-ˌəp\ *n* : SUMMARY

wrap up *vb* **1** : SUMMARIZE, SUM UP **2** : to bring to a usu. successful conclusion

wrasse \'ras\ *n* : any of a large family of usu. brightly colored marine fishes including many food fishes

wrath \'rath\ *n* **1** : violent anger : RAGE **2** : divine punishment ✦ **Synonyms** INDIGNATION, IRE, FURY, ANGER

wrath·ful \-fəl\ *adj* **1** : filled with wrath : very angry **2** : showing, marked by, or arising from anger — **wrath·ful·ly** *adv* — **wrath·ful·ness** *n*

wreak \'rēk\ *vb* [ME *wreken*, fr. OE *wrecan* to drive, punish, avenge] **1** : to exact as a punishment : INFLICT ⟨∼ vengeance on an enemy⟩ **2** : to give free scope or rein to ⟨∼ed his wrath⟩ **3** : BRING ABOUT, CAUSE ⟨∼ havoc⟩

wreath \'rēth\ *n, pl* **wreaths** \'rē<u>th</u>z, 'rēths\ : a circular band of flowers or leaves usu. for decoration; *also* : something having a circular or coiling form ⟨a ∼ of smoke⟩

wreathe \'rē<u>th</u>\ *vb* **wreathed; wreath·ing** **1** : to shape or take on the shape of a wreath **2** : to crown, decorate, or cover with or as if with a wreath ⟨a face *wreathed* in smiles⟩

¹**wreck** \'rek\ *n* **1** : something (as goods) cast up on the land by the sea after a shipwreck **2** : SHIPWRECK **3** : a destructive crash ⟨a car ∼⟩ **4** : the action of breaking up or destroying something **5** : broken remains (as of a vehicle after a crash) **6** : something disabled or in a state of ruin; *also* : an individual broken in health or strength, or spirits ⟨he's a nervous ∼⟩

²**wreck** *vb* **1** : SHIPWRECK **2** : to ruin or damage by breaking up : involve in disaster or ruin

wreck·age \'re-kij\ *n* **1** : the act of wrecking : the state of being wrecked : RUIN **2** : the remains of a wreck

wreck·er \'re-kər\ *n* **1** : one that searches for or works upon the wrecks of ships **2** : TOW TRUCK **3** : one that wrecks; *esp* : one whose work is the demolition of buildings

wren \'ren\ *n* : any of a family of small mostly brown singing birds with short wings and often a tail that points upward

¹**wrench** \'rench\ *vb* **1** : to move with a violent twist **2** : to pull, strain, or tighten with violent twisting or force **3** : to injure or disable by a violent twisting or straining ⟨∼ed her back⟩ **4** : to snatch forcibly : WREST

²**wrench** *n* **1** : a forcible twisting; *also* : an injury (as to one's ankle) by twisting **2** : a tool for holding, twisting, or turning (as nuts or bolts)

¹**wrest** \'rest\ *vb* **1** : to pull or move by a forcible twisting movement **2** : to gain with difficulty by or as if by force or violence ⟨∼ control of the government from the dictator⟩

²**wrest** *n* : a forcible twist : WRENCH

¹**wres·tle** \'re-səl, 'ra-\ *vb* **wres·tled; wres·tling** **1** : to grapple with and try to throw down an opponent **2** : to compete against in wrestling **3** : to struggle for control (as of something difficult) ⟨∼ with a problem⟩ — **wres·tler** \'res-lər, 'ras-\ *n*

²**wrestle** *n* : the action or an instance of wrestling : STRUGGLE

wres·tling \'res-liŋ\ *n* : the sport in which two opponents wrestle each other

wretch \'rech\ *n* [ME *wrecche*, fr. OE *wrecca* outcast, exile] **1** : a miserable unhappy person **2** : a base, despicable, or vile person

wretch·ed \'re-chəd\ *adj* **1** : deeply afflicted, dejected, or distressed : MISERABLE **2** : WOEFUL, GRIEVOUS ⟨a ∼ accident⟩ **3** : DESPICABLE ⟨a ∼ trick⟩ **4** : poor in quality or ability : INFERIOR ⟨∼ workmanship⟩ — **wretch·ed·ly** *adv* — **wretch·ed·ness** *n*

wrig·gle \'ri-gəl\ *vb* **wrig·gled; wrig·gling** **1** : to twist or move to and fro like a worm : SQUIRM ⟨*wriggled* in his chair⟩; *also* : to move along by twisting and turning ⟨a snake *wriggled* along the path⟩ **2** : to extricate oneself as if by wriggling ⟨∼ out of difficulty⟩ — **wriggle** *n*

wrig·gler *n* **1** : one that wriggles **2** : WIGGLER 1

wring \'riŋ\ *vb* **wrung** \'rəŋ\; **wring·ing** \'riŋ-iŋ\ **1** : to squeeze or twist esp. so as to make dry or to extract moisture or liquid ⟨∼ wet clothes⟩ **2** : to get by or as if by twisting or pressing ⟨∼ the truth out of him⟩ **3** : to twist so as to strain or sprain : CONTORT ⟨∼ his neck⟩ **4** : to twist together as a sign of anguish ⟨*wrung* her hands⟩ **5** : to affect painfully as if by wringing : TORMENT ⟨her plight *wrung* my heart⟩

wring·er \'riŋ-ər\ *n* : one that wrings; *esp* : a device for squeezing out liquid or moisture ⟨clothes ∼⟩

¹**wrin·kle** \'riŋ-kəl\ *n* **1** : a crease or small fold on a smooth surface (as in the skin or in cloth) **2** : a clever or new method, trick, or idea — **wrin·kly** \-k(ə-)lē\ *adj*

²**wrinkle** *vb* **wrin·kled; wrin·kling** **1** : to develop or cause to develop wrinkles

wrist \'rist\ *n* : the joint or region between the hand and the arm; *also* : a corresponding part in a lower animal

wrist·band \-ˌband\ *n* : a band or the part of a sleeve encircling the wrist

wrist·let \-lət\ *n* : WRISTBAND; *esp* : a close-fitting knitted band attached to the top of a glove or the end of a sleeve

wrist·watch \-ˌwäch\ *n* : a small watch attached to a bracelet or strap to fasten about the wrist

writ \'rit\ *n* : something written : a written legal order signed by a court officer

writ·able \'rī-tə-bəl\ *adj* : being an electronic storage medium on which it is possible to introduce new data ⟨a ∼ DVD⟩

write \'rīt\ *vb* **wrote** \'rōt\; **writ·ten** \'ri-tᵊn\ *also* **writ** \'rit\; **writ·ing** \'rī-tiŋ\ [ME, fr. OE *wrītan* to scratch, draw, inscribe] **1** : to form characters, letters, or words on a surface ⟨learn to read and ∼⟩ **2** : to form the letters or the words of ⟨∼ your name⟩ ⟨∼ a check⟩ **3** : to put down on paper : express in writing **4** : to make up and set down for others to read ⟨∼ a book⟩ ⟨∼ music⟩ **5** : to write a letter to **6** : to communicate by letter : CORRESPOND

write–in \'rīt-ˌin\ *n* : a vote cast by writing in the name of a candidate; *also* : a candidate whose name is written in

write in *vb* : to insert (a name not listed on a ballot) in an appropriate space; *also* : to cast (a vote) in this manner

write off *vb* : to eliminate (an asset) from a bookkeeping record : enter as a loss or expense

writ•er \'rī-tər\ *n* : one that writes esp. as a business or occupation : AUTHOR

writer's cramp *n* : a painful spasmodic contraction of muscles of the hand or fingers brought on by excessive writing

write–up \'rīt-ˌəp\ *n* : a written account (as in a newspaper); *esp* : a flattering article

writhe \'rī̄th\ *vb* **writhed; writh•ing 1** : to twist and turn this way and that ⟨∼ in pain⟩ **2** : to suffer with shame or confusion

writing *n* **1** : the act of one that writes; *also* : HANDWRITING **2** : something that is written or printed **3** : a style or form of composition **4** : the occupation of a writer

Writings \'rī-tiŋz\ *n pl* : the third part of the Jewish scriptures

wrnt *abbr* warrant

¹**wrong** \'róŋ\ *n* **1** : an injurious, unfair, or unjust act **2** : a violation of the legal rights of another person **3** : something that is wrong : wrong principles, practices, or conduct ⟨know right from ∼⟩ **4** : the state, position, or fact of being wrong

²**wrong** *adj* **wrong•er** \'róŋ-ər\; **wrong•est** \'róŋ-əst\ **1** : SINFUL, IMMORAL **2** : not right according to a standard or code : IMPROPER **3** : INCORRECT ⟨a ∼ solution⟩ **4** : UNSATISFACTORY **5** : UNSUITABLE, INAPPROPRIATE **6** : constituting a surface that is considered the back, bottom, inside, or reverse of something ⟨iron only on the ∼ side of the fabric⟩ ✦ *Synonyms* FALSE, ERRONEOUS, INCORRECT, INACCURATE, UNTRUE — **wrong•ly** *adv*

³**wrong** *adv* **1** : INCORRECTLY **2** : in a wrong direction, manner, or relation

⁴**wrong** *vb* **wronged; wrong•ing** \'róŋ-iŋ\ **1** : to do wrong to : INJURE, HARM **2** : to treat unjustly : DISHONOR, MALIGN ✦ *Synonyms* OPPRESS, PERSECUTE, AGGRIEVE

wrong•do•er \'róŋ-ˌdü-ər\ *n* : a person who does wrong and esp. moral wrong — **wrong•do•ing** \-ˌdü-iŋ\ *n*

wrong•ful \'róŋ-fəl\ *adj* **1** : WRONG, UNJUST **2** : UNLAWFUL — **wrong•ful•ly** *adv* — **wrong•ful•ness** *n*

wrong•head•ed \-'he-dəd\ *adj* : stubborn in clinging to wrong opinion or principles — **wrong•head•ed•ly** *adv* — **wrong•head•ed•ness** *n*

wrote *past of* WRITE

wroth \'róth, 'rōth\ *adj* : filled with wrath : ANGRY

wrought \'rót\ *adj* [ME, fr. pp. of *worken* to work] **1** : FASHIONED, FORMED ⟨carefully ∼ essays⟩ **2** : ORNAMENTED **3** : beaten into shape by tools : HAMMERED ⟨∼ metals⟩ **4** : deeply stirred : EXCITED ⟨gets easily ∼ up⟩

wrung *past and past part of* WRING

wry \'rī\ *adj* **wry•er** \'rī-ər\; **wry•est** \'rī-əst\ **1** : having a bent or twisted shape ⟨a ∼ smile⟩; *also* : turned abnormally to one side : CONTORTED ⟨a ∼ neck⟩ **2** : cleverly and often ironically humorous — **wry•ly** *adv* — **wry•ness** *n*

wry•neck \'rī-ˌnek\ *n* **1** : either of two Old World woodpeckers that differ from typical woodpeckers in having a peculiar manner of twisting the head and neck **2** : an abnormal twisting of the neck and head to one side caused by muscle spasms

WSW *abbr* west-southwest

wt *abbr* weight

wurst \'wərst, 'wu̇rst\ *n* : SAUSAGE

wuss \'wu̇s\ *n* : WIMP — **wussy** \'wu̇-sē\ *adj*

WV *or* **W Va** *abbr* West Virginia

WW *abbr* World War

w/w *abbr* wall-to-wall

WY *or* **Wyo** *abbr* Wyoming

WYS•I•WYG \'wi-zē-ˌwig\ *adj* [what *you see is what you get*] : of, relating to, or being a computer display that shows a document exactly as it will appear when printed out

¹**x** \'eks\ *n, pl* **x's** *or* **xs** \'ek-səz\ *often cap* **1** : the 24th letter of the English alphabet **2** : ten in Roman numerals **3** : an unknown quantity

²**x** *vb* **x-ed** *also* **x'd** *or* **xed** \'ekst\; **x-ing** *or* **x'ing** \'ek-siŋ\ : to cancel or obliterate with a series of *x*'s — usu. used with *out*

³**x** *abbr* **1** ex **2** experimental **3** extra

⁴**x** *symbol* **1** times ⟨3 x 2 is 6⟩ **2** by ⟨a 3 x 5 index card⟩ **3** *often cap* power of magnification

Xan•a•du \'za-nə-ˌdü, -ˌdyü\ *n* [fr. *Xanadu*, locality in *Kubla Khan* (1798), poem by Eng. poet Samuel Taylor Coleridge †1834] : an idyllic, exotic, or luxurious place

Xan•thip•pe \zan-'thi-pē, -'ti-\ *or* **Xan•tip•pe** \-'ti-pē\ *n* [Gk *Xanthippē*, shrewish wife of Socrates] : an ill-tempered woman

x–ax•is \'eks-ˌak-səs\ *n* : the axis of a graph or of a system of coordinates in a plane parallel to which abscissas are measured

X–C *abbr* cross-country

X chromosome *n* : a sex chromosome that usu. occurs paired in each female cell and single in each male cell in organisms (as humans) in which the male normally has two unlike sex chromosomes

Xe *symbol* xenon

xe•non \'zē-ˌnän, 'ze-\ *n* [Gk, neut. of *xenos* strange] : a heavy gaseous chemical element occurring in minute quantities in air

xe•no•pho•bia \ˌze-nə-'fō-bē-ə, ˌzē-\ *n* : fear and hatred of strangers or foreigners or of what is strange or foreign —

xe•no•phobe \'ze-nə-ˌfōb, 'zē-\ *n* — **xe•no•pho•bic** \ˌze-nə-'fō-bik, ˌzē-\ *adj*

xe•ric \'zir-ik, 'zer-\ *adj* : characterized by or requiring only a small amount of moisture ⟨a ∼ habitat⟩

xeri•scape \'zir-ə-ˌskāp, 'zer-\ *n, often cap* : a landscaping method utilizing water-conserving techniques

xe•rog•ra•phy \zə-'rä-grə-fē\ *n* : a process for copying printed matter by the action of light on an electrically charged surface in which the latent image is developed with a powder — **xe•ro•graph•ic** \ˌzir-ə-'gra-fik\ *adj*

xe•ro•phyte \'zir-ə-ˌfīt\ *n* : a plant adapted for growth with a limited water supply — **xe•ro•phyt•ic** \ˌzir-ə-'fi-tik\ *adj*

xi \'zī, 'ksī\ *n* : the 14th letter of the Greek alphabet — Ξ or ξ

XL *abbr* **1** extra large **2** extra long

Xmas \'kris-məs *also* 'eks-məs\ *n* [*X* (symbol for *Christ*, fr. the Gk letter chi (X), initial of *Christos* Christ) + *-mas* (in *Christmas*)] : CHRISTMAS

XML \ˌeks-(ˌ)em-'el\ *n* : a markup language that indicates the structural type of data

XO *abbr* executive officer

x–ra•di•a•tion \ˌeks-ˌrā-dē-'ā-shən\ *n, often cap* **1** : exposure to X-rays **2** : radiation consisting of X-rays

x–ray \'eks-ˌrā\ *vb, often cap* : to examine, treat, or photograph with X-rays

X–ray \'eks-ˌrā\ *n* **1** : a radiation with an extremely short wavelength of less than 100 angstroms that is able to penetrate through various thicknesses of solids and to act on

photographic film **2** : a photograph taken with X-rays —
X–ray *adj*
XS *abbr* extra small
xu \\'sü\ *n, pl* **xu** — see *dong* at MONEY table
xy·lem \\'zī-ləm, -ˌlem\ *n* : a woody tissue of vascular plants
that transports water and dissolved materials upward,
functions in support and storage, and lies central to the
phloem
xy·lo·phone \\'zī-lə-ˌfōn\ *n* [Gk *xylon* wood + *phōnē* voice,
sound] : a musical instrument consisting of a series of
wooden bars graduated in length to produce the musical
scale, supported on belts of straw or felt, and sounded by
striking with two small wooden hammers — **xy·lo·phon-
ist** \-ˌfō-nist\ *n*

xylophone

¹**y** \\'wī\ *n, pl* **y's** *or* **ys** \\'wīz\ *often cap* : the 25th letter of the
English alphabet
²**y** *abbr* **1** yard **2** year
¹**Y** \\'wī\ *n* : YMCA, YWCA
²**Y** *symbol* yttrium
¹**-y** *also* **-ey** \ē\ *adj suffix* **1** : characterized by : full of
⟨dirt*y*⟩ ⟨clay*ey*⟩ **2** : having the character of : composed
of ⟨ic*y*⟩ **3** : like : like that of ⟨home*y*⟩ ⟨wintr*y*⟩ ⟨stag*y*⟩
4 : tending or inclined to ⟨sleep*y*⟩ ⟨chatt*y*⟩ **5** : giving occasion for (specified) action ⟨tear*y*⟩ **6** : performing
(specified) action ⟨curl*y*⟩
²**-y** \ē\ *n suffix, pl* **-ies** **1** : state : condition : quality ⟨beg-
gar*y*⟩ **2** : activity, place of business, or goods dealt with
⟨laundr*y*⟩ **3** : whole body or group ⟨soldier*y*⟩
³**-y** *n suffix, pl* **-ies** : instance of a (specified) action ⟨en-
treat*y*⟩ ⟨inquir*y*⟩
YA *abbr* young adult
¹**yacht** \\'yät\ *n* [obs. D *jaght,* fr. Middle Low German *jacht,*
short for *jachtschip,* lit., hunting ship] : a usu. large recreational watercraft
²**yacht** *vb* : to race or cruise in a yacht
yacht·ing \\'yä-tiŋ\ *n* : the sport of racing or cruising in a
yacht
yachts·man \\'yäts-mən\ *n* : a person who owns or sails a
yacht
ya·hoo \\'yä-hü, 'yä-\ *n, pl* **yahoos** [fr. *Yahoo,* one of a race
of brutes having the form of men in Jonathan Swift's *Gul-
liver's Travels*] : a boorish, crass, or stupid person
Yah·weh \\'yä-ˌwā\ *also* **Yah·veh** \-ˌvā\ *n* : GOD 1 — used
esp. by the Hebrews
¹**yak** \\'yak\ *n, pl* **yaks** *also* **yak** : a large long-haired wild or
domesticated ox of Tibet and adjacent Asian uplands
²**yak** *also* **yack** \\'yak\ *n* : persistent or voluble talk — **yak**
also **yack** *vb*
yam \\'yam\ *n* **1** : the edible starchy root of various twining plants used as a staple food in tropical areas; *also* : a
plant that produces yams **2** : a usu. deep orange sweet
potato
yam·mer \\'ya-mər\ *vb* [ME *yameren,* alter. of *yomeren* to
murmur, be sad, fr. OE *gēomrian*] **1** : WHIMPER **2**
: CHATTER — **yammer** *n*
¹**yank** \\'yaŋk\ *vb* : to pull with a quick vigorous movement
²**yank** *n* : a strong sudden pull : JERK
Yank \\'yaŋk\ *n* : YANKEE
Yan·kee \\'yaŋ-kē\ *n* **1** : a native or inhabitant of New
England; *also* : a native or inhabitant of the northern
U.S. **2** : AMERICAN 2
yan·qui \\'yän-kē\ *n, often cap* [Sp] : a citizen of the U.S. as
distinguished from a Latin American
¹**yap** \\'yap\ *vb* **yapped; yap·ping 1** : BARK, YELP **2** : GAB
²**yap** *n* **1** : a quick sharp bark **2** : CHATTER
¹**yard** \\'yärd\ *n* [ME, fr. OE *geard* enclosure, yard] **1** : a
small enclosed area open to the sky and adjacent to a
building **2** : the grounds of a building **3** : the grounds
surrounding a house usu. covered with grass **4** : an enclosure for livestock **5** : an area set aside for a particular

business or activity **6** : a system of railroad tracks for
storing cars and making up trains
²**yard** *n* [ME *yarde,* fr. OE *gierd* twig, measure, yard] **1** —
see WEIGHT table **2** : a long spar tapered toward the ends
that supports and spreads the head of a sail — **the whole
nine yards** : all of a set of circumstances, conditions, or
details
yard·age \\'yär-dij\ *n* : an aggregate number of yards; *also*
: the length, extent, or volume of something as measured
in yards
yard·arm \\'yärd-ˌärm\ *n* : either end of the yard of a
square-rigged ship
yard·man \-mən, -ˌman\ *n* : a person employed in or about
a yard
yard·mas·ter \-ˌmas-tər\ *n* : the person in charge of a railroad yard
yard·stick \-ˌstik\ *n* **1** : a graduated measuring stick three
feet long **2** : a standard for making a critical judgment
: CRITERION ♦ *Synonyms* GAUGE, TOUCHSTONE,
BENCHMARK, MEASURE
yar·mul·ke \\'yä-mə-kə, 'yär-, -məl-\ *n* [Yiddish *yarmlke*] : a
skullcap worn esp. by Jewish males in the synagogue and
the home
yarn \\'yärn\ *n* **1** : a continuous often plied strand composed of fibers or filaments and used in weaving and knitting to form cloth **2** : STORY; *esp* : a tall tale
yar·row \\'ya-rō\ *n* : a strong-scented herb related to the
daisies that has white or pink flowers in flat clusters
yaw \\'yo\ *vb* : to deviate erratically from a course ⟨the ship
~ed in heavy seas⟩ — **yaw** *n*
yawl \\'yol\ *n* : a 2-masted sailboat with the shorter mast aft
of the rudder
¹**yawn** \\'yon\ *vb* : to open wide; *esp* : to open the mouth
wide and take a deep breath usu. as an involuntary reaction to fatigue or boredom — **yawn·er** *n*
²**yawn** *n* : the act of yawning
yawp *or* **yaup** \\'yop\ *vb* **1** : to make a raucous noise
: SQUAWK **2** : CLAMOR, COMPLAIN — **yawp·er** *n*
yaws \\'yoz\ *n pl* : a contagious tropical disease caused by
a spirochete closely resembling the causative agent of
syphilis and marked by skin lesions
y–ax·is \\'wī-ˌak-səs\ *n* : the axis of a graph or of a system
of coordinates in a plane parallel to which the ordinates
are measured
Yb *symbol* ytterbium
YB *abbr* yearbook
Y chromosome *n* : a sex chromosome that is characteristic of male cells in organisms (as humans) in which the
male typically has two unlike sex chromosomes
yd *abbr* yard
¹**ye** \yē\ *pron* : YOU 1
²**ye** \yē, yə, *originally same as* THE\ *definite article, archaic*
: THE — used by early printers to represent the manuscript word *þe (the)*
¹**yea** \\'yā\ *adv* **1** : YES — used in oral voting **2** : INDEED,
TRULY

²**yea** *n* : an affirmative vote; *also* : a person casting such a vote

yeah \'yeə, 'yaə\ *adv* : YES

year \'yir\ *n* **1** : the period of about 365¼ solar days required for one revolution of the earth around the sun; *also* : the time in which a planet completes a revolution about the sun **2** : a cycle of 365 or 366 days beginning with January 1; *also* : a calendar year specified usu. by a number **3** *pl* : a time of special significance ⟨their glory ∼s⟩ **4** *pl* : AGE ⟨advanced in ∼s⟩ **5** : a period of time other than a calendar year ⟨the school ∼⟩

year·book \-ˌbu̇k\ *n* **1** : a book published annually esp. as a report **2** : a school publication recording the history and activities of a graduating class

year·ling \'yir-liŋ, 'yər-lən\ *n* **1** : one that is a year old **2** : a racehorse between January of the year after the year in which it was born and the next January

year·long \'yir-'lȯŋ\ *adj* : lasting through a year

¹**year·ly** \'yir-lē\ *adj* : ANNUAL

²**yearly** *adv* : every year

yearn \'yərn\ *vb* **1** : to feel a longing or craving **2** : to feel tenderness or compassion ♦ **Synonyms** LONG, PINE, HANKER, HUNGER, THIRST

yearn·ing *n* : a tender or urgent longing

year–round \'yir-'rau̇nd\ *adj* : effective, employed, or operating for the full year : not seasonal ⟨a ∼ resort⟩

yeast \'yēst\ *n* **1** : a surface froth or a sediment in sugary liquids (as fruit juices) that consists largely of cells of a tiny fungus and is used in making alcoholic liquors and as a leaven in baking **2** : a commercial product containing yeast fungi in a moist or dry medium **3** : a minute one-celled fungus present and functionally active in yeast that reproduces by budding; *also* : any of several similar fungi **4** *archaic* : the foam of waves : SPUME **5** : something that causes ferment or activity

yeast infection *n* : infection of the vagina with an excess growth of a normally present fungus that resembles a yeast

yeasty \'yē-stē\ *adj* **yeast·i·er; -est 1** : of, relating to, or resembling yeast **2** : UNSETTLED **3** : full of vitality; *also* : FRIVOLOUS

yegg \'yeg\ *n* : one that breaks open safes to steal; *also* : ROBBER

¹**yell** \'yel\ *vb* : to utter a loud cry or scream : SHOUT — **yell·er** *n*

²**yell** *n* **1** : SHOUT **2** : a cheer used esp. to encourage an athletic team (as at a college)

¹**yel·low** \'ye-lō\ *adj* **1** : of the color yellow **2** : having a yellow complexion or skin **3** : SENSATIONAL ⟨∼ journalism⟩ **4** : COWARDLY — **yel·low·ish** \'ye-lə-wish\ *adj*

²**yellow** *n* **1** : a color between green and orange in the spectrum : the color of ripe lemons or sunflowers **2** : something yellow; *esp* : the yolk of an egg **3** *pl* : any of several plant diseases marked by stunted growth and yellowing of foliage

³**yellow** *vb* : to make or turn yellow

yellow birch *n* : a No. American birch with thin lustrous gray or yellow bark; *also* : its strong hard wood

yellow fever *n* : an acute infectious viral disease marked by prostration, jaundice, fever, and often hemorrhage and transmitted by a mosquito

yellow jack *n* : YELLOW FEVER

yellow jacket *n* : any of various small social wasps having the body barred with bright yellow

yel·low·tail \'ye-lō-ˌtāl\ *n* : any of various fishes with a yellow or yellowish tail including several valuable food fishes

yelp \'yelp\ *vb* [ME, to boast, cry out, fr. OE *gielpan* to boast, exult] : to utter a sharp quick shrill cry — **yelp** *n*

Ye·me·ni \'ye-mə-nē\ *n* : YEMENITE — **Yemeni** *adj*

Ye·men·ite \'ye-mə-ˌnīt\ *n* : a native or inhabitant of Yemen — **Yemenite** *adj*

¹**yen** \'yen\ *n*, *pl* **yen** — see MONEY table

²**yen** *n* [obs. E argot *yen-yen* craving for opium, fr. Chin (Guangdong dial.) *yīn-yáhn*, fr. *yīn* opium + *yáhn* craving] : a strong desire : LONGING

yeo·man \'yō-mən\ *n* **1** : an attendant or officer in a royal or noble household **2** : a naval petty officer who performs clerical duties **3** : a person who owns and cultivates a small farm; *esp* : one of a class of English freeholders below the gentry — **yeo·man·ly** \-lē\ *adj*

yeo·man·ry \-rē\ *n* : the body of yeomen and esp. of small landed proprietors

-yer — see -ER

¹**yes** \'yes\ *adv* — used as a function word esp. to express assent or agreement or to introduce a more emphatic or explicit phrase

²**yes** *n* : an affirmative reply

ye·shi·va *or* **ye·shi·vah** \yə-'shē-və\ *n, pl* **yeshivas** *or* **ye·shi·voth** \-ˌshē-'vōt, -'vōth\ : a Jewish school esp. for religious instruction

yes–man \'yes-ˌman\ *n* : a person who endorses uncritically every opinion or proposal of a superior

¹**yes·ter·day** \'yes-tər-dē, -ˌdā\ *adv* **1** : on the day preceding today **2** : only a short time ago

²**yesterday** *n* **1** : the day last past **2** : time not long past

yes·ter·year \'yes-tər-ˌyir\ *n* **1** : last year **2** : the recent past

¹**yet** \'yet\ *adv* **1** : in addition : BESIDES; *also* : EVEN 6 **2** : up to now; *also* : STILL **3** : so soon as now ⟨not time to go ∼⟩ **4** : EVENTUALLY **5** : NEVERTHELESS, HOWEVER

²**yet** *conj* : but nevertheless : BUT

ye·ti \'ye-tē, 'yā-\ *n* : ABOMINABLE SNOWMAN

yew \'yü\ *n* **1** : any of a genus of evergreen trees and shrubs with dark stiff poisonous needles and fleshy fruits **2** : the wood of a yew; *esp* : that of an Old World yew

Yid·dish \'yi-dish\ *n* [Yiddish *yidish*, short for *yidish daytsh*, lit., Jewish German] : a language derived from medieval German and spoken by Jews esp. of eastern European origin — **Yiddish** *adj*

¹**yield** \'yēld\ *vb* **1** : to give as fitting, owed, or required **2** : GIVE UP; *esp* : to give up possession of on claim or demand **3** : to bear as a natural product **4** : PRODUCE, SUPPLY **5** : to bring in : RETURN **6** : to give way (as to force or influence) **7** : to give place ♦ **Synonyms** RELINQUISH, CEDE, WAIVE, SURRENDER

²**yield** *n* : something yielded; *esp* : the amount or quantity produced or returned

yield·ing \'yēl-diŋ\ *adj* **1** : not rigid or stiff : FLEXIBLE **2** : SUBMISSIVE, COMPLIANT

yikes \'yīks\ *interj* — used to express fear or astonishment

yip \'yip\ *vb* **yipped; yip·ping** : YAP

YK *abbr* Yukon Territory

YMCA \ˌwī-ˌem-(ˌ)sē-'ā\ *n* : Young Men's Christian Association

YMHA \ˌwī-ˌem-ˌāch-'ā\ *n* : Young Men's Hebrew Association

yo \'yō\ *interj* — used to call attention, indicate attentiveness, or express affirmation

YOB *abbr* year of birth

yo·del \'yō-dᵊl\ *vb* **yo·deled** *or* **yo·delled; yo·del·ing** *or* **yo·del·ling** : to sing by suddenly changing from chest voice to falsetto and back; *also* : to shout or call in this manner — **yodel** *n* — **yo·del·er** *n*

yo·ga \'yō-gə\ *n* [Skt. lit., yoking, fr. *yunakti* he yokes] **1** *cap* : a Hindu theistic philosophy teaching the suppression of all activity of body, mind, and will in order that the self may realize its distinction from them and attain liberation **2** : a system of exercises for attaining bodily or mental control and well-being — **yo·gic** \-gik\ *adj, often cap*

yo·gi \'yō-gē\ *also* **yo·gin** \-gən, -ˌgin\ *n* **1** : a person who practices yoga **2** *cap* : an adherent of Yoga philosophy

yo·gurt *also* **yo·ghurt** \'yō-gərt\ *n* [Turk *yoğurt*] : a soured slightly acid often flavored semisolid food made of milk and milk solids to which cultures of bacteria have been added

¹**yoke** \'yōk\ *n, pl* **yokes 1** : a wooden bar or frame by which two draft animals (as oxen) are coupled at the heads or necks for working together; *also* : a frame fitted to a person's shoulders to carry a load in two equal portions **2** : a clamp that embraces two parts to hold or unite them in position **3** *pl usu* **yoke** : two animals yoked together **4** : SERVITUDE, BONDAGE **5** : TIE, LINK ⟨the ∼ of matrimony⟩ **6** : a fitted or shaped piece esp. at the shoulder of a garment ♦ **Synonyms** COUPLE, PAIR, BRACE

²**yoke** *vb* **yoked; yok·ing 1** : to put a yoke on : couple with a yoke **2** : to attach a draft animal to ⟨∼ a plow⟩ **3** : JOIN; *esp* : MARRY

yo·kel \'yō-kəl\ *n* : a naive or gullible country person

yolk \'yōk\ *n* **1** : the yellow rounded inner mass of the egg of a bird or reptile **2** : the stored food material of an egg that supplies nutrients (as proteins and cholesterol) to the developing embryo — **yolked** \'yōkt\ *adj*

Yom Kip·pur \,yŏm-ki-'pŭr, ,yäm-, -'ki-pər\ *n* [Heb *yōm kippūr*, lit., day of atonement] : a Jewish holiday observed in September or October with fasting and prayer as a day of atonement

¹yon \'yän\ *adj* : YONDER

²yon *adv* **1** : YONDER **2** : THITHER ⟨ran hither and ∼⟩

¹yon·der \'yän-dər\ *adv* : at or to that place

²yonder *adj* **1** : more distant ⟨the ∼ side of the river⟩ **2** : being at a distance within view ⟨∼ hills⟩

yore \'yȯr\ *n* [ME, fr. *yore*, adv., long ago, fr. OE *geāra*, fr. *gēar* year] : time long past ⟨in days of ∼⟩

York·ie \'yȯr-kē\ *n* : YORKSHIRE TERRIER

York·shire terrier \'yȯrk-,shir-, -shər-\ *n* : any of a breed of compact toy terriers with long straight silky hair

you \'yü\ *pron* **1** : the person or persons addressed ⟨∼ are a nice person⟩ ⟨∼ are nice people⟩ **2** : ONE 2 ⟨∼ turn this knob to open it⟩

¹young \'yəŋ\ *adj* **youn·ger** \'yəŋ-gər\; **youn·gest** \'yəŋ-gəst\ **1** : being in the first or an early stage of life, growth, or development **2** : having little experience **3** : recently come into being **4** : YOUTHFUL **5** *cap* : belonging to or representing a new or revived usu. political group or movement — **young·ish** \'yəŋ-ish\ *adj*

²young *n, pl* **young** : young persons; *also* : young animals

young·ling \'yəŋ-liŋ\ *n* : one that is young — **youngling** *adj*

young·ster \-stər\ *n* **1** : a young person **2** : CHILD

your \'yùr, 'yȯr, yər\ *adj* : of or relating to you or yourself

yours \'yùrz, 'yȯrz\ *pron* : one or the ones belonging to you

your·self \yər-'self\ *pron, pl* **yourselves** \-'selvz\ : YOU — used reflexively, for emphasis, or in absolute constructions ⟨you'll hurt ∼⟩ ⟨do it ∼⟩

youth \'yüth\ *n, pl* **youths** \'yü<u>t</u>hz, 'yüths\ **1** : the period of life between childhood and maturity **2** : a young man; *also* : young persons **3** : YOUTHFULNESS

youth·ful \'yüth-fəl\ *adj* **1** : of, relating to, or appropriate to youth **2** : being young and not yet mature **3** : FRESH, VIGOROUS — **youth·ful·ly** *adv* — **youth·ful·ness** *n*

youth hostel *n* : HOSTEL 2

yowl \'yaù(-ə)l\ *vb* : to utter a loud long mournful cry : WAIL — **yowl** *n*

yo–yo \'yō-(,)yō\ *n, pl* **yo–yos** [prob. fr. Ilocano (a Philippine language) *yóyo*] : a thick grooved double disk with a string attached to its center that is made to fall and rise to the hand by unwinding and rewinding on the string — **yo–yo** *vb*

yr *abbr* **1** year **2** your

yrbk *abbr* yearbook

YT *abbr* Yukon Territory

yt·ter·bi·um \i-'tər-bē-əm\ *n* : a rare metallic chemical element

yt·tri·um \'i-trē-əm\ *n* : a rare metallic chemical element

yu·an \'yü-ən, yü-'än\ *n, pl* **yuan** **1** — see MONEY table **2** : the dollar of the Republic of China (Taiwan)

yuc·ca \'yə-kə\ *n* : any of a genus of plants related to the agaves that grow esp. in warm dry regions and bear large clusters of white cup-shaped flowers atop a long stiff stalk

yuck *also* **yuk** \'yək\ *interj* — used to express rejection or disgust

yule \'yül\ *n, often cap* : CHRISTMAS

Yule log *n* : a large log formerly put on the hearth on Christmas Eve as the foundation of the fire

yule·tide \'yül-,tīd\ *n, often cap* : CHRISTMASTIDE

yum·my \'yə-mē\ *adj* **yum·mi·er; -est** : highly attractive or pleasing

yup·pie \'yə-pē\ *n* [prob. fr. *y*oung *u*rban *p*rofessional + *-ie* (as in hipp*ie*)] : a young college-educated adult employed in a well-paying profession and living and working in or near a large city — **yup·pie·dom** \-dəm\ *n*

yurt \'yùrt\ *n* : a light round tent of skins or felt stretched over a lattice framework used by pastoral peoples of inner Asia

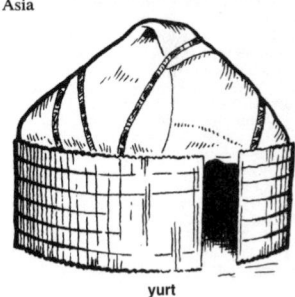

yurt

YWCA \,wī-,də-bəl-yü-(,)sē-'ā\ *n* : Young Women's Christian Association

YWHA \-,āch-'ā\ *n* : Young Women's Hebrew Association

Z

¹z \'zē\ *n, pl* **z's** *or* **zs** \'zēz\ *often cap* : the 26th letter of the English alphabet

²z *abbr* **1** zero **2** zone

Z *symbol* atomic number

Zach *abbr* Zacharias

Zach·a·ri·as \,za-kə-'rī-əs\ *n* : ZECHARIAH

¹za·ny \'zā-nē\ *n, pl* **zanies** [It *zanni*, a traditional masked clown, fr. It dial. *Zanni*, nickname for It *Giovanni* John] **1** : CLOWN, BUFFOON **2** : a silly or foolish person

²zany *adj* **za·ni·er; -est** **1** : characteristic of a zany **2** : CRAZY, FOOLISH ⟨a ∼ movie⟩ — **za·ni·ly** \'zā-nə-lē\ *adv* — **za·ni·ness** \'zā-nē-nəs\ *n*

zap \'zap\ *vb* **zapped; zap·ping** **1** : DESTROY, KILL **2** : to irradiate esp. with microwaves

zeal \'zēl\ *n* : eager and ardent interest in the pursuit of something : FERVOR ✦ *Synonyms* ENTHUSIASM, PASSION, ARDOR

zeal·ot \'ze-lət\ *n* : a zealous person; *esp* : a fanatical partisan ⟨a religious ∼⟩ ✦ *Synonyms* ENTHUSIAST, BIGOT

zeal·ous \'ze-ləs\ *adj* : filled with, characterized by, or due to zeal — **zeal·ous·ly** *adv* — **zeal·ous·ness** *n*

ze·bra \'zē-brə\ *n, pl* **zebras** *also* **zebra** : any of several African mammals related to the horse but conspicuously striped with black or dark brown and white or buff

zebra

zebra mussel *n* : a freshwater Eurasian mollusk introduced into U.S. waterways where it colonizes and clogs water intake pipes

ze·bu \'zē-bü, -byü\ *n* : any of various breeds of domestic oxen developed in India that have a large fleshy hump over the shoulders, a dewlap, drooping ears, and marked resistance to heat and to insect attack

Zech *abbr* Zechariah

Zech·a·ri·ah \ˌze-kə-'rī-ə\ *n* — see BIBLE table

zed \'zed\ *n, chiefly Brit* : the letter *z*

zeit·geist \'tsīt-ˌgīst, 'zīt-\ *n* [G, fr. *Zeit* time + *Geist* spirit] : the general intellectual, moral, and cultural state of an era

Zen \'zen\ *n* : a Japanese Buddhist sect that teaches self-discipline, meditation, and attainment of enlightenment through direct intuitive insight

ze·na·na \zə-'nä-nə\ *n* : HAREM

ze·nith \'zē-nəth\ *n* **1** : the point in the heavens directly overhead **2** : the highest point : ACME ⟨the ~ of her career⟩ ♦ **Synonyms** CULMINATION, PINNACLE, APEX

ze·o·lite \'zē-ə-ˌlīt\ *n* : any of various feldsparlike silicates used esp. as water softeners

Zeph *abbr* Zephaniah

Zeph·a·ni·ah \ˌze-fə-'nī-ə\ *n* — see BIBLE table

zeph·yr \'ze-fər\ *n* : a breeze from the west; *also* : a gentle breeze

zep·pe·lin \'ze-plən, -pə-lən\ *n* [Count Ferdinand von *Zeppelin* †1917 Ger. airship manufacturer] : a cylindrical rigid blimplike airship

¹ze·ro \'zē-rō, 'zir-ō\ *n, pl* zeros *also* zeroes [ultim. fr. Ar *ṣifr*] **1** : the numerical symbol 0 **2** : the number represented by the symbol 0 **3** : the point at which the graduated degrees or measurements on a scale (as of a thermometer) begin **4** : the lowest point

²zero *adj* **1** : of, relating to, or being a zero **2** : having no magnitude or quantity **3** : ABSENT, LACKING; *esp* : having no modified inflectional form

³zero *vb* : to adjust the sights of a firearm to hit the point aimed at — usu. used with *in*

zero hour *n* : the time at which an event (as a military operation) is scheduled to begin

zest \'zest\ *n* **1** : a quality of enhancing enjoyment : PIQUANCY **2** : keen enjoyment : GUSTO — **zest·ful** \-fəl\ *adj* — **zest·ful·ly** *adv* — **zest·ful·ness** *n* — **zesty** \'zes-tē\ *adj*

ze·ta \'zā-tə, 'zē-\ *n* : the 6th letter of the Greek alphabet — Z or ζ

zi·do·vu·dine \zī-'dō-vyü-ˌdēn\ *n* : AZT

¹zig·zag \'zig-ˌzag\ *n* : one of a series of short sharp turns, angles, or alterations in a course; *also* : something marked by such a series

²zigzag *adv* : in or by a zigzag path

³zigzag *adj* : having short sharp turns or angles

⁴zigzag *vb* **zig·zagged; zig·zag·ging** : to form into or proceed along a zigzag

zil·lion \'zil-yən\ *n* : a large indeterminate number

zinc \'ziŋk\ *n* : a bluish-white metallic chemical element that is commonly found in minerals and is used esp. in alloys and as a protective coating for iron and steel

zinc oxide *n* : a white solid used esp. as a pigment, in compounding rubber, and in ointments and sunblocks

zine \'zēn\ *n* : a noncommercial publication usu. devoted to specialized subject matter

zin·fan·del \'zin-fən-ˌdel\ *n, often cap* : a dry red table wine made chiefly in California

zing \'ziŋ\ *n* **1** : a shrill humming noise **2** : VITALITY 4 — **zing** *vb*

zing·er \'ziŋ-ər\ *n* : a pointed witty remark or retort

zin·nia \'zi-nē-ə, 'zēn-yə\ *n* : any of a genus of tropical American herbs or low shrubs related to the daisies and widely grown for their showy long-lasting flowers

Zi·on \'zī-ən\ *n* **1** : the Jewish people **2** : the Jewish homeland as a symbol of Judaism or of Jewish national aspiration **3** : HEAVEN **4** : UTOPIA

Zi·on·ism \'zī-ə-ˌni-zəm\ *n* : an international movement orig. for the establishment of a Jewish national or religious community in Palestine and later for the support of modern Israel — **Zi·on·ist** \-nist\ *adj or n*

¹zip \'zip\ *vb* **zipped; zip·ping** : to move, act, or function with speed or vigor

²zip *n* **1** : a sudden sharp hissing sound **2** : ENERGY, VIM

³zip *n* : NOTHING, ZERO ⟨the score was 27 to ~⟩

⁴zip *vb* **zipped; zip·ping** : to close or open with a zipper

zip code *n, often cap Z&I&P* [*z*one *i*mprovement *p*lan] : a number that identifies each postal delivery area in the U.S.

zip·per \'zi-pər\ *n* : a fastener consisting of two rows of metal or plastic teeth on strips of tape and a sliding piece that closes an opening by drawing the teeth together

zip·py \'zi-pē\ *adj* **zip·pi·er; -est** **1** : very speedy ⟨a ~ car⟩ **2** : strikingly appealing ⟨~ clothes⟩

zir·con \'zər-ˌkän\ *n* : a zirconium-containing mineral transparent varieties of which are used as gems

zir·co·ni·um \ˌzər-'kō-nē-əm\ *n* : a gray corrosion-resistant metallic chemical element used esp. in alloys and ceramics

zit \'zit\ *n* : PIMPLE

zith·er \'zi-thər, -thər\ *n* : a musical instrument having 30 to 40 strings played with plectrum and fingers

zi·ti \'zē-tē\ *n, pl* ziti [It] : medium-size tubular pasta

zlo·ty \'zlȯ-tē\ *n, pl* **zlo·tys** \-tēz\ *or* zloty — see MONEY table

Zn *symbol* zinc

zo·di·ac \'zō-dē-ˌak\ *n* [ME, fr. AF, fr. L *zodiacus*, fr. Gk *zōidiakos*, fr. *zōidion* carved figure, sign of the zodiac, fr. dim. of *zōion* living being, figure] **1** : an imaginary belt in the heavens that encompasses the paths of most of the planets and that is divided into 12 constellations or signs **2** : a figure representing the signs of the zodiac and their symbols — **zo·di·a·cal** \zō-'dī-ə-kəl\ *adj*

zom·bie *also* **zom·bi** \'zäm-bē\ *n* : a person who is believed to have died and been brought back to life without speech or free will

zon·al \'zō-n³l\ *adj* : of, relating to, or having the form of a zone — **zon·al·ly** *adv*

¹zone \'zōn\ *n* [ME, fr. AF, fr. L *zona* belt, zone, fr. Gk *zōnē*] **1** : any of five great divisions of the earth's surface made according to latitude and temperature including the torrid zone, two temperate zones, and two frigid zones **2** : something that forms an encircling band ⟨a ~ of tissue⟩ **3** : a region or area set off as distinct from surrounding parts ⟨business ~⟩ ⟨postal ~⟩

²zone *vb* **zoned; zon·ing** **1** : ENCIRCLE **2** : to arrange in or mark off into zones; *esp* : to divide (as a city) into sections reserved for different purposes

zonked \'zäŋkt\ *adj* : being or acting as if under the influence of alcohol or a drug : HIGH

zoo \'zü\ *n, pl* zoos : a park where wild animals are kept for exhibition

zoo·ge·og·ra·phy \ˌzō-ə-jē-'ä-grə-fē\ *n* : a branch of biogeography concerned with the geographical distribution of animals — **zoo·ge·og·ra·pher** \-fər\ *n* — **zoo·geo·graph·ic** \-jē-ə-'gra-fik\ *also* **zoo·geo·graph·i·cal** \-fi-kəl\ *adj*

zoo·keep·er \'zü-ˌkē-pər\ *n* : a person who cares for animals in a zoo

zool *abbr* zoological; zoology

zoological garden *n* : ZOO

zo·ol·o·gy \zō-'ä-lə-jē\ *n* : a branch of biology that deals with the classification and the properties and vital phenomena of animals — **zo·o·log·i·cal** \ˌzō-ə-'lä-ji-kəl\ *adj* — **zo·ol·o·gist** \zō-'ä-lə-jist\ *n*

zoom \'züm\ *vb* **1** : to move with a loud hum or buzz **2** : to gain altitude quickly **3** : to focus a camera or microscope using a special lens that permits the apparent distance of the object to be varied — **zoom** *n*

zoom lens *n* : a camera lens in which the image size can be varied continuously while the image remains in focus

zoo·mor·phic \ˌzō-ə-'mȯr-fik\ *adj* **1** : having the form of an animal **2** : of, relating to, or being the representation of a deity in the form or with the attributes of an animal

zoo·plank·ton \ˌzō-ə-'plaŋk-tən, -ˌtän\ *n* : plankton composed of animals

zoo·spore \'zō-ə-ˌspȯr\ *n* : a motile spore

zoot suit \'züt-\ *n* : a flashy suit of extreme cut typically consisting of a thigh-length jacket with wide padded shoulders and pants that are wide at the top and narrow at the bottom — **zoot-suit·er** \-ˌsü-tər\ *n*

Zo·ro·as·tri·an·ism \ˌzȯr-ə-'was-trē-ə-ˌni-zəm\ *n* : a religion founded by the Persian prophet Zoroaster — **Zo·ro·as·tri·an** \-trē-ən\ *adj or n*

zounds \'zaúndz\ *interj* [euphemism for *God's wounds*] — used as a mild oath

zoy·sia \\'zȯi-shə, -zhə, -sē-ə, -zē-ə\\ *n* : any of a genus of creeping perennial grasses having fine wiry leaves and including some used as lawn grasses

ZPG *abbr* zero population growth

Zr *symbol* zirconium

zuc·chet·to \\zü-'ke-tō, tsü-\\ *n, pl* **-tos** [It] : a small round skullcap worn by Roman Catholic ecclesiastics

zuc·chi·ni \\zu̇-'kē-nē\\ *n, pl* **-ni** *or* **-nis** [It] : a smooth cylindrical usu. dark green summer squash; *also* : a plant that bears zucchini

Zu·lu \\'zü-,lü\\ *n, pl* **Zulu** *or* **Zulus** : a member of a Bantu‐speaking people of South Africa; *also* : the Bantu language of the Zulus

Zu·ni \\'zü-nē\\ *or* **Zu·ñi** \\-nyē\\ *n, pl* **Zuni** *or* **Zunis** *or* **Zuñi** *or* **Zuñis** : a member of an American Indian people of western New Mexico; *also* : the language of the Zuni people

zwie·back \\'swē-,bak, 'swī-, 'zwē-, 'zwī-, -,bäk\\ *n* [G, lit., twice baked, fr. *zwie-* twice + *backen* to bake] : a usu. sweetened bread that is baked and then sliced and toasted until dry and crisp

Zwing·li·an \\'zwiŋ-glē-ən, 'swiŋ-, -lē-; 'tsfiŋ-lē-\\ *adj* : of or relating to the Swiss religious reformer Ulrich Zwingli or his teachings — **Zwinglian** *n*

zy·de·co \\'zī-də-,kō\\ *n* : popular music of southern Louisiana that combines tunes of French origin with elements of Caribbean music and the blues

zy·gote \\'zī-,gōt\\ *n* : a cell formed by the union of two sexual cells; *also* : the developing individual produced from such a cell — **zy·got·ic** \\zī-'gä-tik\\ *adj*

FOREIGN WORDS & PHRASES

These words and phrases occur frequently enough in English context to be included in a general English dictionary, but they merit a special section because they have not become a part of the English vocabulary.

---

ab·eunt stu·dia in mo·res \'ä-be-ˌu̇nt-'stü-dē-ˌä-ˌin-'mō-ˌräs\ [L] : practices zealously pursued pass into habits

à bien·tôt \ä-byaⁿ-tō\ [F] : so long

ab in·cu·na·bu·lis \ˌäb-ˌin̩-kü-'nä-bü-ˌlēs\ [L] : from the cradle : from infancy

à bon chat, bon rat \ä-bōⁿ-'shä bōⁿ-'rä\ [F] : to a good cat, a good rat : retaliation in kind

à bouche ou·verte \ä-bü-shü-vert\ [F] : with open mouth : eagerly : uncritically

ab ovo us·que ad ma·la \äb-'ō-vō-ˌu̇s-kwe-ˌäd-'mä-lä\ [L] : from egg to apples : from soup to nuts : from beginning to end

à bras ou·verts \ä-brä-zü-ver\ [F] : with open arms : cordially

ab·sit in·vi·dia \'äb-ˌsit-in-'wi-dē-ˌä\ [L] : let there be no envy or ill will

ab uno dis·ce om·nes \äb-'ü-nō-ˌdis-ke-'ȯm-ˌnās\ [L] : from one learn to know all

ab ur·be con·di·ta \äb-'u̇r-be-'kȯn-di-ˌtä\ [L] : from the founding of the city (Rome, founded 753 B.C.) — used by the Romans in reckoning dates

ab·usus non tol·lit usum \'ä-ˌbü-su̇s-ˌnōn-ˌtȯ-lit-'ü-su̇m\ [L] : abuse does not take away use, i.e., is not an argument against proper use

à compte \ä-'kōⁿt\ [F] : on account

à coup sûr \ä-kü-su̇r\ [F] : with sure stroke : surely

acte gra·tuit \äk-tə-grä-twᵉē\ [F] : gratuitous impulsive act

ad ar·bi·tri·um \ˌad-är-'bi-trē-u̇m\ [L] : at will : arbitrarily

ad as·tra per as·pe·ra \ad-'as-trə-ˌpər-'as-pə-rə\ [L] : to the stars by hard ways — motto of Kansas

ad ex·tre·mum \ˌäd-ek-'strä-ˌmu̇m, ˌad-ik-'strē-məm\ [L] : to the extreme : at last

ad ka·len·das Grae·cas \ˌäd-kä-'len-däs-'grī-ˌkäs\ [L] : at the Greek calends : never (since the Greeks had no calends)

ad ma·jo·rem Dei glo·ri·am \ˌäd-mä-'yȯr-ˌem-'de-ˌē-'glȯr-ē-ˌäm\ [L] : to the greater glory of God — motto of the Society of Jesus

ad pa·tres \äd-'pä-ˌträs\ [L] : (gathered) to his fathers : deceased

ad re·fe·ren·dum \ˌäd-ˌre-fe-'ren-du̇m\ [L] : for reference : for further consideration by one having the authority to make a final decision

à droite \ä-drwät\ [F] : to or on the right hand

ad un·guem \äd-'u̇n̩-ˌgwem\ [L] : to the fingernail : to a nicety : exactly (from the use of the fingernail to test the smoothness of marble)

ad utrum·que pa·ra·tus \ˌäd-ü-'tru̇m-kwe-pä-'rä-tu̇s\ [L] : prepared for either (event)

ad vi·vum \äd-'wē-ˌwu̇m\ [L] : to the life

ae·gri som·nia \ˌī-grē-'sȯm-nē-ˌä\ [L] : a sick man's dreams

ae·quam ser·va·re men·tem \'ī-ˌkwäm-ser-ˌwä-rä-'men-ˌtem\ [L] : to preserve a calm mind

ae·quo ani·mo \ˌī-kwō-'ä-ni-ˌmō\ [L] : with even mind : calmly

ae·re per·en·ni·us \'ī-rä-pe-'re-nē-ˌu̇s\ [L] : more lasting than bronze

à gauche \ä-gōsh\ [F] : to or on the left hand

age quod agis \'ä-ge-ˌkwȯd-'ä-ˌgis\ [L] : do what you are doing : to the business at hand

à grands frais \ä-graⁿ-fre\ [F] : at great expense

à huis clos \ä-wᵉē-klō\ [F] : with closed doors : behind closed doors

aide–toi, le ciel t'ai·dera \ed-twä lə-'syel-te-drä\ [F] : help yourself (and) heaven will help you

aî·né \e-nä\ [F] : elder : senior (masc.)

aî·née \e-nä\ [F] : elder : senior (fem.)

à l'aban·don \ä-lä-bäⁿ-dōⁿ\ [F] : carelessly : in disorder

à la belle étoile \ä-lä-bel-ä-twäl\ [F] : under the beautiful star : in the open air at night

à la bonne heure \ä-lä-bȯ-nœr\ [F] : at a good time : well and good : all right

à la fran·çaise \ä-lä-fräⁿ-sez\ [F] : in the French manner

à l'amé·ri·caine \ä-lä-mä-rē-ken\ [F] : in the American manner : of the American kind

à l'an·glaise \ä-läⁿ-glez\ [F] : in the English manner

à la page \ä-lä-päzh\ [F] : at the page : up-to-the-minute

à la russe \ä-lä-rᵫs\ [F] : in the Russian manner

alea jac·ta est \'ä-lē-ˌä-ˌyäk-tä-'est\ [L] : the die is cast

à l'im·pro·viste \ä-laⁿ-prō-vēst\ [F] : unexpectedly

ali·quan·do bo·nus dor·mi·tat Ho·me·rus \ˌä-li-ˌkwän-dō-'bȯ-nu̇s-dȯr-'mē-ˌtät-hō-'mer-u̇s\ [L] : sometimes (even) good Homer nods

alis vo·lat pro·pri·is \'ä-ˌlēs-'wȯ-ˌlät-'prō-prē-ˌēs\ [L] : she flies with her own wings — motto of Oregon

al·ki \'al-ˌkī, -kē\ [Chinook Jargon] : by and by — motto of Washington

alo·ha oe \ä-ˌlō-hä-'ȯi, -'ō-ē\ [Hawaiian] : love to you : greetings : farewell

al·ter idem \ˌȯl-tər-'ī-ˌdem, ˌäl-ter-'ē-\ [L] : second self

à mer·veille \ä-mer-vä\ [F] : marvelously : wonderfully

ami·cus hu·ma·ni ge·ne·ris \ä-'mē-ku̇s-hü-ˌmä-nē-'ge-ne-ris\ [L] : friend of the human race

ami·cus us·que ad aras \-ˌu̇s-kwe-ˌäd-'är-ˌäs\ [L] : a friend as far as to the altars, i.e., except in what is contrary to one's religion; *also* : a friend to the last extremity

ami de cour \ä-ˌmē-də-'ku̇r\ [F] : court friend : insincere friend

amor pa·tri·ae \'ä-ˌmȯr-'pä-trē-ˌī\ [L] : love of one's country

amor vin·cit om·nia \'ä-ˌmȯr-ˌwiŋ-kit-'ȯm-nē-ä\ [L] : love conquers all things

an·cienne no·blesse \äⁿ-syen-nȯ-bles\ [F] : old-time nobility : the French nobility before the Revolution of 1789

an·guis in her·ba \ˌäŋ-gwis-in-'her-ˌbä\ [L] : snake in the grass

ani·mal bi·pes im·plu·me \'ä-ni-ˌmäl-ˌbi-ˌpäs-im-'plü-me\ [L] : two-legged animal without feathers (i.e., the human race)

ani·mis opi·bus·que pa·ra·ti \'ä-ni-ˌmēs-ˌȯ-pi-'bu̇s-kwe-pä-'rä-tē\ [L] : prepared in mind and resources — one of the mottoes of South Carolina

an·no ae·ta·tis su·ae \'ä-nō-'mu̇n-dē\ [L] : in the (specified) year of his (or her) age

an·no mun·di \ä-nō-'mu̇n-dē\ [L] : in the year of the world — used in reckoning dates from the supposed period of the creation of the world, esp. as fixed by James Ussher at 4004 B.C., or by the Jews at 3761 B.C.

an·no ur·bis con·di·tae \ˌä-nō-ˌu̇r-bis-'kȯn-di-ˌtī\ [L] : in the year of the founded city : in the year that the city was founded (Rome, founded 753 B.C.)

an·nu·it coep·tis \ˌä-nü-ˌit-'kȯip-ˌtēs\ [L] : He (God) has approved our beginnings — motto on the reverse of the Great Seal of the United States

à peu près \ä-pœ-pre\ [F] : nearly : approximately

à pied \ä-pyä\ [F] : on foot

à point \ä-pwaⁿ\ [F] : at the right time

après moi le dé·luge \ä-pre-mwä-lə-dä-lᵫezh\ [F] : after me the deluge — attributed to Louis XV

à pro·pos de bottes \ä-prə-pō-də-bȯt\ [F] : apropos of boots — used to change the subject

à pro·pos de rien \-ryaⁿ\ [F] : apropos of nothing

aqua et ig·ni in·ter·dic·tus \ˌä-kwä-et-'ig-nē-ˌin-ter-'dik-tu̇s\ [L] : forbidden to be furnished with water and fire : outlawed

Foreign Words & Phrases

Ar·ca·des am·bo \\'är-kä-ˌdes-'äm-bō\ [L] : both Arcadians : two persons of like occupations or tastes; *also* : two rascals

ar·rec·tis au·ri·bus \ä-'rek-ˌtēs-ˌaù-ri-ˌbùs\ [L] : with ears pricked up : attentively

ar·ri·ve·der·ci \ˌär-ē-vä-'der-chē\ [It] : till we meet again : farewell

ars lon·ga, vi·ta bre·vis \ärs-'lòn-ˌgä ˌwē-ˌtä-'bre-wis\ [L] : art is long, life is short : human life span limits all that might be accomplished

as—sa·laam alai·kum \əs-sə-'läm-ə-'lī-kùm\ [Ar *as-salāmu 'alaykum*] : peace to you — used as a traditional greeting among Muslims

a ter·go \ä-'ter-(ˌ)gō\ [L] : from behind

à tort et à tra·vers \ä-tòr-ā-ä-trä-ver\ [F] : wrong and crosswise : at random : without rhyme or reason

au bout de son la·tin \ō-büd-sòⁿ-lä-taⁿ, -bü-də-\ [F] : at the end of one's Latin : at the end of one's mental resources

au con·traire \ō-kōⁿ-trer\ [F] : on the contrary

au·de·mus ju·ra nos·tra de·fen·de·re \aù-'dā-mùs-ˌyùr-ä-'nò-strä-dā-'fen-de-rä\ [L] : we dare defend our rights — motto of Alabama

au·den·tes for·tu·na ju·vat \aù-'den-ˌtäs-fòr-ˌtü-nä-'yù-ˌwät\ [L] : fortune favors the bold

au·di al·te·ram par·tem \'aù-ˌdē-ˌäl-te-ˌräm-'pär-ˌtem\ [L] : hear the other side

au fait \ō-fet, -fe\ [F] : to the point : fully competent : fully informed : socially correct

au fond \ō-fōⁿ\ [F] : at bottom : fundamentally

au grand sé·rieux \ō-gräⁿ-sä-ryœ\ [F] : in all seriousness

au mieux \ō-myœ\ [F] : on the best terms : on intimate terms

au pays des aveugles les borgnes sont rois \ō-pā-ē-dä-zä-vœglᵊ-lä-bórnʸ-ə-sōⁿ-rwä\ [F] : in the country of the blind the one-eyed men are kings

au·rea me·di·o·cri·tas \'aù-rē-ä-ˌme-dē-'ò-kri-ˌtäs\ [L] : the golden mean

au reste \ō-rest\ [F] : for the rest : besides

au sé·rieux \ō-sä-ryœ\ [F] : seriously

aus·si·tôt dit, aus·si·tôt fait \ō-sē-tō-dē ō-sē-tō-fe\ [F] : no sooner said than done

aut Cae·sar aut ni·hil \aùt-'kī-sär-ˌaùt-'ni-ˌhil\ [L] : either a Caesar or nothing

au·tres temps, au·tres mœurs \ō-trə-täⁿ ō-trə-mœrs\ [F] : other times, other customs

aut vin·ce·re aut mo·ri \aùt-'wiŋ-ke-rä-ˌaùt-'mò-ˌrē\ [L] : either to conquer or to die

aux armes \ō-zärm\ [F] : to arms

avant la lettre \ä-väⁿ-lä-letrᵊ\ [F] : before the letter : before a (specified) name or entity existed

ave at·que va·le \'ä-ˌwä-ˌät-kwe-'wä-ˌlä\ [L] : hail and farewell

à vo·tre san·té \ä-vòt-sä‌ⁿ-tä, -vò-trə-\ [F] : to your health — used as a toast

ax·is mun·di \'ak-səs-'mùn-dē\ [L] : turning point of the world : line through the earth's center around which the universe revolves

bel·la fi·gu·ra \'bel-lə-fē-'gü-rä\ [It] : fine appearance or impression

belle laide \bel-led\ [F] : beautiful ugly woman : woman who is attractive though not conventionally beautiful

bel·lum om·ni·um con·tra om·nes \'be-lùm-'òm-nē-ùm-ˌkòn-trä-'òm-ˌnäs\ [L] : war of all against all

bien en·ten·du \byaⁿ-näⁿ-täⁿ-dœ\ [F] : well understood : of course

bien—pen·sant \byaⁿ-päⁿ-säⁿ\ [F] : right-minded : one who holds orthodox views

bien·sé·ance \byaⁿ-sä-äⁿs\ [F] : propriety

bis dat qui ci·to dat \'bis-ˌdät-kwē-'ki-tō-ˌdät\ [L] : he gives twice who gives promptly

bon ap·pé·tit \bò-nä-pä-tē\ [F] : good appetite : enjoy your meal

bon gré, mal gré \bòⁿ-ˌgrä 'mäl-ˌgrä\ [F] : whether with good grace or bad : willy-nilly

bon·jour \bòⁿ-zhür\ [F] : good day : good morning

bonne foi \bòn-fwä\ [F] : good faith

bon·soir \bōⁿ-swär\ [F] : good evening

bru·tum ful·men \ˌbrü-tùm-'fùl-men\ [L] : insensible thunderbolt : a futile threat or display of force

ca·dit quae·stio \ˌkä-dit-'kwī-stē-ˌō\ [L] : the question drops : the argument collapses

carte d'iden·ti·té \kärt-dē-däⁿ-tē-tä\ [F] : identity card

cau·sa si·ne qua non \'kaù-ˌsä-ˌsi-nä-kwä-'nōn\ [L] : an indispensable cause or condition

ça va sans dire \sä-vä-säⁿ-dir\ [F] : it goes without saying

ca·ve ca·nem \ˌkä-wä-'kä-ˌnem\ [L] : beware of the dog

ce·dant ar·ma to·gae \'kä-ˌdänt-ˌär-mə-'tō-ˌgi\ [L] : let arms yield to the toga : let military power give way to civil power — motto of Wyoming

ce n'est que le pre·mier pas qui coûte \snek-lə-prə-myä-pä-kē-küt\ [F] : it is only the first step that costs

c'est-à-dire \se-tä-dir\ [F] : that is to say : namely

c'est au·tre chose \se-tōt-shōz, -tō-trə-\ [F] : that's a different thing

c'est la guerre \se-lä-ger\ [F] : that's war : it cannot be helped

c'est la vie \se-lä-vē\ [F] : that's life : that's how things happen

c'est plus qu'un crime, c'est une faute \se-plœ-kœⁿ-krēm se-tœn-fōt\ [F] : it is worse than a crime, it is a blunder

ce·te·ra de·sunt \ˌkä-te-ˌrä-'dā-ˌsùnt\ [L] : the rest is missing

cha·cun à son goût \shä-kœⁿ-nä-sōⁿ-gü\ [F] : everyone to his taste

châ·teau en Es·pagne \shä-tō-äⁿ-nes-pänʸ\ [F] : castle in Spain : a visionary project

cher·chez la femme \sher-shä-lä-fäm\ [F] : look for the woman

che sa·rà, sa·rà \ˌkä-sä-ˌrä sä-'rä\ [It] : what will be, will be

che·val de ba·taille \shə-väl-də-bä-täʸ\ [F] : warhorse : argument constantly relied on : favorite subject

co·gi·to, er·go sum \'kō-gi-ˌtō ˌer-gō-'sùm\ [L] : I think, therefore I exist

co·mé·die hu·maine \kò-mä-dē-œ-men\ [F] : human comedy : the whole variety of human life

comme ci, comme ça \kòm-sē kòm-sä\ [F] : so-so

com·pa·gnon de voy·age \kōⁿ-pä-nʸōⁿ-də-vwä-yäzh\ [F] : traveling companion

compte ren·du \kōⁿt-räⁿ-dœ\ [F] : report (as of proceedings in an investigation)

con·cor·dia dis·cors \kòn-'kòr-dē-ä-'dis-ˌkòrs\ [L] : discordant harmony

con·fes·sio fi·dei \kòn-'fe-sē-ō-'fi-dē-ˌē\ [L] : confession of faith

cor·rup·tio op·ti·mi pes·si·ma \kò-'rùp-tē-ˌò-'äp-ti-ˌmē-'pe-si-ˌmä\ [L] : the corruption of the best is the worst of all

coup de maî·tre \küd-metrᵊ, kü-də-\ [F] : masterstroke

coup d'es·sai \kü-dä-se\ [F] : experiment : trial

coûte que coûte \küt-kə-küt\ [F] : cost what it may

cre·do quia ab·sur·dum est \ˌkrä-dō-'kwē-ä-äp-ˌsùr-dùm-'est\ [L] : I believe it because it is absurd

cres·cit eun·do \ˌkres-kit-'eùn-dō\ [L] : it grows as it goes — motto of New Mexico

crise de nerfs *or* **crise des nerfs** \krēz-də-ner\ [F] : crisis of nerves : nervous collapse : hysterical fit

crux cri·ti·co·rum \ˌkrùks-ˌkri-ti-'kòr-ùm\ [L] : crux of critics

cuj·us re·gio, ej·us re·li·gio \ˌkü-yùs-'re-gē-ˌō ˌe-yùs-re-'li-gē-ˌō\ [L] : whose region, his or her religion : subjects are to accept the religion of their ruler

cum gra·no sa·lis \kùm-ˌgrä-nō-'sä-lis\ [L] : with a grain of salt

cur·sus ho·no·rum \'kùr-sùs-hò-'nòr-ùm\ [L] : course of honors : succession of offices of increasing importance

cus·tos mo·rum \ˌkùs-tōs-'mòr-ùm\ [L] : guardian of manners or morals : censor

d'ac·cord \dä-kòr\ [F] : in accord : agreed

dame d'hon·neur \däm-dò-nœr\ [F] : lady-in-waiting

dam·nant quod non in·tel·li·gunt \'däm-ˌnänt-ˌkwòd-ˌnōn-in-'te-li-ˌgùnt\ [L] : they condemn what they do not understand

de bonne grâce \də-bòn-gräs\ [F] : with good grace : willingly

de gus·ti·bus non est dis·pu·tan·dum \dä-'gùs-tə-ˌbùs-ˌnōn-ˌest-ˌdis-pü-'tän-ˌdùm\ [L] : there is no disputing about tastes

Dei gra·tia \ˌdā-ē-'grä-tē-ˌä\ [L] : by the grace of God

de in·te·gro \dä-'in-te-ˌgrō\ [L] : anew : afresh

de·len·da est Car·tha·go \dä-'len-dä-ˌest-kär-'tä-gō\ [L] : Carthage must be destroyed

de·li·ne·a·vit \dä-ˌlē-nä-ˈä-wit\ [L] : he (or she) drew it

de mal en pis \də-mä-läⁿ-ˈpē\ [F] : from bad to worse

de mi·ni·mis non cu·rat lex \dä-ˈmi-ni-ˌmēs-ˌnōn-ˌkü-ˌrät-ˈleks\ [L] : the law takes no account of trifles

de mor·tu·is nil ni·si bo·num \dä-ˈmȯr-tü-ˌēs-ˌnēl-ˌni-sē-ˈbȯ-ˌnùm\ [L] : of the dead (say) nothing but good

de nos jours \də-nō-zhür\ [F] : of our time : contemporary — used postpositively esp. after a proper name

Deo fa·ven·te \ˌdä-ō-fä-ˈven-tä\ [L] : with God's favor

Deo gra·ti·as \ˌdä-ō-ˈgrä-tē-ˌäs\ [L] : thanks (be) to God

de pro·fun·dis \ˌdä-prō-ˈfùn-dēs\ [L] : out of the depths

der Geist der stets ver·neint \dər-ˈgīst-dər-ˌshtäts-fer-ˈnīnt\ [G] : the spirit that ever denies — applied originally to Mephistopheles

de·si·pe·re in lo·co \dā-ˈsi-pe-rä-in-ˈlō-kō\ [L] : to indulge in trifling at the proper time

de te fa·bu·la nar·ra·tur \dä-ˌtā-ˈfä-bù-lä-nä-ˈrä-ˌtùr\ [L] : the story applies to you

De·us ab·scon·di·tus \ˌdä-ùs-ˌäp-ˈskȯn-di-ˌtùs\ [L] : hidden God : God unknowable by the human mind

De·us vult \ˌdä-ùs-ˈwùlt\ [L] : God wills it — rallying cry of the First Crusade

di·es fau·stus \ˌdē-ˌäs-ˈfaù-stùs\ [L] : lucky day

dies in·fau·stus \-ˈin-ˌfaù-stùs\ [L] : unlucky day

dies irae \-ˈē-ˌrī, -ˌrā\ [L] : day of wrath — used of the Judgment Day

Dieu et mon droit \dyœ-ā-mōⁿ-drwä\ [F] : God and my right — motto on the British royal arms

Dieu vous garde \dyœ-vü-gärd\ [F] : God keep you

di·ri·go \ˈdē-ri-ˌgō\ [L] : I direct — motto of Maine

dis ali·ter vi·sum \dēs-ˌä-li-ˌter-ˈwē-ˌsùm\ [L] : the Gods decreed otherwise

di·tat De·us \ˌdē-ˌtät-ˈdä-ˌùs\ [L] : God enriches — motto of Arizona

di·vi·de et im·pe·ra \ˈdē-wi-ˌde-ˌet-ˈim-pe-ˌrä\ [L] : divide and rule

do·cen·do dis·ci·mus \dō-ˌken-dō-ˈdis-ki-ˌmùs\ [L] : we learn by teaching

Do·mi·ne, di·ri·ge nos \ˈdō-mi-ˌne 'dē-ri-ˌge-ˈnōs\ [L] : Lord, direct us — motto of the City of London

Do·mi·nus vo·bis·cum \ˌdō-mi-ˌnùs-wō-ˈbēs-ˌkùm\ [L] : the Lord be with you

dul·ce et de·co·rum est pro pa·tria mo·ri \ˌdùl-ˌke-et-de-ˈkȯr-ùm-ˌest-prō-ˌpä-trē-ä-ˈmȯ-ˌrē\ [L] : it is sweet and seemly to die for one's country

dum spi·ro, spe·ro \ˌdùm-ˈspē-rō ˈspä-rō\ [L] : while I breathe, I hope — one of the mottoes of South Carolina

dum vi·vi·mus vi·va·mus \ˌdùm-ˈwē-wē-ˌmùs-wē-ˈwä-mùs\ [L] : while we live, let us live

d'un cer·tain âge \dœⁿ-ser-te-näzh\ [F] : of a certain age : no longer young

dux fe·mi·na fac·ti \ˌdùks-ˌfā-mi-nä-ˈfäk-ˌtē\ [L] : a woman was leader of the exploit

ec·ce sig·num \ˌe-ke-ˈsig-ˌnùm\ [L] : behold the sign : look at the proof

e con·tra·rio \ˌä-kȯn-ˈträr-ē-ˌō\ [L] : on the contrary

écra·sez l'in·fâme \ā-krä-zä-laⁿ-fäm\ [F] : crush the infamous thing

eheu fu·ga·ces la·bun·tur an·ni \ˌā-ˌheù-fù-ˈgä-ˌkäs-lä-ˈbùn-ˌtùr-ˈä-ˌnē\ [L] : alas! the fleeting years glide on

ein' fes·te Burg ist un·ser Gott \īn-ˌfes-tə-ˈbùrk-ist-ˌùn-zər-ˈgȯt\ [G] : a mighty fortress is our God

em·bar·ras de choix \äⁿ-bä-rä-də-shwä\ or **embarras du choix** \-dœ-shwä\ [F] : embarrassing variety of choice

em·bar·ras de ri·chesses \äⁿ-bä-räd-rē-shes, -rä-də-\ [F] : embarrassing surplus of riches : confusing abundance

en ami \äⁿ-nä-mē\ [F] : as a friend

en ef·fet \äⁿ-nä-fe\ [F] : in fact : indeed

en fa·mille \äⁿ-fä-mē\ [F] : in or with one's family : at home : informally

en·fant ché·ri \äⁿ-fäⁿ-shä-rē\ [F] : loved or pampered child : one that is highly favored

en·fant gâ·té \äⁿ-fäⁿ-gä-tä\ [F] : spoiled child

en·fants per·dus \äⁿ-fäⁿ-per-due\ [F] : lost children : soldiers sent to a dangerous post

en·fin \äⁿ-faⁿ\ [F] : in conclusion : in a word

en gar·çon \äⁿ-gär-sōⁿ\ [F] : as or like a bachelor

en garde \äⁿ-gärd\ [F] : on guard

en pan·tou·fles \äⁿ-päⁿ-tüflᵊ\ [F] : in slippers : at ease : informally

en plein air \äⁿ-ple-ner\ [F] : in the open air

en plein jour \äⁿ-plaⁿ-zhür\ [F] : in broad day

en règle \äⁿ-reglᵊ\ [F] : in order : in due form

en re·tard \äⁿr-(ə-)tär\ [F] : behind time : late

en re·traite \äⁿr-(ə-)tret\ [F] : in retreat : in retirement

en re·vanche \äⁿr-(ə-)väⁿsh\ [F] : in return : in compensation

en se·condes noces \äⁿs-gōⁿd-nós, äⁿ-sə-\ [F] : in a second marriage

en·se pe·tit pla·ci·dam sub li·ber·ta·te qui·e·tem \ˌen-se-ˌpe-tit-ˈplä-ki-ˌdäm-sùb-ˌlē-ber-ˌtä-te-kwē-ˈä-ˌtem\ [L] : with the sword she seeks calm repose under liberty : by the sword we seek peace, but peace only under liberty — motto of Massachusetts

eo ip·so \ä-ō-ˈip-(ˌ)sō\ [L] : by that itself : by that fact alone

épa·ter le bour·geois \ā-pä-tä-lə-bür-zhwä\ or **épater les bourgeois** \-lā-bür-\ [F] : to shock the middle classes

e plu·ri·bus unum \ˌē-ˌplùr-ə-bəs-ˈ(y)ü-nəm, ˌā-ˌplùr-i-bùs-ˈü-nùm\ [L] : one out of many — used on the Great Seal of the U.S. and on several U.S. coins

ep·pur si muo·ve \äp-ˌpür-sē-ˈmwō-vä\ [It] : and yet it does move — attributed to Galileo after recanting his assertion of the earth's motion

Erin go bragh \ˌer-ən-gə-ˈbrȯ, -gō-ˈbrä\ [Ir *go brách* or *go bráth*, lit., till doomsday] : Ireland forever

er·ra·re hu·ma·num est \e-ˈrär-ä-hü-ˌmä-nùm-ˈest\ [L] : to err is human

es·prit de l'es·ca·lier \es-prēd-les-kä-lyä\ or **es·prit d'es·ca·lier** \-prē-des-\ [F] : wit of the staircase : repartee thought of only too late

es·se quam vi·de·ri \ˈe-sä-ˌkwäm-wi-ˈdä-rē\ [L] : to be rather than to seem — motto of North Carolina

est mo·dus in re·bus \est-ˈmȯ-ˌdùs-in-ˈrä-ˌbùs\ [L] : there is a proper measure in things, i.e., the golden mean should always be observed

es·to per·pe·tua \ˈes-ˌtō-per-ˈpe-tù-ˌä\ [L] : may she endure forever — motto of Idaho

et hoc ge·nus om·ne \et-ˌhōk-ˌge-nùs-ˈȯm-ne\ or **et id genus omne** \et-ˌid-\ [L] : and everything of this kind

et in Ar·ca·dia ego \et-in-är-ˌkä-dē-ä-ˈe-gō\ [L] : I too (lived) in Arcadia

et sic de si·mi·li·bus \et-ˌsēk-dä-si-ˈmi-li-ˌbùs\ [L] : and so of like things

et tu Bru·te \et-ˈtü-ˈbrü-te\ [L] : thou too, Brutus — exclamation attributed to Julius Caesar on seeing his friend Brutus among his assassins

eu·re·ka \yù-ˈrē-kä\ [Gk] : I have found it — motto of California

Ewig–Weib·li·che \ˌā-vik-ˈvīp-li-kə\ [G] : eternal feminine

ex ani·mo \eks-ˈä-ni-ˌmō\ [L] : from the heart : sincerely

ex·cel·si·or \ik-ˈsel-sē-ər, eks-ˈkel-sē-ˌȯr\ [L] : still higher — motto of New York

ex·cep·tio pro·bat re·gu·lam de re·bus non ex·cep·tis \eks-ˈkep-tē-ˌō-ˌprō-bät-ˈrā-gù-ˌläm-dä-ˈrä-ˌbùs-ˌnōn-eks-ˈkep-ˌtēs\ [L] : an exception establishes the rule as to things not excepted

ex·cep·tis ex·ci·pi·en·dis \eks-ˈkep-ˌtēs-eks-ˌki-pē-ˈen-ˌdēs\ [L] : with the proper or necessary exceptions

ex·i·tus ac·ta pro·bat \ˈek-si-ˌtùs-ˌäk-tä-ˈprȯ-ˌbät\ [L] : the outcome justifies the deed

ex li·bris \eks-ˈlē-bris\ [L] : from the books of — used on bookplates

ex me·ro mo·tu \ˌeks-ˌmer-ō-ˈmō-tü\ [L] : out of mere impulse : of one's own accord

ex ne·ces·si·ta·te rei \ˌeks-ne-ˌke-si-ˈtä-te-ˈrä(-ˌē)\ [L] : from the necessity of the case

ex ni·hi·lo ni·hil fit \eks-ˈni-hi-ˌlō-ˌni-ˌhil-ˈfit\ [L] : from nothing nothing is produced

ex pe·de Her·cu·lem \eks-ˌpe-de-ˈher-kù-ˌlem\ [L] : from the foot (we may judge of the size of) Hercules : from a part we may judge of the whole

ex·per·to cre·de \eks-ˌper-tō-ˈkrä-de\ or **experto cre·di·te** \-ˈkrä-di-ˌte\ [L] : believe one who has had experience

ex un·gue le·o·nem \eks-ˈùŋ-gwe-le-ˈō-ˌnem\ [L] : from the claw (we may judge of) the lion : from a part we may judge of the whole

ex vi ter·mi·ni \eks-ˌwē-ˈter-mə-ˌnē\ [L] : from the force of the term

fa·ci·le prin·ceps \ˌfä-ki-le-'priŋ-ˌkeps\ [L] : easily first

fa·ci·lis de·scen·sus Aver·no \'fä-ki-ˌlis-dā-ˌskän-ˌsu̇s-ä-'wer-nō\ or facilis descensus Aver·ni \-(ˌ)nē\ [L] : the descent to Avernus is easy : the road to evil is easy

fa·çon de par·ler \fä-sōⁿ-də-pär-lä\ [F] : manner of speaking : figurative or conventional expression

faire suivre \fer-swᵞēvrᵃ\ [F] : have forwarded : please forward

fas est et ab ho·ste do·ce·ri \fäs-'est-et-äb-'hȯ-ste-dȯ-'kā-(ˌ)rē\ [L] : it is right to learn even from an enemy

Fa·ta vi·am in·ve·ni·ent \ˌfä-tä-'wē-ˌäm-in-'we-nē-ˌent\ [L] : the Fates will find a way

fat·ti mas·chii, pa·ro·le fe·mi·ne \ˌfät-tē-'mäs-ˌkē pä-ˌrȯ-lä-'fā-mē-ˌnä\ [It] : deeds are males, words are females : deeds are more effective than words — motto of Maryland, where it is generally interpreted as meaning "manly deeds, womanly words"

faux bon·homme \fō-bȯ-nóm\ [F] : pretended good fellow

faux—naïf \fō-nä-ēf\ [F] : spuriously or affectedly child⁼ like : artfully simple

fe·lix cul·pa \'fä-liks-'kúl-pä\ [L] : fortunate fault — used esp. of original sin in relation to the consequent coming of Christ

femme de cham·bre \fäm-də-shäⁿbrᵃ\ [F] : chambermaid : lady's maid

fe·sti·na len·te \fe-ˌstē-nä-'len-ˌtā\ [L] : make haste slowly

feux d'ar·ti·fice \fœ-där-tē-fēs\ [F] : fireworks : display of wit

fi·at ex·pe·ri·men·tum in cor·po·re vi·li \'fē-ˌät-ek-ˌsper-ē-'men-ˌtùm-in-ˌkȯr-pȯ-re-'wē-lē\ [L] : let experiment be made on a worthless body

fi·at ju·sti·tia, ru·at cae·lum \ˌfē-ˌät-yùs-'ti-tē-ä ˌrù-ˌät-'kī-ˌlùm\ [L] : let justice be done though the heavens fall

fi·at lux \ˌfē-ˌät-'lùks\ [L] : let there be light

Fi·dei De·fen·sor \ˌfi-de-ˌē-dā-'fän-ˌsȯr\ [L] : Defender of the Faith — a title of the sovereigns of England

fille de cham·bre \fē-də-shäⁿbrᵃ\ [F] : lady's maid

fille d'hon·neur \fē-dȯ-nœr\ [F] : maid of honor

fi·nem re·spi·ce \ˌfē-ˌnem-'rä-spi-ˌke\ [L] : consider the end

fi·nis co·ro·nat opus \ˌfē-nis-kȯ-ˌrō-ˌnät-'ō-ˌpús\ [L] : the end crowns the work

flo·re·at \'flō-re-ˌät\ [L] : may (he, she, or it) flourish — usu. followed by a name

fluc·tu·at nec mer·gi·tur \'flùk-tù-ˌät-ˌnek-'mer-gi-ˌtùr\ [L] : it is tossed by the waves but does not sink — motto of Paris

fo·lie de gran·deur or fo·lie des gran·deurs \fȯ-lē-də-gräⁿ-dœr\ [F] : delusion of greatness : megalomania

force de frappe \fȯrs-də-fräp\ [F] : a force equipped to deal a retaliatory blow

fors·an et haec olim me·mi·nis·se ju·va·bit \ˌfȯr-ˌsän-ˌet-'hīk-ˌō-lim-ˌme-mi-'ni-se-yù-'wä-bit\ [L] : perhaps this too will be a pleasure to look back on one day

for·tes for·tu·na ju·vat \'fȯr-ˌtäs-fȯr-ˌtü-nä-'yù-ˌwät\ [L] : fortune favors the brave

fron·ti nul·la fi·des \'frȯn-ˌtē-ˌnù-lä-'fi-ˌdäs\ [L] : no reliance can be placed on appearance

fu·it Ill·um \'fù-it-'i-lē-ùm\ [L] : Troy has been (i.e., is no more)

fu·ror lo·quen·di \ˌfùr-ˌȯr-lȯ-'kwen-(ˌ)dē\ [L] : rage for speaking

furor po·e·ti·cus \-pȯ-'ā-ti-kùs\ [L] : poetic frenzy

furor scri·ben·di \-skrē-'ben-(ˌ)dē\ [L] : rage for writing

Gal·li·ce \'gä-li-ˌke\ [L] : in French : after the French manner

gar·çon d'hon·neur \gär-sōⁿ-dȯ-nœr\ [F] : bridegroom's attendant

garde du corps \gärd-dœ-kȯr\ [F] : bodyguard

gar·dez la foi \gär-dā-lä-fwä\ [F] : keep faith

gau·de·a·mus igi·tur \gaù-dē-'ä-mùs-'i-gi-ˌtùr\ [L] : let us then be merry

gens d'é·glise \zhäⁿ-dā-glēz\ [F] : church people : clergy

gens de guerre \zhäⁿ-də-ger\ [F] : military people : soldiery

gens du monde \zhäⁿ-dœ-mōⁿd\ [F] : people of the world : fashionable people

gno·thi se·au·ton \'gnō-thē-ˌse-aù-'tȯn\ [Gk] : know thyself

goût de ter·roir \gü-də-te-rwär\ [F] : taste of the earth

grand monde \gräⁿ-mōⁿd\ [F] : great world : high society

gros·so mo·do \'grȯs-(ˌ)sȯ-'mō-(ˌ)dȯ\ [It] : roughly

guerre à ou·trance \ger-ä-ü-träⁿs\ [F] : war to the uttermost

gu·ten Tag \ˌgü-tən-'täk\ [G] : good day

has·ta la vis·ta \ˌäs-tə-lä-'vēs-tə\ [Sp] : good-bye

haute vul·ga·ri·sa·tion \ōt-vᵫl-gä-rē-zä-syōⁿ\ [F] : high popularization : effective presentation of a difficult subject to a general audience

haut goût \ō-gü\ [F] : high flavor : slight taint of decay

hic et nunc \'hēk-et-'nùŋk\ [L] : here and now

hic et ubi·que \ˌhēk-et-ù-'bē-kwe\ [L] : here and everywhere

hic ja·cet \hik-'jä-sət, hēk-'yä-ket\ [L] : here lies — used preceding a name on a tombstone

hinc il·lae la·cri·mae \ˌhiŋk-ˌi-ˌlī-'lä-kri-ˌmī\ [L] : hence those tears

hoc age \hōk-'ä-ge\ [L] : do this : apply yourself to what you are about

homme d'af·faires \ȯm-dä-fer\ [F] : man of business : business agent

homme d'es·prit \ȯm-des-prē\ [F] : man of wit

homme moyen sen·suel \ȯm-mwä-yaⁿ-säⁿ-swᵞel\ [F] : the average nonintellectual man

ho·mo sum: hu·ma·ni nil a me ali·e·num pu·to \'hȯ-mō-ˌsùm hü-ˌmä-nē-'nēl-ä-ˌmā-ä-lē-'ä-nùm-'pù-tō\ [L] : I am a human being: I regard nothing of human concern as foreign to my interests

ho·ni soit qui mal y pense \ȯ-nē-swä-kē-mäl-ē-päⁿs\ [F] : shamed be he who thinks evil of it — motto of the Order of the Garter

hors com·merce \ȯr-kȯ-mers\ [F] : outside the trade : not offered through regular commercial channels

hu·ma·num est er·ra·re \hü-ˌmä-nùm-ˌest-e-'rär-ä\ [L] : to err is human

ich dien \ik-'dēn\ [G] : I serve — motto of the Prince of Wales

ici on parle fran·çais \ē-sē-ōⁿ-pärl-fräⁿ-se\ [F] : French is spoken here

idées re·çues \ē-dār-(ə-)sᵫe\ [F] : received ideas : conventional opinions

id est \id-'est\ [L] : that is

ig·no·ran·tia ju·ris ne·mi·nem ex·cu·sat \ˌig-nȯ-ˌrän-tē-ä-'yùr-is-'nä-mi-ˌnem-eks-'kü-ˌsät\ [L] : ignorance of the law excuses no one

ig·no·tum per ig·no·ti·us \ig-'nō-tùm-ˌper-ig-'nō-tē-ùs\ [L] : (explaining) the unknown by means of the more unknown

il faut cul·ti·ver no·tre jar·din \ēl-fō-kᵫel-tē-vä-nȯt-zhär-daⁿ, -nȯ-trə-zhär-\ [F] : we must cultivate our garden : we must tend to our own affairs

in ae·ter·num \in-ī-'ter-ˌnùm\ [L] : forever

in du·bio \in-'dù-bē-ˌō\ [L] : in doubt : undetermined

in fu·tu·ro \in-fü-'tùr-ō\ [L] : in the future

in hoc sig·no vin·ces \in-hōk-'sig-nō-'wiŋ-ˌkäs\ [L] : by this sign (the Cross) you will conquer

in li·mi·ne \in-'lē-mi-ˌne\ [L] : on the threshold : at the beginning

in om·nia pa·ra·tus \in-'ȯm-nē-ä-pä-'rä-ˌtùs\ [L] : ready for all things

in par·ti·bus in·fi·de·li·um \in-'pär-ti-ˌbùs-ˌin-fi-'dā-lē-ˌùm\ [L] : in the regions of the infidels — used of a titular bishop having no diocesan jurisdiction, usu. in non⁼ Christian countries

in prae·sen·ti \in-prī-'sen-ˌtē\ [L] : at the present time

in sae·cu·la sae·cu·lo·rum \in-'sī-kù-ˌlä-ˌsī-kù-'lȯr-ùm, -'sä-kù-ˌlä-ˌsä-\ [L] : for ages of ages : forever and ever

in·shal·lah \ˌin-shä-'lä\ [Ar in shā' Allāh] : if Allah wills : God willing

in sta·tu quo an·te bel·lum \in-'stä-ˌtü-kwō-ˌän-te-'be-lùm\ [L] : in the state before the war

in·te·ger vi·tae sce·le·ris·que pu·rus \in-te-ˌger-'wē-ˌtī-ˌske-le-'ris-kwe-'pü-rùs\ [L] : upright of life and free from wickedness

in·ter nos \in-ter-'nȯs\ [L] : between ourselves

in·tra mu·ros \in-trä-'mù-ˌrȯs\ [L] : within the walls

in utrum·que pa·ra·tus \in-ù-'trùm-kwe-pä-'rä-ˌtùs\ [L] : prepared for either (event)

in·ve·nit \in-'wä-nit\ [L] : he or she devised it

in vi·no ve·ri·tas \in-wē-nō-'wā-ri-ˌtäs\ [L] : there is truth in wine

in·vi·ta Mi·ner·va \in-'wē-ˌtä-mi-'ner-ˌwä\ [L] : Minerva being unwilling : without natural talent or inspiration

ip·sis·si·ma ver·ba \ip-'si-si-ˌmä-'wer-ˌbä\ [L] : the very words

ira fu·ror bre·vis est \ˌē-rä-'fu̇r-ˌȯr-'bre-wis-ˌest\ [L] : anger is a brief madness

j'ac·cuse \zhä-kuez\ [F] : I accuse : bitter denunciation

jac·ta alea est \'yäk-ˌtä-ˌä-lē-ˌä-'est\ [L] : the die is cast

j'adoube \zhä-düb\ [F] : I adjust — used in chess when touching a piece without intending to move it

ja·nu·is clau·sis \ˌyä-nu̇-ˌēs-'klau̇-ˌsēs\ [L] : behind closed doors

je main·tien·drai \zhə-maⁿ-tyaⁿ-drä\ [F] : I will maintain — motto of the Netherlands

jeu de mots \zhœd-mō, zhœe-də-\ [F] : play on words : pun

Jo·an·nes est no·men eius \yō-'ä-näs-est-ˌnō-men-'ä-yu̇s\ [L] : John is his name — motto of Puerto Rico

jo·lie laide \zhȯ-lē-led\ [F] : good-looking ugly woman : woman who is attractive though not conventionally pretty

jour·nal in·time \zhür-näl-aⁿ-tēm\ [F] : intimate journal : private diary

jus di·vi·num \ˌyüs-di-'wē-ˌnu̇m\ [L] : divine law

jus·ti·tia om·ni·bus \yu̇s-ˌti-tē-ˌä-'ȯm-ni-ˌbu̇s\ [L] : justice for all — motto of the District of Columbia

j'y suis, j'y reste \zhē-swʸē zhē-rest\ [F] : here I am, here I remain

Kin·der, Kir·che, Küche \'kin-dər 'kir-ḵə 'ku̇e-ḵə\ [G] : children, church, kitchen

la belle dame sans mer·ci \lä-bel-däm-säⁿ-mer-sē\ [F] : the beautiful lady without mercy

la·bo·ra·re est ora·re \'lä-bȯ-ˌrär-ä-ˌest-'ō-ˌrär-ä\ [L] : to work is to pray

la·bor om·nia vin·cit \'lä-ˌbȯr-ˌȯm-nē-ˌä-'wiŋ-kit\ [L] : labor conquers all things — motto of Oklahoma

la·cri·mae re·rum \ˌlä-kri-ˌmī-'rä-ˌru̇m\ [L] : tears for things : pity for misfortune; also : tears in things : tragedy of life

lais·sez–al·ler or lais·ser–al·ler \le-sä-ä-lä\ [F] : letting go : lack of restraint

lap·sus ca·la·mi \ˌläp-su̇s-'kä-lä-ˌmē\ [L] : slip of the pen

lap·sus lin·guae \-'liŋ-ˌgwī\ [L] : slip of the tongue

la reine le veut \lä-ren-lə-vœ\ [F] : the queen wills it

la·scia·te ogni spe·ran·za, voi ch'en·tra·te \läsh-'shä-tä-ˌō-nʸē-spä-'rän-tsä ˌvō-ē-kän-'trä-tä\ [It] : abandon all hope, ye who enter

lau·da·tor tem·po·ris ac·ti \lau̇-'dä-ˌtȯr-ˌtem-pȯ-ris-'äk-ˌtē\ [L] : one who praises past times

laus Deo \lau̇s-'dä-ō\ [L] : praise (be) to God

Le·bens·welt \'lä-bəns-ˌvelt\ [G] : life world : world of lived experience

le cœur a ses rai·sons que la rai·son ne con·naît point \lə-kœr-ä-sä-re-zōᵏk-lä-re-zōⁿn-kó-ne-pwaⁿ\ [F] : the heart has its reasons that reason knows nothing of

le roi est mort, vive le roi \lə-rwä-e-mȯr vēv-lə-rwä\ [F] : the king is dead, long live the king

le roi le veut \lə-rwä-lə-vœ\ [F] : the king wills it

le roi s'avi·se·ra \lə-rwä-sä-vēz-rä\ [F] : the king will consider

le style, c'est l'homme \lə-stēl se-lóm\ [F] : the style is the man

l'état, c'est moi \lä-tä se-mwä\ [F] : the state, it is I

l'étoile du nord \lä-twäl-due-nór\ [F] : the star of the north — motto of Minnesota

Lie·der·kranz \'lē-dər-ˌkränts\ [G] : wreath of songs : German singing society

lit·tera scrip·ta ma·net \ˌli-te-ˌrä-ˌskrip-tä-'mä-net\ [L] : the written letter abides

lo·cus in quo \ˌlō-kus-in-'kwō\ [L] : place in which

l'union fait la force \lue-nyōⁿ-fe-lä-fȯrs\ [F] : union makes strength — motto of Belgium

lu·sus na·tu·rae \ˌlü-sus-nä-'tu̇r-ē, -'tu̇r-ˌī\ [L] : freak of nature

ma foi \mä-fwä\ [F] : my faith! : indeed

mag·na est ve·ri·tas et prae·va·le·bit \ˌmäg-nä-ˌest-'wä-ri-ˌtäs-et-ˌprī-wä-'lä-bit\ [L] : truth is mighty and will prevail

mag·ni no·mi·nis um·bra \ˌmäg-nē-ˌnō-mi-nis-'u̇m-brä\ [L] : the shadow of a great name

ma·lade ima·gi·naire \mä-läd-ē-mä-zhē-ner\ [F] : imaginary invalid : hypochondriac

mal de siècle \mäl-də-syeklᵃ\ [F] : illness from worldly concerns : world-weariness

ma·lis avi·bus \ˌmä-ˌlēs-'ä-wi-ˌbu̇s\ [L] : under evil auspices

man spricht Deutsch \män-shprikt-'dȯich\ [G] : German spoken

ma·riage de con·ve·nance \mä-ryäzh-də-kōⁿv-näⁿs\ [F] : marriage of convenience

ma·ri com·plai·sant \mä-rē-kōⁿ-ple-zäⁿ\ [F] : complaisant husband : cuckold who accepts his wife's infidelity

mau·vaise honte \mȯ-vez-ōⁿt\ [F] : bad shame : bashfulness

mau·vais quart d'heure \mȯ-ve-kär-dœr\ [F] : bad quarter hour : an uncomfortable though brief experience

me·dio tu·tis·si·mus ibis \'me-dē-ˌō-tü-ˌti-si-mús-'ē-bis\ [L] : you will go most safely by the middle course

me ju·di·ce \mä-'yü-di-ke\ [L] : I being judge : in my judgment

mens sa·na in cor·po·re sa·no \mäns-'sä-nä-in-ˌkȯr-pȯ-re-'sä-nō\ [L] : a sound mind in a sound body

me·um et tu·um \ˌmē-əm-ˌet-'tü-əm, ˌme-üm-ˌet-'tü-ùm\ [L] : mine and thine : distinction of private property

mi·ra·bi·le vi·su \mi-ˌrä-bi-lä-'wē-sü\ [L] : wonderful to behold

mi·ra·bi·lia \ˌmir-ə-'bi-lē-ˌä\ [L] : wonders : miracles

mœurs \mœr(s)\ [F] : mores : attitudes, customs, and manners of a society

mo·le ru·it sua \'mō-le-'rù-it-ˌsù-ä\ [L] : it collapses from its own bigness

monde \mōⁿd\ [F] : world : fashionable world : society

mon·ta·ni sem·per li·be·ri \mȯn-'tä-nē-ˌsem-per-'lē-be-ˌrē\ [L] : mountaineers are always free — motto of West Virginia

mo·nu·men·tum ae·re per·en·ni·us \ˌmȯ-nù-'men-tùm-ˌī-re-pe-'re-nē-ùs\ [L] : a monument more lasting than bronze — used of an immortal work of art or literature

mo·re suo \ˌmȯr-ä-'sü-ō\ [L] : in his (or her) own manner

mo·ri·tu·ri te sa·lu·ta·mus \ˌmȯr-ä-'tu̇r-ē-ˌtä-ˌsä-lü-'tä-mùs\ or morituri te sa·lu·tant \-sä-lù-ˌtänt\ [L] : we (or those) who are about to die salute thee

mul·tum in par·vo \ˌmùl-tùm-in-'pär-vō, -'pär-wō\ [L] : much in little

mu·ta·to no·mi·ne de te fa·bu·la nar·ra·tur \mü-ˌtä-tō-'nō-mi-ne-ˌdä-ˌtä-'fä-bù-lä-nä-'rä-ˌtùr\ [L] : with the name changed the story applies to you

my·ster·i·um tre·men·dum \mi-'ster-ē-ˌùm-tre-'men-dùm\ [L] : overwhelming mystery

na·tu·ram ex·pel·las fur·ca, ta·men us·que re·cur·ret \nä-'tü-ˌräm-ek-ˌspe-läs-'fùr-ˌkä-ˌtä-men-'ùs-kwe-re-'kùr-et\ [L] : you may drive nature out with a pitchfork, but she will keep coming back

na·tu·ra non fa·cit sal·tum \nä-'tü-rä-ˌnōn-ˌfä-kit-'säl-ˌtùm\ [L] : nature makes no leap

ne ce·de ma·lis \nä-ˌkä-de-'mä-ˌlēs\ [L] : yield not to misfortunes

ne·mo me im·pu·ne la·ces·sit \'nä-mō-'mä-im-ˌpü-nä-lä-'ke-sit\ [L] : no one attacks me with impunity — motto of Scotland and of the Order of the Thistle

ne quid ni·mis \ˌnä-ˌkwid-'ni-mis\ [L] : not anything in excess

n'est–ce pas? \nes-pä\ [F] : isn't it so?

nicht wahr? \nikt-'vär\ [G] : not true? : isn't it so?

nil ad·mi·ra·ri \'nēl-ˌäd-mi-'rär-ē\ [L] : to be excited by nothing : equanimity

nil de·spe·ran·dum \'nēl-ˌde-spä-'rän-dùm\ [L] : never despair

nil si·ne nu·mi·ne \ˌnēl-ˌsi-nä-'nü-mi-ne\ [L] : nothing without the divine will — motto of Colorado

n'im·porte \naⁿ-pȯrt\ [F] : it's no matter

no·lens vo·lens \ˌnō-ˌlenz-'vō-ˌlenz\ [L] : unwilling (or) willing : willy-nilly

non om·nia pos·su·mus om·nes \nōn-'ȯm-nē-ä-ˌpȯ-sù-mùs-'ȯm-ˌnäs\ [L] : we can't all (do) all things

non om·nis mo·ri·ar \nōn-'ȯm-nis-'mȯr-ē-ˌär\ [L] : I shall not wholly die

non sans droict \nōⁿ-säⁿ-drwä\ [OF] : not without right — motto on Shakespeare's coat of arms

non sum qua·lis eram \ˌnōn-ˌsùm-ˌkwä-lis-'er-ˌäm\ [L] : I am not what I used to be nos·ce te ip·sum \ˌnòs-ke-ˌtā-ˈip-ˌsùm\ [L] : know thyself

nos·tal·gie de la boue \nòs-täl-zhēd-lä-bü, -zhē-də-\ [F] : yearning for the mud : attraction to what is unworthy, crude, or degrading

nous avons chan·gé tout ce·la \nü-zä-vōⁿ-shäⁿ-zhä-tü-sə-lä\ [F] : we have changed all that

nous ver·rons ce que nous ver·rons \nü-ve-rōⁿs-kə-nü-ve-rōⁿ, -rōⁿ-sə-kə-\ [F] : we shall see what we shall see

no·vus ho·mo \ˌnō-wùs-ˈhò-mō\ [L] : new man : man newly ennobled : upstart

novus or·do se·clo·rum \-ˈòr-ˌdō-sā-ˈklòr-ùm\ [L] : a new cycle of the ages — motto on the reverse of the Great Seal of the United States

nu·gae \ˈnü-ˌgī\ [L] : trifles

nuit blanche \nwᵉē-bläⁿsh\ [F] : white night : a sleepless night

nyet \ˈnyet\ [Russ] : no

ob·iit \ˈò-bē-ˌit\ [L] : he or she died

ob·scu·rum per ob·scu·ri·us \òb-ˈskyùr-ùm-ˌper-òb-ˈskyùr-ē-ùs\ [L] : (explaining) the obscure by means of the more obscure

ode·rint dum me·tu·ant \ˈō-de-ˌrint-ˌdúm-me-tù-ˌänt\ [L] : let them hate, so long as they fear

odi et amo \ˈō-ˌdē-et-ˈä-(ˌ)mō\ [L] : I hate and I love

omer·tà \ò-ˈmer-tä\ [It] : conspiracy of silence

om·ne ig·no·tum pro mag·ni·fi·co \ˌòm-ne-ig-ˈnō-ˌtùm-prō-mäg-ˈni-fi-ˌkō\ [L] : everything unknown (is taken) as grand : the unknown tends to be exaggerated in importance or difficulty

om·nia mu·tan·tur, nos et mu·ta·mur in il·lis \ˌòm-nē-ä-mü-ˈtän-ˌtúr ˌnōs-et-mü-ˌtä-mùr-in-ˈi-ˌlēs\ [L] : all things are changing, and we are changing with them

om·nia vin·cit amor \ˈòm-nē-ä-ˈwin-kit-ˈä-ˌmòr\ [L] : love conquers all

onus pro·ban·di \ˌō-nùs-prō-ˈban-ˌdī, -dē\ [L] : burden of proof

ora pro no·bis \ˌō-rä-prō-ˈnō-ˌbēs\ [L] : pray for us

ore ro·tun·do \ˌōr-ē-rō-ˈtən-dō\ [L] : with round mouth : eloquently

oro y pla·ta \ˌōr-ō-ē-ˈplä-tə\ [Sp] : gold and silver — motto of Montana

o tem·po·ra! o mo·res! \ō-ˈtem-pó-rä ō-ˈmō-ˌräs\ [L] : oh the times! oh the manners!

oti·um cum dig·ni·ta·te \ˈō-tē-ˌùm-kùm-ˌdig-ni-ˈtä-te\ [L] : leisure with dignity

où sont les neiges d'an·tan? \ü-sōⁿ-lā-nezh-däⁿ-täⁿ\ [F] : where are the snows of yesteryear?

outre—mer \ütrᵊ-mer\ [F] : overseas : distant lands

pal·li·da Mors \ˌpa-li-dä-ˈmòrz\ [L] : pale Death

pa·nem et cir·cen·ses \ˈpä-ˌnem-et-kir-ˈkän-ˌsäs\ [L] : bread and circuses : provision of the means of life and recreation by government to appease discontent

pan·ta rhei \ˌpän-ˌtä-ˈrä\ [Gk] : all things are in flux

par avance \ˌpär-ä-väⁿs\ [F] : in advance : by anticipation

par avion \ˌpär-ä-vyōⁿ\ [F] : by airplane — used on airmail

par ex·em·ple \ˌpär-āg-zäⁿplᵊ\ [F] : for example

pars pro to·to \ˈpärs-(ˌ)prō-ˈtō-(ˌ)tō\ [L] : part (taken) for the whole

par·tu·ri·unt mon·tes, nas·ce·tur ri·di·cu·lus mus \ˌpär-ˈtùr-ē-ˌùnt-ˈmòn-ˌtes, näs-ˈkä-ˌtùr-ri-di-kù-lùs-ˈmüs\ [L] : the mountains are in labor, and a ridiculous mouse will be brought forth

pa·ter pa·tri·ae \ˈpä-ˌter-ˈpä-trē-ˌī\ [L] : father of his country

pau·cis ver·bis \ˌpaù-ˌkēs-ˈwer-ˌbēs\ [L] : in a few words

pax vo·bis·cum \ˌpäks-vō-ˈbēs-ˌkúm\ [L] : peace (be) with you

peine forte et dure \pen-fòr-tä-dʉr\ [F] : strong and hard punishment : torture

per an·gus·ta ad au·gus·ta \per-ˈän-ˌgùs-tä-äd-ˈaù-ˌgùs-tä\ [L] : through difficulties to honors

per·fide Al·bion \per-fēd-äl-byōⁿ\ [F] : perfidious Albion (England)

peu à peu \pœ-ä-pœ\ [F] : little by little

peu de chose \pœd-shōz, pœ-də-\ [F] : a trifle

pièce d'oc·ca·sion \pyes-dò-kä-zyōⁿ\ [F] : piece for a special occasion

pinx·it \ˈpiŋk-sit\ [L] : he or she painted it

place aux dames \pläs-ō-däm\ [F] : (make) room for the ladies

ple·no ju·re \ˌplä-nō-ˈyùr-e\ [L] : with full right

plus ça change, plus c'est la même chose \plᴜe-sä-shäⁿzh plᴜe-se-lä-mem-shōz\ [F] : the more that changes, the more it's the same thing — often shortened to *plus ça change*

plus roy·a·liste que le roi \plᴜe-rwä-yä-lēst-kəl-rwä\ [F] : more royalist than the king

po·cas pa·la·bras \ˌpō-käs-pä-ˈlä-vräs\ [Sp] : few words

po·eta nas·ci·tur, non fit \pò-ˌä-tä-ˈnäs-ki-ˌtùr nōn-ˈfit\ [L] : a poet is born, not made

po·ète mau·dit \pò-et-mō-dē\ [F] : accursed poet : a writer dogged by misfortune and lack of recognition

pol·li·ce ver·so \ˌpò-li-ke-ˈwer-sō\ [L] : with thumb turned : with a gesture or expression of condemnation

post hoc, er·go prop·ter hoc \ˈpòst-ˌhòk ˌer-gō-ˈpròp-ter-ˌhòk\ [L] : after this, therefore on account of it (a fallacy of argument)

post ob·itum \ˈpòst-ˈò-bi-ˌtùm\ [L] : after death

pour ac·quit \ˌpür-ä-kē\ [F] : received payment

pour en·cou·ra·ger les autres \ˌpür-äⁿ-kü-rä-zhä-lä-zōtrᵊ\ [F] : in order to encourage the others — said ironically of an action (as an execution) carried out in order to compel others to obey

pour le mé·rite \ˌpür-lə-mä-rēt\ [F] : for merit

pri·mum non no·ce·re \ˌprē-mùm-ˌnōn-nó-ˈkä-rä\ [L] : the first thing (is) to do no harm

pro aris et fo·cis \ˌprō-ˌä-ˌrēs-et-ˈfò-ˌkēs\ [L] : for altars and firesides

pro bo·no pu·bli·co \ˌprō-ˌbò-nō-ˈpü-bli-ˌkō\ [L] : for the public good

pro hac vi·ce \ˌprō-ˌhäk-ˈwi-ke\ [L] : for this occasion

pro pa·tria \ˌprō-ˈpä-trē-ˌä\ [L] : for one's country

pro re·ge, le·ge, et gre·ge \ˌprō-ˈrä-ˌge ˈlä-ˌge et-ˈgre-ˌge\ [L] : for the king, the law, and the people

pro re na·ta \ˌprō-ˌrä-ˈnä-tä\ [L] : for an occasion that has arisen : as needed — used in medical prescriptions

quand même \käⁿ-mem\ [F] : even so : all the same

quan·tum mu·ta·tus ab il·lo \ˌkwän-tùm-mü-ˈtä-tùs-äb-ˈi-lō\ [L] : how changed from what he once was

quan·tum suf·fi·cit \ˌkwän-təm-ˈsə-fə-ˌkit\ [L] : as much as suffices : a sufficient quantity — used chiefly in medical prescriptions

¿quién sa·be? \kyän-ˈsä-vä\ [Sp] : who knows?

qui fa·cit per ali·um fa·cit per se \ˌkwē-ˌfä-kit-ˌper-ˈä-lē-ˌùm-ˌfä-kit-ˌper-ˈsä\ [L] : he who does (something) through another does it through himself

quis cus·to·di·et ip·sos cus·to·des? \ˌkwis-kùs-ˈtō-dē-ˌet-ˌip-ˌsōs-kùs-ˈtō-ˌdäs\ [L] : who will keep the keepers themselves?

qui s'ex·cuse s'ac·cuse \kē-ˈsek-ˌskᴜez-ˈsä-ˌkᴜez\ [F] : he who excuses himself accuses himself

quis se·pa·ra·bit? \ˌkwis-ˌsä-pə-ˈrä-bit\ [L] : who shall separate (us)? — motto of the Order of St. Patrick

qui trans·tu·lit sus·ti·net \kwē-ˈträns-tù-ˌlit-ˈsùs-ti-ˌnet\ [L] : He who transplanted sustains (us) — motto of Connecticut

qui va là? \kē-vä-lä\ [F] : who goes there?

quo·ad hoc \ˌkwó-ˌäd-ˈhòk\ [L] : as far as this : to this extent

quod erat de·mon·stran·dum \ˌkwód-ˈer-ˌät-ˌde-mən-ˈstran-dəm, -ˌä-ˌmòn-ˈsträn-ˌdùm\ [L] : which was to be proved

quod erat fa·ci·en·dum \-ˌfä-kē-ˈen-ˌdùm\ [L] : which was to be done

quod sem·per, quod ubi·que, quod ab om·ni·bus \ˌkwód-ˈsem-ˌper kwód-ˈù-bi-ˌkwä ˌkwód-äb-ˈòm-ni-ˌbùs, -ˌkwód-ù-ˈbē-(ˌ)kwä-\ [L] : what (has been held) always, everywhere, by everybody

quod vi·de \kwód-ˈwi-ˌde\ [L] : which see

quo·rum pars mag·na fui \ˈkwòr-ùm-ˌpärs-ˌmäg-nä-ˈfù-ē\ [L] : in which I played a great part

quos de·us vult per·de·re pri·us de·men·tat \ˌkwōs-ˈdä-ùs-ˌwült-ˈper-de-ˌrä-ˌpri-ùs-dā-ˈmen-ˌtät\ [L] : those whom a god wishes to destroy he first drives mad

quot ho·mi·nes, tot sen·ten·ti·ae \ˌkwōt-ˈhò-mi-ˌnäs ˌtòt-ˌsen-ˈten-tē-ˌī\ [L] : there are as many opinions as there are men

quo va·dis? \kwō-ˈwä-dis, -ˈvä-dəs\ [L] : whither are you going?

rai·son d'état \re-zōⁿ-dä-tä\ [F] : reason of state

re·cu·ler pour mieux sau·ter \rə-kᴜe-lä-pür-myœ-sō-tä\ [F] : to draw back in order to make a better jump

reg·nat po·pu·lus \ˌreg-ˌnät-'pȯ-pu̇-ˌlu̇s\ [L] : the people rule — motto of Arkansas

re in·fec·ta \ˌrä-in-'fek-ˌtä\ [L] : the business being unfinished : without accomplishing one's purpose

re·li·gio lo·ci \re-'li-gē-ˌō-'lō-ˌkē\ [L] : religious sanctity of a place

rem acu te·ti·gis·ti \rem-'ä-ˌkü-ˌte-ti-'gis-tē\ [L] : you have touched the point with a needle : you have hit the nail on the head

ré·pon·dez s'il vous plaît \rä-pōⁿ-dä-sēl-vü-ple\ [F] : reply, if you please

re·qui·es·cat in pa·ce \ˌre-kwē-'es-ˌkät-in-'pä-ˌke, ˌrä-kwē-'es-ˌkät-in-'pä-ˌchä\ [L] : may he or she rest in peace — used on tombstones

re·spi·ce fi·nem \ˌrä-spi-ˌke-'fē-ˌnem\ [L] : look to the end : consider the outcome

re·sur·gam \re-'su̇r-ˌgäm\ [L] : I shall rise again

re·te·nue \rət-nue\ [F] : self-restraint : reserve

re·ve·nons à nos mou·tons \rəv-nōⁿ-ä-nō-mü-tōⁿ\ [F] : let us return to our sheep : let us get back to the subject

ruse de guerre \ru̇z-də-ger\ [F] : war stratagem

rus in ur·be \ˌrüs-in-'u̇r-ˌbe\ [L] : country in the city

sae·va in·dig·na·tio \ˌsī-wä-ˌin-dig-'nä-tē-ō\ [L] : fierce indignation

sal At·ti·cum \sal-'a-ti-kəm\ [L] : Attic salt : wit

salle à man·ger \säl-ä-mäⁿ-zhä\ [F] : dining room

sa·lon des re·fu·sés \sä-lōⁿ-där-(ə-)fu̇e-zä\ [F] : salon of the refused : exhibition of art that has been rejected by an official body

sa·lus po·pu·li su·pre·ma lex es·to \ˌsä-ˌlüs-'pȯ-pu̇-ˌlē-sù-ˌprä-mä-ˌleks-'es-tō\ [L] : let the welfare of the people be the supreme law — motto of Missouri

sanc·ta sim·pli·ci·tas \ˌsäŋk-tä-sim-'pli-ki-ˌtäs\ [L] : holy simplicity — often used ironically in reference to another's naïveté

sans doute \säⁿ-düt\ [F] : without doubt : probably

sans gêne \säⁿ-zhen\ [F] : without embarrassment or constraint

sans peur et sans re·proche \säⁿ-pœr-ā-säⁿ-rə-'prȯsh\ [F] : without fear and without reproach

sans sou·ci \säⁿ-sü-sē\ [F] : without worry

sa·yo·na·ra \ˌsī-ə-'när-ə, ˌsä-yə-\ [Jp] : good-bye

sculp·sit \'skəlp-sət, 'skùlp-sit\ [L] : he or she carved it

scu·to bo·nae vo·lun·ta·tis tu·ae co·ro·nas·ti nos \'skü-ˌtō-'bȯ-ˌnī-ˌvȯ-lùn-ˌtä-tis-'tü-ˌī-'kȯr-ō-ˌnäs-tē-'nōs\ [L] : Thou hast crowned us with the shield of Thy good will — a motto on the Great Seal of Maryland

se·cun·dum ar·tem \sə-ˌkùn-dùm-'är-ˌtem\ [L] : according to the art : according to the accepted practice of a profession or trade

secundum na·tu·ram \-nä-'tü-ˌräm\ [L] : according to nature : naturally

se de·fen·den·do \'sä-ˌdä-ˌfen-'den-dō\ [L] : in self-defense

se ha·bla es·pa·ñol \sä-ˌäv-lä-ˌäs-pä-'nʸȯl\ [Sp] : Spanish spoken

sem·per ea·dem \ˌsem-ˌper-'e-ä-ˌdem\ [L] : always the same (fem.) — motto of Queen Elizabeth I

sem·per fi·de·lis \ˌsem-pər-fə-'dä-ləs\ [L] : always faithful — motto of the U.S. Marine Corps

sem·per idem \ˌsem-ˌper-'ē-ˌdem\ [L] : always the same (masc.)

sem·per pa·ra·tus \ˌsem-pər-pə-'rä-ləs\ [L] : always prepared — motto of the U.S. Coast Guard

se non è ve·ro, è ben tro·va·to \sä-ˌnōn-e-'vä-rō e-ˌben-trō-'vä-tō\ [It] : even if it is not true, it is well conceived

sha·lom alei·chem \shō-ləm-ə-'lä-kəm, ˌshō-, -kəm\ [Heb *shālōm ʿalēkhem*] : peace to you — used as a traditional Jewish greeting

sic itur ad as·tra \sēk-'i-ˌtu̇r-ˌäd-'äs-trə\ [L] : thus one goes to the stars : such is the way to immortality

sic sem·per ty·ran·nis \sik-ˌsem-pər-tə-'ra-nəs\ [L] : thus ever to tyrants — motto of Virginia

sic trans·it glo·ria mun·di \sēk-'trän-sit-ˌglȯr-ē-ä-'mùn-dē\ [L] : so passes away the glory of the world

si jeu·nesse sa·vait, si vieil·lesse pou·vait! \sē-'zhœe-nes-'sä-ve sē-'vye-yes-'pü-ve\ [F] : if youth only knew, if age only could!

si·lent le·ges in·ter ar·ma \ˌsi-ˌlent-'lā-ˌgäs-ˌin-ter-'är-mä\ [L] : the laws are silent in the midst of arms (i.e., in time of war)

s'il vous plaît \sēl-vü-ple\ [F] : if you please

si·mi·lia si·mi·li·bus cu·ran·tur \si-'mi-lē-ä-si-'mi-li-bùs-kü-'rän-ˌtu̇r\ [L] : like is cured by like

si·mi·lis si·mi·li gau·det \'si-mi-lis-'si-mi-lē-'gau̇-ˌdet\ [L] : like takes pleasure in like

si mo·nu·men·tum re·qui·ris, cir·cum·spi·ce \ˌsē-ˌmȯ-nü-ˌmen-tùm-re-'kwē-ris kir-'kùm-spi-ke\ [L] : if you seek this monument, look around — epitaph of Sir Christopher Wren in St. Paul's, London, of which he was architect

sim·pliste \saⁿ-plēst\ [F] : simplistic : overly simple or naïve

si quae·ris pen·in·su·lam amoe·nam, cir·cum·spi·ce \sē-'kwī-ris-pä-'nin-sə-ˌläm-ä-'mȯi-ˌnäm kir-'kùm-spi-ke\ [L] : if you seek a beautiful peninsula, look around — motto of Michigan

sis·te vi·a·tor \ˌsis-te-wē-'ä-ˌtȯr\ [L] : stop, traveler — used on Roman roadside tombs

si vis pa·cem, pa·ra bel·lum \sē-'wēs-'pä-ˌkem 'pä-rä-'be-ˌlùm\ [L] : if you wish peace, prepare for war

sol·vi·tur am·bu·lan·do \'sȯl-wi-ˌtu̇r-ˌäm-bù-'län-dō\ [L] : it is solved by walking : the problem is solved by a practical experiment

spo·lia opi·ma \ˌspō-lē-ä-ō-'pē-mä\ [L] : rich spoils : the arms taken by the victorious from the vanquished general

sta·tus quo an·te bel·lum \'stä-tùs-kwō-ˌän-te-'be-lùm\ [L] : the state existing before the war

sua·vi·ter in mo·do, for·ti·ter in re \'swä-wi-ˌter-in-'mȯ-dō 'fȯr-ti-ˌter-in-'rä\ [L] : gently in manner, strongly in deed

sub ver·bo \sùb-'wer-bō, ˌsəb-'vər-bō\ *or* **sub vo·ce** \sùb-'wō-ke, ˌsəb-'vō-sē\ [L] : under the word — introducing a cross-reference in a dictionary or index

sunt la·cri·mae re·rum \sùnt-ˌlä-kri-ˌmī-'rä-rùm\ [L] : there are tears for things : tears attend trials

suo ju·re \ˌsü-ō-'yùr-e\ [L] : in his or her own right

suo lo·co \-'lō-kō\ [L] : in its proper place

suo Mar·te \-'mär-te\ [L] : by one's own exertions

su·um cui·que \ˌsü-ùm-'kwi-kwe\ [L] : to each his own

tant mieux \täⁿ-myœe\ [F] : so much the better

tant pis \-pē\ [F] : so much the worse : too bad

tem·po·ra mu·tan·tur, nos et mu·ta·mur in il·lis \ˌtem-pȯ-rä-mü-'tän-ˌtu̇r ˌnōs-ˌet-mü-ˌtä-mùr-in-'i-ˌlēs\ [L] : the times are changing, and we are changing with them

tem·pus edax re·rum \'tem-pùs-ˌe-ˌdäks-'rä-rùm\ [L] : time, that devours all things

tem·pus fu·git \ˌtem-pəs-'fyü-jət, ˌtem-pùs-'fü-git\ [L] : time flies

ti·meo Da·na·os et do·na fe·ren·tes \ˌti-mē-ˌō-'dä-nä-ˌōs-ˌet-ˌdō-nä-fe-'ren-ˌtäs\ [L] : I fear the Greeks even when they bring gifts

to·ti·dem ver·bis \ˌtȯ-ti-ˌdem-'wer-ˌbēs\ [L] : in so many words

to·tis vi·ri·bus \ˌtȯ-ˌtēs-'wē-ri-ˌbùs\ [L] : with all one's might

to·to cae·lo \ˌtȯ-tō-'kī-lō\ *or* **toto coe·lo** \-'kȯi-lō\ [L] : by the whole extent of the heavens : diametrically

tou·jours per·drix \tü-zhür-per-drē\ [F] : always partridge : too much of a good thing

tour d'ho·ri·zon \tür-dȯ-rē-zōⁿ\ [F] : circuit of the horizon : general survey

tous frais faits \tü-fre-fe\ [F] : all expenses defrayed

tout à fait \tü-tä-fe\ [F] : altogether : quite

tout au con·traire \tü-tō-kōⁿ-trer\ [F] : quite the contrary

tout à vous \tü-tä-vü\ [F] : wholly yours : at your service

tout bien ou rien \tü-'byaⁿ-nü-'ryaⁿ\ [F] : everything well (done) or nothing (attempted)

tout com·pren·dre c'est tout par·don·ner \'tü-kōⁿ-präⁿ-drə-se-'tü-pär-dȯ-nä\ [F] : to understand all is to forgive all

tout court \tü-kür\ [F] : quite short : and nothing else : simply : just; *also* : brusquely

tout de même \tüt-mem\ [F] : all the same : nevertheless

tout de suite \tüt-swʸēt\ [F] : immediately; *also* : all at once : consecutively

tout en·sem·ble \tü-täⁿ-säⁿblᵉ\ [F] : all together : general effect

tout est per·du fors l'hon·neur \tü-te-per-due-fȯr-lȯ-nœr\ *or* **tout est perdu hors l'honneur** \-due-ȯr-\ [F] : all is lost save honor

tout le monde \tü-lə-mōⁿd\ [F] : all the world : everybody

Foreign Words & Phrases

594

tra·hi·son des clercs \trä-ē-zóⁿ-dā-klerk\ [F] : treason of the intellectuals

tranche de vie \träⁿsh-də-'vē\ [F] : slice of life

trist·esse \trē-stes\ [F] : melancholy

tru·di·tur di·es die \'trü-di-,túr-'di-,ās-'di-,ā\ [L] : day is pushed forth by day : one day hurries on another

tu·e·bor \tú-'ā-,bór\ [L] : I will defend — a motto on the Great Seal of Michigan

ua mau ke ea o ka ai·na i ka po·no \,ú-ä-'mä-ú-kä-'ä-ä-ō-kä-'ä-ē-nä-,ē-kä-'pō-nō\ [Hawaiian] : the life of the land is perpetuated in righteousness — motto of Hawaii

über al·les \,ue-ber-'ä-les\ [G] : above everything else

Über·mensch \'ue-bər-,mench\ [G] : superman

ul·ti·ma ra·tio re·gum \'úl-ti-mä-,rä-tē-ō-'rä-gúm\ [L] : the final argument of kings, i.e., war

und so wei·ter \únt-zō-'vī-tər\ [G] : and so on

uno ani·mo \,ü-nō-'ä-ni-,mō\ [L] : with one mind : unanimously

ur·bi et or·bi \,úr-bē-,et-'ór-bē\ [L] : to the city (Rome) and the world : to everyone

uti·le dul·ci \,ü-ti-le-'dúl-,kē\ [L] : the useful with the agreeable

ut in·fra \út-'in-frä\ [L] : as below

ut su·pra \út-'sü-prä\ [L] : as above

va·de re·tro me, Sa·ta·na \,wä-de-'rä-trō-,mä 'sä-tä-,nä\ [L] : get thee behind me, Satan

vae vic·tis \wī-'wik-,tēs\ [L] : woe to the vanquished

va·ria lec·tio \,wär-ē-ä-'lek-tē-,ō\ pl **va·ri·ae lec·ti·o·nes** \'wär-ē-,ī-,lek-tē-'ō-,nâs\ [L] : variant reading

va·ri·um et mu·ta·bi·le sem·per fe·mi·na \,wär-ē-úm-,et-,mü-'tä-bi-le-,sem-,per-'fä-mi-nä\ [L] : woman is ever a fickle and changeable thing

ve·di Na·po·li e poi mo·ri \,vä-dē-'nä-pō-lē-ä-,pò-ē-'mò-rē\ [It] : see Naples and then die

ve·ni, vi·di, vi·ci \,wä-nē ,wē-dē 'wē-kē, ,vä-nē ,vē-dē 'vē-chē\ [L] : I came, I saw, I conquered

ven·tre à terre \väⁿ-trä-ter\ [F] : belly to the ground : at very great speed

ver·ba·tim ac lit·te·ra·tim \wer-'bä-tim-,äk-,li-te-'rä-tim\ [L] : word for word and letter for letter

ver·bum sat sa·pi·en·ti est \,wer-bùm-'sät-,sä-pē-'en-tē-,est\ [L] : a word to the wise is sufficient

via cru·cis \wē-ä-'krü-sis\ [L] : Way of the Cross : path of suffering

vieux jeu \vyœ-zhœ\ [F] : old game : old hat

vin·cit om·nia ve·ri·tas \,wiŋ-kit-'òm-nē-ä-'wä-ri-,täs\ [L] : truth conquers all things

vin·cu·lum ma·tri·mo·nii \,wiŋ-kú-lùm-,mä-tri-'mō-nē-,ē\ [L] : bond of marriage

vin du pays \vaⁿ-due-pä-ē\ or **vin de pays** \vaⁿ-də-\ [F] : wine of the locality

vir·gi·ni·bus pu·e·ris·que \wir-'gi-ni-bùs-,pù-e-'rēs-kwe\ [L] : for girls and boys

vir·go in·tac·ta \'vir-,gō-in-'täk-tä\ [L] : untouched virgin

vir·tu·te et ar·mis \wir-'tü-te-,et-'är-mēs\ [L] : by valor and arms — motto of Mississippi

vis me·di·ca·trix na·tu·rae \'wēs-,me-di-'kä-triks-nä-'tü-,rī\ [L] : the healing power of nature

vive la dif·fé·rence \vēv-lä-dē-fä-räⁿs\ [F] : long live the difference (between the sexes)

vive la reine \vēv-lä-ren\ [F] : long live the queen

vive le roi \vēv-lə-rwä\ [F] : long live the king

vix·e·re for·tes an·te Aga·mem·no·na \wik-,sä-re-'fòr-,täs-,än-te-,ä-gä-'mem-nò-,nä\ [L] : brave men lived before Agamemnon

vogue la ga·lère \vòg-lä-gä-ler\ [F] : let the galley be kept rowing : keep on, whatever may happen

voi·là tout \vwä-lä-tü\ [F] : that's all

vox et prae·te·rea ni·hil \'wòks-et-prī-'ter-e-ä-'ni-,hil\ [L] : voice and nothing more

vox po·pu·li vox Dei \wòks-'pò-pù-,lē-,wòks-'dä-ē\ [L] : the voice of the people is the voice of God

Wan·der·jahr \'vän-dər-,yär\ [G] : year of wandering

wie geht's? \vē-'gäts\ [G] : how goes it? : how is it going? — used as a greeting

wun·der·bar \'vùn-dər-,bär\ [G] : wonderful

This section gives basic information on many notable figures from contemporary culture, history, legend, mythology, and biblical tradition. Figures from the Bible, myth, and legend are clearly identified as such.

In cases where individuals have alternate names, they are entered under the name by which they are best known. Names are generally alphabetized by the main element of the surname, without regard for connectives such as *da, de, van,* or *von* (as **Gama** . . . Vasco da). Names appearing in the entry in italics are original names, maiden names, or nicknames.

The first dates given in the entry are birth/death dates; other dates refer to terms in office, reigns, achievements, or honors. Abbreviations used here are listed in the front section Abbreviations in This Work.

Aar·on \'er-ən\ brother of Moses and 1st high priest of the Hebrews in the Bible
Aaron Hank 1934– *Henry Louis Aaron* Amer. baseball player
Abel \'ā-bəl\ son of Adam and Eve and brother of Cain in the Bible
Abra·ham \'ā-brə-,ham\ patriarch and founder of the Hebrew people in the Bible; also revered by Muslims
Achil·les \ə-'ki-lēz\ hero of the Trojan War in Greek mythology
Ad·am \'a-dəm\ the 1st man in biblical tradition
Ad·ams \'a-dəmz\ Abigail 1744–1818 née *Smith* Amer. writer; wife of John Adams
Adams Ansel Easton 1902–1984 Amer. photographer
Adams John 1735–1826 2d pres. of the U.S. (1797–1801)
Adams John Quin·cy \'kwin-zē, -sē\ 1767–1848 6th pres. of the U.S. (1825–29); son of John and Abigail Adams
Adams Samuel 1722–1803 patriot in the Amer. Revolution
Ad·dams \'a-dəmz\ Jane 1860–1935 Amer. social worker; Nobel Prize winner (1931)
Ado·nis \ə-'dä-nəs, -'dō-\ youth in Greek mythology loved by Aphrodite
Ae·ne·as \i-'nē-əs\ Trojan hero in Greek and Roman mythology
Ae·o·lus \'ē-ə-ləs\ god of the winds in Greek mythology
Aes·chy·lus \'es-kə-ləs, 'ēs-\ 525–456 B.C. Greek dramatist
Aes·cu·la·pi·us \,es-k(y)ə-'lā-pē-əs\ god of medicine in Roman mythology — compare ASCLEPIUS
Ae·sop \'ē-,säp, -səp\ legendary Greek writer of fables
Ag·a·mem·non \,a-gə-'mem-,nän, -nən\ leader of the Greeks during the Trojan War in Greek mythology
Ag·nes \'ag-nəs\ Saint *died* 304 A.D. Christian martyr
Ahab \'ā-,hab\ king of Israel in the 9th cent. B.C. and husband of Jezebel
Ajax \'ā-jaks\ hero in Greek mythology who kills himself because the armor of Achilles is awarded to Odysseus during the Trojan War
Alad·din \ə-'la-dən\ youth in the *Arabian Nights' Entertainments* who acquires a magic lamp
Al·bright \'ol-,brīt\ Madeleine 1937– née *Korbel* Amer. (Czech-born) diplomat; U.S. secretary of state (1997–2001)
Al·cott \'ol-kət, 'al-, -,kät\ Louisa May 1832–1888 Amer. author
Al·ex·an·der \,a-lig-'zan-dər, ,e-\ name of eight popes: esp. 1431–1503 (pope 1492–1503)
Alexander the Great 356–323 B.C. *Alexander III* king of Macedonia (336–323)
Al·fred \'al-frəd, -fərd\ 849–899 *Alfred the Great* king of the West Saxons (871–899)
Ali \ä-'lē\ Muhammed 1942– orig. *Cassius Clay* Amer. boxer
Ali Ba·ba \,a-lē-'bä-bə, ,ä-lē-\ woodcutter in the *Arabian Nights' Entertainments* who enters the cave of the Forty Thieves by using the password *Sesame*
Al·len \'a-lən\ Ethan 1738–1789 Amer. Revolutionary soldier
Amerigo Vespucci — see VESPUCCI
Am·herst \'a-(,)mərst\ Jeffery 1717–1797 Baron *Amherst* Brit. general in America

Amund·sen \'ä-mən-sən\ Roald 1872–1928 Norwegian explorer
An·a·ni·as \,a-nə-'nī-əs\ early Christian in the Bible struck dead for lying
An·der·sen \'an-dər-sən\ Hans Christian 1805–1875 Danish writer of fairy tales
An·der·son \'an-dər-sən\ Marian 1897–1993 Amer. contralto
An·ge·lou \'an-jə-(,)lō, commonly -,lü\ Maya 1928– orig. *Marguerite Johnson* Amer. author
Anne \'an\ 1665–1714 queen of Great Britain (1702–14)
An·tho·ny \'an(t)-thə-nē\ Susan Brownell 1820–1906 Amer. suffragist
An·tig·o·ne \an-'ti-gə-(,)nē\ daughter of Oedipus and Jocasta in Greek mythology
An·to·ny \'an-tə-nē\ Mark ca 82–30 B.C. *Marc Anthony*; *Marcus An·to·ni·us* \an-'tō-nē-əs\ Roman general and triumvir (43–30)
Aph·ro·di·te \,a-frə-'dī-tē\ goddess of love and beauty in Greek mythology — compare VENUS
Apol·lo \ə-'pä-(,)lō\ god of sunlight, prophecy, music, and poetry in Greek and Roman mythology
Ap·ple·seed \'ap-əl-,sēd\ Johnny 1774–1845 orig. *John Chapman* Amer. pioneer
Aqui·nas \ə-'kwī-nəs\ Saint Thomas 1224/25–1274 Ital. theologian
Ar·chi·me·des \,är-kə-'mē-dēz\ ca 287–212 B.C. Greek mathematician and inventor
Ares \'a-(,)rēz, 'er-(,)ēz\ god of war in Greek mythology — compare MARS
Ar·is·toph·a·nes \,a-rə-'stä-fə-,nēz\ ca 450–ca 388 B.C. Greek playwright
Ar·is·tot·le \'a-rə-,stä-tᵊl\ 384–322 B.C. Greek philosopher
Arm·strong \'ärm-,strȯŋ\ Lance 1971– Amer. cyclist
Armstrong Louis 1901–1971 *Satch·mo* \'sach-,mō\ Amer. jazz musician
Armstrong Neil Alden 1930– Amer. astronaut; 1st man on the moon (1969)
Ar·nold \'är-nᵊld\ Benedict 1741–1801 Amer. Revolutionary general and traitor
Ar·te·mis \'är-tə-məs\ goddess of the moon, wild animals, and hunting in Greek mythology — compare DIANA
Ar·thur \'är-thər\ legendary king of the Britons whose story is based on traditions of a 6th-century military leader — **Ar·thu·ri·an** \är-'thür-ē-ən, -'thyür-\ adj
Arthur Chester Alan 1829–1886 21st pres. of the U.S. (1881–85)
As·cle·pi·us \ə-'sklē-pē-əs\ god of medicine in Greek mythology — compare AESCULAPIUS
As·tor \'as-tər\ John Jacob 1763–1848 Amer. (Ger.-born) fur trader and capitalist
Athe·na \ə-'thē-nə\ or **Athe·ne** \-nē\ goddess of wisdom in Greek mythology — compare MINERVA
At·las \'at-ləs\ Titan in Greek mythology forced to bear the heavens on his shoulders
At·ti·la \'a-tə-lə, ə-'ti-lə\ 406?–453 A.D. king of the Huns
At·tucks \'a-təks\ Crispus 1723?–1770 Amer. patriot
Au·du·bon \'ȯ-də-bən, -,bän\ John James 1785–1851 Amer. (Haitian-born) artist and naturalist

Biographical Names

596

Au·gus·tine \'o-gə-ˌstēn\ o·-'gəs-tən, ə-\ Saint 354–430 A.D. church father; bishop of Hippo (396–430)

Au·gus·tus \o·-'gəs-təs, ə-\ *or* **Caesar Augustus** *or* **Oc·ta·vi·an** \äk-'tā-vē-ən\ 63 B.C.–14 A.D., 1st Roman emperor (27 B.C.–14 A.D.)

Au·ro·ra \ə-'rȯr-ə, o·-\ goddess of the dawn in Roman mythology — compare EOS

Aus·ten \'o·s-tən, 'äs-\ Jane 1775–1817 Eng. author

Bac·chus \'ba-kəs, 'bä-\ — see DIONYSUS

Bach \'bäk, 'bäk\ Johann Sebastian 1685–1750 Ger. composer

Ba·con \'bā-kən\ Francis 1561–1626 Eng. philosopher and author

Ba·den–Pow·ell \'bā-dᵊn-'pō-əl\ Robert Stephenson Smyth 1857–1941 Baron *Baden-Powell* Brit. general and founder of Boy Scout movement

Baf·fin \'ba-fən\ William *ca* 1584–1622 Eng. navigator

Bal·boa \bal-'bō-ə\ Vasco Núñez de 1475–1519 Span. explorer

Bal·ti·more \'bȯl-tə-ˌmȯr, -mər\ Lord — see George CALVERT

Bal·zac \'bȯl-ˌzak, 'bal-\ Honoré de 1799–1850 French author

Ba·rab·bas \bə-'ra-bəs\ prisoner in the Bible released in preference to Jesus at the demand of the multitude

Bar·num \'bär-nəm\ P. T. 1810–1891 *Phineas Taylor Barnum* Amer. showman

Bar·rie \'ba-rē\ Sir James Matthew 1860–1937 Scot. author

Bar·thol·di \bär-'täl-dē, -'tȯl-, -'thäl-, -'thȯl-\ Frédéric-Auguste 1834–1904 French sculptor of the Statue of Liberty

Bar·ton \'bär-tᵊn\ Clara 1821–1912 founder of American Red Cross

Beau·re·gard \'bȯr-ə-ˌgärd\ Pierre Gustave Toutant 1818–1893 Amer. Confederate general

Beck·et \'be-kət\ Saint Thomas *ca* 1118–1170 *Thomas à Becket* archbishop of Canterbury (1162–70)

Beck·ett \'be-kət\ Samuel 1906–1989 Irish playwright in France; Nobel Prize winner (1969)

Bee·tho·ven \'bā-ˌtō-vən\ Ludwig van 1770–1827 Ger. composer

Bell \'bel\ Alexander Graham 1847–1922 Amer. (Scot.-born) inventor of the telephone

Bel·low \'be-(ˌ)lō\ Saul 1915–2005 Amer. (Canad.-born) author

Ben·e·dict \'be-nə-ˌdikt\ name of 15 popes: esp. **XIV** 1675–1758 (pope 1740–58); **XV** 1854–1922 (pope 1914–22); **XVI** 1927– (pope 2005–)

Ben·ja·min \'ben-jə-mən\ youngest son of Jacob and ancestor of one of the 12 tribes of Israel in the Bible

Ben·ton \'ben-tᵊn\ Thomas Hart 1889–1975 Amer. painter

Be·o·wulf \'bā-ə-ˌwu̇lf\ legendary warrior and hero of the Old Eng. poem *Beowulf*

Be·ring \'ber-iŋ, 'bir-\ Vitus 1681–1741 Danish navigator and explorer for Russia

Ber·lin \(ˌ)bər-'lin\ Irving 1888–1989 Amer. (Russ.-born) composer

Ber·ni·ni \ber-'nē-nē\ Gian Lorenzo 1598–1680 Ital. sculptor, architect, and painter

Bes·se·mer \'be-sə-mər\ Sir Henry 1813–1898 Eng. engineer and inventor

Be·thune \bə-'thün, -'thyün\ Mary 1875–1955 née *McLeod* Amer. educator

Bi·zet \bē-'zā\ Georges 1838–1875 French composer

Black Hawk \'blak-ˌhȯk\ 1767–1838 Amer. Indian chief

Black·well \'blak-ˌwel, -wəl\ Elizabeth 1821–1910 Amer. (Eng.-born) physician

Blair \'bler\ Tony 1953– *Anthony Charles Lynton Blair* Brit. prime minister (1997–2007)

Blake \'blāk\ William 1757–1827 Eng. poet and artist

Bloom·er \'blü-mər\ Amelia 1818–1894 née *Jenks* Amer. social reformer

Boc·cac·cio \bō-'kä-ch(ē-ˌ)ō\ Giovanni 1313–1375 Ital. author

Bohr \'bȯr\ Niels 1885–1962 Danish physicist; Nobel Prize winner (1922)

Bo·leyn \bu̇-'lin, -'lēn\ Anne 1507?–1536 2d wife of Henry VIII and mother of Elizabeth I of England

Bo·lí·var \bə-'lē-ˌvär; 'bä-lə-ˌvär, -vər\ Si·món \sē-ˌmōn, ˌsī-mən\ 1783–1830 South Amer. liberator

Bon·i·face \'bä-nə-fəs, -ˌfäs\ name of 9 popes: esp. **VIII** *ca* 1235 (or 1240)–1303 (pope 1294–1303)

Boone \'bün\ Daniel 1734–1820 Amer. pioneer

Booth \'büth\ John Wilkes 1838–1865 Amer. actor; assassin of Abraham Lincoln

Bo·re·as \'bȯr-ē-əs\ god of the north wind in Greek mythology

Bot·ti·cel·li \ˌbä-tə-'che-lē\ Sandro 1445–1510 Ital. painter

Bow·ie \'bü-ē, 'bō-\ Jim 1796–1836 *James Bowie* Amer. popular hero of the Texas revolution

Boyle \'bȯi(-ə)l\ Robert 1627–1691 Eng. physicist and chemist

Brad·bury \'brad-ˌber-ē, -b(ə-)rē\ Ray Douglas 1920– Amer. author

Brad·dock \'bra-dək\ Edward 1695–1755 Brit. general in America

Brad·ford \'brad-fərd\ William 1590–1657 Pilgrim leader

Brad·street \'brad-ˌstrēt\ Anne *ca* 1612–1672 Amer. poet

Bra·dy \'brā-dē\ Mathew B. 1823?–1896 Amer. photographer

Brahe \'brä; 'brä-hē, -hə\ Tycho 1546–1601 Danish astronomer

Brah·ma \'brä-mə\ creator god of the Hindu sacred triad — compare SHIVA; VISHNU

Brahms \'brämz\ Johannes 1833–1897 Ger. composer

Braille \'brāl, 'brī\ Louis 1809–1852 French blind teacher of the blind

Brant \'brant\ Joseph 1742–1807 *Thayendanegea* Mohawk Indian chief

Brant Mary 1736?–1796 *Molly Brant* Mohawk Indian leader; sister of Joseph Brant

Braun \'brau̇n\ Wernher von 1912–1977 Amer. (Ger.⸗born) rocket engineer

Brezh·nev \'brezh-ˌnef\ Leonid Ilich 1906–1982 Soviet leader of the Communist Party (1964–82); pres. of the U.S.S.R. (1960–64; 1977–82)

Bron·të \'brän-tē, -(ˌ)tā\ family of Eng. writers: Charlotte 1816–1855 and her sisters Emily 1818–1848 and Anne 1820–1849

Brooks \'bru̇ks\ Gwendolyn Elizabeth 1917–2000 Amer. poet

Brown \'brau̇n\ John 1800–1859 Amer. abolitionist

Brow·ning \'brau̇-niŋ\ Elizabeth Barrett 1806–1861 Eng. poet

Browning Robert 1812–1889 Eng. poet; husband of the preceding

Bru·tus \'brü-təs\ Marcus Junius 85–42 B.C. Roman politician; one of Julius Caesar's assassins

Bry·an \'brī-ən\ William Jennings 1860–1925 Amer. lawyer and politician

Bu·chan·an \byü-'ka-nən, bə-\ James 1791–1868 15th pres. of the U.S. (1857–61)

Buck \'bək\ Pearl S. 1892–1973 née *Sydenstricker* Amer. author; Nobel Prize winner (1938)

Bud·dha \'bü-də, 'bu̇-\ *ca* 563–*ca* 483 B.C. orig. *Siddhartha Gautama* Indian founder of Buddhism

Buffalo Bill — see W. F. CODY

Bun·yan \'bən-yən\ John 1628–1688 Eng. preacher and author

Bunyan Paul — see PAUL BUNYAN

Bur·bank \'bər-ˌbaŋk\ Luther 1849–1926 Amer. horticulturist

Bur·goyne \(ˌ)bər-'gȯin, 'bər-ˌ\ John 1722–1792 Brit. general in America

Burns \'bərnz\ Robert 1759–1796 Scot. poet

Burn·side \'bərn-ˌsīd\ Ambrose Everett 1824–1881 Amer. general

Burr \'bər\ Aaron 1756–1836 vice pres. of the U.S. (1801–5)

Bush \'bu̇sh\ George (Herbert Walker) 1924– 41st pres. of the U.S. (1989–93)

Bush George W. 1946– *George Walker Bush* 43rd pres. of the U.S. (2001–); son of the preceding

By·ron \'bī-rən\ Lord 1788–1824 *George Gordon Byron*, 6th Baron *Byron* Eng. poet

Cab·ot \'ka-bət\ John *ca* 1450–*ca* 1499 orig. *Giovanni Ca·bo·to* \kä-'bō-tō\ Ital. navigator; explorer for England

Cabot Sebastian 1476?–1557 Eng. navigator; son of J. Cabot

Ca·bri·ni \kə-'brē-nē\ Saint Frances Xavier 1850–1917 *Mother Cabrini* 1st Amer. (Ital.-born) saint (1946)

Cae·sar \\'sē-zər\\ (Gaius) Julius 100?–44 B.C. Roman general, political leader, and writer

Cain \\'kān\\ son of Adam and Eve and brother of Abel in the Bible

Calamity Jane \\kə-'la-mə-tē-\\ 1852?–1903 *Martha Jane Burk* \\'bərk\\ née *Can·nary* \\'ka-nə-rē\\ Amer. frontier figure

Cal·houn \\kal-'hün\\ John Caldwell 1782–1850 vice pres. of the U.S. (1825–32)

Ca·lig·u·la \\kə-'li-gyə-lə\\ 12–41 A.D. Roman emperor (37–41)

Cal·li·ope \\kə-'lī-ə-(ˌ)pē\\ muse of heroic poetry in Greek mythology

Cal·vert \\'kal-vərt\\ George 1580?–1632 Baron *Baltimore* Eng. colonist in America

Cal·vin \\'kal-vən\\ John 1509–1564 *Jean Calvin* or *Cau·vin* \\kō-'vaⁿ\\ French theologian and reformer

Ca·mus \\kä-'mᵫ\\ Albert 1913–1960 French author; Nobel Prize winner (1957)

Ca·nute \\kə-'nüt, -'nyüt\\ *died* 1035 *Canute the Great* Danish king of England (1016–35); of Denmark (1018–35); of Norway (1028–35)

Car·ne·gie \\kär-'ne-gē, 'kär-nə-gē\\ Andrew 1835–1919 Amer. (Scot.-born) industrialist and philanthropist

Car·roll \\'ka-rəl\\ Lewis 1832–1898 pseud. of *Charles Lutwidge Dodgson* Eng. author and mathematician

Car·son \\'kär-sᵊn\\ Kit 1809–1868 *Christopher Carson* Amer. frontiersman and guide

Carson Rachel Louise 1907–1964 Amer. scientist and writer

Car·ter \\'kär-tər\\ Jimmy 1924–   orig. *James Earl Carter, Jr.* 39th pres. of the U.S. (1977–81); Nobel Prize winner (2002)

Car·tier \\kär-'tyā, 'kär-tē-ˌā\\ Jacques 1491–1557 French explorer

Ca·ru·so \\kə-'rü-(ˌ)sō, -(ˌ)zō\\ En·ri·co \\en-'rē-kō\\ 1873–1921 Ital. tenor

Car·ver \\'kär-vər\\ George Washington 1861?–1943 Amer. agricultural chemist and agronomist

Ca·sa·no·va \\ˌka-zə-'nō-və, ˌka-sə-\\ Giovanni Giacomo 1725–1798 Ital. adventurer

Cas·san·dra \\kə-'san-drə, -'sän-\\ daughter of Priam in Greek mythology who is endowed with the gift of prophecy but fated never to be believed

Cas·satt \\kə-'sat\\ Mary 1845–1926 Amer. painter

Cas·tro \\'käs-(ˌ)trō\\ **(Ruz)** \\'rüs\\ Fidel 1926–   Cuban premier (1959–   )

Cath·er \\'ka-thər\\ Willa 1873–1947 Amer. author

Cath·er·ine \\'ka-th(ə-)rən\\ name of 1st, 5th, and 6th wives of Henry VIII of England: Catherine of Aragon 1485–1536; Catherine Howard 1520?–1542; Catherine Parr 1512–1548

Catherine I 1684–1727 wife of Peter the Great; empress of Russia (1725–27)

Catherine II 1729–1796 *Catherine the Great* empress of Russia (1762–96)

Catherine de Mé·di·cis \\-də-ˌmä-dē-'sēs, -'me-də-(ˌ)chē\\ 1519–1589 Ital. *Ca·te·ri·na de' Me·di·ci* \\kä-tā-tā-'rē-nä-dā-'me-dē-(ˌ)chē\\ queen consort of Henry II of France (1547–59) and regent of France (1560–74)

Cav·en·dish \\'ka-vən-(ˌ)dish\\ Henry 1731–1810 Eng. scientist

Ce·ci·lia \\sə-'sēl-yə, -'sil-\\ Saint *fl.* 3d cent. A.D. Christian martyr; patron saint of music

Ce·res \\'sir-(ˌ)ēz\\ goddess of agriculture in Roman mythology — compare DEMETER

Cer·van·tes \\sər-'van-ˌtēz, -'vän-ˌtās\\ Miguel de 1547–1616 Span. author

Cé·zanne \\sā-'zan\\ Paul 1839–1906 French painter

Cha·gall \\shə-'gäl, -'gal\\ Marc 1887–1985 Russ. painter in France

Cham·plain \\ˌsham-'plän, shäⁿ-'plaⁿ\\ Samuel de 1567–1635 French explorer in America

Chap·lin \\'cha-plən\\ Charlie 1889–1977 Sir *Charles Spencer Chaplin* Brit. actor and producer

Chapman \\'chap-mən\\ John — see Johnny APPLESEED

Char·le·magne \\'shär-lə-ˌmān\\ 742–814 A.D. *Charles the Great* or *Charles I* Frankish king (768–814); emperor of the West (800–814)

Charles \\'chärl-(ə)lz\\ name of 10 kings of France: esp. **II** 823–877 A.D. *Charles the Bald* (r. 840–77); Holy Roman emperor (875–77); **IV** 1294–1328 *Charles the Fair* (r. 1322–28); **V** 1337–1380 *Charles the Wise* (r. 1364–80); **VI** 1368–1422 *Charles the Mad* (r. 1380–1422); **VII** 1403–1461 *Charles the Well-Served* or *the Victorious* (r. 1422–61); **IX** 1550–1574 (r. 1560–74); **X** 1757–1836 (r. 1824–30)

Charles name of 2 kings of Great Britain: 1600–1649 (r. 1625–49); 1630–1685 (r. 1660–85); son of Charles I

Charles V 1500–1558 Holy Roman emperor (1519–56); king of Spain as *Charles I* (1516–56)

Charles Edward Stuart — see Charles Edward STUART

Charles Mar·tel \\-mär-'tel\\ *ca* 688–741 A.D. Frankish ruler (719–41); grandfather of Charlemagne

Cha·ryb·dis \\kə-'rib-dəs\\ whirlpool off the coast of Sicily personified in Greek mythology as a female monster

Chau·cer \\'chó-sər\\ Geoffrey *ca* 1342–1400 Eng. poet

Cha·vez \\'chä-ˌväs, -ˌvez\\ Cesar 1927–1993 Amer. labor organizer

Che·khov \\'che-ˌkóf, -ˌkóv\\ Anton Pavlovich 1860–1904 Russ. author

Che·ney \\'chē-nē, *commonly* 'chā-\\ Richard Bruce 1941–   vice pres. of the U.S. (2001–   )

Cheops — see KHUFU

Ches·ter·ton \\'ches-tər-tən\\ G. K. 1874–1936 *Gilbert Keith Chesterton* Eng. author

Cho·pin \\'shō-ˌpan, -ˌpaⁿ\\ Frédéric François 1810–1849 Polish composer

Chou En–lai or **Zhou Enlai** \\'jō-'en-'lī\\ 1898–1976 Chinese Communist politician; premier (1949–76)

Chré·tien \\krā-'tyaⁿ\\ Jean 1934–   Canad. prime minister (1993–2003)

Chris·tie \\'kris-tē\\ Dame Agatha 1890–1976 née *Miller* Eng. author

Chur·chill \\'chər-ˌchil, 'chərch-ˌhil\\ Sir Winston Leonard Spencer 1874–1965 Brit. prime minister (1940–45; 1951–55) Nobel Prize winner (1953)

Clark \\'klärk\\ George Rogers 1752–1818 Amer. soldier and frontiersman

Clark William 1770–1838 Amer. explorer (with Meriwether Lewis)

Clay \\'klā\\ Henry 1777–1852 Amer. politician and orator

Clem·ens \\'kle-mənz\\ Samuel Langhorne — see Mark TWAIN

Cle·o·pa·tra \\ˌklē-ə-'pa-trə, -'pä-\\ 69–30 B.C. queen of Egypt (51–30)

Cleve·land \\'klēv-lənd\\ (Stephen) Grover 1837–1908 22nd and 24th pres. of the U.S. (1885–89; 1893–97)

Clin·ton \\'klin-tᵊn\\ William Jefferson 1946–   *Bill Clinton* 42nd pres. of the U.S. (1993–2001)

Cly·tem·nes·tra \\ˌklī-təm-'nes-trə\\ wife of Agamemnon in Greek mythology

Cobb \\'käb\\ Ty 1886–1961 *Tyrus Raymond Cobb* Amer. baseball player

Co·chise \\kō-'chēs\\ 1812?–1874 Apache Indian chief

Co·dy \\'kō-dē\\ William Frederick 1846–1917 *Buffalo Bill* Amer. hunter, guide, and showman

Co·han \\'kō-ˌhan\\ George Michael 1878–1942 Amer. composer

Cole·ridge \\'kōl-rij, 'kō-lə-rij\\ Samuel Taylor 1772–1834 Eng. poet

Co·lette \\kò-'let\\ 1873–1954 orig. *Sidonie-Gabrielle Colette* French author

Co·lum·bus \\kə-'ləm-bəs\\ Christopher 1451–1506 Ital. navigator and explorer for Spain

Con·fu·cius \\kən-'fyü-shəs\\ 551–479 B.C. Chinese philosopher

Con·rad \\'kän-ˌrad\\ Joseph 1857–1924 Brit. (Polish-born) author

Con·sta·ble \\'kən(t)-stə-bəl, 'kän(t)-\\ John 1776–1837 Eng. painter

Con·stan·tine I \\'kän(t)-stən-ˌtēn, -ˌtīn\\ *after* 280–337 A.D. *Constantine the Great* Roman emperor (306–37)

Cook \\'kúk\\ Captain James 1728–1779 Eng. navigator

Coo·lidge \\'kü-lij\\ (John) Calvin 1872–1933 30th pres. of the U.S. (1923–29)

Coo·per \\'kü-pər, 'kú-\\ James Fenimore 1789–1851 Amer. author

Co·per·ni·cus \\kō-'pər-ni-kəs\\ Nicolaus 1473–1543 Polish astronomer

Cop·land \\'kō-plənd\\ Aaron 1900–1990 Amer. composer

Cop·ley \\'kä-plē\\ John Singleton 1738–1815 Amer. painter

Corn·plan·ter \\'kòrn-ˌplan-tər\\ *ca* 1732–1836 *John O'Bail* Seneca Indian leader of partly European ancestry

Corn·wal·lis \\kòrn-'wä-ləs\\ Charles 1738–1805 1st Marquess *Cornwallis* Brit. general in America

Co·ro·na·do \\ˌkòr-ə-'nä-(ˌ)dō, ˌkär-\\ Francisco Vásquez de *ca* 1510–1554 Span. explorer of southwestern U.S.

Cor·tés \\kòr-'tez, 'kòr-ˌ\\ Hernán *or* Hernando 1485–1547 Span. conqueror of Mexico

Cous·teau \\kü-'stō\\ Jacques-Yves 1910–1997 French marine explorer

Crane \\'krān\\ Stephen 1871–1900 Amer. author

Crazy Horse \\'krā-zē-ˌhòrs\\ 1842?–1877 *Ta-sunko-witko* Sioux Indian chief

Crock·ett \\'krä-kət\\ *Davy* 1786–1836 *David Crockett* Amer. frontiersman

Crom·well \\'kräm-ˌwel, 'kròm-, -wəl\\ Oliver 1599–1658 Eng. general; lord protector of England (1653–58)

Cro·nus \\'krō-nəs, 'krä-\\ Titan in Greek mythology overthrown by his son Zeus

Cum·mings \\'kə-miŋz\\ Edward Estlin 1894–1962 known as *e. e. cummings* Amer. poet

Cu·pid \\'kyü-pəd\\ god of love in Roman mythology — compare EROS

Cu·rie \\kyü-'rē, 'kyur-(ˌ)ē\\ Marie 1867–1934 née *Sklo-dow-ska* \\sklə-'dòf-skə\\ French (Polish-born) chemist; Nobel Prize winner (1903, 1911)

Curie Pierre 1859–1906 French chemist; husband of M. Curie; Nobel Prize winner (1903)

Cus·ter \\'kəs-tər\\ George Armstrong 1839–1876 Amer. general

Cy·ra·no de Ber·ge·rac \\'sir-ə-ˌnō-də-'ber-zhə-ˌrak\\ Savinien 1619–1655 French playwright

Cy·rus II \\'sī-rəs\\ *ca* 585–*ca* 529 B.C. *Cyrus the Great* king of Persia (*ca* 550–529)

Dae·da·lus \\'de-də-ləs, 'dē-\\ builder in Greek mythology of the Cretan labyrinth and inventor of wings by which he and his son Icarus escape imprisonment

Dahl \\'däl\\ Roald 1916–1990 Brit. writer

Da·lí \\'dä-lē, *by himself* dä-'lē\\ Salvador 1904–1989 Span. painter

Dal·ton \\'dòl-tᵊn\\ John 1766–1844 Eng. chemist and physicist

Da·na \\'dä-nə\\ Richard Henry 1815–1882 Amer. author

Dan·iel \\'dan-yəl\\ prophet in the Bible who is held captive in Babylon and delivered from a den of lions

Dan·te \\'dän-(ˌ)tā, 'dan-, -(ˌ)tē\\ 1265–1321 *Dante Ali·ghie·ri* \\ˌa-lə-'gyer-ē\\ Ital. poet

Dare \\'der\\ Virginia 1587–? 1st child born in America of Eng. parents

Da·ri·us I \\də-'rī-əs\\ 550–486 B.C. *Darius the Great* king of Persia (522–486)

Dar·row \\'da-(ˌ)rō\\ Clarence Seward 1857–1938 Amer. lawyer

Dar·win \\'där-wən\\ Charles Robert 1809–1882 Eng. naturalist

Da·vid \\'dā-vəd\\ a youth in the Bible who slays Goliath and succeeds Saul as king of Israel

Da·vis \\'dā-vəs\\ Jefferson 1808–1889 pres. of the Confederate States of America (1861–65)

Dawes \\'dòz\\ William 1745–1799 Amer. patriot

Debs \\'debz\\ Eugene Victor 1855–1926 Amer. socialist and labor organizer

De·bus·sy \\ˌde-byü-'sē, ˌdā-\\ Claude 1862–1918 French composer

De·ca·tur \\di-'kā-tər\\ Stephen 1779–1820 Amer. naval officer

De·foe \\di-'fō\\ Daniel 1660–1731 Eng. author

De·gas \\də-'gä\\ Edgar 1834–1917 French painter

de Gaulle \\di-'gōl, -'gòl\\ Charles 1890–1970 French general; pres. of Fifth Republic (1958–69)

De·li·lah \\di-'lī-lə\\ mistress and betrayer of Samson in the Bible

De·me·ter \\di-'mē-tər\\ goddess of agriculture in Greek mythology — compare CERES

de Mille \\də-'mil\\ Agnes 1905–1993 Amer. dancer and choreographer

De·mos·the·nes \\di-'mäs-thə-ˌnēz\\ 384–322 B.C. Athenian orator and statesman

Demp·sey \\'dem(p)-sē\\ Jack 1895–1983 orig. *William Harrison Dempsey* Amer. boxer

Des·cartes \\dā-'kärt\\ René 1596–1650 French mathematician and philosopher

de So·to \\thə-'sō-(ˌ)tō, di-\\ Hernando *ca* 1496–1542 Span. explorer

Dew·ey \\'dü-ē, 'dyü-\\ George 1837–1917 Amer. admiral

Dewey John 1859–1952 Amer. philosopher and educator

Dewey Melvil 1851–1931 Amer. librarian

Di·ana \\dī-'a-nə\\ ancient Ital. goddess of the forest and of childbirth who was identified with Artemis by the Romans

Dick·ens \\'di-kənz\\ Charles 1812–1870 pseud. *Boz* \\'bäz, 'bòz\\ Eng. author

Dick·in·son \\'di-kən-sən\\ Emily Elizabeth 1830–1886 Amer. poet

Di·do \\'dī-(ˌ)dō\\ legendary queen of Carthage who falls in love with Aeneas and kills herself when he leaves her

Di·Mag·gio \\də-'mä-zhē-(ˌ)ō, -'ma-jē-(ˌ)ō\\ Joe 1914–1999 *Joseph Paul DiMaggio* Amer. baseball player

Di·o·ny·sus \\ˌdī-ə-'nī-səs, -'nē-\\ god of wine and ecstasy in classical mythology

Dis·ney \\'diz-nē\\ Walt 1901–1966 *Walter Elias Disney* Amer. film producer and cartoonist

Dis·rae·li \\diz-'rā-lē\\ Benjamin 1804–1881 Earl of *Beaconsfield* Brit. prime minister (1868; 1874–80)

Dix \\'diks\\ Dorothea Lynde 1802–1887 Amer. social reformer

Dodg·son \\'däd-sən, 'däj-\\ Charles Lutwidge — see Lewis CARROLL

Donne \\'dən\\ John 1572–1631 Eng. poet and clergyman

Don Qui·xote \\ˌdän-kē-'(h)ō-tē, ˌdän-\\ hero of Cervantes' *Don Quixote*

Dos·to·yev·sky \\ˌdäs-tə-'yef-skē, -'yev-\\ Fyodor Mikhaylovich 1821–1881 Russ. novelist

Doug·las \\'də-gləs\\ Stephen Arnold 1813–1861 Amer. politician

Doug·lass \\'də-gləs\\ Frederick 1817–1895 Amer. abolitionist

Doyle \\'dòi(-ə)l\\ Sir Arthur Conan 1859–1930 Brit. physician and author

Drake \\'drāk\\ Sir Francis *ca* 1540–1596 Brit. navigator, explorer, and admiral

Drei·ser \\'drī-sər, -zər\\ Theodore 1871–1945 Amer. author

DuBois \\dü-'bóis, dyü-\\ William Edward Burghardt 1868–1963 Amer. educator and writer

Du·mas \\dü-'mä, dyü-\\ Alexandre 1802–1870 *Dumas père* \\'per\\ French author

Dumas Alexandre 1824–1895 *Dumas fils* \\'fēs\\ French author

Dun·can \\'dəŋ-kən\\ Isadora 1877–1927 Amer. dancer

Dü·rer \\'dùr-ər, 'dyùr-, 'duer-\\ Albrecht 1471–1528 Ger. painter and engraver

Ea·kins \\'ā-kənz\\ Thomas 1844–1916 Amer. artist

Ear·hart \\'er-ˌhärt, 'ir-\\ Amelia 1897–1937 Amer. aviator

Earp \\'ərp\\ Wyatt 1848–1929 Amer. frontiersman and lawman

Ed·dy \\'e-dē\\ Mary Baker 1821–1910 Amer. founder of Christian Science

Ed·i·son \\'e-də-sən\\ Thomas Alva 1847–1931 Amer. inventor

Ed·ward \\'ed-wərd\\ name of 8 post-Norman kings of England: **I** 1239–1307 *Edward Longshanks* (r. 1272–1307); **II** 1284–1327 (r. 1307–27); **III** 1312–1377 (r. 1327–77); **IV** 1442–1483 (r. 1461–70; 1471–83); **V** 1470–1483 (r. 1483); **VI** 1537–1553 (r. 1547–53); son of Henry VIII and Jane Seymour; **VII** 1841–1910 (r. 1901–10); son of Queen Victoria; **VIII** 1894–1972 (r. 1936; abdicated) *Duke of Windsor*; son of George V

Ein·stein \\'īn-ˌstīn\\ Albert 1879–1955 Amer. (Ger.-born) physicist; Nobel Prize winner (1921)

Ei·sen·how·er \\'ī-zᵊn-ˌhaù(-ə)r\\ Dwight David 1890–1969 Amer. general; 34th pres. of the U.S. (1953–61)

Elec·tra \\i-'lek-trə\\ sister of Orestes in Greek mythology who aids him in avenging their father's murder

Eli·jah \\i-'lī-jə\\ Hebrew prophet of the 9th cent. B.C.

El·i·on \\'e-lē-ən\\ Gertrude Belle 1918–1999 Amer. pharmacologist; Nobel Prize winner (1988)

El·iot \\'e-lē-ət, 'el-yət\\ George 1819–1880 pseud. of *Mary Ann Evans* Eng. author

Eliot T. S. 1888–1965 *Thomas Stearns Eliot* Brit. (Amer.-born) poet; Nobel Prize winner (1948)

Eliz·a·beth I \i-'li-zə-bəth\ 1533–1603 queen of England (1558–1603); daughter of Henry VIII and Anne Boleyn

Elizabeth II 1926– queen of the United Kingdom (1952–); daughter of George VI

El·ling·ton \'e-liŋ-tən\ Duke 1899–1974 *Edward Kennedy Ellington* Amer. bandleader and composer

Em·er·son \'e-mər-sən\ Ralph Waldo 1803–1882 Amer. essayist and poet

En·dym·i·on \en-'di-mē-ən\ beautiful youth in Greek mythology loved by the goddess of the moon

Eos \'ē-,äs\ goddess of the dawn in Greek mythology — compare AURORA

Ep·i·cu·rus \,e-pi-'kyùr-əs\ 341–270 B.C. Greek philosopher

Er·ik the Red \'er-ik\ *fl.* 10th cent. orig. *Erik Thorvaldson* Norwegian explorer; father of Leif Eriksson

Eriksson Leif — see LEIF ERIKSSON

Eros \'er-,äs, 'ir-\ god of love in Greek mythology — compare CUPID

Esau \'ē-(,)sò\ son of Isaac and Rebekah and elder twin brother of Jacob in the Bible

Es·ther \'es-tər\ Hebrew woman in the Bible who as the queen of Persia delivers her people from destruction

Eu·clid \'yü-kləd\ *fl. ca* 300 B.C. Greek mathematician

Eu·rip·i·des \yù-'ri-pə-,dēz\ *ca* 484–406 B.C. Greek playwright

Eu·ro·pa \yù-'rō-pə\ princess in Greek mythology who was carried off by Zeus disguised as a white bull

Eu·ryd·i·ce \yù-'ri-də-(,)sē\ wife of Orpheus in Greek mythology

Eve \'ēv\ the 1st woman in biblical tradition; wife of Adam

Eze·kiel \i-'zē-kyəl, -kē-əl\ Hebrew prophet of the 6th cent. B.C.

Fahr·en·heit \'fa-rən-,hīt, 'fär-ən-\ Daniel Gabriel 1686–1736 Ger. physicist

Far·a·day \'fa-rə-,dā, -dē\ Michael 1791–1867 Eng. chemist and physicist

Far·ra·gut \'fa-rə-gət\ David Glasgow 1801–1870 Amer. admiral

Faulk·ner \'fòk-nər\ William 1897–1962 Amer. author; Nobel Prize winner (1949)

Faust \'faùst\ *or* **Fau·stus** \'faù-stəs, 'fò-\ magician in Ger. legend who sells his soul to the devil for knowledge and power

Fawkes \'fòks\ Guy 1570–1606 Eng. conspirator

Fer·di·nand \'fər-də-,nand\ V of Castile *or* II of Aragon 1452–1516 *Ferdinand the Catholic* king of Castile (1474–1504), of Aragon (1479–1516), of Naples (1504–16); husband of Isabella I

Fer·mi \'fer-(,)mē\ Enrico 1901–1954 Amer. (Ital.-born) physicist; Nobel Prize winner (1938)

Fiel·ding \'fēl-diŋ\ Henry 1707–1754 Eng. author

Fill·more \'fil-,mòr\ Millard 1800–1874 13th pres. of the U.S. (1850–53)

Fitz·ger·ald \fits-'jer-əld\ Ella 1917–1996 Amer. singer

Fitzgerald F. Scott 1896–1940 *Francis Scott Key Fitzgerald* Amer. author

Flem·ing \'fle-miŋ\ Sir Alexander 1881–1955 Brit. bacteriologist; Nobel Prize winner (1945)

Flo·ra \'flòr-ə\ goddess of flowers in Roman mythology

Flying Dutchman legendary Dutch mariner condemned to sail the seas until Judgment Day

Ford \'fòrd\ Gerald Rudolph 1913–2007 38th pres. of the U.S. (1974–77)

Ford Henry 1863–1947 Amer. automobile manufacturer

Fos·sey \'fò-sē, 'fä-\ Dian 1932–1985 Amer. zoologist

Fos·ter \'fòs-tər, 'fäs-\ Stephen Collins 1826–1864 Amer. songwriter

Fran·cis of As·si·si \'fran(t)-səs-əv-ə-'si-sē, -'sē-\ Saint 1181/1182–1226 Ital. friar; founder of Franciscan order

Fran·co \'fräŋ-(,)kō, 'fraŋ-\ Francisco 1892–1975 Span. general, dictator, and head of Span. state (1936–75)

Frank \'fraŋk, 'fräŋk\ Anne 1929–1945 Ger.-born diarist during the Holocaust

Frank·lin \'fraŋ-klən\ Benjamin 1706–1790 Amer. patriot, author, and inventor

Fred·er·ick I \'fre-d(ə-)rik\ *ca* 1123–1190 *Frederick Barbarossa* Holy Roman emperor (1152–90)

Frederick II 1712–1786 *Frederick the Great* king of Prussia (1740–86)

Fré·mont \'frē-,mänt\ John Charles 1813–1890 Amer. general and explorer

French \'french\ Daniel Chester 1850–1931 Amer. sculptor

Freud \'fròid\ Sigmund 1856–1939 Austrian neurologist; founder of psychoanalysis

Frig·ga \'fri-gə\ wife of Odin and goddess of married love and the hearth in Norse mythology

Frost \'fròst\ Robert Lee 1874–1963 Amer. poet

Ful·ler \'fù-lər\ (Richard) Buckminster 1895–1983 Amer. engineer and architect

Fuller (Sarah) Margaret 1810–1850 Amer. author and reformer

Ful·ton \'fùl-tᵊn\ Robert 1765–1815 Amer. inventor

Ga·bri·el \'gā-brē-əl\ archangel named in Hebrew tradition — compare MICHAEL; RAPHAEL; URIEL

Ga·ga·rin \gə-'gär-ən\ Yury Alekseyevich 1934–1968 Russ. astronaut; 1st man in space (1961)

Gage \'gāj\ Thomas 1721–1787 Brit. general in America

Gal·a·had \'ga-lə-,had\ knight of the Round Table in medieval legend who finds the Holy Grail

Gal·a·tea \,ga-lə-'tē-ə\ female figure sculpted by Pygmalion in Greek mythology and given life by Aphrodite in answer to the sculptor's prayer

Ga·len \'gā-lən\ 129–*ca* 216 A.D. Greek physician and writer

Ga·li·leo \,ga-lə-'lē-(,)ō, -'lā-\ 1564–1642 *Galileo Galilei* Ital. astronomer and physicist

Gall \'gòl\ 1840?–1894 Sioux Indian leader

Ga·ma \'ga-mə, 'gä-\ Vasco da *ca* 1460–1524 Portuguese navigator and explorer

Gan·dhi \'gän-dē, 'gan-\ Indira 1917–1984 Indian prime minister (1966–77; 1980–84); daughter of Jawaharlal Nehru

Gandhi Mohandas Karamchand 1869–1948 *Ma·hat·ma* \mə-'hät-mə, -'hat-\ Indian leader

Gar·cía Már·quez \gär-'sē-ə-'mär-,kās\ Gabriel 1928– Colombian author

Gar·field \'gär-,fēld\ James Abram 1831–1881 20th pres. of the U.S. (1881)

Gar·i·bal·di \,ga-rə-'bòl-dē\ Giuseppe 1807–1882 Ital. patriot

Gar·ri·son \'ga-rə-sən\ William Lloyd 1805–1879 Amer. abolitionist

Gates \'gāts\ Bill 1955– *William Henry Gates III* Amer. computer software manufacturer

Gau·guin \gō-'gaⁿ\ Paul 1848–1903 French painter

Geh·rig \'ger-ig\ Lou 1903–1941 *Henry Louis Gehrig* Amer. baseball player

Gei·sel \'gī-zəl\ Theodor Seuss 1904–1991 pseud. *Dr. Seuss* Amer. author and illustrator

Gen·ghis Khan \,jeŋ-gəs-'kän, ,geŋ-\ *ca* 1162–1227 Mongol conqueror

George \'jòrj\ name of 6 kings of Great Britain: **I** 1660–1727 (r. 1714–27); **II** 1683–1760 (r. 1727–60); **III** 1738–1820 (r. 1760–1820); **IV** 1762–1830 (r. 1820–30); **V** 1865–1936 (r. 1910–36); **VI** 1895–1952 (r. 1936–52); father of Elizabeth II

Ge·ron·i·mo \jə-'rä-nə-,mō\ 1829–1909 Apache Indian leader

Gersh·win \'gər-shwən\ George 1898–1937 Amer. composer

Gil·bert \'gil-bərt\ Sir William Schwenck 1836–1911 Eng. librettist and poet; collaborator with Sir Arthur Sullivan

Gins·burg \'ginz-,bərg\ Ruth Bader 1933– Amer. jurist

Glad·stone \'glad-,stōn, *chiefly Brit* -stən\ William Ewart 1809–1898 Brit. prime minister (1868–74; 1880–85; 1886; 1892–94)

Glenn \'glen\ John Herschel 1921– Amer. astronaut and politician; 1st Amer. to orbit the earth (1962)

Go·di·va \gə-'dī-və\ an Eng. gentlewoman who in legend rode naked through Coventry to save citizens from a tax

Goe·thals \'gō-thəlz\ George Washington 1858–1928 Amer. engineer who directed the building of the Panama Canal

Goe·the \'gə(r)-tə, 'gœ-tə\ Johann Wolfgang von 1749–1832 Ger. author

Gogh, van \van-'gō, -'gäk\ Vincent Willem 1853–1890 Dutch painter

Gol·ding \'gōl-diŋ\ William Gerald 1911–1993 Eng. author; Nobel Prize winner (1983)

Go·li·ath \gə-'lī-əth\ Philistine giant who is killed by David in the Bible

Gom·pers \'gäm-pərz\ Samuel 1850–1924 Amer. (Brit.‑born) labor leader

Goo·dall \'gu̇-(ˌ)dȯl, -(ˌ)däl\ Jane 1934– Brit. zoologist

Good·year \'gu̇d-ˌyir\ Charles 1800–1860 Amer. inventor

Gor·ba·chev \ˌgȯr-bə-'chȯf, -'chef\ Mikhail Sergeyevich 1931– Soviet leader of Communist party (1985–91); pres. of U.S.S.R. (1990–91); Nobel Prize winner (1990)

Gore \'gȯr\ Albert, Jr. 1948– vice pres. of the U.S. (1993–2001); Nobel Prize winner (2007)

Gor·gas \'gȯr-gəs\ William Crawford 1854–1920 Amer. army surgeon

Gra·ham \'grā-əm, 'gra(-ə)m\ Martha 1893–1991 Amer. dancer and choreographer

Grant \'grant\ Ulysses S. 1822–1885 orig. *Hiram Ulysses Grant* Amer. general; 18th pres. of the U.S. (1869–77)

Gre·co, El \el-'gre-(ˌ)kō\ 1541–1614 *Doménikos Theotokópoulos* Span. (Cretan-born) painter

Gree·ley \'grē-lē\ Horace 1811–1872 Amer. journalist and politician

Greene \'grēn\ (Henry) Graham 1904–1991 Brit. author

Greene Nathanael 1742–1786 Amer. Revolutionary general

Greg·o·ry \'gre-g(ə-)rē\ name of 16 popes: esp. Saint *ca* 540–604 A.D. *Gregory the Great* (pope 590–604); Saint *ca* 1020–1085 (pope 1073–85); 1502–1585 (pope 1572–85)

Grey \'grā\ Lady Jane 1537–1554 queen of England for 9 days (1553)

Grey Zane 1872–1939 Amer. author

Grieg \'grēg\ Edward Hagerup 1843–1907 Norwegian composer

Grimm \'grim\ Jacob 1785–1863 and his brother Wilhelm 1786–1859 Ger. philologists and folklorists

Guin·e·vere \'gwi-nə-ˌvir\ legendary wife of King Arthur and lover of Lancelot

Gu·ten·berg \'gü-tⁿn-ˌbərg\ Johannes *ca* 1400–1468 Ger. inventor of printing method from movable type

Ha·des \'hā-(ˌ)dēz\ — see PLUTO

Ha·dri·an \'hā-drē-ən\ 76–138 A.D. Roman emperor (117–138)

Ha·gar \'hā-ˌgär, -gər\ mistress of Abraham and mother of Ishmael in the Bible

Hai·le Se·las·sie \ˌhī-lē-sə-'la-sē, -'lä-\ 1892–1975 emperor of Ethiopia (1930–36; 1941–74)

Hale Nathan 1755–1776 Amer. Revolutionary hero

Hal·ley \'ha-lē\ Edmond *or* Edmund 1656–1742 Eng. astronomer and mathematician

Hal·sey \'hȯl-sē, -zē\ William Frederick 1882–1959 Amer. admiral

Ham·il·ton \'ha-məl-tən\ Alexander 1755–1804 Amer. political leader

Ham·mu·ra·bi \ˌha-mə-'rä-bē\ *died ca* 1750 B.C. king of Babylon (*ca* 1792–50)

Han·cock \'han-ˌkäk\ John 1737–1793 Amer. Revolutionary patriot

Han·del \'han-dⁿl\ George Frideric 1685–1759 Brit. (Ger.‑born) composer

Han·dy \'han-dē\ W. C. 1873–1958 *William Christopher Handy* Amer. blues musician and composer

Han·ni·bal \'ha-nə-bəl\ 247–183? B.C. Carthaginian general

Har·ding \'här-diŋ\ Warren Gamaliel 1865–1923 29th pres. of the U.S. (1921–23)

Har·dy \'här-dē\ Thomas 1840–1928 Eng. author

Har·per \'här-pər\ Stephen 1959– prime min. of Canada (2006–)

Har·ri·son \'ha-rə-sən\ Benjamin 1833–1901 23rd pres. of the U.S. (1889–93); grandson of W. H. Harrison

Harrison William Henry 1773–1841 Amer. general; 9th pres. of the U.S. (1841)

Harte \'härt\ Bret 1836–1902 orig. *Francis Brett Harte* Amer. author

Har·vey \'här-vē\ William 1578–1657 Eng. physician and anatomist

Haw·thorne \'hȯ-ˌthȯrn\ Nathaniel 1804–1864 Amer. author

Haydn \'hī-dⁿn\ Franz Joseph 1732–1809 Austrian composer

Hayes \'hāz\ Rutherford Birchard 1822–1893 19th pres. of the U.S. (1877–81)

Hearst \'hərst\ William Randolph 1863–1951 Amer. newspaper publisher

Hec·tor \'hek-tər\ son of Priam and Hecuba; Trojan hero slain by Achilles in Greek mythology

Hec·u·ba \'he-kyə-bə\ wife of Priam in Greek mythology

Hel·en of Troy \ˌhe-lən-əv-'trȯi\ wife of Menelaus whose abduction by Paris in Greek mythology causes the Trojan War

He·li·os \'hē-lē-əs, -(ˌ)ōs\ god of the sun in Greek mythology — compare SOL

Hem·ing·way \'he-miŋ-ˌwā\ Ernest Miller 1899–1961 Amer. author; Nobel Prize winner (1954)

Hen·ry \'hen-rē\ name of 8 kings of England: **I** 1068–1135 (r. 1100–35); **II** 1133–1189 (r. 1154–89); **III** 1207–1272 (r. 1216–72); **IV** 1366–1413 (r. 1399–1413); **V** 1387–1422 (r. 1413–22); **VI** 1421–1471 (r. 1422–61; 1470–71); **VII** 1457–1509 (r. 1485–1509); **VIII** 1491–1547 (r. 1509–47)

Henry name of 4 kings of France: **I** *ca* 1008–1060 (r. 1031–60); **II** 1519–1559 (r. 1547–59); **III** 1551–1589 (r. 1574–89); **IV** 1553–1610 *Henry of Navarre* (r. 1589–1610)

Henry O. 1862–1910 pseud. of *William Sydney Porter* Amer. author

Henry Patrick 1736–1799 Amer. patriot and orator

Hen·son \'hen(t)-sən\ Matthew Alexander 1866–1955 Amer. arctic explorer

He·phaes·tus \hi-'fes-təs, -'fēs-\ god of fire and of metalworking in Greek mythology — compare VULCAN

He·ra \'hir-ə, 'he-rə, 'her-ə\ sister and wife of Zeus and goddess of women and marriage in Greek mythology — compare JUNO

Her·cu·les \'hər-kyə-ˌlēz\ *or* **Her·a·cles** \'her-ə-ˌklēz-, 'he-rə-\ hero in Greek mythology noted for his strength

Her·maph·ro·di·tus \(ˌ)hər-ˌma-frə-'dī-təs\ son of Hermes and Aphrodite who in Greek mythology is joined with a nymph into one body

Her·mes \'hər-(ˌ)mēz\ god of commerce, eloquence, invention, travel, and theft who serves as herald and messenger of the other gods in Greek mythology — compare MERCURY

Her·od \'her-əd\ 73–4 B.C. *Herod the Great* Roman king of Judea (37–4)

Herod An·ti·pas \'an-tə-pəs, -ˌpas\ 21 B.C.–39 A.D., Roman governor of Galilee (4 B.C., –39 A.D.); son of Herod the Great

Hes·se \'he-sə\ Hermann 1877–1962 Ger. author; Nobel Prize winner (1946)

Hey·er·dahl \'hā-ər-ˌdäl\ Thor 1914–2002 Norwegian explorer and author

Hi·a·wa·tha \ˌhī-ə-'wȯ-thə, ˌhē-ə-, -'wä-\ legendary Iroquois Indian chief

Hick·ok \'hi-ˌkäk\ Wild Bill 1837–1876 orig. *James Butler Hickok* Amer. frontiersman and U.S. marshal

Hi·dal·go \ē-'thäl-gō\ Miguel 1753–1811 Mexican independence leader

Hil·ton \'hil-tⁿn\ James 1900–1954 Eng. novelist

Hip·poc·ra·tes \hi-'pä-krə-ˌtēz\ *ca* 460–*ca* 377 B.C. Greek physician

Hi·ro·hi·to \ˌhir-ō-'hē-(ˌ)tō\ 1901–1989 emperor of Japan (1926–89)

Hit·ler \'hit-lər\ Adolf 1889–1945 Ger. (Austrian-born) chancellor and dictator (1933–45)

Hodg·kin \'häj-kin\ Dorothy Mary 1910–1994 née *Crowfoot* Brit. physicist; Nobel Prize winner (1964)

Holmes \'hōmz, 'hōlmz\ Oliver Wendell 1809–1894 Amer. physician and author

Holmes Oliver Wendell, Jr. 1841–1935 Amer. jurist; son of the preceding

Ho·mer \'hō-mər\ *fl.* 9th *or* 8th cent. B.C. Greek epic poet

Homer Winslow 1836–1910 Amer. painter

Hooke \'hu̇k\ Robert 1635–1703 Eng. scientist

Hoo·ver \'hü-vər\ Herbert Clark 1874–1964 31st pres. of the U.S. (1929–33)

Hoover John Edgar 1895–1972 Amer. director of the Federal Bureau of Investigation (1924–72)

Hop·per \'hä-pər\ Grace 1906–1992 née *Murray* Amer. admiral, mathematician, and computer scientist

Hou·di·ni \hü-'dē-nē\ Harry 1874–1926 orig. *Erik Weisz* Amer. magician

Hous·ton \'hyü-stən, 'yü-\ Sam 1793–1863 *Samuel Houston* Amer. politician; pres. of the Republic of Texas (1836–38; 1841–44)

Howe \'haù\ Elias 1819–1867 Amer. inventor
Howe Julia 1819–1910 née *Ward* Amer. suffragist and reformer
Hud·son \'həd-sən\ Henry *ca* 1565–1611 Eng. explorer
Hughes \'hyüz\ (James) Langston 1902–1967 Amer. author
Hugo \'hyü-(ˌ)gō, 'yü-\ Victor 1802–1885 French author
Hus·sein I \hü-'sān\ 1935–1999 king of Jordan (1952–99)
Hus·sein Saddam 1937–2006 pres. of Iraq (1979–2003)
Hutch·in·son \'hə-chə(n)-sən\ Anne 1591–1643 née *Marbury* Eng. colonist and religious leader in America
Hutchinson Thomas 1711–1780 Amer. colonial administrator
Ib·sen \'ib-sən, 'ip-\ Henrik 1828–1906 Norwegian playwright
Ic·a·rus \'i-kə-rəs\ son of Daedalus who in Greek mythology falls into the sea when the wax of his artificial wings melts as he flies too near the sun
Ig·na·tius \ig-'nā-sh(ē-)əs\ Saint 1491–1556 *Ignatius of Loyola* Span. priest; founder of Society of Jesus (Jesuits)
In·no·cent \'i-nə-sənt\ name of 13 popes: esp. **II** *died* 1143 (pope 1130–43); **III** 1160/61–1216 (pope 1198–1216); **IV** *died* 1254 (pope 1243–54); **XI** 1611–1689 (pope 1676–89)
Ir·ving \'ər-viŋ\ Washington 1783–1859 Amer. author
Isaac \'ī-zik, -zək\ son of Abraham and father of Jacob in the Bible
Is·a·bel·la I \ˌi-zə-'be-lə\ 1451–1504 queen of Castile (1474–1504) and of Aragon (1479–1504); wife of Ferdinand V
Isa·iah \ī-'zā-ə, *chiefly Brit* -'zī-\ Hebrew prophet of the 8th cent. B.C.
Ish·ma·el \'ish-(ˌ)mā-əl, -mē-\ outcast son of Abraham and Hagar in the Bible
Ives \'īvz\ Charles Edward 1874–1954 Amer. composer
Jack·son \'jak-sən\ Andrew 1767–1845 Amer. general; 7th pres. of the U.S. (1829–37)
Jackson Thomas Jonathan 1824–1863 *Stonewall Jackson* Amer. Confederate general
Ja·cob \'jā-kəb\ son of Isaac and Rebekah and younger twin brother of Esau in the Bible
James \'jāmz\ one of the 12 apostles in the Bible
James *the Less* one of the 12 apostles in the Bible
James name of 2 kings of Great Britain: **I** 1566–1625 (r. 1603–25); king of Scotland as *James VI* (r. 1567–1625); **II** 1633–1701 (r. 1685–88)
James Henry 1843–1916 Brit. (Amer.-born) author
Ja·nus \'jā-nəs\ god of gates and doors and of all beginnings in Roman mythology and that is pictured with two opposite faces
Ja·son \'jā-sⁿn\ hero in Greek mythology noted for his successful quest of the Golden Fleece
Jay \'jā\ John 1745–1829 Amer. jurist and statesman; 1st chief justice of the U.S. Supreme Court (1789–95)
Jef·fer·son \'je-fər-sən\ Thomas 1743–1826 3d pres. of the U.S. (1801–09)
Jer·e·mi·ah \ˌjer-ə-'mī-ə\ Hebrew prophet of the 7th–6th cent. B.C.
Je·sus \'jē-zəs, -zəz\ *or* **Jesus Christ** *ca* 6 B.C.–*ca* 30 A.D. source of the Christian religion and Savior in the Christian faith
Jez·e·bel \'je-zə-ˌbel\ queen of Israel and wife of Ahab who is noted for her wickedness in the Bible
Joan of Arc \ˌjōn-əv-'ärk\ Saint *ca* 1412–1431 *the Maid of Orléans* French national heroine
Job \'jōb\ man in the Bible who has many sufferings but keeps his faith
John \'jän\ one of the 12 apostles believed to be the author of the 4th Gospel, three Epistles, and the Book of Revelation
John name of 21 popes: esp. **XXIII** 1881–1963 (pope 1958–63)
John 1167–1216 *John Lackland* king of England (1199–1216)
John Paul \'pól\ name of 2 popes: esp. **II** (1920–2005) (pope 1978–2005)
John·son \'jän(t)-sən\ Andrew 1808–1875 17th pres. of the U.S. (1865–69)
Johnson Lyndon Baines 1908–1973 36th pres. of the U.S. (1963–69)
Johnson Samuel 1709–1784 *Dr. Johnson* Eng. lexicographer and author

John the Baptist Saint, 1st cent. A.D. prophet and baptizer of Jesus in the Bible
Jol·liet *or* **Jo·liet** \zhòl-'yä\ Louis 1645–1700 French= Canad. explorer
Jo·nah \'jō-nə\ Hebrew prophet who in the Bible spends three days in the belly of a great fish
Jones \'jōnz\ John Paul 1747–1792 Amer. (Scot.-born) naval officer
Jop·lin \'jä-plən\ Scott 1868–1917 Amer. pianist and composer
Jor·dan \'jór-dᵊn\ Michael 1963– Amer. basketball player
Jo·seph \'jō-zəf\ son of Jacob in the Bible who rises to high office in Egypt after being sold into slavery by his brothers
Joseph Chief *ca* 1840–1904 Nez Percé Indian chief
Joseph Saint, husband of Mary, the mother of Jesus, in the Bible
Josh·ua \'jä-sh(ə-)wə\ Hebrew leader in the Bible who succeeds Moses during the settlement of the Israelites in Canaan
Joyce \'jóis\ James Augustine 1882–1941 Irish author
Juan Car·los \'(h)wän-'kär-ˌlōs\ 1938– king of Spain (1975–)
Juá·rez \'hwär-əs, 'wär-\ Benito 1806–1872 pres. of Mexico (1861–65; 1867–72)
Ju·dah \'jü-də\ son of Jacob and ancestor of one of the 12 tribes of Israel in the Bible
Ju·das \'jü-dəs\ *or* **Judas Is·car·i·ot** \-is-'ka-rē-ət\ one of the 12 apostles and the betrayer of Jesus in the Bible
Jung \'yùŋ\ Carl Gustav 1875–1961 Swiss psychologist
Ju·no \'jü-(ˌ)nō\ queen of heaven, wife of Jupiter, and goddess of light, birth, women, and marriage in Roman mythology — compare HERA
Ju·pi·ter \'jü-pə-tər\ chief god and god of light, of the sky and weather, and of the state in Roman mythology — compare ZEUS
Kah·lo \'kä-lō\ Frida 1907–1954 Mex. painter
Ka·me·ha·me·ha I \kə-ˌmä-ə-'mä-(ˌ)hä\ 1758?–1819 orig. *Pai·ea* Hawaiian king (1795–1819)
Keats \'kēts\ John 1795–1821 Eng. poet
Kel·ler \'ke-lər\ Helen Adams 1880–1968 Amer. deaf and blind lecturer and author
Kel·vin \'kel-vən\ 1st Baron 1824–1907 *William Thomson* Brit. mathematician and physicist
Ken·ne·dy \'ke-nə-dē\ John Fitzgerald 1917–1963 35th pres. of the U.S. (1961–63)
Kennedy Robert Francis 1925–1968 attorney general of the U.S. (1961–64); brother of the preceding
Ke·o·kuk \'kē-ə-ˌkək\ 1780?–1848 Amer. Indian chief
Key \'kē\ Francis Scott 1779–1843 Amer. lawyer; author of "The Star-Spangled Banner"
Khayyám Omar — see OMAR KHAYYÁM
Khru·shchev \krùsh-'chóf, -'chóv\ Nikita Sergeyevich 1894–1971 premier of U.S.S.R. (1958–64)
Khu·fu \'kü-(ˌ)fü\ *or* *Greek* **Che·ops** \'kē-ˌäps\ *fl.* 25th cent. B.C. king of Egypt and pyramid builder
Kidd \'kid\ William *ca* 1645–1701 *Captain Kidd* Scot. pirate
Kier·ke·gaard \'kir-kə-ˌgär(d), -ˌgór\ Søren 1813–1855 Danish philosopher
King \'kiŋ\ Billie Jean 1943– Amer. tennis player
King Martin Luther, Jr. 1929–1968 Amer. minister and civil rights leader; Nobel Prize winner (1964)
Kip·ling \'kip-liŋ\ Rudyard 1865–1936 Eng. author; Nobel Prize winner (1907)
Kis·sin·ger \'ki-sⁿn-jər\ Henry Alfred 1923– Amer. (Ger.-born) government official; U.S. secretary of state (1973–77); Nobel Prize winner (1973)
Knox \'näks\ John *ca* 1514–1572 Scot. religious reformer
Koch \'kók, 'kòk, 'kók, 'kōk\ Robert 1843–1910 Ger. bacteriologist; Nobel Prize winner (1905)
Koś·ciusz·ko \kósh-'chùsh-(ˌ)kō, ˌkä-sē-'əs-ˌkō\ Tadeusz 1746–1817 Polish patriot and general in Amer. Revolutionary army
Krish·na \'krish-nə, 'krēsh-\ god worshipped in later Hinduism
Ku·blai Khan \'kü-ˌblə-'kän, -ˌblī-\ 1215–1294 Mongol leader; grandson of Genghis Khan
La·fa·yette \ˌlä-fē-'et, ˌla-\ Marquis de 1757–1834 French general in Amer. Revolutionary army

La·ius \'lä-əs, 'lī-əs\ king of Thebes who in Greek mythology is killed by his son Oedipus

Lan·ce·lot \'lan(t)-sə-ˌlät, 'län(t)-, -s(ə-)lət\ legendary knight of the Round Table and lover of Queen Guinevere

Lange \'laŋ\ Dorothea 1895–1965 Amer. photographer

Lao–tzu \'laud-'zə\ *fl.* 6th cent. B.C. Chinese philosopher

La Salle \lə-'sal\ Sieur de 1643–1687 *René-Robert Cavelier* French explorer

La·voi·sier \ləv-'wä-zē-ˌä\ Antoine-Laurent 1743–1794 French chemist

Law·rence \'lȯr-ən(t)s, 'lär-\ D. H. 1885–1930 *David Herbert Lawrence* Eng. author

Lawrence Thomas Edward 1888–1935 *Lawrence of Arabia* Brit. soldier and author

Laz·a·rus \'laz-rəs, 'la-zə-\ brother of Martha who in the Bible is raised by Jesus from the dead

Lazarus beggar in the biblical parable of the rich man and the beggar

Le·da \'lē-də\ Spartan princess in Greek mythology who is courted by Zeus in the form of a swan

Lee \'lē\ Ann 1736–1784 Eng. mystic; founder of Shaker society in the U.S.

Lee Henry 1756–1818 *Light-Horse Harry* Amer. general

Lee Robert Edward 1807–1870 Amer. Confederate general; son of the preceding

Leeu·wen·hoek \'lā-vən-ˌhu̇k\ Antonie van 1632–1723 Dutch naturalist

Leif Er·iks·son *or* **Er·ics·son** \ˌlāv-'er-ik-sən, ˌlēf-\ *fl.* 1000 Norwegian explorer; son of Erik the Red

Le·nin \'le-nən\ 1870–1924 orig. *Vladimir Ilyich Ul·ya·nov* \u̇l-'yän-əf, -ˌȯf, -ˌȯv\ Russ. Communist leader

Leo \'lē-(ˌ)ō\ name of 13 popes: esp. **I** Saint *died* 461 A.D. *Leo the Great* (pope 440–61); **III** Saint *died* 816 (pope 795–816); **XIII** 1810–1903 (pope 1878–1903)

Le·o·nar·do da Vin·ci \ˌlē-ə-'när-(ˌ)dō-də-'vin-chē, ˌlā-, -'vēn-\ 1452–1519 Ital. painter, sculptor, architect, and engineer

Lew·is \'lü-əs\ C. S. 1898–1963 *Clive Staples Lewis* Brit. author

Lewis John Llewellyn 1880–1969 Amer. labor leader

Lewis Meriwether 1774–1809 Amer. explorer (with William Clark)

Lewis Sinclair 1885–1951 Amer. author; Nobel Prize winner (1930)

Lin·coln \'liŋ-kən\ Abraham 1809–1865 16th pres. of the U.S. (1861–65)

Lind·bergh \'lin(d)-ˌbərg\ Charles Augustus 1902–1974 Amer. aviator

Lin·nae·us \lə-'nē-əs, -'nā-\ Carolus 1707–1778 *Carl von Linné* Swedish botanist

Lis·ter \'lis-tər\ Joseph 1827–1912 Eng. surgeon and medical scientist

Liszt \'list\ Franz 1811–1886 Hungarian pianist and composer

Liv·ing·stone \'li-viŋ-stən\ David 1813–1873 Scot. missionary in Africa

Lon·don \'lən-dən\ Jack 1876–1916 *John Griffith London* Amer. author

Long·fel·low \'lȯŋ-ˌfe-(ˌ)lō\ Henry Wadsworth 1807–1882 Amer. poet

Lou·is \'lü-ē, lü-'ē\ name of 18 kings of France: esp. **IX** Saint 1214–1270 (r. 1226–70); **XI** 1423–1483 (r. 1461–83); **XII** 1462–1515 (r. 1498–1515); **XIII** 1601–1643 (r. 1610–43); **XIV** 1638–1715 (r. 1643–1715); **XV** 1710–1774 (r. 1715–74); **XVI** 1754–1793 (r. 1774–92; guillotined); **XVII** 1785–1795 (r. in name 1793–95); **XVIII** 1755–1824 (r. 1814–15; 1815–24)

Lou·is \'lü-əs\ Joe 1914–1981 orig. *Joseph Louis Barrow* Amer. boxer

Low \'lō\ Juliette 1860–1927 née *Gordon* Amer. founder of the Girl Scouts

Low·ell \'lō-əl\ Amy 1874–1925 Amer. poet

Lowell James Russell 1819–1891 Amer. author

Luke \'lük\ physician and companion of the apostle Paul believed to be the author of the 3d Gospel and the Book of Acts

Lu·ther \'lü-thər\ Martin 1483–1546 Ger. Reformation leader

Ly·on \'lī-ən\ Mary 1797–1849 Amer. educator

Mac·Ar·thur \mə-'kär-thər\ Douglas 1880–1964 Amer. general

Ma·cy \'mā-sē\ Anne Sullivan 1866–1936 née *Sullivan* Amer. educator; teacher of Helen Keller

Mad·i·son \'ma-də-sən\ James 1751–1836 4th pres. of the U.S. (1809–17)

Ma·gel·lan \mə-'je-lən, *chiefly Brit* -'ge-\ Ferdinand *ca* 1480–1521 Portuguese navigator and explorer

Mal·colm X \'mal-kəm-'eks\ 1925–1965 Amer. civil rights leader

Man·dela \man-'de-lə\ Nelson Rolihlahla 1918– pres. of South Africa (1994–99); Nobel Prize winner (1993)

Ma·net \ma-'nā, mä-\ Édouard 1832–1883 French painter

Mann \'man\ Horace 1796–1859 Amer. educator

Mao Tse–tung *or* **Mao Zedong** \'mau̇-(')(d)zə-'du̇ŋ, -(')tsə-\ 1893–1976 Chinese Communist leader of People's Republic of China (1949–76)

Mar·co·ni \mär-'kō-nē\ Guglielmo 1874–1937 Ital. physicist and inventor; Nobel Prize winner (1909)

Marco Polo — see POLO

Ma·rie An·toi·nette \ˌan-twə-'net, -tə-\ 1755–1793 wife of Louis XVI of France

Mar·i·on \'mer-ē-ən\ Francis 1732?–1795 *the Swamp Fox* Amer. commander in Revolution

Mark \'märk\ evangelist believed to be the author of the 2d Gospel

Mark Antony — see ANTONY

Mar·quette \mär-'ket\ Jacques 1637–1675 *Père Marquette* French-born Jesuit missionary and explorer in America

Mars \'märz\ god of war in Roman mythology — compare ARES

Mar·shall \'mär-shəl\ George Catlett 1880–1959 Amer. general and diplomat; Nobel Prize winner (1953)

Marshall John 1755–1835 Amer. jurist; chief justice of the U.S. Supreme Court (1801–35)

Marshall Thurgood 1908–1993 Amer. jurist

Mar·tha \'mär-thə\ sister of Lazarus and friend of Jesus in the Bible

Mar·tin \'mär-tᵊn, mär-'taᵐ\ Saint 316–397 *Martin of Tours* \-'tu̇r\ patron saint of France

Mar·tin \'mär-tᵊn\ Paul (Edgar Phillipe) 1938– Canad. prime minister (2003–06)

Marx \'märks\ Karl 1818–1883 Ger. political philosopher and socialist

Mary \'mer-ē, 'ma-rē, 'mā-rē\ *Saint Mary*; *Virgin Mary* mother of Jesus

Mary I 1516–1558 *Mary Tudor*; *Bloody Mary* queen of England (1553–58)

Mary II 1662–1694 joint Brit. sovereign with William III (1689–94)

Mary Mag·da·lene \'mag-də-lən, -ˌlēn\ woman in the Bible who sees the risen Christ

Mary, Queen of Scots 1542–1587 *Mary Stuart* queen of Scotland (1542–67)

Mas·sa·soit \ˌma-sə-'sȯit\ *died* 1661 Amer. Indian chief

Math·er \'ma-thər, -thər\ Cotton 1663–1728 Amer. religious leader and author

Mather Increase 1639–1723 Amer. minister and author; father of Cotton Mather

Ma·tisse \ma-'tēs, mə-\ Henri 1869–1954 French painter

Mat·thew \'ma-(ˌ)thyü\ apostle believed to be the author of the 1st Gospel

Mau·pas·sant \ˌmō-pə-'säᵑ\ Guy de 1850–1893 French author

Mays \'māz\ Willie Howard 1931– Amer. baseball player

Mc·Au·liffe \mə-'kȯl-əf\ Christa 1948–1986 Amer. teacher; 1st private citizen in space (1986)

Mc·Car·thy \mə-'kär-thē\ Joseph Raymond 1908–1957 Amer. politician

Mc·Clel·lan \mə-'kle-lən\ George Brinton 1826–1885 Amer. general

Mc·Clin·tock \mə-'klin-tək\ Barbara 1902–1992 Amer. botanist; Nobel Prize winner (1983)

Mc·Cor·mick \mə-'kȯr-mik\ Cyrus Hall 1809–1884 Amer. inventor

Mc·Kin·ley \mə-'kin-lē\ William 1843–1901 25th pres. of the U.S. (1897–1901)

Mead \'mēd\ Margaret 1901–1978 Amer. anthropologist

Meade \'mēd\ George Gordon 1815–1872 Amer. Civil War general

Mea·ny \'mē-nē\ George 1894–1980 Amer. labor leader

Me·dea \mə-'dē-ə\ woman with magic powers in Greek

mythology who helps Jason to win the Golden Fleece and who kills her children when he leaves her

Medici Catherine de' — see CATHERINE DE MÉDICIS

Me·di·ci \'me-də-chē\ Lorenzo de' 1449–1492 *Lorenzo the Magnificent* Florentine statesman, ruler, and patron of the arts

Me·du·sa \mi-'dü-sə, -'dyü-, -zə\ Gorgon in Greek mythology slain by Perseus

Me·ir \mā-'ir\ Golda 1898–1978 prime minister of Israel (1969–74)

Mel·ville \'mel-,vil\ Herman 1819–1891 Amer. author

Men·del \'men-dᵊl\ Gregor Johann 1822–1884 Austrian botanist

Men·dels·sohn (**–Bar·thol·dy**) \'men-dᵊl-sən(-bär-'tȯl-dē, -'thȯl-)\ Felix 1809–1847 Ger. composer

Men·e·la·us \,me-nə-'lā-əs\ king of Sparta, brother of Agamemnon, and husband of Helen of Troy in Greek mythology

Meph·is·toph·e·les \,me-fə-'stä-fə-,lēz\ chief devil in the Faust legend

Mer·ca·tor \(,)mər-'kā-tər\ Gerardus 1512–1594 orig. *Gerhard Kremer* Flemish cartographer

Mer·cu·ry \'mər-kyə-rē, -k(ə-)rē\ god of commerce, eloquence, travel, and theft who serves as messenger of the other gods in Roman mythology — compare HERMES

Mer·lin \'mər-lən\ prophet and magician in the legend of King Arthur

Met·a·com \'me-tə-,käm\ or **King Philip** *ca* 1638–1676 *Met·a·com·et* \,me-tə-'käm-ət\ Amer. Indian chief; son of Massasoit

Mi·chael \'mī-kəl\ archangel named in Hebrew tradition — compare GABRIEL; RAPHAEL; URIEL

Mi·chel·an·ge·lo \,mī-kə-'lan-jə-,lō, ,mi-, ,mē-kə-'län-\ 1475–1564 Ital. sculptor, painter, architect, and poet

Mi·das \'mī-dəs\ legendary king having the power to turn everything he touched into gold

Mil·lay \mi-'lā\ Edna St. Vincent 1892–1950 Amer. poet

Mil·ler \'mi-lər\ Arthur 1915–2005 Amer. playwright

Milne \'mil(n)\ A. A. 1882–1956 *Alan Alexander Milne* Eng. author

Mil·ton \'mil-tᵊn\ John 1608–1674 Eng. poet

Mi·ner·va \mə-'nər-və\ goddess of wisdom in Roman mythology — compare ATHENA

Mi·no·taur \'mi-nə-,tȯr, 'mī-\ monster in Greek mythology shaped half like a man and half like a bull

Min·u·it \'min-yə-wət\ Peter *ca* 1580–1638 Dutch colonial administrator in America

Mitch·ell \'mi-chəl\ Maria 1818–1889 Amer. astronomer

Mo·lière \mōl-'yer, 'mōl-,\ 1622–1673 orig. *Jean-Baptiste Poquelin* French actor and playwright

Mo·net \mō-'nā\ Claude 1840–1926 French painter

Mon·roe \mən-'rō\ James 1758–1831 5th pres. of the U.S. (1817–25)

Mont·calm \mänt-'kälm-, -'käm-\ Marquis de 1712–1759 *Louis-Joseph de Montcalm-Grozon* French field marshal in Canada

Mon·tes·so·ri \,män-tə-'sȯr-ē\ Maria 1870–1952 Ital. educator

Mon·te·zu·ma II \,män-tə-'zü-mə\ 1466–1520 last Aztec emperor of Mexico (1502–20)

Moore \'mȯr, 'mȯr\ Marianne 1887–1972 Amer. poet

More \'mȯr\ Sir Thomas 1478–1535 *Saint Thomas More* Eng. public official and author

Mor·gan \'mȯr-gən\ J. P. 1837–1913 *John Pierpont Morgan* Amer. financier

Mor·ri·son \'mȯr-ə-sən, 'mär-\ Toni 1931– orig. *Chloe Anthony Wofford* Amer. author; Nobel Prize winner (1993)

Morse \'mȯrs\ Samuel Finley Breese 1791–1872 Amer. artist and inventor

Mo·ses \'mō-zəz\ Hebrew prophet and lawgiver in the Bible

Moses Grandma 1860–1961 *Anna Mary Moses* née *Robertson* Amer. painter

Mott \'mät\ Lucretia 1793–1880 Amer. reformer

Mo·zart \'mōt-,särt\ Wolfgang Amadeus 1756–1791 Austrian composer

Mu·ham·mad \mō-'ha-məd, -'hä-\ *ca* 570–632 A.D. Arab prophet and founder of Islam

Mus·so·li·ni \,mü-sə-'lē-nē, ,mù-\ Be·ni·to \bə-'nēt-ō\ 1883–1945 *Il Du·ce* \ēl-'dü-chā\ Ital. fascist premier (1922–43)

Na·bo·kov \nə-'bȯ-kəf\ Vladimir 1899–1977 Amer. (Russ.-born) author

Na·po·leon I \nə-'pōl-yən, -'pō-lē-ən\ or **Napoleon Bo·na·parte** \'bō-nə-,pärt\ 1769–1821 French general and emperor of the French (1804–15)

Nar·cis·sus \när-'si-səs\ beautiful youth in Greek mythology who pines away for love of his own reflection and is then turned into the narcissus flower

Nash \'nash\ Ogden 1902–1971 Amer. poet

Na·tion \'nā-shən\ Car·ry \'kar-ē\ Amelia 1846–1911 née *Moore* Amer. temperance agitator

Nav·ra·ti·lo·va \,nav-rə-tə-'lō-və\ Martina 1956– Amer. (Czech-born) tennis player

Neb·u·cha·drez·zar II \,ne-byə-kə-'dre-zər, -bə-\ or **Neb·u·chad·nez·zar** \-kəd-'ne-\ *ca* 561 B.C. Chaldean king of Babylon (605–562)

Neh·ru \'ner-(,)ü, 'nā-(,)rü\ Ja·wa·har·lal \jə-'wä-hər-,läl\ 1889–1964 1st prime minister of Republic of India (1947–64)

Nel·son \'nel-sən\ Horatio 1758–1805 Viscount *Nelson* Brit. admiral

Nem·e·sis \'ne-mə-səs\ goddess of reward and punishment in Greek mythology

Nep·tune \'nep-,tün, -,tyün\ god of the sea in Roman mythology — compare POSEIDON

Ne·ro \'nē-(,)rō, 'nir-(,)ō\ 37–68 A.D. Roman emperor (54–68)

Ne·ru·da \nä-'rü-də\ Pablo 1904–1973 Chilean poet

Nev·el·son \'ne-vəl-sən\ Louise 1900?–1988 Amer. sculptor

New·ton \'nü-tᵊn, 'nyü-\ Sir Isaac 1642–1727 Eng. mathematician and physicist

Nich·o·las \'ni-k(ə-)ləs\ Saint *fl.* 4th cent. A.D. Christian bishop

Nicholas I 1796–1855 czar of Russia (1825–55)

Nicholas II 1868–1918 last czar of Russia (1894–1917)

Nietz·sche \'nē-chə, -chē\ Friedrich Wilhelm 1844–1900 Ger. philosopher

Night·in·gale \'nī-tᵊn-,gäl, -tiŋ-\ Florence 1820–1910 *Lady of the Lamp* Eng. nurse and philanthropist

Ni·ke \'nī-kē\ goddess of victory in Greek mythology

Ni·o·be \'nī-ə-bē\ bereaved mother in Greek mythology who while weeping for her slain children is turned into a stone from which her tears continue to flow

Nix·on \'nik-sən\ Richard Milhous 1913–1994 37th pres. of the U.S. (1969–74)

No·ah \'nō-ə\ biblical builder of the ark in which he, his family, and living creatures of every kind survive the biblical Flood

No·bel \nō-'bel\ Alfred Bernhard 1833–1896 Swedish manufacturer, inventor, and philanthropist

Nor·man \'nȯr-mən\ Jessye 1945– Amer. soprano

Oak·ley \'ōk-lē\ Annie 1860–1926 orig. *Phoebe Anne Oakley Moses* Amer. sharpshooter

O'·Con·nor \ō-'kä-nər\ (Mary) Flannery 1925–1964 Amer. author

O'Connor Sandra Day 1930– Amer. jurist

Odin \'ō-dᵊn\ or **Wo·den** \'wō-dᵊn\ chief god, god of war, and patron of heroes in Norse mythology

Odys·seus \ō-'di-sē-əs, -'dis-yəs, -'di-shəs, -'di-,shüs\ or **Ulys·ses** \yü-'li-(,)sēz\ king of Ithaca and hero in Greek mythology

Oe·di·pus \'e-də-pəs, 'ē-\ son of Laius and Jocasta who in Greek mythology kills his father and marries his mother not knowing their identity

Ogle·thorpe \'ō-gəl-,thȯrp\ James Edward 1696–1785 Eng. general and founder of Georgia

O'·Keeffe \ō-'kēf\ Georgia 1887–1986 Amer. painter

Olaf V \'ō-ləf, -läf, -laf; 'ü-läf\ 1903–1991 king of Norway (1957–91)

Omar Khay·yám \,ō-,mär-,kī-'yäm, ,ō-mər-, -'yam\ 1048–1131 Persian poet and astronomer

O'·Neill \ō-'nēl\ Eugene Gladstone 1888–1953 Amer. playwright; Nobel Prize winner (1936)

Or·pheus \'ȯr-,fyüs, -fē-əs\ poet and musician in Greek mythology

Or·well \'ȯr-,wel, -wəl\ George 1903–1950 pseud. of *Eric Arthur Blair* Eng. author

Osce·o·la \,ä-sē-'ō-lə, ,ō-\ *ca* 1804–1838 Seminole Indian chief

Otis \ 'ō-təs\ James 1725–1783 Amer. Revolutionary patriot

Ov·id \'ä-vəd\ 43 B.C., –17 A.D.? Roman poet

Ow·en \'ō-ən\ Robert 1771–1858 Welsh social reformer

Ow·ens \'ō-ənz\ Jesse 1913–1980 orig. *James Cleveland Owens* Amer. track-and-field athlete

Paine \'pān\ Thomas 1737–1809 Amer. (Eng.-born) political philosopher and author

Pan \'pan\ god of pastures, flocks, and shepherds in Greek mythology who is usu. represented as having the legs, ears, and horns of a goat

Pan·do·ra \pan-'dȯr-ə\ woman in Greek mythology who out of curiosity opens a box and lets loose all of the evils that trouble humans

Pank·hurst \'paŋk-,hərst\ Emmeline 1858–1928 née *Goulden* Eng. suffragist

Par·is \'pa-rəs\ son of Priam whose abduction of Helen of Troy in Greek mythology leads to the Trojan War

Park·man \'pärk-mən\ Francis 1823–1893 Amer. historian

Parks \'pärks\ Rosa 1913–2005 née *McCauley* Amer. civil rights activist

Pas·cal \pa-'skal, päs-'käl\ Blaise 1623–1662 French mathematician and philosopher

Pas·ter·nak \'pas-tər-,nak\ Boris Leonidovich 1890–1960 Russ. author; Nobel Prize winner (1958)

Pas·teur \pas-'tər\ Louis 1822–1895 French chemist and microbiologist

Pat·rick \pa-'trik\ Saint *fl.* 5th cent. A.D. apostle and patron saint of Ireland

Pat·ton \'pa-tᵊn\ George Smith 1885–1945 Amer. general

Paul \'pȯl\ Saint *died ca* 67 A.D. Christian missionary and author of several New Testament epistles

Paul name of 6 popes: esp. **III** 1468–1549 (pope 1534–49); **V** 1552–1621 (pope 1605–21); **VI** 1897–1978 (pope 1963–78)

Paul Bun·yan \'bən-yən\ giant lumberjack in Amer. folklore

Pau·ling \'pȯ-liŋ\ Linus Carl 1901–1994 Amer. chemist; Nobel Prize winner (1954, 1962)

Pav·lov \'päv-,lȯf, 'pav-, -,lȯv\ Ivan Petrovich 1849–1936 Russ. physiologist; Nobel Prize winner (1904)

Pa·vlo·va \'pav-lə-və, pav-'lȯ-\ Anna 1881–1931 Russ. ballerina

Pea·ry \'pir-ē\ Robert Edwin 1856–1920 Amer. arctic explorer

Pe·cos Bill \,pā-kəs-'bil\ cowboy in Amer. folklore known for his extraordinary feats

Peg·a·sus \'pe-gə-səs\ winged horse in Greek mythology

Penn \'pen\ William 1644–1718 Eng. Quaker leader and founder of Pennsylvania

Per·i·cles \'per-ə-,klēz\ *ca* 495–429 B.C. Athenian political leader

Per·ry \'per-ē\ Matthew Calbraith 1794–1858 Amer. commodore

Perry Oliver Hazard 1785–1819 Amer. naval officer; brother of the preceding

Per·seph·o·ne \pər-'se-fə-nē\ daughter of Zeus and Demeter who in Greek mythology is abducted by Pluto to rule with him over the underworld

Per·shing \'pər-shiŋ, -zhiŋ\ John Joseph 1860–1948 Amer. general

Pe·ter \'pē-tər\ Saint *died ca* 64 A.D. orig. *Si·mon* \'sī-mən-\ one of the 12 apostles in the Bible

Peter I 1672–1725 *Peter the Great* czar of Russia (1682–1725)

Phil·ip \'fi-ləp\ Saint, one of the 12 apostles in the Bible

Philip King — see METACOM

Philip name of 6 kings of France: esp. **II** or **Philip Augustus** 1165–1223 (r. 1179–1223); **IV** 1268–1314 *Philip the Fair* (r. 1285–1314); **VI** 1293–1350 (r. 1328–50)

Philip name of 5 kings of Spain: esp. **II** 1527–1598 (r. 1556–98); **V** 1683–1746 (r. 1700–46)

Philip II 382–336 B.C. king of Macedon (359–336); father of Alexander the Great

Pi·cas·so \pi-'kä-(,)sō, -'ka-\ Pablo 1881–1973 Span. painter and sculptor in France

Pic·card \pi-'kär, -'kärd\ Auguste 1884–1962 and his son Jacques 1922–   Swiss scientists and developers of the bathyscaphe

Pick·ett \'pi-kət\ George Edward 1825–1875 Amer. Confederate general

Pierce \'pirs\ Franklin 1804–1869 14th pres. of the U.S. (1853–57)

Pi·late \'pī-lət\ Pon·tius \'pän-chəs, 'pən-chəs\ *died after* 36 A.D. Roman governor of Judea (26–36)

Pinkerton \'piŋ-kər-tᵊn\ Allan 1819–1884 Amer. (Scot.-born) detective

Pis·sar·ro \pə-'sär-(,)ō\ Camille 1830–1903 French (West Indian-born) painter

Pitt \'pit\ William 1759–1806 *the Younger Pitt* Eng. prime minister (1783–1801; 1804–6)

Pi·us \'pī-əs\ name of 12 popes: esp. **VII** 1742–1823 (pope 1800–23); **IX** 1792–1878 (pope 1846–78); **X** Saint 1835–1914 (pope 1903–14); **XI** 1857–1939 (pope 1922–39); **XII** 1876–1958 (pope 1939–58)

Pi·zar·ro \pə-'zär-(,)ō\ Francisco *ca* 1475–1541 Span. conqueror of Peru

Pla·to \'plā-(,)tō\ *ca* 428–348 (*or* 347) B.C. Greek philosopher

Plu·to \'plü-(,)tō\ god of the underworld in Greek mythology

Po·ca·hon·tas \,pō-kə-'hän-təs\ *ca* 1595–1617 Amer. Indian friend of the colonists at Jamestown; daughter of Powhatan

Poe \'pō\ Edgar Allan 1809–1849 Amer. author

Polk \'pōk\ James Knox 1795–1849 11th pres. of the U.S. (1845–49)

Po·lo \'pō-(,)lō\ Marco *ca* 1254–1324 Venetian merchant and traveler

Poly·phe·mus \,päl-ə-lə-'fē-məs\ a one-eyed creature in Greek mythology that is blinded by Odysseus

Ponce de Le·ón \'pän(t)s-ə-,dā-lē-'ōn, ,pänts-də-, -'lē-ən\ Juan 1460–1521 Span. explorer

Pon·ti·ac \'pän-tē-,ak\ *ca* 1720–1769 Ottawa Indian chief

Por·ter \'pȯr-tər\ Cole Albert 1891–1964 Amer. composer

Porter Katherine Anne 1890–1980 Amer. author

Porter William Sydney — see O. HENRY

Po·sei·don \pə-'sī-dᵊn\ god of the sea in Greek mythology — compare NEPTUNE

Pot·ter \'pä-tər\ (Helen) Beatrix 1866–1943 Brit. author and illustrator

Pound \'paund\ Ezra Loomis 1885–1972 Amer. poet

Pound·mak·er \'paund-,mā-kər\ 1826–1886 Cree Indian chief

Pow·ell \'pau(-ə)l\ Colin Luther 1937–   Amer. general; U.S. secretary of state (2001–05)

Pow·ha·tan \,pau-ə-'tan, pau-'ha-tᵊn\ 1550?–1618 Amer. Indian chief of a confederacy of Algonquian-speaking tribes; father of Pocahontas

Pres·ley \'pres-lē, 'prez-\ Elvis Aaron 1935–1977 Amer. popular singer

Pri·am \'prī-əm, -,am\ king of Troy during the Trojan War in Greek mythology

Price \'prīs\ (Mary) Leontyne 1927–   Amer. soprano

Pro·me·theus \prə-'mē-thē-əs, -,thyüs\ Titan in Greek mythology who is punished by Zeus for stealing fire from heaven and giving it to humans

Pro·teus \'prō-tyüs, -tē-əs\ sea god in Greek mythology who is capable of assuming different forms

Ptol·e·my \'tä-lə-mē\ *fl.* 2d cent. A.D. Greco-Egyptian astronomer, geographer, and mathematician in Alexandria

Puc·ci·ni \pü-'chē-nē\ Giacomo 1858–1924 Ital. composer

Pu·las·ki \pə-'las-kē, pyü-\ Kazimierz 1747–1779 Polish soldier in Amer. Revolutionary army

Pu·lit·zer \'pü-lət-sər (*family's pron*), 'pyü-\ Joseph 1847–1911 Amer. (Hungarian-born) journalist

Pu·tin \'pü-tin\ Vladimir Vladimirovich 1952–   pres. of Russia (2000–   )

Pyg·ma·lion \pig-'mäl-yən, -'mä-lē-ən\ sculptor in Greek mythology who creates Galatea

Py·thag·o·ras \pə-'tha-gə-rəs, pī-\ *ca* 580–*ca* 500 B.C. Greek philosopher and mathematician

Ra \'rä\ god of the sun and chief deity of ancient Egypt

Ra·leigh *or* **Ra·legh** \'rȯ-lē, 'rä- *also* 'ra-\ Sir Walter 1554?–1618 Eng. navigator and writer

Ram·ses \'ram-,sēz\ *or* **Ram·e·ses** \'ra-mə-,sēz\ name of 12 kings of Egypt: esp. **II** (r. 1279–1213 B.C.,); **III** (r. 1187–1156 B.C.)

Ran·dolph \'ran-,dälf\ Asa Philip 1889–1979 Amer. labor and civil rights leader

Ra·pha·el \'ra-fē-əl, 'rä-, -,el\ archangel named in Hebrew tradition — compare GABRIEL; MICHAEL; URIEL

Ra·pha·el \'ra-fē-əl, 'rä-, 'rä-\ 1483–1520 orig. *Raffaello Sanzio* or *Santi* Ital. painter

Ras·pu·tin \ra-'spyü-tᵊn, -'spü-, -'spú-\ Grigory Yefimovich 1872–1916 Russ. mystic

Rea·gan \'rā-gən\ Ronald Wilson 1911–2004 40th pres. of the U.S. (1981–89)

Re·bek·ah \ri-'be-kə\ wife of Isaac and mother of Jacob in the Bible

Red Cloud \'red-₁klaúd\ 1822–1909 Sioux Indian chief

Red Jack·et \'red-₁ja-kət\ 1758?–1830 *Sa·go·ye·wa·tha* \sä-₁goi-(y)ə-'wä-thə\ Seneca Indian chief

Reed \'rēd\ Walter 1851–1902 Amer. army surgeon

Rem·brandt \'rem-₁brant *also* -₁bränt\ 1606–1669 *Rembrandt (Harmenszoon) van Rijn* Dutch painter

Rem·ing·ton \'re-miŋ-tən\ Frederic 1861–1909 Amer. painter and sculptor

Re·mus \'rē-məs\ son of Mars who in Roman mythology is killed by his twin brother Romulus

Re·noir \'ren-₁wär, rən-'\ (Pierre-) Auguste 1841–1919 French painter

Re·vere \ri-'vir\ Paul 1735–1818 Amer. patriot and silversmith

Rice \'rīs\ Condoleezza 1954– Am. scholar; U.S. secretary of state (2005–)

Rich·ard \'ri-chərd\ name of 3 kings of England: **I** 1157–1199 *Richard the Lion-Hearted* (r. 1189–99); **II** 1367–1400 (r. 1377–99); **III** 1452–1485 (r. 1483–85)

Ride \'rīd\ Sally Kristen 1951– Amer. astronaut; 1st Amer. woman in space (1983)

Ri·ve·ra \ri-'vir-ə\ Diego 1886–1957 Mex. painter

Rob·in Good·fel·low \'rä-bən-'gúd-₁fe-(₁)lō\ mischievous elf in Eng. folklore

Robin Hood \₁húd\ legendary Eng. outlaw who gave to the poor what he stole from the rich

Rob·in·son \'rä-bən-sən\ Edwin Arlington 1869–1935 Amer. poet

Robinson Jackie 1919–1972 *Jack Roosevelt Robinson* Amer. baseball player

Rob·in·son Cru·soe \'rä-bə(n)-sən-'krü-(₁)sō\ shipwrecked sailor in Daniel Defoe's *Robinson Crusoe* who lives for many years on a desert island

Rocke·fel·ler \'rä-ki-₁fe-lər\ John Davison 1839–1937 and his son John Davison, Jr. 1874–1960 Amer. oil magnates and philanthropists

Ro·ma·nov \rō-'mä-nəf, 'rō-mə-₁näf\ Michael 1596–1645 1st czar (1613–45) of Russ. Romanov dynasty (1613–1917)

Rom·u·lus \'räm-yə-ləs\ son of Mars in Roman mythology who is the twin brother of Remus and the founder of Rome

Rönt·gen *or* **Roent·gen** \'rent-gən, 'rənt-, -jən\ Wilhelm Conrad 1845–1923 Ger. physicist; Nobel Prize winner (1901)

Roo·se·velt \'rō-zə-vəlt, -₁velt\ (Anna) Eleanor 1884–1962 Amer. lecturer and writer; wife of F. D. Roosevelt

Roosevelt Franklin Delano 1882–1945 32nd pres. of the U.S. (1933–45)

Roosevelt Theodore 1858–1919 26th pres. of the U.S. (1901–09); Nobel Prize winner (1906)

Ross \'rós\ Betsy 1752–1836 née *Griscom* reputed maker of 1st Amer. flag

Ros·si·ni \rȯ-'sē-nē, rə-\ Gioacchino Antonio 1792–1868 Ital. composer

Row·ling \'rō-liŋ\ J. K. 1965– *Joanne Kathleen Rowling* Brit. author

Ru·bens \'rü-bənz\ Peter Paul 1577–1640 Flemish painter

Ru·dolph \'rü-₁dȯlf, -₁dälf\ Wilma Glodean 1940–1994 Amer. athlete

Rus·sell \'rə-səl\ Bertrand Arthur William 1872–1970 3d Earl *Russell* Eng. mathematician and philosopher; Nobel Prize winner (1950)

Ruth \'rüth\ woman in the Bible who was one of the ancestors of King David

Ruth Babe 1895–1948 *George Herman Ruth* Amer. baseball player

Ruth·er·ford \'rə-thə(r)-fərd, -thə(r)-\ Ernest 1871–1937 Baron *Rutherford* Brit. physicist; Nobel Prize winner (1908)

Sa·bin \'sā-bin\ Albert Bruce 1906–1993 Amer. (Polish=born) physician and microbiologist

Sac·a·ga·wea \₁sa-kə-jə-'wē-ə\ 1786?–1812 Shoshone Indian guide to Lewis and Clark

Sa·dat \sə-'dat, -'dät\ Anwar el- 1918–1981 pres. of Egypt (1970–81); Nobel Prize winner (1978)

Sa·gan \'sā-gən\ Carl Edward 1934–1996 Amer. astronomer and science writer

Saint Nicholas — see Saint NICHOLAS; SANTA CLAUS

Sal·in·ger \'sa-lən-jər\ J. D. 1919– *Jerome David Salinger* Amer. author

Salk \'sȯ(l)k\ Jonas Edward 1914–1995 Amer. physician and medical researcher

Sa·lo·me \sə-'lō-mē, 'sa-lə-(₁)mä\ niece of Herod Antipas who in the Bible is given the head of John the Baptist as a reward for her dancing

Sa·mo·set \'sa-mə-₁set, sə-'mä-sət\ *died ca* 1653 Amer. Indian leader

Sam·son \'sam(p)-sən\ powerful Hebrew hero in the Bible who fights against the Philistines but is betrayed by Delilah

Sam·u·el \'sam-yə-wəl, -yəl\ Hebrew judge in the Bible who appoints Saul and then David king

Sand·burg \'san(d)-₁bərg\ Carl 1878–1967 Amer. author

Sang·er \'saŋ-ər\ Margaret 1883–1966 née *Higgins* Amer. birth-control activist

San·ta Claus \'san-tə-₁klȯz\ plump white-bearded and red-suited old man in modern folklore who delivers presents to good children at Christmastime

Sap·pho \'sa-(₁)fō\ *fl. ca* 610–*ca* 580 B.C. Greek poet

Sa·rah \'ser-ə, 'sä-rə\ wife of Abraham and mother of Isaac in the Bible

Sar·gent \'sär-jənt\ John Singer 1856–1925 Amer. painter

Sar·tre \'särtrᵊ\ Jean-Paul 1905–1980 French philosopher and author

Sat·urn \'sa-tərn\ god of agriculture in Roman mythology

Saul \'sȯl, 'säl\ 1st king of Israel in the Bible

Saul *or* **Saul of Tarsus** the apostle Paul in the Bible

Sche·her·a·zade \shə-₁her-ə-'zäd\ fictional wife of a sultan and narrator of the tales in the *Arabian Nights' Entertainments*

Schin·dler \'shind-lər\ Oskar 1908–1974 Ger. humanitarian during the Holocaust

Schu·bert \'shü-bərt, -₁bert\ Franz Peter 1797–1828 Austrian composer

Schu·mann \'shü-₁män, -mən\ Clara 1819–1896 née *Wieck* \'vēk\ Ger. pianist; wife of R. Schumann

Schumann Robert Alexander 1810–1856 Ger. composer

Schweit·zer \'shwīt-sər, 'shvīt-, 'swīt-\ Albert 1875–1965 French theologian, philosopher, physician, and music scholar; Nobel Prize winner (1952)

Scott \'skät\ Dred \'dred\ 1795?–1858 Amer. slave

Scott Robert Falcon 1868–1912 Brit. polar explorer

Scott Sir Walter 1771–1832 Scot. author

Scott Winfield 1786–1866 Amer. general

Scyl·la \'si-lə\ nymph in Greek mythology who is changed into a monster and inhabits a cave opposite the whirlpool Charybdis off the coast of Sicily

Se·at·tle \sē-'a-tᵊl\ 1786?–1866 Amer. Indian chief

Se·le·ne \sə-'lē-nē\ goddess of the moon in classical mythology

Se·quoy·ah *or* **Se·quoia** \si-'kwȯi-ə\ *ca* 1760–1843 *George Guess* Cherokee Indian scholar

Ser·ra \'ser-ə\ Junípero 1713–1784 Span. missionary in Mexico and California

Se·ton \'sē-tᵊn\ Saint Elizabeth Ann 1774–1821 *Mother Seton* née *Bayley* Amer. religious leader

Seu·rat \sə-'rä\ Georges 1859–1891 French painter

Sew·ard \'sü-ərd, 'sürd\ William Henry 1801–1872 Amer. politician; U.S. secretary of state (1861–69)

Shack·le·ton \'sha-kəl-tən\ Sir Ernest Henry 1874–1922 Brit. polar explorer

Shake·speare \'shāk-₁spir\ William 1564–1616 Eng. playwright and poet

Shaw \'shȯ\ George Bernard 1856–1950 Brit. playwright; Nobel Prize winner (1925)

Shaw Robert Gould 1837–1863 Amer. soldier

Shel·ley \'she-lē\ Mary Wollstonecraft 1797–1851 née *Godwin* Eng. author; wife of P. B. Shelley

Shelley Percy Bysshe \'bish\ 1792–1822 Eng. poet

Shep·ard \'she-pərd\ Alan Bartlett, Jr. 1923–1998 Amer. astronaut; 1st Amer. in space (1961)

Sher·i·dan \'sher-ə-dən\ Philip Henry 1831–1888 Amer. general

Sher·lock Holmes \'shər-ˌläk-'hōmz, -'hōlmz\ detective in stories by Sir Arthur Conan Doyle
Sher·man \'shər-mən\ John 1823–1900 Amer. statesman; brother of W. T. Sherman
Sherman William Tecumseh 1820–1891 Amer. general
Shi·va \'shi-və, 'shē-\ *or* **Si·va** \'si-və, 'shi-, 'sē-, 'shē-\ god of destruction and regeneration in the Hindu sacred triad — compare BRAHMA; VISHNU
Sieg·fried \'sig-ˌfrēd, 'sēg-\ hero in Germanic legend who kills a dragon guarding a gold hoard
Si·mon \'sī-mən\ *or* **Simon the Zealot** one of the 12 apostles in the Bible
Si·na·tra \sə-'nä-trə\ Frank 1915–1998 *Francis Albert Sinatra* Amer. singer and actor
Sind·bad the Sailor \'sin-ˌbad\ citizen of Baghdad whose adventures are narrated in the *Arabian Nights' Entertainments*
Sis·y·phus \'si-sə-fəs\ king of Corinth who in Greek mythology is condemned to roll a heavy stone up a hill in Hades only to have it roll down again as it nears the top
Sit·ting Bull \ˌsi-tiŋ-'bùl\ *ca* 1831–1890 Sioux Indian chief
Siva — see SHIVA
Smith \'smith\ Bessie 1894?–1937 Amer. blues singer
Smith John *ca* 1580–1631 Eng. colonist in America
Smith Joseph 1805–1844 Amer. founder of the Mormon Church
Soc·ra·tes \'sä-krə-ˌtēz\ *ca* 470–399 B.C. Greek philosopher
Sol \'säl\ god of the sun in Roman mythology — see HELIOS
Sol·o·mon \'sä-lə-mən\ 10th-century B.C. king of Israel noted for his wisdom
Soph·o·cles \'sä-fə-ˌklēz\ *ca* 496–406 B.C. Greek playwright
Sou·sa \'sü-zə, 'sü-sə\ John Philip 1854–1932 Amer. bandmaster and composer
Spar·ta·cus \'spär-tə-kəs\ *died* 71 B.C. Roman slave and gladiator
Sphinx \'sfiŋ(k)s\ monster in Greek mythology having a lion's body, wings, and the head and bust of a woman
Spiel·berg \'spēl-ˌbərg\ Steven 1947– Amer. filmmaker
Squan·to \'skwän-tō\ *died* 1622 Amer. Indian friend of the Pilgrims
Sta·lin \'stä-lən, 'sta-, -ˌlēn\ Joseph 1879–1953 Soviet Communist party leader (1922–53), premier (1941–53), and dictator
Stan·dish \'stan-dish\ Myles *or* Miles 1584?–1656 Amer. colonist
Stan·ley \'stan-lē\ Sir Henry Morton 1841–1904 Brit. explorer in Africa
Stan·ton \'stan-tᵊn\ Elizabeth Cady 1815–1902 Amer. suffragist
Stein \'stīn\ Gertrude 1874–1946 Amer. author
Stein·beck \'stīn-ˌbek\ John Ernst 1902–1968 Amer. author; Nobel Prize winner (1962)
Steu·ben \'stü-bən, 'styü-, 'shtói-\ Friedrich Wilhelm von 1730–1794 Prussian-born general in Amer. Revolution
Ste·ven·son \'stē-vən-sən\ Adlai Ewing 1900–1965 Amer. politician
Stevenson Robert Louis 1850–1894 Scot. author
Sto·ker \'stō-kər\ Bram 1847–1912 *Abraham Stoker* Irish author
Stowe \'stō\ Harriet Beecher 1811–1896 Amer. author
Stra·di·va·ri \ˌstra-də-'vär-ē, -'ver-\ Antonio 1644?–1737 Ital. violin maker
Strauss \'shtraùs, 'straùs\ Johann 1804–1849 and his sons Johann, Jr. 1825–1899 and Josef 1827–1870 Austrian composers
Strauss Richard 1864–1949 Ger. composer
Stra·vin·sky \strə-'vin(t)-skē\ Igor 1882–1971 Amer. (Russ.-born) composer
Stu·art \'stü-ərt, 'styü-; 'st(y)ùrt\ Charles Edward 1720–1788 *the Young Pretender; Bonnie Prince Charlie* claimant to the Brit. throne
Stuart Gilbert Charles 1755–1828 Amer. painter
Stuart Jeb 1833–1864 *James Ewell Brown Stuart* Amer. Confederate general
Stuy·ve·sant \'stī-və-sənt\ Peter *ca* 1610–1672 Dutch colonial administrator in America

Sul·li·van \'sə-lə-vən\ Sir Arthur Seymour 1842–1900 Eng. composer; collaborator with Sir William Gilbert
Sullivan Louis Henri 1856–1924 Amer. architect
Sum·ner \'səm-nər\ Charles 1811–1874 Amer. politician
Sun Yat–sen \'sùn-'yät-'sen\ 1866–1925 Chinese statesman
Sut·ter \'sə-tər, 'sü-\ John Augustus 1803–1880 Amer. (Ger.-born) pioneer in California
Swift \'swift\ Jonathan 1667–1745 Eng. (Irish-born) author
Synge \'siŋ\ John Millington 1871–1909 Irish playwright
Taft \'taft\ William Howard 1857–1930 27th pres. of the U.S. (1909–13); chief justice of the U.S. Supreme Court (1921–30)
Ta·gore \tə-'gòr\ Ra·bin·dra·nath \rə-'bin-drə-ˌnät\ 1861–1941 Indian poet; Nobel Prize winner (1913)
Tall·chief \'tòl-ˌchēf\ Maria 1925– Amer. dancer
Tan \'tan\ Amy 1952– Amer. author
Ta·ney \'tò-nē\ Roger Brooke 1777–1864 Amer. jurist; chief justice of the U.S. Supreme Court (1836–64)
Tan·ta·lus \'tan-tə-ləs\ king in Greek mythology who is condemned to stand up to his chin in a pool of water in Hades and beneath fruit-laden boughs only to have the water or fruit go out of reach at each attempt to drink or eat
Tay·lor \'tā-lər\ Zachary 1784–1850 Amer. general; 12th pres. of the U.S. (1849–50)
Tchai·kov·sky \chī-'kóf-skē, chə-, -'kòv-\ Pyotr Ilich 1840–1893 Russ. composer
Te·cum·seh \tə-'kəm(p)-sə, -sē\ 1768–1813 Shawnee Indian chief
Tek·a·kwitha \ˌte-kə-'kwi-thə\ Kateri 1656–1680 *Lily of the Mohawks* beatified Mohawk Indian religious
Ten·ny·son \'te-nə-sən\ Alfred 1809–1892 Baron *Tennyson* known as *Alfred, Lord Tennyson* Eng. poet
Te·re·sa \tə-'rā-zə, -'rē-sə\ Mother 1910–1997 beatified Albanian religious in India; Nobel Prize winner (1979)
Teresa of Avi·la \'ä-vi-lə\ Saint 1515–1582 Span. nun and mystic
Tes·la \'tes-lə\ Nikola 1856–1943 Amer. (Croatian-born) electrical engineer and inventor
Thatch·er \'tha-chər\ Margaret Hilda 1925– Baroness *Thatcher of Kesteven* née *Roberts* Brit. prime minister (1979–90)
The·seus \'thē-ˌsüs, -sē-əs\ hero in Greek mythology who kills the Minotaur and conquers the Amazons
Thom·as \'tä-məs\ apostle in the Bible who demanded proof of Jesus' resurrection
Thomas à Becket — see Saint Thomas BECKET
Thomas Aquinas Saint — see AQUINAS
Thor \'thòr\ god of thunder, weather, and crops in Norse mythology
Tho·reau \thə-'rō, thò-\ Henry David 1817–1862 Amer. author
Thorpe \'thòrp\ Jim 1888–1953 *James Francis Thorpe* Amer. athlete
Thur·ber \'thər-bər\ James Grover 1894–1961 Amer. author
Ti·be·ri·us \tī-'bir-ē-əs\ 42 B.C., –37 A.D. Roman emperor (14–37)
Tocque·ville \'tōk-ˌvil, 'tòk-, 'täk-, -ˌvēl, -vəl\ Alexis de 1805–1859 French politician and author
Tol·kien \'tòl-ˌkēn\ J. R. R. 1892–1973 *John Ronald Reuel Tolkien* Brit. author
Tol·stoy \'tòl-ˌstòi, tōl-', täl-', 'tòl-ˌ, 'tòl-ˌ, 'täl-ˌ\ Leo 1828–1910 Count *Lev Nikolayevich Tolstoy* Russ. author
Tou·louse–Lau·trec \tù-ˌlüz-lō-'trek\ Henri de 1864–1901 French painter
Tri·ton \'trī-tᵊn\ sea god in Greek mythology who is half man and half fish
Trots·ky \'trät-skē\ Leon 1879–1940 orig. *Lev Davidovich Bronstein* Russ. Communist leader
Tru·deau \'trü-(ˌ)dō, trü-'\ Pierre Elliott 1919–2000 Canad. prime minister (1968–79, 1980–84)
Tru·man \'trü-mən\ Harry S. 1884–1972 33rd pres. of the U.S. (1945–53)
Truth \'trüth\ Sojourner 1797?–1883 Amer. abolitionist
Tub·man \'təb-mən\ Harriet *ca* 1820–1913 Amer. abolitionist
Tut·ankh·a·men \ˌtü-ˌtaŋ-'kä-mən, -ˌtäŋ-\ originally *Tut·ankh·a·ten* \-'kä-tᵊn\ *ca* 1370–1352 B.C., king of Egypt (1361–1352 B.C.)

Twain \'kle-mənz\ Mark 1835–1910 pseud. of *Samuel Langhorne Clem·ens* \'klem-ənz\ Amer. author
Tweed \'twēd\ William Marcy 1823–1878 *Boss Tweed* Amer. politician
Ty·ler \'tī-lər\ John 1790–1862 10th pres. of the U.S. (1841–45)
Ulysses — see ODYSSEUS
Ura·nus \'yùr-ə-nəs, yù-'rā-\ the sky personified as a god and father of the Titans in Greek mythology
Ur·ban \'ər-bən\ name of eight popes: esp. II *ca* 1035–1099 (pope 1088–99)
Uri·el \'yùr-ē-əl\ archangel named in Hebrew tradition — compare GABRIEL; MICHAEL; RAPHAEL
Val·en·tine \'va-lən-ˌtīn\ Saint, 3d cent. Christian martyr
Van Bu·ren \van-'byùr-ən, vən-\ Martin 1782–1862 8th pres. of the U.S. (1837–41)
Van Dyck *or* **Van·dyke** \van-'dīk, vən-\ Sir Anthony 1599–1641 Flemish painter
van Gogh Vincent — see GOGH, VAN
Ve·láz·quez \və-'las-kəs, -'läs-, -kwiz, -(ˌ)kās\ Diego 1599–1660 Span. painter
Ve·nus \'vē-nəs\ goddess of love and beauty in Roman mythology — compare APHRODITE
Ver·di \'ver-dē\ Giuseppe 1813–1901 Ital. composer
Ver·meer \vər-'mer, -'mir\ Jan *or* Johannes 1632–1675 Dutch painter
Verne \'vərn, 'vern\ Jules \'jülz\ 1828–1905 French author
Ves·puc·ci \ve-'spü-chē, -'spyü-\ Ame·ri·go \ə-'mer-i-ˌgō\ 1454–1512 Latin *Amer·i·cus Ves·pu·cius* \ə-'mer-ə-kəs, ˌves-'pyü-sh(ē-)əs\ Ital. navigator for Spain and namesake of America
Vic·to·ria \vik-'tòr-ē-ə\ 1819–1901 *Alexandrina Victoria* queen of the United Kingdom (1837–1901)
Vinci, da Leonardo — see LEONARDO DA VINCI
Vir·gil *also* **Ver·gil** \'vər-jəl\ 70–19 B.C. Roman poet
Vish·nu \'vish-(ˌ)nü\ god of preservation in the Hindu sacred triad — compare BRAHMA; SHIVA
Vol·ta \'vōl-tə, väl-, vòl-\ Alessandro 1745–1827 Ital. physicist
Vol·taire \vōl-'tar, väl-, vòl-, -'ter\ 1694–1778 orig. *François-Marie Arouet* French author
Vul·can \'vəl-kən\ god of fire and metalworking in Roman mythology — compare HEPHAESTUS
Wag·ner \'väg-nər\ Ri·chard \'ri-ˌkärt, -ˌk̲ärt\ 1813–1883 Ger. composer
Walk·er \'wò-kər\ Alice Malsenior 1944–   Amer. writer
Wal·len·berg \'wä-lən-ˌbərg\ Raoul 1912–1947? Swedish diplomat and hero of the Holocaust
War·ren \'wòr-ən, 'wär-\ Earl 1891–1974 Amer. jurist; chief justice of the U.S. Supreme Court (1953–69)
Wash·ing·ton \'wò-shiŋ-tən, 'wä-\ Booker Tal·ia·ferro \'tä-lə-vər\ 1856–1915 Amer. educator
Washington George 1732–1799 Amer. general; 1st pres. of the U.S. (1789–97)
Watt \'wät\ James 1736–1819 Scot. inventor
Wayne \'wān\ Anthony 1745–1796 *Mad Anthony* Amer. general
Web·ster \'web-stər\ Daniel 1782–1852 Amer. politician
Webster Noah 1758–1843 Amer. lexicographer
Wel·ling·ton \'we-liŋ-tən\ Duke of 1769–1852 *Arthur Wellesley; the Iron Duke* Brit. general and statesman
Wells \'welz\ H. G. 1866–1946 *Herbert George Wells* Eng. author and historian
Wel·ty \'wel-tē\ Eudora 1909–2001 Amer. author
Wes·ley \'wes-lē, 'wez-\ John 1703–1791 Eng. founder of Methodism

Wes·ting·house \'wes-tiŋ-ˌhaùs\ George 1846–1914 Amer. inventor and industrialist
Whar·ton \'hwòr-tᵊn, 'wòr-\ Edith 1862–1937 née *Jones* Amer. author
Whis·tler \'hwis-lər, 'wis-\ James (Abbott) McNeill 1834–1903 Amer. artist
Whit·man \'hwit-mən, 'wit-\ Walt 1819–1892 Amer. poet
Whit·ney \'hwit-nē, 'wit-\ Eli 1765–1825 Amer. inventor
Whit·ti·er \'hwi-tē-ər, 'wit-\ John Greenleaf 1807–1892 Amer. poet
Wie·sel \vē-'zel, wē-\ Elie 1928–   Amer. (Romanian-born) author; Nobel Prize winner (1986)
Wilde \'wī(-ə)ld\ Oscar 1854–1900 Irish author
Wil·der \'wī(-ə)l-dər\ Thornton Niven 1897–1975 Amer. author
Wil·liam \'wil-yəm\ name of 4 kings of England: I *ca* 1028–1087 *William the Conqueror* (r. 1066–87); II *ca* 1056–1100 *William Rufus* \'rü-fəs\ (r. 1087–1100); III 1650–1702 (r. 1689–1702); IV 1765–1837 (r. 1830–37)
Wil·liam Tell \'wil-yəm-'tel\ legendary Swiss patriot commanded to shoot an apple off his son's head
Wil·liams \'wil-yəmz\ Roger 1603?–1683 Eng. colonist
Williams Ted 1918–2002 *Theodore Samuel Williams* Amer. baseball player
Williams Tennessee 1911–1983 orig. *Thomas Lanier Williams* Amer. playwright
Williams Venus 1980–   and her sister Serena 1981–   Amer. tennis players
Wil·son \'wil-sən\ (Thomas) Woodrow 1856–1924 28th pres. of the U.S. (1913–21); Nobel Prize winner (1919)
Win·throp \'win(t)-thrəp\ John 1588–1649 1st governor of Massachusetts Bay Colony
Woden — see ODIN
Woll·stone·craft \'wùl-stən-ˌkraft\ Mary 1759–1797 Eng. feminist and writer
Woods \'wùdz\ Tiger 1975–   *Eldrick Woods* Amer. golfer
Woolf \'wùlf\ Virginia 1882–1941 Eng. author
Words·worth \'wərdz-(ˌ)wərth\ William 1770–1850 Eng. poet
Wo·vo·ka \wō-'vō-kə\ 1858?–1932 *Jack Wilson* Paiute Indian mystic
Wren \'ren\ Sir Christopher 1632–1723 Eng. architect
Wright \'rīt\ Frank Lloyd 1867–1959 Amer. architect
Wright Orville 1871–1948 and his brother Wilbur 1867–1912 Amer. pioneers in aviation
Wright Richard 1908–1960 Amer. author
Wy·eth \'wī-əth\ Andrew Newell 1917–   Amer. painter
Yeats \'yāts\ William Butler 1865–1939 Irish author
Yel·tsin \'yelt-sən, 'yel-sin\ Boris Nikolayevich 1931–2007 pres. of Russia (1990–99)
York \'yòrk\ Alvin Cullum 1887–1964 Amer. hero in World War I
Young \'yəŋ\ Brig·ham \'brig-əm\ 1801–1877 Amer. Mormon leader
Za·har·i·as \zə-'ha-rē-əs\ Babe Didrikson 1914–1956 *Mildred Ella Zaharias* née *Didrikson* Amer. athlete
Zech·a·ri·ah \ˌzek-ə-'rī-ə\ Hebrew prophet of the 6th cent. B.C.
Zeng·er \'zeŋ-gər, -ər\ John Peter 1697–1746 Amer. (Ger.-born) journalist and printer
Zeph·y·rus \'ze-fə-rəs\ god of the west wind in Greek mythology
Zeus \'züs\ chief god and ruler of the sky and weather in Greek mythology — compare JUPITER

GEOGRAPHICAL NAMES

This section gives basic information about the world's countries, regions, cities, and major physical features. The latest population figures are given for nations, cities, and some regions. For many of these entries, derived nouns and adjectives are also listed (as **Iceland** . . . **Icelander** . . . *n*). Other derived words not shown here have been separately entered in the main A-Z section, because of the presence of additional senses (as **Chinese**).

Abbreviations used here are listed in the front section Abbreviations in This Work. The capital letters N, E, S, and W, used singly or in combination and without a period, indicate direction. For example, "N India" means "northern India." Where direction is a part of the name, the word is spelled out.

The symbol ✳ denotes a capital. Sizes are given in conventional U.S. units, with metric equivalents following.

Ab·er·deen \ˌa-bər-ˈdēn\ city NE Scotland; *pop* 211,080 — **Ab·er·do·ni·an** \ˌa-bər-ˈdō-nē-ən\ *adj or n*
Ab·i·djan \ˌä-bē-ˈjän, ˌa-bi-\ city, seat of government of Ivory Coast; *pop* 1,934,342
Abilene \ˈa-bə-ˌlēn\ city NW *cen* Texas; *pop* 115,930
Abu Dha·bi \ˌä-bü-ˈdä-bē, -ˈthä-\ city, ✳ of United Arab Emirates; *pop* 347,000
Abu·ja \ä-ˈbü-jä\ city *cen* Nigeria; its ✳; *pop* 423,391
Ab·ys·sin·ia \ˌa-bə-ˈsi-nē-ə, -nyə\ — see ETHIOPIA — **Ab·ys·sin·i·an** \-nē-ən, -nyən\ *adj or n*
Aca·dia \ə-ˈkā-dē-ə\ *or French* **Aca·die** \ä-kä-ˈdē\ NOVA SCOTIA — an early name — **Aca·di·an** \-ē-ən\ *adj or n*
Aca·pul·co \ˌä-kä-ˈpül-(ˌ)kō, ˌa-\ city & port S Mexico on the Pacific; *pop* 687,292
Ac·cra \ˈä-krə, ˈa-; ə-ˈkrä\ city & port, ✳ of Ghana; *pop* 867,459
Acon·ca·gua \ˌä-kōn-ˈkä-gwä\ mountain 22,834 ft. (6960 m.) W Argentina; highest in the Andes & in Western Hemisphere
Ad·dis Aba·ba \ˈä-dis-ˈä-bä-ˌbä, ˌa-dəs-ˈa-bə-bə\ city, ✳ of Ethiopia; *pop* 2,646,000
Ad·e·laide \ˈa-də-ˌlād\ city S Australia, ✳ of South Australia; *pop* 917,000
Aden \ˈä-dᵊn, ˈä-\ city & port S Yemen; *pop* 240,370
Aden, Gulf of arm of Indian Ocean between Yemen (Arabia) & Somalia (Africa)
Adirondack \ˌa-də-ˈrän-ˌdak\ mountains NE New York; highest Mount Marcy 5344 ft. (1629 m.)
Admiralty \ˈad-m(ə-)rəl-tē\ **1** island SE Alaska **2** islands W Pacific N of New Guinea; part of Papua New Guinea
Adri·at·ic Sea \ˌā-drē-ˈa-tik, ˌa-\ arm of Mediterranean between Italy & Balkan Peninsula
Ae·ge·an Sea \i-ˈjē-ən\ arm of Mediterranean between Asia Minor & Greece
Af·ghan·i·stan \af-ˈga-nə-ˌstan, -ˈgä-nə-ˌstän\ country W Asia E of Iran; ✳, Kabul; *pop* (est.) 28,717,000
Af·ri·ca \ˈa-fri-kə\ continent S of the Mediterranean
Aga·na \ä-ˈgä-nyä\ town, ✳ of Guam; *pop* 1139
Agra \ˈä-grə, ˈə-\ city N India SSE of Delhi; *pop* 1,259,979
Aguas·ca·lien·tes \ˌä-gwäs-ˌkäl-ˈyen-ˌtäs\ city *cen* Mexico NE of Guadalajara; metropolitan area *pop* 637,303
Agul·has, Cape \ə-ˈgə-ləs\ cape Republic of South Africa; most southerly point of Africa, at 34° 52′ S latitude
Ahag·gar \ə-ˈhä-gər, ˌä-hə-ˈgär\ mountains S Algeria in W *cen* Sahara
Ah·mad·abad \ˈä-mə-də-ˌbäd, -ˌbad\ city W India N of Bombay; *pop* 3,515,361
Ak·ron \ˈa-krən\ city NE Ohio; *pop* 217,074
Al·a·bama \ˌa-lə-ˈba-mə\ state SE U.S.; ✳, Montgomery; *pop* 4,447,100 — **Al·a·bam·i·an** \-ˈba-mē-ən\ *or* **Al·a·bam·an** \-ˈba-mən\ *adj or n*
Alas·ka \ə-ˈlas-kə\ **1** peninsula SW Alaska SW of Cook Inlet **2** state of U.S. in NW North America; ✳, Juneau; *pop* 626,932 **3** mountain range S Alaska extending from Alaska Peninsula to Yukon boundary — **Alas·kan** \-kən\ *adj or n*

Alaska, Gulf of inlet of Pacific off S Alaska between Alaska Peninsula on W & Alexander Archipelago on E
Al·ba·nia \al-ˈbā-nē-ə, -nyə\ country S Europe in Balkan Peninsula on Adriatic; ✳, Tirane; *pop* 3,069,275
Al·ba·ny \ˈol-bə-nē\ city, ✳ of New York; *pop* 95,658
Albemarle Sound \ˈal-bə-ˌmärl\ inlet of the Atlantic in NE North Carolina
Albert, Lake \ˈal-bərt\ lake E Africa between Uganda & Democratic Republic of the Congo in course of the Nile
Al·ber·ta \al-ˈbər-tə\ province W Canada; ✳, Edmonton; *pop* 2,974,807 — **Al·ber·tan** \-ˈbər-tᵊn\ *adj or n*
Al·bu·quer·que \ˈal-bə-ˌkər-kē\ city *cen* New Mexico; *pop* 448,607
Al·ca·traz \ˈal-kə-ˌtraz\ island California in San Francisco Bay
Al·da·bra \äl-ˈdä-brə\ island NW Indian Ocean N of Madagascar; belongs to Seychelles
Al·der·ney \ˈȯl-dər-nē\ — see CHANNEL
Alep·po \ə-ˈle-(ˌ)pō\ city N Syria; *pop* 1,445,000
Aleu·tian \ə-ˈlü-shən\ islands SW Alaska extending 1700 mi. (2735 km.) W from Alaska Peninsula
Al·ex·an·der \ˌal-ig-ˈzan-dər, ˌel-\ archipelago SE Alaska
Al·ex·an·dria \ˌa-lig-ˈzan-drē-ə, ˌe-\ **1** city N Virginia S of District of Columbia; *pop* 128,283 **2** city N Egypt on the Mediterranean; *pop* 3,170,000 — **Al·ex·an·dri·an** \-drē-ən\ *adj or n*
Al·ge·ria \al-ˈjir-ē-ə\ country NW Africa on Mediterranean; ✳, Algiers; *pop* 22,971,000 — **Al·ge·ri·an** \-ē-ən\ *adj or n*
Al·giers \al-ˈjirz\ city, ✳ of Algeria; *pop* 1,365,400 — **Al·ge·rine** \al-jə-ˈrēn\ *adj or n*
Al·lah·a·bad \ˈä-lä-hä-ˌbäd, ˈa-lə-hə-ˌbad\ city N India on the Ganges; *pop* 990,298
Al·le·ghe·ny \ˌa-lə-ˈgā-nē\ **1** river 325 mi. (523 km.) long W Pennsylvania & SW New York **2** mountains of Appalachian system E U.S. in Pennsylvania, Maryland, Virginia, & West Virginia
Al·len·town \ˈa-lən-ˌtaún\ city E Pennsylvania; *pop* 106,632
Al·maty \əl-ˈmä-tē\ *or* **Al·ma–Ata** \əl-ˈmä-ə-ˈtä; ˌal-mə-ˈä-tə, -ə-ˈtä\ city, former ✳ of Kazakhstan; *pop* 1,156,200
Alps \ˈalps\ mountain system *cen* Europe — see MONT BLANC
Al·tai *or* **Al·tay** \ˌal-ˈtī\ mountain system *cen* Asia between Mongolia & W China & between Kazakhstan & Russia
Ama·ga·sa·ki \ˌä-mä-gä-ˈsä-kē\ city Japan in W *cen* Honshu; *pop* 466,187
Am·a·ril·lo \ˌa-mə-ˈri-(ˌ)lō, -lə\ city NW Texas; *pop* 173,627
Am·a·zon \ˈa-mə-ˌzän, -zən\ river 3900 mi. (6436 km.) long N South America flowing from Peruvian Andes into Atlantic in N Brazil
Amer·i·ca \ə-ˈmer-ə-kə, -ˈme-rə-\ **1** either continent (**North America** or **South America**) of Western Hemisphere **2** *or* the **Amer·i·cas** \-kəz\ lands of Western Hemisphere including North, Central, & South America & West Indies **3** UNITED STATES OF AMERICA — **American** *adj or n*
American Falls — see NIAGARA FALLS

American Samoa or **Eastern Samoa** islands SW cen Pacific; U.S. territory; ✳, Pago Pago (on Tutuila Island); pop 57,291

Am·man \ä-ˈmän, a-, -ˈman\ city, ✳ of Jordan; pop 627,505

Am·ster·dam \ˈam(p)-stər-ˌdam, ˈäm(p)-stər-ˌdäm\ city, official ✳ of the Netherlands; pop 735,526

Amur \ä-ˈmu̇r\ river 1780 mi. (2784 km.) long E Asia flowing into the Pacific & forming part of boundary between China & Russia

An·a·heim \ˈa-nə-ˌhīm\ city SW California E of Long Beach; pop 328,014

An·a·to·lia \ˌa-nə-ˈtō-lē-ə, -ˈtōl-yə\ — see ASIA MINOR — **An·a·to·li·an** \-ˈtō-lē-ən, -ˈtōl-yən\ adj or n

An·chor·age \ˈaŋ-k(ə-)rij\ city S cen Alaska; pop 260,283

An·da·man \ˈan-də-mən, -ˌman\ 1 islands India in Bay of Bengal S of Myanmar & N of Nicobar Islands 2 sea, arm of Bay of Bengal S of Myanmar — **An·da·man·ese** \ˌan-də-mə-ˈnēz, -ˈnēs\ adj or n

An·des \ˈan-(ˌ)dēz\ mountain system W South America extending from Panama to Tierra del Fuego — see ACONCAGUA — **An·de·an** \ˈan-(ˌ)dē-ən, an-ˈ\ adj — **An·dine** \ˈan-ˌdēn, -ˌdīn\ adj

An·dor·ra \an-ˈdȯr-ə, -ˈdär-ə\ country SW Europe in E Pyrenees between France & Spain; ✳, Andorra la Vella; pop 57,110 — **An·dor·ran** \-ən\ adj or n

Andorra la Vel·la \lä-ˈvel-yä\ town, ✳ of Andorra; pop 21,513

An·dros \ˈan-drəs\ island, largest of Bahamas

An·gel Falls \ˈän-jəl\ waterfall 3212 ft. (979 m.) SE Venezuela; world's highest waterfall

Ang·kor \ˈaŋ-ˌkȯr\ ruins of ancient city NW Cambodia

An·gle·sey \ˈaŋ-gəl-sē\ island NW Wales

An·go·la \aŋ-ˈgō-lə, an-\ country SW Africa S of mouth of Congo River; ✳, Luanda; pop 10,609,000 — **An·go·lan** \-lən\ adj or n

An·i·ak·chak Crater \ˌa-nē-ˈak-ˌchak\ volcanic crater SW Alaska on Alaska Peninsula; 6 mi. (10 km.) in diameter

An·ka·ra \ˈaŋ-kə-rə, ˈäŋ-\ city, ✳ of Turkey in N cen Anatolia; pop 2,559,471

An·nap·o·lis \ə-ˈna-pə-lis\ city, ✳ of Maryland; pop 35,838

Ann Ar·bor \(ˌ)an-ˈär-bər\ city SE Michigan; pop 114,024

An·shan \ˈän-ˈshän\ city NE China; pop 1,203,986

An·ta·nan·a·ri·vo \ˌän-tä-ˌnä-nä-ˈrē-(ˌ)vō\ city, ✳ of Madagascar; pop 958,929

Ant·arc·ti·ca \ant-ˈärk-ti-kə, -ˈär-ti-\ body of land around the South Pole; plateau covered by great ice cap

An·ti·gua \an-ˈtē-gə, -gwə\ island West Indies in the Leewards; with Barbuda forms independent **Antigua and Barbuda**; ✳, Saint John's; pop 83,000

An·til·les \an-ˈti-lēz\ the West Indies except for the Bahamas — see GREATER ANTILLES; LESSER ANTILLES — **An·til·le·an** \-lē-ən\ adj

An·trim \ˈan-trəm\ district E Northern Ireland; pop 44,322

Ant·werp \ˈant-ˌwərp, ˈan-ˌtwərp\ city N Belgium; pop 448,709

Aomen — see MACAO

Aorangi — see COOK, MOUNT

Ap·en·nines \ˈa-pə-ˌnīnz\ mountain chain Italy extending length of the peninsula; highest peak Monte Corno (NE of Rome) 9560 ft. (2897 m.) — **Ap·en·nine** \ˈa-pə-ˌnīnz\ adj

Apia \ä-ˈpē-ä\ town, ✳ of Samoa; pop 38,000

Apo, Mount \ˈä-(ˌ)pō\ volcano Philippines in SE Mindanao 9692 ft. (2954 m.); highest peak in the Philippines

Ap·pa·la·chia \ˌa-pə-ˈlä-chə, -ˈla-chə, -ˈlä-shə\ region E U.S. including Appalachian Mountains from S cen New York to cen Alabama — see MITCHELL, MOUNT

Ap·pa·la·chian Mountains \ˌa-pə-ˈlä-ch(ē-)ən, -sh(ē-)ən\ mountain system E North America extending from S Quebec to cen Alabama — see MITCHELL, MOUNT

Aqa·ba, Gulf of \ˈä-kä-bə\ arm of Red Sea E of Sinai Peninsula

Aquid·neck \ə-ˈkwid-ˌnek\ or **Rhode** island SE Rhode Island in Narragansett Bay

Ara·bia \ə-ˈrä-bē-ə\ peninsula of SW Asia including Saudi Arabia, Yemen, Oman, & Persian Gulf States

Ara·bi·an \ə-ˈrä-bē-ən\ 1 desert E Egypt between the Nile & Red Sea 2 sea NW section of Indian Ocean between Arabia & India

Ara·fu·ra \ˌä-rä-ˈfü-rä\ sea between N Australia & W New Guinea

Ar·al Sea \ˈa-rəl\ formerly **Lake Aral** lake W Asia between Kazakhstan & Uzbekistan

Ar·a·rat \ˈa-rə-ˌrat\ mountain 16,946 ft. (5165 m.) E Turkey near border of Iran

Arc·tic \ˈärk-tik, ˈär-tik\ 1 ocean N of Arctic Circle 2 Arctic regions 3 archipelago N Canada in Nunavut & Northwest Territories

Ar·da·bil or **Ar·de·bil** \ˌär-də-ˈbēl\ city NW Iran; pop 281,973

Ards \ˈärdz\ district E Northern Ireland; pop 64,026

Are·ci·bo \ˌä-rä-ˈsē-(ˌ)bō\ city & port N Puerto Rico; pop 100,131

Ar·gen·ti·na \ˌär-jən-ˈtē-nə\ country S South America between the Andes & the Atlantic; ✳, Buenos Aires; pop 33,070,000 — **Ar·gen·tine** \ˈär-jən-ˌtīn, -ˌtēn\ adj or n — **Ar·gen·tin·ean** or **Ar·gen·tin·i·an** \ˌär-jən-ˈti-nē-ən\ adj or n

Ar·gos \ˈär-ˌgȯs, -gəs\ ancient Greek city-state S Greece

Ar·i·zo·na \ˌa-rə-ˈzō-nə\ state SW U.S.; ✳, Phoenix; pop 5,130,632 — **Ar·i·zo·nan** \-nən\ or **Ar·i·zo·nian** \-nē-ən, -nyən\ adj or n

Ar·kan·sas \ˈär-kən-ˌsȯ\ 1 river 1450 mi. (2334 km.) long SW cen U.S. flowing SE into the Mississippi 2 state S cen U.S.; ✳, Little Rock; pop 2,673,400 — **Ar·kan·san** \är-ˈkan-zən\ adj or n

Ar·ling·ton \ˈär-liŋ-tən\ city N Texas; pop 332,969

Ar·magh \är-ˈmä, ˈär-ˌ\ 1 district S Northern Ireland; pop 51,331 2 town cen Armagh district; pop 14,265

Ar·me·nia \är-ˈmē-nē-ə, -nyə\ 1 region W Asia in mountainous area SE of Black Sea & SW of Caspian Sea divided between Iran, Turkey, & Armenia (country) 2 country E Europe; ✳, Yerevan; pop 3,426,000

Arn·hem Land \ˈär-nəm\ region N Australia on N coast of Northern Territory

Ar·no \ˈär-(ˌ)nō\ river 150 mi. (241 km.) long cen Italy flowing through Florence

Aru·ba \ə-ˈrü-bə\ island Netherlands Antilles off coast of NW Venezuela; pop 69,000

Ar·va·da \är-ˈva-də\ city N cen Colorado NW of Denver; pop 102,153

Ash·ga·bat \ˈäsh-gə-ˌbät\ or **Ashkh·a·bad** \ˈash-kə-ˌbad, -ˌbäd\ city, ✳ of Turkmenistan; pop 412,200

Asia \ˈā-zhə, -shə\ continent of Eastern Hemisphere N of the Equator — see EURASIA

Asia Mi·nor \-ˈmī-nər\ or **An·a·to·lia** \ˌa-nə-ˈtō-lē-ə, -ˈtōl-yə\ peninsula in modern Turkey between Black Sea on N & the Mediterranean on S

As·ma·ra \az-ˈmä-rə, -ˈma-rə\ city, ✳ of Eritrea; pop 342,706

As·syr·ia \ə-ˈsir-ē-ə\ ancient empire W Asia extending along the middle Tigris & over foothills to the E — **As·syr·i·an** \-ən\ adj or n

As·ta·na \ä-stä-ˈnä\ city, ✳ of Kazakhstan; pop 319,318

Asun·ción \ä-sün-ˈsyōn\ city, ✳ of Paraguay; pop 502,426

As·wân \a-ˈswän, ä-\ city S Egypt on the Nile near site of Aswân High Dam; pop 191,461

Ata·ca·ma \ˌä-tä-ˈkä-mä\ desert N Chile

Atchaf·a·laya \(ə-)ˌcha-fə-ˈlī-ə\ river 225 mi. (362 km.) long S Louisiana flowing S into Gulf of Mexico

Ath·a·bas·ca or **Ath·a·bas·ka** \ˌa-thə-ˈbas-kə, ˌä-\ river 765 mi. (1231 km.) long NE Alberta flowing into **Lake Athabasca** on Alberta–Saskatchewan border

Ath·ens \ˈa-thənz\ 1 city NE Georgia; pop 101,489 2 city, ✳ of Greece; pop 748,110 — **Athe·nian** \ə-ˈthē-nē-ən, -nyən\ adj or n

At·lan·ta \ət-ˈlan-tə, at-\ city, ✳ of Georgia; pop 416,474

At·lan·tic \ət-ˈlan-tik, at-\ ocean separating North America & South America from Europe & Africa; often divided into **North Atlantic** and **South Atlantic** — **Atlantic** adj

At·las \ˈat-ləs\ mountains NW Africa extending from SW Morocco to N Tunisia

At·ti·ca \ˈa-ti-kə\ ancient state E Greece; chief city Athens — **At·tic** \ˈat-ik\ adj

Auck·land \ˈȯ-klənd\ city N New Zealand on NW North Island; urban area pop 1,074,510

Au·gus·ta \ò-'gəs-tə, ə-\ **1** city E Georgia; *pop* 199,775 **2** city, ✳ of Maine; *pop* 18,560

Au·ro·ra \ə-'ròr-ə, ò-\ **1** city NE *cen* Colorado; *pop* 276,393 **2** city NE Illinois; *pop* 142,990

Auschwitz — see OSWIECIM

Aus·tin \'òs-tən, 'äs-\ city, ✳ of Texas; *pop* 656,562

Aus·tral·asia \,òs-trə-'lä-zhə, ,äs-, -'lä-shə\ Australia, Tasmania, New Zealand, & Melanesia — **Aus·tral·asian** \-zhən, -shən\ *adj or n*

Aus·tra·lia \ò-'sträl-yə, ä-, ə-\ **1** continent of Eastern Hemisphere SE of Asia **2** country including continent of Australia & island of Tasmania; ✳, Canberra; *pop* 17,562,000 — **Aus·tra·lian** \-yən\ *adj or n*

Australian Alps mountain range SE Australia in E Victoria & SE New South Wales; part of Great Dividing Range

Australian Capital Territory district SE Australia including two areas, one containing Canberra (✳ of Australia) & the other on Jervis Bay (inlet of the South Pacific); surrounded by New South Wales

Aus·tria \'òs-trē-ə, 'äs-\ country *cen* Europe; ✳, Vienna; *pop* 7,812,100 — **Aus·tri·an** \-ən\ *adj or n*

Aus·tria–Hun·ga·ry \-'həŋ-gə-rē\ country 1867–1918 *cen* Europe including Bohemia, Moravia, Transylvania, Galicia, and what are now Austria, Hungary, Slovenia, Crotia, & part of NE Italy — **Aus·tro–Hun·gar·i·an** \'òs-(,)trō-,həŋ-'ger-ē-ən, 'äs-\ *adj or n*

Aus·tro·ne·sia \,òs-trə-'nē-zhə, ,äs-, -'nē-shə\ **1** islands of the South Pacific **2** area extending from Madagascar through Malay Peninsula & Malay Archipelago to Hawaii & Easter Island — **Aus·tro·ne·sian** \-zhən, -shən\ *adj or n*

Avon \'ā-vən, 'a-\ river 96 mi. (154 km.) long *cen* England flowing WSW into the Severn

Ayers Rock \'erz\ outcrop *cen* Australia in SW Northern Territory

Ayles·bury \'ālz-b(ə-)rē\ town SE *cen* England; *pop* 41,288

Ayr \'er\ *or* **Ayr·shire** \-,shir, -shər\ former county SW Scotland

Azer·bai·jan \,a-zər-,bī-'jän, ,ä-\ country SE Europe bordering on Caspian Sea; ✳, Baku; *pop* 7,029,000 — **Azer·bai·ja·ni** \,a-zər-,bī-'jä-nē, ,ä-\ *adj or n*

Azores \'ā-,zòrz, ə-'\ islands Portugal in North Atlantic lying 800 mi. (1287 km.) W of Portuguese coast; *pop* 241,763 — **Azor·e·an** *or* **Azor·i·an** \ā-'zòr-ē-ən, ə-\ *adj or n*

Bab·y·lon \'ba-bə-lən, -,län\ ancient city, ✳ of Babylonia; site 55 mi. (89 km.) S of Baghdad near the Euphrates — **Bab·y·lo·nian** \,ba-bə-'lō-nyən, -nē-ən\ *adj or n*

Bab·y·lo·nia \,ba-bə-'lō-nyə, -nē-ə\ ancient country W Asia in valley of lower Euphrates and Tigris rivers

Bac·tria \'bak-trē-ə\ ancient country W Asia in present NE Afghanistan — **Bac·tri·an** \'bak-trē-ən\ *adj or n*

Bad·lands barren region SW South Dakota & NW Nebraska

Baf·fin \'ba-fən\ **1** bay of the Atlantic between W Greenland & E Baffin Island **2** island NE Canada in Arctic Archipelago N of Hudson Strait

Bagh·dad \'bag-,dad, ,bäg-'däd\ city, ✳ of Iraq on the Tigris; *pop* (est.) 5,949,000

Ba·guio \,bä-gē-'ò\ city, former summer ✳ of the Philippines in NW *cen* Luzon; *pop* 183,000

Ba·ha·mas \bə-'hä-məz\ islands in N Atlantic SE of Florida; ✳, Nassau; *pop* 303,611 — **Ba·ha·mi·an** \bə-'hä-mē-ən, -'hä-\ *or* **Ba·ha·man** \-'hä-mən, -'häm-ən\ *adj or n*

Bahia — see SALVADOR

Bah·rain \bä-'rān\ islands in Persian Gulf off coast of Arabia; country; ✳, Manama; *pop* 485,600 — **Bah·raini** \-'rä-nē\ *adj or n*

Bai·kal, Lake *or* **Lake Bay·kal** \bī-'käl, -'kal\ lake Russia, in mountains N of Mongolia

Ba·ja California \'bä-(,)hä\ peninsula NW Mexico W of Gulf of California

Bakersfield \'bā-kərz-,fēld\ city S California; *pop* 247,057

Ba·ku \bä-'kü\ city, ✳ of Azerbaijan on W coast of Caspian Sea; *pop* 1,150,000

Bal·a·ton \'ba-lə-,tän, 'bò-lò-,tòn\ lake W Hungary

Bal·boa Heights \(,)bal-'bō-ə\ town Panama; formerly the center of administration for Canal Zone

Bal·e·ar·ic Islands \,ba-lē-'a-rik\ islands E Spain in the W Mediterranean

Ba·li \'bä-lē, 'ba-\ island Indonesia off E end of Java; *pop* 2,777,811 — **Ba·li·nese** \,bäl-i-nēz, ,bal-, -'nēs\ *adj or n*

Bal·kan \'bòl-kən\ **1** mountains N Bulgaria extending from Serbia border to Black Sea; highest 7793 ft. (2375 m.) **2** peninsula SE Europe between Adriatic & Ionian seas on the W & Aegean & Black seas on the E

Bal·kans \'bòl-kənz\ *or* **Balkan States** countries occupying the Balkan Peninsula: Slovenia, Croatia, Bosnia and Herzegovina, Macedonia, Serbia, Montenegro, Romania, Bulgaria, Albania, Greece, Turkey (in Europe)

Bal·ly·me·na \,ba-lē-'mē-nə\ district NE *cen* Northern Ireland; *pop* 56,032

Bal·ly·mon·ey \,ba-lē-'mə-nē\ district N *cen* Northern Ireland; *pop* 23,984

Bal·tic Sea \'bòl-tik\ arm of the Atlantic N Europe E of Scandinavian Peninsula

Bal·ti·more \'bòl-tə-,mòr, -mər\ city N *cen* Maryland; *pop* 651,154

Ba·ma·ko \'bä-mä-,kō\ city, ✳ of Mali on the Niger; *pop* 745,787

Ban·bridge \ban-'brij\ district SE *cen* Northern Ireland; *pop* 33,102

Ban·dar Se·ri Be·ga·wan \,bən-dər-,ser-ē-bə-'gä-wän\ town, ✳ of Brunei; *pop* 27,285

Ban·dung \'bän-,dùŋ\ city Indonesia in W Java SE of Jakarta; *pop* 2,057,442

Ban·ga·lore \'baŋ-gə-,lòr\ city S India W of Madras; *pop* 4,292,223

Bang·kok \'baŋ-,käk, baŋ-'\ city, ✳ of Thailand; *pop* 6,320,200

Ban·gla·desh \,bäŋ-glə-'desh, ,baŋ-, ,bəŋ-, -'däsh\ country S Asia E of India; ✳, Dhaka; *pop* 115,075,000 — see EAST PAKISTAN — **Ban·gla·deshi** \-'de-shē, -'dä-\ *adj or n*

Ban·gor \'baŋ-,gòr, 'ban-,gòr\ town E Northern Ireland; *pop* 46,585

Ban·gui \bäŋ-'gē\ city, ✳ of Central African Republic; *pop* 300,723

Ban·jul \'bän-,jül\ *formerly* **Bath·urst** \'bath-(,)ərst\ city & port, ✳ of Gambia; *pop* 44,188

Bao·tou *or* **Pao–t'ou** \'baù-'tō\ city N China; *pop* 983,508

Bar·ba·dos \bär-'bā-(,)dōs, -dəs, -(,)dōz\ island West Indies in Lesser Antilles E of Windward Islands; country, ✳, Bridgetown; *pop* 250,010 — **Bar·ba·di·an** \-'bā-dē-ən\ *adj or n*

Bar·bu·da \bär-'bü-də\ island West Indies; part of independent Antigua and Barbuda

Bar·ce·lo·na \,bär-sə-'lō-nə\ city NE Spain on the Mediterranean; chief city of Catalonia; *pop* 1,503,884

Bar·king and Dag·en·ham \'bär-kiŋ-ən(d)-'da-gə-nəm\ borough of E Greater London, England; *pop* 139,900

Bar·na·ul \,bär-nə-'ül\ city S Russia; *pop* 606,000

Bar·net \'bär-nət\ borough of N Greater London, England; *pop* 283,000

Bar·ran·qui·lla \,bär-än-'kē-yä\ city N Colombia; *pop* 1,018,800

Barren Grounds treeless plains N Canada W of Hudson Bay

Bar·rie \'ba-rē\ city Canada in SE Ontario; *pop* 103,710

Bar·row, Point \'ba-(,)rō\ most northerly point of Alaska & of U.S. at about 71°25′ N latitude

Ba·si·lan \bä-'sē-,län\ island S Philippines

Bas·il·don \'ba-zəl-dən\ town SE England; *pop* 157,500

Bass \'bas\ strait separating Tasmania & continent of Australia

Basse·terre \bäs-'ter, bäs-\ seaport Saint Kitts, ✳ of Saint Kitts and Nevis; *pop* 14,725

Basutoland — see LESOTHO

Bathurst — see BANJUL

Bat·on Rouge \,ba-tºn-'rüzh\ city, ✳ of Louisiana; *pop* 227,818

Ba·var·ia \bə-'ver-ē-ə\ *or German* **Bay·ern** \'bī-ərn\ state SE Germany bordering on Czech Republic & Austria; *pop* 11,448,800 — **Ba·var·i·an** \bə-'ver-ē-ən, -'var-\ *adj or n*

Ba·ya·mon \,bī-ä-'mōn\ city NE *cen* Puerto Rico; *pop* 224,004

Beau·fort \'bō-fərt\ sea consisting of part of Arctic Ocean NE of Alaska & NW of Canada

Beau·mont \'bō-ˌmänt, bō-'\ city SE Texas; *pop* 113,866

Bech·u·a·na·land \ˌbech-'wä-nə-ˌland, ˌbe-chə-\ 1 region S Africa N of Orange River 2 — see BOTSWANA — **Bech·u·a·na** \ˌbech-'wä-nə, ˌbe-chə-\ *adj or n*

Bed·ford·shire \'bed-fərd-ˌshir, -shər\ *or* **Bedford** county SE England

Bedloe's — see LIBERTY

Bei·jing \'bā-'jiŋ\ *or* **Pe·king** \'pē-'kiŋ, 'pā-\ city, ✳ of China; *pop* 10,819,407

Bei·rut \bā-'rüt\ city, ✳ of Lebanon; urban area *pop* 1,100,000

Be·la·rus \ˌbel-ə-'rüs, ˌbye-lə-\ country *cen* Europe; ✳, Minsk; *pop* 9,899,000 — **Be·la·ru·si·an** \-'rü-sē-ən, -'rə-shən\ *or* **Be·la·rus·sian** \-'rə-shən\ *adj or n*

Belau — see PALAU

Be·lém \be-'lem\ city N Brazil; *pop* 1,280,614

Bel·fast \'bel-ˌfast, bel-'\ city, ✳ of Northern Ireland; *pop* 295,100

Bel·gium \'bel-jəm\ *or French* **Bel·gique** \bel-'zhēk\ *or Flemish* **Bel·gië** \'bel-ḡē-ə\ country W Europe; ✳, Brussels; *pop* 10,309,725 — **Bel·gian** \'bel-jən\ *adj or n*

Bel·grade \'bel-ˌgräd, -ˌgräd, -ˌgrad, bel-'\ *or* **Beo·grad** \bä-'ō-ˌgräd\ city, ✳ of Serbia on the Danube; *pop* 1,553,854

Be·lize \bə-'lēz\ *formerly* **British Honduras** country Central America on the Caribbean; ✳, Belmopan; *pop* 241,000 — **Be·liz·ean** *adj or n*

Belize City seaport E Belize; *pop* 45,158

Belle·vue \'bel-ˌvyü\ city W Washington E of Seattle; *pop* 109,569

Bel·mo·pan \ˌbel-mō-'pän\ city, ✳ of Belize; *pop* 6500

Be·lo Ho·ri·zon·te \'bä-lō-ˌōr-ē-'zōn-tē\ city E Brazil N of Rio de Janeiro; *pop* 2,238,526

Be·lo·rus·sia \ˌbe-lō-'rə-shə, ˌbye-lō-\ *or* **Bye·lo·rus·sia** \bē-, e-lō-, ˌbye-lō-\ former republic of U.S.S.R.; became independent Belarus in 1991 — **Belo·rus·sian** \ˌbe-lō-'rə-shən, ˌbye-\ *adj or n*

Ben·gal \ben-'gól, beŋ-, -'gäl\ region S Asia including delta of Ganges & Brahmaputra rivers; divided between Bangladesh & India — **Ben·gal·ese** \ˌbeŋ-gə-'lēz, ˌben-, -'lēs\ *adj or n*

Bengal, Bay of arm of Indian Ocean between India & Myanmar

Be·nin \bə-'nēn, -'nin; 'be-nin\ *formerly* **Da·ho·mey** \də-'hō-mē\ country W Africa on Gulf of Guinea; ✳, Porto-Novo; *pop* 5,074,000 — **Ben·i·nese** \bə-ˌni-'nēz, -ˌnē-, -'nēs; ˌbe-ni-'nēz, -'nēs\ *adj or n*

Ben Nev·is \ben-'ne-vəs\ mountain 4406 ft. (1343 m.) W Scotland in the Grampians; highest in Great Britain

Beograd — see BELGRADE

Ber·gen \'bər-gən, 'ber-\ city & port SW Norway; *pop* 209,375

Be·ring \'bir-iŋ, 'ber-\ 1 sea, arm of the North Pacific between Alaska & NE Siberia 2 strait at narrowest point 53 mi. (85 km.) wide between North America (Alaska) and Asia (Russia)

Berke·ley \'bər-klē\ city W California on San Francisco Bay N of Oakland; *pop* 102,743

Berk·shire \'bərk-ˌshir, -shər\ hills W Massachusetts; highest point Mount Greylock 3491 ft. (1064 m.)

Ber·lin \(ˌ)bər-'lin, *G* ber-'lēn\ city, ✳ of Germany; divided 1945–90 into **East Berlin** (✳ of East Germany) & **West Berlin** (city of West Germany lying within East Germany); *pop* 3,392,900 — **Ber·lin·er** \(ˌ)bər-'li-nər\ *n*

Ber·mu·da \(ˌ)bər-'myü-də\ islands W Atlantic ESE of Cape Hatteras; a British colony; ✳, Hamilton; *pop* 62,059 — **Ber·mu·dan** \-dᵊn\ *or* **Ber·mu·di·an** \-dē-ən\ *adj or n*

Bern \'bern, 'bern\ city, ✳ of Switzerland; *pop* 122,469 — **Ber·nese** \(ˌ)bər-'nēz, -'nēs\ *adj or n*

Bes·sa·ra·bia \ˌbe-sə-'rä-bē-ə\ region SE Europe now chiefly in Moldova — **Bes·sa·ra·bi·an** \-bē-ən\ *adj or n*

Beth·le·hem \'beth-li-ˌhem, -lē-həm, -lē-əm\ town of ancient Palestine in Judaea; the present-day town is SW of Jerusalem in the West Bank; *pop* 34,180

Bev·er·ly Hills \'be-vər-lē\ city SW California within Los Angeles; *pop* 33,784

Bex·ley \'bek-slē\ borough of E Greater London, England; *pop* 211,200

Bho·pal \bō-'päl\ city N *cen* India; *pop* 1,433,875

Bhu·tan \bü-'tän, -'tan\ country S Asia in the Himalayas on NE border of India; ✳, Thimphu; *pop* 1,546,000 — **Bhu·ta·nese** \ˌbü-tə-'nēz, -'nēs\ *adj or n*

Bi·ki·ni \bi-'kē-nē\ atoll W Pacific in Marshall Islands

Bil·lings \'bi-liŋz\ city S *cen* Montana; largest in state; *pop* 89,847

Bi·loxi \bə-'lək-sē, -'läk-\ city & port SE Mississippi on Gulf of Mexico; *pop* 50,644

Bi·o·ko \bē-'ō-(ˌ)kō\ *formerly* **Fer·nan·do Póo** \fer-'nän-(ˌ)dō-'pō\ island portion of Equatorial Guinea in Gulf of Guinea

Bir·ken·head \'bər-kən-ˌhed, ˌbər-kən-'\ borough NW England on the Mersey opposite Liverpool; *pop* 123,907

Bir·ming·ham \'bər-miŋ-ˌham\ 1 city N *cen* Alabama; *pop* 242,820 2 city W *cen* England; *pop* 934,900

Bis·cay, Bay of \'bis-ˌkā, -kē\ inlet of the Atlantic between W coast of France & N coast of Spain

Bish·kek \bish-'kek\ *formerly* **1926–91** **Frun·ze** \'frün-zi\ city, ✳ of Kyrgyzstan; *pop* 641,400

Bis·marck \'biz-ˌmärk\ 1 city, ✳ of North Dakota; *pop* 55,532 2 archipelago W Pacific N of E end of New Guinea

Bis·sau \bi-'saù\ city, ✳ of Guinea-Bissau; *pop* 125,000

Bi·thyn·ia \bə-'thi-nē-ə\ ancient country NW Asia Minor bordering on Sea of Marmara and Black Sea — **Bi·thyn·i·an** \-nē-ən\ *adj or n*

Bit·ter·root \'bi-tə(r)-ˌrüt, -ˌrút\ range of the Rockies along Idaho–Montana boundary

Black·burn \'blak-(ˌ)bərn\ town NW England; *pop* 132,800

Black Forest forested mountain region Germany along E bank of the upper Rhine

Black Hills mountains W South Dakota & NE Wyoming

Black·pool \'blak-ˌpül\ town NW England on Irish Sea; *pop* 144,500

Black Sea sea between Europe & Asia connected with Aegean Sea through the Bosporus, Sea of Marmara, & Dardanelles

Blanc, Mont — see MONT BLANC

Blan·tyre \'blan-ˌtī(-ə)r\ city S Malawi; *pop* 554,578

Bloem·fon·tein \'blüm-fən-ˌtān, -ˌfän-\ city Republic of South Africa, judicial ✳ of the country; *pop* 149,836

Blue Ridge E range of the Appalachians E U.S. extending from S Pennsylvania to N Georgia

Bodh Gaya \'bōd-'gī-ä\ village NE India; one of the holiest sites of Buddhism

Boe·o·tia \bē-'ō-sh(ē-)ə\ ancient state E *cen* Greece NW of Attica; chief ancient city, Thebes — **Boe·o·tian** \bē-'ō-shən\ *adj or n*

Bo·go·tá \ˌbō-gō-'tä, -'tò, 'bō-gə-ˌ\ city, ✳ of Colombia; *pop* 4,921,300

Bo Hai *or* **Po Hai** \'bō-'hī\ *or* **Gulf of Chih·li** \'chē-'lē, 'jir-\ arm of Yellow Sea NE China

Bo·he·mia \bō-'hē-mē-ə\ region W Czech Republic; chief city, Prague

Bo·hol \bō-'hól\ island S *cen* Philippines

Boi·se \'bói-sē, -zē\ city, ✳ of Idaho; *pop* 185,787

Bo·liv·ia \bə-'li-vē-ə\ country W *cen* South America; administrative ✳, La Paz; constitutional ✳, Sucre; *pop* 8,274,325 — **Bo·liv·i·an** \-vē-ən\ *adj or n*

Bo·lo·gna \bō-'lō-nyə\ city N Italy; *pop* 379,964

Bol·ton \'bōl-tᵊn\ town NW England; *pop* 253,300

Bom·bay \bäm-'bā\ *or* **Mum·bai** \'məm-ˌbī\ city & port W India; *pop* 11,914,398

Bonn \'bän, 'bón\ city Germany on the Rhine SSE of Cologne, formerly (1949–99) ✳ of West Germany; *pop* 296,244

Boo·thia \'bü-thē-ə\ peninsula N Canada W of Baffin Island; its N tip is most northerly point in mainland North America

Bor·ders \'bór-dərz\ former administrative region SE Scotland

Bor·neo \'bór-nē-ˌō\ island Malay Archipelago SW of the Philippines; divided between Brunei, Indonesia, and Malaysia

Bos·nia \'bäz-nē-ə, 'bóz\ region S Europe; with Herzegovina forms independent **Bosnia and Her·ze·go·vi·na**

\ˌhert-sə-gō-'vē-nə, ˌhərt-, -'gō-və-nə\; ✳, Sarajevo; *pop* 4,422,000 — **Bos·ni·an** \-nē-ən\ *adj or n*
Bos·po·rus \'bäs-p(ə-)rəs\ strait 18 mi. (29 km.) long between Turkey in Europe & Turkey in Asia connecting Sea of Marmara & Black Sea
Bos·ton \'bòs-tən\ city, ✳ of Massachusetts; *pop* 589,141 — **Bos·to·nian** \bò-'stō-nē-ən, -nyən\ *adj or n*
Bot·a·ny Bay \'bä-tə-nē\ inlet of South Pacific SE Australia in New South Wales S of Sydney
Both·nia, Gulf of \'bäth-nē-ə\ arm of Baltic Sea between Sweden & Finland
Bo·tswa·na \bät-'swä-nə\ *formerly* **Bech·u·a·na·land** \ˌbech-'wä-nə-land\ country S Africa; ✳, Gaborone; *pop* 1,611,021
Boul·der \'bōl-dər\ city N *cen* Colorado; *pop* 94,673
Boulder Dam — see HOOVER DAM
Bourne·mouth \'bòrn-məth, 'bùrn-\ town S England on English Channel; *pop* 154,400
Brad·ford \'brad-fərd\ city N England; *pop* 280,691
Brah·ma·pu·tra \ˌbrä-mə-'pü-trə\ river about 1800 mi. (2900 km.) long S Asia flowing from the Himalayas in Tibet to Ganges Delta
Bra·sí·lia \brə-'zil-yə\ city, ✳ of Brazil; *pop* 2,051,146
Bra·ti·sla·va \ˌbra-tə-'slä-və, ˌbrä\ city on the Danube; ✳ of Slovakia; *pop* 428,672
Bra·zil \brə-'zil\ country E & *cen* South America; ✳, Brasília; *pop* 169,799,170 — **Bra·zil·ian** \brə-'zil-yən\ *adj or n*
Braz·za·ville \'bra-zə-ˌvil, 'brä-zə-ˌvēl\ city, ✳ of Republic of the Congo on W bank of lower Congo River; *pop* 937,579
Bre·men \'bre-mən, 'brä-\ city & port NW Germany; *pop* 552,746
Bren·ner \'bre-nər\ pass 4495 ft. (1370 m.) high in the Alps between Austria & Italy
Brent \'brent\ borough of W Greater London, England; *pop* 226,100
Bret·on \'kāp-'bre-tᵊn, kə-'bre-, -'bri-\ cape Canada; most easterly point of Cape Breton Island & of Nova Scotia
Bridge·port \'brij-ˌpòrt\ city SW Connecticut on Long Island Sound; *pop* 139,529
Bridge·town \'brij-ˌtaùn\ city, ✳ of Barbados; *pop* 5996
Brigh·ton \'brī-tᵊn\ town S England on English Channel; *pop* 133,400
Bris·bane \'briz-bən, -ˌbān\ city & port E Australia, ✳ of Queensland; *pop* 751,115
Bris·tol \'bris-tᵊl\ **1** city & port SW England; *pop* 370,300 **2** channel between S Wales & SW England
Brit·ain \'bri-tᵊn\ **1** the island of Great Britain 2 see UNITED KINGDOM
British Columbia province W Canada on Pacific coast; ✳, Victoria; *pop* 3,907,738
British Commonwealth — see COMMONWEALTH, THE
British Empire former empire consisting of Great Britain & the British dominions & dependencies
British Guiana — see GUYANA
British Honduras — see BELIZE
British India the part of India formerly under direct British administration
British Indian Ocean Territory British colony in Indian Ocean consisting of Chagos Archipelago
British Isles island group W Europe consisting of Great Britain, Ireland, & nearby islands
British Virgin Islands E islands of Virgin Islands; a British possession; *pop* 14,786
British West Indies islands of the West Indies including Jamaica, Trinidad and Tobago, & the Bahama & Cayman islands, Windward Islands, Leeward Islands, & British Virgin Islands
Brit·ta·ny \'bri-tə-nē\ region NW France SW of Normandy
Brom·ley \'bräm-lē\ borough of SE Greater London, England; *pop* 281,700
Bronx \'bräŋks\ *or* **The Bronx** borough of New York City NE of Manhattan; *pop* 1,332,650
Brook·lyn \'brùk-lən\ borough of New York City at SW end of Long Island; *pop* 2,465,326
Brooks Range \'brùks\ mountains N Alaska

Browns·ville \'braùnz-ˌvil, -vəl\ city S Texas on the Rio Grande; *pop* 139,722
Bru·nei \brù-'nī, 'brü-ˌnī\ country NE Borneo; ✳, Bandar Seri Begawan; *pop* 332,844 — **Bru·nei·an** \brù-'nī-ən\ *adj or n*
Brus·sels \'brə-səlz\ city, ✳ of Belgium; *pop* 136,730
Bu·cha·rest \'bü-kə-ˌrest, 'byü\ city, ✳ of Romania; *pop* 1,921,751
Buck·ing·ham·shire \'bə-kiŋ-əm-ˌshir\ *or* **Buckingham** county SE *cen* England
Bu·da·pest \'bü-də-ˌpest\ city, ✳ of Hungary; *pop* 2,008,546
Bue·nos Ai·res \ˌbwā-nəs-'a-rēz, Sp ˌbwā-nōs-'ī-rās\ city, ✳ of Argentina; *pop* 2,960,976
Buf·fa·lo \'bə-fə-ˌlō\ city W New York on Lake Erie; *pop* 292,648
Bu·jum·bu·ra \ˌbü-jəm-'bùr-ə\ city, ✳ of Burundi; *pop* 236,334
Bu·ko·vi·na \ˌbü-kō-'vē-nə\ region E *cen* Europe in foothills of E Carpathians
Bul·gar·ia \ˌbəl-'ger-ē-ə, bùl-\ country SE Europe on Black Sea; ✳, Sofia; *pop* 8,466,000 — **Bul·gar·i·an** \ˌbəl-'ger-ē-ən, bùl-\ *adj or n*
Bull Run \'bùl-'rən\ stream NE Virginia
Bun·ker Hill \'bəŋ-kər\ height in Boston, Massachusetts
Bur·bank \'bər-ˌbaŋk\ city SW California; *pop* 100,316
Bur·gun·dy \'bər-gən-dē\ region E France — **Bur·gun·di·an** \(ˌ)bər-'gən-dē-ən\ *adj or n*
Bur·ki·na Fa·so \bùr-'kē-nə-'fä-sō, bər-\ *formerly* **Upper Vol·ta** \'vōl-tə, 'vòl-\ country W Africa N of Ivory Coast, Ghana, & Togo; ✳, Ouagadougou; *pop* 9,780,000
Bur·ling·ton \'bər-liŋ-tən\ city NW Vermont; largest in state; *pop* 38,889
Bur·ma \'bər-mə\ — see MYANMAR — **Bur·mese** \ˌbər-'mēz, -'mēs\ *adj or n*
Bu·run·di \bù-'rün-dē, -'rùn-\ country E *cen* Africa; ✳, Bujumbura; *pop* 5,665,000 — **Bu·run·di·an** \-dē-ən\ *adj or n*
Busan — see PUSAN
Bute \'byüt\ island SW Scotland in Firth of Clyde
Butte \'byüt\ city SW Montana; county *pop* 34,606
Byelorussia — see BELORUSSIA
By·zan·tine Empire \'bi-zᵊn-ˌtēn, 'bī-, -ˌtīn; bə-'zan-ˌtēn, -tīn, bī-\ empire of SE & S Europe and W Asia from 4th to 15th century
By·zan·ti·um \bə-'zan-sh(ē-)əm, -'zant-ē-əm\ ancient city on site of modern Istanbul
Caer·nar·von \kär-'när-vən, kə(r)-\ town & seaport NW Wales; *pop* 9506
Ca·guas \'kä-ˌgwäs\ town E *cen* Puerto Rico; *pop* 140,502
Cai·ro \'kī-(ˌ)rō\ city, ✳ of Egypt; *pop* 6,633,000 — **Cai·rene** \kī-'rēn\ *adj or n*
Ca·la·bria \kə-'lā-brē-ə, -'lä-\ district of ancient Italy consisting of area forming heel of Italian Peninsula — **Ca·la·bri·an** \kə-'lā-brē-ən, -'lä-\ *adj or n*
Cal·cut·ta \kal-'kə-tə\ *or* **Kol·ka·ta** \kōl-'kä-tä\ city E India on Hugli River; *pop* 4,580,544 — **Cal·cut·tan** \-'kə-tᵊn\ *adj or n*
Cal·e·do·nia \ˌka-lə-'dō-nyə, -nē-ə\ — see SCOTLAND — **Cal·e·do·nian** \-nyən, -nē-ən\ *adj or n*
Cal·ga·ry \'kal-gə-rē\ city SW Alberta, Canada; *pop* 878,866
Ca·li \'kä-lē\ city W Colombia; *pop* 1,624,400
Cal·i·for·nia \ˌka-lə-'fòr-nyə\ state SW U.S.; ✳, Sacramento; *pop* 33,871,648 — **Cal·i·for·nian** \-nyən\ *adj or n*
California, Gulf of arm of the Pacific NW Mexico
Cal·va·ry \'kal-v(ə-)rē\ place outside ancient Jerusalem where Jesus was crucified
Cambay, Gulf of — see KHAMBHAT (Gulf of)
Cam·bo·dia \kam-'bō-dē-ə\ *or* **Kam·pu·chea** \ˌkam-pù-'chē-ə\ country SE Asia in S Indochina; ✳, Phnom Penh; *pop* 11,437,656 — **Cam·bo·di·an** \kam-'bō-dē-ən\ *adj or n*
Cam·bria \'kam-brē-ə\ WALES — an old name
Cam·bridge \'kām-brij\ **1** city E Massachusetts W of Boston; *pop* 101,355 **2** city E England; *pop* 92,772
Cam·bridge·shire \'kām-brij-ˌshir, -shər\ *or* **Cambridge** county E England
Cam·den \'kam-dən\ borough of N Greater London, England; *pop* 170,500

Cam·er·oon *or French* **Cam·er·oun** \ˌka-mə-ˈrün\ country W Africa; ✳, Yaoundé; *pop* 13,103,000 — **Cam·er·oo·nian** \-ˈrü-nē-ən, -rü-nyən\ *adj or n*

Ca·mi·guin \ˌkä-mē-ˈgēn\ island S *cen* Philippines

Ca·naan \ˈkä-nən\ ancient region SW Asia; approximately the area later called Palestine — **Ca·naan·ite** \ˈkä-nə-ˌnīt\ *adj or n*

Can·a·da \ˈka-nə-də\ country N North America; ✳, Ottawa; *pop* 27,296,859 — **Ca·na·di·an** \kə-ˈnä-dē-ən\ *adj or n*

Canadian Falls — see NIAGARA FALLS

Canadian Shield *or* **Lau·ren·tian Plateau** \lȯ-ˈren(t)-shən\ plateau region E Canada & NE U.S. extending from Mackenzie River basin E to Davis Strait & S to S Quebec, S *cen* Ontario, NE Minnesota, N Wisconsin, NW Michigan, and NE New York including the Adirondacks

Canal Zone *or* **Panama Canal Zone** strip of territory Panama leased to U.S. (until 1979) for Panama Canal

Ca·nary \kə-ˈner-ē\ islands Spain in the Atlantic off NW coast of Africa; *pop* 1,493,784

Ca·nav·er·al, Cape \kə-ˈnav-rəl, -ˈna-və-\ *or* *1963–73* **Cape Ken·ne·dy** \-ˈken-ə-dē\ cape E Florida in the Atlantic on **Canaveral Peninsula** E of Indian River

Can·ber·ra \ˈkan-brə, -ˌber-ə\ *or* *adj or n* **Can·ber·ra** \ˈkan, ˈkän\ port SE France; *pop* 69,363

Can·ter·bury \ˈkan-tə(r)-ˌber-ē, -b(ə-)rē\ city SE England; *pop* 34,404

Canton — see GUANGZHOU

Cape Bret·on Island \kāp-ˈbre-tⁿn, kə-ˈbre-, -ˈbri-\ island NE Nova Scotia

Cape Coral city SW Florida; *pop* 102,286

Cape Horn — see HORN, CAPE

Cape of Good Hope — see GOOD HOPE, CAPE OF

Cape Province *or* **Cape of Good Hope** *or before 1910* **Cape Colony** former province S Republic of South Africa

Cape Town \ˈkāp-ˌtaún\ city, legislative ✳ of Republic of South Africa and formerly ✳ of Cape Province; *pop* 776,617

Cape Verde \ˈvərd\ islands in the North Atlantic off W Africa; country; ✳, Praia; *pop* 350,000 — **Cape Verd·ean** \ˈvər-dē-ən\ *adj or n*

Cape York Peninsula \ˈyórk\ peninsula NE Australia in N Queensland

Ca·pri \ka-ˈprē, kə-; ˈkä-(ˌ)prē, ˈka-\ island Italy S of Bay of Naples; *pop* 7270

Ca·ra·cas \kä-ˈrä-käs\ city, ✳ of Venezuela; *pop* 1,824,892

Car·diff \ˈkär-dif\ city, ✳ of Wales; *pop* 272,600

Ca·rib·be·an Sea \ˌka-rə-ˈbē-ən, kə-ˈri-bē-\ arm of the Atlantic; on N & E are the West Indies, on S is South America, & on W is Central America — **Caribbean** *adj*

Car·lisle \kär-ˈlī(-ə)l, kər-, ˈkär-ˌ\ city NW England; *pop* 99,800

Carls·bad Caverns \ˈkärlz(-ə)lz-ˌbad\ series of caves SE New Mexico

Car·mar·then \kär-ˈmär-thən, kə(r)-\ port S Wales; *pop* 54,800

Car·o·li·na \ˌka-rə-ˈlī-nə\ English colony on E coast of North America founded 1663 & divided 1729 into North Carolina & South Carolina (the **Carolinas**) — **Car·o·lin·i·an** \ˌka-rə-ˈli-nē-ən, -nyən\ *adj or n*

Ca·ro·li·na \kä-rō-ˈlē-nä\ city NE Puerto Rico; *pop* 186,076

Car·o·line \ˈka-rə-ˌlīn, -lən\ islands W Pacific; comprising Palau & the Federated States of Micronesia

Car·pa·thi·an \kär-ˈpā-thē-ən\ mountains E *cen* Europe along boundary between Slovakia & Poland & in N & *cen* Romania; highest Gerlachovksky 8711 ft. (2655 m.)

Car·pen·tar·ia, Gulf of \ˌkär-pən-ˈter-ē-ə\ inlet of Arafura Sea N of Australia

Car·rick·fer·gus \ˌka-rik-ˈfər-gəs\ district E Northern Ireland; *pop* 32,439

Car·roll·ton \ˈka-rəl-tən\ city N Texas; *pop* 109,576

Car·son City \ˈkär-sⁿn\ city, ✳ of Nevada; *pop* 52,457

Car·thage \ˈkär-thij\ ancient city N Africa NE of modern Tunis; ✳ of an empire that once included much of NW Africa, E Spain, & Sicily — **Car·tha·gin·ian** \ˌkär-thə-ˈji-nyən, -nē-ən\ *adj or n*

Ca·sa·blan·ca \ˌka-sə-ˈblaŋ-kə, ˌkä-sə-ˈbläŋ-, -zə-\ city W Morocco on the Atlantic; *pop* 3,102,000

Cas·cade Range \(ˌ)kas-ˈkād\ mountains NW U.S. in Washington, Oregon, & N California — see RAINIER, MOUNT

Cas·per \ˈkas-pər\ city *cen* Wyoming; *pop* 49,644

Cas·pi·an Sea \ˈkas-pē-ən\ salt lake between Europe and Asia about 90 ft. (27 m.) below sea level

Cas·tile \ka-ˈstēl\ *or in full* **Cas·ti·lla** \kä-ˈstēl-yä, -ˈstē-yä\ region & ancient kingdom *cen* & N Spain

Cas·tle·reagh \ˈka-səl-(ˌ)rā\ district E Northern Ireland; *pop* 60,649

Cas·tries \ˈkas-ˌtrēz, -ˌtrēs\ seaport, ✳ of Saint Lucia; *pop* 1814

Cat·a·lo·nia \ˌka-tə-ˈlō-nyə, -nē-ə\ region NE Spain bordering on France & the Mediterranean; chief city, Barcelona; *pop* 6,059,494 — **Cat·a·lo·nian** \-ˈlō-nyən, -nē-ən\ *adj or n*

Ca·thay \ka-ˈthā\ an old name for China

Cats·kill \ˈkat-ˌskil\ mountains in Appalachian system SE New York W of the Hudson

Cau·ca·sus \ˈkȯ-kə-səs\ mountain system SE Europe between Black & Caspian seas in Russia, Georgia, Azerbaijan, & Armenia

Cay·enne \kī-ˈen, kā-\ city, ✳ of French Guiana; *pop* 37,097

Cay·man \(ˌ)kā-ˈman, *attributively* ˈkā-mən\ islands West Indies NW of Jamaica; a British colony; *pop* 23,881

Ce·bu \sā-ˈbü\ island E *cen* Philippines

Ce·dar Rapids \ˈsē-dər\ city E Iowa; *pop* 120,758

Cel·tic Sea \ˈkel-tik, ˈsel-\ inlet of the Atlantic in British Isles SE of Ireland, SW of Wales, & W of England

Central African Republic country N *cen* Africa; ✳, Bangui; *pop* 2,998,000

Central America narrow portion of North America from S border of Mexico to South America — **Central American** *adj or n*

Central Valley valley of Sacramento & San Joaquin rivers in California between Sierra Nevada & Coast Ranges

Ce·ti·nje \ˈt(t)sē-tē-ˌnyä\ town S Montenegro having some functions of national ✳

Cey·lon \si-ˈlän, sā-\ 1 island in Indian Ocean off S India 2 — see SRI LANKA — **Cey·lon·ese** \ˌsā-lə-ˈnēz, ˌsē-, ˌse-, -ˈnēs\ *adj or n*

Chad \ˈchad\ country N *cen* Africa; ✳, N'Djamena; *pop* 5,200,000 — **Chad·ian** \ˈcha-dē-ən\ *adj or n*

Chad, Lake shallow lake N *cen* Africa at junction of boundaries of Chad, Niger, & Nigeria

Cha·gos Archipelago \ˈchä-gəs\ island group *cen* Indian Ocean; forms British Indian Ocean Territory — see DIEGO GARCIA

Chal·dea \kal-ˈdē-ə\ ancient region SW Asia on Euphrates River & Persian Gulf — **Chal·de·an** \-ˈdē-ən\ *adj or n* — **Chal·dee** \ˈkal-ˌdē\ *n*

Cham·pagne \sham-ˈpān\ region NE France

Cham·plain, Lake \sham-ˈplān\ lake between New York & Vermont extending N into Quebec

Chan·di·garh \ˈchən-dē-gər\ city N India N of Delhi; *pop* 510,565

Chan·dler \ˈchan(d)-lər\ city SW *cen* Arizona; *pop* 176,581

Chang \ˈchäŋ\ *or* **Yang·tze** \ˈyaŋ-ˈsē, ˈyaŋ(k)t-ˈsē; ˈyäŋ-ˈtsə\ river 3434 mi. (5525 km.) long *cen* China flowing into East China Sea

Chang·chun \ˈchäŋ-ˈchùn\ city NE China; *pop* 1,679,270

Chang·sha \ˈchäŋ-ˈshä\ city SE *cen* China; *pop* 1,113,312

Channel islands in English Channel including Jersey, Guernsey, & Alderney & belonging to United Kingdom; *pop* 135,694

Charles \ˈchär(-ə)lz\ river 47 mi. (76 km.) long E Massachusetts flowing into Boston harbor

Charles, Cape cape E Virginia N of entrance to Chesapeake Bay

Charles·ton \ˈchär(-ə)l-stən\ 1 seaport SE South Carolina; *pop* 96,650 2 city, ✳ of West Virginia; *pop* 53,421

Char·lotte \ˈshär-lət\ city S North Carolina; *pop* 540,828

Charlotte Ama·lie \ə-ˈmäl-yə, ˈmäl-ˌyə, ə-ˈmäl-ē\ city, ✳ of Virgin Islands of the U.S.; on island of Saint Thomas; *pop* 12,331

Char·lottes·ville \ˈshär-ləts-ˌvil, -vəl\ city *cen* Virginia; *pop* 45,049

Geographical Names

Char·lotte·town \\'shär-lət-,taún\\ city, ✳ of Prince Edward Island, Canada; *pop* 32,245

Chat·ta·noo·ga \\,cha-tə-'nü-gə\\ city SE Tennessee; *pop* 155,554

Chech·nya \\chech-'nyä, 'chech-nyə\\ republic of SE Russia in Europe; ✳, Grozny

Chelms·ford \\'chemz-fərd\\ town SE England; *pop* 150,000

Che·lya·binsk \\chel-'yä-bən(t)sk\\ city W Russia; *pop* 1,143,000

Cheng–chou — see ZHENGZHOU

Cheng·du *or* **Ch'eng–tu** \\'chən-'dü\\ city SW *cen* China; *pop* 1,713,255

Chennai — see MADRAS

Cher·no·byl \\chər-'nō-bəl, (,)cher-\\ *or* **Chor·no·byl** \\chór-'nō-bəl\\ site N Ukraine of town abandoned after 1986 nuclear accident

Ches·a·peake \\'che-sə-,pēk, 'ches-,pēk\\ city SE Virginia; *pop* 199,184

Chesapeake Bay inlet of the Atlantic in Virginia & Maryland

Chesh·ire \\'che-shər, -,shir\\ *or* **Ches·ter** \\'ches-tər\\ county W England bordering on Wales

Chester \\'ches-tər\\ city NW England; *pop* 58,436

Chev·i·ot \\'chē-vē-ət, 'che-\\ hills along English–Scottish border

Chey·enne \\shī-'an, -'en\\ city, ✳ of Wyoming; *pop* 53,011

Chi·ba \\'chē-bä\\ city E Japan in Honshu on Tokyo Bay E of Tokyo; *pop* 887,164

Chi·ca·go \\shə-'kä-(,)gō, -'kó-, -gə\\ city & port NE Illinois on Lake Michigan; *pop* 2,896,016 — **Chi·ca·go·an** \\-'kä-'gō-ən, -'kó-\\ *n*

Chi·chén Itz·zá \\chē-,chen-ēt-'sä, -'ēt-sə\\ ruined Mayan city SE Mexico in Yucatán Peninsula

Chich·es·ter \\'chi-chəs-tər\\ city S England; *pop* 24,189

Ch'i–ch'i–ha–erh — see QIQIHAR

Chihli, Gulf of — see BO HAI

Chi·le \\'chi-lē, 'chē-(,)lä\\ country SW South America; ✳, Santiago; *pop* 15,116,435 — **Chil·ean** \\'chi-lē-ən, chə-'lā-ən\\ *adj or n*

Chim·bo·ra·zo \\,chēm-bō-'rä-(,)zō\\ mountain 20,561 ft. (6267 m.) W *cen* Ecuador

Chi·na \\'chī-nə\\ **1** country E Asia; ✳, Beijing; *pop* 1,179,467,000 — see TAIWAN **2** sea section of the W Pacific; divided into East China & South China seas

Chin–chou *or* **Chinchow** — see JINZHOU

Chi·si·nau \\,kē-shē-'naú\\ *or* **Ki·shi·nev** \\,ki-shi-'nyóf; 'ki-shə-,nef, -,nev\\ city *cen* Moldova; its ✳; *pop* 665,000

Chit·ta·gong \\'chi-tə-,gäŋ, -,góŋ\\ city SE Bangladesh on Bay of Bengal; *pop* 1,566,070

Chong·qing *or* **Ch'ung–ch'ing** \\'chúŋ-'chiŋ\\ *or* **Chungking** \\'chúŋ-'kiŋ\\ city SW *cen* China; *pop* 2,266,772

Christ·church \\'krīs(t)-,chərch\\ city New Zealand on E coast of South Island; urban area 334,107

Christ·mas \\'kris-məs\\ island E Indian Ocean SW of Java; governed by Australia; *pop* 1000

Chu·la Vis·ta \\,chü-lə-'vis-tə\\ city SW California S of San Diego; *pop* 173,556

Chuuk \\'chúk\\ *or* **Truk** \\'trək, 'trúk\\ islands *cen* Carolines, part of Federated States of Micronesia

Cin·cin·na·ti \\,sin(t)-sə-'na-tē, -'na-tə\\ city SW Ohio; *pop* 331,285

Ci·u·dad Juá·rez \\syü-'thäth-'hwär-es, 'wäs-; ,sē-ù-'dad-\\ city Mexico on Texas border; urban area *pop* 1,011,786

Ciudad Trujillo — see SANTO DOMINGO

Clarks·ville \\'klärks-,vil, -vəl\\ city N Tennessee NW of Nashville; *pop* 103,455

Clear·wa·ter \\'klir-,wó-tər, -,wä-\\ city W Florida NW of St. Petersburg; *pop* 108,787

Cleve·land \\'klēv-lənd\\ city & port NE Ohio on Lake Erie; *pop* 478,403

Clyde \\'klīd\\ river 106 mi. (171 km.) long SW Scotland flowing into **Firth of Clyde** (estuary)

Coast Mountains mountain range W British Columbia, Canada; the N continuation of Cascade Range

Coast Ranges chain of mountain ranges W North America extending along Pacific coast W of Sierra Nevada & Cascade Range & through Vancouver Island into S Alaska to Kenai Peninsula & Kodiak Island

Cod, Cape \\-'käd\\ peninsula SE Massachusetts

Coim·ba·tore \\,kóim-bə-'tór\\ city S India; *pop* 816,321

Cole·raine \\kōl-'rän, 'kōl-,\\ **1** district N Northern Ireland; *pop* 51,062 **2** port in Coleraine district

Co·logne \\kə-'lōn\\ city W Germany on the Rhine; *pop* 956,690

Co·lom·bia \\kə-'ləm-bē-ə\\ country NW South America; ✳, Bogotá; *pop* 26,525,670 — **Co·lom·bi·an** \\-bē-ən\\ *adj or n*

Co·lom·bo \\kə-'ləm-(,)bō\\ city, ✳ of Sri Lanka; *pop* 615,000

Col·o·ra·do \\,kä-lə-'ra-(,)dō\\ **1** river 1450 mi. (2334 km.) long SW U.S. & NW Mexico flowing from N Colorado into Gulf of California **2** desert SE California **3** plateau region SW U.S. W of Rocky Mountains **4** state W U.S.; ✳, Denver; *pop* 4,301,261 — **Col·o·rad·an** \\-'ra-d°n, -'rä-\\ *or* **Co·lo·ra·do·an** \\-'ra-dō-ən, -'rä-\\ *adj or n*

Colorado Springs city *cen* Colorado E of Pikes Peak; *pop* 360,890

Co·lum·bia \\kə-'ləm-bē-ə\\ **1** river 1214 mi. (1953 km.) long SW Canada & NW U.S. flowing S & W from SE British Columbia into the Pacific **2** plateau in Columbia River basin in E Washington, E Oregon, & SW Idaho **3** city, ✳ of South Carolina; *pop* 116,278

Co·lum·bus \\kə-'ləm-bəs\\ **1** city W Georgia; *pop* 186,291 **2** city, ✳ of Ohio; *pop* 711,470

Com·mon·wealth, the \\'käm-ən-,wel(t)th\\ *or* **Commonwealth of Nations** *formerly* **British Commonwealth** the United Kingdom & most of the countries formerly dependent on it

Com·o·ros \\'kä-mə-,rōz\\ islands off SE Africa NW of Madagascar; country (except for Mayotte Island); ✳, Moroni; *pop* 519,527

Con·a·kry \\'kä-nə-krē\\ city, ✳ of Guinea; *pop* 581,000

Con·cord \\'kän-,kórd, 'kän-\\ **1** city W California; *pop* 121,780 **2** town E Massachusetts NW of Boston; *pop* 16,993 **3** city, ✳ of New Hampshire; *pop* 40,687

Con·go \\'käŋ-(,)gō\\ **1** *or* **Zaire** \\zä-'ir\\ river over 2700 mi. (4344 km.) long W Africa flowing into the Atlantic **2** *officially* **Democratic Republic of the Congo** *formerly* *1971–97* **Zaire** country *cen* Africa consisting of most of Congo River basin E of lower Congo River; ✳, Kinshasa; *pop* 43,775,000 **3** *or officially* **Republic of the Congo** country W *cen* Africa W of lower Congo River; ✳, Brazzaville; *pop* 2,775,000 — **Con·go·lese** \\,käŋ-gə-'lēz, -'lēs\\ *adj or n*

Con·nacht \\'kä-,nót\\ province W Ireland; *pop* 422,909

Con·nect·i·cut \\kə-'ne-ti-kət\\ **1** river 407 mi. (655 km.) long NE U.S. flowing S from N New Hampshire into Long Island Sound **2** state NE U.S.; ✳, Hartford; *pop* 3,405,565

Constantinople — see ISTANBUL

Continental Divide line of highest points of land separating the waters flowing W from those flowing N or E and extending SSE from NW Canada across W U.S. through Mexico & Central America to South America where it joins the Andes Mountains

Cook \\'kúk\\ **1** inlet of the Pacific S Alaska W of Kenai Peninsula **2** islands South Pacific SW of Society Islands belonging to New Zealand; *pop* 17,614 **3** strait New Zealand between North Island & South Island

Cook, Mount *formerly* **Ao·rangi** \\aú-'räŋ-ē\\ mountain 12,349 ft. (3764 m.) New Zealand in W *cen* South Island in Southern Alps; highest in New Zealand

Cooks·town \\'kúks-,taún\\ district *cen* Northern Ireland; *pop* 30,808

Co·pen·ha·gen \\,kō-pən-'hā-gən, -'hä-\\ city, ✳ of Denmark; *pop* 501,285

Cor·al Sea \\'kór-əl, 'kär-\\ arm of the W Pacific NE of Australia

Coral Springs city SE Florida; *pop* 117,549

Cór·do·ba \\'kór-də-bə, 'kór-thō-,vä\\ city N *cen* Argentina; *pop* 1,179,067

Cor·inth \\'kór-ən(t)th, 'kär-\\ **1** region of ancient Greece **2** ancient city; site SW of present city of Corinth — **Co·rin·thi·an** \\kə-'rin(t)-thē-ən\\ *adj or n*

Corinth, Gulf of inlet of Ionian Sea *cen* Greece N of the Peloponnese

Cork \\'kórk\\ city S Ireland; *pop* 123,062

Corn·wall \\'kórn-,wól, -wəl\\ *or since 1974* **Cornwall and Isles of Scilly** \\'si-lē\\ county SW England

Co·ro·na \kə-'rō-nə\ city SW California E of Los Angeles; *pop* 124,966

Cor·pus Chris·ti \ˌkȯr-pəs-'kris-tē\ city & port S Texas; *pop* 277,454

Cor·reg·i·dor \kə-'re-gə-ˌdȯr\ island Philippines at entrance to Manila Bay

Cor·si·ca \'kȯr-si-kə\ island France in the Mediterranean N of Sardinia; *pop* 260,149 — **Cor·si·can** \'kȯr-si-kən\ *adj or n*

Cos·ta Me·sa \'mā-sə\ city SW California; *pop* 108,724

Costa Ri·ca \'rē-kə\ country Central America between Nicaragua & Panama; ✳, San José; *pop* 4,075,863 — **Cos·ta Ri·can** \-kən\ *adj or n*

Côte d'Ivoire — see IVORY COAST

Cots·wold \'kät-ˌswōld, -swəld\ hills SW *cen* England

Cov·en·try \'kə-vən-trē\ city *cen* England; *pop* 292,500

Craig·av·on \krā-'ga-vən\ district *cen* Northern Ireland; *pop* 74,494

Cra·ter \'krā-tər\ lake 1932 ft. (589 m.) deep SW Oregon in Cascade Range

Crete \'krēt\ island Greece in E Mediterranean; *pop* 536,980 — **Cre·tan** \'krē-tᵊn\ *adj or n*

Cri·mea \krī-'mē-ə, krə-\ peninsula SE Europe in S Ukraine, extending into Black Sea — **Cri·me·an** \krī-'mē-ən, krə-\ *adj*

Cro·atia \krō-'ā-sh(ē-)ə\ country SE Europe; ✳, Zagreb; *pop* 4,437,460 — **Croat** \'krō-ˌat\ *n*

Croy·don \'krȯi-dᵊn\ borough of S Greater London, England; *pop* 299,600

Cu·ba \'kyü-bə, 'kü-vä\ island in the West Indies; country; ✳, Havana; *pop* 10,892,000 — **Cu·ban** \'kyü-bən\ *adj or n*

Cum·ber·land \'kəm-bər-lənd\ river 687 mi. (1106 km.) long S Kentucky & N Tennessee

Cumberland Gap pass through Cumberland Plateau NE Tennessee

Cumberland Plateau mountain region E U.S.; part of S Appalachian Mountains extending from S West Virginia to NE Alabama

Cum·bria \'kəm-brē-ə\ county NW England; *pop* 486,900

Cum·bri·an \'kəm-brē-ən\ mountains NW England chiefly in Cumbria county

Cu·par \'kü-pər\ town E Scotland; *pop* 6642

Cu·ri·ti·ba \ˌkür-ə-'tē-bə\ city S Brazil SW of São Paulo; *pop* 1,587,315

Cush \'kəsh, 'kush\ ancient country NE Africa in upper Nile valley S of Egypt — **Cush·ite** \'kə-ˌshīt, 'kù-\ *n* — **Cush·it·ic** \ˌkə-'shi-tik, kù-\ *adj*

Cuz·co \'küs-(ˌ)kō\ city S *cen* Peru; *pop* 316,804

Cymru — see WALES

Cy·prus \'sī-prəs\ island E Mediterranean S of Turkey; country; ✳, Nicosia; *pop* 793,100 — **Cyp·ri·ot** \'si-prē-ət, -ˌät\ *or* **Cyp·ri·ote** \-ˌōt, -ət\ *adj or n*

Cy·re·na·ica \ˌsir-ə-'nā-ə-kə, ˌsī-rə-\ ancient region N Africa on coast W of Egypt — **Cy·re·na·i·can** \-'nā-ə-kən\ *adj or n*

Czecho·slo·va·kia \ˌche-kə-slō-'vä-kē-ə, -slə-, -'va-\ former country *cen* Europe divided into the independent states of the Czech Republic & Slovakia — **Czecho·slo·vak** \'slō-ˌväk, -ˌvak\ *adj or n* — **Czecho·slo·va·ki·an** \-slō-'vä-kē-ən, -slə-, -'va-\ *adj or n*

Czech Republic country *cen* Europe; ✳, Prague; *pop* 10,332,000

Daegu — see TAEGU

Daejeon — see TAEJON

Dahomey — see BENIN

Dairen — see DALIAN

Da·kar \'da-ˌkär, dä-'kär\ city, ✳ of Senegal; *pop* 1,729,823

Da·ko·ta 1 *or* **James** river 710 mi. (1143 km.) long North Dakota & South Dakota flowing S into the Missouri 2 territory 1861–89 NW U.S. divided 1889 into states of North Dakota & South Dakota (the **Dakotas** \-təz\ )

Da·lian \'dä-'lyen\ *or* **Ta·lien** \'dä-'lyen\ *or* **Lü·da** *or* **Lü–ta** \'lü-'dä\ *or* **Dai·ren** \'dī-'ren\ city NE China; *pop* 1,723,302

Dal·las \'da-ləs, -lis\ city NE Texas; *pop* 1,188,580

Dal·ma·tia \dal-'mä-sh(ē-)ə\ region W Balkan Peninsula on the Adriatic — **Dal·ma·tian** \-shən\ *adj or n*

Da·ly City \'dā-lē\ city W California S of San Francisco; *pop* 103,621

Da·mas·cus \də-'mas-kəs\ city, ✳ of Syria; *pop* 1,451,000

Dan·ube \'dan-(ˌ)yüb\ river 1771 mi. (2850 km.) long S Europe flowing from SW Germany into Black Sea — **Da·nu·bi·an** \də-'nü-bē-əs, da-, -'nyü-\ *adj*

Dar·da·nelles \ˌdär-də-'nelz\ *or* **Hel·les·pont** \'he-lə-ˌspänt\ strait NW Turkey connecting Sea of Marmara & the Aegean

Dar es Sa·laam \ˌdär-ˌe(s)-sə-'läm\ city, ✳ of Tanzania; *pop* 1,360,850

Dar·ling \'där-liŋ\ river about 1700 mi. (2735 km.) long SE Australia in Queensland & New South Wales flowing SW into the Murray

Dar·win \'där-wən\ city Australia, ✳ of Northern Territory; *pop* 70,071

Da·vao \'dä-ˌvaù, dä-'vaù\ city S Philippines in E Mindanao on Davao Gulf; *pop* 850,000

Dav·en·port \'da-vən-ˌpȯrt\ city E Iowa; *pop* 98,359

Da·vis \'dä-vəs\ strait between SW Greenland & E Baffin Island connecting Baffin Bay & the Atlantic

Day·ton \'dā-tᵊn\ city SW Ohio; *pop* 166,169

Dead Sea salt lake between Israel & Jordan; 1312 ft. (400 m.) below sea level

Death Valley dry valley E California & S Nevada containing lowest point in U.S. (282 ft. *or* 86 m. below sea level)

Dec·can \'de-kən, -ˌkan\ plateau region S India

Del·a·ware \'de-lə-ˌwer, -wər\ **1** river 296 mi. (476 km.) long E U.S. flowing S from S New York into Delaware Bay **2** state E U.S.; ✳, Dover; *pop* 783,600 — **Del·a·war·ean** *or* **Del·a·war·ian** \ˌde-lə-'wer-ē-ən\ *adj or n*

Delaware Bay inlet of the Atlantic between SW New Jersey & E Delaware

Del·hi \'de-lē\ city N India; *pop* 9,817,439 — see NEW DELHI

De·los \'dē-ˌläs\ island Greece — **De·lian** \'dē-lē-ən, 'dēl-yən\ *adj or n*

Del·phi \'del-ˌfī\ ancient town *cen* Greece on slope of Mt. Parnassus

Democratic Republic of the Congo — see CONGO 2

Denali — see MCKINLEY, MOUNT

Den·mark \'den-ˌmärk\ country N Europe occupying most of Jutland & neighboring islands; ✳, Copenhagen; *pop* 5,383,507

Den·ver \'den-vər\ city, ✳ of Colorado; *pop* 554,636

Der·by \'där-bē\ city N *cen* England; *pop* 214,000

Der·by·shire \'där-bē-ˌshir, -shər\ *or* **Derby** county N *cen* England

Der·ry \'der-ē\ *or* **Lon·don·der·ry** \ˌlən-dən-'der-ē\ city & port NW Northern Ireland; *pop* 62,697

Des Moines \di-'mȯin\ city, ✳ of Iowa; *pop* 198,682

De·troit \di-'trȯit\ **1** river 31 mi. (50 km.) long between SE Michigan & Ontario connecting Lake Saint Clair & Lake Erie **2** city SE Michigan; *pop* 951,270

Dev·on \'de-vən\ *or* **De·von·shire** \'de-vən-ˌshir, -shər\ county SW England

Dha·ka \'dä-kə\ city, ✳ of Bangladesh; *pop* 3,637,892

Die·go Gar·cia \dē-ˌā-gō-ˌgär-'sē-ə\ island in Indian Ocean; chief island of Chagos Archipelago

Dili *or* **Dilli** \'di-lē\ city & port N Timor, ✳ of East Timor

Di·nar·ic Alps \də-'na-rik\ range of the E Alps in W Slovenia, W Croatia, Bosnia and Herzegovina, & Montenegro

District of Co·lum·bia \kə-'ləm-bē-ə\ federal district E U.S. coextensive with city of Washington; *pop* 572,059

Djakarta — see JAKARTA

Dji·bou·ti \jə-'bü-tē\ **1** country E Africa on Gulf of Aden; *pop* 510,000 **2** city, its ✳; *pop* 300,000

Dni·pro·pe·trovs'k *or* **Dne·pro·pe·trovsk** \də-ˌnye-prə-pə-'trȯfsk\ city E *cen* Ukraine; *pop* 1,189,000

Dodge City \'däj\ city S Kansas on Arkansas River; *pop* 25,176

Do·do·ma \dō-'dō-(ˌ)mä\ city NE *cen* Tanzania designated as future national ✳; *pop* 203,833

Do·ha \'dō-(ˌ)hä\ city & port, ✳ of Qatar on Persian Gulf; *pop* 217,294

Dom·i·ni·ca \ˌdä-mə-'nē-kə\ island West Indies in the Leeward Islands; country; ✳, Roseau; *pop* 71,242

Do·min·i·can Republic \də-'mi-ni-kən\ country West Indies in E Hispaniola; ✳, Santo Domingo; *pop* 8,533,744 — **Dominican** *adj or n*

Don \'dän\ river 1224 mi. (1969 km.) long SW Russia

Do·nets'k \də-'nyetsk\ city E Ukraine; *pop* 1,121,000
Dor·ches·ter \'dòr-chəs-tər, -,ches-\ town S England; *pop* 14,049
Dor·set \'dòr-sət\ *or* **Dor·set·shire** \-,shir, -shər\ county S England on English Channel
Dort·mund \'dòrt-,mùnt, -mənd\ city W Germany in the Ruhr; *pop* 601,007
Dou·a·la \dü-'ä-lä\ seaport W Cameroon; *pop* 810,000
Dou·ro \'dòr-(,)ü\ *or Spanish* **Due·ro** \'dwe(ə)r-ō\ river 556 mi. (895 km.) long N Spain & N Portugal flowing into the Atlantic
Do·ver \'dō-vər\ city, ✳ of Delaware; *pop* 32,135
Dover, Strait of channel between SE England & N France; the most easterly section of English Channel
Down \'daùn\ district SE Northern Ireland; *pop* 57,511
Downey \'daù-nē\ city SW California SE of Los Angeles; *pop* 107,323
Down·pat·rick \daùn-'pa-trik\ town E Northern Ireland; *pop* 8245
Dra·kens·berg \'drä-kənz-,bərg\ mountain range E Republic of South Africa & Lesotho; highest peak Thabana Ntlenyana 11,425 ft. (3482 m.)
Dres·den \'drez-dən\ city E Germany; *pop* 485,132
Dub·lin \'də-blən\ city, ✳ of Ireland; *pop* 495,781
Dud·ley \'dəd-lē\ town W *cen* England; *pop* 300,000
Duis·burg \'dü-əs-,bərg, 'düz-,\ city W Germany at junction of Rhine & Ruhr rivers; *pop* 537,441
Du·luth \də-'lüth\ city & port NE Minnesota; *pop* 86,918
Dum·fries \dəm-'frēs, -'frēz\ burgh S Scotland; *pop* 32,084
Dumfries and Gal·lo·way \'ga-lə-,wā\ administrative subdivision of S Scotland
Dun·dee \,dən-'dē\ city E Scotland; *pop* 172,860
Dun·gan·non \,dən-'ga-nən\ district W Northern Ireland; *pop* 45,322
Dur·ban \'dər-bən\ city and seaport E Republic of South Africa; *pop* 736,852
Dur·ham \'dər-əm, 'də-rəm, 'dùr-əm\ city N *cen* North Carolina; *pop* 187,035
Du·shan·be \dü-'sham-bə, dyü-, -'shäm-, 'dyü-,; ,dyü-shäm-'bä\ city, ✳ of Tajikistan; *pop* 595,000
Düs·sel·dorf \'dü-səl-,dòrf, 'dyü-, 'düe-\ city W Germany on the Rhine; *pop* 577,561
Ea·ling \'ē-liŋ\ borough of W Greater London, England; *pop* 263,300
East An·glia \'aŋ-glē-ə\ region E England; *pop* 1,366,300
East China Sea — see CHINA
Eas·ter \'ē-stər\ island Chile SE Pacific about 2000 mi. (3200 km.) W of Chilean coast
Eastern Cape province SE Republic of South Africa; *pop* 6,504,000
Eastern Ghats \'gäts, 'gòts, 'gəts\ chain of low mountains SE India along coast
Eastern Hemisphere the half of the earth E of the Atlantic Ocean including Europe, Asia, Australia, and Africa
Eastern Roman Empire the Byzantine Empire from 395 to 474
Eastern Samoa — see AMERICAN SAMOA
East Germany — see GERMANY
East Indies the Malay Archipelago — **East Indian** *adj or n*
East London city S Republic of South Africa; *pop* 119,727
East Pakistan the former E division of Pakistan consisting of E portion of Bengal; now Bangladesh
East River strait SE New York connecting upper New York Bay & Long Island Sound and separating Manhattan & Long Island
East Sea — see JAPAN, SEA OF
East Sus·sex \'sə-siks\ county SE England; *pop* 670,600
East Timor country SE Asia on E Timor; ✳, Dili; *pop* 747,750
Ebro \'ā-(,)brō\ river 565 mi. (909 km.) long NE Spain flowing into the Mediterranean
Ec·ua·dor \'e-kwə-,dòr\ country W South America; ✳, Quito; *pop* 12,156,608 — **Ec·ua·dor·an** \,e-kwə-'dòr-ən\ *or* **Ec·ua·dor·ean** *or* **Ec·ua·dor·ian** \-ē-ən\ *adj or n*
Ed·in·burgh \'e-dən-,bər-ə\ city, ✳ of Scotland; *pop* 434,520

Ed·mon·ton \'ed-mən-tən\ city, ✳ of Alberta, Canada; *pop* 666,104
Edom \'ē-dəm\ ancient country SW Asia S of Judaea & Dead Sea — **Edom·ite** \'ē-də-,mīt\ *n*
Egypt \'ē-jipt\ country NE Africa & Sinai Peninsula of SW Asia bordering on Mediterranean & Red seas; ✳, Cairo; *pop* 67,313,000
Eire — see IRELAND
Elam \'ē-ləm\ ancient country SW Asia at head of Persian Gulf E of Babylonia — **Elam·ite** \'ē-lə-,mīt\ *n*
Elbe \'el-bə, 'elb\ river 720 mi. (1159 km.) long N Czech Republic & NE Germany flowing NW into North Sea
El·bert, Mount \'el-bərt\ mountain 14,433 ft. (4399 m.) W *cen* Colorado; highest in Colorado & the Rocky Mountains
El·brus, Mount \el-'brüz, -'brüs\ mountain 18,510 ft. (5642 m.) Russia; highest in the Caucasus & in Europe
El·burz \el-'bùrz\ mountains N Iran
Eliz·a·beth \i-'li-zə-bəth\ city NE New Jersey; *pop* 120,568
Elles·mere \'elz-,mir\ island N Canada in Nunavut
Ellice — see TUVALU
El·lis Island \'e-ləs\ island SE New York S of Manhattan; served as immigration station 1892–1954
El Mon·te \el-'män-tē\ city SW California E of Los Angeles; *pop* 115,965
El Paso \el-'pa-(,)sō\ city W Texas on Rio Grande; *pop* 563,662
El Sal·va·dor \el-'sal-və-,dòr, -,sal-və-'; ,el-,säl-vä-'thòr\ country Central America bordering on the Pacific; ✳, San Salvador; *pop* 5,517,000
Ely, Isle of \'ē-lē\ area of high ground amid marshes in East Anglia, England
En·field \'en-,fēld\ borough of N Greater London, England; *pop* 248,900
En·gland \'iŋ-glənd, 'iŋ-lənd\ country S Great Britain; a division of United Kingdom; ✳, London; *pop* 49,138,831
English Channel arm of the Atlantic between S England & N France
En·nis·kil·len \,e-nə-'ski-lən\ town SW Northern Ireland in Fermanagh district
Ephra·im \'ē-frē-əm\ **1** hilly region N Jordan E of Jordan River **2** — see ISRAEL — **Ephra·im·ite** \'ē-frē-ə-,mīt\ *n*
Equatorial Guinea *formerly* **Spanish Guinea** country W Africa including Mbini & Bioko; ✳, Malabo; *pop* 376,000
Erie \'ir-ē\ **1** city & port NW Pennsylvania; *pop* 103,717 **2** canal New York between Hudson River at Albany & Lake Erie at Buffalo; now superseded by New York State Barge Canal
Erie, Lake lake E *cen* North America in U.S. & Canada; one of the Great Lakes
Er·in \'er-ən\ poetic name of Ireland
Er·i·trea \,er-ə-'trē-ə, -'trā-\ country NE Africa; ✳, Asmara; *pop* 3,317,611 — **Er·i·tre·an** \-ən\ *adj or n*
Es·con·di·do \,es-kən-'dē-(,)dō\ city SW California N of San Diego; *pop* 133,559
Es·fa·han \,es-fə-'hän, -'han\ *or* **Is·fa·han** \,is-\ city W *cen* Iran; *pop* 986,753
Española — see HISPANIOLA
Es·sen \'e-sªn\ city W Germany in the Ruhr; *pop* 626,989
Es·sex \'e-siks\ county SE England on North Sea
Es·to·nia \e-'stō-nē-ə, -nyə\ country E Europe on Baltic Sea; ✳, Tallinn; *pop* 1,361,242 — **Es·to·nian** \e-'stō-nē-ən, -nyən\ *adj or n*
Ethi·o·pia \,ē-thē-'ō-pē-ə\ *formerly* **Ab·ys·sin·ia** \,a-bə-'si-nē-ə, -nyə\ country E Africa; ✳, Addis Ababa; *pop* 67,220,000 — **Ethi·o·pi·an** \-pē-ən\ *adj or n*
Et·na, Mount \'et-nə\ volcano 10,902 ft. (3323 m.) Italy in NE Sicily
Eto·bi·coke \e-'tō-bi-,kō\ former city Canada in SE Ontario; now part of Toronto
Etru·ria \i-'trùr-ē-ə\ ancient country *cen* peninsula of Italy
Eu·gene \yü-'jēn\ city W Oregon; *pop* 137,893
Eu·phra·tes \yù-'frā-(,)tēz\ river 1700 mi. (2736 km.) long SW Asia flowing from E Turkey & uniting with the Tigris to form the Shatt al Arab
Eur·asia \yù-'rā-zhə, -shə\ landmass consisting of Europe & Asia — **Eur·asian** \-zhən, -shən\ *adj or n*
Eu·rope \'yùr-əp\ continent of the Eastern Hemisphere between Asia & the Atlantic; *pop* 498,000,000

European Union economic, scientific, & political organization consisting of Belgium, France, Italy, Luxembourg, Netherlands, Germany, Denmark, Greece, Ireland, United Kingdom, Spain, Portugal, Austria, Finland, Sweden, Cyprus, Czech Republic, Estonia, Hungary, Latvia, Lithuania, Malta, Poland, Slovakia, Slovenia, Bulgaria, & Romania

Ev·ans·ville \'e-vənz-,vil\ city SW Indiana; *pop* 121,582

Ev·er·est, Mount \'ev-rəst, 'e-və-\ mountain 29,035 ft. (8850 m.) S Asia in the Himalayas on border between Nepal & Tibet; highest in the world

Ev·er·glades \'e-vər-,glādz\ swamp region S Florida

Ex·e·ter \'ek-sə-tər\ city SW England; *pop* 101,100

Faer·oe *or* **Far·oe** \'fer-(,)ō\ islands NE Atlantic NW of the Shetlands belonging to Denmark; *pop* 47,653 — **Faeroese** \,far-ə-'wēz, ,fer-, -'wēs\ *adj or n*

Fair·banks \'fer-,baŋks\ city E *cen* Alaska; *pop* 30,224

Fair·field \'fer-,fēld\ municipality SE Australia in E New South Wales; *pop* 175,099

Fai·sa·la·bad \,fī-,sä-lə-'bäd, -,sa-lə-'bad\ *formerly* **Ly·all·pur** \lē-,äl-'pur\ city NE Pakistan; *pop* 2,008,861

Falk·land Islands \'fò-klənd, 'fòl-\ *or Spanish* **Is·las Mal·vi·nas** \,ēs-läs-mäl-'vē-näs\ island group SW Atlantic E of S end of Argentina; a British colony; ✳, Stanley; *pop* 2100

Far East the countries of E Asia & the Malay Archipelago — usually thought to consist of the Asian countries bordering on the Pacific but sometimes including also India, Sri Lanka, Bangladesh, Tibet, & Myanmar — **Far Eastern** *adj*

Far·go \'fär-(,)gō\ city E North Dakota; largest in state; *pop* 90,599

Faroe — see FAEROE

Fay·ette·ville \'fā-ət-,vil, -vəl\ city SE *cen* North Carolina; *pop* 121,015

Fear, Cape \'fir\ cape SE North Carolina at mouth of Cape Fear River

Fer·man·agh \fər-'ma-nə\ district SW Northern Ireland; *pop* 54,062

Fernando Póo — see BIOKO

Fez \'fez\ city N *cen* Morocco; *pop* 774,574

Fife \'fīf\ administrative subdivision of E Scotland

Fi·ji \'fē-(,)jē\ islands SW Pacific; country; ✳, Suva; *pop* 775,077 — **Fi·ji·an** \'fē-(,)jē-ən, fi-'\ *adj or n*

Fin·land \'fin-lənd\ country NE Europe; ✳, Helsinki; *pop* 5,058,000 — **Fin·land·er** *n*

Flan·ders \'flan-dərz\ **1** region W Belgium & N France on North Sea **2** semiautonomous region W Belgium; *pop* 5,972,781

Flat·tery, Cape \'fla-tə-rē\ cape NW Washington at entrance to Strait of Juan de Fuca

Flint \'flint\ city SE Michigan; *pop* 124,943

Flor·ence \'flòr-ən(t)s, 'flär-\ *or Italian* **Fi·ren·ze** \fē-'rent-sä\ city *cen* Italy; *pop* 374,501 — **Flor·en·tine** \'flòr-ən-,tēn, 'flär-, -,tīn\ *adj or n*

Flor·i·da \'flòr-ə-də, 'flär-\ state SE U.S.; ✳, Tallahassee; *pop* 15,982,378 — **Flo·rid·i·an** \flə-'ri-dē-ən\ *or* **Flor·i·dan** \'flòr-ə-dən, 'flär-\ *adj or n*

Florida, Straits of channel between Florida Keys on NW & Cuba & Bahamas on S & E connecting Gulf of Mexico & the Atlantic

Florida Keys chain of islands off S tip of Florida

Foochow — see FUZHOU

For·a·ker, Mount \'fòr-i-kər, 'fär-\ mountain 17,400 ft. (5304 m.) S *cen* Alaska in Alaska Range

For·mo·sa \fòr-'mō-sə, fər-, -zə\ — see TAIWAN — **For·mo·san** \fòr-'mō-sᵊn, fər-, -zᵊn\ *adj or n*

For·ta·le·za \,fòr-tə-'lä-zə\ city & port NE Brazil on the Atlantic; *pop* 2,141,402

Fort Col·lins \'kä-lənz\ city N Colorado; *pop* 118,652

Fort–de–France \,fòr-də-'fräⁿs\ city West Indies, ✳ of Martinique on W coast; *pop* 93,598

Forth \'fòrth\ river 116 mi. (187 km.) long S *cen* Scotland flowing E into North Sea through **Firth of Forth**

Fort Knox \'näks\ military reservation N *cen* Kentucky; location of U.S. Gold Bullion Depository

Fort Lau·der·dale \'lò-dər-,dāl\ city SE Florida; *pop* 152,397

Fort Wayne \'wān\ city NE Indiana; *pop* 205,727

Fort Worth \'wərth\ city NE Texas; *pop* 534,694

Fox \'fäks\ islands SW Alaska in the E Aleutians

Foxe Basin \'fäks\ inlet of the Atlantic N Canada in E Nunavut W of Baffin Island

France \'fran(t)s, 'fräⁿs\ country W Europe between the English Channel & the Mediterranean; ✳, Paris; *pop* 58,520,688

Frank·fort \'fraŋk-fərt\ city, ✳ of Kentucky; *pop* 27,741

Frank·furt \'fraŋk-fərt, 'fräⁿk-,fúrt\ *or in full* **Frankfurt am Main** \(,)äm-'mīn\ city W Germany on Main River; *pop* 654,679

Frank·lin \'fraŋ-klən\ former district N Canada in Northwest Territories including Arctic Archipelago & Boothia & Melville peninsulas

Fra·ser \'frā-zər, -zhər\ river 850 mi. (1368 km.) long Canada in S *cen* British Columbia flowing into the Pacific

Fred·er·ic·ton \'fre-drik-tən, 'fre-də-rik-\ city, ✳ of New Brunswick, Canada; *pop* 47,560

Free State *formerly* **Or·ange Free State** \'òr-inj, 'är-, -ənj\ province E *cen* Republic of South Africa; *pop* 2,767,000

Free·town \'frē-,taùn\ city, ✳ of Sierra Leone; *pop* 178,600

Fre·mont \'frē-,mänt\ city W California; *pop* 203,413

French Guiana country N South America on the Atlantic; an overseas division of France; ✳, Cayenne; *pop* 128,000

French Indochina — see INDOCHINA

Fres·no \'frez-(,)nō\ city S *cen* California SE of San Francisco; *pop* 427,652

Frunze — see BISHKEK

Fu·ji, Mount \'fü-jē\ *or* **Fu·ji·ya·ma** \,fü-jē-'yä-mä\ mountain 12,388 ft. (3776 m.) Japan in S *cen* Honshu; highest in Japan

Fu·ku·o·ka \,fü-kü-'ō-kä\ city Japan in N Kyushu; *pop* 1,341,470

Ful·ler·ton \'fú-lər-tən\ city SW California; *pop* 126,003

Fu·na·fu·ti \,fü-nä-'fü-tē\ city, ✳ of Tuvalu; *pop* 1328

Fun·dy, Bay of \'fən-dē\ inlet of the Atlantic SE Canada between New Brunswick & Nova Scotia

Fu·shun \'fü-'shùn\ city NE China E of Shenyang; *pop* 1,202,388

Fu·zhou \'fü-'jō\ *or* **Foo·chow** \'fü-'jō, -'chaù\ city & port SE China; *pop* 874,809

Ga·bon \gä-'bōⁿ\ country W Africa on the Equator; ✳, Libreville; *pop* 1,014,976 — **Gab·o·nese** \,ga-bə-'nēz, -'nēs\ *adj or n*

Ga·bo·rone \,gä-bō-'rō-(,)nā, ,kä-\ city, ✳ of Botswana; *pop* 133,468

Gads·den Purchase \'gadz-dən\ area of land S of Gila River in present Arizona & New Mexico purchased 1853 by the U.S. from Mexico

Ga·la·pa·gos Islands \gə-'lä-pə-gəs, -'la-, -,gōs\ island group Ecuador in the Pacific 600 mi. (965 km.) W of South America; *pop* 9785

Ga·la·tia \gə-'lā-sh(ē-)ə\ ancient country *cen* Asia Minor in region around modern Ankara, Turkey — **Ga·la·tian** \-shən\ *adj or n*

Ga·li·cia \gə-'li-sh(ē-)ə\ **1** region E *cen* Europe now divided between Poland & Ukraine **2** region NW Spain on the Atlantic — **Ga·li·cian** \-'li-shən\ *adj or n*

Gal·i·lee \'ga-lə-,lē\ hilly region N Israel — **Gal·i·le·an** \,ga-lə-'lē-ən\ *adj or n*

Galilee, Sea of *or modern* **Lake Ti·be·ri·as** \tī-'bir-ē-əs\ lake N Israel on Syrian border; crossed by Jordan River

Gal·lo·way \'ga-lə-,wā\ former administrative district of SW Scotland — see DUMFRIES AND GALLOWAY

Gam·bia \'gam-bē-ə, 'gäm-\ country W Africa; ✳, Banjul; *pop* 687,817 — **Gam·bi·an** \-bē-ən\ *adj or n*

Gan·ges \'gan-,jēz\ river 1550 mi. (2494 km.) long N India flowing from the Himalayas SE & E to unite with the Brahmaputra and empty into Bay of Bengal through a vast delta — **Gan·get·ic** \gan-'je-tik\ *adj*

Garden Grove city SW California; *pop* 165,196

Gar·land \'gär-lənd\ city NE Texas NNE of Dallas; *pop* 215,768

Ga·ronne \gə-'rän, gä-'rón\ river 355 mi. (571 km.) long SE France flowing into

Gary \'ger-ē\ city NW Indiana on Lake Michigan; *pop* 102,746

Gas·co·ny \'gas-kə-nē\ region SW France — **Gas·con** \'gas-kən\ *adj or n*

Gas·pé \ga-'spā, 'ga-,\ peninsula SE Quebec E of mouth of the Saint Lawrence — **Gas·pe·sian** \ga-'spē-zhən\ adj or n

Gaul \'gȯl\ or Latin **Gal·lia** \'ga-lē-ə\ ancient country W Europe chiefly consisting of region occupied by modern France & Belgium

Gau·teng \'gaú-,teŋ\ province cen NE Republic of South Africa; pop 6,864,000

Ga·za Strip \'gä-zə, 'ga-\ district NE Sinai Peninsula on the Mediterranean

Ge·ne·va \jə-'nē-və\ city SW Switzerland on Lake Geneva; pop 175,998 — **Ge·ne·van** \-vən\ adj or n — **Gen·e·vese** \,je-nə-'vēz, -'vēs\ adj or n

Geneva, Lake lake on border between SW Switzerland & E France

Gen·oa \'je-nō-ə\ or Italian **Ge·no·va** \'je-nō-(,)vä\ city & port NW Italy; pop 632,366 — **Gen·o·ese** \,je-nō-'ēz, -'ēs\ or **Gen·o·vese** \-nə-'vēz, -'vēs\ adj or n

George·town \'jȯrj-,taún\ 1 a W section of Washington, District of Columbia 2 city & port, ✳ of Guyana; pop 162,000

Geor·gia \'jȯr-jə\ 1 state SE U.S.; ✳, Atlanta; pop 8,186,453 2 or **Republic of Georgia** country SE Europe on Black Sea S of Caucasus Mountains; ✳, Tbilisi; pop 5,493,000 — **Geor·gian** \'jȯr-jən\ adj or n

Georgia, Strait of channel Canada & U.S. between Vancouver Island & main part of British Columbia NW of Puget Sound

Georgian Bay inlet of Lake Huron in S Ontario

Ger·man·town \'jər-mən-,taún\ a NW section of Philadelphia, Pennsylvania

Ger·ma·ny \'jər-mə-nē\ country cen Europe bordering on North & Baltic seas; ✳, Berlin; divided 1946–90 into two independent states: the **Federal Republic of Germany** (West Germany; ✳, Bonn) & the **German Democratic Republic** (East Germany; ✳, East Berlin); pop 82,440,000

Get·tys·burg \'ge-tēz-,bərg\ town S Pennsylvania; pop 7490

Gha·na \'gä-nə, 'ga-\ formerly **Gold Coast** country W Africa on Gulf of Guinea; ✳, Accra; pop 15,636,000 — **Gha·na·ian** \gä-'nä-ən, ga-, -'nī-ən\ or **Gha·ni·an** \'gä-nē-ən, 'ga-, -nyən\ adj or n

Ghats \'gȯts\ two mountain chains S India consisting of **Eastern Ghats & Western Ghats**

Ghent \'gent\ city NW cen Belgium; pop 226,220

Gi·bral·tar \jə-'brȯl-tər\ British colony on S coast of Spain including Rock of Gibraltar; pop 29,760

Gibraltar, Rock of cape on S coast of Spain in Gibraltar at E end of Strait of Gibraltar; highest point 1396 ft. (426 m.)

Gibraltar, Strait of passage between Spain & Africa connecting the Atlantic & the Mediterranean

Gi·la \'hē-lə\ river 630 mi. (1014 km.) long SW New Mexico and S Arizona flowing W into the Colorado

Gil·bert \'gil-bərt\ town SW cen Arizona; pop 109,697

Gilbert and El·ice Islands \'e-lis\ island group W Pacific; divided into Kiribati and Tuvalu

Gil·e·ad \'gi-lē-əd\ mountain region of NE ancient Palestine E of Jordan River; now in NW Jordan — **Gil·e·ad·ite** \-lē-ə-,dīt\ n

Gi·za \'gē-zə\ city N Egypt on the Nile SW of Cairo; pop 2,096,000

Gla·cier Bay \'glā-shər\ inlet SE Alaska at S end of Saint Elias Range

Glas·gow \'glas-(,)kō, 'glas-(,)gō, 'glaz-(,)gō\ city S cen Scotland on the Clyde; pop 681,470 — **Glas·we·gian** \gla-'swē-jən, glaz-\ adj or n

Glen·dale \'glen-,dāl\ 1 city cen Arizona NW of Phoenix; pop 218,812 2 city S California NE of Los Angeles; pop 194,973

Glouces·ter \'gläs-tər, 'glȯs\ town SW cen England; pop 91,800

Glouces·ter·shire \'gläs-tər-,shir, -shər, 'glȯs-\ or **Gloucester** county SW cen England

Goa \'gō-ə\ district W India on Malabar coast

Goat Island island W New York in Niagara River — see NIAGARA FALLS

Go·bi \'gō-(,)bē\ desert E cen Asia in Mongolia & N China

Godt·hab — see NUUK

Godwin Austen — see K2

Go·lan Heights \'gō-,län, -lən\ hilly region NE of Sea of Galilee

Gol·con·da \gäl-'kän-də\ ruined city cen India W of Hyderabad

Gold Coast 1 — see GHANA 2 coast region W Africa on N shore of Gulf of Guinea E of Ivory Coast

Golden Gate strait W California connecting San Francisco Bay with Pacific Ocean

Good Hope, Cape of \,gúd-'hōp\ cape S Republic of South Africa on SW coast of Western Cape province

Gorki — see NIZHNIY NOVGOROD

Gö·te·borg \,yœ-tə-'bȯr-ē\ city & port SW Sweden; pop 474,921

Gram·pi·an \'gram-pē-ən\ hills N cen Scotland

Grand Banks shallow area in the W North Atlantic SE of Newfoundland

Grand Canyon gorge of Colorado River NW Arizona

Grand Canyon of the Snake HELLS CANYON

Grande, Rio — see RIO GRANDE

Grand Prairie city NE cen Texas W of Dallas; pop 127,427

Grand Rapids city SW Michigan; pop 197,800

Graz \'gräts\ city S Austria; pop 226,244

Great Australian Bight wide bay on S coast of Australia

Great Barrier Reef coral reef Australia off NE coast of Queensland

Great Basin region W U.S. between Sierra Nevada & Wasatch Range including most of Nevada & parts of California, Idaho, Utah, Wyoming, & Oregon; has no drainage to ocean

Great Bear lake Canada in Northwest Territories draining through Great Bear River into Mackenzie River

Great Brit·ain \'bri-tᵊn\ 1 island W Europe NW of France consisting of England, Scotland, & Wales; pop 53,917,000 2 UNITED KINGDOM

Great Dividing Range mountain system E Australia & Tasmania extending S from Cape York Peninsula — see KOSCIUSKO, MOUNT

Greater Antilles group of islands of the West Indies including Cuba, Hispaniola, Jamaica, & Puerto Rico — see LESSER ANTILLES

Greater London metropolitan county SE England consisting of City of London & 32 surrounding boroughs

Greater Manchester metropolitan county NW England including city of Manchester

Greater Sud·bury \'səd-,ber-ē, -b(ə-)rē\ city SE Ontario, Canada; pop 155,219

Great Lakes chain of five lakes (Superior, Michigan, Huron, Erie, & Ontario) cen North America in U.S. & Canada

Great Plains elevated plains region W cen U.S. & W Canada E of the Rockies; extending from W Texas to NE British Columbia & NW Alberta

Great Rift Valley basin SW Asia & E Africa extending with breaks from valley of the Jordan S to cen Mozambique

Great Salt Lake lake N Utah having no outlet

Great Slave Lake lake NW Canada in S Northwest Territories drained by Mackenzie River

Great Smoky mountains between W North Carolina & E Tennessee; highest Clingmans Dome 6643 ft. (2025 m.)

Greece \'grēs\ country S Europe at S end of Balkan Peninsula; ✳, Athens; pop 10,964,020

Green \'grēn\ 1 mountains E North America in the Appalachians extending from S Quebec S through Vermont into W Massachusetts 2 river 730 mi. (1175 km.) long W U.S. flowing from W Wyoming S into the Colorado in SE Utah

Green Bay 1 inlet of NW Lake Michigan 120 mi. (193 km.) long in NW Michigan & NE Wisconsin 2 city NE Wisconsin on Green Bay; pop 102,313

Green·land \'grēn-lənd, -,land\ island in the North Atlantic off NE North America belonging to Denmark; ✳, Nuuk; pop 55,171

Greens·boro \'grēnz-,bər-ō\ city N cen North Carolina; pop 223,891

Green·wich \'gre-nich, 'grēn-,wich, 'grin-,wich\ borough of SE Greater London, England; pop 200,800

Green·wich Village \'gre-nich\ section of New York City in Manhattan on lower W side

Gre·na·da \grə-'nä-də\ island West Indies in S Windward

Islands; independent country; ✱, Saint George's; *pop* 102,632

Gren·a·dines, the \,gre-nə-'dēnz, 'gre-nə-,\ islands West Indies in *cen* Windward Islands; N islands part of Saint Vincent and the Grenadines; S islands dependency of Grenada

Groz·ny \'gróz-nē, 'gräz-\ city S Russia in Europe; ✱ of Chechnya; *pop* 388,000

Gua·da·la·ja·ra \,gwä-də-lə-'här-ə, ,gwä-thä-lä-'hä-rä\ city W *cen* Mexico; *pop* 2,987,194

Gua·dal·ca·nal \,gwä-dᵊl-kə-'nal, ,gwä-də-kə-\ island W Pacific in the SE Solomons; *pop* 23,922

Gua·dal·qui·vir \,gwä-dᵊl-ki-'vir, -'kwi-vər\ river 408 mi. (656 km.) long S Spain flowing into the Atlantic

Gua·de·loupe \'gwä-də-,lüp\ two islands separated by a narrow channel in West Indies in *cen* Leeward Islands; an overseas division of France; *pop* 418,000

Gua·lla·ti·ri \,gwä-yə-'tir-ē, ,gwī-ə-\ volcano 19,882 ft. (6060 m.) high N Chile

Guam \'gwäm\ island W Pacific in S Marianas belonging to U.S.; ✱, Agana; *pop* 154,805 — **Gua·ma·ni·an** \gwä-'mä-nē-ən\ *adj or n*

Gua·na·ba·ra Bay \,gwä-nä-'bär-ə\ inlet of the Atlantic SE Brazil on which city of Rio de Janeiro is located

Guang·dong \'gwäŋ-'dùŋ\ *or* **Kwang·tung** \'gwäŋ-'dùŋ, 'kwäŋ-, -'tùŋ\ province SE China bordering on South China Sea & Gulf of Tonkin; ✱, Guangzhou; *pop* 62,829,236

Guang·zhou \'gwäŋ-'jō\ *or* **Can·ton** \'kan-,tän, kan-'\ city & port SE China; *pop* 2,914,281

Guan·tá·na·mo Bay \gwän-'tä-nä-,mō\ inlet of the Caribbean in SE Cuba; site of U.S. naval station

Gua·te·ma·la \,gwä-tə-'mä-lə, -tä-'mä-lä\ 1 country Central America; *pop* 9,713,000 2 *or* **Guatemala City** city, its ✱; *pop* 1,132,730 — **Gua·te·ma·lan** \-'mä-lən\ *adj or n*

Gua·ya·quil \,gwī-ə-'kēl, -'kil\ city & port W Ecuador; *pop* 1,508,444

Guay·na·bo \gwī-'nä-(,)bō, -(,)vō\ city NE *cen* Puerto Rico; *pop* 100,053

Guern·sey \'gərn-zē\ — see CHANNEL

Gui·a·na \gē-'a-nə, -'ä-nə; gī-'a-nə\ region N South America on the Atlantic; includes Guyana, French Guiana, Suriname, & nearby parts of Brazil & Venezuela — **Gui·a·nan** \-nən\ *adj or n*

Guin·ea \'gi-nē\ 1 region W Africa on the Atlantic extending along coast from Gambia to Angola 2 country W Africa N of Sierra Leone & Liberia; ✱, Conakry; *pop* 7,300,000 — **Guin·ean** \'gi-nē-ən\ *adj or n*

Guinea, Gulf of arm of the Atlantic W *cen* Africa

Guin·ea–Bis·sau \,gi-nē-bi-'saù\ country W Africa; ✱, Bissau; *pop* 1.036,000

Gui·yang \'gwä-'yäŋ\ *or* **Kuei–yang** \'gwä-'yäŋ\ city S China; *pop* 1,018,619

Gulf States states of U.S. bordering on Gulf of Mexico: Florida, Alabama, Mississippi, Louisiana, and Texas

Gulf Stream warm current of the Atlantic Ocean flowing from Gulf of Mexico NE along coast of U.S. to Nantucket Island and from there eastward

Guy·ana \gī-'an-ə\ *formerly* **British Guiana** country N South America on the Atlantic; ✱, Georgetown; *pop* 755,000 — **Guy·a·nese** \,gī-ə-'nēz, -'nēs\ *adj or n*

Gwangju — see KWANGJU

Gwent \'gwent\ former county SE Wales

Gwyn·edd \'gwi-neth\ former county NW Wales

Hack·ney \'hak-nē\ borough of N Greater London, England; *pop* 164,200

Hague, The \thə-'häg\ city SW Netherlands; seat of government; *pop* 457,726

Hai·kou \'hī-'kō\ city & port SE China; *pop* 280,153

Hai·phong \'hī-'fòŋ, -'fäŋ\ city & port N Vietnam; *pop* 1,726,900

Hai·ti \'hä-tē\ country West Indies in W Hispaniola; ✱, Port-au-Prince; *pop* 6,902,000 — **Hai·tian** \'hä-shən\ *adj or n*

Ha·le·a·ka·la Crater \,hä-lā-,ä-kä-'lä\ crater over 2500 ft. (762 m.) deep Hawaii in E Maui

Hal·i·fax \'ha-lə-,faks\ municipality & port, ✱ of Nova Scotia, Canada; *pop* 359,111

Ham·burg \'ham-,bərg; 'häm-,bùrg, -,bùrk\ city N Ger-

many on the Elbe; *pop* 1,668,800 — **Ham·burg·er** \-,bər-gər, -,bùr-\ *n*

Ham·hung *or* **Ham·heung** \'häm-,hùŋ\ city E *cen* North Korea; *pop* 701,000

Ham·il·ton \'ha-məl-tən\ 1 town, ✱ of Bermuda; *pop* 969 2 city & port, S Ontario, Canada on Lake Ontario; *pop* 490,268

Ham·mer·smith and Ful·ham \'ha-mər-,smith-ənd-'fù-ləm\ borough of SW Greater London, England; *pop* 136,500

Hamp·shire \'hamp-,shir, -shər\ county S England on English Channel

Hamp·ton \'hamp-tən\ city SE Virginia; *pop* 146,437

Hampton Roads channel SE Virginia through which James River flows into Chesapeake Bay

Hang·zhou \'häŋ-'jō\ *or* **Hang·chow** \'haŋ-'chaù, 'häŋ-'jō\ *or* **Hang–chou** \'jō\ city E China; *pop* 1,099,660

Han·ni·bal \'ha-nə-bəl\ city NE Missouri on the Mississippi River; *pop* 17,757

Han·no·ver *or* **Han·o·ver** \'ha-,nō-vər, -nə-vər, *G* hä-'nō-fər\ city N *cen* Germany; *pop* 517,746

Ha·noi \ha-'nói, hə-, hä-\ city, ✱ of Vietnam; *pop* 2,931,400

Ha·ra·re \hə-'rä-(,)rä\ *formerly* **Salis·bury** \'sòlz-,ber-ē, -b(ə-)rē\ city, ✱ of Zimbabwe; *pop* 1,184,169

Har·bin \'här-bən, här-'bin\ *or* **Ha–erh–pin** \'hä-'ər-'bin\ city NE China; *pop* 2,443,398

Har·in·gey \'ha-riŋ-gā\ borough of N Greater London, England; *pop* 187,300

Har·lem \'här-ləm\ section of New York City in N Manhattan

Har·ris·burg \'ha-rəs-,bərg\ city, ✱ of Pennsylvania; *pop* 48,950

Har·row \'ha-(,)rō\ borough of NW Greater London, England; *pop* 194,300

Hart·ford \'härt-fərd\ city, ✱ of Connecticut; *pop* 121,578

Hat·ter·as, Cape \'ha-tə-rəs\ cape North Carolina on **Hatteras Island**

Ha·vana \hə-'va-nə\ city, ✱ of Cuba; *pop* 2,096,054

Hav·ant \'ha-vənt\ town S England; *pop* 117,400

Ha·ver·ing \'hāv-riŋ, 'hä-və-riŋ\ borough of NE Greater London, England; *pop* 224,400

Ha·waii \hə-'wä-yē, -'wä-,ē\ 1 *or* **Ha·wai·ian Islands** *formerly* **Sand·wich Islands** \,san-(d)wich\ group of islands *cen* Pacific belonging to U.S. 2 island, largest of the group 3 state of U.S., ✱, Honolulu; *pop* 1,211,537

Hay·ward \'hā-wərd\ city W California SE of Oakland; *pop* 140,030

Heb·ri·des \'he-brə-,dēz\ islands W Scotland in the North Atlantic consisting of **Outer Hebrides** (to W) and **Inner Hebrides** (to E); *pop* 30,660 — **Heb·ri·de·an** \,he-brə-'dē-ən\ *adj or n*

Hel·e·na \'he-lə-nə\ city, ✱ of Montana; *pop* 25,780

Hellespont — see DARDANELLES

Hells Canyon \'helz\ canyon of Snake River on Idaho–Oregon boundary

Hel·sin·ki \'hel-,siŋ-kē, hel-'\ city, ✱ of Finland; *pop* 559,718

Hen·der·son \'hen-dər-sən\ city S Nevada; *pop* 175,381

Hen·ry, Cape \'hen-rē\ cape E Virginia S of entrance to Chesapeake Bay

Her·e·ford and Wor·ces·ter \'her-ə-fərd-ᵊn-'wùs-tər\ former county W England bordering on Wales

Hert·ford·shire \'här-fərd-,shir, 'härt-, -shər\ *or* **Hertford** county SE England

Her·ze·go·vi·na \,hert-sə-gō-'vē-nə, ,hərt-, -'gō-və-nə\ *or Serb* **Her·ce·go·vi·na** \'kert-sə-gō-vē-nə\ region S Europe S of Bosnia & NW of Montenegro; part of Bosnia and Herzegovina — **Her·ze·go·vi·nian** \,hert-sə-gō-'vē-nē-ən, ,hərt-, -nyən\ *n*

Hi·a·le·ah \,hī-ə-'lē-ə\ city SE Florida; *pop* 226,419

Hi·ber·nia \hī-'bər-nē-ə\ — see IRELAND — **Hi·ber·ni·an** \-ən\ *adj or n*

Hi·ga·shi·ōsa·ka \hē-,gä-shē-'ō-sä-kä\ city Japan in S Honshu E of Osaka; *pop* 515,094

High·land \'hī-lənd\ administrative subdivision of NW Scotland

High·lands \'hī-lənd\ the mountainous N part of Scotland lying N & W of the Lowlands

High Plains the Great Plains esp. from Nebraska southward

Hil·ling·don \'hi-lin-dən\ borough of W Greater London, England; *pop* 225,800

Hi·ma·la·yas, the \,hi-mə-'lā-əz\ *or* **the Himalaya** mountain system S Asia on border between India & Tibet and in Kashmir, Nepal, & Bhutan — see EVEREST, MOUNT — **Hi·ma·la·yan** \,him-ə-'lā-ən, hə-'mäl-(ə-)yən\ *adj*

Hin·du Kush \'hin-(,)dü-'kúsh, -'kȯsh\ mountain range *cen* Asia SW of the Pamirs on border of Kashmir and in Afghanistan

Hin·du·stan \,hin-(,)dü-'stan, -də-, -'stän\ **1** a name for N India **2** the subcontinent of India **3** the country of India

Hi·ro·shi·ma \,hir-ə-'shē-mə, hə-'rō-shə-mə\ city Japan in SW Honshu on Inland Sea; *pop* 1,126,239

His·pan·io·la \,his-pə-'nyō-lə\ *or Spanish* **Es·pa·ño·la** \,es-,pä-'nyō-lä\ island West Indies in Greater Antilles; divided between Haiti on W & Dominican Republic on E

Ho·bart \'hō-bərt\ city Australia, ✳ of Tasmania; *pop* 47,106

Ho Chi Minh City \'hō-,chē-'min\ *formerly* **Sai·gon** \sī-'gän, 'sī-,\ city S Vietnam; *pop* 5,479,000

Hoh·hot \'hō-'hōt\ *or* **Hu·he·hot** \'hü-(,)hä-'hōt\ city N China, ✳ of Inner Mongolia; *pop* 652,534

Hok·kai·do \hó-'kī-(,)dō\ island N Japan N of Honshu; *pop* 5,683,062

Hol·land \'hä-lənd\ **1** county of Holy Roman Empire bordering on North Sea & consisting of area now forming part of W Netherlands **2** — see NETHERLANDS — **Holland·er** \-lən-dər\ *n*

Hol·ly·wood \'hä-lē-,wúd\ **1** section of Los Angeles, California, NW of downtown district **2** city SE Florida; *pop* 139,357

Holy Roman Empire empire consisting mainly of German & Italian territories & existing from 9th or 10th century to 1806

Hon·du·ras \hän-'dúr-əs, -'dyúr-; ȯn-'dü-räs\ country Central America; ✳, Tegucigalpa; *pop* 4,604,800 — **Hon·duran** \-ən\ *adj or n*

Hong Kong \'häŋ-,käŋ, -'käŋ\ *or Chinese* **Xiang·gang** \'shyäŋ-,gäŋ\ special administrative region China on SE coast including Hong Kong Island & Jiulong Peninsula; chief city Victoria; *pop* 6,843,000

Ho·ni·a·ra \,hō-nē-'är-ə\ town, ✳ of Solomon Islands; *pop* 35,288

Ho·no·lu·lu \,hä-nə-'lü-(,)lü, ,hō-nə-\ city, ✳ of Hawaii on Oahu; *pop* 371,657

Hon·shu \'hän-(,)shü, 'hȯn-\ island Japan; largest of the four chief islands; *pop* 102,324,961

Hood, Mount \'hùd\ mountain 11,235 ft. (3424 m.) NW Oregon in Cascade Range

Hoo·ver Dam \'hü-vər\ *or* **Boul·der Dam** \'bōl-dər\ dam 726 ft. (221 m.) high in Colorado River between Arizona & Nevada — see MEAD, LAKE

Hormuz, Strait of \'(h)ȯr-,məz, (h)ȯr-'müz\ strait connecting Persian Gulf & Gulf of Oman

Horn, Cape \'hȯrn\ cape S Chile on an island in Tierra del Fuego; the most southerly point of South America at 56° S latitude

Horn of Africa the easternmost projection of Africa; variously used to refer to Somalia, SE or all of Ethiopia, & sometimes Djibouti

Horseshoe Falls — see NIAGARA FALLS

Houns·low \'haúnz-,lō\ borough of SW Greater London, England; *pop* 193,400

Hous·ton \'hyüs-tən, 'yüs\ city SE Texas; *pop* 1,953,631

How·rah \'haú-rə\ city E India on Hugli River opposite Calcutta; *pop* 1,008,704

Hsi–an — see XI'AN

Huang *or* **Hwang** \'hwäŋ\ *or* **Yellow** river about 3000 mi. (4828 km.) long N China flowing into Bo Hai

Hud·ders·field \'hə-dərz-,fēld\ town N England NE of Manchester; *pop* 123,888

Hud·son \'həd-sən\ **1** river 306 mi. (492 km.) long E New York flowing S **2** bay, inlet of the Atlantic in N Canada **3** strait NE Canada connecting Hudson Bay & the Atlantic

Hu·gli *or* **Hoo·ghly** \'hü-glē\ river 120 mi. (193 km.) long E India flowing S into Bay of Bengal

Huhehot — see HOHHOT

Hull \'həl\ *or* **Kings·ton upon Hull** \'kiŋ-stən\ city & port N England; *pop* 242,200

Hun·ga·ry \'həŋ-gə-rē\ country *cen* Europe; ✳, Budapest; *pop* 10,142,000

Hunt·ing·ton Beach \'hən-tiŋ-tən\ city SW California; *pop* 189,594

Hunts·ville \'hənts-,vil, -vəl\ city N Alabama; *pop* 158,216

Hu·ron, Lake \'hyúr-,än, 'yúr-\ lake E *cen* North America in U.S. & Canada; one of the Great Lakes

Hy·der·abad \'hī-d(ə-)rə-,bad, -,bäd\ **1** city S *cen* India; *pop* 3,449,878 **2** city SE Pakistan on the Indus; *pop* 1,166,894

Iba·dan \i-'bä-dᵊn, -'ba-\ city SW Nigeria; *pop* 1,263,000

Ibe·ri·an \ī-'bir-ē-ə\ peninsula SW Europe occupied by Spain & Portugal

Ice·land \'īs-lənd, 'īs-,land\ island SE of Greenland between Arctic & Atlantic oceans; country; ✳, Reykjavik; *pop* 282,849 — **Ice·land·er** \'īs-,lan-dər, 'īs-lən-\ *n*

Ida·ho \'ī-də-,hō\ state NW U.S.; ✳, Boise; *pop* 1,293,953 — **Ida·ho·an** \,ī-də-'hō-ən\ *adj or n*

Igua·çú *or* **Igua·zú** \,ē-gwə-'sü\ river 745 mi. (1199 km.) long S Brazil flowing W

IJs·sel *or* **Ijs·sel** \'ī-səl, 'ä-\ river 70 mi. (113 km.) long E Netherlands flowing out of Rhine N into IJsselmeer

IJs·sel·meer \'ī-səl-,mer, 'ä-\ *or* **Lake Ijs·sel** freshwater lake N Netherlands separated from North Sea by a dike; part of former Zuider Zee (inlet of North Sea)

Ilium — see TROY

Il·li·nois \,i-lə-'nói\ state N *cen* U.S.; ✳, Springfield; *pop* 12,419,293 — **Il·li·nois·an** \,i-lə-'nói-ən\ *adj or n*

Il·lyr·ia \i-'lir-ē-ə\ ancient country S Europe and Balkan Peninsula on the Adriatic — **Il·lyr·i·an** \-ē-ən\ *adj or n*

Im·pe·ri·al Valley \im-'pir-ē-əl\ valley SE corner of California & partly in NE Baja California, Mexico

In·chon *or* **In·cheon** \'in-,chən\ city South Korea on Yellow Sea; *pop* 2,466,338

In·de·pen·dence \,in-də-'pen-dən(t)s\ city W Missouri E of Kansas City; *pop* 113,288

In·dia \'in-dē-ə\ **1** subcontinent S Asia S of the Himalayas between Bay of Bengal & Arabian Sea **2** country consisting of major portion of the subcontinent; ✳, New Delhi; *pop* 896,567,000 **3** *or* **Indian Empire** before 1947 those parts of the subcontinent of India under British rule or protection

In·di·an \'in-dē-ən\ ocean E of Africa, S of Asia, W of Australia, & N of Antarctica

In·di·ana \,in-dē-'a-nə\ state E *cen* U.S.; ✳, Indianapolis; *pop* 6,080,485 — **In·di·an·an** \-'a-nən\ *or* **In·di·an·i·an** \-'a-nē-ən\ *adj or n*

In·di·a·nap·o·lis \,in-dē-ə-'na-pə-lis\ city, ✳ of Indiana; *pop* 791,926

Indian River lagoon 165 mi. (266 km.) long E Florida between main part of the state & coastal islands

Indian Territory former territory S U.S. in present state of Oklahoma

In·dies \'in-(,)dēz\ **1** EAST INDIES **2** WEST INDIES

In·do·chi·na \,in-(,)dō-'chī-nə\ **1** peninsula SE Asia including Myanmar, Malay Peninsula, Thailand, Cambodia, Laos, & Vietnam **2** *or* **French Indochina** former country SE Asia consisting of area now forming Cambodia, Laos, & Vietnam — **In·do–Chi·nese** \-chī-'nēz, -'nēs\ *adj or n*

In·do·ne·sia \,in-də-'nē-zhə, -shə\ country SE Asia in Malay Archipelago consisting of Sumatra, Java, S & E Borneo, Sulawesi, W New Guinea, & many smaller islands; ✳, Jakarta; *pop* 187,468,250 — **In·do·ne·sian** \-zhən, -shən\ *adj or n*

In·dore \in-'dȯr\ city W *cen* India; *pop* 1,597,441

In·dus \'in-dəs\ river 1800 mi. (2897 km.) long S Asia flowing from Tibet NW & SSW through Pakistan into Arabian Sea

In·gle·wood \'iŋ-gəl-,wúd\ city SW California; *pop* 112,580

In·land Sea \'in-,land, -lənd\ inlet of the Pacific in SW Japan between Honshu on N and Shikoku and Kyushu on S

Inner Hebrides — see HEBRIDES

Inner Mon·go·lia \män-ˈgōl-yə, mäṇ-, -ˈgō-lē-ə\ region N China; *pop* 21,456,798

Inside Passage protected shipping route between Puget Sound, Washington, & Skagway, Alaska

In·ver·ness \ˌin-vər-ˈnes\ town NW Scotland; *pop* 63,090

Io·ni·an \ī-ˈō-nē-ən\ sea, arm of the Mediterranean between SE Italy & W Greece

Io·wa \ˈī-ə-wə\ state N *cen* U.S.; ✳, Des Moines; *pop* 2,926,324 — **Io·wan** \-wən\ *adj or n*

Ips·wich \ˈip-(ˌ)swich\ town SE England; *pop* 115,500

Iqa·lu·it \ē-ˈka-lü-ət\ town Canada, ✳ of Nunavut on Baffin Island; *pop* 5236

Iran \i-ˈrän, -ˈran\ *formerly* **Per·sia** \ˈpər-zhə\ country SW Asia; ✳, Tehran; *pop* 59,570,000 — **Irani** \-ˈrä-nē, -ˈra-\ *adj or n* — **Ira·nian** \i-ˈrä-nē-ən, -ˈran-ē-, -ˈrän-ē-\ *adj or n*

Iraq \i-ˈräk, -ˈrak\ country SW Asia in Mesopotamia; ✳, Baghdad; *pop* (est.) 24,683,000 — **Iraqi** \-ˈräk-ē, -ˈrak-\ *adj or n*

Ire·land \ˈī(-ə)r-lənd\ **1** *or Latin* **Hi·ber·nia** \hī-ˈbər-nē-ə\ island W Europe in the North Atlantic; one of the British Isles **2** *or* **Eire** \ˈer-ə\ country occupying major portion of the Ireland (island); ✳, Dublin; *pop* 3,917,203

Irian Jaya — see WEST PAPUA

Irish Sea arm of the North Atlantic between Great Britain & Ireland

Ir·kutsk \ir-ˈkütsk, ˌər-\ city S Russia near Lake Baikal; *pop* 639,000

Ir·ra·wad·dy \ˌir-ə-ˈwä-dē\ river 1300 mi. (2092 km.) long Myanmar flowing S into Bay of Bengal

Ir·tysh \ir-ˈtish, ˌər-\ river over 2600 mi. (4180 km.) long *cen* Asia flowing NW & N from Altay Mountains in China, through Kazakhstan, & into W *cen* Russia

Ir·vine \ˈər-ˌvīn\ city SW California; *pop* 143,072

Ir·ving \ˈər-viṇ\ city NE Texas NW of Dallas; *pop* 191,615

Isfahan — see ESFAHAN

Is·lam·abad \is-ˈlä-mə-ˌbäd, iz-, -ˈla-mə-ˌbad\ city, ✳ of Pakistan; *pop* 529,180

Islas Malvinas — see FALKLAND ISLANDS

Isle of Man — see MAN, ISLE OF

Isle of Wight \ˈwīt\ island England in English Channel

Isle Roy·ale \ˈī(-ə)l-ˈròi(-ə)l\ island Michigan in Lake Superior

Isles of Scilly 1 — see CORNWALL AND ISLES OF SCILLY **2** — see SCILLY

Is·ling·ton \ˈiz-liṇ-tən\ borough of N Greater London, England; *pop* 155,200

Ispahan — see ESFAHAN

Is·ra·el \ˈiz-rē(-ə)l, -(ˌ)rā(-ə)l\ **1** kingdom in ancient Palestine consisting of lands occupied by the Hebrew people **2** *or* **Ephra·im** \ˈē-frē-əm\ the N part of the Hebrew kingdom after about 933 B.C. **3** country SW Asia; ✳, Jerusalem; *pop* 4,037,620 — **Is·rae·li** \iz-ˈrä-lē\ *adj or n*

Is·tan·bul \ˌis-tən-ˈbül, -ˌtan-, -ˌtän-, -ˈbül, ˈis-tən-ˌ, *or with* m *for* n\ *formerly* **Con·stan·ti·no·ple** \ˌkän-ˌstan-tə-ˈnō-pəl\ city NW Turkey on the Bosporus & Sea of Marmara; *pop* 6,620,241

Is·tria \ˈis-trē-ə\ peninsula in Croatia & Slovenia extending into the N Adriatic — **Is·tri·an** \-trē-ən\ *adj or n*

It·a·ly \ˈi-tə-lē\ country S Europe including a boot-shaped peninsula & the islands of Sicily & Sardinia; ✳, Rome; *pop* 57,844,017

Itas·ca, Lake \ī-ˈtas-kə\ lake NW *cen* Minnesota; source of the Mississippi

Ivory Coast *or* **Côte d'Ivoire** \ˌkōt-dē-ˈvwär\ country W Africa on Gulf of Guinea; official ✳, Yamoussoukro; seat of government, Abidjan; *pop* 13,459,000 — **Ivor·i·an** \(ˌ)ī-ˈvòr-ē-ən\ *adj or n* — **Ivory Coast·er** \ˈkō-stər\ *n*

Iwo Ji·ma \ˌē-(ˌ)wō-ˈjē-mə\ island Japan in W Pacific SSE of Tokyo

Izhevsk \ˈē-ˌzhefsk\ *or 1985–87* **Usti·nov** \ˈüs-ti-ˌnóf, -ˌnòv\ city W Russia; *pop* 651,000

Iz·mir \iz-ˈmir\ *formerly* **Smyr·na** \ˈsmər-nə\ city W Turkey; *pop* 1,757,414

Jack·son \ˈjak-sən\ city, ✳ of Mississippi; *pop* 184,256

Jack·son·ville \ˈjak-sən-ˌvil\ city NE Florida; *pop* 735,617

Jai·pur \ˈjī-ˌpùr\ city NW India; *pop* 2,324,319

Ja·kar·ta *formerly* **Dja·kar·ta** \jə-ˈkär-tə\ city, ✳ of Indonesia in NW Java; *pop* 6,503,449

Ja·mai·ca \jə-ˈmā-kə\ island West Indies in Greater Antilles; country; ✳, Kingston; *pop* 2,599,334 — **Ja·mai·can** \-kən\ *adj or n*

James \ˈjāmz\ **1** — see DAKOTA **2** river 340 mi. (547 km.) long Virginia flowing E into Chesapeake Bay

James Bay the S extension of Hudson Bay between NE Ontario & W Quebec

James·town \ˈjāmz-ˌtaùn\ ruined village E Virginia on James River; first permanent English settlement in America (1607)

Jam·shed·pur \ˈjäm-ˌshed-ˌpùr\ city E India; *pop* 570,349

Ja·pan \jə-ˈpan, ja-\ country E Asia consisting of Honshu, Hokkaido, Kyushu, Shikoku, & other islands in the W Pacific; ✳, Tokyo; *pop* 126,925,843

Japan, Sea of *or* **East Sea** arm of the Pacific between Japan & main part of Asia

Ja·va \ˈjä-və, ˈja-\ island Indonesia SW of Borneo; chief city, Jakarta; *pop* 107,581,306 — **Ja·va·nese** \ˌja-və-ˈnēz, ˌjä-, -ˈnēs\ *n*

Jef·fer·son City \ˈje-fər-sən\ city, ✳ of Missouri; *pop* 39,636

Jer·sey \ˈjər-zē\ — see CHANNEL

Jersey City city NE New Jersey on Hudson River; *pop* 240,055

Je·ru·sa·lem \jə-ˈrü-s(ə-)ləm, -ˈrü-z(ə-)ləm\ city NW of Dead Sea, ✳ of Israel; *pop* 544,200

Jid·da *or* **Jid·dah** \ˈji-də\ *or* **Jed·da** *or* **Jed·dah** \ˈje-də\ city W Saudi Arabia on Red Sea; *pop* 561,104

Ji·lin \ˈjē-ˈlin\ *or* **Ki·rin** \ˈkē-ˈrin\ city NE China; *pop* 1,036,858

Ji·nan *or* **Tsi·nan** \ˈjē-ˈnän\ city E China; *pop* 1,500,000

Jin·zhou *or* **Chin–chou** *or* **Chin·chow** \ˈjin-ˈjò\ city NE China; *pop* 400,000

Jiu·long \ˈjü-ˈlòṇ\ *or* **Kow·loon** \ˈkaù-ˈlün\ **1** peninsula SE China in Hong Kong opposite Hong Kong Island **2** city on Jiulong Peninsula; *pop* 1,975,265

Jo·han·nes·burg \jō-ˈhä-nəs-ˌbərg, -ˈha-\ city NE Republic of South Africa; *pop* 654,232

Jo·li·et \ˌjō-lē-ˈet\ city NE Illinois; *pop* 106,221

Jor·dan \ˈjòr-dᵊn\ **1** river 200 mi. (322 km.) long Israel & Jordan flowing S from Syria into Dead Sea **2** country SW Asia in NW Arabia; ✳, Amman; *pop* 5,182,000 — **Jor·da·ni·an** \jòr-ˈdā-nē-ən\ *adj or n*

Juan de Fu·ca, Strait of \ˌwän-də-ˈfyü-kə, ˌhwän-\ strait 100 mi. (161 km.) long between Vancouver Island, British Columbia, & Olympic Peninsula, Washington

Ju·daea *or* **Ju·dea** \jü-ˈdē-ə, -ˈdā-\ region of ancient Palestine forming its S division under Persian, Greek, & Roman rule — **Ju·dean** \-ən\ *adj or n*

Ju·neau \ˈjü-(ˌ)nō, jü-ˈ\ city, ✳ of Alaska; *pop* 30,711

Ju·ra \ˈjùr-ə\ mountain range extending along boundary between France & Switzerland N of Lake of Geneva

Jut·land \ˈjət-lənd\ **1** peninsula N Europe extending into North Sea and consisting of main part of Denmark & N portion of Germany **2** the main part of Denmark

Ka·bul \ˈkä-bəl, -ˌbül; kə-ˈbül\ city, ✳ of Afghanistan; *pop* (est.) 2,272,000

Ka Lae \kä-ˈlä-ä\ *or* **South Cape** *or* **South Point** most southerly point of Hawaii & of U.S.

Kal·a·ha·ri \ˌka-lə-ˈhär-ē, ˌkä-\ desert region S Africa N of Orange River in S Botswana & NW Republic of South Africa

Kalgan — see ZHANGJIAKOU

Ka·li·man·tan \ˌka-lə-ˈman-ˌtan, ˌkä-lē-ˈmän-ˌtän\ **1** BORNEO — its Indonesian name **2** the S & E portion of Borneo belonging to Indonesia

Ka·li·nin·grad \kə-ˈlē-nən-ˌgrad, -nyən-, -ˌgrät\ *formerly* **Kö·nigs·berg** \ˈkä-nigz-ˌbərg\ city & port W Russia; *pop* 424,000

Kam·chat·ka \kam-ˈchat-kə, -ˈchät-\ peninsula 750 mi. (1207 km.) long E Russia

Kam·pa·la \käm-ˈpä-lä, kam-\ city, ✳ of Uganda; *pop* 773,463

Kampuchea — see CAMBODIA

Kan·da·har \ˈkən-də-ˌhär\ city SE Afghanistan; *pop* (est.) 359,700

Ka·no \ˈkä-(ˌ)nō\ city N *cen* Nigeria; *pop* 594,800

Kan·pur \ˈkän-ˌpùr\ city N India on the Ganges; *pop* 2,532,138

Kan·sas \'kan-zəs\ state W *cen* U.S.; ✳, Topeka; *pop* 2,688,418 — **Kan·san** \'kan-zən\ *adj or n*

Kansas City 1 city NE Kansas bordering on Kansas City, Missouri; *pop* 146,866 **2** city W Missouri; *pop* 441,545

Kao—hsiung \'kaú-'shyúŋ, 'gaú-\ city & port SW Taiwan; *pop* 1,405,860

Ka·ra·chi \kə-'rä-chē\ city S Pakistan on Arabian Sea; *pop* 9,339,023

Ka·ra·gan·da \ˌkär-ə-'gän-də\ *or* **Qa·ra·ghan·dy** \-dē\ city *cen* Kazakhstan *pop* 608,600

Kar·a·ko·ram Pass \ˌkär-ə-'kór-əm\ mountain pass NE Kashmir in **Karakoram Range** (system connecting the Himalayas with the Pamirs)

Ka·re·lia \kə-'rē-lē-ə, -'rēl-yə\ region NE Europe in Finland & Russia; *pop* 800,000 — **Ka·re·lian** \kə-'rē-lē-ən, -'rēl-yən\ *adj or n*

Ka·roo *or* **Kar·roo** \kə-'rü\ plateau region W Republic of South Africa W of Drakensberg Mountains

Kash·mir \'kash-ˌmir, 'kazh-, kash-', kazh-'\ disputed territory N subcontinent of India; claimed by India & Pakistan — **Kash·miri** \kash-'mi(ə)r-ē, kazh-\ *adj or n*

Ka·thi·a·war \ˌkä-tē-ə-'wär\ peninsula W India N of Gulf of Cambay

Kath·man·du *or* **Kat·man·du** \ˌkat-ˌman-'dü, ˌkät-ˌmän-\ city, ✳ of Nepal; metropolitan area *pop* 671,846

Kat·mai, Mount \'kat-ˌmī\ volcano 6715 ft. (2047 m.) S Alaska on Alaska Peninsula

Kat·te·gat \'ka-ti-ˌgat\ arm of North Sea between Sweden & E coast of Jutland Peninsula of Denmark

Kau·ai \kä-'wä-ē\ island Hawaii NW of Oahu

Kau·nas \'kaú-nəs, -ˌnäs\ city *cen* Lithuania; *pop* 378,943

Ka·wa·sa·ki \ˌkä-wä-'sä-kē\ city Japan in E Honshu S of Tokyo; *pop* 1,249,905

Ka·zakh·stan *or* **Ka·zak·stan** \ˌka-(ˌ)zak-'stan\ country NW *cen* Asia; ✳, Astana; *pop* 17,186,000 — **Ka·zakh** *also* **Ka·zak** \kə-'zak, -'zäk\ *n*

Ka·zan \kə-'zan\ city W Russia; *pop* 1,098,000

Kee·wa·tin \kē-'wä-tⁿn, -'wä-\ former district N Canada in E Northwest Territories NW of Hudson Bay; area now part of Nunavut

Ke·me·ro·vo \'kye-mə-rə-və\ city S *cen* Russia; *pop* 521,000

Ke·nai \'kē-ˌnī\ peninsula S Alaska E of Cook Inlet

Kennedy, Cape — see CANAVERAL, CAPE

Ken·sing·ton and Chel·sea \'ken-ziŋ-tən-ənd-'chel-sē, 'ken(t)-siŋ-\ borough of W Greater London, England; *pop* 127,600

Kent \'kent\ county SE England — **Kent·ish** \'ken-tish\ *adj*

Ken·tucky \kən-'tə-kē\ state E *cen* U.S.; ✳, Frankfort; *pop* 4,041,769 — **Ken·tuck·i·an** \-kē-ən\ *adj or n*

Ken·ya \'ke-nyə, 'kē-\ **1** mountain 17,058 ft. (5199 m.) *cen* Kenya **2** country E Africa S of Ethiopia; ✳, Nairobi; *pop* 28,662,239 — **Ken·yan** \-nyən\ *adj or n*

Key West \'west\ city SW Florida on Key West (island); *pop* 25,478

Kha·ba·rovsk \kə-'bär-əfsk, ḵə-\ city SE Russia; *pop* 615,000

Kham·bhat, Gulf of \'kəm-bət\ *or* **Gulf of Cam·bay** \kam-'bä\ inlet of Arabian Sea in India N of Bombay

Khar·kiv \'kär-kəf, 'kär-\ *or* **Khar·kov** \'kär-ˌkóf, 'kär-, -ˌkóv, -kəf\ city NE Ukraine; *pop* 1,623,000

Khar·toum \kär-'tüm\ city, ✳ of Sudan; *pop* 1,950,000

Khy·ber \'kī-bər\ pass 33 mi. (53 km.) long on border between Afghanistan & Pakistan

Ki·bo \'kē-(ˌ)bō\ mountain peak 19,340 ft. (5895 m.) NE Tanzania; highest peak of Kilimanjaro & highest point in Africa

Kiel \'kēl\ — see NORD-OSTSEE

Ki·ev \'kē-ˌef, -ˌev, -if\ *or Ukrainian* **Kyiv** \'kyē-ü\ city, ✳ of Ukraine; *pop* 2,587,000

Ki·ga·li \kē-'gä-lē\ city, ✳ of Rwanda; *pop* 232,733

Ki·lau·ea \ˌkē-ˌlä-'wä-ä\ volcanic crater Hawaii on Hawaii Island on E slope of Mauna Loa

Kil·i·man·ja·ro \ˌki-lə-mən-'jär-(ˌ)ō, -'ja-(ˌ)rō\ mountain NE Tanzania; highest in Africa — see KIBO

Kil·lar·ney, Lakes of \ki-'lär-nē\ three lakes SW Ireland

Kings·ton \'kiŋ-stən\ city & port, ✳ of Jamaica; *pop* 103,771

Kingston upon Hull — see HULL

Kingston upon Thames borough of SW Greater London, England; *pop* 130,600

Kings·town \'kiŋz-ˌtaún\ seaport, ✳ of Saint Vincent and the Grenadines; *pop* 15,670

Kin·sha·sa \kin-'shä-sə\ city, ✳ of Democratic Republic of the Congo; *pop* 3,804,000

Ki·ri·bati \'kir-ə-ˌbas\ island group W Pacific; country; ✳, Tarawa; *pop* 78,600

Kirin — see JILIN

Kirk·wall \'kər-ˌkwól\ town and port N Scotland, ✳ of Orkney Islands; *pop* 5947

Kishinev — see CHIŞINĂU

Ki·ta·kyu·shu \kē-ˌtä-'kyü-(ˌ)shü\ city Japan in N Kyushu; *pop* 1,011,471

Kitch·e·ner \'kich-nər, 'ki-chə-\ city SE Ontario, Canada; *pop* 190,399

Kit·ty Hawk \'kit-ē-ˌhók\ town E North Carolina; *pop* 2991

Klon·dike \'klän-ˌdīk\ region NW Canada in *cen* Yukon Territory in valley of Klondike River

Knox·ville \'näks-ˌvil, -vəl\ city E Tennessee; *pop* 173,890

Ko·be \'kō-bē, -ˌbā\ city Japan in S Honshu; *pop* 1,493,398

Ko·di·ak \'kō-dē-ˌak\ island S Alaska E of Alaska Peninsula

Ko·la \'kō-lə\ peninsula NW Russia

Ko·rea \kə-'rē-ə\ peninsula E Asia between Yellow Sea & Sea of Japan (East Sea); divided 1948 into independent countries of North Korea & South Korea — **Ko·re·an** \kə-'rē-ən\ *adj or n*

Ko·ror \'kór-ˌór\ town, ✳ of Palau; *pop* 13,303

Kos·ci·us·ko, Mount \ˌkä-zē-'əs-(ˌ)kō, ˌkä-sē-\ mountain 7310 ft. (2228 m.) SE Australia in SE New South Wales; highest in Great Dividing Range & in Australia

Ko·so·vo \'kó-sò-ˌvō, 'kä-\ autonomous province S Serbia and Montenegro; *pop* (est.) 2,092,000

Kowloon — see JIULONG

Krak·a·tau \ˌkra-kə-'taú\ *or* **Krak·a·toa** \-'tō-ə\ island & volcano Indonesia between Sumatra & Java

Kra·kow \'krä-ˌkaú, 'kra-, 'krä-, -(ˌ)kó, *Pol* 'krä-ˌküf\ city S Poland; *pop* 748,356

Kras·no·dar \ˌkräs-nə-'där\ city SW Russia; *pop* 635,000

Kras·no·yarsk \ˌkräs-nə-'yärsk\ city S *cen* Russia; *pop* 925,000

Kry·vyy Rih \kri-'vē-'riḵ\ *or* **Kri·voy Rog** \ˌkri-ˌvói-'róg, -'rók\ city SE *cen* Ukraine; *pop* 724,000

K2 \kä-'tü\ *or* **God·win Aus·ten** \gä-dwən-'ós-tən, ˌgó-, -'äs-\ mountain 28,250 ft. (8611 m.) N Kashmir in Karakoram Range; second highest in the world

Kua·la Lum·pur \ˌkwä-lə-'lùm-ˌpúr, -'ləm-, -ˌlùm-'\ city, ✳ of Malaysia; *pop* 1,145,075

Kuei—yang — see GUIYANG

Kun·lun \'kün-'lün\ mountain system W China extending E from the Pamirs; highest peak Ulugh Muztagh 25,340 ft. (7724 m.)

Kun·ming \'kùn-'miŋ\ city S China; *pop* 1,127,411

Kur·di·stan \ˌkùr-də-'stan, ˌkər-, -'stän; 'kər-də-ˌ\ region SW Asia chiefly in E Turkey, NW Iran, & N Iraq — **Kurd** \'kúrd, 'kərd\ *n* — **Kurd·ish** \'kúr-dish, 'kər-\ *adj*

Ku·ril *or* **Ku·rile** \'kyür-ˌēl, 'kúr-; kyü-'rēl, kú-\ islands Russia in W Pacific between Kamchatka Peninsula & Hokkaido Island

Ku·wait \kú-'wät\ **1** country SW Asia in Arabia at head of Persian Gulf; *pop* 1,355,827 **2** city, its ✳; *pop* 181,774 — **Ku·waiti** \-'wä-tē\ *adj or n*

Kuybyshev — see SAMARA

Kuz·netsk Basin \kúz-'netsk\ *or* **Kuz·bas** *or* **Kuz·bass** \'kúz-ˌbas\ basin S *cen* Russia

Kwa·ja·lein \'kwä-jə-lən, -ˌlän\ island W Pacific in Marshall Islands

Kwang·ju *or* **Gwang·ju** \'gwäŋ-(ˌ)jü\ city SW South Korea; *pop* 1,350,948

Kwa·Zu·lu–Na·tal \kwä-'zü-(ˌ)lü-nə-'täl\ province E Republic of South Africa; *pop* 8,553,000

Kyo·to \kē-'ōt-ō\ city Japan in W *cen* Honshu; *pop* 1,467,785

Kyr·gyz·stan \ˌkir-gi-'stan, -'stän\ country W *cen* Asia; ✳, Bishkek; *pop* 4,526,000

Kyu·shu \'kyü-(₁)shü\ island Japan S of W end of Honshu; *pop* 13,445,561

Lab·ra·dor \'la-brə-₁dȯr\ **1** peninsula E Canada between Hudson Bay & the Atlantic divided between the provinces of Quebec & Newfoundland and Labrador **2** the part of the peninsula belonging to the province of Newfoundland and Labrador — **Lab·ra·dor·ean** *or* **Lab·ra·dor·ian** \₁la-brə-'dȯr-ē-ən\ *adj or n*

Lac·ca·dive \'la-kə-₁dēv, -₁dīv, -div\ islands India in Arabian Sea N of Maldive Islands

La·co·nia \lə-'kō-nē-ə, -nyə\ ancient country S Greece in SE Peloponnese; ✳, Sparta — **La·co·nian** \-nē-ən, -nyən\ *adj or n*

La·fay·ette \₁la-fē-'et, ₁lä-\ city S Louisiana; *pop* 110,257

La·gos \'lä-₁gäs, -₁gōs\ city, former ✳ (1960–91) of Nigeria; *pop* 1,340,000

La·hore \lə-'hȯr\ city E Pakistan; *pop* 5,143,495

Lake District region NW England containing many lakes & mountains

Lake·hurst \'lāk-(₁)hərst\ borough E New Jersey; *pop* 2522

Lake·wood \'lāk-₁wu̇d\ city *cen* Colorado; *pop* 144,126

Lam·beth \'lam-bəth, -₁beth\ borough of S Greater London, England; *pop* 220,100

La·nai \lə-'nī, lä-\ island Hawaii W of Maui

Lan·ca·shire \'laŋ-kə-₁shir, -shər\ *or* **Lan·cas·ter** \'laŋ-kəs-tər\ county NW England — **Lan·cas·tri·an** \laŋ-'kas-trē-ən, lan-\ *adj or n*

Lan·cas·ter \'laŋ-kəs-tər, 'lan-₁kas-tər\ city NW England; *pop* 125,600

Land's End \'landz-'end\ cape SW England; most westerly point of England

Lan·sing \'lan-siŋ\ city, ✳ of Michigan; *pop* 119,128

Lan·zhou *or* **Lan–chou** \'län-'jō\ city W China; *pop* 1,194,640

Laos \'lau̇s, 'lä-(₁)ōs, 'lä-₁äs\ country SE Asia in Indochina NE of Thailand; ✳, Vientiane; *pop* 4,533,000 — **Lao·tian** \lä-'ō-shən, 'lau̇-shən\ *adj or n*

La Paz \lä-'päz, -'päs\ city, administrative ✳ of Bolivia; *pop* 711,036

Lap·land \'lap-₁land, -lənd\ region N Europe above the Arctic Circle in N Norway, N Sweden, N Finland, & Kola Peninsula of Russia — **Lap·land·er** \-₁lan-dər, -lən-\ *n*

La·re·do \lə-'rā-(₁)dō\ city S Texas on the Rio Grande; *pop* 176,576

Larne \'lärn\ district NE Northern Ireland; *pop* 29,181

Las·sen Peak \'la-sⁿn\ volcano 10,457 ft. (3187 m.) N California at S end of Cascade Range

Las Ve·gas \läs-'vā-gəs\ city SE Nevada; *pop* 478,434

Latin America 1 Spanish America and Brazil **2** all of the Americas S of the U.S. — **Latin–American** *adj* — **Latin American** *n*

Latin Quarter section of Paris, France S of the Seine

Lat·via \'lat-vē-ə\ country E Europe on Baltic Sea; ✳, Riga; *pop* 2,345,768

Lau·ren·tian Mountains \lȯ-'ren(t)-shən\ hills E Canada in S Quebec N of the Saint Lawrence on S edge of Canadian Shield

Laurentian Plateau — see CANADIAN SHIELD

La·val \lə-'val\ city S Quebec NW of Montreal; *pop* 343,005

Law·rence \'lȯr-ən(t)s, 'lär-\ city NE corner of Massachusetts; *pop* 72,043

League of Nations political organization established at the end of World War I; replaced by United Nations 1946

Leb·a·non \'le-bə-nən\ **1** mountains Lebanon (country) running parallel to coast **2** country SW Asia on the Mediterranean; ✳, Beirut; *pop* 2,909,000 — **Leb·a·nese** \₁le-bə-'nēz, -'nēs\ *adj or n*

Leeds \'lēdz\ city N England; *pop* 674,400

Lee·ward Islands \'lē-wərd, 'lü-ərd\ **1** islands Hawaii extending WNW from main islands of the group **2** islands South Pacific in W Society Islands **3** islands West Indies in N Lesser Antilles extending from Virgin Islands (on N) to Dominica (on S)

Le Ha·vre \lə-'hävrᵊ, -'häv\ city N France on English Channel; *pop* 190,924

Leh·man Caves \'lē-mən\ limestone caverns E Nevada

Leices·ter \'les-tər\ city *cen* England ENE of Birmingham; *pop* 270,600

Leices·ter·shire \'les-tər-₁shir, -shər\ *or* **Leicester** county *cen* England

Lein·ster \'len(t)-stər\ province E Ireland; *pop* 2,105,579

Leip·zig \'līp-sig, -sik\ city E Germany; *pop* 503,191

Le·na \'lē-nə, 'lā-\ river about 2700 mi. (4345 km.) long E Russia, flowing NE & N from mountains W of Lake Baikal into Arctic Ocean

Leningrad — see SAINT PETERSBURG

Le·ón \lā-'ōn\ city *cen* Mexico; metropolitan area *pop* 1,174,180

Ler·wick \'lər-(₁)wik, 'ler-\ town and port N Scotland in the Shetlands; *pop* 7223

Le·so·tho \lə-'sō-(₁)tō, -'sü-(₁)tü\ *formerly* **Ba·su·to·land** \bə-'sü-tō-₁land\ country S Africa surrounded by Republic of South Africa; ✳, Maseru; *pop* 1,903,000

Lesser Antilles islands in the West Indies including Virgin Islands, Leeward Islands, & Windward Islands, Barbados, Trinidad, Tobago, & islands in the S Caribbean N of Venezuela — see GREATER ANTILLES

Le·vant \lə-'vant\ the countries bordering on the E Mediterranean — **Lev·an·tine** \'lev-ən-₁tīn, -₁tēn, lə-'van-\ *adj or n*

Lew·es \'lü-əs\ town S England

Lew·i·sham \'lü-ə-shəm\ borough of SE Greater London, England; *pop* 215,300

Lew·is with Har·ris \'lü-əs-with-'ha-rəs, -with-\ island NW Scotland in Outer Hebrides

Lex·ing·ton \'lek-siŋ-tən\ **1** city NE *cen* Kentucky; county *pop* 260,512 **2** town NE Massachusetts; *pop* 30,355

Ley·te \'lā-tē\ island Philippines S of Samar

Lha·sa \'lä-sə, 'la-\ city SW China; ✳ of Tibet; *pop* 106,885

Li·be·ria \lī-'bir-ē-ə\ country W Africa on the North Atlantic; ✳, Monrovia; *pop* 2,101,628 — **Li·be·ri·an** \-ē-ən\ *adj or n*

Lib·er·ty \'li-bər-tē\ *formerly* **Bed·loe's** \'bed-₁lōz\ island SE New York; site of the Statue of Liberty

Li·bre·ville \'lē-brə-₁vil, -₁vēl\ city, ✳ of Gabon; *pop* 419,596

Lib·ya \'li-bē-ə\ country N Africa on the Mediterranean W of Egypt; ✳, Tripoli; *pop* 4,573,000 — **Lib·y·an** \'li-bē-ən\ *adj or n*

Libyan desert N Africa W of the Nile in Libya, Egypt, & Sudan

Liech·ten·stein \'lik-tən-₁stīn, 'lik-tən-₁shtīn\ country W Europe between Austria & Switzerland; ✳, Vaduz; *pop* 33,525 — **Liech·ten·stein·er** \-₁stī-nər, -₁shtī-\ *n*

Lif·fey \'li-fē\ river 50 mi. (80 km.) long E Ireland

Li·gu·ria \lə-'gyu̇r-ē-ə\ region NW on Ligurian Sea — **Li·gu·ri·an** \-ē-ən\ *adj or n*

Ligurian Sea arm of the Mediterranean N of Corsica

Li·lon·gwe \li-'lȯŋ-(₁)gwā\ city, ✳ of Malawi; *pop* 498,185

Li·ma \'lē-mə\ city, ✳ of Peru; *pop* 5,825,900

Lim·a·vady \₁li-mə-'va-dē\ district NW Northern Ireland; *pop* 29,201

Lim·po·po \lim-'pō-(₁)pō\ river 1000 mi. (1609 km.) long Africa flowing from Republic of South Africa into Indian Ocean in Mozambique

Lin·coln \'liŋ-kən\ **1** city, ✳ of Nebraska; *pop* 225,581 **2** city E England; *pop* 81,900

Lin·coln·shire \'liŋ-kən-₁shir, -shər\ *or* **Lincoln** county E England

Line \'līn\ islands Kiribati S of Hawaii; *pop* 4782

Lis·bon \'liz-bən\ *or Portuguese* **Lis·boa** \lēzh-'vō-ə\ city, ✳ of Portugal; *pop* 564,657

Lis·burn \'liz-(₁)bərn\ district E Northern Ireland; *pop* 99,162

Lith·u·a·nia \₁li-thə-'wā-nē-ə, ₁li-thyə-, -nyə\ country E Europe; ✳, Vilnius; *pop* 3,483,972

Lit·tle Rock \'li-tⁿl-₁räk\ city, ✳ of Arkansas; *pop* 183,133

Liv·er·pool \'li-vər-₁pül\ city NW England; *pop* 448,300

Li·vo·nia \lə-'vō-nē-ə, -nyə\ city SE Michigan; *pop* 100,545

Lju·blja·na \lē-₁ü-blē-'ä-nə\ city, ✳ of Slovenia; *pop* 323,291

Lla·no Es·ta·ca·do \'la-(₁)nō-₁es-tə-'kä-(₁)dō, 'lä-, 'yä-\ *or* **Staked Plain** \'stäk(t)-\ plateau region SE New Mexico & NW Texas

Lo·bam·ba \lō-'bäm-bə\ town, legislative ✳ of Swaziland; *pop* (est.) 10,000

Lodz \'lüj, 'lädz\ city *cen* Poland; *pop* 851,690

Lo·fo·ten \'lō-,fō-t³n\ islands NW Norway

Lo·gan, Mount \'lō-gən\ mountain 19,524 ft. (5951 m.) NW Canada in Saint Elias Range; highest in Canada & second highest in North America

Loire \lə-'wär, 'lwär\ river 634 mi. (1020 km.) long *cen* France flowing NW & W into Bay of Biscay

Lo·mé \lō-'mā\ city, ✻ of Togo; *pop* 229,400

Lo·mond, Loch \'lō-mənd\ lake S *cen* Scotland

Lon·don \'lən-dən\ **1** city SE Ontario, Canada; *pop* 336,539 **2** city, ✻ of England & of United Kingdom on the Thames; consists of **City of London** & Greater London metropolitan county; *pop* 6,377,900 — **Lon·don·er** \-də-nər\ *n*

Londonderry — see DERRY

Long Beach city SW California S of Los Angeles; *pop* 461,522

Long Island island 118 mi. (190 km.) long SE New York S of Connecticut

Long Island Sound inlet of the Atlantic between Connecticut & Long Island, New York

Lon·gueuil \lòn-'gāl\ city Canada in S Quebec E of Montreal; *pop* 128,016

Lor·raine \lə-'rān, lò-\ region NE France

Los An·ge·les \lòs-'an-jə-ləs\ city SW California; *pop* 3,694,820

Lou·ise, Lake \lú-'ēz\ lake SW Alberta, Canada

Lou·i·si·ana \lú-,ē-zē-'a-nə, ,lü-ə-zē-, ,lü-zē-\ state S U.S.; ✻, Baton Rouge; *pop* 4,468,976 — **Lou·i·si·an·ian** \-'a-nē-ən, -'a-nyən\ *or* **Lou·i·si·an·an** \-'a-nən\ *adj or n*

Louisiana Purchase area W *cen* U.S. between Rocky Mountains & the Mississippi purchased 1803 from France

Lou·is·ville \'lü-i,vil, -vəl\ city N Kentucky on the Ohio River; *pop* 256,231

Low Countries region W Europe consisting of modern Belgium, Luxembourg, & the Netherlands

Lowell \'lō-əl\ city NE Massachusetts; *pop* 105,167

Lower 48 the continental states of the U.S. excluding Alaska

Low·lands \'lō-ləndz, -,landz\ the *cen* & E part of Scotland

Lu·an·da \lú-'än-də\ city, ✻ of Angola; *pop* 1,544,400

Lub·bock \'lə-bək\ city NW Texas; *pop* 199,564

Lu·bum·ba·shi \,lü-büm-'bä-shē\ city SE Democratic Republic of the Congo; *pop* (est.) 1,138,000

Luck·now \'lək-,naú\ city N India ESE of Delhi; *pop* 2,207,340

Lüda *or* **Lü–ta** — see DALIAN

Lu·ray Caverns \'lü-,rā, lü-'\ series of caves N Virginia

Lu·sa·ka \lü-'sä-kä\ city, ✻ of Zambia; *pop* 982,362

Lü·shun \'lü-'shùn, 'lue-\ *or* **Port Ar·thur** \-'är-thər\ seaport NE China; part of greater Dalian

Lu·ton \'lü-t³n\ town SE *cen* England; *pop* 167,300

Lux·em·bourg *or* **Lux·em·burg** \'lək-səm-,bərg, 'lúk-səm-,búrk\ **1** country W Europe bordered by Belgium, France, & Germany; *pop* 392,000 **2** city, its ✻; *pop* 75,377 — **Lux·em·bourg·er** \-,bər-gər, -,bùr-\ *n* — **Lux·em·bourg·ian** \,lək-səm-'bər-gē-ən, ,lúk-səm-'búr-\ *adj*

Lu·zon \lü-'zän\ island N Philippines; *pop* 23,900,796

L'viv \lə-'vē-ù, -'vēf\ *or* **L'vov** \lə-'vóf, -'vóv\ *or Polish* **Lwów** \lə-'vúf, -'vúv\ city W Ukraine; *pop* 802,000

Lyallpur — see FAISALABAD

Lyd·ia \'li-dē-ə\ ancient country W Asia Minor on the Aegean — **Lyd·i·an** \-ē-ən\ *adj or n*

Lyon \'lyōⁿ\ *or* **Lyons** \lē-'ōⁿ, 'lī-ənz\ city SE *cen* France; *pop* 445,274

Ma·cao *or Portuguese* **Ma·cau** \mə-'kaú\ *or Chinese* **Ao·men** \'aú-'mən\ **1** special administrative region on coast of SE China W of Hong Kong; *pop* 488,000 **2** city, its ✻; *pop* 161,252 — **Ma·ca·nese** \,mä-kə-'nēz, -'nēs\ *n*

Mac·e·do·nia \,ma·sə-'dō-nē-ə, -nyə\ **1** region S Europe in Balkan Peninsula in NE Greece, the former Yugoslav section & now independent country of Macedonia, & SW Bulgaria including territory of ancient kingdom of Macedonia (**Mac·e·don** \'mas-ə-dən, -ə-,dän\) **2** country S *cen* Balkan Peninsula; ✻, Skopje; a former republic of Yugoslavia; *pop* 2,038,059 — **Mac·e·do·nian** \,mas-ə-'dō-nyən, -nē-ən\ *adj or n*

Mac·gil·li·cud·dy's Reeks \mə-'gi-lə-,kə-dēz-'rēks\ mountains SW Ireland; highest Carrantuohill 3414 ft. (1041 m.)

Ma·chu Pic·chu \,mä-(,)chü-'pē-(,)chü, -'pēk-\ site SE Peru of ancient Inca city

Mac·ken·zie \mə-'ken-zē\ river 1120 mi. (1802 km.) long NW Canada flowing from Great Slave Lake NW into Beaufort Sea

Mack·i·nac, Straits of \'ma-kə-,nò, -,nak\ channel N Michigan connecting Lake Huron & Lake Michigan

Ma·con \'mā-kən\ city *cen* Georgia; *pop* 97,255

Mad·a·gas·car \,ma-də-'gas-kər, -kär\ *formerly* **Mal·a·gasy Re·public** \,ma-lə-'ga-sē\ island country W Indian Ocean off SE Africa; ✻, Antananarivo; *pop* 16,694,272 — **Mad·a·gas·can** \,ma-də-'gas-kən\ *adj or n*

Ma·dei·ra \mə-'dir-ə, -'der-ə\ **1** river 2013 mi. (3239 km.) long W Brazil flowing NE into the Amazon **2** islands Portugal in the North Atlantic N of the Canary Islands; *pop* 245,011 **3** island; chief of the Madeira group — **Ma·dei·ran** \-'dir-ən, -'der-\ *adj or n*

Ma·di·nat ash Sha'b \mə-'dē-,nə-tash-'shab\ city S Yemen

Mad·i·son \'ma-də-sən\ city, ✻ of Wisconsin; *pop* 208,054

Ma·dras \mə-'dras, -'dräs\ *or* **Chen·nai** \'che-,nī\ city SE India; *pop* 4,216,268

Ma·drid \mə-'drid\ city, ✻ of Spain; *pop* 2,938,723

Ma·du·rai \,mä-də-'rī\ city S India; *pop* 922,913

Mag·da·len Islands \'mag-də-lən\ *or F* **Îles de la Ma·de·leine** \,ēl-də-lä-mäd-'len, -mä-də-'len\ islands Canada in Gulf of Saint Lawrence between Newfoundland & Prince Edward Island

Ma·gel·lan, Strait of \mə-'je-lən, *chiefly Brit* -'ge-\ strait at S end of South America between mainland & Tierra del Fuego

Magh·er·a·felt \'mär-ə-,felt, 'ma-kə-rə-,felt\ district *cen* Northern Ireland; *pop* 35,874

Maid·stone \'mād-stən, -,stōn\ town SE England; *pop* 133,200

Main \'mīn, 'mān\ river 325 mi. (523 km.) long S *cen* Germany flowing W into the Rhine

Maine \'mān\ state NE U.S.; ✻, Augusta; *pop* 1,274,923 — **Main·er** \'mā-nər\ *n*

Ma·jor·ca \mä-'jór-kə, mə-, -'yòr-\ *or Spanish* **Ma·llor·ca** \mä-'yòr-kä\ island Spain in W Mediterranean — **Ma·jor·can** \-'jór-kən, -'yòr\ *adj or n*

Ma·ju·ro \mə-'jùr-(,)ō\ atoll, Marshall Islands; contains ✻ of the group; *pop* (est.) 20,000

Mal·a·bar Coast \'ma-lə-,bär\ region SW India on Arabian Sea

Ma·la·bo \mä-'lä-(,)bō\ city, ✻ of Equatorial Guinea; *pop* 37,237

Ma·lac·ca, Strait of \mə-'la-kə, -'lä-\ channel between S Malay Peninsula & island of Sumatra

Ma·la·wi \mə-'lä-wē\ *formerly* **Ny·asa·land** \nī-'a-sə-,land, nē-\ country SE Africa on Lake Nyasa; ✻, Lilongwe; *pop* 10,475,257 — **Ma·la·wi·an** \-ən\ *adj or n*

Malawi, Lake *or* **Lake Ny·asa** \nī-'a-sə, nē-\ lake SE Africa in Malawi, Mozambique, & Tanzania

Ma·lay \mə-'lā, 'mā-(,)lā\ **1** archipelago SE Asia including Sumatra, Java, Borneo, Sulawesi, Moluccas, & Timor; usu. thought to include the Philippines & sometimes New Guinea **2** peninsula SE Asia divided between Thailand & Malaysia (continental)

Ma·laya \mə-'lā-ə, mä-\ **1** the Malay Peninsula **2** former country SE Asia on Malay Peninsula; now part of Malaysia

Ma·lay·sia \mə-'lā-zh(ē-)ə, -sh(ē-)ə\ **1** the Malay Archipelago **2** the Malay Peninsula & Malay Archipelago **3** country SE Asia; ✻, Kuala Lumpur; *pop* 19,077,000 — **Ma·lay·sian** \mə-'lā-zhən, -shən\ *adj or n*

Mal·dives \'mól-,dēvz, -,dīvz\ islands in Indian Ocean SW of Sri Lanka; country; ✻, Male Atoll; *pop* 270,101 — **Mal·div·i·an** \mòl-'di-vē-ən, mal-\ *adj or n*

Ma·le \'mä-lē\ atoll, ✻ of Maldives; *pop* (est.) 63,000

Ma·li \'mä-lē, 'ma-\ country W Africa; ✻, Bamako; *pop* 8,646,000 — **Ma·li·an** \-lē-ən\ *adj or n*

Mal·ta \'mól-tə\ islands in the Mediterranean S of Sicily; country since 1964; ✻, Valletta; *pop* 397,296 — **Mal·tese** \mòl-'tēz, -'tēs\ *adj or n*

Malvinas, Islas — see FALKLAND ISLANDS

Mam·moth Cave \'ma-məth\ limestone caverns SW *cen* Kentucky

Man, Isle of \'man\ island British Isles in Irish Sea; has own legislature & laws; *pop* 60,496

Ma·na·gua \mä-'nä-gwä\ city, ✳ of Nicaragua; *pop* 552,900

Ma·na·ma \mo-'na-mo\ city, ✳ of Bahrain; *pop* 136,999

Man·ches·ter \'man-,ches-tər, -chəs-tər\ **1** city S *cen* New Hampshire; *pop* 107,006 **2** city NW England; *pop* 406,900

Man·chu·ria \man-'chùr-ē-ə\ region NE China S of the Amur — **Man·chu·ri·an** \-ē-ən\ *adj or n*

Man·hat·tan \man-'ha-t⁹n, mən-\ **1** island SE New York in New York City **2** borough of New York City consisting chiefly of Manhattan Island; *pop* 1,537,195

Ma·nila \mo-'ni-lə\ city, ✳ of Philippines in W Luzon; *pop* 1,587,000

Man·i·to·ba \,ma-nə-'tō-bə\ province *cen* Canada; ✳, Winnipeg; *pop* 1,150,034 — **Man·i·to·ban** \-bən\ *adj or n*

Man·i·tou·lin \,ma-nə-'tü-lən\ island 80 mi. (129 km.) long S Ontario in Lake Huron

Ma·pu·to \mä-'pü-(,)tō, -(,)tü\ city, ✳ of Mozambique; *pop* 966,800

Mar·a·cai·bo \,ma-rə-'kī-(,)bō, ,mär-ä-\ city NW Venezuela; *pop* 1,207,513

Maracaibo, Lake extension of a gulf of the Caribbean NW Venezuela

Mar·a·thon \'ma-rə-,thän\ plain E Greece NE of Athens

Mar·i·ana \,mer-ē-'a-nə\ islands W Pacific N of Caroline Islands; comprise Commonwealth of Northern Mariana Islands & Guam

Mariana Trench ocean trench W Pacific extending from SE of Guam to NW of Mariana Islands; deepest in world

Ma·rin·du·que \,ma-rən-'dü-(,)kä, ,mär-ēn-\ island *cen* Philippines; *pop* 173,715

Maritime Provinces the Canadian provinces of New Brunswick, Nova Scotia, & Prince Edward Island & sometimes thought to include Newfoundland and Labrador

Ma·ri·u·pol \,ma-rē-'ü-,pòl, -pəl\ *or 1949–89* **Zhda·nov** \zhə-'dä-nəf\ city E Ukraine; *pop* 417,000

Mar·ma·ra, Sea of \'mär-mə-rə\ sea NW Turkey connected with Black Sea by the Bosporus & with Aegean Sea by the Dardanelles

Marne \'märn\ river 325 mi. (523 km.) long NE France flowing W into the Seine

Mar·que·sas \mär-'kā-zəz, -zəs, -səz, -səs\ islands South Pacific; belonging to France; *pop* 7358 — **Mar·que·san** \-zən, -sən\ *adj or n*

Mar·ra·kech \,ma-rə-'kesh, 'ma-rə-, mə-'rä-kish\ city *cen* Morocco; *pop* 439,728

Mar·seille \mär-'sā\ *or* **Mar·seilles** \mär-'sā, -'sālz\ city SE France; *pop* 797,491

Mar·shall Islands \'mär-shəl\ islands W Pacific E of the Carolines; republic, in association with U.S.; ✳, Majuro; *pop* 70,822

Mar·tha's Vineyard \'mär-thəz\ island SE Massachusetts off SW coast of Cape Cod WNW of Nantucket

Mar·ti·nique \,mär-tə-'nēk\ island West Indies in the Windward Islands; an overseas division of France; ✳, Fort-de-France; *pop* 377,000

Mary·land \'mer-ə-lənd\ state E U.S.; ✳, Annapolis; *pop* 5,296,486 — **Mary·land·er** \-lən-dər, -,lan-\ *n*

Mas·ba·te \mäz-'bä-tē, mäs-\ island *cen* Philippines

Mas·e·ru \'ma-sə-,rü, -zə-\ city, ✳ of Lesotho; *pop* 71,500

Mash·had \mə-'shad\ city NE Iran; *pop* 1,463,508

Ma·son–Dix·on Line \'mä-s⁹n-'dik-sən\ boundary between Maryland & Pennsylvania; often considered the boundary between N & S states

Mas·qat \'mɔs-,kät\ *or* **Mus·cat** \-,kät, -,kat, -kət\ town E Arabia, ✳ of Oman; *pop* 100,000

Mas·sa·chu·setts \,ma-sə-'chü-səts, -zəts\ state NE U.S.; ✳, Boston; *pop* 6,349,097

Mat·a·be·le·land \,ma-tə-'bē-lē-,land, ,mä-tä-'bä-lā-\ region SW Zimbabwe

Mat·lock \'mat-,läk\ town N England; *pop* 20,610

Mat·ter·horn \'ma-tər-,hòrn, 'mä-\ mountain 14,691 ft. (4478 m.) on border between Switzerland & Italy

Maui \'maù-ē\ island Hawaii NW of Hawaii Island

Mau·na Kea \,maù-nä-'kä-ä, ,mò-\ extinct volcano 13,796 ft. (4205 m.) Hawaii in N *cen* Hawaii Island

Mau·na Loa \-'lō-ə\ volcano 13,680 ft. (4170 m.) Hawaii in S *cen* Hawaii Island

Mau·re·ta·nia *or* **Mau·ri·ta·nia** \,mòr-ə-'tā-nē-ə, ,mär-, -nyə\ ancient country NW Africa in modern Morocco & W Algeria — **Mau·re·ta·ni·an** *or* **Mau·ri·ta·ni·an** \-nē-ən, -nyən\ *adj or n*

Mauritania country NW Africa on the Atlantic N of Senegal River; ✳, Nouakchott; *pop* 2,171,000 — **Mauritanian** *adj or n*

Mau·ri·tius \mò-'ri-sh(ē-)əs\ island in Indian Ocean E of Madagascar; country; ✳, Port Louis; *pop* 1,210,196 — **Mau·ri·tian** \-'ri-shən\ *adj or n*

May, Cape \'mā\ cape S New Jersey at entrance to Delaware Bay

Ma·yon, Mount \mä-'yōn\ volcano 8077 ft. (2462 m.) Philippines in SE Luzon

Ma·yotte \mä-'yät, -'yòt\ island Comoros group; French dependency; *pop* 90,000 — see COMOROS

Ma·za·ma, Mount \mo-'zäm-ə\ prehistoric mountain SW Oregon the collapse of whose top formed Crater Lake

Mba·bane \,əm-bä-'bä-nä\ city, ✳ of Swaziland; *pop* 57,992

Mbi·ni \em-'bē-nē\ *formerly* **Río Mu·ni** \,rē-ō-'mü-nē\ mainland portion of Equatorial Guinea

Mc·Al·len \mə-'ka-lən\ city S Texas; *pop* 106,414

Mc·Kin·ley, Mount \mə-'kin-lē\ *or* **De·na·li** \də-'nä-lē\ mountain 20,320 ft. (6194 m.) S *cen* Alaska in Alaska Range; highest in U.S. & North America

Mead, Lake \'mēd\ reservoir NW Arizona & SE Nevada formed by Hoover Dam in Colorado River

Mec·ca \'me-kə\ city W Saudi Arabia containing the Great Mosque of Islam; *pop* 366,801

Me·dan \mā-'dän\ city Indonesia, in N Sumatra; *pop* 1,730,752

Me·de·llín \,me-də-'lēn, ,mä-thā-'yēn\ city NW Colombia; *pop* 1,581,400

Me·di·na \mə-'dī-nə\ city W Saudi Arabia; *pop* 608,295

Med·i·ter·ra·nean \,me-də-tə-'rā-nē-ən, -nyən\ sea 2300 mi. (3700 km.) long between Europe & Africa connecting with the Atlantic through Strait of Gibraltar

Me·kong \'mā-'kòŋ, -'käŋ; 'mā-,\ river 2600 mi. (4184 km.) long SE Asia flowing from E Tibet S & SE into South China Sea in S Vietnam

Mel·a·ne·sia \,me-lə-'nē-zhə, -shə\ islands of the Pacific NE of Australia & S of Micronesia including Bismarck, the Solomons, Vanuatu, New Caledonia, & the Fijis

Mel·bourne \'mel-bərn\ city SE Australia, ✳ of Victoria; metropolitan area *pop* 2,761,995

Melos *see* MÍLOS

Mel·ville \'mel-,vil\ **1** island N Canada, split between Northwest Territories & Nunavut **2** peninsula Canada in Nunavut

Mem·phis \'mem(p)-fəs\ **1** city SW Tennessee; *pop* 650,100 **2** ancient city N Egypt S of modern Cairo

Mem·phre·ma·gog, Lake \,mem(p)-fri-'mā-,gäg\ lake on border between Canada (Quebec) & United States (Vermont)

Men·do·ci·no, Cape \,men-də-'sē-(,)nō\ cape NW California

Mer·cia \'mər-sh(ē-)ə\ ancient Anglo-Saxon kingdom *cen* England — **Mer·cian** \'mər-shən\ *adj or n*

Mer·sey \'mər-zē\ river 70 mi. (113 km.) long NW England flowing NW & W into Irish Sea

Mer·sey·side \'mər-zē-,sīd\ metropolitan county NW England; includes Liverpool

Mer·ton \'mər-t⁹n\ borough of SW Greater London, England; *pop* 161,800

Me·sa \'mā-sə\ city S *cen* Arizona; *pop* 396,375

Me·sa·bi Range \mə-'sä-bē\ region NE Minnesota that contains iron ore

Mes·o·po·ta·mia \,me-s(ə-)pə-'tā-mē-ə, -myə\ **1** region SW Asia between Euphrates & Tigris rivers **2** the entire Tigris–Euphrates valley — **Mes·o·po·ta·mian** \-mē-ən, -myən\ *adj or n*

Mes·quite \mə-'skēt, me-\ city NE Texas E of Dallas; *pop* 124,523

Meuse \'myüz, 'mə(r)z, 'mœz\ river 580 mi. (933 km.)

long W Europe flowing from NE France into North Sea in the Netherlands

Mex·i·co \\'mek-si-ˌkō\\ **1** country S North America; *pop* 89,995,000 **2** *or* **Mexico City** city, its ✻; metropolitan area *pop* 16,674,160 — **Mex·i·can** \\'mek-si-kən\\ *adj or n*

Mexico, Gulf of inlet of the Atlantic SE North America

Mi·ami \\mī-'a-mē\\ city & port SE Florida; *pop* 362,470

Miami Beach city SE Florida; *pop* 87,933

Mich·i·gan \\'mi-shi-gən\\ state N *cen* U.S.; ✻, Lansing; *pop* 9,938,444 — **Mich·i·gan·der** \\ˌmi-shi-'gan-dər\\ *n* — **Mich·i·ga·ni·an** \\ˌmi-shə-'gä-nē-ən, -'ga-\\ *n* — **Mich·i·gan·ite** \\'mi-shi-gə-ˌnīt\\ *n*

Michigan, Lake lake N *cen* U.S.; one of the Great Lakes

Mi·cro·ne·sia \\ˌmī-krə-'nē-zhə, -shə\\ islands of the W Pacific E of the Philippines & N of Melanesia including Caroline, Kiribati, Mariana, & Marshall groups — **Mi·cro·ne·sian** \\-zhən, -shən\\ *adj or n*

Micronesia, Federated States of islands W Pacific in the Carolines; country in association with U.S.; ✻, Palikir; *pop* 134,597

Middle East the countries of SW Asia & N Africa— usually thought to include the countries extending from Libya on the W to Afghanistan on the E — **Middle Eastern** *adj*

Mid·dles·brough \\'mi-dᵊlz-brə\\ town N England; *pop* 141,100

Middle West — see MIDWEST

Mid Gla·mor·gan \\'mid-glə-'mȯr-gən\\ former county SE Wales

Mid·i·an \\'mi-dē-ən\\ ancient region NW Arabia E of Gulf of Aqaba — **Mid·i·an·ite** \\-ē-ə-ˌnīt\\ *n*

Mid·lands \\'mid-ləndz\\ the *cen* counties of England

Mid·way \\'mid-ˌwā\\ islands *cen* Pacific 1300 mi. (2092 km.) WNW of Honolulu belonging to U.S.

Mid·west \\ˌmid-'west\\ *or* **Middle West** region N *cen* U.S. including area around Great Lakes & in upper Mississippi valley from Ohio on the E to North Dakota, South Dakota, Nebraska, & Kansas on the W — **Mid·west·ern** \\ˌmid-'wes-tərn\\ *or* **Middle Western** *adj* — **Mid·west·ern·er** \\ˌmid-'wes-tə(r)-nər\\ *or* **Middle Westerner** *n*

Mi·lan \\mə-'lan, -'län\\ *or Italian* **Mi·la·no** \\mē-'lä-(ˌ)nō\\ city NW Italy; *pop* 1,449,403 — **Mil·a·nese** \\ˌmi-lə-'nēz, -'nēs\\ *adj or n*

Mí·los *or* **Me·los** \\'mē-ˌlòs\\ island Greece

Mil·wau·kee \\mil-'wȯ-kē\\ city SE Wisconsin on Lake Michigan; *pop* 596,974

Mi·nas Basin \\'mī-nəs\\ bay *cen* Nova Scotia; NE extension of Bay of Fundy

Min·da·nao \\ˌmin-də-'nä-ˌō, -'naù\\ island S Philippines; *pop* 13,966,000

Min·do·ro \\min-'dȯr-(ˌ)ō\\ island *cen* Philippines; *pop* 473,940

Min·ne·ap·o·lis \\ˌmi-nē-'a-pə-lis\\ city SE Minnesota; *pop* 382,618

Min·ne·so·ta \\ˌmi-nə-'sō-tə\\ state N *cen* U.S.; ✻, Saint Paul; *pop* 4,919,479 — **Min·ne·so·tan** \\-'sō-tᵊn\\ *adj or n*

Mi·nor·ca \\mə-'nȯr-kə\\ island Spain in W Mediterranean — **Mi·nor·can** \\mə-'nȯr-kən\\ *adj or n*

Minsk \\'min(t)sk\\ city, ✻ of Belarus; *pop* 1,589,000

Mis·sis·sau·ga \\ˌmi-sə-'sȯ-gə\\ city Canada in S Ontario; *pop* 612,925

Mis·sis·sip·pi \\ˌmi-sə-'si-pē\\ **1** river 2340 mi. (3765 km.) long *cen* U.S. flowing into Gulf of Mexico — see ITASCA, LAKE **2** state S U.S.; ✻, Jackson; *pop* 2,844,658

Mis·sou·ri \\mə-'zùr-ē\\ **1** river 2466 mi. (3968 km.) long W U.S. flowing from SW Montana to the Mississippi in E Missouri (state) **2** state *cen* U.S.; ✻, Jefferson City; *pop* 5,595,211 — **Mis·sou·ri·an** \\-'zùr-ē-ən\\ *adj or n*

Mitch·ell, Mount \\'mi-chəl\\ mountain 6684 ft. (2037 m.) W North Carolina in the Appalachians; highest in U.S. E of the Mississippi

Mo·bile \\mō-'bēl, 'mō-ˌbēl\\ city SW Alabama on **Mobile Bay** (inlet of Gulf of Mexico); *pop* 198,915

Mo·des·to \\mə-'des-(ˌ)tō\\ city C California; *pop* 188,856

Mog·a·di·shu \\ˌmä-gə-'di-(ˌ)shü, ˌmō-, -'dē-\\ *or* **Mog·a·di·scio** \\-(ˌ)shō\\ city, ✻ of Somalia; *pop* 349,245

Mo·hawk \\'mō-ˌhȯk\\ river E *cen* New York flowing into the Hudson

Mo·hen·jo Da·ro \\mō-'hen-(ˌ)jō-'där-(ˌ)ō\\ prehistoric city in valley of the Indus NE of modern Karachi, Pakistan

Mo·ja·ve *or* **Mo·ha·ve** \\mə-'hä-vē, mō-\\ desert S California SE of S end of Sierra Nevada

Mol·da·via \\mäl-'dā-vē-ə, -vyə\\ region E Europe in NE Romania & Moldova — **Mol·da·vian** \\-vē-ən, -vyən\\ *adj or n*

Mol·do·va \\mäl-'dō-və, mȯl-\\ country E Europe in E Moldavia region; ✻, Chisinau; *pop* 4,362,000 — **Mol·do·van** \\-vən\\ *adj or n*

Mol·o·kai \\ˌmä-lə-'kī, ˌmō-lō-'kä-ē\\ island Hawaii ESE of Oahu

Mo·luc·cas \\mə-'lə-kəz\\ islands Indonesia E of Sulawesi; *pop* 1,857,790 — **Mo·luc·ca** \\mə-'lə-kə\\ *adj* — **Mo·luc·can** \\-kən\\ *adj or n*

Mom·ba·sa city & port S Kenya; *pop* 665,018

Mo·na·co \\'mä-nə-ˌkō\\ country W Europe on Mediterranean coast of France; ✻, Monaco; *pop* 30,500 — **Mo·na·can** \\'mä-nə-kən, mə-'nä-kən\\ *adj or n* — **Mon·e·gasque** \\ˌmä-ni-'gask\\ *n*

Mon·go·lia \\män-'gōl-yə, mäŋ-, -'gō-lē-ə\\ **1** region E Asia E of Altay Mountains; includes Gobi Desert **2** country E Asia consisting of major portion of Mongolia region; ✻, Ulaanbaatar; *pop* 2,182,000

Mo·non·ga·he·la \\mə-ˌnän-gə-'hē-lə, -ˌnäŋ-gə-, -'hä-lə\\ river N West Virginia & SW Pennsylvania

Mon·ro·via \\(ˌ)mən-'rō-vē-ə\\ city, ✻ of Liberia; *pop* 243,243

Mon·tana \\män-'ta-nə\\ state NW U.S.; ✻, Helena; *pop* 902,195 — **Mon·tan·an** \\-nən\\ *adj or n*

Mont Blanc \\ˌmōⁿ-'bläⁿ\\ mountain 15,771 ft. (4807 m.) SE France on Italian border; highest in the Alps

Mon·te·go Bay \\män-'tē-(ˌ)gō\\ city & port NW Jamaica on Montego Bay (inlet of the Caribbean); *pop* 83,446

Mon·te·ne·gro \\ˌmän-tə-'nē-(ˌ)grō, -'nä-, -'ne-\\ country S Europe on the Adriatic Sea; ✻ Podgorica; a former republic of Yugoslavia; *pop* 616,327

Mon·ter·rey \\ˌmän-tə-'rā\\ city NE Mexico; metropolitan area *pop* 3,022,268

Mon·te·vi·deo \\ˌmän-tə-və-'dā-(ˌ)ō, -'vi-dē-ˌō; ˌmȯn-tä-vē-'thä-ō\\ city, ✻ of Uruguay; *pop* 1,260,753

Mont·gom·ery \\(ˌ)mən(t)-'gə-mə-rē, män(t)-, -'gä-; -'gəm-rē, -'gäm-\\ city, ✻ of Alabama; *pop* 201,568

Mont·pe·lier \\mänt-'pēl-yər, -'pil-\\ city, ✻ of Vermont; *pop* 8035

Mon·tre·al \\ˌmän-trē-'ȯl, ˌmən-\\ city S Quebec, Canada on **Montreal Island** in the Saint Lawrence; *pop* 1,039,534

Mont·ser·rat \\ˌmän(t)-sə-'rat\\ island British West Indies in the Leeward Islands; *pop* 12,100

Mo·ra·via \\mə-'rā-vē-ə\\ region E Czech Republic — **Mo·ra·vi·an** \\mə-'rā-vē-ən\\ *adj or n*

Mo·rea \\mə-'rē-ə\\ PELOPONNESE — an old name

Mo·re·no Valley \\mə-'rē-(ˌ)nō\\ city S California; *pop* 142,381

Mo·roc·co \\mə-'rä-(ˌ)kō\\ country NW Africa; ✻, Rabat; *pop* 29,631,000 — **Mo·roc·can** \\-kən\\ *adj or n*

Mo·ro·ni \\mȯ-'rō-nē\\ city, ✻ of Comoros; *pop* 23,432

Mos·cow \\'mäs-(ˌ)kō, -ˌkaù\\ *or Russian* **Mos·kva** \\mäsk-'vä\\ city, ✻ of Russia; *pop* 8,769,000

Mo·selle \\mō-'zel\\ river about 340 mi. (545 km.) long E France & W Germany

Moyle \\'mȯi(-ə)l\\ district N Northern Ireland; *pop* 14,617

Mo·zam·bique \\ˌmō-zəm-'bēk\\ **1** channel SE Africa between Mozambique (country) & Madagascar **2** country SE Africa; ✻, Maputo; *pop* 16,099,246 — **Mo·zam·bi·can** \\ˌmō-zəm-'bē-kən\\ *adj or n*

Mpu·ma·lan·ga \\əm-ˌpü-mä-'läŋ-gä\\ province NE Republic of South Africa; *pop* 2,911,000

Mukden — see SHENYANG

Mul·tan \\mùl-'tän\\ city NE Pakistan SW of Lahore; *pop* 1,197,384

Mumbai — see BOMBAY

Mu·nich \\'myü-nik\\ *or German* **Mün·chen** \\'mùen-kən\\ city S Germany in Bavaria; *pop* 1,229,052

Mun·ster \\'mən(t)-stər\\ province S Ireland; *pop* 1,100,614

Mur·cia \\'mər-sh(ē-)ə\\ region & ancient kingdom SE Spain — **Mur·cian** \\-shən\\ *adj or n*

Mur·ray \\'mər-ē, 'mə-rē\\ river 1609 mi. (2589 km.) long SE Australia flowing W from E Victoria into Indian Ocean in South Australia

Mur·rum·bidg·ee \ˌmər-əm-ˈbi-jē, ˌmə-rəm-\ river almost 1000 mi. (1609 km.) long SE Australia in New South Wales flowing W into the Murray

Muscat — see MASQAT

Myan·mar \ˈmyän-ˌmär\ or **Bur·ma** \ˈbər-mə\ country SE Asia; ✳, Naypyidaw; pop 45,573,000

My·ce·nae \mī-ˈsē-(ˌ)nē\ ancient city S Greece in NE Peloponnese

Myr·tle Beach \ˈmər-tᵊl\ city E South Carolina on the Atlantic; pop 22,759

My·sore \mī-ˈsȯr\ city S India; pop 742,261

Nab·a·taea or **Nab·a·tea** \ˌna-bə-ˈtē-ə\ ancient Arab kingdom SE of Palestine — **Nab·a·tae·an** or **Nab·a·te·an** \-ˈtē-ən\ adj or n

Na·goya \nə-ˈgȯi-ə, ˈnä-gȯ-(ˌ)yä\ city Japan in S cen Honshu; pop 2,171,557

Nag·pur \ˈnäg-ˌpu̇r\ city E cen India; pop 2,051,320

Nai·ro·bi \nī-ˈrō-bē\ city, ✳ of Kenya; pop 2,083,509

Na·mib·ia \nə-ˈmi-bē-ə\ formerly **South—West Africa** country SW Africa on the Atlantic; ✳, Windhoek; pop 1,511,600 — **Na·mib·ian** \-bē-ən, -byən\ adj or n

Nan·chang \ˈnän-ˈchäŋ\ city SE China; pop 1,086,124

Nan·jing \ˈnän-ˈjiŋ\ or **Nan·king** \ˈnan-ˈkiŋ, ˈnän-\ city E China; pop 2,090,204

Nan·tuck·et \nan-ˈtə-kət\ island SE Massachusetts S of Cape Cod; pop 6012

Na·per·ville \ˈnā-pər-ˌvil\ city NE Illinois; pop 128,358

Na·ples \ˈnā-pəlz\ or Italian **Na·po·li** \ˈnä-pō-lē\ ancient **Ne·ap·o·lis** \nē-ˈa-pə-ləs\ city S Italy on Bay of Naples; pop 1,000,470 — **Ne·a·pol·i·tan** \ˌnē-ə-ˈpäl-ə-tən\ adj or n

Nar·ra·gan·sett Bay \ˌna-rə-ˈgan(t)-sət\ inlet of the Atlantic SE Rhode Island

Nash·ville \ˈnash-ˌvil, -vəl\ city, ✳ of Tennessee; pop 569,891

Nas·sau \ˈna-ˌsȯ\ city, ✳ of Bahamas on New Providence Island; pop 172,196

Na·tal \nə-ˈtal, -ˈtäl\ former province E Republic of South Africa

Na·u·ru \nä-ˈü-(ˌ)rü\ island W Pacific S of the Equator; country; ✳, Yaren; pop 10,000 — **Na·u·ru·an** \-ˈü-rə-wən\ adj or n

Nay·pyi·daw \ˈnē-pyē-ˌdȯ\ site S cen Myanmar to which national ✳ was moved 2006

Naz·a·reth \ˈna-zə-rəth\ town of ancient Palestine in cen Galilee; now a city of N Israel; pop 49,800

N'Dja·me·na \ən-jä-ˈmä-nä, -ˈmē-\ city, ✳ of Chad; pop 687,800

Neagh, Lough \ˌläk-ˈnä\ lake Northern Ireland; largest in British Isles

Near East the countries of NE Africa & SW Asia — **Near Eastern** adj

Ne·bras·ka \nə-ˈbras-kə\ state cen U.S.; ✳, Lincoln; pop 1,711,263 — **Ne·bras·kan** \-kən\ adj or n

Neg·ev \ˈne-ˌgev\ desert region S Israel

Ne·gro \ˈnā-(ˌ)grō, ˈne-\ river 1400 mi. (2253 km.) long in E Colombia & N Brazil flowing into the Amazon

Ne·gros \ˈnā-(ˌ)grōs, ˈne-\ island cen Philippines

Ne·pal \nə-ˈpȯl, nä-\ country Asia on NE border of India in the Himalayas; ✳, Kathmandu; pop 23,151,423 — **Nep·a·lese** \ˌne-pə-ˈlēz, -ˈlēs\ adj or n — **Ne·pali** \nə-ˈpȯl-ē, -ˈpäl-, -ˈpal-\ adj or n

Ness, Loch \ˈnes\ lake NW Scotland

Neth·er·lands \ˈne-thər-ləndz\ 1 or Dutch **Ne·der·land** \ˈnäd-ər-ˌlänt\ also **Holland** country NW Europe on North Sea; ✳, Amsterdam; seat of the government, The Hague; pop 15,009,000 2 LOW COUNTRIES — an historical usage — **Neth·er·land** \ˈne-thər-lənd\ adj — **Neth·er·land·er** \-ˌlan-dər, -lən-\ n — **Neth·er·land·ish** \-ˌlan-dish, -lən-\ adj

Netherlands Antilles islands of the West Indies belonging to the Netherlands; ✳, Willemstad; pop 190,566

Ne·va \ˈnē-və, ˈnä-, nye-ˈvä\ river 40 mi. (64 km.) long W Russia; flows through Saint Petersburg

Ne·vada \nə-ˈva-də\ state W U.S.; ✳, Carson City; pop 1,998,257 — **Ne·vad·an** \-ˈva-dᵊn, -ˈvä-\ or **Ne·vad·i·an** \-ˈva-dē-ən, -ˈvä-\ adj or n

Ne·vis \ˈnē-vəs\ island West Indies in the Leeward Islands — see SAINT KITTS

New Amsterdam town founded 1625 on island of Manhattan by the Dutch; renamed New York 1664 by the British

New·ark \ˈnü-ərk, ˈnyü-\ city NE New Jersey; pop 273,546

New Britain island W Pacific in Bismarck group; pop 263,500

New Bruns·wick \-ˈbrənz-(ˌ)wik\ province SE Canada; ✳, Fredericton; pop 757,077

New Caledonia island SW Pacific SW of Vanuatu; an overseas department of France; ✳, Nouméa; pop 183,100

New·cas·tle \ˈnü-ˌka-səl, ˈnyü-\ city SE Australia in E New South Wales; metropolitan area pop 262,331

Newcastle or **Newcastle upon Tyne** \ˈtīn\ city N England; pop 263,000

New Delhi city, ✳ of India S of Delhi; pop 294,783

New England section of NE U.S. consisting of states of Maine, New Hampshire, Vermont, Massachusetts, Rhode Island, & Connecticut — **New En·gland·er** \ˈiŋ-glən-dər\ n

New·found·land \ˈnü-fən(d)-lənd, ˈnyü-, -ˌland; ˌnü-fən(d)-ˈland, ˌnyü-\ island Canada in the Atlantic — **New·found·land·er** \-lən-dər, -ˌlan-\ n

Newfoundland and Labrador province E Canada consisting of Newfoundland Island and Labrador; ✳, Saint John's; pop 533,761

New France the possessions of France in North America before 1763

New Guinea 1 island W Pacific N of E Australia; divided between West Papua, Indonesia & independent Papua New Guinea 2 NE portion of the island of New Guinea together with some nearby islands; now part of Papua New Guinea — **New Guinean** adj or n

New·ham \ˈnü-əm, ˈnyü-\ borough of E Greater London, England; pop 200,200

New Hamp·shire \ˈhamp-shər, -ˌshir\ state NE U.S.; ✳, Concord; pop 1,235,786 — **New Hamp·shire·man** \-mən\ n — **New Hamp·shir·ite** \-ˌīt\ n

New Ha·ven \ˈhā-vən\ city S Connecticut; pop 123,626

New Hebrides — see VANUATU

New Jersey state E U.S.; ✳, Trenton; pop 8,414,350 — **New Jer·sey·an** \-ən\ n — **New Jer·sey·ite** \-ˌīt\ n

New Mex·i·co \ˈmek-si-ˌkō\ state SW U.S.; ✳, Santa Fe; pop 1,819,046 — **New Mex·i·can** \-si-kən\ adj or n

New Neth·er·land \ˈne-thər-lənd\ former Dutch colony (1613–64) North America along Hudson & lower Delaware rivers

New Or·leans \ˈȯr-lē-ənz, ˈȯr-lənz, ˈȯrl-yənz, (ˌ)ȯr-ˈlēnz\ city SE Louisiana; pop 484,674

New·port \ˈnü-ˌpȯrt, ˈnyü-, -ˌpȯrt\ 1 town S England in Isle of Wight; pop 23,570 2 city SE Wales; pop 129,900

Newport News \ˈnü-ˌpȯrt-ˈnüz, ˈnyü-ˌpȯrt-ˈnyüz, -pərt-\ city SE Virginia; pop 180,150

New Providence island NW cen Bahamas; chief town, Nassau; pop 210,832

New·ry \ˈnü-rē, ˈnyü-\ urban district S Northern Ireland

New South Wales state SE Australia; ✳, Sydney; pop 5,732,032

New Spain former Spanish possessions in North America, Central America, West Indies, & the Philippines

New Sweden former Swedish colony (1638–55) North America on W bank of Delaware River

New·town·ab·bey \ˌnü-tᵊn-ˈa-bē, ˌnyü-\ district E Northern Ireland; pop 73,832

Newtown Saint Bos·wells \ˈnü-ˌtau̇n-sənt-ˈbäz-wəlz, ˈnyü-, -sänt-\ village S Scotland

New World the land of the Western Hemisphere

New York 1 state NE U.S.; ✳, Albany; pop 18,976,457 2 or **New York City** city SE New York (state); pop 8,008,278 — **New York·er** \ˈyȯr-kər\ n

New York State Barge Canal — see ERIE

New Zea·land \ˈzē-lənd\ country SW Pacific ESE of Australia; ✳, Wellington; pop 3,737,277 — **New Zea·land·er** \-lən-dər\ n

Ni·ag·a·ra Falls \(ˌ)nī-ˈa-g(ə-)rə\ falls New York & Ontario in Niagara River (flowing N from Lake Erie into Lake Ontario); divided by Goat Island into Horseshoe Falls, or Canadian Falls (158 ft. or 48 m. high) & American Falls (167 ft. or 51 m. high)

Nia·mey \nē-'ä-(,)mā, nyä-'mā\ city, ✳ of Niger; *pop* 392,165

Ni·caea \nī-'sē-ə\ *or* **Nice** \'nīs\ ancient city W Bithynia; site at modern village in NW Turkey — **Ni·cae·an** \nī-'sē-ən\ *adj or n* — **Ni·cene** \'nī-,sēn, nī-'sēn\ *adj*

Ni·ca·ra·gua \,ni-kə-'rä-gwə, ,nē-kä-'rä-gwä\ **1** lake about 100 mi. (160 km.) long S Nicaragua **2** country Central America; ✳, Managua; *pop* 4,265,000 — **Ni·ca·ra·guan** \-'rä-gwən-'rä-gwən\ *adj or n*

Nice \'nēs\ city & port SE France on the Mediterranean; *pop* 345,892

Nic·o·bar \'ni-kə-,bär\ islands India in Bay of Bengal S of the Andamans; *pop* 14,563

Nic·o·sia \,ni-kə-'sē-ə\ city, ✳ of Cyprus; *pop* 206,200

Ni·ger \'nī-jər, nē-'zher\ **1** river 2600 mi. (4184 km.) long W Africa flowing into Gulf of Guinea **2** country W Africa N of Nigeria; ✳, Niamey; *pop* 8,516,000 — **Ni·ger·ien** \,nī-,jir-ē-'en, nē-'zher-ē-ən\ *adj or n* — **Ni·ger·ois** \,nē-zhər-'wä, -zher-\ *n*

Ni·ge·ria \nī-'jir-ē-ə\ country W Africa on Gulf of Guinea; ✳, Abuja; *pop* 88,514,501 — **Ni·ge·ri·an** \-ē-ən\ *adj or n*

Nii·hau \'nē-,haù\ island Hawaii WSW of Kauai

Nile \'nī(-ə)l\ river 4160 mi. (6693 km.) long E Africa flowing from Lake Victoria in Uganda N into the Mediterranean in Egypt

Nil·gi·ri \'nil-gə-rē\ hills S India

Nin·e·veh \'ni-nə-və\ ancient city, ✳ of Assyria; ruins in Iraq on the Tigris

Nip·i·gon, Lake \'ni-pə-,gän\ lake Canada in W Ontario N of Lake Superior

Nizh·niy Nov·go·rod \'nizh-nē-'näv-gə-,räd, -'nóv-gə-rət\ *formerly 1932–89* **Gor·ki** \'gór-kē\ city W Russia; *pop* 1,433,000

Nord–Ost·see \'nórt-'óst-'zā\ *or* **Kiel** \'kēl\ canal 61 mi. (98 km.) long N Germany across base of Jutland Peninsula connecting Baltic Sea & North Sea

Nor·folk \'nór-fək\ city & port SE Virginia; *pop* 234,403

Nor·man·dy \'nór-mən-dē\ region NW France NE of Brittany

North **1** river estuary of the Hudson between NE New Jersey & SE New York **2** sea, arm of the Atlantic E of Great Britain **3** island N New Zealand; *pop* 2,829,798

North·al·ler·ton \nór-'tha-lər-tən\ town N England; *pop* 9556

North America continent of Western Hemisphere NW of South America & N of the Equator — **North American** *adj or n*

North·amp·ton \nór-'tham(p)-tən, nórth-'ham(p)-\ town *cen* England; *pop* 145,421

North·amp·ton·shire \-,shir, -shər\ *or* **Northampton** county *cen* England

North Cape cape New Zealand at N end of North Island

North Car·o·li·na \,ker(-ə)-'lī-nə, ,ka-rə-\ state E U.S.; ✳, Raleigh; *pop* 8,049,313 — **North Car·o·lin·ian** \-'li-nē-ən, -'li-nyən\ *adj or n*

North Da·ko·ta \də-'kō-tə\ state N U.S.; ✳, Bismarck; *pop* 642,200 — **North Da·ko·tan** \-'kō-tᵊn\ *adj or n*

North Down district E Northern Ireland; *pop* 70,308

Northern Cape province W Republic of South Africa; *pop* 749,000

Northern Cook islands S *cen* Pacific N of Cook Islands

Northern Hemisphere the half of the earth that lies N of the Equator

Northern Ireland region N Ireland comprising 26 districts of Ulster; a division of United Kingdom; ✳, Belfast; *pop* 1,685,267

Northern Mar·i·ana Islands \,mer-ē-'a-nə\ islands W Pacific; commonwealth in association with U.S.; ✳ on Saipan; *pop* 69,221

Northern Rhodesia — SEE ZAMBIA

Northern Territory territory N & *cen* Australia; ✳, Darwin; *pop* 169,300

North Korea *or* **Democratic People's Republic of Korea** country N half of Korean Peninsula in E Asia; ✳, Pyongyang; *pop* 22,646,000

North Las Vegas city SE Nevada; *pop* 115,448

North Slope region N Alaska between Brooks Range & Arctic Ocean

North·um·ber·land \nór-'thəm-bər-lənd\ county N England

North·um·bria \nór-'thəm-brē-ə\ ancient country Great Britain in what is now N England and S Scotland — **North·um·bri·an** \-brē-ən\ *adj or n*

North Vietnam — see VIETNAM

North West province N Republic of South Africa; *pop* 3,349,000

Northwest Passage sea passage between the Atlantic and the Pacific along the N coast of North America

Northwest Territories territory NW Canada consisting of the area of the mainland north of 60° between Yukon Territory & Nunavut; ✳, Yellowknife; *pop* 40,860

North York former city Canada in SE Ontario; now part of Toronto

North Yorkshire county N England

Norwalk \'nór-,wók\ city SW California SE of Los Angeles; *pop* 103,298

Nor·way \'nór-,wā\ country N Europe in Scandinavia; ✳, Oslo; *pop* 4,552,200

Nor·wich \'nór-(,)wich\ city E England; *pop* 120,700

Not·ting·ham \'nä-tiŋ-əm\ city N *cen* England; *pop* 261,500

Not·ting·ham·shire \'nä-tiŋ-əm-,shir, -shər\ *or* **Nottingham** county N *cen* England

Nouak·chott \nú-'äk-,shät\ city, ✳ of Mauritania; *pop* 393,325

Nou·méa \nü-'mā-ə\ city & port, ✳ of New Caledonia; *pop* 65,110

No·va Sco·tia \,nō-və-'skō-shə\ province SE Canada; ✳, Halifax; *pop* 942,691 — **No·va Sco·tian** \-shən\ *adj or n*

No·vo·kuz·netsk \,nō-(,)vō-kùz-'netsk, ,nó-və-küz-'nyetsk\ city S Russia in Asia; *pop* 600,000

No·vo·si·birsk \,nō-(,)vō-sə-'birsk, ,nó-və-\ city S Russia in Asia; *pop* 1,442,000

Nu·bia \'nü-bē-ə, 'nyü-\ region NE Africa in Nile valley in S Egypt & N Sudan — **Nu·bi·an** \'nü-bē-ən, 'nyü-\ *adj or n*

Nu·ku·a·lo·fa \,nü-kü-ä-'lō-fä\ seaport, ✳ of Tonga; *pop* 22,400

Nu·mid·ia \nü-'mi-dē-ə, nyü-\ ancient country N Africa E of Mauretania in modern Algeria — **Nu·mid·i·an** \-dē-ən\ *adj or n*

Nu·na·vut \'nü-nə-,vüt\ semiautonomous territory NE Canada; ✳, Iqaluit; *pop* 28,159

Nu·rem·berg \'nùr-əm-,bərg, 'nyùr-\ *or German* **Nürn·berg** \'nᵘern-,berk\ city S Germany; *pop* 497,496

Nuuk \'nük\ *or* **Godt·häb** \'gót-,hóp\ town, ✳ of Greenland on SW coast; *pop* 12,181

Nyasa, Lake — see MALAWI, LAKE

Nyasaland — see MALAWI

Oa·hu \ō-'ä-(,)hü\ island Hawaii; site of Honolulu

Oak·land \'ō-klənd\ city W California on San Francisco Bay S of San Francisco; *pop* 399,484

Ob' \'äb, 'ób\ river over 2250 mi. (3620 km.) long W Russia in Asia flowing NW & N into Arctic Ocean

Oce·a·nia \,ō-shē-'a-nē-ə, -'ā-\ lands of the *cen* & S Pacific: Micronesia, Melanesia, Polynesia including New Zealand, & sometimes Australia & Malay Archipelago

Ocean·side \'ō-shən-,sīd\ city SW California NNW of San Diego; *pop* 161,029

Oder \'ō-dər\ *or* **Odra** \'ō-drə\ river about 565 mi. (909 km.) long *cen* Europe flowing from Silesia NW into Baltic Sea; forms part of boundary between Poland & Germany

Odes·sa \ō-'de-sə\ city & port S Ukraine on Black Sea; *pop* 1,101,000

Ohio \ō-'hī-(,)ō, ə-, -ə\ **1** river about 981 mi. (1578 km.) long E U.S. flowing from W Pennsylvania into the Mississippi **2** state E *cen* U.S.; ✳, Columbus; *pop* 11,353,140 — **Ohio·an** \-'hī-ō-ən\ *adj or n*

Oka·ya·ma \,ō-kä-'yä-mä\ city Japan in W Honshu on Inland Sea; *pop* 626,642

Okee·cho·bee, Lake \,ō-kə-'chō-bē\ lake S *cen* Florida

Oke·fe·no·kee \,ō-kə-fə-'nō-kē, ,ō-kē-\ swamp SE Georgia & NE Florida

Okhotsk, Sea of \ō-'kätsk, ə-'kotsk\ inlet of the North Pacific E Russia in Asia

Oki·na·wa \,ō-kə-'nä-wə, -'naù-ə\ **1** islands Japan in *cen*

Ryukyus **2** island, chief of group — Oki·na·wan \-'nä-wən, -'naú-ən\ *adj or n*

Okla·ho·ma \ˌō-klə-'hō-mə\ state S *cen* U.S.; ✳, Oklahoma City; *pop* 3,450,654 — Okla·ho·man \-mən\ *adj or n*

Oklahoma City city, ✳ of Oklahoma; *pop* 506,132

Old·ham \'ōl-dəm\ city NW England; *pop* 211,400

Old Point Comfort cape SE Virginia N of entrance to Hampton Roads

Ol·du·vai Gorge \'ōl-də-ˌvī\ canyon N Tanzania SE of Serengeti Plain; site of fossil beds

Old World the half of the earth to the E of the Atlantic Ocean including Europe, Asia, and Africa & esp. the continent of Europe

Olym·pia \ə-'lim-pē-ə, ō-\ **1** city, ✳ of Washington; *pop* 42,514 **2** plain S Greece in NW Peloponnese

Olym·pic \-pik\ mountains NW Washington on Olympic Peninsula; highest Mt. Olympus 7965 ft. (2428 m.)

Olym·pus \ə-'lim-pəs, ō-\ mountains NE Greece

Omagh \'ō-mə, -(ˌ)mä\ **1** district W Northern Ireland; *pop* 45,343 **2** town in Omagh district; *pop* 17,280

Oma·ha \'ō-mə, -(ˌ)mä\ **1** beach NW France in Normandy **2** city E Nebraska on Missouri River; *pop* 390,007

Oman \ō-'män, -'man\ country SW Asia in SE Arabia; ✳, Masqat; *pop* 2,477,687 — Omani \ō-'mä-nē, -'ma-\ *adj or n*

Oman, Gulf of arm of Arabian Sea between Oman & SE Iran

Omsk \'ȯm(p)sk, 'äm(p)sk\ city SW Russia in Asia; *pop* 1,169,000

On·tar·io \än-'ter-ē-ˌō\ **1** city SW California; *pop* 158,007 **2** province E Canada; ✳, Toronto; *pop* 11,874,436 — On·tar·i·an \-ē-ən\ *adj or n*

Ontario, Lake lake E *cen* North America in U.S. & Canada; one of the Great Lakes

Oran \ō-'rän\ city & port NW Algeria; *pop* 628,558

Or·ange \'är-inj, 'ár(-ə)nj, 'ȯr-inj, 'ȯr(-ə)nj\ **1** city SW California; *pop* 128,821 **2** river 1300 mi. (2092 km.) long S Africa flowing W from Drakensberg Mountains into the Atlantic

Orange Free State — see FREE STATE

Or·e·gon \'ȯr-i-gən, 'är-\ state W U.S.; ✳, Salem; *pop* 3,421,399 — Or·e·go·nian \ˌȯr-i-'gō-nē-ən, ˌär-, -nyən\ *adj or n*

Oregon Trail pioneer route to the NW about 2000 mi. (3220 km.) long from Missouri to Washington

Ori·no·co \ˌȯr-ē-'nō-(ˌ)kō\ river 1336 mi. (2150 km.) long Venezuela flowing into the Atlantic

Ork·ney \'ȯrk-nē\ islands N Scotland; *pop* 19,570

Or·lan·do \ȯr-'lan-(ˌ)dō\ city *cen* Florida; *pop* 185,951

Osa·ka \ō-'sä-kä, 'ō-sä-ˌkä\ city Japan in S Honshu; *pop* 2,598,774

Osh·a·wa \'ä-shə-wə, -ˌwä, -ˌwȯ\ city SE Ontario, Canada on Lake Ontario ENE of Toronto; *pop* 139,051

Os·lo \'äz-(ˌ)lō, 'äs-\ city, ✳ of Norway; *pop* 507,831

Oś·wię·cim \ˌȯsh-'fyen-chēm\ *or German* Ausch·witz \'aúsh-ˌvits\ town S Poland W of Krakow; *pop* 45,282

Ot·ta·wa \'ä-tə-wə, -ˌwä, -ˌwȯ\ **1** river 696 mi. (1120 km.) E Canada in SE Ontario & S Quebec flowing E into the Saint Lawrence **2** city, ✳ of Canada in SE Ontario on Ottawa River; *pop* 774,072

Ot·to·man Empire \'ä-tə-mən\ former Turkish sultanate in SE Europe, W Asia, & N Africa

Oua·ga·dou·gou \ˌwä-gä-'dü-(ˌ)gü\ city, ✳ of Burkina Faso; *pop* 366,000

Outer Hebrides — see HEBRIDES

Over·land Park \'ō-vər-lənd\ city NE Kansas; *pop* 149,080

Ox·ford \'äks-fərd\ city *cen* England; *pop* 109,000

Ox·ford·shire \'äks-fərd-ˌshir, -shər\ *or* Oxford county *cen* England

Ox·nard \'äks-ˌnärd\ city SW California; *pop* 170,358

Ozark Plateau \'ō-ˌzärk\ *or* Ozark Mountains eroded plateau N Arkansas, S Missouri, & NE Oklahoma with E extension into S Illinois

Pa·cif·ic \pə-'si-fik\ ocean extending from Arctic Circle to the Equator (**North Pacific**) and from the Equator to the Antarctic regions (**South Pacific**) & from W North America & W South America to E Asia & Australia — Pacific *adj*

Pacific Islands, Trust Territory of the grouping of islands in W Pacific formerly under U.S. administration: the Carolines & the Marshalls

Pacific Rim the countries bordering on or located in the Pacific Ocean — used esp. of Asian countries on the Pacific

Pa·dang \'pä-ˌdäŋ\ city Indonesia in W Sumatra; *pop* 631,543

Pa·dre \'pä-drē, -drä\ island 113 mi. (182 km.) long S Texas in Gulf of Mexico

Pa·go Pa·go \ˌpä-(ˌ)gō-'pä-(ˌ)gō, ˌpäŋ-(ˌ)ō-'päŋ-(ˌ)ō\ town, ✳ of American Samoa on Tutuila Island; *pop* 4278

Painted Desert region N *cen* Arizona

Pak·i·stan \'pa-ki-ˌstan, ˌpä-ki-'stän\ country S Asia NW of India; ✳, Islamabad; *pop* 131,434,000 — see EAST PAKISTAN — Pak·i·stani \ˌpa-ki-'sta-nē, ˌpä-ki-'stä-\ *adj or n*

Pa·lau \pə-'laú\ *or* Be·lau \bə-\ island group W Pacific in the W Carolines in association with U.S.; country; ✳, Koror; *pop* 17,225 — Pa·lau·an \pə-'laú-ən\ *n*

Pa·la·wan \pə-'lä-wən, -ˌwän\ island W Philippines between South China & Sulu seas; *pop* 528,287

Pa·lem·bang \ˌpä-ləm-'bäŋ\ city Indonesia in SE Sumatra; *pop* 1,141,036

Pa·ler·mo \pə-'lər-(ˌ)mō, pä-'ler-\ city Italy, ✳ of Sicily; *pop* 679,290

Pal·es·tine \'pa-lə-ˌstīn\ **1** ancient region SW Asia bordering on E coast of the Mediterranean and extending E of Jordan River **2** region bordering on the Mediterranean on W and Dead Sea on E; now approximately coextensive with Israel & the West Bank — Pal·es·tin·ian \ˌpa-lə-'sti-nē-ən, -nyən\ *adj or n*

Pa·li·kir \ˌpä-lē-'kir\ town, ✳ of Federated States of Micronesia on Pohnpei Island; *pop* 6227

Pal·i·sades \ˌpa-lə-'sādz\ line of high cliffs 15 mi. (24 km.) long on W bank of the Hudson in SE New York & NE New Jersey

Palm·dale \'päm-ˌdāl, 'pälm-\ city SW California NE of Los Angeles; *pop* 116,670

Pa·mirs \pə-'mirz\ elevated mountainous region *cen* Asia in E Tajikistan & on borders of China, India, Pakistan, & Afghanistan; many peaks over 20,000 ft. (6096 m.)

Pam·li·co Sound \'pam-li-ˌkō\ inlet of the North Atlantic E North Carolina between main part of the state & offshore islands

Pam·pa \'pam-pə\ city NW Texas; *pop* 17,887

Pan·a·ma \'pan-ə-ˌmä, -ˌmȯ, ˌpan-ə-'mä, -'mȯ\ **1** country S Central America; *pop* 2,839,177 **2** *or* Panama City city, its ✳ on the Pacific; *pop* 411,549 **3** canal 40 mi. (64 km.) long Panama connecting Atlantic & Pacific oceans — Pan·a·ma·ni·an \ˌpan-ə-'mä-nē-ən\ *adj or n*

Panama, Isthmus of *formerly* Isthmus of Dar·i·en \ˌder-ē-'en\ strip of land *cen* Panama connecting North America & South America

Panama Canal Zone — see CANAL ZONE

Pa·nay \pə-'nī\ island *cen* Philippines

Pan·gaea \pan-'jē-ə\ hypothetical land area believed to have once connected the landmasses of the Southern Hemisphere with those of the Northern Hemisphere

Pan·mun·jom *or* Pan·mun·jeom \ˌpän-ˌmún-'jəm\ village on North Korea–South Korea border

Pao–t'ou — see BAOTOU

Pap·ua, Territory of \'pa-pyù-wə, 'pä-pù-wə\ former British territory consisting of SE New Guinea & offshore islands; now part of Papua New Guinea

Papua New Guinea country SW Pacific combining former territories of Papua & New Guinea; ✳, Port Moresby; *pop* 5,190,736

Par·a·guay \'pa-rə-ˌgwī, -ˌgwä\ **1** river 1584 mi. (2549 km.) long *cen* South America flowing from Brazil S into the Paraná in Paraguay **2** country *cen* South America; ✳, Asunción; *pop* 4,643,000 — Par·a·guay·an \ˌpa-rə-'gwī-ən, -'gwä-\ *adj or n*

Par·a·mar·i·bo \ˌpa-rə-'ma-rə-ˌbō\ city, ✳ of Suriname; *pop* 200,000

Pa·ra·ná \ˌpär-ə-'nä\ river about 2500 mi. (4022 km.) long *cen* South America flowing S from Brazil into Argentina

Pa·ri·cu·tin \pä-ˌrē-kü-'tēn\ **1** former village Mexico **2** volcano on site of former village of Paricutin

Par·is \'pa-rəs\ city, * of France; *pop* 2,125,851 — **Pa·ri·sian** \pə-'ri-zhən, -'rē-\ *adj or n*

Par·nas·sus \pär-'na-səs\ mountain *cen* Greece

Par·os \'pär-,ös\ island Greece — **Par·i·an** \'par-ē-ən, 'per-\ *adj*

Par·ra·mat·ta \,pa-rə-'ma-tə\ city SE Australia in New South Wales NW of Sydney; *pop* 132,798

Par·thia \'pär-thē-ə\ ancient country SW Asia in NE modern Iran — **Par·thi·an** \-thē-ən\ *adj or n*

Pas·a·de·na \,pa-sə-'dē-nə\ **1** city SW California E of Glendale; *pop* 133,936 **2** city SE Texas; *pop* 141,674

Pat·a·go·nia \,pa-tə-'gō-nyə, -nē-ə\ region South America S of about 40° S latitude in S Argentina & S tip of Chile; sometimes thought to include Tierra del Fuego — **Pat·a·go·nian** \-nyən, -nē-ən\ *adj or n*

Pat·er·son \'pa-tər-sən\ city NE New Jersey; *pop* 149,222

Pat·mos \'pat-məs\ island Greece SSW of Samos

Pat·na \'pət-nə\ city NE India on the Ganges; *pop* 1,376,950

Pearl Harbor inlet Hawaii on S coast of Oahu W of Honolulu

Peking — see BEIJING

Pe·li·on \'pē-lē-ən\ mountain 5089 ft. (1551 m.) NE Greece

Pel·o·pon·nese \'pe-lə-pə-,nēz, -,nēs\ *or* **Pel·o·pon·ni·sos** \,pe-lə-pə-'nē-səs\ peninsula forming S part of mainland of Greece

Pem·broke Pines \'pem-,brök\ city SE Florida; *pop* 137,427

Pen·nine Chain \'pe-,nīn\ mountains N England; highest Cross Fell 2930 ft. (893 m.)

Penn·syl·va·nia \,pen(t)-səl-'vā-nyə, -nē-ə\ state E U.S.; *, Harrisburg; *pop* 12,281,054

Pe·o·ria \pē-'òr-ē-ə\ **1** town SW *cen* Arizona; *pop* 108,364 **2** city N *cen* Illinois; *pop* 112,936

Per·ga·mum \'pər-gə-məm\ *or* **Per·ga·mus** \-məs\ ancient Greek kingdom including most of Asia Minor

Perm \'pərm, 'perm\ city E Russia in Europe; *pop* 1,099,000

Pernambuco — see RECIFE

Persia — see IRAN

Per·sian Gulf \'pər-zhən\ arm of Arabian Sea between Iran & Arabia

Perth \'pərth\ city, * of Western Australia; *pop* 80,517

Pe·ru \pə-'rü, pā-\ country W South America; *, Lima; *pop* 22,916,000 — **Pe·ru·vi·an** \-'rü-vē-ən\ *adj or n*

Pe·tra \'pē-trə, 'pe-\ ancient city NW Arabia; site in SW Jordan

Petrograd — see SAINT PETERSBURG

Phil·a·del·phia \,fi-lə-'del-fyə, -fē-ə\ city SE Pennsylvania; *pop* 1,517,550 — **Phil·a·del·phian** \-fyən, -fē-ən\ *adj or n*

Phil·ip·pines \,fi-lə-'pēnz, 'fi-lə-,pēnz\ island group 500 mi. (805 km.) off SE coast of Asia; country; *, Manila; *pop* 64,954,000 — **Phil·ip·pine** \,fi-lə-'pēn, 'fi-lə-,\ *adj*

Phnom Penh \(pə-)'näm-'pen, (pə-)'nòm-\ city, * of Cambodia; *pop* 800,000

Phoe·ni·cia \fi-'ni-sh(ē-)ə, -'nē-\ ancient country SW Asia on the Mediterranean in modern Syria & Lebanon

Phoe·nix \'fē-niks\ city, * of Arizona; *pop* 1,321,045

Phry·gia \'fri-j(ē-)ə\ ancient country W *cen* Asia Minor

Pic·ar·dy \'pi-kər-dē\ *or F* **Pi·car·die** \pē-kär-'dē\ region & former province N France bordering on English Channel N of Normandy — **Pi·card** \'pi-,kärd, -kərd\ *adj or n*

Pied·mont \'pēd-,mänt\ plateau region E U.S. E of the Appalachians between SE New York & NE Alabama

Pierre \'pir\ city, * of South Dakota; *pop* 13,876

Pie·ter·mar·itz·burg \,pē-tər-'ma-rəts-,bərg\ city E Republic of South Africa; *pop* 128,598

Pigs, Bay of \'pigz\ *or* **Ba·hía de Co·chi·nos** \bä-'ē-ä-thä-kō-'chē-nōs\ bay W Cuba on S coast

Pikes Peak \'pīks\ mountain 14,110 ft. (4301 m.) E *cen* Colorado in a range of the Rockies

Pin·dus \'pin-dəs\ mountains W Greece; highest point 8136 ft. (2480 m.)

Pi·sa \'pē-zə, *It* -sä\ city W *cen* Italy; *pop* 91,977

Pit·cairn \'pit-,kern\ island South Pacific; a British colony; *pop* less than 100

Pitts·burgh \'pits-,bərg\ city SW Pennsylvania; *pop* 334,563

Plac·id, Lake \'pla-səd\ lake NE New York

Pla·no \'plā-(,)nō\ city NE Texas N of Dallas; *pop* 222,030

Plov·div \'plòv-,dif, -,div\ city S Bulgaria; *pop* 379,083

Plym·outh \'pli-məth\ **1** town SE Massachusetts; *pop* 51,701 **2** city & port SW England; *pop* 238,800

Po \'pō\ river 405 mi. (652 km.) N Italy flowing into the Adriatic

Pod·go·ri·ca \'pòd-,gòr-ēt-sä\ city * of Montenegro; *pop* 152,242

Po Hai — see BO HAI

Pohn·pei \'pòn-,pā\ *or* **Po·na·pe** \'pō-nə-,pā\ island W Pacific in the E Carolines; part of Federated States of Micronesia

Po·land \'pō-lənd\ country *cen* Europe on Baltic Sea; *, Warsaw; *pop* 38,038,400 — **Pole** n

Pol·y·ne·sia \,pä-lə-'nē-zhə, -shə\ islands of the *cen* & S Pacific including Hawaii, the Line, Tonga, Cook, & Samoa islands, & often New Zealand among others

Pom·er·a·nia \,pä-mə-'rā-nē-ə, -nyə\ region N Europe on Baltic Sea; formerly in Germany, now mostly in Poland

Po·mo·na \pə-'mō-nə\ city SW California E of Los Angeles; *pop* 149,473

Pom·peii \päm-'pā, -'pā-,ē\ ancient city S Italy SE of Naples destroyed 79 A.D. by eruption of Vesuvius — **Pom·pe·ian** \-'pā-ən\ *adj or n*

Pon·ce \'pòn(t)-(,)sä\ city S Puerto Rico; *pop* 186,475

Pon·do·land \'pän-(,)dō-,land\ region S Republic of South Africa

Pon·ta Del·ga·da \,pòn-tə-del-'gä-də\ city & port Portugal, largest in the Azores; *pop* 65,854

Pont·char·train, Lake \'pänt-shər-,trān, ,pänt-shər-'\ lake SE Louisiana E of the Mississippi & N of New Orleans

Pon·tus \'pän-təs\ ancient country NE Asia Minor — **Pon·tic** \'pänt-ik\ *adj or n*

Poole \'pül\ town S England on English Channel; *pop* 130,900

Po·po·ca·te·petl \,pō-pə-'ka-tə-,pe-t⁽°⁾l, -,ka-tə-'\ volcano 17,887 ft. (5452 m.) SE *cen* Mexico

Port Arthur — see LÜSHUN

Port–au–Prince \,pòrt-ō-'prin(t)s, ,pòr-(t)ō-'praⁿs\ city, * of Haiti; *pop* 752,600

Port Jack·son \'jak-sən\ inlet of South Pacific SE Australia in New South Wales; harbor of Sydney

Port·land \'pòrt-lənd\ **1** city SW Maine; largest in state; *pop* 64,249 **2** city NW Oregon; *pop* 529,121

Port Lou·is \'lü-əs, 'lü-ē\ city, * of Mauritius; *pop* 146,876

Port Mores·by \'mòrz-bē\ city, * of Papua New Guinea; *pop* 254,158

Por·to \'pòr-(,)tü\ city & port NW Portugal; *pop* 310,600

Por·to Ale·gre \'pòr-(,)tü-ä-'lā-grē\ city & port S Brazil; *pop* 1,360,590

Port of Spain city NW Trinidad, * of Trinidad and Tobago; *pop* 49,031

Por·to–No·vo \,pòr-tō-'nō-(,)vō\ city, * of Benin; *pop* 192,000

Port Phil·lip Bay \'fi-ləp\ inlet of South Pacific SE Australia in Victoria; harbor of Melbourne

Port Said \sä-'ēd, 'sīd\ city & port NE Egypt on the Mediterranean at N end of the Suez Canal; *pop* 262,760

Ports·mouth \'pòrts-məth\ **1** city SE Virginia; *pop* 100,565 **2** city S England; *pop* 174,400

Por·tu·gal \'pòr-chi-gəl, ,pür-tü-'gäl\ country SW Europe; *, Lisbon; *pop* 10,356,117

Portuguese India former Portuguese possession on W coast of India; became part of India 1962

Port–Vi·la \'pòrt-'vē-lə\ *or* **Vila** city, * of Vanuatu; *pop* 18,905

Po·to·mac \pə-'tō-mək, -mik\ river 287 mi. (462 km.) long flowing from West Virginia into Chesapeake Bay and forming boundary between Maryland & Virginia

Pough·keep·sie \pə-'kip-sē, pò-\ city & river port SE New York on the Hudson; *pop* 29,871

Po·wys \'pō-əs\ administrative subdivision E *cen* Wales

Prague \'präg\ *or Czech* **Pra·ha** \'prä-(,)hä\ city, * of Czech Republic; *pop* 1,162,179

Praia \'prī-ə\ town, * of Cape Verde; *pop* 61,797

Prairie Provinces the Canadian provinces of Alberta, Manitoba, & Saskatchewan

Pres·ton \'pres-tən\ town NW England; *pop* 126,200

Pre·to·ria \pri-ˈtȯr-ē-ə\ city Republic of South Africa, administrative * of the country; *pop* 303,684
Prib·i·lof \ˈpri-bə-ˌlȯf\ islands Alaska in Bering Sea
Prince Ed·ward Island \ˈed-wərd\ island SE Canada in Gulf of Saint Lawrence; a province; *, Charlottetown; *pop* 138,514
Prince Ru·pert's Land \ˈrü-pərts\ historical region N & W Canada consisting of drainage basin of Hudson Bay
Prince·ton \ˈprin(t)-stən\ borough W *cen* New Jersey; *pop* 14,203
Prín·ci·pe \ˈprin(t)-si-pē\ island W Africa in Gulf of Guinea — see SÃO TOMÉ AND PRÍNCIPE
Pro·vence \prə-ˈvän(t)s, prō-ˈväⁿs\ region SE France on the Mediterranean
Prov·i·dence \ˈprä-və-dən(t)s, -ˌden(t)s\ city, * of Rhode Island; *pop* 173,618
Pro·vo \ˈprō-(ˌ)vō\ city N *cen* Utah; *pop* 105,166
Prud·hoe Bay \ˈprü-(ˌ)dō, ˈprə-\ inlet of Beaufort Sea N Alaska
Prus·sia \ˈprə-shə\ former kingdom, & later, state Germany — **Prus·sian** \ˈprə-shən\ *adj or n*
Pueb·lo \ˈpwe-ˌblō\ city SE *cen* Colorado SSE of Colorado Springs; *pop* 102,121
Puer·to Ri·co \ˌpȯr-tə-ˈrē-(ˌ)kō, ˌpwer-tō-\ island West Indies E of Hispaniola; a self-governing commonwealth associated with U.S.; *, San Juan; *pop* 3,808,610 — **Puer·to Ri·can** \ˈrē-kən\ *adj or n*
Pu·get Sound \ˈpyü-jət\ arm of the North Pacific W Washington
Pu·ne \ˈpü-nə\ city W India, ESE of Bombay; *pop* 2,540,069
Pun·jab \ˌpən-ˈjäb, -ˈjab, ˈpən-ˌ\ region in Pakistan & NW India in valley of the Indus
Pu·san \ˈpü-ˌsän, ˈbü-\ *or* **Bu·san** \ˈbü-\ city SE South Korea; *pop* 3,655,437
Pyong·yang *or* **Pyeong·yang** \ˈpyȯŋ-ˈyaŋ, ˈpyəŋ-, -ˈyäŋ\ city, * of North Korea; *pop* 2,355,000
Pyr·e·nees \ˈpir-ə-ˌnēz\ mountains on French–Spanish border extending from Bay of Biscay to the Mediterranean; highest Pico de Aneto 11,168 ft. (3404 m.)
Qaraghandy — see KARAGANDA
Qa·tar \ˈkä-tər, ˈgä-, ˈgə-; kə-ˈtär\ country E Arabia on peninsula extending into Persian Gulf; *, Doha; *pop* 539,000 — **Qa·tari** \kə-ˈtär-ē, gə-\ *adj or n*
Qing·dao \ˈchiŋ-ˈdau\ *or* **Tsing·tao** \ˈchiŋ-ˈdau, ˈ(t)siŋ-ˈdau\ city & port E China; *pop* 1,459,195
Qi·qi·har \ˈchē-ˈchē-ˈhär\ *or* **Ch'i-ch'i-ha-erh** \ˈchē-ˈchē-ˈhä-ˈər\ city NE China; *pop* 1,500,000
Que·bec \kwi-ˈbek, ki-\ *or French* **Qué·bec** \kā-ˈbek\ **1** province E Canada; *pop* 7,410,504 **2** city, its *, on the Saint Lawrence; *pop* 169,076
Queens \ˈkwēnz\ borough of New York City on Long Island E of Brooklyn; *pop* 2,229,379
Queens·land \ˈkwēnz-ˌland, -lənd\ state NE Australia; *, Brisbane; *pop* 3,116,200 — **Queens·land·er** \-ˌlan-dər, -ˌlən-\ *n*
Que·zon City \ˈkā-ˌsȯn\ city Philippines in Luzon; formerly * of the country; *pop* 1,632,000
Qui·to \ˈkē-(ˌ)tō\ city, * of Ecuador; *pop* 1,100,847
Ra·bat \rə-ˈbät\ city, * of Morocco; *pop* 668,000
Rai·nier, Mount \rə-ˈnir, rā-\ mountain 14,410 ft. (4392 m.) W *cen* Washington; highest in Cascade Range
Raj·pu·ta·na \ˌräj-pə-ˈtä-nə\ *or* **Ra·ja·sthan** \ˈräj-ə-ˌstän\ region NW India S of Punjab
Ra·leigh \ˈrȯ-lē, ˈrä-lē\ city, * of North Carolina; *pop* 276,093
Ran·cho Cu·ca·mon·ga \ˈran-(ˌ)chō-ˌkü-kə-ˈməŋ-gə, ˈrän-, -ˈmäŋ-\ city SW California; *pop* 127,743
Rand — see WITWATERSRAND
Rand·wick \ˈran-(ˌ)dwik\ municipality SE Australia in E New South Wales; *pop* 115,349
Rangoon — see YANGON
Ra·wal·pin·di \ˌrä-wəl-ˈpin-dē, raùl-ˈ, rȯl-ˈ\ city NE Pakistan NNW of Lahore; *pop* 1,409,768
Read·ing \ˈre-diŋ\ town S England; *pop* 122,600
Re·ci·fe \ri-ˈsē-fē\ *formerly* **Per·nam·bu·co** \ˌpər-nəm-ˈbü-(ˌ)kō, -ˈbyü-\ city NE Brazil; *pop* 1,422,905
Red \ˈred\ **1** river 1018 mi. (1638 km.) long flowing E on Oklahoma–Texas boundary and into the Atchafalaya &

the Mississippi in Louisiana **2** sea between Arabia & NE Africa
Red·bridge \ˈred-(ˌ)brij\ borough of NE Greater London, England; *pop* 220,600
Re·gi·na \ri-ˈjī-nə\ city, * of Saskatchewan, Canada; *pop* 178,225
Re·no \ˈrē-(ˌ)nō\ city NW Nevada; *pop* 180,480
Republic of the Congo — see CONGO 3
Ré·union \rē-ˈyü-nyən, ˌrä-ue-ˈnyōⁿ\ island W Indian Ocean; an overseas division of France; *, Saint-Denis; *pop* 634,000
Reyk·ja·vik \ˈrā-kyə-ˌvik, -ˌvēk\ city, * of Iceland; *pop* 112,490
Rhine \ˈrīn\ river 820 mi. (1320 km.) long W Europe flowing from SE Switzerland to North Sea in the Netherlands — **Rhen·ish** \ˈre-nish, ˈrē-\ *adj*
Rhine·land \ˈrīn-ˌland, -lənd\ *or German* **Rhein·land** \ˈrīn-ˌlänt\ the part of Germany W of the Rhine — **Rhineland·er** \ˈrīn-ˌlan-dər, -lən-\ *n*
Rhode Is·land \rōd-ˈī-lənd\ **1** *or officially* **Rhode Island and Providence Plantations** state NE U.S.; *, Providence; *pop* 1,048,319 **2** — see AQUIDNECK — **Rhode Is·land·er** \-lən-dər\ *n*
Rhodes \ˈrōdz\ island Greece in the SE Aegean
Rho·de·sia \rō-ˈdē-zh(ē-)ə\ — see ZIMBABWE — **Rho·de·sian** \-zh(ē-)ən\ *adj or n*
Rhone *or French* **Rhône** \ˈrōn\ river 505 mi. (813 km.) long Switzerland & SE France
Rich·mond \ˈrich-mənd\ **1** — see STATEN ISLAND **2** city, * of Virginia; *pop* 197,790
Richmond upon Thames borough of SW Greater London, England; *pop* 154,600
Ri·ga \ˈrē-gə\ city, * of Latvia; *pop* 747,157
Rio de Ja·nei·ro \ˈrē-(ˌ)ō-dā-zhə-ˈner-(ˌ)ō, -dē-\ city SE Brazil on Guanabara Bay; *pop* 5,857,904
Rio Grande \ˌrē-(ˌ)ō-ˈgrand, -ˈgran-dē\ *or Mexican* **Rio Bra·vo** \ˌrē-(ˌ)ō-ˈbrä-(ˌ)vō\ river 1885 mi. (3034 km.) long SW U.S. forming part of U.S.–Mexico boundary and flowing into Gulf of Mexico
Río Muni — see MBINI
Riv·er·side \ˈri-vər-ˌsīd\ city S California; *pop* 255,166
Riv·i·era \ˌri-vē-ˈer-ə\ coast region SE France & NW Italy
Ri·yadh \rē-ˈyäd\ city, * of Saudi Arabia; *pop* 4,700,000
Ro·a·noke \ˈrō-(ə-)ˌnōk\ city W Virginia; *pop* 94,911
Roanoke Island island North Carolina S of entrance to Albemarle Sound
Rob·son, Mount \ˈräb-sən\ mountain 12,972 ft. (3954 m.) W Canada in E British Columbia; highest in the Canadian Rockies
Roch·es·ter \ˈrä-chəs-tər, -ˌches-tər\ city W New York; *pop* 219,773
Rock·ford \ˈräk-fərd\ city N Illinois; *pop* 150,115
Rocky Mountains *or* **Rock·ies** \ˈrä-kēz\ mountains W North America extending SE from N Alaska to *cen* New Mexico
Roman Empire the empire of ancient Rome
Ro·ma·nia \ru̇-ˈmā-nē-ə, rō-, -nyə\ *or* **Ru·ma·nia** \ru̇-\ country SE Europe on Black Sea; *, Bucharest; *pop* 21,698,181
Rom·blon \räm-ˈblōn\ island group *cen* Philippines
Rome \ˈrōm\ *or Italian* **Ro·ma** \ˈrō-mä\ city, * of Italy; *pop* 2,655,970
Ro·sa·rio \rō-ˈzär-ē-ˌō, -ˈsär-\ city E *cen* Argentina on the Paraná; *pop* 591,428
Ro·seau \rō-ˈzō\ seaport, * of Dominica; *pop* 14,847
Ros·tov-on-Don \rə-ˈstȯf-ˌän-ˈdän, -ˈstȯv, -ˌȯn-\ city S Russia in Europe; *pop* 1,027,000
Ros·well \ˈräz-ˌwel, -wəl\ city SE New Mexico; *pop* 45,293
Ro·ta \ˈrō-tə\ island W Pacific in the Marianas
Rot·ter·dam \ˈrä-tər-ˌdam, ˌdäm\ city & port SW Netherlands; *pop* 598,660
Ru·an·da–Urun·di \rü-ˈän-dä-ü-ˈrün-dē\ former trust territory E *cen* Africa bordering on Lake Tanganyika; now divided into Burundi & Rwanda
Rudolf, Lake — see TURKANA, LAKE
Ruhr \ˈru̇r\ **1** river 146 mi. (235 km.) long W Germany flowing NW & W to the Rhine **2** industrial district W Germany E of the Rhine in valley of Ruhr River
Rumania — see ROMANIA

Rupert's Land PRINCE RUPERT'S LAND

Rush·more, Mount \'rash-ˌmȯr\ mountain 5600 ft. (1707 m.) W South Dakota in Black Hills

Rus·sia \'rə-shə\ **1** former empire largely having the same boundaries as U.S.S.R. **2** UNION OF SOVIET SOCIALIST REPUBLICS **3** country E Europe & N Asia; ✳, Moscow; *pop* 148,000,000

Ru·the·nia \rü-'thē-nyə, -nē-ə\ region W Ukraine W of the N Carpathians — **Ru·the·nian** \-'thē-nyən, -nē-ən\ *adj or n*

Ru·wen·zo·ri \ˌrü-ən-'zȯr-ē\ mountain group E *cen* Africa between Uganda & Democratic Republic of the Congo; highest Mount Margherita 16,763 ft. (5109 m.)

Rwan·da *formerly* **Ru·an·da** \rü-'än-dä\ country E *cen* Africa; ✳, Kigali; *pop* 7,584,000 — **Rwan·dan** \-dən\ *adj or n*

Ryu·kyu \rē-'yü-(ˌ)kyü, -(ˌ)kü\ islands Japan extending in an arc from S Japan, to N tip of Taiwan; *pop* 1,222,458 — **Ryu·kyu·an** \-ˌkyü-ən, -ˌkü-\ *adj or n*

Saar \'sär, 'zär\ **1** river about 150 mi. (241 km.) long Europe flowing from E France to W Germany **2** *or* **Saarland** \'sär-ˌland, 'zär-\ region W Europe in valley of Saar River between France & Germany

Sac·ra·men·to \ˌsa-krə-'men-(ˌ)tō\ **1** river 382 mi. (615 km.) long N California flowing S into Suisun Bay **2** city, ✳ of California; *pop* 407,018

Sag·ue·nay \'sa-gə-ˌnā, ˌsa-gə-'\ **1** river 105 mi. (169 km.) long Canada in S Quebec flowing E into the Saint Lawrence **2** city Canada in S Quebec; *pop* 143,692

Sa·ha·ra \sə-'her-ə, -'här-\ desert region N Africa extending from Atlantic coast to Red Sea — **Sa·ha·ran** \-ən\ *adj*

Sa·hel \'sä-hil, sə-'hil\ the S fringe of the Sahara

Saigon — see HO CHI MINH CITY

Saint Al·bans \'ȯl-bənz\ city SE England; *pop* 122,400

Saint Cath·a·rines *usu* St. **Catharines** \'ka-th(ə-)rənz\ city Canada in SE Ontario; *pop* 129,170

Saint Christopher — see SAINT KITTS

Saint Clair, Lake \'kler\ lake SE Michigan & SE Ontario connected by **Saint Clair River** (40 mi. or 64 km. long) with Lake Huron & draining by Detroit River into Lake Erie

Saint Croix \sänt-'krȯi, sənt-\ **1** river 129 mi. (208 km.) long Canada & U.S. on border between New Brunswick & Maine **2** island West Indies; largest of Virgin Islands of the U.S.; *pop* 50,139

Saint Eli·as, Mount \i-'lī-əs\ mountain 18,008 ft. (5489 m.) on Alaska–Canada boundary in **Saint Elias Range**

Saint George's \'jȯr-jəz\ town, ✳ of Grenada; *pop* 29,400

Saint George's Channel channel British Isles between SW Wales & Ireland

Saint Gott·hard \sänt-'gä-tərd, sənt-, 'gät-hərd\ pass S *cen* Switzerland in Saint Gotthard Range of the Alps

Saint He·le·na \ˌsänt-ə-'lē-nə, ˌsänt-hə-'lē-\ island South Atlantic; a British colony; *pop* 5644

Saint Hel·ens, Mount \sänt-'he-lənz, sənt-\ volcano S Washington

Saint John \sänt-'jän, sənt-\ city & port Canada in New Brunswick; *pop* 69,661

Saint John's \sänt-'jänz, sənt-\ **1** city, ✳ of Antigua and Barbuda; *pop* 22,342 **2** *usu* **St. John's** city, ✳ of Newfoundland and Labrador, Canada; *pop* 99,182

Saint Kitts \'kits\ *or* **Saint Chris·to·pher** \'kris-tə-fər\ island West Indies in the Leeward Islands; with Nevis forms independent **Saint Kitts and Nevis**; ✳, Basseterre (on Saint Kitts); *pop* 41,800

Saint Law·rence \sänt-'lȯr-ən(t)s, sənt-, -'lär-\ **1** river 760 mi. (1223 km.) long E Canada in Ontario & Quebec bordering on U.S. in New York and flowing from Lake Ontario NE into the **Gulf of Saint Lawrence** (inlet of the Atlantic) **2** seaway Canada & U.S. in and along the Saint Lawrence between Lake Ontario & Montreal

Saint Lou·is \sänt-'lü-əs, sənt-\ city E Missouri on the Mississippi; *pop* 348,189

Saint Lu·cia \sänt-'lü-shə, sənt-\ island West Indies in the Windwards S of Martinique; country; ✳, Castries; *pop* 157,775

Saint Mo·ritz \ˌsänt-mə-'rits, ˌsaⁿ-mə-\ *or G* **Sankt Mo·ritz** \ˌzäŋkt-mə-'rits\ town E Switzerland; *pop* 5900

Saint Paul \'pȯl\ city, ✳ of Minnesota; *pop* 287,151

Saint Pe·ters·burg \'pē-tərz-ˌbərg\ **1** city W Florida; *pop* 248,232 **2** *formerly* *1914–24* **Pet·ro·grad** \'pe-trə-ˌgrad, -ˌgrät\ *or* *1924–91* **Le·nin·grad** \'le-nən-ˌgrad, -ˌgrät\ city W Russia in Europe; *pop* 4,952,000

Saint Thom·as \'tä-məs\ island West Indies, one of Virgin Islands of the U.S.; chief town, Charlotte Amalie

Saint Vin·cent \sänt-'vin(t)-sənt, sənt-\ island West Indies in the *cen* Windward Islands; with N Grenadines forms independent **Saint Vincent and the Grenadines**; ✳, Kingstown (on Saint Vincent); *pop* 109,000

Sai·pan \sī-'pan, -'pän, 'sī-ˌ\ island W Pacific in S *cen* Marianas; *pop* 38,896

Sa·kai \(ˌ)sä-'kī\ city Japan in S Honshu; *pop* 792,018

Sa·kha·lin \'sa-kə-ˌlēn, -lən; ˌsä-kä-'lēn\ island SE Russia in W Pacific N of Hokkaido, Japan

Sal·a·mis \'sa-lə-məs\ ancient city Cyprus on E coast

Sa·lem \'sä-ləm\ city, ✳ of Oregon; *pop* 136,924

Sa·li·nas \sə-'lē-nəs\ city W California; *pop* 151,060

Salisbury — see HARARE

Salisbury Plain plateau S England; site of Stonehenge

Salop — see SHROPSHIRE

Salt Lake City city, ✳ of Utah; *pop* 181,743

Sal·ton Sea \'sȯl-tᵊn\ saline lake about 235 ft. (72 m.) below sea level SE California; formed by diversion of water from Colorado River

Sal·va·dor \'sal-və-ˌdȯr, ˌsal-və-'\ *or* **Ba·hia** \bä-'ē-ə\ city NE Brazil on the Atlantic; *pop* 2,443,107 — **Sal·va·dor·an** \ˌsal-və-'dȯr-ən\ *or* **Sal·va·dor·ean** *or* **Sal·va·dor·ian** \-ē-ən\ *adj or n*

Sal·ween \'sal-ˌwēn\ river about 1500 mi. (2415 km.) long SE Asia flowing from Tibet S into Bay of Bengal in Myanmar

Sa·mar \'sä-ˌmär\ island *cen* Philippines

Sa·ma·ra \sə-'mär-ə\ *or* *1935–91* **Kuy·by·shev** \'kwē-bə-ˌshef, 'kü-ē-bə-, -ˌshev\ city W Russia, on the Volga; *pop* 1,239,000

Sa·mar·ia \sə-'mer-ē-ə\ district of ancient Palestine W of the Jordan between Galilee & Judaea

Sam·ar·qand *or* **Sam·ar·kand** \'sa-mər-ˌkand\ city E Uzbekistan; *pop* 370,500

Sam·ni·um \'sam-nē-əm\ ancient country S *cen* Italy — **Sam·nite** \'sam-ˌnīt\ *adj or n*

Sa·moa \sə-'mō-ə\ **1** islands SW *cen* Pacific N of Tonga; divided at longitude 171° W into American Samoa (or Eastern Samoa) & independent Samoa **2** *formerly* **Western Samoa** islands Samoa W of 171° W; country; ✳ Apia; *pop* 156,349 — **Sa·mo·an** \sə-'mō-ən\ *adj or n*

Sa·mos \'sä-ˌmäs, 'sä-ˌmȯs\ island Greece in the Aegean off coast of Turkey

San·aa *or* **Sana** \sa-'nä, 'sa-ˌnä\ city SW Arabia, ✳ of Yemen; *pop* 125,093

San An·dre·as Fault \ˌsan-an-'drä-əs\ zone of faults in California extending from N coast toward head of Gulf of California

San An·to·nio \ˌsan-ən-'tō-nē-ˌō\ city S Texas; *pop* 1,144,646

San Ber·nar·di·no \ˌsan-ˌbər-nə(r)-'dē-(ˌ)nō\ city S California; *pop* 185,401

San Di·ego \ˌsan-dē-'ā-(ˌ)gō\ coastal city SW California; *pop* 1,223,400

San·i·bel Island \'sa-nə-bəl, -ˌbel\ island SW Florida

Sand·wich \'san(d)-(ˌ)wich\ town SE England; *pop* 4227

Sandwich Islands — see HAWAII

San Fran·cis·co \ˌsan-frən-'sis-(ˌ)kō\ city W California on San Francisco Bay & Pacific Ocean; *pop* 776,733

San Joa·quin \ˌsan-wä-'kēn, -wò-\ river 350 mi. (563 km.) long *cen* California flowing NW into the Sacramento

San Jo·se \ˌsan-(h)ō-'zā\ city W California SE of San Francisco; *pop* 894,943

San Jo·sé \ˌsän-hō-'sā, ˌsan-(h)ō-'zā\ city, ✳ of Costa Rica; *pop* 330,529

San Juan \san-'wän, ˌsän-'hwän\ city, ✳ of Puerto Rico; *pop* 434,374

San Ma·ri·no \ˌsan-mə-'rē-(ˌ)nō\ **1** small country S Europe surrounded by Italy ENE of Florence near Adriatic Sea; *pop* 24,000 **2** town, its ✳; *pop* 2300 — **Sam·mar·i·nese** \ˌsa(m)-ˌma-rə-'nēz, -'nēs\ *n* — **San Mar·i·nese** \ˌsan-ˌma-\ *adj or n*

633

Geographical Names

San Pe·dro Su·la \sän-'pä-(ˌ)thrō-'sü-lä\ city NW Honduras; *pop* 300,400

San Sal·va·dor \san-'sal-və-ˌdor, ˌsän-'säl-vä-ˌthȯr\ **1** island *cen* Bahamas **2** city, ✻ of El Salvador; *pop* 349,333

San·ta Ana \ˌsan-tə-'a-nə, ˌsän-tä-'ä-nä\ city SW California ESE of Long Beach; *pop* 337,977

San·ta Bar·ba·ra \'bär-b(ə-)rə\ *or* **Channel** islands California off SW coast in the North Pacific

Santa Clara \'kler-ə\ city W California NW of San Jose; *pop* 102,361

Santa Cla·ri·ta \klə-'rē-tə\ city S California N of Los Angeles; *pop* 151,088

San·ta Fe \ˌsan-tə-'fā\ city, ✻ of New Mexico; *pop* 62,203

Santa Fe Trail pioneer route to the SW U.S. about 1200 mi. (1930 km.) long used esp. 1821–80 from vicinity of Kansas City, Missouri, to Santa Fe, New Mexico

Santa Rosa \ˌsan-tə-'rō-zə\ city W California N of San Francisco; *pop* 147,595

San·ti·a·go \ˌsan-tē-'ä-(ˌ)gō, ˌsän-\ city, ✻ of Chile; *pop* 200,792

San·to Do·min·go \ˌsan-tə-də-'miŋ-(ˌ)gō\ *formerly* **Tru·ji·llo** \trü-'hē-(ˌ)yō\ city, ✻ of Dominican Republic; metropolitan area *pop* 2,677,056

São Pau·lo \saůⁿ-'paů-(ˌ)lü, -(ˌ)lō\ city SE Brazil; *pop* 10,434,252

São To·mé \ˌsaůⁿ-tə-'mā\ town, ✻ of São Tomé and Príncipe; *pop* 43,420

São Tomé and Príncipe country W Africa; ✻ São Tomé; *pop* 128,000

Sap·po·ro \'sä-pō-ˌrō; sä-'pȯr-(ˌ)ō\ city Japan on W Hokkaido; *pop* 1,822,368

Sa·ra·je·vo \ˌsa-rə-'yā-(ˌ)vō, ˌsär-ə-\ city SE *cen* Bosnia and Herzegovina, its ✻; *pop* (est.) 602,500

Sa·ra·tov \sə-'rä-təf\ city W Russia, on the Volga; *pop* 909,000

Sar·din·ia \sär-'di-nē-ə, -'di-nyə\ island Italy in the Mediterranean S of Corsica; *pop* 1,648,044 — **Sar·din·ian** \sär-'di-nē-ən, -'din-yən\ *adj or n*

Sar·gas·so Sea \sär-'ga-(ˌ)sō\ area of nearly still water in the North Atlantic lying chiefly between 20° & 35° N latitude & 30° & 70° W longitude

Sas·katch·e·wan \sə-'ska-chə-wən, sa-, -ˌwän\ province W Canada; ✻, Regina; *pop* 1,015,783

Sas·ka·toon \ˌsas-kə-'tün\ city *cen* Saskatchewan, Canada; *pop* 196,811

Sau·di Ara·bia \ˌsaů-dē, 'sȯ-dē, sä-'ü-dē\ country SW Asia occupying largest part of Arabian Peninsula; ✻, Riyadh; *pop* 20,800,000 — **Saudi** *adj or n* — **Saudi Arabian** *adj or n*

Sault Sainte Ma·rie Canals \'sü-(ˌ)sänt-mə-'rē\ *or* **Soo Canals** \ˌsü\ three ship canals, two in U.S. (Michigan) & one in Canada (Ontario), at rapids in river connecting Lake Superior & Lake Huron

Sa·vaii \sə-'vī-ˌē\ island, largest in independent Samoa

Sa·van·nah \sə-'va-nə\ city & port E Georgia; *pop* 131,510

Sa·voy \sə-'voi\ *or French* **Sa·voie** \sä-'vwä\ region SE France SW of Switzerland bordering on Italy — **Sa·voy·ard** \sə-'voi-ˌärd, ˌsa-ˌvoi-'ärd, ˌsa-ˌvwä-'yär(d)\ *adj or n*

Sca·fell Pike \skō-'fel\ mountain 3210 ft. (978 m.) NW England; highest in Cumbrian Mountains & in England

Scan·di·na·via \ˌskan-də-'nā-vē-ə, -vyə\ **1** peninsula N Europe occupied by Norway & Sweden **2** Denmark, Norway, Sweden, & sometimes also Iceland & Finland — **Scan·di·na·vian** \ˌskan-də-'nā-vē-ən, -vyən\ *adj or n*

Scar·bor·ough \'skär-ˌbər-ō\ former city Canada in SE Ontario; now part of Toronto

Schel·de \'skel-də\ *or* **Scheldt** \'skelt\ river 270 mi. (434 km.) long W Europe flowing from N France through Belgium into North Sea in Netherlands

Schuyl·kill \'skü-kᵊl, 'skül-ˌkil\ river 131 mi. (211 km.) long SE Pennsylvania flowing SE into the Delaware River at Philadelphia

Scil·ly, Isles of \'si-lē\ island group SW England off Land's End; *pop* 2900

Sco·tia \'skō-shə\ SCOTLAND — the Medieval Latin name

Scot·land \'skät-lənd\ *or Latin* **Cal·e·do·nia** \ˌka-lə-'dō-nyə, -nē-ə\ country N Great Britain; a division of United Kingdom; ✻, Edinburgh; *pop* 5,062,011

Scotts·dale \'skäts-ˌdāl\ city SW Arizona E of Phoenix; *pop* 202,705

Scyth·ia \'si-thē-ə, -the̱-\ ancient area of Europe & Asia N & NE of Black Sea & E of Aral Sea — **Scyth·i·an** \'si-thē-ən, -the̱-\ *adj or n*

Se·at·tle \sē-'a-tᵊl\ city & port W Washington; *pop* 563,374

Seine \'sän, 'sen\ river 480 mi. (772 km.) long N France flowing NW into English Channel

Sel·kirk \'sel-ˌkərk\ range of the Rocky Mountains SE British Columbia, Canada; highest peak, 11,555 ft. (3522 m.)

Se·ma·rang \sə-'mär-ˌäŋ\ city Indonesia in *cen* Java; *pop* 1,250,971

Sen·dai \(ˌ)sen-'dī\ city Japan in NE Honshu; *pop* 1,008,130

Sen·e·ca Falls \'se-ni-kə\ village W *cen* New York; *pop* 6861

Sen·e·gal \ˌse-ni-'gȯl, -'gäl, 'se-ni-ˌ\ **1** river 1015 mi. (1633 km.) long W Africa flowing N into the North Atlantic **2** country W Africa; ✻, Dakar; *pop* 7,899,000 — **Sen·e·ga·lese** \ˌse-ni-gə-'lēz, -'lēs\ *adj or n*

Seoul \'sōl\ city, ✻ of South Korea; *pop* 9,853,972

Ser·bia \'sər-bē-ə\ country S Europe ✻ Belgrade; a former republic of Yugoslavia; *pop* 9,823,000

Serbia and Montenegro *or 1992–2003* **Yugoslavia** former country S Europe on Balkan Peninsula; ✻, Belgrade

Ser·en·ge·ti Plain \ˌser-ən-'ge-tē\ area N Tanzania

Seven Hills the seven hills upon and about which was built the city of Rome, Italy

Sev·ern \'se-vərn\ river 210 mi. (338 km.) long Wales & England flowing from E Wales into Bristol Channel

Se·ville \sə-'vil\ *or Spanish* **Se·vi·lla** \sā-'vē-(ˌ)yä\ city SW Spain; *pop* 684,633

Sew·ard Peninsula \'sü-ərd\ peninsula 180 mi. (290 km.) long W Alaska projecting into Bering Sea

Sey·chelles \sā-'shel(z)\ islands W Indian Ocean NE of Madagascar; country; ✻, Victoria; *pop* 72,700 — **Sey·chel·lois** \ˌsā-shəl-'wä, -ˌshel-\ *n*

Shang·hai \shaŋ-'hī\ municipality & port E China; *pop* 7,469,509

Shan·non \'sha-nən\ river 230 mi. (370 km.) long W Ireland flowing S & W into the North Atlantic

Sharon, Plain of \'sher-ən\ region Israel on the coast

Shas·ta, Mount \'shas-tə\ mountain 14,162 ft. (4316 m.) N California in Cascade Range

Shatt al Ar·ab \ˌshat-al-'a-rəb\ river 120 mi. (193 km.) long SE Iraq formed by flowing together of Euphrates & Tigris rivers and flowing SE into Persian Gulf

Shef·field \'she-ˌfēld\ city N England; *pop* 499,700

Shen·an·do·ah \ˌshe-nən-'dō-ə, ˌsha-nə-'dō-ə\ valley Virginia between the Allegheny & Blue Ridge mountains

Shen·yang \'shən-'yäŋ\ *or traditionally* **Muk·den** \'mük-dən, 'mək-; mük-'den\ city NE China; chief city of Manchuria; *pop* 3,603,712

Sher·brooke \'shər-ˌbrúk\ city Quebec, Canada SE of Montreal; *pop* 75,916

Sher·wood Forest \'shər-ˌwúd\ ancient royal forest *cen* England

Shet·land \'shet-lənd\ islands N Scotland NE of the Orkneys; *pop* 22,270

Shi·jia·zhuang *or* **Shih–chia–chuang** \'shir-'jyä-'jwäŋ, 'shē-\ city N China; *pop* 1,068,439

Shi·ko·ku \shē-'kō-(ˌ)kü\ island S Japan E of Kyushu; *pop* 4,195,106

Shi·raz \shi-'räz, -'raz\ city SW *cen* Iran; *pop* 848,289

Shreve·port \'shrēv-ˌpȯrt\ city NW Louisiana on Red River; *pop* 200,145

Shrews·bury \'shrü(z)z-ˌber-ē, -b(ə-)rē\ town W England; *pop* 31,640

Shrop·shire \'shräp-shər, -ˌshir\ *or 1974–80* **Sal·op** \'sal-əp\ county W England bordering on Wales

Shu·ma·gin \'shü-mə-gən\ islands SW Alaska S of Alaska Peninsula

Siam — see THAILAND

Siam, Gulf of — see THAILAND, GULF OF

Si·be·ria \sī-'bir-ē-ə\ region N Asia in Russia between the Urals & the North Pacific — **Si·be·ri·an** \-ən\ *adj or n*

Sic·i·ly \'si-s(ə-)lē\ *or Italian* **Si·ci·lia** \sē-'chēl-yä\ island S

Italy SW of toe of peninsula of Italy; ✳, Palermo; *pop* 5,076,700 — **Si·cil·ian** \sə-'sil-yən\ *adj or n*

Si·er·ra Le·one \sē-,er-ə-lē-'ōn, ,sir-ə-, -lē-'ō-nē\ country W Africa on the North Atlantic; ✳, Freetown; *pop* 4,491,000 — **Si·er·ra Le·on·ean** \-'ō-nē-ən\ *adj or n*

Si·er·ra Ma·dre \sē-,er-ə-'mä-drā, 'syer-ä-'mä-thrä\ mountain system Mexico including **Sierra Madre Oc·ci·den·tal** \,äk-sə-,den-'täl, ,ok-sē-,then-'täl\ range W of the *cen* plateau, **Sierra Madre Ori·en·tal** \,ór-ē-,en-'täl\ range E of the plateau, & **Sierra del Sur** \'sùr, 'sür\ range to the S

Sierra Ne·va·da \nə-'va-də, -'vä-\ **1** mountain range E California & W Nevada — see WHITNEY, MOUNT **2** mountain range S Spain

Sik·kim \'si-kəm, -,kim\ former country SE Asia on S slope of the Himalayas between Nepal & Bhutan; part of India (country); *pop* 406,457

Si·le·sia \sī-'lē-zh(ē-)ə, sə-, -sh(ē-)ə\ region E *cen* Europe in valley of the upper Oder; formerly chiefly in Germany now chiefly in E Czech Republic & SW Poland — **Si·le·sian** \-zh(ē-)ən, -sh(ē-)ən\ *adj or n*

Silk Road *or* **Silk Route** ancient trade route that extended from China to the Mediterranean

Sim·coe, Lake \'sim-(,)kō\ lake Canada in SE Ontario

Si·mi Valley \sē-'mē\ city SW California W of Los Angeles; *pop* 111,351

Sim·plon Pass \'sim-,plän\ mountain pass 6590 ft. (2009 m.) between Switzerland & Italy

Si·nai \'sī-,nī\ **1** mountain on Sinai Peninsula where according to the Bible the Law was given to Moses **2** peninsula extension of continent of Asia NE Egypt between Red Sea & the Mediterranean

Sin·ga·pore \'siŋ-ə-,pór\ **1** island off S end of Malay Peninsula; country; *pop* 4,163,700 **2** city, its ✳; *pop* 206,500 — **Sin·ga·por·ean** \,siŋ-ə-'pór-ē-ən\ *adj or n*

Sinkiang Uighur — see XINJIANG UYGUR

Sioux Falls \'sü\ city SE South Dakota; largest in state; *pop* 123,975

Skag·ge·rak \'ska-gə-,rak\ arm of North Sea between S Norway & N Denmark

Skop·je \'skó-pye, -pyə\ city, ✳ of independent Macedonia; *pop* 563,301

Sla·vo·nia \slə-'vō-nē-ə, -nyə\ region E Croatia — **Sla·vo·ni·an** \-nē-ən, -nyən\ *adj or n*

Slo·va·kia \slō-'vä-kē-ə, -'va-\ country *cen* Europe; ✳, Bratislava; *pop* 5,379,455

Slo·ve·nia \slō-'vē-nē-ə, -nyə\ country S Europe; ✳, Ljubljana; *pop* 1,975,164

Smyrna — see IZMIR

Snake \'snāk\ river NW U.S. flowing from NW Wyoming into the Columbia in SE Washington

Snow·don \'snō-dᵊn\ massif 3560 ft. (1085 m.) in **Snow·do·nia** \snō-'dō-nē-ə, -nyə\ (mountainous district) NW Wales; highest point in Wales

So·ci·e·ty \sə-'sī-ə-tē\ islands South Pacific; belonging to France; chief island, Tahiti; *pop* 162,573

So·fia \'sō-fē-ə, 'só-, sō-'\ city, ✳ of Bulgaria; *pop* 1,141,142

So·ho \'sō-,hō\ district of *cen* London, England

So·li·hull \,sō-li-'həl\ city *cen* England; *pop* 194,100

Sol·o·mon \'sä-lə-mən\ **1** islands W Pacific E of New Guinea divided between Papua New Guinea & independent Solomon Islands **2** sea, arm of Coral Sea W of the Solomons

Solomon Islands country, SW Pacific E of New Guinea; ✳, Honiara (on Guadalcanal); *pop* 349,000

So·ma·lia \sō-'mä-lē-ə, sə-, -'mäl-yə\ country E Africa on Gulf of Aden & Indian Ocean; ✳, Mogadishu; *pop* 8,050,000 — **So·ma·li·an** \-'mä-lē-ən, -'mäl-yən\ *adj or n*

So·ma·li·land \sō-'mä-lē-,land, sə-\ region E Africa consisting of Somalia, Djibouti, & part of E Ethiopia — **So·ma·li** \sō-'mä-lē, sə-\ *n*

Som·er·set \'sə-mər-,set, -sət\ *or* **Som·er·set·shire** \-,shir, -shər\ county SW England

So·nor·an \sə-'nór-ən\ *or* **So·no·ra** \sə-'nór-ə\ desert SW U.S. & NW Mexico

Soo Canals — see SAULT SAINTE MARIE CANALS

South island S New Zealand; *pop* 906,756

South Africa, Republic of *formerly* **Union of South Africa** country S Africa; administrative ✳, Pretoria; legislative ✳, Cape Town; judicial ✳, Bloemfontein; *pop* 30,193,000 — **South African** *adj or n*

South America continent of Western Hemisphere SE of North America and chiefly S of the Equator — **South American** *adj or n*

South·amp·ton \saù-'tham(p)-tən, saùth-'ham(p)-\ city S England; *pop* 194,400

South Australia state S Australia; ✳, Adelaide; *pop* 1,462,900 — **South Australian** *adj or n*

South Bend \'bend\ city N Indiana; *pop* 107,789

South Cape *or* **South Point** — see KA LAE

South Car·o·li·na \,ker(-ə)-'lī-nə, ,ka-rə-\ state SE U.S.; ✳, Columbia; *pop* 4,012,012 — **South Car·o·lin·i·an** \-'lī-nē-ən, -'li-nyən\ *adj or n*

South China Sea — see CHINA

South Da·ko·ta \də-'kō-tə\ state NW *cen* U.S.; ✳, Pierre; *pop* 754,844 — **South Da·ko·tan** \-'kō-tᵊn\ *adj or n*

South·end–on–Sea \,saù-,thend-,ón-'sē, -,än-\ seaside resort SE England E of London; *pop* 153,700

Southern Alps mountain range New Zealand in W South Island extending almost the length of the island

Southern Hemisphere the half of the earth that lies S of the Equator

South Georgia island S Atlantic E of Tierra del Fuego; administered by United Kingdom

South Korea *or* **Republic of South Korea** country S half of Korean Peninsula in E Asia; ✳, Seoul; *pop* 45,985,289

South Seas the areas of the Atlantic, Indian, & Pacific oceans in the Southern Hemisphere

South Shields \'shēldz\ seaport N England; *pop* 87,203

South Vietnam — see VIETNAM

South·wark \'sə-thərk, 'saùth-wərk\ borough of S Greater London, England; *pop* 196,500

South–West Africa — see NAMIBIA

South Yorkshire metropolitan county N England; *pop* 1,248,500

Soviet Central Asia portion of *cen* & SW Asia formerly belonging to U.S.S.R. and including the former soviet socialist republics of present-day Kyrgyzstan, Tajikistan, Uzbekistan & sometimes Kazakhstan

Soviet Union — see UNION OF SOVIET SOCIALIST REPUBLICS

So·we·to \sō-'wä-tō, -'we-, -tü\ residential area NE Republic of South Africa adjoining SW Johannesburg

Spain \'spān\ country SW Europe on Iberian Peninsula; ✳, Madrid; *pop* 39,141,000

Spanish America 1 the Spanish-speaking countries of America **2** the parts of America settled and formerly governed by the Spanish

Spanish Guinea — see EQUATORIAL GUINEA

Spanish Sahara — see WESTERN SAHARA

Spar·ta \'spär-tə\ ancient city S Greece in Peloponnese; ✳ of Laconia

Spo·kane \spō-'kan\ city E Washington; *pop* 195,629

Spring·field \'spriŋ-,fēld\ **1** city, ✳ of Illinois; *pop* 111,454 **2** city SW Massachusetts; *pop* 152,082 **3** city SW Missouri; *pop* 151,580

Sri Lan·ka \(,)srē-'läŋ-kə, (,)shrē-, -'laŋ-\ *formerly* **Cey·lon** \si-'län, sā-\ country having the same boundaries as island of Ceylon; ✳, Colombo; *pop* 17,829,500 — **Sri Lan·kan** \-'läŋ-kən, -'laŋ-\ *adj or n*

Sri·na·gar \srē-'nə-gər\ city N India; *pop* 894,940

Staf·ford \'sta-fərd\ town W *cen* England; *pop* 117,000

Staf·ford·shire \'sta-fərd-,shir, -shər\ *or* **Stafford** county W *cen* England

Staked Plain — see LLANO ESTACADO

Stam·ford \'stam-fərd\ city SW Connecticut; *pop* 117,083

Stan·ley \'stan-lē\ town, ✳ of Falkland Islands; *pop* 1559

Stat·en Island \'sta-tᵊn\ **1** island SE New York SW of mouth of the Hudson **2** *formerly* **Rich·mond** \'rich-mənd\ borough of New York City including Staten Island; *pop* 443,728

Ster·ling Heights \'stər-liŋ\ city SE Michigan; *pop* 124,471

Stir·ling \'stər-liŋ\ town *cen* Scotland; *pop* 38,638

Stock·holm \'stäk-,hō(l)m\ city, ✳ of Sweden; *pop* 758,148

Stock·port \'stäk-,pórt\ town NW England; *pop* 276,800

Stock·ton \'stäk-tən\ city *cen* California; *pop* 243,771

Stoke–on–Trent \'stōk-,än-'trent, -,ón-\ city *cen* England; *pop* 244,800

Stone·henge \'stōn-ˌhenj, (ˌ)stōn-'\ prehistoric assemblage of megaliths S England in Wiltshire on Salisbury Plain

Stone Mountain mountain 1686 ft. (514 m.) NW Georgia E of Atlanta

Stor·no·way \'stȯr-nə-ˌwä\ seaport NW Scotland; chief town of Lewis with Harris Island; *pop* 8660

Stra·bane \strə-'ban\ district W Northern Ireland; *pop* 35,668

Strath·clyde \strath-'klīd\ former region SW Scotland; included Glasgow

Strom·bo·li \'sträm-bō-(ˌ)lē\ volcano 2500 ft. (758 m.) Italy on **Stromboli Island** in Tyrrhenian Sea

Stutt·gart \'shtût-ˌgärt, 'stût-, 'stət-\ city SW Germany; *pop* 591,946

Styx \'stiks\ chief river of the underworld in Greek mythology

Süchow — see XUZHOU

Su·cre \'sü-(ˌ)krā\ city, constitutional ✳ of Bolivia; *pop* 130,952

Su·dan \sü-'dan, -'dän\ **1** region N Africa S of the Sahara between the Atlantic & the upper Nile **2** country NE Africa S of Egypt; ✳, Khartoum; *pop* 25,000,000 — **Su·da·nese** \ˌsü-də-'nēz, -'nēs\ *adj or n*

Sudbury, Greater — see GREATER SUDBURY

Su·ez, Gulf of \sü-'ez, 'sü-ˌez\ arm of Red Sea

Suez, Isthmus of isthmus NE Egypt between Mediterranean & Red seas connecting Africa & Asia

Suez Canal canal 100 mi. (161 km.) long NE Egypt across the Isthmus of Suez

Suf·folk \'sə-fək\ county E England on North Sea

Sui·sun Bay \sə-'sün\ inlet of San Francisco Bay, W *cen* California

Su·la·we·si \ˌsü-lä-'wä-sē\ island Indonesia E of Borneo; *pop* 12,520,711

Su·lu \'sü-(ˌ)lü\ **1** archipelago SW Philippines SW of Mindanao **2** sea W Philippines

Su·ma·tra \sù-'mä-trə\ island W Indonesia S of Malay Peninsula — **Su·ma·tran** \-trən\ *adj or n*

Su·mer \'sü-mər\ the S division of ancient Babylonia — **Su·me·ri·an** \sü-'mer-ē-ən, -'mir-\ *adj or n*

Sun·belt \'sən-ˌbelt\ region S & SW U.S.

Sun·da \'sün-də, 'sən-\ strait between Java & Sumatra

Sun·der·land \'sən-dər-lənd\ seaport N England; *pop* 286,800

Sun·ny·vale \'sə-nē-ˌväl\ city W California WNW of San Jose; *pop* 131,760

Sun Valley resort center *cen* Idaho

Su·pe·ri·or, Lake \sù-'pir-ē-ər\ lake E *cen* North America in U.S. & Canada; largest of the Great Lakes

Su·ra·ba·ya \ˌsùr-ə-'bī-ə\ city Indonesia in NE Java; *pop* 2,483,871

Su·ri·na·me \ˌsùr-ə-'nä-mə\ country N South America between Guyana & French Guiana; ✳, Paramaribo; *pop* 403,000 — **Su·ri·nam·er** \'sùr-ə-ˌnä-mər, ˌsùr-ə-'nä-\ *n* — **Su·ri·nam·ese** \ˌsùr-ə-nə-'mēz, -'mēs\ *adj or n*

Sur·rey \'sər-ē, 'sə-rē\ city Canada in SW British Columbia; *pop* 347,825

Sut·ton \'sə-tᵊn\ borough of S Greater London, England; *pop* 164,300

Su·va \'sü-və\ city & port, ✳ of Fiji on Viti Levu Island; *pop* 63,628

Su·wan·nee \sə-'wä-nē, 'swä-\ river 250 mi. (400 km.) SE U.S. flowing SW into Gulf of Mexico

Sverdlovsk — see YEKATERINBURG

Swan·sea \'swän-zē\ city & port SE Wales; *pop* 182,100

Swa·zi·land \'swä-zē-ˌland\ country SE Africa between Republic of South Africa & Mozambique; ✳, Mbabane; *pop* 929,718 — **Swa·zi** \'swä-zē\ *adj or n*

Swe·den \'swē-dᵊn\ country N Europe on Scandinavia (peninsula) bordering on Baltic Sea; ✳, Stockholm; *pop* 8,940,788

Swit·zer·land \'swit-sər-lənd\ country W Europe in the Alps; ✳, Bern; *pop* 6,996,000

Syd·ney \'sid-nē\ city SE Australia, ✳ of New South Wales; metropolitan area *pop* 3,097,956

Syr·a·cuse \'sir-ə-ˌkyüs, -ˌkyüz\ city *cen* New York; *pop* 147,306

Syr·ia \'sir-ē-ə\ **1** ancient region SW Asia bordering on the Mediterranean **2** country S of Turkey; ✳, Damascus; *pop* 13,398,000 — **Syr·i·an** \'sir-ē-ən\ *adj or n*

Syrian Desert desert region between Mediterranean coast & the Euphrates in N Saudi Arabia, SE Syria, W Iraq, & NE Jordan

Table Bay harbor of Cape Town, Republic of South Africa

Ta·briz \tä-'brēz\ city NW Iran; *pop* 971,482

Ta·co·ma \tə-'kō-mə\ city & port W Washington S of Seattle; *pop* 193,556

Tae·gu \'tä-gü, 'dä-\ *or* **Dae·gu** \'dä-\ city SE South Korea; *pop* 2,473,990

Tae·jon \'tä-'jǝn, 'dä-\ *or* **Dae·jeon** \'dä-\ city *cen* South Korea NW of Taegu; *pop* 1,365,961

Ta·gus \'tä-gəs\ *or Spanish* **Ta·jo** \'tä-(ˌ)hō\ *or Portuguese* **Te·jo** \'tä-(ˌ)zhü\ river 626 mi. (1007 km.) long Spain & Portugal flowing W into the North Atlantic

Ta·hi·ti \tə-'hē-tē\ island South Pacific in Society Islands; *pop* 131,309

Tai·bei \'tī-'bä\ *or* **Tai·pei** \'tī-'pā, -'bä\ city, ✳ of (Nationalist) China in N Taiwan; *pop* 2,651,419

T'ai–nan \'tī-'nän\ city SW Taiwan; *pop* 702,237

Tai·wan \'tī-'wän\ *formerly* **For·mo·sa** \fȯr-'mō-sə, fər-, -zə\ **1** island China off SE coast of mainland; seat of government of (Nationalist) Republic of China; ✳, Taibei; *pop* 20,926,000 **2** strait between Taiwan & mainland of China connecting East China & South China seas — **Tai·wan·ese** \ˌtī-wə-'nēz, -'nēs\ *adj or n*

Tai·yuan \'tī-'ywen, -'ywän\ city N China; *pop* 1,533,884

Tai·zhong \'tī-'jùŋ\ *or* **Tai·chung** \'tī-'chùŋ\ city W Taiwan; *pop* 779,370

Ta·jik·i·stan \tä-ji-ki-'stan, tə-, -ˌjē-, -'stän\ country W *cen* Asia bordering on China & Afghanistan; ✳, Dushanbe; *pop* 5,705,000

Ta·kli·ma·kan \ˌtä-klə-mə-'kän\ desert W China

Ta–lien — see DALIAN

Tal·la·has·see \ˌta-lə-'ha-sē\ city, ✳ of Florida; *pop* 150,624

Tal·linn \'ta-lən, 'tä-\ city, ✳ of Estonia; *pop* 398,434

Tam·pa \'tam-pə\ city W Florida on **Tampa Bay** (inlet of Gulf of Mexico); *pop* 303,447

Tan·gan·yi·ka \ˌtan-gə-'nyē-kə, ˌtaŋ-gə-, -'nē-\ former country E Africa S of Kenya; now part of Tanzania

Tanganyika, Lake lake E Africa between Tanzania & Democratic Republic of the Congo

Tang·shan \'däŋ-'shän, 'täŋ-\ city NE China; *pop* 1,044,194

Tan·za·nia \ˌtan-zə-'nē-ə, ˌtän-\ country E Africa on Indian Ocean, including Zanzibar; designated ✳, Dodoma; seat of government, Dar es Salaam; *pop* 26,542,000 — **Tan·za·ni·an** \-'nē-ən\ *adj or n*

Ta·ra·wa \tə-'rä-wə, 'ta-rə-ˌwä\ island *cen* Pacific, contains ✳ of Kiribati; *pop* 28,802

Tar·ry·town \'ta-rē-ˌtaùn\ village SE New York; *pop* 11,090

Tar·sus \'tär-səs\ ancient city of S Asia Minor; now a city in S Turkey

Tash·kent \tash-'kent, täsh-\ city, ✳ of Uzbekistan; *pop* 2,073,000

Tas·ma·nia \taz-'mā-nē-ə, -nyə\ *or earlier* **Van Die·men's Land** \van-'dē-mənz-\ island SE Australia S of Victoria; a state; ✳, Hobart; *pop* 471,400 — **Tas·ma·nian** \taz-'mā-nē-ən, -nyən\ *adj or n*

Tasman Sea \'taz-mən\ the part of the South Pacific between SE Australia & New Zealand

Ta·try \'tä-trē\ *or* **Ta·tra** \'tä-trə\ mountains N Slovakia & S Poland in *cen* Carpathian Mountains

Taun·ton \'tȯn-tᵊn, 'tän-\ town SW England; *pop* 35,326

Tbi·li·si \tə-'bē-lə-sē, tə-bə-'lē-sē\ *or* **Tif·lis** \'ti-fləs, tə-'flēs\ city, ✳ of Republic of Georgia; *pop* 1,260,000

Te·gu·ci·gal·pa \tə-ˌgü-sə-'gal-pə, tä-ˌgü-sē-'gäl-pä\ city, ✳ of Honduras; *pop* 608,100

Teh·ran \ˌtä-(ə-)'ran, te-'ran, -'rän\ city, ✳ of Iran; at foot of S slope of Elburz Mountains; *pop* 6,042,584

Tel Aviv \ˌtel-ə-'vēv\ city W Israel on the Mediterranean; *pop* 353,200

Tem·pe \tem-'pē\ city S *cen* Arizona; *pop* 158,625

Ten·nes·see \ˌte-nə-'sē, 'te-nə-\ **1** river 652 mi. (1049 km.) long in Tennessee, N Alabama, & W Kentucky **2** state E *cen* U.S.; ✳, Nashville; *pop* 5,689,283 — **Ten·nes·se·an** *or* **Ten·nes·see·an** \ˌte-nə-'sē-ən\ *adj or n*

Te·noch·ti·tlan \tä-ˌnöch-tĕt-ˈlän\ ancient name of Mexico City

Tex·as \ˈtek-səs, -siz\ state S U.S.; ✻, Austin; *pop* 20,851,820 — Tex·an \-sən\ *adj or n*

Texas Panhandle the NW projection of land in Texas

Thai·land \ˈtī-ˌland, -lənd\ *formerly* Si·am \sī-ˈam\ country SE Asia on Gulf of Thailand; ✻, Bangkok; *pop* 60,617,200 — Thai·land·er \-ˌlan-dər, -lən-\ *n*

Thailand, Gulf of *formerly* Gulf of Siam arm of South China Sea between Indochina & Malay Peninsula

Thames \ˈtemz\ river over 200 mi. (322 km.) long S England flowing E from the Cotswolds into the North Sea

Thar \ˈtär\ desert E Pakistan & NW India (country) E of Indus River

Thebes \ˈthēbz\ 1 *or* The·bae \ˈthē-ˌbē\ ancient city S Egypt on the Nile 2 ancient city E Greece NNW of Athens — The·ban \ˈthē-bən\ *adj or n*

Thes·sa·lo·ní·ki \ˌthe-sä-lö-ˈnē-kē\ city N Greece; *pop* 402,443

Thim·phu \tim-ˈpü\ city, ✻ of Bhutan; *pop* 45,000

Thousand Islands island group Canada & U.S. in the Saint Lawrence River in Ontario & New York

Thousand Oaks city SW California W of Los Angeles; *pop* 117,005

Thrace \ˈthrās\ *or ancient* Thra·cia \ˈthrä-sh(ē-)ə\ region SE Europe in Balkan Peninsula N of the Aegean now divided between Greece & Turkey; in ancient times extended N to the Danube — Thra·cian \ˈthrä-shən\ *adj or n*

Thunder Bay city SW Ontario, Canada on Lake Superior; *pop* 109,016

Tian·jin \ˈtyän-ˈjin\ *or* Tien·tsin \ˈtyen-ˈtsin, ˈtin-\ city NE China SE of Beijing; *pop* 7,764,141

Tian Shan *or* Tien Shan \ˈtyen-ˈshän, -ˈshan\ mountain system *cen* Asia extending NE from Pamirs

Ti·ber \ˈtī-bər\ *or Italian* Te·ve·re \ˈtä-vā-rä\ river 252 mi. (405 km.) long *cen* Italy flowing through Rome into Tyrrhenian Sea

Tiberias, Lake — see GALILEE, SEA OF

Ti·bes·ti \tə-ˈbes-tē\ mountains N *cen* Africa in *cen* Sahara in NW Chad; highest 11,204 ft. (3415 m.)

Ti·bet \tə-ˈbet\ *or* Xi·zang \ˈshēd-ˈzäng\ region SW China on high plateau at average altitude 16,000 ft. (4877 m.) N of the Himalayas; ✻, Lhasa; *pop* 2,196,010

Tier·ra del Fue·go \tē-ˈer-ə-(ˌ)del-fü-ˈä-(ˌ)gō, ˈtyer-ä-(ˌ)thel-ˈfwä-gō\ 1 island group off S South America 2 chief island of the group; divided between Argentina & Chile

Tiflis — see TBILISI

Ti·gris \ˈtī-grəs\ river 1180 mi. (1899 km.) long Turkey & Iraq flowing SSE and uniting with the Euphrates to form the Shatt al Arab

Ti·jua·na \ˌtē-ə-ˈwä-nə, tē-ˈhwä-nä\ city NW Mexico on the U.S. border; *pop* 991,592

Tim·buk·tu \ˌtim-ˌbək-ˈtü, tim-ˈbək-(ˌ)tü\ *or* Tom·bouc·tou \tōⁿ-bük-ˈtü\ town Mali near Niger River; *pop* 31,925

Ti·mor \ˈtē-ˌmòr, tē-ˈ\ island S Malay archipelago SE of Sulawesi; W half part of Indonesia, E half independent East Timor

Ti·ra·ne *or* Ti·ra·na \ti-ˈrä-nə, tē-\ city, ✻ of Albania; *pop* 519,720

Ti·rol *or* Ty·rol \tə-ˈröl\ *or Italian* Ti·ro·lo \tē-ˈrö-(ˌ)lö\ region in E Alps in W Austria & NE Italy — Ti·ro·le·an \tə-ˈrö-lē-ən, tī-\ *or* Tir·o·lese \ˌtir-ə-ˈlēz, ˌtī-rə-, -ˈlēs\ *adj or n*

Ti·ti·ca·ca, Lake \ˌti-ti-ˈkä-kä, ˌtē-tē-\ lake on Bolivia–Peru boundary at altitude of 12,500 ft. (3810 m.)

To·ba·go \tə-ˈbä-(ˌ)gö\ island West Indies NE of Trinidad; part of independent Trinidad and Tobago; *pop* 54,084 — To·ba·go·ni·an \ˌtō-bə-ˈgö-nē-ən, -nyən\ *n*

To·go \ˈtō-(ˌ)gö\ country W Africa on Gulf of Guinea; ✻, Lomé; *pop* 3,810,000 — To·go·lese \ˌtō-gə-ˈlēz, -ˈlēs\ *adj or n*

To·kyo \ˈtō-kē-ˌō, -ˌkyō\ city, ✻ of Japan in SE Honshu on Tokyo Bay; *pop* 12,064,101 — To·kyo·ite \ˈtō-kē-(ˌ)ö-ˌīt\ *n*

To·le·do \tə-ˈlē-(ˌ)dō, -ˈlē-də\ city NW Ohio; *pop* 313,619

Tol'·yat·ti \tòl-ˈyä-tē\ city W Russia; NW of Samara; *pop* 666,000

Ton·ga \ˈtäŋ-gə, ˈtäŋ-ə, ˈtòŋ-ä\ islands SW Pacific E of Fiji Islands; country; ✻, Nukualofa; *pop* 101,002 — Ton·gan \-(g)ən\ *adj or n*

Tonkin, Gulf of \ˈtäŋ-kən\ arm of South China Sea E of N Vietnam

To·pe·ka \tə-ˈpē-kə\ city, ✻ of Kansas; *pop* 122,377

Tor·bay \(ˌ)tòr-ˈbā\ urban area SW England; *pop* 122,500

To·ron·to \tə-ˈrän-(ˌ)tö, -ˈrän-tə\ city, ✻ of Ontario, Canada; *pop* 2,481,494

Tor·rance \ˈtòr-ən(t)s, ˈtär-\ city SW California; *pop* 137,946

Tor·res \ˈtòr-əs\ strait between New Guinea & Cape York Peninsula, Australia

Tou·louse \tü-ˈlüz\ city SW France; *pop* 390,301

Tower Hamlets borough of E Greater London, England; *pop* 153,500

Trans·vaal \tran(t)s-ˈväl, tranz-\ former province NE Republic of South Africa

Tran·syl·va·nia \ˌtran(t)-səl-ˈvā-nyə, -nē-ə\ region W Romania — Tran·syl·va·nian \-nyən, -nē-ən\ *adj or n*

Transylvanian Alps a S extension of Carpathian Mountains in *cen* Romania

Tren·ton \ˈtren-tⁿn\ city, ✻ of New Jersey; *pop* 85,403

Trin·i·dad \ˈtri-nə-ˌdad\ island West Indies off NE coast of Venezuela; with Tobago forms the independent country of Trinidad and Tobago; ✻, Port of Spain; *pop* 1,262,386 — Trin·i·da·di·an \ˌtri-nə-ˈdä-dē-ən, -ˈdā-\ *adj or n*

Trip·o·li \ˈtri-pə-lē\ 1 city & port NW Lebanon; *pop* 127,611 2 city & port, ✻ of Libya; *pop* 591,062

Tris·tan da Cu·nha \ˌtris-tən-də-ˈkü-nə, -nyə\ island South Atlantic, chief of the Tristan da Cunha Islands (part of British colony of Saint Helena); *pop* 296

Tri·van·drum \tri-ˈvan-drəm\ city S India; *pop* 744,739

Tro·bri·and \ˈtrō-brē-ˌänd, -ˌand\ islands SW Pacific in Solomon Sea belonging to Papua New Guinea

Trond·heim \ˈträn-ˌhäm\ city & port *cen* Norway; *pop* 137,346

Trow·bridge \ˈtrō-(ˌ)brij\ town S England; *pop* 22,984

Troy \ˈtròi\ *or* Il·i·um \ˈi-lē-əm\ *or* Tro·ja \ˈtrö-jə, -yə\ ancient city NW Asia Minor SW of the Dardanelles

Truk — see CHUUK

Tru·ro \ˈtrür-(ˌ)ö\ city SW England; *pop* 16,277

Tsinan — see JINAN

Tsingtao — see QINGDAO

Tuc·son \ˈtü-ˌsän\ city SE Arizona; *pop* 486,699

Tu·la \ˈtü-lä\ city W Russia S of Moscow; *pop* 541,000

Tul·sa \ˈtəl-sə\ city NE Oklahoma; *pop* 393,049

Tu·nis \ˈtü-nəs, ˈtyü-\ city, ✻ of Tunisia; *pop* 620,149

Tu·ni·sia \tü-ˈnē-zh(ē-)ə, tyü-, -ˈni-\ country N Africa on the Mediterranean E of Algeria; ✻, Tunis; *pop* 9,673,600 — Tu·ni·sian \-zh(ē-)ən\ *adj or n*

Tu·rin \ˈtür-ən, ˈtyür-\ city NW Italy on the Po; *pop* 900,987

Tur·ka·na, Lake \tər-ˈka-nə\ *or* Lake Ru·dolf \ˈrü-ˌdòlf, -ˌdälf\ lake N Kenya in Great Rift Valley

Tur·key \ˈtər-kē\ country W Asia & SE Europe between Mediterranean & Black seas; ✻, Ankara; *pop* 50,664,458 — Turk \ˈtərk\ *n*

Turk·men·i·stan \ˌtərk-ˌme-nə-ˈstan, -ˈstän\ country *cen* Asia; ✻, Ashkhabad; *pop* 3,958,000 — Turk·me·ni·an \ˌtərk-ˈmē-nē-ən\ *adj*

Turks and Cai·cos \ˈtərks-ənd-ˈkä-kəs, -ˌkōs\ two groups of islands West Indies at SE end of the Bahamas; a British colony; *pop* 12,350

Tu·tu·ila \ˌtü-tü-ˈwē-lä\ island South Pacific, chief of American Samoa group

Tu·va·lu \tü-ˈvä-(ˌ)lü, -ˈvär-(ˌ)ü\ *formerly* El·lice \ˈe-lis\ islands W Pacific N of Fiji; country; ✻, Funafuti; *pop* 9700 — see GILBERT AND ELLICE ISLANDS

Tyne and Wear \ˈtīn-ənd-ˈwir\ metropolitan county N England

Tyre \ˈtī(-ə)r\ ancient city, ✻ of Phoenicia; now a town of S Lebanon — Tyr·i·an \ˈtir-ē-ən\ *adj or n*

Tyrol — see TIROL — Ty·ro·le·an \tə-ˈrö-lē-ən, tī-\ — Ty·ro·lese \ˌtir-ə-ˈlēz, ˌtī-rə-, -ˈlēs\ *adj or n*

Tyr·rhe·ni·an Sea \tə-ˈrē-nē-ən\ the part of the Mediterranean SW of Italy, N of Sicily, & E of Sardinia & Corsica

Ufa \ü-ˈfä\ city W Russia NE of Samara; *pop* 1,097,000

Ugan·da \ü-ˈgän-də, yü-, -ˈgan-\ country E Africa N of Lake Victoria; ✻, Kampala; *pop* 24,551,021 — Ugan·dan \-dən\ *adj or n*

Ukraine \yü-ˈkrān, ˈyü-ˌ\ country E Europe on N coast of

Black Sea; *, Kiev; *pop* 52,344,000 — Ukrai·ni·an \yü-'krā-nē-ən\ *adj or n*

Ulaan·baa·tar *or* Ulan Ba·tor \ˌü-ˌlän-'bä-ˌtör\ city, * of Mongolia; *pop* 548,400

Ul·san \'ül-'sän\ city SE South Korea; *pop* 1,012,110

Ul·ster \'əl-stər\ 1 region N Ireland (island) consisting of Northern Ireland & N Ireland (country) 2 province N Ireland (country); *pop* 246,714 3 NORTHERN IRELAND

Um·bria \'əm-brē-ə\ region *cen* Italy in the Apennines; *pop* 840,482

Un·ga·va \ˌən-'ga-və\ 1 bay, inlet of Hudson Strait NE Canada 2 peninsula region NE Canada in N Quebec

Union of South Africa — see SOUTH AFRICA, REPUBLIC OF

Union of Soviet Socialist Republics *or* U.S.S.R. *or* Soviet Union country 1922–91 E Europe & N Asia; former union of 15 republics comprising present-day countries of Armenia, Azerbaijan, Belarus, Estonia, Georgia, Kazakhstan, Kyrgyzstan, Latvia, Lithuania, Moldova, Russia, Tajikistan, Turkmenistan, Ukraine, & Uzbekistan

United Arab Emir·ates \'e-mə-rət, -ˌrāts\ country E Arabia on Persian Gulf; composed of seven emirates; *, Abu Dhabi; *pop* 1,986,000

United Kingdom *or in full* United Kingdom of Great Britain and Northern Ireland country W Europe in British Isles consisting of England, Scotland, Wales, Northern Ireland, Channel Islands, & Isle of Man; *, London; *pop* 58,789,194

United Nations international territory; a small area in New York City in E *cen* Manhattan; seat of permanent headquarters of a political organization established in 1945

United States of America *or* United States country North America bordering on Atlantic, Pacific, & Arctic oceans & including Hawaii; *, Washington; *pop* 281,421,906

Upper Volta — see BURKINA FASO — Upper Vol·tan \'väl-tᵊn, 'vōl-, 'vòl-\ *adj or n*

Ural \'yùr-əl\ 1 mountains Russia & Kazakhstan extending about 1640 mi. (2640 km.); usually thought of as dividing line between Europe & Asia; highest about 6214 ft. (1894 m.) 2 river over 1500 mi. (2414 km.) long Russia & Kazakhstan flowing from S end of Ural Mountains into Caspian Sea

Uru·guay \'ùr-ə-ˌgwī, 'yùr-\ 1 river about 1000 mi. (1609 km.) long SE South America 2 country SE South America; *, Montevideo; *pop* 3,149,000 — Uru·guay·an \ˌùr-ə-'gwī-ən, ˌyùr-\ *adj or n*

Ürüm·qi \'ue-'rœm-'chē\ *or* Urum·chi \ù-'rùm-chē, ˌùr-əm-\\ city NW China; *pop* 1,046,898

Us·pa·lla·ta \ˌüs-pä-'yä-tä, -'zhä-\ mountain pass S South America in the Andes between Argentina & Chile

Ustinov — see IZHEVSK

Utah \'yü-ˌtò, -ˌtä\ state W U.S.; *, Salt Lake City; *pop* 2,233,169 — Utah·an \-ˌtò(-ə)n, -ˌtä(-ə)n\ *adj or n* — Utahn \-ˌtò(-ə)n, -ˌtä(-ə)n\ *n*

Uz·bek·i·stan \ˌùz-ˌbe-ki-'stan, ˌəz-, -'stän\ country W *cen* Asia between Aral Sea & Afghanistan; *, Tashkent; *pop* 21,179,000

Va·duz \vä-'düts\ town, * of Liechtenstein; *pop* 4949

Val·dez \val-'dēz\ city & port S Alaska; *pop* 4036

Va·len·cia \və-'len(t)-sh(ē-)ə, -sē-ə\ 1 region & ancient kingdom E Spain 2 city, its *, on the Mediterranean; *pop* 738,441

Val·le·jo \və-'lā-(ˌ)ō\ city W California; *pop* 116,760

Valley Forge locality SE Pennsylvania

Val·let·ta \və-'le-tə\ city, * of Malta; *pop* 9210

Van·cou·ver \van-'kü-vər\ 1 city SW Washington on Columbia River opposite Portland, Oregon; *pop* 143,560 2 island W Canada in SW British Columbia 3 city & port SW British Columbia, Canada; *pop* 545,671

Van Diemen's Land — see TASMANIA

Van·u·atu \ˌvan-ˌwä-'tü, ˌvän-\ *formerly* New Heb·ri·des \'he-brə-ˌdēz\ islands SW Pacific W of Fiji; country; *, Port-Vila; *pop* 142,419

Va·ra·na·si \və-'rä-nə-sē\ city N India; *pop* 1,100,748

Vat·i·can City \'va-ti-kən\ independent state within Rome, Italy; *pop* 911

Ven·e·zu·e·la \ˌve-nə-'zwä-lə, -zə-'wä-; ˌbā-nā-'swä-lä\

country N South America; *, Caracas; *pop* 20,609,000 — Ven·e·zu·e·lan \-lən\ *adj or n*

Ven·ice \'ve-nəs\ *or Italian* Ve·ne·zia \ve-'net-sē-ä\ city N Italy on islands in Lagoon of Venice; *pop* 275,368 — Ve·ne·tian \və-'nē-shən\ *adj or n*

Ven·tu·ra \ven-'tùr-ə, -'tyùr-\ city & port SW California; *pop* 100,916

Ve·ra·cruz \ˌver-ə-'krüz, -'krüs\ city E Mexico; metropolitan area *pop* 560,200

Ver·mont \vər-'mänt\ state NE U.S.; *, Montpelier; *pop* 608,827 — Ver·mont·er \-'män-tər\ *n*

Ve·ro·na \ve-'rō-nä\ city N Italy W of Venice; *pop* 257,477

Ver·sailles \(ˌ)vər-'sī, ver-\ city N France, WSW suburb of Paris; *pop* 91,029

Ve·su·vi·us \və-'sü-vē-əs\ volcano about 4190 ft. (1277 m.) S Italy near Bay of Naples

Vicks·burg \'viks-ˌbərg\ city W Mississippi; *pop* 26,407

Vic·to·ria \vik-'tòr-ē-ə\ 1 city, * of British Columbia, Canada on Vancouver Island; *pop* 74,125 2 island N Canada in Arctic Archipelago 3 state SE Australia; *, Melbourne; *pop* 4,244,221 4 city & port, Hong Kong; *pop* 1,026,870 5 seaport, * of Seychelles; *pop* 28,000 — Vic·to·ri·an \vik-'tòr-ē-ən\ *adj or n*

Victoria, Lake lake E Africa in Tanzania, Kenya, & Uganda

Victoria Falls waterfall 355 ft. (108 m.) S Africa in the Zambezi on border between Zambia & Zimbabwe

Vi·en·na \vē-'e-nə\ *or German* Wien \'vēn\ city, * of Austria on the Danube; *pop* 1,550,123 — Vi·en·nese \ˌvē-ə-'nēz, -'nēs\ *adj or n*

Vien·tiane \(ˌ)vyen-'tyän\ city, * of Laos; *pop* 132,253

Vie·ques \vē-'ä-kās\ island Puerto Rico off E end of main island

Viet·nam \vē-'et-'näm, vyet-, ˌvē-ət-, vēt-, -'näm\ country SE Asia in Indochina; *, Hanoi; divided 1954–75 into the independent states of North Vietnam (*, Hanoi) & South Vietnam (*, Saigon); *pop* 79,727,400 — Viet·nam·ese \vē-ˌet-nə-'mēz, ˌvyet-, ˌvē-ət-, ˌvēt-, -na-, -nä-, -'mēs\ *adj or n*

Vila — see PORT-VILA

Vi·la No·va de Ga·ia \'vē-lə-'nó-və-dē-'gī-ə\ city NW Portugal; *pop* 288,749

Vil·ni·us \'vil-nē-əs\ city, * of Lithuania; *pop* 542,287

Vin·land \'vīn-lənd\ a portion of the coast of North America visited & so called by Norse voyagers about 1000 A.D.; thought to be located along the North Atlantic in what is now E or NE Canada

Vir·gin·ia \vər-'jin-yə, -'ji-nē-ə\ state E U.S.; *, Richmond; *pop* 7,078,515 — Vir·gin·ian \-nyən, -nē-ən\ *adj or n*

Virginia Beach city SE Virginia; *pop* 425,257

Virginia City locality W Nevada

Virgin Islands island group West Indies E of Puerto Rico — see BRITISH VIRGIN ISLANDS; VIRGIN ISLANDS OF THE UNITED STATES

Virgin Islands of the United States the W islands of the Virgin Islands; U.S. territory; *, Charlotte Amalie (on Saint Thomas); *pop* 108,612

Vi·sa·yan \və-'sī-ən\ islands *cen* Philippines

Vi·sa·kha·pat·nam \vi-ˌsä-kə-'pat-nəm\ *or* Vis·a·kha·pat·nam \vi-ˌsä-\ city E India; *pop* 969,608

Vis·tu·la \'vis-chə-lə, 'vish-chə-, 'vis-tə-\ river over 660 mi. (1062 km.) long Poland flowing N from the Carpathians

Vi·ti Le·vu \ˌvē-tē-'le-(ˌ)vü\ island SW South Pacific; largest of the Fiji group

Vlad·i·vos·tok \ˌvla-də-və-'stäk, -'väs-ˌtäk\ city SE Russia on Sea of Japan; *pop* 648,000

Vol·ga \'väl-gə, 'vòl-, 'vōl-\ river about 2300 mi. (3700 km.) long W Russia; longest river in Europe

Vol·go·grad \'väl-gə-ˌgräd, 'vòl-, 'vōl-, -ˌgrät\ city S Russia in Europe, on the Volga; *pop* 1,006,000

Vol·ta \'väl-tə, 'vòl-, 'vōl-\ river about 300 mi. (485 km.) long Ghana flowing from Lake Volta (reservoir) into Gulf of Guinea

Vo·ro·nezh \və-'ró-nish\ city *cen* Russia in Europe; *pop* 902,000

Vosges \'vōzh\ mountains NE France on W side of Rhine valley; highest 4672 ft. (1424 m.)

Wa·co \'wā-(ˌ)kō\ city *cen* Texas; *pop* 113,726

Wad·den·zee \ˌvä-dᵊn-ˈzä\ inlet of the North Sea N Netherlands

Wake \ˈwāk\ island North Pacific N of Marshall Islands; U.S. territory

Wake·field \ˈwāk-ˌfēld\ city N England; *pop* 60,540

Wa·la·chia *or* **Wal·la·chia** \wä-ˈlā-kē-ə\ region S Romania between Transylvanian Alps & the Danube

Wales \ˈwālz\ *or Welsh* **Cym·ru** \ˈkəm-ˌrē\ principality SW Great Britain; a division of United Kingdom; ✱, Cardiff; *pop* 2,903,085

Wal·lo·nia \wä-ˈlō-nē-ə\ semiautonomous region S Belgium; *pop* 3,358,560

Wal·sall \ˈwȯl-ˌsȯl, -səl\ town W *cen* England; *pop* 255,600

Wal·tham Forest \ˈwȯl-thəm\ borough of NE Greater London, England; *pop* 203,400

Wands·worth \ˈwän(d)z-ˌ(ˌ)wərth\ borough of SW Greater London, England; *pop* 237,500

War·ley \ˈwȯr-lē\ town W *cen* England; *pop* 152,455

War·ren \ˈwȯr-lē\ city SE Michigan; *pop* 138,247

War·saw \ˈwȯr-ˌsȯ\ *or Polish* **War·sza·wa** \vär-ˈshä-vä\ city, ✱ of Poland; *pop* 1,655,063

War·wick \ˈwär-ik\ town *cen* England; *pop* 21,936

War·wick·shire \ˈwär-ik-ˌshir, -shər\ *or* **Warwick** county *cen* England

Wa·satch \ˈwȯ-ˌsach\ range of the Rockies SE Idaho & N *cen* Utah; highest Mount Timpanogos 12,008 ft. (3660 m.), in Utah

Wash·ing·ton \ˈwȯ-shiŋ-tən, ˈwä-\ **1** state NW U.S.; ✱, Olympia; *pop* 5,894,121 **2** city, ✱ of U.S.; having the same boundaries as District of Columbia; *pop* 572,059 — **Wash·ing·to·nian** \ˌwȯ-shiŋ-ˈtō-nē-ən, ˌwä-, -nyən\ *adj or n*

Washington, Mount mountain 6288 ft. (1916 m.) N New Hampshire; highest in White Mountains

Wa·ter·bury \ˈwȯ-tə(r)-ˌber-ē, ˈwä-\ city W *cen* Connecticut; *pop* 107,271

Wa·ver·ley \ˈwä-vər-lē\ municipality SE Australia in E New South Wales; *pop* 59,095

Wei·mar Republic \ˈvī-ˌmär, ˈwī-\ the German republic 1919–33

Wel·land \ˈwe-lənd\ canal 27 mi. (44 km.) long SE Ontario connecting Lake Erie & Lake Ontario

Wel·ling·ton \ˈwe-liŋ-tən\ city, ✱ of New Zealand; urban area *pop* 339,747

Wes·sex \ˈwe-siks\ ancient kingdom S England

West Bank area Middle East W of Jordan River; occupied by Israel since 1967 with parts having been transferred to Palestinian administration since 1993

West Brom·wich \ˈbrä-mich\ town W *cen* England; *pop* 154,930

West Co·vi·na \kō-ˈvē-nə\ city SW California; *pop* 105,080

Western Australia state W Australia; ✱, Perth; *pop* 1,676,400 — **Western Australian** *adj or n*

Western Cape province SW Republic of South Africa; *pop* 3,635,000

Western Ghats — see GHATS

Western Hemisphere the half of the earth lying W of the Atlantic Ocean & comprising North America, South America, & surrounding waters

Western Isles English name for the administrative area of W Scotland consisting of the Outer Hebrides

Western Sahara *formerly* **Spanish Sahara** territory NW Africa; occupied by Morocco

Western Samoa — see SAMOA

West Germany — see GERMANY

West Indies islands lying between SE North America & N South America & consisting of the Greater Antilles, Lesser Antilles, & Bahamas — **West Indian** *adj or n*

West Midlands metropolitan county W *cen* England; includes Birmingham

West·min·ster \ˈwes(t)-ˌmin(t)-stər\ city N *cen* Colorado NW of Denver; *pop* 100,940

West Pakistan the former W division of Pakistan now having the same boundaries as Pakistan

West Papua *or formerly* **Iri·an Ja·ya** \ˈir-ē-ˌän-ˈjī-ä\ *or* **West Irian** territory of Indonesia consisting of the W half of New Guinea; *pop* 1,648,708

West·pha·lia \west-ˈfāl-yə, -ˈfā-lē-ə\ region W Germany E

of the Rhine — **West·pha·lian** \west-ˈfāl-yən, -ˈfā-lē-ən\ *adj or n*

West Point U.S. military post SE New York

West Quod·dy Head \ˈkwä-dē\ cape; most easterly point of Maine & of the Lower 48

West Sus·sex \ˈsə-siks\ county SE England

West Valley City city N Utah S of Salt Lake City; *pop* 108,896

West Virginia state E U.S.; ✱, Charleston; *pop* 1,808,344 — **West Virginian** *adj or n*

West York·shire metropolitan county NW England; includes Wakefield

White sea NW Russia in Europe

White·horse \ˈhwīt-ˌhȯrs, ˈwīt-\ city, ✱ of Yukon Territory, Canada; *pop* 19,058

White Mountains mountains N New Hampshire in the Appalachians — see WASHINGTON, MOUNT

Whit·ney, Mount \ˈhwit-nē, ˈwit-\ mountain 14,495 ft. (4418 m.) SE *cen* California in Sierra Nevada; highest in U.S. outside of Alaska

Wich·i·ta \ˈwi-chə-ˌtȯ\ city S Kansas; *pop* 344,284

Wichita Falls city N Texas; *pop* 104,197

Wien — see VIENNA

Wight, Isle of — see ISLE OF WIGHT

Wil·lem·stad \ˈvi-ləm-ˌstät\ city, ✱ of Netherlands Antilles; *pop* 43,547

Wil·liams·burg \ˈwil-yəmz-ˌbərg\ city SE Virginia; *pop* 11,998

Wil·ming·ton \ˈwil-miŋ-tən\ city N Delaware; largest in state; *pop* 72,664

Wilt·shire \ˈwilt-ˌshir, -shər\ county S England

Win·ches·ter \ˈwin-ˌches-tər, -chəs-tər\ city S England; *pop* 30,642

Win·der·mere \ˈwin-də(r)-ˌmir\ lake NW England in Lake District

Wind·hoek \ˈvint-ˌhük\ city, ✱ of Namibia; *pop* 144,558

Wind·sor \ˈwin-zər\ city S Ontario, Canada on Detroit River; *pop* 208,402

Windward Islands \ˈwind-wərd\ islands West Indies in the S Lesser Antilles extending S from Martinique but not including Barbados, Tobago, or Trinidad

Win·ni·peg \ˈwi-nə-ˌpeg\ city, ✱ of Manitoba, Canada; *pop* 619,544

Winnipeg, Lake lake S Manitoba, Canada

Win·ni·pe·sau·kee, Lake \ˌwi-nə-pə-ˈsȯ-kē\ lake *cen* New Hampshire

Win·ston–Sa·lem \ˌwin(t)-stən-ˈsä-ləm\ city N *cen* North Carolina; *pop* 185,776

Wis·con·sin \wi-ˈskän(t)-sən\ state N *cen* U.S.; ✱, Madison; *pop* 5,363,675 — **Wis·con·sin·ite** \-sə-ˌnīt\ *n*

Wit·wa·ters·rand \ˈwit-ˌwȯ-tərz-ˌrand, -ˌwä-, -ˌränd, -ˌränt\ *or* **Rand** ridge of gold-bearing rock NE Republic of South Africa

Wol·lon·gong \ˈwu̇-lən-ˌgäŋ, -ˌgȯŋ\ city SE Australia in E New South Wales S of Sydney; *pop* 211,417

Wol·ver·hamp·ton \ˌwu̇l-vər-ˈham(p)-tən\ town W *cen* England NW of Birmingham; *pop* 236,582

Worces·ter \ˈwu̇s-tər\ city E *cen* Massachusetts; *pop* 172,648

Wran·gell, Mount \ˈraŋ-gəl\ volcano 14,163 ft. (4317 m.) S Alaska in **Wrangell Mountains**

Wro·claw \ˈvrȯt-ˌswäf, -ˌsläv\ city SW Poland in Silesia; *pop* 642,334

Wu·han \ˈwü-ˈhän\ city E *cen* China; *pop* 3,284,229

Wu·xi *or* **Wu–hsi** \ˈwü-ˈshē\ city E China; *pop* 826,833

Wy·o·ming \wī-ˈō-miŋ\ state NW U.S.; ✱, Cheyenne; *pop* 493,782 — **Wy·o·ming·ite** \-miŋ-ˌīt\ *n*

Xi'·an *or* **Hsi–an** \ˈshē-ˈän\ city E *cen* China; *pop* 1,959,044

Xianggang — see HONG KONG

Xin·jiang Uy·gur *or* **Sin·kiang Ui·ghur** \ˈshin-ˈjyäŋ-ˈwē-gər\ region W China between the Kunlun & Altai mountains; *pop* 15,155,778

Xizang — see TIBET

Xu·zhou \ˈshü-ˈjō\ *or* **Sü–chow** \ˈshü-ˈjō, ˈsü-\ city E China; *pop* 805,695

Yak·i·ma \ˈya-kə-ˌmȯ\ city S *cen* Washington; *pop* 71,845

Ya·lu \ˈyä-(ˌ)lü\ river 500 mi. (804 km.) long SE Manchuria & North Korea

Ya·mous·sou·kro \ˌyä-mə-'sü-krō\ town, official ✳ of Ivory Coast; *pop* 110,000

Yan·gon \ˌyän-'gōn\ *formerly* **Ran·goon** \ran-'gün, raŋ-\ city, former ✳ of Myanmar; *pop* 1,717,649

Yangtze — see CHANG

Yaoun·dé \yaùn-'dā\ city, ✳ of Cameroon; *pop* 649,000

Yap \'yap, 'yäp\ island W Pacific in the W Carolines

Ya·ren \'yä-ˌrən\ town, ✳ of Nauru; *pop* 1100

Ya·ro·slavl \ˌyär-ə-'slä-vᵊl\ city *cen* Russia in Europe, NE of Moscow; *pop* 637,000

Yaz·oo \ya-'zü, 'ya-(ˌ)zü\ river W *cen* Mississippi

Ye·ka·te·rin·burg \yi-'ka-tə-rən-ˌbərg, yi-ˌkä-ti-rēm-'bùrk\ *formerly* **Sverd·lovsk** \sverd-'lófsk\ city W Russia, in *cen* Ural Mountains; *pop* 1,371,000

Yellow **1** — see HUANG **2** sea, section of East China Sea between N China, North Korea, & South Korea

Yel·low·knife \'ye-lō-ˌnīf\ town, ✳ of Northwest Territories, Canada; *pop* 16,541

Ye·men \'ye-mən\ country S Arabia bordering on Red Sea & Gulf of Aden; ✳, Sanaa; *pop* 12,961,000 — **Ye·me·ni** \'ye-mə-nē\ *adj or n* — **Ye·men·ite** \-mə-ˌnīt\ *adj or n*

Ye·ni·sey *or* **Ye·ni·sei** \ˌyi-ni-'sā\ river over 2500 mi. (4022 km.) long *cen* Russia, flowing N into Arctic Ocean

Ye·re·van \ˌyer-ə-'vän\ city, ✳ of Armenia; *pop* 1,199,000

Yo·ko·ha·ma \ˌyō-kō-'hä-mä\ city Japan in SE Honshu on Tokyo Bay S of Tokyo; *pop* 3,426,651

Yon·kers \'yäŋ-kərz\ city SE New York N of New York City; *pop* 196,086

York \'yórk\ city N England; *pop* 100,600

York, Cape cape NE Australia in Queensland at N tip of Cape York Peninsula

York·shire \-ˌshir, -shər\ former county N England

Yo·sem·i·te Falls \yō-'se-mə-tē\ waterfall E California in Yosemite Valley; includes two falls, the upper 1430 ft. (436 m.) & the lower 320 ft. (98 m.)

Youngs·town \'yəŋz-ˌtaùn\ city NE Ohio; *pop* 82,026

Yu·ca·tán \ˌyü-kə-'tan, -kä-'tän\ peninsula SE Mexico & N Central America including Belize & N Guatemala

Yu·go·sla·via \ˌyü-gō-'slä-vē-ə, ˌyü-gə-\ **1** former country S Europe including Serbia, Montenegro, Slovenia, Croatia, Bosnia and Herzegovina, & Macedonia; ✳, Belgrade **2** — see SERBIA AND MONTENEGRO — **Yu·go·slav** \ˌyü-gō-'släv, -'slav; 'yü-gō-ˌ\ *or* **Yu·go·sla·vi·an** \ˌyü-gō-'slä-vē-ən, -gə-\ *adj or n*

Yu·kon \'yü-ˌkän\ **1** river 1979 mi. (3185 km.) long NW Canada & Alaska flowing into Bering Sea **2** *or* **Yukon Territory** territory NW Canada; ✳, Whitehorse; *pop* 29,885

Yu·ma \'yü-mə\ city SW corner of Arizona on the Colorado; *pop* 77,515

Za·greb \'zä-ˌgreb\ city, ✳ of Croatia; *pop* 779,145

Zaire \zä-'ir\ **1** river in Africa — see CONGO 1 **2** country in Africa — see CONGO 2 — **Zair·ean** *or* **Zair·ian** \zä-'ir-ē-ən\ *adj or n*

Zam·be·zi *or* **Zam·be·si** \zam-'bē-zē, zäm-'bä-zē\ river about 1700 mi. (2735 km.) long SE Africa flowing from NW Zambia into Mozambique Channel

Zam·bia \'zam-bē-ə\ *formerly* **Northern Rhodesia** country S Africa N of the Zambezi; ✳, Lusaka; *pop* 9,132,000 — **Zam·bi·an** \'zam-bē-ən\ *adj or n*

Zan·zi·bar \'zan-zə-ˌbär\ island Tanzania off NE Tanganyika coast; united 1964 with Tanganyika forming Tanzania

Za·po·rizh·zhya *or* **Za·po·ro·zh'ye** \ˌzä-pə-'rēzh-zhyə\ city SE Ukraine; *pop* 897,000

Zhang·jia·kou \'jäŋ-'jyä-'kō\ *or* **Kal·gan** \'kal-'gan\ city NE China NW of Beijing; *pop* 529,136

Zhdanov — see MARIUPOL

Zheng·zhou *or* **Cheng·chou** \'jəŋ-'jō\ city NE *cen* China; *pop* 1,159,679

Zim·ba·bwe \zim-'bä-bwē, -(ˌ)bwä\ *formerly* **Rhodesia** country S Africa S of Zambezi River; ✳, Harare; *pop* 7,550,000 — **Zim·ba·bwe·an** \-ən\ *adj or n*

Zui·der Zee \ˌzī-dər-'zā, -'zē\ — see IJSSELMEER

Zu·lu·land \'zü-(ˌ)lü-ˌland\ territory E Republic of South Africa on Indian Ocean

Zu·rich \'zùr-ik\ city N Switzerland; *pop* 340,873